P9-ARF-347

WITHDRAWN

2022 County and City Extra

Annual Metro, City, and County Data Book

30th Edition

Edited by Deirdre A. Gaquin
and Mary Meghan Ryan

Bernan Press

Lanham • Boulder • New York • London

Published by Bernan Press
An imprint of The Rowman & Littlefield Publishing Group, Inc.
4501 Forbes Boulevard, Suite 200, Lanham, Maryland 20706
www.rowman.com

86-90 Paul Street, London EC2A 4NE

Copyright © 2023 by The Rowman & Littlefield Publishing Group, Inc.

All rights reserved. No part of this book may be reproduced in any form or by any electronic or mechanical means, including information storage and retrieval systems, without written permission from the publisher, except by a reviewer who may quote passages in a review. The Rowman & Littlefield Publishing Group, Inc., does not claim copyright on U.S. government information.

ISBN 9781636710822 (hardback) | ISBN 9781636710839 (ebook)

∞™ The paper used in this publication meets the minimum requirements of American National Standard for Information Sciences—Permanence of Paper for Printed Library Materials, ANSI/NISO Z39.48-1992.

Contents

INTRODUCTION

County and City Extra is an annual publication that provides the most up-to-date statistical information available for every state, county, metropolitan area, and congressional district, as well as all cities in the United States with a 2020 census population of 25,000 or more. Data for places, including towns and cities with populations of fewer than 25,000 people are published by Bernan Press in a separate companion volume, *Places, Towns and Townships*, now in its seventh edition. These two volumes are designed to meet the needs of libraries, businesses, and other organizations or individuals who desire convenient and timely sources of the most frequently sought information about geographic entities within the United States. The annual updating of *County and City Extra* for 30 years ensures its status as a reliable and authoritative source for statistical information.

Bernan Press also publishes a companion volume, *State and Metropolitan Area Data Book*, previously published by the Census Bureau. The recently published third edition provides an expanded collection of data about states and metropolitan areas, including micropolitan areas and their component counties. Another addition is the *County and City Extra: Special Historical Edition, 1790–2010* with data from the earliest days of the nation and states, counties, and cities from their beginnings.

County and City Extra, Places, Towns and Townships and *State and Metropolitan Area Data Book* are large volumes but not big enough to accommodate the wealth of information from the decennial census and the American Community Survey. Two additional volumes in the County and City Extra series include this information: *County and City Extra—Special 2020 Decennial Census Edition* provides detailed population and housing data from the initial release of the 2020 census and was published by Bernan Press in 2022. *The Who, What, and Where of America—Understanding the American Community Survey*, recently released in its tenth edition, includes social and economic details from the ongoing American Community Survey. The County and City Extra series includes additional books on special topics, such as the recently published *Education and the American Workforce*.

The American Community Survey (ACS) is a national survey that has replaced the census long form as the key source of detailed social and economic data. *County and City Extra* includes data from both the 2020 census and the ACS.

New and Updated Information for the 2022 Edition

This edition includes data from the first release of the 2020 census—the Redistricting Data File—and population estimates derived by the Census Bureau using the new census numbers. Information on COVID-19 from the Centers for Disease Control is included for states and counties in Table B. This includes the number and rate of deaths from COVID-19 in 2020 for each county, as well as the number and rate of persons vaccinated through April 2022. Updated data include 2021 population estimates for states, counties, metropolitan areas, and cities. Also included are the latest available data for education, vital statistics, income and poverty, employment and unemployment, residential construction, production by industry, health resources, land use, city government finances, and many other topics.

Table E (Congressional Districts) includes a wide selection of 2020 ACS data, business patterns, and social security data for the 116th Congress, as well as data from the 2017 Census of Agriculture for the congressional districts of the 116th Congress, along with the 117th Congressional representatives.

In September 2018, the Office of Management and Budget released an updated list of core-based statistical areas (metropolitan and micropolitan areas) based on the 2010 census and some changes in the way these areas are defined. These changes were substantial, resulting in many new names and component counties. Another update was issued in March 2020 with no changes to metropolitan area delineations. The 2021 population estimates, and most key data sources for this book used the new 2018 list of metropolitan areas. For other sources that still used the earlier metropolitan definitions, we aggregated the county data so that all metropolitan area data use the new definitions. Appendixes B and C provide details about the component counties of these metropolitan and micropolitan areas and their 2010 and 2020 census populations. Appendix D lists all the changes made since the earlier delineations and provides a link to a map of the new metropolitan areas.

This edition includes data from the 2010 and 2020 census, 2021 population estimates, and the ACS. In most years, annual ACS data are available for all states and all metropolitan areas (all geographic areas with populations of 65,000 or more), but five years are needed to build a sample large enough for reliable estimates for all counties. The Census Bureau did not release its standard 2020 ACS 1-year estimates because of the impacts of the COVID-19 pandemic. Instead, the Census Bureau released experimental estimates from the 1-year data. These include a limited number of data tables for the nation, states, and the District of Columbia. In this volume, the experimental estimates are used for the state data in Table A. For all other geographic areas, only the 5-year estimates were available for 2016–2020.

Although some of the state data are also included in Table B (States and Counties), the separate state data table offers several important features:

- Additional data not available at the county level are provided. Examples include population projections, health insurance coverage, number of immigrants, personal tax payments, information about health service firms not subject to federal tax, and exports by state of origin.

- Additional data that exceeds the space limitations for counties can be found for states. Examples are: expanded housing finance data, more detailed information about employment in retail trade and services, and detailed government employment and finance data.

- State totals can be found more quickly and compared more readily.

Appendix F, "Source Notes and Explanations," includes internet references for all data sources. This is especially helpful in today's environment where the data sources are updated at a faster pace. The sources referenced here can be used to track down additional information too cumbersome for this book. Some of the data can be directly found in data tables on the websites, some can be assembled through online access tools, others can be obtained by downloading files and processing them with statistical software, and some need to be ordered from the agencies.

Rankings

The rankings present the geography types by various subjects, including population, land area, population density, population change, age, immigration, birth rate, housing characteristics, race, Hispanic origin, educational attainment, income, unemployment rate, per capita local taxes, poverty rate, defense contracts, value of agricultural products, and violent crime rate.

Subjects Covered and Volume Organization

A summary of the **subjects covered** in each of the five tables appears on **page xi**. The **colored map** portfolio begins on **page xv**.

The main body of this volume contains five basic parts. Each part includes a table that is preceded by highlights and rankings, as well as the complete column headings for the table. **Part A**, which begins on **page 1**, contains data for states. **Part B**, beginning on **page 51**, contains information for states and counties. The county geography codes include county typology codes from the Economic Research Service of the Department of Agriculture. These codes characterize counties by size of the largest place as well as by other criteria for nonmetropolitan counties. (See Appendix A for the definition of each code.) **Part C**, beginning on **page 773**, contains information for metropolitan areas. Statistics for cities with a 2020 census population of 25,000 or more can be found in **Part D**, which begins on **page 895**. **Part E**, beginning on **page 1175**, contains data for the congressional districts of the 116th Congress.

A contents page preceding tables B through E lists the page number on which the data for a given geographic area begin. Counties and cities are listed alphabetically by state. Metropolitan areas are listed alphabetically, except that metropolitan divisions are listed alphabetically within the metropolitan statistical area of which they are components. Congressional districts are listed in numeric order within states.

The appendixes include definitions of geographic concepts (**Appendix A**); sources and definitions of each data item included in this volume (**Appendix F**); an alphabetical listing of metropolitan areas with their component counties delineated as of March 2020, with 2010 and 2020 census populations (**Appendix B**); a listing of metropolitan and micropolitan areas and their component counties as of March 2020, with 2010 and 2020 census populations (**Appendix C**); a list of cities by county (**Appendix E**); and a list of the changes resulting in the new set of metropolitan areas (**Appendix D**).

Symbols

D Indicates that the number has been withheld to avoid disclosure of information pertaining to a specific organization or individual, or because the number does not meet statistical standards for publication.

NA Indicates that data are not available.

X Indicates that data are not applicable or are not meaningful for this geographic unit.

In this volume, a figure that is less than half the unit of measure shown will appear as zero.

Sources

All of the data in this volume have been obtained from federal government sources. For a complete list of these sources, see **Appendix F**.

Data included in this volume meet the publication standards established by the U.S. Census Bureau and the other federal statistical agencies from which they were obtained. Every effort has been made to select data that are accurate, meaningful, and useful. All data from censuses, surveys, and administrative records are subject to errors arising from factors such as sampling variability, reporting errors, incomplete coverage, nonresponse, imputations, and processing error. Responsibility of the editors and publishers of this volume is limited to reasonable care in the reproduction and presentation of data obtained from sources believed to be reliable.

County and City Extra: Annual Metro, City, and County Data Book is part of Bernan Press's County and City Extra series. The editors of *County and City Extra* acknowledge the contributions of the late Courtenay Slater and George Hall, the originators of this publication. Their initial contributions continue to enrich the County and City Extra series. As always, we are especially grateful to the many federal agency personnel who assisted us in obtaining the data, provided excellent resources on their websites, and patiently answered questions.

Deirdre A. Gaquin has been a data use consultant to private organizations, government agencies, and universities for more than thirty-five years. Prior to that, she was Director of Data Access Services at Data Use & Access Laboratories, a pioneer in private sector distribution of federal statistical data. A former President of the Association of Public Data Users, Ms. Gaquin has served on numerous boards, panels, and task forces concerned with federal statistical data and has worked on five decennial censuses. She holds a Master of Urban Planning (MUP) degree from Hunter College. Ms. Gaquin is also an editor of Bernan Press's *The Who, What, and Where of America: Understanding the American Community Survey*; *Places, Towns and Townships*; *The Congressional District Atlas*; *The Almanac of American Education*; *Race and Employment in America*; and the *State and Metropolitan Area Data Book*.

Mary Meghan Ryan is the senior research editor for Bernan Press. She is also the editor for the *Handbook of U.S. Labor Statistics*, *State Profiles*, and the associate editor for *Business Statistics of the United States*.

SUBJECTS COVERED, BY GEOGRAPHY TYPE

Subject	Column number				
	Table A. States	**Table B. States and Counties**	**Table C. Metropolitan Areas**	**Table D. Cities**	**Table E. Congressional Districts**
Land area	1	1	1	1	1
Population					
Total persons, 2000	31				
Total persons, 2010	32	20	20	23	
Total persons, 2020	33	21	21	24	
Total persons, 2021	2	2	2	2	
Total persons, 2016–2020					2
Rank, 2021	3	3	3	3	
Persons per square mile	4	4	4	4	3
Race and Hispanic or Latino origin, 2010	45–50				
Race and Hispanic or Latino origin, 2020				5–12	
Race and Hispanic or Latino origin, 2021	5–9	5–9	5–9		
Race and Hispanic or Latino origin, 2016–2020					4–11
Percent female	20,63	19	19	22	12
Foreign–born population	22,51			13	13
Percent born in state of residence	23				14
Immigrants	24				
Age distribution, 2010	52–61				
Age distribution, 2021	10–19	10–18	10–18		
Age distribution, 2016–2020				14–20	15–23
Median age	21, 62			21	24
Percent population change, 2000–2010	34				
Percent population change, 2010–2020	35	22	22	25	
Percent population change, 2020–2021	36	23	23	26	
Components of population change	37–41	24–26	24–26		
Daytime population		33–34	33–34		
Population projections	42–44				
Households					
Total households, 2010	64				
Total households, 2020	25				
Total households, 2016–2020		27	27	27	28
Percent change in number of households	26, 65				
Household type	27–30, 67–68	29–31	29–31	29–33	30–33
Persons per household	66	28	28	28	29
Persons in group quarters		32	32	34	34–39
Housing					
Housing units in 2010	69–78				
Housing units in 2020	79–87				40–45
Housing units in 2021		87–88	87–88		
Housing units in 2016–2020		89–90		50–52	
Percent change in number of housing units	70, 80	88	88		
Housing costs	73–77, 83–87	91–95	91–95	53–54	43–45
Substandard housing units	78	96	96		
Percent with computer and internet access	89–92			57–58	
Commuting patterns				55–56	
Percent who lived in same house one year ago				59	
Percent who lived in different place one year ago	88			60	
New residential construction	93–95	169–170	169–170	69–71	
Manufactured housing	96				

SUBJECTS COVERED, BY GEOGRAPHY TYPE — Continued

State data begin on page 1
County data begin on page 51
Metropolitan area data begin on page 773
City data begin on page 895
Congressional district data begin on page 1175

Subject	Column number				
	Table A. States	Table B. States and Counties	Table C. Metropolitan Areas	Table D. Cities	Table E. Congressional Districts
Vital statistics					
Births	97–98	35–36	35–36		
Deaths	99–103	37–38	37–38		
Health					
Persons in nursing facilities					37
Medicare enrollees	106	41–43	41–43		
Persons lacking health insurance	104–105	39–40	39–40		59
COVID–19 deaths and vaccinations		44–47			
Crime	107–110		44–47	35–38	
Education					
School enrollment	111–112	48–49	48–49		25
Educational attainment	113–116	50–51	50–51	39–41	26–27
Expenditures for education	117–118	52–53	52–53		
Income					
Personal income	134–149	62–71	62–71		
Per capita income	136, 149	54, 64	54, 64		46
Household income	123–126	55–58	55–58	42–44	47–48
Family and non–family income				45–46	
Individual earnings	122			47–49	
Poverty	127–133	59–61	59–61		49–50
Food stamps					51
Personal income by type	138–140	66–70	66–70		
Earnings by industry	150–158	72–83	72–83		
Transfer payments	141–146	71	71		
Gross state product	159				
Personal tax payments	147				
Disposable personal income	148–149				
Social Security	160–162	84–86	84–86		60–62
Individual income taxes		197–199	197–199		
Labor Force and Employment					
Labor force and unemployment	167–171	97–100	97–100	61–68	52–54
Employment in selected occupations	163–166	101–103	101–103		55–58
Employment by industry	172–183, 207–216	104–112	104–112		73–84
Exports of goods produced	119–121				
Establishments, employment, sales, and payroll					
Manufacturing	207–216	151–154	151–154	88–91	
Construction	217–221				
Wholesale trade	222–226	135–138	135–138	72–75	
Retail trade	227–235	139–142	139–142	76–79	
Information	236–246				
Utilities	247–251				
Transportation and warehousing	252–256				
Finance and insurance	257–261				
Real estate and rental and leasing	262–266	143–146	143–146	80–83	

SUBJECTS COVERED, BY GEOGRAPHY TYPE — Continued

State data begin on page 1
County data begin on page 51
Metropolitan area data begin on page 773
City data begin on page 895
Congressional district data begin on page 1175

Subject	Column number				
	Table A. States	Table B. States and Counties	Table C. Metropolitan Areas	Table D. Cities	Table E. Congressional Districts
Professional, scientific, and technical services	267–275	147–150	147–150	84–87	
Health care and social assistance	276–289	159–162	159–162	100–103	
Arts, entertainment and recreation	290–294			96–99	
Accommodation and food services	295–300	155–158	155–158	92–95	
Other services, except public administration	301–308	163–166	163–166	104–107	
Nonemployer businesses		167–168	167–168		
Government employment	309–314	171, 194–196	171, 194–196	108	
Government payroll	315–330	172–179	172–179	109–116	
Government finances	331–350	180–193	180–193	117–139	
Agriculture	184–202	113–132	113–132		63–72
Land and water	203–206	133–134	133–134		
Voting and elections	351–355				

Population Change
2020–2021

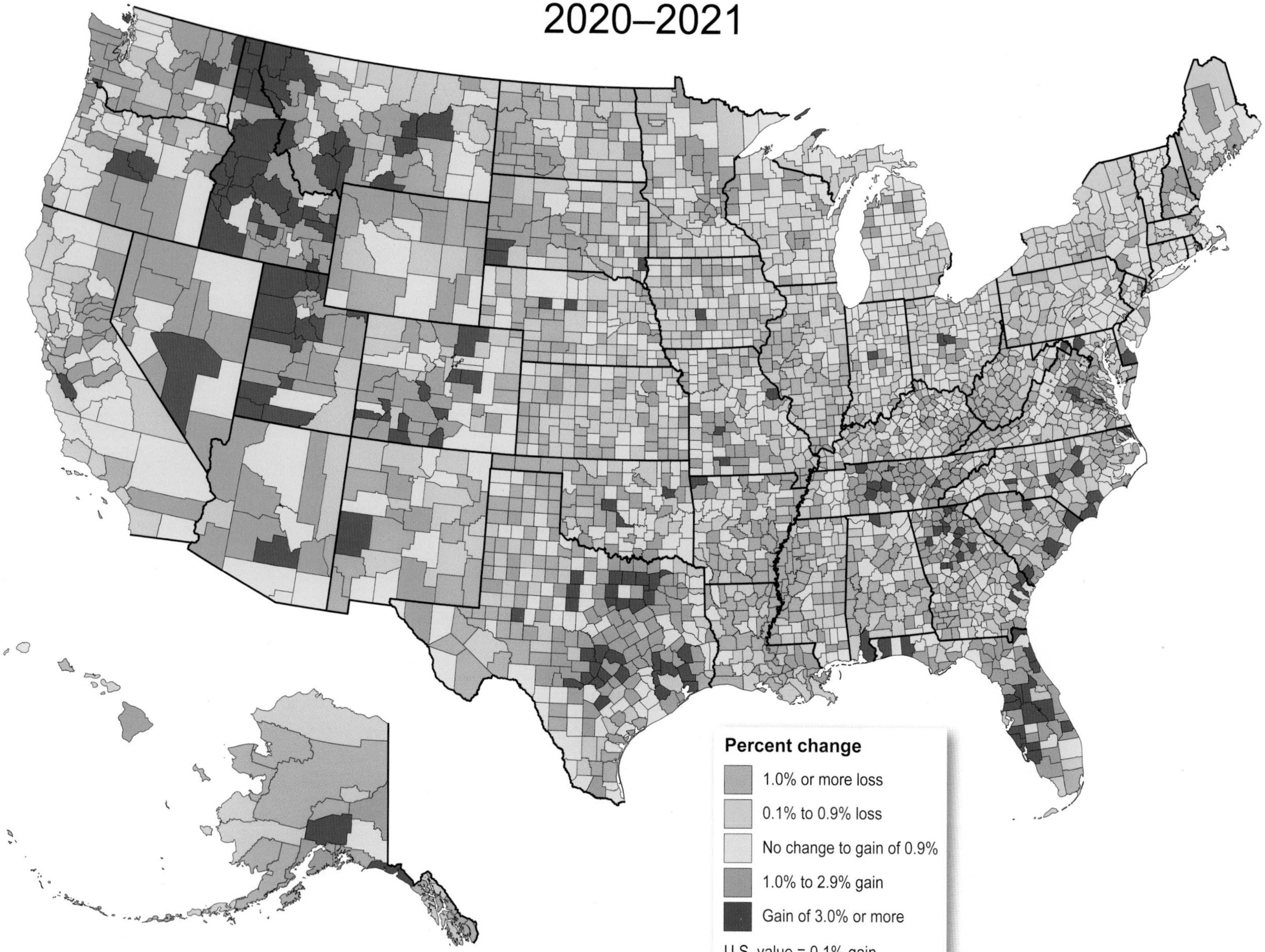

Black, Not Hispanic or Latino, Population

2021

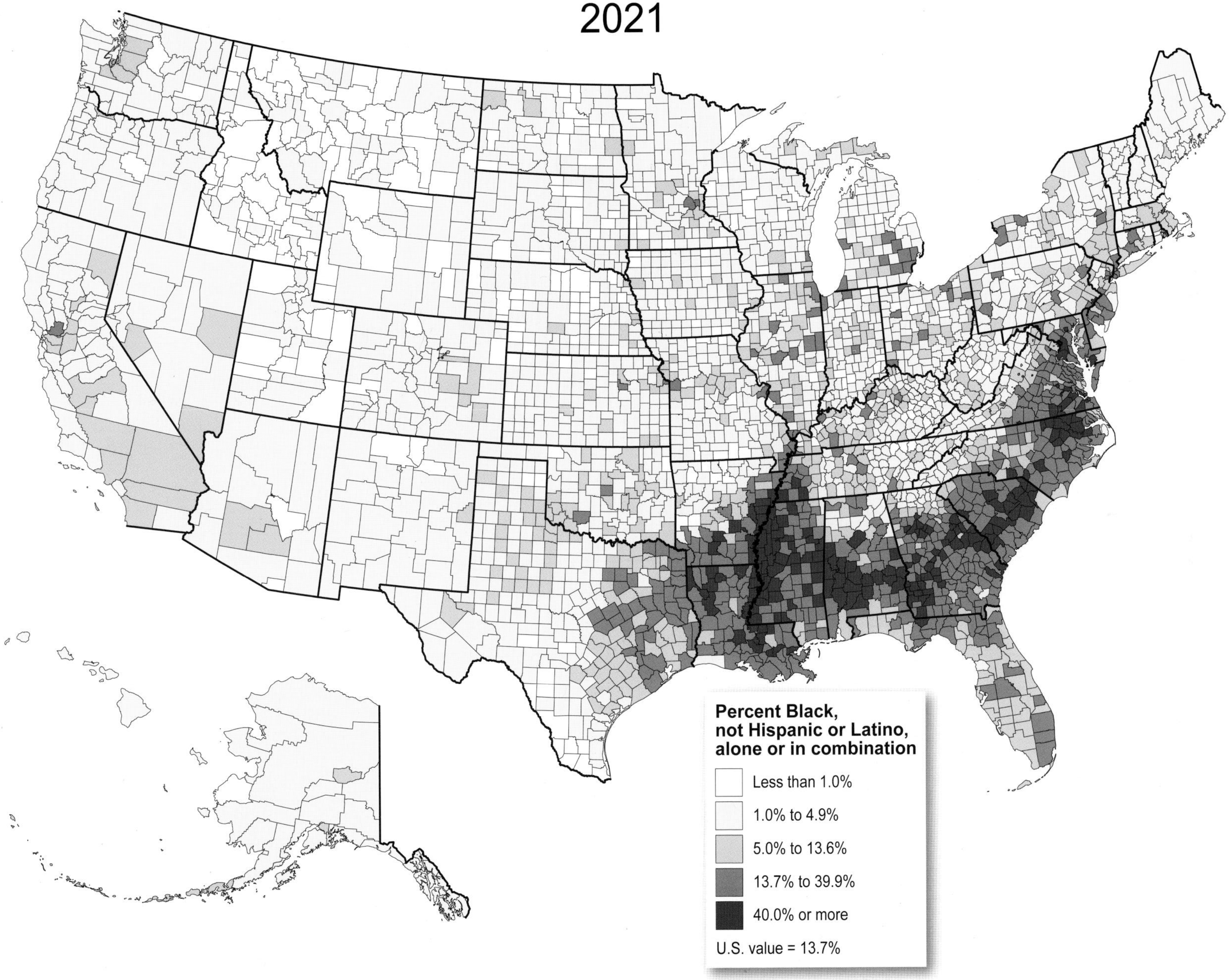

Hispanic or Latino, Population
2021

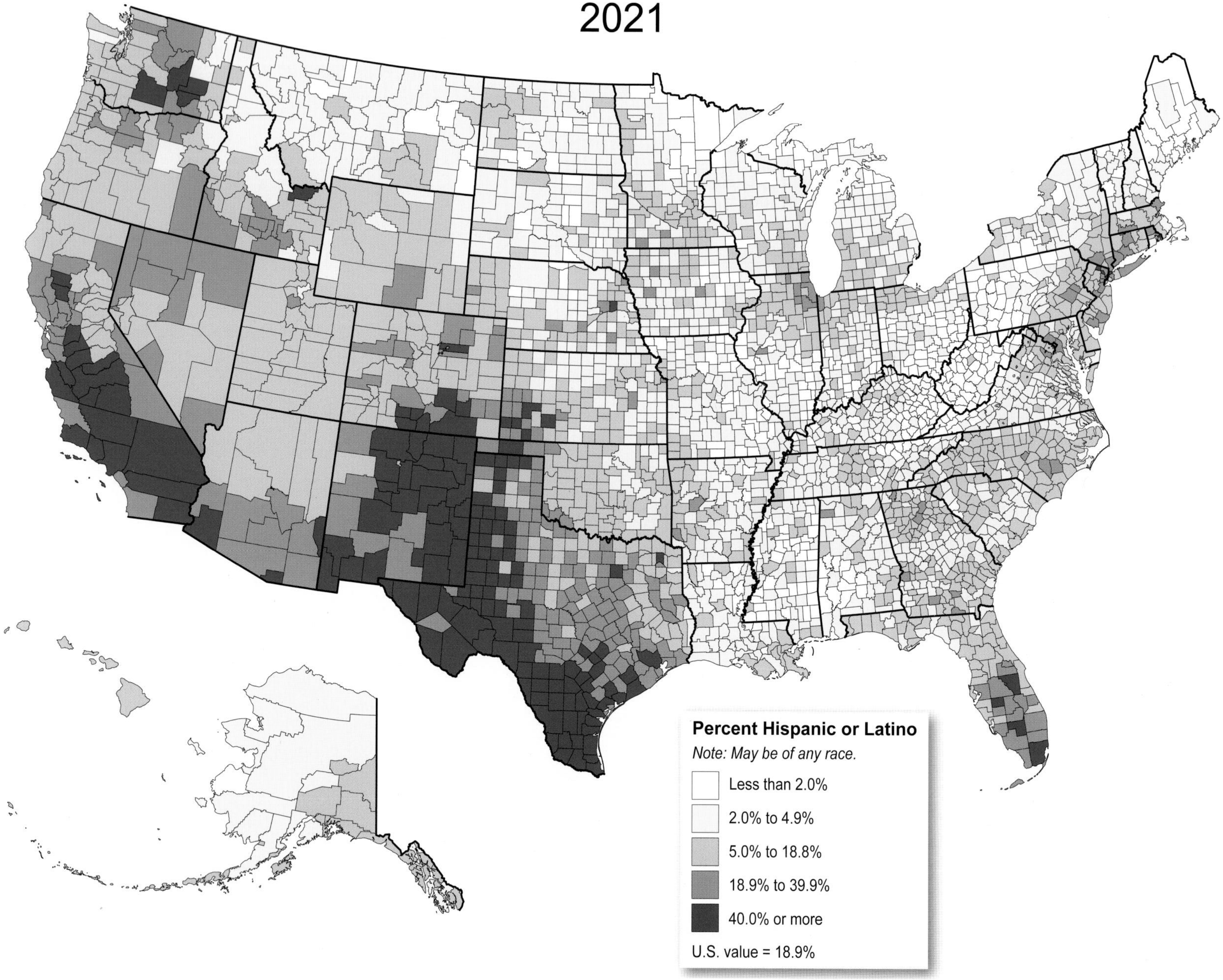

Population Under 15 Years Old

2021

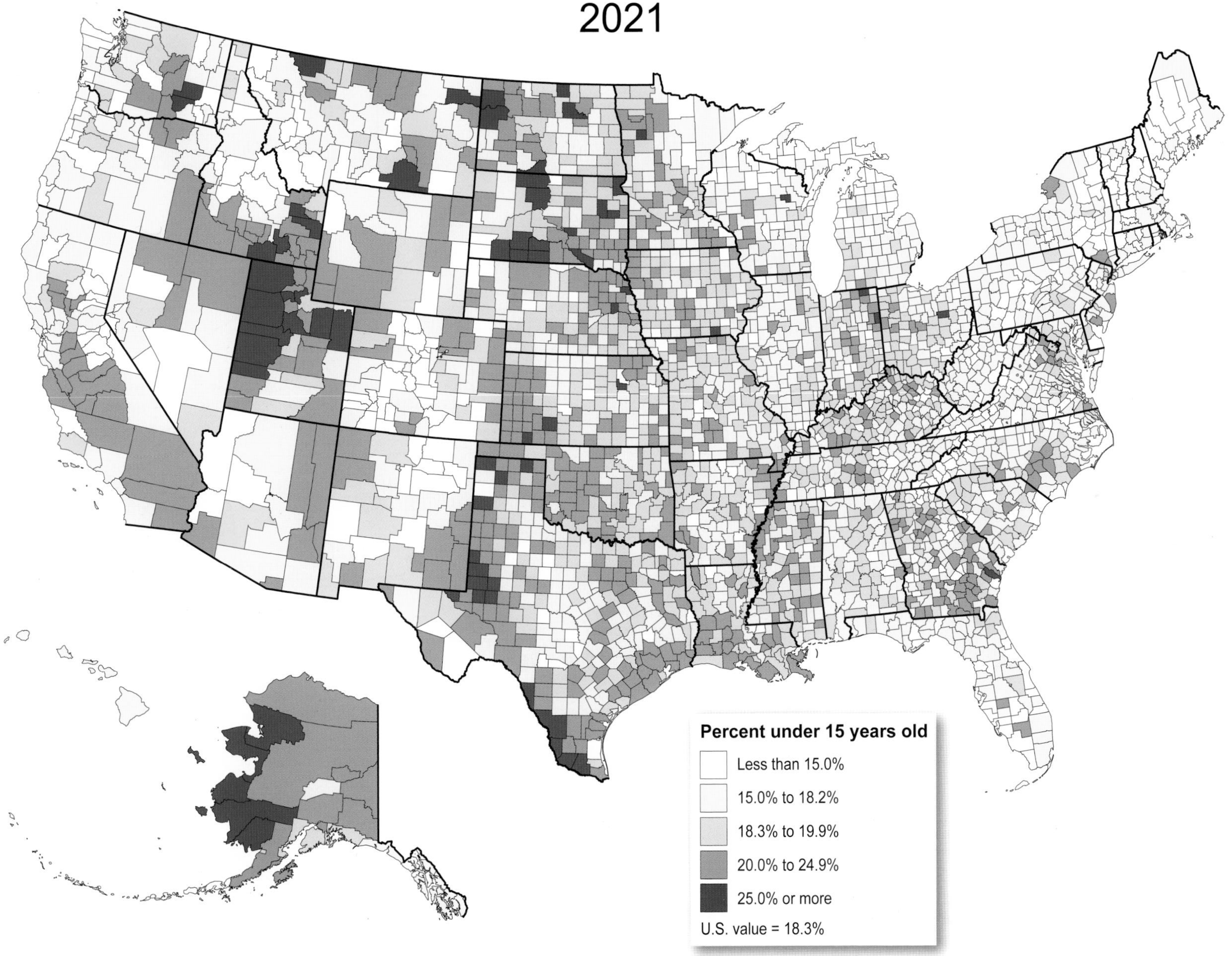

Population 65 Years Old and Over
2021

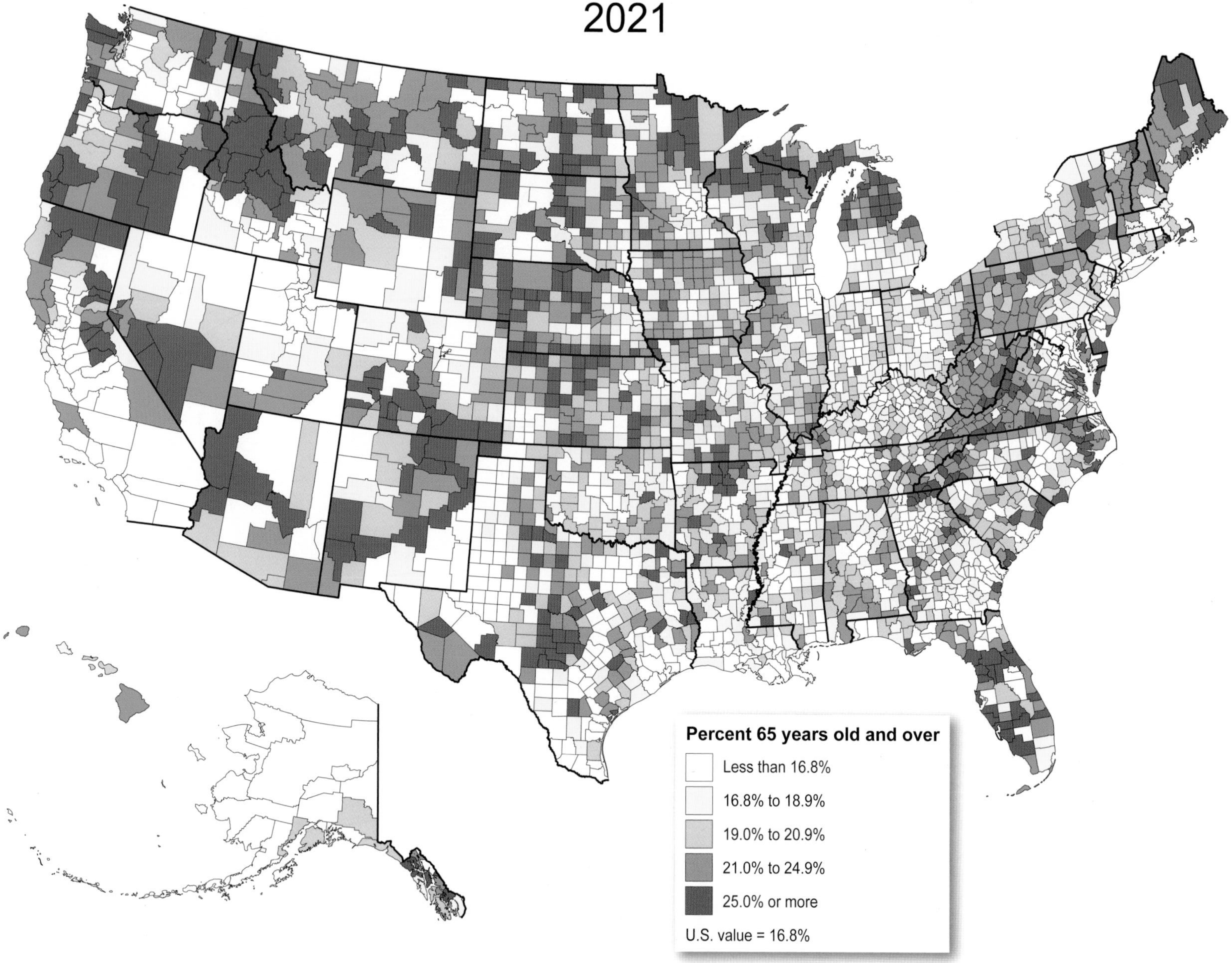

Population Density
2021

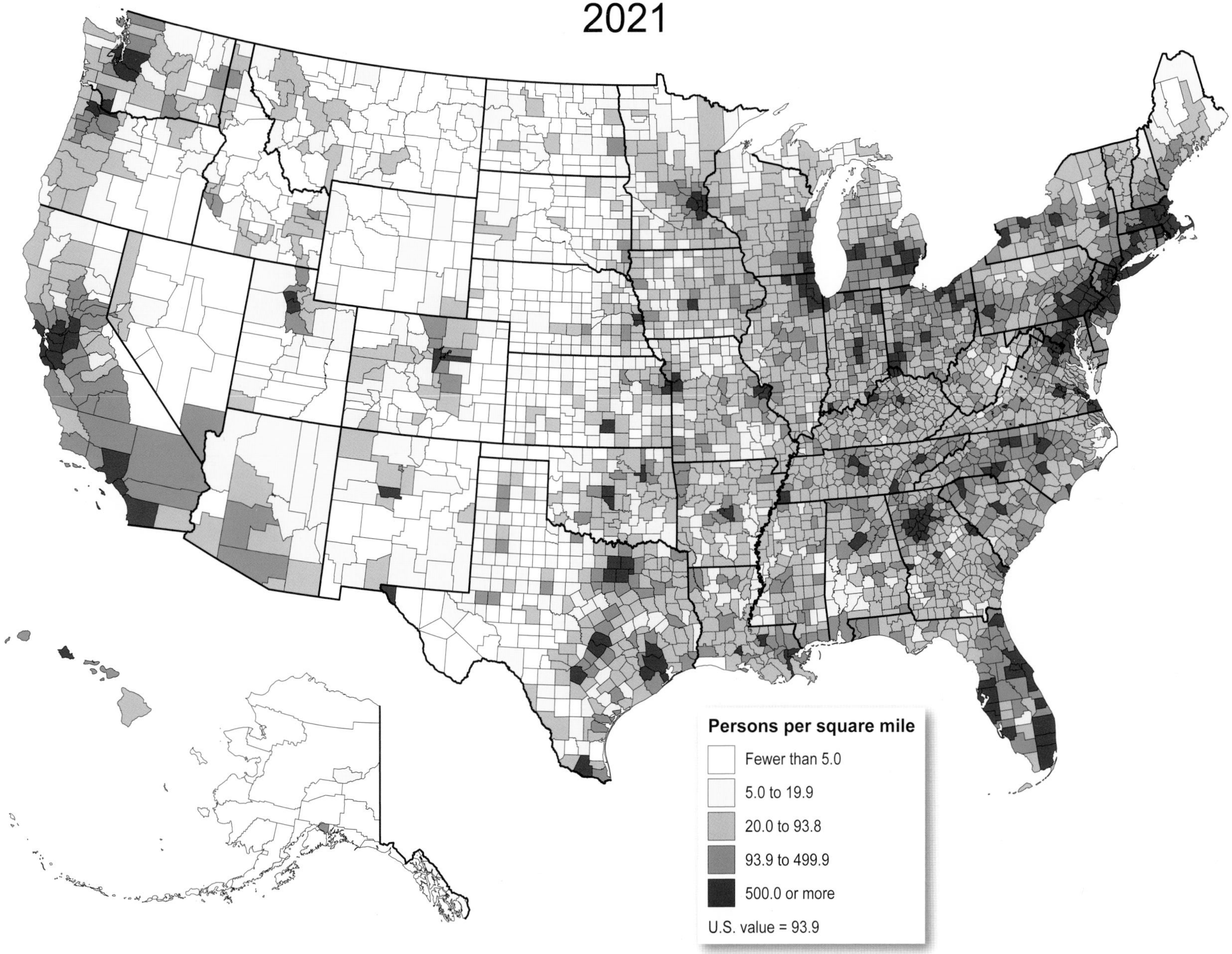

Unemployment Rate
2021

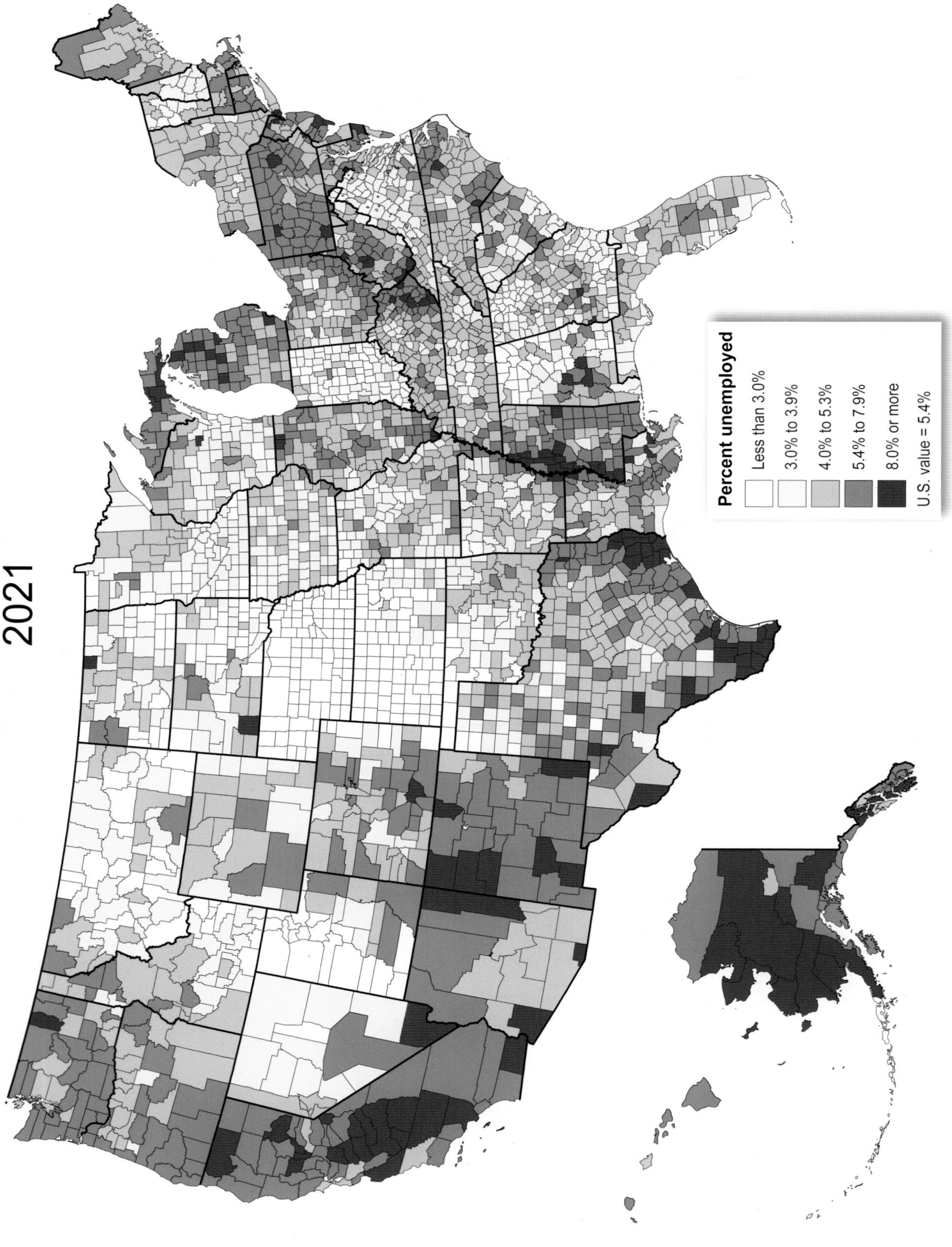

Earnings from Manufacturing

2020

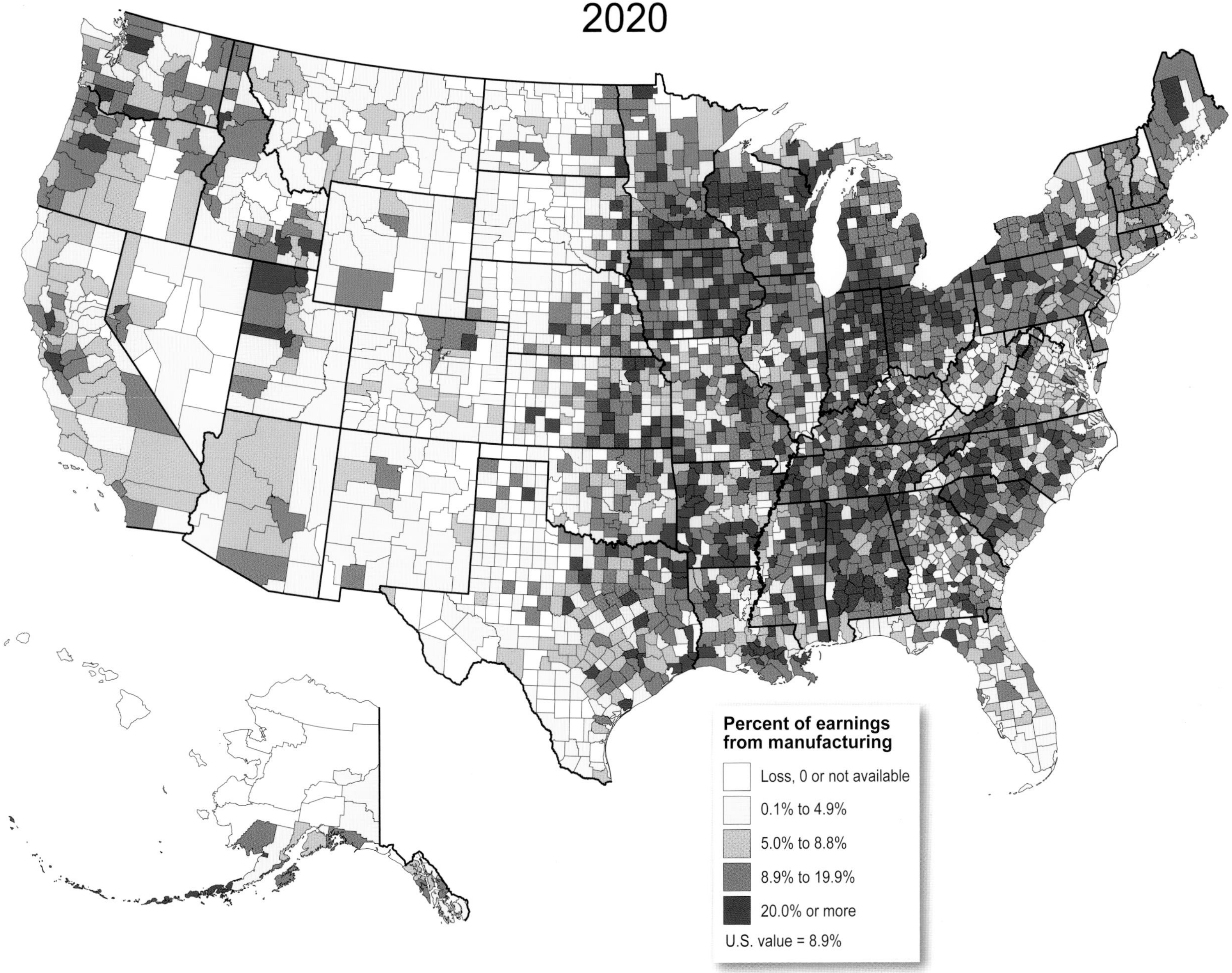

PART A.

States

(For explanation of symbols, see page viii)

Page

State Highlights and Rankings

Figure A-1. Fastest Growing States, 2020–2021

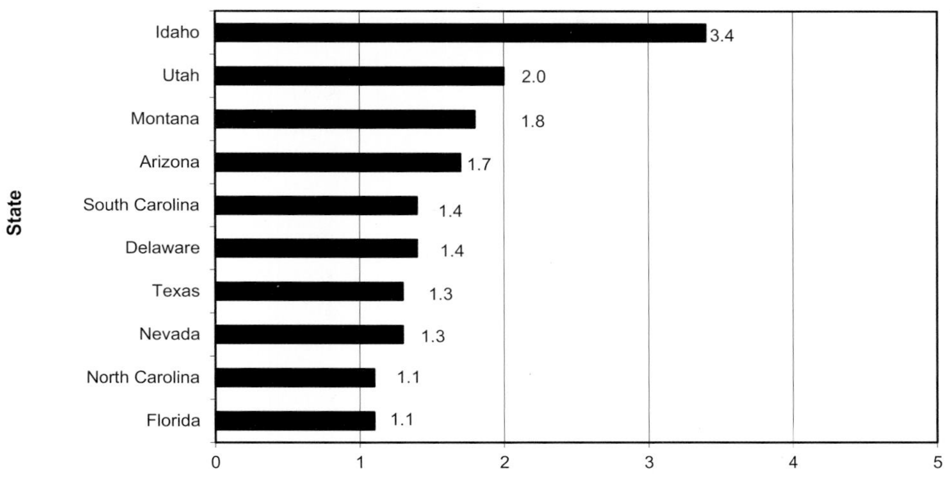

There is no simple relationship between population size and land area for most of the geographic entities included in this publication. According to the Census Bureau's 2021 estimates, state populations ranged from a high of over 39 million in California to a low of 578,803 in Wyoming. (The median population for states—with half having a larger population and half having a smaller population—was over 4.5 million people.) California was also one of the largest states in land area (ranking third). Alaska was by far the largest state in area; it was more than twice the size of Texas, the second-largest state, even though its population rank was close to the bottom (ranked 48th). Texas was also the second-largest state in terms of total population with over 29.0 million residents. At the other end of the geographic size spectrum were many of the New England states (with Rhode Island ranking as the smallest), plus Delaware, Hawaii, and New Jersey. As a consequence of differing area size and population rank, New Jersey was the most densely settled state, with 1,260.0 persons per square mile while Alaska was the least densely settled, with about 1.3 persons per square mile. California, which had the largest population and third-largest land area, ranked 12th in terms of population density (251.8 persons per square mile). The 15 most populous states remained almost unchanged between 2010 and 2021—Arizona moved into the top 15 while Indiana dropped out—but there were changes within their ranks. Florida became the 3rd most populous state, pushing ahead of New York while Georgia became the 8th most populous state. North Carolina moved up to 9th place while Michigan dropped to 10th.

Not surprisingly, states with higher population density also had higher proportions of developed land. According to the Department of Agriculture's most recent National Resources Inventory, 35.7 percent of New Jersey's land was developed. Connecticut had the second-highest proportion with 34.1 percent, followed by Massachusetts at 33.0 percent. Among the reporting states, Nevada had the lowest proportion of developed land, at just 0.8 percent, followed by Wyoming and Montana, with 1.1 percent and 1.2 percent, respectively. Nearly 85 percent of Nevada's land was owned by the federal government, stemming from a provision in Nevada's original constitution of 1864. This was by far the highest percentage in the nation. Federal land accounted for almost 21 percent of the United States' total land area. (Estimates are not available for Alaska and the District of Columbia. See Appendix F for definitions and additional information.)

The total population of the United States increased 7.4 percent between 2010 and 2020, with 22 states matching or exceeding this rate of growth and the remainder growing more slowly. Utah experienced the highest growth rate of any of the states (18.4 percent). Texas, Nevada, North Dakota, and Idaho all had growth rates above 15 percent. The District of Columbia ranked 49th by population size—more than either Vermont or Wyoming—and gained nearly 88,000 residents in the 10-year period. Texas has the second-largest population among all the states and gained nearly 4.0 million residents. North Dakota grew nearly 16 percent between 2010 and 2020. Despite its growth, North Dakota ranked 47th for total population and 48th for density, with only 11.2 persons per square mile. Texas was the only state that ranked among the top five states for total population and for population growth from 2010 to 2020. Florida, with the third-largest population, grew by 14.6 percent, increasing its population by over 2.7 million people. Maine and Wyoming both ranked among the 10 least populous states, as well as among the 10 states with the lowest population growth between 2010 and 2020. While most states have increased their populations in those ten years, the populations of West Virginia, Illinois, and Mississippi all declined. Louisiana's population has rebounded from a loss of about 250,000 residents after Hurricane Katrina hit the state in August 2005. Its 2021 population of over 4.6 million is higher than its 2005 estimated population on July 1 of that year.

States and the District of Columbia, Selected Rankings

Population, 2021			Land Area, 2020				Population density, 2021			
Population rank	State	Population [col 2]	Population rank	Land area	State	Land area (square miles) [col 1]	Population rank	Density rank	State	Density (per square mile) [col 4]
	United States	331,893,745			United States	3,533,044			United States	93.9
1	California	39,237,836	48	1	Alaska	571,017	49	1	District of Columbia	10,966.4
2	Texas	29,527,941	2	2	Texas	261,263	11	2	New Jersey	1,260.0
3	Florida	21,781,128	1	3	California	155,854	44	3	Rhode Island	1,059.7
4	New York	19,835,913	43	4	Montana	145,548	15	4	Massachusetts	895.4
5	Pennsylvania	12,964,056	36	5	New Mexico	121,312	29	5	Connecticut	744.5
6	Illinois	12,671,469	14	6	Arizona	113,653	19	6	Maryland	634.9
7	Ohio	11,780,017	32	7	Nevada	109,860	45	7	Delaware	515.0
8	Georgia	10,799,566	21	8	Colorado	103,638	4	8	New York	420.9
9	North Carolina	10,551,162	51	9	Wyoming	97,089	3	9	Florida	406.0
10	Michigan	10,050,811	27	10	Oregon	95,988	5	10	Pennsylvania	289.8
11	New Jersey	9,267,130	38	11	Idaho	82,645	7	11	Ohio	288.3
12	Virginia	8,642,274	30	12	Utah	82,377	1	12	California	251.8
13	Washington	7,738,692	35	13	Kansas	81,759	6	13	Illinois	228.3
14	Arizona	7,276,316	22	14	Minnesota	79,626	40	14	Hawaii	224.5
15	Massachusetts	6,984,723	37	15	Nebraska	76,817	12	15	Virginia	218.9
16	Tennessee	6,975,218	46	16	South Dakota	75,810	9	16	North Carolina	217.0
17	Indiana	6,805,985	47	17	North Dakota	68,995	17	17	Indiana	190.0
18	Missouri	6,168,187	18	18	Missouri	68,746	8	18	Georgia	187.1
19	Maryland	6,165,129	28	19	Oklahoma	68,596	10	19	Michigan	177.6
20	Wisconsin	5,895,908	13	20	Washington	66,455	23	20	South Carolina	172.7
21	Colorado	5,812,069	8	21	Georgia	57,716	16	21	Tennessee	169.1
22	Minnesota	5,707,390	10	22	Michigan	56,606	41	22	New Hampshire	155.1
23	South Carolina	5,190,705	31	23	Iowa	55,854	13	23	Washington	116.4
24	Alabama	5,039,877	6	24	Illinois	55,514	26	24	Kentucky	114.2
25	Louisiana	4,624,047	20	25	Wisconsin	54,167	2	25	Texas	113.0
26	Kentucky	4,509,394	3	26	Florida	53,648	20	26	Wisconsin	108.8
27	Oregon	4,246,155	33	27	Arkansas	52,038	25	27	Louisiana	107.0
28	Oklahoma	3,986,639	24	28	Alabama	50,647	24	28	Alabama	99.5
29	Connecticut	3,605,597	9	29	North Carolina	48,620	18	29	Missouri	89.7
30	Utah	3,337,975	4	30	New York	47,124	39	30	West Virginia	74.2
31	Iowa	3,193,079	34	31	Mississippi	46,926	22	31	Minnesota	71.7
32	Nevada	3,143,991	5	32	Pennsylvania	44,742	50	32	Vermont	70.0
33	Arkansas	3,025,891	25	33	Louisiana	43,205	14	33	Arizona	64.0
34	Mississippi	2,949,965	16	34	Tennessee	41,238	34	34	Mississippi	62.9
35	Kansas	2,934,582	7	35	Ohio	40,859	33	35	Arkansas	58.1
36	New Mexico	2,115,877	26	36	Kentucky	39,491	28	35	Oklahoma	58.1
37	Nebraska	1,963,692	12	37	Virginia	39,482	31	37	Iowa	57.2
38	Idaho	1,900,923	17	38	Indiana	35,826	21	38	Colorado	56.1
39	West Virginia	1,782,959	42	39	Maine	30,845	42	39	Maine	44.5
40	Hawaii	1,441,553	23	40	South Carolina	30,064	27	40	Oregon	44.2
41	New Hampshire	1,388,992	39	41	West Virginia	24,041	30	41	Utah	40.5
42	Maine	1,372,247	19	42	Maryland	9,711	35	42	Kansas	35.9
43	Montana	1,104,271	50	43	Vermont	9,218	32	43	Nevada	28.6
44	Rhode Island	1,095,610	41	44	New Hampshire	8,953	37	44	Nebraska	25.6
45	Delaware	1,003,384	15	45	Massachusetts	7,801	38	45	Idaho	23.0
46	South Dakota	895,376	11	46	New Jersey	7,355	36	46	New Mexico	17.4
47	North Dakota	774,948	40	47	Hawaii	6,422	46	47	South Dakota	11.8
48	Alaska	732,673	29	48	Connecticut	4,843	47	48	North Dakota	11.2
49	District of Columbia	670,050	45	49	Delaware	1,949	43	49	Montana	7.6
50	Vermont	645,570	44	50	Rhode Island	1,034	51	50	Wyoming	6.0
51	Wyoming	578,803	49	51	District of Columbia	61	48	51	Alaska	1.3

States and the District of Columbia, Selected Rankings

Percent population change, 2010–2020			
Population rank	Percent change rank	State	Percent change [col 35]
		United States	7.4
30	1	Utah	18.4
38	2	Idaho	17.3
2	3	Texas	15.9
47	4	North Dakota	15.8
32	5	Nevada	15.0
21	6	Colorado	14.8
49	7	District of Columbia	14.6
3	7	Florida	14.6
13	7	Washington	14.6
14	10	Arizona	11.9
23	11	South Carolina	10.7
8	12	Georgia	10.6
27	12	Oregon	10.6
45	14	Delaware	10.2
43	15	Montana	9.6
9	16	North Carolina	9.5
46	17	South Dakota	8.9
16	17	Tennessee	8.9
12	19	Virginia	7.9
22	20	Minnesota	7.6
15	21	Massachusetts	7.4
37	21	Nebraska	7.4
40	23	Hawaii	7.0
19	23	Maryland	7.0
1	25	California	6.1
11	26	New Jersey	5.7
28	27	Oklahoma	5.5
24	28	Alabama	5.1
17	29	Indiana	4.7
31	29	Iowa	4.7
41	31	New Hampshire	4.6
44	32	Rhode Island	4.3
4	33	New York	4.2
26	34	Kentucky	3.8
20	35	Wisconsin	3.6
48	36	Alaska	3.3
33	36	Arkansas	3.3
35	38	Kansas	3.0
18	39	Missouri	2.8
36	39	New Mexico	2.8
50	39	Vermont	2.8
25	42	Louisiana	2.7
42	43	Maine	2.6
5	44	Pennsylvania	2.4
7	45	Ohio	2.3
51	45	Wyoming	2.3
10	47	Michigan	2.0
29	48	Connecticut	0.9
6	49	Illinois	-0.1
34	50	Mississippi	-0.2
39	51	West Virginia	-3.2

Percent Under 15 years old, 2021			
Population rank	Under 18 years old rank	State	Percent under 18 years old [cols 10 + 11]
		United States	18.3
30	1	Utah	23.3
2	2	Texas	21.0
48	3	Alaska	20.6
46	4	South Dakota	20.5
37	5	Nebraska	20.4
38	6	Idaho	20.2
47	7	North Dakota	20.1
28	8	Oklahoma	20.0
35	9	Kansas	19.8
25	10	Louisiana	19.5
34	11	Mississippi	19.3
33	12	Arkansas	19.2
8	12	Georgia	19.2
17	12	Indiana	19.2
31	15	Iowa	19.0
22	15	Minnesota	19.0
51	17	Wyoming	18.8
26	18	Kentucky	18.6
18	19	Missouri	18.5
24	20	Alabama	18.4
1	20	California	18.4
32	20	Nevada	18.4
19	23	Maryland	18.3
36	23	New Mexico	18.3
16	23	Tennessee	18.3
14	26	Arizona	18.2
7	26	Ohio	18.2
6	28	Illinois	18.1
12	29	Virginia	18.0
13	29	Washington	18.0
11	31	New Jersey	17.9
9	31	North Carolina	17.9
23	33	South Carolina	17.8
40	34	Hawaii	17.7
20	34	Wisconsin	17.7
21	36	Colorado	17.6
10	36	Michigan	17.6
43	36	Montana	17.6
45	39	Delaware	17.1
4	39	New York	17.1
5	41	Pennsylvania	17.0
27	42	Oregon	16.7
39	43	West Virginia	16.5
49	44	District of Columbia	16.4
29	45	Connecticut	16.3
3	46	Florida	16.2
15	47	Massachusetts	16.0
44	48	Rhode Island	15.6
41	49	New Hampshire	15.0
42	50	Maine	14.9
50	51	Vermont	14.7

Percent 65 years old and over, 2021			
Population rank	65 years old and over rank	State	Percent 65 years old and over [cols 17 + 18 + 19]
		United States	16.8
42	1	Maine	21.6
3	2	Florida	21.2
39	3	West Virginia	20.7
50	4	Vermont	20.6
45	5	Delaware	20.1
43	6	Montana	19.7
40	7	Hawaii	19.6
41	8	New Hampshire	19.3
5	9	Pennsylvania	19.1
27	10	Oregon	18.6
23	10	South Carolina	18.6
36	12	New Mexico	18.5
14	13	Arizona	18.3
10	14	Michigan	18.1
44	14	Rhode Island	18.1
29	16	Connecticut	18.0
51	16	Wyoming	18.0
20	18	Wisconsin	17.9
7	19	Ohio	17.8
24	20	Alabama	17.7
31	20	Iowa	17.7
4	22	New York	17.6
18	23	Missouri	17.5
33	24	Arkansas	17.4
15	24	Massachusetts	17.4
46	24	South Dakota	17.4
26	27	Kentucky	17.1
16	28	Tennessee	17.0
9	29	North Carolina	16.9
11	30	New Jersey	16.8
38	31	Idaho	16.7
35	31	Kansas	16.7
22	31	Minnesota	16.7
34	31	Mississippi	16.7
6	35	Illinois	16.5
25	35	Louisiana	16.5
32	35	Nevada	16.5
17	38	Indiana	16.4
37	38	Nebraska	16.4
19	40	Maryland	16.3
12	40	Virginia	16.3
28	42	Oklahoma	16.2
13	42	Washington	16.2
47	44	North Dakota	16.1
1	45	California	15.2
21	46	Colorado	15.1
8	47	Georgia	14.6
48	48	Alaska	13.3
2	49	Texas	13.2
49	50	District of Columbia	12.9
30	51	Utah	11.7

States and the District of Columbia, Selected Rankings

Percent born in state of residence, 2020

Population rank	Born in state of residence rank	State	Percent born in state of residence [col 23]
		United States	58.2
25	1	Louisiana	77.6
10	2	Michigan	76.7
7	3	Ohio	74.9
5	4	Pennsylvania	71.8
20	5	Wisconsin	71.7
34	6	Mississippi	71.0
31	7	Iowa	70.8
39	8	West Virginia	68.8
24	9	Alabama	68.5
26	10	Kentucky	68.3
22	11	Minnesota	68.2
17	12	Indiana	68.0
6	13	Illinois	67.2
18	14	Missouri	66.6
37	15	Nebraska	65.1
46	16	South Dakota	64.3
47	17	North Dakota	63.5
4	18	New York	62.9
30	19	Utah	62.3
33	20	Arkansas	61.7
42	21	Maine	60.7
28	21	Oklahoma	60.7
2	23	Texas	60.3
35	24	Kansas	59.8
15	25	Massachusetts	59.4
16	26	Tennessee	58.8
1	27	California	56.3
40	28	Hawaii	55.4
9	29	North Carolina	55.3
23	30	South Carolina	55.0
8	31	Georgia	54.9
29	32	Connecticut	54.3
44	32	Rhode Island	54.3
36	34	New Mexico	53.5
43	35	Montana	53.4
11	36	New Jersey	51.9
12	37	Virginia	49.0
13	38	Washington	47.1
19	38	Maryland	47.1
50	40	Vermont	47.0
27	41	Oregon	45.6
38	41	Idaho	45.6
45	43	Delaware	44.7
48	44	Alaska	43.1
21	45	Colorado	42.2
51	46	Wyoming	42.1
41	47	New Hampshire	41.0
14	48	Arizona	39.9
3	49	Florida	36.3
49	50	District of Columbia	34.0
32	51	Nevada	27.1

Number of immigrants, 2020

Population rank	Immigrant rank	State	Number of immigrants [col 24]
		United States	707,362
1	1	California	138,996
4	2	New York	81,755
2	3	Texas	74,565
3	4	Florida	65,799
11	5	New Jersey	30,275
6	6	Illinois	27,377
15	7	Massachusetts	22,107
13	8	Washington	21,549
8	9	Georgia	18,282
12	10	Virginia	18,183
5	11	Pennsylvania	17,398
19	12	Maryland	16,049
9	13	North Carolina	13,989
10	14	Michigan	13,953
7	15	Ohio	12,651
14	16	Arizona	12,516
22	17	Minnesota	9,828
21	18	Colorado	9,223
29	19	Connecticut	7,802
32	20	Nevada	7,040
16	21	Tennessee	6,704
17	22	Indiana	6,551
27	23	Oregon	5,984
18	24	Missouri	5,836
30	25	Utah	5,421
20	26	Wisconsin	4,525
35	27	Kansas	3,943
26	28	Kentucky	3,932
31	29	Iowa	3,907
23	30	South Carolina	3,705
28	31	Oklahoma	3,031
36	32	New Mexico	2,925
24	33	Alabama	2,843
37	34	Nebraska	2,768
40	35	Hawaii	2,709
25	36	Louisiana	2,584
44	37	Rhode Island	2,292
33	38	Arkansas	2,224
38	39	Idaho	1,853
49	40	District of Columbia	1,653
41	41	New Hampshire	1,446
45	42	Delaware	1,301
34	43	Mississippi	1,020
47	44	North Dakota	1,001
42	45	Maine	935
46	46	South Dakota	885
48	47	Alaska	823
39	48	West Virginia	547
43	49	Montana	505
50	50	Vermont	495
51	51	Wyoming	241

Birth rate, 2020

Population rank	Birth rate rank	State	Birth rate (per 1,000 population) [col 98]
		United States	11.0
30	1	Utah	14.1
47	2	North Dakota	13.1
48	3	Alaska	13.0
37	4	Nebraska	12.5
2	4	Texas	12.5
49	6	District of Columbia	12.4
25	7	Louisiana	12.3
46	7	South Dakota	12.3
34	9	Mississippi	12.0
28	9	Oklahoma	12.0
38	11	Idaho	11.8
35	11	Kansas	11.8
24	13	Alabama	11.7
33	14	Arkansas	11.6
17	14	Indiana	11.6
26	16	Kentucky	11.5
8	17	Georgia	11.4
31	17	Iowa	11.4
16	17	Tennessee	11.4
19	20	Maryland	11.3
18	20	Missouri	11.3
40	22	Hawaii	11.2
22	22	Minnesota	11.2
11	24	New Jersey	11.0
9	24	North Carolina	11.0
7	24	Ohio	11.0
12	24	Virginia	11.0
4	28	New York	10.8
13	28	Washington	10.8
1	30	California	10.7
32	30	Nevada	10.7
23	30	South Carolina	10.7
21	33	Colorado	10.6
6	33	Illinois	10.6
45	35	Delaware	10.5
51	35	Wyoming	10.5
14	37	Arizona	10.4
10	37	Michigan	10.4
36	37	New Mexico	10.4
20	37	Wisconsin	10.4
5	41	Pennsylvania	10.2
43	42	Montana	10.0
39	43	West Virginia	9.7
3	44	Florida	9.6
15	44	Massachusetts	9.6
44	44	Rhode Island	9.6
29	47	Connecticut	9.4
27	47	Oregon	9.4
41	49	New Hampshire	8.6
42	50	Maine	8.5
50	51	Vermont	8.2

Figure A-2. States with the Highest Proportion of Foreign-Born Population and States with the Highest Proportion of Population Born in State of Residence, 2020

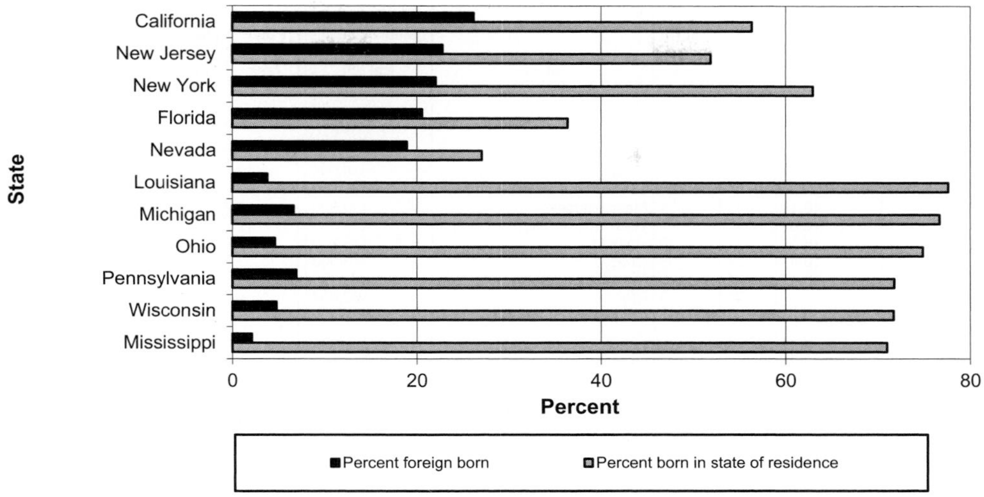

The U.S. median age increased slightly from 37.2 years in 2010 to 38.7 years in 2021, primarily caused by the aging Baby Boomer population. This increase was much less than the jump from 32.1 years to 35.3 years between 1990 and 2000. From 2010 to 2021, the population between 65 and 74 years showed the largest proportional increase, while the proportion between 5 and 17 years showed the largest decrease. The 25–34 Millennial age group grew from 13.3 percent of the population to 13.7 percent of the population, and they outnumber the peak Baby Boomers in the 55–64 age group. The median age by state ranged from 31.6 years in Utah to 45.0 years in Maine. Utah had the highest proportion of young residents; in 2021, 23.3 percent of the state's population was younger than 15 years old. The population age 65 and over ranged from 11.7 percent in Utah to 21.6 percent in Maine. Alaska and North Dakota had the lowest proportions of female residents and were among just sixteen states in which men outnumbered women. The District of Columbia had the highest proportion of female residents with 52.4 percent, followed by Alabama and Delaware at 51.4 percent.

Natural growth is the difference between the number of births and the number of deaths. Vermont had the fewest births from April 2020 to July 2021. During this time period, 25 states had more deaths than births and 26 states had more births than deaths. During the previous decade, from 2010 to 2020, only Maine and West Virginia had more deaths than births. Additionally, due to net migration, 18 states and the District of Columbia experienced a population loss from 2020 to 2021. California, the largest state in the nation, had 115,000 more births than deaths but lost 415,000 residents through net migration. From April 2020 to July 2021, California gained 13,681 residents from foreign countries and lost 429,383 residents to other states. Florida had a net gain of over 305,000 new residents during this period, with 86.5 percent from other states and 13.5 percent from other countries. Texas gained nearly 240,000 new residents, 88 percent of them from other states. Nineteen states had a net loss of residents due to migration including New York, which lost 406,257 residents to other states but gained 18,860 new residents from other countries.

In seven states, 70 percent or more of the residents were born in that same state. Louisiana ranked highest with 77.6 percent. The ten highest rates were mainly in the Midwest and the South. Fourteen states and the District of Columbia had proportions less than 50 percent. Nevada had the lowest proportion by far, with just 27.1 percent of its residents having been born in the state. Nationally, 58.2 percent of Americans lived in the state of their birth.

The U.S. birth rate in 2020 was 11.0 per 1,000 population, the lowest level yet in a steady decrease in the 21st century. Utah had the highest birth rate in the nation, with 14.1 births per 1,000 population. North Dakota had the second highest birth rate at 13.1 followed by Alaska with a birth rate of 13.0. Nine states had birth rates below 10 births per 1,000 population. Utah had the lowest crude death rate with 5.8 deaths per 1,000 population followed by Alaska with a crude death rate of 6.3. However, both states had relatively young populations. (In Utah, 39.7 percent of the population was under 25 years old while 33.7 percent of the population was under 25 in Alaska.) Once adjusted for age, Alaska's death rate increased to 7.0, and Utah's to 6.9, just under the U.S. rate of 7.2. West Virginia, Mississippi, and Maine had the highest crude death rates in the nation. West Virginia and Mississippi had the highest age-adjusted death rate followed by Kentucky, all with a mix of younger and older residents. Maine had the highest proportion of senior citizens followed by Florida. However, Florida also had a high proportion of younger people, which helped give the state a crude death rate of 9.6 per 1,000 population, ranking it 19th, tying with Delaware. When Florida's death rate was age-adjusted, it dropped to 6.5, which was well below the national age-adjusted rate of 7.2 and among the lowest ten states. Hawaii had the lowest age-adjusted death rate at 5.7, one of 13 states with rates below 7.0. Mississippi, Louisiana, and Alabama had the highest infant mortality rates, while New Hampshire, Massachusetts, and California had the lowest infant death rates.

States and the District of Columbia, Selected Rankings

Percent of households with no internet subscription, 2020

Population rank	Lack of internet rank	State	Percent of households with no internet [col 92]
		United States	12.0
34	1	Mississippi	20.3
39	2	West Virginia	18.4
33	3	Arkansas	18.2
36	4	New Mexico	18.1
23	5	South Carolina	16.6
25	6	Louisiana	16.5
24	7	Alabama	16.4
28	8	Oklahoma	15.4
16	9	Tennessee	15.2
50	9	Vermont	15.2
26	11	Kentucky	14.6
18	12	Missouri	14.1
42	13	Maine	14.0
43	14	Montana	13.9
9	14	North Carolina	13.9
31	16	Iowa	13.8
46	16	South Dakota	13.8
5	18	Pennsylvania	13.7
20	19	Wisconsin	13.2
8	20	Georgia	12.7
10	20	Michigan	12.7
17	22	Indiana	12.6
4	23	New York	12.5
7	23	Ohio	12.5
51	25	Wyoming	12.4
47	26	North Dakota	12.3
6	27	Illinois	12.0
35	28	Kansas	11.9
37	29	Nebraska	11.7
2	29	Texas	11.7
49	31	District of Columbia	11.6
14	32	Arizona	11.5
3	32	Florida	11.5
12	32	Virginia	11.5
22	35	Minnesota	11.0
32	36	Nevada	10.9
44	37	Rhode Island	10.8
45	38	Delaware	10.3
29	39	Connecticut	9.9
41	39	New Hampshire	9.9
11	41	New Jersey	9.8
19	42	Maryland	9.7
38	43	Idaho	9.6
15	44	Massachusetts	9.5
27	45	Oregon	9.4
40	46	Hawaii	9.0
48	47	Alaska	8.8
1	48	California	8.6
13	49	Washington	8.4
21	50	Colorado	8.3
30	51	Utah	8.2

Median value of owner-occupied housing units, 2020

Population rank	Median value rank	State	Median value (dollars) [col 85]
		United States	253,600
49	1	District of Columbia	672,700
40	2	Hawaii	648,000
1	3	California	593,400
15	4	Massachusetts	439,800
13	5	Washington	419,500
21	6	Colorado	415,700
27	7	Oregon	373,500
11	8	New Jersey	364,300
30	9	Utah	360,800
4	10	New York	353,100
19	11	Maryland	344,700
32	12	Nevada	333,000
12	13	Virginia	305,100
44	14	Rhode Island	302,200
41	15	New Hampshire	297,800
38	16	Idaho	290,400
48	17	Alaska	288,100
29	18	Connecticut	287,500
14	19	Arizona	278,400
43	20	Montana	272,600
45	21	Delaware	272,200
22	22	Minnesota	263,300
3	23	Florida	261,500
51	24	Wyoming	236,600
50	25	Vermont	235,000
8	26	Georgia	218,600
2	27	Texas	214,400
6	28	Illinois	214,300
20	29	Wisconsin	212,600
42	30	Maine	211,000
9	31	North Carolina	207,300
47	32	North Dakota	205,200
5	33	Pennsylvania	203,800
16	34	Tennessee	203,400
23	35	South Carolina	189,500
46	36	South Dakota	188,900
36	37	New Mexico	188,000
37	38	Nebraska	181,900
10	39	Michigan	179,500
18	40	Missouri	176,000
25	41	Louisiana	174,000
35	42	Kansas	166,200
31	43	Iowa	164,000
7	43	Ohio	164,000
17	45	Indiana	163,500
24	46	Alabama	162,300
26	47	Kentucky	160,700
28	48	Oklahoma	152,500
33	49	Arkansas	141,800
34	50	Mississippi	135,100
39	51	West Virginia	130,500

Median gross rent of renter-occupied housing units, 2020

Population rank	Median rent rank	State	Median rent (dollars) [col 87]
		United States	$1,129
40	1	Hawaii	$1,704
49	2	District of Columbia	$1,701
1	3	California	$1,661
15	4	Massachusetts	$1,449
19	5	Maryland	$1,425
21	6	Colorado	$1,401
13	6	Washington	$1,401
11	8	New Jersey	$1,394
4	9	New York	$1,358
3	10	Florida	$1,270
12	11	Virginia	$1,269
27	12	Oregon	$1,239
32	13	Nevada	$1,229
29	14	Connecticut	$1,217
48	15	Alaska	$1,203
41	16	New Hampshire	$1,179
30	17	Utah	$1,158
14	18	Arizona	$1,149
45	19	Delaware	$1,133
2	20	Texas	$1,113
8	21	Georgia	$1,080
22	22	Minnesota	$1,070
44	23	Rhode Island	$1,069
6	24	Illinois	$1,065
50	25	Vermont	$1,007
5	26	Pennsylvania	$979
9	27	North Carolina	$943
23	28	South Carolina	$937
38	29	Idaho	$923
10	30	Michigan	$908
16	31	Tennessee	$907
42	32	Maine	$903
35	33	Kansas	$877
20	34	Wisconsin	$872
37	35	Nebraska	$870
25	36	Louisiana	$866
43	37	Montana	$854
17	38	Indiana	$850
18	39	Missouri	$841
36	40	New Mexico	$834
7	41	Ohio	$831
28	42	Oklahoma	$811
24	43	Alabama	$800
51	43	Wyoming	$800
26	45	Kentucky	$795
31	46	Iowa	$785
34	47	Mississippi	$779
33	48	Arkansas	$760
47	49	North Dakota	$748
46	50	South Dakota	$724
39	51	West Virginia	$723

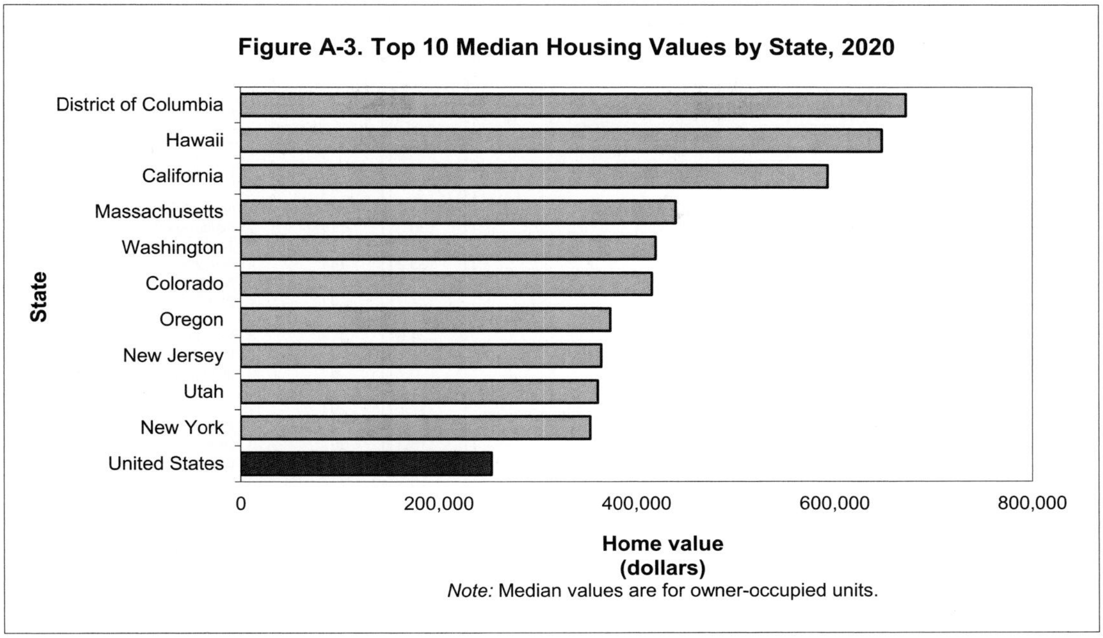

In 2020, the District of Columbia and Maryland had the highest percentage of homeowners with mortgages at 76.9 and 71.1 percent, respectively. Nationally, 60.7 percent of homeowners had mortgages. Twenty-six states and the District of Columbia exceeded this average. Mississippi at 49.7 percent and West Virginia at 46.8 percent were the only two states in the nation where under 50 percent of homeowners had mortgages. Thirteen states and the District of Columbia had median home values exceeding $300,000 in 2020, led by District of Columbia with a median home value of $672,700 and Hawaii with a value of $648,000. Nationally, the median value of owner-occupied housing units was $253,600. Hawaii and the District of Columbia also had the highest median gross rent at $1,704 and $1,701, respectively. Five additional states had rents exceeding $1,400: California, Massachusetts, Maryland, Colorado, and Washington.

Many minority groups had above-average growth rates since 2000. Currently, in five states and the District of Columbia, the minority population outnumbers the non-Hispanic White population. Nationally, 61.4 percent of the U.S. population was non-Hispanic White alone or in combination, but the racial and ethnic compositions of the states varied widely. In Hawaii, the state with the highest proportion of minorities, Asian and Pacific Islander alone or in combination was the largest race group representing 75.4 percent of the state's population. Hispanic or Latino residents made up over 50 percent of New Mexico's population and over 40 percent of residents in both California and Texas. The District of Columbia had the highest proportion of Black residents at 45.7 percent, down from 60.5 percent in 2000. Among the states, Mississippi and Louisiana ranked first and second, with Black populations of 38.3 and 33.4 percent, respectively. Alaska had the highest proportion of American Indians and Alaska Natives, who made up 19.3 percent of the population. Oklahoma, New Mexico, and South Dakota all had high proportions of American Indian populations. As might be expected, the states with the largest number of minorities were among the states with the highest total populations. New York was home to approximately 3.0 million Black residents and California had the largest number of Hispanics, Asian and Pacific Islanders, and American Indians and Alaska Natives. California had over 390,000 non-Hispanic American Indian and Alaska Native residents, though they made up just 1.0 percent of the state's population. Despite having only about 85,000 Native American residents, South Dakota had the second-highest proportion in the nation at 9.6 percent.

States and the District of Columbia, Selected Rankings

Percent White, not Hispanic or Latino, alone or in combination, 2020				Percent Black, not Hispanic or Latino, alone or in combination, 2020				Percent Hispanic or Latino,[1] 2020			
Population rank	Percent White rank	State	Percent White [col 5]	Population rank	Percent Black rank	State	Percent Black [col 6]	Population rank	Hispanic or Latino rank	State	Percent Hispanic or Latino [col 9]
		United States	61.4			United States	13.7			United States	18.9
42	1	Maine	94.2	49	1	District of Columbia	45.7	36	1	New Mexico	50.1
50	2	Vermont	94.1	34	2	Mississippi	38.3	1	2	California	40.2
39	3	West Virginia	93.3	25	3	Louisiana	33.4	2	2	Texas	40.2
41	4	New Hampshire	90.7	8	4	Georgia	33.2	14	4	Arizona	32.3
43	5	Montana	88.0	19	5	Maryland	31.8	32	5	Nevada	29.9
31	6	Iowa	85.9	24	6	Alabama	27.4	3	6	Florida	26.8
26	7	Kentucky	85.4	23	7	South Carolina	27.2	21	7	Colorado	22.3
47	8	North Dakota	85.2	45	8	Delaware	24.0	11	8	New Jersey	21.5
51	8	Wyoming	85.2	9	9	North Carolina	22.6	4	9	New York	19.5
38	10	Idaho	83.2	12	10	Virginia	20.7	6	10	Illinois	18.0
46	11	South Dakota	83.0	16	11	Tennessee	17.7	29	11	Connecticut	17.7
20	12	Wisconsin	81.9	3	12	Florida	16.5	44	12	Rhode Island	17.1
18	13	Missouri	80.9	33	13	Arkansas	16.3	30	13	Utah	14.8
22	14	Minnesota	80.4	4	14	New York	15.5	27	14	Oregon	14.0
7	15	Ohio	79.8	6	15	Illinois	15.1	13	15	Washington	13.7
17	16	Indiana	79.5	10	15	Michigan	15.1	38	16	Idaho	13.3
30	17	Utah	79.4	7	17	Ohio	14.3	15	17	Massachusetts	12.8
37	18	Nebraska	79.3	11	18	New Jersey	13.9	35	18	Kansas	12.7
27	19	Oregon	77.4	2	19	Texas	13.0	37	19	Nebraska	12.0
35	20	Kansas	77.3	18	20	Missouri	12.7	28	20	Oklahoma	11.7
10	21	Michigan	76.5	5	21	Pennsylvania	12.1	49	21	District of Columbia	11.5
5	21	Pennsylvania	76.5	29	22	Connecticut	11.7	40	22	Hawaii	11.1
16	23	Tennessee	74.9	17	23	Indiana	11.1	19	22	Maryland	11.1
33	24	Arkansas	73.2	32	24	Nevada	11.0	51	24	Wyoming	10.6
44	25	Rhode Island	72.3	26	25	Kentucky	9.6	8	25	Georgia	10.2
15	26	Massachusetts	71.9	28	26	Oklahoma	9.1	9	25	North Carolina	10.2
13	27	Washington	70.1	15	27	Massachusetts	8.5	12	25	Virginia	10.2
21	28	Colorado	69.3	22	28	Minnesota	8.4	45	28	Delaware	10.1
28	28	Oklahoma	69.3	44	29	Rhode Island	7.5	5	29	Pennsylvania	8.4
24	30	Alabama	66.4	20	30	Wisconsin	7.4	33	30	Arkansas	8.3
29	31	Connecticut	66.3	35	31	Kansas	7.2	17	31	Indiana	7.7
48	32	Alaska	65.7	1	32	California	6.5	48	32	Alaska	7.5
23	33	South Carolina	65.1	37	33	Nebraska	6.1	20	32	Wisconsin	7.5
9	34	North Carolina	63.7	14	34	Arizona	5.6	31	34	Iowa	6.7
12	35	Virginia	62.9	13	34	Washington	5.6	23	35	South Carolina	6.4
45	36	Delaware	62.8	31	36	Iowa	5.2	16	36	Tennessee	6.1
6	37	Illinois	61.6	21	37	Colorado	5.1	22	37	Minnesota	5.8
25	38	Louisiana	59.3	48	38	Alaska	4.8	25	38	Louisiana	5.6
34	39	Mississippi	57.1	39	39	West Virginia	4.7	10	38	Michigan	5.6
4	40	New York	56.3	47	40	North Dakota	4.0	24	40	Alabama	4.8
14	41	Arizona	55.2	40	41	Hawaii	3.1	18	41	Missouri	4.7
11	42	New Jersey	54.9	46	41	South Dakota	3.1	46	42	South Dakota	4.6
3	43	Florida	54.2	27	43	Oregon	2.9	41	43	New Hampshire	4.4
8	44	Georgia	52.8	36	44	New Mexico	2.5	47	43	North Dakota	4.4
19	45	Maryland	51.2	42	45	Maine	2.3	43	45	Montana	4.3
32	46	Nevada	49.8	41	46	New Hampshire	2.2	7	45	Ohio	4.3
2	47	Texas	41.7	50	47	Vermont	2.0	26	47	Kentucky	4.2
49	48	District of Columbia	39.2	30	48	Utah	1.8	34	48	Mississippi	3.5
1	49	California	37.8	51	49	Wyoming	1.6	50	49	Vermont	2.2
36	50	New Mexico	37.3	38	50	Idaho	1.2	42	50	Maine	2.0
40	51	Hawaii	36.5	43	51	Montana	1.1	39	51	West Virginia	1.9

1. May be of any race.

States and the District of Columbia, Selected Rankings

Percent high school graduates or more,[1] 2020

Population rank	Percent high school graduates rank	State	Percent high school graduates [col 115]
		United States	89.4
43	1	Montana	94.4
50	2	Vermont	94.2
41	3	New Hampshire	94.1
30	4	Utah	94.0
49	5	District of Columbia	93.8
22	6	Minnesota	93.8
51	7	Wyoming	93.8
48	8	Alaska	93.7
42	9	Maine	93.6
47	10	North Dakota	93.5
40	11	Hawaii	93.3
20	12	Wisconsin	93.1
31	13	Iowa	93.1
21	14	Colorado	92.7
46	15	South Dakota	92.2
13	16	Washington	92.1
10	17	Michigan	92.0
27	18	Oregon	91.9
37	19	Nebraska	91.9
35	20	Kansas	91.8
29	21	Connecticut	91.6
5	22	Pennsylvania	91.6
7	23	Ohio	91.5
12	24	Virginia	91.4
18	25	Missouri	91.4
15	26	Massachusetts	91.3
38	27	Idaho	91.3
19	28	Maryland	91.1
45	29	Delaware	91.0
11	30	New Jersey	90.9
6	31	Illinois	90.4
9	32	North Carolina	90.3
17	33	Indiana	90.2
44	34	Rhode Island	90.1
16	35	Tennessee	89.7
3	36	Florida	89.6
23	37	South Carolina	89.4
8	38	Georgia	89.3
28	39	Oklahoma	89.2
39	40	West Virginia	89.1
14	41	Arizona	89.1
26	42	Kentucky	88.7
33	43	Arkansas	88.2
24	44	Alabama	88.0
36	45	New Mexico	87.8
4	46	New York	87.8
32	47	Nevada	87.2
25	48	Louisiana	86.9
34	49	Mississippi	86.8
2	50	Texas	85.8
1	51	California	84.4

Percent college graduates (bachelor's degree or more),[1] 2020

Population rank	Percent college graduates rank	State	Percent college graduates [col 116]
		United States	35.1
49	1	District of Columbia	63.6
15	2	Massachusetts	46.9
21	3	Colorado	44.2
19	4	Maryland	43.1
11	4	New Jersey	43.1
29	6	Connecticut	42.4
50	7	Vermont	42.1
12	8	Virginia	42.0
41	9	New Hampshire	40.2
4	10	New York	39.5
13	11	Washington	38.4
44	12	Rhode Island	38.0
22	13	Minnesota	37.9
6	14	Illinois	37.6
1	15	California	36.9
30	15	Utah	36.9
27	17	Oregon	36.3
40	18	Hawaii	35.5
35	19	Kansas	35.1
8	20	Georgia	34.8
9	20	North Carolina	34.8
45	22	Delaware	34.7
43	23	Montana	34.6
5	24	Pennsylvania	34.0
3	25	Florida	33.7
42	26	Maine	33.5
37	27	Nebraska	33.3
2	28	Texas	33.2
14	29	Arizona	33.0
10	30	Michigan	32.1
48	31	Alaska	31.9
18	31	Missouri	31.9
47	33	North Dakota	31.8
20	33	Wisconsin	31.8
23	35	South Carolina	31.7
38	36	Idaho	30.9
16	37	Tennessee	30.7
7	38	Ohio	30.6
36	39	New Mexico	30.1
31	40	Iowa	29.5
17	41	Indiana	28.9
46	42	South Dakota	28.4
51	43	Wyoming	28.2
32	44	Nevada	28.0
24	45	Alabama	27.8
26	46	Kentucky	27.4
25	47	Louisiana	27.2
28	48	Oklahoma	27.0
33	49	Arkansas	24.9
34	50	Mississippi	24.5
39	51	West Virginia	23.1

Median household income, 2020

Population rank	Median income rank	State	Median income (dollars) [col 123]
		United States	67,340
49	1	District of Columbia	96,762
19	2	Maryland	88,742
15	3	Massachusetts	87,328
11	4	New Jersey	87,016
40	5	Hawaii	86,391
1	6	California	83,056
41	7	New Hampshire	80,972
13	8	Washington	80,408
48	9	Alaska	80,197
29	10	Connecticut	79,719
12	11	Virginia	79,217
30	12	Utah	77,827
21	13	Colorado	77,673
44	14	Rhode Island	75,682
22	15	Minnesota	75,523
4	16	New York	73,398
6	17	Illinois	71,240
45	18	Delaware	70,911
27	19	Oregon	67,927
50	20	Vermont	67,428
51	21	Wyoming	66,432
2	22	Texas	66,031
5	23	Pennsylvania	64,910
20	24	Wisconsin	64,868
14	25	Arizona	64,777
37	26	Nebraska	64,591
32	27	Nevada	64,574
35	28	Kansas	63,321
8	29	Georgia	62,844
38	30	Idaho	62,774
31	31	Iowa	62,209
47	32	North Dakota	61,987
3	33	Florida	61,736
10	34	Michigan	61,497
17	35	Indiana	60,813
46	36	South Dakota	60,643
7	37	Ohio	60,338
9	38	North Carolina	59,580
18	39	Missouri	58,838
42	40	Maine	58,782
43	41	Montana	57,211
23	42	South Carolina	56,973
16	43	Tennessee	56,951
28	44	Oklahoma	54,536
26	45	Kentucky	54,191
24	46	Alabama	53,956
36	47	New Mexico	52,059
25	48	Louisiana	51,730
33	49	Arkansas	51,183
39	50	West Virginia	49,400
34	51	Mississippi	47,247

1. Population 25 years and older.

States and the District of Columbia, Selected Rankings

Unemployment rate, 2021				Per capita state taxes, 2020				Exports of goods by state of origin, 2021			
Population rank	Unemployment rate rank	State	Unemployment rate [col 171]	Population rank	State taxes rank	State	State taxes per capita (dollars) [col 337]	Population rank	Exports rank	State	Exports (milions of dollars) [col 119]
		United States	5.4			United States	X			United States	1,754,578
1	1	California	7.3	47	1	North Dakota	5,666.0	2	1	Texas	375,324
32	2	Nevada	7.2	50	2	Vermont	5,486.5	1	2	California	175,126
4	3	New York	6.9	40	3	Hawaii	5,477.9	4	3	New York	84,874
36	4	New Mexico	6.8	29	4	Connecticut	5,173.0	25	4	Louisiana	76,821
49	5	District of Columbia	6.6	4	5	New York	4,795.1	6	5	Illinois	65,904
48	6	Alaska	6.4	22	6	Minnesota	4,735.6	10	6	Michigan	55,534
29	7	Connecticut	6.3	45	7	Delaware	4,615.8	3	7	Florida	55,462
11	7	New Jersey	6.3	15	8	Massachusetts	4,588.4	13	8	Washington	53,645
5	7	Pennsylvania	6.3	1	9	California	4,368.1	7	9	Ohio	50,422
6	10	Illinois	6.1	11	10	New Jersey	4,270.0	11	10	New Jersey	49,528
10	11	Michigan	5.9	19	11	Maryland	3,943.8	5	11	Pennsylvania	44,725
19	12	Maryland	5.8	13	12	Washington	3,771.1	8	12	Georgia	42,366
40	13	Hawaii	5.7	6	13	Illinois	3,597.6	17	13	Indiana	41,140
15	13	Massachusetts	5.7	42	14	Maine	3,593.1	16	14	Tennessee	34,655
2	13	Texas	5.7	20	15	Wisconsin	3,448.7	9	15	North Carolina	33,446
34	16	Mississippi	5.6	36	16	New Mexico	3,394.5	15	16	Massachusetts	32,453
44	16	Rhode Island	5.6	33	17	Arkansas	3,384.0	23	17	South Carolina	29,673
25	18	Louisiana	5.5	51	18	Wyoming	3,371.7	27	18	Oregon	29,556
21	19	Colorado	5.4	31	19	Iowa	3,370.1	26	19	Kentucky	29,530
45	20	Delaware	5.3	44	20	Rhode Island	3,336.2	20	20	Wisconsin	24,823
27	21	Oregon	5.2	35	21	Kansas	3,315.2	14	21	Arizona	24,083
13	21	Washington	5.2	17	22	Indiana	3,312.3	22	22	Minnesota	23,538
7	23	Ohio	5.1	12	23	Virginia	3,266.8	24	23	Alabama	20,897
39	24	West Virginia	5.0	5	24	Pennsylvania	3,182.6	12	24	Virginia	20,140
14	25	Arizona	4.9	39	25	West Virginia	3,060.2	30	25	Utah	18,060
9	26	North Carolina	4.8	37	26	Nebraska	3,023.0	19	26	Maryland	16,428
26	27	Kentucky	4.7	32	27	Nevada	3,012.1	31	27	Iowa	15,837
3	28	Florida	4.6	27	28	Oregon	3,011.9	18	28	Missouri	15,507
42	28	Maine	4.6	26	29	Kentucky	2,986.3	29	29	Connecticut	14,569
51	30	Wyoming	4.5	43	30	Montana	2,932.1	34	30	Mississippi	12,933
18	31	Missouri	4.4	38	31	Idaho	2,890.0	35	31	Kansas	12,580
16	32	Tennessee	4.3	10	32	Michigan	2,815.6	32	32	Nevada	10,551
31	33	Iowa	4.2	34	33	Mississippi	2,730.2	21	33	Colorado	9,136
33	34	Arkansas	4.0	30	34	Utah	2,686.6	37	34	Nebraska	8,000
23	34	South Carolina	4.0	9	35	North Carolina	2,669.9	41	35	New Hampshire	6,368
8	36	Georgia	3.9	7	36	Ohio	2,615.3	39	36	West Virginia	6,282
12	36	Virginia	3.9	21	37	Colorado	2,595.6	28	37	Oklahoma	6,203
28	38	Oklahoma	3.8	28	38	Oklahoma	2,555.5	48	38	Alaska	6,000
20	38	Wisconsin	3.8	25	39	Louisiana	2,450.0	33	39	Arkansas	5,616
47	40	North Dakota	3.7	24	40	Alabama	2,447.4	36	40	New Mexico	5,379
38	41	Idaho	3.6	16	41	Tennessee	2,435.8	47	41	North Dakota	5,209
17	41	Indiana	3.6	14	42	Arizona	2,378.8	45	42	Delaware	4,724
41	43	New Hampshire	3.5	23	43	South Carolina	2,260.4	38	43	Idaho	3,778
24	44	Alabama	3.4	46	44	South Dakota	2,260.1	42	44	Maine	3,089
22	44	Minnesota	3.4	8	45	Georgia	2,204.3	44	45	Rhode Island	2,963
43	44	Montana	3.4	41	46	New Hampshire	2,092.0	50	46	Vermont	2,582
50	44	Vermont	3.4	2	47	Texas	2,078.1	43	47	Montana	1,974
35	48	Kansas	3.2	18	48	Missouri	2,017.3	46	48	South Dakota	1,859
46	49	South Dakota	3.1	3	49	Florida	1,984.0	49	49	District of Columbia	1,503
30	50	Utah	2.7	48	50	Alaska	1,802.8	51	50	Wyoming	1,425
37	51	Nebraska	2.5	49		District of Columbia	X	40	51	Hawaii	339

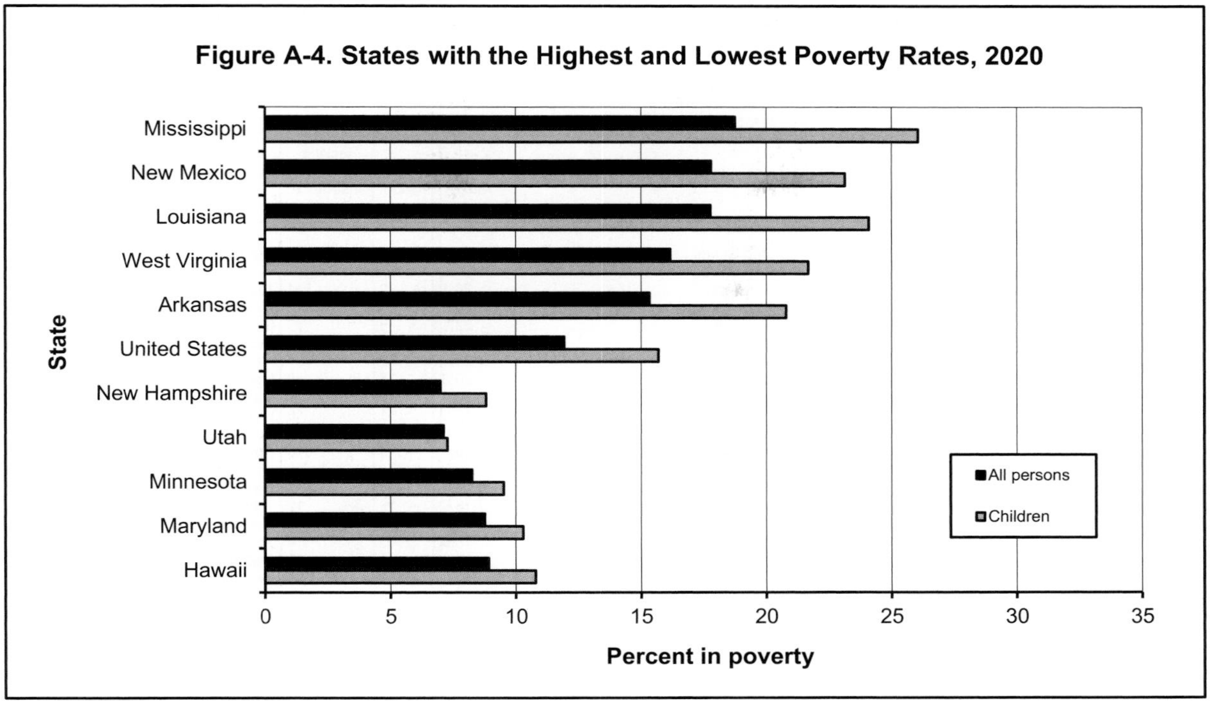

Nationally, 89.4 percent of the population 25 years old and over had graduated from high school. Thirty-three states and the District of Columbia had high school attainment levels of 90 percent or more, led by Montana with 94.4 percent. States in the Midwest and the West tended to have above average high school attainment rates although California had the lowest rate at 84.4 percent, followed by Texas at 85.8 percent. States with above average high school attainment levels do not necessarily have high proportions of college graduates. Nationally, 35.1 percent of the population held bachelor's degrees. In the District of Columbia, 63.6 percent of the population had graduated from college. Even when compared with other large cities, the District of Columbia had among the 10 highest proportions of college graduates in the nation. Of the 50 states, Massachusetts, Colorado, Maryland, Connecticut, New Jersey, Virginia, New Hampshire, and Vermont each had 40 percent or more of their populations holding bachelor's degrees or more. States in the Northeast tended to have above average college attainment levels, while states in the South had below average rates.

Median household income ranged from $47,247 in Mississippi to $96,762 in the District of Columbia. Nationally, the median household income was $67,340. In Mississippi, 22.3 percent of households had incomes below $20,000. The District of Columbia had the highest proportion of households earning $100,000 or more at 49.2 percent, followed by Massachusetts at 44.6 and Maryland at 44.4 percent.

The poverty threshold for an individual was $13,171 in 2020. Mississippi had the highest poverty rate in the nation, with 18.8 percent of its population living in poverty, followed by Louisiana and New Mexico at 17.8 percent. The poverty threshold for a four-person family was $26,496. Among children under 18 years old, 15.7 percent were living in poverty. Over 26 percent of children in Mississippi lived in poverty. Utah had the lowest proportion of children in poverty, at 7.3 percent. New Mexico and Louisiana had the highest proportion of residents 65 years and over living in poverty at 13.6 percent, followed by the District of Columbia at 11.5 percent.

The United States labor force increased by 0.3 percent between 2020 and 2021. From 2000 to 2008, it grew about an average of 1 percent a year but then declined from 2009 to 2011 followed by small increases in recent years. Seventeen states experienced a decline in their labor force between 2020 and 2021 compared with 40 states the previous year. COVID-19 had a major impact on the labor force between 2019 and 2021. For the second year in a row, Vermont experienced the largest proportional decline, dropping 3.8 percent. Meanwhile, the labor force in Texas and Utah grew by 2.5 percent in the same period. In 2021, the unemployment rate was 5.4 percent, a significant decrease from 8.1 percent the year before. Twenty-seven states had an unemployment rate below 5.0 percent compared with just 5 states the previous year. California had the highest unemployment rate in the nation at 7.3 percent followed by Nevada at 7.2 percent and New York at 6.9 percent. Nebraska had the lowest unemployment rate in 2021, at 2.5 percent followed by Utah at 2.7 percent.

States and the District of Columbia, Selected Rankings

Percent of persons below the poverty level, 2020

Population rank	Poverty rate rank	State	Poverty rate [col 127]
		United States	11.9
34	1	Mississippi	18.8
25	2	Louisiana	17.8
36	2	New Mexico	17.8
39	4	West Virginia	16.2
33	5	Arkansas	15.3
26	6	Kentucky	14.8
49	6	District of Columbia	14.8
24	8	Alabama	14.7
28	9	Oklahoma	14.4
23	10	South Carolina	14.0
8	11	Georgia	13.9
16	12	Tennessee	13.7
2	13	Texas	13.5
9	14	North Carolina	13.0
43	14	Montana	13.0
14	16	Arizona	12.8
4	17	New York	12.7
7	17	Ohio	12.7
10	17	Michigan	12.7
3	20	Florida	12.3
32	20	Nevada	12.3
18	22	Missouri	12.1
17	23	Indiana	11.7
46	23	South Dakota	11.7
1	25	California	11.4
45	26	Delaware	11.3
6	27	Illinois	11.0
27	27	Oregon	11.0
47	27	North Dakota	11.0
5	30	Pennsylvania	10.9
35	31	Kansas	10.8
42	32	Maine	10.7
31	33	Iowa	10.4
20	34	Wisconsin	10.1
38	34	Idaho	10.1
29	36	Connecticut	9.8
44	37	Rhode Island	9.7
50	38	Vermont	9.6
11	39	New Jersey	9.5
13	39	Washington	9.5
15	41	Massachusetts	9.4
51	42	Wyoming	9.3
12	43	Virginia	9.2
48	43	Alaska	9.2
21	45	Colorado	9.0
37	45	Nebraska	9.0
40	47	Hawaii	8.9
19	48	Maryland	8.8
22	49	Minnesota	8.3
30	50	Utah	7.1
41	51	New Hampshire	7.0

Percent of children under 18 years old below the poverty level, 2020

Population rank	Poverty rate rank	State	Poverty rate [col 128]
		United States	15.7
34	1	Mississippi	26.1
25	2	Louisiana	24.1
36	3	New Mexico	23.1
39	4	West Virginia	21.7
49	5	District of Columbia	21.1
33	6	Arkansas	20.8
24	7	Alabama	20.4
26	8	Kentucky	19.3
8	9	Georgia	19.0
2	9	Texas	19.0
28	11	Oklahoma	18.9
23	11	South Carolina	18.9
16	13	Tennessee	18.8
9	14	North Carolina	18.5
14	15	Arizona	17.6
10	16	Michigan	17.0
7	17	Ohio	16.8
45	18	Delaware	16.7
4	19	New York	16.6
3	20	Florida	16.5
32	20	Nevada	16.5
17	22	Indiana	15.3
18	22	Missouri	15.3
43	24	Montana	15.0
1	25	California	14.6
5	26	Pennsylvania	14.4
6	27	Illinois	13.8
35	28	Kansas	13.7
46	29	South Dakota	13.5
11	30	New Jersey	13.3
31	31	Iowa	12.4
29	32	Connecticut	12.3
20	33	Wisconsin	12.2
12	34	Virginia	12.1
42	35	Maine	12.0
47	35	North Dakota	12.0
48	37	Alaska	11.8
27	37	Oregon	11.8
38	39	Idaho	11.6
44	40	Rhode Island	11.5
13	41	Washington	11.3
40	42	Hawaii	10.8
15	43	Massachusetts	10.7
21	44	Colorado	10.5
19	45	Maryland	10.3
50	46	Vermont	9.8
22	47	Minnesota	9.5
37	48	Nebraska	9.2
41	49	New Hampshire	8.8
51	50	Wyoming	8.5
30	51	Utah	7.3

Percent of persons lacking health insurance, 2020

Population rank	Percent lacking health insurance rank	State	Percent lacking health insurance [col 104]
		United States	8.8
2	1	Texas	17.5
28	2	Oklahoma	15.3
8	3	Georgia	13.0
3	4	Florida	12.4
32	5	Nevada	12.0
34	6	Mississippi	11.7
48	7	Alaska	11.6
51	8	Wyoming	11.3
14	9	Arizona	11.2
9	10	North Carolina	10.6
23	11	South Carolina	10.5
16	12	Tennessee	10.2
18	13	Missouri	10.1
46	14	South Dakota	9.8
24	15	Alabama	9.7
36	15	New Mexico	9.7
38	17	Idaho	9.6
35	18	Kansas	8.8
43	19	Montana	8.7
33	20	Arkansas	8.5
30	20	Utah	8.5
21	22	Colorado	8.4
25	23	Louisiana	8.2
37	24	Nebraska	8.1
11	25	New Jersey	7.6
17	26	Indiana	7.5
42	26	Maine	7.5
47	28	North Dakota	7.2
12	28	Virginia	7.2
1	30	California	7.1
6	30	Illinois	7.1
7	32	Ohio	6.7
27	33	Oregon	6.6
39	33	West Virginia	6.6
45	35	Delaware	6.3
5	35	Pennsylvania	6.3
13	35	Washington	6.3
41	38	New Hampshire	6.1
26	39	Kentucky	5.8
19	40	Maryland	5.7
20	41	Wisconsin	5.6
10	42	Michigan	5.3
4	43	New York	5.2
31	44	Iowa	4.9
22	44	Minnesota	4.9
29	46	Connecticut	4.6
50	47	Vermont	4.1
40	48	Hawaii	3.9
44	49	Rhode Island	3.7
49	50	District of Columbia	3.5
15	51	Massachusetts	2.6

States and the District of Columbia, Selected Rankings

State government employment, 2020			
Popu-rank	State government employment rank	State	State government employment [col 312]
		United States	4,498,920
1	1	California	438,305
2	2	Texas	323,320
4	3	New York	257,250
3	4	Florida	183,003
5	5	Pennsylvania	157,325
9	6	North Carolina	150,900
10	7	Michigan	150,527
11	8	New Jersey	145,433
7	9	Ohio	134,322
13	10	Washington	133,041
12	11	Virginia	130,965
8	12	Georgia	126,446
6	13	Illinois	125,352
15	14	Massachusetts	105,628
21	15	Colorado	96,760
24	16	Alabama	96,707
19	17	Maryland	96,221
17	18	Indiana	90,341
23	19	South Carolina	85,123
22	20	Minnesota	85,007
18	21	Missouri	83,254
25	22	Louisiana	82,812
26	23	Kentucky	80,803
16	24	Tennessee	79,985
27	25	Oregon	76,004
14	26	Arizona	75,281
20	27	Wisconsin	66,270
30	28	Utah	65,351
28	29	Oklahoma	64,044
33	30	Arkansas	63,474
29	31	Connecticut	59,635
40	32	Hawaii	58,771
35	33	Kansas	55,966
34	34	Mississippi	54,424
31	35	Iowa	51,432
36	36	New Mexico	46,330
39	37	West Virginia	38,801
37	38	Nebraska	36,391
32	39	Nevada	29,893
45	40	Delaware	26,726
38	41	Idaho	24,844
48	42	Alaska	23,739
43	43	Montana	22,957
44	44	Rhode Island	21,138
42	45	Maine	20,695
41	46	New Hampshire	18,573
47	47	North Dakota	18,175
46	48	South Dakota	14,397
50	49	Vermont	13,799
51	50	Wyoming	12,980
49	X	District of Columbia	X

Value of agricultural products sold, 2017			
Population rank	Agricultural sales rank	State	Value of sales (millions of dollars) [col 197]
		United States	388,522.7
1	1	California	45,154.4
31	2	Iowa	28,956.5
2	3	Texas	24,924.0
37	4	Nebraska	21,983.4
35	5	Kansas	18,782.7
22	6	Minnesota	18,395.4
6	7	Illinois	17,010.0
9	8	North Carolina	12,900.7
20	9	Wisconsin	11,427.4
17	10	Indiana	11,107.3
18	11	Missouri	10,525.9
46	12	South Dakota	9,721.5
33	13	Arkansas	9,651.2
13	14	Washington	9,634.5
8	15	Georgia	9,573.3
7	16	Ohio	9,341.2
47	17	North Dakota	8,234.1
10	18	Michigan	8,220.9
5	19	Pennsylvania	7,758.9
38	20	Idaho	7,567.4
21	21	Colorado	7,491.7
28	22	Oklahoma	7,465.5
3	23	Florida	7,357.3
34	24	Mississippi	6,196.0
24	25	Alabama	5,980.6
26	26	Kentucky	5,737.9
4	27	New York	5,369.2
27	28	Oregon	5,006.8
12	29	Virginia	3,960.5
14	30	Arizona	3,852.0
16	31	Tennessee	3,798.9
43	32	Montana	3,520.6
25	33	Louisiana	3,173.0
23	34	South Carolina	3,008.7
36	35	New Mexico	2,582.3
19	36	Maryland	2,472.8
30	37	Utah	1,838.6
51	38	Wyoming	1,472.1
45	39	Delaware	1,466.0
11	40	New Jersey	1,098.0
50	41	Vermont	781.0
39	42	West Virginia	754.3
42	43	Maine	667.0
32	44	Nevada	665.8
29	45	Connecticut	580.1
40	46	Hawaii	563.8
15	47	Massachusetts	475.2
41	48	New Hampshire	187.8
48	49	Alaska	70.5
44	50	Rhode Island	58.0
49	NA	District of Columbia	NA

Violent crime rate, 2020			
Population rank	Violent crime rate rank	State	Violent crime rate (per 100,000 population) [col 108]
		United States	398.5
49	1	District of Columbia	999.8
48	2	Alaska	837.8
36	3	New Mexico	778.3
16	4	Tennessee	672.7
33	5	Arkansas	671.9
25	6	Louisiana	639.4
18	7	Missouri	542.7
23	8	South Carolina	530.7
46	9	South Dakota	501.4
14	10	Arizona	484.8
10	11	Michigan	478.0
43	12	Montana	469.8
32	13	Nevada	460.3
28	14	Oklahoma	458.6
24	15	Alabama	453.6
2	16	Texas	446.5
1	17	California	442.0
45	18	Delaware	431.9
6	19	Illinois	425.9
35	20	Kansas	425.0
21	21	Colorado	423.1
9	22	North Carolina	419.3
8	23	Georgia	400.1
19	24	Maryland	399.9
5	25	Pennsylvania	389.5
3	26	Florida	383.6
4	27	New York	363.8
17	28	Indiana	357.7
39	29	West Virginia	355.9
37	30	Nebraska	334.1
47	31	North Dakota	329.0
20	32	Wisconsin	323.4
7	33	Ohio	308.8
15	33	Massachusetts	308.8
31	35	Iowa	303.5
13	36	Washington	293.7
27	37	Oregon	291.9
34	38	Mississippi	291.2
22	39	Minnesota	277.5
30	40	Utah	260.7
26	41	Kentucky	259.1
40	42	Hawaii	254.2
38	43	Idaho	242.6
51	44	Wyoming	234.2
44	45	Rhode Island	230.8
12	46	Virginia	208.7
11	47	New Jersey	195.4
29	48	Connecticut	181.6
50	49	Vermont	173.4
41	50	New Hampshire	146.4
42	51	Maine	108.6

Table A. States — Land Area and Population Characteristics

State code	STATE	Land area,[1] 2020 (sq mi)	Population, 2021			Population characteristics, 2021										
						Race alone or in combination, not Hispanic or Latino (percent)					Age (percent)					
			Total persons, 2021	Rank	Per square mile	White	Black	American Indian, Alaska Native	Asian and Pacific Islander	Hispanic or Latino[2] (percent)	Under 5 years	5 to 14 years	15 to 24 years	25 to 34 years	35 to 44 years	45 to 54 years
		1	2	3	4	5	6	7	8	9	10	11	12	13	14	15

1. Dry land or land partially or temporarily covered by water. 2. May be of any race.

Table A. States — Population Characteristics, Immigration, and Households

STATE	Population characteristics, 2021 (cont.)								Immigrants admitted to legal status, 2020	Households, 2020					
	Age (percent) (cont.)												Household type		
	55 to 64 years	65 to 74 years	75 to 84 years	85 years and over	Percent female 2021	Median age 2020	Percent foreign born 2020	Percent born in state of residence 2020		Number	Percent change, 2019–2020	Percent with people 60 years and over	Married Couple family	Female house-holder family	House-holder living alone
	16	17	18	19	20	21	22	23	24	25	26	27	28	29	30

Table A. States — Population Change

STATE	Population, 2000–2020			Population change, 2000–2021								Population, 2020–2030		
	Census counts			Percent change			Components of change, April 1, 2020-July 1, 2021					Projections		
									Migration					
	2000	2010	2020	2000–2010	2010–2020	2020–2021	Births	Deaths	Net migration	Inter-national	Net internal	2020	2025	2030
	31	32	33	34	35	36	37	38	39	40	41	42	43	44

Table A. States — Population Characteristics

STATE	Population characteristics, 2010																		
	Race (percent)							Age (percent)											
	White alone	Black alone	American Indian, Alaska Native alone	Asian and Pacific Islander alone	Some other race or two or more races	Percent Hispanic or Latino[1]	Percent foreign born	Under 5 years	5 to 17 years	18 to 24 years	25 to 34 years	35 to 44 years	45 to 54 years	55 to 64 years	65 to 74 years	75 to 84 years	85 years and over	Median age	Percent female
	45	46	47	48	49	50	51	52	53	54	55	56	57	58	59	60	61	62	63

1. May be of any race.

Table A. States — Households and Housing Units

STATE	Households, 2010					Housing units, 2010									
				Percent				Occupied units							
									Owner-occupied				Renter-occupied		
											Median owner cost as a percent of income				
	Number	Percent change, 2000-2010	Persons per house-hold	Female family house-holder[1]	One-person house-holds	Total	Percent change, 2000–2010	Total	Percent	Median value[2] (dollars)	With a mort-gage	Without a mort-gage[3]	Median gross rent[4] (dollars)	Median rent as a percent of income	Sub-standard units[5] (percent)
	64	65	66	67	68	69	70	71	72	73	74	75	76	77	78

1. No spouse present. 2. Specified owner-occupied units. 3. Median monthly costs is often in the minimum category—10.0 percent or less, which is indicated as 10.0 percent.
4. Specified renter-occupied units. 5. Overcrowded or lacking complete plumbing facilities.

Table A. States — Housing Units and Residential Construction

STATE	Housing units 2020													
			Occupied units								Presence of Computer and Internet Subscription			
					Mortgage status by home ownership									
	Total	Percent change, 2019-2020	Total	Percent owner-occupied	With a mort-gage	Without a mort-gage[1]	Median value of units[2] (dollars)	Percent valued over $500,000	Median gross rent[3] (dollars)	Percent living in a different house than 1 year ago	Total house-holds	With a computer (percent)	With an Internet subscription (percent)	With no computer or no internet subscription (percent)
	79	80	81	82	83	84	85	86	87	88	89	90	91	92

1. Median monthly costs is often in the minimum category—10.0 percent or less, which is indicated as 10.0 percent. 2. Specified owner-occupied units. 3. Specified renter-occupied units.

Table A. States — Residential Contruction, Vital Statistics, and Health

STATE	Value of residential construction authorized by building permits, 2021			Manufactured homes placed by state, 2021	Births, 2020		Deaths, 2019					Percent lacking health insurance, 2020		Medicare beneficiaries, 2020
							Number		Rate					
									Total					
	New construction ($1,000)	Number of housing units	Percent single family		Total	Rate[1]	Total	Infant[2]	Crude[1]	Age-adjusted[1]	Infant[3]	All persons	Children under 18 years	
	93	94	95	96	97	98	99	100	101	102	103	104	105	106

1. Per 1,000 resident population. 2. Deaths of infants under 1 year old. 3. Deaths of infants under 1 year old per 1,000 live births.

Table A. States — Crime and Education

STATE	Serious crime known to police,[1] 2020				Public elementary and secondary school enrollment, 2020–2021		Educational attainment[1] (percent)				Local government expenditures for education, 2018–2019	
	Violent crime		Property crime				2010		2020			
	Number	Rate[2]	Number	Rate[2]	Total	Student/ teacher ratio	High school graduate or more	Bach-elor's degree or more	High school graduate or more	Bach-elor's degree or more	Total current expen-ditures (mil dol)	Current expen-ditures per student (dollars)
	107	108	109	110	111	112	113	114	115	116	117	118

1. Data for serious crimes have not been adjusted for underreporting; this may affect comparability between geographic areas and over time. 2. Per 100,000 population estimated by the FBI.

Table A. States — Exports, Income and Poverty

STATE	Exports of goods by state of origin, 2021 (mil dol)			Income and earnings, 2020					Percent below poverty level, 2020						
				Median earnings in the past 12 months (dollars)	Households			Median income of family of four				Families			
	Total	Manu-factured	Non-manu-factured		Median income (dollars)	Percent with income of $20,000 or less	Percent with income of $100,000 or more		All persons	Children under 18 years	Persons 65 years and over	All families	Married-couple families	Male house-holder[1] families	Female house-holder[1] families
	119	120	121	122	123	124	125	126	127	128	129	130	131	132	133

1. No spouse present.

Table A. States — Personal Income

STATE	Personal income												
			Per capita[1], 2021		Sources of personal income (mil dol)								
								Transfer payments, 2020					
									Government payments to individuals				
	Total, 2021 (mil dol)	Percent change, 2020–2021	Dollars	Rank	Wages and salaries[2], 2021	Proprietors' income, 2021	Dividends, interest, and rent, 2021	Total	Total	Social Security	Medical payments	Income main-tenance	Unemploy-ment insurance
	134	135	136	137	138	139	140	141	142	143	144	145	146

1. Based on the resident population estimated as of July 1 of the year shown. 2. Includes supplements to wages and salaries.

Table A. States — Personal Income and Earnings

STATE	Personal tax payments, 2020 (mil dol)	Disposable personal income, 2020		Earnings, 2021									Gross state product, 2021 (mil dol)
					Percent by selected industries								
						Goods-related[2]		Service-related and other[3]					
		Total (mil dol)	Per capita[1] (dollars)	Total (mil dol)	Farm	Total	Manu-facturing	Total	Retail trade	Finance, insurance, real estate, rental and leasing	Health care and social assistance	Govern-ment	
	147	148	149	150	151	152	153	154	155	156	157	158	159

1. Based on the resident population estimated as of July 1 of the year shown. 2. Includes mining, construction, and manufacturing. 3. Includes private sector earnings in forestry, fishing, related activities, and other; utilities; wholesale trade; transportation and warehousing; and information.

Table A. States — Social Security, Employment, and Labor Force

STATE	Social Security beneficiaries, December 2020		Supple-mental Security Income recipients, December 2020	Civilian employment and selected occupations,[2] 2020				Civilian labor force (annual average), 2021				
					Percent						Unemployed	
	Number	Rate[1]		Total	Management, business, science, and arts occupations	Services, sales, and office	Construction and production	Total (1,000)	Percent change, 2020–2021	Employed (1,000)	Total (1,000)	Rate[3]
	160	161	162	163	164	165	166	167	168	169	170	171

1. Per 1,000 resident population estimated as of July 1 of the year shown. 2. Persons 16 years old and over. 3. Percent of civilian labor force.

Table A. States — Nonfarm Employment and Earnings

STATE	Nonfarm employment and earnings, 2021											
	Employed		Manufacturing			Employment (1,000)						
	Total (1,000)	Percent change, 2020–2021	Employment (1,000)	Average earnings of production workers: Hourly	Average earnings of production workers: Weekly	Construction	Transportation and public utilities	Wholesale trade	Retail trade	Information	Financial activities	Services[1]
	172	173	174	175	176	177	178	179	180	181	182	183

1. Includes professional and business services, educational and health services, leisure and hospitality, and other services.

Table A. States — Agriculture

STATE	Agriculture, 2017											
	Farms			Farm producers whose primary occupation is farming (percent)	Government payments, average per farm that recieves payments (dollars)	Land in farms					Value of land and buildings (dollars)	
	Number	Percent with: Fewer than 50 acres	Percent with: 1,000 acres or more			Acreage (1,000)	Percent change, 2012–2017	Acres: Average size of farm	Acres: Total irrigated (1,000)	Acres: Total cropland (1,000)	Average per farm	Average per acre
	184	185	186	187	188	189	190	191	192	193	194	195

Table A. States — Agriculture, Land, and Water

STATE	Agriculture, 2017 (cont.)							Land, 2015			Public water supply withdrawn, 2015 (mil gal per day)
	Value of machinery and equipment, average per farm (dollars)	Value of products sold: Total (mil dol)	Value of products sold: Average per farm (dollars)	Value of products sold: Percent from: Crops	Value of products sold: Percent from: Livestock and poultry products	Organic Farms (number)	Farms with Internet access (percent)	Owned by the federal government (percent)	Developed land (percent)	Rural land (percent)	
	196	197	198	199	200	201	202	203	204	205	206

Table A. States — Manufactures and Construction

STATE	Manufactures, 2020										Construction, 2017				
	All employees			Production workers				Value added by manufacture (mil dol)	Sales, values of shipments or revenue (mil dol)	Total cost of materials (mil dol)	Number of establishments	Employees		Sales, values of shipments or revenue (mil dol)	Annual payroll (mil dol)
	Number (1,000)	Percent change, 2019–2020	Annual payroll (mil dol)	Number (1,000)	Work hours (millions)	Wages: Total (mil dol)	Wages: Average per worker (dollars)					Number	Percent change, 2012–2017		
	207	208	209	210	211	212	213	214	215	216	217	218	219	220	221

Table A. States — Wholesale Trade and Retail Trade

STATE	Wholesale trade, 2017					Retail trade,[1] 2017								
		Employees					Employees							
	Number of estab-lishments	Number	Percent change, 2012–2017	Sales (mil dol)	Annual payroll (mil dol)	Number of estab-lishments	Total	Percent change, 2012–2017	Motor vehicle and parts dealers	Food and beverage stores	Clothing and clothing accessory stores	General merchan-dise stores	Sales (mil dol)	Annual payroll (mil dol)
	222	223	224	225	226	227	228	229	230	231	232	233	234	235

1. Establishments with payroll.

Table A. States — Information

STATE	Information, 2017										
		Employees									
	Number of estab-lishments	Number	Percent change, 2012–2017	Publishing, except Internet	Motion picture and sound recording	Broad-casting, except Internet	Internet publishing and broad-casting and web search portals	Tele-communi-cations	Data processing, hosting, and related services	Sales, values of ship-ments or revenue (mil dol)	Annual payroll (mil dol)
	236	237	238	239	240	241	242	243	244	245	246

Table A. States — Utilities, Transportation and Warehousing, and Finance and Insurance

STATE	Utilities, 2017					Transportation and warehousing, 2017					Finance and insurance, 2017				
		Employees					Employees					Employees			
	Number of estab-lishments	Number	Percent change, 2012–2017	Sales, values of shipments or revenue (mil dol)	Annual payroll (mil dol)	Number of estab-lishments	Number	Percent change, 2012–2017	Receipts (mil dol)	Annual payroll (mil dol)	Number of estab-lishments	Number	Percent change, 2012–2017	Sales, values of ship-ments or revenue (mil dol)	Annual payroll (mil dol)
	247	248	249	250	251	252	253	254	255	256	257	258	259	260	261

Table A. States — Real Estate and Rental and Leasing and Professional, Scientific, and Technical Services

STATE	Real estate and rental and leasing, 2017					Professional, scientific, and technical services, 2017								
		Employees					Employees							
	Number of estab-lishments	Number	Percent change, 2012–2017	Sales, values of shipments or revenue (mil dol)	Annual payroll (mil dol)	Number of estab-lishments	Total	Percent change, 2012–2017	Legal services	Accounting, tax preparation, bookkeeping, and payroll services	Architectural, engineering, and related services	Computer systems design and related services	Sales, values of ship-ments or revenue (mil dol)	Annual payroll (mil dol)
	262	263	264	265	266	267	268	269	270	271	272	273	274	275

Table A. States — **Health Care and Social Assistance**

STATE	Health care and social assistance, 2017													
	Subject to federal tax							Tax-exempt						
		Employees							Employees					
	Number of estab-lishments	Total	Percent change, 2012–2017	Ambulatory health care services	Hospitals	Receipts (mil dol)	Annual payroll (mil dol)	Number of estab-lishments	Total	Percent change, 2012–2017	Ambulatory health care services	Hospitals	Sales, values of ship-ments or revenue (mil dol)	Annual payroll (mil dol)
	276	277	278	279	280	281	282	283	284	285	286	287	288	289

Table A. States — **Arts, Entertainment, and Recreation and Accommodation and Food Services**

STATE	Arts, entertainment, and recreation, 2017					Accommodation and food services, 2017					
		Employees					Employees				
	Number of estab-lishments	Number	Percent change, 2012–2017	Sales, value of shipments, or revenue (mil dol)	Annual payroll (mil dol)	Number of estab-lishments	Total	Percent change, 2012–2017	Food services and drinking places	Sales, values of shipments or revenue (mil dol)	Annual payroll (mil dol)
	290	291	292	293	294	295	296	297	298	299	300

Table A. States — **Other Services, Except Public Administration and Government Employment**

STATE	Other services, except public administration, 2017								Government employment, 2020		
		Employees									
	Number of estab-lishments	Total	Percent change, 2012–2017	Repair and mainte-nance	Personal and laundry services	Religious, civic, and similar services	Sales, values of shipments or revenue (mil dol)	Annual payroll (mil dol)	Federal civilian	Federal military	State and local
	301	302	303	304	305	306	307	308	309	310	311

Table A. States — **State Government Employment and Payroll**

STATE	State government employment and payroll, 2020											
							Full-time payroll					
	State government employment, 2020			State government payroll, 2019			Percent of total for:					
	Full-time equivalent employees	Full-time employees	Part-time employees	Full-time March payroll (1000 dollars)	Part-time March payroll (1000 dollars)	Total March payroll (1000 dollars)[1]	Administration	Judicial and legal	Police	Corrections	Highways	Welfare
	312	313	314	315	316	317	318	319	320	321	322	323

1. Includes program categories not shown separately.

Table A. States — State Government Employment, Payroll and Finances

STATE	State government employment and payroll, 2020 (cont.)							State government finances, 2020							
	Full-time payroll (1000 dollars) (cont.)							General revenue (mil dol)							
	Percent of total for:										From own sources				
									From federal government			Taxes		Taxes per capita[2] (dollars)	
	Health	Hospitals	Social Insurance administration	Natural resources	Sewerge	Elementary and secondary education and libraries	Higher education	Total	Total	Per capita[2] (dollars)	Total	Total	Sales and gross receipts	Total	Sales and gross receipts
	324	325	326	327	328	329	330	331	332	333	334	335	336	337	338

1. Based on resident population estimated as of July 1 of the year shown.

Table A. States — State Government Finances and Voting

STATE	State government finances, 2020 (cont.)												Voting and registration, November 2020		Presidential election, 2020 (percent of vote cast)		
	General expenditures (mil dol) (cont.)										Debt outstanding						
			Direct expenditures		By selected function												
	Total	To local governments	Total	Per capita[1] (dollars)	Education	Health and hospitals	Highways	Public safety	Public welfare	Natural resources, parks, and recreation	Total (mil dol)	Per capita[1]	Percent registered	Percent voted	Democratic	Republican	All other
	339	340	341	342	343	344	345	346	347	348	349	350	351	352	353	354	355

1. Based on resident population estimated as of July 1 of the year shown.

State code	STATE	Land area,[1] 2020 (sq mi)	Population, 2021: Total persons, 2021	Population, 2021: Rank	Population, 2021: Per square mile	Population characteristics, 2021: Race alone or in combination, not Hispanic or Latino (percent): White	Black	American Indian, Alaska Native	Asian and Pacific Islander	Hispanic or Latino[2] (percent)	Age (percent): Under 5 years	5 to 14 years	15 to 24 years	25 to 34 years	35 to 44 years	45 to 54 years
		1	2	3	4	5	6	7	8	9	10	11	12	13	14	15
0	United States	3,533,044	331,893,745	X	93.9	61.4	13.7	1.3	7.2	18.9	5.7	12.6	13.0	13.7	13.1	12.3
01	Alabama	50,647	5,039,877	24	99.5	66.4	27.4	1.2	2.0	4.8	5.8	12.6	13.0	13.0	12.3	12.3
02	Alaska	571,017	732,673	48	1.3	65.7	4.8	19.3	10.6	7.5	6.6	14.0	13.1	15.5	13.9	11.4
04	Arizona	113,653	7,276,316	14	64.0	55.2	5.6	4.4	4.8	32.3	5.5	12.7	13.4	13.8	12.6	11.6
05	Arkansas	52,038	3,025,891	33	58.1	73.2	16.3	1.7	2.6	8.3	6.0	13.2	13.3	13.0	12.5	11.8
06	California	155,854	39,237,836	1	251.8	37.8	6.5	1.0	17.7	40.2	5.7	12.7	13.0	14.9	13.8	12.6
08	Colorado	103,638	5,812,069	21	56.1	69.3	5.1	1.3	4.8	22.3	5.4	12.2	12.9	15.6	14.4	12.2
09	Connecticut	4,843	3,605,597	29	744.5	66.3	11.7	0.7	5.7	17.7	4.9	11.4	13.3	12.6	12.5	12.8
10	Delaware	1,949	1,003,384	45	515.0	62.8	24.0	0.9	4.9	10.1	5.3	11.8	12.0	12.8	12.0	11.6
11	District of Columbia	61	670,050	49	10,966.4	39.2	45.7	0.8	5.6	11.5	6.1	10.3	12.1	21.7	16.5	10.6
12	Florida	53,648	21,781,128	3	406.0	54.2	16.5	0.6	3.8	26.8	5.1	11.1	11.4	12.7	12.5	12.4
13	Georgia	57,716	10,799,566	8	187.1	52.8	33.2	0.7	5.3	10.2	5.9	13.3	13.7	13.8	13.2	12.9
15	Hawaii	6,422	1,441,553	40	224.5	36.5	3.1	1.7	75.4	11.1	5.7	12.0	11.5	13.5	13.2	11.8
16	Idaho	82,645	1,900,923	38	23.0	83.2	1.2	1.9	2.7	13.3	6.0	14.2	13.6	13.1	13.1	11.4
17	Illinois	55,514	12,671,469	6	228.3	61.6	15.1	0.5	6.7	18.0	5.6	12.5	13.0	13.5	13.3	12.5
18	Indiana	35,826	6,805,985	17	190.0	79.5	11.1	0.7	3.2	7.7	6.0	13.2	13.8	13.1	12.6	12.0
19	Iowa	55,854	3,193,079	31	57.2	85.9	5.2	0.7	3.4	6.7	5.9	13.1	14.0	12.5	12.6	11.3
20	Kansas	81,759	2,934,582	35	35.9	77.3	7.2	1.8	4.0	12.7	6.1	13.7	14.2	12.9	12.8	11.2
21	Kentucky	39,491	4,509,394	26	114.2	85.4	9.6	0.7	2.2	4.2	5.9	12.7	13.1	13.1	12.5	12.4
22	Louisiana	43,205	4,624,047	25	107.0	59.3	33.4	1.2	2.3	5.6	6.2	13.3	12.9	13.5	13.2	11.6
23	Maine	30,845	1,372,247	42	44.5	94.2	2.3	1.4	1.9	2.0	4.5	10.4	11.3	12.1	12.0	12.4
24	Maryland	9,711	6,165,129	19	634.9	51.2	31.8	0.8	7.9	11.1	5.8	12.5	12.4	13.3	13.4	12.7
25	Massachusetts	7,801	6,984,723	15	895.4	71.9	8.5	0.6	8.3	12.8	5.0	11.0	13.4	14.1	12.8	12.5
26	Michigan	56,606	10,050,811	10	177.6	76.5	15.1	1.3	4.1	5.6	5.5	12.1	13.1	13.1	12.0	12.2
27	Minnesota	79,626	5,707,390	22	71.7	80.4	8.4	1.8	6.2	5.8	5.9	13.1	12.8	13.1	13.4	11.7
28	Mississippi	46,926	2,949,965	34	62.9	57.1	38.3	0.9	1.5	3.5	6.0	13.3	13.6	12.9	12.5	12.1
29	Missouri	68,746	6,168,187	18	89.7	80.9	12.7	1.2	3.0	4.7	5.8	12.7	13.0	13.2	12.7	11.7
30	Montana	145,548	1,104,271	43	7.6	88.0	1.1	7.6	1.8	4.3	5.3	12.3	12.8	13.0	12.7	10.9
31	Nebraska	76,817	1,963,692	37	25.6	79.3	6.1	1.4	3.4	12.0	6.4	14.0	14.0	12.9	13.0	11.1
32	Nevada	109,860	3,143,991	32	28.6	49.8	11.0	1.5	11.9	29.9	5.7	12.7	11.9	14.5	13.7	12.6
33	New Hampshire	8,953	1,388,992	41	155.1	90.7	2.2	0.8	3.7	4.4	4.5	10.5	12.4	12.8	12.1	12.7
34	New Jersey	7,355	9,267,130	11	1,260.0	54.9	13.9	0.5	11.0	21.5	5.6	12.3	12.3	12.8	13.1	13.1
35	New Mexico	121,312	2,115,877	36	17.4	37.3	2.5	9.5	2.3	50.1	5.4	12.9	13.4	13.3	12.7	11.1
36	New York	47,124	19,835,913	4	420.9	56.3	15.5	0.7	10.1	19.5	5.5	11.6	12.4	14.1	12.8	12.4
37	North Carolina	48,620	10,551,162	9	217.0	63.7	22.6	1.7	4.0	10.2	5.6	12.3	13.3	13.4	12.6	12.8
38	North Dakota	68,995	774,948	47	11.2	85.2	4.0	6.3	2.3	4.4	6.6	13.5	14.6	14.3	12.8	10.1
39	Ohio	40,859	11,780,017	7	288.3	79.8	14.3	0.8	3.2	4.3	5.7	12.5	12.8	13.2	12.4	12.1
40	Oklahoma	68,596	3,986,639	28	58.1	69.3	9.1	12.8	3.4	11.7	6.2	13.8	13.8	13.5	13.0	11.4
41	Oregon	95,988	4,246,155	27	44.2	77.4	2.9	2.4	7.0	14.0	5.0	11.7	12.0	14.1	14.0	12.2
42	Pennsylvania	44,742	12,964,056	5	289.8	76.5	12.1	0.5	4.5	8.4	5.3	11.7	12.4	13.1	12.4	12.1
44	Rhode Island	1,034	1,095,610	44	1,059.7	72.3	7.5	1.0	4.4	17.1	4.9	10.7	13.6	13.9	12.4	12.2
45	South Carolina	30,064	5,190,705	23	172.7	65.1	27.2	0.9	2.5	6.4	5.5	12.3	12.7	13.0	12.3	12.2
46	South Dakota	75,810	895,376	46	11.8	83.0	3.1	9.5	2.3	4.6	6.6	13.9	13.4	12.6	12.5	10.6
47	Tennessee	41,238	6,975,218	16	169.1	74.9	17.7	0.8	2.5	6.1	5.8	12.5	12.7	13.8	12.7	12.5
48	Texas	261,263	29,527,941	2	113.0	41.7	13.0	0.7	6.1	40.2	6.5	14.5	14.1	14.4	14.0	12.3
49	Utah	82,377	3,337,975	30	40.5	79.4	1.8	1.4	5.1	14.8	7.1	16.2	16.4	14.6	14.0	10.7
50	Vermont	9,218	645,570	50	70.0	94.1	2.0	1.1	2.6	2.2	4.4	10.3	13.6	12.0	12.0	12.0
51	Virginia	39,482.1	8,642,274	12	218.9	62.9	20.7	0.8	8.5	10.2	5.7	12.3	13.1	13.6	13.4	12.6
53	Washington	66,455.1	7,738,692	13	116.4	70.1	5.6	2.5	13.1	13.7	5.6	12.4	12.1	15.2	14.2	12.1
54	West Virginia	24,041.1	1,782,959	39	74.2	93.3	4.7	0.8	1.2	1.9	5.0	11.5	12.2	11.9	12.0	12.6
55	Wisconsin	54,167.4	5,895,908	20	108.8	81.9	7.4	1.4	3.7	7.5	5.4	12.3	13.2	12.5	12.7	11.9
56	Wyoming	97,088.7	578,803	51	6.0	85.2	1.6	2.9	1.7	10.6	5.6	13.2	13.1	12.7	13.3	11.1

1. Dry land or land partially or temporarily covered by water. 2. May be of any race.

Table A. States — **Population Characteristics, Immigration, and Households**

STATE	Population characteristics, 2021 (cont.) — Age (percent) (cont.) — 55 to 64 years	65 to 74 years	75 to 84 years	85 years and over	Percent female 2021	Median age 2020	Percent foreign born 2020	Percent born in state of residence 2020	Immigrants admitted to legal status, 2020	Households, 2020 — Number	Percent change, 2019–2020	Percent with people 60 years and over	Household type — Married Couple family	Female house-holder family	House-holder living alone
	16	17	18	19	20	21	22	23	24	25	26	27	28	29	30
United States	12.9	10.1	4.9	1.8	50.5	38.7	13.2	58.2	707,362	124,345,410	1.3	42.0	48.5	11.0	29.2
Alabama	13.3	10.8	5.2	1.7	51.4	39.7	3.5	68.5	2,843	1,895,330	-0.1	43.5	48.7	11.2	32.5
Alaska	12.3	9.1	3.3	0.9	47.6	35.5	7.8	43.1	823	255,456	1.3	38.0	51.1	9.2	27.9
Arizona	12.1	10.8	5.7	1.8	50.1	38.6	12.5	39.9	12,516	2,774,127	3.9	44.4	48.1	10.7	28.5
Arkansas	12.7	10.4	5.2	1.8	50.7	38.5	4.8	61.7	2,224	1,185,599	1.9	42.1	48.9	11.7	30.0
California	12.2	9.1	4.4	1.7	50.0	37.3	26.2	56.3	138,996	13,135,388	-0.2	42.0	50.7	11.4	24.7
Colorado	12.1	9.6	4.1	1.4	49.3	37.2	8.9	42.2	9,223	2,201,823	-1.5	37.5	50.5	7.5	29.4
Connecticut	14.4	10.5	5.3	2.2	50.9	41.2	14.4	54.3	7,802	1,406,237	2.1	43.9	47.2	11.7	29.9
Delaware	14.3	12.4	5.8	1.9	51.4	41.4	8.4	44.7	1,301	387,778	3.1	48.0	45.8	12.0	30.5
District of Columbia	9.9	7.6	3.7	1.6	52.4	34.4	12.8	34.0	1,653	291,687	0.0	29.6	27.7	7.9	49.9
Florida	13.7	11.9	6.8	2.5	50.8	42.7	20.6	36.3	65,799	8,133,696	2.9	48.9	50.0	9.0	30.7
Georgia	12.4	9.1	4.2	1.3	51.2	37.6	10.1	54.9	18,282	3,904,930	1.4	39.0	48.4	12.4	29.6
Hawaii	12.6	11.3	5.6	2.7	49.7	40.0	17.0	55.4	2,709	477,480	2.6	50.8	50.4	12.4	24.2
Idaho	12.0	10.4	4.8	1.5	49.6	37.4	5.5	45.6	1,853	678,555	3.5	41.7	56.7	7.1	24.8
Illinois	13.0	9.9	4.7	1.9	50.6	38.9	13.7	67.2	27,377	4,907,332	0.8	41.1	46.8	11.3	30.8
Indiana	12.8	10.0	4.7	1.7	50.4	38.1	5.3	68.0	6,551	2,642,088	1.7	40.3	48.3	11.0	29.5
Iowa	12.9	10.5	5.0	2.2	49.8	38.7	5.2	70.8	3,907	1,275,934	-0.9	40.8	49.5	9.3	30.3
Kansas	12.5	10.0	4.7	2.0	49.9	37.6	6.5	59.8	3,943	1,151,979	1.2	39.9	50.1	10.4	29.2
Kentucky	13.3	10.6	4.9	1.6	50.5	39.3	3.8	68.3	3,932	1,759,434	0.6	41.2	48.2	11.1	29.7
Louisiana	12.9	10.2	4.7	1.6	51.0	38.0	3.8	77.6	2,584	1,762,869	1.3	41.3	44.6	13.0	32.9
Maine	15.5	13.3	6.1	2.2	50.7	45.0	3.8	60.7	935	584,057	1.8	47.5	46.7	8.6	31.6
Maryland	13.6	9.8	4.7	1.8	51.3	39.2	15.3	47.1	16,049	2,255,168	1.3	41.9	47.7	13.1	28.2
Massachusetts	13.8	10.4	5.0	2.0	51.1	39.8	17.0	59.4	22,107	2,687,421	1.4	43.1	46.9	11.1	28.8
Michigan	13.9	11.1	5.1	1.9	50.4	40.0	6.6	76.7	13,953	4,012,557	1.1	43.3	46.7	10.9	31.0
Minnesota	13.2	10.1	4.7	1.9	49.9	38.7	7.7	68.2	9,828	2,234,764	0.5	39.9	50.8	8.2	29.4
Mississippi	12.9	10.3	4.8	1.6	51.3	38.4	2.1	71.0	1,020	1,126,474	2.4	43.6	44.7	15.8	31.1
Missouri	13.4	10.5	5.1	1.9	50.6	39.1	3.9	66.6	5,836	2,463,458	0.2	41.8	47.9	9.9	31.5
Montana	13.4	12.3	5.5	1.9	49.4	40.6	1.9	53.4	505	446,572	2.0	43.8	48.4	6.9	32.4
Nebraska	12.3	9.9	4.6	1.9	49.7	37.1	7.5	65.1	2,768	774,402	0.4	38.8	49.0	9.2	30.6
Nevada	12.5	10.2	4.9	1.4	49.6	38.9	18.9	27.1	7,040	1,173,874	2.7	41.7	45.6	12.2	28.7
New Hampshire	15.8	12.0	5.3	2.0	50.1	43.3	5.9	41.0	1,446	538,552	-0.5	45.4	53.6	7.6	26.8
New Jersey	13.8	9.9	4.9	2.0	50.8	40.2	22.8	51.9	30,275	3,346,036	1.8	43.7	49.2	13.4	26.8
New Mexico	12.7	11.3	5.4	1.8	50.2	38.6	8.5	53.5	2,925	816,574	2.9	45.7	43.5	11.2	34.2
New York	13.6	10.3	5.1	2.2	51.1	39.5	22.0	62.9	81,755	7,488,719	0.6	44.4	43.3	14.1	29.7
North Carolina	13.0	10.4	4.9	1.6	51.1	39.2	7.7	55.3	13,989	4,088,898	1.1	41.7	49.2	10.2	31.2
North Dakota	11.9	9.5	4.4	2.2	48.6	35.8	4.6	63.5	1,001	321,697	-0.6	36.6	46.9	8.6	33.2
Ohio	13.5	10.9	5.0	1.9	50.7	39.7	4.6	74.9	12,651	4,741,813	0.2	42.7	45.5	11.5	31.7
Oklahoma	12.2	9.7	4.8	1.7	50.2	37.1	5.9	60.7	3,031	1,514,051	1.3	40.8	49.2	10.5	30.1
Oregon	12.4	11.5	5.3	1.8	50.1	40.2	9.3	45.6	5,984	1,688,863	2.4	43.3	47.8	10.1	27.6
Pennsylvania	14.0	11.3	5.5	2.3	50.6	41.0	6.9	71.8	17,398	5,178,588	1.2	44.6	46.7	11.4	30.7
Rhode Island	14.2	10.8	5.1	2.2	51.0	40.4	14.5	54.3	2,292	421,624	3.5	44.4	44.9	12.2	29.8
South Carolina	13.4	11.6	5.4	1.6	51.4	40.2	5.0	55.0	3,705	2,009,401	1.7	44.8	49.2	10.8	31.2
South Dakota	13.0	10.9	4.5	2.0	49.2	37.6	3.7	64.3	885	349,073	-1.3	41.1	49.9	7.6	31.2
Tennessee	13.1	10.4	5.0	1.6	51.0	39.2	4.8	58.8	6,704	2,702,490	1.8	40.7	48.3	11.2	30.6
Texas	11.2	8.2	3.7	1.3	50.1	35.3	16.1	60.3	74,565	10,270,966	2.9	36.1	51.3	11.1	27.6
Utah	9.3	7.3	3.3	1.1	49.4	31.6	7.7	62.3	5,421	1,052,033	2.8	34.0	60.1	9.0	20.2
Vermont	14.9	12.8	5.8	2.0	50.3	42.8	4.3	47.0	495	263,353	0.2	45.6	47.1	8.0	31.0
Virginia	13.0	9.9	4.8	1.6	50.5	38.9	12.2	49.0	18,183	3,213,949	0.7	40.3	51.1	9.9	28.6
Washington	12.3	10.1	4.5	1.6	49.6	38.0	14.5	47.1	21,549	2,987,658	1.9	39.3	50.1	9.2	27.4
West Virginia	14.0	12.7	6.0	2.0	50.1	43.1	1.6	68.8	547	734,080	0.8	48.1	47.2	9.3	33.7
Wisconsin	14.1	11.0	5.0	1.9	49.9	40.0	4.7	71.7	4,525	2,393,344	0.3	41.6	48.0	8.6	31.6
Wyoming	13.0	11.4	4.9	1.7	48.8	38.7	3.8	42.1	241	237,179	1.7	41.5	52.1	8.0	29.1

STATE	Population, 2000–2020			Population change, 2000–2021								Population, 2020–2030		
	Census counts			Percent change			Components of change, April 1, 2020–July 1, 2021					Projections		
									Migration					
	2000	2010	2020	2000–2010	2010–2020	2020–2021	Births	Deaths	Net migration	Inter-national	Net internal	2020	2025	2030
	31	32	33	34	35	36	37	38	39	40	41	42	43	44
United States	281,421,906	308,745,538	331,449,281	9.7	7.4	0.1	4,474,986	4,287,391	256,869	256,869	(X)	335,804,546	349,439,199	363,584,435
Alabama	4,447,100	4,779,736	5,024,279	7.5	5.1	0.3	69,730	81,016	26,717	1,242	25,475	4,728,915	4,800,092	4,874,243
Alaska	626,932	710,231	733,391	13.3	3.3	-0.1	11,687	7,025	-5,365	547	-5,912	774,421	820,881	867,674
Arizona	5,130,632	6,392,017	7,151,502	24.6	11.9	1.7	94,533	94,005	124,295	4,645	119,650	8,456,448	9,531,537	10,712,397
Arkansas	2,673,400	2,915,918	3,011,524	9.1	3.3	0.5	43,575	47,706	18,458	854	17,604	3,060,219	3,151,005	3,240,208
California	33,871,648	37,253,956	39,538,223	10.0	6.1	-0.8	529,290	414,075	-415,522	13,861	-429,383	42,206,743	44,305,177	46,444,861
Colorado	4,301,261	5,029,196	5,773,714	16.9	14.8	0.7	75,917	59,823	21,750	1,716	20,034	5,278,867	5,522,803	5,792,357
Connecticut	3,405,565	3,574,097	3,605,944	4.9	0.9	0.0	40,961	47,074	5,222	4,996	226	3,675,650	3,691,016	3,688,630
Delaware	783,600	897,934	989,948	14.6	10.2	1.4	12,719	14,304	15,039	652	14,387	963,209	990,694	1,012,658
District of Columbia	572,059	601,723	689,545	5.2	14.6	-2.8	10,868	7,939	-22,143	1,179	-23,322	480,540	455,108	433,414
Florida	15,982,378	18,801,310	21,538,187	17.6	14.6	1.1	260,946	319,149	305,218	41,260	263,958	23,406,525	25,912,458	28,685,769
Georgia	8,186,453	9,687,653	10,711,908	18.3	10.6	0.8	150,732	130,940	67,437	7,458	59,979	10,843,753	11,438,622	12,017,838
Hawaii	1,211,537	1,360,301	1,455,271	12.3	7.0	-0.9	19,906	18,421	-15,059	1,115	-16,174	1,412,373	1,438,720	1,466,046
Idaho	1,293,953	1,567,582	1,839,106	21.1	17.3	3.4	26,829	21,368	56,851	412	56,439	1,741,333	1,852,627	1,969,624
Illinois	12,419,293	12,830,632	12,812,508	3.3	-0.1	-1.1	167,169	162,805	-145,656	5,856	-151,512	13,236,720	13,340,507	13,432,892
Indiana	6,080,485	6,483,802	6,785,528	6.6	4.7	0.3	96,817	96,570	19,609	4,994	14,615	6,627,008	6,721,322	6,810,108
Iowa	2,926,324	3,046,355	3,190,369	4.1	4.7	0.1	45,004	44,543	2,025	3,186	-1,161	3,020,496	2,993,222	2,955,172
Kansas	2,688,418	2,853,118	2,937,880	6.1	3.0	-0.1	42,122	39,388	-6,356	1,396	-7,752	2,890,566	2,919,002	2,940,084
Kentucky	4,041,769	4,339,367	4,505,836	7.4	3.8	0.1	63,181	71,410	11,496	1,216	10,280	4,424,431	4,489,662	4,554,998
Louisiana	4,468,976	4,533,372	4,657,757	1.4	2.7	-0.7	69,279	68,795	-34,074	2,780	-36,854	4,719,160	4,762,398	4,802,633
Maine	1,274,923	1,328,361	1,362,359	4.2	2.6	0.7	14,248	22,142	17,912	909	17,003	1,408,665	1,414,402	1,411,097
Maryland	5,296,486	5,773,552	6,177,224	9.0	7.0	-0.2	83,750	76,782	-19,312	7,354	-26,666	6,497,626	6,762,732	7,022,251
Massachusetts	6,349,097	6,547,629	7,029,917	3.1	7.4	-0.6	83,111	87,784	-40,686	13,653	-54,339	6,855,546	6,938,636	7,012,009
Michigan	9,938,444	9,883,640	10,077,331	-0.6	2.0	-0.3	129,524	146,786	-10,254	4,462	-14,716	10,695,993	10,713,730	10,694,172
Minnesota	4,919,479	5,303,925	5,706,494	7.8	7.6	0.0	79,493	66,981	-11,734	4,213	-15,947	5,900,769	6,108,787	6,306,130
Mississippi	2,844,658	2,967,297	2,961,279	4.3	-0.2	-0.4	43,234	47,987	-6,685	447	-7,132	3,044,812	3,069,420	3,092,410
Missouri	5,595,211	5,988,927	6,154,913	7.0	2.8	0.2	86,276	91,907	18,604	3,071	15,533	6,199,882	6,315,366	6,430,173
Montana	902,195	989,415	1,084,225	9.7	9.6	1.8	13,285	15,072	22,062	579	21,483	1,022,735	1,037,387	1,044,898
Nebraska	1,711,263	1,826,341	1,961,504	6.7	7.4	0.1	29,623	24,254	-3,378	1,069	-4,447	1,802,678	1,812,787	1,820,247
Nevada	1,998,257	2,700,551	3,104,614	35.1	15.0	1.3	42,076	39,702	36,605	2,325	34,280	3,452,283	3,863,298	4,282,102
New Hampshire	1,235,786	1,316,470	1,377,529	6.5	4.6	0.8	14,327	18,817	15,977	1,302	14,675	1,524,751	1,586,348	1,646,471
New Jersey	8,414,350	8,791,894	9,288,994	4.5	5.7	-0.2	119,434	112,573	-29,149	10,805	-39,954	9,461,635	9,636,644	9,802,440
New Mexico	1,819,046	2,059,179	2,117,522	13.2	2.8	-0.1	27,543	28,890	-364	1,557	-1,921	2,084,341	2,106,584	2,099,708
New York	18,976,457	19,378,102	20,201,249	2.1	4.2	-1.8	264,380	238,584	-387,397	18,860	-406,257	19,576,920	19,540,179	19,477,429
North Carolina	8,049,313	9,535,483	10,439,388	18.5	9.5	1.1	142,020	144,561	114,080	7,196	106,884	10,709,289	11,449,153	12,227,739
North Dakota	642,200	672,591	779,094	4.7	15.8	-0.5	12,436	9,704	-6,828	291	-7,119	630,112	620,777	606,566
Ohio	11,353,140	11,536,504	11,799,448	1.6	2.3	-0.2	160,886	181,233	-97	7,518	-7,615	11,644,058	11,605,738	11,550,528
Oklahoma	3,450,654	3,751,351	3,959,353	8.7	5.5	0.7	58,736	60,920	29,192	1,603	27,589	3,735,690	3,820,994	3,913,251
Oregon	3,421,399	3,831,074	4,237,256	12.0	10.6	0.2	50,302	55,926	14,491	1,165	13,326	4,260,393	4,536,418	4,833,918
Pennsylvania	12,281,054	12,702,379	13,002,700	3.4	2.4	-0.3	160,565	199,108	-590	7,906	-8,496	12,787,354	12,801,945	12,768,184
Rhode Island	1,048,319	1,052,567	1,097,379	0.4	4.3	-0.2	12,201	15,003	938	647	291	1,154,230	1,157,855	1,152,941
South Carolina	4,012,012	4,625,364	5,118,425	15.3	10.7	1.4	68,052	77,654	82,142	3,330	78,812	4,822,577	4,989,550	5,148,569
South Dakota	754,844	814,180	886,667	7.9	8.9	1.0	13,724	11,671	6,650	1,084	5,566	801,939	801,845	800,462
Tennessee	5,689,283	6,346,105	6,910,840	11.5	8.9	0.9	96,408	106,817	75,259	1,787	73,472	6,780,670	7,073,125	7,380,634
Texas	20,851,820	25,145,561	29,145,505	20.6	15.9	1.3	450,827	308,742	239,792	28,503	211,289	28,634,896	30,865,134	33,317,744
Utah	2,233,169	2,763,885	3,271,616	23.8	18.4	2.0	56,780	27,872	37,304	1,220	36,084	2,990,094	3,225,680	3,485,367
Vermont	608,827	625,741	643,077	2.8	2.8	0.4	6,432	8,688	4,752	282	4,470	690,686	703,288	711,867
Virginia	7,078,515	8,001,024	8,631,393	13.0	7.9	0.1	116,274	105,578	210	11,504	-11,294	8,917,395	9,364,304	9,825,019
Washington	5,894,121	6,724,540	7,705,281	14.1	14.6	0.4	102,270	88,479	19,195	9,787	9,408	7,432,136	7,996,400	8,624,801
West Virginia	1,808,344	1,852,994	1,793,716	2.5	-3.2	-0.6	21,615	34,097	1,704	582	1,122	1,801,112	1,766,435	1,719,959
Wisconsin	5,363,675	5,686,986	5,893,718	6.0	3.6	0.0	76,033	79,179	4,881	2,373	2,508	6,004,954	6,088,374	6,150,764
Wyoming	493,782	563,626	576,851	14.1	2.3	0.3	7,856	7,542	1,651	120	1,531	530,948	529,031	522,979

Table A. States — **Population Characteristics**

STATE	Population characteristics, 2010																		
	Race (percent)							Age (percent)											
	White alone	Black alone	American Indian, Alaska Native alone	Asian and Pacific Islander alone	Some other race or two or more races	Percent Hispanic or Latino[1]	Percent foreign born	Under 5 years	5 to 17 years	18 to 24 years	25 to 34 years	35 to 44 years	45 to 54 years	55 to 64 years	65 to 74 years	75 to 84 years	85 years and over	Median age	Percent female
	45	46	47	48	49	50	51	52	53	54	55	56	57	58	59	60	61	62	63
United States	72.4	12.6	0.9	5.0	9.1	16.3	12.9	6.5	17.5	9.9	13.3	13.3	14.6	11.8	7.0	4.2	1.8	37.2	50.8
Alabama	68.5	26.2	0.6	1.2	3.5	3.9	3.5	6.4	17.3	10.0	12.6	13.0	14.5	12.3	7.8	4.4	1.6	37.9	51.5
Alaska	66.7	3.3	14.8	6.4	8.9	5.5	6.9	7.6	18.8	10.5	14.5	13.1	15.6	12.1	5.0	2.1	0.6	33.8	48.0
Arizona	73.0	4.1	4.6	3.0	15.3	29.6	13.4	7.1	18.4	9.9	13.4	12.9	13.2	11.4	7.8	4.4	1.6	35.9	50.3
Arkansas	77.0	15.4	0.8	1.4	5.4	6.4	4.5	6.8	17.6	9.7	12.6	12.6	14.0	12.0	8.0	4.6	1.8	37.4	50.9
California	57.6	6.2	1.0	13.4	21.9	37.6	27.2	6.8	18.2	10.5	14.2	13.9	14.1	10.8	6.1	3.7	1.6	35.2	50.3
Colorado	81.3	4.0	1.1	2.9	10.6	20.7	9.8	6.8	17.5	9.7	14.4	13.9	14.8	11.9	6.2	3.4	1.4	36.1	49.9
Connecticut	77.6	10.1	0.3	3.8	8.2	13.4	13.6	5.7	17.2	9.1	11.8	13.6	16.1	12.4	7.1	4.6	2.4	40.0	51.3
Delaware	68.9	21.4	0.5	3.2	6.1	8.2	8.0	6.2	16.7	10.1	12.3	12.9	14.9	12.4	8.1	4.5	1.8	38.8	51.6
District of Columbia	38.5	50.7	0.3	3.6	7.0	9.1	13.5	5.4	11.3	14.5	20.9	13.4	12.6	10.6	6.1	3.5	1.8	33.8	52.8
Florida	75.0	16.0	0.4	2.5	6.1	22.5	19.4	5.7	15.6	9.3	12.1	12.9	14.6	12.4	9.2	5.7	2.4	40.7	51.1
Georgia	59.7	30.5	0.3	3.3	6.1	8.8	9.7	7.1	18.6	10.0	13.6	14.4	14.4	11.0	6.3	3.1	1.2	35.3	51.2
Hawaii	24.7	1.6	0.3	48.6	24.8	8.9	18.2	6.4	15.9	9.6	13.3	13.0	14.2	12.9	7.4	4.7	2.3	38.6	49.9
Idaho	89.1	0.6	1.4	1.3	7.6	11.2	5.5	7.8	19.6	9.9	13.3	12.2	13.3	11.5	7.0	3.8	1.7	34.6	49.9
Illinois	71.5	14.5	0.3	4.6	9.0	15.8	13.7	6.5	17.9	9.7	13.9	13.5	14.6	11.5	6.6	4.0	1.9	36.6	51.0
Indiana	84.3	9.1	0.3	1.6	4.7	6.0	4.6	6.7	18.1	10.0	12.7	13.0	14.6	11.9	7.0	4.3	1.7	37.0	50.8
Iowa	91.3	2.9	0.4	1.8	3.6	5.0	4.6	6.6	17.3	10.0	12.6	12.0	14.4	12.2	7.4	5.0	2.5	38.1	50.5
Kansas	83.8	5.9	1.0	2.5	6.9	10.5	6.5	7.2	18.3	10.1	13.0	12.2	14.2	11.6	6.7	4.3	2.1	36.0	50.4
Kentucky	87.8	7.8	0.2	1.2	3.0	3.1	3.2	6.5	17.1	9.5	13.0	13.3	14.8	12.4	7.5	4.2	1.6	38.1	50.8
Louisiana	62.6	32.0	0.7	1.5	3.1	4.2	3.8	6.9	17.7	10.5	13.7	12.5	14.4	11.8	6.9	3.9	1.5	35.8	51.0
Maine	95.2	1.2	0.6	1.0	1.9	1.3	3.4	5.2	15.4	8.7	10.9	12.9	16.5	14.5	8.5	5.3	2.1	42.7	51.1
Maryland	58.2	29.4	0.4	5.6	6.5	8.2	13.9	6.3	17.1	9.7	13.2	13.8	15.6	12.1	6.7	3.9	1.7	38.0	51.6
Massachusetts	80.4	6.6	0.3	5.3	7.3	9.6	15.0	5.6	16.1	10.4	12.9	13.5	15.5	12.3	7.0	4.6	2.2	39.1	51.6
Michigan	78.9	14.2	0.6	2.4	3.8	4.4	6.0	6.0	17.7	9.9	11.7	12.9	15.3	12.7	7.3	4.5	1.9	38.9	50.9
Minnesota	85.3	5.2	1.1	4.0	4.3	4.7	7.1	6.7	17.5	9.5	13.5	12.8	15.2	11.9	6.7	4.2	2.0	37.4	50.4
Mississippi	59.1	37.0	0.5	0.9	2.4	2.7	2.1	7.1	18.4	10.3	12.6	12.6	14.1	11.7	7.2	4.1	1.5	36.0	51.4
Missouri	82.8	11.6	0.5	1.7	3.4	3.5	3.9	6.5	17.3	9.8	12.9	12.5	14.8	12.1	7.5	4.5	2.0	37.9	51.0
Montana	89.4	0.4	6.3	0.7	3.1	2.9	2.0	6.3	16.3	9.6	12.3	11.4	15.1	14.0	8.2	4.7	2.0	39.8	49.8
Nebraska	86.1	4.5	1.0	1.9	6.5	9.2	6.1	7.2	17.9	10.0	13.2	12.1	14.2	11.7	6.7	4.7	2.2	36.2	50.4
Nevada	66.2	8.1	1.2	7.8	16.7	26.5	18.8	6.9	17.7	9.2	14.3	14.2	13.9	11.7	7.3	3.6	1.1	36.3	49.5
New Hampshire	93.9	1.1	0.2	2.2	2.5	2.8	5.3	5.3	16.5	9.4	11.0	13.6	17.2	13.5	7.4	4.4	1.8	41.1	50.7
New Jersey	68.6	13.7	0.3	8.3	9.1	17.7	21.0	6.2	17.3	8.7	12.6	14.1	15.7	11.9	7.0	4.5	2.0	39.0	51.3
New Mexico	68.4	2.1	9.4	1.5	18.7	46.3	9.9	7.0	18.1	9.9	12.8	12.1	14.2	12.5	7.5	4.3	1.5	36.7	50.6
New York	65.7	15.9	0.6	7.3	10.4	17.6	22.2	6.0	16.4	10.2	13.7	13.5	14.9	11.9	7.0	4.5	2.0	38.0	51.6
North Carolina	68.5	21.5	1.3	2.3	6.5	8.4	7.5	6.6	17.3	9.8	13.0	13.9	14.4	11.9	7.3	4.1	1.6	37.4	51.3
North Dakota	90.0	1.2	5.4	1.0	2.3	2.0	2.5	6.6	15.7	12.0	13.1	11.2	14.4	12.2	7.0	5.1	2.5	37.0	49.5
Ohio	82.7	12.2	0.2	1.7	3.2	3.1	4.1	6.2	17.4	9.5	12.4	12.8	15.1	12.6	7.4	4.7	2.0	38.8	51.2
Oklahoma	72.2	7.4	8.6	1.8	10.0	8.9	5.5	7.0	17.7	10.2	13.5	12.3	14.0	11.7	7.5	4.4	1.6	36.2	50.5
Oregon	83.6	1.8	1.4	4.0	9.1	11.7	9.8	6.2	16.4	9.4	13.7	13.0	14.1	13.3	7.6	4.3	2.0	38.4	50.5
Pennsylvania	81.9	10.8	0.2	2.7	4.3	5.7	5.8	5.7	16.2	9.9	11.9	12.7	15.3	12.8	7.7	5.3	2.5	40.1	51.3
Rhode Island	81.4	5.7	0.6	3.0	9.3	12.4	12.8	5.5	15.8	11.4	12.0	13.0	15.4	12.4	7.0	4.9	2.5	39.4	51.7
South Carolina	66.2	27.9	0.4	1.4	4.2	5.1	4.7	6.5	16.8	10.3	12.7	13.0	14.3	12.6	8.0	4.1	1.6	37.9	51.4
South Dakota	85.9	1.3	8.8	0.9	3.0	2.7	2.7	7.3	17.6	10.0	12.8	11.4	14.4	12.0	7.1	4.8	2.4	36.9	50.0
Tennessee	77.6	16.7	0.3	1.5	3.9	4.6	4.5	6.4	17.1	9.6	12.8	13.5	14.6	12.4	7.7	4.2	1.6	38.0	51.3
Texas	70.4	11.8	0.7	3.9	13.2	37.6	16.4	7.7	19.6	10.2	14.3	13.8	13.7	10.3	5.9	3.3	1.2	33.6	50.4
Utah	86.1	1.1	1.2	2.9	8.7	13.0	8.0	9.5	22.0	11.5	16.2	12.0	11.1	8.7	5.0	2.9	1.1	29.2	49.8
Vermont	95.3	1.0	0.4	1.3	2.0	1.5	4.4	5.1	15.5	10.4	11.2	12.5	16.4	14.4	7.9	4.5	2.1	41.5	50.7
Virginia	68.6	19.4	0.4	5.6	6.1	7.9	11.4	6.4	16.8	10	13.6	13.9	15.2	11.9	6.9	3.8	1.5	37.5	50.9
Washington	77.3	3.6	1.5	7.8	9.9	11.2	13.1	6.5	17	9.7	13.9	13.5	14.7	12.4	6.8	3.7	1.8	37.3	50.2
West Virginia	93.9	3.4	0.2	0.7	1.8	1.2	1.2	5.6	15.3	9.1	11.7	12.8	14.9	14.3	8.8	5.2	2	41.3	50.7
Wisconsin	86.2	6.3	1	2.3	4.2	5.9	4.5	6.3	17.3	9.7	12.6	12.8	15.4	12.3	7	4.6	2.1	38.5	50.4
Wyoming	90.7	0.8	2.4	0.9	5.2	8.9	2.8	7.1	16.9	10	13.6	11.9	14.8	13	7	3.8	1.6	36.8	49

1. May be of any race.

Table A. States — **Households and Housing Units**

STATE	Households, 2010: Number	Households, 2010: Percent change, 2000-2010	Households, 2010: Persons per household	Households, 2010: Percent: Female family householder[1]	Households, 2010: Percent: One-person households	Housing units, 2010: Total	Housing units, 2010: Percent change, 2000–2010	Occupied units: Total	Owner-occupied: Percent	Owner-occupied: Median value[2] (dollars)	Median owner cost as a percent of income: With a mortgage	Median owner cost as a percent of income: Without a mortgage[3]	Renter-occupied: Median gross rent[4] (dollars)	Renter-occupied: Median rent as a percent of income	Substandard units[5] (percent)
	64	65	66	67	68	69	70	71	72	73	74	75	76	77	78
United States	116,716,292	10.7	2.58	13.1	26.7	131,791,065	13.7	114,567,419	65.4	179,900	25.1	12.8	855	31.6	3.9
Alabama	1,883,791	8.4	2.48	15.3	27.4	2,174,428	10.7	1,815,152	70.1	123,900	23.0	12.3	667	32.2	2.4
Alaska	258,058	16.5	2.65	10.7	25.6	307,065	17.7	254,610	63.9	241,400	23.3	10.8	981	29	10.2
Arizona	2,380,990	25.2	2.63	12.4	26.1	2,846,738	30.0	2,334,050	65.2	168,800	26.5	11.3	844	31.6	5.1
Arkansas	1,147,084	10.0	2.47	13.4	27.1	1,317,818	12.3	1,114,902	67.4	106,300	21.5	10.9	638	29.9	3.2
California	12,577,498	9.3	2.90	13.3	23.3	13,682,976	12.0	12,406,475	55.6	370,900	30.6	11.4	1,163	33.8	9.1
Colorado	1,972,868	19.0	2.49	10.1	27.9	2,214,262	22.5	1,960,585	65.9	236,600	25.2	10.7	863	31.2	3.2
Connecticut	1,371,087	5.3	2.52	12.9	27.3	1,488,215	7.4	1,358,809	68.0	288,800	26.8	17.6	992	32.1	2.4
Delaware	342,297	14.6	2.55	14.2	25.6	406,489	18.5	328,765	73.0	243,600	24.8	11.8	952	32.3	2.9
District of Columbia	266,707	7.4	2.11	16.4	44.0	296,836	8.0	252,388	42.5	426,900	24.8	11.0	1,198	30.4	3.5
Florida	7,420,802	17.1	2.48	13.5	27.2	8,994,091	23.2	7,035,068	68.1	164,200	29.5	14.4	947	35.5	3.1
Georgia	3,585,584	19.3	2.63	15.8	25.4	4,091,482	24.7	3,482,420	66.2	156,200	25.2	12.3	819	32.4	3.2
Hawaii	455,338	12.9	2.89	12.6	23.3	519,992	12.9	445,812	58.0	525,400	30.1	10.1	1,291	33.5	9.1
Idaho	579,408	23.4	2.66	9.6	23.8	668,634	26.7	576,709	69.6	165,100	24.7	10.6	683	30.5	3.6
Illinois	4,836,972	5.3	2.59	12.9	27.8	5,297,077	8.4	4,752,857	67.7	191,800	25.9	13.8	848	31.5	3.1
Indiana	2,502,154	7.1	2.52	12.4	26.9	2,797,172	10.5	2,470,905	70.3	123,300	21.6	11.0	683	30.8	2.2
Iowa	1,221,576	6.3	2.41	9.3	28.4	1,337,563	8.5	1,223,439	72.4	123,400	21.3	11.5	629	28.1	1.7
Kansas	1,112,096	7.1	2.49	10.4	27.8	1,234,037	9.1	1,101,658	68.1	127,300	21.8	11.8	682	28.1	2.2
Kentucky	1,719,965	8.1	2.45	12.7	27.5	1,928,617	10.1	1,684,348	68.6	121,600	22.2	11.3	613	29.8	2.5
Louisiana	1,728,360	4.4	2.55	17.2	26.9	1,967,947	6.5	1,689,822	67.6	137,500	21.6	10.5	736	31.7	3.7
Maine	557,219	7.5	2.32	10.0	28.6	722,217	10.8	545,417	72.7	179,100	24.1	13.9	707	29.8	2.5
Maryland	2,156,411	8.9	2.61	14.6	26.1	2,380,605	11.0	2,127,439	67.0	301,400	25.4	12.9	1,131	30.8	2.4
Massachusetts	2,547,075	4.2	2.48	12.5	28.7	2,808,727	7.1	2,520,419	62.2	334,100	26.1	15.3	1,009	30.4	2.0
Michigan	3,872,508	2.3	2.49	13.2	27.9	4,531,231	7.0	3,806,621	72.8	123,300	24.6	13.9	730	33.3	2.1
Minnesota	2,087,227	10.1	2.48	9.5	28.0	2,348,242	13.7	2,091,548	73.0	194,300	24.1	11.9	764	30.2	2.3
Mississippi	1,115,768	6.6	2.58	18.5	26.3	1,276,441	9.9	1,079,999	69.8	100,100	23.5	12.0	672	33.2	4.0
Missouri	2,375,611	8.2	2.45	12.3	28.3	2,714,017	11.1	2,350,628	69.0	139,000	22.6	11.7	682	30.1	2.2
Montana	409,607	14.2	2.35	9.0	29.7	483,006	17.1	402,747	69.7	181,200	24.1	11.3	642	28.3	2.8
Nebraska	721,130	8.2	2.46	9.8	28.7	797,677	10.4	719,304	67.4	127,600	21.4	12.6	669	27.7	2.2
Nevada	1,006,250	34.0	2.65	12.7	25.7	1,175,070	42.0	989,811	57.2	174,800	28.1	12.2	952	31.6	5.0
New Hampshire	518,973	9.3	2.46	9.7	25.6	614,996	12.4	515,431	71.7	243,000	26.5	16.5	951	30.3	1.9
New Jersey	3,214,360	4.9	2.68	13.3	25.2	3,554,909	7.4	3,172,421	66.4	339,200	28.7	18.9	1,114	32.4	4.1
New Mexico	791,395	16.7	2.55	14.0	28.0	902,242	15.6	765,183	67.9	161,200	24.3	10.0	699	29.3	4.7
New York	7,317,755	3.7	2.57	14.9	29.1	8,108,211	5.6	7,196,427	54.3	296,500	26.3	15.5	1,020	31.7	5.5
North Carolina	3,745,155	19.6	2.48	13.7	27.0	4,333,479	23.0	3,670,859	67.2	154,200	24.0	12.5	731	31.3	2.8
North Dakota	281,192	9.3	2.30	8.2	31.5	318,099	9.8	280,412	66.9	123,000	19.6	10.0	583	25.8	1.3
Ohio	4,603,435	3.5	2.44	13.1	28.9	5,128,113	7.2	4,525,066	68.4	134,400	23.4	13.1	685	31.1	1.8
Oklahoma	1,460,450	8.8	2.49	12.3	27.5	1,666,205	10.0	1,432,959	67.8	111,400	21.9	11.2	659	28.9	3.0
Oregon	1,518,938	13.9	2.47	10.5	27.4	1,676,476	15.4	1,507,137	62.5	244,500	27.3	12.9	816	32.7	3.4
Pennsylvania	5,018,904	5.1	2.45	12.2	28.6	5,568,820	6.1	4,936,030	70.1	165,500	23.8	13.7	763	30.4	1.6
Rhode Island	413,600	1.3	2.44	13.5	29.6	463,416	5.4	402,295	60.8	254,500	27.7	15.4	868	30.9	2.6
South Carolina	1,801,181	17.4	2.49	15.6	26.5	2,140,337	22.0	1,761,393	68.7	138,100	23.5	12.0	728	32.2	2.7
South Dakota	322,282	11.0	2.42	9.7	29.4	364,031	12.6	318,955	68.0	129,700	21.9	10.9	591	26.9	2.7
Tennessee	2,493,552	11.7	2.48	13.9	26.9	2,815,087	15.4	2,440,663	68.1	139,000	23.7	11.4	697	31.4	2.5
Texas	8,922,933	20.7	2.75	14.1	24.2	9,996,209	22.5	8,738,664	63.6	128,100	23.4	12.5	801	30.2	5.8
Utah	877,692	25.2	3.10	9.7	18.7	981,821	27.7	880,025	69.9	217,200	24.8	10.0	796	29.5	4.6
Vermont	256,442	6.6	2.34	9.6	28.2	322,698	9.6	256,922	70.4	216,800	26.0	16.3	823	31.8	2.2
Virginia	3,056,058	13.2	2.54	12.4	26	3,368,674	16.0	2,992,732	67.7	249,100	24.7	11.4	1,019	30.2	2.6
Washington	2,620,076	15.4	2.51	10.5	27.2	2,888,594	17.9	2,606,863	63.1	271,800	26.7	12.1	908	30.6	3.4
West Virginia	763,831	3.7	2.36	11.2	28.4	882,213	4.5	741,940	74.6	95,100	20.1	10	571	29.7	1.8
Wisconsin	2,279,768	9.4	2.43	10.3	28.2	2,625,477	13.1	2,279,532	68.7	169,400	24.5	14	715	29.8	2.2
Wyoming	226,879	17.2	2.42	8.9	28	262,286	17.2	222,803	69.7	180,100	22	10	693	25.3	2.8

1. No spouse present. 2. Specified owner-occupied units. 3. Median monthly costs is often in the minimum category—10.0 percent or less, which is indicated as 10.0 percent. 4. Specified renter-occupied units. 5. Overcrowded or lacking complete plumbing facilities.

Table A. States — Housing Units and Residential Construction

STATE	Housing units 2020													
	Total	Percent change, 2019-2020	Occupied units								Presence of Computer and Internet Subscription			
			Total	Percent owner-occupied	Mortgage status by home ownership		Median value of units[2] (dollars)	Percent valued over $500,000	Median gross rent[3] (dollars)	Percent living in a different house than 1 year ago	Total households	With a computer (percent)	With an Internet subscription (percent)	With no computer or no internet subscription (percent)
					With a mortgage	Without a mortgage[1]								
	79	80	81	82	83	84	85	86	87	88	89	90	91	92
United States	140,766,987	0.8	124,345,410	57.8	60.7	39.3	253,600	18.6	1,129	12.4	124,345,410	94.0	88.0	12.0
Alabama	2,302,582	0.8	1,895,330	58.4	54.0	46.0	162,300	6.0	800	11.7	1,895,330	91.4	83.6	16.4
Alaska	321,385	0.5	255,456	53.5	60.8	39.2	288,100	11.6	1,203	15.9	255,456	96.6	91.2	8.8
Arizona	3,120,061	1.4	2,774,127	59.7	61.1	38.9	278,400	14.8	1,149	15.2	2,774,127	95.2	88.4	11.5
Arkansas	1,401,087	0.9	1,185,599	57.2	53.2	46.8	141,800	4.3	760	12.6	1,185,599	91.6	81.8	18.2
California	14,383,549	0.1	13,135,388	51.3	67.7	32.3	593,400	59.6	1,661	11.1	13,135,388	96.0	91.4	8.6
Colorado	2,432,832	-1.3	2,201,823	60.4	69.4	30.6	415,700	33.7	1,401	15.8	2,201,823	96.6	91.7	8.3
Connecticut	1,530,056	0.3	1,406,237	60.7	67.1	32.9	287,500	17.9	1,217	10.9	1,406,237	94.2	90.1	9.9
Delaware	449,537	1.3	387,778	62.1	64.2	35.8	272,200	10.1	1,133	10.4	387,778	94.7	89.6	10.3
District of Columbia	327,525	1.5	291,687	36.0	76.9	23.1	672,700	67.2	1,701	19.4	291,687	94.5	88.3	11.6
Florida	9,814,540	1.5	8,133,696	56.6	56.2	43.8	261,500	14.2	1,270	14.1	8,133,696	95.1	88.4	11.5
Georgia	4,426,892	1.1	3,904,930	57.8	62.7	37.3	218,600	10.7	1,080	12.7	3,904,930	94.3	87.3	12.7
Hawaii	554,102	0.7	477,480	55.8	62.6	37.4	648,000	65.4	1,704	12.1	477,480	95.2	91.0	9.0
Idaho	768,816	2.4	678,555	64.2	62.0	38.0	290,400	15.0	923	16.2	678,555	95.5	90.4	9.6
Illinois	5,399,497	0.2	4,907,332	60.7	61.4	38.6	214,300	10.7	1,065	11.2	4,907,332	93.7	88.1	12.0
Indiana	2,940,473	0.7	2,642,088	64.1	64.3	35.7	163,500	4.4	850	12.7	2,642,088	93.1	87.4	12.6
Iowa	1,428,906	0.7	1,275,934	64.7	58.9	41.1	164,000	4.4	785	12.7	1,275,934	93.1	86.2	13.8
Kansas	1,294,032	0.4	1,151,979	60.1	56.9	43.1	166,200	6.0	877	14.5	1,151,979	94.4	88.1	11.9
Kentucky	2,016,609	0.5	1,759,434	59.6	56.3	43.7	160,700	4.8	795	12.6	1,759,434	92.3	85.4	14.6
Louisiana	2,103,943	0.7	1,762,869	57.4	51.4	48.6	174,000	5.7	866	11.3	1,762,869	91.6	83.4	16.5
Maine	755,380	0.6	584,057	57.6	57.1	42.9	211,000	9.9	903	11.5	584,057	92.1	86.0	14.0
Maryland	2,482,043	0.5	2,255,168	60.8	71.1	28.9	344,700	23.0	1,425	12.0	2,255,168	95.4	90.3	9.7
Massachusetts	2,944,398	0.5	2,687,421	56.9	66.3	33.7	439,800	40.7	1,449	11.5	2,687,421	94.7	90.5	9.5
Michigan	4,643,918	0.3	4,012,557	63.3	58.1	41.9	179,500	5.8	908	11.2	4,012,557	93.5	87.2	12.7
Minnesota	2,503,010	1.0	2,234,764	66.0	64.2	35.8	263,300	11.2	1,070	12.1	2,234,764	94.4	89.1	11.0
Mississippi	1,345,251	0.5	1,126,474	58.7	49.7	50.3	135,100	3.5	779	11.0	1,126,474	90.4	79.7	20.3
Missouri	2,833,623	0.5	2,463,458	59.0	60.3	39.7	176,000	6.5	841	12.6	2,463,458	92.9	85.9	14.1
Montana	524,644	0.9	446,572	59.5	53.3	46.7	272,600	16.1	854	13.2	446,572	93.1	86.1	13.9
Nebraska	857,908	0.8	774,402	61.1	56.9	43.1	181,900	4.7	870	13.5	774,402	94.0	88.3	11.7
Nevada	1,305,950	1.6	1,173,874	53.0	66.5	33.5	333,000	18.9	1,229	14.6	1,173,874	95.4	89.2	10.9
New Hampshire	646,849	0.7	538,552	61.0	63.2	36.8	297,800	14.9	1,179	12.5	538,552	94.9	90.1	9.9
New Jersey	3,654,920	0.4	3,346,036	58.3	63.6	36.4	364,300	27.8	1,394	10.1	3,346,036	94.7	90.2	9.8
New Mexico	955,942	0.8	816,574	60.0	50.6	49.4	188,000	7.8	834	11.7	816,574	91.0	81.9	18.1
New York	8,444,156	0.5	7,488,719	48.9	57.8	42.2	353,100	34.7	1,358	9.6	7,488,719	93.0	87.5	12.5
North Carolina	4,813,617	1.4	4,088,898	57.1	60.8	39.2	207,300	9.7	943	12.7	4,088,898	92.6	86.1	13.9
North Dakota	382,115	0.6	321,697	54.4	52.6	47.4	205,200	6.0	748	13.9	321,697	93.6	87.6	12.3
Ohio	5,247,933	0.3	4,741,813	60.7	60.9	39.1	164,000	4.8	831	11.9	4,741,813	93.2	87.5	12.5
Oklahoma	1,759,576	0.6	1,514,051	58.5	52.6	47.4	152,500	4.3	811	14.0	1,514,051	93.0	84.7	15.4
Oregon	1,830,846	1.2	1,688,863	58.4	65.7	34.3	373,500	26.9	1,239	14.5	1,688,863	95.8	90.6	9.4
Pennsylvania	5,753,228	0.4	5,178,588	62.5	58.4	41.6	203,800	9.1	979	10.8	5,178,588	91.7	86.3	13.7
Rhode Island	471,340	0.2	421,624	57.7	67.8	32.2	302,200	15.3	1,069	10.7	421,624	93.2	89.2	10.8
South Carolina	2,386,402	1.5	2,009,401	60.4	56.2	43.8	189,500	10.1	937	12.7	2,009,401	92.0	83.4	16.6
South Dakota	404,906	0.8	349,073	61.1	53.5	46.5	188,900	6.7	724	12.4	349,073	93.3	86.2	13.8
Tennessee	3,065,835	1.2	2,702,490	59.2	58.7	41.3	203,400	9.4	907	13.1	2,702,490	92.4	84.8	15.2
Texas	11,487,050	1.8	10,270,966	56.4	54.9	45.1	214,400	10.5	1,113	13.8	10,270,966	94.9	88.4	11.7
Utah	1,161,907	2.5	1,052,033	64.6	69.1	30.9	360,800	21.6	1,158	13.7	1,052,033	97.0	91.8	8.2
Vermont	341,405	0.6	263,353	56.0	60.8	39.2	235,000	9.3	1,007	13.2	263,353	92.3	84.7	15.2
Virginia	3,586,869	0.7	3,213,949	59.6	67.6	32.4	305,100	23.8	1,269	13.2	3,213,949	94.2	88.5	11.5
Washington	3,242,721	1.5	2,987,658	58.7	67.1	32.9	419,500	37.1	1,401	14.3	2,987,658	96.2	91.6	8.4
West Virginia	896,570	0.2	734,080	60.7	46.8	53.2	130,500	2.3	723	10.8	734,080	88.9	81.6	18.4
Wisconsin	2,738,305	0.5	2,393,344	59.9	62.2	37.8	212,600	7.5	872	11.6	2,393,344	92.6	86.9	13.2
Wyoming	281,946	0.6	237,179	62.3	57.6	42.4	236,600	11.1	800	16.1	237,179	94.5	87.5	12.4

1. Median monthly costs is often in the minimum category—10.0 percent or less, which is indicated as 10.0 percent. 2. Specified owner-occupied units. 3. Specified renter-occupied units.

STATE	Value of residential construction authorized by building permits, 2021			New manufac-tured homes shipped, 2021	Births, 2020		Deaths, 2019					Percent lacking health insurance, 2020		Medicare beneficiaries, 65 years and older, 2020
							Number		Rate					
									Total					
	New construction ($1,000)	Number of housing units	Percent single family		Total	Rate[1]	Total	Infant[2]	Crude[1]	Age-adjusted[1]	Infant[3]	All persons	Children under 19 years	
	93	94	95	96	97	98	99	100	101	102	103	104	105	106
United States	380,036,187	1,736,982	64.2	105,721	3,613,647	11.0	2,854,838	20,921	8.7	7.2	5.6	8.8	5.4	61,551,947
Alabama	4,816,174	22,100	80.9	5,153	57,647	11.7	54,108	449	11.0	9.0	7.7	9.7	3.4	1,062,565
Alaska	413,299	1,552	74.6	13	9,469	13.0	4,613	48	6.3	7.0	4.9	11.6	8.2	104,465
Arizona	15,322,691	65,334	71.3	2,421	76,947	10.4	60,236	429	8.3	6.6	5.4	11.2	9.2	1,370,074
Arkansas	2,857,616	14,198	74.4	2,038	35,251	11.6	32,888	251	10.9	8.8	6.9	8.5	4.2	646,920
California	28,724,878	119,436	55.2	3,344	420,259	10.7	269,831	1,879	6.8	6.0	4.2	7.1	3.4	6,411,106
Colorado	13,743,890	56,524	53.5	1,015	61,494	10.6	39,390	306	6.8	6.5	4.9	8.4	5.3	938,949
Connecticut	1,224,866	4,651	63.2	140	33,460	9.4	31,745	153	8.9	6.5	4.5	4.6	2.8	692,023
Delaware	1,175,682	8,500	85.4	432	10,392	10.5	9,302	66	9.6	7.3	6.3	6.3	3.7	215,724
District of Columbia	625,841	4,740	7.9	0	8,874	12.4	4,927	44	7.0	7.0	4.9	3.5	1.5	94,126
Florida	49,325,935	213,494	69.7	7,601	209,671	9.6	207,002	1,330	9.6	6.5	6.1	12.4	7.1	4,680,137
Georgia	14,437,233	67,223	79.5	4,211	122,473	11.4	85,814	888	8.1	7.7	7.0	13.0	7.4	1,773,148
Hawaii	1,396,040	3,459	70.7	5	15,785	11.2	11,559	85	8.2	5.7	5.1	3.9	3.2	281,164
Idaho	4,949,319	21,732	74.3	575	21,533	11.8	14,430	97	8.1	7.1	4.4	9.6	6.3	349,171
Illinois	4,272,625	19,658	55.6	1,299	133,298	10.6	109,096	794	8.6	7.0	5.7	7.1	3.0	2,265,857
Indiana	7,583,248	29,860	74.4	1,709	78,616	11.6	66,001	525	9.8	8.2	6.5	7.5	6.1	1,283,965
Iowa	3,182,377	13,686	66.9	662	36,114	11.4	30,867	189	9.8	7.3	5.0	4.9	2.7	637,388
Kansas	2,592,906	9,538	68.9	682	34,376	11.8	27,682	201	9.5	7.7	5.7	8.8	5.4	546,423
Kentucky	2,912,471	14,841	68.0	3,884	51,668	11.5	48,990	266	11.0	9.1	5.0	5.8	4.4	943,242
Louisiana	4,054,061	19,147	88.5	5,623	57,328	12.3	45,938	468	9.9	8.6	7.9	8.2	4.4	884,245
Maine	1,593,799	6,530	80.2	787	11,539	8.5	15,065	63	11.2	7.6	5.4	7.5	5.5	347,594
Maryland	4,011,527	18,496	67.7	121	68,554	11.3	50,800	413	8.4	7.0	5.9	5.7	3.5	1,058,229
Massachusetts	4,941,794	19,853	36.4	175	66,428	9.6	58,630	254	8.5	6.6	3.7	2.6	1.7	1,352,786
Michigan	5,684,341	21,732	77.1	4,037	104,074	10.4	99,084	690	9.9	7.7	6.4	5.3	2.7	2,100,420
Minnesota	7,726,133	33,652	49.6	913	63,443	11.2	45,514	302	8.1	6.5	4.6	4.9	3.5	1,046,400
Mississippi	1,541,523	7,988	92.4	4,415	35,473	12.0	32,964	322	11.1	9.5	8.8	11.7	5.5	609,795
Missouri	4,747,590	21,372	65.2	1,594	69,285	11.3	62,401	433	10.2	8.0	6.0	10.1	6.8	1,248,427
Montana	1,411,199	7,272	43.6	361	10,791	10.0	10,402	54	9.7	7.4	4.9	8.7	7.1	237,744
Nebraska	2,016,001	10,723	59.0	277	24,291	12.5	16,970	125	8.8	7.1	5.1	8.1	5.2	353,778
Nevada	5,293,432	23,406	69.6	588	33,653	10.7	25,586	201	8.3	7.4	5.7	12.0	8.3	549,393
New Hampshire	1,260,568	4,892	70.0	324	11,791	8.6	12,744	37	9.4	7.0	3.1	6.1	2.8	307,567
New Jersey	5,234,056	37,094	37.5	415	97,954	11.0	75,010	428	8.4	6.6	4.3	7.6	4.3	1,637,118
New Mexico	1,622,288	7,753	70.5	1,480	21,903	10.4	19,512	129	9.3	7.6	5.6	9.7	5.9	432,470
New York	7,652,184	40,135	27.7	1,678	209,338	10.8	156,375	955	8.0	6.2	4.3	5.2	2.5	3,672,562
North Carolina	20,485,854	94,874	72.3	6,129	116,730	11.0	95,881	808	9.1	7.7	6.8	10.6	5.3	2,035,577
North Dakota	865,569	3,600	62.9	357	10,059	13.1	6,702	77	8.8	7.1	7.4	7.2	6.5	134,332
Ohio	7,339,454	30,418	67.4	1,810	129,191	11.0	123,717	930	10.6	8.3	6.9	6.7	4.7	2,381,221
Oklahoma	3,454,208	14,733	90.4	2,693	47,623	12.0	40,930	343	10.3	8.8	7.0	15.3	9.4	753,478
Oregon	5,128,318	21,916	60.2	1,627	39,820	9.4	37,370	203	8.9	7.0	4.9	6.6	3.6	886,188
Pennsylvania	9,311,131	47,894	39.2	1,779	130,693	10.2	133,983	788	10.5	7.5	5.9	6.3	5.9	2,776,113
Rhode Island	328,495	1,392	74.2	22	10,101	9.6	10,256	61	9.7	7.1	6.0	3.7	3.0	224,732
South Carolina	11,652,262	50,680	85.4	5,216	55,704	10.7	50,962	391	9.9	8.0	6.9	10.5	5.7	1,106,010
South Dakota	1,565,480	7,917	54.6	358	10,960	12.3	8,270	80	9.3	7.4	7.0	9.8	6.2	180,220
Tennessee	11,477,551	57,484	64.3	3,646	78,689	11.4	71,935	563	10.5	8.8	7.0	10.2	6.0	1,385,253
Texas	52,319,224	265,955	67.5	18,478	368,190	12.5	203,362	2,075	7.0	7.2	5.5	17.5	11.6	4,286,051
Utah	9,188,026	39,058	62.5	283	45,702	14.1	18,736	249	5.8	6.9	5.3	8.5	7.1	414,961
Vermont	499,725	2,319	58.7	177	5,133	8.2	5,956	15	9.5	6.8	*	4.1	1.0	151,303
Virginia	7,750,202	39,388	63.8	1,380	94,749	11.0	70,325	570	8.2	7.0	5.9	7.2	4.3	1,545,578
Washington	12,501,328	56,941	44.0	1,445	83,086	10.8	58,263	365	7.7	6.7	4.3	6.3	3.1	1,398,937
West Virginia	778,004	3,692	84.3	1,290	17,323	9.7	23,404	112	13.1	9.5	6.2	6.6	2.8	442,688
Wisconsin	5,985,631	25,444	51.9	841	60,594	10.4	54,189	371	9.3	7.2	5.9	5.6	4.5	1,200,527
Wyoming	1,058,126	2,706	79.7	218	6,128	10.5	5,121	46	8.8	7.4	7.0	11.3	7.8	113,802

1. Per 1,000 resident population. 2. Deaths of infants under 1 year old. 3. Deaths of infants under 1 year old per 1,000 live births.

Table A. States — **Crime and Education**

STATE	Serious crime known to police,[1] 2020				Public elementary and secondary school enrollment, 2020–2021		Educational attainment[3] (percent)				Local government expenditures for education, 2018–2019	
	Violent crime		Property crime				2010		2020			
	Number	Rate[2]	Number	Rate[2]	Total	Student/ teacher ratio	High school graduate or more	Bach-elor's degree or more	High school graduate or more	Bach-elor's degree or more	Total current expen-ditures (mil dol)	Current expen-ditures per student (dollars)
	107	108	109	110	111	112	113	114	115	116	117	118
United States	1,313,105	398.5	6,452,038	1,958.2	49,366,089	16.3	85.6	28.2	89.4	35.1	666,865	13,187
Alabama	22,322	453.6	105,161	2,136.8	734,559	17.4	82.1	21.9	88.0	27.8	7,476	10,107
Alaska	6,126	837.8	16,528	2,260.5	129,872	17.2	91.0	27.9	93.7	31.9	2,409	18,393
Arizona	35,980	484.8	165,323	2,227.7	1,111,500	22.4	85.6	25.9	89.1	33.0	9,828	8,773
Arkansas	20,363	671.9	79,200	2,613.4	486,305	12.6	82.9	19.5	88.2	24.9	5,157	10,412
California	174,026	442.0	842,054	2,138.9	6,064,504	22.5	80.7	30.1	84.4	36.9	86,756	13,831
Colorado	24,570	423.1	164,582	2,833.8	883,199	16.3	89.7	36.4	92.7	44.2	10,093	11,072
Connecticut	6,459	181.6	55,670	1,565.1	509,058	12.0	88.6	35.5	91.6	42.4	11,133	21,140
Delaware	4,262	431.9	19,355	1,961.4	138,092	14.0	87.7	27.8	91.0	34.7	2,205	15,929
District of Columbia	7,127	999.8	24,899	3,493.0	94,573	12.3	87.4	50.1	93.8	63.6	2,020	22,831
Florida	83,368	383.6	384,556	1,769.4	2,791,707	17.3	85.5	25.8	89.6	33.7	28,425	9,986
Georgia	42,850	400.1	214,988	2,007.4	1,730,015	14.7	84.3	27.3	89.3	34.8	19,799	11,203
Hawaii	3,576	254.2	33,928	2,411.4	176,441	14.5	89.9	29.5	93.3	35.5	2,924	16,132
Idaho	4,432	242.6	20,313	1,111.9	307,581	17.5	88.3	24.4	91.3	30.9	2,497	8,043
Illinois	53,612	425.9	196,287	1,559.4	1,886,137	NA	86.9	30.8	90.4	37.6	32,208	16,281
Indiana	24,161	357.7	120,453	1,783.2	1,033,964	15.7	87.0	22.7	90.2	28.9	10,823	10,252
Iowa	9,601	303.5	53,725	1,698.2	506,656	14.1	90.6	24.9	93.1	29.5	6,144	11,933
Kansas	12,385	425.0	64,077	2,199.1	481,750	12.7	89.2	29.8	91.8	35.1	5,638	11,328
Kentucky	11,600	259.1	79,673	1,779.5	658,813	15.5	81.9	20.5	88.7	27.4	7,646	11,280
Louisiana	29,704	639.4	133,989	2,884.4	693,150	18.1	81.9	21.4	86.9	27.2	8,485	11,920
Maine	1,466	108.6	15,610	1,156.2	172,455	11.4	90.3	26.8	93.6	33.5	2,831	15,686
Maryland	24,215	399.9	97,487	1,609.8	882,527	14.2	88.1	36.1	91.1	43.1	13,969	15,576
Massachusetts	21,288	308.8	72,602	1,053.2	921,712	12.3	89.1	39.0	91.3	46.9	18,472	19,196
Michigan	47,641	478.0	135,633	1,360.9	1,434,137	17.0	88.7	25.2	92.0	32.1	18,129	12,052
Minnesota	15,698	277.5	120,212	2,124.9	872,083	16.0	91.8	31.8	93.8	37.9	11,825	13,297
Mississippi	8,638	291.2	62,351	2,101.6	442,627	14.1	81.0	19.5	86.8	24.5	4,361	9,253
Missouri	33,385	542.7	155,698	2,531.0	882,477	12.8	86.9	25.6	91.4	31.9	10,367	11,349
Montana	5,077	469.8	22,917	2,120.8	146,252	13.4	91.7	28.8	94.4	34.6	1,784	11,984
Nebraska	6,473	334.1	36,991	1,909.2	324,697	13.6	90.4	28.6	91.9	33.3	4,160	12,746
Nevada	14,445	460.3	60,462	1,926.6	486,617	20.5	84.7	21.7	87.2	28.0	4,496	9,126
New Hampshire	2,000	146.4	15,014	1,098.9	169,027	11.4	91.5	32.8	94.1	40.2	3,048	17,457
New Jersey	17,353	195.4	102,875	1,158.2	1,373,960	11.8	88.0	35.4	90.9	43.1	29,864	21,331
New Mexico	16,393	778.3	59,859	2,841.9	316,840	14.7	83.3	25.0	87.8	30.1	3,491	10,466
New York	70,339	363.8	272,788	1,410.7	2,606,748	12.2	84.9	32.5	87.8	39.5	65,549	24,882
North Carolina	44,451	419.3	236,026	2,226.5	1,513,677	15.0	84.7	26.5	90.3	34.8	15,213	9,799
North Dakota	2,518	329.0	16,256	2,124.1	114,955	12.1	90.3	27.6	93.5	31.8	1,598	14,033
Ohio	36,104	308.8	216,363	1,850.3	1,645,412	16.3	88.1	24.6	91.5	30.6	22,779	13,433
Oklahoma	18,255	458.6	107,705	2,705.6	694,113	16.1	86.2	22.9	89.2	27.0	6,432	9,203
Oregon	12,380	291.9	112,782	2,659.0	560,917	18.2	88.8	28.8	91.9	36.3	7,247	12,457
Pennsylvania	49,793	389.5	210,167	1,644.1	1,704,396	13.6	88.4	27.1	91.6	34.0	29,235	16,892
Rhode Island	2,440	230.8	13,166	1,245.5	139,184	13.1	83.5	30.2	90.1	38.0	2,516	17,539
South Carolina	27,691	530.7	141,987	2,721.1	766,819	14.3	84.1	24.5	89.4	31.7	8,585	10,994
South Dakota	4,476	501.4	17,468	1,956.7	139,566	13.9	89.6	26.3	92.2	28.4	1,435	10,325
Tennessee	46,328	672.7	171,675	2,492.8	985,207	15.2	83.6	23.1	89.7	30.7	10,017	9,941
Texas	131,084	446.5	659,160	2,245.0	5,372,806	14.5	80.7	25.9	85.8	33.2	53,619	9,868
Utah	8,471	260.7	80,091	2,464.4	680,659	NA	90.6	29.3	94.0	36.9	5,382	7,950
Vermont	1,081	173.4	7,586	1,217.0	82,582	10.3	91.0	33.6	94.2	42.1	1,847	21,217
Virginia	17,925	208.7	125,114	1,456.4	1,251,639	14.4	86.5	34.2	91.4	42.0	16,300	12,642
Washington	22,596	293.7	210,223	2,732.4	1,087,354	17.6	89.8	31.1	92.1	38.4	16,116	14,342
West Virginia	6,352	355.9	24,976	1,399.4	253,930	13.6	83.2	17.5	89.1	23.1	3,288	12,269
Wisconsin	18,861	323.4	86,654	1,485.7	830,066	13.8	90.1	26.3	93.1	31.8	10,905	12,690
Wyoming	1,364	234.2	9,379	1,610.6	92,772	12.3	92.3	24.1	93.8	28.2	1,530	16,228

1. Data for serious crimes have not been adjusted for underreporting; this may affect comparability between geographic areas and over time. 2. Per 100,000 population estimated by the FBI.
3. Persons 25 years old and over.

STATE	Exports of goods by state of origin, 2021 (mil dol)			Income and Earnings, 2020					Percent below poverty level, 2020						
					Households							Families			
	Total	Manu-factured	Non-manu-factured	Median earnings in the past 12 months (dollars)	Median income (dollars)	Percent with income of $20,000 or less	Percent with income of $100,000 or more	Median income of family of four	All persons	Children under 18 years	Persons 65 years and over	All families	Married-couple families	Male house-holder[1] families	Female house-holder[1] families
	119	120	121	122	123	124	125	126	127	128	129	130	131	132	133
United States	1,754,578	1,133,253	315,561	37,138	67,340	13.5	32.7	84,394	11.9	15.7	9.6	8.0	4.3	11.8	23.0
Alabama	20,896	18,286	1,717	32,377	53,956	18.1	24.1	71,781	14.7	20.4	10.9	9.8	4.8	15.9	29.6
Alaska	6,000	864	4,953	41,698	80,197	9.9	38.8	93,751	9.2	11.8	5.7	5.6	2.9	11.0	17.9
Arizona	24,083	13,548	3,500	36,074	64,777	12.8	29.6	79,260	12.8	17.6	8.7	8.8	5.0	15.2	22.9
Arkansas	5,616	3,990	499	31,552	51,183	18.5	21.1	66,166	15.3	20.8	9.3	11.0	5.6	18.2	31.1
California	175,126	109,143	24,306	39,811	83,056	11.2	42.4	96,821	11.4	14.6	10.5	7.7	5.0	10.2	18.9
Colorado	9,136	7,696	454	40,979	77,673	10.2	38.5	97,781	9.0	10.5	7.6	5.4	3.2	9.5	17.8
Connecticut	14,569	11,698	956	42,340	79,719	12.2	40.7	104,535	9.8	12.3	8.0	6.4	2.6	10.2	20.4
Delaware	4,724	3,661	136	36,712	70,911	11.3	33.7	89,996	11.3	16.7	7.5	7.2	4.1	7.1	18.8
District of Columbia	1,503	1,096	355	61,958	96,762	12.8	49.2	160,212	14.8	21.1	11.5	8.0	4.0	11.6	21.0
Florida	55,462	38,262	4,297	32,923	61,736	14.2	28.8	77,200	12.3	16.5	10.6	7.8	5.2	12.4	20.6
Georgia	42,366	31,400	4,822	35,871	62,844	15.0	30.1	78,530	13.9	19.0	10.3	9.3	4.9	14.5	25.0
Hawaii	339	104	149	39,601	86,391	9.2	43.8	102,579	8.9	10.8	8.4	6.0	3.5	9.3	14.7
Idaho	3,778	2,382	671	32,018	62,774	11.8	26.6	75,634	10.1	11.6	7.1	6.7	4.3	8.8	25.0
Illinois	65,904	51,483	3,697	40,345	71,240	13.2	34.5	90,509	11.0	13.8	9.4	7.4	3.5	10.3	22.5
Indiana	41,140	35,830	785	35,397	60,813	13.9	26.5	76,404	11.7	15.3	7.2	8.0	3.3	11.2	27.1
Iowa	15,837	12,740	2,556	36,298	62,209	12.5	27.3	80,513	10.4	12.4	8.1	6.8	3.1	12.2	24.8
Kansas	12,579	8,965	2,651	35,704	63,321	12.8	27.7	78,929	10.8	13.7	7.5	7.4	3.6	9.0	24.9
Kentucky	29,530	22,250	503	32,328	54,191	17.1	23.0	69,485	14.8	19.3	10.6	10.4	5.2	17.5	30.0
Louisiana	76,821	33,229	42,758	33,620	51,730	20.2	24.6	70,245	17.8	24.1	13.6	12.4	5.5	18.3	34.4
Maine	3,089	1,700	1,137	35,015	58,782	15.4	26.1	76,453	10.7	12.0	8.6	6.4	3.4	12.4	20.0
Maryland	16,428	10,220	3,799	47,313	88,742	10.1	44.4	109,898	8.8	10.3	8.1	5.4	2.9	5.9	14.7
Massachusetts	32,453	26,034	1,390	46,684	87,328	12.4	44.6	111,112	9.4	10.7	9.8	6.1	2.8	10.9	18.2
Michigan	55,534	48,112	2,592	35,127	61,497	14.6	27.8	79,736	12.7	17.0	9.1	8.2	4.2	11.9	24.1
Minnesota	23,538	18,820	1,747	41,388	75,523	10.1	36.2	96,184	8.3	9.5	7.1	4.9	2.1	8.9	19.8
Mississippi	12,933	9,686	950	30,807	47,247	22.3	19.9	60,955	18.8	26.1	13.0	14.2	5.7	19.8	36.9
Missouri	15,507	12,591	1,780	35,288	58,838	14.8	26.3	76,700	12.1	15.3	9.2	8.0	4.1	14.0	24.4
Montana	1,974	1,039	856	31,802	57,211	14.4	25.0	74,521	13.0	15.0	10.9	7.4	4.3	13.9	24.9
Nebraska	8,000	6,115	1,539	36,115	64,591	11.8	28.3	81,988	9.0	9.2	7.2	5.8	2.8	11.2	18.6
Nevada	10,551	5,658	805	35,767	64,574	13.0	30.2	76,779	12.3	16.5	9.6	8.0	4.9	7.5	19.9
New Hampshire	6,368	4,400	267	41,850	80,972	9.3	39.7	100,514	7.0	8.8	6.6	4.2	2.1	11.6	15.0
New Jersey	49,528	27,416	7,647	45,503	87,016	10.6	43.9	105,788	9.5	13.3	8.6	7.0	3.4	10.1	19.2
New Mexico	5,379	3,017	336	31,482	52,059	19.6	23.6	67,774	17.8	23.1	13.6	12.5	6.8	22.1	29.9
New York	84,874	45,533	12,821	41,714	73,398	14.4	37.3	91,045	12.7	16.6	11.7	9.3	5.2	12.4	20.7
North Carolina	33,446	26,581	1,783	34,027	59,580	15.4	27.0	76,279	13.0	18.5	9.6	8.5	4.4	13.1	26.8
North Dakota	5,209	3,429	1,652	36,699	61,987	12.8	27.7	82,225	11.0	12.0	6.6	7.4	4.7	9.2	20.9
Ohio	50,422	40,671	4,685	35,720	60,338	15.1	26.4	77,177	12.7	16.8	8.5	8.7	3.6	12.3	27.7
Oklahoma	6,203	4,845	514	32,624	54,536	16.8	23.5	69,656	14.4	18.9	9.2	9.7	5.6	12.2	28.2
Oregon	29,556	22,777	2,789	36,478	67,927	12.5	32.7	83,245	11.0	11.8	8.5	6.6	3.6	9.6	19.4
Pennsylvania	44,725	32,379	5,180	37,724	64,910	13.6	30.4	83,262	10.9	14.4	8.4	7.3	3.4	9.5	22.7
Rhode Island	2,963	1,822	870	40,975	75,682	13.1	36.3	93,564	9.7	11.5	9.8	6.0	2.9	9.3	16.1
South Carolina	29,673	26,494	824	32,748	56,973	16.8	25.3	73,725	14.0	18.9	10.5	9.2	4.8	17.0	26.8
South Dakota	1,859	1,675	121	34,980	60,643	13.6	24.8	76,475	11.7	13.5	10.5	7.3	4.1	14.2	24.4
Tennessee	34,655	24,092	1,739	34,413	56,951	16.0	24.7	72,728	13.7	18.8	10.0	9.1	4.5	14.3	26.7
Texas	375,324	196,318	118,302	35,835	66,031	13.4	31.8	80,872	13.5	19.0	10.5	9.6	5.7	12.9	26.3
Utah	18,060	16,205	693	35,506	77,827	7.7	37.1	88,591	7.1	7.3	5.7	4.7	3.2	8.2	12.4
Vermont	2,582	2,180	60	36,910	67,428	13.2	30.4	87,112	9.6	9.8	7.5	4.3	1.9	11.2	16.1
Virginia	20,140	12,856	5,665	41,510	79,217	10.8	39.8	99,927	9.2	12.1	7.3	5.8	2.9	8.2	19.4
Washington	53,644	29,882	20,129	43,016	80,408	10.3	39.9	97,980	9.5	11.3	7.6	6.1	3.1	8.8	20.9
West Virginia	6,282	3,265	2,783	32,265	49,400	19.7	20.2	65,900	16.2	21.7	9.7	10.9	6.3	25.7	28.0
Wisconsin	24,823	21,259	1,070	37,214	64,868	13.0	28.8	84,243	10.1	12.2	9.0	6.0	3.0	10.4	21.3
Wyoming	1,425	1,275	121	36,811	66,432	12.5	30.1	84,861	9.3	8.5	10.4	5.3	2.6	15.2	17.2

1. No spouse present.

Table A. States — **Personal Income**

STATE	Personal income: Total, 2021 (mil dol)	Percent change, 2020–2021	Per capita[1], 2021: Dollars	Per capita[1], 2021: Rank	Sources of personal income (mil dol): Wages and salaries[2], 2021	Proprietors' income, 2021	Dividends, interest, and rent, 2021	Transfer payments, 2020: Total	Government payments to individuals: Total	Social Security	Medical payments	Income maintenance	Unemployment insurance
	134	135	136	137	138	139	140	141	142	143	144	145	146
United States	21,056,622	7.4	63,444	X	10,309,306	1,829,905	3,661,308	4,241,091	4,050,252	1,077,928	1,504,739	302,583	536,927
Alabama	244,976	7.1	48,608	49	112,713	15,899	39,019	61,243	58,951	19,192	19,959	5,112	3,819
Alaska	49,190	5.9	67,138	11	22,376	3,534	8,372	9,415	8,984	1,738	3,235	835	900
Arizona	395,111	7.2	54,301	42	193,558	26,184	65,656	91,099	87,824	24,729	32,874	5,515	10,705
Arkansas	154,769	8.1	51,148	46	67,532	9,582	33,179	38,638	37,043	11,251	14,441	2,783	2,563
California	2,997,206	8.5	76,386	5	1,544,522	262,907	505,968	552,257	531,274	102,258	198,475	42,543	108,302
Colorado	401,123	8.3	69,016	10	205,233	41,174	76,037	61,654	58,629	15,762	21,052	3,270	7,587
Connecticut	295,956	5.8	82,082	3	128,499	30,292	57,525	47,988	45,468	12,992	18,410	2,708	5,871
Delaware	59,202	6.9	59,002	27	29,709	4,336	10,105	13,861	13,193	4,121	5,421	772	887
District of Columbia	64,909	5.2	96,873	1	84,305	6,886	10,031	10,631	9,580	1,372	4,505	1,040	1,578
Florida	1,323,436	9.4	60,761	21	577,034	76,953	330,094	275,017	265,441	81,590	96,982	19,767	18,511
Georgia	597,101	7.7	55,289	37	302,403	52,762	96,499	118,605	113,580	31,498	34,699	10,002	15,900
Hawaii	87,054	5.5	60,389	23	39,639	7,204	15,285	19,363	18,486	4,785	5,628	1,337	3,895
Idaho	97,668	9.6	51,379	45	42,934	10,738	17,936	19,260	18,425	6,100	6,517	1,132	1,020
Illinois	850,197	7.3	67,095	12	424,748	72,406	152,911	157,539	149,260	39,621	55,999	13,483	20,285
Indiana	382,178	9.0	56,153	34	177,820	39,312	53,472	81,918	78,440	24,239	31,530	5,193	6,135
Iowa	181,919	7.5	56,973	31	84,871	17,810	30,651	37,416	35,252	11,347	13,016	2,188	3,198
Kansas	174,090	6.5	59,324	26	80,086	22,318	30,441	32,319	30,485	9,922	10,855	2,041	2,509
Kentucky	228,620	7.9	50,699	47	105,437	15,431	33,115	62,463	59,792	16,193	24,567	4,446	5,679
Louisiana	251,710	6.5	54,435	41	108,254	25,366	39,697	64,143	61,308	14,638	25,781	5,396	6,506
Maine	78,437	7.2	57,159	30	35,326	5,761	12,650	19,557	18,494	5,644	7,226	1,051	1,550
Maryland	427,034	5.6	69,266	9	203,279	30,542	70,543	74,467	70,605	18,607	27,358	5,005	9,635
Massachusetts	576,064	6.5	82,475	2	312,472	49,245	97,906	105,542	100,085	22,589	38,211	7,922	20,541
Michigan	558,330	5.2	55,551	35	264,563	37,420	89,031	146,541	140,635	40,125	48,091	9,064	25,672
Minnesota	373,754	6.5	65,486	15	192,594	31,637	64,116	71,410	67,618	18,844	25,722	4,331	9,165
Mississippi	134,041	7.2	45,438	51	55,957	10,209	18,590	38,826	37,239	10,707	14,025	3,306	3,282
Missouri	340,232	7.0	55,159	38	168,850	25,792	59,270	73,998	70,355	22,021	27,360	4,574	4,823
Montana	62,582	8.5	56,672	32	26,051	6,630	13,592	13,521	12,780	3,956	4,529	671	1,076
Nebraska	121,935	9.3	62,095	19	57,522	16,214	21,364	20,904	19,644	6,079	6,844	1,251	1,165
Nevada	183,083	8.6	58,233	29	84,284	12,981	37,795	39,268	37,959	9,439	11,635	2,622	8,047
New Hampshire	100,012	9.1	72,003	7	47,918	9,762	14,879	17,296	16,366	5,702	5,822	638	1,559
New Jersey	693,223	6.2	74,805	6	311,234	67,180	106,885	120,949	115,102	31,074	41,570	7,868	19,692
New Mexico	104,356	6.9	49,320	48	45,638	6,197	16,608	28,820	27,687	7,180	11,242	2,585	2,510
New York	1,515,757	5.3	76,415	4	792,600	135,448	278,846	322,884	303,588	64,247	126,278	23,676	55,607
North Carolina	580,767	8.9	55,043	39	292,558	40,888	93,084	124,548	119,495	36,832	41,538	9,092	9,345
North Dakota	50,793	7.9	65,544	14	24,370	8,269	9,631	8,597	7,996	2,284	2,875	431	881
Ohio	665,374	6.1	56,483	33	326,733	49,410	104,778	152,489	145,224	40,179	58,124	10,789	15,955
Oklahoma	211,913	6.7	53,156	43	88,319	27,743	36,894	46,241	44,315	13,351	14,876	3,539	3,613
Oregon	257,641	7.9	60,676	22	126,493	21,762	44,785	56,796	54,499	15,460	21,005	3,517	6,307
Pennsylvania	830,397	5.3	64,054	18	380,212	72,024	131,236	198,663	189,855	50,593	72,166	13,134	31,515
Rhode Island	67,865	5.5	61,942	20	31,241	4,756	10,592	16,038	15,280	3,962	5,780	1,123	2,304
South Carolina	270,299	7.9	52,074	44	120,131	18,712	46,846	64,276	61,911	20,382	21,040	4,290	4,718
South Dakota	57,949	9.5	64,720	17	23,210	11,186	11,468	9,584	8,891	3,027	3,059	666	340
Tennessee	382,749	8.9	54,873	40	186,943	48,076	50,349	83,414	79,605	24,914	28,699	6,674	5,841
Texas	1,762,055	8.9	59,674	25	864,666	214,061	289,761	305,577	292,757	72,726	106,615	25,071	34,746
Utah	184,896	9.0	55,392	36	98,825	14,415	35,097	25,984	24,605	7,408	8,123	1,788	1,656
Vermont	38,543	4.5	59,704	24	17,091	3,231	6,974	9,459	8,927	2,639	3,356	510	1,166
Virginia	565,274	6.2	65,408	16	287,352	32,734	100,967	95,437	91,487	27,589	32,158	5,427	9,215
Washington	556,327	7.7	71,889	8	292,097	43,031	100,716	93,183	88,691	24,861	29,845	5,930	12,306
West Virginia	85,256	6.2	47,817	50	34,626	5,375	11,703	26,723	25,584	7,935	9,712	1,900	1,803
Wisconsin	345,287	6.5	58,564	28	169,122	23,545	58,570	68,767	65,404	22,178	23,993	4,311	4,625
Wyoming	37,985	5.5	65,627	13	15,354	4,578	9,788	6,503	6,154	2,050	1,918	261	419

1. Based on the resident population estimated as of July 1 of the year shown. 2. Includes supplements to wages and salaries.

Table A. States — Personal Income and Earnings

STATE	Personal tax payments, 2020 (mil dol)	Disposable personal income, 2020		Earnings, 2020									Gross state product, 2021 (mil dol)
					Percent by selected industries								
						Goods-related[2]		Service-related and other[3]					
		Total (mil dol)	Per capita[1] (dollars)	Total (mil dol)	Farm	Total	Manu-facturing	Total	Retail trade	Finance, insurance, real estate, rental and leasing	Health care and social assistance	Govern-ment	
	147	148	149	150	151	152	153	154	155	156	157	158	159
United States	2,193,355	17,414,092	52,531	14,381,785	1.0	16.2	8.7	68.0	5.9	9.8	11.3	14.8	22,996,086
Alabama	20,113	208,636	41,521	154,532	0.7	21.0	13.8	59.0	6.8	6.7	11.3	19.3	247,093
Alaska	3,253	43,177	58,950	33,262	0.1	12.9	X	51.1	5.9	4.1	13.7	31.6	54,970
Arizona	34,307	334,151	46,552	259,939	0.7	15.5	7.9	69.7	7.1	11.6	12.6	14.1	411,192
Arkansas	12,583	130,564	43,345	91,383	2.4	19.0	12.2	63.0	6.8	6.3	12.8	15.6	144,545
California	369,903	2,393,408	60,593	2,126,939	0.9	14.5	8.8	70.2	5.1	9.5	9.7	14.4	3,356,631
Colorado	42,751	327,641	56,643	285,830	0.6	18.7	5.6	66.3	5.3	9.2	8.8	14.4	421,941
Connecticut	40,902	238,710	66,304	186,477	0.1	16.0	10.2	71.8	5.6	15.8	12.5	12.1	296,498
Delaware	6,211	49,147	49,549	41,099	1.2	12.5	5.3	70.9	6.0	19.5	14.2	15.3	80,718
District of Columbia	9,265	52,441	75,991	112,625	0.0	1.6	X	59.4	1.0	4.0	5.9	38.3	152,008
Florida	119,105	1,090,891	50,575	768,259	0.4	12.0	4.7	74.8	7.5	10.5	12.6	12.8	1,226,298
Georgia	55,820	498,747	46,500	419,252	0.5	14.4	8.1	70.8	6.1	10.0	10.0	14.3	683,302
Hawaii	8,137	74,391	51,236	58,334	0.4	10.3	1.7	61.4	6.0	7.3	11.4	28.0	90,059
Idaho	8,442	80,636	43,639	63,677	4.9	19.1	9.8	62.1	9.3	7.0	11.8	13.9	94,317
Illinois	94,677	697,458	54,552	589,985	1.9	15.1	10.1	70.5	5.2	11.6	10.5	12.5	938,347
Indiana	34,143	316,617	46,660	258,463	2.3	25.6	18.9	60.5	5.7	10.1	12.7	11.2	420,339
Iowa	16,665	152,517	47,831	123,743	5.9	22.7	15.5	56.0	6.0	9.6	10.4	15.5	219,842
Kansas	16,086	147,376	50,198	120,446	4.1	18.9	11.9	61.6	5.4	11.3	11.2	15.4	192,304
Kentucky	20,678	191,269	42,467	147,317	1.8	20.7	14.1	60.9	6.2	7.4	13.3	16.6	234,498
Louisiana	19,060	217,267	46,712	158,880	0.9	22.8	9.2	60.2	6.6	6.4	13.1	16.1	255,307
Maine	7,118	66,075	48,503	49,543	0.6	17.0	9.3	66.6	7.9	7.7	16.4	15.8	76,057
Maryland	54,322	350,199	56,734	280,285	0.3	11.3	4.4	64.7	5.1	8.6	11.3	23.7	438,235
Massachusetts	79,136	461,719	65,751	424,016	0.0	13.6	7.1	75.6	4.6	11.6	12.8	10.8	636,514
Michigan	52,594	478,214	47,500	361,623	0.7	21.5	15.2	64.9	6.2	7.8	12.5	12.9	568,413
Minnesota	43,007	307,778	53,928	265,170	2.5	19.1	11.9	66.7	5.2	9.7	13.5	11.7	412,001
Mississippi	9,039	115,950	39,214	79,590	2.3	19.9	13.2	56.6	7.7	5.0	12.0	21.2	125,110
Missouri	31,370	286,649	46,576	233,091	2.0	17.2	10.3	67.0	6.2	8.7	13.0	13.8	359,952
Montana	5,655	52,005	47,878	38,758	4.5	16.2	4.2	62.3	8.6	7.3	14.0	17.0	59,303
Nebraska	10,669	100,877	51,429	87,311	8.9	16.2	9.8	60.3	5.3	8.6	11.4	14.6	150,388
Nevada	15,545	153,043	49,146	116,354	0.2	15.1	4.9	70.8	7.4	7.2	9.9	14.0	192,964
New Hampshire	8,720	82,953	60,205	67,634	0.1	17.9	10.2	71.6	7.7	9.1	12.0	10.5	98,242
New Jersey	83,748	568,751	61,290	445,172	0.1	13.6	7.5	73.3	6.2	10.9	11.7	13.0	672,089
New Mexico	7,446	90,158	42,576	62,665	1.5	13.9	3.6	59.2	6.9	5.3	12.4	25.3	108,928
New York	226,218	1,213,832	60,225	1,105,721	0.2	8.4	3.7	75.8	4.5	17.4	11.8	15.6	1,853,926
North Carolina	55,596	477,674	45,679	395,810	0.8	16.9	10.1	66.0	6.3	9.9	10.3	16.3	654,986
North Dakota	3,796	43,293	55,578	38,363	12.0	18.4	6.1	53.4	6.0	6.8	12.7	16.1	63,387
Ohio	61,391	565,841	47,991	450,047	0.9	19.9	13.4	65.2	6.0	7.7	13.4	14.0	736,450
Oklahoma	16,521	182,031	45,944	137,276	1.1	23.5	8.4	56.6	6.3	5.5	10.7	18.9	206,751
Oregon	28,570	210,277	49,576	178,053	1.3	18.1	10.4	64.8	6.7	7.4	12.5	15.8	266,943
Pennsylvania	82,184	706,541	54,393	541,897	0.4	16.6	9.7	71.1	5.5	8.2	14.5	12.0	839,437
Rhode Island	6,571	57,729	52,662	43,295	0.1	14.5	7.9	69.0	6.6	10.2	13.9	16.2	65,939
South Carolina	23,742	226,832	44,210	166,892	0.3	19.9	12.9	61.7	7.0	8.1	9.8	18.1	270,079
South Dakota	3,835	49,086	55,333	39,836	12.4	16.1	8.8	58.1	6.4	11.9	14.3	13.4	61,206
Tennessee	26,541	325,005	46,965	274,501	0.3	18.7	11.1	68.9	7.0	8.5	13.3	12.1	418,294
Texas	135,228	1,483,407	50,771	1,253,773	0.3	22.8	7.8	63.7	5.8	9.3	9.3	13.2	1,985,319
Utah	17,138	152,519	46,476	134,534	0.4	19.5	9.5	65.4	7.6	10.1	8.1	14.7	220,342
Vermont	3,463	33,432	52,034	24,475	0.6	17.8	9.9	64.3	7.4	6.1	15.5	17.3	36,170
Virginia	65,938	466,318	54,022	382,172	0.2	11.4	5.3	66.8	5.0	7.6	9.4	21.6	591,851
Washington	51,223	465,218	60,271	395,287	1.5	14.4	7.1	68.2	9.6	6.5	9.6	15.8	667,577
West Virginia	6,680	73,624	41,135	48,987	0.1	19.7	8.5	59.0	6.8	4.9	17.3	21.3	87,395
Wisconsin	35,086	289,166	49,075	235,130	1.3	24.0	17.2	60.7	5.9	7.7	13.1	13.6	365,931
Wyoming	3,166	32,854	56,913	24,083	1.7	22.0	4.1	51.0	6.0	5.9	7.4	23.5	41,622

1. Based on the resident population estimated as of July 1 of the year shown. 2. Includes mining, construction, and manufacturing. 3. Includes private sector earnings in forestry, fishing, related activities, and other; utilities; wholesale trade; transportation and warehousing; and information.

Table A. States — Social Security, Employment, and Labor Force

STATE	Social Security beneficiaries, December 2020		Supplemental Security Income recipients, December 2020	Civilian employment and selected occupations,[2] 2020				Civilian labor force (annual average), 2021				
					Percent						Unemployed	
	Number	Rate[1]		Total	Management, business, science, and arts occupations	Services, sales, and office	Construction and production	Total (1,000)	Percent change, 2020–2021	Employed (1,000)	Total (1,000)	Rate[3]
	160	161	162	163	164	165	166	167	168	169	170	171
United States	63,281,222	192.1	7,958,723	153,076,251	42.2	36.5	21.3	161,758,337	0.3	153,099,687	8,658,650	5.4
Alabama	1,165,990	236.9	157,314	2,114,666	37.5	36.2	26.3	2,246,993	-0.9	2,169,721	77,272	3.4
Alaska	107,982	147.7	12,424	328,830	38.9	37.6	23.5	354,936	2.3	332,266	22,670	6.4
Arizona	1,433,237	193.1	118,853	3,278,374	40.2	40.3	19.5	3,518,425	1.8	3,346,319	172,106	4.9
Arkansas	707,846	233.6	103,122	1,286,396	37.3	36.4	26.2	1,332,620	-1.8	1,278,984	53,636	4.0
California	6,150,009	156.2	1,192,888	18,090,052	43.3	36.6	20.1	18,923,194	0.0	17,541,944	1,381,250	7.3
Colorado	915,854	157.7	71,971	2,938,263	46.1	35.0	18.9	3,156,110	2.2	2,986,711	169,399	5.4
Connecticut	695,402	195.5	66,925	1,759,017	46.5	35.8	17.7	1,855,923	-2.2	1,739,815	116,108	6.3
Delaware	224,617	227.6	17,143	456,774	40.6	37.7	21.7	496,430	2.2	469,875	26,555	5.3
District of Columbia	83,647	117.3	24,920	378,961	69.9	24.8	5.3	381,673	-2.0	356,578	25,095	6.6
Florida	4,840,275	222.7	575,272	9,760,905	39.5	41.6	19.0	10,312,768	2.2	9,843,057	469,711	4.6
Georgia	1,902,790	177.7	258,304	4,854,858	41.2	36.3	22.5	5,186,969	2.1	4,983,732	203,237	3.9
Hawaii	282,623	200.9	22,412	633,486	38.9	43.5	17.6	668,413	0.9	630,187	38,226	5.7
Idaho	370,385	202.7	30,780	853,075	38.0	36.5	25.5	917,056	2.2	884,328	32,728	3.6
Illinois	2,274,372	180.7	259,810	6,017,115	42.3	36.0	21.7	6,318,915	-0.8	5,935,974	382,941	6.1
Indiana	1,382,024	204.6	127,242	3,180,911	37.4	35.0	27.5	3,321,548	0.0	3,203,166	118,382	3.6
Iowa	663,803	209.8	51,573	1,570,606	38.4	34.0	27.5	1,676,075	-0.4	1,605,206	70,869	4.2
Kansas	569,120	195.3	47,303	1,411,011	40.5	35.6	23.9	1,495,665	0.1	1,447,323	48,342	3.2
Kentucky	1,009,092	225.4	167,786	1,968,308	37.4	36.5	26.1	2,036,942	1.0	1,941,737	95,205	4.7
Louisiana	925,400	199.2	170,026	1,936,063	38.9	38.2	22.8	2,062,492	0.0	1,949,403	113,089	5.5
Maine	355,433	263.3	35,947	657,282	40.1	35.7	24.2	681,884	1.0	650,334	31,550	4.6
Maryland	1,032,078	170.4	120,333	2,972,047	50.2	33.5	16.3	3,175,550	-1.6	2,992,228	183,322	5.8
Massachusetts	1,294,623	187.8	179,322	3,502,108	51.9	33.0	15.1	3,750,870	0.2	3,535,478	215,392	5.7
Michigan	2,250,141	225.8	265,956	4,467,341	40.6	35.7	23.7	4,776,110	-1.4	4,495,651	280,459	5.9
Minnesota	1,069,913	189.1	92,761	2,879,455	45.0	32.9	22.1	3,021,360	-3.3	2,918,393	102,967	3.4
Mississippi	681,219	229.6	114,080	1,223,042	35.0	37.2	27.8	1,254,239	0.9	1,184,401	69,838	5.6
Missouri	1,323,195	215.1	134,636	2,885,886	40.0	36.4	23.7	3,062,449	0.8	2,928,368	134,081	4.4
Montana	244,937	226.7	17,491	516,363	39.0	38.1	22.9	549,743	1.3	531,202	18,541	3.4
Nebraska	357,164	184.3	28,920	978,895	40.9	34.3	24.8	1,049,033	0.4	1,022,662	26,371	2.5
Nevada	565,671	180.2	56,484	1,401,688	34.0	45.2	20.8	1,504,761	0.1	1,395,939	108,822	7.2
New Hampshire	317,389	232.3	17,880	712,111	44.1	35.2	20.7	755,422	-0.6	728,940	26,482	3.5
New Jersey	1,651,408	185.9	173,226	4,281,034	47.0	34.9	18.1	4,661,087	0.4	4,365,397	295,690	6.3
New Mexico	453,282	215.2	60,930	856,371	39.6	38.8	21.7	943,356	0.8	879,329	64,027	6.8
New York	3,680,264	190.3	601,717	8,919,281	46.0	37.8	16.3	9,441,458	-1.4	8,786,280	655,178	6.9
North Carolina	2,183,353	206.0	227,652	4,816,078	42.1	35.7	22.2	4,959,672	2.3	4,721,198	238,474	4.8
North Dakota	138,461	180.9	8,304	395,454	40.2	36.4	23.4	406,187	-1.3	391,255	14,932	3.7
Ohio	2,405,217	205.7	306,163	5,454,898	39.5	36.1	24.4	5,736,882	0.0	5,441,879	295,003	5.1
Oklahoma	811,064	203.7	96,502	1,760,968	37.2	37.8	24.9	1,854,234	1.0	1,783,080	71,154	3.8
Oregon	906,127	213.6	87,980	1,989,206	43.1	36.1	20.8	2,148,333	2.1	2,036,138	112,195	5.2
Pennsylvania	2,877,728	225.1	348,636	6,011,752	42.5	35.4	22.1	6,406,185	-1.2	5,999,442	406,743	6.3
Rhode Island	230,018	217.6	32,124	518,152	43.6	38.4	17.9	571,034	0.7	538,969	32,065	5.6
South Carolina	1,197,138	229.4	113,864	2,305,071	39.0	36.9	24.1	2,364,366	1.4	2,269,813	94,553	4.0
South Dakota	185,752	208.1	14,495	445,810	37.7	35.4	26.9	468,015	1.4	453,511	14,504	3.1
Tennessee	1,496,750	217.3	172,815	3,148,340	39.5	35.7	24.7	3,327,966	0.9	3,185,263	142,703	4.3
Texas	4,421,803	150.6	633,515	13,524,954	40.6	37.3	22.1	14,220,446	2.5	13,413,036	807,410	5.7
Utah	430,247	132.4	31,519	1,585,145	41.7	36.9	21.4	1,681,494	2.5	1,636,150	45,344	2.7
Vermont	156,005	250.3	14,947	318,989	45.5	33.4	21.1	328,216	-3.8	316,941	11,275	3.4
Virginia	1,585,194	184.5	155,200	4,156,509	48.5	34.3	17.2	4,267,656	-2.3	4,100,803	166,853	3.9
Washington	1,401,525	182.2	146,666	3,634,685	45.8	33.8	20.4	3,913,513	-0.4	3,708,738	204,775	5.2
West Virginia	479,303	268.5	69,208	720,778	37.1	37.0	25.9	788,826	0.7	749,132	39,694	5.0
Wisconsin	1,275,932	218.8	116,390	2,938,564	38.9	34.0	27.1	3,134,439	0.9	3,016,039	118,400	3.8
Wyoming	118,420	203.4	6,992	280,323	37.6	34.3	28.1	290,404	-1.1	277,372	13,032	4.5

1. Per 1,000 resident population estimated as of July 1 of the year shown. 2. Persons 16 years old and over. 3. Percent of civilian labor force.

STATE	Nonfarm employment and earnings, 2021											
	Employed		Manufacturing			Employment (1,000)						
	Total (1,000)	Percent change, 2020–2021	Employ-ment (1,000)	Average earnings of production workers: Hourly	Average earnings of production workers: Weekly	Con-struction	Trans-portation and public utilities	Whole-sale trade	Retail trade	Informa-tion	Financial activities	Services[1]
	172	173	174	175	176	177	178	179	180	181	182	183
United States	146,124	3.2	12,346	23.80	985.92	7,413	6,632.7	5,678	15,396	2,831	8,777	64,480
Alabama	2,040	2.7	263.7	21.41	894.94	94.6	89.7	73.3	231.1	20.0	98.0	773.2
Alaska	310	2.9	12.3	26.87	978.07	16.0	20.5	6.2	34.1	4.8	10.8	117.7
Arizona	2,958	3.8	180.8	21.99	864.21	177.6	143.3	101.0	338.3	47.5	245.8	1,304.9
Arkansas	1,282	3.3	157.1	19.74	795.52	55.3	69.4	47.7	139.1	11.7	65.9	523.8
California	16,708	3.5	1,273.2	25.26	1,045.76	880.3	788.2	644.1	1,599.4	566.5	823.1	7,645.1
Colorado	2,744	3.8	148.7	25.40	1,056.64	176.8	103.9	109.7	272.2	76.3	177.7	1,220.7
Connecticut	1,613	3.1	153.4	28.07	1,100.34	59.5	65.5	57.3	166.8	29.8	117.6	738.7
Delaware	450	2.4	24.8	22.22	924.35	23.1	19.9	11.1	49.9	3.6	47.6	203.8
District of Columbia	743	-0.5	1.1	–	–	15.0	4.2	5.0	20.1	19.6	28.1	408.6
Florida	8,913	4.9	388.2	24.82	1,027.55	575.5	388.2	355.5	1,094.8	138.7	622.0	4,252.0
Georgia	4,570	3.7	394.6	22.27	946.48	205.3	252.2	210.9	498.8	123.3	258.4	1,947.5
Hawaii	584	4.7	12.1	22.93	901.15	36.8	29.5	16.3	63.2	7.9	27.1	270.5
Idaho	795	5.3	70.5	20.40	840.48	60.1	32.2	33.1	93.2	8.0	39.1	330.0
Illinois	5,813	2.2	554.0	22.53	955.27	222.3	326.6	282.0	574.3	88.6	406.9	2,571.7
Indiana	3,089	3.4	525.2	21.40	918.06	150.1	174.0	121.8	313.0	26.0	144.4	1,216.4
Iowa	1,536	2.0	217.6	22.51	886.89	77.8	70.3	64.5	173.5	18.9	108.9	548.0
Kansas	1,373	1.1	160.4	20.96	859.36	64.1	69.9	55.6	139.4	16.8	75.8	534.7
Kentucky	1,896	3.3	242.3	23.88	974.30	78.8	130.6	73.9	206.9	20.9	95.6	744.3
Louisiana	1,869	1.7	129.0	21.61	929.23	127.8	81.9	64.4	218	21.0	89.3	796.0
Maine	621	4.1	54.1	22.76	912.68	31.7	18.3	19.1	79.3	6.6	33.0	279.0
Maryland	2,647	2.5	109.1	21.97	911.76	160.2	117.2	81.2	267.6	33.7	137.5	1,235.0
Massachusetts	3,516	4.4	232.5	25.33	1,046.13	164.3	101.3	118.5	332.0	93.2	220.0	1,814.4
Michigan	4,194	4.0	583.7	23.41	955.13	176.3	164.4	164.4	448.5	51.7	232.7	1,791.6
Minnesota	2,842	2.4	312.9	24.75	992.48	129.9	105.1	125.3	281.5	42.3	190.7	1,244.8
Mississippi	1,137	2.5	143.8	20.46	810.22	44.8	65.4	33.9	136.5	9.5	42.4	420.1
Missouri	2,843	2.5	270.1	22.93	901.15	131.7	122.2	120.8	301.2	46.8	178.4	1,241.3
Montana	492	4.8	21.4	21.04	786.90	33.1	18.9	17.4	60.4	5.6	27.0	211.5
Nebraska	1,007	1.8	99.3	21.58	882.62	55.8	50.4	39.4	104.0	17.7	72.8	396.8
Nevada	1,366	7.2	60.7	20.53	882.79	96.9	88.9	38.0	149.1	15.0	70.1	673.2
New Hampshire	663	3.9	67.6	23.77	955.55	29.0	18.1	29.2	91.2	11.7	34.8	295.5
New Jersey	4,021	4.5	240.4	24.86	1,026.72	157.5	232.6	204.8	429	70.5	251.5	1,859.1
New Mexico	813	2.0	27.7	19.46	698.61	47.9	25.8	19.6	90.4	10.1	33.5	362.6
New York	9,045	3.0	408.3	24.30	967.14	374.8	296.6	296.3	830.6	280.9	704.0	4,413.2
North Carolina	4,586	4.7	462.9	19.92	838.63	237.8	191.5	189.4	509.2	77.1	272.5	1,925.2
North Dakota	417	1.2	26.2	23.19	881.22	25.2	21.6	22.7	44.9	5.7	24.6	150.8
Ohio	5,373	2.3	665.1	22.65	937.71	223.5	263.0	228.3	541.0	64.9	308.1	2,319.7
Oklahoma	1,643	1.3	128.9	21.49	893.98	77.2	77.2	53.9	181.3	17.8	78.3	655.5
Oregon	1,874	2.7	187.3	23.61	904.26	111.1	77.2	74.9	210.1	35.1	103.5	783.7
Pennsylvania	5,750	2.6	542.6	23.57	973.44	253.0	310.9	204.7	590.5	86.2	327.1	2,737.6
Rhode Island	480	4.4	39.0	22.01	849.59	20.1	13.1	15.6	46.3	5.5	34.5	242.6
South Carolina	2,146	3.2	249.4	23.63	987.73	104.2	88.7	73.7	251.5	27.3	109.8	870.4
South Dakota	440	3.3	43.8	20.31	844.90	25.1	13.8	21.3	51.4	5.0	28.2	170.8
Tennessee	3,106	3.6	349.4	21.57	916.73	136.7	198.5	121.0	333.5	46.8	172.1	1,313.7
Texas	12,706	3.6	873.5	25.80	1,075.86	736.8	631.7	592.5	1,342.6	207.9	833.0	5,342.0
Utah	1,612	5.2	145.3	22.32	892.80	122.1	69.0	55.4	182.5	41.0	97.2	640.9
Vermont	294	2.4	28.7	21.61	821.18	15.1	7.9	8.7	34.8	4.0	11.9	129.7
Virginia	3,943	2.3	236.3	21.06	878.20	205.2	146.6	107.9	400.6	66.4	209.9	1,853.6
Washington	3,357	2.2	259.1	28.03	1,146.43	223.0	118.6	130.2	403.9	157.1	160.6	1,337.7
West Virginia	685	1.8	45.5	21.20	879.80	30.9	25.8	18.8	78.5	7.2	29.5	285.3
Wisconsin	2,883	2.3	466.6	22.15	925.87	126.6	117.8	120.9	294.2	44.9	154.3	1,163.6
Wyoming	278	1.8	9.7	27.60	1,142.64	21.1	14.1	7.4	29.6	2.9	11.1	99.8

1. Includes professional and business services, educational and health services, leisure and hospitality, and other services.

STATE	Agriculture, 2017											
	Farms			Farm producers whose primary occupation is farming (percent)	Government payments, average per farm that recieves payments (dollars)	Land in farms					Value of land and buildings (dollars)	
		Percent with:						Acres				
	Number	Fewer than 50 acres	1,000 acres or more			Acreage (1,000)	Percent change, 2012–2017	Average size of farm	Total irrigated (1,000)	Total cropland (1,000)	Average per farm	Average per acre
	184	185	186	187	188	189	190	191	192	193	194	195
United States	2,042,220	41.9	8.5	41.1	$13,906	900,218	-1.6	441	58,013.9	396,433.8	$1,311,808	$2,976
Alabama	40,592	40.1	4.2	37.4	$8,892	8,581	-3.6	211	142.0	2,818.8	$630,736	$2,984
Alaska	990	67.0	4.3	41.9	$9,293	850	1.9	858	2.4	83.7	$616,112	$718
Arizona	19,086	69.1	11.0	53.3	$29,735	26,126	-0.5	1,369	910.9	1,286.6	$1,110,303	$811
Arkansas	42,625	30.3	7.2	41.7	$38,624	13,889	0.6	326	4,855.1	7,825.9	$1,030,741	$3,163
California	70,521	64.0	6.3	46.6	$24,112	24,523	-4.1	348	7,833.6	9,597.4	$3,252,414	$9,353
Colorado	38,893	46.2	14.9	38.2	$22,206	31,821	-0.2	818	2,761.2	11,056.3	$1,315,440	$1,608
Connecticut	5,521	70.9	0.7	39.0	$7,551	382	-12.6	69	7.4	148.6	$862,636	$12,483
Delaware	2,302	55.7	6.9	52.8	$18,604	525	3.3	228	163.3	452.2	$1,920,109	$8,414
District of Columbia	NA	NA	NA	NA	NA	NA	NA	NA	NA	NA	NA	NA
Florida	47,590	71.0	3.2	41.3	$14,795	9,732	1.9	204	1,519.4	2,825.8	$1,206,788	$5,901
Georgia	42,439	42.3	5.3	39.4	$18,310	9,954	3.5	235	1,287.5	4,372.1	$822,958	$3,509
Hawaii	7,328	89.5	1.7	46.7	$12,631	1,135	0.5	155	45.5	191.2	$1,445,188	$9,328
Idaho	24,996	56.0	9.7	40.8	$21,306	11,692	-0.6	468	3,398.3	5,894.7	$1,340,738	$2,866
Illinois	72,651	35.6	10.8	43.4	$10,727	27,006	0.3	372	612.5	24,003.1	$2,705,291	$7,278
Indiana	56,649	46.4	7.1	38.1	$12,628	14,970	1.7	264	555.4	12,909.7	$1,737,741	$6,576
Iowa	86,104	31.7	9.8	45.0	$11,146	30,564	-0.2	355	222.0	26,546.0	$2,506,812	$7,062
Kansas	58,569	21.8	20.2	41.9	$14,089	45,759	-0.8	781	2,503.4	29,125.5	$1,443,891	$1,848
Kentucky	75,966	40.1	2.5	36.4	$7,502	12,962	-0.7	171	83.9	6,630.4	$643,019	$3,769
Louisiana	27,386	46.5	7.6	37.7	$22,822	7,998	1.2	292	1,235.8	4,345.8	$889,146	$3,045
Maine	7,600	47.2	2.4	43.2	$10,806	1,308	-10.1	172	32.3	472.5	$446,614	$2,596
Maryland	12,429	54.7	3.2	42.1	$12,471	1,990	-2.0	160	124.8	1,426.7	$1,258,691	$7,861
Massachusetts	7,241	67.8	0.3	42.8	$7,583	492	-6.1	68	23.9	171.5	$739,711	$10,894
Michigan	47,641	46.3	4.5	43.1	$10,892	9,764	-1.9	205	670.2	7,924.5	$1,015,631	$4,955
Minnesota	68,822	28.8	9.3	45.5	$9,568	25,517	-2.0	371	611.6	21,786.8	$1,799,201	$4,853
Mississippi	34,988	31.6	6.4	37.8	$14,986	10,415	-4.7	298	1,814.5	4,960.6	$817,041	$2,745
Missouri	95,320	29.6	6.2	38.8	$10,366	27,782	-1.7	291	1,529.2	15,599.4	$986,481	$3,385
Montana	27,048	30.9	31.7	48.5	$27,014	58,123	-2.7	2,149	2,061.2	16,406.3	$1,968,381	$916
Nebraska	46,332	23.8	23.8	51.6	$20,745	44,987	-0.8	971	8,588.4	22,242.6	$2,674,492	$2,754
Nevada	3,423	51.7	13.7	50.4	$16,183	6,128	3.6	1,790	790.4	794.7	$1,627,858	$909
New Hampshire	4,123	57.1	0.8	38.6	$11,344	425	-10.3	103	2.2	108.0	$539,732	$5,231
New Jersey	9,883	75.2	1.1	39.6	$10,071	734	2.7	74	86.8	463.0	$1,000,464	$13,469
New Mexico	25,044	52.2	18.2	42.1	$18,436	40,660	-5.9	1,624	626.0	1,825.8	$845,740	$521
New York	33,438	36.7	3.3	48.1	$9,162	6,866	-4.4	205	53.3	4,291.4	$663,082	$3,229
North Carolina	46,418	47.9	3.8	42.7	$10,746	8,431	0.2	182	143.4	5,000.7	$843,154	$4,642
North Dakota	26,364	11.7	40.0	54.3	$22,770	39,342	0.2	1,492	263.9	27,951.7	$2,546,783	$1,707
Ohio	77,805	47.4	3.5	37.3	$12,301	13,965	0.0	179	50.7	10,960.7	$1,112,700	$6,199
Oklahoma	78,531	29.6	10.3	37.5	$11,248	34,156	-0.6	435	573.8	11,715.7	$754,099	$1,734
Oregon	37,616	67.1	6.2	40.3	$22,918	15,962	-2.1	424	1,664.9	4,726.1	$1,032,545	$2,433
Pennsylvania	53,157	42.1	1.4	45.7	$6,823	7,279	-5.5	137	32.1	4,651.2	$897,125	$6,552
Rhode Island	1,043	72.5	0.4	38.6	$14,205	57	-18.3	55	3.0	17.7	$897,835	$16,468
South Carolina	24,791	49.8	3.8	36.1	$10,400	4,745	-4.6	191	210.4	2,035.3	$683,873	$3,573
South Dakota	29,968	19.3	32.0	52.4	$19,416	43,244	0.0	1,443	492.5	19,813.5	$2,984,426	$2,068
Tennessee	69,983	45.2	2.3	35.8	$6,254	10,874	0.1	155	184.9	5,286.3	$608,739	$3,918
Texas	248,416	44.1	8.3	35.8	$20,984	127,036	-2.4	511	4,363.3	29,360.2	$980,409	$1,917
Utah	18,409	62.1	6.9	32.1	$12,633	10,812	-1.5	587	1,097.2	1,654.4	$1,067,323	$1,817
Vermont	6,808	41.1	2.3	42.1	$8,355	1,193	-4.7	175	3.0	479.7	$620,691	$3,541
Virginia	43,225	42.2	3.1	40.1	$10,122	7,798	-6.1	180	63.4	3,084.1	$834,254	$4,624
Washington	35,793	66.6	7.2	39.9	$30,692	14,680	-0.5	410	1,689.4	7,488.6	$1,143,889	$2,789
West Virginia	23,622	34.7	1.5	36.7	$4,853	3,662	1.5	155	1.7	947.7	$411,482	$2,654
Wisconsin	64,793	35.3	3.6	45.6	$4,609	14,319	-1.7	221	454.4	10,085.0	$1,083,640	$4,904
Wyoming	11,938	32.7	25.0	43.0	$14,410	29,005	-4.5	2,430	1,567.6	2,587.5	$1,892,340	$779

STATE	Agriculture, 2017 (cont.)							Land, 2015			
	Value of machinery and equipment, average per farm (dollars)	Value of products sold				Organic Farms (number)	Farms with Internet access (percent)	Owned by the federal government (percent)	Developed land (percent)	Rural land (percent)	Public water supply withdrawn, 2015 (mil gal per day)
		Total (mil dol)	Average per farm (dollars)	Percent from:							
				Crops	Livestock and poultry products						
	196	197	198	199	200	201	202	203	204	205	206
United States	133,363	$388,522.7	$190,245	49.8	50.2	20,806	75.4	20.8	5.9	70.6	38,595.83
Alabama	88,528	$5,980.6	$147,334	20.3	79.7	57	72.6	2.8	8.7	84.5	761.53
Alaska	91,623	$70.5	$71,171	42.1	57.9	18	87.9	NA	NA	NA	99.18
Arizona	77,604	$3,852.0	$201,824	54.4	45.6	84	57.4	41.5	2.9	55.4	1,195.15
Arkansas	126,667	$9,651.2	$226,420	37.6	62.4	81	73.6	9.6	5.5	82.3	363.06
California	165,070	$45,154.4	$640,297	73.9	26.1	3,794	82.0	46.7	6.2	45.4	5,147.74
Colorado	117,337	$7,491.7	$192,623	29.9	70.1	323	81.4	36.1	3.0	60.4	843.95
Connecticut	62,250	$580.1	$105,074	72.4	27.6	113	82.4	0.5	34.1	61.4	239.93
Delaware	198,096	$1,466.0	$636,826	22.2	77.8	13	78.7	1.6	19.4	59.2	86.35
District of Columbia	NA	NA	NA	NA	NA	NA	NA	NA	NA	NA	0.00
Florida	72,754	$7,357.3	$154,599	77.5	22.5	251	76.3	10.3	14.7	66.5	2,384.85
Georgia	115,773	$9,573.3	$225,577	34.2	65.8	139	76.0	5.5	12.3	79.3	1,069.91
Hawaii	50,701	$563.8	$76,938	74.0	26.0	167	76.1	14.8	6.0	78.6	266.92
Idaho	$175,951	$7,567.4	$302,746	42.4	57.6	295	83.9	62.5	1.7	34.7	275.79
Illinois	$220,485	$17,010.0	$234,133	81.4	18.6	328	76.9	1.4	9.6	87.0	1,475.66
Indiana	$163,136	$11,107.3	$196,073	64.1	35.9	657	71.9	2.1	11.0	85.3	627.84
Iowa	$230,716	$28,956.5	$336,296	47.8	52.2	785	79.6	0.6	5.4	92.6	390.38
Kansas	$180,725	$18,782.7	$320,694	34.4	65.6	117	76.5	0.9	4.0	94.0	351.15
Kentucky	$82,740	$5,737.9	$75,533	44.3	55.7	227	72.4	4.9	8.2	84.4	552.83
Louisiana	$121,758	$3,173.0	$115,861	65.0	35.0	29	69.9	4.0	6.3	75.2	708.92
Maine	$81,792	$667.0	$87,758	61.3	38.7	621	83.6	1.0	4.1	88.7	84.97
Maryland	$124,871	$2,472.8	$198,955	38.3	61.7	134	76.9	2.1	19.4	57.1	749.52
Massachusetts	$65,382	$475.2	$65,624	76.5	23.5	208	84.1	1.4	33.0	58.6	648.06
Michigan	$154,740	$8,220.9	$172,560	56.5	43.5	764	77.2	8.6	11.2	77.1	1,030.44
Minnesota	$223,666	$18,395.4	$267,289	55.4	44.6	735	79.0	6.4	4.5	83.2	515.24
Mississippi	$109,875	$6,196.0	$177,088	37.0	63.0	37	66.0	5.5	6.3	85.5	400.36
Missouri	$104,066	$10,525.9	$110,427	52.0	48.0	415	72.5	4.5	6.7	86.8	797.09
Montana	$164,524	$3,520.6	$130,162	45.0	55.0	221	81.4	28.7	1.2	69.0	153.19
Nebraska	$268,968	$21,983.4	$474,476	42.4	57.6	292	81.3	1.2	2.6	95.3	275.18
Nevada	$155,033	$665.8	$194,495	41.5	58.5	51	82.9	84.1	0.8	14.6	558.26
New Hampshire	$68,629	$187.8	$45,548	57.4	42.6	156	87.2	13.5	12.3	70.2	95.52
New Jersey	$86,532	$1,098.0	$111,095	89.7	10.3	122	80.9	3.4	35.7	50.1	1,175.42
New Mexico	$63,619	$2,582.3	$103,112	25.2	74.8	183	60.5	33.9	1.7	64.2	254.10
New York	$135,626	$5,369.2	$160,572	39.3	60.7	1,497	77.1	0.7	12.3	82.5	2,424.65
North Carolina	$112,477	$12,900.7	$277,924	29.0	71.0	465	75.2	7.1	14.4	70.2	938.01
North Dakota	$375,872	$8,234.1	$312,324	81.1	18.9	129	78.9	3.9	2.3	91.0	84.18
Ohio	$129,614	$9,341.2	$120,059	58.1	41.9	872	74.6	1.4	15.9	81.1	1,306.28
Oklahoma	$90,442	$7,465.5	$95,065	20.3	79.7	54	72.9	2.7	4.9	90.0	611.24
Oregon	$100,328	$5,006.8	$133,103	65.6	34.4	659	85.7	51.7	2.2	44.7	567.04
Pennsylvania	$109,024	$7,758.9	$145,962	35.8	64.2	1,142	69.3	2.3	15.4	80.6	1,391.70
Rhode Island	$62,786	$58.0	$55,607	70.5	29.5	22	84.1	0.5	28.7	52.1	97.46
South Carolina	$83,077	$3,008.7	$121,364	36.4	63.6	75	72.6	5.3	13.5	77.1	633.39
South Dakota	$282,162	$9,721.5	$324,397	53.1	46.9	87	81.0	5.6	2.0	90.6	71.95
Tennessee	$80,447	$3,798.9	$54,284	57.4	42.6	122	72.7	5.2	11.6	80.3	849.69
Texas	$83,627	$24,924.0	$100,332	27.7	72.3	466	72.6	1.8	5.4	90.3	2,885.33
Utah	$97,789	$1,838.6	$99,876	30.5	69.5	95	77.7	64.1	1.6	31.4	785.91
Vermont	$100,672	$781.0	$114,713	24.0	76.0	679	86.4	7.4	6.5	81.7	42.66
Virginia	$86,136	$3,960.5	$91,625	34.4	65.6	252	74.0	8.7	11.9	72.4	695.63
Washington	$121,662	$9,634.5	$269,172	72.5	27.5	933	84.1	28.5	5.7	62.2	866.53
West Virginia	$56,120	$754.3	$31,931	20.3	79.7	63	70.0	8.2	7.5	83.2	184.96
Wisconsin	$156,689	$11,427.4	$176,368	35.6	64.4	1,708	76.1	5.1	7.8	83.6	479.38
Wyoming	$126,844	$1,472.1	$123,313	21.6	78.4	69	80.5	47.2	1.1	50.9	101.35

Table A. States — **Manufactures and Construction**

STATE	Manufactures, 2020										Construction, 2017				
	All employees			Production workers[1]								Employees			
						Wages									
	Number (1,000)	Percent change, 2019–2020	Annual payroll (mil dol)	Number (1,000)	Work hours (millions)	Total (mil dol)	Average per worker (dollars)	Value added by manufacture (mil dol)	Sales, values of shipments or revenue (mil dol)	Total cost of materials (mil dol)	Number of establishments	Number	Percent change, 2012–2017	Sales, values of shipments or revenue (mil dol)	Annual payroll (mil dol)
	207	208	209	210	211	212	213	214	215	216	217	218	219	220	221
United States	11,353	-1.6	693,181	8,098	15,156	400,410	49,444	2,377,065	5,221,325	2,833,295	715,364	6,647,047	17.2	1,994,166	398,816
Alabama	255	0.0	14,098	195	370	9,137	46,967	48,144	128,151	79,088	7,527	82,090	4.3	22,990	4,133
Alaska	12	0.0	629	10	19	456	46,948	1,700	5,142	3,334	2,456	17,370	-28.2	5,841	1,323
Arizona	147	4.3	9,788	94	172	4,560	48,594	32,537	61,909	29,162	12,397	150,709	21.7	41,597	8,096
Arkansas	155	3.3	7,692	125	239	5,435	43,351	26,921	61,968	34,909	5,427	46,325	7.7	11,083	2,221
California	1,097	-2.2	77,111	703	1,320	36,384	51,749	265,516	507,503	240,989	74,696	779,585	30.5	242,288	49,970
Colorado	122	2.5	7,881	85	157	4,392	51,883	23,580	50,533	26,832	18,531	162,864	31.9	54,261	9,699
Connecticut	153	-2.5	11,442	94	174	5,632	59,807	34,225	58,840	24,133	7,898	58,224	4.1	18,655	3,932
Delaware	27	0.0	1,615	20	40	971	48,321	6,852	16,736	9,715	2,249	21,227	19.4	5,658	1,190
District of Columbia	1	0.0	65	1	2	48	50,921	226	381	156	452	10,386	15.2	3,163	679
Florida	297	-0.7	17,650	204	376	9,394	46,100	56,220	109,607	53,285	53,316	424,041	43.9	118,374	20,555
Georgia	361	-2.4	19,596	274	518	12,338	45,015	74,689	169,850	95,909	18,202	178,499	23.1	63,791	9,988
Hawaii	10	-9.1	496	7	12	299	42,995	1,585	4,853	3,103	2,877	32,115	16.1	10,844	2,232
Idaho	59	-1.7	3,719	44	85	2,386	53,969	10,666	24,474	13,830	6,929	40,671	26.9	10,059	1,870
Illinois	513	-1.5	30,333	375	697	18,080	48,270	100,763	233,451	131,889	29,188	215,621	5.3	74,495	15,550
Indiana	485	-2.0	27,715	373	700	18,415	49,361	96,245	234,514	137,093	13,439	132,101	6.6	36,549	7,818
Iowa	208	-1.9	12,219	155	292	7,605	48,948	46,739	111,259	64,311	8,743	68,457	3.7	20,219	3,950
Kansas	156	-2.5	9,362	115	217	5,774	50,221	28,158	77,506	48,956	7,031	66,965	13.8	18,339	3,597
Kentucky	227	-3.8	12,716	177	326	8,789	49,758	45,883	123,341	77,390	7,327	73,032	14.1	19,305	3,786
Louisiana	114	-2.6	8,428	83	166	5,267	63,540	38,336	130,792	90,668	8,121	138,421	1.5	29,264	7,788
Maine	49	2.1	2,747	37	65	1,788	48,465	8,571	15,663	7,203	5,041	26,421	4.1	6,188	1,414
Maryland	96	1.1	6,507	62	117	3,256	52,780	23,240	41,309	18,010	14,184	154,895	7.5	48,512	9,591
Massachusetts	241	0.8	17,727	141	265	7,513	53,190	47,940	86,701	38,582	19,250	140,470	16.3	51,184	10,416
Michigan	564	-4.1	31,917	413	748	19,743	47,765	95,673	234,622	138,558	19,310	152,413	15.6	46,132	9,724
Minnesota	302	-1.0	18,933	208	396	10,500	50,516	56,250	119,457	62,772	16,546	124,908	9.9	44,435	8,848
Mississippi	136	-2.2	6,884	108	204	4,634	43,046	24,054	58,409	34,043	3,850	43,010	3.5	10,016	2,217
Missouri	263	0.8	15,498	193	352	9,574	49,522	56,574	119,907	63,351	13,505	130,055	17.8	37,872	7,667
Montana	18	5.9	986	13	23	619	49,477	4,612	11,171	6,936	5,466	25,767	7.5	7,041	1,398
Nebraska	96	2.1	5,145	75	152	3,555	47,314	21,444	57,033	35,508	6,472	47,140	16.3	12,497	2,463
Nevada	46	0.0	2,868	33	61	1,790	54,890	9,561	18,336	8,754	4,973	77,924	42.8	20,639	4,231
New Hampshire	64	-3.0	4,073	42	78	2,032	48,900	10,564	20,462	9,862	4,166	28,351	16.0	7,713	1,818
New Jersey	213	-0.5	13,987	145	273	7,389	50,929	46,856	93,071	46,061	21,605	163,968	11.5	51,338	11,359
New Mexico	23	0.0	1,351	17	31	806	48,669	5,236	13,491	8,241	4,338	40,228	6.5	8,698	1,912
New York	383	-3.0	24,420	260	486	13,409	51,619	79,326	150,351	70,502	49,116	375,488	12.5	124,319	25,884
North Carolina	414	-1.9	22,661	309	581	13,777	44,527	100,271	193,810	93,268	23,121	196,113	8.6	58,218	9,998
North Dakota	25	-3.8	1,415	19	36	903	46,708	5,739	13,634	7,916	3,010	24,140	-6.5	7,105	1,607
Ohio	644	-2.0	37,487	471	875	23,072	48,935	119,459	286,256	166,008	19,908	197,082	8.8	58,063	12,097
Oklahoma	122	-3.2	6,813	91	167	4,387	48,387	22,684	54,759	31,460	8,354	73,775	5.9	17,846	3,782
Oregon	183	-1.1	11,810	129	230	6,543	50,528	32,902	66,618	33,633	12,870	95,607	37.0	26,206	5,516
Pennsylvania	521	-3.2	30,332	369	686	18,018	48,802	104,164	205,148	100,610	26,672	242,502	1.8	70,345	15,230
Rhode Island	36	-5.3	2,263	25	46	1,228	48,989	6,568	12,066	5,502	3,165	18,906	8.0	6,008	1,211
South Carolina	229	-1.7	13,372	171	318	8,265	48,381	52,315	118,327	70,570	9,864	87,040	26.7	25,647	4,435
South Dakota	44	-2.2	2,315	33	64	1,528	45,845	6,661	17,533	10,926	3,394	20,493	3.5	5,265	1,042
Tennessee	323	-2.7	18,014	243	453	11,323	46,665	69,740	148,607	78,660	10,051	112,271	10.3	32,115	6,140
Texas	769	-0.4	50,436	537	1,029	27,752	51,710	209,239	493,558	281,098	45,034	717,040	25.1	214,508	42,044
Utah	126	1.6	7,610	88	167	4,300	49,024	26,064	54,467	28,538	9,590	83,923	30.1	24,423	4,386
Vermont	30	0.0	1,805	20	37	937	47,013	4,593	9,057	4,365	2,694	13,757	-13.0	3,182	756
Virginia	228	-2.1	13,475	165	313	8,230	49,853	58,178	101,035	42,560	19,736	186,390	5.2	54,426	10,345
Washington	257	-1.9	18,047	176	320	9,843	56,060	36,857	92,328	55,220	23,619	193,770	39.7	60,286	12,683
West Virginia	46	-4.2	2,738	34	63	1,873	54,535	10,570	22,553	11,770	3,082	24,143	-9.4	5,427	1,290
Wisconsin	454	-1.5	26,269	332	628	15,994	48,122	79,010	173,096	93,577	13,851	112,462	9.7	37,628	7,941
Wyoming	9	-10.0	718	7	14	469	67,518	3,165	7,678	4,480	2,721	17,892	-16.0	4,112	994

1. Production and/or development and exploration workers

Table A. States — **Wholesale Trade and Retail Trade**

STATE	Wholesale trade, 2017					Retail trade,[1] 2017								
		Employees					Employees							
	Number of estab-lishments	Number	Percent change, 2012–2017	Sales (mil dol)	Annual payroll (mil dol)	Number of estab-lishments	Total	Percent change, 2012–2017	Motor vehicle and parts dealers	Food and beverage stores	Clothing and clothing accessory stores	General merchan-dise stores	Sales (mil dol)	Annual payroll (mil dol)
	222	223	224	225	226	227	228	229	230	231	232	233	234	235
United States	408,551	6,527,427	11.0	8,517,446	431,791,587	1,064,210	15,960,369	8.5	2,009,860	3,186,678	1,796,234	2,803,586	4,976,024	442,635
Alabama	5,225	75,178	2.5	88,032	4,115,973	17,958	230,069	5.3	31,412	35,070	22,347	52,669	63,740	5,819
Alaska	748	8,680	-0.7	9,162	537,383	2,480	34,498	2.3	4,268	7,373	2,460	7,520	10,385	1,095
Arizona	6,508	98,089	10.3	113,376	6,359,888	17,918	324,912	13.5	44,267	55,332	33,316	61,354	104,366	9,505
Arkansas	X	X	X	X	X	X	X	X	X	X	X	X	X	X
California	58,772	860,268	2.1	1,192,475	67,632,172	108,233	1,723,278	11.9	204,691	357,427	249,697	262,809	594,861	54,229
Colorado	7,179	102,499	10.6	135,159	7,453,581	19,056	279,982	14.0	36,214	56,152	27,107	44,919	84,931	8,420
Connecticut	4,061	76,120	0.9	149,834	6,361,890	12,391	186,297	2.1	21,461	44,728	23,917	23,526	55,404	5,561
Delaware	1,146	17,586	21.6	21,934	1,836,752	3,648	58,201	12.6	7,336	10,732	6,492	8,853	17,668	1,558
District of Columbia	395	4,540	6.6	5,167	357,039	1,743	23,133	17.0	175	7,152	4,704	2,252	5,534	673
Florida	X	X	X	X	X	X	X	X	X	X	X	X	X	X
Georgia	X	X	X	X	X	X	X	X	X	X	X	X	X	X
Hawaii	1,604	18,963	1.1	16,969	998,662	4,644	72,908	6.7	7,056	13,947	14,591	12,901	21,659	2,185
Idaho	2,141	29,855	13.9	37,786	1,632,433	6,133	82,312	12.8	13,707	12,965	5,326	16,134	24,936	2,312
Illinois	18,068	333,541	6.1	583,865	24,657,027	38,189	629,878	6.2	74,094	142,758	70,734	114,511	173,474	16,247
Indiana	7,585	121,772	9.9	143,451	7,426,911	21,327	336,615	8.7	43,510	52,350	26,526	70,245	102,106	8,660
Iowa	5,019	71,382	6.3	77,650	3,847,452	11,479	181,416	3.9	23,774	40,944	12,213	32,102	50,063	4,519
Kansas	4,416	63,614	-2.3	96,904	3,780,377	10,095	149,845	3.0	19,895	28,887	12,847	28,386	39,338	3,785
Kentucky	4,259	71,042	5.1	125,944	4,022,946	15,021	225,127	11.1	28,368	39,150	17,918	46,827	64,294	5,630
Louisiana	5,330	74,158	-3.4	77,677	4,155,627	16,564	233,385	6.0	30,595	39,555	23,920	50,131	65,001	5,988
Maine	1,517	18,360	9.6	18,858	1,015,627	6,250	81,733	2.0	11,068	18,269	5,632	11,641	23,879	2,250
Maryland	5,401	89,504	4.1	100,900	6,192,615	17,911	291,814	3.6	38,945	63,940	36,634	45,444	84,966	8,241
Massachusetts	7,521	153,303	9.9	214,395	13,078,823	23,928	364,204	3.6	37,828	98,789	46,773	42,020	110,195	10,911
Michigan	X	X	X	X	X	X	X	X	X	X	X	X	X	X
Minnesota	7,901	146,637	8.9	191,615	11,337,187	18,827	302,886	4.8	36,797	57,795	26,556	57,811	91,994	8,118
Mississippi	2,702	37,710	8.5	37,440	1,877,614	11,525	141,410	4.0	18,093	19,821	14,313	35,880	36,921	3,384
Missouri	7,565	126,395	0.1	154,926	7,064,082	20,694	312,616	3.3	41,346	51,652	27,218	62,336	100,394	8,148
Montana	1,597	14,875	3.0	17,276	767,973	4,754	59,032	6.5	8,828	10,613	3,234	9,598	16,936	1,623
Nebraska	3,192	41,471	1.6	63,229	2,442,473	7,154	109,729	3.6	13,622	20,908	8,307	19,779	31,215	2,853
Nevada	3,115	38,586	16.0	34,808	2,286,362	8,745	145,773	12.2	16,174	23,801	26,270	24,292	45,111	4,220
New Hampshire	1,826	26,417	7.6	26,679	1,928,099	6,032	96,591	1.0	12,381	21,789	9,016	13,857	30,039	2,805
New Jersey	13,844	288,082	9.4	463,247	26,201,731	31,200	469,615	7.6	48,577	111,658	61,699	63,997	149,171	13,453
New Mexico	X	X	X	X	X	X	X	X	X	X	X	X	X	X
New York	30,484	374,642	1.5	450,832	25,910,640	78,260	945,360	4.4	81,180	221,446	151,222	122,750	291,725	27,815
North Carolina	11,681	196,695	13.9	218,600	13,588,472	34,926	496,081	11.1	70,495	98,783	49,012	92,173	141,134	12,673
North Dakota	1,733	23,078	7.2	26,258	1,390,598	3,277	49,579	5.1	6,950	7,582	3,601	9,203	19,251	1,454
Ohio	13,630	238,916	4.2	276,251	14,577,328	35,500	588,060	7.1	76,594	123,389	49,953	106,112	174,300	14,861
Oklahoma	X	X	X	X	X	X	X	X	X	X	X	X	X	X
Oregon	5,355	77,990	7.7	80,531	5,041,622	14,318	211,222	12.7	27,054	41,835	19,924	40,269	61,699	6,067
Pennsylvania	14,246	259,620	7.1	310,515	18,332,703	42,514	662,560	2.9	84,065	148,289	65,071	104,995	234,836	17,354
Rhode Island	1,304	21,253	5.0	20,829	1,381,130	3,769	48,753	2.2	5,438	11,265	5,193	6,350	13,844	1,444
South Carolina	5,004	72,946	13.2	78,646	4,314,807	17,700	253,384	14.9	32,022	51,364	26,084	47,880	69,980	6,206
South Dakota	1,566	18,705	5.7	21,755	981,313	3,884	53,134	6.6	7,951	9,472	3,281	9,907	14,674	1,372
Tennessee	6,842	118,612	5.3	165,628	7,111,100	22,593	322,218.0	5.3	43,344	47,069	32,772	64,169	101,978	8,574
Texas	X	X	X	X	X	X	X	X	X	X	X	X	X	X
Utah	3,691	54,922	8.2	55,094	3,372,334	9,995	153,633	15.1	20,468	25,314	14,482	26,155	50,008	4,446
Vermont	777	11,048	2.8	14,273	633,048	3,219	38,390	-1.3	5,241	9,871	2,545	3,157	10,811	1,103
Virginia	6,926	105,989	-0.4	137,827	7,018,515	27,134	429,072	4.4	57,859	86,322	45,845	76,193	120,162	11,476
Washington	9,186	137,876	13.2	163,034	9,012,299	21,751	347,728	13.2	44,014	64,161	34,147	63,369	160,285	11,413
West Virginia	1,406	18,216	-8.5	23,491	890,351	5,963	82,985	-2.7	11,330	12,440	5,414	19,778	23,058	2,004
Wisconsin	6,944	122,143	8.0	117,299	7,335,932	18,908	317,668	7.0	41,782	55,212	22,692	59,776	91,764	8,274
Wyoming	813	6,961	-16.0	7,664	406,997	2,583	29,786	-1.0	4,522	5,228	1,663	5,812	9,124	853

1. Establishments with payroll.

Table A. States — **Information**

STATE	Information, 2017: Number of establishments	Employees: Number	Employees: Percent change, 2012–2017	Employees: Publishing, except Internet	Employees: Motion picture and sound recording	Employees: Broadcasting, except Internet	Employees: Internet publishing and broadcasting and web search portals	Employees: Telecommunications	Employees: Data processing, hosting, and related services	Sales, values of shipments or revenue (mil dol)	Annual payroll (mil dol)
	236	237	238	239	240	241	242	243	244	245	246
United States	154,096	3,719,890	11.4	1,042,420	342,048	275,797	265,848	1,143,243	603,236	175,519	59,956,856
Alabama	1,735	34,078	10.2	8,124	1,937	D	329	15,945	4,569	842	283,180
Alaska	416	6,553	4.3	615	707	D	21	4,186	286	47	14,114
Arizona	2,521	55,357	19.1	13,529	5,503	3,461	899	21,511	10,163	2,065	803,701
Arkansas	X	X	X	X	X	X	X	X	X	X	X
California	25,103	678,261	14.5	192,359	123,009	36,371	116,072	109,847	97,682	35,432	12,305,792
Colorado	3,610	91,856	19.4	22,548	5,185	4,433	3,707	39,292	16,318	4,240	1,211,517
Connecticut	1,796	42,615	7.2	9,348	2,650	7,650	3,003	12,283	6,229	1,915	676,358
Delaware	580	7,169	39.1	1,659	464	232	e	2,912	1,438	337	139,226
District of Columbia	778	23,787	5.0	8,742	964	5,151	3,274	2,232	2,331	497	190,120
Florida	X	X	X	X	X	X	X	X	X	X	X
Georgia	X	X	X	X	X	X	X	X	X	X	X
Hawaii	533	8,218	-1.8	1,366	1,135	D	72	h	672	162	46,559
Idaho	793	13,410	21.3	3,408	847	D	108	5,147	2,846	699	160,421
Illinois	6,010	130,749	11.2	40,010	8,814	7,701	11,633	39,273	21,323	5,356	1,882,723
Indiana	2,440	47,015	11.8	13,327	3,419	3,748	2,133	14,919	9,252	1,538	504,267
Iowa	1,618	29,753	4.7	9,619	1,805	D	e	8,933	6,724	1,019	381,630
Kansas	1,445	30,009	2.8	6,507	1,976	1,925	859	15,352	3,212	662	271,784
Kentucky	1,801	29,021	16.0	5,111	1,978	2,713	625	11,653	6,767	879	340,971
Louisiana	1,537	24,091	7.8	3,096	2,541	D	192	12,482	2,988	518	157,705
Maine	817	11,461	-3.3	3,110	846	1,043	112	4,286	1,465	256	84,844
Maryland	2,550	54,141	7.1	13,280	3,255	4,785	2,005	17,936	11,867	2,678	1,045,571
Massachusetts	3,879	127,108	5.6	57,523	4,716	5,170	12,750	25,659	19,614	5,962	2,469,086
Michigan	X	X	X	X	X	X	X	X	X	X	X
Minnesota	2,788	61,911	5.0	24,483	3,728	4,366	2,426	16,253	10,249	2,144	941,665
Mississippi	1,019	14,262	10.0	2,038	769	D	60	7,783	1,953	193	70,206
Missouri	2,701	60,546	11.5	15,118	3,519	4,482	1,145	26,202	9,677	2,034	696,126
Montana	693	8,637	12.7	2,436	654	D	57	3,656	807	129	55,272
Nebraska	983	20,967	3.0	6,515	1,179	1,593	1,874	5,913	3,851	1,041	334,034
Nevada	1,424	17,896	15.4	3,503	g	1,788	f	6,819	h	X	257,100
New Hampshire	773	16,782	-3.6	6,667	957	537	223	5,274	2,896	491	201,331
New Jersey	3,885	96,288	4.9	23,089	5,650	4,336	3,718	40,914	17,510	5,194	1,742,653
New Mexico	X	X	X	X	X	X	X	X	X	X	X
New York	11,769	298,902	3.8	72,078	37,805	41,500	37,287	64,632	33,810	11,955	4,388,956
North Carolina	3,920	94,977	9.8	29,306	5,942	5,251	1,603	35,114	17,384	5,075	1,339,036
North Dakota	353	7,284	-2.2	2,745	e	D	b	2,183	723	68	32,215
Ohio	4,295	102,069	8.6	35,950	5,154	6,213	7,517	32,531	14,177	3,054	1,346,784
Oklahoma	X	X	X	X	X	X	X	X	X	X	X
Oregon	2,388	39,690	18.8	15,175	3,348	2,492	1,612	11,282	5,625	2,133	453,027
Pennsylvania	5,562	113,792	8.9	31,835	6,681	7,653	4,841	38,621	18,633	5,454	1,783,508
Rhode Island	456	6,863	4.8	2,181	507	482	b	2,649	572	120	43,411
South Carolina	1,639	37,970	14.1	8,614	2,429	2,491	661	18,356	4,992	977	379,536
South Dakota	478	7,254	7.2	1,705	482	1,194	e	h	533	75	25,542
Tennessee	2,788	49,464	12.0	9,548	5,883	5,627	1,881	21,252	5,057	1,523	455,942
Texas	X	X	X	X	X	X	X	X	X	X	X
Utah	1,746	52,159	23.5	19,526	8,365	1,553	2,766	10,931	8,699	1,750	672,201
Vermont	513	8,052	1.2	1,705	416	644	337	1,551	3,088	1,088	260,644
Virginia	4,113	105,182	5.0	27,615	6,203	6,503	5,327	33,077	25,386	11,209	2,537,977
Washington	3,864	139,868	17.8	75,180	5,760	3,893	8,656	29,078	16,292	6,511	1,821,032
West Virginia	677	10,196	0.6	1,564	565	1,092	15	5,544	1,358	256	74,829
Wisconsin	2,634	59,134	14.8	25,848	3,577	4,214	1,141	16,382	7,806	1,208	452,176
Wyoming	401	4,268	21.1	889	427	387	90	1,983	485	83	35,768

STATE	Utilities, 2017					Transportation and warehousing, 2017					Finance and insurance, 2017				
	Number of establishments	Employees: Number	Employees: Percent change, 2012–2017	Sales, value of shipments, or revenue (mil dol)	Annual payroll (mil dol)	Number of establishments	Employees: Number	Employees: Percent change, 2012–2017	Sales, value of shipments, or revenue (mil dol)	Annual payroll (mil dol)	Number of establishments	Employees: Number	Employees: Percent change, 2012–2017	Sales, values of shipments or revenue (mil dol)	Annual payroll (mil dol)
	247	248	249	250	251	252	253	254	255	256	257	258	259	260	261
United States	18,913	658,384	1.1	577,100	67,666,854	237,095	4,954,931	15.1	895,225,411	242,145,488	475,780	6,499,871	7.6	4,340,011	638,823
Alabama	344	13,298	-14.0	Q	1,293,734	3,098	61,687	6.7	8,990,180	2,797,539	7,349	72,311	-0.6	NA	4,949
Alaska	104	2,200	8.6	Q	209,831	1,177	18,923	-0.2	5,609,025	1,358,059	784	7,279	0.9	NA	515
Arizona	290	11,882	-2.5	Q	1,204,829	3,415	92,227	14.2	14,565,768	4,602,977	9,602	161,152	25.2	NA	11,297
Arkansas	331	7,495	6.1	Q	663,572	2,456	51,508	1.4	8,011,461	2,352,309	4,448	38,275	7.8	NA	2,329
California	1,237	62,686	-6.2	Q	7,692,844	24,817	545,870	23.6	99,160,737	28,780,713	50,972	650,176	8.0	NA	73,582
Colorado	401	9,358	10.1	Q	910,091	3,764	70,347	13.5	15,882,039	3,592,089	10,393	111,376	12.8	NA	9,690
Connecticut	131	8,573	-18.7	Q	940,016	1,660	44,938	2.1	5,591,991	1,911,700	5,924	115,871	-2.9	NA	17,038
Delaware	52	2,527	-3.6	Q	241,892	708	10,604	-11.2	1,281,651	467,175	1,925	44,120	21.1	NA	4,030
District of Columbia	55	2,143	X	Q	318,311	159	4,137	-51.2	2,155,311	297,759	997	18,843	4.2	NA	2,948
Florida	860	27,460	0.4	Q	2,795,166	15,619	265,209	26.7	68,145,959	13,283,748	32,200	372,525	9.9	NA	29,569
Georgia	605	24,314	7.5	Q	2,294,017	6,961	194,654	26.2	35,564,898	9,505,164	14,991	187,894	14.3	NA	15,563
Hawaii	68	3,596	6.4	Q	377,019	935	31,863	18.7	6,431,447	1,508,627	1,482	19,718	5.5	NA	1,434
Idaho	211	3,873	4.4	Q	345,445	1,791	19,059	10.8	3,057,829	756,640	2,923	23,040	6.2	NA	1,319
Illinois	512	30,800	2.8	Q	3,561,458	16,223	260,488	12.9	51,368,341	13,137,725	21,302	309,134	4.4	NA	34,782
Indiana	638	16,501	6.1	Q	1,537,932	5,416	128,442	8.6	20,385,955	5,631,026	9,477	102,822	6.1	NA	7,012
Iowa	271	7,716	0.8	Q	702,759	3,677	57,161	2.5	8,913,447	2,521,466	6,357	96,808	5.5	NA	7,069
Kansas	246	7,042	-3.0	Q	692,983	2,637	57,920	15.8	7,839,739	2,481,241	5,997	61,278	3.7	NA	4,226
Kentucky	358	9,275	6.8	Q	821,512	2,951	93,363	10.2	14,378,607	4,884,055	6,355	78,417	15.5	NA	5,271
Louisiana	481	10,653	-4.3	Q	978,709	3,834	67,721	-3.3	14,583,333	3,707,576	7,542	65,556	1.1	NA	4,374
Maine	117	2,437	3.1	Q	215,414	1,238	17,202	15.4	1,846,035	713,950	1,900	27,150	5.7	NA	1,900
Maryland	158	10,259	8.2	Q	1,293,025	3,504	73,564	13.3	11,314,342	3,595,588	7,422	102,326	2.1	NA	10,068
Massachusetts	292	13,284	-0.2	Q	1,294,522	3,973	91,247	17.2	13,596,083	4,261,295	9,630	198,360	-2.2	NA	27,287
Michigan	414	24,691	7.2	Q	2,598,511	6,637	118,638	11.6	25,019,797	5,919,128	12,987	169,105	11.5	NA	12,531
Minnesota	348	12,677	-1.0	Q	1,271,159	4,835	88,812	7.9	18,342,371	4,086,380	9,584	166,181	5.5	NA	15,836
Mississippi	594	9,469	7.6	Q	785,640	2,121	39,819	20.3	5,564,028	1,714,951	4,715	33,499	-2.8	NA	1,931
Missouri	372	15,265	-5.4	Q	1,520,155	4,884	88,413	7.4	15,071,280	3,854,874	10,747	141,494	6.8	NA	10,874
Montana	210	2,882	-1.5	Q	254,931	1,370	11,939	0.7	2,151,726	504,079	1,971	15,804	-2.5	NA	971
Nebraska	116	1,066	14.6	Q	99,896	2,497	29,722	10.6	7,483,576	1,355,937	4,420	68,117	9.1	NA	4,840
Nevada	122	4,460	-10.6	Q	473,186	1,647	55,100	26.0	7,654,009	2,437,670	4,192	37,906	10.2	NA	2,596
New Hampshire	126	3,306	-0.7	Q	325,590	814	13,901	0.8	1,583,610	572,593	2,035	29,386	21.2	NA	2,642
New Jersey	365	22,029	8.5	Q	2,583,564	7,573	177,147	10.5	30,902,528	9,205,205	11,601	198,542	-0.1	NA	23,977
New Mexico	D	h	X	Q	D	1,404	18,165	3.7	2,816,277	806,118	2,715	25,035	10.2	NA	1,417
New York	671	39,488	-7.3	Q	4,070,431	13,083	259,694	7.9	50,015,058	12,357,227	26,296	564,569	4.6	NA	109,705
North Carolina	858	22,509	11.9	Q	2,232,231	6,110	125,437	15.3	16,823,524	5,683,607	13,543	190,259	13.1	NA	18,128
North Dakota	D	h	X	Q	D	1,467	17,380	-7.8	4,367,087	936,199	1,738	17,896	4.1	NA	1,072
Ohio	703	24,526	-6.5	Q	2,496,000	7,698	189,666	19.4	29,460,997	9,020,346	17,229	260,044	7.6	NA	19,921
Oklahoma	368	10,505	28.1	Q	927,214	2,736	51,368	15.4	12,698,585	2,744,277	6,867	59,479	3.0	NA	3,696
Oregon	279	7,818	-3.1	Q	767,993	3,225	60,206	15.0	8,813,005	2,857,091	6,121	63,459	10.5	NA	4,747
Pennsylvania	847	31,639	3.1	Q	3,315,983	8,822	230,350	9.8	28,710,741	10,004,774	17,607	282,836	6.0	NA	25,349
Rhode Island	38	1,300	6.8	Q	129,367	700	11,082	-1.7	1,366,689	467,134	1,452	27,061	7.3	NA	2,419
South Carolina	417	12,951	8.3	Q	1,150,406	2,805	63,980	31.4	7,567,557	2,597,555	7,449	73,990	11.5	NA	4,790
South Dakota	154	2,124	-4.2	Q	186,178	1,259	10,207	6.9	1,686,473	421,105	1,981	26,270	-0.8	NA	1,512
Tennessee	150	3,263	0.2	Q	240,114	4,324	148,152	11.5	22,870,848	6,626,122	10,210	128,741	14.7	NA	9,257
Texas	1,967	58,364	10.3	Q	5,838,442	19,943	485,957	25.6	101,947,033	26,437,929	40,589	551,228	14.4	NA	44,410
Utah	222	3,546	-17.9	Q	338,018	2,342	61,942	34.8	10,193,997	2,816,339	5,289	67,500	27.5	NA	4,628
Vermont	70	1,187	X	Q	124,756	491	6,082	6.1	772,885	246,632	945	8,535	-5.6	NA	646
Virginia	335	16,574	10.0	Q	1,688,285	5,062	104,497	16.0	20,071,064	5,026,540	11,404	154,331	0.7	NA	13,462
Washington	314	9,291	0.8	Q	1,003,750	5,474	100,012	13.8	21,845,661	5,560,125	9,992	104,294	7.2	NA	8,933
West Virginia	229	6,775	15.8	Q	600,615	1,181	15,094	-3.9	3,068,787	692,207	2,087	16,270	-9.0	NA	856
Wisconsin	344	12,182	-13.3	Q	1,239,788	5,635	104,143	6.6	15,551,340	4,504,979	8,972	146,594	4.4	NA	11,019
Wyoming	146	2,615	7.4	Q	233,272	943	9,892	-2.4	2,130,700	539,944	1,070	7,015	4.6	NA	406

Table A. States — Real Estate and Rental and Leasing and Professional, Scientific, and Technical Services

STATE	Real estate and rental and leasing, 2017					Professional, scientific, and technical services, 2017								
		Employees					Employees							
	Number of establishments	Number	Percent change, 2012–2017	Sales, value of shipments, or revenue (mil dol)	Annual payroll (mil dol)	Number of establishments	Total	Percent change, 2012–2017	Legal services	Accounting, tax preparation, bookkeeping, and payroll services	Architectural, engineering, and related services	Computer systems design and related services	Sales, values of shipments or revenue (mil dol)	Annual payroll (mil dol)
	262	263	264	265	266	267	268	269	270	271	272	273	274	275
United States	410,820	2,194,885	14.1	674,147	113,410	913,624	9,015,366	9.9	1,174,350	1,133,903	1,514,699	1,894,668	1,844,781	729,371
Alabama	4,362	22,778	-0.3	5,785	968	9,496	100,857	12.1	13,320	11,627	27,913	22,558	20,681	7,188
Alaska	965	4,622	9.7	1,188	223	1,959	17,869	1.3	1,619	1,639	6,583	2,429	3,235	1,269
Arizona	9,937	48,305	19.3	12,992	2,267	18,100	146,970	21.1	17,326	21,944	27,167	28,543	24,119	10,563
Arkansas	3,115	12,776	-0.7	2,588	473	5,914	38,088	18.2	i	7,251	7,567	5,094	5,565	2,071
California	57,434	314,273	14.9	110,822	18,275	127,023	1,241,452	-4.7	150,205	139,959	186,928	273,580	300,626	118,664
Colorado	12,087	47,642	23.1	12,757	2,388	26,404	192,964	7.2	18,244	20,505	47,612	41,715	39,655	15,801
Connecticut	3,459	20,224	2.3	6,691	1,115	9,184	108,479	11.2	13,331	14,992	13,821	23,127	21,600	9,710
Delaware	1,286	6,096	12.8	5,164	288	2,991	29,716	X	i	2,989	3,623	7,163	7,003	2,942
District of Columbia	1,350	11,000	8.9	4,525	883	5,812	108,016	10.7	31,915	4,257	9,363	17,237	37,245	13,126
Florida	37,660	176,886	26.4	49,175	8,184	79,224	513,798	16.5	97,015	71,989	80,036	89,935	89,601	34,673
Georgia	12,426	63,935	15.1	23,009	3,795	29,737	266,523	X	32,158	41,891	38,896	73,357	55,149	20,189
Hawaii	2,069	13,101	15.2	4,409	675	3,380	22,668	4.8	3,354	3,306	5,345	3,659	3,799	1,466
Idaho	2,644	7,521	20.0	1,635	277	4,686	33,246	3.6	h	4,111	7,364	3,780	5,046	1,921
Illinois	13,589	82,763	7.8	32,355	4,824	38,805	404,450	11.0	58,309	55,152	52,957	80,580	87,119	33,951
Indiana	6,686	34,736	9.5	8,392	1,520	13,061	121,821	21.9	14,188	18,958	23,175	20,766	22,391	8,538
Iowa	3,130	13,999	16.4	2,890	576	6,460	52,607	8.4	7,363	9,299	7,185	10,164	7,937	3,172
Kansas	3,415	14,532	1.9	3,943	586	7,201	65,648	7.6	6,981	9,166	13,696	15,414	10,972	4,174
Kentucky	3,902	18,070	-1.0	5,125	731	8,125	67,615	7.6	10,891	12,984	11,112	12,561	10,272	3,636
Louisiana	5,121	29,345	-6.2	7,301	1,386	12,072	95,652	8.6	19,593	15,134	31,802	8,520	16,082	6,185
Maine	1,821	7,138	14.4	1,484	287	3,543	23,381	1.9	3,966	3,197	4,753	3,303	3,874	1,488
Maryland	6,811	49,157	14.8	18,087	2,852	20,974	283,999	16.1	j	19,575	47,076	89,511	55,405	23,645
Massachusetts	7,584	52,315	22.3	17,912	3,369	21,985	310,313	21.7	29,184	28,962	41,821	69,413	78,598	32,256
Michigan	8,467	54,808	12.5	17,783	2,374	21,832	282,246	X	26,529	34,657	69,425	42,499	39,436	19,670
Minnesota	7,218	38,077	10.4	10,433	1,915	16,689	186,597	32.4	j	19,948	23,440	32,043	34,697	14,712
Mississippi	2,403	9,683	-5.4	1,997	345	4,746	30,477	0.9	7,154	6,993	5,184	3,731	4,598	1,618
Missouri	6,644	37,144	11.1	8,976	1,626	14,171	161,595	17.1	21,788	22,741	24,757	43,618	30,112	11,584
Montana	2,036	5,951	14.3	1,145	206	3,836	17,711	6.3	2,906	3,165	4,789	1,414	2,517	939
Nebraska	2,354	11,293	12.2	2,292	487	4,699	39,566	-46.9	i	6,242	6,470	7,323	6,278	2,385
Nevada	4,684	30,562	36.4	7,359	1,312	9,018	60,168	25.5	9,457	7,337	11,600	8,421	10,816	3,951
New Hampshire	1,523	7,920	12.4	2,000	381	3,674	32,387	7.4	3,888	5,499	5,635	6,863	5,583	2,383
New Jersey	9,622	61,052	13.6	21,184	3,435	28,962	325,516	5.8	38,484	35,573	42,275	99,461	67,232	28,735
New Mexico	2,408	9,229	-5.4	2,186	376	4,728	56,695	28.3	i	4,710	8,315	4,707	10,082	4,190
New York	34,076	193,442	16.3	70,693	11,357	61,744	668,196	13.5	128,077	97,737	67,837	94,294	172,936	60,227
North Carolina	12,450	56,360	19.5	14,647	2,639	24,766	221,438	12.8	24,381	29,133	34,200	44,672	40,878	16,048
North Dakota	1,100	5,440	5.5	1,280	242	1,821	14,880	8.5	2,038	2,071	3,899	2,450	2,425	947
Ohio	10,782	62,902	3.2	20,524	2,986	23,854	250,438	7.1	32,148	37,333	46,869	44,866	43,625	17,059
Oklahoma	4,461	22,135	4.1	4,696	942	9,736	70,920	-1.5	j	14,752	13,173	9,779	11,247	4,456
Oregon	6,771	29,773	14.4	6,774	1,263	12,620	92,358	9.3	11,825	12,272	16,238	12,719	14,720	6,902
Pennsylvania	10,662	66,715	13.9	18,861	3,472	29,991	340,361	7.5	50,588	50,111	65,253	55,904	64,179	26,674
Rhode Island	1,110	5,287	-5.8	1,351	248	3,026	23,910	13.0	4,787	2,899	4,089	4,717	4,043	1,566
South Carolina	5,890	26,764	15.4	6,510	1,128	10,859	100,377	25.7	14,550	11,436	27,015	13,704	17,038	6,498
South Dakota	1,143	4,330	22.8	829	155	1,967	13,063	17.2	1,871	2,668	2,490	1,761	1,763	655
Tennessee	6,048	36,212	18.4	10,679	1,760	11,411	116,205	11.1	j	20,277	19,988	17,191	18,739	7,661
Texas	32,290	198,712	16.9	56,443	10,560	70,033	735,744	15.0	87,848	90,118	156,673	165,740	150,903	59,488
Utah	5,577	19,457	20.1	5,296	877	10,873	92,444	21.1	9,359	12,820	13,900	18,315	15,305	5,610
Vermont	784	2,938	-5.0	652	119	2,096	12,563	-21.2	1,896	1,926	2,224	2,168	2,079	842
Virginia	10,051	55,778	2.8	17,208	2,949	31,431	470,265	9.4	27,806	40,367	67,638	186,672	101,433	41,553
Washington	11,826	53,706	18.8	15,627	2,757	22,144	214,628	28.1	j	21,192	49,424	45,588	42,429	17,333
West Virginia	1,432	6,061	0.8	1,369	229	2,813	22,856	-7.9	5,530	3,671	4,304	2,725	3,295	1,218
Wisconsin	4,956	27,163	14.3	5,908	1,106	11,553	106,041	6.9	14,149	15,987	19,489	18,104	18,880	7,307
Wyoming	1,199	4,777	5.1	1,216	220	2,395	9,589	5.0	g	1,381	2,311	810	1,539	532

STATE	Health care and social assistance, 2017													
	Subject to federal tax							Tax-exempt						
		Employees							Employees					
	Number of estab-lishments	Total	Percent change, 2012–2017	Ambulatory health care services	Hospitals	Sales, value of shipments, or revenue (mil dol)	Annual payroll (mil dol)	Number of estab-lishments	Total	Percent change, 2012–2017	Ambulatory health care services	Hospitals	Sales, values of ship-ments or revenue (mil dol)	Annual payroll (mil dol)
	276	277	278	279	280	281	282	283	284	285	286	287	288	289
United States	744,628	11,103,994	16.4	6,669,762	751,064	1,258,937	514,343	147,617	9,402,508	6.0	893,376	5,423,087	1,268,966	475,713
Alabama	8,794	156,644	10.0	87,140	22,879	17,755	7,038	1,842	101,755	0.9	8,864	67,808	13,484	4,911
Alaska	2,009	22,324	4.4	13,480	2,202	3,381	1,316	670	29,801	9.1	6,093	13,540	4,475	1,732
Arizona	16,871	233,019	26.5	131,519	21,262	26,801	10,435	1,945	145,996	11.5	16,655	84,708	21,329	7,974
Arkansas	6,345	98,148	12.8	49,112	12,964	10,550	4,269	1,533	83,978	5.7	7,430	46,260	9,295	3,692
California	99,272	1,198,086	19.2	740,129	76,748	159,332	63,328	14,118	845,031	9.6	88,774	499,331	151,980	56,173
Colorado	14,297	181,974	29.3	106,304	10,251	20,903	8,265	2,362	138,839	18.5	22,327	80,549	19,153	7,455
Connecticut	8,563	158,995	20.7	84,973	4,028	16,249	7,493	2,502	136,088	-2.5	15,603	64,530	19,054	6,576
Delaware	2,094	34,764	14.4	21,953	g	3,887	1,746	554	33,584	6.6	2,600	j	4,968	1,975
District of Columbia	1,438	30,898	26.9	20,540	X	3,817.001	1,696	765	43,236	-0.3	3,329	j	7,583	2,680
Florida	55,996	718,280	17.0	444,187	82,648	97,268	35,551	5,558	408,875	8.4	39,531	241,661	58,016	19,921
Georgia	22,386	311,585	21.3	202,073	20,983	38,230	15,454	2,874	209,561	9.4	13,688	145,371	30,530	10,317
Hawaii	2,844	29,918	11.7	22,564	X	3,771.589	1,585	833	43,633	9.1	6,514	23,312	6,014	2,414
Idaho	4,725	59,441	19.8	30,208	5,271	5,729	2,234	585	38,659	14.1	2,306	29,506	4,740	2,058
Illinois	28,608	422,680	10.1	251,137	15,018	46,173	19,337	5,627	395,053	2.2	29,205	232,126	51,453	18,752
Indiana	13,698	249,114	20.6	150,472	15,742	26,772	11,332	2,970	187,502	-1.5	16,506	112,181	25,065	8,309
Iowa	5,984	82,550	4.5	46,045	X	8,820.735	3,819	2,626	134,415	5.1	8,763	l	13,599.112	5,422
Kansas	6,195	97,818	5.0	54,150	8,907	11,056	4,410	1,909	98,123	-1.0	6,990	55,588	10,384	4,112
Kentucky	9,600	137,974	8.3	79,800	9,299	14,980	6,411	1,997	130,737	5.1	12,887	88,082	17,389	6,001
Louisiana	10,878	181,347	8.1	97,290	21,048	18,910	7,274	1,807	121,061	3.3	5,411	81,761	15,708	5,639
Maine	3,107	44,753	7.3	24,807	X	3,954.996	1,767	1,664	67,841	0.5	9,032	k	7,822.29	3,233
Maryland	13,949	185,545	10.3	125,549	X	22,447.831	9,526	2,851	198,551	3.7	14,580	m	26,227.901	9,768
Massachusetts	13,717	271,634	14.3	164,867	21,831	31,795	14,422	5,632	363,378	3.9	36,356	170,639	42,229	17,616
Michigan	22,148	317,165	17.2	202,891	16,752	33,917	14,583	4,829	310,643	-1.3	29,288	190,508	40,278	14,727
Minnesota	12,846	212,834	12.4	120,207	X	19,562.022	8,897	4,220	260,504	3.8	25,739	m	30,929.025	12,309
Mississippi	5,356	87,759	3.9	47,881	8,931	9,520	3,654	1,035	81,251	11.0	3,278	60,548	9,232	3,879
Missouri	15,917	213,163	15.3	116,761	12,850	22,077	9,086	3,180	209,894	-2.4	20,948	124,164	26,116	9,596
Montana	2,700	30,706	25.7	18,629	g	3,563	1,514	1,016	42,548	3.2	3,561	j	4,884.756	1,790
Nebraska	4,606	62,134	8.6	34,657	g	6,875	2,831	1,211	73,557	7.8	6,402	k	9,186	3,286
Nevada	6,774	97,187	25.1	49,796	20,450	13,230	4,807	598	34,906	12.9	2,375	22,035	4,882	1,813
New Hampshire	2,863	41,250	16.5	24,837	g	4,920	2,151	874	53,344	3.2	8,059	k	7,011	2,591
New Jersey	24,064	352,009	18.2	231,014	17,104	42,098	16,936	3,941	261,397	7.6	21,211	149,483	32,625	13,198
New Mexico	4,119	73,984	9.6	37,118	7,966	6,894	2,804	1,015	53,824	9.7	5,868	29,685	6,709	2,602
New York	44,830	677,837	25.5	480,628	2,593	69,277	28,220	14,072	976,756	5.1	97,152	483,633	124,231	52,468
North Carolina	20,223	329,678	12.6	195,220	9,644	35,214	14,481	3,857	272,766	15.2	19,344	185,174	37,518	13,146
North Dakota	1,368	16,368	8.8	11,030	X	2,324.254	801	689	46,087	10.8	4,260	j	4,974	2,112
Ohio	23,844	428,546	8.8	254,307	16,318	43,867	18,946	5,751	428,248	5.8	40,316	269,602	53,251	20,523
Oklahoma	9,221	137,610	7.1	71,466	22,221	15,697	5,894	1,814	88,852	4.8	6,962	54,228	11,334	4,059
Oregon	10,959	130,894	24.3	82,937	g	14,414	6,136	2,989	132,384	17.9	14,923	l	18,670	6,970
Pennsylvania	29,203	507,878	17.1	305,298	31,112	53,578	24,403	8,496	528,093	1.2	50,964	256,477	63,044	23,482
Rhode Island	2,458	43,682	22.7	23,589	X	4,493.564	2,028	719	43,864	-9.5	4,870	j	5,080	2,064
South Carolina	8,970	147,388	11.4	79,726	17,490	16,409	6,488	1,618	96,810	20.9	7,180	63,418	13,046	4,562
South Dakota	1,623	21,521	4.9	12,287	g	2,486	968	797	50,300	17.0	2,921	k	6,229	2,490
Tennessee	13,248	249,523	13.3	147,182	27,722	30,270	12,048	2,643	165,075	3.1	11,450	107,960	21,819	8,172
Texas	63,412	1,127,958	19.3	654,109	132,686	119,276	46,467	6,540	453,619	13.4	37,542	305,689	66,833	23,432
Utah	7,490	92,983	20.7	52,728	8,909	10,675	3,970	764	53,382	8.6	5,754	37,205	8,033	2,733
Vermont	1,345	16,268	8.6	9,600	X	1,590.873	706	757	32,017	9.6	6,800	14,913	3,860.753	1,524
Virginia	17,831	276,332	16.9	167,605	17,696	31,163.794	13,461	2,691	178,169	2.0	15,373	103,608	27,629	9,260
Washington	18,081	229,068	18.0	137,208	2,813	24,847	11,014	3,183	209,767	16.5	28,963	123,489	31,594.945	11,836
West Virginia	3,607	59,426	3.5	29,948	5,355	6,403.191	2,460	1,262	73,201	2.1	8,890	45,140	8,834	3,384
Wisconsin	12,596	200,596	14.5	113,937	2,096	20,053	9,188	3,387	216,769	2.7	28,527	114,852	28,425	10,011
Wyoming	1,556	14,756	7.7	8,867	g	1,659	694	445	18,784	6.5	1,012	j	2,213	963

STATE	Arts, entertainment, and recreation, 2017					Accommodation and food services, 2017					
		Employees					Employees				
	Number of estab-lishments	Number	Percent change, 2012–2017	Sales, value of shipments, or revenue (mil dol)	Annual payroll (mil dol)	Number of estab-lishments	Total	Percent change, 2012–2017	Food services and drinking places	Sales, values of shipments or revenue (mil dol)	Annual payroll (mil dol)
	290	291	292	293	294	295	296	297	298	299	300
United States	142,938	2,390,279	14.8	265,620	82,256	726,081	14,002,624	16.6	11,881,174	678,148	202,539
Alabama	1,168	17,939	4.5	1,158	333	9,085	183,590	16.7	164,731	8,201	2,335
Alaska	575	5,433	7.5	449	104	2,214	28,853	7.5	21,693	1,557	505
Arizona	2,041	47,060	11.0	4,812	1,582	13,079	299,628	19.2	244,665	13,483	4,103
Arkansas	787	9,919	11.7	1,057	218	5,977	106,280	10.9	95,188	4,576	1,369
California	26,390	349,752	15.1	53,107	17,209	89,596	1,739,010	24.7	1,467,354	95,667	28,608
Colorado	3,028	58,229	13.7	5,681	1,935	14,121	290,915	21.0	235,601	13,366	4,324
Connecticut	1,744	30,320	14.5	2,406	785	8,762	146,456	8.9	122,550	7,676	2,322
Delaware	440	8,466	4.5	854	224	2,141	39,950	12.2	35,841	2,061	611
District of Columbia	380	9,817	30.7	1,736	830	2,733	72,890	20.7	58,276	4,153	1,370
Florida	8,883	208,733	22.9	23,435	6,639	42,071	955,006	21.5	772,959	45,113	13,288
Georgia	3,452	50,796	18.5	5,245	1,752	21,201	426,884	20.7	381,155	20,818	5,928
Hawaii	510	11,912	12.1	1,026	314	3,865	112,743	14.6	71,189	4,934	1,430
Idaho	804	9,644	7.8	602	174	3,856	65,463	20.7	54,616	2,636	786
Illinois	5,218	91,647	18.8	10,067	2,830	29,025	536,245	14.1	478,471	27,978	8,351
Indiana	2,320	37,937	12.5	3,999	1,119	13,647	280,340	9.8	250,491	11,856	3,586
Iowa	1,451	18,336	-13.6	1,158	315	7,283	123,866	7.6	101,394	4,600	1,405
Kansas	1,092	17,313	20.7	1,231	323	6,253	118,905	11.3	106,572	4,860	1,487
Kentucky	1,406	19,605	12.9	1,965	441	8,228	174,910	11.4	159,803	7,781	2,329
Louisiana	1,526	25,649	9.7	2,789	845	9,877	215,048	10.9	173,404	9,431	2,740
Maine	887	8,027	9.9	677	188	4,257	55,746	12.2	44,641	2,610	831
Maryland	2,172	43,573	21.3	4,970	1,588	12,139	237,730	16.4	207,377	12,732	3,701
Massachusetts	3,477	66,160	19.0	7,037	2,360	17,773	311,058	13.9	278,738	18,222	5,700
Michigan	3,469	49,733	7.5	4,998	1,750	20,696	399,032	14.9	348,803	17,285	5,274
Minnesota	3,012	48,380	14.3	4,162	1,561	12,022	239,194	7.8	202,894	10,353	3,363
Mississippi	694	8,203	-7.2	583	156	5,651	129,836	11.7	96,924	4,517	1,280
Missouri	2,274	40,484	6.0	3,953	1,554	12,896	263,644	10.2	229,465	11,044	3,420
Montana	1,234	10,492	-3.8	877	180	3,568	52,415	13.3	40,479	2,158	632
Nebraska	913	14,879	13.7	891	249	4,621	76,386	8.9	68,262	3,253	979
Nevada	1,635	31,918	19.5	5,143	1,068	6,810	319,584	7.7	128,481	8,817	2,485
New Hampshire	815	12,442	-3.9	978	291	3,784	59,531	10.1	50,102	2,886	905
New Jersey	3,842	65,529	16.1	5,967	1,934	21,495	318,734	9.2	272,795	18,267	4,993
New Mexico	700	12,062	-1.6	1,120	272	4,392	91,601	10.9	72,054	3,610	1,115
New York	13,019	185,076	13.7	29,270	8,695	54,797	824,806	21.4	718,695	50,152	15,216
North Carolina	3,868	69,027	18.6	6,354	2,057	21,437	429,125	19.7	382,079	19,803	5,763
North Dakota	470	5,418	10.5	273	84	2,080	36,648	2.7	27,623	1,342	426
Ohio	3,999	76,914	26.7	8,596	2,832	24,346	474,616	8.5	439,944	21,350	6,390
Oklahoma	1,152	26,523	0.6	3,470	799	8,397	159,826	11.3	137,769	6,752	1,955
Oregon	1,992	29,222	21.6	2,256	776	11,708	182,613	21.4	155,042	8,988	2,837
Pennsylvania	4,862	101,095	1.5	10,655	3,265	28,843	481,682	9.7	424,046	22,462	6,493
Rhode Island	575	8,673	-1.4	739	219	3,167	50,642	14.9	44,151	2,593	805
South Carolina	1,687	28,317	13.6	1,881	542	10,847	223,081	20.4	191,404	10,006	2,917
South Dakota	697	6,799	9.6	541	129	2,495	40,704	7.2	31,118	1,522	462
Tennessee	2,824	37,967	16.9	5,037	1,720	13,518	287,534	19.1	254,036	13,349	4,029
Texas	7,620	153,566	28.9	14,842	4,514	57,098	1,201,419	23.0	1,078,923	60,835	17,640
Utah	1,180	28,240	36.1	1,760	553	5,931	118,734	23.8	98,351	5,098	1,497
Vermont	457	7,739	8.3	517	151	1,979	32,891	4.9	20,555	1,128	370
Virginia	3,071	61,703	13.7	4,447	1,283	18,199	358,010	11.7	311,131	17,107	5,098
Washington	3,097	65,091	10.8	6,483	2,078	17,828	289,371	23.6	246,233	15,680	5,089
West Virginia	775	6,681	-20.0	488	108	3,614	68,102	2.7	55,458	2,655	781
Wisconsin	2,809	47,048	8.0	3,494	1,218	14,840	244,099	10.2	208,576	9,811	2,900
Wyoming	445	4,791	20.6	384	107	1,839	27,248	-1.2	19,072	1,014	315

Table A. States — Other Services, Except Public Administration and Government Employment

STATE	Other services, except public administration, 2017								Government employment, 2020		
	Number of estab-lishments	Employees: Total	Employees: Percent change, 2012–2017	Employees: Repair and mainte-nance	Employees: Personal and laundry services	Employees: Religious, civic, and similar services	Sales, values of shipments or revenue (mil dol)	Annual payroll (mil dol)	Federal civilian	Federal military	State and local
	301	302	303	304	305	306	307	308	309	310	311
United States	560,845	3,696,831	7.8	1,285,621	1,473,881	937,329	544,128	133,751	2,982,000	1,911,000	19,236,000
Alabama	6,149	38,476	3.2	18,544	14,572	5,360	5,844	1,303	55,966	28,942	320,273
Alaska	1,357	7,271	0.5	2,649	2,267	2,355	1,351	270	15,439	26,444	59,072
Arizona	9,271	68,350	10.1	25,735	26,959	15,656	8,727	2,306	58,978	35,315	356,541
Arkansas	3,910	21,132	-3.2	8,685	7,729	4,718	2,874	655	21,274	15,271	185,511
California	62,302	437,372	10.5	154,783	180,043	102,546	64,254	15,638	260,514	197,148	2,277,976
Colorado	11,667	74,317	15.4	25,318	28,209	20,790	10,974	2,785	54,744	55,397	394,406
Connecticut	7,507	46,490	7.2	13,655	22,178	10,657	6,055	1,646	19,235	11,847	206,833
Delaware	1,608	10,252	4.2	3,113	4,976	2,163	1,221	339	6,047	8,795	59,362
District of Columbia	3,502	73,756	25.0	579	6,979	66,198	24,226	5,459	193,423	14,201	42,863
Florida	38,932	222,512	14.0	75,815	94,573	52,124	29,617	6,946	150,018	99,552	948,006
Georgia	14,976	97,721	9.4	39,762	40,576	17,383	14,343	3,348	107,626	94,929	575,231
Hawaii	2,912	20,219	4.5	3,644	8,251	8,324	2,561	652	35,128	50,791	85,634
Idaho	2,749	14,016	15.0	6,719	4,691	2,606	1,574	435	13,721	9,168	111,731
Illinois	24,296	171,261	3.6	58,442	61,347	51,472	29,599	7,164	82,037	46,754	708,808
Indiana	10,777	75,446	3.4	31,173	25,609	18,664	11,121	2,562	41,323	20,416	379,976
Iowa	5,975	31,306	2.1	12,788	11,621	6,897	4,186	1,022	18,155	11,312	235,106
Kansas	5,069	27,987	-5.2	10,906	10,652	6,429	3,986	928	26,202	32,904	233,477
Kentucky	5,900	38,040	-0.8	16,045	15,291	6,704	4,755	1,198	35,509	46,880	260,686
Louisiana	6,531	43,472	-0.1	20,396	15,461	7,615	5,702	1,572	32,741	33,061	283,417
Maine	2,921	14,477	5.2	5,355	4,523	4,599	1,809	475	16,964	5,213	82,549
Maryland	10,355	81,469	2.6	25,123	32,874	23,472	12,118	3,519	178,468	49,165	333,110
Massachusetts	14,810	100,088	7.1	26,498	47,503	26,087	13,094	3,606	47,675	19,180	384,588
Michigan	16,545	104,291	8.5	42,688	40,937	20,666	13,205	3,415	54,175	17,537	519,306
Minnesota	11,339	77,400	6.4	24,362	31,434	21,604	10,077	2,554	33,329	19,685	357,692
Mississippi	3,417	18,345	-4.6	8,375	6,453	3,517	2,279	603	26,409	29,156	212,480
Missouri	10,513	68,206	8.6	28,749	25,796	13,661	8,694	2,297	61,393	36,664	362,687
Montana	2,409	12,077	10.6	5,305	2,920	3,852	1,609	403	13,682	7,998	73,775
Nebraska	4,107	21,757	-0.3	8,606	7,848	5,303	3,608	701	17,454	12,800	142,704
Nevada	4,032	28,825	13.5	10,478	13,898	4,449	3,281	914	20,985	19,762	136,245
New Hampshire	3,011	17,864	7.6	5,908	7,533	4,423	2,096	619	8,306	4,426	78,098
New Jersey	19,162	113,846	5.2	33,372	62,881	17,593	14,026	3,679	50,621	25,473	512,343
New Mexico	2,963	17,547	0.5	7,616	5,413	4,518	2,085	558	30,187	18,074	153,403
New York	48,436	299,209	10.1	60,170	124,431	114,608	51,750	11,846	120,546	54,755	1,288,372
North Carolina	15,118	93,642	16.0	38,832	36,439	18,371	13,022	3,153	77,362	123,536	647,251
North Dakota	1,763	9,706	5.1	3,931	3,215	2,560	1,246	318	9,497	12,118	65,698
Ohio	18,425	126,378	-0.8	44,156	54,558	27,664	15,268	4,044	81,890	35,626	669,734
Oklahoma	5,565	31,947	-1.4	13,379	12,296	6,272	4,934	1,084	51,081	35,914	282,549
Oregon	7,414	43,543	14.8	17,324	15,210	11,009	6,289	1,555	29,271	11,304	245,272
Pennsylvania	26,075	161,337	4.5	51,547	69,740	40,050	22,982	5,137	101,446	34,028	619,415
Rhode Island	2,318	13,882	6.4	4,509	6,091	3,282	1,773	471	11,535	7,229	54,682
South Carolina	7,068	46,847	5.6	19,764	17,125	9,958	5,653	1,529	36,723	48,298	325,400
South Dakota	1,860	8,713	4.1	3,855	2,767	2,091	1,224	278	11,593	8,278	64,557
Tennessee	8,570	61,744	10.3	23,225	26,719	11,800	8,650	2,149	52,377	21,110	377,943
Texas	37,506	285,777	10.3	134,543	107,153	44,081	39,008	10,468	215,186	173,144	1,693,748
Utah	4,763	29,903	14.9	13,638	11,151	5,114	3,527	957	39,375	16,784	209,037
Vermont	1,603	7,339	1.8	2,312	2,073	2,954	922	244	7,376	3,931	44,133
Virginia	15,700	118,537	5.4	35,053	44,371	39,113	20,344	5,188	206,208	121,549	531,839
Washington	13,444	78,480	12.2	26,178	34,251	18,051	14,514	3,005	78,622	68,608	493,152
West Virginia	2,524	14,894	-10.2	6,234	4,989	3,671	1,897	465	25,516	8,473	116,412
Wisconsin	10,351	63,120	1.7	22,858	27,547	12,715	9,241	2,069	30,861	15,828	373,730
Wyoming	1,368	6,245	-6.2	2,927	1,758	1,560	931	221	7,807	6,227	59,187

Table A. States — **State Government Employment and Payroll**

STATE	State government employment and payroll, 2020											
	State government employment, 2020			State government payroll, 2020			Full-time payroll — Percent of total for:					
	Full-time equivalent employees	Full-time employees	Part-time employees	Full-time March payroll (1,000 dollars)	Part-time March payroll (1,000 dollars)	Total March payroll (1,000 dollars)[1]	Administration	Judicial and legal	Police	Corrections	Highways	Welfare
	312	313	314	315	316	317	318	319	320	321	322	323
United States	4,498,920	3,911,456	1,582,095	23,311,325	2,533,826	25,845,151	5.3	4.8	3.1	10.0	4.8	4.8
Alabama	96,707	83,799	35,496	429,055	41,484	470,539	3.1	3.7	1.6	4.7	4.2	3.8
Alaska	23,739	21,956	4,919	139,636	7,794	147,430	7.9	7.7	3.9	10.0	10.1	6.5
Arizona	75,281	62,701	33,139	347,157	38,403	385,560	3.9	3.4	3.3	10.9	3.1	7.0
Arkansas	63,474	58,000	16,112	271,682	17,975	289,657	4.9	2.5	2.3	7.1	5.2	5.8
California	438,305	366,755	181,459	3,007,008	493,122	3,500,130	6.2	1.7	3.2	17.6	6.0	1.1
Colorado	96,760	72,335	45,680	477,306	69,800	547,106	4.5	6.8	2.3	7.6	3.3	2.5
Connecticut	59,635	49,757	25,464	342,879	42,948	385,827	5.5	10.6	4.6	9.6	5.6	9.3
Delaware	26,726	22,998	9,257	122,442	15,596	138,038	4.3	7.4	6.8	11.0	4.6	4.7
District of Columbia	X	X	X	X	X	X	X	X	X	X	X	X
Florida	183,003	163,603	50,554	787,864	70,206	858,071	5.3	11.0	1.7	9.4	3.7	3.7
Georgia	126,446	111,082	51,363	548,836	55,126	603,963	3.7	3.4	0.0	8.1	2.9	4.0
Hawaii	58,771	52,900	19,435	276,960	24,088	301,048	3.0	5.2	1.1	4.9	1.6	0.7
Idaho	24,844	21,645	9,728	127,043	11,319	138,362	7.3	4.8	19.8	11.9	5.0	6.4
Illinois	125,352	105,765	48,266	696,080	96,066	792,146	5.5	4.4	1.5	13.1	5.1	9.7
Indiana	90,341	75,922	44,383	395,166	41,635	436,800	4.5	3.2	1.6	5.4	3.8	7.0
Iowa	51,432	41,363	29,730	292,763	25,377	318,140	3.1	4.5	1.9	4.9	4.1	5.4
Kansas	55,966	49,870	19,001	257,259	23,311	280,569	3.9	3.9	3.6	5.0	3.8	3.3
Kentucky	80,803	70,361	23,949	349,186	29,541	378,727	3.5	5.5	3.5	4.0	4.4	6.6
Louisiana	82,812	74,785	22,253	349,338	21,669	371,007	6.8	2.7	0.9	7.4	5.5	6.4
Maine	20,695	17,566	9,040	89,012	9,132	98,144	10.1	4.8	18.2	6.5	10.5	11.2
Maryland	96,221	79,018	27,331	522,168	46,989	569,156	4.8	5.2	6.4	16.9	5.8	6.4
Massachusetts	105,628	95,853	33,505	644,186	52,777	696,963	5.3	9.9	2.7	11.4	2.9	7.7
Michigan	150,527	120,523	72,461	771,056	151,242	922,298	4.5	1.5	0.8	8.3	1.9	7.0
Minnesota	85,007	72,034	32,851	471,315	56,678	527,993	9.3	5.3	1.1	5.0	6.0	2.6
Mississippi	54,424	49,722	12,627	225,550	13,594	239,143	3.4	1.2	5.0	2.7	4.6	5.7
Missouri	83,254	74,250	26,655	326,519	27,612	354,131	4.4	5.4	0.7	9.9	5.9	6.2
Montana	22,957	19,678	9,627	88,959	11,590	100,549	8.7	5.5	4.7	5.7	11.2	7.4
Nebraska	36,391	30,011	13,268	154,315	13,807	168,122	2.8	3.1	3.7	9.5	5.8	5.8
Nevada	29,893	26,727	9,925	156,544	13,232	169,776	9.0	3.5	2.0	12.2	5.9	7.2
New Hampshire	18,573	14,972	10,013	86,661	13,980	100,641	7.1	4.8	37.2	7.2	7.9	10.7
New Jersey	145,433	132,732	30,264	862,041	61,048	923,088	4.3	9.7	0.3	6.0	3.9	6.5
New Mexico	46,330	41,482	13,599	215,280	19,380	234,660	4.2	8.1	27.6	7.2	4.2	3.7
New York	257,250	239,870	46,784	1,593,193	87,275	1,680,468	7.7	10.0	2.1	12.2	3.6	1.6
North Carolina	150,900	133,714	46,702	732,814	56,673	789,487	4.0	5.0	0.2	10.3	5.5	0.6
North Dakota	18,175	15,395	9,085	81,977	11,266	93,242	4.9	4.9	19.5	5.1	6.1	3.9
Ohio	134,322	108,521	69,148	647,989	84,467	732,456	6.7	3.0	1.6	10.5	4.7	2.5
Oklahoma	64,044	57,109	22,637	275,109	22,352	297,462	4.6	4.7	3.7	6.3	4.6	9.4
Oregon	76,004	66,717	27,816	399,455	55,065	454,519	8.1	5.7	11.6	8.0	5.8	6.9
Pennsylvania	157,325	141,883	49,734	856,571	98,555	955,126	5.7	4.0	0.4	11.9	6.9	5.9
Rhode Island	21,138	19,577	7,219	125,971	8,904	134,875	8.9	6.5	6.9	9.7	4.1	7.6
South Carolina	85,123	76,435	23,031	350,299	27,015	377,314	4.6	1.7	0.5	6.8	4.8	5.4
South Dakota	14,397	12,581	6,503	62,393	5,546	67,939	6.7	6.6	16.1	4.9	7.5	10.8
Tennessee	79,985	71,353	27,085	359,675	27,385	387,059	7.6	5.0	13.9	6.4	4.9	8.6
Texas	323,320	289,873	86,967	1,657,467	114,107	1,771,573	3.6	2.2	0.3	8.9	4.0	6.2
Utah	65,351	55,987	30,177	321,978	37,694	359,672	4.9	2.9	1.3	4.1	2.6	3.4
Vermont	13,799	12,625	4,044	75,914	8,573	84,487	9.5	5.4	23.6	7.5	6.9	10.7
Virginia	130,965	113,117	54,616	650,054	81,454	731,508	4.0	3.3	2.5	7.9	6.4	2.4
Washington	133,041	113,680	51,472	736,310	110,346	846,656	3.6	2.2	0.7	7.4	6.1	8.7
West Virginia	38,801	35,289	11,279	161,441	12,370	173,811	4.8	5.2	3.0	7.2	12.7	6.6
Wisconsin	66,270	55,786	32,933	333,611	64,604	398,215	5.6	4.8	0.3	13.5	2.4	3.0
Wyoming	12,980	11,779	3,509	57,840	3,657	61,497	7.6	6.9	0.0	8.3	12.8	3.9

1. Includes program categories not shown separately.

Table A. States — State Government Employment and Finances

STATE	State government employment and payroll, 2020 (cont.): Full-time payroll (1,000 dollars) (cont.): Percent of total for: Health	Hospitals	Social Insurance administra-tion	Natural resources	Sewerage	Elementary and secondary education and libraries	Higher education	State government finances, 2020: General revenue (mil dol): Total	From federal government: Total	From federal government: Per capita[2] (dollars)	From own sources: Total	Taxes: Total	Taxes: Sales and gross receipts	Taxes per capita[1] (dollars): Total	Taxes per capita[1] (dollars): Sales and gross receipts
	324	325	326	327	328	329	330	331	332	333	334	335	336	337	338
United States	4.2	9.1	1.4	2.7	0.1	1.1	40.5	X	X	X	X	X	X	X	X
Alabama	6.2	14.8	0.8	1.9	0.0	0.0	48.5	36,909	13,657	2,775	19,492,083	12,045	5,904	2,447	1,200
Alaska	3.2	1.0	0.9	8.8	0.0	9.3	16.6	10,421	4,476	6,122	4,330,861	1,318	268	1,803	367
Arizona	3.2	0.8	2.2	1.9	0.0	0.0	53.6	50,548	21,168	2,852	23,453,010	17,654	10,888	2,379	1,467
Arkansas	4.9	11.1	1.8	2.7	0.0	0.0	46.0	28,572	9,365	3,090	14,236,419	10,255	5,138	3,384	1,695
California	3.9	10.5	2.7	3.8	0.2	0.0	37.5	413,373	101,432	2,576	214,425,897	171,964	62,553	4,368	1,589
Colorado	1.9	4.0	1.2	1.3	0.0	0.0	60.1	48,052	11,566	1,991	22,115,710	15,074	6,012	2,596	1,035
Connecticut	5.4	8.9	1.0	1.2	0.1	0.0	28.2	39,646	10,344	2,908	22,436,816	18,401	7,468	5,173	2,100
Delaware	5.9	2.7	0.7	1.7	0.4	0.0	37.9	12,605	4,309	4,367	6,800,959	4,555	586	4,616	593
District of Columbia	X	X	X	X	X	X	X	X	X	X	X	X	X	X	X
Florida	6.7	1.8	1.1	3.6	0.0	0.0	46.6	110,295	36,791	1,693	63,264,942	43,118	35,167	1,984	1,618
Georgia	3.0	6.2	0.6	3.2	0.0	0.0	54.9	61,196	17,800	1,662	30,153,368	23,609	9,539	2,204	891
Hawaii	4.1	6.3	0.3	1.7	0.0	42.0	19.4	18,323	4,205	2,989	11,292,915	7,708	4,924	5,478	3,500
Idaho	7.8	1.8	2.5	8.2	0.0	0.0	31.4	13,348	4,730	2,589	6,783,068	5,280	2,715	2,890	1,486
Illinois	2.2	9.6	1.2	1.6	0.0	0.0	34.3	106,591	26,817	2,130	56,005,438	45,285	20,650	3,598	1,641
Indiana	2.0	1.5	1.0	1.9	0.0	0.0	63.2	52,344	19,472	2,883	29,213,756	22,374	12,507	3,312	1,851
Iowa	1.1	18.1	1.0	3.0	0.0	0.0	47.1	32,304	8,563	2,707	19,887,320	10,661	4,958	3,370	1,567
Kansas	2.2	24.7	0.1	1.3	0.0	0.0	43.9	23,717	6,025	2,068	15,519,148	9,660	4,598	3,315	1,578
Kentucky	5.1	11.7	0.8	2.2	0.0	0.0	47.7	40,266	15,453	3,451	19,235,325	13,371	6,539	2,986	1,461
Louisiana	5.7	13.0	1.1	3.7	0.0	0.0	35.6	38,269	17,247	3,713	15,751,204	11,381	6,060	2,450	1,304
Maine	4.9	2.8	0.8	6.1	0.0	0.2	30.1	12,707	4,778	3,539	6,263,827	4,851	2,402	3,593	1,779
Maryland	6.6	5.1	0.9	1.5	0.0	0.0	31.8	52,423	15,701	2,593	30,647,772	23,883	9,511	3,944	1,571
Massachusetts	7.1	3.8	1.0	1.3	1.0	1.8	26.3	75,908	21,484	3,117	43,072,108	31,630	9,490	4,588	1,377
Michigan	4.0	11.3	0.4	2.4	0.0	0.0	52.3	80,952	26,752	2,684	42,454,187	28,062	13,409	2,816	1,345
Minnesota	4.3	5.3	1.1	3.6	1.0	0.0	44.4	57,362	14,776	2,612	32,142,368	26,791	11,353	4,736	2,007
Mississippi	4.8	22.7	0.9	4.2	0.0	0.7	40.2	24,808	10,177	3,430	11,332,015	8,100	5,264	2,730	1,774
Missouri	3.2	12.7	0.4	2.3	0.0	0.0	39.7	40,228	15,416	2,506	18,491,070	12,410	5,459	2,017	887
Montana	4.0	2.5	3.8	7.2	0.0	0.0	32.8	9,102	3,589	3,322	4,115,618	3,168	679	2,932	628
Nebraska	1.6	5.5	0.6	2.3	0.0	0.0	52.2	13,796	4,710	2,431	7,672,027	5,857	2,813	3,023	1,452
Nevada	5.2	4.8	1.2	3.0	0.0	0.0	35.4	22,026	5,758	1,835	11,043,630	9,453	7,595	3,012	2,420
New Hampshire	5.1	3.1	1.2	2.3	0.0	0.0	35.2	10,405	4,168	3,051	4,621,981	2,858	973	2,092	712
New Jersey	2.3	7.7	0.8	1.6	0.4	11.1	27.1	84,759	20,121	2,265	50,339,898	37,927	16,272	4,270	1,832
New Mexico	5.1	18.3	0.4	2.1	0.0	0.0	37.9	22,755	8,883	4,217	12,368,894	7,150	3,935	3,395	1,868
New York	3.5	16.4	2.6	1.1	0.0	0.0	19.9	211,059	70,869	3,665	117,301,602	92,721	28,388	4,795	1,468
North Carolina	1.1	16.0	0.7	2.2	0.1	0.0	43.3	71,814	22,060	2,081	38,437,183	28,303	12,840	2,670	1,211
North Dakota	8.6	3.7	0.9	6.3	0.0	0.0	40.9	10,214	3,205	4,188	6,022,102	4,336	1,565	5,666	2,045
Ohio	2.8	10.4	1.2	1.9	0.0	0.0	47.5	110,824	30,769	2,631	46,698,773	30,582	20,052	2,615	1,715
Oklahoma	8.1	1.6	1.5	2.2	0.2	0.0	44.7	29,667	9,515	2,390	16,034,342	10,173	4,612	2,556	1,159
Oregon	2.9	10.5	4.4	3.6	0.0	0.0	36.7	43,741	13,116	3,092	22,453,583	12,775	1,928	3,012	455
Pennsylvania	2.8	6.0	1.1	3.0	0.0	0.0	39.7	118,039	37,779	2,955	58,978,102	40,685	21,445	3,183	1,678
Rhode Island	5.1	3.2	1.6	1.9	1.8	13.8	20.8	11,332	4,289	4,057	5,519,577	3,527	1,878	3,336	1,777
South Carolina	6.0	7.0	0.9	2.0	0.0	0.0	46.6	37,278	12,511	2,398	19,896,383	11,795	5,382	2,260	1,031
South Dakota	4.3	3.5	1.4	5.6	0.0	0.0	35.9	6,648	3,087	3,458	2,973,584	2,018	1,679	2,260	1,880
Tennessee	5.6	3.6	0.6	4.5	0.0	0.0	42.8	41,307	14,226	2,066	21,089,936	16,775	13,220	2,436	1,920
Texas	6.3	7.5	1.1	3.2	0.0	0.0	50.4	199,320	66,663	2,270	94,062,952	61,013	53,343	2,078	1,817
Utah	3.3	16.9	1.2	1.8	0.0	0.0	51.7	27,781	5,801	1,785	15,468,919	8,731	4,227	2,687	1,301
Vermont	3.8	1.8	1.4	4.6	0.0	0.0	30.5	8,596	3,422	5,490	4,435,860	3,420	1,165	5,486	1,868
Virginia	5.2	9.5	0.7	2.1	0.0	0.0	49.0	70,083	18,494	2,153	44,662,513	28,064	10,067	3,267	1,172
Washington	6.2	11.1	1.3	3.3	0.4	0.0	40.1	69,823	16,190	2,104	38,787,998	29,013	21,759	3,771	2,828
West Virginia	1.8	2.4	0.9	4.4	0.0	0.0	40.7	16,581	6,723	3,767	8,165,109	5,462	2,819	3,060	1,579
Wisconsin	2.4	4.5	0.9	3.2	0.0	0.0	48.9	64,985	13,305	2,281	28,427,456	20,115	8,698	3,449	1,491
Wyoming	7.2	4.3	0.9	7.6	0.0	0.0	27.5	9,171	3,804	6,532	2,936,572	1,963	951	3,372	1,634

Table A. States — State Government Finances and Voting

STATE	State government finances, 2020 (cont.)												Voting and registration, November 2020		Presidential election, 2020 (percent of vote cast)		
	General expenditures (mil dol) (cont.)										Debt outstanding						
			Direct expenditures		By selected function												
	Total	To local govern-ments	Total	Per capita[1] (dollars)	Educa-tion	Health and hospitals	Highways	Public safety	Public welfare	Natural resources, parks, and recreation	Total (mil dol)	Per capita[1]	Percent registered	Percent voted	Demo-cratic	Repub-lican	All other
	339	340	341	342	343	344	345	346	347	348	349	350	351	352	353	354	355
United States	X	X	X	X	X	X	X	X	X	X	X	X	66.7	61.3	51.0	46.6	2.3
Alabama	35,785	8,341	27,444	5,576	12,883	3,937	1,790	878	7,954	304	9,934	2,019	67.0	59.6	36.6	62.0	1.4
Alaska	12,027	2,261	9,766	13,357	2,401	311	1,137	507	2,900	496	5,849	8,000	72.6	62.4	42.8	52.8	4.4
Arizona	47,170	9,909	37,261	5,021	14,440	644	2,395	1,491	17,456	440	12,947	1,745	68.8	64.7	49.4	49.1	1.6
Arkansas	23,640	5,864	17,776	5,865	8,117	1,510	1,597	457	7,354	333	7,565	2,496	59.6	51.9	34.8	62.4	2.8
California	422,066	116,459	305,607	7,763	109,368	26,713	18,874	12,278	147,237	9,094	144,041	3,659	59.3	55.7	63.5	34.3	2.2
Colorado	42,344	8,411	33,933	5,843	13,543	1,906	2,209	1,509	10,863	510	20,127	3,466	66.2	62.7	55.4	41.9	2.7
Connecticut	30,844	6,305	24,539	6,899	7,743	2,646	1,615	998	4,942	263	41,363	11,629	66.6	60.5	59.3	39.2	1.6
Delaware	11,273	2,015	9,258	9,382	3,990	563	567	524	2,822	143	5,069	5,136	70.8	63.8	58.7	39.8	1.5
District of Columbia	X	X	X	X	X	X	X	X	X	X	X	X	80.5	77.8	92.6	5.4	2.0
Florida	107,660	19,365	88,295	4,063	31,001	7,294	9,022	3,598	29,385	1,982	25,013	1,151	60.9	56.4	47.9	51.2	0.9
Georgia	60,621	14,859	45,762	4,273	22,183	3,387	3,248	1,817	14,154	788	14,116	1,318	65.2	60.9	49.5	49.2	1.3
Hawaii	14,540	323	14,216	10,104	3,718	1,280	529	287	2,992	222	9,430	6,702	63.8	59.7	64.2	34.5	1.3
Idaho	12,089	2,841	9,249	5,062	3,693	226	967	425	3,244	311	3,348	1,833	65.7	61.6	33.1	63.8	3.1
Illinois	99,228	23,266	75,962	6,035	19,484	2,332	6,015	2,195	30,277	554	64,854	5,152	68.2	62.7	57.5	40.6	1.9
Indiana	47,085	10,700	36,385	5,386	16,798	775	3,339	1,047	16,825	516	23,841	3,529	67.0	58.9	41.0	57.0	2.0
Iowa	25,727	5,633	20,095	6,352	7,437	2,689	2,379	421	7,289	482	6,250	1,976	73.8	68.5	44.6	52.8	2.6
Kansas	22,682	5,993	16,689	5,727	8,454	3,407	1,102	519	5,132	281	6,928	2,378	64.8	60.1	41.6	56.2	2.2
Kentucky	38,446	4,910	33,536	7,490	9,961	2,743	2,000	866	13,356	519	14,635	3,269	72.4	65.3	36.2	62.1	1.8
Louisiana	39,439	6,837	32,602	7,018	10,312	862	1,574	1,113	13,535	1,175	16,858	3,629	66.5	59.4	39.9	58.5	1.7
Maine	10,954	1,522	9,432	6,986	2,358	327	908	267	3,874	163	5,151	3,815	76.5	70.5	52.5	43.6	3.9
Maryland	53,538	10,469	43,069	7,112	14,351	4,086	2,641	2,348	14,728	817	29,359	4,848	73.4	68.7	65.4	32.2	2.5
Massachusetts	78,292	10,420	67,873	9,846	13,909	2,617	2,509	2,362	25,868	477	77,321	11,216	64.3	58.9	65.1	31.9	3.0
Michigan	86,679	24,755	61,923	6,213	28,376	7,589	4,145	2,540	21,576	600	34,403	3,452	70.8	64.1	50.6	47.8	1.5
Minnesota	55,575	15,514	40,061	7,081	17,040	1,550	3,308	1,190	17,080	1,049	17,401	3,076	79.2	74.3	52.4	45.3	2.3
Mississippi	23,853	5,515	18,338	6,181	6,067	2,161	1,128	503	6,963	343	7,289	2,457	79.1	69.2	41.1	57.6	1.3
Missouri	38,460	6,829	31,631	5,142	10,324	4,830	1,600	1,059	10,216	442	18,970	3,084	73.1	64.5	41.4	56.8	1.8
Montana	8,602	1,170	7,431	6,877	1,958	245	815	299	2,419	313	2,726	2,523	76.6	72.6	40.6	56.9	2.5
Nebraska	12,048	2,882	9,166	4,731	4,103	500	976	530	2,840	275	2,586	1,335	67.7	62.2	39.2	58.2	2.6
Nevada	20,144	5,028	15,116	4,817	5,872	621	975	456	4,381	197	3,653	1,164	60.6	56.3	50.1	47.7	2.3
New Hampshire	9,975	1,865	8,110	5,936	2,391	201	555	211	2,751	75	7,543	5,521	76.6	72.4	52.7	45.4	1.9
New Jersey	85,380	16,101	69,279	7,800	23,772	4,575	3,331	2,528	20,571	753	64,058	7,212	73.6	68.2	57.3	41.4	1.3
New Mexico	24,002	5,924	18,078	8,583	5,940	1,835	864	692	7,268	290	7,268	3,451	63.9	58.3	54.3	43.5	2.2
New York	227,367	64,784	162,583	8,408	49,557	17,175	5,683	4,657	79,154	1,460	156,004	8,068	62.0	57.0	55.9	34.0	10.0
North Carolina	67,815	16,321	51,494	4,858	23,337	4,519	5,465	2,143	16,976	974	15,099	1,424	63.6	58.9	48.6	49.9	1.5
North Dakota	7,936	2,105	5,831	7,619	2,460	179	754	159	1,680	244	3,018	3,943	75.2	65.3	31.8	65.1	3.1
Ohio	97,459	19,306	78,152	6,684	23,761	6,703	4,703	2,466	30,494	501	30,412	2,601	75.2	68.5	45.2	53.3	1.5
Oklahoma	26,962	4,908	22,054	5,540	8,724	1,309	2,509	856	7,155	324	7,805	1,961	64.0	55.5	32.3	65.4	2.3
Oregon	45,419	7,126	38,293	9,028	12,254	3,755	1,209	1,271	13,136	609	14,600	3,442	76.9	71.3	56.5	40.4	3.2
Pennsylvania	122,554	24,373	98,181	7,680	28,750	10,061	9,169	3,867	39,928	1,140	51,735	4,047	74.1	68.2	50.0	48.8	1.1
Rhode Island	10,549	1,431	9,118	8,625	2,239	435	596	338	3,285	109	9,372	8,865	68.5	61.3	59.4	38.6	2.0
South Carolina	36,903	6,555	30,348	5,816	12,052	3,767	2,072	718	8,629	417	12,896	2,471	67.7	61.3	43.4	55.1	1.5
South Dakota	5,716	923	4,793	5,369	1,672	199	820	183	1,220	203	3,856	4,319	66.3	57.7	35.6	61.8	2.6
Tennessee	35,866	7,774	28,093	4,079	11,310	1,309	2,038	1,253	13,725	596	6,858	996	70.8	63.3	37.5	60.7	1.9
Texas	174,211	35,312	138,899	4,731	61,893	13,388	13,075	5,512	44,073	1,160	57,887	1,972	62.1	55.3	46.5	52.1	1.5
Utah	25,252	4,624	20,628	6,347	9,912	3,238	1,811	572	4,647	346	7,594	2,337	63.3	59.7	37.6	58.1	4.2
Vermont	7,591	1,969	5,622	9,019	2,935	434	466	253	1,955	134	3,563	5,716	72.0	67.5	65.5	30.4	4.2
Virginia	65,338	13,198	52,140	6,069	18,873	7,788	5,318	2,436	15,891	511	29,341	3,415	70.1	66.0	54.1	44.0	1.9
Washington	69,206	18,306	50,901	6,616	24,359	7,925	3,200	1,697	13,853	1,244	29,659	3,855	67.2	64.3	58.0	38.8	3.3
West Virginia	16,560	2,614	13,945	7,813	4,482	509	1,755	468	5,017	346	11,626	6,514	66.4	55.3	30.2	69.8	0.0
Wisconsin	46,107	11,846	34,261	5,874	13,331	3,104	2,855	1,136	12,582	657	22,446	3,848	74.7	71.7	49.5	48.8	1.7
Wyoming	6,356	1,234	5,122	8,795	1,940	320	589	189	865	233	949	1,630	67.9	64.1	26.4	69.5	4.1

1. Based on resident population estimated as of July 1 of the year shown.

States and Counties

(For explanation of symbols, see page viii)

County Highlights and Rankings

Figure B-1. Fastest Growing Counties Among the 75 Largest, 2010–2020

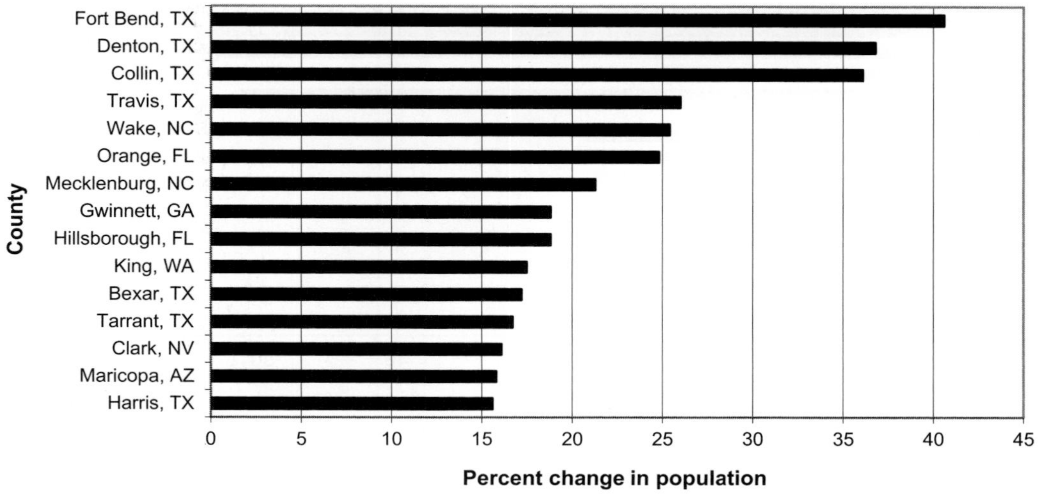

After each decennial census, the Census Bureau produces annual population estimates. The 2021 population estimates show that Los Angeles County, CA, remains, by far, the most populous county with 9.8 million residents. Next is Cook County, IL, which includes Chicago, with over 5.1 million people. Its population had declined 3.4 percent from 2000 to 2010 but increased by 1.6 percent from 2010 to 2020. New York City consists of five counties (the five boroughs), with Kings (Brooklyn) and Queens each with over 2 million residents, New York (Manhattan) with nearly 1.6 million residents, and the Bronx with about 1.4 million. Queens moved out of the top 10 in 2014 but Brooklyn grew by 9.2 percent between 2010 and 2020, keeping Kings the 8th most populous county in the nation.

Among the 75 most populous counties, the highest growth rates from 2010 to 2020 were found in the South, with the top four growth rates in Texas. From 2010 to 2020, the fastest-growing of these large counties was Fort Bend, TX, in the Houston metropolitan area. Its population grew 40.6 percent followed by Denton County, TX, in the Dallas-Fort Worth metropolitan area at 36.8 percent. In 2020, Fort Bend County ranked 72nd among the most populous counties. Seven other counties in Texas also had growth rates over 10 percent: Collin (also Dallas), Travis (Austin), Bexar (San Antonio), Harris (Houston), Tarrant (Fort Worth), Hidalgo (McAllen), and Dallas. Other large counties that experienced more than 10 percent growth in the decade were found mainly in the South and the West. Over 1,600 counties lost population during this period. The largest proportional losses were in counties with very small populations. Among the largest counties, Wayne, MI (Detroit); Cuyahoga, OH (Cleveland); and Milwaukee, WI, declined in population between 2010 and 2020. Four hundred and twenty-three counties had population growth rates at or above 10 percent from 2010 to 2020. Of these counties, 319 had populations of 50,000 or more and 245 had more than 100,000 residents.

Each year, the Census Bureau uses data on births, deaths, and migration to estimate population change since the most recent decennial census. The COVID-19 pandemic introduced difficulties in processing the census and the population estimates. The pandemic caused changes in the birth and death rates, and the long shutdowns contributed to migration, especially from cities with large concentrations of workers in central cities. Between 2020 and 2021, New York County (Manhattan) experienced a decline of 6.9 percent, while Kings (Brooklyn), Queens, and the Bronx each dropped by more than 3 percent. San Francisco County's population dropped by 6.7 percent, while Alameda, San Mateo, and Santa Clara counties in the San Francisco Bay Area each lost more than two percent of their populations. Suffolk County (Boston) declined by 3.3 percent; the District of Columbia lost 2.8 percent; while Cook (Chicago), Los Angeles, and Philadelphia counties all declined by nearly 2 percent. Three of the Texas counties that had the most growth between 2010 and 2020 continued to increase in 2021: Fort Bend, Collin, and Denton counties each grew by 3.9 percent or more.

Within states, the number and physical size of counties varied considerably: Delaware had three counties while Texas had

Figure B-2. Counties Among the 75 Largest with the Highest and Lowest Proportion of Population with a Bachelor's Degree or More, 2016–2020

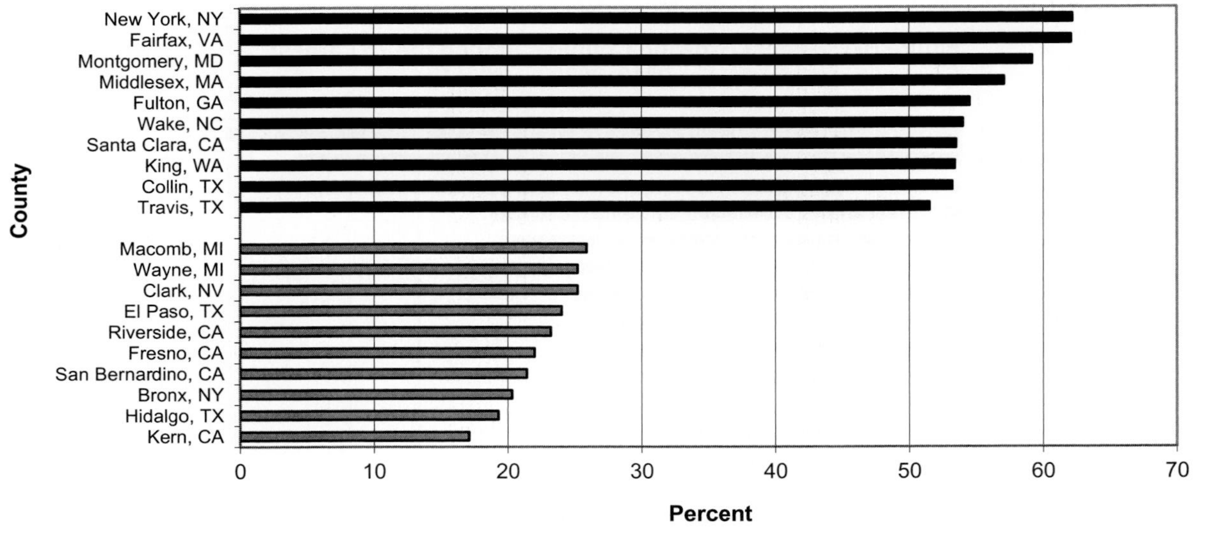

254 counties. For the 3,144 counties (and county equivalents—see Appendix A) in the United States, population in 2021 ranged from more than 9.8 million in Los Angeles, CA, to 57 in Loving County, TX. Other particularly large counties in terms of population are Cook County, IL (encompassing Chicago and its suburbs), with over with 5.1 million people; Harris County, TX (containing Houston), with 4.7 million people; and Maricopa County, AZ (containing Phoenix), with nearly 4.5 million people. There were 47 counties with a population of 1,000,000 or more; these counties combined contain more than one-fourth of the U.S. population. Over half of the U.S. population lived in the 159 largest counties, those with a population of 450,000 or more. At the other extreme, there were 37 counties with fewer than 1,000 people in 2021. The median county population size was 25,787.

In terms of land area, counties range from the nearly 145,576 square miles of Yukon-Koyukuk Census Area, AK; to Kalawao County, HI, with 12 square miles; New York County, NY (Manhattan), with 22.7 square miles; Bristol County, RI, with 24.1 square miles; and Arlington County, VA, with 26 square miles.[1] Counties tend to be larger in the western United States (most of the largest 50 in size are in that region). The median land area for all U.S. counties was about 616 square miles in 2020.

While New York County, NY, had one of the smallest land areas, it had by far the highest population density among U.S. counties in 2021, with over 69,000 persons per square mile. No other county approached that density (although three other New York City boroughs were among the top five counties in population density). San Francisco had the highest population density outside of New York City, with Suffolk County, MA (Boston); Philadelphia County, PA; and Washington, DC, also among the top 10 counties. In 2021, the median county had nearly 45 persons per square mile, with 272 counties having more than 500 persons per square mile. The nation's largest county in terms of population (Los Angeles) had a population density of 2,421.5 persons per square mile. This density ranked 23rd among the 75 most populous U.S. counties.

Proportionally large year-to-year labor force changes are not unusual for counties with small populations. The 2021 annual averages reflect a national labor force that increased by 0.3 percent. Among the 75 most populous counties, 16 counties experienced an increase of the labor force of 2.0 percent or more. Travis County, TX (Austin), experienced the highest increase at 5.5 percent. Five out of the top ten counties with the highest growth in their labor force were in Texas and three were in Florida. Over 1,400 counties experienced a decrease in their labor force in 2021. Among the most populous 75 counties, 35 counties experienced a decrease in their labor force.

The national annual average unemployment rate was 5.3 percent in 2021, significantly lower than in 2020 when it was 8.1 percent. In 2020, unemployment increased drastically as businesses were forced to close due to stay-at-home orders instituted by the states because of COVID-19. Although the unemployment rate decreased

[1] Several independent cities in Virginia, which are treated as counties for tabulation purposes, were excluded here.

in 2021, it was still up from 3.7 percent in 2019, 3.9 percent in 2018, 4.4 percent in 2017, and 4.9 percent in 2016. In 2021, 870 counties had unemployment rates above the national average of 5.3 percent and 37 counties had unemployment rates of 10 percent or greater, down significantly from 1,100 counties in 2010 and 224 counties in 2020. Of the 10 counties with the highest unemployment rates, Imperial County, CA; Bronx County, NY; and Yuma County, AZ, had populations over 100,000. Among the 75 most populous counties, 42 exceeded the national unemployment rate of 5.3 percent and two counties equaled it, with the highest in Bronx County, NY, at 13.6 percent, and 10.1 percent in Kings, NY. Salt Lake County, UT, had the lowest unemployment rate at 2.8 percent, followed by Hennepin, MN (Minneapolis), at 3.4 percent and Gwinnett County, GA (in the Atlanta metropolitan area), at 3.5 percent. Seventy counties had an unemployment rate below 2.0 percent.

Among the 75 largest counties, two counties with high unemployment rates, Fresno and Kern counties in CA, ranked among the top counties for agricultural sales. Meanwhile, Wayne County, MI, which typically has high manufacturing employment, was tied for tenth among the highest unemployment rates among the 75 most populous counties.

Typically, counties with higher levels of educational attainment have lower unemployment rates and higher median household incomes. Of the top ten counties with the highest educational attainment, eight had an unemployment rate lower than the national average and all had median incomes higher than average. Nationally, 35.1 percent of the population held bachelor's degrees or higher in 2020.

75 Largest Counties by 2020 Population

Selected Rankings

Population, 2021			Land area, 2021				Population density, 2021			
Population rank		Population [col 2]	Population rank	Land area rank	County	Land area (Square miles [col 1]	Population rank	Density rank	County	Density (per square kilometer) [col 4]
1	Los Angeles, CA	9,829,544	14	1	San Bernardino, CA	20,068.0	23	1	New York, NY	69,465.9
2	Cook, IL	5,173,146	4	2	Maricopa, AZ	9,201.8	8	2	Kings, NY	38,055.5
3	Harris, TX	4,728,030	45	3	Pima, AZ	9,188.7	28	3	Bronx, NY	33,766.5
4	Maricopa, AZ	4,496,588	63	4	Kern, CA	8,134.6	11	4	Queens, NY	21,445.7
5	San Diego, CA	3,286,069	12	5	Clark, NV	7,891.7	24	5	Philadelphia, PA	11,728.1
6	Orange, CA	3,167,809	10	6	Riverside, CA	7,209.3	73	6	Essex, NJ	6,779.7
7	Miami-Dade, FL	2,662,777	46	7	Fresno, CA	5,958.4	2	7	Cook, IL	5,474.8
8	Kings, NY	2,641,052	5	8	San Diego, CA	4,210.2	30	8	Nassau, NY	4,889.0
9	Dallas, TX	2,586,050	13	9	King, WA	2,115.2	56	9	Bergen, NJ	4,097.2
10	Riverside, CA	2,458,395	26	10	Palm Beach, FL	1,964.3	6	10	Orange, CA	3,995.7
11	Queens, NY	2,331,143	7	11	Miami-Dade, FL	1,899.9	59	11	Milwaukee, WI	3,842.9
12	Clark, NV	2,292,476	75	12	Ventura, CA	1,840.8	54	12	Pinellas, FL	3,495.1
13	King, WA	2,252,305	3	13	Harris, TX	1,707.0	9	13	Dallas, TX	2,961.9
14	San Bernardino, CA	2,194,710	60	14	Pierce, WA	1,668.0	40	14	Fairfax, VA	2,914.9
15	Tarrant, TX	2,126,477	65	15	Hidalgo, TX	1,571.0	19	15	Wayne, MI	2,901.0
16	Bexar, TX	2,028,236	69	16	Worcester, MA	1,510.7	61	16	Du Page, IL	2,821.5
17	Broward, FL	1,930,983	18	17	Santa Clara, CA	1,291.1	70	17	Middlesex, NJ	2,784.0
18	Santa Clara, CA	1,885,508	16	18	Bexar, TX	1,240.3	3	18	Harris, TX	2,769.8
19	Wayne, MI	1,774,816	17	19	Broward, FL	1,202.7	35	19	Cuyahoga, OH	2,732.7
20	Alameda, CA	1,648,556	57	20	Erie, NY	1,042.7	31	20	Franklin, OH	2,482.0
21	Middlesex, MA	1,614,742	27	21	Hillsborough, FL	1,021.9	15	21	Tarrant, TX	2,457.5
22	Sacramento, CA	1,588,921	67	22	El Paso, TX	1,013.2	51	22	Marion, IN	2,448.6
23	New York, NY	1,576,876	32	23	Travis, TX	994.1	1	23	Los Angeles, CA	2,421.5
24	Philadelphia, PA	1,576,251	22	24	Sacramento, CA	965.3	49	24	Westchester, NY	2,316.9
25	Suffolk, NY	1,526,344	2	25	Cook, IL	944.9	34	25	Hennepin, MN	2,287.8
26	Palm Beach, FL	1,497,987	25	26	Suffolk, NY	911.2	52	26	Gwinnett, GA	2,239.0
27	Hillsborough, FL	1,478,194	29	27	Orange, FL	902.0	20	27	Alameda, CA	2,235.3
28	Bronx, NY	1,424,948	58	28	Denton, TX	878.5	41	28	Mecklenburg, NC	2,143.4
29	Orange, FL	1,422,746	9	29	Dallas, TX	873.1	44	29	Montgomery, MD	2,139.2
30	Nassau, NY	1,390,907	33	30	Oakland, MI	867.3	43	30	Fulton, GA	2,022.7
31	Franklin, OH	1,321,414	15	31	Tarrant, TX	865.3	55	31	Prince George's, MD	1,979.1
32	Travis, TX	1,305,154	72	32	Fort Bend, TX	861.7	21	32	Middlesex, MA	1,974.3
33	Oakland, MI	1,270,017	42	33	Collin, TX	841.3	50	33	St. Louis, MO	1,963.4
34	Hennepin, MN	1,267,416	39	34	Wake, NC	834.6	66	34	Macomb, MI	1,829.3
35	Cuyahoga, OH	1,249,387	21	35	Middlesex, MA	817.9	71	35	Montgomery, PA	1,781.7
36	Allegheny, PA	1,238,090	6	36	Orange, CA	792.8	36	36	Allegheny, PA	1,696.0
37	Salt Lake, UT	1,186,421	48	37	Duval, FL	762.6	25	37	Suffolk, NY	1,675.1
38	Contra Costa, CA	1,161,413	62	38	Shelby, TN	760.6	47	38	Honolulu, HI	1,666.5
39	Wake, NC	1,150,204	37	39	Salt Lake, UT	742.1	22	39	Sacramento, CA	1,646.0
40	Fairfax, VA	1,139,720	20	40	Alameda, CA	737.5	16	40	Bexar, TX	1,635.3
41	Mecklenburg, NC	1,122,276	64	41	Hartford, CT	734.9	38	41	Contra Costa, CA	1,620.0
42	Collin, TX	1,109,462	36	42	Allegheny, PA	730.0	17	42	Broward, FL	1,605.5
43	Fulton, GA	1,065,334	38	43	Contra Costa, CA	716.9	37	43	Salt Lake, UT	1,598.7
44	Montgomery, MD	1,054,827	53	44	Fairfield, CT	625.0	29	44	Orange, FL	1,577.3
45	Pima, AZ	1,052,030	19	45	Wayne, MI	611.8	53	45	Fairfield, CT	1,535.6
46	Fresno, CA	1,013,581	68	46	New Haven, CT	604.3	33	46	Oakland, MI	1,464.3
47	Honolulu, HI	1,000,890	47	47	Honolulu, HI	600.6	18	47	Santa Clara, CA	1,460.4
48	Duval, FL	999,935	74	48	Baltimore, MD	598.4	27	48	Hillsborough, FL	1,446.5
49	Westchester, NY	997,895	34	49	Hennepin, MN	554.0	68	49	New Haven, CT	1,429.3
50	St. Louis, MO	997,187	31	50	Franklin, OH	532.4	74	50	Baltimore, MD	1,419.3
51	Marion, IN	971,102	43	51	Fulton, GA	526.7	7	51	Miami-Dade, FL	1,401.5
52	Gwinnett, GA	964,546	41	52	Mecklenburg, NC	523.6	39	52	Wake, NC	1,378.2
53	Fairfield, CT	959,768	50	53	St. Louis, MO	507.9	42	53	Collin, TX	1,318.7
54	Pinellas, FL	956,615	44	54	Montgomery, MD	493.1	32	54	Travis, TX	1,312.9
55	Prince George's, MD	955,306	71	55	Montgomery, PA	483.0	48	55	Duval, FL	1,311.2
56	Bergen, NJ	953,819	55	56	Prince George's, MD	482.7	64	56	Hartford, CT	1,220.4
57	Erie, NY	950,683	66	57	Macomb, MI	479.3	62	57	Shelby, TN	1,215.4
58	Denton, TX	941,647	35	58	Cuyahoga, OH	457.2	58	58	Denton, TX	1,071.9
59	Milwaukee, WI	928,059	52	59	Gwinnett, GA	430.8	13	59	King, WA	1,064.8
60	Pierce, WA	925,708	49	60	Westchester, NY	430.7	72	60	Fort Bend, TX	996.3
61	Du Page, IL	924,885	51	61	Marion, IN	396.6	57	61	Erie, NY	911.8
62	Shelby, TN	924,454	40	62	Fairfax, VA	391.0	67	62	El Paso, TX	856.6
63	Kern, CA	917,673	61	63	Du Page, IL	327.8	5	63	San Diego, CA	780.5
64	Hartford, CT	896,854	70	64	Middlesex, NJ	309.2	26	64	Palm Beach, FL	762.6
65	Hidalgo, TX	880,356	30	65	Nassau, NY	284.5	69	65	Worcester, MA	570.6
66	Macomb, MI	876,792	54	66	Pinellas, FL	273.7	65	66	Hidalgo, TX	560.4
67	El Paso, TX	867,947	59	67	Milwaukee, WI	241.5	60	67	Pierce, WA	555.0
68	New Haven, CT	863,700	56	68	Bergen, NJ	232.8	4	68	Maricopa, AZ	488.7
69	Worcester, MA	862,029	24	69	Philadelphia, PA	134.4	75	69	Ventura, CA	456.2
70	Middlesex, NJ	860,807	73	70	Essex, NJ	126.1	10	70	Riverside, CA	341.0
71	Montgomery, PA	860,578	11	71	Queens, NY	108.7	12	71	Clark, NV	290.5
72	Fort Bend, TX	858,527	8	72	Kings, NY	69.4	46	72	Fresno, CA	170.1
73	Essex, NJ	854,917	28	73	Bronx, NY	42.2	45	73	Pima, AZ	114.5
74	Baltimore, MD	849,316	1	74	Los Angeles, CA	40.3	63	74	Kern, CA	112.8
75	Ventura, CA	839,784	23	75	New York, NY	22.7	14	75	San Bernardino, CA	109.4

75 Largest Counties by 2020 Population

Selected Rankings

Percent population change, 2020–2021				Employment/residence ratio, 2016–2020				Percent White, not Hispanic or Latino, alone or in combination, 2021			
Population rank	Percent change rank	County	Percent change [col 23]	Population rank	Number of employees per resident rank	County	Number of employees per resident [col 34]	Population rank	White rank	County	Percent white [col 5]
72	1	Fort Bend, TX	4.3	23	1	New York, NY	2.85	36	1	Allegheny, PA	79.7
42	2	Collin, TX	4.2	43	2	Fulton, GA	1.73	66	2	Macomb, MI	79.0
58	3	Denton, TX	3.9	34	3	Hennepin, MN	1.32	57	3	Erie, NY	76.2
39	4	Wake, NC	1.8	51	4	Marion, IN	1.27	69	3	Worcester, MA	76.2
4	5	Maricopa, AZ	1.7	41	5	Mecklenburg, NC	1.26	71	5	Montgomery, PA	75.9
10	5	Riverside, CA	1.7	9	6	Dallas, TX	1.25	54	6	Pinellas, FL	75.3
27	7	Hillsborough, FL	1.3	29	6	Orange, FL	1.25	33	7	Oakland, MI	72.9
12	8	Clark, NV	1.2	35	8	Cuyahoga, OH	1.22	21	8	Middlesex, MA	71.9
32	8	Travis, TX	1.2	50	8	St. Louis, MO	1.22	37	8	Salt Lake, UT	71.9
65	10	Hidalgo, TX	1.1	61	10	Du Page, IL	1.21	34	10	Hennepin, MN	70.5
16	11	Bexar, TX	0.9	32	11	Travis, TX	1.20	60	11	Pierce, WA	69.9
63	11	Kern, CA	0.9	48	12	Duval, FL	1.19	25	12	Suffolk, NY	67.0
15	13	Tarrant, TX	0.8	71	12	Montgomery, PA	1.19	50	13	St. Louis, MO	66.8
45	13	Pima, AZ	0.8	62	14	Shelby, TN	1.18	61	14	Du Page, IL	66.7
52	13	Gwinnett, GA	0.8	13	15	King, WA	1.17	31	15	Franklin, OH	63.7
14	16	San Bernardino, CA	0.6	31	16	Franklin, OH	1.16	68	16	New Haven, CT	61.7
41	16	Mecklenburg, NC	0.6	64	16	Hartford, CT	1.16	53	17	Fairfield, CT	61.1
46	18	Fresno, CA	0.5	37	18	Salt Lake, UT	1.15	39	18	Wake, NC	60.9
60	18	Pierce, WA	0.5	3	19	Harris, TX	1.14	13	19	King, WA	60.4
71	18	Montgomery, PA	0.5	18	19	Santa Clara, CA	1.14	64	20	Hartford, CT	60.3
26	21	Palm Beach, FL	0.4	33	19	Oakland, MI	1.14	35	21	Cuyahoga, OH	59.9
48	21	Duval, FL	0.4	36	19	Allegheny, PA	1.14	30	22	Nassau, NY	58.6
67	23	El Paso, TX	0.3	24	23	Philadelphia, PA	1.13	58	23	Denton, TX	57.7
22	24	Sacramento, CA	0.2	21	24	Middlesex, MA	1.09	74	24	Baltimore, MD	56.3
53	24	Fairfield, CT	0.2	39	24	Wake, NC	1.09	51	25	Marion, IN	55.9
37	26	Salt Lake, UT	0.1	19	26	Wayne, MI	1.08	4	26	Maricopa, AZ	55.6
25	27	Suffolk, NY	0.0	2	27	Cook, IL	1.07	42	27	Collin, TX	55.1
69	27	Worcester, MA	0.0	27	27	Hillsborough, FL	1.07	56	28	Bergen, NJ	54.9
3	29	Harris, TX	-0.1	57	27	Erie, NY	1.07	26	29	Palm Beach, FL	54.4
43	29	Fulton, GA	-0.1	6	30	Orange, CA	1.06	49	30	Westchester, NY	53.8
68	29	New Haven, CT	-0.1	7	30	Miami-Dade, FL	1.06	48	31	Duval, FL	53.2
31	32	Franklin, OH	-0.2	40	30	Fairfax, VA	1.06	40	32	Fairfax, VA	52.4
56	32	Bergen, NJ	-0.2	16	33	Bexar, TX	1.05	45	33	Pima, AZ	52.1
30	34	Nassau, NY	-0.3	54	34	Pinellas, FL	1.04	19	34	Wayne, MI	51.4
33	34	Oakland, MI	-0.3	59	34	Milwaukee, WI	1.04	59	35	Milwaukee, WI	51.3
54	34	Pinellas, FL	-0.3	1	36	Los Angeles, CA	1.03	32	36	Travis, TX	50.6
64	34	Hartford, CT	-0.3	26	36	Palm Beach, FL	1.03	27	37	Hillsborough, FL	48.9
70	34	Middlesex, NJ	-0.3	4	38	Maricopa, AZ	1.02	23	38	New York, NY	47.7
5	39	San Diego, CA	-0.4	5	38	San Diego, CA	1.02	41	39	Mecklenburg, NC	47.5
38	39	Contra Costa, CA	-0.4	63	40	Kern, CA	1.01	5	40	San Diego, CA	47.0
57	39	Erie, NY	-0.4	12	41	Clark, NV	1.00	15	41	Tarrant, TX	46.4
29	42	Orange, FL	-0.5	15	41	Tarrant, TX	1.00	22	41	Sacramento, CA	46.4
66	42	Macomb, MI	-0.5	45	41	Pima, AZ	1.00	75	43	Ventura, CA	46.0
75	42	Ventura, CA	-0.5	46	41	Fresno, CA	1.00	44	44	Montgomery, MD	44.8
6	45	Orange, CA	-0.6	47	41	Honolulu, HI	1.00	38	45	Contra Costa, CA	44.7
51	45	Marion, IN	-0.6	67	41	El Paso, TX	1.00	12	46	Clark, NV	44.2
62	45	Shelby, TN	-0.6	53	47	Fairfield, CT	0.99	2	47	Cook, IL	42.9
74	45	Baltimore, MD	-0.6	73	47	Essex, NJ	0.99	6	48	Orange, CA	41.2
17	49	Broward, FL	-0.7	22	49	Sacramento, CA	0.98	70	48	Middlesex, NJ	41.2
44	49	Montgomery, MD	-0.7	70	49	Middlesex, NJ	0.98	29	50	Orange, FL	40.6
49	49	Westchester, NY	-0.7	20	51	Alameda, CA	0.97	43	51	Fulton, GA	40.5
50	49	St. Louis, MO	-0.7	42	52	Collin, TX	0.96	8	52	Kings, NY	38.5
13	53	King, WA	-0.8	49	52	Westchester, NY	0.96	62	53	Shelby, TN	35.8
40	54	Fairfax, VA	-0.9	44	54	Montgomery, MD	0.95	24	54	Philadelphia, PA	35.4
61	54	Du Page, IL	-0.9	65	55	Hidalgo, TX	0.94	52	55	Gwinnett, GA	35.3
19	56	Wayne, MI	-1.0	14	56	San Bernardino, CA	0.93	17	56	Broward, FL	34.7
36	56	Allegheny, PA	-1.0	56	56	Bergen, NJ	0.93	10	57	Riverside, CA	34.2
73	56	Essex, NJ	-1.0	68	56	New Haven, CT	0.93	20	58	Alameda, CA	33.6
9	59	Dallas, TX	-1.1	17	59	Broward, FL	0.91	63	59	Kern, CA	32.8
21	59	Middlesex, MA	-1.1	75	60	Ventura, CA	0.90	18	60	Santa Clara, CA	31.8
34	59	Hennepin, MN	-1.1	74	61	Baltimore, MD	0.89	72	60	Fort Bend, TX	31.8
35	62	Cuyahoga, OH	-1.2	25	62	Suffolk, NY	0.88	47	62	Honolulu, HI	31.7
55	62	Prince George's, MD	-1.2	52	62	Gwinnett, GA	0.88	73	63	Essex, NJ	31.0
59	62	Milwaukee, WI	-1.2	69	64	Worcester, MA	0.87	46	64	Fresno, CA	29.0
7	65	Miami-Dade, FL	-1.4	30	65	Nassau, NY	0.86	3	65	Harris, TX	28.9
47	66	Honolulu, HI	-1.5	60	65	Pierce, WA	0.86	9	66	Dallas, TX	28.5
24	67	Philadelphia, PA	-1.7	66	67	Macomb, MI	0.84	16	67	Bexar, TX	28.0
1	68	Los Angeles, CA	-1.8	10	68	Riverside, CA	0.83	1	68	Los Angeles, CA	27.3
2	69	Cook, IL	-1.9	38	69	Contra Costa, CA	0.75	14	68	San Bernardino, CA	27.3
20	70	Alameda, CA	-2.0	55	69	Prince George's, MD	0.75	11	70	Queens, NY	25.8
18	71	Santa Clara, CA	-2.6	8	71	Kings, NY	0.74	7	71	Miami-Dade, FL	14.0
11	72	Queens, NY	-3.1	11	72	Queens, NY	0.69	55	72	Prince George's, MD	13.3
28	73	Bronx, NY	-3.2	28	72	Bronx, NY	0.69	67	73	El Paso, TX	12.2
8	74	Kings, NY	-3.5	58	72	Denton, TX	0.69	28	74	Bronx, NY	9.7
23	75	New York, NY	-6.9	72	75	Fort Bend, TX	0.60	65	75	Hidalgo, TX	5.9

75 Largest Counties by 2020 Population
Selected Rankings

Percent Black, not Hispanic or Latino, alone or in combination, 2021				Percent American Indian, Alaska Native, alone or in combination, 2021				Percent Asian or Pacific Islander, alone or in combination, 2021			
Population rank	Black rank	County	Percent black [col 6]	Population rank	American Indian Alaska native rank	County	Percent American Indian, Alaska native [col 7]	Population rank	Asian or Pacific Islander rank	County	Percent Asian or Pacific Islander [col 8]
55	1	Prince George's, MD	62.9	45	1	Pima, AZ	3.1	47	1	Honolulu, HI	79.0
62	2	Shelby, TN	55.0	60	2	Pierce, WA	2.7	18	2	Santa Clara, CA	43.0
43	3	Fulton, GA	45.0	4	3	Maricopa, AZ	2.2	20	3	Alameda, CA	36.7
24	4	Philadelphia, PA	41.7	13	4	King, WA	1.6	11	4	Queens, NY	28.5
19	5	Wayne, MI	39.4	22	5	Sacramento, CA	1.5	70	5	Middlesex, NJ	26.3
73	6	Essex, NJ	39.1	47	5	Honolulu, HI	1.5	6	6	Orange, CA	24.9
41	7	Mecklenburg, NC	32.9	34	7	Hennepin, MN	1.4	13	7	King, WA	24.7
74	8	Baltimore, MD	32.0	37	8	Salt Lake, UT	1.2	40	8	Fairfax, VA	23.0
48	9	Duval, FL	31.3	59	8	Milwaukee, WI	1.2	72	9	Fort Bend, TX	22.5
35	10	Cuyahoga, OH	31.1	63	8	Kern, CA	1.2	38	10	Contra Costa, CA	22.4
51	11	Marion, IN	30.7	12	11	Clark, NV	1.1	22	11	Sacramento, CA	21.5
52	12	Gwinnett, GA	30.5	19	11	Wayne, MI	1.1	42	12	Collin, TX	18.9
8	13	Kings, NY	30.4	46	11	Fresno, CA	1.1	56	13	Bergen, NJ	18.2
17	14	Broward, FL	29.9	10	14	Riverside, CA	1.0	44	14	Montgomery, MD	17.4
28	14	Bronx, NY	29.9	38	14	Contra Costa, CA	1.0	1	15	Los Angeles, CA	16.8
59	16	Milwaukee, WI	28.2	55	14	Prince George's, MD	1.0	5	16	San Diego, CA	15.4
50	17	St. Louis, MO	26.1	5	17	San Diego, CA	0.9	21	17	Middlesex, MA	15.2
31	18	Franklin, OH	25.9	11	17	Queens, NY	0.9	52	18	Gwinnett, GA	14.1
2	19	Cook, IL	23.6	14	17	San Bernardino, CA	0.9	61	18	Du Page, IL	14.1
9	19	Dallas, TX	23.6	15	17	Tarrant, TX	0.9	8	20	Kings, NY	13.9
72	21	Fort Bend, TX	21.7	31	17	Franklin, OH	0.9	23	21	New York, NY	13.8
29	22	Orange, FL	21.4	39	17	Wake, NC	0.9	12	22	Clark, NV	13.7
39	23	Wake, NC	21.1	41	17	Mecklenburg, NC	0.9	30	23	Nassau, NY	12.7
44	24	Montgomery, MD	20.3	42	17	Collin, TX	0.9	60	24	Pierce, WA	12.6
3	25	Harris, TX	19.8	57	17	Erie, NY	0.9	46	25	Fresno, CA	12.0
26	26	Palm Beach, FL	19.6	58	17	Denton, TX	0.9	58	26	Denton, TX	11.5
11	27	Queens, NY	19.0	66	17	Macomb, MI	0.9	75	27	Ventura, CA	9.5
15	28	Tarrant, TX	18.4	75	17	Ventura, CA	0.9	14	28	San Bernardino, CA	9.4
27	29	Hillsborough, FL	17.4	20	29	Alameda, CA	0.8	33	29	Oakland, MI	9.3
7	30	Miami-Dade, FL	15.7	24	29	Philadelphia, PA	0.8	39	30	Wake, NC	9.2
34	30	Hennepin, MN	15.7	33	29	Oakland, MI	0.8	71	30	Montgomery, PA	9.2
64	32	Hartford, CT	14.9	48	29	Duval, FL	0.8	43	32	Fulton, GA	8.8
36	33	Allegheny, PA	14.8	74	29	Baltimore, MD	0.8	2	33	Cook, IL	8.7
33	34	Oakland, MI	14.7	9	34	Dallas, TX	0.7	10	34	Riverside, CA	8.6
68	35	New Haven, CT	14.6	32	34	Travis, TX	0.7	24	34	Philadelphia, PA	8.6
49	36	Westchester, NY	14.5	35	34	Cuyahoga, OH	0.7	32	34	Travis, TX	8.6
66	37	Macomb, MI	14.3	43	34	Fulton, GA	0.7	34	34	Hennepin, MN	8.6
23	38	New York, NY	14.0	44	34	Montgomery, MD	0.7	3	38	Harris, TX	7.9
57	38	Erie, NY	14.0	50	34	St. Louis, MO	0.7	37	39	Salt Lake, UT	7.8
12	40	Clark, NV	13.6	51	34	Marion, IN	0.7	9	40	Dallas, TX	7.4
30	41	Nassau, NY	12.3	52	34	Gwinnett, GA	0.7	74	40	Baltimore, MD	7.4
58	41	Denton, TX	12.3	54	34	Pinellas, FL	0.7	41	42	Mecklenburg, NC	7.2
53	43	Fairfield, CT	12.2	1	43	Los Angeles, CA	0.6	49	43	Westchester, NY	7.1
22	44	Sacramento, CA	12.0	6	43	Orange, CA	0.6	15	44	Tarrant, TX	6.9
42	44	Collin, TX	12.0	8	43	Kings, NY	0.6	31	45	Franklin, OH	6.8
20	46	Alameda, CA	11.4	16	43	Bexar, TX	0.6	64	45	Hartford, CT	6.8
54	46	Pinellas, FL	11.4	18	43	Santa Clara, CA	0.6	73	45	Essex, NJ	6.8
40	48	Fairfax, VA	11.1	23	43	New York, NY	0.6	53	48	Fairfield, CT	6.7
70	49	Middlesex, NJ	11.0	27	43	Hillsborough, FL	0.6	29	49	Orange, FL	6.6
71	50	Montgomery, PA	10.9	28	43	Bronx, NY	0.6	48	50	Duval, FL	6.3
60	51	Pierce, WA	10.2	29	43	Orange, FL	0.6	69	50	Worcester, MA	6.3
38	52	Contra Costa, CA	10.0	40	43	Fairfax, VA	0.6	63	52	Kern, CA	6.0
14	53	San Bernardino, CA	9.0	62	43	Shelby, TN	0.6	4	53	Maricopa, AZ	5.9
32	54	Travis, TX	8.9	64	43	Hartford, CT	0.6	50	54	St. Louis, MO	5.8
1	55	Los Angeles, CA	8.7	68	43	New Haven, CT	0.6	59	55	Milwaukee, WI	5.6
13	56	King, WA	8.4	69	43	Worcester, MA	0.6	66	55	Macomb, MI	5.6
25	56	Suffolk, NY	8.4	72	43	Fort Bend, TX	0.6	27	57	Hillsborough, FL	5.4
16	58	Bexar, TX	8.2	73	43	Essex, NJ	0.6	36	58	Allegheny, PA	5.1
10	59	Riverside, CA	7.3	2	59	Cook, IL	0.5	57	58	Erie, NY	5.1
4	60	Maricopa, AZ	6.9	3	59	Harris, TX	0.5	25	60	Suffolk, NY	5.0
21	61	Middlesex, MA	6.2	17	59	Broward, FL	0.5	68	60	New Haven, CT	5.0
56	61	Bergen, NJ	6.2	25	59	Suffolk, NY	0.5	55	62	Prince George's, MD	4.9
69	63	Worcester, MA	6.1	36	59	Allegheny, PA	0.5	17	63	Broward, FL	4.8
63	64	Kern, CA	6.0	49	59	Westchester, NY	0.5	51	64	Marion, IN	4.7
5	65	San Diego, CA	5.8	67	59	El Paso, TX	0.5	19	65	Wayne, MI	4.5
61	66	Du Page, IL	5.7	70	59	Middlesex, NJ	0.5	28	65	Bronx, NY	4.5
46	67	Fresno, CA	5.3	71	59	Montgomery, PA	0.5	54	65	Pinellas, FL	4.5
45	68	Pima, AZ	4.4	21	68	Middlesex, MA	0.4	35	68	Cuyahoga, OH	4.1
47	69	Honolulu, HI	3.7	26	68	Palm Beach, FL	0.4	45	68	Pima, AZ	4.1
67	70	El Paso, TX	3.6	30	68	Nassau, NY	0.4	16	70	Bexar, TX	4.0
18	71	Santa Clara, CA	3.1	53	68	Fairfield, CT	0.4	26	71	Palm Beach, FL	3.6
37	72	Salt Lake, UT	2.5	61	68	Du Page, IL	0.4	62	72	Shelby, TN	3.4
75	73	Ventura, CA	2.4	56	73	Bergen, NJ	0.3	7	73	Miami-Dade, FL	1.9
6	74	Orange, CA	2.3	7	74	Miami-Dade, FL	0.2	67	74	El Paso, TX	1.8
65	75	Hidalgo, TX	0.6	65	75	Hidalgo, TX	0.1	65	75	Hidalgo, TX	1.0

75 Largest Counties by 2020 Population
Selected Rankings

Percent Hispanic or Latino,[1] 2021

Population rank	Hispanic or Latino rank	County	Percent Hispanic or Latino [col 9]
65	1	Hidalgo, TX	92.6
67	2	El Paso, TX	82.9
7	3	Miami-Dade, FL	68.9
16	4	Bexar, TX	60.9
28	5	Bronx, NY	56.4
63	6	Kern, CA	56.1
14	7	San Bernardino, CA	55.8
46	8	Fresno, CA	54.7
10	9	Riverside, CA	51.6
1	10	Los Angeles, CA	49.1
3	11	Harris, TX	44.4
75	12	Ventura, CA	44.1
9	13	Dallas, TX	41.4
45	14	Pima, AZ	38.5
5	15	San Diego, CA	34.8
6	16	Orange, CA	34.1
32	17	Travis, TX	33.3
29	18	Orange, FL	32.9
4	19	Maricopa, AZ	32.0
17	19	Broward, FL	32.0
12	21	Clark, NV	31.8
27	22	Hillsborough, FL	29.9
15	23	Tarrant, TX	29.7
11	24	Queens, NY	28.1
38	25	Contra Costa, CA	26.8
23	26	New York, NY	26.4
2	27	Cook, IL	26.0
49	28	Westchester, NY	25.9
72	29	Fort Bend, TX	25.5
18	30	Santa Clara, CA	25.0
22	31	Sacramento, CA	24.4
73	32	Essex, NJ	24.3
26	33	Palm Beach, FL	23.4
70	34	Middlesex, NJ	22.7
20	35	Alameda, CA	22.2
52	35	Gwinnett, GA	22.2
56	37	Bergen, NJ	22.0
53	38	Fairfield, CT	21.3
25	39	Suffolk, NY	20.7
55	40	Prince George's, MD	20.4
68	41	New Haven, CT	20.2
44	42	Montgomery, MD	20.1
58	43	Denton, TX	20.0
64	44	Hartford, CT	19.4
37	45	Salt Lake, UT	19.3
8	46	Kings, NY	18.8
30	47	Nassau, NY	17.6
40	48	Fairfax, VA	16.6
59	49	Milwaukee, WI	16.4
24	50	Philadelphia, PA	15.9
42	51	Collin, TX	15.8
61	52	Du Page, IL	15.0
41	53	Mecklenburg, NC	13.8
69	54	Worcester, MA	12.8
60	55	Pierce, WA	12.2
48	56	Duval, FL	11.3
51	57	Marion, IN	11.0
39	58	Wake, NC	10.5
13	59	King, WA	10.3
54	59	Pinellas, FL	10.3
47	61	Honolulu, HI	10.2
21	62	Middlesex, MA	8.6
43	63	Fulton, GA	7.3
34	64	Hennepin, MN	7.1
62	65	Shelby, TN	6.9
35	66	Cuyahoga, OH	6.6
19	67	Wayne, MI	6.5
31	68	Franklin, OH	6.2
74	68	Baltimore, MD	6.2
57	70	Erie, NY	6.0
71	71	Montgomery, PA	5.8
33	72	Oakland, MI	4.7
50	73	St. Louis, MO	3.1
66	74	Macomb, MI	2.9
36	75	Allegheny, PA	2.4

Percent under 18 years old, 2021

Population rank	Under 18 years old rank	County	Percent under 18 years old [cols 10 and 11]
65	1	Hidalgo, TX	26.1
63	2	Kern, CA	23.8
46	3	Fresno, CA	23.4
72	4	Fort Bend, TX	22.0
67	5	El Paso, TX	21.9
3	6	Harris, TX	21.8
14	7	San Bernardino, CA	21.5
52	8	Gwinnett, GA	21.3
37	8	Salt Lake, UT	21.3
9	10	Dallas, TX	21.2
15	11	Tarrant, TX	21.1
62	12	Shelby, TN	20.9
51	13	Marion, IN	20.8
16	13	Bexar, TX	20.8
28	15	Bronx, NY	20.5
42	16	Collin, TX	20.4
10	17	Riverside, CA	20.1
59	18	Milwaukee, WI	20.0
73	19	Essex, NJ	19.8
31	20	Franklin, OH	19.6
19	20	Wayne, MI	19.6
60	22	Pierce, WA	19.4
58	23	Denton, TX	19.3
22	24	Sacramento, CA	19.2
8	24	Kings, NY	19.2
48	26	Duval, FL	19.0
41	26	Mecklenburg, NC	19.0
40	26	Fairfax, VA	19.0
39	26	Wake, NC	19.0
4	30	Maricopa, AZ	18.9
44	31	Montgomery, MD	18.8
12	31	Clark, NV	18.8
55	33	Prince George's, MD	18.5
61	34	Du Page, IL	18.2
50	34	St. Louis, MO	18.2
27	34	Hillsborough, FL	18.2
24	34	Philadelphia, PA	18.2
75	38	Ventura, CA	18.1
34	38	Hennepin, MN	18.1
74	40	Baltimore, MD	18.0
38	40	Contra Costa, CA	18.0
29	42	Orange, FL	17.9
47	43	Honolulu, HI	17.8
70	44	Middlesex, NJ	17.7
53	44	Fairfield, CT	17.7
5	44	San Diego, CA	17.7
2	44	Cook, IL	17.7
6	48	Orange, CA	17.6
30	49	Nassau, NY	17.5
71	50	Montgomery, PA	17.4
18	50	Santa Clara, CA	17.4
49	52	Westchester, NY	17.3
43	52	Fulton, GA	17.3
17	52	Broward, FL	17.3
1	52	Los Angeles, CA	17.3
32	56	Travis, TX	17.2
66	57	Macomb, MI	17.0
56	57	Bergen, NJ	17.0
64	59	Hartford, CT	16.9
35	59	Cuyahoga, OH	16.9
69	61	Worcester, MA	16.8
25	61	Suffolk, NY	16.8
11	61	Queens, NY	16.8
33	64	Oakland, MI	16.7
20	64	Alameda, CA	16.7
7	64	Miami-Dade, FL	16.7
57	67	Erie, NY	16.6
45	67	Pima, AZ	16.6
13	69	King, WA	16.5
68	70	New Haven, CT	16.2
21	71	Middlesex, MA	16.1
36	72	Allegheny, PA	15.6
26	73	Palm Beach, FL	15.5
54	74	Pinellas, FL	12.9
23	75	New York, NY	12.4

Percent 65 years old and over, 2021

Population rank	65 years old and over rank	County	Percent 65 years old and over [cols 17 and 18]
54	1	Pinellas, FL	25.9
26	2	Palm Beach, FL	24.6
45	3	Pima, AZ	20.6
36	4	Allegheny, PA	19.7
35	5	Cuyahoga, OH	19.0
47	6	Honolulu, HI	18.8
50	6	St. Louis, MO	18.8
57	6	Erie, NY	18.8
23	9	New York, NY	18.4
30	9	Nassau, NY	18.4
71	9	Montgomery, PA	18.4
68	12	New Haven, CT	18.1
33	13	Oakland, MI	17.9
66	13	Macomb, MI	17.9
49	15	Westchester, NY	17.8
74	15	Baltimore, MD	17.8
56	15	Bergen, NJ	17.8
25	18	Suffolk, NY	17.7
64	18	Hartford, CT	17.7
17	20	Broward, FL	17.5
11	21	Queens, NY	17.4
7	22	Miami-Dade, FL	16.9
61	23	Du Page, IL	16.8
38	24	Contra Costa, CA	16.7
75	24	Ventura, CA	16.7
44	26	Montgomery, MD	16.6
53	27	Fairfield, CT	16.5
69	27	Worcester, MA	16.5
19	29	Wayne, MI	16.2
21	30	Middlesex, MA	16.0
70	31	Middlesex, NJ	15.9
4	32	Maricopa, AZ	15.8
6	32	Orange, CA	15.8
2	34	Cook, IL	15.6
12	35	Clark, NV	15.5
8	36	Kings, NY	15.1
34	36	Hennepin, MN	15.1
20	38	Alameda, CA	14.9
48	38	Duval, FL	14.9
27	38	Hillsborough, FL	14.9
5	41	San Diego, CA	14.8
22	41	Sacramento, CA	14.8
10	41	Riverside, CA	14.8
1	44	Los Angeles, CA	14.7
55	45	Prince George's, MD	14.6
18	46	Santa Clara, CA	14.5
40	46	Fairfax, VA	14.5
62	46	Shelby, TN	14.5
60	49	Pierce, WA	14.4
24	49	Philadelphia, PA	14.4
59	51	Milwaukee, WI	14.3
73	52	Essex, NJ	14.2
28	53	Bronx, NY	14.0
13	54	King, WA	13.7
51	55	Marion, IN	13.2
29	56	Orange, FL	12.8
67	56	El Paso, TX	12.8
31	58	Franklin, OH	12.7
39	59	Wake, NC	12.6
46	59	Fresno, CA	12.6
16	61	Bexar, TX	12.5
43	62	Fulton, GA	12.4
14	63	San Bernardino, CA	12.1
72	63	Fort Bend, TX	12.1
15	65	Tarrant, TX	12.0
41	66	Mecklenburg, NC	11.9
37	67	Salt Lake, UT	11.6
9	68	Dallas, TX	11.5
65	69	Hidalgo, TX	11.4
3	69	Harris, TX	11.4
63	69	Kern, CA	11.4
42	72	Collin, TX	11.3
52	73	Gwinnett, GA	11.1
58	73	Denton, TX	11.1
32	75	Travis, TX	10.7

1. May be of any race.

75 Largest Counties by 2020 Population

Selected Rankings

Percent female-headed family households, 2016–2020			
Population rank	Female households rank	County	Percent female households [col 30]
28	1	Bronx, NY	29.1
65	2	Hidalgo, TX	21.8
24	3	Philadelphia, PA	20.0
62	4	Shelby, TN	19.3
55	5	Prince George's, MD	18.8
67	5	El Paso, TX	18.8
73	7	Essex, NJ	18.6
19	8	Wayne, MI	17.9
7	9	Miami-Dade, FL	17.8
8	10	Kings, NY	17.6
46	11	Fresno, CA	17.1
14	12	San Bernardino, CA	16.9
63	13	Kern, CA	16.1
16	14	Bexar, TX	16.0
59	15	Milwaukee, WI	15.9
11	16	Queens, NY	15.4
3	17	Harris, TX	15.2
9	18	Dallas, TX	15.1
35	18	Cuyahoga, OH	15.1
48	18	Duval, FL	15.1
17	21	Broward, FL	14.9
1	22	Los Angeles, CA	14.7
74	23	Baltimore, MD	14.5
29	24	Orange, FL	14.3
51	25	Marion, IN	14.2
12	26	Clark, NV	14.1
22	26	Sacramento, CA	14.1
43	28	Fulton, GA	14.0
68	28	New Haven, CT	14.0
2	30	Cook, IL	13.9
15	30	Tarrant, TX	13.9
64	32	Hartford, CT	13.8
31	33	Franklin, OH	13.7
52	34	Gwinnett, GA	13.6
27	35	Hillsborough, FL	13.5
50	36	St. Louis, MO	13.3
41	37	Mecklenburg, NC	13.0
57	38	Erie, NY	12.9
10	39	Riverside, CA	12.8
66	40	Macomb, MI	12.7
49	41	Westchester, NY	12.5
45	42	Pima, AZ	12.4
4	43	Maricopa, AZ	12.2
47	43	Honolulu, HI	12.2
72	45	Fort Bend, TX	12.1
38	46	Contra Costa, CA	12.0
53	47	Fairfield, CT	11.9
69	47	Worcester, MA	11.9
75	49	Ventura, CA	11.8
5	50	San Diego, CA	11.6
26	50	Palm Beach, FL	11.6
30	50	Nassau, NY	11.6
6	53	Orange, CA	11.5
70	53	Middlesex, NJ	11.5
60	55	Pierce, WA	11.3
20	56	Alameda, CA	11.2
44	57	Montgomery, MD	11.1
56	57	Bergen, NJ	11.1
23	59	New York, NY	11.0
25	59	Suffolk, NY	11.0
36	61	Allegheny, PA	10.6
39	61	Wake, NC	10.6
54	63	Pinellas, FL	10.4
37	64	Salt Lake, UT	10.1
18	65	Santa Clara, CA	9.9
32	66	Travis, TX	9.8
33	67	Oakland, MI	9.7
42	67	Collin, TX	9.7
58	67	Denton, TX	9.7
21	70	Middlesex, MA	9.4
71	70	Montgomery, PA	9.4
34	72	Hennepin, MN	9.1
61	72	Du Page, IL	9.1
40	74	Fairfax, VA	8.8
13	75	King, WA	8.1

Birth rate, 2021			
Population rank	Live birth rate rank	County	Birth rate [col 36]
65	1	Hidalgo, TX	15.1
9	2	Dallas, TX	13.9
51	3	Marion, IN	13.8
46	4	Fresno, CA	13.7
63	5	Kern, CA	13.5
3	6	Harris, TX	13.4
59	7	Milwaukee, WI	13.3
62	8	Shelby, TN	13.2
8	9	Kings, NY	13.1
31	9	Franklin, OH	13.1
37	11	Salt Lake, UT	12.8
67	12	El Paso, TX	12.7
28	13	Bronx, NY	12.6
41	13	Mecklenburg, NC	12.6
48	15	Duval, FL	12.5
14	16	San Bernardino, CA	12.4
16	16	Bexar, TX	12.4
15	18	Tarrant, TX	12.3
24	18	Philadelphia, PA	12.3
19	20	Wayne, MI	12.0
55	21	Prince George's, MD	11.8
34	22	Hennepin, MN	11.6
60	22	Pierce, WA	11.6
22	24	Sacramento, CA	11.5
32	24	Travis, TX	11.5
5	26	San Diego, CA	11.3
27	26	Hillsborough, FL	11.3
47	26	Honolulu, HI	11.3
12	29	Clark, NV	11.2
40	29	Fairfax, VA	11.2
10	31	Riverside, CA	11.1
29	31	Orange, FL	11.1
43	31	Fulton, GA	11.1
4	34	Maricopa, AZ	11.0
52	34	Gwinnett, GA	11.0
73	34	Essex, NJ	11.0
74	37	Baltimore, MD	10.9
2	38	Cook, IL	10.8
11	38	Queens, NY	10.8
39	40	Wake, NC	10.7
44	40	Montgomery, MD	10.7
58	40	Denton, TX	10.7
35	43	Cuyahoga, OH	10.6
50	43	St. Louis, MO	10.6
7	45	Miami-Dade, FL	10.4
17	45	Broward, FL	10.4
18	45	Santa Clara, CA	10.4
20	45	Alameda, CA	10.4
42	45	Collin, TX	10.4
72	50	Fort Bend, TX	10.3
6	51	Orange, CA	10.2
13	51	King, WA	10.2
61	51	Du Page, IL	10.2
1	54	Los Angeles, CA	10.1
38	55	Contra Costa, CA	10.0
75	55	Ventura, CA	10.0
36	57	Allegheny, PA	9.9
66	57	Macomb, MI	9.9
33	59	Oakland, MI	9.7
57	59	Erie, NY	9.7
21	61	Middlesex, MA	9.6
23	61	New York, NY	9.6
25	61	Suffolk, NY	9.6
26	64	Palm Beach, FL	9.5
30	64	Nassau, NY	9.5
45	64	Pima, AZ	9.5
53	64	Fairfield, CT	9.5
64	64	Hartford, CT	9.5
70	64	Middlesex, NJ	9.5
71	64	Montgomery, PA	9.5
49	71	Westchester, NY	9.4
69	71	Worcester, MA	9.4
68	73	New Haven, CT	9.2
56	74	Bergen, NJ	8.8
54	75	Pinellas, FL	7.8

Percent under 65 who have no health insurance, 2019			
Population rank	No health insurance rank	County	Percent with no health insurance [col 40]
65	1	Hidalgo, TX	33.2
9	2	Dallas, TX	25.1
67	3	El Paso, TX	24.3
3	4	Harris, TX	24.2
7	5	Miami-Dade, FL	19.4
16	6	Bexar, TX	19.1
15	7	Tarrant, TX	18.9
26	8	Palm Beach, FL	17.9
17	9	Broward, FL	17.7
52	9	Gwinnett, GA	17.7
32	11	Travis, TX	16.5
29	12	Orange, FL	15.4
54	12	Pinellas, FL	15.4
72	14	Fort Bend, TX	15.0
27	15	Hillsborough, FL	14.9
48	16	Duval, FL	14.3
12	17	Clark, NV	13.7
58	18	Denton, TX	13.4
4	19	Maricopa, AZ	13.3
45	19	Pima, AZ	13.3
41	21	Mecklenburg, NC	13.2
62	21	Shelby, TN	13.2
43	23	Fulton, GA	12.6
42	24	Collin, TX	12.5
51	25	Marion, IN	12.3
73	26	Essex, NJ	12.0
37	27	Salt Lake, UT	11.4
1	28	Los Angeles, CA	11.1
2	29	Cook, IL	10.9
75	30	Ventura, CA	10.4
11	31	Queens, NY	10.3
55	32	Prince George's, MD	10.2
39	33	Wake, NC	10.1
14	34	San Bernardino, CA	9.9
10	35	Riverside, CA	9.8
46	36	Fresno, CA	9.7
53	37	Fairfield, CT	9.3
63	37	Kern, CA	9.3
40	39	Fairfax, VA	9.1
70	39	Middlesex, NJ	9.1
24	41	Philadelphia, PA	9.0
5	42	San Diego, CA	8.9
31	42	Franklin, OH	8.9
6	44	Orange, CA	8.8
28	45	Bronx, NY	8.5
59	45	Milwaukee, WI	8.5
56	47	Bergen, NJ	8.4
50	48	St. Louis, MO	8.3
44	49	Montgomery, MD	8.1
19	50	Wayne, MI	7.6
60	50	Pierce, WA	7.6
35	52	Cuyahoga, OH	7.3
66	52	Macomb, MI	7.3
8	54	Kings, NY	7.2
68	55	New Haven, CT	7.0
74	56	Baltimore, MD	6.9
22	57	Sacramento, CA	6.8
38	58	Contra Costa, CA	6.5
61	59	Du Page, IL	6.4
13	60	King, WA	6.3
64	61	Hartford, CT	6.0
34	62	Hennepin, MN	5.8
33	63	Oakland, MI	5.7
49	63	Westchester, NY	5.7
23	65	New York, NY	5.6
18	66	Santa Clara, CA	5.5
25	67	Suffolk, NY	5.2
20	68	Alameda, CA	5.1
36	68	Allegheny, PA	5.1
71	70	Montgomery, PA	4.9
30	71	Nassau, NY	4.8
47	72	Honolulu, HI	4.4
57	73	Erie, NY	4.1
69	74	Worcester, MA	3.5
21	75	Middlesex, MA	3.1

75 Largest Counties by 2020 Population
Selected Rankings

Percent college graduates (bachelor's degree or more), 2016–2020				Expenditures per student, 2018–2019				Per capita personal income, 2020			
Population rank	College graduates rank	County	Percent college graduates [col 51]	Population rank	Expenditures rank	County	Expenditures per student (dollars) [col 53]	Population rank	Per capita income rank	County	Per capita income (dollars) [col 64]
23	1	New York, NY	62.2	30	1	Nassau, NY	27,270	23	1	New York, NY	191,220
40	2	Fairfax, VA	62.1	23	2	New York, NY	27,123	18	2	Santa Clara, CA	123,661
44	3	Montgomery, MD	59.2	8	2	Kings, NY	27,123	53	3	Fairfield, CT	120,244
21	4	Middlesex, MA	57.1	11	2	Queens, NY	27,123	49	4	Westchester, NY	115,386
43	5	Fulton, GA	54.5	28	2	Bronx, NY	27,123	13	5	King, WA	96,647
39	6	Wake, NC	54.0	49	6	Westchester, NY	26,963	30	6	Nassau, NY	96,253
18	7	Santa Clara, CA	53.5	25	7	Suffolk, NY	26,514	43	7	Fulton, GA	95,683
13	8	King, WA	53.4	56	8	Bergen, NJ	21,821	38	8	Contra Costa, CA	92,264
42	9	Collin, TX	53.2	64	9	Hartford, CT	21,561	56	9	Bergen, NJ	91,972
32	10	Travis, TX	51.5	53	10	Fairfield, CT	21,004	21	10	Middlesex, MA	90,688
34	11	Hennepin, MN	51.0	68	11	New Haven, CT	20,464	44	11	Montgomery, MD	89,552
56	12	Bergen, NJ	50.7	73	12	Essex, NJ	20,289	40	12	Fairfax, VA	88,971
61	13	Du Page, IL	50.3	71	13	Montgomery, PA	19,393	26	13	Palm Beach, FL	87,478
49	14	Westchester, NY	49.7	70	14	Middlesex, NJ	19,230	20	14	Alameda, CA	87,078
71	15	Montgomery, PA	49.6	36	15	Allegheny, PA	18,474	71	15	Montgomery, PA	86,340
53	16	Fairfield, CT	48.9	21	16	Middlesex, MA	18,340	34	16	Hennepin, MN	79,183
20	17	Alameda, CA	48.7	61	17	Du Page, IL	18,175	61	17	Du Page, IL	79,127
33	18	Oakland, MI	48.0	57	18	Erie, NY	17,767	50	18	St. Louis, MO	78,804
30	19	Nassau, NY	46.7	2	19	Cook, IL	17,549	33	19	Oakland, MI	76,941
72	20	Fort Bend, TX	46.5	44	20	Montgomery, MD	16,490	25	20	Suffolk, NY	76,713
41	21	Mecklenburg, NC	45.8	47	21	Honolulu, HI	16,132	6	21	Orange, CA	74,618
58	21	Denton, TX	45.8	35	22	Cuyahoga, OH	16,124	32	22	Travis, TX	74,032
50	23	St. Louis, MO	44.4	69	23	Worcester, MA	15,809	42	23	Collin, TX	71,246
70	23	Middlesex, NJ	44.4	55	24	Prince George's, MD	15,782	73	24	Essex, NJ	70,497
38	25	Contra Costa, CA	43.3	40	25	Fairfax, VA	15,695	2	25	Cook, IL	69,935
36	26	Allegheny, PA	42.5	24	26	Philadelphia, PA	15,481	36	26	Allegheny, PA	68,777
6	27	Orange, CA	41.2	18	27	Santa Clara, CA	14,996	1	27	Los Angeles, CA	68,272
31	28	Franklin, OH	40.4	13	28	King, WA	14,756	64	28	Hartford, CT	67,938
2	29	Cook, IL	40.0	34	29	Hennepin, MN	14,575	75	29	Ventura, CA	67,422
74	30	Baltimore, MD	39.8	74	30	Baltimore, MD	14,526	70	30	Middlesex, NJ	66,640
5	31	San Diego, CA	39.5	50	31	St. Louis, MO	14,458	74	31	Baltimore, MD	66,585
8	32	Kings, NY	38.8	1	32	Los Angeles, CA	14,288	5	32	San Diego, CA	66,266
64	33	Hartford, CT	38.5	46	33	Fresno, CA	14,128	39	33	Wake, NC	65,450
52	34	Gwinnett, GA	37.4	63	34	Kern, CA	13,842	9	34	Dallas, TX	65,401
25	35	Suffolk, NY	37.3	60	35	Pierce, WA	13,755	41	35	Mecklenburg, NC	65,244
26	36	Palm Beach, FL	37.1	43	36	Fulton, GA	13,728	69	36	Worcester, MA	63,286
69	36	Worcester, MA	37.1	14	37	San Bernardino, CA	13,677	58	37	Denton, TX	63,283
37	38	Salt Lake, UT	36.5	31	38	Franklin, OH	13,635	47	38	Honolulu, HI	62,793
73	39	Essex, NJ	36.3	20	39	Alameda, CA	13,630	72	39	Fort Bend, TX	61,791
68	40	New Haven, CT	36.0	22	40	Sacramento, CA	13,254	3	40	Harris, TX	60,183
47	41	Honolulu, HI	35.7	10	41	Riverside, CA	13,234	68	41	New Haven, CT	60,092
29	42	Orange, FL	35.4	38	42	Contra Costa, CA	13,145	35	42	Cuyahoga, OH	59,923
57	43	Erie, NY	35.1	5	43	San Diego, CA	13,075	8	43	Kings, NY	59,468
27	44	Hillsborough, FL	34.5	6	44	Orange, CA	12,838	51	44	Marion, IN	59,264
55	45	Prince George's, MD	34.4	75	45	Ventura, CA	12,832	54	45	Pinellas, FL	59,178
75	46	Ventura, CA	33.9	33	46	Oakland, MI	12,790	37	46	Salt Lake, UT	59,077
45	47	Pima, AZ	33.6	59	47	Milwaukee, WI	12,668	24	47	Philadelphia, PA	58,941
1	48	Los Angeles, CA	33.5	19	48	Wayne, MI	12,217	22	48	Sacramento, CA	58,307
11	48	Queens, NY	33.5	66	49	Macomb, MI	11,928	7	49	Miami-Dade, FL	57,213
35	48	Cuyahoga, OH	33.5	51	50	Marion, IN	11,179	11	50	Queens, NY	57,085
4	51	Maricopa, AZ	33.4	52	51	Gwinnett, GA	10,997	57	51	Erie, NY	56,748
17	52	Broward, FL	33.1	62	52	Shelby, TN	10,970	60	52	Pierce, WA	56,532
15	53	Tarrant, TX	32.6	65	53	Hidalgo, TX	10,712	17	53	Broward, FL	55,908
9	54	Dallas, TX	32.5	32	54	Travis, TX	10,337	15	54	Tarrant, TX	55,615
54	54	Pinellas, FL	32.5	67	55	El Paso, TX	10,186	31	55	Franklin, OH	55,294
62	56	Shelby, TN	32.4	26	56	Palm Beach, FL	10,145	55	56	Prince George's, MD	54,195
3	57	Harris, TX	32.3	54	57	Pinellas, FL	9,952	62	57	Shelby, TN	53,855
51	58	Marion, IN	32.1	16	58	Bexar, TX	9,921	4	58	Maricopa, AZ	53,521
22	59	Sacramento, CA	31.4	7	59	Miami-Dade, FL	9,888	66	59	Macomb, MI	52,195
59	60	Milwaukee, WI	31.3	29	60	Orange, FL	9,882	27	60	Hillsborough, FL	51,848
24	61	Philadelphia, PA	31.2	17	61	Broward, FL	9,760	12	61	Clark, NV	51,244
7	62	Miami-Dade, FL	30.7	3	62	Harris, TX	9,701	48	62	Duval, FL	51,131
48	62	Duval, FL	30.7	15	63	Tarrant, TX	9,622	59	63	Milwaukee, WI	51,002
16	64	Bexar, TX	28.5	9	64	Dallas, TX	9,613	29	64	Orange, FL	49,390
60	65	Pierce, WA	27.7	72	65	Fort Bend, TX	9,456	19	65	Wayne, MI	48,788
66	66	Macomb, MI	25.9	41	66	Mecklenburg, NC	9,369	16	66	Bexar, TX	48,569
12	67	Clark, NV	25.2	42	67	Collin, TX	9,327	46	67	Fresno, CA	48,495
19	67	Wayne, MI	25.2	39	68	Wake, NC	9,314	45	68	Pima, AZ	48,373
67	69	El Paso, TX	24.0	58	69	Denton, TX	9,310	52	69	Gwinnett, GA	46,886
10	70	Riverside, CA	23.2	48	70	Duval, FL	9,116	10	70	Riverside, CA	45,834
46	71	Fresno, CA	22.0	27	71	Hillsborough, FL	9,077	14	71	San Bernardino, CA	44,831
14	72	San Bernardino, CA	21.4	12	72	Clark, NV	8,937	63	72	Kern, CA	44,721
28	73	Bronx, NY	20.3	45	73	Pima, AZ	8,732	28	73	Bronx, NY	43,919
65	74	Hidalgo, TX	19.3	4	74	Maricopa, AZ	8,515	67	74	El Paso, TX	41,818
63	75	Kern, CA	17.1	37	75	Salt Lake, UT	8,038	65	75	Hidalgo, TX	31,153

75 Largest Counties by 2020 Population
Selected Rankings

Median household income, 2020

Population rank	Median income rank	County	Median income (dollars) [col 58]
18	1	Santa Clara, CA	139,462
40	2	Fairfax, VA	132,509
30	3	Nassau, NY	122,730
44	4	Montgomery, MD	115,394
20	5	Alameda, CA	113,518
21	6	Middlesex, MA	111,158
25	7	Suffolk, NY	109,084
56	8	Bergen, NJ	107,114
38	9	Contra Costa, CA	106,484
49	10	Westchester, NY	103,340
13	11	King, WA	102,620
42	12	Collin, TX	101,560
53	13	Fairfield, CT	98,828
6	14	Orange, CA	98,786
72	15	Fort Bend, TX	97,210
70	16	Middlesex, NJ	95,610
71	17	Montgomery, PA	94,094
61	18	Du Page, IL	92,101
75	19	Ventura, CA	90,961
58	20	Denton, TX	90,880
47	21	Honolulu, HI	89,584
39	22	Wake, NC	88,763
23	23	New York, NY	87,745
5	24	San Diego, CA	87,126
55	25	Prince George's, MD	85,246
33	26	Oakland, MI	82,849
32	27	Travis, TX	82,605
34	28	Hennepin, MN	81,772
60	29	Pierce, WA	80,236
74	30	Baltimore, MD	79,974
37	31	Salt Lake, UT	79,294
11	32	Queens, NY	78,847
69	33	Worcester, MA	77,931
10	34	Riverside, CA	76,409
1	35	Los Angeles, CA	75,624
64	36	Hartford, CT	73,476
52	37	Gwinnett, GA	73,460
22	38	Sacramento, CA	72,953
68	39	New Haven, CT	72,517
41	40	Mecklenburg, NC	72,340
15	41	Tarrant, TX	72,064
4	42	Maricopa, AZ	71,799
2	43	Cook, IL	71,611
43	44	Fulton, GA	71,504
8	45	Kings, NY	70,390
29	46	Orange, FL	69,074
50	47	St. Louis, MO	68,964
26	48	Palm Beach, FL	68,200
14	49	San Bernardino, CA	65,984
9	50	Dallas, TX	65,770
73	51	Essex, NJ	65,528
27	52	Hillsborough, FL	65,272
66	53	Macomb, MI	64,870
36	54	Allegheny, PA	64,236
17	55	Broward, FL	63,901
31	56	Franklin, OH	62,643
12	57	Clark, NV	62,496
3	58	Harris, TX	61,906
54	59	Pinellas, FL	61,532
46	60	Fresno, CA	61,401
16	61	Bexar, TX	60,477
57	62	Erie, NY	59,584
7	63	Miami-Dade, FL	59,259
63	64	Kern, CA	58,583
45	65	Pima, AZ	56,551
51	66	Marion, IN	56,185
48	67	Duval, FL	55,202
35	68	Cuyahoga, OH	55,128
24	69	Philadelphia, PA	55,102
59	70	Milwaukee, WI	52,281
19	71	Wayne, MI	51,777
62	72	Shelby, TN	50,870
67	73	El Paso, TX	48,522
65	74	Hidalgo, TX	46,653
28	75	Bronx, NY	44,906

Median value of owner-occupied housing units, 2016–2020

Population rank	Median value rank	County	Median value (dollars) [col 91]
18	1	Santa Clara, CA	1,061,900
23	2	New York, NY	1,024,500
20	3	Alameda, CA	825,300
8	4	Kings, NY	734,800
6	5	Orange, CA	703,800
47	6	Honolulu, HI	702,300
38	7	Contra Costa, CA	655,500
1	8	Los Angeles, CA	615,500
75	9	Ventura, CA	609,200
13	10	King, WA	601,100
5	11	San Diego, CA	595,600
40	12	Fairfax, VA	576,700
11	13	Queens, NY	575,600
49	14	Westchester, NY	544,100
21	15	Middlesex, MA	540,300
30	16	Nassau, NY	524,400
44	17	Montgomery, MD	491,700
56	18	Bergen, NJ	477,400
53	19	Fairfield, CT	433,000
28	20	Bronx, NY	427,900
25	21	Suffolk, NY	413,900
73	22	Essex, NJ	395,900
22	23	Sacramento, CA	373,000
10	24	Riverside, CA	368,100
70	25	Middlesex, NJ	351,400
14	26	San Bernardino, CA	348,500
32	27	Travis, TX	347,700
42	28	Collin, TX	337,200
60	29	Pierce, WA	336,600
37	30	Salt Lake, UT	336,100
43	31	Fulton, GA	326,700
71	32	Montgomery, PA	326,200
55	33	Prince George's, MD	319,600
61	34	Du Page, IL	315,600
7	35	Miami-Dade, FL	310,700
39	36	Wake, NC	301,600
26	37	Palm Beach, FL	301,000
58	38	Denton, TX	297,100
69	39	Worcester, MA	295,300
34	40	Hennepin, MN	292,100
12	41	Clark, NV	285,100
17	42	Broward, FL	282,400
4	43	Maricopa, AZ	278,700
72	44	Fort Bend, TX	277,600
46	45	Fresno, CA	271,000
74	46	Baltimore, MD	267,400
29	47	Orange, FL	257,800
2	48	Cook, IL	255,500
41	49	Mecklenburg, NC	253,500
33	50	Oakland, MI	252,800
68	51	New Haven, CT	252,300
64	52	Hartford, CT	242,900
52	53	Gwinnett, GA	235,700
27	54	Hillsborough, FL	233,200
63	55	Kern, CA	226,600
54	56	Pinellas, FL	219,800
15	57	Tarrant, TX	209,600
50	58	St. Louis, MO	206,700
45	59	Pima, AZ	199,400
48	60	Duval, FL	195,600
9	61	Dallas, TX	193,900
3	62	Harris, TX	189,400
31	63	Franklin, OH	185,900
66	64	Macomb, MI	174,000
24	65	Philadelphia, PA	171,600
16	66	Bexar, TX	171,200
59	67	Milwaukee, WI	164,200
36	68	Allegheny, PA	161,600
57	69	Erie, NY	160,700
62	70	Shelby, TN	158,700
51	71	Marion, IN	145,200
35	72	Cuyahoga, OH	137,800
67	73	El Paso, TX	126,500
19	74	Wayne, MI	122,700
65	75	Hidalgo, TX	90,000

Median gross rent of renter-occupied housing units, 2016–2020

Population rank	Median rent rank	County	Median rent (dollars) [col 94]
18	1	Santa Clara, CA	2,386
6	2	Orange, CA	1,928
38	2	Contra Costa, CA	1,928
20	4	Alameda, CA	1,904
40	5	Fairfax, VA	1,898
75	6	Ventura, CA	1,854
30	7	Nassau, NY	1,831
25	8	Suffolk, NY	1,810
23	9	New York, NY	1,787
44	10	Montgomery, MD	1,784
47	11	Honolulu, HI	1,779
5	12	San Diego, CA	1,732
21	13	Middlesex, MA	1,714
13	14	King, WA	1,695
11	15	Queens, NY	1,629
49	16	Westchester, NY	1,599
56	17	Bergen, NJ	1,557
1	18	Los Angeles, CA	1,534
53	19	Fairfield, CT	1,511
70	20	Middlesex, NJ	1,495
55	21	Prince George's, MD	1,494
8	22	Kings, NY	1,483
72	23	Fort Bend, TX	1,474
26	24	Palm Beach, FL	1,452
10	25	Riverside, CA	1,447
17	26	Broward, FL	1,433
42	27	Collin, TX	1,428
7	28	Miami-Dade, FL	1,373
61	29	Du Page, IL	1,365
32	30	Travis, TX	1,348
14	31	San Bernardino, CA	1,338
60	31	Pierce, WA	1,338
22	33	Sacramento, CA	1,333
52	34	Gwinnett, GA	1,331
74	35	Baltimore, MD	1,328
71	36	Montgomery, PA	1,323
29	37	Orange, FL	1,284
58	38	Denton, TX	1,269
43	39	Fulton, GA	1,263
28	40	Bronx, NY	1,247
73	41	Essex, NJ	1,211
39	42	Wake, NC	1,204
41	43	Mecklenburg, NC	1,195
27	44	Hillsborough, FL	1,186
4	45	Maricopa, AZ	1,182
12	46	Clark, NV	1,181
34	47	Hennepin, MN	1,176
37	47	Salt Lake, UT	1,176
68	49	New Haven, CT	1,173
54	50	Pinellas, FL	1,165
2	51	Cook, IL	1,160
9	52	Dallas, TX	1,159
15	53	Tarrant, TX	1,142
64	54	Hartford, CT	1,130
3	55	Harris, TX	1,115
33	56	Oakland, MI	1,100
48	57	Duval, FL	1,096
24	58	Philadelphia, PA	1,084
69	59	Worcester, MA	1,074
16	60	Bexar, TX	1,048
46	61	Fresno, CA	1,029
31	62	Franklin, OH	1,002
63	63	Kern, CA	994
50	64	St. Louis, MO	985
66	65	Macomb, MI	977
62	66	Shelby, TN	957
45	67	Pima, AZ	931
36	68	Allegheny, PA	913
51	69	Marion, IN	910
19	70	Wayne, MI	896
59	71	Milwaukee, WI	889
67	72	El Paso, TX	855
57	73	Erie, NY	852
35	74	Cuyahoga, OH	830
65	75	Hidalgo, TX	753

75 Largest Counties by 2020 Population

Selected Rankings

Percent of population below the poverty level, 2020				Percent under 18 years old below the poverty level, 2020				Unemployment rate, 2021			
Population rank	Poverty rate rank	County	Poverty rate [col 59]	Population rank	Poverty rate for children rank	County	Poverty rate for children under 18 years [col 60]	Population rank	Unemployment rate rank	County	Unemployment rate [col 100]
28	1	Bronx, NY	24.4	65	1	Hidalgo, TX	32.5	28	1	Bronx, NY	13.6
65	2	Hidalgo, TX	23.9	28	2	Bronx, NY	30.6	8	2	Kings, NY	10.1
19	3	Wayne, MI	20.0	19	3	Wayne, MI	29.4	63	3	Kern, CA	10.0
24	4	Philadelphia, PA	19.4	62	4	Shelby, TN	27.1	11	4	Queens, NY	9.6
62	5	Shelby, TN	19.1	24	5	Philadelphia, PA	27.0	65	5	Hidalgo, TX	9.3
59	6	Milwaukee, WI	19.0	59	6	Milwaukee, WI	25.5	24	6	Philadelphia, PA	9.2
63	7	Kern, CA	18.3	63	7	Kern, CA	24.6	46	6	Fresno, CA	9.2
8	8	Kings, NY	17.8	8	8	Kings, NY	23.5	1	8	Los Angeles, CA	8.9
67	9	El Paso, TX	17.6	3	9	Harris, TX	23.3	12	9	Clark, NV	8.3
46	10	Fresno, CA	17.1	46	10	Fresno, CA	23.1	19	10	Wayne, MI	8.0
23	11	New York, NY	16.3	67	11	El Paso, TX	22.7	73	10	Essex, NJ	8.0
3	12	Harris, TX	15.9	48	12	Duval, FL	21.1	23	12	New York, NY	7.6
31	13	Franklin, OH	15.4	16	13	Bexar, TX	20.5	55	13	Prince George's, MD	7.5
35	14	Cuyahoga, OH	15.3	31	14	Franklin, OH	20.3	14	14	San Bernardino, CA	7.4
48	15	Duval, FL	15.2	9	15	Dallas, TX	20.1	10	15	Riverside, CA	7.3
7	16	Miami-Dade, FL	15.0	45	16	Pima, AZ	20.0	2	16	Cook, IL	7.0
16	16	Bexar, TX	15.0	7	17	Miami-Dade, FL	19.9	22	16	Sacramento, CA	7.0
45	18	Pima, AZ	14.9	35	17	Cuyahoga, OH	19.9	62	18	Shelby, TN	6.8
51	19	Marion, IN	14.4	14	19	San Bernardino, CA	19.7	68	19	New Haven, CT	6.6
14	20	San Bernardino, CA	14.3	23	20	New York, NY	19.3	3	20	Harris, TX	6.5
73	20	Essex, NJ	14.3	51	21	Marion, IN	19.1	5	20	San Diego, CA	6.5
9	22	Dallas, TX	13.7	73	22	Essex, NJ	18.4	35	20	Cuyahoga, OH	6.5
1	23	Los Angeles, CA	13.2	12	23	Clark, NV	18.0	64	20	Hartford, CT	6.5
12	23	Clark, NV	13.2	57	24	Erie, NY	17.8	38	24	Contra Costa, CA	6.4
57	23	Erie, NY	13.2	43	25	Fulton, GA	17.5	67	25	El Paso, TX	6.2
43	26	Fulton, GA	13.0	1	26	Los Angeles, CA	17.2	75	25	Ventura, CA	6.2
2	27	Cook, IL	12.9	22	27	Sacramento, CA	16.8	20	27	Alameda, CA	6.1
29	28	Orange, FL	12.7	29	28	Orange, FL	16.7	36	27	Allegheny, PA	6.1
22	29	Sacramento, CA	12.5	2	29	Cook, IL	16.6	53	27	Fairfield, CT	6.1
26	30	Palm Beach, FL	12.0	41	30	Mecklenburg, NC	16.3	60	27	Pierce, WA	6.1
27	31	Hillsborough, FL	11.9	26	31	Palm Beach, FL	16.2	6	31	Orange, CA	6.0
4	32	Maricopa, AZ	11.6	4	32	Maricopa, AZ	16.0	56	31	Bergen, NJ	6.0
10	33	Riverside, CA	11.2	54	33	Pinellas, FL	15.8	66	33	Macomb, MI	5.9
68	33	New Haven, CT	11.2	15	34	Tarrant, TX	15.4	69	33	Worcester, MA	5.9
54	35	Pinellas, FL	11.1	10	35	Riverside, CA	14.5	72	33	Fort Bend, TX	5.9
17	36	Broward, FL	11.0	27	36	Hillsborough, FL	14.3	70	36	Middlesex, NJ	5.7
41	36	Mecklenburg, NC	11.0	17	37	Broward, FL	14.1	74	36	Baltimore, MD	5.7
64	38	Hartford, CT	10.7	68	38	New Haven, CT	13.9	9	38	Dallas, TX	5.6
15	39	Tarrant, TX	10.5	64	39	Hartford, CT	13.6	44	39	Montgomery, MD	5.5
36	39	Allegheny, PA	10.5	52	40	Gwinnett, GA	13.5	57	39	Erie, NY	5.5
52	41	Gwinnett, GA	10.4	11	41	Queens, NY	13.0	16	41	Bexar, TX	5.4
11	42	Queens, NY	10.3	36	41	Allegheny, PA	13.0	59	41	Milwaukee, WI	5.4
32	43	Travis, TX	10.2	55	43	Prince George's, MD	12.7	15	43	Tarrant, TX	5.3
5	44	San Diego, CA	9.5	66	44	Macomb, MI	12.6	47	43	Honolulu, HI	5.3
55	44	Prince George's, MD	9.5	75	45	Ventura, CA	11.7	7	45	Miami-Dade, FL	5.2
69	44	Worcester, MA	9.5	50	46	St. Louis, MO	11.6	29	45	Orange, FL	5.2
34	47	Hennepin, MN	9.3	74	47	Baltimore, MD	11.2	31	47	Franklin, OH	5.0
66	48	Macomb, MI	9.2	5	48	San Diego, CA	11.0	45	47	Pima, AZ	5.0
50	49	St. Louis, MO	9.1	32	49	Travis, TX	10.9	71	47	Montgomery, PA	5.0
75	49	Ventura, CA	9.1	53	50	Fairfield, CT	10.8	17	50	Broward, FL	4.9
6	51	Orange, CA	9.0	69	50	Worcester, MA	10.8	41	50	Mecklenburg, NC	4.9
74	52	Baltimore, MD	8.9	34	52	Hennepin, MN	10.5	49	52	Westchester, NY	4.8
53	53	Fairfield, CT	8.8	6	53	Orange, CA	10.3	18	53	Santa Clara, CA	4.7
60	54	Pierce, WA	8.7	72	54	Fort Bend, TX	9.4	33	53	Oakland, MI	4.7
20	55	Alameda, CA	8.6	20	55	Alameda, CA	9.1	43	53	Fulton, GA	4.7
47	56	Honolulu, HI	8.0	47	55	Honolulu, HI	9.1	21	56	Middlesex, MA	4.6
33	57	Oakland, MI	7.8	60	57	Pierce, WA	9.0	25	56	Suffolk, NY	4.6
13	58	King, WA	7.6	49	58	Westchester, NY	8.5	4	58	Maricopa, AZ	4.5
49	58	Westchester, NY	7.6	39	59	Wake, NC	8.3	30	58	Nassau, NY	4.5
39	60	Wake, NC	7.4	70	59	Middlesex, NJ	8.3	48	58	Duval, FL	4.5
70	60	Middlesex, NJ	7.4	13	61	King, WA	8.0	50	58	St. Louis, MO	4.5
72	60	Fort Bend, TX	7.4	38	62	Contra Costa, CA	7.9	61	58	Du Page, IL	4.5
38	63	Contra Costa, CA	7.2	33	63	Oakland, MI	7.8	51	63	Marion, IN	4.4
21	64	Middlesex, MA	7.1	44	64	Montgomery, MD	7.6	58	63	Denton, TX	4.4
37	65	Salt Lake, UT	7.0	58	64	Denton, TX	7.6	13	65	King, WA	4.3
58	66	Denton, TX	6.9	21	66	Middlesex, MA	7.3	26	65	Palm Beach, FL	4.3
44	67	Montgomery, MD	6.7	37	67	Salt Lake, UT	7.2	27	65	Hillsborough, FL	4.3
18	68	Santa Clara, CA	6.6	40	68	Fairfax, VA	7.0	42	65	Collin, TX	4.3
56	69	Bergen, NJ	6.4	42	69	Collin, TX	6.7	32	69	Travis, TX	4.0
42	70	Collin, TX	6.2	56	69	Bergen, NJ	6.7	39	69	Wake, NC	4.0
25	71	Suffolk, NY	6.1	18	71	Santa Clara, CA	6.5	54	69	Pinellas, FL	4.0
61	72	Du Page, IL	5.9	30	72	Nassau, NY	6.3	40	72	Fairfax, VA	3.5
30	73	Nassau, NY	5.7	61	72	Du Page, IL	6.3	52	72	Gwinnett, GA	3.5
71	74	Montgomery, PA	5.6	25	74	Suffolk, NY	6.2	34	74	Hennepin, MN	3.4
40	75	Fairfax, VA	5.3	71	75	Montgomery, PA	5.7	37	75	Salt Lake, UT	2.8

75 Largest Counties by 2020 Population

Selected Rankings

Manufacturing employment as a percent of total nonfarm employment, 2020

Population rank	Manufacturing rank	County	Percent employed in manufacturing [col 107/col 105]
66	1	Macomb, MI	22.7
19	2	Wayne, MI	12.9
20	3	Alameda, CA	11.8
64	4	Hartford, CT	11.4
69	5	Worcester, MA	10.9
15	6	Tarrant, TX	10.4
57	6	Erie, NY	10.4
59	6	Milwaukee, WI	10.4
35	9	Cuyahoga, OH	9.6
75	10	Ventura, CA	9.4
6	11	Orange, CA	9.3
46	11	Fresno, CA	9.3
25	13	Suffolk, NY	9.1
61	14	Du Page, IL	9.0
37	15	Salt Lake, UT	8.8
14	16	San Bernardino, CA	8.4
53	17	Fairfield, CT	8.3
34	18	Hennepin, MN	8.2
71	18	Montgomery, PA	8.2
1	20	Los Angeles, CA	8.0
68	20	New Haven, CT	8.0
5	22	San Diego, CA	7.7
10	22	Riverside, CA	7.7
18	22	Santa Clara, CA	7.7
51	22	Marion, IN	7.7
33	26	Oakland, MI	7.4
54	26	Pinellas, FL	7.4
2	28	Cook, IL	7.3
3	28	Harris, TX	7.3
72	28	Fort Bend, TX	7.3
50	31	St. Louis, MO	7.1
56	32	Bergen, NJ	6.9
52	33	Gwinnett, GA	6.8
58	33	Denton, TX	6.8
9	35	Dallas, TX	6.7
67	35	El Paso, TX	6.7
13	37	King, WA	6.6
45	37	Pima, AZ	6.6
60	37	Pierce, WA	6.6
70	37	Middlesex, NJ	6.6
63	41	Kern, CA	6.5
21	42	Middlesex, MA	6.3
4	43	Maricopa, AZ	6.2
62	44	Shelby, TN	5.6
73	44	Essex, NJ	5.6
48	46	Duval, FL	4.8
36	47	Allegheny, PA	4.7
16	48	Bexar, TX	4.6
38	48	Contra Costa, CA	4.6
31	50	Franklin, OH	4.5
32	50	Travis, TX	4.5
22	52	Sacramento, CA	4.4
42	53	Collin, TX	4.2
74	54	Baltimore, MD	4.1
41	55	Mecklenburg, NC	4.0
27	56	Hillsborough, FL	3.8
7	57	Miami-Dade, FL	3.6
29	57	Orange, FL	3.6
17	59	Broward, FL	3.2
65	59	Hidalgo, TX	3.2
39	61	Wake, NC	3.0
11	62	Queens, NY	2.9
24	63	Philadelphia, PA	2.8
26	64	Palm Beach, FL	2.7
43	64	Fulton, GA	2.7
12	66	Clark, NV	2.6
47	66	Honolulu, HI	2.6
55	66	Prince George's, MD	2.6
8	69	Kings, NY	2.5
30	69	Nassau, NY	2.5
49	69	Westchester, NY	2.5
28	72	Bronx, NY	2.0
44	73	Montgomery, MD	1.3
40	74	Fairfax, VA	0.9
23	75	New York, NY	0.6

Professional, scientific and technical employment as a percent of total nonfarm employment, 2020

Population rank	Professional services rank	County	Percent employed in professional services [col 110/ col 105]
40	1	Fairfax, VA	34.0
44	2	Montgomery, MD	18.0
70	3	Middlesex, NJ	15.7
21	4	Middlesex, MA	15.1
23	5	New York, NY	14.6
33	6	Oakland, MI	14.4
32	7	Travis, TX	13.8
18	8	Santa Clara, CA	13.7
43	9	Fulton, GA	13.5
39	10	Wake, NC	12.5
5	11	San Diego, CA	12.3
66	12	Macomb, MI	11.6
55	13	Prince George's, MD	11.5
42	14	Collin, TX	11.2
20	15	Alameda, CA	10.9
53	16	Fairfield, CT	10.5
2	17	Cook, IL	10.0
13	17	King, WA	10.0
27	19	Hillsborough, FL	9.9
9	20	Dallas, TX	9.2
3	21	Harris, TX	8.8
6	21	Orange, CA	8.8
34	21	Hennepin, MN	8.8
52	21	Gwinnett, GA	8.8
61	25	Du Page, IL	8.7
74	25	Baltimore, MD	8.7
71	27	Montgomery, PA	8.6
75	28	Ventura, CA	8.3
24	29	Philadelphia, PA	8.2
17	30	Broward, FL	8.1
22	30	Sacramento, CA	8.1
26	30	Palm Beach, FL	8.1
50	30	St. Louis, MO	8.1
36	34	Allegheny, PA	8.0
1	35	Los Angeles, CA	7.9
29	36	Orange, FL	7.8
7	37	Miami-Dade, FL	7.7
38	37	Contra Costa, CA	7.7
37	39	Salt Lake, UT	7.6
54	39	Pinellas, FL	7.6
51	41	Marion, IN	7.5
19	42	Wayne, MI	7.4
41	42	Mecklenburg, NC	7.4
73	44	Essex, NJ	7.3
30	45	Nassau, NY	7.1
56	45	Bergen, NJ	7.1
4	47	Maricopa, AZ	7.0
48	47	Duval, FL	7.0
72	47	Fort Bend, TX	7.0
31	50	Franklin, OH	6.8
25	51	Suffolk, NY	6.7
35	51	Cuyahoga, OH	6.7
64	51	Hartford, CT	6.7
69	54	Worcester, MA	6.6
49	55	Westchester, NY	6.4
57	55	Erie, NY	6.4
16	57	Bexar, TX	6.3
45	58	Pima, AZ	5.8
47	59	Honolulu, HI	5.2
15	60	Tarrant, TX	5.1
58	60	Denton, TX	5.1
59	60	Milwaukee, WI	5.1
12	63	Clark, NV	4.6
62	63	Shelby, TN	4.6
63	65	Kern, CA	4.4
68	65	New Haven, CT	4.4
46	67	Fresno, CA	4.0
8	68	Kings, NY	3.6
60	68	Pierce, WA	3.6
67	68	El Paso, TX	3.6
10	71	Riverside, CA	3.5
11	72	Queens, NY	2.9
65	72	Hidalgo, TX	2.9
14	74	San Bernardino, CA	2.8
28	75	Bronx, NY	1.8

Per capita local government taxes, 2017

Population rank	Local taxes rank	County	Per capita local taxes (dollars) [col 183]
23	1	New York, NY	6,557
8	1	Kings, NY	6,557
11	1	Queens, NY	6,557
28	1	Bronx, NY	6,557
30	5	Nassau, NY	5,661
49	6	Westchester, NY	5,592
25	7	Suffolk, NY	4,897
56	8	Bergen, NJ	4,364
44	9	Montgomery, MD	4,149
53	10	Fairfield, CT	3,926
18	11	Santa Clara, CA	3,576
2	12	Cook, IL	3,471
61	13	Du Page, IL	3,400
40	14	Fairfax, VA	3,331
32	15	Travis, TX	3,283
13	16	King, WA	3,282
35	17	Cuyahoga, OH	3,224
20	18	Alameda, CA	3,118
73	19	Essex, NJ	3,095
24	20	Philadelphia, PA	3,079
31	21	Franklin, OH	3,069
71	22	Montgomery, PA	2,963
42	23	Collin, TX	2,953
70	24	Middlesex, NJ	2,922
21	25	Middlesex, MA	2,907
64	26	Hartford, CT	2,897
9	27	Dallas, TX	2,810
57	28	Erie, NY	2,775
3	29	Harris, TX	2,756
43	30	Fulton, GA	2,723
68	31	New Haven, CT	2,680
26	32	Palm Beach, FL	2,672
36	33	Allegheny, PA	2,572
50	34	St. Louis, MO	2,529
55	35	Prince George's, MD	2,422
1	36	Los Angeles, CA	2,401
15	37	Tarrant, TX	2,302
38	38	Contra Costa, CA	2,278
7	39	Miami-Dade, FL	2,255
6	40	Orange, CA	2,214
41	41	Mecklenburg, NC	2,128
74	42	Baltimore, MD	2,116
16	43	Bexar, TX	2,095
5	44	San Diego, CA	2,082
58	45	Denton, TX	2,080
34	46	Hennepin, MN	2,054
29	47	Orange, FL	2,022
17	48	Broward, FL	1,974
69	49	Worcester, MA	1,950
75	50	Ventura, CA	1,866
62	51	Shelby, TN	1,861
37	52	Salt Lake, UT	1,809
60	53	Pierce, WA	1,795
59	54	Milwaukee, WI	1,787
54	55	Pinellas, FL	1,781
72	56	Fort Bend, TX	1,761
39	57	Wake, NC	1,755
47	58	Honolulu, HI	1,662
12	59	Clark, NV	1,657
22	60	Sacramento, CA	1,623
52	60	Gwinnett, GA	1,623
4	62	Maricopa, AZ	1,612
67	63	El Paso, TX	1,585
33	64	Oakland, MI	1,572
48	65	Duval, FL	1,519
10	66	Riverside, CA	1,516
19	67	Wayne, MI	1,513
14	68	San Bernardino, CA	1,502
45	69	Pima, AZ	1,500
27	70	Hillsborough, FL	1,459
63	71	Kern, CA	1,378
46	72	Fresno, CA	1,304
65	73	Hidalgo, TX	1,162
66	74	Macomb, MI	1,112
51	75	Marion, IN	969

75 Largest Counties by 2020 Population
Selected Rankings

Social Security beneficiaries rate per 1,000 population, 2020			
Population rank	Social Security rate rank	County	Social Security rate per 1000 population [col 85]
54	1	Pinellas, FL	269
45	2	Pima, AZ	229
26	3	Palm Beach, FL	223
57	4	Erie, NY	221
36	5	Allegheny, PA	219
66	6	Macomb, MI	215
50	7	St. Louis, MO	210
35	8	Cuyahoga, OH	205
19	9	Wayne, MI	200
25	10	Suffolk, NY	199
33	11	Oakland, MI	197
64	11	Hartford, CT	197
68	13	New Haven, CT	196
71	14	Montgomery, PA	193
30	15	Nassau, NY	190
74	15	Baltimore, MD	190
47	17	Honolulu, HI	184
69	18	Worcester, MA	183
59	19	Milwaukee, WI	179
48	20	Duval, FL	178
62	20	Shelby, TN	178
75	22	Ventura, CA	176
17	23	Broward, FL	175
56	23	Bergen, NJ	175
27	25	Hillsborough, FL	172
49	25	Westchester, NY	172
60	25	Pierce, WA	172
12	28	Clark, NV	168
4	29	Maricopa, AZ	167
61	29	Du Page, IL	167
38	31	Contra Costa, CA	166
7	32	Miami-Dade, FL	165
23	32	New York, NY	165
10	34	Riverside, CA	164
24	34	Philadelphia, PA	164
51	34	Marion, IN	164
53	37	Fairfield, CT	162
22	38	Sacramento, CA	161
5	39	San Diego, CA	160
67	39	El Paso, TX	160
70	41	Middlesex, NJ	159
2	42	Cook, IL	156
16	42	Bexar, TX	156
21	42	Middlesex, MA	156
34	45	Hennepin, MN	155
6	46	Orange, CA	151
11	47	Queens, NY	150
29	48	Orange, FL	145
28	49	Bronx, NY	144
1	50	Los Angeles, CA	143
14	50	San Bernardino, CA	143
46	50	Fresno, CA	143
44	53	Montgomery, MD	140
63	53	Kern, CA	140
73	53	Essex, NJ	140
31	56	Franklin, OH	138
20	57	Alameda, CA	136
13	58	King, WA	135
15	59	Tarrant, TX	134
39	59	Wake, NC	134
55	61	Prince George's, MD	133
8	62	Kings, NY	132
41	62	Mecklenburg, NC	132
43	62	Fulton, GA	132
65	65	Hidalgo, TX	131
18	66	Santa Clara, CA	128
9	67	Dallas, TX	127
37	68	Salt Lake, UT	125
40	69	Fairfax, VA	122
3	70	Harris, TX	121
52	71	Gwinnett, GA	119
72	72	Fort Bend, TX	116
42	73	Collin, TX	110
58	73	Denton, TX	110
32	75	Travis, TX	106

Military as a percent of all federal employment, 2020			
Population rank	Military employment rank	County	Percent military federal employment [col 195/ col 194+195]
60	1	Pierce, WA	73.4
67	2	El Paso, TX	68.6
5	3	San Diego, CA	64.2
72	4	Fort Bend, TX	60.6
47	5	Honolulu, HI	59.6
14	6	San Bernardino, CA	53.9
12	7	Clark, NV	53.2
16	8	Bexar, TX	50.7
42	9	Collin, TX	48.7
52	9	Gwinnett, GA	48.7
48	11	Duval, FL	46.3
71	12	Montgomery, PA	44.3
58	13	Denton, TX	43.7
75	14	Ventura, CA	42.8
56	15	Bergen, NJ	41.3
4	16	Maricopa, AZ	39.6
45	17	Pima, AZ	39.3
70	18	Middlesex, NJ	38.8
69	19	Worcester, MA	38.0
53	20	Fairfield, CT	37.8
50	21	St. Louis, MO	35.3
27	22	Hillsborough, FL	34.4
10	23	Riverside, CA	34.1
28	24	Bronx, NY	33.8
17	25	Broward, FL	33.1
39	25	Wake, NC	33.1
8	27	Kings, NY	32.5
30	28	Nassau, NY	32.0
20	29	Alameda, CA	31.2
6	30	Orange, CA	30.1
33	31	Oakland, MI	29.6
41	32	Mecklenburg, NC	29.5
21	33	Middlesex, MA	28.9
37	34	Salt Lake, UT	28.0
61	35	Du Page, IL	27.9
3	36	Harris, TX	27.1
26	37	Palm Beach, FL	26.5
13	38	King, WA	26.0
65	39	Hidalgo, TX	25.7
63	40	Kern, CA	25.6
38	41	Contra Costa, CA	25.4
1	42	Los Angeles, CA	25.1
34	42	Hennepin, MN	25.1
54	42	Pinellas, FL	25.1
68	45	New Haven, CT	24.8
49	46	Westchester, NY	24.5
15	47	Tarrant, TX	24.4
7	48	Miami-Dade, FL	24.3
64	49	Hartford, CT	23.7
22	50	Sacramento, CA	23.3
18	51	Santa Clara, CA	23.2
62	52	Shelby, TN	22.6
59	53	Milwaukee, WI	21.9
55	54	Prince George's, MD	21.4
31	55	Franklin, OH	21.1
2	56	Cook, IL	21.0
36	57	Allegheny, PA	20.2
11	58	Queens, NY	19.3
40	59	Fairfax, VA	19.1
25	60	Suffolk, NY	18.6
19	61	Wayne, MI	18.2
32	62	Travis, TX	17.3
35	62	Cuyahoga, OH	17.3
9	64	Dallas, TX	17.2
66	65	Macomb, MI	17.1
29	66	Orange, FL	16.6
51	67	Marion, IN	16.5
74	68	Baltimore, MD	16.0
57	69	Erie, NY	15.2
44	70	Montgomery, MD	14.4
73	71	Essex, NJ	14.3
24	72	Philadelphia, PA	12.6
46	73	Fresno, CA	12.3
23	74	New York, NY	10.3
43	75	Fulton, GA	9.8

Mean Income Tax, 2019			
Population rank	Mean income tax rate	County	Mean income tax rate [col 199]
23	1	New York, NY	48,722
53	2	Fairfield, CT	32,036
18	3	Santa Clara, CA	31,254
49	4	Westchester, NY	30,383
13	5	King, WA	22,629
21	6	Middlesex, MA	22,131
40	7	Fairfax, VA	21,006
30	8	Nassau, NY	20,545
26	9	Palm Beach, FL	20,444
43	10	Fulton, GA	20,260
56	11	Bergen, NJ	20,105
32	12	Travis, TX	19,028
44	13	Montgomery, MD	18,821
38	14	Contra Costa, CA	18,537
71	15	Montgomery, PA	17,927
20	16	Alameda, CA	17,865
61	17	Du Page, IL	16,086
42	18	Collin, TX	15,087
73	19	Essex, NJ	14,821
33	20	Oakland, MI	14,817
34	21	Hennepin, MN	14,717
25	22	Suffolk, NY	14,482
6	23	Orange, CA	14,128
50	24	St. Louis, MO	13,994
41	25	Mecklenburg, NC	13,000
72	26	Fort Bend, TX	12,903
39	27	Wake, NC	12,736
58	28	Denton, TX	12,345
9	29	Dallas, TX	11,971
2	30	Cook, IL	11,833
1	31	Los Angeles, CA	11,820
75	32	Ventura, CA	11,618
3	33	Harris, TX	11,583
5	34	San Diego, CA	11,334
74	35	Baltimore, MD	11,162
36	36	Allegheny, PA	10,704
70	37	Middlesex, NJ	10,687
64	38	Hartford, CT	10,571
54	39	Pinellas, FL	10,508
7	40	Miami-Dade, FL	10,487
17	41	Broward, FL	10,181
69	42	Worcester, MA	9,800
4	43	Maricopa, AZ	9,574
68	44	New Haven, CT	9,446
27	45	Hillsborough, FL	9,378
15	46	Tarrant, TX	9,295
8	47	Kings, NY	9,173
37	48	Salt Lake, UT	8,735
35	49	Cuyahoga, OH	8,665
29	50	Orange, FL	8,601
12	51	Clark, NV	8,582
60	52	Pierce, WA	8,232
47	53	Honolulu, HI	8,050
62	54	Shelby, TN	7,992
31	55	Franklin, OH	7,881
57	56	Erie, NY	7,578
48	57	Duval, FL	7,517
22	58	Sacramento, CA	7,513
16	59	Bexar, TX	7,455
45	60	Pima, AZ	6,795
52	61	Gwinnett, GA	6,715
24	62	Philadelphia, PA	6,502
59	63	Milwaukee, WI	6,493
66	64	Macomb, MI	6,187
19	65	Wayne, MI	6,156
51	66	Marion, IN	6,145
11	67	Queens, NY	5,981
55	68	Prince George's, MD	5,900
10	69	Riverside, CA	5,849
46	70	Fresno, CA	5,640
14	71	San Bernardino, CA	5,126
63	72	Kern, CA	5,041
67	73	El Paso, TX	3,857
28	74	Bronx, NY	3,331
65	75	Hidalgo, TX	3,043

75 Largest Counties by 2020 Population
Selected Rankings

Nonemployer businesses, 2019				Value of residential construction authorized by building permits, 2021				Full-time equivalent local government employees, 2017			
Population rank	Nonemployer Businesses rank	County	Nonemployer businesses [col 167]	Population rank	Value ($1,000) rank	County	Value ($1,000) rank [col 169]	Population rank	Government employees rank	County	Government employees rank [col 171]
1	1	Los Angeles, CA	1,112,641	4	1	Maricopa, AZ	9,759,523	23	1	New York, NY	442,294
7	2	Miami-Dade, FL	576,770	3	2	Harris, TX	5,974,645	1	2	Los Angeles, CA	400,857
2	3	Cook, IL	491,217	1	3	Los Angeles, CA	5,090,906	2	3	Cook, IL	205,528
3	4	Harris, TX	480,259	32	4	Travis, TX	4,755,409	3	4	Harris, TX	187,579
4	5	Maricopa, AZ	354,596	42	5	Collin, TX	4,309,408	4	5	Maricopa, AZ	124,148
6	6	Orange, CA	324,958	24	6	Philadelphia, PA	4,144,779	9	6	Dallas, TX	115,153
17	7	Broward, FL	308,930	13	7	King, WA	3,915,263	5	7	San Diego, CA	106,292
5	8	San Diego, CA	292,558	12	8	Clark, NV	3,761,621	7	8	Miami-Dade, FL	93,991
8	9	Kings, NY	284,766	39	9	Wake, NC	3,550,728	6	9	Orange, CA	92,158
11	10	Queens, NY	268,034	15	10	Tarrant, TX	3,463,370	16	10	Bexar, TX	83,813
9	11	Dallas, TX	263,060	7	11	Miami-Dade, FL	3,373,741	15	11	Tarrant, TX	79,300
23	12	New York, NY	219,769	9	12	Dallas, TX	3,217,664	17	12	Broward, FL	78,792
26	13	Palm Beach, FL	205,030	58	13	Denton, TX	2,886,956	10	13	Riverside, CA	78,634
12	14	Clark, NV	203,116	16	14	Bexar, TX	2,842,768	13	14	King, WA	78,547
15	15	Tarrant, TX	194,151	27	15	Hillsborough, FL	2,740,162	14	15	San Bernardino, CA	74,301
10	16	Riverside, CA	183,757	29	16	Orange, FL	2,640,032	41	16	Mecklenburg, NC	70,012
13	17	King, WA	182,281	26	17	Palm Beach, FL	2,523,859	25	17	Suffolk, NY	65,773
29	18	Orange, FL	164,747	72	18	Fort Bend, TX	2,483,299	18	18	Santa Clara, CA	64,447
16	19	Bexar, TX	161,301	10	19	Riverside, CA	2,452,583	20	19	Alameda, CA	64,149
14	20	San Bernardino, CA	159,530	41	20	Mecklenburg, NC	2,406,168	35	20	Cuyahoga, OH	63,287
30	21	Nassau, NY	154,022	37	21	Salt Lake, UT	2,125,291	30	21	Nassau, NY	61,582
27	22	Hillsborough, FL	148,720	5	22	San Diego, CA	2,092,612	12	22	Clark, NV	61,549
21	23	Middlesex, MA	147,204	34	23	Hennepin, MN	1,927,450	24	23	Philadelphia, PA	61,107
20	24	Alameda, CA	145,962	6	24	Orange, CA	1,873,932	21	24	Middlesex, MA	56,125
18	25	Santa Clara, CA	143,404	45	25	Pima, AZ	1,753,992	22	25	Sacramento, CA	54,054
25	26	Suffolk, NY	141,623	22	26	Sacramento, CA	1,504,352	32	26	Travis, TX	51,463
32	27	Travis, TX	138,601	48	27	Duval, FL	1,446,264	26	27	Palm Beach, FL	49,998
19	28	Wayne, MI	137,698	60	28	Pierce, WA	1,339,952	19	28	Wayne, MI	48,307
52	29	Gwinnett, GA	122,611	14	29	San Bernardino, CA	1,294,588	29	29	Orange, FL	47,356
43	30	Fulton, GA	122,228	20	30	Alameda, CA	1,267,192	27	30	Hillsborough, FL	46,480
28	31	Bronx, NY	120,204	31	31	Franklin, OH	1,263,587	31	31	Franklin, OH	46,320
33	32	Oakland, MI	120,182	43	32	Fulton, GA	1,196,669	49	32	Westchester, NY	45,049
44	33	Montgomery, MD	120,068	2	33	Cook, IL	1,184,517	40	33	Fairfax, VA	44,022
22	34	Sacramento, CA	114,724	52	34	Gwinnett, GA	1,099,834	34	34	Hennepin, MN	43,507
40	35	Fairfax, VA	114,617	18	35	Santa Clara, CA	1,070,071	43	35	Fulton, GA	42,801
34	36	Hennepin, MN	110,209	65	36	Hidalgo, TX	1,065,455	36	36	Allegheny, PA	42,657
42	37	Collin, TX	109,863	46	37	Fresno, CA	1,026,920	65	37	Hidalgo, TX	42,017
24	38	Philadelphia, PA	109,486	25	38	Suffolk, NY	995,962	67	38	El Paso, TX	41,955
31	39	Franklin, OH	106,978	21	39	Middlesex, MA	855,370	44	39	Montgomery, MD	38,557
41	40	Mecklenburg, NC	106,579	38	40	Contra Costa, CA	825,987	57	40	Erie, NY	38,244
49	41	Westchester, NY	104,393	8	41	Kings, NY	812,039	46	41	Fresno, CA	36,934
56	42	Bergen, NJ	103,417	17	42	Broward, FL	786,842	42	42	Collin, TX	36,296
38	43	Contra Costa, CA	101,112	33	43	Oakland, MI	784,374	37	43	Salt Lake, UT	35,948
53	44	Fairfield, CT	100,223	19	44	Wayne, MI	763,416	59	44	Milwaukee, WI	35,769
35	45	Cuyahoga, OH	99,039	54	45	Pinellas, FL	722,835	61	45	Du Page, IL	35,243
39	46	Wake, NC	98,720	67	46	El Paso, TX	661,531	50	46	St. Louis, MO	34,807
54	47	Pinellas, FL	95,475	56	47	Bergen, NJ	648,339	63	47	Kern, CA	34,360
37	48	Salt Lake, UT	95,332	28	48	Bronx, NY	615,409	39	48	Wake, NC	33,845
72	49	Fort Bend, TX	89,072	49	49	Westchester, NY	556,260	64	49	Hartford, CT	33,842
55	50	Prince George's, MD	87,879	53	50	Fairfield, CT	538,712	56	50	Bergen, NJ	33,707
61	51	Du Page, IL	86,847	61	51	Du Page, IL	533,886	62	51	Shelby, TN	33,448
36	52	Allegheny, PA	86,412	66	52	Macomb, MI	530,321	51	52	Marion, IN	33,241
62	53	Shelby, TN	86,195	36	53	Allegheny, PA	516,143	55	53	Prince George's, MD	32,780
58	54	Denton, TX	85,626	51	54	Marion, IN	493,331	53	54	Fairfield, CT	32,456
48	55	Duval, FL	81,314	11	55	Queens, NY	486,448	38	55	Contra Costa, CA	31,854
65	56	Hidalgo, TX	81,199	55	56	Prince George's, MD	473,797	45	56	Pima, AZ	31,752
50	57	St. Louis, MO	79,507	47	57	Honolulu, HI	468,350	54	57	Pinellas, FL	31,247
73	58	Essex, NJ	75,412	63	58	Kern, CA	461,218	33	58	Oakland, MI	31,208
71	59	Montgomery, PA	74,394	73	59	Essex, NJ	434,701	75	59	Ventura, CA	30,149
45	60	Pima, AZ	72,626	30	60	Nassau, NY	432,574	68	60	New Haven, CT	29,926
74	61	Baltimore, MD	72,263	50	61	St. Louis, MO	430,148	52	61	Gwinnett, GA	29,474
47	62	Honolulu, HI	71,327	62	62	Shelby, TN	429,254	70	62	Middlesex, NJ	28,682
75	63	Ventura, CA	71,248	57	63	Erie, NY	413,407	74	63	Baltimore, MD	28,278
66	64	Macomb, MI	69,903	69	64	Worcester, MA	407,261	73	64	Essex, NJ	28,131
51	65	Marion, IN	67,767	40	65	Fairfax, VA	398,171	60	65	Pierce, WA	25,902
67	66	El Paso, TX	67,698	71	66	Montgomery, PA	389,500	48	66	Duval, FL	24,856
70	67	Middlesex, NJ	64,680	23	67	New York, NY	362,265	69	67	Worcester, MA	24,532
68	68	New Haven, CT	64,541	75	68	Ventura, CA	343,759	71	68	Montgomery, PA	23,842
64	69	Hartford, CT	62,141	70	69	Middlesex, NJ	308,827	58	69	Denton, TX	23,475
69	70	Worcester, MA	58,690	44	70	Montgomery, MD	300,291	66	70	Macomb, MI	20,652
46	71	Fresno, CA	57,287	35	71	Cuyahoga, OH	279,672	72	71	Fort Bend, TX	20,284
57	72	Erie, NY	54,312	74	72	Baltimore, MD	232,772	47	72	Honolulu, HI	10,620
59	73	Milwaukee, WI	52,074	64	73	Hartford, CT	171,252	8	73	Kings, NY	0
63	74	Kern, CA	50,492	68	74	New Haven, CT	149,328	11	73	Queens, NY	0
60	75	Pierce, WA	49,937	59	75	Milwaukee, WI	89,711	28	73	Bronx, NY	0

75 Largest Counties by Value of Agricultural Sales
Selected Rankings

Value of agricultural sales, 2017			Average agricultural sales per farm, 2017				Number of farms, 2017			
Value of sales rank	County	Value of sales (millions of dollars) [col 125]	Value of sales rank	Average sales rank	County	Average sales per farm (dollars) [col 126]	Value of sales rank	Number of farms rank	County	Number of farms [col 113]
1	Fresno, CA	$5,742.8	21	1	Hartley, TX	$5,930,437	17	1	Lancaster, PA	5,108
2	Tulare, CA	$4,474.8	23	2	Haskell, KS	$5,599,502	41	2	San Diego, CA	5,082
3	Monterey, CA	$4,116.1	25	3	Scott, KS	$4,809,487	1	3	Fresno, CA	4,774
4	Kern, CA	$4,076.8	11	4	Imperial, CA	$4,696,157	2	4	Tulare, CA	4,187
5	Merced, CA	$2,938.4	51	5	Hansford, TX	$4,074,127	8	5	Weld, CO	4,062
6	Stanislaus, CA	$2,526.3	3	6	Monterey, CA	$3,728,396	6	6	Stanislaus, CA	3,621
7	San Joaquin, CA	$2,176.0	39	7	Sherman, TX	$3,420,641	34	7	Sonoma, CA	3,594
8	Weld, CO	$2,047.2	14	8	Deaf Smith, TX	$2,916,004	7	8	San Joaquin, CA	3,430
9	Yakima, WA	$1,988.0	27	9	Castro, TX	$2,728,944	9	9	Yakima, WA	2,952
10	Grant, WA	$1,938.9	43	10	Grant, KS	$2,584,575	49	10	Stearns, MN	2,951
11	Imperial, CA	$1,859.7	4	11	Kern, CA	$2,355,161	53	11	Marion, OR	2,761
12	Sioux, IA	$1,696.1	30	12	Gray, KS	$2,347,519	40	12	Miami-Dade, FL	2,752
13	Kings, CA	$1,649.3	37	13	Parmer, TX	$1,925,302	31	13	Riverside, CA	2,667
14	Deaf Smith, TX	$1,638.8	60	14	Dallam, TX	$1,867,426	53	14	San Luis Obispo, CA	2,349
15	Ventura, CA	$1,633.3	42	15	Finney, KS	$1,829,091	5	15	Merced, CA	2,337
16	Santa Barbara, CA	$1,519.9	13	16	Kings, CA	$1,712,640	15	16	Ventura, CA	2,135
17	Lancaster, PA	$1,507.2	69	17	Morrow, OR	$1,590,632	44	17	Rockingham, VA	2,026
18	Madera, CA	$1,492.6	32	18	Cassia, ID	$1,584,137	70	18	Benton, AR	1,936
19	Duplin, NC	$1,261.7	75	19	Phelps, NE	$1,558,601	22	19	Maricopa, AZ	1,874
20	Sampson, NC	$1,249.1	19	20	Duplin, NC	$1,538,648	4	20	Kern, CA	1,731
21	Hartley, TX	$1,221.7	45	21	Gooding, ID	$1,456,113	12	21	Sioux, IA	1,724
22	Maricopa, AZ	$1,209.1	64	22	Swisher, TX	$1,444,259	52	22	Chester, PA	1,646
23	Haskell, KS	$1,159.1	26	23	Cuming, NE	$1,407,956	29	23	Benton, WA	1,520
24	Texas, OK	$1,135.7	10	24	Grant, WA	$1,400,936	16	24	Santa Barbara, CA	1,467
25	Scott, KS	$1,135.0	24	25	Texas, OK	$1,371,593	18	25	Madera, CA	1,386
26	Cuming, NE	$1,132.0	58	26	Jerome, ID	$1,316,016	10	26	Grant, WA	1,384
27	Castro, TX	$1,121.6	20	27	Sampson, NC	$1,301,188	72	27	Kossuth, IA	1,347
28	Sussex, DE	$1,012.6	5	28	Merced, CA	$1,257,337	36	28	Palm Beach, FL	1,298
29	Benton, WA	$1,005.3	1	29	Fresno, CA	$1,202,926	61	29	Mercer, OH	1,231
30	Gray, KS	$990.7	35	30	Yuma, CO	$1,186,972	50	30	Plymouth, IA	1,219
31	Riverside, CA	$932.0	38	31	Pinal, AZ	$1,131,154	56	31	Twin Falls, ID	1,211
32	Cassia, ID	$926.7	48	32	Dawson, NE	$1,091,000	63	32	Glenn, CA	1,173
33	Lyon, IA	$923.6	18	33	Madera, CA	$1,076,903	74	33	Allegan, MI	1,172
34	Sonoma, CA	$919.1	71	34	Wayne, NC	$1,074,539	66	34	Huron, MI	1,153
35	Yuma, CO	$918.7	2	35	Tulare, CA	$1,068,739	57	35	Washington, IA	1,129
36	Palm Beach, FL	$901.7	16	36	Santa Barbara, CA	$1,036,090	33	36	Lyon, IA	1,122
37	Parmer, TX	$893.3	12	37	Sioux, IA	$983,814	28	37	Sussex, DE	1,119
38	Pinal, AZ	$861.9	68	38	Santa Cruz, CA	$970,464	46	38	Custer, NE	1,108
39	Sherman, TX	$838.1	28	39	Sussex, DE	$904,900	3	39	Monterey, CA	1,104
40	Miami-Dade, FL	$837.7	55	40	Platte, NE	$823,639	47	40	Lincoln, NE	1,040
41	San Diego, CA	$831.4	33	41	Lyon, IA	$823,148	67	41	Renville, MN	1,026
42	Finney, KS	$823.1	61	42	Franklin, WA	$818,132	13	42	Kings, CA	963
43	Grant, KS	$814.1	73	43	Hamilton, IA	$801,623	20	43	Sampson, NC	960
44	Rockingham, VA	$795.9	15	44	Ventura, CA	$765,008	59	44	Martin, MN	911
45	Gooding, ID	$783.4	47	45	Lincoln, NE	$726,188	65	45	Logan, CO	861
46	Custer, NE	$781.2	65	46	Logan, CO	$717,686	55	46	Platte, NE	836
47	Lincoln, NE	$755.2	46	47	Custer, NE	$705,014	24	47	Texas, OK	828
48	Dawson, NE	$748.4	6	48	Stanislaus, CA	$697,690	19	48	Duplin, NC	820
49	Stearns, MN	$748.0	59	49	Martin, MN	$697,610	26	49	Cuming, NE	804
50	Plymouth, IA	$738.2	36	50	Palm Beach, FL	$694,699	35	50	Yuma, CO	774
51	Hansford, TX	$737.4	9	51	Yakima, WA	$673,451	61	51	Franklin, WA	772
52	Chester, PA	$712.5	29	52	Benton, WA	$661,374	38	52	Pinal, AZ	762
53	San Luis Obispo, CA	$701.6	22	53	Maricopa, AZ	$645,215	73	53	Hamilton, IA	732
53	Marion, OR	$701.6	7	54	San Joaquin, CA	$634,404	48	54	Dawson, NE	686
55	Platte, NE	$688.6	50	55	Plymouth, IA	$605,578	68	55	Santa Cruz, CA	625
56	Twin Falls, ID	$680.2	57	56	Washington, IA	$595,126	32	56	Cassia, ID	585
57	Washington, IA	$671.9	67	57	Renville, MN	$593,752	14	57	Deaf Smith, TX	562
58	Jerome, ID	$639.6	56	58	Twin Falls, ID	$561,716	71	58	Wayne, NC	551
59	Martin, MN	$635.5	63	59	Glenn, CA	$536,012	45	59	Gooding, ID	538
60	Dallam, TX	$634.9	66	60	Huron, MI	$529,729	58	60	Jerome, ID	486
61	Mercer, OH	$631.6	61	61	Mercer, OH	$513,089	37	61	Parmer, TX	464
61	Franklin, WA	$631.6	8	62	Weld, CO	$503,982	42	62	Finney, KS	450
63	Glenn, CA	$628.7	74	63	Allegan, MI	$498,612	64	63	Swisher, TX	432
64	Swisher, TX	$623.9	72	64	Kossuth, IA	$436,566	30	64	Gray, KS	422
65	Logan, CO	$617.9	52	65	Chester, PA	$432,848	27	65	Castro, TX	411
66	Huron, MI	$610.8	44	66	Rockingham, VA	$392,852	11	66	Imperial, CA	396
67	Renville, MN	$609.2	31	67	Riverside, CA	$349,450	69	67	Morrow, OR	375
68	Santa Cruz, CA	$606.5	70	68	Benton, AR	$306,494	75	68	Phelps, NE	371
69	Morrow, OR	$596.5	40	69	Miami-Dade, FL	$304,409	60	69	Dallam, TX	340
70	Benton, AR	$593.4	53	70	San Luis Obispo, CA	$298,676	43	70	Grant, KS	315
71	Wayne, NC	$592.1	17	71	Lancaster, PA	$295,068	39	71	Sherman, TX	245
72	Kossuth, IA	$588.1	34	72	Sonoma, CA	$255,719	25	72	Scott, KS	236
73	Hamilton, IA	$586.8	53	73	Marion, OR	$254,104	23	73	Haskell, KS	207
74	Allegan, MI	$584.4	49	74	Stearns, MN	$253,466	21	74	Hartley, TX	206
75	Phelps, NE	$578.2	41	75	San Diego, CA	$163,601	51	75	Hansford, TX	181

75 Largest Counties by Value of Agricultural Sales

Selected Rankings

Average size of farm, 2017

Value of sales rank	Size of farm rank	County	Average size of farm (acres) [col 119]
21	1	Hartley, TX	4,052
51	2	Hansford, TX	3,243
69	3	Morrow, OR	3,003
60	4	Dallam, TX	2,633
39	5	Sherman, TX	2,409
25	6	Scott, KS	1,951
35	7	Yuma, CO	1,809
23	8	Haskell, KS	1,757
42	8	Finney, KS	1,757
14	10	Deaf Smith, TX	1,722
24	11	Texas, OK	1,544
38	12	Pinal, AZ	1,471
46	13	Custer, NE	1,358
27	14	Castro, TX	1,350
4	15	Kern, CA	1,326
65	16	Logan, CO	1,322
30	17	Gray, KS	1,318
11	18	Imperial, CA	1,317
47	19	Lincoln, NE	1,305
64	20	Swisher, TX	1,304
3	21	Monterey, CA	1,214
37	22	Parmer, TX	1,183
43	23	Grant, KS	1,139
32	24	Cassia, ID	1,100
75	25	Phelps, NE	921
48	26	Dawson, NE	889
61	27	Franklin, WA	797
10	28	Grant, WA	753
13	29	Kings, CA	640
67	30	Renville, MN	608
9	31	Yakima, WA	603
8	32	Weld, CO	517
59	33	Martin, MN	493
16	34	Santa Barbara, CA	487
18	35	Madera, CA	466
55	36	Platte, NE	459
26	37	Cuming, NE	452
72	38	Kossuth, IA	441
73	39	Hamilton, IA	431
66	40	Huron, MI	430
50	41	Plymouth, IA	413
5	42	Merced, CA	405
29	43	Benton, WA	404
63	44	Glenn, CA	398
53	45	San Luis Obispo, CA	396
56	46	Twin Falls, ID	387
36	47	Palm Beach, FL	376
58	48	Jerome, ID	353
45	49	Gooding, ID	350
1	50	Fresno, CA	345
20	51	Sampson, NC	314
33	52	Lyon, IA	309
71	53	Wayne, NC	300
2	54	Tulare, CA	299
19	55	Duplin, NC	296
12	56	Sioux, IA	280
57	57	Washington, IA	275
22	58	Maricopa, AZ	253
28	59	Sussex, DE	246
7	60	San Joaquin, CA	225
49	61	Stearns, MN	221
61	62	Mercer, OH	218
6	63	Stanislaus, CA	200
74	64	Allegan, MI	196
34	65	Sonoma, CA	158
70	66	Benton, AR	126
15	67	Ventura, CA	122
44	68	Rockingham, VA	113
53	69	Marion, OR	105
68	70	Santa Cruz, CA	102
31	71	Riverside, CA	99
52	72	Chester, PA	91
17	73	Lancaster, PA	77
41	74	San Diego, CA	44
40	75	Miami-Dade, FL	29

Average value of land and buildings per farm, 2017

Value of sales rank	Value of land and buildings per farm rank	County	Average value per farm (dollars) [col 122]
11	1	Imperial, CA	14,670,312
4	2	Kern, CA	9,787,244
3	3	Monterey, CA	8,944,364
13	4	Kings, CA	6,917,469
5	5	Merced, CA	5,299,308
18	6	Madera, CA	5,102,429
16	7	Santa Barbara, CA	5,060,150
21	8	Hartley, TX	5,028,050
75	9	Phelps, NE	4,707,223
51	10	Hansford, TX	4,353,971
38	11	Pinal, AZ	4,065,306
67	12	Renville, MN	3,990,664
1	13	Fresno, CA	3,917,829
61	14	Franklin, WA	3,662,394
63	15	Glenn, CA	3,547,184
50	16	Plymouth, IA	3,535,476
32	17	Cassia, ID	3,508,509
34	18	Sonoma, CA	3,501,852
2	19	Tulare, CA	3,501,053
73	20	Hamilton, IA	3,495,669
72	21	Kossuth, IA	3,480,288
39	22	Sherman, TX	3,446,896
69	23	Morrow, OR	3,385,469
7	24	San Joaquin, CA	3,384,002
46	25	Custer, NE	3,361,912
59	26	Martin, MN	3,308,478
36	27	Palm Beach, FL	3,149,296
6	28	Stanislaus, CA	3,116,617
15	29	Ventura, CA	3,106,351
33	30	Lyon, IA	3,082,560
48	31	Dawson, NE	3,034,516
53	32	San Luis Obispo, CA	2,991,939
60	33	Dallam, TX	2,986,690
25	34	Scott, KS	2,955,605
35	35	Yuma, CO	2,953,997
12	36	Sioux, IA	2,918,016
55	37	Platte, NE	2,903,960
26	38	Cuming, NE	2,752,249
42	39	Finney, KS	2,749,764
23	40	Haskell, KS	2,682,671
66	41	Huron, MI	2,597,983
10	42	Grant, WA	2,574,272
22	43	Maricopa, AZ	2,338,321
47	44	Lincoln, NE	2,184,451
68	45	Santa Cruz, CA	2,183,024
58	46	Jerome, ID	2,132,761
61	47	Mercer, OH	2,113,330
45	48	Gooding, ID	2,106,203
30	49	Gray, KS	2,103,461
28	50	Sussex, DE	2,085,980
14	51	Deaf Smith, TX	1,942,201
57	52	Washington, IA	1,894,242
27	53	Castro, TX	1,863,235
43	54	Grant, KS	1,794,738
31	55	Riverside, CA	1,794,629
56	56	Twin Falls, ID	1,718,569
9	57	Yakima, WA	1,662,430
29	58	Benton, WA	1,573,284
65	59	Logan, CO	1,570,536
24	60	Texas, OK	1,563,361
20	61	Sampson, NC	1,534,742
71	62	Wayne, NC	1,497,288
19	63	Duplin, NC	1,422,426
17	64	Lancaster, PA	1,410,238
64	65	Swisher, TX	1,364,672
8	66	Weld, CO	1,335,953
37	67	Parmer, TX	1,330,531
53	68	Marion, OR	1,292,998
74	69	Allegan, MI	1,172,374
49	70	Stearns, MN	1,135,611
52	71	Chester, PA	1,110,075
40	72	Miami-Dade, FL	1,068,826
41	73	San Diego, CA	1,014,281
44	74	Rockingham, VA	997,634
70	75	Benton, AR	815,643

Average value of land and buildings per acre, 2017

Value of sales rank	Value of land and buildings per acre rank	County	Average value per acre (dollars) [col 123]
40	1	Miami-Dade, FL	37,450
15	2	Ventura, CA	25,498
41	3	San Diego, CA	23,209
34	4	Sonoma, CA	22,186
68	5	Santa Cruz, CA	21,352
17	6	Lancaster, PA	18,285
31	7	Riverside, CA	18,144
6	8	Stanislaus, CA	15,619
7	9	San Joaquin, CA	15,020
5	10	Merced, CA	13,086
53	11	Marion, OR	12,367
52	12	Chester, PA	12,140
2	13	Tulare, CA	11,726
1	14	Fresno, CA	11,359
11	15	Imperial, CA	11,135
18	16	Madera, CA	10,958
13	17	Kings, CA	10,815
12	18	Sioux, IA	10,405
16	19	Santa Barbara, CA	10,381
33	20	Lyon, IA	9,988
61	21	Mercer, OH	9,673
22	22	Maricopa, AZ	9,236
63	23	Glenn, CA	8,915
44	24	Rockingham, VA	8,844
50	25	Plymouth, IA	8,561
28	26	Sussex, DE	8,473
36	27	Palm Beach, FL	8,379
73	28	Hamilton, IA	8,115
72	29	Kossuth, IA	7,892
53	30	San Luis Obispo, CA	7,547
4	31	Kern, CA	7,380
3	32	Monterey, CA	7,368
57	33	Washington, IA	6,889
59	34	Martin, MN	6,712
67	35	Renville, MN	6,560
70	36	Benton, AR	6,478
55	37	Platte, NE	6,328
26	38	Cuming, NE	6,087
66	39	Huron, MI	6,048
58	40	Jerome, ID	6,039
45	41	Gooding, ID	6,016
74	42	Allegan, MI	5,981
49	43	Stearns, MN	5,149
75	44	Phelps, NE	5,114
71	45	Wayne, NC	4,990
20	46	Sampson, NC	4,891
19	47	Duplin, NC	4,798
61	48	Franklin, WA	4,595
56	49	Twin Falls, ID	4,439
29	50	Benton, WA	3,898
10	51	Grant, WA	3,421
48	52	Dawson, NE	3,412
32	53	Cassia, ID	3,190
38	54	Pinal, AZ	2,764
9	55	Yakima, WA	2,755
8	56	Weld, CO	2,586
46	57	Custer, NE	2,475
47	58	Lincoln, NE	1,674
35	59	Yuma, CO	1,633
30	60	Gray, KS	1,596
43	61	Grant, KS	1,576
42	62	Finney, KS	1,565
23	63	Haskell, KS	1,527
25	64	Scott, KS	1,515
39	65	Sherman, TX	1,431
27	66	Castro, TX	1,380
51	67	Hansford, TX	1,342
21	68	Hartley, TX	1,241
65	69	Logan, CO	1,188
60	70	Dallam, TX	1,134
14	71	Deaf Smith, TX	1,128
69	72	Morrow, OR	1,127
37	73	Parmer, TX	1,125
64	74	Swisher, TX	1,046
24	75	Texas, OK	1,013

Table B. States and Counties — **Land Area and Population**

State / county code	CBSA code[1]	County code[2]	STATE County		Population, 2021			Population and population characteristics, 2021										
								Race alone or in combination, not Hispanic or Latino (percent)					Age (percent)					
				Land area[3] (sq. mi)	Total persons 2021	Rank	Per square mile	White	Black	American Indian, Alaska Native	Asian and Pacific Islancer	Percent Hispanic or Latino[4]	Under 5 years	5 to 17 years	18 to 24 years	25 to 34 years	35 to 44 years	45 to 54 years
				1	2	3	4	5	6	7	8	9	10	11	12	13	14	15

1. CBSA = Core Based Statistical Area. See Appendix A for explanation. See Appendix B for list of metropolitan areas with component counties. 2. County type code from the Economic Research Service of USDA Rural-Urban Continuum Codes. See Appendix A for definition. 3. Dry land or land partially or temporarily covered by water. 4. May be of any race.

Table B. States and Counties — **Population and Households**

STATE County	Population, 2021 (cont.)				Population change, 2000–2021							Households, 2016–2020				
	Age (percent) (cont.)				Total persons		Percent change		Components of change, 2010–2021					Percent		
	55 to 64 years	65 to 74 years	75 years and over	Percent female	2010	2020	2010–2020	2020–2021	Births	Deaths	Net Migration	Number	Persons per household	Family house-holds	Female family house-holder[1]	One person
	16	17	18	19	20	21	22	23	24	25	26	27	28	29	30	31

1. No spouse present.

Table B. States and Counties — **Population, Vital Statistics, and Health**

STATE County	Persons in group quarters, 2021	Daytime Population, 2016–2020		Births, 2021		Deaths, 2021		Persons under 65 with no health insurance, 2019		Medicare, 2021			COVID-19 Deaths, 2020	
		Number	Employment/ residence ratio	Total	Rate[1]	Number	Rate[1]	Number	Percent	Total beneficiaries	Enrolled in Original Medicare	Enrolled in Medicare Advantage	Number	Rate[1]
	32	33	34	35	36	37	38	39	40	41	42	43	44	45

1. Per 1,000 estimated resident population.

Table B. States and Counties — **Health, Education, Money Income, and Poverty**

STATE County	COVID-19 Vaccinations, 2021–2022		Education						Money income, 2016–2020				Income and poverty, 2020			
			School enrollment and attainment, 2015–2019				Local government expenditures,[3] 2018–2019			Households				Percent below poverty level		
			Enrollment[1]		Attainment[2] (percent)						Percent					
	Number	Percent[5]	Total	Percent private	High school graduate or less	Bachelor's degree or more	Total current spending (mil dol)	Current spending per student (dollars)	Per capita income[4]	Median income (dollars)	with income of less than $50,000	with income of $200,000 or more	Median household income (dollars)	All persons	Children under 18 years	Children 5 to 17 years in families
	46	47	48	49	50	51	52	53	54	55	56	57	58	59	60	61

1. All persons 3 years old and over enrolled in nursery school through college. 2. Persons 25 years old and over. 3. Elementary and secondary education expenditures. 4. Based on population estimated by the American Community Survey, 2016–2020. 5. CDC percent based on 2019 population estimate.

Table B. States and Counties — **Personal Income**

STATE County	Personal income, 2020										Earnings, 2020		
	Total (mil dol)	Percent change 2019–2020	Per capita[1] Dollars	Per capita[1] Rank	Wages and salaries (mil dol)	Supplements to wages and salaries, employer contributions (mil dol): Pension and insurance	Supplements to wages and salaries, employer contributions (mil dol): Government social insurance	Proprietors' income (mil dol)	Dividends, interest, and rent (mil dol)	Personal transfer reecipts (mil dol)	Total (mil dol)	Contributions for government social insurance (mil dol): From employee and self-employed	Contributions for government social insurance (mil dol): From employer
	62	63	64	65	66	67	68	69	70	71	72	73	74

1. Based on the resident population estimated as of July 1 of the year shown.

Table B. States and Counties — **Earnings, Social Security, and Housing**

STATE County	Earnings, 2020 (cont.): Percent by selected industries									Social Security beneficiaries, December 2020		Supple-mental Security Income recipients, 2020	Housing units, 2021	
	Farm	Mining, quarrying, and extractions	Construction	Manu-facturing	Information; professional, scientific, technical services	Retail trade	Finance, insurance, real estate, and leasing	Health care and social assistance	Govern-ment	Number	Rate[1]		Total	Percent change, 2010–2021
	75	76	77	78	79	80	81	82	83	84	85	86	87	88

1. Per 1,000 resident population estimated as of July 1 of the year shown.

Table B. States and Counties — **Housing, Labor Force, and Employment**

STATE County	Housing units, 2016–2020								Civilian labor force, 2021				Civilian employment[6], 2016–2020		
	Occupied units: Total	Owner-occupied: Percent	Owner-occupied: Median value[1]	Owner-occupied: Median owner cost as a percent of income: With a mort-gage	Owner-occupied: Median owner cost as a percent of income: Without a mort-gage[2]	Renter-occupied: Median rent[3]	Renter-occupied: Median rent as a percent of income[2]	Sub-standard units[4] (percent)	Total	Percent change, 2020–2021	Unemployment: Total	Unemployment: Rate[5]	Total	Percent: Management, business, science, and arts	Percent: Construction, production, and maintenance occupations
	89	90	91	92	93	94	95	96	97	98	99	100	101	102	103

1. Specified owner-occupied units. 2. A value of 10.0 represents 10 percent or less; a value of 50.0 represents 50 percent or more. 3. Specified renter-occupied units. 4. Overcrowded or lacking complete plumbing facilities. 5. Percent of civilian labor force. 6. Civilian employed persons 16 years old and over.

Table B. States and Counties — **Nonfarm Employment and Agriculture**

STATE County	Private nonfarm establishments, employment and payroll, 2020									Agriculture, 2017			
	Number of establish-ments	Employment: Total	Employment: Health care and social assistance	Employment: Manufac-turing	Employment: Retail trade	Employment: Finance and insurance	Employment: Professional, scientific, and technical services	Annual payroll: Total (mil dol)	Annual payroll: Average per employee (dollars)	Farms: Number	Farms: Percent with: Fewer than 50 acres	Farms: Percent with: 1000 acres or more	Farm producers whose primary occupation is farming (percent)
	104	105	106	107	108	109	110	111	112	113	114	115	116

Table B. States and Counties — **Agriculture**

STATE County	Agriculture, 2017 (cont.)															
	Land in farms					Value of land and buildings (dollars)		Value of machinery and equipment, average per farm (dollars)	Value of products sold:				Organic farms (number)	Farms with internet access (percent)	Government payments	
	Acreage (1,000)	Percent change, 2012–2017	Acres								Percent from:					
			Average size of farm	Total irrigated (1,000)	Total cropland (1,000)	Average per farm	Average per acre		Total (mil dol)	Average per farm (acres)	Crops	Livestock and poultry products			Total ($1,000)	Percent of farms
	117	118	119	120	121	122	123	124	125	126	127	128	129	130	131	132

Table B. States and Counties — **Water Use, Wholesale Trade, Retail Trade, and Real Estate**

STATE County	Water use, 2015		Wholesale Trade[1], 2017				Retail Trade[2], 2017				Real estate and rental and leasing,[2] 2017			
	Public supply water withdrawn (mil gal/ day)	Public supply gallons withdrawn per person per day	Number of establish-ments	Number of employees	Sales (mil dol)	Average payroll (mil dol)	Number of establish-ments	Number of employees	Sales (mil dol)	Average payroll (mil dol)	Number of establish-ments	Number of employees	Sales (mil dol)	Average payroll (mil dol)
	133	134	135	136	137	138	139	140	141	142	143	144	145	146

1 Merchant wholesalers, except manufacturers' sales branches and offices. 2. Employer establishments.

Table B. States and Counties — **Professional Services, Manufacturing, and Accommodation and Food Services**

STATE County	Professional, scientific, and technical services, 2017				Manufacturing, 2017				Accommodation and food services, 2017			
	Number of establish-ments	Number of employees	Sales (mil dol)	Average payroll (mil dol)	Number of establish-ments	Number of employees	Sales (mil dol)	Average payroll (mil dol)	Number of establis-hments	Number of employees	Sales (mil dol)	Annual payroll (mil dol)
	147	148	149	150	151	152	153	154	155	156	157	158

Table B. States and Counties — **Health Care and Social Assistance, Other Services, Nonemployer Businesses, and Residential Construction**

STATE County	Health care and social assistance, 2017				Other services, 2017				Nonemployer businesses, 2019		Value of residential construction authorized by building permits, 2021	
	Number of establish-ments	Number of employees	Receipts (mil dol)	Annual payroll (mil dol)	Number of establish-ments	Number of employees	Receipts (mil dol)	Annual payroll (mil dol)	Number	Receipts (mil dol)	New construction ($1,000)	Number of housing units
	159	160	161	162	163	164	165	166	167	168	169	170

Table B. States and Counties — **Government Employment and Payroll, and Local Government Finances**

STATE County	Government employment and payroll, 2017									Local government finances, 2017				
			March payroll (percent of total)							General revenue				
												Taxes		
													Per capita[1] (dollars)	
	Full-time equivalent employees	March payroll (dollars)	Adminis-tration, judicial, and legal	Police and corrections	Fire protection	Highways and transpor-tation	Health and welfare	Natural resources and utilities	Education and libraries	Total (mil dol)	Inter-govern-mental (mil dol)	Total (mil dol)	Total	Property
	171	172	173	174	175	176	177	178	179	180	181	182	183	184

1. Based on the resident population estimated as of July 1 of the year shown.

Table B. States and Counties — **Local Government Finances, Government Employment, and Income Taxes**

STATE County	Local government finances, 2017 (cont.)									Government employment, 2020			Individual income tax returns, 2019		
	Direct general expenditure							Debt outstanding							
			Percent of total for:												
	Total (mil dol)	Per capita[1] (dollars)	Education	Health and hospitals	Police protection	Public welfare	Highways	Total (mil dol)	Per capita[1] (dollars)	Federal civilian	Federal military	State and local	Number of returns	Mean adjusted gross income	Mean income tax
	185	186	187	188	189	190	191	192	193	194	195	196	197	198	199

1. Based on the resident population estimated as of July 1 of the year shown.

Table B. States and Counties — **Land Area and Population**

State / county code	CBSA code[1]	County Type code[2]	STATE County	Land area[3] (sq. mi)	Population, 2021: Total persons 2021	Population, 2021: Rank	Population, 2021: Per square mile	Population and population characteristics, 2021 — Race alone or in combination, not Hispanic or Latino (percent): White	Black	American Indian, Alaska Native	Asian and Pacific Islancer	Percent Hispanic or Latino[4]	Age (percent): Under 5 years	5 to 17 years	18 to 24 years	25 to 34 years	35 to 44 years	45 to 54 years
				1	2	3	4	5	6	7	8	9	10	11	12	13	14	15
00,000		0	UNITED STATES	3,533,043.7	331,893,745	X	93.9	61.4	13.7	1.3	7.2	18.9	5.7	12.6	13.0	13.7	13.1	12.3
01,000		0	ALABAMA	50,646.6	5,039,877	X	99.5	66.4	27.4	1.2	2.0	4.8	5.8	12.6	13.0	13.0	12.3	12.3
01,001	33,860	2	Autauga	594.5	59,095	888	99.4	74.2	21.8	0.9	1.8	3.3	5.7	13.4	11.9	13.2	13.4	13.1
01,003	19,300	3	Baldwin	1,589.8	239,294	289	150.5	84.9	9.2	1.4	1.6	4.8	5.1	12.2	10.9	11.0	12.1	12.7
01,005	21,640	6	Barbour	885.0	24,964	1,615	28.2	46.5	48.3	0.8	0.8	5.0	5.2	11.7	11.6	13.6	12.8	12.2
01,007	13,820	1	Bibb	622.5	22,477	1,698	36.1	74.8	22.1	0.9	0.5	3.1	5.2	11.2	11.4	14.8	13.4	13.9
01,009	13,820	1	Blount	644.9	59,041	889	91.6	87.5	2.1	1.1	0.6	9.9	5.8	13.1	11.8	12.0	12.0	13.1
01,011		6	Bullock	622.8	10,320	2,389	16.6	22.1	68.7	0.6	0.4	9.1	5.6	12.2	10.8	14.4	14.0	12.3
01,013		6	Butler	776.8	18,884	1,876	24.3	51.7	45.3	0.8	1.6	1.7	5.7	13.0	11.4	11.2	12.3	11.7
01,015	11,500	3	Calhoun	605.9	115,972	543	191.4	73.0	22.5	1.0	1.5	4.2	5.7	12.1	13.3	12.8	12.1	12.1
01,017	29,300	6	Chambers	596.6	34,541	1,313	57.9	55.7	40.8	0.6	1.1	2.9	5.4	11.8	11.0	12.7	11.1	13.1
01,019		6	Cherokee	553.5	24,996	1,611	45.2	92.7	4.9	1.5	0.7	1.9	4.6	10.6	10.5	10.8	10.0	13.3
01,021	13,820	1	Chilton	692.8	45,274	1,072	65.3	81.0	10.6	0.8	0.7	8.1	6.0	13.5	12.1	12.4	12.2	12.8
01,023		9	Choctaw	913.5	12,533	2,242	13.7	57.3	41.5	0.5	0.4	1.2	5.5	10.8	10.7	10.5	10.2	12.4
01,025		7	Clarke	1,238.4	22,760	1,684	18.4	52.5	45.6	0.9	0.7	1.5	5.8	11.8	12.0	11.7	11.3	12.4
01,027		9	Clay	604.0	14,190	2,135	23.5	82.2	15.0	1.0	0.5	3.3	5.2	11.7	11.2	10.8	11.3	13.3
01,029		8	Cleburne	560.1	15,103	2,087	27.0	93.8	3.7	0.9	0.4	2.7	6.0	13.0	11.1	11.5	11.4	13.4
01,031	21,460	4	Coffee	679.0	54,174	937	79.8	71.4	17.9	2.1	2.7	8.8	6.0	13.6	12.2	12.6	12.9	13.1
01,033	22,520	3	Colbert	593.0	57,474	907	96.9	79.2	17.2	1.3	1.0	3.4	5.6	12.0	11.1	12.7	11.7	12.7
01,035		7	Conecuh	850.3	11,328	2,323	13.3	51.3	45.8	1.1	0.5	2.8	5.4	11.3	10.8	10.8	10.3	12.2
01,037	10,760	8	Coosa	650.9	10,450	2,381	16.1	67.4	29.7	1.2	0.4	2.7	4.2	9.1	9.2	10.6	10.3	14.2
01,039		6	Covington	1,030.6	37,524	1,236	36.4	84.2	13.4	1.3	0.7	2.1	5.6	12.5	11.1	11.5	11.3	12.0
01,041		8	Crenshaw	608.9	13,083	2,208	21.5	72.0	25.0	1.4	1.5	2.5	5.5	13.3	11.4	12.5	11.1	12.3
01,043	18,980	4	Cullman	734.7	89,496	663	121.8	92.7	1.7	1.3	0.9	4.7	5.7	12.8	11.5	12.9	12.0	12.6
01,045	37,120	4	Dale	561.1	49,342	1,005	87.9	69.3	22.2	1.5	2.3	7.3	6.6	12.9	12.1	14.6	11.6	11.4
01,047	42,820	4	Dallas	978.7	37,619	1,231	38.4	27.4	71.2	0.5	0.7	1.2	5.8	13.3	12.9	11.2	11.3	11.3
01,049	22,840	6	DeKalb	777.1	71,813	765	92.4	81.0	2.0	2.7	0.6	15.8	5.8	13.8	12.7	11.9	11.9	13.1
01,051	33,860	2	Elmore	618.5	89,304	665	144.4	74.3	22.1	0.9	1.3	3.1	5.5	12.5	12.2	13.8	13.0	13.1
01,053	12,120	6	Escambia	945.4	36,699	1,265	38.8	62.0	32.4	4.4	0.7	2.6	5.9	12.8	11.5	13.4	12.4	12.7
01,055	23,460	3	Etowah	535.1	103,162	595	192.8	78.5	16.4	1.1	1.1	4.6	5.8	12.1	11.8	12.3	11.9	13.3
01,057		6	Fayette	627.7	16,148	2,026	25.7	85.7	12.3	0.9	0.7	2.1	5.4	12.0	11.2	11.4	11.5	12.3
01,059		6	Franklin	633.9	32,013	1,382	50.5	76.2	4.6	1.1	0.5	19.0	6.9	13.8	12.4	12.1	12.0	13.0
01,061	20,020	3	Geneva	574.5	26,701	1,542	46.5	84.8	10.3	1.8	0.7	4.7	5.4	12.4	11.0	11.2	11.6	12.9
01,063	46,220	8	Greene	647.0	7,629	2,603	11.8	18.1	79.7	0.6	0.5	1.9	5.7	12.2	11.2	11.2	10.1	10.7
01,065	46,220	3	Hale	644.0	14,754	2,101	22.9	40.4	57.7	0.6	0.5	1.6	6.5	13.3	11.5	12.1	11.4	10.7
01,067	20,020	3	Henry	561.8	17,459	1,948	31.1	71.5	25.6	1.0	0.7	2.7	5.1	11.7	10.7	10.6	12.2	12.8
01,069	20,020	3	Houston	579.8	107,458	576	185.3	67.1	28.6	1.1	1.7	3.6	6.1	12.7	11.7	12.7	12.5	12.4
01,071	42,460	6	Jackson	1,078.0	52,773	960	49.0	91.3	4.2	3.1	0.8	3.3	5.3	11.6	11.2	11.6	11.6	13.3
01,073	13,820	1	Jefferson	1,111.5	667,820	103	600.8	50.0	44.2	0.6	2.3	4.3	6.2	12.9	12.5	14.2	13.0	11.8
01,075		8	Lamar	604.8	13,689	2,177	22.6	87.3	11.0	0.8	0.4	2.1	5.4	12.0	11.2	10.7	11.1	13.1
01,077	22,520	3	Lauderdale	668.0	94,043	643	140.8	85.8	10.7	1.0	1.2	3.1	5.1	11.1	14.8	12.1	11.0	11.7
01,079	19,460	3	Lawrence	690.7	33,090	1,358	47.9	80.9	11.3	9.3	0.6	2.6	5.3	12.6	11.3	12.1	11.3	13.4
01,081	12,220	3	Lee	607.5	177,218	380	291.7	68.8	23.5	0.7	4.8	3.9	5.4	11.9	20.6	13.7	12.4	11.7
01,083	26,620	2	Limestone	560.0	107,517	575	192.0	77.1	14.8	1.4	2.5	6.5	5.2	12.7	11.6	13.1	13.9	14.0
01,085	33,860	2	Lowndes	716.1	9,965	2,408	13.9	25.5	72.1	0.6	0.5	1.9	6.1	12.4	10.9	12.2	10.8	11.6
01,087		6	Macon	608.7	18,895	1,875	31.0	17.9	79.7	0.7	0.8	2.1	4.6	9.6	20.0	11.2	8.9	10.5
01,089	26,620	2	Madison	801.6	395,211	184	493.0	66.6	25.6	1.6	3.7	5.5	5.6	12.3	12.9	14.2	12.9	12.3
01,091		7	Marengo	976.9	18,996	1,870	19.4	45.1	51.8	0.6	0.5	3.0	5.7	12.8	11.5	12.3	11.0	12.5
01,093		7	Marion	742.3	29,246	1,449	39.4	92.2	4.8	1.0	0.5	2.7	5.4	11.8	11.1	11.6	11.4	13.2
01,095	10,700	4	Marshall	565.8	98,228	624	173.6	80.3	3.3	1.3	1.0	15.6	7.1	14.0	12.4	12.1	11.8	12.3
01,097	33,660	2	Mobile	1,229.4	413,073	173	336.0	57.4	37.2	1.5	2.6	3.1	6.4	13.1	12.6	13.8	12.3	11.7
01,099		7	Monroe	1,025.7	19,648	1,845	19.2	55.3	41.9	2.0	0.7	1.7	5.1	11.8	12.2	11.1	10.7	12.6
01,101	33,860	2	Montgomery	785.4	227,434	307	289.6	32.2	60.9	0.6	3.9	3.9	6.7	13.2	13.4	14.0	12.7	11.7
01,103	19,460	3	Morgan	579.7	123,668	517	213.3	76.5	14.0	1.7	1.1	9.0	6.0	13.0	11.9	12.0	12.3	12.6
01,105		8	Perry	719.7	8,355	2,550	11.6	29.9	67.9	0.6	0.8	1.6	5.4	11.5	17.7	10.7	10.2	10.9
01,107	46,220	3	Pickens	881.4	18,801	1,881	21.3	54.2	40.4	0.6	0.5	5.5	5.1	10.7	11.9	13.2	12.4	12.8
01,109	45,980	6	Pike	672.1	32,991	1,362	49.1	56.9	39.0	1.2	2.2	2.4	5.3	10.8	24.6	12.2	10.1	10.2
01,111		6	Randolph	580.6	21,989	1,713	37.9	77.2	19.7	1.1	0.8	2.9	5.3	12.0	11.8	11.1	10.4	12.9
01,113	17,980	2	Russell	641.2	58,722	893	91.6	46.9	46.9	1.1	1.8	5.9	6.7	13.8	11.7	14.8	12.6	12.0
01,115	13,820	1	St. Clair	631.6	92,748	650	146.8	85.8	11.0	0.9	1.2	2.6	5.5	12.9	11.0	13.0	13.2	13.4
01,117	13,820	1	Shelby	785.4	226,902	309	288.9	77.4	14.6	0.7	2.9	6.0	5.2	13.2	12.6	12.1	13.6	13.9
01,119		8	Sumter	903.8	12,164	2,270	13.5	26.2	71.0	0.5	1.8	1.4	5.5	10.9	20.2	11.8	8.5	10.3
01,121	45,180	4	Talladega	736.8	81,524	706	110.6	63.5	33.9	0.9	0.9	2.6	5.2	11.7	12.3	12.8	12.0	13.0
01,123	10,760	6	Tallapoosa	716.5	41,023	1,162	57.3	69.8	27.3	0.8	0.8	2.6	4.9	11.9	10.7	11.5	10.2	12.5
01,125	46,220	3	Tuscaloosa	1,320.8	227,007	308	171.9	61.2	33.3	0.6	2.1	4.2	5.7	12.0	19.3	14.2	12.1	11.2
01,127	27,530	1	Walker	791.0	64,818	835	81.9	90.0	7.0	1.0	0.7	3.0	6.0	12.7	11.4	12.2	11.2	12.7

1. CBSA = Core Based Statistical Area. See Appendix A for explanation. See Appendix B for list of metropolitan areas with component counties. 2. County type code from the Economic Research Service of USDA Rural-Urban Continuum Codes. See Appendix A for definition. 3. Dry land or land partially or temporarily covered by water. 4. May be of any race.

STATE County	Population, 2021 (cont.)				Population change, 2000–2021							Households, 2016–2020				
	Age (percent) (cont.)				Total persons		Percent change		Components of change, 2020–2021					Percent		
	55 to 64 years	65 to 74 years	75 years and over	Percent female	2010	2020	2010–2020	2020–2021	Births	Deaths	Net Migration	Number	Persons per household	Family house-holds	Female family house-holder[1]	One person
	16	17	18	19	20	21	22	23	24	25	26	27	28	29	30	31
UNITED STATES	12.9	10.1	6.7	50.5	308,745,538	331,449,281	7.4	0.1	4,474,986	4,287,391	256,869	122,354,219	2.60	65.3	12.3	28.0
ALABAMA	13.3	10.8	6.9	51.4	4,779,736	5,024,279	5.1	0.3	69,730	81,016	26,717	1,888,504	2.53	65.4	13.9	30.0
Autauga	13.3	9.5	6.6	51.4	54,571	58,805	7.8	0.5	792	849	339	21,559	2.55	70.1	13.6	26.3
Baldwin	14.6	13.2	8.2	51.3	182,265	231,767	27.2	3.2	2,787	3,528	8,358	84,047	2.56	66.7	8.7	29.0
Barbour	13.0	11.8	8.2	46.7	27,457	25,223	-8.1	-1.0	338	503	-94	9,322	2.37	65.3	20.3	32.8
Bibb	13.3	10.0	6.7	46.0	22,915	22,293	-2.7	0.8	288	372	269	7,259	2.85	72.7	16.4	25.9
Blount	13.4	11.2	7.6	50.2	57,322	59,134	3.2	-0.2	781	1,040	159	21,205	2.70	70.9	10.3	25.9
Bullock	13.2	10.5	7.1	44.6	10,914	10,357	-5.1	-0.4	163	166	-36	3,429	2.84	62.9	21.8	35.4
Butler	13.5	12.0	9.2	53.4	20,947	19,051	-9.1	-0.9	254	353	-66	6,649	2.92	68.8	16.6	28.9
Calhoun	13.5	11.5	7.0	51.6	118,572	116,441	-1.8	-0.4	1,631	2,121	1	44,572	2.50	65.3	14.5	29.0
Chambers	14.7	12.1	8.2	52.1	34,215	34,772	1.6	-0.7	441	633	-42	13,582	2.42	67.2	16.2	27.5
Cherokee	16.2	14.6	9.3	50.2	25,989	24,971	-3.9	0.1	293	587	321	10,836	2.38	68.2	8.1	27.5
Chilton	13.5	10.7	6.8	50.7	43,643	45,014	3.1	0.6	682	728	301	17,140	2.55	70.3	14.1	25.3
Choctaw	16.0	13.4	10.3	52.4	13,859	12,665	-8.6	-1.0	180	271	-41	5,330	2.36	64.8	17.4	32.8
Clarke	14.5	11.5	9.0	52.4	25,833	23,087	-10.6	-1.4	365	495	-198	9,323	2.52	63.0	14.0	35.4
Clay	15.2	12.2	9.0	50.8	13,932	14,236	2.2	-0.3	175	274	51	5,153	2.53	71.4	13.8	25.7
Cleburne	13.9	11.6	8.1	50.7	14,972	15,056	0.6	0.3	183	317	183	5,835	2.53	65.0	10.3	31.6
Coffee	12.4	10.3	6.8	50.5	49,948	53,465	7.0	1.3	804	890	797	19,951	2.59	68.2	13.7	27.9
Colbert	13.9	12.0	8.3	51.8	54,428	57,227	5.1	0.4	745	1,090	592	21,797	2.50	65.2	13.1	29.5
Conecuh	15.0	13.7	10.4	51.8	13,228	11,597	-12.3	-2.3	172	278	-160	4,585	2.66	65.6	20.8	32.8
Coosa	17.7	15.0	9.7	49.2	11,539	10,387	-10.0	0.6	94	186	157	4,016	2.57	64.8	11.1	31.6
Covington	14.4	12.5	9.2	51.5	37,765	37,570	-0.5	-0.1	488	830	298	14,995	2.43	64.7	12.7	31.0
Crenshaw	14.3	12.0	7.6	51.0	13,906	13,194	-5.1	-0.8	182	263	-31	5,011	2.72	66.9	13.2	29.5
Cullman	13.7	11.3	7.4	50.3	80,406	87,866	9.3	1.9	1,152	1,598	2,094	31,733	2.59	69.1	10.4	27.1
Dale	13.0	10.6	7.2	50.8	50,251	49,326	-1.8	0.0	794	822	35	19,405	2.47	64.7	16.4	30.8
Dallas	14.7	12.1	7.5	53.6	43,820	38,462	-12.2	-2.2	538	711	-668	15,409	2.44	59.2	20.4	38.3
DeKalb	13.2	10.8	6.9	50.1	71,109	71,608	0.7	0.3	958	1,245	486	26,365	2.67	73.3	11.2	24.4
Elmore	13.6	10.1	6.2	51.3	79,303	87,977	10.9	1.5	1,133	1,230	1,428	29,794	2.58	73.0	13.5	24.7
Escambia	12.9	10.7	7.7	49.5	38,319	36,757	-4.1	-0.2	527	696	108	12,931	2.61	60.2	13.4	36.4
Etowah	13.6	12.0	7.3	51.3	104,430	103,436	-1.0	-0.3	1,487	2,157	385	38,765	2.62	65.5	15.1	30.8
Fayette	14.3	12.7	9.1	50.9	17,241	16,321	-5.3	-1.1	223	332	-64	6,805	2.37	69.5	10.1	27.3
Franklin	12.8	10.3	6.8	49.9	31,704	32,113	1.3	-0.3	501	562	-46	11,017	2.85	68.7	14.0	28.1
Geneva	14.3	12.5	8.6	50.9	26,790	26,659	-0.5	0.2	334	508	218	10,572	2.47	68.2	9.7	27.4
Greene	14.1	15.1	9.6	53.5	9,045	7,730	-14.5	-1.3	108	133	-76	3,178	2.55	49.2	13.1	48.6
Hale	14.3	12.1	8.1	52.5	15,760	14,785	-6.2	-0.2	227	295	36	5,490	2.65	60.8	18.2	35.1
Henry	13.8	14.0	9.1	51.8	17,302	17,146	-0.9	1.8	211	312	418	6,556	2.56	68.6	11.2	28.7
Houston	13.4	11.0	7.5	51.9	101,547	107,202	5.6	0.2	1,575	1,758	424	39,784	2.62	66.0	14.6	30.5
Jackson	14.4	12.6	8.4	50.6	53,227	52,579	-1.2	0.4	654	1,044	588	20,367	2.51	70.6	11.9	27.8
Jefferson	12.6	10.4	6.3	52.5	658,466	674,721	2.5	-1.0	9,989	10,767	-6,168	263,801	2.44	61.9	16.2	32.7
Lamar	14.2	12.7	9.7	50.5	14,564	13,972	-4.1	-2.0	142	294	-130	5,631	2.43	64.2	10.8	29.8
Lauderdale	13.6	12.2	8.4	51.7	92,709	93,564	0.9	0.5	1,138	1,729	1,075	38,513	2.36	63.1	11.6	30.5
Lawrence	15.1	11.4	7.6	50.8	34,339	33,073	-3.7	0.1	425	646	236	12,551	2.61	70.9	11.1	27.8
Lee	11.2	8.3	4.8	50.7	140,247	174,241	24.2	1.7	2,245	1,851	2,565	60,731	2.59	62.0	12.7	28.8
Limestone	13.9	9.6	5.9	49.7	82,782	103,570	25.1	3.8	1,170	1,362	4,177	32,725	2.87	70.1	10.7	25.9
Lowndes	15.6	11.9	8.4	52.8	11,299	10,311	-8.7	-3.4	167	209	-300	4,213	2.33	65.6	29.9	31.6
Macon	13.5	13.0	8.5	54.5	21,452	19,532	-9.0	-3.3	187	392	-425	7,592	2.14	58.6	19.0	35.5
Madison	14.3	9.3	6.2	50.6	334,811	388,153	15.9	1.8	5,195	5,109	6,968	151,628	2.37	63.5	12.4	31.0
Marengo	13.9	12.0	8.3	52.9	21,027	19,323	-8.1	-1.7	273	380	-219	7,499	2.52	51.2	14.1	47.6
Marion	14.4	11.9	9.2	49.9	30,776	29,341	-4.7	-0.3	400	641	145	11,780	2.48	64.1	10.4	33.1
Marshall	13.1	10.3	6.9	50.5	93,019	97,612	4.9	0.6	1,721	1,688	572	35,115	2.71	69.8	10.9	25.7
Mobile	13.1	10.4	6.6	52.3	412,992	414,809	0.4	-0.4	6,320	6,894	-1,234	157,557	2.58	65.2	16.1	30.6
Monroe	14.8	12.8	8.9	52.1	23,068	19,772	-14.3	-0.6	282	355	-52	8,050	2.58	61.1	16.1	35.4
Montgomery	12.3	9.9	6.1	52.8	229,363	228,954	-0.2	-0.7	3,765	3,195	-2,118	89,511	2.45	60.6	19.2	34.5
Morgan	14.0	10.8	7.3	50.6	119,490	123,421	3.3	0.2	1,717	2,063	582	46,388	2.53	66.2	11.8	29.6
Perry	13.0	11.4	9.2	53.5	10,591	8,511	-19.6	-1.8	122	174	-104	3,140	2.64	48.1	22.3	51.4
Pickens	14.5	11.6	7.9	49.8	19,746	19,123	-3.2	-1.7	223	430	-117	7,731	2.37	67.9	17.8	28.7
Pike	11.0	9.2	6.7	52.1	32,899	33,009	0.3	-0.1	448	467	-6	11,700	2.69	53.2	14.1	37.3
Randolph	15.3	12.7	8.5	51.4	22,913	21,967	-4.1	0.1	292	439	166	8,655	2.57	70.8	13.9	27.4
Russell	13.3	9.5	5.7	52.3	52,947	59,183	11.8	-0.8	999	921	-541	23,694	2.42	63.4	15.6	33.4
St. Clair	13.7	10.7	6.7	50.3	83,593	91,103	9.0	1.8	1,234	1,448	1,867	32,765	2.65	73.2	11.2	23.6
Shelby	12.9	10.3	6.2	51.4	195,085	223,024	14.3	1.7	2,623	2,533	3,794	80,756	2.64	70.9	9.0	25.0
Sumter	12.9	11.8	8.0	53.9	13,763	12,345	-10.3	-1.5	164	233	-112	5,355	2.20	56.3	19.6	36.4
Talladega	14.0	11.8	7.1	51.5	82,291	82,149	-0.2	-0.8	1,035	1,541	-130	31,741	2.42	65.8	16.5	29.6
Tallapoosa	15.5	14.1	8.7	51.3	41,616	41,311	-0.7	-0.7	487	888	114	16,359	2.43	67.5	15.1	29.5
Tuscaloosa	11.2	9.1	5.2	51.8	194,656	227,036	16.6	0.0	3,132	2,722	-492	74,713	2.66	64.2	14.5	28.8
Walker	14.0	12.0	7.8	51.0	67,023	65,342	-2.5	-0.8	952	1,466	-19	25,440	2.47	69.0	12.7	26.4

1. No spouse present.

STATE County	Persons in group quarters, 2021	Daytime Population, 2016–2020		Births, 2021		Deaths, 2021		Persons under 65 with no health insurance, 2019		Medicare, 2021			COVID-19 Deaths, 2020	
		Number	Employment/ residence ratio	Total	Rate[1]	Number	Rate[1]	Number	Percent	Total beneficiaries	Enrolled in Original Medicare	Enrolled in Medicare Advantage	Number	Rate[1]
	32	33	34	35	36	37	38	39	40	41	42	43	44	45
UNITED STATES	7,760,059	326,569,308	1.00	3,581,986	10.8	3,433,943	10.4	28,980,723	10.8	61,521,688	37,063,987	24,457,709	381,310	1.2
ALABAMA	114,572	4,849,490	0.98	56,320	11.2	64,868	12.9	457,718	11.6	1,062,205	576,373	485,833	6,991	1.4
Autauga	442	43,643	0.52	649	11.0	681	11.5	4,366	9.4	11,247	5,593	5,654	59	1.0
Baldwin	2,177	204,552	0.86	2,260	9.6	2,867	12.1	19,085	10.9	55,742	29,149	26,592	179	0.8
Barbour	2,789	24,588	0.95	274	10.9	394	15.7	2,194	13.0	6,189	3,048	3,142	42	1.7
Bibb	2,062	18,472	0.52	226	10.1	282	12.6	1,824	11.0	4,736	2,058	2,678	48	2.2
Blount	449	44,568	0.42	629	10.7	820	13.9	6,663	14.3	13,182	5,739	7,443	97	1.6
Bullock	1,725	9,610	0.86	130	12.6	129	12.5	752	11.1	2,295	1,079	1,216	21	2.0
Butler	241	19,105	0.92	214	11.3	295	15.6	1,755	11.6	4,964	3,106	1,858	55	2.9
Calhoun	3,251	114,402	1.00	1,320	11.4	1,712	14.7	10,767	11.9	26,991	17,248	9,743	190	1.6
Chambers	449	28,100	0.62	356	10.3	512	14.8	3,178	12.2	8,826	5,023	3,803	81	2.3
Cherokee	181	22,099	0.61	238	9.5	473	18.9	2,580	13.0	7,359	4,272	3,087	41	1.6
Chilton	337	36,763	0.58	557	12.3	590	13.1	4,995	13.7	9,666	3,861	5,805	76	1.7
Choctaw	107	12,338	0.90	144	11.5	218	17.3	1,158	12.2	3,820	2,651	1,169	33	2.6
Clarke	189	23,508	0.96	287	12.5	395	17.3	2,209	12.0	6,418	3,084	3,334	45	2.0
Clay	252	12,790	0.91	141	9.9	221	15.6	1,480	14.4	3,678	2,144	1,534	42	3.0
Cleburne	142	12,003	0.48	152	10.1	252	16.7	1,506	12.8	3,541	2,439	1,103	28	1.9
Coffee	515	49,009	0.86	663	12.3	709	13.2	5,604	13.0	10,922	7,241	3,681	77	1.4
Colbert	448	56,933	1.09	578	10.1	877	15.3	4,721	10.8	14,149	9,175	4,974	88	1.5
Conecuh	23	11,497	0.82	137	12.0	230	20.1	1,112	12.2	3,549	2,320	1,229	28	2.4
Coosa	192	8,385	0.43	71	6.8	154	14.8	891	11.3	3,112	1,697	1,415	22	2.1
Covington	517	35,562	0.90	410	10.9	654	17.4	3,608	12.5	9,953	6,776	3,177	95	2.5
Crenshaw	73	12,536	0.77	157	12.0	218	16.6	1,471	13.4	3,413	1,875	1,538	29	2.2
Cullman	1,019	80,005	0.90	907	10.2	1,265	14.3	9,008	13.4	20,104	11,332	8,772	129	1.5
Dale	841	51,040	1.09	637	12.9	652	13.2	4,777	12.0	10,821	6,917	3,904	92	1.9
Dallas	851	37,499	0.95	426	11.2	567	15.0	3,263	11.1	9,737	4,791	4,946	104	2.7
DeKalb	688	66,518	0.84	752	10.5	1,021	14.2	10,814	18.7	15,511	9,619	5,892	130	1.8
Elmore	4,368	66,601	0.57	906	10.2	997	11.2	5,781	8.9	17,506	9,194	8,312	102	1.2
Escambia	2,352	37,652	1.07	429	11.7	564	15.4	3,875	14.2	8,832	4,913	3,919	64	1.7
Etowah	1,975	97,391	0.87	1,200	11.6	1,751	17.0	10,281	12.7	26,225	13,840	12,385	226	2.2
Fayette	252	14,963	0.77	189	11.6	275	16.9	1,508	12.0	4,610	3,042	1,568	45	2.8
Franklin	239	31,046	0.96	400	12.5	448	14.0	3,952	15.4	6,771	4,836	1,936	54	1.7
Geneva	186	21,762	0.56	259	9.7	395	14.8	3,009	14.6	6,946	4,322	2,624	57	2.1
Greene	22	7,858	0.84	84	11.0	109	14.2	708	11.6	2,311	1,421	890	21	2.7
Hale	176	12,606	0.59	181	12.3	250	16.9	1,335	11.6	4,009	2,611	1,398	42	2.8
Henry	158	14,746	0.65	169	9.8	247	14.3	1,632	12.5	4,861	2,515	2,346	25	1.5
Houston	1,298	112,211	1.16	1,291	12.0	1,418	13.2	11,329	13.3	24,387	14,042	10,345	179	1.7
Jackson	554	48,664	0.84	512	9.7	823	15.6	5,584	13.8	13,310	8,549	4,761	71	1.4
Jefferson	16,732	723,131	1.22	8,105	12.1	8,543	12.7	57,398	10.7	132,456	58,127	74,328	798	1.2
Lamar	184	12,194	0.68	108	7.8	234	16.9	1,257	11.9	3,855	2,892	963	50	3.6
Lauderdale	2,299	88,739	0.90	918	9.8	1,407	15.0	8,571	11.9	22,437	14,448	7,989	136	1.5
Lawrence	182	25,130	0.39	337	10.2	511	15.4	3,906	14.8	8,029	4,750	3,279	66	2.0
Lee	5,120	153,313	0.86	1,813	10.3	1,483	8.4	14,928	10.7	25,287	14,775	10,513	153	0.9
Limestone	2,705	84,163	0.70	940	8.9	1,112	10.5	9,428	11.6	18,632	11,659	6,973	105	1.0
Lowndes	92	8,561	0.61	138	13.6	176	17.4	826	10.8	2,924	1,102	1,822	41	4.0
Macon	1,694	17,192	0.82	159	8.3	325	16.9	1,349	10.7	4,621	2,301	2,320	45	2.3
Madison	8,194	401,809	1.19	4,169	10.6	4,067	10.4	28,344	9.2	67,811	45,412	22,400	232	0.6
Marengo	230	18,525	0.91	225	11.8	306	16.0	1,651	11.1	5,427	3,466	1,961	35	1.8
Marion	721	29,371	0.96	322	11.0	510	17.4	2,816	12.3	7,452	5,390	2,063	67	2.3
Marshall	960	97,284	1.03	1,387	14.2	1,323	13.5	12,136	15.4	20,865	13,509	7,356	157	1.6
Mobile	7,156	423,017	1.05	5,081	12.3	5,460	13.2	42,767	12.7	85,179	34,793	50,386	503	1.2
Monroe	126	20,840	0.98	232	11.8	288	14.6	2,083	12.9	5,322	2,828	2,494	30	1.5
Montgomery	8,772	261,693	1.36	3,034	13.3	2,550	11.2	21,123	11.7	43,719	21,322	22,398	356	1.6
Morgan	1,960	121,825	1.05	1,403	11.4	1,620	13.1	12,379	12.8	26,371	16,890	9,481	180	1.5
Perry	643	8,638	0.80	98	11.7	140	16.7	776	12.1	2,616	1,360	1,256	28	3.3
Pickens	1,721	17,242	0.58	177	9.3	342	18.1	1,755	12.4	4,983	3,382	1,601	41	2.2
Pike	1,836	35,513	1.16	365	11.1	386	11.7	3,498	13.5	6,497	3,526	2,970	47	1.4
Randolph	278	19,902	0.67	237	10.8	340	15.5	2,165	12.3	5,910	3,712	2,199	56	2.5
Russell	521	49,678	0.66	826	14.0	763	12.9	5,473	11.3	11,455	6,511	4,944	77	1.3
St. Clair	1,429	73,808	0.61	1,003	10.9	1,180	12.8	7,465	10.2	19,289	8,607	10,682	142	1.6
Shelby	2,433	199,204	0.84	2,143	9.5	2,024	9.0	15,878	8.7	38,893	19,441	19,452	159	0.7
Sumter	749	11,896	0.84	135	11.0	188	15.4	1,218	13.2	3,163	2,007	1,156	27	2.2
Talladega	3,211	83,425	1.10	831	10.2	1,249	15.3	6,969	11.2	19,827	9,823	10,004	137	1.7
Tallapoosa	530	37,712	0.82	390	9.5	709	17.2	3,761	12.1	11,481	6,215	5,267	80	1.9
Tuscaloosa	11,309	217,375	1.09	2,516	11.1	2,230	9.8	17,245	10.1	36,950	20,254	16,697	265	1.2
Walker	824	59,117	0.81	782	12.0	1,143	17.6	6,674	13.2	17,532	8,085	9,447	172	2.6

1. Per 1,000 estimated resident population.

STATE County	COVID-19 Vaccinations, 2021–2022		Education						Money income, 2016–2020				Income and poverty, 2020			
			School enrollment and attainment, 2016–2020				Local government expenditures,[3] 2018–2019			Households				Percent below poverty level		
			Enrollment[1]		Attainment[2] (percent)						Percent					
	Number	Percent[5]	Total	Percent private	High school graduate or less	Bachelor's degree or more	Total current spending (mil dol)	Current spending per student (dollars)	Per capita income[4]	Median income (dollars)	with income of less than $50,000	with income of $200,000 or more	Median household income (dollars)	All persons	Children under 18 years	Children 5 to 17 years in families
	46	47	48	49	50	51	52	53	54	55	56	57	58	59	60	61
UNITED STATES	219,550,028	66.1	80,497,960	16.7	38.1	32.9	657,425.0	13,037	35,384	64,994	39.1	8.3	67,340	11.9	15.7	14.9
ALABAMA	2,503,983	51.1	1,168,551	14.9	43.5	26.2	7,453.7	10,076	28,934	52,035	48.3	4.4	53,958	14.9	20.9	19.7
Autauga	24,701	44.2	13,003	15.8	42.7	28.3	78.2	8,600	29,804	57,982	44.3	4.2	67,565	11.2	14.9	14.5
Baldwin	113,739	51.0	46,076	20.4	36.7	31.9	324.2	10,046	33,751	61,756	41.6	6.6	71,135	8.9	12.4	11.8
Barbour	11,197	45.4	5,332	11.0	61.0	11.6	38.1	6,156	20,074	34,990	62.5	2.6	38,866	25.5	37.5	35.8
Bibb	7,782	34.8	4,192	17.6	64.2	11.3	32.1	9,909	22,626	51,721	48.9	2.2	50,907	17.8	21.9	22.1
Blount	18,346	31.7	12,167	10.6	52.3	13.3	82.8	9,045	25,457	48,922	51.3	2.7	55,203	13.1	18.9	15.8
Bullock	5,403	53.5	2,388	15.3	66.5	10.3	14.7	10,229	20,783	33,866	58.6	2.8	33,124	30.8	38.7	37.0
Butler	7,675	39.5	3,909	18.5	60.1	16.0	28.8	9,541	23,415	44,850	55.3	2.6	42,268	20.6	30.8	29.8
Calhoun	53,369	47.0	27,122	11.3	49.4	18.9	178.7	10,300	26,238	50,128	49.8	2.6	50,259	14.5	16.7	16.7
Chambers	10,467	31.5	6,728	14.3	54.6	14.4	45.6	10,199	24,088	43,875	54.8	1.6	39,318	16.3	26.2	26.1
Cherokee	8,043	30.7	5,061	7.3	56.3	12.9	42.5	10,804	26,231	42,509	54.8	3.3	50,388	14.7	23.3	22.2
Chilton	16,161	36.4	9,646	7.7	61.5	13.6	68.9	8,791	25,894	52,141	48.4	2.3	52,693	13.9	21.0	19.7
Choctaw	8,352	66.3	2,498	30.7	53.4	13.5	14.6	11,225	23,292	36,634	62.0	0.9	41,649	20.4	28.9	27.9
Clarke	12,094	51.2	5,070	12.3	58.9	13.8	38.4	10,601	24,574	37,345	59.1	2.8	44,178	19.5	28.7	28.3
Clay	5,525	41.7	2,752	8.6	58.8	11.8	17.6	9,441	25,337	42,678	56.1	2.8	44,763	14.2	23.8	23.6
Cleburne	4,292	28.8	3,208	11.6	56.2	16.0	24.8	9,872	24,723	46,320	52.8	1.5	50,134	14.2	19.5	19.0
Coffee	24,782	47.3	12,737	10.3	41.8	21.7	92.2	9,468	27,912	56,799	44.9	3.1	54,203	13.9	20.6	19.3
Colbert	26,570	48.1	10,513	9.5	51.3	17.4	89.8	11,182	25,807	47,962	51.6	1.4	54,185	14.4	20.9	20.3
Conecuh	5,274	43.7	2,553	16.4	61.8	13.8	20.8	10,704	20,756	35,444	65.9	2.1	34,664	22.9	35.1	33.2
Coosa	4,337	40.7	1,540	17.0	58.9	11.6	9.8	11,482	25,083	43,571	59.4	1.7	46,509	17.4	28.8	26.5
Covington	14,134	38.1	7,484	5.5	51.9	15.6	60.0	9,736	25,303	42,566	55.9	2.2	43,544	17.1	22.6	21.6
Crenshaw	4,744	34.4	3,050	8.1	59.4	18.5	21.0	9,334	26,351	42,611	57.6	2.7	45,927	16.8	25.6	24.3
Cullman	32,039	38.2	17,453	11.1	50.0	15.4	126.6	9,997	24,770	48,388	51.2	2.1	51,844	12.5	17.4	17.0
Dale	23,607	48.0	10,792	7.1	45.6	18.2	61.7	9,645	24,473	45,644	54.1	2.2	48,493	15.5	26.1	25.2
Dallas	16,938	45.5	9,260	14.1	52.3	16.6	68.0	11,201	19,653	33,317	65.6	1.0	37,679	26.7	42.3	38.6
DeKalb	24,298	34.0	16,320	9.9	54.7	14.0	115.3	9,540	22,511	42,267	56.8	2.2	47,156	15.2	20.2	19.2
Elmore	37,748	46.5	18,202	21.2	44.4	25.8	118.0	8,932	29,585	62,324	39.3	4.4	62,524	11.5	16.6	16.1
Escambia	13,399	36.6	7,615	9.3	62.7	12.5	57.4	10,690	18,587	35,558	64.6	1.4	41,212	20.4	26.1	25.6
Etowah	42,016	41.1	21,923	8.2	48.1	17.7	145.5	9,566	25,094	44,934	54.6	2.1	47,872	15.6	22.9	22.9
Fayette	5,712	35.0	3,575	8.4	58.4	12.3	23.2	10,080	23,389	41,469	56.3	1.6	45,937	16.5	23.7	22.6
Franklin	13,729	43.8	7,371	4.6	60.3	15.0	62.2	10,144	21,503	41,174	57.5	1.3	40,448	17.2	22.9	21.7
Geneva	10,595	40.3	5,729	10.3	54.3	13.1	38.5	9,617	22,415	41,569	57.9	1.4	39,882	21.0	32.0	31.1
Greene	4,124	50.8	1,584	18.2	59.0	10.1	14.0	13,273	16,425	26,688	74.7	1.1	33,609	27.9	43.5	41.1
Hale	8,999	61.4	3,370	12.5	56.5	15.6	24.0	9,637	20,652	30,793	63.3	0.9	41,836	21.9	30.0	28.5
Henry	7,826	45.5	3,403	18.4	51.8	18.9	22.9	9,270	26,011	51,715	48.6	2.9	51,126	16.2	23.5	22.5
Houston	45,813	43.3	24,687	17.4	44.6	22.1	151.6	9,855	27,794	49,069	50.7	4.1	54,391	14.8	23.4	21.2
Jackson	25,537	49.5	10,509	11.4	55.6	16.2	80.8	10,316	23,844	42,578	56.1	2.0	46,606	15.3	23.4	20.2
Jefferson	383,780	58.3	162,114	17.4	35.8	34.1	1,140.1	11,059	33,343	55,088	45.7	6.6	57,802	14.4	20.1	20.2
Lamar	6,076	44.0	2,874	3.4	58.1	11.3	21.7	9,458	22,299	42,688	59.2	1.0	40,204	17.4	21.3	20.6
Lauderdale	43,275	46.7	22,333	11.7	46.3	25.1	133.7	10,670	28,540	48,428	51.1	3.0	52,293	13.9	19.9	17.5
Lawrence	15,531	47.2	7,152	6.6	58.9	15.8	47.0	10,071	24,779	47,125	51.8	2.8	48,924	15.4	21.9	20.8
Lee	66,214	40.2	56,398	12.6	31.9	36.4	230.1	10,106	28,804	52,930	48.0	4.9	58,963	17.9	16.8	14.9
Limestone	38,622	39.0	22,006	14.5	44.1	24.9	132.5	8,896	28,695	64,270	40.2	5.0	70,850	10.4	14.3	12.9
Lowndes	4,971	51.1	2,126	16.6	59.0	14.7	20.5	15,440	21,298	33,634	66.2	1.8	37,499	21.9	38.1	38.5
Macon	8,688	48.1	4,962	48.3	47.0	20.5	23.1	12,362	22,170	35,450	63.8	2.5	37,736	27.9	39.3	40.1
Madison	232,135	62.2	95,682	19.3	27.8	43.8	529.9	9,744	38,192	66,887	38.7	8.0	67,810	10.5	13.5	12.9
Marengo	10,270	54.4	4,224	11.8	52.8	17.1	38.1	10,301	27,975	33,029	60.7	2.6	43,198	18.3	30.2	29.2
Marion	10,862	36.6	5,835	8.1	53.4	13.3	44.6	9,718	22,486	40,978	59.9	2.7	44,333	16.8	23.6	21.5
Marshall	44,260	45.7	23,095	5.2	47.8	20.7	178.1	9,777	25,861	50,216	49.7	4.1	51,417	15.4	24.6	21.3
Mobile	206,515	50.0	97,366	18.5	46.2	24.4	595.8	9,920	26,778	49,625	50.3	3.4	50,871	17.6	27.3	24.9
Monroe	9,058	43.7	3,944	12.2	62.6	13.5	32.9	9,803	21,885	31,969	62.3	2.4	38,812	22.5	29.9	28.3
Montgomery	118,355	52.3	58,027	22.7	37.1	33.7	296.8	9,651	29,543	51,963	48.4	4.4	49,607	20.4	28.4	25.7
Morgan	52,255	43.7	26,920	11.6	47.7	21.3	209.8	10,628	28,474	52,923	47.8	3.9	55,688	14.4	20.1	16.6
Perry	4,346	48.7	2,489	24.1	57.7	17.8	14.4	11,175	13,833	23,875	79.3	0.0	33,712	30.7	44.2	43.8
Pickens	9,896	49.7	3,861	16.5	56.1	14.4	26.2	10,385	23,476	40,362	59.3	2.5	41,870	22.7	31.2	31.5
Pike	13,971	42.2	11,045	8.7	46.0	29.6	43.0	10,610	23,784	39,218	57.7	2.6	43,141	19.7	28.3	27.3
Randolph	7,492	33.0	4,625	12.0	53.5	17.1	36.0	9,793	24,744	45,141	54.5	1.8	46,679	17.5	27.3	26.2
Russell	23,987	41.4	14,801	15.7	44.4	17.5	100.4	9,474	24,300	42,208	56.4	2.9	40,821	20.3	31.7	28.3
St. Clair	35,055	39.2	19,083	11.3	49.1	18.1	123.4	9,130	27,941	62,531	39.6	3.2	61,973	10.5	14.6	13.3
Shelby	78,999	36.3	55,142	18.9	26.2	44.2	310.6	10,333	39,711	78,889	30.0	9.8	88,444	7.0	8.2	8.1
Sumter	6,398	51.5	3,943	7.3	49.3	18.4	19.4	11,815	16,977	26,150	70.9	0.7	32,275	29.2	42.0	41.6
Talladega	29,288	36.6	17,646	9.8	51.7	15.3	116.9	10,108	24,244	43,969	55.0	1.9	44,802	16.9	23.9	22.4
Tallapoosa	15,588	38.6	7,812	5.6	51.7	18.8	57.6	9,707	25,640	48,160	51.5	2.4	46,654	15.2	26.3	25.2
Tuscaloosa	91,592	43.7	61,040	9.0	39.4	31.1	306.4	10,478	27,609	54,283	46.2	4.2	56,610	14.4	17.4	17.7
Walker	30,034	47.3	13,196	8.8	53.3	13.4	105.4	10,281	25,330	45,833	52.9	1.9	46,519	16.4	23.0	21.4

1. All persons 3 years old and over enrolled in nursery school through college. 2. Persons 25 years old and over. 3. Elementary and secondary education expenditures. 4. Based on population estimated by the American Community Survey, 2016–2020. 5. CDC percent based on 2019 population estimate.

STATE County	Personal income, 2020										Earnings, 2020		
			Per capita[1]			Supplements to wages and salaries, employer contributions (mil dol)						Contributions for government social insurance (mil dol)	
	Total (mil dol)	Percent change 2019–2020	Dollars	Rank	Wages and salaries (mil dol)	Pension and insurance	Government social insurance	Proprietors' income (mil dol)	Dividends, interest, and rent (mil dol)	Personal transfer reecipts (mil dol)	Total (mil dol)	From employee and self-employed	From employer
	62	63	64	65	66	67	68	69	70	71	72	73	74
UNITED STATES	19,607,447	6.6	59,147	X	9,425,703	1,455,219	662,382	1,659,171	3,617,027	4,241,091	13,202,475	794,461	662,382
ALABAMA	228,749	5.9	45,524	X	104,935	17,029	7,733	14,211	38,738	61,243	143,909	9,878	7,733
Autauga	2,628	6.2	46,814	1,537	530	89	39	110	377	663	767	60	39
Baldwin	11,683	8.3	50,953	1,037	3,359	496	251	696	2,482	2,818	4,802	368	251
Barbour	931	6.1	37,850	2,702	346	64	27	53	132	356	491	38	27
Bibb	759	7.9	34,300	2,969	239	42	17	26	71	275	324	27	17
Blount	2,246	5.0	38,808	2,591	365	65	28	116	285	656	574	50	28
Bullock	319	11.7	31,944	3,058	117	23	9	26	42	123	176	11	9
Butler	780	5.0	39,988	2,457	265	50	21	54	100	287	390	30	21
Calhoun	4,561	6.0	40,195	2,434	2,000	415	150	189	715	1,536	2,754	198	150
Chambers	1,266	5.4	38,508	2,624	369	68	28	33	175	478	497	43	28
Cherokee	996	4.2	37,869	2,697	199	40	15	50	153	359	304	27	15
Chilton	1,722	6.5	38,778	2,597	410	72	31	101	205	545	614	50	31
Choctaw	524	6.7	42,231	2,163	205	40	15	26	58	204	285	22	15
Clarke	951	8.5	40,822	2,351	366	66	28	41	132	351	500	39	28
Clay	487	7.5	37,179	2,772	172	31	14	33	62	183	250	20	14
Cleburne	565	5.2	37,734	2,711	112	20	8	33	61	182	173	15	8
Coffee	2,409	5.7	45,262	1,759	665	117	51	153	391	682	986	73	51
Colbert	2,324	8.3	41,941	2,207	1,213	212	93	113	339	766	1,632	116	93
Conecuh	437	8.0	36,908	2,791	142	28	11	29	59	190	210	17	11
Coosa	369	6.3	34,683	2,954	60	12	5	11	50	138	87	10	5
Covington	1,401	5.1	37,930	2,693	496	99	38	73	178	534	705	56	38
Crenshaw	522	2.8	38,161	2,670	150	28	12	32	62	196	222	18	12
Cullman	3,605	4.6	42,659	2,107	1,295	210	98	234	497	1,062	1,837	139	98
Dale	1,964	5.3	40,111	2,444	1,375	333	117	66	314	649	1,891	108	117
Dallas	1,487	8.0	41,195	2,305	529	93	40	80	188	629	743	58	40
DeKalb	2,515	5.2	35,100	2,931	945	164	73	107	330	863	1,288	99	73
Elmore	3,884	6.8	47,270	1,480	804	144	61	206	618	1,006	1,214	99	61
Escambia	1,347	7.3	37,137	2,776	572	103	42	57	197	497	774	58	42
Etowah	4,080	5.6	39,852	2,472	1,433	236	111	245	518	1,515	2,024	161	111
Fayette	617	5.7	38,001	2,687	153	33	12	18	71	255	215	23	12
Franklin	1,177	7.0	37,362	2,755	446	85	34	65	154	381	630	48	34
Geneva	1,013	5.6	38,358	2,640	199	40	15	77	133	368	330	29	15
Greene	288	9.1	35,992	2,867	73	16	6	16	34	131	110	9	6
Hale	604	8.9	41,190	2,308	115	22	9	42	70	236	189	16	9
Henry	782	4.4	45,409	1,733	187	30	13	62	115	243	293	24	13
Houston	5,017	6.6	47,072	1,504	2,358	390	174	303	831	1,414	3,226	223	174
Jackson	2,068	5.3	40,089	2,445	644	115	50	110	318	679	919	74	50
Jefferson	38,288	2.7	58,424	501	22,537	3,280	1,601	3,714	7,872	8,115	31,132	2,011	1,601
Lamar	511	7.1	37,161	2,773	154	28	12	25	62	201	219	19	12
Lauderdale	3,803	7.2	40,729	2,368	1,221	209	92	184	682	1,155	1,706	135	92
Lawrence	1,252	7.6	38,098	2,678	219	42	17	28	146	423	306	34	17
Lee	7,085	6.2	42,468	2,134	2,800	500	206	321	1,431	1,522	3,826	252	206
Limestone	4,876	9.7	47,695	1,430	1,371	251	104	226	633	1,064	1,952	138	104
Lowndes	433	7.4	44,921	1,804	118	25	9	34	57	164	185	14	9
Macon	677	9.5	37,834	2,703	230	62	18	11	96	264	321	24	18
Madison	21,677	7.4	57,128	564	14,930	2,235	1,091	1,023	3,925	4,043	19,279	1,204	1,091
Marengo	822	7.8	43,854	1,968	335	60	25	51	106	295	471	35	25
Marion	1,079	8.2	36,330	2,844	417	76	33	59	148	384	585	42	33
Marshall	3,884	5.9	40,045	2,451	1,608	279	123	218	618	1,147	2,229	164	123
Mobile	17,674	6.8	42,823	2,090	9,378	1,451	691	1,346	2,645	5,348	12,866	873	691
Monroe	781	9.5	38,192	2,665	311	54	23	35	105	300	423	33	23
Montgomery	10,732	6.4	47,776	1,421	7,174	1,292	540	641	2,116	2,925	9,647	600	540
Morgan	5,356	6.9	44,679	1,854	2,674	443	199	281	829	1,465	3,596	246	199
Perry	315	9.3	36,217	2,855	77	16	7	31	32	149	130	10	7
Pickens	730	5.8	36,861	2,792	160	34	12	33	108	276	240	21	12
Pike	1,330	5.8	40,342	2,412	677	119	51	69	215	411	916	63	51
Randolph	807	5.1	35,208	2,925	187	36	15	45	113	313	283	25	15
Russell	2,127	8.3	36,526	2,823	610	105	46	53	293	773	814	65	46
St. Clair	3,927	6.7	43,279	2,028	899	143	66	172	486	1,052	1,280	103	66
Shelby	13,194	4.6	59,588	446	5,429	714	374	958	2,397	2,101	7,475	495	374
Sumter	432	9.0	35,310	2,920	133	27	10	34	50	179	204	15	10
Talladega	3,063	6.9	38,300	2,650	1,494	255	113	111	368	1,090	1,972	143	113
Tallapoosa	1,808	5.4	45,058	1,787	525	91	40	108	315	612	765	61	40
Tuscaloosa	9,035	6.5	42,868	2,084	4,849	844	355	458	1,630	2,330	6,505	424	355
Walker	2,784	4.2	44,095	1,931	780	133	59	141	465	963	1,112	93	59

1. Based on the resident population estimated as of July 1 of the year shown.

STATE County	Earnings, 2020 (cont.)									Social Security beneficiaries, December 2020		Supplemental Security Income recipients, 2020	Housing units, 2021	
	Percent by selected industries													
	Farm	Mining, quarrying, and extractions	Construction	Manufacturing	Information; professional, scientific, technical services	Retail trade	Finance, insurance, real estate, and leasing	Health care and social assistance	Government	Number	Rate[1]		Total	Percent change, 2010–2021
	75	76	77	78	79	80	81	82	83	84	85	86	87	88
UNITED STATES	0.8	1.1	6.2	8.9	14.7	5.7	10.0	11.2	15.8	63,281,222	191	7,958,723	142,153,010	1.0
ALABAMA	0.5	0.5	6.6	13.8	10.5	6.6	6.9	11.2	20.2	1,165,990	231	157,314	2,313,642	0.9
Autauga	2.1	0.8	7.2	15.4	D	8.4	5.3	10.0	17.9	12,300	208	1,481	24,773	1.5
Baldwin	0.8	0.3	9.6	5.7	6.4	11.8	8.6	12.8	13.7	60,305	252	3,434	128,519	2.9
Barbour	2.9	1.9	3.5	28.4	D	8.1	3.1	D	19.8	7,160	287	1,370	11,677	0.4
Bibb	0.4	D	23.4	11.9	D	5.9	1.9	9.0	23.5	5,440	242	851	9,077	0.7
Blount	2.3	D	11.1	12.5	5.9	7.6	3.9	D	20.3	13,915	236	1,217	24,752	0.4
Bullock	12.3	0.0	D	20.0	D	3.7	1.3	16.8	21.8	2,180	211	515	4,544	0.5
Butler	0.4	0.0	5.1	20.9	3.7	8.2	2.8	D	12.8	5,515	292	996	9,841	0.3
Calhoun	0.1	D	3.7	16.0	4.4	8.1	4.0	8.8	33.5	30,370	262	4,354	53,205	0.2
Chambers	2.3	0.1	4.4	27.1	D	7.5	2.2	D	22.1	9,800	284	1,375	16,416	0.2
Cherokee	4.4	0.1	4.6	14.9	3.1	11.4	3.2	D	23.7	8,140	326	775	14,616	0.6
Chilton	0.6	D	12.0	19.5	D	11.1	3.3	8.7	17.2	10,705	236	1,358	19,585	0.6
Choctaw	2.5	D	D	D	1.7	4.0	2.5	D	8.5	4,245	339	758	7,146	0.5
Clarke	0.9	D	2.6	26.4	D	9.7	5.5	11.2	19.4	7,235	318	1,286	11,701	0.3
Clay	0.2	0.0	4.3	47.4	1.4	3.4	3.4	D	19.4	4,045	285	467	7,054	0.2
Cleburne	3.6	D	22.7	13.5	D	9.5	2.2	2.7	25.0	3,995	265	488	6,833	0.4
Coffee	1.3	0.0	3.3	17.0	D	10.2	4.8	11.8	17.0	11,995	221	1,441	24,464	1.2
Colbert	0.2	0.6	9.5	25.8	2.0	8.2	4.1	8.0	21.1	15,560	271	1,822	27,888	0.7
Conecuh	4.6	D	2.7	13.7	1.7	5.0	1.2	D	19.0	3,880	343	674	6,426	0.6
Coosa	1.4	0.2	4.7	33.1	D	3.9	D	5.8	19.5	2,990	286	444	6,032	0.5
Covington	2.4	D	5.6	14.7	D	9.7	4.6	D	16.5	11,020	294	1,372	18,664	0.2
Crenshaw	5.0	0.0	5.5	25.0	D	3.8	3.2	D	15.6	4,015	307	571	6,546	0.4
Cullman	0.2	D	8.3	21.5	3.6	8.5	4.7	13.1	13.5	22,435	251	2,499	39,463	0.6
Dale	0.7	D	2.6	20.6	3.0	2.5	1.4	2.4	48.3	12,025	244	1,920	22,873	0.4
Dallas	4.2	D	5.8	25.0	3.0	7.4	4.0	13.3	18.9	11,030	293	3,674	18,917	0.2
DeKalb	-0.6	D	6.5	30.5	3.4	7.9	2.5	10.5	15.3	17,745	247	1,980	30,778	0.5
Elmore	0.2	D	9.3	13.4	4.5	11.3	4.5	12.5	21.6	19,930	223	2,203	37,079	0.6
Escambia	0.9	2.9	5.5	16.8	D	8.3	4.3	D	30.8	9,830	268	1,343	16,727	0.2
Etowah	0.0	D	5.3	14.9	3.5	9.2	4.9	D	15.4	28,955	281	4,245	47,418	0.2
Fayette	1.1	0.9	3.1	24.8	2.0	8.9	3.4	D	29.1	5,420	336	677	7,782	0.2
Franklin	-0.3	1.5	4.0	44.2	2.1	5.7	3.8	7.2	18.3	7,495	234	1,069	13,953	0.3
Geneva	9.2	D	6.1	9.4	D	8.8	5.0	4.3	22.6	7,640	286	1,141	12,517	0.4
Greene	10.2	0.0	2.7	29.1	D	6.6	1.9	D	25.7	2,550	334	689	4,246	0.8
Hale	13.7	D	8.2	18.1	D	4.9	3.5	5.7	23.9	4,565	309	976	7,465	0.7
Henry	8.7	0.1	7.7	11.5	D	4.0	2.5	6.1	13.4	5,350	306	586	9,160	1.0
Houston	0.7	D	5.1	7.4	4.8	10.7	4.9	17.5	18.5	26,710	249	3,950	49,746	0.8
Jackson	2.3	0.2	5.7	31.9	2.9	8.5	3.7	D	19.5	14,830	281	1,579	24,750	0.4
Jefferson	0.0	0.9	7.2	6.4	11.9	4.8	11.2	16.2	15.7	143,810	215	22,121	309,224	0.4
Lamar	1.0	D	3.0	37.0	1.7	4.9	3.2	6.3	14.4	4,315	315	587	7,088	0.2
Lauderdale	0.1	D	8.7	9.0	5.8	10.8	6.0	17.2	19.6	24,750	263	2,501	44,720	0.2
Lawrence	-2.8	D	9.5	3.6	D	10.0	8.0	D	25.4	9,005	272	1,237	15,291	0.4
Lee	0.5	D	7.4	10.8	5.4	7.0	3.9	6.1	33.1	27,700	156	3,166	77,656	3.0
Limestone	1.1	D	12.4	14.8	4.4	9.7	3.1	4.1	32.1	20,510	191	2,026	43,357	1.3
Lowndes	10.2	D	3.7	39.4	D	5.9	2.3	D	16.6	3,145	316	693	4,814	0.6
Macon	0.2	D	D	D	D	3.7	1.1	D	66.4	4,920	260	989	9,634	0.3
Madison	0.0	0.1	3.6	11.4	29.9	4.8	3.8	7.1	25.8	70,885	179	6,639	174,157	2.1
Marengo	2.6	0.4	7.8	20.6	2.7	6.4	4.6	5.9	18.5	5,985	315	1,347	9,814	0.3
Marion	0.9	D	2.5	34.8	1.6	7.1	4.5	D	17.4	7,800	267	968	14,137	0.3
Marshall	-0.5	D	6.7	30.5	4.4	9.3	3.6	6.3	17.3	22,820	232	2,810	41,489	0.5
Mobile	0.4	0.2	8.3	14.2	8.7	6.4	7.3	13.2	14.5	94,200	228	14,923	185,302	0.4
Monroe	2.8	D	6.3	25.1	D	5.6	3.0	D	17.2	5,995	305	873	10,162	0.3
Montgomery	0.2	0.2	4.9	9.7	8.8	5.6	6.0	12.5	30.9	48,010	211	9,497	105,718	0.3
Morgan	-0.1	0.3	10.0	33.5	5.5	6.1	4.6	6.6	12.5	29,110	235	3,265	53,545	0.4
Perry	15.5	0.0	2.4	15.8	D	3.7	2.3	9.0	20.3	2,675	320	923	3,946	0.3
Pickens	4.4	D	5.4	16.2	2.5	5.0	D	D	31.6	5,520	294	1,040	8,688	0.4
Pike	0.2	0.5	3.6	19.7	9.4	6.5	4.2	D	22.2	7,060	214	1,434	16,103	0.6
Randolph	4.2	1.1	6.8	16.4	D	8.9	3.4	D	21.0	6,570	299	826	12,438	0.3
Russell	0.7	0.2	5.2	25.0	3.1	8.5	6.0	13.1	20.8	13,535	230	1,928	27,493	0.7
St. Clair	0.3	D	12.2	18.9	5.1	9.4	4.5	8.4	14.7	20,935	226	1,895	38,505	1.3
Shelby	0.1	1.0	8.4	5.6	10.8	7.7	18.3	8.5	7.7	41,550	183	2,494	90,911	1.7
Sumter	11.6	0.0	2.5	10.1	D	3.7	2.5	D	34.2	3,440	283	985	6,317	0.5
Talladega	0.3	D	6.2	40.0	2.3	4.6	2.4	D	14.8	21,860	268	3,593	38,226	0.6
Tallapoosa	0.7	D	6.2	16.0	5.5	8.5	3.9	16.4	15.7	12,730	310	1,467	22,900	0.8
Tuscaloosa	0.0	2.7	6.2	20.4	6.2	6.2	5.6	7.3	27.1	40,745	179	5,685	103,070	1.2
Walker	0.3	2.2	5.9	12.3	4.0	13.1	5.2	19.2	15.9	19,670	303	2,964	30,167	0.5

1. Per 1,000 resident population estimated as of July 1 of the year shown.

STATE County	Housing units, 2016–2020								Civilian labor force, 2021				Civilian employment[6], 2016–2020		
	Occupied units										Unemployment			Percent	
		Owner-occupied				Renter-occupied									
				Median owner cost as a percent of income											
	Total	Percent	Median value[1]	With a mortgage	Without a mortgage[2]	Median rent[3]	Median rent as a percent of income[2]	Substandard units[4] (percent)	Total	Percent change, 2020–2021	Total	Rate[5]	Total	Management, business, science, and arts	Construction, production, and maintenance occupations
	89	90	91	92	93	94	95	96	97	98	99	100	101	102	103
UNITED STATES	122,354,219	64.4	229,800	21.1	11.1	1,096	29.6	3.7	161,758,337	0.3	8,658,650	5.4	155,888,980	39.5	21.8
ALABAMA	1,888,504	69.2	149,600	19.0	10.0	811	28.8	2.0	2,246,993	-0.9	77,272	3.4	2,119,986	35.7	26.7
Autauga	21,559	74.6	161,200	19.1	10.3	1,011	27.3	2.1	26,341	-0.2	742	2.8	24,580	39.0	24.0
Baldwin	84,047	77.0	211,600	19.9	10.0	1,032	28.2	1.7	99,427	0.5	2,946	3.0	98,768	36.8	22.3
Barbour	9,322	62.0	86,500	18.2	11.1	587	29.3	3.9	8,197	-5.6	469	5.7	8,707	27.4	35.3
Bibb	7,259	74.8	96,400	17.9	10.0	693	32.3	1.8	8,560	-1.7	298	3.5	8,303	22.5	38.3
Blount	21,205	76.1	135,300	19.1	10.0	666	28.4	2.4	25,127	0.0	598	2.4	22,836	29.4	37.5
Bullock	3,429	73.8	74,800	15.5	12.7	559	35.4	1.0	4,606	-5.6	184	4.0	4,007	17.3	49.9
Butler	6,649	73.3	98,100	21.5	10.0	627	29.0	1.2	8,796	-4.8	468	5.3	7,971	27.5	36.4
Calhoun	44,572	70.4	121,600	18.9	10.0	720	26.0	1.5	46,118	-1.9	1,906	4.1	47,905	30.4	30.5
Chambers	13,582	67.2	103,800	20.5	11.2	734	22.3	7.7	15,752	-2.1	579	3.7	14,724	24.3	40.3
Cherokee	10,836	78.2	138,500	19.4	12.0	626	25.7	1.6	11,808	1.2	296	2.5	10,310	31.8	38.0
Chilton	17,140	75.1	104,500	19.0	10.0	683	25.5	3.1	19,811	-0.6	565	2.9	17,752	22.1	41.6
Choctaw	5,330	81.6	75,900	17.9	11.6	560	28.0	2.6	4,591	-2.3	200	4.4	4,427	25.3	35.5
Clarke	9,323	72.5	106,600	19.0	11.5	599	29.1	2.7	7,726	-2.2	462	6.0	8,166	26.7	38.6
Clay	5,153	76.6	116,100	18.7	10.0	482	25.2	1.9	6,095	-0.7	165	2.7	5,389	26.3	44.0
Cleburne	5,835	77.4	118,700	19.4	10.6	659	26.5	2.7	5,890	0.6	151	2.6	5,814	28.6	37.6
Coffee	19,951	67.8	153,700	18.4	10.0	802	24.8	2.5	21,853	-0.7	610	2.8	21,764	33.4	31.5
Colbert	21,797	71.6	125,400	19.3	10.0	712	28.8	0.7	23,460	-1.8	936	4.0	23,563	30.6	33.6
Conecuh	4,585	74.7	83,900	17.4	10.2	545	26.7	0.4	4,376	-4.5	212	4.8	3,972	19.4	44.2
Coosa	4,016	81.1	89,200	19.3	10.8	611	27.3	4.0	4,343	-1.9	134	3.1	4,164	22.8	34.7
Covington	14,995	74.3	99,600	18.2	10.0	611	29.1	3.1	15,215	-0.8	459	3.0	14,880	31.9	34.2
Crenshaw	5,011	76.7	84,400	18.2	11.2	540	21.5	1.7	6,133	-3.7	202	3.3	5,615	25.1	34.1
Cullman	31,733	74.8	135,200	19.0	10.4	721	26.9	2.3	38,858	0.0	915	2.4	35,401	27.5	34.2
Dale	19,405	58.6	113,800	18.2	10.0	753	27.0	1.1	20,915	-0.1	658	3.1	17,282	29.6	32.9
Dallas	15,409	56.7	84,100	19.1	12.1	674	35.0	2.0	13,959	-5.9	1,035	7.4	13,944	26.4	38.2
DeKalb	26,365	73.1	113,600	18.7	10.6	630	27.7	3.1	31,097	-0.6	789	2.5	30,188	25.7	40.6
Elmore	29,794	75.2	171,100	18.4	10.0	900	31.7	1.7	37,582	-0.2	1,022	2.7	34,936	37.5	23.8
Escambia	12,931	66.5	100,800	19.2	10.8	606	28.7	1.5	14,000	-4.1	575	4.1	12,543	25.0	29.0
Etowah	38,765	73.0	124,400	18.7	10.5	676	28.2	1.5	39,262	-5.2	1,604	4.1	43,002	28.1	31.2
Fayette	6,805	75.2	92,400	19.7	10.0	540	27.5	1.3	6,653	-0.2	204	3.1	6,423	25.1	42.5
Franklin	11,017	71.1	103,000	17.5	10.6	561	22.1	3.1	14,304	-1.8	363	2.5	13,019	25.1	43.1
Geneva	10,572	75.2	108,400	18.7	10.0	658	28.3	1.3	10,993	-0.3	309	2.8	10,676	28.9	35.8
Greene	3,178	68.6	76,200	30.5	15.0	559	29.0	2.7	2,897	-6.4	199	6.9	2,401	19.2	43.3
Hale	5,490	75.7	91,500	18.4	13.4	612	37.0	4.1	5,888	-4.5	335	5.7	5,262	36.2	24.7
Henry	6,556	83.5	119,000	18.5	10.0	624	31.5	0.8	6,881	-0.4	219	3.2	6,953	32.1	29.4
Houston	39,784	65.9	141,800	19.0	10.0	769	27.2	1.5	46,880	-0.7	1,594	3.4	44,583	32.9	24.6
Jackson	20,367	77.2	107,900	19.4	10.0	574	27.9	2.6	22,975	-0.5	659	2.9	19,746	33.2	37.3
Jefferson	263,801	63.2	165,000	19.4	10.0	934	29.7	1.9	317,359	-0.9	11,577	3.6	302,092	40.3	20.4
Lamar	5,631	72.8	95,400	15.2	10.7	449	31.0	2.1	5,691	-1.7	170	3.0	5,269	29.5	41.0
Lauderdale	38,513	68.1	149,500	19.0	10.0	669	26.8	1.2	42,080	-1.3	1,335	3.2	41,204	30.5	26.6
Lawrence	12,551	78.4	113,800	18.6	10.0	581	23.7	1.3	14,378	-1.0	422	2.9	13,004	30.2	37.0
Lee	60,731	63.4	173,700	19.0	10.0	856	31.6	3.7	76,658	0.2	2,180	2.8	75,428	43.7	20.3
Limestone	32,725	76.8	167,800	17.6	10.0	723	24.0	2.2	46,572	1.5	1,142	2.5	42,284	34.7	29.4
Lowndes	4,213	75.1	66,500	26.6	14.8	687	41.3	1.7	3,578	-3.9	330	9.2	3,578	22.4	42.3
Macon	7,592	64.8	82,400	19.5	13.3	621	30.3	1.6	7,948	-2.9	477	6.0	7,115	31.9	25.1
Madison	151,628	67.7	190,200	17.6	10.0	887	27.4	1.5	192,204	1.4	5,104	2.7	182,034	48.8	17.5
Marengo	7,499	69.8	82,200	18.1	12.5	565	31.4	0.9	7,709	-2.0	325	4.2	7,067	30.7	32.9
Marion	11,780	75.9	87,700	20.0	11.7	530	27.7	3.5	13,320	0.2	379	2.8	11,851	28.6	37.2
Marshall	35,115	72.9	141,300	19.2	10.0	650	27.5	2.2	44,714	-0.2	1,070	2.4	39,832	32.9	32.2
Mobile	157,557	64.1	138,400	20.0	10.0	869	31.7	2.0	191,711	-1.7	9,039	4.7	175,496	33.9	26.2
Monroe	8,050	67.9	100,900	21.0	11.2	601	28.8	0.6	7,356	-3.5	414	5.6	6,759	25.8	36.0
Montgomery	89,511	57.6	130,000	18.9	10.0	908	30.3	2.3	106,663	-1.5	5,177	4.9	99,636	37.8	21.8
Morgan	46,388	72.2	143,900	18.0	10.0	684	27.7	2.5	59,256	-0.8	1,540	2.6	51,704	30.7	31.8
Perry	3,140	78.3	80,100	37.8	15.4	376	34.4	2.0	3,215	-6.9	267	8.3	2,381	23.9	32.2
Pickens	7,731	75.9	100,000	19.6	10.8	468	30.2	1.0	7,501	-2.4	307	4.1	6,854	29.9	37.6
Pike	11,700	63.5	131,600	18.9	10.7	727	38.3	0.8	16,017	1.1	513	3.2	14,045	33.6	26.0
Randolph	8,655	79.2	119,500	20.8	10.0	640	27.0	3.7	9,408	-1.7	258	2.7	8,795	27.7	41.0
Russell	23,694	60.5	126,300	21.5	11.6	798	31.7	2.2	23,281	-2.3	715	3.1	23,074	29.0	29.3
St. Clair	32,765	80.4	165,900	19.2	10.0	880	25.8	2.0	41,195	-0.5	1,087	2.6	39,664	33.4	30.8
Shelby	80,756	80.4	220,700	18.8	10.0	1,078	26.2	1.2	118,212	0.3	2,529	2.1	107,936	46.8	16.3
Sumter	5,355	62.9	67,300	22.1	13.1	677	40.0	1.5	4,520	-5.4	203	4.5	4,585	21.5	27.0
Talladega	31,741	71.5	112,300	19.1	10.6	666	29.2	2.7	35,695	-2.0	1,480	4.1	32,068	26.9	36.9
Tallapoosa	16,359	74.9	108,300	18.1	10.0	645	28.4	3.6	17,910	-1.6	724	4.0	15,465	25.7	35.7
Tuscaloosa	74,713	62.9	179,000	19.7	10.0	861	30.5	1.7	101,104	-2.6	3,662	3.6	97,448	36.1	26.7
Walker	25,440	77.9	109,600	20.1	10.0	640	26.1	2.2	25,085	-0.5	911	3.6	24,972	28.5	33.0

1. Specified owner-occupied units. 2. A value of 10.0 represents 10 percent or less; a value of 50.0 represents 50 percent or more. 3. Specified renter-occupied units. 4. Overcrowded or lacking complete plumbing facilities. 5. Percent of civilian labor force. 6. Civilian employed persons 16 years old and over.

STATE County	Private nonfarm establishments, employment and payroll, 2020									Agriculture, 2017			
		Employment						Annual payroll		Farms			Farm producers whose primary occupation is farming (percent)
											Percent with:		
	Number of establish-ments	Total	Health care and social assistance	Manufac-turing	Retail trade	Finance and insurance	Professional, scientific, and technical services	Total (mil dol)	Average per employee (dollars)	Number	Fewer than 50 acres	1000 acres or more	
	104	105	106	107	108	109	110	111	112	113	114	115	116
UNITED STATES	8,000,178	134,163,349	21,216,569	11,999,822	15,808,465	6,682,343	9,554,479	7,564,810	56,385	2,042,220	41.9	8.5	41.1
ALABAMA	100,955	1,777,495	271,154	264,687	227,484	69,976	113,667	81,317	45,748	40,592	40.1	4.2	37.4
Autauga	879	11,265	1,635	949	2,434	367	297	386	34,246	371	31.5	6.7	37.1
Baldwin	5,726	66,943	8,578	4,508	13,655	1,695	2,140	2,474	36,951	842	53.8	4.5	45.0
Barbour	431	6,972	576	2,688	762	145	85	246	35,317	498	20.3	5.2	41.4
Bibb	282	4,045	703	605	479	63	70	169	41,885	205	35.6	5.9	32.3
Blount	699	6,764	1,026	1,071	1,164	215	239	244	36,132	1,146	40.8	1.4	43.1
Bullock	110	2,036	325	720	243	43	26	74	36,197	255	18.4	9.4	33.6
Butler	419	6,229	849	1,652	886	146	51	209	33,559	420	30.0	2.4	37.7
Calhoun	2,234	35,684	6,081	6,923	6,238	918	931	1,278	35,819	643	43.4	1.4	34.5
Chambers	539	7,354	817	2,249	1,076	136	203	262	35,616	331	25.4	11.5	28.5
Cherokee	370	4,343	644	950	773	123	67	136	31,399	530	40.4	4.7	38.0
Chilton	768	7,757	856	1,896	1,511	207	120	298	38,423	463	41.9	1.3	42.3
Choctaw	241	2,889	268	1,092	339	73	43	160	55,334	188	30.9	7.4	35.1
Clarke	582	6,610	1,132	1,303	1,445	327	82	242	36,664	320	41.3	5.0	24.4
Clay	190	3,697	525	2,241	282	98	45	132	35,621	381	24.7	2.4	46.5
Cleburne	176	1,604	57	345	331	59	7	73	45,681	319	31.0	0.9	44.7
Coffee	950	14,276	1,991	3,742	2,574	466	732	511	35,773	788	31.5	4.3	41.8
Colbert	1,235	23,985	3,131	6,455	2,741	688	327	968	40,340	591	39.9	8.5	43.1
Conecuh	203	2,594	501	415	345	42	21	93	35,726	344	27.9	6.7	40.7
Coosa	101	1,090	138	378	94	11	31	41	37,974	215	17.2	2.8	32.7
Covington	816	9,727	1,653	1,722	1,697	340	307	358	36,792	907	34.5	3.0	34.4
Crenshaw	220	3,247	385	1,097	245	95	36	118	36,214	543	28.2	4.1	39.7
Cullman	1,747	26,082	4,151	5,219	4,100	800	469	1,032	39,584	1,781	46.7	0.2	40.4
Dale	702	10,759	1,326	435	1,307	383	676	547	50,844	469	27.7	6.6	38.1
Dallas	675	9,312	1,454	2,803	1,415	285	205	352	37,847	528	28.0	16.7	33.8
DeKalb	1,119	18,309	2,671	6,966	2,285	436	332	677	36,983	1,939	44.8	1.5	43.2
Elmore	1,227	14,667	2,180	2,533	2,864	386	428	537	36,608	538	47.2	4.5	33.8
Escambia	750	9,744	1,206	1,978	1,730	332	192	365	37,470	437	46.7	8.0	37.2
Etowah	1,911	29,096	7,137	4,695	4,821	1,012	672	1,007	34,596	817	55.2	0.5	38.2
Fayette	263	3,079	691	1,039	517	73	49	111	35,960	324	28.4	3.4	37.2
Franklin	524	11,329	1,023	6,599	956	409	139	423	37,324	729	26.3	2.6	41.1
Geneva	410	3,761	592	560	692	142	100	126	33,561	820	33.7	4.9	42.5
Greene	101	1,434	110	708	160	34	7	53	37,143	325	24.9	16.9	47.6
Hale	177	1,931	434	488	284	71	29	82	42,213	393	27.7	9.4	37.6
Henry	291	3,323	175	290	309	95	171	249	74,834	455	25.5	9.7	36.9
Houston	2,697	44,738	9,622	4,557	7,385	1,227	1,111	1,785	39,901	698	42.8	5.0	34.4
Jackson	823	12,308	1,550	4,965	1,798	349	201	469	38,079	1,355	44.8	2.4	31.8
Jefferson	16,522	341,139	69,660	23,795	37,477	21,570	17,194	18,439	54,053	387	63.3	1.0	29.1
Lamar	244	3,324	319	1,844	285	120	46	128	38,646	269	29.0	2.6	24.7
Lauderdale	1,943	25,711	5,177	3,001	5,028	1,029	683	856	33,286	1,309	48.1	3.4	33.7
Lawrence	409	3,444	628	230	762	110	217	117	34,076	1,252	46.5	2.4	39.1
Lee	2,979	47,269	6,756	7,204	7,274	1,074	1,810	1,704	36,055	314	43.9	5.7	35.5
Limestone	1,478	19,861	2,395	5,017	2,771	413	979	879	44,278	1,156	52.2	3.5	35.5
Lowndes	109	1,617	135	659	198	25	15	79	48,573	512	35.0	9.2	38.1
Macon	203	4,821	1,606	344	449	34	33	217	44,930	373	26.5	7.5	34.0
Madison	8,658	180,152	27,941	17,197	21,102	3,780	47,030	10,534	58,475	1,021	56.4	4.4	36.3
Marengo	439	6,148	1,024	1,530	812	210	79	265	43,131	471	29.9	5.5	31.5
Marion	534	8,671	1,246	3,140	1,009	409	77	307	35,433	582	30.6	0.9	33.4
Marshall	1,864	35,990	4,256	14,241	4,840	839	643	1,276	35,446	1,444	51.7	0.6	38.7
Mobile	8,771	153,378	21,790	15,208	20,294	5,151	9,643	7,116	46,397	653	60.9	3.1	39.3
Monroe	394	5,297	739	1,300	779	149	38	234	44,126	477	41.5	7.1	34.0
Montgomery	5,493	104,870	18,122	12,672	11,892	4,139	5,946	4,605	43,911	575	27.0	9.7	41.3
Morgan	2,605	46,641	6,209	13,500	5,341	1,318	2,284	2,263	48,514	1,164	51.6	1.1	32.7
Perry	115	1,578	136	455	163	68	17	51	32,405	349	32.1	14.3	41.3
Pickens	250	2,629	536	634	388	138	79	98	37,145	377	31.0	6.9	37.5
Pike	642	12,389	1,098	2,318	1,565	379	1,101	496	40,005	594	26.4	5.2	35.5
Randolph	335	3,985	575	1,260	741	142	35	128	32,083	597	33.3	3.2	38.0
Russell	820	11,292	1,548	2,938	1,966	364	198	421	37,297	296	31.1	10.1	29.6
St. Clair	1,363	18,224	2,187	3,677	3,004	489	646	670	36,774	490	42.0	1.0	34.4
Shelby	5,307	86,433	8,128	5,428	10,587	9,963	5,439	4,737	54,809	447	50.6	1.8	26.3
Sumter	193	2,713	359	191	258	63	16	115	42,255	367	20.2	12.5	39.3
Talladega	1,254	25,351	2,830	9,848	2,839	541	489	1,110	43,796	566	42.2	1.1	40.2
Tallapoosa	767	10,256	1,945	2,149	1,525	279	214	362	35,299	347	25.9	3.2	33.9
Tuscaloosa	4,079	82,006	12,698	18,397	9,906	1,741	2,048	3,643	44,425	557	43.8	3.1	31.9
Walker	1,228	14,351	3,125	2,040	3,039	465	450	556	38,709	501	49.9	2.0	43.2

STATE County	Agriculture, 2017 (cont.) — Land in farms — Acreage (1,000)	Land in farms — Percent change, 2012–2017	Land in farms — Acres — Average size of farm	Land in farms — Acres — Total irrigated (1,000)	Land in farms — Acres — Total cropland (1,000)	Value of land and buildings (dollars) — Average per farm	Value of land and buildings (dollars) — Average per acre	Value of machinery and equipment, average per farm (dollars)	Value of products sold: — Total (mil dol)	Value of products sold: — Average per farm (acres)	Value of products sold: — Percent from: — Crops	Value of products sold: — Percent from: — Livestock and poultry products	Organic farms (number)	Farms with internet access (percent)	Government payments — Total ($1,000)	Government payments — Percent of farms
	117	118	119	120	121	122	123	124	125	126	127	128	129	130	131	132
UNITED STATES	900,218	-1.6	441	58,013.9	396,433.8	1,311,808	2,976	133,363	388,522.7	190,245	49.8	50.2	20,806	75.4	8,943,574	31.5
ALABAMA	8,581	-3.6	211	142.0	2,818.8	630,736	2,984	88,528	5,980.6	147,334	20.3	79.7	57	72.6	134,654	37.3
Autauga	113	1.6	305	1.4	36.9	672,902	2,205	96,682	21.5	57,844	58.4	41.6	NA	76.8	1,069	37.5
Baldwin	175	-9.1	208	7.4	110.4	1,208,662	5,822	136,496	120.4	142,973	84.4	15.6	NA	78.1	6,316	27.3
Barbour	153	-25.2	307	3.6	37.3	684,780	2,233	87,026	105.6	211,978	11.5	88.5	2	60.6	3,003	62.9
Bibb	56	-0.6	273	0.1	15.8	766,325	2,807	68,656	4.2	20,483	53.5	46.5	NA	73.2	395	26.3
Blount	148	1.4	129	0.9	43.8	465,684	3,602	87,452	242.9	211,915	5.5	94.5	3	74.6	3,166	32.3
Bullock	115	-30.0	452	0.1	20.0	968,327	2,142	83,263	D	D	D	D	NA	69.0	1,277	47.1
Butler	84	-4.5	201	0.6	17.7	492,971	2,454	83,737	132.0	314,355	3.5	96.5	NA	73.8	1,160	40.2
Calhoun	89	9.5	138	1.1	28.5	587,727	4,246	74,079	86.8	135,003	15.0	85.0	NA	77.1	913	28.8
Chambers	129	33.5	389	0.2	12.5	976,835	2,513	61,548	9.1	27,369	18.6	81.4	NA	71.9	822	38.4
Cherokee	121	-2.3	229	0.8	72.8	725,287	3,167	125,506	152.1	286,940	25.9	74.1	1	73.2	2,145	38.1
Chilton	76	-16.5	165	0.9	22.0	581,653	3,529	76,741	14.5	31,298	46.2	53.8	NA	73.9	761	19.7
Choctaw	82	20.4	439	0.0	6.6	899,167	2,050	68,483	8.3	43,941	9.6	90.4	NA	66.5	275	41.0
Clarke	65	36.0	202	0.0	11.2	460,092	2,279	61,402	2.9	8,994	42.7	57.3	NA	56.6	264	27.5
Clay	71	-8.5	187	0.0	12.2	525,095	2,807	85,885	81.3	213,462	1.2	98.8	NA	71.7	1,328	42.5
Cleburne	48	-3.6	152	0.4	8.9	524,930	3,460	71,623	117.5	368,197	2.6	97.4	7	76.8	366	21.0
Coffee	177	-12.4	225	4.0	64.3	592,097	2,633	89,163	199.5	253,216	8.6	91.4	4	70.9	5,525	56.9
Colbert	150	-1.6	254	D	85.8	677,872	2,665	105,238	60.2	101,846	62.9	37.1	NA	73.8	3,500	39.6
Conecuh	104	11.0	302	0.1	26.7	647,835	2,142	75,294	21.0	61,125	41.5	58.5	NA	56.7	693	44.2
Coosa	46	27.7	214	0.0	5.2	489,452	2,292	62,564	1.7	7,940	17.6	82.4	NA	72.6	270	27.9
Covington	161	-22.6	178	1.3	54.3	477,739	2,684	79,394	126.5	139,485	16.6	83.4	6	71.6	4,147	47.0
Crenshaw	114	-12.0	211	0.0	23.6	525,225	2,494	97,983	164.9	303,591	2.3	97.7	NA	67.6	1,603	49.7
Cullman	209	7.7	117	1.9	60.9	466,918	3,977	77,508	470.7	264,303	4.0	96.0	NA	75.5	3,139	31.3
Dale	137	5.6	292	2.4	52.5	879,051	3,009	103,692	172.0	366,825	9.9	90.1	NA	77.2	2,946	47.3
Dallas	263	3.1	498	6.4	76.7	934,297	1,875	124,270	64.0	121,212	43.6	56.4	NA	69.3	3,427	51.1
DeKalb	247	7.9	128	1.1	91.5	502,086	3,935	88,244	573.3	295,658	4.4	95.6	2	75.8	4,176	34.6
Elmore	94	3.7	174	2.6	34.9	521,814	2,996	75,563	27.6	51,290	63.0	37.0	3	74.3	855	24.7
Escambia	106	-1.5	242	3.1	55.3	594,861	2,458	92,069	31.0	70,886	88.5	11.5	NA	72.5	3,842	40.7
Etowah	89	3.7	109	0.6	24.8	419,478	3,836	78,981	93.4	114,356	6.7	93.3	NA	73.8	804	21.5
Fayette	68	-15.9	211	0.2	21.0	464,587	2,206	79,352	24.6	75,957	31.9	68.1	NA	75.9	660	48.1
Franklin	130	-13.9	178	D	32.4	435,546	2,451	84,184	139.4	191,202	4.5	95.5	NA	65.8	1,531	40.5
Geneva	183	-16.2	224	5.5	81.7	553,557	2,476	99,070	137.6	167,778	25.0	75.0	1	71.8	4,527	51.7
Greene	153	27.4	472	0.1	20.4	920,549	1,951	95,162	25.9	79,828	4.5	95.5	NA	67.7	1,127	49.2
Hale	158	-1.7	402	1.1	20.7	907,427	2,260	101,638	63.5	161,539	6.6	93.4	2	66.7	1,946	51.1
Henry	174	2.5	382	12.8	74.2	986,630	2,580	147,514	122.9	270,119	22.9	77.1	NA	76.3	3,937	60.2
Houston	149	-25.0	213	10.0	85.9	751,866	3,533	102,777	69.7	99,887	68.1	31.9	NA	71.8	7,557	50.4
Jackson	219	-5.7	161	1.4	95.5	490,606	3,042	86,387	153.5	113,276	19.9	80.1	3	72.5	3,198	36.0
Jefferson	38	-2.8	98	0.2	7.0	432,444	4,413	53,634	4.9	12,770	27.6	72.4	NA	80.1	220	11.1
Lamar	74	-10.5	274	0.3	12.0	508,777	1,859	63,797	10.4	38,509	30.5	69.5	NA	68.4	394	32.7
Lauderdale	211	-0.5	161	0.9	109.0	583,196	3,626	85,411	72.3	55,264	55.7	44.3	NA	69.4	3,934	41.5
Lawrence	214	-12.3	171	6.4	120.8	648,125	3,796	112,499	212.9	170,043	27.7	72.3	NA	70.0	4,147	39.1
Lee	68	14.8	216	0.2	9.0	895,686	4,150	95,632	D	D	D	D	4	79.9	432	26.8
Limestone	225	-8.9	194	10.4	151.1	803,618	4,132	109,978	131.4	113,669	59.8	40.2	NA	75.3	3,378	32.4
Lowndes	203	-6.8	396	6.2	46.5	752,311	1,898	105,508	80.9	157,920	15.7	84.3	NA	60.4	2,573	53.3
Macon	120	16.3	322	2.6	40.8	756,523	2,347	98,817	19.6	52,458	84.2	15.8	NA	66.8	1,238	37.0
Madison	185	-11.7	181	10.7	131.5	961,058	5,306	110,872	70.4	68,913	91.8	8.2	2	77.7	2,670	29.3
Marengo	147	-10.9	313	0.8	28.0	627,909	2,007	79,112	15.9	33,735	32.9	67.1	NA	68.4	1,680	58.2
Marion	83	-27.4	142	D	20.3	331,932	2,339	62,866	105.3	181,003	3.1	96.9	NA	69.9	881	45.2
Marshall	145	-11.0	101	0.3	44.9	445,314	4,431	86,970	283.6	196,403	2.9	97.1	3	78.3	1,729	24.9
Mobile	95	6.9	145	3.1	37.7	688,889	4,738	83,715	90.6	138,712	88.8	11.2	NA	77.0	1,537	15.8
Monroe	141	0.6	297	1.3	42.1	710,642	2,396	90,050	35.4	74,298	59.3	40.7	NA	58.5	2,156	51.4
Montgomery	233	5.9	405	0.1	57.0	1,078,207	2,660	81,751	46.9	81,496	30.8	69.2	NA	73.0	2,808	38.1
Morgan	135	-11.6	116	0.4	45.9	510,162	4,403	65,751	99.7	85,684	10.8	89.2	2	78.4	1,622	26.1
Perry	163	3.8	468	3.0	41.2	1,032,601	2,208	96,333	37.2	106,536	29.9	70.1	1	60.2	1,415	57.3
Pickens	105	2.1	278	2.4	27.1	702,898	2,528	96,970	88.8	235,520	8.9	91.1	NA	68.2	1,346	41.6
Pike	166	-1.0	279	2.9	40.6	730,910	2,620	87,152	138.8	233,722	7.2	92.8	NA	70.9	3,305	54.4
Randolph	120	5.6	202	0.2	19.7	636,356	3,157	97,755	152.7	255,797	1.8	98.2	3	77.2	1,680	36.2
Russell	99	-15.9	333	3.7	31.2	847,048	2,541	90,179	26.1	88,118	47.3	52.7	NA	66.9	2,666	44.9
St. Clair	59	-12.6	120	0.8	14.4	514,787	4,277	77,055	58.3	118,880	13.3	86.7	NA	83.1	565	21.6
Shelby	67	15.0	150	2.0	26.2	597,813	3,976	69,175	16.5	37,007	84.0	16.0	6	77.0	399	17.7
Sumter	180	-24.8	491	1.1	31.1	919,441	1,872	81,695	21.9	59,594	22.1	77.9	NA	75.7	1,987	55.0
Talladega	80	-20.4	140	4.4	30.0	464,811	3,309	89,072	40.4	71,350	29.0	71.0	NA	75.4	1,080	38.0
Tallapoosa	66	8.0	190	D	8.5	541,614	2,855	60,191	16.5	47,640	12.1	87.9	NA	75.5	494	23.6
Tuscaloosa	95	10.4	170	0.4	23.5	573,374	3,364	62,210	38.6	69,284	17.9	82.1	2	77.2	919	30.9
Walker	65	19.2	130	0.1	16.0	391,595	3,019	87,298	55.1	109,928	7.9	92.1	NA	67.5	431	15.8

STATE County	Water use, 2015		Wholesale Trade[1], 2017				Retail Trade[2], 2017				Real estate and rental and leasing,[2] 2017			
	Public supply water withdrawn (mil gal/ day)	Public supply gallons withdrawn per person per day	Number of establish-ments	Number of employees	Sales (mil dol)	Average payroll (mil dol)	Number of establish-ments	Number of employees	Sales (mil dol)	Average payroll (mil dol)	Number of establish-ments	Number of employees	Sales (mil dol)	Average payroll (mil dol)
	133	134	135	136	137	138	139	140	141	142	143	144	145	146
UNITED STATES	38,595.83	120.1	352,065	5,156,359	5,700,966.9	337,908.8	1,064,087	15,938,821	4,949,601.5	441,795.6	410,820	2,194,885	674,147.0	113,409.6
ALABAMA	761.53	156.7	4,410	63,468	66,906.3	3,461.1	17,958	230,069	63,740.4	5,819.1	4,362	22,778	5,785.1	968.2
Autauga	3.64	65.8	24	229	206.2	13.7	170	2,701	666.3	60.1	44	107	22.4	4.0
Baldwin	23.67	116.2	194	2,404	1,447.4	124.6	989	13,735	3,703.4	340.2	365	1,842	369.7	65.2
Barbour	3.23	121.9	12	123	65.1	3.0	91	898	205.8	19.4	D	D	D	D
Bibb	5.18	229.4	13	91	148.3	4.4	48	514	119.8	12.2	9	15	2.0	0.3
Blount	56.86	985.9	36	379	173.4	15.8	131	1,227	340.9	30.5	9	146	11.7	2.0
Bullock	2.11	197.3	6	21	38.8	0.8	26	236	58.7	4.5	3	9	0.5	0.1
Butler	2.28	113.1	13	70	60.3	3.2	100	945	220.6	21.1	21	34	5.4	0.8
Calhoun	25.25	218.4	90	1,614	1,347.9	69.2	466	6,380	1,652.3	151.6	76	307	58.6	10.8
Chambers	4.20	123.1	D	D	D	D	114	1,124	297.1	25.3	17	44	5.8	1.3
Cherokee	3.20	123.7	15	119	68.9	4.3	85	894	207.8	21.7	9	27	6.3	1.4
Chilton	4.40	100.1	24	391	303.3	17.7	148	1,502	510.6	38.7	25	62	8.0	1.4
Choctaw	1.21	91.9	5	D	12.4	D	52	326	90.3	7.0	5	D	0.7	D
Clarke	2.58	104.6	16	142	108.9	6.7	134	1,336	348.2	33.4	20	96	10.6	2.2
Clay	1.78	131.3	NA	NA	NA	NA	36	286	63.0	5.1	7	D	0.8	D
Cleburne	0.48	32.0	6	D	8.5	D	41	333	136.1	9.7	6	8	3.0	0.5
Coffee	6.34	123.8	22	299	196.3	13.7	202	2,456	789.4	65.1	38	167	23.2	6.1
Colbert	8.26	152.0	75	748	547.0	39.4	229	3,037	841.2	83.2	38	115	28.3	4.3
Conecuh	1.32	104.2	6	333	104.8	11.3	37	304	106.9	5.6	5	5	1.0	0.1
Coosa	0.27	25.2	D	D	D	1.4	18	84	21.9	1.6	NA	NA	NA	NA
Covington	4.09	108.1	31	426	463.6	17.1	186	1,827	461.8	44.3	24	92	10.4	2.2
Crenshaw	1.93	138.2	10	472	192.2	23.6	34	274	67.0	6.0	D	D	D	D
Cullman	23.24	283.4	79	1,008	1,006.9	53.3	335	3,996	1,191.3	102.3	57	176	30.1	6.7
Dale	5.90	119.0	16	196	40.1	5.8	145	1,334	373.9	31.8	33	178	38.5	6.9
Dallas	5.91	143.7	21	189	97.6	8.0	159	1,493	360.0	35.3	26	86	10.0	2.0
DeKalb	5.91	83.1	43	595	252.0	26.0	239	2,265	695.9	57.6	24	150	17.8	5.5
Elmore	12.19	149.6	D	D	D	D	206	2,939	774.4	72.1	59	133	25.3	4.1
Escambia	5.00	132.3	27	131	102.3	7.6	166	1,693	426.5	40.1	26	62	10.4	1.7
Etowah	16.85	163.5	70	758	497.3	32.4	393	4,777	1,319.8	114.3	61	232	64.4	7.8
Fayette	1.70	101.4	4	17	8.6	0.7	57	559	134.0	12.8	7	17	2.7	0.4
Franklin	5.94	187.4	16	71	100.5	3.6	99	933	236.4	20.2	D	D	D	0.9
Geneva	1.78	66.5	19	410	417.1	26.7	87	714	162.0	16.0	8	17	3.0	0.4
Greene	1.39	163.9	NA	NA	NA	NA	25	166	36.0	3.0	NA	NA	NA	NA
Hale	3.10	205.7	D	D	D	1.3	40	279	73.3	7.0	4	6	0.5	0.2
Henry	1.66	96.4	11	223	433.3	11.4	50	316	85.8	6.7	5	5	1.3	0.1
Houston	18.94	181.8	158	2,898	10,907.0	156.7	536	7,838	2,218.9	203.0	95	488	99.5	20.1
Jackson	11.79	224.9	D	D	D	D	174	1,832	498.6	45.0	28	76	16.9	2.6
Jefferson	48.98	74.2	911	15,607	17,676.4	921.3	2,666	38,321	10,348.5	1,008.5	779	5,567	1,931.3	313.2
Lamar	1.42	102.3	D	D	D	1.9	49	336	82.7	7.0	5	D	2.2	D
Lauderdale	12.39	133.8	72	1,129	528.8	50.2	400	5,252	1,279.8	124.4	105	413	67.9	13.1
Lawrence	7.73	233.4	16	107	62.3	3.3	82	768	202.9	18.4	7	25	2.0	0.5
Lee	15.83	100.8	83	999	465.5	48.1	478	7,212	1,901.9	169.0	157	678	139.6	25.1
Limestone	11.52	125.7	48	751	455.6	33.9	266	2,790	794.7	72.9	60	183	29.5	6.0
Lowndes	0.95	90.8	NA	NA	NA	NA	27	163	76.3	3.4	6	6	1.6	0.1
Macon	3.31	173.3	D	D	D	0.1	43	469	134.9	7.8	12	31	7.1	0.9
Madison	67.15	190.2	298	4,652	4,906.4	293.3	1,298	19,547	5,427.4	527.9	417	1,804	566.0	72.5
Marengo	2.77	138.3	14	84	51.6	4.4	104	878	220.7	20.5	9	91	29.4	3.1
Marion	6.06	200.9	24	219	199.2	9.6	109	1,096	257.2	25.1	9	16	3.7	0.5
Marshall	23.76	250.8	82	1,238	1,284.8	51.8	396	4,752	1,535.8	122.3	65	574	47.8	11.7
Mobile	66.10	159.1	508	6,103	3,430.8	317.7	1,493	20,361	5,607.8	527.7	438	2,424	565.7	98.4
Monroe	2.31	106.6	18	159	122.1	8.4	91	900	225.4	19.4	D	D	D	D
Montgomery	28.00	123.6	274	5,628	4,338.6	308.4	916	12,601	3,448.9	324.8	257	1,579	341.3	67.9
Morgan	25.60	214.1	D	D	D	95.6	464	5,545	1,774.9	144.3	93	397	107.0	17.8
Perry	2.02	209.3	4	38	18.6	1.1	29	156	33.2	3.2	D	D	D	D
Pickens	3.00	143.8	D	D	D	1.8	52	409	94.5	8.7	3	7	0.5	0.3
Pike	4.58	138.6	31	467	270.2	17.2	136	1,629	416.3	37.3	32	115	21.5	2.8
Randolph	1.22	53.8	6	37	16.2	1.2	82	726	183.4	16.6	D	D	D	0.7
Russell	8.45	141.6	D	D	D	3.5	156	2,091	514.4	45.5	D	D	D	D
St. Clair	8.93	102.6	60	1,154	510.8	50.3	230	2,862	811.5	69.6	42	124	45.6	5.5
Shelby	14.21	68.1	333	4,810	8,118.3	345.4	700	10,386	3,607.4	292.3	236	1,294	559.8	77.0
Sumter	2.06	157.2	10	137	49.5	4.9	50	226	54.0	4.8	D	D	D	D
Talladega	16.00	197.9	D	D	D	27.1	273	2,880	781.9	66.6	D	D	D	D
Tallapoosa	11.87	290.6	15	109	44.9	4.6	156	1,533	415.1	37.9	29	96	30.3	4.2
Tuscaloosa	31.43	154.1	152	1,532	926.0	80.7	719	10,120	2,760.1	248.5	208	1,857	250.1	61.9
Walker	43.88	672.0	37	332	234.2	16.3	281	3,293	949.1	83.9	44	188	32.8	6.6

1 Merchant wholesalers, except manufacturers' sales branches and offices. 2. Employer establishments.

Table B. States and Counties — **Professional Services, Manufacturing, and Accommodation and Food Services**

STATE County	Professional, scientific, and technical services, 2017				Manufacturing, 2017				Accommodation and food services, 2017			
	Number of establish-ments	Number of employees	Sales (mil dol)	Average payroll (mil dol)	Number of establish-ments	Number of employees	Sales (mil dol)	Average payroll (mil dol)	Number of establis-hments	Number of employees	Sales (mil dol)	Annual payroll (mil dol)
	147	148	149	150	151	152	153	154	155	156	157	158
UNITED STATES	908,547	8,759,257	1,795,588.8	707,772.8	291,586	11,522,039	5,548,796.8	670,678.4	726,081	14,002,624	938,237.1	264,603.6
ALABAMA	9,452	99,578	20,370.8	7,087.4	4,133	245,725	137,441.2	12,916.0	9,085	183,590	10,527.7	2,761.5
Autauga	51	266	28.8	10.2	23	1,152	760.1	79.7	D	D	D	D
Baldwin	D	D	D	D	165	4,505	2,616.0	215.9	572	12,977	794.1	228.8
Barbour	32	97	15.2	4.0	28	2,514	809.0	94.9	56	631	29.3	7.5
Bibb	14	64	6.8	2.6	18	309	134.5	14.5	18	267	18.7	3.9
Blount	43	219	34.0	9.6	37	1,041	321.3	37.9	49	677	35.9	9.4
Bullock	D	D	D	1.1	D	D	D	D	9	79	4.6	1.1
Butler	19	61	6.9	2.0	17	1,270	865.6	55.4	D	D	D	D
Calhoun	D	D	D	D	106	5,986	2,699.2	308.1	225	4,642	247.0	66.2
Chambers	32	174	17.9	5.5	24	1,810	880.2	85.5	59	950	43.8	10.6
Cherokee	21	71	6.9	2.1	16	955	328.8	35.6	35	481	21.9	5.6
Chilton	32	88	10.1	3.1	41	1,969	483.0	87.6	55	972	47.1	12.6
Choctaw	20	48	5.6	1.4	D	D	D	D	D	D	D	D
Clarke	29	94	12.6	2.5	23	1,521	648.1	85.4	D	D	D	8.9
Clay	11	50	3.2	1.1	9	2,153	296.3	55.2	11	125	5.4	1.3
Cleburne	8	12	1.2	0.3	9	288	125.1	13.7	D	D	D	D
Coffee	67	758	138.4	55.0	38	3,020	938.9	111.6	106	1,672	82.9	22.1
Colbert	69	278	32.3	10.9	92	6,620	3,691.0	358.0	107	1,966	88.2	23.3
Conecuh	10	21	2.2	0.7	13	463	132.0	19.5	D	D	D	3.0
Coosa	7	24	2.7	1.3	4	471	82.7	18.4	D	D	D	D
Covington	62	283	32.3	11.4	32	2,115	689.7	89.0	D	D	D	D
Crenshaw	14	31	4.1	1.0	6	1,050	308.9	36.7	D	D	D	D
Cullman	101	435	46.5	16.2	98	5,617	2,109.7	257.2	148	2,829	151.5	40.0
Dale	D	D	D	D	29	470	152.7	23.1	77	1,107	58.6	15.0
Dallas	D	D	D	D	41	2,714	1,079.8	131.3	57	853	44.2	10.8
DeKalb	72	324	36.7	11.7	98	6,493	1,442.4	286.2	93	1,576	97.9	25.8
Elmore	99	440	91.5	22.0	57	2,718	890.2	147.6	104	2,773	454.8	59.0
Escambia	42	170	24.0	6.5	36	1,936	758.0	110.3	62	2,113	303.2	46.4
Etowah	127	656	80.8	28.2	89	5,358	1,607.9	231.1	187	3,587	187.6	50.4
Fayette	14	35	4.1	1.3	22	828	170.5	35.0	D	D	D	D
Franklin	25	143	13.2	5.1	40	5,365	1,553.9	206.7	D	D	D	7.1
Geneva	29	98	9.1	2.8	22	698	120.2	23.5	D	D	D	D
Greene	3	8	0.7	0.2	8	408	142.8	16.8	6	41	2.7	0.6
Hale	8	25	2.1	0.4	14	474	148.3	26.0	15	153	7.1	1.6
Henry	25	140	18.9	7.0	13	307	212.2	13.1	D	D	D	D
Houston	D	D	D	D	104	4,667	1,377.1	193.1	256	5,206	280.2	73.1
Jackson	59	242	26.4	9.0	66	5,895	1,515.2	218.0	83	1,295	64.1	16.2
Jefferson	D	D	D	D	543	21,831	8,416.5	1,261.7	1,481	32,014	1,810.1	520.2
Lamar	D	D	D	2.1	22	1,395	440.7	71.9	D	D	D	D
Lauderdale	148	714	73.9	27.5	84	2,392	943.1	100.7	184	4,347	197.4	59.0
Lawrence	31	139	20.9	7.1	23	149	33.3	6.6	D	D	D	D
Lee	254	1,277	163.5	56.6	118	7,008	2,707.0	317.6	363	7,591	371.4	100.0
Limestone	D	D	D	D	66	3,505	1,444.4	160.7	112	2,241	106.7	27.9
Lowndes	5	11	1.4	0.5	11	938	1,169.7	52.3	D	D	D	D
Macon	11	34	6.4	2.2	6	645	456.8	38.2	21	385	20.2	5.1
Madison	1,469	37,711	10,167.3	3,380.3	265	15,834	6,741.9	1,004.9	786	16,885	886.0	253.3
Marengo	16	86	14.0	3.4	22	1,276	578.5	73.6	D	D	D	D
Marion	25	76	6.3	2.2	35	2,482	605.1	103.1	D	D	D	D
Marshall	126	665	84.0	26.8	112	10,255	3,624.4	380.9	185	3,178	166.3	43.4
Mobile	D	D	D	D	323	15,793	10,650.8	1,016.3	705	15,002	791.9	218.0
Monroe	16	41	6.4	1.6	18	1,115	468.4	77.8	D	D	D	D
Montgomery	D	D	D	D	169	12,464	11,183.8	660.0	516	11,673	861.7	186.5
Morgan	193	2,421	529.0	144.8	158	11,931	10,358.9	741.9	D	D	D	D
Perry	6	9	1.8	0.2	5	438	160.0	13.7	11	102	5.8	1.6
Pickens	14	91	7.8	2.5	18	583	114.4	21.1	D	D	D	D
Pike	34	440	39.3	18.5	26	2,306	876.7	122.5	81	1,568	70.4	18.3
Randolph	16	48	4.6	1.3	24	1,060	339.4	40.3	D	D	D	4.3
Russell	46	215	20.0	6.9	34	2,661	1,239.3	142.9	91	1,664	90.4	21.8
St. Clair	101	652	79.1	21.0	71	4,123	1,344.5	194.0	123	2,299	118.1	30.9
Shelby	D	D	D	321.6	158	5,452	1,816.8	305.8	405	8,120	451.8	130.6
Sumter	6	13	2.1	0.4	7	213	67.3	9.2	D	D	D	4.0
Talladega	66	382	41.5	17.7	86	9,360	11,590.0	617.8	D	D	D	D
Tallapoosa	60	206	27.9	9.2	30	2,346	530.3	82.8	69	1,035	52.9	14.3
Tuscaloosa	D	D	D	D	135	14,565	20,691.6	913.3	D	D	D	D
Walker	79	432	39.2	21.7	48	1,890	618.8	77.6	92	1,688	91.2	23.7

STATE County	Health care and social assistance, 2017				Other services, 2017				Nonemployer businesses, 2019		Value of residential construction authorized by building permits, 2021	
	Number of establish-ments	Number of employees	Receipts (mil dol)	Annual payroll (mil dol)	Number of establish-ments	Number of employees	Receipts (mil dol)	Annual payroll (mil dol)	Number	Receipts (mil dol)	New construction ($1,000)	Number of housing units
	159	160	161	162	163	164	165	166	167	168	169	170
UNITED STATES	892,245	20,506,502	2,527,903.3	990,056.2	560,845	3,696,831	544,127.7	133,751.1	27,104,006	1,341,361.7	380,036,187	1,736,982
ALABAMA	10,636	258,399	31,238.9	11,948.8	6,149	38,476	5,844.4	1,302.6	345,095	15,363.2	4,816,174	22,100
Autauga	D	D	D	D	59	256	28.7	6.8	3,522	147.9	91,286	277
Baldwin	503	8,049	848.4	327.8	323	1,544	187.4	46.3	20,803	1,060.6	844,323	3,705
Barbour	D	D	D	D	D	D	D	D	1,512	47.9	3,017	12
Bibb	24	601	55.5	25.4	D	D	D	D	1,126	44.4	2,585	10
Blount	61	976	83.4	35.3	D	D	D	D	3,839	161.3	4,320	26
Bullock	12	422	41.1	14.9	D	D	D	D	528	19.1	0	0
Butler	42	873	84.9	32.3	D	D	D	D	1,085	43.3	1,019	3
Calhoun	275	6,358	622.7	249.8	166	718	79.2	19.7	6,721	264.2	10,515	68
Chambers	55	778	60.6	26.3	37	120	11.9	3.5	2,032	65.7	1,289	9
Cherokee	35	456	36.8	16.0	20	157	9.1	2.5	1,739	81.9	3,633	24
Chilton	72	813	83.8	33.1	D	D	D	D	2,948	125.8	24,619	156
Choctaw	24	356	35.8	13.7	16	58	6.9	2.2	749	28.4	0	0
Clarke	58	897	67.1	29.3	D	D	D	D	1,412	58.1	133	1
Clay	20	515	37.3	17.7	8	37	2.9	0.8	789	38.1	832	5
Cleburne	12	60	5.0	2.1	D	D	D	D	1,028	43.6	170	1
Coffee	104	1,856	173.2	68.4	72	298	30.9	8.8	2,889	107.8	43,812	177
Colbert	118	3,062	333.4	133.5	D	D	D	18.1	3,627	146.8	26,948	221
Conecuh	18	465	34.1	14.1	D	D	D	D	722	23.1	0	0
Coosa	3	D	7.7	D	7	18	2.7	0.5	420	16.6	0	0
Covington	88	1,607	148.4	59.2	50	304	28.5	7.9	2,232	87.6	1,319	5
Crenshaw	15	459	26.9	14.1	13	41	5.4	1.2	840	30.0	0	0
Cullman	194	4,235	398.7	153.0	111	605	66.3	19.9	6,068	296.3	39,521	211
Dale	52	1,150	90.9	40.2	42	185	12.2	4.1	2,778	98.4	6,652	40
Dallas	98	1,765	173.3	66.0	47	322	34.3	8.7	2,202	69.6	3,006	21
DeKalb	134	2,527	216.5	90.6	52	172	17.6	5.0	5,011	239.3	8,558	71
Elmore	122	2,170	176.6	67.5	D	D	D	D	5,498	285.3	26,017	136
Escambia	66	1,065	116.0	36.9	40	171	16.3	3.7	2,063	70.6	1,446	10
Etowah	300	7,233	761.6	303.7	114	779	125.7	24.3	7,632	354.2	28,773	188
Fayette	43	690	56.4	27.3	D	D	D	D	1,042	44.6	0	0
Franklin	48	1,033	80.8	35.1	D	D	D	D	1,856	84.1	1,657	18
Geneva	32	578	44.6	18.1	21	48	6.0	1.2	1,665	71.4	3,294	21
Greene	11	266	16.0	8.1	4	11	1.4	0.3	539	16.3	939	9
Hale	17	385	27.7	11.9	D	D	D	0.2	901	30.3	12,772	119
Henry	21	168	11.8	5.4	D	D	D	D	1,163	49.6	8,132	42
Houston	322	9,826	1,180.0	494.0	185	926	110.0	26.3	7,700	364.5	118,572	431
Jackson	103	1,550	142.8	57.4	D	D	22.0	D	3,209	133.1	13,088	40
Jefferson	1,761	60,705	9,862.6	3,510.6	1,044	9,360	2,377.4	388.6	51,492	2,414.1	543,297	2,121
Lamar	24	368	18.7	8.7	D	D	D	D	901	43.0	0	0
Lauderdale	241	5,150	578.7	203.1	D	D	D	15.1	6,788	339.6	15,619	138
Lawrence	33	787	46.3	21.9	D	D	D	D	1,906	66.8	1,592	13
Lee	258	6,926	697.5	276.4	177	1,068	91.5	26.2	11,110	527.6	461,414	1,851
Limestone	140	2,302	215.8	88.9	78	491	58.5	16.7	6,700	285.8	140,355	631
Lowndes	D	D	D	D	D	D	D	D	667	23.3	0	0
Macon	22	1,719	275.4	117.5	17	43	5.0	1.2	1,038	28.4	1,998	10
Madison	1,021	25,276	3,441.1	1,233.5	500	3,917	498.5	137.8	26,643	1,153.8	929,354	5,541
Marengo	56	1,075	82.6	34.7	25	99	8.8	2.3	1,094	35.2	0	0
Marion	91	1,285	123.1	47.8	D	D	D	D	1,800	94.9	653	3
Marshall	196	3,982	382.4	155.8	87	364	29.5	7.7	7,552	369.5	33,424	154
Mobile	796	21,337	2,651.9	988.4	547	4,061	453.1	121.2	30,889	1,216.8	227,029	1,022
Monroe	30	708	55.9	24.1	D	D	D	D	1,347	48.3	0	0
Montgomery	666	18,304	2,123.7	888.7	439	2,735	412.0	110.1	15,921	680.4	129,596	601
Morgan	349	5,577	517.9	217.6	D	D	D	D	7,805	336.1	57,593	213
Perry	7	128	8.5	3.9	6	21	1.8	0.8	470	15.7	0	0
Pickens	26	543	40.3	16.5	D	D	D	0.7	1,120	37.6	861	7
Pike	55	1,138	110.5	44.9	35	148	11.9	3.4	1,760	74.4	14,633	81
Randolph	27	563	39.8	18.1	D	D	D	D	1,477	56.7	0	0
Russell	D	D	D	D	55	268	28.9	8.2	3,409	108.9	27,437	186
St. Clair	100	2,370	206.9	81.5	89	377	42.4	11.1	6,117	256.8	100,738	517
Shelby	494	7,656	795.7	330.8	319	1,942	244.4	70.1	19,317	1,011.4	376,308	1,154
Sumter	19	353	19.8	9.6	5	33	4.0	1.1	715	27.6	440	4
Talladega	143	D	232.1	D	59	228	22.8	8.8	4,259	173.5	19,633	118
Tallapoosa	79	2,116	194.9	83.4	52	236	26.9	6.8	2,703	138.3	113,032	279
Tuscaloosa	449	13,463	1,478.5	619.0	237	1,452	166.9	46.7	13,408	659.4	282,761	1,361
Walker	172	3,441	316.5	129.9	88	401	52.2	13.7	3,580	154.5	6,161	38

Table B. States and Counties — Government Employment and Payroll, and Local Government Finances

STATE County	Government employment and payroll, 2017									Local government finances, 2017				
			March payroll (percent of total)							General revenue				
												Taxes		
													Per capita[1] (dollars)	
	Full-time equivalent employees	March payroll (dollars)	Administration, judicial, and legal	Police and corrections	Fire protection	Highways and transportation	Health and welfare	Natural resources and utilities	Education and libraries	Total (mil dol)	Intergovernmental (mil dol)	Total (mil dol)	Total	Property
	171	172	173	174	175	176	177	178	179	180	181	182	183	184
UNITED STATES	X	X	X	X	X	X	X	X	X	X	X	X	X	X
ALABAMA	X	X	X	X	X	X	X	X	X	X	X	X	X	X
Autauga	1,734	5,695,272	5.1	10.7	6.8	2.4	0.8	7.3	65.2	140.0	69.5	50.6	914	271
Baldwin	7,998	27,159,727	6.9	8.8	3.3	4.6	13.2	8.1	51.4	778.0	221.7	271.7	1,278	507
Barbour	1,177	3,772,026	3.8	7.2	4.6	2.1	28.5	6.5	45.5	94.1	54.3	22.6	899	300
Bibb	873	2,675,441	2.8	5.2	0.0	2.9	29.7	2.2	55.0	44.7	28.2	8.7	385	216
Blount	1,544	5,111,998	5.5	6.9	1.7	3.3	1.6	5.1	74.3	114.0	70.5	26.7	462	209
Bullock	405	1,232,720	4.9	8.0	0.0	3.6	22.8	2.2	57.1	26.6	17.6	5.7	561	430
Butler	856	3,182,150	4.1	8.4	2.2	4.8	12.8	5.4	60.4	66.9	30.4	18.5	933	370
Calhoun	5,653	18,814,816	3.4	5.0	2.7	2.5	37.3	5.5	41.1	531.6	161.2	130.2	1,135	389
Chambers	1,105	3,409,335	5.5	11.8	4.8	6.0	4.5	8.6	57.1	77.4	41.1	25.1	744	257
Cherokee	1,032	3,120,377	5.3	7.0	0.1	3.1	21.5	2.9	58.8	71.9	30.6	19.6	760	379
Chilton	1,252	3,945,983	7.9	9.4	1.1	4.5	0.8	7.0	68.9	109.4	60.9	31.9	724	360
Choctaw	331	963,611	15.7	6.6	0.0	5.9	0.0	1.2	70.6	25.2	14.0	8.9	689	415
Clarke	1,138	3,692,713	5.0	9.2	0.0	4.0	18.5	11.4	50.9	73.4	36.3	30.5	1,269	384
Clay	702	2,190,795	3.6	7.5	0.1	4.5	38.7	5.7	39.2	48.7	18.7	6.5	490	236
Cleburne	580	2,297,353	2.5	8.1	0.2	3.5	10.8	5.4	68.0	51.2	26.0	7.5	505	263
Coffee	1,961	6,438,467	4.6	7.3	2.2	2.8	12.1	6.5	62.2	160.9	85.9	47.8	922	318
Colbert	2,129	7,472,138	3.6	7.5	3.1	3.6	8.2	18.7	52.9	169.6	79.1	46.2	845	406
Conecuh	565	1,621,775	4.7	13.5	0.0	6.6	2.0	21.2	52.0	35.7	23.1	8.7	704	354
Coosa	240	686,957	8.8	10.9	1.1	6.2	0.8	1.4	69.3	18.3	10.3	5.0	463	301
Covington	1,698	5,041,571	7.2	6.8	1.5	5.8	2.0	21.4	53.5	110.5	57.0	33.2	897	315
Crenshaw	475	1,722,202	4.5	5.4	0.0	6.6	2.1	7.3	73.9	31.3	17.9	8.0	579	232
Cullman	3,867	12,941,467	3.5	6.2	1.7	2.8	30.4	9.8	44.2	239.7	113.1	69.8	842	337
Dale	1,658	5,099,569	3.7	7.4	3.8	2.8	25.6	5.1	50.6	133.8	57.8	32.4	656	286
Dallas	1,571	5,179,439	3.8	7.9	2.1	2.6	2.3	5.2	73.0	117.2	70.1	34.1	870	328
DeKalb	2,270	8,027,316	3.3	7.8	2.1	3.3	4.0	11.1	66.6	188.6	111.4	45.0	630	261
Elmore	2,007	6,738,762	3.3	12.1	2.2	3.7	0.3	6.1	69.3	168.8	93.7	48.1	590	256
Escambia	1,615	4,788,979	4.1	10.1	2.9	4.9	17.9	2.1	55.3	107.4	56.1	34.2	926	410
Etowah	3,617	13,009,490	5.6	11.4	6.0	3.8	7.4	7.0	56.2	298.2	139.3	104.1	1,011	317
Fayette	482	1,481,148	6.5	7.7	1.5	4.5	2.9	6.2	69.1	45.3	26.3	12.5	762	310
Franklin	1,303	4,088,311	4.9	6.2	1.7	3.2	2.4	14.6	65.9	95.2	59.5	17.6	557	267
Geneva	1,068	3,268,649	4.0	5.8	0.3	4.1	29.0	4.7	51.7	83.1	37.0	15.4	585	310
Greene	316	869,694	5.7	10.2	0.0	2.7	3.8	5.6	71.0	29.8	11.6	6.4	770	470
Hale	599	1,933,870	3.9	6.7	0.0	3.4	20.1	4.4	61.4	43.3	22.3	8.2	557	289
Henry	506	1,532,820	6.1	10.0	0.0	5.4	3.6	6.3	68.2	37.6	19.3	10.5	612	285
Houston	5,705	32,358,632	2.5	4.7	2.4	1.5	31.7	4.8	51.0	687.0	134.1	125.4	1,201	386
Jackson	2,502	9,081,304	3.2	5.8	2.1	3.2	26.3	8.2	50.3	221.9	77.8	53.4	1,030	326
Jefferson	26,397	106,388,611	7.8	14.5	7.7	4.3	4.5	10.8	47.5	3,110.8	944.3	1,568.3	2,378	968
Lamar	464	1,463,915	7.4	8.4	1.2	4.7	4.3	9.0	63.8	47.7	26.0	13.0	938	588
Lauderdale	2,917	10,134,952	3.5	8.9	5.4	4.2	1.3	18.4	55.8	237.9	103.7	96.6	1,044	456
Lawrence	1,030	3,487,299	4.1	7.1	0.5	2.3	12.8	4.9	66.7	107.4	44.4	42.4	1,282	372
Lee	7,104	27,907,786	2.7	6.0	2.4	1.6	44.2	5.5	36.9	792.6	189.0	215.4	1,334	592
Limestone	2,212	9,373,150	4.8	8.1	1.7	3.2	0.2	10.7	70.8	247.5	102.6	47.4	504	236
Lowndes	405	1,193,381	10.1	10.0	0.0	5.6	0.4	2.4	70.9	32.1	17.7	10.4	1,029	521
Macon	705	2,144,009	7.4	10.8	3.6	4.4	4.8	7.0	58.0	58.7	28.1	22.7	1,211	373
Madison	18,821	86,685,197	2.9	5.5	2.9	2.6	51.1	5.2	26.3	2,610.2	1,033.3	518.3	1,433	614
Marengo	1,543	6,195,458	2.8	3.9	2.0	2.7	50.3	2.6	34.7	86.1	37.8	19.9	1,025	430
Marion	956	3,067,580	4.4	8.5	1.8	3.0	4.8	12.8	64.4	71.9	39.7	21.6	726	197
Marshall	4,648	16,573,051	2.4	5.3	2.4	1.9	32.4	8.8	45.7	452.0	154.7	88.7	928	392
Mobile	15,404	52,418,321	6.1	13.0	4.7	3.7	11.6	6.9	51.2	1,481.8	632.7	614.0	1,483	580
Monroe	1,076	3,495,389	4.0	7.4	0.7	2.9	35.3	2.3	46.8	78.2	34.3	15.6	733	330
Montgomery	7,810	28,640,171	5.1	14.6	6.9	3.1	3.4	11.5	47.9	1,337.9	303.7	303.3	1,334	364
Morgan	3,972	14,335,679	4.1	9.7	4.0	2.8	1.7	12.3	62.7	385.0	163.8	137.5	1,156	555
Perry	448	1,621,598	1.6	4.3	0.1	5.0	24.2	2.4	61.7	35.5	25.7	6.7	720	385
Pickens	578	1,769,470	7.0	9.8	0.0	5.1	3.7	5.5	65.7	55.3	26.7	8.7	428	270
Pike	1,030	3,548,434	7.9	12.1	3.1	5.2	5.5	10.4	55.4	108.7	43.0	24.0	721	275
Randolph	755	2,605,786	4.4	7.7	0.5	4.9	10.3	2.6	69.2	49.3	30.3	13.4	590	298
Russell	2,161	6,843,660	4.4	11.1	4.0	3.9	2.1	7.4	63.7	167.8	86.5	60.5	1,062	432
St. Clair	2,104	7,818,999	6.7	10.8	4.3	4.3	0.5	4.0	68.8	193.1	100.3	69.3	788	296
Shelby	4,679	17,149,718	6.6	15.8	7.0	3.3	3.1	7.2	55.7	539.4	208.6	236.0	1,105	580
Sumter	966	3,406,938	2.7	3.5	0.9	2.4	62.4	3.2	24.3	34.8	17.9	11.6	911	387
Talladega	3,181	10,111,425	4.4	7.2	2.3	2.6	21.6	7.2	52.4	208.0	100.4	70.1	874	414
Tallapoosa	1,719	5,539,492	4.7	8.6	4.1	2.4	24.5	7.1	47.0	126.9	73.3	32.8	808	402
Tuscaloosa	10,171	39,065,639	3.6	7.7	3.8	3.6	44.9	4.8	30.1	1,109.3	251.9	212.1	1,021	440
Walker	2,038	7,363,701	4.1	8.3	1.5	3.6	1.8	7.2	72.8	170.1	83.9	58.9	922	286

1. Based on the resident population estimated as of July 1 of the year shown.

STATE County	Local government finances, 2017 (cont.)									Government employment, 2020			Individual income tax returns, 2019		
	Direct general expenditure							Debt outstanding							
			Percent of total for:												
	Total (mil dol)	Per capita[1] (dollars)	Education	Health and hospitals	Police protection	Public welfare	Highways	Total (mil dol)	Per capita[1] (dollars)	Federal civilian	Federal military	State and local	Number of returns	Mean adjusted gross income	Mean income tax
	185	186	187	188	189	190	191	192	193	194	195	196	197	198	199
UNITED STATES	X	X	X	X	X	X	X	X	X	2,982,000	1,911,000	19,236,000	157,705,360	75,758	9,886
ALABAMA	X	X	X	X	X	X	X	X	X	55,966	28,942	320,273	2,130,240	60,791	6,408
Autauga	136.8	2,470	59.0	0.1	6.7	0.5	5.1	156.4	2,824	91	272	2,107	25,230	59,390	5,188
Baldwin	833.5	3,922	37.7	18.0	5.7	0.1	8.0	1,143.7	5,382	405	988	9,778	105,840	68,887	7,830
Barbour	96.0	3,816	43.9	21.4	6.6	0.0	1.7	41.8	1,662	63	101	1,581	9,490	41,793	3,313
Bibb	50.3	2,231	63.9	5.4	7.4	0.0	10.0	42.0	1,862	66	83	1,213	8,230	49,189	3,768
Blount	112.6	1,948	77.7	0.5	4.9	0.0	5.7	65.1	1,127	93	239	1,952	23,210	53,631	4,321
Bullock	26.0	2,556	59.1	10.7	2.3	1.0	11.8	9.8	963	39	34	566	3,880	33,152	2,001
Butler	72.8	3,659	45.1	13.0	6.1	0.2	10.7	76.0	3,819	49	80	823	8,190	43,679	3,189
Calhoun	618.0	5,387	32.3	36.7	5.3	0.0	3.4	461.6	4,024	4,276	500	8,363	48,800	48,885	4,049
Chambers	74.2	2,202	60.5	1.0	6.3	0.3	3.6	58.9	1,746	59	135	1,748	14,060	40,956	2,750
Cherokee	75.9	2,940	55.1	0.0	5.1	18.8	5.9	57.6	2,234	55	108	1,227	10,060	48,078	3,744
Chilton	107.1	2,428	64.9	0.2	7.0	0.4	5.8	38.8	880	70	183	1,755	17,770	50,598	4,116
Choctaw	26.8	2,070	58.4	0.6	8.1	0.0	15.0	18.9	1,464	33	51	426	5,000	49,360	3,888
Clarke	77.7	3,229	61.9	0.3	7.4	0.2	5.5	116.6	4,847	76	96	1,632	9,940	49,697	4,141
Clay	49.2	3,682	36.1	38.7	3.4	0.1	3.0	18.9	1,418	50	54	874	5,680	49,622	4,293
Cleburne	53.3	3,575	44.2	0.1	3.7	12.7	9.5	25.5	1,709	52	61	712	5,850	51,713	4,015
Coffee	161.5	3,114	60.4	0.1	5.2	0.4	4.4	138.4	2,669	287	219	2,402	22,360	56,763	5,112
Colbert	179.7	3,285	51.5	7.7	5.0	0.2	5.6	186.0	3,400	621	229	3,987	24,690	54,320	5,131
Conecuh	42.8	3,442	55.2	0.3	6.0	0.0	8.4	62.0	4,985	33	49	699	4,740	40,127	2,804
Coosa	18.6	1,734	54.8	0.2	7.2	0.2	14.4	7.8	728	20	45	306	3,980	46,689	3,684
Covington	124.6	3,363	49.7	0.6	6.1	0.0	12.8	193.3	5,217	137	151	1,914	15,040	50,239	4,255
Crenshaw	36.3	2,622	67.1	6.3	8.8	0.0	3.0	24.5	1,769	48	56	596	5,770	44,564	3,272
Cullman	262.1	3,163	51.1	2.8	8.5	0.9	5.9	332.1	4,008	217	347	4,142	35,500	55,319	5,062
Dale	138.9	2,814	47.7	23.3	5.2	0.2	3.5	62.8	1,272	2,939	4,008	2,085	20,640	47,705	3,790
Dallas	120.6	3,074	58.0	0.2	6.3	0.1	5.9	70.0	1,785	182	147	2,265	14,960	40,600	3,171
DeKalb	190.3	2,664	61.8	4.3	7.1	0.3	7.2	110.2	1,542	179	295	3,308	27,930	44,672	3,459
Elmore	178.5	2,192	67.8	0.4	8.0	0.0	6.1	152.5	1,873	181	324	4,338	37,150	60,563	5,555
Escambia	109.3	2,955	57.2	4.1	8.9	0.6	6.5	95.6	2,584	67	141	3,815	14,350	45,257	3,480
Etowah	302.7	2,939	49.8	2.2	10.0	0.2	4.2	235.4	2,285	315	418	4,878	42,940	49,180	4,204
Fayette	44.2	2,685	55.3	1.7	5.0	0.0	12.1	29.4	1,786	41	68	1,183	6,330	45,933	3,142
Franklin	103.7	3,287	60.6	0.1	6.8	0.0	7.7	82.0	2,599	94	130	1,856	11,960	45,172	3,441
Geneva	85.3	3,234	47.4	26.9	4.0	0.2	5.9	23.3	885	62	109	1,396	10,550	43,911	3,311
Greene	32.0	3,850	43.5	29.6	2.7	0.6	4.4	24.8	2,980	31	33	497	3,300	32,985	1,899
Hale	45.6	3,078	55.3	19.3	5.9	0.0	5.6	21.3	1,437	49	60	790	6,400	42,292	3,048
Henry	38.1	2,225	59.9	0.0	8.5	0.4	8.4	44.1	2,578	48	71	664	7,430	51,509	4,576
Houston	740.4	7,094	20.2	53.1	3.3	0.1	3.1	511.0	4,896	331	486	8,292	46,170	59,113	6,663
Jackson	221.3	4,269	36.9	30.6	5.3	0.3	3.9	138.2	2,666	136	213	2,885	21,480	49,958	4,202
Jefferson	2,939.4	4,456	38.8	3.1	8.0	0.0	5.0	7,200.4	10,916	8,429	2,959	53,742	298,200	73,701	9,582
Lamar	44.4	3,197	53.6	0.1	5.5	0.3	5.6	35.5	2,556	39	56	539	5,420	46,223	3,087
Lauderdale	231.3	2,498	57.3	0.6	6.4	0.1	7.4	225.3	2,434	318	384	4,970	39,380	58,535	5,854
Lawrence	127.8	3,864	40.1	7.1	8.4	0.0	1.1	189.5	5,732	86	136	1,232	13,730	48,229	3,653
Lee	790.2	4,895	32.9	41.4	3.9	0.0	2.8	800.7	4,960	331	726	17,874	66,930	65,264	6,901
Limestone	311.2	3,306	55.3	25.6	5.2	0.3	2.1	507.5	5,391	1,494	414	5,483	43,830	69,932	7,295
Lowndes	33.8	3,350	59.7	0.0	6.8	0.0	12.7	30.0	2,968	38	40	501	4,800	39,188	2,761
Macon	55.8	2,967	50.6	1.6	5.9	0.2	12.3	72.0	3,834	941	79	1,870	7,700	35,990	2,388
Madison	2,623.0	7,251	22.4	52.5	2.8	0.0	2.6	2,849.0	7,875	18,821	2,262	26,393	180,650	77,493	9,308
Marengo	112.1	5,781	34.1	27.3	4.3	0.1	6.3	44.7	2,302	76	93	1,448	8,210	48,397	4,107
Marion	62.5	2,098	74.6	0.0	3.0	0.0	1.6	71.7	2,408	85	120	1,680	11,230	45,117	3,284
Marshall	445.8	4,665	40.7	35.3	3.5	0.1	3.6	275.9	2,887	274	399	5,914	40,120	51,745	4,878
Mobile	1,516.1	3,662	40.6	9.9	7.4	0.2	5.0	1,381.7	3,337	2,806	2,615	21,929	179,630	53,314	5,333
Monroe	75.2	3,533	46.0	28.6	2.0	0.2	6.7	44.7	2,100	58	84	1,275	8,080	45,921	3,555
Montgomery	1,303.1	5,734	23.5	50.1	4.4	0.1	2.0	952.0	4,189	6,462	3,759	25,715	99,780	56,094	5,979
Morgan	430.2	3,618	57.7	0.3	6.2	0.5	3.3	573.0	4,819	287	492	6,645	53,810	59,180	5,808
Perry	35.1	3,772	45.6	26.8	5.2	0.4	6.7	29.2	3,142	25	62	420	3,590	33,114	1,828
Pickens	62.0	3,068	49.5	22.0	6.8	0.1	5.2	31.3	1,551	325	74	750	7,370	47,750	3,936
Pike	149.0	4,469	30.6	19.4	7.0	0.0	10.4	146.5	4,393	107	145	3,444	12,850	46,701	4,100
Randolph	53.0	2,338	68.2	1.7	6.7	0.0	2.8	37.2	1,639	61	94	1,026	9,370	47,161	3,697
Russell	170.4	2,991	59.0	0.1	6.9	0.0	1.6	259.7	4,558	105	240	2,784	23,970	40,823	2,714
St. Clair	201.1	2,287	60.1	0.9	5.1	0.1	4.0	279.0	3,173	132	371	2,889	38,950	59,330	5,275
Shelby	613.9	2,873	62.2	1.5	6.4	0.1	3.4	917.6	4,295	429	910	8,405	100,620	87,879	11,032
Sumter	37.5	2,942	49.2	0.6	8.4	0.0	13.5	42.7	3,350	42	48	1,182	4,830	37,181	2,660
Talladega	214.8	2,681	59.5	0.5	7.9	0.3	5.4	265.2	3,309	464	319	4,256	33,820	46,680	3,615
Tallapoosa	128.8	3,172	47.1	19.9	5.2	0.0	3.6	76.8	1,891	98	164	1,955	17,610	54,651	5,331
Tuscaloosa	1,130.1	5,443	29.9	43.2	4.7	0.0	5.0	1,068.7	5,148	1,751	849	23,476	85,680	60,740	6,348
Walker	173.4	2,715	65.4	0.2	5.3	0.0	7.2	107.3	1,679	204	260	2,869	25,420	58,745	5,103

1. Based on the resident population estimated as of July 1 of the year shown.

State / county code	CBSA code[1]	County Type code[2]	STATE County	Land area[3] (sq. mi)	Population, 2021: Total persons 2021	Population, 2021: Rank	Population, 2021: Per square mile	Race alone or in combination, not Hispanic or Latino (percent): White	Black	American Indian, Alaska Native	Asian and Pacific Islancer	Percent Hispanic or Latino[4]	Age (percent): Under 5 years	5 to 17 years	18 to 24 years	25 to 34 years	35 to 44 years	45 to 54 years
				1	2	3	4	5	6	7	8	9	10	11	12	13	14	15
			ALABAMA—Cont'd															
01129	33660	8	Washington	1,080.2	15,147	2,082	14.0	66.8	23.7	8.3	1.3	1.7	5.5	11.9	12.0	11.3	11.2	12.9
01131		9	Wilcox	887.9	10,446	2,382	11.8	28.3	70.2	0.7	0.6	1.5	6.3	12.4	12.9	11.7	10.4	11.4
01133		6	Winston	613.0	23,652	1,656	38.6	94.6	1.6	1.3	0.6	3.3	5.1	11.4	11.1	10.6	10.9	13.2
02000		0	ALASKA	571,016.9	732,673	X	1.3	65.7	4.8	19.3	10.6	7.5	6.6	14.0	13.1	15.5	13.9	11.4
02013		9	Aleutians East	6,985.2	3,398	2,929	0.5	12.7	10.3	20.9	44.1	16.1	1.6	4.4	9.7	15.7	19.5	23.1
02016		9	Aleutians West	4,393.0	5,059	2,820	1.2	26.0	7.8	13.0	43.6	14.7	3.0	7.1	9.4	17.4	18.9	20.5
02020	11260	2	Anchorage	1,706.8	288,121	246	168.8	62.9	7.5	12.4	16.3	9.7	6.6	13.5	13.3	16.6	14.3	11.5
02050		7	Bethel	40,627.1	18,557	1,895	0.5	11.7	1.5	86.4	1.9	2.1	10.7	19.8	15.8	14.6	11.4	9.2
02060		9	Bristol Bay	482.0	838	3,113	1.7	56.0	4.7	42.1	6.1	9.8	5.4	13.2	8.4	15.5	11.5	11.1
02063		9	Chugach	9,529.8	6,941	2,669	0.7	73.8	1.4	16.4	8.7	6.2	5.8	13.6	10.0	12.9	13.8	11.7
02066		9	Copper River	24,692.1	2,630	2,987	0.1	72.5	2.0	22.9	4.4	5.8	5.9	15.2	11.1	10.5	13.3	10.8
02068		8	Denali	12,641.0	1,593	3,073	0.1	80.7	4.0	9.1	7.1	4.5	4.4	10.7	8.7	16.9	15.8	15.0
02070		9	Dillingham	18,334.0	4,772	2,839	0.3	22.4	1.6	79.0	2.6	3.5	8.9	18.1	13.8	15.8	11.3	8.4
02090	21820	3	Fairbanks North Star	7,334.8	95,593	636	13.0	74.9	6.3	11.2	6.3	8.4	6.9	13.2	16.0	18.2	13.6	9.7
02100		9	Haines	2,343.4	2,071	3,035	0.9	84.0	2.2	14.9	2.9	3.9	4.4	9.7	9.7	10.0	12.6	11.7
02105		9	Hoonah-Angoon	6,555.3	2,332	3,017	0.4	55.6	3.6	41.1	2.0	6.9	4.7	9.6	8.2	10.5	10.2	12.2
02110	27940	5	Juneau	2,704.0	31,973	1,384	11.8	71.1	2.3	17.5	11.8	7.1	5.0	12.1	11.8	14.5	14.6	12.9
02122		7	Kenai Peninsula	16,017.4	59,767	882	3.7	84.4	1.4	11.9	3.7	4.6	5.7	12.8	10.8	12.5	12.7	11.6
02130	28540	7	Ketchikan Gateway	4,856.9	13,754	2,173	2.8	70.6	1.7	20.0	11.0	5.7	4.8	12.0	11.5	13.5	13.8	12.0
02150		7	Kodiak Island	6,688.9	12,787	2,222	1.9	54.0	2.2	16.3	26.3	8.7	6.1	14.4	11.9	16.2	15.2	10.2
02158		0	Kusilvak	17,077.1	8,360	2,549	0.5	5.5	0.9	93.7	1.2	1.6	13.0	23.2	15.8	14.9	9.6	7.9
02164		9	Lake and Peninsula	23,831.8	1,416	3,085	0.1	32.9	3.7	65.1	7.1	3.0	8.7	15.3	12.6	13.0	12.5	11.6
02170	11260	2	Matanuska-Susitna	24,707.0	110,686	560	4.5	84.3	2.3	11.3	4.4	5.6	6.4	15.1	12.5	13.9	14.3	11.7
02180		7	Nome	22,969.5	9,865	2,419	0.4	19.7	1.5	80.5	2.8	2.2	8.7	20.1	15.3	15.0	12.2	9.5
02185		7	North Slope	88,823.6	10,972	2,344	0.1	32.5	2.5	57.2	9.7	4.2	7.1	16.2	12.3	15.4	14.0	12.9
02188		7	Northwest Arctic	35,663.3	7,560	2,611	0.2	15.3	2.1	83.7	2.6	2.6	9.8	21.1	14.8	14.9	11.1	9.5
02195		9	Petersburg	2,900.7	3,356	2,934	1.2	75.7	3.4	14.8	8.1	5.5	5.1	13.1	10.2	11.7	13.0	11.4
02198		9	Prince of Wales-Hyder	5,267.7	5,729	2,759	1.1	52.0	2.1	46.6	4.6	4.2	4.8	13.1	10.5	11.0	11.7	12.3
02220		7	Sitka	2,870.1	8,407	2,541	2.9	68.9	2.0	20.6	10.2	7.6	5.0	11.6	11.2	14.3	14.2	12.2
02230		9	Skagway	433.9	1,132	3,103	2.6	83.0	2.7	7.3	5.5	6.7	3.0	9.5	5.8	15.2	23.8	14.5
02240		9	Southeast Fairbanks	24,831.1	6,970	2,665	0.3	76.4	2.7	14.7	4.2	7.2	7.7	15.1	10.7	13.5	13.5	11.6
02261		9	Valdez-Cordova	NA	NA	NA	NA	74.3	1.4	18.1	6.7	5.6	6.7	13.0	10.7	13.7	12.8	12.0
02275		9	Wrangell	2,556.0	2,055	3,037	0.8	75.4	2.5	25.3	6.4	3.6	5.2	11.8	8.8	12.0	9.7	10.8
02282		9	Yakutat	7,623.3	704	3,126	0.1	44.5	4.7	45.3	12.9	6.5	4.5	12.8	8.1	14.1	11.4	13.5
02290		9	Yukon-Koyukuk	145,575.5	5,275	2,799	0.0	27.1	1.7	72.6	1.9	3.0	7.3	16.8	12.3	11.8	12.0	9.5
04000		0	ARIZONA	113,653.1	7,276,316	X	64.0	55.2	5.6	4.4	4.8	32.3	5.5	12.7	13.4	13.8	12.6	11.6
04001		6	Apache	11,198.3	65,623	820	5.9	19.3	1.2	73.0	0.9	7.1	6.3	15.3	13.9	13.0	11.4	10.8
04003	43420	3	Cochise	6,209.8	126,050	511	20.3	56.7	4.9	1.7	3.7	35.9	5.3	12.1	12.0	12.3	11.6	10.0
04005	22380	3	Coconino	18,616.4	145,052	460	7.8	55.8	2.0	26.6	3.4	14.9	4.9	11.5	23.3	13.9	11.4	9.9
04007	37740	4	Gila	4,757.3	53,589	949	11.3	62.5	0.9	17.4	1.3	19.2	4.6	11.5	9.4	9.9	9.4	9.7
04009	40940	7	Graham	4,621.9	39,050	1,203	8.4	52.0	2.1	12.2	1.4	33.8	6.6	15.3	14.7	14.6	13.6	11.0
04011		7	Greenlee	1,842.1	9,404	2,460	5.1	45.5	2.3	3.6	1.3	49.0	7.1	16.0	12.2	14.9	14.3	10.8
04012		6	La Paz	4,496.6	16,408	2,008	3.6	57.6	1.7	12.9	1.5	28.6	4.4	9.1	8.2	8.6	8.6	8.2
04013	38060	1	Maricopa	9,201.8	4,496,588	4	488.7	55.6	6.9	2.2	5.9	32.0	5.7	13.2	13.4	14.6	13.3	12.3
04015	29420	3	Mohave	13,332.1	217,692	318	16.3	77.4	1.7	3.0	2.2	17.7	4.1	9.4	8.8	10.2	9.4	10.2
04017	43320	4	Navajo	9,949.5	108,147	573	10.9	43.6	1.5	43.4	1.3	12.1	6.1	14.9	12.7	12.0	11.1	10.5
04019	46060	2	Pima	9,188.7	1,052,030	45	114.5	52.1	4.4	3.1	4.1	38.5	5.0	11.6	15.1	13.0	11.7	10.8
04021	38060	1	Pinal	5,366.0	449,557	160	83.8	57.0	6.1	5.0	3.0	31.4	5.4	12.8	11.6	13.2	13.1	11.2
04023	35700	4	Santa Cruz	1,236.2	47,883	1,026	38.7	15.8	0.6	0.5	0.7	82.7	6.6	14.8	13.8	11.7	10.9	11.2
04025	39150	3	Yavapai	8,122.9	242,253	288	29.8	81.0	1.2	2.4	2.0	15.3	3.8	9.0	9.1	9.0	9.0	10.0
04027	49740	3	Yuma	5,513.8	206,990	330	37.5	30.3	2.3	1.4	1.8	65.5	6.9	14.0	14.9	14.0	11.4	9.6
05000		0	ARKANSAS	52,037.5	3,025,891	X	58.1	73.2	16.3	1.7	2.6	8.3	6.0	13.2	13.3	13.0	12.5	11.8
05001		6	Arkansas	992.1	16,722	1,991	16.9	70.0	25.9	1.0	1.1	3.9	6.3	13.2	10.7	11.5	11.8	12.2
05003		7	Ashley	925.5	18,674	1,887	20.2	69.1	24.5	0.9	0.5	6.3	5.7	13.0	11.5	11.0	10.9	12.5
05005	34260	7	Baxter	553.9	42,144	1,143	76.1	95.3	0.8	1.8	0.9	2.8	4.3	10.2	9.3	9.5	9.9	10.9
05007	22220	2	Benton	847.7	293,692	241	346.5	73.7	2.6	2.7	6.0	17.6	6.6	14.7	12.5	14.8	14.9	12.1
05009	25460	7	Boone	589.7	37,830	1,226	64.2	94.9	0.9	2.1	1.0	3.0	5.5	13.1	11.5	11.7	11.6	12.0
05011		7	Bradley	649.2	10,408	2,383	16.0	55.6	27.9	1.1	0.6	16.5	6.4	14.1	11.6	11.6	11.8	12.1
05013	15780	9	Calhoun	628.6	4,741	2,840	7.5	74.2	21.3	1.4	0.7	4.8	4.5	11.0	10.9	11.8	11.3	13.3
05015		6	Carroll	629.9	28,435	1,480	45.1	79.0	1.2	2.4	3.8	15.7	5.4	12.4	11.1	10.5	10.9	11.2
05017		7	Chicot	637.0	10,019	2,402	15.7	39.6	53.4	0.7	0.8	6.5	5.7	12.5	11.8	10.7	10.6	11.8
05019	11660	7	Clark	866.0	21,321	1,745	24.6	69.9	24.4	1.1	1.4	5.1	5.1	11.2	25.2	10.8	9.7	9.9
05021		7	Clay	639.2	14,350	2,126	22.4	95.8	1.6	1.4	0.5	2.4	5.3	12.1	11.3	12.0	11.1	12.5
05023		6	Cleburne	554.0	25,015	1,610	45.2	95.3	1.0	1.7	0.7	3.0	4.5	11.0	9.8	9.6	10.6	11.4

1. CBSA = Core Based Statistical Area. See Appendix A for explanation. See Appendix B for list of metropolitan areas with component counties. 2. County type code from the Economic Research Service of USDA Rural-Urban Continuum Codes. See Appendix A for definition. 3. Dry land or land partially or temporarily covered by water. 4. May be of any race.

STATE County	Population, 2021 (cont.)				Population change, 2000–2021							Households, 2016–2020				
	Age (percent) (cont.)				Total persons		Percent change		Components of change, 2020–2021					Percent		
	55 to 64 years	65 to 74 years	75 years and over	Percent female	2010	2020	2010–2020	2020–2021	Births	Deaths	Net Migration	Number	Persons per household	Family house-holds	Female family house-holder[1]	One person
	16	17	18	19	20	21	22	23	24	25	26	27	28	29	30	31
ALABAMA—Cont'd																
Washington	15.0	12.1	8.0	51.0	17,581	15,388	-12.5	-1.6	189	303	-130	5,830	2.8	71.0	11.1	26.6
Wilcox	13.6	12.6	8.6	52.9	11,670	10,600	-9.2	-1.5	164	214	-104	3,961	2.6	64.7	25.1	30.4
Winston	15.5	12.8	9.4	50.6	24,484	23,540	-3.9	0.5	270	485	333	9,612	2.4	68.1	10.7	28.7
ALASKA	12.3	9.1	4.3	47.6	710,231	733,391	3.3	-0.1	11,687	7,025	-5,365	255,173	2.8	65.8	10.3	26.3
Aleutians East	14.2	6.6	5.1	33.0	3,141	3,420	8.9	-0.6	16	18	-21	988	2.4	60.0	11.3	32.4
Aleutians West	15.5	6.7	1.4	32.6	5,561	5,232	-5.9	-3.3	38	21	-188	1,306	3.4	58.2	6.1	32.2
Anchorage	11.8	8.3	4.2	48.8	291,826	291,247	-0.2	-1.1	4,668	2,740	-5,061	106,970	2.7	65.0	10.7	25.9
Bethel	10.1	5.9	2.5	47.7	17,013	18,666	9.7	-0.6	512	207	-413	4,499	3.8	74.6	19.5	20.0
Bristol Bay	17.3	11.3	6.3	46.1	997	844	-15.3	-0.7	10	12	-4	284	2.3	62.7	6.3	27.8
Chugach	16.6	11.5	4.1	46.6	6,684	7,102	6.3	-2.3	90	49	-201	2,310	2.7	68.3	4.2	26.8
Copper River	14.0	13.0	6.2	45.6	2,952	2,617	-11.3	0.5	33	33	13	1,063	2.7	66.7	7.1	25.0
Denali	15.7	9.4	3.5	45.4	1,826	1,619	-11.3	-1.6	21	4	-41	726	2.2	45.9	3.4	45.5
Dillingham	12.6	7.6	3.4	48.3	4,847	4,857	0.2	-1.8	98	58	-125	1,430	3.2	74.3	23.2	21.6
Fairbanks North Star	10.4	8.2	3.7	45.9	97,581	95,655	-2.0	-0.1	1,628	778	-928	36,199	2.6	65.9	7.9	25.1
Haines	17.8	17.1	7.0	48.8	2,508	2,080	-17.1	-0.4	22	29	-3	917	2.7	58.1	6.9	35.4
Hoonah-Angoon	18.9	17.3	8.3	45.2	2,150	2,365	10.0	-1.4	25	35	-22	755	2.6	57.9	11.0	34.3
Juneau	14.0	10.4	4.8	49.1	31,275	32,255	3.1	-0.9	355	256	-386	12,878	2.5	58.1	8.3	32.0
Kenai Peninsula	14.5	13.2	6.2	47.6	55,400	58,799	6.1	1.6	803	707	880	21,781	2.6	62.9	7.4	30.7
Ketchikan Gateway	14.6	11.6	6.1	48.6	13,477	13,948	3.5	-1.4	148	132	-209	5,299	2.6	66.1	11.0	26.1
Kodiak Island	12.8	8.9	4.2	46.2	13,592	13,101	-3.6	-2.4	159	93	-378	4,231	3.1	68.5	12.5	25.8
Kusilvak	8.9	5.0	1.8	46.8	7,459	8,368	12.2	-0.1	301	107	-203	1,750	4.6	82.7	28.8	12.9
Lake and Peninsula	14.0	8.8	3.6	48.9	1,631	1,476	-9.5	-4.1	28	22	-65	366	2.9	69.7	20.2	25.1
Matanuska-Susitna	12.8	9.3	3.9	48.0	88,995	107,081	20.3	3.4	1,676	1,027	2,980	31,964	3.3	71.0	8.9	23.4
Nome	10.4	6.2	2.5	47.3	9,492	10,046	5.8	-1.8	231	121	-290	2,777	3.4	74.0	22.0	20.2
North Slope	14.2	5.7	2.2	38.5	9,430	11,031	17.0	-0.5	165	76	-151	1,991	3.3	73.7	22.2	18.1
Northwest Arctic	10.4	5.2	3.0	46.0	7,523	7,793	3.6	-3.0	186	76	-339	1,795	4.0	73.1	23.2	20.4
Petersburg	14.1	14.5	6.9	48.3	3,815	3,398	-10.9	-1.2	39	42	-39	1,204	2.7	65.6	11.0	27.0
Prince of Wales-Hyder	16.7	14.3	5.6	45.1	5,559	5,753	3.5	-0.4	70	62	-32	2,353	2.7	63.6	10.1	31.4
Sitka	14.3	10.8	6.4	48.8	8,881	8,458	-4.8	-0.6	109	76	-85	3,572	2.3	62.0	9.2	31.6
Skagway	11.6	10.9	5.8	46.7	968	1,240	28.1	-8.7	6	19	-94	411	2.7	47.7	7.3	39.7
Southeast Fairbanks	12.8	10.4	4.9	44.9	7,029	6,808	-3.1	2.4	132	81	112	2,287	2.9	64.3	8.9	30.7
Valdez-Cordova	16.8	10.6	3.9	47.0	NA	NA	NA	NA	NA	NA	NA	NA	NA	NA	NA	NA
Wrangell	16.6	16.9	8.2	46.9	2,369	2,127	-10.2	-3.4	26	72	-26	989	2.5	65.1	8.0	27.2
Yakutat	16.1	12.6	7.0	43.2	662	662	0.0	6.3	6	2	39	221	2.4	65.2	22.2	32.6
Yukon-Koyukuk	13.6	11.5	5.2	46.7	5,588	5,343	-4.4	-1.3	86	70	-85	1,857	2.6	58.1	18.7	35.8
ARIZONA	12.1	10.8	7.6	50.1	6,392,017	7,151,502	11.9	1.7	94,533	94,005	124,295	2,643,430	2.7	65.1	12.1	27.5
Apache	13.1	10.0	6.3	50.4	71,518	66,021	-7.7	-0.6	1,001	1,247	-165	21,505	3.3	66.9	22.1	31.1
Cochise	13.0	13.8	9.9	48.8	131,346	125,447	-4.5	0.5	1,574	1,986	1,016	50,917	2.3	62.2	10.2	32.9
Coconino	11.1	9.3	4.8	50.6	134,421	145,101	7.9	0.0	1,651	1,430	-306	49,016	2.6	59.4	12.0	26.9
Gila	15.7	17.7	12.2	49.9	53,597	53,272	-0.6	0.6	576	1,208	963	22,523	2.3	62.5	11.9	31.2
Graham	10.1	8.5	5.6	46.2	37,220	38,533	3.5	1.3	585	452	378	11,348	3.1	71.0	14.6	22.7
Greenlee	10.2	8.8	5.6	47.8	8,437	9,563	13.3	-1.7	147	70	-234	3,295	2.8	72.2	8.8	23.7
La Paz	12.1	18.3	22.5	48.5	20,489	16,557	-19.2	-0.9	203	462	116	9,928	2.1	61.1	9.8	34.8
Maricopa	11.7	9.3	6.5	50.3	3,817,117	4,420,568	15.8	1.7	60,751	51,072	65,914	1,596,784	2.7	65.6	12.2	26.6
Mohave	16.2	18.5	13.3	49.2	200,186	213,267	6.5	2.1	2,077	5,051	7,504	90,413	2.3	62.5	10.0	30.6
Navajo	13.4	12.2	7.1	49.6	107,449	106,717	-0.7	1.3	1,638	1,897	1,695	36,406	3.0	70.2	18.8	25.0
Pima	12.1	11.9	8.7	50.5	980,263	1,043,433	6.4	0.8	12,339	15,387	11,592	410,942	2.5	61.0	12.4	31.0
Pinal	11.7	12.5	8.5	48.0	375,770	425,264	13.2	5.7	5,639	5,602	24,553	148,435	2.8	71.4	10.7	22.9
Santa Cruz	11.8	11.2	8.0	51.4	47,420	47,669	0.5	0.4	697	569	79	16,049	2.9	73.3	14.3	24.0
Yavapai	16.5	20.4	13.2	50.8	211,033	236,209	11.9	2.6	2,128	4,646	8,700	101,245	2.2	61.4	7.9	31.8
Yuma	9.7	9.8	9.8	48.2	195,751	203,881	4.2	1.5	3,527	2,926	2,490	74,624	2.8	72.8	14.1	21.9
ARKANSAS	12.7	10.4	7.0	50.7	2,915,918	3,011,524	3.3	0.5	43,575	47,706	18,458	1,170,544	2.5	65.8	13.1	28.7
Arkansas	14.1	12.3	7.9	51.5	19,019	17,149	-9.8	-2.5	267	358	-332	7,416	2.4	63.2	10.8	30.4
Ashley	14.2	12.0	9.2	51.1	21,853	19,062	-12.8	-2.0	276	375	-287	7,716	2.6	68.0	11.1	29.6
Baxter	15.3	16.6	14.0	51.2	41,513	41,627	0.3	1.2	401	1,073	1,213	18,727	2.2	64.7	7.5	30.3
Benton	10.8	8.2	5.4	49.9	221,339	284,333	28.5	3.3	4,279	2,902	8,006	99,661	2.7	73.3	10.3	21.2
Boone	13.9	11.8	9.0	50.5	36,903	37,373	1.3	1.2	456	698	709	15,043	2.5	67.0	8.0	29.1
Bradley	13.3	11.3	7.8	51.2	11,508	10,545	-8.4	-1.3	184	193	-129	4,233	2.5	61.3	11.1	33.5
Calhoun	15.6	13.0	8.7	48.9	5,368	4,739	-11.7	0.0	67	100	35	1,754	2.9	71.3	8.7	28.1
Carroll	14.5	14.6	9.3	49.9	27,446	28,260	3.0	0.6	361	450	269	11,079	2.5	67.1	10.3	27.8
Chicot	14.8	12.6	9.4	48.8	11,800	10,208	-13.5	-1.9	140	247	-82	4,052	2.4	63.8	17.9	33.8
Clark	11.4	9.6	7.2	52.0	22,995	21,446	-6.7	-0.6	274	373	-29	8,336	2.4	61.8	12.8	29.0
Clay	14.2	11.9	9.4	50.3	16,083	14,552	-9.5	-1.4	171	299	-74	6,476	2.3	65.0	12.1	30.2
Cleburne	16.0	14.9	12.2	50.4	25,970	24,711	-4.8	1.2	264	557	610	10,882	2.3	65.2	7.9	30.7

1. No spouse present.

STATE County	Persons in group quarters, 2021	Daytime Population, 2016–2020		Births, 2021		Deaths, 2021		Persons under 65 with no health insurance, 2019		Medicare, 2021			COVID-19 Deaths, 2020	
		Number	Employment/ residence ratio	Total	Rate[1]	Number	Rate[1]	Number	Percent	Total beneficiaries	Enrolled in Original Medicare	Enrolled in Medicare Advantage	Number	Rate[1]
	32	33	34	35	36	37	38	39	40	41	42	43	44	45
ALABAMA—Cont'd														
Washington	74	15,465	0.8	151	9.9	235	15.4	1,781	13.8	4,232	2,599	1,634	25	1.6
Wilcox	104	10,574	1.0	144	13.7	158	15.1	934	11.6	3,165	1,941	1,224	23	2.2
Winston	243	22,129	0.8	216	9.2	401	17.0	2,389	13.0	6,131	3,727	2,403	41	1.7
ALASKA	25,840	744,364	1.0	9,280	12.7	5,641	7.7	79,260	12.7	104,362	102,526	1,836	230	0.3
Aleutians East	1,735	3,476	1.0	14	4.1	14	4.1	691	23.3	163	163	0	D	D
Aleutians West	2,181	6,311	1.2	29	5.7	14	2.7	884	17.7	235	D	D	D	D
Anchorage	7,791	302,231	1.1	3,726	12.9	2,179	7.5	27,810	11.1	39,937	39,199	738	139	0.5
Bethel	337	18,682	1.1	408	21.9	165	8.9	2,755	16.8	1,536	D	D	15	0.8
Bristol Bay	15	883	1.3	8	9.6	11	13.2	103	15.1	157	D	D	D	D
Chugach	183	6,772	1.1	75	10.7	40	5.7	NA	NA	NA	NA	NA	NA	NA
Copper River	9	3,268	1.3	29	11.1	29	11.1	NA	NA	NA	NA	NA	NA	NA
Denali	68	3,001	1.3	14	8.7	2	1.2	206	11.5	274	D	D	D	D
Dillingham	48	5,065	1.1	76	15.8	48	10.0	678	15.5	530	D	D	D	D
Fairbanks North Star	4,562	97,481	1.0	1,276	13.4	641	6.7	9,282	11.3	11,962	11,838	124	21	0.2
Haines	0	2,568	1.0	18	8.7	23	11.1	252	12.6	627	606	21	D	D
Hoonah-Angoon	0	2,130	1.0	17	7.2	24	10.2	323	20.0	517	D	D	D	D
Juneau	956	32,525	1.0	275	8.6	204	6.4	3,070	11.4	5,283	5,233	50	D	D
Kenai Peninsula	1,552	57,914	1.0	663	11.2	582	9.8	6,432	13.8	12,419	12,048	371	21	0.4
Ketchikan Gateway	249	13,947	1.0	113	8.2	106	7.7	1,547	13.5	2,570	2,542	28	D	D
Kodiak Island	366	13,595	1.0	130	10.1	78	6.0	2,047	18.2	1,728	1,710	18	D	D
Kusilvak	9	8,374	1.0	243	29.1	84	10.0	1,197	15.6	565	D	D	NA	NA
Lake and Peninsula	37	1,260	1.2	21	14.6	17	11.8	266	19.1	161	161	0	D	D
Matanuska-Susitna	1,849	95,351	0.7	1,322	12.1	818	7.5	11,867	12.8	15,595	15,238	357	34	0.3
Nome	178	10,113	1.0	176	17.7	99	10.0	1,533	17.2	902	D	D	D	D
North Slope	2,584	15,928	2.3	123	11.2	58	5.3	1,192	13.2	547	D	D	D	D
Northwest Arctic	396	7,953	1.1	150	19.6	57	7.4	1,201	17.5	586	D	D	D	D
Petersburg	43	3,431	1.1	33	9.8	39	11.5	430	16.7	845	834	11	D	D
Prince of Wales-Hyder	19	6,340	1.0	54	9.4	36	6.3	945	18.9	1,056	D	D	D	D
Sitka	241	8,540	1.0	85	10.1	58	6.9	951	13.4	1,496	1,483	13	D	D
Skagway	32	1,301	1.0	6	5.1	19	16.0	112	11.1	194	D	D	D	D
Southeast Fairbanks	325	7,354	1.2	101	14.6	68	9.9	1,044	18.3	1,345	1,316	29	D	D
Valdez-Cordova	NA	NA	NA	NA	NA	NA	NA	1,151	14.7	1,539	1,516	22	D	D
Wrangell	7	2,515	1.0	19	9.1	67	32.0	344	18.4	545	D	D	D	D
Yakutat	19	664	1.2	4	5.8	1	1.4	83	18.2	114	114	0	D	D
Yukon-Koyukuk	49	5,391	1.0	72	13.6	60	11.3	864	20.0	931	D	D	D	D
ARIZONA	145,709	7,145,195	1.0	76,497	10.6	75,665	10.5	789,960	13.6	1,369,035	787,095	581,940	9,177	1.3
Apache	669	70,311	0.9	818	12.4	985	15.0	12,371	21.0	13,310	11,902	1,407	315	4.8
Cochise	5,063	125,360	1.0	1,291	10.3	1,582	12.6	10,599	11.5	33,438	22,351	11,088	181	1.4
Coconino	11,896	142,573	1.0	1,304	9.0	1,182	8.1	17,084	15.2	21,301	17,234	4,067	219	1.5
Gila	682	54,114	1.0	465	8.7	969	18.1	5,535	14.8	17,194	13,162	4,031	131	2.5
Graham	2,692	37,593	1.0	466	12.0	371	9.6	3,591	11.8	5,929	3,443	2,486	54	1.4
Greenlee	35	11,134	1.4	121	12.8	54	5.7	640	7.9	1,301	1,026	276	D	D
La Paz	166	22,033	1.2	167	10.1	392	23.8	2,616	21.2	5,915	4,284	1,631	36	2.2
Maricopa	61,914	4,462,421	1.0	49,202	11.0	41,160	9.2	493,829	13.3	722,323	397,785	324,538	4,829	1.1
Mohave	3,945	200,206	0.9	1,671	7.7	4,021	18.6	19,205	13.6	68,799	44,048	24,751	363	1.7
Navajo	1,830	110,231	1.0	1,273	11.8	1,482	13.8	15,219	17.4	24,710	19,199	5,511	390	3.7
Pima	23,601	1,038,679	1.0	9,925	9.5	12,448	11.9	107,748	13.3	236,346	118,826	117,520	1,268	1.2
Pinal	20,718	387,207	0.6	4,596	10.5	4,496	10.2	43,484	12.8	85,159	45,241	39,919	431	1.0
Santa Cruz	268	45,310	0.9	563	11.8	444	9.3	6,241	16.9	10,198	4,460	5,738	112	2.4
Yavapai	3,740	228,890	1.0	1,740	7.3	3,729	15.6	23,125	14.8	85,203	57,812	27,391	280	1.2
Yuma	8,490	209,133	1.0	2,895	14.1	2,350	11.4	28,673	17.7	37,910	26,323	11,587	568	2.8
ARKANSAS	75,792	3,009,515	1.0	35,021	11.6	38,257	12.7	261,617	10.8	646,559	453,618	192,942	4,004	1.3
Arkansas	169	19,835	1.3	207	12.2	282	16.7	1,338	9.8	4,219	3,376	843	25	1.5
Ashley	124	19,378	0.9	221	11.7	305	16.2	1,710	11.2	5,190	4,250	940	22	1.2
Baxter	483	43,292	1.1	315	7.5	854	20.4	2,924	10.2	15,264	10,164	5,100	80	1.9
Benton	1,813	279,207	1.0	3,445	11.9	2,362	8.1	26,888	11.1	44,485	27,144	17,341	294	1.0
Boone	376	38,165	1.0	375	10.0	565	15.0	2,919	10.0	10,335	7,174	3,162	68	1.8
Bradley	167	10,458	0.9	146	14.0	147	14.1	1,114	13.1	2,538	2,032	507	28	2.7
Calhoun	114	5,606	1.2	55	11.6	75	15.8	372	9.6	1,185	889	296	D	D
Carroll	178	27,955	1.0	295	10.4	356	12.6	3,225	15.1	7,584	4,723	2,860	39	1.4
Chicot	715	10,778	1.1	112	11.1	204	20.2	678	9.4	2,647	1,923	724	30	3.0
Clark	2,733	22,112	1.0	227	10.6	301	14.1	1,471	9.4	4,637	3,303	1,334	21	1.0
Clay	99	13,213	0.8	140	9.7	241	16.7	1,131	10.1	4,005	3,122	883	31	2.1
Cleburne	266	23,361	0.8	211	8.5	432	17.4	1,897	10.6	8,190	6,290	1,900	39	1.6

1. Per 1,000 estimated resident population.

STATE County	COVID-19 Vaccinations, 2021–2022		Education						Money income, 2016–2020				Income and poverty, 2020			
			School enrollment and attainment, 2016–2020				Local government expenditures,[3] 2018–2019			Households				Percent below poverty level		
			Enrollment[1]		Attainment[2] (percent)						Percent					
	Number	Percent[5]	Total	Percent private	High school graduate or less	Bachelor's degree or more	Total current spending (mil dol)	Current spending per student (dollars)	Per capita income[4]	Median income (dollars)	with income of less than $50,000	with income of $200,000 or more	Median household income (dollars)	All persons	Children under 18 years	Children 5 to 17 years in families
	46	47	48	49	50	51	52	53	54	55	56	57	58	59	60	61
ALABAMA—Cont'd																
Washington	7,511	46.0	3,588	20.4	58.3	14.4	25.5	9,587	30,391	42,331	55.7	5.0	36,346	17.5	22.9	22.6
Wilcox	5,591	53.9	2,448	11.8	61.1	11.7	18.7	11,877	19,031	35,063	65.4	1.6	31,909	22.2	29.4	31.4
Winston	5,203	22.0	3,952	3.9	60.3	13.3	42.2	10,559	23,269	40,991	58.7	1.9	46,453	17.4	22.8	21.9
ALASKA	455,411	62.3	180,787	12.8	35.3	30.0	2,408.9	18,394	37,094	77,790	29.8	8.8	79,961	9.6	12.3	11.1
Aleutians East	2,512	75.3	458	9.8	54.1	16.6	8.9	37,898	36,973	75,833	34.2	4.4	79,128	15.1	13.2	12.9
Aleutians West	3,539	62.8	1,052	6.3	50.7	17.0	11.2	22,396	44,164	87,443	16.2	9.3	92,216	8.1	6.0	6.0
Anchorage	195,007	67.7	72,689	12.8	29.7	36.6	720.8	15,453	41,127	84,813	25.7	10.8	84,577	8.3	9.0	8.3
Bethel	12,386	67.4	5,573	1.4	65.2	11.3	174.5	34,313	21,392	54,400	45.6	5.7	52,214	25.3	36.8	36.6
Bristol Bay	917	95.0	116	5.2	36.2	25.8	20.5	44,065	46,950	79,808	25.0	9.5	87,032	10.7	11.8	11.1
Chugach	NA	NA	1,314	20.9	28.4	29.1	NA	NA	42,592	90,776	27.4	9.4	84,063	7.0	7.2	6.8
Copper River	NA	NA	680	25.0	39.1	31.5	NA	NA	33,776	64,745	35.1	8.1	61,215	12.7	16.6	13.9
Denali	1,138	54.3	372	6.7	32.4	39.1	10.6	10,864	35,873	76,364	34.8	5.8	80,192	6.4	7.2	6.3
Dillingham	2,574	52.4	1,268	2.1	53.6	19.4	33.2	31,037	26,381	57,436	44.5	2.4	72,334	18.7	26.5	23.2
Fairbanks North Star	58,331	60.2	25,500	15.2	29.6	32.3	260.6	17,079	38,031	76,464	28.8	8.4	76,650	7.2	7.9	7.8
Haines	1,736	68.6	782	0.0	36.3	27.7	5.5	21,019	30,069	65,014	39.1	4.8	105,044	9.6	18.4	17.2
Hoonah-Angoon	1,510	70.3	303	11.2	42.4	19.6	9.7	33,127	37,200	59,926	42.1	4.6	55,593	12.7	23.2	21.8
Juneau	24,584	76.9	7,150	11.1	25.3	38.8	82.5	17,377	43,074	88,077	22.6	10.0	89,204	8.1	11.9	9.5
Kenai Peninsula	28,397	48.4	12,442	20.1	38.3	25.8	158.1	17,859	35,312	69,245	35.5	7.2	68,448	10.6	14.7	12.3
Ketchikan Gateway	9,136	65.7	2,855	10.1	36.8	25.5	44.3	19,155	38,343	74,678	33.3	7.2	76,780	8.3	9.8	8.9
Kodiak Island	8,485	65.3	3,237	15.8	37.6	29.8	48.8	20,579	32,495	79,173	26.2	5.2	72,028	7.5	8.1	7.0
Kusilvak	5,551	66.8	2,618	0.8	75.6	3.3	79.5	31,375	14,109	37,358	66.1	1.1	37,566	27.9	42.5	41.0
Lake and Peninsula	916	57.5	339	3.5	47.5	23.1	NA	NA	24,983	48,750	50.8	1.1	54,386	17.6	23.0	22.8
Matanuska-Susitna	44,053	40.7	26,926	15.7	40.4	21.9	282.2	14,989	31,963	76,118	32.7	8.1	89,502	8.7	9.5	7.7
Nome	7,067	70.6	2,968	2.2	57.3	17.0	77.5	28,979	24,613	62,843	39.1	6.0	64,309	18.8	23.1	20.6
North Slope	3,832	39.0	2,244	1.3	52.3	15.1	79.9	36,416	45,889	79,083	30.0	7.6	94,759	11.1	14.0	12.5
Northwest Arctic	4,660	61.1	2,240	2.9	62.4	15.0	76.6	36,689	25,601	63,750	40.0	6.6	65,194	18.5	25.4	23.3
Petersburg	2,486	76.1	476	7.8	44.5	25.5	9.6	20,624	34,296	68,667	36.0	8.3	66,096	7.4	9.4	8.7
Prince of Wales-Hyder	3,320	53.5	1,399	6.9	46.9	17.2	37.5	28,342	28,652	54,018	47.0	2.5	53,638	15.9	20.9	17.9
Sitka	6,690	78.8	1,980	12.1	30.1	34.2	36.8	22,273	41,082	81,708	29.2	6.4	79,363	7.4	7.9	6.8
Skagway	833	70.4	193	4.7	41.9	24.2	3.2	22,922	41,842	71,875	32.1	3.4	78,421	3.8	5.0	4.6
Southeast Fairbanks	2,817	40.9	1,666	16.4	44.1	21.2	28.5	23,463	31,885	66,941	40.1	4.4	64,544	11.7	15.2	14.3
Valdez-Cordova	5,802	63.1	NA	NA	NA	NA	32.0	21,637	NA	NA	NA	NA	NA	NA	NA	NA
Wrangell	1,449	57.9	440	4.1	44.3	16.9	6.5	21,393	32,159	58,438	41.8	2.7	64,643	10.6	13.1	10.5
Yakutat	455	78.6	133	8.3	47.2	18.0	2.1	24,149	32,861	59,517	26.7	0.9	68,352	12.4	23.8	22.9
Yukon-Koyukuk	4,050	77.4	1,374	2.0	54.1	13.2	67.9	9,830	24,587	41,728	57.6	2.0	43,060	20.5	27.6	25.4
ARIZONA	4,478,221	61.5	1,760,360	12.4	35.9	30.3	9,727.2	8,689	32,340	61,529	40.6	6.4	64,652	12.8	17.6	16.6
Apache	74,229	95.0	19,576	3.9	49.8	12.5	147.0	14,087	15,781	33,967	64.6	0.6	36,319	32.4	44.4	40.1
Cochise	81,970	65.1	28,273	11.9	35.3	25.6	169.9	9,150	28,021	51,505	48.2	2.8	51,171	14.6	20.7	19.4
Coconino	110,496	77.0	48,201	7.3	30.7	37.6	185.5	10,419	27,631	59,000	42.1	5.2	57,146	17.2	17.3	16.2
Gila	32,065	59.4	9,527	9.9	41.4	19.2	77.2	10,492	26,265	46,907	52.7	2.5	49,280	16.7	26.2	24.6
Graham	24,839	64.0	10,150	7.6	45.0	14.8	58.4	8,554	19,878	55,693	45.3	1.8	55,419	15.2	16.3	15.0
Greenlee	4,191	44.1	2,318	7.3	45.3	16.8	17.3	9,884	27,618	66,368	34.3	2.5	67,530	8.4	9.0	8.6
La Paz	10,237	48.5	3,162	8.0	52.6	11.8	27.1	10,981	24,039	34,956	64.0	1.6	41,637	20.8	26.3	24.4
Maricopa	2,575,090	57.4	1,104,660	13.0	34.0	33.4	6,352.9	8,515	35,090	67,799	36.3	8.1	71,799	11.6	16.0	15.2
Mohave	88,448	41.7	34,836	16.0	47.9	13.4	192.9	8,127	27,968	47,686	52.2	2.5	46,678	15.3	25.5	23.7
Navajo	86,196	77.7	27,318	6.9	45.4	16.1	192.9	10,913	19,623	43,140	56.9	1.4	46,698	23.3	31.5	29.5
Pima	724,561	69.2	261,541	11.3	32.4	33.6	1,260.6	8,732	30,747	55,023	45.6	5.0	56,551	14.9	20.0	17.9
Pinal	249,880	54.0	100,923	14.2	43.3	20.9	453.4	8,441	27,354	60,968	40.2	3.7	66,992	11.1	14.6	13.6
Santa Cruz	52,994	95.0	11,850	8.9	49.6	20.9	86.9	12,707	21,686	41,424	56.9	3.7	44,402	16.8	25.5	24.7
Yavapai	110,056	46.8	43,985	21.3	34.3	26.3	209.5	8,797	31,779	53,329	46.9	4.1	58,860	10.8	15.2	13.2
Yuma	150,437	70.4	54,040	5.2	52.1	15.4	295.8	7,792	23,507	48,790	50.9	2.2	54,278	15.2	20.5	20.6
ARKANSAS	1,641,408	54.4	725,947	11.6	46.7	23.8	5,109.5	10,312	27,724	49,475	50.4	4.0	51,146	15.2	20.8	19.3
Arkansas	9,780	55.9	3,930	11.9	57.0	16.4	28.7	10,033	26,969	51,000	48.2	2.2	51,186	17.2	21.8	21.4
Ashley	9,853	50.1	4,336	6.3	63.4	12.2	34.6	9,596	23,138	43,601	55.3	2.3	44,677	17.1	24.4	21.9
Baxter	19,694	47.0	7,397	9.5	46.3	17.8	47.2	9,256	27,695	43,504	56.3	2.0	44,833	14.4	24.0	23.0
Benton	149,410	53.5	67,567	13.8	39.3	34.6	459.3	9,835	36,597	71,556	32.3	9.2	78,678	9.1	12.5	10.8
Boone	14,033	37.5	7,579	6.8	46.1	17.8	64.1	10,555	24,749	46,392	53.3	2.4	48,153	14.1	19.8	17.7
Bradley	6,137	57.0	2,563	4.2	59.5	13.8	22.3	10,932	22,912	41,808	58.5	1.7	41,578	20.6	28.4	26.8
Calhoun	1,931	37.2	1,076	6.8	61.4	10.7	6.5	11,025	24,823	50,441	49.3	0.2	50,865	16.2	22.3	21.1
Carroll	13,575	47.8	5,923	11.4	49.6	21.2	40.9	10,434	26,445	48,249	51.1	3.9	45,397	14.1	20.6	19.4
Chicot	5,530	54.7	2,275	17.1	59.6	14.6	17.3	12,300	21,418	33,523	65.6	3.7	35,992	26.8	36.7	34.1
Clark	10,926	49.0	7,203	7.3	43.6	25.2	41.5	16,252	21,708	39,500	56.9	2.5	46,464	20.1	22.0	21.3
Clay	6,661	45.8	3,048	10.6	57.9	13.6	22.4	9,284	22,935	37,933	61.1	1.8	43,723	18.1	24.3	23.1
Cleburne	11,100	44.5	3,990	12.3	54.2	16.7	35.3	10,866	27,490	45,563	54.9	3.3	49,964	14.5	20.9	19.7

1. All persons 3 years old and over enrolled in nursery school through college. 2. Persons 25 years old and over. 3. Elementary and secondary education expenditures. 4. Based on population estimated by the American Community Survey, 2016–2020. 5. CDC percent based on 2019 population estimate.

STATE County	Personal income, 2020										Earnings, 2020		
			Per capita[1]			Supplements to wages and salaries, employer contributions (mil dol)						Contributions for government social insurance (mil dol)	
	Total (mil dol)	Percent change 2019–2020	Dollars	Rank	Wages and salaries (mil dol)	Pension and insurance	Government social insurance	Proprietors' income (mil dol)	Dividends, interest, and rent (mil dol)	Personal transfer reecipts (mil dol)	Total (mil dol)	From employee and self-employed	From employer
	62	63	64	65	66	67	68	69	70	71	72	73	74
ALABAMA—Cont'd													
Washington	645	5.5	40,371	2,405	248	52	18	22	66	227	339	26	18
Wilcox	391	10.7	38,273	2,654	139	27	10	33	52	187	209	16	10
Winston	902	7.2	38,382	2,637	343	62	29	60	153	314	494	39	29
ALASKA	46,430	2.5	63,391	X	21,536	5,700	1,569	3,317	8,334	9,415	32,122	1,680	1,569
Aleutians East	203	-1.2	59,574	447	141	30	11	14	14	17	196	10	11
Aleutians West	339	5.6	59,674	441	240	53	18	20	28	32	331	17	18
Anchorage	20,234	1.8	70,477	161	10,402	2,421	779	1,567	3,960	3,745	15,168	815	779
Bethel	884	4.7	47,936	1,401	361	146	24	27	81	294	558	24	24
Bristol Bay	120	-1.4	152,678	5	74	17	6	13	14	13	110	6	6
Chugach	446	D	69,369	172	245	72	16	31	76	80	364	18	16
Copper River	145	D	49,783	1,165	61	19	4	14	31	35	98	6	4
Denali	152	-13.5	72,967	125	73	20	5	6	25	46	105	6	5
Dillingham	294	-2.1	60,792	393	124	39	10	28	47	65	200	10	10
Fairbanks North Star	5,955	3.6	62,254	343	2,781	826	221	216	1,107	1,160	4,043	197	221
Haines	170	-6.3	64,956	264	36	11	3	22	50	41	71	4	3
Hoonah-Angoon	139	-1.1	64,708	275	30	14	2	15	28	43	62	3	2
Juneau	2,362	2.0	74,162	113	1,058	372	67	214	481	362	1,711	77	67
Kenai Peninsula	3,335	4.8	56,139	627	1,145	341	78	247	687	842	1,812	102	78
Ketchikan Gateway	970	-0.8	70,574	158	379	119	27	148	166	208	673	34	27
Kodiak Island	870	2.7	66,988	213	380	122	29	120	142	148	651	31	29
Kusilvak	283	7.4	33,968	2,980	79	48	4	3	24	139	135	5	4
Lake and Peninsula	95	-6.6	63,397	305	35	18	2	7	18	23	63	3	2
Matanuska-Susitna	5,553	5.8	50,386	1,100	1,342	375	102	376	775	1,164	2,195	128	102
Nome	554	3.2	55,950	647	242	83	16	16	61	174	357	16	16
North Slope	844	-3.5	90,809	36	1,288	218	78	14	77	98	1,598	86	78
Northwest Arctic	401	3.8	52,440	896	240	64	16	11	37	137	330	16	16
Petersburg	239	1.9	72,412	132	63	25	4	49	56	57	141	7	4
Prince of Wales-Hyder	301	1.8	48,970	1,261	108	46	7	18	53	87	178	9	7
Sitka	597	-1.8	70,996	152	224	64	16	68	136	113	371	19	16
Skagway	78	-18.9	66,548	231	22	8	2	16	15	18	49	2	2
Southeast Fairbanks	381	6.6	54,808	715	206	51	14	19	63	100	291	17	14
Valdez-Cordova	NA	D	NA	NA	NA	NA	NA	NA	NA	NA	NA	NA	NA
Wrangell	122	-0.2	48,549	1,318	36	12	3	8	27	40	59	4	3
Yakutat	42	11.2	66,119	238	18	6	1	3	7	10	28	1	1
Yukon-Koyukuk	323	2.2	63,675	298	102	58	5	8	45	124	174	7	5
ARIZONA	368,459	10.3	51,332	X	176,179	25,323	12,543	25,639	64,462	91,099	239,683	15,786	12,543
Apache	2,797	14.9	38,915	2,577	907	228	69	43	282	1,424	1,248	86	69
Cochise	5,835	13.1	45,786	1,684	2,243	501	176	264	957	2,181	3,185	221	176
Coconino	7,557	7.5	53,036	855	2,961	591	222	560	1,669	1,837	4,335	266	222
Gila	2,400	11.7	44,201	1,911	712	140	52	88	407	1,133	992	85	52
Graham	1,375	13.4	35,072	2,934	479	99	35	52	137	571	666	45	35
Greenlee	411	5.8	44,050	1,941	359	54	23	15	30	128	452	27	23
La Paz	848	16.0	39,482	2,509	263	53	21	89	141	355	426	29	21
Maricopa	245,078	9.9	53,521	819	132,916	17,403	9,292	17,843	42,574	50,083	177,454	11,290	9,292
Mohave	7,934	8.3	36,529	2,822	2,344	388	175	454	1,277	3,378	3,361	315	175
Navajo	4,055	14.1	36,169	2,859	1,282	267	105	173	507	1,995	1,826	145	105
Pima	51,332	9.6	48,373	1,342	21,306	3,664	1,555	3,264	10,065	14,927	29,789	2,049	1,555
Pinal	17,285	14.5	35,949	2,870	3,256	607	241	775	2,363	5,613	4,879	422	241
Santa Cruz	1,975	10.5	42,204	2,166	738	154	59	241	300	640	1,191	81	59
Yavapai	10,688	10.2	44,490	1,876	3,059	507	227	685	2,633	3,922	4,477	408	227
Yuma	8,887	18.3	40,800	2,354	3,355	667	290	1,092	1,117	2,912	5,404	316	290
ARKANSAS	143,148	5.8	47,522	X	61,910	8,819	4,670	7,421	32,727	38,638	82,821	6,004	4,670
Arkansas	878	9.0	50,534	1,087	487	70	39	103	110	238	699	45	39
Ashley	744	1.0	38,489	2,627	287	45	22	51	79	310	406	32	22
Baxter	1,688	6.2	39,950	2,461	632	103	49	75	311	711	860	80	49
Benton	27,228	3.4	94,289	29	9,146	913	615	373	15,022	2,558	11,047	771	615
Boone	1,434	5.4	38,108	2,673	643	102	50	40	227	520	836	69	50
Bradley	447	6.0	42,037	2,187	156	26	13	27	46	176	222	18	13
Calhoun	197	7.0	38,509	2,623	209	31	16	2	19	65	258	17	16
Carroll	981	5.1	34,692	2,952	403	64	32	2	185	362	501	46	32
Chicot	444	12.0	44,762	1,833	117	18	10	63	50	185	207	14	10
Clark	872	5.6	39,450	2,514	384	63	32	35	125	300	514	38	32
Clay	563	8.0	39,157	2,548	125	21	10	47	69	230	204	17	10
Cleburne	1,039	5.6	41,656	2,244	256	44	20	54	187	385	374	37	20

1. Based on the resident population estimated as of July 1 of the year shown.

STATE County	Earnings, 2020 (cont.)									Social Security beneficiaries, December 2020		Supple-mental Security Income recipients, 2020	Housing units, 2021	
	Percent by selected industries													
	Farm	Mining, quarrying, and extractions	Construction	Manu-facturing	Information; professional, scientific, technical services	Retail trade	Finance, insurance, real estate, and leasing	Health care and social assistance	Govern-ment	Number	Rate[1]		Total	Percent change, 2010–2021
	75	76	77	78	79	80	81	82	83	84	85	86	87	88
ALABAMA—Cont'd														
Washington	2.7	D	4.4	39.9	D	2.8	D	2.0	13.0	4,910	324	652	7,754	0.4
Wilcox	8.5	0.0	3.9	35.8	D	4.6	2.6	D	18.9	3,715	356	1,266	5,297	0.6
Winston	-0.1	D	3.9	42.3	D	5.8	2.8	7.7	12.6	6,795	287	940	13,086	0.4
ALASKA	0.2	6.4	7.1	D	6.4	5.7	4.1	13.0	32.7	107,982	147	12,424	327,890	0.4
Aleutians East	0.0	0.0	D	74.9	D	1.2	D	D	12.0	170	50	15	679	0.0
Aleutians West	1.2	D	2.4	41.8	D	3.2	D	2.5	16.7	245	48	13	1,336	0.3
Anchorage	0.0	3.5	7.0	0.9	9.4	5.6	5.6	15.1	28.9	39,955	139	5,692	119,810	0.8
Bethel	0.0	D	1.2	D	D	5.5	1.7	D	45.1	1,870	101	407	6,000	0.2
Bristol Bay	0.0	D	5.9	40.2	D	3.5	D	D	20.9	150	179	14	860	0.1
Chugach	0.0	0.9	3.4	10.9	4.3	4.1	D	D	30.7	920	133	73	3,582	0.4
Copper River	0.0	0.0	D	1.2	D	4.6	D	D	30.4	665	253	48	2,768	0.0
Denali	0.0	D	3.0	D	0.8	2.6	D	0.7	36.2	285	179	14	1,606	0.0
Dillingham	0.0	D	D	16.0	D	4.0	D	D	29.9	610	128	106	2,404	0.0
Fairbanks North Star	0.1	2.6	8.0	0.9	4.0	5.8	2.9	10.5	48.8	12,375	129	1,117	42,668	0.0
Haines	0.0	D	10.7	D	4.7	9.9	D	11.1	24.3	635	307	41	1,376	0.3
Hoonah-Angoon	0.0	0.0	D	6.7	D	5.6	D	4.5	49.2	515	221	41	1,798	1.1
Juneau	-0.1	D	5.6	1.7	D	5.6	D	7.5	47.6	5,015	157	514	14,177	0.3
Kenai Peninsula	1.9	7.1	6.8	7.0	4.1	7.0	3.1	13.1	30.2	13,100	219	1,004	32,733	0.3
Ketchikan Gateway	0.0	D	5.2	3.8	3.1	9.4	5.5	12.1	33.2	2,640	192	268	6,665	0.6
Kodiak Island	0.0	D	4.8	14.8	1.8	3.3	2.8	9.7	39.3	1,830	143	144	5,848	0.3
Kusilvak	0.0	0.0	D	D	0.1	7.7	D	D	71.7	785	94	187	2,341	0.0
Lake and Peninsula	0.0	-0.1	D	3.9	D	D	D	D	46.9	180	127	24	1,468	-0.1
Matanuska-Susitna	0.7	0.4	18.0	D	6.5	9.9	4.1	15.8	24.8	16,710	151	1,757	51,143	0.1
Nome	0.0	0.0	2.4	D	D	4.7	2.0	D	43.2	1,155	117	224	4,102	0.1
North Slope	0.0	57.7	D	D	2.6	1.0	D	D	14.8	695	63	36	2,655	1.4
Northwest Arctic	0.0	D	2.2	D	D	2.8	D	D	30.6	810	107	88	2,730	0.4
Petersburg	0.0	D	6.2	9.8	D	6.3	2.1	D	37.9	835	249	47	1,748	1.6
Prince of Wales-Hyder	0.0	D	5.0	3.0	D	6.9	3.3	D	50.4	1,115	195	98	3,229	0.0
Sitka	0.0	0.0	6.5	9.6	3.5	6.1	3.4	18.5	30.6	1,485	177	87	4,150	0.2
Skagway	0.0	0.0	D	D	D	15.5	D	D	37.5	145	128	D	765	0.1
Southeast Fairbanks	0.0	32.8	4.7	1.1	4.5	3.7	0.7	6.3	31.5	1,425	204	150	3,512	0.0
Valdez-Cordova	NA	NA	NA	NA	D	NA	D	NA	NA	NA	NA	NA	NA	NA
Wrangell	0.0	0.0	6.0	D	D	9.0	2.0	D	34.0	555	270	36	1,277	0.2
Yakutat	0.0	0.0	D	D	D	D	D	D	35.7	110	156	D	447	1.1
Yukon-Koyukuk	0.0	D	4.9	D	D	2.3	0.1	D	68.0	995	189	170	4,013	0.0
ARIZONA	0.8	0.7	7.0	7.7	10.9	6.8	11.8	12.7	15.2	1,433,237	197	118,853	3,138,871	1.5
Apache	0.2	0.7	1.9	0.9	D	2.9	2.3	14.3	61.1	14,095	215	3,863	28,866	0.4
Cochise	2.1	0.4	8.5	1.3	9.6	6.1	2.6	8.5	45.3	35,400	281	3,158	59,157	0.6
Coconino	0.7	0.0	5.0	8.5	5.1	7.0	5.3	16.7	29.4	22,250	153	2,321	70,056	0.9
Gila	0.9	8.6	5.3	11.6	3.1	7.5	3.4	9.4	36.5	18,400	343	1,337	32,590	0.6
Graham	3.4	D	4.1	2.1	2.0	9.4	D	11.5	31.7	6,660	171	758	13,933	1.4
Greenlee	2.0	D	1.5	0.0	D	2.6	D	D	7.6	1,475	157	111	4,405	0.3
La Paz	18.5	0.4	1.7	1.4	2.8	14.1	D	D	34.1	6,245	381	450	13,685	1.5
Maricopa	0.3	0.3	7.4	7.6	12.1	6.6	13.9	12.5	11.2	748,885	167	60,764	1,849,269	1.6
Mohave	1.6	0.5	8.3	6.1	4.8	12.7	6.4	18.6	16.9	74,085	340	4,642	119,461	1.2
Navajo	0.7	0.6	5.0	1.2	3.2	9.0	3.1	16.1	37.9	26,645	246	4,302	56,810	0.9
Pima	0.2	0.8	5.5	11.4	9.6	6.5	7.2	14.5	23.4	240,875	229	21,066	474,807	0.8
Pinal	5.5	2.2	5.3	6.5	D	8.4	3.9	7.0	31.9	97,200	216	6,440	179,200	2.9
Santa Cruz	1.9	D	2.2	2.7	D	7.7	2.2	4.7	34.7	10,945	229	1,341	18,951	1.0
Yavapai	0.7	2.5	10.2	5.8	6.6	9.8	5.8	15.5	18.9	87,965	363	3,533	123,885	1.8
Yuma	13.4	0.0	4.7	4.1	5.3	7.9	4.1	10.7	26.6	42,110	203	4,767	93,796	1.5
ARKANSAS	0.8	0.4	6.1	12.5	6.3	6.6	6.7	13.3	16.9	707,846	234	103,122	1,380,728	0.9
Arkansas	10.2	D	3.8	31.8	3.6	6.1	4.6	7.8	8.9	4,550	272	656	8,684	0.1
Ashley	7.0	D	9.5	25.0	D	5.8	3.1	12.1	13.1	5,800	311	855	9,383	0.1
Baxter	-0.6	0.4	5.3	16.4	D	9.9	7.1	29.5	11.2	16,220	385	1,049	22,797	0.4
Benton	-0.2	0.0	5.1	7.1	10.2	4.7	2.7	6.1	6.3	48,300	164	3,367	118,234	3.7
Boone	-4.3	D	5.7	12.0	4.7	9.5	4.5	10.2	21.7	11,355	300	1,196	17,386	0.1
Bradley	0.2	D	6.3	26.5	1.7	4.9	3.8	14.0	18.3	2,760	265	491	5,073	0.0
Calhoun	0.0	D	3.3	80.4	D	D	D	1.4	5.3	1,325	279	144	2,451	0.2
Carroll	-9.5	0.2	8.2	34.4	D	7.3	6.0	10.5	13.3	8,240	290	569	13,913	0.3
Chicot	23.0	0.0	5.6	0.3	D	5.3	8.4	15.7	21.7	2,940	293	788	5,107	0.1
Clark	0.0	D	3.0	19.8	3.6	10.3	3.8	D	22.1	5,050	237	741	10,001	0.2
Clay	13.5	0.0	5.4	2.3	2.4	7.1	4.4	12.3	22.9	4,460	311	631	7,474	0.0
Cleburne	-1.2	3.0	9.5	17.4	3.8	11.9	7.0	D	14.2	8,850	354	766	15,657	0.8

1. Per 1,000 resident population estimated as of July 1 of the year shown.

STATE County	Housing units, 2016–2020: Occupied units: Total	Owner-occupied: Percent	Owner-occupied: Median value[1]	Median owner cost as a percent of income: With a mortgage	Median owner cost as a percent of income: Without a mortgage[2]	Renter-occupied: Median rent[3]	Renter-occupied: Median rent as a percent of income[2]	Substandard units[4] (percent)	Civilian labor force, 2021: Total	Percent change, 2020–2021	Unemployment: Total	Unemployment: Rate[5]	Civilian employment[6], 2016–2020: Total	Percent: Management, business, science, and arts	Percent: Construction, production, and maintenance occupations
	89	90	91	92	93	94	95	96	97	98	99	100	101	102	103
ALABAMA—Cont'd															
Washington	5,830	89.5	88,100	16.7	10.7	742	24.8	2.4	6,538	-4.2	305	4.7	5,663	33.0	40.3
Wilcox	3,961	69.9	67,200	19.4	15.7	677	26.9	2.6	2,644	-9.5	291	11.0	3,277	18.1	40.7
Winston	9,612	80.3	87,300	21.0	11.3	558	27.7	2.3	10,110	-1.6	280	2.8	9,430	24.3	43.6
ALASKA	255,173	64.8	275,600	22.0	10.1	1,240	27.5	9.2	354,936	2.3	22,670	6.4	341,492	38.2	23.7
Aleutians East	988	61.4	136,700	14.5	10.0	1,087	19.6	5.4	2,558	1.7	59	2.3	2,328	23.6	50.3
Aleutians West	1,306	27.7	316,700	29.0	10.6	1,476	19.1	14.2	3,625	-5.5	131	3.6	3,805	17.9	48.0
Anchorage	106,970	62.2	320,100	22.4	10.9	1,310	28.3	5.1	150,276	2.1	8,737	5.8	145,816	41.5	19.5
Bethel	4,499	55.8	88,700	17.9	10.8	1,368	20.8	50.2	6,956	-0.4	910	13.1	6,325	34.0	20.2
Bristol Bay	284	51.4	222,200	19.3	12.5	1,208	19.2	11.3	449	14.2	25	5.6	428	31.8	28.7
Chugach	2,310	73.2	234,300	17.5	10.0	1,147	24.6	4.9	3,412	5.0	230	6.7	3,564	32.7	38.2
Copper River	1,063	75.9	234,500	21.6	10.0	757	16.6	11.7	1,356	5.1	121	8.9	1,188	42.9	19.5
Denali	726	82.9	233,700	18.7	10.0	819	25.7	17.6	855	32.6	86	10.1	1,658	17.1	23.2
Dillingham	1,430	60.4	156,000	22.5	12.5	997	24.1	33.0	1,709	-0.7	140	8.2	1,950	44.3	22.1
Fairbanks North Star	36,199	58.9	240,300	21.2	10.0	1,297	27.3	9.5	45,375	1.7	2,276	5.0	44,303	37.2	24.3
Haines	917	60.5	263,900	22.3	12.0	695	14.9	19.2	1,024	0.3	116	11.3	937	33.8	24.5
Hoonah-Angoon	755	73.2	221,600	21.5	10.0	1,009	23.6	11.5	1,156	9.6	107	9.3	1,052	37.0	23.1
Juneau	12,878	64.6	355,100	21.9	10.0	1,262	25.3	3.6	16,734	2.6	794	4.7	16,364	45.9	21.7
Kenai Peninsula	21,781	75.3	245,400	21.4	10.0	1,072	27.7	7.8	27,945	5.0	2,034	7.3	24,668	38.4	25.2
Ketchikan Gateway	5,299	63.9	299,500	21.5	11.0	1,188	31.6	5.2	6,604	1.9	486	7.4	7,064	30.8	25.5
Kodiak Island	4,231	49.7	295,100	23.0	11.0	1,412	26.4	10.0	6,015	-0.9	386	6.4	6,393	28.3	37.2
Kusilvak	1,750	71.7	72,800	16.8	14.4	710	20.6	55.8	2,347	2.6	467	19.9	2,229	29.8	23.8
Lake and Peninsula	366	64.5	120,500	21.0	10.0	775	15.6	24.9	649	5.9	58	8.9	515	45.6	22.3
Matanuska-Susitna	31,964	76.8	257,900	22.8	10.0	1,115	31.7	8.0	49,487	2.3	3,357	6.8	43,444	33.1	28.3
Nome	2,777	61.8	159,600	17.7	12.0	1,232	24.4	44.0	4,088	3.8	395	9.7	3,667	39.8	19.2
North Slope	1,991	46.8	162,500	15.7	10.0	1,050	18.9	38.9	2,918	-7.8	185	6.3	5,172	37.4	34.5
Northwest Arctic	1,795	56.9	125,800	18.0	12.2	1,286	20.6	45.4	2,914	-0.9	336	11.5	2,687	43.1	26.3
Petersburg	1,204	70.6	228,400	21.3	10.0	931	29.0	2.6	1,621	13.4	113	7.0	1,596	23.4	40.7
Prince of Wales-Hyder	2,353	73.6	191,600	18.9	10.0	801	22.7	12.3	2,832	0.0	227	8.0	2,796	34.0	30.8
Sitka	3,572	60.8	365,800	23.1	10.0	1,159	29.9	4.2	4,496	9.1	201	4.5	4,414	42.2	21.7
Skagway	411	64.0	397,200	23.7	10.9	1,090	19.7	5.1	621	-3.1	88	14.2	822	27.6	23.4
Southeast Fairbanks	2,287	73.0	179,300	19.2	10.0	973	21.6	15.1	3,219	9.3	212	6.6	2,712	37.5	30.0
Valdez-Cordova	NA	NA	NA	NA	NA	NA	NA	NA	NA	NA	NA	NA	NA	NA	NA
Wrangell	989	71.3	221,700	22.2	11.4	868	25.9	3.2	946	-0.9	71	7.5	1,067	39.9	24.6
Yakutat	221	51.6	171,200	22.3	10.0	1,071	17.5	9.5	308	10.4	22	7.1	300	33.7	24.7
Yukon-Koyukuk	1,857	74.3	74,700	18.1	11.1	823	20.8	44.5	2,441	4.6	303	12.4	2,228	34.6	27.0
ARIZONA	2,643,430	65.3	242,000	20.9	10.0	1,097	29.0	4.9	3,518,425	1.8	172,106	4.9	3,215,843	37.6	19.8
Apache	21,505	79.7	61,800	19.3	10.0	527	17.5	23.1	18,700	-4.1	1,705	9.1	18,980	32.2	25.3
Cochise	50,917	69.1	150,100	19.8	10.0	803	27.0	2.7	49,027	-2.1	2,360	4.8	44,219	35.7	18.7
Coconino	49,016	60.8	299,100	22.0	10.0	1,185	31.5	9.2	72,223	0.3	4,366	6.0	65,975	37.9	18.0
Gila	22,523	75.2	174,300	22.1	11.6	836	26.9	5.8	20,390	0.2	1,013	5.0	19,246	33.1	22.3
Graham	11,348	71.5	146,600	20.2	10.0	824	23.6	6.6	15,695	1.8	648	4.1	13,390	27.4	31.4
Greenlee	3,295	51.0	91,800	13.5	10.0	468	10.0	5.7	4,343	0.8	174	4.0	4,025	27.3	48.6
La Paz	9,928	71.8	84,600	23.0	10.2	657	22.0	6.2	8,616	-1.3	441	5.1	6,192	23.7	34.3
Maricopa	1,596,784	63.2	278,700	20.6	10.0	1,182	29.0	4.8	2,311,889	2.4	103,031	4.5	2,128,806	39.3	19.1
Mohave	90,413	70.4	172,100	22.0	10.0	839	27.5	4.1	87,215	1.5	4,833	5.5	74,114	26.8	23.8
Navajo	36,406	69.7	135,800	19.8	10.0	712	24.2	13.2	39,276	0.2	2,572	6.5	34,525	32.6	22.1
Pima	410,942	64.0	199,400	20.9	10.4	931	30.6	4.0	480,903	0.3	23,808	5.0	451,995	38.4	17.8
Pinal	148,435	77.4	200,200	21.0	10.0	1,078	28.8	4.3	192,406	2.3	9,072	4.7	167,669	31.5	23.9
Santa Cruz	16,049	67.8	152,700	22.7	10.8	657	31.0	6.2	18,942	0.9	1,644	8.7	17,870	26.4	23.6
Yavapai	101,245	72.6	273,300	23.6	11.1	982	29.0	2.3	105,108	1.6	4,337	4.1	90,114	32.4	20.8
Yuma	74,624	68.6	139,200	22.0	10.0	851	27.2	8.9	93,693	-1.1	12,102	12.9	78,723	25.4	31.3
ARKANSAS	1,170,544	65.8	133,600	18.5	10.0	760	27.2	3.2	1,332,620	-1.8	53,636	4.0	1,309,748	34.9	27.3
Arkansas	7,416	65.9	98,600	18.4	10.0	645	27.2	2.3	9,424	-0.1	316	3.4	7,929	31.3	34.1
Ashley	7,716	77.2	76,200	17.8	10.0	530	28.6	1.5	6,801	-5.3	500	7.4	7,389	25.1	40.5
Baxter	18,727	76.6	134,500	21.4	10.2	722	25.8	2.6	16,287	-1.7	606	3.7	15,355	32.1	30.1
Benton	99,661	65.9	192,900	17.8	10.0	945	22.9	4.3	141,991	0.3	3,998	2.8	132,873	38.7	24.4
Boone	15,043	72.0	127,200	18.6	10.0	638	24.0	2.5	15,782	-0.5	469	3.0	16,152	33.3	25.9
Bradley	4,233	63.1	87,600	17.6	11.1	565	22.7	2.4	4,056	-7.1	191	4.7	4,150	29.5	41.0
Calhoun	1,754	83.5	73,100	16.0	10.0	647	23.9	0.7	2,392	-1.0	80	3.3	2,085	21.4	46.8
Carroll	11,079	75.1	143,600	19.1	10.0	576	23.3	5.8	12,708	-0.2	429	3.4	11,759	29.6	34.1
Chicot	4,052	66.7	68,000	20.0	14.1	568	22.2	2.5	3,084	-4.0	264	8.6	3,282	28.2	36.0
Clark	8,336	59.0	116,100	17.6	10.7	600	28.7	3.0	8,805	-4.9	415	4.7	10,240	29.2	27.2
Clay	6,476	67.4	79,600	17.9	11.0	625	27.3	1.7	5,391	-2.8	213	4.0	6,182	31.5	32.1
Cleburne	10,882	78.1	126,400	19.5	10.0	709	23.9	2.1	8,970	-2.4	411	4.6	10,037	27.5	32.9

1. Specified owner-occupied units. 2. A value of 10.0 represents 10 percent or less; a value of 50.0 represents 50 percent or more. 3. Specified renter-occupied units. 4. Overcrowded or lacking complete plumbing facilities. 5. Percent of civilian labor force. 6. Civilian employed persons 16 years old and over.

STATE County	Private nonfarm establishments, employment and payroll, 2020: Number of establishments	Employment: Total	Employment: Health care and social assistance	Employment: Manufacturing	Employment: Retail trade	Employment: Finance and insurance	Employment: Professional, scientific, and technical services	Annual payroll: Total (mil dol)	Annual payroll: Average per employee (dollars)	Agriculture, 2017: Farms: Number	Farms: Percent with: Fewer than 50 acres	Farms: Percent with: 1000 acres or more	Farm producers whose primary occupation is farming (percent)
	104	105	106	107	108	109	110	111	112	113	114	115	116
ALABAMA—Cont'd													
Washington	199	5,419	291	3,362	265	43	30	429	79,216	435	36.6	5.3	34.1
Wilcox	170	2,117	240	987	238	75	20	102	48,231	318	25.8	19.8	39.1
Winston	425	7,893	697	3,285	727	159	69	288	36,444	484	40.3	1.0	37.1
ALASKA	21,184	266,063	51,984	12,721	33,219	7,195	20,100	16,331	61,380	990	67.0	4.3	41.9
Aleutians East	58	2,327	51	2,145	46	NA	NA	99	42,364	46	65.2	28.3	31.2
Aleutians West	114	3,614	96	2,476	113	NA	12	173	47,795	(1)	(1)	(1)	(1)
Anchorage	8,673	145,986	27,254	2,445	15,141	4,581	14,635	9,287	63,618	350	64.3	0.9	44.4
Bethel	220	2,414	552	NA	853	31	20	121	49,928	(1)	(1)	(1)	(1)
Bristol Bay	103	381	22	56	56	NA	NA	50	132,325	(1)	(1)	(1)	(1)
Chugach	NA	NA	NA	NA	NA	NA	NA	NA	NA	NA	NA	NA	NA
Copper River	NA	NA	NA	NA	NA	NA	NA	NA	NA	NA	NA	NA	NA
Denali	107	992	12	NA	58	NA	361	75	75,479	(1)	(1)	(1)	(1)
Dillingham	103	1,228	666	23	212	13	38	73	59,743	(1)	(1)	(1)	(1)
Fairbanks North Star	2,485	26,391	6,520	503	4,428	615	1,306	1,517	57,491	274	49.6	8.0	45.0
Haines	135	584	111	27	127	NA	21	31	53,063	(1)	(1)	(1)	(1)
Hoonah-Angoon	84	282	32	17	67	NA	NA	12	41,904	(1)	(1)	(1)	(1)
Juneau	1,100	10,957	2,236	292	1,549	336	531	619	56,535	60	96.7	0.0	41.1
Kenai Peninsula	2,215	15,156	3,967	736	2,600	283	581	808	53,330	260	82.7	1.9	37.9
Ketchikan Gateway	589	4,469	767	197	800	200	130	236	52,872	(1)	(1)	(1)	(1)
Kodiak Island	445	4,735	795	1,945	455	77	55	207	43,734	(1)	(1)	(1)	(1)
Kusilvak	73	585	23	NA	314	NA	NA	18	30,410	(1)	(1)	(1)	(1)
Lake and Peninsula	50	288	2	10	24	NA	NA	16	56,819	(1)	(1)	(1)	(1)
Matanuska-Susitna	2,449	20,594	4,940	700	3,838	543	867	1,017	49,400	(1)	(1)	(1)	(1)
Nome	174	2,195	1,094	18	361	29	12	142	64,601	(1)	(1)	(1)	(1)
North Slope	140	5,551	394	NA	304	NA	987	730	131,431	(1)	(1)	(1)	(1)
Northwest Arctic	68	1,727	458	NA	160	NA	NA	171	99,154	(1)	(1)	(1)	(1)
Petersburg	169	931	192	206	176	17	8	46	49,262	(1)	(1)	(1)	(1)
Prince of Wales-Hyder	175	979	142	71	224	29	NA	46	46,492	(1)	(1)	(1)	(1)
Sitka	373	2,762	757	216	403	60	64	148	53,627	(1)	(1)	(1)	(1)
Skagway	92	343	5	NA	68	NA	NA	15	44,257	(1)	(1)	(1)	(1)
Southeast Fairbanks	165	1,420	112	13	212	18	43	119	84,080	(1)	(1)	(1)	(1)
Valdez-Cordova	465	2,518	582	184	357	48	84	182	72,168	(1)	(1)	(1)	(1)
Wrangell	92	472	126	NA	114	15	17	22	46,189	(1)	(1)	(1)	(1)
Yakutat	29	157	21	NA	49	NA	NA	9	58,223	(1)	(1)	(1)	(1)
Yukon-Koyukuk	95	296	25	NA	110	NA	NA	13	42,419	(1)	(1)	(1)	(1)
ARIZONA	149,829	2,644,781	396,025	156,085	335,051	180,224	169,185	134,085	50,698	19,086	69.1	11.0	53.3
Apache	442	6,429	2,429	98	1,337	72	76	268	41,756	5,551	72.3	10.5	55.1
Cochise	2,120	25,545	4,905	340	5,068	479	3,272	1,032	40,402	1,083	39.6	17.7	47.4
Coconino	3,773	55,308	9,441	5,943	7,905	875	1,795	2,383	43,084	2,142	77.8	11.6	55.7
Gila	1,004	10,699	2,144	122	2,038	170	254	442	41,271	298	67.1	5.0	43.8
Graham	529	8,013	2,315	240	1,606	122	513	335	41,755	448	64.3	10.0	34.8
Greenlee	83	3,699	85	NA	260	NA	13	247	66,670	123	52.0	8.1	55.4
La Paz	323	3,717	390	124	1,160	59	16	112	30,011	97	28.9	26.8	54.5
Maricopa	100,346	1,829,257	260,733	112,588	219,996	150,719	128,519	98,731	53,973	1,874	81.7	4.7	44.0
Mohave	3,949	45,156	8,967	3,242	10,467	1,000	1,305	1,702	37,684	317	60.6	17.4	40.7
Navajo	1,788	19,152	4,882	484	3,960	322	381	723	37,734	4,205	67.0	11.8	61.4
Pima	20,408	330,431	65,722	21,689	48,551	13,025	19,064	14,979	45,332	661	79.7	7.9	42.9
Pinal	3,951	54,200	9,314	4,140	9,548	1,168	1,394	2,153	39,721	762	56.2	15.9	55.9
Santa Cruz	1,090	11,120	1,688	347	2,015	182	186	436	39,172	219	47.9	16.4	49.6
Yavapai	6,106	61,828	13,577	3,231	10,398	1,154	2,030	2,407	38,935	850	73.2	8.5	46.2
Yuma	3,116	46,323	8,741	3,480	8,334	1,299	1,272	1,760	37,990	456	60.7	13.2	50.4
ARKANSAS	67,586	1,055,534	185,291	162,692	136,980	40,727	39,683	47,495	44,996	42,625	30.3	7.2	41.7
Arkansas	479	9,092	919	4,397	997	248	63	355	39,048	488	16.2	32.2	43.6
Ashley	368	4,494	725	1,167	597	146	54	209	46,494	353	43.3	11.6	35.8
Baxter	1,071	14,267	4,364	2,680	2,239	625	451	591	41,410	479	35.5	3.8	36.9
Benton	7,046	128,100	10,317	12,577	13,412	3,578	9,233	8,038	62,745	1,936	48.2	1.4	38.7
Boone	856	12,343	2,483	1,707	1,992	376	207	486	39,406	1,313	33.0	4.3	41.9
Bradley	249	2,396	498	609	242	109	37	85	35,680	181	36.5	1.7	32.3
Calhoun	51	383	39	NA	40	13	NA	17	43,178	101	25.7	4.0	35.1
Carroll	694	8,304	670	2,644	1,129	222	159	281	33,838	1,169	25.7	4.0	41.1
Chicot	199	1,763	727	20	202	79	24	66	37,719	291	19.9	36.1	51.3
Clark	520	6,731	1,067	1,331	1,163	193	263	250	37,195	377	27.6	5.8	32.1
Clay	273	2,314	783	84	392	75	46	80	34,391	542	27.1	15.7	42.9
Cleburne	585	5,711	767	1,450	962	214	128	192	33,628	676	27.1	1.8	41.6

1. The Census of Agriculture data for Alaska is combined into regional groups. Aleutians West, Bethel, Bristol Bay, Dillingham, Kodiak Island, Kusilvak, Lake and Peninsula, Nome, North Slope, and Northwest Arctic are included with Aleutians East. Mantanuska-Susitna and Valdez-Cordova included with Anchorage. Denali, Southeast Fairbanks, and Yukon-Koyukuk are included with Fairbanks North Star. Haines, Hoonah-Angoon, Ketchican Gateway, Petersburg, Prince of Wales-Hyder, Sitka, Skagway, Wrangell, and Yakutat are included with Juneau.

STATE County	Agriculture, 2017 (cont.)															
	Land in farms					Value of land and buildings (dollars)		Value of machinery and equipment, average per farm (dollars)	Value of products sold:				Organic farms (number)	Farms with internet access (percent)	Government payments	
	Acreage (1,000)	Percent change, 2012–2017	Acres						Total (mil dol)	Average per farm (acres)	Percent from:				Total ($1,000)	Percent of farms
			Average size of farm	Total irrigated (1,000)	Total cropland (1,000)	Average per farm	Average per acre				Crops	Livestock and poultry products				
	117	118	119	120	121	122	123	124	125	126	127	128	129	130	131	132
ALABAMA—Cont'd																
Washington	120	25.1	275	0.1	22.3	556,827	2,026	72,905	31.3	71,885	23.1	76.9	NA	65.1	1,739	33.8
Wilcox	165	38.2	520	D	26.9	945,109	1,818	66,889	9.1	28,736	26.7	73.3	NA	64.2	1,920	57.5
Winston	57	-1.4	118	0.6	11.9	326,386	2,765	59,645	27.7	57,295	3.5	96.5	NA	70.5	631	43.2
ALASKA	850	1.9	858	2.4	83.7	616,112	718	91,623	70.5	71,171	42.1	57.9	18	87.9	2,091	22.7
Aleutians East	681	2.0	14,811	0.0	1.1	573,623	39	90,364	3.0	64,774	13.1	86.9	1	89.1	193	28.3
Aleutians West	(1)	(1)	(1)	(1)	(1)	(1)	(1)	(1)	(1)	(1)	(1)	(1)	(1)	(1)	(1)	(1)
Anchorage	34	-5.5	98	1.1	15.6	809,796	8,242	106,917	37.5	107,245	45.6	54.4	4	87.7	262	20.6
Bethel	(1)	(1)	(1)	(1)	(1)	(1)	(1)	(1)	(1)	(1)	(1)	(1)	(1)	(1)	(1)	(1)
Bristol Bay	(1)	(1)	(1)	(1)	(1)	(1)	(1)	(1)	(1)	(1)	(1)	(1)	(1)	(1)	(1)	(1)
Chugach	NA	NA	NA	NA	NA	NA	NA	NA	NA	NA	NA	NA	NA	NA	NA	NA
Copper River	NA	NA	NA	NA	NA	NA	NA	NA	NA	NA	NA	NA	NA	NA	NA	NA
Denali	(1)	(1)	(1)	(1)	(1)	(1)	(1)	(1)	(1)	(1)	(1)	(1)	(1)	(1)	(1)	(1)
Dillingham	(1)	(1)	(1)	(1)	(1)	(1)	(1)	(1)	(1)	(1)	(1)	(1)	(1)	(1)	(1)	(1)
Fairbanks North Star	102	2.4	372	1.1	63.2	610,607	1,640	82,638	10.4	37,927	81.6	18.4	5	86.9	1,124	21.9
Haines	(1)	(1)	(1)	(1)	(1)	(1)	(1)	(1)	(1)	(1)	(1)	(1)	(1)	(1)	(1)	(1)
Hoonah-Angoon	(1)	(1)	(1)	(1)	(1)	(1)	(1)	(1)	(1)	(1)	(1)	(1)	(1)	(1)	(1)	(1)
Juneau	1	-0.3	9	0.0	0.0	881,816	100,397	225,293	14.1	235,489	6.5	93.5	1	85.0	11	11.7
Kenai Peninsula	32	8.1	121	0.1	0.2	307,385	2,537	49,878	5.4	20,856	50.0	50.0	6	89.6	502	28.1
Ketchikan Gateway	(1)	(1)	(1)	(1)	(1)	(1)	(1)	(1)	(1)	(1)	(1)	(1)	(1)	(1)	(1)	(1)
Kodiak Island	(1)	(1)	(1)	(1)	(1)	(1)	(1)	(1)	(1)	(1)	(1)	(1)	(1)	(1)	(1)	(1)
Kusilvak	(1)	(1)	(1)	(1)	(1)	(1)	(1)	(1)	(1)	(1)	(1)	(1)	(1)	(1)	(1)	(1)
Lake and Peninsula	(1)	(1)	(1)	(1)	(1)	(1)	(1)	(1)	(1)	(1)	(1)	(1)	(1)	(1)	(1)	(1)
Matanuska-Susitna	(1)	(1)	(1)	(1)	(1)	(1)	(1)	(1)	(1)	(1)	(1)	(1)	(1)	(1)	(1)	(1)
Nome	(1)	(1)	(1)	(1)	(1)	(1)	(1)	(1)	(1)	(1)	(1)	(1)	(1)	(1)	(1)	(1)
North Slope	(1)	(1)	(1)	(1)	(1)	(1)	(1)	(1)	(1)	(1)	(1)	(1)	(1)	(1)	(1)	(1)
Northwest Arctic	(1)	(1)	(1)	(1)	(1)	(1)	(1)	(1)	(1)	(1)	(1)	(1)	(1)	(1)	(1)	(1)
Petersburg	(1)	(1)	(1)	(1)	(1)	(1)	(1)	(1)	(1)	(1)	(1)	(1)	(1)	(1)	(1)	(1)
Prince of Wales-Hyder	(1)	(1)	(1)	(1)	(1)	(1)	(1)	(1)	(1)	(1)	(1)	(1)	(1)	(1)	(1)	(1)
Sitka	(1)	(1)	(1)	(1)	(1)	(1)	(1)	(1)	(1)	(1)	(1)	(1)	(1)	(1)	(1)	(1)
Skagway	(1)	(1)	(1)	(1)	(1)	(1)	(1)	(1)	(1)	(1)	(1)	(1)	(1)	(1)	(1)	(1)
Southeast Fairbanks	(1)	(1)	(1)	(1)	(1)	(1)	(1)	(1)	(1)	(1)	(1)	(1)	(1)	(1)	(1)	(1)
Valdez-Cordova	(1)	(1)	(1)	(1)	(1)	(1)	(1)	(1)	(1)	(1)	(1)	(1)	(1)	(1)	(1)	(1)
Wrangell	(1)	(1)	(1)	(1)	(1)	(1)	(1)	(1)	(1)	(1)	(1)	(1)	(1)	(1)	(1)	(1)
Yakutat	(1)	(1)	(1)	(1)	(1)	(1)	(1)	(1)	(1)	(1)	(1)	(1)	(1)	(1)	(1)	(1)
Yukon-Koyukuk	(1)	(1)	(1)	(1)	(1)	(1)	(1)	(1)	(1)	(1)	(1)	(1)	(1)	(1)	(1)	(1)
ARIZONA	26,126	-0.5	1,369	910.9	1,286.6	1,110,303	811	77,604	3,852.0	201,824	54.4	45.6	84	57.4	22,331	3.9
Apache	5,555	-0.8	1,001	11.9	30.4	275,085	275	30,785	18.0	3,243	20.1	79.9	4	43.6	278	0.6
Cochise	973	6.2	899	86.0	152.9	1,802,553	2,005	99,038	144.7	133,648	56.9	43.1	4	78.9	3,119	10.6
Coconino	6,139	5.6	2,866	1.3	6.9	607,821	212	34,544	23.9	11,162	4.1	95.9	2	43.9	807	0.8
Gila	1,214	2.1	4,074	1.3	2.3	1,583,528	389	51,499	7.3	24,362	7.7	92.3	NA	75.5	143	1.7
Graham	1,290	3.1	2,880	46.7	52.4	1,866,459	648	107,676	62.1	138,558	88.2	11.8	9	73.0	1,083	12.7
Greenlee	66	25.9	536	5.1	5.0	835,412	1,559	76,520	8.7	70,650	24.9	75.1	NA	84.6	87	5.7
La Paz	250	D	2,574	97.1	102.6	5,190,405	2,016	484,196	D	D	D	D	1	71.1	1,280	34.0
Maricopa	474	-0.3	253	180.2	257.2	2,338,321	9,236	171,562	1,209.1	645,215	39.3	60.7	18	85.0	5,310	9.4
Mohave	745	-40.1	2,351	20.9	30.7	1,972,873	839	96,071	32.3	101,871	71.1	28.9	NA	87.4	390	2.8
Navajo	4,413	2.1	1,049	6.7	66.0	231,932	221	26,006	49.9	11,871	8.6	91.4	NA	40.4	340	0.3
Pima	2,618	D	3,960	30.0	40.7	2,088,810	527	79,142	75.5	114,174	84.3	15.7	3	72.0	1,234	5.4
Pinal	1,121	-4.6	1,471	232.2	294.1	4,065,306	2,764	282,808	861.9	1,131,154	35.7	64.3	4	85.4	3,943	20.9
Santa Cruz	198	-8.0	903	2.6	3.2	1,800,767	1,994	62,799	19.6	89,639	48.8	51.2	1	88.1	413	5.0
Yavapai	822	-0.3	967	7.5	8.0	1,596,867	1,651	63,905	35.7	42,036	40.1	59.9	4	86.4	115	1.5
Yuma	247	15.2	542	181.4	234.3	5,006,516	9,235	468,849	D	D	D	D	34	84.4	3,789	14.9
ARKANSAS	13,889	0.6	326	4,855.1	7,825.9	1,030,741	3,163	126,667	9,651.2	226,420	37.6	62.4	81	73.6	321,742	19.5
Arkansas	414	3.0	849	314.3	359.0	2,675,627	3,151	312,157	214.3	439,098	99.6	0.4	NA	68.6	22,110	85.9
Ashley	132	18.3	374	88.9	103.9	1,081,824	2,894	201,843	70.2	198,856	90.4	9.6	NA	64.9	5,447	32.9
Baxter	101	10.4	212	0.0	13.3	569,724	2,690	58,020	31.8	66,309	2.7	97.3	NA	80.6	259	9.6
Benton	244	-20.0	126	0.2	72.9	815,643	6,478	77,246	593.4	306,494	1.3	98.7	8	74.5	456	3.0
Boone	306	19.0	233	0.3	42.3	614,116	2,636	69,650	164.0	124,918	1.9	98.1	NA	76.6	1,492	7.6
Bradley	30	50.4	164	0.5	6.2	539,607	3,287	82,166	42.1	232,503	15.8	84.2	NA	74.0	21	7.2
Calhoun	19	35.1	186	D	3.1	480,703	2,591	61,897	5.5	54,683	6.3	93.7	NA	74.3	48	16.8
Carroll	290	13.3	248	0.0	54.6	683,129	2,750	83,790	363.6	311,050	0.9	99.1	9	76.5	878	8.2
Chicot	307	6.2	1,057	221.3	273.3	3,139,169	2,971	320,397	148.3	509,519	96.6	3.4	NA	72.5	11,746	76.6
Clark	103	14.1	273	2.3	29.6	661,236	2,421	94,828	17.5	46,414	32.4	67.6	NA	70.3	1,237	15.4
Clay	286	-13.6	529	208.8	258.2	2,278,119	4,310	271,792	197.6	364,603	83.2	16.8	NA	70.3	12,965	59.8
Cleburne	129	-17.8	192	0.2	29.2	562,588	2,938	64,986	57.6	85,138	2.6	97.4	NA	73.7	292	8.9

1. The Census of Agriculture data for Alaska is combined into regional groups. Aleutians West, Bethel, Bristol Bay, Dillingham, Kodiak Island, Kusilvak, Lake and Peninsula, Nome, North Slope, and Northwest Arctic are included with Aleutians East. Mantanuska-Susitna and Valdez-Cordova included with Anchorage. Denali, Southeast Fairbanks, and Yukon-Koyukuk are included with Fairbanks North Star. Haines, Hoonah-Angoon, Ketchican Gateway, Petersburg, Prince of Wales-Hyder, Sitka, Skagway, Wrangell, and Yakutat are included with Juneau.

STATE County	Water use, 2015		Wholesale Trade[1], 2017				Retail Trade[2], 2017				Real estate and rental and leasing,[2] 2017			
	Public supply water withdrawn (mil gal/ day)	Public supply gallons withdrawn per person per day	Number of establish- ments	Number of employees	Sales (mil dol)	Average payroll (mil dol)	Number of establish- ments	Number of employees	Sales (mil dol)	Average payroll (mil dol)	Number of establish- ments	Number of employees	Sales (mil dol)	Average payroll (mil dol)
	133	134	135	136	137	138	139	140	141	142	143	144	145	146
ALABAMA—Cont'd														
Washington	2.8	167.2	7	76	94.0	4.0	32	237	70.5	5.6	NA	NA	NA	NA
Wilcox	2.8	253.2	5	29	23.9	1.6	43	240	75.4	5.5	7	D	2.6	D
Winston	0.8	33.9	29	263	294.5	11.7	89	737	158.3	15.8	12	30	12.6	1.6
ALASKA	99.2	134.3	643	7,529	5,557.3	457.5	2,480	34,498	10,384.8	1,095.1	965	4,622	1,188.3	222.8
Aleutians East	1.2	365.2	NA	NA	NA	NA	D	D	D	D	3	41	0.4	0.4
Aleutians West	2.3	398.1	14	142	192.0	10.0	12	124	50.3	4.9	D	D	D	2.1
Anchorage	44.5	148.9	338	5,162	3,807.4	314.0	849	15,445	4,903.2	507.6	437	2,519	681.0	124.4
Bethel	0.3	16.7	4	18	17.8	1.0	51	832	156.2	16.2	9	49	7.2	2.0
Bristol Bay	0.1	78.5	D	D	D	D	10	51	15.1	1.7	D	D	D	0.2
Chugach	NA	NA	NA	NA	NA	NA	NA	NA	NA	NA	NA	NA	NA	NA
Copper River	NA	NA	NA	NA	NA	NA	NA	NA	NA	NA	NA	NA	NA	NA
Denali	0.0	20.8	NA	NA	NA	NA	18	34	18.9	2.0	NA	NA	NA	NA
Dillingham	0.3	50.0	NA	NA	NA	NA	17	202	48.1	5.6	D	D	D	0.8
Fairbanks North Star	14.1	141.7	70	693	470.6	38.4	294	4,749	1,484.8	159.0	158	764	188.3	42.1
Haines	0.3	114.4	NA	NA	NA	NA	19	114	24.6	3.6	6	D	0.5	D
Hoonah-Angoon	0.5	248.5	NA	NA	NA	NA	16	84	16.4	1.7	NA	NA	NA	NA
Juneau	4.8	146.5	33	278	203.1	16.0	148	1,790	464.8	53.3	64	195	60.0	8.0
Kenai Peninsula	3.6	62.5	53	334	207.3	19.6	253	2,607	817.1	84.7	75	267	82.1	14.5
Ketchikan Gateway	5.7	415.8	13	122	99.5	9.0	108	1,037	243.6	33.2	28	91	29.3	4.4
Kodiak Island	7.6	550.1	17	92	44.6	3.3	37	500	125.4	14.1	15	70	12.6	2.7
Kusilvak	0.5	59.1	NA	NA	NA	NA	27	338	65.4	5.9	D	D	D	0.3
Lake and Peninsula	0.1	76.8	NA	NA	NA	NA	D	D	D	0.4	3	4	0.2	0.0
Matanuska-Susitna	2.7	26.6	42	201	91.3	11.5	257	3,909	1,255.5	124.6	81	255	49.4	7.7
Nome	0.7	69.1	D	D	D	2.1	32	336	83.2	7.8	10	50	8.5	0.7
North Slope	0.4	39.2	7	171	133.3	13.3	21	301	85.2	9.1	8	85	20.7	6.1
Northwest Arctic	0.6	73.5	NA	NA	NA	NA	13	187	46.6	4.9	D	D	D	D
Petersburg	0.7	204.6	8	33	18.2	1.9	27	167	38.4	4.9	D	D	D	D
Prince of Wales-Hyder	0.3	53.6	NA	NA	NA	NA	24	222	55.0	6.3	6	31	5.1	0.9
Sitka	1.2	137.7	7	39	27.6	1.8	55	387	107.2	12.4	16	46	8.4	2.4
Skagway	0.2	227.1	NA	NA	NA	NA	46	137	43.0	5.0	NA	NA	NA	NA
Southeast Fairbanks	0.2	35.1	3	68	24.7	2.3	34	253	67.6	7.6	3	8	1.1	0.4
Valdez-Cordova	4.8	515.9	9	35	33.1	2.3	51	348	101.5	10.4	9	20	3.1	0.9
Wrangell	0.6	268.7	NA	NA	NA	NA	15	136	23.4	4.0	4	5	1.2	0.1
Yakutat	0.5	832.0	NA	NA	NA	NA	4	D	5.1	D	NA	NA	NA	NA
Yukon-Koyukuk	0.2	43.4	4	19	21.7	1.1	31	101	27.8	2.1	NA	NA	NA	NA
ARIZONA	1,195.2	175.0	5,508	79,541	71,206.1	4,826.6	17,918	324,912	104,365.6	9,505.5	9,937	48,305	12,992.2	2,267.2
Apache	5.8	80.7	D	D	D	D	94	1,129	280.5	24.6	13	31	4.3	0.7
Cochise	16.2	127.7	D	D	D	11.4	386	5,160	1,324.4	126.6	107	391	57.8	10.8
Coconino	19.9	142.8	96	832	365.3	37.9	580	8,004	2,197.1	207.2	224	884	201.3	30.5
Gila	4.8	90.9	20	140	53.2	7.4	150	2,082	553.0	52.5	69	159	35.8	6.1
Graham	3.8	100.9	D	D	D	D	101	1,546	408.4	40.7	21	65	11.9	2.0
Greenlee	1.7	178.4	D	D	D	0.5	18	188	64.1	5.2	4	D	3.8	D
La Paz	2.9	143.4	D	D	D	5.6	84	951	450.3	24.3	16	D	9.1	D
Maricopa	776.5	186.3	3,956	64,055	61,779.1	4,059.4	10,871	215,452	74,333.1	6,605.7	6,935	35,958	10,576.8	1,830.1
Mohave	47.9	233.8	101	1,217	455.1	53.7	626	9,435	3,063.4	262.1	241	736	150.2	20.1
Navajo	14.5	133.9	D	D	D	D	294	3,991	1,197.2	101.5	102	220	48.1	7.2
Pima	175.4	173.7	666	6,524	3,723.2	321.7	2,721	46,749	12,230.9	1,271.8	1,347	6,396	1,271.3	243.8
Pinal	63.2	155.5	109	1,179	605.9	62.5	507	8,908	2,578.1	227.6	223	1,425	207.4	44.7
Santa Cruz	5.2	111.3	D	D	D	63.8	199	2,205	513.2	51.7	44	127	21.1	3.9
Yavapai	21.1	95.1	141	1,447	952.8	72.9	815	10,820	2,952.7	294.1	414	1,075	245.0	42.3
Yuma	36.3	177.7	128	1,856	1,438.4	102.1	472	8,292	2,219.1	210.0	177	761	148.3	23.3
ARKANSAS	363.1	121.9	2,812	36,528	29,242.1	1,882.8	10,925	142,857	40,174.1	3,665.3	3,115	12,776	2,588.2	473.3
Arkansas	1.2	64.0	31	370	173.6	19.7	87	1,021	302.4	28.7	18	131	16.6	3.7
Ashley	1.2	57.6	16	124	141.7	6.3	67	724	183.0	17.1	8	17	2.7	0.6
Baxter	3.5	84.3	D	D	D	D	190	2,231	571.1	54.3	45	217	26.8	6.2
Benton	64.7	259.3	256	2,849	2,400.1	177.6	755	12,916	3,717.4	345.7	319	1,155	302.9	47.3
Boone	1.0	26.6	D	D	D	D	167	2,062	622.4	54.6	41	100	18.4	2.6
Bradley	0.2	18.9	10	128	75.2	5.0	33	268	71.4	5.9	5	D	0.6	D
Calhoun	0.2	45.9	NA	NA	NA	NA	8	47	12.6	1.0	NA	NA	NA	NA
Carroll	8.6	310.4	9	200	52.3	8.0	149	1,143	250.1	27.1	26	67	10.6	1.6
Chicot	0.6	56.2	12	130	177.8	6.9	43	307	58.3	6.4	9	20	2.2	0.3
Clark	1.8	81.3	D	D	D	2.3	87	1,269	376.9	35.6	28	75	10.7	1.5
Clay	0.9	60.2	15	255	211.7	8.1	50	496	127.7	11.9	6	D	1.3	D
Cleburne	11.2	437.8	18	106	35.7	3.5	92	1,068	412.5	30.1	30	53	8.6	1.5

1 Merchant wholesalers, except manufacturers' sales branches and offices. 2. Employer establishments.

STATE County	Professional, scientific, and technical services, 2017				Manufacturing, 2017				Accommodation and food services, 2017			
	Number of establish-ments	Number of employees	Sales (mil dol)	Average payroll (mil dol)	Number of establish-ments	Number of employees	Sales (mil dol)	Average payroll (mil dol)	Number of establis-hments	Number of employees	Sales (mil dol)	Annual payroll (mil dol)
	147	148	149	150	151	152	153	154	155	156	157	158
ALABAMA—Cont'd												
Washington	10	29	7.4	2.2	14	3,610	5,633.1	326.9	D	D	D	D
Wilcox	10	18	2.2	0.5	D	856	D	62.8	D	D	D	1.4
Winston	25	76	7.4	2.4	46	2,556	738.2	96.6	D	D	D	D
ALASKA	1,932	17,595	3,193.4	1,252.8	535	12,515	8,616.9	585.3	2,214	28,853	2,536.5	741.7
Aleutians East	NA	NA	NA	NA	D	D	D	D	9	62	2.6	0.4
Aleutians West	D	D	D	D	7	2,528	472.7	73.0	7	109	14.8	3.8
Anchorage	1,178	14,141	2,566.7	1,039.8	171	1,675	412.5	89.9	798	15,618	1,224.8	386.2
Bethel	D	D	D	D	D	13	D	0.6	18	40	6.3	0.9
Bristol Bay	NA	NA	NA	NA	9	232	280.7	23.9	21	113	20.1	5.3
Chugach	NA	NA	NA	NA	NA	NA	NA	NA	NA	NA	NA	NA
Copper River	NA	NA	NA	NA	NA	NA	NA	NA	NA	NA	NA	NA
Denali	D	D	D	D	NA	NA	NA	NA	38	507	103.4	20.7
Dillingham	NA	NA	NA	NA	4	48	71.9	8.1	12	45	5.4	0.9
Fairbanks North Star	212	1,356	313.2	91.0	69	454	226.6	24.4	233	3,306	250.7	70.7
Haines	6	8	0.8	0.3	8	83	47.9	4.6	18	84	6.0	1.8
Hoonah-Angoon	NA	NA	NA	NA	NA	NA	NA	NA	15	61	11.0	1.6
Juneau	D	D	D	D	32	258	72.7	14.4	124	1,390	112.9	31.2
Kenai Peninsula	D	D	D	D	D	760	D	67.7	289	1,890	174.8	47.5
Ketchikan Gateway	D	D	D	D	15	380	217.8	25.8	61	554	56.3	15.1
Kodiak Island	22	53	6.1	2.3	25	2,319	591.3	73.3	48	429	34.5	9.6
Kusilvak	NA	NA	NA	NA	NA	NA	NA	NA	NA	NA	NA	NA
Lake and Peninsula	NA	NA	NA	NA	D	D	D	D	10	37	12.6	3.5
Matanuska-Susitna	164	699	104.5	41.0	57	346	64.0	16.3	236	2,490	215.4	51.8
Nome	D	D	D	D	NA	NA	NA	NA	19	156	16.3	4.8
North Slope	D	D	D	D	NA	NA	NA	NA	31	689	115.6	42.0
Northwest Arctic	NA	NA	NA	NA	NA	NA	NA	NA	D	D	D	D
Petersburg	6	14	0.9	0.5	5	D	91.7	9.9	13	69	6.8	1.6
Prince of Wales-Hyder	NA	NA	NA	NA	D	221	D	10.7	22	76	14.1	3.5
Sitka	D	D	D	D	16	448	154.5	16.5	41	378	44.0	11.9
Skagway	NA	NA	NA	NA	D	14	D	0.3	23	78	16.2	5.7
Southeast Fairbanks	11	50	10.6	3.4	D	10	D	D	28	141	14.3	3.9
Valdez-Cordova	D	D	D	D	13	306	534.7	25.2	70	340	39.0	11.4
Wrangell	D	D	D	D	D	D	D	D	5	37	3.5	1.0
Yakutat	NA	NA	NA	NA	NA	NA	NA	NA	6	D	3.3	D
Yukon-Koyukuk	D	D	D	D	NA	NA	NA	NA	D	D	D	0.3
ARIZONA	18,020	145,604	23,838.9	10,455.2	4,343	142,809	56,635.9	9,148.7	13,079	299,628	19,848.7	5,636.1
Apache	D	D	D	D	D	D	D	D	58	933	53.7	14.9
Cochise	223	3,433	501.8	227.8	41	268	118.0	13.6	261	3,522	183.7	55.3
Coconino	349	1,471	190.8	68.8	88	4,893	2,250.3	425.7	601	15,061	1,200.0	323.8
Gila	81	260	30.7	9.4	D	155	D	6.4	139	2,019	124.9	35.4
Graham	29	535	8.0	15.5	D	257	D	9.5	57	1,010	40.4	12.9
Greenlee	4	20	1.5	0.6	NA	NA	NA	NA	10	117	11.9	2.7
La Paz	11	22	2.2	0.7	D	D	D	D	81	1,410	93.8	25.3
Maricopa	D	D	D	D	2,945	100,076	38,022.0	6,055.9	8,004	195,797	13,229.4	3,765.8
Mohave	D	D	D	D	141	2,855	1,027.6	130.0	401	6,670	397.4	110.7
Navajo	D	D	D	D	40	317	83.3	12.8	229	3,924	294.9	73.3
Pima	2,554	17,645	2,636.6	1,069.3	617	23,392	9,958.9	1,965.6	1,852	44,608	2,877.5	808.1
Pinal	D	D	D	D	120	3,613	3,100.9	213.1	369	6,644	328.9	94.9
Santa Cruz	59	187	25.4	8.3	35	388	256.5	15.1	97	1,395	76.4	23.8
Yavapai	565	1,909	235.6	87.9	190	3,261	716.3	160.0	575	9,695	563.9	187.5
Yuma	D	D	D	D	75	3,095	967.4	132.4	345	6,823	371.6	101.7
ARKANSAS	D	D	5,516.4	D	2,571	152,696	58,363.7	7,024.8	5,977	106,280	5,484.8	1,572.8
Arkansas	23	75	9.9	2.7	30	3,894	1,656.0	142.6	42	385	20.5	5.0
Ashley	25	66	6.3	2.0	D	1,600	D	116.6	27	391	18.9	5.2
Baxter	71	449	39.3	15.2	48	2,083	613.3	95.6	106	1,618	73.6	21.2
Benton	D	D	D	D	173	11,608	3,579.3	478.9	512	10,860	610.3	177.9
Boone	D	D	D	D	50	1,697	438.5	70.6	72	1,135	58.1	16.8
Bradley	13	28	2.5	0.7	6	535	146.2	24.3	18	223	9.1	2.3
Calhoun	NA	NA	NA	NA	NA	NA	NA	NA	4	24	1.2	0.3
Carroll	38	692	197.5	67.0	32	3,118	796.6	98.9	144	1,345	69.9	21.2
Chicot	13	38	5.6	1.7	3	7	4.0	0.5	13	126	6.9	1.7
Clark	D	D	D	D	24	1,209	433.1	60.8	62	1,176	55.9	17.3
Clay	14	49	4.2	1.3	13	88	13.7	3.5	23	219	8.6	2.5
Cleburne	36	116	9.3	3.0	30	1,224	256.3	51.9	64	723	35.7	10.2

STATE County	Health care and social assistance, 2017				Other services, 2017				Nonemployer businesses, 2019		Value of residential construction authorized by building permits, 2021	
	Number of establish-ments	Number of employees	Receipts (mil dol)	Annual payroll (mil dol)	Number of establish-ments	Number of employees	Receipts (mil dol)	Annual payroll (mil dol)	Number	Receipts (mil dol)	New construction ($1,000)	Number of housing units
	159	160	161	162	163	164	165	166	167	168	169	170
ALABAMA—Cont'd												
Washington	13	268	18.5	8.4	D	D	D	D	1,004	30.1	0	0
Wilcox	18	269	25.0	8.1	7	15	1.6	0.4	617	21.0	0	0
Winston	45	735	54.7	22.9	D	D	D	D	1,596	84.2	0	0
ALASKA	2,679	52,125	7,856.2	3,048.1	1,357	7,271	1,351.3	269.7	57,896	2,837.6	413,299	1,552
Aleutians East	NA	NA	NA	NA	NA	NA	NA	NA	235	20.0	308	1
Aleutians West	13	108	13.7	5.3	6	28	5.4	1.9	210	13.6	950	4
Anchorage	1,291	27,333	4,482.7	1,673.1	571	3,928	886.5	150.5	21,235	1,087.6	312,471	1,133
Bethel	52	D	127.5	D	24	66	7.8	1.7	607	20.5	4,212	20
Bristol Bay	D	D	D	D	D	D	D	D	230	14.6	1,230	4
Chugach	NA	NA	NA	NA	NA	NA	NA	NA	NA	NA	NA	NA
Copper River	NA	NA	NA	NA	NA	NA	NA	NA	NA	NA	NA	NA
Denali	3	11	0.8	0.5	NA	NA	NA	NA	174	6.2	NA	NA
Dillingham	D	D	D	39.7	D	D	D	0.4	794	34.7	0	0
Fairbanks North Star	313	6,507	890.8	371.6	178	896	121.0	32.9	6,035	245.0	8,033	36
Haines	10	133	8.7	3.9	D	D	D	0.2	416	17.4	1,385	8
Hoonah-Angoon	7	D	1.8	D	NA	NA	NA	NA	284	11.9	615	2
Juneau	133	2,288	310.2	134.4	76	393	62.4	16.6	2,882	148.1	12,930	62
Kenai Peninsula	252	4,062	493.6	198.8	142	533	64.9	18.4	6,923	325.7	27,929	113
Ketchikan Gateway	46	716	109.9	36.0	37	116	14.6	3.9	1,344	85.2	10,371	36
Kodiak Island	43	687	78.0	35.6	24	114	13.8	4.4	1,527	96.2	2,763	8
Kusilvak	D	D	D	D	NA	NA	NA	NA	443	4.6	0	0
Lake and Peninsula	NA	NA	NA	NA	NA	NA	NA	NA	255	11.2	NA	NA
Matanuska-Susitna	331	4,518	569.4	219.5	145	595	101.1	20.7	7,906	375.1	12,327	50
Nome	D	D	D	D	15	67	9.3	1.7	516	15.5	673	8
North Slope	9	D	78.9	D	7	39	7.9	1.6	246	8.0	2,153	7
Northwest Arctic	D	D	D	D	D	D	D	D	240	9.2	2,738	11
Petersburg	9	172	18.7	11.4	D	D	D	D	762	60.9	1,725	6
Prince of Wales-Hyder	12	175	13.5	6.2	12	37	2.1	0.5	553	25.7	0	0
Sitka	22	758	144.0	52.0	25	168	18.6	7.1	1,308	75.6	2,917	14
Skagway	5	D	0.4	D	4	19	1.4	0.4	145	8.1	1,000	3
Southeast Fairbanks	10	101	9.7	4.2	D	D	D	0.2	531	25.7	NA	NA
Valdez-Cordova	27	485	52.3	23.0	25	85	10.4	3.0	1,285	59.6	2,937	13
Wrangell	8	288	28.5	9.8	D	D	D	0.7	328	13.6	2,120	5
Yakutat	D	D	D	0.9	NA	NA	NA	NA	118	9.5	1,513	8
Yukon-Koyukuk	9	D	2.9	D	D	D	D	0.4	364	8.7	0	0
ARIZONA	18,816	379,015	48,130.1	18,409.1	9,271	68,350	8,727.5	2,305.9	530,622	25,448.3	15,322,691	65,334
Apache	71	2,832	370.2	142.0	D	D	D	D	2,670	70.9	25,776	125
Cochise	283	4,921	454.5	188.2	160	661	66.2	16.9	7,191	231.1	58,058	434
Coconino	422	8,994	1,229.8	448.2	249	1,422	143.0	43.3	10,011	429.6	234,809	1,051
Gila	143	2,046	251.6	103.3	56	185	23.5	5.0	3,491	140.6	54,489	204
Graham	72	1,974	219.3	88.0	32	230	28.4	9.8	1,549	64.3	35,241	181
Greenlee	D	D	D	D	NA	NA	NA	NA	240	4.1	5,948	23
La Paz	D	D	D	D	17	66	9.2	1.7	872	37.5	5,237	35
Maricopa	12,396	248,818	32,793.7	12,407.6	5,924	48,349	6,599.8	1,746.5	354,596	18,204.0	9,759,523	42,123
Mohave	500	8,679	1,115.4	403.1	293	1,375	133.7	35.5	12,342	595.7	345,166	1,637
Navajo	253	4,449	623.3	246.5	117	529	49.3	13.3	5,769	219.6	191,542	722
Pima	2,862	61,632	7,137.9	2,861.4	1,485	10,873	1,229.4	305.4	72,626	3,003.4	1,753,992	6,284
Pinal	504	9,830	1,010.9	444.0	254	1,534	131.5	40.3	22,930	872.1	1,895,001	8,458
Santa Cruz	73	1,783	165.4	82.9	54	221	19.0	5.1	4,333	220.6	70,136	285
Yavapai	790	13,844	1,568.4	579.8	390	1,672	178.9	49.5	21,462	935.1	682,637	2,481
Yuma	411	8,367	1,074.7	365.5	214	1,124	102.6	30.6	10,540	419.6	205,136	1,291
ARKANSAS	7,878	182,126	19,845.4	7,960.7	3,910	21,132	2,873.8	655.4	214,924	9,540.8	2,857,616	14,198
Arkansas	48	817	63.3	25.4	28	84	5.8	2.6	1,388	67.2	1,982	18
Ashley	40	893	67.7	31.3	22	91	11.3	2.9	1,003	39.6	0	0
Baxter	176	4,115	441.7	166.9	76	362	27.3	7.5	3,196	152.2	19,620	105
Benton	580	10,426	1,214.8	454.5	296	1,919	287.9	65.2	21,342	1,006.2	1,058,261	4,356
Boone	128	2,572	232.2	93.5	D	D	D	D	2,924	129.2	4,149	28
Bradley	31	527	44.0	16.9	D	D	D	D	546	30.3	260	2
Calhoun	D	D	D	D	D	D	D	D	211	9.6	500	1
Carroll	53	742	75.1	29.4	36	147	14.2	3.4	2,614	96.2	4,606	47
Chicot	33	604	43.4	20.0	14	64	7.4	1.5	568	20.2	0	0
Clark	55	1,126	76.9	33.9	30	84	10.7	2.5	1,330	54.6	12,408	44
Clay	28	707	42.8	20.9	D	D	D	D	854	34.6	1,777	19
Cleburne	50	892	60.8	25.3	31	105	11.1	2.7	2,204	99.9	1,820	7

STATE County	Government employment and payroll, 2017									Local government finances, 2017				
			March payroll (percent of total)							General revenue				
												Taxes		
													Per capita[1] (dollars)	
	Full-time equivalent employees	March payroll (dollars)	Adminis-tration, judicial, and legal	Police and corrections	Fire protection	Highways and transpor-tation	Health and welfare	Natural resources and utilities	Education and libraries	Total (mil dol)	Inter-govern-mental (mil dol)	Total (mil dol)	Total	Property
	171	172	173	174	175	176	177	178	179	180	181	182	183	184
ALABAMA—Cont'd														
Washington	754	2,362,291	4.0	6.3	0.0	12.8	20.3	3.3	53.2	69.6	24.9	13.2	800	536
Wilcox	526	1,505,521	8.9	8.3	0.0	4.0	15.2	4.0	57.5	32.1	17.1	9.6	896	490
Winston	1,347	3,592,965	2.4	4.3	1.3	2.5	31.6	4.2	52.6	86.2	54.4	17.5	738	309
ALASKA	X	X	X	X	X	X	X	X	X	X	X	X	X	X
Aleutians East	141	727,422	20.6	9.0	0.0	14.7	0.0	10.3	38.5	39.1	19.9	12.8	3,714	445
Aleutians West	273	1,510,076	17.0	9.3	4.5	8.2	0.0	20.3	26.6	65.9	23.9	24.5	4,275	1,053
Anchorage	9,451	53,838,637	4.7	8.9	6.8	4.7	3.5	9.8	59.6	1,465.8	643.6	609.3	2,070	1,797
Bethel	302	1,271,943	24.4	15.0	3.4	5.0	23.8	11.3	0.0	48.2	24.2	10.4	578	5
Bristol Bay	68	336,805	14.4	14.0	4.2	12.3	3.1	12.7	38.9	16.8	6.2	7.2	8,307	5,524
Chugach	NA	NA	NA	NA	NA	NA	NA	NA	NA	NA	NA	NA	NA	NA
Copper River	NA	NA	NA	NA	NA	NA	NA	NA	NA	NA	NA	NA	NA	NA
Denali	98	453,460	8.3	0.0	0.0	0.0	0.0	3.9	86.6	15.1	8.3	6.1	2,929	1,138
Dillingham	229	1,071,597	16.0	10.5	0.8	6.1	17.1	4.7	42.0	35.8	23.2	5.7	1,148	467
Fairbanks North Star	3,002	16,676,902	7.1	2.7	3.0	4.7	1.3	2.3	77.7	420.1	226.7	155.1	1,556	1,370
Haines	101	485,115	11.9	8.4	1.6	5.0	0.0	5.3	60.7	18.0	9.4	6.2	2,474	1,197
Hoonah-Angoon	85	381,510	17.4	9.1	1.4	4.6	0.0	16.3	47.1	10.1	5.2	3.1	1,461	545
Juneau	1,882	11,995,964	5.2	5.5	2.7	6.8	32.3	6.9	40.5	355.5	97.8	102.9	3,206	1,520
Kenai Peninsula	2,016	10,480,980	10.5	4.7	7.0	3.3	0.5	4.6	62.5	558.4	145.6	137.3	2,345	1,334
Ketchikan Gateway	749	3,822,292	9.1	5.4	5.0	10.8	0.0	18.5	46.2	145.4	53.3	37.3	2,695	1,103
Kodiak Island	684	3,420,400	10.4	6.3	2.6	3.4	5.0	5.6	65.5	116.6	55.0	29.7	2,198	1,247
Kusilvak	213	728,558	22.4	13.1	0.6	8.1	0.0	22.8	20.3	21.4	14.2	1.8	221	18
Lake and Peninsula	179	756,201	17.1	0.0	0.1	3.5	0.9	3.6	72.3	29.8	17.8	8.9	5,519	3,213
Matanuska-Susitna	3,030	15,877,820	6.6	2.8	1.9	1.5	3.5	2.6	79.2	470.9	262.6	161.1	1,517	1,188
Nome	408	3,363,400	6.1	6.9	0.8	2.1	7.3	11.2	61.7	58.9	33.5	10.3	1,031	323
North Slope	1,780	10,868,287	23.3	6.4	2.8	3.4	12.3	13.3	29.3	602.0	65.8	400.2	40,860	40,759
Northwest Arctic	616	3,233,356	9.6	4.6	2.2	3.3	4.0	4.2	71.8	115.6	81.3	9.5	1,223	610
Petersburg	361	1,882,582	3.3	4.3	0.7	9.4	38.0	7.7	34.2	30.7	14.4	7.2	2,203	1,071
Prince of Wales-Hyder	236	1,050,369	8.2	5.0	0.0	3.7	15.7	9.2	54.7	31.7	20.4	3.9	606	158
Sitka	538	2,929,099	6.3	5.3	0.4	1.9	32.3	10.7	38.7	85.5	24.3	20.2	2,341	757
Skagway	81	480,789	12.4	12.6	4.5	3.4	22.5	8.6	30.1	21.3	7.0	9.9	8,445	1,711
Southeast Fairbanks	11	48,016	49.4	0.0	0.0	4.8	0.0	11.8	22.5	2.6	1.9	0.1	12	2
Valdez-Cordova	485	2,484,899	8.5	9.0	3.6	10.7	17.5	9.9	37.3	165.6	35.0	51.8	5,621	5,101
Wrangell	X	X	X	X	X	X	X	X	X	28.5	8.8	4.5	1,790	683
Yakutat	41	136,787	21.6	29.3	0.0	11.9	0.0	13.8	22.0	4.8	2.3	1.7	2,752	837
Yukon-Koyukuk	399	1,696,302	7.5	1.6	1.4	2.3	0.0	8.9	74.8	57.4	51.6	1.5	281	154
ARIZONA	X	X	X	X	X	X	X	X	X	X	X	X	X	X
Apache	2,561	9,092,298	6.2	5.5	3.1	3.6	2.5	0.7	77.8	239.3	176.1	30.3	424	375
Cochise	4,703	17,332,719	11.3	11.0	5.9	3.1	2.2	4.0	60.1	436.0	208.8	154.2	1,235	895
Coconino	4,429	19,039,894	12.5	13.9	10.9	3.0	3.7	6.5	46.5	547.2	192.8	256.6	1,820	982
Gila	1,844	6,875,652	8.5	14.5	8.8	4.1	3.4	5.1	55.3	226.4	109.7	87.1	1,625	1,157
Graham	1,780	6,231,954	9.2	10.8	0.3	3.4	1.3	8.0	61.4	146.5	86.8	34.3	915	532
Greenlee	438	1,474,480	19.3	16.0	0.0	7.8	4.3	1.9	48.5	39.3	16.0	15.6	1,656	1,465
La Paz	819	2,764,287	12.2	19.2	8.2	4.0	6.2	4.1	43.2	79.6	41.4	22.7	1,099	679
Maricopa	124,148	610,024,911	8.9	14.9	6.5	3.1	6.4	14.3	44.7	16,182.0	5,622.0	6,973.8	1,612	981
Mohave	5,008	18,841,384	14.4	15.1	13.1	5.0	2.0	7.1	41.4	586.3	225.7	230.7	1,114	793
Navajo	3,430	12,806,832	2.5	10.3	6.3	1.5	0.5	4.3	74.1	527.2	226.3	112.3	1,030	712
Pima	31,752	127,346,777	11.2	14.7	7.2	3.8	2.7	7.1	50.9	3,446.6	1,195.6	1,540.0	1,500	1,074
Pinal	9,478	34,939,021	12.0	15.5	6.3	3.5	2.5	6.3	52.6	994.8	427.9	401.7	931	680
Santa Cruz	1,862	6,396,808	10.0	14.5	12.3	1.9	2.7	3.1	53.0	165.6	95.5	54.0	1,160	779
Yavapai	6,183	24,573,588	10.4	15.0	8.4	6.0	4.2	5.0	41.7	671.5	233.0	333.0	1,460	889
Yuma	7,776	27,599,788	11.8	12.2	3.2	2.3	2.4	7.4	59.2	761.8	338.4	336.9	1,608	1,179
ARKANSAS	X	X	X	X	X	X	X	X	X	X	X	X	X	X
Arkansas	744	2,133,165	6.2	10.7	2.2	4.5	0.9	6.3	66.6	71.5	40.2	20.0	1,121	431
Ashley	816	2,164,062	2.6	8.5	3.5	4.8	1.0	6.3	72.8	66.7	37.1	18.1	892	481
Baxter	1,084	3,322,357	5.6	9.8	4.0	6.0	0.2	8.6	64.0	67.4	43.0	14.6	353	180
Benton	7,857	28,010,843	6.2	10.0	5.6	2.4	0.3	7.5	66.3	800.1	441.1	239.3	898	389
Boone	1,418	3,852,255	5.0	7.5	2.9	3.1	2.0	5.1	73.1	95.2	64.6	17.6	470	215
Bradley	488	1,310,975	4.4	5.2	0.8	4.0	1.8	4.1	79.7	36.4	25.4	5.5	511	207
Calhoun	149	456,734	15.6	6.5	4.1	8.8	0.1	4.7	59.1	16.9	7.8	3.2	609	357
Carroll	1,025	2,774,615	5.7	8.8	2.2	5.7	0.2	11.6	63.2	78.5	42.7	20.1	722	340
Chicot	580	1,712,945	7.4	11.3	0.1	3.7	39.3	5.0	32.5	51.7	19.8	10.5	987	412
Clark	937	2,704,581	5.2	7.9	1.5	3.7	0.9	5.3	74.6	66.1	39.5	15.3	690	267
Clay	755	2,196,317	5.3	6.9	0.0	4.3	32.0	5.8	45.5	52.6	24.9	8.6	576	281
Cleburne	805	2,290,053	7.4	10.0	1.1	4.9	0.6	8.1	67.4	63.1	34.0	17.4	693	398

1. Based on the resident population estimated as of July 1 of the year shown.

STATE County	Local government finances, 2017 (cont.)									Government employment, 2020			Individual income tax returns, 2019		
	Direct general expenditure							Debt outstanding							
			Percent of total for:												
	Total (mil dol)	Per capita[1] (dollars)	Education	Health and hospitals	Police protection	Public welfare	Highways	Total (mil dol)	Per capita[1] (dollars)	Federal civilian	Federal military	State and local	Number of returns	Mean adjusted gross income	Mean income tax
	185	186	187	188	189	190	191	192	193	194	195	196	197	198	199
ALABAMA—Cont'd															
Washington	71.7	4,338	40.6	35.0	3.5	0.0	7.1	114.9	6,953	38	66	840	6,480	52,766	4,191
Wilcox	36.8	3,441	55.9	2.3	5.4	0.0	6.9	65.0	6,081	68	42	653	4,290	38,637	2,668
Winston	80.8	3,399	51.1	26.3	2.4	0.0	4.6	55.3	2,326	77	96	1,059	9,330	49,568	4,197
ALASKA	X	X	X	X	X	X	X	X	X	15,439	26,444	59,072	356,530	73,013	8,731
Aleutians East	101.8	29,450	8.1	0.0	1.0	0.1	1.3	16.0	4,635	16	11	242	890	47,592	3,898
Aleutians West	58.4	10,185	15.2	0.3	6.4	0.4	12.1	119.5	20,857	14	28	500	2,100	66,220	7,194
Anchorage	1,453.2	4,937	47.8	1.4	9.1	0.1	8.2	1,638.0	5,565	8,568	12,622	18,247	148,080	81,519	10,833
Bethel	52.4	2,897	5.6	0.1	6.2	0.0	4.5	16.7	925	94	121	2,782	7,090	41,202	3,646
Bristol Bay	12.6	14,455	32.2	0.0	8.5	0.0	7.7	0.4	488	40	5	147	500	67,340	7,554
Chugach	NA	NA	NA	NA	NA	NA	NA	NA	NA	77	187	815	3,560	69,883	7,521
Copper River	NA	NA	NA	NA	NA	NA	NA	NA	NA	66	19	246	1,430	57,162	5,380
Denali	12.7	6,094	76.6	0.1	0.0	0.0	0.0	0.0	0	182	42	146	1,230	66,080	6,887
Dillingham	34.9	7,070	34.6	0.5	4.4	0.0	2.3	19.4	3,919	46	32	644	2,090	46,460	4,281
Fairbanks North Star	387.5	3,888	55.4	1.1	1.9	0.0	6.2	171.3	1,719	3,295	9,656	6,975	46,560	70,844	7,908
Haines	13.6	5,376	39.2	0.7	4.2	0.0	4.2	0.0	0	14	18	165	1,410	57,980	6,429
Hoonah-Angoon	9.6	4,489	46.3	1.6	6.4	0.0	12.6	2.2	1,026	91	14	272	1,010	49,470	4,600
Juneau	343.7	10,707	21.5	30.3	4.1	0.0	3.8	179.4	5,588	716	462	5,780	17,100	78,851	9,133
Kenai Peninsula	541.3	9,244	26.5	44.6	1.7	0.0	2.6	214.8	3,669	399	486	4,218	29,810	70,073	7,864
Ketchikan Gateway	158.8	11,477	22.5	8.2	3.1	0.0	3.4	189.3	13,681	224	286	1,589	7,330	67,992	7,546
Kodiak Island	114.1	8,441	44.4	0.5	4.6	0.0	2.5	155.6	11,516	275	1,046	1,286	6,720	64,749	6,487
Kusilvak	18.6	2,256	44.7	0.6	6.5	0.0	2.9	0.1	10	20	56	1,223	3,120	23,102	1,038
Lake and Peninsula	23.9	14,839	72.0	0.0	0.5	0.0	2.8	32.8	20,372	39	10	360	630	39,227	2,627
Matanuska-Susitna	461.8	4,347	60.6	3.2	2.4	0.0	7.2	425.6	4,007	319	726	4,712	49,190	71,379	7,733
Nome	58.6	5,841	30.8	0.6	9.0	0.0	4.4	27.2	2,717	55	65	1,487	3,700	54,225	5,212
North Slope	402.7	41,116	22.0	6.2	6.3	1.5	4.1	381.7	38,965	19	47	1,980	3,790	55,242	5,587
Northwest Arctic	110.6	14,194	66.1	0.1	1.9	0.0	4.0	51.9	6,656	53	49	954	2,490	56,551	5,443
Petersburg	31.2	9,564	39.2	0.0	4.5	5.0	16.9	15.2	4,667	81	52	419	2,000	60,304	5,822
Prince of Wales-Hyder	32.4	5,024	42.2	2.8	4.6	0.0	7.0	8.6	1,340	84	41	935	2,320	56,992	5,842
Sitka	88.4	10,227	27.0	40.4	5.0	0.0	2.4	165.1	19,102	118	246	724	4,590	69,092	7,846
Skagway	29.2	25,028	11.1	8.4	2.5	0.1	1.7	24.2	20,739	50	8	121	760	68,287	7,639
Southeast Fairbanks	2.4	353	21.5	0.0	0.0	0.0	14.7	0.6	87	347	54	472	3,330	57,830	5,258
Valdez-Cordova	132.0	14,322	16.8	21.1	5.6	0.0	4.6	41.2	4,468	NA	NA	NA	NA	NA	NA
Wrangell	26.4	10,456	21.0	44.0	6.0	0.0	4.1	1.9	743	39	17	165	1,080	57,061	5,231
Yakutat	5.9	9,877	34.2	4.0	19.3	4.6	2.5	0.0	0	25	4	74	280	55,557	4,886
Yukon-Koyukuk	55.1	10,195	87.6	0.1	0.6	0.0	1.6	0.1	18	73	34	1,392	2,450	37,753	2,669
ARIZONA	X	X	X	X	X	X	X	X	X	58,978	35,315	356,541	3,288,210	68,460	8,072
Apache	198.7	2,777	76.5	1.6	2.6	0.1	4.2	186.3	2,603	2,706	154	7,499	26,200	40,192	2,626
Cochise	399.0	3,196	48.4	1.3	10.9	2.7	7.5	162.4	1,301	4,956	4,457	5,830	55,370	50,721	4,347
Coconino	510.3	3,619	36.3	2.7	7.6	0.9	8.5	201.0	1,426	2,727	289	14,651	63,540	62,499	6,681
Gila	179.8	3,356	47.7	1.1	10.2	1.9	5.4	58.4	1,091	298	112	5,023	23,090	51,537	4,572
Graham	165.9	4,425	54.1	1.3	7.8	1.5	3.7	60.5	1,615	408	76	2,339	12,840	52,088	4,076
Greenlee	36.6	3,879	42.4	5.8	14.7	0.7	6.1	1.4	147	37	20	507	3,600	62,642	5,072
La Paz	71.1	3,434	35.4	3.2	10.5	1.1	6.0	45.6	2,200	378	44	1,793	7,180	41,189	3,304
Maricopa	15,034.8	3,474	40.0	5.1	9.3	1.7	3.6	27,893.7	6,446	22,688	14,883	197,970	2,065,850	75,314	9,574
Mohave	532.1	2,570	33.3	4.1	9.9	0.1	6.2	543.6	2,626	551	448	7,482	91,950	48,316	4,402
Navajo	524.9	4,812	41.3	29.9	5.3	2.1	3.7	185.5	1,701	2,010	231	7,436	43,230	45,876	3,500
Pima	3,167.0	3,086	39.3	2.2	12.8	1.8	6.9	5,952.8	5,800	13,387	8,654	66,885	483,760	63,458	6,795
Pinal	969.6	2,247	41.5	3.3	11.4	0.1	7.7	1,061.2	2,459	1,539	964	17,848	177,830	54,727	4,552
Santa Cruz	164.0	3,523	47.3	1.0	7.1	1.8	4.0	93.5	2,009	1,840	98	1,927	22,140	46,209	3,772
Yavapai	710.2	3,114	35.4	3.3	9.4	0.1	10.8	559.6	2,454	1,692	509	8,996	117,170	60,993	6,518
Yuma	662.2	3,161	48.5	1.4	7.5	2.1	4.6	438.5	2,093	3,761	4,376	10,355	94,520	45,331	3,514
ARKANSAS	X	X	X	X	X	X	X	X	X	21,274	15,271	185,511	1,288,340	58,838	6,092
Arkansas	72.9	4,079	44.7	2.0	6.4	0.4	6.6	99.4	5,564	180	66	898	7,680	51,172	5,173
Ashley	62.4	3,074	62.3	0.1	6.8	0.1	6.3	112.9	5,559	78	75	928	7,790	47,851	3,670
Baxter	71.0	1,719	64.6	0.0	5.3	0.0	5.6	175.6	4,250	162	160	1,543	18,810	49,707	4,620
Benton	779.6	2,924	57.6	0.4	5.7	0.0	9.0	1,059.6	3,975	536	1,101	9,972	127,740	98,147	12,711
Boone	109.2	2,914	70.6	0.1	6.5	0.1	5.1	92.1	2,458	147	143	2,966	16,230	49,219	4,149
Bradley	34.6	3,199	71.2	0.6	5.4	0.1	6.6	20.7	1,915	32	40	809	4,150	42,655	3,065
Calhoun	15.4	2,963	37.2	2.1	5.7	0.9	11.2	98.1	18,854	13	19	251	1,950	49,923	3,731
Carroll	72.9	2,617	52.9	0.1	7.0	0.1	6.3	55.5	1,993	93	108	1,127	12,560	43,089	3,421
Chicot	48.9	4,589	32.9	35.9	4.3	0.1	6.5	11.5	1,079	45	35	822	3,860	40,863	3,919
Clark	65.2	2,937	63.5	0.1	8.4	0.2	7.2	40.9	1,842	99	76	2,190	8,520	47,691	3,903
Clay	51.6	3,469	44.6	28.0	6.4	0.3	6.4	20.9	1,404	58	55	838	5,810	41,973	3,204
Cleburne	56.4	2,252	59.6	0.0	8.6	0.3	10.2	63.9	2,549	102	95	862	10,670	50,077	4,298

1. Based on the resident population estimated as of July 1 of the year shown.

State / county code	CBSA code[1]	County Type code[2]	STATE County	Land area[3] (sq. mi)	Population, 2021			Population and population characteristics, 2021										
								Race alone or in combination, not Hispanic or Latino (percent)					Age (percent)					
					Total persons 2021	Rank	Per square mile	White	Black	American Indian, Alaska Native	Asian and Pacific Islancer	Percent Hispanic or Latino[4]	Under 5 years	5 to 17 years	18 to 24 years	25 to 34 years	35 to 44 years	45 to 54 years
				1	2	3	4	5	6	7	8	9	10	11	12	13	14	15
			ARKANSAS—Cont'd															
05025	38220	3	Cleveland	597.9	7,514	2,619	12.6	85.4	11.8	1.2	0.4	2.8	5.2	12.2	11.4	10.5	11.7	12.8
05027	31620	7	Columbia	766.1	22,672	1,690	29.6	60.6	35.7	0.9	1.2	3.1	5.8	12.1	21.1	11.0	10.3	10.3
05029		6	Conway	551.9	20,873	1,768	37.8	82.8	12.5	1.8	0.9	4.4	5.7	13.1	11.0	11.4	11.8	12.3
05031	27860	3	Craighead	707.2	112,218	550	158.7	75.5	18.3	0.8	1.7	5.5	6.5	14.2	15.0	15.0	13.2	11.2
05033	22900	2	Crawford	595.3	60,378	874	101.4	85.7	2.5	4.1	2.1	8.7	6.0	13.7	12.2	12.1	12.3	12.6
05035	32820	1	Crittenden	612.9	47,525	1,031	77.5	40.8	55.8	0.7	1.0	3.1	7.2	15.4	13.3	13.1	12.0	11.7
05037		6	Cross	616.3	16,681	1,993	27.1	73.2	24.0	1.0	1.2	2.3	6.2	13.5	11.5	11.8	12.1	12.7
05039		6	Dallas	667.3	6,308	2,711	9.5	54.9	40.9	1.4	0.7	4.2	4.6	12.5	10.9	9.6	11.1	11.2
05041		6	Desha	741.2	11,090	2,338	15.0	44.4	47.9	1.0	1.1	7.0	6.1	14.7	12.3	10.8	11.2	10.8
05043		6	Drew	828.7	17,110	1,966	20.6	67.1	28.5	0.9	1.0	3.9	6.1	12.1	16.6	12.0	11.4	10.6
05045	30780	2	Faulkner	647.2	125,106	514	193.3	81.0	13.4	1.3	2.1	4.5	5.8	12.9	18.6	13.9	12.9	11.4
05047	22900	6	Franklin	609.0	17,173	1,958	28.2	92.6	1.5	2.5	1.5	3.7	5.4	13.0	12.3	11.2	12.0	12.2
05049		9	Fulton	618.0	12,145	2,274	19.7	95.7	1.5	2.1	0.6	2.3	5.0	12.4	10.3	9.4	10.4	11.6
05051	26300	3	Garland	677.6	100,330	609	148.1	83.4	9.8	1.6	1.4	6.4	5.2	11.1	10.7	11.2	11.3	11.8
05053	30780	2	Grant	631.9	18,090	1,920	28.6	92.9	3.3	1.2	0.8	3.2	5.2	12.7	11.7	12.2	13.0	12.8
05055	37500	4	Greene	577.3	46,317	1,049	80.2	93.2	2.8	1.1	1.1	3.3	6.2	13.8	12.5	13.3	12.9	12.8
05057	26260	6	Hempstead	727.2	19,694	1,842	27.1	55.1	30.9	1.4	1.0	13.9	6.8	14.6	12.0	11.6	11.0	11.2
05059	31680	6	Hot Spring	614.9	33,148	1,354	53.9	84.1	11.7	1.6	0.9	3.8	4.9	11.2	11.9	12.6	12.6	13.1
05061		6	Howard	587.3	12,698	2,229	21.6	63.9	21.4	1.5	0.9	13.9	6.9	14.9	12.6	11.4	11.7	11.3
05063	12900	7	Independence	763.7	37,723	1,229	49.4	88.7	3.2	1.3	1.3	7.3	6.0	13.7	13.0	11.8	12.1	12.3
05065		9	Izard	580.2	13,911	2,156	24.0	93.3	3.0	1.5	0.8	2.8	4.6	10.2	10.4	10.8	11.6	12.4
05067		6	Jackson	633.6	16,811	1,985	26.5	77.8	18.2	1.4	1.0	3.4	5.6	11.3	11.3	14.7	13.3	12.1
05069	38220	3	Jefferson	872.4	65,861	815	75.5	39.0	57.7	0.9	1.3	2.5	5.7	12.0	13.7	12.6	12.0	11.7
05071		7	Johnson	661.0	25,845	1,566	39.1	79.5	2.5	2.2	3.5	14.6	6.5	13.8	13.6	11.9	12.4	11.5
05073		8	Lafayette	529.5	6,163	2,724	11.6	60.6	35.4	1.1	1.0	3.6	5.2	9.8	9.9	11.4	9.8	12.1
05075		6	Lawrence	587.5	16,292	2,016	27.7	95.9	1.9	1.4	0.7	1.8	5.9	12.5	13.8	12.0	11.4	11.7
05077		7	Lee	599.8	8,619	2,524	14.4	42.1	54.2	1.2	0.8	3.2	5.3	9.6	10.9	15.5	12.7	12.8
05079	38220	3	Lincoln	559.5	13,037	2,211	23.3	64.6	30.4	1.0	0.5	4.8	4.1	8.9	13.4	17.0	15.1	13.7
05081	45500	3	Little River	531.3	11,944	2,287	22.5	74.8	20.6	2.4	0.8	3.7	6.0	12.2	11.6	11.5	11.2	12.8
05083		6	Logan	709.1	21,215	1,753	29.9	92.2	1.9	2.1	2.4	3.1	5.6	11.9	11.2	11.2	11.3	13.2
05085	30780	2	Lonoke	771.4	74,722	744	96.9	87.5	7.1	1.2	1.6	4.7	6.3	14.3	12.5	13.9	13.7	12.8
05087	22220	2	Madison	834.2	16,960	1,974	20.3	90.5	0.9	2.6	1.8	6.1	6.1	13.0	11.3	11.8	11.7	12.0
05089		9	Marion	596.7	16,978	1,973	28.5	95.2	1.0	2.2	1.0	2.6	4.5	10.8	8.7	9.0	9.7	10.9
05091	45500	3	Miller	624.0	42,649	1,133	68.3	69.5	26.5	1.4	1.0	3.7	6.2	13.5	11.9	13.0	12.8	12.4
05093	14180	4	Mississippi	902.1	39,661	1,190	44.0	58.7	36.5	0.7	0.7	4.7	7.2	14.4	13.4	12.7	12.2	11.5
05095		7	Monroe	607.5	6,683	2,684	11.0	55.6	41.1	1.3	1.2	2.9	6.7	12.3	9.9	10.3	9.1	11.6
05097		8	Montgomery	780.5	8,611	2,525	11.0	92.6	0.8	2.7	1.6	4.4	4.7	10.2	10.1	9.3	9.3	12.4
05099	26260	7	Nevada	617.8	8,187	2,563	13.3	64.2	31.3	0.9	0.7	4.7	5.6	13.0	11.3	10.4	11.2	12.6
05101	25460	9	Newton	821.1	7,204	2,647	8.8	95.4	1.0	3.1	0.7	2.2	4.9	10.4	10.1	9.6	10.5	11.3
05103	15780	7	Ouachita	732.7	22,306	1,701	30.4	56.7	41.1	1.0	0.8	2.6	5.5	12.7	11.5	11.4	10.9	11.6
05105	30780	2	Perry	551.4	9,964	2,409	18.1	93.6	2.7	2.0	0.7	3.1	5.2	12.7	10.8	10.7	11.3	13.3
05107	25760	6	Phillips	690.4	15,906	2,037	23.0	34.9	62.8	0.7	0.6	2.0	7.4	14.3	12.2	10.7	10.5	10.6
05109		9	Pike	600.3	10,066	2,399	16.8	88.3	4.2	1.7	0.9	6.9	5.1	12.7	11.5	11.3	11.3	13.3
05111	27860	3	Poinsett	758.3	22,660	1,691	29.9	87.6	9.1	0.9	0.6	3.6	6.4	13.4	12.0	12.6	11.5	12.3
05113		7	Polk	856.8	19,353	1,856	22.6	90.2	0.9	3.6	1.2	6.4	5.4	13.0	11.7	10.2	10.4	11.8
05115	40780	5	Pope	811.1	63,789	847	78.6	85.2	3.8	1.7	1.6	9.7	5.8	13.1	16.2	13.2	11.6	11.5
05117		8	Prairie	647.5	8,135	2,569	12.6	86.4	11.5	0.9	0.4	2.0	5.5	11.8	9.6	10.5	10.8	12.5
05119	30780	2	Pulaski	758.3	397,821	182	524.6	52.9	39.2	1.0	2.9	6.3	6.3	13.1	12.4	14.3	13.0	11.8
05121		7	Randolph	651.9	18,865	1,878	28.9	93.0	1.9	1.8	2.9	2.5	7.0	13.8	11.4	12.6	12.0	11.4
05123	22620	6	St. Francis	634.8	22,739	1,685	35.8	40.5	53.3	1.0	1.0	5.7	6.2	11.5	11.1	15.0	14.3	12.4
05125	30780	2	Saline	723.5	125,233	512	173.1	84.2	9.1	1.1	1.8	5.5	5.5	13.5	11.4	12.5	13.7	12.5
05127		6	Scott	892.9	9,822	2,420	11.0	85.9	1.3	3.6	3.5	8.2	5.9	13.0	11.5	11.3	10.7	11.6
05129		9	Searcy	665.8	7,880	2,584	11.8	94.6	0.9	3.1	0.7	3.1	4.8	11.5	9.7	9.9	10.3	11.8
05131	22900	2	Sebastian	531.2	128,400	505	241.7	71.6	8.1	3.5	5.4	14.9	6.4	13.3	13.0	13.4	12.3	12.0
05133		6	Sevier	563.6	15,783	2,045	28.0	58.4	4.6	3.3	1.7	34.2	7.6	16.2	13.6	12.3	11.3	12.1
05135	12900	7	Sharp	604.6	17,622	1,940	29.1	94.7	1.5	2.3	0.8	2.7	5.5	11.6	10.6	10.2	10.1	11.8
05137		9	Stone	606.4	12,481	2,244	20.6	96.3	0.9	2.0	0.7	1.9	5.2	10.7	10.0	9.7	10.0	10.3
05139	20980	7	Union	1,039.1	38,340	1,212	36.9	61.8	33.5	1.0	1.0	4.1	6.0	13.8	12.0	11.7	12.1	11.8
05141		8	Van Buren	709.6	15,694	2,050	22.1	94.6	1.2	2.1	0.6	3.4	4.2	10.9	10.2	8.8	10.4	12.1
05143	22220	2	Washington	941.5	250,057	281	265.6	72.6	4.4	2.3	6.2	17.2	6.3	13.4	18.4	14.8	13.5	11.0
05145	42620	4	White	1,034.1	77,207	733	74.7	89.4	5.5	1.3	1.2	4.6	5.6	13.3	15.2	12.3	11.8	12.1
05147		9	Woodruff	586.0	6,116	2,729	10.4	71.6	27.0	1.0	0.5	1.9	6.1	12.0	10.7	10.2	10.6	12.1
05149	40780	6	Yell	930.2	20,155	1,808	21.7	75.1	2.3	1.3	1.5	21.0	6.1	13.7	12.3	12.0	11.4	12.2

1. CBSA = Core Based Statistical Area. See Appendix A for explanation. See Appendix B for list of metropolitan areas with component counties. 2. County type code from the Economic Research Service of USDA Rural-Urban Continuum Codes. See Appendix A for definition. 3. Dry land or land partially or temporarily covered by water. 4. May be of any race.

STATE County	Population, 2021 (cont.): Age (percent) (cont.): 55 to 64 years	65 to 74 years	75 years and over	Percent female	Population change, 2000–2021: Total persons: 2010	2020	Percent change: 2010–2020	2020–2021	Components of change, 2020–2021: Births	Deaths	Net Migration	Households, 2016–2020: Number	Persons per household	Percent: Family house-holds	Female family house-holder[1]	One person
	16	17	18	19	20	21	22	23	24	25	26	27	28	29	30	31
ARKANSAS—Cont'd																
Cleveland	14.9	12.7	8.6	50.6	8,689	7,550	-13.1	-0.5	98	137	2	3,170	2.5	68.0	12.5	31.3
Columbia	12.0	9.9	7.4	51.6	24,552	22,801	-7.1	-0.6	323	428	-27	8,456	2.6	64.8	13.7	30.2
Conway	14.8	11.6	8.3	50.7	21,273	20,715	-2.6	0.8	251	376	284	8,491	2.4	65.5	15.0	29.8
Craighead	10.8	8.4	5.6	51.3	96,443	111,231	15.3	0.9	1,710	1,478	731	42,203	2.5	65.9	15.1	26.4
Crawford	13.5	10.7	7.0	50.6	61,948	60,133	-2.9	0.4	884	972	323	24,065	2.6	71.6	10.6	24.6
Crittenden	12.7	9.0	5.6	52.3	50,902	48,163	-5.4	-1.3	821	805	-656	19,021	2.5	62.9	21.6	30.6
Cross	13.6	10.7	8.1	51.4	17,870	16,833	-5.8	-0.9	247	323	-77	6,568	2.5	69.8	17.0	25.4
Dallas	14.7	14.5	10.8	50.6	8,116	6,482	-20.1	-2.7	54	127	-101	2,992	2.1	62.3	14.0	35.6
Desha	14.3	12.0	7.8	53.1	13,008	11,395	-12.4	-2.7	164	193	-274	5,059	2.3	65.0	16.7	30.6
Drew	12.9	10.2	7.9	51.1	18,509	17,350	-6.3	-1.4	252	285	-207	7,207	2.4	59.7	11.2	30.6
Faulkner	11.2	8.2	5.0	51.2	113,237	123,498	9.1	1.3	1,780	1,588	1,400	45,091	2.7	65.3	11.0	26.3
Franklin	13.9	11.5	8.5	50.0	18,125	17,097	-5.7	0.4	260	338	153	6,671	2.6	64.4	11.4	29.3
Fulton	15.1	14.6	11.2	50.7	12,245	12,075	-1.4	0.6	157	294	213	5,014	2.4	63.8	9.2	30.0
Garland	14.3	14.3	10.1	51.5	96,024	100,180	4.3	0.1	1,282	2,094	969	40,906	2.4	63.7	13.2	31.1
Grant	14.1	10.7	7.6	50.5	17,853	17,958	0.6	0.7	230	320	223	7,049	2.6	69.9	11.3	27.6
Greene	12.4	9.6	6.6	50.6	42,090	45,736	8.7	1.3	705	738	616	17,587	2.5	72.5	14.6	23.1
Hempstead	13.8	11.0	8.1	51.2	22,609	20,065	-11.3	-1.8	355	351	-373	8,100	2.6	69.3	14.2	26.0
Hot Spring	14.0	12.1	7.6	47.6	32,923	33,040	0.4	0.3	394	609	320	12,515	2.5	68.0	10.7	28.6
Howard	13.2	10.4	7.7	51.2	13,789	12,785	-7.3	-0.7	220	240	-69	5,271	2.5	67.3	17.1	29.3
Independence	12.8	10.7	7.6	50.6	36,647	37,938	3.5	-0.6	532	621	-130	14,325	2.6	68.2	9.7	27.5
Izard	15.1	14.0	10.8	47.4	13,696	13,577	-0.9	2.5	168	293	467	4,911	2.6	62.1	6.6	32.7
Jackson	13.3	10.9	7.4	49.8	17,997	16,755	-6.9	0.3	222	312	146	6,241	2.3	61.8	15.1	33.2
Jefferson	13.5	11.5	7.2	50.3	77,435	67,260	-13.1	-2.1	926	1,168	-1,156	26,630	2.3	62.0	19.0	33.1
Johnson	13.2	10.3	6.9	50.0	25,540	25,749	0.8	0.4	355	407	145	9,792	2.6	67.9	10.2	29.0
Lafayette	16.6	14.0	11.2	50.9	7,645	6,308	-17.5	-2.3	93	147	-89	2,898	2.3	63.8	17.1	32.7
Lawrence	13.7	10.5	8.5	50.4	17,415	16,216	-6.9	0.5	216	345	207	6,584	2.4	69.3	10.8	26.3
Lee	12.9	11.3	8.9	43.0	10,424	8,600	-17.5	0.2	125	166	61	3,202	2.3	60.8	19.5	36.6
Lincoln	12.1	9.0	6.6	37.2	14,134	12,941	-8.4	0.7	106	212	204	3,598	2.3	73.0	9.8	22.9
Little River	13.8	12.0	9.0	51.9	13,171	12,026	-8.7	-0.7	180	272	10	5,292	2.3	64.1	13.6	33.1
Logan	15.4	11.9	8.4	50.4	22,353	21,131	-5.5	0.4	292	429	222	8,359	2.5	69.3	9.2	27.5
Lonoke	12.2	8.8	5.5	50.8	68,356	74,015	8.3	1.0	1,094	1,071	674	27,218	2.7	71.4	12.2	24.0
Madison	14.5	11.8	7.7	50.1	15,717	16,521	5.1	2.7	269	243	419	6,045	2.7	71.1	9.7	26.3
Marion	17.3	17.8	11.3	50.8	16,653	16,826	1.0	0.9	173	378	362	6,918	2.4	64.2	9.9	31.2
Miller	13.0	10.3	7.0	51.0	43,462	42,600	-2.0	0.1	637	714	120	16,237	2.6	66.6	16.6	27.9
Mississippi	13.2	9.6	5.8	51.2	46,480	40,685	-12.5	-2.5	723	747	-994	16,623	2.4	67.5	20.3	27.2
Monroe	15.9	13.6	10.7	52.9	8,149	6,799	-16.6	-1.7	99	137	-79	3,234	2.1	54.5	17.0	43.7
Montgomery	17.4	15.1	11.5	50.6	9,487	8,484	-10.6	1.5	100	211	242	3,706	2.4	74.3	7.4	24.3
Nevada	14.3	12.1	9.5	50.7	8,997	8,310	-7.6	-1.5	97	155	-63	3,188	2.5	67.2	19.0	27.2
Newton	15.7	16.2	11.2	49.6	8,330	7,225	-13.3	-0.3	82	138	36	2,996	2.6	67.2	8.6	30.8
Ouachita	15.2	12.9	8.3	52.4	26,120	22,650	-13.3	-1.5	313	502	-155	9,487	2.5	65.9	20.0	30.8
Perry	15.3	12.2	8.6	50.2	10,445	10,019	-4.1	-0.5	122	204	27	3,700	2.8	76.6	10.6	21.7
Phillips	14.1	12.4	7.8	53.4	21,757	16,568	-23.8	-4.0	321	356	-618	7,561	2.4	62.1	23.4	36.7
Pike	14.3	12.2	8.5	50.2	11,291	10,171	-9.9	-1.0	111	200	-16	4,215	2.5	69.5	6.0	28.3
Poinsett	13.5	10.8	7.5	51.4	24,583	22,965	-6.6	-1.3	351	524	-135	9,567	2.5	66.8	13.0	28.5
Polk	14.5	13.4	9.5	51.2	20,662	19,221	-7.0	0.7	296	413	252	8,114	2.5	66.9	10.4	28.5
Pope	12.3	9.6	6.7	50.5	61,754	63,381	2.6	0.6	795	938	548	22,863	2.7	66.6	12.0	28.2
Prairie	15.1	12.7	11.5	50.0	8,715	8,282	-5.0	-1.8	114	162	-98	3,755	2.1	63.1	11.1	34.5
Pulaski	12.6	10.3	6.2	52.4	382,748	399,125	4.3	-0.3	6,187	5,797	-1,749	161,652	2.4	58.9	16.3	35.1
Randolph	12.7	10.8	8.2	50.5	17,969	18,571	3.4	1.6	321	351	329	7,294	2.4	67.0	12.3	30.3
St. Francis	12.6	10.5	6.4	44.5	28,258	23,090	-18.3	-1.5	404	379	-374	9,313	2.4	63.6	22.0	33.6
Saline	12.7	11.0	7.3	51.2	107,118	123,416	15.2	1.5	1,631	1,783	1,975	45,098	2.7	70.9	11.6	24.8
Scott	15.0	11.9	9.1	49.3	11,233	9,836	-12.4	-0.1	150	176	12	4,114	2.5	66.8	7.8	31.0
Searcy	16.0	15.1	10.7	49.4	8,195	7,828	-4.5	0.7	96	169	127	3,235	2.4	69.9	7.8	27.2
Sebastian	12.8	10.1	6.7	51.0	125,744	127,799	1.6	0.5	2,011	1,918	488	52,026	2.4	64.6	13.4	29.4
Sevier	11.9	9.1	6.0	49.7	17,058	15,839	-7.1	-0.4	320	230	-148	5,690	3.0	75.4	11.9	22.0
Sharp	15.1	14.4	10.7	50.8	17,264	17,271	0.0	2.0	217	420	565	7,315	2.3	63.2	10.4	32.8
Stone	15.9	16.1	12.2	50.6	12,394	12,359	-0.3	1.0	143	240	222	4,866	2.6	66.4	6.8	29.7
Union	13.7	11.4	7.5	51.5	41,639	39,054	-6.2	-1.8	523	755	-479	15,855	2.4	64.3	15.8	31.8
Van Buren	16.7	15.5	11.3	50.4	17,295	15,796	-8.7	-0.6	127	358	130	7,220	2.3	67.0	12.0	29.3
Washington	10.2	7.6	4.7	50.0	203,065	245,871	21.1	1.7	3,803	2,606	2,939	89,094	2.6	62.6	10.5	26.9
White	13.1	9.8	6.8	51.4	77,076	76,822	-0.3	0.5	1,014	1,241	607	28,903	2.6	68.5	12.8	27.4
Woodruff	14.0	14.1	10.2	51.5	7,260	6,269	-13.7	-2.4	73	159	-67	3,002	2.1	63.6	16.0	28.7
Yell	14.2	10.5	7.6	49.7	22,185	20,263	-8.7	-0.5	316	338	-87	7,797	2.7	72.7	14.5	23.7

1. No spouse present.

STATE County	Persons in group quarters, 2021	Daytime Population, 2016–2020		Births, 2021		Deaths, 2021		Persons under 65 with no health insurance, 2019		Medicare, 2021			COVID-19 Deaths, 2020	
		Number	Employment/ residence ratio	Total	Rate[1]	Number	Rate[1]	Number	Percent	Total beneficiaries	Enrolled in Original Medicare	Enrolled in Medicare Advantage	Number	Rate[1]
	32	33	34	35	36	37	38	39	40	41	42	43	44	45
ARKANSAS—Cont'd														
Cleveland	26	6,167	0.4	78	10.4	99	13.1	550	8.8	1,983	1,544	439	21	2.8
Columbia	2,033	22,898	0.9	258	11.4	339	14.9	1,678	9.7	5,168	4,135	1,033	44	1.9
Conway	215	19,011	0.8	185	8.9	296	14.2	1,603	9.7	5,163	3,748	1,415	13	0.6
Craighead	3,734	113,814	1.1	1,356	12.1	1,224	10.9	9,347	10.2	19,074	14,005	5,069	135	1.2
Crawford	381	55,691	0.7	706	11.7	774	12.8	5,805	11.2	13,975	7,958	6,017	65	1.1
Crittenden	921	45,543	0.9	657	13.7	643	13.5	3,647	9.2	9,243	6,531	2,712	90	1.9
Cross	213	15,137	0.8	210	12.6	260	15.5	1,269	9.7	3,974	2,828	1,146	34	2.0
Dallas	291	7,249	1.1	45	7.1	110	17.3	433	8.8	1,896	1,288	608	15	2.3
Desha	48	12,029	1.1	127	11.3	158	14.1	973	10.9	2,788	2,017	771	14	1.2
Drew	615	17,839	0.9	210	12.2	239	13.9	1,222	8.7	3,830	2,973	857	25	1.4
Faulkner	3,706	112,980	0.8	1,451	11.7	1,284	10.3	9,860	9.3	20,522	16,019	4,503	92	0.7
Franklin	344	16,612	0.8	205	12.0	263	15.3	1,518	10.8	4,338	2,754	1,584	28	1.6
Fulton	113	11,293	0.8	131	10.8	236	19.5	1,061	11.7	3,690	2,576	1,113	37	3.1
Garland	2,036	100,739	1.0	1,030	10.3	1,657	16.5	8,848	12.0	28,940	19,585	9,356	152	1.5
Grant	92	15,303	0.6	186	10.3	248	13.8	1,128	7.6	3,975	3,032	943	18	1.0
Greene	532	43,309	0.9	563	12.2	605	13.1	3,253	8.7	9,636	6,866	2,770	61	1.3
Hempstead	145	22,116	1.1	286	14.4	291	14.7	2,170	12.6	4,666	3,284	1,381	21	1.1
Hot Spring	2,023	29,716	0.7	327	9.9	488	14.7	2,291	9.2	7,941	5,559	2,382	59	1.8
Howard	127	15,103	1.3	174	13.7	191	15.0	1,392	13.1	3,044	2,331	713	21	1.6
Independence	883	39,697	1.1	430	11.4	485	12.8	3,028	10.0	8,745	7,012	1,733	83	2.2
Izard	903	12,598	0.8	135	9.8	224	16.3	991	10.8	4,135	3,053	1,083	16	1.2
Jackson	2,057	17,077	1.0	174	10.4	242	14.4	1,080	9.4	3,806	2,860	946	29	1.7
Jefferson	5,368	69,470	1.1	757	11.4	944	14.2	3,927	8.0	15,417	10,498	4,920	139	2.1
Johnson	519	25,975	1.0	291	11.3	326	12.7	2,990	14.1	5,851	3,820	2,031	22	0.9
Lafayette	36	6,102	0.8	77	12.4	121	19.4	583	12.0	1,817	1,429	389	12	1.9
Lawrence	609	15,344	0.8	174	10.7	268	16.5	1,110	8.8	4,302	2,973	1,329	36	2.2
Lee	1,585	8,382	0.8	97	11.3	126	14.7	494	9.4	2,014	1,265	749	18	2.1
Lincoln	3,462	12,936	0.9	85	6.6	158	12.2	745	9.9	2,422	1,826	596	29	2.3
Little River	81	11,206	0.8	147	12.3	224	18.7	925	9.6	3,156	2,346	810	39	3.3
Logan	483	20,033	0.8	235	11.1	343	16.2	1,683	10.1	5,739	3,786	1,953	15	0.7
Lonoke	484	55,427	0.5	867	11.7	839	11.3	5,225	8.3	13,593	9,914	3,679	88	1.2
Madison	58	13,722	0.6	219	13.1	204	12.2	1,918	14.5	4,101	2,380	1,720	11	0.7
Marion	110	15,959	0.9	147	8.7	313	18.5	1,275	10.9	5,420	3,401	2,019	25	1.5
Miller	1,153	39,866	0.8	516	12.1	584	13.7	3,224	9.4	8,880	6,591	2,290	65	1.5
Mississippi	696	44,988	1.2	593	14.8	599	14.9	3,156	9.4	8,365	5,486	2,879	93	2.3
Monroe	80	6,320	0.8	87	12.9	122	18.1	474	9.6	1,979	1,406	573	11	1.6
Montgomery	74	7,778	0.6	85	10.0	165	19.3	973	15.0	2,659	1,960	700	21	2.5
Nevada	146	7,637	0.8	76	9.2	126	15.3	542	8.5	2,178	1,576	602	24	2.9
Newton	29	6,568	0.6	68	9.4	113	15.7	567	10.2	2,305	1,579	726	19	2.6
Ouachita	238	22,491	0.9	248	11.0	405	18.0	1,547	8.6	6,217	4,122	2,095	40	1.8
Perry	88	8,392	0.5	92	9.2	162	16.2	809	9.8	2,639	1,936	704	11	1.1
Phillips	130	18,117	1.0	263	16.3	279	17.2	1,245	9.0	4,244	2,764	1,480	39	2.4
Pike	124	9,451	0.7	87	8.6	177	17.5	1,174	14.1	2,804	2,087	717	18	1.8
Poinsett	257	21,222	0.7	277	12.2	412	18.1	2,010	10.7	5,761	3,708	2,053	56	2.4
Polk	96	19,884	1.0	232	12.0	341	17.7	2,220	14.8	5,453	4,179	1,274	56	2.9
Pope	3,169	66,151	1.1	631	9.9	728	11.5	6,019	11.9	13,007	9,105	3,903	65	1.0
Prairie	126	6,900	0.7	93	11.4	129	15.7	582	9.6	2,203	1,666	538	15	1.8
Pulaski	8,467	466,604	1.4	4,948	12.4	4,632	11.6	31,959	9.9	78,662	56,803	21,858	394	1.0
Randolph	320	17,752	1.0	266	14.2	286	15.3	1,641	11.6	4,552	3,060	1,492	45	2.4
St. Francis	3,721	25,488	1.0	309	13.5	302	13.2	1,482	9.0	4,921	3,239	1,682	36	1.6
Saline	1,276	94,756	0.5	1,321	10.6	1,430	11.5	8,511	8.5	26,769	19,872	6,897	119	1.0
Scott	49	9,540	0.8	118	12.0	128	13.0	968	12.2	2,603	1,677	926	17	1.7
Searcy	49	7,067	0.7	77	9.8	141	18.0	652	11.4	2,540	1,729	811	15	1.9
Sebastian	1,999	142,266	1.3	1,612	12.6	1,542	12.0	14,914	14.2	26,667	16,671	9,996	136	1.1
Sevier	99	15,576	0.8	263	16.7	187	11.9	2,617	18.4	2,963	2,340	623	34	2.2
Sharp	142	15,599	0.7	175	10.0	335	19.2	1,504	11.9	5,807	4,178	1,628	27	1.6
Stone	99	11,980	0.9	114	9.2	191	15.4	1,167	13.2	4,220	3,237	984	31	2.5
Union	476	41,057	1.1	423	10.9	612	15.8	2,847	9.2	9,534	7,270	2,263	80	2.1
Van Buren	128	15,775	0.9	105	6.7	279	17.7	1,442	12.0	5,213	3,703	1,510	13	0.8
Washington	7,966	240,168	1.0	3,029	12.2	2,089	8.4	28,563	14.1	35,382	24,431	10,951	233	0.9
White	2,822	74,997	0.9	832	10.8	1,020	13.2	6,290	10.1	16,846	12,592	4,254	62	0.8
Woodruff	82	6,028	0.8	66	10.7	122	19.8	466	9.8	1,810	1,287	523	D	D
Yell	221	19,260	0.8	246	12.2	273	13.5	2,363	13.7	4,733	3,383	1,349	45	2.2

1. Per 1,000 estimated resident population.

STATE County	COVID-19 Vaccinations, 2021–2022		Education: School enrollment and attainment, 2016–2020: Enrollment[1]		Attainment[2] (percent)		Local government expenditures,[3] 2018–2019		Money income, 2016–2020	Households			Income and poverty, 2020	Percent below poverty level		
	Number	Percent[5]	Total	Percent private	High school graduate or less	Bachelor's degree or more	Total current spending (mil dol)	Current spending per student (dollars)	Per capita income[4]	Median income (dollars)	Percent with income of less than $50,000	Percent with income of $200,000 or more	Median household income (dollars)	All persons	Children under 18 years	Children 5 to 17 years in families
	46	47	48	49	50	51	52	53	54	55	56	57	58	59	60	61
ARKANSAS—Cont'd																
Cleveland	4,226	53.1	1,936	5.8	56.6	15.9	14.4	9,664	23,998	46,349	54.7	1.6	57,697	13.8	19.3	17.3
Columbia	11,432	48.7	6,452	7.2	54.9	20.5	39.6	10,308	23,217	37,609	61.6	3.5	44,925	18.3	25.5	24.9
Conway	11,225	53.8	4,856	9.8	54.6	17.7	57.2	17,151	26,539	44,456	53.9	3.0	47,049	15.8	22.9	20.9
Craighead	50,202	45.5	30,339	6.5	44.2	27.1	189.4	9,498	28,407	49,730	50.2	4.3	51,797	16.8	23.4	23.4
Crawford	29,001	45.8	14,164	5.1	50.5	18.2	104.3	9,543	25,460	48,980	51.0	2.0	54,534	14.4	20.4	18.8
Crittenden	21,618	45.1	12,478	8.1	50.6	17.4	99.5	10,079	24,161	42,384	56.0	2.7	47,545	22.9	35.0	32.0
Cross	8,382	51.1	3,913	6.6	58.9	14.7	32.6	10,120	25,205	44,379	54.6	2.0	40,587	21.2	33.3	33.1
Dallas	3,972	56.7	1,660	40.2	58.4	11.0	10.3	13,028	21,229	35,134	62.6	0.5	34,649	19.5	32.3	30.3
Desha	6,827	60.1	2,759	7.3	65.0	14.0	27.5	11,047	19,090	31,855	65.2	2.0	37,421	22.8	34.0	31.3
Drew	8,757	48.1	5,426	10.9	50.3	22.6	41.4	13,551	26,440	42,924	53.6	2.6	46,787	18.4	24.2	23.9
Faulkner	64,799	51.4	36,688	13.5	38.6	32.1	180.8	9,528	27,414	54,191	47.4	3.8	57,367	12.0	13.3	11.8
Franklin	8,610	48.6	3,822	9.1	56.3	11.3	30.0	10,814	20,639	37,561	59.5	2.0	47,256	15.3	19.9	19.1
Fulton	4,072	32.6	2,312	10.8	52.4	13.2	17.0	9,768	20,564	35,274	63.4	0.6	39,839	17.0	27.7	24.8
Garland	45,317	45.6	19,650	8.8	41.8	22.8	151.9	9,933	27,274	48,150	51.2	2.5	46,459	15.7	22.7	21.9
Grant	8,383	45.9	3,737	9.4	49.3	20.3	40.8	8,528	30,639	59,051	41.6	2.2	62,077	9.9	15.2	14.1
Greene	19,582	43.2	10,666	8.1	55.4	17.3	72.8	9,161	23,978	50,083	49.9	1.8	53,821	17.1	21.4	19.0
Hempstead	8,668	40.3	5,232	9.7	54.5	16.0	40.9	12,181	22,178	45,484	52.3	2.8	42,790	18.7	27.1	25.3
Hot Spring	14,420	42.7	7,159	7.6	51.0	15.3	53.3	9,913	23,498	46,390	52.4	1.9	49,582	14.9	22.5	21.0
Howard	7,196	54.5	3,234	10.0	54.0	13.8	31.8	11,013	23,297	38,038	61.8	2.4	40,566	16.7	24.9	23.2
Independence	15,678	41.4	9,268	7.8	51.4	18.5	64.1	9,400	25,046	48,972	51.8	2.3	50,834	15.0	19.0	17.1
Izard	5,191	38.1	2,293	4.4	53.7	14.5	22.7	12,927	21,189	42,818	59.4	1.2	41,787	20.1	27.3	24.8
Jackson	6,535	39.1	3,196	5.7	60.1	11.7	22.1	10,072	19,901	37,885	63.4	2.1	40,789	23.1	29.6	28.7
Jefferson	29,902	44.7	16,689	12.3	52.8	18.0	119.0	11,604	21,941	40,402	58.6	2.1	40,588	18.9	24.7	25.8
Johnson	13,068	49.2	6,132	17.2	61.6	16.5	43.6	9,477	22,077	39,346	62.1	1.4	39,439	17.3	23.6	21.7
Lafayette	2,773	41.9	1,118	9.9	63.5	14.0	7.3	12,855	22,204	33,763	63.7	0.5	40,007	19.8	29.5	29.4
Lawrence	7,694	46.9	3,765	14.2	53.7	14.4	35.0	11,316	22,113	40,587	57.6	1.2	41,188	19.2	26.1	24.8
Lee	3,016	34.1	1,491	16.1	67.2	8.7	9.7	12,888	20,103	27,902	64.2	2.3	32,502	36.8	45.4	45.1
Lincoln	4,616	35.4	2,171	27.6	68.4	8.5	14.9	9,638	14,182	46,554	53.3	3.8	47,903	23.6	23.2	22.6
Little River	4,877	39.8	2,342	3.0	53.7	14.3	19.3	10,041	27,057	48,966	51.0	1.6	47,125	16.2	24.4	22.8
Logan	10,096	47.0	4,669	10.7	57.0	12.2	38.7	9,986	22,632	44,232	58.0	1.7	43,577	15.8	22.2	22.1
Lonoke	34,942	47.7	17,749	8.9	47.6	20.6	127.7	9,259	28,446	59,278	41.9	3.5	59,623	10.9	14.2	11.9
Madison	7,161	43.2	3,422	13.3	64.4	12.1	23.5	10,254	22,733	41,446	57.8	2.0	45,144	16.9	25.2	24.4
Marion	6,013	36.0	2,742	5.1	48.5	16.1	16.6	9,422	22,113	38,426	64.5	2.1	39,888	19.1	27.6	25.5
Miller	13,690	31.6	10,057	10.1	48.9	18.0	69.9	10,607	23,828	45,391	54.9	2.4	43,634	19.2	24.4	23.1
Mississippi	16,749	41.2	10,247	4.7	56.7	15.6	79.4	11,026	24,825	42,986	56.2	3.0	47,892	21.0	28.0	26.3
Monroe	3,758	56.1	1,412	14.4	64.0	12.6	12.2	12,356	24,610	38,438	59.9	1.9	35,833	23.8	36.5	36.8
Montgomery	3,269	36.4	1,546	4.9	50.7	15.1	11.1	10,627	22,892	41,165	59.7	1.3	42,751	18.8	28.3	27.2
Nevada	3,681	44.6	1,725	7.6	59.6	11.9	14.6	10,632	19,443	39,946	57.2	0.4	41,854	19.1	27.8	25.5
Newton	2,631	33.9	1,407	20.0	51.6	15.9	15.1	11,472	20,768	39,542	59.0	0.5	40,698	18.7	29.8	27.6
Ouachita	12,728	54.4	5,075	6.6	54.4	13.5	45.6	11,618	21,338	38,279	60.5	1.1	46,374	20.5	27.9	25.9
Perry	5,417	51.8	2,195	9.5	52.4	17.8	15.4	9,656	23,030	44,926	55.2	1.4	46,317	14.7	22.7	21.5
Phillips	8,875	49.9	4,543	8.0	49.6	15.5	52.6	14,295	20,379	33,724	63.5	1.4	35,167	22.1	37.0	36.6
Pike	4,501	42.0	2,335	9.7	52.0	18.3	21.1	10,169	24,642	42,983	56.6	3.1	43,133	18.6	24.6	23.1
Poinsett	10,563	44.9	5,086	6.4	64.1	11.5	47.8	11,912	21,154	40,700	58.7	0.9	36,150	21.2	28.9	27.1
Polk	7,106	35.6	3,922	11.7	51.0	15.3	36.2	10,299	24,691	39,084	61.7	3.3	42,915	18.1	28.1	25.8
Pope	31,819	49.7	17,208	5.2	49.0	24.6	102.9	10,160	25,546	46,004	53.9	4.1	46,350	14.1	17.6	16.6
Prairie	3,497	43.4	1,439	5.1	53.1	15.3	11.5	9,679	26,955	42,754	54.8	3.1	48,478	14.5	24.4	24.0
Pulaski	228,986	58.4	95,516	18.6	34.7	35.2	674.7	11,083	33,773	52,930	47.6	6.2	56,171	15.3	22.5	19.9
Randolph	7,319	40.8	3,947	11.1	51.4	13.8	22.9	8,668	23,534	42,844	58.3	1.3	46,495	16.3	23.5	22.4
St. Francis	12,614	50.5	5,341	8.8	55.0	10.9	36.0	10,689	19,743	36,053	67.4	2.2	37,759	30.1	39.6	39.3
Saline	61,998	50.6	28,154	10.5	39.7	27.6	156.1	8,726	31,973	66,876	36.5	4.3	70,550	8.2	10.8	10.3
Scott	4,947	48.1	2,069	1.4	60.8	12.1	24.2	10,139	21,026	42,635	59.3	1.7	41,230	17.5	27.1	25.1
Searcy	3,073	39.0	1,359	5.7	60.6	10.9	17.9	12,160	19,761	35,077	69.1	0.8	33,814	22.3	34.9	32.8
Sebastian	63,612	49.8	31,022	12.4	45.3	23.3	209.5	10,241	28,623	47,878	52.1	3.4	48,627	16.8	24.0	22.3
Sevier	7,789	45.8	4,422	2.2	60.7	13.4	42.7	13,045	23,423	47,872	53.5	2.8	45,838	16.7	24.5	22.3
Sharp	6,784	38.9	3,448	1.9	56.7	10.5	28.2	9,731	21,644	35,573	66.1	1.4	40,437	18.1	28.7	28.0
Stone	4,560	36.5	2,283	10.9	54.6	12.6	17.3	10,257	20,462	36,067	61.8	1.1	36,148	20.1	29.1	29.0
Union	18,986	49.1	9,088	9.0	48.3	21.2	73.3	9,794	27,129	45,293	54.4	3.1	47,857	16.9	21.8	19.7
Van Buren	6,927	41.9	2,966	15.2	56.5	15.8	25.6	11,384	23,244	40,442	60.2	1.3	42,345	16.4	22.6	21.7
Washington	133,386	55.8	70,447	10.0	41.0	33.2	442.3	10,029	29,419	52,380	47.3	5.7	57,712	13.2	14.7	13.1
White	34,966	44.4	21,110	29.0	54.6	20.7	127.4	9,975	23,801	44,000	55.0	2.8	43,765	14.8	19.1	17.6
Woodruff	3,575	56.6	1,197	6.3	60.8	15.1	12.6	11,993	25,677	40,331	60.5	4.6	37,634	22.6	33.1	33.1
Yell	10,429	48.9	4,964	6.2	61.2	13.3	43.2	9,910	23,008	47,981	50.9	1.3	48,728	14.3	21.6	20.1

1. All persons 3 years old and over enrolled in nursery school through college. 2. Persons 25 years old and over. 3. Elementary and secondary education expenditures. 4. Based on population estimated by the American Community Survey, 2016–2020. 5. CDC percent based on 2019 population estimate.

STATE County	Personal income, 2020										Earnings, 2020		
	Total (mil dol)	Percent change 2019–2020	Per capita[1]		Wages and salaries (mil dol)	Supplements to wages and salaries, employer contributions (mil dol)		Proprietors' income (mil dol)	Dividends, interest, and rent (mil dol)	Personal transfer reecipts (mil dol)	Total (mil dol)	Contributions for government social insurance (mil dol)	
			Dollars	Rank		Pension and insurance	Government social insurance					From employee and self-employed	From employer
	62	63	64	65	66	67	68	69	70	71	72	73	74
ARKANSAS—Cont'd													
Cleveland	321	2.0	40,366	2,406	42	8	3	7	33	117	60	7	3
Columbia	905	3.5	38,806	2,593	365	63	29	26	129	323	482	37	29
Conway	855	6.3	40,633	2,381	307	50	24	39	118	293	419	32	24
Craighead	4,572	7.6	40,728	2,369	2,496	361	193	319	580	1,300	3,369	232	193
Crawford	2,278	6.2	35,919	2,872	868	125	71	69	265	790	1,132	92	71
Crittenden	1,975	7.3	41,474	2,273	689	108	55	188	197	668	1,041	74	55
Cross	673	10.4	41,715	2,238	194	31	15	68	73	238	308	22	15
Dallas	276	6.9	40,611	2,383	108	16	9	10	32	120	143	12	9
Desha	499	10.8	44,920	1,806	200	31	15	82	55	192	328	20	15
Drew	732	6.8	40,726	2,370	265	47	20	71	102	254	404	28	20
Faulkner	5,323	7.6	41,943	2,206	2,007	289	149	220	671	1,408	2,666	192	149
Franklin	606	4.1	33,885	2,983	198	40	16	-14	86	231	240	23	16
Fulton	394	10.7	31,840	3,062	86	16	7	3	56	192	111	12	7
Garland	4,426	7.2	44,358	1,897	1,636	227	126	318	835	1,583	2,308	198	126
Grant	769	6.9	41,674	2,241	201	28	15	22	88	226	267	22	15
Greene	1,758	8.2	38,560	2,618	665	104	54	131	205	582	953	70	54
Hempstead	717	4.6	33,760	2,992	321	54	25	12	81	297	412	32	25
Hot Spring	1,152	7.6	34,110	2,974	375	64	30	42	150	446	512	43	30
Howard	456	1.2	34,751	2,949	261	42	22	10	54	181	336	26	22
Independence	1,445	5.3	38,266	2,656	750	115	60	90	199	506	1,015	74	60
Izard	444	6.2	32,606	3,044	111	20	9	15	64	217	155	15	9
Jackson	693	8.5	41,646	2,247	228	38	18	149	69	230	433	28	18
Jefferson	2,579	6.5	39,443	2,516	1,338	236	107	95	355	1,006	1,776	127	107
Johnson	815	6.5	30,728	3,081	318	49	26	16	93	333	409	35	26
Lafayette	253	6.4	38,307	2,648	46	8	4	15	32	99	74	7	4
Lawrence	625	13.1	38,065	2,679	159	27	13	71	75	250	270	21	13
Lee	275	2.4	32,359	3,049	79	14	6	20	33	122	119	10	6
Lincoln	375	4.1	29,008	3,094	121	24	9	21	40	143	175	13	9
Little River	452	6.2	37,075	2,782	193	27	14	16	54	174	250	20	14
Logan	737	5.0	34,433	2,966	204	36	16	16	87	338	272	26	16
Lonoke	3,218	7.0	43,537	2,005	578	84	45	143	438	860	850	72	45
Madison	566	1.1	34,012	2,979	151	24	12	5	78	197	192	22	12
Marion	562	7.3	33,493	3,007	136	26	11	13	96	261	187	21	11
Miller	1,600	6.6	37,065	2,783	586	83	47	83	215	543	799	62	47
Mississippi	1,512	3.4	37,730	2,712	993	140	85	10	159	583	1,228	89	85
Monroe	266	11.7	40,475	2,396	82	12	7	38	29	111	138	10	7
Montgomery	289	7.5	32,125	3,055	47	9	4	10	49	127	69	8	4
Nevada	290	4.1	35,808	2,884	107	17	9	10	34	130	143	12	9
Newton	249	6.6	32,731	3,039	37	8	3	9	42	112	56	8	3
Ouachita	970	7.6	41,877	2,220	286	51	22	22	119	353	380	33	22
Perry	397	5.2	38,404	2,634	51	9	4	22	52	139	85	9	4
Phillips	660	9.1	38,155	2,671	214	37	17	62	69	298	331	24	17
Pike	361	4.4	33,920	2,982	108	18	8	4	52	151	138	14	8
Poinsett	869	6.6	37,307	2,761	249	36	19	95	73	350	399	30	19
Polk	642	5.5	32,573	3,045	223	41	18	35	91	282	316	28	18
Pope	2,356	3.7	36,617	2,811	1,180	195	91	72	313	769	1,538	113	91
Prairie	341	16.3	42,843	2,087	64	10	5	52	41	116	131	9	5
Pulaski	21,835	6.0	55,563	669	15,150	2,197	1,130	1,550	4,408	5,189	20,027	1,309	1,130
Randolph	664	8.7	36,401	2,837	225	37	19	34	78	270	315	27	19
St. Francis	763	6.9	30,903	3,079	326	60	26	51	81	336	463	34	26
Saline	5,664	6.9	45,692	1,698	1,108	151	87	235	717	1,534	1,581	134	87
Scott	328	4.0	32,290	3,051	111	20	9	14	44	138	155	13	9
Searcy	248	11.7	31,657	3,066	52	10	4	9	39	129	75	9	4
Sebastian	5,816	5.2	45,586	1,718	3,187	448	245	573	989	1,621	4,454	312	245
Sevier	550	2.2	32,926	3,032	199	33	17	34	57	184	283	21	17
Sharp	620	4.8	35,612	2,900	126	21	10	38	83	303	195	23	10
Stone	415	5.6	32,753	3,038	92	16	7	23	82	203	138	15	7
Union	1,860	4.4	48,669	1,298	953	154	70	113	351	556	1,289	93	70
Van Buren	570	8.7	34,482	2,962	147	24	11	16	97	265	198	22	11
Washington	10,657	6.9	43,817	1,971	6,045	844	450	804	1,831	2,256	8,144	544	450
White	3,117	6.8	39,598	2,493	1,082	153	85	149	452	999	1,469	115	85
Woodruff	283	17.1	45,248	1,764	78	14	6	53	32	103	150	9	6
Yell	710	0.4	33,506	3,005	255	42	21	21	97	272	339	28	21

1. Based on the resident population estimated as of July 1 of the year shown.

STATE County	Earnings, 2020 (cont.)									Social Security beneficiaries, December 2020		Supple-mental Security Income recipients, 2020	Housing units, 2021	
	Percent by selected industries													
	Farm	Mining, quarrying, and extractions	Construction	Manu-facturing	Information; professional, scientific, technical services	Retail trade	Finance, insurance, real estate, and leasing	Health care and social assistance	Govern-ment	Number	Rate[1]		Total	Percent change, 2010–2021
	75	76	77	78	79	80	81	82	83	84	85	86	87	88
ARKANSAS—Cont'd														
Cleveland	-0.5	0.0	7.9	12.3	D	2.7	D	14.7	28.3	2,115	281	235	3,583	0.3
Columbia	0.5	5.8	2.6	32.6	2.5	6.7	5.0	D	19.7	5,710	252	1,141	11,011	0.1
Conway	3.0	0.4	11.2	17.8	D	8.0	2.4	D	21.3	5,760	276	905	9,669	0.2
Craighead	0.3	D	6.2	14.2	4.6	7.7	5.6	23.8	14.5	21,205	189	4,076	47,884	2.0
Crawford	0.1	0.5	7.8	24.0	D	6.7	3.1	7.0	11.9	15,960	264	1,962	25,460	0.5
Crittenden	5.0	D	5.1	12.9	2.9	6.9	4.7	10.2	14.4	10,710	225	3,058	21,353	0.3
Cross	14.4	0.0	2.3	3.9	2.6	11.1	4.9	D	20.5	4,385	263	768	7,597	0.2
Dallas	1.3	0.0	3.6	22.7	1.3	7.8	3.4	D	11.5	2,130	338	394	3,475	0.2
Desha	22.8	0.0	2.0	22.5	2.3	5.1	3.6	D	15.2	3,150	284	692	5,796	0.0
Drew	6.4	0.0	6.1	13.5	3.2	7.7	4.5	10.0	27.0	4,210	246	680	8,281	0.2
Faulkner	-0.3	1.0	9.8	8.6	12.7	8.5	4.8	16.1	17.1	22,520	180	2,711	52,709	1.8
Franklin	-12.3	2.6	5.4	21.8	D	8.8	1.7	9.6	26.4	4,875	284	555	7,741	0.3
Fulton	-9.4	D	18.5	D	D	5.5	5.6	D	27.0	4,070	335	422	6,203	0.3
Garland	0.1	0.3	10.3	7.3	4.9	11.2	5.6	23.1	12.8	31,020	309	3,743	52,471	0.2
Grant	-0.7	D	8.9	30.5	D	8.2	6.9	D	17.6	4,300	238	413	7,896	0.6
Greene	4.6	D	5.6	31.5	D	8.0	5.2	11.9	13.1	10,905	235	1,716	19,372	0.8
Hempstead	-3.0	D	3.5	31.2	3.0	7.6	3.0	D	22.1	5,195	264	954	9,610	0.1
Hot Spring	-0.5	0.9	4.7	19.3	D	6.4	3.2	D	20.1	8,820	266	1,144	14,280	0.7
Howard	-2.4	D	3.2	45.1	D	6.0	2.6	12.2	13.2	3,380	266	507	6,155	0.0
Independence	1.4	D	6.7	21.9	2.4	7.1	5.3	D	11.4	9,700	257	1,142	16,730	0.3
Izard	-1.5	D	5.8	5.4	1.8	8.7	8.2	19.2	32.9	4,645	334	524	6,737	0.2
Jackson	20.4	0.9	2.2	18.8	3.6	6.5	3.1	D	16.7	4,260	253	663	7,098	0.2
Jefferson	3.0	0.0	2.6	20.2	D	6.0	2.7	14.5	28.2	16,355	248	4,068	30,635	0.2
Johnson	-4.2	D	5.2	28.2	1.9	7.5	3.3	D	16.5	6,525	252	885	11,531	0.4
Lafayette	8.7	1.1	11.7	4.0	D	D	5.6	D	23.3	1,945	316	394	3,930	0.3
Lawrence	17.6	1.3	6.8	5.5	1.3	7.6	3.5	D	21.5	4,730	290	803	7,568	0.8
Lee	10.6	0.0	D	D	2.8	5.0	6.5	D	28.9	2,195	255	641	3,694	0.0
Lincoln	3.6	D	10.1	8.7	D	3.1	2.7	8.5	38.9	2,560	196	449	4,384	0.4
Little River	3.7	D	2.7	50.7	D	5.6	1.3	3.7	17.4	3,495	293	444	6,058	0.2
Logan	-2.1	1.6	6.2	23.5	2.5	9.6	5.1	11.8	25.0	6,395	301	878	9,749	0.0
Lonoke	4.6	D	12.0	8.7	3.8	9.8	7.8	10.1	19.0	15,035	201	1,858	30,623	1.4
Madison	-10.8	0.1	9.8	33.6	D	9.7	3.3	D	18.4	4,510	266	432	7,681	0.9
Marion	-7.3	D	D	41.2	6.0	8.8	5.6	8.0	15.5	6,015	354	491	9,556	0.8
Miller	1.1	1.8	7.9	23.3	D	5.9	3.5	D	15.5	9,675	227	2,099	19,800	0.1
Mississippi	2.5	D	5.8	47.0	1.1	4.2	2.4	D	12.4	9,600	242	2,673	19,105	0.1
Monroe	22.2	0.1	1.8	5.3	D	7.1	5.5	D	14.8	2,130	319	460	3,827	0.0
Montgomery	-5.0	D	11.1	3.4	D	7.1	4.0	4.3	36.0	2,910	338	304	5,453	0.3
Nevada	-0.1	0.1	D	D	D	6.9	2.3	11.0	15.5	2,360	288	425	4,307	0.2
Newton	-8.8	0.1	13.0	3.9	D	7.3	D	D	36.5	2,720	378	313	4,094	0.2
Ouachita	0.1	1.7	4.0	10.2	D	7.9	4.3	D	24.6	6,735	302	1,202	11,846	0.1
Perry	8.4	D	14.0	2.9	D	4.3	D	D	23.4	2,895	291	372	4,951	0.3
Phillips	13.9	0.0	2.1	8.4	D	7.1	4.6	13.5	18.2	4,755	299	1,511	8,367	0.5
Pike	-9.8	D	6.9	18.3	2.3	9.2	11.6	D	22.5	3,065	304	344	5,301	0.2
Poinsett	15.6	D	4.2	14.2	D	5.1	3.0	9.6	15.7	6,290	278	1,393	10,399	0.7
Polk	-0.6	D	6.9	20.2	2.4	8.3	4.9	16.4	18.5	6,035	312	679	9,627	0.1
Pope	-0.7	0.5	7.2	12.4	3.5	7.7	4.8	11.3	16.7	14,345	225	1,971	27,065	0.5
Prairie	30.4	0.0	8.5	2.1	D	5.4	3.2	8.7	15.5	2,355	289	289	4,082	0.2
Pulaski	0.0	0.3	4.8	4.7	9.4	5.3	11.9	14.3	23.6	83,885	211	16,218	191,962	0.6
Randolph	-1.2	0.0	4.7	29.9	D	7.0	4.3	D	17.9	5,080	269	658	8,601	0.4
St. Francis	4.7	0.0	3.6	D	2.2	6.9	3.5	D	32.4	5,525	243	1,685	9,571	0.1
Saline	-0.1	D	14.6	5.8	5.6	13.2	4.5	16.1	15.6	28,440	227	2,463	52,437	0.9
Scott	-0.5	D	3.6	33.0	D	4.8	2.2	D	21.4	2,985	304	432	4,859	0.1
Searcy	-8.9	0.0	D	8.6	D	9.2	4.3	18.1	25.5	2,860	363	390	4,713	0.1
Sebastian	-0.1	0.8	3.9	16.0	4.8	7.0	11.6	18.7	11.4	29,465	229	4,216	57,150	0.6
Sevier	4.3	D	D	D	D	7.7	4.3	7.3	20.5	3,210	203	449	6,757	0.2
Sharp	3.7	D	7.9	3.4	D	12.0	6.4	D	20.3	6,485	368	863	9,514	0.1
Stone	-1.0	0.0	7.2	7.7	D	13.4	5.6	D	21.0	4,665	374	536	6,817	0.4
Union	-0.1	5.0	9.2	21.1	D	6.0	3.9	9.1	10.6	10,505	274	1,652	18,628	0.2
Van Buren	-4.7	D	6.8	4.3	4.0	11.7	6.2	D	17.2	5,760	367	604	9,698	0.3
Washington	-0.6	D	8.0	11.0	6.5	6.4	7.1	13.6	17.7	38,455	154	4,209	103,116	1.9
White	0.5	1.4	8.2	9.4	2.8	9.2	5.5	18.3	12.8	18,770	243	2,590	33,482	0.5
Woodruff	35.4	D	1.8	7.7	D	3.4	1.6	D	16.5	1,975	323	386	3,251	0.1
Yell	0.2	D	6.3	32.5	2.3	5.1	3.1	D	20.8	5,275	262	735	9,268	0.2

1. Per 1,000 resident population estimated as of July 1 of the year shown.

STATE County	Housing units, 2016–2020								Civilian labor force, 2021				Civilian employment[6], 2016–2020		
	Occupied units										Unemployment			Percent	
		Owner-occupied				Renter-occupied									
				Median owner cost as a percent of income											
	Total	Percent	Median value[1]	With a mortgage	Without a mortgage[2]	Median rent[3]	Median rent as a percent of income[2]	Substandard units[4] (percent)	Total	Percent change, 2020–2021	Total	Rate[5]	Total	Management, business, science, and arts	Construction, production, and maintenance occupations
	89	90	91	92	93	94	95	96	97	98	99	100	101	102	103
ARKANSAS—Cont'd															
Cleveland	3,170	77.9	90,400	16.9	10.0	618	20.2	0.9	3,108	-4.4	123	4.0	3,138	34.1	35.6
Columbia	8,456	68.8	87,700	20.1	10.5	681	26.5	5.6	8,814	-2.7	469	5.3	8,843	33.3	32.4
Conway	8,491	70.3	113,500	17.2	10.0	614	27.8	2.1	8,231	-2.2	342	4.2	8,992	28.6	35.7
Craighead	42,203	57.0	149,700	16.8	10.0	780	27.5	2.3	55,682	-1.1	1,821	3.3	51,025	35.5	25.2
Crawford	24,065	75.6	123,800	18.9	10.0	700	29.4	3.3	25,772	-2.8	921	3.6	25,924	29.3	30.7
Crittenden	19,021	56.8	122,700	18.5	10.4	734	30.8	3.1	20,502	-2.8	1,108	5.4	20,641	31.4	31.2
Cross	6,568	66.4	83,800	17.0	10.2	727	28.0	6.5	6,987	-3.8	306	4.4	7,237	24.1	36.2
Dallas	2,992	70.6	78,200	18.6	11.9	689	25.9	0.2	2,770	-1.8	113	4.1	2,794	20.6	36.1
Desha	5,059	62.0	82,500	19.5	12.3	565	28.9	1.9	4,963	-6.2	293	5.9	4,377	28.2	29.8
Drew	7,207	67.2	102,300	16.7	10.0	661	22.1	2.8	7,522	-2.5	377	5.0	7,766	35.7	26.9
Faulkner	45,091	62.4	163,900	18.4	10.0	819	30.1	2.7	61,033	-1.6	2,123	3.5	59,134	40.3	21.1
Franklin	6,671	72.6	96,900	17.9	10.0	607	31.8	3.0	7,267	-2.9	268	3.7	6,898	28.7	37.3
Fulton	5,014	82.5	84,400	20.4	11.1	532	27.5	6.5	4,889	-0.8	178	3.6	4,091	30.0	28.5
Garland	40,906	67.1	142,100	19.8	10.0	791	27.3	3.1	40,528	-1.9	2,028	5.0	40,787	31.9	20.8
Grant	7,049	76.3	122,600	15.2	10.0	700	30.4	2.3	8,146	-1.7	260	3.2	8,048	34.5	31.6
Greene	17,587	66.9	124,800	17.2	10.4	725	28.0	3.0	19,318	-1.4	663	3.4	19,390	30.8	34.5
Hempstead	8,100	68.5	87,700	18.0	10.0	681	28.2	3.9	9,182	-4.6	320	3.5	8,627	25.5	38.5
Hot Spring	12,515	79.5	102,400	18.5	10.0	635	26.4	3.7	13,797	-2.0	533	3.9	13,282	30.5	28.6
Howard	5,271	67.4	101,000	22.5	10.0	649	29.3	4.2	5,455	-1.8	177	3.2	5,544	24.9	43.3
Independence	14,325	72.7	97,900	17.8	10.0	653	24.1	4.2	16,368	-2.2	634	3.9	16,206	30.3	32.1
Izard	4,911	78.1	81,900	19.9	12.1	596	27.1	1.7	4,382	-5.9	236	5.4	4,289	30.5	32.6
Jackson	6,241	70.0	71,300	18.8	10.0	552	27.4	1.7	5,637	-3.7	294	5.2	5,625	25.7	32.0
Jefferson	26,630	61.9	84,900	18.0	10.2	741	29.2	3.0	26,128	-4.2	1,715	6.6	25,271	29.7	31.0
Johnson	9,792	72.5	107,600	20.3	10.0	619	30.2	4.0	9,835	-3.0	462	4.7	10,398	28.5	37.3
Lafayette	2,898	78.2	60,800	20.2	10.0	513	37.8	1.9	2,327	-3.8	135	5.8	2,568	29.0	34.2
Lawrence	6,584	68.9	75,400	18.3	10.0	552	26.0	2.2	6,700	-1.4	286	4.3	6,606	26.4	35.3
Lee	3,202	58.0	76,400	15.0	13.7	522	46.7	3.7	2,554	-7.0	143	5.6	2,697	29.0	35.1
Lincoln	3,598	77.8	90,600	18.1	10.7	550	19.6	1.5	3,729	-3.6	171	4.6	3,347	28.0	34.1
Little River	5,292	77.9	77,400	14.2	10.0	579	25.5	2.5	5,250	-1.9	235	4.5	5,136	32.1	41.2
Logan	8,359	75.2	100,500	18.5	10.0	589	22.2	2.4	8,383	-3.2	350	4.2	8,991	24.7	39.0
Lonoke	27,218	71.1	145,000	18.8	10.0	816	26.1	1.7	33,141	-1.8	1,107	3.3	33,170	35.8	26.6
Madison	6,045	80.3	116,000	19.8	10.0	607	24.5	4.2	7,373	1.1	231	3.1	6,444	26.7	40.1
Marion	6,918	79.5	132,200	22.9	10.2	652	27.7	2.9	6,089	-2.8	260	4.3	5,575	30.5	33.9
Miller	16,237	65.8	113,400	18.7	10.0	742	29.9	4.1	18,987	-1.8	913	4.8	17,026	33.7	28.0
Mississippi	16,623	57.6	93,000	15.6	10.0	655	26.4	4.3	16,310	-5.6	1,169	7.2	17,926	27.5	38.9
Monroe	3,234	61.8	73,500	17.7	10.0	508	30.2	6.1	2,621	-3.7	139	5.3	2,886	23.0	38.2
Montgomery	3,706	84.2	111,600	21.7	10.8	551	23.3	2.8	2,876	-2.8	139	4.8	3,241	29.7	34.0
Nevada	3,188	69.5	66,400	24.3	10.0	716	27.7	4.1	3,373	-4.9	136	4.0	3,103	23.7	38.2
Newton	2,996	83.8	127,100	22.8	10.0	552	35.4	4.3	3,182	-0.1	97	3.0	2,693	25.9	35.4
Ouachita	9,487	70.9	76,900	18.1	10.7	562	29.6	5.0	9,716	-1.3	376	3.9	8,779	33.2	32.2
Perry	3,700	79.7	115,000	18.2	10.0	625	23.9	5.0	4,092	-1.0	168	4.1	3,677	29.2	36.6
Phillips	7,561	46.1	80,800	15.7	10.4	573	29.0	1.6	5,865	-6.9	453	7.7	6,303	27.5	32.3
Pike	4,215	74.4	86,100	17.8	10.0	622	30.7	3.2	4,183	-2.0	184	4.4	4,639	29.1	36.6
Poinsett	9,567	62.8	81,200	18.5	10.1	605	28.8	3.0	9,676	-0.8	377	3.9	9,572	25.5	35.4
Polk	8,114	75.8	103,700	24.0	10.0	657	27.9	4.7	7,771	-2.9	343	4.4	7,335	31.9	32.7
Pope	22,863	72.4	129,000	18.6	10.0	698	29.8	2.0	27,266	-2.2	1,080	4.0	26,827	32.3	29.3
Prairie	3,755	74.9	71,800	21.1	10.7	646	21.8	2.4	3,527	-2.3	130	3.7	3,609	30.8	28.7
Pulaski	161,652	58.1	161,000	18.9	10.0	875	28.5	2.7	184,896	-2.2	9,090	4.9	183,975	42.8	18.2
Randolph	7,294	74.4	92,500	18.4	10.1	637	27.4	3.5	7,313	-1.8	288	3.9	6,993	28.7	40.5
St. Francis	9,313	54.8	65,200	20.4	10.0	688	30.0	3.3	7,675	-4.3	474	6.2	8,791	26.1	39.8
Saline	45,098	78.7	159,300	18.3	10.0	835	25.1	1.7	57,900	-1.5	1,818	3.1	57,987	38.2	23.0
Scott	4,114	73.2	81,900	19.6	10.0	619	29.2	4.3	4,216	-3.0	140	3.3	4,394	27.9	41.0
Searcy	3,235	74.9	99,000	20.3	11.1	536	28.8	1.9	2,920	1.5	124	4.2	3,057	25.0	34.8
Sebastian	52,026	59.3	129,300	18.4	10.0	715	26.4	3.4	54,294	-3.2	2,019	3.7	58,496	33.5	28.1
Sevier	5,690	66.9	95,000	19.5	10.0	601	20.7	8.0	5,368	-3.2	236	4.4	7,091	19.3	50.7
Sharp	7,315	78.7	75,200	20.1	10.6	552	28.7	3.7	5,630	-1.5	277	4.9	6,113	24.6	31.9
Stone	4,866	74.1	135,800	22.6	10.2	636	33.0	4.3	4,531	-2.0	228	5.0	4,197	30.7	34.5
Union	15,855	74.4	89,700	18.8	10.4	707	25.1	5.3	15,025	-3.8	911	6.1	15,928	34.5	27.8
Van Buren	7,220	77.4	105,500	23.6	10.8	600	30.5	3.6	5,803	0.6	282	4.9	5,833	27.8	34.9
Washington	89,094	53.5	184,300	17.9	10.0	819	26.8	4.6	125,728	0.3	3,676	2.9	114,481	40.7	24.0
White	28,903	67.7	125,300	19.1	10.0	692	28.5	1.9	33,712	-0.9	1,351	4.0	32,226	32.9	29.2
Woodruff	3,002	67.8	74,300	15.0	11.1	522	27.8	1.9	2,790	-1.3	139	5.0	2,800	32.9	29.5
Yell	7,797	71.2	110,300	19.4	10.0	591	24.1	5.7	7,831	-1.3	311	4.0	9,476	22.3	39.2

1. Specified owner-occupied units. 2. A value of 10.0 represents 10 percent or less; a value of 50.0 represents 50 percent or more. 3. Specified renter-occupied units. 4. Overcrowded or lacking complete plumbing facilities. 5. Percent of civilian labor force. 6. Civilian employed persons 16 years old and over.

STATE County	Private nonfarm establishments, employment and payroll, 2020: Number of establishments	Employment: Total	Employment: Health care and social assistance	Employment: Manufacturing	Employment: Retail trade	Employment: Finance and insurance	Employment: Professional, scientific, and technical services	Annual payroll: Total (mil dol)	Annual payroll: Average per employee (dollars)	Agriculture, 2017: Farms: Number	Farms: Percent with: Fewer than 50 acres	Farms: Percent with: 1000 acres or more	Farm producers whose primary occupation is farming (percent)
	104	105	106	107	108	109	110	111	112	113	114	115	116
ARKANSAS—Cont'd													
Cleveland	68	643	224	NA	59	NA	NA	16	25,274	205	28.8	1.0	53.8
Columbia	527	7,237	1,015	1,835	947	265	531	287	39,626	297	32.3	2.0	33.3
Conway	406	4,724	832	935	745	105	87	197	41,648	768	28.9	3.4	43.2
Craighead	2,575	46,296	11,530	7,609	6,788	1,277	1,208	1,900	41,040	523	32.3	20.8	43.1
Crawford	1,065	15,608	1,393	5,469	1,975	356	251	559	35,815	799	44.2	2.1	35.4
Crittenden	844	13,834	1,826	2,034	1,928	227	222	487	35,215	262	26.7	34.7	53.6
Cross	370	3,769	942	519	709	212	119	122	32,431	300	18.3	28.0	57.8
Dallas	177	2,216	631	585	309	52	18	81	36,715	126	19.8	3.2	42.2
Desha	290	3,296	506	855	515	125	43	134	40,516	275	19.6	34.9	45.0
Drew	407	5,022	1,176	1,006	837	145	97	177	35,151	318	23.6	10.1	32.7
Faulkner	2,723	35,275	6,437	3,506	5,839	1,267	987	1,375	38,974	1,191	43.7	2.9	35.9
Franklin	284	3,851	391	1,302	598	420	96	144	37,427	752	25.5	5.5	40.9
Fulton	165	1,506	626	105	191	53	53	46	30,798	795	19.2	4.2	40.2
Garland	2,785	34,517	8,197	2,647	5,893	1,020	1,075	1,205	34,901	357	47.6	0.3	38.5
Grant	284	3,579	311	1,157	498	100	156	143	40,071	281	44.1	0.7	31.1
Greene	766	15,207	2,100	5,072	2,086	408	347	575	37,819	631	37.6	10.3	36.5
Hempstead	376	5,841	916	2,112	885	113	187	210	35,936	613	19.7	6.0	47.7
Hot Spring	497	5,833	987	1,517	765	191	93	237	40,558	563	44.2	1.4	36.7
Howard	260	5,679	1,055	2,686	503	120	36	216	38,006	586	27.8	1.9	44.2
Independence	787	15,844	3,486	5,130	1,765	475	207	666	42,063	890	23.6	4.7	37.4
Izard	214	2,048	689	312	354	87	22	60	29,273	632	19.1	6.6	44.3
Jackson	315	3,660	874	973	703	95	72	144	39,431	424	22.9	18.9	54.5
Jefferson	1,251	19,542	4,090	4,414	2,838	716	276	800	40,945	436	36.0	17.4	43.8
Johnson	388	7,196	1,039	2,514	876	114	74	235	32,676	577	26.7	1.9	46.8
Lafayette	105	697	114	91	105	61	42	25	36,184	287	17.4	10.8	43.0
Lawrence	279	3,119	744	372	588	89	33	101	32,284	535	24.3	12.5	43.2
Lee	115	889	282	9	148	38	25	34	38,027	221	14.5	27.1	60.2
Lincoln	154	1,348	269	326	179	51	14	54	40,358	369	33.6	16.3	46.6
Little River	171	2,676	302	1,145	391	59	49	171	63,848	414	17.9	6.5	39.2
Logan	364	3,869	636	1,112	739	135	147	131	33,897	873	24.6	3.2	42.7
Lonoke	1,077	11,539	1,739	1,502	2,200	546	489	382	33,074	702	35.6	13.8	42.7
Madison	219	2,684	212	1,163	401	85	48	103	38,474	1,229	21.2	3.3	45.9
Marion	226	2,810	166	1,530	414	109	68	92	32,573	587	25.4	6.5	43.6
Miller	693	11,772	981	2,542	1,219	254	181	457	38,831	513	37.2	6.0	36.9
Mississippi	746	14,771	1,727	6,705	1,568	213	89	802	54,263	284	16.5	48.6	73.2
Monroe	183	1,627	381	113	256	63	15	55	33,612	186	20.4	35.5	38.3
Montgomery	131	839	64	52	151	28	8	29	34,243	428	30.4	1.2	46.8
Nevada	118	1,875	323	598	288	40	22	72	38,473	355	26.5	3.1	36.6
Newton	84	652	214	63	111	17	6	18	27,324	537	19.4	1.5	38.5
Ouachita	485	7,519	1,394	3,037	849	181	144	351	46,732	205	42.9	0.5	26.9
Perry	108	867	199	19	141	23	12	31	35,537	397	29.2	1.3	42.7
Phillips	348	3,805	839	388	741	115	83	130	34,058	231	10.8	45.5	68.2
Pike	214	1,865	188	353	302	94	44	66	35,405	394	19.5	2.5	44.0
Poinsett	341	3,438	561	712	664	112	41	138	40,179	363	23.1	30.9	59.7
Polk	422	4,840	1,130	1,151	765	160	73	169	34,938	793	32.4	1.1	44.6
Pope	1,557	23,088	3,314	4,671	3,128	516	674	992	42,966	919	39.0	1.7	39.6
Prairie	145	987	222	NA	202	39	39	32	32,538	350	13.7	26.3	49.9
Pulaski	12,258	214,965	47,647	13,072	24,709	15,467	10,956	11,155	51,890	411	56.4	5.4	37.7
Randolph	312	4,046	970	568	610	157	63	124	30,672	657	21.0	7.8	44.3
St. Francis	442	5,421	1,473	745	932	153	112	174	32,122	278	28.1	29.1	55.4
Saline	2,125	22,850	4,775	1,348	4,678	533	820	788	34,484	371	52.3	0.5	32.0
Scott	141	1,946	390	810	201	39	20	64	32,730	528	23.9	1.3	45.0
Searcy	112	1,016	330	140	205	32	20	40	39,228	631	15.1	7.3	44.2
Sebastian	3,337	60,300	11,611	12,505	7,724	1,596	1,651	2,562	42,483	706	43.9	2.3	35.8
Sevier	253	4,173	499	1,431	566	150	63	140	33,555	540	27.0	3.0	44.2
Sharp	309	2,533	778	60	686	171	28	76	29,937	622	18.6	2.9	43.8
Stone	233	2,077	583	227	458	141	32	62	29,808	526	19.0	3.4	40.6
Union	1,044	15,811	1,800	3,083	2,138	412	388	866	54,777	268	39.6	0.4	32.3
Van Buren	298	3,022	664	146	557	105	85	105	34,754	611	22.3	2.1	36.1
Washington	5,752	94,164	16,799	13,402	11,752	2,523	4,495	4,209	44,696	2,279	42.7	1.1	37.6
White	1,593	22,198	4,647	2,145	3,576	605	432	821	36,977	1,613	34.2	3.7	37.7
Woodruff	124	1,235	171	184	155	31	5	50	40,549	187	16.0	36.9	52.5
Yell	321	5,030	1,000	2,093	499	189	87	177	35,149	718	21.2	4.3	46.7

STATE County	Agriculture, 2017 (cont.)															
	Land in farms					Value of land and buildings (dollars)		Value of machinery and equipment, average per farm (dollars)	Value of products sold:				Organic farms (number)	Farms with internet access (percent)	Government payments	
	Acreage (1,000)	Percent change, 2012–2017	Acres: Average size of farm	Acres: Total irrigated (1,000)	Acres: Total cropland (1,000)	Average per farm	Average per acre		Total (mil dol)	Average per farm (acres)	Percent from: Crops	Percent from: Livestock and poultry products			Total ($1,000)	Percent of farms
	117	118	119	120	121	122	123	124	125	126	127	128	129	130	131	132
ARKANSAS—Cont'd																
Cleveland	32	16.2	154	0.1	6.7	652,384	4,232	161,950	128.9	628,927	0.4	99.6	NA	69.3	228	10.7
Columbia	54	19.2	183	0.3	12.1	425,028	2,323	83,478	49.0	164,848	8.0	92.0	NA	66.0	45	4.7
Conway	172	-4.1	224	18.7	79.9	568,722	2,541	89,668	172.3	224,285	8.7	91.3	NA	68.1	838	11.8
Craighead	321	-4.8	615	253.9	293.5	2,835,272	4,613	347,738	195.2	373,256	98.3	1.7	NA	78.4	14,200	54.9
Crawford	122	-2.4	153	2.9	52.2	469,607	3,068	69,950	53.9	67,469	32.7	67.3	3	69.0	416	5.3
Crittenden	315	-6.9	1,201	187.2	292.5	4,625,254	3,851	408,836	165.3	630,737	99.5	0.5	1	69.8	12,248	81.3
Cross	272	-2.4	908	208.6	251.8	3,058,715	3,370	390,962	149.8	499,310	99.6	0.4	1	73.3	17,873	76.7
Dallas	29	38.4	233	0.0	4.2	454,901	1,949	49,777	1.7	13,825	67.5	32.5	NA	66.7	44	10.3
Desha	311	16.6	1,133	249.4	279.1	3,685,791	3,254	552,926	168.1	611,418	95.8	4.2	NA	75.6	9,994	79.3
Drew	134	3.1	421	57.2	77.0	1,217,911	2,893	194,702	60.1	188,858	67.1	32.9	NA	71.4	3,310	34.0
Faulkner	201	8.4	168	7.0	70.0	646,522	3,840	72,429	27.0	22,665	44.0	56.0	1	76.7	2,565	9.2
Franklin	184	15.0	244	1.2	56.5	626,738	2,564	86,566	181.2	240,979	2.8	97.2	2	76.3	520	5.9
Fulton	224	9.6	282	1.4	27.5	526,315	1,867	60,535	29.0	36,434	8.1	91.9	NA	73.2	672	10.9
Garland	34	-4.9	95	0.1	8.2	496,951	5,226	46,231	10.0	27,972	30.5	69.5	NA	74.5	93	5.9
Grant	49	-23.9	175	0.3	7.6	632,688	3,612	70,223	6.3	22,438	15.1	84.9	NA	82.2	36	4.3
Greene	261	0.3	414	164.8	214.7	1,754,440	4,239	169,942	139.3	220,792	91.9	8.1	NA	73.1	10,936	42.6
Hempstead	186	-5.2	304	D	51.5	760,967	2,504	111,077	216.0	352,426	2.4	97.6	NA	70.3	512	10.9
Hot Spring	77	12.5	137	0.4	20.4	382,205	2,783	59,745	29.1	51,675	4.1	95.9	NA	75.0	180	4.3
Howard	150	2.2	256	0.4	34.5	731,438	2,855	98,674	262.1	447,229	0.7	99.3	NA	69.1	83	3.9
Independence	268	7.9	301	27.5	83.4	691,058	2,299	104,678	172.9	194,303	12.2	87.8	NA	73.3	2,947	16.3
Izard	190	9.8	300	0.3	31.7	613,810	2,047	74,547	65.9	104,286	2.0	98.0	1	75.6	438	11.1
Jackson	271	-11.8	639	187.9	243.4	2,151,881	3,369	220,281	125.7	296,552	92.9	7.1	1	71.5	14,540	66.7
Jefferson	292	0.2	671	212.8	253.4	2,190,461	3,267	283,777	169.6	389,021	84.9	15.1	NA	70.0	14,205	60.1
Johnson	104	-12.5	179	1.4	38.8	501,184	2,792	70,205	139.0	240,931	3.0	97.0	2	74.4	116	2.1
Lafayette	133	15.6	464	24.3	67.7	1,182,237	2,547	136,321	119.2	415,411	15.6	84.4	NA	80.5	3,646	33.4
Lawrence	270	6.7	504	147.2	204.1	1,807,457	3,586	203,207	150.6	281,490	66.3	33.7	1	76.4	13,714	40.6
Lee	258	-1.1	1,167	169.5	246.7	3,702,289	3,173	414,909	130.1	588,670	99.8	0.2	NA	69.7	6,534	72.4
Lincoln	209	4.5	566	135.5	161.5	1,743,946	3,082	282,169	179.0	485,000	52.5	47.5	NA	62.6	7,490	51.8
Little River	159	-7.1	385	10.3	58.2	929,079	2,414	114,187	85.5	206,606	19.4	80.6	NA	69.3	1,229	15.5
Logan	187	-5.4	214	D	63.0	535,423	2,499	88,687	225.5	258,293	2.8	97.2	1	73.4	420	6.1
Lonoke	367	8.3	523	224.3	284.9	1,925,684	3,683	222,351	184.2	262,422	85.5	14.5	1	73.9	14,638	40.6
Madison	278	3.1	226	0.7	60.7	707,947	3,133	81,624	279.3	227,291	2.2	97.8	1	74.4	830	19.4
Marion	179	31.1	305	0.4	23.2	744,565	2,438	80,728	52.0	88,608	1.9	98.1	2	78.5	210	9.0
Miller	127	-22.8	247	6.7	58.2	636,224	2,578	93,153	34.9	67,973	45.2	54.8	NA	73.5	1,786	9.7
Mississippi	477	0.2	1,678	350.2	469.3	5,765,623	3,436	743,149	300.9	1,059,602	100.0	0.0	NA	78.2	12,422	78.2
Monroe	203	-24.4	1,091	159.9	189.0	3,078,477	2,823	366,858	D	D	D	D	NA	63.4	8,684	85.5
Montgomery	77	3.8	181	0.3	22.4	469,348	2,599	77,836	27.8	64,895	3.3	96.7	NA	64.3	9	2.1
Nevada	78	16.3	218	0.0	21.5	516,831	2,366	76,092	55.7	156,955	2.8	97.2	NA	67.3	158	9.3
Newton	101	-11.6	188	0.0	14.6	458,102	2,436	55,239	24.0	44,665	3.6	96.4	6	76.0	92	6.9
Ouachita	28	8.8	138	NA	5.4	308,205	2,231	49,231	11.3	55,312	3.1	96.9	NA	63.9	22	3.4
Perry	78	10.3	195	6.6	31.7	539,122	2,758	96,815	56.1	141,340	21.8	78.2	2	75.6	1,013	18.6
Phillips	363	3.1	1,573	273.8	355.3	5,012,409	3,186	499,656	189.7	821,251	99.8	0.2	NA	68.8	11,787	90.0
Pike	82	17.8	209	0.5	23.1	545,769	2,608	79,626	106.5	270,330	0.9	99.1	NA	80.2	177	11.4
Poinsett	317	-17.8	872	256.1	298.8	3,331,838	3,821	442,107	185.8	511,826	99.4	0.6	NA	71.1	16,877	75.2
Polk	140	18.0	177	0.1	37.6	523,224	2,959	79,598	159.0	200,503	1.1	98.9	NA	71.2	331	2.4
Pope	159	3.1	173	6.7	56.8	553,957	3,210	74,378	169.8	184,764	5.8	94.2	2	77.9	909	7.1
Prairie	273	-0.9	779	171.3	213.1	2,274,086	2,920	291,350	127.1	363,197	93.0	7.0	2	76.3	13,847	76.9
Pulaski	79	-5.8	193	20.7	44.6	757,344	3,929	71,002	20.3	49,333	81.1	18.9	7	78.1	1,580	12.7
Randolph	223	5.8	339	59.5	104.3	995,660	2,936	144,033	157.0	238,977	25.7	74.3	5	62.6	7,048	20.2
St. Francis	259	-13.5	933	184.9	231.5	2,899,979	3,108	308,713	125.9	452,763	99.7	0.3	NA	69.1	9,903	61.5
Saline	42	-6.5	113	0.1	12.8	386,927	3,424	54,372	8.2	21,989	13.1	86.9	7	78.4	46	3.0
Scott	93	-6.8	177	D	25.9	434,292	2,454	71,379	136.7	258,813	1.2	98.8	NA	72.0	15	0.8
Searcy	195	15.8	310	0.1	30.1	583,263	1,883	64,568	18.0	28,564	7.4	92.6	2	68.9	579	11.9
Sebastian	101	-15.2	143	0.2	29.1	477,234	3,343	58,679	118.4	167,670	1.4	98.6	NA	80.6	74	2.7
Sevier	142	10.1	263	0.2	30.0	702,812	2,668	96,124	230.8	427,398	0.5	99.5	NA	84.8	184	4.4
Sharp	162	2.2	260	0.3	30.1	554,504	2,132	65,348	146.9	236,125	1.1	98.9	NA	69.9	663	15.6
Stone	160	18.0	303	0.2	31.2	655,942	2,163	74,294	60.2	114,435	1.6	98.4	NA	71.9	370	8.4
Union	36	-14.5	136	0.0	8.2	375,084	2,765	67,177	16.2	60,321	3.7	96.3	NA	74.6	13	2.6
Van Buren	128	3.9	209	0.1	21.6	575,172	2,754	63,590	16.3	26,755	6.6	93.4	NA	77.1	172	7.2
Washington	317	1.6	139	0.3	85.1	713,220	5,132	70,892	509.3	223,456	1.5	98.5	9	78.6	696	2.4
White	344	-3.2	213	41.7	153.2	593,386	2,779	74,101	124.7	77,319	27.4	72.6	2	71.5	7,172	19.5
Woodruff	255	-6.9	1,365	177.8	228.0	4,440,411	3,254	503,337	D	D	D	D	2	64.7	11,420	85.6
Yell	194	21.3	271	1.5	57.4	729,033	2,695	91,819	268.1	373,436	2.2	97.8	NA	73.7	989	13.2

STATE County	Water use, 2015		Wholesale Trade[1], 2017				Retail Trade[2], 2017				Real estate and rental and leasing,[2] 2017			
	Public supply water withdrawn (mil gal/ day)	Public supply gallons withdrawn per person per day	Number of establish-ments	Number of employees	Sales (mil dol)	Average payroll (mil dol)	Number of establish-ments	Number of employees	Sales (mil dol)	Average payroll (mil dol)	Number of establish-ments	Number of employees	Sales (mil dol)	Average payroll (mil dol)
	133	134	135	136	137	138	139	140	141	142	143	144	145	146
ARKANSAS—Cont'd														
Cleveland	0.5	60.2	NA	NA	NA	NA	16	59	16.2	1.0	NA	NA	NA	NA
Columbia	2.2	89.2	D	D	D	D	92	944	199.1	22.3	25	65	12.2	2.2
Conway	4.2	197.9	13	111	62.5	3.9	75	804	241.7	20.9	9	16	2.2	0.6
Craighead	14.1	135.3	127	1,524	1,403.2	69.3	462	6,646	1,828.9	163.8	124	498	119.0	19.0
Crawford	28.9	467.7	64	956	556.6	46.9	160	2,018	500.7	50.9	43	163	25.8	6.1
Crittenden	7.1	145.6	50	1,042	1,469.8	46.2	142	2,125	665.2	49.3	43	221	35.9	6.8
Cross	1.8	104.7	18	276	155.4	13.4	64	735	213.5	19.4	19	77	6.5	1.8
Dallas	0.2	23.7	5	34	5.8	0.6	42	325	77.3	8.3	D	D	D	D
Desha	0.4	35.9	21	241	365.5	12.1	63	566	123.7	11.7	9	63	3.8	1.2
Drew	2.2	118.2	9	127	159.6	7.9	79	953	254.2	22.8	20	61	8.1	1.9
Faulkner	0.2	1.2	79	776	554.8	37.8	408	6,226	1,880.1	165.7	141	514	97.7	16.7
Franklin	3.0	169.5	4	15	8.5	0.6	52	614	203.4	15.0	4	11	2.0	0.4
Fulton	1.4	114.7	D	D	D	0.9	31	180	55.4	4.2	4	D	0.6	D
Garland	16.1	165.4	75	659	460.1	39.1	496	6,194	1,684.3	157.7	130	490	77.5	17.1
Grant	1.0	55.8	D	D	D	4.7	49	463	131.6	12.0	D	D	D	D
Greene	4.4	100.0	D	D	D	D	157	2,022	579.5	52.9	35	75	13.4	1.9
Hempstead	2.8	126.8	D	D	D	3.2	78	915	217.2	21.3	18	58	7.3	1.6
Hot Spring	2.3	67.9	D	D	D	D	89	805	248.2	20.5	12	46	3.9	1.1
Howard	6.1	457.9	11	87	93.0	3.3	53	577	157.0	14.9	6	19	2.1	0.4
Independence	5.8	157.1	D	D	D	D	158	1,871	491.5	44.8	24	96	13.5	3.5
Izard	0.8	58.8	8	35	6.9	0.8	45	371	110.3	9.4	4	37	2.8	0.6
Jackson	0.4	22.5	16	189	135.4	9.3	67	731	229.7	19.3	12	43	3.5	0.9
Jefferson	11.9	166.0	57	465	314.3	21.8	282	3,133	776.8	77.0	56	202	34.5	6.5
Johnson	4.8	183.2	6	24	8.1	0.7	78	948	265.9	24.1	D	D	D	1.2
Lafayette	0.4	52.9	NA	NA	NA	NA	19	144	26.9	2.6	3	D	1.3	D
Lawrence	1.1	65.0	16	153	129.8	6.5	63	688	206.4	18.4	6	27	3.3	0.8
Lee	1.3	132.6	11	136	122.8	7.1	15	158	40.1	3.8	8	D	3.3	D
Lincoln	0.5	36.9	D	D	D	D	28	207	66.8	4.5	D	D	D	D
Little River	2.8	224.5	NA	NA	NA	NA	39	448	129.5	11.3	NA	NA	NA	NA
Logan	3.4	156.1	D	D	D	0.5	68	747	164.8	17.0	14	26	3.6	0.4
Lonoke	6.0	83.9	32	309	218.5	14.0	169	2,061	557.2	52.3	52	138	22.4	5.5
Madison	0.0	0.0	D	D	D	D	32	444	95.9	10.3	D	D	D	D
Marion	0.8	50.0	7	D	4.6	D	39	586	112.8	12.9	10	D	1.4	D
Miller	0.1	2.0	41	407	251.5	17.9	132	1,315	378.8	32.0	D	D	D	D
Mississippi	1.4	32.9	48	487	477.6	25.3	145	1,754	419.5	41.3	36	179	26.4	5.5
Monroe	1.5	205.4	12	177	81.9	8.5	30	266	63.0	6.4	D	D	D	0.2
Montgomery	0.5	58.0	5	45	27.4	1.5	21	120	28.9	3.1	D	D	D	0.2
Nevada	0.2	25.7	D	D	D	0.2	18	273	101.8	5.5	4	11	0.5	0.2
Newton	0.0	2.5	NA	NA	NA	NA	12	132	20.6	1.6	NA	NA	NA	NA
Ouachita	3.3	133.8	D	D	D	D	103	966	242.2	22.6	21	139	20.6	4.1
Perry	0.1	5.9	D	D	D	0.2	17	166	33.7	3.0	D	D	D	D
Phillips	6.1	312.6	29	344	643.5	16.0	73	772	148.1	17.7	17	63	10.0	2.0
Pike	1.1	104.4	7	141	31.7	3.3	34	338	79.8	7.6	6	D	6.8	D
Poinsett	2.2	90.7	24	609	379.0	21.5	66	694	166.2	14.6	8	33	3.9	0.8
Polk	1.7	83.6	15	83	58.2	3.8	80	829	193.8	19.3	14	46	5.7	1.2
Pope	11.0	173.5	64	626	392.0	27.4	272	3,261	895.2	79.6	82	242	46.5	7.2
Prairie	0.4	47.0	D	D	D	D	35	199	51.3	4.4	D	D	D	0.5
Pulaski	39.6	100.8	643	12,040	9,205.7	682.6	1,776	26,282	7,998.1	720.7	703	3,336	776.1	148.8
Randolph	1.3	74.4	10	267	155.7	7.5	62	691	189.5	18.8	15	41	4.1	0.9
St. Francis	3.8	144.4	24	462	512.3	21.8	95	978	254.2	21.7	26	139	21.9	3.3
Saline	29.6	252.3	67	523	558.2	22.1	300	4,187	1,276.9	109.1	86	285	70.9	9.8
Scott	1.6	147.4	D	D	D	3.2	21	191	44.8	4.5	5	16	1.3	0.4
Searcy	0.3	39.4	D	D	D	0.1	28	196	51.3	4.5	7	21	1.8	0.5
Sebastian	0.1	1.0	184	2,729	1,657.8	140.1	573	8,405	2,250.5	206.8	164	1,198	193.5	46.6
Sevier	0.7	42.8	7	56	18.9	3.0	62	654	202.3	16.3	7	21	2.4	0.7
Sharp	1.0	57.9	5	D	2.2	D	59	709	169.4	16.0	8	26	2.3	0.5
Stone	1.8	142.1	5	58	30.3	1.4	45	467	126.4	12.8	6	12	0.9	0.2
Union	4.3	106.9	D	D	D	D	178	2,036	560.1	52.6	36	212	70.7	9.2
Van Buren	2.2	130.6	13	74	36.3	2.9	59	596	159.6	13.7	6	D	1.5	D
Washington	0.2	0.8	226	2,680	2,389.2	148.2	787	12,569	3,587.8	335.9	303	1,219	319.1	46.3
White	7.7	97.5	60	480	350.8	23.8	325	3,777	1,051.9	96.8	69	187	33.1	6.2
Woodruff	0.5	78.6	14	151	105.8	7.4	26	200	44.8	3.6	D	D	D	0.1
Yell	4.8	222.0	D	D	D	D	53	574	125.9	11.9	8	18	2.4	0.3

1 Merchant wholesalers, except manufacturers' sales branches and offices. 2. Employer establishments.

STATE County	Professional, scientific, and technical services, 2017				Manufacturing, 2017				Accommodation and food services, 2017			
	Number of establish-ments	Number of employees	Sales (mil dol)	Average payroll (mil dol)	Number of establish-ments	Number of employees	Sales (mil dol)	Average payroll (mil dol)	Number of establis-hments	Number of employees	Sales (mil dol)	Annual payroll (mil dol)
	147	148	149	150	151	152	153	154	155	156	157	158
ARKANSAS—Cont'd												
Cleveland	NA	NA	NA	NA	4	61	11.6	2.3	NA	NA	NA	NA
Columbia	32	313	35.5	13.4	28	1,613	864.8	102.1	41	720	43.8	10.3
Conway	26	159	8.7	2.5	19	687	475.6	46.9	29	439	29.9	7.6
Craighead	D	D	D	D	91	6,341	2,536.8	301.7	242	5,080	251.5	73.0
Crawford	86	280	33.0	11.8	53	4,525	1,266.8	163.9	89	1,527	73.1	21.5
Crittenden	D	D	D	D	35	1,674	657.3	76.4	93	1,613	90.2	24.6
Cross	25	90	7.5	2.9	11	508	124.1	16.8	D	D	D	D
Dallas	7	34	2.8	0.9	10	532	219.8	24.7	D	D	D	D
Desha	17	47	5.3	1.7	7	696	391.2	45.5	28	312	14.6	3.9
Drew	19	104	9.2	3.5	23	855	228.8	37.9	36	598	29.7	8.5
Faulkner	D	D	D	D	91	2,949	838.0	144.3	227	4,784	234.3	70.1
Franklin	19	78	9.4	2.3	14	1,158	438.2	48.1	27	316	13.5	3.8
Fulton	12	30	2.6	0.8	8	73	7.1	2.3	15	213	9.5	2.6
Garland	D	D	D	D	88	2,427	694.6	115.8	306	5,510	291.2	85.8
Grant	18	109	12.8	5.7	13	D	798.4	D	D	D	D	D
Greene	52	346	32.2	12.8	52	4,933	1,753.3	223.1	70	1,236	59.8	16.5
Hempstead	14	120	9.8	4.6	D	D	D	D	36	554	27.7	7.2
Hot Spring	30	75	6.4	2.0	30	1,391	821.5	69.3	42	592	27.7	7.2
Howard	8	38	3.4	1.1	18	3,126	1,469.3	105.8	17	308	20.8	4.1
Independence	59	194	36.0	7.8	34	3,693	1,467.9	151.6	64	1,267	52.3	13.7
Izard	D	D	1.9	D	6	D	45.8	9.9	14	D	4.9	D
Jackson	D	D	D	D	17	917	340.2	44.4	26	332	16.1	5.0
Jefferson	D	D	D	D	53	4,781	1,582.0	233.8	D	D	D	23.9
Johnson	24	80	8.1	2.9	33	2,641	659.0	83.1	40	595	27.0	7.6
Lafayette	D	D	1.3	D	5	81	16.6	3.3	6	49	4.0	0.8
Lawrence	13	33	4.6	1.0	19	390	75.5	14.4	25	304	14.6	3.8
Lee	8	27	3.2	1.0	NA	NA	NA	NA	4	46	2.7	0.6
Lincoln	D	D	D	D	8	365	85.8	16.1	D	D	D	D
Little River	8	39	5.6	1.4	16	1,098	639.0	84.7	D	D	D	D
Logan	29	122	13.1	4.9	15	1,081	248.5	46.7	30	350	13.6	3.7
Lonoke	89	501	69.0	25.9	28	1,917	407.4	104.0	93	1,562	87.4	23.1
Madison	D	D	D	D	23	957	315.2	36.7	17	191	10.0	2.2
Marion	15	63	4.1	1.6	15	1,138	353.9	43.8	27	198	9.4	2.6
Miller	40	183	17.8	6.5	24	2,265	1,075.4	128.6	D	D	D	D
Mississippi	30	106	10.8	3.5	47	6,325	4,801.8	410.6	80	1,156	60.9	15.4
Monroe	13	19	2.0	0.4	5	94	39.0	3.7	17	241	11.1	3.2
Montgomery	D	D	D	0.3	8	42	21.0	D	14	304	28.9	6.8
Nevada	6	30	1.0	0.4	D	D	D	D	9	90	4.1	1.2
Newton	4	5	0.5	0.1	12	63	13.0	2.3	13	128	7.6	2.2
Ouachita	D	D	D	D	D	D	D	D	35	507	23.2	6.0
Perry	8	13	2.8	1.0	NA	NA	NA	NA	D	D	D	D
Phillips	D	D	D	D	11	284	85.9	11.8	26	273	14.6	3.5
Pike	9	52	5.4	1.4	17	274	84.1	10.9	20	193	10.6	2.7
Poinsett	14	56	4.0	1.3	20	648	264.1	26.7	38	434	20.0	5.7
Polk	D	D	D	D	27	1,103	195.1	43.5	36	411	18.7	5.5
Pope	D	D	D	D	59	4,327	1,729.0	195.7	141	2,846	136.8	40.2
Prairie	7	35	3.3	0.8	3	48	6.5	D	D	D	D	0.8
Pulaski	D	D	D	D	311	12,027	5,425.2	663.9	1,060	20,953	1,127.3	333.2
Randolph	21	62	5.9	2.5	22	231	67.4	10.3	24	387	16.5	4.6
St. Francis	32	112	10.5	3.6	8	722	212.5	24.3	40	603	30.1	7.9
Saline	165	766	120.3	36.7	D	1,401	D	66.1	160	3,083	164.6	47.5
Scott	9	10	1.1	0.3	10	1,040	358.3	35.1	13	221	6.4	3.0
Searcy	5	12	1.1	0.4	12	92	23.6	3.7	D	D	D	1.5
Sebastian	D	D	D	D	163	13,257	4,207.1	564.7	298	6,051	304.3	90.6
Sevier	12	63	3.8	1.4	D	D	D	D	20	267	16.1	3.1
Sharp	12	33	2.4	0.6	14	100	19.7	2.3	28	284	13.2	3.7
Stone	10	41	2.4	0.7	18	99	18.3	3.6	27	444	19.7	5.3
Union	D	D	D	D	46	3,082	1,304.0	178.1	77	1,079	60.0	15.5
Van Buren	17	59	5.6	2.1	8	102	11.9	2.8	20	281	14.5	4.4
Washington	D	D	D	D	203	13,101	4,188.1	555.1	571	11,310	581.7	169.3
White	104	500	54.2	19.9	62	1,858	761.1	83.2	143	2,535	126.2	36.0
Woodruff	D	D	D	0.2	6	190	69.6	7.3	8	75	3.2	0.9
Yell	22	89	8.0	3.2	18	1,786	609.9	65.5	23	350	15.5	4.4

STATE County	Health care and social assistance, 2017				Other services, 2017				Nonemployer businesses, 2019		Value of residential construction authorized by building permits, 2021	
	Number of establish- ments	Number of employees	Receipts (mil dol)	Annual payroll (mil dol)	Number of establish- ments	Number of employees	Receipts (mil dol)	Annual payroll (mil dol)	Number	Receipts (mil dol)	New construction ($1,000)	Number of housing units
	159	160	161	162	163	164	165	166	167	168	169	170
ARKANSAS—Cont'd												
Cleveland	5	150	3.9	2.5	6	20	2.8	0.8	406	14.8	0	0
Columbia	68	1,318	78.6	34.0	33	112	10.3	2.8	1,249	50.6	935	11
Conway	48	716	55.1	23.2	D	D	D	D	1,445	55.7	1,735	14
Craighead	354	10,046	1,184.9	475.1	125	776	81.1	20.5	8,770	434.2	140,871	1,094
Crawford	111	1,584	128.4	57.7	63	281	30.4	8.1	3,996	185.6	19,614	138
Crittenden	126	1,744	129.4	53.2	48	333	31.0	8.8	3,761	139.5	18,014	72
Cross	44	982	55.5	27.2	D	D	D	D	1,330	56.9	1,200	18
Dallas	19	813	42.1	19.5	11	27	3.3	0.9	332	12.4	20	1
Desha	24	489	29.2	11.5	13	38	3.2	0.7	717	29.4	600	1
Drew	43	1,272	104.4	37.2	17	52	7.3	2.0	1,150	49.5	0	0
Faulkner	317	5,737	535.5	217.6	159	734	74.4	19.5	9,093	388.7	131,601	933
Franklin	34	565	47.4	18.6	14	44	3.9	1.1	997	40.2	1,018	11
Fulton	31	581	44.5	17.3	D	D	D	0.3	833	31.0	0	0
Garland	343	8,736	1,069.9	380.5	186	762	67.3	19.5	8,362	365.8	37,597	330
Grant	26	259	15.4	6.9	D	D	4.9	D	1,193	55.6	5,477	35
Greene	103	1,895	187.9	68.3	39	175	16.5	4.3	3,057	140.4	28,870	193
Hempstead	46	1,121	67.0	27.1	28	133	14.1	3.4	1,065	41.5	12	1
Hot Spring	54	1,188	92.9	40.5	24	84	6.6	2.0	2,022	80.3	0	0
Howard	34	918	49.0	24.3	21	100	11.4	2.8	776	33.4	0	0
Independence	99	3,494	343.3	151.3	54	250	19.3	6.1	2,394	107.4	1,820	9
Izard	34	539	30.3	13.4	11	46	3.6	0.9	907	35.8	1,427	10
Jackson	43	808	63.6	25.9	16	88	10.8	1.7	797	30.2	1,140	8
Jefferson	203	3,893	399.0	166.1	70	382	39.5	10.4	3,752	128.9	18,557	44
Johnson	38	907	79.1	35.3	29	123	10.6	3.7	1,382	60.9	7,486	47
Lafayette	7	141	6.3	2.9	3	35	2.0	0.8	343	14.1	418	2
Lawrence	28	656	47.6	23.0	D	D	D	D	1,214	54.9	5,141	71
Lee	18	314	23.2	9.2	6	12	0.9	0.3	620	23.5	0	0
Lincoln	18	320	25.3	10.9	11	33	4.8	1.0	554	28.8	790	2
Little River	21	331	23.5	10.8	D	D	D	D	595	19.7	363	2
Logan	44	674	58.6	24.0	27	74	9.2	2.0	1,231	42.8	674	4
Lonoke	116	1,459	106.6	43.4	58	261	22.5	6.3	4,924	212.2	53,477	256
Madison	15	226	14.6	7.2	D	D	D	1.9	1,325	53.8	13,489	79
Marion	14	297	14.8	5.9	12	28	2.8	0.5	1,231	44.7	16,552	173
Miller	78	1,117	77.0	28.3	D	D	D	D	2,627	125.5	6,685	28
Mississippi	112	1,750	149.4	62.7	43	181	16.3	4.9	2,309	75.8	6,113	43
Monroe	23	526	23.4	11.2	D	D	5.7	D	564	28.2	235	4
Montgomery	11	72	6.2	2.8	D	D	3.1	D	778	32.4	NA	NA
Nevada	15	381	19.6	9.9	11	23	2.4	0.5	457	17.6	0	0
Newton	10	201	8.1	3.7	NA	NA	NA	NA	673	26.8	200	1
Ouachita	D	D	D	D	D	D	10.0	D	1,146	41.4	868	2
Perry	13	184	10.4	4.1	D	D	1.9	D	745	31.9	0	0
Phillips	57	934	75.4	29.9	25	81	6.8	2.0	1,372	46.7	0	0
Pike	18	304	19.5	8.2	3	26	1.5	0.5	851	40.4	NA	NA
Poinsett	43	783	49.1	22.0	D	D	D	D	1,464	57.3	7,336	53
Polk	45	1,009	64.7	32.9	27	121	10.4	2.6	1,574	58.5	836	4
Pope	D	D	D	121.1	94	483	38.8	13.5	3,839	161.3	10,416	102
Prairie	9	188	8.1	4.0	D	D	3.1	D	485	18.9	519	6
Pulaski	1,515	46,881	6,685.8	2,627.9	809	5,543	951.3	210.5	30,586	1,451.7	359,207	1,928
Randolph	43	855	56.2	26.3	15	40	3.8	0.9	1,298	60.5	2,752	35
St. Francis	62	1,494	112.3	45.4	18	53	4.7	1.2	1,713	55.3	547	9
Saline	241	4,292	379.8	150.6	135	1,204	116.4	34.7	8,829	405.3	125,420	483
Scott	23	359	21.9	11.8	D	D	D	D	669	24.9	0	0
Searcy	13	276	13.8	5.7	NA	NA	NA	NA	832	35.8	0	0
Sebastian	428	11,389	1,422.6	551.1	199	906	90.1	25.0	9,111	475.7	61,607	400
Sevier	39	556	47.4	16.7	D	D	D	D	920	43.6	200	6
Sharp	50	643	34.6	16.2	26	157	13.3	3.5	1,263	52.0	972	6
Stone	35	610	39.5	17.7	14	49	4.4	1.3	1,231	44.9	440	3
Union	122	2,265	203.3	82.1	66	340	41.5	10.8	2,753	115.8	2,481	18
Van Buren	30	798	55.5	25.8	D	D	D	D	1,223	40.7	3,431	11
Washington	607	15,329	1,795.3	803.6	332	2,017	488.5	64.3	18,580	866.6	626,820	2,685
White	179	4,860	425.0	165.6	94	534	53.5	16.3	5,413	239.6	23,425	160
Woodruff	13	138	10.2	4.9	4	14	1.1	0.3	425	16.8	0	0
Yell	D	D	D	28.3	13	50	5.3	1.4	1,191	46.3	2,825	25

STATE County	Government employment and payroll, 2017									Local government finances, 2017				
			March payroll (percent of total)							General revenue				
												Taxes		
													Per capita[1] (dollars)	
	Full-time equivalent employees	March payroll (dollars)	Adminis-tration, judicial, and legal	Police and corrections	Fire protection	Highways and transpor-tation	Health and welfare	Natural resources and utilities	Education and libraries	Total (mil dol)	Inter-govern-mental (mil dol)	Total (mil dol)	Total	Property
	171	172	173	174	175	176	177	178	179	180	181	182	183	184
ARKANSAS—Cont'd														
Cleveland	305	798,054	7.6	5.8	0.6	4.1	0.7	2.3	78.6	21.7	15.0	5.5	674	565
Columbia	844	2,253,957	2.7	8.3	2.5	5.0	2.0	6.6	71.9	89.8	41.0	20.1	847	327
Conway	853	2,670,239	4.5	9.4	0.9	4.5	1.8	5.3	72.2	77.7	43.6	19.2	924	533
Craighead	3,526	12,146,858	5.4	9.1	2.8	3.9	1.3	10.5	66.8	330.8	193.4	87.6	817	400
Crawford	2,030	6,952,646	3.7	6.8	2.6	2.5	0.9	4.1	78.8	170.0	106.8	44.9	714	287
Crittenden	2,206	7,455,061	5.4	11.1	4.5	2.4	1.1	6.8	65.9	213.8	120.6	63.5	1,303	537
Cross	689	2,089,801	5.7	9.2	1.3	2.8	1.0	1.8	77.0	51.9	35.4	8.5	505	272
Dallas	258	586,128	10.9	16.4	0.3	4.8	0.2	7.3	59.7	21.1	13.0	4.4	597	161
Desha	761	2,240,254	5.2	7.5	2.4	1.0	24.3	4.1	55.6	64.1	32.8	15.1	1,282	580
Drew	1,073	3,599,821	3.8	2.7	0.9	1.7	33.3	2.0	55.4	97.2	43.3	14.6	794	258
Faulkner	3,353	11,828,937	4.8	9.3	4.1	2.6	0.4	4.8	73.3	352.7	181.7	85.9	695	316
Franklin	664	2,103,759	6.3	5.1	1.2	3.4	0.3	3.7	79.9	54.1	38.0	10.8	609	313
Fulton	479	1,338,215	3.1	4.6	0.6	4.5	30.2	2.0	54.7	38.2	17.6	4.5	370	184
Garland	2,866	10,381,906	5.0	10.8	3.8	3.3	1.5	7.3	67.5	304.8	156.1	87.2	886	270
Grant	747	2,335,417	6.2	6.6	0.0	2.7	0.0	3.4	80.1	59.1	43.4	9.3	513	249
Greene	1,572	5,019,874	3.6	6.2	3.1	3.3	0.9	9.6	67.4	131.4	72.9	26.5	589	229
Hempstead	883	2,974,446	3.4	6.9	1.6	2.9	1.8	8.7	70.1	68.8	45.3	13.9	636	226
Hot Spring	1,015	3,410,812	9.2	2.3	2.1	0.8	1.4	7.7	76.4	85.2	55.2	20.3	605	266
Howard	644	1,981,608	6.0	5.8	0.8	2.9	1.4	10.5	72.6	44.4	30.9	5.4	407	239
Independence	1,475	4,100,818	4.9	7.1	1.2	3.7	3.8	8.7	68.8	137.4	83.0	30.6	817	304
Izard	513	1,366,925	8.2	5.1	0.9	4.7	1.2	3.2	76.5	31.3	23.1	4.4	321	230
Jackson	508	1,537,477	7.9	9.3	3.4	4.6	3.0	6.1	65.1	49.3	26.4	15.5	913	506
Jefferson	2,423	7,522,146	6.1	11.6	3.8	3.7	1.8	1.5	71.4	218.7	128.4	62.7	906	391
Johnson	886	2,790,408	4.5	6.7	0.9	2.5	1.1	8.4	71.0	71.1	47.4	15.5	587	218
Lafayette	259	833,135	9.0	8.5	0.7	7.1	0.1	5.7	68.8	13.9	8.3	3.0	435	213
Lawrence	929	2,618,570	4.5	3.7	1.4	1.9	24.3	3.2	60.5	72.5	40.7	10.4	626	255
Lee	295	770,474	10.0	9.8	3.4	7.8	5.7	9.9	53.1	19.8	12.9	4.4	481	227
Lincoln	318	967,097	6.0	10.1	0.1	4.2	1.7	3.7	73.2	30.0	22.0	4.7	348	172
Little River	656	1,951,349	6.5	4.0	0.5	4.0	37.3	4.2	43.3	76.3	24.2	28.8	2,327	1,888
Logan	753	2,180,723	8.0	8.0	0.4	3.9	4.0	3.3	71.9	51.2	35.9	9.7	444	237
Lonoke	2,432	7,248,544	4.3	6.9	2.1	2.2	1.1	5.8	76.7	190.4	128.3	41.3	568	251
Madison	471	1,252,806	6.4	6.5	0.0	8.9	4.8	5.8	67.3	34.2	23.0	6.8	415	202
Marion	395	1,135,636	9.2	10.7	0.1	8.3	0.5	7.0	63.4	29.6	18.9	7.5	457	245
Miller	1,433	4,198,444	5.8	18.1	6.5	4.2	1.3	0.6	61.1	126.3	79.2	28.0	641	283
Mississippi	1,946	6,023,869	6.2	10.2	3.6	2.9	2.3	7.6	66.3	182.4	89.0	37.4	888	345
Monroe	365	969,748	9.0	9.3	1.3	5.0	4.2	1.3	69.6	23.7	14.9	5.1	730	364
Montgomery	308	758,187	8.9	7.6	0.0	7.0	0.2	7.2	68.3	18.7	13.5	3.2	361	232
Nevada	364	973,929	7.1	8.2	1.0	4.7	1.8	10.8	66.2	23.1	15.5	5.6	672	538
Newton	464	1,314,007	2.7	2.9	0.0	3.2	0.0	2.7	88.0	24.7	21.9	1.3	170	158
Ouachita	1,035	3,046,677	8.8	7.0	3.4	4.0	3.0	4.7	68.1	80.4	49.8	20.5	862	227
Perry	290	964,106	7.6	7.2	0.3	3.0	0.1	3.7	78.1	17.4	14.0	1.9	180	139
Phillips	876	2,488,292	6.7	8.8	3.4	3.5	2.2	6.4	67.4	71.4	48.6	15.7	846	290
Pike	434	1,240,094	5.3	5.4	0.0	3.7	0.6	4.6	79.7	32.9	23.1	6.6	617	241
Poinsett	1,057	3,162,684	5.0	8.8	0.8	2.6	2.7	3.4	76.2	71.6	52.3	9.5	394	185
Polk	827	2,358,009	4.5	7.3	0.8	4.7	1.2	3.3	76.9	85.1	37.9	12.0	597	188
Pope	2,123	6,616,052	3.1	9.1	3.7	2.3	2.5	6.1	70.2	179.0	102.7	50.3	790	324
Prairie	327	898,490	11.0	10.0	0.4	3.6	3.8	7.6	61.0	24.2	12.9	6.1	741	388
Pulaski	14,961	57,806,343	6.2	13.0	6.7	5.4	3.9	11.0	51.8	1,554.1	690.2	522.7	1,329	629
Randolph	727	2,362,081	6.6	4.3	1.1	4.7	35.3	4.0	41.9	57.3	27.0	7.9	447	123
St. Francis	878	2,624,352	6.2	9.3	2.8	2.4	2.4	7.7	68.1	69.9	43.3	17.5	673	177
Saline	2,670	9,187,746	5.6	9.4	5.4	2.3	0.5	3.9	71.3	262.1	159.4	72.6	608	307
Scott	367	1,012,757	4.6	5.2	0.0	4.4	1.1	9.1	72.6	18.1	15.0	1.5	145	72
Searcy	270	681,711	7.8	9.3	0.0	6.3	0.1	4.7	70.7	17.5	12.9	3.1	390	218
Sebastian	4,499	16,611,357	5.6	9.0	4.9	3.6	1.5	9.1	66.0	471.2	238.0	139.0	1,088	387
Sevier	821	2,336,559	4.8	6.0	0.5	2.3	0.9	4.4	81.0	55.5	42.1	6.3	371	150
Sharp	793	1,880,777	7.2	7.5	3.4	6.1	0.1	6.2	67.1	39.8	28.0	6.5	377	178
Stone	396	1,118,159	5.7	7.4	0.0	4.7	0.1	9.5	71.6	25.2	17.4	5.5	441	194
Union	1,547	4,466,114	2.1	10.0	4.5	4.3	0.4	7.3	68.1	128.0	70.7	38.7	981	364
Van Buren	633	1,658,575	8.9	10.9	0.2	4.8	0.3	2.2	71.0	49.4	28.4	14.6	879	535
Washington	7,736	25,196,414	5.5	11.1	4.4	4.8	0.7	5.0	66.9	804.5	444.4	225.6	969	333
White	2,591	8,236,317	4.7	8.2	2.4	2.9	0.8	5.0	74.6	210.9	132.2	49.9	633	236
Woodruff	312	811,976	12.0	6.6	0.3	6.3	3.0	7.7	62.8	25.7	16.4	5.1	779	470
Yell	887	2,628,007	3.2	7.0	0.0	3.7	1.2	3.5	80.6	54.1	42.2	8.4	392	228

1. Based on the resident population estimated as of July 1 of the year shown.

STATE County	Local government finances, 2017 (cont.)									Government employment, 2020			Individual income tax returns, 2019		
	Direct general expenditure							Debt outstanding							
			Percent of total for:												
	Total (mil dol)	Per capita[1] (dollars)	Education	Health and hospitals	Police protection	Public welfare	Highways	Total (mil dol)	Per capita[1] (dollars)	Federal civilian	Federal military	State and local	Number of returns	Mean adjusted gross income	Mean income tax
	185	186	187	188	189	190	191	192	193	194	195	196	197	198	199
ARKANSAS—Cont'd															
Cleveland	25.7	3,145	55.7	0.1	2.8	0.0	5.1	7.3	890	12	30	316	3,130	53,716	4,281
Columbia	88.0	3,716	43.8	25.0	3.8	0.0	6.8	73.9	3,120	44	82	1,866	8,990	51,836	4,520
Conway	94.8	4,555	72.3	0.8	4.9	0.1	5.3	52.1	2,504	62	80	1,587	8,640	49,344	3,904
Craighead	317.1	2,959	58.7	0.4	5.2	0.1	5.3	496.1	4,629	359	421	7,925	45,920	58,633	6,272
Crawford	167.5	2,664	60.0	0.0	5.8	0.1	6.8	237.5	3,776	105	242	2,141	25,140	49,253	3,768
Crittenden	215.9	4,431	60.5	0.7	6.5	0.0	4.5	235.2	4,828	101	179	2,477	21,040	47,105	4,169
Cross	51.6	3,072	63.9	4.6	7.3	0.0	5.0	18.4	1,093	60	84	998	7,110	46,015	3,798
Dallas	19.4	2,662	54.2	0.1	11.9	0.4	8.2	8.1	1,106	22	25	364	2,660	42,361	3,093
Desha	60.9	5,184	44.3	24.7	6.5	0.1	3.5	33.0	2,807	73	42	885	4,860	40,108	3,004
Drew	102.4	5,574	42.3	40.6	3.0	0.1	3.7	57.9	3,152	58	66	1,916	7,160	51,689	4,272
Faulkner	364.2	2,948	49.5	0.1	5.0	0.1	9.7	829.8	6,717	253	477	7,199	53,070	58,736	5,480
Franklin	62.5	3,509	74.9	2.9	3.4	0.3	4.7	71.5	4,016	170	67	907	7,010	46,433	3,470
Fulton	40.9	3,375	41.5	24.6	2.3	0.2	4.0	19.3	1,594	32	47	602	4,570	38,852	2,774
Garland	292.2	2,972	52.9	0.3	5.9	0.1	3.2	550.8	5,602	510	376	3,793	45,410	54,377	5,514
Grant	57.1	3,156	75.4	0.3	3.8	0.1	4.5	88.4	4,883	32	70	776	7,560	58,654	5,055
Greene	127.0	2,823	57.7	0.2	5.3	0.1	5.3	109.7	2,438	103	173	1,973	18,230	51,851	4,420
Hempstead	67.6	3,090	68.2	0.2	4.8	0.1	6.3	47.4	2,165	65	81	1,598	8,570	39,432	2,512
Hot Spring	78.6	2,340	66.5	0.0	3.9	0.1	5.6	90.0	2,678	74	122	1,928	12,970	46,339	3,379
Howard	43.6	3,259	75.2	0.0	3.4	0.0	1.3	111.4	8,332	58	50	754	5,600	42,057	3,161
Independence	124.7	3,334	56.9	0.1	3.8	0.1	4.0	241.3	6,453	104	141	2,056	15,340	55,238	5,356
Izard	32.2	2,358	71.3	1.2	5.6	0.2	5.8	23.2	1,695	37	49	965	5,070	41,618	2,957
Jackson	53.5	3,143	41.1	0.4	6.7	0.5	4.9	46.9	2,755	47	56	1,445	5,930	42,380	3,337
Jefferson	208.0	3,005	55.9	0.1	9.7	0.2	4.2	198.7	2,870	1,395	256	6,309	28,620	43,794	3,535
Johnson	65.4	2,478	64.2	0.2	4.8	0.0	8.4	75.7	2,865	92	99	1,080	10,290	42,400	2,945
Lafayette	13.9	2,049	48.9	0.3	10.9	0.2	10.9	9.5	1,401	31	25	303	2,540	41,222	3,123
Lawrence	70.1	4,233	47.3	24.8	3.4	5.1	3.7	51.3	3,097	50	60	1,094	6,340	41,082	2,988
Lee	19.1	2,094	52.8	0.4	14.4	0.3	13.8	5.9	642	40	26	623	2,800	40,136	3,339
Lincoln	21.4	1,590	65.2	0.1	5.7	0.0	10.2	10.7	793	32	36	1,170	4,070	43,476	3,144
Little River	72.8	5,881	27.5	18.4	3.0	7.0	3.0	58.5	4,729	47	46	763	5,010	44,862	3,201
Logan	49.4	2,272	66.5	3.1	5.8	0.0	7.3	64.3	2,958	104	80	1,273	8,660	42,233	2,856
Lonoke	182.4	2,506	67.8	0.2	5.7	0.1	4.3	182.9	2,513	138	282	2,722	31,550	57,337	4,865
Madison	35.1	2,154	61.7	3.8	6.0	0.0	13.0	33.7	2,069	48	64	579	6,810	46,454	3,799
Marion	32.6	1,984	63.1	0.2	7.4	0.2	10.4	23.1	1,408	38	64	514	6,750	41,050	2,914
Miller	124.9	2,857	53.5	0.4	9.3	0.1	3.8	96.8	2,212	78	161	1,862	18,000	49,415	4,354
Mississippi	179.1	4,254	47.8	2.4	5.9	0.1	3.2	811.3	19,265	115	151	2,678	16,280	45,405	3,670
Monroe	23.8	3,387	53.5	1.4	7.6	0.3	8.8	5.6	804	34	25	380	2,900	35,462	2,626
Montgomery	17.7	1,992	59.9	0.1	4.6	0.0	12.5	12.1	1,362	55	34	419	3,330	40,492	2,827
Nevada	24.3	2,927	60.1	0.3	5.2	0.0	2.6	12.6	1,515	27	31	440	3,410	39,772	2,469
Newton	23.0	2,938	96.5	0.0	0.5	0.0	0.3	35.1	4,486	46	29	365	2,990	40,178	2,608
Ouachita	85.0	3,569	55.6	9.2	4.1	0.1	4.8	67.9	2,849	103	88	1,751	9,730	47,595	3,846
Perry	17.3	1,668	82.5	0.0	1.7	0.0	1.4	10.8	1,045	27	39	344	4,040	48,362	3,671
Phillips	67.4	3,622	63.4	0.2	7.6	0.1	4.7	68.1	3,664	69	66	1,107	6,790	36,481	2,754
Pike	31.5	2,935	75.3	0.1	3.9	0.2	5.4	21.0	1,953	52	43	558	4,220	42,309	3,033
Poinsett	75.8	3,149	72.4	0.1	6.4	0.1	5.5	39.8	1,655	72	88	1,072	9,010	42,979	3,406
Polk	83.0	4,120	42.5	37.6	2.7	0.0	5.1	57.4	2,849	116	91	1,024	7,760	42,845	3,104
Pope	180.3	2,833	60.5	1.7	6.2	0.1	5.6	260.0	4,085	288	236	4,256	26,360	53,645	4,712
Prairie	21.4	2,595	52.7	1.8	10.0	0.0	8.2	13.7	1,663	45	30	332	3,320	48,011	3,821
Pulaski	1,617.9	4,114	42.2	2.6	7.4	0.0	4.9	2,355.1	5,988	9,355	5,270	42,548	185,640	67,107	8,502
Randolph	55.9	3,164	40.2	27.6	5.5	0.1	5.2	21.8	1,237	51	69	1,166	7,320	42,532	3,180
St. Francis	63.7	2,449	56.7	0.5	7.4	0.1	5.2	34.0	1,307	627	79	1,234	8,590	37,949	2,679
Saline	255.1	2,135	57.8	0.2	6.4	0.1	8.9	400.0	3,347	123	471	3,853	54,280	62,998	5,813
Scott	19.2	1,851	81.5	0.5	2.5	0.0	1.5	22.8	2,199	79	39	515	3,970	37,636	2,251
Searcy	19.6	2,474	68.3	0.1	3.8	0.2	8.9	17.5	2,209	42	30	353	3,110	34,480	2,098
Sebastian	452.0	3,537	49.5	0.4	5.0	0.1	9.6	1,147.3	8,978	965	525	6,561	55,040	55,476	5,697
Sevier	54.1	3,161	74.3	0.2	2.2	0.1	4.9	18.7	1,093	69	64	1,108	6,290	40,972	2,713
Sharp	39.9	2,326	68.6	0.1	5.5	0.0	8.6	21.5	1,254	59	66	755	6,740	38,685	2,670
Stone	23.8	1,903	66.2	0.1	6.7	0.3	9.0	14.9	1,189	59	48	465	4,800	40,387	2,857
Union	127.4	3,229	58.5	0.1	5.6	0.0	6.8	128.1	3,245	157	146	2,377	17,180	60,009	6,252
Van Buren	46.4	2,806	57.3	1.1	10.0	0.5	10.0	44.1	2,662	38	63	639	6,420	45,426	3,423
Washington	754.1	3,240	56.2	0.5	5.5	0.0	5.6	1,274.3	5,475	2,266	920	18,509	105,710	64,724	7,521
White	199.8	2,534	64.7	0.1	6.7	0.2	7.4	183.1	2,322	175	294	3,181	31,260	52,695	4,658
Woodruff	29.0	4,409	44.9	0.3	4.4	21.8	6.7	21.3	3,245	40	24	416	2,470	39,989	3,383
Yell	54.3	2,524	81.4	0.0	2.5	0.0	1.9	55.6	2,585	101	80	1,136	8,510	43,997	3,149

1. Based on the resident population estimated as of July 1 of the year shown.

State / county code	CBSA code[1]	County Type code[2]	STATE County	Land area[3] (sq. mi)	Population, 2021: Total persons 2021	Population, 2021: Rank	Population, 2021: Per square mile	Race alone or in combination, not Hispanic or Latino (percent): White	Black	American Indian, Alaska Native	Asian and Pacific Islancer	Percent Hispanic or Latino[4]	Age (percent): Under 5 years	5 to 17 years	18 to 24 years	25 to 34 years	35 to 44 years	45 to 54 years
				1	2	3	4	5	6	7	8	9	10	11	12	13	14	15
06000		0	CALIFORNIA	155,854.0	39,237,836	X	251.8	38.5	6.5	1.0	17.6	39.5	5.7	12.7	13.0	14.9	13.8	12.6
06001	41860	1	Alameda	737.5	1,648,556	20	2,235.3	33.6	11.4	0.8	36.7	22.2	5.3	11.4	11.2	15.8	15.8	13.3
06003		8	Alpine	738.3	1,235	3,097	1.7	65.6	2.0	20.4	2.4	12.6	4.1	9.3	11.9	12.0	9.1	12.1
06005		6	Amador	594.6	41,259	1,159	69.4	78.2	3.5	2.6	2.8	15.5	3.9	8.6	8.0	11.3	12.8	12.4
06007	17020	3	Butte	1,636.5	208,309	328	127.3	72.8	3.0	2.8	7.2	18.4	5.3	11.5	18.1	13.0	11.8	10.2
06009		6	Calaveras	1,020.0	46,221	1,051	45.3	81.5	1.7	2.8	3.4	14.1	4.5	9.6	8.9	9.7	10.8	10.9
06011		6	Colusa	1,150.7	21,917	1,720	19.0	34.4	1.8	1.9	2.2	61.3	6.3	15.3	14.0	13.0	13.1	11.3
06013	41860	1	Contra Costa	716.9	1,161,413	38	1,620.0	44.7	10.0	1.0	22.4	26.8	5.3	12.7	12.1	12.3	14.0	13.6
06015	18860	7	Del Norte	1,006.2	28,100	1,493	27.9	64.5	4.6	9.2	4.7	21.1	4.9	12.3	10.9	13.8	14.7	11.0
06017	40900	1	El Dorado	1,707.9	193,221	354	113.1	79.1	1.6	1.7	7.4	13.8	4.5	11.3	10.5	10.3	12.3	12.4
06019	23420	2	Fresno	5,958.4	1,013,581	46	170.1	29.0	5.3	1.1	12.0	54.7	7.1	16.3	14.4	15.0	13.3	11.0
06021		6	Glenn	1,314.0	28,805	1,463	21.9	50.8	1.6	2.3	3.2	44.0	6.6	15.5	13.6	12.8	12.1	10.6
06023	21700	5	Humboldt	3,568.2	136,310	480	38.2	77.2	2.7	7.1	5.4	12.9	4.9	10.7	15.7	13.0	13.3	11.0
06025	20940	3	Imperial	4,175.5	179,851	373	43.1	9.7	2.6	0.9	1.5	85.8	7.1	16.6	14.6	14.7	12.7	10.7
06027		7	Inyo	10,197.3	18,970	1,871	1.9	61.9	1.8	11.7	2.7	24.5	5.2	12.1	9.7	10.7	12.9	10.7
06029	12540	2	Kern	8,134.6	917,673	63	112.8	32.8	6.0	1.2	6.0	56.1	7.2	16.6	14.8	15.4	13.4	10.9
06031	25260	3	Kings	1,391.0	153,443	446	110.3	32.0	7.1	1.4	5.3	56.6	7.2	15.4	15.0	16.6	14.6	11.1
06033	17340	4	Lake	1,256.6	68,766	783	54.7	69.8	2.8	4.2	3.0	23.9	5.9	12.4	10.1	11.3	11.6	10.9
06035	45000	7	Lassen	4,541.3	33,159	1,353	7.3	66.3	8.8	4.0	3.4	20.5	4.8	10.1	11.9	18.6	15.1	12.3
06037	31080	1	Los Angeles	40.3	9,829,544	1	2,421.5	27.3	8.7	0.6	16.8	49.1	5.3	12.0	12.6	15.9	14.0	13.2
06039	31460	3	Madera	2,136.9	159,410	426	74.6	33.1	3.6	1.7	3.0	60.2	6.8	15.9	13.9	13.8	13.2	11.3
06041	41860	1	Marin	520.4	260,206	272	500.0	73.3	3.4	0.8	9.3	16.8	4.2	11.0	10.8	8.7	11.8	14.8
06043		8	Mariposa	1,448.8	17,147	1,962	11.8	80.2	2.1	4.2	2.7	13.8	4.3	9.7	8.6	11.2	10.6	10.3
06045	46380	4	Mendocino	3,506.8	91,305	657	26.0	65.5	1.6	5.2	3.4	27.2	5.2	12.2	10.7	11.0	12.4	11.6
06047	32900	2	Merced	1,938.0	286,461	248	147.8	26.5	3.7	0.9	8.5	62.5	7.2	16.7	16.3	14.5	12.8	10.9
06049		6	Modoc	3,948.2	8,661	2,517	2.2	78.7	2.4	4.1	2.4	15.4	4.2	11.3	9.0	10.7	10.4	10.5
06051		7	Mono	3,048.9	13,247	2,199	4.3	67.3	1.7	2.6	3.4	27.2	4.3	9.9	11.6	15.2	13.3	12.8
06053	41500	2	Monterey	3,281.7	437,325	164	133.3	30.4	3.1	0.9	7.8	60.4	6.6	14.9	14.1	13.7	13.4	11.7
06055	34900	3	Napa	748.3	136,207	481	182.0	52.7	2.9	1.0	10.6	35.6	4.5	11.3	12.3	12.2	13.0	12.9
06057	46020	4	Nevada	957.8	103,487	592	108.0	86.5	1.2	1.9	3.2	10.1	4.1	9.7	8.8	9.9	12.1	11.2
06059	31080	1	Orange	792.8	3,167,809	6	3,995.7	41.2	2.3	0.6	24.9	34.1	5.5	12.1	12.6	14.3	13.1	13.5
06061	40900	1	Placer	1,407.1	412,300	176	293.0	73.2	2.7	1.3	11.8	15.2	5.0	12.9	11.3	10.9	13.7	13.0
06063		7	Plumas	2,553.1	19,915	1,818	7.8	85.1	2.1	3.5	2.2	10.3	4.3	9.9	8.8	9.7	10.7	9.6
06065	40140	1	Riverside	7,209.3	2,458,395	10	341.0	34.2	7.3	1.0	8.6	51.6	5.9	14.2	13.9	13.9	13.4	12.2
06067	40900	1	Sacramento	965.3	1,588,921	22	1,646.0	46.4	12.0	1.5	21.5	24.4	6.0	13.2	12.2	15.5	14.2	12.1
06069	41940	1	San Benito	1,388.7	66,677	808	48.0	32.1	1.7	1.0	5.1	62.0	6.4	14.7	13.5	13.6	14.4	12.3
06071	40140	1	San Bernardino	20,068.0	2,194,710	14	109.4	27.3	9.0	0.9	9.4	55.8	6.6	14.9	14.4	15.3	13.5	12.0
06073	41740	1	San Diego	4,210.2	3,286,069	5	780.5	47.0	5.8	0.9	15.4	34.8	5.7	12.0	13.4	16.1	14.1	12.1
06075	41860	1	San Francisco	46.9	815,201	78	17,381.7	41.5	6.2	0.8	40.0	15.7	4.3	7.6	8.6	20.3	16.3	13.3
06077	44700	2	San Joaquin	1,392.4	789,410	82	566.9	31.4	8.3	1.2	20.2	43.0	6.6	15.3	14.2	14.0	13.7	12.0
06079	42020	2	San Luis Obispo	3,300.9	283,159	250	85.8	69.9	2.5	1.1	5.5	23.8	4.3	10.0	18.0	11.2	11.8	10.5
06081	41860	1	San Mateo	448.6	737,888	90	1,644.9	40.9	3.1	0.6	35.8	24.0	5.2	11.1	10.6	14.2	14.6	13.6
06083	42200	2	Santa Barbara	2,733.9	446,475	162	163.3	45.0	2.4	1.0	7.1	47.2	6.0	12.5	19.0	13.4	11.7	10.4
06085	41940	1	Santa Clara	1,291.1	1,885,508	18	1,460.4	31.8	3.1	0.6	43.0	25.0	5.4	12.0	12.1	15.8	14.6	13.5
06087	42100	2	Santa Cruz	445.1	267,792	265	601.6	59.1	1.8	1.1	7.0	34.4	4.4	10.7	18.0	11.9	11.9	11.9
06089	39820	3	Shasta	3,775.5	182,139	370	48.2	81.6	2.3	3.8	5.2	11.4	5.5	12.5	11.2	12.7	12.4	10.8
06091		8	Sierra	953.2	3,283	2,942	3.4	83.7	1.5	2.7	1.4	13.0	4.3	9.6	7.5	8.2	11.2	11.5
06093		6	Siskiyou	6,278.8	44,118	1,096	7.0	78.4	2.7	6.2	3.7	13.9	4.8	11.8	10.1	10.1	11.0	10.5
06095	46700	2	Solano	821.8	451,716	159	549.7	39.9	15.9	1.3	20.6	28.6	5.7	12.5	12.1	14.2	13.6	12.0
06097	42220	2	Sonoma	1,575.6	485,887	149	308.4	64.3	2.5	1.6	6.6	28.3	4.6	10.9	11.5	12.4	13.2	12.3
06099	33700	2	Stanislaus	1,496.0	552,999	127	369.7	40.6	3.6	1.2	8.2	49.5	6.8	15.4	14.1	14.3	13.3	11.6
06101	49700	3	Sutter	602.7	99,063	615	164.4	46.5	3.2	1.9	19.4	32.9	6.4	14.5	13.2	13.7	12.8	11.3
06103	39780	4	Tehama	2,949.1	65,498	823	22.2	68.2	1.7	3.2	2.5	27.3	5.8	13.9	11.7	11.9	11.7	10.9
06105		8	Trinity	3,179.3	16,060	2,031	5.1	84.9	1.7	6.9	3.4	7.9	4.3	10.1	8.5	9.1	10.9	11.3
06107	47300	2	Tulare	4,823.9	477,054	151	98.9	27.7	1.8	1.2	4.3	66.7	7.3	17.6	15.4	14.1	13.1	10.9
06109	43760	4	Tuolumne	2,220.9	55,810	925	25.1	80.8	2.9	2.8	2.7	13.7	4.3	9.7	9.3	12.0	12.1	10.7
06111	37100	2	Ventura	1,840.8	839,784	75	456.2	46.0	2.4	0.9	9.5	44.1	5.3	12.8	13.0	13.4	12.8	12.7
06113	40900	1	Yolo	1,014.7	216,986	319	213.8	48.8	3.7	1.3	18.6	32.6	5.0	11.7	23.6	13.5	12.2	10.6
06115	49700	3	Yuba	632.0	83,421	691	132.0	56.1	5.8	3.1	10.0	30.5	7.4	15.8	13.3	15.5	13.7	10.2
08000		0	COLORADO	103,637.5	5,812,069	X	56.1	69.3	5.1	1.3	4.8	22.3	5.4	12.2	12.9	15.6	14.4	12.2
08001	19740	1	Adams	1,166.7	522,140	138	447.5	49.7	4.3	1.1	5.4	41.8	6.3	14.4	13.5	16.1	15.4	12.4
08003		7	Alamosa	722.6	16,547	1,999	22.9	48.0	1.9	2.1	1.6	48.2	6.0	14.3	19.5	13.4	12.1	9.5
08005	19740	1	Arapahoe	797.9	654,900	106	820.8	61.1	12.7	1.1	8.2	20.6	5.7	13.0	12.2	15.6	15.0	12.8
08007		7	Archuleta	1,350.1	13,790	2,167	10.2	78.2	1.3	2.7	1.5	18.5	4.1	10.3	8.2	9.4	11.8	10.9
08009		9	Baca	2,555.0	3,514	2,921	1.4	84.5	2.4	2.5	1.0	12.2	5.7	13.5	10.4	10.4	11.6	9.5
08011		7	Bent	1,512.8	5,759	2,755	3.8	57.1	7.1	2.0	1.5	33.3	4.0	9.0	11.5	15.9	15.0	13.3

1. CBSA = Core Based Statistical Area. See Appendix A for explanation. See Appendix B for list of metropolitan areas with component counties. 2. County type code from the Economic Research Service of USDA Rural-Urban Continuum Codes. See Appendix A for definition. 3. Dry land or land partially or temporarily covered by water. 4. May be of any race.

STATE County	Population, 2021 (cont.): Age (percent) (cont.): 55 to 64 years	65 to 74 years	75 years and over	Percent female	Population change, 2000–2021: Total persons: 2010	2020	Percent change: 2010–2020	2020–2021	Components of change, 2020–2021: Births	Deaths	Net Migration	Households, 2016–2020: Number	Persons per household	Percent: Family house-holds	Female family house-holder[1]	One person
	16	17	18	19	20	21	22	23	24	25	26	27	28	29	30	31
CALIFORNIA	12.2	9.1	6.1	50.3	37,253,956	39,538,223	6.1	-0.8	529,290	414,075	-415,522	13,103,114	2.9	68.6	12.9	23.8
Alameda	12.2	9.0	5.9	50.8	1,510,271	1,682,353	11.4	-2.0	21,798	15,532	-39,716	573,174	2.8	66.5	11.2	24.6
Alpine	16.6	17.6	7.2	47.5	1,175	1,204	2.5	2.6	11	25	45	397	2.8	73.3	6.8	24.4
Amador	15.7	16.7	10.7	45.2	38,091	40,474	6.3	1.9	354	654	1,105	14,844	2.4	66.4	8.4	30.1
Butte	11.8	11.1	7.2	50.3	220,000	211,632	-3.8	-1.6	2,526	2,990	-2,888	83,879	2.6	60.6	11.9	27.5
Calaveras	17.1	17.5	11.1	49.8	45,578	45,292	-0.6	2.1	465	739	1,230	16,958	2.7	71.9	9.3	23.1
Colusa	11.5	9.2	6.2	49.0	21,419	21,839	2.0	0.4	329	197	-59	7,329	2.9	67.4	10.6	28.5
Contra Costa	13.2	9.9	6.8	50.8	1,049,025	1,165,927	11.1	-0.4	14,511	12,046	-7,146	398,299	2.9	71.9	12.0	21.8
Del Norte	13.5	12.1	6.8	45.0	28,610	27,743	-3.0	1.3	305	392	448	9,805	2.5	64.7	13.4	28.3
El Dorado	16.2	14.2	8.4	49.9	181,058	191,185	5.6	1.1	1,845	2,507	2,745	73,078	2.6	69.4	7.0	24.1
Fresno	10.3	7.6	5.0	49.8	930,450	1,008,654	8.4	0.5	17,245	11,142	-1,499	310,097	3.1	72.3	17.1	22.2
Glenn	12.2	10.0	6.7	48.7	28,122	28,917	2.8	-0.4	458	315	-261	10,216	2.7	71.8	11.6	22.5
Humboldt	12.2	12.4	6.8	50.3	134,623	136,463	1.4	-0.1	1,658	1,883	58	54,120	2.4	54.1	10.9	32.5
Imperial	10.1	7.8	5.6	48.5	174,528	179,702	3.0	0.1	2,851	2,034	-722	45,768	3.7	74.7	19.0	22.1
Inyo	14.6	14.0	10.0	49.6	18,546	19,016	2.5	-0.2	220	258	-8	7,954	2.2	55.9	10.1	38.9
Kern	10.3	7.1	4.3	48.6	839,631	909,235	8.3	0.9	15,385	9,696	2,506	273,556	3.2	73.8	16.1	20.9
Kings	9.4	6.4	4.3	44.7	152,982	152,486	-0.3	0.6	2,718	1,345	-466	43,604	3.1	78.3	16.7	17.1
Lake	14.8	14.2	8.9	49.9	64,665	68,163	5.4	0.9	903	1,110	826	25,508	2.5	58.4	11.4	31.7
Lassen	11.3	9.9	6.0	37.8	34,895	32,730	-6.2	1.3	384	305	351	9,172	2.3	67.1	11.9	27.1
Los Angeles	12.4	8.7	6.0	50.4	9,818,605	10,014,009	2.0	-1.8	123,893	103,132	-204,337	3,332,504	3.0	66.4	14.7	25.8
Madera	10.8	8.8	5.4	51.4	150,865	156,255	3.6	2.0	2,603	1,638	2,196	44,479	3.3	78.6	13.5	16.6
Marin	15.1	13.3	10.1	50.6	252,409	262,321	3.9	-0.8	2,566	2,854	-1,830	104,900	2.4	63.0	8.3	29.3
Mariposa	16.5	17.0	11.8	49.3	18,251	17,131	-6.1	0.1	151	247	117	7,846	2.1	60.7	10.6	32.3
Mendocino	13.2	14.9	8.7	50.2	87,841	91,601	4.3	-0.3	1,073	1,280	-89	34,164	2.5	61.6	13.6	30.9
Merced	10.1	7.0	4.5	49.2	255,793	281,202	9.9	1.9	4,713	2,812	3,339	81,306	3.3	76.3	16.9	19.0
Modoc	15.4	16.7	11.8	49.7	9,686	8,700	-10.2	-0.4	54	148	58	3,594	2.3	65.1	8.5	28.7
Mono	15.3	11.7	6.0	46.4	14,202	13,195	-7.1	0.4	137	61	-26	5,196	2.7	54.0	6.6	34.9
Monterey	11.0	8.7	5.8	48.9	415,057	439,035	5.8	-0.4	7,031	3,898	-4,901	128,003	3.3	72.6	12.5	21.4
Napa	13.6	11.6	8.6	49.8	136,484	138,019	1.1	-1.3	1,503	1,706	-1,610	48,484	2.8	68.4	10.2	25.2
Nevada	15.7	17.7	10.8	50.5	98,764	102,241	3.5	1.2	986	1,432	1,733	40,917	2.4	64.5	9.2	29.1
Orange	13.1	9.2	6.6	50.4	3,010,232	3,186,989	5.9	-0.6	40,070	31,088	-28,481	1,040,001	3.0	71.4	11.5	21.2
Placer	13.3	11.5	8.5	50.8	348,432	404,739	16.2	1.9	4,423	4,829	8,055	145,714	2.7	70.5	8.6	23.9
Plumas	16.8	19.1	11.2	49.8	20,007	19,790	-1.1	0.6	186	291	237	8,332	2.2	60.5	9.8	32.7
Riverside	11.7	8.7	6.1	49.8	2,189,641	2,418,185	10.4	1.7	33,756	27,760	34,225	736,413	3.3	73.3	12.8	21.3
Sacramento	12.0	9.1	5.7	50.8	1,418,788	1,585,055	11.7	0.2	22,811	17,746	-1,587	547,519	2.8	66.3	14.1	25.7
San Benito	11.9	8.2	5.0	49.6	55,269	64,209	16.2	3.8	961	521	2,050	18,389	3.3	80.3	12.9	15.4
San Bernardino	11.3	7.7	4.4	49.9	2,035,210	2,181,654	7.2	0.6	33,633	24,061	2,875	640,090	3.3	76.5	16.9	18.4
San Diego	11.8	8.9	5.9	49.3	3,095,313	3,298,634	6.6	-0.4	46,391	32,777	-26,554	1,130,703	2.9	67.2	11.6	23.9
San Francisco	12.2	10.1	7.5	48.9	805,235	873,965	8.5	-6.7	9,976	8,783	-59,025	362,141	2.4	47.1	7.9	36.3
San Joaquin	11.2	7.9	5.1	49.8	685,306	779,233	13.7	1.3	12,218	8,939	6,798	231,092	3.2	74.7	15.1	20.2
San Luis Obispo	12.9	13.1	8.3	49.2	269,637	282,424	4.7	0.3	2,983	3,358	1,099	106,244	2.5	63.2	8.7	26.6
San Mateo	13.2	10.0	7.4	50.2	718,451	764,442	6.4	-3.5	9,783	7,046	-28,885	263,351	2.9	69.9	10.1	22.2
Santa Barbara	11.1	9.2	6.8	49.8	423,895	448,229	5.7	-0.4	6,722	4,541	-3,973	148,309	2.9	65.7	11.0	23.9
Santa Clara	12.3	8.3	6.2	49.1	1,781,642	1,936,259	8.7	-2.6	24,875	15,854	-59,178	635,314	3.0	71.5	9.9	20.4
Santa Cruz	12.8	11.7	6.6	50.3	262,382	270,861	3.2	-1.1	2,848	2,691	-3,230	96,275	2.7	63.2	10.1	25.1
Shasta	13.8	12.6	8.4	50.6	177,223	182,155	2.8	0.0	2,291	3,113	806	70,845	2.5	66.3	11.5	27.1
Sierra	17.3	19.0	11.5	49.3	3,240	3,236	-0.1	1.5	21	48	76	1,250	2.3	66.1	5.5	30.5
Siskiyou	14.7	16.8	10.1	50.0	44,900	44,076	-1.8	0.1	449	759	361	19,195	2.2	59.4	9.8	33.1
Solano	13.1	10.5	6.4	49.8	413,344	453,491	9.7	-0.4	6,217	5,133	-2,921	151,191	2.9	72.3	13.8	21.8
Sonoma	14.0	13.0	8.1	50.8	483,878	488,863	1.0	-0.6	5,430	6,077	-2,361	188,958	2.6	63.6	9.6	27.0
Stanislaus	11.1	8.1	5.3	50.1	514,453	552,878	7.5	0.0	8,935	6,440	-2,524	174,826	3.1	74.4	14.8	20.5
Sutter	12.0	9.3	6.8	50.0	94,737	99,633	5.2	-0.6	1,526	1,187	-922	32,586	2.9	72.8	12.7	21.9
Tehama	13.9	11.8	8.4	50.1	63,463	65,829	3.7	-0.5	911	975	-277	24,661	2.6	65.8	12.4	27.0
Trinity	16.7	18.5	10.6	48.3	13,786	16,112	16.9	-0.3	118	213	49	5,896	2.1	56.1	9.1	35.0
Tulare	9.9	7.1	4.6	49.9	442,179	473,117	7.0	0.8	8,226	4,866	434	139,044	3.3	77.9	17.2	17.7
Tuolumne	14.7	16.4	10.8	47.5	55,365	55,620	0.5	0.3	525	894	573	22,937	2.2	58.7	8.0	34.0
Ventura	13.3	9.9	6.8	50.2	823,318	843,843	2.5	-0.5	10,447	8,931	-5,692	271,639	3.1	72.3	11.8	21.7
Yolo	10.2	8.0	5.2	51.3	200,849	216,403	7.7	0.3	2,463	1,929	-18	74,614	2.8	64.3	11.3	21.6
Yuba	11.0	8.5	4.7	49.2	72,155	81,575	13.1	2.3	1,419	847	1,269	26,434	2.9	68.9	13.0	24.4
COLORADO	12.1	9.6	5.5	49.3	5,029,196	5,773,714	14.8	0.7	75,917	59,823	21,750	2,137,402	2.6	63.6	9.1	27.7
Adams	10.8	7.2	3.9	49.2	441,603	519,572	17.7	0.5	7,842	4,907	-500	167,290	3.0	69.7	12.6	22.8
Alamosa	10.6	9.0	5.7	50.2	15,445	16,376	6.0	1.0	226	158	102	6,240	2.4	61.6	9.7	29.9
Arapahoe	11.8	9.0	5.1	50.0	572,003	655,070	14.5	0.0	9,017	6,486	-2,848	241,889	2.7	65.3	10.5	27.2
Archuleta	18.0	18.8	8.5	49.9	12,084	13,359	10.6	3.2	128	142	452	5,736	2.3	68.5	4.0	25.0
Baca	13.9	13.4	11.6	50.1	3,788	3,506	-7.4	0.2	53	77	33	1,728	2.0	60.8	6.6	35.2
Bent	12.1	11.0	8.2	35.5	6,499	5,650	-13.1	1.9	56	77	132	1,879	2.1	62.2	12.1	30.8

1. No spouse present.

STATE County	Persons in group quarters, 2021	Daytime Population, 2016–2020: Number	Daytime Population, 2016–2020: Employment/ residence ratio	Births, 2021: Total	Births, 2021: Rate[1]	Deaths, 2021: Number	Deaths, 2021: Rate[1]	Persons under 65 with no health insurance, 2019: Number	Persons under 65 with no health insurance, 2019: Percent	Medicare, 2021: Total beneficiaries	Medicare, 2021: Enrolled in Original Medicare	Medicare, 2021: Enrolled in Medicare Advantage	COVID-19 Deaths, 2020: Number	COVID-19 Deaths, 2020: Rate[1]
	32	33	34	35	36	37	38	39	40	41	42	43	44	45
CALIFORNIA	815,696	39,352,174	1.0	424,333	10.8	332,337	8.4	2,947,957	8.9	6,406,280	3,499,131	2,907,149	33,410	0.8
Alameda	36,392	1,638,062	1.0	17,349	10.4	12,705	7.6	72,422	5.1	247,693	135,017	112,676	689	0.4
Alpine	24	1,508	1.9	9	7.4	15	12.3	72	8.7	265	248	17	D	D
Amador	4,415	38,074	0.9	287	7.0	521	12.7	1,851	7.5	11,753	8,920	2,834	37	0.9
Butte	5,112	223,257	1.0	2,022	9.7	2,383	11.4	13,710	7.8	45,888	42,635	3,253	148	0.7
Calaveras	384	39,612	0.6	379	8.3	603	13.2	2,579	7.9	13,379	12,147	1,233	22	0.5
Colusa	230	21,218	1.0	264	12.1	150	6.9	2,195	12.2	3,792	3,529	263	17	0.8
Contra Costa	9,880	1,012,905	0.8	11,600	10.0	9,804	8.4	62,447	6.5	202,459	103,340	99,118	480	0.4
Del Norte	2,996	28,297	1.1	258	9.2	298	10.7	1,652	8.4	6,358	6,181	178	D	D
El Dorado	1,451	169,801	0.8	1,471	7.7	2,051	10.7	9,349	6.2	45,839	29,073	16,766	78	0.4
Fresno	17,384	992,126	1.0	13,817	13.7	8,865	8.8	82,348	9.7	145,804	93,653	52,151	1,017	1.0
Glenn	292	26,898	0.9	361	12.5	260	9.0	2,905	12.4	5,754	5,492	262	22	0.8
Humboldt	5,182	136,510	1.0	1,290	9.5	1,536	11.3	10,146	9.5	29,511	28,269	1,242	25	0.2
Imperial	8,296	177,918	1.0	2,289	12.7	1,567	8.7	14,070	9.6	32,249	24,264	7,985	537	3.0
Inyo	403	18,322	1.1	172	9.1	201	10.6	1,234	9.1	4,548	4,238	310	28	1.5
Kern	30,494	894,422	1.0	12,371	13.5	7,682	8.4	70,588	9.3	120,883	71,492	49,391	761	0.8
Kings	15,702	151,242	1.0	2,176	14.2	1,083	7.1	11,212	9.4	17,921	13,576	4,345	129	0.8
Lake	1,091	59,806	0.8	723	10.6	884	12.9	4,557	9.4	17,316	16,272	1,044	45	0.7
Lassen	7,605	31,855	1.2	292	8.9	242	7.3	914	5.0	5,239	5,085	154	17	0.5
Los Angeles	178,739	10,166,908	1.0	99,716	10.1	82,350	8.3	940,376	11.1	1,523,583	735,371	788,212	11,573	1.2
Madera	6,862	149,254	0.9	2,069	13.1	1,302	8.2	13,807	11.0	24,911	15,639	9,272	184	1.2
Marin	8,396	258,858	1.0	2,034	7.8	2,305	8.8	10,406	5.3	59,640	34,800	24,841	132	0.5
Mariposa	688	17,680	1.1	129	7.5	197	11.5	1,190	9.9	4,947	4,536	411	D	D
Mendocino	1,976	88,170	1.0	869	9.5	1,037	11.4	6,908	10.6	23,347	21,226	2,121	38	0.4
Merced	6,763	256,593	0.8	3,737	13.2	2,224	7.8	26,939	11.4	37,596	31,828	5,768	282	1.0
Modoc	282	8,617	0.9	50	5.8	114	13.2	709	11.5	2,568	2,496	72	D	D
Mono	244	14,462	1.0	111	8.4	49	3.7	1,258	10.6	2,017	1,902	115	D	D
Monterey	17,194	425,939	1.0	5,595	12.8	3,128	7.1	42,273	11.9	66,756	59,648	7,108	265	0.6
Napa	4,960	148,717	1.2	1,214	8.9	1,399	10.2	9,391	8.7	29,865	17,885	11,980	47	0.3
Nevada	1,129	95,206	0.9	783	7.6	1,135	11.0	4,976	7.0	29,958	24,696	5,263	70	0.7
Orange	42,899	3,269,032	1.1	32,347	10.2	25,108	7.9	235,378	8.8	519,799	249,496	270,303	2,647	0.8
Placer	3,718	397,939	1.0	3,510	8.6	3,915	9.6	15,593	4.9	87,193	43,225	43,968	187	0.5
Plumas	275	19,031	1.0	155	7.8	248	12.5	886	6.7	6,361	6,010	352	D	D
Riverside	32,333	2,262,569	0.8	27,110	11.1	22,167	9.1	203,605	9.8	388,660	160,703	227,957	2,849	1.2
Sacramento	23,065	1,526,897	1.0	18,263	11.5	14,293	9.0	89,530	6.8	264,354	126,787	137,566	1,052	0.7
San Benito	326	50,234	0.6	766	11.7	397	6.1	4,869	9.0	9,249	7,859	1,390	35	0.5
San Bernardino	37,626	2,098,980	0.9	27,178	12.4	18,941	8.7	184,915	9.9	306,339	118,403	187,936	2,884	1.3
San Diego	107,528	3,361,529	1.0	37,107	11.3	26,463	8.0	247,271	8.9	544,476	274,208	270,268	1,883	0.6
San Francisco	25,395	1,109,742	1.5	7,944	9.4	7,135	8.5	37,808	5.2	149,174	85,542	63,632	263	0.3
San Joaquin	15,767	715,967	0.9	9,682	12.3	7,059	9.0	53,036	8.2	114,638	64,537	50,101	855	1.1
San Luis Obispo	16,055	283,153	1.0	2,357	8.3	2,671	9.4	14,763	7.0	65,649	53,715	11,934	122	0.4
San Mateo	8,867	777,280	1.0	7,828	10.4	5,754	7.7	37,100	5.8	128,316	68,619	59,697	268	0.4
Santa Barbara	19,813	456,042	1.1	5,303	11.9	3,632	8.1	43,058	12.0	78,006	64,839	13,167	188	0.4
Santa Clara	30,151	2,062,673	1.1	19,843	10.4	13,008	6.8	91,263	5.5	273,330	148,270	125,060	886	0.5
Santa Cruz	13,456	261,860	0.9	2,258	8.4	2,226	8.3	17,026	7.9	52,198	43,837	8,362	129	0.5
Shasta	2,851	179,516	1.0	1,826	10.0	2,480	13.6	11,387	8.1	47,823	44,986	2,838	112	0.6
Sierra	33	2,554	0.7	15	4.6	40	12.3	144	7.1	906	869	37	D	D
Siskiyou	563	43,911	1.0	370	8.4	617	14.0	2,910	9.3	13,715	13,326	389	17	0.4
Solano	11,840	393,918	0.8	4,957	11.0	4,157	9.2	21,935	6.0	81,509	43,610	37,899	198	0.4
Sonoma	10,061	481,971	0.9	4,290	8.8	4,933	10.1	30,207	7.8	108,116	56,246	51,870	221	0.5
Stanislaus	6,164	520,724	0.9	7,180	13.0	5,094	9.2	39,386	8.4	88,425	45,388	43,037	685	1.2
Sutter	692	90,287	0.9	1,218	12.3	964	9.7	7,213	8.9	17,814	16,607	1,207	66	0.7
Tehama	750	61,443	0.9	751	11.5	768	11.7	4,448	8.7	15,149	14,191	958	50	0.8
Trinity	420	12,893	1.1	95	5.9	178	11.1	867	10.1	3,550	3,438	111	D	D
Tulare	4,746	454,584	1.0	6,584	13.8	3,890	8.2	38,062	9.5	64,059	48,976	15,083	533	1.1
Tuolumne	3,965	54,295	1.0	424	7.6	694	12.5	2,498	6.8	16,030	14,871	1,159	41	0.7
Ventura	10,900	804,318	0.9	8,380	10.0	7,178	8.5	72,745	10.4	153,894	97,896	55,998	437	0.5
Yolo	9,714	235,570	1.2	2,004	9.3	1,563	7.2	12,146	6.7	32,665	17,797	14,868	127	0.6
Yuba	1,157	71,025	0.8	1,151	13.9	674	8.2	5,424	8.1	13,032	11,412	1,620	32	0.4
COLORADO	112,718	5,677,174	1.0	60,675	10.5	47,988	8.3	453,100	9.4	938,457	527,427	411,031	4,841	0.8
Adams	3,711	454,372	0.8	6,252	12.0	3,902	7.5	56,098	12.3	63,404	27,326	36,078	502	1.0
Alamosa	824	17,417	1.2	184	11.2	123	7.5	1,686	13.1	3,027	2,157	870	23	1.4
Arapahoe	4,621	637,636	1.0	7,173	11.0	5,228	8.0	54,044	9.6	95,381	48,022	47,359	568	0.9
Archuleta	60	13,335	1.0	98	7.2	116	8.5	1,386	13.8	4,103	3,278	825	D	D
Baca	63	3,527	1.0	38	10.9	56	16.0	413	15.8	961	905	56	D	D
Bent	1,537	5,528	0.9	44	7.7	58	10.2	315	10.9	1,109	1,034	75	12	2.1

1. Per 1,000 estimated resident population.

STATE County	COVID-19 Vaccinations, 2021–2022		Education						Money income, 2016–2020				Income and poverty, 2020			
			School enrollment and attainment, 2016–2020				Local government expenditures,[3] 2018–2019			Households				Percent below poverty level		
			Enrollment[1]		Attainment[2] (percent)						Percent					
	Number	Percent[5]	Total	Percent private	High school graduate or less	Bachelor's degree or more	Total current spending (mil dol)	Current spending per student (dollars)	Per capita income[4]	Median income (dollars)	with income of less than $50,000	with income of $200,000 or more	Median household income (dollars)	All persons	Children under 18 years	Children 5 to 17 years in families
	46	47	48	49	50	51	52	53	54	55	56	57	58	59	60	61
CALIFORNIA	28,448,691	72.0	10,331,447	14.3	36.4	34.7	85,470.1	13,816	38,576	78,672	32.6	13.3	83,001	11.5	14.6	14.2
Alameda	1,371,881	82.1	411,713	15.6	28.2	48.7	3,105.9	13,630	49,883	104,888	24.7	21.7	113,518	8.6	9.1	8.9
Alpine	NA	NA	225	7.6	33.4	38.4	4.5	57,139	37,690	85,750	28.2	7.3	64,542	14.3	24.5	20.0
Amador	21,173	53.3	7,016	11.3	38.8	18.1	52.5	12,626	33,897	65,187	38.5	6.6	68,141	10.3	13.0	12.6
Butte	117,690	53.7	62,563	8.4	32.9	28.3	465.0	14,600	30,700	54,972	46.3	6.3	54,718	17.3	18.7	19.0
Calaveras	24,985	54.4	8,017	13.4	39.3	19.8	80.6	15,107	33,027	67,054	37.5	6.0	66,329	11.6	16.1	15.5
Colusa	13,093	60.8	5,657	3.4	55.7	14.9	68.5	14,323	27,614	59,427	43.9	4.8	59,422	10.3	12.9	12.4
Contra Costa	943,140	81.8	293,319	16.1	27.3	43.3	2,323.7	13,145	50,118	103,997	23.1	20.5	106,484	7.2	7.9	7.2
Del Norte	12,072	43.4	5,989	13.6	52.0	15.4	60.2	14,113	24,361	49,981	50.0	3.6	47,442	18.5	23.4	21.8
El Dorado	120,724	62.6	41,645	12.2	27.0	35.2	378.6	12,622	44,651	83,710	30.3	14.1	87,792	8.4	8.8	7.6
Fresno	611,756	61.2	296,119	7.9	45.3	22.0	2,865.1	14,128	25,757	57,109	44.6	5.7	61,401	17.1	23.1	21.7
Glenn	15,743	55.4	7,024	12.9	53.0	14.4	77.7	14,054	23,715	51,682	48.5	2.9	57,779	12.4	17.2	16.1
Humboldt	89,394	65.9	33,944	9.0	32.4	30.9	270.4	14,777	29,584	49,235	50.6	4.5	56,071	15.8	18.8	17.2
Imperial	168,393	92.9	55,676	4.4	55.3	15.4	583.1	15,466	18,064	46,222	53.4	2.9	47,599	18.1	24.9	24.3
Inyo	NA	NA	3,762	10.0	40.4	26.4	47.5	17,842	33,404	59,296	42.8	3.3	55,981	10.9	14.6	13.8
Kern	483,522	53.7	261,742	9.4	52.2	17.1	2,657.0	13,842	23,855	54,851	45.9	4.7	58,583	18.3	24.6	25.1
Kings	77,143	50.4	44,433	13.6	52.3	15.0	393.3	14,786	22,919	61,556	40.9	4.1	60,319	14.5	17.8	16.3
Lake	38,202	59.3	13,425	9.4	43.9	16.7	133.9	13,941	29,714	49,254	51.0	4.8	52,345	15.9	22.2	22.3
Lassen	11,537	37.7	4,911	13.0	51.4	12.7	53.9	14,042	20,928	56,971	43.5	2.3	63,803	15.5	15.7	15.0
Los Angeles	7,241,868	72.1	2,585,754	15.7	40.6	33.5	20,846.7	14,288	35,685	71,358	36.2	11.1	75,624	13.2	17.2	16.9
Madera	85,031	54.0	44,234	9.1	51.4	15.2	431.6	13,520	23,212	61,924	41.6	4.2	68,744	14.1	18.8	17.9
Marin	229,428	88.6	59,123	23.3	16.6	60.2	559.4	16,728	74,446	121,671	21.3	29.8	127,601	6.0	5.8	4.9
Mariposa	NA	NA	2,877	10.3	31.7	26.9	28.1	14,946	29,882	50,960	48.6	2.9	56,887	13.3	18.5	18.1
Mendocino	58,671	67.6	19,798	9.7	39.6	24.0	210.7	16,134	30,351	52,915	47.0	4.9	53,176	14.3	18.9	17.9
Merced	140,190	50.5	87,116	5.1	55.7	14.1	817.6	13,820	23,677	56,330	44.8	4.7	58,998	16.3	22.8	22.1
Modoc	NA	NA	1,565	16.7	47.1	18.2	22.4	15,339	25,578	51,250	48.6	0.7	46,838	17.9	28.1	26.6
Mono	NA	NA	2,913	1.5	33.8	32.1	35.8	18,710	37,103	64,924	29.6	5.8	73,204	9.0	9.6	9.0
Monterey	315,215	72.6	122,217	9.4	47.1	26.2	1,094.4	14,275	32,122	76,943	31.3	11.1	85,031	11.6	15.0	14.6
Napa	107,323	77.9	32,863	18.6	32.0	37.2	308.9	15,282	46,912	92,219	26.8	16.4	92,149	7.9	8.7	8.2
Nevada	63,654	63.8	18,051	13.2	23.7	37.6	225.7	14,869	41,079	68,333	36.9	9.8	74,158	9.2	11.0	10.7
Orange	2,278,333	71.7	844,632	15.8	31.2	41.2	6,147.0	12,838	43,049	94,441	26.0	16.7	98,786	9.0	10.3	9.6
Placer	269,241	67.6	94,536	12.9	22.5	40.8	833.9	11,885	46,023	93,677	26.2	15.4	100,662	6.5	6.2	6.2
Plumas	NA	NA	3,581	12.1	29.4	24.5	35.9	16,406	34,334	57,233	44.6	4.3	58,489	13.5	18.3	17.2
Riverside	1,457,394	59.0	671,057	11.9	43.9	23.2	5,655.6	13,234	29,913	70,732	35.7	8.4	76,409	11.2	14.5	13.9
Sacramento	1,050,012	67.7	400,583	11.3	34.2	31.4	3,238.1	13,254	34,078	70,684	35.2	8.2	72,953	12.5	16.8	16.4
San Benito	42,002	66.9	17,179	9.8	43.9	20.1	148.2	12,991	33,841	85,808	25.6	11.2	91,185	7.9	9.3	9.2
San Bernardino	1,262,628	57.9	618,051	11.5	45.7	21.4	5,530.5	13,677	26,402	65,761	37.7	6.3	65,984	14.3	19.7	18.6
San Diego	2,535,920	76.0	860,261	14.5	30.2	39.5	6,777.1	13,075	39,737	82,426	30.1	12.9	87,126	9.5	11.0	10.5
San Francisco	735,989	83.5	158,832	32.8	23.0	58.8	1,106.2	18,196	72,041	119,136	25.4	29.0	121,722	10.0	9.4	9.7
San Joaquin	449,377	59.0	210,914	12.1	48.3	19.2	2,001.3	13,581	28,928	68,628	36.1	7.7	70,685	13.9	17.4	17.5
San Luis Obispo	171,661	60.6	76,579	8.1	28.1	36.1	450.9	13,062	38,686	77,948	31.9	10.2	79,455	10.6	9.2	8.8
San Mateo	642,110	83.8	180,734	24.3	24.5	52.1	1,478.3	15,616	64,450	128,091	18.7	30.1	132,369	5.5	5.6	5.3
Santa Barbara	317,213	71.0	135,871	9.6	35.1	35.0	972.7	14,031	38,141	78,925	31.5	13.2	86,136	10.5	12.6	12.1
Santa Clara	1,660,835	86.1	502,252	22.2	25.3	53.5	3,974.7	14,996	59,297	130,890	19.2	30.3	139,462	6.6	6.5	6.5
Santa Cruz	214,469	78.5	80,697	13.1	27.3	41.8	587.0	14,372	44,278	89,986	28.5	16.8	93,015	10.7	10.6	10.2
Shasta	89,879	49.9	40,910	15.1	34.5	22.1	370.2	13,422	31,049	57,139	44.5	5.2	59,108	13.9	18.3	16.1
Sierra	NA	NA	487	9.4	34.3	19.4	8.6	21,167	32,533	52,103	45.8	2.1	59,422	11.5	13.5	13.3
Siskiyou	23,451	53.9	9,234	8.4	35.8	22.1	103.1	16,156	29,381	47,403	52.6	2.3	49,441	14.3	20.2	19.2
Solano	304,662	68.1	106,977	13.7	34.9	27.1	804.6	12,360	36,685	84,638	27.3	10.2	83,678	9.3	10.8	10.1
Sonoma	386,094	78.1	114,484	12.0	29.1	36.4	976.4	13,970	44,071	86,173	27.9	12.3	87,366	7.8	8.6	7.5
Stanislaus	298,297	54.2	152,621	8.5	50.1	17.7	1,497.5	13,627	27,225	62,873	39.7	5.8	64,501	13.0	17.1	16.3
Sutter	59,347	61.2	26,320	7.3	43.2	20.0	306.1	12,982	29,495	63,502	39.1	6.5	65,791	11.5	16.2	15.8
Tehama	27,866	42.8	15,758	8.5	42.7	17.4	156.3	14,325	29,012	48,895	51.2	4.2	61,571	13.3	17.2	17.1
Trinity	NA	NA	2,014	7.4	43.4	19.2	29.6	19,709	26,228	41,780	59.6	1.3	45,113	18.0	26.4	25.0
Tulare	252,584	54.2	140,503	7.6	54.6	14.5	1,480.1	14,241	22,092	52,534	47.4	4.1	62,058	17.1	23.0	22.2
Tuolumne	30,759	56.5	10,218	18.3	34.7	22.3	88.0	16,066	35,694	60,509	41.3	6.1	63,336	12.1	13.4	12.6
Ventura	609,775	72.1	219,446	14.0	33.8	33.9	1,912.3	12,832	39,403	89,295	27.0	14.1	90,961	9.1	11.7	11.8
Yolo	154,825	70.2	81,174	7.8	30.2	42.6	402.1	13,177	36,036	73,746	34.7	11.2	80,668	14.8	11.3	10.0
Yuba	43,112	54.8	21,851	10.7	41.6	18.0	194.7	13,193	25,774	59,424	43.4	3.1	56,278	16.3	19.2	18.4
COLORADO	4,042,299	70.2	1,388,732	13.0	29.1	41.6	9,982.4	10,988	39,545	75,231	32.5	9.6	77,688	9.0	10.6	9.8
Adams	353,216	68.3	131,326	9.9	44.3	25.2	880.3	10,300	31,310	73,817	31.5	6.0	73,615	9.4	12.1	11.0
Alamosa	9,166	56.5	4,996	6.3	41.0	24.5	30.1	11,387	23,020	41,121	60.4	2.7	50,390	16.7	20.9	19.6
Arapahoe	448,225	68.3	160,809	14.0	28.1	43.4	1,376.7	11,633	42,184	80,291	28.9	10.9	82,381	7.0	8.4	7.5
Archuleta	8,056	57.4	2,127	19.0	27.1	39.7	17.0	9,964	32,995	55,658	43.4	5.8	63,961	9.4	16.2	16.5
Baca	1,407	39.3	727	2.1	44.0	21.9	9.6	15,049	24,583	34,655	66.1	2.1	42,531	16.9	24.0	21.9
Bent	1,498	26.9	856	17.6	61.0	15.1	22.0	8,559	15,738	38,083	62.9	0.4	50,688	26.6	27.2	27.7

1. All persons 3 years old and over enrolled in nursery school through college. 2. Persons 25 years old and over. 3. Elementary and secondary education expenditures. 4. Based on population estimated by the American Community Survey, 2016–2020. 5. CDC percent based on 2019 population estimate.

STATE County	Personal income, 2020										Earnings, 2020		
			Per capita[1]			Supplements to wages and salaries, employer contributions (mil dol)						Contributions for government social insurance (mil dol)	
	Total (mil dol)	Percent change 2019–2020	Dollars	Rank	Wages and salaries (mil dol)	Pension and insurance	Government social insurance	Proprietors' income (mil dol)	Dividends, interest, and rent (mil dol)	Personal transfer reecipts (mil dol)	Total (mil dol)	From employee and self-employed	From employer
	62	63	64	65	66	67	68	69	70	71	72	73	74
CALIFORNIA	2,763,312	8.6	69,958	X	1,372,402	207,263	88,184	244,613	498,511	552,257	1,912,462	109,523	88,184
Alameda	144,751	10.0	87,078	51	69,669	10,331	4,597	11,187	21,606	23,110	95,785	5,346	4,597
Alpine	85	-3.9	76,175	99	53	11	4	1	20	23	69	4	4
Amador	1,913	9.6	47,721	1,428	643	174	41	142	359	610	1,000	67	41
Butte	10,697	8.3	50,279	1,112	4,020	862	297	986	1,633	3,421	6,165	384	297
Calaveras	2,456	9.9	53,026	857	484	125	34	188	481	767	830	65	34
Colusa	1,237	29.0	57,382	546	447	98	37	263	215	303	844	37	37
Contra Costa	106,319	9.0	92,264	32	29,077	4,608	1,997	8,560	21,922	15,360	44,242	2,625	1,997
Del Norte	1,124	11.6	40,192	2,435	381	118	25	79	153	474	603	37	25
El Dorado	14,018	6.6	72,662	129	3,375	608	239	986	2,420	2,660	5,209	349	239
Fresno	48,539	13.1	48,495	1,324	20,364	4,388	1,542	5,018	5,955	14,865	31,312	1,746	1,542
Glenn	1,477	20.1	52,219	915	461	107	38	256	216	432	862	43	38
Humboldt	6,773	8.2	50,182	1,128	2,413	578	172	783	1,131	2,114	3,946	241	172
Imperial	8,022	19.5	44,500	1,875	2,973	831	229	980	699	2,984	5,014	258	229
Inyo	1,161	7.1	64,335	282	397	118	26	194	191	338	734	41	26
Kern	40,310	13.4	44,721	1,843	18,026	4,024	1,359	4,347	4,554	11,326	27,756	1,494	1,359
Kings	6,387	14.8	41,829	2,226	2,957	808	232	578	808	1,801	4,575	210	232
Lake	3,040	11.9	47,144	1,494	754	186	57	249	440	1,200	1,245	92	57
Lassen	1,215	11.3	40,490	2,393	541	194	35	62	176	392	832	43	35
Los Angeles	678,829	7.6	68,272	191	326,259	52,017	22,196	69,345	118,855	159,758	469,817	26,871	22,196
Madera	7,025	15.7	44,532	1,868	2,613	610	198	1,177	844	1,973	4,598	231	198
Marin	37,461	4.1	145,575	6	9,511	1,389	605	4,464	11,736	3,488	15,969	911	605
Mariposa	992	7.6	57,828	523	241	74	17	87	167	311	418	27	17
Mendocino	4,716	8.9	54,795	716	1,513	336	111	539	884	1,614	2,500	165	111
Merced	12,263	16.6	43,914	1,963	3,958	928	309	1,429	1,323	3,955	6,625	338	309
Modoc	462	15.0	52,779	870	122	39	9	83	65	166	252	14	9
Mono	793	11.2	54,586	734	323	76	23	127	189	161	549	29	23
Monterey	26,505	8.2	61,510	367	10,711	2,364	859	3,655	5,001	5,671	17,589	883	859
Napa	11,205	10.1	82,408	68	4,722	875	349	1,394	2,564	1,979	7,342	411	349
Nevada	6,462	6.9	64,876	267	1,715	348	123	617	1,478	1,595	2,802	193	123
Orange	236,303	6.5	74,618	109	117,750	17,050	8,298	23,029	50,081	38,574	166,127	9,672	8,298
Placer	29,125	8.0	72,279	134	11,495	1,728	822	2,012	5,128	5,082	16,057	1,011	822
Plumas	1,044	7.3	55,029	702	324	94	23	84	217	370	526	37	23
Riverside	114,090	11.8	45,834	1,678	40,278	7,849	2,959	7,360	15,860	30,575	58,447	3,662	2,959
Sacramento	90,909	10.0	58,307	505	48,384	10,217	3,193	6,561	12,394	23,410	68,354	3,695	3,193
San Benito	3,895	17.4	60,807	391	916	201	69	269	500	748	1,455	84	69
San Bernardino	98,144	11.2	44,831	1,818	44,719	8,551	3,363	6,749	10,684	27,810	63,382	3,801	3,363
San Diego	220,826	9.0	66,266	237	111,843	19,314	7,960	14,921	41,911	44,237	154,038	8,831	7,960
San Francisco	125,500	6.7	144,818	7	113,183	11,262	5,535	11,964	29,636	13,633	141,944	7,831	5,535
San Joaquin	39,793	15.9	51,816	948	14,617	2,823	1,109	3,096	4,484	11,403	21,644	1,263	1,109
San Luis Obispo	17,596	6.0	62,342	339	6,549	1,395	458	1,978	3,967	3,618	10,380	623	458
San Mateo	107,559	6.4	141,841	8	64,004	5,438	3,040	8,839	28,066	8,731	81,321	4,659	3,040
Santa Barbara	30,190	8.1	67,879	196	13,015	2,426	961	3,469	7,951	5,375	19,872	1,097	961
Santa Clara	235,835	7.0	123,661	10	180,418	14,842	8,379	16,435	43,769	22,056	220,074	12,595	8,379
Santa Cruz	20,503	8.9	75,957	103	6,311	1,197	448	2,042	4,039	3,645	9,998	575	448
Shasta	9,247	10.9	51,649	967	3,523	731	263	696	1,333	3,297	5,213	348	263
Sierra	143	6.7	49,139	1,240	26	10	2	11	34	42	48	4	2
Siskiyou	2,148	11.4	49,664	1,179	676	172	53	199	364	850	1,099	75	53
Solano	26,230	13.0	58,688	488	10,042	1,970	712	1,217	3,454	6,337	13,941	838	712
Sonoma	34,966	9.5	71,386	146	13,316	2,214	964	3,784	7,408	6,980	20,277	1,227	964
Stanislaus	26,929	12.9	48,954	1,263	10,635	2,038	807	2,355	3,265	7,650	15,835	922	807
Sutter	4,890	12.0	50,730	1,060	1,552	310	122	528	639	1,398	2,512	151	122
Tehama	2,967	11.6	46,007	1,653	966	205	78	237	500	980	1,486	101	78
Trinity	536	8.7	43,877	1,966	129	38	9	43	115	228	220	17	9
Tulare	21,723	16.5	46,348	1,600	7,677	1,806	596	2,796	2,339	6,790	12,875	651	596
Tuolumne	2,710	8.1	49,708	1,173	866	209	59	172	533	939	1,306	95	59
Ventura	56,728	6.3	67,422	204	21,609	3,693	1,550	4,767	10,925	10,794	31,618	1,856	1,550
Yolo	12,830	7.2	58,391	503	7,418	1,853	483	1,018	2,439	2,505	10,772	532	483
Yuba	3,717	14.4	46,373	1,593	1,440	405	109	202	391	1,346	2,155	115	109
COLORADO	370,392	5.7	64,034	X	187,128	24,092	12,977	36,013	75,070	61,654	260,210	14,944	12,977
Adams	25,014	7.5	48,115	1,368	14,265	1,978	984	1,953	3,008	5,002	19,180	1,022	984
Alamosa	695	11.8	42,974	2,067	371	65	27	65	95	216	528	28	27
Arapahoe	43,846	4.9	66,691	223	26,000	2,850	1,778	3,771	9,156	6,859	34,399	2,002	1,778
Archuleta	657	9.1	46,287	1,609	185	29	13	83	181	199	311	22	13
Baca	189	33.8	53,223	840	49	11	3	45	28	58	109	4	3
Bent	180	10.3	33,591	2,999	50	10	4	22	37	65	86	5	4

1. Based on the resident population estimated as of July 1 of the year shown.

STATE County	Earnings, 2020 (cont.) Percent by selected industries: Farm	Mining, quarrying, and extractions	Construction	Manu-facturing	Information; professional, scientific, technical services	Retail trade	Finance, insurance, real estate, and leasing	Health care and social assistance	Govern-ment	Social Security beneficiaries, December 2020: Number	Rate[1]	Supple-mental Security Income recipients, 2020	Housing units, 2021: Total	Percent change, 2010–2021
	75	76	77	78	79	80	81	82	83	84	85	86	87	88
CALIFORNIA	1.1	0.2	5.5	9.0	20.6	5.0	9.2	9.6	15.7	6,150,009	157	1,192,888	14,512,281	0.7
Alameda	0.1	0.0	7.1	12.8	20.4	4.7	5.9	10.4	15.4	223,525	136	46,979	629,118	0.9
Alpine	0.0	0.0	D	D	D	0.7	D	1.1	40.1	255	206	31	1,549	0.5
Amador	0.7	1.7	7.1	3.9	4.9	7.8	4.0	D	42.8	12,030	292	677	18,875	0.3
Butte	4.1	0.1	7.6	4.9	5.3	9.3	6.2	19.6	21.5	46,535	223	9,420	90,314	0.0
Calaveras	0.1	D	14.8	2.1	D	8.6	5.5	8.7	30.8	13,715	297	989	27,522	0.3
Colusa	27.2	0.1	2.5	13.1	1.1	4.8	5.5	D	18.3	3,955	180	544	8,136	0.3
Contra Costa	0.1	0.3	8.2	5.5	16.7	5.2	13.1	13.9	12.0	192,255	166	24,365	426,356	0.6
Del Norte	3.3	0.0	3.8	1.5	2.7	7.8	2.4	16.8	48.7	6,725	239	1,832	11,146	0.4
El Dorado	0.0	0.1	14.9	4.0	D	7.0	13.0	11.8	18.6	46,235	239	2,842	94,179	0.6
Fresno	6.6	0.2	6.4	6.0	5.4	6.4	5.8	14.6	21.5	145,435	143	42,645	341,686	0.7
Glenn	25.7	0.4	4.8	7.5	3.4	5.0	2.9	D	20.7	6,105	212	1,064	10,944	0.4
Humboldt	2.5	D	8.6	3.8	6.0	9.7	5.6	13.9	28.1	29,490	216	5,533	62,446	0.5
Imperial	13.8	D	2.7	2.7	2.4	7.1	2.5	7.3	37.0	34,750	193	9,816	57,106	0.7
Inyo	0.9	D	4.7	15.6	3.8	6.4	2.1	D	41.3	4,675	246	385	9,497	0.3
Kern	8.4	4.8	5.8	4.0	4.6	6.5	3.5	9.8	24.9	128,525	140	33,197	303,888	0.8
Kings	13.1	D	2.0	7.5	1.7	4.3	1.8	8.2	45.5	19,365	126	4,610	46,758	0.8
Lake	3.5	0.4	9.2	2.2	4.3	9.4	3.7	19.7	24.6	18,300	266	3,533	34,274	0.1
Lassen	4.6	0.0	D	D	D	4.8	1.7	D	68.9	5,560	168	924	12,225	0.1
Los Angeles	0.0	0.1	4.0	7.0	20.3	5.0	10.5	10.5	14.9	1,409,040	143	378,264	3,620,308	0.6
Madera	17.8	D	4.4	5.9	2.3	5.0	2.9	15.2	21.0	26,480	166	4,464	49,982	0.7
Marin	0.3	D	7.6	7.3	19.3	6.4	14.1	10.2	11.5	53,815	207	3,014	111,744	0.1
Mariposa	3.1	D	7.3	1.7	5.2	8.0	D	5.0	46.5	5,090	297	448	9,826	0.6
Mendocino	2.7	0.1	8.9	7.1	4.5	11.0	4.5	13.6	21.4	22,475	246	3,234	41,552	0.3
Merced	17.2	D	4.1	10.3	1.8	6.1	4.0	9.5	24.4	39,985	140	10,561	89,320	1.5
Modoc	27.8	0.0	4.5	0.5	D	4.8	2.8	D	35.9	2,650	306	435	4,760	0.1
Mono	2.0	D	9.2	1.5	D	5.6	6.5	6.8	32.5	1,640	124	88	13,613	0.1
Monterey	11.5	0.3	4.3	2.3	5.1	5.3	5.7	7.9	24.7	66,445	152	7,849	144,403	0.4
Napa	3.4	D	7.6	20.5	6.6	5.0	6.0	9.8	15.7	28,025	206	2,026	55,318	-0.3
Nevada	0.1	0.1	14.9	3.9	9.9	9.0	5.5	12.4	22.0	29,330	283	1,846	53,932	0.5
Orange	0.1	0.0	7.5	10.4	15.2	5.3	14.7	9.1	10.4	479,160	151	71,953	1,138,966	0.6
Placer	0.1	D	12.6	3.3	D	8.0	13.4	17.5	12.1	85,080	206	5,894	174,942	1.2
Plumas	0.2	D	9.3	8.1	3.9	7.3	3.9	5.5	37.9	6,225	313	583	15,437	0.2
Riverside	1.0	0.3	10.9	5.9	5.3	8.2	4.9	11.9	22.4	402,475	164	61,968	858,713	1.0
Sacramento	0.3	D	7.1	3.1	D	4.9	7.7	12.5	33.4	256,575	161	63,170	593,279	0.8
San Benito	5.7	D	11.6	16.6	D	5.5	5.9	4.5	21.9	9,490	142	904	20,960	2.3
San Bernardino	0.3	0.1	7.4	6.8	4.7	7.1	4.7	12.9	21.7	314,725	143	70,204	735,979	0.5
San Diego	0.4	0.0	5.6	9.2	19.5	4.9	8.1	9.0	22.4	525,345	160	79,491	1,237,638	0.6
San Francisco	0.0	D	2.8	1.4	38.9	2.9	16.0	4.5	11.3	127,610	157	39,034	412,268	1.1
San Joaquin	4.5	0.1	6.8	7.6	3.2	6.5	5.2	11.2	20.0	116,600	148	26,768	255,171	1.2
San Luis Obispo	2.5	0.1	10.8	6.1	9.7	8.4	6.7	10.6	20.7	63,625	225	4,182	124,740	0.7
San Mateo	0.1	0.0	3.8	7.5	47.0	2.8	12.3	5.5	5.1	116,940	158	9,219	285,615	0.5
Santa Barbara	4.9	0.8	5.1	6.7	13.2	5.4	8.6	10.8	19.5	75,965	170	8,176	159,798	0.8
Santa Clara	0.1	0.0	3.1	23.0	38.6	2.6	5.5	5.8	5.6	241,015	128	42,149	693,240	0.6
Santa Cruz	4.2	0.0	7.2	6.4	10.6	6.9	8.0	13.1	20.2	50,150	187	5,308	106,543	0.1
Shasta	0.9	0.3	8.2	3.7	6.1	10.1	6.3	19.3	22.1	49,110	270	8,928	79,711	0.4
Sierra	2.5	D	10.0	D	D	2.4	D	D	56.3	895	273	70	2,130	0.1
Siskiyou	9.3	D	5.3	5.9	4.2	7.8	2.8	13.2	31.2	13,975	317	2,524	22,907	-0.1
Solano	0.8	0.3	10.7	13.2	4.0	6.3	4.3	16.9	24.5	82,590	183	11,137	163,356	0.5
Sonoma	1.5	0.1	11.0	13.0	9.7	6.8	7.5	13.6	13.3	103,190	212	8,094	205,903	0.4
Stanislaus	7.0	0.0	6.4	11.6	4.0	7.4	4.9	17.7	17.6	91,355	165	19,915	183,898	0.3
Sutter	8.5	0.3	6.9	4.5	3.7	9.9	5.9	12.8	16.5	18,175	183	3,822	34,639	0.3
Tehama	8.6	D	9.6	8.4	2.2	7.9	2.8	12.3	21.6	15,770	241	2,971	27,429	0.3
Trinity	4.2	D	7.1	7.5	5.3	7.7	1.9	9.8	41.0	3,725	232	608	8,137	-0.6
Tulare	16.1	0.0	5.2	7.7	2.7	5.9	3.7	7.6	22.8	68,015	143	18,525	152,700	1.1
Tuolumne	-1.3	0.6	8.1	5.3	D	9.3	4.6	14.7	34.0	16,495	296	1,554	31,487	0.2
Ventura	3.8	0.6	6.1	8.5	11.2	6.7	9.0	9.7	17.2	148,010	176	15,555	294,681	0.4
Yolo	2.1	0.1	5.6	5.4	5.9	4.2	4.0	6.7	42.3	31,385	145	4,877	81,259	1.1
Yuba	3.5	D	6.1	3.1	2.7	3.2	1.3	D	52.7	13,930	167	3,690	29,978	1.4
COLORADO	0.7	4.4	8.0	5.8	17.0	5.2	9.4	8.9	15.5	915,854	158	71,971	2,540,822	1.6
Adams	0.3	0.6	14.3	6.4	6.3	5.2	4.2	7.4	24.2	64,085	123	6,887	191,383	2.2
Alamosa	8.2	D	5.7	1.5	3.3	9.1	8.3	21.1	23.1	3,120	189	632	7,139	0.9
Arapahoe	0.0	2.0	8.2	2.1	23.9	5.2	13.6	10.6	9.6	91,365	140	7,736	265,888	1.0
Archuleta	1.0	0.3	17.0	1.6	7.7	11.3	6.9	7.4	21.3	4,120	299	108	9,693	1.6
Baca	39.2	D	3.2	0.6	D	4.2	D	0.9	31.0	945	269	70	1,976	0.2
Bent	26.0	D	D	D	0.5	3.9	D	3.1	28.1	1,095	190	247	2,143	0.3

1. Per 1,000 resident population estimated as of July 1 of the year shown.

Table B. States and Counties — **Housing, Labor Force, and Employment**

STATE County	Housing units, 2016–2020								Civilian labor force, 2021				Civilian employment6, 2016–2020		
	Occupied units										Unemployment			Percent	
		Owner-occupied				Renter-occupied									
				Median owner cost as a percent of income											
	Total	Percent	Median value[1]	With a mort- gage	Without a mort- gage[2]	Median rent[3]	Median rent as a percent of income[2]	Sub- standard units[4] (percent)	Total	Percent change, 2020–2021	Total	Rate[5]	Total	Management, business, science, and arts	Construction, production, and maintenance occupations
	89	90	91	92	93	94	95	96	97	98	99	100	101	102	103
CALIFORNIA	13,103,114	55.3	538,500	25.0	10.9	1,586	32.2	8.6	18,923,194	0.0	1,381,250	7.3	18,646,894	40.3	20.6
Alameda	573,174	53.6	825,300	23.7	10.0	1,904	29.3	8.2	809,964	-0.8	49,105	6.1	867,923	51.4	15.7
Alpine	397	80.9	372,500	22.3	10.0	639	25.0	3.8	519	1.2	42	8.1	406	48.3	24.6
Amador	14,844	76.8	329,300	24.6	13.4	1,057	28.3	2.8	14,342	-0.8	997	7.0	14,280	33.6	21.9
Butte	83,879	59.5	304,700	23.2	12.7	1,087	34.3	3.9	92,031	-1.1	6,311	6.9	96,056	38.0	20.2
Calaveras	16,958	79.6	340,000	29.2	14.0	1,354	35.6	2.0	21,402	0.4	1,225	5.7	17,264	32.4	20.8
Colusa	7,329	63.5	274,100	23.1	12.8	918	25.9	6.7	10,740	1.3	1,342	12.5	9,688	24.1	45.3
Contra Costa	398,299	66.8	655,500	24.4	10.7	1,928	31.4	5.4	542,352	-0.6	34,478	6.4	563,813	45.6	16.4
Del Norte	9,805	68.4	227,500	22.6	11.3	946	35.8	4.4	9,314	-1.1	708	7.6	9,161	33.2	19.2
El Dorado	73,078	75.5	479,800	24.7	13.0	1,320	30.8	2.7	91,142	0.5	5,232	5.7	85,899	42.3	16.8
Fresno	310,097	53.7	271,000	22.9	10.0	1,029	33.1	10.0	443,383	-0.4	40,741	9.2	408,625	31.2	28.3
Glenn	10,216	58.4	242,200	24.4	10.5	810	28.3	5.1	12,616	-0.9	876	6.9	11,840	24.8	41.4
Humboldt	54,120	56.8	331,300	25.7	11.2	1,002	36.5	4.6	58,714	-1.6	3,661	6.2	61,137	34.9	20.2
Imperial	45,768	58.1	206,700	24.1	11.6	847	32.1	10.2	69,075	-3.4	11,981	17.3	59,490	25.0	26.6
Inyo	7,954	65.0	258,200	24.2	11.6	938	23.8	2.3	8,229	-0.9	484	5.9	8,061	36.6	20.9
Kern	273,556	58.9	226,600	23.6	11.6	994	32.5	9.6	383,987	-0.5	38,555	10.0	346,787	28.2	33.9
Kings	43,604	53.6	227,400	21.8	10.0	1,030	27.8	8.5	55,930	-1.7	5,386	9.6	53,687	25.2	35.6
Lake	25,508	67.7	238,000	25.1	14.0	1,028	32.4	4.1	28,371	-0.1	2,160	7.6	23,924	26.8	26.6
Lassen	9,172	68.6	207,800	22.0	10.6	928	28.8	2.4	9,159	-2.5	544	5.9	8,256	30.6	25.2
Los Angeles	3,332,504	46.0	615,500	27.2	11.1	1,534	33.8	11.6	4,994,057	0.5	445,205	8.9	4,908,826	38.7	20.8
Madera	44,479	65.8	268,500	23.7	10.0	1,068	30.3	11.1	61,944	0.1	5,476	8.8	58,917	25.8	36.1
Marin	104,900	63.6	1,053,600	25.0	12.6	2,170	30.3	4.8	128,920	-1.1	5,748	4.5	130,038	56.7	10.1
Mariposa	7,846	70.4	290,200	27.9	11.8	1,010	36.6	3.5	7,014	-2.5	558	8.0	6,914	31.5	18.0
Mendocino	34,164	60.3	388,500	27.7	12.0	1,134	34.0	6.2	36,920	-0.5	2,298	6.2	37,369	31.7	22.5
Merced	81,306	52.2	268,800	23.2	11.0	1,054	29.3	8.9	115,158	-0.2	11,935	10.4	107,059	23.7	38.8
Modoc	3,594	76.6	153,600	19.2	11.6	757	26.0	3.2	3,187	0.4	225	7.1	3,166	36.6	24.1
Mono	5,196	68.0	385,500	29.1	16.3	1,248	25.0	9.7	8,340	5.9	569	6.8	8,051	38.9	16.7
Monterey	128,003	51.8	559,400	25.3	10.0	1,600	32.5	13.8	211,858	-0.9	17,548	8.3	188,734	30.4	31.2
Napa	48,484	64.8	666,900	24.6	10.6	1,775	31.4	6.3	68,437	-0.5	4,132	6.0	70,752	37.6	20.9
Nevada	40,917	74.8	446,100	26.9	13.7	1,315	34.2	2.0	47,089	0.8	2,630	5.6	44,843	42.1	16.8
Orange	1,040,001	57.2	703,800	25.3	10.0	1,928	33.0	9.0	1,553,897	-0.5	92,743	6.0	1,592,877	43.6	16.8
Placer	145,714	73.4	495,900	23.9	12.4	1,616	31.0	2.1	188,045	0.7	9,388	5.0	182,516	48.6	13.7
Plumas	8,332	72.9	259,300	22.4	12.2	944	28.6	2.5	7,382	-3.1	700	9.5	7,754	36.5	24.4
Riverside	736,413	67.5	368,100	25.8	12.3	1,447	34.3	7.3	1,129,562	1.1	82,839	7.3	1,050,497	31.2	25.8
Sacramento	547,519	57.4	373,000	23.5	10.2	1,333	32.3	5.5	714,032	0.6	49,679	7.0	715,240	40.0	18.8
San Benito	18,389	65.3	588,500	27.6	12.1	1,533	29.7	7.7	31,976	-1.6	2,318	7.2	29,575	30.7	30.8
San Bernardino	640,090	60.1	348,500	24.6	11.0	1,338	33.6	9.1	988,604	1.8	73,515	7.4	926,877	30.1	28.7
San Diego	1,130,703	53.9	595,600	25.7	10.7	1,732	33.3	7.1	1,543,678	0.1	99,863	6.5	1,589,275	43.4	16.9
San Francisco	362,141	38.0	1,152,300	24.5	10.1	2,010	24.0	8.4	545,953	-2.2	27,519	5.0	521,465	59.1	8.5
San Joaquin	231,092	57.7	367,900	23.9	10.9	1,286	31.9	8.3	334,250	0.0	28,972	8.7	319,808	29.5	31.8
San Luis Obispo	106,244	62.7	605,200	26.5	11.4	1,535	32.5	3.2	135,268	1.0	7,082	5.2	131,426	39.6	19.0
San Mateo	263,351	59.9	1,163,100	24.3	10.0	2,435	29.2	7.8	431,205	-1.5	19,721	4.6	413,687	51.2	13.7
Santa Barbara	148,309	52.3	610,300	24.9	10.5	1,697	32.8	10.6	217,988	-0.1	12,565	5.8	212,400	37.1	22.4
Santa Clara	635,314	56.4	1,061,900	23.8	10.0	2,386	27.9	8.3	1,013,614	-0.8	47,605	4.7	1,003,304	55.5	13.7
Santa Cruz	96,275	60.3	787,000	25.6	11.7	1,843	33.3	7.1	133,351	-0.9	9,185	6.9	137,107	44.2	19.1
Shasta	70,845	65.3	261,000	24.1	13.3	1,075	31.3	3.7	72,809	-0.4	4,975	6.8	73,991	35.1	21.2
Sierra	1,250	73.4	229,400	25.1	14.6	1,032	29.4	1.4	1,304	1.6	78	6.0	1,296	38.8	23.5
Siskiyou	19,195	65.9	214,300	24.0	12.1	878	31.3	3.7	16,561	-2.2	1,339	8.1	16,597	33.4	24.0
Solano	151,191	62.1	437,900	23.7	10.3	1,684	31.6	5.9	199,365	-1.1	14,860	7.5	209,436	33.7	24.2
Sonoma	188,958	61.3	640,000	25.8	11.6	1,743	32.3	5.5	242,752	-1.0	13,313	5.5	253,919	39.6	19.9
Stanislaus	174,826	58.7	314,100	23.8	11.5	1,210	31.2	7.4	239,538	-0.9	20,042	8.4	231,043	29.1	32.1
Sutter	32,586	59.1	306,000	23.0	10.4	1,095	29.7	6.6	45,214	-0.5	4,069	9.0	40,468	29.2	30.7
Tehama	24,661	66.0	231,500	24.2	12.5	972	33.3	5.3	25,443	-0.7	1,826	7.2	24,951	25.2	31.0
Trinity	5,896	68.5	285,700	28.3	11.0	813	35.3	5.5	4,475	-1.3	282	6.3	4,193	32.3	28.6
Tulare	139,044	57.1	223,600	24.4	10.0	974	31.3	10.4	200,896	-0.6	21,435	10.7	183,876	27.0	35.0
Tuolumne	22,937	73.6	314,300	26.2	14.7	1,025	33.8	3.1	20,042	-0.6	1,456	7.3	20,909	34.4	19.9
Ventura	271,639	63.3	609,200	25.8	10.2	1,854	34.2	6.5	404,923	-1.1	24,928	6.2	411,295	38.4	22.4
Yolo	74,614	51.3	456,800	22.5	10.0	1,369	31.2	6.3	106,122	1.4	6,196	5.8	100,638	45.4	20.1
Yuba	26,434	60.9	273,600	24.4	10.7	1,015	30.1	5.3	30,752	0.3	2,604	8.5	29,508	27.9	28.6
COLORADO	2,137,402	66.2	369,900	21.5	10.0	1,335	30.6	2.8	3,156,110	2.2	169,399	5.4	2,937,047	43.5	19.1
Adams	167,290	67.0	335,800	22.4	10.8	1,387	32.4	5.0	276,299	2.2	17,218	6.2	265,445	31.7	28.4
Alamosa	6,240	55.0	153,700	20.1	10.6	696	26.3	6.6	8,533	2.7	471	5.5	7,308	34.3	21.9
Arapahoe	241,889	64.2	385,100	21.6	10.0	1,452	31.3	3.1	367,171	2.0	21,222	5.8	349,502	42.9	18.5
Archuleta	5,736	74.1	331,900	27.5	10.0	997	30.9	3.7	7,300	3.7	357	4.9	6,292	36.9	24.5
Baca	1,728	71.3	98,800	24.8	12.1	432	21.2	2.6	2,118	1.7	45	2.1	1,595	42.0	28.2
Bent	1,879	60.3	82,500	15.8	14.2	668	31.3	3.0	1,886	6.4	115	6.1	1,606	35.5	27.7

1. Specified owner-occupied units. 2. A value of 10.0 represents 10 percent or less; a value of 50.0 represents 50 percent or more. 3. Specified renter-occupied units. 4. Overcrowded or lacking complete plumbing facilities. 5. Percent of civilian labor force. 6. Civilian employed persons 16 years old and over.

STATE County	Private nonfarm establishments, employment and payroll, 2020									Agriculture, 2017			
		Employment						Annual payroll		Farms			Farm producers whose primary occupation is farming (percent)
											Percent with:		
	Number of establish-ments	Total	Health care and social assistance	Manufac-turing	Retail trade	Finance and insurance	Professional, scientific, and technical services	Total (mil dol)	Average per employee (dollars)	Number	Fewer than 50 acres	1000 acres or more	
	104	105	106	107	108	109	110	111	112	113	114	115	116
CALIFORNIA	981,369	15,710,859	2,148,566	1,161,693	1,681,501	638,864	1,318,355	1,132,426	72,079	70,521	64.0	6.3	46.6
Alameda	41,258	719,830	103,185	84,755	70,961	22,299	78,166	57,973	80,537	446	62.6	8.1	35.8
Alpine	46	563	34	NA	19	NA	NA	9	16,829	6	33.3	16.7	40.0
Amador	813	8,351	1,478	740	1,536	172	217	331	39,670	482	54.6	6.2	44.5
Butte	4,646	64,614	15,377	4,437	10,822	2,555	2,561	2,712	41,972	1,912	65.2	2.9	51.3
Calaveras	914	6,621	999	416	1,239	104	335	250	37,821	699	59.7	6.3	35.9
Colusa	373	3,978	433	611	563	91	43	205	51,570	751	29.0	14.9	54.7
Contra Costa	24,822	346,128	61,664	15,773	44,566	22,816	26,603	24,913	71,977	459	75.6	6.1	46.7
Del Norte	397	4,162	1,333	162	915	76	104	154	36,965	90	58.9	4.4	41.6
El Dorado	4,694	49,830	7,260	2,384	6,637	3,075	2,725	2,574	51,661	1,390	83.4	1.3	39.6
Fresno	17,653	284,131	51,046	26,540	37,141	9,190	11,271	13,042	45,902	4,774	54.1	6.6	57.1
Glenn	476	5,347	588	857	902	120	102	289	54,112	1,173	48.3	8.5	53.9
Humboldt	3,192	35,482	7,213	2,194	6,615	1,168	1,881	1,447	40,785	849	46.6	14.6	52.4
Imperial	2,558	32,636	6,308	1,960	8,210	732	859	1,219	37,342	396	24.7	35.1	73.7
Inyo	486	5,141	1,266	206	883	63	153	214	41,652	85	41.2	25.9	37.9
Kern	13,447	203,389	32,910	13,226	30,855	5,091	9,040	9,684	47,611	1,731	40.3	17.6	51.1
Kings	1,707	25,988	5,028	4,457	4,137	502	945	1,095	42,129	963	48.9	9.2	54.1
Lake	1,082	9,897	2,477	378	2,073	195	232	424	42,864	636	69.3	2.8	41.4
Lassen	407	3,680	912	56	798	85	320	149	40,362	377	37.9	17.0	47.7
Los Angeles	291,833	3,914,718	599,257	311,883	415,552	157,889	311,161	244,345	62,417	1,035	89.9	1.0	46.1
Madera	2,095	27,969	6,743	3,848	3,705	444	499	1,374	49,127	1,386	41.6	8.7	52.7
Marin	10,025	103,990	17,020	2,716	14,778	3,662	8,840	7,789	74,903	343	44.9	14.0	42.6
Mariposa	311	2,551	482	90	280	22	91	86	33,822	299	34.8	23.1	46.1
Mendocino	2,432	23,335	4,310	2,336	4,365	441	659	968	41,463	1,128	44.6	11.1	43.2
Merced	3,273	47,847	7,532	9,719	8,345	1,182	828	2,005	41,913	2,337	53.5	7.4	56.3
Modoc	152	1,123	412	15	172	29	37	53	46,752	423	25.1	27.9	55.4
Mono	634	6,734	600	105	662	28	90	229	34,011	65	55.4	23.1	41.7
Monterey	8,883	118,088	17,256	8,484	17,589	2,492	8,218	5,667	47,986	1,104	45.6	20.2	44.3
Napa	4,350	64,556	10,000	11,961	6,663	1,404	2,026	3,515	54,456	1,866	74.9	2.8	32.2
Nevada	3,148	28,120	4,540	1,402	4,287	931	1,526	1,287	45,758	673	81.4	0.9	44.8
Orange	101,681	1,551,280	183,483	143,595	149,379	92,755	136,474	97,481	62,839	193	83.4	1.6	42.6
Placer	11,385	162,738	24,461	4,923	23,508	10,144	10,357	9,340	57,396	1,237	85.0	1.1	36.8
Plumas	610	4,020	941	529	593	124	176	193	48,093	162	45.1	16.0	44.1
Riverside	41,795	622,141	89,209	47,763	95,395	11,517	21,933	26,598	42,752	2,667	87.1	2.1	40.9
Sacramento	31,369	512,205	91,207	22,349	62,381	29,745	41,728	30,652	59,843	1,161	66.8	5.9	48.5
San Benito	1,034	13,019	1,671	3,278	1,381	238	270	624	47,905	610	60.0	10.8	45.5
San Bernardino	38,018	641,517	103,759	53,646	95,771	16,121	18,190	30,426	47,428	1,062	84.4	1.5	41.8
San Diego	88,654	1,333,731	192,379	103,352	147,339	58,951	164,689	84,083	63,043	5,082	90.8	0.8	36.2
San Francisco	34,692	720,508	74,186	7,735	49,806	64,272	134,173	91,390	126,841	10	100.0	NA	27.3
San Joaquin	12,226	200,637	30,473	18,605	27,547	6,178	5,451	9,644	48,066	3,430	62.1	5.4	55.0
San Luis Obispo	8,600	97,529	15,983	7,042	14,350	2,093	5,638	4,626	47,427	2,349	56.4	7.8	40.8
San Mateo	21,477	434,295	38,662	26,779	37,486	19,084	46,684	64,180	147,779	241	66.4	6.2	48.2
Santa Barbara	11,977	156,499	23,832	13,731	18,824	4,463	12,124	8,996	57,484	1,467	60.7	9.5	44.0
Santa Clara	49,013	1,129,499	118,836	86,632	81,366	27,182	154,546	165,114	146,183	890	78.1	5.2	44.9
Santa Cruz	6,985	82,173	14,221	5,351	12,510	2,447	4,701	4,211	51,240	625	80.5	2.1	43.2
Shasta	4,407	51,288	10,826	2,154	9,527	2,074	2,214	2,342	45,660	1,337	71.4	4.6	31.5
Sierra	72	219	49	NA	29	NA	NA	8	34,374	38	23.7	26.3	56.9
Siskiyou	1,052	8,310	1,686	757	1,540	192	278	339	40,845	745	36.4	15.3	49.3
Solano	7,267	118,253	22,974	10,379	18,797	3,441	3,798	6,349	53,690	849	65.3	8.1	44.6
Sonoma	14,242	177,333	27,671	21,999	24,885	6,197	8,681	10,242	57,756	3,594	73.7	3.5	40.6
Stanislaus	9,345	145,654	26,759	19,375	23,665	3,484	6,256	7,194	49,393	3,621	65.3	3.5	51.3
Sutter	1,946	23,073	3,903	1,491	4,392	909	595	1,050	45,493	1,157	49.3	6.1	54.3
Tehama	982	13,429	2,069	1,852	2,096	195	233	646	48,092	1,479	61.9	7.6	44.7
Trinity	246	1,540	319	189	337	39	94	64	41,721	185	64.3	2.2	48.0
Tulare	6,632	100,314	17,702	13,589	16,400	3,061	2,368	4,334	43,209	4,187	57.6	5.4	52.3
Tuolumne	1,247	12,788	2,789	819	2,360	223	467	555	43,383	417	57.3	8.9	37.7
Ventura	21,762	264,604	41,482	24,835	38,844	11,488	21,977	15,045	56,859	2,135	78.4	2.2	43.0
Yolo	4,275	72,490	7,370	6,787	8,037	1,129	4,213	3,750	51,728	949	49.5	9.2	53.5
Yuba	820	12,139	2,893	446	1,458	140	539	595	48,978	764	59.8	3.8	51.0
COLORADO	175,965	2,510,726	330,520	130,080	284,219	126,168	219,296	145,130	57,804	38,893	46.2	14.9	38.2
Adams	10,633	193,760	25,891	13,809	24,696	3,618	7,159	9,721	50,172	905	62.0	10.9	32.2
Alamosa	494	5,795	1,820	108	1,102	386	152	234	40,379	280	23.2	20.7	46.9
Arapahoe	19,441	299,708	42,172	6,360	32,981	26,752	26,666	19,929	66,496	851	73.9	4.8	26.0
Archuleta	513	3,799	607	127	757	88	120	128	33,667	399	41.4	14.3	33.7
Baca	84	516	240	NA	66	19	9	20	38,514	667	3.3	48.4	49.6
Bent	54	579	82	NA	96	48	NA	24	41,817	274	12.8	33.9	47.4

STATE County	Agriculture, 2017 (cont.): Land in farms: Acreage (1,000)	Land in farms: Percent change, 2012–2017	Land in farms: Acres: Average size of farm	Land in farms: Acres: Total irrigated (1,000)	Land in farms: Acres: Total cropland (1,000)	Value of land and buildings (dollars): Average per farm	Value of land and buildings (dollars): Average per acre	Value of machinery and equipment, average per farm (dollars)	Value of products sold: Total (mil dol)	Value of products sold: Average per farm (acres)	Value of products sold: Percent from: Crops	Value of products sold: Percent from: Livestock and poultry products	Organic farms (number)	Farms with internet access (per-cent)	Government payments: Total ($1,000)	Government payments: Percent of farms
	117	118	119	120	121	122	123	124	125	126	127	128	129	130	131	132
CALIFORNIA	24,523	-4.1	348	7,833.6	9,597.4	3,252,414	9,353	165,070	45,154.4	640,297	73.9	26.1	3,794	82.0	127,938	7.5
Alameda	183	3.1	411	7.5	17.3	2,920,388	7,106	58,016	46.2	103,509	77.4	22.6	13	84.5	201	6.3
Alpine	3	D	529	D	D	2,418,390	4,573	104,011	D	D	D	D	NA	83.3	D	16.7
Amador	181	17.0	377	10.4	14.6	1,677,097	4,454	56,975	31.0	64,376	74.8	25.2	13	86.3	146	6.0
Butte	348	-8.6	182	192.5	214.2	2,193,553	12,042	163,066	524.2	274,140	96.8	3.2	100	80.4	6,677	6.1
Calaveras	240	12.9	343	5.8	14.8	1,218,142	3,554	52,629	27.4	39,249	35.0	65.0	11	79.3	1,050	9.3
Colusa	457	0.8	608	233.7	277.5	4,846,803	7,967	320,815	553.9	737,571	98.4	1.6	28	83.1	9,646	31.0
Contra Costa	156	21.9	339	22.6	41.5	2,346,158	6,922	93,600	83.2	181,327	77.4	22.6	9	84.5	503	6.1
Del Norte	20	D	220	9.1	7.9	1,826,521	8,315	157,104	43.4	482,111	25.6	74.4	11	97.8	D	1.1
El Dorado	91	-29.1	65	5.6	8.4	649,878	9,926	41,388	24.5	17,650	87.0	13.0	27	87.6	82	1.3
Fresno	1,647	-4.3	345	972.6	1,142.7	3,917,829	11,359	234,782	5,742.8	1,202,926	71.1	28.9	183	75.6	8,894	7.7
Glenn	467	-30.2	398	243.2	265.1	3,547,184	8,915	248,370	628.7	536,012	82.9	17.1	30	83.3	3,676	15.8
Humboldt	621	4.6	731	20.7	20.6	2,260,162	3,090	89,370	D	D	D	D	123	79.5	626	3.9
Imperial	522	1.2	1,317	456.1	504.0	14,670,312	11,135	884,987	1,859.7	4,696,157	65.7	34.3	45	90.7	3,640	27.5
Inyo	287	-13.3	3,375	17.1	13.6	2,093,360	620	70,430	10.6	124,800	14.3	85.7	1	83.5	1,101	16.5
Kern	2,295	-1.5	1,326	730.7	954.1	9,787,244	7,380	406,230	4,076.8	2,355,161	84.3	15.7	30	82.7	5,101	13.8
Kings	616	-8.6	640	371.7	488.5	6,917,469	10,815	349,654	1,649.3	1,712,640	50.1	49.9	25	80.4	5,849	29.8
Lake	138	-8.2	218	13.9	20.1	1,426,769	6,555	67,768	71.9	113,002	96.5	3.5	101	78.9	106	5.5
Lassen	473	-1.9	1,256	53.6	56.3	2,685,457	2,139	126,819	46.0	121,923	45.0	55.0	16	77.7	1,473	12.5
Los Angeles	58	-37.0	56	13.8	29.6	1,037,785	18,580	56,113	154.6	149,380	86.5	13.5	41	78.7	523	2.1
Madera	645	-1.3	466	300.2	346.1	5,102,429	10,958	229,882	1,492.6	1,076,903	77.4	22.6	74	77.1	2,192	8.4
Marin	140	-18.0	408	5.0	13.7	2,393,811	5,862	102,186	95.3	277,962	11.6	88.4	67	86.9	712	13.1
Mariposa	301	6.3	1,008	2.8	5.8	2,080,275	2,064	55,341	24.7	82,706	7.7	92.3	4	87.3	1,670	23.4
Mendocino	782	1.5	693	27.9	64.3	2,653,485	3,829	87,962	173.0	153,362	86.6	13.4	131	81.6	226	3.3
Merced	946	-3.3	405	493.7	546.5	5,299,308	13,086	334,860	2,938.4	1,257,337	43.9	56.1	68	78.5	8,726	12.5
Modoc	571	9.1	1,350	142.1	159.9	2,640,981	1,956	195,540	114.8	271,357	70.2	29.8	24	82.5	2,537	31.2
Mono	73	29.5	1,124	41.7	7.9	2,158,060	1,921	140,666	9.6	147,277	65.6	34.4	NA	78.5	D	4.6
Monterey	1,340	5.7	1,214	294.6	366.7	8,944,364	7,368	805,557	4,116.1	3,728,396	99.1	0.9	191	75.5	1,269	7.4
Napa	256	1.0	137	60.9	67.7	6,052,361	44,154	94,303	573.2	307,198	97.7	2.3	117	84.7	924	2.1
Nevada	52	23.6	77	5.0	4.8	574,346	7,425	34,251	12.5	18,517	54.5	45.5	58	88.4	173	4.2
Orange	32	-46.4	168	4.2	9.6	3,205,502	19,094	162,436	82.5	427,497	99.5	0.5	7	79.8	6	3.1
Placer	119	29.7	96	20.2	28.5	643,458	6,715	44,969	54.9	44,378	68.4	31.6	26	88.0	327	2.7
Plumas	191	9.6	1,179	18.3	29.2	2,707,681	2,298	86,429	9.6	59,235	35.1	64.9	4	82.1	120	6.8
Riverside	264	-23.3	99	126.2	179.7	1,794,629	18,144	102,551	932.0	349,450	75.9	24.1	228	80.4	1,621	2.4
Sacramento	260	5.4	224	100.4	118.8	2,252,041	10,048	129,041	430.5	370,759	70.1	29.9	27	83.2	1,966	9.7
San Benito	520	-13.9	853	18.1	35.6	3,043,028	3,569	98,840	162.9	267,057	79.9	20.1	75	81.3	575	9.8
San Bernardino	68	-11.6	64	22.2	29.3	1,278,283	19,897	78,028	373.9	352,096	25.2	74.8	25	75.9	647	2.6
San Diego	222	0.3	44	42.7	64.1	1,014,281	23,209	43,529	831.4	163,601	93.5	6.5	419	84.2	558	1.1
San Francisco	0	650.0	9	D	D	699,840	77,760	28,864	D	D	D	D	NA	80.0	NA	NA
San Joaquin	773	-1.8	225	487.1	524.4	3,384,002	15,020	189,084	2,176.0	634,404	74.8	25.2	35	81.7	5,788	6.9
San Luis Obispo	931	-30.4	396	75.8	246.4	2,991,939	7,547	87,783	701.6	298,676	95.2	4.8	132	84.4	4,285	9.4
San Mateo	46	-4.5	191	3.0	6.9	1,863,577	9,769	75,026	79.4	329,560	98.2	1.8	20	88.4	D	0.8
Santa Barbara	715	2.0	487	119.9	146.3	5,060,150	10,381	183,019	1,519.9	1,036,090	98.0	2.0	163	87.7	854	5.2
Santa Clara	288	25.3	324	19.2	34.3	2,633,548	8,136	89,041	310.2	348,525	94.7	5.3	34	86.2	518	3.6
Santa Cruz	64	-36.1	102	20.1	23.5	2,183,024	21,352	116,842	606.5	970,464	98.7	1.3	130	85.1	37	1.9
Shasta	410	8.9	307	48.8	38.9	895,229	2,919	51,324	62.2	46,546	35.0	65.0	16	81.5	547	2.0
Sierra	57	45.7	1,501	10.2	3.7	2,555,225	1,702	115,102	4.0	106,000	17.2	82.8	4	84.2	84	21.1
Siskiyou	687	-4.9	923	115.6	142.8	2,828,476	3,066	142,709	192.4	258,301	81.3	18.7	55	82.8	2,638	14.6
Solano	343	-15.8	404	110.4	152.1	3,691,320	9,148	178,302	296.6	349,337	83.8	16.2	63	85.2	2,554	13.9
Sonoma	567	-3.8	158	86.4	129.9	3,501,852	22,186	77,715	919.1	255,719	66.9	33.1	332	87.7	2,410	3.8
Stanislaus	723	-5.9	200	380.6	404.7	3,116,617	15,619	182,695	2,526.3	697,690	53.0	47.0	35	82.2	5,006	7.5
Sutter	381	1.5	329	198.8	257.3	3,136,319	9,525	240,974	412.2	356,252	99.0	1.0	42	79.0	7,687	14.0
Tehama	614	-0.5	415	72.8	77.2	1,789,414	4,313	80,756	218.4	147,640	74.5	25.5	18	81.6	1,168	4.7
Trinity	66	-62.6	356	D	1.7	683,288	1,921	35,076	D	D	D	100.0	9	82.2	D	2.2
Tulare	1,250	0.9	299	568.2	721.4	3,501,053	11,726	218,462	4,474.8	1,068,739	49.7	50.3	104	78.2	13,824	10.4
Tuolumne	123	39.5	294	2.6	1.5	1,091,612	3,715	52,254	32.3	77,384	3.5	96.5	3	81.5	397	8.4
Ventura	260	-7.5	122	98.1	123.4	3,106,351	25,498	127,982	1,633.3	765,008	99.2	0.8	128	80.6	830	2.5
Yolo	460	-0.3	484	234.7	312.8	4,699,589	9,703	240,642	571.6	602,266	97.1	2.9	98	86.4	2,850	19.2
Yuba	180	-4.3	235	72.5	79.3	1,931,854	8,221	157,292	179.1	234,438	88.9	11.1	21	82.5	2,828	4.6
COLORADO	31,821	-0.2	818	2,761.2	11,056.3	1,315,440	1,608	117,337	7,491.7	192,623	29.9	70.1	323	81.4	198,697	23.0
Adams	705	2.1	779	21.6	586.8	1,256,762	1,613	129,421	126.5	139,779	81.9	18.1	17	80.3	5,037	26.1
Alamosa	192	5.3	686	79.5	81.1	1,453,990	2,120	272,790	89.3	319,050	90.9	9.1	13	83.2	836	22.9
Arapahoe	283	-0.1	332	1.2	136.8	751,389	2,260	63,650	26.7	31,370	78.0	22.0	3	87.7	1,705	15.0
Archuleta	210	0.0	527	18.3	12.5	1,634,748	3,104	67,028	11.2	27,965	12.6	87.4	2	79.4	143	2.5
Baca	1,472	-2.1	2,207	45.5	742.4	1,729,456	784	149,867	114.1	171,039	45.9	54.1	1	77.1	19,467	84.0
Bent	735	1.2	2,681	38.8	93.3	1,850,149	690	166,448	60.8	221,964	27.0	73.0	NA	69.0	1,854	51.5

STATE County	Water use, 2015		Wholesale Trade[1], 2017				Retail Trade[2], 2017				Real estate and rental and leasing,[2] 2017			
	Public supply water withdrawn (mil gal/ day)	Public supply gallons withdrawn per person per day	Number of establish- ments	Number of employees	Sales (mil dol)	Average payroll (mil dol)	Number of establish- ments	Number of employees	Sales (mil dol)	Average payroll (mil dol)	Number of establish- ments	Number of employees	Sales (mil dol)	Average payroll (mil dol)
	133	134	135	136	137	138	139	140	141	142	143	144	145	146
CALIFORNIA	5,147.7	131.5	52,861	735,916	806,282.5	55,597.1	108,233	1,723,278	594,861.4	54,229.4	57,434	314,273	110,821.5	18,275.0
Alameda	168.7	103.0	2,293	42,146	43,709.9	3,185.0	4,318	72,619	26,888.7	2,494.6	2,189	11,182	3,621.8	622.9
Alpine	0.1	90.1	NA	NA	NA	NA	NA	NA	NA	NA	NA	NA	NA	NA
Amador	8.6	233.5	20	87	31.5	4.0	124	1,474	367.6	40.4	45	109	29.4	3.8
Butte	28.8	127.8	144	2,073	975.0	102.1	693	10,652	3,137.5	307.3	262	1,136	207.2	36.2
Calaveras	6.6	147.0	D	D	D	1.8	135	1,213	327.7	34.1	43	96	25.7	3.8
Colusa	2.5	114.5	23	394	579.4	25.5	61	444	159.8	13.0	17	40	10.6	2.4
Contra Costa	140.0	124.2	780	8,912	10,017.1	629.2	2,489	45,970	14,986.4	1,521.1	1,478	7,402	2,767.7	456.2
Del Norte	2.4	88.1	D	D	D	D	59	913	229.9	25.4	31	100	18.7	2.5
El Dorado	27.8	150.7	117	548	272.0	36.3	514	6,612	1,921.0	209.2	269	1,190	277.9	49.4
Fresno	157.1	161.1	827	14,164	10,890.9	780.4	2,438	38,243	11,347.0	1,066.6	852	4,904	1,097.9	207.2
Glenn	2.6	91.0	19	212	148.0	11.3	71	846	262.6	23.5	15	29	3.9	1.2
Humboldt	11.5	84.7	100	992	499.8	48.1	596	7,173	2,055.5	214.6	161	608	135.0	22.3
Imperial	24.5	135.8	202	1,837	1,656.4	87.4	473	8,444	1,815.1	199.7	161	736	136.0	22.6
Inyo	2.4	132.5	18	156	56.2	5.9	90	855	250.4	26.3	28	100	13.8	2.4
Kern	168.9	191.4	561	8,010	6,451.9	443.1	1,960	31,869	9,382.8	860.7	670	3,474	759.1	147.4
Kings	29.1	192.6	61	704	969.0	42.0	292	4,155	1,272.1	117.0	112	436	95.6	14.5
Lake	2.9	45.4	D	D	D	D	166	2,167	614.1	58.5	64	169	30.1	5.6
Lassen	3.8	121.2	9	68	91.7	2.7	76	887	234.1	24.1	27	56	9.4	1.4
Los Angeles	1,256.4	123.5	21,107	241,372	208,449.7	14,003.0	29,356	434,013	150,362.8	13,607.1	16,872	96,996	37,782.5	5,682.8
Madera	15.6	100.8	87	1,032	709.1	59.7	315	3,648	1,157.5	101.3	103	390	68.6	12.7
Marin	28.2	107.9	317	2,332	1,830.8	163.2	1,011	15,549	5,625.2	645.1	642	2,969	1,874.6	229.9
Mariposa	0.7	38.8	D	D	D	0.4	42	339	80.0	8.4	20	D	7.0	D
Mendocino	8.8	100.7	75	860	606.8	39.6	436	4,628	1,270.7	135.9	136	546	97.4	18.0
Merced	50.2	186.9	105	1,759	1,948.0	87.1	544	8,453	2,366.8	214.4	156	569	116.3	18.4
Modoc	0.6	66.9	5	40	85.8	1.8	23	192	48.5	5.0	6	12	2.0	0.4
Mono	2.0	142.4	6	17	15.1	0.7	72	702	164.8	17.8	67	389	54.2	11.5
Monterey	38.2	88.1	349	5,528	8,040.7	353.6	1,292	17,597	5,629.5	529.7	474	1,987	587.0	90.9
Napa	15.3	107.3	D	D	D	D	497	6,742	2,005.4	219.8	219	1,041	256.2	50.0
Nevada	11.4	115.7	71	502	436.5	35.0	383	4,167	1,134.8	127.4	185	868	287.2	46.0
Orange	457.5	144.3	6,681	86,779	107,972.6	6,183.7	9,707	156,535	52,345.3	4,927.0	6,589	45,719	15,227.2	3,118.6
Placer	54.1	144.0	319	4,675	3,572.4	305.9	1,310	23,374	7,799.0	752.3	804	3,658	988.0	198.2
Plumas	2.2	116.8	D	D	D	D	85	583	152.2	16.7	28	69	11.2	1.9
Riverside	440.7	186.7	1,704	25,471	30,247.5	1,510.0	5,305	96,868	31,941.7	2,855.7	2,407	10,120	2,538.3	451.9
Sacramento	231.3	154.1	1,080	16,782	27,125.2	1,030.1	3,536	62,292	19,354.7	1,845.5	1,743	9,009	2,445.2	442.6
San Benito	5.2	89.1	35	543	271.8	43.8	102	1,407	460.5	46.6	55	126	29.7	5.0
San Bernardino	337.7	158.7	2,804	40,924	37,448.3	2,109.0	4,898	94,285	32,452.6	2,747.8	1,820	9,536	2,794.2	425.2
San Diego	408.8	123.9	3,905	46,390	38,374.0	3,219.4	9,455	152,542	46,665.9	4,557.3	6,381	29,423	11,062.2	1,670.4
San Francisco	67.5	78.1	963	14,014	24,706.6	1,245.9	3,396	49,883	19,362.3	2,119.1	2,132	19,351	9,399.2	1,564.4
San Joaquin	93.4	128.6	528	11,280	14,265.8	728.0	1,635	27,256	8,856.3	789.3	566	2,832	634.9	119.8
San Luis Obispo	29.1	103.4	276	2,519	1,282.1	131.0	1,130	14,708	4,372.0	442.0	494	2,024	420.2	80.3
San Mateo	68.4	89.4	969	15,805	16,383.0	1,587.4	2,018	37,611	20,064.3	1,354.4	1,265	7,710	3,367.9	484.2
Santa Barbara	49.9	112.3	405	5,968	5,075.3	490.4	1,479	18,889	5,267.8	547.6	747	3,072	712.4	130.7
Santa Clara	194.6	101.5	2,252	74,332	136,798.9	13,052.5	4,682	86,436	47,472.2	3,353.6	2,776	15,765	6,369.5	1,023.2
Santa Cruz	18.5	67.3	D	D	D	D	893	12,885	4,650.4	364.9	370	1,539	351.3	69.8
Shasta	33.5	186.4	157	1,664	1,056.6	85.1	634	9,391	2,847.7	274.5	220	887	188.2	32.5
Sierra	0.4	124.7	NA	NA	NA	NA	D	D	D	D	NA	NA	NA	NA
Siskiyou	4.6	105.8	27	237	128.7	7.4	171	1,546	476.4	41.3	57	106	13.8	2.9
Solano	52.2	119.7	253	4,043	3,119.4	261.9	1,061	20,104	6,244.8	601.4	393	1,603	503.6	68.8
Sonoma	40.5	80.6	560	8,903	6,419.4	684.6	1,815	25,679	7,760.5	843.1	712	3,334	817.5	152.7
Stanislaus	80.5	149.5	406	6,921	6,198.1	401.0	1,462	24,398	7,486.4	680.1	481	2,047	505.1	85.9
Sutter	13.6	141.1	66	1,325	1,101.1	94.9	287	4,473	1,306.0	124.0	84	369	76.5	12.4
Tehama	5.3	83.1	24	209	100.3	8.3	142	1,963	754.9	56.0	44	115	27.6	3.3
Trinity	1.0	75.8	D	D	D	D	48	402	98.2	10.1	D	D	D	0.3
Tulare	70.3	152.9	338	4,898	8,105.4	270.5	1,098	16,622	4,599.0	429.3	330	1,500	256.8	49.1
Tuolumne	5.5	101.8	D	D	D	D	175	2,484	660.0	69.5	74	202	51.8	6.7
Ventura	130.0	152.9	1,028	15,216	24,894.7	1,221.6	2,569	40,494	13,115.6	1,238.4	1,204	4,751	1,300.4	235.6
Yolo	26.9	126.3	253	6,068	8,608.1	349.2	485	8,138	2,701.8	249.8	305	1,689	338.2	71.0
Yuba	9.0	120.1	27	748	267.4	23.4	121	1,431	489.0	43.5	40	91	15.5	2.7
COLORADO	844.0	154.7	5,953	80,365	83,316.2	5,376.3	19,056	279,982	84,930.6	8,419.7	12,087	47,642	12,757.1	2,387.8
Adams	78.9	160.6	640	15,232	17,240.8	896.1	1,183	20,600	6,974.1	653.1	583	2,855	750.8	132.3
Alamosa	2.1	126.7	12	155	52.0	6.3	84	1,147	317.6	33.8	23	86	13.3	2.9
Arapahoe	141.4	224.0	630	9,086	19,344.0	751.8	1,925	34,509	12,075.7	1,129.1	1,378	5,732	1,674.9	323.8
Archuleta	1.5	122.2	6	20	5.1	0.7	87	805	192.1	22.6	40	184	46.2	6.8
Baca	0.5	124.5	13	D	49.9	D	14	105	29.8	2.3	D	D	D	0.0
Bent	0.8	138.9	NA	NA	NA	NA	15	72	20.8	1.4	NA	NA	NA	NA

1 Merchant wholesalers, except manufacturers' sales branches and offices. 2. Employer establishments.

STATE County	Professional, scientific, and technical services, 2017				Manufacturing, 2017				Accommodation and food services, 2017			
	Number of establish-ments	Number of employees	Sales (mil dol)	Average payroll (mil dol)	Number of establish-ments	Number of employees	Sales (mil dol)	Average payroll (mil dol)	Number of establis-hments	Number of employees	Sales (mil dol)	Annual payroll (mil dol)
	147	148	149	150	151	152	153	154	155	156	157	158
CALIFORNIA	126,250	1,200,190	290,527.7	114,637.8	37,887	1,160,890	510,858.5	76,483.1	89,596	1,739,010	133,716.9	37,677.2
Alameda	6,087	66,185	16,814.0	6,898.5	1,821	80,007	28,157.5	6,799.9	4,191	66,352	5,042.0	1,433.6
Alpine	NA	NA	NA	NA	NA	NA	NA	NA	8	54	7.4	1.8
Amador	71	366	32.5	13.0	48	586	113.6	31.1	109	2,387	290.8	66.0
Butte	D	D	D	D	180	4,287	1,340.8	207.0	452	8,241	498.3	138.1
Calaveras	D	D	D	D	38	325	62.7	12.7	122	1,226	76.1	22.3
Colusa	D	D	4.8	D	23	695	450.4	36.1	36	910	96.3	23.4
Contra Costa	3,499	26,743	5,557.5	2,300.1	530	16,239	28,515.2	1,222.9	2,074	34,165	2,448.6	681.5
Del Norte	22	102	9.4	2.7	12	112	57.4	5.4	64	626	47.2	12.2
El Dorado	D	D	D	D	173	2,514	541.9	145.2	494	7,660	548.1	153.7
Fresno	1,581	10,913	1,576.6	610.6	579	22,774	9,073.4	1,091.3	1,647	30,013	1,783.4	501.2
Glenn	D	D	10.9	D	29	731	358.0	41.9	52	670	41.3	10.5
Humboldt	D	D	D	D	128	2,351	596.2	83.4	403	6,356	400.6	108.2
Imperial	178	826	87.9	34.7	65	2,679	1,291.9	121.7	281	4,212	246.3	69.9
Inyo	D	D	D	D	11	170	100.4	9.5	88	1,412	134.1	30.7
Kern	1,189	9,602	1,542.5	569.4	376	13,484	6,938.0	678.5	1,467	23,929	1,507.6	410.3
Kings	105	965	109.9	44.9	60	4,514	2,819.7	215.2	196	4,210	460.0	97.9
Lake	68	286	35.2	11.8	42	296	70.0	14.2	126	1,535	116.9	30.7
Lassen	23	277	23.1	8.8	4	10	2.9	0.7	49	679	43.2	12.8
Los Angeles	35,978	305,750	69,868.3	25,566.5	11,794	316,464	150,047.8	19,199.0	23,592	456,789	34,725.9	9,833.4
Madera	107	401	45.2	15.7	104	3,517	1,490.1	192.4	210	2,882	200.0	52.1
Marin	1,796	8,000	1,779.5	671.9	232	2,962	780.9	167.4	763	13,685	1,025.8	321.3
Mariposa	D	D	D	D	12	80	13.4	4.4	43	986	102.1	25.9
Mendocino	D	D	D	D	127	2,469	780.2	120.6	341	4,127	266.4	77.2
Merced	157	800	87.6	30.4	116	9,822	5,969.6	459.9	340	5,365	320.4	81.5
Modoc	D	D	4.5	D	D	D	D	D	16	108	8.5	2.6
Mono	34	106	15.0	4.5	9	68	12.2	2.3	144	4,192	451.9	123.4
Monterey	D	D	D	D	280	9,070	4,346.2	429.1	1,095	22,103	1,894.5	524.6
Napa	430	2,044	363.0	130.9	492	13,127	5,873.9	890.0	408	11,705	1,068.5	339.4
Nevada	343	1,358	252.9	94.5	138	1,532	340.8	92.2	245	6,165	339.9	104.3
Orange	15,867	136,767	27,614.5	10,958.5	4,572	146,707	46,800.8	9,553.6	8,230	176,590	13,293.4	3,749.0
Placer	1,352	10,437	1,686.8	670.6	261	4,288	1,136.9	244.7	951	22,782	2,120.4	491.1
Plumas	D	D	D	D	18	470	164.8	25.9	102	447	41.9	10.3
Riverside	3,610	20,461	2,938.3	1,075.2	1,547	43,177	16,073.4	2,229.1	3,934	92,264	6,997.9	1,971.1
Sacramento	3,873	41,600	7,781.1	4,041.1	761	20,006	7,899.3	1,226.6	2,906	55,359	3,462.8	993.9
San Benito	75	273	39.7	15.2	61	3,251	1,037.2	167.5	96	1,418	90.1	26.3
San Bernardino	2,749	19,069	2,750.7	978.9	1,795	50,781	20,023.9	2,719.3	3,652	66,336	4,102.2	1,139.9
San Diego	14,150	143,999	37,220.4	14,266.1	2,972	100,773	31,443.8	7,335.4	7,810	184,771	14,854.7	4,139.0
San Francisco	7,124	115,262	40,464.4	14,240.6	704	8,583	1,983.3	485.9	4,559	89,123	9,426.2	2,717.4
San Joaquin	808	4,858	616.0	259.4	533	19,833	9,574.9	1,001.7	1,185	19,118	1,206.4	332.1
San Luis Obispo	929	4,853	797.0	298.6	453	6,433	2,341.3	343.5	985	17,024	1,148.8	331.1
San Mateo	3,232	43,162	14,613.1	6,440.1	611	32,094	29,757.6	3,380.4	2,167	41,461	3,911.8	1,106.8
Santa Barbara	1,389	10,005	2,285.7	777.4	495	12,939	4,208.2	916.0	1,215	25,145	2,149.9	607.0
Santa Clara	8,759	144,020	42,451.6	18,186.4	2,197	92,225	36,391.1	8,114.1	5,107	90,824	7,261.7	2,143.6
Santa Cruz	878	4,262	648.4	315.9	314	5,049	1,707.6	301.1	711	12,032	831.9	251.5
Shasta	357	2,043	272.7	116.7	130	2,158	656.3	106.5	373	6,351	428.5	118.5
Sierra	D	D	D	D	NA	NA	NA	NA	18	83	6.9	2.6
Siskiyou	90	309	35.7	12.3	31	750	287.5	39.9	146	1,554	101.6	28.4
Solano	590	3,726	627.2	233.5	245	9,085	7,191.2	610.6	775	13,222	848.6	237.8
Sonoma	1,585	8,289	1,357.1	544.3	891	21,445	7,370.0	1,344.2	1,306	24,035	2,085.6	534.8
Stanislaus	682	5,805	761.7	314.5	406	19,982	12,685.7	1,202.1	926	16,562	971.6	273.6
Sutter	124	596	73.2	26.8	56	1,493	576.3	81.7	146	2,343	153.5	40.4
Tehama	55	217	22.1	7.4	43	1,783	605.5	85.5	126	1,986	163.8	43.9
Trinity	D	D	7.6	D	10	208	70.5	12.2	47	260	17.8	4.6
Tulare	D	D	D	D	231	13,534	8,119.7	719.1	640	9,898	641.4	173.1
Tuolumne	86	454	61.8	23.1	45	814	210.3	43.5	169	2,130	172.2	42.7
Ventura	2,816	23,034	3,556.9	2,558.7	872	25,626	9,751.9	1,585.0	1,718	32,483	2,147.4	629.8
Yolo	D	D	D	D	167	6,006	2,528.8	311.7	453	9,599	813.4	227.2
Yuba	86	517	93.3	35.6	36	478	109.8	20.6	87	1,066	72.3	19.2
COLORADO	26,285	187,406	38,429.8	15,299.1	5,111	121,372	50,809.1	7,356.9	14,121	290,915	19,455.8	5,804.1
Adams	D	D	D	D	425	13,055	6,223.2	698.1	814	16,036	1,019.0	296.4
Alamosa	D	D	D	D	16	103	21.1	4.0	52	877	47.7	12.9
Arapahoe	D	D	D	D	417	6,866	2,194.1	401.3	1,417	30,207	1,916.3	589.4
Archuleta	44	111	12.8	4.7	17	94	10.5	2.8	53	687	45.4	14.5
Baca	D	D	D	D	NA	NA	NA	NA	D	D	D	0.3
Bent	D	D	D	0.1	NA	NA	NA	NA	D	D	D	0.6

STATE County	Health care and social assistance, 2017				Other services, 2017				Nonemployer businesses, 2019		Value of residential construction authorized by building permits, 2021	
	Number of establish-ments	Number of employees	Receipts (mil dol)	Annual payroll (mil dol)	Number of establish-ments	Number of employees	Receipts (mil dol)	Annual payroll (mil dol)	Number	Receipts (mil dol)	New construction ($1,000)	Number of housing units
	159	160	161	162	163	164	165	166	167	168	169	170
CALIFORNIA	113,390	2,043,117	311,312.2	119,500.6	62,302	437,372	64,253.9	15,637.9	3,458,667	192,591.1	28,724,878	119,436
Alameda	4,812	99,670	16,159.0	6,593.0	3,104	22,883	3,697.8	963.0	145,962	7,851.2	1,267,192	5,025
Alpine	D	D	D	D	D	D	D	0.3	108	4.3	6,153	12
Amador	107	1,331	198.1	71.5	63	243	30.3	8.9	2,846	133.8	38,688	141
Butte	720	15,210	1,977.3	749.0	334	3,579	221.1	71.1	12,745	674.2	336,723	2,050
Calaveras	90	1,061	140.7	51.1	70	258	24.7	7.0	3,691	179.5	45,386	130
Colusa	26	245	19.5	9.0	D	D	6.7	D	1,039	62.5	10,978	37
Contra Costa	3,233	58,665	10,075.4	3,904.3	1,711	11,985	1,428.0	468.2	101,112	5,954.9	825,987	3,901
Del Norte	63	1,264	151.8	59.9	21	78	8.9	2.4	1,374	57.1	9,445	38
El Dorado	457	6,597	878.6	351.2	317	1,595	161.4	49.0	17,425	951.1	257,013	669
Fresno	2,398	47,713	6,660.5	2,612.0	1,035	8,607	994.0	274.0	57,287	3,096.1	1,026,920	3,902
Glenn	43	492	52.8	23.3	24	105	20.9	4.3	1,458	65.1	4,707	19
Humboldt	425	7,355	904.8	349.4	230	1,276	219.2	42.1	11,150	478.4	56,659	371
Imperial	288	5,327	652.5	237.9	143	695	73.4	20.1	10,075	387.3	79,994	555
Inyo	48	1,151	143.1	56.2	36	148	18.5	5.0	1,357	50.0	2,173	6
Kern	1,684	30,531	4,574.8	1,580.8	865	6,057	671.3	199.2	50,492	2,637.4	461,218	2,293
Kings	213	4,803	631.8	221.0	116	501	59.1	14.2	5,183	233.0	138,977	508
Lake	151	2,462	350.6	123.3	69	278	29.4	7.3	3,964	156.9	15,394	81
Lassen	55	818	98.7	41.8	33	85	8.0	2.1	1,115	41.1	3,038	11
Los Angeles	32,968	568,696	84,372.2	31,197.5	17,225	119,814	17,931.3	4,151.3	1,112,641	62,956.3	5,090,906	23,284
Madera	210	6,171	999.5	387.3	117	576	59.2	16.5	7,775	412.0	274,438	1,066
Marin	1,158	16,799	2,350.7	1,064.8	703	4,890	847.4	203.5	37,149	3,011.5	110,822	265
Mariposa	38	411	39.3	18.6	D	D	D	1.0	1,407	57.1	16,558	85
Mendocino	252	4,475	528.3	209.7	170	709	107.0	22.8	8,293	359.0	21,772	187
Merced	444	7,595	944.4	372.0	188	944	95.5	25.1	12,261	648.7	307,754	1,017
Modoc	20	406	34.1	13.7	D	D	D	D	586	22.9	1,089	6
Mono	36	510	91.7	30.5	51	206	25.5	6.7	1,418	83.3	22,150	81
Monterey	999	17,169	2,803.9	1,072.6	607	4,058	573.0	128.9	26,100	1,521.3	187,665	882
Napa	433	10,558	1,653.4	671.2	264	1,645	203.6	54.3	12,337	800.9	216,261	1,204
Nevada	331	5,790	662.3	266.7	198	1,239	184.1	45.1	12,679	630.1	120,833	443
Orange	12,231	176,838	25,663.6	9,314.5	5,568	39,646	4,742.0	1,311.0	324,958	19,853.1	1,873,932	7,867
Placer	1,272	23,006	4,079.8	1,634.6	656	4,634	565.5	164.9	35,081	2,155.7	1,332,798	4,301
Plumas	52	858	111.1	37.8	37	134	19.8	4.7	1,683	84.7	9,776	54
Riverside	4,754	82,483	10,754.6	4,057.5	2,707	16,881	1,744.7	484.1	183,757	8,457.6	2,452,583	9,264
Sacramento	3,612	89,537	15,276.4	6,122.5	2,348	17,404	2,349.3	698.7	114,724	5,615.2	1,504,352	6,235
San Benito	95	1,411	182.4	80.6	74	319	38.9	8.7	3,964	217.9	128,361	485
San Bernardino	4,287	96,414	14,309.5	5,291.9	2,480	16,673	1,747.0	519.3	159,530	7,266.4	1,294,588	6,342
San Diego	9,592	175,430	26,431.3	10,143.4	5,823	42,595	4,888.7	1,379.5	292,558	15,195.6	2,092,612	10,048
San Francisco	3,330	69,425	13,052.4	5,235.7	2,470	25,451	5,265.1	1,112.6	91,940	6,113.5	819,407	2,519
San Joaquin	1,513	32,650	4,236.8	1,600.6	890	5,434	565.0	163.8	44,792	2,502.2	1,277,507	4,389
San Luis Obispo	1,055	15,066	1,912.6	788.2	450	2,986	265.6	78.7	26,134	1,457.5	249,800	1,120
San Mateo	2,482	39,334	6,048.9	2,538.7	1,498	11,771	3,065.5	595.7	70,889	4,883.2	771,112	1,896
Santa Barbara	1,428	23,163	3,662.0	1,207.5	785	5,846	1,759.0	211.2	35,300	2,156.0	170,755	1,152
Santa Clara	5,898	115,234	22,181.0	9,057.1	3,306	22,499	5,467.5	974.4	143,404	8,907.1	1,070,071	4,044
Santa Cruz	940	15,312	2,175.2	831.2	473	3,232	413.6	127.6	24,733	1,320.0	110,222	598
Shasta	670	11,319	1,553.8	575.1	300	1,659	211.8	51.1	12,028	587.4	106,969	368
Sierra	D	D	D	D	NA	NA	NA	NA	262	9.8	638	4
Siskiyou	105	1,834	217.4	97.6	73	310	25.3	7.1	3,310	135.1	26,937	97
Solano	931	22,704	3,667.2	1,608.3	576	3,920	630.6	159.5	26,856	1,173.8	387,484	1,378
Sonoma	1,537	26,382	3,737.9	1,632.2	959	5,810	684.6	206.7	45,633	2,534.5	709,704	2,618
Stanislaus	1,150	26,140	4,257.6	1,674.9	691	4,587	592.0	171.6	30,847	1,594.0	164,256	811
Sutter	240	3,790	479.9	181.6	126	625	68.4	20.1	6,322	462.8	42,150	142
Tehama	133	2,017	224.3	95.6	65	306	35.1	10.5	3,173	166.5	42,203	226
Trinity	22	303	29.7	12.3	10	36	3.9	1.0	900	38.2	5,933	44
Tulare	884	16,822	1,970.5	745.0	405	2,313	267.4	75.4	21,732	1,097.8	347,316	1,510
Tuolumne	171	2,734	399.0	154.7	78	379	54.6	13.1	4,217	197.7	22,207	110
Ventura	2,785	39,199	5,017.7	1,883.6	1,319	6,955	794.9	205.1	71,248	4,033.1	343,759	1,477
Yolo	422	7,576	1,068.5	384.4	337	2,145	259.1	80.1	13,838	706.3	240,404	1,229
Yuba	83	2,776	458.2	172.5	54	183	19.8	5.1	3,825	151.1	170,150	839
COLORADO	16,659	320,813	40,055.8	15,719.7	11,667	74,317	10,973.6	2,785.1	550,568	27,674.4	13,743,890	56,524
Adams	780	25,410	3,232.4	1,364.4	762	5,516	789.8	208.2	39,079	1,859.1	1,112,766	4,687
Alamosa	78	1,579	157.9	61.7	36	182	15.2	4.1	1,198	53.8	20,984	109
Arapahoe	2,220	42,044	5,093.9	1,978.9	1,297	8,655	1,179.8	349.4	64,225	3,350.3	1,193,788	5,519
Archuleta	36	534	56.5	24.8	27	125	12.2	3.8	2,118	94.8	47,643	193
Baca	D	D	D	D	D	D	1.8	D	353	18.2	261	3
Bent	8	D	7.6	D	D	D	D	0.0	231	8.5	917	8

STATE County	Government employment and payroll, 2017									Local government finances, 2017				
			March payroll (percent of total)							General revenue				
												Taxes		
													Per capita[1] (dollars)	
	Full-time equivalent employees	March payroll (dollars)	Adminis-tration, judicial, and legal	Police and corrections	Fire protection	Highways and transpor-tation	Health and welfare	Natural resources and utilities	Education and libraries	Total (mil dol)	Inter-govern-mental (mil dol)	Total (mil dol)	Total	Property
	171	172	173	174	175	176	177	178	179	180	181	182	183	184
CALIFORNIA	X	X	X	X	X	X	X	X	X	X	X	X	X	X
Alameda	64,149	475,857,164	5.3	11.8	4.5	12.0	18.3	8.9	37.1	14,373.8	5,114.9	5,176.4	3,118	1,931
Alpine	231	1,070,089	11.6	13.3	0.6	7.5	10.7	11.3	43.0	27.1	11.7	9.0	8,109	6,925
Amador	1,294	7,214,202	10.5	17.2	2.0	9.5	7.2	5.6	41.4	169.1	77.7	60.2	1,561	1,297
Butte	8,504	42,774,851	6.8	10.0	1.8	1.9	13.8	4.8	59.1	1,192.9	763.9	283.0	1,237	929
Calaveras	1,697	7,848,362	7.6	10.1	4.4	3.7	11.2	10.7	50.1	223.4	93.0	88.0	1,926	1,484
Colusa	1,140	5,836,524	10.7	11.0	1.8	3.4	8.9	7.9	54.6	160.6	92.8	42.5	1,969	1,639
Contra Costa	31,854	210,481,302	5.0	11.4	4.6	3.2	13.8	6.4	53.5	7,830.5	2,442.7	2,609.8	2,278	1,722
Del Norte	1,235	5,038,894	9.9	10.2	0.4	3.4	13.6	3.9	56.0	142.7	99.3	24.8	907	687
El Dorado	6,359	37,808,926	8.0	11.1	5.9	4.3	8.4	4.8	51.7	1,119.1	502.7	376.1	1,993	1,580
Fresno	36,934	197,609,273	3.7	9.8	2.2	3.1	10.2	4.8	65.2	7,476.9	5,082.5	1,284.5	1,304	863
Glenn	1,414	6,777,443	5.3	8.2	0.6	2.8	13.1	9.2	57.4	177.4	112.0	37.3	1,335	1,074
Humboldt	7,047	33,486,085	5.0	10.8	3.5	3.3	16.5	4.5	53.3	842.2	456.4	199.8	1,464	975
Imperial	11,605	61,911,631	3.6	5.2	1.6	1.1	22.1	13.1	47.5	1,462.1	823.5	203.7	1,121	778
Inyo	1,450	7,655,248	8.3	9.1	0.4	5.3	40.1	3.4	32.6	240.0	76.8	60.1	3,361	2,278
Kern	34,360	176,954,893	4.6	10.6	4.2	2.3	11.2	4.9	61.3	5,452.6	3,333.2	1,223.1	1,378	1,104
Kings	5,524	28,583,504	5.7	10.6	2.5	2.1	9.0	5.0	62.4	740.6	510.5	136.2	910	697
Lake	2,574	13,586,601	12.1	11.3	3.0	2.5	19.1	8.3	42.5	326.6	186.0	82.3	1,283	1,054
Lassen	1,151	5,516,096	9.6	10.3	1.0	3.4	11.8	8.6	53.7	139.9	87.7	32.1	1,039	769
Los Angeles	400,857	2,602,396,081	9.3	12.0	4.1	6.0	15.8	8.9	41.0	76,029.6	33,818.3	24,255.9	2,401	1,555
Madera	5,262	26,791,038	8.4	9.4	1.2	1.9	12.2	3.1	62.3	765.1	488.6	169.1	1,088	800
Marin	8,963	64,533,285	8.9	10.4	7.2	3.3	9.5	10.9	46.6	1,844.1	429.4	992.4	3,820	2,667
Mariposa	1,190	5,377,779	8.7	10.2	0.3	1.9	25.2	3.1	47.2	117.1	46.9	38.7	2,225	1,198
Mendocino	4,443	21,862,401	7.5	9.3	1.6	3.4	17.1	4.7	54.7	598.3	288.5	169.2	1,932	1,421
Merced	11,500	58,776,936	5.1	7.4	1.2	0.8	9.4	5.9	67.6	1,626.6	1,064.3	295.0	1,088	823
Modoc	652	2,830,084	5.3	7.5	1.0	4.7	39.8	3.2	35.5	85.4	45.7	12.4	1,400	1,190
Mono	1,043	6,681,287	5.5	9.9	5.4	6.4	41.1	8.7	22.3	223.5	42.1	96.6	6,729	4,157
Monterey	19,396	124,781,670	5.0	7.7	2.4	3.5	27.9	4.3	45.9	3,511.6	1,416.5	905.1	2,083	1,363
Napa	5,188	34,539,364	11.5	13.0	3.1	2.6	10.1	4.7	51.6	1,003.8	286.8	481.0	3,439	2,612
Nevada	3,579	20,669,561	8.1	9.0	5.0	3.6	27.5	9.5	30.1	623.3	178.3	205.8	2,072	1,681
Orange	92,158	640,816,778	6.4	12.9	4.5	3.4	7.1	5.6	58.9	17,778.6	6,803.8	7,027.1	2,214	1,642
Placer	12,560	81,230,645	8.4	10.8	4.6	2.2	5.7	9.7	55.2	2,568.8	781.5	956.1	2,483	2,009
Plumas	1,602	7,016,012	5.4	6.8	2.2	4.2	38.8	2.8	37.1	178.4	57.4	41.0	2,196	1,842
Riverside	78,634	510,029,742	9.1	10.8	1.6	2.1	13.2	5.3	56.2	13,772.3	6,716.3	3,661.4	1,516	1,075
Sacramento	54,054	337,517,731	5.1	12.8	4.7	4.1	8.2	13.9	48.3	9,780.9	4,722.9	2,478.2	1,623	1,100
San Benito	2,271	13,908,888	4.2	7.1	3.0	2.5	29.0	4.1	48.5	389.8	134.3	98.3	1,634	1,266
San Bernardino	74,301	438,536,700	5.0	10.4	4.1	2.2	13.6	4.7	57.9	17,953.7	11,376.5	3,231.3	1,502	1,057
San Diego	106,292	629,893,092	7.5	10.0	3.7	3.2	10.6	6.2	54.8	19,787.8	7,386.6	6,914.4	2,082	1,537
San Francisco	46,523	341,836,622	9.1	13.1	6.3	19.8	19.6	9.1	21.6	11,180.4	2,928.8	4,565.3	5,199	3,155
San Joaquin	26,849	155,624,972	5.8	10.0	3.2	3.1	16.7	4.3	55.8	4,670.9	2,331.8	1,193.2	1,605	1,058
San Luis Obispo	8,813	50,653,491	7.9	12.7	2.9	2.9	9.1	5.7	55.0	1,483.1	506.8	703.3	2,490	1,941
San Mateo	22,759	158,326,401	7.5	11.8	5.7	4.8	15.0	6.3	45.2	5,510.9	1,257.2	2,768.5	3,601	2,566
Santa Barbara	21,940	144,599,650	4.5	8.3	4.1	2.5	11.8	5.0	62.2	3,756.5	1,907.2	1,050.1	2,358	1,793
Santa Clara	64,447	499,870,139	7.4	9.0	2.9	4.9	23.8	5.0	45.0	16,775.4	4,010.7	6,910.6	3,576	2,611
Santa Cruz	9,852	61,097,077	8.1	9.9	4.0	7.1	13.0	8.3	47.4	1,679.8	750.9	583.8	2,124	1,525
Shasta	7,243	36,294,479	6.8	9.0	2.6	3.2	14.4	8.3	53.1	1,172.7	746.1	233.3	1,300	1,022
Sierra	176	898,827	18.3	11.1	0.1	12.9	19.6	2.9	32.9	32.6	18.6	7.5	2,503	2,286
Siskiyou	2,199	9,992,933	7.8	10.7	0.7	5.6	10.8	5.9	56.7	263.0	162.7	61.2	1,404	1,118
Solano	14,181	85,279,873	8.8	16.3	3.9	2.8	11.4	6.1	48.9	2,297.4	1,058.2	776.7	1,751	1,193
Sonoma	17,488	111,265,857	7.9	11.7	4.0	2.5	14.7	6.4	51.1	3,029.9	1,128.7	1,172.0	2,332	1,749
Stanislaus	21,814	117,420,075	5.4	8.3	2.5	1.5	10.8	8.8	60.3	3,252.8	1,916.6	608.7	1,117	790
Sutter	3,622	18,902,432	8.5	7.5	3.2	2.5	14.2	4.0	57.2	576.2	385.6	121.5	1,263	934
Tehama	2,385	11,043,707	7.6	10.4	1.3	2.9	13.7	2.7	59.4	296.7	202.0	64.5	1,011	762
Trinity	758	3,725,402	13.0	8.5	0.2	4.1	26.3	11.0	31.4	169.3	52.8	18.0	1,416	1,146
Tulare	23,861	111,821,006	5.1	7.4	1.9	1.1	31.0	4.0	48.3	3,798.6	1,982.9	537.8	1,163	700
Tuolumne	1,693	9,306,935	10.7	14.8	1.2	3.0	16.4	4.4	43.3	249.9	129.2	79.4	1,471	1,139
Ventura	30,149	195,583,899	9.7	10.1	4.8	2.6	14.9	6.1	50.1	5,323.1	2,073.3	1,584.4	1,866	1,524
Yolo	6,637	38,527,487	9.8	12.8	4.7	1.8	10.7	5.7	50.1	1,166.9	519.0	370.2	1,694	1,024
Yuba	3,322	18,247,567	4.6	9.1	0.8	1.3	8.4	2.1	71.0	456.6	300.1	82.2	1,074	899
COLORADO	X	X	X	X	X	X	X	X	X	X	X	X	X	X
Adams	14,992	69,690,300	8.7	12.9	5.2	3.2	6.3	8.0	54.1	2,225.9	744.1	1,078.7	2,142	1,310
Alamosa	762	2,550,582	10.8	11.4	0.6	3.8	15.4	6.5	49.7	90.7	45.1	29.2	1,815	941
Arapahoe	22,355	105,178,450	5.8	11.6	7.4	2.4	6.1	7.5	57.7	3,305.1	951.2	1,574.1	2,443	1,631
Archuleta	641	2,961,826	6.0	5.7	1.9	3.4	33.2	8.1	24.0	90.9	23.2	31.0	2,328	1,600
Baca	501	1,750,268	6.6	3.7	0.0	9.0	53.1	2.6	23.8	42.3	11.6	9.2	2,583	2,369
Bent	316	859,960	6.9	8.2	0.0	5.1	27.0	9.8	39.8	66.7	18.9	6.5	1,114	938

1. Based on the resident population estimated as of July 1 of the year shown.

STATE County	Local government finances, 2017 (cont.)									Government employment, 2020			Individual income tax returns, 2019		
	Direct general expenditure							Debt outstanding							
			Percent of total for:												
	Total (mil dol)	Per capita[1] (dollars)	Education	Health and hospitals	Police protection	Public welfare	Highways	Total (mil dol)	Per capita[1] (dollars)	Federal civilian	Federal military	State and local	Number of returns	Mean adjusted gross income	Mean income tax
	185	186	187	188	189	190	191	192	193	194	195	196	197	198	199
CALIFORNIA	X	X	X	X	X	X	X	X	X	260,514	197,148	2,277,976	18,638,060	88,405	12,945
Alameda	14,423.0	8,688	25.2	15.7	5.5	4.4	8.2	28,138.5	16,949	9,176	4,167	104,369	807,540	113,574	17,865
Alpine	25.8	23,218	16.5	11.9	11.9	6.7	6.6	5.6	5,076	2	110	250	510	61,724	5,945
Amador	175.1	4,546	31.7	6.5	7.3	7.4	6.3	92.4	2,398	96	68	4,688	18,110	66,789	7,122
Butte	1,303.8	5,701	50.9	7.0	4.3	9.8	3.6	710.4	3,106	738	310	14,955	90,090	60,805	6,198
Calaveras	209.5	4,586	35.1	10.8	5.3	10.1	5.3	219.1	4,797	149	67	2,629	21,300	68,003	7,198
Colusa	171.4	7,941	41.4	5.9	5.2	5.1	4.7	70.1	3,249	80	31	1,823	10,270	55,889	5,049
Contra Costa	7,425.4	6,482	36.0	19.5	6.6	5.9	3.6	7,724.2	6,743	5,181	1,768	40,253	563,980	118,355	18,537
Del Norte	150.4	5,498	34.9	7.8	3.7	15.2	2.9	77.2	2,821	162	48	3,382	10,510	50,089	4,278
El Dorado	1,095.3	5,805	42.4	3.6	4.8	5.6	4.3	1,027.1	5,444	686	284	9,250	94,320	95,652	13,701
Fresno	7,002.6	7,108	41.9	23.6	5.5	6.2	2.3	5,206.5	5,285	11,020	1,543	61,888	424,470	56,374	5,640
Glenn	182.6	6,538	46.3	8.9	5.1	11.3	5.1	81.7	2,924	198	67	1,817	12,770	51,315	4,073
Humboldt	899.3	6,588	47.0	7.6	4.6	11.5	3.4	424.0	3,106	822	370	12,612	59,960	54,517	5,260
Imperial	1,512.6	8,327	43.0	24.1	3.4	7.9	2.3	1,540.3	8,480	2,342	500	16,158	86,310	42,938	3,170
Inyo	256.3	14,342	28.8	39.4	4.2	3.4	4.3	71.0	3,974	299	303	2,776	8,780	62,945	6,382
Kern	7,088.4	7,988	40.8	3.7	3.6	5.7	1.6	4,158.1	4,686	11,487	3,956	53,810	360,880	54,635	5,041
Kings	800.5	5,349	48.0	4.4	4.9	9.9	2.5	315.7	2,110	1,281	6,976	13,492	58,520	50,579	4,118
Lake	322.7	5,034	41.9	6.6	5.7	13.2	3.8	137.8	2,150	187	103	3,626	26,860	49,761	4,320
Lassen	161.3	5,218	44.3	7.4	5.1	8.9	9.3	102.1	3,301	1,951	40	4,116	10,570	56,676	4,848
Los Angeles	70,277.2	6,956	35.1	12.0	8.8	8.4	2.5	101,862.8	10,082	50,852	17,030	538,503	4,806,030	79,836	11,820
Madera	839.1	5,399	50.1	4.5	3.8	8.2	6.4	657.0	4,227	362	221	10,416	63,010	52,568	4,619
Marin	1,820.9	7,010	33.9	7.4	6.6	3.6	3.4	2,913.7	11,217	756	483	13,900	132,180	196,050	39,280
Mariposa	124.3	7,138	20.5	24.9	6.6	10.4	6.7	38.1	2,189	627	24	1,463	7,830	56,206	5,274
Mendocino	1,357.0	15,496	17.1	6.6	2.4	4.4	1.9	535.6	6,116	290	156	6,089	40,440	55,867	5,589
Merced	1,616.8	5,964	57.0	4.2	4.0	8.9	3.7	974.0	3,593	833	404	16,484	112,450	48,593	3,969
Modoc	89.9	10,126	30.1	31.7	3.8	6.7	10.7	5.1	575	213	51	915	3,530	43,452	3,493
Mono	214.9	14,972	17.1	32.4	4.8	2.4	10.8	79.7	5,549	220	265	1,418	6,780	70,493	8,175
Monterey	3,623.3	8,338	38.0	22.1	4.4	5.0	2.3	2,222.3	5,114	5,722	5,734	28,381	201,650	70,766	8,328
Napa	964.8	6,897	37.4	6.8	8.1	4.4	5.0	1,190.6	8,512	252	192	10,156	69,200	100,314	15,186
Nevada	569.1	5,727	23.4	33.6	5.3	5.8	4.9	495.9	4,990	357	148	5,687	51,960	78,260	9,670
Orange	16,921.3	5,331	45.3	3.6	8.0	5.5	3.9	24,733.3	7,792	11,759	5,066	144,402	1,562,000	95,004	14,128
Placer	2,369.5	6,153	45.4	3.4	5.7	4.8	2.6	3,219.6	8,360	759	612	18,356	194,210	98,203	13,130
Plumas	202.5	10,853	25.1	37.2	3.4	4.8	5.8	67.3	3,605	348	27	1,925	9,200	59,671	5,631
Riverside	14,494.5	6,002	43.7	8.4	7.1	6.8	3.4	18,182.0	7,529	7,810	4,043	120,864	1,083,280	60,062	5,849
Sacramento	9,386.1	6,146	39.1	6.7	6.0	6.9	3.7	20,813.8	13,628	10,120	3,078	167,798	735,090	67,644	7,513
San Benito	408.2	6,784	42.6	29.5	3.2	5.4	1.3	350.4	5,824	133	94	2,844	30,760	77,365	8,109
San Bernardino	17,614.4	8,189	33.3	29.0	5.1	6.1	3.7	10,972.1	5,101	14,645	17,140	109,735	972,810	55,558	5,126
San Diego	20,668.2	6,223	39.3	9.4	5.6	4.4	3.1	41,671.1	12,547	49,309	88,491	192,464	1,646,850	83,984	11,334
San Francisco	12,045.8	13,719	12.8	28.1	4.4	11.8	1.0	22,442.2	25,559	13,550	1,619	94,884	463,200	168,149	34,324
San Joaquin	4,399.2	5,918	46.3	10.7	6.0	7.0	4.7	5,064.4	6,813	3,336	1,171	39,287	338,510	63,048	6,316
San Luis Obispo	1,449.8	5,132	41.1	6.4	6.0	7.8	4.0	1,526.6	5,404	634	554	21,596	135,180	80,955	10,233
San Mateo	4,971.8	6,466	36.9	9.7	8.0	4.1	3.1	7,250.3	9,429	3,690	1,333	27,062	388,090	197,461	39,648
Santa Barbara	3,448.8	7,745	33.0	26.8	4.7	4.2	1.9	1,732.6	3,891	3,604	3,189	32,334	207,530	83,790	11,795
Santa Clara	15,563.6	8,054	30.8	24.8	4.9	5.6	1.9	20,395.8	10,554	10,649	3,214	84,477	938,860	166,462	31,254
Santa Cruz	1,650.8	6,006	38.1	7.8	5.8	7.8	3.0	1,276.1	4,643	603	377	19,601	131,880	96,749	14,138
Shasta	1,007.3	5,615	46.0	8.4	6.0	11.3	2.6	573.9	3,199	1,345	302	11,305	80,280	59,517	5,921
Sierra	28.8	9,599	27.0	11.6	10.3	8.4	14.5	9.6	3,181	42	5	312	1,300	54,275	4,922
Siskiyou	278.8	6,392	47.4	6.1	5.7	7.5	4.7	222.6	5,102	787	63	3,374	19,710	49,513	4,408
Solano	2,261.9	5,100	38.2	8.0	9.9	6.9	4.7	2,036.9	4,593	3,731	7,697	20,732	218,670	72,136	7,757
Sonoma	3,042.2	6,054	40.6	9.0	6.5	6.9	3.8	3,352.6	6,672	1,534	1,479	24,505	249,160	86,214	11,364
Stanislaus	3,266.2	5,996	49.6	7.6	5.3	9.3	2.5	6,781.2	12,449	897	804	28,526	238,950	58,426	5,750
Sutter	639.7	6,650	45.1	9.0	6.3	6.7	2.0	348.7	3,624	80	143	4,332	42,740	56,838	5,237
Tehama	314.4	4,924	48.0	7.3	5.6	12.1	4.3	75.1	1,175	234	94	3,630	26,670	51,248	4,400
Trinity	175.5	13,793	18.3	13.3	2.3	6.2	8.8	54.7	4,301	217	17	809	4,630	47,702	3,960
Tulare	3,763.9	8,141	41.8	26.6	3.2	6.7	3.0	1,853.2	4,009	1,078	683	30,684	191,210	47,860	4,068
Tuolumne	268.5	4,975	34.3	8.2	6.8	7.8	10.0	84.4	1,563	428	75	4,660	24,890	63,567	6,453
Ventura	5,425.7	6,390	40.7	12.5	7.4	4.4	2.7	4,701.3	5,537	7,875	5,898	36,169	415,730	85,387	11,618
Yolo	1,145.2	5,242	35.1	5.0	6.5	7.9	5.2	1,501.7	6,873	3,444	323	39,637	93,680	79,946	9,765
Yuba	454.2	5,931	49.9	2.4	3.8	11.7	1.9	650.2	8,490	1,532	4,138	6,366	32,380	51,643	3,937
COLORADO	X	X	X	X	X	X	X	X	X	54,744	55,397	394,406	2,871,570	83,217	10,943
Adams	2,272.9	4,513	40.5	0.4	5.8	4.2	4.7	3,879.8	7,704	3,232	1,236	45,538	253,510	61,654	6,060
Alamosa	74.2	4,606	39.6	6.1	8.7	19.1	6.7	92.8	5,759	141	41	2,090	7,160	48,783	4,146
Arapahoe	3,090.7	4,796	44.2	0.9	7.2	1.7	6.4	6,725.3	10,435	3,297	4,244	34,293	332,210	87,310	12,000
Archuleta	88.2	6,637	16.1	41.2	2.8	5.1	9.9	74.0	5,568	61	34	866	7,060	64,755	6,802
Baca	40.9	11,513	22.0	37.3	3.4	12.5	7.7	3.0	845	34	9	630	1,560	33,449	3,088
Bent	62.6	10,742	21.0	2.0	3.6	8.1	3.2	6.4	1,097	35	9	442	1,710	37,727	2,703

1. Based on the resident population estimated as of July 1 of the year shown.

State / county code	CBSA code[1]	County Type code[2]	STATE County	Land area[3] (sq. mi)	Population, 2021: Total persons 2021	Population, 2021: Rank	Population, 2021: Per square mile	Race alone or in combination, not Hispanic or Latino (percent): White	Black	American Indian, Alaska Native	Asian and Pacific Islancer	Percent Hispanic or Latino[4]	Age (percent): Under 5 years	5 to 17 years	18 to 24 years	25 to 34 years	35 to 44 years	45 to 54 years
				1	2	3	4	5	6	7	8	9	10	11	12	13	14	15
			COLORADO—Cont'd															
08013	14500	2	Boulder	726.4	329,543	219	453.7	79.5	1.6	0.9	6.4	14.1	4.0	10.5	17.9	13.8	12.8	12.7
08014	19740	1	Broomfield	33.0	75,325	742	2,282.6	77.3	2.0	0.9	8.7	13.5	4.5	12.3	12.2	15.9	14.7	13.8
08015		7	Chaffee	1,013.4	20,074	1,812	19.8	86.0	2.1	1.8	1.3	10.2	3.5	8.5	8.6	12.8	13.5	11.6
08017		9	Cheyenne	1,778.3	1,707	3,066	1.0	82.6	1.8	1.9	2.6	12.5	4.7	15.5	10.5	8.8	14.1	10.0
08019	19740	1	Clear Creek	395.1	9,446	2,456	23.9	89.2	1.6	1.5	1.9	7.7	3.6	7.5	8.0	12.7	13.7	14.7
08021		9	Conejos	1,287.4	7,612	2,604	5.9	46.8	1.0	1.7	0.8	50.9	6.0	14.9	12.5	11.2	11.4	10.5
08023		9	Costilla	1,227.6	3,625	2,917	3.0	36.6	2.3	2.7	2.0	58.5	4.6	10.9	10.1	10.3	10.3	10.5
08025		8	Crowley	787.4	6,012	2,733	7.6	53.8	10.9	2.4	1.5	32.8	2.4	7.0	11.8	20.8	18.2	15.5
08027		8	Custer	738.6	5,045	2,821	6.8	90.6	2.1	2.1	1.0	6.2	4.0	7.5	7.9	7.5	8.9	10.0
08029		6	Delta	1,142.1	31,661	1,388	27.7	82.2	1.0	1.6	1.1	15.6	4.6	11.1	10.2	9.8	11.3	10.6
08031	19740	1	Denver	153.1	711,463	94	4,647.0	57.2	10.2	1.3	5.1	29.0	5.5	10.1	11.0	23.1	16.9	11.7
08033		9	Dolores	1,067.2	2,397	3,008	2.2	88.4	1.0	3.6	0.9	8.0	3.3	11.4	9.4	9.5	11.7	11.7
08035	19740	1	Douglas	840.2	368,990	200	439.2	82.5	2.3	0.7	7.4	9.7	5.3	13.8	12.7	11.9	14.9	15.3
08037	20780	5	Eagle	1,684.5	55,727	926	33.1	68.0	1.3	0.8	1.8	29.3	4.8	11.9	11.2	14.7	15.6	15.0
08039	19740	1	Elbert	1,850.8	27,128	1,524	14.7	88.3	1.9	1.4	1.8	8.6	4.5	12.3	11.2	9.6	12.2	14.3
08041	17820	2	El Paso	2,126.4	737,867	91	347.0	71.4	7.8	1.4	5.4	18.4	6.2	13.3	14.6	16.1	13.7	11.1
08043	15860	4	Fremont	1,533.9	49,661	1,000	32.4	80.0	4.2	2.3	1.3	13.7	4.0	9.1	9.6	14.2	14.0	12.4
08045	24060	5	Garfield	2,947.4	62,161	857	21.1	67.8	1.0	1.2	1.4	30.0	6.3	14.0	12.1	13.5	14.3	12.5
08047	19740	1	Gilpin	150.0	5,873	2,745	39.2	88.0	2.1	2.0	2.6	7.8	2.8	8.2	8.1	10.6	13.9	16.6
08049		7	Grand	1,846.4	15,860	2,041	8.6	87.7	1.2	1.3	1.3	9.9	3.7	9.2	9.6	13.5	14.2	12.8
08051		7	Gunnison	3,239.1	17,281	1,954	5.3	87.7	1.2	1.5	1.4	9.9	3.9	9.3	19.7	14.5	14.1	12.6
08053		9	Hinsdale	1,117.2	781	3,119	0.7	90.9	2.3	2.2	1.3	6.1	3.6	9.2	11.0	8.5	10.0	9.3
08055		6	Huerfano	1,591.0	6,920	2,670	4.3	64.2	1.6	2.1	1.4	32.6	3.5	9.2	8.8	8.8	9.5	10.4
08057		9	Jackson	1,613.7	1,363	3,090	0.8	85.0	0.7	1.4	0.8	12.9	4.6	9.8	7.6	9.4	12.8	13.9
08059	19740	1	Jefferson	764.4	579,581	119	758.2	79.1	1.9	1.1	4.2	15.9	4.8	10.7	10.8	15.3	14.9	12.5
08061		9	Kiowa	1,767.8	1,452	3,081	0.8	88.4	1.3	1.4	0.7	9.6	6.1	13.8	10.1	10.5	10.3	8.9
08063		7	Kit Carson	2,160.8	6,950	2,668	3.2	79.2	1.3	1.3	1.3	18.6	6.0	15.0	11.6	11.2	12.4	9.6
08065		6	Lake	376.9	7,407	2,628	19.7	61.8	1.4	1.7	1.3	35.2	5.6	11.8	12.0	16.6	15.0	12.4
08067	20420	4	La Plata	1,689.7	56,250	920	33.3	79.9	1.1	6.5	1.3	13.0	4.1	10.5	12.1	12.8	13.8	12.3
08069	22660	2	Larimer	2,595.8	362,533	204	139.7	83.6	1.8	1.1	3.5	12.4	4.4	10.8	17.3	14.8	13.0	11.0
08071		7	Las Animas	4,772.9	14,633	2,106	3.1	54.5	2.5	2.0	1.8	40.7	4.2	10.2	12.0	11.3	11.2	10.9
08073		8	Lincoln	2,577.7	5,688	2,763	2.2	76.2	6.2	1.7	1.9	15.8	5.2	11.1	10.8	16.7	14.0	12.0
08075	44540	7	Logan	1,838.6	21,487	1,737	11.7	75.9	4.9	1.5	1.3	17.8	5.0	9.9	13.2	15.9	13.7	11.5
08077	24300	3	Mesa	3,328.7	157,335	435	47.3	82.1	1.4	1.4	1.8	15.3	5.1	12.0	12.4	12.9	13.0	10.7
08079		9	Mineral	875.8	924	3,110	1.1	91.7	1.3	1.1	1.0	6.6	3.5	7.1	8.2	9.3	12.4	14.0
08081	18780	7	Moffat	4,743.2	13,185	2,202	2.8	80.6	1.5	1.5	1.4	16.9	5.7	14.7	12.3	12.2	13.2	11.5
08083		6	Montezuma	2,029.3	26,175	1,556	12.9	73.7	1.0	13.3	1.3	12.8	4.9	12.6	10.4	11.0	11.6	10.9
08085	33940	4	Montrose	2,240.9	43,168	1,123	19.3	76.8	0.9	1.6	1.3	21.1	4.9	12.1	10.5	10.0	11.9	10.9
08087	22820	6	Morgan	1,280.5	29,008	1,456	22.7	57.6	4.2	1.0	1.2	37.3	7.1	14.7	12.4	14.1	12.7	11.0
08089		6	Otero	1,261.9	18,594	1,891	14.7	54.2	1.6	1.5	1.2	43.1	5.7	13.4	13.5	11.2	12.1	10.5
08091	33940	9	Ouray	540.7	5,035	2,822	9.3	91.1	0.8	1.2	1.3	7.3	2.8	8.2	7.2	8.6	11.4	12.5
08093	19740	1	Park	2,193.5	17,720	1,934	8.1	90.1	1.5	1.8	1.8	7.0	3.6	8.2	7.4	9.8	12.7	14.1
08095		9	Phillips	687.9	4,512	2,855	6.6	74.3	1.1	0.9	1.0	23.8	5.8	14.2	12.5	10.1	11.6	10.9
08097	24060	7	Pitkin	970.7	17,348	1,951	17.9	85.4	1.4	0.8	2.7	11.1	3.9	8.2	8.8	14.3	13.6	14.6
08099		7	Prowers	1,638.4	11,996	2,286	7.3	57.7	1.5	1.4	0.9	39.9	6.7	14.8	14.4	11.0	11.8	10.4
08101	39380	3	Pueblo	2,386.6	169,622	395	71.1	52.6	2.5	1.5	1.6	43.7	5.5	12.7	12.6	13.2	12.7	11.4
08103		9	Rio Blanco	3,221.0	6,476	2,701	2.0	85.5	2.2	1.7	1.6	11.3	5.0	14.1	13.5	11.3	13.4	10.1
08105		7	Rio Grande	912.0	11,408	2,319	12.5	53.0	1.3	1.8	0.8	44.4	5.1	12.4	12.0	11.5	12.5	11.0
08107	44460	7	Routt	2,362.0	25,091	1,606	10.6	90.5	1.4	0.8	1.4	7.0	4.0	10.1	10.0	13.8	15.3	14.2
08109		9	Saguache	3,168.6	6,471	2,702	2.0	60.9	1.8	2.7	1.4	35.4	4.3	10.8	10.5	8.4	11.1	11.6
08111		9	San Juan	387.5	733	3,124	1.9	83.6	1.0	1.8	1.5	14.3	1.6	8.2	6.4	13.1	16.0	13.2
08113		9	San Miguel	1,286.7	8,074	2,574	6.3	85.7	1.1	1.3	1.5	11.9	3.7	10.1	8.9	15.4	14.4	15.8
08115		9	Sedgwick	548.0	2,336	3,016	4.3	80.4	1.6	1.2	1.0	17.5	3.8	11.3	10.2	7.9	11.9	9.7
08117	14720	5	Summit	608.3	30,941	1,403	50.9	81.9	1.6	0.7	2.1	15.0	4.1	9.0	8.5	19.1	15.7	14.3
08119	17820	2	Teller	557.1	24,926	1,617	44.7	88.6	1.5	1.9	1.8	8.3	3.6	9.7	8.5	9.7	11.6	12.6
08121		9	Washington	2,518.1	4,861	2,832	1.9	86.8	2.0	0.9	0.8	11.1	5.1	13.5	10.9	11.7	12.4	11.3
08123	24540	2	Weld	3,984.9	340,036	213	85.3	65.5	1.8	1.2	2.6	30.6	6.8	14.5	13.3	15.1	14.7	12.0
08125		7	Yuma	2,364.4	9,941	2,412	4.2	72.2	0.8	0.7	0.6	26.6	6.8	16.0	12.2	11.4	12.1	10.9
09000		0	CONNECTICUT	4,842.7	3,605,597	X	744.5	66.3	11.7	0.7	5.7	17.7	4.9	11.4	13.3	12.6	12.5	12.8
09001	14860	2	Fairfield	625.0	959,768	53	1,535.6	61.1	12.2	0.4	6.7	21.3	5.2	12.5	13.2	11.6	12.9	13.7
09003	25540	1	Hartford	734.9	896,854	64	1,220.4	60.3	14.9	0.6	6.8	19.4	5.2	11.7	12.7	13.3	13.1	12.4
09005	45860	4	Litchfield	920.5	185,000	365	201.0	87.4	2.7	0.6	2.7	8.1	4.1	10.0	10.8	10.9	11.3	13.0
09007	25540	1	Middlesex	369.3	164,759	407	446.1	84.1	6.1	0.6	4.1	7.1	3.9	9.4	12.1	11.7	11.7	13.0
09009	35300	2	New Haven	604.3	863,700	68	1,429.3	61.7	14.6	0.6	5.0	20.2	5.0	11.2	13.4	13.3	12.5	12.4
09011	35980	2	New London	665.1	268,805	263	404.2	76.9	7.4	1.8	5.4	12.0	4.7	10.8	13.3	13.2	11.8	11.9

1. CBSA = Core Based Statistical Area. See Appendix A for explanation. See Appendix B for list of metropolitan areas with component counties. 2. County type code from the Economic Research Service of USDA Rural-Urban Continuum Codes. See Appendix A for definition. 3. Dry land or land partially or temporarily covered by water. 4. May be of any race.

STATE County	Population, 2021 (cont.)				Population change, 2000–2021							Households, 2016–2020				
	Age (percent) (cont.)				Total persons		Percent change		Components of change, 2020–2021					Percent		
	55 to 64 years	65 to 74 years	75 years and over	Percent female	2010	2020	2010–2020	2020–2021	Births	Deaths	Net Migration	Number	Persons per household	Family households	Female family householder[1]	One person
	16	17	18	19	20	21	22	23	24	25	26	27	28	29	30	31
COLORADO—Cont'd																
Boulder	12.4	10.1	5.9	49.4	294,567	330,758	12.3	-0.4	3,020	2,869	-1,416	127,365	2.5	57.5	7.2	29.3
Broomfield	11.6	9.2	5.8	49.7	55,889	74,112	32.6	1.6	783	621	1,040	27,199	2.5	64.0	6.6	27.5
Chaffee	15.4	16.7	9.3	47.1	17,809	19,476	9.4	3.1	171	254	693	8,650	2.1	64.6	8.4	27.6
Cheyenne	14.0	13.5	9.0	48.7	1,836	1,748	-4.8	-2.3	21	29	-32	804	2.4	68.5	4.9	28.1
Clear Creek	17.8	15.4	6.6	47.1	9,088	9,397	3.4	0.5	75	76	51	4,378	2.2	53.6	5.9	38.1
Conejos	13.5	12.3	7.7	49.4	8,256	7,461	-9.6	2.0	117	92	126	3,222	2.5	53.2	8.2	45.5
Costilla	16.9	16.5	9.9	47.7	3,524	3,499	-0.7	3.6	39	39	129	1,620	2.4	60.3	13.8	34.3
Crowley	11.0	7.9	5.4	26.0	5,823	5,922	1.7	1.5	31	85	145	1,421	3.2	62.2	8.1	36.2
Custer	21.0	23.5	9.7	48.4	4,255	4,704	10.6	7.2	52	77	373	2,310	2.1	65.6	1.6	27.5
Delta	15.1	16.8	10.4	49.8	30,952	31,196	0.8	1.5	341	571	707	12,277	2.4	64.9	8.5	29.9
Denver	9.4	7.6	4.5	49.6	600,158	715,522	19.2	-0.6	10,870	7,509	-7,444	287,756	2.4	48.1	8.9	38.4
Dolores	16.8	15.3	10.8	47.1	2,064	2,326	12.7	3.1	17	24	79	930	2.0	60.8	6.1	37.6
Douglas	12.9	8.5	4.7	49.6	285,465	357,978	25.4	3.1	4,266	2,530	9,302	121,492	2.8	76.6	6.3	18.6
Eagle	13.0	9.6	4.2	47.1	52,197	55,731	6.8	0.0	653	198	-471	18,667	2.9	64.0	6.2	24.6
Elbert	17.8	12.6	5.4	48.9	23,086	26,062	12.9	4.1	275	238	1,045	8,816	3.0	80.6	6.4	15.1
El Paso	11.6	8.6	5.0	49.2	622,263	730,395	17.4	1.0	11,029	7,467	3,752	262,780	2.6	68.0	9.7	24.8
Fremont	14.3	13.6	8.8	42.2	46,824	48,939	4.5	1.5	461	780	1,055	17,449	2.1	65.8	8.5	27.6
Garfield	12.7	9.8	4.7	48.5	56,389	61,685	9.4	0.8	922	524	66	21,586	2.7	71.5	8.7	20.8
Gilpin	20.4	14.6	4.9	47.3	5,441	5,808	6.7	1.1	43	47	68	2,860	2.1	58.8	7.0	32.5
Grand	16.9	14.7	5.5	46.6	14,843	15,717	5.9	0.9	155	84	72	6,315	2.4	59.1	5.6	33.0
Gunnison	11.7	9.9	4.4	46.1	15,324	16,918	10.4	2.1	160	122	327	6,824	2.4	52.1	5.4	34.1
Hinsdale	17.3	19.5	11.7	48.9	843	788	-6.5	-0.9	5	5	-6	376	2.1	61.4	13.0	33.8
Huerfano	17.8	19.7	12.3	49.0	6,711	6,820	1.6	1.5	50	166	222	3,057	2.2	59.7	7.9	36.5
Jackson	16.3	16.7	8.9	47.4	1,394	1,379	-1.1	-1.2	9	12	-12	635	2.1	62.4	2.7	33.5
Jefferson	13.7	10.9	6.5	49.7	534,543	582,910	9.0	-0.6	6,920	6,832	-3,479	229,007	2.5	64.3	8.4	27.2
Kiowa	15.8	13.4	11.2	50.2	1,398	1,446	3.4	0.4	16	19	8	615	2.3	61.8	9.6	28.9
Kit Carson	13.7	11.4	9.1	49.5	8,270	7,087	-14.3	-1.9	107	107	-136	3,020	2.3	62.8	6.0	33.7
Lake	12.0	10.1	4.5	46.3	7,310	7,436	1.7	-0.4	89	43	-77	3,275	2.4	50.3	8.8	36.0
La Plata	14.5	13.4	6.5	49.3	51,334	55,638	8.4	1.1	560	575	630	21,370	2.5	62.2	7.0	31.0
Larimer	11.8	10.7	6.2	50.0	299,630	359,066	19.8	1.0	3,691	3,454	3,185	134,185	2.5	62.5	7.0	24.6
Las Animas	14.7	15.5	9.9	47.2	15,507	14,555	-6.1	0.5	134	236	182	6,750	2.0	57.5	11.1	34.5
Lincoln	13.0	8.9	8.2	40.8	5,467	5,675	3.8	0.2	60	66	18	1,513	2.3	58.8	5.9	37.9
Logan	12.6	10.6	7.6	42.7	22,709	21,528	-5.2	-0.2	277	355	33	8,301	2.6	60.1	7.4	35.0
Mesa	13.4	12.6	7.9	50.3	146,723	155,703	6.1	1.0	1,911	2,298	2,019	59,750	2.5	62.8	9.7	29.7
Mineral	16.6	18.7	10.2	49.8	712	865	21.5	6.8	6	11	65	394	2.1	64.0	4.6	33.5
Moffat	13.6	10.8	6.0	48.3	13,795	13,292	-3.6	-0.8	183	171	-120	5,218	2.5	66.0	15.1	28.4
Montezuma	14.6	15.4	8.6	50.3	25,535	25,849	1.2	1.3	290	411	454	10,521	2.5	66.7	9.8	26.8
Montrose	14.7	14.8	10.3	50.4	41,276	42,679	3.4	1.1	493	677	677	17,483	2.4	69.4	8.1	26.8
Morgan	12.0	9.3	6.7	48.6	28,159	29,111	3.4	-0.4	518	402	-222	10,863	2.6	68.6	10.3	24.4
Otero	13.1	11.8	8.7	50.3	18,831	18,690	-0.7	-0.5	246	351	7	7,761	2.3	59.9	11.6	33.7
Ouray	19.0	20.8	9.4	49.4	4,436	4,874	9.9	3.3	30	38	171	2,259	2.2	63.1	4.9	25.4
Park	21.0	17.5	5.6	46.8	16,206	17,390	7.3	1.9	174	166	327	6,987	2.6	74.1	3.9	19.3
Phillips	12.8	11.3	10.8	49.9	4,442	4,530	2.0	-0.4	69	82	-5	1,737	2.5	68.7	7.4	28.8
Pitkin	14.7	13.8	8.1	47.8	17,148	17,358	1.2	-0.1	164	70	-104	7,424	2.4	52.6	8.4	34.5
Prowers	12.6	11.2	7.1	49.8	12,551	11,999	-4.4	0.0	191	191	-5	4,900	2.4	64.3	12.5	31.8
Pueblo	12.8	11.6	7.5	50.4	159,063	168,162	5.7	0.9	2,154	2,873	2,182	65,206	2.5	61.7	13.0	32.6
Rio Blanco	14.4	11.5	6.8	48.1	6,666	6,529	-2.1	-0.8	60	58	-53	2,513	2.4	64.5	8.1	32.8
Rio Grande	13.4	13.7	8.4	49.9	11,982	11,539	-3.7	-1.1	130	175	-86	4,737	2.3	61.7	8.5	34.5
Routt	14.7	12.7	5.2	47.8	23,509	24,829	5.6	1.1	240	163	184	10,100	2.5	62.0	5.9	26.9
Saguache	17.9	17.8	7.6	49.8	6,108	6,368	4.3	1.6	64	109	152	2,803	2.4	63.3	10.5	33.7
San Juan	16.6	16.1	8.7	45.3	699	705	0.9	4.0	1	12	40	297	2.2	49.5	2.7	37.4
San Miguel	14.7	12.4	4.6	46.7	7,359	8,072	9.7	0.0	67	38	-30	3,604	2.3	55.3	4.6	32.7
Sedgwick	15.5	16.5	13.1	50.8	2,379	2,404	1.1	-2.8	16	50	-34	954	2.4	59.9	11.1	37.1
Summit	14.1	11.1	4.2	45.2	27,994	31,055	10.9	-0.4	291	102	-310	11,609	2.6	55.6	3.7	28.5
Teller	19.6	17.9	6.8	49.2	23,350	24,710	5.8	0.9	206	287	303	10,460	2.4	66.5	6.1	28.0
Washington	13.5	12.5	8.9	47.0	4,814	4,817	0.1	0.9	57	89	76	2,081	2.2	69.8	7.6	24.1
Weld	11.0	8.1	4.6	49.2	252,825	328,981	30.1	3.4	5,467	2,898	8,503	102,046	3.0	73.6	10.1	20.8
Yuma	12.0	10.4	8.1	49.4	10,043	9,988	-0.5	-0.5	148	148	-47	4,108	2.4	71.3	10.0	25.1
CONNECTICUT	14.4	10.5	7.5	50.9	3,574,097	3,605,944	0.9	0.0	40,961	47,074	5,222	1,385,437	2.5	65.2	12.5	28.5
Fairfield	14.4	9.5	7.0	51.0	916,829	957,419	4.4	0.2	11,437	10,825	1,566	345,070	2.7	69.4	11.9	25.1
Hartford	13.8	10.2	7.5	51.1	894,014	899,498	0.6	-0.3	10,715	12,429	-1,100	353,653	2.5	63.8	13.8	30.1
Litchfield	17.2	13.6	9.2	50.1	189,927	185,186	-2.5	-0.1	1,670	2,792	943	74,902	2.4	65.1	9.3	28.8
Middlesex	16.5	12.7	9.0	51.0	165,676	164,245	-0.9	0.3	1,546	2,281	1,256	67,765	2.3	63.2	9.6	29.5
New Haven	14.1	10.6	7.5	51.6	862,477	864,835	0.3	-0.1	9,991	11,956	677	332,765	2.5	62.6	14.0	31.0
New London	14.9	11.4	7.9	49.6	274,055	268,555	-2.0	0.1	2,948	3,647	920	109,616	2.3	65.2	11.9	28.1

1. No spouse present.

STATE County	Persons in group quarters, 2021	Daytime Population, 2016–2020		Births, 2021		Deaths, 2021		Persons under 65 with no health insurance, 2019		Medicare, 2021			COVID-19 Deaths, 2020	
		Number	Employment/ residence ratio	Total	Rate[1]	Number	Rate[1]	Number	Percent	Total beneficiaries	Enrolled in Original Medicare	Enrolled in Medicare Advantage	Number	Rate[1]
	32	33	34	35	36	37	38	39	40	41	42	43	44	45
COLORADO—Cont'd														
Boulder	10,435	361,024	1.2	2,415	7.3	2,319	7.0	20,712	7.7	53,602	29,926	23,676	167	0.5
Broomfield	254	75,402	1.2	619	8.3	504	6.7	3,245	5.3	10,980	5,089	5,891	61	0.8
Chaffee	1,221	20,059	1.0	133	6.7	202	10.2	1,539	11.3	5,527	4,163	1,364	18	0.9
Cheyenne	33	2,419	1.4	17	9.9	21	12.2	204	14.6	393	354	40	D	D
Clear Creek	60	8,176	0.8	55	5.8	63	6.7	547	7.2	1,925	1,086	840	D	D
Conejos	7	7,033	0.6	83	11.0	73	9.7	708	11.1	1,951	1,326	625	D	D
Costilla	0	3,539	0.8	29	8.1	27	7.6	419	15.3	1,194	825	369	D	D
Crowley	2,707	5,571	0.9	23	3.9	59	9.9	286	12.5	869	656	213	12	2.0
Custer	107	4,504	0.8	47	9.6	63	12.9	413	12.9	1,827	1,312	514	D	D
Delta	525	28,989	0.8	277	8.8	462	14.7	2,524	11.5	9,488	6,584	2,904	31	1.0
Denver	15,116	863,848	1.4	8,755	12.3	6,019	8.4	63,469	10.1	92,682	42,509	50,173	734	1.0
Dolores	0	1,662	0.7	14	5.9	19	8.0	157	10.5	568	496	72	D	D
Douglas	519	312,057	0.8	3,446	9.5	2,065	5.7	13,403	4.3	48,922	26,470	22,452	193	0.5
Eagle	43	53,756	1.0	513	9.2	163	2.9	6,582	13.7	6,419	5,852	567	14	0.3
Elbert	35	18,271	0.4	231	8.7	200	7.5	1,584	7.1	5,063	3,143	1,920	15	0.6
El Paso	19,435	703,951	1.0	8,819	12.0	5,909	8.0	54,443	9.0	111,603	67,502	44,101	595	0.8
Fremont	8,021	47,437	1.0	386	7.8	628	12.7	2,680	9.2	12,673	7,050	5,623	32	0.7
Garfield	818	55,469	0.9	731	11.8	424	6.8	7,965	15.7	8,910	7,776	1,134	40	0.6
Gilpin	21	7,907	1.5	36	6.2	39	6.7	218	4.3	1,071	646	425	D	D
Grand	179	15,155	1.0	124	7.8	70	4.4	1,427	11.2	2,693	2,104	588	D	D
Gunnison	876	17,371	1.0	129	7.5	100	5.8	1,398	9.9	2,522	2,207	315	D	D
Hinsdale	55	878	1.3	4	5.1	5	6.3	68	12.2	251	217	34	D	D
Huerfano	137	6,811	1.0	42	6.1	128	18.6	399	8.8	2,440	1,768	672	11	1.6
Jackson	2	1,383	1.1	7	5.1	9	6.6	159	15.2	342	303	39	D	D
Jefferson	7,804	533,415	0.9	5,516	9.5	5,518	9.5	35,897	7.5	108,278	45,558	62,720	579	1.0
Kiowa	12	1,474	1.0	14	9.6	14	9.6	111	10.5	348	326	22	D	D
Kit Carson	44	7,304	1.0	85	12.1	78	11.1	811	14.5	1,522	1,376	146	D	D
Lake	92	6,032	0.6	71	9.6	32	4.3	969	14.4	1,029	886	143	D	D
La Plata	1,673	57,366	1.0	462	8.3	477	8.5	5,001	11.3	11,336	9,135	2,201	30	0.5
Larimer	9,675	348,546	1.0	2,960	8.2	2,759	7.6	22,447	7.7	65,205	38,640	26,565	139	0.4
Las Animas	773	14,252	1.0	105	7.2	183	12.5	1,297	13.2	4,283	2,999	1,285	D	D
Lincoln	983	5,998	1.3	48	8.5	55	9.7	382	10.4	1,047	929	119	D	D
Logan	3,302	21,600	0.9	219	10.2	276	12.8	1,627	11.2	4,278	3,331	948	58	2.7
Mesa	4,310	151,697	1.0	1,529	9.8	1,877	12.0	13,094	10.9	35,695	22,687	13,008	141	0.9
Mineral	0	868	1.0	6	6.7	6	6.7	56	11.0	298	242	56	D	D
Moffat	79	11,381	0.7	135	10.2	131	9.9	1,103	10.0	2,368	2,124	244	21	1.6
Montezuma	177	26,061	1.0	235	9.0	341	13.1	2,751	13.9	6,921	5,535	1,386	16	0.6
Montrose	418	41,428	1.0	405	9.4	559	13.0	4,115	12.9	11,510	8,219	3,291	32	0.7
Morgan	488	29,001	1.0	402	13.8	300	10.3	3,547	14.9	5,099	4,108	992	78	2.7
Otero	472	18,457	1.0	202	10.8	290	15.6	1,572	11.4	4,707	3,438	1,269	44	2.4
Ouray	0	4,643	0.9	18	3.6	22	4.4	309	8.6	1,466	1,220	245	D	D
Park	36	14,599	0.6	128	7.3	142	8.1	1,289	8.8	3,824	2,715	1,108	D	D
Phillips	56	4,238	0.9	46	10.2	68	15.0	435	13.5	1,038	959	79	D	D
Pitkin	29	26,156	1.7	133	7.7	55	3.2	1,500	10.6	3,045	2,856	189	D	D
Prowers	264	11,976	1.0	148	12.3	142	11.8	1,383	14.6	2,515	2,299	216	20	1.7
Pueblo	3,791	165,514	1.0	1,723	10.2	2,283	13.5	12,543	9.6	39,116	19,892	19,224	302	1.8
Rio Blanco	258	6,801	1.2	49	7.5	42	6.5	479	9.5	1,221	1,031	190	D	D
Rio Grande	184	11,273	1.0	105	9.2	142	12.4	1,227	14.2	3,289	2,620	669	D	D
Routt	257	26,877	1.1	183	7.3	139	5.6	2,043	9.6	4,227	3,713	514	21	0.8
Saguache	5	6,485	0.9	49	7.6	84	13.1	899	18.1	1,400	1,165	235	D	D
San Juan	0	820	1.5	0	0.0	9	12.5	65	12.2	173	157	16	D	D
San Miguel	7	9,342	1.3	51	6.3	30	3.7	844	12.3	1,141	1,016	125	D	D
Sedgwick	33	2,285	1.0	14	5.9	37	15.7	199	12.4	730	669	61	D	D
Summit	251	33,501	1.2	241	7.8	80	2.6	3,217	12.1	3,669	3,018	651	D	D
Teller	72	22,840	0.8	178	7.2	234	9.4	1,544	8.0	6,698	3,948	2,751	11	0.4
Washington	160	4,368	0.8	43	8.9	71	14.7	386	10.6	1,079	991	88	14	2.9
Weld	5,434	285,728	0.8	4,333	12.9	2,340	7.0	30,273	10.9	46,091	25,768	20,323	295	0.9
Yuma	157	10,361	1.1	115	11.5	118	11.8	1,194	15.1	1,918	1,778	140	12	1.2
CONNECTICUT	109,137	3,528,821	1.0	32,671	9.1	37,646	10.4	201,146	7.0	691,541	381,673	309,868	6,214	1.7
Fairfield	19,219	941,120	1.0	9,146	9.5	8,696	9.1	72,442	9.3	159,488	103,589	55,899	1,726	1.8
Hartford	24,667	961,681	1.2	8,558	9.5	9,904	11.0	43,194	6.0	174,825	84,713	90,112	1,859	2.1
Litchfield	2,394	155,940	0.7	1,331	7.2	2,254	12.2	8,618	6.1	43,407	25,563	17,844	261	1.4
Middlesex	4,870	151,193	0.9	1,225	7.5	1,822	11.1	5,840	4.7	37,212	18,780	18,431	241	1.5
New Haven	28,367	825,058	0.9	7,980	9.2	9,516	11.0	47,465	7.0	167,724	89,020	78,705	1,606	1.9
New London	10,719	265,511	1.0	2,325	8.7	2,938	10.9	12,556	6.1	57,332	33,939	23,393	300	1.1

1. Per 1,000 estimated resident population.

STATE County	COVID-19 Vaccinations, 2021–2022		Education						Money income, 2016–2020				Income and poverty, 2020			
			School enrollment and attainment, 2016–2020				Local government expenditures,[3] 2018–2019			Households				Percent below poverty level		
			Enrollment[1]		Attainment[2] (percent)						Percent					
	Number	Percent[5]	Total	Percent private	High school graduate or less	Bachelor's degree or more	Total current spending (mil dol)	Current spending per student (dollars)	Per capita income[4]	Median income (dollars)	with income of less than $50,000	with income of $200,000 or more	Median household income (dollars)	All persons	Children under 18 years	Children 5 to 17 years in families
	46	47	48	49	50	51	52	53	54	55	56	57	58	59	60	61
COLORADO—Cont'd																
Boulder	256,255	78.6	97,287	10.9	15.8	63.0	743.4	11,651	48,776	87,476	29.7	15.6	88,289	9.5	6.3	5.6
Broomfield	56,854	80.7	17,288	12.0	17.1	56.1	NA	NA	51,461	101,206	20.4	16.3	106,263	4.2	4.1	3.8
Chaffee	13,045	64.1	2,913	8.2	32.5	35.5	28.8	12,235	31,960	55,176	43.0	5.4	64,220	9.6	11.2	10.5
Cheyenne	607	33.2	464	7.8	33.2	23.5	5.4	18,659	31,409	67,763	43.2	5.2	56,383	12.3	18.1	17.1
Clear Creek	4,772	49.2	1,518	8.7	22.8	50.9	10.6	13,922	44,162	71,919	32.9	10.6	79,422	7.3	9.3	8.8
Conejos	4,060	49.5	2,050	9.3	43.2	25.5	16.1	10,395	20,139	33,611	65.8	1.1	39,822	17.6	22.4	20.8
Costilla	2,344	60.3	686	13.8	41.1	23.9	7.3	14,371	21,893	34,732	67.8	3.3	35,639	21.8	32.2	30.5
Crowley	1,321	21.8	1,112	18.2	62.1	8.7	4.5	10,222	16,593	40,785	61.4	1.1	36,836	37.2	29.5	26.2
Custer	2,466	48.7	842	27.0	25.8	34.1	4.3	11,100	31,608	60,361	39.8	3.9	60,485	12.2	23.2	22.6
Delta	14,892	47.8	5,763	9.6	46.7	21.7	48.8	9,763	26,642	47,968	53.6	3.2	53,553	12.1	15.4	13.7
Denver	552,201	75.9	153,405	18.2	28.0	50.3	1,329.6	12,054	45,636	72,661	33.7	11.4	75,355	12.4	17.3	17.8
Dolores	864	42.0	268	16.4	41.4	26.1	3.5	14,870	31,290	56,786	44.4	1.5	50,821	12.5	15.3	13.2
Douglas	258,192	73.5	94,762	15.9	14.4	58.6	682.2	10,094	53,836	121,393	14.8	21.6	122,290	3.0	2.6	2.3
Eagle	45,404	82.4	11,655	11.1	23.4	50.5	85.0	12,360	47,406	85,877	28.5	14.4	94,309	6.4	7.2	6.2
Elbert	10,057	37.6	5,676	17.2	28.3	34.1	34.0	10,383	43,911	104,231	22.1	15.2	107,139	4.8	6.8	6.0
El Paso	465,301	64.6	189,054	14.3	25.5	38.7	1,240.8	10,218	35,177	71,517	33.8	7.4	72,459	9.1	11.4	10.5
Fremont	21,224	44.4	7,368	17.1	49.4	18.5	53.5	10,558	24,703	52,364	47.4	2.7	52,414	15.2	17.7	17.3
Garfield	38,827	64.6	14,555	13.6	37.1	32.0	137.2	11,573	33,826	75,435	28.5	5.5	79,958	6.7	9.4	8.4
Gilpin	3,630	58.1	1,005	4.8	20.9	44.3	5.9	12,193	59,076	90,547	23.9	12.1	79,622	6.6	7.8	5.4
Grand	9,937	63.2	2,596	7.3	31.9	40.1	22.3	12,620	39,547	71,769	36.0	6.2	74,484	6.8	9.0	8.1
Gunnison	12,107	69.3	4,688	10.5	20.0	57.5	22.6	10,913	33,727	60,557	38.9	6.0	68,214	9.6	8.8	7.6
Hinsdale	527	64.3	70	10.0	20.5	43.7	2.0	24,500	34,595	39,038	58.0	7.7	63,034	7.2	18.8	19.3
Huerfano	3,741	54.2	1,240	14.4	34.3	23.6	9.6	12,976	25,839	40,255	58.7	1.4	49,502	19.9	32.3	28.5
Jackson	637	45.8	237	16.5	32.8	31.4	2.5	13,755	30,813	46,157	56.9	3.8	55,430	11.6	16.7	16.6
Jefferson	451,919	77.5	126,303	13.6	25.1	46.4	908.3	10,730	45,581	87,793	26.1	11.8	90,097	6.1	6.6	6.2
Kiowa	528	37.6	340	4.7	33.4	21.1	3.5	13,389	23,275	39,503	60.0	2.9	49,179	12.0	15.9	16.0
Kit Carson	2,765	39.0	1,572	5.7	43.3	17.6	15.7	10,966	29,276	50,411	49.6	2.4	54,642	10.8	15.5	14.6
Lake	4,862	59.8	1,794	19.7	34.3	40.3	14.0	12,969	35,264	65,858	37.7	3.5	61,518	10.6	14.1	13.0
La Plata	39,724	70.7	12,288	15.0	25.0	44.0	94.9	12,625	38,841	69,291	36.8	7.2	66,080	10.0	12.2	11.2
Larimer	242,942	68.1	96,273	11.7	22.4	47.7	512.9	10,737	38,142	76,366	32.6	8.5	80,344	9.9	7.6	6.5
Las Animas	8,945	61.7	2,700	10.2	39.3	20.0	24.7	11,625	26,918	44,159	54.9	3.4	46,281	16.4	23.4	21.6
Lincoln	2,057	36.1	906	2.9	64.9	12.6	14.6	20,069	16,755	47,042	52.1	2.1	50,169	15.6	18.3	18.0
Logan	8,556	38.2	3,892	8.2	45.9	20.6	29.6	9,962	26,281	49,560	50.3	2.3	55,717	13.1	14.7	14.5
Mesa	77,003	49.9	35,695	11.5	37.7	27.4	253.0	11,142	29,783	57,157	44.7	3.7	64,141	11.1	13.6	12.5
Mineral	638	83.0	101	7.9	18.9	54.1	2.3	24,695	30,908	53,571	46.4	2.5	58,004	8.7	15.0	16.0
Moffat	5,773	43.5	2,897	9.5	48.4	21.5	20.5	8,877	29,059	54,583	47.0	3.9	63,128	9.9	12.1	10.5
Montezuma	18,082	69.1	5,190	8.6	40.3	29.2	39.1	9,790	26,564	50,717	49.5	3.1	54,053	12.9	20.0	18.7
Montrose	20,967	49.0	8,444	10.3	43.4	24.6	62.5	9,706	30,017	54,611	46.1	3.0	59,764	10.4	15.1	14.0
Morgan	14,072	48.4	6,663	13.4	51.7	17.3	56.4	9,842	24,800	58,468	43.4	1.7	63,297	10.5	12.4	12.3
Otero	9,021	49.4	4,433	10.1	42.5	20.5	38.6	11,842	23,275	43,075	55.1	1.6	46,235	17.6	24.7	22.6
Ouray	3,255	65.7	743	9.4	15.0	49.1	9.7	17,874	41,481	68,893	37.2	6.9	74,492	6.7	8.0	7.1
Park	8,941	47.4	2,959	12.4	29.0	32.6	18.5	11,502	38,042	76,611	30.0	4.8	77,598	7.8	11.3	9.8
Phillips	2,232	52.3	1,116	4.8	42.6	25.5	14.0	14,990	29,857	50,426	49.1	4.3	57,385	10.2	14.9	14.3
Pitkin	14,766	83.1	2,881	15.1	17.6	61.2	33.2	19,901	61,261	82,455	23.4	15.0	93,634	6.4	5.2	4.9
Prowers	5,239	43.0	2,829	7.1	44.6	18.6	25.2	10,752	23,496	42,648	57.2	2.6	47,463	16.2	21.7	20.1
Pueblo	95,762	56.9	39,754	7.8	39.3	22.9	258.6	9,777	26,504	49,979	50.0	3.2	50,885	14.1	17.9	16.1
Rio Blanco	2,441	38.6	1,595	7.1	39.0	24.8	16.5	13,047	28,287	54,247	45.8	2.3	64,039	9.8	10.9	10.3
Rio Grande	7,134	63.3	2,764	7.1	42.1	26.0	21.1	11,009	27,300	43,570	55.2	2.3	51,416	13.3	19.7	19.6
Routt	19,416	75.7	5,101	7.7	21.9	49.3	47.3	13,681	44,727	76,198	28.0	8.9	82,330	6.3	6.2	5.9
Saguache	2,451	35.9	1,398	13.4	45.6	22.4	15.4	15,441	22,921	45,231	57.5	0.4	56,012	18.6	29.1	23.5
San Juan	690	94.8	131	0.0	35.0	33.5	1.7	24,043	36,454	56,875	46.8	2.7	54,387	11.3	17.0	16.9
San Miguel	6,817	83.3	1,432	14.9	22.4	56.6	17.4	15,610	47,248	66,898	36.4	9.3	77,099	7.6	7.9	7.3
Sedgwick	1,180	52.5	421	3.3	36.8	20.6	6.6	9,639	27,961	43,875	53.8	3.9	43,354	13.2	22.1	21.8
Summit	26,311	84.8	5,202	11.8	21.7	53.6	45.4	12,704	44,973	80,709	25.7	9.6	91,079	6.1	6.4	5.6
Teller	13,753	54.2	4,900	19.1	27.8	35.5	30.9	11,216	34,541	61,463	38.8	5.4	62,845	7.3	11.7	10.9
Washington	1,518	30.9	957	7.5	39.5	21.0	13.3	14,003	28,224	51,181	48.8	2.4	59,174	11.8	17.6	16.6
Weld	198,884	61.3	85,420	9.4	39.8	27.6	459.3	10,253	32,399	74,332	32.2	6.4	77,937	8.9	9.8	9.4
Yuma	4,415	44.1	2,295	11.9	43.7	20.6	21.9	11,723	28,791	54,393	43.3	2.5	82,124	11.5	16.1	15.0
CONNECTICUT	2,821,249	79.1	888,200	20.2	35.4	40.0	10,532.8	20,573	45,668	79,855	32.0	13.2	79,723	9.7	11.8	11.5
Fairfield	770,845	81.7	248,483	24.6	30.6	48.9	3,029.1	21,004	58,851	97,539	27.3	22.2	98,828	8.8	10.8	11.1
Hartford	676,896	75.9	216,858	16.1	36.2	38.5	2,754.4	21,561	41,470	76,259	34.0	10.7	73,476	10.7	13.6	13.0
Litchfield	136,544	75.7	37,487	17.2	35.9	35.9	462.8	21,607	45,702	81,590	30.2	10.3	79,512	7.4	8.2	8.0
Middlesex	135,606	83.5	37,659	23.6	30.2	42.7	437.4	14,462	46,846	84,907	28.7	12.1	89,970	7.7	6.5	6.0
New Haven	665,847	77.9	212,715	23.7	39.7	36.0	2,432.4	20,464	39,134	71,370	35.9	9.7	72,517	11.2	13.9	13.0
New London	210,709	79.5	59,892	18.6	35.7	34.4	721.7	20,553	40,995	75,831	32.0	9.1	77,202	8.0	10.9	10.6

1. All persons 3 years old and over enrolled in nursery school through college. 2. Persons 25 years old and over. 3. Elementary and secondary education expenditures. 4. Based on population estimated by the American Community Survey, 2016–2020. 5. CDC percent based on 2019 population estimate.

STATE County	Personal income, 2020										Earnings, 2020		
			Per capita[1]			Supplements to wages and salaries, employer contributions (mil dol)						Contributions for government social insurance (mil dol)	
	Total (mil dol)	Percent change 2019–2020	Dollars	Rank	Wages and salaries (mil dol)	Pension and insurance	Government social insurance	Proprietors' income (mil dol)	Dividends, interest, and rent (mil dol)	Personal transfer reecipts (mil dol)	Total (mil dol)	From employee and self-employed	From employer
	62	63	64	65	66	67	68	69	70	71	72	73	74
COLORADO—Cont'd													
Boulder	26,059	3.4	79,649	81	14,939	1,729	978	1,931	7,302	3,094	19,576	1,115	978
Broomfield	4,876	5.6	67,495	203	4,068	371	246	-130	939	630	4,555	307	246
Chaffee	1,061	6.6	51,361	990	371	59	25	103	306	256	558	35	25
Cheyenne	111	15.4	61,731	359	38	7	3	29	20	24	76	3	3
Clear Creek	644	6.5	67,132	208	159	23	11	39	168	105	232	14	11
Conejos	324	12.5	39,847	2,473	61	12	5	60	37	112	137	8	5
Costilla	151	16.1	38,430	2,629	35	7	3	18	23	64	62	4	3
Crowley	135	12.5	23,751	3,111	55	10	4	22	21	50	90	4	4
Custer	237	9.2	45,691	1,700	34	6	2	36	72	76	79	7	2
Delta	1,309	10.2	42,127	2,175	363	64	26	102	285	452	555	42	26
Denver	62,823	4.1	85,411	59	43,045	5,069	2,879	13,147	12,376	7,606	64,140	3,452	2,879
Dolores	88	13.9	42,093	2,181	29	4	2	8	16	29	43	3	2
Douglas	28,492	6.0	78,980	86	9,914	1,069	674	950	5,096	2,863	12,607	838	674
Eagle	4,827	2.6	87,872	46	1,790	194	134	582	1,812	462	2,700	148	134
Elbert	1,747	7.8	63,970	291	203	29	14	97	282	254	344	23	14
El Paso	39,439	7.4	54,151	770	19,347	3,237	1,463	2,390	7,021	8,509	26,437	1,475	1,463
Fremont	1,864	8.7	38,952	2,571	681	136	47	122	331	651	985	67	47
Garfield	3,778	4.2	62,581	330	1,420	202	101	311	1,333	588	2,034	116	101
Gilpin	345	9.4	55,256	685	232	19	17	18	72	69	286	17	17
Grand	908	7.0	57,476	540	322	46	23	96	287	156	487	28	23
Gunnison	898	8.4	51,025	1,026	398	64	28	103	245	164	593	32	28
Hinsdale	40	4.9	49,423	1,208	10	2	1	3	15	11	16	1	1
Huerfano	323	14.6	46,859	1,531	77	15	5	24	68	132	121	10	5
Jackson	86	14.7	62,008	349	24	4	2	17	21	17	48	2	2
Jefferson	40,147	4.1	68,829	182	16,549	2,165	1,183	3,148	7,573	6,299	23,045	1,408	1,183
Kiowa	97	29.0	66,839	216	29	5	3	32	13	19	69	2	3
Kit Carson	336	12.0	47,198	1,489	127	22	10	66	64	82	224	11	10
Lake	322	7.6	40,344	2,411	117	20	8	29	60	73	174	10	8
La Plata	3,468	6.4	61,304	375	1,352	191	94	352	1,101	625	1,989	116	94
Larimer	21,166	5.9	58,725	487	9,930	1,394	674	1,462	4,660	3,662	13,460	776	674
Las Animas	622	13.0	43,118	2,046	225	40	17	40	97	252	322	22	17
Lincoln	203	21.0	35,695	2,894	105	21	7	35	33	59	168	7	7
Logan	1,016	6.0	46,217	1,617	381	68	28	165	180	253	641	34	28
Mesa	7,537	6.2	48,435	1,333	3,174	478	236	578	1,311	2,053	4,467	288	236
Mineral	57	3.7	73,101	124	21	3	2	7	16	13	33	2	2
Moffat	624	10.4	47,467	1,452	264	48	19	53	98	168	384	22	19
Montezuma	1,239	9.3	46,919	1,524	390	71	28	88	258	386	578	39	28
Montrose	1,961	9.3	45,262	1,759	721	118	53	197	407	579	1,090	72	53
Morgan	1,409	8.3	48,701	1,294	645	96	49	167	175	319	957	52	49
Otero	752	10.8	41,333	2,286	285	51	23	43	104	300	402	28	23
Ouray	336	6.2	67,263	205	86	12	6	38	117	61	144	9	6
Park	920	6.8	48,514	1,322	126	20	9	62	190	201	216	16	9
Phillips	218	14.1	49,877	1,155	75	15	6	48	38	56	143	7	6
Pitkin	2,775	-1.2	155,067	4	992	101	71	193	1,720	187	1,356	74	71
Prowers	508	7.3	41,990	2,196	179	34	13	64	78	160	291	16	13
Pueblo	7,336	10.2	43,196	2,038	3,208	491	241	352	1,027	2,548	4,291	286	241
Rio Blanco	332	7.2	52,422	898	160	30	11	15	70	76	216	11	11
Rio Grande	606	11.5	53,641	809	190	34	16	97	94	187	336	19	16
Routt	2,194	4.4	85,836	57	791	103	58	185	964	244	1,137	63	58
Saguache	278	18.1	40,032	2,454	68	14	6	59	55	74	146	7	6
San Juan	37	13.5	50,039	1,139	11	2	1	6	9	8	20	1	1
San Miguel	761	3.9	93,954	30	264	31	20	91	350	73	407	22	20
Sedgwick	115	13.0	50,896	1,040	34	7	3	16	20	36	59	3	3
Summit	2,382	5.1	77,754	90	1,022	115	76	359	754	260	1,572	85	76
Teller	1,394	6.8	54,587	733	347	49	24	68	281	353	488	37	24
Washington	240	18.3	49,287	1,219	61	13	5	53	34	55	133	6	5
Weld	17,385	9.4	52,054	932	6,476	873	463	1,744	2,383	3,048	9,556	542	463
Yuma	475	7.6	47,285	1,476	190	31	16	83	86	111	321	15	16
CONNECTICUT	279,612	3.5	77,664	X	120,129	18,209	8,324	27,836	56,824	47,988	174,497	9,888	8,324
Fairfield	113,322	1.2	120,244	12	39,482	4,918	2,404	12,439	32,949	11,496	59,242	3,283	2,404
Hartford	60,412	5.0	67,938	195	38,262	5,707	2,694	6,232	8,008	12,585	52,895	2,964	2,694
Litchfield	12,055	2.7	67,118	209	3,202	578	251	1,351	2,267	2,378	5,383	335	251
Middlesex	11,525	3.7	71,291	149	4,148	719	312	1,095	1,824	2,073	6,274	368	312
New Haven	51,195	5.7	60,092	422	23,492	3,857	1,811	4,452	7,227	12,417	33,611	1,953	1,811
New London	16,216	5.0	61,191	380	7,455	1,489	552	1,172	2,540	3,782	10,668	605	552

1. Based on the resident population estimated as of July 1 of the year shown.

STATE County	Earnings, 2020 (cont.)									Social Security beneficiaries, December 2020		Supplemental Security Income recipients, 2020	Housing units, 2021	
	Percent by selected industries													
	Farm	Mining, quarrying, and extractions	Construction	Manufacturing	Information; professional, scientific, technical services	Retail trade	Finance, insurance, real estate, and leasing	Health care and social assistance	Government	Number	Rate[1]		Total	Percent change, 2010–2021
	75	76	77	78	79	80	81	82	83	84	85	86	87	88
COLORADO—Cont'd														
Boulder	0.1	0.2	3.7	11.7	33.4	4.5	6.2	9.1	14.2	49,545	150	2,163	143,154	1.3
Broomfield	0.0	D	7.9	16.2	38.6	4.1	-3.8	4.5	2.8	10,140	135	400	31,799	1.3
Chaffee	1.3	D	14.3	1.9	7.5	11.9	6.7	4.8	27.8	5,440	271	193	11,271	2.8
Cheyenne	27.2	11.6	D	D	D	3.1	D	D	18.9	365	214	14	933	0.4
Clear Creek	0.0	D	8.1	3.2	6.3	4.9	2.5	2.2	17.7	1,850	196	74	5,773	1.5
Conejos	28.4	1.6	11.8	2.7	D	6.6	D	9.5	19.1	1,980	260	321	4,063	1.4
Costilla	21.1	0.2	D	D	D	5.9	D	5.0	24.7	1,300	359	235	2,427	0.1
Crowley	25.3	D	3.1	0.2	D	3.8	D	D	37.0	890	148	132	1,524	0.9
Custer	8.5	D	22.4	3.6	7.3	9.4	6.0	D	17.2	1,900	377	67	4,310	2.7
Delta	5.4	1.6	9.8	4.9	4.8	9.2	7.5	9.1	29.1	9,750	308	550	14,866	0.4
Denver	0.0	12.9	4.1	2.8	19.1	2.7	12.1	6.4	10.6	87,640	123	13,690	351,868	1.5
Dolores	14.5	2.5	D	D	2.6	22.7	D	D	23.4	600	250	23	1,329	0.6
Douglas	0.1	3.0	9.0	1.4	13.5	6.8	23.6	9.1	7.5	46,950	127	1,156	140,236	2.8
Eagle	0.3	0.1	15.5	0.9	8.3	7.9	10.0	14.0	9.4	5,960	107	112	33,539	1.3
Elbert	0.5	0.1	27.1	2.5	11.9	6.5	6.1	1.9	15.8	4,880	180	99	10,174	3.3
El Paso	0.1	D	7.9	3.8	15.6	5.8	8.0	10.3	30.7	113,750	154	9,165	295,342	2.3
Fremont	0.9	0.6	8.4	5.0	3.9	7.0	3.5	12.2	43.3	13,250	267	1,146	20,432	0.7
Garfield	1.1	4.8	18.1	1.3	7.6	7.8	7.1	11.9	18.1	8,890	143	442	24,600	1.8
Gilpin	0.0	0.1	3.0	D	D	0.7	D	D	12.5	1,075	183	27	3,543	0.5
Grand	2.6	0.3	16.7	1.5	5.6	7.9	9.1	2.5	20.4	2,545	160	58	16,870	1.1
Gunnison	1.0	D	14.4	1.7	7.9	8.0	5.9	3.6	24.8	2,450	142	56	12,386	1.7
Hinsdale	0.1	D	15.6	D	4.5	D	D	D	29.0	240	307	D	1,342	0.8
Huerfano	3.0	D	11.6	4.9	3.9	9.6	3.8	D	20.5	2,515	363	279	4,734	1.0
Jackson	30.5	D	D	D	6.3	6.6	D	D	18.5	330	242	12	1,196	0.4
Jefferson	0.0	1.3	9.1	12.3	18.0	6.2	6.3	10.1	13.8	101,630	175	5,274	250,910	0.8
Kiowa	48.8	0.4	D	1.7	D	7.0	D	1.3	18.1	355	244	20	738	0.1
Kit Carson	26.3	D	6.6	4.0	2.2	5.9	6.5	4.2	17.2	1,460	210	100	3,425	0.4
Lake	0.0	D	13.6	D	D	5.5	2.1	D	23.8	1,045	141	61	4,360	1.1
La Plata	0.5	6.1	10.4	2.3	10.5	7.3	9.7	13.1	19.5	11,235	200	428	28,545	1.0
Larimer	0.4	0.3	9.2	12.9	13.0	6.4	6.4	9.1	21.5	62,495	172	2,537	162,052	1.6
Las Animas	6.0	7.3	4.4	2.5	2.6	11.2	4.5	16.1	25.8	4,280	292	512	8,131	0.5
Lincoln	16.2	0.1	4.0	D	D	7.8	5.0	4.5	38.5	1,040	183	68	2,375	0.6
Logan	8.8	2.8	5.4	7.3	1.9	8.0	5.0	11.3	24.0	4,140	193	376	8,685	0.1
Mesa	0.8	3.7	10.6	4.4	5.9	8.5	8.1	18.5	16.9	35,830	228	2,645	68,652	1.5
Mineral	2.4	0.6	D	D	D	D	D	D	15.4	290	314	D	1,239	1.5
Moffat	4.1	13.7	5.9	1.1	D	9.7	4.2	14.5	17.7	2,530	192	184	6,110	0.2
Montezuma	3.4	1.5	8.9	3.4	4.4	10.8	4.0	15.3	25.0	7,180	274	442	12,345	0.3
Montrose	2.5	0.3	14.3	6.9	4.8	9.3	5.7	11.6	21.4	11,685	271	614	19,350	1.8
Morgan	12.7	2.7	6.3	24.6	D	5.0	3.7	7.5	13.0	5,135	177	439	11,654	1.1
Otero	6.5	0.2	4.8	8.3	4.8	6.8	3.8	18.1	23.7	4,585	247	820	8,721	0.0
Ouray	3.8	D	13.8	3.5	9.8	8.2	7.7	3.2	16.7	1,435	285	17	3,385	1.7
Park	1.2	D	20.4	2.9	10.6	7.6	4.7	2.1	22.2	3,940	222	122	14,357	1.4
Phillips	21.8	D	7.2	1.2	3.8	3.8	4.2	D	24.2	940	208	54	2,031	0.2
Pitkin	0.1	D	6.3	0.4	9.9	6.5	11.8	2.6	15.5	2,850	164	22	13,332	0.6
Prowers	13.1	0.6	6.4	5.9	D	8.1	6.1	8.1	26.3	2,475	206	353	5,454	0.3
Pueblo	0.5	D	8.9	8.4	7.5	8.4	3.8	20.6	20.1	38,455	227	6,018	72,976	1.2
Rio Blanco	4.9	28.5	6.4	1.3	D	3.0	1.8	1.1	33.6	1,225	189	54	3,281	0.2
Rio Grande	19.0	0.2	6.9	2.9	1.8	4.4	4.7	D	17.1	3,470	304	489	6,566	0.5
Routt	1.8	2.5	11.9	0.9	8.1	8.1	11.0	7.5	15.9	3,905	156	78	16,826	1.5
Saguache	39.3	D	4.9	2.7	D	3.2	D	2.5	18.2	1,455	225	105	3,814	1.5
San Juan	0.0	0.5	D	D	D	13.1	D	D	22.2	165	225	D	788	0.9
San Miguel	0.9	0.4	15.0	2.1	10.2	7.6	8.2	3.8	13.4	1,105	137	28	6,603	0.6
Sedgwick	29.4	0.2	1.8	3.3	D	4.0	D	3.2	29.9	740	317	60	1,343	0.0
Summit	0.0	D	16.5	1.2	8.1	8.3	12.1	6.8	11.3	3,340	108	36	31,831	1.3
Teller	0.0	D	8.8	D	8.0	8.4	5.9	4.7	17.8	6,885	276	202	13,494	1.1
Washington	34.6	D	D	D	D	5.3	4.0	0.7	17.5	1,060	218	69	2,287	0.4
Weld	5.8	7.8	14.0	12.1	4.9	6.3	5.2	7.1	11.7	46,630	137	3,553	124,909	3.3
Yuma	24.1	4.0	3.9	4.6	2.2	5.4	6.8	D	18.3	1,900	191	87	4,320	0.1
CONNECTICUT	0.1	D	5.6	10.5	12.6	5.3	16.4	12.2	12.8	695,402	193	66,925	1,536,344	0.3
Fairfield	0.0	-0.1	4.8	7.3	16.8	5.1	24.3	9.6	7.8	155,430	162	12,672	380,686	0.4
Hartford	0.1	0.0	4.5	11.7	12.3	4.4	20.6	12.1	13.2	176,535	197	21,691	386,139	0.2
Litchfield	0.2	D	13.7	14.5	7.4	8.4	5.4	13.1	12.8	43,920	237	1,790	87,827	0.2
Middlesex	0.3	D	9.3	17.5	8.6	6.7	5.0	14.9	14.7	37,225	226	1,671	76,491	0.2
New Haven	0.1	0.0	6.5	8.5	9.9	6.0	6.3	16.3	14.0	169,565	196	21,088	370,802	0.3
New London	0.6	0.1	5.4	21.4	8.5	5.9	3.1	11.8	23.7	59,005	220	4,572	123,392	0.3

1. Per 1,000 resident population estimated as of July 1 of the year shown.

Table B. States and Counties — **Housing, Labor Force, and Employment**

STATE County	Housing units, 2016–2020								Civilian labor force, 2021				Civilian employment[6], 2016–2020		
	Occupied units										Unemployment			Percent	
		Owner-occupied				Renter-occupied									
				Median owner cost as a percent of income											
	Total	Percent	Median value[1]	With a mortgage	Without a mortgage[2]	Median rent[3]	Median rent as a percent of income[2]	Substandard units[4] (percent)	Total	Percent change, 2020–2021	Total	Rate[5]	Total	Management, business, science, and arts	Construction, production, and maintenance occupations
	89	90	91	92	93	94	95	96	97	98	99	100	101	102	103
COLORADO—Cont'd															
Boulder	127,365	63.6	539,100	20.7	10.0	1,582	33.7	1.7	195,616	2.6	8,522	4.4	175,556	54.9	13.0
Broomfield	27,199	66.3	450,600	19.4	10.0	1,711	28.6	1.3	41,167	1.9	1,848	4.5	39,116	55.9	10.9
Chaffee	8,650	71.1	387,300	25.0	11.2	1,104	30.7	3.4	10,248	6.3	413	4.0	9,272	36.0	21.4
Cheyenne	804	74.4	141,700	16.8	10.0	665	16.6	0.2	1,105	2.0	25	2.3	965	42.3	31.6
Clear Creek	4,378	78.4	399,000	22.4	10.0	1,004	29.1	2.0	6,023	1.0	334	5.5	5,547	41.2	18.0
Conejos	3,222	80.0	123,000	24.8	11.1	614	27.2	6.7	4,102	2.4	196	4.8	3,215	35.1	30.3
Costilla	1,620	73.6	123,600	24.4	12.5	569	29.3	7.3	1,885	4.0	114	6.0	1,324	29.2	34.9
Crowley	1,421	73.3	82,900	23.8	11.0	1,060	40.1	2.7	1,465	1.7	76	5.2	1,726	33.3	23.6
Custer	2,310	88.2	249,900	23.4	10.4	655	33.8	3.3	2,325	11.5	93	4.0	1,933	40.7	32.5
Delta	12,277	73.2	253,500	23.6	10.3	837	37.6	2.4	14,360	1.4	761	5.3	11,242	33.4	30.1
Denver	287,756	50.4	427,600	20.7	10.0	1,397	28.8	3.3	427,421	1.8	25,298	5.9	408,318	49.6	15.3
Dolores	930	79.2	167,700	19.6	10.0	0	10.0	1.4	1,176	3.6	55	4.7	822	34.5	23.4
Douglas	121,492	79.2	493,500	20.0	10.0	1,749	29.0	1.4	200,746	2.4	8,183	4.1	185,330	55.6	9.7
Eagle	18,667	69.7	617,200	25.4	10.0	1,611	33.3	4.2	36,813	4.0	1,636	4.4	32,699	37.1	18.7
Elbert	8,816	91.3	492,300	23.7	10.0	1,203	21.9	1.1	15,468	3.1	587	3.8	13,922	44.0	22.8
El Paso	262,780	65.2	300,200	21.4	10.0	1,234	31.3	3.0	350,677	2.5	19,761	5.6	328,734	43.0	18.0
Fremont	17,449	75.7	197,500	21.5	10.0	853	31.0	2.5	15,860	4.2	1,096	6.9	14,700	35.0	22.1
Garfield	21,586	67.5	375,600	23.2	10.0	1,177	26.8	3.7	32,254	2.7	1,505	4.7	31,818	33.6	24.9
Gilpin	2,860	85.7	387,000	19.0	10.0	1,245	27.6	2.7	3,880	-1.3	239	6.2	3,850	49.1	13.0
Grand	6,315	69.9	347,400	21.6	10.9	976	28.8	2.6	9,718	5.1	409	4.2	8,669	32.2	26.2
Gunnison	6,824	65.4	381,900	22.6	10.2	998	29.5	3.3	11,837	4.8	435	3.7	10,074	34.6	20.0
Hinsdale	376	79.0	325,000	29.8	16.4	815	28.3	1.1	450	6.4	16	3.6	349	40.4	14.6
Huerfano	3,057	72.9	183,100	22.1	15.0	633	31.7	1.1	2,645	1.8	217	8.2	2,485	36.2	23.4
Jackson	635	72.0	211,500	36.0	10.0	0	28.1	1.3	988	5.7	33	3.3	624	30.1	28.4
Jefferson	229,007	71.7	433,100	20.7	10.0	1,451	30.9	1.7	334,051	2.0	16,767	5.0	317,720	48.2	15.9
Kiowa	615	74.5	85,900	21.5	12.8	811	26.3	0.0	957	0.4	32	3.3	693	38.2	23.7
Kit Carson	3,020	67.5	127,800	25.1	10.0	803	27.7	1.4	4,261	1.2	126	3.0	3,560	34.2	31.2
Lake	3,275	77.4	258,200	23.7	10.0	1,086	33.7	5.6	4,974	3.6	218	4.4	4,589	47.0	23.6
La Plata	21,370	71.0	415,900	22.6	10.0	1,195	32.5	2.6	31,905	3.2	1,657	5.2	28,564	42.4	17.0
Larimer	134,185	66.3	390,600	21.2	10.0	1,340	32.4	1.5	206,492	2.6	9,617	4.7	185,199	45.2	17.6
Las Animas	6,750	68.5	158,600	25.7	11.0	722	31.6	1.5	6,513	1.8	426	6.5	5,936	30.1	23.1
Lincoln	1,513	72.4	157,500	21.6	10.0	744	29.6	1.1	2,364	1.0	99	4.2	1,454	41.9	13.5
Logan	8,301	66.5	161,800	19.4	11.8	816	28.0	3.9	10,985	1.1	480	4.4	11,234	29.9	33.7
Mesa	59,750	69.1	245,000	22.1	10.0	963	30.0	2.4	77,219	3.3	4,421	5.7	71,273	35.6	24.8
Mineral	394	73.1	329,300	29.7	10.1	750	27.1	0.0	463	-0.2	23	5.0	455	43.3	11.6
Moffat	5,218	63.9	190,600	19.8	10.0	841	31.8	3.7	7,286	1.7	347	4.8	6,133	30.6	33.0
Montezuma	10,521	70.6	238,200	21.5	10.0	802	30.3	2.5	13,215	4.7	735	5.6	11,492	32.2	23.2
Montrose	17,483	73.9	242,300	22.5	10.0	980	29.1	1.6	22,392	4.2	1,122	5.0	18,381	32.0	29.6
Morgan	10,863	62.9	217,200	25.1	10.8	902	28.4	6.5	16,212	2.0	793	4.9	13,276	27.2	40.1
Otero	7,761	66.9	101,000	20.7	10.4	687	27.3	2.5	8,366	2.3	512	6.1	7,109	33.8	30.7
Ouray	2,259	71.7	486,200	28.0	10.0	1,305	28.9	1.1	2,708	9.1	122	4.5	2,334	51.5	16.5
Park	6,987	91.0	367,400	21.8	10.8	1,167	34.3	1.6	11,273	2.8	463	4.1	8,781	37.7	19.8
Phillips	1,737	72.3	191,200	23.3	10.0	750	25.0	4.3	2,490	1.3	71	2.9	1,900	39.8	34.1
Pitkin	7,424	67.4	599,000	25.1	12.5	1,598	28.6	3.5	11,127	0.0	613	5.5	11,728	46.2	14.9
Prowers	4,900	63.1	108,800	21.3	11.3	696	27.9	4.1	6,265	2.5	284	4.5	5,316	32.4	33.3
Pueblo	65,206	65.1	172,500	21.6	11.0	853	31.3	2.7	77,498	1.8	6,151	7.9	69,867	32.2	23.1
Rio Blanco	2,513	74.3	218,500	21.4	10.0	765	25.4	4.0	2,931	0.9	162	5.5	2,749	31.3	27.3
Rio Grande	4,737	68.8	186,700	17.7	11.1	606	27.9	4.9	5,529	3.2	360	6.5	4,691	32.3	29.1
Routt	10,100	74.6	534,100	24.7	10.1	1,365	29.4	2.0	16,024	0.6	681	4.2	14,340	42.9	18.3
Saguache	2,803	72.8	152,400	22.6	11.1	635	25.7	5.5	3,496	2.7	206	5.9	2,900	32.6	34.2
San Juan	297	55.6	348,700	23.8	11.1	1,038	25.9	3.7	608	17.1	21	3.5	340	24.1	20.9
San Miguel	3,604	60.0	448,900	25.9	11.0	1,146	27.7	3.1	5,836	7.6	294	5.0	5,079	42.7	16.5
Sedgwick	954	67.6	111,300	17.5	10.0	600	33.1	2.0	1,185	2.7	44	3.7	1,018	32.4	30.3
Summit	11,609	68.8	596,300	25.4	11.2	1,449	29.7	6.3	22,727	3.5	909	4.0	19,491	36.6	18.5
Teller	10,460	81.2	304,800	23.8	10.0	1,107	36.1	2.4	13,074	1.9	645	4.9	12,029	40.0	19.5
Washington	2,081	69.8	162,200	21.7	10.0	765	24.6	3.6	2,828	-0.6	90	3.2	2,283	42.7	25.0
Weld	102,046	74.5	326,100	22.5	10.0	1,143	30.6	3.6	165,660	0.5	9,478	5.7	156,119	33.7	29.2
Yuma	4,108	70.3	190,400	21.7	10.0	821	24.9	4.1	5,668	2.1	155	2.7	4,976	36.8	31.9
CONNECTICUT	1,385,437	66.1	279,700	22.4	14.4	1,201	30.8	2.2	1,855,923	-2.2	116,108	6.3	1,807,525	44.5	17.4
Fairfield	345,070	66.7	433,000	23.7	15.0	1,511	32.2	3.0	465,448	-1.6	28,397	6.1	476,757	47.2	14.5
Hartford	353,653	64.1	242,900	21.6	14.3	1,130	30.3	2.0	468,861	-2.8	30,681	6.5	449,633	44.6	17.7
Litchfield	74,902	76.1	258,300	22.7	13.8	1,061	29.8	1.4	101,537	-1.9	5,574	5.5	96,144	41.4	20.1
Middlesex	67,765	73.5	293,300	21.6	14.7	1,174	30.4	1.0	91,071	-2.3	4,709	5.2	87,330	46.6	15.5
New Haven	332,765	62.1	252,300	22.9	15.0	1,173	31.1	2.3	453,791	-1.9	29,734	6.6	429,416	43.1	18.8
New London	109,616	67.1	246,800	21.8	13.9	1,144	28.5	1.7	129,504	-3.2	8,873	6.9	132,072	42.1	18.0

1. Specified owner-occupied units. 2. A value of 10.0 represents 10 percent or less; a value of 50.0 represents 50 percent or more. 3. Specified renter-occupied units. 4. Overcrowded or lacking complete plumbing facilities. 5. Percent of civilian labor force. 6. Civilian employed persons 16 years old and over.

STATE County	Private nonfarm establishments, employment and payroll, 2020: Number of establishments	Employment: Total	Employment: Health care and social assistance	Employment: Manufacturing	Employment: Retail trade	Employment: Finance and insurance	Employment: Professional, scientific, and technical services	Annual payroll: Total (mil dol)	Annual payroll: Average per employee (dollars)	Agriculture, 2017: Farms: Number	Farms: Percent with: Fewer than 50 acres	Farms: Percent with: 1000 acres or more	Farm producers whose primary occupation is farming (percent)
	104	105	106	107	108	109	110	111	112	113	114	115	116
COLORADO—Cont'd													
Boulder	13,013	157,780	21,664	14,700	18,673	3,959	26,954	10,802	68,460	1,012	79.0	2.2	33.1
Broomfield	2,296	45,445	2,975	3,059	5,109	2,569	3,878	3,748	82,482	38	76.3	7.9	38.3
Chaffee	986	6,514	977	151	1,277	211	214	245	37,537	289	52.2	4.2	42.4
Cheyenne	68	653	79	NA	42	43	3	29	44,440	377	4.8	53.1	47.2
Clear Creek	333	3,044	65	58	291	15	47	104	34,159	33	42.4	9.1	27.8
Conejos	113	747	192	65	172	NA	20	29	39,368	524	33.4	14.3	49.2
Costilla	50	375	31	95	81	NA	NA	11	29,661	229	51.5	9.6	38.2
Crowley	38	527	72	NA	71	19	NA	22	42,357	246	21.1	30.9	51.7
Custer	150	572	19	43	162	11	14	17	30,205	315	35.6	8.6	39.0
Delta	836	6,448	1,581	413	1,204	211	174	231	35,777	1,615	69.7	2.8	41.8
Denver	26,817	474,978	57,766	16,508	34,064	29,136	53,629	32,812	69,081	12	100.0	NA	60.0
Dolores	60	301	44	22	47	NA	6	12	38,668	313	21.7	10.5	38.1
Douglas	9,947	122,489	15,926	7,543	18,910	7,188	10,052	7,516	61,357	1,223	67.4	3.0	25.0
Eagle	3,578	32,493	2,326	360	4,173	664	1,607	1,496	46,054	257	44.7	7.8	34.2
Elbert	635	3,063	124	193	521	64	235	133	43,561	1,632	43.2	10.5	29.8
El Paso	18,165	257,543	41,285	12,219	31,762	12,793	25,320	12,733	49,440	1,345	45.5	10.6	34.9
Fremont	907	8,345	2,202	384	1,737	204	204	294	35,240	1,034	72.4	6.8	30.9
Garfield	2,529	21,208	3,267	188	3,166	777	1,265	1,031	48,620	661	49.5	13.2	45.1
Gilpin	127	3,991	NA	9	21	NA	20	140	34,987	37	51.4	NA	31.3
Grand	870	8,563	492	157	693	104	723	272	31,808	290	47.9	13.1	31.6
Gunnison	1,167	6,885	682	162	1,153	152	351	258	37,525	309	40.5	18.1	40.0
Hinsdale	62	145	NA	NA	18	NA	NA	5	32,145	26	7.7	15.4	25.7
Huerfano	152	1,161	398	NA	216	17	28	46	39,354	437	21.3	21.7	30.5
Jackson	64	279	NA	NA	54	NA	13	11	38,724	131	15.3	37.4	46.2
Jefferson	17,665	204,788	29,295	8,884	30,638	15,619	24,644	10,517	51,356	597	77.7	2.7	28.6
Kiowa	37	312	126	NA	96	NA	NA	11	34,304	388	3.1	48.2	47.5
Kit Carson	265	1,987	332	112	372	103	31	78	39,267	574	11.0	40.4	47.0
Lake	218	1,504	171	104	181	19	29	47	31,336	33	42.4	6.1	25.0
La Plata	2,428	22,893	4,072	670	3,477	1,472	1,147	1,115	48,687	1,093	53.4	3.9	35.1
Larimer	11,342	133,524	21,170	12,842	19,658	3,544	10,103	6,635	49,692	2,043	71.0	4.4	31.6
Las Animas	365	3,254	820	127	700	126	60	116	35,608	549	19.1	37.7	44.8
Lincoln	142	1,342	257	16	314	65	33	54	40,011	489	8.4	51.5	48.9
Logan	556	5,064	1,097	352	1,032	200	91	194	38,230	861	16.6	33.1	45.7
Mesa	4,549	55,267	12,410	3,177	8,283	1,679	2,600	2,404	43,497	2,465	80.1	2.6	32.1
Mineral	66	198	NA	NA	43	NA	5	8	40,035	19	NA	21.1	21.9
Moffat	388	3,290	591	57	662	97	88	164	49,819	462	24.5	28.1	29.9
Montezuma	749	6,517	1,367	370	1,304	167	252	245	37,560	1,123	49.2	5.9	37.0
Montrose	1,354	12,692	2,796	1,182	2,196	290	580	526	41,435	1,135	55.9	6.1	40.4
Morgan	715	9,893	1,444	2,906	1,178	212	147	445	44,980	740	28.4	19.5	51.8
Otero	397	4,292	1,225	537	689	138	147	154	35,896	444	30.4	16.9	42.7
Ouray	316	1,319	63	94	190	49	74	57	42,859	122	55.7	9.8	44.0
Park	500	1,691	53	73	270	34	113	65	38,700	278	30.2	14.4	30.1
Phillips	130	1,086	303	NA	154	59	39	48	44,007	326	11.3	39.9	56.3
Pitkin	1,669	18,401	812	187	1,581	266	819	764	41,517	112	51.8	8.9	38.8
Prowers	333	2,851	731	181	677	182	77	95	33,341	472	10.2	36.9	47.6
Pueblo	3,178	53,924	13,644	5,025	8,395	1,171	2,377	2,240	41,541	839	41.7	14.2	37.6
Rio Blanco	198	1,883	394	14	239	38	45	113	59,778	320	35.3	22.2	41.4
Rio Grande	361	2,401	481	88	371	87	65	100	41,446	321	27.7	16.2	59.8
Routt	1,801	14,439	1,428	185	1,846	237	656	533	36,941	887	50.3	11.8	30.4
Saguache	129	953	105	104	113	NA	9	32	34,006	288	23.6	25.3	52.4
San Juan	67	223	NA	NA	29	NA	NA	7	30,915	NA	NA	NA	NA
San Miguel	688	5,469	170	124	534	60	178	187	34,179	133	30.1	17.3	35.0
Sedgwick	66	427	152	33	61	22	10	13	30,740	212	8.0	41.0	57.9
Summit	2,312	21,808	1,169	414	3,400	240	638	729	33,428	55	45.5	14.5	30.9
Teller	779	6,151	677	85	903	163	281	237	38,596	159	51.6	10.1	39.8
Washington	110	510	40	75	77	36	17	21	41,080	757	10.2	39.1	52.1
Weld	6,703	96,024	9,210	15,122	10,732	3,051	3,242	4,944	51,491	4,062	46.3	10.2	38.1
Yuma	353	2,458	532	82	402	171	87	105	42,663	774	16.0	42.5	57.9
CONNECTICUT	88,060	1,551,590	299,524	159,874	182,272	114,192	113,200	100,459	64,746	5,521	70.9	0.7	39.0
Fairfield	26,625	426,426	74,303	35,401	49,271	30,392	44,933	35,375	82,957	402	81.8	2.2	49.3
Hartford	22,565	468,738	88,916	53,254	49,944	58,785	31,381	29,935	63,862	786	70.9	0.5	39.3
Litchfield	4,633	53,140	11,200	8,841	8,450	1,333	1,667	2,482	46,707	1,217	67.7	0.7	33.8
Middlesex	4,208	63,268	15,142	9,641	8,453	1,410	2,811	3,345	52,874	441	79.4	0.2	42.1
New Haven	19,176	344,442	77,498	27,467	41,872	12,142	15,124	18,588	53,965	686	81.9	0.3	38.3
New London	5,780	105,420	17,460	14,990	14,745	1,941	7,549	5,596	53,086	823	63.1	0.6	43.3

STATE County	Agriculture, 2017 (cont.)															
	Land in farms					Value of land and buildings (dollars)		Value of machinery and equipment, average per farm (dollars)	Value of products sold:				Organic farms (number)	Farms with internet access (percent)	Government payments	
			Acres								Percent from:					
	Acreage (1,000)	Percent change, 2012–2017	Average size of farm	Total irrigated (1,000)	Total cropland (1,000)	Average per farm	Average per acre		Total (mil dol)	Average per farm (acres)	Crops	Livestock and poultry products			Total ($1,000)	Percent of farms
	117	118	119	120	121	122	123	124	125	126	127	128	129	130	131	132
COLORADO—Cont'd																
Boulder	107	-19.5	106	27.2	38.1	1,329,691	12,571	67,305	43.9	43,378	87.4	12.6	29	90.7	501	5.6
Broomfield	9	-23.8	224	1.2	7.7	1,223,811	5,467	48,312	0.6	16,132	77.5	22.5	NA	63.2	D	2.6
Chaffee	66	-14.6	229	16.5	17.2	1,164,108	5,075	71,744	12.2	42,343	32.7	67.3	NA	83.7	56	3.5
Cheyenne	1,076	10.1	2,853	23.6	599.1	2,389,477	838	260,682	89.2	236,676	76.0	24.0	NA	73.7	10,125	82.0
Clear Creek	10	24.8	314	0.3	0.9	990,682	3,157	54,704	0.2	5,273	30.5	69.5	NA	81.8	NA	NA
Conejos	266	3.3	508	119.5	131.5	857,351	1,687	133,635	53.9	102,939	63.2	36.8	17	64.9	718	18.1
Costilla	358	-4.9	1,562	39.3	50.6	1,898,119	1,215	154,192	22.1	96,328	87.7	12.3	2	59.4	308	9.2
Crowley	484	-3.1	1,969	4.7	31.0	1,002,121	509	88,555	96.3	391,370	1.4	98.6	5	71.5	1,701	48.8
Custer	161	-14.5	512	22.6	29.0	994,967	1,943	81,523	9.7	30,733	47.3	52.7	NA	79.7	173	3.2
Delta	237	-5.5	147	66.8	69.4	705,824	4,813	67,981	67.1	41,559	45.2	54.8	33	83.7	897	6.3
Denver	0	-9.8	11	D	0.0	685,079	63,728	26,067	D	D	D	D	1	75.0	NA	NA
Dolores	158	-1.4	504	7.2	69.9	898,017	1,783	69,774	8.5	27,208	70.9	29.1	5	67.7	1,123	44.4
Douglas	202	0.8	165	2.3	26.5	1,112,035	6,747	50,523	18.9	15,428	62.0	38.0	3	87.3	428	3.4
Eagle	155	19.9	604	14.8	15.4	1,998,474	3,309	83,582	8.2	32,074	23.9	76.1	7	86.0	60	5.1
Elbert	1,018	-2.4	624	6.7	189.9	952,293	1,526	61,221	35.4	21,675	21.2	78.8	1	87.1	3,286	11.9
El Paso	630	-2.9	468	8.9	51.5	659,073	1,407	46,294	31.9	23,716	43.3	56.7	5	80.8	1,300	7.5
Fremont	278	-4.3	269	11.3	15.1	628,195	2,336	48,150	21.8	21,089	23.6	76.4	3	81.1	244	2.0
Garfield	475	52.9	719	52.0	77.4	1,724,785	2,399	89,572	35.9	54,256	24.5	75.5	4	80.0	360	7.3
Gilpin	4	-32.2	106	D	0.5	446,403	4,226	33,954	0.2	5,838	17.1	82.9	NA	81.1	28	16.2
Grand	241	6.2	831	36.3	36.5	1,827,034	2,199	92,591	14.4	49,793	23.5	76.5	NA	76.9	30	1.7
Gunnison	267	40.3	864	57.7	49.3	2,217,820	2,567	107,695	24.1	78,045	22.7	77.3	NA	83.2	51	3.9
Hinsdale	10	2.4	403	2.5	1.1	741,831	1,841	70,145	D	D	D	D	NA	76.9	D	3.8
Huerfano	582	0.1	1,331	8.6	19.4	1,280,062	962	58,781	13.2	30,174	10.8	89.2	1	70.7	311	7.8
Jackson	301	-12.0	2,301	70.4	67.4	3,045,594	1,323	196,274	24.5	186,924	18.5	81.5	3	71.8	35	6.9
Jefferson	69	0.4	115	1.2	5.4	885,635	7,715	36,831	9.0	15,144	77.8	22.2	2	86.1	151	3.0
Kiowa	1,092	-1.9	2,814	2.7	676.3	2,122,946	754	162,846	65.5	168,729	61.8	38.2	NA	72.2	10,450	82.0
Kit Carson	1,358	-1.4	2,366	117.8	890.7	2,883,863	1,219	375,287	474.3	826,268	32.4	67.6	NA	81.2	13,382	71.4
Lake	12	-1.9	362	1.9	0.5	743,849	2,055	46,972	D	D	D	D	NA	84.8	NA	NA
La Plata	549	-7.0	503	58.5	89.7	1,135,305	2,259	74,568	24.4	22,281	38.3	61.7	3	87.5	1,066	8.4
Larimer	482	7.1	236	60.2	98.6	1,095,047	4,637	76,905	150.7	73,772	45.7	54.3	20	85.1	633	5.5
Las Animas	1,796	-16.1	3,272	17.3	75.6	1,968,541	602	80,465	25.8	47,080	14.7	85.3	7	71.8	4,168	27.5
Lincoln	1,500	1.8	3,067	5.8	588.3	2,158,581	704	200,920	67.9	138,855	58.9	41.1	2	74.4	10,318	61.8
Logan	1,138	3.5	1,322	107.1	562.7	1,570,536	1,188	208,745	617.9	717,686	16.0	84.0	2	82.9	11,511	68.8
Mesa	343	-11.5	139	76.2	79.8	767,492	5,523	57,249	94.2	38,209	48.7	51.3	12	86.2	730	3.9
Mineral	8	27.2	444	2.9	0.7	1,526,408	3,441	31,306	D	D	D	100.0	NA	84.2	D	10.5
Moffat	953	2.5	2,063	30.1	123.4	1,648,562	799	107,741	33.1	71,727	11.7	88.3	2	71.9	2,109	26.4
Montezuma	691	0.0	615	79.0	117.2	744,860	1,211	85,128	46.4	41,339	64.3	35.7	6	79.0	1,237	13.3
Montrose	331	0.3	291	79.8	65.6	900,826	3,093	79,919	81.2	71,565	22.7	77.3	10	83.6	792	10.2
Morgan	659	1.9	891	132.3	340.4	1,546,382	1,735	241,369	559.5	756,130	16.1	83.9	5	82.0	6,040	53.9
Otero	688	-2.7	1,548	49.3	78.1	1,162,135	750	148,382	121.5	273,759	25.1	74.9	3	77.9	2,724	48.9
Ouray	85	4.7	698	8.6	8.6	2,130,534	3,054	88,951	4.2	34,459	17.2	82.8	1	89.3	64	4.1
Park	189	5.1	680	12.0	11.2	1,142,769	1,680	55,212	5.1	18,374	7.5	92.5	NA	78.1	26	2.5
Phillips	439	0.6	1,347	79.3	384.4	2,279,496	1,692	324,052	174.2	534,479	50.5	49.5	NA	86.2	8,706	79.4
Pitkin	33	1.9	292	10.1	5.9	2,225,232	7,617	88,246	2.9	26,000	34.9	65.1	NA	70.5	NA	NA
Prowers	1,011	-1.0	2,143	88.3	525.2	1,726,199	806	220,792	310.0	656,875	20.3	79.7	NA	65.7	9,185	75.6
Pueblo	896	0.0	1,067	18.1	72.0	1,097,156	1,028	76,147	52.0	62,033	41.0	59.0	7	77.5	2,117	13.9
Rio Blanco	411	-19.0	1,284	27.1	43.7	1,763,734	1,373	101,073	18.8	58,597	14.8	85.2	2	83.1	390	13.4
Rio Grande	177	-4.3	553	93.6	109.1	1,726,626	3,123	311,844	99.0	308,274	88.7	11.3	9	82.9	998	26.5
Routt	465	-24.1	524	42.7	81.0	1,647,039	3,141	69,340	31.6	35,679	16.2	83.8	4	81.1	962	10.8
Saguache	314	0.8	1,090	118.4	132.7	2,068,512	1,898	218,769	105.4	365,983	85.8	14.2	15	76.4	843	18.8
San Juan	NA	NA	NA	NA	NA	NA	NA	NA	NA	NA	NA	NA	NA	NA	NA	NA
San Miguel	136	7.5	1,023	15.9	14.3	1,524,124	1,490	79,047	6.4	47,925	14.0	86.0	NA	77.4	322	15.0
Sedgwick	349	3.8	1,645	40.4	228.1	2,226,323	1,353	321,028	93.9	442,693	49.3	50.7	2	82.1	4,776	81.6
Summit	27	4.8	483	5.5	6.8	2,041,182	4,225	90,529	1.5	27,127	35.1	64.9	NA	94.5	D	1.8
Teller	71	0.6	449	0.9	5.6	908,034	2,023	40,497	1.2	7,811	12.2	87.8	3	83.0	NA	NA
Washington	1,358	11.6	1,794	40.4	836.2	1,969,481	1,098	221,219	184.6	243,802	50.9	49.1	5	74.4	15,207	72.7
Weld	2,099	7.3	517	323.4	923.0	1,335,953	2,586	159,664	2,047.2	503,982	17.0	83.0	42	82.9	19,375	26.0
Yuma	1,400	3.5	1,809	209.0	628.2	2,953,997	1,633	313,588	918.7	1,186,972	21.8	78.2	4	82.4	19,612	69.8
CONNECTICUT	382	-12.6	69	7.4	148.6	862,636	12,483	62,250	580.1	105,074	72.4	27.6	113	82.4	1,850	4.4
Fairfield	52	-3.2	130	0.2	4.6	1,402,826	10,794	57,696	42.1	104,649	52.7	47.3	9	87.1	33	3.5
Hartford	48	-11.5	61	3.4	26.2	981,893	16,126	64,077	93.9	119,481	95.1	4.9	9	80.9	212	3.8
Litchfield	90	-0.7	74	0.5	37.4	840,256	11,322	56,949	41.1	33,800	51.0	49.0	28	83.3	363	3.8
Middlesex	16	-31.8	37	0.7	6.5	555,077	14,911	66,715	57.1	129,426	96.8	3.2	10	83.9	304	4.8
New Haven	27	-36.3	39	1.3	11.4	922,400	23,490	67,524	111.6	162,720	95.9	4.1	26	78.4	323	5.2
New London	60	-7.7	73	0.6	23.9	837,723	11,467	67,605	135.8	164,989	55.5	44.5	22	88.0	267	6.1

STATE County	Water use, 2015		Wholesale Trade[1], 2017				Retail Trade[2], 2017				Real estate and rental and leasing,[2] 2017			
	Public supply water withdrawn (mil gal/ day)	Public supply gallons withdrawn per person per day	Number of establish- ments	Number of employees	Sales (mil dol)	Average payroll (mil dol)	Number of establish- ments	Number of employees	Sales (mil dol)	Average payroll (mil dol)	Number of establish- ments	Number of employees	Sales (mil dol)	Average payroll (mil dol)
	133	134	135	136	137	138	139	140	141	142	143	144	145	146
COLORADO—Cont'd														
Boulder	48.3	151.2	428	6,066	4,884.6	516.0	1,187	19,230	5,635.2	602.1	775	2,894	754.0	161.8
Broomfield	5.7	87.1	70	845	430.1	55.9	286	5,338	1,280.6	139.7	150	425	170.4	22.9
Chaffee	4.0	212.2	15	117	53.6	4.2	141	1,234	371.1	34.3	79	159	26.9	4.7
Cheyenne	0.4	196.8	6	D	96.7	D	16	52	14.4	1.3	NA	NA	NA	NA
Clear Creek	1.2	125.8	15	D	14.7	D	51	311	84.4	7.7	D	D	D	D
Conejos	3.4	415.7	D	D	D	1.2	22	188	34.0	4.5	NA	NA	NA	NA
Costilla	0.5	125.6	NA	NA	NA	NA	14	73	14.7	1.1	NA	NA	NA	NA
Crowley	1.0	179.8	NA	NA	NA	NA	9	79	18.8	2.5	NA	NA	NA	NA
Custer	0.4	85.5	NA	NA	NA	NA	21	133	49.4	4.7	8	D	3.8	D
Delta	5.0	166.8	26	165	39.4	6.9	115	1,270	326.9	33.4	42	921	19.9	25.3
Denver	163.3	239.2	1,191	20,941	20,105.5	1,388.8	2,471	32,753	9,218.5	1,047.9	2,033	11,307	3,866.6	710.4
Dolores	0.3	126.4	D	D	D	1.4	5	43	10.4	0.8	4	D	0.6	D
Douglas	38.5	119.4	284	2,321	2,462.7	181.5	939	18,587	5,755.5	520.1	761	1,725	577.3	90.7
Eagle	10.3	192.3	78	492	216.9	23.8	410	4,299	1,072.6	143.2	420	2,082	445.9	79.1
Elbert	0.9	34.4	17	61	26.9	2.4	37	450	140.4	12.4	D	D	D	D
El Paso	88.4	131.0	459	4,834	3,005.6	320.3	2,096	31,935	9,701.0	926.1	1,326	4,447	1,015.8	188.2
Fremont	6.4	137.5	20	82	26.1	3.0	134	1,751	487.4	45.8	42	183	18.2	4.5
Garfield	11.6	200.4	55	342	173.3	16.9	277	3,209	1,169.5	109.9	152	582	116.8	25.5
Gilpin	0.7	116.7	NA	NA	NA	NA	10	29	7.6	0.9	8	11	3.6	0.7
Grand	2.3	158.1	D	D	D	0.8	96	706	210.4	21.4	91	457	67.7	14.4
Gunnison	1.9	117.0	7	16	4.4	0.5	134	1,081	243.5	25.7	104	235	45.8	7.6
Hinsdale	0.2	310.1	NA	NA	NA	NA	13	20	5.0	0.6	7	D	4.9	D
Huerfano	3.0	457.5	3	7	0.6	0.1	25	202	50.1	5.0	D	D	D	D
Jackson	0.3	236.0	NA	NA	NA	NA	10	54	16.2	1.3	NA	NA	NA	NA
Jefferson	23.0	40.7	548	4,685	2,929.7	307.6	1,864	29,948	8,899.4	882.2	1,096	3,036	807.1	145.0
Kiowa	0.2	161.6	5	D	16.4	D	8	92	29.8	1.9	NA	NA	NA	NA
Kit Carson	1.3	163.7	21	224	231.7	10.6	38	356	116.3	9.2	11	39	3.2	1.0
Lake	4.5	597.2	4	20	7.8	0.8	31	219	48.0	5.5	D	D	D	D
La Plata	5.7	105.0	51	548	232.6	27.7	306	3,396	989.1	104.5	173	438	105.1	17.2
Larimer	30.6	91.7	336	4,724	3,723.5	349.3	1,266	19,902	5,893.8	574.0	766	2,404	663.9	109.9
Las Animas	3.5	246.1	10	32	13.0	0.8	61	733	193.2	19.7	18	64	8.5	1.8
Lincoln	0.8	140.4	NA	NA	NA	NA	25	322	126.9	8.1	4	7	0.5	0.1
Logan	3.3	147.9	23	102	122.8	5.2	99	1,094	346.8	29.5	17	48	7.1	1.5
Mesa	17.5	117.9	200	1,731	942.8	90.2	572	8,305	2,463.2	237.0	303	936	208.8	39.0
Mineral	0.2	303.0	NA	NA	NA	NA	12	47	10.8	1.2	3	4	1.0	0.1
Moffat	1.7	134.5	24	161	188.4	9.7	63	687	198.0	21.2	11	17	3.8	0.6
Montezuma	4.4	167.0	25	226	131.3	10.9	112	1,309	363.9	37.6	36	127	27.4	4.4
Montrose	9.1	223.0	51	316	120.7	14.4	165	2,148	650.1	62.5	60	154	30.4	5.0
Morgan	6.0	210.2	36	299	236.7	14.2	95	1,064	303.9	28.4	30	74	11.1	2.0
Otero	4.0	217.5	20	126	63.0	4.8	67	700	180.6	17.1	13	78	7.4	2.4
Ouray	1.8	383.7	NA	NA	NA	NA	40	223	37.9	4.9	10	D	3.7	D
Park	0.4	24.2	D	D	D	D	49	254	63.7	7.0	27	D	8.8	D
Phillips	0.8	184.0	D	D	D	4.8	25	179	50.7	4.5	NA	NA	NA	NA
Pitkin	8.1	457.1	16	30	32.8	1.4	234	1,680	404.9	56.0	242	950	238.4	47.6
Prowers	1.9	159.8	15	110	67.4	4.3	57	679	167.3	16.0	D	D	D	D
Pueblo	41.3	252.4	94	1,037	684.5	57.8	506	8,124	2,144.4	214.1	148	658	116.3	19.4
Rio Blanco	1.9	287.6	D	D	D	D	30	207	54.6	5.2	8	19	1.8	0.6
Rio Grande	1.2	104.0	23	322	202.7	14.1	51	406	111.9	11.2	D	D	D	D
Routt	2.9	119.4	50	376	200.3	20.8	193	1,737	417.0	50.8	155	587	97.8	19.5
Saguache	0.7	110.4	11	253	72.4	8.9	21	138	23.9	2.6	D	D	D	D
San Juan	0.2	342.4	NA	NA	NA	NA	17	38	9.5	1.1	D	D	D	0.1
San Miguel	0.7	86.3	9	D	6.0	D	82	548	115.1	15.8	84	264	68.0	11.5
Sedgwick	0.7	287.6	5	D	12.4	D	11	68	26.1	1.8	NA	NA	NA	NA
Summit	6.6	219.1	31	79	29.7	3.9	321	3,423	794.4	90.6	339	1,388	297.6	64.3
Teller	6.2	263.8	11	37	13.7	1.2	70	898	261.3	23.5	54	101	17.4	3.3
Washington	0.4	72.0	5	D	34.2	D	12	79	28.6	2.1	5	D	0.6	D
Weld	28.3	99.2	274	3,365	3,733.5	201.6	668	10,289	3,768.8	327.5	314	1,616	358.6	79.6
Yuma	1.4	140.0	31	342	656.5	20.0	58	425	109.1	10.9	13	35	7.4	1.2
CONNECTICUT	239.9	66.8	3,504	62,298	102,896.5	5,173.7	12,391	186,297	55,404.5	5,560.8	3,459	20,224	6,691.3	1,114.8
Fairfield	88.0	92.8	1,131	19,293	66,731.7	1,916.5	3,368	51,210	16,458.8	1,717.6	1,165	7,605	2,604.5	536.9
Hartford	59.2	66.1	930	19,164	19,181.9	1,276.8	3,127	50,098	14,132.7	1,389.1	892	5,100	1,480.8	259.4
Litchfield	10.2	55.4	139	798	436.3	43.1	673	8,552	2,683.2	268.7	141	414	81.1	17.0
Middlesex	7.3	44.6	157	2,363	1,550.5	159.5	645	8,983	2,588.1	259.2	138	847	195.4	35.7
New Haven	54.5	63.4	880	16,151	12,689.6	1,516.0	2,870	42,459	12,606.7	1,225.2	753	4,825	1,990.9	210.9
New London	8.1	29.8	149	2,638	1,679.6	176.0	1,015	15,140	4,030.8	422.3	228	818	236.0	32.3

1 Merchant wholesalers, except manufacturers' sales branches and offices. 2. Employer establishments.

STATE County	Professional, scientific, and technical services, 2017				Manufacturing, 2017				Accommodation and food services, 2017			
	Number of establish-ments	Number of employees	Sales (mil dol)	Average payroll (mil dol)	Number of establish-ments	Number of employees	Sales (mil dol)	Average payroll (mil dol)	Number of establis-hments	Number of employees	Sales (mil dol)	Annual payroll (mil dol)
	147	148	149	150	151	152	153	154	155	156	157	158
COLORADO—Cont'd												
Boulder	D	D	D	D	561	14,472	5,400.1	939.4	939	19,279	1,157.9	360.1
Broomfield	D	D	D	D	82	3,161	3,441.8	210.6	178	3,689	261.1	77.9
Chaffee	104	203	23.9	8.5	30	131	33.7	6.2	114	1,502	87.3	29.1
Cheyenne	4	6	0.3	0.1	NA	NA	NA	NA	3	22	0.9	0.2
Clear Creek	46	64	12.6	4.2	10	32	4.5	D	54	628	42.8	14.0
Conejos	D	D	1.5	D	7	70	21.0	3.1	13	47	5.1	1.4
Costilla	NA	NA	NA	NA	D	D	D	D	D	D	D	0.8
Crowley	NA	NA	NA	NA	NA	NA	NA	NA	NA	NA	NA	NA
Custer	10	18	4.7	0.8	8	33	10.1	2.1	12	57	3.6	0.9
Delta	63	168	15.3	4.8	52	337	108.4	17.7	82	736	35.7	11.0
Denver	5,110	49,765	12,602.4	4,732.3	773	16,660	5,404.4	836.0	2,354	55,545	4,477.0	1,297.4
Dolores	D	D	D	0.2	4	12	6.3	1.5	7	D	5.2	D
Douglas	D	D	D	D	137	8,329	3,526.8	907.6	571	12,316	742.9	226.7
Eagle	D	D	D	D	58	335	131.9	18.2	295	8,137	680.6	204.9
Elbert	97	230	42.5	12.8	19	200	35.7	8.6	27	196	11.0	3.3
El Paso	2,632	22,760	4,500.5	1,766.2	454	11,012	3,335.0	673.2	1,377	30,711	1,909.3	547.3
Fremont	64	217	19.1	6.7	37	347	135.4	19.4	79	1,149	60.4	18.1
Garfield	D	D	D	D	39	172	45.4	10.5	215	3,223	218.0	69.5
Gilpin	20	36	6.8	2.0	D	36	D	D	13	2,672	433.2	100.9
Grand	81	911	69.7	46.8	17	157	25.6	6.0	136	2,141	130.2	46.7
Gunnison	143	276	40.0	13.2	28	141	24.6	5.1	135	2,531	130.6	41.9
Hinsdale	NA	NA	NA	NA	NA	NA	NA	NA	17	15	3.4	0.8
Huerfano	13	34	3.1	1.8	NA	NA	NA	NA	22	174	10.2	2.3
Jackson	6	13	1.6	0.4	NA	NA	NA	NA	11	55	3.7	1.1
Jefferson	D	D	D	D	463	8,742	4,128.7	555.3	1,245	24,777	1,535.2	462.9
Kiowa	NA	NA	NA	NA	NA	NA	NA	NA	D	D	D	D
Kit Carson	17	34	3.9	1.3	6	93	30.8	3.6	27	314	16.1	4.1
Lake	15	31	4.5	1.2	5	57	8.0	D	34	242	13.6	4.4
La Plata	D	D	D	D	65	567	109.2	23.7	227	4,528	256.3	84.7
Larimer	1,642	9,285	1,637.8	668.0	444	9,931	3,909.8	646.2	949	18,194	1,087.4	338.0
Las Animas	26	65	5.8	2.3	5	28	6.7	1.7	46	593	36.7	9.6
Lincoln	10	40	2.8	1.0	NA	NA	NA	NA	25	261	19.5	4.4
Logan	26	91	12.9	4.1	21	358	208.3	12.4	46	710	33.9	9.8
Mesa	497	3,416	527.2	209.4	150	2,740	552.2	124.2	335	6,462	356.5	117.5
Mineral	D	D	D	0.2	NA	NA	NA	NA	19	79	10.3	3.4
Moffat	D	D	D	D	12	49	18.2	2.0	33	383	19.2	5.7
Montezuma	73	262	30.1	11.3	34	277	53.0	10.6	89	1,368	98.0	25.7
Montrose	D	D	D	D	62	1,292	267.7	49.3	98	1,270	70.5	21.4
Morgan	38	126	14.9	4.8	31	3,061	2,644.4	143.9	65	988	66.1	13.3
Otero	D	D	D	D	16	465	92.0	23.0	49	572	28.9	8.1
Ouray	53	83	13.4	4.0	9	29	8.7	1.9	55	499	35.5	10.6
Park	62	102	12.3	4.3	D	49	D	1.7	43	250	24.5	5.0
Phillips	10	22	5.3	0.9	D	83	D	4.3	15	D	3.3	D
Pitkin	D	D	D	D	20	157	43.8	9.4	161	5,778	502.0	158.7
Prowers	26	98	7.3	2.5	15	184	39.0	6.7	34	360	19.3	4.7
Pueblo	D	D	D	D	94	4,380	2,103.4	256.3	336	5,761	289.7	84.7
Rio Blanco	10	38	3.4	1.4	3	21	3.5	1.0	23	192	9.0	3.8
Rio Grande	22	55	5.6	1.9	12	72	11.1	2.3	43	312	18.8	5.7
Routt	209	636	101.5	37.9	35	158	22.8	6.8	163	5,244	272.4	88.1
Saguache	D	D	D	0.4	5	132	17.9	2.9	7	39	2.7	0.8
San Juan	D	D	0.2	D	NA	NA	NA	NA	22	83	11.0	2.5
San Miguel	80	145	28.4	7.6	13	87	15.5	5.2	74	1,628	132.4	42.8
Sedgwick	D	D	D	0.3	D	D	D	0.8	6	D	1.4	D
Summit	D	D	D	D	25	292	76.7	14.2	271	6,898	491.2	143.6
Teller	122	269	32.0	13.0	10	70	10.4	3.1	65	1,992	129.7	43.8
Washington	D	D	1.9	D	6	67	37.2	3.1	5	29	1.3	0.4
Weld	D	D	D	D	305	11,968	5,959.4	657.2	472	7,843	406.0	117.9
Yuma	D	D	D	D	13	77	122.5	3.1	29	267	12.5	3.6
CONNECTICUT	9,126	107,375	21,342.6	9,625.6	3,986	156,822	57,882.0	11,021.6	8,762	146,456	10,791.5	3,069.7
Fairfield	3,519	47,964	10,735.9	4,661.4	779	34,375	12,255.6	2,634.2	2,438	35,172	2,597.3	767.7
Hartford	D	D	D	D	1,163	51,705	19,350.3	3,875.2	2,154	37,527	2,338.8	694.8
Litchfield	D	D	D	D	326	8,974	2,711.2	513.5	434	4,988	321.1	96.4
Middlesex	D	D	D	D	219	9,702	3,640.9	600.2	441	6,004	400.2	123.7
New Haven	1,814	14,470	2,620.3	1,218.0	1,048	29,004	10,764.2	1,792.6	2,047	29,719	1,854.2	534.1
New London	527	8,313	973.2	972.2	175	14,024	6,228.6	1,105.9	750	25,852	2,816.6	722.2

STATE County	Health care and social assistance, 2017				Other services, 2017				Nonemployer businesses, 2019		Value of residential construction authorized by building permits, 2021	
	Number of establish-ments	Number of employees	Receipts (mil dol)	Annual payroll (mil dol)	Number of establish-ments	Number of employees	Receipts (mil dol)	Annual payroll (mil dol)	Number	Receipts (mil dol)	New construction ($1,000)	Number of housing units
	159	160	161	162	163	164	165	166	167	168	169	170
COLORADO—Cont'd												
Boulder	1,432	21,332	2,566.9	1,012.1	823	5,173	671.5	202.2	41,219	2,223.4	401,188	1,237
Broomfield	197	2,472	287.5	117.3	145	732	158.2	36.2	6,746	303.9	176,997	501
Chaffee	77	966	114.5	46.4	51	188	17.7	5.7	2,764	123.4	90,231	349
Cheyenne	D	D	D	D	NA	NA	NA	NA	216	11.5	1,625	12
Clear Creek	18	92	6.6	2.6	11	83	4.6	2.4	1,092	55.0	17,680	97
Conejos	15	235	20.9	8.8	D	D	D	0.2	672	35.3	13,838	45
Costilla	D	D	D	1.1	NA	NA	NA	NA	312	15.9	0	0
Crowley	3	78	3.6	2.1	NA	NA	NA	NA	193	7.7	1,533	14
Custer	NA	NA	NA	NA	13	39	2.5	0.7	711	37.2	43,149	146
Delta	77	1,701	137.4	61.6	52	174	18.3	4.7	3,180	154.8	39,125	223
Denver	2,302	56,165	8,008.4	3,078.4	1,874	15,112	2,404.0	600.2	76,967	4,318.1	1,514,650	10,000
Dolores	4	D	2.3	D	NA	NA	NA	NA	176	6.2	1,845	6
Douglas	934	13,150	2,257.4	710.1	646	3,907	432.2	133.1	36,132	1,957.2	1,491,515	6,059
Eagle	193	2,058	452.0	137.4	208	1,267	132.6	43.1	7,817	498.4	225,536	439
Elbert	24	140	9.9	4.7	40	104	12.8	3.7	3,031	154.7	139,234	413
El Paso	2,126	39,317	4,488.9	1,848.1	1,264	10,636	2,375.2	452.2	56,516	2,427.4	2,574,547	9,186
Fremont	101	2,204	165.1	78.5	47	196	16.4	5.0	2,990	126.2	47,787	174
Garfield	162	3,170	509.6	202.8	150	677	77.6	23.9	6,739	374.3	183,445	631
Gilpin	D	D	D	0.6	7	51	2.7	0.8	683	27.5	6,099	22
Grand	37	420	53.2	19.2	45	116	17.1	4.1	2,089	116.5	161,097	467
Gunnison	61	561	77.2	27.5	78	251	31.4	6.6	2,653	118.1	76,452	197
Hinsdale	NA	NA	NA	NA	D	D	D	0.3	159	6.9	5,900	14
Huerfano	14	426	32.6	16.0	6	17	1.5	0.2	642	25.1	10,715	57
Jackson	NA	NA	NA	NA	NA	NA	NA	NA	184	7.9	160	2
Jefferson	1,821	32,117	3,636.5	1,458.9	1,216	6,781	804.7	231.7	60,026	2,803.5	525,322	2,515
Kiowa	D	D	D	D	NA	NA	NA	NA	153	7.3	1,024	6
Kit Carson	28	323	27.1	11.9	17	53	9.3	2.2	734	35.3	1,370	6
Lake	11	134	14.4	6.2	17	39	4.4	1.0	700	34.3	13,201	64
La Plata	232	3,351	524.9	176.4	157	643	60.4	19.1	6,837	324.1	161,138	415
Larimer	1,147	19,461	2,304.6	932.0	734	4,247	640.0	141.2	34,654	1,652.3	834,591	3,221
Las Animas	42	814	69.3	30.7	35	154	14.6	3.9	1,042	37.9	6,620	41
Lincoln	11	309	27.7	11.4	D	D	4.2	D	377	17.6	1,321	10
Logan	70	1,152	124.7	47.1	51	187	22.7	5.4	1,402	72.5	3,732	14
Mesa	438	11,405	1,429.2	530.6	315	1,662	188.0	55.8	12,670	591.6	194,944	1,231
Mineral	NA	NA	NA	NA	D	D	D	0.1	163	7.4	2,890	8
Moffat	44	547	72.8	29.0	32	157	11.0	3.6	1,024	42.7	2,726	15
Montezuma	83	1,456	131.0	56.0	54	183	19.9	4.9	2,401	96.5	5,424	22
Montrose	159	3,064	301.9	117.2	83	329	39.6	10.6	4,100	209.0	74,367	451
Morgan	58	1,447	156.6	63.7	44	155	16.9	4.5	2,044	113.9	32,749	195
Otero	55	1,296	92.1	46.0	22	83	8.2	2.3	1,036	37.4	4,008	16
Ouray	D	D	D	1.9	11	77	5.2	1.5	958	58.6	58,301	146
Park	D	D	D	2.6	19	55	5.9	1.6	2,126	93.7	54,176	193
Phillips	9	266	29.4	12.2	D	D	D	0.6	467	25.1	2,064	8
Pitkin	72	767	149.0	56.6	109	824	103.0	32.3	3,802	279.0	165,370	97
Prowers	31	621	55.6	24.4	24	87	11.2	2.5	908	45.9	2,081	8
Pueblo	407	13,427	1,403.4	602.5	235	1,348	125.1	36.1	9,224	394.4	120,065	742
Rio Blanco	D	D	D	D	D	D	D	0.9	603	24.3	3,615	12
Rio Grande	27	435	34.3	15.5	27	94	14.3	3.3	1,094	50.1	6,391	35
Routt	139	1,488	188.7	76.9	114	561	57.4	17.5	4,012	220.8	187,480	215
Saguache	D	D	D	2.1	D	D	D	1.7	631	27.2	12,956	101
San Juan	D	D	D	D	D	D	D	0.8	143	6.4	5,100	17
San Miguel	29	151	13.7	6.8	40	230	44.0	9.8	1,744	108.4	124,467	80
Sedgwick	D	D	D	D	D	D	D	0.2	211	10.0	150	1
Summit	115	1,211	181.3	65.2	144	467	58.1	15.5	4,494	275.5	236,723	407
Teller	62	546	54.5	19.5	51	166	19.2	5.4	2,850	113.1	47,838	149
Washington	7	D	3.2	D	D	D	1.5	D	395	20.6	230	1
Weld	551	8,971	1,127.3	446.2	418	2,212	278.9	74.4	25,419	1,268.5	1,249,558	5,268
Yuma	22	576	58.6	23.3	28	66	9.2	1.8	1,037	51.8	1,190	4
CONNECTICUT	11,065	295,083	35,302.4	14,069.0	7,507	46,490	6,055.5	1,645.5	292,009	17,444.4	1,224,866	4,651
Fairfield	3,071	72,290	10,942.1	3,753.5	2,180	14,442	2,103.2	530.8	100,223	7,174.6	538,712	1,292
Hartford	2,994	89,797	9,665.2	4,186.6	1,971	13,694	1,736.4	523.0	62,141	3,380.6	171,252	835
Litchfield	510	9,674	903.0	391.3	383	1,643	206.0	53.9	17,489	1,017.1	99,022	254
Middlesex	506	16,147	1,681.2	822.4	361	1,791	214.5	58.2	13,550	766.1	59,206	260
New Haven	2,585	76,203	9,164.6	3,610.4	1,772	10,522	1,229.8	347.7	64,541	3,410.6	149,328	983
New London	798	17,766	1,817.6	795.5	483	2,577	312.5	70.6	17,537	871.6	113,505	456

STATE County	Government employment and payroll, 2017: Full-time equivalent employees	Government employment and payroll, 2017: March payroll (dollars)	March payroll (percent of total): Adminis-tration, judicial, and legal	March payroll (percent of total): Police and corrections	March payroll (percent of total): Fire protection	March payroll (percent of total): Highways and transpor-tation	March payroll (percent of total): Health and welfare	March payroll (percent of total): Natural resources and utilities	March payroll (percent of total): Education and libraries	Local government finances, 2017: General revenue: Total (mil dol)	General revenue: Inter-govern-mental (mil dol)	General revenue: Taxes: Total (mil dol)	Taxes: Per capita[1] (dollars): Total	Taxes: Per capita[1] (dollars): Property
	171	172	173	174	175	176	177	178	179	180	181	182	183	184
COLORADO—Cont'd														
Boulder	12,053	61,752,806	8.2	10.5	5.2	2.6	6.2	8.9	54.2	1,954.8	451.4	1,117.5	3,466	2,375
Broomfield	765	4,448,301	17.0	35.1	0.0	2.2	18.5	18.7	3.6	273.2	16.5	152.4	2,232	881
Chaffee	1,135	4,646,831	6.2	7.5	2.1	3.2	53.5	3.6	23.4	132.3	22.6	39.0	1,981	1,067
Cheyenne	169	548,400	9.2	6.3	0.0	7.8	27.9	2.5	42.3	23.6	6.1	7.2	3,864	3,071
Clear Creek	427	1,724,550	16.5	24.0	1.6	8.8	8.7	6.7	32.1	66.0	11.4	42.6	4,445	4,026
Conejos	395	1,321,761	8.4	7.8	0.1	6.0	12.7	2.8	61.8	36.8	22.5	10.5	1,288	676
Costilla	251	708,815	12.3	6.7	0.4	13.7	16.4	4.5	40.8	30.5	15.2	11.1	2,964	2,907
Crowley	150	410,874	13.1	10.8	0.3	6.5	12.7	6.6	46.1	10.7	5.9	3.3	572	460
Custer	171	559,390	16.4	12.3	0.7	9.8	18.9	5.3	32.5	15.7	3.5	9.0	1,862	1,472
Delta	1,739	6,945,583	4.5	5.8	0.3	2.2	46.5	5.1	34.5	170.2	46.8	36.1	1,181	657
Denver	36,005	196,656,831	6.4	13.4	4.4	12.1	25.3	9.5	28.0	7,076.0	1,282.7	2,796.9	3,968	1,774
Dolores	126	375,221	16.8	9.8	0.0	17.6	6.4	2.8	44.2	111.7	4.4	106.0	51,812	51,744
Douglas	9,267	41,903,758	7.5	11.2	2.2	3.1	1.3	6.0	64.9	1,489.9	399.3	759.3	2,261	1,645
Eagle	2,056	10,948,776	10.1	15.1	8.5	10.0	7.7	12.6	29.1	436.2	48.2	284.6	5,180	3,292
Elbert	740	2,611,721	6.9	15.3	6.0	7.8	5.0	3.3	54.8	83.4	38.8	32.5	1,261	1,083
El Paso	21,142	92,207,013	5.4	12.5	5.0	2.8	3.7	16.5	52.2	2,505.7	1,031.1	1,027.5	1,468	741
Fremont	1,458	4,946,191	3.4	13.1	3.6	4.9	8.8	8.1	49.4	144.6	65.4	53.0	1,115	620
Garfield	3,290	14,845,350	6.6	9.6	5.1	2.8	25.3	8.2	39.5	459.3	124.2	219.2	3,713	2,801
Gilpin	348	1,824,112	16.8	31.6	11.2	10.6	3.2	6.8	15.2	68.8	19.7	35.2	5,845	1,587
Grand	973	4,190,299	8.9	8.1	2.1	9.0	35.2	11.9	22.9	145.4	20.2	73.2	4,762	3,288
Gunnison	926	4,431,480	12.3	7.7	2.4	8.3	36.3	8.3	20.1	130.8	29.9	51.4	3,047	2,036
Hinsdale	71	261,394	18.6	8.1	0.0	16.5	21.2	2.7	27.3	7.4	2.1	3.9	4,889	3,826
Huerfano	700	2,721,294	8.5	5.1	0.1	4.9	51.8	4.8	22.2	60.2	14.5	14.4	2,177	1,713
Jackson	98	302,997	14.7	12.1	0.0	9.0	6.3	7.6	48.7	8.5	3.5	3.4	2,456	1,698
Jefferson	17,598	81,941,659	6.8	14.0	6.3	2.2	5.0	6.9	56.3	2,003.7	586.2	1,064.2	1,849	1,404
Kiowa	180	564,349	8.9	5.9	0.1	8.4	45.8	1.3	27.6	18.8	5.4	4.7	3,440	3,197
Kit Carson	608	1,994,649	6.2	6.5	2.1	6.0	35.6	5.2	36.1	54.1	17.4	15.5	2,177	1,921
Lake	1,118	4,657,023	2.0	2.1	1.2	1.5	9.5	1.8	80.4	128.0	30.5	64.7	8,345	8,023
La Plata	2,202	9,074,777	10.6	12.4	7.6	5.9	6.4	6.5	43.8	278.0	81.9	141.6	2,549	1,493
Larimer	11,808	54,787,902	10.2	11.8	1.5	3.1	9.4	17.5	42.7	1,540.8	372.6	770.7	2,240	1,405
Las Animas	709	2,423,976	10.8	9.5	3.1	7.7	8.7	7.6	49.2	80.1	37.3	25.5	1,797	1,084
Lincoln	467	1,624,923	5.3	7.5	0.0	6.9	41.7	3.1	34.4	51.4	17.8	14.2	2,575	1,877
Logan	871	2,830,803	9.0	10.3	4.7	6.5	6.9	7.3	52.2	66.3	28.1	30.2	1,353	1,095
Mesa	5,190	22,403,036	4.9	11.8	4.6	3.6	5.4	9.0	57.7	577.7	216.3	242.8	1,606	965
Mineral	61	209,780	21.3	16.1	0.0	14.2	0.7	9.2	36.7	5.7	1.3	3.0	4,024	3,351
Moffat	604	2,569,544	8.6	13.4	0.2	9.9	5.3	7.6	50.6	71.8	26.9	35.0	2,675	1,998
Montezuma	1,062	3,219,203	7.9	15.7	2.3	5.9	5.3	9.5	45.2	146.6	48.6	63.7	2,439	1,516
Montrose	1,571	5,748,173	9.9	13.0	4.5	6.3	7.2	11.9	43.3	260.5	64.1	69.1	1,654	894
Morgan	1,324	4,512,710	7.0	9.1	0.3	4.3	9.2	11.2	56.4	132.7	42.6	64.3	2,272	1,843
Otero	918	2,842,292	7.6	6.5	2.0	3.0	11.2	10.6	57.7	111.8	43.9	49.9	2,721	768
Ouray	273	1,080,668	26.0	6.3	3.5	2.8	4.7	8.1	46.6	28.1	9.5	13.4	2,780	1,961
Park	500	1,877,930	8.4	11.9	11.3	9.1	8.0	3.3	41.3	57.8	20.8	27.9	1,562	1,305
Phillips	470	1,792,239	5.2	2.6	2.1	4.0	45.7	3.8	36.0	76.8	11.6	35.8	8,339	2,524
Pitkin	1,762	10,803,740	7.6	6.9	2.0	19.6	34.4	8.1	13.5	430.1	33.6	195.5	10,876	4,990
Prowers	905	3,180,058	6.5	5.7	1.3	3.3	33.2	9.6	37.5	94.4	31.5	21.9	1,823	990
Pueblo	5,844	27,151,176	5.3	12.1	10.8	2.9	7.3	6.0	53.1	632.0	278.7	262.3	1,578	1,002
Rio Blanco	833	3,496,255	6.4	6.4	0.8	4.4	51.0	8.7	19.3	126.6	22.5	61.2	9,630	8,689
Rio Grande	590	1,781,261	9.1	10.8	0.5	7.6	7.3	4.4	59.9	63.0	27.8	27.1	2,397	1,001
Routt	1,137	5,312,629	13.1	10.3	4.5	13.5	3.6	8.5	39.4	181.0	38.0	98.9	3,931	2,246
Saguache	371	1,125,818	10.1	11.3	0.8	6.9	8.3	6.3	54.7	29.9	20.0	6.5	984	803
San Juan	45	188,197	26.2	10.9	0.0	14.2	6.3	7.6	34.6	6.0	1.9	3.4	4,756	2,510
San Miguel	506	2,335,059	13.2	12.8	4.6	14.8	8.6	5.5	40.4	112.3	19.6	58.8	7,320	5,091
Sedgwick	248	987,639	12.6	1.7	1.9	4.2	48.6	4.7	24.4	18.5	5.4	9.3	4,045	3,830
Summit	1,494	7,358,035	10.1	11.2	11.6	11.3	10.6	9.1	28.1	270.6	23.2	178.7	5,799	3,071
Teller	911	3,287,414	10.6	16.0	5.2	5.8	11.0	4.7	41.0	108.2	39.5	52.4	2,124	1,450
Washington	317	920,735	9.5	11.0	0.0	10.1	6.2	4.2	57.4	35.7	13.9	11.5	2,336	2,094
Weld	9,283	38,633,927	9.4	12.0	4.9	4.5	6.1	8.0	51.9	1,519.5	370.2	817.7	2,673	1,807
Yuma	811	3,063,690	3.5	4.9	0.0	5.3	41.4	5.1	39.2	99.2	29.6	23.9	2,395	2,047
CONNECTICUT	X	X	X	X	X	X	X	X	X	X	X	X	X	X
Fairfield	32,456	194,415,331	3.6	10.0	5.5	3.2	3.2	2.7	70.4	5,258.8	1,080.1	3,702.6	3,926	3,839
Hartford	33,842	190,339,606	3.1	8.1	3.5	2.5	2.8	4.5	73.2	4,687.9	1,738.5	2,587.4	2,897	2,869
Litchfield	5,925	29,964,946	5.0	6.9	1.8	5.1	1.7	2.4	75.6	786.3	156.1	562.8	3,098	3,078
Middlesex	5,401	28,429,699	4.8	7.3	4.5	3.8	3.4	3.0	71.2	732.7	138.0	509.0	3,124	3,103
New Haven	29,926	153,376,297	3.4	10.0	6.1	3.3	3.0	4.9	68.4	4,281.3	1,605.5	2,298.8	2,680	2,641
New London	9,464	49,779,946	3.9	7.1	3.6	3.2	2.1	5.2	70.6	1,247.5	411.9	703.0	2,629	2,606

1. Based on the resident population estimated as of July 1 of the year shown.

STATE County	Local government finances, 2017 (cont.) — Direct general expenditure — Total (mil dol)	Per capita[1] (dollars)	Percent of total for: Education	Health and hospitals	Police protection	Public welfare	Highways	Debt outstanding — Total (mil dol)	Per capita[1] (dollars)	Government employment, 2020 — Federal civilian	Federal military	State and local	Individual income tax returns, 2019 — Number of returns	Mean adjusted gross income	Mean income tax
	185	186	187	188	189	190	191	192	193	194	195	196	197	198	199
COLORADO—Cont'd															
Boulder	2,018.9	6,261	43.6	1.9	5.4	2.4	6.8	2,807.4	8,707	2,172	845	33,151	164,710	114,568	18,225
Broomfield	178.4	2,613	0.0	1.4	10.0	8.1	5.8	794.6	11,640	179	172	1,430	38,110	101,350	14,088
Chaffee	126.9	6,454	20.5	44.9	3.5	1.3	8.9	94.2	4,791	78	46	2,075	10,350	69,476	7,592
Cheyenne	21.7	11,717	27.0	26.8	3.6	12.6	8.1	0.6	317	14	4	271	790	50,939	4,963
Clear Creek	56.5	5,896	22.6	5.3	9.5	5.4	11.1	16.0	1,672	46	23	564	5,080	90,303	12,664
Conejos	37.4	4,597	43.4	4.7	3.3	3.1	5.0	9.3	1,139	49	19	490	3,190	41,231	2,647
Costilla	29.6	7,893	34.5	7.0	2.0	14.8	13.4	22.5	5,980	11	9	345	1,500	37,507	2,592
Crowley	11.8	2,012	37.1	0.0	4.1	13.1	9.5	0.6	97	10	7	505	1,570	29,435	1,946
Custer	15.2	3,120	28.6	14.7	6.3	3.1	11.1	3.6	736	18	15	243	2,310	64,173	7,369
Delta	171.4	5,618	30.3	42.9	3.5	2.2	3.9	61.4	2,012	175	74	2,417	14,210	49,928	4,226
Denver	6,027.1	8,550	21.7	18.7	3.9	2.3	2.5	15,683.0	22,247	13,275	2,085	58,824	382,040	92,523	14,208
Dolores	10.7	5,229	35.3	5.0	5.9	5.8	23.0	1.1	556	9	5	214	870	48,101	3,746
Douglas	1,411.5	4,203	45.4	0.6	5.3	1.9	10.2	1,862.0	5,545	469	868	13,085	176,430	123,096	18,361
Eagle	413.5	7,528	23.3	3.3	5.8	1.4	9.0	982.1	17,879	133	131	3,180	30,710	108,962	17,079
Elbert	87.4	3,391	39.0	4.7	4.7	5.8	9.3	141.0	5,473	37	65	961	13,050	94,605	11,888
El Paso	2,338.9	3,341	52.0	1.2	7.5	3.0	8.3	4,561.4	6,515	12,596	40,204	40,839	347,560	69,788	7,589
Fremont	123.5	2,597	42.7	0.6	11.8	6.5	5.9	93.7	1,970	993	96	4,249	19,450	51,832	4,458
Garfield	522.4	8,849	40.3	15.0	4.4	3.6	4.7	509.2	8,625	271	142	4,887	29,530	76,972	9,818
Gilpin	58.8	9,777	10.7	3.1	15.8	3.3	18.5	58.5	9,726	16	15	430	2,970	69,568	7,582
Grand	123.9	8,064	15.9	23.8	5.6	2.0	6.2	261.8	17,040	125	37	1,258	8,200	77,506	9,632
Gunnison	125.1	7,417	16.8	22.1	6.0	3.2	16.2	127.1	7,535	175	40	2,166	8,760	72,677	8,536
Hinsdale	7.1	9,005	27.8	19.2	7.2	1.0	18.7	0.4	512	4	2	88	400	64,498	5,793
Huerfano	61.9	9,332	14.0	46.5	2.7	8.6	2.6	45.6	6,873	19	16	441	2,940	44,669	3,693
Jackson	8.4	6,122	36.3	5.1	6.0	5.0	19.1	3.6	2,615	30	3	133	680	44,426	4,165
Jefferson	2,037.4	3,541	45.2	1.2	6.5	2.4	4.7	1,389.2	2,414	8,402	1,441	27,200	309,690	89,300	11,703
Kiowa	15.2	11,116	25.5	41.1	3.4	2.7	10.8	9.2	6,739	17	3	235	650	49,712	4,302
Kit Carson	55.9	7,836	30.0	28.2	5.3	3.4	9.8	23.8	3,331	42	17	703	3,340	49,382	4,793
Lake	153.8	19,851	81.8	5.8	1.2	2.0	1.0	99.2	12,798	54	19	630	3,750	54,618	4,908
La Plata	266.1	4,789	34.5	0.5	6.7	3.8	6.9	295.9	5,326	344	131	5,290	28,200	81,501	10,289
Larimer	1,367.1	3,973	34.9	5.0	7.1	3.4	10.2	1,497.6	4,352	2,657	859	36,926	179,310	81,897	10,513
Las Animas	64.7	4,557	38.8	6.2	4.9	0.0	12.9	52.5	3,697	78	37	1,387	6,420	44,825	3,842
Lincoln	54.4	9,842	31.9	29.8	2.2	5.8	10.4	17.9	3,246	21	12	995	2,150	44,873	3,499
Logan	63.8	2,860	49.0	2.2	3.9	6.7	9.5	62.7	2,811	62	44	2,281	8,900	56,303	5,321
Mesa	590.7	3,907	38.0	2.0	11.7	5.4	9.0	401.0	2,653	1,774	378	8,703	74,150	61,497	6,191
Mineral	4.6	6,173	50.2	0.6	3.6	0.0	11.6	12.3	16,271	6	2	101	470	61,519	6,034
Moffat	70.1	5,354	28.9	0.9	8.7	7.8	17.7	35.2	2,690	135	31	927	6,070	55,123	4,810
Montezuma	128.2	4,908	29.0	4.7	8.1	9.2	9.3	61.1	2,339	329	63	2,190	12,290	53,534	5,201
Montrose	244.0	5,845	24.7	41.6	5.0	2.3	5.5	104.8	2,510	329	102	2,813	20,500	55,554	5,007
Morgan	118.6	4,190	50.6	1.4	5.9	4.3	8.6	133.3	4,711	108	68	2,023	13,820	54,226	4,695
Otero	105.7	5,764	35.5	3.5	4.9	5.1	6.5	41.9	2,284	99	42	1,760	7,740	42,632	3,151
Ouray	26.9	5,584	39.0	3.8	5.3	4.2	10.7	9.3	1,941	18	12	375	2,850	82,944	10,952
Park	52.7	2,945	34.5	3.3	6.8	9.1	10.5	31.4	1,754	60	45	720	8,300	70,163	7,335
Phillips	73.1	17,041	21.9	33.3	3.6	0.9	5.3	29.9	6,969	24	10	563	2,110	55,574	4,700
Pitkin	353.9	19,692	9.6	35.7	4.0	1.8	3.4	352.2	19,597	85	43	2,309	10,700	154,362	32,739
Prowers	89.6	7,469	28.7	33.7	5.9	4.8	5.3	173.9	14,495	37	28	1,324	5,120	43,456	3,466
Pueblo	625.0	3,759	39.5	1.4	7.3	4.1	4.1	578.0	3,476	1,069	413	11,326	75,510	53,068	4,770
Rio Blanco	117.5	18,501	14.5	29.0	3.1	2.2	7.8	83.3	13,109	64	15	1,151	2,740	60,996	5,559
Rio Grande	59.5	5,263	34.6	6.7	6.3	9.4	7.8	27.7	2,450	126	27	820	6,060	50,894	4,610
Routt	156.0	6,199	29.7	1.6	5.2	2.9	10.0	122.5	4,865	125	60	2,312	13,850	126,002	18,645
Saguache	30.4	4,587	48.1	1.4	5.4	15.0	10.4	16.3	2,452	47	17	484	2,220	41,471	4,041
San Juan	5.5	7,721	42.9	2.2	10.0	2.1	0.0	1.4	1,996	3	2	84	370	50,562	4,595
San Miguel	109.2	13,587	21.9	7.6	4.9	1.3	9.3	94.6	11,774	34	19	762	4,470	111,985	20,086
Sedgwick	16.5	7,132	44.0	0.0	3.4	6.6	9.6	9.1	3,928	19	5	315	1,090	42,372	3,312
Summit	244.9	7,947	19.8	4.6	5.0	0.9	6.2	621.2	20,155	70	73	2,338	17,830	96,796	13,928
Teller	105.6	4,279	29.5	6.2	7.5	2.7	7.9	95.2	3,860	65	61	1,334	12,920	69,521	7,040
Washington	31.4	6,382	40.2	3.2	3.4	10.0	11.8	24.2	4,910	42	11	437	2,070	46,741	3,495
Weld	1,346.8	4,403	41.0	1.2	6.1	2.3	8.2	1,730.4	5,657	649	787	16,493	153,010	72,572	7,940
Yuma	95.1	9,551	23.8	40.5	2.5	3.4	5.8	37.3	3,744	46	24	990	4,480	50,449	4,448
CONNECTICUT	X	X	X	X	X	X	X	X	X	19,235	11,847	206,833	1,793,910	100,123	15,746
Fairfield	4,968.1	5,268	53.4	1.0	6.9	0.9	3.8	3,859.8	4,093	3,072	1,868	41,667	467,180	160,632	32,036
Hartford	4,405.9	4,933	57.9	0.9	5.1	0.7	3.4	3,703.3	4,147	5,868	1,820	63,397	456,560	80,533	10,571
Litchfield	772.0	4,250	63.4	1.5	4.1	0.2	7.2	219.8	1,210	491	356	7,016	95,630	84,595	11,224
Middlesex	783.4	4,808	59.2	0.7	4.2	0.3	3.8	394.4	2,420	408	317	9,245	85,590	90,932	12,371
New Haven	4,329.0	5,047	54.3	0.8	5.3	0.3	3.3	3,393.1	3,956	5,815	1,918	41,558	424,220	75,800	9,446
New London	1,142.3	4,271	59.0	0.8	6.3	0.5	6.0	611.7	2,288	2,973	5,024	21,395	138,450	74,413	8,864

1. Based on the resident population estimated as of July 1 of the year shown.

State / county code	CBSA code[1]	County Type code[2]	STATE County	Land area[3] (sq. mi)	Population, 2021: Total persons 2021	Population, 2021: Rank	Population, 2021: Per square mile	Race alone or in combination, not Hispanic or Latino (percent): White	Black	American Indian, Alaska Native	Asian and Pacific Islancer	Percent Hispanic or Latino[4]	Age (percent): Under 5 years	5 to 17 years	18 to 24 years	25 to 34 years	35 to 44 years	45 to 54 years
				1	2	3	4	5	6	7	8	9	10	11	12	13	14	15
			CONNECTICUT—Cont'd															
09013	25540	1	Tolland	410.4	150,293	452	366.2	84.3	4.4	0.5	6.1	6.6	4.0	9.6	21.7	11.5	11.1	11.4
09015	49340	2	Windham	512.9	116,418	539	227.0	83.3	2.9	1.0	1.9	12.7	4.6	11.1	13.2	12.7	12.6	12.9
10000		0	DELAWARE	1,948.5	1,003,384	X	515.0	62.8	24.0	0.9	4.9	10.1	5.3	11.8	12.0	12.8	12.0	11.6
10001	20100	3	Kent	586.1	184,149	367	314.2	61.8	29.4	1.3	3.6	7.8	5.9	13.0	13.6	13.2	12.2	11.1
10003	37980	1	New Castle	426.3	571,708	123	1,341.1	56.8	27.3	0.7	6.7	11.0	5.4	12.0	12.8	14.0	13.0	12.4
10005	41540	2	Sussex	936.2	247,527	282	264.4	77.2	12.5	1.0	1.8	9.6	4.8	10.1	9.0	9.6	9.6	10.3
11000		0	DISTRICT OF COLUMBIA	61.1	670,050	X	10,966.4	39.2	45.7	0.8	5.6	11.5	6.1	10.3	12.1	21.7	16.5	10.6
11001	47900	1	District of Columbia	61.1	670,050	102	10,966.4	39.2	45.7	0.8	5.6	11.5	6.1	10.3	12.1	21.7	16.5	10.6
12000		0	FLORIDA	53,647.9	21,781,128	X	406.0	54.2	16.5	0.6	3.8	26.8	5.1	11.1	11.4	12.7	12.5	12.4
12001	23540	2	Alachua	875.6	279,238	253	318.9	62.3	21.4	0.6	7.4	11.0	4.8	10.3	22.9	14.9	11.7	9.7
12003	27260	1	Baker	585.2	28,715	1,468	49.1	81.0	15.4	1.1	1.2	3.3	6.1	13.6	12.3	14.5	13.5	13.2
12005	37460	3	Bay	758.6	179,168	377	236.2	78.2	12.4	1.4	3.9	7.4	5.5	11.7	11.0	13.2	12.7	12.5
12007		6	Bradford	294.0	28,540	1,475	97.1	73.9	20.9	0.9	1.2	4.9	5.1	11.1	11.2	15.3	13.8	12.7
12009	37340	2	Brevard	1,015.0	616,628	112	607.5	75.1	11.3	0.8	3.8	11.6	4.4	10.5	10.3	11.4	11.2	11.7
12011	33100	1	Broward	1,202.7	1,930,983	17	1,605.5	34.7	29.9	0.5	4.8	32.0	5.5	11.8	11.2	13.0	13.7	13.5
12013		6	Calhoun	567.3	13,641	2,181	24.0	78.9	13.6	2.1	1.3	6.3	4.8	11.5	11.2	13.9	12.8	13.7
12015	39460	3	Charlotte	681.1	194,843	349	286.1	84.5	6.2	0.7	2.0	8.2	2.8	6.8	7.1	7.8	7.8	9.8
12017	26140	3	Citrus	581.9	158,083	432	271.7	88.2	3.7	1.0	2.2	6.7	3.6	8.5	7.9	8.7	8.4	10.2
12019	27260	1	Clay	604.6	222,361	315	367.8	72.7	13.8	1.0	4.7	11.1	5.2	13.4	12.1	12.1	13.5	13.1
12021	34940	2	Collier	1,997.0	385,980	187	193.3	62.5	7.1	0.4	2.1	29.0	4.1	9.4	9.3	9.3	9.8	10.9
12023	29380	4	Columbia	797.6	70,385	774	88.2	73.1	19.3	1.0	1.6	6.9	5.5	12.5	12.4	12.5	12.3	11.6
12027	11580	6	DeSoto	636.7	34,408	1,317	54.0	55.1	12.5	0.6	0.8	32.1	4.9	10.1	12.1	13.2	13.1	11.6
12029		6	Dixie	705.0	17,102	1,967	24.3	84.9	10.4	1.4	0.9	4.5	4.6	10.6	10.1	11.3	12.5	11.9
12031	27260	1	Duval	762.6	999,935	48	1,311.2	53.2	31.3	0.8	6.3	11.3	6.4	12.6	12.1	16.1	13.3	11.8
12033	37860	2	Escambia	657.0	322,390	223	490.7	66.6	24.1	1.5	5.1	6.4	5.8	11.8	14.5	14.6	11.7	10.9
12035	19660	2	Flagler	486.2	120,932	526	248.7	75.7	10.9	0.8	3.3	11.4	3.6	9.5	9.2	8.8	9.8	11.7
12037		6	Franklin	545.0	12,572	2,238	23.1	80.0	14.1	1.0	0.7	6.0	3.8	8.4	9.2	14.6	12.1	12.1
12039	45220	2	Gadsden	516.4	43,714	1,103	84.7	33.6	54.8	0.6	1.0	11.2	5.6	12.0	11.7	11.8	12.2	13.2
12041	23540	2	Gilchrist	349.7	18,360	1,907	52.5	86.6	6.4	0.9	1.0	6.7	5.4	11.5	14.8	10.5	10.8	11.4
12043		6	Glades	806.8	12,234	2,268	15.2	60.2	13.5	4.4	0.9	22.2	2.8	8.5	9.6	12.4	12.8	12.5
12045		3	Gulf	553.5	14,363	2,124	25.9	84.1	12.4	1.5	1.1	3.4	4.1	11.2	9.6	10.4	9.8	12.2
12047		6	Hamilton	514.3	13,993	2,151	27.2	55.4	33.1	1.3	1.1	11.0	5.3	10.6	14.4	13.5	11.8	12.3
12049	48100	6	Hardee	637.6	25,425	1,589	39.9	47.5	7.6	0.7	1.4	44.2	6.5	14.9	14.2	13.3	11.6	11.7
12051	17500	4	Hendry	1,156.0	40,313	1,172	34.9	30.6	11.0	1.6	1.2	56.5	7.0	15.1	13.6	13.6	12.8	12.3
12053	45300	1	Hernando	473.0	200,638	342	424.2	76.4	6.5	0.8	2.0	15.4	4.4	10.7	10.0	10.8	10.9	11.9
12055	42700	3	Highlands	1,017.7	103,296	594	101.5	67.0	10.4	0.8	1.9	21.3	4.1	9.9	8.8	9.6	9.2	9.4
12057	45300	1	Hillsborough	1,021.9	1,478,194	27	1,446.5	48.9	17.4	0.6	5.4	29.9	5.7	12.5	12.4	14.9	14.2	13.1
12059		6	Holmes	478.9	19,784	1,833	41.3	88.2	7.4	2.2	1.1	3.2	5.1	11.6	11.9	12.7	12.0	13.0
12061	42680	3	Indian River	502.8	163,662	411	325.5	76.1	9.7	0.6	2.1	12.9	3.9	8.5	8.8	9.3	9.0	10.4
12063		6	Jackson	918.2	47,694	1,028	51.9	67.3	27.1	1.4	1.2	5.1	5.2	10.4	11.6	13.0	13.7	12.7
12065	45220	2	Jefferson	598.1	14,555	2,111	24.3	62.6	32.5	1.0	1.0	4.4	4.1	9.7	9.0	11.4	11.8	13.8
12067		9	Lafayette	543.3	8,382	2,547	15.4	72.7	13.0	0.8	0.7	14.3	4.1	11.0	14.6	13.4	13.7	13.6
12069	36740	1	Lake	951.6	395,804	183	415.9	69.3	11.7	0.8	2.9	17.1	4.7	11.0	9.9	11.0	11.4	11.7
12071	15980	2	Lee	781.0	787,976	83	1,008.9	66.9	8.8	0.5	2.3	23.0	4.4	9.7	9.8	10.7	10.6	11.3
12073	45220	2	Leon	668.4	292,817	243	438.1	57.4	32.9	0.8	4.5	6.8	4.9	10.6	24.1	13.9	11.5	10.1
12075	23540	6	Levy	1,118.2	44,158	1,095	39.5	80.5	9.7	1.3	1.2	9.1	4.9	11.4	9.5	11.1	10.4	11.4
12077		8	Liberty	835.6	7,900	2,582	9.5	72.7	19.7	1.4	0.7	7.0	4.0	9.5	11.6	16.5	15.9	14.2
12079		6	Madison	696.5	18,288	1,910	26.3	55.7	37.7	1.1	0.7	6.2	5.0	10.5	10.4	13.4	12.6	12.7
12081	35840	2	Manatee	742.8	412,703	175	555.6	72.1	9.4	0.6	2.8	16.8	4.4	10.1	9.6	10.2	10.6	11.7
12083	36100	2	Marion	1,588.4	385,915	188	243.0	70.5	13.5	0.9	2.3	14.7	4.8	10.7	9.9	11.0	10.4	10.8
12085	38940	2	Martin	543.8	159,942	424	294.1	79.0	5.7	0.6	2.0	14.1	3.9	9.1	9.0	9.0	9.8	11.3
12086	33100	1	Miami-Dade	1,899.9	2,662,777	7	1,401.5	14.0	15.7	0.2	1.9	68.9	5.5	11.2	11.5	13.5	13.8	14.3
12087	28580	4	Monroe	983.0	82,170	701	83.6	65.9	7.2	0.9	2.1	25.5	4.2	8.9	8.5	11.5	12.6	13.9
12089	27260	1	Nassau	648.7	94,189	641	145.2	87.7	6.5	0.8	1.7	4.9	4.9	11.3	9.8	11.1	11.8	12.4
12091	18880	3	Okaloosa	930.2	213,255	322	229.3	76.1	11.4	1.3	5.5	10.0	6.2	12.6	12.4	15.4	13.1	10.5
12093	36380	4	Okeechobee	769.2	40,266	1,174	52.3	63.1	9.0	1.2	1.3	26.5	6.1	11.7	11.2	12.9	12.5	12.8
12095	36740	1	Orange	902.0	1,422,746	29	1,577.3	40.6	21.4	0.6	6.6	32.9	5.7	12.2	13.7	16.2	14.8	13.1
12097	36740	1	Osceola	1,327.5	403,282	181	303.8	30.8	10.7	0.5	3.4	56.0	5.9	13.8	13.4	14.1	14.9	13.3
12099	33100	1	Palm Beach	1,964.3	1,497,987	26	762.6	54.4	19.6	0.4	3.6	23.4	4.9	10.6	10.7	11.6	11.8	12.3
12101	45300	1	Pasco	746.6	584,067	117	782.3	73.5	7.0	0.8	3.8	17.1	4.9	11.8	10.6	11.4	12.7	12.9
12103	45300	1	Pinellas	273.7	956,615	54	3,495.1	75.3	11.4	0.7	4.5	10.3	4.0	8.9	9.1	12.1	11.4	12.4
12105	29460	2	Polk	1,797.8	753,520	89	419.1	57.2	15.8	0.7	2.4	25.7	5.6	12.6	12.2	13.3	12.6	11.7

1. CBSA = Core Based Statistical Area. See Appendix A for explanation. See Appendix B for list of metropolitan areas with component counties. 2. County type code from the Economic Research Service of USDA Rural-Urban Continuum Codes. See Appendix A for definition. 3. Dry land or land partially or temporarily covered by water. 4. May be of any race.

STATE County	Population, 2021 (cont.)				Population change, 2000–2021							Households, 2016–2020				
	Age (percent) (cont.)				Total persons		Percent change		Components of change, 2020–2021					Percent		
	55 to 64 years	65 to 74 years	75 years and over	Percent female	2010	2020	2010–2020	2020–2021	Births	Deaths	Net Migration	Number	Persons per household	Family house-holds	Female family house-holder[1]	One person
	16	17	18	19	20	21	22	23	24	25	26	27	28	29	30	31
CONNECTICUT—Cont'd																
Tolland	13.7	10.0	6.9	49.7	152,691	149,788	-1.9	0.3	1,413	1,560	636	56,077	2.4	65.4	8.4	24.0
Windham	15.2	10.9	7.0	50.0	118,428	116,418	-1.7	0.0	1,241	1,584	324	45,589	2.4	65.6	12.6	26.9
DELAWARE	14.3	12.4	7.7	51.4	897,934	989,948	10.2	1.4	12,719	14,304	15,039	370,953	2.5	65.5	12.7	28.1
Kent	13.0	10.7	7.2	51.7	162,310	181,851	12.0	1.3	2,495	2,598	2,394	67,299	2.6	67.6	15.7	25.8
New Castle	13.6	10.1	6.5	51.3	538,479	570,719	6.0	0.2	7,323	7,341	882	209,431	2.6	63.5	12.7	29.6
Sussex	16.8	19.0	10.7	51.5	197,145	237,378	20.4	4.3	2,901	4,365	11,763	94,223	2.4	68.5	10.7	26.6
DISTRICT OF COLUMBIA	9.9	7.6	5.2	52.4	601,723	689,545	14.6	-2.8	10,868	7,939	-22,143	288,307	2.3	42.8	13.3	45.1
District of Columbia	9.9	7.6	5.2	52.4	601,723	689,545	14.6	-2.8	10,868	7,939	-22,143	288,307	2.3	42.8	13.3	45.1
FLORIDA	13.7	11.9	9.2	50.8	18,801,310	21,538,187	14.6	1.1	260,946	319,149	305,218	7,931,313	2.6	64.5	12.7	28.6
Alachua	10.4	9.3	5.9	51.7	247,336	278,468	12.6	0.3	3,206	3,104	596	101,979	2.5	49.8	10.7	37.0
Baker	12.3	8.9	5.7	46.9	27,115	28,259	4.2	1.6	431	389	413	8,828	2.9	73.0	13.5	18.9
Bay	15.0	11.2	7.3	50.2	168,852	175,216	3.8	2.3	2,353	2,763	4,434	73,536	2.4	64.5	12.1	29.0
Bradford	12.7	10.3	7.7	44.2	28,520	28,303	-0.8	0.8	356	458	341	9,318	2.5	63.1	14.1	30.6
Brevard	16.3	13.8	10.4	50.7	543,376	606,612	11.6	1.7	6,156	10,911	14,952	236,005	2.5	63.1	9.8	30.7
Broward	13.9	10.1	7.4	50.9	1,748,066	1,944,375	11.2	-0.7	25,061	24,055	-14,462	704,942	2.7	63.5	14.9	29.8
Calhoun	13.2	10.8	8.2	45.6	14,625	13,648	-6.7	-0.1	152	264	106	4,510	2.7	61.0	10.0	36.0
Charlotte	17.5	22.1	18.4	50.9	159,978	186,847	16.8	4.3	1,261	4,331	11,260	79,789	2.3	63.9	7.5	30.1
Citrus	16.4	20.0	16.3	51.2	141,236	153,843	8.9	2.8	1,298	4,115	7,185	64,621	2.3	62.0	9.0	32.2
Clay	14.0	10.6	6.0	50.5	190,865	218,245	14.3	1.9	2,607	2,930	4,474	75,360	2.8	76.4	12.8	19.9
Collier	14.1	16.3	16.8	50.4	321,520	375,752	16.9	2.7	3,813	5,795	12,384	147,977	2.5	66.3	8.6	28.7
Columbia	13.5	11.8	7.9	48.0	67,531	69,698	3.2	1.0	937	1,261	1,013	25,205	2.6	62.4	12.4	30.6
DeSoto	12.3	11.9	10.7	44.0	34,862	33,976	-2.5	1.3	461	567	538	12,421	2.7	66.9	13.7	26.7
Dixie	15.1	13.8	10.2	44.8	16,422	16,759	2.1	2.0	209	307	447	6,233	2.4	69.3	9.6	26.4
Duval	12.7	9.4	5.5	51.3	864,263	995,567	15.2	0.4	15,486	13,349	2,058	369,704	2.5	60.9	15.1	31.8
Escambia	13.3	10.7	6.7	50.5	297,619	321,905	8.2	0.2	4,583	5,368	1,220	122,169	2.5	60.6	14.8	30.8
Flagler	16.2	18.2	12.9	51.6	95,696	115,378	20.6	4.8	971	2,083	6,773	44,040	2.6	71.7	10.5	22.9
Franklin	15.2	15.4	9.2	43.0	11,549	12,451	7.8	1.0	120	206	211	4,691	2.2	62.4	12.0	31.8
Gadsden	14.1	11.9	7.5	52.5	46,389	43,826	-5.5	-0.3	598	711	2	17,307	2.4	65.1	20.6	31.2
Gilchrist	14.6	12.4	8.6	48.2	16,939	17,864	5.5	2.8	230	288	561	6,701	2.5	66.6	12.1	27.5
Glades	13.3	14.1	14.0	44.0	12,884	12,126	-5.9	0.9	78	229	263	4,859	2.5	66.8	11.6	27.8
Gulf	16.8	15.9	10.1	49.8	15,863	14,192	-10.5	1.2	141	286	320	5,897	2.1	66.8	14.2	26.4
Hamilton	13.3	11.5	7.1	41.5	14,799	14,004	-5.4	-0.1	200	240	28	4,385	2.6	71.3	16.2	22.0
Hardee	11.0	9.3	7.5	46.9	27,731	25,327	-8.7	0.4	415	292	-28	7,991	3.1	73.1	12.8	23.1
Hendry	11.8	7.8	5.9	47.1	39,140	39,619	1.2	1.8	686	486	488	12,878	3.1	72.8	19.3	22.9
Hernando	14.6	14.8	11.8	51.7	172,778	194,515	12.6	3.1	1,982	4,166	8,438	76,708	2.5	67.5	11.5	26.4
Highlands	13.3	17.4	18.3	51.3	98,786	101,235	2.5	2.0	961	2,404	3,573	42,721	2.4	63.6	10.0	31.5
Hillsborough	12.3	9.1	5.8	51.0	1,229,226	1,459,762	18.8	1.3	20,481	17,701	15,407	539,919	2.7	62.7	13.5	28.8
Holmes	13.7	11.3	8.7	46.9	19,927	19,653	-1.4	0.7	234	373	274	7,137	2.5	69.2	16.2	27.7
Indian River	15.7	18.4	15.9	52.0	138,028	159,788	15.8	2.4	1,517	3,196	5,637	60,959	2.6	61.8	6.7	33.2
Jackson	13.2	11.4	8.7	46.0	49,746	47,319	-4.9	0.8	589	971	767	17,533	2.3	65.4	13.4	30.8
Jefferson	15.6	14.6	9.9	47.7	14,761	14,510	-1.7	0.3	152	253	149	5,643	2.2	67.3	12.7	29.4
Lafayette	12.4	9.9	7.3	44.0	8,870	8,226	-7.3	1.9	79	127	206	2,315	3.1	71.5	12.4	24.5
Lake	13.7	14.5	12.0	51.6	297,052	383,956	29.3	3.1	4,155	6,880	14,783	137,446	2.6	68.6	10.3	25.9
Lee	14.4	15.8	13.3	51.1	618,754	760,822	23.0	3.6	8,316	12,139	31,411	288,916	2.6	65.0	9.3	28.8
Leon	10.4	9.1	5.4	52.8	275,487	292,198	6.1	0.2	3,546	3,172	173	116,530	2.4	53.2	13.0	32.0
Levy	15.9	15.2	10.1	51.1	40,801	42,915	5.2	2.9	504	814	1,574	16,971	2.4	63.3	11.8	30.3
Liberty	12.3	9.8	6.1	38.1	8,365	7,974	-4.7	-0.9	88	111	-52	2,513	2.7	63.7	11.5	33.3
Madison	14.2	13.0	8.2	47.1	19,224	17,968	-6.5	1.8	262	373	435	6,891	2.4	59.1	14.9	34.3
Manatee	15.1	15.7	12.7	51.8	322,833	399,710	23.8	3.3	4,235	6,538	15,506	150,345	2.6	66.0	9.7	28.6
Marion	13.8	15.7	13.0	52.0	331,298	375,908	13.5	2.7	4,237	7,861	13,826	145,863	2.4	64.9	11.4	30.0
Martin	15.9	16.2	15.8	50.8	146,318	158,431	8.3	1.0	1,505	3,117	3,180	64,870	2.4	61.9	8.2	31.9
Miami-Dade	13.4	9.3	7.6	51.3	2,496,435	2,701,767	8.2	-1.4	34,623	33,451	-39,861	902,200	3.0	68.7	17.8	25.6
Monroe	16.7	14.4	9.4	48.1	73,090	82,874	13.4	-0.8	819	1,007	-517	32,794	2.2	59.5	7.3	29.2
Nassau	15.6	14.5	8.7	50.8	73,314	90,352	23.2	4.2	1,025	1,518	4,384	33,475	2.5	72.8	10.2	21.3
Okaloosa	13.4	10.0	6.3	49.2	180,822	211,668	17.1	0.7	3,196	2,905	1,267	79,235	2.5	65.3	9.6	28.2
Okeechobee	12.8	11.0	9.0	46.3	39,996	39,644	-0.9	1.6	617	693	705	14,601	2.6	67.4	12.8	25.3
Orange	11.7	7.9	4.9	51.0	1,145,956	1,429,908	24.8	-0.5	19,583	13,216	-13,608	468,075	2.9	66.1	14.3	24.6
Osceola	11.1	8.1	5.3	50.7	268,685	388,656	44.7	3.8	5,525	3,861	13,043	109,642	3.3	74.0	16.9	19.6
Palm Beach	13.6	12.3	12.3	51.6	1,320,134	1,492,191	13.0	0.4	17,607	23,199	11,363	565,598	2.6	62.2	11.6	31.0
Pasco	13.6	12.3	9.7	51.4	464,697	561,891	20.9	3.9	6,242	9,650	25,913	209,483	2.5	66.5	12.0	27.7
Pinellas	16.3	14.4	11.5	52.0	916,542	959,107	4.6	-0.3	9,318	18,191	6,487	413,239	2.3	56.4	10.4	35.7
Polk	12.1	11.3	8.6	51.0	602,095	725,046	20.4	3.9	9,964	11,253	30,129	240,879	2.9	68.6	13.4	25.2

1. No spouse present.

STATE County	Persons in group quarters, 2021	Daytime Population, 2016–2020		Births, 2021		Deaths, 2021		Persons under 65 with no health insurance, 2019		Medicare, 2021			COVID-19 Deaths, 2020	
		Number	Employment/ residence ratio	Total	Rate[1]	Number	Rate[1]	Number	Percent	Total beneficiaries	Enrolled in Original Medicare	Enrolled in Medicare Advantage	Number	Rate[1]
	32	33	34	35	36	37	38	39	40	41	42	43	44	45
CONNECTICUT—Cont'd														
Tolland	14,418	125,300	0.7	1,112	7.4	1,254	8.4	5,013	4.4	27,810	13,094	14,716	128	0.9
Windham	4,483	103,018	0.8	994	8.5	1,262	10.8	6,018	6.5	23,743	12,974	10,769	93	0.8
DELAWARE	24,405	966,777	1.0	10,311	10.3	11,655	11.7	60,910	8.0	215,611	174,723	40,889	1,038	1.0
Kent	4,360	170,776	0.9	2,049	11.2	2,119	11.6	13,058	9.0	38,492	31,219	7,273	197	1.1
New Castle	17,502	574,107	1.1	5,904	10.3	5,936	10.4	30,759	6.8	102,830	81,083	21,747	511	0.9
Sussex	2,543	221,894	0.9	2,358	9.7	3,600	14.8	17,093	10.4	74,288	62,420	11,869	330	1.4
DISTRICT OF COLUMBIA	37,003	1,137,626	2.2	8,723	12.8	6,552	9.6	23,635	4.0	94,033	73,216	20,818	885	1.3
District of Columbia	37,003	1,137,626	2.2	8,723	12.8	6,552	9.6	23,635	4.0	94,032	73,215	20,818	885	1.3
FLORIDA	412,459	21,159,645	1.0	210,305	9.7	255,553	11.8	2,716,165	16.4	4,677,489	2,409,421	2,268,069	21,523	1.0
Alachua	14,882	284,608	1.1	2,573	9.2	2,522	9.0	26,882	12.4	45,840	32,658	13,182	155	0.6
Baker	2,531	25,688	0.7	350	12.3	310	10.9	2,484	11.1	4,993	3,267	1,726	38	1.3
Bay	3,540	182,394	1.0	1,908	10.8	2,238	12.7	20,640	14.8	37,013	26,004	11,009	204	1.2
Bradford	4,127	26,160	0.8	281	9.9	369	13.0	2,568	13.5	5,845	3,695	2,151	20	0.7
Brevard	6,418	584,944	1.0	4,938	8.1	8,659	14.1	62,753	13.9	159,117	90,617	68,500	518	0.9
Broward	15,538	1,860,056	0.9	20,130	10.4	19,099	9.9	282,874	17.7	331,717	137,131	194,586	1,940	1.0
Calhoun	1,531	12,520	0.6	121	8.9	207	15.2	1,559	15.8	3,006	1,721	1,286	22	1.6
Charlotte	2,536	177,938	0.9	1,002	5.2	3,500	18.3	19,097	17.4	71,649	42,202	29,447	268	1.4
Citrus	2,146	141,956	0.9	1,038	6.6	3,242	20.7	15,868	17.1	60,329	33,745	26,584	241	1.6
Clay	1,035	172,843	0.6	2,102	9.5	2,351	10.7	23,029	12.6	43,817	29,529	14,288	157	0.7
Collier	3,956	390,555	1.1	3,036	8.0	4,761	12.5	54,372	21.3	104,801	74,053	30,748	363	1.0
Columbia	5,046	70,569	1.0	755	10.8	1,030	14.7	7,488	14.2	16,604	10,682	5,923	103	1.5
DeSoto	2,966	37,543	1.0	374	10.9	455	13.3	6,914	26.5	7,295	4,412	2,883	58	1.7
Dixie	1,678	15,339	0.7	170	10.0	252	14.9	1,918	17.5	4,291	2,522	1,769	16	1.0
Duval	21,014	1,034,768	1.2	12,525	12.5	10,722	10.7	114,072	14.3	168,337	96,414	71,924	762	0.8
Escambia	17,734	336,673	1.1	3,668	11.4	4,260	13.2	34,595	14.0	71,316	44,657	26,660	341	1.1
Flagler	503	99,135	0.7	796	6.7	1,624	13.7	12,438	15.8	39,414	20,980	18,434	58	0.5
Franklin	1,757	11,657	0.9	96	7.7	152	12.1	1,324	17.9	3,140	1,933	1,207	D	D
Gadsden	2,945	41,681	0.8	489	11.2	570	13.0	5,549	16.3	10,425	4,244	6,181	58	1.3
Gilchrist	1,059	15,117	0.6	186	10.3	229	12.6	2,347	17.2	4,091	2,686	1,405	15	0.8
Glades	1,150	12,626	0.7	66	5.4	195	16.0	2,241	26.5	2,792	1,624	1,168	16	1.3
Gulf	393	14,667	0.9	121	8.5	225	15.8	1,314	13.5	3,834	2,657	1,177	23	1.6
Hamilton	2,522	14,125	0.9	159	11.4	178	12.7	1,369	15.2	2,956	1,936	1,020	22	1.6
Hardee	1,324	25,741	0.9	347	13.7	230	9.1	4,077	19.9	4,505	2,626	1,880	22	0.9
Hendry	477	39,970	0.9	571	14.3	387	9.7	9,450	26.9	6,016	3,579	2,438	55	1.4
Hernando	1,588	174,200	0.8	1,604	8.1	3,324	16.8	21,668	15.6	60,299	25,000	35,299	236	1.2
Highlands	1,354	103,606	1.0	784	7.7	1,880	18.4	13,536	20.4	34,125	19,311	14,814	195	1.9
Hillsborough	22,292	1,501,581	1.1	16,571	11.3	14,264	9.7	184,263	14.9	242,267	112,429	129,838	1,088	0.7
Holmes	1,697	16,828	0.6	193	9.8	298	15.1	2,563	18.4	4,429	2,899	1,530	29	1.5
Indian River	1,147	158,529	1.0	1,237	7.6	2,563	15.8	19,417	18.6	54,766	36,923	17,843	152	0.9
Jackson	6,437	46,384	0.9	486	10.2	762	16.1	4,557	14.9	11,273	7,520	3,753	110	2.3
Jefferson	1,222	11,725	0.5	116	8.0	192	13.2	1,417	14.9	3,695	1,755	1,941	14	1.0
Lafayette	1,177	8,092	0.8	58	7.0	106	12.7	1,115	19.6	1,480	998	482	19	2.3
Lake	3,885	321,103	0.8	3,370	8.6	5,542	14.2	41,405	15.7	107,014	58,966	48,048	321	0.8
Lee	7,712	741,221	1.0	6,677	8.6	9,861	12.7	96,245	17.9	201,807	121,956	79,851	680	0.9
Leon	14,609	311,107	1.1	2,826	9.7	2,503	8.6	28,530	11.9	46,687	22,293	24,394	171	0.6
Levy	307	35,424	0.6	411	9.4	670	15.4	5,879	19.3	12,433	7,312	5,121	33	0.8
Liberty	1,876	8,247	1.0	74	9.3	89	11.2	738	14.6	1,392	675	717	16	2.0
Madison	1,792	18,825	1.0	209	11.5	297	16.4	2,095	16.7	4,554	2,866	1,688	41	2.3
Manatee	4,318	366,023	0.8	3,419	8.4	5,267	12.9	48,162	16.8	104,964	62,059	42,906	450	1.1
Marion	9,187	351,545	0.9	3,442	9.0	6,192	16.2	42,094	16.9	120,124	60,208	59,916	489	1.3
Martin	3,882	166,803	1.1	1,197	7.5	2,501	15.7	17,411	16.2	47,211	31,601	15,610	184	1.2
Miami-Dade	41,295	2,783,378	1.1	27,851	10.4	26,611	9.9	428,190	19.4	475,765	138,854	336,912	4,092	1.5
Monroe	2,105	79,789	1.1	639	7.7	795	9.6	12,047	21.6	17,430	14,577	2,852	42	0.5
Nassau	453	72,468	0.7	812	8.8	1,257	13.6	8,114	11.8	23,249	15,344	7,904	71	0.8
Okaloosa	4,971	216,934	1.1	2,588	12.2	2,288	10.8	24,981	14.5	41,619	31,868	9,751	221	1.0
Okeechobee	2,658	40,315	0.9	500	12.5	554	13.9	6,699	22.0	8,577	4,741	3,836	58	1.5
Orange	35,935	1,546,971	1.3	15,764	11.1	10,606	7.4	183,226	15.4	192,564	90,443	102,122	818	0.6
Osceola	3,101	314,866	0.7	4,423	11.1	3,056	7.7	51,986	16.3	62,680	22,554	40,126	298	0.8
Palm Beach	21,080	1,503,336	1.0	14,241	9.5	18,623	12.5	199,201	17.9	332,132	194,156	137,977	1,806	1.2
Pasco	5,396	473,902	0.7	5,005	8.7	7,781	13.5	66,501	15.7	136,335	55,566	80,770	420	0.7
Pinellas	18,839	989,351	1.0	7,512	7.8	14,614	15.3	110,535	15.4	249,082	118,278	130,804	935	1.0
Polk	13,115	674,420	0.9	8,086	10.9	8,962	12.1	95,885	17.1	160,554	68,277	92,278	760	1.0

1. Per 1,000 estimated resident population.

STATE County	COVID-19 Vaccinations, 2021–2022: Number	COVID-19 Vaccinations, 2021–2022: Percent[5]	Education: School enrollment and attainment, 2016–2020: Enrollment[1]: Total	Enrollment[1]: Percent private	Attainment[2] (percent): High school graduate or less	Attainment[2] (percent): Bachelor's degree or more	Local government expenditures,[3] 2018–2019: Total current spending (mil dol)	Local government expenditures,[3] 2018–2019: Current spending per student (dollars)	Money income, 2016–2020: Per capita income[4]	Households: Median income (dollars)	Households: Percent with income of less than $50,000	Households: Percent with income of $200,000 or more	Income and poverty, 2020: Median household income (dollars)	Percent below poverty level: All persons	Percent below poverty level: Children under 18 years	Percent below poverty level: Children 5 to 17 years in families
	46	47	48	49	50	51	52	53	54	55	56	57	58	59	60	61
CONNECTICUT—Cont'd																
Tolland	101,061	67.1	47,336	8.7	31.7	42.4	389.0	20,476	41,537	87,809	28.2	12.2	87,247	6.9	5.6	5.2
Windham	74,952	64.2	27,770	9.7	46.0	23.7	306.1	19,904	33,337	67,365	36.2	6.9	66,349	10.4	12.5	12.0
DELAWARE	672,434	69.1	225,882	16.0	40.4	32.7	2,202.0	15,910	36,574	69,110	36.1	7.6	71,335	10.9	15.1	14.1
Kent	101,493	56.1	44,836	13.6	45.3	24.5	390.1	14,188	28,911	60,117	42.2	3.0	61,538	13.0	16.4	14.9
New Castle	385,236	68.9	139,216	18.2	38.3	36.7	1,344.6	17,119	38,965	75,275	33.4	9.5	75,145	10.1	13.9	12.7
Sussex	159,836	68.2	41,830	11.3	41.8	29.4	467.4	14,439	36,739	64,905	37.9	6.5	69,829	11.0	17.4	17.0
DISTRICT OF COLUMBIA	522,640	74.1	168,035	40.3	24.7	59.8	1,954.7	22,097	58,659	90,842	30.5	19.8	91,957	15.0	22.3	23.2
District of Columbia	495,217	70.2	168,035	40.3	24.7	59.8	1,954.7	22,097	58,659	90,842	30.5	19.8	91,957	15.0	22.3	23.2
FLORIDA	14,374,253	66.9	4,774,888	18.6	39.7	30.5	27,289.2	9,582	32,848	57,703	43.4	6.4	61,724	12.4	17.2	16.5
Alachua	178,526	66.4	92,393	10.4	27.5	44.1	289.7	9,345	29,821	50,089	49.9	5.6	51,995	17.2	15.1	14.2
Baker	10,641	36.4	6,795	14.9	56.9	14.4	44.7	8,831	24,051	62,299	37.9	3.1	61,514	12.8	17.3	18.6
Bay	93,091	53.3	39,584	15.6	38.6	24.5	241.6	8,589	30,774	56,483	43.6	3.9	61,332	12.4	20.0	18.9
Bradford	12,550	44.5	5,339	19.3	62.6	10.3	35.6	11,272	21,003	43,580	55.4	2.0	48,260	17.5	22.0	21.3
Brevard	389,998	64.8	124,375	20.5	34.5	30.9	673.2	9,130	33,662	59,359	41.9	6.0	65,871	9.9	13.5	13.1
Broward	1,394,706	71.4	472,306	21.1	37.6	33.1	2,659.9	9,760	34,063	60,922	41.5	7.7	63,901	11.0	14.1	13.8
Calhoun	4,913	34.8	2,953	6.2	64.4	9.1	25.2	11,567	19,512	38,037	61.9	1.6	43,994	20.3	28.7	26.0
Charlotte	123,710	65.5	24,026	15.9	42.6	23.8	154.5	9,650	33,275	52,724	47.1	4.2	58,368	9.8	15.8	14.5
Citrus	84,375	56.4	22,302	16.4	48.5	18.9	145.7	9,416	28,174	45,689	54.8	2.7	48,574	12.6	23.1	23.3
Clay	118,767	54.2	55,514	16.8	37.6	26.2	321.4	8,396	32,037	68,657	34.1	5.1	72,520	8.9	12.9	12.3
Collier	269,542	70.0	67,847	18.6	38.0	35.9	534.5	11,268	46,785	70,217	35.5	12.2	81,895	10.1	14.9	14.0
Columbia	30,100	42.0	14,715	17.6	51.4	14.9	93.6	9,225	24,569	44,818	54.1	2.5	46,670	15.6	22.8	21.8
DeSoto	17,646	46.4	6,798	10.1	69.3	12.2	48.7	9,880	18,193	36,360	65.7	0.7	45,807	20.8	27.6	26.9
Dixie	5,790	34.4	2,992	23.4	68.4	9.5	21.7	9,728	19,911	41,674	64.2	2.0	41,450	23.2	31.1	30.2
Duval	585,214	61.1	225,735	20.5	38.0	30.7	1,187.2	9,116	32,233	56,769	43.6	5.2	55,202	15.2	21.1	22.7
Escambia	178,144	56.0	73,894	24.3	36.5	27.2	365.3	9,138	29,166	53,023	46.6	4.3	57,089	13.5	20.4	18.7
Flagler	73,181	63.6	21,207	12.5	41.1	25.6	114.0	8,784	32,722	57,536	43.0	4.7	67,054	9.4	16.3	15.2
Franklin	5,848	48.2	1,832	13.5	55.1	20.4	16.7	12,736	26,211	48,814	51.4	3.6	47,206	19.1	30.8	28.9
Gadsden	26,509	58.1	10,191	16.5	55.0	18.2	63.5	12,121	21,087	41,135	59.8	1.3	42,698	21.9	34.9	32.5
Gilchrist	6,805	36.6	4,186	9.6	57.4	12.3	29.5	10,726	22,775	47,381	52.5	1.3	52,000	14.5	22.5	22.3
Glades	4,692	34.0	2,251	14.8	63.8	11.5	19.3	10,972	22,128	39,709	59.8	1.7	45,328	18.1	23.5	20.7
Gulf	7,082	51.9	2,406	15.8	47.3	23.2	28.3	14,445	27,626	50,640	48.9	4.1	51,593	15.1	25.2	23.0
Hamilton	5,031	34.9	2,824	15.6	71.2	8.2	18.1	11,212	15,532	38,300	61.1	1.3	41,871	24.2	34.5	33.8
Hardee	11,550	42.9	6,386	6.4	72.3	9.1	50.3	9,895	20,181	40,165	60.7	1.9	46,264	21.2	28.0	25.2
Hendry	20,917	49.8	10,165	8.9	64.5	8.2	70.5	9,699	20,122	36,978	60.9	2.4	45,652	22.9	31.4	31.5
Hernando	106,538	54.9	36,451	17.1	45.4	19.1	198.8	8,715	26,520	50,280	49.7	2.5	52,108	12.5	20.1	18.6
Highlands	55,740	52.5	17,405	13.8	51.8	17.5	116.2	9,424	27,979	43,708	55.8	2.7	48,922	16.1	26.6	25.3
Hillsborough	924,574	62.8	362,874	18.6	38.2	34.5	1,999.3	9,077	33,616	60,566	41.5	7.6	65,272	11.9	14.3	14.3
Holmes	5,791	29.5	3,905	6.6	63.7	9.9	32.3	9,848	19,028	39,215	61.4	1.0	41,969	20.5	30.9	29.0
Indian River	107,520	67.2	28,747	19.6	38.7	30.6	175.3	9,817	38,274	57,945	44.3	7.1	72,934	8.7	16.0	16.2
Jackson	20,147	43.4	8,916	16.0	56.1	12.9	65.8	10,170	21,058	40,754	58.5	2.2	44,108	19.5	29.5	28.8
Jefferson	8,514	59.8	2,580	24.7	51.9	23.3	7.4	9,592	25,795	49,081	50.2	2.3	54,354	17.2	26.4	24.9
Lafayette	3,323	39.5	1,949	7.2	68.8	9.3	12.0	9,786	17,022	51,734	41.6	0.4	41,635	20.7	27.7	23.5
Lake	242,117	66.0	70,805	20.5	42.1	24.4	393.0	8,945	29,426	55,792	44.7	3.9	58,501	9.2	14.0	13.1
Lee	477,985	62.0	144,206	14.0	41.9	28.5	911.7	9,657	34,818	59,608	41.4	6.4	66,140	10.5	14.7	13.4
Leon	166,509	56.7	101,960	12.1	25.7	46.6	320.7	8,657	31,778	54,675	46.4	6.0	61,403	17.6	22.0	20.5
Levy	19,608	47.2	7,834	15.7	55.2	14.1	52.7	9,573	22,772	38,951	61.5	1.4	41,894	16.9	27.2	26.3
Liberty	2,861	34.2	1,786	3.6	65.5	13.6	17.5	13,278	19,585	39,121	61.0	1.2	46,734	21.2	24.7	25.0
Madison	8,528	46.1	3,300	11.6	57.1	13.8	27.0	10,331	18,909	35,240	65.3	1.0	41,650	23.8	30.1	29.8
Manatee	248,995	61.7	73,164	17.9	40.5	30.2	505.3	10,248	35,146	59,963	42.1	6.3	63,328	10.9	16.2	15.9
Marion	207,974	56.9	67,411	18.4	48.5	20.7	418.8	9,760	26,990	46,587	53.4	3.0	48,553	15.3	21.7	18.6
Martin	102,503	63.7	28,426	17.4	34.1	33.5	186.8	10,030	43,758	65,821	38.2	9.8	72,736	11.1	17.3	16.5
Miami-Dade	2,307,803	84.9	657,474	20.9	44.9	30.7	3,465.0	9,888	29,598	53,975	46.6	6.7	59,259	15.0	19.9	18.3
Monroe	58,204	78.4	11,711	14.2	35.7	35.3	119.3	13,904	47,382	72,012	34.6	9.7	68,584	10.2	15.3	14.8
Nassau	51,105	57.7	16,774	18.8	40.7	30.5	113.5	9,363	37,787	72,998	32.5	8.9	75,123	8.1	11.6	11.2
Okaloosa	135,207	64.2	46,859	14.6	32.5	32.2	296.8	9,316	34,357	64,373	37.7	6.4	65,977	9.6	14.2	13.2
Okeechobee	19,622	46.5	8,347	14.7	59.0	14.3	59.8	9,223	23,133	46,097	55.6	2.9	48,028	17.7	24.7	24.0
Orange	966,912	69.4	368,715	18.5	35.4	35.4	2,118.0	9,882	31,409	61,416	40.5	6.9	69,074	12.7	16.7	16.2
Osceola	274,154	73.0	92,418	17.3	43.2	23.2	606.1	8,841	24,146	55,538	45.1	3.5	63,018	11.8	17.6	18.0
Palm Beach	992,622	66.3	321,531	19.6	35.2	37.1	1,995.9	10,145	40,957	65,015	39.1	10.4	68,200	12.0	16.2	15.7
Pasco	326,640	59.0	114,214	18.5	44.1	24.6	665.7	8,870	29,498	53,431	47.0	4.1	52,332	11.4	16.3	15.1
Pinellas	630,616	64.7	184,170	19.9	35.6	32.5	1,004.6	9,952	36,754	56,419	44.3	6.2	61,532	11.1	15.8	15.5
Polk	415,330	57.3	160,280	18.8	48.3	20.6	1,004.0	9,503	25,820	51,535	48.5	3.7	54,591	14.4	22.2	22.0

1. All persons 3 years old and over enrolled in nursery school through college. 2. Persons 25 years old and over. 3. Elementary and secondary education expenditures. 4. Based on population estimated by the American Community Survey, 2016–2020. 5. CDC percent based on 2019 population estimate.

STATE County	Personal income, 2020: Total (mil dol)	Personal income, 2020: Percent change 2019–2020	Personal income, 2020: Per capita[1]: Dollars	Personal income, 2020: Per capita[1]: Rank	Personal income, 2020: Wages and salaries (mil dol)	Personal income, 2020: Supplements to wages and salaries, employer contributions (mil dol): Pension and insurance	Personal income, 2020: Supplements to wages and salaries, employer contributions (mil dol): Government social insurance	Personal income, 2020: Proprietors' income (mil dol)	Personal income, 2020: Dividends, interest, and rent (mil dol)	Personal income, 2020: Personal transfer reecipts (mil dol)	Earnings, 2020: Total (mil dol)	Earnings, 2020: Contributions for government social insurance (mil dol): From employee and self-employed	Earnings, 2020: Contributions for government social insurance (mil dol): From employer
	62	63	64	65	66	67	68	69	70	71	72	73	74
CONNECTICUT—Cont'd													
Tolland	8,974	4.6	59,590	445	2,225	560	155	617	1,335	1,645	3,556	202	155
Windham	5,914	7.1	50,747	1,059	1,863	381	146	478	673	1,613	2,868	177	146
DELAWARE	55,357	5.4	55,810	X	27,895	4,785	2,053	3,526	9,964	13,861	38,259	2,441	2,053
Kent	8,558	7.7	46,600	1,562	3,647	885	290	505	1,370	2,522	5,328	325	290
New Castle	33,666	4.7	59,955	427	20,402	3,198	1,460	1,656	5,946	7,325	26,715	1,679	1,460
Sussex	13,133	5.5	54,352	758	3,846	702	304	1,365	2,648	4,014	6,217	438	304
DISTRICT OF COLUMBIA	61,706	7.8	89,417	X	80,053	15,171	5,695	6,086	9,942	10,631	107,005	5,534	5,695
District of Columbia	61,706	7.8	86,567	52	80,053	15,171	5,695	6,086	9,942	10,631	107,005	5,534	5,695
FLORIDA	1,209,996	6.2	56,096	X	510,579	70,235	34,932	73,018	324,682	275,017	688,765	47,103	34,932
Alachua	13,440	6.9	49,556	1,191	7,649	1,372	531	461	2,772	2,939	10,012	616	531
Baker	1,081	8.8	36,552	2,818	311	60	23	36	155	321	430	32	23
Bay	8,685	6.7	50,696	1,065	3,919	657	286	477	1,800	2,324	5,339	357	286
Bradford	1,038	7.8	36,301	2,848	285	54	20	25	146	347	384	30	20
Brevard	31,340	7.4	51,507	978	13,590	1,957	945	1,365	6,531	8,624	17,856	1,290	945
Broward	109,474	5.9	55,908	649	51,901	6,587	3,474	6,231	25,833	21,752	68,193	4,451	3,474
Calhoun	454	10.5	32,264	3,052	119	25	9	21	63	175	173	14	9
Charlotte	8,880	7.5	45,606	1,716	2,338	339	165	429	2,495	3,309	3,270	322	165
Citrus	6,416	7.6	41,933	2,209	1,443	234	102	307	1,515	2,758	2,085	235	102
Clay	10,513	7.1	47,407	1,455	2,548	383	178	375	1,841	2,676	3,484	276	178
Collier	40,816	2.5	103,865	19	8,936	1,075	602	2,234	23,112	5,020	12,847	929	602
Columbia	2,778	8.8	38,243	2,660	1,125	216	82	120	387	976	1,542	112	82
DeSoto	1,073	10.3	27,863	3,102	461	79	35	85	185	429	659	46	35
Dixie	523	8.6	30,651	3,083	113	25	8	17	102	229	164	16	8
Duval	49,430	7.1	51,131	1,014	35,496	4,878	2,478	3,682	8,659	11,498	46,534	2,887	2,478
Escambia	15,274	7.8	47,381	1,464	8,390	1,489	618	713	2,870	4,318	11,210	717	618
Flagler	5,993	6.5	50,599	1,077	1,064	168	75	319	1,568	1,831	1,627	165	75
Franklin	481	6.9	39,452	2,513	134	25	10	35	150	154	205	17	10
Gadsden	1,743	6.9	38,507	2,625	638	116	46	66	300	605	865	59	46
Gilchrist	707	11.7	37,425	2,746	189	36	13	52	93	228	290	21	13
Glades	399	12.2	28,116	3,100	123	25	9	26	72	132	184	11	9
Gulf	672	9.3	49,666	1,178	185	33	13	31	134	202	262	22	13
Hamilton	427	9.7	29,383	3,093	168	37	12	17	52	176	234	18	12
Hardee	852	12.0	31,775	3,064	317	66	24	73	117	272	479	30	24
Hendry	1,522	13.3	35,546	2,903	629	112	50	132	209	442	923	49	50
Hernando	8,227	9.7	41,385	2,280	2,018	309	146	279	1,384	3,171	2,751	268	146
Highlands	3,962	8.7	37,158	2,774	1,157	202	84	169	773	1,702	1,612	150	84
Hillsborough	77,666	8.3	51,848	944	48,550	6,322	3,263	4,538	13,382	16,580	62,672	3,950	3,263
Holmes	679	7.3	34,661	2,955	134	31	10	36	108	271	210	21	10
Indian River	13,750	3.4	84,607	63	2,748	375	190	761	6,361	2,579	4,074	334	190
Jackson	1,784	9.0	38,710	2,604	643	133	46	115	293	677	937	70	46
Jefferson	641	6.7	44,065	1,939	104	20	8	31	135	191	163	15	8
Lafayette	255	12.5	30,032	3,087	57	13	4	27	37	85	101	6	4
Lake	17,484	7.7	46,563	1,568	4,758	720	340	667	3,339	5,561	6,486	572	340
Lee	43,261	6.0	54,707	722	14,566	2,021	1,003	2,847	15,722	10,388	20,437	1,526	1,003
Leon	14,433	6.5	48,850	1,277	8,168	1,437	560	836	2,703	2,983	11,001	670	560
Levy	1,714	10.8	40,598	2,385	368	70	26	124	253	623	588	49	26
Liberty	238	11.2	28,496	3,096	86	19	6	13	34	82	125	9	6
Madison	670	9.7	35,828	2,881	181	39	13	53	110	255	287	23	13
Manatee	21,546	6.7	52,395	901	6,846	926	472	1,499	6,091	5,402	9,742	739	472
Marion	15,520	9.4	41,553	2,263	5,048	783	356	637	3,393	5,842	6,825	597	356
Martin	14,456	2.6	89,185	42	3,609	497	250	623	6,852	2,303	4,979	369	250
Miami-Dade	154,892	5.2	57,213	560	74,381	9,975	5,011	14,547	38,053	32,876	103,914	6,720	5,011
Monroe	7,876	2.1	106,583	17	2,123	318	157	422	4,323	957	3,021	198	157
Nassau	5,899	6.2	64,746	273	1,174	179	82	260	1,533	1,190	1,696	139	82
Okaloosa	11,626	7.1	54,630	729	6,371	1,284	501	781	2,898	2,678	8,938	523	501
Okeechobee	1,480	9.0	34,998	2,937	515	86	37	123	222	525	762	55	37
Orange	69,363	6.6	49,390	1,213	49,540	6,170	3,357	4,745	11,444	14,857	63,812	3,934	3,357
Osceola	15,108	11.4	39,210	2,541	4,335	631	312	807	1,898	4,480	6,084	450	312
Palm Beach	131,881	3.3	87,478	48	40,742	4,924	2,668	8,276	59,694	19,212	56,609	3,839	2,668
Pasco	25,931	10.1	45,461	1,728	6,023	905	424	1,015	3,831	7,579	8,367	722	424
Pinellas	57,805	5.8	59,178	472	26,334	3,582	1,779	2,429	13,668	14,254	34,124	2,379	1,779
Polk	29,604	9.8	39,760	2,480	12,370	1,800	863	1,372	5,622	9,377	16,405	1,214	863

1. Based on the resident population estimated as of July 1 of the year shown.

Table B. States and Counties — **Earnings, Social Security, and Housing**

STATE County	Earnings, 2020 (cont.) — Percent by selected industries: Farm	Mining, quarrying, and extractions	Construction	Manu-facturing	Information; professional, scientific, technical services	Retail trade	Finance, insurance, real estate, and leasing	Health care and social assistance	Govern-ment	Social Security beneficiaries, December 2020: Number	Rate[1]	Supple-mental Security Income recipients, 2020	Housing units, 2021: Total	Percent change, 2010–2021
	75	76	77	78	79	80	81	82	83	84	85	86	87	88
CONNECTICUT—Cont'd														
Tolland	0.6	0.0	8.5	7.5	6.4	6.7	3.9	10.2	38.8	28,350	189	1,246	61,265	0.5
Windham	0.4	0.2	6.4	18.8	4.4	8.3	3.4	16.0	18.3	25,370	218	2,195	49,742	0.3
DELAWARE	0.8	0.2	6.8	5.6	11.8	5.8	20.2	14.1	16.7	224,617	224	17,143	457,954	1.7
Kent	1.9	D	6.2	D	4.6	7.3	4.5	12.4	38.2	40,520	220	3,570	75,086	2.8
New Castle	0.1	D	5.7	D	14.6	4.8	25.7	13.9	13.4	106,360	186	10,296	235,323	0.6
Sussex	2.7	0.1	12.1	10.5	6.0	8.6	9.9	16.1	12.2	77,740	314	3,277	147,545	3.1
DISTRICT OF COLUMBIA	0.0	0.0	1.6	D	28.2	1.0	4.1	5.8	38.7	83,647	125	24,920	357,489	1.7
District of Columbia	0.0	0.0	1.6	D	28.2	1.0	4.1	5.8	38.7	83,647	125	24,920	357,489	1.7
FLORIDA	0.5	0.1	7.3	4.8	13.1	7.3	10.4	12.6	14.0	4,840,275	222	575,272	10,054,457	1.6
Alachua	0.6	0.0	3.6	3.5	8.9	5.4	5.7	18.3	36.3	48,000	172	6,695	125,524	1.3
Baker	1.1	0.0	6.2	D	D	10.2	2.7	9.2	38.1	5,595	195	646	10,002	1.6
Bay	0.1	D	9.6	5.0	8.3	9.6	7.7	D	23.7	40,385	225	4,025	106,152	2.7
Bradford	0.9	D	7.6	3.8	3.2	11.5	3.3	8.2	32.0	6,365	223	869	10,812	0.7
Brevard	0.1	0.0	7.1	19.4	12.1	6.8	5.1	12.3	14.5	169,725	275	12,015	294,224	1.5
Broward	0.0	0.0	7.1	3.4	14.7	8.0	10.5	10.2	13.3	337,650	175	45,595	864,436	0.4
Calhoun	4.6	0.0	9.7	D	2.5	5.9	2.2	D	31.6	3,290	241	526	5,648	0.3
Charlotte	0.8	0.2	10.1	1.6	8.6	12.4	7.0	21.7	13.8	75,025	385	2,948	113,474	2.6
Citrus	0.1	0.3	12.1	1.7	5.8	12.0	5.9	22.1	12.9	64,195	406	3,676	82,832	1.1
Clay	0.0	0.2	9.5	2.9	12.8	10.1	5.9	18.7	14.5	47,290	213	3,299	86,753	1.6
Collier	0.9	0.0	11.7	3.7	12.3	8.6	11.9	14.0	8.5	104,050	270	4,079	233,658	1.9
Columbia	0.8	0.0	4.3	10.2	4.2	10.1	4.4	12.7	25.9	18,155	258	2,752	30,032	0.7
DeSoto	10.5	D	6.7	5.2	D	6.3	2.4	10.1	18.2	7,890	229	1,045	15,692	0.7
Dixie	3.0	0.0	5.5	19.1	D	6.9	D	D	35.8	4,840	283	792	9,347	0.6
Duval	0.0	0.0	6.6	5.0	12.2	5.8	15.2	13.3	13.5	177,890	178	27,052	444,956	1.9
Escambia	0.1	0.1	5.9	4.8	7.7	6.6	11.3	15.5	26.6	75,870	235	9,994	147,734	1.4
Flagler	0.7	D	8.5	2.7	10.4	9.5	6.3	12.6	15.5	41,110	340	1,847	57,815	3.3
Franklin	0.0	0.1	8.1	3.3	6.0	11.5	7.2	D	27.6	3,320	264	319	8,452	1.0
Gadsden	15.0	1.4	10.0	7.8	2.4	4.5	1.4	3.4	28.3	11,575	265	2,534	19,013	0.4
Gilchrist	15.9	0.0	7.1	14.6	2.2	2.8	2.0	D	22.1	4,555	248	516	7,607	1.3
Glades	14.6	D	7.5	8.7	D	2.1	1.7	D	18.6	2,810	230	199	6,557	0.8
Gulf	0.0	D	10.7	3.9	9.6	8.4	6.9	D	23.8	4,130	288	349	9,074	2.7
Hamilton	5.2	0.0	D	D	D	5.1	1.0	D	27.7	3,320	237	665	5,625	0.4
Hardee	14.6	D	5.0	3.6	D	6.2	4.6	D	22.1	4,895	193	746	9,880	0.5
Hendry	24.7	D	5.9	2.6	D	6.3	2.4	4.1	16.6	6,785	168	1,393	15,431	2.7
Hernando	0.3	0.1	6.9	5.5	D	11.3	4.8	21.3	15.2	64,925	324	4,700	90,535	1.2
Highlands	5.5	D	6.0	2.5	4.5	11.2	4.3	23.5	16.1	36,165	350	3,076	57,930	0.7
Hillsborough	0.4	0.0	6.3	3.7	17.7	6.1	14.9	11.1	12.2	253,715	172	41,106	617,907	1.9
Holmes	4.1	D	12.8	2.6	D	6.2	3.0	D	38.5	5,560	281	829	8,640	0.2
Indian River	1.2	D	7.6	5.8	11.9	8.8	10.1	16.7	9.5	57,015	348	2,689	84,973	1.3
Jackson	4.3	0.8	7.4	6.7	D	7.8	3.0	8.5	34.9	12,585	264	1,869	20,043	0.7
Jefferson	8.2	0.1	D	D	D	6.9	5.7	D	19.6	3,980	273	560	6,779	1.1
Lafayette	24.3	D	2.6	3.3	D	5.3	D	D	35.4	1,630	194	165	3,327	1.2
Lake	1.6	0.2	12.3	4.1	6.0	11.8	5.8	20.4	12.6	112,860	285	7,485	182,327	2.2
Lee	0.4	0.1	12.2	2.4	11.5	9.2	8.3	11.8	16.9	208,320	264	12,961	428,910	2.5
Leon	0.0	D	4.4	1.3	16.1	5.7	6.4	14.0	34.9	49,220	168	6,559	135,687	1.3
Levy	13.9	0.7	13.3	7.9	4.2	8.8	3.7	4.9	18.2	13,610	308	1,511	21,177	1.2
Liberty	3.8	0.0	9.3	16.0	D	D	D	D	35.6	1,565	198	289	3,208	0.2
Madison	8.9	D	2.4	10.9	D	7.4	3.7	D	24.9	4,890	267	881	8,375	0.6
Manatee	1.8	D	10.0	6.9	9.8	9.2	9.3	13.1	10.6	109,025	264	6,147	212,675	2.4
Marion	0.6	0.1	8.5	9.4	6.0	10.6	5.4	17.7	14.6	125,085	324	10,638	181,756	2.1
Martin	0.9	D	9.7	5.3	10.3	8.4	8.8	18.8	8.9	48,110	301	1,610	82,018	0.6
Miami-Dade	0.4	0.1	6.6	2.8	14.8	6.5	12.0	11.5	13.2	438,835	165	156,825	1,084,353	0.7
Monroe	0.0	D	8.2	0.7	8.9	8.8	7.7	6.6	22.7	17,740	216	1,247	54,423	0.6
Nassau	0.2	0.0	5.8	9.0	8.0	8.0	4.9	9.5	17.9	24,330	258	1,241	43,392	3.4
Okaloosa	0.1	0.0	4.6	3.5	15.5	7.1	6.0	6.8	40.9	45,095	211	3,425	102,271	0.9
Okeechobee	11.0	D	6.6	3.3	6.4	8.8	3.0	D	20.4	9,415	234	1,174	18,532	0.2
Orange	0.2	0.0	6.6	5.5	15.5	6.1	8.8	10.2	10.4	205,615	145	34,045	575,826	2.0
Osceola	0.7	0.0	8.1	2.0	5.8	10.6	5.0	16.2	15.7	69,465	172	11,202	162,335	3.7
Palm Beach	0.6	0.1	6.0	3.4	14.5	6.5	12.8	12.2	10.2	334,175	223	23,541	713,787	0.9
Pasco	0.3	0.1	9.4	3.4	8.4	13.2	4.7	19.9	13.9	146,645	251	13,197	263,165	2.0
Pinellas	0.0	0.0	6.0	9.2	13.0	7.1	10.8	14.7	10.9	257,290	269	21,148	517,744	0.1
Polk	0.8	0.5	6.9	9.1	5.3	7.9	8.4	13.3	11.9	174,055	231	23,328	327,799	2.9

1. Per 1,000 resident population estimated as of July 1 of the year shown.

STATE County	Housing units, 2016–2020								Civilian labor force, 2021				Civilian employment6, 2016–2020		
		Occupied units									Unemployment			Percent	
		Owner-occupied				Renter-occupied									
				Median owner cost as a percent of income											
	Total	Percent	Median value[1]	With a mort-gage	Without a mort-gage[2]	Median rent[3]	Median rent as a percent of income[2]	Sub-standard units[4] (percent)	Total	Percent change, 2020–2021	Total	Rate[5]	Total	Management, business, science, and arts	Construction, production, and maintenance occupations
	89	90	91	92	93	94	95	96	97	98	99	100	101	102	103
CONNECTICUT—Cont'd															
Tolland	56,077	71.7	259,700	19.9	12.5	1,194	30.2	1.3	83,876	-2.4	4,279	5.1	78,029	47.9	16.8
Windham	45,589	68.1	210,300	22.2	12.2	977	30.3	1.3	61,835	-2.0	3,860	6.2	58,144	34.6	25.3
DELAWARE	370,953	71.4	258,300	20.9	10.0	1,150	29.7	1.8	496,430	2.2	26,555	5.3	456,872	40.8	20.4
Kent	67,299	68.8	226,600	22.7	10.0	1,110	32.0	1.9	81,389	2.0	5,069	6.2	79,624	34.0	24.8
New Castle	209,431	67.9	266,500	20.0	10.0	1,182	28.5	1.6	303,427	1.6	16,129	5.3	276,370	44.8	18.1
Sussex	94,223	81.1	269,700	21.5	10.3	1,049	32.7	2.3	111,615	4.1	5,358	4.8	100,878	35.2	23.2
DISTRICT OF COLUMBIA	288,307	42.5	618,100	20.8	10.0	1,607	28.2	3.9	381,673	-2.0	25,095	6.6	382,108	65.5	6.4
District of Columbia	288,307	42.5	618,100	20.8	10.0	1,607	28.2	3.9	381,673	-2.0	25,095	6.6	382,108	65.5	6.4
FLORIDA	7,931,313	66.2	232,000	23.0	11.9	1,218	33.3	3.2	10,312,768	2.2	469,711	4.6	9,684,712	36.4	19.7
Alachua	101,979	54.6	201,600	19.9	10.6	1,004	36.6	2.2	138,458	3.0	5,142	3.7	127,147	47.8	12.1
Baker	8,828	76.5	158,000	18.5	10.0	784	21.5	2.3	12,089	3.7	449	3.7	11,036	33.6	26.8
Bay	73,536	67.3	195,000	22.8	10.5	1,099	31.3	2.8	85,937	3.9	3,333	3.9	82,380	34.0	22.2
Bradford	9,318	66.0	118,900	22.3	10.0	815	29.5	2.6	10,791	0.7	448	4.2	9,966	26.9	23.9
Brevard	236,005	75.6	220,000	22.3	10.5	1,111	30.7	1.7	289,653	2.9	11,702	4.0	260,668	40.5	19.1
Broward	704,942	62.8	282,400	25.7	14.8	1,433	36.2	4.4	1,029,454	0.8	50,390	4.9	974,826	37.0	18.1
Calhoun	4,510	78.2	91,100	25.6	10.0	539	29.1	1.9	4,866	2.6	218	4.5	4,687	23.1	28.1
Charlotte	79,789	81.6	209,500	23.7	12.7	1,042	35.0	1.6	73,248	2.6	3,188	4.4	64,605	30.6	20.4
Citrus	64,621	83.5	144,100	21.4	10.0	847	32.5	1.1	47,343	1.6	2,687	5.7	47,389	31.2	23.6
Clay	75,360	77.0	195,900	19.7	10.0	1,158	29.4	1.8	107,819	3.1	3,804	3.5	100,004	36.7	21.7
Collier	147,977	74.4	366,600	24.4	12.6	1,374	33.9	4.0	180,891	2.6	6,617	3.7	159,715	32.8	21.2
Columbia	25,205	72.6	128,800	20.7	10.0	821	27.8	3.4	29,220	-0.7	1,324	4.5	26,763	32.0	26.7
DeSoto	12,421	68.9	103,600	23.2	10.4	738	32.1	4.8	14,631	2.0	561	3.8	13,363	18.8	41.6
Dixie	6,233	82.6	85,000	18.3	10.0	628	28.1	8.2	5,910	1.1	257	4.3	5,337	21.9	30.7
Duval	369,704	57.1	195,600	21.5	10.1	1,096	30.1	2.3	492,463	2.5	21,957	4.5	458,848	37.4	20.2
Escambia	122,169	62.8	157,200	20.9	10.2	1,020	29.5	1.9	146,033	1.7	6,613	4.5	136,462	34.6	19.5
Flagler	44,040	76.5	232,700	22.9	12.2	1,327	33.1	0.9	48,309	2.6	2,242	4.6	45,349	34.9	20.6
Franklin	4,691	75.8	193,800	24.5	11.1	806	32.0	3.0	4,719	1.5	179	3.8	4,210	28.4	26.2
Gadsden	17,307	73.1	98,100	22.8	10.0	691	30.8	3.2	19,283	5.9	1,033	5.4	17,332	31.4	25.8
Gilchrist	6,701	82.5	125,900	18.7	10.0	676	24.2	3.1	7,226	2.7	270	3.7	7,272	21.6	35.1
Glades	4,859	80.1	72,100	19.9	10.0	713	27.5	9.8	5,073	0.1	211	4.2	3,798	25.1	38.3
Gulf	5,897	75.6	170,700	19.3	10.6	1,074	32.1	2.8	5,270	3.9	190	3.6	5,638	34.1	25.5
Hamilton	4,385	72.2	85,900	20.8	10.0	676	29.3	5.0	4,137	-1.7	250	6.0	3,969	22.8	24.2
Hardee	7,991	67.0	94,100	19.2	11.1	759	30.2	9.4	8,895	5.1	424	4.8	9,711	23.9	37.4
Hendry	12,878	70.3	105,900	24.9	10.0	833	31.6	8.3	15,734	2.9	952	6.1	18,765	21.4	42.7
Hernando	76,708	79.3	158,400	21.4	10.4	996	33.0	1.7	73,476	2.1	3,742	5.1	72,547	32.5	22.1
Highlands	42,721	77.0	120,500	20.2	10.7	801	29.9	2.3	34,977	1.0	2,058	5.9	34,339	29.8	25.8
Hillsborough	539,919	59.3	233,200	21.5	10.3	1,186	31.4	3.2	769,097	2.0	32,698	4.3	714,057	40.0	18.5
Holmes	7,137	76.0	86,400	22.2	10.3	705	28.5	2.6	6,935	1.8	283	4.1	7,070	26.6	28.8
Indian River	60,959	80.0	220,700	22.6	11.6	994	33.1	1.4	65,119	1.5	3,076	4.7	60,128	35.3	20.1
Jackson	17,533	71.6	101,300	20.0	10.0	691	32.1	2.7	17,202	0.5	789	4.6	16,462	31.6	23.8
Jefferson	5,643	75.0	137,300	23.7	10.0	770	28.5	1.3	5,580	3.1	235	4.2	5,458	35.3	17.0
Lafayette	2,315	77.8	100,600	18.2	10.0	638	18.1	6.9	2,787	0.7	111	4.0	2,756	25.9	26.4
Lake	137,446	75.1	202,500	22.2	11.1	1,111	32.5	2.0	159,493	1.7	7,458	4.7	148,392	33.8	18.9
Lee	288,916	72.7	235,300	23.4	12.3	1,225	31.9	2.7	357,018	3.4	14,901	4.2	323,278	32.1	22.2
Leon	116,530	52.6	212,900	20.7	10.0	1,024	34.2	2.5	154,331	2.4	6,470	4.2	148,372	46.7	12.4
Levy	16,971	79.4	119,000	25.3	11.5	704	31.1	2.7	16,849	2.2	754	4.5	15,607	24.7	29.8
Liberty	2,513	78.7	83,700	23.5	10.6	720	23.9	1.8	2,582	-0.4	108	4.2	2,548	31.4	36.8
Madison	6,891	72.5	89,100	23.0	11.5	726	32.3	3.2	7,720	2.3	381	4.9	6,206	26.4	29.1
Manatee	150,345	73.8	250,700	23.2	11.6	1,185	32.6	2.7	182,554	3.9	7,175	3.9	165,297	35.2	20.5
Marion	145,863	74.8	151,700	21.8	11.1	929	29.7	2.6	141,992	2.2	6,983	4.9	132,240	30.6	22.5
Martin	64,870	79.4	293,000	23.8	11.6	1,152	32.7	1.4	73,492	3.0	2,614	3.6	67,052	38.1	17.2
Miami-Dade	902,200	51.6	310,700	27.1	14.1	1,373	37.6	6.6	1,307,815	2.8	68,341	5.2	1,326,437	33.8	21.5
Monroe	32,794	59.1	558,100	29.9	12.0	1,714	34.1	5.2	45,926	3.3	1,368	3.0	39,263	32.0	21.6
Nassau	33,475	82.0	243,700	20.7	10.0	1,049	28.6	1.6	42,729	2.8	1,461	3.4	38,101	35.7	25.1
Okaloosa	79,235	66.0	234,600	21.8	10.0	1,156	30.7	2.0	99,417	4.4	3,315	3.3	91,880	39.0	18.4
Okeechobee	14,601	74.8	116,500	19.5	10.6	833	31.9	4.3	17,488	2.3	720	4.1	15,648	27.1	32.2
Orange	468,075	56.0	257,800	22.5	10.7	1,284	32.9	3.8	741,002	-0.1	38,318	5.2	697,785	37.9	18.4
Osceola	109,642	64.4	221,600	25.0	11.6	1,261	34.9	3.5	185,839	-2.3	11,669	6.3	173,579	28.4	23.5
Palm Beach	565,598	69.2	301,000	24.5	14.2	1,452	35.6	3.3	734,055	2.6	31,669	4.3	686,067	37.7	17.4
Pasco	209,483	73.2	173,900	22.1	11.3	1,093	31.1	1.8	246,350	2.3	10,866	4.4	224,973	38.1	18.9
Pinellas	413,239	68.1	219,800	22.4	13.4	1,165	32.2	2.2	486,173	2.0	19,465	4.0	458,965	40.7	16.2
Polk	240,879	69.5	162,400	22.0	11.3	1,014	30.2	3.5	328,590	2.8	17,585	5.4	296,493	29.9	25.6

1. Specified owner-occupied units. 2. A value of 10.0 represents 10 percent or less; a value of 50.0 represents 50 percent or more. 3. Specified renter-occupied units. 4. Overcrowded or lacking complete plumbing facilities. 5. Percent of civilian labor force. 6. Civilian employed persons 16 years old and over.

STATE County	Private nonfarm establishments, employment and payroll, 2020: Number of establishments	Employment: Total	Employment: Health care and social assistance	Employment: Manufacturing	Employment: Retail trade	Employment: Finance and insurance	Employment: Professional, scientific, and technical services	Annual payroll: Total (mil dol)	Annual payroll: Average per employee (dollars)	Agriculture, 2017: Farms: Number	Farms: Percent with: Fewer than 50 acres	Farms: Percent with: 1000 acres or more	Farm producers whose primary occupation is farming (percent)
	104	105	106	107	108	109	110	111	112	113	114	115	116
CONNECTICUT—Cont'd													
Tolland	2,365	28,403	5,827	4,397	4,563	523	1,192	1,318	46,394	520	70.6	0.8	34.4
Windham	2,087	30,254	6,975	5,883	4,945	725	578	1,307	43,208	646	63.3	0.6	38.4
DELAWARE	27,472	422,044	75,037	29,718	55,071	41,109	32,771	25,115	59,508	2,302	55.7	6.9	52.8
Kent	4,163	56,012	12,301	4,483	9,628	1,503	2,948	2,496	44,557	822	53.4	6.3	48.5
New Castle	16,874	282,911	49,878	13,879	32,009	36,457	25,994	19,114	67,562	361	66.5	5.8	43.5
Sussex	6,074	74,840	12,663	11,355	13,429	2,070	2,607	3,079	41,141	1,119	54.0	7.6	58.9
DISTRICT OF COLUMBIA	24,083	543,174	73,547	1,048	23,148	20,494	107,658	45,850	84,411	NA	NA	NA	NA
District of Columbia	24,083	543,174	73,547	1,048	23,148	20,494	107,658	45,850	84,411	NA	NA	NA	NA
FLORIDA	591,046	9,084,079	1,200,831	325,068	1,118,138	397,483	565,050	440,383	48,479	47,590	71.0	3.2	41.3
Alachua	6,377	102,496	30,395	3,827	14,240	3,942	6,035	4,594	44,818	1,611	72.1	2.5	34.5
Baker	406	5,876	1,857	201	889	132	111	201	34,187	328	69.2	1.2	35.0
Bay	4,813	60,002	10,383	3,458	11,754	1,590	3,714	2,404	40,059	190	69.5	4.2	23.2
Bradford	427	4,369	746	267	1,070	105	93	149	34,125	490	73.9	3.1	37.2
Brevard	14,646	191,581	31,839	15,688	28,940	5,178	21,218	9,155	47,787	522	81.0	3.1	43.5
Broward	64,660	736,561	105,097	23,900	108,416	34,094	59,404	37,388	50,760	640	97.2	0.2	41.5
Calhoun	186	1,569	550	20	265	61	20	51	32,264	289	56.4	3.8	29.7
Charlotte	4,125	39,684	8,793	412	9,876	1,053	1,528	1,496	37,709	306	66.3	6.2	37.2
Citrus	2,813	30,516	10,551	345	5,684	679	808	1,147	37,585	609	75.2	2.1	43.4
Clay	4,091	45,134	9,894	1,194	8,459	1,271	2,242	1,716	38,015	361	83.4	0.6	41.1
Collier	12,935	140,574	21,640	4,233	24,335	4,189	5,468	6,423	45,693	322	77.3	7.1	36.2
Columbia	1,418	19,443	4,492	845	3,158	477	622	786	40,420	979	66.4	1.7	40.6
DeSoto	492	5,817	1,060	476	1,050	124	140	217	37,290	761	57.4	7.4	44.5
Dixie	198	1,487	112	422	254	23	39	49	32,623	235	60.9	5.5	51.6
Duval	26,700	477,733	67,545	22,843	53,291	45,960	33,439	24,545	51,378	366	81.7	2.7	42.4
Escambia	7,067	115,357	22,456	4,442	16,179	10,835	7,907	5,120	44,380	649	72.7	2.2	36.1
Flagler	2,341	19,482	3,230	494	3,947	599	1,145	662	33,964	116	56.9	15.5	43.0
Franklin	302	2,339	268	65	503	42	73	72	30,994	15	66.7	6.7	20.0
Gadsden	672	8,370	1,528	931	1,191	107	179	371	44,300	522	54.0	1.3	33.6
Gilchrist	260	2,110	606	210	185	44	43	78	36,786	565	67.3	2.1	45.7
Glades	124	1,009	48	162	122	13	5	37	36,826	354	53.7	7.1	48.1
Gulf	336	1,901	210	54	382	97	108	66	34,507	46	30.4	4.3	26.4
Hamilton	162	1,742	225	524	422	19	49	92	53,081	338	43.5	3.0	43.2
Hardee	410	4,755	1,065	394	679	258	80	173	36,356	1,038	56.9	5.5	41.4
Hendry	651	6,966	1,289	741	1,465	236	370	264	37,859	436	50.9	10.8	47.3
Hernando	3,501	37,766	9,526	2,386	7,809	867	1,468	1,351	35,772	747	80.6	0.9	42.9
Highlands	1,994	20,582	5,879	839	4,687	511	679	713	34,644	989	66.4	6.1	45.7
Hillsborough	39,670	643,710	95,465	24,594	75,119	56,031	63,692	34,677	53,870	2,265	83.6	1.0	40.7
Holmes	272	1,827	535	91	388	35	55	57	31,077	721	41.5	1.7	34.5
Indian River	4,449	48,131	9,539	2,206	8,985	1,563	2,643	1,972	40,970	450	76.2	5.1	42.6
Jackson	802	9,622	1,708	760	1,975	262	277	351	36,520	1,154	45.6	4.3	41.5
Jefferson	262	1,560	178	49	319	83	69	53	33,698	592	62.8	4.1	36.3
Lafayette	93	603	138	41	90	19	22	18	30,491	257	43.2	4.7	50.0
Lake	7,892	89,493	19,404	3,544	17,657	2,228	2,369	3,329	37,195	1,703	75.1	2.7	37.6
Lee	20,054	235,798	38,416	5,385	41,511	6,061	13,990	10,277	43,584	800	81.6	2.4	38.5
Leon	7,821	103,435	19,369	1,653	16,388	4,821	10,013	4,671	45,162	325	67.4	3.7	32.5
Levy	780	6,238	510	765	1,469	212	235	211	33,846	1,058	66.4	3.9	49.4
Liberty	87	1,009	267	280	161	NA	19	37	36,669	111	54.1	0.9	28.1
Madison	303	3,006	926	501	526	77	61	104	34,606	669	38.6	4.6	43.5
Manatee	9,760	112,148	16,521	8,485	20,930	3,380	5,862	4,522	40,324	753	66.3	7.0	45.7
Marion	7,471	90,111	16,556	8,881	17,910	1,993	3,285	3,443	38,204	3,985	81.2	1.2	43.8
Martin	5,808	63,057	14,029	2,467	10,411	1,858	3,030	2,645	41,954	594	79.0	5.9	40.5
Miami-Dade	90,482	1,009,024	148,685	36,305	143,447	48,434	77,725	51,382	50,922	2,752	93.2	0.3	47.1
Monroe	3,885	32,757	2,283	303	6,193	658	1,041	1,183	36,113	40	100.0	NA	26.8
Nassau	1,970	19,928	2,929	1,419	3,556	471	687	789	39,576	373	70.2	2.7	37.8
Okaloosa	5,605	63,069	9,088	2,370	12,419	1,849	7,012	2,713	43,011	481	64.4	1.0	33.4
Okeechobee	839	7,282	1,520	204	1,730	201	207	261	35,784	599	48.1	13.9	43.8
Orange	41,172	791,098	85,427	28,690	90,173	24,548	61,398	37,713	47,671	622	83.8	1.9	51.8
Osceola	7,139	90,050	14,151	1,811	16,581	1,443	2,226	2,848	31,630	392	65.1	10.2	37.7
Palm Beach	51,563	554,858	92,489	14,826	80,605	22,005	44,906	28,581	51,510	1,298	89.1	3.0	48.3
Pasco	10,500	108,103	23,533	3,474	24,793	2,520	5,148	4,237	39,193	1,165	71.7	4.0	36.5
Pinellas	29,940	406,468	77,582	30,205	54,127	30,347	30,751	20,241	49,797	148	97.3	0.7	31.2
Polk	12,491	203,461	30,981	17,148	31,020	10,930	7,115	8,889	43,687	2,080	63.2	4.8	37.6

Agriculture, 2017 (cont.)

STATE County	Land in farms: Acreage (1,000)	Land in farms: Percent change, 2012–2017	Land in farms: Acres: Average size of farm	Land in farms: Acres: Total irrigated (1,000)	Land in farms: Acres: Total cropland (1,000)	Value of land and buildings (dollars): Average per farm	Value of land and buildings (dollars): Average per acre	Value of machinery and equipment, average per farm (dollars)	Value of products sold: Total (mil dol)	Value of products sold: Average per farm (acres)	Value of products sold: Percent from: Crops	Value of products sold: Percent from: Livestock and poultry products	Organic farms (number)	Farms with internet access (percent)	Government payments: Total ($1,000)	Government payments: Percent of farms
	117	118	119	120	121	122	123	124	125	126	127	128	129	130	131	132
CONNECTICUT—Cont'd																
Tolland	36	-25.4	69	0.2	16.2	665,187	9,703	62,379	53.4	102,725	62.3	37.7	3	79.2	215	3.5
Windham	52	-10.8	80	0.4	22.4	760,709	9,452	57,273	45.1	69,800	36.9	63.1	6	78.2	132	4.6
DELAWARE	525	3.3	228	163.3	452.2	1,920,109	8,414	198,096	1,466.0	636,826	22.2	77.8	13	78.7	15,162	35.4
Kent	182	5.9	222	57.8	155.7	1,758,029	7,923	179,332	391.3	476,038	27.9	72.1	4	76.6	4,531	34.3
New Castle	67	5.1	187	5.1	53.7	1,775,015	9,499	140,504	62.1	171,986	55.1	44.9	2	80.9	1,342	26.6
Sussex	275	1.2	246	100.3	242.8	2,085,980	8,473	230,459	1,012.6	904,900	18.0	82.0	7	79.4	9,289	39.1
DISTRICT OF COLUMBIA	NA	NA	NA	NA	NA	NA	NA	NA	NA	NA	NA	NA	NA	NA	NA	NA
District of Columbia	NA	NA	NA	NA	NA	NA	NA	NA	NA	NA	NA	NA	NA	NA	NA	NA
FLORIDA	9,732	1.9	204	1,519.4	2,825.8	1,206,788	5,901	72,754	7,357.3	154,599	77.5	22.5	251	76.3	59,120	8.4
Alachua	178	-5.2	111	10.4	55.9	866,214	7,832	55,524	99.9	62,019	75.3	24.7	23	79.1	661	5.6
Baker	33	1.1	102	0.2	3.6	465,756	4,588	38,815	13.2	40,256	16.1	83.9	NA	78.4	72	2.4
Bay	74	601.5	387	1.7	4.6	794,316	2,051	41,297	2.9	15,274	69.6	30.4	NA	73.2	23	3.2
Bradford	59	67.8	120	0.6	12.9	573,623	4,777	61,641	13.1	26,708	27.3	72.7	NA	75.3	85	1.6
Brevard	157	6.9	300	10.5	21.0	1,507,863	5,027	62,406	59.0	112,977	76.9	23.1	1	78.7	186	3.6
Broward	7	-53.5	11	0.7	1.6	348,907	33,140	31,890	24.9	38,883	94.2	5.8	NA	85.5	18	0.6
Calhoun	118	175.5	409	3.3	25.4	880,123	2,154	63,913	22.0	76,163	85.5	14.5	NA	75.4	876	10.7
Charlotte	113	-48.1	368	11.6	18.5	2,644,176	7,176	66,707	43.9	143,402	91.8	8.2	2	73.9	329	5.2
Citrus	56	37.5	92	0.9	9.6	726,032	7,929	49,552	13.5	22,118	67.3	32.7	NA	81.0	197	2.6
Clay	D	D	D	0.3	4.7	366,072	5,726	42,781	5.5	15,111	55.7	44.3	NA	72.9	23	2.2
Collier	148	20.1	461	37.3	82.7	2,189,706	4,749	121,437	189.7	588,994	96.8	3.2	2	83.5	141	5.3
Columbia	107	5.5	109	4.2	33.6	476,995	4,361	52,758	40.2	41,040	41.2	58.8	1	75.5	1,189	10.7
DeSoto	335	10.5	440	57.7	73.5	2,203,290	5,008	100,533	168.3	221,145	72.1	27.9	3	73.2	1,066	13.4
Dixie	56	24.8	240	3.3	16.3	892,927	3,722	65,150	10.8	46,034	84.6	15.4	NA	67.2	273	3.8
Duval	30	6.1	82	2.3	5.9	616,395	7,523	47,364	9.0	24,656	71.5	28.5	4	70.5	135	4.4
Escambia	59	-21.1	91	2.0	33.1	562,575	6,206	75,174	26.9	41,507	91.2	8.8	4	76.9	1,957	11.7
Flagler	79	81.8	683	3.4	5.8	3,801,926	5,565	81,473	14.3	123,388	90.2	9.8	3	73.3	55	8.6
Franklin	D	D	D	NA	0.1	D	D	126,657	D	D	D	D	NA	80.0	56	26.7
Gadsden	66	30.4	127	4.1	19.4	540,049	4,256	62,186	90.5	173,354	81.4	18.6	1	73.6	238	8.6
Gilchrist	82	-2.0	146	10.9	42.0	774,215	5,321	88,720	89.7	158,837	33.9	66.1	NA	73.5	462	8.7
Glades	429	-3.2	1,211	65.8	43.9	5,217,205	4,308	142,023	78.2	220,924	62.7	37.3	NA	66.1	869	12.7
Gulf	D	D	D	0.0	1.6	6,070,106	1,435	47,216	D	D	D	D	NA	56.5	17	8.7
Hamilton	88	22.9	261	8.9	33.6	1,009,713	3,865	157,590	42.4	125,364	69.9	30.1	3	76.6	1,825	18.6
Hardee	377	37.6	363	46.8	68.3	1,937,932	5,337	95,859	204.7	197,171	60.0	40.0	1	70.8	1,611	16.6
Hendry	433	-12.6	993	183.3	203.5	4,867,433	4,900	262,368	329.5	755,716	91.6	8.4	4	78.4	1,163	11.7
Hernando	50	-18.8	67	2.0	8.2	706,024	10,488	41,410	20.4	27,309	73.8	26.2	2	77.9	313	5.1
Highlands	376	-23.3	380	73.3	87.6	1,484,269	3,906	92,897	196.7	198,865	72.5	27.5	2	71.1	2,471	11.0
Hillsborough	180	-16.1	80	25.8	76.3	929,585	11,678	64,339	447.6	197,627	91.6	8.4	25	75.8	584	3.0
Holmes	101	-4.1	140	1.1	36.3	468,245	3,334	53,453	28.2	39,122	34.7	65.3	2	73.0	1,500	32.6
Indian River	183	12.4	406	52.9	55.5	2,330,717	5,745	90,645	106.5	236,611	89.3	10.7	9	68.2	426	7.1
Jackson	275	4.8	238	18.4	152.3	880,430	3,694	101,848	93.3	80,821	87.0	13.0	8	76.4	9,120	28.8
Jefferson	168	29.7	284	2.8	35.6	983,884	3,468	56,238	36.1	60,990	24.2	75.8	4	77.7	1,147	10.8
Lafayette	94	2.6	364	17.0	32.4	1,102,316	3,024	186,306	85.9	334,218	24.6	75.4	NA	68.9	1,200	14.0
Lake	184	20.8	108	19.6	43.5	856,367	7,932	60,783	215.7	126,665	91.1	8.9	21	81.0	890	5.9
Lee	87	0.1	109	10.5	22.2	1,330,329	12,206	53,238	104.4	130,449	93.8	6.2	7	76.0	163	1.8
Leon	92	12.8	282	2.3	7.6	1,204,029	4,266	50,879	5.5	17,034	73.4	26.6	7	84.6	54	4.6
Levy	187	12.0	177	20.8	79.1	816,534	4,608	90,455	131.0	123,818	38.5	61.5	2	83.8	2,571	7.0
Liberty	35	145.3	313	0.0	1.4	1,227,282	3,916	64,185	2.5	22,126	6.8	93.2	NA	79.3	106	19.8
Madison	168	17.3	251	16.4	47.5	884,049	3,527	87,915	88.3	131,945	40.1	59.9	6	65.6	1,002	16.9
Manatee	193	3.4	256	56.5	71.2	1,991,183	7,784	116,597	360.1	478,246	89.3	10.7	3	76.2	151	3.6
Marion	331	2.9	83	13.2	79.3	922,892	11,114	47,624	145.5	36,501	41.1	58.9	5	82.3	813	1.4
Martin	154	10.4	259	28.8	49.6	1,137,728	4,396	88,036	112.6	189,505	91.4	8.6	3	81.5	487	4.2
Miami-Dade	79	-3.4	29	36.8	55.2	1,068,826	37,450	51,638	837.7	304,409	98.8	1.2	35	70.6	1,733	1.8
Monroe	0	-64.9	4	0.0	0.1	D	D	67,514	3.9	98,375	22.1	77.9	NA	90.0	NA	NA
Nassau	55	38.8	146	0.2	4.6	547,982	3,744	52,065	12.9	34,525	5.5	94.5	NA	73.2	236	12.6
Okaloosa	47	-24.2	97	0.4	13.7	461,280	4,763	38,830	8.3	17,318	70.3	29.7	NA	71.9	992	14.3
Okeechobee	297	-32.7	497	23.2	42.2	2,096,854	4,223	135,425	235.9	393,791	13.6	86.4	NA	70.1	2,671	24.4
Orange	109	-17.5	176	8.1	15.7	1,482,493	8,432	70,712	232.0	372,932	96.6	3.4	2	77.0	205	4.5
Osceola	525	-4.0	1,339	36.5	40.2	5,196,486	3,880	121,645	85.4	217,982	52.4	47.6	3	78.6	1,048	9.4
Palm Beach	488	-5.1	376	370.7	438.9	3,149,296	8,379	179,904	901.7	694,699	98.3	1.7	10	84.2	114	1.1
Pasco	192	11.9	164	3.6	25.9	1,177,181	7,161	56,608	65.0	55,766	23.1	76.9	NA	77.8	876	11.8
Pinellas	2	64.3	16	0.1	0.7	943,499	57,464	29,146	1.9	13,068	73.5	26.5	3	81.8	D	1.4
Polk	487	-6.5	234	88.6	131.0	1,420,064	6,064	69,094	297.7	143,136	81.0	19.0	5	71.5	2,242	11.5

STATE County	Water use, 2015		Wholesale Trade[1], 2017				Retail Trade[2], 2017				Real estate and rental and leasing,[2] 2017			
	Public supply water withdrawn (mil gal/ day)	Public supply gallons withdrawn per person per day	Number of establish- ments	Number of employees	Sales (mil dol)	Average payroll (mil dol)	Number of establish- ments	Number of employees	Sales (mil dol)	Average payroll (mil dol)	Number of establish- ments	Number of employees	Sales (mil dol)	Average payroll (mil dol)
	133	134	135	136	137	138	139	140	141	142	143	144	145	146
CONNECTICUT—Cont'd														
Tolland	4.9	32.6	57	561	217.4	28.2	358	4,747	1,468.1	137.8	94	487	74.4	18.3
Windham	7.7	66.1	61	1,330	409.6	57.5	335	5,108	1,436.0	141.0	48	128	28.3	4.4
DELAWARE	86.4	91.3	962	9,315	7,224.6	522.6	3,648	58,201	17,667.9	1,558.0	1,286	6,096	5,163.7	287.7
Kent	11.8	68.1	D	D	D	D	600	9,606	3,059.7	263.9	161	697	225.2	26.9
New Castle	60.6	108.9	D	D	D	D	1,967	35,232	10,672.4	947.7	819	4,088	4,623.7	210.5
Sussex	13.9	64.6	D	D	D	D	1,081	13,363	3,935.9	346.3	306	1,311	314.8	50.3
DISTRICT OF COLUMBIA	0.0	0.0	321	3,851	3,387.1	292.5	1,743	23,133	5,533.9	672.6	1,350	11,000	4,524.7	883.3
District of Columbia	0.0	0.0	321	3,851	3,387.1	292.5	1,743	23,133	5,533.9	672.6	1,350	11,000	4,524.7	883.3
FLORIDA	2,384.9	117.6	27,230	283,295	288,642.2	16,241.2	74,496	1,086,052	333,134.6	29,686.2	37,660	176,886	49,175.2	8,183.6
Alachua	23.4	89.9	187	1,947	1,652.3	112.9	914	14,317	3,726.7	339.1	365	2,033	348.9	74.3
Baker	0.9	32.8	D	D	D	2.4	78	862	283.5	21.8	6	2	0.7	0.1
Bay	47.6	262.2	155	1,728	746.4	81.2	826	11,802	3,219.3	305.2	313	1,138	272.3	37.7
Bradford	1.0	35.3	D	D	D	2.1	79	1,022	343.3	27.1	18	40	11.0	0.9
Brevard	31.5	55.4	454	3,798	2,494.8	207.9	2,026	29,154	7,884.4	747.1	860	2,623	512.5	92.3
Broward	233.7	123.2	3,886	38,460	43,614.1	2,218.3	7,220	107,986	35,031.3	3,159.0	4,042	19,924	6,193.7	936.6
Calhoun	0.6	40.1	D	D	D	0.7	35	281	72.1	6.6	4	7	1.5	0.2
Charlotte	7.5	43.4	102	1,037	578.8	53.3	599	9,574	2,757.2	254.8	304	963	208.8	29.7
Citrus	14.2	100.3	74	527	272.7	24.8	431	5,633	1,864.0	157.5	163	1,014	94.7	21.7
Clay	13.5	66.2	D	D	D	32.3	569	8,396	2,097.1	209.5	230	894	177.6	29.4
Collier	51.8	145.0	309	3,273	3,862.1	269.5	1,499	22,521	7,302.9	693.1	1,189	3,758	863.4	184.6
Columbia	3.3	47.8	D	D	D	D	260	2,694	823.8	71.7	56	158	29.1	5.0
DeSoto	33.2	936.3	14	72	21.9	2.5	83	1,112	282.6	27.8	20	68	8.5	1.3
Dixie	0.6	38.3	D	D	D	D	37	247	73.7	5.3	NA	NA	NA	NA
Duval	109.0	119.4	1,154	22,455	20,621.7	1,393.3	3,381	53,267	17,312.7	1,472.3	1,494	8,805	3,144.4	489.2
Escambia	37.5	120.6	274	2,557	1,547.2	133.8	1,081	15,794	4,534.5	417.2	376	1,679	403.5	60.3
Flagler	9.2	87.0	56	281	138.6	14.6	261	3,821	1,087.4	97.7	168	426	92.4	16.0
Franklin	2.0	167.5	9	162	99.6	5.5	66	433	100.9	9.9	17	90	11.8	3.1
Gadsden	4.1	88.4	33	644	475.8	32.1	127	1,366	386.2	29.5	17	42	6.8	1.2
Gilchrist	0.2	13.4	14	80	72.0	3.4	34	183	51.8	3.5	6	6	1.2	0.1
Glades	0.5	37.3	NA	NA	NA	NA	14	88	28.7	1.8	3	D	1.7	D
Gulf	1.9	118.5	7	17	10.2	0.5	46	326	79.3	7.1	15	50	12.5	1.9
Hamilton	0.9	61.6	NA	NA	NA	NA	44	365	190.8	8.0	7	22	1.2	0.4
Hardee	1.6	59.6	19	132	95.2	6.9	71	717	187.0	15.8	18	39	6.1	1.0
Hendry	3.3	84.6	28	259	177.5	11.2	110	1,481	344.1	31.6	25	66	11.7	1.9
Hernando	18.3	102.3	83	451	209.3	20.8	473	7,896	2,036.5	191.0	187	465	87.1	12.6
Highlands	7.5	75.3	53	434	200.2	20.7	329	4,589	1,261.2	109.9	98	302	60.5	8.3
Hillsborough	196.4	145.6	1,739	27,830	24,464.4	1,608.7	4,661	74,470	24,583.3	2,111.0	2,377	11,801	4,040.4	577.0
Holmes	1.0	52.3	D	D	D	D	54	390	108.3	9.7	6	16	1.3	0.2
Indian River	16.9	114.5	133	856	5,125.0	96.6	684	9,009	2,267.7	222.7	276	1,569	257.8	52.5
Jackson	2.5	50.6	16	145	60.0	4.6	178	1,991	602.0	48.0	30	90	12.6	3.2
Jefferson	0.7	46.2	D	D	D	D	46	381	69.8	6.3	7	21	1.1	0.3
Lafayette	0.2	19.6	7	83	51.0	3.8	16	83	25.8	1.9	NA	NA	NA	NA
Lake	49.3	151.2	234	1,534	713.1	65.7	1,061	16,287	4,938.9	441.6	486	2,065	356.5	69.4
Lee	64.6	92.0	638	5,832	3,164.5	278.6	2,651	39,847	12,227.8	1,071.9	1,562	6,205	1,535.0	384.0
Leon	28.5	99.6	214	2,547	1,942.0	167.0	1,019	16,228	4,081.0	396.5	441	2,832	450.3	97.0
Levy	1.5	37.2	29	164	103.7	6.2	148	1,474	421.9	34.1	28	57	7.5	1.2
Liberty	0.5	55.2	D	D	D	D	18	157	28.2	2.3	NA	NA	NA	NA
Madison	1.2	66.8	9	48	45.3	3.6	59	543	157.4	11.3	8	19	2.4	0.6
Manatee	42.8	117.9	332	3,190	2,148.9	187.2	1,301	19,601	5,421.8	508.6	635	2,122	523.3	82.5
Marion	27.7	80.7	280	3,742	2,243.1	188.1	1,152	16,765	5,080.9	454.7	416	1,614	301.9	47.7
Martin	15.6	99.9	170	1,165	641.5	62.6	768	10,396	3,089.8	274.5	343	1,781	429.1	71.3
Miami-Dade	351.9	130.7	8,150	67,693	80,939.0	3,590.8	10,680	141,982	45,110.7	3,964.1	6,073	25,412	8,315.8	1,227.9
Monroe	0.0	0.0	76	303	514.7	13.9	626	6,105	1,688.5	159.9	383	1,135	290.6	39.4
Nassau	7.0	89.2	D	D	D	11.9	257	3,197	791.3	77.6	117	270	69.7	11.5
Okaloosa	21.8	109.8	125	610	252.0	29.0	871	12,309	3,609.7	322.4	413	1,900	398.5	73.7
Okeechobee	2.7	68.9	25	158	101.8	8.9	139	1,765	625.1	45.4	35	98	13.1	2.7
Orange	221.9	172.3	1,693	26,493	32,960.3	1,847.7	5,020	86,080	26,388.5	2,238.7	2,865	24,857	9,060.4	1,425.3
Osceola	42.2	130.2	147	1,852	4,306.5	82.8	969	15,629	4,128.2	368.4	590	4,330	842.0	147.0
Palm Beach	238.7	167.8	1,992	18,587	17,481.6	1,181.9	5,680	79,430	24,445.7	2,335.5	3,149	14,516	3,696.6	733.4
Pasco	61.2	122.8	296	1,822	1,004.9	92.7	1,511	23,252	7,098.7	615.0	565	2,135	367.5	58.0
Pinellas	23.9	25.1	1,141	12,087	7,620.0	677.8	3,732	53,060	16,891.1	1,530.8	1,928	8,946	1,635.7	348.8
Polk	67.5	103.9	528	7,950	13,505.1	402.1	1,793	27,302	8,333.4	726.9	727	3,332	734.1	127.7

1 Merchant wholesalers, except manufacturers' sales branches and offices. 2. Employer establishments.

STATE County	Professional, scientific, and technical services, 2017				Manufacturing, 2017				Accommodation and food services, 2017			
	Number of establish-ments	Number of employees	Sales (mil dol)	Average payroll (mil dol)	Number of establish-ments	Number of employees	Sales (mil dol)	Average payroll (mil dol)	Number of establis-hments	Number of employees	Sales (mil dol)	Annual payroll (mil dol)
	147	148	149	150	151	152	153	154	155	156	157	158
CONNECTICUT—Cont'd												
Tolland	D	D	D	D	116	3,378	835.7	192.2	245	3,859	259.9	70.0
Windham	D	D	D	D	160	5,660	2,095.6	307.9	253	3,335	203.3	60.8
DELAWARE	2,979	29,589	6,967.0	2,934.2	558	27,536	16,689.2	1,543.9	2,141	39,950	2,554.4	714.1
Kent	D	D	D	D	70	4,635	2,139.3	210.0	285	6,916	476.3	115.0
New Castle	D	D	D	D	354	12,407	10,948.5	902.6	1,214	23,051	1,360.6	387.0
Sussex	D	D	D	D	134	10,494	3,601.4	431.3	642	9,983	717.5	212.1
DISTRICT OF COLUMBIA	5,593	98,614	34,764.8	12,275.9	113	1,092	277.4	49.8	2,733	72,890	6,739.8	2,060.2
District of Columbia	5,593	98,614	34,764.8	12,275.9	113	1,092	277.4	49.8	2,733	72,890	6,739.8	2,060.2
FLORIDA	79,028	508,370	88,907.6	34,319.6	13,471	296,389	106,341.9	16,575.6	42,071	955,006	67,950.4	18,462.3
Alachua	863	5,461	780.2	311.2	170	3,869	1,122.6	250.3	591	13,043	682.2	200.8
Baker	19	98	10.4	3.7	6	153	111.3	8.4	34	773	31.6	8.8
Bay	D	D	D	D	106	3,728	1,488.1	208.0	515	11,608	757.4	215.8
Bradford	32	101	9.6	3.6	13	397	127.5	20.0	41	696	34.5	9.2
Brevard	1,920	19,218	3,795.1	1,440.5	447	19,579	5,939.2	1,622.5	1,202	23,254	1,343.2	384.3
Broward	10,546	54,062	9,519.6	3,632.7	1,432	22,969	6,516.5	1,183.8	4,113	83,312	6,473.1	1,691.1
Calhoun	6	6	0.8	0.3	4	28	5.9	0.7	D	D	D	D
Charlotte	D	D	D	D	78	512	101.9	21.2	294	6,067	336.5	96.2
Citrus	D	D	D	D	55	338	75.1	13.6	235	3,513	175.3	50.8
Clay	D	D	D	D	79	892	329.0	47.6	293	6,148	310.6	93.8
Collier	1,602	5,768	1,103.6	381.5	209	3,397	797.0	173.7	881	24,719	1,957.8	527.6
Columbia	D	D	D	D	38	709	336.5	39.3	126	2,936	150.4	43.1
DeSoto	32	113	16.6	3.9	14	451	246.1	24.0	40	569	33.0	8.1
Dixie	15	32	2.3	0.7	10	587	126.5	19.5	D	D	D	D
Duval	3,408	37,455	6,724.4	2,668.0	593	22,768	11,136.8	1,349.6	2,195	46,414	2,773.1	772.1
Escambia	D	D	D	D	157	3,655	2,866.8	260.8	589	14,086	805.8	223.2
Flagler	223	591	86.7	31.9	44	582	135.7	24.1	180	3,451	250.8	61.1
Franklin	23	74	9.2	3.1	NA	NA	NA	NA	46	602	43.6	14.1
Gadsden	D	D	D	D	25	880	182.0	41.2	51	791	46.1	13.9
Gilchrist	17	44	4.4	1.3	8	128	53.4	5.6	21	272	20.1	4.8
Glades	6	17	0.5	0.3	7	168	126.2	9.8	9	120	5.1	1.3
Gulf	30	162	21.2	6.4	7	49	6.8	1.5	35	421	25.9	7.9
Hamilton	11	40	3.3	1.5	D	D	D	D	D	D	D	D
Hardee	20	67	6.3	2.0	10	325	134.1	13.4	31	433	23.2	5.0
Hendry	D	D	D	D	D	830	D	44.5	60	886	47.8	13.0
Hernando	307	1,340	154.9	52.1	82	1,876	451.1	78.2	270	5,154	254.6	75.8
Highlands	D	D	D	D	46	707	284.3	33.2	143	2,450	125.6	35.8
Hillsborough	5,832	61,813	11,447.1	4,706.0	801	20,022	11,450.1	1,076.0	2,514	57,750	4,268.3	1,098.7
Holmes	14	40	4.7	1.6	10	75	11.0	3.4	D	D	D	D
Indian River	518	2,076	286.9	116.0	87	1,538	362.3	82.6	282	5,660	334.0	97.0
Jackson	47	258	28.5	11.3	22	693	309.4	36.7	80	1,090	56.8	14.0
Jefferson	21	135	12.9	5.0	D	D	D	D	20	164	8.9	2.2
Lafayette	D	D	2.1	D	5	21	5.5	1.0	D	D	D	D
Lake	661	2,303	287.2	100.8	161	2,836	999.7	120.1	552	11,402	646.2	189.2
Lee	D	D	2,197.4	D	366	5,117	1,176.3	249.1	1,432	31,343	1,925.7	566.6
Leon	D	D	D	D	111	1,442	468.4	77.3	722	15,606	830.6	227.1
Levy	53	209	24.6	7.9	20	482	123.9	21.5	65	818	37.4	11.1
Liberty	NA	NA	NA	NA	4	290	197.6	17.4	4	D	1.7	D
Madison	15	111	15.0	6.5	13	401	238.1	17.4	22	304	15.9	4.6
Manatee	D	D	D	D	275	7,264	2,110.5	388.8	679	13,593	766.2	235.3
Marion	D	D	D	D	188	7,109	3,330.8	337.8	516	9,478	531.8	146.7
Martin	763	3,789	515.1	182.1	193	2,558	749.1	141.6	384	7,302	439.7	126.5
Miami-Dade	14,033	71,986	15,104.0	5,282.6	2,157	31,558	7,916.7	1,515.7	5,693	131,647	11,060.0	2,971.1
Monroe	393	981	154.9	49.4	68	264	68.4	14.0	542	12,466	1,229.2	341.4
Nassau	208	681	92.4	34.1	35	1,316	905.4	88.9	175	4,663	324.7	102.4
Okaloosa	D	D	D	D	93	1,565	481.9	81.1	520	11,250	694.9	199.7
Okeechobee	57	256	28.0	9.1	22	373	192.3	17.1	55	875	56.7	13.0
Orange	5,659	50,796	8,330.7	3,635.1	835	26,099	8,135.6	1,652.1	3,221	124,474	11,132.8	2,814.9
Osceola	523	2,029	264.5	90.6	98	1,197	523.2	54.9	684	18,989	1,500.4	390.8
Palm Beach	8,348	43,426	8,585.1	3,051.8	966	13,242	4,082.6	782.3	3,064	68,960	4,656.3	1,349.2
Pasco	D	D	D	D	235	2,934	828.5	147.6	648	12,747	701.1	198.8
Pinellas	D	D	D	D	1,027	28,004	8,845.1	1,582.5	2,294	45,742	3,056.6	840.0
Polk	1,077	6,200	780.3	299.4	408	14,431	8,312.3	772.9	893	18,045	1,019.0	272.7

STATE County	Health care and social assistance, 2017				Other services, 2017				Nonemployer businesses, 2019		Value of residential construction authorized by building permits, 2021	
	Number of establish-ments	Number of employees	Receipts (mil dol)	Annual payroll (mil dol)	Number of establish-ments	Number of employees	Receipts (mil dol)	Annual payroll (mil dol)	Number	Receipts (mil dol)	New construction ($1,000)	Number of housing units
	159	160	161	162	163	164	165	166	167	168	169	170
CONNECTICUT—Cont'd												
Tolland	320	5,852	511.8	213.3	190	1,144	176.4	43.8	9,682	501.3	62,660	413
Windham	281	7,354	616.9	296.0	167	677	76.7	17.6	6,846	322.5	31,183	158
DELAWARE	2,648	68,348	8,855.3	3,720.5	1,608	10,252	1,220.8	339.1	73,918	4,941.6	1,175,682	8,500
Kent	433	10,827	1,248.9	497.3	248	1,249	124.2	37.3	12,047	883.3	270,500	1,873
New Castle	1,651	45,968	6,099.3	2,652.7	1,014	7,184	906.7	247.1	42,665	2,903.5	207,792	1,822
Sussex	564	11,553	1,507.1	570.5	346	1,819	189.9	54.7	19,206	1,154.8	697,390	4,805
DISTRICT OF COLUMBIA	2,203	74,134	11,400.2	4,376.0	3,502	73,756	24,225.6	5,459.1	61,721	3,292.1	625,841	4,740
District of Columbia	2,203	74,134	11,400.2	4,376.0	3,502	73,756	24,225.6	5,459.1	61,721	3,292.1	625,841	4,740
FLORIDA	61,554	1,127,155	155,283.6	55,472.2	38,932	222,512	29,616.9	6,946.2	2,508,552	114,386.0	49,325,935	213,494
Alachua	807	26,051	3,922.9	1,462.7	413	3,892	568.1	126.6	20,648	800.2	339,678	2,179
Baker	37	1,882	128.0	80.8	D	D	D	3.0	1,479	56.3	22,190	116
Bay	549	10,448	1,288.9	495.7	319	1,922	176.4	47.3	15,550	826.2	683,169	2,610
Bradford	40	822	83.6	26.9	26	89	9.3	2.4	1,345	53.1	13,174	66
Brevard	1,600	32,031	3,775.1	1,369.8	1,023	4,793	466.5	135.2	48,279	1,957.3	1,537,334	5,174
Broward	6,614	95,619	13,231.2	4,736.4	4,538	22,941	2,920.0	750.2	308,930	13,592.7	786,842	4,069
Calhoun	22	632	44.5	21.1	D	D	D	D	806	32.4	1,855	17
Charlotte	514	8,529	1,259.5	400.0	335	1,418	146.7	39.7	15,697	730.0	1,246,156	4,830
Citrus	393	9,117	940.2	381.0	225	964	70.3	19.9	10,763	446.0	434,456	1,983
Clay	512	9,445	1,174.4	437.7	D	D	D	36.5	15,433	620.9	491,689	2,273
Collier	1,143	20,535	2,704.8	980.5	1,011	6,309	662.8	191.7	46,683	3,037.2	1,990,454	6,766
Columbia	185	4,270	584.6	244.9	83	310	33.5	7.6	4,422	211.9	61,709	258
DeSoto	46	1,140	102.5	43.3	26	95	8.7	2.5	1,870	88.0	22,157	127
Dixie	11	148	9.2	3.7	D	D	4.4	D	872	36.7	5,256	52
Duval	2,861	71,476	10,405.2	3,809.1	1,791	11,787	1,591.2	408.2	81,314	3,252.6	1,446,264	10,104
Escambia	834	21,902	2,968.5	1,142.0	453	3,230	312.0	87.1	23,860	1,046.3	329,074	1,960
Flagler	230	3,762	499.9	166.6	162	670	61.5	16.4	10,933	529.0	810,754	3,018
Franklin	19	163	16.0	6.9	24	60	5.8	1.9	1,311	60.7	25,190	115
Gadsden	56	2,329	163.9	108.4	36	115	13.3	3.5	3,271	106.2	30,903	92
Gilchrist	21	621	61.7	24.9	13	30	4.3	1.0	1,107	47.2	74,883	313
Glades	D	D	D	D	6	18	1.4	0.3	583	21.6	15,570	104
Gulf	25	225	14.4	6.5	12	41	4.0	0.6	1,247	66.8	80,773	293
Hamilton	D	D	D	6.1	D	D	D	D	694	26.7	5,628	25
Hardee	64	1,096	84.1	38.3	26	63	5.6	1.7	1,497	57.9	12,549	61
Hendry	61	1,261	99.7	45.4	44	170	20.3	4.7	3,339	127.1	106,266	685
Hernando	550	8,989	1,247.9	394.8	237	1,223	96.9	30.4	14,049	559.0	464,376	1,905
Highlands	309	6,442	729.3	284.6	125	403	39.6	9.5	6,638	284.3	137,252	644
Hillsborough	4,107	83,163	13,642.4	4,492.1	2,364	17,128	2,235.3	505.5	148,720	6,597.6	2,740,162	11,281
Holmes	28	509	39.2	14.9	D	D	D	D	1,259	47.6	1,730	13
Indian River	495	9,718	1,155.2	454.1	313	1,726	167.0	51.2	15,714	861.7	614,021	1,592
Jackson	83	1,723	164.4	70.4	52	236	28.4	7.1	2,864	111.6	23,363	103
Jefferson	D	D	D	D	13	48	2.8	1.0	1,162	45.4	24,360	112
Lafayette	10	132	8.6	3.5	D	D	1.0	D	388	15.9	3,081	36
Lake	950	19,135	2,211.1	823.4	521	2,529	250.2	67.7	30,282	1,238.3	1,192,697	4,505
Lee	1,700	38,678	5,215.6	2,158.8	1,425	7,305	834.2	222.8	79,000	3,950.3	2,671,616	13,394
Leon	783	18,888	2,413.6	941.8	615	4,473	728.7	194.5	23,134	933.6	344,906	2,211
Levy	63	687	46.6	21.5	52	151	16.8	3.6	3,171	136.0	25,217	251
Liberty	D	D	D	D	D	D	D	0.4	404	15.6	155	2
Madison	41	684	58.3	24.0	D	D	D	D	1,094	46.1	10,618	52
Manatee	963	16,571	1,943.6	725.7	656	2,970	301.2	85.3	37,089	1,871.6	1,576,889	8,119
Marion	909	15,902	2,033.6	716.2	516	2,545	263.3	71.9	28,673	1,293.6	1,208,547	6,229
Martin	585	11,069	1,257.1	517.8	430	2,212	238.5	70.0	17,542	1,010.7	328,141	942
Miami-Dade	9,159	144,441	21,236.1	7,238.0	5,335	31,051	3,952.6	909.2	576,770	25,840.3	3,373,741	13,393
Monroe	228	2,093	341.7	110.2	284	1,121	160.4	39.1	13,956	871.2	189,101	515
Nassau	186	2,449	267.9	97.1	137	543	66.9	19.5	7,391	347.4	501,918	1,855
Okaloosa	590	8,400	1,141.5	397.9	371	1,496	158.2	43.4	18,215	922.1	424,748	1,351
Okeechobee	117	1,510	214.1	71.3	69	284	33.4	9.2	2,471	98.6	4,107	13
Orange	3,581	74,659	11,145.8	3,816.0	2,327	19,594	3,802.3	664.1	164,747	7,012.6	2,640,032	12,890
Osceola	671	12,936	2,032.1	663.3	424	2,078	219.4	59.9	44,815	1,614.9	1,868,280	10,003
Palm Beach	5,903	87,245	12,287.3	4,300.0	3,725	20,953	2,620.0	676.6	205,030	10,825.1	2,523,859	7,851
Pasco	1,320	21,001	2,968.7	1,027.3	702	3,131	327.1	91.7	45,519	1,807.1	1,874,055	8,905
Pinellas	3,506	72,361	9,734.2	3,602.0	2,132	11,092	1,237.4	342.0	95,475	4,664.5	722,835	2,740
Polk	1,148	27,693	3,505.9	1,282.2	717	3,805	460.2	122.5	54,665	2,109.1	2,708,544	13,071

STATE County	Government employment and payroll, 2017		March payroll (percent of total)							Local government finances, 2017 — General revenue				
	Full-time equivalent employees	March payroll (dollars)	Adminis-tration, judicial, and legal	Police and corrections	Fire protection	Highways and transpor-tation	Health and welfare	Natural resources and utilities	Education and libraries	Total (mil dol)	Inter-govern-mental (mil dol)	Taxes: Total (mil dol)	Taxes: Per capita[1] (dollars): Total	Taxes: Per capita[1] (dollars): Property
	171	172	173	174	175	176	177	178	179	180	181	182	183	184
CONNECTICUT—Cont'd														
Tolland	4,812	22,573,034	5.3	3.0	1.3	4.4	2.1	2.9	79.5	565.4	166.0	355.5	2,354	2,328
Windham	4,280	19,365,768	4.5	2.2	1.3	3.7	1.6	2.2	82.2	470.0	202.8	232.7	1,999	1,987
DELAWARE	X	X	X	X	X	X	X	X	X	X	X	X	X	X
Kent	4,452	19,533,638	5.1	6.3	0.1	0.8	1.8	5.1	79.4	513.1	312.8	109.2	619	544
New Castle	13,758	68,584,293	5.3	10.4	1.5	3.5	2.2	4.2	71.3	2,025.0	893.9	754.9	1,358	1,110
Sussex	5,620	25,192,097	5.1	4.7	0.0	1.2	3.0	4.1	80.6	778.5	394.2	223.2	995	758
DISTRICT OF COLUMBIA	X	X	X	X	X	X	X	X	X	X	X	X	X	X
District of Columbia	52,851	365,723,937	11.0	13.7	4.0	26.1	14.2	7.0	16.9	13,246.4	4,230.7	7,455.9	10,729	3,500
FLORIDA	X	X	X	X	X	X	X	X	X	X	X	X	X	X
Alachua	9,388	36,390,714	11.6	16.6	5.0	5.0	3.8	11.7	43.8	964.9	331.4	356.8	1,340	1,075
Baker	895	2,640,778	6.4	3.9	1.5	2.9	2.3	6.2	76.3	95.3	47.5	19.8	699	497
Bay	8,252	28,582,062	5.1	9.8	2.7	3.8	24.7	5.2	47.3	727.1	246.4	300.1	1,625	1,070
Bradford	829	2,600,500	11.9	12.6	2.6	2.7	5.3	3.1	58.3	70.2	37.7	20.1	742	535
Brevard	19,876	71,754,734	7.2	12.8	6.8	4.6	7.5	8.1	51.1	2,102.4	685.7	749.1	1,275	944
Broward	78,792	389,220,424	5.0	13.2	5.4	3.7	32.3	6.1	32.6	12,006.7	2,460.8	3,819.2	1,974	1,586
Calhoun	513	1,282,306	5.4	4.0	0.2	6.0	0.0	4.7	79.5	51.3	38.9	9.1	628	475
Charlotte	4,751	17,974,279	14.2	16.9	10.5	6.1	1.4	9.3	39.5	618.7	101.2	291.7	1,607	1,248
Citrus	3,578	11,361,255	9.3	10.8	0.3	3.5	2.1	4.9	64.4	336.2	116.8	150.9	1,038	922
Clay	6,503	21,317,220	4.6	11.7	4.3	1.2	0.2	4.6	71.4	605.5	265.1	186.8	880	650
Collier	10,447	46,883,097	6.7	17.1	7.6	3.2	5.8	8.0	48.7	1,526.6	242.6	884.1	2,372	2,131
Columbia	2,321	6,980,424	2.7	2.9	4.1	4.8	0.6	4.2	74.5	216.5	115.2	60.4	863	586
DeSoto	1,357	4,556,679	3.8	10.1	5.2	2.6	26.0	5.2	46.1	131.5	47.3	34.1	916	685
Dixie	497	1,302,803	5.3	1.2	1.4	6.5	9.6	7.5	67.8	48.8	29.9	12.2	734	608
Duval	24,856	100,025,694	5.9	14.4	6.6	2.8	1.4	8.4	55.1	3,573.5	1,256.5	1,424.5	1,519	1,040
Escambia	10,448	35,675,524	5.8	14.8	3.2	2.8	2.7	10.5	57.0	1,196.2	415.4	375.5	1,199	750
Flagler	3,121	11,214,768	13.1	10.3	7.2	4.8	1.7	8.4	51.9	340.4	100.6	160.2	1,457	1,232
Franklin	406	1,170,228	7.7	10.5	1.8	8.5	3.3	13.4	50.7	60.5	18.7	27.8	2,370	1,981
Gadsden	1,599	4,603,867	10.2	11.9	2.1	7.2	5.1	4.2	56.9	110.0	62.3	31.7	690	492
Gilchrist	601	1,591,452	4.9	0.6	0.6	3.2	1.1	3.5	77.7	55.7	34.8	15.1	842	615
Glades	599	2,023,704	8.3	23.3	0.3	2.4	3.4	5.9	55.1	79.2	22.4	12.5	922	817
Gulf	574	1,787,849	13.1	12.7	0.2	4.9	5.8	8.7	51.0	59.9	21.9	28.8	1,790	1,416
Hamilton	590	1,857,007	5.1	15.9	0.6	5.0	3.6	21.4	45.0	68.3	36.7	24.4	1,695	1,312
Hardee	748	2,319,628	5.9	4.0	0.0	0.8	0.2	5.0	83.5	105.5	53.9	30.9	1,138	955
Hendry	1,627	5,855,789	10.9	8.7	1.1	3.8	23.3	9.8	40.2	185.4	78.0	54.4	1,327	982
Hernando	5,021	18,120,327	6.4	11.5	8.6	1.9	0.5	19.0	50.2	540.1	171.4	256.1	1,371	1,219
Highlands	3,221	10,134,596	7.5	15.0	2.0	3.4	1.9	4.9	63.1	302.8	127.4	101.8	980	722
Hillsborough	46,480	191,019,225	6.7	13.8	5.9	5.6	3.1	6.8	55.7	5,912.8	2,418.9	2,081.3	1,459	1,059
Holmes	866	2,311,727	6.1	5.9	0.0	4.4	24.9	2.4	53.6	77.3	49.3	9.9	512	379
Indian River	4,114	16,229,719	5.2	17.3	4.8	4.9	3.8	12.9	48.2	515.4	108.8	297.9	1,931	1,523
Jackson	2,613	8,483,063	4.3	5.6	2.7	2.7	34.0	2.4	46.1	239.2	100.8	41.7	863	469
Jefferson	325	834,386	9.1	5.8	2.5	10.1	6.7	9.7	53.0	32.7	12.5	13.6	957	634
Lafayette	289	851,769	6.4	11.1	0.0	3.3	2.5	3.6	68.0	21.4	14.4	4.6	536	472
Lake	10,219	34,465,237	6.4	13.3	7.7	2.4	0.9	8.0	57.1	1,031.6	329.0	396.8	1,149	840
Lee	33,112	154,572,301	3.8	7.4	4.9	3.0	47.3	4.2	28.2	4,646.6	703.6	1,284.1	1,735	1,464
Leon	10,881	43,682,389	11.3	12.5	4.1	4.4	3.2	16.6	43.8	1,141.1	385.1	396.5	1,363	930
Levy	1,384	4,036,870	4.9	14.1	1.5	5.6	6.2	3.4	60.8	115.5	56.7	36.2	899	697
Liberty	361	949,943	2.1	0.1	0.2	4.3	5.4	3.4	83.8	28.2	20.4	4.9	596	460
Madison	966	2,812,310	4.8	8.6	1.3	3.2	16.6	4.4	57.9	81.8	42.0	17.7	958	662
Manatee	11,742	43,798,961	8.5	15.5	5.9	4.3	2.7	5.6	54.2	1,621.6	387.7	743.5	1,929	1,635
Marion	10,693	35,122,480	4.8	11.0	9.8	2.1	0.8	6.7	62.3	962.8	383.9	311.7	882	738
Martin	4,598	17,470,072	9.1	12.8	13.8	2.5	0.8	6.9	49.2	590.0	114.2	354.1	2,217	1,997
Miami-Dade	93,991	469,157,165	7.3	16.4	6.7	8.4	14.5	8.1	35.3	14,969.4	3,265.1	6,118.7	2,255	1,664
Monroe	3,903	18,227,562	9.3	19.0	8.7	3.9	4.4	19.6	31.8	657.8	128.3	317.3	4,149	2,611
Nassau	2,061	7,376,121	4.4	2.6	12.3	4.2	1.0	5.2	65.5	256.9	67.6	142.4	1,717	1,372
Okaloosa	7,072	25,149,599	5.4	11.0	5.4	3.1	2.3	7.6	62.0	694.5	252.3	258.8	1,272	1,009
Okeechobee	1,602	4,781,680	7.2	16.2	6.5	2.6	1.2	4.1	58.1	127.6	62.5	47.6	1,153	668
Orange	47,356	187,768,001	6.4	13.0	7.6	5.4	2.5	9.0	50.9	6,687.2	1,776.9	2,741.4	2,022	1,417
Osceola	12,048	43,029,385	7.4	13.3	6.6	2.3	0.7	9.0	57.0	1,423.1	490.2	507.4	1,435	910
Palm Beach	49,998	226,983,697	8.2	17.4	9.4	2.1	4.2	12.1	43.4	7,208.5	1,451.4	3,928.2	2,672	2,261
Pasco	15,712	51,647,343	6.3	11.7	7.1	2.3	2.7	5.6	62.3	1,509.9	621.2	521.2	993	718
Pinellas	31,247	129,067,444	9.1	18.1	6.3	3.6	2.9	12.1	43.4	3,760.3	955.5	1,724.8	1,781	1,359
Polk	24,085	82,688,018	8.2	12.8	5.3	2.2	2.2	10.4	55.7	2,121.7	833.2	708.7	1,034	683

1. Based on the resident population estimated as of July 1 of the year shown.

STATE County	Local government finances, 2017 (cont.)									Government employment, 2020			Individual income tax returns, 2019		
	Direct general expenditure							Debt outstanding							
			Percent of total for:												
	Total (mil dol)	Per capita[1] (dollars)	Education	Health and hospitals	Police protection	Public welfare	Highways	Total (mil dol)	Per capita[1] (dollars)	Federal civilian	Federal military	State and local	Number of returns	Mean adjusted gross income	Mean income tax
	185	186	187	188	189	190	191	192	193	194	195	196	197	198	199
CONNECTICUT—Cont'd															
Tolland	563.8	3,733	64.8	0.6	2.3	0.5	5.2	175.1	1,160	301	319	16,033	69,550	85,597	10,623
Windham	477.8	4,105	72.9	0.8	2.8	0.2	3.8	122.9	1,056	307	225	6,522	56,740	61,948	6,141
DELAWARE	X	X	X	X	X	X	X	X	X	6,047	8,795	59,362	485,450	71,348	8,394
Kent	520.7	2,950	74.0	1.3	5.4	0.0	1.4	371.1	2,103	1,775	4,572	17,448	86,400	55,363	4,985
New Castle	2,033.5	3,657	59.7	0.9	8.5	0.0	4.7	1,908.6	3,433	3,581	2,919	33,690	277,840	76,337	9,510
Sussex	757.2	3,375	71.3	1.9	4.1	0.1	1.5	432.8	1,929	691	1,304	8,224	121,200	71,311	8,266
DISTRICT OF COLUMBIA	X	X	X	X	X	X	X	X	X	193,423	14,201	42,863	351,550	107,044	18,155
District of Columbia	13,255.1	19,075	21.9	5.0	4.8	29.6	3.4	17,640.3	25,385	193,423	14,201	42,863	351,550	107,044	18,155
FLORIDA	X	X	X	X	X	X	X	X	X	150,018	99,552	948,006	10,635,580	74,096	10,259
Alachua	994.2	3,733	37.3	2.9	7.9	1.7	4.3	2,434.8	9,143	4,888	537	37,260	119,740	67,215	8,281
Baker	100.6	3,561	44.1	4.7	9.3	0.8	4.2	33.7	1,194	69	56	2,596	11,610	52,804	4,134
Bay	718.8	3,891	43.3	2.6	8.1	0.0	4.5	596.2	3,227	3,971	2,747	8,596	85,660	60,706	6,903
Bradford	68.7	2,530	49.0	5.7	10.0	0.0	7.2	8.0	293	37	45	1,936	10,760	47,607	3,756
Brevard	2,232.0	3,797	35.9	9.2	7.0	0.2	4.6	1,844.7	3,138	6,900	2,952	22,000	305,340	66,971	8,078
Broward	11,894.2	6,148	25.1	28.0	9.9	1.2	1.3	11,449.4	5,919	7,601	3,764	96,778	996,250	71,681	10,181
Calhoun	61.8	4,282	56.7	1.5	4.7	0.5	19.2	0.6	43	25	46	869	4,980	44,600	3,382
Charlotte	621.4	3,423	26.1	3.8	10.9	1.3	15.4	578.0	3,184	380	332	5,698	93,520	65,185	7,368
Citrus	372.5	2,562	41.6	6.4	9.6	0.6	8.5	478.1	3,288	236	257	4,084	71,910	53,896	5,436
Clay	587.4	2,768	53.4	2.7	8.2	0.7	5.0	436.2	2,055	427	378	6,903	107,270	63,472	6,331
Collier	1,422.5	3,817	38.1	3.4	12.7	0.5	5.2	1,944.8	5,219	813	663	12,388	198,250	161,646	30,328
Columbia	209.4	2,992	55.4	2.3	6.7	0.2	8.3	130.0	1,857	1,276	143	4,140	30,220	46,852	4,094
DeSoto	134.4	3,610	36.2	25.9	5.7	0.4	3.7	54.6	1,465	63	60	1,750	13,350	44,554	3,658
Dixie	53.1	3,195	50.3	9.1	6.4	0.0	10.6	12.1	726	15	27	1,001	5,460	54,217	6,431
Duval	3,286.7	3,504	42.7	2.5	11.3	0.4	1.6	9,891.8	10,546	17,968	15,486	37,134	487,950	62,461	7,517
Escambia	1,280.6	4,088	37.7	1.8	6.4	0.0	3.6	4,176.3	13,332	6,071	13,075	15,162	154,460	57,978	6,371
Flagler	358.7	3,261	34.5	1.7	6.0	0.2	9.5	505.1	4,591	186	201	3,530	58,820	64,323	7,354
Franklin	58.0	4,946	27.5	17.3	8.2	0.2	9.3	25.0	2,129	21	18	952	4,810	63,975	8,707
Gadsden	123.7	2,689	49.6	4.8	7.9	1.3	8.7	49.8	1,083	95	72	4,002	20,610	42,625	3,231
Gilchrist	54.1	3,024	56.1	5.3	5.1	0.6	9.7	4.8	268	38	30	1,041	7,340	52,477	4,928
Glades	78.1	5,754	22.3	0.9	5.1	0.0	5.2	171.7	12,643	12	22	526	4,560	52,274	5,405
Gulf	79.1	4,912	27.1	29.7	4.9	0.1	10.6	36.5	2,265	13	22	957	6,150	61,235	6,747
Hamilton	88.3	6,146	45.8	2.8	3.9	0.2	3.2	3.3	227	32	20	1,037	5,030	40,596	2,901
Hardee	110.6	4,075	44.6	4.3	9.9	0.2	4.8	20.9	768	60	44	1,659	10,270	43,717	3,440
Hendry	192.4	4,691	37.5	18.0	6.8	0.4	7.5	76.9	1,875	93	151	2,081	17,610	45,340	4,103
Hernando	566.9	3,037	35.2	3.4	8.3	0.1	4.7	301.1	1,613	400	338	5,375	90,530	49,476	4,411
Highlands	317.5	3,058	44.6	3.2	10.1	0.6	5.4	109.0	1,050	313	180	3,816	44,520	47,026	4,185
Hillsborough	5,977.9	4,190	37.7	2.8	6.8	0.7	2.7	6,717.3	4,708	16,299	8,550	64,134	714,530	71,339	9,378
Holmes	101.4	5,220	56.8	13.7	3.9	0.1	6.1	24.5	1,260	67	34	1,302	7,070	44,358	3,866
Indian River	533.9	3,462	35.9	4.1	7.3	0.9	7.3	253.7	1,645	406	275	4,514	81,830	116,349	18,779
Jackson	231.7	4,797	36.3	34.9	3.4	0.0	8.5	47.9	992	448	68	4,716	18,890	44,628	3,613
Jefferson	32.8	2,315	29.8	7.0	11.4	0.8	7.6	12.4	874	33	23	506	6,170	59,296	5,864
Lafayette	21.4	2,485	56.6	5.8	7.8	0.1	11.7	0.2	24	13	12	571	2,720	41,097	3,036
Lake	1,055.3	3,055	41.1	4.6	9.0	0.5	3.7	940.7	2,723	675	635	11,745	182,520	60,435	6,283
Lee	4,462.4	6,030	24.7	37.4	5.2	0.2	2.4	4,561.8	6,165	2,633	1,410	40,843	375,900	84,490	11,941
Leon	1,118.6	3,844	39.5	2.4	8.5	0.3	7.3	4,855.4	16,687	1,977	525	50,230	135,100	64,688	7,759
Levy	115.8	2,876	48.0	6.2	8.3	0.9	4.9	21.9	544	80	100	1,740	18,720	45,242	4,217
Liberty	28.8	3,500	55.6	7.9	5.2	0.5	10.6	4.1	494	39	11	714	2,760	45,966	3,095
Madison	83.3	4,507	47.3	13.3	6.1	0.4	9.6	31.5	1,705	45	28	1,221	7,360	41,980	3,258
Manatee	1,400.8	3,634	41.4	2.2	8.3	0.5	4.9	1,651.1	4,283	1,056	727	12,384	197,310	81,014	11,207
Marion	965.7	2,733	49.5	3.7	7.4	0.9	5.5	629.5	1,782	885	625	14,472	176,180	53,122	5,519
Martin	620.3	3,884	34.0	6.0	8.9	1.9	4.7	239.7	1,501	305	271	5,578	80,850	126,933	21,003
Miami-Dade	14,469.2	5,333	28.2	13.3	9.2	3.4	1.6	28,281.1	10,423	21,994	7,052	119,512	1,387,160	68,290	10,487
Monroe	708.9	9,268	19.7	5.8	9.3	0.5	3.3	1,611.0	21,063	1,210	1,608	4,777	46,370	130,254	22,652
Nassau	269.6	3,251	48.8	4.8	8.8	0.2	3.8	164.6	1,985	538	155	2,985	45,330	91,306	12,481
Okaloosa	716.2	3,520	47.8	2.0	7.4	0.3	3.9	449.9	2,211	9,300	18,822	8,086	107,660	67,888	8,033
Okeechobee	125.7	3,046	50.5	3.0	8.7	0.6	5.3	32.2	781	82	67	2,103	16,330	46,467	4,195
Orange	6,836.2	5,042	38.6	1.6	6.7	0.2	3.0	10,178.6	7,507	12,998	2,587	68,963	697,940	66,557	8,601
Osceola	1,330.3	3,762	44.5	0.5	8.7	1.5	5.3	2,606.1	7,370	587	707	12,764	192,450	44,672	3,669
Palm Beach	6,984.6	4,750	30.3	4.6	10.4	1.7	2.1	5,584.1	3,798	7,392	2,666	54,508	755,370	115,786	20,444
Pasco	1,577.8	3,005	51.7	2.4	8.5	0.2	3.5	1,241.2	2,364	993	979	15,417	264,590	59,256	6,166
Pinellas	3,845.9	3,972	32.7	5.4	11.5	1.6	3.3	3,338.4	3,448	8,089	2,710	36,967	504,070	76,553	10,508
Polk	2,193.4	3,200	47.9	2.6	8.2	1.4	4.0	2,340.3	3,415	1,411	1,259	27,660	336,020	52,426	4,872

1. Based on the resident population estimated as of July 1 of the year shown.

State / county code	CBSA code[1]	County Type code[2]	STATE County	Land area[3] (sq. mi)	Population, 2021: Total persons 2021	Population, 2021: Rank	Population, 2021: Per square mile	Race alone or in combination, not Hispanic or Latino (percent): White	Black	American Indian, Alaska Native	Asian and Pacific Islancer	Percent Hispanic or Latino[4]	Age (percent): Under 5 years	5 to 17 years	18 to 24 years	25 to 34 years	35 to 44 years	45 to 54 years
				1	2	3	4	5	6	7	8	9	10	11	12	13	14	15
			FLORIDA—Cont'd															
12107	37260	4	Putnam	728.4	74,167	746	101.8	72.5	16.7	1.0	1.0	10.4	5.5	12.2	10.7	11.3	10.3	10.9
12109	27260	1	St. Johns	600.6	292,466	244	487.0	83.1	6.0	0.6	4.5	7.9	4.6	12.9	10.9	9.2	13.7	13.8
12111	38940	2	St. Lucie	571.7	343,579	212	601.0	56.7	21.7	0.6	2.7	20.3	4.9	11.2	10.6	11.5	11.4	11.7
12113	37860	2	Santa Rosa	1,012.4	193,998	352	191.6	84.6	7.3	1.6	3.9	6.1	5.3	12.6	11.5	13.5	13.8	12.8
12115	35840	2	Sarasota	556.0	447,057	161	804.1	83.8	5.0	0.6	2.4	9.7	3.3	8.0	8.3	8.4	8.6	10.5
12117	36740	1	Seminole	309.4	470,093	153	1,519.4	60.0	12.8	0.6	6.0	22.9	5.0	11.9	11.8	14.2	14.5	13.3
12119	45540	3	Sumter	557.1	135,638	483	243.5	86.0	7.0	0.7	1.3	6.0	1.7	4.1	4.0	5.8	6.1	6.4
12121		6	Suwannee	688.6	44,485	1,086	64.6	76.7	12.7	1.0	0.9	10.2	5.3	12.2	11.2	11.9	11.7	11.5
12123		6	Taylor	1,043.3	21,815	1,724	20.9	74.3	20.4	1.6	1.3	4.3	5.1	11.4	10.5	14.0	12.3	12.5
12125		6	Union	243.6	16,335	2,012	67.1	70.9	23.2	0.7	0.9	5.8	5.2	11.7	12.1	15.2	13.5	13.4
12127	19660	2	Volusia	1,101.3	564,412	124	512.5	71.0	11.6	0.8	2.6	16.1	4.5	10.0	10.9	11.7	10.9	11.7
12129	45220	2	Wakulla	606.4	34,690	1,308	57.2	80.6	14.6	1.3	1.2	4.4	5.0	11.8	10.9	13.6	14.3	14.3
12131	18880	3	Walton	1,038.3	80,069	715	77.1	86.0	5.8	1.6	2.1	6.8	5.4	11.8	9.6	11.5	12.9	12.7
12133		6	Washington	584.7	25,436	1,587	43.5	79.2	15.6	2.1	1.6	4.1	5.1	11.1	11.6	14.0	13.2	13.4
13000		0	GEORGIA	57,716.3	10,799,566	X	187.1	52.8	33.2	0.7	5.3	10.2	5.9	13.3	13.7	13.8	13.2	12.9
13001		7	Appling	508.3	18,488	1,899	36.4	69.9	20.0	0.6	0.9	10.3	6.2	14.1	12.4	11.6	11.9	11.9
13003	20060	9	Atkinson	342.7	8,391	2,545	24.5	55.9	16.6	1.0	0.8	27.5	6.9	14.3	13.9	13.5	12.3	12.9
13005		7	Bacon	284.1	11,079	2,339	39.0	74.5	17.4	0.4	0.9	8.8	6.7	14.2	13.0	12.2	12.2	13.0
13007		3	Baker	342.0	2,819	2,975	8.2	50.0	42.0	1.2	1.7	6.8	4.8	11.0	10.6	11.0	10.3	11.7
13009	33300	4	Baldwin	258.7	43,781	1,100	169.2	53.5	42.6	0.5	2.1	2.7	4.5	10.5	22.1	11.4	10.8	10.9
13011		8	Banks	232.6	18,562	1,894	79.8	87.7	3.6	0.9	1.4	8.0	5.5	11.8	12.4	12.0	12.4	13.7
13013	12060	1	Barrow	161.0	86,658	672	538.2	68.1	14.6	0.7	4.6	14.1	6.3	14.7	12.7	14.7	14.3	12.9
13015	12060	1	Bartow	458.9	110,843	558	241.5	77.7	12.0	0.8	1.6	9.8	6.0	13.3	12.5	14.0	12.6	13.5
13017	22340	7	Ben Hill	250.1	17,158	1,960	68.6	55.3	37.5	0.8	1.0	6.9	6.2	14.2	12.4	11.8	11.9	11.8
13019		6	Berrien	453.4	18,147	1,918	40.0	81.5	12.0	0.8	1.5	5.8	6.1	13.3	12.2	12.3	12.1	12.8
13021	31420	3	Bibb	249.4	156,762	437	628.6	37.5	57.0	0.5	2.7	3.9	6.3	13.7	14.4	13.9	11.9	11.3
13023		6	Bleckley	215.9	12,607	2,236	58.4	68.9	27.1	0.5	1.4	3.5	5.0	11.1	18.8	11.9	11.0	11.5
13025	15260	3	Brantley	443.2	18,101	1,919	40.8	92.6	4.6	1.2	0.6	2.7	5.8	13.2	12.0	12.3	11.6	13.3
13027	46660	3	Brooks	493.2	16,270	2,020	33.0	57.2	35.0	0.9	1.7	6.6	5.3	12.6	10.7	11.7	11.1	12.6
13029	42340	2	Bryan	437.6	46,938	1,038	107.3	73.8	16.6	0.9	3.4	8.4	6.9	17.2	12.8	13.5	16.7	12.1
13031	44340	4	Bulloch	676.0	82,442	699	122.0	64.7	30.2	0.7	1.9	4.5	5.4	11.1	27.0	13.0	11.1	10.1
13033	12260	2	Burke	827.0	24,310	1,635	29.4	49.5	46.4	0.9	0.9	3.8	6.0	14.5	12.6	12.0	11.8	11.9
13035	12060	1	Butts	183.7	25,781	1,573	140.3	67.4	28.7	0.7	1.0	3.8	5.3	11.6	13.0	14.8	13.2	13.1
13037		8	Calhoun	280.4	5,509	2,776	19.6	32.8	61.4	0.5	1.2	5.2	4.2	8.9	12.5	15.4	15.6	14.4
13039	41220	4	Camden	630.4	55,664	927	88.3	71.8	19.7	1.1	2.8	7.7	6.7	13.9	14.6	16.0	12.3	10.0
13043		7	Candler	243.1	11,037	2,341	45.4	62.0	25.6	0.5	1.0	12.2	6.3	14.8	12.7	11.7	10.9	12.3
13045	12060	1	Carroll	499.1	121,968	522	244.4	71.4	21.2	0.7	1.5	7.5	6.2	13.2	16.7	13.5	12.3	12.2
13047	16860	2	Catoosa	162.2	68,397	788	421.7	91.4	3.9	0.9	2.0	3.6	5.1	12.9	12.0	12.2	12.5	13.5
13049		6	Charlton	780.1	12,766	2,227	16.4	62.8	30.0	2.3	1.3	6.0	4.5	10.7	11.2	17.4	14.0	13.3
13051	42340	2	Chatham	433.1	296,329	240	684.2	49.1	41.7	0.7	3.9	6.8	5.7	11.5	14.2	15.6	13.0	11.3
13053	17980	2	Chattahoochee	248.7	9,048	2,483	36.4	60.2	19.0	1.8	5.4	17.7	8.3	12.2	29.1	25.4	11.2	4.5
13055	44900	6	Chattooga	313.3	24,932	1,616	79.6	83.7	10.7	0.8	0.8	5.7	5.9	12.5	11.9	12.8	12.1	12.9
13057	12060	1	Cherokee	421.1	274,615	255	652.1	78.6	8.3	0.7	3.1	11.3	5.3	13.2	12.7	11.9	13.6	14.5
13059	12020	3	Clarke	119.2	128,711	502	1,079.8	57.0	28.4	0.5	4.8	11.2	4.7	9.5	28.3	15.9	11.4	9.3
13061		9	Clay	195.4	2,882	2,968	14.7	37.7	58.9	0.6	1.5	2.3	5.2	11.1	10.4	10.0	11.5	9.1
13063	12060	1	Clayton	141.7	297,100	239	2,096.7	9.9	72.6	0.7	5.5	13.5	6.9	15.6	14.4	15.6	13.0	12.6
13065		6	Clinch	815.0	6,725	2,680	8.3	66.2	28.1	1.1	0.7	5.7	6.6	14.2	12.8	12.7	11.5	12.8
13067	12060	1	Cobb	339.8	766,802	86	2,256.6	52.2	29.4	0.7	6.5	13.7	5.6	12.8	13.2	14.5	14.2	13.9
13069	20060	7	Coffee	592.3	43,386	1,116	73.3	58.0	29.4	0.6	1.0	12.4	6.5	13.8	13.7	14.5	13.0	12.6
13071	34220	6	Colquitt	547.0	45,812	1,065	83.8	55.1	23.8	0.6	1.1	20.5	6.4	14.6	13.1	12.7	12.9	12.3
13073	12260	2	Columbia	290.2	159,639	425	550.1	68.2	20.6	0.8	6.0	7.6	5.9	14.6	12.3	13.5	14.8	12.6
13075		6	Cook	228.5	17,225	1,955	75.4	64.6	28.6	0.7	1.0	6.6	5.9	14.9	12.7	12.3	12.1	12.9
13077	12060	1	Coweta	441.1	149,956	453	340.0	71.1	19.5	0.7	3.0	7.7	5.5	13.3	12.6	12.5	13.3	14.3
13079	31420	3	Crawford	324.9	12,153	2,273	37.4	74.0	21.5	1.1	1.1	3.8	4.4	11.9	10.9	11.4	11.3	13.0
13081	18380	6	Crisp	272.7	19,879	1,823	72.9	50.5	44.9	0.6	1.3	4.1	5.8	13.6	12.1	11.5	11.8	11.8
13083	16860	2	Dade	174.0	16,326	2,013	93.8	94.4	2.1	1.2	1.4	2.6	4.7	11.1	14.9	11.6	11.5	11.9
13085	12060	1	Dawson	210.8	28,497	1,477	135.2	90.9	1.9	1.0	1.4	6.3	5.4	11.2	11.1	12.8	11.4	13.0
13087	12460	6	Decatur	597.2	29,038	1,455	48.6	50.2	42.8	0.6	0.8	6.9	6.7	13.4	13.1	12.7	11.8	12.4
13089	12060	1	DeKalb	267.7	757,718	87	2,830.5	31.0	54.6	0.7	7.3	8.6	6.5	12.5	11.8	16.5	14.4	12.7
13091		6	Dodge	496.0	19,759	1,835	39.8	65.4	30.5	0.7	0.8	4.1	4.9	10.7	11.5	13.0	12.8	14.2
13093		6	Dooly	392.6	10,885	2,353	27.7	43.3	48.8	0.7	1.0	7.5	4.0	8.7	11.1	12.0	13.2	13.7
13095	10500	3	Dougherty	328.6	84,844	678	258.2	24.4	71.9	0.5	1.3	3.2	6.5	13.4	15.7	13.3	11.4	10.9
13097	12060	1	Douglas	200.1	145,814	457	728.7	36.3	52.0	0.9	2.4	11.1	6.0	14.6	14.1	13.0	13.4	14.4
13099		6	Early	512.6	10,619	2,368	20.7	44.3	52.5	0.8	1.1	2.5	6.3	13.8	12.7	10.8	10.9	12.4
13101	46660	3	Echols	420.4	3,699	2,910	8.8	60.7	7.5	2.2	1.2	30.4	6.4	15.7	12.9	11.6	14.5	13.0

1. CBSA = Core Based Statistical Area. See Appendix A for explanation. See Appendix B for list of metropolitan areas with component counties. 2. County type code from the Economic Research Service of USDA Rural-Urban Continuum Codes. See Appendix A for definition. 3. Dry land or land partially or temporarily covered by water. 4. May be of any race.

STATE County	Population, 2021 (cont.): Age (percent) (cont.): 55 to 64 years	Population, 2021 (cont.): Age (percent) (cont.): 65 to 74 years	Population, 2021 (cont.): Age (percent) (cont.): 75 years and over	Population, 2021 (cont.): Percent female	Population change, 2000–2021: Total persons: 2010	Population change, 2000–2021: Total persons: 2020	Population change, 2000–2021: Percent change: 2010–2020	Population change, 2000–2021: Percent change: 2020–2021	Population change, 2000–2021: Components of change, 2020–2021: Births	Population change, 2000–2021: Components of change, 2020–2021: Deaths	Population change, 2000–2021: Components of change, 2020–2021: Net Migration	Households, 2016–2020: Number	Households, 2016–2020: Persons per household	Households, 2016–2020: Percent: Family house-holds	Households, 2016–2020: Percent: Female family house-holder[1]	Households, 2016–2020: Percent: One person
	16	17	18	19	20	21	22	23	24	25	26	27	28	29	30	31
FLORIDA—Cont'd																
Putnam	15.5	14.3	9.4	50.7	74,364	73,321	-1.4	1.2	986	1,517	1,391	29,822	2.4	61.0	14.1	31.8
St. Johns	14.3	12.7	7.9	51.3	190,039	273,425	43.9	7.0	2,721	3,266	19,857	91,253	2.8	74.0	8.8	20.7
St. Lucie	14.2	13.8	10.7	51.2	277,789	329,226	18.5	4.4	3,751	5,442	16,272	118,527	2.7	68.9	12.6	25.1
Santa Rosa	14.2	10.4	6.0	49.0	151,372	188,000	24.2	3.2	2,342	2,502	6,211	65,697	2.6	72.9	11.0	21.3
Sarasota	15.7	19.2	18.0	52.4	379,448	434,006	14.4	3.0	3,372	9,340	19,359	189,228	2.2	62.1	8.5	30.9
Seminole	12.9	9.8	6.6	51.6	422,718	470,856	11.4	-0.2	5,544	5,407	-977	178,094	2.6	67.4	12.0	25.5
Sumter	13.8	31.4	26.8	50.4	93,420	129,752	38.9	4.5	549	3,338	8,846	59,076	2.0	67.0	4.8	28.9
Suwannee	14.3	12.6	9.2	48.7	41,551	43,474	4.6	2.3	542	871	1,358	15,149	2.8	70.3	11.7	25.2
Taylor	13.2	12.3	8.7	45.5	22,570	21,796	-3.4	0.1	254	413	178	7,172	2.5	71.3	14.7	26.5
Union	13.9	8.8	6.1	35.5	15,535	16,147	3.9	1.2	179	367	380	4,008	2.4	71.7	15.3	23.5
Volusia	15.3	14.5	10.5	51.0	494,593	553,543	11.9	2.0	5,818	10,709	15,960	220,386	2.4	61.9	10.5	30.3
Wakulla	14.0	10.5	5.6	45.8	30,776	33,764	9.7	2.7	379	489	1,044	11,382	2.6	73.5	10.1	21.4
Walton	16.1	12.9	7.2	49.5	55,043	75,305	36.8	6.3	1,023	1,121	4,931	28,635	2.4	70.0	10.4	24.2
Washington	13.9	10.6	6.9	45.6	24,896	25,318	1.7	0.5	315	439	239	9,037	2.5	65.8	16.1	28.2
GEORGIA	12.4	9.1	5.5	51.2	9,687,653	10,711,908	10.6	0.8	150,732	130,940	67,437	3,830,264	2.7	67.0	14.9	27.3
Appling	13.2	11.2	7.3	49.9	18,236	18,444	1.1	0.2	267	310	85	6,650	2.7	73.2	14.2	25.3
Atkinson	12.4	8.6	5.2	49.2	8,375	8,286	-1.1	1.3	160	95	37	2,953	2.8	69.6	14.2	26.9
Bacon	11.5	10.9	6.3	51.2	11,096	11,140	0.4	-0.5	172	184	-51	3,743	2.8	65.1	15.1	28.7
Baker	15.8	15.6	9.3	49.9	3,451	2,876	-16.7	-2.0	25	54	-27	1,448	2.1	58.8	13.7	38.1
Baldwin	12.8	10.5	6.5	49.0	45,720	43,799	-4.2	0.0	481	732	227	16,698	2.4	61.2	15.7	31.3
Banks	14.1	11.3	6.9	48.8	18,395	18,035	-2.0	2.9	247	233	520	6,941	2.7	75.3	7.9	23.6
Barrow	11.7	8.2	4.7	50.7	69,367	83,505	20.4	3.8	1,316	962	2,819	27,268	3.0	75.7	12.7	20.5
Bartow	13.5	9.2	5.4	50.5	100,157	108,901	8.7	1.8	1,606	1,556	1,888	37,905	2.8	73.4	13.2	22.2
Ben Hill	13.4	11.4	6.9	52.8	17,634	17,194	-2.5	-0.2	249	339	52	6,612	2.5	63.4	22.0	32.2
Berrien	14.0	10.3	7.1	50.5	19,286	18,160	-5.8	-0.1	273	341	53	7,391	2.6	66.9	13.3	29.1
Bibb	12.4	9.9	6.3	53.0	155,547	157,346	1.2	-0.4	2,430	2,584	-460	58,154	2.5	59.6	19.9	35.3
Bleckley	13.4	9.4	7.9	51.8	13,063	12,583	-3.7	0.2	164	215	74	4,250	2.7	72.1	14.1	23.5
Brantley	14.3	10.8	6.6	50.4	18,411	18,021	-2.1	0.4	250	328	156	6,763	2.8	62.9	10.6	34.4
Brooks	15.7	12.6	7.8	51.6	16,243	16,301	0.4	-0.2	199	291	60	6,392	2.4	64.4	13.4	32.3
Bryan	10.0	6.8	3.9	50.5	30,233	44,738	48.0	4.9	711	420	1,929	13,503	2.8	77.1	13.2	17.7
Bulloch	10.2	7.7	4.4	51.0	70,217	81,099	15.5	1.7	1,048	860	1,143	27,967	2.5	60.8	14.1	27.3
Burke	14.0	11.0	6.2	52.2	23,316	24,596	5.5	-1.2	335	388	-232	7,953	2.8	69.5	16.5	28.7
Butts	13.4	9.6	6.0	46.6	23,655	25,434	7.5	1.4	329	429	446	8,342	2.6	73.6	18.6	22.0
Calhoun	12.5	9.5	7.1	38.7	6,694	5,573	-16.7	-1.1	62	76	-50	1,726	2.6	70.5	28.4	22.7
Camden	11.7	9.3	5.5	48.5	50,513	54,768	8.4	1.6	886	566	569	19,746	2.7	72.3	15.7	22.5
Candler	12.8	11.4	7.1	51.0	10,998	10,981	-0.2	0.5	170	218	102	4,042	2.6	67.3	18.2	30.7
Carroll	11.9	8.6	5.3	51.2	110,527	119,148	7.8	2.4	1,910	1,627	2,548	42,196	2.7	71.7	16.2	22.3
Catoosa	13.2	11.1	7.5	51.4	63,942	67,872	6.1	0.8	794	1,025	757	25,151	2.7	72.0	10.8	24.4
Charlton	12.8	9.0	7.0	41.1	12,171	12,518	2.9	2.0	136	184	298	3,826	3.1	68.6	10.3	25.0
Chatham	12.2	10.2	6.4	51.8	265,128	295,291	11.4	0.4	4,262	3,772	532	109,868	2.5	60.9	16.3	30.4
Chattahoochee	4.2	2.9	2.2	35.1	11,267	9,565	-15.1	-5.4	196	47	-659	2,550	2.8	76.1	19.4	20.7
Chattooga	13.6	11.1	7.3	48.9	26,015	24,965	-4.0	-0.1	342	448	72	9,106	2.5	62.7	11.6	32.5
Cherokee	13.3	9.9	5.5	50.5	214,346	266,620	24.4	3.0	3,272	2,607	7,362	90,372	2.8	75.6	9.3	19.2
Clarke	8.9	7.5	4.5	52.5	116,714	128,671	10.2	0.0	1,537	1,126	-394	50,284	2.3	48.3	13.4	34.3
Clay	14.0	17.0	11.7	52.5	3,183	2,848	-10.5	1.2	34	49	50	1,313	2.2	51.1	14.9	44.6
Clayton	11.5	7.2	3.2	53.2	259,424	297,595	14.7	-0.2	4,837	2,867	-2,533	96,826	2.9	67.1	26.6	27.7
Clinch	12.7	10.3	6.3	51.6	6,798	6,749	-0.7	-0.4	117	123	-19	2,387	2.6	69.9	18.3	21.1
Cobb	12.5	8.5	4.8	51.3	688,078	766,149	11.3	0.1	10,469	7,084	-2,913	283,359	2.6	67.2	12.8	25.7
Coffee	11.9	8.9	5.3	48.3	42,356	43,092	1.7	0.7	651	653	289	14,832	2.7	68.1	14.8	28.1
Colquitt	11.8	9.6	6.5	50.1	45,498	45,898	0.9	-0.2	708	732	-71	15,865	2.8	64.4	16.7	29.4
Columbia	11.9	9.2	5.2	50.9	124,053	156,010	25.8	2.3	2,115	1,606	3,127	48,233	3.2	75.3	10.8	21.8
Cook	12.6	10.0	6.6	51.7	17,212	17,229	0.1	0.0	237	296	52	6,202	2.8	69.1	12.8	27.5
Coweta	13.6	9.4	5.5	51.3	127,317	146,158	14.8	2.6	1,906	1,676	3,583	53,104	2.7	74.7	13.0	20.4
Crawford	17.2	12.6	7.4	49.7	12,630	12,130	-4.0	0.2	116	206	114	4,573	2.7	71.3	12.1	24.5
Crisp	13.4	12.2	7.7	52.4	23,439	20,128	-14.1	-1.2	306	412	-146	8,479	2.6	70.1	25.5	26.6
Dade	14.0	12.7	7.7	50.7	16,633	16,251	-2.3	0.5	176	304	204	6,155	2.4	71.3	9.3	25.3
Dawson	14.8	12.9	7.4	50.1	22,330	26,798	20.0	6.3	369	338	1,690	9,521	2.6	73.7	9.8	22.4
Decatur	13.0	9.9	7.0	51.0	27,842	29,367	5.5	-1.1	428	544	-215	9,684	2.6	69.3	18.9	27.9
DeKalb	11.9	8.6	4.9	52.6	691,893	764,382	10.5	-0.9	12,347	7,600	-11,353	283,799	2.6	57.9	16.6	33.9
Dodge	13.8	11.1	8.0	47.5	21,796	19,925	-8.6	-0.8	237	399	-6	7,530	2.5	69.6	14.4	26.7
Dooly	15.3	13.0	8.9	44.9	14,918	11,208	-24.9	-2.9	135	259	-197	4,979	2.4	69.7	21.0	26.4
Dougherty	12.2	10.4	6.4	53.8	94,565	85,790	-9.3	-1.1	1,418	1,504	-875	34,233	2.5	58.9	24.1	36.1
Douglas	12.4	7.9	4.3	52.4	132,403	144,237	8.9	1.1	2,038	1,604	1,122	49,788	2.9	71.0	17.8	23.3
Early	13.4	10.8	8.8	53.4	11,008	10,854	-1.4	-2.2	151	205	-180	4,196	2.4	65.6	23.6	32.3
Echols	12.5	8.8	4.6	48.4	4,034	3,697	-8.4	0.1	57	44	-11	1,497	2.6	73.3	11.8	25.3

1. No spouse present.

STATE County	Persons in group quarters, 2021	Daytime Population, 2016–2020: Number	Daytime Population, 2016–2020: Employment/ residence ratio	Births, 2021: Total	Births, 2021: Rate[1]	Deaths, 2021: Number	Deaths, 2021: Rate[1]	Persons under 65 with no health insurance, 2019: Number	Persons under 65 with no health insurance, 2019: Percent	Medicare, 2021: Total beneficiaries	Medicare, 2021: Enrolled in Original Medicare	Medicare, 2021: Enrolled in Medicare Advantage	COVID-19 Deaths, 2020: Number	COVID-19 Deaths, 2020: Rate[1]
	32	33	34	35	36	37	38	39	40	41	42	43	44	45
FLORIDA—Cont'd														
Putnam	1,210	67,423	0.8	811	11.0	1,188	16.1	9,959	18.2	20,044	11,513	8,531	78	1.1
St. Johns	2,707	235,022	0.8	2,145	7.5	2,673	9.4	22,830	10.9	60,527	41,223	19,304	111	0.4
St. Lucie	2,719	286,223	0.7	3,035	9.0	4,429	13.1	44,138	18.1	82,954	44,890	38,064	381	1.2
Santa Rosa	6,042	146,579	0.6	1,877	9.8	2,023	10.6	17,956	12.0	36,535	23,331	13,204	134	0.7
Sarasota	5,512	455,357	1.2	2,725	6.2	7,520	17.0	43,250	16.0	149,539	98,404	51,135	447	1.0
Seminole	3,119	439,616	0.9	4,491	9.5	4,367	9.3	45,093	11.4	82,284	43,862	38,422	284	0.6
Sumter	7,704	140,663	1.4	434	3.3	2,687	20.2	5,957	12.5	74,807	40,166	34,641	129	1.0
Suwannee	2,287	41,707	0.9	460	10.5	684	15.5	5,457	17.0	11,010	7,110	3,900	74	1.7
Taylor	2,394	22,245	1.1	212	9.7	315	14.5	2,149	14.8	5,002	3,348	1,654	33	1.5
Union	5,108	15,432	1.0	144	8.9	294	18.1	1,046	12.5	2,196	1,430	766	66	4.1
Volusia	13,860	520,476	0.9	4,650	8.3	8,523	15.2	66,872	16.6	152,020	70,988	81,032	446	0.8
Wakulla	3,182	26,109	0.5	316	9.2	402	11.7	3,131	12.4	6,424	2,890	3,533	30	0.9
Walton	1,889	73,099	1.1	844	10.8	884	11.3	9,397	16.4	16,802	11,444	5,357	53	0.7
Washington	2,488	23,448	0.8	264	10.4	339	13.3	3,248	17.7	5,694	3,823	1,872	33	1.3
GEORGIA	253,468	10,518,780	1.0	121,269	11.3	105,276	9.8	1,387,604	15.7	1,772,282	1,011,229	761,053	10,209	1.0
Appling	367	18,615	1.0	210	11.4	251	13.6	3,001	20.6	3,895	2,247	1,648	49	2.7
Atkinson	16	7,604	0.8	129	15.5	68	8.1	1,615	23.8	1,378	739	640	11	1.3
Bacon	264	10,950	1.0	127	11.4	143	12.9	1,743	19.6	2,253	1,342	911	26	2.3
Baker	0	2,604	0.5	20	7.1	36	12.7	411	18.1	706	332	374	D	D
Baldwin	5,508	42,584	0.9	399	9.1	579	13.2	5,396	16.9	9,135	4,541	4,594	52	1.2
Banks	0	15,565	0.6	192	10.5	179	9.8	3,350	21.3	3,596	1,981	1,615	21	1.2
Barrow	267	65,736	0.6	1,065	12.5	785	9.2	12,872	17.8	13,495	7,413	6,082	68	0.8
Bartow	892	101,219	0.9	1,272	11.6	1,252	11.4	16,360	18.0	19,013	10,912	8,101	121	1.1
Ben Hill	284	17,674	1.1	202	11.8	270	15.7	2,279	17.1	3,846	2,056	1,791	50	2.9
Berrien	109	16,472	0.6	220	12.1	278	15.3	3,313	21.1	3,816	2,362	1,454	32	1.8
Bibb	6,788	172,936	1.3	1,970	12.6	2,051	13.1	17,632	14.6	31,208	16,991	14,216	208	1.3
Bleckley	1,273	10,788	0.6	123	9.8	167	13.3	1,343	14.5	2,570	1,746	823	32	2.5
Brantley	45	14,502	0.3	203	11.2	277	15.3	2,899	18.6	3,581	2,213	1,368	32	1.8
Brooks	51	12,603	0.5	171	10.5	226	13.9	2,317	19.2	3,996	2,373	1,623	31	1.9
Bryan	118	28,985	0.5	580	12.6	327	7.1	4,479	12.6	5,986	3,516	2,470	21	0.5
Bulloch	6,499	74,501	0.9	835	10.2	724	8.8	10,565	16.7	10,973	6,719	4,254	57	0.7
Burke	292	25,689	1.3	266	10.9	313	12.8	2,775	15.1	4,789	2,374	2,415	28	1.1
Butts	2,961	22,818	0.8	265	10.3	348	13.6	2,762	15.3	4,833	2,386	2,447	43	1.7
Calhoun	1,437	6,208	1.0	54	9.8	44	8.0	636	18.4	1,194	666	528	10	1.8
Camden	1,894	51,256	0.9	709	12.8	464	8.4	6,350	14.2	9,186	6,262	2,924	23	0.4
Candler	235	9,812	0.8	140	12.7	170	15.4	1,883	22.2	2,421	1,275	1,146	35	3.2
Carroll	3,877	112,210	0.9	1,555	12.9	1,318	10.9	16,536	16.7	21,544	12,138	9,407	128	1.1
Catoosa	395	53,553	0.6	623	9.1	830	12.2	6,996	12.7	14,120	8,926	5,193	63	0.9
Charlton	2,261	11,603	0.7	114	9.0	147	11.6	1,777	20.3	2,169	1,355	814	19	1.5
Chatham	14,823	325,327	1.3	3,447	11.7	3,039	10.3	37,624	16.4	51,262	28,463	22,800	212	0.7
Chattahoochee	2,294	18,547	2.3	152	16.4	43	4.6	826	10.7	611	336	275	D	D
Chattooga	1,219	22,841	0.8	285	11.4	350	14.0	3,309	17.3	5,799	3,162	2,637	39	1.6
Cherokee	1,525	208,049	0.6	2,588	9.5	2,132	7.9	31,738	14.3	43,730	26,217	17,513	132	0.5
Clarke	10,378	145,254	1.3	1,224	9.5	914	7.1	17,173	16.8	17,308	10,320	6,987	53	0.4
Clay	50	2,704	0.8	27	9.4	35	12.2	343	17.3	774	415	359	D	D
Clayton	4,723	276,755	0.9	3,853	13.0	2,227	7.5	46,395	18.2	37,074	16,716	20,358	213	0.7
Clinch	121	6,817	1.1	92	13.7	92	13.7	962	17.9	1,469	824	645	15	2.2
Cobb	9,402	744,645	1.0	8,419	11.0	5,819	7.6	94,503	14.4	106,424	64,235	42,188	503	0.7
Coffee	3,149	44,102	1.1	517	12.0	514	11.9	6,927	20.7	7,327	4,251	3,076	101	2.3
Colquitt	1,133	43,561	0.9	558	12.2	578	12.6	8,674	23.5	8,848	5,071	3,777	57	1.2
Columbia	538	123,361	0.6	1,676	10.6	1,296	8.2	16,534	12.2	24,439	16,221	8,218	110	0.7
Cook	101	15,858	0.8	191	11.1	240	13.9	2,638	18.7	3,495	2,052	1,442	34	2.0
Coweta	458	122,935	0.7	1,524	10.3	1,343	9.1	15,969	12.5	24,596	14,109	10,488	112	0.8
Crawford	99	9,844	0.5	85	7.0	161	13.3	1,717	17.4	2,751	1,473	1,278	D	D
Crisp	281	22,933	1.1	240	12.0	321	16.1	2,888	16.7	4,480	2,313	2,167	47	2.3
Dade	956	14,090	0.7	138	8.5	237	14.6	1,972	16.5	3,737	2,317	1,421	D	D
Dawson	90	23,385	0.9	312	11.2	280	10.1	3,496	16.8	5,412	3,304	2,108	19	0.7
Decatur	1,105	25,736	0.9	331	11.3	429	14.7	3,810	18.3	5,801	3,503	2,298	46	1.6
DeKalb	11,569	727,069	0.9	10,049	13.2	6,134	8.1	109,204	16.9	106,989	53,718	53,271	522	0.7
Dodge	1,664	18,715	0.8	194	9.8	317	16.0	2,518	16.8	4,188	2,570	1,618	71	3.6
Dooly	1,480	13,364	1.0	108	9.8	210	19.1	1,612	18.7	2,214	1,175	1,039	20	1.8
Dougherty	4,313	101,492	1.4	1,152	13.5	1,190	14.0	11,325	16.5	17,469	9,237	8,232	199	2.3
Douglas	998	126,142	0.7	1,631	11.2	1,269	8.7	18,875	14.8	21,224	11,123	10,101	113	0.8
Early	133	9,918	0.9	126	11.8	168	15.7	1,238	15.5	2,425	1,401	1,023	36	3.3
Echols	0	2,913	0.4	47	12.7	26	7.0	793	23.4	562	357	205	D	D

1. Per 1,000 estimated resident population.

STATE County	COVID-19 Vaccinations, 2021–2022: Number	COVID-19 Vaccinations, 2021–2022: Percent[5]	Education: School enrollment and attainment, 2016–2020: Enrollment[1]: Total	Enrollment[1]: Percent private	Attainment[2] (percent): High school graduate or less	Attainment[2] (percent): Bachelor's degree or more	Local government expenditures,[3] 2018–2019: Total current spending (mil dol)	Local government expenditures,[3] 2018–2019: Current spending per student (dollars)	Money income, 2016–2020: Per capita income[4]	Households: Median income (dollars)	Households: Percent with income of less than $50,000	Households: Percent with income of $200,000 or more	Income and poverty, 2020: Median household income (dollars)	Percent below poverty level: All persons	Percent below poverty level: Children under 18 years	Percent below poverty level: Children 5 to 17 years in families
	46	47	48	49	50	51	52	53	54	55	56	57	58	59	60	61
FLORIDA—Cont'd																
Putnam	31,353	42.1	15,187	18.0	59.6	13.6	112.7	10,250	22,257	40,068	61.1	1.9	36,527	24.3	33.0	31.7
St. Johns	186,238	70.4	61,195	16.2	27.1	44.5	362.9	8,554	43,433	83,803	27.9	13.0	94,343	8.1	9.3	8.2
St. Lucie	192,160	58.5	67,895	17.7	44.9	22.5	390.3	9,425	28,426	55,237	45.7	3.8	59,023	13.8	21.2	20.2
Santa Rosa	99,981	54.2	41,289	14.0	35.7	27.3	255.3	8,967	32,322	70,663	35.3	5.8	71,583	9.4	11.8	11.3
Sarasota	303,100	69.9	65,654	16.9	34.5	36.4	499.9	11,595	44,402	64,644	37.9	8.7	66,138	8.7	13.8	13.6
Seminole	292,914	62.1	117,706	17.6	26.0	41.0	589.5	8,634	36,016	70,297	35.2	8.0	71,930	8.0	10.4	10.1
Sumter	106,141	80.2	9,736	17.6	38.3	32.0	87.7	9,925	35,879	59,618	40.5	3.3	60,278	12.3	34.8	32.0
Suwannee	16,965	38.2	9,285	19.0	58.7	15.7	56.9	9,547	23,389	46,280	52.8	2.3	46,264	17.7	28.3	27.3
Taylor	8,685	40.3	4,012	23.6	65.5	10.8	28.3	10,185	19,492	38,295	59.2	1.7	45,527	19.3	25.8	25.7
Union	5,469	35.9	2,330	8.5	60.9	10.5	21.0	8,936	20,663	55,139	47.0	1.9	49,313	20.7	20.3	19.6
Volusia	330,394	59.7	111,383	20.8	40.7	24.4	563.2	8,908	29,859	52,407	47.5	4.1	55,463	11.6	14.0	14.8
Wakulla	15,178	45.0	7,046	12.0	47.1	18.6	45.0	8,899	28,320	67,480	36.1	4.1	64,671	10.3	15.7	14.5
Walton	36,466	49.2	14,369	12.0	39.6	30.0	99.5	10,132	35,996	67,390	38.2	6.7	74,108	11.4	18.0	17.3
Washington	8,302	32.6	4,573	13.0	60.5	12.1	35.4	10,273	19,375	37,260	60.3	1.3	44,661	20.4	28.7	26.6
GEORGIA	5,805,736	54.7	2,743,653	15.0	39.6	32.2	19,759.8	11,182	32,427	61,224	41.5	7.1	62,800	14.0	19.5	18.8
Appling	6,599	35.9	4,427	7.7	60.3	9.5	40.0	11,153	21,675	37,924	59.9	1.8	44,871	19.9	29.9	29.0
Atkinson	3,237	39.6	1,983	1.3	66.5	12.2	18.7	11,034	20,887	35,703	62.3	2.1	39,633	21.6	33.8	32.4
Bacon	3,418	30.6	2,281	5.7	62.3	9.3	23.8	11,113	19,882	36,692	60.6	0.6	41,756	21.1	29.0	27.0
Baker	1,574	51.8	588	13.9	52.2	21.4	5.4	19,039	25,691	34,034	61.9	0.5	43,696	23.7	39.5	40.6
Baldwin	19,852	44.2	13,545	13.2	46.1	24.3	57.4	11,169	26,934	46,250	53.3	2.3	49,350	22.6	30.9	29.9
Banks	5,863	30.5	4,227	11.9	58.5	15.8	30.9	11,232	24,303	50,912	49.3	3.1	62,836	11.6	17.2	15.9
Barrow	33,363	40.1	21,043	15.8	47.7	20.2	144.8	10,298	25,849	62,990	38.7	3.1	64,460	10.1	13.0	13.4
Bartow	40,238	37.3	24,295	13.0	49.6	19.8	184.2	10,248	27,047	61,226	41.3	4.1	64,980	10.2	15.3	14.5
Ben Hill	6,438	38.6	3,867	9.1	62.6	11.0	34.6	11,060	18,241	32,077	69.2	1.0	39,305	22.3	32.7	31.0
Berrien	6,566	33.9	4,113	6.5	61.0	13.2	30.8	9,734	20,545	42,089	56.3	0.7	45,094	18.9	26.6	25.8
Bibb	70,441	46.0	40,122	24.2	44.6	25.3	282.7	11,585	25,519	41,317	56.8	4.0	44,467	28.0	37.4	35.3
Bleckley	4,700	36.5	3,405	3.4	48.9	17.9	26.7	10,403	20,502	46,992	52.7	1.5	51,448	18.5	28.1	28.0
Brantley	4,986	26.1	4,112	11.2	65.1	6.9	36.2	10,466	18,883	34,679	61.7	0.0	39,256	17.8	26.6	25.6
Brooks	7,448	48.2	3,294	5.3	49.9	16.5	27.4	12,618	26,115	37,516	60.3	4.1	42,973	20.6	32.5	32.1
Bryan	21,407	54.0	12,137	15.3	33.2	33.0	87.4	9,070	32,825	76,121	30.7	6.6	81,890	8.0	9.8	9.8
Bulloch	27,373	34.4	28,774	6.2	40.4	27.6	123.3	11,395	25,121	48,786	51.5	3.3	48,629	20.7	23.1	23.8
Burke	12,791	57.1	5,823	18.6	55.1	14.5	62.7	15,085	24,050	45,699	54.9	3.5	44,870	20.0	31.6	30.2
Butts	8,459	33.9	4,806	14.8	61.2	11.1	38.2	10,971	25,343	48,282	51.7	2.1	52,720	20.8	37.0	40.3
Calhoun	2,999	48.5	1,359	11.7	61.4	11.8	13.9	12,226	15,461	41,962	57.8	1.4	37,984	34.4	35.9	34.0
Camden	30,992	56.7	13,082	10.4	40.2	22.5	92.2	9,858	29,449	60,594	43.2	3.0	67,525	9.4	12.9	14.2
Candler	4,560	42.2	2,803	7.4	62.3	11.4	28.6	9,155	20,897	36,955	60.1	1.7	42,583	20.1	31.8	29.8
Carroll	45,445	37.9	32,871	9.0	48.4	22.1	205.9	10,115	26,495	59,197	43.7	3.2	64,554	16.8	21.5	19.1
Catoosa	29,868	44.2	15,824	11.5	43.6	23.0	121.2	11,273	28,537	58,932	43.1	4.0	61,906	10.1	14.2	13.1
Charlton	3,387	25.3	2,978	10.5	61.7	12.8	18.3	10,655	19,228	42,743	57.3	1.7	46,061	25.5	30.6	26.9
Chatham	163,012	56.3	76,926	27.3	34.0	34.4	437.7	11,650	33,106	57,739	43.3	6.1	56,357	15.6	24.5	24.2
Chattahoochee	28,773	95.0	2,320	17.1	36.7	27.0	10.4	11,379	23,894	45,700	56.0	1.6	51,811	15.6	14.7	15.9
Chattooga	9,444	38.1	5,241	8.1	66.1	9.7	45.6	11,082	18,523	37,351	64.4	0.8	44,399	18.8	26.7	25.8
Cherokee	128,629	49.7	65,592	16.3	31.3	36.9	442.6	10,237	38,153	84,817	27.0	9.8	90,675	6.7	8.8	8.4
Clarke	59,831	46.6	49,915	7.9	30.4	45.4	193.1	14,288	25,343	40,363	57.6	3.8	46,693	24.6	23.1	21.7
Clay	1,829	64.5	711	2.8	51.2	16.9	4.0	19,866	22,389	32,434	72.0	0.8	35,937	24.1	43.3	43.4
Clayton	127,479	43.6	82,912	11.5	48.5	19.1	635.3	9,476	21,804	49,460	50.7	1.6	49,370	16.8	25.0	24.3
Clinch	2,649	40.0	1,680	0.1	64.0	10.8	15.8	11,697	17,539	38,844	59.7	1.1	43,088	20.4	29.9	28.4
Cobb	444,128	58.4	201,138	16.8	25.8	48.4	1,343.8	11,094	41,480	80,830	29.2	11.9	81,517	9.2	10.6	10.0
Coffee	16,130	37.3	10,294	9.4	62.8	12.2	81.2	10,514	20,659	42,526	58.1	1.8	44,520	23.1	32.7	32.2
Colquitt	18,304	40.1	11,293	5.1	63.7	13.7	102.4	10,695	20,530	36,799	60.8	2.0	41,673	20.4	28.9	27.7
Columbia	79,499	50.7	41,617	14.8	31.4	36.5	270.5	9,584	35,349	82,251	25.9	9.0	87,489	6.7	8.5	8.1
Cook	7,106	41.1	4,139	6.0	52.1	15.7	37.4	11,922	20,769	40,943	58.6	2.1	35,225	19.5	29.8	27.5
Coweta	66,273	44.6	36,233	19.4	36.9	33.3	248.4	10,384	36,884	79,795	29.9	8.0	84,121	8.6	11.8	10.5
Crawford	5,077	40.9	2,539	10.6	58.2	10.6	18.5	10,670	24,404	47,917	51.7	2.1	48,184	16.1	25.1	23.5
Crisp	9,797	43.8	5,638	8.3	57.1	13.7	45.6	11,532	25,402	38,272	60.2	4.5	36,871	24.5	36.0	34.6
Dade	7,399	45.9	3,919	34.7	55.1	15.8	23.0	10,566	24,964	40,384	57.8	3.7	41,069	13.0	15.5	15.6
Dawson	10,388	39.8	5,021	8.9	38.0	33.6	47.7	13,283	36,110	72,260	34.7	7.9	75,081	8.7	12.6	12.1
Decatur	12,964	49.1	5,739	4.2	53.7	14.0	52.4	10,333	21,810	40,567	60.2	1.5	42,996	25.6	36.8	35.8
DeKalb	428,342	56.4	195,443	22.2	30.3	45.6	1,332.7	12,565	37,523	65,116	38.9	9.9	69,545	15.8	23.8	26.6
Dodge	7,308	35.5	4,016	7.4	55.6	15.3	38.7	12,543	21,144	42,211	58.4	2.8	42,683	21.4	27.8	27.4
Dooly	5,007	37.4	2,702	12.3	61.6	12.9	14.9	12,072	25,198	48,039	51.7	3.0	45,112	27.0	35.2	32.2
Dougherty	43,307	49.2	26,195	10.0	44.9	22.2	174.7	12,360	22,647	40,947	60.1	2.3	40,793	27.4	38.1	37.9
Douglas	67,911	46.4	41,421	14.4	42.2	28.1	281.5	10,600	29,083	67,651	37.5	4.7	65,269	11.5	16.5	14.7
Early	4,983	48.9	2,357	11.5	57.5	13.7	24.0	11,908	21,992	34,811	64.2	1.1	39,697	24.0	36.2	34.8
Echols	1,247	31.1	863	4.6	70.2	7.8	9.5	10,849	23,768	44,454	54.8	2.4	45,378	20.6	31.2	28.7

1. All persons 3 years old and over enrolled in nursery school through college. 2. Persons 25 years old and over. 3. Elementary and secondary education expenditures. 4. Based on population estimated by the American Community Survey, 2016–2020. 5. CDC percent based on 2019 population estimate.

STATE County	Personal income, 2020										Earnings, 2020		
			Per capita[1]			Supplements to wages and salaries, employer contributions (mil dol)						Contributions for government social insurance (mil dol)	
	Total (mil dol)	Percent change 2019–2020	Dollars	Rank	Wages and salaries (mil dol)	Pension and insurance	Government social insurance	Proprietors' income (mil dol)	Dividends, interest, and rent (mil dol)	Personal transfer reecipts (mil dol)	Total (mil dol)	From employee and self-employed	From employer
	62	63	64	65	66	67	68	69	70	71	72	73	74
FLORIDA—Cont'd													
Putnam	2,720	8.5	36,354	2,842	779	141	54	107	447	1,142	1,082	95	54
St. Johns	20,609	8.6	73,944	118	4,362	587	302	786	5,405	3,037	6,038	452	302
St. Lucie	14,826	9.0	43,970	1,951	4,022	632	284	608	2,980	4,618	5,546	457	284
Santa Rosa	9,357	8.4	49,472	1,200	2,002	348	148	437	1,627	2,186	2,934	227	148
Sarasota	31,434	4.7	70,884	153	9,502	1,218	651	1,977	13,618	6,924	13,348	1,048	651
Seminole	25,322	4.0	53,403	826	12,006	1,494	810	1,133	4,585	5,019	15,444	1,009	810
Sumter	7,581	6.1	54,533	737	1,630	280	118	671	2,457	3,003	2,699	304	118
Suwannee	1,614	8.9	35,987	2,868	474	88	34	143	205	619	739	58	34
Taylor	718	8.7	33,227	3,018	300	54	21	28	108	288	403	31	21
Union	373	9.1	24,593	3,110	151	38	11	14	55	137	213	15	11
Volusia	26,096	6.0	46,475	1,581	8,433	1,247	591	1,213	5,715	8,104	11,484	929	591
Wakulla	1,371	8.5	39,938	2,463	286	57	20	53	188	345	416	34	20
Walton	5,355	9.4	69,862	169	1,358	183	96	448	1,846	857	2,084	148	96
Washington	852	8.8	32,862	3,033	258	49	18	37	128	320	362	29	18
GEORGIA	554,566	7.0	51,704	X	275,344	41,461	18,581	47,953	95,493	118,605	383,339	22,736	18,581
Appling	718	9.9	39,199	2,543	415	98	28	61	68	240	602	34	28
Atkinson	268	7.2	31,938	3,060	100	20	8	19	26	93	147	9	8
Bacon	422	16.1	38,281	2,651	163	34	12	36	40	150	244	14	12
Baker	128	5.4	43,156	2,041	23	4	2	16	19	41	45	2	2
Baldwin	1,642	7.7	36,399	2,838	623	147	41	46	279	629	857	55	41
Banks	722	4.7	37,333	2,758	150	28	10	39	103	212	228	14	10
Barrow	3,461	11.0	40,435	2,398	1,016	166	70	188	422	846	1,441	98	70
Bartow	4,676	9.2	42,734	2,102	2,080	356	147	229	631	1,228	2,812	177	147
Ben Hill	602	10.7	36,234	2,854	236	48	18	26	84	242	327	24	18
Berrien	684	8.4	35,260	2,923	144	33	10	41	102	245	229	17	10
Bibb	6,847	7.7	44,830	1,819	4,260	670	289	391	1,185	2,214	5,610	355	289
Bleckley	476	6.8	36,712	2,803	97	25	6	18	79	155	146	11	6
Brantley	576	9.7	30,007	3,088	109	26	8	36	56	222	179	14	8
Brooks	618	8.3	40,221	2,429	145	27	10	45	99	216	228	16	10
Bryan	2,309	8.9	56,648	592	396	79	27	99	308	445	601	41	27
Bulloch	2,860	9.6	35,376	2,915	1,100	231	73	130	463	816	1,534	91	73
Burke	951	10.0	41,973	2,202	1,434	207	89	86	100	308	1,816	103	89
Butts	951	9.8	37,403	2,751	325	59	24	30	126	304	438	32	24
Calhoun	177	11.4	28,426	3,098	42	11	3	25	21	76	80	5	3
Camden	2,175	7.8	39,262	2,540	928	235	72	37	374	606	1,273	74	72
Candler	402	10.3	36,613	2,813	115	27	8	34	53	148	184	12	8
Carroll	5,116	7.2	42,058	2,185	2,118	365	148	250	787	1,401	2,881	187	148
Catoosa	2,639	8.4	38,815	2,589	649	112	46	143	269	771	950	66	46
Charlton	365	10.5	27,192	3,103	94	18	6	10	37	133	128	10	6
Chatham	14,996	6.4	51,805	950	8,800	1,444	634	995	3,109	3,583	11,873	693	634
Chattahoochee	350	4.6	33,166	3,019	1,020	323	102	2	137	58	1,448	50	102
Chattooga	841	9.0	33,855	2,985	202	48	14	37	93	352	301	26	14
Cherokee	14,929	7.0	56,278	619	3,428	509	235	999	2,081	2,528	5,172	344	235
Clarke	4,804	7.2	37,588	2,729	3,726	758	236	278	1,019	1,226	4,998	265	236
Clay	111	12.0	38,731	2,601	21	5	2	7	17	50	35	2	2
Clayton	9,570	15.5	32,702	3,041	7,628	1,444	497	408	1,009	3,314	9,977	560	497
Clinch	291	13.8	44,238	1,906	104	21	8	47	25	97	181	11	8
Cobb	48,229	4.9	63,214	311	26,007	3,141	1,718	3,697	8,637	7,170	34,562	2,021	1,718
Coffee	1,535	7.8	35,507	2,906	725	135	53	76	189	516	988	61	53
Colquitt	1,704	10.7	37,418	2,747	636	131	45	150	224	577	962	58	45
Columbia	8,728	7.8	54,420	749	1,714	290	118	409	1,442	1,668	2,532	173	118
Cook	628	8.4	36,301	2,848	167	37	12	21	86	221	236	17	12
Coweta	7,860	7.9	52,106	928	1,980	329	138	236	1,176	1,527	2,683	180	138
Crawford	459	7.5	37,563	2,732	52	12	4	17	59	155	84	6	4
Crisp	821	6.9	37,250	2,766	348	66	25	43	109	307	481	31	25
Dade	599	6.4	37,327	2,760	161	33	12	42	83	194	247	19	12
Dawson	1,306	8.6	48,170	1,362	351	58	25	76	222	286	510	37	25
Decatur	1,082	9.7	40,879	2,346	343	71	24	93	171	363	531	33	24
DeKalb	42,999	6.9	56,428	615	20,400	2,870	1,387	2,746	8,132	8,037	27,402	1,631	1,387
Dodge	683	6.3	33,419	3,011	186	46	12	23	93	261	267	20	12
Dooly	456	3.0	34,582	2,959	146	29	12	47	68	151	233	16	12
Dougherty	3,473	10.0	40,161	2,438	2,332	426	163	161	532	1,316	3,081	189	163
Douglas	5,959	10.5	40,264	2,423	2,128	332	148	207	680	1,592	2,815	182	148
Early	430	7.8	42,889	2,076	221	46	15	29	52	152	311	19	15
Echols	128	13.5	31,945	3,057	20	5	1	6	16	35	33	2	1

1. Based on the resident population estimated as of July 1 of the year shown.

STATE County	Earnings, 2020 (cont.) — Percent by selected industries: Farm	Mining, quarrying, and extractions	Construction	Manu-facturing	Information; professional, scientific, technical services	Retail trade	Finance, insurance, real estate, and leasing	Health care and social assistance	Govern-ment	Social Security beneficiaries, December 2020: Number	Rate[1]	Supple-mental Security Income recipients, 2020	Housing units, 2021: Total	Percent change, 2010–2021
	75	76	77	78	79	80	81	82	83	84	85	86	87	88
FLORIDA—Cont'd														
Putnam	2.2	D	7.0	13.2	D	9.4	3.6	13.0	23.4	22,070	298	3,081	36,206	0.5
St. Johns	0.5	D	7.6	7.4	11.0	8.5	10.0	11.0	12.2	62,510	214	2,507	125,222	4.1
St. Lucie	1.0	0.0	8.0	5.0	6.9	8.9	5.1	15.5	18.4	88,720	258	7,241	153,312	3.1
Santa Rosa	0.6	0.2	9.3	3.1	9.4	9.0	5.9	12.4	23.3	39,880	206	2,624	78,344	2.8
Sarasota	0.1	0.0	10.9	4.6	13.5	8.6	9.4	18.2	8.9	150,765	337	4,708	258,634	1.6
Seminole	0.1	0.0	12.1	3.8	17.5	8.5	12.8	9.3	7.7	85,870	183	7,577	196,649	1.2
Sumter	1.0	0.3	24.3	4.9	5.0	7.4	7.4	D	15.7	77,025	568	1,693	79,678	4.8
Suwannee	9.5	0.6	6.1	13.7	2.5	11.9	2.4	7.7	21.5	12,360	278	1,523	18,986	0.6
Taylor	1.1	D	5.8	28.7	D	8.9	2.2	D	19.6	5,595	256	772	11,133	0.3
Union	1.7	0.0	6.8	0.5	D	D	1.3	D	56.3	2,540	155	390	4,767	0.9
Volusia	0.9	0.0	8.0	7.0	7.7	9.9	7.1	18.4	13.1	162,365	288	12,698	277,289	1.6
Wakulla	0.3	0.1	9.9	12.8	7.4	7.3	11.6	4.8	28.1	7,170	207	660	14,112	3.0
Walton	0.6	0.1	13.0	1.3	10.1	10.4	12.0	8.8	11.7	17,405	217	961	58,570	3.0
Washington	2.1	D	8.5	2.5	D	7.4	2.7	D	32.8	6,365	250	813	10,931	0.6
GEORGIA	0.4	0.2	6.0	8.1	15.9	5.9	10.2	9.8	15.3	1,902,790	176	258,304	4,475,274	1.2
Appling	6.5	0.0	4.8	7.7	1.4	8.4	1.9	D	12.8	4,280	232	623	8,527	0.3
Atkinson	8.9	D	2.4	44.3	1.4	2.8	3.1	4.6	15.5	1,550	185	348	3,512	1.2
Bacon	10.9	D	D	14.4	D	4.4	4.1	D	14.6	2,395	216	379	4,821	0.2
Baker	35.1	0.0	0.2	0.5	D	3.2	D	D	14.3	780	277	115	1,452	0.3
Baldwin	0.0	D	3.8	9.2	D	10.3	4.4	15.9	35.9	9,955	227	1,515	20,112	0.5
Banks	3.4	0.0	11.6	10.1	D	8.0	D	D	21.3	4,170	225	326	7,327	1.3
Barrow	-0.8	D	12.7	11.7	4.3	14.1	4.7	8.1	14.7	14,900	172	1,888	31,151	3.1
Bartow	0.1	0.4	8.0	25.8	4.4	7.4	2.7	7.8	12.4	21,165	191	2,268	43,469	2.0
Ben Hill	2.7	0.0	1.7	24.7	1.8	7.0	3.2	D	17.0	4,045	236	900	8,133	0.1
Berrien	11.0	0.0	4.0	27.3	D	6.9	D	D	22.7	4,220	233	757	8,054	0.7
Bibb	0.0	0.4	3.3	7.9	6.5	7.5	15.2	22.4	11.5	33,330	213	7,971	71,919	0.0
Bleckley	7.1	0.0	6.9	2.1	2.7	11.1	5.5	5.8	39.3	2,745	218	395	5,194	0.3
Brantley	0.9	D	10.7	9.1	4.6	4.6	D	4.3	24.4	3,855	213	528	8,205	0.7
Brooks	16.6	0.0	3.2	6.1	D	5.6	2.9	8.0	15.5	3,975	244	741	7,331	0.6
Bryan	0.6	0.0	10.1	9.8	4.9	10.1	9.1	8.0	24.8	6,780	144	645	17,348	3.0
Bulloch	0.7	D	7.8	7.6	D	8.0	6.9	12.9	31.0	11,870	144	1,704	33,609	1.5
Burke	2.3	0.0	D	2.0	4.1	1.8	1.2	D	5.5	5,420	223	1,011	11,209	0.5
Butts	0.6	D	6.7	14.1	D	7.7	3.4	D	21.5	5,580	216	758	9,624	1.7
Calhoun	30.5	D	D	D	D	4.6	D	D	29.1	1,300	236	288	2,027	0.3
Camden	0.0	0.0	4.8	7.4	D	6.3	4.1	4.5	54.6	10,285	185	877	23,039	1.9
Candler	7.2	0.1	9.0	3.3	D	9.4	D	D	22.9	2,640	239	459	4,645	0.3
Carroll	0.4	D	8.7	19.5	D	7.1	4.2	16.2	16.1	24,090	198	3,463	46,998	1.3
Catoosa	0.5	D	9.1	11.2	D	16.5	7.8	10.3	17.7	15,065	220	846	28,302	0.9
Charlton	0.7	D	5.4	19.3	D	5.5	D	3.3	21.1	2,460	193	364	4,694	0.6
Chatham	0.0	0.0	4.7	14.7	6.0	7.0	6.0	13.6	16.9	54,705	185	6,874	135,928	1.1
Chattahoochee	0.0	0.0	D	D	D	0.1	D	0.1	90.6	765	85	156	3,243	0.1
Chattooga	-0.3	0.0	6.7	31.1	D	8.1	5.8	D	23.9	6,595	265	1,018	10,868	0.1
Cherokee	0.1	0.1	15.7	8.5	8.0	8.8	7.0	10.2	12.3	46,090	168	2,499	103,714	2.3
Clarke	0.0	D	3.8	8.0	4.8	6.7	8.3	17.9	33.7	18,605	145	3,011	56,658	1.0
Clay	10.1	0.0	D	D	D	5.0	D	10.1	33.9	820	285	137	1,969	0.4
Clayton	0.0	D	4.5	4.8	1.7	5.5	2.3	5.6	10.9	41,655	140	9,106	115,055	0.7
Clinch	9.5	0.0	1.2	34.7	D	4.3	D	2.4	15.8	1,640	244	351	3,038	0.4
Cobb	0.0	0.0	9.8	5.8	18.8	6.8	10.6	9.8	8.0	109,150	142	9,483	311,450	0.7
Coffee	2.5	0.0	6.4	18.6	2.8	10.3	4.1	13.6	15.5	8,125	187	1,599	17,415	0.4
Colquitt	9.9	0.1	3.9	16.8	D	8.9	6.7	D	25.1	9,725	212	1,939	19,291	0.9
Columbia	0.0	D	9.9	10.1	D	11.8	8.0	12.0	17.7	26,925	169	1,765	60,366	2.3
Cook	3.1	D	10.2	13.2	D	9.3	3.0	D	29.5	3,950	229	721	7,322	0.7
Coweta	0.2	D	6.5	13.9	5.0	11.3	5.2	17.5	14.6	26,665	178	2,242	58,000	1.7
Crawford	16.6	D	11.3	1.3	D	3.3	D	8.1	30.5	2,925	241	238	5,211	0.9
Crisp	3.6	D	2.4	14.4	D	9.9	4.9	D	17.0	4,865	245	986	9,889	0.3
Dade	0.8	0.1	D	28.3	2.9	6.3	D	7.4	13.3	4,140	254	337	7,413	0.3
Dawson	1.2	0.0	8.4	13.0	5.6	19.9	6.0	8.9	15.3	5,865	206	461	12,437	3.5
Decatur	10.8	D	3.9	9.4	3.2	9.3	8.0	5.4	22.2	6,340	218	1,339	13,069	0.2
DeKalb	0.0	0.2	4.6	3.8	14.1	6.0	9.0	12.1	14.3	108,280	143	18,156	328,290	0.5
Dodge	4.5	0.0	3.8	11.4	D	9.6	3.4	D	36.1	4,645	235	820	8,583	0.4
Dooly	15.6	0.0	D	D	0.5	4.2	2.8	D	17.7	2,630	242	666	4,765	0.1
Dougherty	0.7	0.0	4.0	9.8	5.7	6.8	5.0	19.1	22.4	19,055	225	4,926	40,698	0.2
Douglas	0.0	D	7.7	9.7	3.9	10.5	4.1	10.7	15.0	23,620	162	3,103	54,817	1.5
Early	7.2	0.0	D	D	D	3.7	4.0	D	23.1	2,600	245	574	4,935	0.3
Echols	7.1	0.0	D	D	0.2	2.2	D	D	30.6	600	162	41	1,547	0.9

1. Per 1,000 resident population estimated as of July 1 of the year shown.

Table B. States and Counties — **Housing, Labor Force, and Employment**

STATE County	Housing units, 2016–2020: Occupied units: Total	Owner-occupied: Percent	Owner-occupied: Median value[1]	Median owner cost as a percent of income: With a mortgage	Median owner cost as a percent of income: Without a mortgage[2]	Renter-occupied: Median rent[3]	Renter-occupied: Median rent as a percent of income[2]	Substandard units[4] (percent)	Civilian labor force, 2021: Total	Percent change, 2020–2021	Unemployment: Total	Unemployment: Rate[5]	Civilian employment[6], 2016–2020: Total	Percent: Management, business, science, and arts	Percent: Construction, production, and maintenance occupations
	89	90	91	92	93	94	95	96	97	98	99	100	101	102	103
FLORIDA—Cont'd															
Putnam	29,822	71.4	103,400	22.0	10.0	742	30.2	3.1	27,149	2.8	1,648	6.1	26,512	24.6	34.1
St. Johns	91,253	81.4	326,300	20.9	10.2	1,355	32.8	1.3	141,901	3.1	4,310	3.0	116,238	46.3	14.4
St. Lucie	118,527	75.1	209,700	24.4	12.8	1,214	33.3	2.8	150,366	2.3	7,364	4.9	137,781	30.0	23.3
Santa Rosa	65,697	77.1	214,900	20.5	10.0	1,163	29.2	2.2	84,880	2.4	2,938	3.5	75,974	38.2	20.9
Sarasota	189,228	76.2	269,300	23.2	11.8	1,342	32.3	1.6	191,384	4.0	7,365	3.8	174,884	36.3	17.9
Seminole	178,094	65.8	263,700	21.2	10.0	1,323	29.9	2.6	244,546	2.9	9,956	4.1	240,266	45.5	14.6
Sumter	59,076	88.6	267,100	23.6	10.0	935	38.7	0.9	34,621	6.0	1,831	5.3	26,114	31.5	21.4
Suwannee	15,149	76.8	107,100	19.5	10.0	713	24.5	4.1	17,414	-1.3	777	4.5	17,024	31.2	28.8
Taylor	7,172	78.1	81,900	18.8	10.2	679	32.1	4.4	8,112	-0.5	404	5.0	6,218	29.0	29.1
Union	4,008	70.5	112,600	19.9	10.0	671	22.4	4.6	4,546	0.3	170	3.7	3,892	33.5	23.8
Volusia	220,386	71.2	194,900	22.7	12.4	1,097	33.4	1.2	255,093	2.6	11,790	4.6	234,106	32.6	21.1
Wakulla	11,382	84.4	171,200	18.3	10.0	918	24.4	2.7	15,429	2.9	488	3.2	14,752	40.2	21.1
Walton	28,635	76.0	245,400	21.8	10.0	1,012	32.5	2.6	33,792	4.5	1,195	3.5	31,844	37.5	18.8
Washington	9,037	78.9	120,800	22.9	11.2	686	30.3	2.9	9,507	0.7	428	4.5	8,867	28.0	31.7
GEORGIA	3,830,264	64.0	190,200	19.9	10.0	1,042	29.6	2.5	5,186,969	2.1	203,237	3.9	4,910,269	38.5	23.4
Appling	6,650	74.8	87,100	19.3	11.3	571	27.8	2.7	9,288	1.0	332	3.6	7,563	28.5	42.2
Atkinson	2,953	71.4	63,400	18.6	10.6	478	24.1	6.3	4,503	1.1	131	2.9	3,475	24.6	46.0
Bacon	3,743	74.6	82,300	19.2	10.0	534	23.9	2.8	4,837	-0.2	157	3.2	4,112	25.9	38.1
Baker	1,448	68.4	108,100	24.8	11.0	532	19.2	1.9	1,135	0.8	56	4.9	1,023	32.0	26.1
Baldwin	16,698	59.4	128,800	19.0	10.9	717	33.8	2.5	17,731	0.4	846	4.8	18,449	35.5	26.6
Banks	6,941	74.1	164,500	21.0	10.8	713	26.3	3.2	10,116	3.0	262	2.6	8,073	31.8	34.7
Barrow	27,268	76.7	169,900	20.5	10.0	1,020	28.7	2.5	42,115	3.1	1,233	2.9	39,491	32.1	29.3
Bartow	37,905	67.8	178,500	19.5	10.0	935	27.9	2.6	51,257	2.5	1,801	3.5	49,642	30.7	29.0
Ben Hill	6,612	57.6	85,500	22.5	13.6	677	28.4	2.3	5,568	1.3	292	5.2	6,642	23.4	37.8
Berrien	7,391	65.8	95,200	19.8	10.0	660	24.0	2.3	7,648	3.0	285	3.7	7,703	24.9	41.0
Bibb	58,154	51.7	125,300	19.9	11.1	834	33.6	2.3	67,875	1.0	3,404	5.0	63,027	33.6	20.8
Bleckley	4,250	72.8	101,900	17.9	10.8	624	27.3	2.2	4,622	2.5	229	5.0	4,700	30.9	32.1
Brantley	6,763	78.8	92,800	19.0	17.5	627	28.8	1.7	7,296	4.0	266	3.6	6,593	24.1	39.3
Brooks	6,392	69.9	94,200	19.4	12.4	615	38.4	3.5	6,821	1.1	255	3.7	6,331	21.9	30.5
Bryan	13,503	70.8	227,400	20.3	10.0	1,322	29.3	1.3	19,894	4.1	573	2.9	17,206	40.7	22.6
Bulloch	27,967	54.3	147,100	19.7	10.0	815	30.2	2.0	38,062	2.4	1,567	4.1	35,303	32.1	28.7
Burke	7,953	73.1	89,900	18.9	10.0	691	29.5	3.1	9,156	1.3	535	5.8	9,510	23.9	41.5
Butts	8,342	71.3	156,700	19.0	10.1	907	29.4	2.3	11,132	2.7	405	3.6	9,347	27.8	30.2
Calhoun	1,726	68.0	48,700	19.9	11.6	596	24.5	1.3	2,228	-0.4	90	4.0	1,735	30.0	30.0
Camden	19,746	61.9	171,400	19.8	10.0	970	27.6	1.7	21,658	2.6	685	3.2	21,320	33.8	26.9
Candler	4,042	57.6	89,800	19.7	10.0	606	30.5	5.4	6,009	4.8	182	3.0	4,468	24.6	37.8
Carroll	42,196	68.8	147,400	19.5	10.0	901	26.7	2.1	56,140	2.6	2,067	3.7	53,930	31.4	30.3
Catoosa	25,151	74.4	151,300	18.5	10.0	767	25.0	3.0	33,457	2.6	906	2.7	31,971	32.2	27.8
Charlton	3,826	71.2	87,200	21.7	10.4	533	22.7	3.0	4,959	1.8	157	3.2	4,328	26.2	38.0
Chatham	109,868	55.6	209,200	22.0	11.4	1,115	29.6	2.2	143,877	3.0	6,233	4.3	138,257	37.6	20.8
Chattahoochee	2,550	24.3	82,000	21.5	15.4	1,135	27.2	2.8	1,912	-0.4	86	4.5	1,889	37.7	23.1
Chattooga	9,106	68.8	77,200	19.4	10.6	573	30.1	5.9	9,562	-2.0	455	4.8	9,086	18.3	44.3
Cherokee	90,372	76.4	271,300	19.9	10.0	1,304	30.2	1.4	139,406	3.2	3,645	2.6	129,683	43.4	17.0
Clarke	50,284	40.5	186,800	19.2	10.1	872	34.3	2.1	59,167	2.0	2,245	3.8	61,052	43.9	18.5
Clay	1,313	76.1	70,500	27.3	15.2	337	29.2	0.8	884	-1.9	90	10.2	949	21.9	38.4
Clayton	96,826	50.3	122,100	22.2	10.0	1,024	31.2	3.8	140,309	1.2	9,189	6.5	132,229	24.8	31.3
Clinch	2,387	78.8	71,800	21.7	10.1	509	25.9	5.9	3,022	2.1	89	2.9	2,149	29.3	42.7
Cobb	283,359	65.8	273,900	18.9	10.0	1,264	28.2	1.8	423,126	2.7	13,807	3.3	396,989	47.8	16.6
Coffee	14,832	65.0	106,400	21.8	10.0	624	24.4	3.0	18,845	-0.5	766	4.1	17,636	27.5	34.1
Colquitt	15,865	62.3	92,600	18.6	10.8	664	28.5	3.8	22,227	1.7	713	3.2	18,851	25.2	36.3
Columbia	48,233	79.5	215,200	18.9	10.0	1,172	25.8	1.1	76,478	1.6	2,058	2.7	70,487	42.6	18.3
Cook	6,202	65.6	93,400	23.3	12.3	802	34.5	2.3	8,237	1.7	280	3.4	7,273	27.1	33.7
Coweta	53,104	75.1	225,000	19.0	10.0	1,124	29.7	2.0	76,218	2.4	2,557	3.4	72,242	38.9	23.8
Crawford	4,573	77.4	121,500	20.1	11.9	685	23.7	1.3	5,523	2.0	204	3.7	4,816	24.0	33.0
Crisp	8,479	56.8	83,100	18.7	10.5	641	33.5	2.7	10,068	3.6	862	8.6	9,051	28.2	29.1
Dade	6,155	71.0	128,500	21.1	11.2	663	21.5	4.1	8,049	3.4	210	2.6	7,113	23.8	32.3
Dawson	9,521	81.5	241,900	19.7	10.0	1,039	28.1	3.8	13,115	3.6	350	2.7	12,706	41.0	21.0
Decatur	9,684	61.3	115,000	21.5	11.6	681	25.6	6.8	11,338	0.2	415	3.7	10,351	26.3	30.5
DeKalb	283,799	55.7	235,300	20.3	10.0	1,224	31.5	2.6	400,667	1.8	18,524	4.6	384,519	46.3	17.8
Dodge	7,530	69.8	86,600	22.6	10.9	596	27.3	2.2	7,005	1.2	296	4.2	7,980	29.0	35.2
Dooly	4,979	70.9	81,400	16.9	10.1	626	22.7	5.0	4,936	-0.8	359	7.3	5,075	25.7	33.8
Dougherty	34,233	45.9	106,200	21.3	12.0	774	31.6	2.0	37,494	0.0	2,384	6.4	35,499	30.4	24.6
Douglas	49,788	65.5	171,300	19.1	10.0	1,143	29.0	2.7	74,001	2.2	3,230	4.4	69,763	36.2	25.5
Early	4,196	67.5	120,700	27.2	12.5	689	29.7	4.8	4,338	-1.8	217	5.0	3,690	27.8	38.2
Echols	1,497	71.3	76,000	19.4	10.4	670	24.2	3.0	1,897	0.8	52	2.7	1,730	17.3	43.2

1. Specified owner-occupied units. 2. A value of 10.0 represents 10 percent or less; a value of 50.0 represents 50 percent or more. 3. Specified renter-occupied units. 4. Overcrowded or lacking complete plumbing facilities. 5. Percent of civilian labor force. 6. Civilian employed persons 16 years old and over.

STATE County	Private nonfarm establishments, employment and payroll, 2020									Agriculture, 2017			
		Employment						Annual payroll		Farms			Farm producers whose primary occupation is farming (percent)
											Percent with:		
	Number of establish-ments	Total	Health care and social assistance	Manufac-turing	Retail trade	Finance and insurance	Professional, scientific, and technical services	Total (mil dol)	Average per employee (dollars)	Number	Fewer than 50 acres	1000 acres or more	
	104	105	106	107	108	109	110	111	112	113	114	115	116
FLORIDA—Cont'd													
Putnam	1,236	13,059	2,698	1,960	2,797	288	244	482	36,937	564	68.1	2.8	38.2
St. Johns	7,088	67,854	9,197	2,251	12,267	1,928	3,897	2,792	41,150	253	68.8	3.2	47.9
St. Lucie	6,407	67,708	13,221	4,165	12,445	1,322	2,554	2,523	37,256	415	55.7	13.3	49.2
Santa Rosa	3,040	29,954	4,738	932	5,888	950	1,492	1,109	37,032	699	63.2	2.9	38.6
Sarasota	14,480	149,279	29,008	6,883	24,940	4,955	9,393	6,888	46,141	292	71.2	5.8	41.7
Seminole	14,251	188,461	21,362	7,489	28,737	18,115	14,393	9,101	48,293	403	86.4	0.7	40.1
Sumter	1,706	27,829	5,360	1,091	4,421	786	665	1,062	38,179	1,307	75.7	1.9	37.0
Suwannee	676	9,038	1,345	2,268	1,997	148	178	301	33,348	1,079	56.3	2.8	48.2
Taylor	406	4,768	500	1,730	905	58	100	190	39,927	240	41.3	9.2	39.5
Union	126	1,623	328	142	225	10	10	63	38,832	308	62.7	3.6	40.5
Volusia	13,395	158,984	28,281	9,307	28,329	5,695	8,203	6,247	39,291	1,575	83.1	1.5	39.7
Wakulla	456	3,682	190	465	923	68	185	132	35,798	209	71.8	1.0	32.9
Walton	2,736	23,278	2,076	271	5,001	456	820	899	38,623	598	50.0	3.3	42.8
Washington	412	4,358	781	284	751	78	303	140	32,087	437	59.7	0.9	34.4
GEORGIA	244,668	4,107,151	544,603	391,620	487,658	183,954	303,779	216,568	52,730	42,439	42.3	5.3	39.4
Appling	380	5,623	990	593	1,003	148	38	310	55,149	548	43.8	6.6	39.2
Atkinson	87	1,461	33	647	133	58	NA	55	37,520	215	34.4	11.6	45.3
Bacon	232	3,223	579	725	308	145	61	110	34,280	273	38.1	4.8	39.5
Baker	31	281	23	NA	34	25	NA	11	40,160	147	29.3	21.8	56.1
Baldwin	831	12,914	4,091	1,038	2,398	332	221	485	37,569	139	36.0	6.5	23.4
Banks	289	3,357	173	253	802	26	55	99	29,441	463	40.0	0.9	48.9
Barrow	1,334	18,737	1,641	3,075	2,997	321	751	723	38,612	288	58.0	0.3	37.4
Bartow	2,181	35,653	3,374	8,695	4,311	589	923	1,522	42,685	469	56.5	1.9	39.9
Ben Hill	287	4,492	518	1,780	743	133	40	159	35,479	217	41.0	5.5	40.9
Berrien	249	2,800	300	1,251	372	150	36	101	35,966	349	33.5	8.6	48.4
Bibb	4,150	77,258	16,086	5,703	11,653	9,839	2,382	3,408	44,116	98	55.1	1.0	44.6
Bleckley	168	1,770	286	59	487	72	20	48	27,233	231	43.7	5.2	21.6
Brantley	210	1,461	166	163	319	36	31	54	36,686	235	49.4	NA	33.9
Brooks	207	2,047	548	153	339	65	48	73	35,844	360	31.1	11.9	43.8
Bryan	719	6,795	814	358	1,375	169	273	231	33,937	95	58.9	8.4	35.8
Bulloch	1,531	18,838	3,556	1,542	3,505	512	713	625	33,153	478	30.5	11.9	38.3
Burke	354	11,440	642	333	835	122	107	870	76,081	467	25.3	14.6	43.7
Butts	387	5,466	610	905	921	98	68	213	38,982	173	37.0	1.7	44.6
Calhoun	65	703	74	NA	72	34	3	27	38,410	169	20.1	16.0	40.1
Camden	852	9,605	1,010	234	1,986	284	1,415	334	34,754	47	70.2	2.1	28.4
Candler	221	2,384	468	284	405	95	133	81	33,772	197	32.0	6.1	30.5
Carroll	2,189	38,806	5,908	10,136	5,249	686	682	1,688	43,489	867	53.1	0.9	38.8
Catoosa	946	12,617	1,484	1,803	3,407	411	311	427	33,879	250	48.8	0.4	39.5
Charlton	149	1,755	77	342	249	39	72	69	39,276	120	50.8	5.0	28.1
Chatham	8,211	146,460	20,129	16,407	19,326	2,522	5,443	6,474	44,206	67	73.1	NA	44.0
Chattahoochee	108	1,792	46	NA	66	16	634	75	41,738	12	58.3	NA	22.7
Chattooga	320	5,002	392	2,397	684	120	73	161	32,216	323	36.8	1.2	43.1
Cherokee	5,834	61,204	8,564	6,416	11,070	1,446	4,229	2,396	39,142	430	73.3	NA	39.3
Clarke	3,119	49,313	11,026	5,344	8,004	1,155	1,627	2,039	41,345	91	62.6	1.1	28.4
Clay	42	284	14	NA	64	NA	NA	10	35,658	67	14.9	20.9	42.5
Clayton	3,934	73,303	7,787	4,837	10,395	1,383	868	3,004	40,979	19	89.5	NA	47.2
Clinch	136	1,865	250	835	176	35	23	74	39,625	113	39.8	8.8	47.1
Cobb	21,492	358,927	39,229	19,122	38,626	18,622	43,701	21,780	60,682	116	92.2	NA	37.5
Coffee	835	14,241	2,180	3,767	1,961	287	260	532	37,376	608	34.7	9.2	40.2
Colquitt	900	11,897	2,548	3,312	1,908	270	218	442	37,176	498	31.9	8.8	47.7
Columbia	2,620	32,816	4,237	2,858	6,676	747	1,666	1,317	40,129	183	56.3	2.7	29.7
Cook	308	3,392	410	773	685	130	90	112	32,892	239	45.6	14.6	41.7
Coweta	2,718	38,325	5,533	5,591	6,331	726	1,662	1,525	39,794	368	56.3	1.6	35.0
Crawford	120	539	71	48	115	25	11	18	33,703	192	35.4	3.6	37.1
Crisp	488	7,259	1,307	1,419	1,190	173	149	256	35,202	236	32.6	14.0	33.1
Dade	219	2,982	242	707	508	90	38	109	36,428	198	41.9	1.5	40.6
Dawson	765	8,813	642	1,001	3,461	160	207	239	27,170	192	60.4	NA	38.4
Decatur	604	7,287	885	1,595	1,409	242	96	266	36,486	337	24.3	21.7	45.1
DeKalb	17,869	283,367	47,960	11,051	33,658	14,244	22,130	16,074	56,725	34	97.1	NA	42.3
Dodge	302	3,296	1,023	503	649	142	56	106	32,100	391	24.8	6.1	33.3
Dooly	150	2,863	43	1,560	280	55	15	90	31,453	297	30.3	18.9	45.8
Dougherty	2,231	36,907	8,693	2,931	5,756	968	1,960	1,483	40,184	110	40.0	10.0	38.9
Douglas	2,737	40,404	4,979	4,188	8,632	685	1,119	1,608	39,786	93	67.7	NA	34.7
Early	203	3,328	374	1,118	364	109	81	148	44,349	321	14.6	17.4	44.7
Echols	29	136	5	NA	13	NA	NA	6	41,588	66	37.9	13.6	43.4

STATE County	Agriculture, 2017 (cont.) — Land in farms: Acreage (1,000)	Land in farms: Percent change, 2012–2017	Land in farms — Acres: Average size of farm	Acres: Total irrigated (1,000)	Acres: Total cropland (1,000)	Value of land and buildings (dollars): Average per farm	Value of land and buildings (dollars): Average per acre	Value of machinery and equipment, average per farm (dollars)	Value of products sold: Total (mil dol)	Value of products sold: Average per farm (acres)	Percent from: Crops	Percent from: Livestock and poultry products	Organic farms (number)	Farms with internet access (percent)	Government payments: Total ($1,000)	Government payments: Percent of farms
	117	118	119	120	121	122	123	124	125	126	127	128	129	130	131	132
FLORIDA—Cont'd																
Putnam	85	20.3	150	6.7	13.5	596,965	3,977	65,825	46.1	81,681	76.0	24.0	NA	74.8	466	6.4
St. Johns	34	2.3	136	14.4	17.5	1,156,661	8,507	130,543	61.4	242,605	95.3	4.7	2	85.4	D	2.8
St. Lucie	226	15.8	545	48.2	68.7	3,254,221	5,976	109,557	139.6	336,446	89.3	10.7	2	68.9	947	14.5
Santa Rosa	85	-12.9	122	1.2	52.8	652,601	5,362	61,267	38.5	55,117	89.1	10.9	NA	79.3	4,549	23.2
Sarasota	71	-11.2	244	5.2	11.0	2,240,920	9,195	63,666	23.1	79,092	77.4	22.6	1	76.7	348	5.1
Seminole	35	61.0	87	1.2	7.1	716,815	8,271	38,395	21.3	52,965	91.2	8.8	5	78.7	136	3.2
Sumter	177	-3.4	135	2.0	21.3	816,314	6,025	50,217	54.5	41,666	36.7	63.3	8	74.7	1,099	16.7
Suwannee	170	-12.2	157	27.4	78.5	695,473	4,418	83,821	258.9	239,981	21.5	78.5	9	76.6	1,988	6.8
Taylor	59	56.8	245	0.2	4.5	892,861	3,650	55,626	11.8	49,113	21.1	78.9	NA	75.0	10	3.8
Union	54	16.3	175	1.5	10.3	649,755	3,722	54,492	7.7	25,010	47.7	52.3	NA	74.0	93	3.6
Volusia	114	7.8	73	9.2	25.1	748,025	10,309	51,317	196.4	124,693	93.4	6.6	6	76.3	1,139	5.8
Wakulla	24	-23.4	113	0.1	2.0	387,249	3,420	38,983	2.4	11,431	22.9	77.1	NA	65.6	161	7.7
Walton	89	-39.7	149	1.2	23.1	562,514	3,771	45,630	30.6	51,186	19.6	80.4	NA	80.1	1,007	16.7
Washington	45	-22.4	104	0.9	16.0	395,545	3,820	53,771	8.9	20,471	66.5	33.5	2	71.9	458	18.1
GEORGIA	9,954	3.5	235	1,287.5	4,372.1	822,958	3,509	115,773	9,573.3	225,577	34.2	65.8	139	76.0	247,428	31.8
Appling	128	4.4	234	13.7	85.1	760,709	3,249	136,171	166.6	303,936	36.6	63.4	7	71.5	2,462	31.9
Atkinson	72	-17.2	334	9.1	40.8	971,298	2,904	192,878	71.1	330,563	38.6	61.4	NA	72.1	2,132	34.0
Bacon	62	7.6	228	6.1	38.6	937,359	4,116	144,034	63.2	231,440	50.5	49.5	1	80.2	1,141	20.9
Baker	131	-10.6	891	26.2	53.2	1,980,216	2,222	343,799	57.0	387,469	63.5	36.5	2	62.6	5,182	59.9
Baldwin	34	81.5	244	0.1	8.0	527,772	2,165	66,743	1.4	10,216	33.7	66.3	NA	79.9	93	12.9
Banks	56	-5.5	122	0.5	12.1	655,689	5,381	95,826	169.5	366,194	2.3	97.7	NA	76.9	943	27.2
Barrow	22	-25.0	78	0.4	6.1	508,793	6,557	50,503	36.0	124,844	2.4	97.6	5	78.8	161	12.5
Bartow	77	21.2	165	1.0	16.9	994,446	6,025	65,838	71.4	152,292	12.5	87.5	NA	77.8	919	22.2
Ben Hill	53	-8.3	242	5.3	22.4	597,934	2,469	111,377	20.9	96,244	69.0	31.0	NA	71.0	891	44.2
Berrien	117	-18.6	335	21.4	61.2	1,046,386	3,128	170,691	85.5	244,931	70.7	29.3	NA	77.7	5,470	44.1
Bibb	9	-38.2	93	0.1	4.1	371,840	4,006	77,778	4.8	49,429	6.4	93.6	NA	83.7	27	9.2
Bleckley	48	-26.8	209	8.1	23.2	539,162	2,580	59,016	12.4	53,654	93.6	6.4	NA	58.9	638	53.7
Brantley	24	4.5	104	0.9	5.7	304,091	2,919	47,411	D	D	D	D	NA	78.7	127	17.4
Brooks	178	20.4	496	22.1	91.6	1,733,285	3,496	215,239	118.9	330,253	63.2	36.8	NA	72.5	3,288	55.0
Bryan	26	69.8	272	0.0	3.5	837,457	3,077	67,866	3.0	31,400	33.1	66.9	NA	74.7	33	7.4
Bulloch	197	9.4	413	17.7	126.1	1,181,592	2,864	202,153	89.9	187,992	82.2	17.8	1	76.8	9,661	46.9
Burke	223	38.3	478	43.2	123.3	1,357,912	2,843	266,151	118.1	252,972	57.2	42.8	3	76.4	7,072	45.6
Butts	31	48.0	181	0.0	6.4	704,674	3,897	61,476	4.3	24,694	37.7	62.3	NA	68.8	112	16.8
Calhoun	116	7.8	686	38.0	66.3	2,067,724	3,014	298,570	63.5	375,917	79.9	20.1	NA	66.3	6,347	72.2
Camden	6	-64.8	118	0.1	2.1	337,997	2,865	59,431	0.7	15,809	32.6	67.4	1	80.9	22	10.6
Candler	55	2.4	278	3.9	24.5	879,763	3,160	95,491	21.8	110,853	72.9	27.1	1	69.5	796	37.1
Carroll	85	-0.8	98	D	18.2	470,633	4,786	69,536	186.0	214,525	4.0	96.0	1	81.2	519	11.6
Catoosa	24	17.0	97	0.1	7.5	531,318	5,503	69,075	26.7	106,880	16.5	83.5	NA	78.0	360	25.2
Charlton	21	54.9	173	D	2.3	418,803	2,427	55,039	3.8	31,842	13.9	86.1	NA	66.7	41	18.3
Chatham	5	22.0	70	0.7	1.7	354,509	5,078	129,996	12.2	182,448	95.7	4.3	1	85.1	NA	NA
Chattahoochee	2	-57.4	145	D	0.1	428,469	2,958	70,000	D	D	100.0	D	NA	75.0	D	16.7
Chattooga	55	10.3	171	0.0	15.9	605,993	3,542	72,635	74.2	229,836	2.8	97.2	NA	78.0	403	25.4
Cherokee	24	-4.5	56	0.1	6.6	484,880	8,675	56,805	21.7	50,484	22.8	77.2	NA	89.8	182	10.0
Clarke	8	-9.5	88	0.1	1.6	683,725	7,735	52,373	44.7	491,385	9.5	90.5	NA	90.1	59	9.9
Clay	45	12.9	674	6.6	23.0	1,596,179	2,367	277,136	15.8	236,239	88.1	11.9	1	83.6	1,883	58.2
Clayton	1	-29.3	31	0.0	0.2	259,453	8,355	26,985	0.2	12,842	48.4	51.6	NA	89.5	D	5.3
Clinch	27	3.0	243	3.7	8.9	967,887	3,983	179,959	33.9	299,876	89.8	10.2	NA	72.6	290	31.0
Cobb	3	-50.9	22	0.0	0.4	248,584	11,425	38,141	D	D	D	D	NA	92.2	D	1.7
Coffee	189	12.6	311	35.3	103.5	938,419	3,016	187,887	185.5	305,051	39.0	61.0	4	75.8	8,386	37.2
Colquitt	186	-1.4	373	45.4	120.8	1,235,184	3,308	224,282	295.9	594,273	66.5	33.5	NA	72.7	8,659	55.6
Columbia	23	74.5	125	0.1	3.4	555,982	4,452	39,103	2.8	15,208	51.0	49.0	2	84.7	50	8.7
Cook	79	15.4	330	15.9	48.9	1,004,035	3,038	167,271	88.1	368,544	63.1	36.9	NA	70.7	4,636	50.2
Coweta	53	-3.8	145	0.3	12.5	699,043	4,825	67,682	11.7	31,793	36.4	63.6	NA	81.0	136	9.5
Crawford	35	3.9	184	2.7	10.7	739,529	4,029	103,828	61.0	317,745	20.6	79.4	3	82.8	243	18.8
Crisp	108	-7.8	458	20.2	66.9	1,403,992	3,065	198,462	60.0	254,085	82.0	18.0	NA	77.5	3,815	55.9
Dade	29	-10.6	147	0.0	4.8	584,184	3,981	58,107	25.1	126,631	3.2	96.8	3	68.7	198	24.7
Dawson	19	49.1	99	0.0	3.9	689,160	6,983	66,115	46.8	243,880	2.0	98.0	2	77.6	134	12.0
Decatur	192	-3.6	569	82.9	133.4	1,855,602	3,260	315,713	179.5	532,591	83.7	16.3	3	68.2	15,914	70.0
DeKalb	0	-84.1	14	0.0	0.0	646,015	46,933	17,575	0.5	16,059	71.1	28.9	NA	97.1	NA	NA
Dodge	103	14.4	264	11.6	36.3	685,800	2,600	81,427	30.5	78,115	73.9	26.1	NA	73.7	1,767	52.7
Dooly	186	46.6	626	29.7	121.2	1,830,024	2,922	240,010	99.2	334,020	86.0	14.0	1	76.1	4,446	67.3
Dougherty	64	-1.4	586	18.4	24.0	2,267,228	3,869	167,695	40.3	366,355	89.6	10.4	NA	85.5	1,747	38.2
Douglas	7	-15.1	76	0.2	1.9	509,840	6,695	49,702	0.7	7,398	46.4	53.6	NA	67.7	9	5.4
Early	168	-1.0	522	32.2	80.0	1,341,069	2,569	186,003	59.3	184,629	91.7	8.3	NA	73.5	4,866	74.5
Echols	23	71.6	346	3.4	9.2	965,776	2,791	147,334	17.9	271,697	82.0	18.0	NA	74.2	215	37.9

STATE County	Water use, 2015		Wholesale Trade[1], 2017				Retail Trade[2], 2017				Real estate and rental and leasing,[2] 2017			
	Public supply water withdrawn (mil gal/ day)	Public supply gallons withdrawn per person per day	Number of establish-ments	Number of employees	Sales (mil dol)	Average payroll (mil dol)	Number of establish-ments	Number of employees	Sales (mil dol)	Average payroll (mil dol)	Number of establish-ments	Number of employees	Sales (mil dol)	Average payroll (mil dol)
	133	134	135	136	137	138	139	140	141	142	143	144	145	146
FLORIDA—Cont'd														
Putnam	2.1	29.2	D	D	D	D	227	2,867	737.4	65.9	45	118	17.1	3.3
St. Johns	16.8	74.3	184	1,792	1,550.3	116.2	882	11,538	3,214.8	285.3	470	1,405	327.4	56.1
St. Lucie	29.4	98.4	211	1,683	790.9	78.2	746	11,839	3,794.9	332.7	319	1,341	241.1	40.7
Santa Rosa	15.0	89.6	63	521	427.3	23.1	373	5,294	1,508.1	132.7	200	441	101.3	13.8
Sarasota	20.2	49.7	428	4,165	2,809.4	211.7	1,753	23,507	7,397.3	680.2	1,028	3,337	734.5	151.3
Seminole	57.6	128.2	614	5,162	2,685.3	282.7	1,706	27,111	9,607.0	765.7	866	3,732	824.7	154.4
Sumter	24.1	203.0	49	450	267.0	22.4	241	3,726	1,089.7	88.2	137	652	90.5	18.3
Suwannee	1.2	27.2	34	359	238.0	12.1	136	2,007	572.4	51.4	26	61	12.6	1.7
Taylor	1.8	77.8	17	51	110.7	2.6	87	872	268.1	20.2	12	24	6.0	0.6
Union	0.2	14.4	D	D	D	0.8	29	191	63.9	5.6	D	D	D	0.3
Volusia	55.5	107.1	399	2,842	1,426.2	136.7	1,981	26,960	7,739.6	706.8	754	2,752	597.5	97.4
Wakulla	2.3	73.3	D	D	D	D	65	865	236.5	18.3	21	27	6.8	0.9
Walton	11.2	175.9	55	665	418.3	29.2	416	4,802	1,122.1	114.6	305	1,211	303.4	51.9
Washington	1.0	38.5	12	145	147.3	7.0	67	813	203.9	18.2	9	13	2.4	0.5
GEORGIA	1,069.9	104.7	10,832	165,088	188,899.2	10,594.4	34,100	485,505	148,624.6	12,560.5	12,426	63,935	23,009.0	3,795.4
Appling	0.8	41.2	19	170	129.7	8.3	79	1,173	578.7	36.8	10	25	3.2	0.5
Atkinson	0.4	51.2	5	94	47.4	3.6	23	141	41.7	3.2	NA	NA	NA	NA
Bacon	1.0	86.7	14	201	180.0	8.6	44	324	81.2	6.6	NA	NA	NA	NA
Baker	0.2	47.2	3	D	7.7	D	4	28	4.1	0.4	NA	NA	NA	NA
Baldwin	3.8	84.0	D	D	D	D	182	2,401	674.2	58.5	D	D	D	D
Banks	2.6	141.1	12	98	88.1	3.9	49	838	223.6	19.1	7	31	3.3	0.6
Barrow	4.5	59.2	61	1,232	765.4	63.1	168	2,870	993.6	82.7	56	116	32.5	4.2
Bartow	52.4	510.1	128	2,375	1,066.5	111.0	330	4,163	1,330.7	104.8	106	435	87.7	16.3
Ben Hill	2.5	141.4	7	38	18.9	1.8	74	769	207.0	17.4	13	26	4.0	0.7
Berrien	0.8	41.1	19	194	96.7	6.8	52	439	100.3	8.9	7	12	2.0	0.2
Bibb	24.1	157.0	178	2,913	1,943.5	149.2	761	10,330	2,685.4	259.1	203	1,050	208.6	40.3
Bleckley	0.2	16.3	6	38	22.4	1.6	41	458	93.8	9.5	4	D	1.5	D
Brantley	0.2	13.0	5	13	1.6	0.5	40	261	70.9	5.4	NA	NA	NA	NA
Brooks	0.9	57.5	11	103	107.3	4.9	40	350	93.4	7.6	D	D	D	0.3
Bryan	2.6	73.7	19	299	512.8	20.1	104	1,221	373.4	25.8	39	101	41.3	4.7
Bulloch	4.8	65.7	46	257	207.6	12.6	264	3,407	957.5	83.5	81	319	50.5	10.2
Burke	0.9	37.4	26	546	395.9	23.9	58	818	221.2	20.0	12	21	6.0	0.7
Butts	2.7	116.1	9	253	402.3	11.6	75	868	316.0	19.9	17	24	6.1	0.7
Calhoun	0.4	67.9	3	36	28.0	2.0	13	90	13.9	1.6	NA	NA	NA	NA
Camden	3.9	75.6	D	D	D	D	151	1,941	600.9	45.0	27	127	27.3	3.2
Candler	0.4	37.7	7	63	27.0	1.9	49	401	145.7	10.1	3	5	0.4	0.1
Carroll	11.3	98.8	82	824	538.0	38.7	376	5,369	1,556.9	129.8	97	347	66.9	9.7
Catoosa	4.7	70.9	43	487	412.7	23.0	185	3,050	948.3	82.9	37	148	27.7	4.5
Charlton	0.8	58.6	6	82	37.3	3.2	33	247	61.0	4.7	4	32	1.9	0.5
Chatham	28.1	97.9	332	4,916	5,884.0	288.9	1,321	19,102	5,006.2	473.7	464	2,376	567.2	91.6
Chattahoochee	0.3	27.3	NA	NA	NA	NA	16	94	14.8	1.6	NA	NA	NA	NA
Chattooga	2.8	112.4	D	D	D	D	74	703	159.9	15.3	10	34	3.9	0.7
Cherokee	19.3	81.8	254	2,350	1,347.2	145.0	660	10,814	2,977.0	270.7	292	707	210.9	31.1
Clarke	11.5	92.6	94	2,042	2,980.2	95.9	513	8,212	1,982.0	195.5	202	1,392	242.9	54.2
Clay	0.3	79.6	NA	NA	NA	NA	11	52	7.8	0.9	NA	NA	NA	NA
Clayton	10.8	39.3	214	4,698	4,813.8	262.0	700	10,714	3,454.9	285.6	180	1,019	331.3	50.6
Clinch	0.5	65.3	7	120	19.8	3.2	27	153	36.9	3.0	NA	NA	NA	NA
Cobb	42.2	57.0	1,049	17,683	25,968.6	1,263.9	2,261	39,473	18,543.7	1,066.1	1,257	6,174	1,911.4	343.9
Coffee	4.1	94.0	45	503	467.9	25.3	188	1,910	542.1	46.2	28	74	10.6	2.0
Colquitt	3.1	67.8	49	453	456.1	21.3	198	2,047	528.2	50.9	30	92	14.1	2.7
Columbia	15.9	110.5	84	1,038	477.8	51.1	323	6,455	2,111.5	191.8	120	499	147.6	21.4
Cook	1.4	81.8	10	72	23.0	3.4	65	692	200.1	16.0	7	46	4.2	1.3
Coweta	7.5	53.8	99	1,171	1,899.0	59.7	390	6,192	1,943.1	155.3	170	370	109.3	18.8
Crawford	0.4	32.3	NA	NA	NA	NA	21	95	21.8	2.3	NA	NA	NA	NA
Crisp	2.0	87.8	31	347	376.2	18.4	115	1,237	315.9	28.6	22	194	15.1	5.2
Dade	2.0	124.2	NA	NA	NA	NA	61	510	153.9	11.1	5	5	1.4	0.2
Dawson	1.5	64.8	18	158	38.6	5.5	200	3,364	747.6	66.7	25	55	18.4	2.1
Decatur	2.4	89.4	28	251	186.0	10.3	119	1,341	378.4	32.1	26	68	10.0	1.9
DeKalb	0.0	0.0	717	10,312	13,007.6	592.9	2,231	34,345	10,567.2	946.9	1,064	4,685	1,298.4	245.6
Dodge	1.4	66.6	11	44	9.3	1.1	62	708	160.7	14.1	D	D	D	D
Dooly	2.3	162.5	12	84	47.1	3.7	35	307	127.6	8.6	3	4	0.2	0.1
Dougherty	11.6	126.7	114	1,997	1,189.7	93.7	443	5,959	1,578.7	135.0	117	484	106.1	17.0
Douglas	17.5	124.5	116	2,209	2,721.6	139.7	416	8,318	2,760.6	221.2	140	605	141.6	22.4
Early	1.2	114.4	12	69	66.3	3.2	52	413	92.4	7.6	4	9	0.9	0.2
Echols	0.1	12.4	NA	NA	NA	NA	5	12	4.2	0.2	NA	NA	NA	NA

1 Merchant wholesalers, except manufacturers' sales branches and offices. 2. Employer establishments.

STATE County	Professional, scientific, and technical services, 2017				Manufacturing, 2017				Accommodation and food services, 2017			
	Number of establish-ments	Number of employees	Sales (mil dol)	Average payroll (mil dol)	Number of establish-ments	Number of employees	Sales (mil dol)	Average payroll (mil dol)	Number of establis-hments	Number of employees	Sales (mil dol)	Annual payroll (mil dol)
	147	148	149	150	151	152	153	154	155	156	157	158
FLORIDA—Cont'd												
Putnam	D	D	D	D	38	1,514	932.0	94.3	95	1,313	69.4	18.0
St. Johns	D	D	D	D	116	1,933	570.9	86.8	600	12,316	824.6	232.7
St. Lucie	549	2,367	313.8	105.4	152	3,100	817.1	142.4	444	8,381	456.7	127.8
Santa Rosa	324	1,687	258.9	101.6	54	665	547.9	36.2	218	4,863	238.4	65.6
Sarasota	D	D	D	D	353	6,921	1,667.2	367.9	957	18,847	1,151.7	343.2
Seminole	2,038	12,586	1,979.1	786.7	375	6,585	1,902.1	317.5	877	17,286	1,038.1	290.9
Sumter	160	753	103.6	40.1	39	943	474.7	49.1	143	3,614	177.1	56.6
Suwannee	43	165	17.9	5.4	16	1,959	597.7	63.0	56	963	51.0	12.3
Taylor	28	77	7.9	2.9	20	1,617	546.7	94.1	36	429	21.7	5.9
Union	D	D	D	0.3	D	D	D	D	4	55	3.0	0.9
Volusia	D	D	D	D	372	9,074	2,391.4	440.2	1,187	22,605	1,293.3	366.1
Wakulla	D	D	D	D	D	D	D	D	44	576	32.6	8.0
Walton	265	655	114.8	32.6	40	202	63.9	8.7	237	6,326	526.7	146.7
Washington	31	290	39.9	14.7	D	257	D	6.7	37	436	23.1	5.9
GEORGIA	29,635	265,189	54,903.5	20,100.5	7,510	368,836	169,058.5	19,071.6	21,201	426,884	26,010.1	6,999.7
Appling	16	41	5.4	1.3	26	597	222.3	30.0	34	508	25.6	6.5
Atkinson	NA	NA	NA	NA	12	647	249.8	29.0	8	66	2.5	0.6
Bacon	16	59	6.0	2.0	13	947	220.3	33.6	D	D	D	D
Baker	NA	NA	NA	NA	NA	NA	NA	NA	NA	NA	NA	NA
Baldwin	D	D	D	D	D	D	D	D	D	D	D	D
Banks	14	43	6.4	2.6	11	262	47.1	11.6	47	1,005	59.8	16.1
Barrow	115	785	77.6	29.5	72	2,350	1,008.2	113.9	100	2,385	177.5	38.7
Bartow	D	D	D	D	117	7,853	4,466.2	416.8	197	4,081	234.5	64.2
Ben Hill	D	D	D	D	28	1,348	508.7	63.1	29	298	17.8	4.9
Berrien	14	38	6.1	1.4	D	1,237	D	52.8	24	225	11.5	2.8
Bibb	D	D	D	D	119	5,179	2,443.3	297.1	444	8,531	451.0	122.9
Bleckley	8	14	2.2	1.0	7	66	12.9	3.4	16	D	12.4	D
Brantley	9	17	1.6	0.6	9	91	53.7	5.2	13	132	5.7	1.7
Brooks	13	45	3.6	1.2	6	186	95.7	9.2	14	166	7.7	2.1
Bryan	74	262	40.1	12.4	12	270	160.1	16.6	81	1,243	65.1	16.7
Bulloch	D	D	D	D	43	1,332	416.1	56.4	153	4,021	173.6	47.4
Burke	D	D	D	D	9	291	65.6	13.0	26	402	22.0	5.8
Butts	22	71	6.9	2.5	12	842	420.7	29.8	37	426	26.4	6.7
Calhoun	3	2	0.3	0.1	NA	NA	NA	NA	4	D	0.4	D
Camden	D	D	D	D	14	D	111.9	D	118	2,108	107.1	29.7
Candler	26	90	11.7	3.4	8	163	47.3	4.4	D	D	D	D
Carroll	145	595	101.9	30.3	108	8,686	5,937.5	417.7	215	4,122	215.8	55.7
Catoosa	D	D	D	D	47	1,403	484.2	72.5	100	2,225	122.0	32.7
Charlton	D	D	D	D	6	237	66.7	11.3	13	178	8.8	2.3
Chatham	D	D	D	D	182	16,361	10,193.1	1,407.2	1,018	22,190	1,492.3	383.6
Chattahoochee	D	D	D	D	NA	NA	NA	NA	6	73	3.1	0.8
Chattooga	D	D	9.4	D	14	2,412	614.2	84.8	27	314	16.9	3.5
Cherokee	791	3,015	546.4	164.1	170	4,510	1,221.0	209.1	380	7,874	420.4	122.8
Clarke	318	1,510	192.2	71.2	92	5,698	2,376.5	261.8	360	7,878	396.0	110.0
Clay	NA	NA	NA	NA	NA	NA	NA	NA	NA	NA	NA	NA
Clayton	221	952	145.1	48.3	90	4,457	1,893.6	221.2	410	8,801	585.6	153.4
Clinch	D	D	D	D	D	672	D	D	13	D	4.0	D
Cobb	3,463	32,471	6,500.9	2,369.0	497	19,472	8,818.9	1,362.6	1,649	34,784	2,056.6	565.8
Coffee	51	241	27.0	11.2	45	3,178	910.0	127.5	60	1,625	75.0	19.4
Colquitt	64	214	26.1	7.3	40	2,754	944.9	94.7	D	D	D	D
Columbia	216	1,224	204.3	67.0	58	3,168	2,485.7	146.8	225	4,871	242.2	65.2
Cook	17	60	6.7	2.2	30	637	516.5	29.7	36	550	30.9	6.6
Coweta	D	D	D	D	83	5,044	2,426.7	258.7	188	4,500	235.2	68.2
Crawford	D	D	D	0.5	D	30	D	1.6	D	D	D	D
Crisp	26	153	19.3	7.5	19	1,012	538.3	52.4	50	1,030	59.2	12.4
Dade	11	39	3.2	1.0	11	452	185.8	24.2	D	D	D	D
Dawson	55	198	25.3	8.5	24	1,115	211.1	33.0	58	1,191	66.4	17.3
Decatur	30	107	12.6	3.7	28	1,191	724.3	59.1	47	689	34.9	8.9
DeKalb	2,951	22,022	3,898.6	1,594.3	408	11,374	4,013.1	573.4	1,561	27,441	1,768.1	490.7
Dodge	18	72	10.1	3.9	14	294	133.9	12.9	25	416	16.1	4.3
Dooly	D	D	D	D	8	D	398.9	D	13	158	9.2	1.7
Dougherty	212	2,000	269.0	104.0	57	2,910	2,729.2	176.2	221	4,431	235.8	63.6
Douglas	218	970	123.3	43.8	91	3,804	1,043.9	162.1	241	5,171	287.3	74.6
Early	15	74	8.6	3.2	5	785	647.9	60.4	D	D	D	D
Echols	NA	NA	NA	NA	NA	NA	NA	NA	NA	NA	NA	NA

STATE County	Health care and social assistance, 2017				Other services, 2017				Nonemployer businesses, 2019		Value of residential construction authorized by building permits, 2021	
	Number of establish-ments	Number of employees	Receipts (mil dol)	Annual payroll (mil dol)	Number of establish-ments	Number of employees	Receipts (mil dol)	Annual payroll (mil dol)	Number	Receipts (mil dol)	New construction ($1,000)	Number of housing units
	159	160	161	162	163	164	165	166	167	168	169	170
FLORIDA—Cont'd												
Putnam	159	2,213	236.4	83.8	104	372	38.5	9.3	4,532	160.9	20,484	109
St. Johns	660	8,990	1,013.8	367.9	413	5,020	1,828.8	192.6	26,484	1,417.6	1,876,365	8,390
St. Lucie	788	13,396	1,853.0	616.2	421	1,685	166.5	46.6	31,365	1,162.0	1,493,427	7,461
Santa Rosa	285	3,931	512.9	173.0	165	598	63.8	16.0	13,689	592.0	428,460	2,091
Sarasota	1,589	28,231	3,766.3	1,300.3	1,015	5,093	717.0	157.2	48,314	2,668.8	2,342,630	7,805
Seminole	1,411	20,780	2,625.8	933.6	912	4,645	478.0	139.9	47,771	2,060.0	619,016	3,220
Sumter	202	4,682	635.1	217.7	82	436	34.6	11.4	8,147	364.3	1,203,827	4,611
Suwannee	70	1,357	114.5	45.3	39	188	23.7	5.4	2,875	124.7	24,470	144
Taylor	37	572	50.0	20.9	D	D	D	3.6	1,090	42.2	8,159	32
Union	10	350	29.6	12.8	D	D	1.5	D	662	26.9	500	46
Volusia	1,452	28,599	3,465.8	1,273.6	1,049	4,675	697.6	150.2	47,548	1,975.6	1,335,899	5,196
Wakulla	D	D	D	D	37	108	9.9	2.7	2,366	97.7	90,878	490
Walton	135	2,054	250.5	96.9	112	525	58.1	16.3	9,774	661.8	1,094,511	2,541
Washington	44	753	72.2	26.5	D	D	D	2.8	1,765	68.5	14,985	90
GEORGIA	25,260	521,146	68,759.7	25,771.5	14,976	97,721	14,342.5	3,347.6	1,000,184	42,095.4	14,437,233	67,223
Appling	D	D	D	D	23	74	7.9	2.1	1,219	48.9	556	5
Atkinson	5	23	1.0	0.6	3	14	0.9	0.2	613	26.8	2,500	15
Bacon	19	513	44.7	17.5	D	D	D	D	612	30.5	0	0
Baker	D	D	D	1.4	D	D	D	D	189	6.5	0	0
Baldwin	101	3,547	345.2	137.4	53	268	21.5	6.3	3,460	117.6	43,845	235
Banks	15	150	17.6	7.8	D	D	D	D	1,347	67.0	15,418	103
Barrow	104	1,471	135.7	55.9	93	475	60.0	15.2	7,604	322.5	149,705	1,134
Bartow	214	3,349	449.3	159.6	131	718	110.1	26.3	8,983	412.0	151,997	1,133
Ben Hill	27	468	36.1	15.8	23	87	7.8	1.6	1,034	37.7	1,804	11
Berrien	25	286	22.0	8.5	11	37	4.0	0.8	1,183	55.2	8,768	34
Bibb	619	16,894	2,123.3	756.1	245	1,633	217.1	58.6	13,761	451.5	31,112	177
Bleckley	17	248	17.5	6.8	D	D	D	D	851	27.3	11,854	80
Brantley	D	D	D	D	12	28	2.9	0.7	1,082	42.2	14,328	67
Brooks	20	558	39.9	19.2	D	D	D	D	972	40.3	0	0
Bryan	62	688	57.2	21.3	48	488	37.1	13.0	3,176	152.5	170,368	574
Bulloch	204	3,328	354.0	125.2	95	469	50.8	12.4	5,346	216.3	88,543	585
Burke	31	648	38.9	19.1	D	D	D	D	1,622	59.9	16,722	69
Butts	31	487	42.9	19.0	D	D	D	D	1,819	71.2	54,017	176
Calhoun	9	69	6.3	2.3	NA	NA	NA	NA	300	14.4	1,958	9
Camden	100	1,023	105.4	38.2	60	277	22.7	6.6	2,848	97.4	120,563	712
Candler	20	512	30.7	15.2	7	33	2.3	0.4	856	39.4	395	3
Carroll	214	5,294	785.2	314.3	119	610	69.1	17.2	9,147	351.7	296,790	1,251
Catoosa	108	2,325	231.8	75.2	49	303	31.0	8.2	4,490	209.6	55,703	272
Charlton	13	73	4.4	2.6	D	D	D	D	558	16.9	8,526	32
Chatham	761	21,255	2,541.9	977.6	467	3,587	436.1	128.4	24,074	1,099.0	405,624	1,904
Chattahoochee	D	D	D	D	D	D	D	D	246	4.6	182	1
Chattooga	27	385	31.3	12.7	D	D	D	D	1,408	76.3	0	0
Cherokee	507	7,011	980.3	315.9	356	1,838	203.2	61.2	27,574	1,261.5	801,814	2,754
Clarke	456	10,263	1,666.8	621.3	196	1,403	275.9	48.3	9,477	348.6	145,120	1,166
Clay	4	20	0.9	0.4	NA	NA	NA	NA	190	6.4	925	4
Clayton	413	8,536	924.3	397.7	281	1,678	201.4	57.1	33,121	862.2	195,509	929
Clinch	12	222	16.2	6.4	D	D	1.5	D	394	12.8	742	5
Cobb	2,134	39,978	5,569.5	2,444.9	1,384	10,745	1,045.6	353.6	86,497	3,916.7	761,058	3,247
Coffee	107	2,342	281.5	98.4	46	233	21.3	7.4	3,240	137.8	9,450	72
Colquitt	93	1,961	239.7	88.8	53	221	21.3	5.5	2,983	125.6	19,012	142
Columbia	268	4,211	387.6	162.8	183	1,097	110.9	34.5	11,583	501.1	293,774	1,548
Cook	40	427	36.2	15.6	D	D	D	D	1,181	51.3	50,048	209
Coweta	264	5,616	1,103.4	286.8	150	783	77.1	22.6	12,770	475.5	569,102	1,712
Crawford	D	D	D	D	10	45	5.3	1.6	828	29.6	2,025	9
Crisp	63	1,147	170.4	47.4	32	151	20.2	5.1	1,464	55.9	4,744	29
Dade	D	D	D	D	D	D	D	D	1,105	50.4	0	0
Dawson	48	521	62.9	19.5	36	177	18.6	5.4	2,608	149.4	145,830	581
Decatur	53	840	72.2	32.5	43	151	14.2	3.1	1,871	73.2	17,818	142
DeKalb	2,078	47,637	5,974.3	2,416.6	1,142	7,483	1,120.3	296.6	86,762	3,119.3	679,809	2,862
Dodge	52	974	71.3	27.2	D	D	9.5	D	1,504	48.8	513	5
Dooly	11	46	3.3	1.3	9	30	3.1	0.6	663	25.0	0	0
Dougherty	313	8,489	1,158.0	457.9	134	906	83.3	25.5	6,561	211.6	8,413	25
Douglas	283	4,710	557.8	205.3	189	978	116.4	32.0	14,885	489.8	301,796	1,639
Early	D	D	D	D	13	30	3.9	0.9	637	29.4	1,523	7
Echols	NA	NA	NA	NA	NA	NA	NA	NA	213	8.8	265	3

STATE County	Government employment and payroll, 2017									Local government finances, 2017				
			March payroll (percent of total)							General revenue				
												Taxes		
													Per capita[1] (dollars)	
	Full-time equivalent employees	March payroll (dollars)	Adminis-tration, judicial, and legal	Police and corrections	Fire protection	Highways and transpor-tation	Health and welfare	Natural resources and utilities	Education and libraries	Total (mil dol)	Inter-govern-mental (mil dol)	Total (mil dol)	Total	Property
	171	172	173	174	175	176	177	178	179	180	181	182	183	184
FLORIDA—Cont'd														
Putnam	3,479	13,112,988	7.6	7.0	1.1	1.6	2.9	25.2	53.4	376.7	160.4	158.0	2,153	1,944
St. Johns	7,186	26,903,374	6.5	13.1	7.2	1.8	1.5	5.5	58.9	892.9	224.0	373.4	1,532	1,301
St. Lucie	9,995	39,089,749	5.6	13.6	8.1	1.8	2.1	7.9	56.2	1,233.7	354.0	481.5	1,537	1,305
Santa Rosa	4,207	14,416,778	9.4	14.5	1.9	1.2	0.5	3.0	69.1	437.9	208.1	149.9	861	674
Sarasota	17,288	78,763,540	6.7	9.0	5.7	3.0	37.1	5.9	29.2	2,415.6	267.3	869.1	2,071	1,600
Seminole	13,454	52,063,875	6.8	15.3	6.8	2.3	0.9	6.6	59.4	1,543.0	567.5	635.9	1,374	997
Sumter	1,805	6,376,591	5.2	22.2	6.8	3.6	0.3	3.5	57.8	324.6	40.6	147.5	1,180	970
Suwannee	1,197	3,723,646	3.6	1.8	4.9	6.2	0.6	2.5	75.4	133.6	77.9	36.7	831	608
Taylor	789	2,322,312	10.4	15.2	3.4	3.6	0.6	5.4	59.3	65.8	29.8	26.6	1,221	958
Union	458	1,208,109	4.9	0.0	0.0	3.5	6.5	4.7	79.3	37.5	26.0	6.6	430	264
Volusia	15,886	61,497,255	8.2	16.3	5.4	3.3	3.7	9.0	50.9	2,518.3	603.8	818.9	1,522	1,139
Wakulla	828	2,436,692	6.0	0.3	5.9	0.0	1.4	1.9	82.7	81.8	44.9	23.9	747	540
Walton	2,607	9,053,017	9.8	15.2	13.3	6.1	0.9	2.3	45.9	299.8	56.1	203.9	2,998	2,197
Washington	914	2,754,142	8.1	9.4	0.3	3.8	0.6	3.3	73.2	80.8	48.3	20.8	846	605
GEORGIA	X	X	X	X	X	X	X	X	X	X	X	X	X	X
Appling	1,086	3,342,587	6.1	8.6	0.2	3.5	32.0	1.7	46.6	102.4	29.0	37.2	2,017	1,350
Atkinson	387	1,735,046	12.3	1.5	0.2	1.4	0.2	2.5	79.5	29.6	15.8	6.7	823	591
Bacon	409	1,529,007	7.4	6.4	0.4	3.3	2.1	0.9	78.7	36.3	19.0	12.0	1,074	685
Baker	108	297,903	11.0	14.3	0.0	3.6	0.0	0.3	70.0	8.8	3.9	4.0	1,269	1,032
Baldwin	1,778	5,432,600	6.3	9.3	4.4	2.0	33.9	4.7	37.6	127.0	50.2	53.5	1,189	682
Banks	698	2,400,762	6.9	7.3	3.3	1.4	0.4	2.7	75.9	49.6	20.3	22.5	1,209	685
Barrow	2,202	8,733,548	5.0	11.5	5.9	1.2	1.0	2.7	70.8	231.3	102.4	91.5	1,159	715
Bartow	3,757	13,895,285	7.5	8.7	5.1	2.0	2.4	7.7	65.5	366.7	121.3	185.2	1,762	1,084
Ben Hill	984	3,377,220	3.2	13.7	2.1	2.6	23.0	7.1	44.3	80.3	27.8	21.4	1,255	746
Berrien	769	2,162,144	8.7	10.1	0.2	4.4	5.2	2.5	66.4	51.5	27.3	17.6	919	626
Bibb	5,503	21,076,493	6.9	10.9	6.6	2.0	4.6	6.0	60.1	496.0	236.8	147.4	965	668
Bleckley	506	1,546,372	5.4	6.5	1.9	2.9	1.1	2.0	79.2	50.5	22.9	12.3	960	650
Brantley	727	2,183,628	4.6	7.2	1.1	3.6	3.8	0.6	79.0	51.0	30.1	15.1	800	553
Brooks	526	1,838,263	7.0	9.5	2.6	3.3	1.3	2.0	71.7	43.0	20.0	16.8	1,074	805
Bryan	1,278	4,501,314	6.6	8.0	2.8	1.4	2.9	1.3	74.8	126.1	52.7	55.4	1,496	916
Bulloch	2,971	9,601,219	4.9	9.6	1.3	2.5	11.3	7.2	61.5	217.6	83.3	89.1	1,173	620
Burke	1,327	4,425,013	6.6	9.5	11.8	4.3	1.1	3.2	61.4	121.9	26.0	85.6	3,798	3,136
Butts	814	2,725,650	9.8	12.2	6.4	3.5	0.8	6.4	60.4	64.4	23.7	30.9	1,285	754
Calhoun	218	687,826	14.0	11.0	0.3	3.3	3.3	5.6	58.7	20.6	8.3	5.1	799	543
Camden	1,951	7,933,054	5.7	7.5	6.1	2.1	0.1	3.8	71.6	167.0	62.6	70.9	1,337	865
Candler	593	1,891,822	5.5	6.0	1.3	1.5	30.0	4.0	50.9	52.5	21.2	11.3	1,051	581
Carroll	3,751	13,069,947	4.9	10.1	4.6	1.9	0.8	7.6	68.4	347.9	148.3	137.3	1,170	667
Catoosa	2,056	7,580,949	4.8	6.3	2.5	2.2	0.7	3.3	78.6	375.1	78.8	72.4	1,089	625
Charlton	565	1,709,347	8.1	7.2	0.2	2.9	28.1	3.2	48.9	37.1	14.5	16.2	1,264	946
Chatham	10,284	40,221,481	9.9	15.3	4.9	6.0	3.4	8.4	47.8	1,791.9	329.5	666.3	2,303	1,474
Chattahoochee	222	618,747	7.8	5.5	0.0	4.0	0.5	3.7	77.5	14.0	8.5	3.7	366	173
Chattooga	833	2,858,771	7.1	8.6	0.5	3.2	1.5	10.5	67.1	73.5	35.6	21.2	856	506
Cherokee	7,585	27,818,955	5.2	8.4	6.7	1.4	0.7	4.0	72.1	720.1	235.5	354.2	1,430	1,009
Clarke	4,590	17,021,391	7.3	12.9	4.9	2.6	7.2	9.0	51.4	858.6	139.6	176.8	1,394	995
Clay	123	336,328	16.3	9.1	0.0	6.1	6.9	5.7	53.2	15.6	4.1	6.1	2,064	1,723
Clayton	10,560	39,755,068	6.7	13.9	5.5	1.0	2.3	3.3	64.1	970.9	408.0	420.7	1,480	853
Clinch	411	1,464,990	8.8	6.4	1.6	2.4	27.5	2.8	50.6	38.1	11.4	10.6	1,590	1,274
Cobb	23,528	98,376,437	7.2	8.7	4.8	1.1	1.6	5.3	70.1	2,465.8	764.5	1,279.6	1,700	1,123
Coffee	1,553	4,931,558	4.3	8.1	2.8	2.2	1.1	3.4	75.2	131.2	66.7	41.0	955	516
Colquitt	3,145	10,521,532	3.5	3.9	1.3	1.5	41.9	1.8	44.2	266.6	83.0	51.7	1,137	661
Columbia	4,609	16,921,276	5.1	8.7	4.4	2.0	0.6	4.9	72.4	427.3	162.2	200.6	1,324	802
Cook	785	2,201,477	8.0	11.1	2.5	3.0	0.0	5.7	66.9	55.1	24.4	19.4	1,129	640
Coweta	4,327	18,142,647	5.4	10.0	5.4	1.9	0.6	4.7	67.7	380.3	133.8	197.7	1,381	870
Crawford	405	906,421	23.0	8.0	1.8	4.0	1.4	1.1	59.3	25.9	13.0	10.3	838	642
Crisp	1,102	3,736,914	6.6	10.8	3.9	2.5	2.3	12.4	58.3	92.9	39.0	35.2	1,552	868
Dade	469	1,393,274	2.2	10.4	0.3	2.0	1.6	7.0	75.5	35.2	15.9	16.2	999	585
Dawson	830	3,226,303	9.9	10.6	5.8	1.7	1.2	3.9	64.0	82.4	20.5	52.8	2,165	1,173
Decatur	1,626	5,616,306	4.4	8.5	1.3	2.1	31.4	2.8	47.4	142.0	40.5	41.4	1,550	1,012
DeKalb	26,965	181,019,159	4.5	4.7	1.6	0.4	23.7	2.6	61.7	3,353.9	815.6	1,202.8	1,601	1,144
Dodge	1,053	3,799,900	2.7	4.3	0.8	1.4	27.3	1.4	61.2	124.3	32.9	18.1	872	513
Dooly	452	1,485,388	12.1	18.9	0.5	5.1	6.1	5.1	52.1	39.7	12.3	16.4	1,200	806
Dougherty	4,459	14,873,418	6.7	11.0	4.7	2.8	7.3	9.4	55.6	360.7	141.6	134.9	1,508	932
Douglas	4,718	18,148,063	7.4	10.3	4.0	1.5	0.8	4.6	68.7	459.2	185.2	194.5	1,357	891
Early	535	1,742,905	6.9	3.7	2.8	3.9	5.1	4.7	70.3	36.7	17.5	15.4	1,492	1,063
Echols	160	484,584	5.8	5.7	0.0	3.8	1.3	2.1	81.2	12.3	7.1	4.5	1,144	846

1. Based on the resident population estimated as of July 1 of the year shown.

STATE County	Local government finances, 2017 (cont.) — Direct general expenditure — Total (mil dol)	Per capita[1] (dollars)	Percent of total for: Education	Health and hospitals	Police protection	Public welfare	Highways	Debt outstanding — Total (mil dol)	Per capita[1] (dollars)	Government employment, 2020 — Federal civilian	Federal military	State and local	Individual income tax returns, 2019 — Number of returns	Mean adjusted gross income	Mean income tax
	185	186	187	188	189	190	191	192	193	194	195	196	197	198	199
FLORIDA—Cont'd															
Putnam	363.4	4,952	40.6	2.6	5.0	0.0	3.7	76.6	1,044	153	125	3,577	31,430	42,025	3,275
St. Johns	911.8	3,742	44.8	2.1	8.8	0.9	4.7	1,335.0	5,478	678	478	9,758	133,270	111,647	17,060
St. Lucie	1,195.1	3,816	40.7	0.9	8.5	1.1	9.1	2,143.9	6,846	816	643	12,578	161,470	54,976	5,471
Santa Rosa	425.7	2,446	57.6	1.6	10.2	0.0	3.8	320.3	1,840	912	1,498	5,973	85,510	69,877	7,586
Sarasota	2,329.3	5,550	24.9	33.8	5.7	0.0	3.9	1,745.3	4,159	1,114	798	13,589	226,620	98,022	15,068
Seminole	1,548.5	3,346	46.8	1.8	8.7	0.6	7.8	836.5	1,807	1,106	803	15,610	236,320	72,689	9,155
Sumter	307.7	2,461	27.6	1.1	7.3	0.5	7.7	579.9	4,640	1,748	232	3,126	65,400	86,555	11,166
Suwannee	132.9	3,012	48.3	4.6	5.7	0.7	11.8	25.2	571	117	72	2,320	17,940	42,959	3,613
Taylor	72.1	3,310	46.7	2.7	8.8	0.5	6.5	7.4	340	42	33	1,310	8,370	48,410	3,826
Union	36.0	2,332	59.1	5.4	6.1	0.7	5.8	2.6	169	20	18	1,940	5,090	45,352	3,151
Volusia	2,354.4	4,377	29.1	27.0	7.0	0.3	3.9	2,352.3	4,373	1,442	1,053	19,596	274,990	59,004	6,634
Wakulla	81.4	2,540	54.9	4.5	14.2	0.1	3.1	5.9	183	92	53	1,817	14,630	55,862	4,833
Walton	290.9	4,277	36.2	5.4	11.8	0.1	8.1	108.8	1,599	182	127	3,355	36,290	113,176	19,422
Washington	92.2	3,755	55.1	3.4	4.3	0.0	10.7	11.1	453	38	47	1,774	10,260	44,925	3,421
GEORGIA	X	X	X	X	X	X	X	X	X	107,626	94,929	575,231	4,751,840	67,630	8,162
Appling	102.1	5,538	40.4	32.1	3.5	0.0	7.3	31.6	1,714	52	47	1,260	7,350	47,852	3,862
Atkinson	31.3	3,822	57.4	0.9	3.8	0.1	4.9	6.5	790	18	28	396	3,120	35,175	2,142
Bacon	36.8	3,288	59.8	2.0	5.7	0.1	6.7	35.9	3,203	47	29	578	4,280	42,114	3,150
Baker	9.6	3,032	62.8	1.2	7.0	0.0	11.2	0.0	0	2	8	124	1,170	37,493	3,583
Baldwin	117.1	2,604	51.0	8.3	8.3	0.0	3.5	44.2	983	86	130	5,140	17,750	46,652	4,041
Banks	45.0	2,416	70.1	0.3	8.7	0.0	3.3	28.6	1,536	21	51	844	7,660	50,661	3,883
Barrow	228.8	2,900	63.2	2.3	6.4	0.2	5.1	237.0	3,003	179	224	2,982	37,890	53,305	4,592
Bartow	343.2	3,265	56.3	1.7	8.8	0.2	5.5	214.2	2,038	218	286	4,834	48,750	56,336	5,346
Ben Hill	84.6	4,966	41.8	30.5	4.5	0.3	3.3	9.0	530	27	43	965	6,640	40,972	2,986
Berrien	50.1	2,624	61.1	2.3	5.4	0.3	4.8	20.1	1,052	39	51	881	6,980	43,793	3,762
Bibb	529.8	3,466	54.8	7.6	5.1	0.0	0.8	365.4	2,391	1,047	389	8,673	66,960	52,762	5,547
Bleckley	48.5	3,802	51.6	21.8	3.6	0.0	5.5	14.3	1,117	30	30	1,064	4,900	48,336	3,789
Brantley	54.0	2,869	73.8	3.4	3.1	0.1	5.1	7.1	379	26	50	784	6,950	42,015	2,725
Brooks	43.9	2,811	53.8	1.1	7.4	0.1	9.7	5.4	344	23	42	632	6,320	42,362	3,449
Bryan	123.7	3,343	64.8	2.3	6.8	0.0	3.9	64.1	1,732	187	107	1,919	19,050	66,909	6,830
Bulloch	221.4	2,914	51.0	11.6	6.6	0.0	3.8	271.8	3,577	166	220	7,511	29,020	51,836	5,092
Burke	118.1	5,240	54.9	8.9	3.7	0.0	6.5	19.9	883	47	60	1,446	9,710	47,628	4,173
Butts	64.3	2,672	55.0	1.1	9.5	0.1	6.4	25.9	1,076	55	59	1,480	10,180	52,912	4,938
Calhoun	21.2	3,312	49.5	15.0	5.2	0.8	5.3	11.8	1,851	22	12	424	1,990	34,994	2,413
Camden	162.3	3,061	53.2	3.7	5.6	0.1	5.8	134.7	2,542	2,624	2,842	2,286	23,510	55,174	4,567
Candler	52.5	4,905	38.5	30.5	5.4	0.0	4.9	23.6	2,200	23	28	694	4,270	43,567	3,389
Carroll	367.6	3,131	62.2	0.5	6.2	0.0	2.9	446.1	3,800	256	309	6,960	50,330	55,977	5,212
Catoosa	244.5	3,677	50.4	28.3	3.3	0.2	2.5	151.2	2,274	89	178	2,585	28,730	53,375	4,464
Charlton	40.1	3,130	43.5	5.7	7.3	0.1	7.0	6.8	527	33	29	409	3,810	43,401	2,948
Chatham	1,846.5	6,382	27.6	30.7	6.4	0.8	5.3	535.1	1,850	2,770	5,580	16,210	132,790	65,686	7,665
Chattahoochee	15.0	1,473	66.7	0.0	0.0	0.0	3.0	4.4	428	54	15,855	218	3,160	40,170	1,914
Chattooga	77.4	3,128	60.8	0.4	4.9	0.2	4.9	61.9	2,500	42	62	1,163	9,640	42,653	3,040
Cherokee	666.1	2,689	64.8	0.5	5.2	0.1	4.5	788.3	3,182	408	693	8,404	124,060	80,367	9,453
Clarke	892.9	7,041	22.4	50.5	3.5	0.1	1.4	638.1	5,031	934	370	23,552	49,010	57,143	6,496
Clay	16.2	5,472	25.4	32.0	5.2	0.5	4.8	7.1	2,405	39	7	147	1,170	39,021	2,730
Clayton	1,003.6	3,532	58.4	1.4	7.7	0.2	4.0	348.4	1,226	1,565	807	12,729	137,410	34,556	2,151
Clinch	33.0	4,969	46.2	28.1	3.6	0.4	3.8	14.1	2,117	15	17	510	2,410	45,649	3,821
Cobb	2,828.5	3,758	50.1	1.4	5.8	0.0	5.8	3,892.4	5,172	2,741	2,290	33,293	364,560	86,149	11,753
Coffee	134.3	3,132	62.4	1.1	5.8	0.0	6.5	19.3	449	114	105	2,669	16,330	41,614	3,756
Colquitt	175.6	3,860	63.1	5.1	4.3	0.1	3.8	108.7	2,389	118	122	3,534	17,210	45,059	3,820
Columbia	422.9	2,791	66.2	0.5	4.4	0.0	5.5	366.8	2,421	500	422	5,647	68,370	78,299	8,661
Cook	53.1	3,083	53.2	1.3	8.7	0.5	7.0	26.8	1,558	31	45	1,219	6,680	41,688	3,278
Coweta	401.5	2,805	60.7	1.5	7.3	0.0	6.3	203.0	1,418	294	395	5,033	67,650	73,587	8,157
Crawford	26.1	2,125	65.2	0.4	5.3	0.0	5.5	9.4	766	10	58	443	5,140	43,879	2,987
Crisp	96.1	4,230	50.5	1.0	7.0	0.0	9.0	34.4	1,516	48	57	1,327	8,200	41,796	3,367
Dade	38.7	2,378	64.4	1.2	6.3	0.2	5.1	11.5	707	26	40	582	6,260	51,022	4,118
Dawson	80.6	3,302	58.5	4.0	5.7	0.0	5.9	83.1	3,405	46	71	1,221	12,230	68,797	7,625
Decatur	144.4	5,406	36.2	32.4	5.5	0.0	3.1	71.6	2,680	51	67	2,073	11,160	42,293	3,498
DeKalb	3,396.2	4,521	39.0	25.5	5.0	0.3	1.8	2,576.9	3,430	11,393	1,992	33,683	361,560	72,406	9,605
Dodge	91.2	4,394	43.9	25.4	3.0	0.0	3.3	15.2	734	46	51	1,668	7,240	39,980	2,940
Dooly	39.6	2,894	42.0	3.1	11.5	1.0	8.5	26.0	1,898	61	30	639	3,780	41,197	3,091
Dougherty	383.7	4,290	47.5	3.3	6.7	0.0	2.7	142.2	1,589	2,626	533	6,193	35,690	43,580	4,035
Douglas	432.8	3,019	62.7	1.7	5.6	0.0	2.9	355.3	2,478	258	386	5,538	68,140	50,889	4,506
Early	42.2	4,090	56.3	6.1	5.0	0.0	5.4	8.5	820	39	26	1,218	4,170	39,212	3,140
Echols	12.0	3,072	74.2	2.0	1.9	0.0	8.6	5.6	1,431	1	13	194	1,350	39,303	2,564

1. Based on the resident population estimated as of July 1 of the year shown.

State / county code	CBSA code[1]	County Type code[2]	STATE County	Land area[3] (sq. mi)	Population, 2021: Total persons 2021	Population, 2021: Rank	Population, 2021: Per square mile	Race alone or in combination, not Hispanic or Latino (percent): White	Black	American Indian, Alaska Native	Asian and Pacific Islancer	Percent Hispanic or Latino[4]	Age (percent): Under 5 years	5 to 17 years	18 to 24 years	25 to 34 years	35 to 44 years	45 to 54 years
				1	2	3	4	5	6	7	8	9	10	11	12	13	14	15
			GEORGIA—Cont'd															
13103	42340	2	Effingham	478.8	66,741	807	139.4	77.5	16.0	0.9	1.9	5.9	6.4	15.4	12.4	13.5	14.8	12.9
13105		6	Elbert	351.1	19,579	1,848	55.8	64.0	29.0	0.7	1.4	6.3	5.6	12.8	11.0	12.2	11.4	11.7
13107		7	Emanuel	680.6	22,716	1,686	33.4	60.0	34.6	0.6	1.0	4.9	6.5	14.4	13.2	12.8	12.7	11.2
13109		6	Evans	182.9	10,672	2,364	58.3	56.9	30.8	0.7	1.1	12.0	6.0	14.6	13.7	12.2	12.4	12.3
13111		8	Fannin	387.1	25,817	1,568	66.7	95.0	1.4	1.2	1.0	2.8	3.7	8.9	9.1	8.7	9.5	11.6
13113	12060	1	Fayette	194.6	120,574	527	619.6	60.4	27.2	0.7	6.1	7.9	4.3	13.5	13.4	9.0	11.9	13.7
13115	40660	3	Floyd	509.8	98,771	620	193.7	71.6	15.6	0.7	1.9	12.1	5.7	13.0	14.2	13.0	12.1	12.4
13117	12060	1	Forsyth	224.6	260,206	272	1,158.5	67.4	5.2	0.6	18.8	9.8	5.5	15.6	13.0	9.4	16.2	16.3
13119		8	Franklin	261.4	23,785	1,651	91.0	83.4	10.0	0.8	1.9	5.6	5.8	12.4	13.6	12.4	10.8	12.5
13121	12060	1	Fulton	526.7	1,065,334	43	2,022.7	40.5	45.0	0.7	8.8	7.3	5.4	11.9	13.8	17.1	14.4	13.6
13123		6	Gilmer	426.2	32,026	1,381	75.1	85.6	1.2	0.9	0.8	12.5	4.9	10.4	9.7	9.4	10.2	12.5
13125		9	Glascock	143.7	2,919	2,963	20.3	88.4	9.6	1.1	0.9	1.7	5.0	11.7	13.3	9.7	12.2	14.4
13127	15260	3	Glynn	419.6	84,739	680	202.0	65.1	26.7	0.7	2.3	6.9	5.2	12.0	11.8	11.6	11.7	12.1
13129	15660	4	Gordon	356.4	58,237	901	163.4	77.3	4.9	0.7	1.7	17.1	5.7	13.3	13.4	12.8	12.7	14.0
13131		6	Grady	454.5	25,918	1,564	57.0	58.5	28.7	1.0	0.8	12.1	6.1	13.9	12.0	11.1	11.9	12.0
13133		6	Greene	387.5	19,536	1,850	50.4	60.6	31.5	0.7	1.5	6.8	4.3	10.5	9.3	9.1	9.9	10.5
13135	12060	1	Gwinnett	430.8	964,546	52	2,239.0	35.3	30.5	0.7	14.1	22.2	6.1	15.2	14.2	12.9	14.2	14.3
13137	18460	6	Habersham	276.9	46,774	1,041	168.9	77.0	4.5	0.8	2.7	16.6	5.5	12.7	13.6	12.6	12.0	12.2
13139	23580	3	Hall	393.0	207,369	329	527.7	60.6	8.2	0.6	2.6	29.5	6.1	13.5	13.8	12.9	12.4	13.1
13141	33300	7	Hancock	471.1	8,630	2,522	18.3	26.8	69.0	0.7	1.3	3.1	3.1	8.8	10.3	14.3	11.7	11.5
13143	12060	1	Haralson	282.2	30,572	1,419	108.3	91.8	5.6	0.9	1.3	2.3	6.4	13.7	12.2	12.9	12.6	13.5
13145	17980	2	Harris	463.8	35,626	1,293	76.8	77.5	16.7	1.0	2.3	4.7	4.8	12.9	11.4	10.6	12.5	13.8
13147		6	Hart	232.4	26,409	1,548	113.6	76.3	19.4	0.5	1.5	3.9	5.0	11.7	11.1	11.6	10.7	12.7
13149	12060	1	Heard	296.0	11,565	2,311	39.1	86.1	11.1	1.0	1.0	3.0	5.2	13.2	12.1	12.3	11.5	13.6
13151	12060	1	Henry	318.7	245,235	284	769.5	37.6	52.3	0.8	4.2	7.9	5.6	14.4	14.6	12.6	13.2	14.7
13153	47580	3	Houston	376.0	166,829	405	443.7	56.3	34.8	0.8	4.5	6.9	6.3	15.0	13.1	14.2	14.0	11.7
13155		7	Irwin	354.4	9,618	2,443	27.1	67.9	27.4	0.3	0.9	4.5	5.1	11.5	12.9	14.3	13.5	12.8
13157	27600	4	Jackson	339.7	80,286	711	236.3	80.1	8.7	0.7	2.8	9.6	6.2	14.7	11.9	13.2	14.3	13.3
13159	12060	1	Jasper	368.4	15,278	2,072	41.5	77.6	18.5	0.8	0.7	4.1	5.4	13.4	11.9	12.0	11.8	13.4
13161		7	Jeff Davis	330.9	14,872	2,096	44.9	71.2	15.6	0.5	0.9	13.0	6.3	15.0	13.4	11.8	12.2	12.6
13163		6	Jefferson	526.6	15,524	2,059	29.5	43.5	52.3	0.5	0.8	4.1	6.0	13.4	12.1	12.6	12.0	11.8
13165		6	Jenkins	347.3	8,639	2,520	24.9	51.0	41.3	0.7	1.3	6.9	5.3	11.2	13.3	15.1	12.8	12.3
13167	20140	7	Johnson	303.0	9,160	2,478	30.2	62.2	34.9	0.6	0.7	3.0	5.4	9.7	11.0	13.1	13.3	14.1
13169	31420	3	Jones	393.9	28,400	1,484	72.1	71.7	26.0	0.7	1.0	2.2	5.0	13.2	12.5	11.6	12.5	13.1
13171	12060	1	Lamar	183.5	19,080	1,867	104.0	67.3	29.6	0.8	1.1	3.1	5.6	11.8	16.7	13.0	10.9	12.0
13173	46660	3	Lanier	196.5	9,907	2,417	50.4	68.7	23.5	1.4	1.9	7.4	6.1	13.5	12.8	14.3	13.7	11.5
13175	20140	5	Laurens	807.3	49,547	1,003	61.4	58.3	38.5	0.5	1.3	2.9	6.3	14.0	12.3	12.3	12.0	12.2
13177	10500	3	Lee	355.9	33,411	1,345	93.9	69.2	25.1	0.6	3.0	3.4	5.8	15.2	13.0	12.8	14.8	13.5
13179	25980	3	Liberty	516.5	65,711	818	127.2	40.7	46.2	1.1	3.9	12.6	10.0	15.0	16.6	19.2	11.7	8.3
13181	12260	2	Lincoln	210.4	7,749	2,592	36.8	69.1	28.6	1.0	0.9	2.2	4.9	11.0	9.1	11.2	10.4	11.9
13183	25980	3	Long	400.4	17,152	1,961	42.8	59.0	28.8	1.6	3.0	11.6	7.3	16.0	12.5	15.8	15.3	11.9
13185	46660	3	Lowndes	497.2	119,276	532	239.9	54.0	38.4	0.7	2.9	6.3	6.7	13.9	20.1	14.5	11.8	10.0
13187		6	Lumpkin	282.9	34,278	1,322	121.2	91.6	2.2	1.3	1.3	5.2	4.3	9.6	22.0	11.1	10.2	11.0
13189	12260	2	McDuffie	257.4	21,633	1,730	84.0	54.5	42.2	0.6	0.9	3.6	6.3	14.4	12.4	11.7	11.2	11.9
13191	15260	3	McIntosh	431.4	11,123	2,336	25.8	64.4	32.4	1.0	1.0	2.9	4.2	8.1	9.0	10.8	9.3	12.9
13193		6	Macon	400.7	12,004	2,285	30.0	33.8	60.2	0.6	1.8	4.7	4.9	10.5	12.3	14.9	12.8	11.9
13195	12020	3	Madison	282.3	30,885	1,406	109.4	81.2	10.8	0.6	2.4	6.7	6.0	13.3	11.5	12.8	12.3	12.6
13197	17980	2	Marion	365.7	7,440	2,624	20.3	60.3	30.3	1.6	1.8	8.2	5.0	11.6	11.1	10.7	10.5	12.9
13199	12060	1	Meriwether	500.9	20,793	1,773	41.5	59.1	38.0	0.8	1.0	2.9	5.6	11.7	11.5	12.0	10.9	12.0
13201		8	Miller	282.4	5,919	2,741	21.0	67.6	29.0	0.9	0.8	3.4	6.1	12.8	11.3	10.4	11.5	11.5
13205		6	Mitchell	512.2	21,521	1,734	42.0	46.4	47.8	0.7	1.2	5.3	5.2	13.0	12.2	13.5	12.7	12.7
13207	31420	3	Monroe	396.1	28,712	1,469	72.5	74.5	22.4	0.6	1.4	2.6	4.9	12.1	11.7	11.9	12.5	13.1
13209	47080	9	Montgomery	241.1	8,653	2,519	35.9	66.8	26.2	0.6	1.0	7.0	5.3	11.6	15.3	12.3	11.7	12.8
13211	12060	1	Morgan	347.4	20,635	1,783	59.4	75.1	21.4	0.7	1.0	3.4	5.7	12.6	11.6	10.8	11.7	12.7
13213	19140	3	Murray	344.5	39,951	1,182	116.0	82.1	1.6	0.7	0.8	16.0	6.0	13.2	13.2	12.9	12.2	13.7
13215	17980	2	Muscogee	216.5	205,617	336	949.7	41.3	48.6	1.0	4.1	8.2	6.9	14.1	13.5	15.9	13.2	10.9
13217	12060	1	Newton	273.8	115,355	544	421.3	43.2	50.0	0.7	1.8	6.5	6.1	14.6	14.6	12.7	12.7	13.9
13219	12020	3	Oconee	184.3	43,023	1,126	233.4	84.6	5.6	0.5	5.1	5.9	5.1	15.9	13.3	8.5	14.3	14.1
13221	12020	3	Oglethorpe	439.1	15,140	2,083	34.5	76.0	18.1	0.9	1.4	5.8	5.2	11.8	10.9	12.4	12.3	13.1
13223	12060	1	Paulding	312.4	173,780	388	556.3	67.1	24.5	0.8	2.1	8.0	6.0	14.8	13.2	13.6	14.3	14.8
13225	47580	3	Peach	150.3	28,417	1,483	189.1	46.1	45.0	0.8	1.6	8.4	5.8	11.6	17.3	12.0	11.3	11.2
13227	12060	1	Pickens	232.1	34,024	1,330	146.6	94.3	1.9	0.9	1.1	3.4	4.5	10.8	10.8	11.4	10.7	13.0
13229	48180	6	Pierce	340.5	19,976	1,814	58.7	85.1	9.7	1.0	1.2	5.1	6.4	13.7	12.7	11.6	12.4	13.0
13231	12060	1	Pike	216.1	19,477	1,852	90.1	88.6	9.5	0.8	0.9	2.0	5.5	13.3	12.8	11.3	13.1	14.4
13233	16340	4	Polk	310.3	43,496	1,113	140.2	72.4	13.7	0.6	1.0	14.1	6.7	14.3	13.0	13.2	12.4	12.2
13235		3	Pulaski	249.3	9,917	2,414	39.8	63.0	32.8	0.6	1.6	3.8	4.5	9.9	11.1	12.4	12.0	13.0

1. CBSA = Core Based Statistical Area. See Appendix A for explanation. See Appendix B for list of metropolitan areas with component counties. 2. County type code from the Economic Research Service of USDA Rural-Urban Continuum Codes. See Appendix A for definition. 3. Dry land or land partially or temporarily covered by water. 4. May be of any race.

STATE County	Population, 2021 (cont.)				Population change, 2000–2021							Households, 2016–2020				
	Age (percent) (cont.)				Total persons		Percent change		Components of change, 2020–2021					Percent		
	55 to 64 years	65 to 74 years	75 years and over	Percent female	2010	2020	2010–2020	2020–2021	Births	Deaths	Net Migration	Number	Persons per household	Family house-holds	Female family house-holder[1]	One person
	16	17	18	19	20	21	22	23	24	25	26	27	28	29	30	31
GEORGIA—Cont'd																
Effingham	12.4	7.9	4.3	50.1	52,250	64,769	24.0	3.0	984	704	1,701	21,828	2.8	72.4	11.7	24.2
Elbert	14.1	12.3	8.8	52.0	20,166	19,637	-2.6	-0.3	244	430	127	7,695	2.5	66.7	14.8	28.2
Emanuel	12.6	10.1	6.4	50.3	22,598	22,768	0.8	-0.2	337	434	41	8,273	2.6	68.2	22.1	27.6
Evans	12.7	9.5	6.7	50.7	11,000	10,774	-2.1	-0.9	164	192	-73	4,006	2.5	69.6	22.1	26.4
Fannin	17.8	19.1	11.7	50.7	23,682	25,319	6.9	2.0	224	521	806	11,174	2.3	69.1	8.7	27.2
Fayette	14.8	11.8	7.7	51.4	106,567	119,194	11.8	1.2	1,055	1,351	1,695	40,792	2.8	77.9	10.0	19.2
Floyd	12.6	10.1	6.9	51.1	96,317	98,584	2.4	0.2	1,324	1,669	515	36,192	2.6	70.2	16.0	25.4
Forsyth	11.7	7.4	4.9	50.0	175,511	251,283	43.2	3.6	2,791	2,074	8,267	80,319	2.9	81.0	7.0	15.1
Franklin	13.4	11.3	7.8	50.9	22,084	23,424	6.1	1.5	355	477	488	8,425	2.7	73.2	13.3	22.8
Fulton	11.6	7.7	4.7	51.5	920,581	1,066,710	15.9	-0.1	14,484	11,011	-5,056	427,379	2.4	53.7	14.0	37.8
Gilmer	16.6	16.7	9.6	49.5	28,292	31,353	10.8	2.1	372	556	868	12,423	2.5	68.0	9.7	26.6
Glascock	15.1	10.8	7.8	50.5	3,082	2,884	-6.4	1.2	35	50	51	1,118	2.6	65.0	13.1	31.4
Glynn	14.1	12.9	8.5	52.9	79,626	84,499	6.1	0.3	1,017	1,414	631	34,191	2.4	66.0	14.9	29.1
Gordon	12.9	9.5	5.9	50.5	55,186	57,544	4.3	1.2	816	854	724	20,446	2.8	72.9	11.2	23.0
Grady	13.7	11.5	7.8	51.5	25,011	26,236	4.9	-1.2	357	374	-300	9,116	2.7	70.7	15.2	24.3
Greene	16.5	18.2	11.6	50.8	15,994	18,915	18.3	3.3	191	348	789	7,371	2.4	68.3	13.0	28.8
Gwinnett	12.0	7.3	3.8	51.0	805,321	957,062	18.8	0.8	13,306	7,274	1,225	299,683	3.1	75.2	13.6	20.8
Habersham	13.1	11.0	7.4	52.0	43,041	46,031	6.9	1.6	585	723	886	15,258	2.8	67.3	7.6	27.8
Hall	12.3	9.5	6.4	50.0	179,684	203,136	13.1	2.1	3,117	2,544	3,662	65,555	3.1	74.7	12.9	20.5
Hancock	15.5	14.8	9.9	43.6	9,429	8,735	-7.4	-1.2	67	218	47	3,072	2.0	62.8	23.0	34.3
Haralson	12.8	9.5	6.4	50.9	28,780	29,919	4.0	2.2	464	581	778	11,454	2.6	72.6	10.8	23.2
Harris	15.0	12.2	6.8	49.6	32,024	34,668	8.3	2.8	358	462	1,074	12,429	2.7	80.0	8.4	18.6
Hart	14.8	13.3	9.2	50.5	25,213	25,828	2.4	2.2	292	481	781	10,271	2.4	65.9	11.3	29.4
Heard	14.6	10.8	6.7	50.2	11,834	11,412	-3.6	1.3	155	168	164	4,649	2.5	69.8	14.4	26.6
Henry	12.7	8.0	4.3	52.4	203,922	240,712	18.0	1.9	3,177	2,540	3,886	78,204	2.9	75.3	16.8	21.1
Houston	12.4	8.4	4.9	51.6	139,900	163,633	17.0	2.0	2,392	1,995	2,798	58,042	2.7	70.2	13.6	25.1
Irwin	12.0	10.0	8.0	47.2	9,538	9,666	1.3	-0.5	124	162	-13	3,477	2.7	65.0	14.1	33.0
Jackson	12.1	8.8	5.5	50.2	60,485	75,907	25.5	5.8	1,118	976	4,286	24,268	2.9	79.1	11.5	16.1
Jasper	14.5	11.0	6.4	50.6	13,900	14,588	4.9	4.7	177	235	760	5,326	2.6	78.4	15.0	17.9
Jeff Davis	12.7	9.8	6.4	50.5	15,068	14,779	-1.9	0.6	233	257	114	5,139	2.9	75.0	21.5	20.6
Jefferson	13.4	11.7	7.1	51.3	16,930	15,709	-7.2	-1.2	214	342	-58	5,583	2.7	67.8	17.4	28.0
Jenkins	12.9	10.4	6.7	46.4	8,340	8,674	4.0	-0.4	106	155	13	3,392	2.5	60.9	11.6	31.7
Johnson	13.5	11.6	8.3	42.9	9,980	9,189	-7.9	-0.3	130	174	15	3,483	2.5	64.4	18.4	34.1
Jones	13.8	11.3	6.9	51.3	28,669	28,347	-1.1	0.2	290	419	182	10,914	2.6	73.0	11.8	23.0
Lamar	13.3	10.3	6.5	51.9	18,317	18,500	1.0	3.1	247	329	670	6,658	2.6	56.0	8.9	38.8
Lanier	13.4	9.3	5.4	49.5	10,078	9,877	-2.0	0.3	157	158	28	3,825	2.7	66.4	10.4	30.6
Laurens	12.7	10.6	7.5	52.3	48,434	49,570	2.3	0.0	695	884	158	17,159	2.7	67.1	16.8	29.7
Lee	11.3	9.1	4.5	49.8	28,298	33,163	17.2	0.7	403	400	240	10,550	2.7	78.6	14.1	19.2
Liberty	9.0	6.7	3.6	49.2	63,453	65,256	2.8	0.7	1,770	560	-764	24,053	2.5	69.6	18.8	25.4
Lincoln	16.6	15.1	9.8	51.3	7,996	7,690	-3.8	0.8	81	137	117	3,277	2.4	67.9	15.9	27.8
Long	10.9	7.1	3.3	49.8	14,464	16,168	11.8	6.1	314	171	852	6,006	3.2	69.6	14.1	25.6
Lowndes	10.2	7.9	4.9	51.7	109,233	118,251	8.3	0.9	1,952	1,457	501	42,755	2.6	62.8	15.9	28.9
Lumpkin	13.2	11.6	6.9	50.4	29,966	33,488	11.8	2.4	333	436	900	11,866	2.7	65.6	7.6	25.7
McDuffie	13.5	11.3	7.3	52.6	21,875	21,632	-1.1	0.0	317	367	49	8,238	2.6	70.1	19.7	25.3
McIntosh	16.8	17.0	11.8	51.5	14,333	10,975	-23.4	1.3	121	227	258	6,343	2.2	68.2	13.5	28.9
Macon	14.2	11.8	6.6	44.3	14,740	12,082	-18.0	-0.6	159	205	-33	4,648	2.4	62.7	20.7	35.0
Madison	13.8	10.9	6.8	50.6	28,120	30,120	7.1	2.5	474	431	727	10,622	2.8	76.0	17.0	19.6
Marion	16.7	12.8	8.7	51.0	8,742	7,498	-14.2	-0.8	98	125	-29	3,423	2.4	73.8	15.1	23.5
Meriwether	15.1	12.7	8.4	51.9	21,992	20,613	-6.3	0.9	297	392	278	8,255	2.5	68.1	23.6	29.8
Miller	14.2	11.5	10.7	52.2	6,125	6,000	-2.0	-1.4	75	109	-45	2,339	2.4	68.1	18.0	28.3
Mitchell	13.3	10.2	7.2	47.8	23,498	21,755	-7.4	-1.1	273	388	-123	8,018	2.5	65.8	25.7	23.6
Monroe	14.4	11.8	7.6	50.0	26,424	27,957	5.8	2.7	299	499	969	10,177	2.6	67.5	9.9	28.8
Montgomery	13.3	10.9	6.7	48.9	9,123	8,610	-5.6	0.5	114	139	68	3,061	2.7	72.4	14.5	23.7
Morgan	14.2	12.1	8.5	51.6	17,868	20,097	12.5	2.7	243	292	595	7,040	2.7	76.6	14.4	21.2
Murray	13.4	9.5	5.9	50.3	39,628	39,973	0.9	-0.1	534	632	67	14,520	2.7	75.3	12.6	20.0
Muscogee	11.4	8.7	5.5	51.3	189,885	206,922	9.0	-0.6	3,411	2,827	-1,906	73,648	2.6	60.9	18.9	34.2
Newton	12.2	8.4	4.9	52.7	99,958	112,483	12.5	2.6	1,627	1,463	2,730	37,543	2.9	73.9	17.5	20.8
Oconee	12.3	9.9	6.4	50.7	32,808	41,799	27.4	2.9	422	413	1,228	13,773	2.8	81.8	9.1	16.7
Oglethorpe	14.9	11.5	7.7	50.3	14,899	14,825	-0.5	2.1	176	249	392	5,477	2.7	68.7	13.8	29.2
Paulding	12.1	7.4	3.9	51.0	142,324	168,661	18.5	3.0	2,339	1,722	4,520	54,993	3.0	78.3	13.5	17.6
Peach	14.0	10.6	6.2	51.7	27,695	27,981	1.0	1.6	418	393	410	10,215	2.5	65.0	18.5	31.1
Pickens	16.2	14.5	8.2	50.5	29,431	33,216	12.9	2.4	345	535	1,010	12,129	2.6	72.5	10.4	23.7
Pierce	12.7	10.5	7.0	50.3	18,758	19,716	5.1	1.3	274	339	326	7,178	2.7	68.6	15.9	28.4
Pike	13.5	9.7	6.3	50.8	17,869	18,889	5.7	3.1	250	265	612	6,163	3.0	72.9	8.7	24.1
Polk	12.7	9.4	6.1	51.0	41,475	42,853	3.3	1.5	708	720	656	15,425	2.7	69.5	14.2	25.2
Pulaski	14.1	12.9	10.1	57.1	12,010	9,855	-17.9	0.6	126	184	120	3,803	2.5	64.4	20.1	32.6

1. No spouse present.

STATE County	Persons in group quarters, 2021	Daytime Population, 2016–2020		Births, 2021		Deaths, 2021		Persons under 65 with no health insurance, 2019		Medicare, 2021			COVID-19 Deaths, 2020	
		Number	Employment/ residence ratio	Total	Rate[1]	Number	Rate[1]	Number	Percent	Total beneficiaries	Enrolled in Original Medicare	Enrolled in Medicare Advantage	Number	Rate[1]
	32	33	34	35	36	37	38	39	40	41	42	43	44	45
GEORGIA—Cont'd														
Effingham	523	46,836	0.5	773	11.7	589	8.9	7,337	13.0	9,711	5,645	4,066	32	0.5
Elbert	246	17,988	0.9	211	10.8	337	17.2	2,691	18.2	5,185	2,857	2,328	30	1.5
Emanuel	1,307	21,718	0.9	272	12.0	352	15.5	3,044	17.4	4,959	2,632	2,328	51	2.2
Evans	392	11,094	1.1	131	12.2	152	14.2	1,575	18.9	2,147	1,171	976	12	1.1
Fannin	90	25,941	1.0	180	7.0	400	15.6	3,493	19.4	8,416	5,548	2,868	30	1.2
Fayette	449	114,944	1.0	851	7.1	1,082	9.0	10,537	11.3	24,228	15,127	9,101	74	0.6
Floyd	3,551	99,919	1.1	1,076	10.9	1,349	13.7	14,101	18.1	20,813	12,918	7,895	120	1.2
Forsyth	559	217,993	0.8	2,224	8.7	1,716	6.7	23,650	10.9	32,265	19,470	12,795	81	0.3
Franklin	745	22,595	1.0	288	12.2	369	15.6	3,484	19.3	5,475	3,070	2,406	35	1.5
Fulton	33,377	1,444,766	1.7	11,798	11.1	9,072	8.5	114,040	12.6	139,258	76,162	63,096	753	0.7
Gilmer	114	27,530	0.7	305	9.6	451	14.2	5,046	21.8	8,912	5,900	3,012	35	1.1
Glascock	64	2,101	0.3	29	10.0	36	12.4	338	14.0	599	383	217	11	3.8
Glynn	1,313	91,140	1.2	835	9.9	1,134	13.4	12,217	18.5	19,413	12,635	6,778	118	1.4
Gordon	537	57,946	1.0	655	11.3	684	11.8	9,421	19.6	10,906	7,043	3,864	65	1.1
Grady	196	20,841	0.6	291	11.2	322	12.4	3,997	20.4	5,457	3,179	2,278	40	1.5
Greene	143	19,359	1.2	162	8.4	295	15.3	2,295	18.0	6,167	3,928	2,238	27	1.4
Gwinnett	4,760	874,059	0.9	10,585	11.0	5,835	6.1	147,535	17.7	110,107	58,245	51,862	586	0.6
Habersham	2,303	41,806	0.8	460	9.9	551	11.9	7,023	20.3	9,947	5,638	4,309	79	1.7
Hall	2,663	203,563	1.0	2,503	12.2	2,022	9.8	36,780	21.6	36,023	21,578	14,444	220	1.1
Hancock	1,305	8,355	0.9	53	6.1	167	19.2	669	13.1	2,307	1,061	1,246	41	4.7
Haralson	269	27,143	0.8	379	12.5	438	14.5	4,091	16.6	6,275	3,480	2,795	52	1.7
Harris	305	25,179	0.4	286	8.1	406	11.5	3,082	10.9	7,271	4,673	2,598	31	0.9
Hart	564	24,158	0.8	235	9.0	402	15.4	3,845	19.5	6,760	4,115	2,645	39	1.5
Heard	59	9,582	0.5	111	9.6	136	11.8	1,536	16.0	2,277	1,230	1,047	D	D
Henry	887	198,363	0.7	2,560	10.5	2,081	8.5	25,109	12.2	34,973	17,890	17,083	158	0.7
Houston	1,481	155,911	1.0	1,922	11.6	1,593	9.6	17,854	13.2	26,029	18,311	7,717	118	0.7
Irwin	1,141	7,822	0.6	100	10.4	128	13.3	1,037	15.7	1,955	1,121	834	19	2.0
Jackson	639	69,158	1.0	905	11.5	796	10.1	9,513	15.3	13,733	7,836	5,896	82	1.1
Jasper	77	10,723	0.4	147	9.8	185	12.4	2,005	17.3	3,029	1,611	1,418	17	1.2
Jeff Davis	51	14,328	0.9	193	13.0	196	13.2	2,410	19.5	2,809	1,727	1,082	30	2.0
Jefferson	579	14,328	0.8	174	11.2	260	16.7	2,187	18.5	3,891	2,057	1,834	41	2.6
Jenkins	1,112	8,364	0.9	95	11.0	130	15.0	1,053	17.7	1,791	912	880	26	3.0
Johnson	1,502	8,351	0.6	110	12.0	137	14.9	1,031	16.6	1,899	1,043	856	29	3.2
Jones	195	21,400	0.4	237	8.4	328	11.6	3,307	14.2	5,892	3,192	2,701	21	0.7
Lamar	1,013	17,069	0.8	199	10.6	267	14.2	1,920	13.1	4,016	2,056	1,960	33	1.8
Lanier	153	8,518	0.5	130	13.1	137	13.8	1,298	15.1	1,642	1,078	564	12	1.2
Laurens	1,157	48,679	1.1	557	11.2	688	13.9	5,843	15.5	10,946	6,399	4,547	107	2.2
Lee	941	22,430	0.5	324	9.7	301	9.0	2,969	11.7	5,029	3,157	1,872	35	1.1
Liberty	2,375	67,250	1.2	1,445	22.1	424	6.5	6,540	12.2	7,811	5,022	2,789	37	0.6
Lincoln	38	6,398	0.5	67	8.7	116	15.0	1,029	17.5	2,173	1,242	931	18	2.3
Long	177	14,070	0.3	245	14.7	140	8.4	2,987	17.4	1,831	1,196	635	D	D
Lowndes	5,899	123,356	1.1	1,587	13.4	1,154	9.7	16,602	17.3	18,731	12,654	6,077	111	0.9
Lumpkin	2,940	28,387	0.7	266	7.8	345	10.2	4,668	19.0	6,783	4,288	2,495	22	0.7
McDuffie	235	20,576	0.9	259	12.0	297	13.7	2,770	16.3	4,974	2,304	2,670	24	1.1
McIntosh	17	11,409	0.6	102	9.2	192	17.4	1,668	16.4	3,251	1,746	1,505	14	1.3
Macon	1,663	12,610	0.9	132	11.0	159	13.2	1,522	17.6	2,565	1,269	1,296	11	0.9
Madison	193	21,779	0.4	381	12.5	356	11.6	4,470	18.3	6,560	3,692	2,868	27	0.9
Marion	17	6,834	0.5	82	11.0	103	13.8	1,231	19.0	1,682	928	754	D	D
Meriwether	173	17,859	0.6	240	11.6	312	15.1	2,851	17.4	5,408	2,574	2,834	21	1.0
Miller	124	5,413	0.9	63	10.6	89	15.0	749	17.2	1,390	863	527	D	D
Mitchell	2,041	21,238	0.9	206	9.5	296	13.7	2,932	18.4	4,592	2,468	2,124	54	2.5
Monroe	1,057	24,827	0.8	236	8.3	405	14.3	2,895	13.5	6,220	3,707	2,513	49	1.7
Montgomery	698	7,259	0.5	92	10.7	118	13.7	1,187	17.8	1,778	1,018	760	17	2.0
Morgan	145	20,469	1.2	187	9.2	222	10.9	2,266	14.8	4,729	2,571	2,157	13	0.6
Murray	211	32,706	0.6	433	10.8	490	12.3	6,817	20.4	7,818	5,492	2,326	43	1.1
Muscogee	7,075	219,002	1.3	2,720	13.2	2,283	11.1	21,415	13.3	35,598	21,237	14,361	218	1.1
Newton	1,484	91,020	0.6	1,293	11.3	1,168	10.2	15,821	16.7	18,967	9,344	9,623	117	1.0
Oconee	125	38,279	1.0	322	7.6	331	7.8	3,401	9.9	7,092	4,597	2,495	31	0.7
Oglethorpe	141	10,151	0.3	136	9.1	201	13.4	2,374	19.6	3,368	1,958	1,411	D	D
Paulding	383	120,476	0.5	1,851	10.8	1,385	8.1	20,564	13.7	22,485	12,711	9,774	112	0.7
Peach	1,415	26,142	0.9	333	11.8	305	10.8	3,800	17.7	5,671	3,482	2,189	36	1.3
Pickens	346	28,332	0.8	277	8.2	440	13.1	4,086	16.2	9,356	5,816	3,540	25	0.8
Pierce	122	16,778	0.7	214	10.8	264	13.3	2,854	18.0	4,187	2,610	1,577	38	1.9
Pike	196	14,078	0.4	202	10.5	218	11.4	2,361	15.0	3,665	2,035	1,630	33	1.7
Polk	305	39,243	0.8	565	13.1	600	13.9	6,337	17.9	8,840	5,084	3,756	51	1.2
Pulaski	985	10,462	0.8	104	10.5	154	15.6	1,161	15.8	2,106	1,323	783	23	2.3

1. Per 1,000 estimated resident population.

STATE County	COVID-19 Vaccinations, 2021–2022		Education: School enrollment and attainment, 2016–2020				Education: Local government expenditures,[3] 2018–2019		Money income, 2016–2020	Money income, 2016–2020: Households			Income and poverty, 2020	Percent below poverty level		
			Enrollment[1]		Attainment[2] (percent)						Percent					
	Number	Percent[5]	Total	Percent private	High school graduate or less	Bachelor's degree or more	Total current spending (mil dol)	Current spending per student (dollars)	Per capita income[4]	Median income (dollars)	with income of less than $50,000	with income of $200,000 or more	Median household income (dollars)	All persons	Children under 18 years	Children 5 to 17 years in families
	46	47	48	49	50	51	52	53	54	55	56	57	58	59	60	61
GEORGIA—Cont'd																
Effingham	24,855	38.7	16,043	12.1	48.4	23.9	127.9	10,040	32,608	67,050	35.3	4.5	77,690	8.1	11.3	10.9
Elbert	8,074	42.1	4,234	9.3	62.3	11.8	35.8	11,754	23,368	39,323	59.1	1.2	43,553	23.8	38.0	39.7
Emanuel	9,110	40.2	5,099	17.3	63.7	11.4	45.4	10,602	19,310	38,423	63.5	1.3	36,243	26.4	34.3	33.2
Evans	4,335	40.7	2,726	17.4	61.8	16.1	20.2	10,658	20,990	46,392	54.4	0.7	51,018	19.6	29.5	26.9
Fannin	11,008	42.0	4,228	16.3	46.2	22.1	38.8	12,968	29,845	46,028	53.8	4.8	44,730	15.6	24.1	23.1
Fayette	71,274	62.3	30,412	17.1	25.7	46.8	233.2	11,247	44,668	93,777	21.5	14.5	98,623	5.3	7.2	6.6
Floyd	41,796	42.4	24,112	20.7	49.7	21.4	193.5	11,915	27,418	50,657	49.5	3.8	47,423	18.4	26.2	25.6
Forsyth	129,654	53.1	67,646	16.6	21.9	54.8	487.7	9,884	46,470	112,834	19.3	20.2	116,690	5.1	5.4	4.8
Franklin	8,395	36.0	5,191	16.8	54.5	17.1	42.6	11,802	24,338	47,821	50.8	3.3	47,706	16.3	23.7	23.7
Fulton	600,621	56.5	274,762	21.4	24.2	54.5	2,052.0	13,728	49,369	72,741	35.8	14.9	71,504	13.0	17.5	15.9
Gilmer	12,830	40.9	5,482	9.2	51.1	21.4	50.8	12,117	27,789	57,376	44.8	2.8	66,066	14.0	23.5	22.2
Glascock	984	33.1	776	3.7	61.6	10.3	7.2	12,579	24,258	46,500	52.0	2.2	50,800	15.5	18.5	17.5
Glynn	43,927	51.5	19,262	14.3	38.3	29.7	147.0	11,064	33,975	56,952	43.9	5.5	59,286	15.5	24.5	22.0
Gordon	21,835	37.7	12,876	11.4	56.7	15.9	108.5	10,070	25,114	48,662	51.7	3.1	54,915	11.8	15.0	15.7
Grady	10,853	44.1	6,733	12.6	57.2	15.3	46.3	9,918	24,272	48,047	51.6	2.9	54,601	18.7	27.4	26.6
Greene	10,013	54.6	3,280	6.0	43.9	30.5	38.2	14,669	42,339	57,880	45.3	10.6	61,857	15.3	28.5	26.8
Gwinnett	517,190	55.2	267,514	13.6	34.6	37.4	2,086.4	10,997	31,935	72,787	32.9	7.8	73,460	10.4	13.5	13.2
Habersham	18,216	40.2	11,011	20.0	54.2	21.1	81.1	11,710	24,060	54,147	45.6	3.6	61,071	13.7	16.8	16.3
Hall	92,410	45.2	50,271	10.8	48.9	24.0	369.1	10,516	30,459	63,651	38.1	6.3	67,735	12.7	19.6	19.0
Hancock	4,085	48.3	910	7.4	67.2	9.3	14.6	17,427	17,802	32,914	68.9	2.5	36,424	30.7	41.2	39.3
Haralson	9,964	33.4	7,141	7.6	54.2	17.3	61.9	10,941	27,507	52,021	47.8	3.0	51,431	15.5	20.0	18.0
Harris	17,065	48.4	8,067	12.6	32.2	32.4	59.2	10,859	37,882	79,860	28.1	8.5	81,151	9.0	11.1	10.5
Hart	10,038	38.3	5,921	13.3	52.8	17.2	38.2	10,711	24,443	45,874	52.2	1.9	52,401	14.4	22.0	21.6
Heard	3,377	28.3	2,673	10.7	60.0	9.2	23.9	11,315	23,498	50,583	49.4	1.8	51,532	16.4	21.2	19.8
Henry	104,059	44.4	62,961	15.4	39.5	28.1	440.3	10,331	31,173	71,110	32.3	5.7	69,620	8.7	13.1	12.4
Houston	80,045	50.7	43,827	13.5	34.3	31.0	323.5	10,867	30,616	65,870	38.4	4.5	69,442	10.8	15.6	15.3
Irwin	3,448	36.6	2,043	9.5	55.4	17.2	20.2	11,775	21,123	41,484	56.6	3.5	47,492	20.9	30.9	30.4
Jackson	30,886	42.3	17,836	11.5	46.8	23.5	138.7	10,296	29,724	68,307	34.1	4.7	70,960	9.1	11.4	11.0
Jasper	4,956	34.9	3,054	21.9	57.1	14.6	26.4	11,097	24,270	52,409	48.5	2.2	57,796	14.0	21.6	20.8
Jeff Davis	4,693	31.0	3,763	8.7	58.7	11.0	31.4	10,122	18,452	36,987	64.4	0.8	44,417	20.0	29.4	29.0
Jefferson	8,323	54.2	3,618	17.1	61.9	10.7	27.5	11,059	21,178	37,009	59.9	1.5	40,333	21.1	33.1	31.7
Jenkins	3,288	37.9	1,754	7.7	68.9	5.2	15.2	13,064	14,212	25,712	74.1	0.1	38,306	28.0	35.7	34.4
Johnson	3,414	35.4	1,601	8.6	74.1	7.0	12.9	11,456	21,093	42,421	56.4	0.3	36,358	25.9	30.7	30.9
Jones	12,611	43.9	6,943	11.7	46.9	20.8	55.0	10,377	27,555	63,046	40.5	2.6	64,812	11.6	16.6	15.6
Lamar	6,645	34.8	5,290	4.6	52.9	14.0	27.7	10,344	24,576	50,088	49.9	2.4	55,024	13.8	20.9	20.8
Lanier	2,824	27.1	2,368	5.7	52.6	19.7	19.2	11,156	18,788	32,158	63.3	2.1	35,215	19.6	31.9	30.0
Laurens	22,148	46.6	11,002	12.0	55.1	17.1	94.5	10,549	23,694	39,476	60.1	3.4	46,690	20.7	31.0	32.5
Lee	13,869	46.2	8,782	12.0	37.2	27.1	61.4	9,447	29,379	68,338	33.5	3.4	74,640	10.1	14.7	14.1
Liberty	38,029	61.9	16,637	12.6	37.7	19.3	113.1	11,185	24,121	50,411	49.5	1.6	49,788	14.7	22.6	23.8
Lincoln	3,650	46.1	1,561	4.2	59.1	13.9	14.0	12,301	24,074	42,036	58.5	2.6	47,883	16.5	27.5	29.2
Long	4,179	21.4	4,756	8.1	55.1	14.7	34.5	9,094	22,553	52,099	48.9	2.4	53,841	16.7	23.5	22.5
Lowndes	46,981	40.0	34,552	9.2	44.4	26.2	193.8	9,866	24,580	46,113	52.2	2.9	48,864	20.3	27.3	25.2
Lumpkin	11,561	34.4	9,473	6.1	42.2	31.4	43.0	11,168	29,361	52,872	48.0	3.8	63,822	12.5	16.2	16.1
McDuffie	9,589	45.0	4,701	8.9	56.0	15.0	43.3	11,371	23,355	47,327	53.3	1.6	48,392	16.7	27.8	29.5
McIntosh	5,949	41.4	2,523	25.1	52.1	17.5	16.3	12,357	28,352	56,262	47.7	1.9	48,097	19.9	32.0	30.9
Macon	5,607	43.3	2,721	15.3	60.1	10.1	16.5	12,887	20,198	31,910	65.7	2.4	35,997	31.1	38.0	37.1
Madison	12,969	43.4	6,375	15.2	52.4	19.2	74.5	11,150	24,772	51,142	48.9	2.5	50,619	14.5	19.7	19.0
Marion	3,465	41.5	1,899	6.3	57.4	13.4	15.2	11,284	23,617	52,450	47.9	2.1	46,792	20.6	31.8	29.9
Meriwether	8,797	41.6	4,396	9.0	58.8	10.8	30.7	11,954	22,905	40,769	57.0	2.4	45,095	22.1	33.3	30.1
Miller	3,107	54.3	1,136	16.5	44.0	18.6	10.8	11,755	24,492	49,771	50.2	0.9	51,855	19.8	29.0	28.5
Mitchell	10,420	47.7	4,905	6.6	59.1	11.7	46.0	12,463	19,377	39,404	60.3	2.5	38,256	38.2	50.1	46.3
Monroe	11,625	42.2	6,024	22.6	47.1	26.6	49.1	12,103	34,630	60,491	40.9	8.8	65,599	12.8	17.9	17.5
Montgomery	3,286	35.8	2,351	24.3	54.8	16.5	10.9	12,212	23,744	45,230	52.4	3.5	47,074	19.3	26.0	25.2
Morgan	8,763	45.5	4,119	9.9	47.9	24.2	39.3	12,744	34,205	68,669	34.7	6.7	68,343	11.6	18.1	17.6
Murray	14,913	37.2	9,337	5.2	61.9	10.6	67.7	9,323	23,208	51,133	49.0	3.0	58,761	15.9	23.3	20.4
Muscogee	87,735	44.8	53,742	12.1	38.3	27.5	338.8	10,636	26,709	47,418	52.1	3.9	44,959	21.1	29.8	28.1
Newton	47,166	42.2	30,072	13.3	45.3	20.9	214.4	10,865	25,394	59,178	41.9	3.4	62,183	14.4	21.4	20.9
Oconee	23,023	57.2	11,123	16.4	24.7	50.6	82.6	10,297	49,099	95,064	26.4	14.9	104,519	6.0	6.8	5.9
Oglethorpe	6,461	42.3	3,410	9.2	54.5	19.6	24.2	11,530	25,884	52,816	46.7	3.2	55,678	13.4	20.6	20.2
Paulding	63,059	37.4	43,806	11.7	40.1	23.9	302.6	10,100	29,766	74,154	29.6	4.1	77,755	7.3	9.9	9.5
Peach	12,529	45.5	8,424	8.7	47.3	22.0	37.3	10,388	25,929	50,267	49.7	3.6	51,531	19.2	28.6	26.3
Pickens	13,566	41.6	6,379	11.2	45.7	22.7	53.4	12,329	32,501	68,365	37.8	4.8	69,781	10.5	18.0	17.4
Pierce	6,497	33.4	4,092	8.1	59.2	13.4	37.8	10,434	23,832	48,969	52.1	2.2	51,696	16.5	24.0	22.8
Pike	6,185	32.6	4,537	12.1	50.6	19.5	31.5	9,575	29,024	68,138	34.3	5.6	64,986	10.1	12.5	12.1
Polk	16,566	38.9	9,553	11.2	58.1	12.7	77.4	9,790	24,258	46,846	52.3	1.9	51,040	16.3	22.6	23.0
Pulaski	4,139	37.2	2,314	7.9	56.1	13.1	14.6	10,851	20,693	42,213	56.2	0.3	44,019	20.4	27.6	27.0

1. All persons 3 years old and over enrolled in nursery school through college. 2. Persons 25 years old and over. 3. Elementary and secondary education expenditures. 4. Based on population estimated by the American Community Survey, 2016–2020. 5. CDC percent based on 2019 population estimate.

STATE County	Personal income, 2020										Earnings, 2020		
			Per capita[1]			Supplements to wages and salaries, employer contributions (mil dol)						Contributions for government social insurance (mil dol)	
	Total (mil dol)	Percent change 2019–2020	Dollars	Rank	Wages and salaries (mil dol)	Pension and insurance	Government social insurance	Proprietors' income (mil dol)	Dividends, interest, and rent (mil dol)	Personal transfer reecipts (mil dol)	Total (mil dol)	From employee and self-employed	From employer
	62	63	64	65	66	67	68	69	70	71	72	73	74
GEORGIA—Cont'd													
Effingham	2,964	9.7	45,069	1,786	541	112	35	86	291	642	775	53	35
Elbert	743	7.7	38,414	2,632	243	52	17	39	123	289	351	27	17
Emanuel	848	12.1	37,678	2,716	284	61	20	53	98	332	418	27	20
Evans	398	9.6	37,408	2,750	171	33	13	25	52	132	241	16	13
Fannin	1,055	6.2	39,796	2,477	256	45	18	118	212	397	437	37	18
Fayette	8,268	5.0	71,384	147	2,431	355	164	428	1,590	1,324	3,378	218	164
Floyd	4,066	7.1	41,238	2,297	1,905	321	135	290	589	1,338	2,651	170	135
Forsyth	17,022	7.2	67,859	198	4,561	638	308	948	2,616	1,833	6,455	378	308
Franklin	826	1.8	35,134	2,927	322	55	23	59	121	310	459	32	23
Fulton	103,090	4.1	95,683	26	80,204	9,099	5,108	20,805	23,041	10,844	115,215	6,349	5,108
Gilmer	1,201	5.7	37,542	2,735	281	55	20	110	221	437	466	38	20
Glascock	109	6.8	36,615	2,812	14	4	1	2	14	36	21	2	1
Glynn	4,319	5.9	50,480	1,093	1,847	333	130	240	1,174	1,128	2,549	164	130
Gordon	2,219	6.6	37,759	2,709	1,167	180	82	119	249	657	1,547	100	82
Grady	924	6.8	37,725	2,713	261	53	19	95	113	296	428	28	19
Greene	1,155	3.9	61,326	372	286	47	20	93	471	292	445	33	20
Gwinnett	44,196	8.2	46,886	1,528	22,543	2,987	1,500	3,997	5,977	8,109	31,026	1,808	1,500
Habersham	1,690	6.0	36,691	2,805	613	131	43	88	282	539	875	61	43
Hall	10,073	6.2	48,759	1,287	5,116	764	339	716	1,849	2,190	6,936	425	339
Hancock	285	8.7	33,557	3,001	61	16	4	7	37	130	88	8	4
Haralson	1,197	7.3	39,401	2,523	342	65	23	52	134	388	482	34	23
Harris	1,846	7.0	51,168	1,005	221	44	15	60	301	412	341	29	15
Hart	1,040	4.3	39,402	2,522	286	57	21	82	175	348	446	33	21
Heard	411	8.2	34,362	2,967	112	30	8	19	43	138	169	12	8
Henry	10,477	10.8	43,812	1,972	3,148	519	224	360	1,241	2,544	4,251	280	224
Houston	7,458	8.0	46,579	1,565	3,602	911	273	241	1,261	1,835	5,026	282	273
Irwin	360	9.8	38,364	2,639	92	20	7	33	50	127	152	9	7
Jackson	3,436	9.6	45,099	1,780	1,452	230	106	149	420	786	1,936	137	106
Jasper	587	7.6	40,541	2,390	91	20	6	26	79	172	143	14	6
Jeff Davis	522	8.3	34,341	2,968	183	39	14	32	62	185	268	18	14
Jefferson	604	13.2	39,544	2,498	217	44	16	41	79	244	318	22	16
Jenkins	293	9.9	33,497	3,006	60	14	5	19	39	111	97	7	5
Johnson	270	9.7	27,965	3,101	55	14	4	8	31	118	81	8	4
Jones	1,193	7.0	41,436	2,276	187	37	13	28	160	340	264	19	13
Lamar	718	9.7	37,303	2,763	175	37	12	32	86	241	256	19	12
Lanier	333	10.1	31,021	3,076	57	15	4	14	40	117	90	6	4
Laurens	1,979	8.8	41,650	2,245	852	182	60	125	261	673	1,220	78	60
Lee	1,569	9.0	51,908	940	300	54	20	55	174	325	429	28	20
Liberty	2,526	8.8	40,087	2,446	1,892	570	169	32	464	750	2,662	117	169
Lincoln	325	7.8	40,424	2,399	52	12	3	17	45	111	84	8	3
Long	600	9.0	29,738	3,090	46	14	3	14	86	180	77	7	3
Lowndes	4,863	8.4	41,117	2,319	2,463	526	181	241	817	1,350	3,411	193	181
Lumpkin	1,408	7.0	41,181	2,311	351	83	24	70	247	396	529	36	24
McDuffie	870	8.1	41,111	2,321	287	55	22	31	114	305	395	28	22
McIntosh	496	9.3	34,500	2,961	74	18	5	18	105	177	115	11	5
Macon	432	4.8	33,955	2,981	124	25	9	58	59	157	215	11	9
Madison	1,184	5.2	38,890	2,582	153	36	10	59	162	373	258	23	10
Marion	269	7.3	31,621	3,067	41	10	3	5	55	96	58	6	3
Meriwether	828	10.1	39,121	2,554	204	45	15	33	104	318	296	23	15
Miller	280	7.1	49,844	1,161	80	20	5	35	40	81	140	7	5
Mitchell	858	7.7	39,711	2,483	267	55	20	105	136	282	448	27	20
Monroe	1,374	6.6	48,985	1,256	370	88	24	49	208	345	531	33	24
Montgomery	307	11.1	34,061	2,976	63	14	4	14	32	106	95	6	4
Morgan	1,081	6.9	55,032	701	339	57	24	59	220	249	479	33	24
Murray	1,355	8.7	33,841	2,986	326	61	23	66	133	469	476	37	23
Muscogee	9,445	7.3	48,080	1,377	5,349	1,034	381	364	2,243	2,720	7,128	414	381
Newton	4,334	11.2	38,256	2,657	1,304	232	88	117	516	1,289	1,741	120	88
Oconee	2,951	2.3	71,768	139	673	102	45	302	639	373	1,123	68	45
Oglethorpe	588	3.8	38,236	2,661	83	18	6	31	90	177	138	10	6
Paulding	7,384	11.0	42,595	2,117	1,164	209	78	232	816	1,525	1,684	112	78
Peach	1,172	8.7	41,931	2,211	434	85	32	65	201	374	615	42	32
Pickens	1,685	6.0	50,868	1,045	416	66	28	87	307	467	597	48	28
Pierce	780	8.8	39,979	2,459	178	34	13	34	113	262	259	20	13
Pike	847	7.2	44,311	1,901	132	26	9	41	111	206	209	17	9
Polk	1,550	8.7	36,190	2,857	491	91	36	50	163	567	668	51	36
Pulaski	388	9.0	34,636	2,957	117	24	8	18	77	132	167	12	8

1. Based on the resident population estimated as of July 1 of the year shown.

STATE County	Earnings, 2020 (cont.) — Percent by selected industries: Farm	Mining, quarrying, and extractions	Construction	Manu-facturing	Information; professional, scientific, technical services	Retail trade	Finance, insurance, real estate, and leasing	Health care and social assistance	Govern-ment	Social Security beneficiaries, December 2020: Number	Rate[1]	Supple-mental Security Income recipients, 2020	Housing units, 2021: Total	Percent change, 2010–2021
	75	76	77	78	79	80	81	82	83	84	85	86	87	88
GEORGIA—Cont'd														
Effingham	1.1	D	6.8	19.3	6.5	5.8	3.6	D	27.5	10,915	164	889	25,244	3.1
Elbert	-1.0	2.2	4.3	29.1	2.1	6.8	D	5.6	23.8	5,770	295	805	9,334	0.9
Emanuel	2.1	0.0	3.3	26.7	D	7.3	3.5	D	27.2	5,460	240	1,013	9,967	0.1
Evans	4.0	0.0	5.0	37.9	2.0	6.3	D	D	15.8	2,370	222	383	4,676	0.5
Fannin	0.8	0.0	12.1	D	5.1	12.9	9.7	13.4	13.5	9,080	352	663	18,076	2.1
Fayette	0.1	D	9.1	13.1	8.6	7.1	8.3	14.7	12.5	24,840	206	1,155	45,843	1.2
Floyd	0.3	D	3.0	17.4	D	6.5	5.6	25.8	13.8	22,795	231	3,217	40,751	0.6
Forsyth	0.1	0.1	11.9	10.4	15.5	6.6	6.8	11.5	9.8	31,600	121	1,145	90,456	2.8
Franklin	1.1	0.1	5.1	19.1	6.5	8.4	3.9	D	14.4	6,195	260	868	10,726	1.2
Fulton	0.0	0.1	2.7	2.6	31.5	3.0	16.9	7.4	9.2	140,130	132	26,622	498,665	0.7
Gilmer	3.6	D	11.1	15.1	6.5	10.5	6.1	6.5	16.5	9,675	302	613	18,093	1.8
Glascock	-1.4	0.1	D	0.4	2.3	5.2	D	D	39.8	665	228	98	1,408	0.3
Glynn	0.0	D	5.0	6.1	5.6	7.9	5.5	16.3	24.9	20,655	244	1,886	42,638	0.9
Gordon	0.6	0.0	5.0	41.6	D	5.1	3.4	9.5	11.5	12,115	208	1,515	23,029	1.0
Grady	8.3	0.2	6.0	16.8	D	6.5	3.9	D	17.5	5,815	224	992	11,583	0.3
Greene	1.4	D	14.6	8.5	7.3	7.4	12.8	9.4	12.2	6,370	326	600	10,443	2.3
Gwinnett	0.0	D	10.5	8.2	15.3	7.8	8.5	7.2	9.3	115,145	119	12,667	335,964	1.3
Habersham	1.2	D	5.2	25.1	D	8.2	5.8	5.4	20.1	10,960	234	952	18,635	1.4
Hall	-0.1	D	7.4	18.9	5.0	7.0	7.2	17.0	10.5	39,155	189	3,151	79,005	2.3
Hancock	3.7	D	D	D	D	3.9	D	D	42.7	2,605	302	415	4,927	0.5
Haralson	0.3	0.3	9.3	25.6	3.9	6.4	4.4	D	20.1	7,025	230	1,052	12,450	1.1
Harris	0.3	0.0	11.6	20.6	D	2.4	11.0	D	22.2	7,680	216	458	14,498	1.6
Hart	2.5	0.1	5.0	30.8	D	7.8	5.7	5.5	15.6	7,250	275	590	12,968	1.4
Heard	3.2	0.0	9.7	19.8	D	1.6	2.7	2.4	23.3	2,550	220	342	4,786	0.8
Henry	0.1	0.5	6.3	6.9	7.1	10.1	4.3	14.1	17.8	39,550	161	4,626	88,845	2.1
Houston	0.1	D	3.5	7.4	9.8	5.6	2.6	5.9	54.7	28,080	168	3,687	68,070	1.7
Irwin	15.8	0.0	10.7	D	D	4.5	D	2.4	24.2	2,225	231	351	4,187	0.6
Jackson	0.3	D	7.8	22.1	D	11.0	6.5	2.9	10.5	14,860	185	1,789	29,101	4.3
Jasper	0.2	0.0	12.3	17.0	D	4.8	4.3	D	25.5	3,405	223	338	6,395	1.7
Jeff Davis	2.8	0.0	2.3	25.7	D	6.9	2.5	D	19.3	3,225	217	496	6,369	0.2
Jefferson	8.4	D	6.8	19.0	D	6.1	2.8	D	17.7	4,230	272	816	7,150	0.0
Jenkins	15.0	0.0	4.0	3.8	D	5.2	D	D	22.5	1,940	225	441	4,096	0.6
Johnson	-0.8	0.0	5.3	6.2	D	6.5	D	18.0	35.7	2,185	239	537	3,552	0.3
Jones	0.2	0.0	18.2	0.7	9.6	6.4	3.1	D	26.0	6,515	229	371	11,728	1.0
Lamar	2.8	D	4.0	20.6	D	7.1	4.9	4.8	26.3	4,420	232	575	7,706	1.6
Lanier	5.2	0.1	6.7	11.4	D	D	D	2.2	39.5	1,855	187	343	4,129	1.2
Laurens	1.5	D	5.5	13.2	D	8.3	4.0	D	31.1	11,965	241	2,012	21,996	0.3
Lee	7.7	D	11.8	5.5	D	8.8	5.4	D	20.2	5,685	170	516	12,905	1.3
Liberty	0.0	D	0.8	7.8	D	3.2	1.5	1.9	74.0	9,185	140	1,444	27,171	1.6
Lincoln	1.5	0.0	22.0	2.4	3.0	7.4	7.9	1.7	24.9	2,380	307	226	4,447	1.1
Long	3.2	D	10.2	D	1.0	2.6	D	D	55.8	2,240	131	278	6,545	5.0
Lowndes	0.5	D	6.1	8.5	6.2	7.4	5.0	8.7	35.2	21,065	177	4,314	50,220	2.5
Lumpkin	-0.4	D	8.5	7.3	3.1	6.7	5.5	9.5	41.0	7,395	216	498	13,291	1.8
McDuffie	4.4	D	6.7	23.1	D	9.1	5.0	D	20.6	5,365	248	920	9,451	0.6
McIntosh	1.2	D	11.2	D	D	7.5	2.4	2.6	31.7	3,545	319	389	6,723	1.3
Macon	18.5	D	3.2	27.5	D	4.4	2.2	D	18.9	2,515	210	380	5,126	0.3
Madison	5.7	1.3	16.9	6.8	D	5.8	5.2	D	27.3	7,300	236	981	12,356	2.0
Marion	-0.5	D	D	D	D	5.7	2.2	D	30.5	1,830	246	273	3,525	0.7
Meriwether	1.4	0.0	15.4	18.0	D	5.7	2.3	D	22.9	5,820	280	797	9,543	0.7
Miller	21.5	0.0	2.6	1.1	D	5.7	6.8	3.9	44.4	1,450	245	291	2,859	0.2
Mitchell	19.0	D	D	D	D	5.7	5.3	D	17.3	4,960	230	971	9,040	0.0
Monroe	-0.4	D	8.6	2.4	5.7	4.9	3.2	5.6	32.1	6,610	230	536	11,320	1.8
Montgomery	8.2	0.0	4.6	6.1	D	4.1	5.1	D	21.6	1,965	227	325	3,770	0.7
Morgan	0.4	0.0	7.1	25.5	D	7.7	10.0	D	13.9	5,035	244	416	8,793	5.2
Murray	1.8	D	4.2	30.8	D	9.4	5.1	D	18.6	8,585	215	1,181	16,139	0.5
Muscogee	0.0	0.1	3.5	7.4	7.0	5.3	17.4	12.5	28.3	40,135	195	7,789	91,617	1.3
Newton	0.0	0.0	10.1	19.4	D	6.7	4.2	8.9	18.2	21,190	184	3,234	42,721	2.0
Oconee	0.8	D	7.3	6.6	10.0	6.9	11.3	10.1	9.7	7,550	175	324	15,320	1.8
Oglethorpe	14.3	2.9	17.3	7.8	D	3.1	5.2	D	22.1	3,630	240	281	6,431	1.2
Paulding	0.0	0.2	13.4	5.6	5.2	11.4	5.7	13.2	23.7	25,220	145	1,753	61,417	3.1
Peach	5.1	0.0	D	D	2.8	7.8	D	4.9	20.7	5,930	209	1,117	12,092	0.7
Pickens	-0.5	D	8.9	10.7	5.0	8.6	8.3	23.0	14.3	10,055	296	611	15,162	1.5
Pierce	5.3	0.0	8.8	8.1	D	8.7	3.7	D	18.6	4,325	217	707	8,446	0.8
Pike	1.1	D	25.6	9.7	4.4	5.3	5.7	D	20.5	4,080	209	389	7,228	1.9
Polk	1.7	D	5.9	29.8	2.7	10.3	2.3	9.3	17.8	9,870	227	1,675	17,277	-0.1
Pulaski	6.9	0.0	D	D	4.4	7.4	D	31.8	19.5	2,270	229	386	4,305	0.5

1. Per 1,000 resident population estimated as of July 1 of the year shown.

STATE County	Housing units, 2016–2020: Total	Occupied units: Owner-occupied: Percent	Owner-occupied: Median value[1]	Median owner cost as a percent of income: With a mortgage	Median owner cost as a percent of income: Without a mortgage[2]	Renter-occupied: Median rent[3]	Renter-occupied: Median rent as a percent of income[2]	Substandard units[4] (percent)	Civilian labor force, 2021: Total	Percent change, 2020–2021	Unemployment: Total	Unemployment: Rate[5]	Civilian employment[6], 2016–2020: Total	Percent: Management, business, science, and arts	Percent: Construction, production, and maintenance occupations
	89	90	91	92	93	94	95	96	97	98	99	100	101	102	103
GEORGIA—Cont'd															
Effingham	21,828	77.3	170,600	19.8	10.0	1,009	24.5	1.6	33,266	4.4	974	2.9	29,166	35.3	32.5
Elbert	7,695	71.6	87,400	23.8	11.2	674	26.0	4.0	7,810	-1.5	381	4.9	7,760	22.8	39.6
Emanuel	8,273	58.9	74,700	19.4	10.0	633	23.7	3.4	8,698	1.5	458	5.3	8,437	27.0	36.6
Evans	4,006	59.8	97,700	18.4	11.8	642	21.8	5.0	5,179	3.4	181	3.5	4,358	24.0	40.5
Fannin	11,174	77.8	206,900	24.1	10.0	680	30.2	1.8	11,797	6.0	334	2.8	9,986	29.8	24.8
Fayette	40,792	81.5	293,400	20.4	10.0	1,396	27.7	1.2	58,170	2.8	1,695	2.9	53,738	47.9	18.6
Floyd	36,192	62.5	137,600	19.4	10.0	786	29.3	3.3	43,891	1.8	1,614	3.7	42,403	29.2	31.9
Forsyth	80,319	84.2	362,300	18.7	10.0	1,432	27.9	1.4	127,031	3.3	3,157	2.5	120,236	53.3	12.7
Franklin	8,425	70.1	120,500	19.3	10.0	671	24.7	1.7	10,111	2.2	371	3.7	9,504	30.0	34.5
Fulton	427,379	52.9	326,700	19.6	10.0	1,263	29.3	2.3	569,144	1.9	26,480	4.7	545,793	53.1	12.1
Gilmer	12,423	73.4	205,800	20.3	10.0	785	27.4	4.1	12,343	2.7	374	3.0	13,004	28.0	31.5
Glascock	1,118	73.3	82,600	18.6	11.7	628	27.8	5.8	1,263	1.4	33	2.6	1,359	24.4	35.3
Glynn	34,191	65.0	194,300	20.2	10.0	899	28.0	1.8	39,201	2.4	1,474	3.8	39,008	34.8	21.4
Gordon	20,446	66.7	148,300	18.7	10.8	738	27.9	4.0	28,846	2.7	923	3.2	26,465	25.9	36.9
Grady	9,116	65.8	121,700	18.8	13.9	740	31.5	4.5	11,040	3.9	345	3.1	10,741	32.3	34.5
Greene	7,371	76.8	241,300	23.5	12.0	743	27.8	0.6	7,231	0.6	270	3.7	6,775	32.7	24.6
Gwinnett	299,683	66.5	235,700	20.7	10.0	1,331	31.6	3.0	492,181	2.5	17,181	3.5	464,715	39.3	21.7
Habersham	15,258	79.8	155,200	20.7	10.3	778	26.1	2.3	18,592	-0.7	662	3.6	19,545	31.9	32.2
Hall	65,555	68.9	212,700	20.2	10.0	987	29.0	5.3	104,792	2.4	2,792	2.7	95,737	31.1	33.1
Hancock	3,072	73.4	80,400	31.2	13.3	689	35.2	1.1	2,530	-0.4	161	6.4	2,350	22.6	23.2
Haralson	11,454	68.7	144,200	17.6	11.6	706	27.8	1.2	12,750	3.1	447	3.5	13,622	31.0	34.9
Harris	12,429	89.3	230,400	20.5	10.0	874	25.4	1.1	16,881	0.2	484	2.9	15,853	40.7	23.3
Hart	10,271	73.4	149,100	21.9	10.0	710	29.4	2.8	11,640	2.7	456	3.9	10,343	28.1	32.4
Heard	4,649	68.0	114,500	21.4	10.9	695	24.8	1.9	5,239	2.6	203	3.9	4,872	24.3	40.6
Henry	78,204	70.9	189,600	21.1	10.0	1,203	28.0	1.5	118,685	2.0	4,992	4.2	112,967	35.0	25.0
Houston	58,042	66.5	157,200	18.5	10.0	936	28.2	2.8	71,710	1.7	2,568	3.6	71,751	36.7	22.4
Irwin	3,477	69.3	83,200	19.1	10.5	582	26.0	4.3	3,568	2.4	161	4.5	3,773	26.5	42.5
Jackson	24,268	79.0	210,100	19.1	10.1	854	25.6	2.4	42,806	6.9	1,019	2.4	33,267	36.3	26.3
Jasper	5,326	80.0	145,000	22.2	11.2	926	24.6	2.6	7,065	3.6	227	3.2	5,835	26.7	35.7
Jeff Davis	5,139	65.4	85,900	19.9	12.1	568	26.4	4.1	6,100	-0.5	242	4.0	5,551	26.8	35.5
Jefferson	5,583	63.9	85,600	16.6	10.3	575	28.7	3.9	6,979	4.6	327	4.7	6,030	31.1	40.0
Jenkins	3,392	75.4	61,300	23.5	18.4	574	28.8	1.7	3,217	0.9	151	4.7	3,296	30.3	30.4
Johnson	3,483	70.9	68,900	19.0	10.9	513	32.8	4.9	4,150	3.7	147	3.5	3,581	20.9	47.8
Jones	10,914	80.3	149,700	19.0	10.0	796	32.5	2.7	13,642	2.1	418	3.1	12,961	35.5	26.3
Lamar	6,658	71.8	145,800	20.2	10.0	764	28.5	1.4	8,249	3.3	345	4.2	7,190	26.9	27.6
Lanier	3,825	62.7	117,800	23.4	12.0	734	32.2	1.9	3,850	1.3	147	3.8	3,840	33.4	22.9
Laurens	17,159	63.0	99,600	19.3	10.4	622	29.3	2.9	19,818	2.8	844	4.3	17,939	31.5	29.8
Lee	10,550	76.7	166,900	20.0	10.0	916	23.5	1.4	15,173	1.0	466	3.1	13,795	39.9	23.4
Liberty	24,053	46.0	133,700	19.3	10.8	1,064	28.9	2.5	26,349	2.5	1,045	4.0	22,707	31.0	28.9
Lincoln	3,277	72.4	132,300	23.0	11.7	712	33.6	1.3	3,558	1.4	143	4.0	3,222	27.9	34.2
Long	6,006	62.7	129,800	19.4	10.0	776	35.9	2.7	8,467	3.5	257	3.0	6,780	26.4	36.1
Lowndes	42,755	52.5	145,900	19.9	10.0	813	30.2	2.9	51,719	0.4	2,103	4.1	48,334	30.7	24.0
Lumpkin	11,866	72.6	199,100	21.3	10.8	878	32.1	1.5	17,402	5.1	479	2.8	15,677	28.7	27.7
McDuffie	8,238	68.0	115,100	22.3	10.0	719	29.7	0.8	8,554	0.0	447	5.2	8,752	28.0	36.0
McIntosh	6,343	82.1	152,700	24.0	10.6	798	32.1	0.6	6,129	3.1	225	3.7	6,292	24.5	28.8
Macon	4,648	61.4	68,600	22.0	12.4	582	29.9	1.9	4,684	0.7	295	6.3	4,424	21.9	37.2
Madison	10,622	73.3	143,200	19.3	10.0	745	29.2	3.2	13,599	2.9	415	3.1	13,587	28.6	32.6
Marion	3,423	75.9	109,400	21.2	10.9	565	22.0	1.0	3,257	0.6	118	3.6	3,291	23.6	40.8
Meriwether	8,255	66.1	112,500	23.8	13.7	734	31.0	1.7	8,897	1.8	468	5.3	8,273	26.1	41.4
Miller	2,339	66.5	99,400	18.9	12.0	562	23.0	6.5	2,782	0.4	84	3.0	2,322	36.5	25.2
Mitchell	8,018	62.8	94,200	26.3	13.6	664	24.8	3.0	8,228	-0.7	415	5.0	8,180	25.4	32.8
Monroe	10,177	81.9	175,000	19.0	10.0	728	29.4	2.1	13,124	1.7	410	3.1	12,054	36.8	23.9
Montgomery	3,061	75.3	92,200	19.4	10.0	660	34.0	1.9	3,858	0.7	159	4.1	3,400	32.5	35.6
Morgan	7,040	74.0	230,400	19.6	10.3	837	19.2	2.5	9,521	3.2	309	3.2	9,020	32.6	33.3
Murray	14,520	70.4	122,100	18.9	10.0	690	23.3	4.1	15,477	0.6	665	4.3	17,817	19.3	42.0
Muscogee	73,648	49.1	142,900	20.7	10.1	925	29.4	2.5	76,629	-0.8	4,076	5.3	78,784	34.2	21.9
Newton	37,543	71.2	159,200	21.5	10.0	1,071	35.9	1.7	53,410	2.5	2,346	4.4	49,853	31.5	31.4
Oconee	13,773	82.6	304,400	19.2	10.0	1,098	24.4	1.3	20,285	3.4	443	2.2	19,259	52.4	14.9
Oglethorpe	5,477	77.2	133,200	20.6	10.9	684	30.4	3.5	7,027	2.7	201	2.9	7,181	33.4	29.7
Paulding	54,993	77.6	184,000	19.8	10.0	1,198	25.3	1.5	89,362	2.9	2,694	3.0	80,574	35.8	25.4
Peach	10,215	63.2	140,100	18.3	10.0	750	31.0	1.8	12,060	1.9	562	4.7	11,059	26.8	33.3
Pickens	12,129	78.5	196,400	19.9	10.4	874	28.9	3.6	15,533	3.3	434	2.8	14,539	28.4	29.1
Pierce	7,178	76.0	101,700	19.2	12.2	704	29.6	1.5	8,623	1.3	269	3.1	7,958	25.7	42.3
Pike	6,163	84.7	181,700	19.3	10.0	910	28.0	1.7	8,981	3.3	253	2.8	8,062	39.2	28.3
Polk	15,425	64.8	121,900	20.1	10.5	720	30.7	3.9	18,480	1.1	657	3.6	18,682	20.5	42.5
Pulaski	3,803	64.2	109,500	19.2	10.0	732	34.4	5.8	4,048	2.4	146	3.6	4,030	29.4	34.5

1. Specified owner-occupied units. 2. A value of 10.0 represents 10 percent or less; a value of 50.0 represents 50 percent or more. 3. Specified renter-occupied units. 4. Overcrowded or lacking complete plumbing facilities. 5. Percent of civilian labor force. 6. Civilian employed persons 16 years old and over.

STATE County	Private nonfarm establishments, employment and payroll, 2020: Number of establishments	Employment: Total	Employment: Health care and social assistance	Employment: Manufacturing	Employment: Retail trade	Employment: Finance and insurance	Employment: Professional, scientific, and technical services	Annual payroll: Total (mil dol)	Annual payroll: Average per employee (dollars)	Agriculture, 2017: Farms: Number	Farms: Percent with: Fewer than 50 acres	Farms: Percent with: 1000 acres or more	Farm producers whose primary occupation is farming (percent)
	104	105	106	107	108	109	110	111	112	113	114	115	116
GEORGIA—Cont'd													
Effingham	815	8,614	1,015	1,705	1,589	158	242	379	44,010	254	55.5	6.7	35.4
Elbert	426	4,671	492	2,049	569	177	53	158	33,797	453	34.0	4.2	39.4
Emanuel	374	5,292	840	1,878	796	186	88	191	36,068	465	28.4	8.4	34.9
Evans	216	4,114	410	1,935	456	76	47	134	32,640	143	31.5	6.3	39.8
Fannin	643	5,441	947	301	1,441	155	220	180	33,127	211	64.0	0.9	44.2
Fayette	3,689	44,684	7,416	2,916	7,298	1,141	2,350	1,925	43,080	148	58.1	NA	53.4
Floyd	2,023	36,680	8,718	6,749	4,165	718	768	1,505	41,038	547	51.7	2.0	35.2
Forsyth	6,971	78,470	10,256	8,281	10,926	1,657	6,703	3,798	48,401	291	63.2	NA	49.9
Franklin	454	6,523	650	1,493	887	150	125	240	36,787	753	47.7	0.4	52.4
Fulton	39,155	849,093	93,614	22,805	56,060	60,095	114,774	65,541	77,189	195	75.9	NA	38.8
Gilmer	596	6,298	477	1,515	1,259	115	210	213	33,871	330	56.4	0.3	49.7
Glascock	26	202	81	NA	34	NA	6	6	31,693	76	35.5	3.9	38.2
Glynn	2,583	31,651	5,532	1,941	5,220	702	997	1,188	37,550	53	71.7	NA	25.0
Gordon	1,024	19,493	2,162	5,623	2,465	272	218	975	50,001	740	52.6	1.2	39.5
Grady	420	4,669	441	1,170	724	139	93	171	36,727	415	29.9	9.2	33.7
Greene	460	5,702	789	515	805	180	413	269	47,119	248	27.8	7.3	40.2
Gwinnett	25,682	347,324	34,732	23,719	46,989	15,366	30,426	17,837	51,355	177	67.2	0.6	39.7
Habersham	886	11,832	1,271	3,452	1,951	361	296	419	35,428	379	63.6	NA	42.2
Hall	4,602	86,434	15,109	23,841	9,379	2,090	2,223	4,179	48,351	551	63.5	0.4	38.1
Hancock	62	627	150	172	90	24	NA	20	32,242	145	20.0	3.4	36.2
Haralson	476	5,756	806	1,769	1,014	145	69	216	37,601	321	49.2	NA	38.2
Harris	470	4,170	285	1,052	341	81	100	126	30,244	289	47.4	2.4	40.0
Hart	418	5,863	354	2,536	939	130	148	213	36,260	516	40.3	0.6	50.7
Heard	119	1,272	89	551	108	16	17	60	47,403	227	30.0	1.8	37.2
Henry	4,159	56,503	9,452	2,860	10,533	1,327	2,098	2,183	38,643	240	72.9	NA	39.7
Houston	2,625	41,739	6,982	4,721	7,722	1,141	4,146	1,533	36,726	277	55.2	2.9	21.5
Irwin	117	1,399	395	198	116	31	35	57	40,701	348	29.9	10.1	46.2
Jackson	1,438	29,687	1,164	7,311	3,356	219	489	1,251	42,128	734	52.7	0.8	38.2
Jasper	186	1,526	238	363	258	66	32	50	33,029	251	51.4	3.6	37.0
Jeff Davis	233	3,824	344	1,472	618	72	34	139	36,412	197	41.1	11.7	37.5
Jefferson	310	3,691	421	831	586	160	62	146	39,518	318	25.2	12.6	43.5
Jenkins	101	1,052	254	14	144	32	15	36	33,747	210	35.2	11.4	33.9
Johnson	123	874	207	123	209	32	21	26	29,341	284	28.9	7.4	28.5
Jones	329	2,725	384	36	551	78	83	96	35,225	165	33.3	5.5	29.3
Lamar	265	3,164	389	709	509	103	64	124	39,264	220	52.3	0.9	38.7
Lanier	95	840	174	215	113	62	21	27	32,685	103	45.6	19.4	38.1
Laurens	1,071	15,693	3,052	2,475	2,484	562	399	622	39,641	626	30.4	4.2	29.0
Lee	415	4,599	468	436	742	140	111	222	48,305	206	40.8	13.6	33.7
Liberty	868	13,972	2,217	2,792	2,254	346	431	594	42,548	69	63.8	1.4	23.3
Lincoln	153	786	33	37	144	41	38	27	34,882	104	40.4	1.9	25.6
Long	87	446	61	NA	89	21	5	13	30,081	85	44.7	NA	28.9
Lowndes	2,799	42,031	7,985	3,358	6,561	1,200	1,295	1,562	37,165	380	52.6	3.2	30.9
Lumpkin	543	5,095	853	415	864	103	230	178	34,886	240	60.8	1.3	45.3
McDuffie	425	6,003	908	1,408	1,026	149	95	216	35,964	269	46.8	3.0	31.1
McIntosh	178	1,161	44	12	250	65	37	37	31,817	32	68.8	6.3	33.3
Macon	177	1,607	421	429	194	40	18	81	50,526	339	34.2	5.9	43.1
Madison	387	2,619	199	210	440	71	188	90	34,393	673	51.0	1.0	44.4
Marion	79	1,226	148	NA	120	13	16	37	30,423	222	29.3	6.8	46.1
Meriwether	285	2,878	840	251	574	54	50	110	38,193	344	34.9	4.1	39.0
Miller	127	1,309	608	20	163	42	47	51	39,290	144	27.1	15.3	45.7
Mitchell	363	5,220	496	2,414	616	125	147	174	33,371	425	31.5	11.8	48.9
Monroe	536	6,077	1,108	521	963	138	205	255	42,041	219	38.8	4.1	35.9
Montgomery	107	1,109	108	163	136	49	21	44	39,482	179	27.4	10.1	32.3
Morgan	513	6,422	482	1,536	1,012	194	224	245	38,204	513	37.8	1.8	46.6
Murray	399	5,921	539	1,982	890	103	54	223	37,736	278	45.0	1.4	37.9
Muscogee	4,403	83,288	15,840	6,648	11,008	12,915	2,509	3,828	45,964	37	35.1	2.7	40.8
Newton	1,510	19,655	2,520	3,791	3,187	518	368	912	46,420	292	50.3	1.4	36.5
Oconee	1,251	14,015	2,119	1,771	2,392	509	1,034	560	39,987	329	49.2	1.2	29.7
Oglethorpe	179	1,193	124	92	105	35	29	42	35,534	427	38.6	2.8	39.9
Paulding	2,165	21,338	3,523	956	5,076	449	790	737	34,541	212	60.4	NA	26.3
Peach	474	7,246	608	2,629	1,033	113	165	275	37,964	228	51.3	3.5	43.9
Pickens	717	6,797	1,415	842	1,256	275	191	294	43,250	258	62.4	0.4	45.1
Pierce	334	3,274	127	487	462	83	49	116	35,377	352	46.6	6.5	36.6
Pike	277	1,969	234	180	184	164	66	72	36,495	286	45.1	1.0	30.2
Polk	605	10,380	1,288	3,854	1,448	151	100	389	37,495	401	51.4	3.0	38.8
Pulaski	169	2,068	910	130	302	69	47	78	37,922	189	41.8	7.9	40.5

STATE County	Agriculture, 2017 (cont.) — Land in farms: Acreage (1,000)	Land in farms: Percent change, 2012–2017	Land in farms: Acres: Average size of farm	Land in farms: Acres: Total irrigated (1,000)	Land in farms: Acres: Total cropland (1,000)	Value of land and buildings (dollars): Average per farm	Value of land and buildings (dollars): Average per acre	Value of machinery and equipment, average per farm (dollars)	Value of products sold: Total (mil dol)	Value of products sold: Average per farm (acres)	Value of products sold: Percent from: Crops	Value of products sold: Percent from: Livestock and poultry products	Organic farms (number)	Farms with internet access (percent)	Government payments: Total ($1,000)	Government payments: Percent of farms
	117	118	119	120	121	122	123	124	125	126	127	128	129	130	131	132
GEORGIA—Cont'd																
Effingham	50	24.9	199	2.8	28.4	646,043	3,250	104,350	16.3	64,063	92.0	8.0	4	82.7	369	22.0
Elbert	79	39.3	175	1.0	19.2	687,827	3,925	83,075	107.1	236,494	4.9	95.1	4	64.7	919	28.3
Emanuel	139	-8.7	298	4.8	45.7	622,886	2,091	95,023	33.0	71,013	85.0	15.0	1	74.4	2,565	40.9
Evans	36	-1.2	249	5.6	14.4	671,882	2,699	104,565	32.2	224,979	60.7	39.3	NA	79.0	567	29.4
Fannin	16	17.9	78	0.2	4.0	457,536	5,902	48,477	23.0	109,175	21.7	78.3	NA	84.4	239	16.6
Fayette	11	-1.8	76	0.1	3.5	415,120	5,441	42,880	4.1	27,432	79.0	21.0	1	86.5	13	5.4
Floyd	75	6.7	137	0.7	21.7	665,897	4,866	88,749	53.4	97,700	10.2	89.8	NA	77.3	442	13.5
Forsyth	18	12.1	62	0.3	5.3	488,028	7,879	64,873	45.9	157,732	11.1	88.9	1	74.2	93	9.6
Franklin	79	1.9	105	0.2	21.0	601,312	5,748	100,018	371.8	493,734	0.6	99.4	1	78.6	928	27.5
Fulton	12	-13.3	63	0.2	2.2	1,195,368	19,063	42,330	2.3	11,641	39.9	60.1	7	91.8	110	10.8
Gilmer	28	11.0	86	0.1	6.9	658,366	7,657	86,301	205.4	622,530	1.5	98.5	NA	87.3	402	30.6
Glascock	21	-10.6	283	D	6.1	449,699	1,592	52,828	2.0	26,947	82.0	18.0	NA	86.8	187	23.7
Glynn	2	-46.5	36	0.1	0.2	559,751	15,411	68,477	0.3	5,887	26.0	74.0	1	54.7	8	9.4
Gordon	75	-12.1	101	1.0	29.8	660,422	6,545	73,663	294.2	397,519	2.9	97.1	1	73.1	1,580	29.5
Grady	124	-5.0	298	13.2	69.6	1,120,918	3,760	138,658	100.7	242,636	66.8	33.2	NA	69.2	5,132	52.0
Greene	76	55.8	305	0.2	9.0	1,094,410	3,586	98,364	79.1	319,073	3.0	97.0	NA	74.2	1,429	12.9
Gwinnett	11	1.9	60	0.1	3.0	563,058	9,339	53,633	16.8	95,068	96.5	3.5	NA	78.5	D	4.5
Habersham	26	-32.2	68	0.1	9.7	485,967	7,160	99,560	123.0	324,485	1.5	98.5	1	81.3	269	16.1
Hall	41	-21.7	74	0.1	13.8	689,173	9,332	79,541	128.5	233,156	2.3	97.7	1	80.9	789	20.3
Hancock	39	21.3	267	0.5	5.7	559,388	2,092	60,754	4.4	30,297	29.7	70.3	1	74.5	134	19.3
Haralson	27	0.5	84	0.2	7.7	398,850	4,750	59,412	75.4	234,754	1.8	98.2	NA	69.8	194	15.3
Harris	42	29.2	145	0.3	12.2	626,701	4,322	54,841	5.1	17,550	72.5	27.5	1	72.0	68	9.3
Hart	66	-2.9	129	2.2	26.1	722,492	5,622	116,647	215.1	416,953	6.2	93.8	NA	75.8	1,103	38.2
Heard	38	42.0	169	0.3	7.6	611,638	3,611	77,480	43.3	190,767	8.4	91.6	NA	84.1	346	18.9
Henry	12	-42.4	52	0.1	3.4	389,536	7,482	33,481	2.8	11,654	59.0	41.0	8	80.0	126	4.2
Houston	39	-17.5	141	7.6	18.3	567,998	4,021	86,680	18.2	65,588	55.0	45.0	NA	82.7	445	19.9
Irwin	123	-17.3	353	31.4	73.3	1,146,611	3,249	180,086	63.1	181,417	81.2	18.8	2	75.0	5,680	59.2
Jackson	75	-3.5	102	1.4	19.8	647,798	6,370	76,784	197.6	269,181	5.2	94.8	1	76.6	711	19.2
Jasper	43	-2.2	171	0.3	8.0	594,493	3,481	58,915	27.0	107,641	7.2	92.8	1	77.3	40	8.8
Jeff Davis	72	-9.2	363	10.3	46.3	910,689	2,505	215,420	40.6	205,914	70.9	29.1	NA	80.2	1,831	36.5
Jefferson	125	-14.2	393	33.6	69.7	1,017,736	2,590	140,667	58.5	183,912	73.0	27.0	NA	65.7	2,413	45.9
Jenkins	79	-13.2	378	7.3	33.4	989,382	2,620	96,519	21.6	103,071	87.2	12.8	NA	79.5	2,721	46.2
Johnson	75	31.2	263	9.1	25.0	551,537	2,093	59,306	12.3	43,447	82.2	17.8	NA	71.5	1,340	35.2
Jones	36	58.3	221	D	7.1	619,706	2,806	67,284	5.5	33,448	14.3	85.7	3	81.8	115	15.8
Lamar	32	-8.9	147	0.2	10.2	514,385	3,501	87,640	46.5	211,136	8.5	91.5	2	79.5	84	10.0
Lanier	47	12.4	454	7.3	25.4	1,376,047	3,030	220,587	22.9	222,184	98.9	1.1	NA	74.8	1,027	33.0
Laurens	155	-16.0	247	9.3	42.7	518,267	2,096	73,721	25.7	41,003	71.6	28.4	NA	74.3	2,465	57.2
Lee	120	14.1	584	19.1	60.1	1,976,595	3,384	150,525	60.4	293,097	77.3	22.7	NA	69.9	3,101	46.1
Liberty	6	2.5	92	0.1	1.0	488,481	5,289	36,656	0.5	6,986	61.0	39.0	NA	75.4	19	11.6
Lincoln	18	-22.5	176	D	3.3	549,595	3,125	64,987	4.2	40,346	17.0	83.0	NA	67.3	177	20.2
Long	10	-0.8	120	0.1	3.0	402,578	3,361	71,266	7.3	85,518	8.8	91.2	NA	85.9	63	9.4
Lowndes	62	-4.8	163	7.0	24.4	886,787	5,451	79,945	35.5	93,363	85.7	14.3	3	73.4	1,121	31.8
Lumpkin	27	55.1	112	0.2	6.9	665,565	5,925	82,836	51.3	213,658	7.6	92.4	NA	80.4	227	19.2
McDuffie	44	15.0	162	0.6	11.0	486,078	2,994	72,590	D	D	D	D	NA	74.0	255	20.4
McIntosh	10	-42.9	305	D	1.0	722,542	2,372	84,945	D	D	D	D	1	87.5	NA	NA
Macon	111	10.1	328	25.2	59.5	1,056,552	3,217	182,358	271.6	801,212	20.0	80.0	1	71.1	2,615	48.7
Madison	69	-3.7	102	0.3	23.0	577,100	5,664	83,713	239.6	355,947	1.7	98.3	1	77.4	569	21.2
Marion	64	35.0	288	1.8	14.4	684,034	2,375	99,628	20.6	92,599	24.6	75.4	NA	72.1	777	42.3
Meriwether	71	14.5	206	1.0	13.9	673,529	3,262	85,309	12.5	36,445	75.5	24.5	NA	75.9	261	15.7
Miller	80	-16.3	557	26.6	54.6	1,805,529	3,242	327,966	47.9	332,486	87.9	12.1	NA	75.0	6,028	70.1
Mitchell	190	-0.8	446	66.6	121.8	1,651,849	3,702	281,683	262.7	618,111	44.7	55.3	NA	72.7	6,948	51.1
Monroe	49	40.9	222	0.0	5.6	727,734	3,279	79,453	51.2	233,685	1.9	98.1	NA	84.0	94	10.5
Montgomery	60	3.2	333	7.2	22.5	859,810	2,584	96,589	15.5	86,732	87.2	12.8	NA	58.1	1,018	39.1
Morgan	88	-6.6	172	1.1	26.0	803,842	4,673	74,639	121.0	235,889	4.8	95.2	NA	76.8	922	19.1
Murray	47	0.5	170	0.9	11.9	860,300	5,068	105,708	122.7	441,428	3.5	96.5	NA	76.3	470	31.7
Muscogee	9	117.3	251	D	2.9	1,255,529	5,003	50,172	0.2	5,324	79.2	20.8	NA	94.6	D	2.7
Newton	43	5.0	146	0.1	8.5	655,436	4,475	74,446	12.4	42,308	15.1	84.9	2	79.8	245	12.0
Oconee	36	-21.2	108	0.6	7.9	784,386	7,235	69,487	42.2	128,210	33.7	66.3	1	79.6	383	26.1
Oglethorpe	73	-9.7	171	1.6	17.9	743,571	4,353	76,951	198.4	464,553	7.1	92.9	4	84.8	934	31.4
Paulding	15	77.2	70	0.1	4.1	404,436	5,781	52,413	9.5	44,967	5.7	94.3	NA	77.8	34	10.4
Peach	58	64.5	255	16.4	33.8	1,469,850	5,766	191,004	65.4	286,654	88.1	11.9	NA	81.6	254	14.5
Pickens	17	-1.5	64	0.1	4.0	548,090	8,529	101,132	77.1	298,841	1.2	98.8	NA	71.7	215	20.5
Pierce	81	3.4	230	8.3	47.6	661,340	2,877	151,848	42.1	119,608	82.5	17.5	NA	70.7	1,653	34.1
Pike	41	7.4	143	0.7	8.6	699,823	4,897	65,136	18.8	65,881	14.2	85.8	NA	78.7	225	18.2
Polk	62	38.4	155	0.1	28.7	561,506	3,616	116,950	46.0	114,691	29.2	70.8	1	73.3	232	15.7
Pulaski	53	-15.8	278	14.0	28.8	743,749	2,671	115,184	49.7	262,937	38.9	61.1	NA	87.3	703	57.1

STATE County	Water use, 2015		Wholesale Trade[1], 2017				Retail Trade[2], 2017				Real estate and rental and leasing,[2] 2017			
	Public supply water withdrawn (mil gal/ day)	Public supply gallons withdrawn per person per day	Number of establish- ments	Number of employees	Sales (mil dol)	Average payroll (mil dol)	Number of establish- ments	Number of employees	Sales (mil dol)	Average payroll (mil dol)	Number of establish- ments	Number of employees	Sales (mil dol)	Average payroll (mil dol)
	133	134	135	136	137	138	139	140	141	142	143	144	145	146
GEORGIA—Cont'd														
Effingham	35.8	626.9	18	108	129.2	7.1	103	1,626	444.5	34.9	32	90	23.5	2.5
Elbert	1.6	82.1	40	229	97.6	8.2	72	581	126.0	12.6	NA	NA	NA	NA
Emanuel	1.6	70.0	17	83	96.7	3.6	81	792	245.6	19.5	13	32	13.8	0.9
Evans	0.5	50.1	5	19	6.8	0.7	61	454	166.0	11.8	4	14	1.5	0.3
Fannin	1.8	72.0	18	122	45.4	3.7	127	1,400	377.7	31.6	D	D	D	D
Fayette	9.5	85.4	171	2,181	1,692.4	144.5	435	7,502	1,725.0	163.0	225	596	151.8	25.1
Floyd	11.8	122.3	67	1,010	655.3	50.1	389	4,269	1,214.8	106.6	83	260	56.2	9.3
Forsyth	20.6	97.0	417	5,823	4,457.7	361.9	677	9,901	3,037.0	273.0	344	908	216.0	37.6
Franklin	2.0	87.4	22	188	90.0	8.6	91	893	293.1	20.3	11	23	14.7	0.9
Fulton	196.3	194.3	1,514	29,384	40,998.6	2,272.3	3,599	55,155	16,815.9	1,592.5	2,598	23,538	12,563.1	1,968.0
Gilmer	2.5	85.0	19	99	44.3	3.5	99	1,192	328.0	30.1	38	143	21.0	4.0
Glascock	0.1	22.8	NA	NA	NA	NA	4	19	6.1	0.3	NA	NA	NA	NA
Glynn	9.3	111.4	81	747	769.0	31.3	468	5,607	1,498.9	132.5	165	510	98.0	18.0
Gordon	10.4	184.4	75	1,096	519.9	60.7	230	2,520	660.1	54.5	41	126	42.3	4.4
Grady	1.7	68.6	29	365	443.5	18.4	69	778	214.6	18.5	20	39	5.4	1.2
Greene	1.2	73.6	18	101	57.3	5.5	74	780	271.9	20.5	25	55	17.2	2.2
Gwinnett	0.6	0.7	1,772	30,291	39,243.9	2,351.1	2,821	46,440	15,083.3	1,342.0	1,206	5,857	1,636.6	306.9
Habersham	5.7	128.6	D	D	D	D	174	1,906	512.0	45.3	D	D	D	D
Hall	88.2	455.6	261	4,205	7,901.5	236.0	619	9,240	2,948.9	268.3	220	549	180.7	25.3
Hancock	1.2	140.3	NA	NA	NA	NA	22	78	22.7	2.0	NA	NA	NA	NA
Haralson	2.5	87.7	18	126	36.6	7.4	88	992	398.6	29.2	12	11	1.4	0.3
Harris	6.3	187.5	D	D	D	D	47	308	73.4	5.6	D	D	D	D
Hart	1.5	57.2	12	71	43.6	2.8	76	1,032	213.6	20.3	9	62	11.7	1.3
Heard	1.2	105.7	NA	NA	NA	NA	20	99	23.0	2.0	3	D	0.2	D
Henry	34.1	156.7	123	1,918	1,313.0	110.8	589	10,479	2,947.9	245.3	177	567	164.4	24.7
Houston	23.8	158.3	43	320	175.8	13.7	486	7,535	2,075.9	182.5	124	455	114.3	15.7
Irwin	0.4	47.6	8	68	29.3	2.5	27	161	32.0	2.8	D	D	D	0.3
Jackson	9.5	150.3	74	1,686	1,935.7	101.1	242	3,590	1,578.6	109.4	68	159	42.5	4.8
Jasper	0.8	55.0	NA	NA	NA	NA	22	207	54.2	4.0	5	5	2.1	0.4
Jeff Davis	0.9	60.3	13	104	78.8	4.9	66	678	164.3	14.8	D	D	D	D
Jefferson	1.3	82.0	10	204	191.7	5.1	64	584	136.8	12.6	9	47	2.2	1.2
Jenkins	0.5	50.2	D	D	D	D	18	146	32.9	2.7	NA	NA	NA	NA
Johnson	0.5	54.9	3	14	11.8	0.6	25	158	40.9	2.8	NA	NA	NA	NA
Jones	2.7	95.8	D	D	D	D	44	518	107.0	10.3	D	D	D	D
Lamar	1.9	102.7	7	260	143.1	12.3	45	525	116.9	11.0	4	8	1.0	0.1
Lanier	0.4	34.9	NA	NA	NA	NA	18	154	33.7	2.9	NA	NA	NA	NA
Laurens	3.5	74.2	40	368	278.1	15.7	233	2,579	754.2	56.3	D	D	D	D
Lee	1.9	64.0	17	291	768.6	35.6	65	726	224.9	17.7	20	53	12.5	2.0
Liberty	6.4	102.8	D	D	D	D	185	2,122	598.6	52.2	D	D	D	5.3
Lincoln	0.0	1.3	5	D	7.4	D	20	169	41.1	3.5	6	12	2.1	0.4
Long	0.5	28.8	NA	NA	NA	NA	14	74	19.1	1.5	D	D	D	0.3
Lowndes	13.2	116.6	109	1,113	904.7	51.5	523	6,980	2,098.9	167.1	143	701	124.2	22.7
Lumpkin	1.3	40.4	13	234	73.2	15.6	77	886	236.4	22.1	D	D	D	D
McDuffie	2.6	120.2	D	D	D	D	86	1,106	335.5	27.1	13	46	5.5	1.3
McIntosh	1.0	74.5	7	97	13.9	2.0	43	315	90.9	6.6	D	D	D	D
Macon	1.0	75.6	10	99	264.0	5.0	40	267	43.7	5.2	4	D	0.3	D
Madison	0.5	18.6	D	D	D	2.6	58	450	116.1	8.8	D	D	D	D
Marion	1.4	160.9	NA	NA	NA	NA	24	118	28.8	2.6	NA	NA	NA	NA
Meriwether	0.3	14.6	D	D	D	0.8	70	546	104.7	11.2	NA	NA	NA	NA
Miller	0.3	44.4	9	97	61.1	3.9	22	171	57.6	4.7	3	3	0.2	0.0
Mitchell	3.8	167.0	21	194	222.4	7.9	82	677	139.5	13.6	D	D	D	D
Monroe	1.6	58.3	D	D	D	5.0	78	903	226.7	20.3	21	39	7.6	1.2
Montgomery	0.2	20.1	NA	NA	NA	NA	24	165	32.2	3.2	NA	NA	NA	NA
Morgan	1.3	74.3	16	134	139.1	5.8	69	984	258.8	22.3	D	D	D	D
Murray	1.9	47.8	27	556	332.8	38.6	92	867	190.1	17.1	D	D	D	7.2
Muscogee	36.8	183.3	152	1,978	1,683.1	109.0	794	11,547	2,979.2	268.9	242	1,314	342.8	54.5
Newton	13.7	130.2	59	924	2,501.7	76.5	218	3,266	950.7	80.4	64	233	54.1	8.6
Oconee	0.4	9.7	29	215	110.3	12.4	116	2,246	566.9	51.9	88	479	96.6	29.5
Oglethorpe	0.3	17.5	D	D	D	4.0	19	118	31.3	2.7	D	D	D	D
Paulding	0.1	0.7	62	282	146.7	14.0	271	4,863	1,472.7	121.0	83	427	92.3	25.4
Peach	2.3	86.5	D	D	D	D	101	1,020	356.7	26.6	24	59	13.0	2.5
Pickens	2.8	91.4	34	144	72.4	4.7	100	1,223	417.4	33.1	35	54	10.3	1.8
Pierce	0.6	29.8	13	360	330.9	14.0	66	409	123.5	9.1	9	59	32.7	1.9
Pike	3.0	165.5	8	172	41.6	8.0	36	173	39.3	3.9	9	12	3.6	0.4
Polk	5.6	134.9	19	225	332.4	9.6	132	1,485	377.8	36.6	D	D	D	D
Pulaski	1.1	95.6	NA	NA	NA	NA	38	306	82.4	7.8	5	9	0.7	0.2

1 Merchant wholesalers, except manufacturers' sales branches and offices. 2. Employer establishments.

STATE County	Professional, scientific, and technical services, 2017				Manufacturing, 2017				Accommodation and food services, 2017			
	Number of establish-ments	Number of employees	Sales (mil dol)	Average payroll (mil dol)	Number of establish-ments	Number of employees	Sales (mil dol)	Average payroll (mil dol)	Number of establis-hments	Number of employees	Sales (mil dol)	Annual payroll (mil dol)
	147	148	149	150	151	152	153	154	155	156	157	158
GEORGIA—Cont'd												
Effingham	D	D	D	D	24	1,669	832.2	106.9	59	809	40.2	9.9
Elbert	20	67	5.1	1.6	83	1,803	311.1	77.6	D	D	D	4.1
Emanuel	21	92	13.0	4.1	33	1,827	790.6	69.5	37	422	23.1	5.6
Evans	15	59	11.8	2.5	13	1,838	471.7	64.4	12	204	8.3	2.4
Fannin	43	219	19.1	7.5	28	290	39.8	9.6	64	914	52.2	13.9
Fayette	D	D	D	D	100	2,836	1,269.6	144.8	258	6,095	325.9	94.9
Floyd	178	808	123.2	31.6	98	6,153	3,872.4	358.9	202	4,241	227.3	64.8
Forsyth	1,325	6,253	1,141.5	388.1	231	8,010	2,375.0	375.9	349	6,999	364.8	101.5
Franklin	28	150	13.4	4.5	32	1,570	419.5	69.5	44	755	43.1	10.6
Fulton	7,614	110,359	28,924.9	10,416.8	602	19,877	10,427.0	1,149.7	3,407	85,340	6,380.6	1,745.6
Gilmer	D	D	D	D	31	1,252	346.1	40.3	63	922	48.1	13.4
Glascock	NA	NA	NA	NA	NA	NA	NA	NA	3	33	0.7	0.2
Glynn	D	D	D	D	50	2,026	969.5	140.7	287	7,637	594.2	165.7
Gordon	50	357	33.6	10.2	94	6,483	2,280.3	303.9	91	1,572	89.2	22.7
Grady	17	79	6.6	2.2	19	981	242.5	37.3	30	345	19.4	4.2
Greene	42	268	55.1	22.9	12	449	516.4	23.5	37	1,639	197.7	46.7
Gwinnett	3,312	28,939	5,504.1	2,013.5	705	22,058	7,837.2	1,211.4	1,942	31,382	1,910.3	483.3
Habersham	66	274	42.0	10.7	54	4,158	1,191.9	171.5	72	1,413	71.0	19.7
Hall	410	1,919	331.0	107.0	223	20,766	8,353.0	932.3	312	5,862	338.5	93.2
Hancock	NA	NA	NA	NA	D	D	D	D	D	D	D	D
Haralson	30	78	8.1	2.7	31	1,553	957.8	99.9	41	513	27.8	6.3
Harris	37	76	12.4	3.1	14	1,204	436.9	40.7	D	D	D	8.8
Hart	40	167	20.8	7.9	28	2,582	621.8	114.5	D	D	D	D
Heard	D	D	D	D	11	531	193.2	23.3	D	D	D	D
Henry	314	1,460	256.5	69.3	66	2,729	1,962.3	149.3	379	7,164	396.5	105.2
Houston	D	D	D	D	56	4,714	2,558.9	200.4	329	7,252	347.1	92.4
Irwin	D	D	D	D	NA	NA	NA	NA	5	68	2.1	0.5
Jackson	101	400	58.5	23.0	76	6,367	2,925.5	311.5	78	1,318	68.9	18.3
Jasper	11	25	2.8	1.0	15	433	141.6	20.2	11	146	6.2	2.0
Jeff Davis	12	32	3.1	1.4	28	1,324	323.2	54.2	24	335	16.2	4.3
Jefferson	11	62	7.1	2.0	25	979	277.1	50.0	31	303	15.3	3.4
Jenkins	6	13	1.4	0.5	5	20	20.6	1.6	14	145	7.5	1.7
Johnson	6	12	0.9	0.3	5	83	17.1	3.6	9	46	1.6	0.4
Jones	13	68	5.4	1.6	D	38	D	2.2	D	D	D	D
Lamar	15	67	5.6	1.9	12	550	299.6	29.5	43	524	21.3	4.9
Lanier	5	21	1.2	0.3	D	D	D	D	D	D	D	D
Laurens	59	386	54.5	20.3	41	2,253	925.2	116.4	104	2,025	101.1	26.7
Lee	30	254	16.8	6.4	14	423	100.4	14.8	25	322	19.4	4.7
Liberty	D	D	D	D	19	1,904	1,276.2	123.5	114	2,078	104.3	26.4
Lincoln	D	D	D	D	4	77	19.1	3.3	10	90	3.7	1.1
Long	NA	NA	NA	NA	NA	NA	NA	NA	D	D	D	D
Lowndes	D	D	D	D	91	3,150	2,777.5	162.7	276	5,921	307.6	81.4
Lumpkin	66	192	22.8	8.2	30	537	108.8	23.6	63	1,165	63.8	18.4
McDuffie	D	D	11.3	D	28	1,595	585.5	69.3	41	679	34.6	8.1
McIntosh	14	39	4.3	1.3	4	8	2.3	0.6	31	390	22.9	5.7
Macon	8	19	1.7	0.5	13	514	338.4	39.1	15	177	8.8	2.1
Madison	26	87	8.9	2.7	23	166	23.0	6.8	23	146	9.4	2.5
Marion	4	10	1.3	0.4	D	D	D	D	D	D	D	0.4
Meriwether	11	43	5.6	1.7	17	627	208.1	29.7	27	239	11.3	2.8
Miller	D	D	3.7	D	3	11	2.4	0.6	8	D	3.5	D
Mitchell	22	208	21.1	9.1	13	2,176	881.4	78.2	29	360	20.1	5.6
Monroe	47	208	26.6	10.3	15	584	164.0	19.3	42	643	32.8	8.9
Montgomery	6	20	1.5	0.6	8	156	50.9	5.9	9	79	3.5	0.9
Morgan	46	282	52.4	15.7	27	1,315	428.5	67.9	57	884	47.0	14.6
Murray	16	76	17.8	6.6	57	3,485	1,012.0	132.7	43	622	29.5	7.8
Muscogee	D	D	D	D	116	6,683	2,208.9	353.0	474	10,818	574.5	162.6
Newton	102	405	53.5	15.6	78	3,694	2,412.4	199.5	133	2,251	131.8	36.4
Oconee	169	915	121.6	44.3	26	2,258	584.6	117.7	79	1,749	78.1	21.7
Oglethorpe	12	32	2.6	0.8	10	81	9.2	2.8	6	142	4.9	2.2
Paulding	203	756	146.2	36.8	50	801	283.0	42.6	158	3,743	205.5	55.7
Peach	28	134	15.5	5.8	D	D	D	D	D	D	D	11.4
Pickens	80	180	25.1	6.9	42	776	139.0	36.4	49	909	52.8	15.1
Pierce	17	48	3.6	1.1	13	436	181.6	20.0	26	340	16.1	4.4
Pike	25	66	8.3	2.3	10	195	85.8	6.9	D	D	D	D
Polk	31	108	11.7	3.0	29	3,841	1,100.6	171.4	66	1,223	61.1	16.3
Pulaski	13	38	4.7	2.1	NA	NA	NA	NA	D	D	D	3.4

STATE County	Health care and social assistance, 2017				Other services, 2017				Nonemployer businesses, 2019		Value of residential construction authorized by building permits, 2021	
	Number of establish-ments	Number of employees	Receipts (mil dol)	Annual payroll (mil dol)	Number of establish-ments	Number of employees	Receipts (mil dol)	Annual payroll (mil dol)	Number	Receipts (mil dol)	New construction ($1,000)	Number of housing units
	159	160	161	162	163	164	165	166	167	168	169	170
GEORGIA—Cont'd												
Effingham	70	890	95.5	38.6	56	503	63.1	21.1	4,413	183.0	168,723	749
Elbert	31	512	38.0	16.0	D	D	D	D	1,493	57.9	12,460	103
Emanuel	44	870	66.8	29.9	24	96	12.2	2.6	1,749	79.0	7,060	33
Evans	16	426	31.8	14.3	14	88	8.6	3.0	724	23.0	3,012	25
Fannin	61	902	112.4	40.0	33	218	19.0	5.5	3,098	184.2	96,355	447
Fayette	430	6,561	880.0	327.6	249	1,732	155.9	51.4	12,203	600.3	272,204	762
Floyd	322	8,395	1,147.7	397.0	115	808	79.6	23.5	7,095	290.8	61,657	204
Forsyth	562	9,270	1,334.7	495.4	388	2,365	298.0	88.4	24,458	1,299.8	368,568	2,359
Franklin	38	626	54.5	23.4	29	189	35.7	7.1	1,775	77.4	19,768	142
Fulton	3,950	86,258	14,367.1	4,845.8	2,372	22,826	5,613.3	900.1	122,228	6,317.3	1,196,669	5,170
Gilmer	48	507	41.0	16.8	36	196	19.8	5.3	2,976	138.9	62,379	414
Glascock	D	D	D	D	3	5	0.4	0.1	185	7.1	NA	NA
Glynn	257	5,461	670.2	260.3	147	913	99.2	23.3	7,529	353.4	212,728	576
Gordon	78	2,313	247.0	90.7	45	234	24.6	6.9	3,717	182.0	64,737	480
Grady	35	504	57.1	18.0	30	115	12.2	2.7	1,538	67.6	11,966	48
Greene	45	745	70.3	25.9	29	177	13.7	3.9	1,889	106.4	291,408	417
Gwinnett	2,114	31,297	3,716.0	1,507.7	1,565	8,763	1,068.5	300.4	122,611	5,386.2	1,099,834	4,735
Habersham	91	1,311	120.0	52.2	62	252	24.6	7.2	3,351	144.4	63,946	395
Hall	488	13,913	1,965.5	721.0	282	1,514	177.5	51.0	17,795	852.5	432,875	2,249
Hancock	7	136	9.6	4.6	5	10	0.9	0.3	648	17.2	6,743	31
Haralson	43	583	184.1	74.1	D	D	D	D	2,272	101.3	20,755	89
Harris	30	246	16.9	7.0	D	D	D	1.0	2,767	129.4	64,082	242
Hart	33	340	33.7	13.9	D	D	D	D	1,990	82.9	74,057	253
Heard	D	D	D	D	D	D	D	0.6	837	29.3	7,890	34
Henry	477	8,458	1,079.1	432.0	256	1,186	128.0	35.1	24,597	846.2	579,575	2,486
Houston	341	7,395	750.1	269.9	166	976	86.8	25.7	11,133	367.7	274,506	1,389
Irwin	11	343	24.1	9.4	D	D	D	D	619	21.4	2,875	33
Jackson	112	1,473	102.8	45.2	84	513	37.8	21.0	6,528	277.8	312,986	1,782
Jasper	D	D	D	D	D	D	D	D	1,250	51.4	35,813	152
Jeff Davis	23	327	21.6	8.9	D	D	D	D	976	36.3	150	2
Jefferson	23	480	30.7	13.8	D	D	D	D	1,375	42.6	313	3
Jenkins	12	258	18.7	7.2	6	15	5.2	0.6	515	20.1	9,650	71
Johnson	14	206	15.5	7.1	D	D	D	D	564	23.1	1,523	7
Jones	38	446	33.2	13.4	22	58	9.8	1.7	2,125	78.7	28,147	137
Lamar	D	D	D	8.5	16	173	16.4	5.3	1,271	44.5	37,328	184
Lanier	D	D	D	D	NA	NA	NA	NA	600	28.3	4,443	35
Laurens	152	3,081	498.3	184.0	D	D	D	D	3,984	184.2	3,637	17
Lee	41	379	33.3	13.7	28	234	27.1	8.2	2,338	88.6	17,199	164
Liberty	91	2,157	259.7	104.0	D	D	D	D	3,341	93.5	104,222	488
Lincoln	6	43	3.3	1.7	D	D	D	D	640	25.0	22,418	82
Long	5	25	2.7	1.1	D	D	D	D	885	28.6	83,496	349
Lowndes	459	7,871	901.8	327.8	147	670	70.0	17.4	7,950	385.5	268,389	1,497
Lumpkin	56	725	96.7	26.1	D	D	D	D	2,726	116.7	61,700	240
McDuffie	51	955	73.9	29.9	D	D	22.4	D	1,897	55.7	14,754	54
McIntosh	D	D	D	D	13	71	5.8	1.4	1,041	45.3	18,810	80
Macon	21	463	31.8	12.5	11	50	5.3	1.4	808	25.9	2,718	13
Madison	23	201	13.0	5.4	D	D	D	0.8	2,480	99.3	44,739	187
Marion	D	D	D	D	D	D	D	D	462	17.7	3,571	18
Meriwether	23	965	74.7	30.4	D	D	D	D	1,644	54.6	23,744	115
Miller	15	572	57.3	22.4	D	D	1.9	D	345	12.0	85	1
Mitchell	34	556	46.4	17.9	24	80	8.3	2.1	1,382	51.5	2,615	8
Monroe	D	D	D	D	36	141	19.5	5.6	2,386	106.6	52,520	230
Montgomery	D	D	D	D	D	D	D	D	602	24.6	3,359	24
Morgan	D	D	D	D	30	126	14.0	3.3	2,257	100.6	60,587	224
Murray	D	D	D	D	27	109	13.5	3.3	1,959	79.1	14,115	59
Muscogee	666	15,924	1,829.0	701.9	D	D	D	62.2	13,379	468.5	118,533	675
Newton	137	2,426	252.1	109.5	79	318	35.4	9.5	11,191	355.8	190,827	1,150
Oconee	161	1,830	188.6	81.5	55	445	65.4	18.3	4,431	236.4	184,289	418
Oglethorpe	10	117	7.5	3.4	D	D	D	0.7	1,150	41.1	1,155	77
Paulding	177	3,538	427.9	167.3	153	652	59.5	16.6	15,168	539.4	225,152	2,143
Peach	41	565	46.9	16.8	25	127	17.3	3.7	2,014	76.8	25,588	145
Pickens	69	1,327	173.6	69.4	51	433	43.4	12.9	3,282	161.4	87,863	341
Pierce	22	194	10.0	4.5	18	50	4.6	1.1	1,241	48.7	11,579	89
Pike	D	D	D	7.9	D	D	D	1.0	1,719	79.0	44,739	187
Polk	60	1,086	106.2	40.0	39	324	33.0	9.1	2,755	99.0	1,630	9
Pulaski	24	866	69.9	37.2	8	23	1.7	0.5	742	25.1	7,305	44

Table B. States and Counties — **Government Employment and Payroll, and Local Government Finances**

STATE County	Government employment and payroll, 2017									Local government finances, 2017				
			March payroll (percent of total)							General revenue				
												Taxes		
													Per capita[1] (dollars)	
	Full-time equivalent employees	March payroll (dollars)	Adminis-tration, judicial, and legal	Police and corrections	Fire protection	Highways and transpor-tation	Health and welfare	Natural resources and utilities	Education and libraries	Total (mil dol)	Inter-govern-mental (mil dol)	Total (mil dol)	Total	Property
	171	172	173	174	175	176	177	178	179	180	181	182	183	184
GEORGIA—Cont'd														
Effingham	2,530	9,080,471	3.6	7.9	3.3	0.3	16.3	1.7	65.9	309.6	84.7	77.1	1,284	814
Elbert	896	2,970,610	6.2	7.8	2.0	1.7	20.2	7.3	52.5	75.9	26.0	23.1	1,209	835
Emanuel	1,261	4,150,130	4.9	7.6	1.3	3.5	30.0	2.6	48.4	102.6	38.6	24.9	1,104	674
Evans	422	1,286,946	7.8	7.6	0.9	3.0	5.2	6.0	68.8	45.3	17.6	11.0	1,024	575
Fannin	769	2,585,142	6.7	7.4	1.9	5.6	5.3	4.4	68.0	70.6	21.5	40.9	1,613	900
Fayette	4,117	16,713,945	6.0	9.2	7.0	1.7	0.2	2.8	69.9	390.4	113.5	204.2	1,814	1,311
Floyd	3,978	13,144,682	5.5	10.4	4.8	3.7	2.2	6.5	65.2	377.8	154.9	149.8	1,537	984
Forsyth	7,135	29,839,562	5.0	7.0	3.1	1.1	0.7	3.7	77.7	787.1	261.5	401.3	1,753	1,192
Franklin	813	2,679,239	7.3	11.5	0.2	2.5	5.3	5.3	66.3	69.1	29.8	28.8	1,259	769
Fulton	42,801	177,707,903	10.3	12.6	4.9	15.0	2.3	8.6	45.6	5,704.3	1,290.5	2,829.1	2,723	1,993
Gilmer	1,014	3,339,978	6.6	11.8	6.5	2.2	0.4	4.9	65.8	82.8	30.0	41.8	1,374	907
Glascock	155	449,339	13.2	0.0	5.4	4.1	0.6	1.9	72.9	9.2	5.0	3.4	1,121	779
Glynn	5,449	23,453,893	3.7	5.6	3.0	1.4	51.6	2.8	30.6	646.3	95.8	166.8	1,970	1,270
Gordon	1,956	7,118,689	6.8	9.3	4.7	2.8	0.9	5.4	67.0	188.7	76.4	80.5	1,408	848
Grady	1,026	3,285,875	5.2	8.1	1.9	2.9	0.9	6.2	68.7	77.2	39.9	24.9	1,004	660
Greene	705	2,544,629	9.2	9.3	0.0	1.9	5.3	3.1	68.1	70.6	17.0	44.4	2,584	1,740
Gwinnett	29,474	120,526,583	6.0	7.6	4.0	0.7	1.6	4.1	75.1	3,209.4	1,189.1	1,490.4	1,623	1,143
Habersham	2,098	7,199,487	4.7	5.7	2.3	1.5	28.7	4.0	50.7	178.4	56.4	53.7	1,206	708
Hall	6,731	25,935,061	6.3	9.9	7.4	1.6	4.5	5.5	63.2	690.5	254.6	301.9	1,518	931
Hancock	373	1,041,916	6.1	11.4	0.0	2.9	4.6	5.2	67.2	36.2	10.8	16.3	1,906	1,560
Haralson	1,199	4,193,572	7.0	8.5	4.9	2.4	3.1	4.4	69.1	96.5	47.8	37.0	1,264	843
Harris	1,107	3,723,319	4.3	10.2	0.0	1.9	3.4	5.1	72.6	87.1	31.4	43.6	1,286	931
Hart	810	2,529,596	5.8	8.0	1.1	3.8	6.2	4.4	69.2	70.8	30.6	30.2	1,175	769
Heard	481	1,604,121	7.1	7.8	9.0	2.5	2.4	4.7	63.9	42.1	13.8	24.7	2,105	1,020
Henry	8,159	29,035,197	7.8	7.6	5.5	1.3	1.3	3.9	69.5	734.4	268.8	359.7	1,597	1,063
Houston	5,858	21,180,489	4.8	8.7	3.3	1.8	1.4	3.6	73.8	499.9	208.4	210.1	1,371	786
Irwin	532	1,604,996	6.2	3.8	1.0	1.9	21.1	1.0	58.1	68.2	16.3	9.7	1,039	768
Jackson	2,489	8,810,842	5.3	10.7	0.4	1.8	2.7	4.9	70.6	239.9	80.4	118.3	1,749	1,150
Jasper	495	1,474,019	6.3	7.0	0.8	3.9	4.2	4.1	73.1	50.0	18.7	17.1	1,232	974
Jeff Davis	678	2,258,153	5.7	5.5	2.2	2.0	20.6	3.4	59.6	47.0	23.8	17.4	1,157	586
Jefferson	787	2,446,812	1.8	11.2	1.8	3.1	19.6	4.3	56.1	62.2	24.2	20.8	1,328	875
Jenkins	336	1,040,123	7.2	9.2	2.4	4.7	3.6	5.3	67.0	32.6	19.0	9.6	1,089	691
Johnson	458	1,259,519	5.0	6.4	1.0	1.5	5.3	1.3	79.2	23.5	12.1	7.6	777	502
Jones	1,120	3,183,020	5.1	7.9	0.3	3.1	0.3	4.3	78.9	78.9	38.3	32.9	1,154	879
Lamar	619	1,781,815	9.3	13.6	1.7	3.3	1.3	6.4	61.9	50.0	20.3	20.0	1,077	784
Lanier	268	837,866	6.2	5.8	0.1	3.0	0.4	1.4	82.5	24.9	15.2	8.3	796	590
Laurens	2,010	7,072,670	5.6	8.0	2.4	2.6	6.2	4.7	68.5	181.6	91.0	62.7	1,324	703
Lee	1,242	3,793,199	5.8	8.2	2.9	2.2	3.3	1.8	73.6	94.7	39.7	41.9	1,423	1,002
Liberty	2,654	8,935,784	5.5	9.6	2.1	0.9	19.3	1.8	56.9	235.8	92.9	64.3	1,044	724
Lincoln	331	996,570	9.2	9.9	0.0	2.7	7.4	2.8	65.3	28.4	11.5	11.5	1,461	1,059
Long	530	1,540,782	5.8	5.9	1.3	2.4	0.0	2.0	82.6	50.4	34.5	12.8	679	534
Lowndes	6,117	22,966,286	3.4	6.7	2.0	1.2	45.2	3.0	38.1	682.2	148.6	151.5	1,313	833
Lumpkin	901	2,978,044	9.0	9.7	5.0	2.6	0.3	4.7	67.0	71.5	24.4	36.5	1,113	737
McDuffie	951	2,939,097	6.2	7.6	4.1	1.8	2.2	5.4	70.7	71.6	33.9	28.4	1,322	763
McIntosh	456	1,345,123	11.3	17.8	0.0	3.1	4.1	4.9	56.7	34.8	10.9	16.8	1,191	842
Macon	396	1,181,723	8.9	11.4	0.9	3.8	4.8	6.8	62.4	34.1	12.7	15.8	1,188	881
Madison	1,010	3,188,661	5.5	7.3	0.0	1.9	4.0	1.2	77.9	76.6	42.4	25.0	854	611
Marion	270	959,139	6.9	7.5	0.0	4.4	3.8	3.8	72.7	21.1	10.8	7.7	914	622
Meriwether	805	2,343,467	7.3	11.0	1.1	3.7	6.2	2.5	65.8	61.4	26.6	24.5	1,165	855
Miller	730	2,625,098	4.8	3.8	0.2	0.8	63.4	2.2	24.3	70.1	44.9	9.3	1,606	1,250
Mitchell	956	2,922,809	8.0	11.9	2.7	2.3	3.1	4.4	64.5	80.6	33.4	30.4	1,363	983
Monroe	1,099	3,677,674	4.3	11.0	1.8	3.3	15.3	3.5	58.0	65.8	21.0	26.6	977	779
Montgomery	232	670,711	6.8	6.5	0.5	3.4	2.2	2.5	76.4	21.1	11.2	7.4	825	549
Morgan	924	3,191,062	7.4	6.4	0.9	2.5	17.6	6.5	56.9	84.7	24.5	36.0	1,960	1,286
Murray	1,158	4,056,208	4.4	7.6	3.3	2.4	0.9	1.8	74.6	99.6	55.2	33.1	833	437
Muscogee	8,905	30,532,915	4.4	12.3	5.0	2.3	10.2	7.3	55.0	735.2	271.0	279.8	1,443	978
Newton	3,939	13,566,867	6.2	9.2	3.9	1.5	0.8	5.3	70.7	407.0	153.8	127.3	1,181	787
Oconee	1,258	4,271,841	7.0	7.4	0.4	2.2	0.4	5.1	73.5	124.4	43.1	65.8	1,725	1,077
Oglethorpe	444	1,472,805	4.5	9.3	0.0	4.3	3.4	3.2	75.3	33.8	15.7	14.4	967	746
Paulding	4,614	16,994,666	3.6	7.4	3.1	1.4	0.5	2.7	80.5	418.6	199.9	173.4	1,087	714
Peach	1,076	3,658,633	7.8	11.0	3.6	0.7	2.3	7.2	59.7	107.4	25.9	37.8	1,401	910
Pickens	1,035	3,467,071	11.4	10.9	8.0	2.5	0.7	4.3	61.7	96.1	31.4	50.0	1,586	1,085
Pierce	645	2,462,438	6.8	4.5	0.2	1.7	3.4	1.9	77.6	52.7	28.4	18.6	967	633
Pike	616	1,844,937	6.8	10.0	0.0	3.6	0.2	1.7	76.4	43.0	21.4	18.5	1,017	780
Polk	1,416	4,844,573	4.5	11.6	2.6	2.3	0.7	3.6	71.5	129.6	63.4	45.6	1,090	687
Pulaski	330	1,035,204	12.7	7.8	3.8	4.0	1.3	5.4	65.0	24.6	11.1	10.7	957	655

1. Based on the resident population estimated as of July 1 of the year shown.

STATE County	Local government finances, 2017 (cont.)									Government employment, 2020			Individual income tax returns, 2019		
	Direct general expenditure							Debt outstanding							
			Percent of total for:												
	Total (mil dol)	Per capita[1] (dollars)	Education	Health and hospitals	Police protection	Public welfare	Highways	Total (mil dol)	Per capita[1] (dollars)	Federal civilian	Federal military	State and local	Number of returns	Mean adjusted gross income	Mean income tax
	185	186	187	188	189	190	191	192	193	194	195	196	197	198	199
GEORGIA—Cont'd															
Effingham	246.9	4,109	51.8	22.6	4.0	0.0	2.9	244.8	4,074	80	172	3,120	28,410	61,803	5,459
Elbert	74.7	3,911	43.2	19.6	4.2	0.7	2.3	11.1	580	125	50	1,195	8,320	43,900	3,265
Emanuel	103.2	4,578	42.1	32.1	2.8	0.0	7.5	21.3	947	62	56	1,941	8,940	40,550	2,891
Evans	46.3	4,311	41.0	26.8	4.7	0.0	7.2	11.8	1,097	47	27	606	4,410	41,887	3,192
Fannin	65.6	2,589	58.3	3.9	4.8	0.1	8.7	23.4	924	66	69	895	11,310	56,422	5,872
Fayette	389.5	3,460	62.8	1.0	6.8	0.0	5.4	197.3	1,753	543	354	4,627	56,450	97,990	13,321
Floyd	407.1	4,176	48.2	8.6	5.5	0.1	2.8	185.7	1,904	226	253	5,367	41,560	57,662	5,750
Forsyth	808.5	3,532	63.1	0.4	4.5	0.0	2.0	715.3	3,125	271	658	8,006	109,900	107,278	14,388
Franklin	65.2	2,852	59.6	3.3	10.4	0.0	5.7	33.0	1,444	54	60	1,039	9,770	44,824	3,239
Fulton	5,537.5	5,330	38.8	2.5	6.5	0.5	3.8	20,584.7	19,813	27,782	3,005	79,763	501,280	115,114	20,260
Gilmer	82.0	2,694	64.1	0.3	5.9	0.0	2.9	91.4	3,002	90	84	1,167	13,590	54,375	5,240
Glascock	10.4	3,420	63.8	1.4	6.9	0.0	13.2	0.2	61	4	8	178	1,100	46,859	3,206
Glynn	655.5	7,741	24.1	51.9	3.0	0.0	3.7	373.4	4,410	2,005	286	5,170	38,890	69,605	8,330
Gordon	172.0	3,008	64.1	1.3	6.3	0.3	4.1	115.4	2,019	104	153	2,567	24,200	50,517	4,207
Grady	100.5	4,058	53.3	2.0	3.9	0.0	6.2	43.1	1,739	81	64	1,110	9,690	44,647	3,457
Greene	66.7	3,875	51.4	1.0	7.4	0.2	10.9	33.8	1,965	53	55	822	8,740	110,029	17,659
Gwinnett	3,193.9	3,478	59.1	1.5	5.3	0.1	4.2	3,329.3	3,626	2,708	2,570	34,915	439,900	62,460	6,715
Habersham	134.1	3,011	55.4	3.9	5.9	0.0	3.6	143.8	3,229	108	115	2,707	19,210	52,259	4,344
Hall	705.1	3,544	54.9	6.3	5.7	0.3	3.3	1,794.7	9,021	535	536	10,478	94,240	66,181	7,438
Hancock	38.1	4,457	42.8	12.2	3.7	1.5	8.9	21.4	2,506	15	19	668	3,240	36,962	2,592
Haralson	97.2	3,324	64.5	2.9	6.2	0.1	2.7	40.2	1,373	55	79	1,470	12,380	51,945	4,129
Harris	81.4	2,399	67.2	3.3	5.5	0.0	2.2	39.6	1,166	69	94	1,223	15,330	75,255	8,204
Hart	74.7	2,907	62.7	3.6	5.1	0.1	4.6	446.1	17,353	85	68	1,105	10,940	51,063	4,687
Heard	40.4	3,441	56.1	8.0	4.9	0.1	6.4	9.3	788	15	31	649	4,450	47,973	3,804
Henry	764.6	3,395	62.2	0.2	7.6	0.0	6.2	723.5	3,213	994	629	8,439	113,480	55,393	5,108
Houston	481.7	3,144	61.8	1.7	6.5	0.0	3.4	144.8	945	15,813	3,932	9,535	73,170	57,774	5,322
Irwin	44.1	4,714	46.1	32.8	5.2	0.1	4.1	7.8	834	23	22	627	3,620	42,941	3,194
Jackson	248.7	3,677	51.6	3.1	5.1	0.0	3.4	406.8	6,014	165	199	3,015	33,600	61,375	5,830
Jasper	49.9	3,594	51.7	23.7	4.2	0.3	5.4	6.9	495	29	38	647	6,120	55,279	4,958
Jeff Davis	49.2	3,270	62.4	2.7	4.7	0.1	11.4	19.6	1,306	29	40	879	5,600	41,872	3,173
Jefferson	65.2	4,172	42.7	21.7	4.8	0.0	8.1	48.6	3,112	55	39	959	6,820	39,756	2,817
Jenkins	32.5	3,682	66.2	3.4	4.3	0.5	7.6	14.2	1,612	25	20	382	3,030	40,838	3,032
Johnson	24.2	2,489	56.4	2.6	5.2	0.4	3.7	1.7	176	19	21	530	3,080	39,240	2,458
Jones	77.0	2,704	66.9	0.5	5.4	0.2	4.6	18.2	640	37	75	1,057	12,330	56,493	4,753
Lamar	50.9	2,734	51.9	0.2	7.1	0.0	4.9	66.4	3,570	47	48	1,006	7,570	49,218	3,925
Lanier	25.3	2,424	72.1	0.8	7.3	0.1	6.0	6.3	605	15	28	633	3,550	40,816	2,626
Laurens	182.0	3,841	50.9	12.5	5.5	0.0	7.7	45.5	960	1,759	123	2,946	20,400	48,619	4,295
Lee	100.1	3,404	69.2	0.6	9.7	0.0	3.6	68.0	2,311	47	77	1,470	14,000	62,899	5,974
Liberty	249.5	4,049	46.7	20.7	5.4	0.1	1.9	125.9	2,043	3,750	15,855	3,165	28,290	41,259	2,649
Lincoln	28.6	3,637	49.5	4.2	3.8	0.2	5.6	33.9	4,318	18	21	389	3,450	52,799	4,539
Long	50.0	2,660	78.1	0.7	5.3	0.0	1.9	11.2	596	20	52	741	6,260	41,429	2,298
Lowndes	769.1	6,664	29.8	48.5	3.8	0.0	2.2	530.1	4,594	1,164	4,984	10,004	47,610	51,627	5,005
Lumpkin	72.4	2,206	56.0	1.0	7.1	0.0	5.5	51.1	1,558	82	299	2,955	13,490	55,950	5,049
McDuffie	68.6	3,190	61.3	8.0	6.4	0.2	2.5	23.2	1,076	27	171	1,133	9,550	46,442	3,798
McIntosh	35.7	2,539	53.0	3.6	9.4	0.2	3.2	17.7	1,257	61	41	535	5,310	49,582	4,822
Macon	38.2	2,882	62.5	3.1	4.8	0.3	5.3	18.5	1,398	30	28	705	4,440	37,824	2,491
Madison	77.6	2,648	69.5	2.9	3.8	0.1	3.9	39.5	1,350	45	80	1,173	13,120	51,649	4,250
Marion	21.5	2,553	67.8	2.5	3.3	1.2	2.9	20.9	2,486	17	22	318	2,800	46,177	3,899
Meriwether	63.1	2,999	49.4	3.1	8.1	0.0	3.5	62.3	2,964	51	57	1,145	9,260	47,151	4,278
Miller	65.9	11,343	16.2	64.6	1.9	5.0	2.1	24.1	4,149	20	14	886	2,310	42,993	3,935
Mitchell	86.9	3,895	57.2	1.0	6.4	0.0	7.0	41.4	1,854	65	51	1,290	8,240	39,430	2,637
Monroe	96.1	3,537	51.0	13.5	8.3	0.1	4.1	33.9	1,248	37	72	2,547	11,970	72,319	8,247
Montgomery	22.5	2,489	55.2	1.1	5.6	0.2	8.2	3.7	412	17	22	377	3,190	47,047	3,774
Morgan	82.6	4,496	53.2	19.8	2.1	0.9	3.5	183.3	9,974	42	51	1,117	9,200	69,915	7,943
Murray	96.0	2,412	69.0	3.3	4.1	0.0	3.8	47.3	1,188	105	105	1,252	15,970	42,905	2,803
Muscogee	808.5	4,171	45.6	8.7	6.3	4.6	4.5	618.0	3,188	6,472	6,999	12,434	85,720	55,271	5,915
Newton	393.3	3,647	50.9	18.8	5.2	0.0	3.7	151.9	1,409	270	294	4,222	51,390	46,614	3,767
Oconee	120.6	3,165	64.3	0.5	4.1	0.2	7.8	152.0	3,986	74	108	1,545	18,220	116,536	17,047
Oglethorpe	33.5	2,252	66.1	3.3	3.8	0.1	6.9	15.3	1,030	14	40	594	6,510	48,204	3,769
Paulding	393.1	2,465	73.0	0.2	5.0	0.0	6.4	747.8	4,688	157	506	5,203	76,700	59,152	5,295
Peach	87.3	3,236	42.9	13.8	7.5	0.0	3.2	12.3	457	116	74	1,942	11,840	49,413	3,945
Pickens	88.4	2,801	58.0	0.5	5.9	0.0	6.6	32.2	1,022	64	86	1,189	15,710	66,558	6,958
Pierce	53.2	2,772	70.4	2.1	4.8	0.1	4.8	4.5	235	54	51	709	8,000	49,589	4,240
Pike	49.1	2,699	73.6	0.9	3.6	0.1	8.5	20.9	1,146	35	50	695	8,360	64,615	5,914
Polk	127.6	3,051	65.6	0.5	6.5	0.1	4.6	116.9	2,795	79	112	1,673	17,420	44,556	3,231
Pulaski	25.6	2,287	54.0	2.6	10.5	0.0	5.4	2.3	209	16	26	570	3,770	46,653	4,020

1. Based on the resident population estimated as of July 1 of the year shown.

State / county code	CBSA code[1]	County Type code[2]	STATE County	Land area[3] (sq. mi)	Population, 2021: Total persons 2021	Population, 2021: Rank	Population, 2021: Per square mile	Race alone or in combination, not Hispanic or Latino (percent): White	Black	American Indian, Alaska Native	Asian and Pacific Islancer	Percent Hispanic or Latino[4]	Age (percent): Under 5 years	5 to 17 years	18 to 24 years	25 to 34 years	35 to 44 years	45 to 54 years
				1	2	3	4	5	6	7	8	9	10	11	12	13	14	15
			GEORGIA—Cont'd															
13237		6	Putnam	344.7	22,585	1,694	65.5	67.2	26.5	0.6	1.0	6.2	4.8	10.9	10.4	10.3	10.5	12.0
13239	21640	9	Quitman	151.2	2,243	3,024	14.8	50.2	47.5	1.2	0.7	2.1	5.3	9.8	8.6	9.0	8.3	10.2
13241		7	Rabun	370.1	17,119	1,964	46.3	89.0	2.2	1.1	1.3	7.9	4.2	8.7	9.5	10.6	10.1	12.5
13243		6	Randolph	428.2	6,287	2,713	14.7	36.3	60.8	0.4	0.7	2.8	4.6	12.2	12.1	9.8	10.4	9.9
13245	12260	2	Richmond	324.3	205,673	335	634.2	34.7	59.0	0.9	2.8	5.3	6.5	12.5	14.8	16.1	12.2	10.5
13247	12060	1	Rockdale	129.8	94,082	642	724.8	27.5	60.9	0.7	2.6	10.7	5.3	13.8	13.8	12.2	11.7	13.7
13249	11140	8	Schley	166.9	4,478	2,858	26.8	73.2	20.5	0.6	1.4	6.2	5.5	12.9	13.5	9.8	11.7	16.0
13251		6	Screven	645.8	14,105	2,145	21.8	56.1	41.1	0.7	0.9	2.6	5.7	11.3	10.9	13.0	11.7	12.4
13253		6	Seminole	237.5	9,197	2,472	38.7	62.8	33.1	0.7	0.9	3.8	5.2	11.3	11.2	10.7	10.3	12.3
13255	12060	1	Spalding	196.0	67,909	789	346.5	57.4	36.9	0.8	1.4	5.5	6.4	12.9	12.2	13.6	11.7	11.8
13257	45740	7	Stephens	178.9	26,865	1,533	150.2	84.0	12.4	0.8	1.5	4.1	5.8	12.6	13.3	11.6	11.1	11.7
13259	17980	8	Stewart	458.7	5,341	2,790	11.6	23.5	38.9	0.9	3.2	34.9	2.8	6.1	13.5	27.6	16.0	10.0
13261	11140	6	Sumter	482.9	29,283	1,448	60.6	39.8	53.1	0.6	1.5	6.1	5.9	12.9	17.4	12.2	10.7	11.1
13263	17980	8	Talbot	391.4	5,742	2,758	14.7	41.9	54.3	1.1	0.7	3.4	4.4	9.1	9.8	10.1	9.6	12.3
13265		8	Taliaferro	194.6	1,558	3,075	8.0	40.4	54.0	0.6	2.9	5.1	4.2	9.7	8.4	10.0	10.5	11.1
13267		6	Tattnall	480.8	23,052	1,676	47.9	58.1	28.9	0.6	1.0	12.7	4.9	11.8	13.2	15.7	14.0	13.2
13269		8	Taylor	376.7	7,799	2,589	20.7	59.2	37.7	0.6	1.3	2.7	5.0	11.2	11.0	12.0	10.5	13.3
13271		7	Telfair	437.3	12,414	2,248	28.4	49.4	34.5	0.5	1.1	15.8	4.4	8.8	10.4	15.0	16.2	13.7
13273	10500	3	Terrell	335.8	8,964	2,489	26.7	37.4	59.6	0.7	0.7	2.9	5.5	12.8	11.9	12.6	11.2	10.6
13275	45620	4	Thomas	544.6	45,842	1,064	84.2	58.3	37.0	0.8	1.3	4.0	6.0	13.7	12.1	11.7	12.1	11.8
13277	45700	5	Tift	260.9	41,212	1,160	158.0	55.2	31.2	0.5	1.7	12.8	6.5	13.9	15.0	13.0	12.4	11.6
13279	47080	7	Toombs	364.0	26,911	1,530	73.9	60.5	27.3	0.5	1.2	11.9	7.0	14.8	13.2	12.5	12.3	11.3
13281		9	Towns	166.5	12,875	2,219	77.3	94.4	1.7	0.8	1.2	3.1	3.5	6.7	15.2	7.6	6.9	9.5
13283	20140	7	Treutlen	199.4	6,306	2,712	31.6	64.7	31.9	0.7	0.7	3.7	5.4	13.2	13.8	12.7	12.3	11.0
13285	29300	4	Troup	414.0	69,720	776	168.4	57.1	37.3	0.6	2.8	4.0	6.4	13.6	13.7	13.9	12.3	12.2
13287		6	Turner	285.4	8,966	2,488	31.4	54.2	40.2	0.6	1.2	4.9	6.7	13.9	13.3	12.3	11.8	11.0
13289	31420	3	Twiggs	359.3	7,856	2,587	21.9	56.2	40.5	1.0	0.8	3.1	4.6	11.1	9.4	10.7	10.9	12.2
13291		9	Union	322.1	25,521	1,584	79.2	94.2	1.3	1.0	0.8	3.9	3.6	8.8	8.6	8.3	8.6	10.5
13293	45580	6	Upson	323.5	27,720	1,511	85.7	68.2	29.1	0.8	1.0	2.6	5.8	13.0	11.8	12.6	11.3	12.6
13295	16860	2	Walker	446.4	68,510	787	153.5	91.6	5.5	0.8	1.1	2.8	5.5	12.3	11.3	12.5	12.7	12.9
13297	12060	1	Walton	326.8	99,853	611	305.5	72.6	20.4	0.7	2.3	5.8	5.8	13.6	12.8	12.4	12.6	13.6
13299	48180	5	Ware	899.2	36,033	1,282	40.1	63.9	31.0	0.7	1.5	4.8	6.6	14.0	12.3	13.3	12.0	11.9
13301		8	Warren	284.4	5,240	2,804	18.4	40.4	57.6	0.6	1.0	2.0	5.5	11.5	10.7	11.8	10.0	11.7
13303		7	Washington	678.5	19,785	1,832	29.2	43.5	53.8	0.4	0.8	2.8	5.2	12.6	11.9	13.5	12.3	12.0
13305	27700	6	Wayne	641.8	30,380	1,424	47.3	72.5	20.7	0.9	1.2	6.7	6.0	13.9	11.9	13.6	13.3	12.6
13307		8	Webster	209.7	2,367	3,013	11.3	52.2	42.6	0.6	1.0	5.2	4.7	9.8	11.8	10.1	9.5	12.8
13309		9	Wheeler	295.5	7,471	2,620	25.3	56.6	38.0	0.5	0.6	5.7	3.9	9.0	13.4	17.1	15.2	14.2
13311		6	White	240.7	28,442	1,479	118.2	93.3	2.9	1.1	0.9	3.6	4.7	11.0	13.0	10.8	10.5	12.4
13313	19140	3	Whitfield	290.4	102,848	598	354.2	57.3	4.3	0.6	1.8	37.3	6.2	14.5	14.4	13.1	12.7	12.8
13315		8	Wilcox	377.8	8,739	2,507	23.1	60.1	34.4	0.7	1.2	5.0	4.5	10.9	12.1	14.6	14.2	13.3
13317		6	Wilkes	469.5	9,513	2,450	20.3	53.8	40.9	0.6	1.0	5.8	5.1	11.8	11.3	10.4	10.4	12.0
13319		8	Wilkinson	449.2	8,831	2,500	19.7	58.9	38.2	0.8	0.7	3.1	5.5	12.5	11.8	10.7	11.7	11.2
13321	10500	3	Worth	570.7	20,554	1,788	36.0	68.4	28.7	0.7	1.1	2.4	5.3	12.4	11.5	12.1	11.4	12.5
15000		0	HAWAII	6,422.4	1,441,553	X	224.5	36.2	3.0	1.7	75.6	10.9	5.7	12.0	11.5	13.5	13.2	11.8
15001	25900	5	Hawaii	4,028.4	202,906	339	50.4	48.0	1.8	2.3	68.1	13.5	5.4	12.4	10.4	11.3	12.5	11.4
15003	46520	2	Honolulu	600.6	1,000,890	47	1,666.5	31.7	3.7	1.5	79.0	10.2	5.9	11.9	12.1	14.4	13.3	11.7
15005		3	Kalawao	12.0	82	3,142	6.8	40.2	2.3	5.7	66.7	1.1	0.0	0.0	0.0	4.9	12.2	13.4
15007	28180	5	Kauai	619.9	73,454	752	118.5	44.7	1.4	1.8	68.4	11.6	5.4	12.7	10.0	11.8	13.2	12.0
15009	27980	3	Maui	1,161.5	164,221	410	141.4	44.0	1.5	1.8	68.0	11.9	5.6	12.4	10.2	11.5	13.8	12.7
16000		0	IDAHO	82,645.1	1,900,923	X	23.0	83.5	1.2	1.9	2.7	13.0	6.0	14.2	13.6	13.1	13.1	11.4
16001	14260	2	Ada	1,052.0	511,931	141	486.6	86.5	1.9	1.1	4.5	8.8	5.1	13.1	12.8	13.9	14.6	12.8
16003		9	Adams	1,362.8	4,625	2,846	3.4	93.6	0.7	2.4	1.8	3.7	4.1	9.8	8.0	8.6	9.4	10.7
16005	38540	3	Bannock	1,112.5	88,263	669	79.3	85.1	1.4	3.6	2.9	9.2	6.3	14.7	14.7	14.0	13.7	10.6
16007		9	Bear Lake	975.7	6,545	2,695	6.7	94.2	0.6	1.2	0.9	4.3	6.8	15.5	11.8	11.0	11.5	10.2
16009		6	Benewah	776.9	9,931	2,413	12.8	88.0	1.1	9.6	1.1	4.2	5.4	13.0	10.0	10.3	10.7	11.2
16011	13940	4	Bingham	2,093.7	48,876	1,009	23.3	75.4	0.6	5.9	1.5	18.1	6.8	17.5	14.3	11.8	13.0	10.5
16013	25200	7	Blaine	2,637.7	24,766	1,622	9.4	74.6	0.9	0.7	1.5	23.5	4.1	11.6	11.3	10.5	12.6	13.1
16015	14260	2	Boise	1,899.6	8,094	2,572	4.3	91.6	0.8	2.2	2.0	5.4	3.7	8.6	8.7	8.6	11.0	12.1
16017	41760	6	Bonner	1,733.2	49,491	1,004	28.6	94.6	0.5	2.1	1.4	3.6	4.7	11.3	9.3	9.7	11.5	11.5
16019	26820	3	Bonneville	1,866.0	127,930	507	68.6	83.9	1.0	1.3	2.0	13.6	7.6	17.6	13.5	13.6	13.7	10.2
16021		7	Boundary	1,268.7	12,561	2,239	9.9	91.3	1.0	2.6	1.8	5.3	5.9	13.2	10.7	9.8	11.2	11.2
16023	26820	3	Butte	2,236.5	2,654	2,985	1.2	93.1	0.6	1.8	1.1	5.3	4.6	13.4	11.5	8.3	11.9	10.0
16025	25200	9	Camas	1,074.2	1,139	3,102	1.1	91.7	0.7	3.0	1.2	6.4	4.1	13.3	9.1	7.2	13.4	12.8
16027	14260	2	Canyon	587.1	243,115	287	414.1	72.1	1.1	1.5	2.1	25.5	6.7	15.6	14.1	13.9	13.1	11.3

1. CBSA = Core Based Statistical Area. See Appendix A for explanation. See Appendix B for list of metropolitan areas with component counties. 2. County type code from the Economic Research Service of USDA Rural-Urban Continuum Codes. See Appendix A for definition. 3. Dry land or land partially or temporarily covered by water. 4. May be of any race.

STATE County	Population, 2021 (cont.)				Population change, 2000–2021							Households, 2016–2020				
	Age (percent) (cont.)				Total persons		Percent change		Components of change, 2020–2021					Percent		
	55 to 64 years	65 to 74 years	75 years and over	Percent female	2010	2020	2010–2020	2020–2021	Births	Deaths	Net Migration	Number	Persons per household	Family house-holds	Female family house-holder[1]	One person
	16	17	18	19	20	21	22	23	24	25	26	27	28	29	30	31
GEORGIA—Cont'd																
Putnam	16.3	15.6	9.2	51.7	21,218	22,047	3.9	2.4	248	409	708	9,457	2.3	66.2	13.5	29.0
Quitman	16.5	19.0	13.2	51.9	2,513	2,235	-11.1	0.4	27	45	27	958	2.4	59.1	10.2	36.6
Rabun	15.7	17.4	11.3	50.8	16,276	16,883	3.7	1.4	193	383	432	7,022	2.3	63.3	8.5	31.0
Randolph	15.3	14.4	11.3	53.5	7,719	6,425	-16.8	-2.1	81	138	-78	2,704	2.5	62.5	25.5	33.4
Richmond	12.3	9.5	5.5	51.3	200,549	206,607	3.0	-0.5	3,378	3,053	-1,295	72,526	2.7	59.1	21.6	35.0
Rockdale	14.2	9.9	5.4	53.0	85,215	93,570	9.8	0.5	1,164	1,150	488	31,465	2.8	72.1	20.2	24.6
Schley	12.9	9.8	8.0	51.5	5,010	4,547	-9.2	-1.5	66	59	-76	1,861	2.8	79.6	12.5	19.8
Screven	14.9	12.7	7.5	50.7	14,593	14,067	-3.6	0.3	208	257	85	4,939	2.7	64.5	18.5	32.9
Seminole	15.2	13.5	10.3	52.0	8,729	9,147	4.8	0.5	116	157	93	3,364	2.4	64.4	18.7	30.7
Spalding	12.7	11.4	7.4	52.0	64,073	67,306	5.0	0.9	1,034	1,250	817	25,693	2.5	68.8	20.3	26.1
Stephens	13.7	12.6	7.7	51.6	26,175	26,784	2.3	0.3	362	498	216	9,977	2.5	66.2	11.0	30.6
Stewart	9.9	7.8	6.3	31.1	6,058	5,314	-12.3	0.5	43	89	72	1,845	2.3	59.6	21.8	37.7
Sumter	12.3	10.5	7.0	52.8	32,819	29,616	-9.8	-1.1	415	493	-256	11,419	2.4	62.3	18.0	33.3
Talbot	17.9	16.9	9.9	52.1	6,865	5,733	-16.5	0.2	56	120	75	2,891	2.2	66.7	20.6	28.7
Taliaferro	17.3	16.6	12.1	49.2	1,717	1,559	-9.2	-0.1	13	39	25	662	2.4	66.8	18.0	30.2
Tattnall	12.1	9.3	5.7	42.5	25,520	22,842	-10.5	0.9	298	344	255	8,345	2.3	69.2	16.8	25.7
Taylor	15.2	12.5	9.3	52.2	8,906	7,816	-12.2	-0.2	106	133	11	3,623	2.2	63.9	16.8	31.1
Telfair	12.6	10.8	8.0	40.6	16,500	12,477	-24.4	-0.5	167	254	23	4,481	2.8	69.6	21.0	28.0
Terrell	14.6	12.3	8.5	51.7	9,315	9,185	-1.4	-2.4	122	152	-188	3,355	2.5	66.2	23.5	28.0
Thomas	13.7	11.1	7.8	52.4	44,720	45,798	2.4	0.1	647	746	139	17,750	2.5	69.2	18.2	26.3
Tift	11.7	9.5	6.2	51.5	40,118	41,344	3.1	-0.3	648	586	-197	14,868	2.6	66.1	16.6	28.3
Toombs	12.2	9.7	7.0	52.4	27,223	27,030	-0.7	-0.4	470	510	-83	9,792	2.7	66.0	15.2	29.3
Towns	15.8	19.8	15.0	52.4	10,471	12,493	19.3	3.1	108	266	549	5,006	2.2	68.0	7.9	25.5
Treutlen	13.3	11.0	7.3	49.4	6,885	6,406	-7.0	-1.6	85	125	-59	2,395	2.6	66.1	14.8	32.0
Troup	12.7	9.6	5.8	52.0	67,044	69,426	3.6	0.4	1,055	1,117	346	24,982	2.8	68.4	19.5	28.5
Turner	12.1	10.3	8.5	51.5	8,930	9,006	0.9	-0.4	137	134	-45	3,208	2.4	67.9	17.0	29.3
Twiggs	17.2	14.3	9.5	50.6	9,023	8,022	-11.1	-2.1	78	213	-31	3,080	2.6	64.9	14.1	33.1
Union	17.5	20.6	13.5	51.2	21,356	24,632	15.3	3.6	194	533	1,249	10,231	2.3	67.9	8.3	28.5
Upson	14.4	11.2	7.4	52.3	27,153	27,700	2.0	0.1	375	595	238	10,399	2.5	57.4	13.4	38.5
Walker	13.7	11.3	7.7	50.5	68,756	67,654	-1.6	1.3	911	1,204	1,158	26,306	2.6	70.7	13.5	25.7
Walton	13.0	9.7	6.3	51.0	83,768	96,673	15.4	3.3	1,343	1,364	3,230	32,094	2.9	75.7	14.0	18.9
Ware	12.2	10.3	7.3	49.7	36,312	36,251	-0.2	-0.6	596	703	-116	13,657	2.4	60.9	15.3	34.3
Warren	15.6	13.3	9.9	52.8	5,834	5,215	-10.6	0.5	74	104	55	2,261	2.3	67.2	24.5	31.4
Washington	14.7	10.7	7.2	48.6	21,187	19,988	-5.7	-1.0	243	386	-65	7,719	2.4	67.7	22.0	28.2
Wayne	12.6	9.9	6.3	48.7	30,099	30,144	0.1	0.8	423	485	298	10,479	2.7	69.1	12.8	26.9
Webster	16.9	13.7	10.6	50.6	2,799	2,348	-16.1	0.8	20	22	21	1,115	2.3	58.2	6.3	39.0
Wheeler	11.6	9.1	6.5	34.7	7,421	7,471	0.7	0.0	70	97	27	1,774	4.4	58.4	10.8	40.7
White	15.0	13.4	9.2	50.7	27,144	28,003	3.2	1.6	319	506	633	11,727	2.5	74.5	13.4	20.8
Whitfield	11.8	8.5	6.0	50.0	102,599	102,864	0.3	0.0	1,504	1,251	-298	36,412	2.8	71.6	14.5	24.1
Wilcox	11.8	10.5	8.2	39.4	9,255	8,766	-5.3	-0.3	84	161	49	2,542	2.6	69.0	14.9	26.7
Wilkes	15.1	13.1	10.7	51.7	10,593	9,565	-9.7	-0.5	104	193	38	4,115	2.4	61.5	14.8	36.8
Wilkinson	15.6	12.3	8.7	51.9	9,563	8,877	-7.2	-0.5	120	163	-4	3,301	2.7	61.4	16.4	33.0
Worth	14.8	11.8	8.3	52.3	21,679	20,784	-4.1	-1.1	239	318	-152	7,982	2.5	75.1	18.3	19.9
HAWAII	12.6	11.3	8.3	49.9	1,360,301	1,455,271	7.0	-0.9	19,906	18,421	-15,059	467,932	2.9	69.3	12.4	24.3
Hawaii	13.9	14.6	8.1	50.5	185,079	200,629	8.4	1.1	2,559	2,979	2,714	71,747	2.8	67.2	12.8	26.1
Honolulu	12.0	10.3	8.5	49.7	953,207	1,016,508	6.6	-1.5	14,250	12,457	-17,266	316,928	3.0	69.4	12.2	24.5
Kalawao	18.3	26.8	24.4	52.9	90	82	-8.9	0.0	0	0	0	306	1.4	53.6	0.0	46.1
Kauai	13.5	13.1	8.3	50.5	67,091	73,298	9.3	0.2	904	926	171	23,331	3.1	70.3	11.1	22.3
Maui	14.0	12.3	7.5	50.4	154,834	164,754	6.4	-0.3	2,193	2,059	-678	55,620	3.0	71.3	13.2	21.6
IDAHO	12.0	10.4	6.2	49.9	1,567,582	1,839,106	17.3	3.4	26,829	21,368	56,851	649,299	2.7	68.0	8.7	25.7
Ada	12.1	9.8	5.7	49.9	392,365	494,967	26.1	3.4	6,062	5,140	16,144	179,708	2.6	64.8	8.2	27.8
Adams	18.4	21.0	10.1	48.1	3,976	4,379	10.1	5.6	47	54	257	1,726	2.4	67.8	4.8	28.7
Bannock	10.9	9.8	5.4	50.2	82,839	87,018	5.0	1.4	1,334	1,103	1,007	31,669	2.6	64.0	9.1	29.1
Bear Lake	13.0	12.2	8.1	49.9	5,986	6,372	6.4	2.7	101	107	183	2,455	2.5	75.1	8.8	21.7
Benewah	16.1	14.9	8.5	49.1	9,285	9,530	2.6	4.2	138	156	427	3,564	2.6	68.0	8.8	24.6
Bingham	11.4	9.2	5.5	50.0	45,607	47,992	5.2	1.8	785	569	667	15,612	2.9	74.4	10.3	23.1
Blaine	15.7	13.1	8.0	50.2	21,376	24,272	13.5	2.0	203	193	486	8,318	2.7	64.7	10.1	31.5
Boise	19.5	19.4	8.3	48.4	7,028	7,610	8.3	6.4	55	105	545	3,351	2.3	67.8	5.6	26.1
Bonner	16.2	16.9	9.0	49.9	40,877	47,110	15.2	5.1	495	661	2,590	17,998	2.5	68.7	7.3	25.9
Bonneville	10.2	8.4	5.1	50.1	104,234	123,964	18.9	3.2	2,228	1,387	3,142	40,946	2.8	70.3	10.9	25.1
Boundary	14.7	14.8	8.6	49.5	10,972	12,056	9.9	4.2	170	204	546	4,596	2.6	66.4	4.9	29.2
Butte	15.1	15.2	9.9	49.0	2,891	2,574	-11.0	3.1	35	37	83	966	2.7	64.2	6.1	34.3
Camas	16.3	16.2	7.6	49.1	1,117	1,077	-3.6	5.8	13	11	61	391	2.7	58.6	5.9	36.1
Canyon	11.0	8.9	5.3	50.3	188,923	231,105	22.3	5.2	3,880	2,518	10,756	75,494	2.9	71.3	10.6	22.4

1. No spouse present.

STATE County	Persons in group quarters, 2021	Daytime Population, 2016–2020		Births, 2021		Deaths, 2021		Persons under 65 with no health insurance, 2019		Medicare, 2021			COVID-19 Deaths, 2020	
		Number	Employment/ residence ratio	Total	Rate[1]	Number	Rate[1]	Number	Percent	Total beneficiaries	Enrolled in Original Medicare	Enrolled in Medicare Advantage	Number	Rate[1]
	32	33	34	35	36	37	38	39	40	41	42	43	44	45
GEORGIA—Cont'd														
Putnam	90	19,824	0.8	210	9.4	339	15.2	2,988	18.2	6,026	3,627	2,398	31	1.4
Quitman	0	2,132	0.8	22	9.9	32	14.3	308	19.7	721	384	336	D	D
Rabun	372	17,156	1.1	152	8.9	294	17.3	2,592	21.5	5,298	3,609	1,689	26	1.5
Randolph	261	6,522	0.9	67	10.6	99	15.6	777	16.4	1,624	813	811	25	3.9
Richmond	12,956	243,745	1.5	2,750	13.3	2,468	12.0	22,751	14.3	37,523	20,606	16,917	259	1.3
Rockdale	721	91,899	1.0	911	9.7	901	9.6	12,249	16.1	16,014	7,824	8,190	76	0.8
Schley	0	4,572	0.7	50	11.1	49	10.9	634	14.8	813	425	388	D	D
Screven	441	11,808	0.6	176	12.5	199	14.1	1,658	15.5	3,410	1,759	1,652	18	1.3
Seminole	52	7,929	0.9	92	10.0	126	13.7	1,026	16.9	2,209	1,376	833	15	1.6
Spalding	1,267	62,366	0.9	815	12.0	990	14.6	8,962	17.0	15,321	7,919	7,402	95	1.4
Stephens	567	26,539	1.1	300	11.2	413	15.4	3,227	16.1	6,900	4,085	2,815	43	1.6
Stewart	1,233	6,175	0.8	35	6.6	74	13.9	726	18.5	1,103	502	601	13	2.5
Sumter	1,548	30,740	1.1	342	11.6	386	13.1	3,632	16.2	6,202	3,101	3,101	73	2.5
Talbot	0	4,395	0.3	44	7.7	107	18.7	733	16.1	1,662	797	865	D	D
Taliaferro	7	1,219	0.4	12	7.7	29	18.6	189	17.5	491	233	258	D	D
Tattnall	3,888	24,224	0.9	238	10.4	282	12.3	3,326	19.7	4,096	2,250	1,846	35	1.5
Taylor	137	7,498	0.8	86	11.0	104	13.3	978	15.8	1,825	945	880	20	2.6
Telfair	2,358	16,099	1.1	135	10.9	209	16.8	1,637	16.8	2,414	1,388	1,026	35	2.8
Terrell	264	8,045	0.8	97	10.7	108	11.9	1,106	17.1	2,215	1,088	1,127	31	3.4
Thomas	614	47,560	1.2	538	11.7	608	13.3	5,679	16.1	10,317	6,006	4,311	79	1.7
Tift	1,540	46,582	1.3	518	12.5	464	11.2	6,242	19.2	7,783	4,417	3,366	78	1.9
Toombs	342	29,239	1.2	363	13.5	395	14.6	4,238	19.4	5,734	3,436	2,298	56	2.1
Towns	1,176	11,402	0.9	87	6.8	209	16.4	1,272	18.9	5,012	3,158	1,854	27	2.2
Treutlen	386	5,648	0.5	65	10.2	98	15.4	986	19.0	1,399	714	684	15	2.3
Troup	1,973	78,765	1.3	864	12.4	895	12.9	9,452	16.6	13,185	7,623	5,562	112	1.6
Turner	405	7,111	0.7	118	13.2	93	10.4	902	15.1	1,962	910	1,052	26	2.9
Twiggs	78	7,557	0.8	68	8.6	167	21.1	1,026	16.8	2,349	1,158	1,191	22	2.8
Union	231	24,552	1.1	160	6.4	412	16.4	3,005	18.8	9,124	5,825	3,300	35	1.4
Upson	402	24,388	0.8	306	11.0	471	17.0	2,876	13.7	6,674	3,304	3,370	63	2.3
Walker	1,148	56,750	0.6	744	10.9	981	14.4	8,359	15.1	14,969	9,254	5,715	64	0.9
Walton	697	78,289	0.7	1,089	11.1	1,099	11.2	12,001	15.2	17,779	9,770	8,010	103	1.1
Ware	2,399	40,597	1.4	484	13.4	563	15.6	4,500	16.7	8,147	4,860	3,287	80	2.2
Warren	71	4,307	0.6	62	11.9	76	14.6	596	15.1	1,452	687	765	D	D
Washington	1,766	20,449	1.0	192	9.7	317	16.0	2,312	15.6	4,562	2,313	2,248	57	2.9
Wayne	1,995	29,442	1.0	319	10.5	389	12.9	4,052	17.6	6,083	3,594	2,489	46	1.5
Webster	0	2,215	0.6	17	7.2	15	6.4	330	16.8	578	285	293	D	D
Wheeler	2,360	6,738	0.6	60	8.1	73	9.8	645	15.5	1,164	640	524	15	2.0
White	668	26,538	0.7	264	9.3	405	14.3	4,283	18.8	7,434	4,159	3,275	40	1.4
Whitfield	952	114,969	1.2	1,206	11.7	995	9.7	20,150	22.9	17,308	13,003	4,305	150	1.5
Wilcox	1,865	7,631	0.6	70	8.0	130	14.9	816	15.6	1,718	985	733	25	2.9
Wilkes	137	9,120	0.8	73	7.7	157	16.5	1,429	19.7	2,720	1,565	1,155	12	1.3
Wilkinson	158	8,726	0.9	87	9.8	117	13.2	1,134	16.3	2,337	1,313	1,024	16	1.8
Worth	166	16,071	0.5	185	9.0	236	11.4	2,746	17.2	4,380	2,464	1,916	44	2.1
HAWAII	42,136	1,421,144	1.0	15,904	11.0	14,648	10.1	53,289	4.8	280,940	147,885	133,055	375	0.3
Hawaii	3,449	201,425	1.0	2,048	10.1	2,358	11.7	8,771	5.6	46,305	29,323	16,982	54	0.3
Honolulu	35,294	980,834	1.0	11,366	11.3	9,898	9.8	33,662	4.4	187,165	94,183	92,982	300	0.3
Kalawao	3	96	0.2	0	0.0	NA	NA	NA	NA	NA	D	D	NA	NA
Kauai	1,077	71,987	1.0	724	9.9	764	10.4	2,952	5.2	15,825	9,052	6,773	D	D
Maui	2,313	166,802	1.0	1,766	10.7	1,628	9.9	7,904	5.9	31,643	15,326	16,317	21	0.1
IDAHO	28,962	1,732,985	1.0	21,316	11.4	16,918	9.0	187,336	12.7	349,014	219,432	129,582	1,441	0.8
Ada	11,167	492,611	1.1	4,814	9.5	4,135	8.2	38,528	9.5	85,153	41,856	43,297	364	0.7
Adams	16	3,652	0.7	37	8.2	44	9.7	487	16.4	1,405	1,052	353	D	D
Bannock	1,781	85,297	1.0	1,072	12.2	864	9.8	8,817	12.1	15,611	10,004	5,607	71	0.8
Bear Lake	28	5,352	0.7	77	11.9	82	12.7	532	11.0	1,471	1,422	49	D	D
Benewah	54	9,707	1.1	104	10.7	128	13.1	1,055	14.9	2,774	2,657	117	D	D
Bingham	297	42,273	0.8	632	13.0	442	9.1	5,725	14.6	8,195	5,869	2,325	44	0.9
Blaine	249	24,056	1.1	171	7.0	153	6.2	3,511	19.0	5,164	4,198	966	15	0.6
Boise	25	6,799	0.8	45	5.7	91	11.6	696	12.1	2,294	1,248	1,046	D	D
Bonner	350	43,265	0.9	387	8.0	549	11.3	4,535	13.4	13,283	8,868	4,415	21	0.4
Bonneville	1,222	123,294	1.1	1,791	14.2	1,109	8.8	11,095	10.9	19,475	13,824	5,650	121	1.0
Boundary	34	12,124	1.0	143	11.6	162	13.1	1,526	16.5	3,532	2,481	1,051	10	0.8
Butte	10	4,812	3.2	27	10.3	25	9.6	206	10.5	679	654	24	D	D
Camas	0	855	0.5	10	9.0	9	8.1	95	11.4	259	203	56	D	D
Canyon	3,212	202,591	0.8	3,102	13.0	1,980	8.3	29,380	15.3	39,962	18,080	21,882	228	1.0

1. Per 1,000 estimated resident population.

STATE County	COVID-19 Vaccinations, 2021–2022		Education: School enrollment and attainment, 2016–2020: Enrollment[1]		Attainment[2] (percent)		Local government expenditures,[3] 2018–2019		Money income, 2016–2020	Households			Income and poverty, 2020	Percent below poverty level		
	Number	Percent[5]	Total	Percent private	High school graduate or less	Bachelor's degree or more	Total current spending (mil dol)	Current spending per student (dollars)	Per capita income[4]	Median income (dollars)	Percent with income of less than $50,000	Percent with income of $200,000 or more	Median household income (dollars)	All persons	Children under 18 years	Children 5 to 17 years in families
	46	47	48	49	50	51	52	53	54	55	56	57	58	59	60	61
GEORGIA—Cont'd																
Putnam	9,580	43.3	4,246	17.9	49.2	23.5	38.4	13,024	34,294	52,910	46.1	5.5	56,104	16.3	27.3	26.0
Quitman	761	33.1	337	9.2	62.3	11.5	5.9	18,667	22,827	34,394	68.5	2.8	37,735	23.1	40.3	41.2
Rabun	7,919	46.2	2,851	19.7	44.3	28.4	31.3	14,012	30,875	44,871	55.5	4.0	53,038	13.8	22.6	22.7
Randolph	3,149	46.5	1,948	6.1	58.9	12.3	16.3	13,801	15,931	29,400	79.7	0.3	36,064	27.4	38.9	37.1
Richmond	100,556	49.7	49,621	13.1	46.3	22.5	322.9	10,196	23,842	43,882	54.4	2.6	43,942	25.5	38.7	38.8
Rockdale	46,104	50.7	24,499	12.1	40.7	27.2	195.2	11,633	29,098	62,505	39.4	5.0	61,332	12.7	20.5	18.9
Schley	1,831	34.8	1,465	5.1	48.8	12.1	16.3	12,496	21,857	49,105	51.7	1.0	53,163	15.0	21.8	20.1
Screven	6,737	48.2	2,981	12.9	56.5	14.6	25.4	11,022	23,912	39,852	55.8	2.6	44,061	20.7	30.5	32.7
Seminole	3,686	45.6	1,599	8.0	53.2	15.4	16.5	11,308	28,132	35,286	64.8	1.1	41,778	22.9	34.2	33.1
Spalding	27,023	40.5	14,478	9.1	58.1	18.1	118.8	11,480	30,491	48,970	50.9	3.7	51,019	17.9	25.6	26.5
Stephens	10,693	41.2	6,099	16.1	58.1	18.0	41.7	10,595	22,975	46,766	52.9	1.2	46,626	16.9	22.9	22.2
Stewart	2,157	32.6	872	12.0	63.2	13.6	8.5	18,704	17,244	34,028	70.4	2.6	40,205	31.3	31.6	31.0
Sumter	15,323	51.9	8,688	8.2	51.3	20.0	49.4	11,005	21,927	37,174	59.7	2.0	42,653	24.3	36.4	33.6
Talbot	3,002	48.5	1,185	16.8	61.0	12.6	8.0	17,706	23,687	40,020	59.8	1.6	44,458	20.8	35.9	37.0
Taliaferro	781	50.8	181	7.2	72.4	5.7	5.1	NA	20,979	37,717	71.5	0.6	28,004	23.2	33.2	36.2
Tattnall	8,351	33.0	5,577	12.5	62.3	14.0	37.9	10,056	19,245	44,053	55.8	3.2	45,191	20.7	28.1	26.5
Taylor	3,667	45.7	1,517	10.9	59.5	12.5	16.1	11,294	21,770	28,550	70.8	2.2	38,783	23.2	32.5	32.3
Telfair	4,630	29.2	2,565	14.4	77.9	7.0	19.7	11,425	17,518	32,764	65.2	2.2	38,161	29.9	32.8	31.7
Terrell	4,965	58.2	2,168	10.8	57.1	10.2	16.7	13,049	19,987	35,335	59.8	1.5	39,433	27.8	45.0	42.6
Thomas	21,772	49.0	10,865	9.6	44.9	24.1	99.3	11,396	27,937	47,133	51.8	3.3	57,969	16.2	23.6	22.5
Tift	16,415	40.4	11,048	10.7	50.8	17.3	84.6	10,725	24,191	44,827	54.3	2.9	45,093	20.5	29.9	29.6
Toombs	11,279	42.0	7,073	12.1	52.6	16.6	59.2	10,720	24,797	41,244	59.0	1.8	42,165	22.2	33.2	31.9
Towns	5,870	48.8	2,242	32.9	35.9	32.6	15.1	15,900	27,763	51,257	48.3	2.4	43,640	13.2	19.8	20.9
Treutlen	2,427	35.2	1,678	9.5	64.6	16.3	11.9	10,631	24,390	32,072	60.0	3.8	40,834	23.4	31.2	29.2
Troup	25,815	36.9	17,267	13.1	49.8	20.1	134.3	11,082	24,660	46,796	51.8	3.9	51,799	16.4	23.1	23.1
Turner	3,984	49.9	1,683	4.3	55.3	10.8	15.8	12,754	19,653	34,514	64.1	0.7	46,042	22.2	37.9	38.7
Twiggs	4,388	54.0	1,557	23.1	62.3	10.3	11.1	13,987	22,534	43,477	58.2	1.3	46,444	20.0	29.0	28.2
Union	11,166	45.6	3,571	13.0	47.0	22.7	35.1	12,119	30,885	49,703	50.2	5.4	50,653	12.9	21.4	20.8
Upson	11,997	45.6	5,826	12.6	54.5	13.6	43.7	10,693	22,423	39,221	59.8	1.5	48,233	15.2	28.0	27.7
Walker	28,897	41.4	15,268	10.8	51.0	19.2	116.1	11,614	25,157	46,601	53.1	3.4	49,388	14.1	18.7	17.9
Walton	39,079	41.3	23,248	16.9	47.7	22.5	163.7	10,331	28,436	65,491	37.1	4.8	71,390	11.4	15.8	14.9
Ware	13,758	38.5	7,666	8.5	59.1	15.2	72.5	11,787	20,221	37,041	62.0	1.7	39,994	26.0	39.8	35.7
Warren	2,524	48.0	948	6.1	66.2	10.5	9.4	15,081	24,547	38,250	63.2	1.5	40,422	23.4	39.1	39.4
Washington	8,992	44.1	4,644	7.2	62.4	15.1	37.3	11,992	20,535	36,402	63.2	1.6	43,309	21.3	28.8	27.9
Wayne	12,610	42.1	7,119	6.0	57.8	12.6	56.2	10,451	21,763	45,773	54.9	1.7	48,885	19.7	27.8	27.1
Webster	1,149	44.1	662	10.3	52.7	11.0	4.3	13,756	22,034	31,629	66.0	1.1	45,381	18.6	28.0	27.4
Wheeler	2,084	26.5	1,609	6.7	66.0	15.1	12.2	12,127	15,186	28,864	63.6	0.2	36,671	35.6	33.7	32.3
White	10,999	35.7	6,053	16.9	46.9	20.2	75.6	12,838	28,340	55,788	45.1	2.4	58,831	12.5	19.5	17.8
Whitfield	45,413	43.4	26,538	3.2	59.3	16.4	226.8	10,861	24,361	50,055	49.9	3.7	56,249	13.0	17.7	16.2
Wilcox	3,155	36.5	1,653	2.4	59.8	12.0	15.2	12,661	16,471	39,216	58.5	1.1	40,856	27.9	31.8	30.9
Wilkes	4,708	48.2	2,218	10.2	64.2	11.4	18.3	12,319	23,265	36,486	58.5	1.5	42,071	20.2	31.9	31.6
Wilkinson	4,563	51.0	2,233	16.7	64.0	11.2	16.8	12,722	22,987	36,896	61.0	1.9	44,068	20.1	32.0	31.0
Worth	8,434	41.7	4,354	8.4	58.3	10.3	32.3	9,951	26,533	50,913	48.9	1.9	47,907	18.2	29.2	28.9
HAWAII	1,107,310	78.2	318,529	22.5	34.8	33.6	2,924.3	16,132	37,013	83,173	29.0	11.3	86,878	8.9	10.4	9.8
Hawaii	NA	NA	42,641	17.0	37.4	29.5	(6)	(6)	31,863	65,401	39.1	6.3	70,313	12.2	16.1	16.0
Honolulu	NA	NA	228,611	24.5	33.3	35.7	2,924.3	16,132	38,288	87,722	26.7	12.7	89,584	8.0	9.1	8.4
Kalawao	NA	NA	3	66.7	31.9	39.5	(6)	(6)	48,687	76,465	2.3	0.0	0	0.0	0.0	0.0
Kauai	NA	NA	14,549	16.5	38.5	28.5	(6)	(6)	34,324	82,818	31.4	8.7	80,517	9.9	10.1	10.3
Maui	NA	NA	32,725	18.7	38.9	28.3	(6)	(6)	36,872	84,363	28.5	10.7	80,763	9.5	10.6	9.8
IDAHO	965,384	54.0	456,826	15.6	35.4	28.7	2,449.0	7,905	29,494	58,915	41.8	4.7	62,603	10.1	11.6	10.4
Ada	309,736	64.3	121,933	14.4	25.5	40.1	628.3	7,804	37,333	69,952	33.8	8.2	73,324	7.7	7.0	6.2
Adams	1,887	43.9	649	9.1	43.4	18.8	4.7	10,687	30,136	50,309	49.4	8.2	49,967	13.7	22.3	21.2
Bannock	46,027	52.4	25,004	9.5	34.8	27.0	106.9	7,097	25,044	51,977	48.1	2.6	54,538	12.2	13.7	13.0
Bear Lake	2,835	46.3	1,377	11.8	42.4	18.3	9.2	7,593	27,596	52,829	45.9	2.7	55,689	9.5	11.8	11.4
Benewah	4,835	52.0	1,754	13.7	48.8	17.9	15.1	10,915	24,737	47,983	53.3	2.4	53,014	12.5	17.7	15.8
Bingham	22,654	48.4	12,499	10.6	43.7	20.5	77.4	7,274	24,947	58,260	42.0	3.2	65,658	11.1	12.2	10.8
Blaine	18,932	82.2	4,685	16.1	34.3	39.3	55.2	15,422	36,232	64,627	38.3	6.6	76,301	6.9	7.7	6.8
Boise	2,646	33.8	1,180	14.2	36.0	28.4	9.6	11,297	33,384	51,760	47.5	3.9	55,583	11.5	17.2	15.7
Bonner	19,759	43.2	8,352	21.8	37.9	26.6	48.4	9,504	28,527	51,594	48.8	3.6	55,241	12.6	17.1	15.8
Bonneville	63,833	53.6	33,064	14.2	32.8	30.9	180.0	7,073	28,171	61,435	40.0	5.2	67,294	9.7	12.5	11.2
Boundary	4,317	35.3	2,371	26.1	51.5	18.0	12.8	8,741	26,796	45,319	54.1	4.8	52,193	14.0	20.3	20.3
Butte	1,280	49.3	515	10.3	40.7	17.2	4.0	9,226	31,659	37,404	55.8	3.2	52,081	14.2	17.6	15.0
Camas	477	43.1	219	14.2	50.4	22.1	2.3	13,333	31,291	36,908	57.5	10.2	59,409	8.3	9.6	7.2
Canyon	106,882	46.5	61,070	14.9	44.8	20.2	311.6	7,382	23,919	56,916	42.4	2.9	57,886	10.6	12.5	10.9

1. All persons 3 years old and over enrolled in nursery school through college. 2. Persons 25 years old and over. 3. Elementary and secondary education expenditures. 4. Based on population estimated by the American Community Survey, 2016–2020. 5. CDC percent based on 2019 population estimate. 6. Hawaii, Kalawao, Kauai, and Maui counties are included with Honolulu county

STATE County	Personal income, 2020										Earnings, 2020		
			Per capita[1]			Supplements to wages and salaries, employer contributions (mil dol)						Contributions for government social insurance (mil dol)	
	Total (mil dol)	Percent change 2019–2020	Dollars	Rank	Wages and salaries (mil dol)	Pension and insurance	Government social insurance	Proprietors' income (mil dol)	Dividends, interest, and rent (mil dol)	Personal transfer reecipts (mil dol)	Total (mil dol)	From employee and self-employed	From employer
	62	63	64	65	66	67	68	69	70	71	72	73	74
GEORGIA—Cont'd													
Putnam	1,092	8.9	48,498	1,323	232	48	16	43	261	312	339	26	16
Quitman	79	10.9	34,810	2,946	14	4	1	2	10	38	21	3	1
Rabun	763	7.9	44,160	1,916	201	37	15	41	245	250	294	24	15
Randolph	249	8.8	37,204	2,770	78	17	6	20	32	97	121	8	6
Richmond	8,487	8.3	41,999	2,194	6,460	1,447	477	584	1,374	2,788	8,968	475	477
Rockdale	3,642	10.3	40,051	2,449	1,837	276	124	148	483	1,099	2,384	151	124
Schley	185	5.8	35,588	2,902	43	12	3	15	23	50	73	5	3
Screven	528	8.6	37,694	2,714	117	26	8	14	74	202	165	14	8
Seminole	388	4.5	48,082	1,376	107	21	8	74	44	130	210	13	8
Spalding	2,615	10.0	38,792	2,594	985	193	66	110	369	926	1,354	93	66
Stephens	1,048	7.7	40,153	2,441	374	68	26	37	164	387	505	39	26
Stewart	168	11.5	25,041	3,109	78	15	5	10	21	70	108	7	5
Sumter	1,183	8.7	40,387	2,404	479	109	35	79	180	425	701	43	35
Talbot	237	9.4	38,621	2,613	33	8	2	8	34	95	51	6	2
Tali(2)erro	58	0.7	36,860	2,793	9	3	1	3	9	23	15	1	1
Tattnall	767	6.4	30,222	3,085	249	57	17	75	101	260	399	24	17
Taylor	272	4.9	33,630	2,997	72	16	5	11	39	111	104	8	5
Telfair	357	8.5	22,644	3,112	92	20	6	27	44	167	145	10	6
Terrell	383	8.0	44,976	1,795	83	17	6	26	62	139	131	9	6
Thomas	2,194	8.6	49,443	1,203	1,002	166	70	149	419	653	1,388	88	70
Tift	1,722	10.4	42,279	2,157	953	195	62	149	250	514	1,359	75	62
Toombs	1,080	12.0	40,041	2,453	489	93	36	53	124	374	671	45	36
Towns	525	9.1	42,908	2,073	133	30	9	33	140	220	206	20	9
Treutlen	218	9.6	31,899	3,061	43	11	3	11	24	87	68	6	3
Troup	2,873	9.5	40,920	2,343	1,943	306	136	100	416	925	2,485	154	136
Turner	310	8.1	39,281	2,536	82	18	6	20	35	126	126	9	6
Twiggs	362	8.4	44,686	1,852	79	13	7	37	38	136	136	10	7
Union	1,010	7.2	39,839	2,475	304	62	20	56	242	403	441	38	20
Upson	1,045	8.1	39,391	2,525	284	54	20	43	151	382	401	31	20
Walker	2,535	7.2	36,157	2,860	574	127	42	130	322	876	873	74	42
Walton	4,357	7.9	44,977	1,794	1,220	198	84	245	611	1,077	1,748	128	84
Ware	1,337	10.6	37,306	2,762	686	131	57	70	178	551	944	63	57
Warren	207	10.1	39,545	2,497	67	12	5	5	25	87	89	7	5
Washington	789	8.0	39,151	2,549	287	62	20	24	159	283	392	27	20
Wayne	1,047	9.3	34,877	2,940	403	82	27	48	111	390	561	38	27
Webster	94	8.5	36,032	2,865	24	5	2	6	15	29	37	3	2
Wheeler	163	9.6	21,087	3,113	47	10	3	13	15	71	73	5	3
White	1,208	7.3	38,858	2,585	332	62	24	63	223	389	481	38	24
Whitfield	4,512	6.5	43,456	2,016	2,776	420	197	427	927	1,147	3,820	230	197
Wilcox	254	3.2	29,895	3,089	49	12	3	30	33	102	94	7	3
Wilkes	408	1.0	42,093	2,181	111	25	8	30	66	154	173	13	8
Wilkinson	354	6.4	40,158	2,439	162	28	13	20	46	134	224	16	13
Worth	781	6.7	39,102	2,556	132	28	9	39	103	251	209	16	9
HAWAII	82,527	5.1	56,840	X	36,490	7,943	2,951	6,894	15,174	19,363	54,278	3,336	2,951
Hawaii	9,411	9.4	46,281	1,610	3,212	719	257	859	1,890	3,046	5,047	346	257
Honolulu	60,522	4.8	62,793	322	28,500	6,299	2,314	4,644	10,929	12,702	41,757	2,499	2,314
Kalawao	(2)	(2)	(2)	(2)	(2)	(2)	(2)	(2)	(2)	(2)	(2)	(2)	(2)
Kauai	3,886	5.6	54,089	775	1,459	296	115	390	740	1,159	2,259	150	115
Maui	(2)8708	(2) 2.7	(2) 51838	(2) 945	(2)3320	(2) 629	(2) 265	(2)1001	(2)1615	(2)2455	(2)5215	(2) 341	(2) 265
IDAHO	89,078	8.9	48,208	X	38,231	5,968	3,261	10,245	17,640	19,260	57,705	3,755	3,261
Ada	28,287	7.7	57,215	559	15,521	2,139	1,245	2,439	5,926	4,823	21,344	1,411	1,245
Adams	183	9.4	41,066	2,330	57	11	5	18	52	59	91	7	5
Bannock	3,665	8.1	41,272	2,292	1,550	288	137	166	535	983	2,141	150	137
Bear Lake	285	10.3	46,370	1,595	66	15	6	36	44	78	123	8	6
Benewah	404	10.1	42,803	2,093	165	32	15	37	69	137	249	18	15
Bingham	2,008	13.7	42,541	2,121	636	117	57	328	278	480	1,137	65	57
Blaine	2,757	2.8	117,681	13	650	82	56	335	1,504	267	1,123	72	56
Boise	366	8.2	45,422	1,731	55	13	5	24	72	101	97	8	5
Bonner	2,095	8.5	44,751	1,836	648	113	57	150	591	602	969	78	57
Bonneville	6,669	5.7	54,601	731	2,522	390	221	1,252	1,343	1,216	4,385	276	221
Boundary	497	8.3	39,272	2,537	167	32	16	44	98	160	258	20	16
Butte	136	18.9	51,370	989	913	74	67	25	18	35	1,079	69	67
Camas	60	7.3	53,373	828	20	3	2	18	11	12	43	2	2
Canyon	8,916	11.8	37,611	2,725	3,226	517	292	867	1,206	2,325	4,902	340	292

1. Based on the resident population estimated as of July 1 of the year shown. 2. Kalawao county is included with Maui county.

STATE County	Earnings, 2020 (cont.)									Social Security beneficiaries, December 2020		Supple-mental Security Income recipients, 2020	Housing units, 2021	
	Percent by selected industries													
	Farm	Mining, quarrying, and extractions	Construction	Manu-facturing	Information; professional, scientific, technical services	Retail trade	Finance, insurance, real estate, and leasing	Health care and social assistance	Govern-ment	Number	Rate[1]		Total	Percent change, 2010–2021
	75	76	77	78	79	80	81	82	83	84	85	86	87	88
GEORGIA—Cont'd														
Putnam	2.0	0.0	9.8	11.7	D	8.3	8.7	D	25.4	6,375	282	533	13,267	1.6
Quitman	5.2	0.0	0.4	D	D	5.0	D	D	34.5	790	352	130	1,688	0.4
Rabun	0.2	D	12.4	5.9	4.2	14.5	5.5	D	18.1	5,695	333	404	12,081	0.8
Randolph	9.4	0.0	D	D	D	5.4	D	D	23.1	1,760	280	370	3,449	0.3
Richmond	0.0	D	2.9	7.9	6.8	4.5	6.0	13.6	42.5	41,670	203	8,191	92,622	0.5
Rockdale	0.0	0.0	D	16.0	7.6	8.7	8.4	11.8	13.0	17,595	187	2,108	35,725	0.7
Schley	5.2	0.1	D	30.0	D	4.1	D	D	28.0	930	208	135	1,981	0.9
Screven	3.3	0.0	5.2	23.3	D	7.6	D	D	31.2	3,730	264	652	6,535	0.4
Seminole	12.5	0.0	1.7	14.2	D	9.2	4.6	13.0	11.6	2,580	281	412	5,058	0.1
Spalding	0.1	0.0	4.4	14.3	3.6	7.8	4.6	16.3	23.3	16,730	246	2,757	28,263	1.4
Stephens	0.3	D	5.5	26.4	3.5	9.6	4.0	D	19.8	7,570	282	1,214	12,336	0.1
Stewart	4.5	0.0	D	D	0.6	1.7	D	D	24.7	1,150	215	249	2,106	0.1
Sumter	6.0	D	2.0	21.5	D	6.1	4.2	D	20.7	6,690	228	1,287	13,468	0.1
Talbot	4.3	19.4	21.8	0.1	D	1.7	D	D	25.2	1,765	307	292	3,054	0.3
Tali[2]erro	13.1	0.0	D	D	0.5	2.1	D	D	49.1	500	321	91	912	0.3
Tattnall	16.5	0.0	6.3	3.2	3.2	4.1	3.0	D	24.6	4,535	197	916	9,352	0.5
Taylor	3.4	D	7.2	2.7	D	6.9	3.5	13.6	22.6	1,985	255	390	3,912	0.4
Telfair	7.3	0.0	4.9	4.7	D	6.8	4.3	6.5	27.1	2,735	220	567	4,717	0.2
Terrell	13.1	0.0	2.6	4.9	D	11.7	8.9	D	22.3	2,425	271	502	4,245	0.0
Thomas	1.0	D	3.3	17.0	4.0	6.6	8.8	21.7	14.6	11,255	246	2,139	20,846	0.8
Tift	1.7	0.0	4.3	5.9	3.3	8.5	7.8	6.9	33.6	8,565	208	1,584	17,547	0.7
Toombs	3.5	0.0	4.7	15.3	D	9.4	4.6	21.2	13.5	6,285	234	1,241	12,055	0.2
Towns	-0.1	D	D	5.1	D	5.5	7.6	D	13.7	5,350	416	214	8,694	0.9
Treutlen	5.5	0.0	3.4	10.9	D	9.8	D	D	30.1	1,555	247	315	2,891	0.7
Troup	0.0	D	5.8	32.8	2.6	8.3	4.3	9.7	10.3	14,905	214	2,277	29,393	2.0
Turner	13.4	0.0	0.7	11.6	D	8.3	4.5	4.2	23.4	2,110	235	449	3,923	0.1
Twiggs	0.8	D	D	D	D	D	D	D	12.1	2,615	333	384	4,044	0.3
Union	0.2	D	8.3	5.0	D	9.7	5.1	D	26.4	9,830	385	468	14,927	1.6
Upson	2.5	0.0	4.9	16.3	3.8	8.0	6.2	21.2	20.5	7,340	265	1,163	12,400	0.7
Walker	0.8	0.0	6.4	30.5	D	5.5	9.2	D	20.5	16,830	246	2,068	29,383	0.7
Walton	0.2	0.1	17.2	14.0	3.2	6.2	5.4	8.7	15.2	19,555	196	2,597	36,456	2.2
Ware	1.3	0.0	3.3	13.3	D	10.2	3.0	16.6	20.3	8,200	228	1,685	15,895	0.2
Warren	1.5	D	2.0	37.8	D	3.6	D	D	15.5	1,585	302	254	2,519	0.3
Washington	1.1	3.2	6.5	8.2	3.7	6.0	3.9	D	26.9	5,065	256	824	8,679	1.1
Wayne	1.4	0.0	14.6	19.8	1.9	7.9	3.1	D	28.6	6,785	223	1,078	12,561	0.7
Webster	11.1	D	0.2	D	0.0	D	1.4	0.1	18.2	615	260	83	1,205	0.6
Wheeler	9.0	0.0	D	D	D	3.1	D	D	21.0	1,275	171	210	2,426	0.2
White	0.5	0.0	14.4	10.3	D	10.1	4.9	D	15.9	8,080	284	599	13,719	1.1
Whitfield	-0.1	D	2.6	31.5	9.3	5.7	6.8	10.9	9.9	19,390	189	2,500	39,294	0.9
Wilcox	26.4	0.0	D	D	D	D	D	5.0	30.9	1,810	207	330	3,451	0.3
Wilkes	12.8	D	11.1	10.9	D	7.0	4.5	5.0	24.0	3,025	318	442	5,208	0.7
Wilkinson	0.3	37.7	10.5	5.8	D	2.4	D	3.1	10.0	2,650	300	366	4,302	0.3
Worth	15.4	0.0	4.8	5.0	D	7.6	D	8.8	24.3	4,610	224	642	9,283	0.3
HAWAII	0.5	0.1	8.8	1.8	7.6	5.8	7.4	11.5	29.9	282,623	196	22,412	564,908	0.5
Hawaii	2.7	0.0	D	D	5.8	9.3	5.6	D	26.0	48,660	240	4,978	89,750	0.9
Honolulu	0.2	0.1	8.5	1.8	8.2	4.9	7.6	11.5	32.6	184,365	184	14,635	372,626	0.4
Kalawao	[2]	[2]	[2]	[2]	[2]	[2]	[2]	[2]	[2]	32,905	200	1,960	72,086	0.7
Kauai	0.9	D	D	D	5.3	8.4	6.6	D	21.7	16,680	227	D	30,332	0.4
Maui	[2]0.5	[2]D	[2]10.8	[2]1.4	[2]5.7	[2]8.3	[2]7.5	[2]12.2	[2]15.9	10	122	D	114	0.0
IDAHO	5.9	0.4	8.1	10.2	8.8	8.8	7.0	11.6	15.1	370,385	195	30,780	775,267	2.5
Ada	0.4	0.1	8.0	10.5	10.8	8.1	9.7	13.1	13.0	89,025	174	6,740	204,585	3.0
Adams	7.6	0.0	8.4	10.5	D	5.6	2.5	D	24.1	1,480	320	56	2,655	0.4
Bannock	0.9	D	6.0	7.4	4.5	7.9	6.5	16.1	23.5	16,045	182	2,021	35,737	2.2
Bear Lake	18.0	D	3.1	3.4	D	7.5	4.3	D	32.8	1,555	238	89	3,923	1.6
Benewah	4.0	D	4.4	15.8	2.3	4.0	2.7	D	32.6	3,015	304	241	4,689	1.1
Bingham	19.9	0.1	7.2	12.1	D	4.4	5.7	9.2	19.3	9,040	185	1,002	17,274	1.8
Blaine	1.1	D	15.4	2.2	14.2	7.3	17.4	6.9	9.0	5,005	202	89	15,679	1.4
Boise	1.8	0.3	11.9	2.3	D	5.5	D	D	33.7	2,500	309	107	5,587	2.3
Bonner	0.3	1.5	9.8	14.9	8.3	9.6	6.8	7.9	17.4	14,155	286	819	26,557	0.8
Bonneville	2.0	D	6.3	8.6	6.7	23.3	5.0	15.7	10.2	20,875	163	2,411	46,282	1.9
Boundary	5.1	D	11.1	13.0	4.8	6.6	5.0	5.9	26.3	3,720	296	248	5,493	1.4
Butte	2.1	D	D	D	D	0.2	D	D	1.3	745	281	88	1,292	0.2
Camas	33.5	0.2	9.1	D	D	D	D	D	15.6	280	246	D	700	1.0
Canyon	5.1	0.0	15.2	15.0	4.8	8.4	3.9	11.4	11.9	43,050	177	4,403	85,195	4.1

1. Per 1,000 resident population estimated as of July 1 of the year shown. 2. Kalawao county is included with Maui county.

STATE County	Housing units, 2016–2020: Total	Occupied units: Owner-occupied: Percent	Owner-occupied: Median value[1]	Median owner cost as a percent of income: With a mortgage	Median owner cost as a percent of income: Without a mortgage[2]	Renter-occupied: Median rent[3]	Renter-occupied: Median rent as a percent of income[2]	Sub-standard units[4] (percent)	Civilian labor force, 2021: Total	Percent change, 2020–2021	Unemployment: Total	Unemployment: Rate[5]	Civilian employment[6], 2016–2020: Total	Percent: Management, business, science, and arts	Percent: Construction, production, and maintenance occupations
	89	90	91	92	93	94	95	96	97	98	99	100	101	102	103
GEORGIA—Cont'd															
Putnam	9,457	74.9	165,800	21.1	10.5	808	27.6	3.2	8,661	4.5	347	4.0	8,637	28.1	33.7
Quitman	958	78.5	70,200	17.5	18.2	661	18.0	3.0	768	-3.4	38	4.9	702	21.4	29.6
Rabun	7,022	73.9	185,500	22.8	10.0	810	39.6	1.7	7,528	4.0	236	3.1	6,484	30.2	23.3
Randolph	2,704	50.0	76,100	27.9	13.5	570	30.1	4.5	2,373	-3.8	123	5.2	2,425	19.3	35.1
Richmond	72,526	51.6	115,300	20.1	11.5	908	33.4	1.9	84,416	0.4	4,515	5.3	83,015	31.4	23.2
Rockdale	31,465	66.5	170,100	22.1	10.0	1,105	29.7	3.7	44,591	2.2	2,062	4.6	41,213	35.1	25.9
Schley	1,861	77.1	134,800	21.1	13.8	636	32.3	1.5	2,134	-0.6	79	3.7	2,255	29.4	30.2
Screven	4,939	70.5	85,700	22.2	10.5	570	26.2	3.9	5,122	1.5	288	5.6	5,594	25.7	35.2
Seminole	3,364	66.0	92,100	25.7	13.7	737	29.8	5.1	3,059	-1.2	114	3.7	2,810	35.0	32.4
Spalding	25,693	64.0	134,800	19.8	12.0	879	30.9	1.3	28,984	2.3	1,357	4.7	27,407	28.6	35.0
Stephens	9,977	72.9	123,800	20.6	11.1	758	30.1	1.1	10,512	0.8	453	4.3	10,862	25.4	31.5
Stewart	1,845	70.5	44,100	27.0	13.1	803	28.8	2.5	2,562	1.9	98	3.8	1,710	20.1	38.8
Sumter	11,419	57.7	122,000	21.4	14.6	713	29.5	1.9	12,334	-2.0	707	5.7	12,490	33.4	30.3
Talbot	2,891	78.5	98,800	24.7	10.9	665	23.6	2.5	2,775	0.7	126	4.5	2,582	27.2	40.5
Taliaferro	662	76.4	63,500	32.9	11.9	693	32.1	2.0	535	0.4	27	5.0	660	15.5	39.2
Tattnall	8,345	67.2	89,800	17.7	10.0	532	22.5	4.5	9,621	-0.5	308	3.2	8,313	32.4	33.8
Taylor	3,623	60.2	87,100	19.9	14.2	670	39.8	0.6	2,950	6.6	168	5.7	3,140	27.7	32.6
Telfair	4,481	70.3	69,300	25.4	10.0	524	31.1	5.0	3,735	-1.7	268	7.2	4,797	25.0	44.2
Terrell	3,355	56.0	93,400	20.3	12.3	636	33.9	4.7	3,568	1.2	221	6.2	3,372	18.4	38.1
Thomas	17,750	62.3	150,300	20.2	12.5	871	29.9	2.6	17,576	3.4	735	4.2	19,860	36.3	26.4
Tift	14,868	61.6	123,000	23.3	10.0	661	27.8	1.5	21,225	3.4	724	3.4	18,137	33.6	27.0
Toombs	9,792	62.7	97,800	21.2	10.8	592	24.6	3.9	12,171	0.1	544	4.5	10,415	25.3	34.5
Towns	5,006	80.4	241,900	23.3	10.0	776	24.8	1.2	4,055	4.8	160	3.9	4,479	31.2	19.4
Treutlen	2,395	62.7	71,900	27.9	14.3	587	19.9	1.7	2,630	-1.1	112	4.3	2,421	35.3	34.2
Troup	24,982	60.0	138,300	20.9	11.5	849	32.9	3.0	37,678	0.2	1,648	4.4	30,644	27.8	35.2
Turner	3,208	64.4	73,600	19.1	13.3	547	23.9	0.7	3,283	0.6	210	6.4	3,081	28.6	26.5
Twiggs	3,080	86.2	71,800	21.0	13.5	682	27.2	2.8	2,804	0.6	143	5.1	2,980	18.8	34.5
Union	10,231	78.4	199,000	23.9	10.0	705	27.8	4.2	11,094	5.2	300	2.7	8,612	35.6	28.7
Upson	10,399	65.2	102,800	19.8	11.2	652	31.9	1.7	11,628	2.3	466	4.0	10,885	29.6	32.6
Walker	26,306	73.0	121,600	20.1	11.8	754	29.7	2.0	31,304	2.4	977	3.1	30,447	30.9	33.0
Walton	32,094	76.1	210,500	20.4	10.2	1,023	30.4	2.2	46,945	3.1	1,497	3.2	43,728	31.1	29.8
Ware	13,657	63.7	86,800	20.1	11.7	674	31.1	1.4	15,404	0.7	567	3.7	13,375	26.3	32.9
Warren	2,261	66.4	64,600	22.9	13.4	571	25.3	1.1	2,684	1.7	126	4.7	2,161	20.1	40.1
Washington	7,719	66.7	92,500	22.0	14.2	691	28.5	2.4	6,875	-0.7	343	5.0	7,338	27.5	35.4
Wayne	10,479	62.8	116,000	18.9	11.5	682	22.2	2.9	11,919	3.1	446	3.7	11,277	25.5	35.3
Webster	1,115	87.2	69,700	30.8	10.9	350	34.7	0.0	992	-2.3	44	4.4	939	25.3	31.3
Wheeler	1,774	69.4	55,500	20.6	10.3	428	29.2	1.5	1,637	1.6	90	5.5	2,804	14.8	65.2
White	11,727	76.2	182,700	20.0	10.0	844	26.9	2.8	16,616	2.3	422	2.5	13,498	32.6	25.5
Whitfield	36,412	65.9	142,800	19.3	10.6	737	25.0	5.4	43,361	0.6	1,697	3.9	47,358	25.2	43.1
Wilcox	2,542	76.6	62,000	17.7	10.0	513	27.1	1.6	2,778	0.9	129	4.6	2,728	28.2	39.7
Wilkes	4,115	64.0	79,000	22.2	14.7	694	35.1	1.1	3,657	0.4	171	4.7	3,876	22.5	34.8
Wilkinson	3,301	77.2	70,100	18.4	12.8	662	33.9	2.5	3,657	-3.8	152	4.2	3,243	25.5	39.4
Worth	7,982	69.6	93,400	20.1	10.0	734	27.7	1.2	8,888	0.9	352	4.0	8,849	26.0	38.6
HAWAII	467,932	60.3	636,400	25.5	10.0	1,651	32.5	9.3	668,413	0.9	38,226	5.7	674,453	35.7	18.5
Hawaii	71,747	69.3	364,100	24.7	10.0	1,214	29.7	9.3	93,848	2.4	5,169	5.5	89,750	33.1	21.3
Honolulu	316,928	57.5	702,300	25.5	10.0	1,779	33.4	9.3	451,661	0.5	23,881	5.3	464,037	37.5	17.8
Kalawao	306	0.0	0	0.0	0.0	1,122	17.4	0.0	NA	NA	NA	NA	425	2.6	18.8
Kauai	23,331	65.1	606,900	26.8	10.0	1,423	28.2	8.5	35,949	-1.0	2,796	7.8	36,395	29.2	19.3
Maui	55,620	62.5	657,400	26.3	10.0	1,543	30.6	9.8	86,954	2.2	6,379	7.3	83,846	31.2	18.7
IDAHO	649,299	70.8	235,600	20.7	10.0	887	27.9	3.0	917,056	2.2	32,728	3.6	818,085	36.0	25.3
Ada	179,708	70.2	298,600	19.9	10.0	1,062	27.7	1.8	266,936	2.9	8,696	3.3	242,385	45.0	16.8
Adams	1,726	82.3	228,500	21.7	10.0	702	24.0	2.7	1,804	1.6	119	6.6	1,578	29.7	30.0
Bannock	31,669	68.5	167,300	19.2	10.0	703	27.5	2.6	42,735	1.0	1,520	3.6	36,687	37.4	21.3
Bear Lake	2,455	78.5	154,500	20.1	10.0	577	29.0	3.3	3,121	1.1	94	3.0	2,609	28.6	35.0
Benewah	3,564	73.7	177,500	23.2	10.8	699	25.5	5.1	4,092	-1.7	228	5.6	3,629	23.9	34.0
Bingham	15,612	78.2	168,200	19.4	10.0	680	26.2	3.6	24,278	1.5	775	3.2	20,031	32.8	29.9
Blaine	8,318	72.6	458,100	24.9	11.7	1,002	25.7	2.9	12,885	0.7	469	3.6	12,388	29.8	24.1
Boise	3,351	82.7	234,900	22.5	10.0	717	25.9	2.4	3,734	2.4	202	5.4	3,370	41.6	19.9
Bonner	17,998	76.2	275,700	24.8	10.2	913	26.6	3.8	21,552	1.8	1,033	4.8	18,601	29.9	31.5
Bonneville	40,946	69.8	202,100	19.2	10.0	814	26.9	3.7	60,471	3.4	1,749	2.9	53,056	36.8	23.2
Boundary	4,596	76.3	235,000	22.7	10.7	689	26.9	4.6	5,597	1.1	244	4.4	4,712	26.7	28.2
Butte	966	78.9	146,600	23.1	11.1	683	29.6	1.2	1,447	3.8	55	3.8	1,019	32.5	36.0
Camas	391	75.4	164,900	27.2	10.0	844	32.0	2.0	704	1.9	24	3.4	489	38.4	24.9
Canyon	75,494	72.1	211,600	21.0	10.0	937	28.2	3.9	110,244	2.8	4,359	4.0	100,721	27.6	31.7

1. Specified owner-occupied units. 2. A value of 10.0 represents 10 percent or less; a value of 50.0 represents 50 percent or more. 3. Specified renter-occupied units. 4. Overcrowded or lacking complete plumbing facilities. 5. Percent of civilian labor force. 6. Civilian employed persons 16 years old and over.

STATE County	Private nonfarm establishments, employment and payroll, 2020									Agriculture, 2017			
		Employment						Annual payroll		Farms			Farm producers whose primary occupation is farming (percent)
											Percent with:		
	Number of establish-ments	Total	Health care and social assistance	Manufac-turing	Retail trade	Finance and insurance	Professional, scientific, and technical services	Total (mil dol)	Average per employee (dollars)	Number	Fewer than 50 acres	1000 acres or more	
	104	105	106	107	108	109	110	111	112	113	114	115	116
GEORGIA—Cont'd													
Putnam	461	4,901	506	1,165	838	129	93	177	36,185	186	24.7	2.2	42.6
Quitman	37	204	14	NA	30	10	NA	6	31,789	37	8.1	10.8	22.2
Rabun	503	4,685	535	311	1,078	119	151	148	31,602	135	68.9	0.7	34.2
Randolph	129	1,425	265	164	159	37	25	47	32,962	153	5.9	21.6	42.5
Richmond	4,272	87,323	25,892	6,486	10,964	1,399	4,077	3,881	44,449	118	63.6	0.8	34.2
Rockdale	2,167	33,193	4,240	5,723	5,123	645	821	1,585	47,740	74	75.7	1.4	42.6
Schley	59	751	30	433	72	NA	7	28	37,422	89	12.4	7.9	30.9
Screven	222	2,318	259	834	413	111	43	74	31,749	352	22.2	12.8	41.4
Seminole	174	1,609	454	19	290	71	41	61	37,832	157	25.5	12.1	68.4
Spalding	1,143	17,622	4,413	3,190	2,878	409	372	669	37,959	225	66.2	0.4	36.9
Stephens	521	8,135	1,235	2,498	1,227	177	128	309	38,018	227	45.8	NA	44.5
Stewart	56	732	112	NA	73	17	8	29	39,585	104	13.5	8.7	22.9
Sumter	607	8,681	2,534	1,171	1,408	222	244	313	36,063	371	18.9	12.4	35.2
Talbot	64	533	17	NA	74	62	NA	23	43,328	102	22.5	4.9	38.3
Taliaferro	17	218	NA	NA	18	NA	NA	2	11,381	48	4.2	4.2	40.5
Tattnall	304	3,796	811	120	464	129	54	135	35,462	547	37.7	3.3	44.8
Taylor	126	921	221	22	128	43	5	42	45,161	224	13.4	5.4	32.4
Telfair	173	2,566	167	1,034	310	65	24	81	31,703	255	25.5	3.5	41.6
Terrell	166	1,702	147	359	314	65	37	60	35,428	256	22.3	16.4	42.5
Thomas	1,146	17,366	3,615	2,359	2,399	717	388	785	45,199	408	31.1	12.5	41.3
Tift	1,086	17,972	3,322	1,419	2,886	462	699	733	40,781	306	38.2	16.3	44.0
Toombs	663	9,622	2,002	1,738	1,787	283	191	344	35,759	320	36.6	6.9	35.3
Towns	290	2,767	574	83	380	49	80	91	32,965	105	61.0	NA	46.8
Treutlen	83	691	111	150	205	42	7	22	31,378	148	26.4	4.7	26.8
Troup	1,459	33,949	3,710	11,307	3,554	937	453	1,498	44,116	261	46.7	1.5	36.0
Turner	156	1,586	189	358	276	106	33	53	33,551	246	30.1	9.3	35.2
Twiggs	75	1,699	161	NA	74	8	NA	64	37,832	116	43.1	12.1	30.8
Union	596	6,381	1,476	498	1,188	146	157	265	41,582	251	61.8	NA	36.0
Upson	451	5,541	1,414	1,255	983	176	107	206	37,095	235	46.0	1.7	34.2
Walker	687	11,486	932	4,886	1,359	258	171	386	33,613	624	44.9	1.6	35.7
Walton	1,771	18,260	2,273	2,596	2,757	420	493	713	39,067	437	55.8	0.7	41.5
Ware	867	12,148	2,582	1,906	2,290	246	216	432	35,558	248	50.4	7.7	40.3
Warren	82	1,066	129	229	86	5	11	49	45,689	135	19.3	4.4	42.4
Washington	344	5,190	882	566	747	142	230	218	42,057	383	26.4	6.8	35.7
Wayne	590	6,287	1,213	1,032	1,202	167	160	252	40,009	316	46.8	3.8	36.9
Webster	32	365	NA	NA	36	6	NA	15	40,997	109	18.3	20.2	45.2
Wheeler	53	659	NA	NA	86	NA	NA	25	38,002	143	21.7	10.5	33.5
White	655	6,549	698	679	1,208	160	128	213	32,523	301	67.4	0.3	40.4
Whitfield	2,208	55,660	5,451	20,814	4,886	645	1,966	2,298	41,288	386	52.3	0.5	36.9
Wilcox	86	820	153	9	80	62	5	22	26,332	287	30.0	9.1	41.0
Wilkes	183	1,878	263	333	357	72	30	71	37,732	277	25.3	5.1	39.3
Wilkinson	140	2,163	146	212	179	43	34	104	47,967	140	22.1	3.6	24.0
Worth	267	2,942	388	617	500	125	61	95	32,456	469	32.0	15.4	44.9
HAWAII	32,627	549,375	73,273	12,778	69,668	21,863	23,664	23,756	43,242	7,328	89.5	1.7	46.7
Hawaii	4,178	55,669	7,684	1,713	10,072	1,119	1,491	2,107	37,855	4,220	89.4	1.4	46.4
Honolulu	21,237	364,092	55,287	9,617	45,977	18,724	19,009	16,854	46,290	927	91.3	1.7	55.4
Kalawao	NA	NA	NA	NA	NA	NA	NA	NA	NA	NA	NA	NA	NA
Kauai	2,143	27,104	3,152	420	3,997	420	731	919	33,903	773	87.8	2.2	44.0
Maui	4,798	67,107	7,042	1,028	9,579	914	1,931	2,403	35,813	1,408	89.6	2.3	43.8
IDAHO	51,957	637,810	107,514	63,808	85,559	23,947	38,826	28,807	45,165	24,996	56.0	9.7	40.8
Ada	15,311	221,629	39,566	15,388	26,500	10,312	15,521	11,970	54,010	1,304	86.8	2.1	28.8
Adams	107	531	52	120	124	11	28	19	35,923	232	42.2	13.8	49.2
Bannock	2,203	25,799	5,693	2,458	4,552	2,594	920	986	38,226	757	51.9	9.0	35.1
Bear Lake	128	1,060	302	55	282	34	27	33	30,909	395	25.8	14.4	39.3
Benewah	254	2,151	340	539	295	44	56	88	40,712	288	42.7	8.7	41.2
Bingham	933	11,096	2,126	2,218	1,319	219	332	458	41,245	1,177	59.8	13.7	42.9
Blaine	1,569	12,137	821	332	1,385	255	924	516	42,478	190	47.4	23.2	42.8
Boise	178	762	15	32	129	8	6	20	26,745	90	68.9	7.8	45.0
Bonner	1,733	13,401	1,771	1,804	2,157	292	538	518	38,634	1,213	72.2	0.6	29.7
Bonneville	3,761	56,964	11,225	3,308	7,607	1,523	9,759	2,863	50,265	1,109	67.1	8.4	31.0
Boundary	411	2,751	516	512	508	52	120	104	37,852	348	48.9	4.6	39.1
Butte	57	372	152	NA	114	8	4	11	28,761	189	24.3	27.0	58.1
Camas	34	169	9	30	15	NA	6	5	29,402	151	18.5	27.2	47.0
Canyon	4,973	61,203	9,009	10,688	8,796	1,048	1,608	2,340	38,238	2,289	77.7	2.6	36.8

STATE County	Agriculture, 2017 (cont.)															
	Land in farms					Value of land and buildings (dollars)		Value of machinery and equipment, average per farm (dollars)	Value of products sold:				Organic farms (number)	Farms with internet access (percent)	Government payments	
			Acres								Percent from:					
	Acreage (1,000)	Percent change, 2012–2017	Average size of farm	Total irrigated (1,000)	Total cropland (1,000)	Average per farm	Average per acre		Total (mil dol)	Average per farm (acres)	Crops	Livestock and poultry products			Total ($1,000)	Percent of farms
	117	118	119	120	121	122	123	124	125	126	127	128	129	130	131	132
GEORGIA—Cont'd																
Putnam	38	34.3	206	1.8	14.7	865,498	4,206	100,518	34.7	186,780	20.0	80.0	NA	71.5	333	16.1
Quitman	19	111.8	521	D	4.2	1,201,990	2,307	64,583	D	D	D	D	NA	56.8	265	56.8
Rabun	8	-5.7	56	D	3.1	464,254	8,240	94,314	D	D	D	D	3	84.4	149	11.9
Randolph	122	2.2	797	33.6	66.3	2,256,188	2,832	275,608	43.4	283,784	85.0	15.0	NA	57.5	4,997	77.8
Richmond	13	-4.4	113	0.1	4.1	414,735	3,680	64,945	D	D	100.0	D	3	76.3	D	1.7
Rockdale	4	-22.8	57	0.0	1.0	402,413	7,060	38,569	0.5	6,108	49.6	50.4	NA	78.4	D	1.4
Schley	35	-1.5	392	D	8.5	1,116,611	2,848	60,512	14.8	166,843	18.9	81.1	NA	51.7	474	70.8
Screven	187	3.7	532	32.4	80.9	1,169,455	2,200	206,003	50.6	143,838	95.7	4.3	2	80.4	4,807	58.8
Seminole	105	19.0	669	41.0	79.5	2,100,309	3,141	286,662	61.9	394,401	92.3	7.7	1	69.4	6,536	65.6
Spalding	17	-9.5	76	0.1	4.8	387,738	5,121	32,050	9.3	41,338	34.9	65.1	NA	78.7	107	5.3
Stephens	20	6.0	86	0.0	4.8	496,202	5,774	112,819	114.3	503,595	0.3	99.7	NA	76.7	359	37.4
Stewart	51	-13.8	491	0.3	7.6	1,016,280	2,069	71,304	5.1	48,692	23.4	76.6	NA	59.6	534	56.7
Sumter	175	9.0	471	41.3	96.7	1,346,756	2,859	258,509	133.2	359,005	54.5	45.5	1	76.3	4,274	58.8
Talbot	30	-10.9	296	0.0	4.8	809,499	2,735	70,159	1.1	10,520	35.3	64.7	NA	79.4	242	18.6
Taliaferro	18	30.2	374	0.1	2.2	1,231,989	3,292	81,632	24.3	505,479	0.9	99.1	NA	70.8	323	39.6
Tattnall	114	5.7	208	14.6	52.5	804,395	3,874	140,385	387.7	708,722	28.7	71.3	5	77.3	1,663	32.7
Taylor	64	4.3	286	4.1	20.2	595,317	2,079	82,999	27.7	123,790	37.0	63.0	NA	72.8	686	52.2
Telfair	52	-21.7	205	6.4	17.5	452,315	2,210	59,880	10.3	40,475	91.7	8.3	NA	71.8	725	48.2
Terrell	134	11.1	524	32.0	88.2	1,468,061	2,803	285,046	53.1	207,543	92.9	7.1	NA	78.9	7,191	74.2
Thomas	187	8.1	459	11.4	85.3	1,670,886	3,640	166,382	78.7	192,958	68.1	31.9	1	78.9	5,807	52.2
Tift	121	42.8	394	33.3	77.0	1,251,034	3,174	203,433	84.0	274,425	95.4	4.6	3	79.4	6,522	56.2
Toombs	81	10.1	252	16.5	39.4	700,382	2,780	153,211	83.2	260,081	88.9	11.1	4	70.6	572	37.2
Towns	7	-20.0	64	0.0	2.0	352,577	5,497	70,921	2.2	21,257	70.8	29.2	NA	80.0	85	27.6
Treutlen	37	5.2	250	1.4	11.5	470,130	1,883	73,055	6.1	40,939	95.1	4.9	NA	62.2	233	34.5
Troup	45	38.2	172	0.2	6.4	557,147	3,246	64,542	5.9	22,778	46.6	53.4	6	83.1	288	15.7
Turner	92	6.4	376	27.9	58.2	1,159,576	3,084	220,779	65.2	265,240	57.1	42.9	1	76.8	4,558	58.1
Twiggs	39	1.4	338	3.5	14.0	817,257	2,417	82,020	7.1	61,362	88.8	11.2	1	69.8	495	35.3
Union	19	-6.1	77	0.0	7.3	446,988	5,771	77,107	37.4	148,940	15.0	85.0	5	74.9	158	27.9
Upson	32	-29.3	135	0.6	9.5	532,497	3,954	76,595	42.9	182,468	6.2	93.8	NA	77.4	113	10.2
Walker	91	13.9	145	0.2	26.1	616,558	4,239	72,803	152.4	244,223	3.1	96.9	1	80.9	1,100	27.7
Walton	47	-9.6	109	0.8	13.4	614,553	5,664	57,774	26.6	60,899	23.0	77.0	1	75.7	276	19.7
Ware	63	12.0	256	4.3	22.6	656,805	2,565	103,573	31.7	127,879	74.3	25.7	NA	71.0	1,210	20.6
Warren	38	10.7	282	D	11.3	841,802	2,982	57,368	3.1	22,807	48.2	51.8	NA	63.7	444	25.2
Washington	96	-3.8	251	8.8	35.1	528,574	2,106	87,028	19.9	51,893	65.0	35.0	1	70.2	1,684	47.5
Wayne	63	0.4	198	5.8	20.3	411,476	2,080	89,301	27.5	86,889	48.4	51.6	NA	72.2	539	19.0
Webster	60	24.3	548	10.4	33.3	1,338,185	2,442	377,331	22.8	209,394	79.6	20.4	NA	67.0	1,529	79.8
Wheeler	57	11.8	396	0.7	7.3	724,035	1,829	51,312	3.4	23,853	90.7	9.3	NA	74.1	269	54.5
White	19	-20.3	62	0.1	6.2	505,000	8,126	77,920	92.8	308,399	1.8	98.2	NA	84.1	388	13.6
Whitfield	37	-6.5	95	D	9.1	585,687	6,185	64,119	136.8	354,433	1.3	98.7	NA	79.0	565	33.7
Wilcox	91	-21.4	316	19.0	54.1	824,117	2,608	132,330	98.6	343,700	37.7	62.3	NA	72.1	3,486	71.1
Wilkes	91	-2.8	329	0.6	18.9	1,133,797	3,447	67,477	154.8	558,939	3.5	96.5	1	72.6	536	26.4
Wilkinson	30	90.8	217	0.4	11.0	444,442	2,050	50,675	6.2	44,186	40.0	60.0	1	52.9	183	20.7
Worth	218	-5.1	464	49.2	129.9	1,394,353	3,003	249,754	104.3	222,354	83.9	16.1	NA	77.0	9,709	54.2
HAWAII	1,135	0.5	155	45.5	191.2	1,445,188	9,328	50,701	563.8	76,938	74.0	26.0	167	76.1	8,362	9.0
Hawaii	664	-3.3	157	6.7	82.3	1,091,739	6,934	41,883	269.2	63,789	59.5	40.5	89	75.9	5,339	7.9
Honolulu	72	3.8	77	11.7	23.1	1,920,259	24,794	92,036	151.4	163,305	90.4	9.6	25	71.1	350	10.8
Kalawao	NA	NA	NA	NA	NA	NA	NA	NA	NA	NA	NA	NA	NA	NA	NA	NA
Kauai	150	4.2	194	22.3	29.3	1,744,739	8,982	47,852	61.0	78,946	75.2	24.8	13	70.4	499	12.5
Maui	249	8.6	177	4.8	56.6	2,027,299	11,466	51,466	82.2	58,385	90.3	9.7	40	83.5	2,174	9.4
IDAHO	11,692	-0.6	468	3,398.3	5,894.7	1,340,738	2,866	175,951	7,567.4	302,746	42.4	57.6	295	83.9	129,605	24.3
Ada	112	-22.0	86	57.3	62.9	819,575	9,511	80,276	131.6	100,936	32.5	67.5	9	88.3	471	4.4
Adams	163	19.7	703	22.2	16.9	1,089,369	1,550	83,372	12.6	54,306	25.4	74.6	NA	78.9	93	7.8
Bannock	315	6.8	416	40.0	181.5	812,963	1,953	97,293	37.8	49,943	56.8	43.2	1	81.6	5,606	33.9
Bear Lake	297	15.2	752	54.7	108.3	1,081,929	1,439	141,605	36.5	92,443	47.9	52.1	15	76.5	1,549	37.5
Benewah	140	-4.6	486	0.2	82.1	940,817	1,936	128,882	19.1	66,358	96.6	3.4	2	76.7	1,931	34.4
Bingham	933	7.3	793	333.9	397.7	2,016,632	2,544	258,056	453.1	384,999	77.8	22.2	6	84.9	13,317	24.8
Blaine	211	17.9	1,112	37.3	52.1	2,813,206	2,530	179,893	27.2	142,905	61.4	38.6	15	90.0	800	20.5
Boise	53	D	591	1.3	1.7	847,323	1,433	52,205	2.6	28,733	59.8	40.2	NA	75.6	6	3.3
Bonner	89	10.8	74	1.2	32.8	370,858	5,036	42,446	10.2	8,406	60.2	39.8	10	79.7	224	2.9
Bonneville	419	2.3	378	131.6	260.6	1,100,960	2,915	130,606	167.9	151,363	66.0	34.0	2	82.8	7,179	22.4
Boundary	69	-8.4	198	2.3	44.5	946,934	4,784	100,250	30.8	88,509	87.4	12.6	4	79.3	1,129	16.7
Butte	130	4.1	690	69.4	78.6	1,415,857	2,053	212,368	42.2	223,169	84.6	15.4	6	92.6	1,877	52.9
Camas	193	14.9	1,276	27.4	98.6	1,710,551	1,341	171,377	24.7	163,490	82.9	17.1	39	74.2	826	42.4
Canyon	275	-9.5	120	213.4	219.4	989,782	8,240	161,943	574.8	251,095	54.7	45.3	11	86.4	2,463	8.0

STATE County	Water use, 2015		Wholesale Trade[1], 2017				Retail Trade[2], 2017				Real estate and rental and leasing,[2] 2017			
	Public supply water withdrawn (mil gal/ day)	Public supply gallons withdrawn per person per day	Number of establish-ments	Number of employees	Sales (mil dol)	Average payroll (mil dol)	Number of establish-ments	Number of employees	Sales (mil dol)	Average payroll (mil dol)	Number of establish-ments	Number of employees	Sales (mil dol)	Average payroll (mil dol)
	133	134	135	136	137	138	139	140	141	142	143	144	145	146
GEORGIA—Cont'd														
Putnam	3.8	176.1	22	141	92.5	7.0	79	1,004	219.6	20.6	20	46	11.8	2.7
Quitman	0.2	73.8	NA	NA	NA	NA	13	62	13.2	1.1	NA	NA	NA	NA
Rabun	1.6	98.3	NA	NA	NA	NA	75	1,039	272.8	27.8	D	D	D	D
Randolph	0.9	122.3	9	77	86.0	3.6	25	130	30.3	2.9	3	4	1.3	0.1
Richmond	39.2	194.1	172	1,995	1,162.3	104.9	769	11,085	2,842.6	265.1	197	837	230.7	37.6
Rockdale	11.8	132.3	76	574	456.6	36.0	303	4,896	1,285.0	121.2	83	505	156.8	28.8
Schley	0.5	87.1	4	80	22.5	3.0	10	73	13.5	1.5	NA	NA	NA	NA
Screven	0.7	52.3	4	12	5.2	0.4	50	384	95.4	8.3	4	8	1.1	0.4
Seminole	0.5	57.8	11	68	78.3	4.1	41	286	69.8	5.5	NA	NA	NA	NA
Spalding	6.8	106.6	45	619	372.5	38.9	225	3,025	850.0	72.9	42	141	23.0	3.9
Stephens	3.4	132.1	D	D	D	D	103	1,157	273.3	28.3	12	47	13.2	1.8
Stewart	0.8	133.3	NA	NA	NA	NA	13	66	19.8	1.5	NA	NA	NA	NA
Sumter	2.5	80.6	29	423	125.6	13.5	134	1,402	295.3	30.1	D	D	D	D
Talbot	1.3	209.9	NA	NA	NA	NA	12	57	16.3	1.2	NA	NA	NA	NA
Taliaferro	0.1	30.5	NA	NA	NA	NA	3	15	2.8	0.3	NA	NA	NA	NA
Tattnall	1.2	48.4	17	495	244.4	23.2	63	460	104.8	9.2	6	18	1.5	0.3
Taylor	0.6	74.4	D	D	D	D	21	113	45.1	3.2	3	8	0.7	0.1
Telfair	1.2	74.4	6	33	18.9	1.2	43	324	78.7	5.9	NA	NA	NA	NA
Terrell	1.4	158.0	8	D	347.0	D	41	368	92.6	10.0	D	D	D	D
Thomas	5.6	125.2	D	D	D	27.8	212	2,332	642.5	56.8	50	144	36.3	4.8
Tift	4.8	117.3	66	1,436	1,230.2	69.8	231	2,894	882.4	71.2	45	179	34.7	7.1
Toombs	2.8	104.3	D	D	D	D	148	1,764	510.2	44.1	D	D	D	D
Towns	1.5	137.7	8	15	2.2	0.3	62	406	83.3	7.6	17	47	9.5	1.7
Treutlen	0.3	44.2	NA	NA	NA	NA	23	222	42.6	4.1	NA	NA	NA	NA
Troup	8.5	122.4	53	583	495.4	26.5	264	3,278	923.8	83.2	73	202	56.6	7.8
Turner	0.8	96.2	14	214	92.5	7.7	40	270	91.9	6.8	D	D	D	1.3
Twiggs	0.5	53.6	NA	NA	NA	NA	13	65	21.3	1.1	NA	NA	NA	NA
Union	1.8	81.7	9	76	42.3	3.1	95	1,250	321.4	27.8	34	56	11.8	2.0
Upson	3.0	114.5	7	15	9.6	0.5	89	1,048	223.9	23.2	D	D	D	D
Walker	6.6	97.3	36	229	123.5	10.4	148	1,391	335.6	28.9	15	30	3.8	0.7
Walton	3.2	35.7	60	636	329.6	36.7	199	2,740	894.1	71.5	84	218	44.1	10.0
Ware	2.7	77.5	36	269	452.5	11.0	199	2,463	699.7	60.8	32	101	14.5	2.4
Warren	0.3	58.6	4	52	25.0	2.2	12	69	13.4	1.7	5	D	2.7	D
Washington	2.0	96.1	13	101	168.4	4.5	70	788	171.6	17.0	13	46	20.5	2.6
Wayne	1.5	50.8	D	D	D	D	116	1,135	290.5	25.6	12	55	6.6	1.3
Webster	0.1	37.8	3	D	1.8	D	6	46	9.2	1.1	NA	NA	NA	NA
Wheeler	0.2	22.8	NA	NA	NA	NA	14	61	17.5	1.2	NA	NA	NA	NA
White	1.5	51.9	13	78	36.4	2.3	114	1,222	346.7	31.2	28	83	14.8	2.8
Whitfield	24.0	229.9	218	3,518	1,201.4	150.5	396	4,678	1,413.3	119.1	D	D	D	8.6
Wilcox	0.4	49.7	5	D	18.2	D	23	80	19.3	1.4	NA	NA	NA	NA
Wilkes	1.0	102.4	7	70	31.3	2.1	41	386	73.7	7.7	3	7	0.4	0.1
Wilkinson	0.7	76.5	5	D	6.2	D	25	165	32.6	2.9	4	D	0.3	D
Worth	1.0	48.8	27	257	213.7	10.0	47	567	135.0	13.7	5	11	5.1	0.2
HAWAII	266.9	186.4	1,423	16,829	11,342.6	858.8	4,644	72,908	21,658.9	2,184.7	2,069	13,101	4,409.0	675.2
Hawaii	39.7	202.1	169	1,696	760.7	72.8	629	10,232	3,086.0	307.8	281	1,280	339.4	56.5
Honolulu	168.8	169.0	1,036	13,217	9,376.4	689.4	2,856	48,609	14,266.1	1,437.5	1,288	8,864	3,150.9	483.1
Kalawao	0.0	112.4	NA	NA	NA	NA	NA	NA	NA	NA	NA	NA	NA	NA
Kauai	16.3	227.8	72	562	376.8	33.0	356	4,170	1,253.1	127.4	157	973	267.3	48.1
Maui	42.1	255.7	146	1,354	828.7	63.7	D	D	D	D	343	1,984	651.4	87.5
IDAHO	275.8	166.6	1,870	23,878	23,736.5	1,259.7	6,133	82,312	24,936.1	2,312.2	2,644	7,521	1,635.4	276.7
Ada	72.7	167.5	587	9,095	9,627.7	558.3	1,505	24,520	7,401.4	742.7	968	3,285	764.3	134.2
Adams	0.5	137.9	NA	NA	NA	NA	D	D	D	D	4	D	0.9	D
Bannock	16.9	201.9	82	859	616.8	37.9	321	4,601	1,290.2	114.2	99	270	55.0	7.6
Bear Lake	0.4	62.5	D	D	D	D	27	241	58.3	4.9	5	12	1.3	0.2
Benewah	0.5	57.4	D	D	D	D	32	301	73.6	7.1	D	D	D	0.1
Bingham	2.0	44.2	48	811	473.1	35.7	118	1,203	312.1	29.2	30	71	9.8	2.0
Blaine	5.4	251.9	35	299	252.5	17.3	176	1,427	375.1	49.4	D	D	D	D
Boise	0.5	68.0	NA	NA	NA	NA	16	100	22.4	1.8	D	D	D	0.4
Bonner	1.7	40.9	33	203	68.7	8.5	216	2,194	585.9	58.7	93	251	43.9	9.5
Bonneville	36.6	332.6	184	2,305	2,841.8	112.5	515	7,783	2,247.5	201.7	151	477	124.9	19.4
Boundary	0.4	34.5	8	56	31.0	2.7	48	469	116.9	10.6	10	15	2.0	0.3
Butte	1.4	571.8	5	D	37.8	D	11	116	19.2	2.3	NA	NA	NA	NA
Camas	0.1	131.3	NA	NA	NA	NA	3	23	7.0	0.5	NA	NA	NA	NA
Canyon	15.9	76.7	166	1,881	1,445.1	89.5	509	7,976	2,764.2	234.7	183	507	91.7	17.2

1 Merchant wholesalers, except manufacturers' sales branches and offices. 2. Employer establishments.

STATE County	Professional, scientific, and technical services, 2017				Manufacturing, 2017				Accommodation and food services, 2017			
	Number of establish-ments	Number of employees	Sales (mil dol)	Average payroll (mil dol)	Number of establish-ments	Number of employees	Sales (mil dol)	Average payroll (mil dol)	Number of establis-hments	Number of employees	Sales (mil dol)	Annual payroll (mil dol)
	147	148	149	150	151	152	153	154	155	156	157	158
GEORGIA—Cont'd												
Putnam	31	62	14.1	2.8	30	701	193.1	35.3	D	D	D	D
Quitman	NA	NA	NA	NA	NA	NA	NA	NA	NA	NA	NA	NA
Rabun	48	137	15.2	5.1	21	397	184.9	15.6	69	1,173	74.0	20.9
Randolph	6	28	2.9	0.8	D	D	D	D	14	74	4.4	1.2
Richmond	464	4,935	877.2	282.2	104	7,900	4,281.4	501.2	466	10,315	562.8	149.2
Rockdale	D	D	D	D	81	4,621	2,375.3	250.4	208	4,733	253.2	72.7
Schley	NA	NA	NA	NA	5	255	100.1	13.6	3	22	1.0	0.3
Screven	12	46	4.5	2.1	9	707	148.7	33.0	16	178	8.9	2.1
Seminole	D	D	D	D	4	9	5.9	0.7	17	119	8.0	1.3
Spalding	82	396	60.1	19.7	53	2,833	1,467.7	152.4	108	1,799	102.0	26.0
Stephens	37	129	15.8	4.7	49	2,075	711.6	85.8	38	736	30.7	8.5
Stewart	D	D	D	D	D	11	D	0.5	NA	NA	NA	NA
Sumter	D	D	D	D	31	1,025	330.3	36.9	51	855	40.6	11.6
Talbot	NA	NA	NA	NA	NA	NA	NA	NA	NA	NA	NA	NA
Taliaferro	NA	NA	NA	NA	NA	NA	NA	NA	NA	NA	NA	NA
Tattnall	17	57	5.3	1.3	8	91	10.8	3.7	23	275	12.7	3.3
Taylor	NA	NA	NA	NA	6	62	40.0	2.1	6	36	2.1	0.4
Telfair	7	28	1.8	0.7	D	D	D	D	20	149	7.9	1.8
Terrell	13	39	3.7	1.3	11	373	162.0	14.2	D	D	D	D
Thomas	76	417	57.9	16.7	46	2,174	718.1	114.4	104	1,784	91.3	24.5
Tift	79	623	69.7	29.9	33	1,318	487.3	60.2	100	2,463	119.1	33.1
Toombs	53	197	18.4	6.8	28	1,120	682.5	43.0	70	1,132	59.7	15.5
Towns	D	D	6.4	D	11	33	5.9	1.5	38	481	39.3	6.6
Treutlen	NA	NA	NA	NA	4	D	8.7	D	5	37	1.7	0.5
Troup	98	501	71.9	25.9	91	12,465	11,966.6	631.1	135	2,373	121.7	32.3
Turner	9	66	5.1	1.5	9	328	159.1	14.8	17	222	9.5	2.4
Twiggs	D	D	D	0.4	NA	NA	NA	NA	6	D	1.6	D
Union	42	144	19.5	6.2	29	344	83.3	16.6	50	687	36.2	9.8
Upson	26	84	17.9	3.7	20	1,199	441.9	51.2	47	603	31.3	8.4
Walker	47	181	21.8	7.9	41	4,047	1,513.4	156.2	57	703	32.7	8.5
Walton	150	451	53.3	20.1	47	2,514	1,107.1	135.9	118	2,100	109.0	31.4
Ware	56	275	22.2	7.9	30	1,347	470.2	59.0	75	1,537	78.3	20.0
Warren	D	D	1.0	D	5	439	106.6	19.4	NA	NA	NA	NA
Washington	20	225	18.7	11.6	17	596	269.9	28.0	29	432	18.1	5.3
Wayne	32	146	13.3	6.8	24	943	751.8	72.9	51	720	41.8	9.7
Webster	NA	NA	NA	NA	NA	NA	NA	NA	NA	NA	NA	NA
Wheeler	NA	NA	NA	NA	NA	NA	NA	NA	3	20	0.2	0.1
White	52	136	15.8	5.0	35	736	131.4	33.6	90	1,138	82.8	22.7
Whitfield	D	D	D	D	246	17,470	6,817.6	735.6	178	3,533	212.2	55.4
Wilcox	3	4	0.3	0.1	D	11	D	D	NA	NA	NA	NA
Wilkes	11	32	3.4	1.0	13	411	211.6	18.4	16	170	7.8	2.1
Wilkinson	D	D	3.1	D	10	424	129.4	26.8	4	15	0.6	0.1
Worth	15	75	6.1	2.3	9	534	315.9	23.7	D	D	D	D
HAWAII	3,347	22,058	3,701.3	1,423.2	783	11,850	6,055.9	558.5	3,865	112,743	12,101.8	3,296.8
Hawaii	D	D	D	D	110	1,433	447.3	66.7	477	13,731	1,363.8	396.8
Honolulu	2,473	18,527	3,231.9	1,238.8	501	9,240	5,325.4	439.0	2,569	67,611	6,805.4	1,767.8
Kalawao	NA	NA	NA	NA	NA	NA	NA	NA	NA	NA	NA	NA
Kauai	D	D	D	D	52	332	62.7	12.0	273	9,430	1,002.9	319.8
Maui	D	D	D	D	120	845	220.4	40.8	546	21,971	2,929.7	812.5
IDAHO	D	D	D	D	1,877	58,746	20,263.4	3,486.1	3,856	65,463	3,598.1	1,006.2
Ada	1,882	13,732	2,179.5	815.1	423	14,550	3,307.2	1,400.9	1,049	21,248	1,132.3	336.7
Adams	7	11	1.1	0.3	7	113	13.5	4.7	15	42	2.5	0.7
Bannock	D	D	D	D	51	2,082	921.9	120.5	201	3,462	176.7	47.4
Bear Lake	7	8	1.0	0.3	4	25	3.7	0.8	21	159	8.2	1.7
Benewah	D	D	D	1.0	D	532	D	D	24	152	7.6	2.0
Bingham	62	225	26.6	8.0	38	2,156	655.0	93.8	48	639	28.5	7.3
Blaine	169	831	116.2	60.7	39	306	63.8	14.7	113	3,128	178.0	60.5
Boise	D	D	D	D	D	D	D	1.1	D	D	D	D
Bonner	155	437	56.6	20.8	75	1,501	485.6	65.4	127	1,993	89.6	27.2
Bonneville	D	D	D	D	140	3,026	810.7	129.2	237	5,065	257.2	77.1
Boundary	D	D	10.0	D	27	451	172.9	20.4	D	D	D	D
Butte	4	6	0.3	0.1	NA	NA	NA	NA	D	D	D	D
Camas	NA	NA	NA	NA	NA	NA	NA	NA	D	D	D	0.4
Canyon	D	D	D	D	225	8,812	3,186.0	399.0	282	5,348	265.2	72.5

STATE County	Health care and social assistance, 2017				Other services, 2017				Nonemployer businesses, 2019		Value of residential construction authorized by building permits, 2021	
	Number of establish-ments	Number of employees	Receipts (mil dol)	Annual payroll (mil dol)	Number of establish-ments	Number of employees	Receipts (mil dol)	Annual payroll (mil dol)	Number	Receipts (mil dol)	New construction ($1,000)	Number of housing units
	159	160	161	162	163	164	165	166	167	168	169	170
GEORGIA—Cont'd												
Putnam	35	418	35.0	13.9	23	85	10.6	2.0	2,154	97.4	82,880	276
Quitman	NA	NA	NA	NA	NA	NA	NA	NA	143	4.1	440	4
Rabun	38	586	43.2	21.2	38	111	10.5	3.2	2,040	89.9	73,716	181
Randolph	10	288	25.4	11.7	6	12	1.1	0.3	434	11.6	1,265	9
Richmond	608	24,655	3,883.8	1,371.0	293	1,799	220.3	59.1	13,693	440.2	112,770	689
Rockdale	262	4,060	484.6	169.9	144	733	105.1	24.5	9,927	312.2	54,901	218
Schley	5	27	4.4	0.7	D	D	D	D	333	11.6	3,830	18
Screven	15	302	23.3	9.9	24	75	11.0	2.2	992	33.5	4,613	23
Seminole	25	439	39.0	19.3	D	D	D	D	605	27.1	1,576	18
Spalding	141	3,050	318.1	130.2	72	385	39.5	11.5	5,450	185.3	128,558	555
Stephens	55	1,232	110.3	46.6	30	151	14.1	4.9	1,672	67.5	3,074	16
Stewart	8	D	8.4	D	D	D	D	0.1	237	4.9	951	4
Sumter	81	2,645	428.5	107.0	D	D	D	D	1,938	71.1	5,146	25
Talbot	4	D	0.6	D	3	3	0.2	0.1	461	11.9	1,632	7
Taliaferro	NA	NA	NA	NA	NA	NA	NA	NA	118	4.7	NA	NA
Tattnall	28	787	117.0	29.5	D	D	D	D	1,363	58.5	5,116	37
Taylor	19	214	11.8	5.4	D	D	D	0.8	504	20.1	3,263	15
Telfair	15	205	11.9	5.3	16	63	8.3	1.8	763	29.1	155	2
Terrell	D	D	D	D	D	D	D	D	678	26.0	887	7
Thomas	141	3,748	502.3	181.6	64	462	53.7	10.7	3,254	153.5	45,241	346
Tift	101	3,260	517.7	197.4	51	319	31.9	10.4	3,198	141.6	19,315	177
Toombs	D	D	D	D	D	D	D	D	1,953	85.1	1,825	24
Towns	30	573	43.0	19.4	8	24	2.0	0.5	1,292	54.7	32,346	98
Treutlen	8	128	9.3	3.9	D	D	D	D	492	19.9	393	4
Troup	133	2,671	396.0	171.6	83	349	44.4	10.8	5,278	177.3	59,330	297
Turner	10	142	8.4	3.6	5	14	1.3	0.3	721	25.4	850	4
Twiggs	D	D	D	D	4	9	1.7	0.3	615	22.4	355	10
Union	69	1,380	121.0	52.6	37	173	24.3	4.7	2,554	113.1	83,198	251
Upson	63	1,350	139.1	57.1	45	168	21.8	5.5	1,745	63.5	10,698	36
Walker	52	922	66.2	27.3	40	212	20.8	6.4	4,287	198.5	50,271	342
Walton	154	2,131	240.9	82.7	110	396	40.7	10.5	9,118	364.7	179,428	1,144
Ware	125	2,727	186.3	85.7	52	307	31.0	9.0	1,969	83.7	7,007	48
Warren	7	135	7.3	3.8	3	4	0.2	0.1	506	13.1	7,454	73
Washington	38	914	50.7	24.7	27	84	12.5	2.7	1,246	38.8	12,634	115
Wayne	74	1,202	131.4	46.0	36	133	13.3	3.2	1,805	75.5	21,933	119
Webster	NA	NA	NA	NA	NA	NA	NA	NA	159	6.9	1,044	5
Wheeler	NA	NA	NA	NA	3	3	0.5	0.1	368	15.3	0	0
White	39	921	66.5	27.1	46	182	18.2	4.7	2,725	125.0	47,284	231
Whitfield	D	D	D	D	125	857	114.2	31.1	6,149	321.9	88,271	673
Wilcox	9	64	3.1	1.4	D	D	2.1	D	480	18.7	NA	NA
Wilkes	18	331	12.7	5.6	D	D	D	D	679	23.2	7,512	50
Wilkinson	14	154	10.4	4.4	D	D	2.5	D	659	22.2	1,190	6
Worth	D	D	D	D	22	69	7.9	2.1	1,423	63.5	5,794	28
HAWAII	3,677	73,551	9,785.7	3,998.4	2,912	20,219	2,561.2	652.4	116,783	5,887.2	1,396,040	3,459
Hawaii	476	8,222	917.2	420.1	290	1,379	204.4	46.5	19,339	905.3	401,325	971
Honolulu	2,578	54,227	7,522.5	2,994.2	2,064	15,687	1,965.5	500.9	71,327	3,675.4	468,350	1,438
Kalawao	NA	NA	NA	NA	NA	NA	NA	NA	NA	NA	NA	NA
Kauai	192	3,324	413.3	180.2	149	761	91.9	25.7	7,450	355.5	130,159	170
Maui	431	7,778	932.7	403.9	409	2,392	299.4	79.2	18,667	951.0	396,207	880
IDAHO	5,310	98,100	10,469.0	4,292.3	2,749	14,016	1,574.0	434.6	142,798	6,748.2	4,949,319	21,732
Ada	1,558	35,758	4,249.2	1,814.5	850	4,988	599.6	170.9	43,771	2,162.2	1,925,077	7,487
Adams	6	D	3.4	D	D	D	D	0.3	407	19.2	8,641	13
Bannock	386	5,589	621.3	214.2	114	506	70.3	15.9	5,619	230.3	91,627	489
Bear Lake	11	305	42.3	12.6	3	11	1.3	0.2	480	20.3	30,413	89
Benewah	14	360	31.3	14.3	17	78	10.1	2.6	680	29.7	16,721	71
Bingham	115	1,855	210.0	90.0	54	289	40.2	10.0	3,019	141.1	46,229	251
Blaine	79	858	105.9	45.8	95	382	54.1	14.2	3,817	259.8	220,433	290
Boise	6	22	2.0	0.7	D	D	D	D	760	32.0	35,517	105
Bonner	144	1,830	156.0	68.4	88	364	37.0	9.5	4,498	196.6	65,155	326
Bonneville	578	9,005	1,077.5	365.9	D	D	D	D	9,324	468.8	220,003	1,100
Boundary	27	686	49.5	25.6	25	56	5.0	1.3	1,081	45.2	27,164	120
Butte	D	D	D	4.2	D	D	D	D	213	7.4	169	1
Camas	D	D	D	D	NA	NA	NA	NA	102	4.3	1,467	10
Canyon	404	7,256	631.9	270.9	226	1,253	118.9	36.3	15,307	650.6	636,620	4,257

STATE County	Government employment and payroll, 2017									Local government finances, 2017				
			March payroll (percent of total)							General revenue				
												Taxes		
													Per capita[1] (dollars)	
	Full-time equivalent employees	March payroll (dollars)	Adminis-tration, judicial, and legal	Police and corrections	Fire protection	Highways and transpor-tation	Health and welfare	Natural resources and utilities	Education and libraries	Total (mil dol)	Inter-govern-mental (mil dol)	Total (mil dol)	Total	Property
	171	172	173	174	175	176	177	178	179	180	181	182	183	184
GEORGIA—Cont'd														
Putnam	881	3,538,894	6.2	7.9	2.1	1.8	12.8	3.2	61.7	65.5	18.6	38.9	1,793	1,367
Quitman	122	349,836	12.7	5.9	0.0	5.7	5.9	5.3	64.1	7.3	5.0	1.1	490	418
Rabun	673	2,344,388	8.2	11.1	2.4	3.9	6.0	6.9	60.0	77.5	24.3	44.9	2,713	2,004
Randolph	512	1,450,960	7.1	7.3	2.0	3.0	35.0	2.3	39.4	36.2	11.4	8.9	1,281	947
Richmond	8,236	26,032,382	7.5	11.6	4.8	2.7	4.9	6.8	60.7	725.4	288.5	251.4	1,247	793
Rockdale	3,741	12,706,963	7.1	9.9	4.1	1.3	0.9	2.4	72.2	308.4	121.5	123.7	1,377	966
Schley	218	765,828	2.2	3.2	0.9	3.3	0.0	6.5	83.8	20.0	12.0	5.2	985	710
Screven	593	1,723,859	7.4	9.7	3.7	3.4	3.3	6.4	63.2	42.9	19.2	16.9	1,208	865
Seminole	314	1,210,782	6.2	8.6	2.7	4.3	0.0	4.9	73.1	27.7	12.0	12.8	1,553	1,128
Spalding	2,703	9,580,057	6.0	13.0	5.1	1.7	7.6	6.7	57.9	233.8	102.5	81.5	1,247	851
Stephens	918	3,145,718	6.2	9.5	2.5	2.4	2.6	5.3	69.4	120.8	37.3	32.5	1,264	810
Stewart	214	662,289	14.8	9.7	7.8	3.7	2.1	2.3	59.6	19.2	9.9	5.9	933	670
Sumter	1,277	4,584,282	6.1	12.1	4.9	2.1	9.6	2.2	60.6	119.4	52.9	39.7	1,328	835
Talbot	170	542,906	15.2	11.0	0.9	7.1	5.1	4.8	55.9	15.4	4.7	8.8	1,403	1,018
Taliaferro	102	290,207	10.8	14.2	0.0	4.0	0.2	1.8	65.6	11.9	5.6	3.8	2,326	1,895
Tattnall	773	2,319,640	7.4	5.8	5.9	2.7	1.4	2.5	73.1	63.0	31.8	23.1	910	521
Taylor	334	1,035,828	7.3	9.5	0.5	4.9	1.7	3.0	72.5	26.7	13.2	10.0	1,228	793
Telfair	451	1,273,226	9.4	9.9	1.3	3.4	5.9	4.4	64.8	35.2	15.3	14.4	901	595
Terrell	402	1,272,609	2.9	15.0	3.6	4.1	4.0	2.8	66.6	29.3	12.4	12.0	1,382	972
Thomas	2,432	8,226,021	5.8	8.0	3.5	3.5	11.5	6.8	54.1	239.8	81.1	70.4	1,578	1,018
Tift	3,567	17,141,046	2.2	3.3	0.8	0.9	69.8	0.7	21.2	437.6	62.7	53.0	1,311	580
Toombs	1,296	4,145,016	4.7	11.1	1.5	1.8	3.4	2.0	75.0	255.8	52.0	33.8	1,259	672
Towns	545	1,581,012	6.2	7.5	0.8	2.1	0.0	25.2	49.2	30.0	6.1	18.0	1,556	885
Treutlen	236	727,124	8.1	7.8	2.8	3.1	3.0	2.6	72.1	18.5	10.3	4.9	725	473
Troup	3,172	11,325,815	5.0	12.0	4.6	1.8	10.2	7.2	54.8	269.0	96.5	100.4	1,434	889
Turner	381	1,245,789	15.4	9.4	1.8	6.0	8.2	3.6	54.5	33.1	12.6	11.3	1,425	984
Twiggs	316	948,450	8.4	21.9	0.0	6.9	0.0	1.8	56.2	21.0	8.0	10.4	1,263	1,014
Union	1,436	4,910,401	2.3	5.6	1.7	1.3	49.4	3.8	34.8	64.9	23.0	37.4	1,599	965
Upson	994	3,137,963	10.3	9.5	1.5	2.7	1.8	3.4	70.0	80.2	39.9	29.0	1,109	739
Walker	2,516	8,497,959	5.8	5.3	3.2	1.4	9.0	4.8	68.8	168.2	109.7	29.4	427	318
Walton	3,207	11,641,649	7.0	8.5	4.5	1.9	2.7	5.6	66.7	285.0	104.0	126.2	1,383	959
Ware	1,754	5,525,840	5.7	9.9	3.8	2.0	14.3	2.5	57.0	142.9	64.6	47.5	1,332	772
Warren	178	576,699	9.1	7.1	0.0	3.2	5.8	6.2	63.4	29.2	16.1	8.4	1,588	1,130
Washington	1,050	3,510,831	5.7	8.4	1.0	3.5	29.8	3.4	46.3	114.5	25.8	32.3	1,589	1,046
Wayne	1,443	5,278,781	3.6	5.9	0.8	3.1	32.7	2.1	50.2	167.8	43.9	41.7	1,401	782
Webster	89	326,252	19.3	0.0	0.0	3.3	3.2	3.6	70.6	7.5	4.2	2.7	1,061	847
Wheeler	239	548,888	9.8	9.1	0.0	4.6	4.2	3.0	67.8	21.2	12.0	6.9	865	649
White	959	3,298,378	5.4	10.6	1.9	1.7	0.4	3.8	72.9	90.8	30.9	41.0	1,391	850
Whitfield	4,150	15,747,724	3.6	7.3	4.9	3.2	5.5	6.1	63.8	438.7	191.0	143.1	1,373	862
Wilcox	265	790,584	7.2	6.4	0.0	1.9	0.7	2.1	81.4	28.3	17.9	7.9	902	667
Wilkes	651	2,382,391	4.7	3.5	1.5	3.1	27.4	5.1	54.2	40.2	15.5	15.8	1,598	1,124
Wilkinson	402	1,138,739	9.9	16.2	0.7	7.7	0.0	1.3	63.2	33.5	13.8	17.3	1,936	1,288
Worth	737	2,288,460	5.9	9.4	4.8	4.0	1.6	2.7	70.4	60.4	28.8	20.7	1,009	744
HAWAII	X	X	X	X	X	X	X	X	X	X	X	X	X	X
Hawaii	2,603	13,993,658	20.0	24.2	18.6	5.1	5.4	20.3	0.0	431.6	77.9	313.8	1,569	1,333
Honolulu	10,620	59,188,205	13.8	33.1	16.0	4.1	4.2	22.8	0.0	2,959.6	435.8	1,639.6	1,662	1,115
Kalawao	X	X	X	X	X	X	X	X	X	X	X	X	X	X
Kauai	1,280	7,098,138	18.8	20.4	16.1	10.7	2.7	26.7	0.0	220.1	47.9	143.6	2,000	1,680
Maui	2,489	15,157,755	20.1	26.1	17.0	6.5	3.3	24.9	0.0	479.7	60.6	331.2	1,994	1,641
IDAHO	X	X	X	X	X	X	X	X	X	X	X	X	X	X
Ada	13,487	49,826,035	10.4	13.0	6.1	4.5	2.9	5.2	55.2	1,472.9	569.1	542.9	1,189	1,098
Adams	143	495,412	15.9	18.3	0.0	12.1	2.2	5.2	42.2	22.5	7.2	13.5	3,280	3,070
Bannock	2,787	10,399,001	7.8	15.0	5.6	5.2	3.7	7.9	51.7	252.4	111.2	86.8	1,015	978
Bear Lake	236	719,522	10.0	11.5	0.2	8.7	0.1	8.6	54.9	23.6	9.9	4.4	729	697
Benewah	499	1,677,766	4.3	6.0	2.1	4.0	42.0	2.7	38.0	27.5	15.4	8.7	945	894
Bingham	1,540	4,733,371	6.4	10.9	3.1	4.3	0.3	5.2	68.9	127.9	76.7	32.1	699	678
Blaine	949	4,578,178	11.2	9.9	6.3	3.5	0.9	6.1	59.1	132.4	29.3	71.1	3,176	2,943
Boise	267	908,437	14.7	9.2	1.9	5.4	0.8	2.8	64.1	25.1	11.9	8.2	1,122	1,112
Bonner	1,321	4,417,721	11.7	16.3	3.8	6.0	0.2	7.5	51.5	122.9	45.7	54.1	1,240	1,164
Bonneville	3,793	12,587,349	7.5	11.1	6.4	4.9	2.2	11.1	55.5	352.2	180.0	100.2	876	830
Boundary	552	1,761,941	6.8	7.1	0.6	3.5	38.3	7.0	36.0	44.8	16.2	10.2	849	840
Butte	234	1,127,536	3.1	3.5	0.0	3.3	62.6	3.9	23.5	19.0	5.6	3.9	1,508	1,438
Camas	60	195,129	17.6	11.0	0.0	20.5	0.0	7.2	43.6	6.2	3.7	1.8	1,623	1,599
Canyon	6,362	22,467,284	8.4	13.1	3.7	2.1	3.4	4.6	61.4	589.3	301.3	187.6	865	795

1. Based on the resident population estimated as of July 1 of the year shown.

STATE County	Local government finances, 2017 (cont.)									Government employment, 2020			Individual income tax returns, 2019		
	Direct general expenditure							Debt outstanding							
			Percent of total for:												
	Total (mil dol)	Per capita[1] (dollars)	Education	Health and hospitals	Police protection	Public welfare	Highways	Total (mil dol)	Per capita[1] (dollars)	Federal civilian	Federal military	State and local	Number of returns	Mean adjusted gross income	Mean income tax
	185	186	187	188	189	190	191	192	193	194	195	196	197	198	199
GEORGIA—Cont'd															
Putnam	63.1	2,909	58.1	5.0	7.1	0.3	4.8	22.4	1,032	72	59	1,339	10,090	65,663	7,546
Quitman	9.2	3,946	62.4	3.8	4.3	0.0	5.7	13.3	5,684	8	6	132	870	37,575	2,479
Rabun	65.9	3,983	56.3	5.2	5.2	0.2	4.5	51.1	3,087	61	44	807	8,040	59,162	6,538
Randolph	36.8	5,275	31.9	37.1	4.3	0.0	4.9	12.3	1,760	27	17	524	2,510	37,432	2,646
Richmond	765.6	3,796	46.4	4.0	5.7	0.2	5.3	1,279.5	6,344	7,981	12,404	24,229	88,780	45,179	3,982
Rockdale	316.3	3,521	58.9	0.6	6.4	0.4	6.6	180.5	2,009	128	238	4,271	42,500	48,496	4,125
Schley	23.7	4,529	70.4	2.6	3.6	0.1	6.4	16.3	3,115	8	14	320	1,750	46,125	2,942
Screven	42.3	3,032	56.2	3.8	4.8	0.0	7.4	9.1	655	38	36	885	5,730	43,668	3,443
Seminole	30.3	3,671	56.3	0.5	7.2	0.0	12.0	5.5	669	24	21	426	3,340	42,058	3,281
Spalding	233.3	3,569	54.7	10.1	6.3	0.1	2.8	109.7	1,679	138	174	4,984	29,480	47,651	4,050
Stephens	119.4	4,638	33.3	41.4	3.6	0.4	2.9	46.3	1,798	70	67	1,543	11,060	48,610	4,264
Stewart	18.6	2,939	62.3	0.3	9.4	0.0	8.4	8.2	1,299	113	13	260	1,520	36,673	2,286
Sumter	115.2	3,854	47.1	13.3	6.2	0.0	3.8	25.7	858	118	73	2,377	11,600	42,944	3,595
Talbot	14.0	2,245	50.1	3.5	9.0	0.1	9.1	3.5	556	11	16	239	2,500	39,078	2,713
Tali[2]erro	12.1	7,514	35.3	0.4	9.7	0.0	4.4	0.7	436	4	4	144	640	39,358	2,570
Tattnall	64.0	2,519	58.9	2.4	4.8	0.0	12.0	17.5	688	58	55	1,675	8,230	44,853	3,747
Taylor	26.4	3,257	60.9	2.2	7.4	0.1	7.7	4.3	533	23	21	397	3,190	46,392	3,535
Telfair	36.1	2,267	50.1	5.2	6.2	0.0	7.7	9.4	590	34	33	679	3,950	37,610	2,836
Terrell	31.2	3,590	52.3	3.6	7.6	0.1	6.1	6.7	772	54	22	491	3,760	41,747	3,395
Thomas	223.5	5,008	45.9	12.6	5.5	0.0	5.1	284.7	6,382	167	116	3,014	19,250	55,645	5,635
Tift	447.4	11,066	19.8	67.1	2.8	0.0	0.9	152.7	3,777	198	103	5,974	17,300	49,008	4,628
Toombs	273.9	10,199	28.0	57.6	1.9	0.0	2.4	180.9	6,735	74	70	1,567	10,960	47,899	4,273
Towns	28.1	2,429	50.7	4.8	5.7	0.0	5.2	27.1	2,348	32	29	476	5,780	56,934	5,409
Treutlen	18.9	2,796	59.4	2.6	6.0	2.2	5.1	8.9	1,319	17	17	356	2,480	40,884	2,802
Troup	275.3	3,929	49.6	8.8	7.3	0.1	3.4	83.9	1,197	144	179	3,750	29,720	51,415	4,802
Turner	31.9	4,038	43.9	4.1	10.4	0.4	10.0	7.4	943	30	20	450	3,570	36,383	2,530
Twiggs	21.9	2,653	58.3	0.3	12.4	0.3	7.1	9.4	1,141	12	21	294	3,470	39,857	2,601
Union	54.0	2,310	69.0	2.7	6.6	0.0	0.5	22.0	943	62	66	1,873	11,450	56,521	5,310
Upson	81.8	3,122	54.0	3.4	5.3	0.2	2.9	25.1	957	43	69	1,314	11,110	46,305	3,574
Walker	211.7	3,067	55.4	11.0	4.7	0.0	3.4	112.8	1,635	116	181	2,812	27,190	47,476	3,717
Walton	268.7	2,944	57.7	0.5	6.1	0.2	5.0	266.7	2,922	162	253	3,566	43,170	61,242	5,852
Ware	148.3	4,157	48.8	17.2	4.9	0.4	4.5	42.6	1,195	87	89	3,239	14,170	43,915	3,625
Warren	22.9	4,349	36.1	2.7	4.8	0.5	8.9	4.9	934	23	14	249	2,260	37,202	2,488
Washington	94.5	4,653	38.1	28.9	4.5	0.0	6.0	59.7	2,937	55	48	1,893	7,940	44,801	3,351
Wayne	171.3	5,750	36.4	39.7	3.6	0.0	7.6	53.7	1,803	384	74	1,874	11,380	48,625	3,839
Webster	6.9	2,657	69.0	6.0	4.7	0.3	5.4	1.7	664	8	7	120	940	38,388	3,096
Wheeler	21.6	2,718	54.7	2.3	5.0	0.0	4.7	8.5	1,073	12	14	288	1,940	35,047	2,314
White	90.0	3,057	65.9	1.4	5.8	0.1	6.0	33.3	1,132	56	80	1,124	12,490	53,397	4,735
Whitfield	437.3	4,196	54.7	12.4	4.0	0.0	4.5	83.0	796	168	270	5,426	43,860	53,178	5,138
Wilcox	28.4	3,228	70.1	3.2	4.7	0.6	6.5	9.0	1,020	29	18	517	2,790	33,652	2,397
Wilkes	38.9	3,946	48.9	3.4	7.9	0.0	4.2	35.7	3,625	32	25	715	4,070	44,672	3,541
Wilkinson	34.4	3,841	54.6	1.9	9.4	0.5	8.9	22.6	2,524	20	23	424	3,900	42,477	2,943
Worth	64.7	3,150	60.2	0.3	6.9	0.1	7.3	53.5	2,604	36	52	795	8,340	44,117	3,386
HAWAII	X	X	X	X	X	X	X	X	X	35,128	50,791	85,634	714,750	68,779	7,562
Hawaii	496.7	2,484	0.0	0.0	12.8	1.5	7.8	510.8	2,554	1,356	1,411	12,820	94,640	56,735	5,676
Honolulu	1,981.5	2,009	0.0	2.2	14.5	1.1	9.1	6,208.2	6,294	32,296	47,560	60,496	496,000	71,953	8,050
Kalawao	X	X	X	X	X	X	X	X	X	[2]881	[2]1213	[2]7852	NA	NA	NA
Kauai	220.5	3,070	0.0	0.0	15.0	5.2	11.1	204.1	2,842	595	607	4,466	37,490	66,028	7,129
Maui	467.9	2,816	0.0	0.0	11.5	13.0	10.1	336.6	2,026	[2]	[2]	[2]	86,620	64,950	7,015
IDAHO	X	X	X	X	X	X	X	X	X	13,721	9,168	111,731	824,000	65,152	6,853
Ada	1,348.1	2,953	40.4	2.4	9.0	0.6	6.9	674.3	1,477	6,190	1,560	30,477	235,440	81,900	10,271
Adams	12.2	2,950	37.5	0.0	12.4	0.0	13.3	3.5	836	113	14	212	1,970	51,642	4,867
Bannock	231.6	2,710	41.8	2.2	8.8	0.6	6.9	66.9	783	595	266	7,838	37,470	54,550	4,507
Bear Lake	26.0	4,316	35.0	25.0	2.5	0.5	0.9	8.0	1,322	46	19	647	2,660	51,806	3,809
Benewah	50.9	5,558	28.1	43.0	3.5	0.5	5.1	38.9	4,252	60	28	1,276	4,380	47,184	3,512
Bingham	122.8	2,676	55.4	0.3	8.7	0.4	6.5	74.3	1,619	210	143	3,824	20,020	51,370	4,216
Blaine	118.8	5,311	46.3	2.3	8.2	2.7	5.2	51.8	2,316	108	70	1,214	13,160	143,827	24,418
Boise	19.6	2,672	44.5	1.3	0.9	1.0	10.3	11.1	1,512	161	24	347	3,670	67,334	6,682
Bonner	123.6	2,831	36.9	5.9	16.1	0.1	10.9	30.9	707	214	141	2,232	22,150	63,739	6,569
Bonneville	323.4	2,824	45.1	4.3	8.3	0.3	4.5	206.1	1,800	740	390	5,923	52,960	66,046	6,148
Boundary	46.2	3,865	26.9	28.9	10.0	1.0	8.7	14.7	1,231	149	38	931	5,760	51,277	4,173
Butte	17.3	6,693	20.8	37.5	4.0	0.0	4.9	5.0	1,946	64	8	159	1,040	50,612	4,078
Camas	5.4	4,955	37.8	1.4	8.0	1.6	17.6	2.6	2,354	23	3	93	520	57,446	5,675
Canyon	542.1	2,500	50.2	1.7	7.5	0.6	4.4	345.4	1,593	384	716	8,938	101,010	53,453	4,332

1. Based on the resident population estimated as of July 1 of the year shown. 2. Kalawao county is included with Maui county.

State / county code	CBSA code[1]	County Type code[2]	STATE County	Land area[3] (sq. mi)	Population, 2021: Total persons 2021	Population, 2021: Rank	Population, 2021: Per square mile	Race alone or in combination, not Hispanic or Latino (percent): White	Black	American Indian, Alaska Native	Asian and Pacific Islancer	Percent Hispanic or Latino[4]	Age (percent): Under 5 years	5 to 17 years	18 to 24 years	25 to 34 years	35 to 44 years	45 to 54 years
				1	2	3	4	5	6	7	8	9	10	11	12	13	14	15
			IDAHO—Cont'd															
16029		6	Caribou	1,764.2	7,111	2,653	4.0	91.8	0.3	1.2	1.0	6.9	6.7	16.5	12.4	10.5	14.1	10.2
16031	15420	7	Cassia	2,565.6	25,164	1,601	9.8	70.5	0.6	1.2	1.3	27.6	7.9	17.5	14.7	12.2	12.3	10.1
16033		9	Clark	1,763.1	792	3,117	0.4	55.4	2.1	0.8	1.3	41.7	7.4	12.9	11.7	11.0	13.1	12.1
16035		6	Clearwater	2,457.3	8,895	2,499	3.6	92.2	0.9	3.7	1.6	4.0	3.7	8.2	8.7	11.1	11.4	12.3
16037		8	Custer	4,922.2	4,428	2,861	0.9	93.5	0.8	2.1	0.9	4.9	3.5	9.9	7.8	8.5	11.0	11.1
16039	34300	6	Elmore	3,075.1	28,827	1,462	9.4	75.4	3.6	2.0	4.7	17.8	7.2	13.7	14.9	16.5	12.1	9.5
16041	30860	3	Franklin	663.0	14,666	2,104	22.1	91.8	0.5	1.3	0.7	6.8	7.4	17.3	15.1	11.1	12.6	11.0
16043	39940	6	Fremont	1,864.0	13,592	2,185	7.3	86.2	0.5	1.3	1.0	12.0	5.9	12.9	13.9	11.8	12.8	11.7
16045	14260	2	Gem	559.8	19,792	1,830	35.4	89.0	0.5	1.9	1.8	8.8	5.3	12.9	11.0	10.7	11.4	11.1
16047		7	Gooding	729.3	15,772	2,046	21.6	68.7	0.5	1.5	1.2	29.5	6.2	15.5	13.2	11.9	11.6	11.4
16049		6	Idaho	8,477.5	17,040	1,969	2.0	92.5	0.9	4.2	1.1	3.7	4.7	11.3	10.0	8.8	10.3	10.0
16051	26820	3	Jefferson	1,093.7	32,202	1,378	29.4	87.8	0.5	1.2	1.3	10.6	7.5	19.6	14.3	11.5	14.1	10.5
16053	46300	7	Jerome	597.5	24,662	1,627	41.3	60.8	0.5	1.1	0.8	37.8	7.1	17.2	13.9	13.0	13.2	10.7
16055	17660	3	Kootenai	1,237.8	179,789	374	145.2	92.3	0.8	2.2	2.0	5.1	5.6	13.1	11.2	12.8	12.9	11.7
16057	34140	4	Latah	1,075.9	40,313	1,172	37.5	91.0	1.5	1.8	3.9	4.6	5.0	10.8	24.8	14.3	11.0	9.3
16059		7	Lemhi	4,563.7	8,162	2,565	1.8	95.1	0.7	2.1	0.8	3.3	4.4	10.1	8.5	8.9	11.1	9.4
16061		8	Lewis	478.8	3,715	2,908	7.8	86.6	1.6	7.5	3.0	5.1	4.8	13.3	10.7	8.6	10.8	9.4
16063		9	Lincoln	1,201.4	5,282	2,797	4.4	65.3	1.0	2.0	1.0	32.5	6.2	15.1	13.8	12.9	13.4	10.9
16065	39940	4	Madison	469.3	53,881	943	114.8	88.8	1.0	0.8	2.5	8.5	8.8	13.2	33.6	15.6	8.2	6.6
16067	15420	7	Minidoka	757.0	21,955	1,717	29.0	62.4	0.7	1.4	0.9	36.0	7.1	16.8	13.3	12.8	11.7	10.5
16069	30300	3	Nez Perce	848.3	42,454	1,137	50.0	88.6	0.9	6.6	1.9	4.6	5.5	12.1	12.1	12.7	11.9	11.5
16071		8	Oneida	1,199.0	4,611	2,847	3.8	94.0	0.8	0.9	1.1	4.5	6.4	15.5	12.2	9.2	12.2	10.3
16073	14260	2	Owyhee	7,668.2	12,336	2,256	1.6	70.8	0.7	3.4	1.0	25.7	6.1	14.4	12.9	11.7	11.9	11.7
16075	36620	6	Payette	406.9	26,350	1,552	64.8	79.3	0.9	2.1	1.8	18.3	6.6	14.8	11.8	11.6	11.9	11.7
16077	38540	6	Power	1,403.8	7,950	2,579	5.7	62.0	0.9	2.9	1.1	34.9	7.3	18.1	13.4	11.8	11.8	9.4
16079		6	Shoshone	2,637.4	13,612	2,184	5.2	93.1	1.1	3.0	1.1	4.1	5.8	11.6	9.8	11.6	10.8	11.7
16081	27220	9	Teton	449.1	12,267	2,263	27.3	82.5	0.6	0.9	1.0	16.0	5.0	13.7	10.6	12.8	16.5	15.1
16083	46300	5	Twin Falls	1,921.7	92,243	654	48.0	78.9	1.1	1.3	2.5	17.8	6.6	15.7	12.9	13.5	13.6	10.4
16085		8	Valley	3,665.1	12,241	2,266	3.3	93.2	0.7	1.5	1.1	5.1	3.9	10.4	8.1	9.5	12.8	12.5
16087		6	Washington	1,452.9	10,898	2,351	7.5	81.0	0.9	2.0	1.4	16.7	5.0	12.8	11.8	9.2	10.5	10.9
17000		0	ILLINOIS	55,513.7	12,671,469	X	228.3	61.6	15.1	0.5	6.7	18.0	5.6	12.5	13.0	13.5	13.3	12.5
17001	39500	5	Adams	855.1	64,954	833	76.0	93.0	5.5	0.4	1.3	1.9	5.9	12.8	11.6	11.8	12.0	11.2
17003	16020	3	Alexander	235.4	5,030	2,823	21.4	66.4	32.1	1.2	0.9	2.2	5.0	12.7	9.7	9.5	10.3	11.8
17005	41180	1	Bond	380.3	16,596	1,995	43.6	88.4	7.3	0.9	1.2	3.9	4.4	10.7	11.1	13.3	14.0	12.1
17007	40420	2	Boone	280.7	53,159	953	189.4	72.1	3.1	0.7	1.7	23.9	5.2	13.7	13.9	11.2	12.1	13.8
17009		7	Brown	305.7	6,421	2,703	21.0	71.1	21.5	0.4	0.5	7.3	4.5	8.8	13.2	18.9	16.7	12.9
17011	36837	7	Bureau	869.1	32,883	1,365	37.8	87.6	1.6	0.6	1.3	10.1	5.1	11.8	11.5	10.7	11.6	12.1
17013	41180	1	Calhoun	253.8	4,369	2,864	17.2	97.1	0.8	0.5	0.5	1.7	4.6	11.9	9.9	9.1	10.6	13.1
17015		7	Carroll	445.4	15,698	2,049	35.2	93.4	2.0	0.6	1.0	4.3	4.5	11.2	10.5	9.9	10.9	11.7
17017		6	Cass	375.8	12,773	2,226	34.0	73.6	5.0	0.4	1.2	20.7	6.8	13.7	12.1	11.0	12.6	12.2
17019	16580	3	Champaign	996.1	205,943	334	206.7	68.5	15.4	0.5	12.1	6.6	5.2	10.6	25.7	13.5	11.6	9.6
17021	45380	6	Christian	709.5	33,662	1,341	47.4	95.6	2.4	0.5	1.0	1.7	5.0	11.3	11.3	12.1	12.4	12.6
17023		6	Clark	501.4	15,300	2,071	30.5	97.1	0.9	0.6	0.6	1.8	5.8	12.9	11.1	11.0	12.0	12.0
17025		7	Clay	468.4	13,143	2,204	28.1	96.5	1.1	0.6	1.1	1.8	5.8	13.0	11.1	11.7	11.4	12.1
17027	41180	1	Clinton	473.9	36,793	1,261	77.6	92.1	4.4	0.4	1.0	3.4	5.6	11.9	11.2	12.7	13.6	12.2
17029	16660	5	Coles	508.3	46,765	1,042	92.0	91.5	5.0	0.6	1.6	3.1	4.9	10.1	20.2	12.6	11.3	10.8
17031	16980	1	Cook	944.9	5,173,146	2	5,474.8	42.9	23.6	0.5	8.7	26.0	5.6	12.1	12.2	15.7	14.0	12.4
17033		7	Crawford	443.6	18,659	1,888	42.1	91.0	6.1	0.6	0.9	2.6	5.2	11.4	10.7	13.4	13.5	12.2
17035	16660	9	Cumberland	345.9	10,345	2,387	29.9	97.1	1.2	0.6	0.9	1.4	5.5	13.0	10.8	10.7	12.4	11.9
17037	16980	1	DeKalb	631.3	100,414	606	159.1	75.9	9.7	0.5	3.3	12.6	5.4	12.4	22.7	13.1	11.7	10.3
17039		3	De Witt	397.6	15,341	2,068	38.6	95.1	1.7	0.6	0.8	3.1	5.5	11.9	11.2	11.1	12.4	12.5
17041		6	Douglas	416.6	19,722	1,839	47.3	90.8	1.4	0.6	1.0	7.6	6.4	13.8	12.7	12.2	12.0	11.4
17043	16980	1	DuPage	327.8	924,885	61	2,821.5	66.7	5.7	0.4	14.1	15.0	5.6	12.6	12.5	12.3	13.6	12.8
17045		6	Edgar	623.3	16,520	2,001	26.5	97.3	1.3	0.5	0.6	1.3	5.0	11.0	10.7	10.6	12.1	12.3
17047		9	Edwards	222.4	6,075	2,732	27.3	97.3	1.2	0.7	0.7	1.3	5.4	12.6	11.0	9.7	11.5	12.7
17049	20820	7	Effingham	478.8	34,430	1,315	71.9	96.1	1.1	0.3	1.0	2.3	6.3	13.5	11.5	12.5	12.2	11.0
17051		6	Fayette	716.4	21,384	1,740	29.8	92.8	5.1	0.6	0.6	2.0	5.4	11.6	11.9	12.7	12.8	12.3
17053		3	Ford	485.6	13,511	2,190	27.8	93.6	2.1	0.7	1.1	4.4	5.9	12.7	12.0	11.4	12.2	11.9
17055		4	Franklin	408.9	37,442	1,238	91.6	96.5	1.4	0.8	0.7	2.1	5.8	12.4	11.1	11.4	11.6	12.8
17057	37900	6	Fulton	865.7	33,197	1,351	38.3	91.8	4.9	0.6	0.6	3.2	4.5	11.1	11.4	12.1	13.1	12.7
17059		8	Gallatin	322.9	4,903	2,828	15.2	96.9	1.7	1.1	0.7	1.7	4.4	11.8	10.0	10.2	11.6	12.8
17061		6	Greene	543.0	11,843	2,294	21.8	96.6	1.9	0.5	0.5	1.3	5.2	12.2	11.2	11.2	11.9	12.7
17063	16980	1	Grundy	418.1	52,989	958	126.7	85.7	2.5	0.4	1.4	11.2	5.9	14.1	12.8	12.3	14.1	13.3
17065		7	Hamilton	434.6	7,911	2,581	18.2	96.2	1.2	0.8	1.0	2.1	5.6	12.2	11.0	11.0	11.8	11.7
17067	22800	7	Hancock	793.7	17,400	1,949	21.9	96.7	1.4	0.6	0.7	1.8	5.0	12.4	10.4	10.2	11.3	11.4

1. CBSA = Core Based Statistical Area. See Appendix A for explanation. See Appendix B for list of metropolitan areas with component counties. 2. County type code from the Economic Research Service of USDA Rural-Urban Continuum Codes. See Appendix A for definition. 3. Dry land or land partially or temporarily covered by water. 4. May be of any race.

STATE County	Population, 2021 (cont.) — Age (percent) (cont.) — 55 to 64 years	Population, 2021 (cont.) — Age (percent) (cont.) — 65 to 74 years	Population, 2021 (cont.) — Age (percent) (cont.) — 75 years and over	Population, 2021 (cont.) — Percent female	Population change, 2000–2021 — Total persons — 2010	Population change, 2000–2021 — Total persons — 2020	Population change, 2000–2021 — Percent change — 2010–2020	Population change, 2000–2021 — Percent change — 2020–2021	Population change, 2000–2021 — Components of change, 2020–2021 — Births	Population change, 2000–2021 — Components of change, 2020–2021 — Deaths	Population change, 2000–2021 — Components of change, 2020–2021 — Net Migration	Households, 2016–2020 — Number	Households, 2016–2020 — Persons per household	Households, 2016–2020 — Percent — Family households	Households, 2016–2020 — Percent — Female family householder[1]	Households, 2016–2020 — Percent — One person
	16	17	18	19	20	21	22	23	24	25	26	27	28	29	30	31
IDAHO—Cont'd																
Caribou	11.4	10.9	7.3	49.3	6,963	7,027	0.9	1.2	110	101	74	2,562	2.7	74.6	5.0	23.5
Cassia	10.5	8.9	5.9	49.0	22,952	24,655	7.4	2.1	472	272	309	7,832	3.0	77.8	9.3	18.9
Clark	12.2	10.6	8.8	47.9	982	790	-19.6	0.3	11	4	-5	332	2.6	53.9	1.8	45.5
Clearwater	16.8	16.5	11.4	44.6	8,761	8,734	-0.3	1.8	88	167	244	3,547	2.2	55.5	3.1	38.3
Custer	17.3	19.9	11.0	47.7	4,368	4,275	-2.1	3.6	27	58	188	1,889	2.2	63.2	4.2	35.4
Elmore	11.7	9.0	5.5	47.7	27,038	28,666	6.0	0.6	520	297	-64	10,885	2.4	62.9	9.9	28.3
Franklin	10.9	8.8	5.9	48.9	12,786	14,194	11.0	3.3	261	120	333	4,432	3.1	79.7	6.7	17.7
Fremont	13.2	11.0	6.8	47.6	13,242	13,388	1.1	1.5	204	160	161	4,464	2.8	79.6	8.4	17.7
Gem	15.2	13.5	8.9	49.8	16,719	19,123	14.4	3.5	255	331	751	6,822	2.6	71.9	10.7	23.9
Gooding	12.0	10.9	7.3	49.0	15,464	15,598	0.9	1.1	225	228	176	5,615	2.7	68.4	10.7	24.6
Idaho	16.0	17.6	11.3	47.5	16,267	16,541	1.7	3.0	165	275	621	6,462	2.5	69.2	6.3	26.6
Jefferson	10.4	7.9	4.2	48.8	26,140	30,891	18.2	4.2	547	246	1,023	8,825	3.3	80.0	5.4	15.5
Jerome	11.5	8.4	4.9	48.5	22,374	24,237	8.3	1.8	392	235	265	8,004	3.0	75.2	12.2	18.6
Kootenai	13.4	12.2	7.3	50.5	138,494	171,362	23.7	4.9	2,269	2,278	8,543	64,475	2.5	69.6	8.4	23.8
Latah	10.0	9.2	5.6	49.1	37,244	39,517	6.1	2.0	526	352	622	15,737	2.3	54.7	5.1	31.0
Lemhi	16.1	18.7	12.7	49.7	7,936	7,974	0.5	2.4	82	153	266	3,717	2.1	57.5	6.0	41.4
Lewis	14.8	16.4	11.3	49.4	3,821	3,533	-7.5	5.2	46	56	196	1,649	2.3	56.0	4.9	37.1
Lincoln	12.7	9.8	5.1	47.8	5,208	5,127	-1.6	3.0	78	57	135	1,804	2.9	68.6	8.6	26.9
Madison	6.2	4.7	3.0	49.0	37,536	52,913	41.0	1.8	1,380	227	-199	11,858	3.3	81.8	4.0	11.7
Minidoka	11.7	9.3	6.9	49.7	20,069	21,613	7.7	1.6	361	258	237	7,456	2.8	72.6	10.0	23.9
Nez Perce	13.5	12.0	8.8	50.6	39,265	42,090	7.2	0.9	551	688	502	16,548	2.4	65.3	9.4	29.1
Oneida	13.0	12.3	9.0	49.3	4,286	4,564	6.5	1.0	59	46	33	1,715	2.6	69.0	8.0	28.6
Owyhee	13.6	11.1	6.7	49.0	11,526	11,913	3.4	3.6	175	171	424	4,429	2.6	71.6	8.6	24.2
Payette	12.7	11.1	7.9	49.6	22,623	25,386	12.2	3.8	404	353	921	9,086	2.6	69.1	10.8	25.8
Power	11.9	9.9	6.4	49.2	7,817	7,878	0.8	0.9	116	92	48	2,693	2.8	65.6	9.5	31.0
Shoshone	15.4	14.5	8.7	49.0	12,765	13,169	3.2	3.4	174	260	540	5,436	2.3	59.0	9.5	32.5
Teton	12.7	10.0	3.6	47.7	10,170	11,630	14.4	5.5	152	73	563	4,290	2.7	64.0	5.7	26.6
Twin Falls	11.3	9.7	6.4	50.4	77,230	90,046	16.6	2.4	1,415	1,273	2,064	31,758	2.7	69.1	8.6	24.6
Valley	16.0	18.4	8.3	48.6	9,862	11,746	19.1	4.2	110	125	520	3,920	2.8	73.4	8.1	19.9
Washington	14.1	15.5	10.1	49.8	10,198	10,500	3.0	3.8	108	167	466	4,263	2.3	64.1	9.8	30.2
ILLINOIS	13.0	9.9	6.6	50.6	12,830,632	12,812,508	-0.1	-1.1	167,169	162,805	-145,656	4,884,061	2.5	63.8	12.1	29.8
Adams	13.9	11.5	9.3	50.4	67,103	65,737	-2.0	-1.2	902	1,174	-511	27,199	2.4	64.0	9.8	30.5
Alexander	16.8	14.5	9.7	50.9	8,238	5,240	-36.4	-4.0	68	134	-141	2,252	2.6	59.3	14.3	37.8
Bond	14.5	11.8	8.1	47.4	17,768	16,725	-5.9	-0.8	181	263	-50	6,359	2.3	63.4	7.4	29.9
Boone	13.4	9.8	6.8	49.6	54,165	53,448	-1.3	-0.5	662	590	-368	18,799	2.8	72.2	10.6	23.3
Brown	11.0	8.1	5.9	33.4	6,937	6,244	-10.0	2.8	60	76	195	2,090	2.3	58.7	6.8	35.3
Bureau	14.7	12.8	9.8	50.4	34,978	33,244	-5.0	-1.1	398	609	-153	13,801	2.4	66.4	10.1	28.4
Calhoun	16.6	13.6	10.7	49.5	5,089	4,437	-12.8	-1.5	47	94	-20	1,661	2.8	73.1	5.4	24.3
Carroll	15.3	15.0	11.1	49.6	15,387	15,702	2.0	0.0	151	270	118	6,511	2.1	61.2	7.4	32.7
Cass	13.4	10.8	7.5	49.6	13,642	13,042	-4.4	-2.1	216	213	-271	5,068	2.4	65.1	11.4	30.4
Champaign	10.0	8.4	5.3	50.2	201,081	205,865	2.4	0.0	2,686	2,150	-517	83,059	2.3	51.3	9.4	36.3
Christian	14.9	11.6	8.9	48.5	34,800	34,032	-2.2	-1.1	419	632	-160	13,977	2.2	58.8	9.4	34.2
Clark	15.0	11.5	8.6	50.2	16,335	15,455	-5.4	-1.0	205	289	-72	6,726	2.3	73.3	11.6	22.4
Clay	14.1	12.2	8.6	50.3	13,815	13,288	-3.8	-1.1	191	229	-107	5,607	2.3	64.5	8.8	28.9
Clinton	14.7	10.7	7.4	47.8	37,762	36,899	-2.3	-0.3	466	522	-58	14,596	2.4	66.1	8.5	28.3
Coles	12.5	10.6	7.2	51.1	53,873	46,863	-13.0	-0.2	570	765	90	20,972	2.3	56.8	11.4	33.5
Cook	12.3	9.3	6.3	51.2	5,194,675	5,275,541	1.6	-1.9	70,461	62,236	-109,966	1,991,474	2.6	59.4	13.9	33.2
Crawford	14.2	11.5	8.0	47.1	19,817	18,679	-5.7	-0.1	221	303	62	7,704	2.1	65.4	10.1	29.7
Cumberland	15.0	12.4	8.4	49.9	11,048	10,450	-5.4	-1.0	152	161	-95	4,229	2.5	68.0	3.9	27.7
DeKalb	11.1	8.2	5.1	50.2	105,160	100,420	-4.5	0.0	1,379	1,102	-303	38,616	2.6	59.5	11.3	29.2
De Witt	15.4	12.0	8.1	50.0	16,561	15,516	-6.3	-1.1	192	318	-50	6,732	2.3	61.7	8.5	34.8
Douglas	12.8	10.7	7.9	50.0	19,980	19,740	-1.2	-0.1	310	261	-69	7,600	2.6	67.6	7.3	27.3
DuPage	13.8	10.3	6.5	50.5	916,924	932,877	1.7	-0.9	11,965	9,818	-10,227	344,314	2.7	69.9	9.1	24.9
Edgar	15.1	13.5	9.7	50.5	18,576	16,866	-9.2	-2.1	187	356	-175	7,851	2.2	65.6	10.6	29.8
Edwards	14.3	13.3	9.5	51.4	6,721	6,245	-7.1	-2.7	63	120	-112	2,756	2.3	64.6	9.7	29.8
Effingham	14.3	11.0	7.6	49.6	34,242	34,668	1.2	-0.7	495	523	-213	13,856	2.4	66.3	8.5	27.1
Fayette	13.7	11.1	8.4	46.6	22,140	21,488	-2.9	-0.5	269	334	-41	7,918	2.5	66.9	8.3	28.2
Ford	14.1	11.0	8.7	50.1	14,081	13,534	-3.9	-0.2	166	239	50	5,824	2.2	61.4	10.1	35.0
Franklin	14.0	12.0	8.9	50.3	39,561	37,804	-4.4	-1.0	494	790	-71	16,207	2.4	61.2	11.3	33.7
Fulton	13.9	12.4	8.8	47.3	37,069	33,609	-9.3	-1.2	339	691	-64	14,072	2.3	61.5	8.3	32.6
Gallatin	14.7	13.8	10.6	50.6	5,589	4,946	-11.5	-0.9	53	98	2	2,274	2.2	64.0	14.6	33.2
Greene	15.4	11.8	8.4	49.1	13,886	11,985	-13.7	-1.2	131	223	-50	4,984	2.6	66.6	9.0	29.5
Grundy	12.7	9.1	5.8	49.9	50,063	52,533	4.9	0.9	720	641	372	20,071	2.5	71.0	10.0	24.4
Hamilton	14.4	12.5	9.6	50.6	8,457	7,993	-5.5	-1.0	107	146	-43	3,366	2.4	70.0	10.1	24.4
Hancock	15.2	14.0	10.1	50.0	19,104	17,620	-7.8	-1.2	215	287	-147	7,542	2.3	64.8	7.3	31.3

1. No spouse present.

STATE County	Persons in group quarters, 2021	Daytime Population, 2016–2020: Number	Daytime Population, 2016–2020: Employment/ residence ratio	Births, 2021: Total	Births, 2021: Rate[1]	Deaths, 2021: Number	Deaths, 2021: Rate[1]	Persons under 65 with no health insurance, 2019: Number	Persons under 65 with no health insurance, 2019: Percent	Medicare, 2021: Total beneficiaries	Medicare, 2021: Enrolled in Original Medicare	Medicare, 2021: Enrolled in Medicare Advantage	COVID-19 Deaths, 2020: Number	COVID-19 Deaths, 2020: Rate[1]
	32	33	34	35	36	37	38	39	40	41	42	43	44	45
IDAHO—Cont'd														
Caribou	20	7,620	1.2	88	12.5	82	11.6	620	10.5	1,404	1,355	49	D	D
Cassia	244	24,976	1.1	377	15.1	214	8.6	3,414	17.1	4,065	3,063	1,002	19	0.8
Clark	1	892	1.0	7	8.8	2	2.5	196	29.7	143	101	42	D	D
Clearwater	699	8,652	1.0	65	7.4	130	14.7	805	14.4	2,834	2,755	79	D	D
Custer	19	4,141	1.0	21	4.8	47	10.8	436	14.6	1,368	1,333	34	D	D
Elmore	696	26,463	1.0	408	14.2	228	7.9	3,386	15.0	4,735	3,383	1,352	15	0.5
Franklin	79	11,253	0.6	215	14.9	92	6.4	1,546	13.2	2,385	1,957	428	D	D
Fremont	437	11,697	0.7	163	12.1	127	9.4	1,742	17.0	2,608	2,018	590	14	1.0
Gem	131	15,101	0.7	192	9.8	260	13.3	2,034	14.7	4,987	2,448	2,539	20	1.0
Gooding	23	14,511	0.9	183	11.7	174	11.1	2,424	19.9	3,133	2,195	937	22	1.4
Idaho	473	16,010	0.9	136	8.1	210	12.5	1,834	16.2	5,113	4,957	156	17	1.0
Jefferson	159	24,976	0.7	425	13.4	188	5.9	3,555	13.6	4,276	3,195	1,081	16	0.5
Jerome	101	24,542	1.0	310	12.7	181	7.4	4,349	21.1	3,702	2,378	1,324	18	0.7
Kootenai	1,384	155,624	0.9	1,782	10.1	1,815	10.3	16,442	12.4	40,392	26,300	14,092	128	0.7
Latah	2,569	36,840	0.8	407	10.2	272	6.8	3,462	10.8	6,623	5,623	1,000	D	D
Lemhi	56	7,781	1.0	67	8.3	110	13.7	738	13.5	2,720	2,650	70	11	1.4
Lewis	24	4,063	1.2	33	9.1	42	11.6	417	15.2	1,446	1,404	42	D	D
Lincoln	17	4,498	0.7	59	11.3	46	8.8	918	20.4	899	698	202	D	D
Madison	758	40,237	1.0	1,092	20.5	196	3.7	3,395	9.4	3,349	2,489	860	16	0.3
Minidoka	68	19,657	0.9	290	13.3	192	8.8	3,090	17.9	3,929	2,822	1,107	26	1.2
Nez Perce	1,026	43,229	1.2	438	10.4	524	12.4	3,851	12.2	10,412	7,777	2,636	46	1.1
Oneida	43	3,956	0.8	53	11.6	30	6.5	464	13.1	1,035	1,014	22	D	D
Owyhee	115	10,424	0.7	146	12.0	136	11.2	2,167	23.1	2,398	1,281	1,117	18	1.5
Payette	141	21,196	0.8	319	12.3	291	11.2	3,063	16.0	5,805	3,253	2,552	27	1.1
Power	45	7,916	1.1	91	11.5	74	9.3	1,164	18.4	1,420	1,055	365	D	D
Shoshone	137	12,208	0.9	132	9.9	217	16.2	1,374	14.2	3,899	3,523	376	28	2.1
Teton	2	9,817	0.7	116	9.7	60	5.0	1,663	15.8	1,572	1,503	68	D	D
Twin Falls	903	86,454	1.0	1,120	12.3	981	10.7	10,179	14.1	16,836	10,345	6,491	111	1.2
Valley	44	12,010	1.2	80	6.6	98	8.1	1,163	13.8	3,125	2,025	1,100	D	D
Washington	103	9,553	0.9	89	8.3	126	11.8	1,257	17.1	3,147	2,116	1,031	15	1.4
ILLINOIS	289,121	12,694,698	1.0	133,097	10.5	130,319	10.2	907,738	8.7	2,265,099	1,581,792	683,306	17,233	1.3
Adams	1,909	68,221	1.1	750	11.5	942	14.4	3,118	6.1	15,041	12,272	2,769	85	1.3
Alexander	69	5,068	0.5	54	10.6	106	20.8	336	7.7	1,620	1,393	228	13	2.5
Bond	1,581	15,135	0.8	145	8.7	209	12.6	835	7.1	3,614	2,750	865	15	0.9
Boone	259	45,607	0.7	529	9.9	481	9.0	3,785	8.5	9,935	6,479	3,456	65	1.2
Brown	1,830	8,656	1.9	52	8.2	61	9.7	158	4.3	1,080	837	244	10	1.6
Bureau	419	29,930	0.8	312	9.5	456	13.8	1,837	7.3	8,150	6,637	1,514	67	2.0
Calhoun	47	3,719	0.5	37	8.4	81	18.5	254	7.1	1,189	925	264	D	D
Carroll	221	13,567	0.9	126	8.0	217	13.8	778	7.4	4,232	3,006	1,226	32	2.0
Cass	181	11,698	0.9	178	13.8	161	12.5	997	10.2	2,521	1,923	598	28	2.2
Champaign	15,917	219,099	1.1	2,143	10.4	1,707	8.3	11,815	7.1	30,217	15,258	14,959	78	0.4
Christian	1,618	29,244	0.8	343	10.2	505	14.9	1,663	6.8	7,674	5,574	2,100	65	1.9
Clark	186	13,800	0.8	152	9.9	231	15.0	792	6.5	3,700	2,826	874	22	1.4
Clay	278	13,294	1.0	155	11.7	188	14.2	734	7.1	3,272	2,952	319	38	2.9
Clinton	1,925	31,354	0.7	367	10.0	426	11.6	1,737	6.0	7,575	5,908	1,667	46	1.2
Coles	2,895	51,528	1.0	445	9.5	601	12.9	2,904	7.4	9,851	7,506	2,345	59	1.3
Cook	92,570	5,336,413	1.1	56,201	10.8	50,008	9.6	466,676	10.9	830,121	560,562	269,558	8,046	1.5
Crawford	1,442	19,461	1.1	177	9.5	250	13.4	939	6.8	4,457	3,896	562	32	1.7
Cumberland	83	8,683	0.6	123	11.8	128	12.3	607	7.1	2,459	1,822	637	20	1.9
DeKalb	5,202	95,782	0.8	1,089	10.9	884	8.8	6,473	7.5	15,992	11,762	4,231	68	0.7
De Witt	202	14,632	0.9	147	9.6	247	16.0	806	6.5	3,596	2,567	1,029	25	1.6
Douglas	142	19,138	1.0	258	13.1	206	10.4	1,718	10.9	3,952	2,542	1,410	33	1.7
DuPage	12,537	1,027,536	1.2	9,480	10.2	7,878	8.5	49,519	6.4	159,928	116,854	43,074	881	0.9
Edgar	223	17,389	1.0	157	9.4	276	16.6	921	7.0	4,322	3,435	887	40	2.4
Edwards	37	6,150	0.9	52	8.5	87	14.2	306	6.2	1,499	1,336	164	11	1.8
Effingham	394	39,341	1.3	400	11.6	412	11.9	1,666	6.0	7,468	6,420	1,049	56	1.6
Fayette	1,608	19,155	0.7	216	10.1	271	12.7	1,463	9.3	4,513	3,777	736	42	2.0
Ford	396	11,997	0.8	125	9.2	193	14.3	737	7.1	3,089	2,264	824	30	2.2
Franklin	428	33,409	0.7	411	10.9	634	16.9	2,400	8.0	9,668	7,408	2,260	70	1.9
Fulton	2,562	30,175	0.7	275	8.3	551	16.5	1,946	7.9	8,231	6,040	2,190	43	1.3
Gallatin	25	4,401	0.7	41	8.3	86	17.5	256	7.1	1,410	1,193	217	D	D
Greene	204	10,475	0.6	113	9.5	178	15.0	711	7.0	2,982	2,423	558	38	3.2
Grundy	228	47,526	0.9	568	10.8	510	9.7	2,385	5.5	8,971	7,667	1,304	49	0.9
Hamilton	80	7,163	0.7	93	11.7	120	15.1	419	6.7	1,926	1,653	273	11	1.4
Hancock	183	14,465	0.6	165	9.4	231	13.2	921	6.9	4,706	3,956	750	34	1.9

1. Per 1,000 estimated resident population.

STATE County	COVID-19 Vaccinations, 2021–2022		Education						Money income, 2016–2020				Income and poverty, 2020			
			School enrollment and attainment, 2016–2020				Local government expenditures,[3] 2018–2019			Households				Percent below poverty level		
			Enrollment[1]		Attainment[2] (percent)						Percent					
	Number	Percent[5]	Total	Percent private	High school graduate or less	Bachelor's degree or more	Total current spending (mil dol)	Current spending per student (dollars)	Per capita income[4]	Median income (dollars)	with income of less than $50,000	with income of $200,000 or more	Median household income (dollars)	All persons	Children under 18 years	Children 5 to 17 years in families
	46	47	48	49	50	51	52	53	54	55	56	57	58	59	60	61
IDAHO—Cont'd																
Caribou	2,880	40.3	1,908	6.7	43.3	17.5	13.8	8,524	26,640	58,099	42.6	2.4	63,719	7.9	11.9	10.8
Cassia	9,823	40.9	6,965	8.4	43.7	19.4	43.2	7,772	23,406	52,256	46.5	3.3	64,591	10.1	12.5	11.6
Clark	365	43.2	220	1.4	67.0	16.7	2.3	20,339	20,733	36,429	62.3	0.0	52,182	11.6	20.2	19.7
Clearwater	3,733	42.6	1,383	8.5	42.6	17.3	14.9	12,711	25,357	42,413	54.5	2.7	45,377	14.0	23.6	22.1
Custer	2,048	47.5	740	2.2	34.6	29.7	6.3	10,811	24,082	44,757	57.6	0.4	53,278	12.7	19.3	18.6
Elmore	15,458	56.2	6,246	17.2	38.2	20.7	35.0	7,117	23,772	45,656	55.6	1.0	49,450	11.7	15.5	15.5
Franklin	6,233	44.9	4,104	9.5	51.4	17.1	21.9	6,766	25,825	59,934	38.0	4.3	65,396	7.7	9.7	9.5
Fremont	5,937	45.3	3,337	16.6	41.0	19.6	17.4	7,773	23,970	56,825	43.0	1.8	58,658	12.6	17.0	14.8
Gem	7,251	40.0	3,832	21.9	48.7	18.9	21.3	8,002	26,671	53,720	47.2	3.8	60,526	11.0	15.6	14.6
Gooding	6,724	44.3	3,591	15.0	56.3	16.9	26.5	8,212	24,388	50,057	50.0	3.1	57,728	11.2	16.5	15.4
Idaho	5,132	30.8	3,151	16.6	42.9	20.7	19.8	11,420	24,811	44,951	54.3	2.3	51,201	13.1	18.5	17.4
Jefferson	12,866	43.1	9,415	21.3	33.6	25.2	49.2	6,600	25,639	65,577	31.7	5.1	66,806	8.5	9.8	9.2
Jerome	11,276	46.2	6,497	9.2	52.3	14.8	35.4	7,154	23,417	55,521	43.4	4.0	57,342	12.3	15.3	14.9
Kootenai	76,851	46.4	35,337	17.9	32.9	26.6	180.3	7,742	30,912	60,903	40.1	3.7	66,959	8.6	9.9	8.2
Latah	23,615	58.9	15,439	10.0	23.8	44.4	51.0	10,786	27,644	51,312	48.7	4.9	59,834	15.3	10.7	9.6
Lemhi	3,813	47.5	1,424	11.9	35.5	23.4	9.2	8,984	25,417	38,819	61.3	2.0	48,908	15.3	22.3	20.8
Lewis	2,013	52.4	813	20.9	38.5	19.1	9.5	12,699	24,994	42,370	56.4	1.8	52,255	12.9	19.5	17.4
Lincoln	2,230	41.6	1,367	5.8	52.3	11.1	9.4	10,066	22,250	52,363	46.2	1.4	58,806	11.4	15.7	14.2
Madison	21,888	54.8	19,234	49.3	19.1	38.6	46.5	6,670	21,943	44,419	55.3	3.6	53,727	14.3	10.5	11.0
Minidoka	8,717	41.4	5,292	8.7	53.3	13.8	36.1	8,200	24,423	53,011	47.4	2.4	56,022	14.0	19.0	17.3
Nez Perce	22,722	56.2	8,842	11.2	38.1	24.1	56.3	10,406	30,103	57,099	44.7	3.5	57,839	11.6	12.7	11.6
Oneida	2,087	46.1	1,077	9.2	42.0	22.2	13.2	5,345	24,294	54,484	47.5	3.1	69,357	9.7	12.5	12.0
Owyhee	4,215	35.7	2,715	12.3	57.3	12.5	20.2	8,472	23,798	48,601	51.2	3.3	53,910	13.6	19.2	18.2
Payette	7,646	31.9	5,532	11.2	50.9	16.4	31.5	7,179	26,028	52,788	47.6	3.8	60,177	11.5	14.4	13.5
Power	3,972	51.7	2,055	8.8	55.4	15.7	17.2	10,332	24,775	51,014	49.2	2.6	45,404	12.4	16.8	16.0
Shoshone	5,551	43.1	2,116	7.8	50.8	10.6	20.3	11,832	24,564	40,483	57.9	1.3	44,336	14.4	21.0	19.6
Teton	7,563	62.3	2,900	23.3	23.8	41.4	16.8	9,155	34,905	73,274	29.6	2.9	74,935	7.4	10.1	9.0
Twin Falls	43,710	50.3	22,679	14.4	39.3	23.3	126.3	7,652	27,018	53,363	45.7	2.8	54,995	11.1	13.3	11.5
Valley	7,083	62.2	1,826	15.2	33.1	30.3	16.8	11,119	31,192	63,115	39.8	4.0	62,600	8.7	11.3	10.6
Washington	4,129	40.5	2,117	10.0	42.9	19.0	15.9	8,492	24,216	42,126	58.1	2.1	49,186	14.2	20.0	18.0
ILLINOIS	8,708,021	68.7	3,166,891	18.9	35.9	35.5	31,831.6	16,244	37,306	68,428	37.2	8.8	71,243	11.0	13.9	13.4
Adams	34,299	52.4	14,497	20.3	42.2	25.2	110.8	12,030	31,035	55,052	45.2	4.1	57,434	10.7	13.2	12.6
Alexander	1,918	33.3	1,315	3.5	53.0	11.5	13.7	18,892	20,450	34,709	67.1	1.8	38,315	24.2	36.5	36.9
Bond	9,083	55.3	4,083	19.4	43.2	21.7	27.6	12,358	27,274	53,568	46.5	2.4	58,209	10.8	14.7	13.4
Boone	32,951	61.5	14,114	17.8	45.6	24.2	144.4	15,275	32,659	70,396	35.7	7.2	82,318	6.8	10.6	9.5
Brown	3,544	53.9	1,370	19.5	56.8	12.8	10.5	14,596	22,835	60,694	42.8	1.7	52,277	16.7	11.3	11.5
Bureau	18,605	57.0	7,069	15.9	45.4	20.7	75.8	15,350	29,700	55,549	44.6	3.4	57,728	10.0	14.1	13.1
Calhoun	2,467	52.1	1,014	15.5	48.0	15.7	8.6	14,204	30,282	66,602	37.3	4.9	61,648	9.2	11.9	11.0
Carroll	9,362	65.4	2,531	8.8	47.5	19.7	30.2	14,016	30,090	52,813	47.4	2.3	53,965	10.5	15.1	14.2
Cass	7,546	62.1	2,756	12.4	57.2	16.0	26.6	11,685	26,747	53,899	45.2	1.5	54,205	12.2	15.5	15.1
Champaign	137,066	65.4	78,078	8.5	27.0	45.0	396.2	15,765	31,254	53,936	46.9	5.9	64,387	15.1	15.4	14.5
Christian	15,901	49.2	6,724	13.2	51.6	17.9	81.0	15,330	28,959	52,120	46.7	2.0	56,656	9.9	14.9	14.1
Clark	7,649	49.5	2,955	6.6	45.9	21.8	30.5	11,685	30,649	59,481	41.0	2.1	59,633	10.4	14.8	14.5
Clay	5,078	38.5	2,820	6.6	50.5	15.3	22.3	9,514	29,950	52,167	47.9	3.5	59,602	13.3	18.5	18.9
Clinton	22,498	59.9	7,705	15.2	42.1	21.7	63.9	12,278	33,231	67,179	36.3	4.7	71,883	7.1	7.5	8.0
Coles	23,425	46.3	14,782	6.9	40.2	26.1	96.8	15,560	28,495	46,411	53.0	2.5	46,900	17.5	17.5	18.1
Cook	3,750,317	72.8	1,258,897	23.9	35.0	40.0	12,828.1	17,549	39,239	67,886	38.0	10.1	71,611	12.9	16.6	16.5
Crawford	9,588	51.4	3,725	18.6	42.8	16.5	34.5	12,130	27,211	50,968	48.6	3.5	57,632	11.0	14.6	14.8
Cumberland	4,232	39.3	2,226	10.0	48.3	18.9	18.3	11,280	29,426	59,271	43.8	3.5	68,683	8.9	11.3	10.5
DeKalb	59,672	56.9	35,101	9.9	33.3	32.4	262.3	15,762	29,780	62,353	40.7	4.8	68,546	10.8	11.2	10.8
De Witt	8,283	53.0	3,373	15.0	46.9	20.4	35.7	14,184	30,910	57,727	43.6	3.7	65,526	9.9	13.2	12.7
Douglas	9,547	49.0	4,082	13.7	49.7	20.1	46.1	13,233	28,603	59,620	41.6	3.9	63,003	8.2	11.5	10.6
DuPage	713,775	77.3	239,333	22.1	24.9	50.3	2,746.5	18,175	47,501	94,930	24.4	15.5	92,101	5.9	6.3	5.9
Edgar	8,370	48.8	3,114	8.9	48.6	18.0	33.6	11,556	27,775	48,543	50.9	2.1	52,668	11.7	17.6	17.5
Edwards	2,580	40.3	1,297	5.1	42.1	13.3	10.8	12,075	27,847	53,801	45.4	1.0	55,832	10.7	13.9	13.7
Effingham	16,706	49.1	7,496	17.4	40.8	23.2	55.0	11,013	32,901	59,932	41.2	5.3	65,172	9.3	11.4	10.5
Fayette	7,735	36.3	4,309	16.2	53.5	12.4	35.5	13,350	23,920	45,634	53.3	1.6	49,030	14.7	18.6	17.9
Ford	7,523	58.0	2,794	12.1	44.7	21.6	43.7	16,044	29,288	50,582	49.5	3.5	58,478	9.5	13.5	12.2
Franklin	17,320	45.0	7,774	7.8	44.1	17.0	70.7	11,581	24,642	43,671	55.8	1.4	49,834	15.5	21.0	20.9
Fulton	19,855	57.8	7,342	5.6	47.0	18.3	54.1	12,149	29,850	52,243	47.5	3.7	48,828	13.2	16.5	15.9
Gallatin	2,661	55.1	948	4.7	52.2	11.5	9.5	12,621	31,693	43,092	54.1	3.3	44,282	15.6	21.1	20.3
Greene	5,736	44.2	2,614	15.3	53.7	15.3	23.4	12,676	27,105	51,746	48.1	3.2	51,242	13.3	17.3	16.6
Grundy	29,646	58.1	12,680	8.1	38.2	25.4	174.6	12,977	35,483	75,767	30.8	6.1	74,935	5.9	7.4	7.1
Hamilton	3,191	39.3	1,763	19.9	43.9	21.2	14.4	11,975	28,046	55,977	43.6	2.8	49,302	13.0	19.1	17.5
Hancock	8,599	48.6	3,614	9.2	42.7	22.3	38.1	13,375	30,405	55,818	45.0	2.9	54,076	11.2	15.6	15.0

1. All persons 3 years old and over enrolled in nursery school through college. 2. Persons 25 years old and over. 3. Elementary and secondary education expenditures. 4. Based on population estimated by the American Community Survey, 2016–2020. 5. CDC percent based on 2019 population estimate.

Table B. States and Counties — **Personal Income**

STATE County	Personal income, 2020										Earnings, 2020		
			Per capita[1]			Supplements to wages and salaries, employer contributions (mil dol)						Contributions for government social insurance (mil dol)	
	Total (mil dol)	Percent change 2019–2020	Dollars	Rank	Wages and salaries (mil dol)	Pension and insurance	Government social insurance	Proprietors' income (mil dol)	Dividends, interest, and rent (mil dol)	Personal transfer reecipts (mil dol)	Total (mil dol)	From employee and self-employed	From employer
	62	63	64	65	66	67	68	69	70	71	72	73	74
IDAHO—Cont'd													
Caribou	346	16.8	48,595	1,309	216	41	19	60	48	78	336	19	19
Cassia	1,242	12.2	51,149	1,009	497	81	46	353	164	238	977	45	46
Clark	41	16.8	47,615	1,437	16	3	1	10	5	6	31	1	1
Clearwater	346	10.6	39,140	2,551	119	27	11	24	68	136	180	15	11
Custer	207	10.9	48,718	1,293	59	13	5	27	51	60	104	7	5
Elmore	1,154	6.6	42,033	2,188	529	143	51	115	248	296	837	41	51
Franklin	576	13.2	40,495	2,391	140	30	13	76	75	125	258	16	13
Fremont	539	10.4	40,803	2,353	143	28	13	90	98	134	274	16	13
Gem	NA	NA	NA	NA	NA	NA	NA	NA	NA	NA	NA	NA	NA
Gooding	1,071	17.6	68,597	185	268	44	26	441	109	180	779	23	26
Idaho	659	12.2	39,182	2,545	193	41	17	72	146	213	323	24	17
Jefferson	1,232	11.5	40,288	2,421	283	52	25	203	164	244	563	33	25
Jerome	1,040	11.8	42,332	2,152	418	67	39	275	129	215	799	38	39
Kootenai	8,353	7.8	48,953	1,264	3,130	496	276	615	1,715	2,036	4,517	333	276
Latah	1,794	7.2	43,944	1,955	613	141	52	173	392	361	979	62	52
Lemhi	386	11.0	47,981	1,396	111	23	10	37	97	130	180	14	10
Lewis	211	12.4	54,918	706	63	13	6	30	29	92	112	9	6
Lincoln	244	13.8	45,593	1,717	71	15	7	92	26	51	184	8	7
Madison	1,243	8.8	30,838	3,080	638	118	57	190	163	322	1,003	58	57
Minidoka	992	15.8	46,743	1,545	366	63	33	191	148	207	652	33	33
Nez Perce	2,060	9.6	50,550	1,084	1,030	173	92	198	388	540	1,493	102	92
Oneida	195	12.8	43,117	2,047	43	10	4	25	26	54	82	5	4
Owyhee	517	13.3	42,616	2,114	116	21	11	125	73	123	274	12	11
Payette	1,098	10.6	44,312	1,900	296	52	27	143	180	292	518	35	27
Power	404	24.6	52,807	867	178	32	16	125	48	79	351	15	16
Shoshone	529	13.9	40,953	2,339	211	36	18	18	93	194	282	24	18
Teton	544	9.0	43,521	2,009	161	24	15	71	136	87	271	17	15
Twin Falls	3,900	8.9	44,112	1,927	1,651	268	146	589	621	954	2,655	165	146
Valley	617	7.1	52,298	910	203	35	18	59	209	146	315	23	18
Washington	415	12.2	40,050	2,450	109	22	10	35	82	144	176	14	10
ILLINOIS	792,135	5.8	61,957	X	394,161	62,664	26,329	61,447	151,530	157,539	544,601	31,225	26,329
Adams	3,354	7.8	51,779	951	1,594	292	112	276	588	889	2,274	137	112
Alexander	238	9.4	43,272	2,030	50	14	3	17	27	122	83	6	3
Bond	679	8.5	41,745	2,236	208	53	14	48	101	215	323	21	14
Boone	2,695	5.2	51,066	1,018	862	168	69	102	379	607	1,201	75	69
Brown	269	10.6	41,094	2,323	233	44	16	21	40	62	315	17	16
Bureau	1,521	10.1	47,081	1,503	546	103	41	71	245	427	760	50	41
Calhoun	220	7.4	47,665	1,433	27	8	2	21	30	66	58	4	2
Carroll	724	13.9	50,871	1,042	202	49	16	98	119	216	366	23	16
Cass	573	14.7	48,079	1,378	263	51	19	56	65	162	390	22	19
Champaign	10,289	7.7	49,187	1,231	5,572	1,321	342	680	1,971	1,887	7,915	382	342
Christian	1,503	10.0	46,873	1,529	434	92	31	163	200	473	720	45	31
Clark	711	9.5	46,560	1,569	192	46	14	65	104	215	318	20	14
Clay	596	14.1	45,559	1,721	207	52	15	39	79	222	312	19	15
Clinton	1,911	6.3	51,095	1,017	477	104	34	147	279	451	762	44	34
Coles	2,316	8.3	45,967	1,658	1,105	250	73	230	353	629	1,658	91	73
Cook	357,246	5.5	69,935	167	199,451	28,475	13,067	31,408	76,721	69,020	272,401	15,460	13,067
Crawford	944	8.2	50,986	1,033	382	114	26	91	142	254	612	34	26
Cumberland	853	8.5	80,116	79	119	26	10	387	56	132	542	12	10
DeKalb	4,760	8.0	45,555	1,723	1,930	437	128	299	775	1,062	2,794	151	128
De Witt	820	12.2	53,339	832	301	70	20	83	118	207	474	27	20
Douglas	1,087	9.4	55,721	660	364	78	27	190	135	230	658	36	27
DuPage	72,597	3.1	79,127	85	44,713	6,093	3,048	6,156	14,319	9,568	60,010	3,390	3,048
Edgar	816	14.2	48,411	1,337	329	70	24	78	100	257	501	30	24
Edwards	288	10.6	45,295	1,754	94	22	7	39	43	79	162	10	7
Effingham	1,868	8.0	54,838	711	1,038	176	77	183	334	423	1,474	86	77
Fayette	867	12.2	40,786	2,356	213	51	15	87	123	280	366	22	15
Ford	758	12.5	58,512	495	237	51	16	140	92	178	444	23	16
Franklin	1,584	9.2	41,625	2,250	380	86	28	90	192	623	585	44	28
Fulton	1,424	9.4	42,264	2,159	341	88	23	95	196	483	548	37	23
Gallatin	234	13.4	48,856	1,276	44	9	3	34	33	86	91	6	3
Greene	539	16.3	42,437	2,139	103	25	7	71	58	173	207	13	7
Grundy	3,155	4.1	61,862	354	1,349	269	95	499	439	538	2,212	122	95
Hamilton	390	10.6	48,255	1,354	86	20	6	49	63	122	162	9	6
Hancock	895	13.7	51,388	988	162	40	11	143	121	256	356	21	11

1. Based on the resident population estimated as of July 1 of the year shown.

STATE County	Earnings, 2020 (cont.) — Percent by selected industries: Farm	Mining, quarrying, and extractions	Construction	Manu-facturing	Information; professional, scientific, technical services	Retail trade	Finance, insurance, real estate, and leasing	Health care and social assistance	Govern-ment	Social Security beneficiaries, December 2020: Number	Rate[1]	Supple-mental Security Income recipients, 2020	Housing units, 2021: Total	Percent change, 2010–2021
	75	76	77	78	79	80	81	82	83	84	85	86	87	88
IDAHO—Cont'd														
Caribou	11.6	18.0	7.2	26.0	3.0	2.8	1.5	7.6	12.9	1,495	210	72	3,131	0.6
Cassia	32.9	0.6	5.6	9.6	2.9	6.4	4.6	7.6	8.5	4,515	179	400	8,970	1.3
Clark	35.3	0.1	D	D	D	D	D	D	23.6	145	183	D	485	0.2
Clearwater	3.1	D	5.8	12.3	2.6	5.2	2.8	D	33.3	3,000	337	246	4,598	0.9
Custer	18.3	7.1	8.0	D	4.8	4.4	2.3	D	24.2	1,450	327	72	3,078	1.7
Elmore	12.1	0.0	2.9	4.7	1.8	4.8	2.0	5.2	55.6	5,195	180	615	12,159	0.8
Franklin	20.0	1.1	8.4	7.2	D	7.4	5.1	D	21.6	2,610	178	162	5,096	1.8
Fremont	22.4	D	14.0	2.2	D	4.8	D	3.6	22.3	2,780	205	171	8,623	1.6
Gem	NA	NA	NA	NA	NA	NA	NA	NA	NA	5,345	270	408	7,746	2.0
Gooding	61.0	D	2.5	7.6	D	2.0	D	D	6.3	3,285	208	298	6,078	0.6
Idaho	8.9	2.2	9.4	9.9	3.4	5.1	4.3	9.2	26.2	4,725	277	319	8,887	0.1
Jefferson	18.6	0.2	12.0	12.8	2.7	7.7	5.0	4.4	11.7	4,755	148	340	10,489	2.8
Jerome	32.2	0.0	4.5	14.2	D	6.0	D	3.6	7.9	4,025	163	392	8,685	1.1
Kootenai	0.2	0.6	10.4	8.1	8.2	9.7	7.9	12.8	19.0	42,655	237	2,538	78,262	3.9
Latah	3.9	D	5.8	2.3	8.4	7.5	4.8	10.7	39.3	7,045	175	528	17,413	0.7
Lemhi	11.0	0.6	9.3	2.6	7.9	6.6	3.8	D	33.2	2,865	351	174	4,620	0.9
Lewis	18.2	D	6.0	8.2	D	6.5	D	5.0	22.5	2,285	615	268	1,821	0.6
Lincoln	52.0	0.0	5.0	6.6	D	D	D	3.7	15.4	965	183	72	1,969	0.9
Madison	6.5	0.1	5.3	5.5	7.0	8.0	3.8	D	13.9	3,490	65	331	14,850	4.5
Minidoka	26.4	D	5.6	13.8	3.5	5.4	3.7	D	13.8	4,075	186	377	8,408	2.1
Nez Perce	2.3	D	5.8	20.9	4.6	7.4	9.4	15.2	17.3	11,015	259	973	18,491	0.6
Oneida	25.7	D	D	2.1	3.2	5.9	D	2.9	28.8	1,115	242	63	2,035	1.1
Owyhee	46.8	D	5.7	3.6	3.6	3.6	2.4	D	12.6	2,635	214	246	4,773	0.9
Payette	15.3	0.2	6.2	13.7	D	5.2	D	13.1	10.7	6,390	243	539	9,953	2.6
Power	36.7	0.0	1.4	24.3	D	D	D	D	10.0	1,505	189	126	2,953	0.4
Shoshone	-0.1	D	5.4	3.1	5.7	19.2	3.5	8.1	18.9	4,230	311	437	7,028	0.4
Teton	7.7	D	20.6	2.7	10.6	6.7	3.4	7.5	12.3	1,585	129	44	6,099	4.2
Twin Falls	11.5	D	5.3	13.1	5.1	8.2	5.6	16.0	11.1	18,105	196	1,824	35,826	2.7
Valley	1.8	D	10.3	1.1	D	10.2	8.7	11.1	23.4	3,245	265	120	12,524	2.3
Washington	14.7	D	5.0	17.3	7.0	6.7	3.4	D	23.8	3,365	309	292	4,569	1.0
ILLINOIS	1.0	0.2	4.8	10.3	14.6	5.0	11.9	10.5	13.5	2,274,372	179	259,810	5,440,401	0.2
Adams	3.6	0.8	5.4	14.8	4.2	7.5	7.5	20.3	10.9	15,495	239	1,347	30,268	0.1
Alexander	14.5	D	1.3	11.6	D	2.3	D	D	30.1	1,615	321	310	2,944	0.0
Bond	7.8	0.0	5.9	18.5	D	3.7	2.7	D	26.2	3,800	229	307	6,866	0.1
Boone	1.4	D	10.4	44.2	2.4	3.9	2.7	4.9	14.1	10,575	199	558	20,191	0.1
Brown	3.6	D	4.7	0.7	D	1.3	D	D	11.2	1,105	172	68	2,329	0.0
Bureau	2.5	D	6.2	15.7	3.3	5.4	3.8	11.4	18.7	8,305	253	444	15,684	0.5
Calhoun	25.0	D	8.0	D	D	7.6	5.8	D	26.9	1,285	294	89	2,289	0.3
Carroll	18.2	D	5.5	12.9	D	3.7	5.9	D	25.6	4,210	268	236	8,182	0.3
Cass	11.4	0.0	D	D	D	3.7	4.1	D	13.2	2,635	206	233	5,678	0.1
Champaign	2.0	D	4.7	6.0	7.0	5.2	5.1	15.6	37.8	28,970	141	3,262	94,741	1.5
Christian	12.8	D	4.9	14.7	D	6.3	4.0	D	14.9	8,250	245	628	15,174	-0.1
Clark	13.7	1.2	6.9	25.5	4.4	5.6	4.5	3.8	16.0	3,940	258	285	7,322	0.0
Clay	7.5	1.7	2.0	33.7	D	5.7	3.2	D	20.3	3,405	259	289	6,152	0.1
Clinton	7.2	0.2	12.1	10.4	2.8	9.5	5.1	10.0	21.7	7,740	210	290	15,697	0.6
Coles	3.2	0.2	4.7	7.3	D	10.2	8.6	15.3	23.4	10,020	214	1,199	22,712	-0.1
Cook	0.0	0.1	3.4	6.4	20.5	4.0	16.3	10.1	11.6	805,045	156	141,768	2,268,057	0.1
Crawford	4.9	1.3	5.6	42.1	6.4	5.1	3.3	D	16.1	4,685	251	343	8,462	-0.1
Cumberland	69.0	D	D	D	0.3	3.0	D	4.0	6.0	2,575	249	151	4,725	0.0
DeKalb	3.4	D	9.8	12.0	D	8.0	4.1	11.6	28.3	16,180	161	1,157	41,437	0.3
De Witt	11.3	D	7.0	8.6	D	8.0	2.4	D	15.1	3,715	242	235	7,318	0.1
Douglas	10.0	D	10.4	37.3	D	4.6	3.7	3.0	10.2	4,110	208	245	8,485	0.2
DuPage	0.0	0.1	6.2	9.4	15.6	4.9	10.3	10.4	7.8	154,575	167	7,906	366,283	0.3
Edgar	10.7	0.0	3.1	33.0	2.8	4.1	9.1	D	13.2	4,500	272	397	8,224	-0.1
Edwards	12.6	D	D	D	D	4.1	D	1.5	10.2	1,600	263	72	3,041	0.0
Effingham	4.1	D	8.6	13.9	D	7.7	4.3	17.5	8.2	7,830	227	441	15,375	0.3
Fayette	14.1	1.5	6.6	5.8	3.0	7.6	6.7	D	21.5	4,850	227	384	8,828	0.0
Ford	16.1	D	6.6	14.9	3.0	4.5	2.3	D	11.5	3,135	232	206	6,268	0.0
Franklin	4.7	6.7	8.0	6.0	D	7.9	3.9	13.0	25.3	10,360	277	1,295	18,472	0.0
Fulton	10.4	0.0	4.6	3.1	4.3	7.7	5.5	17.3	26.6	8,680	261	670	15,868	0.1
Gallatin	34.2	D	1.9	1.7	D	3.2	D	D	15.5	1,515	309	201	2,499	0.1
Greene	28.2	0.0	4.4	2.1	2.2	5.8	D	D	20.6	3,035	256	364	5,782	0.0
Grundy	2.3	2.6	13.1	19.4	D	8.6	2.7	7.1	10.4	9,805	185	414	21,363	0.7
Hamilton	20.4	D	6.6	3.5	D	4.1	4.4	4.1	19.7	1,970	249	184	3,807	0.0
Hancock	26.8	0.5	5.7	5.2	5.2	4.1	5.7	D	16.5	4,870	280	276	8,941	-0.1

1. Per 1,000 resident population estimated as of July 1 of the year shown.

STATE County	Housing units, 2016–2020: Total	Occupied units: Owner-occupied: Percent	Owner-occupied: Median value[1]	Median owner cost as a percent of income: With a mortgage	Median owner cost as a percent of income: Without a mortgage[2]	Renter-occupied: Median rent[3]	Renter-occupied: Median rent as a percent of income[2]	Sub-standard units[4] (percent)	Civilian labor force, 2021: Total	Percent change, 2020–2021	Unemployment: Total	Unemployment: Rate[5]	Civilian employment[6], 2016–2020: Total	Percent: Management, business, science, and arts	Percent: Construction, production, and maintenance occupations
	89	90	91	92	93	94	95	96	97	98	99	100	101	102	103
IDAHO—Cont'd															
Caribou	2,562	78.1	151,100	18.2	10.0	625	20.0	3.6	4,128	0.1	128	3.1	3,233	28.2	39.7
Cassia	7,832	69.1	168,400	19.5	10.0	701	22.4	3.8	12,613	1.3	365	2.9	10,376	30.1	38.4
Clark	332	54.5	122,900	41.7	10.1	669	31.7	2.4	377	-0.3	12	3.2	341	18.8	51.6
Clearwater	3,547	76.0	167,700	23.8	10.2	748	29.4	2.4	3,033	-0.4	196	6.5	2,962	27.6	26.3
Custer	1,889	79.7	216,700	30.8	15.0	707	36.0	1.1	2,279	1.8	106	4.7	1,610	34.9	18.4
Elmore	10,885	61.0	164,400	22.8	10.0	869	27.8	2.3	12,015	0.9	449	3.7	9,612	24.8	37.2
Franklin	4,432	83.8	222,200	20.5	10.0	745	33.6	4.9	7,369	2.6	182	2.5	6,241	27.6	39.6
Fremont	4,464	81.3	168,400	20.8	10.1	713	29.6	5.2	8,191	3.4	236	2.9	5,318	26.7	37.6
Gem	6,822	75.5	198,700	21.1	10.0	664	26.7	4.9	8,739	2.6	359	4.1	7,765	28.3	33.7
Gooding	5,615	69.7	156,500	18.7	10.0	736	27.6	3.5	8,381	1.0	264	3.1	6,775	27.8	39.2
Idaho	6,462	77.5	197,200	25.0	10.0	711	23.7	3.5	6,822	1.2	335	4.9	6,314	30.9	29.3
Jefferson	8,825	81.2	223,900	21.5	10.0	853	20.9	5.1	14,673	3.3	399	2.7	13,489	37.7	29.1
Jerome	8,004	68.1	178,300	21.5	10.0	761	24.6	3.7	12,348	1.4	412	3.3	11,289	28.4	41.5
Kootenai	64,475	71.3	294,100	22.3	10.0	1,037	29.3	2.1	82,719	1.0	3,540	4.3	75,049	34.5	23.2
Latah	15,737	55.4	245,200	20.0	10.0	728	30.6	3.0	19,857	0.6	660	3.3	20,139	43.1	20.0
Lemhi	3,717	78.9	192,100	23.2	11.5	627	35.6	3.7	3,713	1.6	198	5.3	3,251	33.9	26.8
Lewis	1,649	74.6	150,000	22.3	10.6	585	25.8	3.3	1,661	0.2	94	5.7	1,379	31.3	29.9
Lincoln	1,804	69.3	152,500	25.9	10.0	660	24.1	5.3	2,698	1.5	120	4.4	2,632	22.3	40.9
Madison	11,858	41.7	229,800	20.5	10.0	775	37.8	10.1	23,322	4.1	512	2.2	19,046	40.5	19.4
Minidoka	7,456	71.0	155,600	19.3	10.0	717	25.2	4.9	11,852	1.4	372	3.1	9,327	23.7	46.4
Nez Perce	16,548	73.0	205,600	19.7	10.0	731	32.0	2.4	20,918	0.1	683	3.3	19,082	32.2	28.4
Oneida	1,715	82.0	182,700	22.5	11.0	731	27.5	2.0	2,578	9.8	64	2.5	1,896	34.4	34.2
Owyhee	4,429	71.9	160,900	23.4	10.0	662	23.6	7.2	5,604	0.9	243	4.3	5,135	26.5	43.5
Payette	9,086	70.7	183,600	20.0	10.2	740	23.5	6.0	12,081	0.6	483	4.0	10,341	27.4	38.1
Power	2,693	66.1	149,100	18.9	10.0	647	18.6	2.3	4,159	0.5	160	3.8	3,543	28.8	45.0
Shoshone	5,436	71.9	133,000	20.1	12.5	722	26.5	1.9	5,499	0.5	364	6.6	5,095	24.3	32.5
Teton	4,290	78.1	358,100	21.9	10.9	968	23.3	1.3	7,105	6.0	207	2.9	6,332	42.4	18.1
Twin Falls	31,758	69.6	182,100	21.3	10.8	828	28.2	2.7	42,103	1.3	1,503	3.6	40,519	32.9	32.2
Valley	3,920	82.9	306,900	23.0	10.5	851	35.6	2.7	5,784	1.6	304	5.3	4,772	30.5	16.8
Washington	4,263	72.6	163,000	22.6	12.3	700	34.7	2.5	4,838	1.4	211	4.4	3,947	25.6	32.9
ILLINOIS	4,884,061	66.3	202,100	21.0	12.6	1,038	28.7	2.7	6,318,915	-0.8	382,941	6.1	6,236,755	39.8	22.0
Adams	27,199	71.6	130,500	18.2	10.0	692	28.2	2.1	30,856	-0.9	1,209	3.9	32,800	32.9	26.0
Alexander	2,252	74.8	56,100	24.7	13.4	643	26.9	1.1	1,831	-0.2	149	8.1	1,943	25.7	26.7
Bond	6,359	73.3	116,900	19.1	12.5	603	22.9	5.0	7,425	0.4	341	4.6	7,066	28.9	30.5
Boone	18,799	82.4	160,600	20.9	11.0	927	28.4	2.8	24,982	-1.3	2,133	8.5	25,691	31.5	31.6
Brown	2,090	76.6	99,800	16.5	10.5	485	25.0	2.7	3,012	1.0	75	2.5	2,307	30.4	32.8
Bureau	13,801	75.3	103,900	18.5	11.1	693	24.7	1.2	16,347	-0.2	811	5.0	15,846	27.1	33.6
Calhoun	1,661	88.7	131,800	18.0	10.3	546	29.1	1.9	2,164	-0.3	103	4.8	2,029	45.1	23.3
Carroll	6,511	75.8	102,200	18.3	12.0	621	22.3	0.5	7,545	1.5	319	4.2	6,444	31.7	35.5
Cass	5,068	75.4	81,700	18.1	11.7	627	21.7	1.8	5,667	-2.5	278	4.9	5,761	22.4	40.4
Champaign	83,059	53.1	166,600	18.8	10.7	873	31.8	3.7	108,489	1.5	5,259	4.8	102,846	47.6	16.9
Christian	13,977	73.9	93,200	17.9	11.8	677	26.1	1.3	13,401	-0.7	730	5.4	14,879	33.4	28.6
Clark	6,726	78.0	94,900	17.6	10.3	697	23.8	1.3	7,233	-0.7	363	5.0	7,521	29.6	35.5
Clay	5,607	74.3	84,400	17.6	10.3	625	19.7	2.2	5,900	-4.7	326	5.5	6,042	30.5	38.1
Clinton	14,596	79.6	145,700	18.7	11.8	777	25.6	2.1	19,742	0.5	681	3.4	18,409	39.0	29.4
Coles	20,972	60.1	105,100	18.9	11.3	678	27.8	2.3	22,756	-1.3	1,165	5.1	25,085	34.2	27.3
Cook	1,991,474	57.2	255,500	23.1	14.0	1,160	29.0	3.5	2,594,101	-1.1	182,546	7.0	2,560,882	42.4	19.4
Crawford	7,704	76.8	94,100	16.5	11.2	650	25.1	2.7	8,469	1.0	426	5.0	7,962	28.8	32.4
Cumberland	4,229	81.2	106,300	17.8	11.0	589	18.6	1.7	5,920	-0.1	246	4.2	5,665	26.9	36.0
DeKalb	38,616	57.9	182,300	20.5	13.1	917	30.2	1.6	53,006	0.3	2,994	5.6	54,162	33.7	24.7
De Witt	6,732	76.2	103,600	18.5	10.6	686	27.3	0.7	7,094	1.4	346	4.9	7,715	30.8	30.4
Douglas	7,600	75.9	120,500	18.1	10.9	734	26.2	3.1	10,153	1.9	375	3.7	9,573	27.8	34.8
DuPage	344,314	73.0	315,600	21.6	13.1	1,365	27.5	2.5	499,576	-0.7	22,481	4.5	489,746	47.3	16.7
Edgar	7,851	74.4	82,800	16.6	11.8	653	26.4	0.7	8,931	0.6	359	4.0	8,109	30.0	37.2
Edwards	2,756	80.3	81,000	17.0	10.0	609	25.7	1.7	2,550	-3.8	130	5.1	2,852	28.8	42.8
Effingham	13,856	76.7	151,700	18.8	10.8	654	21.8	3.2	19,397	1.1	753	3.9	17,278	32.0	29.1
Fayette	7,918	81.3	93,200	17.7	12.2	610	27.0	2.0	9,804	1.1	501	5.1	8,794	26.3	32.0
Ford	5,824	74.2	98,600	18.2	12.3	645	28.9	0.8	6,207	0.8	275	4.4	6,384	34.3	30.1
Franklin	16,207	75.0	77,000	18.9	11.4	645	30.9	2.3	15,656	-1.8	1,038	6.6	15,961	28.2	31.7
Fulton	14,072	78.8	92,600	17.8	11.1	650	27.4	0.8	14,421	-0.9	820	5.7	14,753	32.7	29.7
Gallatin	2,274	77.0	76,400	16.6	11.8	460	28.6	0.9	1,954	-2.7	119	6.1	1,950	27.5	39.4
Greene	4,984	77.5	83,400	17.0	10.7	607	27.5	1.0	5,874	-0.1	273	4.6	6,045	27.1	30.7
Grundy	20,071	72.8	199,800	20.5	12.7	987	24.2	1.4	25,122	-1.0	1,326	5.3	25,456	32.0	31.7
Hamilton	3,366	77.7	104,900	18.2	10.3	660	22.6	1.5	4,208	0.2	183	4.3	3,448	34.8	33.9
Hancock	7,542	81.6	88,500	17.1	10.3	652	22.7	1.3	8,079	0.2	348	4.3	8,151	30.9	33.5

1. Specified owner-occupied units. 2. A value of 10.0 represents 10 percent or less; a value of 50.0 represents 50 percent or more. 3. Specified renter-occupied units. 4. Overcrowded or lacking complete plumbing facilities. 5. Percent of civilian labor force. 6. Civilian employed persons 16 years old and over.

STATE County	Private nonfarm establishments, employment and payroll, 2020: Number of establish-ments	Employment: Total	Employment: Health care and social assistance	Employment: Manufac-turing	Employment: Retail trade	Employment: Finance and insurance	Employment: Professional, scientific, and technical services	Annual payroll: Total (mil dol)	Annual payroll: Average per employee (dollars)	Agriculture, 2017: Farms: Number	Farms: Percent with: Fewer than 50 acres	Farms: Percent with: 1000 acres or more	Farm producers whose primary occupation is farming (percent)
	104	105	106	107	108	109	110	111	112	113	114	115	116
IDAHO—Cont'd													
Caribou	181	1,760	316	467	290	43	55	92	52,385	411	28.2	23.6	48.2
Cassia	714	8,417	1,390	1,416	1,142	160	194	312	37,036	585	44.3	25.3	51.7
Clark	13	90	NA	NA	NA	NA	NA	4	44,133	68	19.1	38.2	52.1
Clearwater	228	1,724	497	207	229	45	37	75	43,430	312	50.6	3.8	36.9
Custer	183	760	99	16	174	16	23	31	41,371	267	34.8	12.0	50.6
Elmore	455	4,444	746	662	1,037	181	184	153	34,330	340	59.4	14.1	41.5
Franklin	332	2,470	456	359	576	69	50	87	35,064	787	44.7	7.6	33.9
Fremont	325	1,929	261	133	295	28	32	74	38,511	513	37.4	9.7	36.9
Gem	425	3,049	861	238	491	58	127	109	35,775	860	77.4	3.4	39.7
Gooding	351	2,970	739	720	339	62	70	125	42,176	538	58.6	7.6	50.9
Idaho	502	3,585	732	620	488	134	73	149	41,698	708	32.1	17.1	45.5
Jefferson	578	4,713	325	977	641	89	152	173	36,771	750	60.0	10.0	41.7
Jerome	571	6,926	513	1,823	952	104	89	286	41,327	486	49.8	7.8	55.3
Kootenai	5,372	57,834	10,949	5,161	8,913	2,354	2,897	2,506	43,334	1,073	68.7	2.1	32.1
Latah	955	9,394	1,643	310	1,851	199	641	296	31,462	1,041	48.7	9.1	34.3
Lemhi	292	1,969	586	86	359	36	77	64	32,703	351	48.1	8.8	42.8
Lewis	106	844	30	182	222	42	NA	28	33,408	197	26.9	27.9	50.0
Lincoln	89	567	94	157	64	6	28	21	37,651	276	32.6	13.0	59.4
Madison	994	19,738	2,083	1,110	1,808	355	802	506	25,612	454	50.7	10.8	47.3
Minidoka	469	5,761	625	1,153	768	157	133	272	47,238	620	51.8	9.0	49.5
Nez Perce	1,138	16,755	2,938	3,400	2,441	1,151	488	733	43,744	446	47.3	24.2	42.4
Oneida	99	762	196	49	183	63	6	25	32,920	422	28.7	23.0	36.1
Owyhee	218	2,061	285	158	233	24	110	69	33,429	565	46.2	15.2	55.6
Payette	554	5,976	903	1,437	494	167	240	251	41,954	640	70.3	3.1	40.6
Power	176	2,259	166	688	171	48	36	92	40,540	295	29.2	39.3	52.6
Shoshone	341	4,011	687	162	958	57	151	165	41,136	48	75.0	NA	30.0
Teton	562	2,859	326	146	398	40	127	124	43,405	277	38.6	12.3	44.0
Twin Falls	2,778	32,298	6,457	3,780	5,292	863	1,205	1,185	36,691	1,211	51.6	5.9	49.6
Valley	686	4,431	546	91	599	63	105	155	35,054	188	57.4	6.4	33.4
Washington	210	2,066	362	609	309	32	66	68	32,770	535	49.7	15.0	50.2
ILLINOIS	318,689	5,545,538	829,966	542,154	583,926	344,625	413,214	329,401	59,399	72,651	35.6	10.8	43.4
Adams	1,746	31,217	6,599	5,474	4,549	1,440	759	1,399	44,826	1,308	26.8	9.9	42.8
Alexander	83	895	178	146	61	13	9	37	41,834	126	30.2	11.9	36.5
Bond	307	3,572	476	748	343	117	49	131	36,727	637	46.3	7.4	36.7
Boone	837	15,449	944	8,138	1,286	190	529	815	52,735	457	54.5	5.5	47.4
Brown	110	3,711	144	139	133	42	24	175	47,199	419	25.3	7.2	30.2
Bureau	701	9,439	2,119	1,523	1,022	314	156	444	47,069	1,038	28.9	13.8	46.5
Calhoun	70	467	88	NA	92	52	9	12	26,368	474	25.7	5.3	34.2
Carroll	358	3,197	453	843	429	179	50	124	38,936	627	31.6	9.4	47.3
Cass	234	4,608	332	2,279	413	161	48	208	45,214	429	29.1	14.5	36.9
Champaign	4,216	69,928	14,703	6,131	9,506	3,228	2,603	3,227	46,154	1,214	33.1	16.0	50.0
Christian	700	7,315	1,447	787	1,283	333	141	313	42,802	794	33.8	16.5	48.2
Clark	333	3,669	242	1,087	442	156	165	134	36,580	733	37.8	10.8	38.2
Clay	336	4,880	681	2,308	515	114	105	205	41,917	732	37.8	8.6	37.4
Clinton	862	8,948	1,859	849	1,686	293	199	315	35,224	831	32.4	6.0	39.1
Coles	1,113	19,137	4,831	2,639	2,435	754	464	765	39,975	701	39.8	10.4	39.1
Cook	133,921	2,448,843	386,104	179,149	226,169	197,167	245,217	165,872	67,735	182	78.6	0.5	34.7
Crawford	411	6,187	846	2,133	713	221	223	283	45,782	566	38.0	11.3	41.4
Cumberland	186	1,960	334	616	218	88	18	63	31,919	724	40.2	4.8	34.3
DeKalb	1,963	28,276	5,071	4,024	4,317	766	1,079	1,215	42,983	779	35.3	14.2	53.7
De Witt	351	4,318	508	502	659	101	212	244	56,419	504	44.6	12.5	43.4
Douglas	560	6,743	326	2,869	811	201	103	307	45,602	600	45.5	12.5	40.5
DuPage	33,953	585,430	68,925	52,753	56,235	33,148	51,050	37,027	63,248	77	87.0	NA	41.8
Edgar	327	6,110	1,055	2,504	582	194	77	249	40,778	637	30.3	16.6	48.2
Edwards	142	1,892	79	1,127	149	68	28	82	43,437	291	31.3	11.3	40.8
Effingham	1,241	28,511	3,022	3,350	2,759	434	442	1,199	42,050	1,193	37.6	6.1	35.5
Fayette	476	4,647	827	318	750	239	115	155	33,294	1,239	38.7	8.2	37.1
Ford	337	4,277	1,307	781	514	114	100	183	42,877	564	29.8	13.8	49.5
Franklin	688	6,801	903	557	1,343	224	153	235	34,599	596	41.4	7.6	38.1
Fulton	592	5,837	1,706	132	1,225	342	197	199	34,175	973	27.9	12.7	45.4
Gallatin	78	518	94	17	50	20	20	24	45,905	165	20.0	21.8	60.6
Greene	213	1,646	332	92	373	124	72	57	34,403	733	25.9	14.2	43.0
Grundy	1,170	17,728	2,558	1,618	2,273	310	680	929	52,400	412	29.6	19.2	49.7
Hamilton	185	1,566	440	73	140	42	41	59	37,365	552	30.4	10.5	32.8
Hancock	368	2,788	486	372	447	159	202	118	42,410	1,109	26.1	12.4	47.5

STATE County	Agriculture, 2017 (cont.) — Land in farms — Acreage (1,000)	Land in farms — Percent change, 2012–2017	Land in farms — Acres — Average size of farm	Land in farms — Acres — Total irrigated (1,000)	Land in farms — Acres — Total cropland (1,000)	Value of land and buildings (dollars) — Average per farm	Value of land and buildings (dollars) — Average per acre	Value of machinery and equipment, average per farm (dollars)	Value of products sold: — Total (mil dol)	Value of products sold: — Average per farm (acres)	Value of products sold: — Percent from: — Crops	Value of products sold: — Percent from: — Livestock and poultry products	Organic farms (number)	Farms with internet access (percent)	Government payments — Total ($1,000)	Government payments — Percent of farms
	117	118	119	120	121	122	123	124	125	126	127	128	129	130	131	132
IDAHO—Cont'd																
Caribou	366	-7.1	892	61.1	217.1	1,654,989	1,856	219,066	90.3	219,757	62.2	37.8	1	81.8	3,905	52.8
Cassia	643	5.3	1,100	259.3	385.0	3,508,509	3,190	512,076	926.7	1,584,137	27.6	72.4	4	87.9	11,088	38.6
Clark	149	-1.2	2,197	31.6	40.7	3,856,994	1,755	320,235	25.9	380,309	74.4	25.6	2	75.0	1,490	55.9
Clearwater	57	-22.1	181	D	24.8	447,579	2,469	54,776	7.3	23,487	46.8	53.2	NA	79.5	639	18.3
Custer	148	3.5	554	60.1	49.7	1,509,320	2,726	169,068	36.4	136,468	23.7	76.3	3	90.3	343	13.1
Elmore	358	4.0	1,054	113.2	148.9	2,626,980	2,492	400,675	429.9	1,264,462	27.8	72.2	7	82.6	684	11.5
Franklin	228	-13.0	290	65.3	132.1	674,740	2,325	128,763	82.8	105,187	31.1	68.9	26	83.5	2,730	39.6
Fremont	280	-11.6	545	101.9	171.0	1,507,845	2,767	225,633	138.2	269,419	84.7	15.3	NA	80.7	4,130	38.8
Gem	183	2.3	213	29.9	28.3	599,509	2,815	69,848	39.2	45,560	39.6	60.4	8	85.2	834	10.9
Gooding	188	-21.4	350	121.8	125.3	2,106,203	6,016	286,549	783.4	1,456,113	9.3	90.7	9	83.3	2,416	16.5
Idaho	537	-15.9	759	2.7	180.6	1,248,054	1,644	112,824	43.7	61,689	54.8	45.2	NA	79.2	3,060	36.4
Jefferson	334	3.3	445	198.3	228.3	1,566,390	3,522	264,821	294.6	392,743	58.7	41.3	6	86.9	4,603	24.4
Jerome	172	-8.7	353	134.9	134.6	2,132,761	6,039	418,233	639.6	1,316,016	18.9	81.1	16	84.2	2,050	33.5
Kootenai	140	12.4	130	13.7	62.2	719,383	5,525	49,847	21.5	20,057	81.0	19.0	3	81.7	1,211	9.9
Latah	350	-16.1	336	0.2	254.7	853,388	2,542	126,243	78.0	74,900	94.3	5.7	7	82.9	7,066	35.4
Lemhi	174	-7.2	496	72.2	46.4	1,251,971	2,526	116,297	33.3	94,818	16.6	83.4	3	89.7	295	10.0
Lewis	200	-9.4	1,017	D	151.1	1,997,866	1,964	238,202	37.8	191,787	90.2	9.8	NA	86.3	2,929	70.1
Lincoln	135	4.0	489	77.3	84.9	1,784,513	3,651	226,469	203.1	735,830	21.0	79.0	8	83.7	1,163	35.9
Madison	196	-2.6	432	125.9	160.0	1,797,444	4,162	289,620	157.0	345,855	93.2	6.8	1	90.3	3,919	39.0
Minidoka	268	9.6	432	232.7	242.6	1,958,696	4,539	300,481	354.4	571,692	73.4	26.6	6	81.9	4,319	40.2
Nez Perce	382	18.4	856	1.1	233.8	1,779,079	2,079	230,280	74.3	166,632	81.4	18.6	1	84.1	7,319	43.0
Oneida	320	-2.7	758	25.7	151.3	1,256,611	1,658	138,236	36.2	85,863	44.9	55.1	2	80.6	5,063	55.2
Owyhee	727	-2.9	1,287	119.0	137.8	2,096,160	1,628	232,705	273.4	483,851	22.6	77.4	7	82.8	2,365	21.4
Payette	163	3.5	254	59.2	57.4	890,516	3,505	141,684	167.4	261,563	30.0	70.0	3	88.1	900	12.0
Power	486	4.1	1,649	147.7	381.4	4,068,136	2,467	438,509	235.4	798,108	89.6	10.4	3	86.1	10,617	59.3
Shoshone	2	D	51	0.1	0.6	340,665	6,715	42,286	0.2	4,479	30.2	69.8	NA	77.1	NA	NA
Teton	117	-11.9	424	48.9	84.4	1,675,941	3,954	180,866	45.3	163,679	90.4	9.6	16	89.9	865	28.9
Twin Falls	469	-3.1	387	241.5	257.3	1,718,569	4,439	225,875	680.2	561,716	24.8	75.2	26	88.2	4,456	29.7
Valley	51	-16.8	271	22.1	4.3	703,011	2,594	62,528	10.5	56,069	8.7	91.3	1	67.6	84	4.3
Washington	468	9.8	876	38.8	80.4	1,185,859	1,354	132,560	50.2	93,918	41.8	58.2	6	80.7	1,591	28.4
ILLINOIS	27,006	0.3	372	612.5	24,003.1	2,705,291	7,278	220,485	17,010.0	234,133	81.4	18.6	328	76.9	521,229	66.9
Adams	478	22.9	365	11.0	382.8	2,376,117	6,506	227,632	269.4	205,979	73.2	26.8	9	75.7	4,870	60.0
Alexander	50	-19.1	401	2.6	43.1	1,371,640	3,423	144,673	16.6	131,889	98.5	1.5	NA	81.0	1,130	61.9
Bond	173	-12.9	271	0.0	149.8	1,865,147	6,874	180,014	84.8	133,047	89.7	10.3	2	76.9	3,877	60.3
Boone	114	-15.8	248	0.9	106.0	1,939,825	7,811	171,009	78.4	171,589	75.5	24.5	6	84.2	3,291	38.5
Brown	142	3.0	338	0.2	88.2	1,892,515	5,598	125,319	49.8	118,947	78.6	21.4	4	70.4	3,224	83.1
Bureau	437	-2.9	421	13.5	408.2	3,460,532	8,219	290,184	360.0	346,795	89.4	10.6	12	79.3	17,896	79.8
Calhoun	115	30.6	242	D	68.7	1,013,115	4,189	98,750	38.7	81,584	72.8	27.2	NA	63.5	2,393	68.6
Carroll	246	-4.1	392	10.6	210.0	3,150,456	8,039	269,522	216.8	345,845	69.0	31.0	NA	80.1	4,490	75.6
Cass	198	8.1	461	30.5	169.8	2,946,206	6,398	268,331	121.9	284,096	79.2	20.8	2	73.7	5,151	84.4
Champaign	583	-5.5	480	14.2	566.4	4,471,916	9,317	322,994	375.6	309,349	96.2	3.8	5	80.3	5,861	82.3
Christian	403	7.8	507	0.0	382.6	4,381,139	8,638	311,771	278.7	351,029	90.7	9.3	2	76.8	10,174	79.5
Clark	261	-2.1	356	11.8	227.7	2,032,961	5,708	205,302	163.3	222,795	73.9	26.1	1	71.8	4,408	77.8
Clay	294	8.9	402	D	258.7	2,058,866	5,121	214,709	116.1	158,626	86.9	13.1	NA	73.1	5,966	76.2
Clinton	236	-17.4	284	1.2	214.9	1,965,321	6,928	263,352	247.0	297,197	45.1	54.9	NA	78.1	6,067	74.8
Coles	237	-11.2	338	0.1	219.9	2,660,833	7,875	196,323	133.9	191,073	95.7	4.3	1	77.5	4,071	75.5
Cook	12	40.1	65	0.1	10.8	1,349,568	20,635	77,634	19.7	108,187	89.5	10.5	3	89.0	81	17.0
Crawford	220	2.2	388	9.1	193.5	2,039,041	5,254	213,282	108.4	191,594	90.4	9.6	NA	77.0	5,598	77.0
Cumberland	172	0.9	237	1.0	145.7	1,504,990	6,344	141,060	120.6	166,609	65.3	34.7	1	71.7	6,191	82.6
DeKalb	372	-6.5	477	0.5	362.6	4,495,730	9,420	299,674	384.2	493,178	60.9	39.1	11	87.2	8,773	71.6
De Witt	186	-4.9	369	0.2	177.1	3,094,024	8,387	202,905	120.4	238,875	91.6	8.4	5	79.6	4,331	69.0
Douglas	245	-6.9	408	0.0	236.6	3,701,396	9,071	203,298	159.5	265,888	93.9	6.1	7	64.3	3,836	57.2
DuPage	2	-70.2	28	0.0	1.6	471,456	16,807	38,061	3.9	50,377	97.6	2.4	NA	92.2	89	10.4
Edgar	318	-9.5	499	D	299.5	3,708,748	7,425	289,955	D	D	D	D	NA	80.4	7,464	82.4
Edwards	112	4.7	384	D	98.6	2,062,863	5,372	228,647	61.1	209,842	76.2	23.8	NA	78.0	3,203	80.4
Effingham	299	4.3	251	0.4	260.7	1,657,000	6,603	179,393	195.1	163,505	64.8	35.2	NA	79.2	9,626	73.8
Fayette	349	15.1	282	0.2	297.8	1,520,838	5,398	170,568	164.9	133,117	88.9	11.1	NA	70.2	6,528	63.9
Ford	270	-12.3	479	1.0	262.7	3,722,553	7,769	260,649	190.7	338,188	83.1	16.9	4	80.1	3,095	70.0
Franklin	174	-4.2	292	0.1	148.8	1,300,260	4,460	160,135	83.7	140,460	77.6	22.4	NA	67.6	3,569	54.4
Fulton	402	13.4	414	1.0	305.5	2,561,328	6,193	194,999	220.4	226,489	77.0	23.0	2	76.1	4,859	59.8
Gallatin	178	-4.5	1,078	28.0	161.3	5,719,128	5,307	451,878	92.4	559,933	97.9	2.1	NA	79.4	4,534	80.6
Greene	328	13.1	448	0.8	257.8	2,768,122	6,184	222,206	183.4	250,139	78.7	21.3	5	77.5	4,745	72.7
Grundy	233	7.4	566	D	224.9	5,018,301	8,868	344,786	135.5	328,791	97.6	2.4	NA	84.7	1,375	49.3
Hamilton	201	-10.2	363	NA	174.4	1,747,933	4,810	179,660	86.2	156,243	95.1	4.9	1	61.4	6,053	83.5
Hancock	455	17.9	411	6.8	378.2	2,911,061	7,091	222,490	320.2	288,772	69.7	30.3	NA	71.6	4,399	59.0

STATE County	Water use, 2015		Wholesale Trade[1], 2017				Retail Trade[2], 2017				Real estate and rental and leasing,[2] 2017			
	Public supply water withdrawn (mil gal/ day)	Public supply gallons withdrawn per person per day	Number of establish- ments	Number of employees	Sales (mil dol)	Average payroll (mil dol)	Number of establish- ments	Number of employees	Sales (mil dol)	Average payroll (mil dol)	Number of establish- ments	Number of employees	Sales (mil dol)	Average payroll (mil dol)
	133	134	135	136	137	138	139	140	141	142	143	144	145	146
IDAHO—Cont'd														
Caribou	1.6	230.4	13	61	169.4	2.5	33	290	92.4	7.7	5	D	1.5	D
Cassia	3.7	155.7	27	451	909.5	24.7	121	1,180	341.0	29.7	28	51	9.2	0.9
Clark	0.2	193.2	NA	NA	NA	NA	NA	NA	NA	NA	NA	NA	NA	NA
Clearwater	1.0	122.4	6	126	60.2	7.6	37	279	71.0	6.6	D	D	D	0.4
Custer	1.0	232.4	NA	NA	NA	NA	27	221	40.5	3.8	9	9	3.4	0.2
Elmore	5.6	217.2	17	104	61.3	4.2	77	991	285.4	25.7	17	34	5.8	0.9
Franklin	11.6	888.8	12	142	293.7	7.5	45	575	136.8	11.3	13	17	1.9	0.2
Fremont	1.3	104.5	13	115	108.5	4.8	43	290	91.3	7.8	16	18	4.0	0.7
Gem	0.9	51.0	D	D	D	1.5	46	467	123.3	11.7	16	26	4.8	0.7
Gooding	3.6	234.9	20	163	277.2	9.1	45	351	95.3	8.3	10	18	4.4	0.4
Idaho	0.9	57.2	14	58	57.1	2.5	65	529	98.0	12.0	13	D	1.3	D
Jefferson	1.1	39.4	27	D	1,597.0	D	60	644	209.6	17.7	D	D	D	D
Jerome	3.7	160.9	31	319	496.7	18.3	72	881	281.7	26.3	15	18	4.7	0.5
Kootenai	34.7	230.7	135	1,540	1,066.9	77.1	600	8,570	2,942.5	255.1	301	731	181.1	28.7
Latah	4.2	108.3	18	377	247.0	22.0	131	1,838	352.6	41.5	50	165	19.6	3.9
Lemhi	1.6	210.7	6	54	45.5	2.4	39	396	109.3	11.0	13	22	3.0	0.7
Lewis	0.5	139.9	7	D	81.2	D	20	202	39.5	3.6	4	11	1.2	0.3
Lincoln	0.4	75.5	NA	NA	NA	NA	13	47	16.2	1.4	NA	NA	NA	NA
Madison	3.4	88.6	42	729	343.7	27.3	191	1,749	496.0	45.6	59	261	32.8	5.4
Minidoka	2.8	137.3	49	774	533.2	38.3	61	751	215.4	18.5	12	32	7.4	1.5
Nez Perce	10.1	251.4	48	560	487.5	25.4	205	2,557	717.6	71.2	45	139	27.2	4.6
Oneida	0.7	168.2	NA	NA	NA	NA	18	162	37.9	2.7	5	D	1.6	D
Owyhee	0.7	64.5	D	D	D	D	24	160	41.2	4.6	D	D	D	0.1
Payette	1.9	84.7	22	167	86.4	6.6	56	480	158.5	13.1	29	41	7.3	1.1
Power	2.2	281.1	14	220	200.9	9.0	17	175	31.9	3.5	9	D	1.9	D
Shoshone	2.5	199.5	10	D	36.5	D	56	1,096	730.0	44.3	D	D	D	0.7
Teton	0.8	73.8	7	42	33.8	1.6	44	385	99.4	9.5	38	45	14.1	2.1
Twin Falls	15.7	191.1	132	1,309	836.6	63.1	371	5,189	1,549.2	138.9	142	352	70.5	10.5
Valley	1.6	153.4	13	59	24.2	2.9	76	457	123.8	11.8	56	122	28.4	3.7
Washington	0.7	74.1	8	147	183.4	4.5	31	289	102.2	6.8	7	8	2.0	0.4
ILLINOIS	1,475.7	114.7	15,409	272,391	311,140.6	19,071.8	38,189	629,878	173,473.9	16,246.9	13,589	82,763	32,355.2	4,824.5
Adams	10.4	154.4	D	D	D	D	286	4,946	1,095.9	115.6	64	263	42.9	7.3
Alexander	1.6	237.5	D	D	D	0.7	18	87	18.6	1.6	NA	NA	NA	NA
Bond	1.3	76.7	19	267	211.9	11.1	37	377	101.3	7.1	7	16	1.2	0.2
Boone	3.6	66.4	29	280	132.8	13.7	99	1,326	395.8	34.4	25	60	12.3	1.8
Brown	0.0	5.9	D	D	D	D	15	133	29.2	2.9	NA	NA	NA	NA
Bureau	3.0	88.1	48	950	1,461.4	45.3	89	1,067	262.9	25.0	D	D	D	0.7
Calhoun	0.4	83.7	D	D	D	0.2	14	95	24.5	2.5	NA	NA	NA	NA
Carroll	1.0	70.5	29	211	362.7	11.3	57	495	98.7	10.5	10	D	2.6	D
Cass	1.1	85.6	14	147	279.6	8.0	44	440	114.1	10.2	5	19	3.2	0.6
Champaign	24.4	116.9	165	2,935	2,433.6	134.6	615	9,880	2,470.0	232.5	231	2,083	388.5	85.4
Christian	2.6	75.8	42	621	792.1	32.2	116	1,437	425.3	35.7	19	106	12.3	3.1
Clark	1.6	100.1	20	236	225.3	8.9	45	443	137.0	11.3	6	34	5.9	1.1
Clay	0.0	0.7	24	217	163.2	8.5	53	547	125.2	12.5	7	50	8.6	0.9
Clinton	7.0	184.7	44	385	298.3	15.9	131	1,745	485.5	49.4	19	198	46.1	7.4
Coles	4.1	78.1	46	474	692.8	24.8	188	2,860	861.6	69.8	D	D	D	D
Cook	834.1	159.2	5,775	96,186	104,269.8	7,100.3	14,620	245,527	66,513.5	6,535.4	6,605	47,645	19,438.6	3,040.5
Crawford	2.2	112.3	18	184	186.7	7.7	71	748	183.4	18.2	18	75	9.8	2.6
Cumberland	0.3	24.8	D	D	D	D	29	284	63.5	4.3	NA	NA	NA	NA
DeKalb	7.6	73.2	75	884	1,039.8	45.0	251	4,426	1,043.9	97.4	76	391	80.3	13.4
De Witt	1.3	80.6	26	325	849.6	21.1	55	704	232.0	19.4	9	24	1.3	0.3
Douglas	0.7	33.8	31	327	388.5	16.4	126	1,194	204.7	20.8	9	34	4.5	1.2
DuPage	6.8	7.3	2,325	49,609	66,305.4	3,795.2	3,144	63,797	19,876.7	1,790.7	1,508	10,695	6,075.0	727.4
Edgar	1.6	89.4	10	651	277.1	22.8	54	672	183.5	16.6	10	28	3.4	0.8
Edwards	0.0	6.1	13	174	135.5	6.3	24	179	42.5	3.5	3	D	0.8	D
Effingham	2.1	59.9	63	1,416	853.5	70.1	201	2,976	875.6	73.8	35	374	50.1	13.2
Fayette	1.3	57.6	26	361	635.8	14.9	78	798	224.2	20.1	8	25	2.3	0.7
Ford	1.4	104.8	33	372	381.4	16.7	49	561	125.9	11.8	D	D	D	D
Franklin	15.4	389.8	23	229	105.4	9.5	131	1,537	392.7	36.0	13	52	6.1	1.5
Fulton	2.6	71.4	21	204	221.2	9.5	105	1,396	305.4	29.3	14	52	5.8	1.0
Gallatin	3.3	617.3	5	D	24.2	D	12	51	9.4	1.1	NA	NA	NA	NA
Greene	0.7	52.9	20	183	174.0	7.9	42	391	117.2	8.4	3	1	0.2	0.0
Grundy	3.4	67.5	42	503	562.7	29.5	146	2,498	711.4	56.9	33	99	18.5	3.1
Hamilton	0.0	0.0	8	83	79.1	4.0	32	160	43.8	3.5	5	20	2.0	0.7
Hancock	1.3	71.2	31	315	352.5	15.2	59	545	100.8	11.3	5	20	1.4	0.2

1 Merchant wholesalers, except manufacturers' sales branches and offices. 2. Employer establishments.

STATE County	Professional, scientific, and technical services, 2017				Manufacturing, 2017				Accommodation and food services, 2017			
	Number of establish-ments	Number of employees	Sales (mil dol)	Average payroll (mil dol)	Number of establish-ments	Number of employees	Sales (mil dol)	Average payroll (mil dol)	Number of establis-hments	Number of employees	Sales (mil dol)	Annual payroll (mil dol)
	147	148	149	150	151	152	153	154	155	156	157	158
IDAHO—Cont'd												
Caribou	8	29	2.3	0.7	8	D	524.2	D	18	112	3.9	1.2
Cassia	49	168	15.2	5.4	32	1,208	909.5	61.5	D	D	D	D
Clark	NA	NA	NA	NA	NA	NA	NA	NA	NA	NA	NA	NA
Clearwater	10	37	2.4	1.0	17	219	42.5	7.1	28	191	8.4	2.4
Custer	5	24	1.9	0.4	3	D	2.4	0.5	33	162	14.2	4.1
Elmore	23	110	13.8	4.0	15	581	301.3	22.2	52	665	34.6	9.4
Franklin	24	50	5.4	1.7	21	347	56.3	16.6	19	264	7.2	2.3
Fremont	10	39	2.7	1.1	10	24	7.2	1.4	35	186	17.5	4.1
Gem	31	95	12.1	4.2	16	102	9.7	3.1	24	267	13.6	3.6
Gooding	33	117	14.2	6.2	23	602	833.5	40.3	32	239	10.1	2.7
Idaho	24	64	5.5	1.7	26	524	222.3	24.4	44	243	13.5	3.6
Jefferson	35	119	14.8	3.8	D	D	D	D	D	D	D	D
Jerome	28	98	14.7	4.4	23	1,467	1,017.6	62.8	34	392	23.8	5.7
Kootenai	499	2,576	388.7	138.5	262	4,995	1,241.2	238.2	416	7,789	502.1	141.2
Latah	68	478	51.2	18.4	30	306	97.3	15.1	117	1,870	82.3	24.2
Lemhi	27	59	4.4	1.4	7	75	25.9	3.4	35	283	14.1	4.0
Lewis	D	D	0.3	D	5	147	56.6	5.4	17	D	6.6	D
Lincoln	D	D	D	D	D	D	D	D	D	D	D	0.3
Madison	D	D	D	D	30	1,076	217.5	33.6	65	1,301	53.5	14.1
Minidoka	D	D	D	D	30	989	488.4	52.3	D	D	D	D
Nez Perce	D	D	D	D	39	3,838	1,483.2	219.4	108	1,935	100.2	28.9
Oneida	5	9	0.9	0.3	5	D	9.7	2.4	D	D	D	0.9
Owyhee	9	22	4.4	0.7	D	D	D	6.2	D	D	D	D
Payette	41	175	16.2	6.4	33	1,459	300.0	42.1	30	306	11.3	3.1
Power	10	28	3.4	1.1	D	D	D	D	14	61	3.0	0.6
Shoshone	23	138	14.3	6.0	14	144	33.6	5.5	D	D	D	8.2
Teton	47	111	17.8	5.4	14	102	20.9	4.3	45	300	19.6	5.8
Twin Falls	231	1,073	138.8	47.0	93	3,691	1,605.6	172.2	202	3,687	180.1	50.1
Valley	44	96	13.0	4.3	16	78	5.7	1.9	79	995	73.7	23.4
Washington	16	60	4.6	1.5	14	537	128.2	21.5	23	221	7.9	2.1
ILLINOIS	38,649	394,230	85,306.7	33,131.2	13,162	527,862	241,484.3	30,116.3	29,025	536,245	35,314.4	10,188.5
Adams	D	D	73.8	D	80	D	3,070.5	D	D	D	D	D
Alexander	D	D	D	D	D	142	D	6.8	D	D	D	D
Bond	26	77	7.1	2.4	16	861	286.3	45.4	35	386	17.7	4.6
Boone	D	D	D	D	79	7,262	4,699.6	571.6	64	932	46.2	11.6
Brown	5	16	1.3	0.5	6	129	21.7	6.1	D	D	D	D
Bureau	43	156	18.7	6.1	39	1,589	580.6	86.4	73	727	33.5	9.1
Calhoun	NA	NA	NA	NA	3	8	2.0	0.5	D	D	D	D
Carroll	20	56	9.4	2.3	21	925	178.0	32.8	41	302	20.9	3.9
Cass	8	51	8.5	1.7	D	D	D	D	32	256	10.8	3.1
Champaign	D	D	D	D	118	6,336	2,578.8	313.1	570	11,228	574.4	169.5
Christian	37	498	21.6	8.1	20	710	471.1	44.0	74	948	39.3	11.2
Clark	20	176	22.8	12.3	17	1,202	768.9	54.9	38	427	18.6	5.0
Clay	15	85	4.8	2.0	19	2,029	973.0	102.9	26	259	11.8	3.1
Clinton	D	D	D	D	36	756	198.1	31.2	93	1,082	49.8	13.0
Coles	61	411	39.3	15.6	D	D	D	D	128	2,124	89.9	25.1
Cook	19,322	245,667	60,906.8	23,107.3	4,745	181,875	74,966.9	10,425.4	12,521	250,110	19,616.0	5,708.6
Crawford	29	265	23.2	9.3	D	1,871	D	139.3	36	555	23.0	5.6
Cumberland	6	17	1.2	0.4	D	D	D	D	13	122	3.3	1.1
DeKalb	153	1,071	180.3	53.8	113	3,564	1,308.4	181.3	210	3,331	166.4	46.2
De Witt	27	259	32.4	13.1	12	567	275.8	31.3	47	435	23.0	6.3
Douglas	28	96	8.0	2.6	76	2,647	1,010.2	139.4	66	760	36.7	9.7
DuPage	D	D	D	D	1,640	55,728	18,792.6	3,300.0	2,231	44,640	2,932.1	850.4
Edgar	28	96	10.6	3.5	20	2,884	936.8	110.8	38	364	16.8	4.5
Edwards	D	D	2.0	D	D	D	D	D	D	D	D	0.4
Effingham	68	425	52.3	18.7	63	3,204	791.0	145.1	116	2,099	109.1	30.2
Fayette	24	119	10.2	4.1	16	276	89.3	10.4	44	606	24.3	7.6
Ford	17	106	12.4	4.2	19	727	529.7	34.5	34	321	14.1	4.3
Franklin	45	213	27.7	7.9	39	510	122.4	23.1	83	966	42.6	10.7
Fulton	36	233	23.2	9.9	16	D	19.5	4.6	76	829	33.4	9.4
Gallatin	8	21	1.9	0.8	5	10	1.9	0.5	5	D	1.9	D
Greene	11	98	8.7	4.7	11	79	38.4	4.9	23	186	6.8	2.0
Grundy	91	1,008	118.5	58.7	48	1,387	1,696.9	117.7	133	1,891	101.6	26.4
Hamilton	14	37	2.9	1.0	7	58	11.7	2.4	9	130	4.8	1.5
Hancock	20	166	52.3	12.4	21	622	400.2	26.9	35	184	10.3	2.9

STATE County	Health care and social assistance, 2017				Other services, 2017				Nonemployer businesses, 2019		Value of residential construction authorized by building permits, 2021	
	Number of establish-ments	Number of employees	Receipts (mil dol)	Annual payroll (mil dol)	Number of establish-ments	Number of employees	Receipts (mil dol)	Annual payroll (mil dol)	Number	Receipts (mil dol)	New construction ($1,000)	Number of housing units
	159	160	161	162	163	164	165	166	167	168	169	170
IDAHO—Cont'd												
Caribou	21	310	27.7	12.9	D	D	D	D	505	20.4	3,487	15
Cassia	81	1,317	123.7	43.5	D	D	D	D	1,634	96.3	27,406	141
Clark	NA	NA	NA	NA	NA	NA	NA	NA	59	1.9	75	1
Clearwater	23	527	49.3	25.9	10	26	3.5	1.0	522	22.3	3,119	24
Custer	11	D	4.0	D	D	D	1.3	D	460	15.3	3,053	13
Elmore	45	759	73.7	28.1	31	106	8.7	2.3	1,393	54.3	20,777	105
Franklin	27	437	33.1	15.0	D	D	D	D	1,160	51.4	43,173	172
Fremont	22	254	19.2	8.5	15	53	8.4	1.9	1,266	63.9	34,646	180
Gem	38	757	56.8	26.7	25	78	8.3	2.2	1,395	54.7	44,133	251
Gooding	35	537	45.1	20.3	22	95	11.1	2.8	929	46.2	8,919	57
Idaho	28	822	67.7	31.0	D	D	D	D	1,356	59.2	1,880	7
Jefferson	D	D	D	7.7	D	D	D	D	2,598	129.0	69,826	377
Jerome	39	506	40.8	18.3	40	185	21.4	5.1	1,200	61.1	23,651	169
Kootenai	528	10,600	1,069.8	492.9	284	1,450	139.3	41.4	14,546	698.2	538,557	2,426
Latah	93	1,569	137.4	56.8	64	384	34.1	10.1	2,799	116.3	41,816	182
Lemhi	29	494	46.6	20.4	20	73	7.8	2.1	789	32.7	6,164	48
Lewis	13	D	4.0	D	NA	NA	NA	NA	309	12.4	505	4
Lincoln	D	D	D	D	D	D	D	D	273	13.6	5,055	21
Madison	111	1,846	170.0	55.9	35	163	13.8	3.5	3,220	138.1	80,090	342
Minidoka	32	462	39.1	17.3	D	D	D	D	1,208	65.3	51,288	304
Nez Perce	139	3,288	309.4	124.4	71	473	39.9	13.3	2,166	88.5	40,542	96
Oneida	11	176	13.9	5.4	D	D	D	D	364	14.7	23,180	85
Owyhee	20	229	12.5	5.7	D	D	D	D	767	41.0	24,368	96
Payette	53	628	52.5	23.6	D	D	D	D	1,589	76.8	41,308	229
Power	15	162	13.6	5.7	11	41	5.1	1.2	406	16.4	5,152	21
Shoshone	31	531	41.0	17.3	17	47	3.9	1.3	807	27.0	5,913	35
Teton	35	291	29.0	12.7	24	82	10.9	3.4	1,754	75.1	112,813	389
Twin Falls	393	6,474	682.8	245.1	154	921	88.8	27.2	6,206	294.0	197,186	899
Valley	31	499	54.2	23.8	31	138	15.0	3.2	1,437	70.4	157,308	375
Washington	24	421	30.7	11.6	D	D	D	D	603	24.3	8,693	59
ILLINOIS	34,235	817,733	97,626.1	38,088.6	24,296	171,261	29,599.4	7,164.3	994,233	45,420.6	4,272,625	19,658
Adams	D	D	D	313.6	D	D	95.2	D	3,910	163.8	15,070	70
Alexander	D	D	D	D	D	D	D	D	245	7.4	0	0
Bond	D	D	D	D	D	D	D	D	899	30.7	3,565	26
Boone	64	947	87.7	32.0	71	343	38.7	10.2	3,043	139.8	16,010	108
Brown	10	185	12.5	6.4	11	21	2.4	0.5	305	10.9	0	0
Bureau	70	2,049	200.8	83.5	D	D	D	D	1,768	71.1	2,723	12
Calhoun	D	D	D	D	NA	NA	NA	NA	295	11.1	1,524	6
Carroll	23	489	24.4	9.9	29	161	14.1	4.0	972	40.3	10,835	40
Cass	13	333	14.2	7.2	D	D	7.5	D	660	21.2	672	4
Champaign	D	D	D	D	301	2,176	749.9	84.3	12,465	500.5	116,331	594
Christian	55	1,685	136.8	52.9	57	277	18.5	5.3	1,709	61.9	5,888	28
Clark	24	301	18.8	7.6	19	71	5.2	1.1	958	38.5	960	6
Clay	44	787	54.7	26.8	31	88	8.8	1.8	901	35.1	915	5
Clinton	92	1,854	157.6	60.6	78	276	27.6	7.2	2,290	90.7	24,261	84
Coles	161	4,918	485.4	193.3	86	374	32.0	10.2	2,579	99.9	2,915	11
Cook	15,121	382,756	45,827.4	18,285.6	10,518	83,813	18,747.7	4,054.0	491,217	22,652.4	1,184,517	6,789
Crawford	39	853	67.0	31.4	31	151	13.0	3.5	1,230	46.7	1,970	6
Cumberland	17	519	18.4	8.4	18	60	4.7	1.1	685	24.4	0	0
DeKalb	220	4,937	570.2	203.4	152	766	69.9	19.3	6,066	229.1	47,253	240
De Witt	25	508	41.0	16.5	20	70	7.6	1.5	900	30.2	3,350	10
Douglas	31	285	21.2	9.6	34	160	16.5	5.3	1,560	72.1	6,026	29
DuPage	3,509	66,417	8,717.6	3,477.7	2,142	18,378	2,422.5	809.5	86,847	4,868.3	533,886	1,554
Edgar	31	926	76.6	37.2	24	93	10.1	2.5	856	30.3	0	0
Edwards	12	96	4.3	2.3	17	54	5.5	1.3	407	14.2	NA	NA
Effingham	134	2,859	393.6	120.6	106	1,034	75.8	39.1	2,598	126.0	8,753	32
Fayette	47	833	54.4	23.9	34	120	14.6	3.2	1,234	48.7	510	3
Ford	35	1,162	126.8	50.9	30	110	11.1	2.6	886	35.4	2,000	8
Franklin	67	975	87.1	33.1	54	187	23.7	4.7	2,050	72.6	2,298	13
Fulton	69	1,904	160.5	71.9	45	179	17.0	4.4	1,531	53.8	5,731	34
Gallatin	8	88	4.3	2.0	D	D	3.2	D	295	12.0	NA	NA
Greene	17	334	22.4	11.2	15	44	4.8	1.0	746	27.3	791	2
Grundy	145	2,271	298.0	107.2	102	1,140	149.6	59.9	3,072	134.6	21,686	78
Hamilton	22	444	30.7	13.8	20	74	7.3	2.1	537	15.3	NA	NA
Hancock	29	507	46.6	19.7	D	D	D	D	1,227	49.8	430	1

STATE County	Government employment and payroll, 2017									Local government finances, 2017				
			March payroll (percent of total)							General revenue				
												Taxes		
													Per capita[1] (dollars)	
	Full-time equivalent employees	March payroll (dollars)	Adminis-tration, judicial, and legal	Police and corrections	Fire protection	Highways and transpor-tation	Health and welfare	Natural resources and utilities	Education and libraries	Total (mil dol)	Inter-govern-mental (mil dol)	Total (mil dol)	Total	Property
	171	172	173	174	175	176	177	178	179	180	181	182	183	184
IDAHO—Cont'd														
Caribou	572	1,914,185	6.3	6.5	0.8	4.7	45.7	2.6	32.8	34.1	14.6	11.8	1,696	1,650
Cassia	991	2,996,775	7.0	10.5	1.8	4.2	0.1	7.9	64.5	99.4	43.8	23.6	999	781
Clark	75	232,218	8.2	10.3	0.0	11.7	0.0	4.2	47.4	5.5	2.2	3.0	3,416	3,206
Clearwater	394	1,125,348	14.2	11.9	0.2	6.6	2.3	7.2	50.6	37.5	15.0	16.8	1,943	1,848
Custer	196	574,965	18.3	8.6	0.2	10.2	1.3	7.2	49.7	16.0	9.3	4.0	957	942
Elmore	863	2,481,291	9.8	13.7	0.8	6.9	0.7	7.6	57.9	76.7	36.9	23.5	873	845
Franklin	650	2,076,070	4.6	5.0	0.0	3.0	34.8	3.4	48.5	35.5	24.0	7.3	542	514
Fremont	535	1,694,793	11.3	18.2	2.5	5.7	2.5	7.2	51.5	41.5	17.2	19.2	1,461	1,373
Gem	552	1,556,250	10.0	12.9	1.5	3.8	0.2	9.2	61.5	43.9	21.6	17.2	993	961
Gooding	630	1,677,452	10.4	10.2	2.1	4.8	3.5	7.5	59.6	45.5	26.9	12.0	793	760
Idaho	583	2,063,196	5.1	6.8	0.0	8.7	29.3	3.0	42.7	53.6	22.5	12.6	772	765
Jefferson	1,004	2,656,177	5.5	8.7	2.3	3.0	0.2	2.3	77.1	62.2	44.8	13.8	484	481
Jerome	735	2,359,346	10.4	10.8	3.0	5.1	0.5	5.7	63.0	71.5	36.6	19.9	837	801
Kootenai	7,757	33,973,530	5.6	7.5	3.1	2.0	43.3	3.4	34.7	903.2	235.7	172.7	1,098	1,032
Latah	1,054	4,213,007	10.8	11.5	0.8	5.6	1.2	7.5	60.1	101.0	40.2	38.9	979	922
Lemhi	405	1,523,806	6.3	7.1	1.2	4.3	47.3	5.0	24.7	41.9	15.7	4.9	628	557
Lewis	247	708,412	12.5	8.3	0.0	8.9	0.3	5.5	63.9	18.5	11.0	4.5	1,160	1,151
Lincoln	212	611,303	11.7	7.9	0.7	8.8	0.3	5.8	61.8	16.1	9.9	3.8	710	679
Madison	1,187	3,602,076	7.3	15.1	0.5	4.2	3.8	4.2	62.9	188.3	82.1	37.3	948	912
Minidoka	985	3,305,590	5.5	7.1	2.1	0.9	28.7	11.8	42.3	69.4	33.4	12.6	610	586
Nez Perce	1,420	5,752,990	8.6	12.6	6.6	3.8	3.9	7.3	51.8	146.3	62.4	52.8	1,310	1,245
Oneida	171	533,003	12.7	8.6	0.2	5.9	0.4	10.8	59.3	19.5	8.3	7.4	1,676	1,648
Owyhee	397	1,244,002	10.1	10.8	1.6	5.5	0.2	4.6	66.7	41.2	24.2	10.6	912	896
Payette	839	2,498,050	9.3	11.4	0.9	4.6	0.4	6.3	66.0	63.2	32.4	21.6	932	816
Power	503	1,520,346	4.3	5.9	0.2	7.8	24.2	4.4	52.2	46.0	19.4	16.7	2,197	2,168
Shoshone	634	2,055,612	7.9	7.7	5.0	7.5	21.1	6.6	43.5	57.1	21.8	16.0	1,277	1,232
Teton	337	1,217,589	12.3	5.8	7.6	3.9	0.0	5.1	63.1	51.0	16.6	15.6	1,360	1,244
Twin Falls	3,370	11,792,355	9.0	10.1	2.7	3.0	3.4	4.8	65.7	334.9	158.4	104.5	1,225	1,142
Valley	584	2,091,242	14.1	12.9	9.0	8.7	8.2	9.3	36.7	51.5	15.1	26.6	2,491	2,362
Washington	495	1,799,937	7.5	9.3	0.2	5.2	27.4	6.8	41.8	53.7	19.9	12.0	1,197	1,141
ILLINOIS	X	X	X	X	X	X	X	X	X	X	X	X	X	X
Adams	2,643	9,098,939	5.8	9.6	4.6	4.8	5.3	5.0	63.7	224.4	101.1	88.0	1,333	1,136
Alexander	305	979,817	8.5	11.0	0.0	13.3	6.9	2.0	54.8	21.8	13.9	5.1	806	733
Bond	530	1,889,362	10.2	12.9	1.5	5.9	5.8	4.7	58.5	47.0	18.6	18.2	1,093	1,021
Boone	1,618	7,647,159	6.0	10.3	2.5	1.9	1.1	3.9	72.4	181.0	69.6	95.1	1,778	1,649
Brown	225	848,596	12.4	7.8	0.6	8.0	5.8	1.8	63.4	16.3	5.9	7.5	1,140	937
Bureau	1,597	6,419,293	6.4	7.1	2.1	3.5	24.1	5.7	50.1	161.3	47.6	55.3	1,668	1,625
Calhoun	153	520,148	10.7	6.9	5.2	9.0	6.9	0.7	60.6	14.2	7.3	5.4	1,103	1,073
Carroll	510	1,913,321	10.1	11.2	3.0	5.1	1.3	4.8	63.6	54.7	16.8	30.8	2,125	2,082
Cass	521	1,645,754	9.1	6.5	0.9	6.3	1.2	4.4	68.7	49.2	25.0	16.0	1,283	1,219
Champaign	7,428	31,761,851	6.9	10.0	4.4	6.9	6.0	5.4	58.4	800.2	271.0	407.2	1,935	1,617
Christian	1,367	4,737,664	7.8	8.5	2.2	4.6	1.5	4.9	69.5	100.5	45.5	41.4	1,254	1,213
Clark	603	2,100,872	6.9	8.2	4.0	6.3	2.0	11.0	58.8	56.7	30.5	17.4	1,103	998
Clay	738	3,020,248	4.9	4.4	0.0	3.5	40.7	5.3	40.6	47.0	27.8	13.0	982	931
Clinton	1,017	4,028,845	9.3	11.1	0.2	4.9	3.6	7.4	62.7	88.7	31.2	43.5	1,155	1,129
Coles	2,736	10,830,347	5.2	7.0	3.9	2.1	1.7	2.8	76.5	177.8	65.9	63.8	1,243	1,137
Cook	205,528	1,216,640,423	5.4	14.9	5.4	10.0	5.1	6.3	49.8	36,045.1	11,878.6	18,051.5	3,471	2,414
Crawford	965	3,932,672	3.5	5.7	1.2	4.0	45.2	1.6	38.0	104.9	20.9	30.2	1,593	1,577
Cumberland	341	1,506,830	9.1	5.3	3.0	5.7	2.3	3.2	71.0	28.6	14.4	10.4	954	932
DeKalb	3,861	16,075,945	5.7	12.8	5.5	3.7	5.5	4.7	61.0	445.5	134.4	243.6	2,336	1,993
De Witt	693	2,635,487	7.4	7.0	2.2	3.0	21.6	3.6	53.1	78.9	16.5	36.8	2,315	2,262
Douglas	708	2,533,662	12.4	7.5	0.9	3.4	0.8	2.7	72.2	70.7	25.4	38.5	1,962	1,878
DuPage	35,243	186,878,707	4.3	9.7	4.6	2.4	2.8	8.2	66.2	4,840.5	983.3	3,163.1	3,400	3,022
Edgar	693	2,517,272	6.7	9.4	3.4	4.5	3.8	3.6	68.2	55.7	25.2	24.6	1,415	1,273
Edwards	194	602,546	7.0	7.5	6.7	2.6	2.8	4.1	69.0	14.1	7.0	4.8	750	734
Effingham	1,157	4,609,810	7.7	10.5	2.7	4.5	1.6	3.9	68.0	106.9	44.0	46.0	1,347	1,283
Fayette	744	2,354,663	9.7	10.9	0.0	4.6	4.4	4.7	65.0	56.9	26.8	18.6	865	848
Ford	637	2,097,747	4.4	7.0	0.0	3.8	3.4	2.7	75.8	57.3	20.0	31.5	2,367	2,302
Franklin	1,590	6,048,883	2.8	5.4	11.6	2.4	15.2	7.4	54.4	152.4	70.8	35.4	908	797
Fulton	1,476	5,334,986	6.7	6.2	2.9	3.5	6.7	4.3	69.2	134.6	56.2	52.4	1,492	1,444
Gallatin	212	610,109	22.1	6.7	1.9	4.3	3.1	2.6	58.1	14.7	7.9	5.2	1,024	974
Greene	497	1,565,591	6.9	9.6	1.8	10.1	3.8	8.9	57.9	35.1	15.6	14.1	1,075	1,024
Grundy	2,319	8,628,263	6.9	8.5	3.4	2.8	2.3	2.4	71.3	245.3	63.3	156.2	3,085	2,993
Hamilton	399	1,349,402	7.5	3.5	0.0	3.5	38.5	4.4	41.2	38.1	11.6	6.7	825	824
Hancock	727	2,287,973	8.0	5.8	2.3	5.6	6.9	4.2	65.4	56.2	20.2	27.9	1,552	1,498

1. Based on the resident population estimated as of July 1 of the year shown.

STATE County	Local government finances, 2017 (cont.)									Government employment, 2020			Individual income tax returns, 2019		
	Direct general expenditure							Debt outstanding							
			Percent of total for:												
	Total (mil dol)	Per capita[1] (dollars)	Education	Health and hospitals	Police protection	Public welfare	Highways	Total (mil dol)	Per capita[1] (dollars)	Federal civilian	Federal military	State and local	Number of returns	Mean adjusted gross income	Mean income tax
	185	186	187	188	189	190	191	192	193	194	195	196	197	198	199
IDAHO—Cont'd															
Caribou	32.1	4,598	41.8	0.5	10.5	0.5	14.0	11.3	1,618	40	22	707	2,950	54,801	4,680
Cassia	98.3	4,157	58.8	0.2	3.5	0.6	4.5	106.2	4,489	138	73	1,361	10,240	50,964	4,252
Clark	2.9	3,341	78.8	0.0	1.1	0.0	2.7	1.0	1,091	27	6	97	320	39,619	2,106
Clearwater	64.8	7,495	23.2	0.8	3.3	0.4	45.1	8.7	1,011	145	42	765	3,670	50,663	4,201
Custer	17.2	4,152	39.7	1.9	5.8	0.0	18.3	0.9	223	143	13	288	2,050	47,741	3,887
Elmore	68.9	2,563	47.0	1.5	8.9	1.0	9.1	15.8	589	878	3,623	1,095	12,230	45,594	3,291
Franklin	34.3	2,550	63.9	1.7	7.1	0.5	6.8	6.6	491	37	43	1,042	5,790	52,213	3,697
Fremont	44.5	3,389	36.4	1.4	6.5	0.2	12.9	28.8	2,191	82	39	949	5,660	46,907	3,481
Gem	37.0	2,139	56.4	2.0	6.0	1.6	5.0	19.8	1,141	82	56	864	8,520	52,542	4,356
Gooding	49.0	3,238	46.2	1.9	4.6	0.5	9.2	45.1	2,981	52	47	884	6,660	38,457	3,643
Idaho	51.2	3,128	39.5	5.3	4.5	1.4	15.7	7.3	444	334	50	878	6,830	51,608	4,542
Jefferson	51.1	1,797	83.9	0.0	1.3	0.0	0.6	64.0	2,252	54	92	1,366	12,190	59,361	4,477
Jerome	78.3	3,293	50.9	0.7	5.6	0.7	1.7	87.2	3,670	62	74	1,009	9,870	47,146	3,431
Kootenai	909.8	5,783	24.0	51.5	3.8	0.2	2.5	282.6	1,796	699	514	11,010	84,360	66,780	7,083
Latah	99.8	2,511	45.7	0.3	8.4	0.4	9.1	40.2	1,012	177	136	6,350	17,020	60,693	5,616
Lemhi	35.4	4,523	21.8	46.0	4.2	0.8	6.2	16.3	2,079	215	24	601	3,830	46,650	3,990
Lewis	18.7	4,818	50.4	0.9	6.2	0.9	14.0	4.9	1,260	80	11	368	1,820	48,502	3,645
Lincoln	16.8	3,123	54.2	2.1	3.2	0.5	10.7	7.8	1,456	86	16	388	2,080	41,045	2,642
Madison	163.9	4,163	27.0	42.0	4.0	0.0	5.2	95.1	2,416	70	122	2,240	14,940	44,952	3,202
Minidoka	65.9	3,178	47.5	0.0	5.8	0.3	1.8	47.1	2,271	91	64	1,403	9,260	48,852	3,665
Nez Perce	143.3	3,557	37.2	6.2	8.4	0.2	7.5	115.4	2,863	211	122	3,894	19,200	57,618	5,107
Oneida	17.3	3,945	39.7	2.8	6.6	0.2	6.0	2.7	612	22	15	434	1,980	44,343	3,252
Owyhee	38.5	3,318	51.6	0.2	5.5	0.8	5.6	14.2	1,222	45	36	634	5,190	43,045	3,555
Payette	59.3	2,558	53.5	1.9	6.9	0.7	6.7	17.1	737	39	75	1,016	10,860	54,146	4,539
Power	40.8	5,366	39.9	19.6	3.6	0.2	8.5	4.7	615	21	23	668	3,330	45,890	3,517
Shoshone	55.3	4,415	35.2	21.4	4.9	0.2	11.2	30.8	2,459	75	39	824	5,820	45,290	3,559
Teton	43.8	3,826	35.2	2.4	2.7	0.1	5.6	19.6	1,710	45	38	451	5,530	69,214	7,595
Twin Falls	339.7	3,979	56.0	2.5	4.2	1.1	6.8	321.2	3,763	396	266	4,603	39,320	53,266	4,914
Valley	53.7	5,039	30.4	0.2	7.5	0.1	14.5	39.8	3,735	261	36	720	5,990	76,332	8,985
Washington	51.3	5,105	28.9	33.1	6.1	0.3	5.7	18.5	1,843	57	31	711	4,490	46,239	3,354
ILLINOIS	X	X	X	X	X	X	X	X	X	82,037	46,754	708,808	6,173,840	78,283	10,416
Adams	271.0	4,103	48.8	2.9	5.2	0.3	3.9	180.9	2,738	244	134	3,367	31,470	61,864	6,315
Alexander	24.7	3,936	49.0	1.0	6.6	0.0	7.1	4.5	711	26	15	312	2,290	41,096	2,818
Bond	42.5	2,554	48.0	7.0	7.3	0.2	7.9	44.9	2,698	301	30	708	6,930	55,266	4,769
Boone	175.9	3,286	58.6	1.5	6.6	0.7	6.7	124.3	2,323	73	106	2,055	25,840	67,781	7,470
Brown	17.9	2,713	52.8	1.1	6.3	0.0	11.5	11.0	1,658	43	9	411	2,400	51,534	4,195
Bureau	166.9	5,035	36.8	25.8	4.4	0.9	5.6	96.1	2,899	111	64	2,023	16,570	55,299	5,003
Calhoun	14.3	2,939	43.1	0.2	3.3	0.0	29.2	7.5	1,553	20	9	242	2,060	59,149	5,277
Carroll	53.6	3,702	50.3	0.6	5.3	1.2	10.3	42.1	2,911	474	28	658	7,440	56,521	5,336
Cass	46.6	3,734	46.3	11.0	4.5	0.2	5.9	28.6	2,288	54	24	781	6,230	49,638	3,643
Champaign	798.4	3,794	50.3	2.7	6.2	2.4	5.6	724.3	3,442	1,313	423	35,350	86,530	68,637	7,846
Christian	116.1	3,518	58.5	1.2	5.5	0.1	7.1	64.4	1,952	76	62	1,511	15,080	56,135	4,907
Clark	58.2	3,679	39.6	1.9	6.0	0.2	18.6	44.3	2,801	50	30	800	7,250	56,244	4,878
Clay	38.6	2,908	48.9	0.0	7.1	0.4	13.5	36.2	2,729	42	26	894	6,170	49,075	3,708
Clinton	92.0	2,444	54.3	2.8	8.3	0.0	7.8	42.9	1,139	103	75	2,105	17,510	70,950	7,463
Coles	236.0	4,596	59.4	0.7	8.1	0.6	5.5	151.0	2,940	147	99	5,041	21,100	55,108	5,274
Cook	32,809.7	6,309	38.3	5.9	7.7	1.1	3.7	68,769.6	13,223	39,932	10,608	268,871	2,553,690	81,433	11,833
Crawford	105.1	5,541	24.9	52.0	3.6	0.2	5.8	50.4	2,656	59	34	1,435	8,460	58,450	5,538
Cumberland	28.9	2,656	46.3	1.3	5.1	0.1	20.5	8.0	740	32	31	426	4,880	56,043	4,590
DeKalb	464.3	4,451	48.5	4.5	8.1	0.4	4.8	351.9	3,373	253	203	10,532	46,900	61,220	5,929
De Witt	72.5	4,559	38.9	23.3	5.5	0.1	6.6	35.7	2,246	44	31	1,032	7,550	60,447	5,594
Douglas	66.7	3,399	52.3	2.7	5.8	0.3	9.0	17.5	893	58	39	991	9,960	56,909	5,042
DuPage	4,926.8	5,296	52.3	0.7	7.3	1.0	6.9	4,689.0	5,040	4,949	1,913	43,709	469,110	105,237	16,086
Edgar	54.7	3,146	55.3	3.2	6.6	0.1	9.7	32.2	1,850	52	33	936	7,940	52,779	4,610
Edwards	14.4	2,228	53.1	1.6	5.7	0.1	8.2	4.8	740	24	13	277	2,840	53,032	3,826
Effingham	108.1	3,169	46.3	2.2	8.2	0.9	11.3	67.0	1,965	160	70	1,539	17,390	68,379	7,332
Fayette	57.8	2,685	52.3	5.9	7.7	0.0	6.5	45.6	2,119	51	40	1,050	9,020	51,193	4,099
Ford	55.8	4,199	59.5	1.3	6.6	0.1	11.4	80.8	6,076	50	25	739	6,470	57,692	5,198
Franklin	159.7	4,095	42.2	12.3	6.5	0.2	5.1	41.2	1,057	185	76	1,883	16,440	48,767	3,881
Fulton	128.3	3,655	57.1	5.7	5.3	0.3	5.1	65.1	1,854	99	63	2,035	15,250	51,353	4,332
Gallatin	13.9	2,741	49.4	0.0	2.6	0.7	11.7	7.8	1,533	19	10	230	2,130	54,037	4,622
Greene	34.4	2,618	54.4	4.4	7.0	0.4	11.9	20.3	1,544	51	25	670	5,510	49,080	3,740
Grundy	260.9	5,154	61.7	0.8	5.3	0.5	5.6	283.3	5,597	114	103	2,932	25,870	73,296	7,994
Hamilton	38.9	4,749	28.6	44.1	2.7	0.4	7.4	27.9	3,408	38	16	506	3,630	51,347	4,001
Hancock	54.8	3,053	57.3	0.0	4.8	6.7	8.9	27.9	1,556	74	35	942	8,420	55,067	4,564

1. Based on the resident population estimated as of July 1 of the year shown.

State / county code	CBSA code[1]	County Type code[2]	STATE County	Land area[3] (sq. mi)	Population, 2021: Total persons 2021	Population, 2021: Rank	Population, 2021: Per square mile	Race alone or in combination, not Hispanic or Latino (percent): White	Black	American Indian, Alaska Native	Asian and Pacific Islancer	Percent Hispanic or Latino[4]	Age (percent): Under 5 years	5 to 17 years	18 to 24 years	25 to 34 years	35 to 44 years	45 to 54 years
				1	2	3	4	5	6	7	8	9	10	11	12	13	14	15
			ILLINOIS—Cont'd															
17069		9	Hardin	177.4	3,650	2,915	20.6	95.7	1.5	1.3	0.9	2.2	4.4	9.6	9.8	9.2	10.7	13.1
17071	15460	9	Henderson	378.8	6,312	2,710	16.7	96.6	1.4	0.7	0.9	1.9	4.8	10.7	9.0	9.6	10.3	11.8
17073	19340	2	Henry	823.1	48,907	1,008	59.4	91.0	2.7	0.4	0.9	6.4	5.1	12.5	11.4	10.7	12.4	12.4
17075		6	Iroquois	1,117.4	26,827	1,536	24.0	90.2	1.9	0.5	0.8	7.7	5.7	11.8	11.4	10.4	11.5	11.6
17077	16060	3	Jackson	583.6	52,565	963	90.1	76.1	16.6	0.9	4.4	4.8	5.2	10.4	24.5	12.6	10.3	9.4
17079		7	Jasper	494.6	9,193	2,473	18.6	97.6	0.7	0.4	0.5	1.4	6.1	12.8	10.8	10.3	12.1	11.3
17081	34500	7	Jefferson	571.2	36,877	1,256	64.6	86.8	9.8	0.6	1.7	3.1	5.9	12.6	11.1	12.7	12.6	12.3
17083	41180	1	Jersey	369.7	21,333	1,744	57.7	96.5	1.5	0.7	1.2	1.5	4.9	11.3	13.3	10.7	11.9	12.2
17085		6	Jo Daviess	600.9	21,939	1,718	36.5	95.1	1.3	0.5	0.7	3.4	4.0	10.6	10.0	8.7	10.1	11.2
17087	16060	8	Johnson	343.7	13,463	2,192	39.2	87.9	8.6	0.7	0.6	3.3	4.1	10.4	11.2	13.1	12.8	12.6
17089	16980	1	Kane	519.4	515,588	140	992.7	57.4	6.0	0.4	4.9	32.7	5.9	13.8	13.8	11.9	13.3	13.6
17091	28100	3	Kankakee	676.5	106,601	578	157.6	72.3	16.0	0.5	1.5	11.6	5.8	12.6	15.2	12.2	12.0	12.0
17093	16980	1	Kendall	320.2	134,867	486	421.2	66.4	9.0	0.4	4.4	21.7	6.1	16.2	13.7	12.2	16.1	14.4
17095	23660	4	Knox	716.4	49,268	1,006	68.8	84.0	10.2	0.6	1.4	6.4	5.5	11.0	13.1	11.7	11.7	11.3
17097	16980	1	Lake	443.6	711,239	95	1,603.3	60.9	7.7	0.5	9.7	23.1	5.4	13.5	14.7	11.2	12.8	13.3
17099	36837	4	LaSalle	1,135.2	108,965	566	96.0	85.4	3.5	0.5	1.4	10.6	5.2	12.0	12.1	11.9	12.4	12.0
17101		7	Lawrence	372.2	15,152	2,080	40.7	83.9	11.6	0.5	0.7	4.2	4.5	10.9	12.0	15.3	14.2	12.5
17103	19940	6	Lee	724.8	34,049	1,329	47.0	85.6	6.9	0.6	1.1	7.2	4.8	11.3	10.7	12.7	12.7	12.6
17105	38700	4	Livingston	1,043.6	35,664	1,290	34.2	89.4	5.3	0.4	1.0	5.2	5.7	12.1	11.9	12.4	12.4	11.6
17107	30660	6	Logan	618.1	27,992	1,498	45.3	86.5	9.7	0.6	1.1	3.8	4.9	10.8	13.5	14.1	13.9	11.7
17109	31380	5	McDonough	589.3	26,828	1,535	45.5	88.6	6.3	0.8	2.9	3.1	4.5	9.6	26.0	10.6	10.1	9.2
17111	16980	1	McHenry	603.4	311,122	230	515.6	80.4	2.2	0.5	3.8	14.7	5.2	13.1	12.7	11.6	13.0	13.7
17113	14010	3	McLean	1,183.2	170,889	391	144.4	80.9	10.0	0.5	5.8	5.4	5.4	12.0	21.2	12.6	12.3	10.9
17115	19500	3	Macon	580.6	102,432	600	176.4	77.8	20.6	0.5	1.8	2.6	6.0	12.6	12.5	11.8	11.6	11.3
17117	41180	1	Macoupin	863.0	44,406	1,088	51.5	96.8	1.7	0.7	0.7	1.3	5.1	11.8	11.7	10.5	12.3	12.2
17119	41180	1	Madison	715.5	264,490	267	369.7	85.9	10.3	0.6	1.7	3.7	5.3	12.5	11.9	12.9	12.8	12.2
17121	16460	4	Marion	572.5	37,390	1,239	65.3	92.2	5.9	0.6	1.0	2.3	6.1	13.6	11.0	11.8	11.6	11.7
17123	37900	2	Marshall	386.8	11,663	2,302	30.2	95.1	1.4	0.6	1.0	3.3	5.1	11.7	10.1	11.2	11.0	11.6
17125		6	Mason	539.4	12,881	2,218	23.9	96.6	1.5	0.7	0.9	1.6	5.1	11.5	11.4	10.3	11.4	12.4
17127	37140	7	Massac	237.2	13,960	2,153	58.9	89.4	7.7	0.9	0.9	3.4	5.4	12.0	11.3	10.0	11.5	13.1
17129	44100	3	Menard	314.4	12,164	2,270	38.7	96.6	1.9	0.8	0.8	1.6	5.1	12.4	10.6	11.0	12.6	12.0
17131	19340	2	Mercer	561.2	15,582	2,056	27.8	95.5	1.3	0.6	0.8	3.1	4.8	12.2	11.1	10.2	12.4	12.4
17133	41180	1	Monroe	385.3	34,932	1,305	90.7	96.9	0.9	0.5	1.0	1.7	5.4	12.6	10.8	10.2	13.7	12.7
17135		6	Montgomery	703.8	28,084	1,496	39.9	93.2	4.6	0.4	0.8	1.9	5.1	11.5	11.1	12.3	12.9	11.9
17137	27300	4	Morgan	568.9	32,606	1,369	57.3	88.8	8.3	0.6	1.2	2.9	5.0	10.5	13.6	12.2	12.7	11.5
17139		6	Moultrie	336.0	14,510	2,115	43.2	96.7	1.4	0.5	0.6	1.8	5.9	14.8	12.3	11.1	12.3	11.4
17141	40300	4	Ogle	758.7	51,449	977	67.8	86.9	2.0	0.5	0.9	11.1	5.4	12.7	11.7	11.4	12.1	12.5
17143	37900	2	Peoria	618.7	179,432	375	290.0	71.4	20.7	0.6	5.0	5.4	6.6	13.4	12.7	13.1	12.4	11.6
17145		6	Perry	441.9	20,985	1,763	47.5	86.0	10.8	0.6	0.9	3.5	4.6	10.8	12.8	13.9	13.1	12.4
17147	16580	3	Piatt	439.2	16,753	1,988	38.1	96.8	1.4	0.5	1.0	1.6	5.6	12.6	10.8	11.0	12.9	11.8
17149		7	Pike	831.4	14,618	2,107	17.6	96.1	2.0	0.6	0.6	1.6	6.2	12.8	10.9	11.5	11.7	11.7
17151		8	Pope	368.9	3,779	2,902	10.2	91.1	6.4	1.3	0.8	2.0	3.1	5.0	11.6	8.0	10.3	12.5
17153		8	Pulaski	199.3	5,065	2,818	25.4	66.8	30.7	1.4	1.3	2.8	5.1	11.5	11.5	10.6	11.1	11.2
17155	36837	8	Putnam	160.1	5,566	2,772	34.8	92.0	1.1	0.4	0.9	6.4	4.4	11.6	10.6	10.0	11.9	11.4
17157		6	Randolph	575.4	30,142	1,434	52.4	84.2	11.8	0.5	0.9	3.7	4.9	10.9	11.1	13.7	13.6	12.4
17159		7	Richland	360.0	15,796	2,042	43.9	95.9	1.6	0.6	1.2	1.9	5.8	13.2	10.9	11.3	12.0	11.6
17161	19340	2	Rock Island	427.5	142,909	469	334.3	72.1	13.1	0.6	3.3	13.7	5.8	12.8	12.5	12.1	12.1	11.4
17163	41180	1	St. Clair	657.7	254,796	278	387.4	63.1	31.8	0.7	2.7	4.6	5.9	13.4	12.0	12.7	13.2	12.0
17165		6	Saline	380.0	23,320	1,666	61.4	93.1	4.9	0.9	1.2	1.8	5.7	11.4	11.4	11.7	11.8	12.4
17167	44100	3	Sangamon	868.3	194,734	350	224.3	81.5	15.1	0.5	2.9	2.6	5.6	12.4	12.1	12.1	12.8	12.1
17169		7	Schuyler	437.3	6,843	2,671	15.6	92.2	5.2	0.4	0.5	2.4	4.6	10.4	9.4	10.8	12.9	13.5
17171	27300	9	Scott	250.8	4,836	2,834	19.3	96.5	1.2	0.6	1.5	1.4	4.5	12.2	11.7	10.5	11.8	12.3
17173		6	Shelby	758.5	20,789	1,774	27.4	97.5	1.0	0.6	0.7	1.3	5.4	12.2	10.3	10.5	11.6	11.6
17175	37900	2	Stark	288.1	5,294	2,795	18.4	95.6	1.6	0.6	1.2	2.5	5.3	12.5	11.1	10.1	11.4	12.3
17177	23300	4	Stephenson	564.2	44,021	1,098	78.0	84.1	12.6	0.5	1.3	4.8	5.4	12.0	11.2	10.4	10.7	11.5
17179	37900	2	Tazewell	646.5	130,413	496	201.7	94.6	2.2	0.5	1.5	2.6	5.3	12.9	11.4	11.7	13.3	12.5
17181		6	Union	413.4	16,923	1,978	40.9	92.2	2.0	0.9	0.9	5.5	5.4	11.7	10.8	11.3	11.6	12.8
17183	19180	3	Vermilion	898.3	73,095	754	81.4	79.5	15.4	0.5	1.3	5.6	6.0	13.3	11.8	11.7	11.9	11.5
17185		7	Wabash	223.3	11,202	2,330	50.2	95.3	1.4	0.7	1.6	2.5	5.6	12.7	11.0	11.3	11.4	11.0
17187		6	Warren	542.4	16,531	2,000	30.5	84.0	3.7	0.6	2.7	10.5	5.7	12.1	15.9	10.3	11.3	11.1
17189		6	Washington	562.6	13,655	2,180	24.3	96.5	1.6	0.5	0.8	1.6	5.4	11.4	10.8	11.1	12.1	12.2
17191		7	Wayne	713.8	15,963	2,033	22.4	96.7	1.2	0.5	0.8	1.8	6.0	12.9	10.7	10.9	11.6	11.6
17193		6	White	495.0	13,784	2,170	27.8	96.8	1.2	0.6	0.8	1.6	5.0	13.3	10.4	10.7	12.4	11.5
17195	44580	4	Whiteside	684.1	55,305	931	80.8	84.8	2.4	0.5	0.8	12.9	5.5	12.5	11.6	11.2	11.1	12.2
17197	16980	1	Will	835.9	697,252	98	834.1	62.6	12.8	0.4	7.0	18.9	5.5	13.7	13.9	12.0	13.5	14.3
17199	16060	3	Williamson	420.2	66,879	803	159.2	90.6	5.9	0.7	1.7	2.9	5.4	12.5	10.7	12.5	13.2	12.5

1. CBSA = Core Based Statistical Area. See Appendix A for explanation. See Appendix B for list of metropolitan areas with component counties. 2. County type code from the Economic Research Service of USDA Rural-Urban Continuum Codes. See Appendix A for definition. 3. Dry land or land partially or temporarily covered by water. 4. May be of any race.

STATE County	Population, 2021 (cont.)				Population change, 2000–2021							Households, 2016–2020				
	Age (percent) (cont.)				Total persons		Percent change		Components of change, 2020–2021					Percent		
	55 to 64 years	65 to 74 years	75 years and over	Percent female	2010	2020	2010–2020	2020–2021	Births	Deaths	Net Migration	Number	Persons per household	Family house-holds	Female family house-holder[1]	One person
	16	17	18	19	20	21	22	23	24	25	26	27	28	29	30	31
ILLINOIS—Cont'd																
Hardin	16.1	16.5	10.8	49.3	4,320	3,649	-15.5	0.0	35	82	48	1,515	2.5	62.6	4.2	34.6
Henderson	16.9	14.7	12.3	50.1	7,331	6,387	-12.9	-1.2	58	118	-14	3,028	2.2	67.3	7.8	27.9
Henry	14.4	12.4	8.8	50.0	50,486	49,284	-2.4	-0.8	630	811	-198	19,996	2.4	68.1	9.5	28.6
Iroquois	15.2	12.5	9.8	50.6	29,718	27,077	-8.9	-0.9	397	515	-135	11,845	2.3	65.9	10.1	29.1
Jackson	10.9	10.1	6.6	50.1	60,218	52,974	-12.0	-0.8	683	732	-365	24,208	2.2	51.1	12.5	38.3
Jasper	15.9	12.4	8.3	49.4	9,698	9,287	-4.2	-1.0	127	136	-86	3,791	2.5	70.4	8.8	25.1
Jefferson	13.4	11.5	7.8	48.2	38,827	37,113	-4.4	-0.6	535	679	-95	14,792	2.4	66.9	13.3	29.1
Jersey	15.6	11.8	8.2	50.7	22,985	21,512	-6.4	-0.8	232	382	-30	8,158	2.6	66.7	7.5	28.8
Jo Daviess	16.1	17.2	12.1	49.5	22,678	22,035	-2.8	-0.4	198	344	53	10,069	2.1	64.8	8.1	29.3
Johnson	14.4	12.3	9.1	44.0	12,582	13,308	5.8	1.2	117	201	242	4,174	2.4	72.7	11.3	24.1
Kane	13.0	9.2	5.7	49.9	515,269	516,522	0.2	-0.2	7,141	5,200	-2,983	181,845	2.9	73.1	11.5	21.8
Kankakee	13.0	10.2	7.1	50.4	113,449	107,502	-5.2	-0.8	1,498	1,696	-719	40,297	2.6	65.7	11.7	29.0
Kendall	10.4	6.9	4.0	50.1	114,736	131,869	14.9	2.3	1,873	957	2,079	41,398	3.1	79.1	11.5	18.0
Knox	13.6	12.7	9.4	48.8	52,919	49,967	-5.6	-1.4	595	957	-336	20,428	2.2	55.9	10.0	37.9
Lake	13.7	9.4	5.9	49.7	703,462	714,342	1.5	-0.4	8,405	7,252	-4,367	248,684	2.7	72.5	9.9	22.8
LaSalle	14.9	11.5	8.1	49.1	113,924	109,658	-3.7	-0.6	1,348	1,917	-139	45,089	2.3	65.1	11.7	29.5
Lawrence	12.9	10.2	7.5	42.9	16,833	15,280	-9.2	-0.8	158	276	-10	6,166	2.2	63.0	10.2	28.2
Lee	14.8	12.1	8.4	46.2	36,031	34,145	-5.2	-0.3	353	604	156	13,634	2.3	59.0	10.1	34.2
Livingston	14.4	11.3	8.2	49.1	38,950	35,815	-8.0	-0.4	481	625	-13	14,366	2.3	65.9	11.1	29.8
Logan	12.7	10.5	8.0	48.8	30,305	27,987	-7.6	0.0	331	482	155	10,958	2.3	63.6	8.2	28.5
McDonough	11.7	10.6	7.7	50.5	32,612	27,238	-16.5	-1.5	290	467	-236	11,573	2.3	49.7	6.6	39.8
McHenry	14.8	10.0	5.9	49.9	308,760	310,229	0.5	0.3	3,652	3,248	440	113,269	2.7	74.7	10.0	20.6
McLean	11.4	8.7	5.5	51.2	169,572	170,954	0.8	0.0	2,129	1,847	-393	66,225	2.5	59.9	9.2	29.9
Macon	13.4	12.1	8.6	51.9	110,768	103,998	-6.1	-1.5	1,476	1,805	-1,232	43,810	2.3	59.7	11.8	34.9
Macoupin	15.3	12.8	8.4	50.5	47,765	44,967	-5.9	-1.2	479	830	-214	18,577	2.4	67.4	11.4	26.5
Madison	14.2	10.9	7.2	51.0	269,282	265,859	-1.3	-0.5	3,283	4,308	-391	108,429	2.4	65.3	12.0	27.8
Marion	14.2	11.6	8.5	50.6	39,437	37,729	-4.3	-0.9	540	680	-204	16,126	2.3	61.1	12.3	33.1
Marshall	15.4	13.5	10.5	50.0	12,640	11,742	-7.1	-0.7	130	209	-1	4,922	2.3	64.1	8.1	30.6
Mason	15.1	12.9	9.9	50.3	14,666	13,086	-10.8	-1.6	179	249	-136	5,917	2.2	64.5	9.9	28.1
Massac	15.2	11.6	10.0	51.6	15,429	14,169	-8.2	-1.5	173	270	-111	5,619	2.4	67.8	9.5	27.6
Menard	15.8	12.2	8.3	50.9	12,705	12,297	-3.2	-1.1	147	178	-103	5,211	2.3	73.2	11.5	23.6
Mercer	15.0	12.6	9.4	49.7	16,434	15,699	-4.5	-0.7	162	247	-33	6,477	2.4	67.9	6.6	27.4
Monroe	15.6	11.4	7.6	49.9	32,957	34,962	6.1	-0.1	385	506	87	13,576	2.5	75.5	7.3	21.6
Montgomery	14.6	11.9	8.7	46.8	30,104	28,288	-6.0	-0.7	326	551	18	11,619	2.2	61.7	8.7	32.5
Morgan	14.1	11.5	8.8	48.9	35,547	32,915	-7.4	-0.9	422	600	-135	13,560	2.3	60.8	11.8	33.2
Moultrie	13.4	10.8	8.0	50.8	14,846	14,526	-2.2	-0.1	214	265	36	6,043	2.4	67.3	8.5	27.2
Ogle	14.8	11.2	8.2	50.0	53,497	51,788	-3.2	-0.7	655	748	-252	20,967	2.4	65.9	9.2	29.6
Peoria	12.3	10.6	7.3	51.3	186,494	181,830	-2.5	-1.3	2,798	2,663	-2,534	73,519	2.4	59.3	13.4	35.4
Perry	13.2	11.3	7.9	44.1	22,350	20,945	-6.3	0.2	225	336	151	8,504	2.2	66.8	14.2	29.0
Piatt	14.9	12.2	8.0	50.0	16,729	16,673	-0.3	0.5	219	253	114	6,755	2.4	70.6	8.4	26.0
Pike	13.7	12.2	9.4	49.7	16,430	14,739	-10.3	-0.8	212	292	-41	6,258	2.4	62.6	10.3	32.5
Pope	20.1	17.0	12.5	48.5	4,470	3,763	-15.8	0.4	40	52	28	1,618	2.4	63.9	11.2	35.9
Pulaski	15.2	14.8	9.0	51.5	6,161	5,193	-15.7	-2.5	65	104	-89	2,050	2.6	59.7	14.1	35.8
Putnam	16.5	14.6	9.1	49.0	6,006	5,637	-6.1	-1.3	53	88	-36	2,435	2.4	68.5	7.9	28.3
Randolph	14.1	11.1	8.2	44.0	33,476	30,163	-9.9	-0.1	358	539	159	12,047	2.3	65.4	11.6	30.0
Richland	14.2	11.3	9.7	50.5	16,233	15,813	-2.6	-0.1	213	271	39	6,527	2.4	65.6	10.0	30.2
Rock Island	13.1	11.9	8.3	50.5	147,546	144,672	-1.9	-1.2	1,925	2,237	-1,451	60,607	2.3	61.5	12.0	33.2
St. Clair	13.9	10.4	6.5	51.5	270,056	257,400	-4.7	-1.0	3,577	3,961	-2,251	104,631	2.5	63.3	15.0	32.2
Saline	14.7	12.2	8.7	50.3	24,913	23,768	-4.6	-1.9	338	519	-266	10,140	2.3	65.3	12.6	31.5
Sangamon	14.0	11.5	7.3	51.7	197,465	196,343	-0.6	-0.8	2,493	3,046	-1,081	84,093	2.3	59.5	13.3	33.8
Schuyler	14.8	13.5	10.0	47.0	7,544	6,902	-8.5	-0.9	79	111	-27	2,730	2.2	57.0	8.6	34.7
Scott	16.6	11.6	8.8	50.3	5,355	4,949	-7.6	-2.3	48	91	-69	1,973	2.5	72.3	9.4	25.0
Shelby	15.0	13.4	10.0	49.9	22,363	20,990	-6.1	-1.0	243	378	-67	9,158	2.3	68.3	7.5	26.1
Stark	14.4	13.4	9.6	49.6	5,994	5,400	-9.9	-2.0	71	93	-83	2,304	2.3	65.3	8.8	31.4
Stephenson	15.0	13.4	10.3	51.1	47,711	44,630	-6.5	-1.4	560	821	-346	19,741	2.2	64.2	12.9	31.7
Tazewell	13.5	11.4	8.1	50.4	135,394	131,343	-3.0	-0.7	1,615	2,110	-450	53,997	2.4	65.5	8.8	29.2
Union	14.3	12.8	9.5	49.6	17,808	17,244	-3.2	-1.9	193	324	-187	6,813	2.4	65.2	7.8	30.3
Vermilion	13.7	11.7	8.3	49.8	81,625	74,188	-9.1	-1.5	1,050	1,385	-757	31,013	2.4	61.4	14.5	33.3
Wabash	14.7	13.0	9.3	50.0	11,947	11,361	-4.9	-1.4	141	193	-108	4,780	2.4	64.3	9.3	32.4
Warren	13.2	11.9	8.5	50.2	17,707	16,835	-4.9	-1.8	198	267	-235	6,789	2.3	66.8	13.1	28.9
Washington	15.6	12.2	9.1	49.4	14,716	13,761	-6.5	-0.8	172	196	-84	6,020	2.3	67.8	8.7	28.4
Wayne	14.4	12.1	9.7	50.2	16,760	16,179	-3.5	-1.3	232	296	-150	7,114	2.3	64.8	9.2	31.4
White	15.2	12.0	9.5	50.4	14,665	13,877	-5.4	-0.7	163	313	57	6,040	2.2	64.6	13.0	33.5
Whiteside	14.3	12.6	9.1	50.3	58,498	55,691	-4.8	-0.7	730	955	-165	23,225	2.4	63.8	11.7	30.3
Will	13.1	8.8	5.3	50.0	677,560	696,355	2.8	0.1	8,674	7,316	-611	232,395	2.9	75.0	11.2	20.6
Williamson	13.5	11.5	8.2	49.8	66,357	67,153	1.2	-0.4	853	1,077	-57	27,937	2.3	62.4	11.4	31.9

1. No spouse present.

STATE County	Persons in group quarters, 2021	Daytime Population, 2016–2020		Births, 2021		Deaths, 2021		Persons under 65 with no health insurance, 2019		Medicare, 2021			COVID-19 Deaths, 2020	
		Number	Employment/ residence ratio	Total	Rate[1]	Number	Rate[1]	Number	Percent	Total beneficiaries	Enrolled in Original Medicare	Enrolled in Medicare Advantage	Number	Rate[1]
	32	33	34	35	36	37	38	39	40	41	42	43	44	45
ILLINOIS—Cont'd														
Hardin	6	3,296	0.6	31	8.5	66	18.1	225	8.1	1,090	919	171	10	2.8
Henderson	30	5,042	0.5	48	7.6	95	15.0	385	7.8	1,678	1,333	344	15	2.4
Henry	674	41,748	0.7	503	10.3	640	13.1	2,607	6.8	11,595	7,818	3,777	70	1.4
Iroquois	418	24,038	0.7	308	11.4	418	15.5	1,823	8.7	6,894	5,665	1,229	53	2.0
Jackson	3,135	60,064	1.1	519	9.8	579	11.0	3,691	8.3	10,281	7,373	2,908	74	1.4
Jasper	31	7,871	0.6	98	10.6	110	11.9	530	6.9	2,243	1,880	363	15	1.6
Jefferson	2,031	43,101	1.3	413	11.2	567	15.3	2,066	7.3	8,460	7,104	1,355	79	2.1
Jersey	721	17,848	0.6	192	9.0	286	13.4	995	5.9	5,159	3,771	1,388	39	1.8
Jo Daviess	155	19,018	0.8	161	7.3	277	12.6	1,210	8.0	6,540	3,234	3,306	25	1.1
Johnson	1,322	11,737	0.8	90	6.7	164	12.3	617	7.3	2,993	2,197	796	20	1.5
Kane	6,123	494,397	0.9	5,633	10.9	4,230	8.2	46,080	10.2	81,566	57,986	23,580	558	1.1
Kankakee	5,940	106,091	0.9	1,207	11.3	1,366	12.8	6,322	7.4	21,977	16,455	5,523	142	1.3
Kendall	165	99,793	0.6	1,492	11.2	771	5.8	7,377	6.4	16,166	11,958	4,208	78	0.6
Knox	3,882	49,610	1.0	463	9.4	745	15.0	2,578	7.3	12,239	7,914	4,326	115	2.3
Lake	18,893	712,147	1.0	6,681	9.4	5,809	8.2	47,402	8.2	113,825	90,291	23,534	749	1.1
LaSalle	3,275	104,144	0.9	1,055	9.7	1,519	13.9	5,551	6.5	24,391	20,238	4,153	207	1.9
Lawrence	2,317	14,533	0.8	123	8.1	225	14.8	786	7.4	3,253	2,896	357	34	2.2
Lee	2,977	34,064	1.0	285	8.4	490	14.4	1,536	6.2	7,791	6,021	1,770	75	2.2
Livingston	2,236	36,516	1.1	385	10.8	510	14.3	1,752	6.5	7,945	5,895	2,051	58	1.6
Logan	3,950	27,254	0.9	263	9.4	366	13.1	1,082	5.5	6,056	4,205	1,852	48	1.7
McDonough	2,968	31,065	1.1	233	8.6	364	13.5	1,563	7.4	5,854	4,140	1,714	44	1.6
McHenry	1,530	260,790	0.7	2,901	9.3	2,560	8.2	18,546	7.1	53,469	42,414	11,055	251	0.8
McLean	10,311	176,020	1.1	1,663	9.7	1,474	8.6	7,970	5.8	27,167	18,010	9,157	131	0.8
Macon	3,859	110,904	1.1	1,191	11.6	1,430	13.9	4,788	6.0	24,263	19,173	5,090	159	1.5
Macoupin	796	37,418	0.6	385	8.6	674	15.1	2,355	6.7	11,140	8,702	2,437	71	1.6
Madison	3,786	245,184	0.9	2,598	9.8	3,461	13.1	13,796	6.4	55,288	33,224	22,064	330	1.2
Marion	704	36,546	0.9	422	11.3	527	14.1	2,057	7.0	9,342	8,175	1,167	95	2.5
Marshall	241	9,869	0.7	109	9.3	173	14.8	572	6.6	3,017	2,294	723	D	D
Mason	154	11,441	0.7	141	10.9	193	14.9	704	6.9	3,390	2,695	696	35	2.7
Massac	274	12,414	0.7	150	10.7	228	16.2	764	7.1	3,687	3,264	424	28	2.0
Menard	129	8,551	0.4	123	10.1	145	11.9	563	5.8	2,789	1,733	1,057	13	1.1
Mercer	159	12,112	0.5	124	7.9	202	12.9	764	6.4	3,822	2,399	1,424	19	1.2
Monroe	296	26,786	0.6	325	9.3	393	11.3	1,092	3.8	7,169	4,049	3,120	48	1.4
Montgomery	2,383	27,735	0.9	254	9.0	413	14.7	1,431	7.0	6,737	5,439	1,297	31	1.1
Morgan	3,143	34,704	1.1	338	10.3	461	14.1	1,470	6.1	7,774	5,809	1,965	77	2.3
Moultrie	348	13,662	0.9	166	11.4	209	14.4	993	8.6	3,125	2,591	533	21	1.4
Ogle	486	44,595	0.7	513	9.9	594	11.5	2,926	7.2	11,011	7,674	3,337	63	1.2
Peoria	4,741	199,203	1.2	2,249	12.5	2,124	11.8	10,443	7.3	36,351	22,814	13,537	227	1.3
Perry	2,435	19,382	0.8	176	8.4	276	13.2	1,008	6.9	4,632	3,401	1,230	35	1.7
Piatt	59	12,582	0.5	174	10.4	196	11.7	744	5.7	3,701	2,062	1,639	10	0.6
Pike	389	14,026	0.8	169	11.6	229	15.7	916	7.7	3,788	3,167	621	41	2.8
Pope	207	3,754	0.6	37	9.8	37	9.8	246	8.4	1,142	893	250	D	D
Pulaski	17	5,650	1.1	49	9.6	78	15.3	342	8.4	1,426	1,228	199	D	D
Putnam	1	4,742	0.7	40	7.1	74	13.2	276	6.3	1,413	1,071	342	D	D
Randolph	4,022	32,153	1.0	283	9.4	419	13.9	1,426	6.6	6,894	4,820	2,074	56	1.9
Richland	330	15,530	1.0	168	10.6	212	13.4	926	7.7	3,755	3,185	569	30	1.9
Rock Island	4,560	151,590	1.1	1,548	10.8	1,768	12.3	8,856	8.1	31,140	17,718	13,422	230	1.6
St. Clair	4,231	241,780	0.8	2,864	11.2	3,146	12.3	15,294	7.2	49,451	29,363	20,088	350	1.4
Saline	852	22,882	0.9	281	12.0	402	17.1	1,366	7.5	6,093	4,914	1,179	44	1.9
Sangamon	3,846	209,938	1.2	1,980	10.1	2,462	12.6	10,156	6.5	41,685	24,333	17,352	204	1.0
Schuyler	452	6,195	0.8	64	9.3	94	13.7	376	7.3	1,658	1,308	350	14	2.0
Scott	29	4,016	0.6	39	8.0	64	13.1	226	5.7	1,126	869	257	D	D
Shelby	141	17,770	0.6	195	9.4	313	15.0	1,004	6.1	5,360	4,616	744	35	1.7
Stark	84	4,800	0.8	57	10.7	79	14.8	293	7.2	1,304	950	355	12	2.2
Stephenson	769	43,529	0.9	449	10.1	651	14.7	2,211	6.6	11,688	6,430	5,258	68	1.5
Tazewell	2,426	126,560	0.9	1,245	9.5	1,645	12.6	5,767	5.5	28,902	19,554	9,348	202	1.5
Union	555	15,446	0.8	157	9.2	260	15.2	1,080	8.4	4,497	3,339	1,158	29	1.7
Vermilion	2,701	76,202	1.0	863	11.7	1,093	14.9	3,829	6.6	17,556	10,070	7,486	94	1.3
Wabash	68	10,045	0.7	104	9.2	158	14.0	606	6.7	2,813	2,445	368	18	1.6
Warren	950	16,246	0.9	160	9.6	209	12.5	1,059	8.5	3,940	3,004	937	36	2.1
Washington	206	14,209	1.0	145	10.6	160	11.7	611	5.6	3,222	2,633	589	21	1.5
Wayne	56	14,378	0.7	186	11.6	231	14.4	1,054	8.4	3,899	3,525	374	38	2.4
White	370	12,965	0.9	128	9.3	244	17.7	749	7.2	3,638	3,148	491	32	2.3
Whiteside	951	52,449	0.9	598	10.8	770	13.9	2,895	6.8	13,964	10,769	3,195	159	2.9
Will	8,515	622,694	0.8	6,866	9.9	5,915	8.5	40,663	6.9	107,466	76,580	30,886	701	1.0
Williamson	1,933	68,188	1.0	683	10.2	876	13.1	3,504	6.7	15,250	11,919	3,331	91	1.4

1. Per 1,000 estimated resident population.

STATE County	COVID-19 Vaccinations, 2021–2022: Number	COVID-19 Vaccinations, 2021–2022: Percent[5]	Education: School enrollment and attainment, 2016–2020: Enrollment[1]: Total	Enrollment[1]: Percent private	Attainment[2] (percent): High school graduate or less	Attainment[2] (percent): Bachelor's degree or more	Local government expenditures,[3] 2018–2019: Total current spending (mil dol)	Local government expenditures,[3] 2018–2019: Current spending per student (dollars)	Money income, 2016–2020: Per capita income[4]	Households: Median income (dollars)	Households: Percent with income of less than $50,000	Households: Percent with income of $200,000 or more	Income and poverty, 2020: Median household income (dollars)	Percent below poverty level: All persons	Percent below poverty level: Children under 18 years	Percent below poverty level: Children 5 to 17 years in families
	46	47	48	49	50	51	52	53	54	55	56	57	58	59	60	61
ILLINOIS—Cont'd																
Hardin	1,600	41.9	535	2.8	49.4	11.2	6.1	11,206	27,720	50,847	49.3	2.2	39,674	18.0	27.8	26.5
Henderson	3,278	49.3	1,193	16.0	49.8	17.5	10.5	13,715	31,645	55,759	44.8	1.3	58,577	10.6	14.5	14.4
Henry	28,852	59.0	10,966	7.9	41.6	23.7	109.4	13,056	31,763	60,000	42.2	4.3	63,859	9.6	12.4	11.3
Iroquois	13,928	51.4	5,803	11.9	51.3	15.4	63.9	15,162	28,790	54,445	47.1	2.9	53,633	11.2	14.0	13.8
Jackson	29,780	52.5	19,933	7.3	31.7	35.5	109.4	15,836	26,656	39,689	59.4	3.8	45,608	17.2	24.2	24.0
Jasper	4,054	42.2	2,033	13.9	44.3	18.8	22.4	17,499	27,877	55,911	43.2	2.2	57,969	9.6	12.8	12.4
Jefferson	17,782	47.2	7,858	12.0	42.1	17.4	75.6	12,961	26,742	51,662	48.5	3.5	58,114	12.5	18.8	19.3
Jersey	12,193	56.0	5,056	26.9	43.1	24.3	30.1	11,818	32,544	67,845	38.1	6.7	69,341	8.5	11.8	11.2
Jo Daviess	16,595	78.1	4,018	11.1	42.4	26.4	57.1	17,437	34,974	59,223	42.2	3.7	56,446	9.1	11.6	11.5
Johnson	6,489	52.3	2,253	3.2	50.6	16.0	22.1	12,353	23,548	55,363	45.5	2.3	51,607	14.9	16.5	15.5
Kane	359,223	67.5	144,730	15.3	37.2	34.7	1,406.0	14,526	37,548	83,374	28.6	10.8	83,784	7.3	8.9	8.1
Kankakee	57,695	52.5	27,114	21.1	46.4	20.6	257.1	14,731	28,445	59,370	42.5	3.8	57,413	13.6	17.3	17.3
Kendall	88,960	69.0	37,383	13.5	31.0	35.9	382.4	14,101	36,504	96,854	17.9	10.1	97,263	3.9	4.0	3.9
Knox	29,512	59.4	11,380	21.0	46.6	19.2	92.6	12,864	24,804	44,464	54.3	1.9	52,881	13.4	18.3	18.2
Lake	546,694	78.5	187,215	17.2	29.3	46.1	2,583.8	19,797	47,223	92,654	26.8	17.7	100,325	7.0	8.3	8.5
LaSalle	63,411	58.4	23,371	13.8	46.1	18.4	246.0	15,832	31,020	60,069	41.9	3.5	62,714	11.4	15.5	14.3
Lawrence	6,428	41.0	2,667	4.0	51.6	14.0	23.9	11,376	26,233	53,087	47.7	3.6	47,408	16.5	17.7	18.2
Lee	20,399	59.8	6,936	18.6	44.7	18.7	63.0	15,217	29,343	59,986	43.2	3.8	64,310	10.6	12.7	12.4
Livingston	18,142	50.9	6,967	10.8	52.3	16.6	90.8	15,792	29,646	58,676	42.0	2.8	66,274	9.9	12.9	12.8
Logan	15,531	54.3	6,670	21.9	46.6	19.5	48.0	14,887	29,377	58,122	43.3	4.1	65,255	11.6	14.6	14.3
McDonough	14,261	48.0	10,421	5.5	35.6	32.4	59.5	17,958	25,219	43,591	54.7	2.6	52,155	16.8	18.8	17.1
McHenry	207,083	67.3	77,468	12.6	32.5	35.2	1,087.8	15,747	40,545	90,014	25.4	10.7	89,730	6.3	7.3	6.4
McLean	109,526	63.9	56,942	11.9	27.9	44.6	348.4	13,866	34,496	68,037	38.5	7.0	71,919	10.7	9.8	9.2
Macon	55,673	53.5	22,817	17.5	43.0	23.6	205.5	12,798	30,681	53,725	47.4	4.2	57,601	12.8	18.0	18.1
Macoupin	24,702	55.0	10,229	15.7	48.5	18.5	97.9	12,037	28,726	56,264	45.4	2.0	53,312	10.8	14.5	13.9
Madison	163,923	62.3	65,283	14.1	36.2	27.8	518.9	13,030	33,599	64,045	38.8	5.3	63,903	11.0	12.6	11.6
Marion	17,067	45.9	8,244	13.7	44.7	16.2	87.7	13,106	26,853	49,925	50.1	2.5	52,019	14.2	20.9	18.2
Marshall	6,581	57.5	2,089	11.3	45.8	18.2	16.9	13,667	29,533	57,303	44.5	2.0	54,022	9.3	12.3	12.0
Mason	7,198	53.9	2,744	13.7	51.0	16.5	34.3	13,438	30,144	50,883	48.9	4.0	53,503	13.4	20.0	18.7
Massac	5,667	41.1	2,830	3.9	46.9	13.8	31.5	13,651	24,624	51,195	49.4	1.0	49,054	14.8	22.9	22.2
Menard	6,999	57.4	2,715	8.4	39.6	23.3	27.7	11,245	39,221	77,550	30.2	4.0	69,749	7.9	10.8	10.2
Mercer	9,367	60.7	3,206	12.1	48.0	18.0	35.3	13,028	30,493	57,182	42.0	2.1	62,857	8.8	12.1	11.5
Monroe	21,672	62.6	7,713	19.6	30.5	36.6	60.0	11,829	43,435	89,648	26.5	10.2	90,880	4.1	3.5	3.1
Montgomery	14,724	51.8	5,721	13.0	51.5	18.1	49.0	11,833	27,510	54,886	45.6	2.3	59,497	13.5	17.1	16.1
Morgan	18,423	54.7	7,596	27.4	49.9	20.0	71.3	15,630	29,047	53,002	47.2	3.0	54,764	12.4	15.1	15.1
Moultrie	6,411	44.2	3,205	16.8	48.6	20.5	18.7	11,250	30,734	64,033	39.4	3.8	61,022	9.1	11.8	11.0
Ogle	29,446	58.1	11,630	11.2	43.6	21.8	136.3	15,578	31,974	63,643	38.4	3.7	71,470	8.3	11.1	10.5
Peoria	110,411	61.6	44,637	24.1	36.4	31.1	405.8	14,676	32,371	55,729	44.8	5.2	53,506	14.2	19.7	18.1
Perry	10,636	50.9	3,894	6.7	53.6	11.6	29.7	11,147	24,442	51,616	49.2	1.8	55,132	15.1	16.5	14.6
Piatt	10,184	62.3	3,499	14.8	39.4	29.8	36.8	13,854	34,674	73,668	35.4	4.4	69,521	6.4	7.1	6.6
Pike	6,432	41.3	3,274	11.8	51.4	15.6	31.9	12,920	26,185	46,605	52.3	3.0	48,815	13.5	18.1	17.9
Pope	1,503	36.0	562	3.4	55.2	16.5	6.4	12,797	22,690	43,140	56.1	0.9	49,071	15.6	22.9	24.8
Pulaski	2,280	42.7	1,198	6.2	50.2	11.7	15.2	18,366	20,898	37,308	59.5	1.3	40,481	20.4	31.6	28.8
Putnam	3,296	57.4	1,041	6.8	43.8	19.2	13.0	15,251	32,902	64,694	37.5	2.4	70,070	7.3	11.5	10.8
Randolph	16,699	52.5	6,122	21.4	53.9	12.9	56.7	14,223	27,206	55,319	43.5	2.7	56,867	12.0	15.5	14.8
Richland	7,460	48.1	3,399	12.0	38.0	21.0	26.1	11,124	28,457	55,032	46.5	2.8	56,900	11.9	15.7	15.0
Rock Island	83,086	58.6	32,267	18.6	40.3	23.8	294.5	13,863	30,380	55,980	43.7	3.4	58,022	13.5	18.8	18.2
St. Clair	164,918	63.5	65,295	17.1	36.1	29.0	608.7	15,257	31,511	57,473	44.5	5.0	61,863	13.8	19.3	18.0
Saline	11,436	48.7	4,859	9.4	40.6	19.9	45.3	11,608	27,421	43,928	56.3	3.4	45,793	15.3	21.4	21.5
Sangamon	126,761	65.1	46,721	16.4	35.1	34.1	395.6	13,646	35,549	61,743	41.0	5.5	60,541	12.8	16.2	15.3
Schuyler	3,795	56.1	1,263	9.8	44.0	20.5	12.6	12,299	26,479	51,376	48.2	2.2	53,686	11.7	14.6	14.5
Scott	2,093	42.3	1,076	17.0	53.1	21.0	10.8	12,737	29,120	59,352	43.5	1.9	59,285	10.8	17.3	16.6
Shelby	9,102	42.1	4,571	14.6	51.1	16.6	28.0	12,257	28,234	59,134	41.1	1.9	64,508	8.9	12.0	11.4
Stark	2,863	53.6	1,042	13.4	50.3	18.3	11.4	13,434	29,007	53,828	46.7	2.4	54,219	10.8	15.4	14.7
Stephenson	27,200	61.1	9,141	13.3	41.7	20.8	98.5	15,697	28,893	50,466	49.6	2.8	57,952	11.2	17.2	16.5
Tazewell	78,236	59.4	30,088	14.0	38.7	26.0	268.6	13,684	33,854	66,220	37.5	4.9	69,874	7.6	9.3	8.6
Union	9,500	57.0	3,326	9.4	45.7	23.1	39.9	13,814	27,778	51,655	47.5	3.2	55,736	14.0	18.6	17.6
Vermilion	34,764	45.9	17,411	6.7	51.7	15.5	185.7	14,983	25,484	46,842	52.8	2.1	49,678	18.6	29.2	25.2
Wabash	5,680	49.3	2,536	16.4	39.3	18.9	19.2	11,730	29,252	48,878	50.9	3.5	56,190	11.7	13.9	13.3
Warren	8,408	49.9	4,698	28.4	45.3	22.7	32.0	12,381	27,899	54,291	43.9	3.3	57,964	10.7	14.2	14.9
Washington	8,157	58.7	2,792	29.7	40.2	20.9	20.8	11,479	32,687	64,390	37.9	1.8	69,386	7.6	9.1	8.8
Wayne	6,400	39.5	3,164	14.2	47.5	14.2	27.4	11,256	26,502	50,205	49.9	1.3	49,649	12.9	19.0	18.3
White	7,058	52.1	2,738	6.8	43.8	17.1	36.1	14,643	27,449	48,303	52.1	2.6	46,080	15.4	20.4	18.9
Whiteside	31,976	58.0	11,887	11.5	46.3	18.9	131.3	14,826	31,185	57,172	44.4	3.1	64,413	9.1	13.8	13.6
Will	470,317	68.1	184,547	15.2	34.8	34.8	1,751.6	15,867	37,967	90,800	25.4	11.0	90,349	7.2	9.0	8.4
Williamson	37,046	55.6	14,551	10.2	37.4	25.6	130.3	12,692	29,092	52,076	48.2	3.5	59,174	13.9	18.0	17.3

1. All persons 3 years old and over enrolled in nursery school through college. 2. Persons 25 years old and over. 3. Elementary and secondary education expenditures. 4. Based on population estimated by the American Community Survey, 2016–2020. 5. CDC percent based on 2019 population estimate.

STATE County	Personal income, 2020: Total (mil dol)	Personal income, 2020: Percent change 2019–2020	Personal income, 2020: Per capita[1]: Dollars	Personal income, 2020: Per capita[1]: Rank	Personal income, 2020: Wages and salaries (mil dol)	Personal income, 2020: Supplements to wages and salaries, employer contributions (mil dol): Pension and insurance	Personal income, 2020: Supplements to wages and salaries, employer contributions (mil dol): Government social insurance	Personal income, 2020: Proprietors' income (mil dol)	Personal income, 2020: Dividends, interest, and rent (mil dol)	Personal income, 2020: Personal transfer reecipts (mil dol)	Earnings, 2020: Total (mil dol)	Earnings, 2020: Contributions for government social insurance (mil dol): From employee and self-employed	Earnings, 2020: Contributions for government social insurance (mil dol): From employer
	62	63	64	65	66	67	68	69	70	71	72	73	74
ILLINOIS—Cont'd													
Hardin	155	8.2	40,720	2,371	27	8	2	12	21	69	49	4	2
Henderson	319	15.1	48,805	1,280	45	13	3	49	45	91	109	6	3
Henry	2,474	9.7	51,103	1,016	641	141	44	184	393	610	1,010	63	44
Iroquois	1,384	15.8	51,824	946	329	70	24	222	198	399	645	35	24
Jackson	2,284	7.6	40,297	2,418	1,298	345	80	131	411	680	1,854	95	80
Jasper	455	15.0	48,090	1,374	102	28	7	68	76	121	205	11	7
Jefferson	1,644	8.8	44,163	1,915	946	176	67	108	231	551	1,297	78	67
Jersey	1,012	9.3	46,828	1,534	221	52	15	51	124	299	340	26	15
Jo Daviess	1,134	10.1	53,399	827	309	67	22	77	257	302	475	33	22
Johnson	492	8.6	39,793	2,479	96	28	6	21	67	159	150	12	6
Kane	29,724	6.1	55,976	644	11,832	2,122	810	1,574	4,748	5,356	16,338	926	810
Kankakee	5,103	8.7	46,988	1,520	2,199	450	155	236	693	1,495	3,041	184	155
Kendall	7,054	8.2	53,998	782	1,384	276	93	266	882	1,049	2,020	120	93
Knox	2,204	12.1	44,921	1,804	827	172	73	162	329	791	1,234	82	73
Lake	59,066	2.6	85,159	60	29,535	4,623	1,892	3,810	14,742	7,164	39,860	2,221	1,892
LaSalle	5,302	7.6	49,292	1,217	2,095	426	148	324	723	1,434	2,992	183	148
Lawrence	555	15.9	35,878	2,876	194	47	13	57	86	219	311	19	13
Lee	1,590	10.7	47,249	1,483	593	118	41	132	227	450	884	55	41
Livingston	1,845	15.7	52,100	929	651	130	45	314	232	441	1,140	59	45
Logan	1,183	11.3	41,682	2,240	405	88	29	132	160	352	654	38	29
McDonough	1,221	8.8	41,685	2,239	494	138	30	117	219	350	779	39	30
McHenry	18,383	4.7	60,097	421	4,977	919	347	767	2,896	3,138	7,011	446	347
McLean	9,357	9.8	54,639	728	5,553	913	343	730	1,423	1,613	7,539	417	343
Macon	5,377	7.4	52,196	918	2,786	492	199	369	822	1,531	3,846	236	199
Macoupin	2,048	8.9	45,948	1,661	471	108	32	134	279	634	746	51	32
Madison	13,508	6.2	51,433	986	5,186	1,013	373	783	1,910	3,448	7,356	456	373
Marion	1,740	9.4	46,966	1,522	585	128	45	98	242	652	856	60	45
Marshall	579	11.9	51,165	1,006	135	30	10	61	83	165	236	15	10
Mason	621	14.0	47,178	1,491	125	34	8	80	85	203	247	15	8
Massac	601	10.2	44,089	1,934	152	37	10	25	87	239	224	17	10
Menard	616	8.5	51,028	1,023	73	21	5	54	93	150	152	10	5
Mercer	822	13.0	53,966	784	126	31	9	105	109	211	271	16	9
Monroe	2,132	4.7	61,366	369	373	73	26	98	333	386	570	40	26
Montgomery	1,127	10.9	40,180	2,436	355	81	25	117	187	394	578	37	25
Morgan	1,462	9.0	43,763	1,978	659	129	45	119	230	466	953	58	45
Moultrie	994	0.1	69,297	174	243	44	18	381	112	181	686	36	18
Ogle	2,521	6.5	50,110	1,132	851	178	59	144	365	615	1,231	76	59
Peoria	9,701	6.8	54,609	730	6,846	1,083	455	481	1,616	2,382	8,865	522	455
Perry	855	8.2	41,366	2,283	204	55	13	115	110	291	387	24	13
Piatt	981	10.7	59,952	428	158	38	10	101	133	185	308	18	10
Pike	717	12.6	47,052	1,508	172	40	13	106	98	218	331	19	13
Pope	138	12.1	33,286	3,016	20	6	1	7	22	60	34	3	1
Pulaski	226	12.9	43,533	2,007	68	23	4	15	28	102	111	6	4
Putnam	382	3.9	66,839	216	99	19	7	108	49	74	233	13	7
Randolph	1,314	9.2	41,919	2,214	519	119	35	94	198	407	767	48	35
Richland	718	10.9	46,318	1,605	269	53	20	64	111	220	407	25	20
Rock Island	6,833	8.5	48,492	1,325	5,009	856	321	263	1,224	1,854	6,448	387	321
St. Clair	12,811	6.9	49,646	1,182	5,186	1,119	389	546	2,003	3,662	7,241	430	389
Saline	1,027	8.6	44,321	1,899	327	78	23	71	149	422	500	34	23
Sangamon	10,255	6.6	52,891	861	5,350	1,055	353	695	1,788	2,482	7,453	420	353
Schuyler	334	11.0	49,505	1,196	75	19	5	52	41	86	151	8	5
Scott	233	15.2	47,152	1,493	43	13	3	41	27	58	99	5	3
Shelby	974	12.9	45,745	1,694	223	49	16	130	133	280	419	26	16
Stark	270	19.9	51,267	998	69	15	5	51	39	72	140	7	5
Stephenson	2,040	6.6	46,534	1,574	861	162	61	146	338	618	1,230	81	61
Tazewell	6,790	6.6	51,920	939	2,346	428	168	361	1,084	1,643	3,302	214	168
Union	792	10.1	48,028	1,390	196	51	14	46	112	286	308	21	14
Vermilion	3,334	10.9	44,533	1,867	1,333	293	94	250	438	1,102	1,970	121	94
Wabash	532	8.3	47,543	1,444	153	40	10	34	96	158	237	15	10
Warren	789	15.8	47,232	1,484	280	55	20	129	109	210	483	26	20
Washington	740	10.5	53,789	795	343	82	25	109	118	179	559	31	25
Wayne	707	12.1	44,127	1,925	165	42	12	104	100	229	323	19	12
White	698	5.6	52,223	914	168	37	12	105	116	216	322	20	12
Whiteside	2,665	9.3	48,757	1,288	976	230	68	163	417	811	1,437	87	68
Will	39,739	5.7	57,700	531	13,857	2,410	988	1,831	5,426	7,013	19,086	1,122	988
Williamson	3,229	6.7	48,625	1,305	1,318	303	94	165	434	923	1,879	115	94

1. Based on the resident population estimated as of July 1 of the year shown.

STATE County	Earnings, 2020 (cont.) — Percent by selected industries: Farm	Mining, quarrying, and extractions	Construction	Manu-facturing	Information; professional, scientific, technical services	Retail trade	Finance, insurance, real estate, and leasing	Health care and social assistance	Govern-ment	Social Security beneficiaries, December 2020: Number	Rate[1]	Supple-mental Security Income recipients, 2020	Housing units, 2021: Total	Percent change, 2010–2021
	75	76	77	78	79	80	81	82	83	84	85	86	87	88
ILLINOIS—Cont'd														
Hardin	8.1	D	D	D	D	D	D	26.1	23.7	1,180	323	155	2,196	0.0
Henderson	40.3	D	5.0	1.3	D	2.5	D	5.6	20.9	1,725	273	113	3,364	0.2
Henry	9.7	D	10.8	8.4	D	6.4	5.9	10.5	22.1	11,895	243	633	22,201	-0.1
Iroquois	27.5	D	7.4	6.3	2.1	6.7	5.7	D	13.7	7,120	265	553	12,786	0.1
Jackson	0.8	D	4.7	3.4	D	5.7	2.8	19.7	41.4	10,345	197	1,641	27,729	0.0
Jasper	26.7	1.4	6.5	4.7	1.1	4.4	4.8	1.1	19.9	2,405	262	138	4,227	0.0
Jefferson	1.5	0.5	2.8	23.2	D	6.8	5.4	19.1	13.1	8,905	241	894	16,643	0.0
Jersey	5.7	D	8.6	5.5	6.7	8.8	4.8	D	26.6	5,590	262	326	9,862	1.0
Jo Daviess	7.5	D	9.6	11.4	4.0	7.0	5.5	D	18.7	6,650	303	182	13,428	0.1
Johnson	4.3	D	5.3	2.1	3.2	3.8	D	8.3	46.8	3,215	239	267	5,530	0.1
Kane	0.1	0.1	7.9	16.5	9.0	5.5	6.2	10.0	17.6	81,200	157	5,095	189,742	0.5
Kankakee	2.4	D	4.2	24.3	D	6.5	4.3	16.0	15.3	23,025	216	2,596	45,332	0.1
Kendall	1.3	0.1	9.2	13.5	6.2	9.5	4.9	5.5	23.8	17,525	130	811	45,704	1.3
Knox	6.9	D	3.7	6.7	D	6.9	4.3	D	17.6	12,115	246	1,272	23,793	-0.1
Lake	0.0	0.0	3.9	22.2	9.7	6.7	7.1	6.2	14.0	111,430	157	8,180	270,019	0.2
LaSalle	4.3	2.3	6.0	18.7	3.7	6.8	5.1	8.1	15.1	25,920	238	1,712	49,839	0.0
Lawrence	7.6	9.7	3.3	22.0	1.8	4.0	10.1	9.5	19.2	3,475	229	295	6,344	0.9
Lee	6.9	0.5	3.0	26.1	2.7	5.6	4.9	15.8	15.5	8,280	243	494	14,988	0.0
Livingston	16.4	D	5.5	17.1	5.2	8.4	4.0	7.3	14.5	8,300	233	496	15,915	0.0
Logan	13.8	0.0	3.2	18.1	2.8	5.6	4.0	12.2	16.0	6,415	229	394	11,970	-0.1
McDonough	9.8	0.0	4.5	13.8	2.4	6.0	2.7	5.6	42.6	5,835	217	570	13,590	-0.1
McHenry	0.3	0.1	11.9	15.2	6.8	8.1	4.1	9.5	16.4	54,800	176	2,146	120,239	0.4
McLean	2.3	D	3.3	3.7	D	5.5	38.3	D	14.5	28,265	165	1,931	75,077	0.3
Macon	1.8	0.0	7.2	29.4	4.4	5.2	5.2	12.9	11.0	24,990	244	3,183	49,678	-0.1
Macoupin	8.1	D	7.8	7.3	D	7.6	5.8	D	21.5	11,975	270	983	21,101	0.3
Madison	0.5	0.1	8.1	15.3	6.6	6.8	4.2	11.8	16.3	57,730	218	5,542	118,943	0.2
Marion	3.3	1.8	5.4	17.5	2.8	5.0	3.9	17.9	18.4	9,530	255	1,243	17,370	0.1
Marshall	19.0	D	7.5	27.7	2.3	3.4	1.6	7.3	13.2	3,220	276	154	5,820	-0.1
Mason	24.0	D	4.1	3.2	1.9	4.3	4.9	6.0	30.7	3,550	276	306	6,622	0.0
Massac	3.5	D	3.0	D	1.5	5.6	2.3	D	27.4	4,035	289	446	6,827	0.5
Menard	21.8	0.0	7.2	1.2	7.2	5.6	D	D	26.5	2,990	246	169	5,596	0.1
Mercer	30.6	0.0	5.0	11.2	2.1	4.8	4.9	D	18.0	4,235	272	153	7,286	0.0
Monroe	3.9	0.4	12.1	4.1	11.3	8.8	9.8	7.9	17.2	7,340	210	154	14,690	0.8
Montgomery	11.6	1.9	6.2	8.5	3.0	9.3	6.2	14.4	18.5	7,125	254	612	12,522	0.1
Morgan	5.8	0.0	4.0	24.6	D	7.1	6.6	11.4	15.3	8,240	253	858	15,035	0.0
Moultrie	7.1	3.6	6.8	49.9	6.9	2.8	1.6	3.1	5.2	3,225	222	167	6,182	0.2
Ogle	5.0	D	8.4	17.3	D	4.3	5.1	D	16.0	11,545	224	584	22,646	0.1
Peoria	0.5	D	4.1	23.6	8.4	4.4	7.4	20.6	9.2	38,210	213	4,968	84,992	-0.1
Perry	4.6	D	3.6	19.9	D	5.0	9.2	D	27.9	4,970	237	442	9,148	0.2
Piatt	21.1	0.1	5.9	5.7	3.7	5.4	6.8	D	21.2	3,665	219	119	7,392	0.4
Pike	21.8	D	5.5	2.2	D	5.6	10.9	11.1	18.3	3,850	263	324	7,278	0.2
Pope	5.3	D	3.6	D	D	D	D	D	41.1	1,225	324	96	2,357	0.1
Pulaski	9.4	D	D	D	-0.1	3.6	D	D	54.8	1,575	311	239	2,842	0.3
Putnam	11.4	0.9	D	24.6	D	2.2	4.0	5.7	8.0	1,495	269	57	3,073	0.5
Randolph	4.1	D	5.0	19.0	D	7.9	3.3	8.3	23.5	7,305	242	476	13,397	0.1
Richland	9.4	1.8	3.0	8.2	2.0	6.5	5.6	13.8	15.8	3,970	251	414	7,360	0.0
Rock Island	0.5	0.1	3.6	10.6	7.2	5.0	3.8	8.8	19.4	32,115	225	2,728	66,735	0.0
St. Clair	0.5	0.1	5.5	6.2	11.7	6.4	3.9	12.1	30.1	51,375	202	7,427	115,117	0.4
Saline	2.9	0.5	9.1	4.4	6.8	9.2	6.2	D	23.7	6,500	279	1,032	11,569	0.0
Sangamon	1.5	D	4.3	3.0	10.1	6.0	8.6	21.9	24.2	44,350	228	4,529	93,260	0.2
Schuyler	23.2	D	6.6	5.7	D	4.2	3.7	5.9	25.3	1,640	240	85	3,317	-0.1
Scott	29.9	0.0	4.2	D	D	2.7	D	D	17.9	1,085	224	69	2,386	0.0
Shelby	21.1	D	4.7	20.5	6.8	4.9	4.1	D	12.6	5,425	261	308	10,063	0.4
Stark	30.5	0.0	10.7	14.2	D	6.0	D	3.2	12.1	1,370	259	65	2,575	0.0
Stephenson	4.2	0.0	15.3	18.7	4.3	5.3	8.4	13.1	14.5	12,040	274	1,058	21,345	-0.1
Tazewell	2.2	D	9.6	15.1	5.4	9.0	7.1	6.8	16.1	30,735	236	1,862	58,608	0.1
Union	5.2	D	3.8	5.4	3.7	7.6	3.9	D	31.4	4,785	283	567	7,856	0.2
Vermilion	5.9	D	3.2	19.9	2.0	5.6	4.6	9.3	22.7	18,495	253	2,603	34,356	-0.1
Wabash	6.6	8.7	11.4	4.2	D	6.0	4.3	D	32.6	2,930	262	191	5,413	0.0
Warren	19.6	0.0	4.2	29.9	1.9	4.4	3.1	D	13.1	3,575	216	290	7,589	-0.1
Washington	5.5	D	4.3	19.8	D	9.5	3.9	D	8.7	3,290	241	143	6,407	0.3
Wayne	18.8	3.9	4.9	1.5	3.0	6.8	3.8	D	18.9	4,025	252	282	7,682	0.0
White	16.5	12.8	5.9	4.8	2.3	7.8	5.6	D	15.3	3,915	284	397	6,746	-0.1
Whiteside	5.7	D	4.2	20.8	4.7	6.2	3.3	7.1	27.1	14,670	265	1,022	25,829	-0.1
Will	0.2	0.1	8.6	10.8	6.7	6.9	4.4	10.3	14.6	109,225	157	7,023	252,679	0.7
Williamson	0.3	D	4.4	11.0	4.1	7.8	8.0	18.6	26.5	16,050	240	1,595	32,009	0.5

1. Per 1,000 resident population estimated as of July 1 of the year shown.

STATE County	Housing units, 2016–2020: Occupied units: Total	Owner-occupied: Percent	Owner-occupied: Median value[1]	Median owner cost as a percent of income: With a mortgage	Median owner cost as a percent of income: Without a mortgage[2]	Renter-occupied: Median rent[3]	Renter-occupied: Median rent as a percent of income[2]	Sub-standard units[4] (percent)	Civilian labor force, 2021: Total	Civilian labor force, 2021: Percent change, 2020–2021	Unemployment: Total	Unemployment: Rate[5]	Civilian employment[6], 2016–2020: Total	Percent: Management, business, science, and arts	Percent: Construction, production, and maintenance occupations
	89	90	91	92	93	94	95	96	97	98	99	100	101	102	103
ILLINOIS—Cont'd															
Hardin	1,515	78.8	77,500	19.9	11.0	350	23.1	3.0	1,322	2.6	89	6.7	1,422	32.7	36.4
Henderson	3,028	83.1	85,800	15.7	10.0	638	26.8	2.0	3,543	0.3	142	4.0	3,243	35.4	32.2
Henry	19,996	78.8	122,200	17.2	12.6	692	25.1	1.0	23,644	-0.2	1,153	4.9	23,169	32.3	27.7
Iroquois	11,845	76.3	107,300	19.5	11.3	690	27.2	1.4	13,086	-3.4	616	4.7	12,584	30.8	30.7
Jackson	24,208	50.4	114,300	18.5	10.4	682	33.2	1.7	27,201	0.2	1,471	5.4	24,568	37.8	20.5
Jasper	3,791	83.2	99,900	19.9	10.0	645	24.5	2.9	4,723	3.3	201	4.3	4,542	27.0	33.3
Jefferson	14,792	71.8	97,100	18.9	10.7	717	26.3	2.2	16,498	-2.6	1,022	6.2	16,391	28.4	32.6
Jersey	8,158	82.1	148,800	18.2	11.2	632	27.3	0.5	10,545	-0.3	462	4.4	10,538	36.8	27.7
Jo Daviess	10,069	76.7	156,300	20.1	12.8	699	26.6	2.0	10,552	1.1	465	4.4	10,679	33.5	27.2
Johnson	4,174	83.3	117,500	18.7	10.3	637	36.3	1.1	4,088	0.1	245	6.0	3,830	37.0	19.6
Kane	181,845	74.6	245,500	22.2	13.0	1,187	29.8	3.4	259,900	-0.5	15,345	5.9	270,509	35.9	24.7
Kankakee	40,297	67.1	152,800	19.9	13.5	906	30.3	2.2	52,515	-2.5	3,415	6.5	50,893	30.7	30.0
Kendall	41,398	83.5	243,700	22.7	13.2	1,487	29.2	1.9	69,542	-1.0	3,258	4.7	66,161	41.0	22.1
Knox	20,428	66.5	83,700	18.2	12.0	623	30.7	1.6	20,453	-2.8	1,343	6.6	20,893	32.6	28.8
Lake	248,684	73.5	271,700	21.2	13.4	1,216	28.4	2.4	365,816	0.5	19,256	5.3	350,463	44.8	18.4
LaSalle	45,089	72.3	130,600	19.2	11.2	785	27.1	1.6	52,681	0.0	3,145	6.0	51,973	28.1	32.9
Lawrence	6,166	71.5	80,500	16.5	10.0	717	26.3	1.8	5,602	-2.5	341	6.1	6,415	31.7	34.8
Lee	13,634	69.6	122,600	18.4	11.4	671	27.3	0.7	16,913	-1.0	769	4.5	15,058	35.3	29.0
Livingston	14,366	71.9	114,000	19.0	12.0	745	24.4	2.0	15,499	-2.4	760	4.9	15,966	28.4	33.7
Logan	10,958	71.3	107,600	17.2	10.0	714	24.9	0.6	11,820	-2.0	567	4.8	12,463	31.7	26.7
McDonough	11,573	63.3	91,700	18.0	11.0	714	35.8	1.8	12,693	-0.6	624	4.9	13,445	32.2	23.7
McHenry	113,269	80.1	234,000	21.6	12.9	1,200	29.0	1.6	163,096	-1.0	7,707	4.7	164,018	38.7	22.5
McLean	66,225	64.9	166,400	18.2	10.0	842	26.2	1.6	85,656	1.0	3,910	4.6	86,450	43.7	15.8
Macon	43,810	69.1	103,100	17.9	10.0	690	28.2	1.4	46,552	-1.1	3,563	7.7	46,000	33.4	27.3
Macoupin	18,577	75.3	102,900	18.3	10.5	727	29.2	1.4	21,984	0.4	996	4.5	20,263	30.3	29.7
Madison	108,429	72.3	138,500	18.2	11.3	835	29.7	1.4	130,828	0.0	6,403	4.9	128,229	36.2	23.8
Marion	16,126	74.6	81,600	18.6	10.9	639	26.5	2.1	16,810	-1.4	975	5.8	16,390	28.2	32.4
Marshall	4,922	80.6	105,700	18.4	12.3	661	24.7	2.0	5,092	0.6	286	5.6	5,148	30.8	32.7
Mason	5,917	77.5	87,600	17.1	12.3	655	26.2	0.7	5,904	-0.1	320	5.4	6,094	28.9	30.7
Massac	5,619	77.1	88,500	20.3	11.0	719	31.9	2.9	5,368	-0.8	309	5.8	5,655	27.7	25.0
Menard	5,211	78.6	151,900	17.4	10.0	750	19.9	0.7	6,145	1.7	252	4.1	6,139	40.8	21.3
Mercer	6,477	78.7	111,000	18.1	10.2	688	27.4	1.0	7,555	-0.6	371	4.9	7,339	28.3	33.0
Monroe	13,576	84.9	220,600	18.7	11.0	846	28.5	0.3	18,465	0.5	579	3.1	18,476	44.8	18.8
Montgomery	11,619	76.4	90,300	16.8	10.4	628	28.4	1.5	11,279	-1.3	611	5.4	11,682	32.2	26.7
Morgan	13,560	69.5	109,700	18.7	10.3	684	24.8	1.2	15,739	-0.7	781	5.0	15,120	30.7	28.2
Moultrie	6,043	76.2	108,300	18.8	10.4	695	22.1	2.4	7,337	1.3	260	3.5	6,782	29.9	40.9
Ogle	20,967	71.9	150,400	19.2	10.8	763	24.6	2.4	23,645	-1.9	1,368	5.8	24,572	31.7	31.2
Peoria	73,519	65.1	130,700	19.1	11.5	813	28.1	2.1	82,725	-0.8	5,961	7.2	80,540	40.1	18.9
Perry	8,504	73.7	85,700	17.8	10.7	593	28.9	1.6	7,928	-1.7	456	5.8	7,942	26.8	33.7
Piatt	6,755	82.3	143,000	18.4	10.7	865	24.7	0.7	8,495	1.7	342	4.0	8,228	37.5	25.5
Pike	6,258	79.4	83,500	18.7	12.3	554	25.9	1.8	6,787	0.8	277	4.1	6,746	28.8	31.7
Pope	1,618	79.5	114,600	19.5	10.6	325	26.4	0.8	1,676	2.3	85	5.1	1,138	31.5	36.4
Pulaski	2,050	74.6	61,300	18.6	10.6	518	24.5	1.3	1,702	-3.1	158	9.3	1,819	29.2	25.7
Putnam	2,435	81.1	134,800	19.9	10.4	682	27.0	1.4	2,956	0.6	148	5.0	2,844	27.1	37.8
Randolph	12,047	73.4	110,900	17.4	10.0	674	23.0	1.2	13,674	-0.4	592	4.3	13,202	23.9	32.9
Richland	6,527	73.2	88,800	16.1	10.0	569	22.5	1.6	7,057	-4.0	304	4.3	7,382	28.4	35.5
Rock Island	60,607	67.9	123,100	18.5	12.2	753	27.1	1.9	67,709	-1.1	3,785	5.6	66,791	32.6	28.3
St. Clair	104,631	65.9	134,800	19.7	11.8	881	29.8	1.6	123,792	-0.2	7,570	6.1	122,448	36.4	21.8
Saline	10,140	74.3	77,900	18.6	10.4	664	31.2	2.5	9,274	-2.4	613	6.6	9,837	32.9	25.7
Sangamon	84,093	70.0	144,100	18.8	10.5	829	28.7	1.7	97,844	1.3	5,421	5.5	93,173	43.4	16.7
Schuyler	2,730	76.9	96,900	20.7	11.2	766	23.0	0.9	3,150	0.8	124	3.9	2,850	30.9	27.5
Scott	1,973	82.5	91,800	16.6	10.5	538	20.4	1.9	2,296	-2.2	117	5.1	2,356	37.3	30.1
Shelby	9,158	80.3	105,500	17.5	10.9	707	20.2	3.7	10,192	-0.2	424	4.2	10,428	28.5	33.5
Stark	2,304	80.3	87,500	17.9	11.7	672	26.4	0.1	2,362	0.4	129	5.5	2,470	32.6	34.6
Stephenson	19,741	69.9	99,600	18.4	12.7	671	28.2	1.2	20,851	-1.0	1,146	5.5	20,370	32.3	30.9
Tazewell	53,997	76.4	142,300	18.9	11.3	751	25.5	1.1	61,358	-0.8	3,053	5.0	62,193	35.7	24.2
Union	6,813	78.0	110,500	19.7	10.3	639	25.6	1.9	7,169	-0.1	406	5.7	6,904	31.2	29.5
Vermilion	31,013	70.8	80,900	17.4	11.1	683	27.0	1.7	31,753	-1.7	2,064	6.5	31,356	28.2	31.5
Wabash	4,780	80.5	80,900	17.1	10.3	664	27.6	2.2	5,409	-4.7	244	4.5	5,308	28.2	33.0
Warren	6,789	75.4	86,900	18.0	10.1	608	23.2	3.5	7,782	-3.3	357	4.6	7,943	30.5	30.5
Washington	6,020	78.9	117,400	17.9	13.1	723	22.2	1.6	9,551	0.2	287	3.0	7,068	31.7	34.7
Wayne	7,114	76.7	89,000	18.5	10.7	577	23.9	4.0	6,766	0.1	317	4.7	7,222	27.1	37.2
White	6,040	79.9	75,400	19.3	11.3	560	25.9	1.3	5,956	-2.1	296	5.0	5,923	28.7	35.4
Whiteside	23,225	74.3	107,800	17.6	11.1	711	27.8	1.8	27,339	-1.0	1,324	4.8	26,273	27.9	32.0
Will	232,395	81.4	239,400	21.8	12.9	1,183	30.3	2.1	354,842	-1.1	20,390	5.7	353,027	37.4	24.7
Williamson	27,937	70.6	120,900	18.5	11.3	725	27.5	0.8	31,145	-0.7	1,726	5.5	29,669	35.3	22.8

1. Specified owner-occupied units. 2. A value of 10.0 represents 10 percent or less; a value of 50.0 represents 50 percent or more. 3. Specified renter-occupied units. 4. Overcrowded or lacking complete plumbing facilities. 5. Percent of civilian labor force. 6. Civilian employed persons 16 years old and over.

STATE County	Private nonfarm establishments, employment and payroll, 2020									Agriculture, 2017			
		Employment						Annual payroll		Farms			Farm producers whose primary occupation is farming (percent)
											Percent with:		
	Number of establish-ments	Total	Health care and social assistance	Manufac-turing	Retail trade	Finance and insurance	Professional, scientific, and technical services	Total (mil dol)	Average per employee (dollars)	Number	Fewer than 50 acres	1000 acres or more	
	104	105	106	107	108	109	110	111	112	113	114	115	116
ILLINOIS—Cont'd													
Hardin	56	545	283	NA	58	14	22	19	34,594	161	21.7	3.1	30.6
Henderson	107	651	128	NA	75	85	25	22	33,661	438	23.3	11.4	58.8
Henry	1,016	13,157	1,578	4,378	1,801	505	268	547	41,589	1,353	37.0	10.7	45.5
Iroquois	638	5,659	1,568	608	880	334	93	211	37,267	1,516	26.2	14.7	48.3
Jackson	1,220	15,838	3,804	1,083	3,184	575	604	610	38,518	772	34.7	6.9	40.4
Jasper	216	1,548	147	172	182	112	30	63	40,880	913	36.0	6.9	39.2
Jefferson	914	18,231	3,611	5,065	2,171	405	386	857	46,994	1,099	41.4	5.2	34.5
Jersey	401	4,569	935	200	838	205	112	148	32,399	519	35.5	9.2	43.2
Jo Daviess	670	6,042	737	722	947	183	145	237	39,146	947	31.0	6.0	42.3
Johnson	165	1,319	261	33	244	61	99	36	27,108	653	34.2	2.6	36.3
Kane	12,951	190,960	25,162	30,561	24,003	7,503	9,911	9,413	49,294	605	53.1	7.9	47.9
Kankakee	2,277	37,296	8,082	6,131	5,672	1,024	685	1,643	44,056	756	36.6	12.3	46.9
Kendall	2,301	24,083	1,795	2,382	5,547	744	940	924	38,354	313	39.9	13.7	52.5
Knox	974	14,736	3,375	1,030	3,308	406	265	472	32,054	853	22.5	14.3	50.7
Lake	19,769	320,154	37,516	38,768	36,091	14,897	32,000	24,772	77,374	302	77.8	2.6	40.6
LaSalle	2,565	36,007	4,812	5,701	5,953	1,239	1,257	1,589	44,140	1,496	33.4	11.4	45.9
Lawrence	237	3,309	411	1,033	344	336	39	122	36,984	426	34.7	15.3	44.0
Lee	700	10,501	2,050	3,434	1,210	263	286	461	43,861	832	33.5	14.5	50.8
Livingston	841	11,563	1,448	3,488	1,496	427	186	498	43,026	1,313	29.9	14.3	49.2
Logan	549	7,040	1,412	1,083	916	245	231	263	37,408	683	30.7	19.0	51.6
McDonough	620	8,264	1,891	1,476	1,371	284	218	290	35,053	760	29.3	13.2	47.2
McHenry	8,016	87,256	12,235	13,943	13,734	2,024	3,249	4,255	48,768	881	58.2	6.5	50.7
McLean	3,461	72,607	8,488	3,494	8,770	18,750	2,530	4,092	56,357	1,416	33.9	13.8	46.4
Macon	2,353	45,126	8,123	8,234	4,890	1,547	1,318	2,398	53,139	589	41.8	16.0	49.9
Macoupin	820	7,621	1,436	511	1,216	381	119	278	36,524	1,169	31.7	9.9	43.2
Madison	5,544	88,571	14,293	10,087	11,689	2,852	3,682	3,981	44,943	1,079	47.1	8.4	36.7
Marion	864	10,843	2,770	2,838	1,145	355	203	414	38,191	1,004	39.1	4.7	32.5
Marshall	237	2,470	451	845	245	86	30	102	41,330	472	21.2	11.0	45.6
Mason	257	2,049	535	110	364	125	23	76	37,065	548	25.2	18.4	47.8
Massac	228	3,092	762	363	342	107	109	124	40,234	417	34.3	7.9	50.3
Menard	195	1,101	81	56	229	91	81	44	39,833	386	32.4	12.7	46.5
Mercer	252	2,192	382	527	321	126	31	78	35,757	748	33.2	10.8	46.0
Monroe	821	8,328	967	293	1,342	378	700	314	37,648	568	46.0	10.9	41.2
Montgomery	681	7,164	1,437	642	1,375	391	158	256	35,699	1,067	33.3	13.8	47.9
Morgan	789	13,056	2,295	2,329	1,744	1,092	453	534	40,867	693	29.0	13.3	44.2
Moultrie	324	5,006	667	2,324	363	133	125	223	44,573	526	50.2	10.3	35.6
Ogle	1,012	13,015	1,550	2,868	1,362	459	291	630	48,431	1,011	43.0	10.8	46.7
Peoria	4,256	99,362	24,926	5,886	10,154	3,557	4,703	6,126	61,653	884	37.8	7.7	38.4
Perry	381	4,158	1,186	422	589	153	67	148	35,557	572	34.4	7.9	40.6
Piatt	329	2,364	461	226	432	158	108	91	38,480	422	36.0	21.1	53.6
Pike	349	2,983	687	135	519	199	70	112	37,575	956	24.7	15.2	40.4
Pope	49	361	93	NA	55	NA	7	6	17,753	322	25.2	2.5	32.9
Pulaski	84	577	125	NA	109	37	NA	17	29,901	222	26.1	15.3	38.6
Putnam	121	1,174	27	439	87	35	21	78	66,044	147	19.7	10.2	43.1
Randolph	626	10,503	2,055	2,708	1,314	302	327	405	38,559	808	34.7	7.9	36.7
Richland	436	5,362	1,073	487	628	174	153	211	39,334	596	41.9	8.4	35.9
Rock Island	3,067	61,704	9,756	6,936	7,437	2,544	3,191	3,612	58,541	649	38.1	6.0	42.5
St. Clair	5,037	72,933	13,763	4,999	12,886	2,013	4,426	3,026	41,490	793	46.0	9.5	42.3
Saline	530	6,292	2,211	374	1,093	365	139	233	36,999	452	39.6	9.5	36.6
Sangamon	4,820	81,131	22,523	2,417	11,709	5,347	4,127	3,667	45,201	1,083	46.4	13.0	44.5
Schuyler	155	1,099	346	57	176	56	37	40	36,791	544	21.5	11.2	33.5
Scott	77	558	13	NA	67	50	6	26	46,740	300	25.0	15.0	45.3
Shelby	417	4,296	615	1,161	525	176	280	157	36,514	1,197	36.9	7.7	43.4
Stark	108	986	97	249	134	75	29	48	48,324	362	30.9	18.2	51.3
Stephenson	1,020	15,792	2,554	3,271	1,728	1,049	414	766	48,515	965	43.7	7.5	48.7
Tazewell	2,741	42,318	5,120	6,277	6,855	1,912	1,502	1,776	41,961	857	35.9	10.2	44.7
Union	358	3,267	1,055	311	647	132	108	105	32,225	590	30.7	5.4	37.2
Vermilion	1,338	23,491	5,046	4,536	3,356	1,127	367	1,038	44,184	1,049	38.9	14.1	47.8
Wabash	249	2,936	906	258	298	111	109	121	41,062	208	38.0	17.3	37.7
Warren	359	6,072	611	2,102	551	212	101	244	40,200	711	28.4	14.9	55.9
Washington	378	7,266	335	2,362	620	172	102	326	44,876	715	23.9	15.2	48.6
Wayne	366	3,081	1,018	93	595	146	48	100	32,453	1,025	31.6	11.0	42.8
White	346	3,090	698	266	481	141	72	113	36,480	496	34.9	17.3	46.3
Whiteside	1,145	17,661	3,409	4,124	2,340	524	521	714	40,412	959	33.5	10.4	45.6
Will	15,842	246,188	28,735	19,435	29,876	4,604	8,478	11,720	47,607	801	56.4	7.2	42.3
Williamson	1,545	23,636	6,613	3,044	3,613	1,377	593	942	39,872	610	45.7	4.6	28.7

STATE County	Agriculture, 2017 (cont.)															
	Land in farms					Value of land and buildings (dollars)		Value of machinery and equipment, average per farm (dollars)	Value of products sold:				Organic farms (number)	Farms with internet access (percent)	Government payments	
	Acreage (1,000)	Percent change, 2012–2017	Acres: Average size of farm	Acres: Total irrigated (1,000)	Acres: Total cropland (1,000)	Average per farm	Average per acre		Total (mil dol)	Average per farm (acres)	Percent from: Crops	Percent from: Livestock and poultry products			Total ($1,000)	Percent of farms
	117	118	119	120	121	122	123	124	125	126	127	128	129	130	131	132
ILLINOIS—Cont'd																
Hardin	37	10.2	227	NA	21.2	745,489	3,281	84,639	D	D	D	D	1	90.1	679	38.5
Henderson	193	12.4	440	12.7	165.1	3,065,949	6,961	208,592	122.3	279,297	83.4	16.6	5	84.5	3,938	76.9
Henry	484	1.0	358	7.4	440.8	2,828,369	7,902	225,411	353.0	260,897	77.2	22.8	7	81.1	15,746	72.4
Iroquois	681	1.8	449	5.7	655.9	3,302,325	7,348	249,933	420.5	277,400	84.4	15.6	11	77.8	8,969	61.8
Jackson	222	3.5	287	1.7	176.8	1,546,191	5,386	149,783	87.2	112,920	85.9	14.1	3	69.3	4,446	47.8
Jasper	250	-0.5	273	D	218.7	1,540,385	5,634	162,342	165.9	181,690	61.6	38.4	2	75.0	7,045	84.2
Jefferson	269	25.9	245	0.1	222.6	1,019,111	4,158	108,307	94.6	86,101	82.8	17.2	6	69.9	5,256	64.8
Jersey	190	22.0	366	0.0	152.1	2,314,178	6,330	220,839	82.1	158,143	95.3	4.7	NA	75.0	4,326	64.5
Jo Daviess	289	6.5	306	0.8	202.1	1,867,551	6,110	196,260	151.9	160,415	65.0	35.0	3	75.1	6,275	67.9
Johnson	105	17.6	162	0.5	55.8	597,733	3,701	66,612	18.2	27,824	80.0	20.0	NA	65.4	2,524	45.2
Kane	170	1.0	281	1.3	161.9	2,971,109	10,558	229,206	181.3	299,633	84.8	15.2	10	83.6	3,782	45.6
Kankakee	313	-8.7	414	18.4	300.4	3,237,465	7,822	285,392	221.1	292,508	91.3	8.7	3	75.5	2,346	45.4
Kendall	138	6.3	441	D	133.6	3,991,102	9,059	260,029	101.6	324,655	92.4	7.6	3	85.6	2,128	60.7
Knox	414	19.1	485	0.0	355.5	3,553,390	7,319	247,401	284.4	333,419	78.5	21.5	2	82.6	7,150	73.0
Lake	31	1.8	101	0.4	23.9	1,230,772	12,149	102,194	39.1	129,364	85.2	14.8	8	77.8	423	10.9
LaSalle	573	-4.9	383	6.1	545.4	3,495,212	9,125	265,453	370.9	247,958	94.1	5.9	3	81.6	12,749	72.1
Lawrence	225	22.2	528	29.1	205.5	2,983,608	5,650	327,369	156.4	367,045	71.4	28.6	1	71.1	7,260	71.8
Lee	392	6.2	471	23.9	374.4	4,085,091	8,668	320,174	278.9	335,184	89.8	10.2	6	81.3	9,291	70.9
Livingston	601	-8.5	457	0.1	581.3	3,764,261	8,230	280,950	408.4	311,023	85.2	14.8	9	84.3	6,848	57.9
Logan	354	-2.5	518	2.6	338.1	4,343,867	8,380	297,104	245.7	359,712	90.5	9.5	2	79.9	4,262	79.8
McDonough	315	7.8	414	0.1	272.5	3,037,172	7,334	233,227	214.1	281,663	82.9	17.1	1	79.7	3,359	66.8
McHenry	208	-11.0	236	9.6	189.7	2,256,366	9,541	174,498	163.8	185,871	75.3	24.7	5	80.6	4,201	30.6
McLean	620	-10.4	438	3.2	599.9	4,310,555	9,844	280,498	457.1	322,784	85.0	15.0	3	81.1	9,368	73.0
Macon	277	-17.6	471	0.1	268.0	4,356,859	9,250	281,637	180.0	305,610	97.7	2.3	5	84.6	4,815	69.4
Macoupin	421	-4.1	360	0.0	355.3	2,589,379	7,195	203,190	236.5	202,305	82.6	17.4	1	74.7	4,907	63.5
Madison	319	3.8	295	0.5	287.8	2,571,906	8,706	176,232	174.7	161,912	89.9	10.1	6	79.0	6,378	56.1
Marion	249	-6.8	248	0.2	203.7	1,210,249	4,885	147,171	111.9	111,406	70.8	29.2	5	73.4	6,728	76.1
Marshall	199	-5.0	421	2.9	180.7	3,396,974	8,075	245,161	119.5	253,275	96.7	3.3	3	82.4	4,124	79.4
Mason	312	7.6	569	136.9	289.3	3,974,753	6,983	352,375	192.9	352,035	88.9	11.1	1	73.9	6,447	86.7
Massac	119	16.0	284	10.4	95.5	1,100,621	3,871	176,306	45.8	109,928	86.5	13.5	NA	77.7	3,252	63.1
Menard	168	6.5	435	3.8	139.0	3,399,115	7,807	261,654	89.7	232,267	93.2	6.8	NA	80.6	3,801	71.0
Mercer	282	12.0	377	7.8	247.3	2,471,925	6,551	197,201	217.5	290,807	71.9	28.1	3	78.2	6,604	76.7
Monroe	176	-8.8	310	3.2	151.0	2,065,789	6,659	215,520	88.2	155,195	74.5	25.5	NA	75.7	4,205	59.5
Montgomery	439	14.8	411	D	398.1	2,992,259	7,276	254,828	263.0	246,517	85.6	14.4	NA	79.9	6,978	76.9
Morgan	300	-2.9	433	7.7	265.2	3,573,396	8,247	266,790	172.0	248,221	88.5	11.5	11	81.8	4,846	75.8
Moultrie	202	-1.6	384	0.0	194.9	3,351,079	8,737	205,183	141.2	268,365	93.6	6.4	9	67.5	2,939	56.7
Ogle	355	-5.8	351	0.8	326.8	3,015,903	8,599	246,650	276.4	273,371	75.4	24.6	1	85.3	3,708	61.4
Peoria	250	-0.1	283	3.5	216.3	2,232,609	7,892	180,266	145.2	164,249	90.6	9.4	5	77.4	2,517	64.1
Perry	184	2.0	322	0.2	153.5	1,539,778	4,782	174,881	66.3	115,955	92.3	7.7	NA	62.9	3,806	73.8
Piatt	256	-1.2	607	1.1	251.2	5,617,953	9,260	341,248	165.3	391,673	99.5	0.5	2	85.5	3,844	68.0
Pike	447	8.6	468	3.1	342.9	2,766,090	5,916	203,650	278.9	291,705	64.8	35.2	NA	72.4	5,868	74.4
Pope	66	-15.3	205	D	30.9	715,861	3,491	75,796	8.9	27,503	76.5	23.5	NA	65.8	1,815	59.0
Pulaski	101	23.3	456	5.2	83.1	1,871,568	4,103	181,600	40.1	180,450	96.8	3.2	NA	68.9	2,466	64.9
Putnam	50	-17.3	339	0.2	43.7	2,833,889	8,372	272,212	D	D	D	D	NA	76.2	837	80.3
Randolph	262	-6.0	324	D	216.5	1,757,514	5,423	158,325	98.5	121,881	85.7	14.3	NA	73.0	5,839	66.2
Richland	178	-5.5	299	1.0	158.2	1,581,240	5,280	158,267	119.8	201,000	57.6	42.4	NA	82.0	5,629	76.2
Rock Island	160	7.0	246	4.8	132.4	1,712,532	6,965	179,885	99.9	153,954	80.3	19.7	2	76.6	3,685	60.9
St. Clair	237	-5.8	299	0.5	218.8	2,218,716	7,417	183,236	135.6	171,019	83.1	16.9	4	77.3	4,907	62.3
Saline	145	3.6	321	D	122.3	1,546,065	4,824	155,847	73.6	162,761	75.9	24.1	NA	72.1	3,646	51.5
Sangamon	531	3.4	491	0.8	496.8	4,381,113	8,931	259,349	352.6	325,599	92.4	7.6	3	78.8	6,498	63.3
Schuyler	212	16.3	389	2.4	153.8	2,135,913	5,484	176,634	116.3	213,836	64.6	35.4	NA	69.1	2,423	78.1
Scott	155	5.4	518	6.3	131.8	3,367,008	6,498	237,953	84.7	282,197	82.0	18.0	NA	70.7	1,621	65.3
Shelby	362	-10.7	303	D	325.7	2,133,632	7,047	191,064	219.1	183,081	79.9	20.1	1	75.1	8,283	75.1
Stark	179	6.3	494	D	169.2	4,103,207	8,314	302,743	117.0	323,246	96.1	3.9	1	79.3	3,618	82.9
Stephenson	305	-13.5	316	0.3	277.9	2,662,038	8,424	231,782	288.5	298,940	53.2	46.8	13	81.7	9,220	66.5
Tazewell	304	-9.8	355	39.7	282.2	2,938,881	8,272	216,559	220.4	257,216	82.6	17.4	19	78.5	3,523	58.0
Union	151	24.3	255	4.5	110.7	1,084,536	4,248	113,939	47.9	81,264	90.3	9.7	1	72.5	3,589	55.4
Vermilion	471	8.5	449	0.8	443.7	3,686,595	8,203	261,347	283.0	269,783	95.2	4.8	6	77.8	5,125	56.7
Wabash	115	8.5	555	2.7	105.6	3,070,471	5,533	310,687	52.6	252,793	96.1	3.9	NA	76.0	2,768	75.0
Warren	341	0.8	480	0.2	301.4	3,880,818	8,092	284,489	253.6	356,689	79.1	20.9	3	81.6	2,469	74.5
Washington	349	-1.7	488	1.8	325.7	3,134,730	6,422	325,140	203.8	284,987	69.0	31.0	NA	69.2	8,727	81.3
Wayne	368	-0.1	359	1.2	319.6	1,710,457	4,764	188,596	188.3	183,664	72.6	27.4	NA	72.4	10,861	76.5
White	289	-6.9	584	21.1	256.8	2,908,130	4,983	282,694	141.1	284,377	93.2	6.8	NA	73.6	7,825	71.8
Whiteside	371	-8.1	387	60.4	340.4	3,051,253	7,892	283,093	301.0	313,911	69.9	30.1	8	78.6	12,909	74.1
Will	217	-7.5	270	0.5	208.2	2,403,429	8,888	163,473	133.5	166,674	92.3	7.7	6	81.5	1,014	30.6
Williamson	104	0.4	170	0.0	73.3	673,017	3,953	94,199	34.7	56,907	74.4	25.6	NA	70.7	2,137	39.7

STATE County	Water use, 2015		Wholesale Trade[1], 2017				Retail Trade[2], 2017				Real estate and rental and leasing,[2] 2017			
	Public supply water withdrawn (mil gal/ day)	Public supply gallons withdrawn per person per day	Number of establish- ments	Number of employees	Sales (mil dol)	Average payroll (mil dol)	Number of establish- ments	Number of employees	Sales (mil dol)	Average payroll (mil dol)	Number of establish- ments	Number of employees	Sales (mil dol)	Average payroll (mil dol)
	133	134	135	136	137	138	139	140	141	142	143	144	145	146
ILLINOIS—Cont'd														
Hardin	0.1	31.4	NA	NA	NA	NA	11	64	13.6	1.2	3	4	0.2	0.1
Henderson	8.8	1,260.9	D	D	D	D	13	97	19.0	1.5	3	2	0.2	0.0
Henry	4.0	80.2	D	D	D	D	153	1,836	481.2	45.8	24	65	12.3	1.4
Iroquois	2.0	69.4	55	512	518.7	23.6	78	994	291.3	22.2	20	45	9.1	1.2
Jackson	6.0	100.4	27	274	169.4	12.4	217	3,527	904.6	77.0	77	362	63.8	8.3
Jasper	1.8	184.2	21	219	180.4	7.4	24	166	65.0	4.7	4	D	0.5	D
Jefferson	0.0	0.0	D	D	D	36.6	158	2,165	596.2	53.1	28	77	18.7	2.6
Jersey	1.1	48.3	24	194	232.1	5.9	57	847	217.5	22.2	14	32	3.3	0.9
Jo Daviess	2.0	91.9	23	129	197.0	6.8	108	957	332.6	23.8	21	118	57.7	5.7
Johnson	0.9	67.4	5	D	14.2	D	32	238	91.3	5.4	4	D	1.1	D
Kane	61.8	116.3	742	11,620	13,711.5	761.0	1,495	25,639	6,686.0	632.4	479	2,585	1,265.4	137.2
Kankakee	13.3	119.6	116	2,199	1,384.6	110.9	366	5,932	1,516.0	134.1	89	331	68.4	12.2
Kendall	7.7	62.1	61	1,265	2,084.1	58.2	241	5,803	1,434.9	135.0	79	172	40.6	6.1
Knox	0.5	9.5	45	706	555.2	35.4	178	3,582	862.3	96.0	36	115	17.8	3.0
Lake	59.7	84.7	1,071	29,609	31,296.7	2,787.0	2,204	38,507	12,816.9	1,047.9	837	3,736	1,881.8	240.0
LaSalle	9.1	81.5	110	1,881	2,658.7	109.7	404	6,246	1,710.6	153.5	73	355	55.1	11.7
Lawrence	0.6	37.6	12	218	124.0	7.9	32	389	82.0	8.2	D	D	D	D
Lee	3.9	113.9	D	D	D	D	105	1,340	408.5	35.0	22	90	16.7	3.0
Livingston	5.7	154.3	D	D	D	D	124	1,487	418.9	39.7	19	70	9.4	2.6
Logan	2.9	97.6	37	508	694.9	30.1	84	1,028	302.8	25.0	20	61	6.5	1.6
McDonough	2.6	83.9	28	219	274.3	9.4	109	1,597	319.9	33.6	30	118	16.7	3.0
McHenry	18.7	60.8	381	5,182	3,114.1	316.5	849	14,300	3,898.2	368.9	240	704	142.3	26.8
McLean	10.5	60.6	165	2,108	7,165.7	150.4	523	9,562	2,301.8	211.7	154	754	151.1	26.2
Macon	20.0	186.6	95	1,303	1,363.5	74.8	395	5,594	1,515.3	143.5	88	484	78.7	14.9
Macoupin	3.0	64.3	43	584	831.3	28.1	132	1,370	385.8	34.4	15	45	4.5	1.0
Madison	52.4	196.8	204	3,258	2,977.0	181.2	772	12,202	3,599.7	317.1	235	963	220.4	36.5
Marion	1.0	25.8	D	D	D	D	131	1,334	340.1	34.8	23	108	11.4	2.3
Marshall	1.7	139.4	D	D	D	9.2	37	274	53.4	5.8	D	D	D	D
Mason	0.6	41.6	26	304	791.3	16.4	43	418	90.5	7.3	7	17	1.9	0.6
Massac	4.7	320.3	D	D	D	4.1	36	316	98.1	8.2	D	D	D	0.7
Menard	0.8	65.1	10	71	50.6	3.2	27	266	65.5	5.4	3	8	0.6	0.2
Mercer	0.9	55.5	D	D	D	D	37	347	73.7	7.2	4	6	0.5	0.2
Monroe	0.4	10.9	D	D	D	17.0	93	1,307	457.9	39.4	36	163	57.3	8.7
Montgomery	2.7	93.1	39	371	382.9	16.5	125	1,407	395.3	33.9	20	79	7.9	1.7
Morgan	0.3	8.9	D	D	D	18.9	141	1,884	473.5	42.8	25	100	14.6	3.2
Moultrie	0.2	11.4	11	80	240.7	4.8	44	366	102.5	7.3	3	D	1.3	D
Ogle	5.1	98.5	D	D	D	D	123	1,514	430.5	35.3	36	103	23.8	4.5
Peoria	24.0	128.8	187	2,906	1,517.5	146.5	679	11,032	2,544.7	260.8	190	1,019	186.6	39.7
Perry	0.7	32.5	14	103	67.2	4.1	54	632	183.6	19.0	5	14	1.8	0.4
Piatt	1.1	68.3	24	286	286.1	15.9	40	405	131.7	11.4	D	D	D	D
Pike	1.9	118.8	26	244	254.7	12.5	53	625	141.8	12.9	8	95	39.6	3.4
Pope	0.0	0.0	NA	NA	NA	NA	10	46	9.0	0.9	4	D	0.8	D
Pulaski	0.2	29.9	D	D	D	4.5	15	88	38.1	2.3	NA	NA	NA	NA
Putnam	0.5	81.5	10	48	165.6	2.4	12	133	24.9	2.5	D	D	D	0.1
Randolph	2.4	74.0	26	513	473.4	25.6	101	1,305	360.2	33.9	11	27	8.5	1.1
Richland	1.4	88.6	24	294	198.8	13.2	60	754	171.5	16.0	7	31	3.6	1.0
Rock Island	17.4	119.0	140	2,769	2,567.4	163.3	426	7,912	1,993.9	199.8	125	520	103.1	17.1
St. Clair	17.3	65.6	180	2,236	2,868.2	109.3	863	13,465	3,272.6	333.3	229	936	185.2	35.4
Saline	0.0	0.0	12	159	97.1	9.0	101	1,266	344.3	31.4	13	67	21.0	2.7
Sangamon	23.2	116.8	175	2,446	3,128.9	129.9	723	12,124	3,024.0	289.8	243	887	227.4	29.6
Schuyler	0.9	130.8	D	D	D	2.1	22	210	33.6	4.8	3	D	3.1	D
Scott	4.8	946.6	D	D	D	3.5	7	64	22.0	1.7	NA	NA	NA	NA
Shelby	1.7	75.8	27	225	210.7	9.4	61	627	137.3	11.8	D	D	D	D
Stark	0.6	101.9	D	D	D	6.0	19	154	51.5	5.6	NA	NA	NA	NA
Stephenson	3.9	84.2	D	D	D	D	156	1,978	560.3	49.2	33	95	11.5	2.6
Tazewell	14.7	109.2	121	2,153	1,905.5	113.9	388	7,392	2,172.4	206.0	95	349	64.6	12.6
Union	1.3	73.5	10	94	46.7	4.0	59	687	177.2	17.3	5	19	2.8	0.6
Vermilion	9.0	112.9	D	D	D	91.7	247	3,709	934.8	84.3	46	153	38.3	5.9
Wabash	1.8	151.6	12	162	141.4	11.4	42	369	88.7	7.3	12	28	6.1	0.9
Warren	2.8	156.9	28	253	416.8	11.6	53	610	135.8	12.3	10	19	1.6	0.3
Washington	0.6	44.1	32	870	384.7	39.0	57	587	293.4	19.9	9	12	1.4	0.2
Wayne	1.1	68.2	14	125	172.4	5.3	61	595	155.1	14.9	7	24	7.9	0.5
White	1.1	75.4	30	265	139.2	10.0	59	544	140.2	12.3	10	24	5.7	0.8
Whiteside	3.6	63.4	67	629	732.5	28.6	180	2,643	623.0	62.4	36	95	14.7	2.4
Will	35.1	51.0	777	17,101	23,383.3	1,091.2	1,640	31,930	8,424.0	763.5	542	2,128	554.5	109.0
Williamson	1.2	18.1	57	650	250.6	27.9	249	3,669	1,175.0	99.2	60	185	34.1	5.7

1 Merchant wholesalers, except manufacturers' sales branches and offices. 2. Employer establishments.

STATE County	Professional, scientific, and technical services, 2017				Manufacturing, 2017				Accommodation and food services, 2017			
	Number of establish-ments	Number of employees	Sales (mil dol)	Average payroll (mil dol)	Number of establish-ments	Number of employees	Sales (mil dol)	Average payroll (mil dol)	Number of establis-hments	Number of employees	Sales (mil dol)	Annual payroll (mil dol)
	147	148	149	150	151	152	153	154	155	156	157	158
ILLINOIS—Cont'd												
Hardin	NA	NA	NA	NA	NA	NA	NA	NA	D	D	D	D
Henderson	8	28	2.2	0.7	NA	NA	NA	NA	14	46	2.1	0.4
Henry	65	309	24.7	9.1	50	4,441	2,594.6	169.9	93	1,119	46.8	13.3
Iroquois	33	90	10.3	3.5	23	516	381.0	22.7	55	437	20.2	5.2
Jackson	D	D	D	D	45	890	208.6	33.4	149	2,640	104.6	30.6
Jasper	9	23	2.3	0.9	10	185	41.4	6.3	16	140	5.3	1.5
Jefferson	63	403	50.2	20.6	D	3,311	D	189.7	86	1,720	82.8	23.1
Jersey	17	100	10.8	5.5	15	131	28.4	5.3	58	704	33.1	10.2
Jo Daviess	49	182	28.9	8.5	40	871	354.8	45.0	99	1,333	82.1	24.6
Johnson	10	160	4.7	1.3	11	40	9.2	1.9	D	D	D	D
Kane	D	D	D	D	777	30,913	12,294.9	1,761.5	949	18,433	1,058.3	308.4
Kankakee	143	767	89.4	35.3	109	5,400	5,619.1	331.0	243	4,101	187.0	56.8
Kendall	222	858	117.2	39.9	78	2,311	683.0	123.2	197	3,504	189.3	50.9
Knox	59	290	33.7	12.3	33	1,015	344.9	43.0	128	1,768	83.7	22.8
Lake	D	D	D	D	817	28,356	10,863.9	1,751.5	1,563	28,143	1,677.7	489.3
LaSalle	D	D	D	D	144	5,277	2,708.6	312.1	310	4,079	216.9	58.3
Lawrence	8	39	4.5	1.8	D	D	D	42.9	20	252	10.6	3.0
Lee	29	284	40.0	14.0	35	3,240	1,432.6	163.7	74	895	42.2	11.4
Livingston	45	212	32.7	9.7	61	3,225	1,121.4	179.9	72	767	34.8	9.3
Logan	32	229	20.9	9.0	14	1,198	766.0	59.1	61	970	35.0	10.7
McDonough	44	231	21.5	8.0	16	1,399	349.9	69.4	88	1,309	52.9	14.6
McHenry	D	D	D	D	455	13,071	4,155.5	730.0	592	10,042	544.9	156.8
McLean	D	D	D	D	81	4,592	993.1	185.3	417	8,518	413.1	123.6
Macon	142	1,099	146.8	54.3	101	6,731	6,948.0	460.3	255	4,345	206.4	62.5
Macoupin	38	116	13.2	3.7	34	404	199.7	23.2	D	D	D	D
Madison	D	D	D	D	183	9,719	12,113.7	625.0	583	11,077	525.4	155.2
Marion	54	287	19.7	8.8	43	2,800	771.9	127.5	83	934	43.9	12.3
Marshall	12	73	8.2	2.5	9	840	251.1	45.6	29	226	7.5	2.2
Mason	11	27	2.8	0.8	9	91	28.3	4.7	34	249	9.8	2.8
Massac	10	185	26.4	10.6	D	D	D	D	D	D	D	D
Menard	15	115	9.5	3.8	8	43	7.3	1.4	20	161	6.6	1.9
Mercer	D	D	D	D	12	478	103.8	24.0	25	212	7.6	2.3
Monroe	73	655	109.2	46.9	21	226	57.0	12.5	76	1,338	60.8	17.9
Montgomery	36	204	18.5	8.5	23	660	351.1	33.1	71	1,013	45.6	13.5
Morgan	39	630	55.5	29.0	D	D	D	D	87	1,531	74.2	18.2
Moultrie	13	116	14.8	5.8	42	2,083	606.0	99.2	25	251	10.8	2.9
Ogle	74	386	55.4	22.5	65	3,388	1,165.8	163.4	115	1,251	60.0	15.4
Peoria	D	D	D	D	137	5,392	2,453.2	365.1	458	7,790	404.7	120.1
Perry	25	87	11.1	2.6	15	345	249.3	18.4	43	516	19.2	5.6
Piatt	24	114	10.3	4.8	17	190	37.0	9.2	37	307	13.3	4.0
Pike	18	98	12.9	4.8	12	131	43.4	5.2	28	343	14.8	4.0
Pope	D	D	D	0.2	NA	NA	NA	NA	D	D	D	0.2
Pulaski	NA	NA	NA	NA	NA	NA	NA	NA	D	D	D	0.4
Putnam	D	D	D	D	5	384	788.1	23.9	16	87	3.3	0.7
Randolph	28	276	33.2	10.6	28	2,607	639.1	81.2	69	980	41.5	11.8
Richland	29	81	10.1	3.5	23	421	160.1	20.4	37	536	22.2	6.5
Rock Island	D	D	D	D	134	8,809	2,958.2	381.9	351	6,301	342.6	96.8
St. Clair	D	D	D	D	141	5,127	2,607.9	273.0	542	10,972	612.0	167.8
Saline	42	163	16.6	5.7	22	308	55.0	12.2	49	877	42.3	9.8
Sangamon	497	5,245	755.3	320.4	89	2,699	847.3	138.9	552	10,006	490.8	148.3
Schuyler	8	36	3.7	1.3	D	D	D	D	12	111	5.8	1.8
Scott	4	7	0.8	0.2	NA	NA	NA	NA	8	42	2.1	0.4
Shelby	22	253	31.3	12.4	21	1,138	413.9	58.9	38	429	16.0	4.6
Stark	8	40	4.1	1.3	5	202	54.3	11.3	3	24	0.8	0.1
Stephenson	69	401	64.3	20.6	63	2,711	961.6	159.4	90	1,384	63.1	17.6
Tazewell	182	1,410	166.0	74.5	113	5,589	2,667.5	330.3	322	6,290	353.7	98.4
Union	22	88	8.5	3.3	13	234	78.4	10.7	37	421	13.3	4.0
Vermilion	76	385	57.8	17.6	80	4,496	1,881.2	244.5	152	2,338	101.6	28.0
Wabash	24	110	11.4	4.8	10	307	62.8	16.5	17	281	10.1	3.4
Warren	19	115	10.7	3.0	13	1,920	834.9	94.1	36	450	20.6	6.1
Washington	23	107	19.2	5.7	13	1,701	588.9	94.3	29	367	15.8	4.4
Wayne	20	83	7.8	2.9	17	122	48.7	5.8	26	345	15.4	4.2
White	16	68	7.6	2.7	13	273	77.6	13.2	25	321	13.4	4.1
Whiteside	75	397	61.9	19.3	87	3,540	1,334.1	207.5	135	1,769	74.6	21.4
Will	D	D	D	D	588	19,153	15,580.8	1,229.2	1,194	23,183	1,500.8	399.3
Williamson	D	D	D	D	42	3,226	1,212.7	147.3	159	2,979	147.1	41.1

STATE County	Health care and social assistance, 2017				Other services, 2017				Nonemployer businesses, 2019		Value of residential construction authorized by building permits, 2021	
	Number of establish-ments	Number of employees	Receipts (mil dol)	Annual payroll (mil dol)	Number of establish-ments	Number of employees	Receipts (mil dol)	Annual payroll (mil dol)	Number	Receipts (mil dol)	New construction ($1,000)	Number of housing units
	159	160	161	162	163	164	165	166	167	168	169	170
ILLINOIS—Cont'd												
Hardin	11	277	18.1	9.5	NA	NA	NA	NA	159	4.1	0	0
Henderson	7	132	8.0	4.0	6	14	3.2	0.6	351	16.8	1,646	9
Henry	79	1,632	160.2	58.2	90	279	38.0	8.1	2,773	99.3	8,577	54
Iroquois	70	1,617	106.5	52.2	46	117	14.2	3.2	1,786	66.7	4,485	26
Jackson	154	4,373	665.8	192.2	93	534	57.6	11.2	3,005	114.5	870	6
Jasper	19	184	11.5	3.9	17	49	5.6	1.1	804	27.1	300	3
Jefferson	144	4,053	518.8	185.8	73	522	62.1	15.5	2,135	97.4	1,653	11
Jersey	35	1,144	85.1	36.4	37	121	11.2	3.2	1,315	43.6	29,193	123
Jo Daviess	44	793	53.9	22.8	53	240	28.1	7.1	1,881	81.8	12,195	41
Johnson	18	230	12.8	5.2	D	D	5.2	D	764	24.7	0	0
Kane	1,224	24,156	3,291.4	1,233.3	911	6,364	722.3	214.4	36,249	1,624.4	326,199	1,333
Kankakee	290	7,298	720.7	336.0	175	846	92.4	27.1	5,773	216.4	34,567	140
Kendall	181	1,555	144.4	54.7	181	774	76.9	22.2	9,361	379.8	116,988	684
Knox	134	3,593	353.0	116.0	70	469	132.7	15.3	2,140	74.4	504	3
Lake	2,077	36,794	5,359.2	1,818.9	1,403	8,027	918.2	271.2	56,410	3,225.5	294,892	902
LaSalle	272	5,359	521.3	191.1	225	1,040	122.5	33.3	5,571	207.1	21,403	77
Lawrence	23	526	34.8	14.6	19	73	7.6	1.7	695	25.5	11,040	64
Lee	88	2,381	262.7	96.0	60	341	32.8	9.4	1,838	71.8	5,615	26
Livingston	67	1,501	146.6	46.6	69	339	36.7	9.5	1,871	71.7	4,834	22
Logan	58	1,572	132.9	50.1	44	187	17.7	4.3	1,353	49.8	1,997	9
McDonough	66	1,822	170.9	71.5	D	D	D	5.1	1,518	50.0	870	2
McHenry	772	11,931	1,547.5	571.8	685	3,465	338.1	104.5	23,120	1,036.7	237,356	1,374
McLean	377	8,713	1,061.4	402.1	272	2,436	262.9	85.3	9,674	409.1	56,741	283
Macon	287	8,451	1,014.4	362.8	172	1,030	293.2	35.5	5,047	177.4	9,057	33
Macoupin	81	1,724	121.9	51.1	79	270	25.6	6.3	2,401	92.7	15,054	71
Madison	686	14,455	1,350.4	532.0	472	2,893	312.6	90.2	14,710	612.1	115,443	399
Marion	107	2,905	274.2	99.7	67	256	25.3	6.5	1,932	71.5	761	8
Marshall	17	454	20.9	11.6	D	D	D	D	612	19.7	979	4
Mason	19	505	38.6	17.9	19	84	8.3	1.9	631	25.0	1,713	7
Massac	D	D	D	D	D	D	D	D	805	28.7	490	15
Menard	8	135	6.4	4.0	16	67	10.0	2.3	747	24.7	3,872	15
Mercer	21	296	28.4	12.1	18	93	7.2	2.0	894	30.2	1,357	8
Monroe	91	1,049	71.5	30.7	76	396	35.7	13.6	2,286	98.7	34,697	117
Montgomery	68	1,451	158.1	50.4	47	194	24.9	5.5	1,459	48.3	5,385	22
Morgan	103	2,597	239.0	98.4	D	D	D	D	1,813	68.9	169	2
Moultrie	32	716	39.3	19.0	19	66	6.4	1.7	1,003	45.8	23,730	97
Ogle	84	1,526	115.4	49.4	81	329	37.5	9.7	3,101	117.4	8,473	32
Peoria	514	24,940	3,301.2	1,375.5	298	4,335	454.6	203.8	9,455	382.4	25,433	76
Perry	46	973	76.2	31.2	46	184	14.2	3.6	938	30.2	4,616	22
Piatt	D	D	D	D	20	60	5.7	1.7	1,169	44.7	7,696	22
Pike	23	702	62.1	24.3	27	68	7.6	1.7	955	41.6	3,585	17
Pope	9	74	3.6	1.5	D	D	D	0.2	292	8.2	0	0
Pulaski	13	148	5.0	1.7	D	D	3.8	D	275	9.0	3,427	14
Putnam	5	25	1.8	0.6	D	D	D	D	355	16.8	2,784	19
Randolph	76	1,886	182.1	77.8	65	322	49.0	12.2	1,355	50.8	9,441	44
Richland	54	1,170	88.2	40.1	43	164	20.6	4.9	1,055	44.3	275	2
Rock Island	406	9,287	980.8	387.9	220	1,514	149.2	46.7	6,752	267.8	26,851	145
St. Clair	603	14,766	1,501.4	626.2	384	2,244	209.2	66.1	14,139	485.1	146,747	542
Saline	83	2,720	225.0	82.3	40	168	20.7	4.5	1,357	51.7	0	0
Sangamon	470	22,478	3,032.8	1,050.0	467	3,250	402.8	131.2	11,978	478.6	62,409	317
Schuyler	12	338	29.6	12.5	13	30	4.9	0.9	439	15.4	0	0
Scott	7	14	1.3	0.5	NA	NA	NA	NA	320	11.8	NA	NA
Shelby	31	651	37.3	18.4	29	98	13.9	3.1	1,222	44.9	6,893	28
Stark	7	109	7.4	3.3	NA	NA	NA	NA	362	20.4	140	1
Stephenson	102	2,535	337.9	105.7	89	396	36.2	10.3	2,649	97.5	6,068	20
Tazewell	275	5,116	442.7	168.1	222	1,192	129.7	40.3	6,435	253.3	27,992	222
Union	61	1,300	80.3	32.9	26	104	9.9	3.0	1,012	37.4	1,084	8
Vermilion	146	5,046	578.9	265.4	112	509	53.0	14.3	3,910	137.0	1,103	6
Wabash	20	861	65.9	25.6	22	94	7.2	1.5	715	25.2	615	4
Warren	38	586	49.8	17.5	36	102	11.4	1.9	878	34.6	761	3
Washington	22	400	33.0	12.1	28	61	6.4	1.3	890	36.3	8,140	28
Wayne	42	947	62.3	29.2	24	113	14.1	3.5	1,262	44.5	0	0
White	38	707	57.4	19.6	29	132	18.4	4.3	1,024	40.2	734	3
Whiteside	98	3,423	253.6	112.9	99	542	49.0	12.9	2,668	105.9	4,904	23
Will	1,551	27,115	2,757.6	1,123.0	1,160	7,504	992.3	250.7	51,484	2,352.7	446,735	1,970
Williamson	212	7,024	913.4	304.4	96	501	49.1	13.3	4,123	160.3	15,796	93

STATE County	Government employment and payroll, 2017									Local government finances, 2017				
			March payroll (percent of total)							General revenue				
												Taxes		
													Per capita[1] (dollars)	
	Full-time equivalent employees	March payroll (dollars)	Adminis-tration, judicial, and legal	Police and corrections	Fire protection	Highways and transpor-tation	Health and welfare	Natural resources and utilities	Education and libraries	Total (mil dol)	Inter-govern-mental (mil dol)	Total (mil dol)	Total	Property
	171	172	173	174	175	176	177	178	179	180	181	182	183	184
ILLINOIS—Cont'd														
Hardin	355	964,662	4.8	3.6	0.1	67.0	2.4	1.9	20.2	11.7	8.6	1.6	397	394
Henderson	259	794,157	14.4	7.2	0.6	7.5	12.6	1.1	56.2	20.1	7.1	9.7	1,426	1,331
Henry	2,305	8,261,504	5.7	8.4	1.8	3.2	22.2	5.0	53.1	213.8	62.0	79.6	1,618	1,542
Iroquois	913	3,709,326	9.8	7.1	1.2	5.1	0.1	2.7	72.9	88.2	33.1	43.8	1,579	1,529
Jackson	2,296	7,460,282	7.1	10.1	3.1	5.0	9.8	7.0	57.0	194.5	82.7	80.7	1,393	1,067
Jasper	432	1,484,947	9.8	6.5	0.5	5.8	9.2	4.1	63.9	35.3	16.7	14.8	1,553	1,523
Jefferson	1,644	6,130,923	6.1	7.1	3.2	2.8	2.3	2.1	75.4	160.2	85.3	51.9	1,365	1,060
Jersey	864	3,597,723	4.3	7.3	0.3	2.7	46.9	2.8	34.2	96.2	21.3	25.3	1,154	1,020
Jo Daviess	765	3,218,722	9.5	10.0	0.5	5.3	1.7	2.3	69.9	89.9	21.7	55.6	2,586	2,420
Johnson	315	1,048,861	8.9	6.6	0.3	2.5	1.7	5.0	75.0	31.6	15.9	8.6	694	693
Kane	23,307	119,685,773	5.1	8.6	4.9	1.9	1.5	6.0	70.9	3,136.7	933.2	1,815.4	3,411	3,119
Kankakee	4,432	18,124,649	7.1	11.6	4.2	3.3	1.1	3.4	67.9	414.1	162.1	176.4	1,596	1,513
Kendall	4,540	19,788,537	4.2	9.3	3.0	1.1	1.2	4.0	76.8	518.1	169.8	289.8	2,297	2,210
Knox	2,096	8,569,394	6.4	10.6	3.9	3.1	9.3	5.2	60.3	204.4	73.6	90.3	1,786	1,567
Lake	29,578	152,226,049	4.8	8.4	4.0	2.3	3.2	5.9	70.2	4,064.7	1,048.8	2,555.2	3,637	3,411
LaSalle	4,070	17,042,807	6.3	11.5	3.2	3.6	3.2	3.3	67.6	434.5	146.0	224.5	2,048	1,856
Lawrence	637	2,603,378	5.2	4.6	0.0	3.1	44.1	4.3	38.3	34.7	20.0	9.3	583	562
Lee	1,093	4,234,740	7.8	5.9	4.3	3.8	2.3	3.3	71.4	114.7	35.6	59.7	1,727	1,645
Livingston	1,606	6,248,617	6.4	8.5	1.8	4.4	3.1	2.8	72.2	148.2	51.3	69.8	1,931	1,905
Logan	857	3,071,770	8.8	11.1	4.2	5.4	2.9	2.8	62.2	82.8	30.5	35.3	1,216	1,141
McDonough	1,763	7,331,926	3.9	6.9	1.8	2.5	50.9	2.2	31.1	180.5	37.6	37.6	1,238	1,187
McHenry	11,450	51,968,532	6.0	10.6	5.1	2.8	2.4	5.1	66.5	1,368.0	327.1	853.5	2,773	2,571
McLean	6,093	27,474,898	6.9	11.6	5.5	5.0	3.2	7.0	58.0	710.8	161.0	421.6	2,440	1,942
Macon	3,903	16,584,624	6.5	13.5	5.1	3.4	3.3	7.1	58.7	459.7	187.3	179.9	1,707	1,439
Macoupin	1,653	6,375,505	7.8	8.5	1.0	2.5	2.9	4.3	72.3	134.0	67.7	45.9	1,008	981
Madison	8,747	37,036,497	7.7	11.8	4.2	3.9	2.2	6.4	61.9	1,040.8	419.6	447.2	1,686	1,525
Marion	1,918	7,344,248	5.0	6.5	1.7	7.3	2.0	3.7	72.8	172.0	96.7	48.9	1,296	1,243
Marshall	337	1,117,988	11.6	9.5	0.0	6.6	0.0	4.9	65.4	37.9	10.4	24.3	2,081	1,983
Mason	921	3,116,994	6.9	6.0	1.2	5.5	34.8	1.8	43.6	73.4	20.8	23.6	1,726	1,654
Massac	699	2,610,477	4.8	7.7	3.3	2.2	30.4	5.6	45.9	76.2	28.9	15.0	1,049	1,010
Menard	584	1,894,919	5.0	8.0	0.2	3.3	19.9	3.7	58.7	49.9	15.2	22.1	1,796	1,702
Mercer	579	2,003,713	12.5	9.1	0.0	4.3	3.1	2.9	66.8	58.0	19.1	31.4	2,015	1,977
Monroe	1,165	4,473,031	6.0	9.5	3.8	2.6	11.6	6.0	60.2	108.2	27.3	52.7	1,542	1,469
Montgomery	998	3,803,424	8.5	8.7	2.8	7.2	5.1	5.8	61.2	89.9	39.1	38.0	1,322	1,218
Morgan	1,605	5,143,648	4.6	8.3	1.8	3.1	3.9	3.8	73.9	104.5	45.3	48.0	1,401	1,282
Moultrie	430	1,479,487	14.0	9.8	4.2	4.1	1.2	10.0	51.6	37.3	13.6	19.1	1,299	1,259
Ogle	2,519	10,005,346	4.9	8.9	3.1	3.1	0.8	6.4	72.3	253.4	74.0	135.1	2,650	2,523
Peoria	7,199	29,894,387	5.5	13.1	5.3	5.3	4.3	7.0	57.7	789.4	287.3	349.9	1,917	1,574
Perry	795	3,003,562	3.7	8.6	1.5	3.4	31.0	5.3	44.9	76.1	26.8	15.7	740	705
Piatt	646	2,360,752	6.1	9.2	1.1	5.1	19.3	3.5	54.0	69.2	23.1	29.6	1,800	1,746
Pike	632	2,444,120	6.8	6.8	0.0	6.5	5.9	6.7	64.2	51.2	22.6	18.5	1,179	1,125
Pope	135	415,660	15.1	7.7	0.0	1.6	3.8	7.7	64.1	13.9	5.4	4.3	1,038	862
Pulaski	386	1,105,044	8.6	9.0	0.0	19.5	1.8	1.9	58.6	36.9	21.2	4.2	760	725
Putnam	233	671,429	16.2	13.2	0.0	6.9	3.9	4.1	54.4	23.1	11.0	9.7	1,704	1,671
Randolph	1,559	6,096,504	5.2	5.7	0.1	2.9	36.8	4.0	44.3	154.5	45.5	34.4	1,065	1,025
Richland	889	3,418,270	4.4	5.0	0.4	2.4	0.9	2.7	83.8	51.4	24.3	15.2	962	892
Rock Island	5,593	24,550,254	5.5	11.1	4.6	6.9	5.2	6.0	59.2	641.0	245.2	281.6	1,958	1,716
St. Clair	8,822	37,845,721	5.8	10.1	2.3	3.3	2.8	3.4	70.2	1,174.6	618.8	385.0	1,466	1,326
Saline	1,033	4,590,790	5.0	7.0	0.9	3.6	2.0	4.1	77.0	93.2	49.2	27.2	1,135	1,045
Sangamon	8,122	38,176,352	4.7	9.9	4.6	5.3	2.1	15.0	58.2	836.8	305.4	387.8	1,968	1,666
Schuyler	432	1,599,283	9.0	5.5	1.8	4.4	47.8	4.3	26.3	44.3	8.6	10.1	1,452	1,433
Scott	217	643,991	11.1	6.8	0.0	3.3	3.7	4.9	70.3	16.9	6.8	5.8	1,155	1,065
Shelby	566	2,072,677	12.4	9.0	2.0	8.3	3.6	4.7	57.8	49.8	22.8	20.4	936	905
Stark	211	748,119	18.3	1.8	0.0	6.6	0.0	1.4	71.8	20.9	5.7	12.7	2,333	2,301
Stephenson	2,026	7,213,358	5.0	9.1	4.2	3.0	5.7	3.7	68.9	183.6	67.5	81.4	1,810	1,664
Tazewell	4,866	20,502,398	5.1	10.5	3.8	2.6	2.2	5.8	69.1	562.7	186.8	261.2	1,957	1,719
Union	680	2,600,080	10.9	6.2	0.3	5.0	3.8	3.6	69.3	62.7	34.3	20.8	1,228	1,189
Vermilion	3,100	11,926,933	8.2	8.8	2.8	3.9	4.1	4.3	64.0	364.0	228.8	92.7	1,193	1,097
Wabash	712	2,806,713	2.5	4.1	1.4	1.6	51.1	2.6	36.5	70.4	14.6	10.3	894	854
Warren	588	2,061,899	7.5	10.1	4.3	4.6	2.8	2.3	68.1	52.8	22.0	24.5	1,429	1,322
Washington	516	2,031,972	7.3	8.5	1.3	4.6	28.1	4.1	44.5	56.8	14.1	18.9	1,354	1,343
Wayne	625	2,027,975	8.6	8.9	1.5	3.7	2.8	9.1	63.3	58.3	37.2	15.5	943	876
White	840	2,861,503	5.9	7.1	0.7	2.9	2.0	5.6	75.1	51.3	29.1	15.3	1,101	1,061
Whiteside	3,520	15,743,468	4.3	4.2	1.1	2.0	52.8	2.7	32.4	435.9	86.1	81.8	1,461	1,368
Will	23,275	114,026,103	4.8	11.3	6.0	2.1	2.5	4.7	67.5	2,958.3	810.0	1,726.1	2,500	2,290
Williamson	2,486	9,699,278	4.3	9.1	3.8	3.5	0.8	5.3	71.6	249.9	118.8	96.8	1,443	1,274

1. Based on the resident population estimated as of July 1 of the year shown.

STATE County	Local government finances, 2017 (cont.)									Government employment, 2020			Individual income tax returns, 2019		
	Direct general expenditure							Debt outstanding							
			Percent of total for:												
	Total (mil dol)	Per capita[1] (dollars)	Education	Health and hospitals	Police protection	Public welfare	Highways	Total (mil dol)	Per capita[1] (dollars)	Federal civilian	Federal military	State and local	Number of returns	Mean adjusted gross income	Mean income tax
	185	186	187	188	189	190	191	192	193	194	195	196	197	198	199
ILLINOIS—Cont'd															
Hardin	8.7	2,206	54.1	0.7	2.4	0.1	8.4	8.3	2,107	11	8	173	1,490	48,991	4,341
Henderson	19.0	2,793	45.2	5.0	7.3	0.1	9.4	6.5	957	39	18	355	3,130	49,260	3,842
Henry	238.9	4,853	43.6	22.3	5.6	0.2	4.9	164.0	3,331	124	97	3,371	23,860	61,029	5,757
Iroquois	92.8	3,340	65.1	1.7	4.0	0.1	6.9	50.4	1,815	95	53	1,347	13,040	55,745	4,868
Jackson	197.5	3,410	46.6	4.2	7.9	0.1	6.4	116.0	2,004	159	117	10,833	22,160	54,312	5,505
Jasper	33.8	3,551	50.2	4.5	8.6	0.4	12.8	9.3	973	37	26	576	4,580	55,859	4,589
Jefferson	149.7	3,934	62.3	0.6	5.8	0.1	7.4	162.8	4,278	142	71	2,104	16,540	52,213	4,691
Jersey	94.6	4,316	24.8	44.6	3.9	0.1	4.3	45.1	2,058	43	42	1,157	10,230	59,268	5,293
Jo Daviess	92.2	4,288	44.6	1.6	6.7	0.1	11.1	28.6	1,333	67	43	1,236	11,960	60,206	6,635
Johnson	28.9	2,327	57.8	1.4	5.0	0.0	6.9	22.0	1,776	79	22	777	5,040	53,797	4,291
Kane	2,961.8	5,564	57.5	0.2	7.1	0.7	4.7	5,354.6	10,060	1,647	1,060	28,905	253,810	78,326	9,557
Kankakee	447.3	4,046	52.8	0.5	6.7	0.1	5.4	491.0	4,442	250	211	5,770	50,670	58,281	5,460
Kendall	502.9	3,986	60.4	1.4	5.7	0.4	4.7	715.8	5,674	174	264	5,682	62,390	74,375	8,021
Knox	204.3	4,039	49.3	7.0	5.7	0.2	6.3	253.8	5,017	176	91	2,840	23,000	52,847	4,794
Lake	4,040.8	5,752	56.9	2.0	5.9	0.1	5.0	3,441.8	4,900	5,465	17,391	34,998	346,020	114,928	18,898
LaSalle	427.2	3,897	52.5	3.2	6.3	0.1	6.3	325.9	2,972	358	212	5,612	54,280	58,741	5,782
Lawrence	36.5	2,275	49.5	3.9	6.3	1.0	11.3	33.9	2,114	40	26	832	6,250	50,253	3,985
Lee	118.1	3,418	55.3	1.5	7.5	0.1	8.4	89.5	2,590	84	63	1,761	16,310	59,628	5,751
Livingston	151.6	4,198	53.8	3.2	5.8	0.1	9.7	49.4	1,366	94	67	2,096	17,030	60,369	5,650
Logan	81.4	2,803	46.7	3.3	5.4	0.1	6.9	37.8	1,304	95	49	1,339	12,450	56,809	5,042
McDonough	186.5	6,140	23.7	49.7	3.8	0.6	4.6	80.4	2,645	98	55	4,295	11,710	54,370	4,983
McHenry	1,398.3	4,543	51.3	2.3	7.2	0.4	6.6	1,098.7	3,569	502	615	13,785	157,630	78,574	9,291
McLean	716.1	4,145	43.6	1.2	7.8	1.4	6.3	932.9	5,400	440	331	14,317	77,550	76,828	9,045
Macon	452.0	4,288	47.3	1.2	10.4	1.1	5.4	425.2	4,034	313	202	5,110	48,200	60,818	6,389
Macoupin	132.1	2,903	58.4	3.6	6.0	0.1	6.2	89.6	1,969	124	88	2,284	21,210	55,826	4,833
Madison	970.5	3,659	46.4	1.1	8.2	1.9	5.8	909.3	3,428	587	528	15,175	127,130	66,081	7,064
Marion	161.0	4,268	65.7	0.8	3.2	0.1	3.3	97.1	2,573	104	73	2,106	17,520	49,999	4,159
Marshall	39.7	3,404	48.7	1.3	5.4	0.0	12.0	17.2	1,471	37	22	449	5,770	57,524	5,217
Mason	73.9	5,403	35.7	31.8	3.4	1.2	4.4	29.9	2,189	58	26	1,065	6,220	53,314	4,741
Massac	82.3	5,758	31.1	31.3	4.3	0.3	4.5	41.2	2,886	34	27	865	6,160	49,570	4,057
Menard	51.8	4,217	45.5	16.1	4.6	0.6	10.8	26.5	2,157	27	24	630	6,060	69,541	6,773
Mercer	55.4	3,550	49.3	1.7	5.5	0.1	10.0	33.3	2,134	54	30	766	7,640	60,030	5,352
Monroe	100.0	2,926	50.0	9.5	8.6	0.7	9.0	139.3	4,075	68	70	1,297	17,500	84,087	9,761
Montgomery	90.5	3,144	49.0	0.2	3.7	0.1	6.9	52.5	1,825	94	52	1,454	12,420	57,221	5,065
Morgan	124.5	3,634	61.3	1.2	5.9	1.9	6.5	106.7	3,115	74	61	1,904	15,390	56,562	5,231
Moultrie	37.6	2,556	46.8	1.8	4.9	0.0	13.9	14.9	1,014	31	28	489	6,670	59,858	5,688
Ogle	262.9	5,155	57.1	0.0	5.1	1.0	8.1	256.0	5,020	118	101	2,754	25,400	61,473	5,731
Peoria	761.9	4,174	41.8	0.9	7.5	1.9	6.9	757.5	4,150	1,513	394	8,500	86,900	69,556	8,514
Perry	73.5	3,455	33.6	35.0	7.1	0.1	5.0	48.2	2,264	45	37	1,291	8,740	50,872	3,889
Piatt	64.0	3,896	43.0	15.3	5.8	2.3	9.5	21.5	1,308	41	33	953	8,240	70,392	7,192
Pike	56.4	3,597	44.7	4.0	5.4	0.4	11.4	29.7	1,894	60	30	888	6,680	51,926	4,944
Pope	13.8	3,296	33.7	0.0	2.3	0.0	8.0	1.3	299	20	8	193	1,540	49,751	4,001
Pulaski	33.4	6,047	52.1	1.1	2.0	0.1	5.3	13.0	2,347	54	16	810	2,290	43,590	3,145
Putnam	23.6	4,151	45.0	2.6	5.2	0.0	15.5	4.2	746	14	12	310	2,890	64,901	6,188
Randolph	166.8	5,165	31.6	36.9	3.7	0.8	4.6	76.7	2,376	90	61	2,283	13,620	56,005	4,904
Richland	81.6	5,151	76.9	0.5	3.9	0.1	4.9	48.6	3,071	46	31	907	7,340	52,315	4,296
Rock Island	680.4	4,731	45.1	3.5	7.9	0.6	5.4	822.9	5,721	5,097	639	7,247	69,860	57,479	5,583
St. Clair	1,086.2	4,136	53.4	1.5	7.9	1.0	5.1	903.4	3,440	5,490	5,191	12,401	122,390	61,663	6,388
Saline	96.2	4,017	60.8	0.0	5.5	0.1	6.1	81.1	3,385	104	45	1,727	9,970	53,145	4,959
Sangamon	878.1	4,456	45.6	1.6	9.1	0.1	8.1	3,122.8	15,846	1,790	445	17,741	99,200	71,163	8,311
Schuyler	43.2	6,222	24.1	55.3	3.0	0.0	6.4	6.1	874	23	13	548	3,330	50,205	4,232
Scott	17.9	3,591	51.9	2.0	3.2	16.0	7.0	13.4	2,694	15	10	327	2,420	54,786	4,527
Shelby	50.3	2,312	40.5	3.4	6.6	0.0	16.1	19.1	879	97	43	760	10,130	56,216	4,765
Stark	19.9	3,641	53.8	0.5	4.8	0.8	11.9	6.4	1,170	28	10	272	2,610	54,451	4,665
Stephenson	179.9	3,998	54.4	5.2	6.4	0.2	5.4	109.7	2,438	128	87	2,552	21,930	53,587	4,893
Tazewell	569.1	4,263	58.3	1.5	6.6	0.2	6.6	369.4	2,767	506	286	6,734	63,380	68,398	7,230
Union	69.0	4,066	66.1	0.1	6.2	0.0	5.5	31.5	1,854	66	32	1,221	7,640	51,515	4,337
Vermilion	307.4	3,957	52.9	0.9	5.4	0.1	7.9	108.9	1,402	1,390	145	4,298	33,090	49,246	4,217
Wabash	70.5	6,114	22.8	51.8	2.3	0.0	2.4	10.6	917	26	22	1,060	5,060	62,247	6,383
Warren	54.3	3,167	49.0	2.2	5.3	1.7	10.3	49.6	2,893	66	32	945	7,710	52,836	4,400
Washington	56.9	4,075	31.7	27.3	3.6	2.7	11.1	36.8	2,635	47	27	713	6,920	65,785	6,488
Wayne	57.0	3,470	54.4	0.3	4.1	1.3	12.8	37.6	2,289	60	32	916	7,150	50,401	3,774
White	53.1	3,818	54.9	1.8	4.6	0.1	9.5	19.8	1,426	51	26	783	6,120	54,945	4,740
Whiteside	434.6	7,767	24.7	52.7	2.5	0.7	2.6	122.8	2,194	157	108	4,747	27,430	55,066	4,928
Will	2,807.8	4,066	52.3	2.1	7.9	0.0	5.4	4,430.4	6,416	1,092	1,377	31,445	342,850	78,757	9,354
Williamson	253.1	3,774	57.8	0.2	6.7	0.1	5.7	320.5	4,781	1,692	130	4,029	30,630	58,278	5,774

1. Based on the resident population estimated as of July 1 of the year shown.

State / county code	CBSA code[1]	County Type code[2]	STATE County	Land area[3] (sq. mi)	Population, 2021: Total persons 2021	Population, 2021: Rank	Population, 2021: Per square mile	Race alone or in combination, not Hispanic or Latino (percent): White	Black	American Indian, Alaska Native	Asian and Pacific Islancer	Percent Hispanic or Latino[4]	Age (percent): Under 5 years	5 to 17 years	18 to 24 years	25 to 34 years	35 to 44 years	45 to 54 years
				1	2	3	4	5	6	7	8	9	10	11	12	13	14	15
			ILLINOIS—Cont'd															
17201	40420	2	Winnebago	513.1	283,119	251	551.8	68.8	15.4	0.6	3.5	14.4	6.1	13.2	12.3	12.6	11.9	12.1
17203	37900	2	Woodford	527.5	38,225	1,216	72.5	96.2	1.5	0.5	1.2	2.0	5.7	13.8	12.9	10.3	12.8	11.9
18000		0	INDIANA	35,826.4	6,805,985	X	190.0	79.5	11.1	0.7	3.2	7.7	6.0	13.2	13.8	13.1	12.6	12.0
18001	19540	6	Adams	338.9	35,961	1,283	106.1	94.1	1.1	0.5	0.5	4.6	8.8	17.6	13.5	11.6	10.6	10.6
18003	23060	2	Allen	657.3	388,608	186	591.2	74.9	13.6	0.8	5.8	8.1	6.8	14.4	13.4	14.1	12.7	11.7
18005	18020	3	Bartholomew	406.9	82,475	698	202.7	81.4	3.0	0.7	8.5	8.0	6.2	13.7	12.0	14.1	12.8	12.3
18007	29200	3	Benton	406.4	8,714	2,509	21.4	92.6	1.7	0.7	0.6	6.0	6.1	13.8	12.4	11.6	12.0	12.0
18009		6	Blackford	165.1	12,091	2,276	73.2	96.3	1.6	0.8	0.9	1.9	5.5	12.8	11.0	11.5	10.6	12.7
18011	26900	1	Boone	422.9	73,052	755	172.7	89.8	3.2	0.6	4.4	3.6	6.3	15.0	12.2	12.1	14.3	13.2
18013	26900	1	Brown	312.0	15,552	2,058	49.8	96.5	1.3	1.0	0.7	1.9	3.8	9.8	9.6	9.6	10.4	13.5
18015	29200	3	Carroll	372.2	20,444	1,794	54.9	93.9	1.3	0.6	0.4	4.8	5.4	12.4	11.4	11.5	11.6	12.8
18017	30900	4	Cass	412.1	37,563	1,234	91.2	78.2	2.7	0.8	2.1	17.4	5.6	12.7	12.3	11.6	12.4	12.8
18019	31140	1	Clark	372.8	122,738	519	329.2	84.3	10.0	0.8	1.8	6.0	5.9	12.6	11.5	14.1	13.4	13.0
18021	45460	3	Clay	357.6	26,410	1,547	73.9	96.6	1.5	0.8	0.6	1.9	6.1	12.9	11.1	12.0	12.4	12.4
18023	23140	6	Clinton	405.1	33,065	1,359	81.6	81.4	1.3	0.5	0.6	17.1	6.8	14.9	12.9	12.0	11.9	11.7
18025		8	Crawford	305.6	10,514	2,375	34.4	96.7	1.3	1.1	0.6	1.8	5.7	11.8	10.8	10.4	11.4	13.0
18027	47780	7	Daviess	429.5	33,397	1,346	77.8	91.5	2.9	0.5	0.6	5.7	8.3	16.4	13.3	12.4	11.5	10.5
18029	17140	1	Dearborn	305.1	50,816	987	166.6	97.0	1.3	0.6	0.7	1.5	5.4	12.3	12.3	11.0	12.1	13.3
18031	24700	6	Decatur	372.6	26,320	1,553	70.6	95.4	1.2	0.5	1.6	2.3	6.2	13.3	12.5	12.3	12.1	12.4
18033	12140	4	DeKalb	362.8	43,333	1,119	119.4	95.5	1.2	0.5	0.8	3.1	6.3	13.6	12.2	12.6	12.3	12.3
18035	34620	3	Delaware	392.1	111,871	552	285.3	88.4	8.5	0.7	2.1	2.8	4.6	10.2	22.7	11.7	10.4	11.0
18037	27540	5	Dubois	427.3	43,549	1,109	101.9	89.3	1.2	0.4	0.8	9.0	6.2	13.9	12.1	11.0	11.7	11.8
18039	21140	3	Elkhart	463.2	206,921	331	446.7	75.3	7.1	0.7	1.7	17.6	7.3	15.3	13.9	12.8	12.1	11.7
18041	18220	6	Fayette	215.0	23,360	1,665	108.7	96.4	2.1	0.7	0.5	1.5	5.6	12.2	11.8	11.4	11.4	13.0
18043	31140	1	Floyd	148.5	80,454	710	541.8	88.9	7.0	0.7	1.8	3.9	5.7	12.9	12.1	12.7	13.2	12.6
18045		6	Fountain	395.7	16,427	2,006	41.5	95.7	1.1	0.8	0.7	2.9	5.7	12.1	11.6	11.7	11.1	12.9
18047	17140	6	Franklin	384.4	22,842	1,680	59.4	97.4	0.7	0.5	0.9	1.3	6.1	12.3	11.9	10.9	11.5	12.9
18049		7	Fulton	368.4	20,386	1,799	55.3	92.3	1.6	0.9	0.9	5.6	5.7	13.6	11.7	11.1	11.9	11.8
18051		6	Gibson	487.4	32,924	1,364	67.6	94.4	4.0	0.7	1.0	2.1	6.1	13.4	12.3	12.0	12.3	12.1
18053	31980	4	Grant	414.1	66,263	810	160.0	86.6	8.9	0.8	1.4	4.9	5.6	11.9	16.4	11.0	10.4	11.5
18055		6	Greene	542.5	30,786	1,409	56.7	96.9	0.7	0.8	0.6	2.0	5.6	12.1	11.1	11.8	11.4	12.8
18057	26900	1	Hamilton	394.4	356,650	205	904.3	83.6	5.6	0.4	8.0	4.6	5.9	15.1	12.7	11.9	15.1	14.0
18059	26900	1	Hancock	306.0	81,789	705	267.3	92.0	4.3	0.7	1.5	3.1	5.6	13.5	11.5	12.1	13.6	13.2
18061	31140	1	Harrison	484.1	39,761	1,188	82.1	96.3	1.3	0.7	0.9	2.2	5.3	12.7	11.1	11.3	13.1	12.8
18063	26900	1	Hendricks	406.9	179,355	376	440.8	82.4	10.4	0.5	4.1	4.7	5.3	14.4	12.7	12.6	14.7	13.4
18065	35220	4	Henry	391.9	48,935	1,007	124.9	94.3	3.5	0.6	0.9	2.1	5.1	11.4	11.9	13.0	12.1	13.2
18067	29020	3	Howard	293.1	83,687	687	285.5	86.4	9.8	0.9	1.9	3.9	6.1	12.9	12.0	12.4	11.4	11.8
18069	26540	6	Huntington	382.6	36,717	1,263	96.0	95.2	1.2	0.9	1.0	2.9	5.7	12.2	13.4	12.1	12.0	12.1
18071	42980	4	Jackson	510.0	46,067	1,058	90.3	87.3	1.8	0.7	3.0	8.4	6.7	13.6	11.8	11.9	12.8	12.7
18073	16980	1	Jasper	559.7	33,091	1,357	59.1	91.7	1.4	0.6	0.8	6.6	5.4	12.9	13.9	11.4	12.0	12.4
18075		6	Jay	383.9	20,248	1,803	52.7	95.2	1.1	0.8	0.7	3.4	6.9	14.1	12.2	11.6	10.8	12.3
18077	31500	6	Jefferson	360.6	33,141	1,355	91.9	93.5	2.7	0.7	1.3	3.1	5.6	11.1	13.3	12.0	12.1	12.5
18079	35860	6	Jennings	376.6	27,409	1,520	72.8	95.4	1.4	0.8	0.7	3.1	5.8	13.3	11.9	12.8	11.1	13.9
18081	26900	1	Johnson	320.4	164,298	409	512.8	87.8	3.9	0.6	5.6	4.0	6.0	14.1	12.6	13.5	13.8	12.6
18083	47180	5	Knox	515.8	35,956	1,284	69.7	93.0	3.7	0.7	1.4	2.7	5.5	12.2	15.9	11.4	12.0	10.7
18085	47700	4	Kosciusko	531.4	80,106	713	150.7	88.5	1.7	0.6	1.9	8.6	6.1	13.3	13.1	12.6	12.0	11.5
18087		6	LaGrange	379.6	40,524	1,169	106.8	94.4	0.8	0.4	0.7	4.4	8.8	17.6	15.1	11.6	10.9	10.8
18089	16980	1	Lake	498.7	498,558	144	999.7	54.4	24.3	0.7	2.1	20.4	5.8	13.2	12.8	12.2	13.0	12.3
18091	33140	3	LaPorte	598.3	112,390	549	187.8	80.5	13.0	0.8	1.1	7.1	5.6	12.2	11.6	13.4	12.4	12.3
18093	13260	6	Lawrence	449.1	45,070	1,075	100.4	96.6	0.9	1.0	0.9	1.8	5.7	11.6	11.7	11.4	11.8	12.9
18095	26900	1	Madison	451.9	130,782	493	289.4	86.2	9.6	0.7	1.0	4.5	5.4	12.0	12.5	12.9	12.4	12.7
18097	26900	1	Marion	396.6	971,102	51	2,448.6	55.9	30.7	0.7	4.7	11.0	6.9	13.9	13.3	16.6	13.4	11.2
18099	38500	6	Marshall	443.6	46,121	1,055	104.0	88.0	1.2	0.7	0.9	10.6	6.0	14.1	13.0	11.1	11.5	12.2
18101		7	Martin	335.8	9,780	2,428	29.1	97.6	0.6	0.6	0.8	1.3	5.8	12.3	11.6	11.0	11.6	12.3
18103	37940	6	Miami	373.8	36,081	1,281	96.5	90.1	5.9	1.6	0.8	3.6	5.3	11.8	12.3	13.4	13.0	13.0
18105	14020	3	Monroe	394.5	139,875	470	354.6	85.4	4.8	0.7	8.1	3.7	4.1	8.8	28.7	13.8	11.0	9.5
18107	18820	6	Montgomery	504.6	38,063	1,223	75.4	92.6	1.7	0.7	1.2	5.1	5.8	13.1	13.3	11.9	11.3	12.0
18109	26900	1	Morgan	403.8	72,206	762	178.8	96.6	1.0	0.8	1.0	1.8	5.4	12.6	11.9	11.6	12.1	13.4
18111	16980	1	Newton	401.8	13,808	2,166	34.4	90.9	1.3	0.8	0.7	7.3	5.3	11.9	10.8	11.8	12.2	12.3
18113	28340	6	Noble	410.8	47,227	1,035	115.0	87.7	1.3	0.7	0.9	10.5	6.4	13.6	12.5	12.2	12.1	12.3
18115	17140	1	Ohio	86.2	5,978	2,735	69.4	96.7	1.3	0.8	0.6	1.9	5.0	11.7	9.5	10.8	11.0	12.3
18117		6	Orange	398.4	19,830	1,826	49.8	95.7	2.2	1.0	0.7	1.8	6.2	12.7	11.5	11.3	11.2	11.9
18119	14020	3	Owen	385.3	21,446	1,738	55.7	97.1	1.0	1.0	1.0	1.3	5.3	11.5	10.9	11.2	11.4	12.7
18121	45460	6	Parke	444.7	16,407	2,009	36.9	95.1	3.1	0.7	0.3	1.6	5.7	12.2	11.2	12.8	11.7	12.1
18123		6	Perry	381.7	19,316	1,859	50.6	94.4	3.4	0.6	1.0	1.5	5.3	11.8	11.6	13.4	13.1	11.9

1. CBSA = Core Based Statistical Area. See Appendix A for explanation. See Appendix B for list of metropolitan areas with component counties. 2. County type code from the Economic Research Service of USDA Rural-Urban Continuum Codes. See Appendix A for definition. 3. Dry land or land partially or temporarily covered by water. 4. May be of any race.

STATE County	Population, 2021 (cont.)				Population change, 2000–2021							Households, 2016–2020				
	Age (percent) (cont.)				Total persons		Percent change		Components of change, 2020–2021					Percent		
	55 to 64 years	65 to 74 years	75 years and over	Percent female	2010	2020	2010–2020	2020–2021	Births	Deaths	Net Migration	Number	Persons per household	Family house-holds	Female family house-holder[1]	One person
	16	17	18	19	20	21	22	23	24	25	26	27	28	29	30	31
ILLINOIS—Cont'd																
Winnebago	13.4	10.9	7.4	51.0	295,266	285,350	-3.4	-0.8	4,133	4,321	-2,077	115,768	2.4	64.1	14.5	29.8
Woodford	13.8	11.1	7.7	49.9	38,664	38,467	-0.5	-0.6	520	566	-200	14,652	2.6	72.2	7.8	23.5
INDIANA	12.8	10.0	6.4	50.4	6,483,802	6,785,528	4.7	0.3	96,817	96,570	19,609	2,602,770	2.5	64.5	11.5	29.0
Adams	11.3	9.2	6.9	49.8	34,387	35,809	4.1	0.4	816	455	-214	12,512	2.8	70.1	9.5	25.6
Allen	11.8	9.4	5.8	50.7	355,329	385,410	8.5	0.8	6,365	5,021	1,778	147,043	2.5	63.4	12.2	30.1
Bartholomew	12.1	9.8	6.8	49.5	76,794	82,208	7.1	0.3	1,234	1,139	161	31,772	2.6	65.6	10.0	28.4
Benton	14.3	10.2	7.6	49.3	8,854	8,719	-1.5	-0.1	134	120	-20	3,435	2.5	65.3	11.6	28.6
Blackford	14.0	12.7	9.1	50.6	12,766	12,112	-5.1	-0.2	148	200	32	5,105	2.3	64.9	10.4	31.1
Boone	12.6	8.8	5.4	50.0	56,640	70,812	25.0	3.2	1,038	806	2,021	25,822	2.6	72.9	7.9	21.7
Brown	17.6	16.5	9.3	49.9	15,242	15,475	1.5	0.5	113	244	212	6,372	2.4	77.7	7.7	18.7
Carroll	14.9	11.9	8.0	49.1	20,155	20,306	0.7	0.7	259	261	141	8,123	2.5	66.1	7.0	28.1
Cass	13.9	10.9	7.7	49.6	38,966	37,870	-2.8	-0.8	546	612	-244	14,950	2.4	63.3	11.9	32.6
Clark	13.3	10.3	6.0	50.9	110,232	121,093	9.9	1.4	1,700	1,815	1,755	45,024	2.6	65.5	11.2	28.9
Clay	14.1	11.5	7.3	50.2	26,890	26,466	-1.6	-0.2	376	423	-15	10,454	2.5	72.0	13.2	23.6
Clinton	12.7	9.8	7.2	49.9	33,224	33,190	-0.1	-0.4	554	483	-202	12,144	2.6	64.5	9.9	28.4
Crawford	16.5	13.0	7.4	48.9	10,713	10,526	-1.7	-0.1	155	188	21	4,117	2.5	65.1	9.4	30.4
Daviess	12.0	9.3	6.3	49.4	31,648	33,381	5.5	0.0	700	491	-199	11,354	2.9	68.7	7.9	26.9
Dearborn	14.9	11.8	6.9	49.8	50,047	50,679	1.3	0.3	617	717	232	19,279	2.5	72.0	9.2	22.6
Decatur	14.0	10.4	6.7	50.1	25,740	26,472	2.8	-0.6	359	427	-87	10,241	2.6	65.2	6.8	26.0
DeKalb	13.7	10.4	6.5	50.1	42,223	43,265	2.5	0.2	644	626	41	16,904	2.5	69.7	9.5	25.8
Delaware	12.1	10.0	7.3	51.7	117,671	111,903	-4.9	0.0	1,258	1,935	636	46,632	2.3	58.4	12.5	31.1
Dubois	14.7	11.0	7.5	49.5	41,889	43,637	4.2	-0.2	628	621	-101	16,691	2.5	64.4	8.5	30.5
Elkhart	11.7	9.0	6.2	50.3	197,559	207,047	4.8	-0.1	3,657	2,551	-1,269	72,362	2.8	69.4	12.8	25.7
Fayette	13.8	12.6	8.2	50.6	24,277	23,398	-3.6	-0.2	283	450	129	9,686	2.3	67.7	13.8	26.2
Floyd	13.8	10.7	6.2	51.0	74,578	80,484	7.9	0.0	1,029	1,300	228	29,264	2.6	66.5	11.5	28.4
Fountain	14.6	11.5	8.8	50.0	17,240	16,479	-4.4	-0.3	223	348	71	6,982	2.3	65.7	9.8	28.0
Franklin	14.9	12.0	7.6	50.0	23,087	22,785	-1.3	0.3	304	341	93	8,867	2.6	71.7	11.0	25.4
Fulton	13.8	12.0	8.3	49.6	20,836	20,480	-1.7	-0.5	273	329	-39	7,840	2.5	64.2	10.3	30.6
Gibson	13.9	10.7	7.1	49.6	33,503	33,011	-1.5	-0.3	449	522	-20	13,551	2.4	69.4	10.2	24.5
Grant	13.6	11.4	8.1	51.9	70,061	66,674	-4.8	-0.6	890	1,224	-88	26,896	2.2	64.7	13.6	30.1
Greene	15.1	12.0	8.1	49.8	33,165	30,803	-7.1	-0.1	392	601	192	12,988	2.5	68.0	9.4	26.9
Hamilton	12.1	8.3	4.9	50.7	274,569	347,467	26.5	2.6	4,455	2,958	7,702	123,066	2.7	74.8	8.0	20.6
Hancock	13.7	10.2	6.5	50.5	70,002	79,840	14.1	2.4	1,030	1,072	2,011	29,627	2.6	71.7	7.8	22.4
Harrison	14.9	11.7	7.0	49.7	39,364	39,654	0.7	0.3	482	617	241	14,534	2.7	67.9	6.2	26.9
Hendricks	12.3	9.1	5.4	49.6	145,448	174,788	20.2	2.6	2,024	1,860	4,434	60,307	2.7	75.0	9.3	19.7
Henry	14.1	11.4	7.9	47.2	49,462	48,914	-1.1	0.0	538	885	367	18,387	2.4	65.9	10.6	27.9
Howard	13.6	11.4	8.3	51.3	82,752	83,658	1.1	0.0	1,217	1,562	369	34,632	2.4	63.6	14.3	32.0
Huntington	14.6	10.8	7.0	50.2	37,124	36,662	-1.2	0.2	481	613	185	14,790	2.4	65.2	10.3	30.0
Jackson	13.5	10.0	6.9	49.7	42,376	46,428	9.6	-0.8	743	748	-360	16,923	2.6	69.9	11.7	24.6
Jasper	13.9	11.0	7.3	49.9	33,478	32,918	-1.7	0.5	435	507	244	12,676	2.6	68.6	10.3	28.0
Jay	13.5	11.2	7.4	49.5	21,253	20,478	-3.6	-1.1	333	327	-235	8,293	2.5	65.1	9.9	28.7
Jefferson	14.7	11.6	7.1	51.4	32,428	33,147	2.2	0.0	465	537	61	12,833	2.3	62.5	10.4	31.8
Jennings	14.3	10.4	6.6	49.5	28,525	27,613	-3.2	-0.7	375	469	-114	10,776	2.5	70.6	11.7	24.4
Johnson	12.3	9.2	5.9	50.3	139,654	161,765	15.8	1.6	2,248	2,119	2,398	57,872	2.7	70.9	10.0	23.7
Knox	13.8	10.9	7.6	49.0	38,440	36,282	-5.6	-0.9	492	649	-171	15,186	2.3	64.4	11.4	31.3
Kosciusko	13.6	10.9	6.8	49.7	77,358	80,240	3.7	-0.2	1,150	1,145	-153	31,462	2.5	67.7	10.5	26.5
LaGrange	11.0	8.8	5.5	48.8	37,128	40,446	8.9	0.2	911	410	-427	12,547	3.1	78.9	9.1	17.3
Lake	13.4	10.5	6.7	51.3	496,005	498,700	0.5	0.0	6,774	7,797	796	188,646	2.6	65.6	15.6	29.2
LaPorte	13.9	11.6	7.1	48.4	111,467	112,417	0.9	0.0	1,413	1,838	386	42,725	2.4	64.7	12.9	28.3
Lawrence	14.5	12.1	8.2	50.4	46,134	45,011	-2.4	0.1	620	839	276	18,968	2.4	66.7	9.6	27.7
Madison	13.5	11.2	7.5	49.9	131,636	130,129	-1.1	0.5	1,685	2,249	1,215	51,276	2.4	64.7	14.4	29.7
Marion	11.7	8.3	4.9	51.8	903,393	977,203	8.2	-0.6	16,733	12,317	-10,587	377,695	2.5	54.9	14.2	37.0
Marshall	13.5	11.0	7.7	50.1	47,051	46,095	-2.0	0.1	607	681	98	17,430	2.6	69.9	8.2	25.6
Martin	14.7	12.6	8.1	49.5	10,334	9,812	-5.1	-0.3	142	158	-18	4,095	2.4	61.2	7.2	32.1
Miami	13.1	10.7	7.3	46.1	36,903	35,962	-2.5	0.3	469	521	170	13,531	2.5	66.5	9.9	27.8
Monroe	10.0	8.6	5.4	50.3	137,974	139,718	1.3	0.1	1,301	1,470	285	56,399	2.3	52.5	9.7	33.1
Montgomery	14.2	10.6	7.8	49.4	38,124	37,936	-0.5	0.3	539	622	206	15,618	2.4	64.9	8.8	28.9
Morgan	15.2	11.3	6.6	50.4	68,894	71,780	4.2	0.6	910	1,089	604	26,460	2.6	72.9	9.4	21.8
Newton	15.3	12.2	8.1	49.3	14,244	13,830	-2.9	-0.2	173	236	39	5,599	2.5	69.2	11.5	25.0
Noble	13.8	10.8	6.2	49.7	47,536	47,457	-0.2	-0.5	742	715	-263	18,133	2.6	68.9	9.9	25.8
Ohio	16.9	13.2	9.6	51.0	6,128	5,940	-3.1	0.6	59	116	97	2,623	2.2	67.6	9.1	28.3
Orange	14.8	12.4	8.0	50.1	19,840	19,867	0.1	-0.2	280	355	36	7,988	2.4	68.1	12.5	27.4
Owen	16.7	13.0	7.3	49.7	21,575	21,321	-1.2	0.6	259	369	237	8,830	2.3	65.3	8.7	28.2
Parke	14.5	12.1	7.6	52.9	17,339	16,156	-6.8	1.6	207	246	293	6,005	2.6	73.8	7.7	22.6
Perry	14.0	11.7	7.3	46.0	19,338	19,170	-0.9	0.8	220	292	219	7,713	2.3	62.4	7.5	30.8

1. No spouse present.

STATE County	Persons in group quarters, 2021	Daytime Population, 2016–2020: Number	Daytime Population, 2016–2020: Employment/ residence ratio	Births, 2021: Total	Births, 2021: Rate[1]	Deaths, 2021: Number	Deaths, 2021: Rate[1]	Persons under 65 with no health insurance, 2019: Number	Persons under 65 with no health insurance, 2019: Percent	Medicare, 2021: Total beneficiaries	Medicare, 2021: Enrolled in Original Medicare	Medicare, 2021: Enrolled in Medicare Advantage	COVID-19 Deaths, 2020: Number	COVID-19 Deaths, 2020: Rate[1]
	32	33	34	35	36	37	38	39	40	41	42	43	44	45
ILLINOIS—Cont'd														
Winnebago	4,564	288,242	1.0	3,257	11.5	3,426	12.1	18,485	8.1	59,232	35,022	24,210	371	1.3
Woodford	932	32,233	0.7	418	10.9	452	11.8	1,746	5.7	7,966	5,885	2,081	53	1.4
INDIANA	181,555	6,644,210	1.0	77,598	11.4	76,906	11.3	565,717	10.3	1,283,388	822,981	460,407	9,322	1.4
Adams	346	34,878	1.0	647	18.0	353	9.8	4,240	14.3	6,201	3,928	2,273	46	1.3
Allen	5,905	386,156	1.1	5,090	13.1	3,989	10.3	33,536	10.6	67,968	32,178	35,789	482	1.2
Bartholomew	935	93,567	1.3	975	11.8	898	10.9	6,827	9.8	15,717	11,487	4,230	115	1.4
Benton	67	7,378	0.7	103	11.8	93	10.7	816	11.5	1,884	1,424	460	13	1.5
Blackford	152	10,393	0.7	130	10.7	162	13.4	889	9.9	3,135	2,093	1,043	24	2.0
Boone	531	60,847	0.8	828	11.5	659	9.1	4,192	7.1	11,573	7,710	3,863	86	1.2
Brown	143	11,394	0.5	94	6.1	194	12.5	1,177	10.5	4,227	2,688	1,539	22	1.4
Carroll	81	15,994	0.6	212	10.4	209	10.3	1,720	10.7	4,462	3,166	1,296	19	0.9
Cass	991	35,141	0.9	440	11.7	479	12.7	4,250	14.1	8,088	5,469	2,618	84	2.2
Clark	1,256	111,998	0.9	1,359	11.1	1,432	11.7	8,738	8.9	23,864	16,364	7,500	140	1.2
Clay	294	22,250	0.7	307	11.6	341	12.9	1,862	8.8	5,999	4,320	1,679	39	1.5
Clinton	785	29,058	0.8	439	13.3	374	11.3	3,138	11.8	6,534	4,267	2,267	39	1.2
Crawford	31	8,916	0.6	114	10.8	150	14.2	1,039	12.5	2,674	1,920	754	13	1.2
Daviess	496	31,296	0.9	554	16.6	399	11.9	5,235	18.8	5,608	4,642	966	78	2.3
Dearborn	491	40,812	0.6	494	9.7	588	11.6	3,329	8.3	10,867	7,406	3,461	59	1.2
Decatur	301	28,827	1.2	299	11.3	352	13.3	1,938	8.9	5,536	3,848	1,688	63	2.4
DeKalb	490	45,313	1.1	519	12.0	510	11.8	3,316	9.2	8,897	4,244	4,653	70	1.6
Delaware	8,316	113,950	1.0	1,003	9.0	1,502	13.4	8,911	10.3	23,875	15,762	8,113	141	1.3
Dubois	842	48,897	1.3	503	11.5	499	11.5	3,026	8.7	8,959	7,527	1,433	61	1.4
Elkhart	3,489	234,476	1.3	2,927	14.1	1,999	9.7	25,976	15.1	35,101	21,881	13,220	349	1.7
Fayette	353	20,100	0.7	225	9.6	357	15.3	1,775	9.8	6,360	4,895	1,466	47	2.0
Floyd	1,265	70,543	0.8	826	10.3	988	12.3	5,223	8.0	16,291	11,613	4,678	107	1.3
Fountain	134	14,377	0.7	170	10.3	268	16.3	1,229	9.5	4,010	2,888	1,122	28	1.7
Franklin	150	17,847	0.6	248	10.9	277	12.1	1,719	9.3	5,075	3,452	1,624	32	1.4
Fulton	194	17,904	0.8	230	11.3	253	12.4	1,999	12.6	4,695	2,783	1,912	35	1.7
Gibson	614	40,436	1.4	353	10.7	417	12.6	2,099	7.7	7,062	4,827	2,235	73	2.2
Grant	4,825	66,926	1.0	718	10.8	959	14.5	4,732	9.8	15,843	10,401	5,442	129	1.9
Greene	185	26,280	0.6	314	10.2	475	15.4	2,644	10.5	7,396	5,532	1,864	65	2.1
Hamilton	1,737	310,002	0.9	3,572	10.1	2,390	6.8	17,843	6.0	48,779	32,363	16,416	305	0.9
Hancock	580	64,822	0.7	822	10.2	856	10.6	4,734	7.2	15,524	9,337	6,187	85	1.1
Harrison	344	33,619	0.6	378	9.5	488	12.3	2,981	9.1	8,785	6,429	2,356	43	1.1
Hendricks	4,004	153,594	0.9	1,623	9.1	1,473	8.3	11,029	7.7	28,404	17,537	10,866	205	1.2
Henry	3,573	42,514	0.7	441	9.0	733	15.0	3,180	9.0	11,476	6,975	4,501	69	1.4
Howard	1,196	85,929	1.1	953	11.4	1,250	14.9	6,419	9.9	19,535	12,687	6,848	150	1.8
Huntington	1,271	33,153	0.8	378	10.3	490	13.4	2,802	9.6	8,357	4,074	4,284	48	1.3
Jackson	578	46,608	1.1	603	13.0	592	12.8	4,071	11.2	9,095	5,725	3,370	58	1.3
Jasper	836	30,891	0.8	336	10.2	415	12.6	2,931	11.0	7,045	5,249	1,796	39	1.2
Jay	199	19,556	0.9	266	13.1	257	12.6	1,832	11.2	4,575	3,058	1,517	39	1.9
Jefferson	2,045	31,593	1.0	371	11.2	415	12.5	2,218	9.1	7,294	5,270	2,024	52	1.6
Jennings	243	23,367	0.7	301	11.0	379	13.8	2,219	9.8	6,036	3,951	2,085	35	1.3
Johnson	2,314	135,329	0.7	1,809	11.1	1,674	10.3	11,109	8.3	28,513	18,174	10,340	240	1.5
Knox	1,776	38,165	1.1	391	10.8	531	14.7	2,644	9.4	8,133	6,445	1,688	77	2.1
Kosciusko	1,520	80,473	1.0	901	11.3	898	11.2	8,085	12.5	15,876	8,336	7,540	76	0.9
LaGrange	291	39,107	1.0	732	18.1	337	8.3	9,514	27.9	5,820	3,450	2,370	76	1.9
Lake	6,364	466,003	0.9	5,436	10.9	6,146	12.3	39,323	9.9	95,353	62,504	32,849	695	1.4
LaPorte	6,488	104,018	0.9	1,137	10.1	1,464	13.0	8,550	10.3	23,751	17,238	6,513	140	1.2
Lawrence	541	40,304	0.8	482	10.7	673	14.9	3,570	10.0	10,832	7,577	3,255	88	2.0
Madison	6,119	116,874	0.8	1,365	10.5	1,771	13.6	10,641	10.7	29,612	16,188	13,424	242	1.9
Marion	18,193	1,080,125	1.3	13,434	13.8	9,904	10.2	100,212	12.3	147,109	85,426	61,683	1,356	1.4
Marshall	580	46,348	1.0	499	10.8	528	11.5	5,495	14.7	9,552	5,317	4,234	84	1.8
Martin	85	13,707	1.7	113	11.6	125	12.8	752	9.4	2,350	1,941	408	14	1.4
Miami	3,352	31,787	0.7	370	10.3	418	11.6	2,850	11.1	7,486	5,139	2,347	47	1.3
Monroe	13,948	155,904	1.1	1,045	7.5	1,191	8.5	10,733	9.4	21,863	15,825	6,038	121	0.9
Montgomery	1,074	37,414	1.0	434	11.4	501	13.2	3,368	11.1	8,129	5,240	2,889	65	1.7
Morgan	542	55,627	0.6	738	10.2	876	12.2	5,814	10.0	15,470	9,562	5,908	98	1.4
Newton	119	11,429	0.6	141	10.2	191	13.8	1,462	13.2	3,229	2,402	827	26	1.9
Noble	696	44,448	0.9	601	12.7	557	11.8	4,980	12.7	9,280	4,528	4,752	55	1.2
Ohio	35	4,451	0.5	50	8.4	96	16.1	387	8.5	1,526	986	540	16	2.7
Orange	220	18,834	0.9	235	11.8	289	14.6	1,746	11.3	4,806	3,406	1,400	37	1.9
Owen	170	16,974	0.6	206	9.6	297	13.9	2,091	12.7	5,016	3,330	1,686	34	1.6
Parke	1,460	14,730	0.7	164	10.1	207	12.7	1,494	12.5	3,681	2,584	1,098	12	0.7
Perry	1,528	17,873	0.9	174	9.0	236	12.3	1,135	8.1	4,309	3,265	1,044	28	1.5

1. Per 1,000 estimated resident population.

STATE County	COVID-19 Vaccinations, 2021–2022: Number	COVID-19 Vaccinations, 2021–2022: Percent[5]	Education: School enrollment and attainment, 2016–2020: Enrollment[1]: Total	Education: School enrollment and attainment, 2016–2020: Enrollment[1]: Percent private	Education: School enrollment and attainment, 2016–2020: Attainment[2] (percent): High school graduate or less	Education: School enrollment and attainment, 2016–2020: Attainment[2] (percent): Bachelor's degree or more	Education: Local government expenditures,[3] 2018–2019: Total current spending (mil dol)	Education: Local government expenditures,[3] 2018–2019: Current spending per student (dollars)	Money income, 2016–2020: Per capita income[4]	Money income, 2016–2020: Households: Median income (dollars)	Money income, 2016–2020: Households: Percent with income of less than $50,000	Money income, 2016–2020: Households: Percent with income of $200,000 or more	Income and poverty, 2020: Median household income (dollars)	Income and poverty, 2020: Percent below poverty level: All persons	Income and poverty, 2020: Percent below poverty level: Children under 18 years	Income and poverty, 2020: Percent below poverty level: Children 5 to 17 years in families
	46	47	48	49	50	51	52	53	54	55	56	57	58	59	60	61
ILLINOIS—Cont'd																
Winnebago	164,792	58.3	66,111	18.7	43.0	23.0	653.7	14,457	29,894	55,310	45.3	3.9	54,971	14.6	20.1	18.6
Woodford	21,075	54.8	9,952	16.7	35.8	33.8	104.9	13,986	37,751	74,777	31.5	8.9	72,980	6.2	6.7	6.2
INDIANA	3,688,866	54.8	1,654,841	16.7	43.9	27.2	10,787.3	10,237	30,693	58,235	42.9	4.5	60,794	11.6	14.9	13.7
Adams	11,847	33.1	8,846	21.1	57.1	15.0	46.2	10,698	22,617	52,712	47.4	1.5	58,602	11.8	20.9	20.6
Allen	198,902	52.4	95,832	24.6	38.7	28.9	551.9	10,015	29,951	57,104	43.4	4.0	61,039	11.4	15.9	14.1
Bartholomew	50,024	59.7	19,130	17.1	41.0	33.9	130.0	10,459	32,371	66,978	37.9	5.4	70,545	9.1	11.1	10.2
Benton	3,673	42.0	2,074	13.8	49.9	18.4	21.8	12,431	27,353	52,656	47.5	2.0	59,663	10.7	16.6	13.2
Blackford	5,487	46.7	2,318	12.4	56.3	13.7	16.4	10,354	25,287	44,341	56.0	1.4	49,105	13.4	19.4	19.5
Boone	47,975	70.7	17,170	13.3	24.0	50.8	122.7	9,860	48,835	89,444	26.5	15.2	92,302	5.2	4.6	4.2
Brown	7,686	50.9	2,777	13.1	39.7	29.3	23.5	12,317	35,000	66,833	38.5	5.3	70,930	9.9	14.5	13.6
Carroll	7,207	35.6	3,938	14.4	53.0	15.4	25.3	10,283	29,527	56,159	44.9	3.0	62,388	7.8	10.4	10.1
Cass	17,216	45.7	8,637	8.8	55.5	13.0	70.1	10,573	25,184	49,020	51.4	1.1	50,419	10.7	14.9	13.6
Clark	71,345	60.3	26,695	13.6	45.4	20.7	167.5	9,753	29,279	57,111	42.8	3.0	65,555	8.6	9.8	9.6
Clay	14,729	56.2	5,809	9.2	51.4	16.5	43.1	10,307	27,298	59,398	42.2	1.8	56,422	9.8	16.7	15.3
Clinton	15,648	48.3	7,748	12.7	58.2	14.6	59.7	9,408	24,678	53,750	46.1	1.4	59,503	10.0	13.4	12.3
Crawford	3,950	37.3	2,189	8.1	64.5	10.5	15.3	10,109	23,001	41,761	55.6	1.5	46,884	15.6	23.1	21.1
Daviess	11,046	33.1	7,425	31.9	59.6	12.8	45.8	9,747	23,600	53,800	45.3	2.1	53,101	10.9	14.9	13.9
Dearborn	30,544	61.8	10,838	8.4	47.5	25.7	81.6	10,068	31,992	70,779	35.5	4.9	73,459	7.8	9.5	8.7
Decatur	12,795	48.2	6,107	11.4	53.9	19.5	44.9	10,941	28,190	60,794	40.3	3.0	61,561	10.0	11.7	10.7
DeKalb	18,453	42.4	10,539	19.1	52.9	18.0	90.6	12,831	28,782	58,415	41.8	2.9	62,411	8.8	11.4	10.2
Delaware	55,340	48.5	34,215	7.0	44.1	24.9	156.0	9,845	25,718	45,910	53.5	2.9	46,612	19.4	20.9	20.1
Dubois	24,490	57.3	9,927	11.8	48.3	25.5	73.8	10,310	31,605	62,846	38.1	2.8	64,120	6.7	7.0	6.4
Elkhart	88,772	43.0	49,053	17.0	53.4	19.5	374.4	10,330	26,806	58,509	42.3	3.5	66,801	9.8	12.7	11.7
Fayette	9,256	40.1	4,714	12.6	61.0	14.8	39.1	11,178	23,839	47,465	51.6	1.0	53,616	13.5	17.7	16.2
Floyd	44,435	56.6	18,833	17.2	39.3	30.1	122.0	10,008	34,609	67,603	36.4	6.4	70,610	11.5	17.0	13.1
Fountain	7,660	46.9	3,453	9.9	55.6	14.0	27.3	10,475	26,636	52,334	47.4	2.1	55,627	10.9	13.2	12.3
Franklin	8,610	37.8	4,980	24.7	52.4	20.4	46.4	10,433	32,095	68,180	35.0	4.0	71,828	7.7	10.3	9.7
Fulton	7,985	40.0	4,445	8.9	53.0	14.5	24.8	10,076	26,865	50,597	49.2	1.2	55,895	12.0	19.8	19.2
Gibson	15,672	46.6	7,868	16.0	48.9	18.6	51.1	10,418	28,105	56,638	44.5	2.3	59,074	9.3	11.6	10.9
Grant	27,635	42.0	17,469	34.4	50.4	18.3	111.2	10,187	24,255	46,900	52.8	1.5	49,788	16.7	23.8	20.6
Greene	13,195	41.3	6,578	9.5	52.2	14.8	51.3	10,329	26,236	51,777	48.1	2.3	55,213	11.2	16.1	15.3
Hamilton	240,962	71.3	90,302	17.1	17.7	59.4	634.5	9,261	49,196	98,880	20.5	16.2	96,359	4.2	4.6	3.9
Hancock	52,950	67.7	17,396	12.6	38.1	31.8	129.2	9,443	36,450	75,647	29.6	6.5	77,916	5.1	5.8	5.4
Harrison	20,637	50.9	8,676	11.6	51.8	18.4	57.7	9,540	28,056	59,169	40.7	2.6	62,082	8.8	11.5	10.8
Hendricks	122,556	72.0	43,146	16.5	32.6	38.9	289.4	9,445	37,815	84,754	24.7	6.9	86,905	5.2	5.5	5.0
Henry	25,046	52.2	9,717	8.9	53.5	16.4	72.9	10,361	25,417	51,104	48.6	1.6	54,002	10.8	13.2	12.2
Howard	39,130	47.4	18,626	8.8	46.6	21.1	137.0	9,859	29,647	56,387	44.5	3.0	59,309	11.5	16.2	15.7
Huntington	18,408	50.4	8,463	16.9	49.8	21.0	50.4	9,840	27,441	54,286	45.4	2.4	59,252	9.1	11.0	10.5
Jackson	23,501	53.1	10,042	15.7	51.7	17.9	68.7	9,747	26,997	55,097	45.9	3.0	62,415	10.3	11.2	10.8
Jasper	15,926	47.5	7,703	15.5	55.2	15.1	49.6	9,941	28,434	61,889	40.5	3.4	70,662	8.3	10.5	10.0
Jay	7,931	38.8	4,515	7.7	59.1	12.5	34.5	10,890	24,165	45,864	54.4	1.2	42,504	13.9	22.5	21.0
Jefferson	18,096	56.0	7,241	29.1	52.2	17.3	46.6	10,908	27,845	51,981	47.8	2.7	55,588	12.7	15.9	15.4
Jennings	11,264	40.6	6,010	10.0	56.6	12.8	46.2	11,022	26,879	61,610	38.9	1.7	60,526	10.8	16.3	15.5
Johnson	92,572	58.5	38,582	18.6	39.2	32.3	257.5	9,458	35,048	72,928	32.1	6.5	76,868	6.7	7.9	7.0
Knox	18,049	49.3	9,087	8.4	47.9	16.5	56.0	10,526	27,521	47,394	51.4	4.1	44,842	15.9	19.0	17.2
Kosciusko	32,349	40.7	17,168	16.0	47.4	24.3	120.3	10,276	30,951	62,789	39.7	3.9	62,269	8.2	10.1	9.6
LaGrange	8,935	22.6	8,170	31.1	69.0	11.5	58.1	10,779	25,588	69,331	34.1	3.9	72,513	8.8	12.5	12.2
Lake	274,941	56.6	115,622	14.0	46.4	23.1	814.3	10,276	29,951	57,530	43.8	4.1	59,158	15.8	25.2	23.3
LaPorte	61,706	56.2	21,559	13.3	50.1	19.1	183.6	10,550	27,706	57,010	44.2	2.9	63,999	12.1	17.6	16.2
Lawrence	22,436	49.5	9,507	14.8	52.2	18.8	70.7	11,226	28,561	57,740	43.7	2.5	63,904	11.8	15.3	14.2
Madison	68,004	52.5	27,579	14.9	50.9	18.3	185.7	9,963	26,379	51,476	48.7	2.1	51,718	12.1	15.6	14.7
Marion	539,635	55.9	238,635	18.4	40.8	32.1	1,763.3	11,179	30,013	51,219	48.8	4.6	56,185	14.4	19.1	17.9
Marshall	20,696	44.7	10,974	20.5	53.2	19.7	71.9	9,695	26,590	54,207	45.3	2.0	57,657	9.3	11.8	10.7
Martin	4,641	45.3	2,152	8.0	55.9	12.6	14.1	9,516	26,576	55,378	44.6	1.3	46,486	11.2	14.1	13.5
Miami	14,300	40.3	8,179	10.4	55.4	13.7	47.3	9,143	24,439	50,616	49.5	2.3	54,439	13.1	18.7	16.6
Monroe	87,287	58.8	57,576	6.8	29.0	45.3	157.9	10,891	29,675	52,229	48.1	5.2	61,808	18.2	13.7	13.5
Montgomery	17,515	45.7	8,600	18.9	50.1	20.8	63.9	10,396	29,257	56,408	43.4	3.6	58,867	10.8	13.6	12.6
Morgan	38,095	54.0	15,762	12.3	52.1	18.6	100.9	9,418	31,856	67,680	34.9	4.9	67,004	8.5	11.1	10.5
Newton	4,459	31.9	2,731	7.1	59.2	11.9	22.7	10,926	27,742	57,866	42.2	3.2	59,246	10.5	14.8	14.3
Noble	18,460	38.7	10,456	9.1	56.1	15.4	71.2	9,920	27,532	58,947	40.9	2.3	62,173	9.9	12.8	12.0
Ohio	4,438	75.5	1,147	3.4	53.8	14.4	9.1	11,443	31,873	63,649	40.3	1.1	63,210	9.8	14.6	12.8
Orange	10,939	55.7	3,933	7.8	60.5	12.9	34.9	11,328	26,600	52,164	48.5	2.5	52,029	13.0	18.7	18.3
Owen	8,859	42.6	4,015	14.3	57.2	14.7	25.5	10,197	25,602	52,204	48.3	0.8	53,893	11.7	17.0	16.2
Parke	6,703	39.6	3,053	19.8	55.0	12.5	22.9	10,325	25,056	55,853	43.9	2.1	54,125	14.3	20.6	19.7
Perry	10,866	56.7	3,854	13.1	55.6	16.0	28.1	9,455	25,436	51,496	48.4	1.6	44,011	12.3	13.1	12.1

1. All persons 3 years old and over enrolled in nursery school through college. 2. Persons 25 years old and over. 3. Elementary and secondary education expenditures. 4. Based on population estimated by the American Community Survey, 2016–2020. 5. CDC percent based on 2019 population estimate.

STATE County	Personal income, 2020										Earnings, 2020		
			Per capita[1]			Supplements to wages and salaries, employer contributions (mil dol)						Contributions for government social insurance (mil dol)	
	Total (mil dol)	Percent change 2019–2020	Dollars	Rank	Wages and salaries (mil dol)	Pension and insurance	Government social insurance	Proprietors' income (mil dol)	Dividends, interest, and rent (mil dol)	Personal transfer reecipts (mil dol)	Total (mil dol)	From employee and self-employed	From employer
	62	63	64	65	66	67	68	69	70	71	72	73	74
ILLINOIS—Cont'd													
Winnebago	13,334	7.4	47,404	1,458	6,556	1,192	462	627	1,842	3,862	8,837	546	462
Woodford	2,163	6.7	56,797	585	490	97	35	169	371	415	791	47	35
INDIANA	350,760	6.4	51,691	X	162,612	26,248	12,296	34,281	52,924	81,918	235,436	14,921	12,296
Adams	1,521	6.6	42,452	2,137	610	110	49	296	202	362	1,063	62	49
Allen	19,234	6.1	50,327	1,109	10,292	1,581	783	1,475	3,164	4,496	14,130	903	783
Bartholomew	4,713	5.2	55,804	655	3,012	458	226	350	749	947	4,045	253	226
Benton	424	16.2	48,450	1,329	105	20	8	76	56	104	210	12	8
Blackford	490	7.8	41,561	2,261	123	25	9	34	62	189	191	15	9
Boone	5,570	5.6	80,314	77	1,833	235	143	326	1,227	634	2,536	159	143
Brown	778	4.0	51,505	980	95	20	8	47	136	210	170	17	8
Carroll	947	8.3	46,792	1,540	258	42	19	97	127	235	416	26	19
Cass	1,656	9.0	44,305	1,902	641	116	48	100	222	555	905	62	48
Clark	5,750	7.6	48,210	1,357	2,678	453	210	319	678	1,486	3,660	244	210
Clay	1,101	9.4	41,941	2,207	304	63	25	63	133	358	455	33	25
Clinton	1,386	7.9	43,027	2,059	525	89	40	86	180	396	740	51	40
Crawford	407	10.4	38,276	2,653	78	17	6	21	41	161	122	10	6
Daviess	1,606	8.9	47,919	1,404	567	94	43	296	215	380	1,001	57	43
Dearborn	2,630	5.7	52,778	871	656	111	50	118	391	621	935	70	50
Decatur	1,277	8.6	48,033	1,388	714	119	58	97	167	346	988	63	58
DeKalb	2,137	5.6	48,937	1,265	1,159	181	90	185	320	530	1,614	104	90
Delaware	4,646	7.0	40,948	2,340	2,180	402	165	226	673	1,618	2,973	204	165
Dubois	2,532	4.5	59,524	450	1,365	210	106	202	590	495	1,884	119	106
Elkhart	10,282	6.4	49,875	1,156	7,156	1,131	567	962	1,628	2,285	9,816	602	567
Fayette	1,039	8.5	45,375	1,739	268	49	21	58	119	411	395	33	21
Floyd	4,755	5.7	60,233	414	1,496	250	114	313	928	1,010	2,172	146	114
Fountain	738	10.8	44,685	1,853	187	39	15	72	91	228	314	23	15
Franklin	1,168	8.2	51,316	994	189	39	15	82	198	292	325	28	15
Fulton	933	7.8	46,613	1,560	280	51	21	123	141	262	476	31	21
Gibson	1,657	7.4	48,976	1,258	1,176	210	100	118	220	432	1,604	99	100
Grant	2,870	7.2	43,997	1,948	1,233	214	98	148	374	1,071	1,693	121	98
Greene	1,431	8.1	44,437	1,884	268	56	21	81	188	456	426	34	21
Hamilton	27,686	4.6	80,426	75	9,532	1,208	683	2,143	5,597	2,686	13,565	832	683
Hancock	4,382	7.5	55,084	698	1,353	226	102	228	661	872	1,909	132	102
Harrison	1,890	6.7	46,468	1,584	451	87	34	91	252	493	663	51	34
Hendricks	9,558	9.0	55,169	691	3,616	532	285	465	1,457	1,564	4,897	319	285
Henry	2,066	8.0	43,016	2,061	548	105	42	124	257	704	819	63	42
Howard	3,718	6.1	44,945	1,800	1,933	324	159	157	506	1,244	2,574	179	159
Huntington	1,673	7.4	45,969	1,657	600	109	46	73	255	486	828	61	46
Jackson	2,108	7.1	47,673	1,432	1,124	208	91	97	298	525	1,519	99	91
Jasper	1,638	8.3	48,987	1,255	515	98	40	181	204	413	834	54	40
Jay	861	11.2	42,194	2,168	286	54	22	153	92	259	515	31	22
Jefferson	1,543	7.6	48,068	1,381	564	115	43	131	201	485	854	59	43
Jennings	1,249	8.1	45,380	1,738	345	59	27	68	130	452	499	37	27
Johnson	8,525	6.4	53,081	852	2,756	420	216	513	1,274	1,669	3,904	264	216
Knox	1,795	9.2	49,156	1,235	795	162	61	157	238	578	1,174	73	61
Kosciusko	4,083	5.1	51,687	963	2,118	415	165	300	620	898	2,998	187	165
LaGrange	1,810	6.5	45,115	1,778	678	117	57	298	222	343	1,150	65	57
Lake	24,001	7.4	49,229	1,228	9,988	1,661	758	1,286	3,089	6,748	13,694	929	758
LaPorte	5,075	7.1	46,274	1,613	1,894	329	147	279	740	1,466	2,648	187	147
Lawrence	2,088	8.0	45,897	1,665	636	109	48	85	247	651	878	68	48
Madison	5,483	7.5	42,283	2,156	1,846	304	142	272	662	1,878	2,564	195	142
Marion	57,260	5.4	59,264	464	40,294	5,841	2,918	13,938	7,250	11,469	62,991	3,597	2,918
Marshall	2,088	7.1	45,277	1,756	800	138	61	142	301	542	1,142	77	61
Martin	445	8.9	44,160	1,916	621	180	50	39	65	129	889	49	50
Miami	1,331	5.8	37,669	2,717	412	87	34	97	187	440	631	44	34
Monroe	6,921	6.1	46,693	1,551	3,472	760	254	476	1,477	1,358	4,961	295	254
Montgomery	1,704	8.4	44,415	1,888	758	130	59	119	218	478	1,065	71	59
Morgan	3,386	5.3	47,894	1,407	717	127	55	166	398	871	1,065	86	55
Newton	643	12.3	46,215	1,619	144	27	12	68	71	172	251	15	12
Noble	2,125	6.9	44,436	1,885	786	143	63	183	265	552	1,175	77	63
Ohio	263	7.0	44,555	1,866	42	8	3	11	33	74	65	6	3
Orange	818	9.1	41,640	2,248	284	47	22	87	98	297	441	33	22
Owen	940	8.3	45,143	1,775	243	64	19	54	115	295	380	29	19
Parke	701	9.4	41,554	2,262	126	29	10	95	95	230	259	17	10
Perry	769	5.7	40,140	2,442	283	56	21	61	102	247	422	29	21

1. Based on the resident population estimated as of July 1 of the year shown.

STATE County	Earnings, 2020 (cont.) — Percent by selected industries: Farm	Mining, quarrying, and extractions	Construction	Manu-facturing	Information; professional, scientific, technical services	Retail trade	Finance, insurance, real estate, and leasing	Health care and social assistance	Govern-ment	Social Security beneficiaries, December 2020: Number	Rate[1]	Supple-mental Security Income recipients, 2020	Housing units, 2021: Total	Percent change, 2010–2021
	75	76	77	78	79	80	81	82	83	84	85	86	87	88
ILLINOIS—Cont'd														
Winnebago	0.3	0.0	5.1	20.4	4.6	6.4	5.4	20.4	13.1	62,580	221	7,454	124,990	0.0
Woodford	10.4	0.0	12.1	12.8	D	7.4	5.0	8.0	16.7	8,200	215	243	15,731	0.1
INDIANA	1.3	D	6.5	18.7	7.3	5.6	10.5	13.0	12.1	1,382,024	203	127,242	2,950,185	0.8
Adams	7.0	D	17.1	30.4	D	6.3	3.4	3.9	12.3	6,625	184	371	13,250	0.5
Allen	0.3	D	8.0	16.0	6.2	6.6	8.6	20.4	9.1	73,195	188	8,028	164,369	0.9
Bartholomew	1.0	D	3.9	44.4	5.2	4.8	4.0	7.4	9.1	16,800	204	1,215	35,500	0.4
Benton	27.8	0.0	6.0	11.3	D	3.2	D	2.5	14.3	2,080	239	174	3,779	-0.1
Blackford	8.4	D	6.4	30.2	D	4.6	4.4	10.4	14.2	3,415	282	276	5,852	-0.1
Boone	1.5	D	9.2	8.2	12.8	6.5	5.6	5.8	11.1	12,010	164	504	28,945	2.4
Brown	0.6	0.0	14.5	8.3	D	7.2	D	8.3	21.7	4,520	291	197	8,508	0.7
Carroll	12.7	D	7.3	D	D	4.1	4.5	D	10.3	4,880	239	206	9,525	0.4
Cass	4.7	D	6.4	28.8	2.1	6.0	4.6	D	21.7	8,710	232	786	16,389	0.1
Clark	0.5	0.2	6.8	15.0	3.9	8.0	7.4	11.5	12.4	25,815	210	2,210	53,746	2.6
Clay	5.9	D	4.0	37.0	D	7.8	3.3	D	14.3	6,735	255	666	11,635	0.0
Clinton	6.5	0.0	5.6	37.0	D	4.8	D	6.7	12.8	7,100	215	509	13,483	0.2
Crawford	1.9	D	5.3	D	2.0	D	D	5.6	19.2	3,055	291	335	5,885	0.2
Daviess	8.5	D	21.9	15.8	5.3	7.8	4.2	D	11.3	5,855	175	515	12,767	0.2
Dearborn	0.3	D	9.2	14.8	D	10.9	5.3	9.9	19.2	11,820	233	630	20,997	0.6
Decatur	4.3	D	3.5	44.2	D	4.5	3.4	4.2	10.8	6,005	228	424	11,605	0.7
DeKalb	1.5	0.3	4.1	49.7	2.6	3.9	2.7	5.0	7.8	9,690	224	656	18,250	0.7
Delaware	0.8	D	4.5	8.1	6.4	8.0	6.8	22.4	21.4	25,825	231	2,946	51,578	0.2
Dubois	2.5	D	4.6	36.5	3.7	6.8	4.5	13.2	6.7	9,560	220	383	18,724	0.4
Elkhart	1.0	D	4.1	48.6	2.2	4.3	3.4	7.5	5.5	37,085	179	2,969	80,101	0.6
Fayette	2.9	D	3.6	23.6	D	6.9	4.1	22.1	14.5	6,970	298	910	10,892	0.1
Floyd	0.0	D	7.7	20.2	7.6	5.1	3.7	22.1	12.0	17,310	215	1,354	34,619	0.7
Fountain	12.4	0.0	3.2	34.3	2.9	6.7	5.0	D	13.5	4,445	271	328	7,824	0.7
Franklin	7.7	0.3	10.6	16.6	D	7.9	5.1	D	16.2	6,245	273	422	9,721	0.7
Fulton	7.9	D	13.3	23.4	D	7.0	6.6	D	17.4	5,080	249	357	9,545	0.1
Gibson	3.3	3.4	1.9	55.4	D	3.6	1.9	D	4.9	7,530	229	488	14,728	1.1
Grant	2.0	D	3.5	18.7	3.5	6.9	4.5	D	15.2	17,325	261	2,100	29,863	0.2
Greene	8.6	1.2	7.4	7.0	4.5	8.0	3.1	D	26.8	8,110	263	714	14,341	0.1
Hamilton	0.3	0.1	8.8	4.6	14.8	6.2	17.7	10.3	7.4	49,810	140	1,704	139,519	2.7
Hancock	1.7	-0.1	10.0	25.2	8.4	5.6	4.4	6.7	14.8	16,630	203	719	32,982	2.3
Harrison	2.7	1.1	7.4	16.4	3.1	7.5	4.8	D	18.7	9,680	243	597	16,805	0.6
Hendricks	0.4	D	7.0	6.0	3.6	12.0	4.1	7.2	14.0	29,710	166	986	68,435	2.0
Henry	4.2	D	7.0	21.6	2.5	7.6	4.4	D	23.2	12,670	259	1,095	20,992	0.2
Howard	1.0	D	4.0	41.1	2.7	6.6	4.4	13.5	10.5	21,610	258	2,252	39,768	0.3
Huntington	3.2	D	5.8	27.1	D	5.3	6.3	9.6	10.2	9,055	247	620	16,283	0.3
Jackson	2.2	D	4.3	38.0	1.8	6.0	3.5	D	14.9	9,900	215	785	19,278	0.9
Jasper	11.1	D	7.4	14.7	2.6	6.4	4.7	6.5	10.0	8,045	243	471	13,676	1.0
Jay	19.8	D	7.9	32.7	D	3.9	3.0	D	9.5	5,010	247	378	8,900	0.1
Jefferson	1.1	0.0	3.8	26.0	D	13.8	3.8	13.1	14.8	8,215	248	690	14,445	0.3
Jennings	5.1	D	15.3	23.6	2.0	5.4	2.6	D	14.4	6,665	243	674	11,684	0.8
Johnson	0.4	D	8.8	10.1	6.0	9.0	6.9	12.7	13.3	30,550	186	1,730	64,653	1.7
Knox	6.2	6.6	5.0	10.8	2.7	5.9	3.5	12.3	24.0	8,710	242	954	16,968	0.3
Kosciusko	2.6	D	4.4	45.9	2.9	5.0	4.0	6.6	5.9	16,925	211	892	38,531	0.9
LaGrange	8.6	D	7.4	44.6	1.9	6.3	2.7	D	6.4	6,195	153	293	14,993	0.8
Lake	0.1	0.1	8.5	17.8	4.8	6.7	4.8	17.4	10.9	103,150	207	12,435	216,228	0.6
LaPorte	2.3	0.1	8.5	21.4	3.5	6.8	4.7	13.8	15.0	25,640	228	2,166	49,860	0.1
Lawrence	1.3	1.3	6.5	24.0	6.9	7.9	5.5	16.1	12.6	11,815	262	1,041	20,522	0.2
Madison	1.4	D	6.7	16.2	3.5	6.6	6.8	17.0	14.6	32,100	245	3,342	59,046	0.4
Marion	0.0	0.0	5.3	10.9	11.2	3.5	22.6	13.7	10.7	159,365	164	26,050	439,283	0.4
Marshall	5.1	D	4.8	35.9	3.6	6.4	4.9	8.1	10.1	10,265	223	619	19,907	1.2
Martin	1.5	0.0	1.2	3.5	10.2	1.4	0.6	0.8	75.9	2,535	259	191	4,579	0.0
Miami	7.8	0.7	5.5	17.0	2.5	5.4	4.7	7.8	26.8	7,590	210	775	14,871	0.1
Monroe	0.0	0.7	4.8	12.0	10.1	4.8	5.0	14.0	32.2	22,850	163	1,835	64,362	0.9
Montgomery	4.3	D	3.5	36.6	D	5.4	3.1	D	11.2	8,880	233	631	16,537	0.4
Morgan	2.0	0.3	14.1	14.9	4.8	7.2	6.6	10.7	13.9	16,980	235	945	29,730	1.1
Newton	21.1	D	6.7	14.3	D	3.0	D	5.1	14.1	3,205	232	191	6,044	0.4
Noble	4.1	D	5.7	48.0	D	5.8	2.8	5.1	9.1	10,340	219	637	20,205	0.7
Ohio	1.6	0.0	8.6	D	D	2.1	D	5.2	27.0	1,530	256	74	2,751	0.8
Orange	3.2	D	24.9	11.9	2.1	4.7	2.8	D	10.9	5,255	265	470	9,088	0.2
Owen	2.8	0.0	6.1	48.0	2.8	4.8	2.8	5.4	11.2	5,585	260	363	9,845	0.4
Parke	8.9	D	13.0	15.3	D	6.6	5.9	2.7	21.0	3,935	240	254	7,586	0.6
Perry	2.6	0.4	6.5	33.6	D	5.9	7.9	5.4	20.8	4,780	247	351	8,545	0.4

1. Per 1,000 resident population estimated as of July 1 of the year shown.

STATE County	Housing units, 2016–2020: Total	Occupied units: Owner-occupied: Percent	Owner-occupied: Median value[1]	Median owner cost as a percent of income: With a mortgage	Median owner cost as a percent of income: Without a mortgage[2]	Renter-occupied: Median rent[3]	Renter-occupied: Median rent as a percent of income[2]	Sub-standard units[4] (percent)	Civilian labor force, 2021: Total	Percent change, 2020–2021	Unemployment: Total	Unemployment: Rate[5]	Civilian employment[6], 2016–2020: Total	Percent: Management, business, science, and arts	Percent: Construction, production, and maintenance occupations
	89	90	91	92	93	94	95	96	97	98	99	100	101	102	103
ILLINOIS—Cont'd															
Winnebago	115,768	65.5	121,400	19.1	12.0	817	28.3	2.2	133,417	-1.5	11,256	8.4	131,614	30.8	30.0
Woodford	14,652	80.6	170,800	18.7	10.9	754	26.5	0.8	18,001	0.3	712	4.0	18,574	41.6	22.8
INDIANA	2,602,770	69.5	148,900	18.0	10.0	844	28.3	2.0	3,321,548	0.0	118,382	3.6	3,219,679	35.1	28.2
Adams	12,512	77.8	142,100	18.9	10.0	640	26.4	9.7	16,691	-0.5	365	2.2	15,503	24.4	40.7
Allen	147,043	68.6	136,700	17.7	10.0	789	26.8	1.7	184,097	-0.7	6,771	3.7	183,580	35.1	26.8
Bartholomew	31,772	70.9	163,400	18.1	10.0	940	23.5	2.4	42,821	-2.0	1,227	2.9	40,240	41.4	27.0
Benton	3,435	74.1	98,900	18.0	10.0	721	28.7	2.8	4,199	0.9	114	2.7	4,134	26.2	36.2
Blackford	5,105	72.0	73,500	18.0	11.4	635	32.0	1.1	4,685	-3.0	173	3.7	4,962	31.9	35.2
Boone	25,822	78.6	245,200	18.1	10.0	1,044	24.4	0.8	36,964	2.4	774	2.1	34,716	52.0	18.7
Brown	6,372	85.4	206,600	19.1	10.4	822	33.6	4.2	7,637	1.4	248	3.2	7,437	33.8	26.4
Carroll	8,123	79.2	133,600	17.7	10.8	710	21.7	1.6	9,497	0.9	278	2.9	9,578	26.5	40.5
Cass	14,950	73.4	91,500	17.2	10.1	660	24.4	2.0	17,216	-2.4	622	3.6	17,788	23.5	41.7
Clark	45,024	72.6	152,000	18.7	10.1	868	28.3	1.6	61,556	-0.2	1,976	3.2	58,594	31.4	29.3
Clay	10,454	78.3	104,200	17.0	10.0	717	24.1	2.1	11,473	-1.0	410	3.6	11,977	27.4	37.3
Clinton	12,144	70.1	119,000	17.8	10.0	752	27.8	2.2	16,723	-0.1	462	2.8	15,260	23.0	43.4
Crawford	4,117	82.2	89,500	19.4	12.6	663	29.9	3.1	4,788	-1.7	175	3.7	4,292	18.7	46.6
Daviess	11,354	70.3	139,800	17.3	10.0	683	28.9	5.8	16,405	-0.9	375	2.3	14,719	25.2	39.1
Dearborn	19,279	81.4	174,500	19.2	10.0	740	31.3	1.0	25,257	-0.4	757	3.0	24,921	34.4	27.4
Decatur	10,241	70.4	139,500	17.5	10.0	777	22.3	0.8	14,786	-1.1	418	2.8	13,250	31.4	37.0
DeKalb	16,904	79.2	129,100	17.7	10.0	707	23.8	1.6	22,028	-0.8	594	2.7	21,594	26.4	43.1
Delaware	46,632	64.5	96,600	17.1	10.6	725	32.3	1.7	51,868	-1.1	2,026	3.9	52,838	35.0	22.7
Dubois	16,691	78.6	162,400	17.8	10.0	646	25.9	1.1	22,020	-2.5	530	2.4	21,849	31.6	35.1
Elkhart	72,362	70.4	149,300	17.7	10.0	820	27.1	2.7	115,907	4.9	2,900	2.5	98,737	28.0	37.0
Fayette	9,686	69.0	84,000	17.0	10.5	701	29.0	2.0	8,393	-2.4	370	4.4	10,309	23.9	38.4
Floyd	29,264	74.3	179,100	18.1	10.0	812	27.2	0.7	41,370	0.1	1,149	2.8	38,626	39.6	24.4
Fountain	6,982	74.2	107,600	18.4	10.0	691	25.5	1.0	7,628	-1.3	219	2.9	7,429	28.1	43.1
Franklin	8,867	81.5	167,200	18.3	10.0	634	23.7	2.5	11,196	-1.1	303	2.7	11,594	28.7	33.5
Fulton	7,840	76.3	109,200	18.1	10.0	691	26.9	1.0	9,445	-2.4	312	3.3	9,147	25.6	38.5
Gibson	13,551	75.4	123,900	17.3	10.2	691	24.0	3.1	19,133	-2.3	480	2.5	16,702	26.3	41.0
Grant	26,896	69.6	96,300	18.6	10.4	704	27.9	2.0	31,094	-1.6	1,155	3.7	29,038	29.6	30.9
Greene	12,988	78.4	101,300	18.5	11.1	625	28.0	4.3	13,423	1.2	456	3.4	14,299	30.0	33.4
Hamilton	123,066	76.7	282,700	17.7	10.0	1,188	25.2	1.0	188,744	2.1	4,141	2.2	175,992	55.4	10.6
Hancock	29,627	80.1	179,300	18.1	10.0	919	25.8	1.0	41,318	1.4	1,059	2.6	39,551	40.1	23.8
Harrison	14,534	83.1	159,500	18.9	10.2	784	26.0	1.8	20,019	0.3	534	2.7	17,836	31.0	32.0
Hendricks	60,307	78.4	205,300	17.4	10.0	1,097	25.4	1.5	91,963	1.9	2,298	2.5	88,514	42.9	21.3
Henry	18,387	74.4	101,800	17.8	10.1	697	25.6	1.9	21,673	-1.0	702	3.2	20,014	30.0	31.3
Howard	34,632	72.1	113,900	17.0	10.0	743	25.9	1.4	34,727	-6.5	2,136	6.2	37,368	30.6	32.4
Huntington	14,790	75.5	109,200	18.0	10.0	697	28.0	1.4	18,004	-0.3	532	3.0	18,271	28.9	34.9
Jackson	16,923	70.9	131,000	17.3	10.8	780	24.8	1.7	23,214	0.5	692	3.0	21,198	28.5	37.9
Jasper	12,676	77.7	158,300	17.6	10.0	786	27.4	0.9	15,355	-1.2	541	3.5	15,051	26.8	34.6
Jay	8,293	75.2	90,800	19.1	10.9	685	22.1	3.9	8,746	-0.8	234	2.7	9,571	25.8	42.2
Jefferson	12,833	69.3	139,000	18.2	11.7	716	26.5	3.2	14,891	-0.4	469	3.1	14,331	30.0	35.7
Jennings	10,776	77.6	111,000	18.9	10.0	836	21.7	2.2	13,342	-1.6	490	3.7	14,035	25.0	38.3
Johnson	57,872	72.8	178,500	17.3	10.0	986	25.8	1.1	84,093	1.3	2,161	2.6	79,362	41.3	21.5
Knox	15,186	62.9	97,900	16.8	10.0	684	26.9	1.8	18,090	-1.0	514	2.8	17,744	29.7	29.6
Kosciusko	31,462	74.7	153,500	17.5	10.0	800	25.2	2.6	40,499	-2.1	1,107	2.7	40,239	28.8	39.2
LaGrange	12,547	84.5	194,600	17.2	10.0	730	22.2	3.5	20,421	5.8	404	2.0	16,864	22.7	50.2
Lake	188,646	70.1	156,100	18.8	11.0	885	29.6	2.4	222,818	-1.5	13,520	6.1	219,358	31.4	28.4
LaPorte	42,725	73.3	139,900	17.9	10.0	763	28.4	2.8	46,208	-2.4	2,335	5.1	48,248	28.1	30.2
Lawrence	18,968	79.7	126,200	18.6	10.0	678	25.4	2.2	20,729	0.2	722	3.5	20,987	27.9	34.5
Madison	51,276	69.1	103,800	17.9	10.2	798	30.3	1.5	58,663	0.4	2,406	4.1	57,780	29.9	28.4
Marion	377,695	54.6	145,200	18.6	10.4	910	30.3	2.0	497,073	0.9	22,097	4.4	469,219	37.2	24.5
Marshall	17,430	74.9	144,400	18.5	10.0	760	28.3	2.6	22,445	-1.1	595	2.7	21,418	25.5	42.3
Martin	4,095	78.8	125,400	18.2	10.0	554	21.7	2.7	5,389	-0.3	137	2.5	4,739	28.2	42.9
Miami	13,531	72.3	91,100	16.9	10.0	713	28.1	2.4	14,721	-3.0	645	4.4	15,475	22.5	42.3
Monroe	56,399	55.2	189,900	18.0	10.0	949	34.4	1.4	69,181	1.9	2,015	2.9	73,614	46.6	15.1
Montgomery	15,618	74.5	132,200	17.7	10.2	702	26.4	1.4	18,414	-1.0	481	2.6	18,965	26.6	38.6
Morgan	26,460	79.2	165,300	18.1	10.0	822	25.1	1.8	36,205	2.0	1,052	2.9	33,935	30.3	34.4
Newton	5,599	80.6	116,000	19.4	10.8	710	21.1	1.1	6,526	-0.5	246	3.8	6,263	21.4	44.8
Noble	18,133	76.4	132,400	18.1	10.0	687	24.4	3.0	21,988	-3.8	715	3.3	22,958	25.2	45.7
Ohio	2,623	76.2	146,500	19.5	10.0	713	21.8	1.8	3,121	-1.2	79	2.5	2,873	27.0	34.0
Orange	7,988	75.3	102,400	18.3	10.2	634	26.4	2.1	8,149	-4.2	345	4.2	9,019	23.7	39.7
Owen	8,830	77.6	125,200	20.0	11.0	708	29.6	3.7	9,156	1.6	326	3.6	9,836	24.7	42.1
Parke	6,005	79.1	96,400	18.1	10.0	759	24.5	5.4	6,916	0.9	201	2.9	6,476	23.4	35.8
Perry	7,713	74.9	114,600	16.8	10.0	550	23.1	3.4	8,766	-3.4	271	3.1	8,185	26.8	41.6

1. Specified owner-occupied units. 2. A value of 10.0 represents 10 percent or less; a value of 50.0 represents 50 percent or more. 3. Specified renter-occupied units. 4. Overcrowded or lacking complete plumbing facilities. 5. Percent of civilian labor force. 6. Civilian employed persons 16 years old and over.

STATE County	Private nonfarm establishments, employment and payroll, 2020									Agriculture, 2017			
		Employment						Annual payroll		Farms			Farm producers whose primary occupation is farming (percent)
											Percent with:		
	Number of establish-ments	Total	Health care and social assistance	Manufac-turing	Retail trade	Finance and insurance	Professional, scientific, and technical services	Total (mil dol)	Average per employee (dollars)	Number	Fewer than 50 acres	1000 acres or more	
	104	105	106	107	108	109	110	111	112	113	114	115	116
ILLINOIS—Cont'd													
Winnebago	6,193	117,134	20,411	24,519	14,497	3,326	4,248	5,287	45,134	736	50.5	6.5	39.6
Woodford	743	8,538	1,405	1,943	1,090	239	186	348	40,734	920	35.8	8.2	41.4
INDIANA	148,724	2,821,903	450,974	510,695	328,151	107,274	133,188	133,253	47,221	56,649	46.4	7.1	38.1
Adams	724	12,060	1,603	5,003	1,559	270	238	484	40,130	1,450	62.8	2.8	34.2
Allen	9,352	182,488	36,851	26,731	23,219	8,855	6,302	8,472	46,427	1,548	58.1	4.5	33.0
Bartholomew	1,889	46,272	5,229	12,677	4,918	958	2,835	2,417	52,232	564	47.0	8.7	36.6
Benton	177	1,320	124	399	143	96	33	52	39,615	358	30.2	23.2	52.2
Blackford	240	2,562	527	905	260	62	90	104	40,701	234	30.8	9.0	44.2
Boone	1,655	27,497	3,116	3,179	6,396	418	824	1,184	43,064	626	57.5	11.3	40.3
Brown	354	2,088	266	125	336	30	110	58	27,955	182	46.7	NA	31.2
Carroll	380	5,182	305	2,684	389	94	142	203	39,158	573	43.8	14.0	43.1
Cass	649	12,472	2,619	4,023	1,442	297	185	472	37,868	642	40.5	8.1	38.0
Clark	2,515	50,152	6,599	7,208	10,793	2,583	1,046	2,123	42,328	483	44.9	4.6	32.1
Clay	466	6,140	726	2,352	954	134	63	227	36,928	585	49.6	8.9	37.6
Clinton	609	9,918	1,257	4,348	1,026	216	120	406	40,948	560	41.6	15.4	48.7
Crawford	130	1,358	131	384	151	18	21	51	37,895	391	33.8	0.8	26.8
Daviess	908	11,463	1,414	2,652	1,429	331	432	462	40,291	1,230	62.4	4.7	28.3
Dearborn	937	12,912	2,424	2,164	1,925	274	434	471	36,500	598	38.5	0.8	30.6
Decatur	623	11,575	1,448	4,309	1,189	352	124	507	43,843	581	31.3	8.6	48.0
DeKalb	977	20,164	1,822	9,361	1,454	294	482	972	48,215	771	48.6	6.9	33.3
Delaware	2,356	40,708	10,619	3,740	5,801	2,154	1,275	1,592	39,108	546	52.9	8.1	45.0
Dubois	1,278	28,219	4,037	10,261	3,125	589	410	1,266	44,870	757	37.1	4.8	37.5
Elkhart	4,989	133,932	11,511	73,473	10,323	1,931	1,935	6,408	47,844	1,667	64.1	1.9	34.8
Fayette	398	4,698	1,185	1,021	762	168	94	176	37,428	343	39.9	7.3	39.3
Floyd	1,856	29,038	6,941	6,074	2,996	684	1,275	1,204	41,449	229	61.6	1.7	32.6
Fountain	309	3,749	318	1,697	532	141	78	144	38,452	497	35.4	12.5	42.5
Franklin	431	5,914	773	903	686	186	60	257	43,513	704	34.5	2.6	36.2
Fulton	443	5,133	690	1,633	994	178	88	193	37,570	635	42.8	11.5	44.4
Gibson	689	17,843	1,435	9,164	1,459	126	345	878	49,213	513	38.2	12.7	40.3
Grant	1,245	28,316	5,745	4,765	2,720	645	342	1,012	35,745	494	40.5	13.0	47.5
Greene	528	4,443	945	568	819	125	326	152	34,202	828	43.4	4.5	37.4
Hamilton	9,519	155,119	21,448	4,927	16,685	20,281	18,243	8,549	55,116	585	62.6	4.8	33.8
Hancock	1,451	23,589	3,101	3,919	3,418	363	2,622	1,173	49,733	551	56.4	10.2	34.7
Harrison	678	8,831	1,654	1,518	1,309	243	142	317	35,870	1,054	51.0	2.7	30.5
Hendricks	3,504	68,302	10,684	3,109	13,045	1,073	1,845	2,910	42,598	658	62.9	6.4	41.6
Henry	833	11,204	2,449	2,593	1,589	254	136	398	35,529	636	50.2	6.3	40.3
Howard	1,774	30,733	5,293	8,559	4,641	787	717	1,281	41,689	422	36.3	10.0	49.1
Huntington	845	12,462	1,810	3,939	1,189	314	301	450	36,140	611	41.6	10.8	33.7
Jackson	984	20,931	2,780	8,003	1,951	397	332	937	44,750	665	38.3	8.4	40.1
Jasper	752	8,945	1,008	1,548	1,600	279	211	360	40,240	611	39.1	13.7	47.5
Jay	413	5,862	751	2,721	612	138	136	219	37,441	770	45.3	8.3	37.4
Jefferson	661	11,516	2,011	3,207	1,797	174	197	452	39,268	684	39.8	2.2	30.5
Jennings	416	6,668	814	2,110	663	94	100	286	42,847	510	46.3	5.3	34.4
Johnson	3,309	52,587	8,485	6,078	9,498	1,306	1,286	1,974	37,528	642	62.9	5.9	37.8
Knox	837	14,019	3,432	1,935	1,845	299	270	560	39,920	496	30.0	19.8	53.4
Kosciusko	1,973	37,048	4,003	12,517	3,664	780	627	2,044	55,179	1,042	55.6	6.9	32.2
LaGrange	898	14,263	924	8,286	1,336	207	219	619	43,384	2,144	62.0	1.7	34.0
Lake	10,059	171,960	36,115	22,036	24,195	4,161	6,006	8,024	46,660	384	52.3	6.3	42.0
LaPorte	2,207	35,745	5,474	7,839	5,532	829	780	1,438	40,218	740	42.4	9.5	45.4
Lawrence	887	11,285	2,655	2,612	1,824	322	444	481	42,654	840	42.4	3.0	31.1
Madison	2,249	35,025	6,657	4,860	4,398	816	652	1,386	39,572	667	51.3	9.7	41.7
Marion	23,484	531,508	93,372	40,923	47,070	25,246	39,624	30,494	57,373	192	79.7	3.1	26.2
Marshall	1,063	17,822	2,511	6,154	1,908	478	309	717	40,236	829	47.8	6.4	39.3
Martin	202	2,168	139	380	291	31	706	109	50,330	260	39.2	7.3	29.2
Miami	557	6,286	910	1,723	838	311	104	222	35,329	629	37.8	7.9	43.5
Monroe	3,081	53,522	11,137	8,414	6,388	1,699	1,889	2,247	41,977	490	50.0	0.6	30.0
Montgomery	835	13,334	1,331	5,238	1,539	242	167	639	47,939	634	38.0	14.5	44.3
Morgan	1,190	13,152	1,725	2,485	2,154	404	400	506	38,444	501	49.1	7.0	38.1
Newton	246	2,265	239	512	262	102	48	86	38,122	358	28.2	17.3	50.7
Noble	882	18,025	1,368	10,233	1,663	251	226	685	37,999	1,015	52.4	5.6	33.6
Ohio	77	849	89	18	45	13	22	22	25,764	158	31.6	1.3	27.7
Orange	368	7,166	749	1,688	578	124	69	292	40,718	448	37.1	5.1	37.2
Owen	314	3,358	509	1,244	490	102	88	117	34,703	649	45.6	3.7	31.9
Parke	266	2,155	112	328	465	49	156	75	34,823	597	37.0	8.7	42.5
Perry	340	5,352	941	2,026	669	131	247	213	39,719	445	29.4	2.5	28.4

STATE County	Agriculture, 2017 (cont.)															
	Land in farms					Value of land and buildings (dollars)		Value of machinery and equipment, average per farm (dollars)	Value of products sold:				Organic farms (number)	Farms with internet access (percent)	Government payments	
	Acreage (1,000)	Percent change, 2012–2017	Acres: Average size of farm	Acres: Total irrigated (1,000)	Acres: Total cropland (1,000)	Average per farm	Average per acre		Total (mil dol)	Average per farm (acres)	Percent from: Crops	Percent from: Livestock and poultry products			Total ($1,000)	Percent of farms
	117	118	119	120	121	122	123	124	125	126	127	128	129	130	131	132
ILLINOIS—Cont'd																
Winnebago	179	-2.3	243	1.6	161.0	1,732,196	7,137	145,947	107.2	145,644	78.1	21.9	9	81.7	6,961	54.9
Woodford	283	-12.3	308	D	259.0	2,761,299	8,972	205,867	216.1	234,897	75.2	24.8	23	77.6	3,479	73.6
INDIANA	14,970	1.7	264	555.4	12,909.7	1,737,741	6,576	163,136	11,107.3	196,073	64.1	35.9	657	71.9	342,914	47.9
Adams	213	1.3	147	0.5	194.4	1,215,197	8,274	101,610	283.1	195,266	34.9	65.1	15	50.8	3,926	35.4
Allen	282	4.0	182	0.4	249.5	1,446,442	7,950	113,983	175.8	113,581	71.1	28.9	19	65.6	5,389	47.2
Bartholomew	160	-6.5	284	15.5	142.2	1,902,512	6,688	159,738	93.0	164,929	88.3	11.7	NA	79.3	3,919	55.7
Benton	251	-1.3	701	6.6	246.4	5,422,824	7,734	405,595	178.9	499,765	86.9	13.1	NA	80.7	4,100	81.6
Blackford	92	4.7	394	NA	86.3	2,601,618	6,605	219,419	63.5	271,265	74.8	25.2	NA	76.5	1,567	67.9
Boone	230	3.8	367	0.1	219.9	2,800,238	7,621	206,909	134.6	215,045	92.9	7.1	3	89.8	6,471	42.0
Brown	15	1.4	81	0.1	5.7	356,748	4,390	44,535	1.9	10,527	85.4	14.6	1	81.9	162	18.7
Carroll	224	9.9	391	1.6	213.4	2,949,885	7,539	249,168	250.0	436,283	55.0	45.0	8	71.6	4,972	59.9
Cass	199	-0.4	311	0.8	182.7	1,939,195	6,243	212,168	149.5	232,807	66.4	33.6	2	77.4	3,933	66.5
Clark	94	19.6	195	0.7	68.6	1,072,932	5,515	113,762	41.7	86,244	84.3	15.7	NA	71.4	1,746	37.7
Clay	162	-0.5	277	0.6	139.1	1,412,114	5,100	142,144	76.2	130,309	96.4	3.6	1	72.6	3,616	63.8
Clinton	247	10.6	441	D	238.8	3,162,178	7,169	282,883	184.7	329,836	78.4	21.6	4	86.3	7,274	65.5
Crawford	53	13.4	135	D	18.7	416,192	3,094	51,196	9.3	23,754	41.1	58.9	NA	73.4	475	23.0
Daviess	225	0.0	183	4.8	193.2	1,395,457	7,620	144,028	270.9	220,211	41.6	58.4	1	52.3	6,725	23.3
Dearborn	65	14.2	108	0.1	29.8	525,303	4,861	56,517	12.2	20,390	69.6	30.4	NA	80.4	278	20.2
Decatur	202	8.3	348	0.0	179.2	2,461,834	7,083	231,518	178.9	307,904	57.8	42.2	NA	76.4	5,753	67.6
DeKalb	159	-1.2	206	3.6	140.1	1,143,430	5,547	121,735	93.8	121,624	65.3	34.7	NA	74.8	5,313	60.3
Delaware	168	-4.3	307	0.6	157.6	2,038,398	6,633	188,657	92.2	168,773	92.9	7.1	NA	83.5	4,044	56.4
Dubois	179	2.4	236	0.7	133.4	1,289,755	5,455	169,974	248.8	328,690	28.1	71.9	NA	71.9	6,327	60.1
Elkhart	175	1.2	105	25.0	146.5	1,173,021	11,178	98,422	298.3	178,936	23.4	76.6	86	45.5	3,082	16.3
Fayette	86	9.8	251	0.2	72.2	1,416,832	5,656	164,773	45.8	133,458	85.0	15.0	NA	73.8	2,463	51.9
Floyd	25	16.5	109	0.1	13.8	595,936	5,456	71,967	7.1	31,162	90.8	9.2	NA	72.5	335	18.3
Fountain	212	-1.1	427	D	187.4	2,871,619	6,732	224,601	112.7	226,809	94.0	6.0	3	77.7	4,181	66.6
Franklin	133	6.5	189	D	92.2	1,071,362	5,670	102,977	67.1	95,261	76.8	23.2	NA	69.2	3,190	50.4
Fulton	214	13.8	338	25.1	197.5	2,131,615	6,312	233,337	140.2	220,855	78.1	21.9	2	75.0	5,859	58.9
Gibson	220	-17.8	430	7.8	203.1	2,785,651	6,484	297,121	149.0	290,458	85.6	14.4	NA	76.4	6,226	64.9
Grant	190	3.7	385	D	181.4	2,716,186	7,059	216,027	118.6	240,095	83.3	16.7	3	82.4	1,747	60.1
Greene	169	-6.7	204	2.2	124.2	1,010,049	4,952	110,938	108.4	130,965	56.6	43.4	10	78.9	4,026	30.9
Hamilton	127	-2.7	218	D	117.4	1,903,729	8,750	168,283	104.6	178,853	97.5	2.5	2	83.9	1,209	39.5
Hancock	170	2.3	308	0.0	161.2	2,322,612	7,543	185,610	115.7	210,031	72.1	27.9	3	89.3	4,498	45.2
Harrison	149	10.1	141	0.3	100.7	644,972	4,575	84,004	88.7	84,114	51.9	48.1	NA	71.5	2,627	26.7
Hendricks	153	-30.0	232	0.1	141.5	1,774,141	7,638	128,330	84.4	128,293	96.2	3.8	6	82.1	3,541	36.9
Henry	168	-4.5	265	0.1	151.9	1,586,242	5,987	174,623	122.9	193,259	65.0	35.0	NA	80.3	5,297	51.3
Howard	146	1.1	345	D	138.0	2,681,236	7,765	219,981	97.1	230,078	83.1	16.9	3	79.9	4,286	68.2
Huntington	197	4.4	323	D	181.4	2,212,369	6,854	221,979	160.2	262,116	56.5	43.5	NA	81.7	2,019	62.7
Jackson	201	9.5	303	11.1	155.9	1,602,696	5,295	202,939	186.5	280,451	40.6	59.4	NA	73.1	4,533	56.2
Jasper	270	-4.5	442	25.9	251.6	2,854,205	6,456	251,325	298.7	488,939	47.7	52.3	1	78.4	4,951	67.6
Jay	208	18.1	270	D	190.3	2,044,970	7,585	180,334	372.6	483,891	23.7	76.3	2	75.2	3,566	60.8
Jefferson	107	11.7	156	0.0	66.9	645,429	4,141	87,775	31.4	45,975	84.6	15.4	1	74.4	1,417	33.0
Jennings	128	3.8	251	0.5	91.1	1,146,513	4,564	142,906	63.3	124,141	70.2	29.8	NA	73.1	2,427	39.8
Johnson	141	-2.4	220	2.4	122.0	1,482,614	6,745	148,278	75.3	117,271	88.6	11.4	2	82.7	4,292	37.9
Knox	311	-5.5	627	32.1	289.9	3,905,102	6,224	365,221	245.3	494,635	79.7	20.3	3	85.7	10,316	70.8
Kosciusko	262	2.7	251	30.1	229.7	1,788,066	7,120	177,429	298.0	286,019	42.0	58.0	7	68.2	8,572	43.7
LaGrange	195	-4.3	91	38.9	144.1	842,807	9,249	75,820	275.6	128,536	29.9	70.1	271	19.8	2,970	9.9
Lake	112	-15.5	293	4.7	106.0	2,040,013	6,966	155,636	65.4	170,253	93.0	7.0	NA	78.4	2,032	44.3
LaPorte	249	9.2	336	68.5	230.0	2,473,619	7,355	210,852	166.4	224,842	82.2	17.8	7	79.6	8,644	58.4
Lawrence	147	9.4	175	0.1	82.3	651,657	3,716	72,451	43.5	51,751	69.4	30.6	2	71.0	3,141	35.6
Madison	208	1.3	312	1.5	198.0	2,526,028	8,108	205,713	129.5	194,096	92.6	7.4	2	81.3	5,002	53.4
Marion	17	-13.5	90	0.1	15.5	955,725	10,564	62,277	12.1	62,844	92.2	7.8	3	81.8	423	19.3
Marshall	199	-3.5	240	16.5	177.3	1,503,166	6,259	151,905	145.2	175,111	65.2	34.8	21	63.3	5,212	45.7
Martin	62	-0.5	239	D	35.3	930,286	3,886	144,218	60.8	233,777	29.6	70.4	NA	62.3	879	35.4
Miami	194	10.4	308	3.4	175.1	2,076,888	6,750	165,044	179.5	285,297	51.5	48.5	1	80.1	5,973	71.1
Monroe	48	-9.5	97	0.1	22.2	640,303	6,569	62,244	9.4	19,196	73.7	26.3	16	83.3	493	19.8
Montgomery	282	-1.7	445	2.1	260.0	3,108,274	6,984	270,937	162.7	256,550	94.4	5.6	3	81.7	6,451	66.6
Morgan	137	-0.5	273	D	111.4	1,713,947	6,289	140,341	65.5	130,812	87.4	12.6	NA	79.0	2,760	41.9
Newton	181	-5.8	506	4.7	161.3	3,403,798	6,733	335,472	196.2	547,925	48.6	51.4	NA	84.4	1,666	57.0
Noble	200	10.2	197	21.1	172.3	1,259,845	6,394	141,041	158.5	156,156	53.2	46.8	35	69.1	5,315	46.5
Ohio	24	11.9	152	0.0	11.1	663,843	4,368	71,293	4.6	29,051	76.2	23.8	NA	75.3	445	17.7
Orange	102	4.3	229	0.1	72.2	1,026,470	4,489	136,262	122.5	273,498	31.1	68.9	NA	77.2	4,352	41.3
Owen	112	17.2	172	0.2	73.6	783,546	4,543	73,005	34.1	52,582	84.7	15.3	3	71.0	1,857	33.4
Parke	181	2.4	303	3.9	139.9	1,768,164	5,840	173,611	92.7	155,295	84.4	15.6	23	62.1	3,317	47.6
Perry	77	16.0	173	0.5	42.2	693,181	4,013	91,796	40.1	90,036	39.3	60.7	1	71.2	1,039	34.2

STATE County	Water use, 2015		Wholesale Trade[1], 2017				Retail Trade[2], 2017				Real estate and rental and leasing,[2] 2017			
	Public supply water withdrawn (mil gal/ day)	Public supply gallons withdrawn per person per day	Number of establish-ments	Number of employees	Sales (mil dol)	Average payroll (mil dol)	Number of establish-ments	Number of employees	Sales (mil dol)	Average payroll (mil dol)	Number of establish-ments	Number of employees	Sales (mil dol)	Average payroll (mil dol)
	133	134	135	136	137	138	139	140	141	142	143	144	145	146
ILLINOIS—Cont'd														
Winnebago	29.2	101.8	308	4,281	2,788.2	230.7	927	14,085	3,946.2	349.8	231	1,316	281.1	57.3
Woodford	7.3	185.1	D	D	D	36.4	88	1,014	414.5	31.3	15	32	2.5	0.9
INDIANA	627.8	94.8	6,271	96,880	87,596.7	5,505.8	21,327	336,615	102,106.0	8,660.1	6,686	34,736	8,392.2	1,519.7
Adams	2.3	66.0	32	285	176.6	10.8	141	1,511	413.2	35.4	21	81	8.1	2.9
Allen	35.7	96.9	473	7,968	8,489.9	424.7	1,270	22,962	6,972.1	632.0	445	2,215	541.5	89.4
Bartholomew	9.5	116.9	D	D	D	D	315	5,106	1,311.6	112.8	75	355	91.4	12.4
Benton	0.4	46.1	12	243	279.1	10.6	29	157	46.4	3.5	3	4	0.4	0.1
Blackford	1.0	84.6	9	90	156.3	3.9	33	310	80.3	6.1	12	22	3.7	0.5
Boone	2.0	31.7	69	1,149	1,920.7	71.8	167	5,585	2,803.6	179.0	82	305	57.6	12.4
Brown	0.0	0.0	5	18	10.0	0.8	75	331	54.5	6.6	14	66	5.0	1.7
Carroll	1.3	66.0	24	171	153.4	7.3	51	376	97.8	8.7	11	16	2.8	0.6
Cass	5.9	156.4	35	418	465.8	19.1	113	1,560	360.9	33.5	17	59	11.7	1.8
Clark	22.1	191.6	98	1,339	1,699.3	72.7	421	10,327	3,354.3	277.9	111	467	110.8	18.2
Clay	0.3	12.5	11	84	39.3	3.4	79	993	292.8	22.2	D	D	D	D
Clinton	3.7	112.9	28	179	202.4	8.3	97	1,007	270.4	23.9	12	31	3.2	0.7
Crawford	1.6	156.4	NA	NA	NA	NA	25	183	71.8	4.2	4	5	1.4	0.2
Daviess	3.6	107.9	31	341	162.5	14.9	124	1,498	586.4	44.5	19	56	7.0	1.3
Dearborn	4.4	89.2	34	D	281.1	D	140	2,079	682.0	52.5	35	139	20.6	3.4
Decatur	2.6	97.7	D	D	D	D	109	1,306	348.5	29.7	16	46	8.5	1.5
DeKalb	3.2	74.4	D	D	D	D	109	1,476	465.4	38.8	32	128	19.6	5.2
Delaware	9.6	82.0	89	829	520.8	35.7	430	5,983	1,662.1	144.3	104	430	91.5	16.7
Dubois	5.8	137.5	76	1,204	594.6	56.8	228	3,336	1,005.8	91.3	33	115	14.0	3.0
Elkhart	13.0	63.6	317	6,495	4,827.8	332.6	705	9,603	2,889.9	262.5	181	767	167.3	28.7
Fayette	2.4	103.3	10	143	104.3	6.6	72	1,041	230.4	21.6	20	53	8.9	1.2
Floyd	1.2	15.8	59	562	299.1	26.6	201	3,402	908.2	83.1	95	280	54.9	9.1
Fountain	0.9	53.0	13	81	244.3	4.0	62	572	141.7	11.0	6	22	1.4	0.4
Franklin	2.6	114.6	D	D	D	D	63	882	205.0	17.6	13	31	3.9	0.5
Fulton	1.1	52.7	18	162	146.7	7.7	83	1,037	289.5	24.3	12	20	3.3	0.6
Gibson	1.7	50.6	23	349	569.0	16.1	117	1,597	501.7	39.3	24	73	14.1	2.1
Grant	4.0	58.1	40	385	287.2	18.5	222	2,810	763.8	63.1	53	196	23.6	4.7
Greene	2.9	88.5	19	90	46.1	3.5	93	996	293.6	23.2	10	26	3.6	0.5
Hamilton	35.7	115.2	388	5,238	3,744.7	372.1	896	17,614	5,631.6	478.8	537	2,995	1,144.7	219.1
Hancock	3.2	43.8	43	1,030	1,863.7	51.2	161	2,267	800.0	63.0	55	156	42.4	7.1
Harrison	2.6	66.7	D	D	D	10.8	108	1,287	557.3	34.4	26	59	8.1	1.4
Hendricks	5.1	32.2	117	3,332	4,285.6	177.3	442	12,750	4,672.0	382.4	148	410	113.3	16.1
Henry	4.7	95.5	29	D	846.0	D	142	1,668	538.8	40.8	29	70	8.7	1.6
Howard	8.5	102.6	D	D	D	D	341	5,141	1,382.5	117.8	78	300	62.9	9.9
Huntington	3.7	101.8	41	374	292.8	12.2	135	1,335	324.0	30.9	36	96	14.1	2.3
Jackson	5.4	122.3	35	641	879.4	30.0	179	1,998	621.9	53.1	53	163	27.4	4.2
Jasper	0.9	27.2	34	225	391.8	12.5	126	1,584	507.6	33.9	22	103	26.7	2.5
Jay	1.5	72.0	16	168	233.7	7.7	57	756	145.8	14.6	13	21	2.9	0.4
Jefferson	5.6	173.7	17	253	334.2	11.3	119	1,633	437.6	45.1	31	98	10.9	2.7
Jennings	1.0	36.9	16	234	99.1	9.6	57	716	194.3	18.7	9	54	8.9	2.2
Johnson	10.0	67.1	92	2,269	1,579.8	135.2	487	9,952	3,248.9	255.9	151	461	127.5	16.9
Knox	4.2	110.7	51	545	331.0	24.6	154	1,936	507.6	44.9	40	189	30.7	5.2
Kosciusko	3.3	42.4	D	D	D	D	278	4,012	1,099.7	99.4	83	198	35.4	6.2
LaGrange	1.0	25.0	31	326	137.6	12.6	152	1,297	343.9	32.3	31	95	11.6	1.7
Lake	76.1	155.9	370	4,017	3,769.5	227.1	1,539	24,996	7,473.7	625.4	411	1,921	396.3	76.4
LaPorte	9.4	84.3	92	1,254	756.2	53.1	428	5,969	1,507.0	131.8	84	343	67.0	13.6
Lawrence	5.1	111.0	24	178	76.9	7.4	170	1,970	589.9	50.5	27	90	14.2	3.1
Madison	15.0	115.5	77	914	1,423.1	53.9	317	4,897	1,508.0	116.2	92	390	86.7	11.7
Marion	111.3	118.5	1,225	26,017	22,159.4	1,717.1	2,933	49,975	15,372.5	1,347.2	1,429	11,817	3,291.7	591.8
Marshall	2.9	60.8	55	697	405.4	34.1	164	2,094	666.1	50.7	29	98	15.6	2.9
Martin	0.6	61.6	D	D	D	1.2	33	325	154.8	8.0	4	D	4.0	D
Miami	2.7	74.2	D	D	D	D	93	925	263.9	21.3	20	54	7.2	1.8
Monroe	15.8	109.0	D	D	D	D	436	6,467	1,853.5	157.5	193	1,037	193.6	36.8
Montgomery	3.6	94.4	D	D	D	D	134	1,675	489.3	40.3	31	107	14.8	2.3
Morgan	10.5	151.0	38	502	243.4	23.5	169	2,205	671.2	58.0	62	140	24.0	4.9
Newton	0.6	40.0	18	132	218.8	7.4	36	256	72.6	5.0	6	14	1.4	0.3
Noble	2.3	48.2	38	469	756.7	22.9	139	1,650	475.4	41.7	35	102	14.7	3.2
Ohio	0.7	124.6	D	D	D	D	8	56	11.7	1.0	3	8	0.8	0.1
Orange	0.0	0.0	12	96	80.4	3.1	64	622	168.1	14.8	10	30	3.5	0.6
Owen	1.4	67.1	D	D	D	D	47	571	128.9	12.3	6	12	1.3	0.2
Parke	0.9	55.0	13	101	63.2	3.9	39	350	92.9	7.1	10	21	2.5	0.6
Perry	0.3	17.1	8	59	11.9	2.0	69	726	166.6	15.1	13	34	5.0	0.9

1 Merchant wholesalers, except manufacturers' sales branches and offices. 2. Employer establishments.

Table B. States and Counties — **Professional Services, Manufacturing, and Accommodation and Food Services**

STATE County	Professional, scientific, and technical services, 2017				Manufacturing, 2017				Accommodation and food services, 2017			
	Number of establish-ments	Number of employees	Sales (mil dol)	Average payroll (mil dol)	Number of establish-ments	Number of employees	Sales (mil dol)	Average payroll (mil dol)	Number of establis-hments	Number of employees	Sales (mil dol)	Annual payroll (mil dol)
	147	148	149	150	151	152	153	154	155	156	157	158
ILLINOIS—Cont'd												
Winnebago	577	5,044	817.5	286.8	564	24,052	9,218.4	1,493.9	579	11,359	587.5	171.5
Woodford	55	218	21.7	9.1	42	1,777	622.6	106.7	63	875	32.9	9.8
INDIANA	13,003	121,271	22,318.0	8,504.6	8,064	496,083	246,671.7	28,131.2	13,647	280,340	15,250.0	4,288.5
Adams	45	245	23.3	10.8	65	5,498	2,290.9	255.0	54	952	35.4	10.1
Allen	817	5,643	871.8	307.3	468	26,533	18,954.5	1,548.3	746	16,830	822.2	244.1
Bartholomew	D	D	D	D	140	12,239	5,531.9	637.4	176	4,414	216.3	62.5
Benton	9	27	2.2	0.9	D	D	D	D	6	46	2.0	0.4
Blackford	11	104	14.5	4.2	20	976	325.8	47.7	D	D	D	D
Boone	185	803	174.6	47.2	74	2,037	674.6	96.7	130	2,103	103.5	30.3
Brown	D	D	D	D	17	88	14.4	3.0	44	533	23.6	7.9
Carroll	18	152	9.3	2.9	D	D	D	D	35	528	25.6	7.7
Cass	38	190	18.1	5.8	45	4,304	1,658.9	175.0	70	1,083	45.6	12.8
Clark	D	D	D	D	142	7,569	2,468.5	360.5	235	5,966	297.8	88.0
Clay	23	71	6.5	2.5	28	2,266	650.2	107.4	46	615	25.7	6.9
Clinton	35	127	11.5	4.2	40	3,638	3,253.4	186.0	54	779	33.5	9.8
Crawford	D	D	0.7	D	D	393	D	D	D	D	D	D
Daviess	50	475	49.8	22.2	96	2,126	793.9	81.1	62	934	40.2	10.9
Dearborn	59	334	27.1	10.5	46	1,455	503.9	78.2	D	D	D	D
Decatur	31	114	13.6	4.9	49	4,661	5,622.6	273.6	50	947	48.4	14.4
DeKalb	67	469	54.5	21.9	120	9,664	5,787.2	555.4	89	1,388	66.8	18.7
Delaware	D	D	D	D	118	4,234	1,723.0	219.5	220	5,143	225.4	66.9
Dubois	82	345	39.3	13.7	95	11,152	2,846.1	447.5	104	1,727	72.9	22.1
Elkhart	D	D	D	D	819	70,059	24,520.9	3,763.1	378	7,145	369.0	97.5
Fayette	28	172	17.3	5.0	28	1,484	438.1	74.9	45	605	28.1	7.8
Floyd	D	D	D	D	106	5,128	1,664.3	290.4	159	3,166	150.3	43.1
Fountain	17	76	7.4	2.2	23	1,325	290.2	67.3	D	D	D	D
Franklin	23	47	4.8	1.6	20	782	359.1	38.3	41	808	42.2	11.4
Fulton	21	95	24.7	3.5	39	1,503	355.7	71.8	38	447	20.2	5.4
Gibson	49	329	57.9	16.7	42	8,454	11,193.6	565.6	62	1,195	52.6	16.4
Grant	69	318	36.6	12.5	63	4,443	1,807.4	268.8	133	2,343	107.2	31.9
Greene	D	D	D	D	24	452	121.3	20.7	49	612	25.2	7.4
Hamilton	D	D	D	D	201	4,536	1,552.9	259.6	702	17,827	975.4	300.3
Hancock	141	1,949	159.0	216.2	67	3,175	1,217.2	161.6	119	2,543	116.8	34.0
Harrison	44	158	13.6	5.9	42	1,685	561.6	82.0	55	2,416	310.0	60.3
Hendricks	300	1,526	179.4	62.0	96	3,068	1,402.4	175.4	330	7,632	371.7	109.1
Henry	44	138	14.7	4.7	47	2,217	723.3	121.2	73	1,199	54.8	16.1
Howard	118	714	93.0	29.8	62	9,251	4,005.0	629.8	195	4,095	185.4	54.0
Huntington	53	214	26.9	8.4	61	3,835	2,051.1	180.6	89	1,206	54.3	15.2
Jackson	53	277	33.3	10.1	62	7,969	3,037.8	468.9	88	1,431	71.3	20.4
Jasper	D	D	D	D	37	1,428	737.9	73.8	66	931	42.3	10.8
Jay	26	98	6.8	2.9	32	2,856	923.3	127.5	31	483	20.5	5.4
Jefferson	37	230	24.3	8.7	47	3,209	1,575.2	175.4	73	1,143	53.3	14.6
Jennings	20	93	12.8	4.4	41	1,802	439.6	79.0	24	450	19.9	5.3
Johnson	289	1,575	211.8	71.7	134	6,191	2,223.5	324.9	295	6,596	337.8	97.9
Knox	42	236	25.2	9.3	36	2,122	708.8	90.6	80	1,562	67.9	20.4
Kosciusko	145	547	69.3	22.3	177	10,861	6,565.7	635.5	179	2,704	140.5	40.1
LaGrange	32	170	16.9	7.1	166	7,087	2,108.6	378.8	67	771	44.3	12.0
Lake	D	D	D	D	341	22,241	20,585.0	1,714.1	1,019	20,007	1,206.1	321.3
LaPorte	145	706	89.6	32.7	166	7,181	2,445.0	373.8	228	5,006	367.7	88.1
Lawrence	62	718	95.0	38.1	59	3,040	719.1	177.8	64	1,284	59.5	16.8
Madison	163	641	68.6	24.2	101	4,446	2,222.6	260.2	229	4,301	194.2	58.8
Marion	2,742	50,117	11,154.9	4,510.8	839	43,459	21,231.2	3,074.1	2,308	53,348	3,276.2	931.4
Marshall	65	298	27.6	10.0	139	5,622	1,536.6	263.3	87	1,596	77.1	22.9
Martin	36	874	147.0	57.3	10	353	150.9	20.6	23	199	8.0	2.4
Miami	32	112	16.4	6.5	36	1,919	598.4	74.4	53	901	32.7	9.8
Monroe	275	1,830	241.1	93.7	97	7,432	1,424.5	375.5	395	8,100	423.3	119.2
Montgomery	46	167	16.4	5.2	52	4,928	3,316.4	311.4	82	1,365	66.5	18.0
Morgan	99	420	64.5	24.1	66	2,628	808.1	111.9	79	1,673	78.2	24.0
Newton	14	50	4.5	1.6	18	549	134.3	23.3	27	365	23.7	6.4
Noble	53	196	32.2	8.9	117	8,594	2,823.7	400.8	74	1,143	49.7	13.5
Ohio	D	D	1.8	D	D	15	D	0.5	D	D	D	D
Orange	16	61	5.2	1.8	22	1,257	300.0	55.1	39	640	30.4	7.9
Owen	23	107	9.5	4.6	28	1,055	194.8	47.2	22	281	13.9	3.8
Parke	10	93	20.9	8.4	16	365	124.8	16.3	D	D	D	2.9
Perry	26	194	19.1	8.8	23	2,084	941.8	126.5	39	574	25.5	7.5

STATE County	Health care and social assistance, 2017				Other services, 2017				Nonemployer businesses, 2019		Value of residential construction authorized by building permits, 2021	
	Number of establish-ments	Number of employees	Receipts (mil dol)	Annual payroll (mil dol)	Number of establish-ments	Number of employees	Receipts (mil dol)	Annual payroll (mil dol)	Number	Receipts (mil dol)	New construction ($1,000)	Number of housing units
	159	160	161	162	163	164	165	166	167	168	169	170
ILLINOIS—Cont'd												
Winnebago	655	20,279	2,635.3	1,015.1	499	3,092	343.3	90.1	17,316	644.5	30,330	172
Woodford	51	1,335	85.8	37.5	45	203	28.6	7.7	2,519	102.4	14,092	42
INDIANA	16,668	436,616	51,837.3	19,641.2	10,777	75,446	11,120.7	2,561.7	428,052	18,583.1	7,583,248	29,860
Adams	54	1,611	113.2	54.0	75	359	34.7	9.2	3,218	200.4	18,545	80
Allen	1,043	36,047	4,501.6	1,698.5	668	5,046	550.3	167.3	24,991	1,079.3	493,512	1,863
Bartholomew	217	5,146	608.5	229.4	112	729	87.2	21.5	4,356	184.6	63,407	231
Benton	12	69	4.8	2.0	D	D	D	D	570	23.8	393	3
Blackford	35	508	55.2	19.0	20	55	5.4	1.5	609	18.5	470	3
Boone	131	2,420	244.1	103.7	94	623	46.5	14.6	5,865	291.6	401,442	900
Brown	20	258	10.4	6.3	13	66	7.4	2.0	1,507	67.7	24,972	88
Carroll	34	266	20.6	8.1	D	D	D	D	1,352	62.2	9,231	50
Cass	69	2,619	200.9	91.9	56	259	28.6	6.4	1,796	67.0	5,864	31
Clark	261	6,386	693.7	277.7	167	1,318	154.8	41.8	7,471	323.3	287,341	1,626
Clay	49	592	56.8	20.1	34	169	23.9	6.3	1,400	50.1	2,245	14
Clinton	58	1,114	77.3	33.9	42	316	37.3	9.9	1,706	65.8	12,867	53
Crawford	18	126	8.0	3.3	8	31	3.6	0.7	621	27.0	610	3
Daviess	80	1,373	113.9	47.3	67	412	121.8	17.7	2,281	109.5	10,024	39
Dearborn	126	2,718	248.2	104.4	66	267	28.2	7.4	3,052	130.2	40,569	127
Decatur	58	1,425	159.2	52.3	45	271	36.4	6.5	1,572	68.9	21,377	129
DeKalb	83	1,798	149.2	61.4	70	292	25.3	6.3	2,495	108.5	44,352	138
Delaware	379	10,377	1,061.6	418.1	169	1,102	133.5	31.5	5,714	214.2	30,192	113
Dubois	132	3,672	417.2	163.7	91	468	57.7	15.4	2,890	122.3	28,842	121
Elkhart	373	11,322	1,394.3	488.3	345	2,646	334.3	98.6	13,076	603.8	114,735	458
Fayette	54	1,437	128.3	47.0	35	151	13.1	3.8	1,054	47.3	3,679	27
Floyd	269	6,982	728.4	281.2	122	673	77.1	19.6	5,473	246.3	81,098	248
Fountain	19	456	33.5	12.0	29	83	9.7	2.0	946	40.7	8,054	73
Franklin	52	552	48.5	23.3	46	142	16.1	3.7	1,596	69.1	24,114	78
Fulton	41	1,049	87.3	39.0	40	166	20.1	4.3	1,298	53.7	9,550	42
Gibson	69	1,357	99.9	40.9	50	259	25.6	7.1	1,674	64.1	30,335	184
Grant	173	4,669	416.2	163.5	103	471	47.2	14.0	3,189	115.3	9,392	32
Greene	61	996	87.3	34.5	42	174	17.7	4.1	1,793	53.2	NA	NA
Hamilton	1,101	20,604	2,519.0	968.3	555	4,097	373.3	118.9	32,092	1,698.4	1,402,874	4,806
Hancock	151	2,734	298.6	115.6	96	369	37.7	10.1	5,491	232.4	400,142	1,597
Harrison	80	1,432	144.8	52.2	34	163	19.9	5.0	2,597	104.2	39,027	156
Hendricks	333	8,433	973.6	386.1	247	1,924	180.8	62.7	12,496	518.8	413,548	1,370
Henry	97	2,316	226.9	81.5	65	330	45.7	8.0	2,426	99.5	12,959	48
Howard	233	5,323	589.4	222.2	126	705	88.2	17.4	4,168	148.0	46,559	190
Huntington	70	1,823	145.4	62.5	76	395	32.3	9.1	1,961	81.4	21,849	73
Jackson	98	2,690	266.3	111.7	76	440	40.1	11.8	2,158	90.1	23,074	99
Jasper	51	1,430	91.4	43.3	D	D	D	D	1,883	85.5	45,800	165
Jay	32	914	83.1	33.8	35	118	11.6	2.1	1,359	64.1	4,802	17
Jefferson	86	2,073	245.7	90.6	47	239	19.6	5.8	1,822	77.4	16,612	65
Jennings	82	827	65.1	28.2	24	105	9.4	2.2	1,483	57.3	12,279	53
Johnson	338	8,458	758.5	333.1	236	1,461	147.1	47.2	11,403	563.3	410,927	1,460
Knox	92	3,462	359.0	147.7	60	320	32.5	8.5	1,856	75.1	10,526	43
Kosciusko	159	4,448	357.3	146.6	137	1,001	138.5	35.4	5,042	214.2	75,825	369
LaGrange	40	1,072	86.2	32.8	51	262	33.2	8.7	3,724	169.7	27,179	138
Lake	1,305	33,653	4,638.8	1,608.7	857	6,614	690.6	226.2	29,921	1,218.7	496,149	1,755
LaPorte	229	5,904	777.2	299.5	198	1,031	133.0	29.0	6,072	225.0	47,719	138
Lawrence	130	2,896	232.9	100.3	61	338	31.8	9.0	2,578	96.1	6,555	33
Madison	280	6,683	729.3	273.2	170	967	89.8	23.6	6,851	255.5	68,359	293
Marion	2,837	90,422	12,707.3	4,909.0	1,658	17,871	4,220.9	783.5	67,767	2,960.9	493,331	2,251
Marshall	84	2,285	207.3	74.8	77	770	83.6	24.3	2,854	113.9	39,571	245
Martin	11	149	7.3	3.5	13	41	5.2	0.9	631	21.7	734	3
Miami	42	970	103.3	39.8	46	215	26.8	5.9	1,646	65.8	3,505	18
Monroe	416	10,565	977.0	419.6	212	1,533	429.8	55.5	9,419	379.8	263,430	2,053
Montgomery	95	1,380	125.2	54.3	68	268	27.8	6.5	2,206	93.5	17,278	79
Morgan	121	2,236	251.6	93.5	97	454	47.1	13.0	4,589	197.5	109,899	404
Newton	12	238	13.6	7.3	D	D	D	D	775	30.8	12,297	42
Noble	67	1,371	148.6	52.6	73	280	40.5	6.5	2,670	118.4	37,072	133
Ohio	10	97	7.5	2.6	D	D	D	0.4	318	10.6	6,820	26
Orange	51	802	71.1	25.9	29	148	14.3	3.6	1,202	48.2	1,927	10
Owen	37	547	36.8	16.0	27	66	6.2	1.2	1,437	57.2	8,109	33
Parke	18	180	10.6	4.6	27	83	10.0	2.1	1,159	59.8	11,133	86
Perry	40	872	81.9	28.6	22	79	6.2	2.0	851	37.4	7,092	37

STATE County	Government employment and payroll, 2017: Full-time equivalent employees	Government employment and payroll, 2017: March payroll (dollars)	March payroll (percent of total): Adminis-tration, judicial, and legal	March payroll (percent of total): Police and corrections	March payroll (percent of total): Fire protection	March payroll (percent of total): Highways and transpor-tation	March payroll (percent of total): Health and welfare	March payroll (percent of total): Natural resources and utilities	March payroll (percent of total): Education and libraries	Local government finances, 2017, General revenue: Total (mil dol)	General revenue: Inter-govern-mental (mil dol)	Taxes: Total (mil dol)	Taxes: Per capita[1] (dollars): Total	Taxes: Per capita[1] (dollars): Property
	171	172	173	174	175	176	177	178	179	180	181	182	183	184
ILLINOIS—Cont'd														
Winnebago	10,108	44,836,553	5.1	12.7	6.4	3.8	4.4	7.2	59.3	1,312.2	577.3	543.2	1,908	1,647
Woodford	1,499	5,765,466	4.7	6.6	0.6	4.4	1.8	3.1	78.6	134.5	43.5	75.8	1,961	1,944
INDIANA	X	X	X	X	X	X	X	X	X	X	X	X	X	X
Adams	1,650	6,028,628	4.5	5.6	0.8	2.0	48.1	3.5	34.8	155.3	42.9	31.8	899	864
Allen	11,137	44,759,235	6.4	13.3	4.4	4.4	2.2	5.4	62.8	1,165.8	549.6	465.5	1,252	957
Bartholomew	4,111	16,129,167	3.8	7.4	3.0	1.4	41.3	4.3	37.9	614.4	104.8	80.3	977	940
Benton	510	1,372,200	8.0	7.0	0.0	6.2	4.0	3.9	70.0	35.0	18.5	12.5	1,449	1,427
Blackford	455	1,477,437	7.4	11.6	2.1	4.5	0.9	4.9	66.6	35.8	18.6	10.7	890	831
Boone	2,824	12,455,140	4.4	5.8	4.6	1.5	32.3	3.8	47.0	336.7	101.6	82.4	1,254	1,158
Brown	531	1,549,624	11.9	12.7	0.1	3.8	2.4	3.2	62.6	42.4	20.6	15.9	1,056	985
Carroll	617	1,867,416	8.6	11.2	0.0	4.7	2.0	6.1	66.9	64.3	26.5	31.5	1,572	1,512
Cass	2,218	7,871,513	4.7	5.4	1.7	2.2	35.1	8.4	41.2	214.1	68.1	52.9	1,399	1,338
Clark	4,970	19,005,482	3.8	8.7	3.3	2.3	35.3	3.7	42.3	443.8	214.5	135.9	1,166	990
Clay	895	2,956,288	7.5	9.7	2.1	3.0	2.0	3.4	71.3	77.5	39.9	23.7	907	594
Clinton	1,276	4,458,361	4.8	9.9	7.6	3.3	0.9	11.1	60.4	144.6	65.7	59.9	1,860	1,773
Crawford	366	927,209	12.9	8.0	0.0	7.1	3.7	3.7	62.7	54.6	18.3	32.3	3,069	3,040
Daviess	1,409	5,500,456	5.1	7.3	1.2	2.8	41.3	6.9	34.7	114.7	43.9	48.4	1,459	801
Dearborn	1,792	6,094,969	8.8	11.8	2.4	2.5	0.8	6.4	64.5	387.3	101.7	92.6	1,869	1,838
Decatur	1,159	4,643,596	4.4	5.1	2.2	2.7	44.5	3.6	37.4	180.5	44.4	48.6	1,825	1,648
DeKalb	1,668	5,500,156	7.7	7.8	2.3	3.4	0.8	8.7	60.7	165.9	78.1	47.1	1,101	1,079
Delaware	3,844	13,695,351	5.6	8.5	3.6	3.7	3.0	4.5	69.0	411.1	185.8	88.7	769	723
Dubois	1,617	5,303,292	8.0	8.8	0.6	5.9	2.2	17.8	55.8	432.2	98.9	73.0	1,717	1,055
Elkhart	7,096	28,545,949	5.0	8.8	4.0	2.1	1.6	3.1	72.4	664.7	333.5	219.8	1,077	1,000
Fayette	775	2,716,489	5.6	12.0	4.3	2.8	1.3	6.9	61.2	53.5	36.5	12.0	519	495
Floyd	2,198	8,020,054	6.9	11.6	6.7	2.5	3.5	3.7	64.5	251.0	102.4	82.1	1,066	941
Fountain	608	1,865,542	8.9	8.6	1.8	5.6	5.6	6.3	63.0	46.3	26.3	14.0	854	831
Franklin	488	1,612,210	9.1	10.3	0.2	5.2	1.7	2.7	69.5	38.3	21.4	12.3	544	497
Fulton	1,010	4,020,897	4.0	4.9	1.5	2.2	50.7	2.2	33.0	52.2	27.7	13.8	691	638
Gibson	1,180	3,779,902	8.4	7.7	2.8	4.0	4.0	5.2	66.7	118.5	54.8	43.6	1,294	1,255
Grant	2,178	6,806,498	7.1	16.1	4.3	4.3	2.0	2.2	63.5	191.2	108.8	56.0	844	823
Greene	1,388	4,795,988	5.2	6.2	1.5	2.3	22.7	3.8	57.0	89.8	46.1	26.0	808	614
Hamilton	11,180	46,901,560	5.6	7.3	7.0	1.8	13.0	4.3	59.4	1,579.9	431.8	523.3	1,621	1,294
Hancock	2,973	11,331,967	5.7	7.4	4.9	1.6	31.4	3.5	44.0	346.2	106.5	80.0	1,066	861
Harrison	1,449	5,427,289	5.5	4.9	0.0	2.3	38.3	3.0	44.6	242.7	198.7	22.0	552	496
Hendricks	6,012	25,797,353	1.8	3.2	5.6	0.5	32.4	2.5	53.8	1,123.8	250.6	246.2	1,505	1,160
Henry	2,426	9,309,783	4.2	5.2	2.5	2.2	42.6	3.4	38.9	260.9	93.7	94.6	1,964	1,746
Howard	3,042	10,199,579	6.3	12.7	4.2	3.2	3.2	3.4	65.3	262.2	141.0	92.8	1,129	1,108
Huntington	1,056	3,701,086	6.5	8.3	4.1	4.8	1.2	4.1	67.3	86.1	41.5	30.0	827	803
Jackson	2,284	9,879,858	3.1	6.8	3.4	1.4	47.6	1.9	34.7	269.6	56.5	34.4	784	656
Jasper	1,147	3,521,843	9.2	13.1	0.1	4.0	1.3	8.4	63.1	112.3	45.4	55.2	1,651	1,295
Jay	1,038	3,710,595	6.1	6.3	1.7	2.7	34.7	2.2	45.1	67.0	33.0	21.9	1,048	1,000
Jefferson	937	3,151,949	10.0	11.3	0.2	4.3	1.1	5.5	67.5	87.0	43.5	27.6	862	841
Jennings	904	2,910,827	5.9	9.9	0.7	3.9	2.4	5.6	69.8	72.6	39.4	15.5	562	556
Johnson	5,177	19,308,878	5.2	8.2	3.1	2.1	23.1	3.5	52.9	828.1	232.2	162.0	1,053	946
Knox	2,859	12,155,381	2.7	4.6	1.3	1.1	72.7	1.4	16.1	376.5	57.1	39.6	1,068	1,009
Kosciusko	2,847	9,243,126	6.2	8.7	2.3	3.3	1.3	3.7	73.7	283.8	145.5	87.8	1,111	1,055
LaGrange	1,108	3,552,148	5.6	6.9	0.4	3.1	0.6	2.9	78.8	88.7	49.7	28.5	727	656
Lake	17,781	66,212,636	10.8	11.0	4.9	5.6	2.6	8.5	55.1	1,999.5	909.7	681.5	1,406	1,358
LaPorte	4,410	14,500,631	6.4	12.0	4.0	3.7	2.8	6.2	63.3	390.5	185.2	125.9	1,146	1,100
Lawrence	1,538	5,349,008	5.2	9.5	3.3	3.7	9.0	4.9	63.7	156.2	61.6	34.8	764	692
Madison	3,950	14,479,297	8.4	13.9	4.7	4.1	2.2	10.8	54.4	433.7	172.4	193.6	1,496	1,073
Marion	33,241	142,174,649	4.1	7.5	7.3	2.7	18.2	7.4	51.9	4,655.4	1,870.7	920.8	969	812
Marshall	1,537	5,374,932	7.2	11.1	1.8	4.2	1.1	5.4	67.8	196.2	62.4	105.1	2,264	2,219
Martin	333	1,020,519	9.9	14.7	1.2	4.5	0.1	5.2	60.6	31.8	17.3	9.3	914	878
Miami	1,211	4,312,290	4.8	8.7	3.0	4.2	1.2	5.8	69.5	118.3	65.7	27.4	765	729
Monroe	3,742	13,600,022	11.4	13.3	5.5	5.1	2.5	7.1	53.1	404.3	152.3	174.8	1,192	1,133
Montgomery	1,253	4,400,029	6.4	11.3	6.6	3.5	1.0	8.6	61.8	112.8	56.1	39.4	1,029	1,009
Morgan	2,165	6,661,029	6.7	10.1	5.0	2.9	1.2	3.0	70.4	177.2	96.3	60.2	863	804
Newton	555	1,682,981	12.2	10.2	0.0	3.3	4.6	1.7	66.6	83.5	23.4	45.5	3,242	3,206
Noble	1,436	4,855,396	9.2	11.3	1.4	3.6	1.0	5.0	68.2	126.3	62.2	45.8	968	951
Ohio	222	764,712	11.3	9.1	0.0	5.9	2.0	8.5	56.9	26.7	14.4	7.4	1,257	1,008
Orange	659	2,044,620	9.1	9.3	0.5	6.1	0.5	5.4	68.7	52.2	30.4	17.2	885	753
Owen	516	1,573,362	5.9	12.0	4.0	5.2	0.5	1.7	70.8	37.9	22.1	12.1	583	543
Parke	613	1,570,005	9.0	10.2	0.9	5.0	4.2	4.3	64.2	40.9	25.5	10.9	644	602
Perry	912	3,316,555	5.3	5.5	0.5	4.7	39.6	5.6	38.2	61.5	32.0	15.6	823	743

1. Based on the resident population estimated as of July 1 of the year shown.

STATE County	Local government finances, 2017 (cont.)									Government employment, 2020			Individual income tax returns, 2019		
	Direct general expenditure							Debt outstanding							
			Percent of total for:												
	Total (mil dol)	Per capita[1] (dollars)	Education	Health and hospitals	Police protection	Public welfare	Highways	Total (mil dol)	Per capita[1] (dollars)	Federal civilian	Federal military	State and local	Number of returns	Mean adjusted gross income	Mean income tax
	185	186	187	188	189	190	191	192	193	194	195	196	197	198	199
ILLINOIS—Cont'd															
Winnebago	1,376.8	4,836	51.3	0.8	9.5	2.6	6.4	965.8	3,393	891	591	12,783	137,350	56,231	5,517
Woodford	141.3	3,654	63.8	1.1	4.0	0.0	7.7	66.6	1,722	75	75	1,922	18,130	82,254	9,436
INDIANA	X	X	X	X	X	X	X	X	X	41,323	20,416	379,976	3,216,070	62,295	6,623
Adams	160.8	4,543	27.3	44.3	1.8	0.4	3.5	134.5	3,802	65	104	2,105	15,330	54,236	4,723
Allen	1,076.3	2,895	51.0	1.2	8.3	0.0	6.4	1,152.5	3,100	2,203	1,152	16,593	187,000	62,455	6,816
Bartholomew	629.6	7,658	19.8	63.2	2.4	0.1	2.0	281.4	3,422	201	245	6,001	40,160	69,987	7,647
Benton	34.0	3,942	58.6	1.0	3.2	0.6	8.1	44.5	5,158	27	25	557	4,260	50,173	4,009
Blackford	30.3	2,520	51.2	0.6	4.4	0.1	8.2	28.5	2,371	25	34	457	5,840	44,748	3,293
Boone	323.8	4,926	35.0	33.6	4.2	0.1	1.6	414.9	6,313	119	203	3,832	33,800	114,597	17,648
Brown	43.7	2,911	57.8	1.4	1.9	0.1	4.4	27.4	1,826	21	44	653	7,980	58,596	5,789
Carroll	63.6	3,169	37.8	2.0	3.0	0.8	7.8	20.3	1,012	69	59	720	9,950	55,940	4,791
Cass	194.8	5,149	36.0	38.5	2.7	0.0	4.5	90.8	2,399	95	107	2,966	18,080	47,252	3,617
Clark	378.1	3,244	43.2	0.5	5.3	0.1	3.3	505.8	4,340	2,591	349	4,194	60,080	57,781	5,412
Clay	86.9	3,320	51.5	0.5	2.1	0.0	8.4	89.3	3,413	67	76	1,167	12,280	50,011	3,943
Clinton	112.1	3,481	50.7	1.4	5.1	0.4	7.5	104.2	3,238	61	92	1,541	15,500	50,162	3,841
Crawford	29.8	2,833	49.9	2.7	1.7	0.0	13.5	12.9	1,221	26	31	435	4,690	43,484	2,913
Daviess	117.2	3,538	43.1	0.6	2.6	0.0	9.6	106.9	3,226	78	98	1,837	14,960	54,462	4,679
Dearborn	339.0	6,840	23.3	51.1	2.3	0.0	2.3	156.3	3,154	117	145	2,490	25,410	63,412	6,059
Decatur	151.0	5,672	27.4	52.7	1.6	0.0	3.0	138.4	5,197	72	77	1,552	13,200	53,559	4,597
DeKalb	157.3	3,674	56.5	0.2	5.0	0.2	3.0	96.5	2,254	91	127	1,990	21,270	56,676	5,018
Delaware	644.3	5,590	24.6	0.6	2.4	0.0	1.8	330.8	2,870	327	316	10,525	48,720	50,679	4,706
Dubois	332.3	7,812	21.5	62.2	1.5	0.0	2.9	242.2	5,693	109	124	2,135	22,580	68,069	7,417
Elkhart	693.5	3,396	57.5	1.1	4.4	0.0	4.3	677.6	3,318	300	597	8,180	97,630	59,097	5,964
Fayette	74.4	3,215	55.0	3.5	5.6	1.8	6.4	27.9	1,203	45	66	947	10,560	44,233	3,344
Floyd	196.0	2,546	59.9	0.3	4.0	0.0	2.5	338.1	4,391	241	229	4,122	39,320	72,702	8,262
Fountain	42.5	2,591	60.2	0.9	2.9	0.8	9.8	24.1	1,469	64	48	699	7,960	50,120	3,887
Franklin	45.7	2,014	57.1	0.7	4.9	0.0	6.7	17.0	751	50	67	867	10,790	61,969	5,751
Fulton	54.1	2,705	54.1	0.9	2.4	0.0	8.2	54.9	2,744	42	58	1,265	9,500	52,291	4,529
Gibson	99.0	2,936	51.2	2.2	4.1	0.0	6.7	140.6	4,170	100	97	1,273	16,170	56,912	4,909
Grant	173.8	2,622	55.2	0.7	7.8	0.1	5.9	108.9	1,642	1,130	178	2,700	29,470	45,905	3,606
Greene	85.9	2,670	61.3	2.4	3.8	0.0	5.8	80.4	2,498	79	94	1,801	14,680	50,558	3,991
Hamilton	1,475.2	4,568	37.8	29.2	4.5	0.0	3.6	2,786.9	8,630	453	1,009	13,733	165,250	116,675	17,706
Hancock	313.5	4,180	38.5	33.8	2.7	0.0	3.3	302.0	4,027	132	232	4,133	39,480	70,642	7,194
Harrison	100.2	2,520	57.3	1.5	1.4	0.0	4.1	97.7	2,457	106	119	1,946	18,780	57,739	5,090
Hendricks	946.0	5,782	28.0	50.3	2.0	0.1	1.4	911.9	5,573	282	499	9,144	84,930	72,460	7,469
Henry	203.4	4,223	36.5	36.9	2.9	0.0	2.5	114.6	2,378	99	131	2,836	22,570	49,550	4,088
Howard	263.3	3,202	53.5	0.4	6.4	0.1	2.3	246.6	2,999	186	241	4,739	41,260	54,695	4,915
Huntington	67.5	1,862	75.3	0.0	5.4	0.0	1.1	34.2	944	101	103	1,318	17,980	53,013	4,694
Jackson	244.7	5,568	28.7	57.2	2.0	0.0	1.3	132.7	3,018	98	132	3,130	21,660	55,912	4,927
Jasper	87.4	2,615	57.8	2.0	2.1	0.1	1.2	184.1	5,509	104	96	1,423	15,860	56,647	5,204
Jay	73.1	3,500	47.9	2.2	3.1	0.6	5.9	65.4	3,130	49	59	787	9,280	44,337	3,345
Jefferson	83.7	2,614	57.0	1.1	3.4	0.0	5.5	38.0	1,187	80	89	2,271	14,970	54,425	5,051
Jennings	73.9	2,672	60.1	1.2	4.5	0.6	6.1	58.5	2,114	84	80	1,148	12,910	46,935	3,546
Johnson	898.6	5,842	28.6	39.7	1.4	0.1	2.2	571.6	3,716	450	799	6,984	78,170	70,442	7,601
Knox	348.2	9,399	17.5	64.7	1.4	0.0	2.1	305.6	8,249	160	102	4,768	16,800	52,332	4,559
Kosciusko	270.4	3,422	53.4	0.4	2.9	0.1	5.0	320.9	4,061	177	228	2,799	39,200	66,444	7,103
LaGrange	92.1	2,345	62.9	0.5	3.0	0.6	4.5	53.9	1,374	60	117	1,190	17,690	56,113	4,531
Lake	1,737.0	3,584	44.1	0.5	6.6	0.1	3.3	2,491.0	5,140	1,580	1,422	21,703	236,480	58,754	5,979
LaPorte	385.7	3,511	46.8	0.7	5.0	0.1	3.5	349.2	3,179	192	324	6,186	52,840	55,101	5,339
Lawrence	126.8	2,781	49.9	17.8	4.6	0.0	1.2	90.5	1,984	135	132	1,707	21,780	51,679	4,435
Madison	454.0	3,508	36.0	0.4	4.6	0.0	5.2	559.3	4,322	271	365	5,639	61,120	49,054	4,054
Marion	4,333.5	4,559	37.1	30.7	5.4	0.0	0.1	7,535.8	7,928	15,772	3,109	67,254	470,680	56,328	6,145
Marshall	111.0	2,391	64.4	0.8	4.8	0.6	1.7	87.0	1,874	105	134	1,941	22,280	56,263	5,962
Martin	31.2	3,065	46.7	0.4	3.5	0.1	6.4	16.8	1,654	5,021	95	446	4,780	52,949	4,242
Miami	111.5	3,109	59.5	0.4	2.2	0.0	6.3	111.1	3,097	633	109	1,853	15,720	47,110	3,548
Monroe	506.3	3,453	29.3	0.4	3.2	0.1	3.1	595.1	4,058	351	411	24,032	58,270	66,467	7,798
Montgomery	100.5	2,621	62.9	0.3	4.8	0.0	2.1	156.9	4,092	79	110	1,937	18,500	51,606	4,207
Morgan	171.8	2,461	60.6	1.0	2.9	0.2	3.5	153.2	2,195	106	207	2,482	34,980	60,357	5,646
Newton	62.9	4,481	40.2	0.4	2.0	0.9	3.9	52.1	3,713	28	48	680	6,700	53,766	4,671
Noble	116.4	2,459	61.4	0.0	3.5	0.1	4.8	186.4	3,938	91	139	1,700	22,440	51,893	4,050
Ohio	21.9	3,749	37.9	0.7	5.0	0.0	4.7	8.9	1,525	14	17	300	2,820	54,282	4,591
Orange	47.7	2,453	69.9	0.3	2.3	0.0	6.2	71.6	3,688	49	57	809	9,040	44,509	3,385
Owen	39.2	1,887	65.8	3.4	0.1	0.0	8.1	32.4	1,557	36	61	748	9,900	48,300	3,664
Parke	39.0	2,304	58.2	1.3	3.5	0.0	10.1	31.1	1,841	51	45	982	6,930	51,067	4,272
Perry	47.8	2,520	54.8	0.5	3.1	0.0	9.8	44.5	2,347	78	52	1,372	8,650	49,826	3,869

1. Based on the resident population estimated as of July 1 of the year shown.

State / county code	CBSA code[1]	County Type code[2]	STATE County	Land area[3] (sq. mi)	Population, 2021: Total persons 2021	Population, 2021: Rank	Population, 2021: Per square mile	Race alone or in combination, not Hispanic or Latino (percent): White	Black	American Indian, Alaska Native	Asian and Pacific Islancer	Percent Hispanic or Latino[4]	Age (percent): Under 5 years	5 to 17 years	18 to 24 years	25 to 34 years	35 to 44 years	45 to 54 years
				1	2	3	4	5	6	7	8	9	10	11	12	13	14	15
			INDIANA—Cont'd															
18125	27540	8	Pike	334.3	12,144	2,275	36.3	96.8	1.0	0.7	0.8	1.6	5.8	12.3	10.8	11.5	11.4	12.5
18127	16980	1	Porter	418.1	174,243	384	416.7	83.4	4.9	0.6	2.0	10.7	5.0	12.4	13.0	12.0	13.6	12.8
18129	21780	2	Posey	409.4	25,116	1,603	61.3	96.8	1.8	0.6	0.8	1.3	5.2	13.0	10.7	11.2	12.3	12.0
18131		6	Pulaski	433.7	12,339	2,255	28.5	94.3	1.3	1.0	1.0	3.5	5.3	12.4	11.6	11.3	11.8	12.2
18133	26900	1	Putnam	480.5	36,979	1,254	77.0	92.6	4.4	0.7	1.7	2.1	4.9	11.1	16.6	13.2	11.9	12.1
18135		6	Randolph	452.4	24,387	1,632	53.9	94.6	1.3	0.7	0.7	3.9	5.5	12.8	11.9	11.0	11.3	12.7
18137		6	Ripley	446.4	29,081	1,453	65.1	96.6	0.8	0.7	1.1	1.9	6.3	12.9	12.4	11.4	11.5	12.8
18139		6	Rush	408.1	16,672	1,994	40.9	96.5	1.6	0.6	0.6	1.8	5.6	12.7	11.8	11.9	11.4	12.7
18141	43780	2	St. Joseph	457.8	272,212	258	594.6	74.2	15.2	1.0	3.4	9.4	6.2	13.1	15.1	13.4	12.2	11.4
18143	42500	1	Scott	190.4	24,355	1,634	127.9	95.7	1.0	0.6	1.2	2.5	5.5	12.9	12.0	12.7	12.1	13.7
18145	26900	1	Shelby	411.1	45,039	1,077	109.6	92.7	1.9	0.6	1.1	4.9	5.6	12.8	11.9	12.1	11.9	12.9
18147		8	Spencer	396.9	19,798	1,829	49.9	95.4	1.3	0.6	0.6	3.2	5.1	12.5	11.4	10.7	11.6	12.4
18149		6	Starke	309.1	23,372	1,664	75.6	94.5	0.8	0.9	0.6	4.4	5.8	13.0	11.5	11.6	11.5	12.5
18151	11420	7	Steuben	308.8	34,632	1,310	112.2	94.3	1.2	0.6	1.1	3.9	5.4	11.1	13.6	10.7	10.2	12.1
18153	45460	3	Sullivan	447.2	20,758	1,776	46.4	92.8	5.4	0.9	0.5	1.8	4.9	10.4	11.6	14.4	13.6	13.4
18155		8	Switzerland	220.7	9,790	2,424	44.4	96.3	1.5	0.5	0.5	2.0	5.5	14.2	11.3	10.6	12.2	13.0
18157	29200	3	Tippecanoe	498.9	187,076	362	375.0	76.7	6.9	0.6	9.1	8.9	5.5	11.4	26.9	14.1	10.9	9.6
18159		6	Tipton	260.5	15,372	2,065	59.0	95.4	1.2	0.6	0.9	3.1	5.1	11.5	11.3	11.6	10.9	13.1
18161	17140	1	Union	161.2	7,047	2,658	43.7	95.7	1.5	0.8	1.0	2.5	5.7	11.7	11.8	11.3	11.5	12.7
18163	21780	2	Vanderburgh	233.4	179,987	372	771.2	85.2	11.9	0.6	2.2	3.0	5.8	12.2	13.4	14.1	12.5	11.2
18165	45460	3	Vermillion	256.9	15,341	2,068	59.7	97.3	1.2	0.7	0.7	1.5	5.1	12.5	12.0	11.4	11.7	12.9
18167	45460	3	Vigo	403.6	105,994	581	262.6	87.2	8.7	0.8	2.8	3.0	5.3	11.5	18.4	13.1	11.8	11.2
18169	47340	6	Wabash	412.5	30,816	1,408	74.7	94.9	1.5	1.1	0.8	2.9	5.2	11.7	13.9	11.1	11.2	11.7
18171	29200	8	Warren	364.7	8,475	2,535	23.2	95.9	1.1	0.8	0.8	2.6	4.9	12.9	11.1	10.9	11.6	12.6
18173	21780	2	Warrick	384.8	64,514	841	167.7	92.7	2.8	0.5	3.3	2.3	5.1	13.7	11.8	11.5	13.2	12.9
18175	31140	1	Washington	513.7	28,102	1,492	54.7	97.5	1.1	0.6	0.5	1.4	5.7	12.7	11.7	12.0	12.0	12.8
18177	39980	5	Wayne	401.8	66,456	809	165.4	90.1	7.0	0.8	1.9	3.4	5.9	12.4	13.3	11.7	11.4	12.2
18179		2	Wells	368.1	28,197	1,488	76.6	94.6	1.6	0.6	0.8	3.5	6.2	14.3	11.8	11.7	12.0	11.4
18181		6	White	505.1	24,651	1,628	48.8	89.5	1.1	0.7	0.7	9.1	5.9	13.0	11.8	11.1	10.9	12.2
18183	23060	2	Whitley	335.6	34,430	1,315	102.6	96.0	1.2	0.8	0.9	2.5	5.7	13.1	11.6	12.1	11.7	12.5
19000		0	IOWA	55,853.7	3,193,079	X	57.2	85.9	5.2	0.7	3.4	6.7	5.9	13.1	14.0	12.5	12.6	11.3
19001		8	Adair	569.3	7,541	2,615	13.2	95.4	1.3	0.6	0.7	3.0	6.5	12.5	10.3	11.2	11.3	10.5
19003		9	Adams	423.4	3,641	2,916	8.6	96.4	1.0	1.0	0.9	1.6	5.2	13.1	9.4	10.3	11.0	9.7
19005		6	Allamakee	639.0	13,926	2,155	21.8	89.7	2.0	0.5	0.8	7.7	7.0	13.2	10.4	10.1	10.6	10.5
19007		7	Appanoose	497.3	12,257	2,264	24.6	95.4	1.4	1.1	1.1	2.6	5.6	12.9	10.8	10.0	11.2	11.5
19009		8	Audubon	443.0	5,635	2,768	12.7	96.1	0.9	0.6	0.9	2.3	5.6	12.3	9.9	10.2	10.4	10.7
19011	16300	2	Benton	716.1	25,691	1,579	35.9	96.7	1.4	0.6	0.7	1.8	5.9	13.0	11.4	10.8	11.9	12.4
19013	47940	3	Black Hawk	565.8	130,368	497	230.4	82.2	11.3	0.6	3.9	4.9	6.1	12.2	17.8	12.8	11.8	10.2
19015	11180	6	Boone	570.5	26,723	1,540	46.8	94.9	1.8	0.7	0.9	2.9	5.2	11.5	11.2	12.5	13.4	12.1
19017	47940	3	Bremer	435.5	25,081	1,607	57.6	95.3	2.0	0.5	1.6	1.9	5.4	13.0	16.0	10.5	12.5	11.1
19019		6	Buchanan	571.1	20,657	1,781	36.2	96.6	1.3	0.5	0.9	1.9	6.5	14.5	12.3	10.7	12.7	11.2
19021	44740	7	Buena Vista	574.9	20,771	1,775	36.1	55.9	4.0	0.5	13.3	27.5	7.2	14.8	15.1	11.9	12.6	9.9
19023		8	Butler	580.1	14,332	2,127	24.7	96.7	0.9	0.5	1.2	1.8	5.3	13.2	11.0	10.2	12.2	11.5
19025		9	Calhoun	569.8	9,915	2,415	17.4	94.1	3.4	0.8	0.5	2.4	5.2	12.6	11.2	12.1	11.5	10.4
19027	16140	7	Carroll	569.5	20,692	1,778	36.3	94.7	1.7	0.5	0.7	3.4	6.0	14.3	11.5	10.7	11.4	10.7
19029		6	Cass	564.3	13,050	2,209	23.1	94.5	1.0	0.4	1.6	3.3	5.4	13.0	10.8	10.5	11.7	10.8
19031		6	Cedar	579.5	18,410	1,904	31.8	95.7	1.6	0.6	1.0	2.5	4.9	12.6	11.1	10.5	12.8	12.3
19033	32380	5	Cerro Gordo	568.3	42,706	1,131	75.1	90.7	3.1	0.6	1.8	5.7	5.2	12.1	11.3	11.1	11.5	10.9
19035		6	Cherokee	576.9	11,503	2,313	19.9	92.7	1.7	0.7	1.0	4.9	5.3	13.2	9.9	10.5	11.3	10.3
19037		6	Chickasaw	504.3	11,887	2,292	23.6	95.5	1.1	0.4	0.6	3.3	5.9	13.4	11.5	10.3	11.2	10.8
19039		6	Clarke	431.1	9,785	2,425	22.7	80.5	1.4	0.7	1.6	16.8	6.4	14.8	12.5	10.6	11.6	11.8
19041	43980	7	Clay	567.2	16,440	2,005	29.0	93.6	1.5	0.7	1.1	4.4	5.7	13.1	11.2	11.1	12.2	10.9
19043		8	Clayton	778.5	16,998	1,972	21.8	96.4	1.5	0.5	0.6	2.2	5.5	12.1	10.3	10.1	10.6	11.0
19045	17540	4	Clinton	695.0	46,463	1,046	66.9	92.4	4.4	0.8	1.1	3.6	5.8	13.2	11.2	11.4	11.8	11.6
19047		7	Crawford	714.2	16,193	2,023	22.7	63.3	3.6	0.6	2.8	30.4	6.4	14.2	13.6	11.9	11.4	11.6
19049	19780	2	Dallas	588.3	103,796	591	176.4	84.8	3.8	0.5	6.0	6.5	6.8	15.7	11.8	14.2	16.5	12.4
19051		9	Davis	502.2	9,138	2,479	18.2	97.3	0.6	0.8	0.7	1.8	8.5	16.5	12.7	10.3	11.0	10.5
19053		9	Decatur	531.9	7,659	2,601	14.4	92.8	2.6	1.2	1.4	3.4	5.6	12.7	20.1	9.9	9.6	9.6
19055		6	Delaware	577.7	17,510	1,944	30.3	96.9	1.3	0.4	0.6	1.7	5.8	13.3	11.8	9.5	11.3	11.4
19057	15460	5	Des Moines	416.1	38,491	1,208	92.5	88.6	7.9	0.8	1.5	3.8	5.4	13.1	11.3	11.1	12.2	11.6
19059	44020	7	Dickinson	380.5	17,851	1,929	46.9	95.3	1.2	0.5	1.3	2.9	4.9	11.1	10.1	10.0	10.8	11.1
19061	20220	3	Dubuque	608.3	98,718	621	162.3	91.2	4.7	0.5	2.5	2.9	6.0	12.9	13.7	12.8	11.8	10.8
19063		7	Emmet	395.9	9,321	2,464	23.5	87.3	1.7	0.9	0.9	10.3	5.0	10.4	13.5	10.9	12.2	11.1
19065		6	Fayette	730.8	19,258	1,861	26.4	94.1	2.3	0.6	1.4	3.0	5.5	12.0	12.8	10.7	10.8	10.8
19067		7	Floyd	500.6	15,413	2,064	30.8	91.4	3.3	0.5	1.8	4.4	5.9	13.1	11.3	10.7	11.1	11.3

1. CBSA = Core Based Statistical Area. See Appendix A for explanation. See Appendix B for list of metropolitan areas with component counties. 2. County type code from the Economic Research Service of USDA Rural-Urban Continuum Codes. See Appendix A for definition. 3. Dry land or land partially or temporarily covered by water. 4. May be of any race.

STATE County	Population, 2021 (cont.): Age (percent) (cont.): 55 to 64 years	Population, 2021 (cont.): Age (percent) (cont.): 65 to 74 years	Population, 2021 (cont.): Age (percent) (cont.): 75 years and over	Population, 2021 (cont.): Percent female	Population change, 2000–2021: Total persons: 2010	Population change, 2000–2021: Total persons: 2020	Population change, 2000–2021: Percent change: 2010–2020	Population change, 2000–2021: Percent change: 2020–2021	Population change, 2000–2021: Components of change, 2020–2021: Births	Population change, 2000–2021: Components of change, 2020–2021: Deaths	Population change, 2000–2021: Components of change, 2020–2021: Net Migration	Households, 2016–2020: Number	Households, 2016–2020: Persons per household	Households, 2016–2020: Percent: Family house-holds	Households, 2016–2020: Percent: Female family house-holder[1]	Households, 2016–2020: Percent: One person
	16	17	18	19	20	21	22	23	24	25	26	27	28	29	30	31
INDIANA—Cont'd																
Pike	15.4	12.0	8.3	49.8	12,845	12,250	-4.6	-0.9	156	232	-31	5,294	2.3	62.2	6.1	32.5
Porter	13.6	11.1	6.4	50.7	164,343	173,215	5.4	0.6	1,959	2,419	1,483	65,153	2.5	67.4	9.9	26.2
Posey	15.3	12.5	7.7	50.2	25,910	25,222	-2.7	-0.4	309	377	-39	10,361	2.4	71.3	8.9	23.7
Pulaski	15.0	12.0	8.4	49.0	13,402	12,514	-6.6	-1.4	160	248	-87	5,113	2.4	63.0	12.5	32.7
Putnam	13.4	10.0	6.8	47.5	37,963	36,726	-3.3	0.7	439	567	383	13,651	2.4	70.3	9.0	24.6
Randolph	14.3	11.7	9.0	50.5	26,171	24,502	-6.4	-0.5	296	424	12	10,358	2.4	65.2	11.2	29.9
Ripley	14.1	11.0	7.6	50.3	28,818	28,995	0.6	0.3	443	408	47	11,243	2.5	70.1	10.6	25.6
Rush	14.9	11.2	7.8	50.8	17,392	16,752	-3.7	-0.5	247	300	-29	6,648	2.5	68.3	9.2	25.5
St. Joseph	12.1	10.1	6.4	51.2	266,931	272,912	2.2	-0.3	4,131	3,988	-896	104,380	2.5	61.0	12.5	33.0
Scott	14.3	10.5	6.3	51.0	24,181	24,384	0.8	-0.1	323	487	133	9,228	2.5	63.5	11.4	30.5
Shelby	14.8	11.0	7.0	50.4	44,436	45,055	1.4	0.0	579	703	101	17,902	2.5	65.2	8.2	27.9
Spencer	15.9	12.4	8.1	49.6	20,952	19,810	-5.5	-0.1	257	314	44	8,321	2.4	68.2	8.3	27.9
Starke	14.5	12.3	7.2	50.0	23,363	23,371	0.0	0.0	318	428	111	8,490	2.7	68.0	10.8	24.7
Steuben	15.4	13.5	8.1	49.5	34,185	34,435	0.7	0.6	447	531	281	14,449	2.3	65.1	8.0	27.0
Sullivan	13.2	11.1	7.4	45.3	21,475	20,817	-3.1	-0.3	245	323	17	7,806	2.4	69.0	11.8	25.8
Switzerland	14.8	11.0	7.4	48.1	10,613	9,737	-8.3	0.5	136	152	69	4,430	2.4	63.5	10.8	30.4
Tippecanoe	9.5	7.4	4.7	49.0	172,780	186,251	7.8	0.4	2,462	1,842	146	71,686	2.5	56.4	9.6	31.0
Tipton	14.7	12.3	9.5	50.0	15,936	15,359	-3.6	0.1	177	247	82	6,360	2.4	72.3	7.0	22.1
Union	14.9	12.6	7.7	51.3	7,516	7,087	-5.7	-0.6	116	113	-42	2,848	2.5	71.6	7.5	24.5
Vanderburgh	13.3	10.7	6.9	51.5	179,703	180,136	0.2	-0.1	2,593	3,017	246	76,094	2.3	59.9	13.2	32.4
Vermillion	13.9	12.4	8.1	50.1	16,212	15,439	-4.8	-0.6	169	316	48	6,557	2.3	71.7	12.2	22.3
Vigo	11.8	9.9	6.8	49.2	107,848	106,153	-1.6	-0.1	1,409	1,707	120	42,657	2.3	58.1	12.0	33.4
Wabash	14.2	11.8	9.2	51.0	32,888	30,976	-5.8	-0.5	396	699	144	12,705	2.3	67.8	10.8	26.9
Warren	15.0	11.9	9.2	49.8	8,508	8,440	-0.8	0.4	94	121	64	3,383	2.4	75.8	7.8	20.8
Warrick	13.7	11.0	7.0	50.5	59,689	63,898	7.1	1.0	737	960	842	24,607	2.5	73.6	8.1	21.6
Washington	14.9	11.5	6.7	49.9	28,262	28,182	-0.3	-0.3	398	450	-32	10,820	2.6	69.3	10.8	27.6
Wayne	13.7	11.4	8.0	51.3	68,917	66,553	-3.4	-0.1	942	1,258	213	27,435	2.3	64.0	14.2	28.9
Wells	13.9	11.0	7.7	50.1	27,636	28,180	2.0	0.1	407	404	13	11,122	2.5	69.8	8.9	26.9
White	14.3	12.7	8.2	49.7	24,643	24,688	0.2	-0.1	361	424	25	9,792	2.4	68.0	10.4	26.8
Whitley	14.4	11.7	7.2	49.8	33,292	34,191	2.7	0.7	455	473	255	13,822	2.4	70.1	9.2	24.1
IOWA	12.9	10.5	7.2	49.8	3,046,355	3,190,369	4.7	0.1	45,004	44,543	2,025	1,273,941	2.4	62.9	9.1	29.8
Adair	15.4	12.1	10.1	49.5	7,682	7,496	-2.4	0.6	120	128	56	3,217	2.2	62.7	6.2	30.8
Adams	17.5	12.9	11.0	50.3	4,029	3,704	-8.1	-1.7	52	48	-68	1,627	2.2	62.0	4.2	30.8
Allamakee	15.0	13.8	9.5	48.8	14,330	14,061	-1.9	-1.0	235	272	-97	5,947	2.3	61.5	5.8	31.7
Appanoose	14.5	13.9	9.7	50.0	12,887	12,317	-4.4	-0.5	162	259	38	5,196	2.4	62.7	9.7	33.9
Audubon	15.8	13.5	11.6	51.0	6,119	5,674	-7.3	-0.7	69	102	-6	2,691	2.0	58.4	6.8	36.1
Benton	15.7	10.8	8.1	49.4	26,076	25,575	-1.9	0.5	319	360	160	10,306	2.5	70.5	7.9	24.2
Black Hawk	11.6	10.6	6.8	50.6	131,090	131,144	0.0	-0.6	2,016	1,888	-912	53,321	2.4	58.8	9.9	31.8
Boone	15.0	12.0	7.1	48.8	26,306	26,715	1.6	0.0	301	422	128	10,801	2.4	65.5	7.6	28.8
Bremer	12.1	10.7	8.8	50.2	24,276	24,988	2.9	0.4	307	389	173	9,680	2.4	69.7	6.9	26.5
Buchanan	13.7	10.9	7.5	49.9	20,958	20,565	-1.9	0.4	338	299	50	8,027	2.6	70.1	8.6	26.2
Buena Vista	12.3	9.6	6.6	48.6	20,260	20,823	2.8	-0.2	362	245	-170	7,584	2.5	60.7	7.0	31.8
Butler	13.8	13.0	9.9	50.0	14,867	14,334	-3.6	0.0	188	254	64	6,153	2.3	68.6	6.9	27.1
Calhoun	13.7	12.9	10.5	47.2	9,670	9,927	2.7	-0.1	117	154	24	4,103	2.2	65.2	9.6	30.6
Carroll	14.5	11.6	9.4	49.8	20,816	20,760	-0.3	-0.3	287	358	3	8,651	2.3	62.4	8.4	33.4
Cass	14.6	13.1	10.1	50.0	13,956	13,127	-5.9	-0.6	153	287	58	5,901	2.2	59.8	6.7	35.5
Cedar	15.4	12.1	8.4	49.8	18,499	18,505	0.0	-0.5	222	279	-37	7,472	2.4	66.5	7.1	28.0
Cerro Gordo	15.0	13.4	9.5	50.8	44,151	43,127	-2.3	-1.0	523	755	-190	19,452	2.1	59.3	8.9	34.6
Cherokee	15.1	13.2	11.2	49.7	12,072	11,658	-3.4	-1.3	156	236	-73	5,297	2.0	59.0	8.1	34.8
Chickasaw	15.4	12.5	8.9	48.8	12,439	12,012	-3.4	-1.0	160	186	-99	5,107	2.3	65.0	4.3	30.1
Clarke	13.4	11.3	7.6	48.6	9,286	9,748	5.0	0.4	145	138	29	3,950	2.3	61.7	4.4	30.5
Clay	13.9	12.4	9.4	50.4	16,667	16,384	-1.7	0.3	205	251	103	7,381	2.1	59.2	8.5	34.6
Clayton	15.9	14.2	10.4	49.2	18,129	17,043	-6.0	-0.3	232	303	27	7,563	2.3	62.4	6.3	32.0
Clinton	14.9	11.7	8.5	50.6	49,116	46,460	-5.4	0.0	663	759	94	19,477	2.4	61.9	10.9	32.2
Crawford	12.8	10.5	7.6	48.5	17,096	16,525	-3.3	-2.0	253	241	-341	6,388	2.6	70.7	11.7	22.7
Dallas	10.1	7.6	4.9	50.3	66,135	99,678	50.7	4.1	1,547	834	3,422	35,383	2.5	66.4	6.4	26.2
Davis	12.5	10.7	7.4	49.4	8,753	9,110	4.1	0.3	181	115	-38	3,182	2.8	75.4	5.6	22.8
Decatur	11.9	11.4	9.2	49.6	8,457	7,645	-9.6	0.2	93	122	45	3,242	2.2	62.7	8.5	26.9
Delaware	16.3	12.1	8.4	49.0	17,764	17,488	-1.6	0.1	237	267	52	6,915	2.4	68.7	5.0	26.1
Des Moines	14.0	12.4	8.9	50.9	40,325	38,910	-3.5	-1.1	539	625	-334	16,850	2.3	62.3	12.5	31.7
Dickinson	14.9	16.4	10.7	50.1	16,667	17,703	6.2	0.8	200	275	227	8,479	2.0	59.0	7.9	35.8
Dubuque	13.4	11.0	7.7	50.4	93,653	99,266	6.0	-0.6	1,368	1,341	-579	38,655	2.4	65.2	8.5	28.7
Emmet	14.7	13.0	9.2	49.7	10,302	9,388	-8.9	-0.7	119	186	-1	4,023	2.1	57.8	9.1	34.2
Fayette	15.3	12.6	9.5	49.2	20,880	19,509	-6.6	-1.3	251	364	-140	8,215	2.3	61.3	6.2	33.1
Floyd	14.5	12.4	9.8	50.2	16,303	15,627	-4.1	-1.4	209	290	-133	6,899	2.2	60.0	8.0	36.9

1. No spouse present.

STATE County	Persons in group quarters, 2021	Daytime Population, 2016–2020: Number	Daytime Population, 2016–2020: Employment/ residence ratio	Births, 2021: Total	Births, 2021: Rate[1]	Deaths, 2021: Number	Deaths, 2021: Rate[1]	Persons under 65 with no health insurance, 2019: Number	Persons under 65 with no health insurance, 2019: Percent	Medicare, 2021: Total beneficiaries	Medicare, 2021: Enrolled in Original Medicare	Medicare, 2021: Enrolled in Medicare Advantage	COVID-19 Deaths, 2020: Number	COVID-19 Deaths, 2020: Rate[1]
	32	33	34	35	36	37	38	39	40	41	42	43	44	45
INDIANA—Cont'd														
Pike	161	10,085	0.6	123	10.1	184	15.1	996	10.2	2,927	1,968	960	27	2.2
Porter	3,338	157,127	0.8	1,581	9.1	1,961	11.3	10,367	7.4	34,221	23,553	10,668	200	1.2
Posey	180	23,706	0.9	257	10.2	296	11.8	1,483	7.3	5,649	3,925	1,724	22	0.9
Pulaski	173	11,819	0.9	137	11.0	193	15.5	1,049	10.8	3,074	2,255	819	32	2.6
Putnam	4,632	35,855	0.9	357	9.7	455	12.4	2,249	8.5	7,450	4,804	2,645	43	1.2
Randolph	288	21,857	0.8	247	10.1	332	13.6	2,242	11.7	5,926	4,487	1,439	57	2.3
Ripley	406	26,445	0.9	345	11.9	319	11.0	2,288	10.0	6,370	4,521	1,849	48	1.7
Rush	143	15,096	0.8	192	11.5	226	13.5	1,464	11.0	3,724	2,633	1,091	18	1.1
St. Joseph	11,445	273,136	1.0	3,291	12.1	3,170	11.6	22,075	10.2	50,362	30,049	20,313	417	1.5
Scott	285	22,854	0.9	273	11.2	393	16.1	1,794	9.2	5,570	3,792	1,778	44	1.8
Shelby	611	42,065	0.9	466	10.3	549	12.2	3,296	9.0	9,377	5,762	3,615	69	1.5
Spencer	295	18,009	0.8	204	10.3	266	13.4	1,438	8.9	4,585	3,436	1,149	12	0.6
Starke	15	18,698	0.5	251	10.7	326	14.0	1,949	10.6	5,804	3,938	1,866	52	2.2
Steuben	1,232	33,470	0.9	343	9.9	423	12.2	2,729	10.5	8,133	4,155	3,978	33	1.0
Sullivan	2,241	18,972	0.8	193	9.3	259	12.5	1,379	9.4	4,447	3,228	1,220	28	1.3
Switzerland	39	8,648	0.5	103	10.6	127	13.0	1,092	12.5	2,090	1,489	600	D	D
Tippecanoe	15,528	206,229	1.1	1,949	10.4	1,467	7.9	15,778	10.1	25,622	18,302	7,321	100	0.5
Tipton	174	13,766	0.8	150	9.8	198	12.9	1,080	9.1	3,629	2,370	1,259	40	2.6
Union	45	5,314	0.5	89	12.6	95	13.4	603	10.7	1,684	1,258	426	D	D
Vanderburgh	6,692	200,389	1.2	2,114	11.7	2,385	13.2	15,281	10.6	37,708	24,742	12,966	261	1.4
Vermillion	171	13,715	0.7	131	8.5	261	17.0	1,070	8.7	3,873	2,932	941	26	1.7
Vigo	9,398	114,767	1.2	1,133	10.7	1,368	12.9	8,240	10.3	22,187	16,182	6,005	157	1.5
Wabash	1,768	30,512	1.0	310	10.0	560	18.2	2,421	10.5	8,055	4,459	3,596	56	1.8
Warren	74	6,747	0.6	78	9.2	92	10.9	539	8.3	1,920	1,496	424	D	D
Warrick	657	52,469	0.7	588	9.2	765	11.9	3,948	7.6	13,199	9,165	4,034	95	1.5
Washington	209	22,690	0.6	320	11.4	367	13.0	2,491	10.9	6,234	4,025	2,210	20	0.7
Wayne	2,627	68,246	1.1	762	11.5	997	15.0	5,788	11.4	15,964	13,142	2,821	143	2.2
Wells	407	25,982	0.9	316	11.2	331	11.7	2,000	8.8	6,049	3,217	2,832	50	1.8
White	275	23,442	0.9	294	11.9	319	12.9	2,413	12.7	5,753	4,211	1,543	31	1.3
Whitley	363	30,574	0.8	379	11.0	398	11.6	2,386	8.7	7,307	3,255	4,052	27	0.8
IOWA	91,659	3,151,599	1.0	35,771	11.2	35,538	11.1	144,986	5.7	637,150	477,159	159,991	4,725	1.5
Adair	148	6,626	0.9	98	13.1	100	13.3	280	5.1	1,901	1,613	288	21	2.8
Adams	68	3,347	0.8	43	11.7	35	9.5	163	6.0	1,017	988	29	D	D
Allamakee	191	12,314	0.8	173	12.4	227	16.2	900	8.7	3,397	2,840	557	33	2.3
Appanoose	71	12,048	0.9	134	10.9	215	17.5	598	6.3	3,373	2,451	922	42	3.4
Audubon	106	4,927	0.8	55	9.7	85	15.0	283	6.9	1,587	1,508	79	D	D
Benton	257	19,315	0.5	255	10.0	298	11.6	930	4.5	5,376	3,860	1,517	52	2.0
Black Hawk	4,115	140,771	1.1	1,589	12.2	1,525	11.7	5,945	5.7	26,841	16,309	10,532	255	1.9
Boone	679	23,432	0.8	247	9.2	348	13.0	945	4.5	6,008	4,669	1,339	17	0.6
Bremer	1,494	23,276	0.9	244	9.7	296	11.8	701	3.7	5,445	3,997	1,448	49	2.0
Buchanan	204	18,523	0.8	266	12.9	233	11.3	828	4.8	4,314	2,910	1,404	24	1.2
Buena Vista	809	20,609	1.1	302	14.5	175	8.4	1,581	10.2	3,538	3,212	326	34	1.6
Butler	167	11,622	0.6	152	10.6	206	14.4	585	5.3	3,746	2,912	834	25	1.7
Calhoun	713	8,639	0.8	92	9.3	118	11.9	355	5.2	2,576	2,327	249	D	D
Carroll	377	21,230	1.1	229	11.1	293	14.2	715	4.5	4,905	4,295	610	42	2.0
Cass	263	13,194	1.0	114	8.7	217	16.6	705	7.3	3,635	3,140	496	43	3.3
Cedar	269	14,008	0.5	175	9.5	232	12.6	621	4.2	4,065	3,063	1,002	19	1.0
Cerro Gordo	1,089	45,726	1.1	435	10.2	593	13.8	1,537	4.8	11,145	9,907	1,238	78	1.8
Cherokee	346	10,958	0.9	122	10.5	176	15.2	449	5.4	3,053	2,672	381	31	2.7
Chickasaw	73	11,616	0.9	129	10.8	148	12.4	625	6.7	2,831	2,492	338	12	1.0
Clarke	149	9,482	1.0	113	11.6	104	10.7	535	7.2	2,110	1,772	339	D	D
Clay	188	16,750	1.1	169	10.3	197	12.0	737	5.9	4,001	3,788	214	20	1.2
Clayton	178	15,886	0.8	185	10.9	249	14.6	964	7.3	4,648	3,399	1,249	51	3.0
Clinton	548	45,856	1.0	529	11.4	634	13.7	1,928	5.2	10,903	7,918	2,985	78	1.7
Crawford	427	16,493	0.9	213	13.0	188	11.5	1,569	11.5	3,356	2,933	423	26	1.6
Dallas	649	83,049	0.9	1,209	11.8	672	6.6	3,257	3.9	13,145	9,702	3,443	74	0.7
Davis	66	8,175	0.8	141	15.5	82	9.0	746	10.2	1,731	1,353	377	21	2.3
Decatur	600	7,144	0.8	76	10.0	95	12.4	399	7.1	1,815	1,498	317	D	D
Delaware	196	15,945	0.9	189	10.8	222	12.7	753	5.5	3,812	2,798	1,014	36	2.1
Des Moines	551	42,027	1.2	418	10.8	514	13.3	1,531	5.1	9,619	7,955	1,664	46	1.2
Dickinson	149	17,492	1.0	163	9.2	212	11.9	581	4.6	5,250	4,845	406	32	1.8
Dubuque	4,071	105,429	1.2	1,112	11.2	1,100	11.1	3,726	4.9	20,642	9,402	11,240	161	1.6
Emmet	415	8,773	0.9	98	10.5	143	15.3	490	7.1	2,343	2,201	143	34	3.6
Fayette	779	18,715	0.9	195	10.1	276	14.3	839	5.7	4,947	3,873	1,074	28	1.4
Floyd	187	15,320	1.0	167	10.8	219	14.1	760	6.3	3,955	3,416	539	38	2.4

1. Per 1,000 estimated resident population.

STATE County	COVID-19 Vaccinations, 2021–2022		Education						Money income, 2016–2020				Income and poverty, 2020			
			School enrollment and attainment, 2016–2020				Local government expenditures,[3] 2018–2019			Households				Percent below poverty level		
			Enrollment[1]		Attainment[2] (percent)						Percent					
	Number	Percent[5]	Total	Percent private	High school graduate or less	Bachelor's degree or more	Total current spending (mil dol)	Current spending per student (dollars)	Per capita income[4]	Median income (dollars)	with income of less than $50,000	with income of $200,000 or more	Median household income (dollars)	All persons	Children under 18 years	Children 5 to 17 years in families
	46	47	48	49	50	51	52	53	54	55	56	57	58	59	60	61
INDIANA—Cont'd																
Pike	7,147	57.7	2,474	3.1	57.1	15.5	19.7	10,730	27,889	55,022	46.8	0.6	58,220	9.7	11.4	10.6
Porter	97,104	57.0	40,513	19.5	40.8	28.6	271.7	10,091	35,672	72,255	34.2	6.6	78,732	8.6	9.9	9.3
Posey	12,067	47.5	6,009	22.1	44.0	23.0	39.3	11,422	32,136	64,983	37.7	2.5	63,801	9.3	10.2	9.3
Pulaski	5,616	45.5	2,856	6.4	55.9	12.9	21.4	10,793	26,171	49,140	52.2	0.8	52,609	11.2	15.5	14.4
Putnam	16,037	42.7	9,593	30.5	52.9	16.9	60.5	10,983	25,686	61,505	39.4	2.0	66,613	11.3	13.0	12.1
Randolph	11,244	45.6	5,420	10.3	53.3	16.4	54.3	7,348	26,960	53,322	46.8	2.3	67,178	12.4	18.5	17.5
Ripley	13,653	48.2	6,115	12.3	51.7	19.6	38.7	12,737	30,800	60,055	41.9	3.6	58,849	9.5	12.3	11.5
Rush	7,778	46.9	3,350	11.0	58.1	15.2	24.3	10,654	27,133	56,814	41.5	2.1	67,318	9.7	13.1	13.0
St. Joseph	158,874	58.4	73,597	34.6	40.2	31.0	385.5	9,909	29,635	54,433	46.3	4.3	60,070	12.7	16.0	15.5
Scott	10,510	44.0	4,561	14.3	61.4	13.2	39.7	10,287	23,820	45,123	54.3	1.3	59,286	13.9	18.1	17.2
Shelby	25,891	57.9	9,536	11.0	55.2	19.0	71.6	9,497	29,452	59,712	40.6	3.5	59,252	9.4	11.8	11.0
Spencer	9,023	44.5	4,295	7.2	51.6	17.3	29.6	9,004	32,105	56,919	44.5	2.9	66,667	7.9	9.3	8.5
Starke	8,580	37.3	4,903	14.9	58.7	11.6	34.5	10,285	24,105	49,705	50.4	1.5	51,996	14.2	20.2	19.4
Steuben	16,418	47.5	7,808	24.2	47.9	22.5	38.4	10,261	31,000	58,905	40.8	3.2	62,273	9.6	13.4	12.9
Sullivan	10,223	49.5	4,075	10.2	55.0	12.7	31.6	10,013	25,021	49,449	50.5	1.7	45,227	15.5	18.4	17.2
Switzerland	3,341	31.1	2,299	5.6	67.8	9.4	14.6	9,571	26,288	51,270	49.3	2.7	55,618	14.0	20.7	18.3
Tippecanoe	112,494	57.5	74,088	8.0	35.1	39.7	246.3	10,216	27,622	51,926	48.4	4.3	52,806	16.1	14.5	12.6
Tipton	6,843	45.2	2,997	12.8	49.1	25.9	22.5	9,692	32,880	68,707	37.6	3.0	76,368	7.3	8.8	8.5
Union	3,509	49.7	1,307	5.8	53.0	19.2	15.2	11,760	28,820	55,278	41.3	3.3	59,098	10.0	15.1	14.3
Vanderburgh	104,151	57.4	42,673	21.7	41.2	26.9	255.4	11,012	29,731	51,179	48.8	3.3	49,482	14.6	17.6	16.4
Vermillion	7,270	46.9	3,169	4.2	50.8	15.7	25.1	10,348	26,955	54,361	47.4	1.5	52,433	11.9	15.9	14.7
Vigo	53,186	49.7	29,502	13.8	42.9	24.9	160.6	10,910	26,380	47,261	52.4	3.1	45,897	20.7	28.4	24.7
Wabash	12,785	41.2	7,194	19.3	53.2	18.9	53.6	10,064	27,170	56,573	44.6	1.7	55,750	10.6	13.6	12.3
Warren	3,782	45.8	1,697	5.1	47.9	18.5	12.3	9,316	34,291	65,614	36.5	3.3	68,135	8.1	12.3	11.0
Warrick	39,352	62.5	15,334	16.6	34.4	33.0	98.6	9,629	40,276	79,079	31.0	8.0	82,453	6.4	7.5	6.8
Washington	11,242	40.1	5,884	15.8	57.4	12.4	42.4	10,312	25,047	50,459	49.5	1.8	49,494	13.4	18.0	16.8
Wayne	32,842	49.8	14,704	16.4	48.6	19.8	98.7	9,551	26,605	47,756	52.8	2.4	49,798	15.1	21.8	19.6
Wells	11,808	41.7	6,430	10.6	48.1	18.7	47.5	9,514	28,828	57,565	43.7	2.7	66,597	8.2	10.7	9.6
White	13,166	54.6	5,200	9.8	51.1	16.7	47.4	10,198	27,948	53,865	45.6	2.0	57,787	9.0	13.0	12.1
Whitley	15,986	47.1	7,473	18.0	45.0	22.4	56.3	9,159	32,020	64,992	38.6	3.6	61,841	7.2	8.6	8.3
IOWA	1,953,232	61.9	785,736	14.9	38.3	29.3	6,130.2	11,907	33,021	61,836	40.1	5.0	62,362	10.2	12.0	11.1
Adair	3,532	49.4	1,352	7.4	45.6	19.5	9.8	11,824	30,662	55,700	45.4	1.3	55,265	10.8	14.3	14.4
Adams	2,030	56.4	624	15.7	45.4	17.3	5.7	14,029	29,079	52,287	47.7	2.8	56,291	10.8	16.0	14.9
Allamakee	7,332	53.6	3,036	24.3	50.0	18.2	25.9	11,609	28,546	55,523	45.1	4.0	55,320	10.9	16.6	16.4
Appanoose	5,906	47.5	2,517	12.9	44.5	18.4	21.3	10,682	25,455	39,693	58.6	1.8	49,737	14.6	19.7	18.3
Audubon	3,205	58.3	933	6.8	45.2	18.8	6.1	11,175	29,132	49,245	51.0	2.2	56,338	9.6	14.7	14.0
Benton	15,007	58.5	5,592	9.5	43.5	20.4	40.1	11,003	32,221	66,046	36.5	3.7	72,308	7.5	8.2	7.5
Black Hawk	79,025	60.2	36,779	11.0	38.1	29.2	260.9	13,793	31,347	54,774	45.3	4.5	56,091	12.2	14.0	13.1
Boone	16,932	64.5	5,673	10.8	38.3	25.4	41.3	10,833	34,016	67,442	36.7	4.4	70,656	6.9	8.0	7.6
Bremer	15,026	60.0	7,033	31.9	34.7	33.0	61.0	10,713	33,510	72,209	31.4	3.2	74,596	5.6	5.7	5.6
Buchanan	11,362	53.7	5,129	15.4	42.4	22.1	32.9	10,181	33,287	67,252	37.7	3.9	66,852	8.3	12.8	12.4
Buena Vista	13,342	68.0	5,401	14.9	52.2	20.8	53.3	11,176	26,230	54,014	47.0	2.5	61,189	9.1	12.0	11.9
Butler	8,298	57.5	3,086	6.0	43.5	18.2	20.2	11,099	30,186	56,473	43.2	2.6	54,822	8.4	9.1	8.2
Calhoun	5,772	59.7	1,975	10.4	44.1	19.7	17.9	10,054	29,557	55,285	47.1	4.5	62,000	10.0	12.3	11.7
Carroll	12,483	61.9	4,251	24.2	39.8	23.4	36.5	10,815	32,274	59,198	43.5	2.6	61,701	7.0	8.1	7.6
Cass	7,467	58.2	2,867	4.5	43.5	23.0	32.8	10,623	30,479	52,005	47.8	3.4	55,301	10.8	13.9	12.7
Cedar	11,208	60.2	3,947	4.4	44.0	21.0	36.0	11,060	32,122	69,259	34.6	3.4	68,592	7.3	7.5	6.9
Cerro Gordo	26,822	63.2	8,731	14.1	40.4	23.2	72.8	11,974	33,567	56,082	44.1	5.0	57,659	10.6	13.1	12.1
Cherokee	5,961	53.1	2,136	10.4	43.8	22.7	15.2	10,136	33,882	56,302	43.6	4.6	61,360	9.0	10.8	10.1
Chickasaw	6,571	55.1	2,376	10.2	51.1	17.8	17.9	10,672	31,027	61,239	41.4	2.3	63,869	8.3	10.2	9.8
Clarke	5,164	55.0	1,934	15.0	54.8	15.9	19.1	11,225	28,723	55,078	42.4	2.2	69,923	11.1	15.4	13.7
Clay	8,322	52.0	3,346	12.3	38.2	23.9	27.0	11,222	29,707	51,259	49.1	2.2	59,940	8.1	10.5	9.5
Clayton	8,413	47.9	3,332	15.8	54.4	17.1	51.9	18,323	29,586	56,456	44.8	3.0	56,256	10.4	12.7	11.4
Clinton	25,405	54.7	10,187	9.6	46.8	19.3	88.7	11,468	28,761	52,221	47.1	2.3	56,017	12.5	16.4	14.1
Crawford	9,094	54.1	4,582	10.1	57.1	15.1	32.3	10,616	30,228	54,849	43.7	3.4	56,707	12.5	14.4	13.3
Dallas	62,566	66.9	23,602	14.8	22.8	50.5	204.7	10,180	45,319	88,368	24.5	12.2	92,025	4.4	4.5	4.2
Davis	3,315	36.8	1,763	22.1	49.0	18.7	14.2	11,057	28,818	67,627	36.0	4.5	57,225	11.7	17.2	17.1
Decatur	3,232	41.1	2,243	27.8	48.0	26.5	13.0	12,269	23,469	48,154	51.5	1.9	46,373	16.9	22.8	22.0
Delaware	9,308	54.7	3,880	19.8	52.1	17.4	23.8	10,869	34,681	63,877	38.8	3.6	66,364	8.4	9.8	9.3
Des Moines	20,144	51.7	8,474	11.6	40.9	19.8	71.7	11,420	31,046	51,784	47.9	3.8	55,153	13.0	18.6	15.2
Dickinson	10,070	58.3	3,197	9.4	30.4	32.2	29.0	10,512	39,366	60,975	39.6	5.5	67,477	6.7	7.9	6.7
Dubuque	62,771	64.5	24,422	29.3	39.4	31.4	173.8	11,847	34,275	64,493	38.4	5.4	65,986	8.9	10.4	9.4
Emmet	4,836	52.5	2,302	6.0	42.3	18.6	19.8	11,784	30,110	56,708	44.6	2.9	57,652	10.2	14.1	14.2
Fayette	10,723	54.6	4,454	19.2	49.8	18.3	40.5	12,119	28,269	49,834	50.2	3.1	53,254	11.8	14.5	13.6
Floyd	8,307	53.1	3,443	13.2	45.3	19.6	23.4	11,394	30,547	51,768	48.3	4.5	60,790	9.3	14.3	13.9

1. All persons 3 years old and over enrolled in nursery school through college. 2. Persons 25 years old and over. 3. Elementary and secondary education expenditures. 4. Based on population estimated by the American Community Survey, 2016–2020. 5. CDC percent based on 2019 population estimate.

STATE County	Personal income, 2020										Earnings, 2020		
			Per capita[1]			Supplements to wages and salaries, employer contributions (mil dol)						Contributions for government social insurance (mil dol)	
	Total (mil dol)	Percent change 2019–2020	Dollars	Rank	Wages and salaries (mil dol)	Pension and insurance	Government social insurance	Proprietors' income (mil dol)	Dividends, interest, and rent (mil dol)	Personal transfer reecipts (mil dol)	Total (mil dol)	From employee and self-employed	From employer
	62	63	64	65	66	67	68	69	70	71	72	73	74
INDIANA—Cont'd													
Pike	552	7.1	44,603	1,861	171	38	13	26	63	179	246	18	13
Porter	9,858	5.4	57,654	534	3,061	488	235	558	1,519	2,063	4,342	296	235
Posey	1,381	5.2	54,646	724	569	122	40	133	204	315	864	53	40
Pulaski	626	12.9	50,558	1,083	223	41	17	72	90	179	354	22	17
Putnam	1,551	7.1	41,404	2,278	569	99	46	83	206	429	797	55	46
Randolph	1,065	11.0	44,027	1,945	288	55	22	112	132	351	478	34	22
Ripley	1,337	9.2	46,992	1,519	653	111	49	75	214	341	887	57	49
Rush	831	8.0	49,889	1,152	215	43	16	93	103	232	368	24	16
St. Joseph	13,884	5.9	51,141	1,011	6,449	995	495	1,267	2,319	3,349	9,207	592	495
Scott	999	8.0	41,981	2,199	348	66	27	38	106	342	479	36	27
Shelby	2,182	7.9	48,628	1,303	868	144	66	144	299	588	1,222	81	66
Spencer	969	4.3	47,890	1,409	310	61	23	79	123	250	473	32	23
Starke	897	9.9	38,910	2,578	167	34	14	65	95	350	280	23	14
Steuben	1,673	5.7	48,032	1,389	670	120	53	92	320	438	936	66	53
Sullivan	821	9.0	39,903	2,465	272	60	21	51	107	281	405	28	21
Switzerland	382	8.6	35,647	2,897	74	13	6	23	57	115	115	9	6
Tippecanoe	8,128	5.5	41,446	2,275	4,685	897	355	468	1,450	1,683	6,405	387	355
Tipton	763	7.1	50,127	1,131	265	46	21	65	125	207	398	26	21
Union	311	9.9	43,626	1,991	50	11	4	32	39	90	96	7	4
Vanderburgh	9,128	5.8	50,033	1,141	5,590	872	421	557	1,609	2,469	7,440	487	421
Vermillion	644	9.4	41,997	2,195	233	45	18	25	80	233	322	24	18
Vigo	4,466	6.8	41,895	2,218	2,242	409	172	217	702	1,500	3,040	207	172
Wabash	1,442	8.2	46,847	1,532	507	89	39	92	249	501	727	53	39
Warren	408	11.3	49,845	1,160	87	16	7	56	47	102	166	9	7
Warrick	3,808	3.3	60,188	418	917	149	68	238	623	758	1,372	97	68
Washington	1,228	9.4	43,519	2,010	243	46	19	103	139	365	411	29	19
Wayne	2,993	7.0	45,499	1,725	1,336	244	101	193	388	1,027	1,874	130	101
Wells	1,286	7.0	45,704	1,697	476	81	38	102	198	328	696	47	38
White	1,151	8.7	47,633	1,436	421	76	33	98	182	320	628	43	33
Whitley	1,693	6.3	49,256	1,224	645	119	49	114	240	396	927	63	49
IOWA	169,182	6.0	53,057	X	79,968	14,028	6,313	13,104	30,474	37,416	113,413	7,476	6,313
Adair	398	8.0	56,422	616	126	25	11	26	60	94	189	13	11
Adams	214	3.4	59,569	448	51	11	4	52	29	52	118	7	4
Allamakee	697	6.1	51,107	1,015	192	44	16	105	125	171	357	23	16
Appanoose	524	7.4	42,125	2,176	183	41	16	33	76	185	273	22	16
Audubon	298	5.9	54,313	762	68	15	5	70	53	74	158	9	5
Benton	1,456	6.2	57,277	555	264	55	21	220	237	302	560	37	21
Black Hawk	6,426	6.3	49,133	1,242	3,742	635	301	304	1,172	1,669	4,982	335	301
Boone	1,367	5.8	52,028	933	429	87	36	84	235	335	635	45	36
Bremer	1,332	7.7	52,608	883	444	87	35	79	243	303	644	46	35
Buchanan	1,087	6.2	51,065	1,019	282	59	23	121	211	242	485	32	23
Buena Vista	951	9.6	48,077	1,379	495	93	42	102	150	224	731	47	42
Butler	708	5.2	49,428	1,207	154	34	13	66	123	189	267	21	13
Calhoun	498	5.4	52,585	885	118	25	9	70	86	132	223	15	9
Carroll	1,120	4.4	56,244	620	480	89	37	164	213	251	771	49	37
Cass	652	5.1	50,849	1,048	238	51	19	61	122	189	370	26	19
Cedar	1,045	4.3	56,528	607	221	45	18	84	195	202	367	26	18
Cerro Gordo	2,259	4.8	53,643	808	1,138	192	91	160	419	603	1,582	111	91
Cherokee	681	7.0	60,881	388	224	43	18	147	114	156	432	28	18
Chickasaw	704	6.2	59,495	453	223	41	18	144	122	150	426	28	18
Clarke	410	7.5	43,807	1,974	185	37	15	17	56	123	253	18	15
Clay	869	5.7	54,395	750	389	72	31	116	167	205	607	39	31
Clayton	929	7.3	53,657	805	292	57	25	129	181	242	503	34	25
Clinton	2,242	7.2	48,328	1,346	899	167	77	116	338	641	1,259	91	77
Crawford	761	7.0	45,230	1,767	326	61	27	93	123	191	507	32	27
Dallas	6,870	8.1	70,851	154	2,922	389	214	371	1,145	742	3,897	249	214
Davis	377	5.9	41,649	2,246	88	20	7	78	46	99	193	14	7
Decatur	298	8.2	38,347	2,642	87	21	8	14	46	104	130	11	8
Delaware	929	8.4	54,843	710	316	65	26	135	166	203	542	33	26
Des Moines	2,001	3.4	51,704	961	937	170	81	193	335	579	1,381	96	81
Dickinson	1,111	4.5	63,319	308	387	75	33	115	302	245	611	43	33
Dubuque	5,343	6.8	54,751	720	2,907	466	230	365	1,129	1,214	3,968	267	230
Emmet	424	1.2	46,654	1,558	151	31	12	28	76	124	222	17	12
Fayette	912	6.6	47,373	1,467	279	60	24	95	168	277	458	32	24
Floyd	777	5.1	50,215	1,122	266	59	21	65	129	224	411	28	21

1. Based on the resident population estimated as of July 1 of the year shown.

STATE County	Earnings, 2020 (cont.) — Percent by selected industries: Farm	Mining, quarrying, and extractions	Construction	Manu-facturing	Information; professional, scientific, technical services	Retail trade	Finance, insurance, real estate, and leasing	Health care and social assistance	Govern-ment	Social Security beneficiaries, December 2020: Number	Rate[1]	Supple-mental Security Income recipients, 2020	Housing units, 2021: Total	Percent change, 2010–2021
	75	76	77	78	79	80	81	82	83	84	85	86	87	88
INDIANA—Cont'd														
Pike	5.2	D	D	4.8	D	2.9	D	D	14.2	3,230	266	226	5,581	0.0
Porter	0.6	D	9.9	19.3	6.7	6.9	5.5	13.9	9.8	36,955	212	2,038	72,138	0.7
Posey	4.8	1.7	5.8	42.6	4.0	5.1	2.6	D	7.5	6,120	244	346	11,074	0.4
Pulaski	15.3	D	3.7	30.2	D	4.7	4.2	D	18.1	3,370	273	278	5,834	0.3
Putnam	2.7	0.7	8.1	17.9	3.6	5.4	4.0	6.9	17.7	8,055	218	481	15,152	1.0
Randolph	10.2	D	12.6	24.5	D	3.9	3.3	D	13.0	6,490	266	500	11,397	0.0
Ripley	3.9	0.1	5.0	14.3	4.1	4.0	3.7	D	8.1	6,345	218	325	12,371	0.8
Rush	12.4	D	8.2	19.1	4.3	6.1	4.7	D	17.3	4,055	243	280	7,361	0.1
St. Joseph	0.3	D	5.6	13.1	10.0	6.6	5.6	16.3	9.2	53,490	197	5,672	118,288	0.1
Scott	1.1	D	3.4	40.3	D	7.2	3.2	D	14.3	6,255	257	852	10,768	0.4
Shelby	3.0	0.7	8.6	29.8	D	4.9	3.4	6.8	14.4	10,190	226	713	19,487	0.3
Spencer	6.8	D	7.0	19.8	D	3.1	3.4	D	11.0	4,975	251	254	8,654	0.8
Starke	10.4	0.0	4.5	15.2	2.7	8.1	3.2	D	17.4	6,570	281	514	11,190	0.5
Steuben	1.5	0.1	4.8	34.8	4.1	7.4	3.5	D	8.7	8,800	254	432	19,035	0.9
Sullivan	6.4	D	2.7	8.9	3.3	4.9	2.6	3.5	28.1	4,905	236	428	8,794	0.1
Switzerland	3.4	D	D	D	1.6	D	D	5.9	22.5	2,085	213	212	4,379	1.7
Tippecanoe	0.5	D	4.8	22.5	6.0	5.2	4.5	13.8	27.0	27,260	146	2,378	79,337	1.6
Tipton	7.8	0.0	8.2	35.1	3.1	5.4	4.2	D	10.3	3,855	251	166	6,824	0.3
Union	12.8	0.0	7.2	13.1	D	8.0	D	D	20.2	1,665	236	126	3,251	0.3
Vanderburgh	0.2	-0.1	7.8	13.2	7.8	6.6	5.7	19.8	9.2	40,450	225	4,429	84,675	0.7
Vermillion	2.7	0.3	19.7	21.6	1.7	7.0	D	D	11.5	4,295	280	344	7,317	0.3
Vigo	0.5	0.6	6.6	13.6	4.0	7.8	5.5	20.6	18.7	23,810	225	3,196	46,920	0.0
Wabash	5.2	D	7.4	26.3	3.1	7.5	4.9	D	11.2	8,805	286	576	14,059	0.1
Warren	26.9	D	5.2	17.7	1.9	D	D	11.3	12.0	2,065	244	90	3,688	0.7
Warrick	1.2	0.7	8.9	18.3	5.7	4.8	7.1	24.9	9.5	14,135	219	684	26,538	1.2
Washington	10.4	D	11.9	20.1	2.6	10.6	4.0	9.2	15.8	6,915	246	623	12,171	0.6
Wayne	2.0	0.1	4.2	20.4	3.3	7.0	5.1	23.1	13.4	17,340	261	2,172	30,743	0.0
Wells	6.3	D	6.1	23.7	D	5.7	5.5	D	10.5	6,390	227	314	11,994	0.4
White	9.6	D	10.2	27.0	D	6.7	4.9	6.6	11.1	6,225	253	350	12,905	0.3
Whitley	3.6	0.0	7.0	45.6	D	6.2	3.6	D	9.2	7,950	231	360	14,938	0.5
IOWA	3.0	0.2	7.2	16.1	6.7	6.0	10.3	10.5	16.6	663,803	208	51,573	1,426,108	0.8
Adair	6.6	D	12.9	17.1	D	7.3	4.3	6.9	14.5	1,830	243	93	3,587	0.0
Adams	20.9	D	4.2	21.6	3.6	D	D	13.5	10.9	1,000	275	62	1,892	0.2
Allamakee	16.2	0.3	6.9	17.3	2.3	7.2	3.7	6.0	18.4	3,600	259	150	7,716	0.5
Appanoose	0.8	D	4.2	20.3	D	7.7	3.5	D	15.9	3,565	291	424	6,313	0.1
Audubon	34.9	0.0	5.1	7.9	4.1	3.4	3.7	5.0	15.2	1,615	287	75	2,788	0.0
Benton	12.5	D	9.0	23.5	D	6.8	5.3	D	17.9	5,790	225	334	11,084	0.0
Black Hawk	0.5	D	4.4	26.8	4.9	6.8	5.7	13.5	15.1	28,055	215	3,244	58,827	0.3
Boone	4.4	D	8.9	6.6	D	6.4	4.1	7.8	25.3	6,150	230	312	11,959	0.3
Bremer	3.2	D	6.4	16.6	3.3	7.1	15.9	D	20.1	5,675	226	195	10,547	0.4
Buchanan	13.8	D	9.4	19.9	D	6.7	4.8	4.2	20.6	4,635	224	281	8,934	0.5
Buena Vista	4.5	0.0	5.5	34.6	2.7	5.5	4.1	D	16.3	3,670	177	264	8,154	0.2
Butler	9.6	D	7.1	20.6	D	4.8	5.6	D	16.7	3,940	275	174	6,557	0.3
Calhoun	23.1	0.0	4.2	2.6	D	6.5	4.6	D	17.9	2,700	272	159	4,783	0.2
Carroll	10.6	D	6.5	12.8	3.3	7.1	9.0	D	10.1	5,010	242	259	9,512	0.2
Cass	7.3	D	9.1	11.5	4.2	7.7	6.3	8.6	26.0	3,815	292	275	6,398	0.0
Cedar	8.8	D	8.9	10.6	5.3	5.4	4.4	D	17.8	4,255	231	161	8,241	0.5
Cerro Gordo	1.1	D	6.1	11.6	6.0	7.9	6.4	25.7	12.7	11,650	273	815	22,746	0.6
Cherokee	7.4	0.2	7.1	20.9	5.8	4.7	3.4	D	15.5	3,090	269	124	5,557	0.0
Chickasaw	8.3	D	6.4	29.2	4.4	7.0	3.5	D	9.3	2,945	248	125	5,532	0.0
Clarke	0.7	D	D	37.4	1.7	6.6	2.6	D	21.9	2,230	228	134	4,394	2.4
Clay	6.9	D	6.9	6.5	D	13.5	3.5	12.2	18.1	4,195	255	213	8,142	0.1
Clayton	13.0	D	16.3	13.4	2.9	5.2	3.2	D	16.6	4,885	287	220	8,775	0.2
Clinton	2.2	D	5.3	28.6	3.7	7.0	4.3	14.0	12.6	11,570	249	1,100	21,551	0.1
Crawford	9.1	0.0	5.9	30.1	2.8	4.4	4.2	6.0	17.7	3,550	219	208	6,853	0.0
Dallas	1.0	0.1	4.6	4.1	6.5	6.2	41.8	10.3	7.7	13,330	128	497	42,843	3.5
Davis	3.2	D	15.3	19.9	D	7.3	3.9	6.6	21.0	1,835	201	132	3,580	0.0
Decatur	0.2	D	D	D	3.3	6.0	D	D	25.4	1,870	244	191	3,652	0.0
Delaware	12.0	0.1	8.7	26.4	2.7	4.7	5.8	D	16.8	3,950	226	237	8,130	0.3
Des Moines	0.9	D	5.1	28.1	3.7	7.0	3.6	17.1	12.5	9,890	257	1,039	18,805	0.1
Dickinson	4.6	D	9.0	19.2	5.5	10.1	6.1	6.6	13.8	5,450	305	179	13,924	1.4
Dubuque	1.9	D	5.8	20.2	7.2	6.0	11.5	13.8	8.3	21,985	223	1,654	42,899	0.5
Emmet	2.1	D	7.0	20.3	4.1	6.8	4.6	D	19.3	2,435	261	146	4,479	0.1
Fayette	10.9	D	8.9	11.7	2.6	5.6	4.0	D	15.7	5,115	266	519	9,306	0.1
Floyd	9.1	0.0	4.6	30.8	2.5	7.5	5.3	D	16.2	4,115	267	298	7,315	0.0

1. Per 1,000 resident population estimated as of July 1 of the year shown.

STATE County	Housing units, 2016–2020: Total	Occupied units: Owner-occupied: Percent	Owner-occupied: Median value[1]	Median owner cost as a percent of income: With a mortgage	Median owner cost as a percent of income: Without a mortgage[2]	Renter-occupied: Median rent[3]	Renter-occupied: Median rent as a percent of income[2]	Sub-standard units[4] (percent)	Civilian labor force, 2021: Total	Percent change, 2020–2021	Unemployment: Total	Unemployment: Rate[5]	Civilian employment[6], 2016–2020: Total	Percent: Management, business, science, and arts	Percent: Construction, production, and maintenance occupations
	89	90	91	92	93	94	95	96	97	98	99	100	101	102	103
INDIANA—Cont'd															
Pike	5,294	84.2	109,400	15.9	11.8	596	24.9	2.7	5,782	-6.3	196	3.4	5,685	24.9	46.9
Porter	65,153	74.9	193,500	18.3	10.2	947	28.4	1.8	83,182	-1.3	3,208	3.9	80,640	37.6	27.6
Posey	10,361	80.5	150,900	17.4	10.0	667	22.0	1.1	12,821	0.4	337	2.6	12,286	31.9	29.7
Pulaski	5,113	73.9	114,100	19.1	10.0	633	24.3	1.2	6,276	-2.0	185	2.9	5,816	27.5	38.4
Putnam	13,651	74.0	144,900	18.1	10.5	784	24.4	2.7	16,353	1.0	499	3.1	16,965	31.2	33.8
Randolph	10,358	78.5	83,700	16.6	10.0	693	26.1	2.1	11,874	6.1	350	2.9	11,633	30.1	37.3
Ripley	11,243	76.0	156,400	18.0	10.0	656	26.7	3.9	13,534	-2.8	375	2.8	14,310	28.5	37.9
Rush	6,648	68.6	115,900	17.6	10.3	721	22.2	1.8	8,755	-0.1	244	2.8	7,439	26.4	39.3
St. Joseph	104,380	67.9	134,800	17.6	10.0	825	28.4	2.0	130,947	-1.9	5,493	4.2	129,334	37.4	24.7
Scott	9,228	67.2	107,800	19.5	11.8	736	28.8	3.2	10,362	-1.0	401	3.9	9,971	26.2	40.5
Shelby	17,902	73.2	139,300	18.0	10.0	794	25.9	2.6	23,037	0.1	700	3.0	21,973	32.8	31.1
Spencer	8,321	79.6	133,200	17.4	10.0	673	27.3	1.4	10,418	0.8	285	2.7	9,975	31.4	38.1
Starke	8,490	82.0	111,100	18.9	10.3	684	27.9	1.6	9,555	-2.0	413	4.3	9,268	25.8	38.9
Steuben	14,449	78.7	154,300	19.1	10.0	793	23.2	0.7	19,886	-0.1	500	2.5	17,052	27.5	36.8
Sullivan	7,806	75.7	89,400	18.2	10.7	660	27.9	3.8	7,836	-1.6	301	3.8	8,656	28.0	34.8
Switzerland	4,430	77.8	116,000	18.8	12.4	624	25.2	4.8	4,666	-2.9	161	3.5	4,585	18.9	44.2
Tippecanoe	71,686	55.2	160,900	17.5	10.0	880	32.9	1.7	93,208	1.6	3,037	3.3	95,059	42.1	23.3
Tipton	6,360	81.8	123,900	16.6	10.0	771	22.5	1.0	8,960	-0.8	269	3.0	7,703	36.5	35.6
Union	2,848	76.3	128,200	19.6	10.0	825	25.3	1.8	3,471	0.1	82	2.4	3,575	30.1	34.6
Vanderburgh	76,094	64.8	136,100	19.0	11.8	815	29.6	1.5	91,401	-0.8	3,306	3.6	88,141	34.3	25.1
Vermillion	6,557	75.3	83,900	16.3	10.0	681	27.2	3.4	6,480	-1.8	258	4.0	6,754	27.6	37.4
Vigo	42,657	63.4	105,200	18.0	10.0	761	33.1	2.9	45,481	-1.6	1,958	4.3	48,945	33.6	24.8
Wabash	12,705	76.0	109,600	16.5	10.0	710	26.9	1.6	14,406	-0.4	420	2.9	14,463	26.6	34.9
Warren	3,383	81.7	120,300	17.0	10.0	794	33.5	1.7	3,973	0.2	103	2.6	4,062	30.9	39.1
Warrick	24,607	81.5	173,900	17.1	10.0	895	24.9	1.2	31,859	0.1	831	2.6	31,459	42.9	23.6
Washington	10,820	80.4	120,100	17.4	12.2	658	28.6	2.4	13,510	-0.4	422	3.1	12,627	26.8	44.2
Wayne	27,435	66.8	102,400	18.5	10.0	704	26.4	1.6	29,433	-2.3	1,054	3.6	30,613	31.5	30.7
Wells	11,122	77.4	132,500	17.6	10.0	688	24.0	1.0	13,851	-0.1	355	2.6	14,196	33.1	32.3
White	9,792	78.5	119,200	18.4	10.8	714	27.5	1.6	13,117	-0.4	342	2.6	11,024	28.3	38.3
Whitley	13,822	81.4	151,900	18.0	10.0	767	24.9	0.6	17,253	-0.1	460	2.7	17,068	30.2	35.5
IOWA	1,273,941	71.2	153,900	18.7	11.1	806	26.7	1.9	1,676,075	-0.4	70,869	4.2	1,611,524	37.2	26.6
Adair	3,217	69.9	111,100	17.6	10.0	575	22.0	0.8	4,307	1.6	133	3.1	3,416	34.0	34.2
Adams	1,627	80.8	81,400	18.3	11.5	679	19.8	2.0	2,027	-1.5	61	3.0	1,701	37.2	29.6
Allamakee	5,947	80.1	133,400	20.9	11.3	629	20.9	2.1	7,039	-0.8	321	4.6	6,804	29.5	35.6
Appanoose	5,196	72.4	85,000	19.2	14.3	661	28.8	2.4	5,961	0.5	255	4.3	4,908	28.9	32.0
Audubon	2,691	75.0	84,300	17.7	10.3	606	24.8	0.7	3,034	0.3	96	3.2	2,858	33.2	35.2
Benton	10,306	81.8	158,700	18.7	12.0	695	23.6	0.9	12,847	-0.5	573	4.5	13,472	30.3	33.6
Black Hawk	53,321	65.6	150,200	18.9	10.7	818	28.0	2.1	67,282	-0.8	3,088	4.6	68,084	33.0	27.2
Boone	10,801	78.2	141,000	18.7	11.3	747	24.0	1.5	14,563	-0.1	507	3.5	14,169	33.5	28.8
Bremer	9,680	83.1	169,000	18.9	10.7	677	24.4	1.1	13,793	0.1	442	3.2	13,056	38.1	26.7
Buchanan	8,027	80.0	143,200	18.0	10.5	691	21.3	2.3	11,178	-0.3	414	3.7	10,682	34.4	31.8
Buena Vista	7,584	64.5	120,300	17.1	10.0	706	23.6	4.9	11,628	-1.0	368	3.2	10,159	26.3	43.6
Butler	6,153	77.3	120,100	18.3	11.3	628	23.5	1.0	7,883	1.8	296	3.8	6,989	31.0	33.6
Calhoun	4,103	78.7	85,600	16.1	10.0	591	26.7	2.1	4,061	-1.0	160	3.9	4,318	36.9	28.3
Carroll	8,651	76.2	138,700	16.2	10.0	610	28.3	0.6	10,559	-0.5	327	3.1	10,672	31.8	29.3
Cass	5,901	72.7	107,200	17.8	11.2	633	26.2	1.3	6,768	-0.5	248	3.7	6,389	31.7	30.8
Cedar	7,472	80.4	163,100	18.4	11.5	700	21.1	1.2	10,351	-1.1	389	3.8	9,762	31.3	32.2
Cerro Gordo	19,452	69.6	130,400	17.6	11.2	711	24.9	1.6	22,505	-3.2	971	4.3	22,045	31.8	30.6
Cherokee	5,297	73.7	117,400	15.2	10.0	536	23.7	1.4	6,119	-1.9	207	3.4	5,884	31.7	34.1
Chickasaw	5,107	82.1	122,000	18.1	10.7	638	23.7	0.7	6,373	0.7	227	3.6	6,395	30.2	37.9
Clarke	3,950	69.3	115,400	18.3	14.7	601	27.0	6.5	4,833	0.6	209	4.3	4,467	31.7	40.1
Clay	7,381	67.5	129,700	19.2	11.9	693	26.1	0.7	8,479	0.5	309	3.6	8,037	36.9	28.2
Clayton	7,563	73.4	131,600	19.2	11.0	656	22.2	2.9	9,632	-1.1	493	5.1	9,118	26.8	37.9
Clinton	19,477	74.1	120,200	20.1	12.7	659	29.6	1.1	21,967	-1.0	1,169	5.3	21,615	29.9	33.7
Crawford	6,388	69.4	101,100	17.0	10.0	643	22.7	7.3	7,867	-1.6	407	5.2	7,971	23.8	46.3
Dallas	35,383	72.2	258,300	18.4	11.3	1,064	24.1	2.0	51,851	1.5	1,500	2.9	48,784	54.5	15.3
Davis	3,182	84.6	117,900	19.5	10.5	722	23.5	6.2	4,168	0.4	139	3.3	4,147	38.7	30.5
Decatur	3,242	64.6	82,800	20.3	12.5	568	21.8	3.6	4,271	0.9	143	3.3	3,625	35.7	26.3
Delaware	6,915	82.9	141,300	17.9	11.8	621	24.4	0.9	10,412	-0.6	345	3.3	9,387	32.4	34.9
Des Moines	16,850	69.7	111,600	18.4	12.9	808	34.0	1.6	18,427	-1.6	1,165	6.3	18,810	29.9	30.6
Dickinson	8,479	77.9	199,800	20.3	10.9	833	32.0	1.1	10,128	2.8	400	3.9	9,228	35.1	28.8
Dubuque	38,655	73.4	175,300	19.1	11.3	802	26.6	1.7	54,963	-0.9	2,432	4.4	50,479	37.3	25.0
Emmet	4,023	78.8	90,000	17.8	11.5	637	22.0	3.2	4,928	-2.9	201	4.1	4,747	30.9	35.8
Fayette	8,215	74.2	106,200	19.5	13.5	645	26.3	0.9	10,172	-1.5	478	4.7	9,422	30.3	33.3
Floyd	6,899	73.2	107,700	17.0	10.8	537	25.4	1.2	8,197	-1.2	354	4.3	7,750	34.7	32.5

1. Specified owner-occupied units. 2. A value of 10.0 represents 10 percent or less; a value of 50.0 represents 50 percent or more. 3. Specified renter-occupied units. 4. Overcrowded or lacking complete plumbing facilities. 5. Percent of civilian labor force. 6. Civilian employed persons 16 years old and over.

STATE County	Private nonfarm establishments, employment and payroll, 2020									Agriculture, 2017			
		Employment						Annual payroll		Farms			Farm producers whose primary occupation is farming (percent)
											Percent with:		
	Number of establish- ments	Total	Health care and social assistance	Manufac- turing	Retail trade	Finance and insurance	Professional, scientific, and technical services	Total (mil dol)	Average per employee (dollars)	Number	Fewer than 50 acres	1000 acres or more	
	104	105	106	107	108	109	110	111	112	113	114	115	116
INDIANA—Cont'd													
Pike	190	2,096	394	154	182	30	32	97	46,484	327	36.4	5.8	24.1
Porter	3,610	55,648	8,896	10,602	7,466	1,149	2,283	2,557	45,949	445	48.1	7.0	42.6
Posey	511	9,662	388	3,041	776	136	316	600	62,074	491	38.1	13.6	49.3
Pulaski	306	3,803	638	1,506	433	124	78	178	46,721	547	41.0	13.9	44.4
Putnam	717	11,042	1,968	2,222	1,188	236	207	403	36,496	828	44.8	4.5	30.8
Randolph	466	5,305	775	1,664	594	116	145	217	40,846	754	43.1	9.4	46.6
Ripley	632	8,745	1,481	1,497	844	272	141	386	44,136	879	36.9	4.7	34.3
Rush	376	3,953	578	565	453	80	166	143	36,251	557	30.9	9.2	51.3
St. Joseph	5,867	122,326	19,749	14,382	16,226	3,899	4,986	5,410	44,225	629	56.0	5.7	41.1
Scott	397	6,998	1,429	2,521	823	105	116	253	36,083	315	46.7	4.1	34.1
Shelby	924	15,595	2,120	5,080	1,472	223	293	699	44,804	567	44.4	11.8	44.8
Spencer	426	5,041	226	1,533	648	170	138	229	45,456	665	37.4	5.4	40.5
Starke	304	3,153	343	975	550	61	66	110	34,881	507	47.1	8.9	37.3
Steuben	939	14,856	1,541	5,185	2,121	184	225	532	35,841	472	40.3	6.1	35.4
Sullivan	321	3,812	547	361	560	98	103	158	41,325	450	30.7	9.3	43.5
Switzerland	130	1,514	104	114	154	25	16	41	27,214	410	38.3	1.0	30.5
Tippecanoe	3,660	71,317	12,706	17,367	9,263	1,739	3,156	3,110	43,612	693	53.7	9.1	35.4
Tipton	311	4,361	577	1,927	457	63	65	179	40,951	404	43.8	11.1	43.4
Union	119	1,012	96	281	207	24	76	32	31,538	238	26.5	9.2	51.2
Vanderburgh	5,061	105,927	20,821	11,979	12,500	4,885	5,698	4,843	45,717	251	47.8	6.4	43.4
Vermillion	262	3,860	625	692	578	41	43	221	57,201	283	36.7	14.5	49.8
Vigo	2,362	42,933	9,980	6,492	6,566	1,102	967	1,694	39,455	477	55.6	6.9	37.7
Wabash	721	10,585	2,129	2,419	1,326	282	191	413	38,988	724	41.0	7.6	40.6
Warren	125	1,718	231	938	97	30	15	64	37,391	417	37.9	11.5	36.4
Warrick	1,194	16,000	4,206	2,829	1,578	418	525	825	51,570	364	53.0	9.1	41.7
Washington	448	4,500	631	1,482	928	124	130	155	34,409	865	36.8	5.4	40.1
Wayne	1,430	25,408	5,722	5,617	3,551	756	338	1,044	41,075	768	38.5	4.2	40.4
Wells	628	10,903	1,720	2,956	1,045	156	264	459	42,063	581	39.1	14.3	44.9
White	583	7,486	824	3,055	1,022	176	119	301	40,202	539	37.3	14.8	48.8
Whitley	684	12,252	1,262	5,568	1,367	222	231	533	43,472	696	48.3	7.8	31.6
IOWA	82,440	1,390,551	218,777	216,348	184,211	96,947	60,098	65,641	47,205	86,104	31.7	9.8	45.0
Adair	202	1,887	346	NA	228	75	35	69	36,649	738	22.2	14.5	44.4
Adams	100	992	235	232	109	25	24	37	36,897	509	21.2	10.4	51.2
Allamakee	375	3,752	908	923	552	195	76	142	37,886	997	26.7	6.0	38.2
Appanoose	283	3,768	741	1,068	592	99	65	150	39,786	675	35.9	6.4	36.4
Audubon	186	1,301	292	158	181	57	21	50	38,664	628	29.1	13.9	47.8
Benton	535	4,599	828	894	811	185	75	177	38,521	1,148	33.3	11.8	49.3
Black Hawk	3,144	62,771	11,075	11,289	9,192	2,204	3,020	2,884	45,940	968	42.3	8.9	42.5
Boone	583	7,025	1,622	528	1,030	165	141	301	42,879	967	44.0	10.2	36.5
Bremer	577	9,204	2,006	1,507	1,285	1,068	244	405	44,008	963	35.7	6.3	40.5
Buchanan	492	5,438	1,080	1,443	816	223	130	212	38,989	1,057	35.3	8.0	49.5
Buena Vista	527	8,978	1,152	3,563	1,083	243	221	392	43,700	802	24.9	12.7	52.4
Butler	345	2,507	504	755	375	135	49	96	38,225	1,074	40.3	8.8	46.9
Calhoun	279	2,224	605	121	395	115	42	90	40,523	813	33.1	16.1	52.0
Carroll	845	10,041	2,051	1,422	1,598	762	186	394	39,262	1,074	35.2	7.3	45.6
Cass	450	4,708	956	672	872	195	149	177	37,546	643	28.1	14.3	48.0
Cedar	451	4,144	566	591	524	131	98	156	37,640	933	37.6	9.4	45.9
Cerro Gordo	1,397	20,175	4,331	3,091	3,514	976	659	880	43,622	760	33.6	12.6	46.2
Cherokee	332	3,959	826	337	566	153	80	168	42,554	863	21.7	8.9	55.4
Chickasaw	381	3,999	562	1,595	422	155	67	180	45,041	973	33.4	7.5	44.4
Clarke	171	3,459	515	1,205	524	75	46	126	36,523	624	23.2	6.3	31.6
Clay	577	7,074	1,398	528	1,341	328	190	285	40,234	716	26.0	15.4	50.4
Clayton	496	5,208	1,066	884	715	203	94	220	42,157	1,525	26.8	5.0	42.2
Clinton	1,116	16,869	2,768	4,185	2,476	523	303	682	40,406	1,169	30.8	9.8	44.7
Crawford	412	5,823	933	2,161	704	203	95	247	42,364	915	26.6	12.0	49.3
Dallas	2,243	41,358	3,906	2,009	6,850	14,343	1,479	2,446	59,149	924	41.0	8.2	35.9
Davis	177	1,451	427	247	220	58	34	62	42,442	826	30.4	4.6	35.8
Decatur	136	1,771	368	56	244	42	32	46	25,794	659	25.2	9.0	39.1
Delaware	509	6,150	1,158	2,167	699	253	93	259	42,167	1,331	30.2	5.2	49.7
Des Moines	1,081	19,783	3,528	5,014	3,218	483	320	826	41,776	593	32.5	7.6	40.7
Dickinson	766	7,447	917	1,764	1,220	212	178	303	40,753	411	29.7	15.8	51.7
Dubuque	2,747	55,313	8,464	9,473	7,183	4,320	1,700	2,542	45,962	1,402	30.5	3.4	42.8
Emmet	283	2,974	737	727	464	96	56	107	36,015	488	26.2	13.9	56.7
Fayette	537	5,777	1,052	681	723	195	116	204	35,319	1,265	31.2	6.7	46.9
Floyd	380	4,814	1,119	1,162	768	199	71	217	45,061	917	33.9	10.9	45.2

STATE County	Agriculture, 2017 (cont.): Land in farms: Acreage (1,000)	Land in farms: Percent change, 2012–2017	Land in farms: Acres: Average size of farm	Land in farms: Acres: Total irrigated (1,000)	Land in farms: Acres: Total cropland (1,000)	Value of land and buildings (dollars): Average per farm	Value of land and buildings (dollars): Average per acre	Value of machinery and equipment, average per farm (dollars)	Value of products sold: Total (mil dol)	Value of products sold: Average per farm (acres)	Value of products sold: Percent from: Crops	Value of products sold: Percent from: Livestock and poultry products	Organic farms (number)	Farms with internet access (percent)	Government payments: Total ($1,000)	Government payments: Percent of farms
	117	118	119	120	121	122	123	124	125	126	127	128	129	130	131	132
INDIANA—Cont'd																
Pike	81	0.7	246	D	63.3	1,214,424	4,931	138,768	42.6	130,343	68.1	31.9	NA	75.8	2,207	65.1
Porter	123	1.6	275	10.4	114.7	1,862,858	6,766	198,333	77.3	173,742	88.4	11.6	NA	79.6	3,698	53.9
Posey	194	-15.3	395	13.0	175.2	2,396,308	6,073	274,785	118.2	240,717	92.7	7.3	2	74.7	7,423	68.2
Pulaski	232	7.1	424	29.9	217.7	2,607,043	6,150	185,625	188.2	344,108	68.0	32.0	NA	73.9	5,770	72.2
Putnam	185	-6.4	223	0.5	140.4	1,437,116	6,435	103,171	85.1	102,793	84.7	15.3	NA	78.1	5,065	47.3
Randolph	242	0.3	321	0.2	224.5	2,057,555	6,417	207,262	213.1	282,635	55.4	44.6	10	75.9	5,720	59.3
Ripley	176	5.6	200	0.1	132.1	1,034,225	5,163	123,313	86.5	98,396	78.3	21.7	8	72.8	3,808	58.7
Rush	211	1.8	379	0.1	195.5	2,752,265	7,255	243,945	165.1	296,497	67.1	32.9	NA	79.4	4,579	63.4
St. Joseph	150	-1.3	238	28.1	133.8	1,928,345	8,087	164,410	103.9	165,261	80.0	20.0	3	74.4	4,335	44.7
Scott	59	15.2	188	3.7	45.7	1,010,422	5,368	116,543	23.8	75,695	88.9	11.1	NA	74.0	1,843	38.7
Shelby	220	-5.4	389	5.2	207.4	2,700,637	6,945	229,128	135.6	239,138	88.3	11.7	1	76.4	6,523	56.1
Spencer	169	-0.6	255	0.7	133.5	1,174,320	4,609	174,957	92.9	139,705	75.0	25.0	1	73.1	4,531	62.0
Starke	146	9.2	287	38.7	130.6	1,438,032	5,004	146,138	69.2	136,578	94.9	5.1	1	68.6	6,179	73.8
Steuben	120	15.1	255	13.0	101.7	1,411,595	5,537	144,619	64.0	135,672	71.0	29.0	NA	74.4	2,336	63.1
Sullivan	160	-6.0	356	7.1	139.6	1,770,624	4,977	190,307	88.9	197,533	90.3	9.7	2	82.2	4,194	69.3
Switzerland	55	8.9	134	D	27.8	549,933	4,098	67,288	14.8	36,127	74.6	25.4	9	68.0	711	24.4
Tippecanoe	222	0.9	321	4.6	197.0	2,893,652	9,027	188,551	143.0	206,338	83.1	16.9	1	85.6	3,070	51.9
Tipton	161	11.1	399	D	155.9	3,261,470	8,167	274,856	114.9	284,366	82.1	17.9	NA	85.6	2,684	67.6
Union	83	11.5	349	NA	71.0	2,211,666	6,340	200,911	41.9	175,992	91.5	8.5	NA	79.0	2,457	69.3
Vanderburgh	64	-16.5	255	1.3	61.0	2,013,091	7,906	184,217	39.0	155,339	98.0	2.0	NA	74.9	1,620	61.4
Vermillion	123	4.0	435	0.3	104.4	2,467,818	5,674	233,387	76.8	271,247	76.8	23.2	NA	71.0	1,888	53.7
Vigo	120	2.1	252	1.6	100.9	1,364,518	5,425	135,673	55.4	116,216	98.9	1.1	2	75.7	1,454	55.1
Wabash	211	6.9	292	1.8	190.3	1,835,188	6,290	192,429	161.2	222,664	59.1	40.9	2	76.8	3,814	62.3
Warren	188	6.8	450	7.1	167.9	3,057,183	6,786	239,741	130.6	313,293	79.7	20.3	2	78.9	4,075	62.8
Warrick	105	5.6	289	0.1	86.4	1,569,892	5,429	175,673	49.4	135,821	92.6	7.4	NA	77.2	2,445	46.4
Washington	212	6.2	245	0.2	147.0	1,102,858	4,501	129,743	160.6	185,609	42.5	57.5	2	70.4	3,910	36.0
Wayne	163	4.9	213	0.9	131.5	1,169,226	5,492	110,988	100.1	130,385	68.6	31.4	31	71.1	3,878	48.6
Wells	225	12.3	387	0.0	215.4	2,922,012	7,544	255,414	192.1	330,707	62.5	37.5	4	79.9	3,224	70.7
White	283	-1.8	525	5.0	266.5	4,101,696	7,815	319,127	256.8	476,384	61.8	38.2	NA	86.3	3,750	67.7
Whitley	176	25.8	253	1.6	154.1	1,606,248	6,343	187,714	120.9	173,774	65.3	34.7	NA	78.4	3,103	51.1
IOWA	30,564	-0.2	355	222.0	26,546.0	2,506,812	7,062	230,716	28,956.5	336,296	47.8	52.2	785	79.6	682,995	71.2
Adair	335	3.5	454	0.1	261.5	2,372,891	5,230	223,107	188.0	254,749	54.9	45.1	9	77.8	7,583	75.7
Adams	223	-2.5	439	D	174.1	2,189,535	4,987	197,021	108.3	212,764	59.2	40.8	NA	76.8	6,239	79.8
Allamakee	292	0.9	293	0.0	188.8	1,564,078	5,345	172,462	200.5	201,062	33.3	66.7	18	75.4	6,176	81.4
Appanoose	179	-4.5	266	NA	108.3	1,079,752	4,065	87,526	44.5	65,901	59.4	40.6	1	76.3	3,894	55.9
Audubon	276	-1.7	439	D	253.4	3,012,527	6,866	285,066	276.6	440,482	47.0	53.0	2	76.9	9,364	83.9
Benton	421	-0.4	366	0.2	384.2	2,706,668	7,387	245,776	347.7	302,895	62.8	37.2	11	80.7	7,127	77.0
Black Hawk	292	-1.6	302	0.4	275.6	2,632,645	8,723	250,907	261.2	269,871	61.9	38.1	5	84.2	6,532	73.1
Boone	315	0.5	326	0.2	288.7	2,595,336	7,966	205,330	218.4	225,806	73.9	26.1	4	83.1	5,716	70.4
Bremer	262	-3.5	272	0.5	240.8	2,174,810	7,991	227,554	229.9	238,769	59.4	40.6	10	81.0	5,871	77.8
Buchanan	330	-3.5	312	0.1	309.5	2,459,772	7,884	252,896	366.4	346,651	50.9	49.1	33	79.6	8,083	70.3
Buena Vista	357	-1.2	445	D	334.9	3,577,469	8,045	302,722	537.2	669,864	32.9	67.1	4	81.9	6,426	84.4
Butler	359	-1.0	334	1.6	333.5	2,397,864	7,169	202,064	291.5	271,395	62.8	37.2	3	81.3	11,840	80.4
Calhoun	351	-2.0	432	0.7	334.0	3,429,727	7,942	290,880	321.6	395,549	54.8	45.2	7	79.1	5,250	65.6
Carroll	349	-2.8	325	0.5	319.5	2,608,918	8,030	239,347	573.0	533,488	31.1	68.9	10	80.4	5,341	55.5
Cass	285	-1.8	443	D	241.9	2,610,781	5,895	236,918	203.4	316,264	56.9	43.1	7	77.1	5,293	73.4
Cedar	340	8.9	365	0.3	307.8	2,866,790	7,858	275,263	321.5	344,610	58.5	41.5	4	80.6	4,563	73.1
Cerro Gordo	320	-2.2	421	0.5	305.2	3,088,779	7,341	250,319	226.6	298,208	74.6	25.4	1	89.1	7,612	80.0
Cherokee	339	0.4	392	0.0	299.4	3,105,879	7,914	300,575	387.1	448,583	41.9	58.1	1	83.2	5,329	47.6
Chickasaw	293	-2.0	301	0.3	269.2	2,248,034	7,463	227,181	303.0	311,375	48.9	51.1	1	71.2	6,716	63.7
Clarke	193	14.1	309	D	112.2	1,319,833	4,271	98,535	123.2	197,500	17.4	82.6	1	71.8	7,147	68.6
Clay	329	3.2	460	0.7	306.8	3,670,430	7,985	310,588	348.7	487,042	46.9	53.1	1	85.9	9,744	84.8
Clayton	413	3.7	271	0.4	305.5	1,500,568	5,545	166,778	364.2	238,852	39.1	60.9	30	72.0	12,580	81.6
Clinton	403	-3.5	345	0.4	358.9	2,599,062	7,544	252,926	339.8	290,686	61.9	38.1	2	80.8	9,749	76.6
Crawford	440	-2.5	481	0.5	391.0	3,255,634	6,774	269,409	400.3	437,461	55.3	44.7	4	76.6	8,356	59.8
Dallas	293	-4.2	318	0.8	257.6	2,594,337	8,169	186,706	237.6	257,187	60.5	39.5	20	82.1	4,422	48.6
Davis	199	-7.2	240	0.1	121.8	941,546	3,916	125,282	91.9	111,274	31.0	69.0	39	59.9	2,701	50.6
Decatur	236	2.0	358	D	142.6	1,377,822	3,845	129,758	103.4	156,869	34.6	65.4	3	72.1	7,942	67.1
Delaware	365	-0.3	274	0.3	321.6	2,129,527	7,773	261,745	534.6	401,616	35.2	64.8	8	81.1	13,135	83.1
Des Moines	175	1.1	295	4.5	143.9	2,035,386	6,910	183,368	108.3	182,639	80.8	19.2	2	79.4	3,495	65.6
Dickinson	187	0.0	456	1.0	176.5	3,389,715	7,439	285,670	179.3	436,195	49.2	50.8	2	83.7	4,070	76.6
Dubuque	313	7.6	224	0.4	258.5	1,930,243	8,633	188,850	440.1	313,898	29.2	70.8	15	82.0	5,667	73.5
Emmet	230	4.9	471	0.8	211.9	3,382,133	7,182	356,936	234.9	481,395	49.9	50.1	1	86.3	4,554	83.4
Fayette	385	-0.9	304	1.3	337.6	2,183,246	7,176	222,654	372.9	294,761	46.1	53.9	9	79.5	14,587	84.3
Floyd	311	-2.2	339	2.1	286.3	2,493,726	7,359	238,169	281.0	306,482	55.1	44.9	6	79.6	10,269	77.1

STATE County	Water use, 2015		Wholesale Trade[1], 2017				Retail Trade[2], 2017				Real estate and rental and leasing,[2] 2017			
	Public supply water withdrawn (mil gal/ day)	Public supply gallons withdrawn per person per day	Number of establish- ments	Number of employees	Sales (mil dol)	Average payroll (mil dol)	Number of establish- ments	Number of employees	Sales (mil dol)	Average payroll (mil dol)	Number of establish- ments	Number of employees	Sales (mil dol)	Average payroll (mil dol)
	133	134	135	136	137	138	139	140	141	142	143	144	145	146
INDIANA—Cont'd														
Pike	1.0	80.2	7	D	64.7	D	28	214	63.6	4.5	8	58	4.7	1.8
Porter	15.8	94.5	148	2,215	1,822.8	128.1	460	7,862	2,183.2	191.8	164	762	155.7	28.6
Posey	1.0	39.2	15	214	297.5	11.7	58	729	342.7	20.6	13	56	10.1	2.6
Pulaski	0.4	29.5	25	176	529.5	8.1	47	367	161.4	10.6	D	D	D	D
Putnam	4.0	107.2	18	115	50.8	6.7	97	1,281	400.0	33.8	30	115	12.0	2.5
Randolph	2.2	86.6	14	121	110.9	4.5	71	647	206.2	14.3	12	46	4.7	0.6
Ripley	1.2	41.5	24	189	101.9	6.5	103	764	233.5	22.3	20	31	4.8	0.8
Rush	1.0	59.4	30	689	515.7	39.1	45	430	118.4	9.9	D	D	D	D
St. Joseph	21.8	81.1	292	4,437	3,881.1	253.9	914	16,377	5,381.5	439.8	236	1,604	282.0	60.4
Scott	3.3	140.2	9	166	39.2	8.0	79	826	237.0	20.0	22	55	7.5	1.4
Shelby	5.7	127.3	35	504	293.9	22.9	124	1,589	512.5	41.2	44	148	23.2	4.8
Spencer	2.0	95.1	18	304	184.7	12.1	67	676	155.9	14.1	9	31	4.3	1.5
Starke	0.6	26.6	10	75	52.1	2.8	60	606	174.1	15.6	13	25	1.9	0.4
Steuben	1.4	39.6	42	336	191.6	13.8	174	2,157	623.0	45.3	43	107	15.3	3.3
Sullivan	1.4	65.0	18	146	144.5	6.5	48	527	173.5	12.7	6	14	0.9	0.2
Switzerland	1.0	98.8	D	D	D	D	19	143	43.8	3.0	NA	NA	NA	NA
Tippecanoe	12.8	69.1	112	1,434	1,211.3	74.9	553	9,689	2,707.4	234.5	209	1,218	209.6	45.1
Tipton	0.9	59.6	16	133	173.0	6.9	42	430	140.7	10.3	10	22	2.4	0.5
Union	0.4	48.7	NA	NA	NA	NA	22	199	33.9	3.7	NA	NA	NA	NA
Vanderburgh	17.4	95.7	255	3,880	2,689.5	208.8	760	13,106	3,570.8	330.0	220	1,274	297.1	48.4
Vermillion	1.3	79.7	10	68	136.5	2.7	50	612	191.1	14.9	D	D	D	D
Vigo	12.2	113.1	91	1,152	450.4	48.5	417	6,558	1,683.5	152.6	92	576	103.7	18.2
Wabash	3.5	108.3	26	328	317.3	17.6	116	1,359	345.4	32.7	27	120	8.6	2.6
Warren	0.4	52.0	8	109	100.3	5.0	15	102	19.5	1.2	3	6	0.3	0.0
Warrick	2.7	43.6	36	256	306.6	12.7	129	1,519	425.1	37.3	51	165	33.8	4.3
Washington	2.4	87.7	12	45	16.2	1.6	76	909	274.4	22.7	15	55	5.3	1.0
Wayne	5.0	74.8	50	802	984.3	36.3	251	3,768	957.1	85.8	56	212	42.4	8.2
Wells	2.4	87.3	28	529	941.9	38.2	80	985	250.6	24.5	31	102	11.8	2.6
White	1.0	39.9	23	210	308.7	10.0	93	1,116	316.4	28.3	23	35	6.6	1.0
Whitley	1.4	41.3	24	443	271.8	20.6	103	1,367	397.0	39.8	19	87	27.7	5.1
IOWA	390.4	125.0	4,426	62,658	64,162.6	3,389.3	11,479	181,416	50,063.1	4,518.5	3,130	13,999	2,890.1	575.6
Adair	0.7	92.7	D	D	D	5.3	29	259	49.6	4.7	7	D	4.8	D
Adams	1.0	263.4	D	D	D	D	13	118	22.2	2.4	NA	NA	NA	NA
Allamakee	0.9	65.5	29	281	217.3	13.2	62	627	141.7	13.6	14	36	2.7	0.7
Appanoose	6.7	530.8	15	105	67.5	3.5	51	651	140.6	15.9	6	10	1.8	0.2
Audubon	0.2	41.6	D	D	D	5.7	15	155	39.0	3.4	NA	NA	NA	NA
Benton	1.3	49.1	34	418	403.5	20.0	83	811	205.7	19.5	D	D	D	D
Black Hawk	16.6	124.1	144	2,591	2,150.4	137.7	506	8,863	2,213.9	222.1	152	786	143.2	26.8
Boone	2.4	89.7	D	D	D	D	64	1,037	261.0	26.2	18	53	5.2	1.2
Bremer	1.5	61.1	23	198	165.0	9.8	80	1,404	290.4	33.5	D	D	D	D
Buchanan	1.2	57.0	31	303	214.1	14.3	74	853	218.7	20.2	10	D	3.4	D
Buena Vista	3.6	174.2	D	D	D	D	83	1,073	241.2	25.6	18	74	11.0	2.7
Butler	0.8	55.6	27	186	222.6	8.9	51	411	102.4	8.6	NA	NA	NA	NA
Calhoun	1.0	103.9	20	228	247.8	10.9	45	350	160.9	10.3	D	D	D	D
Carroll	2.0	99.5	57	1,303	1,001.3	51.8	140	1,559	372.1	40.8	20	107	23.7	4.2
Cass	1.2	91.6	20	232	318.5	9.5	72	927	199.6	21.1	15	71	14.8	3.2
Cedar	1.0	56.7	27	443	367.0	22.0	58	597	189.0	13.1	13	21	3.6	0.7
Cerro Gordo	6.5	151.1	93	1,071	924.7	56.1	212	3,596	912.4	85.1	66	160	32.7	4.8
Cherokee	1.9	166.8	19	175	201.3	8.5	52	602	133.3	14.5	D	D	D	0.1
Chickasaw	1.1	87.6	35	382	363.7	18.8	52	454	114.2	10.0	8	10	1.1	0.3
Clarke	1.2	128.5	8	72	48.8	3.0	29	563	130.3	12.6	5	11	1.1	0.1
Clay	2.3	137.5	49	658	450.4	23.8	100	1,419	478.2	37.9	23	102	14.3	2.9
Clayton	0.7	41.4	22	336	529.0	17.3	86	747	225.8	18.5	10	D	4.2	D
Clinton	3.9	81.0	38	329	302.9	17.3	181	2,570	591.0	58.1	36	112	23.8	4.2
Crawford	3.0	173.2	21	251	326.9	13.0	47	788	174.2	17.0	10	D	2.5	D
Dallas	1.5	18.3	64	841	491.1	55.2	281	6,246	1,527.1	145.9	126	973	152.3	61.1
Davis	0.0	0.0	10	82	38.8	2.9	29	282	66.2	6.4	6	11	1.7	0.3
Decatur	0.6	66.9	9	83	36.1	2.5	22	224	40.2	4.7	4	8	1.4	0.3
Delaware	0.9	50.6	29	332	385.5	17.4	60	682	197.8	17.3	8	35	4.4	1.1
Des Moines	5.8	143.8	53	657	723.3	26.8	197	3,285	911.2	83.4	47	639	105.2	27.2
Dickinson	2.1	121.0	D	D	D	D	109	1,168	340.4	34.7	36	50	16.5	1.7
Dubuque	7.7	79.4	156	2,348	2,185.6	122.0	424	7,233	1,763.9	175.4	121	400	94.9	14.4
Emmet	1.2	119.8	19	152	132.7	8.8	41	440	87.0	9.1	NA	NA	NA	NA
Fayette	1.1	55.3	39	369	317.9	17.8	98	866	193.9	19.4	15	28	15.7	1.0
Floyd	2.2	139.1	23	382	276.9	20.4	59	810	215.0	18.1	9	22	2.6	0.5

1 Merchant wholesalers, except manufacturers' sales branches and offices. 2. Employer establishments.

STATE County	Professional, scientific, and technical services, 2017				Manufacturing, 2017				Accommodation and food services, 2017			
	Number of establishments	Number of employees	Sales (mil dol)	Average payroll (mil dol)	Number of establishments	Number of employees	Sales (mil dol)	Average payroll (mil dol)	Number of establishments	Number of employees	Sales (mil dol)	Annual payroll (mil dol)
	147	148	149	150	151	152	153	154	155	156	157	158
INDIANA—Cont'd												
Pike	8	31	3.3	1.0	6	178	85.5	9.9	14	232	8.0	2.3
Porter	D	D	D	D	153	10,337	9,156.2	860.1	321	6,263	315.5	91.2
Posey	39	307	45.1	16.8	31	3,322	3,816.0	291.5	31	558	21.7	6.6
Pulaski	23	69	6.6	1.5	17	1,387	499.6	79.1	D	D	D	D
Putnam	41	170	14.1	5.8	28	3,011	1,192.7	146.6	82	1,299	58.0	16.1
Randolph	34	128	20.5	4.4	47	1,671	560.0	81.8	39	514	21.7	6.2
Ripley	35	126	12.1	4.7	37	1,496	730.5	69.8	43	641	25.5	8.6
Rush	32	138	14.5	4.9	25	662	252.5	26.2	24	350	17.9	5.1
St. Joseph	501	4,779	1,569.3	296.4	336	15,133	6,184.5	845.7	568	11,392	591.2	166.6
Scott	22	117	10.9	3.8	19	2,076	962.5	110.2	D	D	D	D
Shelby	57	235	55.7	11.9	81	5,560	2,796.9	289.3	80	1,579	69.4	20.4
Spencer	24	223	33.4	13.1	23	1,488	1,296.3	77.1	28	334	16.8	4.5
Starke	17	106	9.1	3.2	22	734	225.5	31.1	D	D	D	D
Steuben	62	217	19.5	6.7	89	5,078	1,435.2	229.1	90	1,400	72.2	21.2
Sullivan	21	98	7.9	3.6	18	497	103.5	18.3	36	486	19.4	6.4
Switzerland	10	15	1.3	0.5	D	81	D	D	D	D	D	D
Tippecanoe	335	2,869	439.4	173.9	124	17,647	14,562.9	1,054.5	451	9,044	475.7	128.8
Tipton	D	D	D	D	16	1,034	326.7	50.9	25	443	16.7	5.0
Union	D	D	1.9	D	D	238	D	12.1	D	D	D	1.5
Vanderburgh	D	D	D	D	240	11,605	4,073.2	537.1	471	11,279	640.0	174.4
Vermillion	10	30	2.0	0.6	15	748	708.5	58.8	29	389	22.2	5.4
Vigo	D	D	D	D	111	6,828	3,641.3	363.8	276	5,623	276.8	78.8
Wabash	49	204	36.2	8.6	57	2,545	1,407.5	148.3	68	1,008	45.6	12.4
Warren	D	D	1.4	D	12	668	154.9	28.1	D	D	D	D
Warrick	103	416	61.2	22.0	48	2,057	1,099.8	143.0	75	1,210	56.4	15.9
Washington	37	121	10.2	3.6	34	1,478	388.1	66.7	30	452	18.4	5.5
Wayne	D	D	D	D	96	5,100	1,989.4	253.7	149	2,834	136.3	41.9
Wells	35	262	29.4	10.6	54	2,732	1,118.8	122.4	41	572	24.1	6.6
White	29	99	12.1	3.7	42	2,695	1,227.0	111.0	61	665	28.9	7.8
Whitley	41	212	21.0	7.4	63	4,744	2,143.9	267.3	60	985	37.8	10.8
IOWA	6,426	52,390	7,907.3	3,160.8	3,489	210,722	109,727.8	11,373.9	7,283	123,866	7,110.7	1,897.4
Adair	12	42	2.9	1.2	NA	NA	NA	NA	18	218	8.3	2.2
Adams	7	26	3.3	0.8	D	201	D	9.9	D	D	D	0.4
Allamakee	19	79	13.8	3.4	24	956	271.4	42.3	35	235	10.4	2.5
Appanoose	21	89	8.3	3.2	19	1,088	336.2	46.3	32	547	26.3	7.7
Audubon	D	D	D	D	9	153	57.9	7.2	9	62	2.0	0.5
Benton	28	72	8.1	2.7	24	631	301.4	33.9	33	277	11.5	3.3
Black Hawk	D	D	D	D	144	13,259	5,936.3	650.3	318	6,704	363.7	97.4
Boone	38	134	16.5	6.3	34	476	129.9	28.1	42	528	22.5	6.4
Bremer	33	225	23.2	7.1	34	1,352	575.3	78.8	52	571	25.3	6.8
Buchanan	22	114	24.1	4.0	39	1,331	582.8	61.8	38	348	14.8	3.9
Buena Vista	35	211	28.2	10.7	27	3,601	1,757.3	155.4	42	677	28.5	7.4
Butler	19	49	5.3	1.4	24	732	379.9	29.0	19	122	3.6	0.8
Calhoun	13	35	6.3	1.4	13	82	11.2	3.9	14	110	3.6	1.0
Carroll	40	174	24.9	8.0	40	1,411	769.0	70.7	53	719	30.3	9.0
Cass	24	140	14.8	5.9	22	506	138.1	23.3	30	346	14.5	4.0
Cedar	23	101	13.2	4.1	27	506	176.6	23.9	35	300	11.4	3.2
Cerro Gordo	D	D	D	D	59	3,321	1,561.0	161.5	126	2,062	100.0	29.8
Cherokee	16	79	11.8	2.9	16	328	359.6	14.5	27	293	13.2	3.4
Chickasaw	19	60	7.6	2.3	39	1,391	662.1	67.9	27	247	9.0	2.5
Clarke	11	37	8.7	1.9	9	1,309	854.8	62.2	19	538	86.3	11.3
Clay	37	180	24.6	9.3	29	636	285.5	31.2	53	738	32.5	9.2
Clayton	24	94	8.9	3.0	28	924	202.3	38.1	52	341	13.1	3.4
Clinton	60	273	29.2	12.2	54	4,230	3,596.9	251.0	107	1,812	100.9	23.7
Crawford	21	97	9.1	3.0	18	2,171	943.2	104.2	35	412	17.9	4.6
Dallas	248	1,425	243.7	91.6	39	2,042	608.1	87.9	170	3,245	192.7	56.5
Davis	12	54	6.5	1.9	10	119	44.0	5.9	D	D	D	D
Decatur	7	30	2.3	0.6	5	D	11.9	D	9	88	3.8	1.1
Delaware	25	99	11.5	4.9	43	2,204	807.0	116.7	D	D	D	D
Des Moines	53	362	37.9	13.9	48	4,568	1,629.2	249.9	106	2,077	93.3	29.7
Dickinson	50	179	22.4	7.3	35	1,537	698.1	72.5	105	1,019	73.9	23.0
Dubuque	D	D	D	D	148	9,356	4,987.4	463.1	251	4,953	270.8	78.0
Emmet	16	60	7.2	2.9	17	614	188.8	29.0	20	240	9.9	2.9
Fayette	31	116	10.8	4.4	22	459	123.8	20.5	42	411	17.6	4.9
Floyd	24	75	7.4	2.9	19	1,264	809.9	73.3	31	350	16.1	3.9

STATE County	Health care and social assistance, 2017				Other services, 2017				Nonemployer businesses, 2019		Value of residential construction authorized by building permits, 2021	
	Number of establish-ments	Number of employees	Receipts (mil dol)	Annual payroll (mil dol)	Number of establish-ments	Number of employees	Receipts (mil dol)	Annual payroll (mil dol)	Number	Receipts (mil dol)	New construction ($1,000)	Number of housing units
	159	160	161	162	163	164	165	166	167	168	169	170
INDIANA—Cont'd												
Pike	14	299	17.1	5.8	20	64	8.2	2.6	558	22.5	0	0
Porter	389	8,715	959.2	369.0	292	1,837	191.5	54.7	10,567	478.3	206,126	653
Posey	44	395	27.2	11.1	49	177	20.8	5.3	1,377	52.4	11,454	47
Pulaski	17	535	43.8	19.3	28	86	8.6	2.1	811	30.2	3,352	17
Putnam	74	1,909	133.8	58.5	58	253	23.4	5.8	2,002	88.9	41,604	151
Randolph	47	801	58.4	24.5	37	124	12.7	2.9	1,364	54.1	3,118	19
Ripley	79	1,548	148.7	61.5	60	185	21.8	5.0	1,752	81.2	21,883	99
Rush	33	622	61.3	23.7	24	107	12.2	2.4	1,106	47.7	6,628	23
St. Joseph	663	19,436	2,404.8	829.9	431	3,025	354.6	99.3	16,229	675.6	132,673	364
Scott	59	1,306	91.2	34.4	D	D	D	D	1,115	39.7	17,720	77
Shelby	89	1,979	236.8	90.0	61	405	52.0	13.1	2,797	133.6	32,553	131
Spencer	29	220	22.3	6.6	30	188	20.9	6.6	1,177	46.9	16,062	62
Starke	26	424	55.5	20.0	26	85	14.7	2.4	1,204	47.5	13,390	80
Steuben	75	1,359	132.6	48.8	85	439	62.0	16.4	2,265	106.7	56,103	145
Sullivan	29	614	55.8	22.1	28	119	8.2	2.0	930	29.7	660	6
Switzerland	15	124	7.6	3.4	10	42	3.8	0.9	557	23.1	4,428	76
Tippecanoe	478	12,733	1,627.6	612.3	249	2,110	491.8	74.0	9,717	430.1	217,584	1,129
Tipton	34	593	73.0	25.2	26	92	15.3	2.6	1,031	45.1	6,664	32
Union	11	90	4.7	2.6	D	D	D	1.2	440	20.6	1,565	8
Vanderburgh	617	20,158	2,479.5	879.0	357	2,901	334.5	89.0	9,949	409.9	179,929	870
Vermillion	24	574	75.2	25.3	23	63	5.5	1.2	738	23.2	6,112	27
Vigo	371	9,441	1,268.8	440.5	172	1,053	124.8	29.2	4,908	188.5	6,443	37
Wabash	75	2,225	156.0	64.2	55	321	39.1	6.9	1,758	61.6	9,913	45
Warren	13	269	26.4	11.1	D	D	5.2	D	503	20.9	8,549	30
Warrick	151	3,806	485.9	172.3	98	524	51.4	14.6	4,093	185.3	124,665	374
Washington	57	680	52.7	21.4	31	142	15.1	3.2	1,711	72.9	10,415	49
Wayne	201	5,563	728.7	250.2	105	542	54.9	13.4	3,663	161.0	10,566	54
Wells	57	1,367	109.3	42.5	60	301	31.3	8.6	1,704	68.1	13,708	56
White	37	874	66.8	25.7	36	138	14.4	3.4	1,450	75.4	12,146	42
Whitley	62	1,323	120.9	45.6	66	408	43.4	11.6	2,104	83.8	35,060	115
IOWA	8,610	216,965	22,419.8	9,241.6	5,975	31,306	4,186.5	1,021.5	212,431	9,833.5	3,182,377	13,686
Adair	26	336	22.6	9.6	D	D	2.1	D	598	26.1	4,845	19
Adams	14	423	67.2	22.2	11	26	2.2	0.5	336	15.8	590	2
Allamakee	43	894	57.8	29.0	D	D	D	D	1,136	54.6	14,721	66
Appanoose	31	688	60.2	25.3	22	82	8.2	1.9	865	43.6	100	1
Audubon	17	305	24.0	10.2	18	48	7.0	1.4	459	21.6	1,749	5
Benton	51	815	73.0	26.3	D	D	D	3.7	1,816	75.8	12,432	41
Black Hawk	373	11,246	1,179.9	485.6	211	1,507	154.9	41.9	7,460	361.0	52,891	138
Boone	53	1,613	114.6	52.7	46	146	19.5	5.3	1,780	63.8	14,248	63
Bremer	63	1,756	133.0	63.2	55	206	21.5	6.2	1,776	83.2	18,405	49
Buchanan	40	937	72.4	35.5	24	83	6.8	2.0	1,511	74.6	5,069	20
Buena Vista	51	1,312	108.9	44.7	34	129	17.0	3.6	1,218	56.0	13,871	117
Butler	28	514	23.4	12.5	D	D	D	2.6	1,052	47.0	9,406	30
Calhoun	31	658	56.9	22.5	D	D	D	2.1	713	29.1	5,700	20
Carroll	110	2,246	199.8	83.2	65	285	27.0	6.4	1,951	100.2	12,554	56
Cass	47	1,174	98.7	42.3	40	252	18.6	4.6	1,131	46.6	1,924	6
Cedar	52	606	33.0	16.0	36	89	13.4	2.7	1,338	55.6	9,716	48
Cerro Gordo	138	4,072	391.7	181.4	D	D	D	D	2,802	115.5	13,802	40
Cherokee	43	861	78.0	38.0	23	57	7.8	1.7	842	37.0	2,375	6
Chickasaw	33	647	62.2	22.4	26	90	10.0	2.3	916	45.4	3,395	13
Clarke	27	521	47.3	18.2	15	53	6.4	1.1	558	23.0	15,363	120
Clay	63	1,485	171.9	68.5	42	227	20.9	5.7	1,333	77.8	4,764	20
Clayton	69	1,145	69.1	32.4	D	D	11.3	D	1,464	61.9	10,203	40
Clinton	128	3,359	255.0	107.2	97	317	33.8	8.3	2,645	109.6	10,851	67
Crawford	38	941	77.4	33.6	27	106	12.3	2.9	880	44.0	1,820	6
Dallas	202	3,989	402.1	170.7	119	476	39.5	12.2	7,151	381.2	380,716	1,481
Davis	20	435	40.0	16.7	11	29	2.8	0.6	733	52.1	971	57
Decatur	16	343	29.2	13.4	D	D	D	D	558	28.1	60	1
Delaware	37	1,109	89.9	40.9	41	147	16.5	4.1	1,324	75.0	7,874	48
Des Moines	148	3,534	402.5	166.8	84	396	44.5	10.2	2,375	86.9	4,633	40
Dickinson	63	951	84.7	31.9	41	196	18.9	5.1	1,749	91.2	99,306	385
Dubuque	283	8,469	943.9	405.4	205	1,118	135.7	31.4	6,472	303.4	109,497	537
Emmet	34	781	54.0	20.8	26	83	9.0	2.9	643	26.5	7,234	75
Fayette	53	1,302	91.3	43.1	49	219	28.1	7.0	1,311	53.8	4,504	23
Floyd	49	929	65.6	30.5	38	106	13.0	2.6	1,083	40.6	7,361	19

STATE County	Government employment and payroll, 2017									Local government finances, 2017				
			March payroll (percent of total)							General revenue				
												Taxes		
													Per capita[1] (dollars)	
	Full-time equivalent employees	March payroll (dollars)	Adminis-tration, judicial, and legal	Police and corrections	Fire protection	Highways and transpor-tation	Health and welfare	Natural resources and utilities	Education and libraries	Total (mil dol)	Inter-govern-mental (mil dol)	Total (mil dol)	Total	Property
	171	172	173	174	175	176	177	178	179	180	181	182	183	184
INDIANA—Cont'd														
Pike	376	1,267,623	15.7	9.9	0.0	4.7	4.6	3.9	61.1	47.2	17.8	26.4	2,144	1,901
Porter	5,027	18,091,151	5.3	10.3	4.0	3.2	0.9	5.1	69.2	545.8	244.5	213.1	1,265	1,187
Posey	873	2,782,425	8.1	8.2	1.0	6.0	5.3	5.9	63.3	71.4	31.2	29.1	1,138	1,119
Pulaski	761	2,900,049	6.3	6.4	0.7	2.1	48.4	2.8	33.0	106.3	21.3	11.1	889	851
Putnam	1,541	5,175,859	5.5	6.3	1.4	2.7	25.6	1.8	54.9	116.6	69.2	30.9	828	720
Randolph	917	2,927,259	9.3	9.1	3.5	3.4	2.7	2.9	67.3	82.0	36.9	36.8	1,479	1,469
Ripley	1,144	4,018,061	6.8	6.0	0.7	3.0	2.2	4.7	75.7	122.0	61.2	46.6	1,638	1,477
Rush	959	2,631,447	6.7	4.4	4.5	4.2	39.4	2.5	38.0	82.4	33.5	35.4	2,127	1,980
St. Joseph	8,426	31,242,839	6.0	13.1	8.2	4.8	2.4	7.1	57.0	1,052.2	450.4	395.1	1,463	1,159
Scott	971	3,502,719	8.3	7.3	0.2	1.8	20.4	9.5	51.0	63.9	36.2	18.1	761	717
Shelby	2,332	8,734,101	3.2	7.2	4.0	1.7	40.8	2.0	40.6	305.0	133.0	46.2	1,042	907
Spencer	735	2,727,729	6.8	7.5	0.1	2.9	1.4	4.6	75.5	51.8	27.7	14.1	691	661
Starke	720	2,236,687	9.2	10.2	0.2	4.9	4.1	2.5	67.4	73.3	34.9	30.3	1,323	1,279
Steuben	1,033	3,461,764	11.8	11.4	2.4	4.2	5.4	6.5	57.0	103.3	50.0	32.9	957	917
Sullivan	901	2,822,687	6.5	5.8	2.0	3.7	34.8	2.7	43.9	99.4	25.8	35.7	1,722	1,714
Switzerland	376	1,180,396	9.7	9.0	0.0	4.8	1.6	4.0	61.5	44.8	31.4	8.4	781	541
Tippecanoe	4,813	18,962,006	7.7	11.8	5.4	4.6	1.8	5.5	61.8	572.0	262.5	175.4	917	873
Tipton	976	3,778,449	5.5	4.2	1.6	1.6	46.3	5.3	34.7	87.2	23.4	50.7	3,348	3,121
Union	369	1,190,233	12.2	4.3	12.1	3.3	1.2	1.9	64.3	28.8	13.0	10.7	1,501	1,096
Vanderburgh	5,246	21,088,289	6.4	14.4	6.5	5.0	2.1	6.8	56.5	623.8	279.8	199.4	1,102	1,043
Vermillion	522	1,635,207	9.3	8.6	1.4	4.1	1.6	3.0	71.3	45.1	21.8	17.1	1,103	1,073
Vigo	3,041	12,168,829	7.9	11.1	6.8	4.5	2.2	4.0	62.3	354.2	164.1	107.7	1,001	869
Wabash	1,039	2,928,878	7.5	12.2	6.2	3.8	0.8	4.8	62.8	100.0	49.4	34.6	1,101	905
Warren	249	839,058	11.8	10.1	0.0	8.0	0.0	7.1	62.6	33.2	13.6	14.1	1,715	1,025
Warrick	1,874	6,732,032	7.6	6.2	0.8	2.6	1.0	4.4	76.9	189.5	92.4	54.2	869	821
Washington	1,007	3,213,506	6.6	6.9	1.0	2.9	2.0	2.9	76.9	84.9	37.8	41.7	1,502	1,312
Wayne	2,582	8,382,351	8.8	11.8	3.5	3.3	3.9	12.8	54.5	214.4	101.3	72.0	1,089	1,056
Wells	1,007	3,432,160	6.4	11.5	1.0	3.1	0.8	5.3	71.5	83.6	38.4	31.6	1,129	743
White	1,085	3,734,602	6.7	8.0	3.4	3.8	0.5	5.7	70.0	97.2	44.5	28.3	1,171	1,137
Whitley	934	3,049,878	6.9	15.4	0.0	6.3	1.7	2.6	65.1	91.5	44.6	27.9	827	782
IOWA	X	X	X	X	X	X	X	X	X	X	X	X	X	X
Adair	354	1,285,189	7.2	8.9	0.0	9.0	29.6	2.9	42.0	47.0	12.3	16.6	2,349	2,103
Adams	157	536,007	6.4	8.7	0.0	14.6	5.9	3.8	58.4	16.9	7.2	8.0	2,191	1,957
Allamakee	696	2,613,749	5.1	4.8	0.1	6.7	28.3	2.0	51.8	70.8	34.8	22.0	1,593	1,327
Appanoose	487	1,695,790	8.2	7.5	1.0	7.1	1.5	2.5	71.5	40.1	22.4	14.2	1,150	952
Audubon	329	1,358,335	6.5	4.5	0.0	6.9	37.5	1.4	42.6	28.3	11.2	12.0	2,168	1,909
Benton	947	3,311,970	5.1	7.1	0.3	6.3	1.2	8.0	71.6	93.9	44.1	39.5	1,539	1,375
Black Hawk	5,888	25,785,248	3.3	8.3	3.8	3.9	4.2	8.5	66.6	632.3	290.7	225.2	1,703	1,428
Boone	1,215	5,162,400	4.1	5.3	1.0	4.6	35.3	4.8	44.5	129.6	40.4	39.8	1,505	1,282
Bremer	1,085	4,122,991	6.2	7.2	0.0	5.1	2.4	3.7	73.9	174.1	50.8	47.5	1,914	1,644
Buchanan	918	3,620,791	4.4	5.5	0.6	4.6	28.2	4.7	51.2	96.9	31.7	29.3	1,388	1,210
Buena Vista	1,352	5,090,475	4.6	4.7	0.3	3.9	32.3	3.9	49.5	147.2	44.9	38.8	1,926	1,633
Butler	294	1,055,541	15.9	11.9	0.1	16.9	5.6	6.5	39.7	77.3	47.4	20.5	1,408	1,249
Calhoun	436	1,312,852	8.3	8.1	0.0	11.1	8.7	4.7	58.1	41.9	17.4	18.7	1,924	1,721
Carroll	863	3,050,468	6.9	6.8	0.1	7.3	4.3	8.9	63.6	94.9	34.5	38.2	1,883	1,533
Cass	847	3,327,200	4.3	3.9	0.5	4.6	48.0	2.5	35.0	109.5	27.2	30.5	2,320	2,039
Cedar	836	2,809,400	6.7	7.4	0.1	6.4	2.8	6.1	70.4	74.0	32.0	34.1	1,842	1,622
Cerro Gordo	1,648	6,969,938	4.9	9.0	3.3	8.9	4.0	6.8	61.9	207.4	72.8	81.2	1,889	1,558
Cherokee	412	1,513,267	10.4	8.1	0.6	9.1	0.4	6.7	64.0	44.6	18.5	20.5	1,809	1,506
Chickasaw	414	1,499,116	7.6	5.1	2.5	8.2	4.9	6.4	63.5	43.6	19.2	19.4	1,615	1,288
Clarke	569	1,988,284	4.8	6.3	0.0	5.1	30.2	3.3	49.5	64.1	20.2	16.8	1,784	1,545
Clay	1,189	4,750,090	3.8	4.5	0.6	6.4	41.5	8.7	31.9	171.3	30.6	31.5	1,951	1,618
Clayton	933	3,473,585	4.8	4.9	0.0	5.3	15.5	3.1	65.7	113.5	40.9	28.7	1,625	1,427
Clinton	1,789	6,779,889	5.3	8.4	3.6	6.0	2.3	4.4	66.8	199.2	83.7	85.7	1,828	1,486
Crawford	911	3,895,378	3.8	3.8	0.1	5.3	35.1	5.8	44.0	110.7	39.5	30.7	1,800	1,623
Dallas	2,920	12,020,235	4.6	4.2	0.7	2.3	5.1	2.6	79.3	348.1	145.8	153.2	1,757	1,655
Davis	430	1,804,127	4.8	4.9	0.4	5.0	39.5	2.6	42.5	54.3	17.0	11.2	1,252	1,119
Decatur	459	1,645,151	4.6	6.2	0.0	7.5	24.3	2.3	54.3	45.9	17.3	11.5	1,451	1,299
Delaware	1,012	4,298,102	3.6	3.6	0.0	4.1	47.3	1.6	39.5	120.6	28.4	33.4	1,949	1,687
Des Moines	1,812	7,541,692	4.6	7.2	3.2	3.8	1.6	3.4	74.8	195.4	87.2	67.3	1,711	1,383
Dickinson	882	3,384,380	8.1	6.7	0.1	4.5	28.3	6.2	45.3	120.7	17.3	54.4	3,173	2,769
Dubuque	3,536	14,203,131	6.2	8.7	3.8	7.3	5.2	4.6	62.8	432.9	186.4	173.0	1,782	1,463
Emmet	710	2,757,375	4.6	5.0	0.2	5.0	1.5	3.4	79.4	79.3	33.9	25.5	2,707	2,459
Fayette	867	2,840,894	4.8	9.5	0.4	6.9	1.6	4.8	70.6	80.6	37.9	31.0	1,576	1,356
Floyd	760	3,203,579	6.3	5.2	0.6	6.4	30.1	2.7	48.1	102.8	36.5	22.7	1,438	1,248

1. Based on the resident population estimated as of July 1 of the year shown.

STATE County	Local government finances, 2017 (cont.)									Government employment, 2020			Individual income tax returns, 2019		
	Direct general expenditure							Debt outstanding							
	Total (mil dol)	Per capita[1] (dollars)	Percent of total for: Education	Health and hospitals	Police protection	Public welfare	Highways	Total (mil dol)	Per capita[1] (dollars)	Federal civilian	Federal military	State and local	Number of returns	Mean adjusted gross income	Mean income tax
	185	186	187	188	189	190	191	192	193	194	195	196	197	198	199
INDIANA—Cont'd															
Pike	37.2	3,019	46.8	0.5	2.6	0.0	6.5	18.4	1,492	37	36	626	5,710	53,179	4,094
Porter	488.5	2,899	57.1	0.9	4.2	0.1	4.8	656.5	3,896	468	494	6,359	85,560	74,246	8,586
Posey	54.8	2,144	72.1	0.1	2.0	0.1	1.9	55.3	2,161	75	74	1,059	12,150	72,008	7,540
Pulaski	55.5	4,431	45.6	25.5	3.3	0.0	5.7	39.3	3,136	45	36	978	6,000	50,624	4,119
Putnam	94.8	2,537	64.8	1.3	2.6	0.1	7.1	89.2	2,387	85	96	2,280	16,310	55,390	4,818
Randolph	70.0	2,812	62.6	0.2	3.6	2.2	2.4	48.1	1,931	65	70	1,128	11,450	45,208	3,328
Ripley	88.1	3,101	71.0	0.1	1.9	0.0	4.7	91.0	3,201	76	82	1,200	13,980	55,643	5,053
Rush	75.8	4,553	28.1	0.8	2.8	0.1	12.1	48.4	2,911	41	49	1,017	8,100	50,954	4,124
St. Joseph	871.5	3,227	43.1	1.4	6.4	0.0	4.4	651.7	2,413	904	850	12,498	128,950	59,267	6,202
Scott	84.5	3,553	45.4	7.2	3.5	0.0	5.0	44.7	1,879	86	69	1,088	10,820	46,730	3,452
Shelby	261.2	5,886	26.4	60.4	2.8	0.0	0.4	219.7	4,951	129	130	2,538	21,850	57,354	5,188
Spencer	54.5	2,669	57.3	0.6	2.8	0.0	5.5	29.0	1,420	66	59	918	9,830	57,656	5,022
Starke	57.6	2,513	60.1	2.4	1.8	0.0	6.5	46.1	2,009	45	68	864	10,650	48,106	3,780
Steuben	102.0	2,966	46.3	3.9	4.9	0.0	3.7	87.7	2,550	63	99	1,385	16,860	60,310	6,220
Sullivan	138.9	6,712	19.4	24.0	2.7	0.0	3.6	80.8	3,903	57	55	1,879	8,880	49,692	3,811
Switzerland	35.1	3,288	47.6	1.9	2.7	0.0	7.0	9.0	838	22	31	451	4,330	47,335	3,573
Tippecanoe	495.3	2,591	50.5	0.5	5.0	0.6	7.0	455.2	2,381	460	607	24,025	78,040	63,201	6,662
Tipton	84.0	5,551	30.7	0.3	1.2	0.0	4.7	75.1	4,964	38	44	711	7,760	57,992	5,127
Union	30.0	4,187	54.0	0.8	3.0	0.0	7.3	14.6	2,036	14	21	365	3,340	48,219	3,499
Vanderburgh	561.4	3,103	43.3	1.8	8.0	0.3	3.0	993.1	5,488	1,140	568	9,401	87,710	58,439	6,182
Vermillion	57.9	3,737	51.7	0.3	3.0	0.1	3.9	44.2	2,849	32	45	655	7,330	48,750	3,703
Vigo	323.4	3,007	46.1	0.8	6.9	0.0	2.8	295.7	2,749	1,094	304	7,637	46,710	51,696	4,855
Wabash	100.7	3,209	50.3	0.8	5.3	0.0	9.4	64.3	2,050	79	85	1,410	15,020	55,735	5,226
Warren	26.1	3,184	52.4	1.7	4.0	0.1	7.3	17.1	2,087	12	24	335	4,020	57,442	4,950
Warrick	181.1	2,902	55.1	0.5	3.3	0.0	3.6	86.1	1,380	125	184	2,011	31,090	81,697	10,392
Washington	69.4	2,498	70.8	0.4	3.9	0.0	5.8	55.1	1,986	67	82	1,063	12,870	46,549	3,495
Wayne	211.2	3,192	45.6	3.7	5.2	0.0	3.8	140.7	2,127	174	187	4,536	30,460	48,372	4,211
Wells	84.1	3,007	52.4	0.6	5.4	0.0	5.2	62.5	2,234	54	82	1,216	13,470	57,301	4,787
White	98.9	4,095	50.3	0.3	2.4	0.0	5.3	74.4	3,081	59	70	1,263	12,240	53,446	4,732
Whitley	83.1	2,463	48.8	0.6	3.8	0.0	6.6	74.7	2,216	83	100	1,356	17,100	60,816	5,627
IOWA	X	X	X	X	X	X	X	X	X	18,155	11,312	235,106	1,489,240	66,348	6,927
Adair	41.2	5,850	43.7	17.2	3.6	0.3	20.8	45.4	6,434	32	25	431	3,550	51,342	4,108
Adams	20.5	5,618	34.7	6.1	7.5	0.9	20.0	12.1	3,299	24	13	188	1,770	48,989	3,976
Allamakee	72.3	5,235	39.4	27.9	3.8	0.3	12.9	30.9	2,241	70	48	1,012	6,600	49,192	4,090
Appanoose	43.9	3,557	57.5	2.3	8.2	1.5	11.9	14.2	1,149	48	44	613	5,490	45,936	3,650
Audubon	39.6	7,137	31.4	36.7	4.0	0.2	14.0	11.5	2,063	33	19	344	2,750	57,173	4,880
Benton	92.1	3,590	47.8	3.7	4.5	0.2	13.0	114.3	4,456	60	90	1,436	11,990	66,336	5,897
Black Hawk	672.1	5,082	54.9	3.3	4.9	1.3	5.4	488.7	3,696	561	485	10,302	59,970	62,143	6,338
Boone	134.2	5,075	36.6	33.4	4.0	1.0	10.1	189.6	7,171	115	92	2,155	12,770	64,133	5,813
Bremer	118.1	4,756	58.0	5.4	4.4	0.1	7.0	96.1	3,870	61	85	1,829	11,250	71,869	6,915
Buchanan	110.9	5,252	33.0	36.1	3.4	0.1	8.5	86.2	4,079	54	75	1,417	9,530	60,623	5,426
Buena Vista	149.2	7,408	38.7	30.8	3.1	0.1	5.9	129.6	6,435	86	69	1,632	9,660	56,460	4,686
Butler	76.7	5,255	28.8	37.1	3.8	0.3	10.8	30.6	2,094	42	51	688	6,690	59,872	5,029
Calhoun	44.6	4,582	48.7	7.7	4.5	0.8	14.2	16.8	1,722	32	31	594	4,480	55,549	4,441
Carroll	85.9	4,239	44.9	3.1	4.3	0.4	14.0	44.7	2,206	76	71	1,194	10,050	64,678	6,106
Cass	112.4	8,551	32.4	42.6	2.7	0.2	7.5	108.9	8,282	67	45	1,321	6,170	55,459	5,018
Cedar	77.1	4,167	52.1	5.8	4.8	0.1	15.0	47.0	2,540	85	65	975	9,020	62,936	5,643
Cerro Gordo	207.0	4,813	51.8	4.7	6.4	0.4	6.5	139.0	3,232	169	147	2,634	20,850	63,384	6,433
Cherokee	46.0	4,068	48.3	3.5	4.4	0.1	16.7	23.4	2,070	41	39	969	5,570	58,211	4,932
Chickasaw	42.4	3,536	49.6	5.1	4.9	0.1	17.4	34.4	2,867	52	42	561	5,680	57,939	5,291
Clarke	67.6	7,197	32.5	38.8	3.5	0.3	9.0	27.6	2,935	34	33	795	4,490	49,197	3,719
Clay	174.3	10,801	19.4	52.3	2.0	0.3	5.7	160.9	9,965	59	57	1,488	7,910	62,477	5,976
Clayton	126.4	7,161	43.9	25.9	3.1	0.3	9.6	40.7	2,309	79	61	1,162	8,360	53,060	4,838
Clinton	191.6	4,087	50.0	0.3	5.7	0.0	10.3	260.8	5,563	110	165	2,396	22,330	55,613	4,804
Crawford	104.4	6,113	35.2	35.6	2.9	0.1	9.5	56.6	3,313	58	59	1,171	7,690	54,294	4,364
Dallas	355.6	4,078	66.2	6.3	3.3	0.3	6.5	470.3	5,392	112	356	4,070	46,790	104,188	14,455
Davis	53.1	5,925	28.2	47.1	3.3	0.3	9.6	19.1	2,129	34	32	527	3,670	49,362	3,577
Decatur	46.6	5,867	41.5	29.8	3.9	0.2	10.4	30.7	3,867	29	26	516	3,040	46,376	4,016
Delaware	118.5	6,911	28.2	46.0	2.8	0.1	7.9	68.5	3,996	34	64	1,278	8,300	57,253	4,880
Des Moines	213.3	5,423	66.0	2.1	4.4	0.2	5.0	106.4	2,705	209	138	2,358	19,050	57,208	5,408
Dickinson	109.2	6,372	28.9	34.5	4.2	0.3	8.5	128.4	7,489	79	62	1,168	9,250	76,289	8,710
Dubuque	417.0	4,296	46.7	1.8	5.2	0.3	5.1	473.0	4,873	286	356	4,373	47,890	68,985	7,641
Emmet	88.2	9,365	72.7	3.1	3.0	0.2	6.1	67.0	7,109	35	31	659	4,430	52,621	3,996
Fayette	85.8	4,360	57.0	2.9	5.0	0.2	12.3	49.5	2,513	77	66	1,081	8,850	48,750	4,168
Floyd	86.2	5,465	36.1	33.2	3.6	0.5	9.4	42.8	2,713	48	55	917	7,380	53,753	4,566

1. Based on the resident population estimated as of July 1 of the year shown.

Table B. States and Counties — **Land Area and Population**

State / county code	CBSA code[1]	County Type code[2]	STATE County	Land area[3] (sq. mi)	Population, 2021: Total persons 2021	Population, 2021: Rank	Population, 2021: Per square mile	Race alone or in combination, not Hispanic or Latino (percent): White	Black	American Indian, Alaska Native	Asian and Pacific Islancer	Percent Hispanic or Latino[4]	Age (percent): Under 5 years	5 to 17 years	18 to 24 years	25 to 34 years	35 to 44 years	45 to 54 years
				1	2	3	4	5	6	7	8	9	10	11	12	13	14	15
			IOWA—Cont'd															
19069		7	Franklin	582.0	9,952	2,410	17.1	84.6	1.3	0.6	0.8	13.7	6.1	13.1	11.3	9.9	12.0	10.8
19071		8	Fremont	511.2	6,567	2,694	12.8	95.0	1.6	0.9	0.7	3.2	5.2	12.7	10.8	10.2	11.2	11.6
19073		6	Greene	569.6	8,717	2,508	15.3	94.9	1.3	0.8	1.0	3.3	5.4	13.0	11.1	10.1	11.3	10.9
19075	47940	3	Grundy	501.9	12,347	2,253	24.6	97.2	1.1	0.5	0.6	1.6	5.4	13.6	11.3	10.7	12.5	11.4
19077	19780	2	Guthrie	590.6	10,567	2,372	17.9	95.6	1.3	0.8	0.7	2.9	4.8	11.8	11.1	9.5	11.6	11.6
19079		6	Hamilton	576.7	14,887	2,093	25.8	89.1	1.8	0.8	2.8	7.1	6.0	12.9	11.0	10.4	11.8	11.6
19081		7	Hancock	571.0	10,663	2,365	18.7	93.1	1.2	0.5	0.9	5.3	5.6	11.8	11.2	10.3	11.7	10.6
19083		6	Hardin	569.3	16,708	1,992	29.3	92.5	2.0	0.7	1.3	4.7	4.8	10.4	12.0	10.6	12.2	11.3
19085	36540	2	Harrison	696.9	14,669	2,103	21.0	96.5	1.0	0.7	0.7	2.3	5.9	13.7	10.9	10.6	11.9	12.2
19087		6	Henry	434.3	20,387	1,798	46.9	89.0	3.5	0.8	2.9	5.4	5.2	12.2	13.6	11.6	12.2	11.8
19089		6	Howard	473.2	9,478	2,452	20.0	96.4	1.3	0.5	0.8	2.0	6.8	13.9	11.7	10.6	11.8	10.5
19091		7	Humboldt	434.4	9,634	2,442	22.2	93.0	1.4	0.5	0.9	5.3	6.1	13.7	11.0	10.7	12.5	9.8
19093		8	Ida	431.5	6,956	2,667	16.1	94.5	1.1	0.6	1.0	4.0	5.7	14.9	12.2	9.9	11.7	10.5
19095		6	Iowa	586.5	16,568	1,996	28.2	95.3	1.2	0.5	0.8	3.3	5.5	13.5	11.0	10.8	12.3	11.5
19097		6	Jackson	636.0	19,368	1,855	30.5	95.9	1.4	0.6	1.5	1.8	5.7	12.6	11.0	10.3	10.9	11.6
19099	19780	6	Jasper	730.4	37,764	1,228	51.7	93.5	2.8	0.7	1.1	3.0	5.4	12.5	11.4	12.3	13.0	12.2
19101	21840	7	Jefferson	435.5	15,647	2,052	35.9	83.1	2.9	1.1	11.3	3.7	4.2	8.9	13.4	13.7	11.6	10.6
19103	26980	3	Johnson	613.0	154,748	443	252.4	79.3	9.0	0.7	7.5	6.0	5.4	11.0	23.6	15.0	12.5	10.0
19105	16300	2	Jones	575.6	20,805	1,771	36.1	94.1	3.0	0.6	0.8	2.4	4.9	11.9	11.0	11.2	12.9	12.0
19107		8	Keokuk	579.2	9,914	2,416	17.1	96.4	1.4	0.4	0.6	2.4	5.5	13.0	11.2	10.7	12.0	11.1
19109		7	Kossuth	972.7	14,529	2,113	14.9	93.7	1.4	0.4	0.9	4.6	5.7	12.1	10.9	10.2	10.9	10.1
19111	22800	5	Lee	517.6	33,215	1,350	64.2	92.0	4.2	0.8	1.2	3.8	5.5	12.1	10.8	11.6	12.1	11.7
19113	16300	2	Linn	717.1	228,939	303	319.3	87.0	8.1	0.6	3.6	3.7	5.9	12.8	13.0	13.2	13.5	12.1
19115		8	Louisa	401.8	10,749	2,363	26.8	78.6	1.7	0.7	3.8	16.2	5.4	12.4	11.4	11.1	12.8	11.7
19117		6	Lucas	430.7	8,710	2,512	20.2	96.0	0.9	0.7	0.6	2.8	6.2	13.1	10.6	10.9	10.4	11.1
19119		8	Lyon	587.6	12,011	2,284	20.4	95.6	0.9	0.5	1.0	3.2	7.3	15.7	12.9	10.5	12.4	10.4
19121	19780	2	Madison	561.0	16,773	1,987	29.9	95.6	1.1	0.7	1.3	2.6	5.5	14.6	12.1	9.9	13.4	13.4
19123	36820	7	Mahaska	570.9	21,984	1,714	38.5	93.3	2.7	0.6	2.2	2.5	6.2	13.4	14.6	11.2	12.1	11.2
19125	37800	6	Marion	554.5	33,380	1,348	60.2	95.2	1.5	0.5	1.8	2.3	5.4	13.6	14.6	10.4	12.2	11.4
19127	32260	4	Marshall	572.5	39,853	1,187	69.6	68.6	2.8	0.8	4.4	24.9	6.3	14.5	13.1	11.9	11.8	11.2
19129	36540	2	Mills	437.4	14,465	2,122	33.1	94.5	1.2	1.0	0.9	3.7	5.0	13.5	11.4	9.8	12.3	13.5
19131		7	Mitchell	469.3	10,555	2,374	22.5	96.7	0.9	0.4	0.8	2.0	5.8	13.8	11.7	10.7	11.1	10.8
19133		6	Monona	694.1	8,574	2,530	12.4	95.0	1.4	2.2	0.5	2.2	5.7	12.0	11.3	10.8	10.5	10.6
19135		7	Monroe	433.7	7,610	2,605	17.5	96.0	1.7	0.5	0.7	2.5	6.1	13.2	11.8	10.9	11.7	12.0
19137		6	Montgomery	424.1	10,322	2,388	24.3	94.0	1.2	0.8	0.8	4.3	5.8	13.0	11.4	10.7	10.8	11.6
19139	34700	4	Muscatine	437.4	42,688	1,132	97.6	77.1	3.3	0.7	1.5	18.8	5.9	14.1	12.5	12.3	12.3	11.9
19141		7	O'Brien	573.0	14,015	2,150	24.5	91.9	1.7	0.4	1.1	6.0	6.3	13.4	12.4	11.1	12.0	10.4
19143		7	Osceola	398.7	6,159	2,725	15.4	87.8	1.6	0.8	1.6	9.5	5.9	13.1	11.3	10.3	10.9	10.7
19145		6	Page	534.9	15,197	2,078	28.4	91.2	3.8	1.1	1.5	3.9	4.3	10.1	11.2	12.5	13.0	12.1
19147		7	Palo Alto	563.9	8,906	2,496	15.8	93.6	2.1	0.7	1.4	3.3	6.0	12.9	12.2	11.0	11.4	10.1
19149		3	Plymouth	862.8	25,650	1,581	29.7	90.6	2.5	0.8	1.4	6.0	5.9	14.5	12.2	10.6	12.6	11.4
19151		9	Pocahontas	577.2	7,074	2,656	12.3	92.5	1.5	0.8	1.5	5.0	6.2	12.5	10.7	9.9	10.5	10.0
19153	19780	2	Polk	572.2	496,844	145	868.3	78.0	8.9	0.6	6.0	9.1	6.5	13.8	12.8	15.2	14.3	12.1
19155	36540	2	Pottawattamie	951.3	93,304	647	98.1	87.9	2.7	1.0	1.6	8.7	5.8	13.3	12.5	11.8	12.4	11.8
19157		7	Poweshiek	584.9	18,586	1,893	31.8	92.6	2.0	0.7	2.8	3.5	4.6	11.5	18.1	9.7	11.0	10.5
19159		9	Ringgold	535.5	4,639	2,845	8.7	95.3	1.0	0.6	1.1	2.8	5.3	12.6	12.4	9.0	11.2	10.2
19161		9	Sac	575.0	9,752	2,431	17.0	94.5	1.1	0.5	0.9	4.1	5.9	12.5	10.8	10.4	10.6	10.6
19163	19340	2	Scott	458.1	174,170	385	380.2	81.4	9.8	0.9	3.8	7.4	5.9	13.4	12.4	12.6	13.6	12.1
19165		6	Shelby	590.8	11,770	2,297	19.9	94.6	1.5	0.8	1.0	3.5	5.6	13.2	11.4	9.6	10.2	11.4
19167		7	Sioux	767.9	35,893	1,286	46.7	86.7	0.9	0.4	1.0	11.7	7.0	15.4	17.9	10.4	12.0	9.6
19169	11180	3	Story	572.5	99,472	613	173.8	85.0	3.6	0.5	8.6	4.0	4.2	9.3	32.2	13.2	10.2	8.4
19171		6	Tama	721.0	16,867	1,982	23.4	80.4	1.6	7.2	1.0	11.9	6.0	13.6	12.2	10.3	11.2	11.8
19173		9	Taylor	531.9	5,868	2,746	11.0	90.2	1.0	0.6	0.7	8.7	5.8	13.7	11.4	9.7	12.4	10.2
19175		6	Union	423.6	12,018	2,283	28.4	94.3	1.7	0.7	1.1	3.2	5.4	12.7	13.5	10.6	12.2	11.2
19177		9	Van Buren	484.8	7,243	2,644	14.9	97.2	0.9	0.5	0.9	1.7	6.6	12.8	11.1	9.8	11.2	11.5
19179	36900	5	Wapello	431.8	35,256	1,300	81.6	80.0	4.7	0.7	4.3	11.8	6.4	13.0	12.3	12.8	12.4	11.5
19181	19780	2	Warren	569.8	53,402	951	93.7	94.5	1.6	0.6	1.5	3.4	5.8	14.4	13.6	11.4	13.6	12.4
19183	26980	3	Washington	568.8	22,491	1,697	39.5	90.8	1.5	0.5	1.1	7.4	6.6	14.1	11.5	11.7	11.7	11.0
19185		9	Wayne	525.5	6,508	2,699	12.4	96.6	1.2	0.6	1.0	2.1	7.2	14.8	11.5	10.2	10.4	9.7
19187	22700	5	Webster	715.7	37,147	1,249	51.9	87.4	6.5	0.7	1.6	6.2	5.9	12.0	15.3	12.7	11.5	10.4
19189		7	Winnebago	400.5	10,656	2,366	26.6	91.9	2.2	0.6	1.4	5.4	5.2	12.9	14.0	10.1	11.4	10.7
19191		7	Winneshiek	689.8	19,892	1,822	28.8	95.4	1.3	0.3	1.3	2.4	4.5	10.3	18.6	9.0	10.2	10.5
19193	43580	3	Woodbury	872.9	105,607	582	121.0	71.4	6.4	2.2	4.2	18.6	6.8	14.8	14.4	12.7	12.8	11.4
19195	32380	9	Worth	400.1	7,385	2,631	18.5	94.9	1.3	0.6	0.9	3.5	5.7	11.7	10.3	11.5	12.0	12.1
19197		7	Wright	580.4	12,785	2,223	22.0	84.2	1.5	0.7	0.9	13.9	6.5	13.8	11.3	10.1	11.1	10.6

1. CBSA = Core Based Statistical Area. See Appendix A for explanation. See Appendix B for list of metropolitan areas with component counties. 2. County type code from the Economic Research Service of USDA Rural-Urban Continuum Codes. See Appendix A for definition. 3. Dry land or land partially or temporarily covered by water. 4. May be of any race.

STATE County	Population, 2021 (cont.)				Population change, 2000–2021							Households, 2016–2020				
	Age (percent) (cont.)				Total persons		Percent change		Components of change, 2020–2021					Percent		
	55 to 64 years	65 to 74 years	75 years and over	Percent female	2010	2020	2010–2020	2020–2021	Births	Deaths	Net Migration	Number	Persons per household	Family house-holds	Female family house-holder[1]	One person
	16	17	18	19	20	21	22	23	24	25	26	27	28	29	30	31
IOWA—Cont'd																
Franklin	14.3	12.9	9.5	48.9	10,680	10,019	-6.2	-0.7	171	182	-58	4,195	2.4	68.1	8.1	27.7
Fremont	15.2	13.6	9.5	48.9	7,441	6,605	-11.2	-0.6	74	115	3	2,952	2.3	64.6	7.5	27.7
Greene	14.7	13.2	10.2	50.1	9,336	8,771	-6.1	-0.6	98	139	-14	4,037	2.2	61.6	10.4	32.3
Grundy	14.0	11.8	9.3	50.3	12,453	12,329	-1.0	0.1	153	189	55	5,164	2.3	69.6	6.0	25.5
Guthrie	16.0	13.7	9.8	49.6	10,954	10,623	-3.0	-0.5	111	197	30	4,478	2.4	69.4	7.5	26.2
Hamilton	15.2	11.8	9.2	49.8	15,673	15,039	-4.0	-1.0	215	246	-121	6,122	2.4	65.1	7.8	32.0
Hancock	15.1	13.6	10.0	49.5	11,341	10,795	-4.8	-1.2	141	177	-96	4,787	2.2	69.2	7.0	25.3
Hardin	15.4	13.2	10.1	49.4	17,534	16,878	-3.7	-1.0	173	305	-39	7,185	2.2	61.7	7.5	33.7
Harrison	15.4	11.7	7.9	49.3	14,928	14,582	-2.3	0.6	207	296	178	6,094	2.3	69.4	7.7	25.2
Henry	13.7	11.3	8.3	47.8	20,145	20,482	1.7	-0.5	236	330	-1	7,591	2.4	67.2	10.1	28.8
Howard	14.6	11.4	8.8	49.5	9,566	9,469	-1.0	0.1	155	156	10	3,754	2.4	68.1	8.4	28.4
Humboldt	14.9	12.0	9.3	50.1	9,815	9,597	-2.2	0.4	140	157	54	4,195	2.2	61.6	8.2	32.4
Ida	13.7	12.2	9.1	49.8	7,089	7,005	-1.2	-0.7	88	148	13	2,972	2.3	64.0	5.4	31.3
Iowa	15.8	11.1	8.3	49.4	16,355	16,662	1.9	-0.6	201	276	-20	6,646	2.4	67.7	7.2	26.4
Jackson	16.3	12.7	8.9	49.6	19,848	19,485	-1.8	-0.6	251	329	-38	8,183	2.3	66.9	8.1	26.8
Jasper	13.9	11.0	8.3	48.1	36,842	37,813	2.6	-0.1	482	603	67	14,644	2.4	68.4	9.7	26.9
Jefferson	13.2	16.7	7.7	45.8	16,843	15,663	-7.0	-0.1	176	271	81	6,855	2.5	55.9	6.9	37.6
Johnson	9.6	8.1	4.7	50.3	130,882	152,854	16.8	1.2	2,074	1,182	962	60,430	2.4	54.1	7.1	29.2
Jones	14.8	12.3	8.9	47.7	20,638	20,646	0.0	0.8	233	302	230	8,186	2.4	63.9	9.3	30.2
Keokuk	14.4	12.8	9.3	49.3	10,511	10,033	-4.5	-1.2	123	179	-65	4,330	2.3	61.2	6.9	33.4
Kossuth	15.4	13.2	11.5	48.8	15,543	14,828	-4.6	-2.0	192	239	-248	6,575	2.2	61.1	6.7	33.6
Lee	14.8	13.0	8.4	49.3	35,862	33,555	-6.4	-1.0	414	589	-168	14,338	2.3	65.5	9.1	29.2
Linn	12.8	9.9	6.7	50.5	211,226	230,299	9.0	-0.6	3,291	2,943	-1,723	91,304	2.4	62.5	9.2	29.4
Louisa	15.3	11.7	8.1	48.9	11,387	10,837	-4.8	-0.8	134	140	-83	4,343	2.5	70.5	6.0	24.5
Lucas	15.5	12.6	9.5	48.7	8,898	8,634	-3.0	0.9	126	137	88	3,718	2.3	68.3	9.3	27.8
Lyon	11.9	10.5	8.2	48.7	11,581	11,934	3.0	0.6	208	171	40	4,593	2.5	73.2	5.8	23.4
Madison	13.7	10.6	6.7	49.9	15,679	16,548	5.5	1.4	222	201	204	6,619	2.4	74.5	7.0	22.9
Mahaska	13.2	10.5	7.6	48.6	22,381	22,190	-0.9	-0.9	311	339	-179	8,947	2.4	66.0	8.5	28.1
Marion	13.7	10.7	7.9	49.6	33,309	33,414	0.3	-0.1	434	476	7	13,532	2.3	69.0	7.7	25.6
Marshall	13.1	10.5	7.6	49.0	40,648	40,105	-1.3	-0.6	604	688	-172	15,388	2.5	65.1	9.1	28.6
Mills	14.7	12.6	7.2	49.4	15,059	14,484	-3.8	-0.1	191	199	-11	5,442	2.7	67.5	7.3	27.3
Mitchell	15.3	11.2	9.6	49.7	10,776	10,565	-2.0	-0.1	150	175	14	4,472	2.3	65.9	7.8	31.9
Monona	15.0	12.7	11.4	51.1	9,243	8,751	-5.3	-2.0	109	229	-55	3,988	2.1	60.1	8.0	35.3
Monroe	14.5	11.7	8.2	50.2	7,970	7,577	-4.9	0.4	123	139	48	3,243	2.4	61.6	4.8	33.4
Montgomery	14.7	12.7	9.4	50.8	10,740	10,330	-3.8	-0.1	127	214	80	4,479	2.2	63.3	11.3	30.8
Muscatine	13.3	10.8	6.8	49.8	42,745	43,235	1.1	-1.3	562	586	-523	16,543	2.5	67.2	12.8	26.7
O'Brien	13.5	11.6	9.2	48.8	14,398	14,182	-1.5	-1.2	208	286	-89	5,976	2.3	60.5	4.4	32.5
Osceola	14.9	12.3	10.5	49.1	6,462	6,192	-4.2	-0.5	79	113	-1	2,664	2.2	61.6	7.0	29.8
Page	13.9	13.3	9.6	45.9	15,932	15,211	-4.5	-0.1	160	271	98	6,414	2.2	60.5	7.0	35.6
Palo Alto	14.0	12.5	9.9	49.7	9,421	8,996	-4.5	-1.0	124	160	-54	3,712	2.3	58.7	5.8	36.7
Plymouth	13.7	11.3	7.9	49.5	24,986	25,698	2.8	-0.2	338	370	-17	10,298	2.4	72.3	7.4	23.5
Pocahontas	16.5	13.0	10.7	50.0	7,310	7,078	-3.2	-0.1	101	119	14	3,127	2.1	59.4	6.4	32.1
Polk	11.7	8.6	5.1	50.3	430,640	492,401	14.3	0.9	7,851	5,653	2,168	191,125	2.5	61.3	11.3	30.2
Pottawattamie	14.0	11.2	7.0	50.5	93,158	93,667	0.5	-0.4	1,288	1,514	-153	36,875	2.5	64.1	12.2	29.6
Poweshiek	13.6	11.8	9.2	51.2	18,914	18,662	-1.3	-0.4	187	285	19	7,827	2.1	60.1	8.3	33.8
Ringgold	15.3	12.9	11.1	49.8	5,131	4,663	-9.1	-0.5	51	99	23	1,843	2.6	67.0	8.0	29.7
Sac	15.3	13.5	10.4	49.9	10,350	9,814	-5.2	-0.6	121	167	-15	4,344	2.2	63.9	6.6	32.0
Scott	12.9	10.4	6.7	50.6	165,224	174,669	5.7	-0.3	2,484	2,383	-632	67,437	2.5	63.4	11.2	30.0
Shelby	15.8	12.2	10.5	50.3	12,167	11,746	-3.5	0.2	147	216	96	5,066	2.2	63.4	6.1	30.7
Sioux	11.4	9.0	7.2	49.7	33,704	35,872	6.4	0.1	600	413	-168	12,379	2.6	72.4	3.6	23.2
Story	9.3	7.8	5.2	47.8	89,542	98,537	10.0	0.9	983	769	700	37,997	2.3	49.8	5.2	31.5
Tama	14.6	11.8	8.6	49.5	17,767	17,135	-3.6	-1.6	241	310	-198	6,736	2.5	65.2	8.6	29.8
Taylor	14.1	12.6	10.1	48.6	6,317	5,896	-6.7	-0.5	75	108	5	2,567	2.4	62.0	5.1	31.2
Union	13.5	11.8	9.1	51.0	12,534	12,138	-3.2	-1.0	148	214	-56	5,199	2.3	60.4	8.8	31.9
Van Buren	14.8	13.6	8.6	48.8	7,570	7,203	-4.8	0.6	119	122	42	2,969	2.4	65.0	6.8	30.0
Wapello	13.1	11.1	7.3	49.7	35,625	35,437	-0.5	-0.5	553	620	-118	14,404	2.4	64.8	11.3	29.8
Warren	12.7	9.9	6.3	50.3	46,225	52,403	13.4	1.9	676	668	997	19,320	2.5	69.2	8.2	25.2
Washington	13.6	11.4	8.4	50.0	21,704	22,565	4.0	-0.3	367	348	-95	8,876	2.5	70.8	10.0	24.1
Wayne	14.2	12.0	9.9	49.8	6,403	6,497	1.5	0.2	115	121	18	2,620	2.4	64.2	6.9	31.0
Webster	13.6	11.0	7.6	47.1	38,013	36,999	-2.7	0.4	546	667	267	15,605	2.1	56.9	9.6	36.2
Winnebago	13.8	12.5	9.5	50.1	10,866	10,679	-1.7	-0.2	128	183	31	4,533	2.2	58.0	10.3	36.2
Winneshiek	14.9	12.8	9.3	49.8	21,056	20,070	-4.7	-0.9	216	267	-127	8,265	2.2	63.8	6.8	30.5
Woodbury	11.9	9.5	5.8	49.8	102,172	105,941	3.7	-0.3	1,764	1,478	-640	39,523	2.5	65.3	13.7	27.7
Worth	14.6	13.0	9.1	48.5	7,598	7,443	-2.0	-0.8	104	102	-59	3,199	2.3	65.6	7.3	29.9
Wright	13.4	12.8	10.4	49.1	13,229	12,943	-2.2	-1.2	201	241	-116	5,582	2.2	61.3	8.5	32.7

1. No spouse present.

STATE County	Persons in group quarters, 2021	Daytime Population, 2016–2020		Births, 2021		Deaths, 2021		Persons under 65 with no health insurance, 2019		Medicare, 2021			COVID-19 Deaths, 2020	
		Number	Employment/ residence ratio	Total	Rate[1]	Number	Rate[1]	Number	Percent	Total beneficiaries	Enrolled in Original Medicare	Enrolled in Medicare Advantage	Number	Rate[1]
	32	33	34	35	36	37	38	39	40	41	42	43	44	45
IOWA—Cont'd														
Franklin	149	9,707	0.9	135	13.5	138	13.8	557	7.1	2,388	2,216	172	19	1.9
Fremont	84	6,007	0.7	55	8.4	90	13.7	275	5.2	1,757	1,529	228	D	D
Greene	63	8,333	0.9	77	8.8	111	12.7	345	5.1	2,333	1,863	469	D	D
Grundy	118	10,357	0.7	128	10.4	146	11.8	397	4.1	2,895	2,211	684	31	2.5
Guthrie	121	9,144	0.7	91	8.6	162	15.3	521	6.4	2,756	2,124	633	25	2.4
Hamilton	171	13,813	0.9	172	11.5	208	13.9	627	5.4	3,401	2,887	514	35	2.3
Hancock	166	10,673	1.0	100	9.3	140	13.1	420	5.2	2,692	2,572	120	26	2.4
Hardin	730	16,809	1.0	129	7.7	252	15.0	732	5.9	4,180	3,535	645	32	1.9
Harrison	268	11,091	0.6	161	11.0	234	16.0	576	5.2	3,311	2,742	569	65	4.5
Henry	1,569	20,539	1.1	197	9.7	260	12.7	758	5.2	4,498	3,925	573	35	1.7
Howard	177	8,832	0.9	120	12.7	130	13.7	435	6.1	2,230	2,096	134	20	2.1
Humboldt	82	9,169	0.9	111	11.5	131	13.6	420	5.7	2,233	2,093	140	23	2.4
Ida	93	7,595	1.2	68	9.7	117	16.8	276	5.2	1,680	1,482	198	32	4.6
Iowa	262	16,829	1.1	142	8.5	223	13.4	535	4.1	3,593	2,795	798	23	1.4
Jackson	159	17,169	0.8	198	10.2	265	13.7	820	5.4	4,904	3,199	1,705	35	1.8
Jasper	1,774	30,644	0.6	370	9.8	489	12.9	1,260	4.4	8,259	6,238	2,021	62	1.6
Jefferson	1,325	18,760	1.1	144	9.2	221	14.1	1,134	9.1	4,614	3,496	1,118	28	1.8
Johnson	8,210	158,070	1.1	1,640	10.7	979	6.4	7,387	5.9	21,338	16,424	4,913	58	0.4
Jones	1,142	17,539	0.7	181	8.7	251	12.1	844	5.5	4,706	3,413	1,293	51	2.5
Keokuk	102	8,310	0.6	97	9.7	141	14.2	481	6.1	2,472	1,914	558	26	2.6
Kossuth	185	14,929	1.0	156	10.6	185	12.6	536	4.8	3,895	3,705	189	48	3.2
Lee	1,197	35,749	1.1	328	9.8	468	14.0	1,351	5.3	8,512	7,752	761	39	1.2
Linn	5,026	236,385	1.1	2,615	11.4	2,365	10.3	8,883	4.8	42,398	27,356	15,043	292	1.3
Louisa	80	10,234	0.8	110	10.2	108	10.0	786	8.9	2,375	1,852	524	35	3.2
Lucas	44	8,692	1.0	100	11.5	104	12.0	372	5.6	2,129	1,639	490	13	1.5
Lyon	139	10,905	0.9	172	14.4	150	12.5	618	6.5	2,344	2,110	234	39	3.3
Madison	111	12,578	0.6	172	10.3	171	10.2	661	4.9	3,294	2,387	907	11	0.7
Mahaska	908	20,278	0.8	258	11.7	269	12.2	963	5.5	4,669	3,608	1,061	42	1.9
Marion	1,272	35,484	1.1	339	10.2	369	11.1	1,090	4.2	7,206	5,812	1,394	58	1.7
Marshall	1,190	39,847	1.0	480	12.0	547	13.7	2,374	7.6	8,589	6,366	2,223	65	1.6
Mills	434	11,979	0.6	148	10.3	161	11.2	570	4.8	3,296	2,658	638	17	1.2
Mitchell	174	9,857	0.9	115	10.9	137	13.0	627	7.6	2,450	2,328	122	38	3.6
Monona	166	8,080	0.9	83	9.6	187	21.6	381	5.9	2,360	1,820	540	18	2.1
Monroe	64	7,580	1.0	101	13.3	103	13.6	361	5.9	1,787	1,348	439	19	2.5
Montgomery	177	10,078	1.0	98	9.5	178	17.2	468	6.1	2,727	2,299	429	31	3.0
Muscatine	503	44,671	1.1	459	10.7	457	10.7	2,119	6.1	8,642	6,063	2,579	86	2.0
O'Brien	395	13,151	0.9	159	11.3	235	16.7	666	6.2	3,336	3,089	247	56	4.0
Osceola	101	5,390	0.8	58	9.4	82	13.3	347	7.6	1,421	1,321	100	12	1.9
Page	1,485	15,675	1.1	141	9.3	222	14.6	604	5.9	3,961	3,482	479	16	1.1
Palo Alto	228	8,376	0.9	109	12.2	116	13.0	389	5.7	2,267	2,166	101	12	1.3
Plymouth	248	24,168	0.9	260	10.1	286	11.1	1,079	5.3	5,286	4,307	979	71	2.8
Pocahontas	92	6,398	0.9	80	11.3	98	13.9	352	7.0	1,810	1,680	131	15	2.1
Polk	8,966	522,248	1.2	6,288	12.7	4,480	9.1	24,317	5.8	77,265	52,988	24,276	484	1.0
Pottawattamie	1,877	86,818	0.9	1,028	11.0	1,193	12.8	4,487	6.0	19,937	13,284	6,653	125	1.3
Poweshiek	1,612	19,643	1.1	146	7.8	238	12.8	683	5.2	4,246	3,476	770	27	1.4
Ringgold	132	4,483	0.8	33	7.1	69	14.9	261	7.2	1,291	1,176	115	10	2.2
Sac	145	8,615	0.8	102	10.4	141	14.4	411	5.6	2,575	2,445	129	15	1.5
Scott	3,234	178,199	1.1	1,959	11.2	1,905	10.9	7,743	5.5	33,556	22,284	11,272	189	1.1
Shelby	179	11,895	1.1	124	10.6	156	13.3	490	5.6	3,058	2,700	358	29	2.5
Sioux	2,235	37,033	1.1	481	13.4	339	9.4	1,775	6.5	6,085	5,637	448	66	1.8
Story	10,515	102,425	1.1	766	7.7	624	6.3	4,788	6.4	14,002	11,341	2,660	40	0.4
Tama	260	15,134	0.8	203	12.0	246	14.5	1,121	8.4	3,896	2,877	1,019	58	3.4
Taylor	31	5,760	0.9	60	10.2	85	14.5	390	8.3	1,533	1,508	25	10	1.7
Union	403	12,955	1.1	118	9.8	159	13.2	590	6.3	2,941	2,511	430	26	2.1
Van Buren	49	6,609	0.8	95	13.2	93	12.9	410	7.6	1,828	1,448	380	16	2.2
Wapello	865	36,145	1.1	435	12.3	492	13.9	2,229	8.1	7,775	5,316	2,459	97	2.7
Warren	1,375	38,147	0.5	547	10.3	534	10.1	1,614	3.8	9,658	6,882	2,776	50	1.0
Washington	262	20,776	0.9	302	13.4	260	11.6	1,141	6.5	4,964	4,060	903	33	1.5
Wayne	80	5,994	0.8	85	13.1	102	15.7	382	7.8	1,536	1,178	358	21	3.2
Webster	2,745	38,133	1.1	426	11.5	527	14.2	1,732	6.5	8,119	6,486	1,633	80	2.2
Winnebago	480	10,801	1.1	104	9.8	144	13.5	386	5.0	2,547	2,348	199	29	2.7
Winneshiek	1,889	20,801	1.1	168	8.4	214	10.7	666	4.8	4,740	3,970	771	25	1.2
Woodbury	2,496	101,365	1.0	1,376	13.0	1,141	10.8	6,474	7.6	18,786	12,951	5,835	188	1.8
Worth	60	5,985	0.6	82	11.1	79	10.7	299	5.2	1,740	1,559	181	D	D
Wright	193	13,044	1.1	155	12.1	204	15.9	639	6.7	3,051	2,815	236	26	2.0

1. Per 1,000 estimated resident population.

STATE County	COVID-19 Vaccinations, 2021–2022		Education: School enrollment and attainment, 2016–2020: Enrollment[1]		Education: School enrollment and attainment, 2016–2020: Attainment[2] (percent)		Education: Local government expenditures,[3] 2018–2019		Money income, 2016–2020	Money income, 2016–2020: Households			Income and poverty, 2020	Income and poverty, 2020: Percent below poverty level		
	Number	Percent[5]	Total	Percent private	High school graduate or less	Bachelor's degree or more	Total current spending (mil dol)	Current spending per student (dollars)	Per capita income[4]	Median income (dollars)	Percent with income of less than $50,000	Percent with income of $200,000 or more	Median household income (dollars)	All persons	Children under 18 years	Children 5 to 17 years in families
	46	47	48	49	50	51	52	53	54	55	56	57	58	59	60	61
IOWA—Cont'd																
Franklin	5,509	54.7	2,078	3.6	45.3	18.6	17.8	11,807	28,650	55,630	45.7	2.1	59,596	10.5	14.9	14.3
Fremont	3,680	52.9	1,388	8.9	40.9	18.8	13.6	11,135	31,173	59,688	43.2	3.2	62,234	9.1	13.2	12.6
Greene	5,191	58.4	1,908	12.2	45.0	19.8	17.2	11,498	29,356	51,098	48.7	2.1	54,857	10.7	12.9	11.5
Grundy	7,606	62.2	2,802	8.0	36.6	27.2	30.3	11,024	37,360	71,760	32.5	5.9	71,837	5.5	6.0	5.7
Guthrie	6,236	58.3	2,280	3.8	43.2	20.0	26.7	11,132	33,818	62,644	40.6	5.4	65,344	8.5	10.8	10.0
Hamilton	9,405	63.7	3,307	8.7	38.3	24.0	30.8	11,728	31,397	60,248	40.3	3.2	61,650	8.1	10.8	10.4
Hancock	5,296	49.8	2,056	4.6	43.8	22.1	18.4	10,990	31,178	61,957	37.0	3.0	58,053	8.1	10.2	9.7
Hardin	9,467	56.2	3,629	11.1	42.2	21.5	35.8	11,232	28,189	54,930	44.7	2.1	58,502	9.6	12.4	12.5
Harrison	7,311	52.0	2,978	6.3	46.4	19.1	30.3	10,916	33,333	64,154	37.9	3.7	63,118	8.3	11.2	10.5
Henry	10,764	53.9	4,354	16.1	43.7	22.5	37.4	10,708	26,840	54,490	44.3	1.8	56,260	10.8	13.3	12.2
Howard	4,753	51.9	1,921	21.2	47.6	18.6	18.0	12,153	28,351	56,709	41.5	1.9	60,034	10.5	13.4	12.3
Humboldt	4,778	50.0	2,117	14.6	44.2	20.1	18.6	11,118	30,396	55,707	44.0	3.6	62,071	8.8	11.3	10.2
Ida	3,356	48.9	1,408	3.8	47.7	17.6	16.2	10,973	31,481	54,219	46.8	3.4	56,096	10.3	13.6	12.3
Iowa	10,176	62.9	3,578	7.2	42.7	21.9	28.4	10,803	33,910	62,660	36.1	3.5	67,820	6.4	6.8	6.2
Jackson	10,338	53.2	4,075	12.0	48.2	19.7	32.8	11,415	30,694	59,042	43.2	3.0	61,538	11.4	14.9	14.1
Jasper	21,799	58.6	8,084	10.1	47.4	19.2	62.3	10,679	29,576	59,481	41.0	3.6	63,458	8.5	9.7	9.3
Jefferson	8,807	48.1	4,555	31.3	33.5	36.5	27.1	11,458	28,849	47,401	51.7	3.9	52,830	14.8	18.3	17.5
Johnson	109,827	72.7	54,704	8.3	20.1	54.3	225.3	11,716	35,875	63,062	41.4	7.9	68,790	14.1	10.0	9.0
Jones	12,132	58.7	4,131	13.1	45.8	19.9	32.9	11,352	29,560	57,134	42.4	4.0	61,736	9.9	10.9	9.9
Keokuk	4,786	46.7	2,222	6.5	48.5	18.4	12.3	10,718	30,097	52,012	48.5	3.1	54,790	13.7	17.8	15.7
Kossuth	7,705	52.0	2,997	18.1	43.0	18.2	22.0	11,886	31,475	56,156	44.8	3.0	65,006	10.0	11.6	10.8
Lee	17,232	51.2	7,027	17.9	45.1	18.5	53.9	10,977	27,834	52,072	47.9	2.1	58,619	11.5	16.2	15.7
Linn	151,323	66.7	55,752	18.7	31.7	34.1	485.9	12,674	36,321	67,301	36.3	6.5	69,559	8.1	9.5	8.9
Louisa	5,854	53.0	2,307	3.7	53.5	16.9	26.1	11,373	29,762	63,034	40.9	4.1	72,404	9.1	11.5	11.0
Lucas	3,900	45.3	1,857	12.0	49.4	16.6	14.0	10,986	30,003	53,967	44.7	2.7	48,662	13.5	21.4	21.4
Lyon	4,868	41.4	2,792	11.0	46.4	19.2	23.6	10,752	29,410	65,959	36.1	2.0	67,280	6.3	7.3	7.3
Madison	8,840	54.1	3,850	9.9	38.4	25.3	34.5	10,559	37,951	71,811	34.1	6.9	75,563	7.5	8.8	7.8
Mahaska	9,811	44.4	5,421	22.1	49.0	21.3	31.2	11,162	28,511	56,417	43.5	2.3	59,704	10.2	11.2	10.2
Marion	17,639	53.0	8,288	30.4	38.6	30.8	60.6	10,739	33,571	64,136	36.3	5.4	64,327	8.0	8.3	7.7
Marshall	26,024	66.1	9,112	7.6	48.7	20.8	78.4	11,184	28,152	58,735	41.3	2.5	64,341	10.1	12.8	11.8
Mills	8,545	56.6	3,565	10.2	39.3	26.0	28.0	10,788	35,711	75,137	30.2	6.7	76,010	8.3	10.0	8.2
Mitchell	5,173	48.9	2,176	12.7	44.9	22.1	17.5	10,964	31,327	60,260	41.9	2.5	67,127	8.9	13.9	13.1
Monona	4,647	53.9	1,753	4.6	46.7	15.7	18.1	11,669	30,221	51,866	47.3	3.1	58,079	11.0	14.2	13.7
Monroe	3,574	46.4	1,493	5.5	48.9	19.9	12.3	10,280	30,732	59,489	41.0	2.7	58,297	11.4	15.1	14.2
Montgomery	5,616	56.6	2,122	2.7	42.8	19.8	18.5	11,313	34,545	55,761	43.1	3.9	54,767	11.6	17.4	16.1
Muscatine	25,988	60.9	9,890	7.2	45.8	21.8	80.4	10,959	30,902	60,435	40.1	3.3	62,877	10.2	12.5	11.2
O'Brien	6,929	50.4	3,009	17.3	44.7	21.8	27.1	11,197	31,149	57,200	43.2	3.1	63,559	8.4	9.8	9.1
Osceola	2,692	45.2	1,311	13.0	48.1	15.0	8.5	10,634	31,097	61,167	39.2	2.8	63,695	7.9	10.9	10.6
Page	8,077	53.5	2,866	8.6	43.9	20.3	29.3	10,922	27,800	51,196	48.6	1.7	52,739	13.2	17.2	15.6
Palo Alto	4,532	51.0	2,043	13.1	37.0	24.8	19.5	11,424	29,636	56,437	43.4	3.3	63,164	9.5	11.6	11.1
Plymouth	13,230	52.5	5,840	18.4	41.0	22.3	47.3	10,517	35,078	71,147	33.4	5.1	72,261	6.0	8.0	7.4
Pocahontas	3,460	52.3	1,351	13.0	47.0	15.9	33.9	39,417	30,428	53,573	45.6	2.7	56,360	10.2	14.7	14.2
Polk	331,865	67.7	119,309	17.7	32.6	37.6	1,016.9	12,810	36,290	69,747	35.1	6.7	67,821	11.5	13.8	12.8
Pottawattamie	53,740	57.7	21,962	11.4	43.4	21.9	216.8	13,690	30,466	59,901	41.7	3.9	61,607	9.2	11.8	10.4
Poweshiek	10,833	58.5	4,769	38.6	44.8	28.1	31.2	10,924	34,576	53,925	44.7	6.8	60,023	11.6	11.3	10.0
Ringgold	2,567	52.5	1,147	8.5	45.3	19.6	9.4	12,229	27,414	55,970	46.0	3.7	53,466	13.3	21.5	19.9
Sac	5,135	52.8	2,029	4.0	43.6	17.8	14.9	11,362	32,704	57,446	43.4	3.5	54,107	10.5	14.0	12.5
Scott	105,452	61.0	42,225	17.0	35.1	32.6	359.8	12,465	34,792	63,876	39.1	6.5	67,038	12.1	16.0	14.0
Shelby	6,790	59.3	2,538	9.6	43.3	21.1	21.2	10,783	34,617	60,139	43.2	5.6	54,234	8.3	9.4	8.6
Sioux	14,553	41.8	10,468	41.1	37.4	29.5	60.0	10,898	30,044	73,260	31.1	5.0	74,868	6.5	6.2	5.8
Story	61,390	63.2	41,981	4.0	20.3	51.9	129.6	10,868	31,037	58,302	43.4	5.4	61,341	12.4	7.2	6.1
Tama	10,574	62.7	3,923	6.7	49.8	15.6	27.9	10,878	28,623	54,749	44.5	2.6	58,329	10.8	15.9	14.3
Taylor	2,878	47.0	1,313	3.2	48.9	14.8	11.1	11,132	31,551	57,768	44.3	4.1	70,519	10.5	14.3	12.9
Union	6,280	51.3	2,899	18.7	42.3	22.4	22.9	11,450	27,212	50,375	49.6	2.1	48,862	12.1	16.2	14.7
Van Buren	2,969	42.1	1,348	31.8	48.1	16.4	10.5	12,118	28,466	49,898	50.2	2.8	51,908	14.4	23.5	23.1
Wapello	17,514	50.1	8,128	12.7	47.8	19.7	94.4	14,240	25,760	46,433	53.3	1.6	49,060	15.5	18.0	17.7
Warren	30,888	60.0	13,160	20.9	35.6	31.3	100.2	9,805	35,966	80,309	29.3	6.2	82,206	4.9	5.5	4.9
Washington	12,472	56.8	4,981	6.6	48.1	22.0	43.7	11,375	30,390	63,532	37.6	3.2	65,061	7.1	12.4	11.8
Wayne	2,706	42.0	1,247	14.0	54.6	14.3	12.5	11,099	26,026	47,543	52.2	1.7	52,016	13.0	21.3	20.8
Webster	20,703	57.7	8,149	12.7	42.6	21.1	58.3	11,627	28,116	51,909	48.1	2.4	58,355	12.4	10.6	12.0
Winnebago	5,424	52.4	2,508	12.7	40.5	23.1	27.5	11,526	28,927	51,581	48.2	1.7	52,706	9.3	12.9	12.1
Winneshiek	12,504	62.5	5,669	42.2	38.3	29.8	32.7	12,194	32,383	63,162	38.5	4.2	61,813	9.2	8.4	7.9
Woodbury	58,307	56.5	26,773	15.7	44.1	23.5	237.5	12,499	28,919	60,768	40.9	3.9	60,553	11.3	12.8	12.2
Worth	3,840	52.0	1,566	7.0	45.0	18.2	15.3	11,156	32,381	60,442	40.5	4.0	54,474	8.5	11.9	12.0
Wright	7,236	57.6	2,648	4.4	45.8	16.3	32.1	11,925	29,142	51,221	48.9	2.1	57,133	10.7	15.3	14.7

1. All persons 3 years old and over enrolled in nursery school through college. 2. Persons 25 years old and over. 3. Elementary and secondary education expenditures. 4. Based on population estimated by the American Community Survey, 2016–2020. 5. CDC percent based on 2019 population estimate.

STATE County	Personal income, 2020										Earnings, 2020		
			Per capita[1]			Supplements to wages and salaries, employer contributions (mil dol)						Contributions for government social insurance (mil dol)	
	Total (mil dol)	Percent change 2019–2020	Dollars	Rank	Wages and salaries (mil dol)	Pension and insurance	Government social insurance	Proprietors' income (mil dol)	Dividends, interest, and rent (mil dol)	Personal transfer reecipts (mil dol)	Total (mil dol)	From employee and self-employed	From employer
	62	63	64	65	66	67	68	69	70	71	72	73	74
IOWA—Cont'd													
Franklin	509	7.3	51,028	1,023	180	37	14	70	95	127	302	19	14
Fremont	342	3.7	50,870	1,043	127	24	10	34	52	96	195	13	10
Greene	463	8.6	52,647	879	152	34	12	52	85	130	251	16	12
Grundy	679	7.2	55,615	666	213	37	17	66	125	142	334	22	17
Guthrie	588	6.8	54,755	719	140	29	11	65	113	142	246	17	11
Hamilton	759	1.5	51,584	975	246	49	19	93	140	185	407	26	19
Hancock	571	4.2	54,318	760	275	55	23	56	99	139	409	26	23
Hardin	834	4.2	50,328	1,108	287	60	23	94	170	219	463	32	23
Harrison	692	3.9	49,678	1,176	180	36	14	48	97	181	278	21	14
Henry	917	5.6	46,541	1,572	407	78	33	66	154	243	585	41	33
Howard	484	8.9	52,726	877	165	36	14	68	91	119	283	17	14
Humboldt	495	4.6	52,298	910	173	37	14	55	83	121	279	18	14
Ida	392	10.6	57,429	542	187	35	15	46	88	92	282	18	15
Iowa	948	6.9	58,759	486	408	98	39	86	196	198	631	38	39
Jackson	958	7.5	49,878	1,154	241	48	20	85	160	272	394	30	20
Jasper	1,726	6.3	46,473	1,582	491	98	40	95	278	449	723	53	40
Jefferson	783	5.3	42,674	2,104	331	74	26	50	211	218	481	35	26
Johnson	8,697	4.1	56,573	603	4,672	1,231	349	481	1,989	1,311	6,734	385	349
Jones	979	6.8	47,506	1,449	258	54	21	82	172	252	415	30	21
Keokuk	490	8.3	48,599	1,308	96	21	8	74	76	129	199	14	8
Kossuth	784	5.3	53,422	823	304	56	24	116	147	198	500	33	24
Lee	1,525	5.5	45,548	1,724	749	140	68	94	256	477	1,051	76	68
Linn	12,895	5.9	56,592	600	7,472	1,154	585	541	2,471	2,654	9,752	649	585
Louisa	494	4.3	44,821	1,820	182	35	15	46	63	128	279	19	15
Lucas	381	4.5	44,707	1,846	175	29	14	30	65	111	248	18	14
Lyon	679	3.1	57,766	527	187	36	14	159	116	114	396	21	14
Madison	880	7.4	53,244	837	165	34	14	51	135	187	263	20	14
Mahaska	1,038	6.5	46,388	1,592	354	73	30	68	170	278	525	36	30
Marion	1,779	5.5	53,648	807	938	162	71	79	344	399	1,251	85	71
Marshall	1,884	9.2	47,696	1,429	804	148	67	117	346	536	1,136	78	67
Mills	892	0.6	60,384	410	175	40	14	166	118	192	394	27	14
Mitchell	661	-0.2	62,037	347	203	39	17	159	103	126	418	27	17
Monona	437	7.9	50,807	1,054	102	22	8	49	70	128	182	13	8
Monroe	376	8.1	48,423	1,336	200	34	17	19	62	103	271	18	17
Montgomery	454	7.0	45,665	1,706	179	38	14	34	77	154	265	19	14
Muscatine	2,168	5.7	51,135	1,013	1,184	199	96	125	375	521	1,604	107	96
O'Brien	788	4.4	57,629	535	269	54	21	103	159	175	447	28	21
Osceola	304	5.3	50,706	1,064	99	21	8	42	53	71	170	10	8
Page	713	9.7	47,321	1,474	250	55	20	57	130	223	382	27	20
Palo Alto	457	1.9	51,679	965	148	33	12	68	81	123	262	16	12
Plymouth	1,500	5.1	59,460	455	611	103	53	169	290	283	935	59	53
Pocahontas	351	-0.1	53,074	854	143	25	12	62	53	92	243	14	12
Polk	28,214	6.3	57,080	570	19,101	2,682	1,437	1,668	4,911	5,309	24,888	1,604	1,437
Pottawattamie	4,472	4.9	47,921	1,403	1,864	321	156	203	655	1,202	2,544	181	156
Poweshiek	922	8.5	50,139	1,130	483	80	39	63	188	217	665	45	39
Ringgold	241	6.3	50,196	1,126	56	14	4	42	45	71	116	7	4
Sac	573	5.0	59,653	442	134	28	11	151	96	125	324	20	11
Scott	10,127	6.0	58,465	497	4,392	704	356	622	1,863	2,123	6,075	413	356
Shelby	631	5.1	55,229	686	236	47	19	72	119	168	373	24	19
Sioux	1,935	6.0	55,209	689	950	178	77	301	380	332	1,506	87	77
Story	4,514	5.0	45,951	1,660	2,514	595	187	302	1,019	793	3,598	217	187
Tama	879	11.5	52,315	909	249	50	21	82	157	214	402	27	21
Taylor	273	6.2	44,763	1,832	81	17	7	43	38	82	147	10	7
Union	532	5.9	43,735	1,983	258	58	22	25	87	171	362	26	22
Van Buren	295	4.0	41,781	2,231	78	19	7	26	54	96	130	11	7
Wapello	1,500	7.9	42,889	2,076	735	136	64	83	198	491	1,017	72	64
Warren	2,835	5.9	54,251	765	530	102	43	152	414	526	828	64	43
Washington	1,310	-2.3	59,565	449	336	69	28	298	212	276	730	47	28
Wayne	300	9.7	46,743	1,545	83	21	7	47	47	87	158	11	7
Webster	1,756	4.8	48,862	1,275	878	168	70	152	278	476	1,268	83	70
Winnebago	470	7.1	45,722	1,696	177	35	14	33	82	140	259	19	14
Winneshiek	1,073	8.2	54,036	779	453	89	37	121	215	247	700	46	37
Woodbury	4,923	6.8	47,731	1,426	2,381	412	196	387	699	1,224	3,376	226	196
Worth	335	8.5	45,566	1,719	93	19	8	31	52	91	150	11	8
Wright	656	7.1	52,825	864	283	59	24	52	112	183	417	29	24

1. Based on the resident population estimated as of July 1 of the year shown.

STATE County	Earnings, 2020 (cont.)									Social Security beneficiaries, December 2020		Supple-mental Security Income recipients, 2020	Housing units, 2021	
	Percent by selected industries													
	Farm	Mining, quarrying, and extractions	Construction	Manu-facturing	Information; professional, scientific, technical services	Retail trade	Finance, insurance, real estate, and leasing	Health care and social assistance	Govern-ment	Number	Rate[1]		Total	Percent change, 2010–2021
	75	76	77	78	79	80	81	82	83	84	85	86	87	88
IOWA—Cont'd														
Franklin	13.1	D	7.0	24.7	2.1	4.1	4.9	4.9	14.7	2,450	246	103	4,647	-0.2
Fremont	11.8	0.0	8.4	20.0	2.5	6.0	D	D	12.6	1,840	280	103	3,119	0.3
Greene	12.9	D	4.0	23.1	D	4.9	5.3	D	20.9	2,440	280	146	4,318	0.1
Grundy	9.9	0.0	20.9	5.5	3.0	4.6	D	D	12.6	3,025	245	95	5,480	0.2
Guthrie	14.6	-0.1	9.6	5.8	6.8	3.7	D	D	22.4	3,045	288	150	5,806	0.5
Hamilton	13.4	D	6.3	13.4	3.7	5.8	7.7	D	19.6	3,550	238	188	7,035	0.0
Hancock	6.8	D	3.0	44.0	1.8	3.4	2.3	D	10.5	2,670	250	80	5,123	0.2
Hardin	10.5	D	9.1	7.7	3.9	6.9	5.0	D	21.3	4,315	258	255	8,032	0.0
Harrison	6.0	0.0	5.2	10.3	4.2	8.5	4.3	D	18.8	3,435	234	257	6,690	0.3
Henry	3.4	D	3.1	26.5	D	5.1	3.2	D	18.9	4,640	228	307	8,422	0.3
Howard	14.5	0.0	7.0	27.9	1.9	6.6	4.4	D	16.7	2,290	242	112	4,316	0.1
Humboldt	10.9	D	7.6	22.9	2.9	5.1	3.4	D	17.2	2,305	239	153	4,580	0.2
Ida	10.7	0.0	5.6	41.3	1.3	4.7	6.3	D	7.6	1,710	246	69	3,363	0.3
Iowa	6.4	D	6.4	45.9	2.7	5.7	2.1	4.6	10.9	3,825	231	169	7,358	0.2
Jackson	9.1	D	7.5	14.8	5.3	9.2	6.6	D	17.1	5,155	266	364	9,270	0.2
Jasper	5.8	D	9.3	21.3	4.7	7.3	3.9	9.4	19.1	8,825	234	580	16,236	0.6
Jefferson	1.6	D	4.5	12.4	7.7	6.9	20.3	D	17.7	4,555	291	343	7,707	0.1
Johnson	0.4	0.1	4.5	6.0	4.7	5.3	4.4	7.3	48.9	21,400	138	1,798	67,075	1.4
Jones	8.8	D	13.0	11.2	3.6	6.7	4.6	9.6	20.4	5,000	240	303	8,886	0.1
Keokuk	19.5	D	5.4	6.4	2.9	3.8	4.2	D	17.5	2,615	264	204	4,648	-0.1
Kossuth	11.5	0.0	6.2	19.9	5.1	5.1	11.8	D	14.1	4,125	284	159	7,218	0.0
Lee	0.9	D	7.1	34.4	3.2	5.6	4.1	10.3	13.8	8,870	267	895	15,839	-0.1
Linn	0.3	0.1	7.0	21.0	9.4	5.3	10.4	11.4	10.5	44,485	194	3,962	101,901	0.5
Louisa	10.9	D	2.9	39.7	D	2.0	2.8	4.5	15.1	2,485	231	163	4,733	0.4
Lucas	0.4	0.0	D	8.6	1.9	4.5	5.5	D	17.1	2,260	259	175	4,056	0.0
Lyon	28.2	D	6.8	9.1	8.3	3.4	4.5	D	10.1	2,305	192	53	4,837	0.3
Madison	2.9	D	16.7	4.5	5.9	7.1	7.0	6.0	24.8	3,480	207	143	7,030	1.4
Mahaska	5.0	0.0	5.5	28.9	4.2	6.6	3.5	6.0	19.0	4,870	222	441	9,710	0.3
Marion	0.9	D	4.1	50.3	3.1	4.4	3.2	10.5	9.0	7,555	226	418	14,303	1.5
Marshall	4.0	D	5.1	30.3	3.6	5.9	3.1	10.3	19.3	9,035	227	618	16,775	0.2
Mills	4.4	D	4.0	15.2	D	16.1	3.4	D	26.0	3,435	237	210	6,111	0.0
Mitchell	7.4	D	13.9	33.7	D	2.3	2.9	D	11.1	2,520	239	97	4,903	1.0
Monona	18.7	0.0	D	3.4	D	6.4	5.1	19.6	17.3	2,515	293	159	4,375	0.0
Monroe	2.3	D	7.8	42.4	D	3.1	D	D	14.9	1,885	248	105	3,648	0.3
Montgomery	3.4	D	8.6	15.5	D	5.9	5.2	7.9	25.4	2,865	278	274	5,007	0.0
Muscatine	0.9	0.1	3.7	41.0	5.4	4.3	2.6	6.4	11.2	9,220	216	857	18,379	0.0
O'Brien	14.7	D	4.5	11.7	4.8	5.6	5.6	14.5	13.5	3,420	244	177	6,550	0.4
Osceola	19.5	0.2	6.3	11.3	2.4	D	D	10.2	11.0	1,465	238	48	2,873	-0.2
Page	8.5	D	4.5	16.6	D	6.3	4.1	D	24.9	4,205	277	352	6,980	0.0
Palo Alto	14.0	0.1	3.6	19.1	2.7	4.7	4.6	D	21.8	2,210	248	130	4,517	0.0
Plymouth	8.0	D	4.9	30.3	D	4.3	3.7	D	11.2	5,550	216	206	10,877	0.3
Pocahontas	19.7	D	14.1	11.5	2.0	4.3	D	D	14.4	1,855	262	101	3,659	-0.1
Polk	0.1	0.0	7.6	5.6	11.4	5.3	20.4	10.5	12.9	80,670	162	8,133	214,991	1.9
Pottawattamie	1.7	0.2	9.6	13.4	5.4	7.8	3.6	13.8	16.1	20,420	219	2,191	40,029	0.4
Poweshiek	3.4	D	9.9	15.4	2.5	4.6	14.8	D	8.1	4,415	238	214	8,926	0.2
Ringgold	28.4	D	7.3	D	D	3.6	4.3	6.9	28.1	1,330	287	92	2,673	0.0
Sac	19.6	D	3.2	24.9	4.6	3.0	D	7.2	10.5	2,625	269	97	5,114	-0.1
Scott	0.3	D	10.2	16.3	6.2	8.0	6.0	14.3	10.9	34,940	201	4,020	78,231	0.4
Shelby	11.7	0.0	3.5	11.8	6.9	5.4	6.9	D	17.5	3,165	269	188	5,435	0.1
Sioux	11.2	0.2	9.8	25.9	3.2	4.2	5.3	6.8	10.1	6,130	171	191	13,144	1.0
Story	0.8	D	6.2	12.5	9.2	5.2	4.4	7.8	37.8	14,065	141	748	41,660	0.4
Tama	13.9	D	5.2	23.3	D	4.1	3.6	D	27.7	4,120	244	181	7,581	0.1
Taylor	18.0	0.0	7.2	23.0	D	3.2	3.2	4.7	15.2	1,595	272	93	2,887	0.1
Union	-0.1	D	7.0	20.1	D	7.1	3.8	6.9	29.7	3,140	261	260	5,778	-0.1
Van Buren	3.0	0.9	12.9	26.5	2.0	4.3	3.7	3.7	24.5	1,950	269	128	3,499	0.0
Wapello	0.4	D	5.4	30.2	2.3	7.6	3.4	13.0	16.1	8,210	233	1,076	15,735	0.0
Warren	1.0	-0.1	16.0	7.9	8.0	9.0	6.3	9.5	20.6	10,090	189	431	21,448	2.4
Washington	9.3	D	12.2	18.0	4.0	5.7	3.3	5.6	13.7	5,235	233	340	9,635	0.5
Wayne	5.7	0.0	19.1	19.8	2.9	4.3	D	4.3	26.8	1,640	252	132	3,022	-0.1
Webster	4.9	D	10.0	17.9	3.2	7.0	3.3	13.6	15.7	8,545	230	766	17,062	0.7
Winnebago	4.4	D	7.3	17.5	6.1	9.8	6.7	D	16.3	2,690	252	118	5,071	-0.1
Winneshiek	5.8	D	9.4	15.5	D	6.6	4.2	D	17.5	4,820	242	149	8,997	0.8
Woodbury	1.4	D	9.8	15.2	4.5	7.8	4.3	15.8	14.5	19,950	189	1,962	43,279	1.2
Worth	8.2	1.0	9.8	21.6	D	2.9	D	4.6	14.8	1,805	244	77	3,477	0.0
Wright	0.2	D	4.6	35.1	4.0	3.4	3.1	5.3	25.8	3,155	247	171	6,267	0.1

1. Per 1,000 resident population estimated as of July 1 of the year shown.

STATE County	Housing units, 2016–2020: Total	Occupied units: Owner-occupied: Percent	Owner-occupied: Median value[1]	Median owner cost as a percent of income: With a mortgage	Median owner cost as a percent of income: Without a mortgage[2]	Renter-occupied: Median rent[3]	Renter-occupied: Median rent as a percent of income[2]	Sub-standard units[4] (percent)	Civilian labor force, 2021: Total	Percent change, 2020–2021	Unemployment: Total	Unemployment: Rate[5]	Civilian employment[6], 2016–2020: Total	Percent: Management, business, science, and arts	Percent: Construction, production, and maintenance occupations
	89	90	91	92	93	94	95	96	97	98	99	100	101	102	103
IOWA—Cont'd															
Franklin	4,195	70.5	93,200	16.2	10.6	647	19.1	0.9	5,617	-0.2	210	3.7	4,593	29.7	36.7
Fremont	2,952	76.7	113,200	17.6	10.6	640	20.2	1.6	3,720	-0.1	107	2.9	3,335	35.3	28.7
Greene	4,037	72.9	93,500	19.3	10.9	693	23.1	3.0	5,336	-0.3	184	3.4	4,479	36.2	32.2
Grundy	5,164	82.0	138,100	17.3	10.0	698	22.0	0.5	6,337	0.0	231	3.6	6,234	39.9	27.6
Guthrie	4,478	81.3	129,000	19.2	11.9	704	24.6	2.0	5,491	1.1	233	4.2	5,365	33.8	29.0
Hamilton	6,122	74.6	105,200	16.5	11.9	762	22.2	0.6	6,826	0.0	288	4.2	7,295	34.4	29.5
Hancock	4,787	79.5	100,900	16.8	10.0	755	24.3	1.1	5,718	-1.3	218	3.8	5,709	34.3	34.4
Hardin	7,185	74.1	95,100	16.8	11.4	693	25.7	1.8	7,790	-0.6	324	4.2	8,352	31.4	33.1
Harrison	6,094	73.8	124,000	16.5	10.1	729	23.6	0.8	7,029	0.0	274	3.9	7,356	35.8	30.7
Henry	7,591	72.9	118,500	19.1	11.4	665	24.9	1.7	9,502	-0.3	398	4.2	9,235	28.3	34.3
Howard	3,754	77.2	105,800	18.0	10.0	660	22.0	1.8	5,126	-0.2	196	3.8	4,690	31.3	36.7
Humboldt	4,195	74.9	109,200	15.8	10.9	586	21.9	0.5	4,946	-0.6	171	3.5	4,639	33.4	33.9
Ida	2,972	75.6	102,400	16.0	10.0	562	23.4	2.5	3,978	-0.7	126	3.2	3,462	32.6	33.9
Iowa	6,646	80.4	156,000	19.8	12.3	615	19.0	0.9	9,966	-1.7	376	3.8	8,468	35.1	31.7
Jackson	8,183	80.9	127,600	17.3	10.0	616	28.0	0.5	10,589	-0.8	530	5.0	9,581	31.4	34.1
Jasper	14,644	74.8	137,200	18.7	11.5	734	26.3	1.4	19,128	-1.0	829	4.3	18,038	30.4	31.7
Jefferson	6,855	69.6	120,600	21.0	12.1	756	30.1	1.2	9,849	-0.2	414	4.2	8,368	37.4	26.2
Johnson	60,430	58.6	238,600	19.7	10.0	984	34.9	2.4	84,310	-1.0	3,150	3.7	83,477	48.9	16.0
Jones	8,186	78.6	140,000	19.5	11.4	659	26.6	1.4	10,185	-1.1	457	4.5	9,843	32.0	30.8
Keokuk	4,330	78.3	95,800	18.4	11.2	711	28.7	1.6	5,181	0.0	228	4.4	4,820	32.1	37.1
Kossuth	6,575	74.4	109,400	17.7	10.6	710	28.1	0.9	8,089	-1.0	265	3.3	7,169	29.8	35.0
Lee	14,338	74.0	98,400	18.5	12.2	711	27.3	0.9	15,340	-2.7	909	5.9	15,559	31.3	33.6
Linn	91,304	74.3	161,600	19.2	11.4	778	27.1	1.6	118,805	-1.3	5,980	5.0	119,793	39.6	23.0
Louisa	4,343	76.5	107,900	17.9	11.6	647	17.4	2.7	5,903	-1.4	253	4.3	5,468	28.1	41.5
Lucas	3,718	76.5	94,200	17.4	11.9	659	27.5	1.6	4,606	-0.8	143	3.1	4,033	26.1	37.3
Lyon	4,593	85.4	160,700	19.5	10.6	714	19.7	1.4	6,941	0.8	159	2.3	6,029	37.9	28.0
Madison	6,619	79.4	186,700	19.6	12.6	827	25.1	0.4	8,486	0.8	381	4.5	9,005	41.4	26.8
Mahaska	8,947	68.0	113,100	17.4	11.3	673	22.2	1.5	11,953	0.2	441	3.7	11,123	34.4	30.9
Marion	13,532	73.7	160,100	18.7	11.0	721	20.8	1.7	18,549	2.6	579	3.1	16,702	36.3	29.5
Marshall	15,388	71.9	104,400	17.9	11.4	725	25.9	4.2	17,329	-1.9	1,122	6.5	18,825	29.7	35.9
Mills	5,442	79.0	178,500	18.6	10.0	837	28.1	1.9	6,992	-0.3	243	3.5	7,429	35.9	27.1
Mitchell	4,472	80.1	120,400	17.9	10.0	610	21.0	1.0	5,812	-4.7	176	3.0	5,463	33.5	33.8
Monona	3,988	73.7	90,000	17.7	10.4	635	28.4	0.9	4,416	0.3	194	4.4	4,216	29.0	31.9
Monroe	3,243	78.4	113,800	16.8	11.6	598	30.7	2.8	3,946	-0.7	162	4.1	3,759	34.5	35.1
Montgomery	4,479	72.3	85,300	16.8	10.8	656	22.0	1.6	4,880	-0.2	201	4.1	4,873	31.2	31.5
Muscatine	16,543	74.4	135,400	18.5	12.0	829	25.3	2.5	20,871	-2.7	981	4.7	21,276	31.0	36.3
O'Brien	5,976	74.6	116,300	18.0	10.0	576	23.9	3.3	8,082	-0.9	245	3.0	7,149	32.3	33.4
Osceola	2,664	77.0	96,600	17.5	10.0	672	22.2	1.4	3,530	0.1	85	2.4	3,085	30.4	39.6
Page	6,414	70.3	96,400	17.4	11.3	663	25.7	1.1	6,279	0.6	257	4.1	7,066	36.2	31.4
Palo Alto	3,712	75.6	107,300	17.2	11.7	545	21.3	0.8	4,486	-2.1	150	3.3	4,726	33.1	32.0
Plymouth	10,298	76.7	172,600	17.7	10.0	714	18.8	1.1	14,441	0.1	436	3.0	13,457	32.6	29.8
Pocahontas	3,127	76.3	81,900	15.8	10.4	630	28.0	0.5	4,228	-0.3	129	3.1	3,329	29.2	37.5
Polk	191,125	67.1	190,400	19.2	11.4	938	26.8	2.7	267,873	0.6	12,050	4.5	257,853	42.6	19.4
Pottawattamie	36,875	68.8	141,300	18.8	11.7	850	27.8	2.3	47,038	-0.8	2,002	4.3	46,531	32.7	26.3
Poweshiek	7,827	66.3	148,200	19.6	12.2	734	24.0	1.4	10,031	2.0	445	4.4	9,376	35.0	28.1
Ringgold	1,843	74.9	113,000	17.8	12.6	636	28.7	1.4	2,383	-0.2	80	3.4	2,172	40.2	27.5
Sac	4,344	79.2	101,200	16.9	10.0	606	19.0	2.9	5,209	0.1	173	3.3	4,903	29.4	35.5
Scott	67,437	70.1	167,900	18.7	10.7	812	28.5	1.5	87,116	-0.3	4,734	5.4	84,844	39.2	24.1
Shelby	5,066	74.9	120,700	18.6	10.1	701	28.2	1.0	6,327	-1.0	203	3.2	5,919	40.7	27.4
Sioux	12,379	80.8	182,500	18.7	10.0	693	26.5	1.8	21,797	2.3	521	2.4	18,830	39.6	27.5
Story	37,997	54.5	195,200	18.8	10.9	921	33.5	0.7	57,384	0.5	1,701	3.0	51,405	45.9	16.8
Tama	6,736	76.1	114,400	19.7	12.6	729	27.3	3.1	9,146	-1.6	427	4.7	8,249	25.9	35.1
Taylor	2,567	81.5	84,100	17.4	10.6	581	17.9	0.9	3,100	0.2	97	3.1	3,076	34.2	35.1
Union	5,199	72.3	109,600	18.8	13.7	610	24.6	3.3	6,088	-1.9	271	4.5	5,846	32.1	32.7
Van Buren	2,969	80.8	91,200	20.0	11.4	571	26.5	5.6	3,626	-1.8	137	3.8	3,115	31.7	37.5
Wapello	14,404	67.7	87,400	19.0	12.3	767	29.0	2.4	16,957	-2.9	840	5.0	16,349	25.9	38.8
Warren	19,320	80.4	196,100	18.8	11.8	833	27.2	1.7	28,292	1.3	1,057	3.7	26,965	38.8	24.6
Washington	8,876	68.7	158,600	20.1	10.3	784	23.7	0.7	11,446	-0.3	430	3.8	11,530	30.5	31.0
Wayne	2,620	80.5	79,900	22.0	10.1	543	21.4	4.2	2,817	0.3	103	3.7	2,819	29.1	41.1
Webster	15,605	68.3	107,900	18.4	10.9	667	25.5	1.8	18,473	-1.6	856	4.6	17,032	32.1	29.3
Winnebago	4,533	77.8	96,200	18.5	10.8	617	23.5	1.1	4,949	-2.5	208	4.2	5,482	31.1	37.4
Winneshiek	8,265	78.0	183,300	20.0	10.9	723	26.5	0.8	11,385	1.7	472	4.1	11,463	37.2	27.0
Woodbury	39,523	67.4	131,300	17.9	10.3	802	25.7	2.6	54,789	-0.2	2,358	4.3	51,839	30.8	31.4
Worth	3,199	79.6	107,600	15.0	10.4	586	18.6	1.9	4,016	-2.4	170	4.2	4,017	30.8	35.6
Wright	5,582	73.1	86,100	18.3	10.2	644	24.5	1.2	6,679	-4.8	277	4.1	5,686	31.4	35.8

1. Specified owner-occupied units. 2. A value of 10.0 represents 10 percent or less; a value of 50.0 represents 50 percent or more. 3. Specified renter-occupied units. 4. Overcrowded or lacking complete plumbing facilities. 5. Percent of civilian labor force. 6. Civilian employed persons 16 years old and over.

STATE County	Private nonfarm establishments, employment and payroll, 2020									Agriculture, 2017			
		Employment						Annual payroll		Farms			Farm producers whose primary occupation is farming (percent)
											Percent with:		
	Number of establish-ments	Total	Health care and social assistance	Manufac-turing	Retail trade	Finance and insurance	Professional, scientific, and technical services	Total (mil dol)	Average per employee (dollars)	Number	Fewer than 50 acres	1000 acres or more	
	104	105	106	107	108	109	110	111	112	113	114	115	116
IOWA—Cont'd													
Franklin	303	3,135	504	946	364	120	57	131	41,930	835	35.2	12.5	44.1
Fremont	193	1,842	292	232	545	63	41	85	46,082	527	25.4	17.6	45.4
Greene	254	3,145	540	557	447	142	234	146	46,446	700	25.7	18.3	50.8
Grundy	292	3,182	610	357	466	198	38	171	53,774	760	36.2	9.6	45.5
Guthrie	307	2,223	436	200	414	134	76	82	37,068	802	25.8	10.8	37.0
Hamilton	377	4,422	661	780	675	192	68	193	43,703	732	39.8	13.3	44.3
Hancock	324	4,014	787	1,143	380	88	598	174	43,284	801	30.5	13.5	48.0
Hardin	515	4,851	943	650	877	258	109	195	40,117	837	35.4	14.7	50.1
Harrison	342	2,940	694	292	441	146	57	121	41,295	794	29.5	16.4	48.8
Henry	471	7,440	1,058	2,426	898	144	156	290	38,964	908	30.1	5.9	34.6
Howard	255	3,083	534	1,258	424	117	39	117	38,018	879	32.5	7.7	46.2
Humboldt	283	3,344	397	886	503	103	70	144	43,203	572	31.1	14.3	51.4
Ida	254	3,246	410	1,458	321	180	30	168	51,622	525	31.2	17.1	49.8
Iowa	476	8,148	734	4,313	1,236	95	224	335	41,152	970	32.0	7.8	41.4
Jackson	515	4,859	600	962	905	235	118	172	35,479	1,107	30.3	5.7	45.4
Jasper	769	8,917	1,358	2,080	1,448	230	543	349	39,137	986	34.3	10.0	47.0
Jefferson	659	7,160	751	776	987	1,167	429	288	40,222	636	31.4	6.3	38.1
Johnson	3,346	66,755	18,869	4,709	9,910	2,806	2,765	3,013	45,139	1,257	38.0	5.3	46.5
Jones	507	4,611	795	1,129	655	196	101	168	36,448	1,110	34.5	8.6	45.1
Keokuk	228	1,633	332	144	194	89	35	63	38,818	927	25.2	9.6	47.3
Kossuth	552	5,502	677	1,381	824	515	227	246	44,728	1,347	25.2	13.4	53.4
Lee	844	14,396	2,089	4,013	1,987	367	1,820	640	44,446	837	32.6	5.1	38.5
Linn	5,693	120,299	16,292	16,571	15,948	8,955	7,802	6,388	53,097	1,374	44.0	5.9	38.2
Louisa	221	3,122	361	1,505	182	50	29	144	46,038	576	32.5	11.5	40.7
Lucas	190	4,117	494	132	530	94	39	147	35,730	567	25.7	7.9	38.0
Lyon	395	3,795	631	860	387	145	137	177	46,699	1,122	26.1	7.4	55.0
Madison	407	2,662	503	161	535	138	111	103	38,678	977	40.4	7.6	34.0
Mahaska	550	6,695	918	1,384	1,106	180	141	251	37,471	943	31.0	9.2	43.9
Marion	836	16,508	2,085	7,894	1,630	279	372	794	48,107	1,030	39.1	6.5	35.2
Marshall	791	13,143	1,844	4,427	1,863	351	263	573	43,594	886	38.6	10.7	43.6
Mills	287	1,954	327	55	282	85	118	83	42,732	520	38.8	13.1	41.6
Mitchell	313	3,392	622	1,056	374	121	78	137	40,259	789	29.0	10.6	52.6
Monona	219	1,902	572	91	333	109	28	70	36,764	619	20.8	17.6	53.3
Monroe	181	2,293	405	902	285	74	47	101	44,084	618	24.6	6.1	30.3
Montgomery	288	3,101	750	534	501	122	55	131	42,084	516	20.0	14.0	50.7
Muscatine	928	20,284	1,935	7,321	2,076	374	755	1,024	50,479	714	33.3	8.0	47.5
O'Brien	490	5,388	1,400	694	829	224	223	196	36,407	876	23.2	7.3	58.5
Osceola	191	1,751	397	216	147	82	28	73	41,462	591	26.7	11.0	55.7
Page	401	5,172	1,555	1,422	602	170	100	205	39,691	715	22.7	15.8	51.3
Palo Alto	284	2,948	767	568	369	124	33	112	37,863	785	28.9	13.6	45.1
Plymouth	684	10,702	1,213	3,308	1,100	277	316	537	50,179	1,219	24.6	10.7	54.3
Pocahontas	211	1,829	254	461	232	94	35	75	41,103	730	25.2	14.2	55.6
Polk	13,496	282,508	39,337	17,143	32,736	32,719	20,708	15,798	55,922	755	56.6	9.1	38.5
Pottawattamie	1,958	31,473	4,955	5,604	5,651	612	628	1,300	41,301	1,114	30.8	15.3	51.4
Poweshiek	561	9,740	1,019	1,755	1,335	969	121	414	42,527	852	29.5	10.3	47.8
Ringgold	143	1,121	348	44	232	40	67	38	33,522	675	12.9	11.0	41.9
Sac	329	2,289	490	487	292	110	36	97	42,346	889	31.3	12.9	47.5
Scott	4,452	85,454	13,655	11,196	12,388	2,920	2,641	3,764	44,044	684	35.4	8.8	46.6
Shelby	386	4,938	796	754	496	285	111	221	44,739	890	27.2	12.0	48.3
Sioux	1,325	19,713	3,106	5,794	1,515	647	680	827	41,961	1,724	35.6	4.9	48.6
Story	2,104	32,362	5,635	5,529	4,982	658	1,129	1,535	47,431	955	48.2	10.8	37.8
Tama	302	4,062	457	1,161	437	120	97	168	41,283	1,072	27.1	10.0	47.6
Taylor	137	1,521	170	709	142	38	22	64	42,229	667	21.9	12.0	41.2
Union	310	4,711	919	1,222	760	143	57	165	34,953	627	31.4	10.8	40.6
Van Buren	142	1,462	256	589	228	44	38	56	38,302	690	25.7	9.4	39.1
Wapello	704	13,510	2,401	3,326	2,258	404	212	587	43,468	715	33.7	6.9	38.1
Warren	947	9,084	1,161	578	1,868	398	254	313	34,452	1,214	45.3	5.7	31.0
Washington	684	6,638	1,382	714	1,069	206	178	234	35,178	1,129	31.0	4.3	46.2
Wayne	142	1,358	402	345	194	31	61	52	38,410	743	24.1	8.7	39.0
Webster	1,021	16,395	2,565	1,780	2,437	372	766	722	44,052	960	35.7	14.8	47.4
Winnebago	312	5,870	362	2,740	528	184	159	258	43,941	571	31.5	12.3	41.6
Winneshiek	608	9,090	1,440	1,639	1,061	272	170	346	38,012	1,458	30.1	5.5	46.7
Woodbury	2,597	47,940	9,813	7,650	7,320	1,134	1,114	2,005	41,816	1,037	30.9	13.1	42.5
Worth	186	1,912	217	511	136	53	15	70	36,560	582	33.5	15.6	48.3
Wright	375	4,746	876	2,023	427	127	170	216	45,570	735	35.9	16.9	50.6

STATE County	Agriculture, 2017 (cont.)															
	Land in farms					Value of land and buildings (dollars)		Value of machinery and equipment, average per farm (dollars)	Value of products sold:				Organic farms (number)	Farms with internet access (percent)	Government payments	
	Acreage (1,000)	Percent change, 2012–2017	Acres			Average per farm	Average per acre		Total (mil dol)	Average per farm (acres)	Percent from:				Total ($1,000)	Percent of farms
			Average size of farm	Total irrigated (1,000)	Total cropland (1,000)						Crops	Livestock and poultry products				
	117	118	119	120	121	122	123	124	125	126	127	128	129	130	131	132
IOWA—Cont'd																
Franklin	349	-1.7	418	0.2	330.0	3,267,910	7,814	267,635	382.7	458,354	49.9	50.1	2	79.9	9,716	85.4
Fremont	274	-4.6	520	17.1	247.2	3,123,290	6,002	290,739	150.7	286,046	86.8	13.2	1	75.1	5,143	78.9
Greene	351	-1.6	502	0.1	323.0	4,163,712	8,297	298,887	299.4	427,783	58.3	41.7	13	84.0	4,531	63.9
Grundy	308	-3.1	405	0.0	296.3	3,682,729	9,086	287,687	266.7	350,933	70.8	29.2	NA	81.1	10,419	78.9
Guthrie	332	1.4	414	D	268.4	2,610,011	6,301	239,048	227.1	283,158	54.6	45.4	1	80.8	8,954	71.3
Hamilton	315	-3.6	431	D	296.2	3,495,669	8,115	303,864	586.8	801,623	28.7	71.3	5	86.1	5,877	59.2
Hancock	345	-2.2	431	3.6	334.9	3,286,656	7,621	331,122	422.6	527,586	44.7	55.3	NA	79.9	9,659	86.1
Hardin	337	1.3	402	D	310.6	3,142,054	7,813	299,034	484.6	578,983	39.0	61.0	5	82.2	4,740	79.3
Harrison	380	-3.6	478	43.4	336.2	2,945,210	6,161	275,156	216.2	272,293	81.1	18.9	NA	81.6	5,349	78.6
Henry	262	-2.9	288	0.0	213.8	1,807,194	6,267	167,085	177.8	195,843	58.8	41.2	7	74.2	6,564	73.2
Howard	299	-0.3	340	0.5	273.7	2,537,364	7,455	246,741	285.0	324,225	52.1	47.9	27	73.7	6,702	75.4
Humboldt	240	2.0	419	0.3	230.8	3,387,096	8,088	295,137	180.9	316,248	69.4	30.6	NA	79.0	4,733	83.0
Ida	263	0.8	501	D	239.3	3,681,819	7,347	326,692	222.8	424,358	63.3	36.7	11	78.5	3,738	77.9
Iowa	347	3.1	357	D	283.4	2,291,958	6,415	209,704	227.9	234,951	61.6	38.4	11	81.2	7,532	73.5
Jackson	316	2.2	285	0.2	228.4	1,703,564	5,973	189,407	264.1	238,539	37.5	62.5	7	78.1	7,264	73.4
Jasper	378	1.2	384	0.6	320.0	2,497,555	6,512	256,238	252.8	256,395	70.7	29.3	3	84.0	3,560	51.8
Jefferson	206	3.9	324	0.1	170.4	1,792,949	5,538	161,501	108.6	170,704	62.6	37.4	25	71.9	5,626	70.0
Johnson	304	-7.4	242	0.9	264.9	1,945,168	8,037	174,726	219.6	174,717	65.3	34.7	94	75.6	10,976	63.2
Jones	344	9.5	310	0.1	285.9	2,155,654	6,962	232,937	288.0	259,458	54.3	45.7	2	80.5	8,615	74.4
Keokuk	318	7.7	343	0.1	262.9	2,003,712	5,837	195,144	216.3	233,309	52.0	48.0	13	79.0	10,997	79.6
Kossuth	594	-0.9	441	2.1	573.4	3,480,288	7,892	300,789	588.1	436,566	54.3	45.7	15	80.3	14,891	87.8
Lee	220	-6.6	263	1.1	166.4	1,360,388	5,166	124,972	122.7	146,585	61.3	38.7	3	75.9	3,860	62.5
Linn	325	-4.4	236	0.7	284.6	1,966,919	8,328	167,553	218.8	159,214	74.0	26.0	1	84.2	7,745	63.5
Louisa	190	12.7	330	16.9	165.3	2,187,445	6,631	230,894	205.9	357,387	45.4	54.6	2	79.7	4,825	80.7
Lucas	175	-1.1	309	0.0	106.9	1,055,881	3,413	108,610	50.1	88,383	45.3	54.7	NA	74.3	4,943	65.8
Lyon	346	-6.4	309	1.4	318.2	3,082,560	9,988	287,450	923.6	823,148	20.6	79.4	4	83.1	3,718	75.7
Madison	271	-1.8	277	0.5	179.3	1,572,389	5,668	140,797	119.3	122,129	60.0	40.0	4	76.3	5,316	59.3
Mahaska	311	-3.7	330	0.1	262.9	2,043,469	6,193	198,211	280.7	297,707	43.4	56.6	1	80.2	7,046	76.6
Marion	255	-3.7	248	0.1	195.7	1,428,870	5,771	129,159	110.6	107,378	76.1	23.9	9	79.6	6,125	58.5
Marshall	316	1.3	357	0.0	289.6	2,714,523	7,600	259,796	266.0	300,265	65.9	34.1	4	84.2	4,640	49.8
Mills	208	0.6	399	1.9	188.9	2,391,040	5,992	221,104	98.8	189,944	97.9	2.1	2	82.5	5,150	73.1
Mitchell	289	-2.4	367	1.8	272.0	2,883,359	7,865	275,666	315.9	400,393	47.7	52.3	9	80.1	5,099	77.1
Monona	334	-1.3	539	60.4	293.2	3,107,691	5,762	317,189	192.6	311,189	80.1	19.9	NA	77.9	8,869	82.1
Monroe	193	-1.0	312	D	113.9	1,314,106	4,206	119,256	61.6	99,710	48.0	52.0	1	75.2	6,442	65.7
Montgomery	245	0.0	475	D	213.2	2,695,892	5,680	266,552	155.7	301,806	71.6	28.4	3	83.3	4,661	82.8
Muscatine	219	2.0	307	10.4	187.4	2,063,703	6,720	204,328	185.4	259,639	55.8	44.2	4	77.0	3,374	70.0
O'Brien	314	3.2	359	0.8	294.0	3,489,359	9,727	273,559	501.2	572,092	35.5	64.5	7	83.7	6,056	81.4
Osceola	235	-1.4	397	1.5	225.0	3,481,261	8,762	297,874	459.0	776,591	27.4	72.6	NA	85.3	5,537	83.9
Page	325	2.6	455	0.5	272.6	2,444,334	5,370	212,178	168.1	235,057	80.1	19.9	4	84.5	3,359	66.4
Palo Alto	342	-4.7	436	6.8	329.4	3,491,702	8,014	322,625	468.3	596,596	38.9	61.1	15	81.4	11,659	87.4
Plymouth	503	-7.1	413	2.8	452.6	3,535,476	8,561	285,527	738.2	605,578	33.9	66.1	5	80.3	7,240	79.2
Pocahontas	329	-0.8	451	0.4	319.5	3,638,642	8,064	311,860	356.0	487,684	48.3	51.7	5	78.6	5,254	89.5
Polk	194	-1.9	257	0.8	173.9	2,269,262	8,841	163,985	110.9	146,873	88.1	11.9	2	83.7	2,098	33.0
Pottawattamie	512	-4.0	459	2.6	465.2	3,116,311	6,784	285,570	409.3	367,376	69.8	30.2	9	80.6	4,495	48.1
Poweshiek	340	1.5	399	0.1	293.7	2,673,805	6,708	240,513	314.5	369,148	47.9	52.1	2	77.8	4,962	74.4
Ringgold	303	12.4	449	D	208.9	1,731,086	3,854	142,521	121.4	179,914	41.3	58.7	9	74.7	10,630	75.9
Sac	353	-1.1	397	0.7	330.7	3,155,661	7,943	295,984	459.5	516,830	39.9	60.1	11	81.2	5,280	64.0
Scott	220	-0.3	322	1.9	201.7	3,083,078	9,588	263,956	223.8	327,151	58.0	42.0	6	82.7	3,084	73.4
Shelby	371	-0.5	416	D	343.5	2,853,345	6,853	242,943	305.4	343,181	64.2	35.8	9	79.9	7,416	83.9
Sioux	484	-0.2	280	9.6	453.5	2,918,016	10,405	297,115	1,696.1	983,814	16.4	83.6	5	86.9	4,371	46.1
Story	304	-0.6	318	0.4	284.2	3,013,807	9,467	199,884	224.9	235,519	73.0	27.0	12	86.4	4,910	51.8
Tama	407	1.1	380	0.1	362.2	2,754,577	7,256	245,618	288.0	268,670	68.4	31.6	8	77.5	7,483	61.1
Taylor	289	3.6	433	D	225.3	2,081,546	4,812	169,533	128.0	191,942	65.8	34.2	2	72.4	10,007	77.4
Union	246	14.8	392	D	176.6	1,749,559	4,458	169,761	129.2	206,137	41.9	58.1	15	80.7	6,028	66.8
Van Buren	210	-1.4	305	0.0	139.8	1,424,733	4,674	130,212	97.8	141,791	40.4	59.6	5	70.1	5,276	57.2
Wapello	199	5.6	279	0.0	153.0	1,359,960	4,876	148,496	78.1	109,175	72.7	27.3	1	78.3	4,434	61.8
Warren	247	-6.2	204	0.0	181.7	1,147,348	5,636	105,972	79.0	65,045	85.0	15.0	3	78.3	6,028	48.2
Washington	310	-1.3	275	0.3	263.7	1,894,242	6,889	209,805	671.9	595,126	20.5	79.5	38	75.6	9,990	74.7
Wayne	285	4.2	384	0.0	201.8	1,632,207	4,252	159,124	91.8	123,524	57.9	42.1	7	64.6	7,493	71.3
Webster	409	0.1	426	0.0	387.1	3,388,576	7,948	258,965	320.7	334,043	67.0	33.0	1	79.8	11,444	83.4
Winnebago	246	4.5	431	0.0	234.5	3,012,461	6,989	297,495	239.9	420,168	54.5	45.5	1	83.0	8,604	84.9
Winneshiek	391	4.0	268	0.1	322.6	1,718,306	6,401	199,801	337.4	231,388	41.9	58.1	33	82.7	8,883	74.7
Woodbury	451	1.1	435	4.6	395.6	3,205,600	7,375	255,301	368.8	355,602	54.1	45.9	1	81.6	12,463	74.3
Worth	239	1.6	410	1.5	223.1	2,854,365	6,956	308,236	144.4	248,129	86.1	13.9	6	79.7	7,896	84.2
Wright	356	-0.9	485	NA	340.6	3,671,012	7,573	344,709	481.9	655,631	38.9	61.1	NA	81.0	9,844	84.5

STATE County	Water use, 2015		Wholesale Trade[1], 2017				Retail Trade[2], 2017				Real estate and rental and leasing,[2] 2017			
	Public supply water withdrawn (mil gal/ day)	Public supply gallons withdrawn per person per day	Number of establish-ments	Number of employees	Sales (mil dol)	Average payroll (mil dol)	Number of establish-ments	Number of employees	Sales (mil dol)	Average payroll (mil dol)	Number of establish-ments	Number of employees	Sales (mil dol)	Average payroll (mil dol)
	133	134	135	136	137	138	139	140	141	142	143	144	145	146
IOWA—Cont'd														
Franklin	0.7	65.1	28	306	910.5	16.6	35	312	69.8	7.7	11	23	5.5	0.6
Fremont	0.5	72.4	15	133	140.8	6.9	30	580	160.6	14.1	D	D	D	0.1
Greene	0.7	73.1	16	375	1,211.6	19.0	40	463	96.6	10.1	6	8	1.3	0.2
Grundy	0.3	20.9	20	245	217.7	13.5	43	439	93.5	9.2	D	D	D	D
Guthrie	0.9	79.6	15	140	129.7	7.3	38	326	115.5	9.5	D	D	D	D
Hamilton	1.1	75.0	32	936	796.8	47.9	52	697	190.2	14.9	9	19	2.2	0.4
Hancock	0.6	52.9	24	185	232.8	9.7	44	427	228.4	11.6	8	41	5.1	2.0
Hardin	1.5	84.6	D	D	D	D	86	909	201.9	22.5	15	45	8.9	1.6
Harrison	0.9	64.5	D	D	D	26.7	44	463	273.2	14.1	7	14	2.9	0.3
Henry	2.0	102.3	24	245	153.2	9.3	60	885	244.5	21.7	11	32	4.3	0.6
Howard	0.5	57.4	17	123	167.7	6.6	47	444	116.9	10.1	4	3	1.9	0.2
Humboldt	0.9	98.4	27	276	321.4	15.7	42	524	102.3	10.8	4	D	0.9	D
Ida	0.4	59.8	23	339	307.8	18.6	33	326	58.9	6.6	8	15	2.1	0.2
Iowa	1.1	64.0	22	257	1,698.5	19.6	122	1,351	251.7	22.3	D	D	D	0.4
Jackson	1.1	56.6	32	223	163.8	10.7	73	923	281.7	24.0	8	11	1.8	0.3
Jasper	5.0	134.7	D	D	D	D	97	1,424	386.9	32.3	24	49	7.0	1.4
Jefferson	1.6	91.1	D	D	D	16.4	88	1,047	223.2	26.6	29	39	6.4	1.3
Johnson	10.0	69.6	99	1,343	1,391.7	75.3	470	9,142	2,264.7	236.6	149	702	147.9	31.4
Jones	0.9	43.5	25	252	183.6	10.7	72	834	257.0	25.2	D	D	D	D
Keokuk	1.2	122.0	28	200	149.1	8.0	35	246	53.5	4.1	7	D	1.8	D
Kossuth	1.3	82.4	36	404	289.7	23.6	84	890	237.8	21.9	D	D	D	D
Lee	12.4	352.8	35	451	395.3	24.4	126	1,881	440.3	43.7	26	72	9.1	1.9
Linn	41.9	190.5	305	5,149	3,401.3	327.9	679	15,106	6,405.8	369.6	251	1,123	256.0	47.3
Louisa	0.5	43.8	10	317	324.3	11.2	24	224	60.3	4.7	6	D	1.2	D
Lucas	0.5	54.1	6	31	10.6	0.8	34	517	95.1	11.3	4	12	1.5	0.5
Lyon	2.4	205.2	24	221	283.3	10.5	54	402	89.4	7.8	10	41	10.6	3.4
Madison	0.4	22.9	19	224	187.2	12.4	53	564	104.5	11.6	13	18	7.5	0.7
Mahaska	2.6	115.6	33	395	273.6	17.4	92	1,066	205.2	23.2	15	39	7.4	1.1
Marion	2.9	87.4	41	D	283.7	D	121	1,542	385.9	39.4	32	56	12.1	1.6
Marshall	5.0	123.0	43	376	311.2	20.7	135	2,024	493.8	46.7	27	478	100.1	17.1
Mills	0.9	58.6	D	D	D	6.1	35	329	85.4	7.7	14	34	5.3	0.7
Mitchell	0.8	69.2	20	274	333.3	14.8	52	450	72.7	8.3	4	D	1.5	D
Monona	0.8	91.3	18	159	205.0	7.4	38	354	102.7	7.5	4	D	0.6	D
Monroe	0.0	0.0	9	67	45.2	2.2	24	261	60.2	6.1	6	14	2.2	0.3
Montgomery	1.5	141.7	13	128	191.0	5.4	44	498	96.7	10.5	11	43	5.0	1.1
Muscatine	28.9	672.9	D	D	D	D	128	2,108	535.6	51.4	47	171	32.8	5.4
O'Brien	2.3	165.2	34	441	494.8	22.0	88	778	162.5	16.5	7	22	4.3	0.7
Osceola	4.3	698.7	11	115	207.6	7.0	28	153	118.9	4.0	NA	NA	NA	NA
Page	1.8	114.6	21	192	147.1	7.4	66	619	122.1	14.0	10	15	2.9	0.2
Palo Alto	0.8	85.4	18	174	236.3	8.7	39	348	78.1	7.8	6	13	1.1	0.3
Plymouth	3.3	134.7	D	D	D	D	94	1,019	327.2	25.0	27	62	12.0	1.7
Pocahontas	0.5	68.5	15	169	258.0	7.6	35	224	48.2	5.3	NA	NA	NA	NA
Polk	56.1	119.9	698	13,485	16,611.0	834.1	1,495	30,271	8,958.0	840.0	684	3,765	900.9	167.8
Pottawattamie	15.0	160.3	94	1,485	1,441.6	85.4	265	5,815	1,575.9	138.4	93	392	71.7	14.6
Poweshiek	1.3	71.7	22	160	136.1	7.7	78	1,605	584.4	61.3	D	D	D	D
Ringgold	0.0	0.0	D	D	D	D	23	211	48.9	4.6	NA	NA	NA	NA
Sac	1.1	113.8	31	306	259.6	16.1	52	306	95.7	7.7	NA	NA	NA	NA
Scott	17.8	103.5	253	3,698	2,221.0	195.7	633	11,830	3,209.8	308.2	199	821	189.7	31.4
Shelby	2.0	164.3	27	333	256.2	13.6	50	528	148.1	10.9	9	16	1.8	0.4
Sioux	9.1	261.3	85	1,632	1,309.9	76.2	159	1,599	423.2	37.8	33	157	35.9	7.3
Story	8.4	87.7	78	1,444	1,083.4	56.5	281	5,073	1,193.9	119.7	117	522	90.8	23.1
Tama	2.7	153.4	26	201	183.7	8.5	58	564	156.6	13.0	5	11	2.3	0.3
Taylor	0.0	0.0	D	D	D	2.9	15	152	40.0	2.5	5	D	1.2	D
Union	4.2	332.8	17	238	231.9	12.6	51	778	172.1	17.9	8	D	2.0	D
Van Buren	0.0	0.0	D	D	D	1.4	24	225	45.7	4.5	3	4	0.2	0.1
Wapello	7.9	225.7	30	220	267.3	10.8	136	2,315	592.7	58.4	26	124	24.8	3.8
Warren	1.0	20.6	42	388	197.7	18.4	103	1,739	409.7	43.3	D	D	D	D
Washington	1.8	81.4	45	639	365.1	33.3	87	1,006	201.1	24.0	9	13	1.8	0.3
Wayne	0.0	0.0	D	D	D	3.7	25	213	50.2	4.4	NA	NA	NA	NA
Webster	11.0	297.0	63	771	390.6	45.4	160	2,555	596.8	60.6	42	227	36.2	6.2
Winnebago	0.9	83.9	25	273	250.9	15.0	52	546	173.5	13.9	3	6	0.9	0.1
Winneshiek	1.3	64.2	41	350	249.3	15.6	116	1,201	300.3	29.5	14	23	2.3	0.4
Woodbury	14.0	135.9	163	2,368	2,167.6	123.5	407	7,373	2,009.5	176.1	95	497	81.0	15.6
Worth	0.5	59.5	13	106	131.8	4.9	26	189	37.6	3.9	3	2	0.3	0.0
Wright	1.2	97.1	19	319	556.9	18.0	54	533	89.9	11.2	8	12	1.9	0.3

1 Merchant wholesalers, except manufacturers' sales branches and offices. 2. Employer establishments.

STATE County	Professional, scientific, and technical services, 2017				Manufacturing, 2017				Accommodation and food services, 2017			
	Number of establish-ments	Number of employees	Sales (mil dol)	Average payroll (mil dol)	Number of establish-ments	Number of employees	Sales (mil dol)	Average payroll (mil dol)	Number of establis-hments	Number of employees	Sales (mil dol)	Annual payroll (mil dol)
	147	148	149	150	151	152	153	154	155	156	157	158
IOWA—Cont'd												
Franklin	14	59	5.3	1.6	25	860	249.3	35.6	16	172	6.6	1.7
Fremont	9	37	4.1	1.2	10	960	332.4	24.8	19	193	9.5	2.6
Greene	18	65	6.9	3.4	11	498	141.5	23.3	20	161	9.1	2.6
Grundy	8	33	4.8	1.0	13	418	141.8	21.1	20	161	5.8	1.3
Guthrie	20	75	14.4	3.7	8	495	350.0	17.2	D	D	D	D
Hamilton	22	82	16.7	5.4	22	779	303.4	35.5	26	238	11.2	2.9
Hancock	18	504	34.7	23.0	26	1,002	379.3	52.2	16	140	4.9	1.5
Hardin	33	131	13.3	4.2	28	567	974.0	30.9	31	316	13.7	3.7
Harrison	18	49	8.3	1.8	16	235	96.5	12.3	29	289	14.4	3.6
Henry	35	127	17.2	5.1	32	2,423	858.2	111.9	D	D	D	D
Howard	D	D	D	D	22	1,004	271.0	42.7	D	D	D	D
Humboldt	16	58	6.5	2.3	19	877	241.0	43.6	19	208	8.0	2.2
Ida	11	54	3.3	1.2	14	1,463	575.6	78.6	12	66	3.4	0.8
Iowa	25	194	34.6	21.5	24	4,376	1,777.8	185.9	36	455	19.7	6.4
Jackson	D	D	D	D	31	904	241.4	36.2	43	497	20.7	5.4
Jasper	50	480	131.5	25.0	36	1,945	518.8	90.0	60	779	40.8	10.9
Jefferson	132	502	87.6	29.2	31	864	203.3	46.5	41	482	24.6	7.3
Johnson	291	2,899	367.3	144.5	82	5,024	6,863.4	261.0	D	D	D	D
Jones	23	105	11.3	3.5	25	690	194.1	29.3	39	386	19.9	5.6
Keokuk	D	D	7.3	D	12	141	56.0	6.6	13	D	3.6	D
Kossuth	38	257	36.0	11.2	28	1,415	889.8	72.4	32	347	15.4	4.5
Lee	41	261	24.4	9.8	63	4,107	2,331.1	239.5	95	1,072	49.5	13.1
Linn	526	6,517	1,041.2	468.8	206	16,906	10,451.7	1,448.7	540	9,764	480.5	148.8
Louisa	12	32	3.3	0.8	D	1,489	D	65.5	16	D	3.6	D
Lucas	15	45	3.7	1.2	7	119	26.0	6.9	D	D	D	D
Lyon	24	131	23.2	13.8	27	623	133.5	32.9	20	602	70.6	12.5
Madison	29	95	10.2	3.5	19	159	38.7	7.6	D	D	D	D
Mahaska	27	132	14.2	5.7	29	1,234	756.6	62.0	38	540	23.8	6.3
Marion	57	403	65.3	18.3	41	6,668	2,143.2	375.5	71	1,099	45.1	11.9
Marshall	41	323	58.1	14.2	38	4,551	2,485.0	278.4	78	1,035	49.7	14.3
Mills	32	119	12.2	5.4	9	37	7.7	1.4	D	D	D	D
Mitchell	13	70	6.0	2.3	19	848	646.9	46.0	19	158	6.9	1.7
Monona	12	39	4.2	1.9	6	49	18.9	2.7	20	150	8.0	2.0
Monroe	13	42	6.8	1.5	12	763	618.4	45.0	21	168	6.6	1.7
Montgomery	17	61	10.0	2.8	12	543	238.5	27.5	22	270	10.3	3.2
Muscatine	D	D	D	D	70	8,104	4,472.0	452.0	103	1,221	60.4	15.3
O'Brien	29	174	26.7	7.1	25	589	685.9	31.5	D	D	D	D
Osceola	10	30	4.5	1.0	17	282	170.0	13.7	10	73	2.8	0.7
Page	20	119	7.4	3.0	16	1,246	346.1	70.9	26	289	13.2	4.1
Palo Alto	14	56	6.5	2.4	20	639	562.0	36.3	32	481	41.1	7.2
Plymouth	37	303	24.0	17.0	32	3,143	1,210.7	148.6	D	D	D	D
Pocahontas	15	42	2.9	1.2	12	400	90.7	18.3	13	D	3.2	D
Polk	1,602	16,639	3,136.8	1,175.8	343	16,918	8,337.4	921.3	1,205	24,155	1,485.0	426.6
Pottawattamie	D	D	D	D	61	4,966	3,442.5	224.7	209	5,738	601.5	116.2
Poweshiek	39	125	13.3	4.1	26	1,555	416.0	61.8	48	597	24.7	7.3
Ringgold	8	48	6.6	1.6	5	D	3.1	D	13	D	3.0	D
Sac	17	37	4.4	1.0	21	417	262.3	17.5	D	D	D	1.3
Scott	D	D	D	D	158	11,233	6,399.0	705.0	449	9,733	575.9	150.0
Shelby	21	171	19.9	7.1	17	739	323.5	35.6	26	236	8.9	2.3
Sioux	79	916	132.5	41.2	89	4,974	1,890.8	234.2	70	1,103	45.0	12.9
Story	D	D	D	D	76	4,599	3,279.3	269.0	248	5,077	244.7	69.8
Tama	17	53	6.7	1.8	18	1,190	746.0	57.0	27	1,062	118.1	24.3
Taylor	D	D	2.8	D	6	621	230.0	27.0	5	37	1.4	0.4
Union	18	67	6.5	2.5	12	1,474	364.7	49.5	29	429	16.7	4.6
Van Buren	7	32	2.9	1.2	12	580	129.4	27.7	12	D	2.8	D
Wapello	D	D	D	D	27	3,391	1,740.9	188.2	D	D	D	D
Warren	72	271	47.2	11.5	27	430	133.5	27.5	67	854	36.4	11.0
Washington	53	173	18.9	7.3	35	666	206.9	24.7	D	D	D	D
Wayne	9	45	4.6	1.5	5	344	61.0	14.2	D	D	D	0.4
Webster	67	1,253	33.8	76.7	46	1,863	1,793.2	117.3	95	1,390	71.2	20.0
Winnebago	18	137	11.4	3.5	19	3,169	1,007.6	152.3	21	191	6.1	1.8
Winneshiek	D	D	D	D	30	1,360	344.9	66.9	64	752	39.1	9.8
Woodbury	D	D	D	D	87	5,692	3,518.7	261.5	266	5,708	378.5	90.7
Worth	7	15	0.9	0.4	13	454	238.5	19.4	D	D	D	D
Wright	20	142	16.3	3.0	22	1,461	1,024.6	70.3	36	264	9.2	2.4

STATE County	Health care and social assistance, 2017				Other services, 2017				Nonemployer businesses, 2019		Value of residential construction authorized by building permits, 2021	
	Number of establish-ments	Number of employees	Receipts (mil dol)	Annual payroll (mil dol)	Number of establish-ments	Number of employees	Receipts (mil dol)	Annual payroll (mil dol)	Number	Receipts (mil dol)	New construction ($1,000)	Number of housing units
	159	160	161	162	163	164	165	166	167	168	169	170
IOWA—Cont'd												
Franklin	27	465	35.6	12.9	25	74	8.3	2.0	774	35.9	385	2
Fremont	16	314	25.5	10.6	D	D	D	0.3	461	20.1	2,918	11
Greene	32	575	40.8	16.8	31	96	13.0	2.4	698	28.0	2,620	12
Grundy	26	504	41.2	16.4	15	49	4.7	1.0	922	41.1	5,196	18
Guthrie	27	347	21.6	10.2	29	93	11.6	2.7	1,049	43.7	5,278	15
Hamilton	36	733	57.8	31.7	31	114	22.3	3.9	1,018	43.8	5,015	35
Hancock	21	547	44.5	16.1	26	203	28.6	7.7	922	38.2	1,285	4
Hardin	50	974	70.1	30.3	46	155	17.9	4.5	1,226	51.7	2,105	8
Harrison	32	843	80.1	31.2	22	52	5.7	1.3	1,059	55.0	4,116	14
Henry	59	1,149	92.2	36.0	43	143	10.7	4.1	1,284	47.3	8,300	39
Howard	20	550	41.2	15.0	16	38	5.5	1.0	845	44.5	2,200	9
Humboldt	23	513	32.8	15.3	17	49	9.8	1.9	760	36.2	2,659	12
Ida	20	491	39.2	16.8	D	D	D	1.0	557	26.6	3,458	15
Iowa	38	736	59.2	25.5	28	88	11.2	3.0	1,154	47.0	3,086	13
Jackson	42	609	47.3	19.7	48	122	16.2	3.3	1,487	59.3	4,847	32
Jasper	72	1,519	108.9	46.7	63	214	22.7	5.7	2,237	87.4	16,350	54
Jefferson	48	849	79.5	28.7	45	193	30.8	7.1	1,782	62.8	2,191	17
Johnson	437	18,459	2,629.6	972.6	223	1,417	303.6	52.0	10,429	506.4	263,241	1,104
Jones	41	855	60.9	25.8	D	D	D	2.7	1,359	68.1	2,689	12
Keokuk	17	317	24.2	11.6	D	D	D	1.7	716	38.1	873	3
Kossuth	34	717	61.9	23.1	45	128	14.7	3.3	1,361	64.5	2,559	12
Lee	100	2,235	171.9	79.7	71	246	23.8	5.8	1,750	67.3	2,567	11
Linn	661	15,576	1,839.9	709.5	383	2,815	303.6	92.0	13,667	623.7	121,332	845
Louisa	26	415	17.3	9.4	D	D	D	0.8	663	25.3	3,080	16
Lucas	24	522	35.1	17.0	14	47	6.0	1.6	629	29.0	535	4
Lyon	24	520	46.2	13.9	27	98	16.1	3.0	1,018	49.6	10,683	35
Madison	30	531	42.5	18.3	32	100	13.9	3.0	1,424	69.5	28,943	90
Mahaska	48	1,014	96.5	46.0	42	144	16.0	4.2	1,419	56.7	4,097	25
Marion	94	2,117	207.0	87.9	59	197	17.0	4.9	2,252	92.8	34,332	152
Marshall	95	2,442	204.7	88.5	58	247	26.6	6.7	1,865	71.4	12,825	61
Mills	35	603	34.9	18.2	22	65	9.3	2.0	964	41.5	3,180	23
Mitchell	25	583	46.0	16.5	32	89	8.2	2.1	851	40.3	14,676	76
Monona	26	674	54.1	24.7	14	55	7.9	1.9	603	27.7	2,648	12
Monroe	D	D	D	D	11	25	3.9	0.7	532	22.7	1,913	10
Montgomery	29	796	68.4	30.4	26	94	11.9	2.9	705	27.7	1,612	6
Muscatine	99	2,127	159.9	71.6	64	444	75.8	14.7	2,161	99.2	26,031	199
O'Brien	48	1,410	92.6	35.9	45	149	18.7	4.1	949	48.1	6,161	25
Osceola	12	245	19.2	7.4	D	D	D	D	402	17.7	890	3
Page	60	1,490	134.8	59.4	23	63	6.5	1.4	861	31.2	3,119	13
Palo Alto	32	747	52.9	22.2	D	D	D	D	744	31.4	450	2
Plymouth	58	1,070	78.7	31.2	57	225	27.5	6.7	1,842	97.1	16,257	45
Pocahontas	18	266	20.9	9.9	D	D	1.8	D	500	24.7	0	0
Polk	1,304	35,596	4,322.6	1,857.5	1,036	7,898	1,239.2	328.1	34,441	1,692.6	1,170,828	4,785
Pottawattamie	235	5,267	563.5	215.0	139	664	105.4	20.3	5,135	233.3	32,472	143
Poweshiek	53	1,049	106.7	48.8	29	89	13.2	3.0	1,235	50.5	10,337	45
Ringgold	12	344	30.5	12.1	15	56	6.5	1.3	451	21.5	490	2
Sac	32	513	33.9	15.2	19	45	4.5	1.1	850	39.3	2,945	10
Scott	533	12,882	1,288.1	536.0	301	2,121	199.1	61.9	10,813	527.5	102,021	422
Shelby	38	813	74.5	27.0	29	94	10.4	2.4	951	45.3	3,630	13
Sioux	92	2,786	200.0	83.3	97	305	36.1	8.6	2,787	132.7	29,176	117
Story	217	6,102	701.7	285.0	160	1,164	274.7	36.7	5,638	240.0	79,770	331
Tama	28	476	25.7	12.5	19	62	6.0	1.5	1,060	49.3	2,357	25
Taylor	D	D	D	D	D	D	6.0	D	522	22.0	1,018	5
Union	42	982	89.1	36.7	24	152	31.8	6.1	731	31.1	908	4
Van Buren	12	276	20.7	9.5	D	D	2.3	D	594	31.2	1,160	3
Wapello	95	2,924	255.6	99.5	44	210	18.2	5.3	1,589	61.8	5,143	23
Warren	77	1,260	88.0	41.1	77	284	27.2	7.6	3,762	169.3	142,817	544
Washington	66	1,381	104.1	44.3	50	113	17.4	3.3	1,802	75.1	13,798	63
Wayne	19	365	37.0	14.9	D	D	D	0.6	601	52.2	0	0
Webster	122	2,921	289.2	123.6	67	386	46.7	15.7	2,023	84.8	5,672	28
Winnebago	30	452	23.8	10.0	D	D	D	D	856	34.0	1,706	5
Winneshiek	57	1,557	126.1	58.1	48	205	21.7	6.0	1,833	72.2	22,774	106
Woodbury	336	9,461	1,051.2	411.8	173	1,110	115.9	30.2	5,465	261.1	48,123	235
Worth	10	191	9.4	4.7	D	D	D	D	564	19.6	1,400	5
Wright	28	835	135.2	41.1	27	68	10.1	1.8	848	38.7	4,182	19

Table B. States and Counties — **Government Employment and Payroll, and Local Government Finances**

STATE County	Government employment and payroll, 2017									Local government finances, 2017				
			March payroll (percent of total)							General revenue				
												Taxes		
													Per capita[1] (dollars)	
	Full-time equivalent employees	March payroll (dollars)	Adminis-tration, judicial, and legal	Police and corrections	Fire protection	Highways and transpor-tation	Health and welfare	Natural resources and utilities	Education and libraries	Total (mil dol)	Inter-govern-mental (mil dol)	Total (mil dol)	Total	Property
	171	172	173	174	175	176	177	178	179	180	181	182	183	184
IOWA—Cont'd														
Franklin	730	2,473,290	5.0	4.0	0.0	6.0	26.0	2.6	54.1	58.5	25.8	24.1	2,375	2,081
Fremont	330	980,119	11.7	10.5	0.0	12.2	0.3	2.4	57.7	33.0	15.7	15.2	2,189	1,933
Greene	642	2,310,941	4.8	4.0	0.2	6.4	34.8	4.2	44.9	77.5	17.9	19.0	2,122	1,805
Grundy	568	2,237,450	6.0	4.3	0.0	2.9	33.5	4.6	48.2	87.4	22.5	21.8	1,773	1,504
Guthrie	732	2,681,463	4.8	3.0	0.0	5.3	26.4	3.5	56.6	77.1	24.3	29.0	2,723	2,430
Hamilton	937	3,558,349	5.5	6.1	0.9	5.2	35.5	4.4	41.5	101.6	32.2	31.3	2,079	1,814
Hancock	523	2,009,716	5.3	5.5	0.0	7.1	34.2	2.2	44.5	66.7	16.8	19.9	1,854	1,634
Hardin	785	2,773,954	6.1	8.6	0.6	6.7	2.6	5.8	69.4	111.5	33.9	36.4	2,131	1,839
Harrison	678	2,337,407	7.1	5.5	0.0	6.7	2.9	3.1	72.3	63.7	28.0	28.1	1,993	1,792
Henry	1,053	4,316,495	4.3	4.6	0.2	2.9	27.8	4.6	53.5	109.1	35.9	29.8	1,487	1,282
Howard	540	1,907,281	6.4	2.9	0.2	6.9	33.2	3.9	45.8	80.0	15.9	18.2	1,970	1,793
Humboldt	535	2,050,493	7.4	4.6	0.1	5.9	29.6	2.8	48.0	65.3	18.6	19.3	2,012	1,766
Ida	318	1,172,919	6.0	5.6	0.0	7.5	0.0	3.8	77.0	27.9	13.0	11.9	1,739	1,487
Iowa	847	3,089,125	4.2	5.6	0.0	6.3	25.7	2.3	55.2	95.8	26.8	29.9	1,855	1,506
Jackson	703	2,797,720	6.5	9.2	0.0	6.5	17.5	6.7	52.9	87.2	31.3	31.7	1,637	1,355
Jasper	1,190	4,811,184	6.7	7.7	3.0	6.0	1.8	4.5	68.5	133.7	62.4	54.0	1,458	1,290
Jefferson	764	3,055,439	4.6	7.0	0.6	4.6	46.0	4.7	32.2	101.9	19.0	25.8	1,414	1,242
Johnson	4,304	18,758,728	6.6	8.3	2.2	5.6	4.8	6.2	62.9	578.7	198.4	290.9	1,948	1,752
Jones	694	2,531,220	4.8	7.1	0.0	9.4	2.7	4.7	70.9	74.2	33.7	32.0	1,554	1,293
Keokuk	591	2,136,703	4.9	3.1	0.0	6.8	24.0	2.3	58.4	56.9	18.8	17.6	1,736	1,588
Kossuth	756	3,193,530	7.9	4.7	0.8	6.2	33.9	3.9	41.4	112.0	22.9	28.2	1,885	1,615
Lee	1,283	4,891,782	4.7	7.2	3.4	4.7	4.1	9.1	63.3	132.8	58.5	47.5	1,388	1,122
Linn	9,297	42,529,348	3.7	8.5	2.7	4.3	2.6	5.6	71.2	1,225.4	483.6	472.9	2,107	1,750
Louisa	528	1,907,077	5.4	7.4	0.0	4.7	1.9	2.1	77.8	57.5	26.1	20.8	1,861	1,527
Lucas	567	2,212,003	3.2	2.9	0.0	4.7	37.7	14.5	36.5	49.3	17.1	11.1	1,302	1,186
Lyon	456	1,705,855	5.7	7.4	0.0	8.0	2.3	4.8	69.1	64.6	26.9	23.7	2,014	1,736
Madison	750	2,843,194	5.6	4.1	0.0	5.2	20.6	7.1	57.3	90.5	34.3	28.7	1,794	1,602
Mahaska	929	4,381,532	1.0	2.0	0.9	1.0	56.4	1.2	36.6	123.5	32.8	30.6	1,376	1,161
Marion	1,294	4,521,779	6.4	7.7	0.0	5.8	3.3	8.6	66.7	132.3	56.7	53.8	1,627	1,428
Marshall	2,003	7,151,943	4.2	7.8	2.1	4.3	0.2	4.3	75.4	179.6	83.2	61.5	1,535	1,257
Mills	605	2,098,241	6.2	6.9	0.0	8.0	3.9	1.3	70.7	55.2	25.6	24.8	1,644	1,435
Mitchell	558	2,106,103	5.4	4.5	0.1	4.7	37.2	3.2	43.0	39.7	16.7	14.0	1,321	1,122
Monona	456	1,498,814	11.4	6.5	0.0	1.5	2.2	6.4	61.8	37.0	14.4	17.5	2,001	1,883
Monroe	420	1,624,442	5.6	4.4	0.2	6.0	41.6	1.3	40.3	31.0	15.3	13.9	1,781	1,582
Montgomery	694	2,965,707	3.5	3.4	1.5	4.4	53.2	3.2	29.3	86.3	20.4	21.1	2,091	1,845
Muscatine	1,830	8,225,672	4.1	7.2	2.6	3.3	1.6	24.0	53.1	205.2	83.8	72.0	1,680	1,448
O'Brien	738	2,672,396	4.5	7.0	0.2	6.1	0.8	5.6	74.9	88.4	33.6	33.8	2,453	2,119
Osceola	205	739,165	10.8	9.0	0.0	14.8	0.0	8.4	56.0	29.2	6.2	10.0	1,655	1,512
Page	744	2,874,743	5.4	5.3	0.7	5.0	26.7	3.1	52.6	92.7	27.9	25.7	1,689	1,452
Palo Alto	660	2,358,550	5.2	3.6	0.8	6.3	30.0	3.3	49.8	73.6	18.3	22.5	2,488	2,246
Plymouth	1,185	4,839,864	4.5	5.8	0.5	5.9	26.5	4.1	52.2	185.6	42.7	47.0	1,877	1,670
Pocahontas	353	1,372,747	9.0	7.1	0.0	8.4	28.0	7.9	38.9	37.8	13.9	17.7	2,594	2,435
Polk	18,292	91,866,993	5.2	8.5	3.7	4.4	9.3	5.8	61.6	2,662.3	963.7	1,059.4	2,205	2,004
Pottawattamie	4,139	17,992,820	4.7	11.8	3.7	3.2	1.9	2.8	71.0	509.9	221.8	209.6	2,244	1,841
Poweshiek	617	2,484,969	5.8	7.7	1.1	6.3	0.7	7.0	70.5	73.5	29.2	33.7	1,837	1,590
Ringgold	398	1,587,151	4.8	3.2	0.3	4.9	40.1	1.5	45.0	45.8	11.8	10.4	2,075	1,892
Sac	427	1,636,145	8.3	7.7	0.0	9.0	1.8	10.3	60.9	41.7	18.0	17.9	1,831	1,639
Scott	6,416	29,440,373	5.0	8.2	3.6	3.5	1.6	5.3	70.0	821.4	348.6	341.7	1,981	1,677
Shelby	747	2,290,978	6.2	4.7	0.2	6.8	59.6	6.3	14.2	78.1	16.1	16.8	1,450	1,286
Sioux	1,589	6,244,439	6.2	4.9	0.1	4.0	31.3	5.1	47.3	192.7	52.7	58.2	1,674	1,406
Story	2,794	12,489,459	6.8	7.5	2.7	7.8	7.4	10.3	54.3	525.8	110.4	157.1	1,615	1,375
Tama	888	3,064,417	4.9	6.6	0.0	7.2	4.2	4.8	70.1	79.6	40.3	31.7	1,859	1,630
Taylor	269	882,058	10.7	5.8	0.0	10.5	7.3	2.6	62.7	27.2	14.5	9.8	1,613	1,430
Union	995	4,230,257	2.4	3.0	0.6	2.8	45.7	1.3	43.9	140.1	39.1	24.8	1,988	1,760
Van Buren	370	1,423,594	4.8	3.1	0.0	5.2	47.1	3.1	36.3	36.4	9.6	9.8	1,365	1,188
Wapello	2,085	8,499,871	2.7	4.5	1.8	2.8	2.2	4.4	80.9	188.5	82.6	51.4	1,467	1,210
Warren	1,616	6,933,651	4.8	6.0	1.6	3.6	2.4	5.2	75.0	202.9	91.7	76.6	1,529	1,349
Washington	1,143	4,532,672	4.5	5.5	0.4	3.8	31.6	4.4	49.5	135.6	38.4	39.8	1,792	1,505
Wayne	461	1,828,631	3.8	4.0	0.0	4.9	57.2	2.3	27.5	71.7	8.9	9.5	1,466	1,296
Webster	2,010	8,073,006	4.5	5.0	2.0	4.2	2.7	4.5	76.1	214.8	76.5	66.0	1,802	1,466
Winnebago	592	2,060,290	6.5	5.5	0.3	5.1	4.9	5.3	70.9	58.9	23.5	25.6	2,419	2,167
Winneshiek	1,424	5,316,173	3.2	3.5	0.4	3.7	34.6	2.8	51.3	181.8	46.9	43.9	2,178	1,924
Woodbury	4,357	20,192,238	4.3	8.9	3.8	5.0	2.4	4.9	69.5	520.8	255.6	182.2	1,784	1,389
Worth	333	1,159,232	10.3	8.6	0.2	10.3	4.0	2.7	62.3	38.7	14.8	17.2	2,303	1,999
Wright	1,003	4,509,426	3.8	3.7	0.1	3.9	51.5	1.9	34.2	159.5	31.6	27.6	2,162	1,959

1. Based on the resident population estimated as of July 1 of the year shown.

STATE County	Local government finances, 2017 (cont.)									Government employment, 2020			Individual income tax returns, 2019		
	Direct general expenditure							Debt outstanding							
			Percent of total for:												
	Total (mil dol)	Per capita[1] (dollars)	Education	Health and hospitals	Police protection	Public welfare	Highways	Total (mil dol)	Per capita[1] (dollars)	Federal civilian	Federal military	State and local	Number of returns	Mean adjusted gross income	Mean income tax
	185	186	187	188	189	190	191	192	193	194	195	196	197	198	199
IOWA—Cont'd															
Franklin	83.1	8,178	35.3	31.1	2.7	0.1	8.6	49.4	4,857	38	35	681	4,490	59,165	5,270
Fremont	39.5	5,703	45.2	5.6	4.8	0.1	22.3	10.2	1,468	26	25	402	3,130	60,040	5,131
Greene	68.5	7,649	28.7	43.3	2.9	0.1	9.0	33.5	3,744	31	31	795	4,130	54,035	4,615
Grundy	77.2	6,281	37.4	36.3	3.0	0.0	8.3	70.6	5,742	30	43	702	5,800	70,686	6,768
Guthrie	78.4	7,368	40.0	24.7	2.4	0.1	10.5	54.8	5,145	54	38	815	5,180	69,737	7,239
Hamilton	114.8	7,636	35.7	30.3	3.1	0.1	12.0	99.5	6,619	41	52	1,172	7,070	58,028	5,180
Hancock	69.4	6,453	36.6	32.9	3.8	0.1	11.2	29.9	2,782	46	37	640	5,130	59,602	5,426
Hardin	110.7	6,484	39.9	22.5	3.7	0.0	10.9	72.0	4,216	69	57	1,541	7,830	55,343	4,831
Harrison	64.3	4,557	55.7	6.4	4.2	0.4	13.3	24.3	1,726	71	49	805	6,780	60,411	5,424
Henry	118.1	5,891	37.6	32.1	2.7	0.1	6.2	297.7	14,853	71	65	1,516	8,920	53,299	4,207
Howard	68.0	7,367	34.7	32.2	2.8	0.0	9.3	37.3	4,044	34	32	735	4,590	49,541	3,987
Humboldt	62.8	6,561	32.7	34.0	3.6	0.2	10.4	29.4	3,071	45	34	721	4,520	62,162	5,784
Ida	31.2	4,546	53.5	1.7	8.3	1.0	16.5	17.8	2,598	31	24	351	3,340	68,757	7,633
Iowa	101.4	6,282	34.8	36.2	3.5	0.4	9.7	78.2	4,846	69	57	965	8,010	61,729	5,440
Jackson	87.7	4,524	43.0	16.9	4.1	0.1	8.8	27.7	1,430	81	68	974	9,520	52,516	4,553
Jasper	142.6	3,853	51.3	0.9	4.9	0.0	2.9	121.6	3,287	98	127	1,879	17,170	60,406	5,285
Jefferson	97.3	5,343	22.5	44.7	3.0	0.2	8.8	103.0	5,656	67	60	1,214	7,500	52,767	5,170
Johnson	614.8	4,117	47.2	2.6	5.6	0.5	8.1	732.8	4,907	2,094	571	37,293	67,870	78,749	9,639
Jones	81.7	3,962	56.2	6.3	4.4	0.1	12.9	64.9	3,150	51	70	1,223	9,120	59,651	5,485
Keokuk	51.9	5,122	46.6	21.4	2.6	0.1	12.5	24.3	2,401	45	36	506	4,490	51,031	4,093
Kossuth	107.3	7,183	27.6	34.5	2.4	0.1	11.0	56.8	3,803	68	52	1,015	7,350	59,630	5,341
Lee	126.9	3,709	47.1	5.5	5.6	0.6	7.8	114.0	3,331	101	132	1,866	15,370	57,406	5,841
Linn	1,263.4	5,630	51.1	1.5	5.2	0.8	3.5	1,327.9	5,918	1,072	805	12,131	110,790	70,549	7,580
Louisa	53.8	4,807	60.7	2.4	5.0	0.2	9.9	75.2	6,720	61	39	611	5,040	54,756	4,318
Lucas	48.1	5,634	30.5	43.5	2.4	0.3	9.8	68.8	8,058	45	30	581	3,970	51,196	4,155
Lyon	53.6	4,545	47.1	1.0	5.9	0.7	19.2	32.0	2,715	37	42	667	5,250	65,135	5,853
Madison	86.6	5,410	48.6	25.4	2.7	0.1	8.3	121.1	7,571	41	59	943	7,680	72,292	7,176
Mahaska	125.2	5,635	31.2	43.0	2.4	0.2	7.2	37.6	1,694	54	77	1,290	9,720	59,287	5,107
Marion	135.3	4,087	59.9	3.6	4.8	0.1	8.8	124.2	3,753	142	115	1,621	15,210	71,774	7,295
Marshall	186.7	4,659	64.6	1.8	5.1	0.2	8.7	120.2	3,000	108	138	3,038	18,060	56,586	4,672
Mills	56.0	3,715	53.9	2.7	6.2	0.8	13.5	32.4	2,152	39	51	1,404	6,740	71,015	7,164
Mitchell	50.4	4,775	43.3	2.1	5.4	1.4	14.1	69.1	6,546	36	38	666	4,870	58,249	5,065
Monona	39.3	4,503	54.2	0.8	4.9	0.0	17.8	14.7	1,681	39	30	520	4,050	55,376	4,945
Monroe	57.0	7,309	23.7	38.6	4.3	0.0	1.1	18.4	2,360	40	28	531	3,440	54,904	4,728
Montgomery	83.3	8,236	25.9	50.4	3.0	0.1	6.6	28.0	2,769	44	35	875	4,710	53,990	4,355
Muscatine	184.3	4,300	47.7	2.3	5.2	0.5	5.9	78.6	1,834	86	151	2,444	20,830	58,876	5,307
O'Brien	90.0	6,531	60.8	2.9	3.8	0.1	9.8	41.7	3,026	46	48	1,035	6,590	61,832	5,615
Osceola	32.2	5,348	28.1	0.6	6.6	0.7	13.1	8.1	1,343	26	21	289	2,860	52,860	4,364
Page	86.0	5,654	36.2	39.5	3.1	0.0	7.6	29.6	1,943	72	49	1,255	6,580	53,121	4,361
Palo Alto	72.8	8,043	32.0	35.0	2.8	0.2	10.4	34.1	3,763	39	31	963	4,220	54,010	4,669
Plymouth	201.3	8,032	26.7	46.7	2.5	0.1	6.5	129.3	5,158	85	90	1,470	12,420	67,405	6,649
Pocahontas	33.7	4,934	39.9	3.6	4.8	0.5	14.5	32.4	4,749	37	23	534	3,250	53,626	4,310
Polk	2,663.1	5,542	49.0	8.5	4.7	1.1	3.6	2,914.1	6,065	6,133	1,852	29,659	238,480	74,416	8,789
Pottawattamie	488.4	5,228	59.5	1.5	5.1	0.6	4.6	394.2	4,219	221	329	5,338	43,970	59,825	5,624
Poweshiek	78.9	4,301	45.9	0.9	5.6	0.0	25.1	55.5	3,028	60	60	804	8,300	61,952	5,809
Ringgold	48.1	9,583	26.9	41.9	2.3	0.1	12.3	40.5	8,065	27	17	450	2,050	46,323	4,379
Sac	44.4	4,527	50.2	7.8	5.2	0.2	16.5	9.4	957	39	35	554	4,790	57,916	4,856
Scott	823.8	4,777	58.0	0.8	5.5	0.5	3.7	602.0	3,491	664	614	7,880	83,840	71,579	8,274
Shelby	87.2	7,530	20.4	47.4	2.2	0.0	8.7	40.5	3,502	37	40	991	5,790	63,905	6,512
Sioux	191.4	5,503	32.2	31.7	3.3	0.1	6.9	146.2	4,202	88	118	2,331	14,640	71,624	7,529
Story	502.7	5,168	30.3	42.8	3.3	0.5	2.6	467.5	4,806	947	345	18,419	38,540	72,444	7,950
Tama	82.7	4,859	61.4	5.6	3.9	0.1	12.9	41.7	2,449	61	59	1,840	8,340	53,224	4,313
Taylor	31.4	5,145	43.4	5.2	4.5	0.2	28.4	14.0	2,291	39	22	373	2,730	45,747	3,509
Union	135.2	10,853	35.9	43.0	1.5	0.1	4.9	45.3	3,636	55	42	1,387	5,600	49,775	4,044
Van Buren	41.7	5,829	36.1	40.3	0.5	0.0	9.9	12.9	1,808	36	25	489	3,160	48,134	3,918
Wapello	223.4	6,379	69.2	0.7	3.7	0.5	4.1	80.6	2,301	117	123	2,343	15,670	49,996	3,875
Warren	186.8	3,731	58.7	2.8	6.1	0.4	8.5	248.6	4,964	99	183	2,365	24,650	76,260	7,893
Washington	130.9	5,895	40.9	31.0	3.2	0.2	7.3	139.4	6,278	61	78	1,450	10,410	61,144	5,224
Wayne	73.4	11,311	15.0	68.1	2.3	0.4	6.3	19.2	2,953	30	23	616	2,720	42,491	3,181
Webster	264.7	7,224	60.6	2.5	2.6	0.2	4.7	218.9	5,974	181	119	2,753	16,560	57,061	5,320
Winnebago	63.4	5,994	50.1	5.4	4.4	0.1	19.2	37.5	3,544	44	38	642	5,030	54,345	4,461
Winneshiek	181.6	9,023	45.4	33.3	2.0	0.1	6.1	88.0	4,374	80	65	1,893	9,250	60,839	5,956
Woodbury	530.3	5,193	56.4	1.8	5.0	0.7	3.9	434.4	4,253	636	363	5,818	48,820	56,110	5,136
Worth	37.6	5,049	46.8	2.8	7.1	0.1	15.4	25.8	3,460	28	26	346	3,560	55,164	4,265
Wright	125.5	9,829	27.9	45.3	2.3	0.3	6.3	71.1	5,572	71	44	1,432	5,770	55,135	4,360

1. Based on the resident population estimated as of July 1 of the year shown.

State / county code	CBSA code[1]	County Type code[2]	STATE County	Land area[3] (sq. mi)	Population, 2021: Total persons 2021	Population, 2021: Rank	Population, 2021: Per square mile	Race alone or in combination, not Hispanic or Latino (percent): White	Black	American Indian, Alaska Native	Asian and Pacific Islancer	Percent Hispanic or Latino[4]	Age (percent): Under 5 years	5 to 17 years	18 to 24 years	25 to 34 years	35 to 44 years	45 to 54 years
				1	2	3	4	5	6	7	8	9	10	11	12	13	14	15
20000		0	KANSAS	81,758.5	2,934,582	X	35.9	77.3	7.2	1.8	4.0	12.7	6.1	13.7	14.2	12.9	12.8	11.2
20001		7	Allen	500.3	12,464	2,246	24.9	91.8	3.5	1.9	1.4	4.1	6.0	12.1	13.0	11.4	11.8	11.1
20003		6	Anderson	579.6	7,778	2,590	13.4	95.1	1.7	1.7	1.1	2.5	6.5	14.6	12.0	10.1	10.7	11.4
20005	11860	6	Atchison	431.2	16,239	2,022	37.7	90.7	6.0	1.5	1.1	3.3	5.6	12.7	18.0	10.8	11.1	10.6
20007		9	Barber	1,134.1	4,110	2,876	3.6	92.5	1.8	1.8	1.0	4.9	6.0	13.2	10.2	9.9	11.1	9.5
20009	24460	7	Barton	895.3	25,216	1,599	28.2	81.5	2.2	1.3	0.6	16.0	6.0	13.8	12.6	11.4	12.0	9.7
20011		6	Bourbon	635.5	14,323	2,129	22.5	91.5	4.1	2.1	1.6	3.3	6.5	14.9	13.6	10.9	11.3	10.2
20013		6	Brown	570.9	9,455	2,454	16.6	84.3	2.9	8.6	1.2	5.8	6.7	14.8	10.9	10.4	11.8	10.5
20015	48620	2	Butler	1,429.7	67,889	790	47.5	89.9	3.1	2.0	2.1	5.5	5.6	14.7	13.3	11.9	13.7	11.7
20017	21380	9	Chase	773.1	2,598	2,989	3.4	91.2	2.5	1.7	0.6	6.2	5.1	12.2	10.6	12.2	10.5	11.1
20019		8	Chautauqua	638.9	3,395	2,930	5.3	88.2	2.9	8.0	1.1	4.9	5.9	11.8	10.4	10.0	11.0	9.8
20021		6	Cherokee	587.6	19,130	1,865	32.6	90.3	1.8	7.4	1.3	3.3	5.8	12.9	11.8	10.7	12.0	12.4
20023		9	Cheyenne	1,019.9	2,633	2,986	2.6	89.7	0.8	1.0	1.4	7.8	5.9	12.5	9.4	10.7	10.6	10.2
20025		9	Clark	974.6	1,977	3,043	2.0	84.6	1.7	2.1	1.9	12.5	6.0	14.4	11.7	11.1	11.8	9.6
20027		6	Clay	645.3	8,077	2,573	12.5	94.1	1.8	1.5	1.0	3.6	5.5	13.8	10.8	9.5	12.7	11.0
20029		7	Cloud	715.3	8,928	2,493	12.5	93.4	1.9	1.1	1.4	4.0	5.9	13.4	13.6	10.7	11.2	10.5
20031		6	Coffey	626.9	8,338	2,551	13.3	93.6	1.4	1.7	1.1	3.7	5.1	12.7	10.7	11.2	11.5	11.8
20033		9	Comanche	788.3	1,670	3,070	2.1	91.2	1.3	1.0	0.6	7.8	3.8	14.9	11.3	8.5	10.0	11.1
20035	49060	4	Cowley	1,125.7	34,496	1,314	30.6	81.4	4.0	3.2	2.9	11.7	5.7	13.7	14.2	11.6	12.3	11.3
20037	38260	4	Crawford	589.8	39,110	1,201	66.3	88.0	3.3	2.2	2.7	6.5	5.6	12.5	21.5	11.5	11.5	10.2
20039		9	Decatur	893.5	2,751	2,980	3.1	94.1	1.9	1.4	0.4	4.0	5.8	12.0	8.5	10.0	10.0	8.6
20041		7	Dickinson	847.1	18,459	1,900	21.8	91.5	2.3	1.6	1.3	5.6	5.2	13.5	11.3	11.1	12.3	11.6
20043	41140	3	Doniphan	393.5	7,471	2,620	19.0	91.8	4.1	2.1	0.8	3.3	5.3	12.3	14.8	10.5	11.3	11.6
20045	29940	3	Douglas	455.8	119,363	531	261.9	81.8	6.2	3.5	6.1	6.7	4.5	10.2	26.0	13.8	12.4	9.7
20047		9	Edwards	621.9	2,832	2,971	4.6	75.5	2.2	2.0	0.5	21.8	5.4	12.9	11.8	8.8	11.2	11.3
20049		8	Elk	644.3	2,441	3,001	3.8	92.7	1.5	4.0	1.2	4.5	4.9	13.2	10.2	8.5	8.8	10.8
20051	25700	5	Ellis	899.9	28,790	1,464	32.0	90.2	2.1	0.8	1.9	6.6	5.0	12.2	20.6	12.5	12.1	9.7
20053		7	Ellsworth	715.6	6,336	2,707	8.9	86.5	6.2	1.5	0.8	6.4	4.1	10.4	11.4	13.5	13.6	11.2
20055	23780	5	Finney	1,302.0	38,107	1,221	29.3	40.3	4.5	0.8	4.2	51.4	8.0	16.9	15.6	13.9	12.2	10.9
20057	19980	5	Ford	1,098.3	34,159	1,326	31.1	38.7	2.8	0.8	1.7	57.0	8.5	16.7	15.0	13.6	12.1	11.4
20059	36840	6	Franklin	571.8	25,986	1,563	45.4	92.7	2.4	2.0	0.9	4.7	5.8	13.3	12.9	12.0	12.1	11.7
20061	31740	4	Geary	384.7	35,934	1,285	93.4	61.0	19.4	2.1	6.5	16.9	11.5	16.6	17.5	21.1	12.5	6.2
20063		9	Gove	1,071.7	2,755	2,979	2.6	94.6	1.0	0.6	1.0	3.8	7.3	14.3	11.0	9.3	11.1	9.7
20065		9	Graham	898.5	2,400	3,007	2.7	89.6	4.8	2.0	2.1	4.5	4.6	12.3	9.8	9.7	11.5	9.6
20067		7	Grant	574.8	7,324	2,637	12.7	48.8	1.1	1.1	0.9	49.5	7.4	17.3	14.4	11.5	11.8	11.3
20069		9	Gray	868.9	5,644	2,767	6.5	81.1	1.3	0.9	0.8	17.1	6.8	16.9	13.7	11.3	12.0	11.1
20071		9	Greeley	778.4	1,304	3,092	1.7	77.8	0.8	1.2	0.6	20.3	7.1	16.5	10.2	10.1	14.0	6.8
20073		6	Greenwood	1,143.3	5,939	2,737	5.2	93.5	1.4	2.7	0.8	4.1	4.6	12.5	10.5	8.6	10.4	10.6
20075		9	Hamilton	996.5	2,484	2,998	2.5	60.7	1.4	1.8	0.8	37.0	6.4	16.1	12.5	12.5	12.6	10.8
20077		8	Harper	801.3	5,331	2,791	6.7	90.7	1.4	2.1	0.8	6.8	5.9	15.0	10.3	9.7	11.4	10.8
20079	48620	2	Harvey	539.8	33,817	1,336	62.6	83.9	2.8	1.7	1.5	12.6	5.5	13.9	14.2	11.0	12.3	10.4
20081		9	Haskell	577.5	3,668	2,911	6.4	66.7	1.1	1.2	1.1	31.5	7.4	14.7	14.6	11.6	11.5	11.2
20083		9	Hodgeman	860.0	1,710	3,065	2.0	86.6	2.7	1.2	3.6	7.5	5.0	13.3	11.5	10.6	11.1	10.1
20085	45820	3	Jackson	656.2	13,261	2,198	20.2	86.0	2.0	9.1	0.9	5.4	6.6	14.0	12.3	10.5	11.5	12.0
20087	45820	3	Jefferson	532.6	18,411	1,903	34.6	94.6	1.4	2.1	0.7	3.2	5.2	12.6	11.4	10.2	12.0	12.5
20089		9	Jewell	910.0	2,937	2,961	3.2	95.7	1.1	1.2	0.6	2.6	4.5	12.7	9.6	8.8	9.6	8.8
20091	28140	1	Johnson	473.6	613,219	113	1,294.8	81.0	6.1	0.9	6.4	8.2	5.9	13.5	12.2	13.5	14.5	12.6
20093	23780	9	Kearny	870.5	3,891	2,895	4.5	64.8	2.1	2.0	0.9	32.2	7.1	17.3	12.6	12.2	12.4	10.1
20095		2	Kingman	863.4	7,392	2,630	8.6	93.6	1.1	1.7	0.9	4.5	5.4	12.3	11.2	10.6	11.6	11.1
20097		9	Kiowa	722.6	2,392	3,009	3.3	90.9	2.3	1.7	2.1	5.1	5.4	13.9	14.3	10.2	10.2	9.9
20099	37660	7	Labette	645.4	19,912	1,820	30.9	88.2	5.6	3.8	1.1	5.3	6.6	13.8	11.5	11.3	11.1	11.2
20101		9	Lane	717.4	1,565	3,074	2.2	86.4	1.9	2.5	1.1	11.1	5.2	14.2	10.3	10.7	9.2	11.8
20103	28140	1	Leavenworth	463.4	82,184	700	177.4	81.1	10.0	1.7	2.9	7.7	6.1	13.5	11.8	13.6	14.8	12.2
20105		9	Lincoln	719.4	2,903	2,965	4.0	93.9	1.3	1.0	0.9	4.1	4.4	13.3	11.6	7.9	11.7	9.9
20107	28140	1	Linn	594.1	9,747	2,433	16.4	94.9	1.4	2.2	0.8	3.0	5.2	12.5	11.2	9.0	11.3	12.2
20109		9	Logan	1,073.0	2,722	2,982	2.5	91.4	1.6	1.3	1.4	6.4	7.6	12.8	10.8	12.1	11.1	9.1
20111	21380	4	Lyon	847.5	31,998	1,383	37.8	72.8	3.2	1.4	2.9	22.1	5.8	12.5	21.1	12.1	10.9	9.8
20113	32700	7	McPherson	898.3	30,146	1,433	33.6	92.5	2.1	1.1	1.4	4.7	5.3	13.1	13.1	11.5	12.5	10.4
20115		6	Marion	944.3	11,712	2,301	12.4	93.6	1.4	1.7	1.0	4.1	4.8	12.1	14.2	9.3	10.6	10.3
20117		6	Marshall	900.2	9,979	2,406	11.1	95.8	1.3	1.2	0.9	2.6	6.2	14.1	10.9	9.8	12.1	9.7
20119		9	Meade	978.1	4,022	2,888	4.1	77.5	1.5	1.6	1.1	19.5	6.8	15.0	12.2	11.7	10.7	11.4
20121	28140	1	Miami	575.9	34,593	1,312	60.1	93.9	2.0	1.5	1.1	3.4	5.5	13.8	12.2	10.4	12.8	12.8
20123		7	Mitchell	701.8	5,748	2,756	8.2	95.6	0.6	1.1	1.4	2.6	6.3	13.2	13.4	9.1	11.1	10.0
20125	17700	5	Montgomery	643.6	31,156	1,397	48.4	83.3	6.6	6.2	1.8	7.4	5.5	13.6	13.5	10.8	11.4	10.8
20127		8	Morris	695.3	5,356	2,787	7.7	92.8	1.2	1.7	1.3	5.5	5.2	11.7	10.0	10.3	11.6	9.7
20129		9	Morton	729.7	2,692	2,983	3.7	72.7	1.7	2.3	1.8	23.2	6.2	14.3	12.5	9.0	11.7	11.6
20131		6	Nemaha	717.4	10,216	2,394	14.2	96.0	1.2	1.2	0.7	2.3	6.8	15.7	12.4	10.3	11.2	10.1

1. CBSA = Core Based Statistical Area. See Appendix A for explanation. See Appendix B for list of metropolitan areas with component counties. 2. County type code from the Economic Research Service of USDA Rural-Urban Continuum Codes. See Appendix A for definition. 3. Dry land or land partially or temporarily covered by water. 4. May be of any race.

STATE County	Population, 2021 (cont.): Age (percent) (cont.): 55 to 64 years	Population, 2021 (cont.): Age (percent) (cont.): 65 to 74 years	Population, 2021 (cont.): Age (percent) (cont.): 75 years and over	Population, 2021 (cont.): Percent female	Population change, 2000–2021: Total persons: 2010	Population change, 2000–2021: Total persons: 2020	Population change, 2000–2021: Percent change: 2010–2020	Population change, 2000–2021: Percent change: 2020–2021	Population change, 2000–2021: Components of change, 2020–2021: Births	Population change, 2000–2021: Components of change, 2020–2021: Deaths	Population change, 2000–2021: Components of change, 2020–2021: Net Migration	Households, 2016–2020: Number	Households, 2016–2020: Persons per household	Households, 2016–2020: Percent: Family house-holds	Households, 2016–2020: Percent: Female family house-holder[1]	Households, 2016–2020: Percent: One person
	16	17	18	19	20	21	22	23	24	25	26	27	28	29	30	31
KANSAS	12.5	10.0	6.7	49.9	2,853,118	2,937,880	3.0	-0.1	42,122	39,388	-6,356	1,141,985	2.5	64.6	9.8	29.1
Allen	13.4	12.1	9.1	50.6	13,371	12,526	-6.3	-0.5	162	226	1	5,125	2.4	63.5	12.5	30.5
Anderson	13.9	11.3	9.6	49.4	8,102	7,836	-3.3	-0.7	99	145	-14	3,154	2.5	69.6	9.5	29.0
Atchison	13.2	10.1	7.9	51.2	16,924	16,348	-3.4	-0.7	222	243	-92	6,039	2.4	65.0	11.7	31.8
Barber	15.0	15.1	9.9	49.0	4,861	4,228	-13.0	-2.8	53	79	-90	1,931	2.3	63.0	6.9	32.0
Barton	14.4	11.8	8.3	50.3	27,674	25,493	-7.9	-1.1	364	434	-208	10,628	2.4	64.3	8.0	29.8
Bourbon	12.5	11.8	8.3	50.5	15,173	14,360	-5.4	-0.3	236	240	-34	5,921	2.4	64.7	8.8	29.5
Brown	13.8	12.8	8.2	49.9	9,984	9,508	-4.8	-0.6	135	198	8	3,757	2.5	66.3	7.8	29.0
Butler	13.2	9.9	6.2	49.3	65,880	67,380	2.3	0.8	849	969	625	24,833	2.6	71.8	8.0	23.7
Chase	13.9	13.2	11.1	48.7	2,790	2,572	-7.8	1.0	26	30	33	1,082	2.3	66.0	6.7	31.7
Chautauqua	15.5	13.5	12.0	48.9	3,669	3,379	-7.9	0.5	37	56	38	1,418	2.3	67.0	10.1	28.6
Cherokee	15.0	11.6	7.8	50.0	21,603	19,362	-10.4	-1.2	249	433	-48	7,954	2.5	61.8	9.3	33.5
Cheyenne	13.1	14.8	12.8	49.3	2,726	2,616	-4.0	0.6	39	48	26	1,263	2.1	51.5	8.1	45.7
Clark	13.6	10.9	11.0	50.9	2,215	1,991	-10.1	-0.7	32	34	-11	890	2.2	60.6	8.1	33.3
Clay	13.2	12.8	10.7	50.0	8,535	8,117	-4.9	-0.5	90	139	10	3,741	2.1	63.4	6.7	35.2
Cloud	13.4	11.7	9.6	49.7	9,533	9,032	-5.3	-1.2	128	179	-54	3,641	2.3	62.6	7.1	30.0
Coffey	14.9	12.8	9.3	50.1	8,601	8,360	-2.8	-0.3	114	147	11	3,648	2.2	67.7	9.8	26.0
Comanche	13.2	14.4	12.6	50.9	1,891	1,689	-10.7	-1.1	17	34	-1	818	2.1	56.0	7.6	40.5
Cowley	13.0	10.4	7.8	49.8	36,311	34,549	-4.9	-0.2	454	694	186	13,800	2.4	62.7	11.1	32.2
Crawford	11.2	9.3	6.6	49.8	39,134	38,972	-0.4	0.4	511	583	204	15,603	2.4	61.4	12.8	30.5
Decatur	16.0	15.8	13.2	49.7	2,961	2,764	-6.7	-0.5	28	60	21	1,414	2.0	54.3	6.3	40.8
Dickinson	14.7	11.5	8.8	49.7	19,754	18,402	-6.8	0.3	240	322	141	7,933	2.3	62.6	6.9	33.1
Doniphan	14.0	11.9	8.3	49.1	7,945	7,510	-5.5	-0.5	86	123	-3	3,003	2.3	64.2	7.1	29.8
Douglas	9.9	8.6	4.9	50.2	110,826	118,785	7.2	0.5	1,303	1,044	282	47,972	2.4	54.8	6.7	28.9
Edwards	16.0	13.1	9.5	48.3	3,037	2,907	-4.3	-2.6	33	52	-55	1,285	2.1	62.9	6.3	34.2
Elk	15.1	15.6	12.9	49.8	2,882	2,483	-13.8	-1.7	20	48	-12	1,150	2.2	67.5	6.4	30.3
Ellis	11.2	10.0	6.8	49.8	28,452	28,934	1.7	-0.5	329	356	-121	11,686	2.4	58.8	8.5	31.3
Ellsworth	14.4	12.4	9.0	41.9	6,497	6,376	-1.9	-0.6	63	98	-5	2,390	2.2	66.0	5.2	30.2
Finney	10.8	7.2	4.6	48.4	36,776	38,470	4.6	-0.9	677	321	-723	12,494	2.9	70.7	12.1	24.3
Ford	10.9	7.1	4.7	47.8	33,848	34,287	1.3	-0.4	761	356	-538	11,237	2.9	69.8	11.6	23.9
Franklin	14.5	10.7	6.9	49.8	25,992	25,996	0.0	0.0	321	393	57	10,190	2.5	66.9	8.6	27.5
Geary	5.6	5.1	3.9	47.4	34,362	36,739	6.9	-2.2	1,097	300	-1,578	12,866	2.5	70.2	14.3	24.5
Gove	14.2	11.8	11.3	49.6	2,695	2,718	0.9	1.4	48	54	44	1,260	2.1	60.2	3.1	35.3
Graham	16.0	13.5	13.0	49.9	2,597	2,415	-7.0	-0.6	22	39	2	1,252	1.9	55.6	8.9	42.3
Grant	11.3	9.2	5.7	48.7	7,829	7,352	-6.1	-0.4	116	64	-82	2,561	2.8	62.6	6.3	32.4
Gray	12.5	8.8	6.9	48.6	6,006	5,653	-5.9	-0.2	94	85	-19	2,150	2.8	75.6	5.8	22.2
Greeley	15.9	10.9	8.4	49.4	1,247	1,284	3.0	1.6	19	17	18	491	2.3	68.4	11.0	29.5
Greenwood	16.1	15.5	11.2	49.2	6,689	6,016	-10.1	-1.3	65	113	-29	2,695	2.2	63.2	8.9	34.9
Hamilton	13.2	9.5	6.4	47.9	2,690	2,518	-6.4	-1.4	50	24	-60	818	3.1	58.8	6.5	38.6
Harper	13.2	13.1	10.6	49.6	6,034	5,485	-9.1	-2.8	80	128	-105	2,367	2.3	63.0	7.6	33.4
Harvey	13.0	10.8	9.0	50.0	34,684	34,024	-1.9	-0.6	458	553	-116	13,396	2.5	69.9	9.7	26.1
Haskell	12.6	10.0	6.4	49.4	4,256	3,780	-11.2	-3.0	80	40	-149	1,401	2.8	71.4	5.4	24.4
Hodgeman	16.3	12.2	9.9	48.6	1,916	1,723	-10.1	-0.8	15	48	19	790	2.3	67.8	4.6	29.1
Jackson	13.8	11.5	7.9	49.2	13,462	13,232	-1.7	0.2	204	186	8	5,429	2.4	68.9	9.5	26.6
Jefferson	16.1	12.0	8.0	49.0	19,126	18,368	-4.0	0.2	200	249	91	7,619	2.5	71.8	7.1	22.9
Jewell	15.2	16.9	14.0	47.8	3,077	2,932	-4.7	0.2	24	43	25	1,386	2.0	62.1	5.1	35.9
Johnson	12.3	9.6	5.9	50.6	544,179	609,863	12.1	0.6	8,362	6,488	1,338	233,599	2.5	67.8	8.2	25.9
Kearny	11.9	9.3	7.2	49.7	3,977	3,983	0.2	-2.3	73	48	-116	1,270	3.0	65.8	10.8	27.8
Kingman	16.4	11.8	9.5	49.6	7,858	7,470	-4.9	-1.0	89	187	22	3,253	2.2	63.5	7.4	31.6
Kiowa	12.8	14.1	9.3	51.0	2,553	2,460	-3.6	-2.8	16	38	-45	975	2.3	59.3	4.0	36.4
Labette	14.5	11.6	8.5	49.6	21,607	20,184	-6.6	-1.3	309	362	-218	8,270	2.4	64.4	9.8	31.5
Lane	15.2	13.4	10.0	49.9	1,750	1,574	-10.1	-0.6	9	33	14	737	2.1	55.1	0.8	43.7
Leavenworth	12.7	9.6	5.8	46.4	76,227	81,881	7.4	0.4	1,044	988	233	27,645	2.7	72.0	9.6	23.7
Lincoln	15.3	15.5	10.3	49.8	3,241	2,939	-9.3	-1.2	23	46	-13	1,305	2.3	59.9	5.4	37.6
Linn	16.3	13.2	9.1	48.9	9,656	9,591	-0.7	1.6	126	153	186	4,509	2.1	69.7	7.9	26.8
Logan	14.5	12.3	9.7	49.8	2,756	2,762	0.2	-1.4	36	31	-45	1,144	2.4	67.9	8.8	29.1
Lyon	11.5	9.8	6.5	51.2	33,690	32,179	-4.5	-0.6	437	422	-200	13,561	2.4	56.3	8.5	31.7
McPherson	13.7	11.3	9.1	50.7	29,180	30,223	3.6	-0.3	352	507	75	12,479	2.2	66.0	6.5	28.4
Marion	15.1	12.5	11.0	50.1	12,660	11,823	-6.6	-0.9	134	221	-25	4,838	2.3	64.3	7.6	31.2
Marshall	14.5	12.7	10.1	50.2	10,117	10,038	-0.8	-0.6	132	191	0	4,128	2.3	62.0	5.4	35.1
Meade	13.2	10.1	8.9	48.9	4,575	4,055	-11.4	-0.8	74	50	-58	1,715	2.3	66.2	12.6	29.2
Miami	14.7	10.5	7.3	50.0	32,787	34,191	4.3	1.2	380	428	452	13,000	2.5	72.9	7.1	23.0
Mitchell	13.7	12.9	10.3	49.2	6,373	5,796	-9.1	-0.8	94	138	-4	2,593	2.3	61.1	10.1	31.3
Montgomery	13.8	11.8	8.8	50.3	35,471	31,486	-11.2	-1.0	386	577	-142	13,767	2.3	61.3	11.0	34.0
Morris	16.0	14.7	10.8	50.1	5,923	5,386	-9.1	-0.6	39	99	31	2,344	2.3	71.6	9.0	25.2
Morton	14.0	10.8	9.9	50.4	3,233	2,701	-16.5	-0.3	67	61	-14	1,036	2.5	57.4	6.5	34.8
Nemaha	13.7	10.1	9.7	49.0	10,178	10,273	0.9	-0.6	144	163	-40	4,069	2.4	66.5	5.0	29.3

1. No spouse present.

STATE County	Persons in group quarters, 2021	Daytime Population, 2016–2020		Births, 2021		Deaths, 2021		Persons under 65 with no health insurance, 2019		Medicare, 2021			COVID-19 Deaths, 2020	
		Number	Employment/ residence ratio	Total	Rate[1]	Number	Rate[1]	Number	Percent	Total beneficiaries	Enrolled in Original Medicare	Enrolled in Medicare Advantage	Number	Rate[1]
	32	33	34	35	36	37	38	39	40	41	42	43	44	45
KANSAS	74,847	2,930,643	1.0	33,670	11.5	31,407	10.7	254,180	10.7	546,213	429,673	116,539	3,413	1.2
Allen	349	12,405	1.0	121	9.7	196	15.7	927	9.8	3,114	2,723	390	D	D
Anderson	71	6,828	0.7	75	9.6	122	15.6	654	10.8	1,852	1,628	225	D	D
Atchison	1,368	15,240	0.9	179	11.0	188	11.6	1,041	8.6	3,405	2,843	563	D	D
Barber	23	4,125	0.8	43	10.4	64	15.4	473	14.1	1,200	1,149	51	D	D
Barton	582	26,286	1.0	285	11.3	353	13.9	2,597	12.9	5,667	5,506	161	40	1.6
Bourbon	355	14,600	1.0	185	12.9	189	13.2	1,204	10.8	3,252	2,415	838	17	1.2
Brown	91	10,116	1.1	108	11.4	154	16.3	819	10.9	2,350	2,233	117	31	3.3
Butler	2,209	56,783	0.7	655	9.7	781	11.5	4,801	8.8	12,450	9,312	3,138	43	0.6
Chase	133	2,314	0.8	25	9.7	23	8.9	211	11.5	663	618	45	D	D
Chautauqua	76	3,040	0.8	30	8.8	43	12.7	372	16.1	941	863	78	D	D
Cherokee	141	17,296	0.7	204	10.6	356	18.5	1,746	11.1	4,625	3,618	1,006	31	1.6
Cheyenne	43	2,647	1.0	31	11.8	43	16.4	299	15.7	752	688	64	12	4.6
Clark	52	2,023	1.0	26	13.2	22	11.1	178	11.5	471	453	18	D	D
Clay	112	7,434	0.8	80	9.9	116	14.3	580	9.6	2,083	1,970	113	17	2.1
Cloud	491	8,409	0.9	100	11.2	138	15.4	624	9.6	2,277	2,171	106	22	2.4
Coffey	115	8,317	1.0	90	10.8	125	15.0	525	8.2	2,065	1,864	201	11	1.3
Comanche	58	1,712	1.0	12	7.2	25	14.9	171	13.9	502	482	20	D	D
Cowley	1,895	34,725	1.0	359	10.4	574	16.6	2,825	10.6	7,422	6,367	1,055	70	2.0
Crawford	1,710	39,483	1.0	411	10.5	466	11.9	3,638	11.7	7,444	6,087	1,357	56	1.4
Decatur	68	2,477	0.7	22	8.0	48	17.5	267	13.3	808	745	63	D	D
Dickinson	264	16,833	0.8	193	10.5	249	13.5	1,600	11.0	4,386	4,075	311	26	1.4
Doniphan	401	6,546	0.7	74	9.9	96	12.9	574	10.1	1,680	1,539	142	10	1.3
Douglas	8,352	113,441	0.9	1,009	8.5	854	7.2	9,568	9.7	18,145	14,566	3,578	63	0.5
Edwards	33	2,518	0.8	25	8.7	46	16.1	355	16.4	718	698	20	12	4.1
Elk	29	2,331	0.8	18	7.3	35	14.2	288	16.4	787	713	75	D	D
Ellis	998	29,689	1.1	252	8.7	289	10.0	2,333	10.1	5,321	5,121	200	60	2.1
Ellsworth	988	6,052	1.0	48	7.6	71	11.2	369	9.4	1,439	1,383	57	17	2.7
Finney	550	36,735	1.0	550	14.4	250	6.5	5,443	17.4	4,759	4,563	196	64	1.7
Ford	686	34,453	1.0	604	17.7	286	8.4	5,301	18.4	4,201	4,044	157	45	1.3
Franklin	445	23,570	0.8	241	9.3	334	12.8	1,867	9.0	5,425	4,481	944	25	1.0
Geary	895	41,207	1.5	878	24.2	228	6.3	2,249	8.1	4,135	3,653	482	27	0.7
Gove	53	2,711	1.1	44	16.1	37	13.6	318	16.2	660	640	20	20	7.4
Graham	35	2,546	1.1	17	7.1	33	13.7	226	12.8	716	674	42	D	D
Grant	75	6,938	0.9	93	12.7	52	7.1	1,005	16.7	1,163	1,100	63	16	2.2
Gray	45	6,000	1.0	76	13.5	68	12.1	896	17.8	1,059	1,023	36	12	2.1
Greeley	24	1,271	1.2	17	13.2	13	10.1	133	13.6	284	D	D	D	D
Greenwood	74	5,178	0.7	52	8.7	86	14.4	495	11.3	1,802	1,651	152	D	D
Hamilton	0	2,481	0.9	39	15.7	16	6.4	455	21.4	410	394	16	D	D
Harper	116	5,652	1.1	62	11.5	106	19.6	634	15.5	1,400	1,291	109	16	2.9
Harvey	1,206	33,039	0.9	369	10.9	436	12.9	2,884	10.8	7,862	6,000	1,862	44	1.3
Haskell	17	3,999	1.0	65	17.5	26	7.0	691	20.9	613	589	24	D	D
Hodgeman	8	1,689	0.8	15	8.8	35	20.4	189	14.0	423	411	12	D	D
Jackson	111	11,041	0.6	170	12.8	155	11.7	1,209	11.5	2,885	2,288	597	12	0.9
Jefferson	160	13,662	0.4	166	9.0	190	10.4	1,432	9.3	4,167	3,283	884	23	1.3
Jewell	25	2,615	0.8	20	6.8	36	12.3	242	12.2	899	857	42	D	D
Johnson	4,817	626,762	1.1	6,675	10.9	5,164	8.4	36,800	7.1	99,855	66,483	33,372	512	0.8
Kearny	78	3,766	0.9	51	13.0	38	9.7	562	17.8	648	627	21	10	2.5
Kingman	186	6,424	0.8	67	9.0	156	21.0	548	9.9	1,899	1,759	140	34	4.6
Kiowa	148	2,568	1.1	12	5.0	33	13.6	272	15.5	575	560	15	D	D
Labette	455	20,197	1.0	255	12.7	278	13.9	1,961	12.6	4,858	4,045	812	32	1.6
Lane	3	1,453	0.9	6	3.8	27	17.2	147	12.7	440	427	14	D	D
Leavenworth	6,363	74,704	0.8	835	10.2	771	9.4	5,102	8.0	14,050	10,746	3,304	65	0.8
Lincoln	36	2,771	0.8	19	6.5	41	14.0	290	13.3	820	798	22	D	D
Linn	42	8,579	0.7	98	10.1	123	12.7	884	12.0	2,488	1,642	846	D	D
Logan	37	2,879	1.1	27	9.9	21	7.7	228	10.4	675	642	33	D	D
Lyon	1,270	33,247	1.0	353	11.0	333	10.4	3,679	13.8	6,077	5,425	652	71	2.2
McPherson	927	30,378	1.1	289	9.6	402	13.3	1,989	8.9	6,663	5,885	777	50	1.7
Marion	687	10,431	0.7	113	9.6	168	14.3	1,011	11.8	3,031	2,907	124	10	0.9
Marshall	154	9,778	1.0	112	11.2	160	16.0	668	8.9	2,513	2,313	199	24	2.4
Meade	105	3,835	0.9	63	15.6	31	7.7	542	17.1	804	765	39	D	D
Miami	554	26,537	0.6	305	8.9	338	9.8	2,087	7.4	6,850	4,769	2,080	24	0.7
Mitchell	197	6,489	1.2	81	14.1	108	18.8	442	10.1	1,587	1,527	60	D	D
Montgomery	1,022	33,029	1.1	313	10.0	457	14.6	3,220	13.3	7,646	6,354	1,292	46	1.5
Morris	38	4,907	0.8	31	5.8	80	14.9	480	11.4	1,437	1,365	71	15	2.8
Morton	80	2,550	0.9	51	18.9	38	14.1	313	15.8	579	551	29	D	D
Nemaha	228	10,450	1.1	121	11.8	112	11.0	655	8.0	2,260	2,174	86	46	4.5

1. Per 1,000 estimated resident population.

STATE County	COVID-19 Vaccinations, 2021–2022: Number	COVID-19 Vaccinations, 2021–2022: Percent[5]	Education: School enrollment and attainment, 2016–2020: Enrollment[1]: Total	Enrollment[1]: Percent private	Attainment[2] (percent): High school graduate or less	Attainment[2] (percent): Bachelor's degree or more	Local government expenditures,[3] 2018–2019: Total current spending (mil dol)	Local government expenditures,[3] 2018–2019: Current spending per student (dollars)	Money income, 2016–2020: Per capita income[4]	Money income, 2016–2020: Households: Median income (dollars)	Households: Percent with income of less than $50,000	Households: Percent with income of $200,000 or more	Income and poverty, 2020: Median household income (dollars)	Percent below poverty level: All persons	Percent below poverty level: Children under 18 years	Percent below poverty level: Children 5 to 17 years in families
	46	47	48	49	50	51	52	53	54	55	56	57	58	59	60	61
KANSAS	1,787,573	61.4	758,270	13.9	34.5	33.9	5,951.0	11,957	32,798	61,091	41.1	5.7	63,214	10.6	13.0	11.9
Allen	5,734	46.4	2,873	4.7	43.6	18.2	40.8	16,636	23,493	47,983	51.7	1.2	48,616	14.5	19.7	18.7
Anderson	3,405	43.3	1,805	16.3	51.0	18.6	14.2	11,371	26,290	52,995	46.3	3.4	53,936	12.7	15.9	14.7
Atchison	7,497	46.6	4,942	44.8	49.4	20.8	26.4	12,012	24,250	50,683	49.7	2.4	56,691	13.1	14.9	13.8
Barber	2,083	47.1	960	16.1	42.1	20.6	9.4	12,275	28,934	49,668	50.3	3.0	52,749	12.0	18.2	17.4
Barton	11,171	43.3	5,983	7.6	42.0	21.3	53.2	12,662	27,333	48,863	51.3	2.0	51,149	12.7	15.0	13.3
Bourbon	5,356	36.9	3,476	8.6	41.7	21.0	26.2	10,990	24,198	46,369	52.4	1.1	49,821	14.5	21.0	19.0
Brown	5,840	61.1	2,281	14.3	45.7	19.1	22.4	14,792	25,183	50,649	49.5	1.9	49,483	13.0	16.4	16.1
Butler	32,618	48.7	17,998	12.8	35.2	30.4	171.8	9,226	30,689	66,405	37.9	4.1	71,827	8.7	9.4	8.4
Chase	1,228	46.4	616	2.1	35.4	27.1	4.8	12,320	29,645	48,906	50.6	3.0	57,338	10.1	12.8	12.2
Chautauqua	1,342	41.3	672	8.5	48.1	14.5	7.3	13,650	23,909	39,500	61.4	2.8	43,155	18.3	25.9	26.8
Cherokee	9,162	46.0	4,574	9.8	44.5	19.9	44.3	12,574	23,238	41,936	56.8	1.0	48,336	14.3	19.6	18.5
Cheyenne	1,219	45.9	559	2.1	36.9	26.0	6.0	15,284	29,914	42,802	55.3	3.9	50,623	11.8	20.0	19.7
Clark	927	46.5	416	9.9	29.9	30.4	6.9	15,142	29,227	52,500	47.2	3.0	58,365	11.0	14.3	12.7
Clay	4,843	60.5	1,950	9.9	41.8	27.6	19.0	14,082	28,784	47,880	50.5	3.1	53,119	9.8	12.5	11.9
Cloud	4,214	48.0	1,937	11.2	38.0	24.0	25.8	15,349	25,589	48,295	51.0	1.5	55,001	12.1	15.3	14.6
Coffey	4,372	53.5	1,629	8.2	39.8	23.6	23.8	15,761	33,494	59,405	41.9	3.5	59,142	9.6	10.6	9.6
Comanche	782	46.0	320	4.7	41.2	17.3	4.9	14,522	29,271	48,125	51.1	1.5	49,314	11.2	17.2	14.3
Cowley	16,892	48.4	8,955	16.6	38.3	22.7	77.8	12,767	26,743	50,786	49.1	2.2	51,398	14.0	18.7	16.8
Crawford	18,297	47.1	11,639	8.1	37.8	29.5	128.5	21,058	23,936	42,615	57.9	2.4	46,714	16.6	19.2	18.7
Decatur	1,144	40.5	490	3.5	43.8	20.2	4.6	13,085	29,659	44,125	54.2	1.8	48,189	12.4	19.4	19.2
Dickinson	10,422	56.4	4,246	14.8	39.1	24.3	39.6	11,342	31,153	53,864	46.9	3.9	56,755	9.8	12.7	11.7
Doniphan	3,675	48.4	1,953	5.0	41.7	20.5	17.9	13,330	26,916	51,953	48.8	2.8	57,012	12.9	12.9	12.2
Douglas	75,831	62.0	42,844	10.3	23.2	51.2	168.8	11,108	32,776	61,020	42.0	6.3	65,149	11.8	9.1	8.3
Edwards	1,364	48.7	563	3.0	41.3	20.1	6.3	13,376	27,487	50,028	50.0	3.3	51,756	10.8	15.3	13.7
Elk	860	34.0	503	4.8	51.2	17.5	10.1	21,584	25,374	42,564	55.3	2.1	45,974	15.1	25.5	24.9
Ellis	14,196	49.7	9,000	14.3	30.3	38.0	50.4	12,822	30,625	57,053	44.8	2.9	55,505	16.0	11.8	10.6
Ellsworth	3,447	56.5	1,279	4.9	40.2	23.7	14.8	12,246	27,402	56,306	42.8	0.9	53,443	10.6	12.0	11.4
Finney	17,095	46.9	11,116	4.9	52.0	17.7	91.9	10,702	25,204	60,498	40.4	2.3	65,023	12.2	15.8	14.8
Ford	15,145	45.0	8,947	3.6	51.6	17.0	86.3	11,108	24,364	53,743	45.7	3.3	54,442	10.3	11.7	11.7
Franklin	13,107	51.3	6,398	15.7	45.1	20.1	52.1	11,773	27,534	55,873	45.9	2.3	60,899	8.9	10.9	10.8
Geary	28,454	89.8	10,123	10.1	28.9	22.8	87.9	11,790	24,177	52,019	47.2	0.6	50,102	12.5	17.4	18.6
Gove	1,271	48.2	510	10.2	44.9	19.9	8.1	15,294	32,012	53,906	44.9	2.5	57,676	10.1	17.5	17.0
Graham	1,226	49.4	561	7.7	41.5	26.3	5.1	12,244	26,616	40,890	61.6	1.1	47,104	12.5	14.5	12.0
Grant	3,402	47.6	2,123	12.6	48.5	20.5	27.8	16,658	31,400	60,625	39.4	4.5	67,764	10.1	15.0	14.3
Gray	2,757	46.0	1,458	16.1	44.2	23.4	30.6	24,021	31,151	70,457	30.4	4.5	72,095	7.0	8.4	7.1
Greeley	633	51.4	277	1.4	39.7	26.7	3.2	12,004	27,300	53,750	44.8	2.6	66,089	10.0	14.0	12.9
Greenwood	2,963	49.5	1,184	6.7	44.8	20.1	13.3	13,903	28,912	43,320	55.5	2.1	50,399	12.7	20.5	17.7
Hamilton	1,057	41.6	693	18.8	61.0	18.6	6.4	11,381	22,558	44,894	52.9	0.1	61,342	10.4	15.7	14.2
Harper	2,622	48.2	1,235	12.2	48.7	16.4	13.0	12,733	25,119	49,283	50.7	3.7	48,275	13.2	18.2	17.0
Harvey	16,070	46.7	8,584	21.0	32.0	32.0	69.3	11,581	29,169	58,782	41.0	2.6	63,861	9.3	10.2	9.1
Haskell	1,554	39.2	955	14.8	50.0	17.5	17.5	24,503	31,535	54,638	45.5	6.9	66,053	10.2	15.6	13.8
Hodgeman	799	44.5	327	2.4	30.7	32.5	3.6	12,699	30,218	60,703	42.7	0.9	60,414	9.1	8.3	7.8
Jackson	8,462	64.2	3,236	8.5	46.3	20.1	32.0	13,147	28,853	59,686	39.7	3.2	57,871	9.3	12.0	11.7
Jefferson	10,384	54.5	4,164	15.3	45.0	24.5	62.7	17,271	33,441	67,429	33.5	3.7	63,712	7.2	9.4	8.3
Jewell	1,344	46.7	439	6.2	44.4	19.9	4.5	13,959	27,982	38,188	61.5	2.1	46,688	13.0	21.9	21.4
Johnson	455,825	75.7	152,933	18.7	17.8	56.1	1,014.6	10,788	47,997	91,650	24.2	13.9	91,799	4.6	4.1	3.6
Kearny	2,059	53.6	925	7.4	57.3	16.7	11.0	12,473	22,971	46,464	55.2	1.4	66,713	9.4	13.2	12.2
Kingman	3,366	47.1	1,450	14.2	39.3	23.7	14.3	12,178	35,664	57,304	41.8	5.5	58,678	9.8	15.0	14.5
Kiowa	1,268	51.2	628	17.8	41.6	23.9	6.7	11,397	25,889	53,107	45.9	2.3	56,664	12.3	15.5	14.8
Labette	9,719	49.5	4,297	11.1	40.8	21.6	45.7	11,764	24,963	47,922	52.5	2.4	50,222	14.0	19.7	18.8
Lane	660	43.0	270	0.7	37.8	22.8	4.6	15,029	28,775	41,318	54.8	3.9	60,530	9.6	15.3	14.5
Leavenworth	48,157	58.9	20,837	16.0	35.5	33.5	147.1	10,815	32,893	76,307	32.2	5.6	76,429	8.5	8.9	8.5
Lincoln	1,301	43.9	720	2.1	32.9	25.8	8.4	13,786	26,545	46,523	54.3	1.3	50,231	12.7	17.1	15.6
Linn	3,437	35.4	2,024	7.6	48.8	17.4	24.8	13,144	30,070	48,325	50.8	4.3	55,006	12.5	16.0	14.3
Logan	1,309	46.9	661	7.3	37.4	18.4	20.1	37,429	28,078	51,136	48.7	3.7	56,833	9.1	13.3	14.2
Lyon	19,125	57.6	10,280	6.1	43.3	26.9	72.9	13,191	26,429	50,141	49.9	2.4	56,290	12.6	13.9	13.0
McPherson	15,854	55.5	6,562	29.5	35.8	28.8	64.1	12,323	31,579	59,928	42.5	4.2	68,904	7.7	7.7	6.7
Marion	5,830	49.1	3,050	22.5	38.1	28.2	36.5	16,270	26,282	50,816	49.0	2.1	53,709	10.1	10.3	9.5
Marshall	6,257	64.5	2,024	13.1	49.8	19.2	24.1	12,585	29,502	52,293	47.0	3.0	56,429	8.7	11.4	11.3
Meade	1,649	40.9	922	11.1	40.9	21.1	7.5	13,341	30,774	56,817	40.3	4.2	52,590	9.3	12.2	10.7
Miami	16,309	47.6	7,967	9.7	36.5	31.2	107.1	11,616	35,642	75,635	30.4	6.4	78,717	7.6	8.1	7.5
Mitchell	3,196	53.5	1,408	15.3	34.7	26.1	19.8	17,498	26,117	47,375	52.9	2.6	53,745	10.0	13.5	13.3
Montgomery	14,598	45.9	7,753	12.9	41.1	20.2	74.6	13,247	25,719	45,288	54.2	2.5	44,071	17.8	24.8	22.7
Morris	3,149	56.0	1,121	5.9	43.0	26.5	13.6	12,513	29,407	52,792	46.7	4.3	53,793	10.5	15.5	15.2
Morton	1,085	41.9	567	0.0	46.7	16.3	12.0	8,791	23,754	41,866	56.6	2.0	56,878	12.1	17.9	16.8
Nemaha	5,581	54.5	2,521	12.4	43.2	26.9	21.2	11,917	31,715	61,382	43.3	3.2	62,744	8.3	9.0	8.9

1. All persons 3 years old and over enrolled in nursery school through college. 2. Persons 25 years old and over. 3. Elementary and secondary education expenditures. 4. Based on population estimated by the American Community Survey, 2016–2020. 5. CDC percent based on 2019 population estimate.

STATE County	Personal income, 2020: Total (mil dol)	Personal income, 2020: Percent change 2019–2020	Personal income, 2020: Per capita[1]: Dollars	Personal income, 2020: Per capita[1]: Rank	Personal income, 2020: Wages and salaries (mil dol)	Personal income, 2020: Supplements to wages and salaries, employer contributions (mil dol): Pension and insurance	Personal income, 2020: Supplements to wages and salaries, employer contributions (mil dol): Government social insurance	Personal income, 2020: Proprietors' income (mil dol)	Personal income, 2020: Dividends, interest, and rent (mil dol)	Personal income, 2020: Personal transfer reecipts (mil dol)	Earnings, 2020: Total (mil dol)	Earnings, 2020: Contributions for government social insurance (mil dol): From employee and self-employed	Earnings, 2020: Contributions for government social insurance (mil dol): From employer
	62	63	64	65	66	67	68	69	70	71	72	73	74
KANSAS	163,462	5.5	55,677	X	75,798	11,710	5,801	18,870	30,284	32,319	112,180	6,914	5,801
Allen	568	7.2	45,840	1,677	229	44	18	54	95	183	345	23	18
Anderson	349	12.6	43,864	1,967	92	17	8	59	48	102	176	11	8
Atchison	688	7.3	42,974	2,067	257	42	20	57	104	199	377	25	20
Barber	217	11.7	49,804	1,164	68	13	5	31	43	64	118	8	5
Barton	1,268	3.1	49,436	1,206	527	91	40	141	229	327	800	52	40
Bourbon	643	6.1	44,521	1,872	257	46	20	71	87	187	394	27	20
Brown	455	5.2	48,026	1,391	225	38	17	44	80	132	323	21	17
Butler	3,402	5.5	50,789	1,055	867	178	67	320	527	720	1,432	95	67
Chase	147	11.6	56,852	582	37	8	3	23	42	30	71	4	3
Chautauqua	145	9.1	44,908	1,807	28	6	2	9	30	51	46	4	2
Cherokee	881	5.7	44,739	1,838	287	54	21	125	114	263	488	33	21
Cheyenne	142	17.9	54,465	745	35	6	3	42	20	38	86	4	3
Clark	119	9.1	60,647	399	37	7	3	15	21	30	62	3	3
Clay	378	8.5	47,126	1,497	112	22	9	50	76	106	193	12	9
Cloud	384	9.9	44,452	1,882	127	23	10	60	63	119	219	14	10
Coffey	465	8.3	56,988	573	256	64	18	44	63	113	381	22	18
Comanche	78	12.0	46,141	1,629	23	5	2	8	15	26	37	3	2
Cowley	1,466	6.2	42,334	2,150	626	109	49	109	234	461	892	61	49
Crawford	1,664	8.5	42,963	2,070	739	137	58	140	320	464	1,074	71	58
Decatur	142	14.5	51,018	1,028	31	6	2	33	24	40	72	4	2
Dickinson	865	9.7	47,348	1,470	264	52	22	80	143	248	419	29	22
Doniphan	336	4.0	44,885	1,811	100	20	8	38	49	92	166	11	8
Douglas	5,819	5.4	47,494	1,451	2,299	428	173	438	1,152	1,073	3,337	208	173
Edwards	170	14.2	61,904	351	42	7	3	48	23	37	101	4	3
Elk	106	9.4	42,431	2,140	20	4	2	10	22	42	36	3	2
Ellis	1,456	8.0	50,785	1,056	680	128	51	190	232	329	1,048	64	51
Ellsworth	285	1.4	47,276	1,477	101	19	8	35	55	76	163	10	8
Finney	1,684	6.3	46,899	1,527	911	143	68	190	217	331	1,312	77	68
Ford	1,492	11.4	45,081	1,784	887	131	62	157	181	278	1,236	74	62
Franklin	1,194	6.1	46,437	1,587	440	59	36	104	162	315	640	44	36
Geary	1,761	5.8	54,663	723	1,659	491	156	49	327	359	2,356	100	156
Gove	160	6.6	61,150	381	52	9	4	49	25	35	114	6	4
Graham	134	10.1	56,190	625	37	7	3	32	18	39	78	4	3
Grant	317	1.5	44,835	1,817	128	24	10	57	44	66	220	12	10
Gray	359	3.6	60,355	411	130	21	11	90	56	52	251	12	11
Greeley	107	34.1	89,737	40	26	5	2	58	9	15	90	2	2
Greenwood	270	7.6	46,032	1,649	61	12	5	22	46	92	100	8	5
Hamilton	184	30.9	75,840	105	46	7	4	84	17	26	140	3	4
Harper	309	7.5	57,870	520	110	20	9	66	49	77	205	12	9
Harvey	1,601	6.1	46,698	1,549	650	105	55	146	241	429	956	67	55
Haskell	221	5.3	56,311	617	80	14	7	63	32	35	163	6	7
Hodgeman	109	15.9	61,030	385	24	5	2	31	16	21	62	3	2
Jackson	613	7.8	46,523	1,576	166	28	12	42	101	160	248	18	12
Jefferson	915	7.1	48,099	1,371	165	28	14	66	118	213	273	21	14
Jewell	158	12.2	55,860	652	27	6	2	41	30	40	76	4	2
Johnson	48,991	3.3	80,681	72	23,839	2,730	1,727	6,651	9,824	5,505	34,947	2,115	1,727
Kearny	232	15.1	61,932	350	57	11	5	71	34	45	144	6	5
Kingman	355	8.7	50,889	1,041	148	23	12	46	58	93	229	15	12
Kiowa	119	19.1	48,250	1,355	40	8	3	30	19	30	81	4	3
Labette	923	9.1	47,114	1,501	389	73	31	89	128	321	583	38	31
Lane	110	8.8	72,211	136	28	5	2	30	20	22	66	3	2
Leavenworth	3,798	5.2	46,176	1,623	1,517	382	131	167	654	853	2,197	127	131
Lincoln	156	20.1	52,328	907	47	11	4	21	29	43	82	5	4
Linn	426	7.8	44,155	1,919	113	26	8	39	64	128	186	13	8
Logan	158	18.1	57,732	529	52	11	4	34	25	38	101	5	4
Lyon	1,422	10.2	43,035	2,057	658	120	49	87	220	383	914	59	49
McPherson	1,662	4.0	58,438	498	807	164	61	239	259	369	1,272	78	61
Marion	543	7.7	46,588	1,564	137	26	11	74	79	153	249	17	11
Marshall	467	9.8	48,358	1,343	220	38	19	44	94	133	321	22	19
Meade	264	9.1	65,633	247	70	13	6	75	52	46	165	7	6
Miami	1,813	6.2	52,811	866	395	63	32	146	280	367	636	45	32
Mitchell	373	3.6	63,384	306	134	25	10	119	47	89	288	16	10
Montgomery	1,281	7.5	40,651	2,380	596	122	48	89	188	447	855	60	48
Morris	268	10.8	48,171	1,361	62	12	5	44	46	75	123	8	5
Morton	137	20.5	54,151	770	44	8	4	41	21	33	97	4	4
Nemaha	567	8.8	56,013	640	225	37	18	69	152	113	349	22	18

1. Based on the resident population estimated as of July 1 of the year shown.

STATE County	Earnings, 2020 (cont.)									Social Security beneficiaries, December 2020		Supple-mental Security Income recipients, 2020	Housing units, 2021	
	Percent by selected industries													
	Farm	Mining, quarrying, and extractions	Construction	Manu-facturing	Information; professional, scientific, technical services	Retail trade	Finance, insurance, real estate, and leasing	Health care and social assistance	Govern-ment	Number	Rate[1]		Total	Percent change, 2010–2021
	75	76	77	78	79	80	81	82	83	84	85	86	87	88
KANSAS	2.4	0.9	5.8	12.2	9.0	5.3	11.5	11.4	16.2	569,120	194	47,303	1,284,344	0.6
Allen	4.6	D	3.6	31.7	3.4	5.8	4.1	D	19.8	3,365	270	348	6,058	0.0
Anderson	19.7	2.9	14.1	4.9	1.8	10.5	D	11.3	14.8	1,920	247	124	3,572	0.4
Atchison	7.1	D	5.7	16.8	3.0	5.1	11.4	D	12.7	3,430	211	360	6,809	0.0
Barber	7.3	9.6	7.3	11.8	D	6.6	D	D	27.7	1,240	302	60	2,570	-0.1
Barton	2.8	8.3	10.4	7.2	3.5	7.8	10.2	D	14.9	5,900	234	468	12,369	0.0
Bourbon	4.8	D	6.0	19.6	D	4.8	11.9	D	14.4	3,585	250	350	6,763	-0.1
Brown	8.3	D	2.1	25.4	4.8	4.9	4.1	11.2	21.5	2,460	260	212	4,477	-0.1
Butler	2.4	1.2	10.0	14.9	D	5.8	7.2	15.2	20.4	13,565	200	811	27,250	1.1
Chase	18.1	D	3.5	16.0	D	1.9	D	D	14.9	600	231	33	1,396	-0.1
Chautauqua	11.8	D	D	7.8	D	4.6	4.5	15.5	24.8	1,080	318	108	1,976	0.0
Cherokee	6.1	D	9.0	27.6	D	4.4	10.5	D	12.3	5,045	264	596	9,130	0.2
Cheyenne	39.9	D	2.7	1.5	D	1.9	6.8	13.2	11.9	785	298	19	1,462	-0.1
Clark	18.2	0.7	D	D	D	4.3	D	0.2	39.2	475	240	27	1,041	-0.1
Clay	16.9	0.0	8.3	7.8	2.8	7.9	5.7	6.7	24.9	2,095	259	100	3,940	0.2
Cloud	13.0	D	3.7	8.2	D	7.2	D	D	17.2	2,385	267	199	4,493	-0.2
Coffey	6.9	0.7	2.1	2.0	1.3	3.4	D	D	16.3	2,335	280	153	3,995	0.8
Comanche	-3.4	2.7	4.7	6.7	D	7.2	D	D	31.8	495	296	35	936	-0.1
Cowley	2.3	0.7	4.0	33.4	3.1	5.6	6.3	D	21.4	7,965	231	702	15,610	0.2
Crawford	2.1	D	5.5	14.9	4.0	6.5	5.1	13.7	22.5	7,895	202	1,021	18,079	0.4
Decatur	28.7	D	D	D	D	5.4	D	11.5	13.3	855	311	46	1,637	-0.1
Dickinson	8.1	0.6	4.6	21.6	D	5.7	5.6	D	21.0	4,520	245	295	8,791	0.1
Doniphan	15.0	D	8.1	16.0	D	2.6	6.8	4.9	24.7	1,730	232	95	3,372	0.2
Douglas	0.5	0.0	5.5	9.5	11.2	6.9	7.5	7.6	32.0	18,825	158	1,371	53,310	0.7
Edwards	43.6	D	1.2	5.8	D	2.3	2.7	9.0	11.3	735	260	49	1,547	-0.1
Elk	5.2	10.0	D	D	2.9	6.6	4.4	D	33.8	860	352	55	1,490	-0.1
Ellis	1.9	5.2	5.2	5.3	6.3	7.4	9.2	19.5	19.8	5,575	194	321	13,213	0.3
Ellsworth	11.5	D	2.8	12.6	8.6	4.1	D	6.6	30.7	1,500	237	54	3,091	0.4
Finney	3.8	1.5	6.0	21.9	2.3	7.3	6.1	10.5	13.3	5,155	135	542	14,276	0.5
Ford	2.6	D	4.2	38.4	3.3	5.6	5.0	D	12.6	4,465	131	423	12,646	0.7
Franklin	4.8	0.6	7.1	8.7	D	8.1	5.6	D	13.9	5,810	224	485	11,241	0.7
Geary	0.3	0.0	0.8	3.9	D	2.0	1.9	1.2	79.9	4,585	128	574	15,935	0.1
Gove	10.3	1.6	4.7	7.7	1.6	15.8	9.0	4.3	18.4	655	238	15	1,323	-0.1
Graham	21.0	11.7	D	D	3.8	4.3	D	4.5	20.8	790	329	38	1,422	0.1
Grant	13.8	3.7	6.9	5.1	D	4.1	6.8	7.0	13.5	1,200	164	71	2,936	0.2
Gray	28.0	0.0	10.7	2.9	2.8	3.6	5.6	2.7	16.2	1,050	186	23	2,337	0.4
Greeley	64.9	D	1.5	0.1	D	4.3	D	D	7.4	275	211	D	638	0.0
Greenwood	14.7	5.0	6.2	6.9	D	4.4	D	11.9	21.1	1,890	318	183	3,666	0.0
Hamilton	63.7	D	0.5	0.0	D	1.9	7.0	D	8.6	430	173	17	1,107	0.0
Harper	8.2	2.6	1.4	23.6	D	6.4	D	1.7	18.5	1,465	275	89	3,022	-0.1
Harvey	2.4	0.9	7.4	28.6	3.2	5.5	5.8	D	11.1	7,885	233	521	14,607	0.2
Haskell	36.4	3.3	4.5	5.0	D	2.0	D	D	17.7	605	165	20	1,549	0.2
Hodgeman	42.8	D	1.6	D	D	3.1	4.6	D	22.1	435	254	D	841	-0.1
Jackson	4.1	D	7.5	8.2	3.0	5.6	7.3	12.2	37.9	3,155	238	167	5,613	0.5
Jefferson	8.4	D	23.2	7.4	D	4.2	2.3	D	19.9	4,415	240	243	7,987	0.8
Jewell	43.9	0.4	D	1.1	D	3.5	4.6	D	22.1	930	317	40	1,761	-0.1
Johnson	0.0	0.1	5.4	6.2	15.7	4.6	21.8	11.1	6.4	99,065	162	3,969	255,159	1.1
Kearny	35.4	0.4	D	D	D	2.3	12.0	0.4	25.3	675	173	47	1,586	0.2
Kingman	10.3	1.8	33.4	12.0	D	3.8	4.4	7.7	11.6	1,975	267	91	3,669	0.6
Kiowa	26.4	2.0	D	D	D	2.9	2.5	D	17.2	605	253	51	1,153	-0.1
Labette	6.6	0.0	2.5	18.0	2.1	5.7	3.8	13.7	27.2	5,125	257	693	9,519	0.0
Lane	44.1	D	D	0.3	D	D	7.3	0.1	17.1	440	281	15	894	-0.1
Leavenworth	0.2	D	5.6	3.5	5.3	3.5	5.7	4.5	60.4	14,645	178	889	31,591	1.0
Lincoln	18.3	0.2	5.5	D	D	2.4	3.7	4.1	22.8	845	291	41	1,669	-0.1
Linn	8.8	2.3	7.4	5.4	D	5.2	5.2	D	20.4	2,655	272	184	5,142	1.3
Logan	22.1	D	D	D	D	3.6	D	1.5	34.5	685	252	30	1,373	0.3
Lyon	3.0	D	3.3	28.8	D	6.5	3.9	6.6	25.6	6,415	200	626	14,998	0.2
McPherson	1.7	0.9	6.0	38.2	D	3.3	3.9	8.2	8.1	6,955	231	291	13,129	0.8
Marion	14.1	0.2	5.6	12.2	4.0	6.3	4.6	D	17.4	3,075	263	158	5,681	0.2
Marshall	3.8	D	4.8	26.9	5.9	5.9	9.1	D	10.7	2,410	242	119	4,757	-0.1
Meade	33.0	0.3	7.8	1.0	D	D	10.1	D	16.0	830	206	28	1,901	0.1
Miami	1.8	0.6	14.1	6.8	3.8	7.6	11.5	11.6	20.0	6,935	200	382	14,041	1.0
Mitchell	6.6	D	5.5	6.8	D	5.5	6.8	D	17.3	1,565	272	99	3,119	-0.1
Montgomery	2.4	0.4	5.8	29.2	2.8	6.7	4.2	D	14.7	8,280	266	1,069	15,553	-0.1
Morris	19.1	0.2	7.4	9.2	9.1	4.4	8.2	D	20.7	1,430	267	73	2,998	0.1
Morton	40.7	4.6	D	D	3.9	3.7	D	3.3	20.0	635	236	30	1,315	-0.1
Nemaha	8.3	D	5.6	20.6	3.3	4.4	D	12.6	10.5	2,225	218	82	4,495	0.0

1. Per 1,000 resident population estimated as of July 1 of the year shown.

STATE County	Housing units, 2016–2020								Civilian labor force, 2021				Civilian employment[6], 2016–2020		
	Occupied units										Unemployment			Percent	
		Owner-occupied				Renter-occupied									
				Median owner cost as a percent of income											
	Total	Percent	Median value[1]	With a mortgage	Without a mortgage[2]	Median rent[3]	Median rent as a percent of income[2]	Substandard units[4] (percent)	Total	Percent change, 2020–2021	Total	Rate[5]	Total	Management, business, science, and arts	Construction, production, and maintenance occupations
	89	90	91	92	93	94	95	96	97	98	99	100	101	102	103
KANSAS	1,141,985	66.2	157,600	19.3	11.3	863	27.0	2.4	1,495,665	0.1	48,342	3.2	1,444,074	39.2	24.0
Allen	5,125	70.4	80,300	19.2	10.2	678	28.2	1.1	6,524	2.0	198	3.0	5,822	26.6	37.5
Anderson	3,154	72.4	100,300	18.6	11.9	686	22.4	2.3	4,655	8.7	115	2.5	3,377	33.5	33.1
Atchison	6,039	71.4	108,700	18.6	12.4	702	24.8	1.3	6,742	-1.6	257	3.8	7,815	31.8	25.7
Barber	1,931	74.2	74,400	20.3	10.0	585	23.0	3.9	2,301	-0.5	44	1.9	2,140	36.9	32.9
Barton	10,628	67.4	97,100	19.7	10.9	676	26.1	1.4	13,371	-2.0	388	2.9	12,831	31.0	28.1
Bourbon	5,921	73.1	83,900	21.0	11.9	700	27.1	4.4	6,513	-2.6	241	3.7	6,473	28.7	35.6
Brown	3,757	70.9	87,000	17.9	10.0	647	27.9	1.7	5,143	0.1	137	2.7	4,433	33.0	27.6
Butler	24,833	74.9	150,300	20.0	12.1	831	29.1	2.0	32,456	0.2	1,141	3.5	30,659	40.5	23.0
Chase	1,082	78.4	102,500	20.5	14.0	576	23.3	0.9	1,385	-4.6	33	2.4	1,162	31.1	38.6
Chautauqua	1,418	75.9	51,700	21.3	13.1	628	26.4	6.3	1,458	-1.4	59	4.0	1,331	33.1	31.7
Cherokee	7,954	71.2	80,700	20.5	11.6	572	26.8	2.1	9,907	-0.7	290	2.9	8,760	29.8	33.0
Cheyenne	1,263	79.4	84,200	19.0	12.9	614	24.8	1.6	1,299	-0.2	23	1.8	1,251	38.3	26.6
Clark	890	77.1	74,300	18.6	12.9	671	15.7	3.1	1,139	0.4	21	1.8	973	37.8	29.0
Clay	3,741	72.0	105,500	19.1	12.0	608	29.2	3.7	3,795	-0.3	97	2.6	3,746	38.7	29.4
Cloud	3,641	72.4	77,800	21.0	11.0	670	24.4	0.6	3,902	1.6	108	2.8	4,311	37.5	28.6
Coffey	3,648	76.3	124,300	17.8	10.4	694	22.3	2.5	3,960	0.7	128	3.2	4,000	34.7	30.7
Comanche	818	69.6	72,500	17.5	12.5	562	28.2	2.2	891	3.0	19	2.1	923	38.5	28.7
Cowley	13,800	68.4	88,600	18.9	12.0	670	24.2	2.1	16,678	-0.6	572	3.4	15,562	32.6	32.1
Crawford	15,603	59.9	96,900	19.7	11.4	723	31.7	2.9	18,935	0.0	601	3.2	18,894	34.5	26.6
Decatur	1,414	74.4	68,400	17.7	11.3	666	22.8	0.6	1,205	-1.6	31	2.6	1,342	29.8	34.1
Dickinson	7,933	73.3	116,400	19.0	12.3	677	28.2	1.9	9,097	2.6	269	3.0	9,147	33.3	28.8
Doniphan	3,003	76.7	100,000	18.3	13.3	653	25.4	2.1	4,124	-0.3	113	2.7	3,869	29.9	32.3
Douglas	47,972	50.7	212,400	19.2	10.7	952	29.4	2.0	64,611	1.0	2,030	3.1	68,255	45.5	16.9
Edwards	1,285	78.2	60,700	20.6	10.0	597	18.8	0.2	1,464	0.3	31	2.1	1,414	33.3	29.6
Elk	1,150	81.4	49,400	17.4	13.5	483	19.3	2.2	1,158	-0.8	33	2.8	948	32.2	29.1
Ellis	11,686	62.8	172,700	19.7	11.1	730	28.1	1.1	17,158	0.7	332	1.9	16,120	36.9	21.1
Ellsworth	2,390	79.4	110,100	18.2	11.0	619	22.4	2.8	2,701	-0.1	60	2.2	2,695	37.4	24.9
Finney	12,494	64.5	159,300	20.0	12.0	831	21.7	8.3	20,305	-1.2	428	2.1	18,467	24.0	40.6
Ford	11,237	63.1	109,800	20.1	10.5	770	22.5	6.4	17,686	2.5	377	2.1	16,658	25.0	45.0
Franklin	10,190	73.2	138,500	19.8	13.6	773	27.0	2.8	14,521	2.1	452	3.1	12,809	27.9	36.3
Geary	12,866	41.7	143,100	22.0	13.0	954	26.1	3.1	11,402	-2.0	486	4.3	12,772	31.6	29.1
Gove	1,260	73.3	99,800	19.1	12.6	692	24.4	1.8	1,465	0.3	28	1.9	1,278	39.7	27.9
Graham	1,252	77.2	77,500	20.6	12.0	625	29.7	0.0	1,132	-0.2	33	2.9	1,179	33.0	26.5
Grant	2,561	68.4	137,000	16.7	10.0	589	18.4	6.1	2,963	-4.3	90	3.0	3,167	29.3	38.0
Gray	2,150	80.9	142,600	18.3	10.0	663	20.3	2.9	3,229	-0.2	55	1.7	3,287	33.6	32.2
Greeley	491	63.7	112,100	19.8	10.4	600	16.8	0.0	822	0.5	10	1.2	579	28.3	26.6
Greenwood	2,695	76.8	64,500	19.2	10.8	566	24.6	2.4	3,011	-3.0	85	2.8	2,883	29.2	34.7
Hamilton	818	77.4	75,000	21.1	13.4	705	24.9	3.1	1,620	0.3	22	1.4	1,187	26.1	38.2
Harper	2,367	71.5	75,200	17.4	13.1	664	23.8	2.3	2,774	-0.3	73	2.6	2,303	28.4	37.4
Harvey	13,396	69.9	131,000	19.9	11.5	729	28.0	3.1	16,918	0.9	497	2.9	17,316	37.6	27.6
Haskell	1,401	78.0	96,300	19.3	10.0	619	17.0	2.9	2,223	-0.8	40	1.8	1,904	31.8	41.0
Hodgeman	790	78.7	93,400	18.1	12.5	750	22.9	1.0	1,036	2.1	19	1.8	979	46.3	28.4
Jackson	5,429	74.5	139,400	20.8	11.1	699	22.2	2.4	7,236	0.0	188	2.6	6,247	28.8	32.5
Jefferson	7,619	85.5	163,400	19.5	12.4	759	21.5	0.9	10,332	1.0	307	3.0	9,628	37.5	30.8
Jewell	1,386	82.8	56,300	19.3	11.2	516	33.3	1.0	1,235	-1.1	27	2.2	1,230	38.2	26.9
Johnson	233,599	69.0	277,500	18.8	10.0	1,147	25.9	1.5	343,991	0.7	9,240	2.7	327,842	53.2	12.6
Kearny	1,270	71.3	91,200	19.4	11.7	849	23.8	1.3	2,048	1.1	33	1.6	1,739	30.9	43.7
Kingman	3,253	74.4	92,500	19.8	10.0	766	21.0	1.4	3,272	0.7	100	3.1	3,566	36.5	32.3
Kiowa	975	69.5	132,500	24.0	10.3	619	26.3	0.6	1,220	-2.0	26	2.1	1,174	34.4	26.8
Labette	8,270	71.0	76,500	19.5	11.9	652	28.0	2.5	9,413	-2.4	320	3.4	9,533	35.5	30.3
Lane	737	72.2	75,100	17.3	12.9	503	22.4	8.5	747	-1.1	15	2.0	795	35.6	34.3
Leavenworth	27,645	67.1	195,000	19.6	10.3	991	24.7	2.0	36,842	0.6	1,218	3.3	34,763	40.4	21.3
Lincoln	1,305	78.5	75,400	18.0	12.2	550	25.2	1.1	1,689	-2.6	37	2.2	1,463	38.7	24.0
Linn	4,509	79.3	112,000	19.3	14.8	661	25.2	6.1	4,331	0.0	186	4.3	4,273	27.0	36.3
Logan	1,144	66.0	89,600	16.2	11.9	701	28.3	1.1	1,632	1.5	26	1.6	1,406	36.0	24.1
Lyon	13,561	57.7	113,700	20.8	10.8	654	27.8	4.0	16,921	1.9	481	2.8	17,585	30.5	30.9
McPherson	12,479	69.3	154,700	19.6	10.0	749	24.6	1.0	17,164	0.0	362	2.1	14,849	34.6	29.1
Marion	4,838	79.6	96,600	19.9	12.0	615	19.7	1.0	6,005	0.9	145	2.4	5,643	34.4	33.2
Marshall	4,128	78.5	101,600	18.7	12.0	572	25.6	2.4	5,436	-0.8	105	1.9	4,955	32.9	34.2
Meade	1,715	66.4	101,800	18.8	10.0	640	18.1	0.8	2,187	1.8	48	2.2	2,032	45.3	25.1
Miami	13,000	80.0	212,500	21.5	12.8	955	27.7	1.6	17,750	1.0	519	2.9	16,563	35.5	26.3
Mitchell	2,593	69.5	92,100	19.8	12.4	563	18.9	1.1	3,434	0.2	67	2.0	2,803	35.1	30.4
Montgomery	13,767	69.5	78,900	19.9	12.4	672	28.3	2.6	14,715	-1.0	575	3.9	14,077	29.4	31.3
Morris	2,344	77.2	94,400	18.7	10.0	606	19.5	0.3	3,053	-0.8	72	2.4	2,791	37.9	29.3
Morton	1,036	64.1	90,300	28.8	10.0	603	22.5	0.0	1,135	0.5	29	2.6	1,172	34.0	41.1
Nemaha	4,069	73.2	150,400	17.2	10.0	674	24.0	0.7	5,553	-0.5	98	1.8	5,093	38.6	29.0

1. Specified owner-occupied units. 2. A value of 10.0 represents 10 percent or less; a value of 50.0 represents 50 percent or more. 3. Specified renter-occupied units. 4. Overcrowded or lacking complete plumbing facilities. 5. Percent of civilian labor force. 6. Civilian employed persons 16 years old and over.

STATE County	Private nonfarm establishments, employment and payroll, 2020									Agriculture, 2017			
		Employment						Annual payroll		Farms			Farm producers whose primary occupation is farming (percent)
											Percent with:		
	Number of establish-ments	Total	Health care and social assistance	Manufac-turing	Retail trade	Finance and insurance	Professional, scientific, and technical services	Total (mil dol)	Average per employee (dollars)	Number	Fewer than 50 acres	1000 acres or more	
	104	105	106	107	108	109	110	111	112	113	114	115	116
KANSAS	73,982	1,207,003	195,983	166,901	146,028	65,011	67,042	58,374	48,363	58,569	21.8	20.2	41.9
Allen	352	4,059	589	1,462	580	116	193	151	37,200	505	24.0	13.5	41.3
Anderson	189	1,563	359	97	486	104	35	57	36,376	611	18.7	16.5	43.7
Atchison	347	5,094	873	847	590	128	81	192	37,732	595	17.5	9.1	44.4
Barber	172	1,175	246	163	218	33	30	49	41,544	362	11.6	36.7	54.7
Barton	912	10,377	2,691	1,177	1,462	525	431	433	41,683	628	19.9	24.8	46.0
Bourbon	343	4,476	564	1,382	708	193	106	151	33,746	813	18.0	10.6	41.9
Brown	268	3,494	721	973	332	192	92	143	40,831	510	22.4	19.2	47.5
Butler	1,310	14,060	2,807	1,958	2,112	444	650	546	38,834	1,471	38.0	12.8	33.4
Chase	64	501	NA	165	40	11	26	17	34,675	238	13.4	33.6	51.4
Chautauqua	64	461	125	61	83	37	NA	13	28,599	351	16.2	21.4	45.8
Cherokee	326	5,152	840	1,646	388	132	81	264	51,249	756	29.6	12.4	42.4
Cheyenne	110	574	211	23	80	35	20	21	35,744	384	11.2	31.8	40.6
Clark	61	445	217	NA	42	34	20	20	46,047	230	2.2	33.5	41.7
Clay	260	2,111	406	326	393	109	58	71	33,812	547	19.6	22.5	42.7
Cloud	284	2,607	652	273	461	84	79	86	33,113	412	18.7	23.3	42.9
Coffey	211	2,748	453	119	320	98	42	188	68,475	699	16.5	15.2	38.3
Comanche	66	386	158	38	65	21	8	12	30,775	197	0.5	53.8	54.9
Cowley	680	12,206	2,085	5,043	1,369	330	217	475	38,956	921	24.1	15.0	44.2
Crawford	931	14,792	2,709	2,867	1,756	317	329	528	35,668	777	25.6	11.2	37.3
Decatur	97	563	159	NA	80	30	36	16	28,313	270	12.6	40.0	52.4
Dickinson	437	5,053	870	1,489	765	183	138	190	37,508	919	22.0	18.2	43.4
Doniphan	151	1,648	154	476	150	45	14	67	40,575	430	23.3	13.3	45.2
Douglas	2,724	37,380	6,479	4,261	6,178	1,272	2,480	1,409	37,694	998	44.7	5.6	33.5
Edwards	74	516	107	109	72	22	10	20	38,855	249	6.8	32.9	49.0
Elk	57	297	17	NA	47	18	8	8	26,865	318	12.6	22.3	48.3
Ellis	1,106	12,362	2,955	1,113	2,027	438	327	470	38,016	603	16.1	20.6	37.3
Ellsworth	162	1,649	235	310	211	101	75	84	51,016	384	10.7	28.6	45.5
Finney	1,007	14,697	1,474	3,757	2,671	449	263	592	40,307	450	11.3	41.8	55.7
Ford	771	14,695	1,166	5,762	1,630	316	480	711	48,407	505	11.9	32.9	44.1
Franklin	533	9,054	1,576	776	1,147	145	126	354	39,071	1,020	37.5	9.1	37.4
Geary	561	7,935	1,366	704	1,181	273	258	275	34,622	213	19.2	27.2	41.4
Gove	122	964	210	95	150	40	12	36	37,673	350	7.7	40.3	46.2
Graham	85	518	184	NA	76	25	6	19	35,836	429	12.1	27.5	38.7
Grant	224	2,022	194	157	262	105	37	94	46,415	315	7.6	27.0	40.0
Gray	231	1,526	180	112	171	73	49	69	45,431	422	13.3	29.9	49.7
Greeley	44	330	137	NA	81	26	11	14	42,212	227	4.0	45.8	52.8
Greenwood	158	1,163	309	87	177	51	45	44	37,433	540	16.3	26.1	48.1
Hamilton	74	553	33	NA	76	71	NA	24	42,736	353	4.8	37.1	41.8
Harper	189	1,863	383	553	267	98	45	76	40,699	477	13.2	29.8	45.3
Harvey	740	12,904	2,913	3,574	1,381	312	244	503	38,978	752	38.2	14.2	40.5
Haskell	117	857	198	102	103	34	22	37	42,600	207	8.2	43.0	70.9
Hodgeman	47	259	71	NA	37	26	NA	10	37,780	351	4.0	38.7	50.6
Jackson	255	3,049	535	283	374	101	72	97	31,729	972	23.7	8.1	34.9
Jefferson	301	2,056	305	236	270	63	107	86	41,809	1,012	33.1	6.1	33.7
Jewell	77	428	80	NA	51	24	10	12	28,827	455	12.1	30.3	53.3
Johnson	18,150	344,495	42,872	23,029	38,424	31,829	33,368	20,711	60,121	564	60.5	4.1	28.8
Kearny	80	716	308	NA	100	56	11	28	39,803	299	6.4	34.1	45.4
Kingman	212	1,794	336	378	253	96	29	72	39,977	740	16.4	19.9	40.2
Kiowa	89	753	189	NA	102	26	NA	27	36,142	359	6.4	25.9	39.9
Labette	427	7,180	2,305	2,062	779	273	92	287	39,959	997	26.5	11.4	38.0
Lane	59	293	66	NA	33	27	13	12	39,833	242	8.3	39.3	48.4
Leavenworth	1,244	14,229	2,486	1,226	2,214	677	1,176	613	43,048	1,213	44.8	2.5	29.5
Lincoln	83	580	147	NA	50	51	12	18	31,622	392	18.4	26.0	44.0
Linn	181	1,326	56	158	236	77	20	73	54,974	864	21.6	7.2	33.4
Logan	107	694	177	NA	91	57	22	30	42,589	270	7.8	45.9	54.9
Lyon	808	12,449	1,957	3,876	1,705	348	189	467	37,485	867	22.8	16.1	40.1
McPherson	886	14,602	2,429	5,304	1,240	622	323	665	45,526	988	25.0	17.8	40.2
Marion	274	2,492	613	301	243	86	94	77	31,066	892	26.3	17.3	40.5
Marshall	361	3,910	493	1,342	554	190	123	169	43,165	802	15.1	21.6	42.0
Meade	122	824	163	17	121	73	30	33	40,465	407	11.1	32.9	48.1
Miami	747	7,014	2,166	450	964	230	305	284	40,439	1,400	45.6	5.1	35.4
Mitchell	233	2,430	564	275	355	142	72	91	37,244	365	18.9	36.7	53.2
Montgomery	743	11,595	2,865	3,682	1,324	339	202	461	39,721	1,006	28.1	7.4	33.8
Morris	129	1,208	311	226	137	49	48	47	38,814	430	17.4	23.0	52.4
Morton	73	677	152	NA	69	46	9	28	41,099	323	4.3	28.8	42.7
Nemaha	365	4,291	856	1,014	433	177	107	188	43,723	809	16.8	13.0	46.8

STATE County	Agriculture, 2017 (cont.): Land in farms: Acreage (1,000)	Land in farms: Percent change, 2012–2017	Land in farms: Acres: Average size of farm	Land in farms: Acres: Total irrigated (1,000)	Land in farms: Acres: Total cropland (1,000)	Value of land and buildings (dollars): Average per farm	Value of land and buildings (dollars): Average per acre	Value of machinery and equipment, average per farm (dollars)	Value of products sold: Total (mil dol)	Value of products sold: Average per farm (acres)	Value of products sold: Percent from: Crops	Value of products sold: Percent from: Livestock and poultry products	Organic farms (number)	Farms with internet access (percent)	Government payments: Total ($1,000)	Government payments: Percent of farms
	117	118	119	120	121	122	123	124	125	126	127	128	129	130	131	132
KANSAS	45,759	-0.8	781	2,503.4	29,125.5	1,443,891	1,848	180,725	18,782.7	320,694	34.4	65.6	117	76.5	509,205	61.7
Allen	240	-2.2	475	0.5	133.0	964,120	2,029	104,166	47.9	94,921	65.1	34.9	NA	74.7	1,578	53.7
Anderson	365	-0.5	597	2.9	242.1	1,216,033	2,038	170,102	108.8	178,031	74.3	25.7	2	68.4	2,651	65.5
Atchison	236	7.0	396	1.0	174.3	1,205,388	3,040	161,609	85.2	143,200	78.5	21.5	NA	73.4	2,051	58.8
Barber	632	6.9	1,745	14.2	236.5	2,506,422	1,436	218,751	93.6	258,472	40.8	59.2	NA	79.8	4,125	60.8
Barton	558	-1.4	888	28.9	425.3	1,395,047	1,570	191,756	365.7	582,280	20.5	79.5	NA	72.1	7,953	75.8
Bourbon	336	0.5	413	0.6	132.0	830,177	2,008	97,866	78.9	97,090	31.6	68.4	NA	75.8	1,658	40.3
Brown	312	5.7	611	8.0	258.6	2,142,870	3,507	234,470	131.8	258,516	85.0	15.0	NA	81.0	5,985	75.3
Butler	798	3.9	543	2.7	323.5	1,231,054	2,268	125,659	266.2	180,942	29.7	70.3	4	78.9	3,696	31.2
Chase	360	-8.3	1,513	D	65.3	2,891,131	1,911	199,983	85.4	358,954	21.9	78.1	NA	89.9	650	51.7
Chautauqua	288	-7.1	822	0.0	41.6	1,340,024	1,631	97,412	31.3	89,268	32.9	67.1	NA	67.8	507	23.9
Cherokee	319	3.6	422	1.0	234.9	934,030	2,211	141,016	107.0	141,476	75.9	24.1	NA	77.2	2,126	48.0
Cheyenne	529	-3.2	1,378	43.6	340.7	2,035,736	1,477	237,954	132.8	345,714	51.1	48.9	3	67.4	2,764	77.6
Clark	434	-13.7	1,888	2.7	156.2	2,241,930	1,187	150,734	111.4	484,439	13.5	86.5	NA	59.6	6,014	87.8
Clay	386	6.5	706	30.9	259.7	1,914,257	2,712	226,844	121.2	221,528	67.5	32.5	NA	80.6	5,062	75.5
Cloud	322	0.0	782	16.9	203.2	1,799,344	2,302	219,484	77.5	188,070	73.8	26.2	NA	74.0	3,234	71.4
Coffey	386	17.3	553	1.1	219.0	1,008,529	1,825	128,316	71.7	102,564	65.4	34.6	1	76.5	3,260	68.5
Comanche	454	-6.5	2,302	5.0	152.3	2,669,162	1,159	228,061	51.8	262,959	31.6	68.4	NA	76.1	3,306	79.2
Cowley	563	-1.9	612	1.8	232.9	1,131,273	1,849	130,373	96.5	104,794	55.9	44.1	1	76.8	3,311	55.4
Crawford	335	3.7	431	1.4	208.4	868,757	2,014	127,884	85.9	110,605	72.6	27.4	NA	80.2	2,304	57.4
Decatur	420	-9.2	1,556	6.6	254.3	2,267,881	1,458	261,822	233.4	864,559	20.3	79.7	4	80.7	2,069	61.9
Dickinson	519	1.8	565	4.4	364.4	1,209,027	2,140	176,779	149.5	162,723	51.0	49.0	2	75.7	7,399	76.8
Doniphan	177	-1.1	413	1.8	144.9	1,416,197	3,431	214,601	81.2	188,902	94.3	5.7	NA	75.1	4,128	71.6
Douglas	230	9.3	231	3.5	159.3	939,826	4,072	94,196	65.9	65,999	76.7	23.3	11	78.3	1,316	38.8
Edwards	392	-0.6	1,574	71.3	275.1	2,902,328	1,843	359,573	228.8	918,795	30.5	69.5	NA	85.9	7,290	91.2
Elk	247	-22.0	777	0.0	56.9	1,199,924	1,545	92,972	37.7	118,428	21.6	78.4	NA	73.3	461	34.9
Ellis	502	1.0	832	1.6	270.4	1,122,301	1,349	133,106	65.0	107,813	48.9	51.1	NA	71.3	4,333	65.8
Ellsworth	390	2.3	1,016	0.5	200.0	1,632,908	1,608	200,669	48.3	125,828	55.6	44.4	NA	82.3	3,065	83.1
Finney	791	-3.1	1,757	186.4	679.5	2,749,764	1,565	507,327	823.1	1,829,091	22.0	78.0	NA	75.8	14,410	74.9
Ford	670	-4.3	1,326	67.1	529.2	2,051,886	1,547	293,262	515.3	1,020,301	21.1	78.9	NA	79.2	9,951	77.6
Franklin	355	-1.8	348	4.3	222.5	837,366	2,403	110,830	140.9	138,123	53.8	46.2	NA	76.4	1,602	37.1
Geary	155	6.5	728	2.8	65.1	1,676,183	2,301	148,272	31.8	149,451	46.7	53.3	NA	72.3	934	63.4
Gove	567	-1.9	1,621	13.4	362.3	2,108,777	1,301	243,452	201.5	575,757	29.7	70.3	NA	76.6	5,853	81.7
Graham	470	-2.6	1,097	12.3	278.7	1,409,160	1,285	160,299	58.2	135,676	76.5	23.5	NA	72.5	5,961	83.7
Grant	359	-1.3	1,139	83.2	304.6	1,794,738	1,576	356,803	814.1	2,584,575	9.9	90.1	1	78.4	5,423	86.3
Gray	556	1.6	1,318	116.9	439.4	2,103,461	1,596	317,212	990.7	2,347,519	12.0	88.0	NA	80.8	11,783	76.1
Greeley	475	-4.5	2,092	19.8	437.2	2,962,429	1,416	335,255	251.3	1,107,084	23.9	76.1	1	74.4	6,405	78.9
Greenwood	616	-12.1	1,141	D	112.4	1,901,459	1,667	128,315	105.5	195,311	16.4	83.6	NA	75.2	1,120	37.4
Hamilton	544	-14.3	1,541	20.5	435.4	1,642,940	1,066	242,221	335.7	950,878	12.3	87.7	NA	67.7	9,079	87.3
Harper	489	-3.3	1,026	3.3	337.1	1,684,429	1,642	198,557	93.1	195,279	50.3	49.7	NA	72.5	2,397	71.9
Harvey	344	1.3	457	40.4	297.9	1,448,397	3,167	188,621	140.0	186,137	57.4	42.6	11	82.0	7,020	59.8
Haskell	364	0.0	1,757	117.0	320.9	2,682,671	1,527	589,216	1,159.1	5,599,502	9.2	90.8	NA	84.1	8,597	90.8
Hodgeman	495	-8.8	1,410	27.3	319.9	1,658,340	1,176	271,148	191.9	546,698	20.8	79.2	NA	78.6	8,878	86.9
Jackson	335	1.6	344	0.9	168.6	921,574	2,677	103,920	71.0	73,086	56.6	43.4	NA	79.8	2,468	44.7
Jefferson	255	4.8	252	4.1	153.3	732,914	2,904	86,460	75.7	74,833	59.3	40.7	5	72.9	1,968	37.0
Jewell	463	-0.1	1,018	5.6	293.5	2,097,604	2,060	271,175	149.5	328,574	57.2	42.8	NA	79.8	5,204	80.7
Johnson	87	-12.3	154	0.5	56.4	582,891	3,773	81,219	D	D	D	D	NA	82.1	390	22.0
Kearny	516	-5.6	1,727	53.2	416.0	2,490,399	1,442	287,798	281.0	939,726	27.2	72.8	NA	83.6	8,766	86.3
Kingman	517	-4.7	698	16.6	316.5	1,130,791	1,619	137,458	78.8	106,458	62.8	37.2	NA	72.4	6,379	76.6
Kiowa	443	-2.7	1,234	56.8	256.3	1,938,782	1,571	193,895	72.3	201,340	74.2	25.8	NA	68.0	5,038	84.7
Labette	399	7.8	400	0.3	220.2	849,632	2,121	129,803	176.0	176,565	37.3	62.7	1	72.3	2,239	40.5
Lane	417	-7.8	1,723	10.2	311.4	2,195,555	1,274	220,218	D	D	D	D	NA	61.2	6,680	93.0
Leavenworth	195	5.5	160	0.1	112.0	548,881	3,421	69,466	44.0	36,235	70.3	29.7	1	77.8	1,027	22.5
Lincoln	385	-3.1	981	0.5	199.6	1,695,466	1,727	161,747	58.2	148,347	54.1	45.9	NA	76.3	3,203	72.7
Linn	302	-14.8	350	D	156.9	892,889	2,554	91,016	60.3	69,764	68.3	31.7	NA	73.5	2,040	51.4
Logan	605	6.7	2,239	11.3	340.1	3,014,159	1,346	268,005	70.9	262,481	67.3	32.7	NA	84.4	4,466	75.2
Lyon	523	-2.2	603	D	267.5	1,199,352	1,988	150,828	134.4	155,065	44.9	55.1	NA	76.2	3,709	58.7
McPherson	558	-2.4	565	39.3	415.5	1,547,157	2,739	198,986	155.0	156,919	60.8	39.2	3	81.4	9,838	71.2
Marion	568	-4.8	637	3.3	334.7	1,299,945	2,042	163,154	146.5	164,247	45.7	54.3	3	82.6	5,929	69.3
Marshall	500	14.0	623	5.0	361.5	1,928,648	3,094	224,692	125.4	156,353	74.1	25.9	1	80.5	6,159	74.1
Meade	588	-4.9	1,445	93.8	331.6	2,131,999	1,476	304,190	233.4	573,428	38.7	61.3	NA	77.9	10,913	76.9
Miami	296	0.0	211	1.6	181.6	653,977	3,095	85,262	71.8	51,285	73.9	26.1	2	81.1	1,356	28.3
Mitchell	414	-5.6	1,135	6.7	297.8	2,119,970	1,868	258,391	126.5	346,474	54.0	46.0	NA	79.5	5,379	79.5
Montgomery	366	8.9	364	2.8	202.9	730,827	2,010	112,280	95.3	94,683	58.6	41.4	NA	72.9	1,761	31.2
Morris	409	5.2	952	0.8	170.7	1,543,925	1,622	184,687	138.6	322,360	26.6	73.4	1	76.5	2,094	67.0
Morton	401	-12.2	1,242	32.0	331.0	1,272,145	1,024	161,831	134.8	417,381	29.7	70.3	NA	70.9	8,627	83.0
Nemaha	400	4.6	495	1.0	286.1	1,487,190	3,006	225,584	197.4	244,049	38.6	61.4	4	78.1	5,377	69.8

STATE County	Water use, 2015		Wholesale Trade[1], 2017				Retail Trade[2], 2017				Real estate and rental and leasing,[2] 2017			
	Public supply water withdrawn (mil gal/ day)	Public supply gallons withdrawn per person per day	Number of establish-ments	Number of employees	Sales (mil dol)	Average payroll (mil dol)	Number of establish-ments	Number of employees	Sales (mil dol)	Average payroll (mil dol)	Number of establish-ments	Number of employees	Sales (mil dol)	Average payroll (mil dol)
	133	134	135	136	137	138	139	140	141	142	143	144	145	146
KANSAS	351.2	120.6	3,755	52,611	61,889.4	3,159.9	10,095	149,845	39,337.5	3,784.9	3,415	14,532	3,942.5	586.4
Allen	1.8	140.0	22	149	79.7	8.1	51	588	146.7	13.2	31	52	3.2	0.6
Anderson	0.6	76.8	10	44	42.8	2.0	30	377	131.4	12.1	3	D	0.5	D
Atchison	4.2	258.0	18	360	247.3	15.3	46	577	142.7	14.1	8	27	4.1	0.8
Barber	0.6	130.6	10	80	53.5	4.2	29	199	74.3	5.1	5	D	4.5	D
Barton	2.4	89.3	62	552	319.9	26.1	122	1,577	382.9	38.7	36	115	15.8	4.1
Bourbon	2.1	141.4	D	D	D	13.5	52	607	152.7	15.5	8	26	2.9	0.6
Brown	0.9	96.2	13	178	315.2	10.5	41	371	84.1	8.7	5	14	0.9	0.2
Butler	9.8	147.4	51	543	406.6	32.4	168	2,227	654.1	55.9	67	168	24.9	5.4
Chase	0.2	63.5	D	D	D	0.7	7	55	13.2	0.9	NA	NA	NA	NA
Chautauqua	0.4	123.5	NA	NA	NA	NA	12	89	16.1	1.2	NA	NA	NA	NA
Cherokee	1.8	89.1	21	183	243.0	9.6	48	414	114.2	9.6	5	12	1.3	0.2
Cheyenne	0.5	175.4	10	98	93.0	5.0	20	100	18.5	1.8	D	D	D	0.0
Clark	0.3	143.1	3	18	2.9	0.8	5	38	7.9	0.9	NA	NA	NA	NA
Clay	0.9	105.4	17	130	98.2	5.5	39	409	87.8	8.8	4	10	2.2	0.3
Cloud	0.9	96.5	21	305	321.8	15.1	48	484	103.3	11.3	D	D	D	0.2
Coffey	0.5	62.0	13	103	96.7	4.3	42	384	92.9	8.2	5	D	0.3	D
Comanche	0.4	195.3	NA	NA	NA	NA	14	78	16.5	1.6	NA	NA	NA	NA
Cowley	5.4	150.9	19	178	83.1	9.0	116	1,438	323.8	36.2	26	61	8.7	1.4
Crawford	4.9	124.9	43	853	449.3	37.8	141	1,895	428.4	40.3	36	99	15.0	2.5
Decatur	0.4	126.2	12	95	94.2	3.7	16	75	17.7	1.7	4	10	1.8	0.2
Dickinson	1.9	100.0	17	315	312.7	15.8	70	703	175.7	17.0	9	15	1.4	0.2
Doniphan	0.2	26.9	D	D	D	4.9	21	144	47.1	3.5	D	D	D	D
Douglas	12.7	107.3	78	619	464.2	29.0	371	6,373	1,529.3	146.7	156	711	114.2	24.2
Edwards	0.3	84.2	9	88	251.7	5.1	10	76	13.6	1.3	NA	NA	NA	NA
Elk	0.1	34.5	NA	NA	NA	NA	12	57	14.9	1.0	NA	NA	NA	NA
Ellis	2.5	87.2	54	476	224.4	20.2	177	2,151	570.1	51.7	48	130	21.3	3.8
Ellsworth	1.4	220.7	D	D	D	3.3	31	210	45.8	3.8	NA	NA	NA	NA
Finney	7.6	205.3	D	D	D	D	175	2,855	717.0	66.1	38	140	25.9	4.5
Ford	6.8	196.6	64	895	541.9	43.1	118	1,762	476.3	41.8	31	87	27.4	3.3
Franklin	1.9	75.4	19	188	215.0	12.4	85	1,200	281.1	27.4	23	45	7.7	1.3
Geary	4.5	121.3	D	D	D	D	88	1,327	324.3	30.7	52	265	77.6	9.9
Gove	0.3	113.6	10	85	79.8	3.9	18	190	83.4	5.6	NA	NA	NA	NA
Graham	0.5	208.4	8	D	22.2	D	17	100	24.5	2.3	NA	NA	NA	NA
Grant	1.2	157.8	13	210	162.2	10.2	32	232	59.7	5.5	D	D	D	D
Gray	0.7	109.2	25	165	384.3	8.3	25	170	37.7	4.3	7	D	1.4	D
Greeley	0.3	188.0	D	D	D	1.3	8	68	14.8	1.9	NA	NA	NA	NA
Greenwood	0.6	100.9	9	78	13.0	2.0	32	198	34.6	3.5	NA	NA	NA	NA
Hamilton	0.7	282.9	6	56	45.4	3.3	11	75	25.1	1.6	NA	NA	NA	NA
Harper	0.9	147.8	12	81	75.8	3.6	39	244	50.2	5.7	3	7	0.7	0.1
Harvey	9.1	260.6	19	192	92.5	7.1	108	1,451	340.5	32.2	29	56	8.1	1.3
Haskell	0.5	132.9	17	126	201.5	6.8	11	70	17.5	1.1	NA	NA	NA	NA
Hodgeman	0.2	79.2	5	32	66.5	1.4	7	27	5.4	0.6	NA	NA	NA	NA
Jackson	1.1	79.5	14	107	56.9	5.2	40	370	86.9	8.8	8	31	4.5	1.0
Jefferson	1.2	63.4	D	D	D	2.0	51	291	69.4	5.5	NA	NA	NA	NA
Jewell	0.6	198.7	9	D	23.2	D	13	56	11.1	1.0	NA	NA	NA	NA
Johnson	11.5	19.9	905	16,313	25,385.5	1,173.2	1,846	37,452	10,360.8	1,046.5	1,088	5,204	2,000.9	264.8
Kearny	0.6	139.0	NA	NA	NA	NA	13	74	16.6	1.6	3	D	0.5	D
Kingman	0.9	110.6	22	123	153.9	5.1	27	210	49.4	4.7	7	13	1.2	0.3
Kiowa	0.3	128.7	6	D	18.8	D	12	50	11.3	1.3	NA	NA	NA	NA
Labette	2.6	125.9	D	D	D	D	84	812	184.2	19.0	14	47	4.3	0.9
Lane	0.3	161.7	11	D	58.0	D	9	31	6.7	0.7	NA	NA	NA	NA
Leavenworth	28.8	362.6	22	69	64.0	3.3	156	2,155	631.2	56.1	66	222	60.4	6.5
Lincoln	0.2	48.3	5	D	30.4	D	10	61	7.9	0.8	NA	NA	NA	NA
Linn	1.1	114.3	D	D	D	1.5	33	243	59.7	4.9	D	D	D	D
Logan	0.6	205.3	13	93	309.1	4.8	12	103	31.1	2.9	NA	NA	NA	NA
Lyon	4.0	120.9	23	433	301.6	17.6	141	1,731	459.4	38.2	44	174	23.1	4.1
McPherson	4.3	149.6	38	317	200.2	15.1	116	1,250	338.9	29.2	26	54	10.4	1.5
Marion	1.0	81.8	17	127	59.5	6.5	39	277	61.6	5.5	9	12	2.8	0.3
Marshall	1.1	111.7	24	220	183.4	9.5	68	679	229.9	16.0	5	3	0.4	0.1
Meade	0.7	150.1	D	D	D	8.7	17	130	22.5	2.3	NA	NA	NA	NA
Miami	5.7	174.2	17	55	85.8	2.4	78	1,030	294.4	26.7	D	D	D	D
Mitchell	1.2	194.2	23	200	499.6	10.1	46	405	128.2	10.6	6	36	3.8	0.6
Montgomery	5.2	155.2	32	293	135.9	12.7	121	1,359	300.3	32.5	29	76	9.5	1.7
Morris	1.6	287.0	5	D	2.9	D	23	160	35.7	3.3	NA	NA	NA	NA
Morton	0.6	206.2	10	64	50.6	3.2	11	77	15.3	2.1	NA	NA	NA	NA
Nemaha	1.3	130.0	28	274	210.2	13.7	55	468	137.7	12.2	NA	NA	NA	NA

1 Merchant wholesalers, except manufacturers' sales branches and offices. 2. Employer establishments.

STATE County	Professional, scientific, and technical services, 2017				Manufacturing, 2017				Accommodation and food services, 2017			
	Number of establish-ments	Number of employees	Sales (mil dol)	Average payroll (mil dol)	Number of establish-ments	Number of employees	Sales (mil dol)	Average payroll (mil dol)	Number of establis-hments	Number of employees	Sales (mil dol)	Annual payroll (mil dol)
	147	148	149	150	151	152	153	154	155	156	157	158
KANSAS	7,162	65,238	10,824.0	4,151.0	2,760	155,968	83,418.1	9,032.0	6,253	118,905	5,907.5	1,723.7
Allen	27	107	8.9	3.6	26	1,743	442.3	78.0	28	332	14.8	3.9
Anderson	16	32	4.1	0.9	10	154	117.7	7.8	D	D	D	D
Atchison	21	80	6.1	2.5	19	814	678.5	63.7	31	484	19.3	5.8
Barber	D	D	D	1.6	D	153	D	10.2	14	D	4.9	D
Barton	61	332	32.0	12.3	38	1,086	403.4	45.7	62	895	39.2	10.3
Bourbon	26	96	11.1	4.4	24	1,201	202.6	47.6	33	365	17.4	4.5
Brown	D	D	D	D	19	843	411.7	52.0	D	D	D	D
Butler	D	D	D	D	44	1,399	4,649.7	100.2	114	1,773	77.2	21.6
Chase	5	13	3.2	0.7	D	D	D	7.1	7	D	2.7	D
Chautauqua	NA	NA	NA	NA	D	67	D	2.1	3	33	1.1	0.3
Cherokee	23	84	7.5	2.0	29	1,400	439.2	64.7	32	357	16.7	4.5
Cheyenne	7	19	2.2	0.6	4	24	3.1	0.6	8	56	1.5	0.3
Clark	6	18	4.5	1.0	NA	NA	NA	NA	D	D	D	0.1
Clay	15	58	4.3	2.0	11	265	59.6	13.1	18	205	7.4	2.0
Cloud	12	68	7.0	2.6	10	294	72.5	16.8	25	432	16.4	4.5
Coffey	15	47	4.5	1.5	8	123	24.5	4.9	15	133	5.0	1.4
Comanche	4	6	0.3	0.1	5	23	8.3	1.4	3	27	0.9	0.3
Cowley	D	D	D	D	39	3,680	2,691.9	206.1	68	1,171	52.9	15.2
Crawford	D	D	D	D	50	2,435	1,050.4	103.2	80	1,985	93.8	24.3
Decatur	8	33	2.4	0.7	NA	NA	NA	NA	9	51	2.3	0.6
Dickinson	26	110	14.7	3.8	15	1,166	353.3	53.3	39	400	17.8	4.9
Doniphan	D	D	D	D	10	370	94.6	19.9	7	46	2.1	0.6
Douglas	304	4,993	331.9	131.3	65	3,723	1,499.1	183.9	327	7,255	326.0	96.0
Edwards	5	9	0.9	0.5	6	95	24.8	4.1	5	D	0.9	D
Elk	8	14	1.5	0.3	NA	NA	NA	NA	8	D	7.0	D
Ellis	D	D	D	D	30	768	207.2	34.6	96	1,891	75.6	24.3
Ellsworth	10	71	9.9	4.3	7	259	46.5	10.1	D	D	D	D
Finney	57	384	44.1	15.8	30	4,240	2,506.2	168.8	90	1,615	89.5	23.6
Ford	D	D	D	D	25	5,727	5,520.4	261.3	92	1,523	99.9	27.0
Franklin	28	144	15.3	5.5	24	658	323.8	34.6	52	762	35.6	9.4
Geary	D	D	D	D	8	611	299.4	28.2	80	1,577	70.0	19.2
Gove	D	D	1.2	D	7	101	104.6	4.8	7	D	2.5	D
Graham	D	D	D	0.4	NA	NA	NA	NA	5	D	0.8	D
Grant	7	35	3.1	0.9	9	151	93.4	8.7	22	247	9.8	2.7
Gray	18	57	7.1	2.9	5	74	10.9	3.7	D	D	D	0.6
Greeley	4	13	1.1	0.4	NA	NA	NA	NA	NA	NA	NA	NA
Greenwood	15	33	3.4	1.0	6	57	41.6	4.7	9	76	3.0	0.9
Hamilton	NA	NA	NA	NA	NA	NA	NA	NA	9	50	2.1	0.6
Harper	D	D	1.8	D	19	496	170.9	21.9	17	128	4.6	1.3
Harvey	45	272	26.2	8.9	58	3,297	1,022.9	157.8	67	1,030	42.6	12.6
Haskell	9	26	3.4	0.9	6	79	79.7	4.7	D	D	D	0.3
Hodgeman	NA	NA	NA	NA	NA	NA	NA	NA	3	12	0.4	0.1
Jackson	17	68	5.6	1.3	7	236	92.1	11.3	24	972	144.8	26.4
Jefferson	D	D	D	D	D	292	D	13.3	D	D	D	D
Jewell	4	11	0.6	0.2	NA	NA	NA	NA	D	D	D	0.4
Johnson	2,777	30,470	6,128.3	2,346.8	446	21,797	8,772.1	1,361.9	1,223	29,848	1,637.9	510.1
Kearny	5	13	1.5	0.5	NA	NA	NA	NA	10	70	2.0	0.6
Kingman	12	52	4.9	1.6	12	263	47.7	14.0	16	404	26.1	6.5
Kiowa	NA	NA	NA	NA	NA	NA	NA	NA	D	D	D	0.7
Labette	22	87	11.7	3.3	39	2,106	473.5	91.4	40	547	20.7	5.6
Lane	4	14	1.2	0.6	NA	NA	NA	NA	NA	NA	NA	NA
Leavenworth	D	D	D	D	35	1,340	222.6	55.3	110	1,913	92.3	29.4
Lincoln	8	13	1.2	0.6	NA	NA	NA	NA	NA	NA	NA	NA
Linn	D	D	D	D	13	D	48.7	D	13	43	2.6	0.7
Logan	7	20	3.0	0.6	NA	NA	NA	NA	11	77	3.2	1.1
Lyon	D	D	D	D	40	3,513	1,973.6	156.1	102	1,531	64.2	16.9
McPherson	57	258	33.5	12.3	54	4,441	3,982.7	283.8	73	987	45.2	14.1
Marion	15	82	17.5	3.6	24	378	255.8	19.2	24	D	7.8	D
Marshall	26	108	14.9	4.3	17	1,182	320.0	62.8	23	211	12.4	2.8
Meade	7	23	5.1	0.7	NA	NA	NA	NA	D	D	D	0.4
Miami	D	D	D	D	23	465	110.8	26.4	48	689	32.3	8.8
Mitchell	14	62	6.6	2.1	9	231	58.5	10.6	19	168	6.7	1.7
Montgomery	46	243	22.7	8.1	50	3,180	6,658.4	181.6	72	1,026	43.5	11.9
Morris	10	56	4.9	1.6	6	161	97.8	9.1	13	D	4.3	D
Morton	4	12	0.9	0.3	NA	NA	NA	NA	6	D	1.8	D
Nemaha	D	D	D	D	21	1,112	443.8	57.7	22	228	8.3	2.4

STATE County	Health care and social assistance, 2017: Number of establish-ments	Health care and social assistance, 2017: Number of employees	Health care and social assistance, 2017: Receipts (mil dol)	Health care and social assistance, 2017: Annual payroll (mil dol)	Other services, 2017: Number of establish-ments	Other services, 2017: Number of employees	Other services, 2017: Receipts (mil dol)	Other services, 2017: Annual payroll (mil dol)	Nonemployer businesses, 2019: Number	Nonemployer businesses, 2019: Receipts (mil dol)	Value of residential construction authorized by building permits, 2021: New construction ($1,000)	Value of residential construction authorized by building permits, 2021: Number of housing units
	159	160	161	162	163	164	165	166	167	168	169	170
KANSAS	8,104	195,941	21,439.7	8,522.4	5,069	27,987	3,986.2	927.7	203,283	9,680.9	2,592,906	9,538
Allen	38	521	46.7	17.1	22	71	7.9	1.7	784	30.6	2,099	11
Anderson	18	357	32.3	12.5	9	22	3.0	0.5	667	29.3	3,627	15
Atchison	42	813	75.5	34.8	25	72	7.6	1.9	840	31.9	1,815	4
Barber	14	230	17.5	7.9	15	33	3.1	0.9	507	20.0	0	0
Barton	109	2,061	123.7	55.2	76	277	36.6	9.1	2,173	102.0	524	4
Bourbon	41	920	62.1	30.3	28	97	9.5	2.3	973	40.8	250	8
Brown	34	773	76.8	32.1	20	62	6.0	1.3	713	26.0	0	0
Butler	162	2,920	270.2	106.3	89	299	37.9	10.9	4,342	189.0	51,407	169
Chase	D	D	D	D	D	D	2.2	D	239	9.1	0	0
Chautauqua	8	146	10.1	4.5	NA	NA	NA	NA	293	14.8	0	0
Cherokee	36	942	80.0	29.0	19	47	4.6	1.1	1,097	47.5	583	6
Cheyenne	11	201	15.7	7.4	D	D	D	0.2	257	10.0	0	0
Clark	D	D	D	D	NA	NA	NA	NA	213	7.5	368	2
Clay	23	556	38.6	18.4	23	78	8.5	1.8	653	25.7	4,800	17
Cloud	32	700	45.1	18.6	D	D	D	D	640	25.6	0	0
Coffey	30	462	32.9	17.0	15	89	27.0	7.3	644	28.5	2,274	15
Comanche	4	147	8.8	4.8	D	D	0.8	D	166	6.4	0	0
Cowley	104	1,965	155.7	62.1	50	210	25.0	5.3	1,944	73.7	8,084	67
Crawford	121	2,800	241.9	101.3	61	232	20.3	5.8	2,116	85.1	19,725	86
Decatur	6	D	10.6	D	D	D	1.7	D	236	12.1	150	1
Dickinson	38	832	59.0	26.1	37	108	18.5	2.7	1,156	48.1	4,735	26
Doniphan	D	D	D	D	D	D	3.0	D	464	18.5	1,085	4
Douglas	316	6,533	649.4	260.4	197	1,251	226.5	42.9	8,669	358.5	106,087	518
Edwards	8	D	9.8	D	D	D	1.3	D	192	9.8	0	0
Elk	NA	NA	NA	NA	D	D	D	0.4	243	13.3	NA	NA
Ellis	126	3,016	307.7	130.6	80	403	62.0	10.5	2,837	132.9	28,315	98
Ellsworth	23	323	20.2	9.3	D	D	5.3	D	450	15.5	15,062	62
Finney	89	1,794	206.5	79.7	73	369	49.2	12.5	2,349	167.1	9,100	57
Ford	79	1,155	138.0	47.6	53	270	36.5	7.9	1,912	114.2	16,043	84
Franklin	72	1,503	112.4	52.6	50	240	21.9	7.3	1,684	67.7	19,306	87
Geary	42	1,481	169.1	71.3	48	278	20.0	7.0	1,391	49.7	4,147	16
Gove	8	212	16.3	6.3	D	D	D	D	322	18.2	180	2
Graham	9	189	12.4	5.8	10	20	2.2	0.5	293	11.7	0	0
Grant	14	191	22.7	8.2	15	43	5.0	1.2	494	30.6	320	2
Gray	10	175	8.2	4.1	D	D	6.9	D	605	39.2	4,332	17
Greeley	NA	NA	NA	NA	D	D	D	D	136	5.3	0	0
Greenwood	17	305	26.9	12.1	D	D	1.7	D	527	19.1	0	0
Hamilton	7	D	1.3	D	4	15	1.7	0.3	185	8.8	0	0
Harper	16	296	24.0	10.5	D	D	D	0.3	484	20.2	500	2
Harvey	103	2,779	254.9	110.2	54	270	28.1	8.3	2,340	83.2	10,102	50
Haskell	D	D	D	D	D	D	D	0.9	404	26.0	0	0
Hodgeman	D	D	D	D	D	D	0.8	D	163	9.0	0	0
Jackson	25	496	44.5	19.0	24	109	10.1	2.3	826	27.8	10,251	43
Jefferson	30	408	21.6	10.8	D	D	D	D	1,265	50.0	15,146	64
Jewell	D	D	D	D	D	D	1.6	D	240	10.5	0	0
Johnson	1,904	39,937	5,792.6	2,018.8	1,038	7,674	901.1	278.9	52,476	2,954.0	1,163,186	3,660
Kearny	D	D	D	D	5	18	2.0	0.5	321	19.1	180	1
Kingman	18	334	21.6	10.7	14	31	1.6	0.5	616	24.0	4,232	18
Kiowa	9	196	12.6	6.2	D	D	D	0.4	263	8.3	0	0
Labette	69	2,203	176.4	83.2	31	193	22.8	5.7	1,132	53.0	20	1
Lane	D	D	D	D	D	D	0.4	D	200	9.1	0	0
Leavenworth	138	3,355	347.9	143.0	104	445	38.8	11.9	4,109	156.5	78,698	361
Lincoln	6	D	10.4	D	7	20	1.5	0.3	242	6.7	250	1
Linn	D	D	D	D	D	D	D	D	736	24.0	17,018	114
Logan	D	D	D	D	15	27	3.5	0.7	273	11.8	0	0
Lyon	109	2,050	182.7	71.2	58	211	24.0	5.7	1,718	65.9	10,501	73
McPherson	87	2,406	150.5	69.4	73	289	44.1	9.0	2,355	102.2	17,256	97
Marion	30	548	43.5	16.7	22	95	23.0	3.1	924	31.3	5,196	22
Marshall	36	539	42.5	19.3	26	85	7.8	1.9	740	30.3	0	0
Meade	12	D	14.8	D	D	D	D	0.6	382	18.5	85	1
Miami	70	2,015	150.9	73.2	D	D	D	D	2,614	126.3	35,012	128
Mitchell	20	594	44.5	20.9	21	52	9.1	1.4	581	24.5	63	1
Montgomery	100	2,964	146.0	75.1	D	D	D	D	1,729	59.4	842	6
Morris	16	271	25.0	8.5	D	D	1.9	D	449	20.9	400	1
Morton	D	D	D	D	4	8	0.9	0.2	214	5.0	0	0
Nemaha	43	874	60.0	28.3	24	72	9.0	1.9	839	37.8	5,734	17

STATE County	Government employment and payroll, 2017									Local government finances, 2017				
			March payroll (percent of total)							General revenue				
												Taxes		
													Per capita[1] (dollars)	
	Full-time equivalent employees	March payroll (dollars)	Adminis-tration, judicial, and legal	Police and corrections	Fire protection	Highways and transpor-tation	Health and welfare	Natural resources and utilities	Education and libraries	Total (mil dol)	Inter-govern-mental (mil dol)	Total (mil dol)	Total	Property
	171	172	173	174	175	176	177	178	179	180	181	182	183	184
KANSAS	X	X	X	X	X	X	X	X	X	X	X	X	X	X
Allen	1,206	3,386,282	6.4	5.7	4.0	3.5	1.1	8.7	68.7	72.3	33.7	26.6	2,120	1,732
Anderson	339	1,143,624	11.1	12.1	1.2	8.1	0.8	10.8	52.8	22.7	12.5	7.7	977	682
Atchison	689	2,141,245	7.6	8.8	3.1	4.1	11.7	6.3	55.8	56.3	23.5	23.6	1,448	1,004
Barber	443	1,439,745	7.6	3.1	0.1	7.3	48.3	3.7	28.6	45.4	7.2	18.2	3,978	3,138
Barton	1,621	5,594,991	5.1	6.4	2.4	3.4	6.3	5.1	71.0	134.9	58.1	41.5	1,573	1,088
Bourbon	825	2,577,083	7.0	4.6	3.0	4.8	0.9	4.5	73.8	68.0	30.4	25.7	1,756	1,407
Brown	504	1,480,659	8.7	10.8	0.7	4.1	1.8	5.1	67.9	69.8	15.7	48.5	5,050	4,889
Butler	3,820	13,594,071	5.2	6.4	1.9	2.6	1.8	3.9	76.3	344.1	149.9	119.6	1,790	1,532
Chase	133	400,846	19.1	17.4	1.1	8.5	5.6	1.4	46.0	13.9	5.6	5.5	2,085	1,915
Chautauqua	187	585,546	9.5	8.1	0.0	7.9	4.7	10.3	57.9	13.9	6.4	6.4	1,926	1,541
Cherokee	796	3,157,542	10.6	14.1	1.3	6.0	2.2	3.1	61.6	67.0	39.3	20.6	1,023	746
Cheyenne	159	418,712	11.2	5.0	0.0	7.9	2.0	6.5	64.9	13.4	4.8	6.8	2,519	2,092
Clark	324	1,163,469	4.6	3.5	0.0	3.3	62.1	3.3	23.0	31.0	4.5	7.4	3,699	3,481
Clay	814	2,573,844	4.2	3.5	1.0	4.4	42.0	7.0	36.2	54.3	13.9	14.3	1,783	1,412
Cloud	863	2,648,207	3.1	6.5	1.7	4.6	1.2	3.0	78.7	48.2	20.0	17.2	1,927	1,559
Coffey	721	2,935,460	6.3	5.5	0.0	7.3	38.8	4.8	35.4	72.2	14.4	30.2	3,671	3,518
Comanche	171	551,982	7.0	6.7	0.0	6.9	42.4	3.7	31.4	21.3	5.3	10.8	6,136	5,927
Cowley	2,518	8,522,490	5.0	5.5	2.3	1.8	21.8	6.3	56.2	172.5	77.3	47.0	1,330	1,037
Crawford	2,951	8,874,046	5.2	6.1	2.8	1.9	13.9	3.9	65.2	159.5	82.1	49.8	1,278	803
Decatur	129	411,896	16.1	6.0	0.3	11.4	5.4	6.8	47.1	18.3	9.9	6.5	2,287	1,992
Dickinson	1,316	4,765,557	5.2	5.5	1.1	2.9	35.8	3.2	45.5	131.5	40.4	33.0	1,753	1,383
Doniphan	705	2,334,745	3.7	3.4	0.1	3.3	2.1	4.0	82.9	48.5	25.0	12.9	1,682	1,460
Douglas	5,231	23,730,724	5.5	10.3	4.9	3.3	33.9	8.7	31.5	655.6	134.8	204.1	1,697	1,155
Edwards	171	531,403	18.9	6.3	0.6	15.7	3.2	5.6	49.2	15.9	5.5	8.1	2,817	2,523
Elk	248	634,742	9.0	4.1	0.4	6.7	4.2	2.8	71.2	13.6	7.2	4.5	1,796	1,552
Ellis	1,047	3,344,250	8.4	10.2	3.1	6.1	4.7	6.8	56.9	104.0	34.0	51.6	1,797	1,152
Ellsworth	359	1,095,132	16.1	3.1	0.0	7.5	5.1	8.2	59.4	26.8	10.2	13.3	2,120	1,799
Finney	2,241	7,951,552	6.0	10.9	2.1	1.9	2.5	6.6	68.4	225.6	100.7	71.4	1,943	1,425
Ford	2,552	7,227,791	5.1	7.8	3.3	2.6	2.6	3.3	73.2	210.6	104.6	59.3	1,733	1,155
Franklin	1,523	6,868,830	5.0	6.2	1.3	1.7	27.0	4.7	52.0	133.1	45.9	37.5	1,465	1,145
Geary	2,182	7,774,641	3.9	8.4	3.6	1.7	20.2	1.3	59.9	223.4	104.1	52.2	1,544	959
Gove	287	1,056,581	5.3	1.7	0.0	2.9	44.5	1.6	42.8	26.2	7.2	7.7	2,942	2,483
Graham	217	944,986	7.1	4.1	0.5	7.7	34.2	3.3	41.5	19.5	3.9	7.4	2,976	2,622
Grant	642	2,042,378	3.2	4.9	0.1	4.9	3.8	4.1	78.1	49.5	19.9	25.5	3,400	3,111
Gray	331	1,148,498	8.3	7.6	0.0	6.8	1.6	6.0	66.7	29.3	12.9	11.9	1,979	1,801
Greeley	89	275,669	10.9	7.8	0.1	8.9	7.2	7.5	54.5	4.3	2.3	1.6	1,330	1,293
Greenwood	348	1,033,163	9.3	7.5	1.0	6.7	3.8	4.3	66.6	28.1	11.8	14.7	2,428	2,402
Hamilton	115	383,001	16.0	9.0	1.4	8.7	3.3	9.3	41.5	14.9	5.5	8.6	3,287	3,068
Harper	557	1,854,247	5.7	4.5	0.0	6.1	49.8	5.8	26.3	57.4	13.6	17.4	3,121	2,895
Harvey	1,515	5,347,985	8.9	8.9	5.3	4.0	3.0	5.8	62.3	138.4	57.3	50.4	1,466	964
Haskell	390	1,604,338	6.9	6.3	0.0	7.3	33.2	1.2	44.7	37.3	8.8	16.7	4,152	3,877
Hodgeman	169	392,549	12.6	7.8	0.0	10.8	7.8	13.2	42.4	18.7	4.9	11.9	6,386	6,176
Jackson	1,193	3,448,832	3.9	5.1	0.5	3.3	0.5	4.8	80.5	48.9	26.8	17.9	1,339	1,125
Jefferson	1,064	3,187,375	4.2	6.2	0.1	3.7	4.7	3.6	75.2	81.3	38.1	24.6	1,299	1,209
Jewell	227	656,812	7.5	3.7	0.4	14.0	32.6	7.0	29.9	15.7	3.8	7.1	2,471	2,208
Johnson	22,476	95,446,190	7.0	9.7	3.9	2.4	5.0	7.4	63.0	2,929.7	836.6	1,369.1	2,315	1,502
Kearny	522	1,977,242	3.9	3.5	1.2	3.4	57.9	3.6	25.2	48.5	9.5	14.6	3,702	3,540
Kingman	313	1,057,325	10.2	8.9	0.5	9.6	4.0	5.7	57.6	32.3	12.6	15.5	2,125	1,876
Kiowa	175	522,866	13.9	11.1	0.3	13.4	2.5	8.3	43.7	14.9	4.4	8.5	3,409	3,206
Labette	1,562	5,650,058	3.1	4.6	1.2	2.3	39.0	3.1	44.5	145.7	42.1	26.0	1,294	874
Lane	191	585,401	9.4	5.7	0.4	7.8	35.8	3.3	36.9	13.8	3.0	9.8	6,318	5,994
Leavenworth	2,831	9,904,997	6.6	9.7	2.6	3.0	3.2	5.4	68.1	261.2	131.7	90.3	1,113	809
Lincoln	287	873,911	5.1	4.6	0.1	6.8	36.1	4.5	42.1	17.2	6.0	8.6	2,826	2,435
Linn	512	1,578,522	12.2	8.0	3.9	4.9	2.1	7.4	60.5	48.6	19.5	25.5	2,634	2,538
Logan	506	1,674,444	2.9	2.8	0.1	2.9	32.5	1.9	56.9	18.0	9.7	6.0	2,139	1,796
Lyon	2,381	8,466,398	4.0	7.5	2.8	3.7	29.1	3.3	47.6	205.0	66.5	50.6	1,522	1,126
McPherson	1,681	6,302,623	4.9	6.8	1.5	4.1	1.4	14.0	64.4	113.4	41.5	48.5	1,690	1,348
Marion	797	2,604,278	5.4	5.2	0.1	4.5	19.6	5.4	58.7	61.1	23.6	21.3	1,786	1,490
Marshall	521	1,631,580	7.8	6.8	0.3	8.2	2.2	4.2	67.9	45.2	16.6	22.2	2,293	2,053
Meade	415	1,383,508	5.3	3.8	1.0	5.1	54.6	4.3	24.8	39.9	9.4	13.7	3,248	2,923
Miami	1,389	4,586,183	7.1	10.7	0.8	4.2	3.7	4.0	66.6	121.8	50.8	49.2	1,473	1,088
Mitchell	593	1,586,312	6.7	6.5	0.0	6.4	2.9	12.0	61.8	44.4	15.2	18.6	3,028	2,154
Montgomery	2,150	6,554,386	5.0	7.5	4.1	3.1	1.1	7.9	70.3	176.0	89.8	54.8	1,693	1,230
Morris	241	681,932	15.0	9.4	0.1	12.0	0.0	7.6	54.4	19.8	7.1	10.4	1,906	1,557
Morton	254	932,368	7.1	4.1	0.3	6.3	31.0	3.5	42.5	27.4	12.9	12.3	4,461	4,133
Nemaha	466	1,441,764	8.3	6.7	0.1	7.1	1.7	10.0	65.3	35.9	14.0	17.0	1,692	1,397

1. Based on the resident population estimated as of July 1 of the year shown.

STATE County	Local government finances, 2017 (cont.)									Government employment, 2020			Individual income tax returns, 2019		
	Direct general expenditure							Debt outstanding							
			Percent of total for:												
	Total (mil dol)	Per capita[1] (dollars)	Education	Health and hospitals	Police protection	Public welfare	Highways	Total (mil dol)	Per capita[1] (dollars)	Federal civilian	Federal military	State and local	Number of returns	Mean adjusted gross income	Mean income tax
	185	186	187	188	189	190	191	192	193	194	195	196	197	198	199
KANSAS	X	X	X	X	X	X	X	X	X	26,202	32,904	233,477	1,367,720	68,830	7,837
Allen	77.9	6,207	62.4	2.0	3.4	0.7	3.3	63.8	5,086	49	44	1,434	5,940	44,303	3,385
Anderson	32.2	4,115	41.9	2.9	3.9	0.0	9.8	23.4	2,990	35	30	521	3,590	47,808	3,688
Atchison	55.8	3,426	44.8	1.2	5.8	5.8	10.2	99.7	6,115	48	54	856	7,020	52,371	4,382
Barber	46.3	10,141	19.3	44.1	2.5	0.0	11.7	30.7	6,726	29	16	627	2,110	41,470	3,876
Barton	151.8	5,752	65.8	3.2	2.9	0.0	5.5	55.0	2,085	72	92	2,312	11,910	52,700	4,603
Bourbon	94.9	6,493	69.0	0.3	2.2	0.0	4.9	80.5	5,512	82	52	1,137	6,240	44,084	3,200
Brown	39.0	4,057	65.6	0.1	5.0	0.0	5.7	37.5	3,902	103	35	1,344	4,440	49,823	3,833
Butler	328.7	4,918	69.5	1.2	3.1	0.0	5.4	875.2	13,093	138	239	5,374	30,190	69,561	7,333
Chase	26.7	10,053	62.3	0.6	1.6	0.0	5.2	29.1	10,978	17	9	213	1,150	59,035	5,637
Chautauqua	13.6	4,103	49.0	6.2	4.2	0.0	11.0	8.6	2,585	19	12	237	1,470	42,384	3,193
Cherokee	71.1	3,533	63.7	2.1	4.4	0.0	8.0	35.8	1,779	62	72	1,147	8,540	48,861	4,139
Cheyenne	13.5	5,032	44.0	4.8	3.4	0.0	10.7	1.0	357	17	9	232	1,240	44,016	3,403
Clark	33.9	16,979	18.7	61.9	2.2	0.0	4.5	5.8	2,912	13	7	416	910	52,592	4,433
Clay	54.5	6,809	34.1	38.2	3.4	0.0	5.2	59.3	7,411	39	30	917	3,940	51,412	3,743
Cloud	53.4	5,991	63.4	2.7	3.3	0.1	6.8	21.1	2,363	39	30	745	4,070	45,897	3,374
Coffey	61.0	7,415	39.7	38.3	0.9	0.0	12.2	27.9	3,387	58	30	1,059	4,030	60,523	5,710
Comanche	13.6	7,716	31.8	36.1	0.9	0.0	1.6	7.2	4,084	6	6	254	810	43,416	3,394
Cowley	171.8	4,868	56.4	9.8	4.4	0.0	5.6	211.7	5,997	111	120	3,398	15,270	52,037	4,253
Crawford	200.9	5,161	58.8	12.0	4.6	0.0	3.2	187.7	4,823	94	139	4,991	16,400	52,767	4,893
Decatur	13.6	4,761	32.0	3.1	3.9	0.0	13.9	5.1	1,787	17	10	235	1,350	40,787	3,196
Dickinson	116.9	6,211	40.8	29.1	3.1	0.0	6.4	95.9	5,093	97	66	1,610	8,990	51,909	3,978
Doniphan	45.9	5,990	75.0	2.1	3.0	0.0	6.4	11.2	1,463	30	26	895	3,310	53,473	4,320
Douglas	638.1	5,305	25.4	35.8	4.3	0.0	3.0	783.8	6,517	471	463	17,576	53,160	68,458	7,814
Edwards	14.3	4,973	42.7	4.2	5.1	0.0	13.7	7.1	2,456	19	10	215	1,370	49,109	3,927
Elk	14.9	5,942	62.2	2.0	3.4	0.7	13.4	3.0	1,205	11	9	293	1,130	41,339	3,200
Ellis	108.3	3,767	41.2	3.5	4.5	0.0	6.7	47.2	1,642	152	102	4,208	13,200	58,147	5,704
Ellsworth	26.8	4,259	52.9	4.1	5.0	0.0	12.9	17.3	2,754	30	19	881	2,620	53,036	4,693
Finney	209.0	5,692	51.9	1.9	7.1	0.0	3.7	168.8	4,598	120	131	2,939	17,720	53,637	4,761
Ford	294.3	8,600	68.1	1.7	2.5	1.0	2.5	436.5	12,756	213	120	2,445	14,960	50,524	4,051
Franklin	164.4	6,414	41.1	28.5	2.9	0.0	3.7	143.5	5,599	72	93	1,521	12,220	53,929	4,439
Geary	203.4	6,021	43.8	22.2	6.7	0.0	3.3	296.9	8,791	3,159	15,917	2,400	17,680	44,007	2,655
Gove	27.9	10,625	25.8	51.6	1.9	0.0	8.0	2.4	924	17	9	412	1,340	46,354	3,922
Graham	22.2	8,929	21.2	38.3	2.9	0.0	8.8	12.1	4,851	26	9	306	1,190	39,797	3,158
Grant	47.4	6,329	53.9	4.0	4.0	0.0	6.0	18.7	2,499	21	26	553	3,170	56,439	4,728
Gray	29.4	4,877	52.7	2.9	0.8	0.0	13.1	15.2	2,531	22	22	884	2,710	56,520	6,445
Greeley	4.0	3,226	77.3	0.0	1.2	0.0	4.3	3.6	2,955	9	5	177	590	53,944	4,203
Greenwood	17.3	2,846	76.9	0.1	0.0	0.0	9.7	5.0	817	39	21	480	2,800	44,259	3,413
Hamilton	18.3	6,982	67.0	1.4	4.4	0.0	5.8	7.7	2,950	12	9	250	1,040	27,210	3,491
Harper	49.4	8,845	25.8	37.7	2.3	7.2	10.0	17.3	3,100	34	19	711	2,480	43,980	3,477
Harvey	133.3	3,877	51.1	1.4	6.4	0.0	6.9	425.5	12,379	76	122	1,916	16,000	58,642	5,146
Haskell	38.1	9,471	33.3	36.2	3.6	0.0	11.6	4.3	1,061	16	14	518	1,720	62,397	4,988
Hodgeman	11.4	6,121	34.0	2.3	4.4	0.0	13.4	9.2	4,954	19	7	263	860	50,853	3,767
Jackson	56.4	4,233	63.6	1.3	4.7	0.0	8.6	39.2	2,938	52	48	1,796	6,310	52,160	4,071
Jefferson	85.1	4,495	70.1	2.6	4.5	0.0	9.8	46.4	2,453	78	69	1,007	8,910	60,281	5,307
Jewell	15.2	5,306	25.2	21.5	2.5	0.0	17.8	0.8	286	31	10	344	1,390	46,616	3,312
Johnson	2,698.6	4,564	44.1	2.2	7.8	0.9	9.6	5,985.2	10,122	2,852	2,258	28,355	300,030	107,690	15,953
Kearny	45.3	11,503	22.9	51.4	2.8	0.0	4.9	6.1	1,550	13	14	648	1,760	56,740	4,882
Kingman	21.7	2,984	68.1	0.5	0.3	0.0	9.2	15.5	2,125	36	31	536	3,560	49,651	4,225
Kiowa	16.3	6,575	37.8	2.8	4.9	0.0	16.2	6.8	2,722	13	10	309	1,080	49,967	3,877
Labette	146.0	7,255	35.4	43.4	2.8	0.0	3.0	91.2	4,530	90	71	2,834	8,990	45,321	3,405
Lane	13.9	8,961	32.3	1.8	1.2	0.0	1.3	13.8	8,892	9	6	245	830	40,922	4,218
Leavenworth	258.4	3,185	55.1	1.7	5.9	0.7	6.5	395.3	4,874	4,493	3,698	3,892	35,260	67,183	6,336
Lincoln	17.5	5,737	43.8	7.4	2.8	0.0	13.1	1.0	337	31	11	350	1,400	42,627	3,190
Linn	60.2	6,212	59.7	2.2	3.8	0.0	6.9	45.7	4,712	48	35	697	4,530	50,224	4,054
Logan	21.9	7,797	82.5	0.0	3.4	0.0	2.8	3.5	1,233	22	21	675	1,400	52,798	4,626
Lyon	195.9	5,889	37.4	33.9	3.8	0.4	4.5	94.8	2,849	99	117	4,620	14,760	50,546	4,015
McPherson	111.8	3,897	52.1	1.9	4.6	0.4	11.1	191.4	6,672	94	102	1,853	14,110	63,952	6,149
Marion	62.0	5,187	44.8	17.2	2.7	0.0	15.0	36.1	3,024	65	40	917	5,240	53,679	4,000
Marshall	48.7	5,032	62.0	2.7	3.7	0.0	9.1	31.5	3,248	53	35	785	4,950	54,900	4,628
Meade	39.7	9,389	18.1	40.8	2.8	3.9	7.4	11.4	2,692	19	14	522	1,940	61,037	5,202
Miami	116.9	3,496	55.8	2.4	5.0	0.0	7.3	112.6	3,367	76	124	2,174	16,170	71,401	7,478
Mitchell	44.6	7,273	61.9	4.9	3.9	0.0	9.6	33.6	5,467	32	21	984	2,880	50,592	4,343
Montgomery	164.9	5,090	60.0	2.4	3.6	0.0	4.7	203.2	6,273	120	112	2,453	13,450	48,375	3,986
Morris	19.4	3,543	44.9	8.2	3.5	0.0	15.2	13.8	2,521	35	20	484	2,610	52,028	4,678
Morton	23.9	8,687	47.4	1.9	1.0	0.0	4.3	2.7	978	21	9	369	1,330	51,395	4,280
Nemaha	32.3	3,212	59.7	1.3	2.7	0.0	11.6	25.7	2,550	53	36	747	4,950	63,669	5,745

1. Based on the resident population estimated as of July 1 of the year shown.

State / county code	CBSA code[1]	County Type code[2]	STATE County	Land area[3] (sq. mi)	Population, 2021: Total persons 2021	Population, 2021: Rank	Population, 2021: Per square mile	Race alone or in combination, not Hispanic or Latino (percent): White	Black	American Indian, Alaska Native	Asian and Pacific Islancer	Percent Hispanic or Latino[4]	Age (percent): Under 5 years	5 to 17 years	18 to 24 years	25 to 34 years	35 to 44 years	45 to 54 years
				1	2	3	4	5	6	7	8	9	10	11	12	13	14	15
			KANSAS— Cont'd															
20133		7	Neosho	571.5	15,784	2,044	27.6	90.7	1.9	2.0	1.2	6.4	5.9	14.2	13.0	11.0	11.3	11.0
20135		9	Ness	1,074.7	2,672	2,984	2.5	87.2	1.0	1.1	0.4	11.4	5.7	12.6	10.5	9.4	10.4	9.5
20137		7	Norton	878.0	5,342	2,789	6.1	89.5	4.1	1.1	1.7	5.5	5.0	10.7	10.8	13.7	13.0	12.6
20139	45820	3	Osage	705.5	15,768	2,047	22.4	94.6	1.4	1.5	0.8	3.6	5.5	13.0	11.5	10.5	11.7	11.6
20141		9	Osborne	892.5	3,498	2,923	3.9	95.0	1.3	1.3	1.5	2.4	5.8	12.7	9.3	10.5	10.7	9.1
20143	41460	9	Ottawa	720.7	5,838	2,750	8.1	94.9	1.9	0.9	0.7	2.9	5.4	13.5	11.8	10.2	11.8	11.4
20145		7	Pawnee	754.3	6,225	2,718	8.3	85.3	6.5	1.4	0.8	7.8	4.0	7.8	11.3	12.8	13.8	12.7
20147		7	Phillips	885.9	4,815	2,836	5.4	94.4	0.9	1.0	1.4	3.5	5.6	12.6	11.1	9.8	10.5	10.7
20149	31740	3	Pottawatomie	840.7	25,790	1,571	30.7	91.6	2.0	1.4	1.8	5.4	7.2	16.8	12.8	11.8	14.0	10.4
20151		7	Pratt	735.0	9,181	2,475	12.5	89.5	2.4	1.5	1.3	7.3	5.7	14.1	13.9	10.8	11.9	9.7
20153		9	Rawlins	1,069.4	2,549	2,994	2.4	90.4	1.6	1.0	0.9	7.9	6.8	12.2	8.8	10.1	10.6	9.9
20155	26740	4	Reno	1,255.3	61,414	865	48.9	85.6	4.3	1.4	1.1	10.0	5.2	12.5	13.1	11.8	12.3	11.2
20157		9	Republic	717.4	4,662	2,844	6.5	96.0	1.4	0.7	0.9	2.4	5.3	12.6	9.8	9.5	10.9	9.1
20159		7	Rice	726.2	9,390	2,461	12.9	84.9	2.2	1.8	1.6	11.8	5.5	13.5	16.2	11.0	11.2	9.7
20161	31740	3	Riley	609.7	72,208	761	118.4	79.4	7.9	1.2	6.3	8.6	5.1	9.0	33.5	16.3	11.1	7.1
20163		9	Rooks	890.5	4,831	2,835	5.4	95.5	1.5	0.9	0.9	2.4	5.8	12.3	10.7	10.4	11.3	10.9
20165		9	Rush	717.8	2,953	2,960	4.1	93.1	1.0	1.5	0.7	5.0	4.8	11.4	9.8	9.5	10.5	12.2
20167		7	Russell	886.3	6,703	2,682	7.6	93.0	2.4	1.6	0.9	4.2	5.5	13.5	9.6	10.3	10.9	10.4
20169	41460	5	Saline	720.2	53,888	942	74.8	82.0	4.9	1.1	3.0	12.0	5.9	12.9	12.9	12.2	12.0	11.5
20171		7	Scott	717.6	5,131	2,811	7.2	78.6	1.0	1.0	1.3	19.1	6.5	15.4	12.7	12.0	10.8	10.7
20173	48620	2	Sedgwick	996.9	523,828	136	525.5	70.3	10.6	1.9	5.5	15.4	6.4	14.5	13.6	14.0	12.9	11.1
20175	30580	5	Seward	639.7	21,747	1,726	34.0	29.9	4.0	0.8	2.9	63.7	8.5	17.3	16.2	13.9	11.8	11.2
20177	45820	3	Shawnee	544.0	178,264	378	327.7	76.4	10.0	2.1	2.3	13.1	5.8	13.3	12.8	12.0	12.5	11.2
20179		9	Sheridan	896.0	2,478	2,999	2.8	92.7	1.1	0.8	0.6	6.0	6.5	14.3	11.8	9.6	10.8	9.1
20181		7	Sherman	1,056.1	5,895	2,743	5.6	85.6	2.0	0.8	0.9	12.5	6.3	14.2	12.5	11.1	12.3	9.6
20183		9	Smith	895.5	3,576	2,918	4.0	95.8	1.6	1.4	0.9	2.7	4.7	12.0	9.8	8.6	10.4	9.8
20185		9	Stafford	792.0	4,034	2,885	5.1	84.5	1.5	1.7	0.9	13.5	6.1	14.1	11.7	9.6	11.4	9.8
20187		9	Stanton	680.4	2,044	3,038	3.0	57.4	2.4	2.3	1.4	40.1	5.5	18.3	13.7	9.9	12.0	10.9
20189		7	Stevens	727.3	5,293	2,796	7.3	59.0	1.2	1.4	0.6	39.0	6.2	17.4	13.8	10.8	12.1	11.5
20191	48620	2	Sumner	1,181.7	22,385	1,700	18.9	90.8	2.3	2.6	1.0	6.1	5.8	14.0	12.0	11.0	12.0	11.1
20193		7	Thomas	1,074.7	7,877	2,585	7.3	89.8	1.7	1.0	1.1	7.9	6.3	14.1	16.1	12.3	11.0	9.5
20195		9	Trego	889.5	2,793	2,978	3.1	95.2	1.2	1.3	0.7	3.2	4.5	10.7	8.4	10.1	11.5	10.7
20197	45820	3	Wabaunsee	794.3	6,966	2,666	8.8	93.5	1.8	1.9	0.8	4.4	5.7	13.2	11.5	10.1	11.0	10.9
20199		9	Wallace	913.7	1,508	3,077	1.7	90.9	1.7	1.1	0.4	7.5	9.1	13.9	11.5	10.3	9.7	8.2
20201		9	Washington	894.8	5,511	2,775	6.2	93.9	1.0	0.7	0.9	4.6	7.1	13.4	10.4	9.9	10.4	10.1
20203		9	Wichita	718.6	2,082	3,034	2.9	69.2	1.4	1.0	0.5	28.9	6.0	15.3	12.5	10.2	11.1	10.3
20205		7	Wilson	570.4	8,526	2,534	14.9	93.9	1.5	2.5	1.0	3.7	5.8	13.7	11.4	9.5	11.8	10.6
20207		9	Woodson	497.8	3,102	2,952	6.2	94.8	2.0	2.4	0.6	3.3	4.6	11.4	10.3	9.4	11.8	9.9
20209	28140	1	Wyandotte	151.6	167,046	404	1,101.9	41.9	22.6	1.4	6.2	30.8	7.4	15.5	13.3	14.4	13.3	11.3
21000		0	KENTUCKY	39,491.4	4,509,394	X	114.2	85.4	9.6	0.7	2.2	4.2	5.9	12.7	13.1	13.1	12.5	12.4
21001		7	Adair	405.3	18,932	1,873	46.7	93.5	3.9	0.8	0.7	2.7	4.8	11.0	16.2	11.5	10.5	12.4
21003	14540	3	Allen	344.3	20,797	1,772	60.4	95.5	2.0	0.9	0.5	2.5	5.9	13.0	11.2	12.7	11.7	13.4
21005	23180	6	Anderson	202.2	24,035	1,641	118.9	94.5	3.2	0.8	1.0	2.4	5.7	13.5	11.4	12.1	12.1	14.3
21007	37140	9	Ballard	246.9	7,695	2,597	31.2	93.9	4.9	1.0	0.8	1.7	4.8	11.9	11.5	10.8	11.9	13.1
21009	23980	6	Barren	487.6	44,544	1,085	91.4	91.3	5.1	0.7	1.0	3.6	6.2	13.4	11.5	12.1	12.4	12.5
21011	34460	8	Bath	278.8	12,778	2,224	45.8	96.1	2.1	0.5	0.8	1.9	6.8	14.1	12.0	11.8	11.4	13.0
21013	33180	7	Bell	359.1	23,858	1,646	66.4	95.2	3.5	1.3	0.7	1.4	6.0	11.7	11.7	12.5	11.5	12.7
21015	17140	1	Boone	246.3	137,412	476	557.9	88.0	5.4	0.6	3.5	4.7	6.3	14.6	12.8	12.1	13.7	13.4
21017	30460	2	Bourbon	289.7	20,229	1,804	69.8	86.6	6.8	0.7	0.7	7.2	5.5	13.0	11.4	12.1	11.1	12.8
21019	26580	2	Boyd	159.9	47,899	1,025	299.6	94.4	3.6	0.8	0.9	1.9	5.4	12.2	10.8	11.9	12.6	12.7
21021	19220	7	Boyle	180.4	30,747	1,413	170.4	87.3	9.4	0.8	1.4	3.5	5.3	11.6	15.2	12.2	11.6	12.0
21023	17140	1	Bracken	202.7	8,439	2,539	41.6	96.7	1.6	0.8	0.4	2.0	5.8	13.5	11.4	11.3	12.5	12.8
21025		7	Breathitt	492.4	13,553	2,187	27.5	97.1	1.0	0.6	0.9	1.4	6.1	11.3	10.7	12.3	12.4	13.4
21027		8	Breckinridge	569.8	20,651	1,782	36.2	94.8	3.3	0.9	0.6	2.1	5.8	12.3	11.8	10.9	11.6	12.3
21029	31140	1	Bullitt	297.1	82,918	695	279.1	94.8	2.2	0.9	1.1	2.7	5.1	12.2	11.3	13.0	13.2	13.8
21031	14540	3	Butler	426.1	12,294	2,260	28.9	95.0	1.4	0.8	0.4	3.7	6.0	12.8	10.9	11.6	12.9	12.5
21033		7	Caldwell	344.8	12,624	2,234	36.6	91.9	6.2	0.8	0.8	2.0	5.8	13.1	10.9	11.6	11.3	12.5
21035	34660	7	Calloway	385.0	37,560	1,235	97.6	91.0	5.1	0.8	2.2	2.8	4.6	10.6	22.2	12.0	10.7	10.6
21037	17140	1	Campbell	151.3	93,050	648	615.0	93.4	3.9	0.6	1.4	2.4	5.5	11.6	13.0	14.4	13.0	11.7
21039		9	Carlisle	189.4	4,791	2,838	25.3	95.0	3.0	1.3	0.7	2.6	5.8	13.3	11.1	11.0	11.3	12.8
21041		6	Carroll	128.7	10,863	2,354	84.4	90.5	3.2	1.0	0.6	6.9	7.0	15.1	11.7	12.5	12.2	11.9
21043	26580	6	Carter	409.5	26,412	1,546	64.5	97.2	1.1	0.7	0.4	1.5	5.5	12.9	12.4	11.4	11.4	13.0
21045		9	Casey	444.2	15,866	2,040	35.7	95.4	1.5	0.8	0.5	2.9	5.9	13.2	11.2	11.8	11.4	12.3
21047	17300	2	Christian	717.5	72,357	759	100.8	67.9	23.4	1.1	2.7	8.5	9.4	14.6	19.2	16.9	10.3	8.4
21049	30460	2	Clark	252.5	36,871	1,257	146.0	91.0	5.8	0.6	1.0	3.4	5.8	12.7	11.3	12.6	12.1	13.3

1. CBSA = Core Based Statistical Area. See Appendix A for explanation. See Appendix B for list of metropolitan areas with component counties. 2. County type code from the Economic Research Service of USDA Rural-Urban Continuum Codes. See Appendix A for definition. 3. Dry land or land partially or temporarily covered by water. 4. May be of any race.

STATE County	Population, 2021 (cont.)				Population change, 2000–2021							Households, 2016–2020				
	Age (percent) (cont.)				Total persons		Percent change		Components of change, 2020–2021					Percent		
	55 to 64 years	65 to 74 years	75 years and over	Percent female	2010	2020	2010–2020	2020–2021	Births	Deaths	Net Migration	Number	Persons per household	Family house-holds	Female family house-holder[1]	One person
	16	17	18	19	20	21	22	23	24	25	26	27	28	29	30	31
KANSAS— Cont'd																
Neosho	13.6	11.4	8.7	50.2	16,512	15,904	-3.7	-0.8	225	278	-68	6,462	2.4	65.9	9.6	30.0
Ness	16.4	14.1	11.6	51.2	3,107	2,687	-13.5	-0.6	27	50	7	1,260	2.2	66.3	4.3	30.1
Norton	13.4	10.9	10.0	44.0	5,671	5,459	-3.7	-2.1	61	105	-72	1,865	2.4	62.8	6.1	31.3
Osage	15.9	12.4	8.1	49.9	16,295	15,766	-3.2	0.0	192	279	90	6,624	2.4	67.4	9.5	28.0
Osborne	15.8	13.6	12.6	49.8	3,858	3,500	-9.3	-0.1	47	54	6	1,687	2.0	57.6	8.4	37.3
Ottawa	15.3	12.4	8.3	48.1	6,091	5,735	-5.8	1.8	76	106	135	2,433	2.3	71.3	9.1	23.9
Pawnee	15.3	12.9	9.3	43.9	6,973	6,253	-10.3	-0.4	80	123	16	2,447	2.3	56.4	9.3	39.8
Phillips	14.8	14.8	10.1	49.9	5,642	4,981	-11.7	-3.3	59	105	-118	2,406	2.2	57.7	7.5	36.3
Pottawatomie	11.8	9.3	5.8	50.3	21,604	25,348	17.3	1.7	400	270	312	8,883	2.7	72.3	7.4	24.9
Pratt	12.9	11.9	9.1	50.4	9,656	9,157	-5.2	0.3	114	159	70	3,733	2.4	62.1	6.9	30.2
Rawlins	13.8	14.8	12.9	49.1	2,519	2,561	1.7	-0.5	28	42	2	1,169	2.1	65.6	2.8	31.1
Reno	13.5	11.5	8.8	49.7	64,511	61,898	-4.1	-0.8	759	1,069	-179	24,970	2.4	62.3	10.4	31.1
Republic	15.3	14.9	12.6	50.5	4,980	4,674	-6.1	-0.3	58	109	40	2,176	2.1	61.2	5.3	37.3
Rice	13.1	11.4	8.5	49.4	10,083	9,427	-6.5	-0.4	112	148	-2	3,939	2.2	65.8	7.7	31.2
Riley	7.6	6.4	4.0	47.7	71,115	71,959	1.2	0.3	945	556	-156	26,878	2.4	53.3	6.7	31.2
Rooks	15.4	13.2	10.1	51.2	5,181	4,919	-5.1	-1.8	51	108	-30	2,167	2.2	64.1	5.9	32.5
Rush	15.9	14.6	11.3	48.9	3,307	2,956	-10.6	-0.1	37	59	19	1,448	2.0	49.9	5.1	45.9
Russell	14.7	13.7	11.4	50.8	6,970	6,691	-4.0	0.2	78	142	79	3,005	2.3	60.1	6.0	34.8
Saline	13.6	11.0	7.9	50.3	55,606	54,303	-2.3	-0.8	843	831	-428	22,251	2.4	60.0	10.2	34.8
Scott	12.3	10.7	8.8	49.4	4,936	5,151	4.4	-0.4	90	75	-37	2,062	2.3	69.4	5.8	26.4
Sedgwick	12.2	9.6	5.8	50.6	498,365	523,824	5.1	0.0	8,050	6,963	-1,174	199,320	2.6	63.3	12.1	30.7
Seward	10.1	6.5	4.5	48.9	22,952	21,964	-4.3	-1.0	446	182	-483	7,183	3.0	69.3	12.8	25.9
Shawnee	13.3	11.5	7.6	51.7	177,934	178,909	0.5	-0.4	2,506	2,820	-361	72,962	2.4	62.1	11.2	32.1
Sheridan	14.2	12.7	10.9	49.1	2,556	2,447	-4.3	1.3	44	40	28	1,080	2.3	61.9	8.1	33.1
Sherman	13.6	11.5	8.8	49.2	6,010	5,927	-1.4	-0.5	94	110	-16	2,569	2.2	66.4	6.6	30.2
Smith	15.9	16.1	12.7	49.8	3,853	3,570	-7.3	0.2	40	65	32	1,664	2.1	66.5	6.3	28.2
Stafford	15.4	11.8	10.0	48.9	4,437	4,072	-8.2	-0.9	65	68	-35	1,758	2.3	65.4	5.8	29.7
Stanton	12.0	9.9	7.7	49.2	2,235	2,084	-6.8	-1.9	25	24	-41	850	2.4	58.5	6.7	31.1
Stevens	12.9	8.5	6.9	51.0	5,724	5,250	-8.3	0.8	68	53	29	1,770	3.0	74.4	8.5	21.8
Sumner	14.4	11.8	8.0	49.6	24,132	22,382	-7.3	0.0	323	374	52	9,462	2.4	65.8	10.1	29.6
Thomas	12.0	10.5	8.0	50.3	7,900	7,930	0.4	-0.7	111	113	-52	3,294	2.2	64.9	7.0	25.9
Trego	17.7	15.8	10.7	48.7	3,001	2,808	-6.4	-0.5	36	50	0	1,353	2.0	65.9	5.7	31.5
Wabaunsee	16.3	13.1	8.3	48.7	7,053	6,877	-2.5	1.3	98	88	80	2,722	2.5	70.5	8.7	27.4
Wallace	14.0	12.4	10.9	49.9	1,485	1,512	1.8	-0.3	19	15	-7	651	2.4	68.8	6.1	30.0
Washington	14.6	12.6	11.4	48.9	5,799	5,530	-4.6	-0.3	85	97	-8	2,412	2.2	59.8	4.9	35.4
Wichita	13.0	12.2	9.4	46.2	2,234	2,152	-3.7	-3.3	29	20	-78	935	2.2	60.7	8.3	33.8
Wilson	14.1	13.6	9.6	50.1	9,409	8,624	-8.3	-1.1	118	155	-57	3,627	2.3	68.5	10.6	27.7
Woodson	17.0	15.7	9.9	48.8	3,309	3,115	-5.9	-0.4	39	55	4	1,390	2.2	60.1	10.1	35.8
Wyandotte	11.7	8.3	4.8	50.0	157,505	169,245	7.5	-1.3	3,068	2,170	-3,089	60,400	2.7	64.2	16.4	30.4
KENTUCKY	13.3	10.6	6.5	50.5	4,339,367	4,505,836	3.8	0.1	63,181	71,410	11,496	1,748,053	2.5	65.2	12.2	28.7
Adair	14.6	11.6	7.3	49.9	18,656	18,903	1.3	0.2	239	377	167	6,991	2.6	67.1	10.2	29.6
Allen	14.2	10.9	7.0	50.0	19,956	20,588	3.2	1.0	302	359	267	7,816	2.7	72.6	13.3	24.7
Anderson	14.3	10.4	6.2	50.4	21,421	23,852	11.3	0.8	307	353	229	8,757	2.6	67.6	11.6	26.4
Ballard	14.3	12.7	8.9	49.9	8,249	7,728	-6.3	-0.4	87	132	11	3,052	2.6	68.3	8.6	28.2
Barren	13.9	10.8	7.2	51.4	42,173	44,485	5.5	0.1	616	799	236	17,392	2.5	66.3	12.6	26.5
Bath	13.7	10.7	6.5	50.4	11,591	12,750	10.0	0.2	198	240	68	4,885	2.5	71.4	14.9	21.8
Bell	14.2	12.0	7.8	50.6	28,691	24,097	-16.0	-1.0	337	567	-11	10,504	2.4	67.5	15.9	29.2
Boone	12.6	9.1	5.2	50.1	118,811	135,968	14.4	1.1	2,031	1,506	892	47,391	2.8	72.6	11.7	22.5
Bourbon	14.0	11.7	8.2	50.5	19,985	20,252	1.3	-0.1	232	320	63	7,990	2.5	64.7	11.8	28.2
Boyd	14.0	12.2	8.2	50.2	49,542	48,261	-2.6	-0.8	624	927	-66	18,213	2.5	65.8	13.6	30.0
Boyle	12.7	11.1	8.1	49.9	28,432	30,614	7.7	0.4	361	526	296	11,079	2.4	66.3	13.3	30.0
Bracken	14.8	11.4	6.4	49.8	8,488	8,400	-1.0	0.5	124	135	50	3,197	2.6	68.4	6.5	25.5
Breathitt	15.3	12.1	6.2	49.9	13,878	13,718	-1.2	-1.2	199	279	-86	5,281	2.4	67.2	13.7	30.0
Breckinridge	15.2	12.6	7.5	49.4	20,059	20,432	1.9	1.1	304	355	272	7,731	2.6	65.7	9.3	28.1
Bullitt	14.4	10.5	6.3	50.1	74,319	82,217	10.6	0.9	996	1,079	780	29,940	2.7	74.1	11.2	21.5
Butler	14.2	11.6	7.7	49.2	12,690	12,371	-2.5	-0.6	170	233	-15	4,823	2.6	71.5	11.7	22.8
Caldwell	13.5	12.6	8.6	51.0	12,984	12,649	-2.6	-0.2	160	238	52	5,215	2.4	68.6	12.1	26.0
Calloway	11.9	10.3	7.1	50.9	37,191	37,103	-0.2	1.2	395	614	681	15,492	2.3	58.4	8.2	34.2
Campbell	13.9	10.6	6.3	50.5	90,336	93,076	3.0	0.0	1,251	1,294	6	37,197	2.4	61.9	11.8	31.9
Carlisle	13.9	11.6	9.2	49.6	5,104	4,826	-5.4	-0.7	65	86	-14	1,925	2.4	67.6	9.1	28.5
Carroll	13.5	9.7	6.4	49.8	10,811	10,810	0.0	0.5	190	185	46	4,176	2.5	67.4	16.9	26.6
Carter	13.8	11.7	7.8	50.4	27,720	26,627	-3.9	-0.8	349	503	-64	9,624	2.7	69.4	10.6	28.7
Casey	13.7	12.4	8.1	51.1	15,955	15,941	-0.1	-0.5	204	344	65	6,048	2.6	65.8	12.2	28.3
Christian	8.7	7.3	5.3	46.9	73,955	72,748	-1.6	-0.5	1,862	989	-1,260	26,097	2.5	66.9	14.9	26.7
Clark	13.9	11.0	7.2	51.1	35,613	36,972	3.8	-0.3	495	573	-29	14,576	2.5	68.7	13.4	25.8

1. No spouse present.

STATE County	Persons in group quarters, 2021	Daytime Population, 2016–2020		Births, 2021		Deaths, 2021		Persons under 65 with no health insurance, 2019		Medicare, 2021			COVID-19 Deaths, 2020	
		Number	Employment/ residence ratio	Total	Rate[1]	Number	Rate[1]	Number	Percent	Total beneficiaries	Enrolled in Original Medicare	Enrolled in Medicare Advantage	Number	Rate[1]
	32	33	34	35	36	37	38	39	40	41	42	43	44	45
KANSAS— Cont'd														
Neosho	399	16,286	1.0	176	11.1	230	14.5	1,186	9.6	3,631	3,279	353	18	1.1
Ness	50	2,749	0.9	23	8.6	43	16.1	326	16.5	779	749	29	15	5.6
Norton	810	5,474	1.0	46	8.5	77	14.3	391	11.3	1,149	1,094	54	24	4.4
Osage	151	11,712	0.4	157	10.0	221	14.0	1,247	10.0	3,981	3,325	656	23	1.5
Osborne	91	3,445	1.0	40	11.4	42	12.0	327	13.0	968	935	34	D	D
Ottawa	79	4,622	0.6	61	10.5	87	15.0	430	9.7	1,390	1,344	46	12	2.1
Pawnee	957	6,851	1.1	62	9.9	94	15.1	386	9.5	1,485	1,431	54	10	1.6
Phillips	41	5,289	1.0	48	9.8	81	16.6	423	10.9	1,473	1,418	55	16	3.2
Pottawatomie	270	23,251	0.9	321	12.5	212	8.3	1,808	8.7	4,248	3,694	554	16	0.6
Pratt	350	9,593	1.1	93	10.1	135	14.7	799	11.6	2,090	2,031	59	26	2.8
Rawlins	37	2,402	0.9	22	8.6	30	11.8	265	14.7	724	677	47	D	D
Reno	2,989	61,803	1.0	601	9.8	840	13.6	5,664	12.2	14,325	12,410	1,915	107	1.7
Republic	93	4,405	0.9	42	9.0	100	21.4	390	11.8	1,384	1,322	61	11	2.4
Rice	616	9,157	0.9	87	9.3	111	11.8	822	11.6	2,122	2,032	90	12	1.3
Riley	8,932	70,308	0.9	742	10.3	446	6.2	5,883	10.3	8,057	7,524	533	23	0.3
Rooks	61	4,809	0.9	39	8.0	94	19.3	433	11.6	1,290	1,230	60	10	2.0
Rush	51	2,672	0.8	27	9.2	47	15.9	254	11.3	877	840	37	13	4.4
Russell	57	6,500	0.9	59	8.8	115	17.2	607	12.0	1,813	1,759	54	20	3.0
Saline	1,395	56,632	1.1	664	12.3	663	12.3	4,599	10.7	11,671	10,600	1,071	84	1.5
Scott	102	4,960	1.0	72	14.0	59	11.5	530	13.9	1,042	999	43	18	3.5
Sedgwick	6,952	530,806	1.1	6,527	12.5	5,570	10.6	53,090	12.3	91,128	64,930	26,199	550	1.0
Seward	474	22,557	1.1	360	16.5	138	6.3	3,648	19.7	2,477	2,379	99	40	1.8
Shawnee	4,274	191,120	1.2	1,992	11.2	2,255	12.6	12,400	8.8	39,376	31,967	7,409	262	1.5
Sheridan	24	2,405	0.9	37	15.0	29	11.8	277	14.5	599	585	14	10	4.1
Sherman	95	5,863	1.0	77	13.1	85	14.4	423	9.1	1,310	1,261	49	11	1.9
Smith	48	3,526	1.0	29	8.1	46	12.9	298	11.7	1,167	1,115	53	D	D
Stafford	58	3,637	0.8	50	12.3	48	11.9	460	14.6	973	932	41	D	D
Stanton	45	2,138	1.1	23	11.2	15	7.3	258	15.9	346	334	12	D	D
Stevens	47	5,711	1.1	55	10.4	43	8.2	874	19.4	851	817	34	D	D
Sumner	325	20,482	0.8	253	11.3	305	13.6	1,807	9.9	5,093	3,971	1,122	44	2.0
Thomas	348	7,962	1.1	92	11.7	92	11.7	653	10.7	1,563	1,478	86	10	1.3
Trego	60	2,593	0.9	27	9.6	43	15.4	224	11.1	799	780	18	D	D
Wabaunsee	75	5,292	0.5	75	10.8	73	10.5	459	8.5	1,579	1,369	211	D	D
Wallace	14	1,518	0.9	14	9.3	13	8.6	122	10.7	343	D	D	D	D
Washington	100	5,103	0.9	70	12.7	80	14.5	520	12.8	1,463	1,403	60	10	1.8
Wichita	24	2,105	1.0	22	10.4	16	7.6	288	17.3	451	D	D	D	D
Wilson	112	8,627	1.0	90	10.5	125	14.6	747	11.5	2,338	2,108	230	10	1.2
Woodson	37	2,746	0.7	28	9.0	47	15.1	306	13.3	821	741	81	D	D
Wyandotte	1,245	183,341	1.2	2,452	14.6	1,725	10.3	23,968	17.0	24,605	13,215	11,390	227	1.3
KENTUCKY	125,165	4,476,649	1.0	50,725	11.3	56,853	12.6	275,158	7.6	942,915	578,633	364,282	4,483	1.0
Adair	1,357	16,800	0.7	193	10.2	282	14.9	1,213	8.5	4,444	3,112	1,332	46	2.4
Allen	112	18,595	0.7	237	11.5	302	14.6	1,454	8.5	4,538	2,876	1,661	34	1.7
Anderson	97	17,003	0.5	240	10.0	277	11.6	1,271	6.7	4,787	2,509	2,278	13	0.5
Ballard	87	6,532	0.6	70	9.1	115	14.9	438	7.2	2,089	1,455	633	D	D
Barren	623	43,415	1.0	512	11.5	628	14.1	2,866	8.1	10,249	6,711	3,538	54	1.2
Bath	89	9,783	0.4	165	12.9	183	14.4	885	8.7	2,909	1,610	1,299	10	0.8
Bell	759	27,384	1.1	273	11.4	449	18.8	1,765	8.9	6,794	4,557	2,237	43	1.8
Boone	752	156,168	1.4	1,624	11.9	1,264	9.2	6,474	5.6	21,582	11,933	9,649	93	0.7
Bourbon	208	18,135	0.8	188	9.3	264	13.0	1,465	9.4	4,616	2,579	2,036	D	D
Boyd	1,898	53,602	1.4	501	10.4	719	15.0	2,519	7.1	11,904	7,178	4,726	58	1.2
Boyle	3,148	33,088	1.3	283	9.2	408	13.3	1,385	6.6	7,048	4,377	2,672	51	1.7
Bracken	26	6,347	0.4	92	10.9	105	12.5	501	7.4	2,029	1,202	827	D	D
Breathitt	327	11,697	0.7	164	12.0	212	15.6	780	7.8	3,486	2,042	1,443	D	D
Breckinridge	245	16,925	0.5	234	11.4	274	13.3	1,427	8.9	4,975	3,478	1,497	16	0.8
Bullitt	281	68,171	0.7	784	9.5	861	10.4	4,141	6.1	16,286	9,732	6,553	70	0.9
Butler	138	11,299	0.7	133	10.8	181	14.7	992	9.7	2,939	1,748	1,191	24	1.9
Caldwell	109	11,583	0.8	124	9.8	186	14.7	785	7.9	3,330	2,298	1,031	16	1.3
Calloway	2,920	40,205	1.1	306	8.2	502	13.4	2,618	9.0	8,072	5,086	2,986	41	1.1
Campbell	3,023	79,064	0.7	998	10.7	1,048	11.3	4,324	5.7	17,378	9,540	7,838	65	0.7
Carlisle	53	3,763	0.4	50	10.4	60	12.5	350	9.5	1,257	827	429	D	D
Carroll	292	13,598	1.7	155	14.3	156	14.4	713	8.2	2,333	1,378	955	16	1.5
Carter	535	24,206	0.7	277	10.5	411	15.5	1,860	8.9	6,821	4,126	2,695	25	0.9
Casey	402	14,686	0.8	162	10.2	275	17.3	1,327	10.8	3,969	2,699	1,270	27	1.7
Christian	6,159	91,195	1.6	1,484	20.5	811	11.2	4,739	8.5	11,567	8,198	3,369	73	1.0
Clark	413	34,587	0.9	403	10.9	462	12.5	1,981	6.8	8,216	4,511	3,705	19	0.5

1. Per 1,000 estimated resident population.

STATE County	COVID-19 Vaccinations, 2021–2022: Number	COVID-19 Vaccinations, 2021–2022: Percent[5]	Education: School enrollment and attainment, 2016–2020: Enrollment[1]: Total	Education: Enrollment[1]: Percent private	Education: Attainment[2] (percent): High school graduate or less	Education: Attainment[2] (percent): Bachelor's degree or more	Education: Local government expenditures,[3] 2018–2019: Total current spending (mil dol)	Education: Local government expenditures,[3] 2018–2019: Current spending per student (dollars)	Money income, 2016–2020: Per capita income[4]	Money income, 2016–2020: Households: Median income (dollars)	Money income, 2016–2020: Households: Percent with income of less than $50,000	Money income, 2016–2020: Households: Percent with income of $200,000 or more	Income and poverty, 2020: Median household income (dollars)	Income and poverty, 2020: Percent below poverty level: All persons	Income and poverty, 2020: Percent below poverty level: Children under 18 years	Income and poverty, 2020: Percent below poverty level: Children 5 to 17 years in families
	46	47	48	49	50	51	52	53	54	55	56	57	58	59	60	61
KANSAS— Cont'd																
Neosho	4,487	28.0	4,306	9.2	40.3	20.0	27.0	11,046	24,975	49,493	50.4	1.5	56,085	13.8	19.9	16.9
Ness	1,446	52.6	581	23.9	39.4	21.9	5.7	13,320	31,999	57,222	44.0	2.5	55,311	9.6	13.6	12.8
Norton	2,837	52.9	959	8.9	40.3	19.5	10.9	12,723	27,752	48,486	51.7	3.1	47,512	12.9	16.1	16.1
Osage	8,156	51.1	3,515	5.6	48.2	19.4	41.7	14,997	28,945	58,927	43.2	2.5	55,287	10.1	12.5	11.8
Osborne	1,434	41.9	644	5.0	38.8	21.0	6.2	14,533	30,453	50,774	49.6	1.5	47,811	11.7	15.3	15.2
Ottawa	2,518	44.1	1,222	9.0	39.5	23.9	18.7	15,649	33,655	59,607	41.7	3.6	60,560	10.0	13.4	11.7
Pawnee	3,464	54.0	1,150	8.7	43.6	19.0	16.7	16,136	25,746	46,559	52.3	0.8	53,821	14.9	17.3	17.4
Phillips	2,266	43.3	1,100	7.9	41.4	23.2	17.3	22,713	29,527	51,820	46.6	2.0	56,047	10.9	14.4	13.9
Pottawatomie	10,067	41.3	6,574	13.1	34.9	34.4	51.3	12,247	30,763	70,064	35.1	4.1	75,476	6.9	8.2	7.6
Pratt	4,505	49.2	2,445	9.4	33.1	29.5	30.8	17,656	29,607	54,644	45.6	5.7	62,958	9.6	13.6	12.5
Rawlins	1,089	43.0	557	6.8	34.0	21.7	4.3	11,590	30,651	57,281	45.2	1.7	54,417	11.1	15.8	16.3
Reno	30,712	49.5	14,341	14.3	39.3	20.0	120.4	12,602	27,613	51,520	48.1	3.1	57,611	10.6	13.3	12.1
Republic	2,354	50.8	1,001	6.7	35.0	28.2	9.4	12,392	28,100	50,411	49.4	2.2	52,537	9.9	12.7	12.3
Rice	4,175	43.8	2,583	20.6	38.2	21.8	26.6	14,881	26,324	49,688	50.4	1.4	59,659	10.3	12.1	12.9
Riley	29,184	39.3	28,776	5.4	20.2	47.2	81.6	10,371	27,975	51,098	49.0	4.5	56,333	19.2	17.9	15.0
Rooks	2,389	48.6	1,188	9.3	39.8	24.3	10.7	13,393	27,023	51,362	48.0	1.3	51,376	9.6	12.5	12.5
Rush	1,542	50.8	636	3.3	38.0	21.9	7.2	13,553	27,291	46,333	52.3	1.8	50,673	11.2	15.9	15.0
Russell	2,954	43.1	1,454	2.6	34.5	23.6	11.2	13,105	26,921	50,630	49.0	3.6	56,536	12.9	18.5	17.7
Saline	27,342	50.4	12,529	16.4	37.6	27.2	124.2	14,444	29,509	51,830	47.9	3.0	56,928	9.8	13.4	12.5
Scott	2,319	48.1	1,111	8.6	44.3	24.8	11.0	10,792	28,965	55,625	48.4	3.0	68,514	7.3	10.0	9.2
Sedgwick	280,201	54.3	136,816	16.8	36.5	31.4	967.0	11,330	30,340	57,540	43.9	4.5	59,789	13.4	17.3	15.7
Seward	9,861	46.0	6,423	3.3	60.7	11.2	62.8	11,327	21,434	49,395	50.9	1.9	54,330	11.5	15.0	13.6
Shawnee	108,887	61.6	40,590	12.2	39.0	31.3	321.5	11,512	31,574	58,652	43.0	4.0	56,191	10.5	13.1	11.9
Sheridan	895	35.5	546	1.8	40.7	23.8	8.1	12,430	39,170	62,105	41.7	9.3	58,186	10.5	17.0	15.6
Sherman	2,620	44.3	1,455	7.1	38.1	21.8	10.6	10,676	36,495	57,005	39.1	5.3	52,718	13.0	18.0	17.0
Smith	1,606	44.8	649	7.6	42.6	21.1	9.2	14,383	29,017	42,098	56.3	3.4	49,114	10.3	15.2	15.3
Stafford	1,934	46.5	897	4.6	35.1	27.9	12.7	14,801	27,897	51,857	48.5	3.9	55,004	11.0	17.2	16.2
Stanton	1,022	50.9	560	9.3	53.0	17.9	5.8	13,143	29,716	57,741	42.6	3.5	68,439	10.2	14.7	12.8
Stevens	2,144	39.1	1,337	3.9	48.4	12.4	16.0	13,002	23,355	59,044	42.7	1.5	66,592	9.7	13.4	11.8
Sumner	9,931	43.5	5,779	12.1	41.6	23.6	48.7	12,923	27,499	53,578	47.0	1.9	56,609	11.3	14.2	12.9
Thomas	3,234	41.6	1,756	21.3	29.7	25.1	12.2	10,923	34,865	68,313	34.6	5.7	65,158	9.1	9.3	8.5
Trego	1,102	39.3	527	4.6	34.8	22.4	4.9	12,027	36,415	59,420	39.2	4.8	60,246	10.4	15.4	16.4
Wabaunsee	3,310	47.8	1,480	13.2	39.9	24.0	12.9	14,492	30,047	65,742	36.3	3.9	64,886	8.5	8.6	7.6
Wallace	568	37.4	347	3.7	36.9	29.4	4.5	15,027	25,262	49,632	51.2	0.8	57,386	12.5	23.3	24.3
Washington	2,924	54.1	1,053	32.2	48.5	21.0	9.8	12,272	28,646	52,172	47.8	2.4	51,751	9.9	11.7	11.5
Wichita	1,089	51.4	462	2.8	38.7	23.3	5.3	12,881	30,803	58,299	45.6	2.6	61,326	10.6	14.4	12.7
Wilson	3,763	44.1	1,632	5.2	45.6	19.4	20.4	12,427	27,661	49,682	50.4	2.2	50,472	14.3	18.3	17.1
Woodson	1,325	42.2	596	1.5	45.9	20.0	6.3	13,072	26,969	42,692	56.4	2.9	45,357	14.0	21.4	19.5
Wyandotte	95,387	57.7	42,980	9.8	52.3	18.3	387.3	11,898	23,111	48,093	52.1	1.9	52,223	16.9	24.5	23.3
KENTUCKY	2,561,976	57.3	1,043,315	16.0	45.5	25.0	7,684.4	11,287	29,123	52,238	47.9	4.2	54,074	14.9	19.4	18.2
Adair	7,563	39.4	4,984	28.9	57.0	18.4	28.1	10,646	22,751	43,026	57.1	1.9	42,429	22.1	33.3	31.1
Allen	8,465	39.7	4,349	18.1	56.4	17.3	31.0	10,103	23,299	44,180	55.5	2.0	49,980	15.3	23.1	20.7
Anderson	12,605	55.4	5,066	18.6	45.4	22.7	35.6	9,568	28,143	54,413	46.3	3.5	65,443	10.0	13.1	11.7
Ballard	3,031	38.4	1,736	5.8	50.5	15.7	13.2	10,506	26,911	45,517	51.7	3.3	48,623	14.2	22.4	20.8
Barren	20,386	46.1	9,353	8.6	59.4	16.2	88.5	10,721	22,502	41,674	60.8	2.0	45,298	17.3	25.2	25.3
Bath	6,753	54.0	2,672	5.4	63.9	15.5	20.5	10,258	24,167	44,893	53.9	2.0	41,778	22.5	33.3	29.4
Bell	11,932	45.8	5,250	5.3	68.1	9.5	49.6	11,019	16,416	28,442	72.6	0.8	30,202	29.8	38.3	35.1
Boone	83,193	62.3	35,040	15.6	35.4	32.2	242.5	10,772	36,371	82,838	28.6	8.2	82,393	6.5	8.0	7.2
Bourbon	11,501	58.1	4,129	19.9	51.3	23.0	37.9	10,613	27,676	47,024	52.2	3.2	52,368	14.1	21.6	20.3
Boyd	23,013	49.3	10,051	8.0	45.4	20.2	84.3	11,570	26,055	51,019	48.9	2.6	54,694	15.8	21.9	20.3
Boyle	17,135	57.0	7,263	26.9	45.7	25.8	56.8	11,910	26,575	51,562	48.2	3.6	53,374	14.0	18.3	17.1
Bracken	3,928	47.3	1,731	18.8	60.2	12.5	16.3	10,432	25,587	60,053	45.8	1.9	55,112	13.2	19.9	18.6
Breathitt	6,660	52.7	2,288	17.7	61.1	16.1	26.4	11,784	20,325	29,538	65.2	1.6	33,852	27.9	37.0	36.8
Breckinridge	10,082	49.2	4,376	14.0	55.9	14.4	33.8	10,897	24,458	47,236	51.8	2.1	50,292	17.1	22.6	21.8
Bullitt	37,152	45.5	17,021	15.6	52.7	15.7	130.8	9,939	30,075	65,531	36.9	3.1	71,835	8.7	11.2	10.6
Butler	5,844	45.4	2,641	11.7	63.0	14.0	22.3	9,804	22,672	45,955	54.0	1.9	44,933	17.1	22.2	21.3
Caldwell	6,674	52.4	2,738	9.1	54.4	16.8	20.0	10,069	32,439	48,281	50.9	5.1	47,670	15.3	23.3	22.0
Calloway	17,830	45.7	12,150	10.5	40.4	32.0	52.4	10,940	23,984	41,841	56.1	2.4	47,438	15.6	17.6	17.3
Campbell	59,714	63.8	22,624	20.8	36.0	37.5	141.0	12,109	35,124	63,152	40.4	6.8	64,151	10.6	11.5	11.4
Carlisle	1,956	41.1	1,088	10.5	58.9	14.3	8.7	11,063	29,638	41,222	56.7	4.4	46,935	14.4	23.3	22.0
Carroll	4,965	46.7	2,616	9.9	60.6	7.4	26.9	12,476	25,084	41,014	56.0	4.3	52,640	16.2	23.9	22.8
Carter	13,204	49.3	5,687	15.2	60.1	13.8	45.6	10,380	20,672	39,492	59.6	1.7	44,720	18.5	23.4	22.9
Casey	5,873	36.3	3,202	17.8	65.9	11.2	26.3	11,176	18,384	33,004	69.3	0.9	35,069	22.7	32.9	32.0
Christian	25,723	36.5	17,468	18.5	43.2	18.7	87.8	10,082	24,489	44,279	56.4	3.1	46,950	16.9	21.8	21.9
Clark	19,848	54.7	7,501	14.3	48.6	20.1	58.8	10,870	30,194	54,871	45.5	3.4	58,340	14.4	20.9	19.6

1. All persons 3 years old and over enrolled in nursery school through college. 2. Persons 25 years old and over. 3. Elementary and secondary education expenditures. 4. Based on population estimated by the American Community Survey, 2016–2020. 5. CDC percent based on 2019 population estimate.

STATE County	Personal income, 2020										Earnings, 2020		
			Per capita[1]			Supplements to wages and salaries, employer contributions (mil dol)						Contributions for government social insurance (mil dol)	
	Total (mil dol)	Percent change 2019–2020	Dollars	Rank	Wages and salaries (mil dol)	Pension and insurance	Government social insurance	Proprietors' income (mil dol)	Dividends, interest, and rent (mil dol)	Personal transfer reecipts (mil dol)	Total (mil dol)	From employee and self-employed	From employer
	62	63	64	65	66	67	68	69	70	71	72	73	74
KANSAS— Cont'd													
Neosho	694	8.0	43,566	2,000	266	48	21	53	101	211	388	27	21
Ness	167	14.5	60,508	406	50	9	4	37	36	44	99	6	4
Norton	254	10.0	47,679	1,431	101	20	8	43	50	59	172	10	8
Osage	736	8.2	46,698	1,549	104	21	8	55	102	202	188	16	8
Osborne	177	8.7	51,423	987	57	10	4	30	31	46	101	6	4
Ottawa	261	9.5	45,692	1,698	48	10	4	26	35	70	88	6	4
Pawnee	280	6.7	43,986	1,949	121	23	9	48	44	78	202	12	9
Phillips	293	8.7	56,496	610	92	22	7	45	59	75	168	10	7
Pottawatomie	1,421	8.2	57,495	538	444	77	35	100	181	235	656	41	35
Pratt	491	8.2	53,750	800	198	34	15	78	92	120	326	19	15
Rawlins	164	16.1	65,230	257	42	7	3	50	27	40	102	5	3
Reno	2,752	6.6	44,529	1,869	1,169	201	87	245	476	775	1,701	117	87
Republic	223	10.3	49,163	1,233	67	13	5	35	37	68	121	8	5
Rice	433	5.1	46,275	1,612	157	30	12	43	65	116	243	15	12
Riley	3,307	5.6	45,177	1,772	1,349	283	101	167	764	552	1,899	114	101
Rooks	226	15.7	46,817	1,536	74	15	6	33	40	68	129	8	6
Rush	174	14.3	59,190	471	43	9	4	40	29	44	96	6	4
Russell	330	6.9	48,430	1,335	95	20	7	42	56	95	164	11	7
Saline	2,875	6.0	53,320	833	1,319	212	101	417	489	684	2,048	130	101
Scott	290	6.7	60,520	403	97	16	8	58	58	66	180	9	8
Sedgwick	29,401	4.7	56,550	605	13,812	2,122	1,062	3,436	6,770	5,789	20,431	1,268	1,062
Seward	917	12.0	43,606	1,995	566	91	40	91	105	193	788	46	40
Shawnee	9,014	6.1	51,216	1,002	5,222	811	403	680	1,474	2,339	7,115	465	403
Sheridan	128	12.9	50,691	1,066	47	9	4	24	25	29	85	5	4
Sherman	280	11.2	48,439	1,332	100	18	8	44	46	76	170	10	8
Smith	193	16.1	54,497	742	51	10	4	45	36	53	110	6	4
Stafford	205	8.5	50,623	1,074	50	10	4	40	36	54	105	6	4
Stanton	169	14.7	85,633	58	47	7	4	80	26	20	138	5	4
Stevens	262	12.2	48,686	1,296	97	18	8	64	39	48	187	9	8
Sumner	1,002	6.3	44,392	1,893	282	49	24	86	147	277	441	30	24
Thomas	396	7.3	51,457	983	169	27	13	76	60	83	285	17	13
Trego	155	14.1	56,311	617	51	12	4	31	23	43	97	5	4
Wabaunsee	376	6.4	54,428	748	54	10	4	20	92	81	88	7	4
Wallace	91	19.3	59,159	473	24	4	2	29	13	19	59	3	2
Washington	286	14.5	52,731	876	78	16	6	50	48	74	150	9	6
Wichita	127	-3.4	61,032	383	40	7	3	33	25	27	84	4	3
Wilson	379	5.9	45,341	1,746	139	30	11	39	58	131	219	15	11
Woodson	131	8.2	43,381	2,020	25	6	2	15	22	43	48	4	2
Wyandotte	6,108	7.1	36,961	2,788	5,510	772	451	513	573	1,870	7,246	454	451
KENTUCKY	211,948	8.0	47,058	X	97,175	17,339	7,536	13,898	32,828	62,463	135,948	8,953	7,536
Adair	702	12.4	35,880	2,875	166	35	13	46	71	301	261	20	13
Allen	756	7.4	35,499	2,907	193	36	16	53	86	281	298	23	16
Anderson	1,005	8.1	44,009	1,946	200	41	15	32	130	275	288	24	15
Ballard	351	10.5	45,124	1,777	90	18	7	46	44	120	161	10	7
Barren	1,819	8.9	41,057	2,331	629	121	48	187	235	639	985	69	48
Bath	441	11.4	35,333	2,919	83	17	7	20	42	186	127	12	7
Bell	882	12.0	34,618	2,958	295	66	24	29	89	500	414	34	24
Boone	7,231	7.8	53,405	825	5,006	749	392	346	903	1,353	6,493	407	392
Bourbon	1,027	3.2	51,624	969	318	56	26	170	164	268	570	31	26
Boyd	2,043	8.5	43,917	1,962	1,274	256	95	86	244	794	1,712	116	95
Boyle	1,307	8.9	43,024	2,060	634	123	51	99	216	420	908	62	51
Bracken	350	9.6	42,258	2,161	57	12	4	17	37	118	91	8	4
Breathitt	477	11.0	38,011	2,686	97	23	8	10	36	283	138	13	8
Breckinridge	803	11.6	39,084	2,560	144	31	11	63	129	296	249	21	11
Bullitt	3,831	8.6	46,618	1,559	1,185	173	98	160	383	971	1,616	114	98
Butler	495	9.1	38,969	2,567	110	26	8	41	47	195	186	14	8
Caldwell	512	13.5	40,364	2,407	174	33	15	41	61	201	263	19	15
Calloway	1,518	7.6	38,629	2,612	625	145	48	96	241	481	915	59	48
Campbell	5,025	6.3	53,445	822	1,459	254	110	169	767	1,113	1,992	139	110
Carlisle	229	8.1	48,900	1,269	39	8	3	42	33	74	92	6	3
Carroll	446	9.9	41,568	2,260	432	73	33	16	50	154	555	35	33
Carter	956	11.9	36,002	2,866	213	43	17	43	94	440	317	29	17
Casey	585	14.0	36,436	2,831	147	33	12	40	54	264	231	18	12
Christian	3,065	9.0	42,884	2,078	3,314	937	314	278	504	912	4,843	216	314
Clark	1,603	8.4	43,952	1,953	659	125	52	67	227	500	902	64	52

1. Based on the resident population estimated as of July 1 of the year shown.

STATE County	Earnings, 2020 (cont.)									Social Security beneficiaries, December 2020		Supple-mental Security Income recipients, 2020	Housing units, 2021	
	Percent by selected industries													
	Farm	Mining, quarrying, and extractions	Construction	Manu-facturing	Information; professional, scientific, technical services	Retail trade	Finance, insurance, real estate, and leasing	Health care and social assistance	Govern-ment	Number	Rate[1]		Total	Percent change, 2010–2021
	75	76	77	78	79	80	81	82	83	84	85	86	87	88
KANSAS— Cont'd														
Neosho	4.1	1.7	6.9	20.0	D	7.5	6.5	11.0	26.0	3,845	244	384	7,215	0.1
Ness	21.5	14.6	3.0	1.3	2.9	2.7	D	D	22.4	770	288	22	1,546	-0.1
Norton	17.1	D	2.5	9.4	3.5	5.4	5.7	8.4	24.5	1,190	223	51	2,458	-0.1
Osage	12.4	D	10.0	4.7	D	6.1	7.6	D	28.8	3,945	250	315	7,285	0.6
Osborne	17.2	1.9	D	D	D	5.7	7.7	7.6	17.2	1,030	294	45	2,042	0.0
Ottawa	17.6	0.0	1.9	11.1	2.5	2.3	10.9	11.3	23.1	1,455	249	83	2,686	0.2
Pawnee	15.6	D	6.0	1.2	D	4.7	5.6	9.0	42.2	1,510	243	83	3,051	-0.1
Phillips	16.2	1.8	2.3	13.0	4.1	4.4	D	2.1	24.4	1,525	317	59	2,791	-0.1
Pottawatomie	2.5	0.0	10.9	22.6	5.4	7.8	8.2	D	10.6	4,485	174	196	10,073	1.6
Pratt	12.3	3.7	2.8	3.2	4.0	9.4	8.2	D	17.2	2,160	235	114	4,378	-0.1
Rawlins	21.1	0.3	4.4	3.4	4.9	14.2	D	4.0	13.7	765	300	27	1,362	-0.1
Reno	1.8	0.5	5.7	11.6	5.9	6.6	8.1	14.4	16.4	15,205	248	1,243	28,296	0.0
Republic	22.7	D	3.0	8.3	4.0	6.3	5.8	D	16.9	1,420	305	74	2,670	-0.2
Rice	14.2	6.3	4.4	11.7	5.0	3.9	D	D	19.6	2,205	235	133	4,377	0.0
Riley	0.7	D	6.0	2.0	7.3	6.8	8.7	11.6	39.0	8,390	116	640	30,709	0.7
Rooks	11.1	7.1	D	D	3.4	3.6	4.9	4.1	26.5	1,365	283	65	2,635	-0.1
Rush	23.2	D	2.2	13.5	5.1	3.2	7.2	D	22.2	880	298	52	1,660	-0.1
Russell	9.2	11.3	5.5	13.1	D	4.1	6.5	D	16.3	1,885	281	128	3,674	0.0
Saline	0.8	D	6.1	14.8	7.1	7.1	5.7	18.2	12.0	12,355	229	1,039	24,110	0.1
Scott	20.6	0.6	3.9	2.9	D	5.0	4.6	D	20.6	1,055	206	44	2,266	0.0
Sedgwick	0.1	2.3	6.2	20.3	7.7	6.0	7.4	12.4	12.4	97,595	186	11,012	225,426	0.6
Seward	2.8	2.4	D	D	1.7	6.2	5.4	D	18.8	2,695	124	306	8,293	0.3
Shawnee	0.1	D	5.0	7.3	9.5	4.9	11.5	16.6	21.3	40,300	226	4,688	80,835	0.4
Sheridan	18.2	0.6	3.6	7.7	D	3.8	D	0.8	25.7	585	236	15	1,150	-0.2
Sherman	19.6	D	2.5	2.9	D	8.0	9.0	D	22.7	1,370	232	114	2,931	-0.1
Smith	33.7	D	3.2	1.1	1.6	5.4	3.2	11.8	14.9	1,200	336	62	2,022	-0.1
Stafford	27.7	9.0	D	D	D	1.9	D	5.2	21.3	1,035	257	56	2,098	0.4
Stanton	40.1	1.0	3.8	1.7	D	2.5	5.2	0.5	11.9	340	166	20	934	0.3
Stevens	20.5	13.5	4.6	2.1	D	4.7	D	D	19.0	895	169	36	2,248	0.3
Sumner	9.3	0.7	4.8	10.3	4.6	5.0	6.7	7.8	23.0	5,415	242	339	10,378	0.5
Thomas	9.5	D	6.2	2.2	4.5	8.1	12.4	D	12.4	1,570	199	62	3,571	-0.1
Trego	23.2	D	3.1	2.5	D	3.7	D	D	26.8	825	295	30	1,609	-0.1
Wabaunsee	9.6	3.6	13.2	13.8	D	2.9	D	D	22.5	1,700	244	75	3,122	0.3
Wallace	38.3	0.3	D	D	D	4.2	D	0.3	14.6	370	245	20	740	0.0
Washington	23.9	D	8.9	6.8	D	3.2	D	4.2	21.3	1,505	273	49	2,722	-0.1
Wichita	40.8	0.2	D	D	D	2.1	D	D	18.1	440	211	17	999	0.0
Wilson	7.9	D	10.4	29.4	1.4	3.7	3.8	6.1	22.4	2,480	291	220	4,497	0.3
Woodson	8.7	11.4	D	D	D	5.3	5.4	6.6	24.6	815	263	55	1,834	0.3
Wyandotte	0.0	0.1	6.9	11.9	5.6	4.5	3.0	17.9	16.2	26,660	160	4,878	68,625	0.2
KENTUCKY	1.3	0.5	6.2	14.2	7.4	6.1	7.6	12.9	17.5	1,009,092	224	167,786	2,008,239	0.6
Adair	7.4	D	7.6	6.7	D	12.2	6.0	D	19.2	4,855	256	906	8,623	0.2
Allen	2.6	0.1	7.3	25.5	D	5.7	3.5	D	15.2	5,010	241	790	9,248	0.4
Anderson	-1.0	D	D	26.1	5.4	10.2	4.3	D	17.0	5,240	218	427	10,143	0.8
Ballard	13.7	0.0	11.5	29.8	D	4.5	1.3	D	12.2	2,165	281	266	3,697	0.3
Barren	3.7	D	5.7	13.4	4.6	10.3	4.6	17.0	13.1	11,245	252	1,648	20,059	1.2
Bath	1.7	0.0	22.8	D	D	3.8	2.5	D	22.2	3,190	250	783	5,476	0.5
Bell	-0.2	3.0	3.6	16.0	D	12.9	5.2	D	21.3	7,270	305	2,650	11,575	0.4
Boone	0.1	0.0	4.9	16.5	5.5	6.0	5.5	5.7	8.0	22,910	167	1,660	52,371	1.5
Bourbon	26.3	D	4.3	12.1	2.2	8.7	4.1	7.0	9.4	4,900	242	574	9,155	0.4
Boyd	-0.1	0.8	8.5	13.7	6.8	7.3	3.5	25.4	12.0	12,660	264	2,383	21,739	0.0
Boyle	0.0	D	4.0	16.8	D	7.4	5.1	D	11.9	7,385	240	1,117	12,968	0.3
Bracken	2.6	0.0	7.1	D	D	2.7	2.3	10.5	23.7	2,205	261	321	3,852	0.3
Breathitt	0.0	D	1.5	D	1.8	10.5	4.3	30.1	35.1	3,805	281	1,731	6,590	0.5
Breckinridge	9.5	D	13.4	7.8	D	8.1	5.3	D	18.2	5,575	270	746	10,749	0.3
Bullitt	-0.1	D	12.3	14.4	2.4	5.9	3.1	4.7	11.1	17,955	217	1,213	33,243	1.4
Butler	9.4	D	8.1	30.3	1.5	4.0	6.0	D	17.2	3,285	267	447	5,443	0.4
Caldwell	4.7	D	6.4	23.6	D	9.7	D	D	12.4	3,485	276	449	6,089	0.1
Calloway	3.2	D	5.6	16.8	D	7.2	5.4	3.8	29.1	8,585	229	867	17,960	0.4
Campbell	0.1	D	7.8	8.3	10.5	8.2	5.7	13.4	20.4	17,930	193	1,707	41,559	0.3
Carlisle	29.1	0.0	7.4	2.9	2.7	3.5	D	8.6	12.5	1,385	289	150	2,301	0.3
Carroll	0.3	D	D	50.8	D	4.2	1.1	D	7.7	2,680	247	493	4,682	0.4
Carter	0.0	1.2	10.4	14.6	3.1	9.8	4.6	D	20.9	7,285	276	1,484	12,272	0.5
Casey	3.2	D	8.6	24.0	2.7	5.4	D	11.5	15.5	4,225	266	815	7,395	0.3
Christian	1.6	0.1	1.9	7.8	2.7	2.6	1.7	4.9	66.0	12,815	177	2,260	29,299	0.2
Clark	-0.2	D	6.4	23.2	5.1	7.1	4.0	11.0	10.6	8,855	240	1,321	16,257	0.7

1. Per 1,000 resident population estimated as of July 1 of the year shown.

STATE County	Housing units, 2016–2020: Occupied units: Total	Owner-occupied: Percent	Owner-occupied: Median value[1]	Median owner cost as a percent of income: With a mortgage	Median owner cost as a percent of income: Without a mortgage[2]	Renter-occupied: Median rent[3]	Renter-occupied: Median rent as a percent of income[2]	Sub-standard units[4] (percent)	Civilian labor force, 2021: Total	Percent change, 2020–2021	Unemployment: Total	Unemployment: Rate[5]	Civilian employment[6], 2016–2020: Total	Percent: Management, business, science, and arts	Percent: Construction, production, and maintenance occupations
	89	90	91	92	93	94	95	96	97	98	99	100	101	102	103
KANSAS— Cont'd															
Neosho	6,462	73.5	83,800	18.8	12.1	600	22.8	3.4	6,093	-2.0	259	4.3	7,115	31.4	30.7
Ness	1,260	85.2	74,100	16.5	10.0	624	15.8	0.1	1,312	-2.7	29	2.2	1,426	33.2	35.1
Norton	1,865	76.7	79,100	17.0	10.0	604	23.4	0.6	2,669	0.9	47	1.8	2,267	30.5	25.0
Osage	6,624	75.8	123,600	21.1	12.8	722	27.6	1.5	8,001	0.6	237	3.0	7,538	32.8	29.6
Osborne	1,687	77.4	66,100	15.0	11.1	555	22.4	1.7	1,961	-0.6	36	1.8	1,748	41.0	22.9
Ottawa	2,433	78.8	117,300	20.8	11.2	677	24.5	1.3	2,967	-0.1	82	2.8	2,913	36.7	26.8
Pawnee	2,447	61.9	78,800	15.4	11.0	647	27.4	0.2	2,831	-0.7	63	2.2	2,859	33.9	27.0
Phillips	2,406	71.2	82,700	17.6	10.0	577	19.9	4.0	2,637	-0.2	56	2.1	2,665	35.4	32.6
Pottawatomie	8,883	76.4	176,700	20.0	10.0	928	27.5	3.4	12,242	0.9	307	2.5	11,197	43.5	24.7
Pratt	3,733	67.3	107,500	17.4	10.0	697	25.0	3.1	4,913	-0.2	110	2.2	4,457	38.1	24.0
Rawlins	1,169	71.9	101,000	18.5	10.8	558	20.4	2.1	1,632	5.7	26	1.6	1,346	41.8	27.3
Reno	24,970	69.9	106,100	19.3	11.9	742	28.1	2.6	29,772	0.1	947	3.2	28,927	30.7	28.9
Republic	2,176	71.8	67,100	19.2	11.4	649	22.7	0.8	2,356	1.9	54	2.3	2,227	42.5	26.4
Rice	3,939	73.3	79,500	17.6	10.0	604	21.4	1.5	5,315	4.6	128	2.4	4,715	34.6	30.2
Riley	26,878	43.6	205,900	19.9	10.5	943	31.6	2.7	33,731	0.5	942	2.8	36,863	43.1	15.3
Rooks	2,167	73.4	77,300	19.4	11.7	585	20.2	0.6	2,437	-2.6	59	2.4	2,338	32.4	27.8
Rush	1,448	73.1	70,100	15.0	12.6	611	30.3	0.5	1,583	0.7	38	2.4	1,503	32.6	28.3
Russell	3,005	78.3	99,900	20.0	13.5	650	26.7	2.4	3,361	1.6	81	2.4	3,186	34.5	24.6
Saline	22,251	65.3	141,300	20.5	11.5	774	31.0	1.1	29,373	-0.4	879	3.0	27,488	32.9	25.3
Scott	2,062	60.8	134,000	22.6	10.0	631	19.0	1.7	2,833	0.3	45	1.6	2,489	32.1	31.0
Sedgwick	199,320	62.3	146,300	18.8	11.2	837	27.7	2.8	255,086	-0.9	11,695	4.6	249,898	36.4	25.6
Seward	7,183	62.4	111,200	24.3	12.0	769	23.0	3.4	9,863	0.7	275	2.8	10,536	22.2	44.9
Shawnee	72,962	66.3	135,100	18.8	11.5	825	27.7	2.3	91,236	0.2	2,837	3.1	84,733	39.0	23.0
Sheridan	1,080	79.7	119,000	18.8	10.2	652	20.4	0.5	1,465	0.0	27	1.8	1,404	38.5	28.6
Sherman	2,569	65.8	107,500	18.8	10.0	803	21.5	0.4	2,856	-0.5	72	2.5	3,060	37.2	29.8
Smith	1,664	77.5	75,300	20.3	12.2	463	20.8	1.5	2,012	1.1	35	1.7	1,701	34.9	28.0
Stafford	1,758	79.1	73,900	16.6	10.0	616	18.8	1.8	1,980	-2.1	44	2.2	1,998	35.3	26.0
Stanton	850	76.8	63,200	15.7	10.0	631	23.3	0.8	1,108	3.1	21	1.9	898	33.2	35.4
Stevens	1,770	68.2	104,200	17.7	11.1	728	25.9	3.3	2,884	2.9	60	2.1	2,360	25.1	42.2
Sumner	9,462	71.1	94,800	18.4	12.6	744	24.5	1.4	10,735	-1.0	442	4.1	10,293	31.1	31.3
Thomas	3,294	73.0	129,600	17.7	10.2	663	22.3	0.3	4,259	0.6	78	1.8	4,264	35.7	17.9
Trego	1,353	77.2	103,600	17.2	10.0	594	29.1	0.2	1,419	-1.9	30	2.1	1,530	24.8	34.6
Wabaunsee	2,722	83.0	153,700	21.9	10.6	678	19.2	3.0	3,711	1.0	91	2.5	3,443	38.5	31.4
Wallace	651	67.9	84,500	19.0	10.4	482	16.2	1.2	887	6.1	15	1.7	719	49.0	20.9
Washington	2,412	77.4	84,100	18.0	12.5	450	16.7	1.3	3,063	0.0	53	1.7	2,589	35.1	34.2
Wichita	935	74.5	101,500	18.7	13.6	690	32.7	2.2	1,179	-5.1	23	2.0	1,093	44.4	24.2
Wilson	3,627	73.6	82,200	16.8	11.8	663	29.1	2.7	3,837	-1.7	154	4.0	3,977	34.5	33.5
Woodson	1,390	84.6	68,700	19.1	12.0	593	23.1	1.5	1,528	-2.1	53	3.5	1,305	35.6	32.4
Wyandotte	60,400	58.9	107,000	21.9	14.1	884	29.7	5.1	77,532	-0.2	3,627	4.7	76,763	25.5	35.3
KENTUCKY	1,748,053	67.6	147,100	18.9	10.1	783	27.1	2.4	2,036,942	1.0	95,205	4.7	1,993,889	35.2	27.4
Adair	6,991	77.3	105,400	19.4	10.0	621	27.6	3.5	7,267	3.5	361	5.0	7,796	30.9	35.6
Allen	7,816	75.5	123,300	19.1	10.2	680	28.5	4.1	8,894	2.7	360	4.0	8,864	27.5	35.4
Anderson	8,757	75.5	158,100	18.7	10.0	729	32.5	1.0	11,983	1.9	475	4.0	10,368	35.7	29.5
Ballard	3,052	78.7	103,800	18.8	10.0	659	19.4	3.4	3,447	3.7	173	5.0	3,195	31.1	30.2
Barren	17,392	65.6	127,100	20.3	10.7	681	29.5	3.5	18,032	-0.2	959	5.3	18,412	29.2	36.0
Bath	4,885	71.6	83,900	18.2	10.0	496	21.7	1.9	4,632	2.1	267	5.8	4,793	27.7	36.0
Bell	10,504	63.1	62,800	19.6	10.3	559	33.5	3.0	8,225	0.5	469	5.7	7,455	25.7	34.4
Boone	47,391	75.9	194,700	17.4	10.0	1,029	25.8	2.0	71,482	1.3	2,701	3.8	67,197	38.1	24.8
Bourbon	7,990	62.9	155,300	18.5	10.0	725	24.7	1.6	9,663	1.0	375	3.9	9,250	32.6	26.9
Boyd	18,213	67.6	110,000	19.2	10.0	694	26.2	1.6	17,284	-1.0	1,076	6.2	18,223	39.6	22.5
Boyle	11,079	68.9	144,000	18.8	10.9	715	27.8	0.8	12,657	0.8	630	5.0	12,623	34.4	29.2
Bracken	3,197	75.9	102,700	17.4	11.7	624	24.5	2.1	3,775	1.7	178	4.7	3,611	27.7	38.5
Breathitt	5,281	71.7	53,000	17.6	11.3	473	35.0	5.4	3,261	0.3	282	8.6	3,890	36.8	27.1
Breckinridge	7,731	81.8	104,500	18.7	10.2	618	25.9	3.8	8,021	2.6	420	5.2	7,630	28.6	38.8
Bullitt	29,940	81.4	171,300	19.0	11.2	849	25.5	2.4	42,784	1.5	1,984	4.6	40,657	29.2	35.5
Butler	4,823	72.2	92,000	18.6	10.0	604	24.4	2.8	4,945	1.8	226	4.6	5,077	26.0	42.7
Caldwell	5,215	74.3	89,600	18.5	10.0	657	29.0	1.6	5,910	5.8	249	4.2	5,284	26.2	33.6
Calloway	15,492	62.8	141,200	19.6	10.8	669	28.9	1.3	17,608	-0.9	801	4.5	18,079	34.5	23.8
Campbell	37,197	70.4	173,400	18.9	10.7	843	29.1	1.7	50,276	1.5	2,034	4.0	47,301	43.9	20.1
Carlisle	1,925	81.7	83,200	20.0	11.0	651	29.9	2.3	2,244	3.8	86	3.8	1,751	31.0	35.4
Carroll	4,176	65.8	105,800	18.6	11.9	676	27.1	5.5	5,391	1.9	222	4.1	4,514	17.7	40.3
Carter	9,624	78.7	109,500	19.9	10.0	585	28.8	2.3	9,695	1.8	755	7.8	8,983	28.4	28.9
Casey	6,048	76.6	97,600	21.9	10.0	524	27.6	3.3	6,766	1.7	280	4.1	5,410	26.1	37.7
Christian	26,097	46.9	121,000	20.0	10.0	858	29.2	2.1	24,795	1.4	1,444	5.8	23,349	27.6	29.6
Clark	14,576	69.0	151,300	19.8	10.4	724	27.7	2.0	17,054	0.6	750	4.4	16,363	35.4	28.7

1. Specified owner-occupied units. 2. A value of 10.0 represents 10 percent or less; a value of 50.0 represents 50 percent or more. 3. Specified renter-occupied units. 4. Overcrowded or lacking complete plumbing facilities. 5. Percent of civilian labor force. 6. Civilian employed persons 16 years old and over.

STATE County	Private nonfarm establishments, employment and payroll, 2020									Agriculture, 2017			
		Employment						Annual payroll		Farms			Farm producers whose primary occupation is farming (percent)
											Percent with:		
	Number of establish-ments	Total	Health care and social assistance	Manufac-turing	Retail trade	Finance and insurance	Professional, scientific, and technical services	Total (mil dol)	Average per employee (dollars)	Number	Fewer than 50 acres	1000 acres or more	
	104	105	106	107	108	109	110	111	112	113	114	115	116
KANSAS— Cont'd													
Neosho	412	4,718	1,124	984	748	215	140	180	38,066	687	25.5	9.3	36.3
Ness	127	873	254	23	60	41	21	34	38,907	523	8.2	33.8	39.8
Norton	174	1,710	519	242	185	96	34	68	39,504	328	14.0	39.6	52.1
Osage	243	1,550	361	149	324	114	60	47	30,273	1,042	24.8	12.7	36.1
Osborne	130	979	183	107	129	83	46	33	33,450	319	10.7	36.1	46.3
Ottawa	136	808	224	45	77	73	56	27	33,783	438	18.9	28.1	45.7
Pawnee	134	1,831	1,067	45	180	55	70	75	40,906	362	10.8	31.5	39.1
Phillips	221	1,501	282	174	236	120	92	60	39,923	415	11.8	33.3	50.1
Pottawatomie	640	9,823	1,576	1,929	1,752	264	228	400	40,692	774	27.4	14.6	34.4
Pratt	357	3,263	663	106	588	140	107	127	38,818	481	8.9	27.7	46.1
Rawlins	98	706	188	52	116	49	15	28	40,166	298	9.4	49.3	60.3
Reno	1,546	21,957	4,164	3,432	3,065	916	639	874	39,788	1,552	21.1	13.0	37.6
Republic	166	1,130	294	128	199	57	30	34	29,765	561	13.2	23.0	53.6
Rice	254	2,399	236	429	238	120	132	86	35,641	470	17.9	26.6	43.3
Riley	1,622	20,411	3,578	435	3,833	817	1,076	694	34,000	504	31.7	11.7	33.1
Rooks	168	1,259	298	108	197	67	46	47	37,482	412	10.9	32.3	45.5
Rush	95	808	134	236	84	47	15	29	35,480	488	10.5	25.4	38.9
Russell	242	1,754	325	244	227	75	48	67	38,275	500	15.0	23.0	38.1
Saline	1,456	24,832	4,422	4,285	3,750	787	1,184	1,012	40,766	609	25.1	17.1	41.5
Scott	197	1,453	497	49	162	98	50	58	39,751	236	17.8	39.4	58.9
Sedgwick	12,283	233,148	34,829	44,567	28,718	7,097	11,693	11,112	47,662	1,360	40.7	11.4	33.6
Seward	525	8,914	1,145	2,959	1,168	166	106	448	50,213	282	7.1	27.0	44.8
Shawnee	4,044	75,422	18,657	7,529	9,487	5,708	3,347	3,632	48,157	847	41.4	5.5	34.8
Sheridan	112	698	179	NA	76	50	25	31	43,708	318	2.8	49.1	65.0
Sherman	259	1,893	371	63	341	88	41	67	35,161	386	10.6	33.7	54.5
Smith	127	772	232	13	165	57	16	27	35,609	425	11.1	33.9	55.9
Stafford	121	601	176	NA	92	45	16	22	36,145	466	12.0	29.2	44.5
Stanton	58	482	116	NA	58	45	8	24	50,141	220	2.7	42.3	51.2
Stevens	135	1,073	233	67	111	58	15	44	41,268	377	7.4	27.1	37.9
Sumner	464	4,330	909	875	637	197	96	152	35,051	953	21.9	24.3	43.3
Thomas	331	2,825	538	67	618	155	82	112	39,777	402	8.2	45.8	57.7
Trego	114	713	204	39	113	33	19	25	34,386	343	9.9	37.0	50.1
Wabaunsee	128	867	89	170	98	41	NA	31	35,328	638	21.0	16.1	35.3
Wallace	53	299	46	NA	57	21	15	11	37,475	281	5.0	39.9	47.0
Washington	194	1,396	369	171	175	68	32	44	31,714	694	13.0	23.2	50.0
Wichita	86	481	119	54	72	23	3	20	41,017	254	10.2	46.9	55.2
Wilson	208	3,507	560	1,077	222	88	39	147	41,886	420	14.3	21.7	49.6
Woodson	75	392	77	NA	54	24	6	14	36,003	289	16.3	23.5	55.1
Wyandotte	3,016	72,875	15,058	9,872	7,047	1,173	1,515	3,636	49,899	158	74.7	2.5	32.1
KENTUCKY	90,922	1,666,427	266,526	248,033	215,525	75,843	76,806	75,360	45,222	75,966	40.1	2.5	36.4
Adair	326	4,040	537	341	776	245	68	125	30,879	1,154	30.4	1.1	37.1
Allen	240	3,707	368	984	384	140	67	158	42,712	1,127	36.6	1.8	43.0
Anderson	338	3,925	392	1,347	766	125	79	161	41,121	774	45.7	0.6	31.4
Ballard	140	1,336	130	536	148	40	128	69	51,291	295	33.6	8.1	42.9
Barren	840	14,315	2,268	3,055	2,500	394	534	494	34,533	1,899	42.5	1.5	38.3
Bath	131	1,533	209	452	134	61	27	55	35,950	728	30.1	1.4	33.2
Bell	465	6,628	1,368	1,175	1,450	238	141	216	32,652	110	49.1	1.8	24.0
Boone	3,110	87,329	5,133	12,036	12,166	3,556	2,753	4,193	48,011	721	54.5	1.0	25.7
Bourbon	370	5,214	651	1,389	1,012	217	103	234	44,898	915	38.6	2.1	45.1
Boyd	1,205	21,899	6,855	1,980	3,418	492	739	1,052	48,026	203	46.8	NA	33.6
Boyle	746	13,744	3,199	3,027	1,698	334	314	521	37,875	602	45.0	2.3	39.5
Bracken	89	844	114	255	134	28	15	33	38,759	531	29.0	0.6	35.8
Breathitt	156	1,995	794	NA	371	94	13	57	28,523	160	36.9	1.3	29.2
Breckinridge	284	2,551	566	261	508	165	64	88	34,584	1,357	31.9	2.8	35.8
Bullitt	1,158	21,991	1,409	4,354	5,974	325	274	868	39,474	486	58.4	1.0	31.7
Butler	182	1,810	245	672	234	81	27	72	39,770	642	29.3	4.5	25.3
Caldwell	271	3,369	523	756	645	129	35	122	36,145	475	36.4	5.3	33.5
Calloway	845	12,678	1,722	2,541	1,819	460	363	443	34,956	710	48.9	3.8	36.9
Campbell	1,670	24,334	3,343	2,202	4,001	503	1,211	1,054	43,308	577	54.8	0.3	32.3
Carlisle	88	657	104	45	101	68	12	22	32,932	273	40.3	7.0	41.7
Carroll	229	6,153	369	3,305	559	65	86	395	64,250	308	25.6	1.0	32.5
Carter	402	5,099	622	750	964	183	103	150	29,350	718	27.7	0.4	38.3
Casey	223	3,222	522	1,384	374	72	200	100	31,137	1,106	33.3	2.1	40.7
Christian	1,272	24,055	3,791	6,774	3,137	564	955	952	39,565	1,137	33.3	6.9	42.4
Clark	739	12,478	1,761	2,612	1,564	284	549	505	40,458	871	41.8	2.3	37.7

STATE County	Agriculture, 2017 (cont.)															
	Land in farms					Value of land and buildings (dollars)		Value of machinery and equipment, average per farm (dollars)	Value of products sold:				Organic farms (number)	Farms with internet access (percent)	Government payments	
	Acreage (1,000)	Percent change, 2012–2017	Acres			Average per farm	Average per acre		Total (mil dol)	Average per farm (acres)	Percent from:				Total ($1,000)	Percent of farms
			Average size of farm	Total irrigated (1,000)	Total cropland (1,000)						Crops	Livestock and poultry products				
	117	118	119	120	121	122	123	124	125	126	127	128	129	130	131	132
KANSAS— Cont'd																
Neosho	323	4.8	470	0.8	169.9	923,397	1,963	93,313	81.9	119,167	56.0	44.0	2	72.9	1,845	49.5
Ness	668	-1.4	1,278	3.7	404.6	1,385,852	1,084	159,980	60.8	116,216	61.4	38.6	NA	73.0	8,605	91.6
Norton	495	-1.4	1,509	20.3	284.0	2,053,567	1,361	299,003	143.3	436,744	43.0	57.0	NA	69.8	2,110	74.1
Osage	440	-0.6	422	1.3	252.6	840,108	1,992	126,651	92.4	88,677	72.4	27.6	NA	72.6	2,606	52.3
Osborne	437	-0.7	1,370	5.6	228.6	1,932,419	1,410	206,187	62.5	195,922	71.3	28.7	NA	75.5	2,266	81.8
Ottawa	439	4.6	1,003	6.5	242.2	2,017,300	2,011	217,607	108.4	247,436	46.7	53.3	2	74.7	3,278	74.9
Pawnee	474	-1.3	1,310	60.7	397.9	2,171,753	1,658	243,559	307.9	850,519	25.1	74.9	1	68.2	6,089	77.3
Phillips	497	0.5	1,198	6.4	254.1	1,728,534	1,442	208,663	107.6	259,294	54.5	45.5	NA	75.4	1,925	68.4
Pottawatomie	406	-0.9	525	19.6	158.7	1,290,997	2,461	124,388	101.4	130,961	41.3	58.7	NA	80.2	2,520	52.2
Pratt	465	0.1	967	63.8	366.5	1,987,147	2,055	245,812	271.3	564,046	33.6	66.4	NA	72.8	9,324	83.4
Rawlins	604	-0.9	2,025	14.3	356.0	3,123,663	1,542	323,136	100.4	336,748	66.6	33.4	1	84.2	3,971	79.5
Reno	789	-0.1	508	54.1	590.7	1,087,423	2,139	154,602	216.7	139,645	53.5	46.5	NA	69.3	14,557	69.5
Republic	373	3.4	665	40.2	269.1	1,720,315	2,586	200,912	187.5	334,275	51.9	48.1	2	73.4	5,249	77.4
Rice	463	1.2	986	29.9	366.1	2,006,778	2,036	254,152	235.5	501,162	36.0	64.0	1	81.5	6,079	73.8
Riley	214	-1.8	425	3.8	106.1	1,285,194	3,022	137,948	51.2	101,532	63.6	36.4	3	82.7	1,107	49.2
Rooks	559	1.3	1,356	5.7	320.2	1,696,528	1,251	189,770	76.6	185,934	64.1	35.9	NA	77.7	4,218	81.3
Rush	448	-1.1	919	8.6	323.2	1,193,377	1,299	146,600	59.5	121,994	69.4	30.6	NA	68.4	8,957	82.0
Russell	492	13.1	985	0.5	263.3	1,318,319	1,339	125,089	50.1	100,106	65.9	34.1	NA	70.4	5,057	79.6
Saline	358	-1.7	588	4.9	223.3	1,394,788	2,371	157,229	73.6	120,823	52.8	47.2	1	77.0	4,352	71.8
Scott	460	1.5	1,951	29.1	365.7	2,955,605	1,515	503,414	1,135.0	4,809,487	7.7	92.3	7	79.2	6,872	74.2
Sedgwick	497	2.0	365	40.4	408.9	1,264,948	3,464	135,560	118.9	87,440	79.9	20.1	1	79.9	7,283	52.6
Seward	361	-10.2	1,279	95.5	263.7	1,803,833	1,410	305,603	424.7	1,506,021	18.9	81.1	NA	69.9	7,997	76.2
Shawnee	202	3.8	238	14.7	126.5	712,656	2,993	88,748	49.2	58,035	79.8	20.2	2	81.3	1,312	33.4
Sheridan	512	-8.9	1,610	68.4	358.5	2,518,737	1,564	431,777	348.9	1,097,022	25.4	74.6	1	83.6	6,021	87.4
Sherman	618	4.0	1,602	97.1	491.6	2,821,024	1,761	358,514	139.2	360,567	72.8	27.2	4	74.6	8,255	78.2
Smith	541	8.2	1,274	7.4	363.2	2,431,582	1,909	275,597	129.3	304,144	75.9	24.1	5	84.0	4,089	86.4
Stafford	494	-1.0	1,059	76.4	393.0	1,909,862	1,803	300,164	198.6	426,120	41.5	58.5	NA	74.2	8,445	83.9
Stanton	435	1.4	1,978	54.3	396.1	2,105,893	1,064	364,126	133.5	606,786	54.5	45.5	NA	80.5	9,689	88.2
Stevens	455	0.0	1,208	138.4	370.0	1,675,641	1,387	330,668	340.6	903,358	32.3	67.7	NA	71.6	9,552	86.5
Sumner	758	5.3	795	25.7	630.3	1,461,530	1,838	204,872	155.7	163,348	87.8	12.2	NA	77.8	8,737	70.3
Thomas	670	-0.8	1,667	81.4	569.5	2,911,418	1,747	417,933	251.1	624,515	52.6	47.4	NA	84.8	6,720	79.6
Trego	515	15.4	1,503	5.5	276.3	1,714,222	1,141	222,541	57.2	166,706	59.5	40.5	NA	73.2	4,819	82.2
Wabaunsee	379	-4.4	594	8.7	114.2	1,144,196	1,927	113,289	63.1	98,975	40.0	60.0	NA	80.9	1,949	48.9
Wallace	446	-8.6	1,587	33.9	303.1	2,144,593	1,352	252,476	81.8	291,050	68.3	31.7	2	74.0	5,388	81.5
Washington	526	7.3	757	13.9	336.7	1,837,799	2,426	218,194	182.0	262,218	47.9	52.1	NA	76.9	4,929	80.3
Wichita	438	-5.6	1,724	40.9	367.9	2,416,112	1,401	385,925	559.3	2,202,157	12.8	87.2	16	76.0	6,749	84.3
Wilson	287	12.6	683	1.8	180.2	1,329,365	1,947	182,949	62.3	148,298	79.8	20.2	NA	71.2	1,941	51.0
Woodson	283	-4.0	979	D	135.4	1,627,566	1,662	184,288	52.6	181,834	52.8	47.2	2	78.2	1,573	55.4
Wyandotte	12	3.2	78	0.6	8.8	528,919	6,742	73,098	5.3	33,380	90.5	9.5	2	82.9	52	4.4
KENTUCKY	12,962	-0.7	171	83.9	6,630.4	643,019	3,769	82,740	5,737.9	75,533	44.3	55.7	227	72.4	126,697	22.2
Adair	172	1.1	149	0.0	76.8	448,542	3,008	72,779	69.4	60,101	26.2	73.8	1	68.5	2,151	33.6
Allen	169	15.8	150	0.2	74.2	518,199	3,462	70,602	88.6	78,613	26.4	73.6	8	68.1	2,489	24.2
Anderson	82	1.0	106	0.0	29.1	392,778	3,713	53,625	12.3	15,926	34.6	65.4	6	67.8	276	4.9
Ballard	94	-12.0	320	D	75.3	1,155,670	3,614	205,371	70.6	239,366	54.0	46.0	NA	87.5	1,653	49.8
Barren	254	2.1	134	0.1	141.4	481,503	3,602	90,193	127.2	66,982	38.3	61.7	NA	77.6	2,218	26.1
Bath	127	-10.6	175	0.0	46.7	412,199	2,360	61,331	18.3	25,161	30.8	69.2	4	76.2	217	6.2
Bell	15	87.3	137	0.0	3.4	273,172	1,990	43,893	0.5	4,591	48.5	51.5	NA	68.2	10	9.1
Boone	79	17.2	109	0.1	36.6	655,823	6,004	58,670	15.4	21,315	75.2	24.8	2	73.0	440	9.0
Bourbon	171	-7.0	187	0.6	74.9	1,061,516	5,684	104,627	209.6	229,030	21.9	78.1	3	76.2	695	17.9
Boyd	19	-10.7	96	0.0	3.5	230,681	2,405	57,311	1.2	5,842	38.0	62.0	NA	83.3	5	3.0
Boyle	89	-12.7	147	0.0	36.8	547,715	3,720	64,909	31.3	52,056	20.6	79.4	7	71.9	251	12.5
Bracken	87	0.0	164	0.1	32.4	408,483	2,498	60,419	10.7	20,190	60.2	39.8	1	64.6	84	10.0
Breathitt	23	4.4	145	0.0	3.6	227,411	1,569	54,188	0.5	3,175	59.4	40.6	NA	72.5	21	13.8
Breckinridge	275	5.9	203	0.1	126.8	625,871	3,087	92,986	99.4	73,279	47.0	53.0	6	68.8	3,162	37.1
Bullitt	44	-3.7	91	D	19.3	471,740	5,161	46,835	6.2	12,848	69.8	30.2	NA	78.8	41	2.5
Butler	147	-3.8	229	0.2	75.6	605,594	2,648	78,210	48.9	76,221	55.8	44.2	NA	65.1	2,423	34.6
Caldwell	130	-2.5	274	6.2	86.5	915,071	3,339	122,658	45.1	95,038	89.0	11.0	NA	71.8	2,555	40.8
Calloway	136	-23.0	191	2.9	102.5	786,844	4,122	115,703	97.7	137,631	60.0	40.0	NA	77.9	2,938	57.3
Campbell	46	9.3	80	0.0	15.9	404,186	5,060	51,900	7.1	12,334	48.3	51.7	NA	77.8	28	3.6
Carlisle	88	-10.8	322	1.7	73.1	1,224,443	3,798	170,980	67.6	247,681	56.3	43.7	NA	68.1	1,602	65.2
Carroll	51	-5.0	165	0.0	17.9	560,794	3,393	55,839	5.8	18,867	57.6	42.4	NA	68.8	140	10.4
Carter	92	-13.1	128	0.0	23.4	247,720	1,933	49,400	6.9	9,586	31.9	68.1	4	68.4	153	5.0
Casey	179	0.1	162	0.1	65.4	379,677	2,343	60,628	32.2	29,071	50.2	49.8	14	66.3	581	23.1
Christian	346	-4.1	304	5.1	245.8	1,464,184	4,817	152,416	205.3	180,542	81.1	18.9	13	56.6	6,215	42.9
Clark	147	7.2	169	0.1	66.4	749,313	4,431	74,443	34.0	39,068	45.5	54.5	2	78.5	289	10.1

STATE County	Water use, 2015		Wholesale Trade[1], 2017				Retail Trade[2], 2017				Real estate and rental and leasing,[2] 2017			
	Public supply water withdrawn (mil gal/ day)	Public supply gallons withdrawn per person per day	Number of establish-ments	Number of employees	Sales (mil dol)	Average payroll (mil dol)	Number of establish-ments	Number of employees	Sales (mil dol)	Average payroll (mil dol)	Number of establish-ments	Number of employees	Sales (mil dol)	Average payroll (mil dol)
	133	134	135	136	137	138	139	140	141	142	143	144	145	146
KANSAS— Cont'd														
Neosho	1.1	66.1	32	284	162.1	11.7	79	843	219.6	21.6	19	41	6.8	1.2
Ness	0.3	106.5	17	108	127.6	5.0	12	71	11.9	1.5	NA	NA	NA	NA
Norton	0.8	135.1	9	77	39.0	3.0	27	191	50.1	4.6	NA	NA	NA	NA
Osage	1.5	95.9	12	54	38.4	1.8	46	349	76.1	6.5	6	16	1.4	0.3
Osborne	0.5	122.2	D	D	D	5.5	22	160	30.6	2.9	NA	NA	NA	NA
Ottawa	0.5	88.7	8	143	64.1	7.1	14	91	13.8	1.2	5	7	2.1	0.2
Pawnee	0.9	137.5	7	63	69.5	3.9	24	191	46.4	3.8	D	D	D	D
Phillips	1.0	180.5	14	67	40.2	3.0	31	230	40.9	4.1	NA	NA	NA	NA
Pottawatomie	6.2	267.0	32	614	195.6	26.4	80	1,602	346.7	46.8	27	85	17.0	2.8
Pratt	1.7	172.3	21	243	356.2	14.1	51	645	166.3	16.8	12	26	3.3	0.6
Rawlins	0.3	119.7	D	D	D	8.3	17	103	22.0	2.0	NA	NA	NA	NA
Reno	7.6	119.4	81	1,036	1,149.4	43.8	240	3,085	764.3	73.1	77	221	35.3	7.0
Republic	0.7	137.6	16	128	91.9	4.5	30	207	55.0	4.4	D	D	D	D
Rice	1.2	116.3	23	109	125.0	5.5	40	287	49.3	4.9	5	13	2.0	0.3
Riley	3.0	40.3	32	280	152.4	12.2	246	4,206	904.5	93.2	125	619	80.6	19.9
Rooks	0.7	131.4	17	163	141.9	7.3	26	206	48.6	3.2	3	5	0.9	0.1
Rush	0.5	162.9	11	D	28.8	D	10	65	24.4	2.0	NA	NA	NA	NA
Russell	0.4	62.5	18	137	103.7	4.8	39	255	68.5	5.1	6	D	1.1	D
Saline	5.9	105.9	89	1,229	813.9	66.9	237	4,021	1,094.8	93.9	64	205	50.4	6.6
Scott	0.8	169.2	12	119	146.6	6.0	33	226	47.1	4.3	NA	NA	NA	NA
Sedgwick	52.0	101.6	589	8,732	8,030.5	527.5	1,718	29,929	8,082.9	773.3	617	3,195	764.6	122.8
Seward	4.9	210.3	38	279	185.5	13.3	93	1,282	335.5	31.5	21	60	12.3	2.2
Shawnee	14.3	80.2	154	2,070	1,972.0	116.7	600	9,622	2,395.4	227.0	222	952	175.4	32.1
Sheridan	0.5	191.1	11	119	147.4	7.9	17	86	17.1	1.7	NA	NA	NA	NA
Sherman	1.3	224.0	21	251	493.0	12.8	34	408	110.8	9.4	4	6	1.5	0.2
Smith	0.5	132.3	10	136	83.0	4.8	29	180	58.0	4.2	3	3	0.3	0.0
Stafford	0.4	82.6	8	D	31.6	D	20	86	28.3	2.0	NA	NA	NA	NA
Stanton	0.4	193.1	D	D	D	2.8	14	63	25.4	1.8	NA	NA	NA	NA
Stevens	1.4	236.0	13	113	126.2	5.9	17	120	35.6	3.1	NA	NA	NA	NA
Sumner	2.1	89.2	19	123	114.0	6.4	70	630	168.2	14.7	16	44	4.3	1.0
Thomas	1.3	160.7	30	339	458.7	17.4	64	634	197.2	16.2	9	31	7.9	0.7
Trego	0.7	232.3	8	65	80.3	2.6	20	130	41.7	2.6	D	D	D	D
Wabaunsee	0.5	77.7	D	D	D	1.4	20	94	29.0	2.0	D	D	D	D
Wallace	0.2	144.9	D	D	D	D	8	42	7.0	1.1	NA	NA	NA	NA
Washington	0.8	139.3	17	106	86.3	4.4	35	176	35.3	3.9	4	8	0.6	0.1
Wichita	0.3	134.4	11	71	231.7	3.2	12	60	14.8	1.5	NA	NA	NA	NA
Wilson	1.4	153.6	D	D	D	0.6	31	244	48.2	4.7	5	D	0.4	D
Woodson	0.3	96.3	5	84	54.6	2.4	13	73	20.3	1.7	NA	NA	NA	NA
Wyandotte	62.2	380.4	220	6,602	8,955.5	442.3	442	7,813	2,158.2	212.9	130	706	138.7	29.6
KENTUCKY	552.8	124.9	3,646	55,784	80,128.5	3,171.6	15,021	225,127	64,294.3	5,630.0	3,902	18,070	5,125.3	731.1
Adair	0.0	0.0	16	81	29.1	2.1	55	782	223.1	19.6	D	D	D	D
Allen	1.0	46.0	8	221	63.1	11.2	49	430	117.0	10.3	10	66	2.9	1.3
Anderson	2.2	100.6	9	67	23.5	2.0	59	843	237.8	20.1	16	66	6.8	1.2
Ballard	0.6	70.6	D	D	D	3.1	24	150	40.6	3.2	D	D	D	D
Barren	7.8	178.1	D	D	D	D	182	2,503	734.6	61.0	27	83	11.7	2.1
Bath	0.0	0.0	3	10	6.2	0.2	28	164	40.3	4.0	D	D	D	D
Bell	3.8	140.1	11	149	155.4	5.3	114	1,459	396.1	34.3	17	93	8.2	2.1
Boone	0.0	0.3	178	7,394	37,571.3	635.5	467	14,413	4,772.0	363.9	144	765	207.1	31.6
Bourbon	2.1	104.4	9	141	32.7	10.1	61	945	430.4	30.6	12	26	5.1	0.6
Boyd	11.1	229.5	63	682	583.7	30.4	223	3,505	855.4	74.9	43	257	56.7	11.8
Boyle	5.6	187.2	19	155	110.1	7.1	126	1,773	527.8	43.5	21	134	14.5	1.9
Bracken	0.7	78.1	NA	NA	NA	NA	19	135	28.1	2.4	NA	NA	NA	NA
Breathitt	1.4	104.6	NA	NA	NA	NA	40	437	112.3	10.5	D	D	D	D
Breckinridge	1.8	89.9	9	D	35.5	D	53	543	160.4	13.1	D	D	D	0.8
Bullitt	0.0	0.0	30	1,148	935.0	49.6	170	5,350	1,505.3	151.2	42	188	31.3	6.5
Butler	1.2	93.5	D	D	D	D	31	250	61.7	5.1	D	D	D	D
Caldwell	0.0	0.0	D	D	D	D	64	727	190.8	17.2	6	D	1.6	D
Calloway	3.5	90.5	29	328	193.1	13.9	160	1,978	610.5	47.3	31	272	15.6	6.5
Campbell	26.3	286.1	53	829	1,492.8	47.5	242	4,851	1,187.8	102.9	83	613	144.1	46.4
Carlisle	0.1	28.7	D	D	D	0.7	14	100	20.6	1.9	3	7	1.0	0.2
Carroll	1.9	174.8	D	D	D	1.7	41	608	177.1	15.3	6	31	9.3	1.3
Carter	4.1	150.6	9	280	46.0	7.2	102	939	256.1	19.2	18	32	5.6	1.0
Casey	1.0	63.9	13	96	64.3	3.1	57	396	104.0	8.5	3	8	0.9	0.1
Christian	12.2	166.3	65	743	804.0	35.5	247	3,183	927.2	78.3	62	334	57.4	15.3
Clark	6.9	193.0	36	627	823.1	30.7	121	1,582	480.1	40.6	30	109	24.4	3.7

1 Merchant wholesalers, except manufacturers' sales branches and offices. 2. Employer establishments.

STATE County	Professional, scientific, and technical services, 2017				Manufacturing, 2017				Accommodation and food services, 2017			
	Number of establish-ments	Number of employees	Sales (mil dol)	Average payroll (mil dol)	Number of establish-ments	Number of employees	Sales (mil dol)	Average payroll (mil dol)	Number of establis-hments	Number of employees	Sales (mil dol)	Annual payroll (mil dol)
	147	148	149	150	151	152	153	154	155	156	157	158
KANSAS— Cont'd												
Neosho	29	111	18.0	5.7	33	750	214.7	42.3	D	D	D	D
Ness	D	D	D	0.6	5	20	9.3	1.0	6	D	0.7	D
Norton	14	31	4.0	0.9	7	278	47.8	15.0	14	207	8.2	2.5
Osage	17	63	6.0	2.6	D	D	D	D	19	145	6.5	1.7
Osborne	7	27	1.9	0.7	5	113	21.1	4.8	9	D	1.3	D
Ottawa	13	37	6.5	1.9	5	36	5.0	1.6	10	37	1.4	0.4
Pawnee	16	79	7.4	2.6	NA	NA	NA	NA	13	161	9.2	2.4
Phillips	D	D	19.0	D	9	197	239.8	15.2	17	98	4.8	1.2
Pottawatomie	D	D	D	D	33	1,513	390.9	94.6	40	575	27.9	8.3
Pratt	30	115	12.8	4.6	8	99	117.6	5.3	40	457	18.9	4.9
Rawlins	9	14	1.0	0.3	6	25	8.2	1.6	5	34	1.0	0.3
Reno	D	D	D	D	89	3,499	1,152.4	169.4	132	2,578	110.4	33.4
Republic	9	38	5.2	1.1	8	153	46.3	5.8	7	D	2.8	D
Rice	15	143	12.5	2.8	16	399	298.3	22.6	D	D	D	D
Riley	D	D	D	D	26	490	135.6	19.2	177	4,427	177.6	54.4
Rooks	11	47	4.9	1.7	7	110	18.7	4.1	12	D	2.5	D
Rush	D	D	D	D	6	269	90.4	13.2	7	D	1.4	D
Russell	13	48	5.4	1.4	D	136	D	5.4	17	218	11.5	2.7
Saline	D	D	D	D	72	5,017	1,336.9	222.4	146	3,014	140.4	39.1
Scott	18	55	7.4	2.0	6	26	19.7	1.6	16	176	7.5	2.2
Sedgwick	1,189	11,563	1,919.5	716.3	501	41,132	16,434.6	2,920.7	1,177	24,300	1,166.6	346.1
Seward	28	110	21.6	4.5	D	D	D	D	53	891	43.8	12.5
Shawnee	D	D	D	D	112	6,691	3,344.3	353.8	D	D	D	D
Sheridan	4	24	3.4	0.6	NA	NA	NA	NA	D	D	D	0.3
Sherman	17	63	5.6	1.5	4	89	59.0	3.7	26	314	14.0	4.1
Smith	8	21	1.5	0.4	4	9	2.8	0.4	D	D	D	0.7
Stafford	D	D	1.8	D	NA	NA	NA	NA	9	D	1.9	D
Stanton	6	18	1.3	0.4	NA	NA	NA	NA	4	36	0.9	0.3
Stevens	8	27	2.9	0.8	D	62	D	2.9	15	128	6.0	1.5
Sumner	30	76	9.2	3.0	29	714	152.3	38.3	35	446	19.9	5.5
Thomas	24	56	6.4	2.1	11	73	27.0	3.2	30	472	21.5	5.4
Trego	7	11	1.0	0.3	7	34	4.9	1.3	12	79	2.9	0.7
Wabaunsee	D	D	D	D	D	D	D	D	D	D	D	D
Wallace	D	D	D	D	NA	NA	NA	NA	NA	NA	NA	NA
Washington	12	116	12.9	4.8	9	169	39.9	5.9	D	D	D	D
Wichita	4	7	0.4	0.1	4	54	21.2	2.2	3	11	0.6	0.2
Wilson	11	36	4.9	1.6	19	935	237.4	50.4	D	D	D	D
Woodson	5	8	0.9	0.1	NA	NA	NA	NA	D	D	D	0.5
Wyandotte	D	D	D	D	178	10,742	8,310.9	668.0	277	6,065	347.0	97.6
KENTUCKY	8,091	66,995	10,185.0	3,605.7	3,699	234,010	133,415.5	12,768.7	8,228	174,910	9,191.2	2,621.2
Adair	16	53	6.4	1.5	21	374	50.2	12.6	D	D	D	D
Allen	11	67	5.9	1.8	12	D	237.0	D	23	347	20.5	5.4
Anderson	29	106	9.5	3.2	23	1,029	825.3	58.6	32	D	24.5	D
Ballard	12	124	22.1	9.8	D	184	D	9.7	D	D	D	0.4
Barren	42	438	32.2	11.6	47	3,605	920.6	168.1	89	1,890	91.3	25.0
Bath	D	D	D	D	D	D	D	D	D	D	D	D
Bell	25	130	14.2	5.3	17	1,045	327.9	39.4	53	1,092	47.2	12.0
Boone	245	1,783	327.7	99.5	169	11,471	4,702.5	666.6	309	6,882	403.1	110.5
Bourbon	30	306	27.1	12.3	23	1,352	1,106.1	71.2	D	D	D	D
Boyd	D	D	D	D	35	1,825	6,621.9	157.1	129	3,117	147.7	41.4
Boyle	56	374	65.9	19.7	27	2,444	696.3	108.0	66	1,515	75.3	20.9
Bracken	D	D	3.3	D	D	D	D	D	D	D	D	D
Breathitt	D	D	D	D	4	19	3.7	0.9	D	D	D	D
Breckinridge	15	64	6.1	2.0	15	261	39.1	11.5	16	189	9.6	2.7
Bullitt	81	283	30.1	10.4	52	2,372	1,368.6	123.7	96	2,066	109.6	29.6
Butler	9	39	2.5	1.0	D	591	D	26.6	D	D	D	D
Caldwell	23	47	5.0	1.2	16	848	461.5	37.5	31	409	17.6	4.7
Calloway	63	335	35.8	12.1	25	2,457	1,138.8	106.3	D	D	D	D
Campbell	D	D	D	D	72	2,199	771.0	112.8	223	4,585	231.8	67.0
Carlisle	4	12	1.0	0.3	5	67	12.1	1.8	8	43	1.6	0.4
Carroll	15	88	9.3	4.7	17	2,612	3,854.4	212.1	26	515	30.9	7.8
Carter	25	111	8.7	2.9	D	620	D	23.9	41	726	32.7	9.2
Casey	D	D	9.9	D	30	954	257.9	36.5	15	217	9.1	3.3
Christian	D	D	D	D	82	6,271	2,447.7	298.4	121	2,460	120.7	34.9
Clark	48	1,188	174.3	30.2	41	2,854	1,172.4	140.5	64	1,685	64.9	18.4

STATE County	Health care and social assistance, 2017				Other services, 2017				Nonemployer businesses, 2019		Value of residential construction authorized by building permits, 2021	
	Number of establish-ments	Number of employees	Receipts (mil dol)	Annual payroll (mil dol)	Number of establish-ments	Number of employees	Receipts (mil dol)	Annual payroll (mil dol)	Number	Receipts (mil dol)	New construction ($1,000)	Number of housing units
	159	160	161	162	163	164	165	166	167	168	169	170
KANSAS— Cont'd												
Neosho	50	1,151	112.7	42.3	26	76	6.3	1.3	1,073	39.5	1,394	11
Ness	10	D	20.4	D	D	D	D	1.5	277	13.4	150	1
Norton	22	469	31.1	15.6	D	D	D	D	409	17.2	0	0
Osage	28	420	23.0	10.6	16	44	5.7	1.2	1,007	47.1	11,017	48
Osborne	13	263	13.5	6.6	D	D	5.5	D	315	10.4	0	0
Ottawa	12	254	15.0	6.9	14	34	3.2	0.8	490	17.9	4,717	20
Pawnee	18	1,055	99.9	45.8	14	29	3.7	0.5	408	20.3	240	1
Phillips	16	274	21.7	9.0	26	72	47.3	2.1	461	16.1	0	0
Pottawatomie	58	1,534	102.6	39.5	50	159	17.6	4.2	1,874	84.9	54,500	180
Pratt	35	696	87.4	37.5	31	103	10.3	2.9	777	33.7	410	1
Rawlins	10	173	13.4	5.5	D	D	1.1	D	249	9.6	50	1
Reno	167	4,304	473.0	182.7	109	503	57.7	12.8	3,806	146.5	12,890	62
Republic	18	306	23.3	10.1	13	44	4.1	1.1	416	15.6	0	0
Rice	21	351	20.9	8.5	18	50	7.6	1.3	624	24.1	5,928	26
Riley	215	3,673	389.9	137.5	119	1,108	293.5	48.3	3,509	153.4	24,828	82
Rooks	13	270	22.6	9.5	13	35	5.4	0.8	514	16.9	175	1
Rush	6	156	8.9	4.8	D	D	D	0.1	257	9.4	0	0
Russell	15	368	27.4	13.2	D	D	D	D	801	39.3	1,885	10
Saline	156	4,993	563.9	230.0	108	581	105.3	16.9	3,369	169.2	15,076	75
Scott	16	D	35.7	D	18	47	9.5	1.7	444	17.7	0	0
Sedgwick	1,493	37,305	4,197.1	1,678.6	779	5,283	730.5	165.4	34,011	1,647.6	615,965	2,124
Seward	70	1,064	112.6	40.2	46	172	20.5	4.3	1,202	85.8	3,020	27
Shawnee	492	16,848	1,984.7	832.2	349	2,381	325.8	94.5	9,563	447.5	104,190	540
Sheridan	D	D	D	D	8	27	1.9	0.5	264	13.9	NA	NA
Sherman	32	417	34.7	15.1	22	78	8.5	2.7	520	20.6	490	2
Smith	8	228	21.0	7.6	D	D	D	0.7	328	10.2	245	1
Stafford	15	178	13.4	4.6	8	18	2.3	0.4	377	17.7	734	3
Stanton	D	D	D	D	D	D	D	D	192	11.7	0	0
Stevens	D	D	D	D	11	26	4.8	1.0	386	21.6	1,435	6
Sumner	54	959	64.1	26.9	38	108	11.1	2.9	1,376	48.0	5,960	41
Thomas	24	415	45.1	18.4	24	70	7.1	2.0	807	28.6	3,635	16
Trego	D	D	D	D	10	20	2.3	0.5	309	11.8	0	0
Wabaunsee	9	114	5.0	2.4	D	D	D	D	507	20.7	4,995	22
Wallace	4	59	2.6	1.1	D	D	0.7	D	161	5.9	0	0
Washington	22	334	19.1	9.2	D	D	6.1	D	433	21.6	238	1
Wichita	D	D	D	D	D	D	D	0.3	180	7.6	0	0
Wilson	35	678	50.6	21.9	D	D	10.7	D	591	22.0	1,481	7
Woodson	4	D	4.0	D	7	7	0.5	0.1	252	13.3	1,231	11
Wyandotte	297	16,184	1,915.6	843.2	206	1,447	364.3	50.6	8,703	363.6	36,938	179
KENTUCKY	11,597	268,711	32,369.5	12,412.1	5,900	38,040	4,755.2	1,198.2	299,477	13,553.3	2,912,471	14,841
Adair	38	500	46.0	17.6	D	D	D	D	1,568	71.1	0	0
Allen	D	D	D	D	18	43	4.6	1.3	1,535	70.7	1,050	9
Anderson	35	359	24.3	10.4	29	100	15.5	2.9	1,517	55.8	26,864	178
Ballard	D	D	D	D	D	D	D	D	456	15.0	NA	NA
Barren	97	2,397	295.5	110.1	64	249	21.6	5.9	3,384	177.5	65,910	302
Bath	8	101	8.3	3.6	D	D	D	D	811	33.6	0	0
Bell	68	1,363	145.1	51.2	28	108	10.9	2.6	1,270	46.6	5,053	47
Boone	281	4,843	516.7	209.7	194	1,780	164.1	55.5	8,468	388.4	172,995	1,107
Bourbon	52	742	61.8	24.2	21	101	7.2	1.9	1,347	64.7	14,554	41
Boyd	195	7,103	812.7	348.7	83	659	60.5	24.6	2,405	100.5	0	0
Boyle	137	2,692	336.5	113.1	53	266	26.6	6.8	2,076	74.7	8,668	62
Bracken	7	129	11.3	4.6	D	D	D	0.8	545	17.1	NA	NA
Breathitt	47	737	82.6	28.8	D	D	D	D	571	17.9	0	0
Breckinridge	31	540	46.7	18.2	D	D	D	D	1,363	62.8	375	3
Bullitt	115	1,441	112.9	50.5	96	1,187	62.5	36.6	4,660	195.0	143,276	432
Butler	D	D	D	D	14	75	6.7	1.8	767	31.5	0	0
Caldwell	38	532	38.9	15.2	D	D	D	D	770	27.5	1,882	9
Calloway	99	1,730	185.4	78.1	50	214	17.5	5.1	2,488	113.1	9,814	137
Campbell	170	3,607	368.9	150.0	121	988	138.0	34.6	5,859	240.8	140,121	664
Carlisle	8	79	5.8	2.2	4	11	0.9	0.4	416	17.2	NA	NA
Carroll	24	411	37.4	16.3	15	70	7.6	1.9	528	21.7	225	6
Carter	34	592	42.4	16.6	30	106	13.4	2.3	1,577	63.4	1,932	9
Casey	D	D	D	D	D	D	D	0.7	1,211	59.1	0	0
Christian	153	3,457	373.9	137.6	93	472	44.3	12.8	3,750	166.0	10,152	91
Clark	118	1,642	182.5	69.5	49	216	20.6	5.5	2,225	104.7	25,894	165

STATE County	Government employment and payroll, 2017		March payroll (percent of total)							Local government finances, 2017 General revenue		Taxes		
	Full-time equivalent employees	March payroll (dollars)	Adminis-tration, judicial, and legal	Police and corrections	Fire protection	Highways and transpor-tation	Health and welfare	Natural resources and utilities	Education and libraries	Total (mil dol)	Inter-govern-mental (mil dol)	Total (mil dol)	Per capita[1] (dollars) Total	Per capita[1] (dollars) Property
	171	172	173	174	175	176	177	178	179	180	181	182	183	184
KANSAS— Cont'd														
Neosho	1,297	4,801,938	3.0	4.4	1.4	2.8	39.4	8.0	38.6	120.4	29.8	22.5	1,398	1,037
Ness	353	1,117,456	5.7	3.8	0.0	7.3	52.0	1.9	27.7	27.8	5.2	9.7	3,409	3,248
Norton	415	1,502,007	19.4	1.7	0.1	1.6	37.4	5.4	34.1	23.9	9.5	10.5	1,931	1,643
Osage	681	2,328,841	6.6	8.3	0.2	4.4	1.4	7.7	69.7	54.7	29.6	19.3	1,221	1,010
Osborne	190	579,543	9.9	8.7	0.0	9.0	5.6	14.1	49.4	13.5	3.7	7.3	2,062	1,718
Ottawa	360	1,026,767	7.3	5.9	0.4	7.2	4.4	6.2	65.2	25.8	13.4	10.8	1,860	1,781
Pawnee	516	1,671,513	7.5	7.9	0.1	5.2	3.4	6.3	67.1	31.4	12.1	15.7	2,350	1,938
Phillips	490	1,755,399	5.9	2.7	0.0	4.5	4.5	4.9	76.1	24.5	10.8	9.7	1,808	1,558
Pottawatomie	1,086	3,349,875	6.0	8.3	0.6	5.4	1.3	6.0	69.0	87.2	35.4	37.4	1,564	1,300
Pratt	1,145	2,943,117	4.5	6.0	0.7	4.6	3.1	7.3	72.8	57.5	20.2	26.6	2,797	2,290
Rawlins	141	412,477	14.2	8.8	5.6	13.6	4.3	5.8	47.7	10.7	4.0	5.3	2,140	1,677
Reno	3,405	11,880,654	4.4	9.9	3.6	4.2	2.2	4.6	69.6	296.9	118.3	123.3	1,966	1,387
Republic	265	785,802	8.5	9.5	0.1	12.9	6.3	14.0	44.1	25.5	9.6	12.5	2,677	2,391
Rice	713	2,394,086	5.6	6.4	1.8	4.6	26.0	3.9	51.0	60.3	22.9	18.6	1,940	1,739
Riley	2,444	8,630,897	9.2	12.1	6.1	4.6	2.9	8.6	55.7	251.1	74.8	132.7	1,794	1,119
Rooks	436	1,399,610	6.4	5.4	0.0	5.9	41.2	4.0	35.9	45.0	12.5	13.0	2,566	2,272
Rush	244	772,126	6.0	3.8	0.0	9.0	27.1	7.8	42.9	20.1	5.5	6.9	2,264	2,211
Russell	432	1,355,647	10.1	9.1	3.0	10.6	6.4	15.1	45.0	31.7	11.3	14.2	2,055	1,922
Saline	2,668	9,840,370	4.9	9.6	5.0	4.2	2.8	5.9	65.7	234.4	97.0	98.0	1,798	1,108
Scott	257	752,664	11.3	9.5	0.2	6.8	2.9	5.8	62.9	25.2	7.8	14.9	3,016	2,370
Sedgwick	19,778	74,886,985	6.5	11.9	4.8	3.1	4.6	5.1	62.0	2,058.2	954.7	660.8	1,288	924
Seward	1,967	6,874,718	4.4	5.1	1.6	2.1	27.3	5.1	52.2	184.4	73.7	35.4	1,590	1,087
Shawnee	8,734	32,886,735	5.1	11.3	4.8	2.8	2.4	5.2	67.6	788.7	323.9	316.0	1,775	1,198
Sheridan	269	807,205	4.8	5.0	0.0	4.8	59.3	3.4	22.2	24.4	4.7	7.9	3,111	2,610
Sherman	565	1,972,655	6.5	4.0	0.8	4.7	35.9	5.0	38.9	31.2	13.1	11.3	1,907	1,503
Smith	261	796,134	12.9	3.6	4.6	10.1	4.6	7.7	52.6	25.6	7.9	14.9	4,114	3,559
Stafford	275	1,012,071	11.0	5.7	0.6	9.8	3.4	4.8	61.9	29.2	9.8	12.2	2,918	2,649
Stanton	250	919,988	4.9	3.7	0.0	6.2	42.7	5.0	28.0	16.4	4.4	10.5	5,109	4,866
Stevens	516	1,791,369	4.3	5.4	0.3	5.7	39.0	5.0	38.1	57.8	12.3	22.6	4,075	3,789
Sumner	1,337	4,256,344	5.8	8.0	2.2	5.5	17.1	5.8	52.4	102.9	42.7	37.3	1,616	1,280
Thomas	574	1,857,168	17.9	3.7	1.2	2.5	1.0	5.1	66.2	52.2	14.5	22.7	2,906	2,208
Trego	348	1,157,339	7.9	4.7	0.2	5.2	59.5	2.8	18.1	13.4	3.6	7.9	2,780	2,419
Wabaunsee	273	775,032	17.0	9.0	0.0	6.6	2.3	7.5	55.7	24.7	10.1	11.3	1,652	1,561
Wallace	107	308,513	8.6	10.2	0.0	10.2	1.5	3.9	61.4	9.0	3.0	5.2	3,437	3,356
Washington	357	1,093,990	6.7	5.7	0.0	7.6	19.8	5.9	51.0	30.7	10.5	13.4	2,447	2,288
Wichita	254	742,160	4.0	3.4	0.1	6.1	47.2	4.4	34.5	19.2	3.8	7.7	3,612	3,096
Wilson	645	2,126,416	4.4	8.6	0.7	3.5	31.0	6.7	42.2	45.5	17.4	13.3	1,529	1,306
Woodson	165	496,876	11.0	8.9	0.3	9.4	5.4	8.1	50.4	12.9	5.4	6.4	2,036	1,771
Wyandotte	8,721	39,159,416	3.6	11.1	9.4	2.5	2.8	10.8	56.5	853.3	419.3	287.6	1,742	920
KENTUCKY	X	X	X	X	X	X	X	X	X	X	X	X	X	X
Adair	672	1,911,619	4.8	5.8	0.0	1.5	2.9	6.2	77.6	54.2	23.9	10.4	540	368
Allen	694	1,911,037	2.2	11.0	0.0	1.2	7.3	6.9	70.6	44.3	25.8	13.2	632	375
Anderson	708	2,270,158	6.2	6.3	0.2	2.1	4.7	4.9	74.8	51.4	23.5	20.9	926	700
Ballard	312	902,100	4.7	11.1	0.1	2.5	4.8	5.1	71.2	22.5	12.0	7.6	953	722
Barren	1,798	5,562,968	2.0	6.1	2.2	1.4	1.3	13.4	71.2	131.2	71.1	41.7	953	579
Bath	440	1,283,556	6.7	2.8	0.0	1.9	3.4	5.3	78.8	28.4	18.3	6.3	512	324
Bell	1,028	2,854,698	2.9	7.9	4.4	2.8	3.1	1.1	76.8	74.4	45.7	18.1	672	359
Boone	4,012	15,531,882	2.2	9.7	7.7	1.5	0.6	2.8	72.6	382.2	117.4	238.7	1,823	1,071
Bourbon	1,007	2,702,469	4.9	5.0	4.8	3.2	1.9	5.5	73.4	55.8	26.6	22.9	1,142	634
Boyd	2,240	7,334,452	3.2	9.5	7.5	4.4	4.9	10.1	55.5	157.3	71.4	63.2	1,322	685
Boyle	1,169	4,242,008	3.9	8.1	3.3	1.6	4.1	3.0	74.6	88.9	34.1	43.5	1,451	796
Bracken	360	1,060,350	8.3	8.2	0.0	2.4	5.1	6.1	67.1	21.0	12.3	6.5	785	558
Breathitt	517	1,741,469	4.8	4.6	1.3	5.3	10.1	2.6	70.0	39.1	25.6	8.0	617	288
Breckinridge	646	1,872,417	5.7	10.5	0.0	2.0	2.2	1.8	77.2	43.7	27.1	12.8	635	471
Bullitt	2,632	8,353,177	2.0	9.0	4.0	1.2	3.4	1.9	78.0	183.5	74.3	87.7	1,093	786
Butler	467	1,484,940	3.0	5.3	0.0	5.4	9.3	2.9	72.8	22.8	16.3	5.4	423	206
Caldwell	446	1,290,394	6.2	6.0	2.9	2.7	10.4	2.8	68.5	30.8	17.0	9.8	771	288
Calloway	2,192	7,589,227	2.2	4.3	2.0	1.6	52.2	1.9	35.3	186.4	37.3	28.7	739	533
Campbell	2,556	9,933,993	5.0	14.6	6.9	2.6	2.0	0.7	67.3	254.5	81.5	143.6	1,546	965
Carlisle	196	529,702	7.0	2.7	0.0	3.8	0.0	3.5	75.2	38.9	7.8	3.3	689	533
Carroll	489	1,542,741	6.6	11.6	0.9	1.2	2.7	4.8	71.7	46.3	16.1	13.4	1,254	592
Carter	1,032	2,802,794	2.1	4.3	0.0	1.9	10.7	4.2	74.9	55.4	39.3	11.6	425	218
Casey	766	2,410,352	2.4	5.7	0.0	1.1	37.6	2.6	50.4	54.0	25.0	7.3	462	323
Christian	1,508	5,687,041	3.4	11.0	6.8	1.4	4.6	12.3	51.9	147.9	73.5	61.5	866	415
Clark	1,224	4,097,901	3.7	9.0	9.0	1.9	5.8	4.5	63.3	105.5	39.2	43.9	1,224	674

1. Based on the resident population estimated as of July 1 of the year shown.

STATE County	Local government finances, 2017 (cont.)									Government employment, 2020			Individual income tax returns, 2019		
	Direct general expenditure							Debt outstanding							
			Percent of total for:												
	Total (mil dol)	Per capita[1] (dollars)	Education	Health and hospitals	Police protection	Public welfare	Highways	Total (mil dol)	Per capita[1] (dollars)	Federal civilian	Federal military	State and local	Number of returns	Mean adjusted gross income	Mean income tax
	185	186	187	188	189	190	191	192	193	194	195	196	197	198	199
KANSAS— Cont'd															
Neosho	135.7	8,431	30.4	44.7	2.1	0.0	2.9	174.8	10,859	55	57	1,761	7,070	47,682	3,886
Ness	27.8	9,748	22.0	55.5	2.5	0.0	8.0	1.2	436	28	10	411	1,340	52,263	4,465
Norton	31.5	5,808	54.4	4.8	3.6	0.0	5.7	17.9	3,305	24	17	742	2,300	50,710	4,606
Osage	52.6	3,319	59.3	1.2	5.9	0.0	10.5	43.2	2,726	73	58	1,100	7,450	51,574	3,891
Osborne	13.8	3,899	29.1	8.8	8.0	0.0	14.8	2.6	732	29	12	326	1,740	44,456	3,411
Ottawa	27.4	4,706	66.9	2.4	4.0	0.0	9.7	40.0	6,884	22	21	441	2,760	49,691	3,837
Pawnee	53.2	7,979	63.4	4.2	2.4	0.0	7.2	41.0	6,151	39	20	1,366	2,820	48,746	3,974
Phillips	30.6	5,698	54.1	3.3	3.3	0.0	11.1	9.3	1,737	38	19	875	2,550	44,123	3,447
Pottawatomie	86.5	3,618	58.9	7.0	3.7	0.6	8.6	147.3	6,159	63	93	1,313	11,460	66,829	5,947
Pratt	66.9	7,047	63.8	3.1	4.4	0.0	7.7	24.2	2,543	38	32	1,020	4,250	57,089	5,235
Rawlins	11.8	4,756	32.7	5.4	4.0	0.0	11.8	11.6	4,707	19	9	304	1,220	54,301	6,243
Reno	328.2	5,234	53.1	1.7	4.2	0.0	6.6	329.2	5,250	179	217	4,966	28,690	53,216	4,711
Republic	21.9	4,702	40.2	6.4	4.2	0.0	10.7	8.5	1,834	31	16	448	2,310	45,203	3,292
Rice	57.3	5,992	46.8	27.2	2.9	0.0	5.2	67.1	7,018	37	32	1,008	4,160	52,796	4,152
Riley	227.3	3,072	37.1	2.4	15.6	0.0	7.5	516.9	6,988	670	270	13,159	26,330	62,734	6,541
Rooks	45.6	9,020	22.2	34.9	3.0	0.0	6.1	23.1	4,574	34	18	655	2,400	44,275	3,705
Rush	19.9	6,524	33.5	32.7	0.0	0.0	10.4	8.1	2,646	24	66	334	1,560	43,474	3,274
Russell	36.1	5,216	31.8	5.9	3.0	0.0	13.5	15.4	2,222	32	25	620	3,200	46,154	3,681
Saline	237.0	4,349	53.0	1.8	5.7	0.0	6.6	274.4	5,034	246	195	4,068	26,920	58,295	5,750
Scott	23.7	4,813	41.2	4.0	6.7	2.7	8.8	54.4	11,043	26	17	610	2,330	73,464	8,277
Sedgwick	2,036.5	3,968	48.5	3.4	6.2	0.1	6.6	4,317.8	8,414	5,128	4,805	28,077	247,290	65,952	7,285
Seward	235.2	10,572	52.2	19.8	1.9	0.2	2.7	168.6	7,580	90	76	2,372	9,520	49,144	3,957
Shawnee	852.3	4,787	51.0	1.6	6.5	0.1	6.8	1,169.8	6,570	3,362	743	18,351	86,160	59,078	5,867
Sheridan	22.0	8,694	18.7	51.2	1.2	0.0	8.6	1.9	753	16	9	399	1,250	43,694	5,112
Sherman	33.9	5,713	54.8	5.5	3.6	0.1	6.1	24.6	4,136	51	21	694	2,650	51,078	4,067
Smith	21.4	5,932	40.3	2.7	3.5	0.0	13.0	8.2	2,282	37	13	337	1,800	44,862	3,422
Stafford	29.7	7,101	43.3	4.1	3.5	0.0	12.8	1.4	328	43	15	485	1,910	42,384	3,395
Stanton	14.5	7,042	39.6	1.4	1.6	0.0	5.7	14.4	6,991	10	7	314	900	61,187	4,916
Stevens	51.7	9,307	28.3	34.6	4.1	0.0	9.8	17.6	3,168	24	20	657	2,310	59,342	5,345
Sumner	110.0	4,757	52.6	11.7	3.6	0.0	7.1	101.6	4,394	80	82	1,898	10,510	54,832	4,547
Thomas	47.2	6,030	60.4	1.8	3.3	0.0	7.9	29.9	3,817	32	27	747	3,700	54,545	5,225
Trego	13.3	4,675	34.8	5.5	2.9	0.6	15.0	13.0	4,558	19	10	512	1,450	48,483	3,776
Wabaunsee	25.1	3,676	47.9	1.3	4.6	0.0	14.1	21.6	3,159	18	25	441	3,270	59,203	4,899
Wallace	10.3	6,800	39.6	2.9	3.8	2.4	13.6	4.6	3,036	11	6	208	670	52,724	4,027
Washington	29.6	5,408	44.0	18.2	2.3	0.0	10.8	11.0	2,007	46	20	696	2,700	50,247	4,122
Wichita	19.9	9,384	26.4	37.0	3.3	0.0	7.5	5.0	2,341	19	8	268	1,050	53,467	4,820
Wilson	46.9	5,384	42.2	27.4	5.6	0.0	5.2	50.4	5,790	38	30	912	3,850	47,611	3,801
Woodson	13.3	4,240	44.4	2.4	6.6	0.0	13.8	2.3	725	14	11	255	1,420	42,689	3,113
Wyandotte	891.3	5,399	48.2	2.6	6.3	0.0	1.6	2,776.8	16,820	1,309	605	13,829	74,040	43,934	3,206
KENTUCKY	X	X	X	X	X	X	X	X	X	35,509	46,880	260,686	1,966,680	58,910	6,062
Adair	48.9	2,538	46.6	31.5	1.9	0.0	4.4	92.7	4,807	53	54	835	7,280	37,519	2,626
Allen	49.3	2,361	56.6	8.7	5.5	0.1	3.9	81.3	3,889	47	64	779	8,140	46,105	3,566
Anderson	46.0	2,039	58.6	6.7	2.5	0.1	4.1	156.8	6,953	42	68	836	10,920	54,894	4,399
Ballard	22.5	2,805	62.0	6.2	1.7	0.0	6.0	17.9	2,231	28	23	351	3,380	51,202	4,054
Barren	125.0	2,858	58.5	11.9	3.7	0.5	3.3	184.9	4,227	107	130	2,083	18,820	46,523	3,849
Bath	25.7	2,077	69.1	4.9	1.4	0.0	6.5	89.0	7,186	30	37	480	4,830	40,201	2,689
Bell	70.8	2,637	58.8	7.7	3.3	0.0	3.6	68.0	2,532	121	73	1,461	8,700	36,435	2,353
Boone	320.2	2,445	62.5	0.3	5.3	0.0	4.6	1,384.5	10,572	1,470	428	5,418	64,700	72,942	8,088
Bourbon	63.1	3,138	58.8	3.6	4.5	0.1	2.6	34.5	1,717	40	59	914	8,990	51,503	5,189
Boyd	143.5	3,001	54.4	4.8	4.4	0.1	5.3	320.0	6,693	407	134	2,903	19,310	54,227	5,073
Boyle	86.5	2,886	60.0	3.6	4.3	0.3	3.5	380.6	12,697	70	81	1,794	12,470	56,960	5,789
Bracken	20.6	2,487	63.0	7.0	2.7	0.0	7.3	16.5	1,987	17	25	417	3,770	47,228	3,387
Breathitt	35.5	2,748	61.5	10.9	2.4	0.3	7.7	31.9	2,467	56	36	741	4,410	41,165	2,674
Breckinridge	54.2	2,692	71.6	2.9	1.3	0.1	4.5	321.5	15,973	63	61	785	8,350	46,285	3,439
Bullitt	183.5	2,286	62.0	3.1	4.8	0.0	4.9	230.7	2,874	78	244	2,775	39,440	59,221	5,237
Butler	21.7	1,696	78.4	4.8	1.6	0.0	1.8	41.3	3,230	32	38	592	5,050	45,416	3,133
Caldwell	33.0	2,607	44.9	14.5	5.5	0.0	5.7	15.6	1,232	37	37	582	5,520	46,576	3,499
Calloway	178.4	4,595	23.9	61.6	2.4	0.0	2.2	209.2	5,387	82	110	4,531	15,360	50,688	4,635
Campbell	238.1	2,564	54.4	0.6	6.8	0.1	4.3	277.7	2,990	317	272	5,976	44,680	72,471	8,460
Carlisle	18.4	3,836	67.1	6.5	0.8	0.0	4.9	24.3	5,069	12	14	218	2,050	53,567	4,100
Carroll	143.1	13,361	15.4	0.7	0.8	0.0	0.8	3,436.3	320,729	36	31	695	4,800	49,178	3,767
Carter	53.1	1,953	68.0	3.0	3.2	0.0	5.0	61.9	2,274	62	77	1,156	10,370	46,097	3,442
Casey	55.2	3,490	42.1	34.0	0.8	0.0	3.5	54.9	3,469	30	49	697	5,980	37,296	2,510
Christian	131.2	1,847	55.6	3.2	5.0	0.1	3.6	433.2	6,099	3,408	28,533	3,172	30,040	44,908	3,519
Clark	100.7	2,805	49.4	7.3	3.5	0.0	2.7	199.1	5,546	109	111	1,465	16,470	54,611	4,852

1. Based on the resident population estimated as of July 1 of the year shown.

State / county code	CBSA code[1]	County Type code[2]	STATE County	Land area[3] (sq. mi)	Population, 2021: Total persons 2021	Population, 2021: Rank	Population, 2021: Per square mile	Race alone or in combination, not Hispanic or Latino (percent): White	Black	American Indian, Alaska Native	Asian and Pacific Islancer	Percent Hispanic or Latino[4]	Age (percent): Under 5 years	5 to 17 years	18 to 24 years	25 to 34 years	35 to 44 years	45 to 54 years
				1	2	3	4	5	6	7	8	9	10	11	12	13	14	15
			KENTUCKY—Cont'd															
21051	30940	7	Clay	469.3	20,206	1,805	43.1	93.7	4.3	0.7	0.4	2.1	5.6	11.5	10.6	15.4	13.6	13.7
21053		9	Clinton	197.3	9,265	2,469	47.0	95.2	1.3	1.1	0.7	3.2	5.4	12.4	11.6	11.6	11.5	13.1
21055		7	Crittenden	360.0	8,947	2,491	24.9	96.7	1.8	1.0	0.5	1.5	5.5	12.9	11.3	10.9	11.6	12.3
21057		9	Cumberland	305.2	5,879	2,744	19.3	94.6	4.2	0.8	0.5	1.9	5.8	12.4	9.8	11.0	10.9	11.5
21059	36980	3	Daviess	458.4	103,063	596	224.8	89.3	6.6	0.4	2.5	3.5	6.3	13.8	12.4	12.8	12.2	11.7
21061	14540	3	Edmonson	302.9	12,291	2,261	40.6	95.4	2.6	1.0	0.7	1.6	4.4	10.0	11.8	12.2	12.2	13.2
21063		9	Elliott	234.3	7,381	2,632	31.5	94.3	4.1	0.6	0.5	1.4	4.0	10.5	10.5	14.1	13.1	13.9
21065	40080	6	Estill	253.1	14,092	2,146	55.7	97.7	0.9	0.7	0.3	1.5	5.1	12.4	10.8	11.7	12.1	13.6
21067	30460	2	Fayette	283.6	321,793	224	1,134.7	72.4	17.2	0.7	5.2	7.5	5.6	11.5	17.5	14.9	13.1	11.5
21069		7	Fleming	348.5	15,224	2,076	43.7	96.6	2.2	0.5	0.4	1.6	6.6	13.7	11.9	11.5	11.3	13.2
21071		7	Floyd	393.3	35,274	1,299	89.7	97.4	1.4	0.5	0.4	1.0	5.8	12.5	11.6	11.4	12.3	12.9
21073	23180	4	Franklin	207.8	51,682	971	248.7	83.6	11.8	0.8	2.4	3.9	5.2	11.8	12.8	12.8	12.4	13.0
21075		9	Fulton	205.9	6,512	2,698	31.6	72.1	25.9	1.0	1.0	2.8	5.5	12.3	10.9	13.7	11.5	10.7
21077	17140	1	Gallatin	98.4	8,775	2,506	89.2	92.2	3.0	1.0	0.8	5.3	6.1	13.4	12.3	13.3	11.7	13.9
21079		6	Garrard	230.1	17,362	1,950	75.5	94.8	3.1	0.8	0.5	2.4	5.3	12.8	10.6	11.1	11.9	13.3
21081	17140	1	Grant	258.0	25,244	1,596	97.8	94.9	1.7	0.6	0.7	3.2	7.2	14.6	13.1	12.7	12.1	13.2
21083	32460	7	Graves	551.8	36,615	1,268	66.4	87.5	5.8	0.7	0.8	7.6	6.5	13.6	11.4	12.0	11.8	12.0
21085		6	Grayson	499.9	26,524	1,545	53.1	96.7	1.8	0.8	0.6	1.5	6.0	13.0	11.6	12.4	12.0	12.5
21087	15820	8	Green	286.0	11,291	2,326	39.5	95.2	2.7	1.0	0.6	2.2	5.5	12.1	10.3	11.3	11.6	12.9
21089	26580	2	Greenup	344.5	35,649	1,291	103.5	97.0	1.3	0.9	0.7	1.2	5.1	12.3	11.0	11.1	11.8	13.0
21091	36980	3	Hancock	187.7	9,064	2,482	48.3	95.9	2.1	0.6	0.6	2.0	5.6	14.1	12.6	11.2	12.1	13.2
21093	21060	3	Hardin	623.4	111,607	554	179.0	79.0	13.9	1.1	3.9	6.1	6.3	14.1	13.1	13.3	13.5	12.1
21095		7	Harlan	465.8	26,164	1,558	56.2	96.2	2.6	0.6	0.7	1.1	5.9	13.6	10.5	12.2	11.8	12.6
21097		6	Harrison	306.4	18,950	1,872	61.8	94.8	2.9	0.7	0.6	2.6	6.0	12.7	11.5	12.2	11.4	13.3
21099		8	Hart	412.6	19,460	1,853	47.2	92.9	5.2	0.7	0.7	2.1	6.6	13.6	12.1	12.1	11.0	12.6
21101	21780	2	Henderson	436.3	44,329	1,091	101.6	87.7	9.9	0.5	0.9	3.1	5.7	12.9	11.8	12.0	12.3	12.3
21103	31140	1	Henry	286.3	15,657	2,051	54.7	92.5	4.2	1.0	0.7	3.7	5.5	13.1	12.0	11.8	11.7	12.9
21105		9	Hickman	242.3	4,424	2,862	18.3	87.6	10.3	0.7	0.8	2.5	4.2	11.2	10.2	10.0	10.5	12.9
21107	31580	5	Hopkins	542.1	45,138	1,073	83.3	90.2	8.4	0.7	1.0	2.3	6.0	13.0	11.4	12.3	12.2	12.3
21109		9	Jackson	345.2	12,984	2,214	37.6	98.2	0.7	0.6	0.4	0.9	6.2	13.1	10.9	11.5	12.5	13.6
21111	31140	1	Jefferson	380.8	777,874	84	2,042.7	67.5	24.1	0.6	4.0	6.6	6.0	12.3	12.3	14.6	13.0	11.8
21113	30460	2	Jessamine	172.2	53,626	946	311.4	89.6	5.7	0.8	2.0	4.1	5.9	13.7	13.3	12.4	12.8	12.5
21115		7	Johnson	262.0	22,556	1,695	86.1	97.9	0.8	0.7	0.7	1.0	5.3	12.8	11.9	11.2	12.6	13.1
21117	17140	1	Kenton	160.3	169,495	396	1,057.4	89.7	6.4	0.5	2.0	3.7	6.3	13.1	12.1	14.8	13.4	11.9
21119		9	Knott	351.5	14,053	2,147	40.0	97.6	1.4	0.5	0.4	1.0	4.9	11.7	13.3	10.4	10.9	13.3
21121	30940	7	Knox	386.3	29,909	1,438	77.4	96.3	1.9	0.8	0.6	1.6	6.3	13.2	12.9	12.7	11.6	12.9
21123	21060	3	Larue	261.6	15,028	2,088	57.4	93.1	4.0	0.8	0.7	3.4	5.9	12.7	11.7	12.2	12.8	12.1
21125	30940	5	Laurel	434.0	62,561	854	144.1	96.6	1.4	0.8	0.8	1.6	5.9	12.9	11.9	12.8	12.7	13.1
21127		6	Lawrence	415.6	16,290	2,018	39.2	97.7	1.0	0.6	0.6	1.4	6.3	13.9	11.0	11.5	12.0	12.8
21129		9	Lee	208.9	7,451	2,623	35.7	94.6	3.5	0.8	0.4	1.6	4.6	10.3	10.0	14.9	13.4	13.6
21131		9	Leslie	400.9	10,278	2,391	25.6	98.2	0.9	0.5	0.5	0.9	5.1	12.8	10.1	12.4	11.8	13.1
21133		9	Letcher	337.9	21,253	1,751	62.9	97.8	1.1	0.5	0.5	1.0	5.4	12.5	10.6	10.9	12.3	12.7
21135		8	Lewis	482.8	12,987	2,213	26.9	98.2	1.1	0.6	0.3	0.9	6.0	12.4	11.4	11.4	11.3	13.0
21137	19220	7	Lincoln	332.8	24,243	1,639	72.8	95.3	3.0	0.8	0.5	1.9	6.6	13.4	11.5	11.8	11.3	12.9
21139	37140	9	Livingston	313.3	8,959	2,490	28.6	96.0	1.2	1.1	0.7	2.6	4.8	12.3	9.9	11.3	10.6	13.1
21141		6	Logan	552.2	27,771	1,507	50.3	90.2	7.2	0.7	0.6	3.3	6.5	13.5	11.7	11.9	12.0	12.0
21143		9	Lyon	213.8	8,803	2,504	41.2	90.8	6.4	0.9	0.9	2.4	3.0	8.3	9.7	11.8	11.9	13.3
21145	37140	5	McCracken	248.7	67,454	798	271.2	84.8	12.5	0.9	1.4	2.9	5.7	12.7	11.1	12.1	12.1	12.1
21147		9	McCreary	426.8	16,892	1,979	39.6	90.3	6.2	1.4	0.8	2.7	5.7	12.3	11.9	14.5	13.9	13.0
21149	36980	3	McLean	252.5	9,100	2,480	36.0	96.5	1.6	0.8	0.5	2.1	5.7	13.3	12.1	10.6	11.5	12.8
21151	40080	4	Madison	437.4	94,666	640	216.4	91.3	5.5	0.9	1.7	2.8	5.5	11.6	20.7	13.0	11.7	11.8
21153		9	Magoffin	308.4	11,497	2,315	37.3	97.9	0.7	0.7	0.3	1.3	5.9	12.6	11.0	11.6	11.6	13.8
21155		7	Marion	343.0	19,725	1,838	57.5	89.4	8.1	0.6	1.0	2.9	6.1	13.8	12.1	11.9	12.5	12.2
21157		7	Marshall	302.2	31,748	1,386	105.1	96.9	0.9	0.7	0.7	1.9	4.8	11.6	10.7	10.9	11.6	12.7
21159		9	Martin	229.6	11,140	2,333	48.5	89.0	7.3	0.8	0.4	3.5	4.8	11.1	10.7	15.8	13.8	13.3
21161	32500	6	Mason	240.1	16,931	1,977	70.5	90.5	7.8	0.8	1.2	2.3	6.1	13.2	11.5	12.4	11.0	12.7
21163	21060	3	Meade	305.4	30,131	1,435	98.7	90.3	4.8	1.2	1.6	4.2	5.1	13.2	11.8	13.0	14.3	13.1
21165	34460	9	Menifee	203.6	6,194	2,719	30.4	94.9	3.4	0.8	0.5	1.6	4.8	9.2	12.6	10.8	11.3	14.0
21167		6	Mercer	249.1	22,850	1,679	91.7	92.3	4.6	0.7	1.0	3.3	5.6	12.8	11.0	12.0	11.4	12.6
21169	23980	9	Metcalfe	289.6	10,349	2,386	35.7	95.6	2.5	0.7	0.5	2.1	5.8	13.8	11.2	11.7	11.5	12.4
21171		8	Monroe	329.4	11,233	2,328	34.1	94.3	2.7	0.6	0.5	3.2	6.2	13.0	11.3	11.2	11.7	12.5
21173	34460	6	Montgomery	197.4	28,219	1,487	143.0	94.0	3.1	0.6	0.6	3.0	6.2	13.1	11.6	13.1	12.3	13.9
21175		9	Morgan	381.1	13,820	2,164	36.3	92.9	5.2	0.7	1.1	1.1	4.4	10.1	11.3	15.0	13.9	14.3
21177	16420	6	Muhlenberg	467.4	30,694	1,415	65.7	92.9	5.4	0.6	0.5	1.8	5.5	11.4	12.6	12.2	12.1	12.7
21179	12680	6	Nelson	417.5	47,098	1,037	112.8	91.8	6.2	0.6	0.9	2.4	5.9	13.3	11.6	13.1	12.4	12.7
21181		8	Nicholas	195.2	7,712	2,595	39.5	96.4	1.2	0.4	0.4	2.4	5.8	14.6	12.0	11.6	12.1	13.3

1. CBSA = Core Based Statistical Area. See Appendix A for explanation. See Appendix B for list of metropolitan areas with component counties. 2. County type code from the Economic Research Service of USDA Rural-Urban Continuum Codes. See Appendix A for definition. 3. Dry land or land partially or temporarily covered by water. 4. May be of any race.

STATE County	Population, 2021 (cont.)				Population change, 2000–2021							Households, 2016–2020				
	Age (percent) (cont.)				Total persons		Percent change		Components of change, 2020–2021					Percent		
	55 to 64 years	65 to 74 years	75 years and over	Percent female	2010	2020	2010–2020	2020–2021	Births	Deaths	Net Migration	Number	Persons per household	Family house-holds	Female family house-holder[1]	One person
	16	17	18	19	20	21	22	23	24	25	26	27	28	29	30	31
KENTUCKY—Cont'd																
Clay	13.8	10.0	5.9	47.6	21,730	20,345	-6.4	-0.7	269	356	-55	7,432	2.5	73.7	16.1	23.7
Clinton	14.7	12.0	7.9	51.1	10,272	9,253	-9.9	0.1	124	202	91	4,023	2.5	61.7	10.7	35.6
Crittenden	14.4	12.5	8.8	49.3	9,315	8,990	-3.5	-0.5	119	160	-1	3,588	2.4	67.2	10.8	29.2
Cumberland	16.1	13.5	8.9	50.3	6,856	5,888	-14.1	-0.2	86	155	61	2,642	2.5	56.9	11.1	40.0
Daviess	13.2	10.5	7.0	50.9	96,656	103,312	6.9	-0.2	1,479	1,545	-198	40,229	2.4	66.7	11.9	27.4
Edmonson	15.1	12.7	8.3	49.7	12,161	12,126	-0.3	1.4	129	211	250	5,028	2.4	68.9	9.0	26.2
Elliott	12.9	12.2	8.9	42.6	7,852	7,354	-6.3	0.4	58	98	68	2,412	2.5	72.6	8.0	23.6
Estill	15.1	11.7	7.5	50.2	14,672	14,163	-3.5	-0.5	169	268	26	5,640	2.5	65.3	15.7	30.1
Fayette	11.3	9.0	5.4	50.9	295,803	322,570	9.0	-0.2	4,558	3,789	-1,596	130,926	2.4	56.9	11.3	32.4
Fleming	13.4	11.4	6.9	50.7	14,348	15,082	5.1	0.9	229	265	180	5,890	2.5	71.3	9.9	23.5
Floyd	14.3	12.3	6.8	51.1	39,451	35,942	-8.9	-1.9	490	846	-314	14,700	2.4	69.5	15.1	25.9
Franklin	13.6	11.5	6.9	51.4	49,285	51,541	4.6	0.3	630	819	322	21,278	2.3	62.9	14.8	31.6
Fulton	13.8	12.9	8.6	49.8	6,813	6,515	-4.4	0.0	81	134	52	2,550	2.2	61.9	18.9	35.0
Gallatin	14.9	9.6	4.9	49.2	8,589	8,690	1.2	1.0	122	123	89	3,088	2.8	66.7	12.2	27.0
Garrard	16.2	11.6	7.2	50.0	16,912	16,953	0.2	2.4	216	295	495	6,779	2.6	72.2	10.8	23.1
Grant	12.9	8.8	5.4	49.7	24,662	24,941	1.1	1.2	415	372	258	9,210	2.7	71.8	13.9	21.5
Graves	13.7	11.3	7.6	50.8	37,121	36,649	-1.3	-0.1	514	678	128	14,402	2.5	64.8	8.4	29.9
Grayson	14.3	11.5	6.8	49.5	25,746	26,420	2.6	0.4	385	479	198	9,753	2.7	66.2	11.0	29.1
Green	15.6	12.5	8.2	50.1	11,258	11,107	-1.3	1.7	136	206	259	4,440	2.5	67.3	11.3	28.4
Greenup	13.9	12.9	8.8	51.1	36,910	35,962	-2.6	-0.9	388	692	-12	14,314	2.4	68.5	11.3	26.9
Hancock	13.4	10.6	7.2	48.4	8,565	9,095	6.2	-0.3	107	151	11	3,364	2.6	73.7	9.3	21.2
Hardin	12.9	9.1	5.6	49.9	105,543	110,702	4.9	0.8	1,700	1,556	750	42,059	2.5	67.8	12.3	26.8
Harlan	14.1	12.4	6.8	51.8	29,278	26,831	-8.4	-2.5	381	679	-368	10,745	2.4	69.2	14.0	27.3
Harrison	14.9	11.2	6.8	50.6	18,846	18,692	-0.8	1.4	261	318	316	7,474	2.5	71.0	11.1	25.5
Hart	14.9	10.6	6.3	50.3	18,199	19,288	6.0	0.9	298	326	200	7,256	2.6	63.3	10.8	32.6
Henderson	14.1	11.6	7.2	51.3	46,250	44,793	-3.2	-1.0	603	809	-263	18,762	2.4	66.7	12.9	29.2
Henry	14.9	11.6	6.6	50.2	15,416	15,678	1.7	-0.1	208	249	19	6,154	2.6	68.3	13.3	25.2
Hickman	15.2	14.2	11.6	51.9	4,902	4,521	-7.8	-2.1	34	92	-38	1,724	2.5	63.3	11.6	31.4
Hopkins	13.8	11.5	7.5	51.1	46,920	45,423	-3.2	-0.6	630	878	-41	18,619	2.4	65.4	12.7	27.7
Jackson	14.2	11.5	6.5	49.8	13,494	12,955	-4.0	0.2	196	260	93	5,417	2.5	69.0	10.9	27.3
Jefferson	13.1	10.5	6.4	51.4	741,096	782,969	5.7	-0.7	11,486	12,184	-4,476	316,411	2.4	59.0	13.9	34.0
Jessamine	13.2	9.9	6.3	51.2	48,586	52,991	9.1	1.2	734	697	596	18,888	2.7	71.9	14.8	21.5
Johnson	14.1	11.9	7.1	50.4	23,356	22,680	-2.9	-0.5	268	420	25	8,528	2.6	70.9	12.0	25.9
Kenton	13.2	9.8	5.5	50.3	159,720	169,064	5.9	0.3	2,732	2,181	-152	64,544	2.5	62.7	11.2	28.9
Knott	15.4	12.8	7.3	50.4	16,346	14,251	-12.8	-1.4	154	274	-79	6,319	2.3	66.4	13.2	28.5
Knox	13.0	10.3	7.1	51.0	31,883	30,193	-5.3	-0.9	469	647	-109	12,075	2.5	67.3	14.6	29.5
Larue	14.6	10.9	7.2	50.0	14,193	14,867	4.7	1.1	197	228	195	5,779	2.4	67.0	10.7	25.5
Laurel	13.5	10.7	6.4	50.7	58,849	62,613	6.4	-0.1	869	1,075	141	22,665	2.6	71.1	13.1	24.8
Lawrence	13.8	11.9	6.7	49.9	15,860	16,293	2.7	0.0	231	288	51	5,583	2.8	68.2	7.5	29.3
Lee	15.3	11.8	6.0	43.3	7,887	7,395	-6.2	0.8	79	172	151	2,884	2.3	54.6	16.4	40.1
Leslie	15.6	11.9	7.2	49.9	11,310	10,513	-7.0	-2.2	131	210	-155	4,156	2.4	69.2	12.0	27.6
Letcher	15.1	13.2	7.3	50.5	24,519	21,548	-12.1	-1.4	257	456	-98	9,599	2.3	67.7	13.2	28.7
Lewis	15.0	12.0	7.5	49.8	13,870	13,080	-5.7	-0.7	191	237	-47	5,226	2.5	66.7	12.7	30.3
Lincoln	13.9	11.2	7.4	50.9	24,742	24,275	-1.9	-0.1	365	462	64	9,677	2.5	69.9	11.1	25.8
Livingston	15.8	13.5	8.8	50.6	9,519	8,888	-6.6	0.8	99	212	188	3,803	2.4	65.0	10.3	31.1
Logan	13.9	10.8	7.7	50.2	26,835	27,432	2.2	1.2	449	460	352	10,459	2.6	67.3	11.1	27.6
Lyon	16.2	15.8	9.8	43.8	8,314	8,680	4.4	1.4	59	190	259	3,266	2.1	60.1	5.4	34.0
McCracken	13.6	12.2	8.5	52.0	65,565	67,875	3.5	-0.6	857	1,231	-55	27,787	2.3	60.7	11.9	32.7
McCreary	12.6	9.9	6.2	45.1	18,306	16,888	-7.7	0.0	236	281	47	6,187	2.5	65.8	8.7	27.7
McLean	14.0	11.7	8.3	50.5	9,531	9,152	-4.0	-0.6	120	196	22	3,747	2.4	71.1	9.2	26.8
Madison	11.4	8.9	5.4	51.4	82,916	92,701	11.8	2.1	1,213	1,286	2,046	33,876	2.5	64.0	12.2	27.1
Magoffin	14.9	11.7	6.9	49.8	13,333	11,637	-12.7	-1.2	175	216	-100	4,989	2.5	69.5	12.7	29.2
Marion	14.3	10.3	6.7	50.0	19,820	19,581	-1.2	0.7	265	330	209	7,433	2.5	61.2	14.2	33.7
Marshall	15.0	13.4	9.1	50.3	31,448	31,659	0.7	0.3	355	632	370	13,119	2.3	69.8	10.3	26.1
Martin	12.9	11.3	6.3	44.6	12,929	11,287	-12.7	-1.3	132	199	-81	4,045	2.5	68.0	5.7	27.9
Mason	14.0	12.1	6.9	50.9	17,490	17,120	-2.1	-1.1	243	303	-131	6,523	2.6	66.6	13.9	29.1
Meade	14.1	9.9	5.5	49.3	28,602	30,003	4.9	0.4	323	362	166	10,690	2.6	71.4	8.6	22.4
Menifee	16.5	13.3	7.4	49.4	6,306	6,113	-3.1	1.3	90	133	125	2,464	2.6	64.6	4.6	28.0
Mercer	15.5	11.6	7.4	50.6	21,331	22,641	6.1	0.9	280	393	325	8,718	2.5	63.1	8.4	33.3
Metcalfe	14.1	11.5	7.9	49.8	10,099	10,286	1.9	0.6	136	216	146	4,187	2.4	71.9	10.2	24.6
Monroe	14.7	11.5	8.0	49.5	10,963	11,338	3.4	-0.9	141	212	-35	4,533	2.3	65.7	11.3	30.9
Montgomery	13.1	10.3	6.4	51.0	26,499	28,114	6.1	0.4	387	441	157	10,653	2.6	72.5	15.9	20.6
Morgan	13.7	11.2	6.1	42.4	13,923	13,726	-1.4	0.7	153	224	166	4,796	2.4	67.4	11.2	26.4
Muhlenberg	13.7	11.6	8.1	48.6	31,499	30,928	-1.8	-0.8	401	578	-62	11,539	2.6	68.8	8.3	25.1
Nelson	14.2	10.8	6.0	50.3	43,437	46,738	7.6	0.8	637	680	399	17,991	2.5	68.4	10.8	26.6
Nicholas	14.4	9.7	6.4	49.8	7,135	7,537	5.6	2.3	97	140	222	2,714	2.6	69.1	11.7	25.6

1. No spouse present.

STATE County	Persons in group quarters, 2021	Daytime Population, 2016–2020: Number	Daytime Population, 2016–2020: Employment/ residence ratio	Births, 2021: Total	Births, 2021: Rate[1]	Deaths, 2021: Number	Deaths, 2021: Rate[1]	Persons under 65 with no health insurance, 2019: Number	Persons under 65 with no health insurance, 2019: Percent	Medicare, 2021: Total beneficiaries	Medicare, 2021: Enrolled in Original Medicare	Medicare, 2021: Enrolled in Medicare Advantage	COVID-19 Deaths, 2020: Number	COVID-19 Deaths, 2020: Rate[1]
	32	33	34	35	36	37	38	39	40	41	42	43	44	45
KENTUCKY—Cont'd														
Clay	1,625	18,947	0.8	221	10.9	285	14.1	1,382	9.3	4,847	2,399	2,448	22	1.1
Clinton	80	10,715	1.2	102	11.0	160	17.3	723	9.1	2,480	1,750	731	22	2.4
Crittenden	187	8,094	0.8	98	10.9	119	13.3	553	8.2	2,224	1,558	665	11	1.2
Cumberland	42	6,313	0.9	73	12.4	125	21.3	408	8.1	1,812	1,226	586	D	D
Daviess	2,656	102,841	1.0	1,206	11.7	1,209	11.7	6,033	7.4	22,216	14,714	7,502	104	1.0
Edmonson	312	9,602	0.4	112	9.2	167	13.7	888	9.4	2,982	1,864	1,118	20	1.6
Elliott	986	6,681	0.6	43	5.8	76	10.3	336	6.8	1,426	686	740	D	D
Estill	103	11,996	0.5	139	9.8	206	14.6	929	8.4	3,675	2,420	1,255	11	0.8
Fayette	12,705	356,156	1.2	3,631	11.3	2,945	9.1	23,429	8.8	50,444	28,573	21,871	168	0.5
Fleming	19	12,897	0.7	179	11.8	221	14.6	1,220	10.3	3,508	2,140	1,368	18	1.2
Floyd	638	34,484	0.9	405	11.4	671	18.9	2,465	8.7	10,336	6,497	3,839	54	1.5
Franklin	1,821	59,989	1.4	499	9.7	658	12.7	3,134	7.8	14,244	7,572	6,672	44	0.9
Fulton	446	6,157	1.0	70	10.8	109	16.8	290	6.8	1,776	1,129	647	21	3.2
Gallatin	57	7,180	0.6	95	10.9	93	10.7	696	9.2	1,627	861	767	14	1.6
Garrard	55	12,754	0.4	169	9.9	219	12.8	1,336	9.3	4,018	2,549	1,469	25	1.5
Grant	368	20,583	0.6	327	13.0	309	12.3	1,414	6.7	4,984	2,523	2,461	13	0.5
Graves	377	34,518	0.8	410	11.2	531	14.5	2,607	8.7	8,720	5,376	3,344	74	2.0
Grayson	694	24,086	0.8	308	11.6	380	14.4	1,850	8.9	6,346	4,271	2,075	44	1.7
Green	89	9,113	0.5	108	9.6	160	14.3	887	10.4	2,847	1,847	1,000	18	1.6
Greenup	425	30,210	0.6	328	9.2	560	15.7	1,802	6.6	9,539	5,896	3,643	42	1.2
Hancock	86	9,661	1.3	88	9.7	123	13.5	438	6.1	2,002	1,476	526	D	D
Hardin	2,995	113,551	1.1	1,334	12.0	1,213	10.9	5,818	6.3	20,664	14,512	6,152	98	0.9
Harlan	616	26,042	1.0	302	11.4	525	19.9	1,670	8.2	7,412	4,713	2,699	36	1.3
Harrison	214	16,687	0.8	211	11.2	259	13.8	1,177	7.7	4,257	2,719	1,539	11	0.6
Hart	199	17,780	0.9	231	11.9	254	13.1	1,376	8.9	4,224	2,759	1,465	36	1.9
Henderson	1,054	45,213	1.0	478	10.7	654	14.7	2,556	7.1	10,284	6,250	4,034	65	1.5
Henry	47	12,723	0.5	167	10.7	189	12.1	1,240	9.5	3,587	1,893	1,694	10	0.6
Hickman	207	3,920	0.7	28	6.3	77	17.2	271	8.8	1,272	855	417	10	2.2
Hopkins	1,029	44,406	1.0	512	11.3	690	15.2	2,419	6.8	10,843	7,186	3,658	103	2.3
Jackson	62	11,332	0.5	161	12.4	211	16.3	899	8.4	3,195	1,969	1,226	23	1.8
Jefferson	16,932	858,045	1.2	9,278	11.9	9,686	12.4	44,606	7.1	150,001	90,471	59,529	838	1.1
Jessamine	1,464	49,861	0.9	591	11.1	551	10.3	3,632	8.2	9,911	5,569	4,343	53	1.0
Johnson	505	21,182	0.8	220	9.7	349	15.4	1,359	7.8	6,079	3,822	2,257	24	1.1
Kenton	2,545	147,063	0.8	2,188	12.9	1,757	10.4	9,138	6.5	29,461	16,138	13,322	119	0.7
Knott	667	13,325	0.6	129	9.1	213	15.1	964	8.6	3,937	2,284	1,653	11	0.8
Knox	542	30,042	0.9	391	13.0	522	17.4	1,982	8.0	7,826	4,966	2,860	36	1.2
Larue	299	10,811	0.5	158	10.6	179	12.0	968	8.4	3,421	2,238	1,183	10	0.7
Laurel	659	63,582	1.1	709	11.3	858	13.7	4,115	8.3	14,055	8,708	5,348	31	0.5
Lawrence	105	14,105	0.7	188	11.5	228	14.0	1,077	8.7	3,979	2,565	1,415	14	0.9
Lee	986	6,576	0.8	62	8.4	136	18.4	371	7.4	1,820	1,154	666	17	2.3
Leslie	225	8,501	0.5	99	9.5	165	15.9	647	8.3	2,866	1,470	1,395	D	D
Letcher	206	20,308	0.8	212	9.9	352	16.5	1,355	8.0	6,066	3,654	2,412	25	1.2
Lewis	88	11,321	0.5	153	11.7	192	14.7	950	9.0	3,167	1,968	1,199	32	2.5
Lincoln	164	20,389	0.6	296	12.2	370	15.3	1,863	9.5	6,004	3,864	2,140	39	1.6
Livingston	41	7,879	0.7	80	9.0	165	18.5	552	7.8	2,622	1,852	770	21	2.4
Logan	230	25,749	0.9	344	12.4	358	13.0	1,811	8.3	6,218	4,191	2,027	43	1.6
Lyon	1,152	8,117	1.0	49	5.6	160	18.3	422	8.5	2,374	1,617	758	16	1.8
McCracken	1,157	76,507	1.4	679	10.0	980	14.5	3,612	7.0	16,434	11,212	5,222	82	1.2
McCreary	1,807	15,674	0.7	195	11.6	228	13.5	1,090	8.7	3,883	2,592	1,291	11	0.7
McLean	59	7,783	0.6	98	10.8	154	16.9	543	7.4	2,385	1,499	886	16	1.8
Madison	6,263	89,114	0.9	979	10.4	1,029	11.0	5,166	7.0	17,034	9,376	7,659	70	0.8
Magoffin	86	11,378	0.7	142	12.3	171	14.8	982	10.0	3,255	1,855	1,401	12	1.0
Marion	466	20,419	1.2	211	10.7	262	13.3	1,175	7.5	4,190	2,831	1,359	28	1.4
Marshall	423	30,556	1.0	271	8.5	499	15.7	1,723	7.2	8,633	5,872	2,761	38	1.2
Martin	1,360	11,508	1.0	104	9.3	145	13.0	617	7.9	2,788	1,763	1,025	D	D
Mason	253	18,258	1.2	200	11.8	227	13.3	1,114	8.2	4,026	2,495	1,531	24	1.4
Meade	207	21,637	0.5	268	8.9	281	9.3	1,548	6.4	5,494	3,726	1,768	15	0.5
Menifee	216	5,303	0.5	72	11.7	106	17.2	406	8.1	1,750	922	828	D	D
Mercer	112	19,694	0.8	226	9.9	308	13.5	1,401	7.9	5,350	3,252	2,098	28	1.2
Metcalfe	106	8,515	0.6	110	10.7	169	16.4	652	8.2	2,566	1,557	1,009	18	1.8
Monroe	140	9,668	0.8	117	10.4	171	15.2	867	10.3	2,709	1,886	823	38	3.4
Montgomery	295	28,437	1.0	321	11.4	360	12.8	1,738	7.5	6,045	3,386	2,660	20	0.7
Morgan	1,848	13,115	1.0	119	8.6	176	12.8	844	9.4	3,041	1,650	1,390	D	D
Muhlenberg	2,017	28,820	0.8	321	10.4	479	15.6	1,934	8.3	7,703	4,742	2,961	43	1.4
Nelson	433	41,322	0.8	519	11.1	546	11.6	2,420	6.3	10,040	6,778	3,262	39	0.8
Nicholas	91	5,433	0.4	79	10.4	118	15.5	610	10.3	1,742	1,130	612	D	D

1. Per 1,000 estimated resident population.

STATE County	COVID-19 Vaccinations, 2021–2022: Number	COVID-19 Vaccinations, 2021–2022: Percent[5]	Education: School enrollment and attainment, 2016–2020: Enrollment[1]: Total	Enrollment[1]: Percent private	Attainment[2] (percent): High school graduate or less	Attainment[2] (percent): Bachelor's degree or more	Local government expenditures,[3] 2018–2019: Total current spending (mil dol)	Local government expenditures,[3] 2018–2019: Current spending per student (dollars)	Money income, 2016–2020: Per capita income[4]	Households: Median income (dollars)	Households: Percent with income of less than $50,000	Households: Percent with income of $200,000 or more	Income and poverty, 2020: Median household income (dollars)	Percent below poverty level: All persons	Percent below poverty level: Children under 18 years	Percent below poverty level: Children 5 to 17 years in families
	46	47	48	49	50	51	52	53	54	55	56	57	58	59	60	61
KENTUCKY—Cont'd																
Clay	8,865	44.5	3,593	7.8	71.1	9.5	35.3	10,895	15,905	27,479	70.2	1.0	26,866	37.3	47.5	45.1
Clinton	4,182	40.9	2,021	5.2	64.6	12.3	20.1	11,129	21,730	33,092	68.3	1.8	37,428	21.5	31.7	28.9
Crittenden	3,608	41.0	1,965	12.8	60.6	13.6	14.0	10,007	24,732	46,354	53.8	2.6	46,844	16.8	26.9	24.4
Cumberland	2,964	44.8	1,099	13.8	61.0	14.9	11.2	11,740	20,685	35,030	63.1	1.1	38,275	21.0	31.0	29.8
Daviess	55,094	54.3	24,128	15.8	42.9	24.4	185.9	11,108	30,186	54,881	45.9	3.6	54,948	13.4	16.0	14.6
Edmonson	4,211	34.7	2,086	9.4	61.1	10.4	19.6	10,069	22,818	44,229	54.3	0.9	44,459	15.8	22.0	22.0
Elliott	2,681	35.7	1,304	3.6	69.2	9.3	11.2	10,849	13,857	36,950	62.0	0.2	35,030	28.8	35.5	34.7
Estill	7,327	51.9	2,738	5.4	69.6	11.5	24.0	9,994	18,609	32,800	66.2	0.6	39,719	20.6	28.8	27.2
Fayette	215,606	66.7	90,082	15.4	27.1	45.0	538.8	12,832	35,466	58,954	42.8	6.9	60,215	14.6	16.3	14.8
Fleming	7,560	51.8	3,211	7.9	59.2	15.3	23.8	10,526	23,512	42,087	56.3	2.4	44,691	14.6	23.9	23.7
Floyd	20,344	57.2	7,302	11.0	62.5	11.9	65.0	11,207	19,932	35,096	65.5	1.4	35,087	28.3	40.9	37.2
Franklin	31,337	61.5	11,727	17.6	39.4	30.7	78.3	10,707	31,994	59,056	41.5	3.9	59,911	12.8	18.3	17.3
Fulton	3,519	59.0	1,191	3.4	58.1	13.4	11.7	11,995	19,149	31,587	72.4	0.5	36,421	25.2	38.4	36.1
Gallatin	3,654	41.2	1,817	7.7	65.7	9.6	17.7	11,227	23,057	55,113	43.4	0.3	55,650	13.3	19.6	18.5
Garrard	8,533	48.3	3,311	11.1	52.6	20.1	28.5	10,732	27,179	55,369	45.5	3.2	54,951	14.0	18.3	16.9
Grant	12,295	49.0	5,996	12.4	59.7	13.8	47.8	10,511	25,292	56,746	45.4	2.6	56,274	12.8	18.1	16.9
Graves	17,021	45.7	8,170	7.9	53.4	16.5	64.4	10,309	25,557	45,614	52.8	2.7	44,475	18.2	24.0	22.8
Grayson	13,591	51.4	5,471	9.0	62.1	10.9	43.2	10,145	21,339	38,262	62.6	2.3	42,297	20.5	25.2	23.3
Green	4,783	43.7	2,001	11.2	64.6	11.6	17.6	10,536	23,407	33,846	63.5	1.6	41,322	20.1	26.0	24.6
Greenup	18,348	52.3	7,911	5.6	47.3	16.4	64.4	10,418	27,496	52,337	46.7	4.1	55,777	13.0	17.6	16.4
Hancock	5,171	59.3	2,106	8.8	57.1	14.2	18.6	11,101	25,891	56,265	44.0	0.9	57,111	14.4	18.9	14.3
Hardin	69,852	63.0	26,909	13.0	38.2	22.0	182.0	10,480	30,779	57,101	44.3	3.6	56,557	11.2	14.3	13.6
Harlan	12,070	46.4	5,622	9.9	59.9	10.4	48.9	10,500	17,385	28,261	70.5	1.1	30,745	28.0	36.5	33.7
Harrison	9,479	50.2	3,498	7.6	56.0	16.6	30.1	10,165	25,226	50,270	49.7	2.1	55,934	13.5	18.6	18.1
Hart	6,796	35.7	3,610	7.9	65.0	11.4	27.2	11,285	21,542	39,834	59.9	2.5	41,608	22.1	27.6	26.8
Henderson	23,130	51.2	9,801	9.7	50.2	18.2	76.8	10,328	27,490	50,471	49.4	2.6	54,701	13.4	18.9	16.6
Henry	8,687	53.9	3,306	15.2	59.3	12.9	32.9	10,948	24,823	52,550	48.7	1.4	53,170	14.2	17.9	15.7
Hickman	1,642	37.5	865	2.1	53.0	22.7	9.1	11,801	30,609	44,063	52.4	7.5	46,553	20.9	33.7	31.6
Hopkins	23,159	51.8	9,923	11.8	52.2	16.1	74.9	10,161	24,883	47,014	53.6	2.0	47,631	18.1	23.6	20.1
Jackson	4,899	36.8	2,726	7.0	72.6	10.2	25.6	11,994	17,573	31,515	67.1	1.1	35,889	24.0	33.8	31.9
Jefferson	490,947	64.0	175,576	25.3	35.3	33.9	1,392.0	14,151	34,365	58,196	42.8	5.7	62,067	11.4	15.4	15.1
Jessamine	29,171	53.9	13,928	24.9	42.7	29.2	87.2	10,360	33,110	64,855	38.6	7.1	67,610	10.5	15.6	14.3
Johnson	11,179	50.4	4,969	8.8	58.1	15.5	48.6	11,131	22,196	38,333	60.0	1.9	40,455	22.5	28.0	27.1
Kenton	101,088	60.5	40,712	23.9	36.9	33.8	251.5	10,920	34,936	66,541	37.3	6.2	66,015	11.0	13.6	12.5
Knott	7,101	48.0	3,314	22.7	57.5	15.7	26.7	11,715	18,723	32,531	68.3	1.0	33,253	27.7	35.5	32.1
Knox	11,380	36.5	7,239	11.2	63.1	15.1	58.0	11,467	17,665	30,257	67.3	1.3	31,568	27.8	36.1	33.8
Larue	6,304	43.8	2,907	15.4	52.5	15.3	26.3	11,150	24,231	48,495	51.5	2.2	50,980	14.7	19.5	19.0
Laurel	24,674	40.6	13,641	10.4	56.0	16.1	94.2	9,800	23,283	43,745	54.8	2.4	50,743	17.9	25.1	24.1
Lawrence	7,428	48.5	2,989	8.7	68.2	9.2	26.5	10,513	17,882	32,856	66.3	1.1	38,213	22.3	29.7	27.8
Lee	3,697	49.9	1,346	11.1	68.7	7.5	9.8	10,505	17,946	24,699	74.2	1.5	30,575	32.1	40.7	39.5
Leslie	5,162	52.3	1,817	7.8	62.4	9.4	19.1	10,663	18,011	36,038	67.1	0.2	39,098	25.8	31.8	30.1
Letcher	11,464	53.2	4,656	12.6	58.2	10.8	40.8	11,794	22,103	33,181	67.2	1.4	36,259	24.4	28.8	27.7
Lewis	5,198	39.2	2,619	6.2	65.3	8.7	23.1	10,291	18,853	29,844	65.5	0.7	39,288	22.2	32.1	31.9
Lincoln	10,065	41.0	5,155	12.2	62.0	12.6	41.3	10,933	21,716	42,231	58.3	1.7	43,748	18.4	22.8	22.0
Livingston	4,547	49.5	1,690	17.6	54.9	14.5	15.6	12,932	28,504	52,795	48.2	1.9	52,994	14.0	20.1	18.8
Logan	13,803	50.9	5,985	5.9	56.5	17.2	49.2	10,837	25,026	48,912	51.2	2.1	51,905	15.1	21.1	20.0
Lyon	4,793	58.4	1,269	5.7	52.4	15.5	9.5	9,967	26,993	49,286	50.6	1.0	51,970	14.4	18.8	16.9
McCracken	36,529	55.8	14,093	8.8	40.0	25.6	110.0	10,679	30,044	47,011	52.0	3.7	50,650	15.5	21.2	19.5
McCreary	6,760	39.2	3,625	15.8	63.2	8.5	31.8	11,066	16,016	29,499	69.3	1.1	31,453	36.2	40.9	38.8
McLean	4,707	51.1	2,080	11.7	52.0	14.6	16.0	10,206	27,855	54,181	46.0	1.7	48,088	13.6	18.0	16.0
Madison	44,665	48.0	27,774	15.7	38.4	32.1	128.4	9,930	26,528	51,649	48.2	3.2	55,336	15.5	16.9	14.6
Magoffin	6,237	51.3	2,402	11.9	65.9	10.5	23.4	11,056	17,939	27,807	71.2	1.3	32,389	30.9	38.6	33.5
Marion	9,743	50.6	4,520	10.0	60.5	14.3	35.9	10,943	22,747	43,587	54.3	1.3	57,062	15.7	20.4	20.1
Marshall	16,704	53.7	6,002	9.2	45.1	20.8	50.0	10,477	30,564	57,348	44.0	3.7	56,286	10.3	14.8	13.6
Martin	6,071	54.2	2,154	12.3	59.2	10.7	21.1	11,143	19,063	42,894	59.5	0.8	30,320	31.9	37.2	33.4
Mason	8,707	51.0	3,853	10.1	47.0	21.4	29.1	10,819	29,371	46,241	52.4	3.5	49,216	15.7	22.8	21.3
Meade	11,223	39.3	6,408	10.5	46.0	18.4	46.3	9,497	29,173	61,500	39.0	2.6	56,845	11.6	15.3	13.6
Menifee	2,888	44.5	1,290	5.7	67.7	11.9	11.6	11,631	20,283	46,746	54.2	0.3	40,773	22.7	35.4	34.6
Mercer	11,972	54.6	4,655	10.1	49.5	18.7	36.8	11,037	27,748	52,312	46.6	2.9	53,743	13.1	18.6	17.8
Metcalfe	4,091	40.6	2,048	12.0	61.1	13.1	17.0	10,846	20,182	40,391	62.3	0.8	39,993	21.4	33.6	31.9
Monroe	4,928	46.3	2,092	7.1	62.3	13.4	22.8	12,652	24,007	35,078	60.9	2.9	38,449	22.5	32.1	30.6
Montgomery	13,147	46.7	5,998	10.4	56.2	15.6	46.4	9,920	22,437	46,998	51.1	1.3	51,234	15.7	20.5	19.0
Morgan	6,424	48.3	2,201	7.9	63.6	15.0	21.3	10,845	18,919	37,399	62.7	1.9	38,274	24.5	30.2	27.9
Muhlenberg	15,646	51.1	6,094	8.4	59.1	13.1	51.7	11,116	25,692	45,937	53.7	4.6	45,599	16.9	21.9	20.8
Nelson	24,205	52.4	10,355	19.1	43.8	19.3	79.0	10,699	30,856	63,032	39.4	3.2	68,264	9.2	13.6	12.5
Nicholas	3,861	53.1	1,436	13.0	65.0	8.9	11.3	10,059	24,356	47,665	53.1	2.5	48,290	16.8	26.8	25.1

1. All persons 3 years old and over enrolled in nursery school through college. 2. Persons 25 years old and over. 3. Elementary and secondary education expenditures. 4. Based on population estimated by the American Community Survey, 2016–2020. 5. CDC percent based on 2019 population estimate.

STATE County	Personal income, 2020										Earnings, 2020		
			Per capita[1]			Supplements to wages and salaries, employer contributions (mil dol)						Contributions for government social insurance (mil dol)	
	Total (mil dol)	Percent change 2019–2020	Dollars	Rank	Wages and salaries (mil dol)	Pension and insurance	Government social insurance	Proprietors' income (mil dol)	Dividends, interest, and rent (mil dol)	Personal transfer reecipts (mil dol)	Total (mil dol)	From employee and self-employed	From employer
	62	63	64	65	66	67	68	69	70	71	72	73	74
KENTUCKY—Cont'd													
Clay	692	13.0	35,259	2,924	162	40	12	29	56	394	243	21	12
Clinton	360	11.8	35,609	2,901	133	30	12	19	34	179	193	15	12
Crittenden	353	10.4	39,879	2,469	68	17	5	31	44	138	121	9	5
Cumberland	291	22.1	44,628	1,857	84	18	6	37	25	135	145	11	6
Daviess	4,729	8.9	46,373	1,593	2,136	378	164	276	745	1,444	2,954	199	164
Edmonson	455	9.4	37,223	2,769	62	17	5	25	48	182	109	9	5
Elliott	199	15.2	27,001	3,104	31	9	2	6	20	111	49	4	2
Estill	516	10.6	36,569	2,816	93	20	8	14	45	237	135	14	8
Fayette	17,803	5.7	54,824	714	10,544	1,888	777	1,291	4,184	3,478	14,499	849	777
Fleming	582	13.9	39,846	2,474	137	29	11	63	58	215	240	18	11
Floyd	1,445	9.6	41,330	2,287	431	89	33	115	148	764	668	53	33
Franklin	2,403	8.5	47,009	1,513	1,556	339	109	97	426	770	2,102	128	109
Fulton	237	12.1	39,745	2,481	76	18	7	21	30	111	122	9	7
Gallatin	335	10.8	38,178	2,668	140	25	10	10	31	104	186	13	10
Garrard	688	9.6	38,822	2,587	89	19	7	34	87	230	150	15	7
Grant	1,035	10.1	40,772	2,363	220	41	17	46	104	341	325	28	17
Graves	1,556	8.2	42,264	2,159	493	97	39	149	197	567	778	54	39
Grayson	1,032	11.6	38,959	2,569	302	63	24	63	125	406	453	35	24
Green	439	14.1	39,882	2,468	67	15	5	36	43	188	124	11	5
Greenup	1,600	8.0	45,897	1,665	339	68	30	61	176	598	498	43	30
Hancock	352	-1.2	40,261	2,424	292	48	21	8	39	116	369	26	21
Hardin	5,329	8.0	47,873	1,410	2,630	640	220	372	827	1,531	3,861	226	220
Harlan	916	12.2	35,824	2,882	224	51	17	26	83	558	318	30	17
Harrison	777	12.0	41,079	2,326	231	49	18	48	98	260	345	27	18
Hart	711	9.3	37,418	2,747	203	42	17	124	84	260	385	27	17
Henderson	2,004	7.1	44,793	1,825	853	160	67	112	262	652	1,192	81	67
Henry	698	8.9	43,426	2,019	117	26	9	37	92	216	189	17	9
Hickman	203	7.4	46,425	1,590	32	8	3	47	25	80	90	4	3
Hopkins	1,917	6.7	42,918	2,072	758	137	60	113	262	697	1,069	76	60
Jackson	442	10.9	33,106	3,022	61	18	5	15	40	205	98	10	5
Jefferson	44,407	6.5	57,863	521	28,648	4,186	2,160	3,335	8,179	10,368	38,329	2,445	2,160
Jessamine	2,671	5.7	49,406	1,210	777	134	61	297	415	593	1,268	81	61
Johnson	831	8.7	37,769	2,708	198	43	15	26	99	416	282	25	15
Kenton	10,497	6.5	62,500	333	4,379	675	317	894	2,366	1,980	6,264	402	317
Knott	518	10.6	35,697	2,893	86	19	7	17	40	296	128	14	7
Knox	1,048	12.8	33,797	2,989	286	65	22	44	93	554	417	33	22
Larue	611	10.7	42,333	2,151	97	21	8	33	78	209	159	13	8
Laurel	2,319	11.2	37,869	2,697	1,049	190	88	138	224	903	1,464	102	88
Lawrence	563	10.6	36,446	2,829	137	28	12	21	54	278	198	18	12
Lee	238	11.8	32,694	3,042	65	13	5	9	21	136	92	8	5
Leslie	373	10.7	38,666	2,610	60	14	5	13	26	219	92	10	5
Letcher	759	11.5	35,770	2,887	161	35	12	26	59	456	235	24	12
Lewis	488	14.0	36,806	2,797	75	17	6	27	41	220	124	12	6
Lincoln	913	10.9	37,303	2,763	159	34	12	60	115	365	265	25	12
Livingston	392	10.9	43,379	2,022	137	25	11	25	50	150	199	15	11
Logan	1,123	11.8	40,963	2,338	430	81	34	134	133	389	680	46	34
Lyon	332	6.4	40,843	2,348	92	22	7	13	53	126	133	11	7
McCracken	3,425	7.6	52,171	923	1,870	330	144	269	594	1,024	2,612	174	144
McCreary	528	14.8	30,943	3,078	119	33	10	18	54	305	179	16	10
McLean	392	7.4	43,162	2,040	68	15	5	45	43	141	133	10	5
Madison	3,685	10.0	39,093	2,559	1,493	308	118	118	452	1,110	2,037	137	118
Magoffin	457	12.6	38,033	2,681	64	15	5	15	44	255	100	11	5
Marion	796	9.7	41,225	2,300	353	70	29	55	94	282	508	34	29
Marshall	1,433	8.3	45,975	1,656	615	114	48	76	209	483	852	62	48
Martin	357	8.7	32,383	3,048	90	25	7	8	52	218	130	12	7
Mason	775	9.7	45,488	1,727	367	80	29	53	115	256	528	35	29
Meade	1,280	7.9	44,720	1,844	188	41	14	51	178	349	295	23	14
Menifee	231	12.2	35,489	2,908	36	9	3	7	21	113	56	6	3
Mercer	898	8.1	41,025	2,335	310	67	26	58	122	311	461	34	26
Metcalfe	360	11.7	35,804	2,885	76	18	6	23	35	165	123	11	6
Monroe	450	12.8	42,638	2,111	126	27	10	60	40	189	223	16	10
Montgomery	1,115	9.4	39,549	2,496	429	78	36	62	124	379	604	44	36
Morgan	414	10.0	31,500	3,068	111	30	8	22	45	196	171	14	8
Muhlenberg	1,137	6.5	37,328	2,759	337	72	27	49	137	474	484	38	27
Nelson	2,220	8.9	47,784	1,420	763	139	60	100	273	598	1,062	76	60
Nicholas	286	11.6	39,531	2,499	32	8	3	16	29	115	58	6	3

1. Based on the resident population estimated as of July 1 of the year shown.

STATE County	Earnings, 2020 (cont.) — Percent by selected industries: Farm	Mining, quarrying, and extractions	Construction	Manu-facturing	Information; professional, scientific, technical services	Retail trade	Finance, insurance, real estate, and leasing	Health care and social assistance	Govern-ment	Social Security beneficiaries, December 2020: Number	Rate[1]	Supple-mental Security Income recipients, 2020	Housing units, 2021: Total	Percent change, 2010–2021
	75	76	77	78	79	80	81	82	83	84	85	86	87	88
KENTUCKY—Cont'd														
Clay	0.7	0.6	3.0	3.1	3.2	7.4	2.9	D	38.1	5,295	262	2,777	8,626	0.4
Clinton	3.7	-0.2	3.7	38.6	1.2	5.4	D	15.0	15.0	2,735	295	740	4,857	0.3
Crittenden	10.9	D	D	19.3	D	6.8	4.9	13.8	17.4	2,440	273	252	4,338	0.1
Cumberland	1.9	0.1	D	5.9	D	3.5	3.2	49.7	12.4	1,960	333	379	3,388	0.2
Daviess	2.4	0.4	4.9	16.6	4.3	7.2	9.5	20.7	11.1	24,070	234	3,187	44,193	0.6
Edmonson	7.9	0.0	17.1	4.1	D	5.4	D	D	37.3	3,230	263	356	6,394	0.5
Elliott	1.3	0.0	4.8	0.3	D	3.8	D	9.5	59.7	1,760	238	420	3,049	0.7
Estill	-0.4	2.0	5.5	D	2.6	7.3	4.6	19.6	25.2	3,800	270	1,175	6,840	0.2
Fayette	1.2	0.2	7.0	7.0	10.9	5.8	5.9	12.8	25.8	51,555	160	6,485	147,594	0.8
Fleming	6.8	D	13.4	12.4	2.1	7.3	8.1	D	15.4	4,050	266	643	6,762	0.4
Floyd	0.1	3.9	6.4	5.2	9.1	8.1	2.1	24.2	18.1	11,505	326	3,623	17,429	0.5
Franklin	0.2	D	3.2	10.1	6.9	4.3	4.6	D	43.4	14,570	282	1,432	24,073	0.3
Fulton	14.8	D	3.3	17.6	D	11.1	D	D	21.4	1,880	289	415	3,171	-0.2
Gallatin	1.3	0.0	2.6	D	D	3.4	D	6.8	12.7	1,300	148	178	3,756	1.7
Garrard	-0.6	D	24.5	D	6.2	4.9	4.3	D	23.1	4,390	253	608	7,262	0.1
Grant	-1.1	0.0	D	13.3	D	11.1	3.6	D	20.2	5,930	235	799	10,143	0.7
Graves	9.4	D	5.3	15.6	4.5	8.1	5.1	11.2	14.8	9,365	256	1,380	16,502	0.2
Grayson	2.4	D	9.8	26.2	D	7.3	3.3	D	20.4	7,180	271	1,217	13,325	0.3
Green	11.1	0.1	D	3.5	5.2	6.5	5.3	19.6	20.2	3,130	277	510	5,283	0.2
Greenup	-0.1	D	D	12.1	9.4	6.8	3.6	18.2	16.8	9,275	260	1,305	16,246	0.1
Hancock	1.5	-1.0	3.3	77.9	D	1.2	0.6	D	6.6	2,260	249	270	3,908	0.3
Hardin	0.4	D	3.2	13.8	7.2	6.1	4.5	6.8	43.0	22,910	205	3,309	47,324	1.2
Harlan	-0.1	D	2.4	1.3	5.4	8.7	2.4	24.2	27.7	8,200	313	2,466	12,993	0.2
Harrison	1.1	0.0	9.1	31.4	3.6	6.3	1.7	D	13.2	4,710	249	703	8,130	0.7
Hart	4.3	D	D	41.1	D	4.1	1.6	D	11.6	4,595	236	836	8,875	0.6
Henderson	3.5	0.2	5.6	29.0	3.1	6.0	5.5	D	12.4	11,100	250	1,547	20,109	0.2
Henry	3.9	D	8.9	16.0	D	5.0	3.8	D	23.9	3,950	252	488	6,666	0.9
Hickman	44.8	0.0	D	D	D	D	D	8.3	13.1	1,365	309	162	2,154	0.1
Hopkins	3.7	D	8.5	14.5	D	7.0	4.0	17.4	15.7	11,720	260	1,802	20,985	0.3
Jackson	-0.3	D	7.5	3.8	D	5.2	3.9	14.4	33.0	3,465	267	1,133	5,978	0.3
Jefferson	0.0	0.0	5.0	12.6	10.3	5.0	13.5	13.8	10.0	155,210	200	24,242	357,918	0.1
Jessamine	8.0	D	9.6	13.8	5.0	11.3	3.5	5.8	11.2	10,625	198	1,276	20,883	1.0
Johnson	-0.4	D	4.9	0.4	7.7	16.2	4.4	D	26.5	6,720	298	1,860	10,528	0.3
Kenton	0.0	0.0	9.9	8.6	8.0	4.3	12.7	15.9	10.8	30,565	180	3,493	72,766	0.2
Knott	-0.2	D	5.9	0.3	14.1	5.4	D	D	28.3	4,130	294	1,344	6,689	0.6
Knox	-0.1	0.4	3.7	13.4	8.2	10.5	3.3	D	20.6	8,080	270	2,854	13,803	0.5
Larue	8.9	0.0	11.1	15.2	D	4.7	5.8	9.6	21.5	3,765	251	491	6,516	0.5
Laurel	0.1	0.7	4.3	15.7	D	10.9	4.7	13.9	11.4	14,955	239	2,910	26,668	0.4
Lawrence	-0.1	D	6.4	1.0	D	9.7	D	34.0	18.5	4,380	269	1,277	7,567	0.5
Lee	-0.6	3.3	D	D	D	7.4	2.2	20.7	21.3	1,910	256	703	3,225	0.4
Leslie	-0.1	D	D	D	D	7.1	D	D	29.1	3,175	309	955	4,906	0.6
Letcher	-0.1	5.8	2.8	1.2	D	11.5	2.5	30.4	22.8	7,170	337	1,855	10,575	0.4
Lewis	2.4	0.0	13.9	10.8	D	3.8	D	15.7	24.6	3,315	255	886	6,048	0.3
Lincoln	4.5	0.2	D	10.6	9.2	7.0	4.1	11.1	19.1	6,460	266	1,434	10,857	0.6
Livingston	3.8	19.7	20.2	3.1	D	2.9	D	8.0	15.7	2,850	318	276	4,609	0.4
Logan	7.8	D	8.1	41.5	2.8	5.2	2.8	5.1	9.7	6,830	246	878	12,465	0.0
Lyon	1.6	-0.3	7.2	D	D	5.5	2.4	D	38.8	2,570	292	189	4,814	0.6
McCracken	0.2	D	6.2	5.4	10.5	8.4	5.2	22.6	11.0	17,330	257	2,105	32,148	0.3
McCreary	-1.2	D	D	10.7	2.0	6.3	3.4	6.9	51.0	4,245	251	1,585	6,917	0.3
McLean	26.2	D	4.9	7.3	D	5.7	D	5.2	18.3	2,595	285	272	4,167	0.1
Madison	0.1	D	6.8	16.8	11.8	8.5	3.7	9.1	24.2	18,485	195	2,923	39,811	1.1
Magoffin	-1.0	D	D	D	D	7.9	D	17.0	28.7	3,620	315	1,358	5,454	0.8
Marion	3.3	0.0	D	47.2	D	4.5	3.1	D	10.0	4,560	231	866	8,426	0.8
Marshall	1.4	D	18.5	33.7	D	6.7	4.0	D	11.2	9,325	294	736	16,461	0.6
Martin	-0.1	D	2.2	D	D	7.4	D	10.4	53.2	3,165	284	1,074	4,828	0.6
Mason	2.1	0.0	9.1	19.3	D	8.0	3.1	D	12.4	4,420	261	620	8,180	0.3
Meade	2.8	3.5	12.7	15.1	5.3	9.4	5.6	5.7	18.8	6,215	206	525	12,108	1.2
Menifee	-0.4	D	D	12.8	D	4.4	D	D	34.3	1,975	319	486	3,295	0.5
Mercer	0.9	D	7.4	37.0	D	5.5	2.7	D	10.6	5,840	256	673	10,409	0.6
Metcalfe	5.6	0.1	D	33.4	2.7	4.0	2.9	7.2	19.7	2,885	279	551	4,708	0.3
Monroe	11.4	0.0	11.2	15.1	2.6	6.7	5.1	D	13.5	2,900	258	588	5,248	0.2
Montgomery	0.5	D	D	33.1	D	9.7	5.2	D	11.2	6,685	237	1,193	12,201	0.5
Morgan	0.7	D	D	11.1	D	6.3	D	10.2	32.7	3,295	238	866	5,644	0.4
Muhlenberg	4.8	5.8	3.8	11.7	3.8	8.5	2.9	16.3	24.6	8,325	271	1,207	13,532	0.3
Nelson	1.1	D	10.1	34.6	3.2	7.1	4.6	9.6	10.5	11,025	234	1,168	20,049	1.3
Nicholas	10.1	0.0	16.4	6.2	D	4.2	D	13.8	26.4	1,865	242	287	3,325	0.2

1. Per 1,000 resident population estimated as of July 1 of the year shown.

STATE County	Housing units, 2016–2020: Total	Occupied units: Owner-occupied: Percent	Owner-occupied: Median value[1]	Median owner cost as a percent of income: With a mortgage	Median owner cost as a percent of income: Without a mortgage[2]	Renter-occupied: Median rent[3]	Renter-occupied: Median rent as a percent of income[2]	Sub-standard units[4] (percent)	Civilian labor force, 2021: Total	Percent change, 2020–2021	Unemployment: Total	Unemployment: Rate[5]	Civilian employment[6], 2016–2020: Total	Percent: Management, business, science, and arts	Percent: Construction, production, and maintenance occupations
	89	90	91	92	93	94	95	96	97	98	99	100	101	102	103
KENTUCKY—Cont'd															
Clay	7,432	68.9	61,300	19.5	10.9	535	29.8	3.7	5,187	0.4	352	6.8	5,722	23.2	33.9
Clinton	4,023	69.9	77,900	22.6	11.3	511	21.5	2.5	3,960	0.2	176	4.4	3,808	28.0	31.0
Crittenden	3,588	82.7	97,200	19.3	11.5	630	23.0	1.4	3,809	3.7	165	4.3	3,604	23.4	39.3
Cumberland	2,642	72.3	110,000	23.0	11.5	467	23.2	2.0	3,307	1.6	116	3.5	2,628	29.7	40.6
Daviess	40,229	66.6	143,500	19.7	10.0	809	26.3	3.0	46,297	1.0	2,007	4.3	46,273	33.2	29.0
Edmonson	5,028	84.4	91,900	18.7	11.0	624	22.0	4.4	4,655	1.4	237	5.1	4,669	27.4	33.1
Elliott	2,412	77.6	76,600	18.1	11.4	801	19.7	2.8	1,892	-3.0	158	8.4	1,762	27.6	42.4
Estill	5,640	69.6	78,200	19.1	11.5	610	26.6	4.1	5,137	0.0	266	5.2	4,806	20.8	40.5
Fayette	130,926	54.6	200,900	18.3	10.0	920	28.8	2.4	173,189	0.8	6,796	3.9	168,366	44.8	17.0
Fleming	5,890	72.9	91,100	18.4	10.0	588	24.7	3.6	6,049	-1.0	299	4.9	5,726	32.0	36.5
Floyd	14,700	71.4	74,000	21.2	12.0	644	29.6	1.9	10,797	1.4	764	7.1	11,076	30.4	24.9
Franklin	21,278	62.4	149,900	18.7	10.0	792	23.6	2.2	25,190	1.9	1,109	4.4	24,045	39.6	21.0
Fulton	2,550	65.9	63,800	19.9	13.2	593	33.5	4.2	2,075	4.5	110	5.3	2,088	25.6	30.2
Gallatin	3,088	73.2	135,100	19.3	10.2	711	24.1	2.3	4,000	1.3	172	4.3	3,890	19.8	41.2
Garrard	6,779	85.0	144,900	19.6	10.4	718	30.5	1.3	7,629	1.5	340	4.5	7,773	31.3	30.8
Grant	9,210	70.0	141,600	18.3	10.0	727	24.1	2.1	11,637	0.4	524	4.5	11,307	21.9	41.4
Graves	14,402	74.2	109,000	17.7	11.3	660	29.8	3.3	15,892	2.1	706	4.4	15,559	29.7	35.2
Grayson	9,753	73.6	118,100	22.1	11.2	583	30.4	3.1	10,512	-1.2	589	5.6	10,669	23.7	42.9
Green	4,440	72.2	80,600	24.5	10.0	515	26.8	2.4	5,177	0.6	193	3.7	4,184	21.8	37.9
Greenup	14,314	78.0	114,900	18.0	10.0	732	27.3	1.4	13,020	-1.0	890	6.8	13,934	37.1	25.9
Hancock	3,364	81.0	113,600	16.5	10.0	671	25.7	1.2	3,848	0.9	168	4.4	3,742	23.2	44.0
Hardin	42,059	61.0	157,700	18.7	10.0	811	23.4	2.1	47,078	-1.2	2,233	4.7	47,832	33.9	27.5
Harlan	10,745	69.4	64,100	21.6	11.7	541	31.6	3.2	6,466	-0.6	558	8.6	6,804	27.9	30.0
Harrison	7,474	70.4	146,800	19.3	10.7	621	25.4	3.4	8,766	1.1	340	3.9	8,573	26.6	40.2
Hart	7,256	74.1	93,000	18.0	10.9	559	27.7	3.1	7,645	0.1	338	4.4	7,607	23.6	39.5
Henderson	18,762	63.6	133,200	18.3	10.0	692	26.9	1.0	20,775	0.5	932	4.5	20,452	30.0	32.8
Henry	6,154	70.6	134,100	19.8	11.1	842	29.9	3.8	8,151	1.6	326	4.0	6,907	21.5	32.9
Hickman	1,724	80.2	85,000	21.5	10.0	572	22.4	3.2	1,719	0.1	77	4.5	1,655	33.7	30.9
Hopkins	18,619	68.1	107,100	17.6	10.0	745	24.8	2.9	18,031	0.1	925	5.1	18,643	31.8	31.8
Jackson	5,417	77.5	83,100	22.7	11.2	526	27.7	3.3	4,097	1.5	257	6.3	4,033	20.3	44.4
Jefferson	316,411	61.5	178,100	19.3	11.1	901	27.1	2.2	394,151	1.2	18,941	4.8	385,423	38.7	24.4
Jessamine	18,888	67.3	186,400	18.7	10.0	812	24.4	1.5	26,219	1.1	1,054	4.0	25,154	34.3	23.9
Johnson	8,528	70.9	115,800	20.3	11.3	623	31.2	2.4	6,659	1.1	489	7.3	6,980	35.8	23.3
Kenton	64,544	67.7	167,100	17.7	10.0	821	25.7	1.8	87,115	1.3	3,636	4.2	86,893	40.8	22.1
Knott	6,319	73.2	52,300	19.4	10.0	509	24.8	7.1	4,275	-0.3	309	7.2	4,518	31.8	22.9
Knox	12,075	66.6	87,000	19.5	11.5	551	28.3	2.1	10,049	1.8	622	6.2	9,677	33.2	23.6
Larue	5,779	76.2	125,100	20.6	10.0	711	24.0	2.0	5,803	-0.7	286	4.9	6,411	31.6	40.0
Laurel	22,665	70.5	116,300	18.7	10.5	680	28.0	3.4	25,250	1.3	1,139	4.5	23,932	30.1	30.2
Lawrence	5,583	75.3	91,800	20.3	11.8	632	36.0	2.3	5,340	2.6	342	6.4	4,602	26.2	35.6
Lee	2,884	68.7	65,800	19.1	14.2	504	34.5	5.3	2,009	-1.6	113	5.6	2,127	24.8	37.0
Leslie	4,156	85.3	69,000	23.7	11.7	491	32.6	5.9	2,534	-1.7	206	8.1	3,336	25.6	34.7
Letcher	9,599	73.9	54,700	22.7	11.1	529	30.8	3.7	6,038	-0.4	459	7.6	7,303	32.8	26.6
Lewis	5,226	76.8	68,300	22.2	12.5	491	29.1	2.0	4,703	1.1	359	7.6	4,041	24.1	46.5
Lincoln	9,677	78.3	106,100	19.0	11.0	604	28.1	2.8	9,278	0.7	519	5.6	9,857	31.3	33.2
Livingston	3,803	84.6	90,600	18.5	10.3	670	24.0	0.7	3,632	3.8	223	6.1	3,856	30.3	38.3
Logan	10,459	71.0	108,900	19.4	11.2	622	25.0	1.6	12,296	1.6	467	3.8	11,553	30.4	36.2
Lyon	3,266	83.6	149,100	18.2	10.0	602	28.8	1.8	3,113	1.9	139	4.5	2,960	29.4	30.9
McCracken	27,787	64.5	145,200	19.4	10.0	744	27.8	2.6	29,655	3.2	1,495	5.0	29,366	33.7	21.7
McCreary	6,187	67.5	76,700	20.4	10.0	543	28.1	3.4	4,886	1.3	280	5.7	4,914	30.6	31.7
McLean	3,747	78.3	111,800	18.2	10.0	521	26.9	2.1	4,021	1.4	172	4.3	3,755	29.8	39.1
Madison	33,876	60.6	161,400	18.7	10.6	728	27.6	1.8	46,664	1.8	1,922	4.1	43,048	37.4	22.8
Magoffin	4,989	74.3	71,100	23.4	13.8	604	36.7	3.9	3,242	2.0	406	12.5	3,411	27.8	35.8
Marion	7,433	73.3	112,900	19.3	10.0	656	32.4	1.9	9,285	0.8	405	4.4	7,609	31.5	40.6
Marshall	13,119	83.3	138,000	17.9	10.0	724	33.1	1.6	14,446	-2.4	672	4.7	13,207	31.7	30.8
Martin	4,045	77.2	78,100	20.3	11.2	611	28.4	3.0	2,350	-5.0	218	9.3	3,271	30.1	25.0
Mason	6,523	69.1	144,200	18.6	10.0	654	24.2	1.5	6,796	-0.8	375	5.5	7,323	31.6	33.2
Meade	10,690	74.5	154,200	17.5	10.0	856	23.2	3.1	11,679	-0.6	618	5.3	12,676	34.6	34.6
Menifee	2,464	75.4	83,200	21.1	10.4	592	19.4	2.6	2,309	2.6	159	6.9	2,285	30.0	38.4
Mercer	8,718	73.3	148,900	19.2	10.0	622	24.8	1.3	9,932	0.7	452	4.6	9,641	32.5	32.4
Metcalfe	4,187	78.3	76,900	17.6	11.0	557	19.6	2.9	3,980	-0.1	216	5.4	4,138	26.9	43.1
Monroe	4,533	69.9	97,000	17.2	11.2	546	33.9	3.0	4,637	1.7	185	4.0	4,644	31.1	38.7
Montgomery	10,653	67.5	124,600	20.0	10.0	697	23.5	3.2	11,543	1.9	615	5.3	11,796	24.1	37.2
Morgan	4,796	76.7	79,900	19.9	10.6	581	24.9	3.6	4,326	-1.6	249	5.8	3,876	31.8	30.0
Muhlenberg	11,539	81.1	96,000	19.9	10.0	610	24.5	1.0	9,822	-0.9	651	6.6	12,120	29.0	32.7
Nelson	17,991	78.1	164,200	18.3	10.0	799	24.1	1.6	23,223	2.3	1,010	4.3	22,054	30.6	37.2
Nicholas	2,714	69.7	86,500	16.0	11.0	565	21.9	1.8	3,314	1.3	143	4.3	2,956	21.7	40.1

1. Specified owner-occupied units. 2. A value of 10.0 represents 10 percent or less; a value of 50.0 represents 50 percent or more. 3. Specified renter-occupied units. 4. Overcrowded or lacking complete plumbing facilities. 5. Percent of civilian labor force. 6. Civilian employed persons 16 years old and over.

STATE County	Private nonfarm establishments, employment and payroll, 2020									Agriculture, 2017			
		Employment						Annual payroll		Farms			Farm producers whose primary occupation is farming (percent)
											Percent with:		
	Number of establish-ments	Total	Health care and social assistance	Manufac-turing	Retail trade	Finance and insurance	Professional, scientific, and technical services	Total (mil dol)	Average per employee (dollars)	Number	Fewer than 50 acres	1000 acres or more	
	104	105	106	107	108	109	110	111	112	113	114	115	116
KENTUCKY—Cont'd													
Clay	236	2,620	963	222	590	74	85	82	31,320	233	28.3	3.0	33.6
Clinton	177	2,653	456	1,211	319	72	24	83	31,224	512	40.6	1.0	32.2
Crittenden	153	1,577	319	368	239	72	25	51	32,147	575	23.7	6.1	33.0
Cumberland	97	1,100	375	161	126	65	60	42	38,258	395	27.1	3.5	31.0
Daviess	2,304	41,593	7,912	5,669	5,278	2,803	869	1,780	42,798	919	52.6	7.7	39.9
Edmonson	108	863	201	NA	178	61	13	25	28,975	578	37.0	0.5	33.1
Elliott	43	329	149	NA	76	12	NA	9	27,246	363	25.1	NA	41.8
Estill	181	1,588	381	215	250	87	40	49	30,637	367	31.1	1.4	37.9
Fayette	8,835	167,728	33,825	7,602	21,273	4,939	12,737	7,797	46,487	622	51.8	3.2	40.2
Fleming	226	2,115	419	529	429	110	35	78	36,647	1,013	32.0	1.8	39.8
Floyd	688	8,060	2,719	183	1,357	179	157	305	37,820	136	58.8	NA	31.7
Franklin	1,203	16,456	2,538	2,672	2,590	934	947	696	42,268	599	40.7	0.3	34.9
Fulton	121	1,436	116	592	214	67	11	49	34,243	146	41.1	19.9	53.6
Gallatin	88	1,157	237	42	197	26	14	45	38,690	235	43.8	3.0	25.5
Garrard	220	1,367	237	199	191	60	24	50	36,231	793	37.6	1.9	42.4
Grant	361	4,457	493	1,414	908	65	79	162	36,270	811	36.1	0.9	34.3
Graves	677	9,113	1,412	2,555	1,431	330	316	341	37,404	1,104	43.2	6.3	39.3
Grayson	430	6,366	1,018	1,738	975	224	63	215	33,803	1,339	33.8	2.1	35.9
Green	167	1,253	537	21	208	40	38	37	29,260	1,004	33.4	1.5	28.8
Greenup	453	5,218	1,134	625	931	224	155	181	34,760	584	37.0	0.9	34.4
Hancock	126	3,688	114	2,775	117	83	42	234	63,448	321	35.8	0.9	26.5
Hardin	2,169	39,566	8,818	6,643	6,284	1,247	1,277	1,539	38,898	1,305	49.0	2.9	34.3
Harlan	368	4,197	1,220	97	851	111	169	144	34,374	39	51.3	5.1	21.1
Harrison	278	4,409	1,103	1,424	554	84	55	190	43,158	1,138	36.7	1.1	39.0
Hart	259	3,930	346	2,353	437	99	44	149	37,797	1,287	40.9	1.2	36.7
Henderson	977	15,696	2,103	5,415	1,920	372	468	690	43,983	458	46.7	12.4	39.4
Henry	209	1,936	234	370	327	78	65	69	35,708	771	35.3	2.2	41.7
Hickman	69	841	162	111	189	56	14	31	36,785	246	34.6	10.2	54.8
Hopkins	909	14,289	2,847	1,829	2,796	368	390	598	41,834	656	43.9	5.0	34.6
Jackson	97	1,065	253	90	168	46	16	38	35,376	551	36.7	0.7	33.6
Jefferson	19,902	459,956	68,991	51,865	44,888	31,057	24,941	24,857	54,043	343	70.0	NA	35.8
Jessamine	1,193	17,071	1,275	2,250	2,638	229	1,422	658	38,563	671	56.9	1.2	35.7
Johnson	352	3,727	601	21	1,232	101	202	131	35,164	224	34.8	NA	24.8
Kenton	3,160	60,728	11,884	5,517	5,044	5,380	3,456	3,219	53,003	506	54.3	0.2	24.4
Knott	146	1,339	281	NA	243	46	47	61	45,668	62	38.7	3.2	50.0
Knox	447	8,828	1,480	1,483	1,129	153	1,785	220	24,913	336	50.9	0.9	34.3
Larue	193	1,991	304	530	193	411	44	92	46,122	718	49.7	2.1	38.0
Laurel	1,170	22,788	2,832	3,922	3,374	929	1,355	812	35,653	955	48.6	0.3	33.0
Lawrence	198	2,514	771	NA	538	49	64	87	34,735	284	25.4	2.1	32.8
Lee	90	1,205	315	NA	178	13	17	42	34,845	144	36.8	2.8	38.4
Leslie	95	1,141	333	NA	203	66	29	47	41,600	26	53.8	NA	12.5
Letcher	283	2,823	976	61	555	92	94	106	37,375	103	68.9	NA	27.3
Lewis	122	1,255	275	307	247	96	12	41	32,586	550	21.5	1.5	37.9
Lincoln	292	2,549	604	321	504	86	122	82	32,126	1,090	42.8	2.0	42.8
Livingston	143	1,742	355	77	172	35	33	73	41,789	365	20.3	5.5	36.3
Logan	471	7,694	675	3,918	918	171	157	389	50,512	1,078	37.9	4.0	41.6
Lyon	159	1,373	263	13	243	20	35	43	31,133	208	31.7	2.4	33.1
McCracken	2,030	33,778	6,716	2,082	5,771	1,242	1,174	1,472	43,579	318	52.5	6.3	36.8
McCreary	152	1,567	258	438	323	84	80	44	28,073	173	49.1	NA	35.5
McLean	157	1,163	142	130	203	52	24	42	36,197	439	42.8	8.4	39.5
Madison	1,711	24,892	4,066	4,651	4,178	548	1,168	931	37,395	1,187	37.3	1.9	38.6
Magoffin	150	1,121	305	NA	217	46	115	37	33,323	335	36.7	0.9	30.4
Marion	331	8,384	1,530	4,373	602	146	116	296	35,295	954	35.6	1.5	38.0
Marshall	674	8,995	976	2,243	1,412	449	206	454	50,479	699	49.4	2.3	27.9
Martin	129	1,148	214	22	315	59	13	34	29,749	30	30.0	6.7	39.5
Mason	421	6,554	1,374	870	1,255	160	85	259	39,565	680	32.5	2.6	36.6
Meade	341	3,390	335	437	690	141	263	134	39,542	781	51.3	3.3	31.7
Menifee	55	488	172	139	67	NA	NA	18	36,453	283	36.7	0.4	27.8
Mercer	343	4,596	448	1,889	595	109	80	195	42,514	1,108	43.4	1.2	33.0
Metcalfe	113	1,274	150	655	124	42	21	47	36,795	945	38.7	1.6	40.4
Monroe	200	2,653	491	724	474	75	24	95	35,853	765	30.5	3.7	37.1
Montgomery	532	8,576	928	3,299	1,532	274	177	308	35,922	659	38.7	3.2	32.6
Morgan	152	1,831	337	276	353	105	97	63	34,648	657	26.2	2.1	37.5
Muhlenberg	512	6,156	1,383	835	1,142	144	222	220	35,719	549	32.8	4.0	37.6
Nelson	964	15,458	1,342	5,936	1,970	330	212	688	44,527	1,434	54.0	2.0	38.6
Nicholas	76	426	132	NA	79	21	11	13	29,343	556	26.3	0.9	44.7

STATE County	Agriculture, 2017 (cont.) — Land in farms — Acreage (1,000)	Land in farms — Percent change, 2012–2017	Land in farms — Acres — Average size of farm	Acres — Total irrigated (1,000)	Acres — Total cropland (1,000)	Value of land and buildings (dollars) — Average per farm	Value of land and buildings (dollars) — Average per acre	Value of machinery and equipment, average per farm (dollars)	Value of products sold: — Total (mil dol)	Value of products sold: — Average per farm (acres)	Percent from: — Crops	Percent from: — Livestock and poultry products	Organic farms (number)	Farms with internet access (percent)	Government payments — Total ($1,000)	Government payments — Percent of farms
	117	118	119	120	121	122	123	124	125	126	127	128	129	130	131	132
KENTUCKY—Cont'd																
Clay	44	26.3	190	0.0	8.3	345,381	1,814	53,754	5.2	22,399	75.2	24.8	2	74.7	9	3.9
Clinton	65	-12.0	127	0.0	23.8	354,745	2,788	72,223	40.6	79,334	7.5	92.5	NA	76.6	358	17.8
Crittenden	158	6.2	275	D	79.2	754,514	2,747	84,792	39.3	68,289	69.8	30.2	4	51.5	2,296	42.8
Cumberland	82	24.6	207	0.0	22.6	423,878	2,053	57,763	10.7	26,965	46.1	53.9	3	66.6	118	8.4
Daviess	238	0.3	259	10.9	190.8	1,291,082	4,986	163,634	185.9	202,262	64.4	35.6	NA	71.7	4,337	44.0
Edmonson	82	-4.0	141	0.0	38.1	448,629	3,178	75,656	27.5	47,500	40.9	59.1	NA	74.7	1,188	26.8
Elliott	55	-2.4	152	0.0	15.1	245,278	1,619	49,503	3.1	8,628	32.0	68.0	NA	79.3	72	9.9
Estill	53	1.6	145	0.0	14.2	347,874	2,404	48,838	4.1	11,183	35.4	64.6	1	75.5	126	16.1
Fayette	115	-0.2	184	0.3	33.7	2,694,042	14,619	122,300	215.5	346,492	5.9	94.1	6	90.0	576	10.1
Fleming	171	-6.4	169	D	77.3	447,405	2,643	71,101	48.8	48,124	38.3	61.7	2	68.4	783	46.5
Floyd	9	12.0	67	D	2.1	207,547	3,088	34,195	0.6	4,294	59.8	40.2	NA	88.2	D	1.5
Franklin	75	-5.1	124	0.2	29.4	493,851	3,967	53,515	18.9	31,482	42.3	57.7	10	77.6	666	7.3
Fulton	98	17.1	669	7.0	86.6	2,456,571	3,674	304,536	62.1	425,521	71.5	28.5	NA	76.7	2,263	73.3
Gallatin	33	17.0	138	0.0	14.2	393,568	2,845	61,824	7.7	32,936	85.7	14.3	NA	70.2	6	4.7
Garrard	141	10.8	178	0.0	56.8	518,773	2,917	76,025	35.4	44,608	32.0	68.0	5	70.6	345	12.4
Grant	97	-1.6	119	D	35.5	394,863	3,309	54,915	10.1	12,486	58.3	41.7	1	73.0	67	6.2
Graves	251	-13.9	228	5.1	194.8	870,326	3,825	144,824	346.2	313,547	29.7	70.3	NA	70.4	5,088	50.5
Grayson	212	5.7	159	0.2	95.3	468,818	2,956	64,374	59.6	44,494	37.4	62.6	11	65.1	2,219	30.1
Green	156	2.4	156	0.1	76.1	403,864	2,595	76,652	53.2	53,021	59.4	40.6	2	65.9	3,100	39.4
Greenup	74	-6.2	126	0.1	19.0	312,060	2,471	57,719	5.8	9,911	50.4	49.6	2	74.7	132	3.6
Hancock	48	-8.6	149	0.0	21.4	442,673	2,977	78,019	11.6	36,131	71.9	28.1	NA	80.1	472	38.9
Hardin	199	-1.9	153	D	109.6	701,236	4,594	81,201	59.2	45,396	70.1	29.9	1	73.9	1,777	22.1
Harlan	7	7.7	173	D	0.5	270,697	1,564	32,631	0.2	5,436	68.9	31.1	NA	79.5	D	5.1
Harrison	168	1.9	147	1.2	71.2	456,684	3,100	75,066	35.1	30,850	57.8	42.2	3	74.2	300	12.0
Hart	170	-6.9	132	0.2	73.8	406,053	3,078	59,043	36.8	28,584	51.6	48.4	3	65.3	3,457	29.1
Henderson	181	2.7	394	9.2	156.8	2,010,156	5,096	193,308	97.7	213,312	88.9	11.1	NA	83.2	4,739	53.1
Henry	131	1.9	170	0.2	65.2	656,023	3,861	79,554	30.6	39,696	53.9	46.1	2	73.9	195	10.1
Hickman	118	-16.1	482	9.5	103.9	1,933,385	4,014	317,655	159.6	648,817	35.7	64.3	NA	72.4	3,156	65.4
Hopkins	146	-10.2	223	0.1	91.0	752,392	3,372	98,293	119.6	182,309	32.6	67.4	2	73.6	1,661	31.9
Jackson	75	-3.3	136	0.0	26.1	321,560	2,356	50,666	5.7	10,430	35.2	64.8	4	73.7	55	6.4
Jefferson	20	-12.4	59	0.1	7.6	725,049	12,296	43,708	6.4	18,551	78.5	21.5	3	80.5	99	2.9
Jessamine	76	-8.8	114	0.0	32.4	754,661	6,640	57,978	79.9	119,028	7.4	92.6	1	85.5	387	7.7
Johnson	22	-9.4	98	0.0	3.8	294,847	3,001	37,113	0.7	3,152	29.7	70.3	NA	82.1	10	3.6
Kenton	37	-3.7	73	0.0	15.9	406,271	5,597	54,195	5.4	10,652	53.3	46.7	NA	77.7	38	5.3
Knott	13	89.1	206	D	0.6	263,055	1,279	38,779	0.4	6,581	8.6	91.4	NA	88.7	NA	NA
Knox	39	15.5	115	0.0	12.0	275,946	2,394	58,675	2.5	7,542	53.2	46.8	2	70.5	54	3.6
Larue	110	-1.4	154	0.0	67.7	545,514	3,549	93,130	41.1	57,259	78.9	21.1	NA	81.2	986	20.6
Laurel	90	-6.6	94	0.0	35.1	313,976	3,343	59,396	15.4	16,153	43.2	56.8	NA	69.0	147	7.0
Lawrence	51	22.9	180	D	7.9	288,449	1,599	47,327	1.3	4,423	40.8	59.2	NA	79.2	19	3.5
Lee	25	12.8	174	NA	8.5	356,475	2,047	49,063	1.4	9,667	25.2	74.8	NA	70.1	55	19.4
Leslie	2	D	63	0.0	0.2	242,308	3,820	23,981	0.0	1,269	69.7	30.3	NA	69.2	NA	NA
Letcher	6	95.5	55	NA	0.4	163,784	3,000	31,980	0.1	1,340	44.2	55.8	NA	82.5	NA	NA
Lewis	117	-0.5	213	D	41.7	447,476	2,096	58,968	12.7	23,065	68.7	31.3	NA	71.6	338	13.3
Lincoln	163	-9.7	150	0.0	69.0	486,123	3,246	73,186	59.0	54,136	31.5	68.5	20	70.1	939	21.8
Livingston	122	-1.2	333	0.0	61.6	937,557	2,812	108,341	24.2	66,178	63.8	36.2	NA	67.9	1,309	51.2
Logan	276	0.2	256	4.8	195.2	1,237,795	4,829	133,156	152.2	141,154	68.8	31.2	5	71.1	6,869	46.0
Lyon	33	-21.5	157	D	17.6	490,391	3,121	61,700	6.7	32,029	80.2	19.8	NA	64.4	391	28.8
McCracken	62	-7.6	195	0.2	50.6	869,914	4,456	123,106	28.9	90,953	77.4	22.6	NA	84.6	821	33.0
McCreary	18	1.3	106	D	3.8	259,977	2,455	59,199	2.6	14,740	23.6	76.4	1	63.0	44	21.4
McLean	129	4.0	295	D	108.1	1,315,544	4,466	184,326	190.8	434,711	29.7	70.3	NA	83.6	2,369	58.8
Madison	230	-1.3	194	0.1	74.8	671,408	3,468	71,336	50.6	42,592	15.3	84.7	6	72.4	361	14.7
Magoffin	44	-1.5	131	0.0	7.1	270,577	2,070	54,356	1.4	4,269	55.7	44.3	NA	76.7	7	3.3
Marion	163	-2.1	171	0.0	85.2	594,733	3,482	86,494	60.2	63,134	45.3	54.7	2	76.8	893	36.2
Marshall	85	-10.8	121	0.1	52.9	459,882	3,796	82,985	51.4	73,504	33.2	66.8	NA	73.8	1,139	40.1
Martin	11	D	368	NA	2.3	1,270,003	3,451	72,023	0.2	7,133	10.7	89.3	NA	70.0	NA	NA
Mason	132	4.3	194	0.0	68.7	574,464	2,957	76,841	31.3	46,081	63.5	36.5	4	75.3	557	25.3
Meade	141	18.0	181	0.0	80.4	781,623	4,328	98,021	45.8	58,634	61.2	38.8	NA	83.1	1,798	31.6
Menifee	35	-13.7	125	0.0	8.2	241,589	1,933	44,239	2.4	8,449	27.7	72.3	NA	73.5	6	1.8
Mercer	136	-5.4	123	0.0	59.7	483,392	3,925	61,328	45.9	41,428	26.2	73.8	3	73.6	2,019	12.4
Metcalfe	138	10.5	147	0.0	58.6	392,272	2,677	74,723	43.1	45,654	47.4	52.6	2	77.6	1,290	24.2
Monroe	160	-7.2	209	0.1	61.1	594,999	2,847	83,370	102.5	133,949	16.6	83.4	2	73.1	754	28.8
Montgomery	103	3.6	156	0.0	41.0	547,952	3,505	74,291	21.4	32,461	26.6	73.4	NA	71.9	114	13.1
Morgan	107	-10.3	162	0.1	23.2	315,781	1,948	55,320	5.8	8,804	38.4	61.6	NA	68.9	139	7.0
Muhlenberg	128	-1.0	232	0.0	69.3	695,899	2,996	102,576	94.5	172,069	30.3	69.7	NA	70.1	1,142	28.8
Nelson	214	13.7	149	0.2	114.0	604,664	4,061	76,095	67.1	46,791	62.7	37.3	NA	73.4	927	10.0
Nicholas	93	-9.1	167	0.0	39.4	387,800	2,322	66,211	25.9	46,653	49.3	50.7	1	60.1	139	8.6

Table B. States and Counties — **Water Use, Wholesale Trade, Retail Trade, and Real Estate**

STATE County	Water use, 2015		Wholesale Trade[1], 2017				Retail Trade[2], 2017				Real estate and rental and leasing,[2] 2017			
	Public supply water withdrawn (mil gal/ day)	Public supply gallons withdrawn per person per day	Number of establish-ments	Number of employees	Sales (mil dol)	Average payroll (mil dol)	Number of establish-ments	Number of employees	Sales (mil dol)	Average payroll (mil dol)	Number of establish-ments	Number of employees	Sales (mil dol)	Average payroll (mil dol)
	133	134	135	136	137	138	139	140	141	142	143	144	145	146
KENTUCKY—Cont'd														
Clay	5.2	247.5	NA	NA	NA	NA	58	635	204.7	15.1	8	D	2.0	D
Clinton	3.8	368.6	8	D	20.5	D	43	323	73.8	6.8	4	13	1.8	0.3
Crittenden	0.5	51.2	D	D	D	D	28	258	54.6	5.8	7	D	1.3	D
Cumberland	0.6	93.2	NA	NA	NA	NA	24	174	51.2	3.9	5	D	1.8	D
Daviess	13.4	134.6	97	1,267	1,008.3	65.5	400	5,513	1,505.5	132.2	97	549	90.2	15.7
Edmonson	1.7	139.1	NA	NA	NA	NA	23	154	44.9	3.8	NA	NA	NA	NA
Elliott	0.2	24.8	NA	NA	NA	NA	12	67	16.4	1.4	NA	NA	NA	NA
Estill	1.3	91.1	D	D	D	3.1	39	269	66.1	5.9	D	D	D	0.2
Fayette	35.2	112.0	328	4,645	3,402.9	258.8	1,211	23,102	6,341.8	597.9	486	2,223	580.8	86.3
Fleming	0.2	14.3	9	42	14.1	1.6	54	492	144.0	14.5	8	D	1.8	D
Floyd	4.5	119.7	33	366	237.8	14.1	148	1,462	473.5	37.6	27	113	26.6	4.1
Franklin	16.1	319.6	56	522	523.5	30.2	190	2,688	809.9	67.6	43	192	28.4	5.5
Fulton	1.2	189.2	D	D	D	3.0	32	205	45.0	3.8	D	D	D	0.1
Gallatin	0.6	69.5	NA	NA	NA	NA	17	152	67.7	3.1	D	D	D	0.2
Garrard	1.4	83.0	D	D	D	0.7	30	153	56.0	3.7	5	D	1.5	D
Grant	1.7	68.7	10	145	83.0	6.3	70	959	348.5	26.5	19	31	5.6	0.9
Graves	2.6	70.0	D	D	D	D	134	1,515	564.1	43.4	30	85	12.2	2.0
Grayson	2.6	100.7	D	D	D	D	100	992	279.5	23.2	15	211	9.8	5.4
Green	0.8	76.3	D	D	D	1.0	26	234	59.0	5.9	D	D	D	D
Greenup	3.8	105.4	D	D	D	D	85	946	271.8	20.5	13	31	7.0	0.7
Hancock	0.5	61.0	NA	NA	NA	NA	17	127	34.4	2.8	D	D	D	D
Hardin	14.3	134.6	64	594	477.2	27.1	391	6,326	1,744.6	157.5	116	556	86.8	15.3
Harlan	3.4	122.7	D	D	D	4.1	84	886	204.6	20.5	13	36	4.6	0.9
Harrison	2.8	148.2	9	46	28.5	1.3	49	590	145.8	13.5	9	37	5.1	0.8
Hart	4.1	222.2	7	29	18.9	1.3	63	495	147.8	8.7	7	15	1.9	0.3
Henderson	8.7	187.0	37	444	237.8	24.2	149	1,944	663.9	50.2	53	200	24.7	5.7
Henry	0.0	0.0	D	D	D	D	35	349	168.1	7.1	4	4	0.8	0.1
Hickman	0.1	28.2	8	62	65.8	2.0	17	239	60.4	6.0	NA	NA	NA	NA
Hopkins	9.6	208.3	D	D	D	D	164	2,583	955.8	70.5	31	105	15.4	3.1
Jackson	1.5	110.1	NA	NA	NA	NA	21	148	34.8	2.8	3	8	0.8	0.2
Jefferson	133.8	175.2	983	15,570	10,876.9	971.9	2,669	44,590	12,543.4	1,182.5	1,062	5,688	2,649.4	290.2
Jessamine	5.3	102.8	38	930	1,463.9	44.1	154	2,850	986.1	77.3	44	157	22.8	5.3
Johnson	2.5	107.0	10	72	36.6	2.6	84	1,350	385.0	33.4	16	50	7.9	1.4
Kenton	0.0	0.0	131	2,313	1,317.0	121.4	390	6,337	1,601.6	148.0	140	809	195.5	35.7
Knott	1.8	117.2	NA	NA	NA	NA	29	258	61.0	5.3	NA	NA	NA	NA
Knox	0.3	9.5	12	45	20.3	1.2	109	1,370	294.9	28.7	17	65	8.1	1.7
Larue	0.7	47.0	4	14	6.7	0.6	28	200	56.7	5.0	NA	NA	NA	NA
Laurel	8.9	148.1	55	680	505.0	31.4	246	3,376	1,086.6	88.4	48	265	39.3	6.8
Lawrence	1.5	94.6	7	189	113.2	8.7	48	711	161.3	14.4	9	21	4.0	0.4
Lee	1.0	140.7	D	D	D	0.8	19	171	36.9	3.9	3	5	0.3	0.0
Leslie	1.1	99.0	NA	NA	NA	NA	27	236	55.6	4.4	NA	NA	NA	NA
Letcher	1.6	69.6	10	151	247.8	6.1	57	635	138.8	16.1	10	33	6.2	1.1
Lewis	2.4	176.9	D	D	D	0.5	30	278	63.0	5.1	NA	NA	NA	NA
Lincoln	2.1	86.3	10	42	11.3	1.1	61	551	146.3	11.9	4	5	1.0	0.1
Livingston	1.7	178.2	D	D	D	2.8	27	206	45.5	4.2	NA	NA	NA	NA
Logan	0.0	0.0	26	208	147.7	9.4	98	961	276.1	24.8	13	31	5.3	1.0
Lyon	2.7	321.5	D	D	D	D	25	230	65.3	6.2	5	5	3.5	0.5
McCracken	8.2	126.3	103	1,377	4,324.5	63.1	399	6,077	1,715.6	155.7	68	393	90.5	11.9
McCreary	2.0	109.6	NA	NA	NA	NA	44	338	88.4	8.0	D	D	D	0.3
McLean	0.7	72.5	D	D	D	D	31	236	78.6	6.2	NA	NA	NA	NA
Madison	11.4	130.0	38	347	216.1	13.1	298	4,314	1,232.2	103.7	80	241	54.0	7.7
Magoffin	0.8	60.9	3	15	3.6	0.5	32	199	58.2	5.0	NA	NA	NA	NA
Marion	4.1	213.3	12	77	34.9	2.4	62	669	176.3	14.9	5	16	2.0	0.7
Marshall	4.1	131.8	25	193	112.3	9.3	125	1,395	453.1	37.2	22	89	30.6	5.5
Martin	4.5	361.6	5	D	49.5	D	38	394	106.0	7.9	3	D	1.4	D
Mason	2.7	159.7	15	253	86.4	12.3	97	1,479	383.3	32.3	12	77	9.8	2.0
Meade	0.8	26.9	9	73	121.6	3.8	61	660	225.8	16.3	D	D	D	D
Menifee	1.1	169.9	NA	NA	NA	NA	12	64	17.5	1.3	NA	NA	NA	NA
Mercer	2.9	137.3	D	D	D	1.2	52	644	172.0	16.2	7	14	1.8	0.4
Metcalfe	0.0	0.0	NA	NA	NA	NA	22	172	46.5	3.7	3	4	0.5	0.1
Monroe	1.4	132.2	6	D	24.2	D	46	485	118.7	10.9	7	35	2.2	0.9
Montgomery	3.0	108.7	18	249	65.9	6.8	124	1,534	467.2	36.9	19	40	6.0	1.0
Morgan	1.0	75.3	NA	NA	NA	NA	33	355	85.9	7.4	NA	NA	NA	NA
Muhlenberg	3.5	111.3	D	D	D	D	108	1,275	310.1	28.6	11	54	3.8	1.0
Nelson	5.5	121.9	34	414	251.0	20.1	161	2,036	590.3	53.8	34	98	15.9	2.1
Nicholas	1.7	239.8	NA	NA	NA	NA	12	76	16.2	1.3	NA	NA	NA	NA

1 Merchant wholesalers, except manufacturers' sales branches and offices. 2. Employer establishments.

STATE County	Professional, scientific, and technical services, 2017				Manufacturing, 2017				Accommodation and food services, 2017			
	Number of establish-ments	Number of employees	Sales (mil dol)	Average payroll (mil dol)	Number of establish-ments	Number of employees	Sales (mil dol)	Average payroll (mil dol)	Number of establis-hments	Number of employees	Sales (mil dol)	Annual payroll (mil dol)
	147	148	149	150	151	152	153	154	155	156	157	158
KENTUCKY—Cont'd												
Clay	D	D	12.2	D	6	133	28.0	6.2	19	328	15.5	4.5
Clinton	12	21	1.8	0.5	D	1,587	D	45.6	D	D	D	D
Crittenden	13	33	2.8	1.0	11	470	160.3	17.0	12	263	7.1	2.5
Cumberland	D	D	D	0.6	7	175	29.3	4.8	11	90	6.6	1.9
Daviess	D	D	D	D	97	5,070	3,078.5	285.5	D	D	D	D
Edmonson	6	16	1.7	0.4	NA	NA	NA	NA	D	D	D	D
Elliott	NA	NA	NA	NA	NA	NA	NA	NA	D	D	D	0.8
Estill	9	43	2.2	0.5	9	139	12.2	4.2	18	255	13.4	3.0
Fayette	1,158	11,056	2,000.7	698.3	219	7,509	2,739.9	385.9	849	20,035	1,112.4	325.4
Fleming	14	38	3.2	1.0	20	459	103.0	17.4	D	D	D	D
Floyd	D	D	D	D	12	172	33.4	6.1	58	849	40.9	10.8
Franklin	130	1,086	140.2	51.5	38	2,538	1,605.1	138.3	110	D	120.6	D
Fulton	4	23	1.6	0.6	7	450	198.4	19.2	D	D	D	D
Gallatin	D	D	5.0	D	D	D	D	D	D	D	D	D
Garrard	17	38	2.9	1.1	13	190	34.6	7.4	D	D	D	D
Grant	30	75	9.6	2.8	D	779	D	45.5	D	D	D	D
Graves	48	263	23.8	9.6	39	2,482	909.9	91.7	51	817	38.8	10.6
Grayson	18	57	6.5	2.3	28	1,682	434.6	68.1	31	551	26.0	6.8
Green	12	32	2.6	0.8	7	72	8.2	1.8	8	153	6.0	1.7
Greenup	26	152	13.7	5.3	D	546	D	29.9	D	D	D	D
Hancock	8	50	4.2	1.9	16	2,333	2,239.3	177.8	D	D	D	D
Hardin	162	1,044	185.4	66.5	66	6,183	2,438.9	331.5	194	4,763	232.5	66.6
Harlan	25	139	9.7	4.8	7	52	17.5	2.9	36	573	23.9	6.1
Harrison	16	54	6.2	1.2	20	1,236	756.2	72.9	D	D	D	D
Hart	18	53	5.1	1.6	21	2,560	876.9	102.0	18	309	14.2	3.7
Henderson	73	434	37.9	14.0	68	5,451	2,662.4	269.9	77	1,384	71.5	18.6
Henry	18	50	5.2	1.7	5	368	359.3	17.2	D	D	D	D
Hickman	D	D	D	D	4	143	24.3	3.2	NA	NA	NA	NA
Hopkins	D	D	D	D	44	1,719	755.2	98.4	65	1,274	58.9	16.6
Jackson	D	D	1.0	D	7	21	4.9	0.8	7	51	4.4	0.7
Jefferson	2,264	24,439	4,188.0	1,546.4	690	49,360	37,068.9	3,037.4	1,830	43,548	2,517.3	720.2
Jessamine	98	850	142.8	46.4	69	2,364	837.7	108.6	82	1,754	77.6	23.7
Johnson	21	125	24.3	5.7	8	44	7.4	1.5	34	576	25.9	7.3
Kenton	D	D	D	D	99	4,738	2,537.5	307.6	317	6,987	405.6	117.9
Knott	11	56	10.3	2.6	NA	NA	NA	NA	10	97	5.8	1.4
Knox	D	D	D	D	17	1,350	244.3	51.9	44	959	48.8	12.6
Larue	15	41	3.2	1.1	D	495	D	D	10	105	5.5	1.5
Laurel	93	1,513	145.5	33.3	51	3,831	1,026.3	163.4	101	2,587	128.2	36.2
Lawrence	12	70	6.2	2.7	NA	NA	NA	NA	D	D	D	4.7
Lee	5	14	2.2	0.3	NA	NA	NA	NA	D	D	D	0.6
Leslie	D	D	D	D	NA	NA	NA	NA	7	77	4.1	1.2
Letcher	D	D	D	D	7	69	26.6	D	D	D	D	D
Lewis	D	D	D	0.3	15	349	104.6	13.0	6	72	3.5	0.9
Lincoln	19	98	9.9	3.4	16	368	71.0	14.8	17	438	11.5	3.7
Livingston	8	37	5.6	2.1	D	D	D	D	D	D	D	D
Logan	29	170	16.0	7.3	37	2,913	2,129.4	166.5	32	572	25.8	6.7
Lyon	10	31	2.7	0.9	NA	NA	NA	NA	24	327	19.1	5.2
McCracken	D	D	D	D	51	2,269	547.4	108.4	220	4,650	218.2	64.2
McCreary	8	98	5.7	1.5	9	241	46.6	7.9	22	283	10.2	2.8
McLean	8	23	2.3	0.8	8	135	123.2	6.7	13	72	3.4	0.9
Madison	D	D	D	D	60	4,957	3,059.3	273.8	159	3,755	184.7	54.1
Magoffin	16	137	21.3	5.4	NA	NA	NA	NA	10	191	8.3	2.1
Marion	22	108	16.7	4.3	31	4,245	1,286.2	198.0	34	567	23.6	6.3
Marshall	44	241	39.3	14.5	40	2,349	2,840.1	204.8	80	1,425	58.6	16.0
Martin	8	19	2.5	0.5	NA	NA	NA	NA	10	148	6.2	1.6
Mason	22	99	11.4	3.9	15	1,223	773.4	60.9	41	856	39.3	11.8
Meade	16	276	10.8	4.0	D	522	D	D	31	554	23.3	6.2
Menifee	NA	NA	NA	NA	D	D	D	D	NA	NA	NA	NA
Mercer	25	56	5.2	1.7	11	1,854	1,270.7	112.1	31	458	23.5	6.6
Metcalfe	10	15	1.4	0.4	8	646	382.6	23.3	10	115	4.6	1.2
Monroe	D	D	D	0.7	17	667	104.7	25.0	D	D	D	D
Montgomery	35	165	19.4	5.2	29	3,423	1,012.8	153.0	D	D	D	D
Morgan	16	83	5.2	2.1	5	43	8.0	1.6	11	165	6.9	2.0
Muhlenberg	27	355	27.4	7.6	33	D	210.6	D	49	727	32.8	8.9
Nelson	D	D	D	D	60	5,104	2,152.7	292.2	71	1,264	65.3	17.9
Nicholas	7	13	1.3	0.5	D	D	D	D	4	16	0.9	0.1

STATE County	Health care and social assistance, 2017				Other services, 2017				Nonemployer businesses, 2019		Value of residential construction authorized by building permits, 2021	
	Number of establish- ments	Number of employees	Receipts (mil dol)	Annual payroll (mil dol)	Number of establish- ments	Number of employees	Receipts (mil dol)	Annual payroll (mil dol)	Number	Receipts (mil dol)	New construction ($1,000)	Number of housing units
	159	160	161	162	163	164	165	166	167	168	169	170
KENTUCKY—Cont'd												
Clay	40	852	81.1	29.8	D	D	D	1.0	1,141	33.2	0	0
Clinton	26	484	49.2	16.7	D	D	1.5	D	754	30.2	0	0
Crittenden	16	401	25.9	11.7	D	D	D	D	639	26.9	150	1
Cumberland	13	382	28.2	13.1	D	D	2.7	D	575	23.2	263	1
Daviess	334	9,664	1,080.4	474.3	146	1,072	87.9	30.9	5,935	273.3	36,118	388
Edmonson	D	D	D	D	7	24	2.6	0.6	970	41.4	NA	NA
Elliott	11	D	12.4	D	3	7	0.4	0.1	367	13.2	NA	NA
Estill	D	D	D	18.0	12	34	4.1	0.8	780	21.0	0	0
Fayette	1,154	32,976	4,708.5	1,706.1	595	4,860	961.7	165.0	24,941	1,253.6	260,249	1,655
Fleming	17	495	40.6	16.6	19	55	6.0	1.5	1,338	72.5	0	0
Floyd	124	2,079	251.9	85.7	36	169	21.0	5.5	2,272	99.9	2,975	7
Franklin	160	2,301	333.6	101.9	121	659	100.6	27.1	3,548	130.4	26,126	114
Fulton	D	D	D	D	D	D	D	D	275	9.5	0	0
Gallatin	6	185	14.4	6.1	D	D	6.6	D	413	15.0	7,768	59
Garrard	25	317	17.0	8.8	D	D	D	D	1,379	56.5	0	0
Grant	39	505	56.9	23.4	D	D	D	D	1,428	70.6	19,898	92
Graves	76	1,466	153.5	56.8	D	D	35.3	D	2,572	122.9	1,523	7
Grayson	60	1,076	93.9	36.3	D	D	D	D	1,890	123.1	1,220	6
Green	23	543	41.8	18.5	D	D	6.8	D	924	38.4	75	1
Greenup	77	1,123	102.1	47.9	D	D	D	D	1,893	73.9	7,812	21
Hancock	16	131	9.9	3.2	D	D	D	0.3	472	20.0	2,018	10
Hardin	303	8,248	860.6	383.9	138	785	79.7	22.1	5,934	242.2	74,759	353
Harlan	45	1,318	145.3	48.5	20	64	6.9	1.6	1,290	39.3	0	0
Harrison	43	1,086	101.7	41.4	D	D	D	D	1,081	46.1	14,635	70
Hart	28	389	45.1	14.3	19	67	5.3	1.4	1,718	99.4	6,681	63
Henderson	145	2,521	226.7	91.6	62	414	83.3	17.9	2,352	94.9	14,976	58
Henry	D	D	D	6.9	D	D	D	D	1,056	46.9	14,980	53
Hickman	8	D	11.2	D	3	9	1.1	0.4	341	11.0	NA	NA
Hopkins	151	3,163	332.9	132.1	75	410	50.4	14.0	2,341	91.5	11,743	62
Jackson	19	219	16.3	6.9	4	12	1.4	0.2	918	28.0	0	0
Jefferson	2,472	69,939	9,367.8	3,580.8	1,339	11,113	1,497.6	382.1	58,524	2,781.9	362,802	1,917
Jessamine	124	1,368	101.6	47.2	85	313	27.8	7.6	4,605	221.0	103,990	367
Johnson	44	705	84.3	28.2	D	D	D	2.6	1,309	53.7	0	0
Kenton	372	13,524	1,964.5	736.7	220	1,785	150.9	47.2	10,202	488.0	180,613	653
Knott	24	205	20.0	6.3	D	D	D	D	818	31.3	NA	NA
Knox	70	1,222	103.6	41.2	D	D	D	D	1,997	82.0	0	0
Larue	D	D	D	D	18	75	6.0	1.7	1,077	41.5	14,072	60
Laurel	148	2,600	344.4	137.2	D	D	D	D	4,159	198.4	1,180	11
Lawrence	23	617	77.5	28.8	D	D	D	D	712	21.1	NA	NA
Lee	19	742	30.8	12.3	NA	NA	NA	NA	385	11.9	NA	NA
Leslie	15	309	26.5	10.2	3	17	1.1	0.4	467	19.2	NA	NA
Letcher	57	963	116.6	44.5	D	D	D	D	1,090	35.4	0	0
Lewis	12	453	50.6	22.6	D	D	1.8	D	850	35.0	0	0
Lincoln	37	564	39.7	15.8	D	D	D	D	1,675	70.6	19,700	71
Livingston	16	333	27.1	10.7	D	D	1.2	D	520	17.4	NA	NA
Logan	47	693	62.9	23.4	31	120	14.3	3.9	1,895	98.0	1,644	12
Lyon	20	289	20.4	8.3	6	14	1.2	0.3	496	18.9	3,017	14
McCracken	279	7,108	920.6	312.7	129	821	113.7	25.2	4,607	200.9	32,520	134
McCreary	27	266	21.4	8.4	9	22	2.6	0.5	861	34.0	0	0
McLean	12	136	10.3	4.2	D	D	D	D	515	17.5	0	0
Madison	253	3,714	386.4	147.2	104	602	72.0	17.2	6,025	259.2	76,695	455
Magoffin	21	285	31.4	11.3	D	D	D	0.5	633	24.1	NA	NA
Marion	39	1,077	98.3	36.1	23	96	14.3	3.1	1,220	52.6	6,385	39
Marshall	D	D	D	D	44	263	31.8	8.5	2,194	86.1	31,973	93
Martin	18	227	18.1	8.4	D	D	8.7	D	426	12.4	NA	NA
Mason	57	1,220	137.8	54.8	35	160	11.1	3.0	1,148	56.5	5,795	29
Meade	D	D	D	D	24	146	12.9	4.0	1,610	70.5	22,355	113
Menifee	9	152	11.2	5.1	NA	NA	NA	NA	418	13.4	NA	NA
Mercer	39	579	41.7	20.0	31	99	11.0	2.6	1,632	72.4	8,165	39
Metcalfe	16	90	7.3	2.7	D	D	D	D	853	29.7	NA	NA
Monroe	26	474	38.6	17.0	9	33	4.7	1.0	894	40.2	NA	NA
Montgomery	68	963	119.2	41.4	27	124	12.8	3.5	1,766	71.9	9,902	47
Morgan	18	359	43.8	15.9	12	66	9.1	2.3	740	26.4	115	3
Muhlenberg	80	1,291	97.5	48.4	38	136	14.6	4.1	1,577	54.6	1,277	6
Nelson	105	1,371	142.8	50.5	47	180	18.8	4.2	3,099	134.8	63,094	313
Nicholas	12	169	13.4	6.5	D	D	2.7	D	514	21.5	0	0

STATE County	Government employment and payroll, 2017: Full-time equivalent employees	Government employment and payroll, 2017: March payroll (dollars)	March payroll (percent of total): Adminis-tration, judicial, and legal	March payroll (percent of total): Police and corrections	March payroll (percent of total): Fire protection	March payroll (percent of total): Highways and transpor-tation	March payroll (percent of total): Health and welfare	March payroll (percent of total): Natural resources and utilities	March payroll (percent of total): Education and libraries	Local government finances, 2017, General revenue: Total (mil dol)	General revenue: Inter-govern-mental (mil dol)	Taxes: Total (mil dol)	Taxes: Per capita[1] (dollars): Total	Taxes: Per capita[1] (dollars): Property
	171	172	173	174	175	176	177	178	179	180	181	182	183	184
KENTUCKY—Cont'd														
Clay	859	2,375,911	5.0	5.6	0.0	2.3	4.5	4.4	77.8	44.3	31.9	7.6	373	215
Clinton	398	1,121,150	2.1	4.3	0.0	2.4	5.6	1.4	83.8	23.2	15.2	5.9	582	291
Crittenden	298	866,183	5.8	13.4	0.0	1.8	0.0	6.3	71.5	20.5	13.7	5.3	588	348
Cumberland	451	1,495,373	3.2	1.9	0.3	1.6	46.9	4.1	40.1	29.6	17.1	4.6	683	311
Daviess	4,180	14,060,220	3.8	7.2	4.1	3.8	4.8	13.0	59.1	336.4	122.9	120.0	1,195	713
Edmonson	423	1,188,212	3.3	4.5	0.4	2.0	3.9	8.6	77.1	22.9	14.9	6.1	498	384
Elliott	263	721,216	4.3	0.5	0.0	3.7	11.3	2.9	71.9	14.5	11.5	2.3	301	176
Estill	550	1,582,577	1.9	5.5	1.0	2.2	7.7	5.4	73.2	33.5	22.4	7.0	493	315
Fayette	9,865	41,635,220	4.8	14.0	9.4	2.7	3.3	6.4	56.0	1,138.7	245.8	687.2	2,134	1,001
Fleming	478	1,690,476	4.4	3.2	1.1	2.3	5.2	3.9	79.5	58.4	21.8	8.9	619	406
Floyd	1,297	3,808,363	2.3	5.6	2.8	1.8	5.2	4.6	76.6	82.8	53.6	18.1	498	381
Franklin	1,723	6,510,417	4.0	6.7	10.0	3.1	0.9	12.4	50.1	176.9	46.4	75.0	1,485	755
Fulton	412	1,101,709	9.6	16.5	5.3	8.6	3.1	8.8	46.2	28.1	16.0	5.6	917	552
Gallatin	329	988,148	7.6	2.4	0.0	2.3	2.3	4.1	81.1	24.3	13.4	8.6	989	598
Garrard	483	1,479,069	4.4	2.3	0.2	2.3	6.1	2.4	82.0	41.1	21.7	12.3	705	468
Grant	934	2,920,679	4.4	7.4	1.7	2.1	0.0	6.0	77.1	63.5	39.0	16.0	640	464
Graves	1,238	3,892,508	3.6	8.9	4.4	2.7	0.0	2.7	76.6	79.4	47.5	25.5	685	409
Grayson	978	2,948,785	4.3	17.1	0.3	2.1	0.1	4.9	68.3	71.5	43.9	19.5	741	393
Green	386	1,076,131	3.8	3.0	0.0	2.0	4.8	4.6	80.8	23.2	15.0	5.9	533	333
Greenup	1,163	3,780,181	4.1	7.1	0.7	2.4	0.2	4.9	79.0	85.7	43.5	33.5	943	750
Hancock	416	1,244,317	9.1	3.7	0.0	2.3	3.9	4.4	70.6	24.8	11.4	10.8	1,227	658
Hardin	5,558	22,988,923	1.3	3.3	1.6	1.1	51.5	3.8	36.5	586.1	125.3	105.6	977	545
Harlan	1,155	3,185,246	3.0	7.1	0.3	2.3	8.2	5.7	71.8	78.9	52.2	13.7	514	369
Harrison	644	1,959,248	6.6	10.6	3.7	2.9	0.1	3.4	70.9	41.4	21.3	16.1	858	387
Hart	508	1,727,761	5.1	7.0	0.1	2.1	5.1	10.1	68.9	40.6	23.1	11.7	626	318
Henderson	1,909	6,339,040	6.8	12.3	4.7	4.1	1.8	13.5	55.6	133.7	65.2	52.2	1,138	664
Henry	595	1,840,305	10.3	3.8	0.0	1.5	1.8	5.6	77.0	37.6	21.2	12.0	749	576
Hickman	175	523,679	5.9	5.5	0.0	5.6	0.2	0.8	78.6	11.6	7.3	3.4	761	567
Hopkins	1,826	5,753,345	4.9	9.9	4.7	3.6	3.1	9.8	62.9	125.6	61.0	46.7	1,032	515
Jackson	528	1,248,716	4.0	7.5	0.0	3.0	0.0	2.2	80.3	33.3	25.3	5.6	415	229
Jefferson	24,734	113,244,260	3.2	10.3	4.3	4.0	5.6	9.2	61.8	2,682.0	667.8	1,404.9	1,825	929
Jessamine	1,768	5,333,658	5.4	8.0	4.3	1.4	4.9	5.3	67.2	130.3	48.4	68.8	1,292	772
Johnson	925	2,854,090	3.6	2.5	0.9	2.0	7.5	1.3	81.1	63.4	35.7	15.8	701	416
Kenton	5,801	23,671,220	2.9	9.6	5.9	15.5	3.6	9.3	52.5	687.9	177.3	254.0	1,534	892
Knott	533	1,546,838	5.4	1.3	0.0	1.9	0.0	5.1	81.7	31.0	22.2	7.0	460	392
Knox	1,143	3,414,140	2.4	2.7	0.1	1.7	12.0	0.9	80.0	85.3	54.2	15.2	483	252
Larue	504	1,104,219	5.1	7.6	0.0	2.6	0.3	5.2	71.4	31.0	20.0	8.6	605	442
Laurel	1,952	5,552,219	3.1	7.6	0.7	2.7	2.9	5.7	76.2	134.3	74.5	46.0	763	351
Lawrence	567	1,592,040	5.9	3.3	1.1	2.3	5.0	3.1	78.9	33.5	22.1	8.6	543	415
Lee	243	764,630	10.4	3.5	0.0	4.3	1.4	6.9	73.4	15.6	9.9	3.9	586	413
Leslie	421	1,213,626	5.4	3.2	0.0	3.2	0.0	4.8	77.1	26.6	20.4	5.2	509	344
Letcher	732	2,218,820	1.6	2.7	0.6	0.8	0.0	5.7	88.2	53.2	35.2	11.8	531	340
Lewis	575	1,833,270	3.6	5.3	0.2	1.7	1.0	4.3	82.3	31.0	20.8	7.5	563	422
Lincoln	836	2,289,112	2.1	4.8	0.5	2.0	2.5	3.7	83.9	59.6	38.7	13.3	542	357
Livingston	321	886,221	4.4	4.8	2.2	3.9	7.1	5.1	69.1	24.0	13.0	8.7	943	630
Logan	1,001	2,855,484	4.5	7.7	1.4	1.8	0.0	5.0	77.6	65.8	35.9	25.3	937	489
Lyon	243	717,253	9.1	6.6	0.4	4.8	10.4	5.7	57.7	18.1	7.0	7.9	951	709
McCracken	2,315	10,412,476	3.0	7.4	3.6	3.7	6.8	10.2	62.4	205.9	78.8	84.0	1,285	662
McCreary	620	1,867,437	2.1	5.1	0.0	1.8	8.4	4.4	77.0	44.3	28.0	14.8	854	743
McLean	377	975,438	7.1	2.0	0.0	2.3	0.0	6.6	75.0	29.8	15.6	9.3	1,014	501
Madison	2,654	8,082,172	2.1	4.0	3.3	2.3	9.0	3.2	72.3	216.5	94.7	90.3	990	478
Magoffin	497	1,549,269	4.5	3.8	0.9	3.8	4.6	2.8	79.6	33.8	24.7	5.5	442	216
Marion	756	2,298,284	3.3	14.6	0.4	2.4	2.3	9.4	66.7	50.2	24.4	18.5	958	640
Marshall	1,244	5,690,803	2.0	3.2	0.0	1.7	16.5	4.9	71.3	109.3	39.7	42.3	1,352	722
Martin	490	1,622,222	7.1	2.9	0.0	2.3	2.7	4.4	80.2	30.3	20.2	6.6	571	375
Mason	912	2,313,200	5.6	11.3	4.5	2.9	5.1	9.5	59.5	50.4	22.1	20.2	1,173	558
Meade	893	2,746,337	3.8	6.0	0.0	1.6	3.4	5.0	79.4	61.6	36.5	18.7	666	514
Menifee	236	632,187	2.9	0.9	0.0	3.5	0.4	4.5	85.5	14.3	10.6	2.7	421	240
Mercer	705	2,044,636	6.4	7.6	3.3	2.5	0.0	4.4	72.0	52.0	23.1	22.8	1,057	650
Metcalfe	316	999,594	4.1	3.7	0.0	5.1	0.6	6.0	80.5	22.6	15.6	5.9	589	309
Monroe	549	1,359,308	6.7	7.5	0.0	1.8	2.3	10.3	71.0	39.8	17.7	7.7	723	396
Montgomery	902	3,035,358	3.3	6.6	6.5	3.0	6.6	0.9	73.1	69.2	39.1	23.5	841	426
Morgan	448	1,238,906	5.1	5.0	0.0	2.1	5.2	5.7	76.4	33.2	18.6	7.8	592	261
Muhlenberg	1,070	3,150,997	3.5	5.2	1.5	1.1	2.6	8.3	76.1	73.5	43.3	17.4	563	437
Nelson	1,438	4,943,456	2.2	6.2	1.6	1.4	2.5	8.0	76.3	123.4	45.5	44.8	983	750
Nicholas	210	598,380	8.6	4.7	0.1	3.1	0.0	9.8	71.8	16.9	12.1	2.6	362	270

1. Based on the resident population estimated as of July 1 of the year shown.

STATE County	Local government finances, 2017 (cont.)									Government employment, 2020			Individual income tax returns, 2019		
	Direct general expenditure							Debt outstanding							
			Percent of total for:												
	Total (mil dol)	Per capita[1] (dollars)	Education	Health and hospitals	Police protection	Public welfare	Highways	Total (mil dol)	Per capita[1] (dollars)	Federal civilian	Federal military	State and local	Number of returns	Mean adjusted gross income	Mean income tax
	185	186	187	188	189	190	191	192	193	194	195	196	197	198	199
KENTUCKY—Cont'd															
Clay	42.2	2,085	68.2	3.0	2.2	0.0	5.2	33.3	1,645	354	54	1,016	6,240	36,564	2,060
Clinton	23.4	2,287	68.1	4.7	2.4	0.0	5.3	28.1	2,756	41	30	555	3,770	34,993	1,966
Crittenden	19.7	2,194	53.9	0.9	3.1	0.1	11.0	30.1	3,340	19	26	416	3,550	45,106	3,244
Cumberland	31.1	4,638	29.5	51.5	2.7	0.0	4.4	15.8	2,357	12	19	336	2,540	38,900	2,482
Daviess	319.5	3,180	47.7	6.7	3.4	0.1	3.8	916.4	9,122	279	320	4,946	46,610	58,541	5,667
Edmonson	22.5	1,844	70.2	5.3	3.2	0.0	4.0	40.6	3,318	210	35	477	4,860	45,633	3,108
Elliott	14.3	1,906	66.5	0.9	1.3	0.0	10.7	17.8	2,381	11	19	567	2,280	39,032	2,437
Estill	40.5	2,857	67.2	7.1	1.3	0.0	3.0	43.0	3,030	22	42	614	5,470	41,170	2,764
Fayette	1,061.7	3,298	42.6	1.5	5.7	1.0	1.6	1,535.9	4,770	4,382	1,004	40,505	146,590	69,705	8,706
Fleming	70.1	4,854	39.8	38.6	0.8	0.0	2.6	211.0	14,616	46	43	598	6,130	42,445	2,929
Floyd	108.8	2,999	72.8	2.7	1.3	0.1	0.7	160.7	4,427	125	103	2,129	12,650	43,769	3,484
Franklin	166.5	3,298	38.2	4.0	5.5	0.2	3.3	146.6	2,904	465	165	13,042	25,870	54,759	4,844
Fulton	42.5	6,889	23.5	0.0	2.4	0.0	1.4	23.1	3,753	31	33	465	2,360	38,627	2,795
Gallatin	23.4	2,688	64.9	3.3	2.5	0.1	5.2	362.6	41,582	35	26	417	3,750	49,848	3,792
Garrard	38.3	2,193	55.0	20.0	2.2	0.0	3.6	51.8	2,971	23	53	616	7,210	49,161	3,730
Grant	65.0	2,602	63.9	0.4	3.4	0.0	2.8	101.8	4,075	52	74	1,132	11,120	49,872	3,850
Graves	77.7	2,088	70.0	3.4	2.2	0.3	6.4	125.2	3,365	207	108	1,657	15,370	48,937	3,971
Grayson	68.4	2,601	50.5	1.6	1.8	0.0	5.6	91.0	3,461	91	77	1,556	10,750	44,001	3,188
Green	26.0	2,355	67.5	5.5	1.7	0.0	6.3	44.6	4,039	23	32	464	4,450	38,996	2,504
Greenup	83.1	2,340	66.7	4.9	3.1	0.0	5.1	69.8	1,966	63	103	1,432	14,930	55,904	5,188
Hancock	25.5	2,907	58.7	3.0	2.2	0.4	6.1	1,321.1	150,506	23	26	402	3,890	52,029	3,822
Hardin	577.7	5,341	26.6	56.0	1.5	0.0	2.2	423.2	3,912	5,239	5,431	7,591	50,600	54,246	4,647
Harlan	74.6	2,795	54.1	15.2	2.9	0.6	3.8	51.0	1,913	69	74	1,773	8,620	36,315	2,478
Harrison	40.7	2,170	59.5	1.2	4.1	0.2	6.7	33.9	1,810	44	56	744	8,120	49,332	3,878
Hart	43.2	2,303	59.3	5.5	3.1	0.0	4.9	114.9	6,130	45	56	779	7,560	40,308	2,611
Henderson	124.5	2,715	51.0	0.2	5.7	0.3	3.8	965.7	21,054	102	131	2,304	19,930	54,747	4,909
Henry	36.6	2,291	71.2	2.2	2.7	0.0	3.5	44.5	2,785	101	48	668	7,290	49,947	4,012
Hickman	11.2	2,477	62.7	0.0	3.7	0.2	8.6	6.1	1,358	20	12	205	1,810	48,144	3,676
Hopkins	119.6	2,642	51.2	3.3	6.1	1.7	4.4	84.7	1,871	174	130	2,758	19,210	54,192	4,746
Jackson	34.4	2,563	60.7	15.7	0.4	0.0	3.5	30.0	2,239	40	39	621	4,660	39,004	2,261
Jefferson	2,871.6	3,730	42.0	4.2	7.1	0.6	3.2	5,585.4	7,255	7,143	2,479	38,267	381,720	68,284	8,236
Jessamine	116.4	2,186	56.3	4.8	5.3	0.1	3.2	204.2	3,834	78	156	2,246	23,330	67,905	8,043
Johnson	61.4	2,718	66.3	5.7	2.0	0.0	4.3	59.0	2,610	51	64	1,338	7,800	50,740	4,494
Kenton	627.6	3,790	37.0	3.1	4.9	0.0	6.3	1,835.7	11,085	2,491	492	6,372	81,460	72,980	8,904
Knott	29.4	1,928	75.7	0.2	0.5	0.1	6.0	22.6	1,484	40	41	630	4,700	46,313	4,156
Knox	81.9	2,605	55.8	10.5	1.2	0.0	2.7	121.0	3,849	130	91	1,286	11,320	38,499	2,465
Larue	35.1	2,471	70.6	1.9	1.9	0.0	4.1	45.6	3,214	42	42	551	6,460	46,768	3,528
Laurel	129.0	2,138	61.8	2.5	2.5	0.0	3.4	294.9	4,889	248	181	2,507	24,560	47,069	3,989
Lawrence	33.2	2,104	64.5	5.3	1.1	0.0	6.6	314.1	19,936	38	46	646	5,610	45,273	3,213
Lee	16.5	2,496	51.3	1.3	4.3	0.2	14.6	16.9	2,561	13	19	381	2,210	37,412	2,649
Leslie	28.4	2,757	57.0	0.3	0.3	0.0	7.3	25.1	2,433	17	28	501	3,320	40,669	2,541
Letcher	49.1	2,202	68.0	0.2	2.0	0.1	3.9	38.1	1,709	38	63	995	7,170	42,379	2,926
Lewis	28.8	2,157	65.2	4.9	2.2	0.0	5.2	38.2	2,860	24	39	590	4,890	40,510	2,463
Lincoln	62.6	2,557	63.0	18.1	1.2	0.0	3.1	44.9	1,834	59	72	871	9,650	42,652	2,975
Livingston	35.5	3,838	34.0	37.5	1.8	0.0	5.1	26.0	2,808	98	27	434	3,880	49,469	3,974
Logan	73.6	2,727	68.8	0.5	5.1	0.1	3.6	88.4	3,274	66	81	1,144	11,820	49,866	4,015
Lyon	18.8	2,280	39.0	4.7	4.9	0.0	7.9	17.5	2,117	36	21	832	3,320	51,111	4,796
McCracken	195.9	2,998	46.6	0.1	4.0	0.1	7.4	855.8	13,093	569	221	3,553	30,710	64,335	7,349
McCreary	46.5	2,675	75.6	1.0	0.4	0.0	2.1	37.5	2,160	506	45	684	5,010	33,453	1,708
McLean	29.9	3,248	43.5	4.1	0.2	0.8	6.6	36.5	3,961	33	27	469	3,890	51,807	4,040
Madison	187.7	2,059	54.2	10.1	4.5	0.0	3.6	389.7	4,274	1,241	270	6,465	38,590	54,801	4,809
Magoffin	35.0	2,792	64.9	3.7	2.1	0.1	4.2	46.9	3,743	16	36	531	3,980	40,159	2,497
Marion	55.7	2,888	49.9	1.2	2.3	0.0	4.2	221.3	11,481	48	56	865	8,670	48,282	3,812
Marshall	113.5	3,623	38.6	21.8	4.0	0.5	3.9	892.8	28,506	92	92	1,523	14,360	57,316	5,252
Martin	32.5	2,828	72.5	7.0	0.5	0.0	5.5	76.5	6,657	392	29	445	3,040	39,166	2,924
Mason	45.5	2,645	54.7	5.9	5.3	0.0	8.4	181.3	10,545	50	50	1,232	7,450	50,890	4,397
Meade	63.2	2,254	69.5	2.5	0.9	0.0	2.2	90.1	3,213	37	85	943	13,350	54,532	4,342
Menifee	13.7	2,120	69.1	0.3	1.5	0.0	6.3	8.9	1,383	47	19	312	2,350	38,084	2,157
Mercer	54.6	2,537	51.0	3.6	2.4	0.0	3.4	121.3	5,629	48	65	810	10,010	50,777	4,038
Metcalfe	24.0	2,375	66.4	1.7	2.2	0.0	4.7	33.8	3,354	23	30	431	4,100	35,782	2,171
Monroe	32.1	3,029	54.2	7.1	2.4	1.1	4.8	39.9	3,766	25	31	572	4,230	41,721	3,245
Montgomery	66.1	2,367	61.8	6.6	3.4	0.0	3.7	65.9	2,361	68	83	1,079	11,980	50,447	4,463
Morgan	37.5	2,832	75.3	0.5	1.7	0.0	3.2	93.3	7,050	34	34	1,013	4,250	42,647	3,076
Muhlenberg	71.2	2,303	55.8	8.1	3.5	0.1	4.1	102.0	3,298	266	85	1,556	12,030	48,009	3,694
Nelson	131.1	2,875	53.0	2.1	2.9	0.1	3.0	385.7	8,459	84	137	1,704	22,660	58,017	5,488
Nicholas	26.1	3,647	75.9	2.1	0.2	0.2	3.2	33.4	4,669	15	21	285	3,060	39,169	2,613

1. Based on the resident population estimated as of July 1 of the year shown.

State / county code	CBSA code[1]	County Type code[2]	STATE County	Land area[3] (sq. mi)	Population, 2021: Total persons 2021	Population, 2021: Rank	Population, 2021: Per square mile	Race alone or in combination, not Hispanic or Latino (percent): White	Black	American Indian, Alaska Native	Asian and Pacific Islancer	Percent Hispanic or Latino[4]	Age (percent): Under 5 years	5 to 17 years	18 to 24 years	25 to 34 years	35 to 44 years	45 to 54 years
				1	2	3	4	5	6	7	8	9	10	11	12	13	14	15
			KENTUCKY—Cont'd															
21183		6	Ohio	587.3	23,688	1,654	40.3	95.0	1.6	0.6	0.4	3.4	5.8	13.6	12.2	11.6	12.4	12.4
21185	31140	1	Oldham	187.2	68,685	784	366.9	89.6	5.0	0.7	2.4	4.1	5.0	14.8	13.4	10.0	14.9	15.1
21187		8	Owen	351.1	11,294	2,325	32.2	95.7	1.7	0.6	0.4	2.6	5.1	12.4	11.8	11.3	11.8	13.8
21189		9	Owsley	197.4	3,953	2,890	20.0	97.0	1.2	0.8	0.2	1.8	6.3	12.0	10.8	11.6	11.7	12.7
21191	17140	1	Pendleton	277.2	14,607	2,109	52.7	96.9	1.7	0.8	0.6	1.5	6.0	13.1	11.4	12.4	11.0	13.1
21193		7	Perry	339.7	27,929	1,501	82.2	96.0	2.3	0.6	1.2	1.1	6.1	13.2	10.7	12.1	12.4	13.2
21195		7	Pike	786.7	57,391	910	73.0	97.5	1.1	0.5	0.7	1.0	5.1	11.7	11.8	11.2	12.0	13.7
21197		6	Powell	179.0	13,133	2,205	73.4	96.6	1.6	0.6	0.6	1.7	6.0	14.1	11.5	12.7	12.9	13.0
21199	43700	5	Pulaski	658.4	65,423	824	99.4	94.9	1.7	0.8	1.1	2.7	5.7	12.5	11.2	11.9	12.1	13.1
21201		8	Robertson	99.9	2,257	3,022	22.6	96.9	1.5	0.9	0.4	1.9	5.5	12.7	9.8	10.3	10.7	12.5
21203		7	Rockcastle	316.5	16,115	2,027	50.9	97.8	0.9	1.1	0.4	1.1	5.0	12.2	11.1	11.9	11.6	14.1
21205		7	Rowan	279.8	24,861	1,619	88.9	95.2	2.5	0.6	1.1	2.0	5.3	11.0	25.5	12.4	10.0	10.3
21207		9	Russell	253.7	18,156	1,917	71.6	94.6	1.4	0.7	0.7	3.9	5.9	13.3	10.7	11.3	10.5	12.8
21209	30460	2	Scott	281.8	58,252	900	206.7	88.4	6.7	0.6	1.8	4.6	6.2	14.1	13.5	14.1	14.0	13.6
21211	31140	1	Shelby	379.8	48,461	1,014	127.6	82.2	8.2	0.8	1.6	9.7	5.7	12.4	12.3	12.6	13.2	13.4
21213		6	Simpson	234.2	19,718	1,840	84.2	87.0	10.2	0.8	1.0	2.9	6.0	13.6	12.0	13.2	11.9	12.5
21215	31140	1	Spencer	186.7	19,916	1,817	106.7	94.8	2.5	0.7	0.7	2.7	5.4	12.9	10.9	10.8	13.8	15.0
21217	15820	7	Taylor	266.4	26,235	1,554	98.5	91.2	6.6	0.6	1.1	2.6	6.2	12.7	15.1	12.5	11.4	10.7
21219		8	Todd	374.5	12,285	2,262	32.8	86.9	8.7	0.8	0.6	5.0	7.1	15.1	12.9	11.6	11.6	12.0
21221	17300	2	Trigg	441.5	14,192	2,132	32.1	89.5	8.5	1.0	0.8	2.6	5.5	12.0	10.9	9.9	10.4	12.7
21223		1	Trimble	151.6	8,530	2,533	56.3	94.6	1.4	0.9	1.0	3.6	5.5	12.7	11.1	11.9	11.3	14.5
21225		6	Union	342.8	13,544	2,188	39.5	83.8	14.2	0.7	0.9	2.1	4.6	9.5	19.1	11.5	11.8	12.0
21227	14540	3	Warren	541.7	137,212	477	253.3	78.9	11.0	0.7	6.2	5.7	6.3	12.9	19.4	13.6	12.3	11.3
21229		9	Washington	297.0	12,072	2,278	40.6	89.6	6.6	0.5	0.9	4.2	6.1	13.3	11.5	11.5	11.8	12.6
21231		7	Wayne	458.2	19,540	1,849	42.6	94.0	2.3	0.8	0.5	3.7	5.5	11.2	10.9	11.7	11.3	12.7
21233		8	Webster	332.1	12,813	2,221	38.6	89.5	4.5	0.7	0.8	6.0	6.3	13.3	11.2	11.5	13.0	12.6
21235	30940	7	Whitley	437.8	36,939	1,255	84.4	96.7	1.4	0.8	0.7	1.6	7.1	14.5	15.3	12.4	11.2	11.5
21237		9	Wolfe	222.2	6,507	2,700	29.3	97.9	0.9	0.8	0.4	1.1	6.3	12.0	11.7	10.6	12.2	12.3
21239	30460	2	Woodford	190.1	27,075	1,526	142.4	87.9	5.6	0.5	1.0	6.6	5.2	12.7	12.2	10.2	12.2	12.4
22000		0	LOUISIANA	43,204.5	4,624,047	X	107.0	59.3	33.4	1.2	2.3	5.6	6.2	13.3	12.9	13.5	13.2	11.6
22001	29180	2	Acadia	655.2	57,288	911	87.4	78.3	18.7	0.7	0.6	3.4	6.7	14.4	12.9	12.9	12.4	11.4
22003		6	Allen	762.1	22,687	1,688	29.8	71.3	23.9	2.9	1.0	2.9	5.9	12.4	11.9	15.8	14.3	12.8
22005	12940	2	Ascension	290.0	128,369	506	442.7	67.7	24.9	0.7	1.8	6.4	6.6	15.2	12.6	13.2	14.8	12.8
22007	12940	6	Assumption	344.0	20,689	1,780	60.1	66.1	29.8	1.0	0.7	3.4	5.1	11.7	11.4	12.3	11.9	12.5
22009		6	Avoyelles	831.9	39,236	1,198	47.2	65.9	30.9	1.8	1.0	2.3	6.2	13.4	12.1	13.4	12.8	11.7
22011	19760	6	Beauregard	1,157.5	36,584	1,270	31.6	82.5	12.7	1.9	1.3	4.1	6.7	14.2	12.3	13.5	12.7	12.3
22013		6	Bienville	811.3	12,776	2,225	15.7	56.1	41.7	1.1	0.7	2.2	5.8	12.8	11.0	11.3	11.4	11.5
22015	43340	2	Bossier	839.5	129,144	501	153.8	66.7	25.0	1.1	2.8	7.0	6.4	14.2	13.0	14.1	14.2	11.2
22017	43340	2	Caddo	879.5	233,092	295	265.0	44.9	50.8	1.0	1.9	3.1	6.2	13.4	12.2	13.0	12.6	11.4
22019	29340	3	Calcasieu	1,064.1	205,282	337	192.9	68.9	26.0	1.1	1.9	4.2	6.9	13.8	12.3	13.9	12.9	11.4
22021		8	Caldwell	529.8	9,571	2,446	18.1	79.7	16.5	0.9	0.6	3.7	5.7	12.6	12.1	13.3	12.4	12.2
22023	29340	3	Cameron	1,284.6	5,080	2,816	4.0	90.6	4.7	1.6	0.8	4.4	6.0	12.5	11.4	12.4	12.2	11.5
22025		9	Catahoula	708.0	8,805	2,503	12.4	66.1	32.0	1.0	0.3	1.9	5.7	11.8	11.7	13.5	13.5	11.0
22027		6	Claiborne	754.8	14,038	2,149	18.6	45.2	52.7	1.0	0.8	1.7	4.5	10.4	10.7	15.7	12.8	12.4
22029	35020	7	Concordia	697.1	18,376	1,905	26.4	57.1	40.5	0.8	0.7	1.9	6.2	13.3	12.6	13.6	12.2	10.8
22031	43340	2	De Soto	876.4	26,919	1,529	30.7	61.2	34.9	1.6	0.7	3.3	5.8	13.9	11.6	11.9	13.0	12.0
22033	12940	2	East Baton Rouge	455.5	453,301	158	995.2	44.7	47.7	0.6	3.9	4.6	6.2	12.8	17.2	13.8	12.6	10.5
22035		7	East Carroll	420.9	7,220	2,645	17.2	28.6	68.2	0.7	0.6	2.9	4.9	13.4	13.1	15.9	12.6	11.1
22037	12940	2	East Feliciana	453.3	19,338	1,857	42.7	55.5	42.5	1.0	0.6	1.9	4.8	9.7	11.0	12.6	13.3	13.7
22039		6	Evangeline	662.4	32,215	1,376	48.6	67.5	28.1	0.8	0.7	4.3	6.9	14.1	13.2	13.7	12.2	11.4
22041		7	Franklin	624.3	19,668	1,843	31.5	65.8	32.3	0.5	0.6	1.8	6.6	13.8	12.3	12.1	12.1	11.0
22043	10780	3	Grant	643.2	22,236	1,704	34.6	77.3	16.2	1.7	0.9	5.5	5.5	11.9	10.9	17.0	15.0	11.9
22045	29180	2	Iberia	573.7	68,975	782	120.2	59.9	33.7	0.8	3.1	4.4	6.5	14.4	12.8	12.7	12.1	11.3
22047	12940	2	Iberville	618.7	29,824	1,440	48.2	48.6	48.1	0.7	0.6	3.2	5.5	11.0	11.6	14.6	13.8	12.8
22049		6	Jackson	569.4	14,876	2,095	26.1	69.2	29.0	0.9	0.9	1.9	4.7	12.2	11.6	12.4	12.5	12.2
22051	35380	1	Jefferson	300.9	433,688	165	1,441.3	52.2	28.3	0.9	5.0	15.3	6.2	12.4	10.9	13.5	13.1	11.8
22053	27660	6	Jefferson Davis	651.5	32,345	1,372	49.6	79.7	18.0	1.2	0.9	2.5	6.5	14.6	12.2	12.9	12.4	11.2
22055	29180	2	Lafayette	268.8	244,205	285	908.5	65.9	28.0	0.7	2.4	4.7	6.4	13.5	12.7	15.2	14.2	11.5
22057	26380	3	Lafourche	1,067.8	97,504	628	91.3	78.1	14.5	3.6	1.2	4.6	5.9	13.2	12.1	13.5	13.0	11.9
22059		6	La Salle	624.9	14,834	2,097	23.7	83.1	12.6	1.6	0.6	3.1	5.8	13.3	12.5	13.8	13.6	11.8
22061	40820	4	Lincoln	471.6	48,152	1,019	102.1	54.7	40.8	0.7	1.8	3.2	5.1	11.1	28.5	11.6	10.7	8.9
22063	12940	2	Livingston	648.1	145,830	456	225.0	85.7	9.0	0.8	1.1	4.7	6.3	14.7	12.4	14.1	14.3	12.6
22065		7	Madison	624.2	9,799	2,422	15.7	34.2	63.2	0.8	0.5	2.6	6.6	13.1	12.2	17.0	11.6	12.3
22067	33740	6	Morehouse	795.0	25,025	1,609	31.5	49.9	48.3	0.7	0.8	1.6	6.3	13.5	11.9	11.5	11.7	11.7
22069	35060	6	Natchitoches	1,253.3	37,026	1,252	29.5	54.4	42.3	1.9	1.1	2.6	5.8	12.8	20.8	11.2	10.4	10.3

1. CBSA = Core Based Statistical Area. See Appendix A for explanation. See Appendix B for list of metropolitan areas with component counties. 2. County type code from the Economic Research Service of USDA Rural-Urban Continuum Codes. See Appendix A for definition. 3. Dry land or land partially or temporarily covered by water. 4. May be of any race.

STATE County	Population, 2021 (cont.) — Age (percent) (cont.) — 55 to 64 years	65 to 74 years	75 years and over	Percent female	Population change, 2000–2021 — Total persons — 2010	2020	Percent change — 2010–2020	2020–2021	Components of change, 2020–2021 — Births	Deaths	Net Migration	Households, 2016–2020 — Number	Persons per household	Percent — Family house-holds	Female family house-holder[1]	One person
	16	17	18	19	20	21	22	23	24	25	26	27	28	29	30	31
KENTUCKY—Cont'd																
Ohio	13.5	11.2	7.3	49.6	23,842	23,772	-0.3	-0.4	319	410	4	9,226	2.6	69.8	11.9	24.4
Oldham	12.7	9.1	5.1	47.4	60,316	67,607	12.1	1.6	665	669	1,088	21,259	3.0	83.1	8.6	14.4
Owen	14.7	12.1	7.0	50.0	10,841	11,278	4.0	0.1	108	196	105	4,246	2.5	67.1	6.8	29.3
Owsley	14.4	12.1	8.3	50.5	4,755	4,051	-14.8	-2.4	47	117	-28	1,655	2.6	66.1	18.1	30.6
Pendleton	16.0	10.9	6.1	48.7	14,877	14,644	-1.6	-0.3	205	240	-3	5,250	2.7	72.0	11.3	25.6
Perry	14.3	11.6	6.3	50.4	28,712	28,473	-0.8	-1.9	376	631	-289	11,334	2.3	69.1	18.6	25.6
Pike	14.6	12.6	7.3	50.8	65,024	58,669	-9.8	-2.2	676	1,247	-706	25,506	2.3	67.7	12.5	29.0
Powell	13.6	10.5	5.8	49.9	12,613	13,129	4.1	0.0	191	218	28	4,698	2.6	70.9	13.8	27.4
Pulaski	14.1	11.9	7.5	50.8	63,063	65,034	3.1	0.6	847	1,273	819	25,572	2.5	64.0	11.6	29.9
Robertson	15.6	11.9	10.9	49.4	2,282	2,193	-3.9	2.9	26	54	95	859	2.4	62.3	8.5	27.5
Rockcastle	15.3	11.6	7.2	50.8	17,056	16,037	-6.0	0.5	184	317	212	6,609	2.5	69.3	13.1	28.2
Rowan	11.1	8.6	5.8	51.4	23,333	24,662	5.7	0.8	312	322	206	8,747	2.5	58.8	11.0	30.4
Russell	14.8	12.6	8.0	50.8	17,565	17,991	2.4	0.9	226	374	315	7,122	2.5	65.2	9.1	29.1
Scott	11.7	8.4	4.4	50.6	47,173	57,155	21.2	1.9	867	652	871	21,186	2.6	73.8	11.2	19.9
Shelby	14.0	10.4	6.1	51.1	42,074	48,065	14.2	0.8	688	629	328	16,801	2.8	72.6	9.4	21.9
Simpson	14.1	10.3	6.5	51.2	17,327	19,594	13.1	0.6	289	308	141	7,181	2.5	66.5	10.7	28.3
Spencer	15.9	10.1	5.2	49.0	17,061	19,490	14.2	2.2	221	246	455	6,899	2.7	81.8	9.5	13.5
Taylor	13.1	10.9	7.3	50.9	24,512	26,023	6.2	0.8	385	486	314	9,659	2.5	68.1	10.8	27.3
Todd	13.2	9.9	6.6	49.6	12,460	12,243	-1.7	0.3	201	190	29	4,655	2.6	71.5	10.3	23.5
Trigg	15.8	13.9	9.0	49.8	14,339	14,061	-1.9	0.9	200	297	231	5,916	2.5	67.0	8.2	30.5
Trimble	15.0	11.1	6.8	49.4	8,809	8,474	-3.8	0.7	99	151	110	3,398	2.5	65.3	12.4	27.6
Union	13.3	12.1	6.1	47.5	15,007	13,668	-8.9	-0.9	186	244	-64	5,176	2.5	72.8	9.4	24.4
Warren	10.9	8.2	5.1	50.6	113,792	134,554	18.2	2.0	2,097	1,626	2,179	49,880	2.5	62.3	12.5	28.0
Washington	14.6	11.2	7.4	50.6	11,717	12,027	2.6	0.4	158	213	99	4,702	2.5	64.0	10.7	28.3
Wayne	14.5	13.4	8.8	50.3	20,813	19,555	-6.0	-0.1	262	371	93	8,298	2.4	66.8	12.1	30.0
Webster	13.8	11.4	7.0	49.8	13,621	13,017	-4.4	-1.6	187	265	-126	5,001	2.5	66.5	10.3	30.2
Whitley	11.9	9.7	6.4	50.6	35,637	36,712	3.0	0.6	637	692	279	12,685	2.7	70.8	11.7	23.9
Wolfe	15.0	12.4	7.5	50.5	7,355	6,562	-10.8	-0.8	101	150	-6	2,991	2.4	59.9	13.8	35.9
Woodford	14.9	12.9	7.3	51.7	24,939	26,871	7.7	0.8	297	352	259	10,399	2.5	71.3	11.8	24.8
LOUISIANA	12.9	10.2	6.3	51.0	4,533,372	4,657,757	2.7	-0.7	69,279	68,795	-34,074	1,751,956	2.6	63.7	15.5	30.7
Acadia	13.2	9.9	6.3	50.8	61,773	57,576	-6.8	-0.5	989	1,037	-251	22,598	2.7	70.7	13.6	25.5
Allen	12.0	8.9	6.1	42.6	25,764	22,750	-11.7	-0.3	368	368	-68	8,137	2.6	72.2	14.5	25.5
Ascension	11.9	8.3	4.5	50.6	107,215	126,500	18.0	1.5	1,948	1,226	1,121	44,029	2.8	75.3	12.9	19.9
Assumption	15.1	12.0	7.9	51.1	23,421	21,039	-10.2	-1.7	281	340	-289	8,941	2.5	69.9	14.8	26.2
Avoyelles	12.9	10.5	7.1	49.1	42,073	39,693	-5.7	-1.2	567	725	-302	15,217	2.4	63.7	16.7	30.6
Beauregard	12.5	9.9	6.0	48.8	35,654	36,549	2.5	0.1	562	560	28	13,812	2.7	68.2	12.6	27.5
Bienville	14.8	11.7	9.7	51.5	14,353	12,981	-9.6	-1.6	161	287	-80	5,855	2.2	58.5	18.6	38.9
Bossier	11.7	9.2	6.0	50.5	116,979	128,746	10.1	0.3	1,953	1,740	155	49,600	2.5	65.4	13.2	28.6
Caddo	12.9	11.2	7.2	52.5	254,969	237,848	-6.7	-2.0	3,711	4,042	-4,390	96,043	2.5	59.7	18.2	35.4
Calcasieu	12.7	9.9	6.1	50.8	192,768	216,785	12.5	-5.3	3,525	3,092	-11,736	78,427	2.5	65.9	14.9	27.3
Caldwell	12.8	11.5	7.2	48.2	10,132	9,645	-4.8	-0.8	123	182	-17	3,899	2.5	72.2	11.9	22.6
Cameron	16.1	11.0	6.9	49.2	6,839	5,617	-17.9	-9.6	85	85	-530	2,902	2.4	82.9	18.3	14.6
Catahoula	14.1	11.7	7.0	46.3	10,407	8,906	-14.4	-1.1	149	144	-107	3,394	2.5	73.8	10.0	23.2
Claiborne	13.4	11.8	8.3	42.8	17,195	14,170	-17.6	-0.9	176	282	-28	5,808	2.4	60.2	15.5	36.6
Concordia	12.4	11.6	7.3	48.8	20,822	18,687	-10.3	-1.7	272	353	-231	6,694	2.7	69.1	20.0	27.2
De Soto	13.5	11.1	7.2	51.4	26,656	26,812	0.6	0.4	395	464	172	10,951	2.5	67.6	21.5	29.3
East Baton Rouge	11.5	9.6	5.8	52.2	440,171	456,781	3.8	-0.8	6,816	5,966	-4,372	164,641	2.6	60.0	15.6	32.7
East Carroll	12.9	9.7	6.3	43.7	7,759	7,459	-3.9	-3.2	85	111	-211	1,688	2.5	56.4	21.0	37.0
East Feliciana	15.7	12.3	7.0	44.7	20,267	19,539	-3.6	-1.0	210	369	-44	7,010	2.2	67.3	16.0	28.4
Evangeline	12.8	9.4	6.3	48.7	33,984	32,350	-4.8	-0.4	549	568	-122	12,393	2.6	64.2	18.8	31.3
Franklin	13.3	11.0	7.7	50.9	20,767	19,774	-4.8	-0.5	309	341	-78	7,503	2.5	70.9	17.8	27.1
Grant	12.1	9.5	6.1	43.5	22,309	22,169	-0.6	0.3	317	297	42	7,054	2.7	67.1	12.1	31.0
Iberia	13.9	10.1	6.1	50.9	73,240	69,929	-4.5	-1.4	1,104	1,094	-964	26,776	2.6	71.3	15.2	24.0
Iberville	13.7	10.4	6.6	49.1	33,387	30,241	-9.4	-1.4	408	489	-338	11,105	2.6	73.1	24.0	23.7
Jackson	13.9	11.4	9.0	48.5	16,274	15,031	-7.6	-1.0	150	287	-18	5,859	2.5	66.6	15.6	30.4
Jefferson	13.8	11.2	7.2	51.5	432,552	440,781	1.9	-1.6	6,769	6,543	-7,248	170,398	2.5	61.3	14.5	33.3
Jefferson Davis	13.5	10.0	6.7	50.7	31,594	32,250	2.1	0.3	496	563	159	11,565	2.7	68.4	16.3	29.3
Lafayette	12.3	9.2	5.1	51.3	221,578	241,753	9.1	1.0	3,742	2,928	1,594	92,476	2.6	63.9	13.2	28.4
Lafourche	14.1	9.8	6.6	50.7	96,318	97,557	1.3	-0.1	1,370	1,407	-39	36,645	2.6	69.4	13.4	25.4
La Salle	11.8	10.5	6.9	47.9	14,890	14,791	-0.7	0.3	197	231	74	4,868	2.8	75.2	14.5	22.4
Lincoln	9.7	8.5	5.9	51.0	46,735	48,396	3.6	-0.5	555	613	-199	17,861	2.5	55.4	18.1	32.5
Livingston	11.9	8.6	5.1	50.7	128,026	142,282	11.1	2.5	2,081	1,716	3,203	48,690	2.9	74.2	15.6	20.7
Madison	11.8	9.9	5.6	50.6	12,093	10,017	-17.2	-2.2	159	197	-179	3,729	2.4	65.6	26.0	31.9
Morehouse	13.4	12.4	7.7	51.6	27,979	25,629	-8.4	-2.4	358	551	-409	9,738	2.5	60.1	14.8	36.5
Natchitoches	11.3	10.2	7.1	51.9	39,566	37,515	-5.2	-1.3	535	608	-419	14,324	2.6	53.2	12.9	36.8

1. No spouse present.

STATE County	Persons in group quarters, 2021	Daytime Population, 2016–2020		Births, 2021		Deaths, 2021		Persons under 65 with no health insurance, 2019		Medicare, 2021			COVID-19 Deaths, 2020	
		Number	Employment/ residence ratio	Total	Rate[1]	Number	Rate[1]	Number	Percent	Total beneficiaries	Enrolled in Original Medicare	Enrolled in Medicare Advantage	Number	Rate[1]
	32	33	34	35	36	37	38	39	40	41	42	43	44	45
KENTUCKY—Cont'd														
Ohio	238	23,126	0.9	263	11.1	342	14.4	1,501	7.8	5,705	3,515	2,190	29	1.2
Oldham	4,336	53,876	0.6	539	7.9	528	7.7	2,356	4.3	10,368	6,752	3,616	60	0.9
Owen	0	8,639	0.5	87	7.7	152	13.5	741	8.5	2,388	1,308	1,080	11	1.0
Owsley	44	4,065	0.7	41	10.3	91	22.8	253	7.3	1,155	757	399	12	3.0
Pendleton	183	10,875	0.4	169	11.6	197	13.5	962	8.0	3,152	1,733	1,419	D	D
Perry	618	28,716	1.3	287	10.2	505	17.9	1,657	8.0	6,932	4,277	2,655	38	1.3
Pike	1,419	61,383	1.2	538	9.3	998	17.2	4,051	9.0	16,661	10,434	6,227	49	0.8
Powell	186	10,424	0.6	159	12.1	163	12.4	754	7.5	3,154	1,768	1,387	D	D
Pulaski	853	66,645	1.1	684	10.5	1,003	15.4	4,845	9.4	17,037	10,438	6,599	75	1.2
Robertson	55	1,775	0.6	21	9.5	43	19.4	136	8.4	570	368	203	D	D
Rockcastle	215	15,619	0.8	150	9.3	273	17.0	1,004	7.6	4,092	2,652	1,440	16	1.0
Rowan	2,961	26,187	1.2	232	9.4	251	10.1	1,431	8.0	4,866	2,520	2,345	11	0.4
Russell	135	17,648	1.0	176	9.7	284	15.7	1,394	9.9	4,626	3,195	1,431	37	2.1
Scott	983	58,931	1.1	673	11.6	498	8.6	3,076	6.3	8,685	4,737	3,948	25	0.4
Shelby	1,565	43,341	0.8	560	11.6	512	10.6	3,759	9.4	9,033	5,532	3,501	50	1.0
Simpson	322	19,880	1.2	232	11.8	255	13.0	1,129	7.5	4,110	2,691	1,420	25	1.3
Spencer	78	12,252	0.3	176	8.9	205	10.4	1,029	6.2	3,562	2,194	1,369	16	0.8
Taylor	1,305	26,950	1.1	295	11.3	394	15.1	1,442	7.3	6,171	4,205	1,966	34	1.3
Todd	142	10,299	0.6	157	12.8	158	12.9	1,266	12.6	2,469	1,793	677	15	1.2
Trigg	38	12,905	0.7	167	11.8	240	17.0	943	8.5	3,928	2,717	1,211	11	0.8
Trimble	23	6,488	0.4	80	9.4	126	14.8	495	7.2	1,986	1,228	757	11	1.3
Union	1,496	14,198	0.9	148	10.9	192	14.1	998	8.4	3,202	1,905	1,297	13	1.0
Warren	6,392	138,936	1.1	1,712	12.6	1,301	9.6	9,688	9.0	21,237	13,559	7,678	108	0.8
Washington	163	10,912	0.8	124	10.3	168	13.9	852	8.7	2,721	1,899	822	28	2.3
Wayne	242	19,499	0.9	209	10.7	300	15.4	1,298	8.4	5,173	3,489	1,684	27	1.4
Webster	362	11,431	0.7	146	11.3	210	16.3	1,057	10.3	3,109	1,933	1,176	25	1.9
Whitley	1,844	37,222	1.1	516	14.0	570	15.5	2,178	7.6	8,658	5,739	2,919	35	1.0
Wolfe	80	6,880	0.8	84	12.9	123	18.8	438	7.9	1,965	1,099	867	D	D
Woodford	491	25,088	0.9	235	8.7	288	10.7	1,652	7.8	5,922	3,197	2,725	D	D
LOUISIANA	121,748	4,676,854	1.0	55,942	12.1	55,335	11.9	391,933	10.3	883,811	512,547	371,264	7,066	1.5
Acadia	759	53,549	0.6	820	14.3	833	14.5	5,206	10.1	12,140	9,247	2,893	136	2.4
Allen	3,638	25,665	1.0	301	13.3	291	12.8	1,784	10.1	4,566	3,623	944	57	2.5
Ascension	636	112,411	0.8	1,570	12.3	1,039	8.1	8,059	7.3	18,222	7,322	10,900	125	1.0
Assumption	116	17,963	0.6	218	10.5	282	13.5	1,771	10.1	4,956	2,780	2,177	27	1.3
Avoyelles	3,160	36,317	0.7	453	11.5	584	14.8	3,206	10.6	8,958	6,575	2,383	74	1.9
Beauregard	1,115	33,221	0.7	476	13.0	464	12.7	3,327	11.0	7,260	5,832	1,427	57	1.6
Bienville	250	12,454	0.8	141	11.0	235	18.3	971	9.5	3,408	2,372	1,036	50	3.9
Bossier	2,427	120,069	0.9	1,581	12.3	1,400	10.9	10,025	9.4	21,573	15,371	6,202	191	1.5
Caddo	5,959	257,773	1.2	2,991	12.7	3,302	14.0	18,842	9.8	50,479	33,333	17,146	501	2.1
Calcasieu	3,883	213,959	1.1	2,826	13.4	2,468	11.7	16,151	9.6	36,363	27,564	8,799	273	1.3
Caldwell	515	8,926	0.7	91	9.5	147	15.3	879	11.6	2,244	1,584	660	23	2.4
Cameron	9	10,972	2.3	71	13.3	67	12.5	591	10.2	1,201	946	255	D	D
Catahoula	761	8,504	0.6	116	13.1	114	12.9	708	10.2	2,286	1,677	609	25	2.8
Claiborne	2,547	14,694	0.8	141	10.0	213	15.1	1,040	10.7	3,387	2,481	906	47	3.3
Concordia	1,348	18,818	0.9	212	11.5	292	15.8	1,409	9.8	4,233	3,222	1,011	47	2.5
De Soto	126	24,332	0.7	321	11.9	380	14.1	2,383	10.7	6,127	4,334	1,792	54	2.0
East Baton Rouge	11,341	494,304	1.2	5,476	12.0	4,757	10.5	38,246	10.5	76,280	36,598	39,682	537	1.2
East Carroll	1,147	7,114	1.2	73	10.0	88	12.1	411	8.8	1,373	934	439	21	2.8
East Feliciana	2,445	18,977	1.0	172	8.9	282	14.5	1,222	9.2	4,240	2,285	1,956	70	3.6
Evangeline	1,190	30,020	0.7	436	13.5	471	14.6	2,885	10.8	7,133	5,573	1,560	57	1.8
Franklin	648	18,284	0.7	258	13.1	294	14.9	1,871	11.9	4,577	3,277	1,300	61	3.1
Grant	2,881	18,311	0.5	265	11.9	240	10.8	1,676	10.5	4,238	3,056	1,181	39	1.8
Iberia	847	69,507	1.0	884	12.7	857	12.4	6,592	11.4	14,429	9,594	4,835	90	1.3
Iberville	3,578	40,155	1.6	345	11.5	402	13.4	2,043	8.7	6,278	2,527	3,751	71	2.4
Jackson	871	14,694	0.8	122	8.2	237	15.9	1,134	9.8	3,629	2,569	1,060	23	1.5
Jefferson	3,159	426,911	1.0	5,422	12.4	5,246	12.0	45,498	12.9	88,616	32,654	55,962	647	1.5
Jefferson Davis	537	28,397	0.7	406	12.6	446	13.8	2,632	10.2	6,584	5,383	1,201	59	1.8
Lafayette	4,733	270,486	1.2	3,063	12.6	2,380	9.8	19,679	9.5	40,130	29,979	10,152	176	0.7
Lafourche	1,499	91,168	0.8	1,090	11.2	1,126	11.5	9,931	12.3	18,897	10,610	8,287	152	1.6
La Salle	1,137	14,354	0.9	161	10.9	186	12.5	1,299	11.6	3,077	2,484	594	25	1.7
Lincoln	5,024	47,455	1.0	442	9.2	477	9.9	4,094	11.5	7,443	5,044	2,399	72	1.5
Livingston	1,036	107,163	0.5	1,708	11.8	1,375	9.5	11,767	9.7	22,329	9,394	12,935	121	0.8
Madison	1,342	11,152	1.0	133	13.5	160	16.2	707	9.1	2,020	1,549	471	20	2.0
Morehouse	758	22,776	0.7	290	11.5	427	16.9	1,837	9.5	6,475	4,149	2,327	46	1.8
Natchitoches	2,062	39,149	1.1	429	11.5	476	12.8	3,042	10.3	7,666	5,793	1,872	60	1.6

1. Per 1,000 estimated resident population.

STATE County	COVID-19 Vaccinations, 2021–2022: Number	COVID-19 Vaccinations, 2021–2022: Percent[5]	Education: School enrollment and attainment, 2016–2020: Enrollment[1]: Total	Enrollment[1]: Percent private	Attainment[2] (percent): High school graduate or less	Attainment[2] (percent): Bachelor's degree or more	Local government expenditures,[3] 2018–2019: Total current spending (mil dol)	Local government expenditures: Current spending per student (dollars)	Money income, 2016–2020: Per capita income[4]	Households: Median income (dollars)	Households: Percent with income of less than $50,000	Households: Percent with income of $200,000 or more	Income and poverty, 2020: Median household income (dollars)	Percent below poverty level: All persons	Percent below poverty level: Children under 18 years	Percent below poverty level: Children 5 to 17 years in families
	46	47	48	49	50	51	52	53	54	55	56	57	58	59	60	61
KENTUCKY—Cont'd																
Ohio	9,543	39.8	5,272	8.6	58.3	13.0	41.9	9,832	24,728	45,773	57.0	1.7	48,621	15.0	21.5	19.5
Oldham	38,316	57.4	18,484	18.6	25.4	43.0	128.2	10,076	44,186	103,761	21.5	17.8	105,897	5.0	4.5	3.7
Owen	4,116	37.8	2,186	10.2	61.9	16.3	19.6	10,372	25,997	50,553	48.6	3.0	45,177	15.1	19.9	18.7
Owsley	2,102	47.6	683	3.2	70.3	14.5	11.0	13,715	18,917	29,406	67.3	0.2	25,997	30.6	44.0	41.9
Pendleton	6,449	44.2	3,326	10.1	57.8	14.2	23.6	9,951	25,647	56,000	46.1	2.2	60,824	13.6	20.1	19.2
Perry	16,037	62.3	5,592	7.9	53.9	14.3	54.6	10,891	24,466	39,594	59.0	2.2	35,555	22.0	29.5	26.8
Pike	30,606	52.9	13,100	11.1	61.5	13.9	109.7	11,188	22,515	34,700	64.6	1.6	38,917	23.7	27.7	26.7
Powell	6,538	52.9	2,833	9.8	59.6	17.6	23.9	10,410	21,484	41,071	54.9	1.3	40,215	20.5	30.6	29.3
Pulaski	30,111	46.3	13,852	11.1	50.1	16.8	108.2	10,243	26,063	40,658	56.6	2.3	44,717	19.1	26.5	25.5
Robertson	815	38.7	495	4.8	54.4	13.8	5.1	11,130	23,794	53,074	46.1	2.8	49,529	17.9	23.6	22.1
Rockcastle	6,763	40.5	3,715	8.6	62.5	12.9	30.3	10,738	22,597	38,744	58.9	1.6	42,205	22.4	28.2	24.7
Rowan	12,792	52.3	8,307	5.5	47.0	25.8	34.2	9,858	23,985	42,754	57.4	5.3	46,535	24.4	28.8	27.5
Russell	8,222	45.9	3,609	7.1	55.0	15.5	32.6	10,412	22,956	41,731	56.6	2.7	41,088	18.1	26.6	25.3
Scott	31,804	55.8	14,510	21.7	36.9	30.4	90.3	9,538	33,535	71,750	33.2	6.2	70,526	8.0	10.3	9.3
Shelby	23,013	46.9	10,652	21.7	41.7	28.0	76.8	10,629	33,189	72,564	35.6	7.3	75,600	8.4	11.8	11.5
Simpson	9,408	50.7	3,966	9.2	58.9	12.0	33.3	11,093	24,402	50,159	49.8	2.2	56,107	12.0	18.8	17.4
Spencer	5,822	30.1	4,066	12.0	44.3	21.4	29.5	9,617	35,209	85,488	29.5	5.0	83,583	6.8	8.2	7.5
Taylor	12,410	48.2	6,678	21.2	49.7	23.5	41.4	10,683	25,441	50,266	49.9	2.5	48,384	15.9	22.5	22.9
Todd	5,213	42.4	2,805	21.2	61.3	14.5	20.2	10,089	23,971	47,229	50.6	2.9	50,393	17.3	24.8	23.4
Trigg	6,901	47.1	2,975	17.0	44.1	19.1	22.0	10,825	26,953	50,980	48.2	2.5	50,258	16.7	27.1	24.2
Trimble	3,710	43.8	1,677	12.3	61.2	15.1	13.2	10,581	27,194	57,589	46.2	2.1	64,971	12.2	16.0	15.2
Union	6,065	42.2	2,637	15.3	54.9	11.1	24.1	10,854	23,705	49,812	50.3	2.1	53,064	17.5	21.7	19.4
Warren	51,431	38.7	38,731	8.7	38.5	32.2	207.7	10,101	30,138	54,325	46.3	4.6	56,552	18.7	23.7	20.7
Washington	6,186	51.1	2,631	23.6	55.0	20.3	19.5	11,262	27,448	55,321	44.9	4.6	51,897	14.2	17.5	16.8
Wayne	8,565	42.1	3,624	4.9	65.4	13.3	35.6	11,092	26,172	37,678	60.4	1.7	36,628	23.6	32.9	31.1
Webster	5,962	46.1	2,498	9.2	62.1	10.4	22.9	10,186	24,341	44,540	55.1	2.8	52,901	15.6	19.3	19.1
Whitley	16,127	44.5	9,591	22.6	56.9	20.0	88.9	10,710	21,535	39,258	58.8	1.8	34,559	21.7	28.7	27.4
Wolfe	3,856	53.9	1,360	13.6	64.0	6.6	16.1	12,542	14,162	22,292	77.7	0.2	33,757	29.7	41.0	39.0
Woodford	17,702	66.2	6,054	18.7	36.8	36.8	43.9	10,757	32,847	66,442	38.9	3.8	69,544	9.1	10.9	10.2
LOUISIANA	2,484,925	53.5	1,145,889	19.6	47.4	24.9	8,381.1	11,787	29,522	50,800	49.2	4.7	51,730	17.8	24.3	23.0
Acadia	32,866	53.0	14,372	18.2	61.7	15.2	92.9	9,512	25,174	44,412	54.7	2.5	45,183	20.7	33.1	28.3
Allen	9,247	36.1	5,213	11.9	61.6	12.3	47.6	11,180	21,829	48,328	52.0	1.5	49,671	21.1	24.5	22.2
Ascension	64,518	51.0	32,883	19.5	40.2	27.6	261.7	11,611	35,699	82,594	30.2	8.4	88,680	9.6	12.9	12.0
Assumption	9,527	43.5	4,755	16.3	64.9	12.9	37.4	11,149	26,952	44,742	53.0	4.5	52,046	15.8	26.1	24.8
Avoyelles	18,729	46.7	10,263	21.1	58.6	12.3	56.8	9,440	21,049	35,530	63.1	2.6	40,448	21.6	31.0	28.9
Beauregard	13,445	35.9	8,555	10.7	49.9	18.3	60.7	10,333	27,626	49,256	50.5	3.1	53,708	14.5	19.2	17.9
Bienville	6,508	49.2	3,045	13.4	60.3	12.3	39.8	18,446	21,513	27,815	68.4	2.0	39,695	22.8	38.0	35.4
Bossier	64,284	50.6	30,764	10.9	37.8	25.4	252.2	11,166	42,337	55,448	45.4	5.6	53,225	17.8	24.7	18.6
Caddo	116,592	48.5	59,335	13.7	44.6	24.5	462.3	12,101	27,967	42,003	56.4	4.3	43,216	20.9	25.7	23.5
Calcasieu	86,565	42.6	49,245	16.0	46.2	21.9	415.3	12,198	29,866	52,866	47.0	4.7	57,252	16.6	23.2	22.2
Caldwell	3,839	38.7	2,067	19.9	67.2	14.6	20.7	13,683	27,121	40,690	57.5	2.6	42,490	21.4	28.6	25.3
Cameron	1,246	17.9	1,315	12.9	52.1	16.6	24.8	18,521	28,341	56,902	46.4	4.5	60,887	13.1	17.7	17.7
Catahoula	3,860	40.7	2,034	14.1	64.3	15.4	15.5	12,942	21,815	40,973	57.3	3.5	39,222	28.4	41.2	37.5
Claiborne	6,415	40.9	2,802	10.0	64.3	12.8	21.4	12,674	15,149	26,849	75.3	0.4	37,407	31.9	38.4	35.1
Concordia	8,391	43.6	4,336	4.5	59.5	13.3	45.1	11,813	19,963	36,294	62.1	1.6	37,546	28.6	38.8	36.9
De Soto	11,792	42.9	6,270	7.8	59.9	14.2	77.8	15,463	25,926	44,436	53.6	2.9	43,733	19.8	25.2	24.8
East Baton Rouge	246,556	56.0	128,492	21.0	36.1	36.6	857.1	13,195	33,813	56,076	44.6	7.2	57,099	16.4	20.8	19.9
East Carroll	3,189	46.5	1,381	11.0	70.4	9.3	12.7	13,401	18,059	24,551	69.6	1.9	32,813	37.6	50.9	45.5
East Feliciana	7,804	40.8	3,627	22.4	62.1	13.2	22.6	12,010	25,718	54,187	46.0	3.7	52,158	19.9	22.8	21.2
Evangeline	12,925	38.7	7,587	16.9	65.0	12.7	59.9	10,290	19,578	31,427	67.1	2.1	38,415	24.5	34.1	32.4
Franklin	7,406	37.0	4,441	16.7	65.2	13.2	33.2	11,064	21,370	35,759	61.1	1.9	42,706	24.1	37.4	35.1
Grant	9,538	42.6	4,745	15.4	59.2	10.0	30.7	10,167	24,228	51,449	49.1	7.6	56,380	18.2	22.4	21.1
Iberia	32,915	47.1	17,767	12.6	60.4	15.3	130.1	10,361	25,580	50,602	49.2	2.1	50,449	22.5	33.9	32.7
Iberville	18,280	56.2	7,267	19.4	61.2	16.0	78.9	15,600	24,771	49,539	50.3	3.1	36,990	23.7	31.7	30.7
Jackson	6,727	42.7	3,321	9.4	59.9	13.5	25.2	11,154	21,937	41,760	57.0	2.5	41,940	20.9	27.2	24.1
Jefferson	283,066	65.4	99,903	31.3	43.9	27.6	585.5	11,725	32,939	54,825	45.0	4.9	58,586	16.1	25.2	25.7
Jefferson Davis	11,584	36.9	7,685	12.2	59.2	18.4	62.5	10,810	25,821	42,716	53.7	3.8	47,924	17.6	23.1	22.2
Lafayette	122,750	50.2	61,802	20.4	40.7	33.1	343.1	10,275	33,254	58,761	44.2	6.5	59,362	16.2	19.3	18.6
Lafourche	44,185	45.3	21,966	16.4	61.6	16.9	142.3	9,801	28,220	54,530	47.6	4.2	56,743	14.5	18.7	17.9
La Salle	6,713	45.1	3,082	10.3	63.7	15.6	30.3	11,500	25,656	51,141	47.4	4.2	48,306	17.3	20.4	19.2
Lincoln	20,241	43.3	17,094	8.1	39.0	35.2	80.0	12,418	22,379	36,496	61.9	3.7	44,728	21.7	26.9	25.0
Livingston	56,170	39.9	33,661	14.6	52.5	19.6	253.4	9,928	30,317	67,365	37.8	4.1	61,680	11.7	16.0	13.9
Madison	5,019	45.8	2,579	22.2	57.5	15.1	15.5	12,457	17,831	32,585	64.9	2.0	33,841	33.6	47.4	44.5
Morehouse	11,445	46.0	5,079	15.2	59.2	12.5	47.0	12,520	19,566	33,780	64.1	1.4	36,290	23.3	40.7	43.1
Natchitoches	16,527	43.3	11,753	13.3	50.1	19.9	75.2	11,946	20,219	30,625	66.9	1.9	44,720	21.7	31.6	28.2

1. All persons 3 years old and over enrolled in nursery school through college. 2. Persons 25 years old and over. 3. Elementary and secondary education expenditures. 4. Based on population estimated by the American Community Survey, 2016–2020. 5. CDC percent based on 2019 population estimate.

STATE County	Personal income, 2020: Total (mil dol)	Personal income, 2020: Percent change 2019–2020	Per capita[1]: Dollars	Per capita[1]: Rank	Wages and salaries (mil dol)	Supplements to wages and salaries, employer contributions (mil dol): Pension and insurance	Supplements to wages and salaries, employer contributions (mil dol): Government social insurance	Proprietors' income (mil dol)	Dividends, interest, and rent (mil dol)	Personal transfer receipts (mil dol)	Earnings, 2020: Total (mil dol)	Contributions for government social insurance (mil dol): From employee and self-employed	Contributions for government social insurance (mil dol): From employer
	62	63	64	65	66	67	68	69	70	71	72	73	74
KENTUCKY—Cont'd													
Ohio	875	9.8	36,606	2,814	275	61	22	47	97	373	405	30	22
Oldham	4,622	3.9	68,986	178	845	141	61	237	899	611	1,283	85	61
Owen	413	11.8	37,464	2,743	63	16	5	17	50	151	100	9	5
Owsley	160	12.3	36,830	2,796	23	6	2	5	11	101	35	4	2
Pendleton	679	2.7	46,524	1,575	103	22	8	28	88	191	162	14	8
Perry	1,111	11.3	43,661	1,987	469	94	36	61	106	566	661	49	36
Pike	2,251	8.5	39,450	2,514	920	173	72	-13	278	1,117	1,152	99	72
Powell	455	13.8	37,224	2,768	96	22	8	18	38	208	143	13	8
Pulaski	2,752	10.0	41,989	2,197	1,030	205	84	165	300	1,208	1,484	110	84
Robertson	84	15.0	39,137	2,553	11	3	1	4	9	32	19	2	1
Rockcastle	600	11.0	35,809	2,883	144	36	12	18	48	274	210	17	12
Rowan	853	9.9	34,561	2,960	385	86	30	34	108	339	535	36	30
Russell	732	8.9	40,672	2,376	207	46	17	139	81	296	410	29	17
Scott	2,778	9.6	47,509	1,448	1,579	259	136	128	297	566	2,101	131	136
Shelby	2,510	9.8	50,602	1,076	738	135	59	180	409	518	1,112	74	59
Simpson	793	9.8	42,537	2,122	381	68	31	81	90	257	561	37	31
Spencer	961	9.2	49,066	1,251	85	17	6	37	92	218	146	15	6
Taylor	1,015	11.5	39,488	2,508	469	86	39	46	119	405	639	45	39
Todd	519	8.5	41,672	2,242	100	23	8	85	59	158	216	13	8
Trigg	613	9.5	41,497	2,269	103	24	8	44	86	217	179	15	8
Trimble	375	9.4	44,227	1,908	63	16	5	11	43	119	95	8	5
Union	594	12.9	41,157	2,315	242	44	20	73	76	217	379	24	20
Warren	5,475	8.1	40,705	2,373	2,979	541	231	357	761	1,548	4,108	269	231
Washington	509	10.4	41,902	2,217	146	28	12	34	74	172	221	16	12
Wayne	672	13.7	33,258	3,017	199	44	17	30	83	322	290	23	17
Webster	549	6.4	42,496	2,131	135	30	11	65	62	190	240	17	11
Whitley	1,394	11.7	38,256	2,657	516	105	41	62	164	683	724	60	41
Wolfe	259	15.1	36,449	2,828	47	12	4	8	19	147	70	7	4
Woodford	1,470	3.7	54,911	707	433	79	36	156	245	327	704	43	36
LOUISIANA	236,327	6.4	50,810	X	101,801	17,696	6,697	22,446	39,575	64,143	148,640	8,782	6,697
Acadia	2,533	9.1	40,916	2,344	609	118	41	231	317	833	998	67	41
Allen	943	5.2	37,054	2,784	335	86	20	62	115	319	503	28	20
Ascension	6,999	7.1	54,395	750	2,828	452	186	365	875	1,310	3,830	229	186
Assumption	1,115	3.8	51,585	973	186	37	12	91	137	311	325	23	12
Avoyelles	1,678	8.3	41,977	2,200	392	87	25	118	209	636	622	41	25
Beauregard	1,781	8.7	47,003	1,516	417	79	27	49	240	527	572	42	27
Bienville	550	6.9	42,372	2,145	186	41	12	18	72	237	256	17	12
Bossier	6,225	7.3	48,907	1,268	2,448	515	180	340	1,058	1,596	3,483	196	180
Caddo	13,073	7.9	55,047	700	5,672	994	383	1,181	2,971	3,721	8,230	490	383
Calcasieu	10,368	2.5	50,994	1,030	5,187	962	341	724	1,502	2,830	7,214	424	341
Caldwell	381	9.9	38,705	2,605	87	21	6	25	42	161	138	10	6
Cameron	345	2.4	49,224	1,229	686	80	44	16	58	74	826	46	44
Catahoula	363	10.5	39,357	2,528	83	21	5	28	40	146	137	10	5
Claiborne	563	4.9	36,281	2,851	148	37	9	41	84	213	235	15	9
Concordia	736	13.1	38,891	2,581	215	48	14	79	93	300	356	21	14
De Soto	1,261	8.6	45,615	1,713	400	78	24	37	214	392	540	37	24
East Baton Rouge	24,838	5.7	56,484	612	15,515	2,527	984	2,422	4,744	5,737	21,448	1,178	984
East Carroll	276	14.4	41,875	2,221	62	15	4	47	42	111	127	6	4
East Feliciana	846	3.8	44,787	1,827	240	64	12	28	125	283	343	21	12
Evangeline	1,259	12.9	37,820	2,705	297	65	20	118	168	509	500	33	20
Franklin	745	13.0	37,754	2,710	183	46	12	75	80	337	315	19	12
Grant	776	9.3	34,870	2,941	171	47	12	24	80	279	254	20	12
Iberia	3,052	6.9	44,242	1,904	1,330	215	87	206	499	1,059	1,838	118	87
Iberville	1,490	5.3	46,461	1,586	1,122	218	70	95	207	468	1,505	85	70
Jackson	587	7.9	37,665	2,719	166	38	10	29	66	232	243	16	10
Jefferson	23,940	6.2	55,373	678	10,839	1,508	712	2,402	4,439	6,050	15,460	958	712
Jefferson Davis	1,424	6.5	45,620	1,711	349	74	22	109	195	443	555	33	22
Lafayette	12,944	6.5	52,507	888	6,835	1,004	460	1,257	2,583	2,916	9,557	562	460
Lafourche	4,757	6.2	48,741	1,291	1,970	343	128	540	816	1,219	2,981	179	128
La Salle	543	7.6	36,116	2,862	215	47	14	24	64	194	299	18	14
Lincoln	2,092	5.9	44,944	1,801	788	164	50	293	396	569	1,295	71	50
Livingston	6,557	7.4	45,620	1,711	1,258	230	83	324	794	1,561	1,894	129	83
Madison	408	13.6	38,337	2,645	124	32	9	44	40	169	208	11	9
Morehouse	1,071	9.7	44,187	1,912	270	52	19	99	116	477	439	30	19
Natchitoches	1,646	4.8	43,702	1,986	564	132	34	169	230	549	899	52	34

1. Based on the resident population estimated as of July 1 of the year shown.

STATE County	Earnings, 2020 (cont.) — Percent by selected industries: Farm	Mining, quarrying, and extractions	Construction	Manu-facturing	Information; professional, scientific, technical services	Retail trade	Finance, insurance, real estate, and leasing	Health care and social assistance	Govern-ment	Social Security beneficiaries, December 2020: Number	Rate[1]	Supple-mental Security Income recipients, 2020	Housing units, 2021: Total	Percent change, 2010–2021
	75	76	77	78	79	80	81	82	83	84	85	86	87	88
KENTUCKY—Cont'd														
Ohio	4.5	0.3	4.8	32.3	D	6.8	2.2	D	21.7	6,350	268	916	10,209	0.4
Oldham	0.8	D	10.2	6.2	12.1	5.2	17.9	11.5	16.3	10,755	157	466	23,539	1.8
Owen	3.0	0.0	5.8	D	D	5.8	D	6.3	24.3	2,780	246	375	5,360	0.6
Owsley	0.5	0.0	D	D	D	D	D	28.5	35.5	1,155	292	733	2,053	0.4
Pendleton	-0.1	D	D	12.5	D	3.5	4.6	8.2	19.8	3,500	240	493	6,280	0.2
Perry	0.0	D	2.3	0.4	D	9.2	3.0	D	18.8	7,615	273	2,612	13,266	0.3
Pike	0.0	D	3.3	3.0	4.3	11.0	5.2	D	14.9	17,915	312	4,226	28,885	0.6
Powell	0.1	D	D	15.3	D	8.0	2.6	D	25.3	3,530	269	952	5,608	0.3
Pulaski	1.1	D	5.6	14.1	4.1	9.3	4.7	22.9	13.6	18,790	287	3,710	31,733	0.5
Robertson	6.6	0.1	D	D	D	D	D	15.9	35.3	530	235	99	1,040	0.2
Rockcastle	0.3	D	D	2.7	D	4.8	2.9	D	18.9	4,455	276	1,027	7,354	0.4
Rowan	0.0	D	3.6	10.3	D	9.5	4.2	D	28.6	5,290	213	1,158	10,569	0.4
Russell	2.4	0.7	D	30.8	5.3	6.8	3.9	D	13.3	4,995	275	1,033	10,137	0.4
Scott	0.9	D	3.9	48.1	3.2	3.3	2.1	D	6.8	9,480	163	1,058	23,224	1.5
Shelby	2.0	0.0	6.9	24.1	D	7.4	5.5	6.3	12.0	9,540	197	709	19,162	1.6
Simpson	5.4	-0.2	8.5	34.5	D	11.8	2.8	5.0	8.8	4,485	227	500	8,455	1.9
Spencer	3.4	0.0	15.9	D	D	6.6	8.1	D	25.5	3,940	198	270	7,619	2.1
Taylor	1.0	0.0	D	10.9	D	8.6	4.9	D	18.5	6,720	256	1,170	11,201	0.0
Todd	20.3	D	9.4	14.8	D	7.2	4.0	D	13.4	2,720	221	363	5,132	0.2
Trigg	8.3	D	10.1	10.4	D	7.9	5.3	D	21.9	4,200	296	404	7,632	1.3
Trimble	2.1	D	7.9	D	D	2.7	6.4	4.8	17.3	2,215	260	231	3,861	0.4
Union	12.1	D	2.2	14.1	D	4.6	3.4	D	9.9	3,525	260	395	5,857	-0.1
Warren	1.0	0.1	7.4	16.6	5.5	7.5	5.4	15.0	13.5	22,575	165	3,440	57,960	1.6
Washington	3.6	0.0	14.2	34.1	D	4.0	D	8.4	12.4	3,065	254	394	5,214	0.3
Wayne	3.9	D	3.8	18.2	D	8.0	D	10.5	18.4	5,605	287	1,615	10,136	0.3
Webster	15.2	0.3	22.1	10.0	D	3.7	3.0	D	14.3	3,400	265	480	5,722	0.3
Whitley	0.1	D	3.3	9.3	D	7.6	4.2	D	15.6	9,445	256	3,655	15,544	0.4
Wolfe	-0.4	D	D	2.4	D	7.3	4.4	18.6	29.4	2,150	330	1,108	3,040	0.5
Woodford	15.9	D	5.7	15.5	7.6	4.6	3.3	D	12.5	6,305	233	383	11,601	0.7
LOUISIANA	0.7	4.6	8.1	9.5	8.5	6.4	6.8	12.8	17.1	925,400	200	170,026	2,093,393	0.8
Acadia	7.4	3.0	9.8	8.0	4.3	8.3	4.7	14.9	15.9	12,575	220	2,449	24,977	0.6
Allen	1.9	3.1	1.4	12.0	D	4.6	2.0	9.7	47.5	5,060	223	711	9,530	0.4
Ascension	0.0	0.5	20.2	27.1	4.3	6.3	5.0	5.4	10.0	19,865	155	2,128	50,902	2.0
Assumption	2.3	D	13.9	14.3	D	4.6	10.5	D	17.2	5,210	252	900	10,009	0.7
Avoyelles	7.5	D	10.1	2.6	4.5	9.3	6.8	15.5	27.0	9,605	245	2,387	18,389	1.4
Beauregard	-0.2	0.3	6.1	19.2	D	7.5	8.3	12.7	18.0	7,755	212	1,072	15,941	0.8
Bienville	0.0	10.5	1.4	20.7	D	3.9	4.7	D	23.9	3,540	277	781	6,862	0.6
Bossier	0.0	4.4	5.1	5.3	5.9	8.5	4.8	8.8	35.2	22,310	173	3,367	56,032	1.2
Caddo	-0.1	4.4	4.5	5.7	6.7	7.0	6.7	22.5	18.8	52,130	224	12,974	112,515	0.1
Calcasieu	0.0	0.4	13.9	20.8	6.5	7.1	4.2	12.0	13.4	39,560	193	5,633	94,433	1.0
Caldwell	1.6	2.4	D	2.4	D	5.5	D	27.6	24.9	2,330	243	487	4,638	1.0
Cameron	0.7	0.3	71.0	11.8	D	D	D	0.7	5.9	1,255	247	74	3,953	-5.7
Catahoula	10.4	D	D	D	D	7.5	D	D	26.2	2,430	276	500	4,435	0.5
Claiborne	5.3	16.9	3.3	4.0	D	4.5	D	D	33.2	3,515	250	763	6,804	0.4
Concordia	10.8	1.9	3.2	3.1	D	9.9	6.1	D	25.5	4,585	250	1,144	9,012	0.3
De Soto	-0.6	18.1	6.7	18.3	1.8	6.3	2.8	D	21.3	6,570	244	1,207	12,546	1.3
East Baton Rouge	0.0	0.3	12.2	6.7	D	5.3	8.7	13.7	17.8	76,400	169	14,126	205,673	0.5
East Carroll	33.7	D	D	D	D	4.6	D	D	23.6	1,370	190	551	2,792	0.1
East Feliciana	-1.0	1.1	4.5	8.7	D	3.9	5.5	11.8	50.5	4,345	225	792	8,161	1.0
Evangeline	9.2	1.3	4.3	9.7	3.1	8.2	4.6	D	18.0	7,480	232	1,999	14,544	0.7
Franklin	13.2	0.5	3.6	2.8	2.6	11.1	5.9	D	27.7	4,810	245	1,192	8,932	0.5
Grant	-0.9	D	5.9	8.9	D	3.6	D	D	53.2	4,540	204	744	9,064	0.9
Iberia	0.8	17.5	6.4	12.8	3.6	7.3	9.9	7.7	14.2	15,915	231	3,111	31,048	0.3
Iberville	0.5	D	11.5	44.8	1.8	2.4	4.8	D	14.6	6,730	226	1,230	13,354	1.0
Jackson	2.2	D	D	D	D	6.5	3.2	8.9	30.4	3,725	250	665	7,212	0.3
Jefferson	0.0	0.4	7.5	4.8	8.7	7.8	9.6	16.8	9.6	90,125	208	12,576	194,137	0.1
Jefferson Davis	12.2	2.4	5.2	4.8	1.8	8.3	5.8	15.7	22.4	6,605	204	1,008	14,085	0.9
Lafayette	0.1	9.4	6.0	6.8	11.4	7.2	6.8	18.1	11.0	42,000	172	6,157	110,258	1.9
Lafourche	0.7	7.1	6.3	9.7	2.8	4.4	3.7	10.1	12.7	20,310	208	3,033	41,402	0.9
La Salle	-0.5	8.0	3.1	10.3	D	6.0	3.6	D	30.4	3,190	215	500	6,181	0.4
Lincoln	1.2	2.2	5.7	7.7	8.0	7.5	9.8	13.3	21.5	7,335	152	1,496	20,753	1.5
Livingston	0.4	0.7	14.4	9.1	5.6	10.8	9.2	7.3	19.2	24,040	165	2,700	58,821	1.9
Madison	14.6	D	0.8	9.8	D	6.3	4.1	D	24.7	2,115	216	686	4,378	0.0
Morehouse	13.6	D	7.2	11.6	2.1	7.0	4.2	D	13.4	6,990	279	1,707	11,876	0.1
Natchitoches	1.4	0.6	4.1	23.6	D	6.3	5.1	6.5	29.4	8,030	217	2,005	18,646	0.6

1. Per 1,000 resident population estimated as of July 1 of the year shown.

STATE County	Housing units, 2016–2020								Civilian labor force, 2021				Civilian employment[6], 2016–2020		
	Occupied units										Unemployment			Percent	
		Owner-occupied				Renter-occupied									
				Median owner cost as a percent of income											
	Total	Percent	Median value[1]	With a mortgage	Without a mortgage[2]	Median rent[3]	Median rent as a percent of income[2]	Sub-standard units[4] (percent)	Total	Percent change, 2020–2021	Total	Rate[5]	Total	Management, business, science, and arts	Construction, production, and maintenance occupations
	89	90	91	92	93	94	95	96	97	98	99	100	101	102	103
KENTUCKY—Cont'd															
Ohio	9,226	77.8	90,400	20.1	10.0	633	22.0	2.3	9,010	-2.8	498	5.5	10,146	26.6	39.8
Oldham	21,259	86.4	299,300	18.4	10.0	964	23.8	1.4	33,100	2.0	1,185	3.6	31,990	47.4	17.4
Owen	4,246	80.8	116,300	23.0	11.8	631	22.9	4.1	5,092	0.1	217	4.3	4,650	32.9	36.3
Owsley	1,655	63.5	67,400	18.7	10.0	325	28.4	2.8	1,054	-2.2	74	7.0	1,222	34.7	28.7
Pendleton	5,250	70.8	130,100	19.2	10.2	758	32.2	3.0	6,897	2.0	285	4.1	6,606	25.5	36.6
Perry	11,334	77.5	78,900	17.4	11.6	703	27.2	2.3	7,994	-1.7	503	6.3	9,687	31.1	23.1
Pike	25,506	72.3	82,700	22.1	11.9	702	32.0	2.0	19,105	0.0	1,214	6.4	19,320	36.1	26.0
Powell	4,698	70.1	105,000	17.4	10.6	693	32.5	6.9	5,135	1.8	247	4.8	4,830	25.1	37.2
Pulaski	25,572	70.4	113,900	19.2	10.0	706	30.0	1.4	25,971	1.0	1,279	4.9	26,344	31.0	27.8
Robertson	859	72.6	101,900	19.1	13.6	480	17.3	9.2	801	1.8	34	4.2	826	24.5	40.2
Rockcastle	6,609	76.5	88,500	19.0	11.4	573	26.3	2.7	6,457	1.3	320	5.0	6,252	31.1	34.3
Rowan	8,747	60.4	126,900	18.6	10.0	648	28.8	1.8	9,943	-0.2	526	5.3	10,574	40.5	24.6
Russell	7,122	75.0	99,000	19.0	10.0	571	25.9	2.6	6,118	0.8	333	5.4	7,157	30.6	32.4
Scott	21,186	72.3	197,900	18.0	10.0	934	24.6	2.5	29,876	0.0	1,091	3.7	28,483	36.9	31.2
Shelby	16,801	70.9	202,000	18.9	10.0	833	24.2	3.0	25,837	1.7	980	3.8	24,005	34.4	30.1
Simpson	7,181	64.0	141,400	20.3	12.1	844	25.8	1.9	8,850	3.9	371	4.2	7,929	24.1	37.4
Spencer	6,899	86.9	227,000	17.7	10.0	726	23.4	2.4	10,529	1.8	447	4.2	9,875	34.0	30.9
Taylor	9,659	63.6	122,800	16.7	10.0	650	28.5	0.6	12,363	-4.7	484	3.9	11,323	28.4	33.8
Todd	4,655	67.1	112,500	17.1	10.1	666	23.9	3.7	5,521	2.4	201	3.6	4,942	31.3	41.8
Trigg	5,916	79.0	156,000	19.7	11.4	567	25.1	1.7	6,062	1.6	307	5.1	5,943	30.8	35.5
Trimble	3,398	77.7	129,700	19.6	11.9	741	19.5	5.5	3,834	1.4	185	4.8	3,810	26.9	39.5
Union	5,176	71.2	90,900	16.1	10.0	615	23.1	0.7	6,021	1.6	262	4.4	6,292	24.0	40.5
Warren	49,880	57.6	180,000	19.1	10.0	822	28.4	3.6	64,517	1.7	2,749	4.3	66,821	33.8	25.8
Washington	4,702	75.2	123,600	16.4	10.0	633	19.5	1.7	6,177	1.6	240	3.9	5,704	31.5	37.4
Wayne	8,298	73.9	90,300	19.7	10.0	584	23.8	2.3	7,410	0.9	375	5.1	7,433	23.1	36.0
Webster	5,001	72.8	76,200	18.9	11.1	641	18.7	2.1	5,344	-1.2	241	4.5	5,104	27.4	45.4
Whitley	12,685	68.4	104,200	18.4	10.0	610	24.7	4.6	14,007	1.6	698	5.0	13,004	34.0	26.4
Wolfe	2,991	62.8	66,300	22.9	12.8	390	35.8	7.7	2,222	6.9	130	5.9	1,478	17.4	32.9
Woodford	10,399	69.5	212,100	19.1	10.0	800	26.9	1.8	15,053	1.4	510	3.4	13,214	39.9	23.2
LOUISIANA	1,751,956	66.6	168,100	19.6	10.0	876	32.3	2.7	2,062,492	0.0	113,089	5.5	2,023,915	35.3	24.2
Acadia	22,598	69.1	130,300	17.6	10.0	659	32.6	2.7	23,518	0.9	1,163	4.9	24,086	25.4	32.3
Allen	8,137	75.7	107,400	17.3	10.0	664	22.3	4.6	8,137	-3.0	450	5.5	9,012	27.2	30.4
Ascension	44,029	82.5	224,300	17.5	10.0	1,030	28.8	2.1	64,756	0.7	2,706	4.2	60,122	38.0	26.3
Assumption	8,941	77.6	118,900	20.4	10.0	721	36.1	2.8	8,713	-0.7	625	7.2	9,708	29.4	33.1
Avoyelles	15,217	69.7	103,900	19.5	11.6	667	33.1	2.5	14,753	-1.2	771	5.2	15,080	32.8	24.3
Beauregard	13,812	79.4	141,600	17.9	10.0	734	25.8	2.5	14,628	1.7	598	4.1	14,695	33.5	32.9
Bienville	5,855	70.4	73,700	21.8	10.0	474	30.6	4.2	5,244	-2.4	299	5.7	4,548	26.2	33.7
Bossier	49,600	63.7	176,700	20.9	10.0	989	31.8	1.5	57,066	0.6	2,199	3.9	53,972	39.4	20.8
Caddo	96,043	61.4	150,200	21.5	10.4	806	35.5	2.6	101,475	0.0	6,303	6.2	101,111	34.8	21.7
Calcasieu	78,427	68.5	160,800	18.1	10.0	850	29.6	2.5	95,934	-1.4	5,393	5.6	90,319	32.4	27.3
Caldwell	3,899	71.4	79,100	20.7	10.0	732	26.9	6.5	3,670	0.6	170	4.6	3,314	26.7	38.1
Cameron	2,902	88.5	124,300	20.3	10.0	857	20.7	4.7	3,503	0.0	122	3.5	3,078	33.3	29.2
Catahoula	3,394	79.6	90,600	19.4	10.7	657	36.7	6.5	3,483	1.0	179	5.1	3,172	31.1	28.0
Claiborne	5,808	68.2	75,500	24.9	11.0	624	40.9	0.9	5,456	0.0	266	4.9	5,082	22.5	38.8
Concordia	6,694	73.1	94,500	19.0	11.6	668	37.1	3.3	6,906	0.2	406	5.9	6,137	24.7	27.0
De Soto	10,951	72.1	116,500	18.6	10.0	629	27.5	2.7	10,738	0.5	520	4.8	10,876	29.0	35.2
East Baton Rouge	164,641	60.1	201,100	19.5	10.0	936	32.3	2.8	227,407	0.6	11,943	5.3	215,335	40.4	19.7
East Carroll	1,688	56.8	62,800	14.8	13.6	596	48.8	4.9	1,745	-3.8	172	9.9	1,099	31.5	15.6
East Feliciana	7,010	80.1	153,800	19.8	10.0	712	23.6	2.7	7,654	1.2	348	4.5	6,588	28.6	30.3
Evangeline	12,393	62.0	99,500	19.2	11.2	573	29.3	4.6	11,985	0.4	652	5.4	11,924	25.9	34.2
Franklin	7,503	72.3	86,600	21.1	10.0	627	40.1	3.7	7,420	1.4	431	5.8	6,917	28.8	28.8
Grant	7,054	76.2	122,600	17.2	10.0	718	30.0	1.6	8,207	1.1	330	4.0	7,837	25.3	35.5
Iberia	26,776	67.8	120,500	19.5	10.0	811	31.6	4.2	27,669	0.6	1,912	6.9	29,434	28.1	30.4
Iberville	11,105	74.9	139,100	19.9	10.0	748	25.3	2.8	13,659	0.1	980	7.2	12,900	33.4	25.2
Jackson	5,859	69.4	85,700	19.5	10.0	575	26.7	1.8	6,745	0.4	253	3.8	5,510	33.8	27.5
Jefferson	170,398	62.7	193,600	21.0	10.0	986	31.4	2.8	208,446	-0.5	12,446	6.0	208,512	35.4	23.2
Jefferson Davis	11,565	75.5	110,800	17.1	10.0	635	33.2	2.3	12,658	-0.5	601	4.7	11,608	26.3	29.3
Lafayette	92,476	66.8	189,700	18.8	10.0	871	29.6	3.2	115,123	0.9	5,167	4.5	119,445	38.8	20.1
Lafourche	36,645	76.1	158,800	19.0	10.0	820	30.4	2.3	40,657	-1.2	1,852	4.6	41,452	29.6	31.8
La Salle	4,868	83.7	107,000	14.8	10.0	640	30.5	5.8	6,677	-2.2	219	3.3	5,788	31.4	34.5
Lincoln	17,861	51.5	152,400	17.0	10.0	733	35.6	3.0	21,118	0.6	903	4.3	20,576	36.1	20.3
Livingston	48,690	83.2	173,200	18.6	10.0	966	24.2	2.7	69,221	0.7	2,610	3.8	63,576	35.6	28.5
Madison	3,729	56.0	77,600	19.8	10.0	612	31.1	10.0	3,478	-1.5	234	6.7	3,172	34.2	24.1
Morehouse	9,738	66.9	94,500	19.1	10.0	565	37.4	3.2	9,942	-0.7	728	7.3	8,810	24.9	34.5
Natchitoches	14,324	50.0	148,300	18.1	10.0	725	40.3	1.4	16,341	1.6	766	4.7	12,931	31.7	28.8

1. Specified owner-occupied units. 2. A value of 10.0 represents 10 percent or less; a value of 50.0 represents 50 percent or more. 3. Specified renter-occupied units. 4. Overcrowded or lacking complete plumbing facilities. 5. Percent of civilian labor force. 6. Civilian employed persons 16 years old and over.

STATE County	Private nonfarm establishments, employment and payroll, 2020: Number of establishments	Employment: Total	Employment: Health care and social assistance	Employment: Manufacturing	Employment: Retail trade	Employment: Finance and insurance	Employment: Professional, scientific, and technical services	Annual payroll: Total (mil dol)	Annual payroll: Average per employee (dollars)	Agriculture, 2017: Farms: Number	Farms: Percent with: Fewer than 50 acres	Farms: Percent with: 1000 acres or more	Farm producers whose primary occupation is farming (percent)
	104	105	106	107	108	109	110	111	112	113	114	115	116
KENTUCKY—Cont'd													
Ohio	362	6,793	1,136	1,943	617	117	96	237	34,944	813	35.1	2.8	39.3
Oldham	1,286	13,740	2,815	998	1,608	1,923	666	628	45,723	466	54.3	1.5	28.0
Owen	121	893	126	32	148	43	13	31	35,231	821	28.4	2.9	33.7
Owsley	43	390	239	NA	99	NA	NA	12	29,590	153	20.9	2.6	35.3
Pendleton	177	1,694	188	553	177	55	50	73	43,096	919	33.7	0.3	29.2
Perry	542	9,107	3,178	85	1,617	289	399	349	38,321	63	31.7	9.5	34.5
Pike	1,127	17,111	4,782	702	3,631	773	498	719	42,045	85	23.5	2.4	51.0
Powell	165	1,610	215	262	393	59	12	49	30,181	194	36.1	1.5	29.5
Pulaski	1,388	20,771	4,945	3,855	3,726	671	419	741	35,652	1,704	41.4	0.8	37.8
Robertson	20	172	114	NA	NA	NA	NA	4	25,070	245	20.4	NA	35.8
Rockcastle	197	2,928	1,141	115	249	83	163	99	33,699	681	37.7	0.9	26.8
Rowan	498	7,597	1,906	943	1,346	224	67	263	34,589	329	45.3	0.3	34.7
Russell	331	4,771	876	1,236	716	140	48	150	31,383	672	45.5	1.9	37.7
Scott	956	23,274	1,658	11,977	1,925	291	447	1,179	50,656	851	47.5	2.1	38.1
Shelby	1,048	16,223	1,402	4,484	2,767	350	411	630	38,808	1,548	55.1	2.3	37.3
Simpson	386	8,432	491	3,433	1,066	146	52	349	41,369	471	53.1	6.6	40.9
Spencer	224	1,353	220	28	333	54	28	37	27,530	606	49.3	1.0	34.3
Taylor	621	10,639	1,664	1,322	2,492	222	123	333	31,319	803	47.3	1.9	34.1
Todd	188	1,500	181	308	352	75	45	50	33,381	593	27.7	6.6	49.4
Trigg	212	2,275	331	543	377	87	43	62	27,371	405	34.1	4.7	40.1
Trimble	74	753	79	123	78	53	5	49	65,278	469	43.3	2.1	37.5
Union	249	4,086	918	533	481	93	55	171	41,795	284	41.2	16.2	45.3
Warren	2,849	55,903	8,682	9,970	7,705	1,345	3,371	2,373	42,445	1,755	49.9	2.1	30.9
Washington	244	2,961	568	1,065	300	75	39	119	40,184	1,102	34.1	0.5	33.4
Wayne	264	4,279	678	1,372	594	157	47	122	28,553	710	39.2	1.1	39.1
Webster	201	1,587	250	212	275	78	56	65	41,242	499	33.9	8.2	34.5
Whitley	589	10,631	2,733	958	1,476	235	522	374	35,221	548	45.1	0.5	33.1
Wolfe	94	851	250	73	128	17	7	25	29,445	294	32.3	0.3	33.8
Woodford	574	7,796	627	1,994	962	171	648	313	40,135	689	44.8	2.8	46.3
LOUISIANA	106,230	1,703,353	299,719	119,276	221,245	64,340	100,746	79,848	46,877	27,386	46.5	7.6	37.7
Acadia	1,115	12,170	2,237	1,372	2,249	415	301	404	33,205	964	50.0	8.8	40.2
Allen	297	3,567	748	755	658	106	64	129	36,134	420	47.4	5.2	37.0
Ascension	2,438	42,939	3,147	5,852	6,297	895	1,869	2,378	55,375	221	69.7	6.8	31.5
Assumption	240	2,521	289	370	425	171	77	126	49,968	103	35.9	36.9	48.4
Avoyelles	681	7,958	2,130	216	1,408	384	234	262	32,909	770	40.1	8.6	38.0
Beauregard	608	6,618	1,209	844	1,221	684	272	278	41,959	730	40.8	3.4	31.2
Bienville	216	3,306	471	1,031	261	163	14	153	46,407	221	41.6	1.8	41.2
Bossier	2,540	36,243	4,764	2,345	6,556	1,168	1,221	1,331	36,723	519	54.5	5.6	44.2
Caddo	6,065	96,854	26,200	5,225	12,346	2,691	4,671	4,365	45,069	706	54.1	8.9	34.7
Calcasieu	4,659	80,323	13,824	9,142	10,845	2,121	5,504	3,662	45,588	931	50.2	7.0	28.2
Caldwell	168	1,634	657	33	317	90	93	58	35,378	329	42.9	4.0	30.4
Cameron	136	2,134	NA	NA	119	15	152	201	94,164	294	24.8	17.0	31.5
Catahoula	169	1,478	417	NA	275	94	91	46	31,191	433	26.6	14.3	33.6
Claiborne	218	2,238	704	105	340	69	35	88	39,166	255	32.5	6.3	37.0
Concordia	352	3,529	837	131	760	215	88	130	36,947	371	24.0	22.6	36.3
De Soto	421	4,853	672	700	815	157	116	258	53,198	599	41.1	5.8	41.7
East Baton Rouge	12,326	247,474	36,341	9,917	25,980	11,914	22,360	12,583	50,848	449	58.4	1.3	40.5
East Carroll	109	1,144	295	63	82	23	21	44	38,590	209	18.2	35.9	62.4
East Feliciana	242	3,314	1,635	261	331	119	79	142	42,773	412	50.5	9.2	38.3
Evangeline	506	6,513	2,620	978	989	245	99	220	33,801	596	45.1	7.7	38.0
Franklin	383	3,753	1,099	198	823	224	105	98	26,177	797	31.0	8.7	36.7
Grant	183	1,859	269	378	307	57	19	65	35,073	207	35.7	8.2	28.4
Iberia	1,515	22,156	3,427	3,412	3,037	793	698	1,005	45,342	334	64.1	10.2	40.5
Iberville	547	11,699	830	4,155	1,087	285	398	815	69,646	151	31.8	27.2	55.6
Jackson	227	2,623	724	494	446	110	50	119	45,540	191	46.1	0.5	46.0
Jefferson	11,644	178,451	31,785	6,274	27,874	9,016	10,756	8,751	49,038	52	59.6	1.9	21.1
Jefferson Davis	621	6,344	1,468	428	1,322	283	222	240	37,841	703	37.8	12.4	37.7
Lafayette	8,559	128,637	26,608	6,822	16,943	4,035	8,750	6,111	47,506	549	73.4	2.9	33.3
Lafourche	1,698	26,677	4,400	1,811	3,789	813	898	1,361	51,030	379	53.0	6.9	27.1
La Salle	351	3,647	866	242	462	145	169	145	39,819	235	48.5	0.4	32.7
Lincoln	1,100	15,378	3,186	1,071	2,509	611	839	561	36,464	378	39.9	1.6	37.7
Livingston	1,910	24,268	2,286	1,615	5,150	704	1,136	880	36,277	436	74.5	0.2	38.0
Madison	190	2,551	1,027	193	327	67	14	89	34,811	250	16.4	32.4	50.2
Morehouse	432	5,596	1,959	482	825	285	76	179	31,942	409	27.1	18.6	49.0
Natchitoches	805	11,620	1,922	2,511	1,745	531	226	458	39,387	627	35.2	7.5	38.8

STATE County	Agriculture, 2017 (cont.)															
	Land in farms					Value of land and buildings (dollars)		Value of machinery and equipment, average per farm (dollars)	Value of products sold:				Organic farms (number)	Farms with internet access (percent)	Government payments	
	Acreage (1,000)	Percent change, 2012–2017	Acres: Average size of farm	Acres: Total irrigated (1,000)	Acres: Total cropland (1,000)	Average per farm	Average per acre		Total (mil dol)	Average per farm (acres)	Percent from: Crops	Percent from: Livestock and poultry products			Total ($1,000)	Percent of farms
	117	118	119	120	121	122	123	124	125	126	127	128	129	130	131	132
KENTUCKY—Cont'd																
Ohio	158	-0.4	194	D	86.4	662,879	3,418	96,947	135.8	166,998	27.8	72.2	3	67.2	1,810	29.5
Oldham	51	-14.7	110	0.1	21.3	879,589	7,964	66,919	18.5	39,730	46.2	53.8	1	80.3	252	4.7
Owen	157	19.3	192	0.5	61.7	542,771	2,831	72,383	23.9	29,107	54.9	45.1	NA	69.7	158	5.7
Owsley	29	5.7	190	D	10.3	255,706	1,342	37,727	1.3	8,458	64.0	36.0	NA	74.5	41	5.2
Pendleton	111	9.9	121	0.5	38.2	344,033	2,840	55,326	9.4	10,282	64.2	35.8	NA	71.3	112	8.7
Perry	16	49.3	260	0.0	5.6	297,441	1,146	49,250	0.3	5,175	27.6	72.4	NA	77.8	D	1.6
Pike	19	45.5	229	0.0	3.4	324,062	1,414	56,010	0.7	8,753	49.6	50.4	NA	85.9	NA	NA
Powell	28	-6.8	144	0.0	9.6	336,855	2,334	46,794	2.7	13,938	73.4	26.6	NA	64.9	32	8.2
Pulaski	226	-0.9	133	0.2	100.3	429,851	3,238	67,220	55.5	32,570	45.2	54.8	2	69.2	632	21.0
Robertson	42	8.8	172	0.0	14.5	377,155	2,187	51,275	3.5	14,473	31.5	68.5	3	64.1	22	5.3
Rockcastle	81	-11.2	119	0.0	27.8	258,213	2,179	41,923	7.3	10,742	39.5	60.5	NA	71.5	215	13.1
Rowan	40	-6.4	120	0.0	13.1	333,138	2,770	56,262	4.1	12,605	40.1	59.9	NA	66.9	126	17.6
Russell	92	3.5	138	0.0	42.2	425,730	3,093	68,898	37.5	55,823	22.0	78.0	NA	69.8	456	20.7
Scott	131	2.4	153	0.3	56.1	858,492	5,595	78,301	51.7	60,734	30.2	69.8	1	78.7	224	6.8
Shelby	201	0.8	130	0.9	124.4	753,848	5,809	85,413	72.1	46,577	67.6	32.4	5	77.1	1,603	14.6
Simpson	111	9.2	235	0.3	88.3	1,335,785	5,675	146,265	79.0	167,658	64.5	35.5	NA	77.5	1,628	39.9
Spencer	74	7.3	122	0.1	34.8	556,079	4,542	62,736	18.3	30,163	75.1	24.9	NA	75.1	255	7.4
Taylor	112	-2.5	139	0.0	61.1	422,767	3,038	82,616	46.1	57,365	49.3	50.7	2	71.9	1,440	35.4
Todd	168	-7.2	283	0.8	127.5	1,468,492	5,185	159,843	175.6	296,152	47.2	52.8	13	50.3	2,136	43.2
Trigg	122	-5.3	302	2.2	75.9	1,239,797	4,110	130,967	58.8	145,183	74.6	25.4	5	60.2	2,747	35.8
Trimble	66	18.6	141	D	30.4	456,362	3,245	57,517	12.1	25,823	80.0	20.0	NA	65.9	356	8.3
Union	195	-0.1	685	3.8	172.8	3,453,444	5,039	337,598	108.9	383,285	92.5	7.5	NA	79.2	4,606	53.9
Warren	262	6.3	149	0.2	156.6	796,970	5,334	85,047	110.9	63,189	54.5	45.5	NA	75.6	5,481	21.8
Washington	161	14.5	147	0.1	67.5	470,574	3,212	62,124	34.4	31,208	34.9	65.1	2	68.1	459	18.2
Wayne	96	-25.3	135	0.1	34.5	360,738	2,666	63,632	58.0	81,655	17.2	82.8	NA	74.1	371	15.1
Webster	163	6.9	327	0.6	123.0	1,202,901	3,683	145,475	141.9	284,333	37.5	62.5	NA	73.9	4,513	64.5
Whitley	59	1.0	108	0.0	20.2	272,502	2,532	52,085	6.1	11,057	34.2	65.8	1	65.3	206	13.7
Wolfe	34	-20.6	115	0.0	10.2	231,135	2,016	53,278	1.5	5,044	56.4	43.6	NA	70.4	17	9.2
Woodford	112	0.2	163	0.0	42.0	1,320,705	8,111	92,879	132.6	192,441	9.7	90.3	2	88.2	403	9.3
LOUISIANA	7,998	1.2	292	1,235.8	4,345.8	889,146	3,045	121,758	3,173.0	115,861	65.0	35.0	29	69.9	177,399	28.4
Acadia	266	11.5	275	86.1	207.9	760,885	2,762	166,113	100.7	104,466	84.7	15.3	NA	62.1	13,935	59.1
Allen	95	7.9	226	18.9	46.4	580,390	2,566	68,258	19.8	47,055	71.2	28.8	NA	64.8	3,122	31.2
Ascension	38	-23.9	174	0.0	26.3	629,741	3,626	104,541	13.1	59,217	89.4	10.6	3	72.4	198	10.0
Assumption	92	47.8	892	D	86.5	2,626,865	2,944	469,713	45.6	442,806	98.8	1.2	NA	83.5	427	27.2
Avoyelles	282	-5.7	366	26.0	201.1	931,760	2,544	158,024	104.3	135,473	89.9	10.1	NA	69.5	7,776	39.0
Beauregard	148	0.9	202	3.3	39.1	614,319	3,039	69,645	15.8	21,705	45.4	54.6	1	76.7	2,855	12.9
Bienville	34	-39.0	154	D	10.0	392,811	2,547	59,842	32.3	146,068	2.6	97.4	NA	69.7	116	7.7
Bossier	107	31.4	206	2.0	34.0	642,592	3,122	73,951	14.4	27,825	65.7	34.3	NA	76.7	398	13.7
Caddo	199	42.5	282	22.6	84.7	841,843	2,983	110,644	61.1	86,482	62.7	37.3	NA	71.2	2,145	10.8
Calcasieu	354	4.8	380	13.1	77.5	1,323,640	3,480	77,967	25.8	27,676	51.6	48.4	NA	75.8	3,924	20.4
Caldwell	68	8.8	206	3.6	21.8	515,954	2,507	60,462	18.7	56,714	38.6	61.4	NA	60.2	1,822	36.2
Cameron	188	-20.1	639	5.9	50.9	1,584,171	2,478	87,142	12.0	40,667	46.1	53.9	NA	72.4	1,266	28.9
Catahoula	210	-6.3	485	58.5	145.7	1,309,375	2,702	184,305	70.6	163,046	97.6	2.4	NA	62.8	6,969	66.1
Claiborne	63	10.8	249	2.2	12.9	594,447	2,389	78,967	77.9	305,533	2.5	97.5	NA	60.4	324	7.8
Concordia	281	17.1	759	46.3	206.5	2,125,125	2,802	219,661	100.3	270,415	97.7	2.3	NA	66.0	8,888	78.7
De Soto	137	-16.9	228	0.2	28.3	676,324	2,966	97,326	20.6	34,347	12.6	87.4	NA	74.8	182	2.7
East Baton Rouge	58	1.3	130	0.5	13.4	1,071,013	8,251	89,008	12.6	28,058	22.3	77.7	1	83.1	132	5.8
East Carroll	221	-11.8	1,059	128.4	193.4	3,932,394	3,713	491,558	116.5	557,191	99.9	0.1	NA	76.6	9,631	86.6
East Feliciana	131	16.4	318	0.0	24.7	889,716	2,799	75,308	9.2	22,303	18.2	81.8	NA	80.3	511	11.2
Evangeline	159	-17.2	267	45.9	113.5	650,632	2,441	100,421	54.7	91,851	84.7	15.3	NA	74.2	6,872	41.4
Franklin	255	3.5	320	103.8	178.4	906,715	2,836	122,690	115.3	144,689	94.5	5.5	NA	64.0	8,085	64.9
Grant	51	6.0	246	D	17.0	672,574	2,738	75,464	7.7	37,411	74.8	25.2	NA	71.0	506	21.7
Iberia	115	7.0	344	2.6	88.2	985,830	2,868	215,874	57.9	173,263	96.5	3.5	NA	71.3	846	14.1
Iberville	182	11.2	1,203	D	76.8	2,159,687	1,796	484,293	48.3	320,126	95.3	4.7	NA	84.1	501	21.2
Jackson	21	10.5	108	0.2	3.2	431,104	4,003	76,776	42.8	223,874	1.1	98.9	NA	73.8	82	23.0
Jefferson	8	5.1	157	0.0	0.5	365,529	2,334	58,697	0.7	13,115	46.5	53.5	NA	75.0	11	9.6
Jefferson Davis	243	-8.1	346	68.2	167.7	771,190	2,227	119,746	73.3	104,239	78.3	21.7	NA	69.4	13,380	48.6
Lafayette	50	-10.8	90	5.1	29.9	504,748	5,581	86,348	21.4	38,998	79.0	21.0	2	71.8	1,039	8.2
Lafourche	157	-0.7	414	0.3	58.6	1,200,913	2,899	125,407	39.0	102,821	66.8	33.2	NA	72.8	124	3.2
La Salle	24	20.9	100	D	4.5	319,962	3,185	67,387	1.6	6,817	27.3	72.7	NA	74.9	166	24.3
Lincoln	72	28.6	190	0.6	14.8	609,592	3,210	84,608	134.2	354,944	1.0	99.0	NA	75.7	282	6.9
Livingston	30	7.5	68	0.1	5.8	363,820	5,351	57,006	10.6	24,232	8.2	91.8	NA	67.4	239	5.7
Madison	245	9.2	981	83.4	190.9	2,697,499	2,749	404,533	106.8	427,108	99.4	0.6	NA	63.2	8,445	84.0
Morehouse	257	-8.1	627	144.6	196.1	1,994,849	3,180	255,996	129.4	316,421	97.1	2.9	NA	71.4	10,044	63.6
Natchitoches	213	6.2	340	14.1	81.1	794,915	2,335	111,180	98.5	157,166	30.3	69.7	NA	67.5	2,910	37.8

STATE County	Water use, 2015		Wholesale Trade[1], 2017				Retail Trade[2], 2017				Real estate and rental and leasing,[2] 2017			
	Public supply water withdrawn (mil gal/ day)	Public supply gallons withdrawn per person per day	Number of establish- ments	Number of employees	Sales (mil dol)	Average payroll (mil dol)	Number of establish- ments	Number of employees	Sales (mil dol)	Average payroll (mil dol)	Number of establish- ments	Number of employees	Sales (mil dol)	Average payroll (mil dol)
	133	134	135	136	137	138	139	140	141	142	143	144	145	146
KENTUCKY—Cont'd														
Ohio	2.6	108.2	D	D	D	3.8	70	776	207.7	19.5	10	35	4.0	1.0
Oldham	3.9	60.6	47	319	131.8	16.7	100	1,467	493.0	41.5	61	141	41.1	6.8
Owen	0.0	0.0	5	D	18.9	D	23	167	63.6	4.3	D	D	D	D
Owsley	0.5	118.8	NA	NA	NA	NA	12	112	20.2	2.5	4	9	1.0	0.2
Pendleton	1.0	67.3	D	D	D	1.7	24	206	41.5	3.6	D	D	D	D
Perry	4.2	151.6	22	267	143.0	13.2	112	1,586	467.3	39.8	18	77	28.6	3.1
Pike	6.1	98.6	36	295	282.8	14.5	263	3,813	1,001.1	91.4	38	118	16.2	3.6
Powell	1.5	118.2	D	D	D	4.7	39	379	97.8	7.4	4	14	3.6	0.3
Pulaski	7.6	118.5	63	914	695.7	32.1	308	3,844	1,171.1	98.7	52	210	36.7	6.1
Robertson	0.0	0.0	NA	NA	NA	NA	3	24	2.7	0.3	NA	NA	NA	NA
Rockcastle	2.0	115.1	6	35	11.0	1.1	38	277	69.0	6.9	5	16	2.6	0.5
Rowan	6.0	252.4	D	D	D	6.2	98	1,428	380.4	32.5	22	101	13.9	2.5
Russell	2.0	113.8	D	D	D	D	86	741	206.0	16.1	3	8	0.6	0.2
Scott	2.9	55.1	30	692	1,771.2	49.9	115	1,835	597.9	43.8	52	164	35.2	4.9
Shelby	2.9	64.2	37	606	251.2	28.4	191	2,719	724.6	58.5	42	183	34.1	5.0
Simpson	1.7	91.6	16	215	281.5	10.1	68	1,133	365.5	26.9	14	40	6.0	0.9
Spencer	0.0	0.0	NA	NA	NA	NA	25	221	83.4	5.0	D	D	D	D
Taylor	5.2	204.6	18	157	185.5	6.2	119	2,581	732.5	70.0	25	104	15.5	2.6
Todd	0.0	0.0	D	D	D	2.1	40	350	92.8	7.9	D	D	D	0.1
Trigg	2.1	146.8	5	38	13.0	1.1	46	343	104.0	7.8	8	35	5.5	1.6
Trimble	2.8	313.6	NA	NA	NA	NA	13	65	20.4	1.1	NA	NA	NA	NA
Union	1.9	124.3	17	388	226.6	15.7	51	526	130.8	12.3	6	D	9.9	D
Warren	17.5	142.2	145	2,031	2,476.8	104.1	502	7,917	1,968.8	190.0	144	582	122.1	19.0
Washington	1.2	97.0	12	68	41.7	2.4	35	324	99.5	8.4	4	D	0.6	D
Wayne	2.8	134.9	11	97	35.5	3.2	59	700	162.2	15.9	NA	NA	NA	NA
Webster	2.0	153.4	D	D	D	4.9	39	273	62.2	6.3	3	6	0.6	0.1
Whitley	4.8	134.0	19	278	151.5	12.5	125	1,550	422.6	38.2	22	60	15.3	2.7
Wolfe	0.5	64.7	NA	NA	NA	NA	23	138	52.4	3.5	D	D	D	D
Woodford	3.1	121.0	15	304	134.5	15.1	73	894	271.8	21.7	19	30	7.7	1.2
LOUISIANA	708.9	151.8	4,673	63,503	59,523.7	3,493.7	16,564	233,385	65,000.8	5,988.4	5,121	29,345	7,300.6	1,386.0
Acadia	5.6	89.8	49	758	462.3	28.7	185	2,557	575.4	58.0	39	380	62.5	17.1
Allen	4.2	165.1	D	D	D	D	71	702	204.5	15.7	D	D	D	0.3
Ascension	2.7	22.2	133	2,105	1,208.0	123.3	373	6,371	2,031.2	167.5	138	847	302.5	50.7
Assumption	4.2	183.4	9	51	87.5	1.5	40	450	117.6	10.6	5	D	4.5	D
Avoyelles	4.1	98.5	17	308	454.7	13.2	149	1,408	378.7	33.7	22	56	9.7	1.6
Beauregard	4.4	121.2	11	63	41.3	3.4	105	1,273	337.3	29.8	24	52	10.4	2.1
Bienville	2.7	197.3	D	D	D	D	37	296	77.9	6.1	7	78	15.8	3.5
Bossier	12.9	102.9	106	1,682	1,047.4	85.3	440	7,643	2,182.4	187.7	137	600	145.1	22.8
Caddo	43.3	172.1	322	4,997	7,739.1	277.0	887	12,909	3,729.0	343.8	341	1,841	380.7	73.4
Calcasieu	27.5	138.4	D	D	D	113.3	790	11,232	3,622.5	288.6	D	D	D	D
Caldwell	1.0	103.1	D	D	D	1.3	26	296	76.9	6.8	NA	NA	NA	NA
Cameron	1.5	220.0	D	D	D	2.6	18	152	37.4	2.9	D	D	D	D
Catahoula	1.2	115.3	9	67	36.4	2.9	32	285	54.4	5.6	NA	NA	NA	NA
Claiborne	3.0	184.7	10	64	138.0	3.9	43	336	87.9	8.4	3	5	0.6	0.1
Concordia	2.6	130.6	18	270	512.3	14.5	77	822	228.6	22.3	12	112	10.3	3.3
De Soto	3.1	113.9	13	37	22.5	1.7	72	814	288.8	21.9	8	39	8.5	2.1
East Baton Rouge	72.1	161.4	571	8,111	5,706.2	496.8	1,834	28,939	8,006.5	779.5	632	3,270	823.8	148.5
East Carroll	0.9	124.5	D	D	D	D	20	120	25.5	2.6	6	8	1.5	0.3
East Feliciana	2.2	112.2	5	162	80.5	8.7	44	306	78.5	7.1	7	8	1.1	0.1
Evangeline	6.5	192.6	16	118	85.2	2.9	113	971	224.5	21.7	23	65	6.2	1.4
Franklin	2.0	95.5	19	137	214.3	6.7	74	866	258.0	20.6	11	30	4.1	0.9
Grant	4.5	203.2	NA	NA	NA	NA	29	269	89.0	7.7	NA	NA	NA	NA
Iberia	8.7	116.7	85	1,153	701.1	60.0	269	3,275	1,003.6	89.2	91	985	288.7	58.5
Iberville	2.0	59.8	26	269	147.6	12.1	81	1,104	291.9	27.7	25	179	73.1	10.7
Jackson	1.7	109.1	D	D	D	0.3	46	502	129.7	11.3	6	6	0.9	0.1
Jefferson	61.8	141.6	680	10,121	7,582.7	568.7	1,760	29,102	8,987.6	811.3	601	3,812	1,036.2	165.4
Jefferson Davis	3.8	121.5	D	D	D	D	122	1,404	380.8	32.6	18	176	35.5	5.6
Lafayette	25.4	105.9	459	6,489	3,658.9	357.9	1,090	17,143	4,471.0	447.5	503	3,007	831.1	169.2
Lafourche	25.7	261.0	D	D	D	D	300	4,022	1,042.2	95.5	64	210	43.6	8.9
La Salle	1.7	114.9	7	167	364.8	6.1	46	472	132.3	12.2	4	12	2.0	0.3
Lincoln	7.2	150.3	35	546	308.5	27.2	170	2,458	611.6	59.2	68	430	42.0	11.8
Livingston	11.5	83.8	41	554	541.1	32.4	319	5,322	1,493.2	125.8	79	283	46.1	12.0
Madison	1.7	143.3	14	140	212.2	6.8	28	363	108.9	7.6	D	D	D	D
Morehouse	3.5	131.5	19	257	111.0	10.8	73	900	196.6	20.8	25	47	9.2	1.3
Natchitoches	7.7	197.0	21	153	365.4	6.4	137	1,687	442.6	37.9	48	198	35.0	5.3

1 Merchant wholesalers, except manufacturers' sales branches and offices. 2. Employer establishments.

STATE County	Professional, scientific, and technical services, 2017				Manufacturing, 2017				Accommodation and food services, 2017			
	Number of establish-ments	Number of employees	Sales (mil dol)	Average payroll (mil dol)	Number of establish-ments	Number of employees	Sales (mil dol)	Average payroll (mil dol)	Number of establis-hments	Number of employees	Sales (mil dol)	Annual payroll (mil dol)
	147	148	149	150	151	152	153	154	155	156	157	158
KENTUCKY—Cont'd												
Ohio	24	111	11.8	3.7	20	2,368	732.3	82.1	31	395	19.3	5.5
Oldham	173	661	97.0	35.6	40	1,303	519.2	75.4	69	1,507	78.2	21.4
Owen	6	9	2.0	0.3	D	D	D	D	15	205	8.5	2.2
Owsley	NA	NA	NA	NA	NA	NA	NA	NA	NA	NA	NA	NA
Pendleton	11	53	4.2	1.7	13	D	158.9	D	D	D	D	D
Perry	D	D	D	D	7	74	15.0	4.2	44	881	46.2	11.7
Pike	92	583	80.6	28.2	23	550	183.4	28.2	100	2,002	103.3	28.7
Powell	7	12	0.7	0.2	7	92	32.1	5.2	18	271	14.7	3.9
Pulaski	D	D	D	D	77	4,093	1,369.0	171.2	99	2,443	115.4	33.0
Robertson	NA	NA	NA	NA	NA	NA	NA	NA	NA	NA	NA	NA
Rockcastle	16	209	12.9	6.8	9	105	14.9	4.4	19	245	13.0	3.1
Rowan	D	D	D	D	21	1,157	381.6	45.6	50	1,259	57.5	16.2
Russell	21	48	4.0	1.1	24	1,251	350.4	38.3	32	404	22.0	5.9
Scott	88	382	52.9	19.0	41	11,077	10,376.6	797.5	107	2,252	127.1	35.8
Shelby	95	320	41.2	12.7	56	3,861	1,656.0	194.5	D	D	D	D
Simpson	15	64	8.2	2.2	35	2,695	1,414.5	160.5	50	994	49.5	13.6
Spencer	D	D	5.0	D	D	D	D	D	D	D	D	D
Taylor	56	110	13.8	4.0	29	1,208	288.6	43.4	47	933	47.0	11.9
Todd	11	41	4.0	1.7	19	298	111.1	12.0	10	113	4.0	1.1
Trigg	11	35	4.2	1.5	12	545	135.2	20.9	20	357	18.5	4.9
Trimble	D	D	0.4	D	D	D	D	D	D	D	D	D
Union	9	46	5.4	1.8	13	439	175.8	20.2	D	D	D	D
Warren	D	D	D	D	106	9,632	5,906.2	556.2	293	6,870	352.1	107.9
Washington	10	44	3.0	0.9	14	1,163	412.5	56.5	16	182	8.2	2.1
Wayne	20	43	2.8	1.2	23	1,224	138.3	40.3	D	D	D	D
Webster	10	32	3.9	1.1	11	224	140.6	8.4	D	D	D	D
Whitley	45	830	48.7	20.7	16	817	236.2	36.2	65	1,211	63.1	18.2
Wolfe	3	5	0.7	0.2	4	23	2.8	0.6	4	55	2.1	0.6
Woodford	80	437	78.0	29.5	33	2,839	788.4	149.1	D	D	D	D
LOUISIANA	12,010	94,813	15,935.7	6,130.5	3,190	117,910	187,439.9	8,257.3	9,877	215,048	14,553.0	3,808.8
Acadia	121	293	38.5	11.4	44	988	372.6	41.3	80	1,273	60.0	15.9
Allen	D	D	D	D	9	700	367.4	38.6	30	378	22.1	4.8
Ascension	204	2,272	279.5	158.4	100	5,970	9,047.0	603.6	230	4,051	217.9	61.0
Assumption	31	70	8.2	2.5	13	357	157.7	19.5	12	149	4.8	1.4
Avoyelles	57	214	34.9	8.5	20	253	41.0	12.8	43	1,663	127.3	32.8
Beauregard	54	215	22.0	7.8	18	905	919.0	70.1	46	710	39.6	10.1
Bienville	6	18	2.1	0.7	8	1,269	354.5	37.4	D	D	D	D
Bossier	D	D	D	D	63	1,444	654.2	73.9	263	8,989	777.1	168.1
Caddo	D	D	D	D	160	5,097	3,150.9	329.7	509	12,034	772.7	197.9
Calcasieu	471	4,473	661.2	299.8	D	D	D	D	451	14,129	1,374.8	296.1
Caldwell	30	75	8.7	2.3	3	36	5.5	1.1	D	D	D	1.7
Cameron	18	227	60.2	23.8	NA	NA	NA	NA	6	31	2.2	0.3
Catahoula	28	82	11.3	3.9	NA	NA	NA	NA	D	D	D	D
Claiborne	8	29	4.4	1.2	5	108	49.6	5.5	D	D	D	1.3
Concordia	27	81	11.7	3.4	10	118	56.5	7.1	26	326	17.5	4.2
De Soto	28	127	14.1	4.7	D	D	D	D	30	369	21.3	5.0
East Baton Rouge	D	D	D	D	325	10,327	31,999.7	779.2	1,066	26,112	1,553.1	419.5
East Carroll	4	16	1.4	0.5	5	65	25.6	1.7	8	67	2.9	0.6
East Feliciana	D	D	5.1	D	D	D	D	D	16	185	7.5	2.3
Evangeline	39	99	11.5	3.3	15	675	302.5	42.1	D	D	D	D
Franklin	34	121	12.2	3.4	8	392	57.0	6.5	D	D	D	D
Grant	6	3	1.5	0.4	D	D	D	D	D	D	D	0.5
Iberia	139	770	127.2	44.7	110	3,076	1,259.5	181.8	108	1,726	83.3	23.1
Iberville	57	473	72.0	30.6	36	4,629	8,228.6	463.8	39	633	38.2	9.4
Jackson	18	41	5.5	1.5	D	D	D	D	D	D	D	D
Jefferson	D	D	D	D	288	6,620	2,486.9	373.4	1,127	21,335	1,394.8	370.4
Jefferson Davis	67	254	35.5	11.2	21	431	100.6	18.3	46	670	33.7	9.1
Lafayette	1,286	8,329	1,518.1	534.8	268	6,356	1,812.9	333.7	759	16,127	1,027.0	265.6
Lafourche	172	1,298	133.5	67.9	55	2,111	678.3	114.9	156	2,419	128.8	32.9
La Salle	D	D	D	D	6	57	19.0	3.4	21	220	12.1	3.1
Lincoln	97	750	113.2	48.6	39	1,236	467.5	69.2	94	2,165	115.4	31.8
Livingston	D	D	D	D	55	1,795	559.7	90.5	170	3,316	164.5	43.2
Madison	9	22	2.2	0.5	D	166	D	9.3	18	211	12.2	2.7
Morehouse	20	84	8.9	3.1	18	626	183.6	18.1	30	D	24.0	D
Natchitoches	54	207	32.2	8.0	18	2,459	1,474.8	128.1	85	1,495	76.8	19.4

STATE County	Health care and social assistance, 2017				Other services, 2017				Nonemployer businesses, 2019		Value of residential construction authorized by building permits, 2021	
	Number of establish-ments	Number of employees	Receipts (mil dol)	Annual payroll (mil dol)	Number of establish-ments	Number of employees	Receipts (mil dol)	Annual payroll (mil dol)	Number	Receipts (mil dol)	New construction ($1,000)	Number of housing units
	159	160	161	162	163	164	165	166	167	168	169	170
KENTUCKY—Cont'd												
Ohio	46	1,161	79.7	39.4	35	93	10.4	2.7	1,094	43.6	951	5
Oldham	145	2,828	309.5	106.0	75	315	30.7	9.6	5,526	287.6	152,924	399
Owen	12	181	15.8	7.0	D	D	4.0	D	750	29.4	6,090	28
Owsley	11	202	14.0	5.6	NA	NA	NA	NA	268	9.2	NA	NA
Pendleton	16	235	16.7	7.4	D	D	D	D	743	30.8	0	0
Perry	113	2,905	351.7	128.9	24	100	10.2	2.4	1,315	47.4	0	0
Pike	183	5,226	763.6	291.8	70	302	27.1	8.1	2,762	111.1	2,995	8
Powell	16	203	16.5	7.1	6	12	1.1	0.3	786	29.1	175	2
Pulaski	228	4,985	551.0	223.8	62	307	34.9	8.4	4,640	206.5	0	0
Robertson	NA	NA	NA	NA	NA	NA	NA	NA	126	3.8	NA	NA
Rockcastle	25	990	83.8	35.8	6	25	2.6	0.6	922	33.6	NA	NA
Rowan	85	2,028	235.5	89.5	22	111	6.7	1.7	1,394	58.2	1,018	16
Russell	41	887	67.5	29.2	D	D	D	D	1,316	52.7	600	3
Scott	126	1,824	180.2	69.9	64	373	35.9	10.2	3,747	156.0	104,492	591
Shelby	98	1,532	151.6	57.1	66	549	53.0	17.2	3,682	183.1	116,285	451
Simpson	33	443	52.5	16.2	23	107	10.9	3.4	1,330	66.7	20,690	130
Spencer	D	D	D	7.3	D	D	4.1	D	1,338	59.7	40,876	177
Taylor	83	1,605	157.2	62.9	D	D	D	D	1,758	70.4	3,171	10
Todd	16	189	11.5	5.1	D	D	D	0.9	928	55.8	8,107	38
Trigg	27	357	31.6	12.8	16	97	6.3	1.9	1,017	44.7	2,108	10
Trimble	6	104	11.5	4.6	D	D	1.9	D	481	16.2	NA	NA
Union	33	864	69.7	28.6	11	42	7.4	1.4	694	26.6	NA	NA
Warren	400	9,097	1,196.9	438.1	217	1,273	116.1	32.7	10,407	617.1	335,448	2,128
Washington	27	430	32.0	13.3	D	D	D	D	833	38.9	595	15
Wayne	37	595	42.4	19.8	D	D	D	D	1,226	46.7	0	0
Webster	25	276	17.4	8.0	D	D	D	1.2	656	19.9	653	3
Whitley	95	2,940	333.9	124.5	D	D	D	D	2,349	100.3	4,138	44
Wolfe	12	245	18.1	6.4	3	16	1.3	0.4	438	15.9	NA	NA
Woodford	64	664	63.4	24.5	33	136	14.3	3.6	2,334	104.1	33,128	124
LOUISIANA	12,685	302,408	34,618.0	12,912.7	6,531	43,472	5,702.0	1,571.6	392,105	17,350.0	4,054,061	19,147
Acadia	125	2,475	206.8	76.3	60	259	27.7	6.2	4,535	201.1	22,622	135
Allen	41	770	66.7	25.2	D	D	12.9	D	1,170	37.4	5,959	46
Ascension	203	3,496	300.5	120.4	173	1,820	272.6	90.2	9,685	426.8	187,353	1,061
Assumption	16	436	19.6	8.9	20	55	13.4	1.9	1,596	57.5	9,475	28
Avoyelles	90	2,267	154.1	60.8	42	138	18.2	3.2	2,452	101.0	765	13
Beauregard	63	1,249	88.8	37.5	32	152	16.9	4.4	2,105	75.8	4,849	138
Bienville	20	526	45.2	14.8	9	16	2.2	0.4	785	28.9	3,136	15
Bossier	242	4,864	518.0	200.9	130	1,055	107.0	31.0	9,444	430.5	181,702	785
Caddo	876	28,411	4,122.4	1,490.0	D	D	D	D	21,253	902.7	61,160	228
Calcasieu	553	13,776	1,429.0	553.2	D	D	D	D	13,577	590.8	170,195	1,020
Caldwell	25	710	57.8	24.8	11	42	4.5	1.1	721	24.0	3,544	11
Cameron	3	117	8.4	4.1	D	D	D	D	654	30.5	19,238	44
Catahoula	17	365	21.1	9.6	D	D	D	0.8	612	20.7	475	3
Claiborne	24	770	48.7	20.8	9	38	2.5	0.6	786	32.4	344	4
Concordia	40	763	63.9	26.2	24	90	6.2	2.4	1,175	43.4	3,400	26
De Soto	D	D	D	D	D	D	D	D	2,203	84.9	32,926	123
East Baton Rouge	1,433	40,379	4,979.8	1,735.7	890	6,557	1,008.3	257.9	40,618	1,838.1	407,162	1,452
East Carroll	10	318	20.7	8.9	D	D	D	D	378	14.7	0	0
East Feliciana	31	1,521	120.8	65.1	18	60	7.8	2.2	1,462	56.2	15,709	73
Evangeline	101	2,521	188.8	74.8	D	D	D	D	1,662	66.6	12,720	54
Franklin	46	1,063	79.6	34.0	27	81	8.9	1.7	1,428	57.3	5,300	17
Grant	24	266	19.4	6.8	9	28	3.6	0.7	1,111	38.2	625	2
Iberia	200	3,804	322.8	116.6	110	668	92.7	27.7	6,056	230.1	3,188	67
Iberville	45	842	85.9	25.3	35	262	34.2	10.8	2,332	72.5	45,166	201
Jackson	29	639	53.4	19.8	15	87	8.1	2.7	866	36.3	5,212	17
Jefferson	1,389	31,801	4,091.2	1,643.8	782	5,061	657.3	180.7	46,954	2,325.9	215,668	995
Jefferson Davis	65	1,566	138.6	59.6	38	135	16.3	3.9	1,915	71.0	28,190	139
Lafayette	1,212	25,143	2,980.6	1,066.1	451	3,231	381.0	104.6	25,113	1,281.3	509,384	2,371
Lafourche	188	4,168	446.2	184.8	106	548	72.1	18.2	7,163	317.6	81,347	379
La Salle	22	835	61.6	26.0	D	D	48.3	D	939	38.7	3,735	13
Lincoln	129	2,965	253.2	95.5	53	243	20.3	5.5	3,127	153.1	13,953	98
Livingston	149	1,947	146.5	59.4	127	534	59.3	16.9	10,430	455.7	268,933	1,239
Madison	28	1,055	58.8	24.8	D	D	D	D	672	18.9	510	2
Morehouse	74	1,960	126.2	48.9	33	116	8.5	2.2	1,712	54.5	1,060	4
Natchitoches	95	2,073	192.4	63.8	42	135	14.9	3.3	2,515	103.4	15,024	58

STATE County	Government employment and payroll, 2017: Full-time equivalent employees	Government employment and payroll, 2017: March payroll (dollars)	March payroll (percent of total): Adminis-tration, judicial, and legal	March payroll (percent of total): Police and corrections	March payroll (percent of total): Fire protection	March payroll (percent of total): Highways and transpor-tation	March payroll (percent of total): Health and welfare	March payroll (percent of total): Natural resources and utilities	March payroll (percent of total): Education and libraries	Local government finances, 2017, General revenue: Total (mil dol)	General revenue: Inter-govern-mental (mil dol)	Taxes: Total (mil dol)	Taxes: Per capita[1] (dollars): Total	Taxes: Per capita[1] (dollars): Property
	171	172	173	174	175	176	177	178	179	180	181	182	183	184
KENTUCKY—Cont'd														
Ohio	1,341	3,789,958	3.2	4.4	0.2	1.5	39.8	3.0	47.8	55.0	33.9	16.0	662	349
Oldham	1,966	6,901,073	3.1	3.6	1.2	1.0	3.4	1.5	85.5	160.9	64.6	77.5	1,164	877
Owen	344	892,449	8.5	4.4	0.0	3.0	7.9	0.7	75.3	23.5	14.3	7.0	651	490
Owsley	258	647,309	6.0	3.1	0.1	6.7	0.0	1.9	79.7	13.1	10.0	1.7	388	256
Pendleton	536	1,655,442	4.8	4.1	0.1	2.1	15.0	5.3	66.3	36.4	22.2	9.4	641	512
Perry	1,400	4,272,954	3.5	3.5	1.7	2.4	12.1	4.4	71.8	85.3	50.7	22.2	835	475
Pike	1,971	6,872,000	3.8	4.3	1.8	3.2	4.9	2.7	78.9	164.4	91.5	53.4	907	527
Powell	554	1,636,898	9.8	8.1	0.1	0.8	4.4	4.5	70.6	32.1	22.9	6.3	511	274
Pulaski	2,449	7,448,220	4.1	5.7	3.1	1.7	12.2	6.2	66.9	152.2	76.4	56.9	884	543
Robertson	84	240,471	9.8	5.0	0.0	5.1	0.0	1.4	78.2	8.1	5.8	1.4	655	415
Rockcastle	706	1,557,825	7.6	8.9	0.0	2.1	3.2	0.9	73.3	36.7	27.1	8.1	485	190
Rowan	790	2,523,845	3.3	7.9	0.4	3.7	10.2	3.6	69.7	63.0	26.2	25.1	1,024	441
Russell	908	2,789,361	3.5	5.7	0.0	1.0	33.4	3.4	52.0	111.1	24.3	14.6	824	491
Scott	1,731	5,777,032	3.5	9.1	7.1	1.9	8.9	0.9	67.3	159.7	53.0	81.9	1,495	587
Shelby	1,713	6,943,492	2.5	5.4	1.7	1.4	4.9	1.3	81.4	106.0	42.1	54.3	1,150	795
Simpson	715	2,207,301	8.7	11.3	1.4	2.4	6.1	3.7	65.5	56.9	26.6	20.2	1,121	578
Spencer	511	1,635,338	5.9	3.9	1.0	1.4	2.7	2.6	82.1	35.4	19.2	13.3	716	550
Taylor	1,428	5,528,404	2.0	2.6	0.9	1.0	57.1	0.9	34.7	147.5	63.8	23.7	928	493
Todd	443	1,285,695	3.1	6.5	1.7	1.8	5.8	8.5	72.5	32.0	19.9	8.2	671	352
Trigg	600	1,948,983	2.9	5.2	0.5	2.7	28.5	7.9	51.8	29.2	15.5	12.0	829	521
Trimble	294	914,679	6.1	3.0	2.6	2.2	0.0	6.8	78.6	17.0	8.3	7.5	878	593
Union	558	1,747,883	6.8	6.7	1.7	4.3	0.7	6.7	70.7	36.1	19.9	12.3	844	606
Warren	4,152	13,982,618	2.6	9.4	4.7	1.8	4.5	9.2	63.5	330.8	120.6	163.7	1,269	609
Washington	362	1,217,688	3.2	2.5	6.7	1.9	3.1	6.6	73.8	32.0	16.6	10.4	874	440
Wayne	686	1,957,101	3.2	7.1	0.2	2.0	4.0	1.4	79.9	43.9	29.5	11.0	532	324
Webster	516	1,504,866	5.3	11.0	3.2	2.8	0.7	9.0	64.5	33.6	21.6	8.8	673	517
Whitley	1,666	4,944,984	2.7	5.4	2.3	2.1	9.3	5.5	71.3	117.7	72.6	26.8	743	340
Wolfe	323	905,288	3.4	1.8	0.0	1.4	0.2	3.4	86.1	18.1	14.4	2.3	323	185
Woodford	855	2,924,644	3.9	12.7	3.0	3.1	4.3	4.7	67.1	69.8	23.0	38.2	1,448	824
LOUISIANA	X	X	X	X	X	X	X	X	X	X	X	X	X	X
Acadia	1,865	5,132,550	7.7	6.0	2.5	3.4	0.8	5.6	73.0	169.8	77.3	68.7	1,099	431
Allen	1,217	3,011,014	8.7	15.0	0.5	3.2	16.4	1.2	54.8	267.5	110.5	85.2	3,330	1,784
Ascension	4,015	15,039,268	7.3	9.2	2.6	2.5	3.0	4.0	69.2	465.0	161.7	259.1	2,104	858
Assumption	1,168	4,001,399	7.8	6.0	0.7	15.6	15.7	6.0	47.4	63.7	30.9	26.6	1,179	644
Avoyelles	1,505	3,666,589	8.2	23.1	1.7	1.0	13.8	5.7	46.2	109.9	45.5	22.0	540	132
Beauregard	1,523	4,885,820	3.1	2.7	1.6	1.8	35.8	1.4	52.8	143.8	44.1	53.8	1,461	689
Bienville	652	2,118,412	15.2	15.6	0.0	5.0	0.1	3.1	60.7	57.7	16.8	39.3	2,885	2,130
Bossier	4,800	16,718,972	8.1	14.2	5.7	3.3	0.3	2.9	64.6	474.7	161.6	239.7	1,888	815
Caddo	10,182	35,717,990	6.9	16.7	7.8	2.2	3.1	5.0	55.4	1,104.5	336.7	572.6	2,328	1,246
Calcasieu	9,753	32,272,710	5.9	12.9	3.8	5.4	9.4	5.0	54.9	1,094.7	277.6	593.2	2,930	1,002
Caldwell	351	883,483	7.9	0.7	0.1	4.0	0.0	2.7	83.8	35.3	17.9	16.2	1,630	1,319
Cameron	469	1,641,476	6.8	0.0	0.3	7.9	10.9	3.7	70.4	46.9	12.6	28.9	4,168	4,125
Catahoula	504	1,610,614	10.2	10.1	0.5	4.4	0.0	3.2	70.4	29.4	17.6	7.8	792	256
Claiborne	703	2,118,405	5.7	2.4	0.2	2.5	55.0	1.8	32.3	71.5	18.6	13.8	864	502
Concordia	1,215	3,846,133	5.2	22.1	2.4	2.9	18.8	5.7	42.7	108.1	31.6	43.6	2,197	585
De Soto	1,230	4,077,671	3.7	19.0	0.9	6.1	1.1	5.6	63.2	113.9	21.8	80.3	2,944	1,980
East Baton Rouge	14,509	57,542,743	7.2	13.3	6.7	5.4	8.4	5.0	53.9	1,882.7	474.8	1,033.1	2,324	998
East Carroll	326	915,955	5.6	6.1	0.9	1.7	42.3	2.8	40.1	47.2	23.4	8.3	1,164	583
East Feliciana	588	1,575,919	11.9	28.9	0.2	2.6	0.5	5.9	49.7	46.9	22.2	19.7	1,014	397
Evangeline	1,505	4,498,451	5.1	7.6	2.8	3.2	16.2	6.2	57.9	129.4	52.4	42.4	1,261	597
Franklin	1,063	3,246,498	5.1	13.9	1.1	1.7	35.0	1.9	41.3	97.0	34.3	26.0	1,283	480
Grant	536	1,408,063	9.7	2.7	0.0	2.1	3.1	5.9	76.0	47.9	27.2	14.6	655	353
Iberia	3,364	11,267,277	3.2	9.1	2.8	2.7	26.7	2.7	52.1	335.0	128.8	102.9	1,429	625
Iberville	1,420	4,860,218	7.6	15.9	1.3	5.5	1.5	5.5	61.4	172.8	32.8	124.9	3,797	1,710
Jackson	927	2,823,927	4.3	17.0	1.6	5.1	28.1	4.9	38.1	63.8	17.7	30.1	1,894	1,216
Jefferson	12,733	58,502,045	9.8	14.0	3.4	2.8	16.6	7.5	43.9	1,960.3	534.4	797.7	1,829	825
Jefferson Davis	1,389	3,649,957	4.4	11.4	2.1	2.3	1.2	2.8	75.3	126.0	48.3	55.6	1,766	640
Lafayette	8,689	26,026,218	7.5	14.2	4.9	3.7	1.2	9.4	58.1	814.0	210.7	478.2	1,978	829
Lafourche	4,703	18,572,811	6.0	10.7	0.0	3.8	35.6	3.2	38.8	639.0	210.9	204.4	2,083	1,459
La Salle	1,090	3,428,899	2.1	12.0	0.3	0.6	46.6	2.9	35.0	89.8	21.7	21.5	1,441	703
Lincoln	1,670	4,901,269	8.2	10.3	5.5	3.9	1.0	10.0	60.5	146.8	50.6	78.0	1,642	735
Livingston	4,347	31,808,462	58.0	4.0	0.4	0.8	0.2	1.7	34.6	424.4	223.5	156.6	1,137	366
Madison	571	1,239,152	10.5	36.2	0.0	5.0	0.3	1.7	45.6	58.8	20.3	19.7	1,733	1,052
Morehouse	1,147	3,631,339	4.9	13.6	4.3	2.1	26.2	1.3	46.5	108.4	42.5	31.4	1,223	546
Natchitoches	2,527	8,229,190	6.7	10.8	2.2	2.0	39.9	5.3	31.4	168.2	57.3	61.1	1,566	612

1. Based on the resident population estimated as of July 1 of the year shown.

STATE County	Local government finances, 2017 (cont.)									Government employment, 2020			Individual income tax returns, 2019		
	Direct general expenditure							Debt outstanding							
	Total (mil dol)	Per capita[1] (dollars)	Percent of total for: Education	Health and hospitals	Police protection	Public welfare	Highways	Total (mil dol)	Per capita[1] (dollars)	Federal civilian	Federal military	State and local	Number of returns	Mean adjusted gross income	Mean income tax
	185	186	187	188	189	190	191	192	193	194	195	196	197	198	199
KENTUCKY—Cont'd															
Ohio	53.1	2,201	64.8	0.5	4.5	0.1	6.6	256.1	10,621	73	70	1,519	9,570	45,437	3,066
Oldham	162.5	2,442	68.7	1.7	4.3	0.1	2.8	709.0	10,652	79	188	3,120	29,630	106,340	15,074
Owen	23.0	2,127	74.7	4.8	1.2	2.5	5.5	207.1	19,183	21	33	413	4,490	48,782	3,566
Owsley	12.6	2,863	71.8	0.1	1.7	0.0	7.6	4.9	1,118	13	13	256	1,310	35,675	2,150
Pendleton	36.1	2,470	53.3	15.5	3.4	0.0	5.6	42.4	2,902	32	43	550	6,410	52,638	4,174
Perry	122.3	4,601	51.5	28.0	2.0	0.0	2.9	363.2	13,663	150	74	2,172	9,900	45,705	3,809
Pike	176.2	2,991	63.8	3.1	1.7	0.2	3.8	190.9	3,240	195	166	2,738	19,920	49,719	4,574
Powell	37.1	3,016	67.4	5.3	2.1	0.0	3.3	31.3	2,543	34	36	718	5,030	40,190	2,548
Pulaski	147.7	2,296	58.2	1.5	3.6	0.0	4.4	197.7	3,073	221	194	3,539	26,760	47,617	4,282
Robertson	6.7	3,151	52.5	1.8	2.9	0.1	5.2	22.3	10,497	2	6	147	840	44,258	2,880
Rockcastle	36.3	2,163	66.8	8.3	2.6	0.0	3.1	39.2	2,336	33	49	792	6,170	41,496	2,603
Rowan	68.4	2,792	41.0	10.9	2.8	0.4	4.1	92.3	3,764	97	68	2,824	8,930	47,316	3,822
Russell	62.0	3,498	41.3	35.6	2.0	0.0	3.0	72.0	4,064	72	53	940	7,300	41,095	2,902
Scott	139.7	2,551	51.0	8.4	5.0	0.1	2.7	615.6	11,237	66	171	2,388	26,210	66,741	6,599
Shelby	104.3	2,210	63.7	2.5	3.4	0.2	2.9	159.5	3,378	86	143	2,250	22,240	68,532	7,400
Simpson	47.8	2,649	54.6	4.0	6.6	0.1	4.8	76.6	4,246	37	55	794	8,620	46,332	3,629
Spencer	46.8	2,512	78.8	2.3	3.0	0.1	1.7	46.9	2,520	30	59	603	8,950	69,490	6,425
Taylor	161.4	6,320	32.9	52.6	1.0	0.0	1.4	194.0	7,596	93	73	1,737	10,750	44,487	3,304
Todd	28.9	2,371	57.8	5.5	3.2	0.0	5.3	127.1	10,441	37	37	565	4,910	47,817	3,531
Trigg	30.1	2,090	57.5	4.8	4.5	0.1	8.4	35.0	2,429	83	44	557	6,250	47,817	3,800
Trimble	24.3	2,849	45.9	2.6	1.0	0.0	4.1	557.0	65,374	19	25	284	3,730	51,348	3,934
Union	39.6	2,710	50.8	0.6	4.4	1.4	4.7	20.2	1,383	53	38	629	5,800	52,223	4,317
Warren	280.5	2,174	56.4	0.1	5.6	0.1	5.2	618.5	4,792	388	392	8,823	57,040	57,193	5,854
Washington	32.8	2,760	53.0	6.0	1.9	0.1	7.4	80.5	6,776	32	36	452	5,410	48,005	3,691
Wayne	41.7	2,024	65.8	3.3	2.6	0.1	4.8	45.9	2,223	42	59	934	7,600	38,240	2,435
Webster	34.9	2,684	55.0	3.4	3.0	0.1	6.2	120.2	9,241	44	37	628	5,350	50,592	3,911
Whitley	122.0	3,382	64.8	6.4	3.1	0.0	3.9	226.9	6,290	99	103	2,035	13,800	43,015	3,301
Wolfe	20.8	2,869	76.0	0.1	0.6	0.0	6.8	34.0	4,685	24	21	378	2,370	36,078	2,012
Woodford	63.4	2,405	55.7	4.6	9.7	0.0	3.1	76.2	2,887	46	78	1,397	12,890	63,276	6,937
LOUISIANA	X	X	X	X	X	X	X	X	X	32,741	33,061	283,417	2,049,470	59,697	6,757
Acadia	192.1	3,071	49.0	17.9	8.3	0.3	4.8	37.1	593	101	231	2,473	25,010	50,308	4,362
Allen	272.2	10,640	17.3	2.3	12.9	0.8	2.2	352.6	13,784	583	81	2,984	8,700	48,935	3,712
Ascension	615.4	4,996	52.9	1.0	1.4	0.0	25.0	737.2	5,985	191	484	5,070	56,990	74,967	8,342
Assumption	64.7	2,866	67.1	0.1	5.3	0.7	2.6	11.9	529	37	81	835	9,420	55,751	5,070
Avoyelles	100.0	2,448	53.8	11.9	14.5	0.0	3.3	14.2	348	91	138	2,885	16,260	45,525	3,748
Beauregard	139.7	3,791	44.7	27.3	8.2	0.0	1.4	85.2	2,313	75	139	1,659	14,320	59,942	5,248
Bienville	49.3	3,614	69.9	0.4	3.6	0.0	8.8	26.1	1,912	46	48	848	5,610	44,702	3,325
Bossier	444.3	3,499	60.3	1.3	5.3	0.2	2.6	854.8	6,733	2,021	5,718	6,187	56,750	60,824	6,045
Caddo	1,111.6	4,520	45.1	2.6	8.6	0.0	2.7	418.8	1,703	2,928	921	14,572	108,980	57,450	6,830
Calcasieu	998.4	4,931	39.1	8.6	7.2	0.4	7.5	1,108.5	5,475	578	833	12,736	88,280	62,160	6,656
Caldwell	26.1	2,624	74.6	0.0	0.9	0.0	4.3	14.0	1,405	30	35	600	3,800	53,166	4,586
Cameron	54.2	7,798	45.5	10.4	16.4	0.0	6.8	3.8	543	15	26	717	2,890	70,100	8,201
Catahoula	33.2	3,373	51.9	13.2	3.4	0.0	5.7	9.7	990	49	32	543	3,440	45,355	3,625
Claiborne	67.9	4,254	28.4	53.2	1.9	0.4	4.2	7.7	485	53	49	1,146	5,460	48,273	4,068
Concordia	86.6	4,366	45.0	19.9	5.0	0.0	2.2	41.6	2,098	69	66	1,364	7,210	44,922	3,590
De Soto	109.1	4,001	77.3	4.3	0.9	2.2	0.8	103.5	3,798	54	104	1,607	12,250	56,732	5,698
East Baton Rouge	1,988.9	4,474	38.0	7.3	8.2	0.3	2.5	1,561.7	3,513	2,395	1,806	46,278	202,480	70,177	9,149
East Carroll	61.7	8,683	20.6	17.9	2.8	0.0	3.7	35.2	4,954	25	21	468	2,420	34,629	2,976
East Feliciana	54.9	2,833	52.2	0.3	9.0	0.4	13.8	11.1	573	34	62	2,258	8,440	53,560	4,874
Evangeline	137.6	4,089	41.8	24.6	5.3	0.0	7.5	46.8	1,391	53	120	1,479	12,730	48,886	3,986
Franklin	98.6	4,868	33.1	34.6	7.2	0.0	3.3	49.7	2,452	62	72	1,424	8,150	39,796	3,322
Grant	44.1	1,977	70.1	0.1	6.5	0.0	2.5	18.5	832	706	81	773	8,020	50,318	3,975
Iberia	337.5	4,689	41.2	22.9	6.7	0.1	2.9	189.4	2,631	115	332	3,785	30,980	50,466	4,739
Iberville	157.1	4,774	54.3	0.5	7.6	1.3	5.5	131.8	4,005	92	118	2,862	14,090	53,807	5,364
Jackson	64.5	4,059	40.0	31.0	2.7	0.0	7.3	13.5	852	38	55	1,156	6,160	49,461	3,760
Jefferson	1,960.7	4,496	29.8	21.5	9.6	2.1	4.7	978.7	2,244	1,553	1,752	16,575	210,850	59,683	7,000
Jefferson Davis	118.0	3,747	54.6	3.5	5.1	0.0	5.3	162.8	5,171	96	116	1,906	13,560	53,446	4,860
Lafayette	836.9	3,462	46.0	0.2	12.4	0.1	6.9	1,034.4	4,279	1,078	962	12,741	112,640	66,646	8,181
Lafourche	462.4	4,712	34.9	35.5	1.6	1.1	2.9	180.4	1,838	156	383	5,331	40,860	27,778	6,197
La Salle	94.1	6,322	30.6	0.4	12.9	0.0	1.4	12.2	817	56	52	1,414	5,410	56,850	4,744
Lincoln	144.2	3,038	55.9	0.5	6.9	0.5	7.3	75.8	1,597	151	171	4,389	17,900	57,983	6,001
Livingston	399.8	2,903	75.1	0.4	4.0	0.0	4.5	278.6	2,023	168	538	5,623	61,320	59,252	5,375
Madison	52.3	4,613	33.2	30.3	8.3	0.0	5.8	57.2	5,039	38	34	738	4,100	31,961	2,510
Morehouse	100.0	3,898	50.2	19.1	2.9	0.1	2.9	88.1	3,435	55	89	951	10,600	41,018	3,098
Natchitoches	169.1	4,331	42.6	19.6	5.9	0.4	2.9	49.4	1,265	177	137	3,855	15,170	52,664	5,149

1. Based on the resident population estimated as of July 1 of the year shown.

State / county code	CBSA code[1]	County Type code[2]	STATE County	Land area[3] (sq. mi)	Population, 2021: Total persons 2021	Population, 2021: Rank	Population, 2021: Per square mile	Race alone or in combination, not Hispanic or Latino (percent): White	Black	American Indian, Alaska Native	Asian and Pacific Islancer	Percent Hispanic or Latino[4]	Age (percent): Under 5 years	5 to 17 years	18 to 24 years	25 to 34 years	35 to 44 years	45 to 54 years
				1	2	3	4	5	6	7	8	9	10	11	12	13	14	15
			LOUISIANA—Cont'd															
22071	35380	1	Orleans	169.5	376,971	194	2,224.0	32.3	59.4	0.8	3.5	5.7	5.5	11.1	11.4	15.9	15.1	11.6
22073	33740	3	Ouachita	610.3	158,768	429	260.1	58.3	38.5	0.6	1.4	2.4	6.4	13.9	13.8	13.6	12.8	11.7
22075	35380	1	Plaquemines	780.2	23,303	1,667	29.9	64.9	21.7	2.3	5.2	8.4	6.3	14.7	12.7	12.7	13.6	12.6
22077	12940	2	Pointe Coupee	556.9	20,356	1,801	36.6	61.6	35.2	0.5	0.6	3.2	5.7	12.2	11.3	11.1	11.4	11.1
22079	10780	3	Rapides	1,320.4	128,654	504	97.4	62.2	32.9	1.5	1.9	3.5	6.4	14.0	12.8	12.8	12.6	11.4
22081		8	Red River	389.0	7,564	2,610	19.4	56.4	40.2	0.9	0.4	3.0	6.2	13.5	11.4	11.6	11.0	12.3
22083		6	Richland	555.6	19,805	1,828	35.6	61.7	35.8	0.6	0.6	2.4	6.3	13.1	12.3	12.8	12.7	11.2
22085		6	Sabine	866.6	22,135	1,707	25.5	70.6	17.3	10.7	0.7	4.1	5.5	13.4	11.7	11.1	11.6	11.3
22087	35380	1	St. Bernard	377.5	44,258	1,093	117.2	62.6	24.7	1.3	2.8	10.6	6.4	15.4	11.9	14.9	14.7	11.2
22089	35380	1	St. Charles	277.7	52,282	966	188.3	66.0	26.7	0.8	1.6	6.5	5.7	14.2	12.5	12.4	13.8	12.3
22091	12940	2	St. Helena	408.5	10,912	2,349	26.7	45.0	52.5	0.9	0.5	2.3	5.1	11.7	11.4	13.5	11.7	11.5
22093	35380	1	St. James	237.9	19,742	1,836	83.0	49.3	48.6	0.5	0.5	1.8	5.6	12.7	11.6	12.8	12.3	11.0
22095	35380	1	St. John the Baptist	214.5	42,094	1,145	196.2	33.2	58.8	0.6	1.6	7.0	6.1	13.7	13.0	12.8	12.7	12.0
22097	36660	4	St. Landry	924.0	82,071	703	88.8	55.2	42.3	0.6	0.7	2.4	6.8	15.2	12.8	12.3	11.7	11.1
22099	29180	2	St. Martin	737.5	51,540	974	69.9	65.7	30.5	0.8	1.3	3.1	6.1	13.8	11.7	13.2	12.8	12.0
22101	34020	4	St. Mary	555.8	48,232	1,018	86.8	57.9	32.6	2.4	2.0	7.2	6.5	13.5	11.4	12.3	11.4	11.8
22103	35380	1	St. Tammany	845.3	269,388	261	318.7	79.0	13.8	1.0	2.0	6.0	5.7	13.6	12.0	11.2	13.3	12.5
22105	25220	3	Tangipahoa	791.2	135,217	485	170.9	64.0	31.0	0.8	1.1	4.6	6.8	13.8	13.5	14.4	12.9	11.2
22107		9	Tensas	603.0	4,043	2,882	6.7	42.5	55.0	0.6	0.6	2.6	5.0	13.0	10.6	8.4	10.1	10.1
22109	26380	3	Terrebonne	1,229.9	108,708	568	88.4	68.5	20.5	7.0	1.7	5.3	6.4	14.3	12.4	13.1	13.3	11.7
22111	33740	3	Union	876.9	21,091	1,759	24.1	69.8	24.8	0.7	0.4	5.1	5.7	12.1	11.4	11.4	11.3	11.7
22113	29180	2	Vermilion	1,173.6	57,204	914	48.7	79.6	15.0	0.7	2.4	3.7	6.3	14.6	12.3	12.0	13.1	11.7
22115	22860	5	Vernon	1,326.7	48,027	1,020	36.2	72.9	15.3	2.1	3.6	9.7	7.7	13.4	17.4	17.6	12.4	9.4
22117	14220	6	Washington	669.6	45,133	1,074	67.4	66.4	31.0	0.9	0.6	2.7	6.1	13.4	12.2	12.0	12.4	11.6
22119	33380	2	Webster	593.3	36,184	1,278	61.0	62.7	34.8	1.0	0.7	2.2	6.0	12.6	11.5	11.9	11.7	11.8
22121	12940	2	West Baton Rouge	192.3	27,792	1,506	144.5	55.6	40.8	0.6	1.0	3.5	6.6	13.8	11.7	14.5	14.5	11.0
22123		9	West Carroll	359.7	9,594	2,444	26.7	78.9	16.7	0.9	0.4	4.2	5.0	13.0	12.5	11.9	12.2	11.8
22125	12940	2	West Feliciana	403.3	15,494	2,060	38.4	53.1	44.7	0.5	1.0	1.7	3.6	9.4	8.3	13.3	18.9	17.5
22127		6	Winn	950.0	13,488	2,191	14.2	66.0	31.7	1.4	0.7	2.0	5.0	11.9	11.7	13.5	13.0	12.9
23000		0	MAINE	30,844.8	1,372,247	X	44.5	94.2	2.3	1.4	1.9	2.0	4.5	10.4	11.3	12.1	12.0	12.4
23001	30340	3	Androscoggin	468.0	111,034	557	237.3	91.8	5.9	1.0	1.7	2.1	5.4	12.2	12.3	12.5	12.4	12.3
23003		7	Aroostook	6,671.1	66,859	805	10.0	94.8	1.5	2.7	0.9	1.6	4.6	10.5	10.6	10.0	10.6	12.4
23005	38860	2	Cumberland	836.2	305,231	231	365.0	91.5	4.0	0.9	3.4	2.3	4.7	10.2	11.7	13.8	13.2	12.6
23007		6	Franklin	1,697.0	29,687	1,441	17.5	96.8	1.0	1.4	0.9	1.6	4.1	10.2	12.7	10.9	10.7	11.7
23009		6	Hancock	1,587.1	56,192	921	35.4	95.4	1.4	1.2	1.7	1.7	3.9	9.5	9.5	11.2	11.1	12.2
23011	12300	4	Kennebec	867.5	124,486	515	143.5	95.8	1.3	1.4	1.6	1.9	4.7	10.9	11.7	12.0	12.0	12.5
23013		7	Knox	365.1	41,084	1,161	112.5	96.3	1.2	1.3	1.0	1.8	3.8	10.0	9.8	10.3	11.4	12.0
23015		8	Lincoln	455.9	35,828	1,288	78.6	96.6	1.0	1.1	1.2	1.5	4.1	9.6	8.8	10.2	10.4	11.9
23017		6	Oxford	2,077.0	58,629	895	28.2	96.4	1.0	1.5	1.3	1.7	4.2	10.2	10.0	10.9	11.5	12.8
23019	12620	3	Penobscot	3,397.2	152,765	449	45.0	94.8	1.5	2.1	1.7	1.7	4.3	9.9	13.8	13.0	12.0	12.4
23021		8	Piscataquis	3,960.9	17,165	1,959	4.3	94.8	1.1	1.5	1.5	2.8	5.0	9.3	9.5	8.8	10.4	12.6
23023	38860	2	Sagadahoc	254.0	37,071	1,251	145.9	95.6	1.5	1.0	1.4	2.1	4.2	10.6	9.7	11.3	12.3	12.4
23025		6	Somerset	3,924.3	50,592	989	12.9	96.7	1.1	1.4	1.0	1.4	4.5	10.3	10.5	11.0	11.4	13.5
23027		6	Waldo	730.0	39,912	1,186	54.7	96.5	1.0	1.4	0.9	1.7	4.5	10.4	10.2	10.5	12.0	12.5
23029		7	Washington	2,562.7	31,121	1,399	12.1	90.8	1.1	6.4	0.8	3.0	4.6	11.0	10.1	9.7	10.7	11.8
23031	38860	2	York	991.2	214,591	321	216.5	95.1	1.6	1.0	2.0	2.0	4.5	10.2	10.5	12.5	12.2	12.4
24000		0	MARYLAND	9,711.1	6,165,129	X	634.9	51.2	31.8	0.8	7.9	11.1	5.8	12.5	12.4	13.3	13.4	12.7
24001	19060	3	Allegany	422.2	67,729	794	160.4	88.1	9.9	0.5	1.5	2.1	4.6	9.7	15.3	12.9	11.9	11.9
24003	12580	1	Anne Arundel	414.8	590,336	115	1,423.2	67.8	19.9	0.8	5.9	9.0	5.9	12.7	12.1	13.8	14.1	12.5
24005	12580	1	Baltimore	598.4	849,316	74	1,419.3	56.3	32.0	0.8	7.4	6.2	5.7	12.3	12.5	13.2	12.8	12.1
24009	47900	1	Calvert	213.2	93,928	644	440.6	79.2	15.0	1.0	3.4	4.8	5.3	13.5	12.3	11.6	13.2	13.0
24011		6	Caroline	319.4	33,386	1,347	104.5	77.0	15.1	0.7	1.5	8.1	6.1	13.4	11.6	12.5	12.3	12.2
24013	12580	1	Carroll	447.6	173,873	387	388.5	89.1	4.9	0.5	3.2	4.3	5.4	12.4	12.1	11.3	12.8	13.1
24015	37980	1	Cecil	346.3	103,905	590	300.0	85.9	8.7	0.7	2.2	4.9	5.6	12.6	11.9	12.7	12.2	13.1
24017	47900	1	Charles	457.8	168,698	400	368.5	37.5	53.2	1.5	4.7	7.0	5.8	13.8	12.7	12.7	13.4	14.3
24019	15700	6	Dorchester	540.8	32,489	1,371	60.1	64.0	29.5	0.8	1.6	6.2	5.3	12.0	10.4	11.9	10.9	11.3
24021	47900	1	Frederick	660.6	279,835	252	423.6	71.9	12.4	0.7	6.8	11.3	5.8	13.3	12.3	12.5	14.3	13.2
24023		6	Garrett	649.1	28,702	1,470	44.2	96.8	1.6	0.4	0.8	1.3	4.6	10.0	10.4	11.3	11.2	12.7
24025	12580	1	Harford	437.1	262,977	269	601.6	76.4	16.5	0.7	4.2	5.1	5.4	12.8	11.8	12.4	13.3	12.8
24027	12580	1	Howard	251.0	334,529	217	1,332.8	51.7	21.8	0.7	21.9	7.6	5.5	14.1	12.4	11.8	14.6	13.8
24029		6	Kent	277.0	19,270	1,860	69.6	79.6	15.1	0.6	1.8	4.9	4.1	8.6	14.2	10.4	9.9	10.2
24031	47900	1	Montgomery	493.1	1,054,827	44	2,139.2	44.8	20.3	0.7	17.4	20.1	5.8	13.0	11.8	12.1	14.0	13.6
24033	47900	1	Prince George's	482.7	955,306	55	1,979.1	13.3	62.9	1.0	4.9	20.4	6.2	12.3	12.8	14.0	13.6	13.1
24035	12580	1	Queen Anne's	371.7	50,798	988	136.7	87.7	7.1	0.7	2.0	4.6	5.2	12.0	11.4	10.4	11.5	13.3

1. CBSA = Core Based Statistical Area. See Appendix A for explanation. See Appendix B for list of metropolitan areas with component counties. 2. County type code from the Economic Research Service of USDA Rural-Urban Continuum Codes. See Appendix A for definition. 3. Dry land or land partially or temporarily covered by water. 4. May be of any race.

STATE County	Population, 2021 (cont.)				Population change, 2000–2021							Households, 2016–2020				
	Age (percent) (cont.)				Total persons		Percent change		Components of change, 2020–2021					Percent		
	55 to 64 years	65 to 74 years	75 years and over	Percent female	2010	2020	2010–2020	2020–2021	Births	Deaths	Net Migration	Number	Persons per household	Family house-holds	Female family house-holder[1]	One person
	16	17	18	19	20	21	22	23	24	25	26	27	28	29	30	31
LOUISIANA—Cont'd																
Orleans	12.9	10.7	5.9	52.7	343,829	383,997	11.7	-1.8	5,455	5,328	-7,087	154,826	2.4	46.2	16.9	46.5
Ouachita	12.1	9.6	6.1	51.9	153,720	160,368	4.3	-1.0	2,384	2,472	-1,530	56,956	2.6	61.8	16.2	33.5
Plaquemines	12.9	8.7	5.7	49.9	23,042	23,515	2.1	-0.9	319	283	-253	8,600	2.7	74.8	15.5	22.8
Pointe Coupee	15.2	13.3	8.6	51.6	22,802	20,758	-9.0	-1.9	304	405	-298	9,056	2.4	59.2	15.4	35.7
Rapides	13.0	10.1	6.9	51.6	131,613	130,023	-1.2	-1.1	1,926	2,210	-1,102	49,075	2.6	66.2	17.9	29.8
Red River	14.5	11.5	8.1	51.9	9,091	7,620	-16.2	-0.7	135	141	-51	3,282	2.5	63.9	14.1	32.8
Richland	13.5	11.2	7.0	51.3	20,725	20,043	-3.3	-1.2	292	368	-163	7,563	2.5	68.1	16.7	29.5
Sabine	13.9	12.6	8.9	50.7	24,233	22,155	-8.6	-0.1	272	384	92	9,370	2.5	60.8	12.2	35.4
St. Bernard	12.7	8.4	4.2	50.9	35,897	43,764	21.9	1.1	676	579	389	15,165	3.1	68.3	19.4	26.6
St. Charles	14.5	9.7	5.0	51.1	52,780	52,549	-0.4	-0.5	647	676	-241	19,308	2.7	73.6	16.3	22.0
St. Helena	14.2	12.4	8.4	51.8	11,203	10,920	-2.5	-0.1	98	162	56	3,885	2.6	73.0	18.4	25.7
St. James	15.2	11.6	7.2	51.6	22,102	20,192	-8.6	-2.2	279	328	-397	7,907	2.7	73.7	18.9	24.6
St. John the Baptist	14.3	10.0	5.4	51.4	45,924	42,477	-7.5	-0.9	650	621	-418	15,251	2.8	72.5	20.0	22.8
St. Landry	13.2	10.4	6.5	51.8	83,384	82,540	-1.0	-0.6	1,306	1,560	-229	30,496	2.7	68.9	17.5	28.4
St. Martin	14.0	10.4	6.2	50.8	52,160	51,767	-0.8	-0.4	762	766	-233	19,655	2.7	69.6	15.8	26.7
St. Mary	15.0	10.9	7.2	50.8	54,650	49,406	-9.6	-2.4	772	791	-1,144	19,633	2.5	54.4	13.1	41.9
St. Tammany	13.8	11.4	6.6	51.4	233,740	264,570	13.2	1.8	3,345	3,700	5,222	95,054	2.7	70.6	13.2	24.3
Tangipahoa	12.2	9.8	5.4	51.6	121,097	133,157	10.0	1.5	2,259	1,986	1,774	48,548	2.7	66.3	17.2	28.0
Tensas	16.2	15.7	10.9	51.1	5,252	4,147	-21.0	-2.5	57	95	-65	1,814	2.4	56.1	10.5	40.4
Terrebonne	13.4	9.5	5.9	50.8	111,860	109,580	-2.0	-0.8	1,603	1,612	-881	40,374	2.7	67.6	15.5	24.5
Union	14.8	12.8	8.7	50.6	22,721	21,107	-7.1	-0.1	304	402	80	8,399	2.6	63.4	13.2	33.7
Vermilion	13.8	9.9	6.3	51.7	57,999	57,359	-1.1	-0.3	854	876	-141	22,180	2.7	70.6	13.2	23.8
Vernon	9.2	7.8	5.2	46.8	52,334	48,750	-6.8	-1.5	1,007	569	-1,153	17,516	2.7	68.7	10.4	28.3
Washington	13.2	11.7	7.3	50.8	47,168	45,463	-3.6	-0.7	712	955	-93	17,794	2.5	67.2	17.7	28.7
Webster	14.0	11.8	8.7	51.3	41,207	36,967	-10.3	-2.1	583	726	-633	16,320	2.3	62.5	13.1	31.4
West Baton Rouge	13.1	9.4	5.4	51.1	23,788	27,199	14.3	2.2	433	318	480	9,610	2.7	75.1	12.8	19.6
West Carroll	13.8	11.4	8.4	49.4	11,604	9,751	-16.0	-1.6	134	210	-83	4,126	2.6	66.7	16.5	30.5
West Feliciana	13.3	9.7	6.1	34.8	15,625	15,310	-2.0	1.2	89	182	279	4,202	2.8	59.6	11.1	37.1
Winn	12.9	11.0	8.1	46.3	15,313	13,755	-10.2	-1.9	147	284	-130	5,361	2.3	62.8	16.1	34.3
MAINE	15.5	13.3	8.3	50.7	1,328,361	1,362,359	2.6	0.7	14,248	22,142	17,912	569,551	2.3	61.4	8.9	29.8
Androscoggin	14.5	11.2	7.1	50.8	107,702	111,139	3.2	-0.1	1,364	1,749	268	45,906	2.3	60.5	10.3	29.8
Aroostook	16.2	14.8	10.3	50.0	71,870	67,105	-6.6	-0.4	738	1,339	362	29,594	2.2	61.5	8.2	33.6
Cumberland	14.4	11.9	7.6	51.2	281,674	303,069	7.6	0.7	3,401	4,178	2,918	123,384	2.3	59.6	7.8	30.2
Franklin	16.5	14.6	8.7	50.6	30,768	29,456	-4.3	0.8	254	478	463	12,426	2.3	60.4	7.9	31.6
Hancock	16.5	16.3	9.9	51.4	54,418	55,478	1.9	1.3	495	970	1,209	24,116	2.2	60.9	8.0	30.5
Kennebec	15.6	12.8	7.9	51.0	122,151	123,642	1.2	0.7	1,328	2,094	1,617	52,506	2.3	60.8	10.1	31.3
Knox	15.6	16.5	10.5	50.1	39,736	40,607	2.2	1.2	336	691	847	17,497	2.2	60.4	9.1	32.9
Lincoln	16.4	17.1	11.6	50.8	34,457	35,237	2.3	1.7	288	684	1,006	15,665	2.2	61.8	9.7	31.6
Oxford	17.6	14.5	8.3	50.0	57,833	57,777	-0.1	1.5	623	1,035	1,282	22,359	2.6	64.6	8.6	27.9
Penobscot	15.1	12.1	7.3	50.1	153,923	152,199	-1.1	0.4	1,482	2,555	1,645	63,073	2.3	60.4	9.9	29.3
Piscataquis	17.6	16.7	10.2	49.2	17,535	16,800	-4.2	2.2	133	336	579	7,180	2.3	61.6	9.8	30.1
Sagadahoc	15.9	14.1	9.5	50.8	35,293	36,699	4.0	1.0	373	584	590	16,024	2.2	65.4	7.6	26.9
Somerset	16.5	14.0	8.4	49.9	52,228	50,477	-3.4	0.2	537	896	478	21,645	2.3	61.7	9.9	29.1
Waldo	15.8	15.8	8.4	50.4	38,786	39,607	2.1	0.8	430	658	538	17,427	2.2	64.8	9.3	25.7
Washington	16.3	16.1	9.5	50.7	32,856	31,095	-5.4	0.1	320	695	405	13,830	2.2	63.4	10.4	30.5
York	16.1	13.4	8.2	50.9	197,131	211,972	7.5	1.2	2,146	3,200	3,705	86,919	2.3	63.6	8.7	27.6
MARYLAND	13.6	9.8	6.5	51.3	5,773,552	6,177,224	7.0	-0.2	83,750	76,782	-19,312	2,230,527	2.6	66.3	14.0	27.5
Allegany	13.2	11.5	9.0	47.4	75,087	68,106	-9.3	-0.6	779	1,340	179	27,369	2.3	60.6	11.3	32.0
Anne Arundel	13.4	9.3	6.1	50.3	537,656	588,261	9.4	0.4	8,142	6,982	782	213,122	2.6	69.5	11.6	24.8
Baltimore	13.5	10.5	7.3	52.5	805,029	854,535	6.1	-0.6	11,487	12,653	-4,168	315,347	2.6	64.4	14.5	29.4
Calvert	15.3	9.6	6.2	50.2	88,737	92,783	4.6	1.2	1,095	1,200	1,258	32,558	2.8	75.4	10.8	19.7
Caroline	14.8	10.4	6.6	50.9	33,066	33,293	0.7	0.3	483	489	93	12,160	2.7	71.4	14.2	22.1
Carroll	15.3	10.4	7.1	50.1	167,134	172,891	3.4	0.6	1,996	2,419	1,406	61,261	2.7	74.3	8.2	21.7
Cecil	15.3	10.6	6.1	50.1	101,108	103,725	2.6	0.2	1,400	1,569	332	37,293	2.7	70.4	12.2	23.9
Charles	14.1	8.2	5.0	51.6	146,551	166,617	13.7	1.2	2,239	1,835	1,665	57,388	2.8	73.2	16.7	21.8
Dorchester	15.7	13.3	9.2	52.5	32,618	32,531	-0.3	-0.1	400	587	145	13,433	2.3	64.3	15.6	31.2
Frederick	13.5	9.1	5.9	50.5	233,385	271,717	16.4	3.0	3,547	2,951	7,591	94,299	2.7	72.2	10.5	22.0
Garrett	16.4	13.8	9.6	50.2	30,097	28,806	-4.3	-0.4	322	528	101	12,745	2.2	66.0	10.7	29.4
Harford	14.5	10.3	6.5	50.8	244,826	260,924	6.6	0.8	3,260	3,367	2,151	95,094	2.7	72.6	10.4	22.3
Howard	13.1	8.9	5.8	50.8	287,085	332,317	15.8	0.7	3,969	2,787	975	116,457	2.8	73.4	11.2	21.4
Kent	15.6	15.1	11.9	51.9	20,197	19,198	-4.9	0.4	202	405	280	8,274	2.2	59.8	10.2	32.5
Montgomery	13.2	9.6	7.0	51.3	971,777	1,062,061	9.3	-0.7	14,332	9,464	-12,115	372,825	2.8	69.9	11.1	24.5
Prince George's	13.5	9.3	5.3	51.7	863,420	967,201	12.0	-1.2	14,070	10,217	-15,683	315,634	2.8	64.6	18.8	29.4
Queen Anne's	16.5	11.7	8.0	50.1	47,798	49,874	4.3	1.9	627	658	965	19,000	2.6	72.6	8.4	22.6

1. No spouse present.

STATE County	Persons in group quarters, 2021	Daytime Population, 2016–2020		Births, 2021		Deaths, 2021		Persons under 65 with no health insurance, 2019		Medicare, 2021			COVID-19 Deaths, 2020	
		Number	Employment/ residence ratio	Total	Rate[1]	Number	Rate[1]	Number	Percent	Total beneficiaries	Enrolled in Original Medicare	Enrolled in Medicare Advantage	Number	Rate[1]
	32	33	34	35	36	37	38	39	40	41	42	43	44	45
LOUISIANA—Cont'd														
Orleans	12,960	440,607	1.3	4,448	11.7	4,295	11.3	32,121	10.2	64,567	27,804	36,763	578	1.5
Ouachita	5,682	161,633	1.1	1,913	12.0	1,969	12.4	11,677	9.4	28,829	18,779	10,050	303	1.9
Plaquemines	238	30,122	1.7	255	10.9	227	9.7	2,231	11.3	3,746	1,561	2,185	22	0.9
Pointe Coupee	63	18,318	0.6	246	12.0	326	15.9	1,721	10.2	5,084	2,366	2,717	54	2.6
Rapides	4,361	135,269	1.1	1,555	12.0	1,781	13.8	11,205	10.7	28,011	20,652	7,358	223	1.7
Red River	71	8,295	0.9	97	12.8	116	15.3	638	9.6	1,780	1,269	511	29	3.8
Richland	950	19,347	0.9	229	11.5	294	14.8	1,730	11.1	4,420	3,042	1,378	46	2.3
Sabine	240	22,802	0.9	206	9.3	306	13.8	2,353	12.7	5,560	4,262	1,298	49	2.2
St. Bernard	173	40,697	0.7	556	12.6	469	10.6	4,446	10.8	6,740	2,838	3,902	43	1.0
St. Charles	487	55,701	1.1	523	10.0	534	10.2	3,228	7.2	9,176	3,325	5,852	64	1.2
St. Helena	117	8,404	0.5	71	6.5	125	11.5	918	11.6	2,988	1,551	1,436	D	D
St. James	127	22,215	1.1	215	10.8	274	13.7	1,370	8.0	4,493	1,889	2,604	44	2.2
St. John the Baptist	380	41,483	0.9	511	12.1	494	11.7	3,243	9.0	8,325	3,212	5,113	100	2.4
St. Landry	984	77,120	0.8	1,049	12.8	1,242	15.1	7,016	10.4	18,524	13,347	5,177	192	2.3
St. Martin	557	46,476	0.7	615	11.9	613	11.9	4,678	10.6	10,797	7,541	3,257	93	1.8
St. Mary	805	52,323	1.1	615	12.6	622	12.8	4,450	11.1	10,696	6,445	4,251	95	1.9
St. Tammany	1,122	240,490	0.9	2,696	10.1	2,991	11.2	19,767	9.2	53,851	24,800	29,052	275	1.0
Tangipahoa	3,350	123,993	0.8	1,863	13.9	1,617	12.0	11,986	10.8	24,079	13,084	10,996	173	1.3
Tensas	11	4,138	0.8	43	10.5	77	18.9	333	10.5	1,157	841	316	D	D
Terrebonne	1,292	119,277	1.2	1,301	11.9	1,309	12.0	11,841	12.8	21,223	13,829	7,394	128	1.2
Union	352	19,563	0.7	243	11.5	331	15.7	1,750	10.3	5,303	3,639	1,664	72	3.4
Vermilion	384	51,198	0.6	686	12.0	709	12.4	5,413	10.9	11,373	8,455	2,918	74	1.3
Vernon	3,324	49,256	1.0	814	16.9	450	9.3	3,566	9.2	7,754	6,507	1,247	70	1.4
Washington	1,446	42,902	0.8	575	12.7	782	17.3	3,744	10.4	10,569	6,082	4,487	84	1.9
Webster	1,031	37,767	0.9	468	12.8	565	15.5	3,199	10.9	9,503	6,496	3,008	80	2.2
West Baton Rouge	534	28,629	1.2	359	13.0	248	9.0	1,769	8.0	4,588	1,921	2,667	46	1.7
West Carroll	292	9,939	0.8	99	10.3	169	17.5	998	12.0	2,623	1,774	849	35	3.6
West Feliciana	5,258	15,598	1.0	71	4.6	134	8.7	667	8.2	2,210	1,301	909	27	1.8
Winn	1,673	13,288	0.8	116	8.5	228	16.8	957	9.9	3,028	2,226	802	33	2.4
MAINE	35,169	1,326,309	1.0	11,291	8.3	17,635	12.9	104,963	10.2	347,452	202,526	144,926	460	0.3
Androscoggin	3,135	104,825	0.9	1,094	9.9	1,384	12.5	8,323	9.7	25,081	12,421	12,660	45	0.4
Aroostook	2,092	67,082	1.0	591	8.8	1,093	16.3	6,194	12.7	20,366	14,283	6,083	24	0.4
Cumberland	9,295	322,399	1.2	2,704	8.9	3,324	10.9	18,262	7.8	66,621	34,722	31,900	112	0.4
Franklin	951	28,541	0.9	204	6.9	377	12.8	2,685	12.1	8,148	4,016	4,132	10	0.3
Hancock	861	54,051	1.0	370	6.6	777	13.9	4,621	11.4	15,803	10,509	5,294	27	0.5
Kennebec	3,644	126,028	1.1	1,048	8.4	1,680	13.5	9,885	10.5	32,065	17,016	15,049	36	0.3
Knox	1,389	41,254	1.1	276	6.8	558	13.7	3,227	11.5	12,155	7,188	4,967	D	D
Lincoln	463	31,983	0.9	233	6.6	531	15.0	3,345	13.6	11,343	6,282	5,060	D	D
Oxford	841	51,997	0.8	486	8.3	842	14.5	5,035	11.4	16,046	9,103	6,943	34	0.6
Penobscot	7,170	155,295	1.1	1,164	7.6	2,029	13.3	13,631	11.7	37,389	23,162	14,228	37	0.2
Piscataquis	198	16,405	0.9	117	6.9	258	15.2	1,504	12.7	5,415	3,640	1,775	D	D
Sagadahoc	240	33,596	0.9	296	8.0	470	12.7	2,470	8.9	9,838	5,472	4,367	D	D
Somerset	650	46,956	0.8	418	8.3	705	14.0	4,684	12.1	14,231	9,094	5,137	20	0.4
Waldo	518	35,765	0.8	334	8.4	525	13.2	3,393	11.4	11,156	6,606	4,550	22	0.6
Washington	272	31,140	1.0	249	8.0	527	16.9	3,679	16.2	9,624	7,541	2,082	D	D
York	3,450	178,992	0.8	1,707	8.0	2,555	12.0	14,025	8.6	52,171	31,472	20,699	93	0.4
MARYLAND	137,754	5,783,104	0.9	66,906	10.8	61,654	10.0	345,782	7.0	1,057,571	919,440	138,132	6,706	1.1
Allegany	7,198	74,644	1.1	609	9.0	1,070	15.8	2,842	5.8	16,994	16,181	813	173	2.5
Anne Arundel	14,037	569,051	1.0	6,484	11.0	5,641	9.6	23,587	4.9	96,978	85,798	11,180	398	0.7
Baltimore	21,627	780,853	0.9	9,250	10.9	10,074	11.8	46,135	6.9	162,576	138,899	23,677	1,024	1.2
Calvert	517	71,200	0.6	885	9.5	976	10.5	3,299	4.2	16,423	15,307	1,116	55	0.6
Caroline	341	28,082	0.7	376	11.3	406	12.2	2,354	8.5	6,669	6,331	338	16	0.5
Carroll	3,303	139,309	0.7	1,579	9.1	1,933	11.1	6,153	4.5	33,653	30,313	3,340	196	1.1
Cecil	1,226	88,314	0.7	1,137	11.0	1,255	12.1	4,944	5.8	19,513	18,017	1,496	100	1.0
Charles	1,297	126,175	0.6	1,832	10.9	1,474	8.8	6,710	4.8	24,441	22,312	2,129	165	1.0
Dorchester	453	29,771	0.8	327	10.1	488	15.0	1,735	7.1	8,237	7,871	365	34	1.0
Frederick	4,305	234,991	0.8	2,783	10.1	2,371	8.6	12,034	5.5	43,691	39,132	4,558	207	0.8
Garrett	453	29,393	1.0	253	8.8	438	15.2	1,665	7.5	7,279	6,445	833	58	2.0
Harford	2,617	226,757	0.8	2,582	9.9	2,683	10.2	9,770	4.6	49,154	44,188	4,966	178	0.7
Howard	1,534	322,010	1.0	3,136	9.4	2,266	6.8	12,605	4.5	49,440	43,630	5,810	210	0.6
Kent	1,430	20,034	1.1	164	8.5	330	17.2	1,084	8.3	5,685	5,333	353	37	1.9
Montgomery	8,362	1,021,201	1.0	11,367	10.7	7,706	7.3	70,658	8.1	170,566	146,711	23,855	1,213	1.1
Prince George's	21,021	791,344	0.8	11,328	11.8	8,244	8.6	77,960	10.2	134,973	110,926	24,047	1,355	1.4
Queen Anne's	317	42,192	0.7	488	9.7	510	10.1	2,307	5.7	10,562	9,910	652	29	0.6

1. Per 1,000 estimated resident population.

STATE County	COVID-19 Vaccinations, 2021–2022		Education						Money income, 2016–2020				Income and poverty, 2020			
			School enrollment and attainment, 2016–2020				Local government expenditures,[3] 2018–2019			Households				Percent below poverty level		
			Enrollment[1]		Attainment[2] (percent)						Percent					
	Number	Percent[5]	Total	Percent private	High school graduate or less	Bachelor's degree or more	Total current spending (mil dol)	Current spending per student (dollars)	Per capita income[4]	Median income (dollars)	with income of less than $50,000	with income of $200,000 or more	Median household income (dollars)	All persons	Children under 18 years	Children 5 to 17 years in families
	46	47	48	49	50	51	52	53	54	55	56	57	58	59	60	61
LOUISIANA—Cont'd																
Orleans	272,696	69.9	96,278	31.7	35.1	38.0	699.7	13,441	32,764	43,258	54.5	6.2	51,704	21.1	29.9	28.1
Ouachita	69,508	45.3	39,443	15.5	46.8	25.1	304.5	10,985	26,310	44,934	55.2	3.6	45,251	23.7	33.4	33.7
Plaquemines	16,035	69.1	6,467	24.6	50.0	18.2	80.4	16,200	30,788	65,234	38.9	6.1	55,861	16.6	20.1	18.2
Pointe Coupee	12,069	55.5	4,703	25.8	57.7	15.3	33.7	11,757	26,972	44,201	53.2	3.3	49,583	17.3	26.1	24.8
Rapides	64,666	49.9	32,923	16.9	49.8	21.7	249.5	10,765	27,291	48,013	52.0	3.7	45,130	18.7	22.7	21.0
Red River	3,105	36.8	2,063	12.0	66.6	13.1	23.6	16,379	21,264	33,817	60.5	4.3	42,135	23.7	36.8	32.6
Richland	8,681	43.1	4,205	9.4	60.2	15.7	40.7	11,076	20,644	40,491	57.1	1.3	43,794	22.5	34.5	31.1
Sabine	9,158	38.3	5,191	8.5	61.9	13.1	49.2	11,205	23,260	39,755	59.5	2.4	38,833	22.1	26.0	20.3
St. Bernard	23,229	49.2	12,536	15.9	51.5	13.9	86.7	11,183	22,999	47,873	51.7	3.2	50,790	21.3	31.3	26.2
St. Charles	30,201	56.9	13,382	15.7	42.6	28.3	155.1	16,628	34,193	68,113	36.8	6.4	69,889	11.3	15.6	14.2
St. Helena	3,193	31.5	2,367	16.8	61.3	16.5	13.9	11,793	23,403	45,063	54.5	1.5	40,709	22.7	34.9	37.6
St. James	10,946	51.9	4,815	17.1	54.8	16.8	63.4	16,523	28,944	53,209	47.9	3.9	58,309	13.0	21.4	20.5
St. John the Baptist	25,668	59.9	11,600	20.9	49.9	17.2	83.0	13,980	26,683	55,429	47.0	2.9	56,697	16.9	24.5	23.8
St. Landry	34,278	41.7	19,714	20.4	62.6	15.1	148.6	10,932	21,416	40,859	59.5	1.8	39,153	22.6	29.7	29.7
St. Martin	21,571	40.4	12,444	18.6	61.7	15.0	80.8	10,315	25,515	48,884	51.2	3.1	48,524	17.0	24.7	23.7
St. Mary	22,270	45.1	10,738	11.3	69.0	9.8	97.1	11,032	23,306	40,218	60.5	2.1	47,236	19.8	29.0	28.5
St. Tammany	148,010	56.8	62,597	24.9	34.7	34.3	460.7	12,110	35,263	70,730	36.2	8.0	67,462	10.0	12.8	12.3
Tangipahoa	62,727	46.5	33,222	18.0	53.0	22.0	202.6	10,334	25,628	48,745	50.7	3.1	47,272	20.1	29.1	26.1
Tensas	2,724	62.9	974	10.4	61.0	18.9	7.6	17,022	18,435	29,767	69.5	1.3	33,294	30.8	51.4	46.1
Terrebonne	50,314	45.5	26,598	21.5	58.3	15.8	183.5	10,634	27,495	52,224	48.3	3.9	55,402	15.7	19.7	19.9
Union	10,058	45.5	4,768	12.0	59.5	17.0	32.1	10,812	25,598	45,094	53.5	2.8	42,342	26.7	37.2	36.6
Vermilion	22,771	38.3	13,634	17.4	61.5	16.2	93.9	9,804	26,503	52,219	48.2	3.2	52,709	15.4	21.6	20.3
Vernon	26,826	56.6	11,513	8.4	51.3	17.8	92.3	10,630	25,378	50,267	49.6	2.3	55,124	16.1	21.1	19.8
Washington	19,450	42.1	10,427	14.8	62.1	11.8	81.9	11,424	21,384	39,185	60.8	1.6	38,604	22.5	35.8	34.3
Webster	16,536	43.1	8,331	9.6	56.7	15.0	63.4	10,321	20,094	30,324	71.3	1.4	41,747	19.7	28.1	26.1
West Baton Rouge	14,229	53.8	6,349	20.0	49.6	22.7	56.0	14,730	29,195	67,813	34.8	3.7	62,919	14.6	20.2	20.0
West Carroll	4,413	40.7	2,208	8.6	67.4	11.5	22.0	11,072	23,400	42,545	60.3	1.8	38,513	20.8	29.9	27.8
West Feliciana	13,948	89.6	2,958	10.4	51.7	23.5	32.5	14,349	27,279	59,688	41.5	7.3	58,499	21.9	18.7	16.7
Winn	6,634	47.7	2,955	23.4	60.7	16.7	25.7	11,868	22,259	37,764	61.2	3.1	42,991	22.6	28.1	26.5
MAINE	1,068,476	79.5	278,782	18.9	38.1	32.5	2,691.0	14,954	33,774	59,489	42.3	4.9	59,145	10.6	12.8	12.2
Androscoggin	76,063	70.2	24,710	19.8	44.3	22.7	233.8	13,546	29,947	55,002	46.1	3.1	57,723	11.7	15.6	15.0
Aroostook	46,444	69.3	12,771	15.2	47.4	19.8	136.1	14,772	26,774	43,791	55.8	2.5	45,523	15.3	18.8	18.5
Cumberland	259,187	87.9	65,303	22.4	26.3	48.1	607.7	16,073	41,822	76,014	32.3	8.9	75,455	8.6	8.8	8.5
Franklin	19,431	64.3	6,408	8.1	45.1	26.3	49.0	14,679	29,905	51,630	48.3	4.8	49,317	12.9	16.2	15.1
Hancock	42,330	77.0	9,992	14.9	36.8	35.2	113.8	16,749	35,345	58,345	41.8	5.1	58,466	10.3	12.9	12.0
Kennebec	88,046	72.0	26,810	21.1	40.1	29.3	212.6	13,653	31,486	55,368	45.7	3.8	53,876	11.2	13.8	13.0
Knox	33,510	84.3	6,617	18.5	38.8	34.2	104.2	17,467	34,420	57,794	42.0	4.6	66,058	10.2	13.6	12.3
Lincoln	28,052	81.0	5,539	23.2	39.3	36.1	58.9	15,667	35,114	58,125	42.6	4.3	64,825	8.8	13.8	13.2
Oxford	39,676	68.4	10,835	16.2	49.6	20.6	128.6	14,425	26,799	49,761	50.2	2.3	47,611	13.0	16.9	16.2
Penobscot	108,514	71.3	36,421	14.9	40.5	28.6	298.4	13,745	29,603	52,128	48.4	3.4	52,079	12.1	13.1	12.4
Piscataquis	10,418	62.1	2,943	22.5	49.9	18.7	19.4	11,040	25,511	42,083	58.6	2.0	48,769	14.6	21.2	22.2
Sagadahoc	28,659	79.9	6,720	14.6	35.9	37.4	72.4	16,221	35,226	68,039	36.9	3.2	68,433	9.2	10.9	9.8
Somerset	31,265	61.9	9,626	12.9	51.1	17.9	112.3	14,540	25,023	45,382	54.0	1.4	43,694	14.5	18.5	17.9
Waldo	28,446	71.6	7,661	23.4	39.0	31.6	58.7	16,564	31,091	58,034	43.2	3.4	56,085	11.6	15.6	15.0
Washington	22,717	72.4	6,263	12.0	47.0	23.8	71.9	17,694	26,049	44,847	54.3	1.7	48,582	12.0	17.7	18.4
York	165,330	79.6	40,163	21.0	35.8	32.2	413.2	14,725	37,009	68,932	35.1	5.8	67,965	8.1	8.9	8.4
MARYLAND	4,567,278	75.5	1,520,676	19.4	33.6	40.9	13,581.6	15,144	43,352	87,063	28.2	13.4	88,589	9.0	11.2	10.8
Allegany	39,158	55.6	16,412	7.5	50.7	19.3	121.5	14,230	24,776	49,449	50.4	2.1	53,023	14.7	18.6	17.6
Anne Arundel	445,271	76.9	144,455	21.1	29.5	43.0	1,169.0	14,028	48,125	103,225	20.4	15.9	105,979	5.2	6.3	6.1
Baltimore	601,337	72.7	206,170	22.1	33.6	39.8	1,653.3	14,526	41,089	78,724	30.7	9.9	79,974	8.9	11.2	10.2
Calvert	65,526	70.8	22,574	14.5	34.8	34.2	231.6	14,534	47,066	112,696	18.0	17.7	111,665	5.3	5.3	5.4
Caroline	19,108	57.2	7,902	9.2	55.0	19.0	83.2	14,278	29,814	59,042	40.4	4.3	60,617	12.4	17.9	16.4
Carroll	121,502	72.1	41,362	23.2	35.6	37.0	357.9	14,216	43,183	99,569	23.9	13.0	104,817	5.2	5.6	5.2
Cecil	60,241	58.6	23,703	17.3	45.2	25.3	220.5	14,403	35,887	79,415	31.4	7.1	84,248	8.8	12.4	11.4
Charles	115,005	70.4	42,901	14.7	37.5	30.0	399.4	14,732	42,737	103,678	20.1	13.8	102,681	7.4	9.3	8.2
Dorchester	18,984	59.5	6,773	7.9	51.4	19.9	75.3	15,742	29,860	52,799	48.3	3.7	54,846	14.9	23.8	22.6
Frederick	204,135	78.7	66,252	17.9	31.2	41.7	573.8	13,434	44,273	100,685	22.1	13.7	99,254	6.2	7.2	7.4
Garrett	14,819	51.1	5,537	11.3	52.5	23.5	56.3	14,657	34,006	54,542	45.5	5.6	56,929	12.8	16.7	17.0
Harford	178,557	69.9	61,515	17.6	32.9	36.9	521.5	13,786	42,744	94,003	25.4	12.5	102,537	6.2	7.2	6.6
Howard	279,504	85.8	89,025	16.1	17.8	62.7	931.4	16,084	55,873	124,042	16.8	25.6	124,042	5.5	5.8	5.3
Kent	12,740	65.6	4,394	34.4	41.9	36.3	31.7	16,566	37,699	60,208	41.5	7.8	64,437	12.0	17.2	17.0
Montgomery	914,578	87.0	269,177	21.9	22.0	59.2	2,682.6	16,490	55,643	111,812	20.5	23.5	115,394	6.7	7.6	7.0
Prince George's	680,136	74.8	237,553	16.9	38.1	34.4	2,093.6	15,782	38,502	86,994	25.5	10.9	85,246	9.5	12.7	14.0
Queen Anne's	33,939	67.4	11,248	16.1	35.8	36.5	106.0	13,683	45,228	96,467	24.1	13.4	93,427	6.9	7.9	7.5

1. All persons 3 years old and over enrolled in nursery school through college. 2. Persons 25 years old and over. 3. Elementary and secondary education expenditures. 4. Based on population estimated by the American Community Survey, 2016–2020. 5. CDC percent based on 2019 population estimate.

STATE County	Personal income, 2020: Total (mil dol)	Personal income, 2020: Percent change 2019–2020	Per capita[1]: Dollars	Per capita[1]: Rank	Wages and salaries (mil dol)	Supplements to wages and salaries, employer contributions (mil dol): Pension and insurance	Supplements to wages and salaries, employer contributions (mil dol): Government social insurance	Proprietors' income (mil dol)	Dividends, interest, and rent (mil dol)	Personal transfer reecipts (mil dol)	Earnings, 2020: Total (mil dol)	Contributions for government social insurance (mil dol): From employee and self-employed	Contributions for government social insurance (mil dol): From employer
	62	63	64	65	66	67	68	69	70	71	72	73	74
LOUISIANA—Cont'd													
Orleans	22,364	7.6	57,421	543	11,628	1,849	787	2,416	4,793	5,567	16,680	945	787
Ouachita	6,960	7.6	45,661	1,708	3,171	552	210	577	1,045	2,227	4,511	271	210
Plaquemines	1,189	5.4	51,456	984	877	183	56	115	190	271	1,231	67	56
Pointe Coupee	1,127	6.5	52,332	905	273	54	19	114	161	324	460	30	19
Rapides	6,457	6.6	50,226	1,117	2,712	526	181	738	997	2,072	4,157	244	181
Red River	379	5.6	45,680	1,704	112	24	7	38	64	129	182	11	7
Richland	853	8.9	42,644	2,110	255	49	18	62	86	338	383	25	18
Sabine	909	4.9	38,190	2,666	228	50	15	86	133	346	379	26	15
St. Bernard	1,720	10.6	36,093	2,863	580	148	36	92	190	582	856	51	36
St. Charles	2,816	5.8	53,148	847	1,806	384	113	142	379	625	2,445	137	113
St. Helena	491	8.2	48,743	1,290	66	17	4	9	58	194	96	7	4
St. James	1,179	4.2	56,880	578	611	137	39	154	129	306	941	54	39
St. John the Baptist	1,953	7.7	45,927	1,663	872	198	55	102	224	629	1,227	74	55
St. Landry	3,757	7.9	46,131	1,631	1,042	211	67	293	529	1,387	1,613	108	67
St. Martin	2,235	6.3	42,203	2,167	552	97	36	136	290	713	821	57	36
St. Mary	2,212	7.1	45,760	1,691	1,112	193	73	187	364	772	1,564	96	73
St. Tammany	18,491	2.7	70,190	165	4,864	783	310	3,958	3,007	3,378	9,915	569	310
Tangipahoa	5,716	8.8	41,792	2,230	1,976	408	123	305	715	1,932	2,812	170	123
Tensas	184	1.7	44,043	1,942	35	8	2	29	35	74	75	4	2
Terrebonne	5,047	7.2	45,942	1,662	2,659	395	177	377	805	1,515	3,608	226	177
Union	967	6.6	43,609	1,994	188	39	13	66	112	348	306	23	13
Vermilion	2,525	5.7	42,526	2,128	599	118	38	190	349	774	944	60	38
Vernon	2,171	5.6	45,320	1,750	1,105	317	96	76	377	602	1,595	76	96
Washington	1,763	8.4	38,515	2,622	430	97	28	71	208	805	626	47	28
Webster	1,711	7.6	45,088	1,783	514	98	34	101	244	626	747	54	34
West Baton Rouge	1,387	6.6	51,758	958	733	132	50	128	144	320	1,044	60	50
West Carroll	395	12.7	37,148	2,775	83	21	5	29	45	171	139	10	5
West Feliciana	636	3.7	41,145	2,317	357	95	20	55	128	143	527	25	20
Winn	574	6.4	41,491	2,270	190	40	13	89	60	202	332	20	13
MAINE	73,193	7.9	53,728	X	32,289	5,577	2,377	5,267	12,521	19,557	45,509	3,155	2,377
Androscoggin	5,032	8.8	46,357	1,598	2,512	412	189	267	591	1,578	3,381	235	189
Aroostook	3,180	11.1	47,605	1,439	1,189	252	89	264	384	1,192	1,794	126	89
Cumberland	20,342	6.8	68,237	193	11,685	1,672	840	1,615	4,016	3,872	15,812	1,039	840
Franklin	1,298	6.8	43,276	2,029	430	89	32	89	214	444	640	49	32
Hancock	3,051	6.5	55,393	677	1,023	178	79	342	719	813	1,623	122	79
Kennebec	6,205	8.8	50,469	1,094	3,136	622	220	387	860	1,805	4,365	286	220
Knox	2,172	5.6	54,363	754	812	143	60	245	522	597	1,261	93	60
Lincoln	1,888	5.5	54,300	763	473	83	35	150	478	529	741	62	35
Oxford	2,461	9.0	42,327	2,153	739	139	55	156	360	883	1,089	89	55
Penobscot	7,176	9.7	47,315	1,475	3,524	658	256	316	974	2,237	4,754	321	256
Piscataquis	723	8.8	42,527	2,127	236	48	18	49	113	283	351	29	18
Sagadahoc	2,017	6.8	55,965	645	855	168	70	102	422	502	1,195	83	70
Somerset	2,184	10.1	43,134	2,044	743	140	56	154	280	842	1,093	82	56
Waldo	1,896	8.1	47,495	1,450	541	96	40	141	351	592	818	67	40
Washington	1,434	12.3	45,558	1,722	457	101	35	141	200	592	733	54	35
York	12,134	7.3	58,038	510	3,932	775	302	848	2,035	2,797	5,858	418	302
MARYLAND	404,521	6.1	65,534	X	189,437	31,073	13,621	28,509	70,043	74,467	262,639	15,740	13,621
Allegany	3,080	7.3	43,970	1,951	1,408	293	114	123	413	1,204	1,937	133	114
Anne Arundel	42,075	6.2	72,197	137	23,703	4,474	1,761	2,303	7,694	6,365	32,241	1,845	1,761
Baltimore	55,000	6.1	66,585	230	24,877	3,778	1,775	4,119	10,027	11,096	34,549	2,129	1,775
Calvert	6,186	5.6	66,469	234	1,270	230	91	239	986	1,028	1,830	125	91
Caroline	1,621	5.9	48,393	1,339	477	91	36	116	198	507	720	49	36
Carroll	11,312	5.7	66,901	215	2,999	471	219	605	1,612	1,957	4,295	282	219
Cecil	5,363	6.5	51,853	942	1,971	371	154	255	722	1,341	2,750	178	154
Charles	10,084	7.7	61,324	373	2,243	457	169	238	1,512	1,817	3,107	203	169
Dorchester	1,590	7.3	49,921	1,150	592	115	44	99	252	558	851	58	44
Frederick	17,677	8.0	66,664	224	6,433	1,023	469	1,107	2,533	2,736	9,031	555	469
Garrett	1,403	5.9	48,630	1,302	494	93	38	136	212	450	762	51	38
Harford	16,290	6.8	63,432	302	6,029	1,149	456	665	2,338	3,087	8,299	519	456
Howard	26,902	5.8	81,969	69	14,538	1,597	975	1,663	4,539	3,014	18,772	1,130	975
Kent	1,235	5.2	64,331	283	358	65	27	117	357	327	568	39	27
Montgomery	94,192	3.9	89,552	41	41,772	6,281	2,904	10,062	20,711	10,609	61,019	3,515	2,904
Prince George's	49,296	8.3	54,195	767	21,679	4,197	1,607	1,976	6,869	10,291	29,459	1,751	1,607
Queen Anne's	3,472	5.6	67,861	197	744	127	55	283	603	604	1,208	79	55

1. Based on the resident population estimated as of July 1 of the year shown.

STATE County	Earnings, 2020 (cont.)									Social Security beneficiaries, December 2020		Supple-mental Security Income recipients, 2020	Housing units, 2021	
	Percent by selected industries													
	Farm	Mining, quarrying, and extractions	Construction	Manu-facturing	Information; professional, scientific, technical services	Retail trade	Finance, insurance, real estate, and leasing	Health care and social assistance	Govern-ment	Number	Rate[1]		Total	Percent change, 2010–2021
	75	76	77	78	79	80	81	82	83	84	85	86	87	88
LOUISIANA—Cont'd														
Orleans	0.0	2.3	2.7	2.7	17.5	3.6	7.2	11.2	20.0	65,165	173	19,067	194,697	0.4
Ouachita	0.3	0.2	5.7	8.8	8.7	9.1	6.6	19.2	15.9	30,370	191	6,917	70,613	0.7
Plaquemines	0.5	12.9	3.5	18.7	D	2.4	3.2	1.6	15.9	3,925	168	573	9,624	1.6
Pointe Coupee	6.7	2.0	5.0	6.4	D	7.7	13.4	6.5	14.4	5,035	247	914	11,027	0.8
Rapides	1.6	1.4	6.7	7.6	4.9	10.4	5.2	19.0	21.4	29,135	226	6,522	58,267	0.5
Red River	5.3	15.7	4.0	13.5	3.2	4.6	3.4	D	22.0	1,720	227	459	3,588	0.6
Richland	7.1	1.0	6.5	10.3	D	8.2	4.9	D	15.7	4,645	235	1,105	8,682	0.5
Sabine	8.0	1.6	5.7	15.7	4.8	7.5	5.2	D	20.1	5,835	264	991	13,586	1.5
St. Bernard	0.2	D	8.8	31.2	3.0	7.1	2.3	7.0	17.7	7,405	167	1,676	18,015	1.8
St. Charles	0.0	D	11.1	33.1	5.4	2.6	3.3	3.1	10.5	9,870	189	1,089	20,612	0.7
St. Helena	1.2	D	4.6	20.7	D	4.8	D	D	37.8	3,370	309	919	5,317	1.2
St. James	0.5	D	2.2	49.8	D	2.2	2.7	D	11.5	4,845	245	676	8,623	0.7
St. John the Baptist	-0.1	D	10.1	35.3	3.8	5.4	3.5	5.1	13.0	9,065	215	1,704	17,845	0.5
St. Landry	2.5	1.8	7.0	7.0	5.0	10.6	7.3	14.4	20.4	20,360	248	5,163	36,970	0.6
St. Martin	1.0	3.2	7.9	21.9	4.5	9.1	7.3	7.4	15.0	11,785	229	1,688	23,692	0.6
St. Mary	0.8	12.4	6.1	19.5	D	5.0	8.6	4.6	15.5	11,915	247	2,207	22,465	0.2
St. Tammany	0.0	28.6	6.7	2.5	7.2	5.8	7.1	10.0	11.4	55,730	207	4,967	112,406	1.5
Tangipahoa	0.3	0.7	6.2	6.2	4.5	10.4	6.2	11.5	28.3	25,320	187	4,890	58,591	2.9
Tensas	28.4	0.5	D	1.7	D	D	D	D	20.4	1,210	299	342	2,787	0.3
Terrebonne	0.3	13.0	6.6	10.4	6.4	7.4	6.1	13.0	9.9	23,635	217	4,604	47,562	0.4
Union	7.9	0.4	8.6	19.6	D	7.8	6.7	10.5	17.1	5,665	269	920	10,397	0.6
Vermilion	8.1	9.4	7.8	4.4	4.7	7.9	4.6	D	21.6	12,405	217	1,925	25,997	0.8
Vernon	0.2	0.1	2.4	1.1	7.8	3.3	2.3	6.2	67.3	8,070	168	1,164	22,037	0.3
Washington	0.9	0.3	8.3	14.5	2.3	7.4	3.7	D	26.7	11,535	256	2,751	21,415	0.3
Webster	0.1	6.1	8.9	12.5	3.3	9.6	4.7	D	17.3	10,045	278	1,870	18,332	0.3
West Baton Rouge	0.8	D	19.9	26.7	D	4.7	D	1.8	11.3	4,905	176	775	11,795	2.1
West Carroll	13.9	D	4.8	3.6	2.0	9.5	D	D	35.0	2,760	288	466	4,688	0.6
West Feliciana	0.1	D	4.9	D	D	2.9	7.2	D	31.8	2,205	142	276	5,117	1.3
Winn	-0.2	2.1	4.0	13.7	D	4.5	14.1	D	17.7	3,120	231	551	6,351	0.2
MAINE	0.8	0.0	7.4	9.2	8.9	7.7	7.7	16.6	16.8	355,433	259	35,947	745,334	0.7
Androscoggin	0.9	D	8.0	10.7	7.1	8.1	5.8	20.2	11.2	26,620	240	4,052	50,149	0.5
Aroostook	7.2	0.0	4.7	11.3	2.9	8.8	4.9	18.2	23.1	20,990	314	2,504	38,396	0.2
Cumberland	0.1	D	5.8	7.1	14.4	6.3	13.4	17.2	9.7	65,375	214	5,166	151,443	1.0
Franklin	0.6	0.0	8.1	11.9	D	12.1	5.3	D	19.7	8,400	283	940	20,978	0.5
Hancock	1.3	0.1	11.0	3.4	14.2	9.3	4.8	13.5	13.7	15,745	280	1,021	40,433	0.6
Kennebec	0.3	D	5.8	5.2	5.7	8.5	3.9	16.4	29.5	32,705	263	3,935	63,025	0.6
Knox	1.0	0.0	9.6	8.8	6.2	9.6	5.7	15.6	14.4	12,320	300	809	24,411	0.5
Lincoln	1.3	0.0	12.4	D	7.5	10.5	5.9	14.7	14.0	11,300	315	649	23,782	0.6
Oxford	1.0	0.1	10.3	16.4	4.3	9.4	3.4	14.0	17.3	17,290	295	2,041	36,516	1.0
Penobscot	0.3	D	6.2	4.2	5.2	8.7	4.7	24.4	19.6	38,945	255	5,379	75,281	0.5
Piscataquis	0.8	D	7.6	24.3	2.5	10.4	2.5	D	17.3	5,505	321	662	14,622	0.3
Sagadahoc	0.3	0.0	9.4	D	6.7	6.2	2.8	5.8	14.3	9,925	268	595	19,081	0.6
Somerset	2.9	D	12.8	17.2	3.8	8.4	3.8	14.9	14.7	15,375	304	2,174	29,973	0.6
Waldo	1.0	D	10.7	9.1	D	8.3	9.6	14.8	11.9	11,580	290	1,228	22,097	0.7
Washington	6.0	D	6.0	11.0	2.7	8.7	3.7	14.1	24.2	10,030	322	1,315	21,664	0.3
York	0.2	0.1	9.6	11.8	6.5	7.6	4.8	11.0	27.5	53,330	249	3,477	113,483	1.0
MARYLAND	0.2	0.0	6.9	4.5	16.8	4.9	8.9	11.2	24.6	1,032,078	167	120,333	2,546,344	0.5
Allegany	0.1	D	4.5	5.6	3.7	7.6	4.4	21.3	32.4	17,535	259	2,330	32,803	-0.3
Anne Arundel	0.0	0.0	6.8	6.0	15.2	4.4	4.1	7.8	35.2	96,030	163	7,615	235,208	0.7
Baltimore	0.1	0.0	7.7	4.7	12.8	6.1	14.9	13.4	17.3	161,385	190	16,510	350,956	0.2
Calvert	-0.1	0.2	12.8	3.0	7.8	6.9	5.4	14.0	20.9	16,490	176	1,071	36,046	0.8
Caroline	4.0	D	12.3	10.4	D	8.8	D	D	19.0	7,435	223	813	13,487	0.3
Carroll	0.9	D	14.4	8.1	11.2	7.7	5.6	13.6	15.1	33,680	194	1,568	66,197	0.5
Cecil	1.2	D	D	21.1	D	6.8	2.6	9.2	23.8	20,655	199	1,868	44,114	0.3
Charles	0.0	D	10.6	1.5	7.4	10.7	4.0	10.9	34.8	24,605	146	2,405	62,937	1.0
Dorchester	1.0	0.2	D	19.8	D	4.8	4.3	18.3	22.7	8,770	270	1,325	16,403	0.1
Frederick	0.6	D	D	D	D	7.3	D	D	19.5	43,860	157	2,409	106,417	2.3
Garrett	2.5	3.0	11.4	8.1	D	9.5	D	12.6	15.2	7,750	270	598	18,503	0.4
Harford	0.2	D	7.3	5.2	13.7	6.2	5.1	10.0	33.2	50,075	190	3,469	104,488	1.0
Howard	0.1	D	7.2	5.2	34.4	4.4	7.0	7.0	8.9	44,915	134	3,585	124,252	0.7
Kent	5.6	D	8.5	12.0	D	7.3	8.0	10.7	14.0	5,770	299	374	10,307	0.2
Montgomery	0.0	0.0	4.8	3.8	23.2	3.8	12.7	9.6	23.1	147,995	140	13,859	405,744	0.2
Prince George's	0.0	D	11.4	2.2	11.0	5.8	3.6	8.0	38.7	126,670	133	14,321	362,351	0.5
Queen Anne's	2.7	D	10.9	9.6	9.9	7.3	4.6	5.6	17.0	10,765	212	363	21,613	1.2

1. Per 1,000 resident population estimated as of July 1 of the year shown.

STATE County	Housing units, 2016–2020: Occupied units: Total	Owner-occupied: Percent	Owner-occupied: Median value[1]	Median owner cost as a percent of income: With a mortgage	Median owner cost as a percent of income: Without a mortgage[2]	Renter-occupied: Median rent[3]	Median rent as a percent of income[2]	Substandard units[4] (percent)	Civilian labor force, 2021: Total	Percent change, 2020–2021	Unemployment: Total	Unemployment: Rate[5]	Civilian employment[6], 2016–2020: Total	Percent: Management, business, science, and arts	Percent: Construction, production, and maintenance occupations
	89	90	91	92	93	94	95	96	97	98	99	100	101	102	103
LOUISIANA—Cont'd															
Orleans	154,826	49.8	250,000	25.7	12.9	1,025	36.3	1.6	177,776	-1.1	14,796	8.3	178,975	43.7	14.5
Ouachita	56,956	60.0	150,200	18.7	10.0	775	33.9	2.9	69,404	0.0	3,480	5.0	65,345	35.3	21.0
Plaquemines	8,600	73.0	202,700	19.3	10.0	1,312	29.6	4.7	9,539	0.1	413	4.3	9,901	36.0	28.6
Pointe Coupee	9,056	76.1	157,900	21.1	10.5	835	34.0	2.6	9,544	1.0	547	5.7	9,184	24.2	32.5
Rapides	49,075	64.2	147,200	18.7	10.0	825	32.9	2.7	55,425	1.4	2,228	4.0	55,199	34.4	23.2
Red River	3,282	71.7	77,900	18.3	14.3	521	29.3	1.8	3,668	2.3	159	4.3	3,069	22.6	34.9
Richland	7,563	65.7	107,700	18.8	10.0	644	31.9	4.9	8,117	0.2	422	5.2	7,855	27.6	29.1
Sabine	9,370	70.0	87,600	17.8	10.0	594	34.2	2.7	9,271	0.8	342	3.7	8,031	28.8	35.3
St. Bernard	15,165	71.4	152,600	19.3	10.0	952	36.5	4.2	19,908	-0.4	1,359	6.8	19,455	29.1	26.4
St. Charles	19,308	80.5	205,600	19.2	10.0	1,004	33.2	1.4	24,370	0.0	1,220	5.0	24,555	39.4	25.6
St. Helena	3,885	77.8	115,500	19.0	11.1	706	27.9	1.9	4,257	0.4	390	9.2	3,855	33.3	32.3
St. James	7,907	80.7	168,700	16.4	10.0	614	31.6	3.7	8,845	0.0	652	7.4	9,096	28.4	35.7
St. John the Baptist	15,251	80.2	155,900	19.2	10.1	915	28.3	3.4	19,155	-0.2	1,634	8.5	18,375	29.8	29.3
St. Landry	30,496	69.1	122,900	19.3	10.0	621	29.2	4.3	32,024	-0.5	2,016	6.3	31,471	29.0	30.0
St. Martin	19,655	78.7	123,700	19.2	10.0	686	31.0	4.0	21,901	0.6	1,233	5.6	22,352	24.8	34.0
St. Mary	19,633	60.7	105,800	20.2	10.5	784	30.4	1.5	19,192	-1.0	1,295	6.7	19,415	22.3	34.9
St. Tammany	95,054	78.5	223,300	20.5	10.1	1,143	32.9	1.3	116,814	0.1	4,492	3.8	118,423	41.4	19.8
Tangipahoa	48,548	70.3	167,900	19.1	10.0	828	32.3	3.3	56,131	0.0	3,607	6.4	55,975	33.7	26.9
Tensas	1,814	70.3	78,900	20.7	12.7	582	26.9	5.8	1,318	-1.8	78	5.9	1,266	31.3	28.1
Terrebonne	40,374	71.8	155,600	20.2	10.0	862	29.9	3.6	45,015	-1.4	2,597	5.8	47,216	30.0	29.2
Union	8,399	80.6	94,700	16.8	10.0	559	25.0	3.5	8,993	0.1	436	4.8	8,710	24.9	39.0
Vermilion	22,180	74.4	127,700	18.2	10.0	676	28.1	2.8	23,846	1.1	1,201	5.0	24,213	30.8	29.4
Vernon	17,516	52.7	126,000	16.6	10.0	921	24.7	1.5	16,011	1.4	729	4.6	16,299	30.4	28.5
Washington	17,794	71.1	114,900	20.8	10.0	648	31.7	2.6	16,870	1.6	988	5.9	17,126	24.5	29.3
Webster	16,320	66.3	85,300	21.6	11.0	665	41.3	3.2	14,001	0.4	766	5.5	14,182	30.7	31.5
West Baton Rouge	9,610	75.3	197,000	18.1	10.0	883	28.7	3.2	13,611	0.9	662	4.9	11,982	37.8	23.7
West Carroll	4,126	77.4	85,800	17.1	10.0	583	27.1	3.4	3,508	-4.0	222	6.3	4,026	36.2	31.9
West Feliciana	4,202	72.6	230,400	19.1	10.0	819	29.6	0.6	5,253	1.6	193	3.7	5,741	35.5	20.6
Winn	5,361	66.9	77,000	17.4	10.0	577	27.1	0.4	4,602	-1.8	221	4.8	4,897	30.6	33.4
MAINE	569,551	72.9	198,000	20.8	12.3	873	28.6	2.0	681,884	1.0	31,550	4.6	675,784	38.8	22.8
Androscoggin	45,906	64.9	166,600	20.1	13.4	771	28.1	2.0	54,219	-0.1	2,643	4.9	54,139	34.9	23.9
Aroostook	29,594	73.2	102,600	18.8	11.4	589	28.5	1.6	29,056	-0.5	1,648	5.7	29,147	31.0	28.9
Cumberland	123,384	70.0	288,800	20.9	12.8	1,193	28.9	2.1	162,433	1.0	6,491	4.0	164,003	47.7	15.6
Franklin	12,426	77.5	146,900	19.4	10.8	719	26.2	2.7	13,839	0.8	730	5.3	14,531	30.9	29.6
Hancock	24,116	76.7	218,000	20.6	11.5	838	27.6	2.2	28,376	2.4	1,423	5.0	28,029	37.4	24.5
Kennebec	52,506	70.7	164,000	19.8	11.3	777	28.9	1.7	61,360	0.0	2,638	4.3	60,412	39.6	21.0
Knox	17,497	78.6	209,900	23.0	13.3	855	27.7	0.6	19,881	1.6	873	4.4	19,699	34.6	28.2
Lincoln	15,665	78.6	220,000	22.9	11.4	817	27.0	1.5	16,707	2.0	740	4.4	16,306	38.3	28.5
Oxford	22,359	80.5	150,700	19.7	11.9	718	32.3	2.4	26,298	2.0	1,470	5.6	26,029	31.2	29.8
Penobscot	63,073	70.1	148,300	19.4	11.8	823	29.3	2.1	74,855	0.9	3,543	4.7	73,848	36.5	21.2
Piscataquis	7,180	77.0	110,100	24.4	12.5	649	26.2	2.9	7,440	4.0	373	5.0	6,626	32.2	31.6
Sagadahoc	16,024	75.4	222,900	23.1	12.6	896	28.6	0.9	19,159	-0.5	711	3.7	18,880	39.5	24.4
Somerset	21,645	76.5	122,400	20.5	13.0	758	27.7	3.3	22,318	1.4	1,398	6.3	22,318	25.8	33.0
Waldo	17,427	80.4	169,400	20.6	11.6	795	27.3	2.8	20,249	1.3	951	4.7	19,057	39.9	23.5
Washington	13,830	77.6	115,200	21.2	11.6	582	28.6	2.2	13,452	0.8	869	6.5	12,694	31.1	33.4
York	86,919	74.4	260,800	22.0	13.0	1,022	28.4	1.7	112,246	1.5	5,049	4.5	110,066	38.3	24.1
MARYLAND	2,230,527	67.1	325,400	21.3	10.2	1,415	29.7	2.5	3,175,550	-1.6	183,322	5.8	3,076,280	47.2	16.7
Allegany	27,369	69.1	126,500	18.8	11.5	719	30.5	1.0	30,504	-2.8	1,966	6.4	27,491	31.5	23.3
Anne Arundel	213,122	74.3	370,100	21.1	10.0	1,690	28.9	1.8	312,621	-1.5	14,844	4.7	293,748	49.0	15.8
Baltimore	315,347	66.1	267,400	20.5	10.5	1,328	30.0	2.0	444,930	-1.6	25,203	5.7	420,275	45.5	16.7
Calvert	32,558	84.7	364,800	21.1	10.0	1,461	29.9	0.8	48,774	-1.9	2,237	4.6	47,021	45.3	19.8
Caroline	12,160	71.0	213,400	24.3	11.4	1,003	32.0	3.6	17,435	-1.5	826	4.7	16,078	32.1	27.6
Carroll	61,261	82.1	343,400	20.8	10.0	1,121	27.2	0.8	93,816	-1.3	3,920	4.2	88,204	46.7	18.9
Cecil	37,293	74.6	250,400	21.7	11.6	1,151	29.4	2.8	52,338	-1.8	2,743	5.2	50,643	35.5	27.3
Charles	57,388	76.9	326,800	22.3	10.0	1,686	29.5	2.2	86,208	-2.2	4,940	5.7	81,467	43.2	18.1
Dorchester	13,433	67.5	187,300	23.1	12.9	865	32.3	1.1	16,235	-1.9	914	5.6	14,706	31.0	26.0
Frederick	94,299	75.9	341,800	20.8	10.0	1,427	29.3	1.5	134,802	-2.0	6,468	4.8	135,563	47.9	16.6
Garrett	12,745	79.3	194,600	22.3	10.4	629	24.6	1.4	15,365	-1.7	804	5.2	13,894	35.2	28.0
Harford	95,094	79.0	302,900	20.1	10.0	1,294	27.5	1.8	139,296	-1.5	6,671	4.8	131,679	45.9	17.5
Howard	116,457	72.7	464,500	20.4	10.0	1,731	27.6	1.9	186,574	-1.2	8,105	4.3	170,492	63.9	9.1
Kent	8,274	69.2	258,500	23.6	13.7	969	34.5	1.0	9,609	-2.3	524	5.5	9,422	38.1	23.3
Montgomery	372,825	65.6	491,700	21.0	10.0	1,784	30.2	3.4	547,389	-1.6	30,031	5.5	559,029	57.3	11.5
Prince George's	315,634	62.1	319,600	23.1	10.5	1,494	30.4	4.6	502,972	-1.9	37,514	7.5	483,654	40.9	19.9
Queen Anne's	19,000	80.2	363,300	22.4	11.8	1,553	29.6	1.0	27,745	-1.3	1,211	4.4	25,678	44.0	18.1

1. Specified owner-occupied units. 2. A value of 10.0 represents 10 percent or less; a value of 50.0 represents 50 percent or more. 3. Specified renter-occupied units. 4. Overcrowded or lacking complete plumbing facilities. 5. Percent of civilian labor force. 6. Civilian employed persons 16 years old and over.

STATE County	Private nonfarm establishments, employment and payroll, 2020									Agriculture, 2017			
		Employment						Annual payroll		Farms			Farm producers whose primary occupation is farming (percent)
											Percent with:		
	Number of establish-ments	Total	Health care and social assistance	Manufac-turing	Retail trade	Finance and insurance	Professional, scientific, and technical services	Total (mil dol)	Average per employee (dollars)	Number	Fewer than 50 acres	1000 acres or more	
	104	105	106	107	108	109	110	111	112	113	114	115	116
LOUISIANA—Cont'd													
Orleans	9,789	180,995	27,197	3,757	13,978	5,892	13,374	8,388	46,345	39	94.9	NA	55.6
Ouachita	4,188	60,030	13,337	4,427	8,863	3,324	2,691	2,383	39,689	488	54.1	3.7	35.1
Plaquemines	624	8,186	322	1,612	479	92	411	563	68,731	113	52.2	11.5	38.3
Pointe Coupee	334	3,913	786	294	868	198	96	171	43,573	482	45.4	10.2	43.2
Rapides	3,143	46,079	14,265	2,821	7,442	1,346	1,855	1,958	42,491	856	51.1	6.2	45.1
Red River	124	1,704	496	325	133	77	27	68	39,907	197	25.9	13.2	46.8
Richland	415	5,480	1,787	640	767	312	100	201	36,612	626	33.1	10.5	30.2
Sabine	470	4,236	708	1,099	801	201	137	168	39,549	442	39.1	1.4	47.2
St. Bernard	699	8,055	595	1,517	1,668	185	160	374	46,429	33	30.3	21.2	28.6
St. Charles	972	21,218	2,009	4,714	1,420	546	1,212	1,572	74,071	67	32.8	NA	47.3
St. Helena	118	1,185	428	292	179	24	37	47	39,282	348	45.1	1.1	42.0
St. James	320	6,885	558	2,495	559	211	95	536	77,837	56	50.0	32.1	77.4
St. John the Baptist	717	17,139	895	2,285	1,689	347	351	912	53,194	22	45.5	31.8	62.5
St. Landry	1,572	21,300	6,096	1,479	3,870	653	546	810	38,048	1,200	53.7	6.5	37.1
St. Martin	936	11,170	1,243	1,687	1,802	235	319	455	40,760	360	70.0	6.7	34.1
St. Mary	1,112	19,468	1,954	3,678	1,909	475	662	946	48,587	98	48.0	36.7	50.0
St. Tammany	6,653	80,129	16,994	2,673	13,173	4,020	4,892	3,764	46,977	994	80.7	0.4	30.7
Tangipahoa	2,506	37,878	9,058	2,493	6,747	1,210	1,173	1,389	36,677	967	55.0	1.1	37.4
Tensas	64	388	62	NA	61	53	NA	13	34,160	231	16.9	24.7	42.5
Terrebonne	2,681	44,208	7,638	3,176	6,249	1,052	2,320	2,101	47,531	213	55.9	8.5	42.6
Union	341	4,241	759	1,337	580	107	58	145	34,169	426	36.6	3.1	36.4
Vermilion	962	9,496	1,810	496	2,226	330	293	376	39,561	1,304	41.9	8.5	34.6
Vernon	673	7,435	1,693	108	1,566	252	388	280	37,669	432	57.6	1.2	35.5
Washington	610	7,625	1,912	1,125	1,274	330	650	288	37,799	735	55.5	1.6	44.7
Webster	756	9,902	2,351	1,450	1,739	330	170	392	39,615	431	42.0	1.9	33.0
West Baton Rouge	561	11,400	517	2,508	1,181	100	492	530	46,509	111	61.3	11.7	44.3
West Carroll	171	1,547	549	74	316	62	19	48	31,284	548	27.7	8.2	34.9
West Feliciana	188	3,365	485	288	352	70	176	214	63,740	153	34.6	17.0	30.6
Winn	264	3,640	927	683	425	101	63	152	41,738	184	31.5	2.2	34.4
MAINE	41,646	520,969	112,097	51,482	81,612	28,877	23,961	24,650	47,317	7,600	47.2	2.4	43.2
Androscoggin	2,808	44,668	9,829	5,421	5,978	3,352	1,561	1,989	44,525	496	58.7	1.0	61.0
Aroostook	1,853	19,996	5,910	2,525	3,839	834	337	800	40,006	766	21.5	10.6	46.4
Cumberland	11,730	175,362	35,685	10,825	22,537	14,487	11,532	9,493	54,136	668	66.8	0.6	43.3
Franklin	887	8,858	1,810	868	1,696	607	139	311	35,074	354	49.4	2.0	38.1
Hancock	2,277	16,676	2,838	870	3,287	521	1,998	744	44,590	416	45.7	1.7	44.0
Kennebec	3,209	49,572	13,298	2,924	8,569	1,287	1,511	2,161	43,602	642	49.4	1.2	35.0
Knox	1,762	14,565	2,966	1,749	2,665	648	493	606	41,617	308	58.1	NA	44.4
Lincoln	1,370	8,878	1,908	700	1,678	297	322	365	41,082	309	53.4	0.3	45.5
Oxford	1,318	14,165	2,691	2,558	2,332	334	333	582	41,056	545	46.8	0.7	36.2
Penobscot	4,073	57,767	14,866	2,827	10,594	1,912	1,849	2,623	45,404	601	41.3	3.2	44.6
Piscataquis	452	4,714	1,239	1,198	949	70	73	185	39,256	188	29.8	3.7	45.7
Sagadahoc	974	14,596	1,164	6,569	1,887	302	742	657	45,031	209	49.3	1.0	52.1
Somerset	1,174	12,756	2,560	2,638	2,357	247	314	556	43,576	467	29.3	5.4	43.2
Waldo	988	9,566	1,679	1,052	1,680	699	244	423	44,188	517	49.1	0.6	42.5
Washington	790	7,221	1,713	1,161	1,612	328	131	293	40,611	379	44.6	1.6	33.8
York	5,618	56,727	11,589	7,593	9,945	1,766	1,758	2,519	44,414	735	59.0	0.8	43.0
MARYLAND	139,734	2,405,968	402,187	99,306	293,568	100,191	295,991	139,313	57,903	12,429	54.7	3.2	42.1
Allegany	1,461	22,432	5,854	2,041	3,965	825	542	806	35,927	290	43.8	0.3	35.5
Anne Arundel	14,405	247,265	29,478	12,017	32,806	7,010	36,000	14,862	60,107	390	67.7	0.3	38.2
Baltimore	20,012	337,934	64,459	13,840	50,608	18,785	29,424	18,284	54,105	708	67.1	1.7	40.0
Calvert	1,716	19,118	3,638	451	2,996	328	1,595	901	47,115	280	67.1	1.4	37.3
Caroline	610	7,293	744	1,191	1,197	164	253	309	42,303	588	48.3	4.9	50.7
Carroll	4,188	52,600	10,279	3,869	8,414	1,129	3,149	2,303	43,779	1,174	61.0	2.1	40.5
Cecil	1,738	28,041	4,456	4,699	4,026	378	571	1,379	49,191	533	55.7	1.7	42.3
Charles	2,646	34,230	5,224	369	8,328	728	1,712	1,341	39,169	385	58.7	1.3	44.3
Dorchester	682	10,004	1,757	2,957	1,324	202	302	394	39,378	371	39.1	11.1	53.1
Frederick	6,242	91,924	13,899	7,423	13,131	4,618	9,887	4,613	50,187	1,373	53.5	2.5	40.8
Garrett	893	10,622	1,834	1,040	1,643	295	407	376	35,423	707	37.3	0.8	32.7
Harford	5,539	76,214	12,881	4,983	12,686	1,889	9,001	3,567	46,805	628	64.0	1.6	38.4
Howard	9,605	182,310	19,158	6,528	15,862	7,416	41,965	13,002	71,317	321	72.9	1.6	35.9
Kent	579	6,591	1,113	796	811	182	218	252	38,181	346	32.9	11.6	48.2
Montgomery	27,498	451,660	78,450	5,950	46,937	21,425	81,147	31,226	69,136	558	69.7	2.3	39.2
Prince George's	15,716	274,678	34,665	7,229	37,829	5,475	31,642	13,593	49,487	367	71.9	2.2	31.5
Queen Anne's	1,381	12,523	1,234	1,593	2,297	275	676	528	42,155	483	40.2	8.9	47.3

STATE County	Agriculture, 2017 (cont.) Land in farms: Acreage (1,000)	Land in farms: Percent change, 2012–2017	Land in farms, Acres: Average size of farm	Land in farms, Acres: Total irrigated (1,000)	Land in farms, Acres: Total cropland (1,000)	Value of land and buildings (dollars): Average per farm	Value of land and buildings (dollars): Average per acre	Value of machinery and equipment, average per farm (dollars)	Value of products sold: Total (mil dol)	Value of products sold: Average per farm (acres)	Value of products sold, Percent from: Crops	Value of products sold, Percent from: Livestock and poultry products	Organic farms (number)	Farms with internet access (percent)	Government payments: Total ($1,000)	Government payments: Percent of farms
	117	118	119	120	121	122	123	124	125	126	127	128	129	130	131	132
LOUISIANA—Cont'd																
Orleans	1	376.6	14	0.0	0.0	140,455	10,355	17,365	0.2	5,231	92.2	7.8	NA	87.2	8	10.3
Ouachita	93	0.1	191	16.1	49.0	813,699	4,261	89,169	45.3	92,887	52.5	47.5	3	81.6	2,315	22.7
Plaquemines	94	5.8	833	0.1	8.0	1,174,762	1,411	60,963	10.8	95,478	45.5	54.5	1	75.2	NA	NA
Pointe Coupee	188	3.0	389	5.9	132.7	1,203,401	3,091	191,613	80.2	166,309	89.8	10.2	NA	73.0	3,798	27.4
Rapides	203	-3.7	237	26.3	131.8	889,536	3,747	134,402	147.5	172,346	91.3	8.7	1	73.6	3,482	23.8
Red River	95	-29.5	485	2.4	26.8	1,084,557	2,238	150,566	17.6	89,589	38.6	61.4	NA	71.1	1,147	29.9
Richland	218	-21.7	349	73.0	135.5	987,603	2,831	141,410	74.7	119,335	94.3	5.7	NA	62.9	9,359	61.7
Sabine	62	20.0	141	0.1	14.9	531,768	3,779	81,312	145.9	330,118	1.2	98.8	NA	64.3	1,411	25.3
St. Bernard	32	1.7	983	NA	2.8	1,722,736	1,752	116,121	4.0	121,939	1.8	98.2	NA	78.8	D	3.0
St. Charles	14	-11.6	214	0.0	2.9	746,957	3,491	60,454	1.4	21,537	17.0	83.0	NA	61.2	D	3.0
St. Helena	37	-30.5	106	0.2	12.2	441,244	4,159	50,934	20.6	59,075	5.3	94.7	NA	62.4	102	12.1
St. James	51	26.6	903	D	45.0	2,765,668	3,062	645,194	27.0	481,393	99.7	0.3	NA	76.8	49	7.1
St. John the Baptist	20	84.8	904	0.0	18.0	3,163,313	3,500	651,269	7.2	328,364	99.5	0.5	NA	59.1	NA	NA
St. Landry	267	-11.1	223	24.3	195.2	650,514	2,919	110,986	93.1	77,605	85.4	14.6	2	65.9	6,348	28.0
St. Martin	83	10.0	232	3.9	63.7	743,147	3,205	182,286	39.6	109,994	88.3	11.7	NA	66.1	1,723	16.4
St. Mary	80	5.4	818	D	72.2	2,697,959	3,298	552,607	45.1	460,510	99.0	1.0	NA	73.5	368	15.3
St. Tammany	43	26.2	43	0.4	7.7	464,732	10,731	39,617	10.0	10,063	55.7	44.3	1	77.4	NA	NA
Tangipahoa	98	-8.1	101	1.2	29.6	513,368	5,061	63,007	42.4	43,845	47.3	52.7	5	67.6	208	5.0
Tensas	202	2.7	874	55.5	166.0	2,450,887	2,803	324,337	93.5	404,827	99.7	0.3	NA	64.5	7,907	82.3
Terrebonne	79	-15.2	370	0.1	35.8	1,523,117	4,118	175,237	30.1	141,479	56.8	43.2	NA	75.1	131	3.8
Union	75	20.2	177	0.0	19.5	538,032	3,044	85,109	121.1	284,319	1.5	98.5	NA	70.7	185	3.5
Vermilion	410	44.4	314	68.1	217.0	903,947	2,877	117,984	117.3	89,923	57.1	42.9	NA	61.8	13,719	53.5
Vernon	41	-16.5	95	0.3	8.1	350,847	3,703	53,429	25.5	59,113	2.7	97.3	NA	70.4	184	15.3
Washington	81	-0.9	110	0.5	30.8	396,447	3,612	80,648	32.4	44,020	36.4	63.6	8	69.5	255	4.6
Webster	58	11.0	135	0.2	11.7	395,957	2,939	68,771	9.4	21,717	13.6	86.4	NA	66.6	74	4.4
West Baton Rouge	34	12.5	307	0.1	29.8	865,851	2,820	203,536	25.6	230,991	63.0	37.0	NA	80.2	225	18.0
West Carroll	168	1.4	307	69.8	111.1	1,010,538	3,296	115,396	62.5	114,117	96.2	3.8	NA	54.9	5,591	79.4
West Feliciana	86	-14.8	564	0.1	24.7	1,655,865	2,935	110,413	9.2	60,261	42.3	57.7	1	72.5	329	20.3
Winn	30	21.1	164	0.0	5.1	460,561	2,804	97,682	20.2	110,049	2.5	97.5	NA	76.1	282	11.4
MAINE	1,308	-10.1	172	32.3	472.5	446,614	2,596	81,792	667.0	87,758	61.3	38.7	621	83.6	8,947	10.9
Androscoggin	56	-6.4	112	1.0	24.6	395,349	3,526	68,417	40.5	81,726	37.6	62.4	18	85.1	481	10.5
Aroostook	317	-9.6	414	12.7	174.0	720,511	1,741	194,251	202.0	263,674	92.9	7.1	49	79.6	2,817	28.6
Cumberland	50	-20.2	75	0.8	15.3	511,437	6,830	59,232	25.6	38,389	60.8	39.2	38	90.6	539	5.1
Franklin	47	-4.5	133	0.1	11.1	331,253	2,484	59,248	D	D	D	D	37	87.0	277	15.5
Hancock	65	22.2	157	0.2	15.2	438,042	2,794	65,383	18.4	44,163	57.0	43.0	65	80.8	247	7.2
Kennebec	82	5.2	128	0.2	36.5	386,694	3,023	77,600	49.0	76,333	23.4	76.6	48	83.5	422	10.6
Knox	26	-12.9	83	0.3	9.9	392,714	4,725	49,648	9.1	29,597	69.9	30.1	25	78.9	46	3.6
Lincoln	25	-19.3	82	0.1	6.5	382,809	4,644	50,811	12.9	41,689	35.2	64.8	32	86.7	177	5.5
Oxford	77	2.1	141	0.8	17.5	410,809	2,914	65,022	24.1	44,253	78.5	21.5	31	85.7	836	13.8
Penobscot	105	-6.6	175	1.6	41.1	432,698	2,466	93,820	50.9	84,717	35.6	64.4	33	79.0	603	9.2
Piscataquis	51	9.4	272	0.0	8.7	382,344	1,408	84,800	9.1	48,447	47.2	52.8	24	79.8	107	16.0
Sagadahoc	18	-12.0	85	0.1	5.2	349,864	4,134	52,958	D	D	D	D	31	85.2	379	8.1
Somerset	146	4.1	312	0.3	35.8	460,950	1,476	117,809	83.9	179,724	66.3	33.7	53	84.2	475	13.7
Waldo	57	-56.7	109	D	21.5	327,769	2,998	52,008	23.0	44,400	36.9	63.1	81	85.9	908	9.5
Washington	125	-16.2	329	D	31.2	505,172	1,534	65,445	D	D	D	D	19	78.6	55	3.2
York	61	-5.4	83	1.6	18.3	425,179	5,120	60,944	28.6	38,846	82.5	17.5	37	83.9	578	5.4
MARYLAND	1,990	-2.0	160	124.8	1,426.7	1,258,691	7,861	124,871	2,472.8	198,955	38.3	61.7	134	76.9	44,410	28.7
Allegany	35	-2.7	122	0.0	13.2	680,294	5,592	53,733	4.2	14,362	73.0	27.0	1	61.4	245	22.8
Anne Arundel	27	-3.9	69	0.2	14.6	713,958	10,312	65,583	18.2	46,549	70.7	29.3	1	85.9	322	7.2
Baltimore	76	8.1	108	0.7	50.5	1,594,001	14,825	103,714	67.5	95,367	86.9	13.1	10	82.5	1,327	14.8
Calvert	25	-23.6	90	0.3	12.7	921,361	10,257	67,836	6.3	22,579	90.2	9.8	NA	76.4	147	9.6
Caroline	128	-14.8	218	32.4	109.0	1,551,852	7,126	175,992	277.4	471,815	25.5	74.5	3	68.5	3,482	46.8
Carroll	147	10.7	125	1.6	109.4	1,022,466	8,178	117,957	110.4	94,078	65.6	34.4	5	81.9	3,501	33.4
Cecil	74	-3.7	138	1.5	54.6	1,109,934	8,017	139,348	136.8	256,700	57.0	43.0	8	79.5	1,475	22.1
Charles	41	-12.1	107	0.5	26.0	1,007,714	9,458	100,760	14.1	36,532	88.4	11.6	4	76.1	789	17.7
Dorchester	132	4.5	356	29.9	97.0	2,022,110	5,676	229,945	188.7	508,553	30.5	69.5	NA	70.4	4,484	70.6
Frederick	189	3.9	137	1.2	140.7	1,307,843	9,522	122,029	131.6	95,835	48.3	51.7	31	80.3	3,980	26.5
Garrett	90	-5.1	128	0.1	42.7	582,887	4,561	82,214	29.0	41,068	42.4	57.6	11	63.6	260	7.4
Harford	74	13.4	118	0.6	51.7	1,289,892	10,906	107,318	45.9	73,065	74.3	25.7	2	84.7	1,411	20.7
Howard	32	-13.4	101	0.4	17.8	925,165	9,156	86,214	27.3	84,919	86.3	13.7	NA	85.7	240	10.6
Kent	134	0.8	388	10.1	109.2	2,564,409	6,609	248,381	111.2	321,428	61.6	38.4	16	82.1	3,429	69.7
Montgomery	66	3.2	117	1.2	48.7	964,640	8,213	102,089	42.6	76,310	88.8	11.2	4	90.0	1,179	14.3
Prince George's	34	5.5	94	0.8	17.7	762,242	8,132	76,284	17.6	47,872	86.8	13.2	NA	80.4	135	8.4
Queen Anne's	163	3.9	337	16.7	135.8	2,476,771	7,339	191,888	180.6	373,822	50.7	49.3	15	84.7	4,235	59.2

STATE County	Water use, 2015		Wholesale Trade[1], 2017				Retail Trade[2], 2017				Real estate and rental and leasing,[2] 2017			
	Public supply water withdrawn (mil gal/ day)	Public supply gallons withdrawn per person per day	Number of establish- ments	Number of employees	Sales (mil dol)	Average payroll (mil dol)	Number of establish- ments	Number of employees	Sales (mil dol)	Average payroll (mil dol)	Number of establish- ments	Number of employees	Sales (mil dol)	Average payroll (mil dol)
	133	134	135	136	137	138	139	140	141	142	143	144	145	146
LOUISIANA—Cont'd														
Orleans	140.9	361.6	255	3,124	2,506.4	187.2	1,327	14,795	3,499.1	387.0	470	2,327	573.6	99.7
Ouachita	24.2	154.2	182	2,148	1,700.6	102.8	681	9,452	2,410.5	229.6	216	1,317	267.9	49.9
Plaquemines	7.1	303.9	60	929	1,366.3	57.4	63	504	113.6	11.1	28	291	76.5	17.1
Pointe Coupee	3.5	159.1	11	157	182.4	7.9	76	909	231.8	22.1	11	37	5.9	1.4
Rapides	18.9	143.1	D	D	D	D	550	7,461	2,100.4	193.7	D	D	D	D
Red River	1.0	116.4	5	44	16.3	1.8	19	120	34.1	2.5	4	9	1.2	0.4
Richland	3.6	177.4	23	255	427.4	12.3	59	692	222.2	17.8	D	D	D	D
Sabine	2.3	96.8	12	110	62.7	4.2	80	941	247.7	22.6	11	23	2.6	0.6
St. Bernard	7.2	157.7	25	239	77.8	9.5	134	1,716	401.2	40.4	23	44	15.8	2.6
St. Charles	9.1	172.1	67	1,611	1,451.1	94.0	115	1,487	403.8	37.5	37	268	96.2	23.9
St. Helena	0.9	85.2	NA	NA	NA	NA	24	223	44.0	4.1	3	18	0.9	0.1
St. James	4.0	185.5	9	39	114.8	2.5	49	608	138.1	12.6	8	95	9.1	3.3
St. John the Baptist	7.5	170.8	31	568	307.5	48.4	115	1,698	412.3	38.0	38	510	85.9	25.1
St. Landry	10.3	123.0	56	738	940.4	33.0	311	3,921	1,087.5	100.8	52	174	26.0	5.6
St. Martin	4.7	86.7	58	749	355.3	33.8	150	1,643	581.0	37.4	42	695	222.1	51.6
St. Mary	9.3	176.5	65	795	412.4	42.7	183	2,203	529.5	55.2	78	595	119.6	31.7
St. Tammany	23.6	94.5	235	2,359	8,962.2	154.7	920	14,341	4,018.1	352.2	278	1,011	238.7	46.5
Tangipahoa	15.1	117.0	89	2,288	1,747.3	111.0	454	6,671	1,984.3	168.0	113	541	86.5	20.8
Tensas	1.2	244.7	11	85	137.3	3.9	16	93	23.8	1.9	NA	NA	NA	NA
Terrebonne	1.9	16.5	195	1,750	824.5	87.2	470	6,758	1,860.4	177.7	158	1,501	476.1	102.0
Union	4.4	195.8	9	53	109.3	2.8	59	553	175.2	15.3	13	16	2.0	0.4
Vermilion	7.1	118.1	33	299	213.8	14.7	188	2,325	566.4	54.3	31	191	22.8	7.7
Vernon	4.4	85.6	D	D	D	D	131	1,574	437.4	37.0	35	215	75.8	9.2
Washington	4.6	99.8	19	118	95.3	4.8	144	1,459	334.2	31.5	11	32	5.0	0.7
Webster	5.4	133.9	20	312	144.9	14.5	155	2,090	512.8	54.3	28	93	14.2	3.5
West Baton Rouge	7.2	282.9	38	699	1,030.8	38.5	92	1,183	340.0	27.5	14	182	47.2	10.1
West Carroll	1.4	123.1	D	D	D	D	25	333	80.9	7.9	D	D	D	D
West Feliciana	1.7	108.5	D	D	D	D	31	345	88.4	7.4	12	32	6.9	1.1
Winn	2.0	138.0	9	60	29.2	2.3	43	516	117.6	13.9	7	26	4.5	0.9
MAINE	85.0	63.9	1,309	15,527	13,951.8	803.4	6,250	81,733	23,878.7	2,249.6	1,821	7,138	1,484.2	287.4
Androscoggin	7.9	73.9	104	1,274	559.5	64.1	431	5,933	1,816.8	162.8	130	466	86.1	17.1
Aroostook	4.1	59.9	70	494	346.7	24.9	327	4,036	1,059.3	96.2	76	303	37.7	7.5
Cumberland	25.4	87.4	437	5,773	5,520.2	346.3	1,460	22,472	7,031.7	650.5	659	3,050	642.1	142.6
Franklin	1.4	45.3	D	D	D	2.3	175	1,779	428.6	43.8	D	D	D	D
Hancock	6.7	122.4	61	344	341.6	16.6	339	3,259	948.6	95.1	89	244	47.0	8.6
Kennebec	6.2	51.3	91	3,101	2,488.5	138.2	527	8,659	2,485.5	249.7	110	543	81.8	19.2
Knox	3.0	75.8	51	280	248.0	11.6	252	2,873	720.2	79.0	70	187	38.2	7.7
Lincoln	0.7	21.5	31	276	130.3	10.0	211	1,647	484.9	47.9	48	94	17.0	3.3
Oxford	2.9	49.8	D	D	D	7.8	234	2,361	698.0	63.6	49	185	22.8	6.7
Penobscot	4.8	31.4	156	1,816	1,056.4	93.9	697	10,573	3,261.5	276.5	184	924	270.0	29.3
Piscataquis	0.9	52.0	6	8	4.1	0.2	85	947	249.8	26.9	D	D	D	D
Sagadahoc	1.4	40.1	18	84	39.5	3.4	140	1,827	545.2	50.0	35	65	15.9	2.6
Somerset	1.8	35.6	29	164	77.5	7.1	208	2,270	649.0	59.9	34	208	55.8	9.8
Waldo	1.0	25.3	24	319	2,151.2	14.8	165	1,614	395.3	41.9	D	D	D	D
Washington	1.6	49.6	D	D	D	7.0	148	1,663	415.5	43.8	D	D	D	D
York	15.3	76.2	135	1,138	747.3	55.1	851	9,820	2,688.7	262.2	248	618	141.0	25.9
MARYLAND	749.5	124.8	4,598	73,388	62,762.8	4,872.3	17,911	291,814	84,966.2	8,240.9	6,811	49,157	18,087.4	2,851.5
Allegany	0.7	9.2	43	449	141.0	19.6	270	3,856	1,018.1	90.4	61	192	35.8	6.7
Anne Arundel	39.5	70.0	465	7,006	7,067.3	436.3	1,959	33,976	9,441.6	934.8	628	4,376	1,447.4	223.4
Baltimore	209.5	252.0	700	11,309	6,870.4	735.2	2,662	46,685	13,216.5	1,309.8	988	7,618	4,077.8	446.9
Calvert	2.5	27.5	32	D	109.6	D	210	3,182	938.1	89.2	87	278	66.2	11.3
Caroline	1.0	30.1	23	145	78.0	6.8	80	1,147	377.2	32.1	17	67	9.9	2.3
Carroll	7.1	42.1	141	1,197	735.1	67.9	506	8,205	2,387.9	216.2	139	488	100.4	20.8
Cecil	3.6	35.2	D	D	D	D	243	3,803	1,179.9	93.3	89	241	47.1	8.5
Charles	7.3	46.9	54	460	800.6	27.5	467	8,248	2,318.6	222.3	113	462	128.1	19.6
Dorchester	2.7	81.8	28	385	191.4	18.4	90	1,289	489.6	38.2	34	141	12.0	2.9
Frederick	13.8	56.2	232	2,703	1,672.7	163.1	732	12,831	3,906.5	363.8	280	1,024	255.5	49.4
Garrett	2.7	93.0	20	95	38.3	3.4	144	1,589	491.8	43.0	34	420	40.3	13.0
Harford	9.8	39.3	162	2,320	2,563.2	140.0	689	13,882	3,897.3	383.5	245	944	233.3	39.7
Howard	0.0	0.0	474	13,365	11,476.8	959.3	867	16,013	4,643.6	465.8	442	3,969	1,163.8	249.6
Kent	1.1	55.1	28	156	115.4	6.5	90	902	196.0	20.8	23	78	24.0	2.9
Montgomery	354.9	341.3	647	8,452	7,355.0	767.1	2,567	46,463	14,659.2	1,502.6	1,463	12,197	5,976.1	877.7
Prince George's	52.3	57.5	528	11,030	8,127.0	639.0	2,268	37,683	10,485.3	1,081.7	752	8,804	2,240.5	459.6
Queen Anne's	1.8	36.2	63	873	734.5	61.0	226	2,619	623.9	58.2	54	165	43.0	6.7

1 Merchant wholesalers, except manufacturers' sales branches and offices. 2. Employer establishments.

STATE County	Professional, scientific, and technical services, 2017				Manufacturing, 2017				Accommodation and food services, 2017			
	Number of establish-ments	Number of employees	Sales (mil dol)	Average payroll (mil dol)	Number of establish-ments	Number of employees	Sales (mil dol)	Average payroll (mil dol)	Number of establis-hments	Number of employees	Sales (mil dol)	Annual payroll (mil dol)
	147	148	149	150	151	152	153	154	155	156	157	158
LOUISIANA—Cont'd												
Orleans	D	D	D	D	180	3,395	2,462.0	211.8	1,510	42,732	3,768.7	1,026.2
Ouachita	428	2,681	410.5	139.6	D	D	D	271.8	D	D	D	D
Plaquemines	D	D	D	D	D	1,745	D	166.7	55	852	54.2	15.6
Pointe Coupee	27	87	14.6	4.8	6	319	176.4	14.9	30	323	18.4	4.0
Rapides	271	1,823	240.6	86.0	D	D	D	D	250	5,012	271.7	74.3
Red River	8	33	3.1	0.8	6	340	110.1	17.8	9	91	4.3	1.3
Richland	29	89	14.6	3.3	D	D	D	D	26	341	17.8	4.4
Sabine	46	110	14.3	4.9	11	825	201.1	40.6	D	D	D	D
St. Bernard	43	173	20.6	6.6	33	1,382	9,273.2	153.0	80	1,288	66.4	17.7
St. Charles	104	1,550	219.3	101.4	45	4,938	23,469.7	571.1	83	1,004	56.6	14.0
St. Helena	D	D	4.5	D	D	232	D	13.4	D	D	D	0.1
St. James	D	D	D	D	28	2,535	10,036.6	268.6	27	376	19.3	5.7
St. John the Baptist	D	D	D	D	24	2,375	17,844.4	247.0	79	1,213	62.2	16.0
St. Landry	151	702	99.5	34.5	62	1,184	2,078.5	61.2	102	1,641	96.0	23.4
St. Martin	79	263	39.3	12.3	71	1,552	426.5	76.3	70	1,167	55.7	14.9
St. Mary	98	665	100.7	39.8	76	3,228	1,381.4	191.7	104	2,256	129.5	41.6
St. Tammany	D	D	D	D	D	2,638	D	125.4	611	11,444	594.0	177.7
Tangipahoa	209	1,142	174.4	60.4	77	2,023	625.2	87.3	252	4,913	238.7	67.2
Tensas	NA	NA	NA	NA	D	22	D	1.0	D	D	D	D
Terrebonne	254	2,868	388.6	177.1	127	3,912	936.0	227.7	249	4,752	259.9	77.2
Union	15	48	5.7	2.0	D	D	D	33.5	D	D	D	D
Vermilion	110	311	34.9	13.3	36	543	220.7	31.3	76	970	45.3	12.4
Vernon	82	373	43.5	15.3	9	131	45.6	4.8	78	1,138	57.0	16.3
Washington	41	1,632	157.3	19.0	26	1,098	843.5	81.6	61	872	38.6	9.4
Webster	43	183	19.5	6.2	D	D	D	D	63	739	37.6	9.4
West Baton Rouge	35	310	55.0	21.3	42	2,798	5,682.6	172.4	61	1,063	56.5	13.5
West Carroll	D	D	D	0.4	D	D	D	D	12	D	7.9	D
West Feliciana	22	264	26.5	11.3	D	D	D	D	D	D	D	7.6
Winn	15	42	5.4	1.5	12	702	342.0	37.8	16	180	9.2	2.2
MAINE	3,506	21,683	3,484.8	1,361.9	1,691	48,620	15,089.2	2,598.7	4,257	55,746	4,017.7	1,167.1
Androscoggin	D	D	D	D	152	5,665	1,693.9	263.2	238	3,455	207.1	61.3
Aroostook	D	D	D	D	78	2,736	1,072.9	138.7	140	2,054	93.8	29.7
Cumberland	D	D	D	D	410	10,418	3,307.5	578.6	1,096	17,219	1,177.5	364.9
Franklin	D	D	D	D	31	1,203	461.4	49.4	111	1,187	58.8	17.0
Hancock	D	D	D	D	85	920	231.7	44.4	334	2,404	319.3	77.5
Kennebec	268	1,404	209.7	79.5	92	2,540	675.5	130.0	293	4,860	315.9	91.5
Knox	D	D	D	D	92	1,615	559.9	86.9	175	1,612	128.5	39.3
Lincoln	D	D	D	D	72	659	108.7	29.3	167	1,232	113.9	33.7
Oxford	75	347	38.0	16.7	58	2,095	787.3	121.5	149	3,012	222.3	54.2
Penobscot	D	D	D	D	147	2,881	686.3	142.8	332	6,001	365.7	102.4
Piscataquis	10	49	3.8	1.3	22	936	175.5	38.0	57	303	21.9	5.7
Sagadahoc	D	D	D	D	D	D	D	D	86	1,127	73.9	23.0
Somerset	50	524	61.0	31.8	66	2,478	1,076.9	148.0	97	851	54.3	15.6
Waldo	65	221	22.2	9.8	60	898	168.3	39.7	93	863	56.3	17.3
Washington	D	D	D	D	39	895	486.0	45.8	82	608	33.3	9.7
York	424	1,756	260.5	96.4	D	D	D	D	807	8,958	774.9	224.2
MARYLAND	20,776	270,959	52,615.5	22,323.3	2,967	97,992	41,776.9	6,343.2	12,139	237,730	16,930.7	4,624.5
Allegany	D	D	D	D	51	2,691	1,192.5	119.0	D	D	D	55.2
Anne Arundel	2,277	34,752	8,176.0	3,447.1	241	11,289	5,065.7	1,102.6	1,280	32,200	2,613.1	636.3
Baltimore	D	D	D	D	417	14,707	7,606.6	980.5	1,711	29,741	1,876.1	519.6
Calvert	D	D	D	D	42	372	79.5	17.6	153	3,177	192.8	51.9
Caroline	36	226	18.2	7.8	23	1,345	362.7	58.7	D	D	D	6.1
Carroll	D	D	D	D	120	3,977	1,283.2	234.7	278	6,440	318.7	94.7
Cecil	D	D	D	D	51	4,360	1,974.6	324.9	174	3,410	221.4	56.6
Charles	D	D	D	D	47	397	107.5	22.4	262	5,459	312.0	85.6
Dorchester	D	D	D	D	41	2,538	818.5	110.2	61	1,301	69.7	24.8
Frederick	865	8,819	1,307.6	604.6	166	6,991	3,175.9	448.4	489	9,826	569.5	165.9
Garrett	54	434	51.9	23.4	43	867	176.0	33.2	83	1,370	61.5	19.0
Harford	D	D	D	D	127	4,661	2,179.4	289.3	408	8,638	472.5	137.6
Howard	D	D	D	D	178	5,848	1,738.3	339.7	615	13,048	782.6	232.7
Kent	52	263	35.1	14.2	29	602	322.0	39.9	D	D	D	13.8
Montgomery	5,753	79,924	14,769.5	6,583.2	357	7,081	2,098.8	540.3	1,936	34,764	2,561.3	726.1
Prince George's	1,869	28,347	5,512.9	2,188.7	262	6,665	2,041.5	382.1	1,427	33,174	2,877.1	746.8
Queen Anne's	161	686	97.0	41.4	60	1,595	329.6	70.7	101	2,150	136.9	40.6

STATE County	Health care and social assistance, 2017				Other services, 2017				Nonemployer businesses, 2019		Value of residential construction authorized by building permits, 2021	
	Number of establish-ments	Number of employees	Receipts (mil dol)	Annual payroll (mil dol)	Number of establish-ments	Number of employees	Receipts (mil dol)	Annual payroll (mil dol)	Number	Receipts (mil dol)	New construction ($1,000)	Number of housing units
	159	160	161	162	163	164	165	166	167	168	169	170
LOUISIANA—Cont'd												
Orleans	994	26,020	3,804.3	1,273.3	722	5,256	751.2	181.7	41,521	1,806.5	298,269	1,576
Ouachita	671	14,356	1,487.5	546.2	D	D	D	D	12,554	538.3	124,080	614
Plaquemines	22	426	38.0	17.3	D	D	D	D	2,441	135.6	37,863	126
Pointe Coupee	36	741	60.6	23.6	D	D	D	D	1,585	64.7	20,312	64
Rapides	537	13,681	1,712.3	627.9	180	1,040	125.2	33.3	8,231	382.8	70,129	287
Red River	14	454	43.5	15.9	8	55	3.0	1.4	492	16.5	1,500	6
Richland	73	1,693	121.5	50.5	13	52	4.5	1.2	1,511	58.4	8,214	25
Sabine	49	708	55.7	21.4	27	100	16.3	2.8	1,372	54.7	15,773	84
St. Bernard	61	966	73.0	32.5	D	D	D	D	4,141	166.2	66,830	324
St. Charles	78	1,469	127.5	54.9	51	423	70.4	19.4	4,202	174.0	41,518	163
St. Helena	D	D	D	11.7	D	D	D	D	951	23.2	3,569	20
St. James	26	500	53.0	19.6	D	D	D	D	1,224	36.6	17,659	56
St. John the Baptist	75	991	78.2	32.3	D	D	D	D	3,309	110.0	15,711	82
St. Landry	269	6,737	610.1	236.0	74	410	31.6	11.6	5,909	218.0	34,506	179
St. Martin	82	1,363	100.9	40.5	46	160	22.7	6.0	4,627	165.3	27,080	114
St. Mary	109	2,186	166.2	67.6	69	343	54.1	14.3	3,800	131.4	11,728	69
St. Tammany	848	16,034	1,881.0	739.9	396	2,113	235.7	66.9	26,927	1,426.6	482,505	1,960
Tangipahoa	321	8,978	880.7	357.3	160	1,207	127.0	37.2	11,167	416.4	229,453	1,508
Tensas	8	71	4.5	2.0	NA	NA	NA	NA	342	14.0	435	2
Terrebonne	276	7,323	773.6	319.0	158	1,263	192.8	66.2	8,326	370.8	50,295	208
Union	29	722	65.5	22.9	D	D	D	D	1,558	62.6	180	2
Vermilion	97	1,843	153.0	59.0	60	257	26.7	8.3	4,645	177.5	62,733	357
Vernon	65	1,679	200.3	78.3	37	163	15.3	3.6	2,131	78.9	15,308	86
Washington	82	1,908	153.7	64.0	29	130	16.1	3.2	3,209	118.6	0	0
Webster	D	D	D	D	39	174	20.0	4.9	2,546	112.5	11,160	39
West Baton Rouge	27	454	27.1	10.3	43	320	70.4	18.0	2,002	75.2	48,486	276
West Carroll	19	596	47.0	18.5	D	D	5.5	D	649	21.3	1,740	8
West Feliciana	D	D	D	16.1	D	D	D	D	845	38.0	15,913	46
Winn	38	913	73.0	31.2	D	D	D	D	682	37.3	1,088	5
MAINE	4,771	112,594	11,777.3	5,000.0	2,921	14,477	1,809.2	474.8	117,912	5,638.7	15,670	118
Androscoggin	380	10,347	1,145.9	488.6	212	1,029	103.3	30.8	6,579	299.4	47,003	221
Aroostook	223	5,842	549.2	246.7	126	444	55.7	11.5	3,878	168.8	11,814	79
Cumberland	1,372	33,663	4,053.5	1,622.2	792	4,782	638.1	169.6	30,487	1,670.8	532,826	1,944
Franklin	107	1,798	147.3	66.3	49	191	21.2	5.1	2,405	89.7	55,261	214
Hancock	168	3,225	303.9	138.4	149	767	123.9	27.7	7,730	374.0	92,102	338
Kennebec	469	14,228	1,410.9	632.1	287	1,463	177.2	48.8	8,555	361.8	105,554	436
Knox	167	2,977	260.9	113.8	145	671	82.6	24.0	5,871	313.7	41,387	154
Lincoln	108	1,852	186.5	64.0	90	450	54.3	16.1	4,599	200.0	44,633	170
Oxford	135	2,947	227.9	104.6	93	374	31.4	8.9	4,539	195.0	96,007	351
Penobscot	541	15,666	1,719.6	776.9	274	1,425	189.9	44.6	9,498	403.5	77,353	368
Piscataquis	41	1,419	112.1	51.9	21	58	7.9	1.4	1,226	47.1	9,363	42
Sagadahoc	115	1,130	78.2	33.2	72	369	50.5	13.4	3,302	134.8	36,467	162
Somerset	132	2,946	232.1	104.7	85	262	29.4	6.8	3,204	126.7	14,965	134
Waldo	115	1,766	174.8	76.3	82	353	35.7	11.0	4,064	157.8	31,540	140
Washington	103	1,816	148.5	66.7	52	196	33.6	5.8	3,711	175.2	10,588	53
York	595	10,972	1,025.8	413.6	392	1,643	174.6	49.3	18,264	920.5	371,265	1,606
MARYLAND	16,800	384,096	48,675.7	19,294.2	10,355	81,469	12,118.3	3,518.8	527,410	23,970.9	4,011,527	18,496
Allegany	235	5,814	665.8	250.6	133	749	66.4	19.7	2,955	115.2	8,786	36
Anne Arundel	1,390	28,993	3,448.7	1,433.7	1,151	8,972	1,075.8	331.5	46,506	2,321.8	305,090	1,745
Baltimore	2,723	62,797	7,069.8	2,887.2	1,439	10,460	1,348.4	380.1	72,263	3,380.0	232,772	986
Calvert	200	3,889	424.7	183.2	128	819	86.4	29.4	6,665	300.1	57,035	240
Caroline	51	843	70.4	31.5	44	264	33.2	10.3	2,612	115.6	19,311	95
Carroll	470	9,927	952.9	417.8	361	2,231	234.7	72.6	12,865	596.2	119,050	481
Cecil	204	5,314	555.2	254.8	170	1,005	98.7	28.9	5,764	282.4	77,463	366
Charles	323	5,020	544.5	223.6	222	1,442	149.1	46.7	12,632	440.6	333,777	931
Dorchester	74	1,835	170.3	72.4	57	316	22.9	5.5	2,506	102.6	15,541	69
Frederick	680	13,050	1,475.2	635.5	448	2,996	421.4	117.1	21,796	1,033.5	660,167	2,803
Garrett	79	1,959	144.5	65.0	57	301	26.7	7.5	2,302	111.5	85,258	153
Harford	621	11,750	1,330.8	543.0	436	2,526	232.0	83.3	18,001	819.8	238,153	902
Howard	1,048	17,547	2,137.6	894.2	552	4,423	611.3	186.3	30,160	1,531.1	232,034	1,735
Kent	74	1,165	121.4	39.7	43	357	33.9	8.6	1,780	87.5	14,373	48
Montgomery	3,726	71,254	9,203.0	3,955.6	1,947	20,029	4,498.3	1,259.9	120,068	6,400.7	300,291	1,857
Prince George's	1,967	33,146	3,958.5	1,549.8	1,184	9,453	1,140.9	382.0	87,879	2,854.1	473,797	2,459
Queen Anne's	102	1,116	117.5	47.3	107	498	53.5	14.3	5,108	296.4	97,783	428

STATE County	Government employment and payroll, 2017: Full-time equivalent employees	Government employment and payroll, 2017: March payroll (dollars)	March payroll (percent of total): Adminis-tration, judicial, and legal	March payroll (percent of total): Police and corrections	March payroll (percent of total): Fire protection	March payroll (percent of total): Highways and transpor-tation	March payroll (percent of total): Health and welfare	March payroll (percent of total): Natural resources and utilities	March payroll (percent of total): Education and libraries	Local government finances, 2017, General revenue: Total (mil dol)	General revenue: Inter-govern-mental (mil dol)	Taxes: Total (mil dol)	Taxes: Per capita[1] (dollars): Total	Taxes: Per capita[1] (dollars): Property
	171	172	173	174	175	176	177	178	179	180	181	182	183	184
LOUISIANA—Cont'd														
Orleans	7,488	35,682,619	11.9	38.7	8.7	3.0	7.4	16.4	7.5	1,989.3	464.0	925.8	2,365	1,080
Ouachita	6,979	21,934,354	7.7	10.6	6.3	2.0	4.1	5.0	63.5	637.1	248.3	308.1	1,977	711
Plaquemines	1,446	5,546,053	9.3	17.1	0.6	7.7	4.3	8.6	49.3	169.5	74.6	80.7	3,457	2,061
Pointe Coupee	945	3,003,522	8.0	14.2	0.7	1.0	25.1	5.5	45.4	87.5	26.5	36.1	1,630	950
Rapides	5,625	17,644,805	8.9	14.5	5.6	3.3	0.8	6.8	58.4	429.2	188.0	194.6	1,482	556
Red River	485	1,561,297	2.9	35.8	0.0	0.5	0.0	1.0	58.2	42.3	15.3	25.0	2,933	2,190
Richland	1,287	4,862,880	4.5	9.5	0.1	2.4	39.8	1.3	42.3	60.4	27.5	27.1	1,326	566
Sabine	932	2,481,071	6.8	15.6	0.0	4.3	3.3	8.6	49.2	83.9	45.3	33.0	1,381	636
St. Bernard	1,733	5,768,654	9.7	14.3	4.7	5.3	2.2	5.9	55.0	256.2	135.6	85.8	1,860	893
St. Charles	2,873	11,610,582	5.7	15.3	0.0	1.5	6.6	7.7	61.7	264.7	50.1	149.9	2,848	1,906
St. Helena	450	1,367,476	9.1	11.0	0.0	0.9	41.7	1.3	35.6	41.8	25.2	11.7	1,134	678
St. James	1,315	5,199,157	6.2	10.1	0.0	2.5	20.1	6.1	50.4	175.3	34.4	84.1	3,933	2,657
St. John the Baptist	1,521	6,556,079	8.8	14.4	0.0	9.9	1.0	2.5	62.1	188.5	54.4	97.1	2,241	1,052
St. Landry	4,353	13,939,901	7.5	9.2	4.3	2.7	28.7	4.0	42.6	386.9	151.4	110.0	1,317	459
St. Martin	1,699	5,351,403	8.4	14.9	0.1	2.3	1.3	3.1	69.0	140.1	62.7	62.6	1,158	590
St. Mary	3,036	9,397,015	6.2	10.1	1.6	2.8	11.4	10.8	55.3	236.8	84.5	104.1	2,053	1,182
St. Tammany	11,627	46,247,933	4.1	9.2	0.2	1.9	35.5	1.4	46.3	1,348.0	307.5	506.8	1,980	1,112
Tangipahoa	6,779	25,167,545	4.7	6.0	1.3	2.0	46.1	2.3	36.2	779.7	229.4	257.9	1,949	370
Tensas	280	767,261	12.5	18.0	0.0	3.8	0.5	6.6	57.9	22.6	6.8	9.7	2,119	1,299
Terrebonne	5,488	19,422,115	5.2	7.7	1.2	1.3	33.3	4.7	46.5	655.8	190.0	166.1	1,485	548
Union	687	2,277,187	5.4	18.1	0.4	3.0	14.8	5.9	51.4	78.6	40.4	25.8	1,151	515
Vermilion	2,457	8,494,425	5.1	8.5	1.8	3.0	24.7	8.0	48.9	221.7	85.4	79.5	1,326	616
Vernon	2,374	4,433,559	6.9	12.9	1.9	4.2	0.1	2.3	71.0	138.8	79.6	47.7	959	359
Washington	1,764	6,180,189	5.1	8.2	2.1	3.1	16.5	2.2	62.4	120.7	67.8	44.3	950	405
Webster	1,467	4,469,650	6.8	15.2	1.4	5.6	0.9	6.1	62.7	123.3	49.4	60.5	1,541	700
West Baton Rouge	1,289	4,372,750	5.8	3.1	0.8	21.0	0.7	11.4	53.2	116.4	30.9	67.9	2,594	1,197
West Carroll	374	1,208,152	2.4	1.9	0.0	3.5	0.2	5.4	86.3	34.8	18.3	12.5	1,139	354
West Feliciana	736	2,986,222	7.7	10.3	0.2	1.8	19.4	5.0	55.1	63.0	17.3	30.0	1,954	1,068
Winn	623	1,659,435	9.0	15.3	2.4	4.0	1.1	10.6	57.0	43.3	23.2	16.8	1,168	502
MAINE	X	X	X	X	X	X	X	X	X	X	X	X	X	X
Androscoggin	4,097	15,739,689	4.1	8.0	5.5	4.7	2.1	5.4	68.8	419.1	171.6	196.9	1,833	1,822
Aroostook	3,200	11,361,475	4.7	5.3	2.6	4.1	17.8	3.5	61.2	303.1	109.6	100.0	1,479	1,473
Cumberland	11,250	47,445,493	5.7	8.9	5.8	5.6	4.6	6.8	59.1	1,250.5	267.8	748.8	2,563	2,523
Franklin	1,047	4,032,002	6.4	7.6	1.0	4.7	0.1	5.0	73.2	102.3	32.2	61.2	2,053	2,048
Hancock	2,225	7,597,830	7.6	7.2	2.6	3.7	1.1	3.4	73.2	210.9	30.7	161.4	2,959	2,922
Kennebec	4,188	14,675,209	5.3	7.1	3.5	3.4	1.3	5.1	73.2	370.3	132.0	188.9	1,549	1,540
Knox	1,325	5,194,338	8.4	9.0	2.7	5.0	1.1	4.9	67.2	146.7	18.3	101.2	2,545	2,526
Lincoln	1,294	4,530,885	6.7	6.2	1.1	2.1	0.5	5.8	75.6	154.5	41.9	100.2	2,928	2,912
Oxford	2,266	7,726,655	5.2	5.4	2.1	5.3	0.1	3.1	77.8	210.2	71.0	120.2	2,090	2,068
Penobscot	4,862	18,469,574	6.5	8.5	5.4	7.2	2.8	5.2	62.9	493.2	177.7	234.2	1,544	1,531
Piscataquis	1,041	4,537,173	3.8	4.4	0.1	2.3	54.6	3.1	31.2	120.2	34.9	30.7	1,827	1,820
Sagadahoc	1,157	4,864,484	5.8	7.1	3.3	3.7	1.1	4.0	72.2	124.5	33.2	79.5	2,243	2,220
Somerset	2,578	8,814,246	4.1	5.6	1.1	2.8	0.1	2.0	83.0	220.2	93.3	111.9	2,223	2,218
Waldo	827	3,030,537	15.0	9.7	2.2	4.5	0.3	4.1	60.7	114.6	37.3	68.9	1,732	1,724
Washington	956	2,995,324	10.1	9.8	2.5	4.5	6.1	2.9	62.4	99.6	32.7	57.2	1,822	1,818
York	7,092	29,054,999	5.7	9.4	4.4	4.1	0.9	6.3	68.0	739.6	176.8	485.7	2,378	2,340
MARYLAND	X	X	X	X	X	X	X	X	X	X	X	X	X	X
Allegany	2,446	12,517,043	3.6	7.6	2.0	3.9	1.3	5.2	74.5	307.4	159.1	93.0	1,303	816
Anne Arundel	18,444	92,732,222	4.8	9.5	6.4	4.6	2.8	3.7	66.1	2,522.4	685.9	1,434.8	2,511	1,362
Baltimore	28,278	139,892,085	4.1	11.9	5.1	1.3	3.0	2.5	69.7	3,266.2	1,046.8	1,753.5	2,116	1,147
Calvert	3,174	15,760,271	6.0	8.9	0.2	2.1	2.4	5.8	70.5	415.7	119.5	246.1	2,691	1,687
Caroline	1,357	5,637,819	5.4	8.4	0.0	2.6	2.7	2.7	76.4	141.7	72.3	54.8	1,654	1,092
Carroll	5,634	25,017,473	6.1	6.8	0.0	2.7	0.8	3.6	76.4	662.3	194.3	400.5	2,391	1,329
Cecil	3,515	15,724,891	4.0	6.2	0.0	2.4	3.7	2.4	78.2	407.3	161.9	190.6	1,861	1,183
Charles	6,140	30,314,851	5.2	13.5	0.0	0.8	2.8	4.6	70.9	730.8	235.9	385.2	2,416	1,427
Dorchester	1,266	5,345,396	5.2	12.5	0.0	2.7	3.8	3.0	68.5	145.0	68.7	55.8	1,737	1,178
Frederick	9,651	48,627,596	5.0	7.3	6.0	2.5	4.5	4.1	69.0	1,239.6	355.8	687.1	2,742	1,683
Garrett	1,635	5,678,012	5.6	5.1	0.0	9.6	12.4	4.3	62.1	191.8	42.8	71.9	2,458	1,740
Harford	8,074	39,526,360	5.7	9.3	1.1	3.0	1.3	4.5	74.0	988.5	290.4	580.9	2,306	1,295
Howard	12,539	72,691,324	4.3	7.5	2.5	1.0	3.9	4.2	75.1	1,787.5	407.1	1,177.5	3,688	1,927
Kent	641	2,955,712	8.8	12.1	0.0	4.9	0.0	8.2	58.7	80.6	25.1	49.9	2,564	1,712
Montgomery	38,557	270,040,080	3.6	7.9	4.3	3.2	7.0	3.4	65.7	7,013.3	1,284.1	4,343.4	4,149	2,071
Prince George's	32,780	177,507,257	3.2	11.3	2.5	0.8	2.3	11.0	67.5	4,203.7	1,609.2	2,203.2	2,422	1,388
Queen Anne's	2,044	9,249,932	6.4	6.0	0.0	2.7	6.4	6.4	71.2	216.5	60.9	127.4	2,570	1,403

1. Based on the resident population estimated as of July 1 of the year shown.

STATE County	Local government finances, 2017 (cont.) — Direct general expenditure — Total (mil dol)	Per capita[1] (dollars)	Percent of total for: Education	Health and hospitals	Police protection	Public welfare	Highways	Debt outstanding — Total (mil dol)	Per capita[1] (dollars)	Government employment, 2020 — Federal civilian	Federal military	State and local	Individual income tax returns, 2019 — Number of returns	Mean adjusted gross income	Mean income tax
	185	186	187	188	189	190	191	192	193	194	195	196	197	198	199
LOUISIANA—Cont'd															
Orleans	1,775.9	4,536	23.3	2.6	4.9	0.0	3.2	2,802.7	7,159	10,480	3,145	23,431	171,530	65,449	9,050
Ouachita	614.2	3,941	55.1	0.8	7.4	0.3	3.3	614.2	3,941	463	560	9,876	66,510	54,982	5,637
Plaquemines	192.9	8,260	37.4	3.6	1.3	0.4	2.1	255.6	10,948	630	270	1,488	10,630	64,810	7,158
Pointe Coupee	78.7	3,552	41.9	19.4	6.5	0.4	2.0	20.6	931	72	81	948	9,830	56,203	6,148
Rapides	483.5	3,684	51.2	0.0	10.3	0.0	2.6	455.0	3,466	2,084	477	9,869	56,050	55,553	5,477
Red River	38.6	4,530	56.5	0.0	2.5	0.0	2.4	2.0	239	23	31	539	3,420	57,957	5,767
Richland	79.6	3,901	42.7	0.2	7.7	0.0	33.1	62.8	3,078	82	72	851	8,360	48,086	4,462
Sabine	81.4	3,405	65.3	0.2	7.0	0.0	6.5	30.2	1,262	42	88	1,292	9,040	56,262	5,128
St. Bernard	282.8	6,134	41.6	16.0	4.4	0.0	0.3	118.2	2,563	64	179	2,104	18,820	43,338	3,411
St. Charles	284.4	5,404	63.0	0.0	14.1	0.0	11.0	834.5	15,859	173	198	3,148	25,140	66,085	6,927
St. Helena	37.2	3,601	38.5	31.0	5.1	0.0	6.2	30.0	2,902	14	38	599	5,390	42,223	3,112
St. James	239.9	11,221	34.6	23.1	3.2	0.7	2.1	1,264.4	59,139	47	77	1,423	9,820	60,574	5,912
St. John the Baptist	233.8	5,396	40.1	1.0	12.2	0.0	4.9	1,335.2	30,816	111	159	2,019	20,320	48,865	4,173
St. Landry	390.1	4,669	36.6	31.9	5.0	1.1	2.6	161.3	1,931	187	304	4,876	36,160	49,052	4,411
St. Martin	137.7	2,548	67.5	0.7	7.0	0.2	4.6	199.5	3,689	73	197	1,824	23,610	50,380	4,416
St. Mary	256.9	5,066	40.8	10.8	6.4	0.1	3.7	100.4	1,980	139	260	3,639	21,400	49,158	4,438
St. Tammany	1,074.1	4,197	46.5	17.0	5.8	0.2	5.3	1,012.0	3,954	577	991	13,971	123,250	79,693	10,673
Tangipahoa	688.6	5,203	29.1	46.7	3.7	0.0	2.2	306.9	2,318	409	504	10,633	55,840	51,607	4,881
Tensas	23.8	5,196	37.6	2.3	10.5	0.0	5.3	2.7	592	24	16	250	1,690	46,129	4,154
Terrebonne	719.0	6,429	25.7	38.8	5.5	0.4	4.7	164.6	1,472	289	502	4,778	47,410	55,601	5,981
Union	102.1	4,558	52.7	24.8	5.2	0.0	3.1	64.0	2,858	98	82	713	9,180	48,358	3,929
Vermilion	230.0	3,837	41.4	20.3	5.7	2.1	4.8	35.6	594	163	233	2,958	24,830	54,165	4,909
Vernon	138.7	2,786	68.2	0.3	6.1	0.1	4.8	61.5	1,235	2,105	8,182	2,184	20,050	50,193	3,686
Washington	117.7	2,523	65.6	0.6	4.6	0.0	4.7	30.8	661	108	167	2,490	17,000	41,383	2,905
Webster	118.2	3,011	57.8	0.4	7.1	0.1	4.3	86.8	2,210	107	139	1,953	16,430	49,784	4,739
West Baton Rouge	130.2	4,973	40.5	1.0	8.5	0.2	4.6	173.1	6,612	98	99	1,528	12,500	61,349	6,151
West Carroll	33.7	3,071	66.8	2.0	6.7	0.0	8.1	3.1	281	33	39	712	4,190	45,896	3,674
West Feliciana	77.6	5,050	39.4	39.3	1.2	0.0	3.8	38.3	2,495	19	38	2,161	5,060	71,718	9,021
Winn	54.8	3,818	46.7	0.4	9.4	0.0	3.3	15.6	1,087	58	46	928	4,970	49,354	4,120
MAINE	X	X	X	X	X	X	X	X	X	16,964	5,213	82,549	677,780	63,795	6,756
Androscoggin	392.1	3,651	53.5	0.3	3.8	0.3	4.7	282.6	2,631	393	320	5,123	52,160	53,237	4,692
Aroostook	316.3	4,678	43.0	20.8	3.0	0.5	6.4	96.7	1,430	1,204	196	4,676	30,170	48,132	3,810
Cumberland	1,247.1	4,268	44.5	1.0	4.6	3.1	4.7	1,161.5	3,975	1,981	1,137	17,932	160,300	83,788	10,791
Franklin	87.9	2,950	50.4	0.9	5.2	0.3	11.5	85.7	2,877	143	87	1,974	13,500	50,291	4,212
Hancock	201.1	3,687	54.3	0.3	3.3	0.3	7.7	143.7	2,634	359	282	2,840	28,390	61,513	6,219
Kennebec	373.6	3,064	55.8	0.3	4.3	0.2	6.4	196.9	1,615	2,282	363	14,001	60,920	57,202	5,329
Knox	146.9	3,694	46.1	2.3	5.3	0.3	8.4	65.9	1,657	134	196	2,328	20,720	63,305	6,594
Lincoln	132.3	3,867	63.7	1.1	3.8	0.3	7.9	60.0	1,753	95	127	1,482	18,530	62,899	6,503
Oxford	217.2	3,775	62.9	0.5	3.5	0.3	8.0	96.1	1,670	145	173	2,887	27,200	48,895	4,016
Penobscot	508.2	3,352	50.2	1.4	5.1	0.3	5.1	383.0	2,526	1,195	444	12,541	69,830	56,281	5,463
Piscataquis	103.4	6,154	27.0	48.9	2.7	0.2	5.2	28.9	1,722	66	51	932	7,520	48,769	4,062
Sagadahoc	130.4	3,681	57.7	0.3	3.9	0.2	6.5	67.2	1,897	415	211	1,447	19,290	65,171	6,330
Somerset	197.3	3,919	64.2	0.2	3.1	0.2	7.2	87.5	1,738	211	161	2,256	22,950	48,129	3,897
Waldo	104.0	2,615	57.0	2.3	3.7	0.5	11.5	72.0	1,810	100	129	1,434	19,130	52,573	4,537
Washington	98.7	3,146	55.7	3.4	2.7	0.1	9.7	32.1	1,022	374	161	2,247	14,370	44,519	3,469
York	772.0	3,779	59.7	0.5	5.8	0.3	6.3	635.5	3,111	7,867	1,175	8,449	112,830	66,982	7,135
MARYLAND	X	X	X	X	X	X	X	X	X	178,468	49,165	333,110	3,046,680	83,466	10,928
Allegany	307.9	4,316	55.9	0.8	5.5	0.0	5.3	214.6	3,008	513	1,271	5,320	28,910	50,804	4,358
Anne Arundel	2,479.8	4,340	54.5	2.4	6.5	0.6	3.8	2,203.5	3,857	42,907	15,743	33,455	297,890	93,092	12,500
Baltimore	3,662.9	4,420	53.7	1.6	5.8	0.3	2.5	4,519.6	5,454	14,239	2,711	39,371	422,790	83,587	11,162
Calvert	396.9	4,341	58.5	0.9	6.2	0.0	1.9	211.7	2,316	173	297	4,075	46,330	90,984	10,927
Caroline	137.2	4,144	57.6	0.6	4.8	0.0	4.0	68.4	2,066	75	106	1,704	15,940	52,433	4,500
Carroll	657.5	3,924	57.9	0.9	4.0	0.0	5.0	435.3	2,598	362	542	7,455	85,220	86,323	10,249
Cecil	397.5	3,882	60.9	1.1	6.3	0.0	3.9	298.3	2,914	2,151	328	4,125	48,790	66,467	6,835
Charles	715.6	4,488	64.3	0.9	9.6	0.0	2.9	387.4	2,429	2,698	1,132	7,299	85,240	74,051	7,771
Dorchester	134.0	4,174	54.5	0.6	7.5	0.0	5.0	49.3	1,535	187	101	2,061	15,760	49,964	4,544
Frederick	1,170.8	4,672	57.4	3.0	5.3	0.0	5.3	1,093.6	4,364	3,793	2,154	11,412	134,260	84,061	10,050
Garrett	185.8	6,354	38.0	29.8	2.1	0.0	10.6	93.3	3,190	77	91	1,541	13,670	56,890	5,560
Harford	917.7	3,644	62.9	0.4	7.4	0.0	3.8	900.3	3,575	11,377	1,664	8,937	131,460	80,578	9,473
Howard	1,874.6	5,872	56.7	0.6	5.9	0.5	2.9	3,003.3	9,407	742	1,246	15,479	160,690	116,121	17,158
Kent	77.7	3,996	39.8	0.9	5.7	0.0	6.2	39.7	2,042	69	57	957	9,420	71,718	8,183
Montgomery	7,716.2	7,371	40.5	1.6	3.7	1.1	2.8	12,338.3	11,786	48,872	8,253	42,789	534,130	116,612	18,821
Prince George's	4,371.0	4,805	52.3	1.6	9.1	0.7	2.4	1,835.7	2,018	27,553	7,502	63,320	494,590	60,381	5,900
Queen Anne's	226.4	4,566	54.7	1.0	4.9	0.0	4.0	204.0	4,115	111	163	2,412	25,630	93,730	12,382

1. Based on the resident population estimated as of July 1 of the year shown.

State / county code	CBSA code[1]	County Type code[2]	STATE County	Land area[3] (sq. mi)	Population, 2021: Total persons 2021	Population, 2021: Rank	Population, 2021: Per square mile	Race alone or in combination, not Hispanic or Latino (percent): White	Black	American Indian, Alaska Native	Asian and Pacific Islancer	Percent Hispanic or Latino[4]	Age (percent): Under 5 years	5 to 17 years	18 to 24 years	25 to 34 years	35 to 44 years	45 to 54 years
				1	2	3	4	5	6	7	8	9	10	11	12	13	14	15
			MARYLAND— Cont'd															
24,037	15,680	3	St. Mary's	358.6	114,468	545	319.2	76.0	16.6	0.9	4.4	5.7	6.0	13.7	13.3	14.2	13.2	12.4
24,039	41,540	2	Somerset	319.7	24,584	1,630	76.9	54.0	42.1	1.0	1.7	4.1	4.4	9.8	19.6	12.8	11.8	11.1
24,041	20,660	6	Talbot	268.6	37,626	1,230	140.1	78.8	13.2	0.6	1.9	7.4	4.5	10.3	9.5	9.7	9.6	11.0
24,043	25,180	2	Washington	457.8	154,937	442	338.4	78.6	14.7	0.6	2.7	6.5	5.4	12.2	12.1	13.0	12.8	13.1
24,045	41,540	2	Wicomico	374.4	103,980	589	277.7	63.7	28.8	0.6	4.0	5.8	6.1	12.3	18.5	12.1	11.2	10.9
24,047	41,540	2	Worcester	468.4	53,132	954	113.4	81.8	13.3	0.6	2.1	3.9	3.8	10.2	9.7	10.5	10.2	11.4
24,510	12,580	1	Baltimore city	80.9	576,498	120	7,126.1	29.1	62.7	0.9	3.5	6.0	5.9	11.2	12.4	18.3	13.8	10.8
25,000		0	MASSACHUSETTS	7,801.0	6,984,723	X	895.4	71.9	8.5	0.6	8.3	12.8	5.0	11.0	13.4	14.1	12.8	12.5
25,001	12,700	3	Barnstable	394.2	232,411	297	589.6	90.6	4.2	1.1	2.3	3.6	3.5	8.1	9.7	9.3	9.2	10.7
25,003	38,340	3	Berkshire	926.9	128,657	503	138.8	89.1	4.6	0.6	2.5	5.5	3.9	9.1	12.3	10.9	11.2	11.8
25,005	39,300	1	Bristol	553.1	580,164	118	1,048.9	81.9	6.9	0.7	3.3	9.3	5.1	11.7	12.5	13.0	12.7	13.2
25,007	47,240	7	Dukes	103.2	21,097	1,758	204.4	88.6	5.9	2.1	2.3	3.8	4.7	9.8	9.0	10.8	11.5	12.2
25,009	14,460	1	Essex	492.5	807,074	79	1,638.7	69.0	4.6	0.4	4.3	23.3	5.4	11.7	12.8	12.5	12.6	12.8
25,011	44,140	4	Franklin	699.2	71,015	770	101.6	91.5	2.2	1.0	2.7	4.7	3.8	9.8	9.9	11.5	12.6	12.2
25,013	44,140	2	Hampden	617.0	462,718	155	749.9	61.7	9.1	0.7	3.1	27.3	5.3	11.9	13.8	13.4	12.3	12.0
25,015	44,140	2	Hampshire	527.2	161,572	417	306.5	84.7	3.8	0.6	6.8	6.4	3.2	8.2	26.0	10.4	10.2	10.4
25,017	14,460	1	Middlesex	817.9	1,614,742	21	1,974.3	71.9	6.2	0.4	15.2	8.6	5.0	11.1	13.1	15.1	13.9	12.8
25,019		7	Nantucket	46.2	14,491	2,118	313.7	72.3	11.1	0.4	2.3	15.5	5.9	11.2	10.0	13.6	15.0	14.9
25,021	14,460	1	Norfolk	396.1	724,505	92	1,829.1	73.7	8.6	0.4	13.9	5.5	5.1	11.6	12.5	12.9	13.3	13.2
25,023	14,460	1	Plymouth	658.5	533,003	135	809.4	81.8	12.5	0.7	2.5	4.5	5.0	11.8	12.4	11.2	12.0	13.3
25,025	14,460	1	Suffolk	58.3	771,245	85	13,228.9	46.4	21.3	0.7	10.2	23.8	4.9	8.7	16.1	22.3	13.6	10.7
25,027	49,340	2	Worcester	1,510.7	862,029	69	570.6	76.2	6.1	0.6	6.3	12.8	5.1	11.7	13.2	13.1	12.8	13.2
26,000		0	MICHIGAN	56,605.9	10,050,811	X	177.6	76.5	15.1	1.3	4.1	5.6	5.5	12.1	13.1	13.1	12.0	12.2
26,001		9	Alcona	674.7	10,235	2,393	15.2	96.0	1.3	1.4	0.8	2.1	3.2	6.9	7.2	8.0	7.9	10.7
26,003		7	Alger	915.0	8,821	2,502	9.6	85.1	8.7	6.3	1.0	2.2	3.5	8.4	10.4	11.6	11.7	11.2
26,005	26,090	4	Allegan	825.3	120,950	525	146.6	89.4	2.2	1.2	1.2	7.9	5.8	13.5	11.9	12.0	12.4	12.3
26,007	10,980	7	Alpena	571.9	28,893	1,459	50.5	96.4	1.3	1.3	0.8	1.6	4.6	10.6	10.2	10.7	11.3	11.3
26,009		9	Antrim	475.7	23,813	1,648	50.1	95.7	0.9	1.9	0.7	2.4	3.8	9.9	9.7	9.6	10.1	10.9
26,011		8	Arenac	363.2	14,975	2,090	41.2	95.2	1.3	2.1	0.9	2.4	4.5	10.5	9.3	10.0	10.3	11.2
26,013		9	Baraga	898.4	8,215	2,562	9.1	76.1	9.5	16.0	1.0	1.9	3.9	9.5	11.7	12.6	11.7	12.6
26,015		2	Barry	553.1	62,992	849	113.9	94.8	1.4	1.2	0.8	3.5	5.3	12.5	11.5	11.6	11.9	12.4
26,017	13,020	3	Bay	442.4	102,985	597	232.8	91.2	2.9	1.2	0.9	5.8	4.7	11.1	11.5	12.3	11.8	12.1
26,019	45,900	9	Benzie	319.7	18,223	1,913	57.0	94.9	1.4	2.1	0.7	2.5	4.5	9.9	9.4	10.1	11.1	10.7
26,021	35,660	3	Berrien	567.8	153,101	448	269.6	77.1	15.5	1.2	2.8	6.1	5.4	12.2	12.0	11.5	11.8	12.0
26,023	17,740	6	Branch	506.4	44,985	1,078	88.8	90.8	2.9	1.0	1.2	5.8	6.1	13.0	11.7	11.6	12.4	12.0
26,025	12,980	3	Calhoun	706.3	133,819	488	189.5	80.0	13.1	1.4	3.4	5.8	5.7	13.0	12.8	12.4	12.2	12.1
26,027	43,780	2	Cass	490.1	51,483	976	105.0	88.7	6.6	2.1	1.3	4.4	4.8	11.8	11.1	10.4	11.5	12.7
26,029		7	Charlevoix	416.3	26,086	1,561	62.7	94.8	1.0	2.4	1.1	2.5	4.2	10.1	10.4	10.3	10.6	11.2
26,031		7	Cheboygan	715.3	25,752	1,574	36.0	94.0	1.5	4.7	0.8	1.7	3.9	8.7	9.7	9.7	10.1	12.2
26,033	42,300	7	Chippewa	1,558.5	36,816	1,260	23.6	73.5	8.0	20.1	1.7	2.2	4.3	10.4	14.5	13.2	13.3	11.9
26,035		6	Clare	564.4	31,065	1,400	55.0	95.6	1.2	1.7	0.5	2.5	5.1	11.3	9.9	10.6	10.0	11.9
26,037	29,620	2	Clinton	566.3	79,426	722	140.3	91.0	2.8	1.0	2.3	4.9	5.3	12.2	12.3	12.0	12.9	12.8
26,039		7	Crawford	556.4	13,204	2,200	23.7	95.2	1.4	1.5	1.1	2.4	4.4	10.0	9.2	10.0	10.3	11.8
26,041	21,540	5	Delta	1,171.1	36,826	1,259	31.4	94.6	1.2	4.3	1.0	1.5	4.6	11.1	10.7	9.9	11.0	11.7
26,043	27,020	7	Dickinson	760.9	25,787	1,572	33.9	95.9	1.1	1.7	1.1	1.8	4.9	11.3	10.5	10.5	11.4	11.4
26,045	29,620	2	Eaton	575.2	108,944	567	189.4	84.1	8.3	1.2	3.1	5.9	5.2	11.7	12.0	12.9	12.6	11.9
26,047		7	Emmet	467.5	34,225	1,325	73.2	92.5	1.4	4.9	1.1	2.2	4.2	10.7	11.0	11.1	11.5	11.9
26,049	22,420	2	Genesee	636.9	404,208	180	634.6	74.4	21.8	1.3	1.6	3.9	5.7	12.6	12.4	12.8	11.7	12.5
26,051		6	Gladwin	501.8	25,485	1,586	50.8	96.3	0.9	1.2	0.7	2.1	4.9	10.7	9.2	9.3	9.8	11.6
26,053		7	Gogebic	1,102.1	14,361	2,125	13.0	93.7	1.2	4.1	0.8	2.1	4.2	9.6	9.3	9.7	10.2	11.4
26,055	45,900	5	Grand Traverse	464.3	95,860	634	206.5	94.0	1.5	1.8	1.4	3.2	4.7	11.4	11.1	12.3	12.7	11.7
26,057	10,940	6	Gratiot	568.4	41,544	1,155	73.1	85.9	6.7	1.0	0.8	6.8	5.0	11.0	14.7	13.3	13.1	12.2
26,059	25,880	6	Hillsdale	598.2	45,546	1,069	76.1	95.5	1.3	1.2	0.8	2.7	5.4	12.0	13.5	10.7	11.0	11.8
26,061	26,340	5	Houghton	1,009.1	37,313	1,241	37.0	93.8	1.4	1.4	3.0	1.8	5.0	11.7	24.6	10.2	9.7	9.3
26,063		7	Huron	836.0	31,252	1,395	37.4	95.6	0.9	0.8	0.8	2.7	4.7	10.8	10.2	9.6	10.2	11.4
26,065	29,620	2	Ingham	556.1	284,034	249	510.8	72.9	14.3	1.3	7.6	8.2	5.3	11.1	21.9	14.3	11.7	10.4
26,067	24,340	4	Ionia	571.3	67,197	802	117.6	89.1	5.5	1.0	0.9	5.2	5.4	12.3	12.9	14.1	13.1	13.1
26,069		7	Iosco	549.1	25,369	1,592	46.2	94.7	1.5	1.7	1.2	2.7	4.8	9.4	8.7	9.4	9.5	10.4
26,071		7	Iron	1,166.0	11,635	2,304	10.0	95.3	1.0	2.2	0.9	2.2	4.3	10.1	8.6	8.3	10.0	10.2
26,073	34,380	4	Isabella	572.7	64,813	836	113.2	87.7	3.9	4.5	2.5	4.5	4.5	10.0	28.9	12.0	10.4	9.5
26,075	27,100	3	Jackson	701.9	160,050	423	228.0	86.9	10.0	1.0	1.4	3.9	5.4	12.1	12.1	12.9	11.9	12.5
26,077	28,020	2	Kalamazoo	562.0	261,108	271	464.6	79.7	13.6	1.2	3.6	5.6	5.7	12.1	18.7	13.7	12.1	10.7
26,079	45,900	7	Kalkaska	559.7	17,979	1,925	32.1	95.2	1.5	2.0	1.1	2.3	4.9	11.9	10.3	11.7	11.7	12.2
26,081	24,340	2	Kent	848.9	658,046	105	775.2	75.1	11.6	1.0	4.0	11.3	6.2	13.4	13.2	15.8	13.3	11.4

1. CBSA = Core Based Statistical Area. See Appendix A for explanation. See Appendix B for list of metropolitan areas with component counties. 2. County type code from the Economic Research Service of USDA Rural-Urban Continuum Codes. See Appendix A for definition. 3. Dry land or land partially or temporarily covered by water. 4. May be of any race.

STATE County	Population, 2021 (cont.)				Population change, 2000–2021							Households, 2016–2020				
	Age (percent) (cont.)				Total persons		Percent change		Components of change, 2020–2021					Percent		
	55 to 64 years	65 to 74 years	75 years and over	Percent female	2010	2020	2010–2020	2020–2021	Births	Deaths	Net Migration	Number	Persons per household	Family house-holds	Female family house-holder[1]	One person
	16	17	18	19	20	21	22	23	24	25	26	27	28	29	30	31
MARYLAND— Cont'd																
St. Mary's	13.5	8.3	5.3	49.8	105,151	113,777	8.2	0.6	1,667	1,337	330	41,280	2.7	71.4	13.4	23.3
Somerset	13.1	10.6	6.8	45.7	26,470	24,620	-7.0	-0.1	267	409	104	8,509	2.3	67.1	17.7	28.9
Talbot	15.5	15.8	14.1	52.2	37,782	37,526	-0.7	0.3	395	747	463	16,810	2.2	62.2	10.3	32.2
Washington	13.8	10.3	7.3	48.8	147,430	154,705	4.9	0.1	1,961	2,420	673	56,367	2.5	67.3	12.2	27.7
Wicomico	12.5	10.1	6.4	52.5	98,733	103,588	4.9	0.4	1,610	1,607	371	38,142	2.6	63.5	15.2	26.6
Worcester	16.2	16.2	12.0	51.0	51,454	52,460	2.0	1.3	358	961	1,299	22,661	2.3	64.0	11.4	30.1
Baltimore city	12.6	9.3	5.7	53.1	620,961	585,708	-5.7	-1.6	9,142	9,850	-8,509	242,499	2.4	49.2	20.9	40.8
MASSACHUSETTS	13.8	10.4	7.0	51.1	6,547,629	7,029,917	7.4	-0.6	83,111	87,784	-40,686	2,646,980	2.5	63.2	12.0	28.4
Barnstable	18.0	18.7	13.1	51.8	215,888	228,996	6.1	1.5	1,781	4,127	5,872	95,859	2.2	62.2	8.2	31.3
Berkshire	16.3	14.5	10.2	51.3	131,219	129,026	-1.7	-0.3	1,116	2,086	603	54,786	2.2	58.0	11.4	34.3
Bristol	14.3	10.4	7.1	51.2	548,285	579,200	5.6	0.2	6,800	8,198	2,280	220,365	2.5	65.8	14.7	28.2
Dukes	16.5	16.1	9.4	50.7	16,535	20,600	24.6	2.4	225	212	491	6,887	2.5	59.8	9.2	32.3
Essex	14.4	10.7	7.1	51.5	743,159	809,829	9.0	-0.3	10,136	10,518	-2,470	297,254	2.6	66.6	13.7	27.4
Franklin	16.1	15.7	8.4	50.9	71,372	71,029	-0.5	0.0	601	1,071	459	30,790	2.2	58.1	10.8	32.1
Hampden	13.7	10.6	7.1	51.4	463,490	465,825	0.5	-0.7	5,874	7,006	-2,048	180,492	2.5	63.9	17.3	30.1
Hampshire	12.9	11.7	7.0	53.2	158,080	162,308	2.7	-0.5	1,148	1,953	52	59,607	2.3	60.1	10.5	29.6
Middlesex	13.2	9.5	6.5	50.6	1,503,085	1,632,002	8.6	-1.1	19,631	17,784	-19,149	611,850	2.5	64.2	9.4	26.0
Nantucket	13.6	10.0	5.9	48.6	10,172	14,255	40.1	1.7	162	98	171	3,709	3.0	68.2	6.0	26.1
Norfolk	14.1	10.1	7.2	51.5	670,850	725,981	8.2	-0.2	8,680	8,799	-1,466	267,967	2.6	66.6	9.5	26.3
Plymouth	15.1	11.6	7.5	51.1	494,919	530,819	7.3	0.4	6,249	7,387	3,280	190,355	2.7	70.3	12.1	24.8
Suffolk	10.8	7.7	5.2	51.7	722,023	797,936	10.5	-3.3	10,578	7,872	-29,028	312,978	2.4	49.0	14.9	35.6
Worcester	14.5	10.1	6.4	50.4	798,552	862,111	8.0	0.0	10,130	10,673	267	314,081	2.5	65.4	11.9	27.3
MICHIGAN	13.9	11.1	7.0	50.4	9,883,640	10,077,331	2.0	-0.3	129,524	146,786	-10,254	3,980,408	2.5	63.5	11.8	29.9
Alcona	20.7	20.3	15.3	49.4	10,942	10,167	-7.1	0.7	65	270	280	5,115	2.0	61.6	7.1	33.3
Alger	16.6	16.8	9.9	44.1	9,601	8,842	-7.9	-0.2	71	167	76	3,246	2.5	61.8	4.1	32.5
Allegan	14.5	11.1	6.5	49.7	111,408	120,502	8.2	0.4	1,563	1,578	442	43,927	2.6	73.0	8.9	21.7
Alpena	16.8	14.4	10.1	50.2	29,598	28,907	-2.3	0.0	312	512	188	12,769	2.2	60.6	9.9	32.1
Antrim	17.9	17.1	11.1	50.0	23,580	23,431	-0.6	1.6	190	412	616	10,166	2.3	69.3	8.1	25.9
Arenac	17.6	16.5	10.0	48.8	15,899	15,002	-5.6	-0.2	153	309	130	6,585	2.3	62.2	7.7	31.3
Baraga	15.1	14.0	9.1	44.8	8,860	8,158	-7.9	0.7	63	179	176	3,188	2.3	66.3	10.1	29.9
Barry	15.6	12.0	7.2	49.3	59,173	62,423	5.5	0.9	721	860	709	24,342	2.5	69.0	8.5	26.2
Bay	15.1	12.9	8.6	50.5	107,771	103,856	-3.6	-0.8	1,105	1,939	-47	44,627	2.3	62.2	12.1	32.4
Benzie	17.0	16.4	10.9	49.7	17,525	17,970	2.5	1.4	204	343	399	6,940	2.5	66.4	6.6	25.8
Berrien	14.4	12.4	8.3	50.7	156,813	154,316	-1.6	-0.8	1,941	2,536	-626	63,136	2.4	64.4	12.8	29.4
Branch	14.3	11.5	7.3	47.9	45,248	44,862	-0.9	0.3	657	714	178	16,716	2.5	65.7	10.6	26.4
Calhoun	13.5	11.2	7.2	50.7	136,146	134,310	-1.3	-0.4	1,745	2,203	-53	54,124	2.4	61.6	13.6	33.1
Cass	15.6	13.8	8.3	49.4	52,293	51,589	-1.3	-0.2	585	818	128	21,226	2.4	69.1	10.3	25.4
Charlevoix	17.2	16.0	10.0	49.9	25,949	26,054	0.4	0.1	255	449	228	11,725	2.2	65.5	7.8	27.1
Cheboygan	17.3	17.4	11.0	49.5	26,152	25,579	-2.2	0.7	272	522	430	11,219	2.2	64.4	7.4	30.1
Chippewa	13.5	11.5	7.4	44.4	38,520	36,785	-4.5	0.1	363	548	215	14,323	2.4	60.5	11.5	32.9
Clare	16.6	15.7	9.0	49.8	30,926	30,856	-0.2	0.7	395	683	505	12,247	2.5	65.0	9.5	30.3
Clinton	14.1	11.4	6.9	50.4	75,382	79,128	5.0	0.4	935	947	300	30,182	2.6	68.7	9.2	24.8
Crawford	18.4	15.8	10.2	48.6	14,074	12,988	-7.7	1.7	132	293	384	6,155	2.2	64.7	8.6	28.9
Delta	15.7	15.5	9.9	49.8	37,069	36,903	-0.4	-0.2	393	670	203	16,154	2.2	64.0	7.9	30.7
Dickinson	16.1	14.1	9.9	49.3	26,168	25,947	-0.8	-0.6	266	430	4	11,491	2.2	64.7	11.5	29.9
Eaton	14.3	12.0	7.5	50.6	107,759	109,175	1.3	-0.2	1,300	1,593	47	45,037	2.4	65.1	10.6	28.8
Emmet	15.5	15.0	9.0	50.1	32,694	34,112	4.3	0.3	312	540	346	14,197	2.3	65.3	8.7	28.1
Genesee	14.1	11.1	7.1	51.5	425,790	406,211	-4.6	-0.5	5,458	7,058	-477	170,581	2.4	63.6	15.6	30.4
Gladwin	17.3	16.6	10.6	49.3	25,692	25,386	-1.2	0.4	280	544	369	11,181	2.2	64.1	7.7	30.3
Gogebic	16.8	17.1	11.7	48.8	16,427	14,380	-12.5	-0.1	137	305	154	6,896	2.0	54.3	10.7	39.8
Grand Traverse	14.8	13.4	8.0	50.5	86,986	95,238	9.5	0.7	992	1,330	962	37,939	2.4	62.5	7.7	28.9
Gratiot	13.2	10.1	7.5	45.9	42,476	41,761	-1.7	-0.5	496	711	-10	15,084	2.3	66.1	11.1	27.1
Hillsdale	15.0	12.8	7.9	49.9	46,688	45,746	-2.0	-0.4	562	790	24	18,180	2.4	65.8	9.1	27.5
Houghton	11.4	10.6	7.4	45.8	36,628	37,361	2.0	-0.1	388	543	104	13,805	2.4	55.0	6.7	34.1
Huron	16.6	15.9	10.6	49.9	33,118	31,407	-5.2	-0.5	331	645	161	13,908	2.2	61.2	7.5	33.7
Ingham	11.0	9.1	5.3	51.1	280,895	284,900	1.4	-0.3	3,710	3,415	-1,224	113,678	2.4	53.8	10.8	34.3
Ionia	13.5	9.9	5.7	45.9	63,905	66,804	4.5	0.6	838	810	355	23,071	2.6	69.5	9.3	23.9
Iosco	17.8	18.0	12.1	49.7	25,887	25,237	-2.5	0.5	302	614	455	11,772	2.1	58.7	8.9	34.9
Iron	17.6	18.5	12.6	49.8	11,817	11,631	-1.6	0.0	127	276	156	5,150	2.1	56.2	8.8	38.8
Isabella	10.9	8.8	5.0	51.1	70,311	64,394	-8.4	0.7	731	696	373	24,981	2.6	56.5	10.7	29.1
Jackson	14.4	11.5	7.2	48.7	160,248	160,366	0.1	-0.2	2,012	2,502	148	62,216	2.4	64.1	12.0	30.8
Kalamazoo	11.3	9.6	6.2	50.9	250,331	261,670	4.5	-0.2	3,647	3,349	-902	104,278	2.5	60.1	10.8	29.9
Kalkaska	16.3	13.4	7.6	48.8	17,153	17,939	4.6	0.2	218	305	128	7,173	2.5	65.8	9.2	25.9
Kent	12.1	9.0	5.5	50.4	602,622	657,974	9.2	0.0	9,901	7,358	-2,596	244,795	2.6	66.6	10.7	25.9

1. No spouse present.

STATE County	Persons in group quarters, 2021	Daytime Population, 2016–2020: Number	Daytime Population, 2016–2020: Employment/ residence ratio	Births, 2021: Total	Births, 2021: Rate[1]	Deaths, 2021: Number	Deaths, 2021: Rate[1]	Persons under 65 with no health insurance, 2019: Number	Persons under 65 with no health insurance, 2019: Percent	Medicare, 2021: Total beneficiaries	Medicare, 2021: Enrolled in Original Medicare	Medicare, 2021: Enrolled in Medicare Advantage	COVID-19 Deaths, 2020: Number	COVID-19 Deaths, 2020: Rate[1]
	32	33	34	35	36	37	38	39	40	41	42	43	44	45
MARYLAND— Cont'd														
St. Mary's	2,561	108,735	0.9	1,337	11.7	1,067	9.3	4,997	5.2	17,047	16,589	458	97	0.9
Somerset	5,005	24,185	0.8	216	8.8	332	13.5	1,209	7.5	5,242	4,803	440	22	0.9
Talbot	320	40,985	1.2	312	8.3	605	16.1	2,074	8.0	11,443	10,808	635	10	0.3
Washington	8,374	152,697	1.0	1,555	10.0	1,913	12.4	7,906	6.7	31,690	27,532	4,158	200	1.3
Wicomico	4,670	103,464	1.0	1,327	12.8	1,290	12.4	6,984	8.5	20,156	18,796	1,360	90	0.9
Worcester	619	54,205	1.1	274	5.2	756	14.3	2,747	7.4	15,307	13,967	1,340	56	1.1
Baltimore city	26,167	703,512	1.4	7,305	12.6	7,826	13.5	34,023	7.0	99,854	79,643	20,211	783	1.3
MASSACHUSETTS	246,722	6,949,567	1.0	66,197	9.5	70,431	10.1	195,726	3.5	1,352,025	988,677	363,348	10,093	1.4
Barnstable	4,238	208,803	1.0	1,419	6.2	3,360	14.6	5,496	3.8	78,016	64,380	13,636	213	0.9
Berkshire	5,846	127,419	1.0	865	6.7	1,663	12.9	3,482	3.9	35,270	31,640	3,630	127	1.0
Bristol	14,921	510,114	0.8	5,410	9.3	6,514	11.2	17,581	3.9	122,595	94,553	28,042	868	1.5
Dukes	121	17,906	1.1	182	8.7	167	8.0	651	5.1	5,082	4,845	238	D	D
Essex	19,391	717,907	0.8	8,105	10.0	8,406	10.4	24,645	3.9	161,477	119,160	42,318	1,354	1.7
Franklin	1,433	63,489	0.8	483	6.8	869	12.2	1,783	3.3	19,091	14,746	4,345	78	1.1
Hampden	14,058	466,206	1.0	4,695	10.1	5,619	12.1	15,798	4.3	103,062	65,601	37,461	832	1.8
Hampshire	23,067	156,995	1.0	937	5.8	1,537	9.5	3,540	3.2	34,679	26,609	8,070	167	1.0
Middlesex	55,016	1,680,770	1.1	15,629	9.6	14,205	8.8	41,317	3.1	274,646	198,701	75,945	2,274	1.4
Nantucket	57	11,914	1.1	130	9.0	82	5.7	400	4.1	2,026	1,929	97	D	D
Norfolk	16,547	690,372	1.0	6,919	9.5	7,135	9.8	13,598	2.4	133,898	101,686	32,213	1,000	1.4
Plymouth	11,238	462,336	0.8	4,924	9.3	5,969	11.2	12,445	3.0	114,440	90,154	24,287	787	1.5
Suffolk	52,366	1,061,130	1.6	8,436	10.8	6,326	8.1	31,313	4.8	107,480	73,037	34,443	1,172	1.5
Worcester	28,423	774,206	0.9	8,063	9.4	8,579	10.0	23,677	3.5	160,262	101,638	58,624	1,221	1.4
MICHIGAN	211,749	9,937,760	1.0	102,983	10.2	117,336	11.7	564,804	7.0	2,099,584	1,095,821	1,003,763	12,426	1.2
Alcona	77	9,219	0.7	51	5.0	211	20.7	635	9.7	4,374	2,567	1,807	20	2.0
Alger	942	9,019	1.0	55	6.2	140	15.9	484	8.3	2,676	1,568	1,108	D	D
Allegan	883	107,917	0.8	1,259	10.4	1,263	10.5	6,888	7.1	24,220	9,663	14,557	81	0.7
Alpena	476	29,435	1.1	241	8.3	421	14.6	1,501	7.0	8,922	6,072	2,850	25	0.9
Antrim	177	20,893	0.8	151	6.4	315	13.3	1,536	9.2	7,658	4,322	3,335	10	0.4
Arenac	166	13,941	0.8	119	7.9	243	16.2	1,001	9.2	4,824	2,682	2,142	16	1.1
Baraga	969	8,438	1.0	50	6.1	143	17.5	498	9.2	2,197	1,405	792	27	3.3
Barry	553	47,993	0.5	575	9.2	703	11.2	3,186	6.4	13,851	6,147	7,705	42	0.7
Bay	1,347	94,291	0.8	875	8.5	1,521	14.7	5,631	7.0	26,776	14,635	12,142	173	1.7
Benzie	210	14,899	0.7	171	9.4	271	15.0	1,099	8.5	5,582	3,113	2,469	25	1.4
Berrien	3,335	151,528	1.0	1,564	10.2	2,027	13.2	10,145	8.5	36,249	21,594	14,654	195	1.3
Branch	1,858	41,257	0.9	522	11.6	543	12.1	2,877	8.6	9,651	5,762	3,889	78	1.7
Calhoun	4,121	139,348	1.1	1,419	10.6	1,769	13.2	7,646	7.2	30,566	19,215	11,351	178	1.3
Cass	416	42,063	0.6	449	8.7	680	13.2	3,207	8.0	12,968	7,922	5,046	68	1.3
Charlevoix	218	25,064	0.9	205	7.9	368	14.1	1,597	8.2	7,529	4,523	3,007	13	0.5
Cheboygan	355	22,986	0.8	222	8.6	433	16.9	1,626	9.1	8,292	4,952	3,340	42	1.6
Chippewa	4,518	37,503	1.0	291	7.9	444	12.1	2,568	10.0	8,271	4,648	3,623	22	0.6
Clare	335	28,240	0.8	312	10.1	564	18.2	2,229	9.7	9,445	5,256	4,189	45	1.5
Clinton	514	63,845	0.6	734	9.3	761	9.6	3,811	5.8	15,681	6,949	8,732	52	0.7
Crawford	99	13,761	1.0	111	8.5	239	18.3	802	7.8	4,092	2,364	1,727	D	D
Delta	610	35,259	1.0	308	8.4	529	14.4	2,023	7.6	10,813	6,562	4,251	68	1.8
Dickinson	405	26,993	1.1	206	8.0	350	13.5	1,224	6.3	7,002	4,472	2,529	73	2.8
Eaton	1,648	107,164	1.0	1,032	9.5	1,296	11.9	5,201	5.9	24,174	10,882	13,292	83	0.8
Emmet	469	36,395	1.2	240	7.0	434	12.7	2,058	8.1	9,253	5,740	3,513	33	1.0
Genesee	5,412	387,756	0.9	4,387	10.8	5,581	13.8	21,718	6.6	90,711	40,826	49,885	528	1.3
Gladwin	231	22,462	0.7	232	9.1	445	17.5	1,725	9.4	8,304	4,404	3,900	38	1.5
Gogebic	355	14,663	1.0	116	8.1	232	16.2	836	8.5	4,501	2,828	1,673	49	3.4
Grand Traverse	1,439	101,356	1.2	816	8.5	1,079	11.3	5,245	7.2	22,492	11,549	10,942	45	0.5
Gratiot	5,525	39,306	0.9	393	9.4	557	13.4	1,878	6.6	8,777	4,965	3,813	57	1.4
Hillsdale	1,607	41,834	0.8	440	9.6	601	13.2	2,843	8.1	10,845	6,511	4,334	68	1.5
Houghton	2,883	35,795	1.0	311	8.4	404	10.8	2,243	8.4	7,562	4,321	3,241	29	0.8
Huron	486	31,481	1.0	254	8.1	522	16.7	1,883	8.3	9,488	6,232	3,256	50	1.6
Ingham	16,743	320,472	1.2	2,937	10.3	2,705	9.5	17,593	7.5	48,702	25,839	22,863	175	0.6
Ionia	5,171	55,738	0.7	666	9.9	668	10.0	3,465	7.0	11,810	5,178	6,632	40	0.6
Iosco	342	25,933	1.1	234	9.3	492	19.5	1,546	9.0	9,020	5,338	3,682	46	1.8
Iron	346	10,734	0.9	97	8.3	221	19.0	629	8.4	3,916	2,457	1,459	29	2.5
Isabella	4,205	74,290	1.1	598	9.2	583	9.0	5,189	9.3	11,273	6,634	4,639	34	0.5
Jackson	7,734	152,195	0.9	1,575	9.8	2,025	12.6	8,320	6.9	34,986	21,058	13,929	198	1.2
Kalamazoo	7,704	270,943	1.1	2,901	11.1	2,650	10.1	14,695	6.8	49,789	23,993	25,796	212	0.8
Kalkaska	101	15,460	0.7	162	9.0	235	13.1	1,329	9.4	4,750	2,712	2,038	15	0.8
Kent	10,882	707,759	1.2	7,808	11.9	5,820	8.8	41,382	7.4	109,847	42,754	67,094	511	0.8

1. Per 1,000 estimated resident population.

STATE County	COVID-19 Vaccinations, 2021–2022		Education						Money income, 2016–2020				Income and poverty, 2020			
			School enrollment and attainment, 2016–2020				Local government expenditures,[3] 2018–2019			Households				Percent below poverty level		
			Enrollment[1]		Attainment[2] (percent)						Percent					
	Number	Percent[5]	Total	Percent private	High school graduate or less	Bachelor's degree or more	Total current spending (mil dol)	Current spending per student (dollars)	Per capita income[4]	Median income (dollars)	with income of less than $50,000	with income of $200,000 or more	Median household income (dollars)	All persons	Children under 18 years	Children 5 to 17 years in families
	46	47	48	49	50	51	52	53	54	55	56	57	58	59	60	61
MARYLAND— Cont'd																
St. Mary's	75,542	66.6	29,775	16.9	40.2	32.0	241.9	13,438	41,430	95,864	24.4	11.9	105,197	7.3	9.2	8.4
Somerset	12,873	50.3	6,936	8.9	53.5	15.8	51.9	17,717	19,507	44,980	54.2	1.3	51,787	22.2	26.6	25.7
Talbot	27,385	73.7	7,321	20.7	32.0	39.7	64.0	13,686	49,193	73,102	33.6	11.1	69,311	9.6	14.7	14.1
Washington	90,386	59.8	33,531	14.3	47.8	22.4	314.3	13,859	31,525	63,510	40.4	5.5	63,237	12.3	16.9	16.0
Wicomico	57,968	55.9	29,558	11.9	45.4	28.0	218.4	14,607	29,049	60,366	42.5	4.1	59,387	14.2	19.2	17.8
Worcester	37,617	72.0	9,698	15.5	38.6	29.8	122.7	18,015	41,055	65,396	39.0	7.9	62,481	11.7	18.6	17.3
Baltimore city	380,685	64.1	146,904	24.7	43.0	32.9	1,259.9	15,807	32,699	52,164	48.2	6.2	51,485	20.0	26.8	26.1
MASSACHUSETTS	5,438,006	78.9	1,702,976	27.4	32.5	44.5	16,925.2	17,785	45,555	84,385	31.3	14.3	87,288	9.4	10.9	10.5
Barnstable	NA	NA	37,386	16.4	26.9	45.0	490.5	20,040	47,315	76,863	31.7	10.7	76,287	7.7	9.5	8.9
Berkshire	73,488	58.8	26,213	21.9	37.0	35.3	298.0	19,079	37,025	62,166	40.7	6.5	65,458	10.0	14.6	14.2
Bristol	372,351	65.9	129,577	16.4	44.1	29.2	1,254.7	15,795	36,900	71,450	36.8	8.1	71,998	10.1	12.6	12.8
Dukes	NA	NA	3,127	17.5	27.7	44.0	72.8	31,080	43,994	77,318	30.1	12.3	80,459	7.5	10.0	9.9
Essex	585,198	74.2	185,188	22.5	34.8	40.6	1,956.4	16,894	43,948	82,225	32.1	14.3	88,269	9.0	11.2	10.8
Franklin	47,978	68.4	14,120	14.5	34.6	38.3	175.5	18,999	35,919	61,198	41.2	5.0	62,920	10.7	13.7	12.8
Hampden	307,326	65.9	115,064	17.0	44.3	27.4	1,287.6	17,929	31,483	57,623	44.2	5.9	61,600	14.3	20.4	20.0
Hampshire	107,675	66.9	54,976	24.2	27.5	48.9	313.1	17,392	36,600	73,518	35.5	8.9	73,864	9.3	8.4	8.0
Middlesex	1,282,903	79.6	409,377	32.5	24.9	57.1	4,016.8	18,340	54,433	106,202	23.9	20.8	111,158	7.1	7.3	7.1
Nantucket	NA	NA	1,924	23.3	22.2	47.5	39.5	23,672	57,246	112,306	21.9	23.0	95,713	5.3	4.6	4.5
Norfolk	559,194	79.1	175,337	30.4	24.7	54.6	1,851.2	17,967	55,860	105,320	23.4	21.2	106,348	5.9	4.7	4.7
Plymouth	365,594	70.1	125,596	17.1	34.7	38.1	1,340.9	16,198	45,378	92,906	26.9	14.6	88,420	7.2	7.3	6.5
Suffolk	590,001	73.4	218,711	46.7	34.2	47.7	1,825.0	22,343	44,723	74,881	37.4	13.2	85,221	16.5	20.5	20.7
Worcester	582,335	70.1	206,380	22.3	36.1	37.1	2,003.3	15,809	39,113	77,155	33.6	10.3	77,931	9.5	10.8	10.4
MICHIGAN	6,002,679	60.1	2,400,867	13.4	37.2	30.0	18,107.6	12,429	32,854	59,234	42.6	5.7	61,352	12.6	16.8	15.8
Alcona	6,062	58.3	1,289	9.5	48.8	18.4	7.8	11,418	27,171	43,341	57.4	1.7	45,573	14.0	25.5	25.0
Alger	5,689	62.5	1,535	11.7	55.3	19.3	12.8	12,051	21,675	45,184	54.0	1.3	51,126	12.1	16.3	15.6
Allegan	61,692	52.2	27,050	14.4	45.6	23.6	208.8	11,645	30,057	65,071	38.2	4.3	63,732	7.3	8.4	7.8
Alpena	15,835	55.7	5,055	7.3	42.0	18.0	47.9	12,758	25,989	42,603	57.7	1.8	40,442	15.6	19.7	20.1
Antrim	13,564	58.2	4,208	9.9	37.9	29.6	35.4	10,983	32,096	57,256	43.1	3.8	58,738	11.3	19.7	16.6
Arenac	7,628	51.3	2,525	8.5	51.0	12.9	20.8	10,506	25,556	45,679	54.4	1.7	50,286	12.8	21.3	20.6
Baraga	5,005	61.0	1,348	9.4	50.8	15.2	12.1	12,592	23,960	46,581	54.7	2.8	48,846	12.7	16.1	15.6
Barry	30,220	49.1	13,212	13.5	43.9	23.0	92.1	10,415	34,002	65,557	36.7	4.6	68,693	7.6	9.3	9.1
Bay	59,116	57.3	21,763	12.6	43.9	19.7	166.9	12,191	28,331	48,290	51.6	2.5	55,860	12.7	16.4	15.8
Benzie	11,193	63.0	3,255	13.3	35.4	32.5	21.1	11,288	31,452	64,257	40.0	3.5	64,526	9.5	12.7	12.1
Berrien	86,055	56.1	34,183	19.0	38.0	27.6	317.7	12,527	30,839	52,500	48.0	4.6	56,346	15.1	22.1	21.1
Branch	19,738	45.4	9,181	12.9	52.0	15.0	80.9	12,401	25,754	52,782	46.9	2.2	51,757	14.1	18.6	17.3
Calhoun	70,151	52.3	31,066	12.8	45.0	21.5	273.9	14,172	27,939	50,219	49.8	3.4	52,310	15.1	21.5	18.9
Cass	22,572	43.6	10,595	12.5	44.3	20.7	75.4	11,433	32,835	57,514	42.5	4.9	61,180	11.1	16.1	14.1
Charlevoix	16,775	64.2	5,103	9.5	34.2	32.4	61.5	17,449	36,132	60,433	40.8	5.4	66,728	8.7	12.8	11.8
Cheboygan	14,186	56.1	4,279	14.4	45.6	21.8	38.5	15,247	27,589	49,624	50.4	2.3	50,788	12.7	21.7	20.3
Chippewa	26,063	69.8	8,154	15.6	41.0	22.6	70.0	15,392	28,203	50,454	49.3	2.8	52,579	13.9	18.4	16.7
Clare	14,334	46.3	5,580	10.8	52.7	12.1	57.5	13,715	23,067	41,163	59.4	1.9	43,726	18.0	26.7	26.2
Clinton	45,775	57.5	19,314	11.9	31.6	32.1	120.4	11,600	37,513	72,490	33.5	7.1	76,367	7.9	8.7	8.3
Crawford	7,172	51.1	2,427	9.1	41.5	19.1	16.5	10,511	26,628	49,987	50.0	1.1	49,625	13.6	23.9	21.9
Delta	22,054	61.6	6,894	10.1	42.4	19.2	57.6	12,697	27,494	47,008	52.6	2.0	49,414	11.3	15.4	15.4
Dickinson	16,772	66.5	4,891	14.3	38.5	24.4	47.6	12,828	30,798	51,704	47.8	2.6	59,408	9.7	13.4	13.0
Eaton	62,974	57.1	24,881	18.2	32.2	29.2	208.0	11,536	34,282	67,440	35.4	3.9	67,658	7.8	10.3	9.8
Emmet	24,208	72.4	6,593	9.5	30.4	34.7	55.1	11,873	35,306	55,947	43.2	6.1	60,401	8.7	12.1	11.4
Genesee	205,516	50.6	94,933	10.6	41.0	21.5	768.8	12,208	28,696	50,269	49.7	3.6	48,721	18.3	24.3	23.3
Gladwin	12,192	47.9	4,365	13.7	51.6	14.3	27.5	10,278	26,521	45,957	54.5	1.6	48,694	16.6	28.2	28.3
Gogebic	8,902	63.7	2,356	9.0	40.6	19.8	18.9	11,862	27,877	38,625	60.4	3.1	48,975	12.5	22.5	22.0
Grand Traverse	62,605	67.3	20,604	15.2	27.1	38.4	185.8	15,023	35,705	66,457	37.6	6.3	67,290	8.7	10.0	8.6
Gratiot	18,774	46.1	9,713	25.7	48.3	16.5	84.7	14,536	24,623	49,795	50.2	3.0	54,161	13.7	15.7	14.9
Hillsdale	17,673	38.8	10,127	27.6	49.2	18.9	70.0	12,454	26,265	51,535	48.6	2.7	54,974	12.6	19.4	18.6
Houghton	18,669	52.3	12,425	7.5	37.8	33.6	63.9	12,061	24,881	44,839	54.2	3.5	47,399	15.0	13.6	12.6
Huron	16,761	54.1	5,646	13.8	51.6	16.0	66.7	14,466	28,598	49,541	50.6	2.9	53,616	11.6	13.5	12.3
Ingham	167,106	57.1	96,354	7.6	28.5	39.2	534.1	12,984	30,721	55,253	45.5	4.9	62,711	13.8	14.9	14.7
Ionia	30,537	47.2	14,686	13.2	47.5	17.0	96.9	12,309	25,997	60,139	41.0	1.6	58,371	9.6	11.4	10.7
Iosco	14,134	56.3	3,946	11.6	48.2	15.4	43.7	12,014	25,022	42,628	59.5	1.1	43,450	13.8	24.2	24.4
Iron	6,185	55.9	1,714	7.6	50.7	18.9	14.1	11,099	28,556	44,183	53.8	1.3	45,098	14.2	22.8	21.4
Isabella	31,236	44.7	26,528	8.2	39.8	29.5	69.9	10,879	24,297	46,783	52.8	3.1	53,607	17.4	17.0	17.0
Jackson	83,182	52.5	35,772	13.7	41.4	22.5	303.4	13,202	29,141	54,511	45.8	3.4	57,267	12.6	16.8	15.9
Kalamazoo	163,041	61.5	76,631	12.1	28.7	39.8	459.5	13,221	33,450	58,836	42.4	5.9	63,279	12.0	14.0	13.1
Kalkaska	8,416	46.7	3,515	11.5	52.2	14.4	22.2	10,866	25,301	49,402	50.5	2.0	52,903	12.0	19.3	17.9
Kent	403,296	61.4	165,549	20.0	32.8	36.8	1,307.5	12,257	33,629	65,722	37.7	6.3	65,012	11.1	12.6	11.3

1. All persons 3 years old and over enrolled in nursery school through college. 2. Persons 25 years old and over. 3. Elementary and secondary education expenditures. 4. Based on population estimated by the American Community Survey, 2016–2020. 5. CDC percent based on 2019 population estimate.

STATE County	Personal income, 2020										Earnings, 2020		
	Total (mil dol)	Percent change 2019–2020	Per capita[1]		Wages and salaries (mil dol)	Supplements to wages and salaries, employer contributions (mil dol)		Proprietors' income (mil dol)	Dividends, interest, and rent (mil dol)	Personal transfer reecipts (mil dol)	Total (mil dol)	Contributions for government social insurance (mil dol)	
			Dollars	Rank		Pension and insurance	Government social insurance					From employee and self-employed	From employer
	62	63	64	65	66	67	68	69	70	71	72	73	74
MARYLAND— Cont'd													
St. Mary's	7,012	6.5	61,144	382	3,945	816	301	263	1,123	1,222	5,325	303	301
Somerset	828	5.6	32,531	3,047	356	86	26	22	121	373	490	33	26
Talbot	2,829	4.6	76,528	96	867	133	63	219	836	602	1,283	89	63
Washington	7,632	7.3	50,493	1,092	3,269	529	246	485	1,002	2,088	4,528	296	246
Wicomico	4,595	7.4	44,184	1,913	2,298	422	168	296	648	1,493	3,185	201	168
Worcester	3,138	6.2	59,881	432	982	165	79	276	689	894	1,502	108	79
Baltimore city	31,708	6.7	54,097	773	26,132	4,110	1,846	2,841	4,046	10,805	34,928	2,069	1,846
MASSACHUSETTS	540,855	6.8	77,021	X	285,365	40,116	18,726	44,814	96,771	105,542	389,021	21,062	18,726
Barnstable	17,143	6.9	80,420	76	5,085	932	378	1,601	4,279	4,323	7,996	497	378
Berkshire	7,707	7.4	61,872	353	3,070	559	227	532	1,431	2,429	4,388	262	227
Bristol	34,590	10.5	61,031	384	12,573	2,295	923	2,594	3,820	9,824	18,385	1,047	923
Dukes	1,567	3.0	89,757	39	503	87	37	289	480	279	915	50	37
Essex	58,964	8.4	74,519	110	21,042	3,435	1,490	4,237	10,190	12,452	30,204	1,687	1,490
Franklin	4,206	7.1	59,853	435	1,213	267	89	297	697	1,318	1,866	114	89
Hampden	26,828	8.9	57,821	525	11,243	2,173	822	1,473	3,029	9,432	15,711	888	822
Hampshire	9,205	5.8	57,030	572	3,486	838	227	712	1,639	2,060	5,263	267	227
Middlesex	145,951	4.7	90,688	37	90,463	10,492	5,823	11,139	29,235	19,697	117,917	6,386	5,823
Nantucket	1,306	0.0	114,832	15	467	67	37	332	335	150	903	44	37
Norfolk	69,535	5.2	98,019	23	25,010	3,526	1,734	4,776	14,638	9,189	35,045	1,902	1,734
Plymouth	38,774	8.0	74,034	114	11,347	2,023	808	3,079	5,566	8,276	17,256	969	808
Suffolk	72,600	6.9	90,571	38	78,373	9,496	4,602	10,246	14,923	13,844	102,717	5,302	4,602
Worcester	52,478	8.7	63,286	309	21,492	3,926	1,529	3,506	6,509	12,270	30,453	1,645	1,529
MICHIGAN	530,809	7.9	52,724	X	242,644	38,263	17,928	34,496	88,455	146,541	333,331	22,062	17,928
Alcona	472	11.3	44,953	1,798	74	16	6	20	97	212	115	14	6
Alger	342	10.7	37,951	2,691	103	22	8	11	63	144	143	13	8
Allegan	5,957	9.3	50,091	1,135	2,128	373	158	389	940	1,492	3,049	197	158
Alpena	1,290	10.3	45,685	1,702	505	97	42	69	189	548	713	55	42
Antrim	1,231	8.8	52,490	890	203	41	17	89	317	420	350	32	17
Arenac	650	12.6	43,466	2,013	168	32	13	48	83	286	261	23	13
Baraga	316	11.9	38,750	2,598	115	29	9	8	54	130	161	12	9
Barry	3,055	8.2	49,232	1,227	595	128	45	187	483	793	954	71	45
Bay	4,893	9.1	47,786	1,418	1,724	315	130	233	701	1,764	2,402	177	130
Benzie	902	10.6	50,509	1,089	167	30	13	56	242	301	267	24	13
Berrien	8,018	8.4	52,395	901	3,258	623	246	472	1,366	2,338	4,599	313	246
Branch	1,839	11.6	42,356	2,146	660	120	50	133	272	617	963	68	50
Calhoun	5,975	10.5	44,729	1,841	3,092	520	232	231	899	2,114	4,074	277	232
Cass	2,598	10.8	50,365	1,101	439	87	33	134	422	763	692	55	33
Charlevoix	1,496	7.4	57,289	553	487	91	38	101	415	423	716	53	38
Cheboygan	1,136	11.8	44,801	1,824	243	45	21	45	235	477	354	32	21
Chippewa	1,467	11.5	39,693	2,484	524	133	41	76	240	557	775	54	41
Clare	1,189	11.2	38,655	2,611	306	64	24	71	168	558	465	43	24
Clinton	4,072	8.0	51,053	1,020	816	131	63	232	631	894	1,242	89	63
Crawford	551	11.6	39,405	2,520	189	37	15	23	92	236	264	21	15
Delta	1,612	10.1	45,260	1,761	629	116	50	63	235	616	858	67	50
Dickinson	1,344	8.4	53,526	818	710	140	54	29	249	446	933	63	54
Eaton	5,222	8.9	47,407	1,455	2,206	368	161	223	785	1,469	2,958	209	161
Emmet	2,098	7.5	62,918	319	845	136	67	134	581	582	1,182	83	67
Genesee	18,682	9.8	46,152	1,627	6,625	1,095	505	931	2,551	6,800	9,156	678	505
Gladwin	1,037	9.3	40,772	2,363	179	35	14	51	147	451	279	31	14
Gogebic	663	8.4	47,894	1,407	225	48	18	20	139	270	311	25	18
Grand Traverse	5,322	8.7	56,861	581	2,553	413	193	506	1,202	1,364	3,664	245	193
Gratiot	1,695	11.0	42,067	2,184	622	121	48	122	218	616	914	63	48
Hillsdale	1,799	10.3	39,404	2,521	578	109	45	97	250	652	828	61	45
Houghton	1,506	8.5	42,884	2,078	560	124	43	56	306	527	783	55	43
Huron	1,644	15.8	53,638	810	488	96	38	218	318	578	840	55	38
Ingham	13,065	8.6	44,957	1,797	8,406	1,531	611	700	2,187	3,650	11,248	695	611
Ionia	2,541	10.7	39,366	2,527	729	154	56	103	294	773	1,042	75	56
Iosco	1,097	11.5	43,618	1,992	403	70	30	37	179	507	541	48	30
Iron	544	8.3	49,153	1,236	148	30	12	13	91	245	203	18	12
Isabella	2,782	10.1	40,021	2,455	1,197	260	91	146	438	991	1,694	106	91
Jackson	7,044	10.1	44,889	1,810	2,976	583	223	380	1,020	2,329	4,162	287	223
Kalamazoo	13,939	6.5	52,403	899	6,896	1,167	510	925	2,537	3,345	9,498	602	510
Kalkaska	748	15.3	41,545	2,264	232	40	17	51	118	297	340	27	17
Kent	37,808	7.0	57,397	545	22,171	3,330	1,632	3,100	7,644	7,799	30,233	1,870	1,632

1. Based on the resident population estimated as of July 1 of the year shown.

STATE County	Earnings, 2020 (cont.) — Percent by selected industries: Farm	Mining, quarrying, and extractions	Construction	Manu-facturing	Information; professional, scientific, technical services	Retail trade	Finance, insurance, real estate, and leasing	Health care and social assistance	Govern-ment	Social Security beneficiaries, December 2020: Number	Rate[1]	Supple-mental Security Income recipients, 2020	Housing units, 2021: Total	Percent change, 2010–2021
	75	76	77	78	79	80	81	82	83	84	85	86	87	88
MARYLAND— Cont'd														
St. Mary's	0.1	0.0	4.4	1.2	25.8	3.7	1.8	6.5	46.0	17,475	153	1,695	46,196	1.1
Somerset	-0.1	0.0	4.7	D	D	4.5	D	D	50.9	5,565	226	947	10,887	-0.1
Talbot	1.4	D	7.2	D	13.0	8.7	9.1	14.8	12.8	11,420	304	548	19,559	0.1
Washington	1.4	D	6.0	11.6	5.2	9.5	8.9	16.0	15.0	33,780	218	3,756	63,935	0.2
Wicomico	0.8	D	6.5	6.1	5.9	9.2	5.2	21.3	18.8	21,555	207	2,755	43,936	0.5
Worcester	0.5	D	7.4	3.0	6.3	10.6	9.0	10.2	18.2	16,250	306	839	56,492	0.3
Baltimore city	0.0	D	3.1	2.8	14.3	1.7	11.0	18.6	20.3	101,650	176	35,310	293,513	0.2
MASSACHUSETTS	0.0	0.0	6.1	7.3	22.2	4.5	12.1	12.8	11.5	1,294,623	185	179,322	3,017,901	0.5
Barnstable	0.1	D	12.7	2.5	8.8	9.7	8.1	15.7	18.2	74,660	321	3,046	165,524	0.3
Berkshire	0.0	0.1	8.4	6.9	11.3	7.5	6.3	20.0	14.8	35,070	273	3,778	69,984	0.2
Bristol	0.0	D	7.9	D	7.0	7.8	4.5	15.2	14.6	124,285	214	18,060	244,231	0.2
Dukes	0.1	0.0	D	D	D	9.3	4.0	10.3	15.5	4,730	224	118	17,677	0.6
Essex	0.0	0.0	7.9	16.1	12.3	5.7	5.7	15.1	12.9	154,405	191	21,387	328,580	0.3
Franklin	0.9	D	D	13.7	5.8	7.5	3.2	13.5	19.6	18,295	258	1,954	34,436	0.2
Hampden	0.0	0.1	6.2	9.5	5.5	6.0	10.1	21.3	18.1	103,325	223	30,149	197,318	0.1
Hampshire	0.2	D	5.4	5.1	7.1	6.6	4.5	12.4	31.0	32,950	204	2,932	66,624	0.4
Middlesex	0.1	0.0	5.2	9.0	34.9	3.2	6.4	8.2	8.2	252,355	156	24,177	663,691	0.6
Nantucket	0.0	0.0	24.0	D	D	8.2	9.7	5.9	10.6	1,840	127	43	12,397	1.6
Norfolk	0.0	0.0	8.7	7.1	17.3	5.9	12.1	11.3	10.3	125,075	173	10,660	293,463	0.5
Plymouth	0.1	0.0	12.0	5.9	8.5	7.6	8.1	13.1	17.6	112,060	210	9,047	216,266	0.6
Suffolk	0.0	D	2.9	1.1	26.0	2.6	25.5	14.5	9.6	97,690	127	31,956	353,826	1.0
Worcester	0.0	0.1	7.3	11.6	10.8	5.9	7.4	16.5	16.1	157,885	183	22,015	353,884	0.5
MICHIGAN	0.7	0.2	5.6	15.4	12.6	6.0	8.0	12.6	13.7	2,250,141	224	265,956	4,590,528	0.4
Alcona	3.2	0.0	5.3	11.3	3.5	9.2	4.0	D	16.7	4,795	468	337	10,303	0.3
Alger	0.3	0.0	4.8	24.5	D	4.9	4.9	7.7	29.8	3,035	344	159	6,188	0.3
Allegan	3.8	0.2	8.8	37.9	3.8	5.0	3.5	4.2	12.1	26,210	217	1,616	52,267	0.7
Alpena	1.5	0.4	5.3	18.3	4.9	10.8	4.7	10.0	26.4	10,060	348	1,090	15,666	0.1
Antrim	4.5	D	13.9	12.7	6.1	6.8	6.2	4.7	21.2	8,145	342	462	17,634	0.4
Arenac	6.2	D	4.1	20.1	D	9.1	D	D	14.3	5,385	360	595	9,523	0.2
Baraga	0.3	D	4.7	21.1	D	3.7	D	D	49.0	2,220	270	156	5,064	0.2
Barry	5.0	D	8.0	31.3	D	4.4	8.1	6.8	16.8	14,695	233	741	27,577	0.7
Bay	1.3	0.1	4.9	19.3	8.4	8.1	4.5	15.4	16.1	29,570	287	3,080	48,652	0.2
Benzie	1.7	D	15.0	9.1	3.6	7.3	9.1	10.6	16.8	5,945	326	292	12,198	0.7
Berrien	2.1	0.2	4.5	28.9	3.9	5.7	5.9	12.4	13.0	38,475	251	4,468	77,040	0.3
Branch	3.3	0.0	7.6	20.3	2.7	6.6	5.7	4.8	20.8	10,880	242	887	20,806	0.2
Calhoun	0.7	0.1	4.1	20.6	9.5	5.5	2.5	14.2	21.2	33,385	249	4,707	59,558	0.1
Cass	5.4	D	6.5	20.7	4.7	4.6	D	D	19.9	13,480	262	945	25,576	1.0
Charlevoix	0.6	0.0	9.1	26.5	D	5.0	6.0	D	17.4	8,045	308	458	17,570	0.6
Cheboygan	0.3	D	14.7	3.4	6.1	11.4	7.2	7.8	21.9	9,095	353	673	17,703	0.4
Chippewa	0.8	D	4.0	5.3	2.6	7.3	3.3	4.9	54.8	9,100	247	870	20,325	0.2
Clare	1.6	D	9.1	12.8	D	9.7	4.4	9.7	24.0	10,615	342	1,232	21,929	0.4
Clinton	4.4	0.4	13.2	9.0	D	8.7	9.3	7.4	13.8	16,645	210	660	33,219	1.0
Crawford	0.0	D	4.2	19.6	D	7.4	3.9	D	21.4	4,405	334	368	10,219	0.4
Delta	0.6	D	8.2	20.2	D	9.6	4.6	12.9	16.3	11,795	320	929	19,814	0.1
Dickinson	0.1	0.0	18.8	22.7	3.5	7.2	2.6	6.4	24.4	7,670	297	471	13,941	0.2
Eaton	0.8	0.1	5.7	16.9	D	7.2	18.5	5.5	14.1	26,380	242	1,764	47,611	0.2
Emmet	0.1	0.0	9.5	10.6	D	10.2	5.6	19.5	13.9	9,625	281	505	21,858	0.3
Genesee	0.2	0.0	6.4	12.0	5.1	9.0	6.6	19.1	15.9	101,520	251	16,108	183,563	0.2
Gladwin	1.6	D	13.7	17.1	2.0	11.9	5.3	8.1	19.3	9,145	359	846	16,969	0.6
Gogebic	0.1	0.0	4.9	14.7	3.5	7.4	2.8	D	32.5	4,925	343	480	10,399	0.1
Grand Traverse	0.5	0.9	8.4	9.1	9.1	9.1	10.9	21.6	11.9	24,205	253	1,385	46,351	1.0
Gratiot	6.9	D	5.7	15.1	D	5.6	4.3	D	17.8	9,775	235	1,084	16,056	0.1
Hillsdale	4.5	D	4.0	31.4	D	7.5	3.9	D	18.7	11,545	253	1,104	21,475	0.3
Houghton	0.2	D	6.4	6.4	7.9	7.2	3.8	D	40.3	8,285	222	538	18,663	0.1
Huron	17.7	D	5.0	13.0	D	5.2	5.2	D	13.9	10,175	326	684	20,344	0.1
Ingham	0.3	0.0	4.3	8.0	10.2	4.7	8.5	14.9	30.3	52,805	186	7,700	125,766	0.3
Ionia	4.0	D	7.6	24.0	2.8	6.4	6.3	6.2	22.7	13,300	198	1,212	24,744	0.3
Iosco	0.8	0.4	5.5	14.8	3.3	7.2	3.8	D	18.2	9,885	390	787	19,914	0.3
Iron	0.5	D	6.6	5.9	D	15.5	4.5	11.5	27.0	4,355	374	289	9,009	1.4
Isabella	1.7	1.7	8.8	9.6	4.0	7.0	5.8	8.5	34.8	12,200	188	1,207	28,616	0.4
Jackson	0.3	0.2	5.0	17.4	4.7	6.6	5.5	15.6	13.8	38,345	240	4,496	69,210	0.2
Kalamazoo	1.0	D	6.8	23.1	6.7	6.1	8.5	16.6	11.3	53,115	203	6,350	114,532	0.3
Kalkaska	1.2	9.1	18.1	5.2	D	5.6	2.7	2.5	22.5	5,120	285	356	11,633	0.5
Kent	0.3	0.4	6.0	18.5	9.2	5.6	8.6	16.6	7.2	115,460	175	12,816	267,016	0.5

1. Per 1,000 resident population estimated as of July 1 of the year shown.

STATE County	Housing units, 2016–2020								Civilian labor force, 2021				Civilian employment[6], 2016–2020		
	Occupied units														
		Owner-occupied				Renter-occupied					Unemployment			Percent	
				Median owner cost as a percent of income											
	Total	Percent	Median value[1]	With a mort-gage	Without a mort-gage[2]	Median rent[3]	Median rent as a percent of income[2]	Sub-standard units[4] (percent)	Total	Percent change, 2020–2021	Total	Rate[5]	Total	Management, business, science, and arts	Construction, production, and maintenance occupations
	89	90	91	92	93	94	95	96	97	98	99	100	101	102	103
MARYLAND— Cont'd															
St. Mary's	41,280	70.3	318,500	20.3	10.0	1,436	26.5	1.9	57,574	-1.6	2,579	4.5	55,942	46.2	21.4
Somerset	8,509	65.9	131,500	21.3	13.7	766	37.2	2.9	8,824	1.1	670	7.6	9,395	29.8	22.0
Talbot	16,810	71.2	334,000	23.1	11.7	1,122	29.5	1.8	17,647	-1.9	929	5.3	17,311	44.9	18.0
Washington	56,367	66.6	221,700	20.1	10.1	931	28.4	1.6	72,458	-0.8	3,884	5.4	68,853	35.6	24.4
Wicomico	38,142	58.7	185,000	19.7	11.2	1,059	29.8	2.4	49,998	0.3	3,066	6.1	49,592	34.0	22.1
Worcester	22,661	75.7	267,400	22.9	12.6	1,020	31.6	2.4	24,913	-1.8	2,052	8.2	24,238	36.8	16.8
Baltimore city	242,499	47.7	167,300	21.7	13.1	1,094	30.2	2.3	277,525	-1.7	21,223	7.6	281,905	44.3	16.5
MASSACHUSETTS	2,646,980	62.5	398,800	22.2	13.7	1,336	29.6	2.3	3,750,870	0.2	215,392	5.7	3,615,725	48.0	15.9
Barnstable	95,859	79.6	414,000	24.8	13.6	1,362	32.8	1.4	112,478	1.8	7,553	6.7	105,798	40.6	18.0
Berkshire	54,786	70.0	221,000	21.7	13.6	894	29.9	0.6	62,666	0.5	4,175	6.7	62,805	41.6	19.0
Bristol	220,365	62.8	317,800	21.8	13.8	934	28.7	1.8	299,547	-0.1	19,607	6.5	283,747	38.1	22.4
Dukes	6,887	72.5	794,000	34.0	17.2	1,589	35.0	2.6	9,640	1.0	630	6.5	8,902	42.8	23.4
Essex	297,254	63.8	436,600	22.9	14.2	1,298	32.1	3.3	423,777	-0.1	27,018	6.4	409,549	43.6	18.2
Franklin	30,790	69.0	239,900	23.5	14.2	959	30.9	1.4	40,785	1.4	2,028	5.0	36,423	42.8	21.2
Hampden	180,492	61.6	216,100	21.7	14.3	920	31.5	2.2	227,099	0.5	17,157	7.6	215,515	36.7	21.7
Hampshire	59,607	67.9	289,300	22.1	12.7	1,095	31.7	1.2	89,375	1.1	4,169	4.7	83,877	48.4	15.1
Middlesex	611,850	62.1	540,300	21.7	13.5	1,714	27.8	2.1	906,656	0.6	41,897	4.6	888,786	58.2	11.6
Nantucket	3,709	69.1	1,117,300	29.7	13.3	1,781	27.6	1.3	7,733	1.5	595	7.7	6,419	35.3	30.6
Norfolk	267,967	68.8	491,000	22.2	13.7	1,682	29.5	2.1	390,570	0.1	20,099	5.1	376,643	55.5	11.5
Plymouth	190,355	77.2	386,600	23.2	14.4	1,324	30.7	1.6	283,684	0.0	17,400	6.1	269,959	41.5	19.0
Suffolk	312,978	36.3	547,300	22.6	12.2	1,657	29.8	4.1	453,174	-0.7	26,998	6.0	442,673	49.3	11.9
Worcester	314,081	65.7	295,300	21.4	13.9	1,074	29.1	2.0	443,682	0.4	26,065	5.9	424,629	43.1	19.4
MICHIGAN	3,980,408	71.7	162,600	19.2	11.8	892	29.3	1.9	4,776,110	-1.4	280,459	5.9	4,658,357	37.6	24.4
Alcona	5,115	88.2	118,700	21.2	12.2	643	31.5	1.0	3,725	-3.0	263	7.1	3,499	28.4	30.0
Alger	3,246	80.4	141,900	24.4	12.2	631	29.4	2.7	3,089	-1.0	248	8.0	2,999	28.2	27.2
Allegan	43,927	84.4	174,000	19.6	11.2	838	27.5	2.5	60,557	-2.3	2,822	4.7	55,405	31.6	34.7
Alpena	12,769	78.4	104,900	19.4	11.1	580	28.4	0.7	13,183	-0.2	725	5.5	12,246	31.6	26.5
Antrim	10,166	87.6	161,700	21.4	11.4	761	27.6	1.8	9,865	-2.4	693	7.0	10,338	29.2	29.2
Arenac	6,585	84.8	98,600	21.4	11.9	550	25.9	1.0	5,709	-3.9	475	8.3	6,045	24.4	35.7
Baraga	3,188	78.6	108,200	18.3	12.5	556	23.1	2.4	3,006	-4.5	237	7.9	3,008	29.0	27.5
Barry	24,342	84.0	171,800	19.6	11.2	909	26.4	1.9	30,851	-1.7	1,408	4.6	28,707	31.7	33.9
Bay	44,627	76.1	106,400	19.5	12.1	679	27.8	1.3	47,921	-2.9	2,918	6.1	46,970	31.3	26.8
Benzie	6,940	90.9	195,400	20.3	11.5	803	30.1	1.6	8,453	-2.4	504	6.0	8,028	35.2	24.4
Berrien	63,136	71.2	157,500	19.6	10.9	757	29.6	1.7	69,898	-3.5	4,055	5.8	71,218	35.2	25.8
Branch	16,716	75.8	118,200	19.6	12.2	746	25.5	2.9	19,085	-2.9	945	5.0	18,480	24.2	40.0
Calhoun	54,124	69.5	115,500	18.8	12.0	776	29.5	1.6	59,357	-3.9	3,898	6.6	59,819	31.1	30.3
Cass	21,226	81.3	155,600	18.7	11.0	724	27.9	2.5	23,154	-4.9	1,174	5.1	23,914	31.7	35.9
Charlevoix	11,725	81.7	171,100	19.7	10.8	782	29.0	1.7	12,219	-2.3	735	6.0	12,434	34.0	26.7
Cheboygan	11,219	84.0	141,800	20.9	11.5	732	28.2	2.0	9,941	-3.6	828	8.3	10,318	26.8	29.8
Chippewa	14,323	69.9	121,600	18.1	10.0	700	27.8	1.7	15,786	-0.7	1,032	6.5	16,049	29.6	21.9
Clare	12,247	83.6	91,900	21.0	11.9	660	34.0	2.6	11,148	-4.7	897	8.0	11,037	28.2	32.1
Clinton	30,182	82.1	185,500	18.6	11.3	846	26.5	1.2	38,904	-3.2	1,725	4.4	39,086	41.4	21.3
Crawford	6,155	81.5	111,800	19.2	12.3	752	30.5	2.8	5,359	-4.1	378	7.1	5,461	30.0	27.0
Delta	16,154	77.6	115,400	19.0	11.1	548	26.2	1.9	16,243	-3.4	999	6.2	14,882	27.1	33.4
Dickinson	11,491	79.4	109,300	16.5	11.3	653	29.9	1.8	12,132	0.1	580	4.8	11,569	33.9	28.0
Eaton	45,037	72.6	160,000	18.4	10.9	888	24.9	1.7	54,084	-3.6	2,873	5.3	54,085	36.7	26.3
Emmet	14,197	74.2	206,900	20.8	11.6	829	26.4	1.3	16,348	-4.7	1,043	6.4	16,426	34.9	20.9
Genesee	170,581	70.0	119,500	19.8	12.7	781	30.9	1.6	174,492	-2.8	13,251	7.6	171,063	33.0	26.8
Gladwin	11,181	86.4	111,000	20.1	12.3	593	28.2	3.5	9,595	-2.4	677	7.1	8,972	27.8	36.4
Gogebic	6,896	77.6	73,500	17.4	13.2	476	26.6	0.3	5,582	-4.0	309	5.5	6,083	29.7	31.3
Grand Traverse	37,939	76.5	225,400	19.7	10.0	965	31.1	1.7	47,928	-2.2	2,410	5.0	47,221	39.5	20.3
Gratiot	15,084	75.9	97,600	18.6	12.0	688	29.2	1.0	17,041	-4.2	947	5.6	16,562	30.5	27.6
Hillsdale	18,180	77.4	131,800	19.1	11.5	704	26.5	3.6	19,704	-1.9	1,074	5.5	19,511	30.3	35.0
Houghton	13,805	66.7	113,700	18.3	10.5	639	33.4	2.3	15,678	-1.3	790	5.0	15,222	39.7	19.2
Huron	13,908	80.5	109,000	19.0	11.7	637	26.3	1.3	14,854	-3.6	796	5.4	13,669	29.3	34.2
Ingham	113,678	58.8	143,900	18.9	11.9	906	30.4	1.9	141,678	-3.2	7,915	5.6	144,573	41.3	17.8
Ionia	23,071	76.4	140,800	19.2	11.0	781	24.7	1.7	29,513	-2.0	1,408	4.8	29,585	27.4	36.3
Iosco	11,772	80.8	98,200	19.7	11.6	650	25.6	1.6	9,819	-2.8	709	7.2	9,275	25.2	34.4
Iron	5,150	82.6	79,500	20.6	11.6	562	27.6	1.5	4,742	-3.8	288	6.1	4,317	26.4	30.3
Isabella	24,981	62.8	136,900	19.9	11.3	737	33.3	1.5	31,774	-3.6	1,676	5.3	33,763	31.1	22.3
Jackson	62,216	74.3	138,900	19.8	10.7	800	28.8	1.5	71,993	-3.1	4,130	5.7	69,089	33.3	27.6
Kalamazoo	104,278	64.5	168,500	18.5	11.3	846	28.9	1.5	128,630	-2.3	6,441	5.0	132,109	40.9	20.5
Kalkaska	7,173	85.0	127,600	20.6	11.2	690	29.1	2.5	7,632	-3.0	554	7.3	7,387	23.1	33.7
Kent	244,795	70.4	188,500	18.4	10.0	928	29.0	2.3	349,167	-1.8	16,429	4.7	336,145	38.7	24.3

1. Specified owner-occupied units. 2. A value of 10.0 represents 10 percent or less; a value of 50.0 represents 50 percent or more. 3. Specified renter-occupied units. 4. Overcrowded or lacking complete plumbing facilities. 5. Percent of civilian labor force. 6. Civilian employed persons 16 years old and over.

STATE County	Private nonfarm establishments, employment and payroll, 2020									Agriculture, 2017			
		Employment						Annual payroll		Farms			Farm producers whose primary occupation is farming (percent)
											Percent with:		
	Number of establish-ments	Total	Health care and social assistance	Manufac-turing	Retail trade	Finance and insurance	Professional, scientific, and technical services	Total (mil dol)	Average per employee (dollars)	Number	Fewer than 50 acres	1000 acres or more	
	104	105	106	107	108	109	110	111	112	113	114	115	116
MARYLAND— Cont'd													
St. Mary's	2,006	34,465	4,638	504	5,003	460	11,543	1,956	56,764	615	57.2	1.5	43.7
Somerset	349	4,118	1,404	435	462	79	87	156	37,833	255	42.4	3.9	56.2
Talbot	1,448	17,117	3,789	644	2,524	626	1,128	751	43,887	317	44.5	10.4	43.7
Washington	3,442	61,034	10,683	6,757	9,677	4,906	1,678	2,598	42,568	877	50.3	1.1	45.1
Wicomico	2,450	35,493	8,692	2,121	6,317	993	1,252	1,523	42,896	494	53.0	4.9	48.6
Worcester	2,143	19,815	2,599	541	3,614	625	680	698	35,244	369	49.3	7.9	45.9
Baltimore city	12,261	302,260	78,485	11,328	21,064	16,417	21,729	19,698	65,169	NA	NA	NA	NA
MASSACHUSETTS	179,456	3,390,833	624,149	234,714	364,738	185,235	326,716	242,545	71,530	7,241	67.8	0.3	42.8
Barnstable	8,560	76,154	15,945	2,075	15,051	1,961	4,747	3,652	47,961	321	93.5	0.0	46.5
Berkshire	3,728	51,747	11,593	4,837	7,836	1,676	2,755	2,419	46,752	475	50.9	1.3	42.6
Bristol	12,817	205,568	42,575	27,285	33,883	4,301	5,535	10,106	49,160	688	75.9	NA	50.7
Dukes	1,124	5,529	867	121	937	207	225	352	63,603	108	90.7	0.9	45.5
Essex	19,208	298,034	66,264	44,453	38,994	10,685	14,776	16,680	55,967	419	78.0	0.5	46.9
Franklin	1,540	19,892	3,655	4,149	2,799	454	590	853	42,877	830	46.7	0.5	41.6
Hampden	9,367	174,790	44,190	18,538	21,048	8,724	6,781	8,250	47,197	523	64.1	0.4	37.0
Hampshire	3,483	50,373	10,436	2,953	7,595	1,494	1,679	2,031	40,325	692	59.2	NA	41.2
Middlesex	44,475	935,073	121,932	58,685	83,356	29,773	140,919	80,800	86,410	620	73.9	NA	41.3
Nantucket	1,153	4,862	560	69	905	89	227	357	73,515	21	90.5	NA	59.7
Norfolk	20,191	337,184	53,941	18,309	44,116	24,878	21,763	21,635	64,164	197	81.2	0.5	41.0
Plymouth	12,780	176,822	36,545	9,920	28,769	7,783	12,456	8,621	48,758	758	74.8	0.8	47.4
Suffolk	21,943	672,796	143,725	8,905	40,185	73,430	88,113	64,956	96,546	21	100.0	NA	43.8
Worcester	18,347	315,898	68,127	34,415	39,127	14,702	20,958	16,752	53,030	1,568	67.7	0.1	38.6
MICHIGAN	221,060	4,000,120	645,908	598,098	466,976	178,883	293,997	201,871	50,466	47,641	46.3	4.5	43.1
Alcona	187	1,116	176	150	327	33	29	36	32,027	223	37.7	1.3	51.4
Alger	233	1,840	218	433	269	55	21	73	39,574	126	48.4	4.8	39.4
Allegan	2,437	40,983	2,987	14,617	3,984	402	1,816	1,947	47,503	1,172	52.2	5.0	43.9
Alpena	795	9,832	2,787	1,328	1,784	291	260	375	38,153	415	38.6	2.4	38.1
Antrim	548	4,454	359	1,429	530	110	102	150	33,644	333	37.8	2.4	47.4
Arenac	318	3,433	559	978	487	77	150	137	39,911	350	34.0	5.7	36.7
Baraga	173	1,884	295	685	257	38	16	73	38,882	65	29.2	7.7	40.8
Barry	910	10,899	1,199	3,667	1,143	700	306	444	40,705	938	48.8	4.1	34.2
Bay	2,040	29,293	6,412	4,323	5,065	863	1,176	1,240	42,330	726	36.8	8.8	48.8
Benzie	455	3,496	377	501	526	160	53	120	34,377	197	59.9	0.5	38.7
Berrien	3,453	52,675	9,394	9,099	6,921	1,264	2,590	2,593	49,226	872	57.8	3.3	48.8
Branch	797	11,602	1,448	2,494	1,702	414	700	482	41,536	789	38.7	7.5	39.9
Calhoun	2,409	50,383	9,313	13,446	5,918	1,027	1,822	2,580	51,199	958	42.6	5.8	44.2
Cass	742	8,118	964	2,867	815	191	250	313	38,616	747	51.1	5.2	43.1
Charlevoix	802	8,094	1,263	1,970	858	180	225	350	43,241	271	45.8	1.1	39.0
Cheboygan	735	4,333	704	294	1,051	192	98	164	37,934	330	37.0	0.9	32.3
Chippewa	765	8,374	2,055	555	1,570	278	280	267	31,844	427	26.7	3.5	36.1
Clare	571	6,100	1,172	1,113	1,068	114	181	240	39,322	396	40.9	2.3	48.5
Clinton	1,336	16,613	1,953	2,345	2,239	1,129	1,023	698	42,045	1,017	46.7	5.9	41.5
Crawford	295	3,257	1,001	566	538	44	73	129	39,741	45	62.2	NA	19.2
Delta	978	11,712	1,870	2,158	2,092	659	386	431	36,767	253	29.2	5.5	41.6
Dickinson	802	12,003	2,389	2,180	1,554	311	511	610	50,789	158	32.9	1.3	34.9
Eaton	2,139	41,332	3,753	7,760	5,816	4,219	1,073	1,934	46,782	962	41.6	5.0	42.2
Emmet	1,534	15,683	3,188	1,416	2,737	335	495	646	41,194	324	43.8	0.9	33.5
Genesee	7,528	119,084	26,264	11,698	18,665	3,892	4,010	5,138	43,144	820	59.4	3.4	46.2
Gladwin	405	4,111	784	1,041	573	94	74	152	36,926	459	37.5	1.5	39.6
Gogebic	349	3,832	567	675	664	93	104	121	31,503	54	51.9	1.9	18.8
Grand Traverse	3,395	46,560	9,718	5,475	7,927	2,530	1,905	2,088	44,853	497	57.3	0.8	38.4
Gratiot	713	11,105	2,397	2,566	1,359	339	288	442	39,787	812	38.3	9.7	49.8
Hillsdale	746	10,469	1,491	3,652	1,337	278	196	401	38,274	1,205	44.3	5.8	40.8
Houghton	866	9,076	1,892	838	1,637	436	519	324	35,647	208	36.5	0.5	38.7
Huron	902	10,716	1,825	3,522	1,357	374	219	418	39,015	1,153	29.7	14.0	52.0
Ingham	6,092	113,825	23,254	8,119	13,413	9,636	6,820	5,446	47,846	912	60.2	4.4	39.6
Ionia	859	11,416	1,161	4,038	1,704	559	164	455	39,815	954	44.3	5.6	46.3
Iosco	600	6,210	899	1,049	1,196	240	170	269	43,272	244	42.2	0.8	37.0
Iron	343	2,540	344	385	469	123	91	88	34,630	133	32.3	2.3	49.0
Isabella	1,343	25,057	2,947	2,786	3,312	497	619	941	37,543	959	36.9	3.6	42.1
Jackson	2,994	52,350	10,880	9,595	7,106	1,665	2,749	2,559	48,881	923	52.1	3.9	41.5
Kalamazoo	5,574	111,428	20,231	17,730	14,130	4,872	4,483	5,520	49,541	707	61.8	5.1	43.2
Kalkaska	330	3,774	655	384	584	65	41	201	53,326	225	39.1	1.3	35.5
Kent	16,961	375,791	54,516	69,635	37,051	16,035	16,949	18,778	49,970	1,010	54.1	3.5	43.1

STATE County	Agriculture, 2017 (cont.)															
	Land in farms					Value of land and buildings (dollars)		Value of machinery and equipment, average per farm (dollars)	Value of products sold:				Organic farms (number)	Farms with internet access (percent)	Government payments	
	Acreage (1,000)	Percent change, 2012–2017	Acres: Average size of farm	Acres: Total irrigated (1,000)	Acres: Total cropland (1,000)	Average per farm	Average per acre		Total (mil dol)	Average per farm (acres)	Percent from: Crops	Percent from: Livestock and poultry products			Total ($1,000)	Percent of farms
	117	118	119	120	121	122	123	124	125	126	127	128	129	130	131	132
MARYLAND— Cont'd																
St. Mary's	62	-7.9	100	0.7	37.0	999,805	9,949	75,425	26.0	42,203	78.8	21.2	2	58.0	970	19.5
Somerset	59	-8.9	233	0.3	38.0	1,334,676	5,726	173,390	262.2	1,028,239	8.4	91.6	2	76.9	1,875	51.8
Talbot	94	-21.6	295	8.3	81.1	2,075,678	7,028	158,736	68.5	216,199	63.0	37.0	3	80.4	3,891	58.4
Washington	119	-8.0	136	0.6	82.2	1,095,597	8,057	121,316	153.7	175,285	24.8	75.2	12	69.1	995	17.8
Wicomico	89	5.8	179	11.0	65.6	1,261,012	7,034	158,378	304.0	615,350	22.5	77.5	3	75.3	2,410	44.1
Worcester	99	-0.1	269	5.9	71.6	1,425,500	5,300	184,865	249.1	675,154	15.1	84.9	1	72.1	3,630	51.8
Baltimore city	NA	NA	NA	NA	NA	NA	NA	NA	NA	NA	NA	NA	NA	NA	NA	NA
MASSACHUSETTS	492	-6.1	68	23.9	171.5	739,711	10,894	65,382	475.2	65,624	76.5	23.5	208	84.1	4,004	7.3
Barnstable	7	40.4	20	1.1	1.6	624,807	30,555	60,762	23.1	72,019	40.4	59.6	11	90.0	197	4.7
Berkshire	59	-4.9	123	0.3	19.1	943,835	7,644	72,649	23.5	49,453	42.8	57.2	16	85.5	447	7.8
Bristol	32	-8.2	47	2.0	13.0	846,518	18,186	68,617	35.0	50,901	79.0	21.0	18	75.3	429	12.6
Dukes	8	-39.3	71	0.3	0.8	816,456	11,429	88,694	5.4	49,917	61.5	38.5	5	91.7	NA	NA
Essex	21	-7.5	49	1.3	11.0	863,169	17,450	69,643	32.9	78,439	86.6	13.4	6	89.7	54	2.1
Franklin	88	-1.7	106	1.8	24.6	682,435	6,419	67,251	68.9	83,000	73.0	27.0	32	84.3	476	8.6
Hampden	36	-7.0	69	1.0	12.0	711,793	10,343	55,643	25.9	49,507	83.3	16.7	7	79.3	362	6.3
Hampshire	51	-6.1	73	0.8	20.2	560,780	7,662	75,215	46.0	66,512	76.8	23.2	28	85.7	473	9.0
Middlesex	27	-3.2	44	1.2	13.0	702,873	15,944	61,303	63.4	102,177	88.1	11.9	26	84.5	172	4.8
Nantucket	1	-37.6	37	0.3	0.5	1,432,672	39,124	53,243	D	D	D	D	2	42.9	NA	NA
Norfolk	8	-19.3	39	0.5	3.1	663,973	17,150	57,310	D	D	D	D	6	85.8	64	5.1
Plymouth	60	-6.2	79	11.9	18.2	758,347	9,575	73,670	71.9	94,900	86.4	13.6	20	89.3	316	5.7
Suffolk	0	-12.5	1	0.0	0.0	229,899	229,899	12,756	0.5	24,810	96.7	3.3	5	95.2	NA	NA
Worcester	95	-6.4	61	1.5	34.5	747,474	12,297	57,372	65.2	41,579	70.9	29.1	26	82.7	1,015	8.4
MICHIGAN	9,764	-1.9	205	670.2	7,924.5	1,015,631	4,955	154,740	8,220.9	172,560	56.5	43.5	764	77.2	167,189	32.2
Alcona	36	-4.9	163	0.1	24.1	423,042	2,590	106,156	11.5	51,543	43.6	56.4	8	65.9	268	21.5
Alger	21	17.9	166	0.0	9.9	339,285	2,040	69,429	4.2	33,532	29.9	70.1	3	81.0	12	6.3
Allegan	230	-15.0	196	24.8	196.9	1,172,374	5,981	223,117	584.4	498,612	30.2	69.8	12	80.5	4,521	24.2
Alpena	65	-5.6	158	0.0	42.2	401,054	2,545	95,421	25.9	62,400	29.5	70.5	8	74.9	861	23.1
Antrim	56	-13.4	167	4.0	34.2	701,340	4,203	107,992	35.5	106,520	81.7	18.3	9	73.3	226	14.7
Arenac	87	6.7	249	0.2	73.0	835,592	3,355	186,941	43.0	122,860	67.5	32.5	12	74.3	2,256	71.4
Baraga	18	-0.7	271	0.0	9.5	592,800	2,189	89,014	2.2	34,000	58.4	41.6	3	67.7	7	26.2
Barry	155	-6.4	165	4.9	119.2	791,437	4,801	119,827	139.7	148,915	30.9	69.1	6	82.2	2,959	28.1
Bay	210	8.3	289	5.2	197.1	1,460,329	5,052	242,520	116.5	160,519	88.3	11.7	NA	69.3	4,501	67.8
Benzie	19	-10.3	94	0.7	8.7	372,275	3,961	66,072	10.0	50,898	78.5	21.5	2	84.8	189	12.2
Berrien	145	-7.6	166	20.0	123.5	1,068,559	6,445	142,166	171.3	196,501	91.4	8.6	15	76.4	2,594	20.6
Branch	239	-2.0	303	55.7	204.3	1,285,432	4,236	207,759	162.3	205,697	65.9	34.1	6	73.9	5,703	45.5
Calhoun	214	-4.9	223	13.3	174.6	1,185,546	5,309	139,254	113.9	118,861	61.1	38.9	20	71.5	4,522	36.7
Cass	199	5.2	266	71.2	163.7	1,228,314	4,622	191,044	153.4	205,339	65.1	34.9	10	79.8	4,103	42.6
Charlevoix	30	-20.2	110	0.1	14.1	416,535	3,770	59,479	8.4	31,052	59.3	40.7	6	69.0	104	11.8
Cheboygan	44	-3.4	133	D	22.1	341,794	2,562	72,788	7.1	21,655	58.8	41.2	7	69.1	112	10.9
Chippewa	89	-4.3	209	0.0	53.2	451,403	2,164	75,495	10.7	25,000	37.7	62.3	1	79.9	447	23.7
Clare	55	-12.6	138	D	30.4	415,261	3,011	76,135	22.1	55,705	21.9	78.1	13	56.6	384	21.7
Clinton	230	-5.8	226	2.6	200.9	1,277,549	5,655	194,330	224.3	220,535	32.2	67.8	20	80.3	4,392	41.7
Crawford	3	6.8	65	NA	0.3	228,867	3,502	36,385	0.2	4,778	10.2	89.8	NA	71.1	NA	NA
Delta	59	-17.0	232	0.8	29.0	414,631	1,785	89,494	10.8	42,688	59.9	40.1	4	75.5	133	24.1
Dickinson	22	-23.0	140	0.3	8.7	380,435	2,727	84,219	4.4	27,671	54.4	45.6	NA	77.8	33	11.4
Eaton	210	-5.9	218	0.7	177.1	912,095	4,176	132,342	83.3	86,595	89.3	10.7	20	74.1	4,192	37.6
Emmet	39	-1.4	121	0.3	20.5	456,379	3,767	63,450	8.7	26,895	70.3	29.7	15	78.1	97	12.7
Genesee	124	0.5	151	1.5	104.3	795,230	5,262	103,908	70.4	85,871	86.5	13.5	11	84.8	2,561	25.0
Gladwin	59	-12.8	128	0.1	36.5	498,882	3,909	74,943	15.8	34,333	56.1	43.9	3	63.6	680	34.6
Gogebic	6	-8.9	103	D	1.8	266,642	2,601	41,304	0.7	13,833	29.0	71.0	NA	83.3	D	1.9
Grand Traverse	51	-6.7	102	2.8	36.1	651,401	6,362	85,866	34.1	68,610	83.2	16.8	3	81.7	501	17.3
Gratiot	297	2.5	365	15.9	272.4	1,984,846	5,432	280,110	281.4	346,607	43.3	56.7	13	80.9	5,365	60.7
Hillsdale	254	-3.1	211	8.8	212.3	909,201	4,309	149,441	165.1	137,021	51.4	48.6	18	73.0	7,375	50.0
Houghton	26	-4.3	125	0.0	13.4	294,396	2,354	49,491	6.3	30,322	36.3	63.7	4	70.2	52	13.0
Huron	495	9.5	430	3.1	458.8	2,597,983	6,048	360,764	610.8	529,729	43.1	56.9	20	76.6	12,201	75.5
Ingham	178	-11.2	195	1.8	152.2	1,040,491	5,325	143,901	113.8	124,780	64.1	35.9	12	85.1	3,921	19.7
Ionia	234	-5.8	245	5.1	200.1	1,215,280	4,955	206,048	382.9	401,410	21.9	78.1	15	79.5	5,053	45.5
Iosco	34	-11.0	139	0.2	22.9	437,110	3,153	103,020	14.9	61,037	27.3	72.7	6	69.7	503	33.2
Iron	23	2.2	176	0.5	10.6	348,316	1,976	64,714	3.7	27,564	88.6	11.4	NA	74.4	38	7.5
Isabella	212	12.4	221	2.9	174.2	905,013	4,099	156,666	116.8	121,844	52.8	47.2	27	75.2	3,450	41.8
Jackson	160	-12.4	174	4.7	125.8	866,522	4,986	116,065	70.8	76,714	61.6	38.4	6	78.2	3,526	25.9
Kalamazoo	139	-3.5	196	43.0	111.8	1,382,696	7,055	206,186	236.9	335,109	74.5	25.5	2	83.7	2,664	21.6
Kalkaska	27	5.1	121	1.6	16.3	320,046	2,654	88,846	8.3	37,000	92.3	7.7	4	83.1	170	20.0
Kent	157	0.0	156	15.3	124.8	1,150,595	7,380	134,311	262.8	260,213	77.0	23.0	12	85.0	2,199	18.7

STATE County	Water use, 2015		Wholesale Trade[1], 2017				Retail Trade[2], 2017				Real estate and rental and leasing,[2] 2017			
	Public supply water withdrawn (mil gal/ day)	Public supply gallons withdrawn per person per day	Number of establish- ments	Number of employees	Sales (mil dol)	Average payroll (mil dol)	Number of establish- ments	Number of employees	Sales (mil dol)	Average payroll (mil dol)	Number of establish- ments	Number of employees	Sales (mil dol)	Average payroll (mil dol)
	133	134	135	136	137	138	139	140	141	142	143	144	145	146
MARYLAND— Cont'd														
St. Mary's	4.2	37.2	37	D	131.0	D	306	4,740	1,370.3	125.0	88	274	95.6	11.5
Somerset	1.1	42.3	D	D	D	D	56	482	121.9	10.5	15	31	2.9	0.7
Talbot	2.2	59.7	52	458	302.9	25.1	216	2,750	716.7	66.9	69	199	51.1	8.3
Washington	17.3	115.5	136	2,065	2,279.7	109.1	602	10,208	2,618.6	239.0	146	893	210.4	33.6
Wicomico	6.9	67.0	102	1,051	1,110.8	49.6	362	6,450	1,794.3	160.1	130	649	113.6	23.4
Worcester	7.7	149.0	D	D	D	9.5	387	3,747	897.9	93.3	166	540	105.6	18.8
Baltimore city	0.0	0.0	508	7,678	9,253.2	509.0	1,912	21,064	7,175.3	600.3	748	5,107	1,607.3	314.5
MASSACHUSETTS	648.1	95.4	6,324	120,957	137,010.9	10,129.9	23,928	364,204	110,194.5	10,911.5	7,584	52,315	17,912.1	3,369.5
Barnstable	31.8	148.6	D	D	D	D	1,450	16,168	4,537.5	500.4	386	1,533	361.5	66.0
Berkshire	14.3	112.1	98	1,276	491.8	66.1	653	8,151	2,049.7	221.0	116	496	92.7	18.7
Bristol	26.6	47.8	510	12,278	13,332.2	790.1	2,101	33,691	9,616.4	943.3	453	2,126	439.7	75.9
Dukes	3.1	177.5	D	D	D	D	203	1,258	430.4	56.3	73	193	54.5	10.1
Essex	77.2	99.4	677	10,236	16,291.1	882.6	2,642	39,713	11,318.8	1,173.2	689	2,962	784.5	147.4
Franklin	3.7	52.8	D	D	D	D	252	2,860	741.9	81.4	39	101	28.8	3.0
Hampden	45.4	96.4	358	6,524	5,771.8	389.8	1,552	22,417	6,014.7	612.5	400	2,699	561.2	104.6
Hampshire	18.1	112.2	92	1,598	3,281.8	84.5	493	7,543	1,877.8	206.5	117	432	95.8	15.8
Middlesex	70.3	44.3	1,694	38,971	49,659.9	3,834.7	5,044	81,645	24,988.1	2,509.4	1,845	14,522	6,350.3	977.6
Nantucket	2.0	183.1	D	D	D	D	161	1,034	379.5	49.2	66	148	74.9	10.2
Norfolk	35.9	51.6	834	15,675	16,604.8	1,118.6	2,512	45,268	13,773.2	1,385.8	937	7,751	2,323.8	547.2
Plymouth	68.1	133.4	466	6,905	8,658.6	509.7	1,883	28,193	8,039.7	842.9	439	1,643	453.5	87.2
Suffolk	0.0	0.0	623	13,681	13,536.5	1,594.5	2,456	36,618	13,173.4	1,208.1	1,337	14,358	5,477.9	1,139.2
Worcester	251.6	307.3	740	11,938	8,117.7	739.2	2,526	39,645	13,253.5	1,121.5	687	3,351	813.0	166.6
MICHIGAN	1,030.4	103.8	9,173	147,939	138,545.8	9,136.3	34,201	469,987	143,437.1	12,481.8	8,467	54,808	17,782.6	2,374.4
Alcona	0.1	5.8	NA	NA	NA	NA	32	291	62.9	6.8	D	D	D	0.2
Alger	0.4	43.7	NA	NA	NA	NA	45	269	65.4	6.4	D	D	D	D
Allegan	4.0	35.2	D	D	D	D	349	3,848	1,324.8	108.4	70	233	43.3	10.4
Alpena	2.0	70.1	29	524	310.1	26.2	140	1,887	498.9	49.3	21	124	9.8	2.6
Antrim	1.2	51.4	9	41	22.7	1.9	93	684	188.9	16.7	21	60	7.7	1.4
Arenac	42.2	2,762.6	D	D	D	5.2	67	473	192.0	12.0	D	D	D	D
Baraga	0.5	59.5	NA	NA	NA	NA	29	288	50.7	6.7	3	6	0.4	0.1
Barry	1.6	26.5	36	256	178.8	12.4	125	1,309	326.5	30.5	26	107	15.1	4.2
Bay	9.0	84.9	80	1,168	691.9	50.3	385	5,258	1,465.6	139.5	60	182	26.3	4.4
Benzie	0.7	39.0	D	D	D	D	71	520	142.2	13.6	20	32	5.1	1.0
Berrien	12.4	80.3	D	D	D	78.1	553	7,053	1,781.5	171.4	156	656	277.4	23.3
Branch	2.8	63.4	27	381	172.8	17.3	143	1,656	508.9	45.2	32	71	14.8	2.1
Calhoun	12.5	93.3	83	808	1,385.5	43.5	467	6,105	1,855.4	157.7	82	387	59.1	12.5
Cass	1.2	22.3	31	240	210.2	14.0	121	871	289.7	22.5	29	53	13.7	1.9
Charlevoix	2.7	101.4	12	53	11.5	1.9	121	892	258.0	24.8	30	156	26.1	6.9
Cheboygan	1.0	38.5	D	D	D	3.1	129	1,206	337.3	31.7	D	D	D	3.2
Chippewa	2.7	70.7	27	311	89.6	10.7	144	1,641	494.1	42.8	25	80	12.5	2.1
Clare	1.1	36.7	D	D	D	7.8	114	1,091	306.9	28.2	D	D	D	0.6
Clinton	1.2	15.0	52	1,007	1,281.3	53.0	173	2,430	912.3	65.0	67	327	63.2	12.7
Crawford	0.7	47.8	5	41	21.5	1.9	45	543	182.9	13.4	15	29	5.2	1.2
Delta	2.8	77.2	42	395	216.2	15.7	170	2,073	555.8	51.7	29	56	7.5	1.3
Dickinson	2.4	91.1	D	D	D	D	137	1,725	440.9	42.3	28	89	13.6	2.2
Eaton	2.6	24.2	64	1,528	1,125.3	65.9	334	5,796	1,727.4	143.8	95	416	110.7	17.8
Emmet	3.8	115.8	32	268	140.3	12.9	280	2,837	792.1	79.0	50	210	35.7	5.8
Genesee	4.2	10.3	269	4,989	3,403.5	270.6	1,355	19,591	8,429.7	497.7	328	2,107	338.1	73.5
Gladwin	0.5	17.9	11	47	14.7	1.9	89	677	174.2	17.2	16	98	9.6	3.5
Gogebic	1.5	95.9	13	63	58.8	2.5	64	735	164.2	16.2	D	D	D	D
Grand Traverse	7.3	80.0	127	1,249	601.9	64.1	572	8,460	2,311.7	240.9	163	591	121.8	21.6
Gratiot	1.6	38.5	D	D	D	D	128	1,419	407.0	34.2	19	53	7.1	1.4
Hillsdale	2.0	43.8	30	253	252.9	12.2	124	1,497	415.7	37.6	21	33	7.3	0.9
Houghton	3.9	106.4	D	D	D	D	138	1,729	390.1	38.7	D	D	D	D
Huron	2.6	80.9	34	398	398.4	21.6	157	1,483	398.8	36.1	15	24	4.1	0.6
Ingham	26.1	91.2	208	2,957	8,573.0	157.5	923	13,908	3,576.0	340.5	265	2,133	292.7	92.0
Ionia	5.0	77.7	23	259	160.4	11.7	148	1,903	528.3	43.5	23	58	7.1	1.5
Iosco	1.2	47.3	D	D	D	0.3	111	1,296	334.9	33.1	22	59	7.6	1.8
Iron	1.3	111.0	9	111	18.3	2.1	55	588	107.6	13.0	20	47	4.2	0.8
Isabella	3.0	42.6	49	556	289.0	23.5	211	3,491	910.6	85.8	63	1,160	99.3	32.3
Jackson	10.8	68.0	128	1,327	1,023.5	78.3	497	7,174	2,031.9	187.5	109	573	104.9	19.7
Kalamazoo	24.4	93.6	243	4,193	2,158.4	235.8	876	13,882	3,706.7	350.7	224	2,412	297.0	86.6
Kalkaska	0.4	23.8	16	192	187.6	12.7	59	648	186.6	15.7	8	94	20.5	5.8
Kent	9.0	14.2	983	24,306	19,309.7	1,429.8	2,214	35,681	11,021.5	981.6	688	4,153	967.0	183.1

1 Merchant wholesalers, except manufacturers' sales branches and offices. 2. Employer establishments.

STATE County	Professional, scientific, and technical services, 2017				Manufacturing, 2017				Accommodation and food services, 2017			
	Number of establish-ments	Number of employees	Sales (mil dol)	Average payroll (mil dol)	Number of establish-ments	Number of employees	Sales (mil dol)	Average payroll (mil dol)	Number of establis-hments	Number of employees	Sales (mil dol)	Annual payroll (mil dol)
	147	148	149	150	151	152	153	154	155	156	157	158
MARYLAND— Cont'd												
St. Mary's	D	D	D	D	27	409	117.5	24.1	190	3,797	215.6	60.3
Somerset	19	112	12.6	4.9	14	358	204.9	15.9	29	401	19.5	5.1
Talbot	141	1,128	211.6	66.1	35	671	164.5	34.2	143	2,652	158.4	49.5
Washington	D	D	D	D	131	5,748	3,910.0	346.6	319	5,807	314.0	90.2
Wicomico	D	D	D	D	71	2,662	1,085.1	144.0	212	4,168	215.5	58.6
Worcester	150	708	87.3	34.7	39	622	259.9	30.2	455	6,205	680.5	196.8
Baltimore city	1,663	24,412	5,489.4	2,262.5	395	11,536	5,482.7	634.0	1,542	25,190	1,980.5	550.7
MASSACHUSETTS	21,741	297,565	75,346.9	31,147.6	6,437	231,593	82308.5	15749.4	17,773	311,058	22892.8	6,857.1
Barnstable	D	D	D	D	188	2,046	645.3	129.0	1,112	14,179	1,266.5	386.3
Berkshire	D	D	D	D	142	5,115	1,554.7	324.2	516	7,311	487.9	156.4
Bristol	1,039	5,992	858.6	338.7	617	26,859	8,909.8	1,643.0	1,266	21,685	1,198.4	370.2
Dukes	65	253	49.9	16.2	22	143	26.7	7.8	145	944	159.8	47.6
Essex	2,073	15,287	3,714.6	1,280.6	856	39,878	12797.5	2,983.5	1,886	29,227	2,008.2	599.0
Franklin	D	D	D	D	107	3,534	1,683.4	199.4	149	1,856	96.1	31.6
Hampden	780	6,365	943.7	381.4	544	18,712	6,164.1	1,077.3	912	14,904	838.3	250.6
Hampshire	362	1,726	265.9	99.8	137	2,920	848.2	163.5	397	5,847	314.3	105.2
Middlesex	6,909	125,269	32,570.6	14,474.8	1,550	58,446	22733.0	4,509.7	3,971	72,065	5,085.2	1,556.3
Nantucket	D	D	D	D	14	59	15.3	3.0	124	1,168	182.8	48.0
Norfolk	2,659	22,041	5,046.6	1,901.4	565	18,299	8,217.9	1,201.5	1,679	30,121	2,117.0	615.0
Plymouth	1,242	10,104	1,544.3	605.1	449	10,348	2,659.8	605.0	1,142	20,602	1,235.5	396.9
Suffolk	3,519	83,941	24,823.6	9,761.7	319	10,594	4,079.7	623.1	2,680	64,498	6,270.4	1,821.6
Worcester	1,833	18,742	4,100.8	1,706.7	927	34,640	11973.1	2,279.4	1,794	26,651	1,632.5	472.5
MICHIGAN	21,713	280,247	39,125.1	19,529.8	12,418	582,365	262495.4	33349.3	20,696	399,032	23056.4	6,562.7
Alcona	D	D	5.6	D	17	200	28.5	9.8	18	75	5.4	1.4
Alger	10	28	3.4	1.5	D	445	D	D	46	309	28.7	6.8
Allegan	D	D	D	D	223	14,158	5,606.3	708.2	216	3,006	167.8	49.8
Alpena	D	D	D	D	50	1,304	416.8	75.1	74	958	46.0	13.4
Antrim	31	112	11.2	3.9	42	954	199.7	47.0	66	1,124	56.7	19.8
Arenac	D	D	20.9	D	30	910	200.1	44.1	46	417	25.2	7.1
Baraga	3	16	1.3	0.5	19	439	133.6	23.1	21	190	6.5	2.0
Barry	61	308	28.4	12.5	58	3,449	1,555.9	171.7	76	1,158	52.1	16.1
Bay	143	1,201	100.4	51.5	116	3,824	1,209.0	242.1	225	3,858	176.3	50.1
Benzie	29	69	7.4	2.4	22	418	115.3	18.3	63	1,136	74.4	24.0
Berrien	D	D	D	D	281	8,819	2,277.9	455.5	379	6,404	331.2	101.2
Branch	47	580	118.9	34.8	66	2,550	813.3	122.4	82	1,264	63.7	16.6
Calhoun	D	D	D	D	149	14,437	6,760.7	781.4	272	6,655	567.1	126.1
Cass	52	183	17.3	6.8	68	2,697	870.7	123.4	64	800	34.5	9.6
Charlevoix	60	222	26.1	9.2	42	2,247	550.4	118.4	73	1,665	85.1	28.8
Cheboygan	32	103	12.3	4.3	37	294	59.8	12.1	122	825	92.6	21.6
Chippewa	D	D	D	D	28	450	79.0	20.5	104	3,581	401.1	97.0
Clare	33	162	21.5	7.8	24	804	249.5	40.1	69	879	42.2	11.5
Clinton	123	940	120.6	41.7	49	2,150	706.4	105.2	113	1,645	76.2	21.1
Crawford	22	72	23.4	4.1	21	563	251.5	32.2	43	525	30.3	8.5
Delta	D	D	D	D	66	1,959	815.9	131.0	102	1,304	53.1	16.4
Dickinson	53	377	46.3	16.1	34	1,965	866.8	111.8	71	855	37.9	10.5
Eaton	172	1,051	159.6	62.3	95	7,369	8,953.9	414.3	220	4,479	228.3	67.0
Emmet	115	458	71.4	29.5	63	1,302	331.1	64.7	153	2,701	159.9	55.5
Genesee	D	D	D	D	279	11,516	13080.7	738.1	730	14,666	707.3	209.7
Gladwin	17	49	4.9	1.5	26	1,027	266.9	53.7	39	461	20.9	5.8
Gogebic	17	94	6.9	3.2	21	661	103.0	28.2	51	960	51.2	13.8
Grand Traverse	D	D	D	D	187	4,933	1,197.0	237.4	282	6,108	441.9	125.7
Gratiot	27	247	22.3	10.1	51	2,378	695.6	129.2	67	1,013	45.8	13.9
Hillsdale	D	D	D	D	72	3,611	1,471.4	184.5	65	856	39.6	11.1
Houghton	D	D	D	D	42	746	215.4	27.5	106	1,630	63.7	18.3
Huron	45	259	40.8	20.8	60	3,993	1,091.9	174.6	98	880	42.5	11.5
Ingham	704	6,528	1,091.8	413.6	195	8,591	5,338.5	531.2	648	12,887	607.9	189.8
Ionia	46	162	17.4	7.1	70	3,746	1,252.0	176.7	79	1,217	51.5	15.4
Iosco	31	181	11.9	7.2	32	1,143	395.3	49.5	83	796	39.5	11.2
Iron	29	109	12.8	4.9	17	526	111.5	21.8	35	345	17.3	4.2
Isabella	D	D	D	D	55	2,814	773.0	112.5	140	6,331	444.1	114.9
Jackson	D	D	D	D	248	9,000	3,017.6	486.8	272	4,870	243.9	69.4
Kalamazoo	543	4,855	723.1	282.0	294	17,105	8,166.0	1,137.7	598	13,151	622.3	198.8
Kalkaska	27	74	15.3	3.9	13	436	86.0	20.7	31	482	24.6	6.8
Kent	D	D	D	D	1,106	65,939	18311.2	3,627.5	1,326	30,415	1,540.6	488.4

STATE County	Health care and social assistance, 2017				Other services, 2017				Nonemployer businesses, 2019		Value of residential construction authorized by building permits, 2021	
	Number of establish-ments	Number of employees	Receipts (mil dol)	Annual payroll (mil dol)	Number of establish-ments	Number of employees	Receipts (mil dol)	Annual payroll (mil dol)	Number	Receipts (mil dol)	New construction ($1,000)	Number of housing units
	159	160	161	162	163	164	165	166	167	168	169	170
MARYLAND— Cont'd												
St. Mary's	181	4,735	528.0	201.5	140	816	83.4	29.8	7,211	305.9	114,067	359
Somerset	43	1,156	75.4	35.1	29	90	18.3	2.1	1,502	53.8	9,076	62
Talbot	184	4,341	567.2	194.8	124	669	112.5	23.3	4,515	246.9	68,163	167
Washington	439	9,539	1,088.1	442.5	256	1,706	148.6	52.2	9,145	407.9	85,071	332
Wicomico	339	8,973	1,010.0	429.5	188	1,356	137.3	41.5	6,814	317.6	39,264	223
Worcester	153	2,425	259.8	108.7	143	808	89.7	26.6	5,523	293.0	110,439	462
Baltimore city	1,494	77,508	12756.8	4,397.6	996	9,183	1,395.2	359.6	40,838	1,556.6	314,765	1,557
MASSACHUSETTS	19,349	635,012	74024.0	32038.2	14,810	100,088	13093.7	3,605.7	576,528	31364.3	4,941,794	19,853
Barnstable	795	17,032	2,064.8	858.8	627	3,498	395.6	125.5	27,736	1,543.0	410,195	672
Berkshire	436	11,773	1,277.1	569.5	267	1,591	166.8	44.2	10,512	498.3	78,486	193
Bristol	1,434	41,959	4,402.1	1,912.9	1,112	5,879	561.0	170.1	37,188	1,764.2	163,275	866
Dukes	57	879	132.8	55.7	72	288	42.6	11.7	4,223	274.8	135,673	188
Essex	2,195	63,832	6,148.5	2,781.5	1,625	9,004	868.2	260.1	71,971	3,748.0	466,353	1,703
Franklin	178	3,965	325.3	145.5	137	508	50.6	15.2	6,406	235.1	20,767	84
Hampden	1,202	43,673	4,805.2	2,045.0	759	5,779	676.4	173.4	26,877	1,310.3	66,732	263
Hampshire	452	9,667	965.6	454.2	336	1,803	212.2	64.9	13,507	575.8	84,508	398
Middlesex	4,791	121,315	13898.7	6,000.2	3,649	24,713	3,487.9	1,002.5	147,204	8,531.4	855,370	4,671
Nantucket	31	521	101.1	30.6	47	235	36.8	10.9	2,744	230.6	270,768	275
Norfolk	2,423	78,250	6,218.9	2,910.3	1,629	11,232	1,496.5	414.1	63,952	3,941.4	619,075	2,418
Plymouth	1,284	35,925	3,535.6	1,545.9	1,069	6,594	635.7	200.5	41,471	2,236.3	483,522	2,489
Suffolk	1,943	137,719	21688.3	9,447.6	2,020	20,551	3,556.6	849.9	64,047	3,617.1	879,811	3,738
Worcester	2,128	68,502	8,460.0	3,280.6	1,461	8,413	906.7	262.9	58,690	2,858.1	407,261	1,895
MICHIGAN	26,977	627,808	74194.5	29309.9	16,545	104,291	13205.0	3,415.1	741,509	33409.0	13,330	71
Alcona	D	D	D	6.8	D	D	D	0.4	669	25.8	9,791	40
Alger	18	251	22.2	10.6	15	35	6.4	1.2	568	21.4	9,619	32
Allegan	180	3,346	273.4	120.0	178	784	92.4	24.2	8,318	389.2	115,411	328
Alpena	83	2,673	277.0	107.7	71	389	39.6	8.3	1,869	78.8	5,995	30
Antrim	49	303	20.7	9.9	41	157	17.8	5.2	2,107	93.5	16,074	99
Arenac	35	589	48.8	19.6	22	67	5.8	1.9	912	41.0	5,133	21
Baraga	16	280	38.4	12.2	16	37	5.4	0.9	390	17.8	1,394	8
Barry	87	1,323	130.0	52.6	90	462	57.9	14.6	3,910	179.6	58,385	233
Bay	339	6,674	706.0	257.4	168	900	81.1	23.0	5,670	234.8	20,613	74
Benzie	27	367	36.0	15.7	D	D	D	D	1,797	79.1	26,093	107
Berrien	387	9,499	987.6	414.4	258	1,325	158.5	40.3	10,233	442.3	123,870	331
Branch	89	1,663	136.1	60.0	56	261	19.2	7.1	2,464	128.8	10,741	35
Calhoun	321	9,318	1,138.8	443.5	215	1,304	519.5	57.0	6,648	259.3	20,922	108
Cass	65	1,074	75.8	35.7	56	291	29.6	9.4	3,036	143.4	39,072	128
Charlevoix	69	1,322	134.2	62.0	60	211	31.5	7.1	2,641	127.6	27,001	117
Cheboygan	51	828	96.2	29.3	72	197	22.7	5.5	1,994	79.8	28,569	78
Chippewa	83	2,113	205.6	80.2	67	224	22.1	5.0	1,915	58.1	12,701	58
Clare	74	1,197	114.3	38.3	37	173	14.7	3.6	1,763	90.0	6,368	53
Clinton	113	1,926	163.4	66.0	101	598	50.7	16.1	5,538	236.5	50,935	188
Crawford	33	973	113.3	45.5	17	71	7.2	1.5	887	37.6	6,977	40
Delta	102	1,958	201.0	63.2	89	410	45.4	10.5	1,959	67.7	10,485	37
Dickinson	101	2,673	361.1	155.6	63	214	23.9	5.6	1,444	57.0	8,132	36
Eaton	234	3,775	342.5	153.0	170	1,186	154.3	49.0	7,095	291.2	31,272	108
Emmet	177	3,125	423.2	164.3	107	554	68.3	19.9	3,570	173.7	60,520	138
Genesee	1,286	27,955	3,165.7	1,254.4	569	3,886	606.1	116.9	28,457	1,065.0	125,172	510
Gladwin	38	699	62.5	19.8	28	154	12.2	3.2	1,616	89.3	21,159	89
Gogebic	34	645	86.6	31.6	37	111	11.1	2.8	899	30.8	2,585	13
Grand Traverse	417	9,529	1,290.2	490.1	234	1,446	179.5	50.4	9,967	481.8	100,203	553
Gratiot	107	2,362	252.5	90.3	46	201	42.8	7.2	2,146	94.9	8,383	43
Hillsdale	94	1,325	122.3	48.4	53	273	19.8	5.4	2,755	117.4	16,864	69
Houghton	91	1,935	214.6	85.3	D	D	D	D	1,988	64.8	22,303	169
Huron	94	1,911	199.5	70.0	53	182	21.1	4.9	2,162	101.0	11,414	37
Ingham	783	22,927	2,730.5	1,083.3	560	4,929	768.1	211.6	19,656	928.5	119,867	665
Ionia	98	1,294	127.5	52.0	67	304	29.0	7.8	3,343	125.6	29,850	105
Iosco	61	1,007	85.9	35.9	50	179	14.0	3.5	1,561	59.7	17,163	181
Iron	26	418	55.1	19.9	25	152	11.1	3.2	741	25.0	9,218	157
Isabella	218	3,103	263.8	95.6	105	562	59.7	16.2	3,689	168.9	13,903	57
Jackson	361	9,998	1,123.1	492.2	211	1,210	152.8	37.1	8,844	366.5	41,766	176
Kalamazoo	685	21,274	2,818.2	1,154.6	421	3,340	410.2	101.4	16,903	744.9	123,085	419
Kalkaska	21	551	54.1	22.9	D	D	D	D	1,190	48.6	6,616	41
Kent	1,650	55,229	6,984.5	2,609.0	1,204	9,907	1,004.5	293.0	50,382	2,551.7	489,348	1,891

Table B. States and Counties — **Government Employment and Payroll, and Local Government Finances**

STATE County	Government employment and payroll, 2017									Local government finances, 2017				
			March payroll (percent of total)							General revenue				
												Taxes		
													Per capita[1] (dollars)	
	Full-time equivalent employees	March payroll (dollars)	Adminis-tration, judicial, and legal	Police and corrections	Fire protection	Highways and transpor-tation	Health and welfare	Natural resources and utilities	Education and libraries	Total (mil dol)	Inter-govern-mental (mil dol)	Total (mil dol)	Total	Property
	171	172	173	174	175	176	177	178	179	180	181	182	183	184
MARYLAND— Cont'd														
St. Mary's	3,228	15,729,729	6.4	10.5	0.0	2.2	1.2	4.4	72.5	423.1	139.9	222.2	1,975	1,009
Somerset	889	3,682,461	7.3	9.6	0.0	2.7	3.0	4.9	69.6	92.9	54.5	28.0	1,080	760
Talbot	1,296	6,122,919	6.6	12.4	0.0	3.5	4.0	9.0	52.5	172.1	31.5	98.6	2,662	1,398
Washington	5,565	24,234,522	4.1	6.2	1.9	3.1	2.4	5.3	74.2	591.0	251.1	256.8	1,710	1,016
Wicomico	4,036	17,547,154	4.4	11.8	1.9	1.8	0.5	4.2	73.8	428.6	210.3	155.3	1,519	894
Worcester	2,840	13,064,394	8.0	16.4	1.1	3.3	3.9	12.3	51.0	374.0	45.5	260.2	5,036	3,501
Baltimore city	26,369	141,757,363	6.5	17.3	8.5	3.0	6.2	8.5	48.1	3,818.8	1,751.2	1,488.2	2,438	1,405
MASSACHUSETTS	X	X	X	X	X	X	X	X	X	X	X	X	X	X
Barnstable	8,286	44,597,245	6.6	11.6	9.9	4.4	3.2	6.7	55.0	1,119.8	177.1	766.0	3,587	3,359
Berkshire	4,678	20,287,892	4.8	7.3	3.1	4.6	2.3	4.1	72.2	589.6	246.5	294.0	2,326	2,238
Bristol	18,103	90,434,250	3.1	10.3	6.8	2.2	3.5	3.8	68.5	2,292.9	968.1	1,022.4	1,823	1,745
Dukes	1,098	5,345,754	7.2	10.0	3.4	6.9	5.0	6.0	59.2	167.4	27.3	113.2	6,537	6,246
Essex	24,071	128,610,626	3.6	9.1	6.8	2.6	3.1	4.9	67.7	3,461.2	1,235.5	1,798.7	2,293	2,216
Franklin	2,970	13,630,074	4.9	6.3	3.2	4.7	2.3	3.6	64.2	338.8	122.6	164.9	2,336	2,290
Hampden	19,157	91,093,159	3.1	9.6	6.1	2.4	2.6	7.0	67.4	2,085.5	1,015.3	830.3	1,775	1,714
Hampshire	6,083	29,149,694	5.0	9.8	7.6	3.2	3.1	4.9	64.1	538.9	184.5	288.8	1,793	1,734
Middlesex	56,125	305,641,359	3.9	8.9	6.9	2.7	8.1	3.7	63.6	8,055.5	2,092.0	4,661.9	2,907	2,786
Nantucket	584	3,800,935	4.9	8.7	5.6	10.9	11.6	6.4	48.8	151.4	8.5	103.3	9,217	6,940
Norfolk	23,735	132,202,384	3.4	8.6	7.1	2.7	2.3	4.9	68.5	3,218.7	670.2	2,090.6	2,984	2,886
Plymouth	18,407	93,269,080	3.7	8.6	6.3	2.6	2.0	4.1	71.1	2,256.2	774.2	1,251.0	2,427	2,343
Suffolk	23,532	152,449,799	3.5	19.7	10.7	1.8	8.7	4.7	49.6	4,645.7	1,501.5	2,556.7	3,193	2,870
Worcester	24,532	121,122,757	4.7	10.4	6.6	3.5	2.8	4.1	66.5	3,385.5	1,371.0	1,610.5	1,950	1,895
MICHIGAN	X	X	X	X	X	X	X	X	X	X	X	X	X	X
Alcona	217	864,091	20.4	10.7	3.7	11.9	6.8	1.7	38.5	25.4	7.3	12.7	1,235	1,233
Alger	306	1,216,793	11.3	7.1	0.5	17.9	3.3	3.2	54.9	36.7	17.4	10.4	1,132	1,101
Allegan	3,057	11,712,420	9.5	7.1	1.1	3.0	8.4	1.9	68.3	367.8	194.7	125.2	1,076	1,055
Alpena	1,467	5,723,752	7.4	3.5	3.5	7.0	20.8	1.0	55.8	150.7	89.0	30.4	1,068	1,052
Antrim	742	2,734,139	16.9	7.3	2.7	7.8	3.5	3.7	55.3	99.8	25.6	45.0	1,935	1,900
Arenac	374	1,470,122	17.0	6.7	1.8	6.6	0.0	2.9	60.6	45.5	22.2	16.0	1,066	1,032
Baraga	389	1,704,033	10.1	3.6	0.0	8.2	41.8	7.9	27.9	58.7	19.2	9.1	1,083	1,081
Barry	1,420	5,620,614	8.6	7.3	1.3	4.7	18.0	2.0	55.8	181.7	83.4	51.6	850	842
Bay	4,219	17,395,958	6.6	5.0	2.0	4.1	15.6	3.4	61.1	526.0	268.5	126.8	1,219	1,193
Benzie	469	1,875,231	12.3	7.1	1.4	12.6	9.4	4.2	50.6	66.4	17.9	30.5	1,728	1,707
Berrien	4,916	20,205,038	9.5	10.0	1.7	2.9	2.8	4.4	66.9	642.6	301.4	220.9	1,433	1,406
Branch	1,900	7,881,188	5.8	4.4	1.1	3.6	31.6	3.8	47.3	254.2	102.6	44.6	1,028	1,012
Calhoun	3,902	17,403,464	10.1	10.3	3.5	2.2	6.9	4.6	59.9	615.2	302.7	179.7	1,339	1,163
Cass	1,414	5,442,148	10.0	6.8	0.6	3.7	1.8	1.9	73.7	186.7	94.4	53.6	1,041	1,023
Charlevoix	1,353	5,458,888	5.4	4.4	0.5	5.1	27.2	3.3	53.3	180.2	45.3	72.1	2,751	2,725
Cheboygan	697	2,909,603	14.7	8.9	0.6	7.8	0.3	2.0	64.5	91.8	36.3	40.4	1,587	1,582
Chippewa	1,232	4,686,385	10.5	7.1	2.4	13.2	5.6	4.4	55.0	152.7	72.6	38.6	1,023	1,019
Clare	1,153	4,629,928	8.0	5.4	1.5	4.4	0.6	1.4	72.7	141.7	76.8	32.4	1,061	1,048
Clinton	1,641	6,877,274	11.2	9.5	0.9	3.5	0.2	3.0	68.9	215.8	119.6	63.4	807	787
Crawford	385	1,534,085	16.4	10.7	2.3	18.1	4.6	1.4	45.3	48.3	23.6	15.5	1,117	1,061
Delta	1,271	5,378,133	8.5	7.7	0.2	5.4	3.5	6.3	67.0	145.1	78.3	40.9	1,139	1,131
Dickinson	1,731	7,856,461	4.0	4.6	0.7	2.6	57.2	1.7	28.2	210.6	44.2	36.4	1,431	1,416
Eaton	2,770	11,226,348	8.4	8.8	3.4	4.1	2.5	4.2	65.6	336.6	166.9	106.1	969	931
Emmet	1,178	5,264,795	10.8	7.1	0.7	4.9	19.9	5.2	48.0	200.9	72.4	75.4	2,280	2,243
Genesee	14,500	64,991,149	5.0	5.5	1.6	4.1	26.9	2.5	53.4	2,164.1	1,125.9	370.3	909	840
Gladwin	549	2,201,794	12.0	6.1	1.2	11.4	6.3	2.2	57.5	67.0	32.8	22.3	883	865
Gogebic	575	2,483,667	10.5	6.5	0.3	10.1	2.0	7.0	61.2	90.5	30.2	18.3	1,192	1,182
Grand Traverse	4,372	17,331,924	6.7	5.0	1.4	4.8	17.7	2.9	60.1	502.7	207.2	165.9	1,807	1,786
Gratiot	1,416	5,098,790	9.6	6.3	0.3	5.3	0.8	3.1	74.1	159.2	86.2	46.5	1,134	1,122
Hillsdale	1,043	4,049,058	9.8	9.6	1.6	5.7	0.1	3.2	68.1	140.9	70.0	30.6	668	660
Houghton	998	3,962,541	10.2	6.3	0.4	9.5	6.1	4.2	62.9	165.5	82.9	33.9	936	924
Huron	1,157	4,639,308	11.7	6.8	0.4	6.0	16.2	3.7	53.9	157.0	54.5	62.4	1,993	1,964
Ingham	10,811	51,980,691	7.4	6.7	3.2	4.5	11.9	9.4	51.2	1,387.5	599.7	470.9	1,612	1,451
Ionia	1,907	7,894,357	7.0	6.0	0.4	4.0	2.3	2.1	77.5	202.0	118.5	50.4	785	724
Iosco	1,235	4,090,829	9.1	3.9	0.6	4.5	35.2	1.5	43.3	129.2	59.8	34.6	1,377	1,364
Iron	348	1,361,315	16.8	8.6	0.0	10.2	11.0	10.3	42.9	73.5	40.3	17.4	1,565	1,552
Isabella	1,787	6,981,989	9.1	6.1	1.3	6.4	29.6	3.6	41.9	255.4	159.1	49.4	695	679
Jackson	4,580	19,841,345	6.9	7.2	1.5	4.1	4.5	2.4	72.5	658.3	378.1	159.5	1,006	930
Kalamazoo	7,505	31,550,062	7.4	11.7	2.4	2.8	2.4	2.9	69.1	1,031.0	525.6	328.5	1,249	1,210
Kalkaska	724	2,976,208	6.8	4.6	0.3	5.6	57.2	2.9	22.2	89.4	19.8	20.4	1,163	1,142
Kent	17,290	79,275,077	6.9	10.0	2.7	5.0	2.2	3.7	66.9	2,821.1	1,438.1	862.3	1,328	1,121

1. Based on the resident population estimated as of July 1 of the year shown.

STATE County	Local government finances, 2017 (cont.)									Government employment, 2020			Individual income tax returns, 2019		
	Direct general expenditure							Debt outstanding							
			Percent of total for:												
	Total (mil dol)	Per capita[1] (dollars)	Education	Health and hospitals	Police protection	Public welfare	Highways	Total (mil dol)	Per capita[1] (dollars)	Federal civilian	Federal military	State and local	Number of returns	Mean adjusted gross income	Mean income tax
	185	186	187	188	189	190	191	192	193	194	195	196	197	198	199
MARYLAND— Cont'd															
St. Mary's	391.5	3,481	59.9	2.0	7.1	0.0	4.1	366.3	3,256	10,457	2,706	4,689	54,070	83,972	9,763
Somerset	149.4	5,769	33.4	0.7	3.2	0.0	2.7	65.7	2,537	57	96	2,688	9,190	43,316	3,297
Talbot	143.1	3,865	39.6	2.0	8.1	0.0	7.4	118.3	3,194	208	136	1,686	19,640	94,773	14,101
Washington	583.6	3,886	57.2	0.7	4.8	0.0	4.8	427.3	2,845	495	468	7,534	72,120	59,508	5,818
Wicomico	447.4	4,375	55.5	1.0	6.2	1.9	4.3	307.7	3,009	326	325	7,265	47,630	52,942	5,000
Worcester	355.1	6,874	33.4	1.9	8.2	0.0	4.4	247.2	4,785	196	196	3,066	29,590	67,401	7,841
Baltimore city	3,906.1	6,398	35.4	3.0	12.7	0.0	2.5	1,009.0	1,653	10,830	1,877	54,470	263,810	56,301	6,395
MASSACHUSETTS	X	X	X	X	X	X	X	X	X	47,675	19,180	384,588	3,486,200	100,976	15,378
Barnstable	1,227.3	5,746	47.1	1.0	5.2	0.4	3.7	916.3	4,290	1,670	1,219	12,671	129,610	86,539	11,530
Berkshire	681.9	5,397	58.0	0.3	3.3	0.4	6.4	435.0	3,443	414	287	7,439	64,700	68,577	8,070
Bristol	2,297.4	4,096	59.2	0.8	5.4	0.8	3.1	1,270.0	2,264	1,278	1,295	26,825	283,670	69,706	7,959
Dukes	189.1	10,923	47.8	2.9	5.4	0.1	3.6	74.8	4,323	50	62	1,460	11,450	103,849	15,044
Essex	3,542.6	4,516	56.6	0.3	4.6	0.3	3.3	2,102.2	2,680	3,663	1,893	35,338	410,530	93,194	13,582
Franklin	379.2	5,371	59.1	0.8	2.8	0.3	5.2	115.4	1,634	228	161	4,657	36,060	62,754	6,327
Hampden	2,094.3	4,478	57.1	0.7	5.1	0.3	3.1	1,364.2	2,917	3,797	1,229	27,847	223,550	60,863	6,408
Hampshire	581.0	3,607	58.1	0.5	4.0	0.5	5.0	226.1	1,404	1,466	334	17,889	72,770	76,677	9,029
Middlesex	8,127.0	5,067	51.0	7.8	4.3	0.2	3.3	5,173.1	3,225	11,977	4,876	76,697	808,050	131,702	22,131
Nantucket	154.6	13,800	43.5	0.5	3.8	5.0	0.6	248.2	22,153	50	52	749	7,880	110,752	16,981
Norfolk	3,449.2	4,923	53.9	0.5	4.7	0.2	3.4	2,246.2	3,206	1,626	1,619	32,824	362,740	139,782	24,686
Plymouth	2,496.0	4,842	60.5	0.4	5.1	0.3	3.2	1,641.9	3,185	3,544	1,276	26,715	271,880	95,833	13,775
Suffolk	4,402.2	5,497	37.9	6.5	9.1	0.1	3.0	2,769.9	3,459	14,813	2,981	63,667	389,320	100,250	16,687
Worcester	3,673.1	4,448	60.9	0.6	4.3	0.3	4.1	2,567.2	3,109	3,099	1,896	49,810	414,050	78,776	9,800
MICHIGAN	X	X	X	X	X	X	X	X	X	54,175	17,537	519,306	4,850,130	65,853	7,632
Alcona	28.3	2,747	29.1	5.1	4.8	0.5	27.2	1.8	173	26	16	310	5,040	47,912	4,194
Alger	35.6	3,895	36.6	3.6	1.7	0.0	21.2	27.7	3,029	77	16	601	4,140	50,473	4,552
Allegan	396.2	3,405	53.5	8.4	3.4	3.3	10.7	521.6	4,482	195	187	5,265	58,190	63,963	6,437
Alpena	144.7	5,089	42.6	23.8	3.1	0.6	6.7	24.4	859	156	44	2,411	14,200	48,619	4,398
Antrim	99.8	4,287	37.8	2.9	4.3	18.5	11.4	57.9	2,488	62	38	1,054	12,030	63,710	6,879
Arenac	45.4	3,023	47.3	1.9	2.9	0.0	17.4	26.8	1,784	46	23	535	7,280	46,656	3,735
Baraga	55.1	6,533	22.4	44.8	2.0	0.2	8.6	20.1	2,379	32	11	1,298	3,530	46,946	3,573
Barry	206.4	3,401	41.9	6.0	3.4	17.3	9.2	215.1	3,545	93	97	2,256	30,070	64,038	6,343
Bay	486.0	4,671	50.5	10.2	3.8	5.7	5.8	292.8	2,814	268	224	5,250	53,240	53,444	5,081
Benzie	62.9	3,569	34.5	19.3	2.7	0.3	13.2	24.9	1,410	39	28	683	9,550	58,805	5,879
Berrien	712.3	4,622	50.9	8.7	3.9	1.3	5.1	534.7	3,469	362	258	8,385	75,010	62,385	7,184
Branch	283.3	6,530	30.6	24.0	1.6	5.2	6.0	163.2	3,762	94	66	2,644	19,470	50,871	4,291
Calhoun	634.2	4,727	46.9	2.5	5.8	5.4	12.5	651.6	4,856	2,984	255	7,450	62,180	52,720	4,689
Cass	197.3	3,833	51.1	7.2	3.1	4.8	7.0	207.6	4,033	82	82	2,018	24,080	64,995	7,431
Charlevoix	186.3	7,106	39.0	9.6	2.2	15.4	8.3	114.1	4,353	66	67	1,688	14,090	67,820	8,361
Cheboygan	88.9	3,494	51.8	0.9	4.7	1.1	13.6	32.2	1,264	68	106	946	12,980	53,422	5,383
Chippewa	138.3	3,670	45.0	3.7	3.5	0.4	11.0	107.7	2,859	525	232	5,468	16,240	47,252	3,827
Clare	142.5	4,663	63.7	0.5	3.1	0.4	7.8	46.4	1,520	98	55	1,538	13,630	44,438	3,387
Clinton	213.4	2,718	54.3	0.4	4.4	0.6	10.1	255.2	3,250	241	133	2,013	38,520	70,536	7,683
Crawford	62.4	4,491	37.0	2.2	2.8	0.8	14.1	37.3	2,684	161	22	640	6,310	45,928	3,557
Delta	168.2	4,687	51.7	2.1	1.6	0.8	9.9	89.6	2,496	220	55	1,755	17,820	52,898	4,671
Dickinson	213.3	8,390	22.3	53.5	2.6	0.0	5.0	103.5	4,071	805	60	1,893	12,920	54,953	5,037
Eaton	367.8	3,361	51.7	4.6	5.4	4.9	8.0	450.3	4,114	195	210	5,360	55,120	59,427	5,510
Emmet	227.6	6,882	32.9	20.9	1.8	6.4	6.5	113.3	3,424	117	52	2,222	18,500	72,383	8,984
Genesee	2,110.3	5,179	40.0	28.9	4.1	1.6	3.9	912.4	2,239	1,132	634	17,955	195,710	53,368	5,197
Gladwin	65.5	2,596	42.8	1.2	3.5	0.4	18.2	36.2	1,435	54	40	767	11,460	49,867	4,179
Gogebic	92.1	6,005	32.0	8.5	2.9	12.6	9.9	71.6	4,671	180	22	1,419	6,730	45,542	3,777
Grand Traverse	517.5	5,638	48.5	14.8	2.7	6.3	5.4	327.7	3,570	584	265	5,403	50,560	75,085	9,370
Gratiot	161.7	3,947	57.0	0.5	3.7	0.7	9.4	135.0	3,295	75	55	2,159	17,210	49,629	4,252
Hillsdale	152.7	3,333	46.1	1.1	2.8	13.4	7.5	103.6	2,262	90	70	2,266	20,140	49,330	3,954
Houghton	161.8	4,469	45.2	3.2	2.1	13.2	9.5	172.5	4,767	194	89	3,544	15,250	52,238	4,489
Huron	152.6	4,875	38.4	2.9	3.2	8.9	17.4	94.4	3,017	107	48	1,692	16,390	50,821	4,463
Ingham	1,495.7	5,122	46.5	11.4	6.0	2.7	4.2	1,640.5	5,618	1,613	597	38,574	127,740	63,048	7,086
Ionia	203.0	3,157	58.5	1.7	2.3	0.5	11.3	260.8	4,057	122	94	2,990	28,610	53,683	4,656
Iosco	130.0	5,172	38.9	19.4	2.5	11.8	6.0	52.1	2,073	136	59	1,394	12,250	45,846	3,781
Iron	74.4	6,700	18.1	5.3	2.1	32.4	12.6	45.8	4,121	39	21	856	5,670	46,683	4,043
Isabella	261.6	3,680	28.7	33.2	2.8	6.2	7.0	143.8	2,023	170	109	9,001	27,220	53,269	4,848
Jackson	668.6	4,217	50.5	11.8	4.6	3.8	6.7	543.5	3,428	344	238	7,242	72,880	56,281	5,409
Kalamazoo	1,030.7	3,919	55.8	9.5	3.4	0.4	5.5	1,217.5	4,629	743	420	13,038	124,330	70,072	8,249
Kalkaska	84.5	4,810	18.8	53.7	2.4	0.5	5.7	26.2	1,491	31	29	1,115	8,600	46,996	3,813
Kent	3,032.9	4,671	51.6	6.0	4.4	0.9	7.5	3,759.1	5,790	2,966	1,075	23,981	322,230	71,660	8,329

1. Based on the resident population estimated as of July 1 of the year shown.

State / county code	CBSA code[1]	County Type code[2]	STATE County	Land area[3] (sq. mi)	Population, 2021: Total persons 2021	Population, 2021: Rank	Population, 2021: Per square mile	Race alone or in combination, not Hispanic or Latino (percent): White	Black	American Indian, Alaska Native	Asian and Pacific Islancer	Percent Hispanic or Latino[4]	Age (percent): Under 5 years	5 to 17 years	18 to 24 years	25 to 34 years	35 to 44 years	45 to 54 years
				1	2	3	4	5	6	7	8	9	10	11	12	13	14	15
			MICHIGAN— Cont'd															
26083	26340	9	Keweenaw	540.1	2,107	3,033	3.9	97.2	1.1	1.0	0.6	1.8	3.9	8.8	8.5	7.9	8.4	10.3
26085		9	Lake	567.6	12,308	2,258	21.7	88.7	8.4	1.9	0.9	3.0	4.2	9.4	7.7	7.4	9.4	12.1
26087	19820	1	Lapeer	647.0	88,513	667	136.8	92.6	1.7	1.1	1.0	5.1	4.7	11.4	11.7	11.2	11.5	13.3
26089	45900	9	Leelanau	347.2	22,623	1,693	65.2	91.7	1.0	3.4	1.0	4.4	3.8	8.8	8.8	8.3	10.1	9.9
26091	10300	4	Lenawee	749.6	98,956	616	132.0	87.8	3.5	1.1	0.9	8.6	5.1	11.7	13.0	11.7	12.0	12.7
26093	19820	1	Livingston	565.3	195,014	348	345.0	95.1	1.0	0.9	1.6	2.8	4.8	11.7	11.8	11.2	11.9	13.6
26095		7	Luce	899.1	5,309	2,794	5.9	80.3	13.1	7.8	1.0	1.8	4.6	9.2	10.4	13.4	13.2	12.9
26097		7	Mackinac	1,021.9	10,906	2,350	10.7	77.0	4.3	19.8	1.6	2.4	4.4	8.1	9.6	9.6	9.6	12.4
26099	19820	1	Macomb	479.3	876,792	66	1,829.3	79.0	14.3	0.9	5.6	2.9	5.3	11.7	11.6	13.8	12.1	13.1
26101		7	Manistee	542.3	25,350	1,593	46.7	90.2	4.2	3.1	0.7	3.7	4.1	9.3	10.8	10.7	10.4	11.3
26103	32100	5	Marquette	1,809.1	66,103	813	36.5	93.8	2.3	2.9	1.3	1.7	4.4	10.3	18.0	11.7	11.8	10.4
26105	31220	7	Mason	495.0	29,383	1,446	59.4	92.4	1.8	1.5	1.3	4.8	4.8	11.7	10.3	10.6	10.8	10.9
26107	13660	6	Mecosta	555.2	40,031	1,179	72.1	92.8	3.7	1.6	1.4	2.8	5.0	10.1	21.6	10.7	9.6	10.1
26109	31940	7	Menominee	1,044.0	23,299	1,669	22.3	93.6	1.4	3.4	0.8	2.3	4.1	10.1	10.1	9.9	10.8	11.9
26111	33220	3	Midland	517.5	83,457	690	161.3	92.5	2.1	1.0	2.8	3.3	5.4	11.8	12.2	12.4	12.4	12.1
26113	15620	9	Missaukee	564.8	15,130	2,084	26.8	94.9	1.2	1.3	0.9	3.2	5.5	12.9	10.7	11.7	11.1	11.1
26115	33780	3	Monroe	549.4	155,274	439	282.6	92.2	3.7	0.9	1.1	4.0	5.1	12.1	11.6	12.0	11.9	12.9
26117	24340	2	Montcalm	705.3	67,220	801	95.3	92.6	3.2	1.3	0.8	3.9	5.4	12.4	11.6	12.7	12.5	12.6
26119		9	Montmorency	546.7	9,297	2,467	17.0	96.6	1.2	1.7	0.7	1.6	4.0	8.5	7.8	7.8	8.7	10.8
26121	34740	3	Muskegon	503.9	176,511	382	350.3	78.9	15.3	1.6	1.2	6.2	5.8	13.0	11.9	13.1	12.5	11.7
26123		6	Newaygo	838.9	50,296	993	60.0	91.6	1.8	1.4	0.8	6.1	5.4	12.5	11.4	11.7	11.3	11.7
26125	19820	1	Oakland	867.3	1,270,017	33	1,464.3	72.9	14.7	0.8	9.3	4.7	5.2	11.5	11.7	13.5	12.8	13.3
26127		6	Oceana	538.1	26,815	1,537	49.8	82.3	1.6	1.7	0.5	15.5	4.9	12.5	11.7	10.9	11.4	11.1
26129		9	Ogemaw	563.5	20,726	1,777	36.8	95.4	1.0	1.7	1.0	2.3	4.4	10.3	9.6	9.7	10.2	10.9
26131		9	Ontonagon	1,311.0	5,868	2,746	4.5	95.3	1.0	2.4	1.1	1.8	2.6	6.9	7.7	6.3	8.0	11.0
26133		9	Osceola	566.3	23,105	1,675	40.8	95.6	1.8	1.6	0.7	2.3	5.4	12.4	11.5	11.2	11.1	11.4
26135		9	Oscoda	565.7	8,311	2,556	14.7	96.2	1.3	1.5	0.6	2.0	4.9	11.2	9.0	8.8	9.1	9.9
26137		7	Otsego	515.0	25,289	1,595	49.1	95.9	1.4	1.6	1.1	1.9	5.0	12.1	11.0	11.5	11.0	12.0
26139	24340	2	Ottawa	563.5	299,157	235	530.9	84.7	2.5	0.7	3.5	10.4	5.7	13.6	17.2	12.2	12.3	11.1
26141		7	Presque Isle	658.7	13,093	2,207	19.9	96.0	1.2	1.4	0.9	1.8	3.6	8.4	8.8	8.1	9.3	10.3
26143		7	Roscommon	519.9	23,633	1,657	45.5	95.6	1.2	1.6	1.0	2.1	3.5	8.6	7.7	8.4	8.5	10.7
26145	40980	3	Saginaw	800.8	189,591	359	236.8	70.6	20.0	0.9	1.7	9.2	5.7	12.0	13.1	12.7	11.2	11.6
26147	19820	1	St. Clair	721.5	160,053	422	221.8	92.8	3.6	1.1	1.0	3.7	4.9	11.6	11.6	11.5	11.3	13.2
26149	44780	4	St. Joseph	500.6	60,758	871	121.4	87.7	3.8	1.0	1.1	8.8	6.1	13.9	12.1	12.0	11.8	11.4
26151		6	Sanilac	962.6	40,506	1,170	42.1	94.3	1.0	1.0	0.6	4.2	5.0	12.2	11.2	10.3	10.8	11.9
26153		7	Schoolcraft	1,171.9	8,030	2,576	6.9	88.8	1.6	11.2	0.6	1.5	4.4	9.8	9.1	8.6	9.3	11.8
26155	29620	4	Shiawassee	531.0	67,877	791	127.8	95.2	1.3	1.1	0.9	3.0	5.1	11.7	12.0	12.2	11.5	12.8
26157		6	Tuscola	804.9	52,917	959	65.7	93.8	1.7	1.3	0.6	3.9	5.0	11.1	11.1	11.3	11.4	12.6
26159		2	Van Buren	607.8	75,658	741	124.5	82.7	4.7	1.6	1.2	12.3	5.8	13.3	11.6	11.4	11.9	12.0
26161	11460	2	Washtenaw	706.0	369,390	198	523.2	73.2	13.7	1.0	10.7	5.2	4.7	10.3	21.3	14.1	11.8	11.3
26163	19820	1	Wayne	611.8	1,774,816	19	2,901.0	51.4	39.4	1.1	4.5	6.5	6.3	13.3	12.3	14.4	11.9	12.4
26165	15620	7	Wexford	564.9	33,901	1,332	60.0	95.4	1.4	1.4	1.1	2.5	5.8	13.2	11.1	11.7	11.8	11.7
27000		0	MINNESOTA	79,625.9	5,707,390	X	71.7	80.4	8.4	1.8	6.2	5.8	5.9	13.1	12.8	13.1	13.4	11.7
27001		8	Aitkin	1,821.8	15,887	2,038	8.7	95.0	1.3	3.1	0.7	1.5	3.5	9.2	8.6	7.3	9.0	10.0
27003	33460	1	Anoka	422.0	367,018	202	869.7	79.9	9.8	1.4	6.7	5.3	6.0	13.5	11.9	12.9	14.0	12.7
27005		6	Becker	1,315.1	35,219	1,301	26.8	89.2	1.2	9.5	1.1	2.4	5.8	13.8	11.6	10.1	11.7	10.6
27007	13420	7	Beltrami	2,504.7	46,380	1,048	18.5	74.4	1.7	23.2	1.5	2.6	6.6	14.6	16.9	12.0	11.7	9.5
27009	41060	3	Benton	408.3	41,459	1,158	101.5	89.6	6.7	1.0	1.9	3.2	6.6	14.5	12.3	14.2	14.6	11.6
27011		9	Big Stone	499.2	5,145	2,810	10.3	95.9	0.9	1.1	0.7	2.5	6.1	12.5	9.8	9.5	10.6	9.1
27013	31860	3	Blue Earth	747.8	69,280	778	92.6	88.2	5.8	0.7	3.2	4.3	5.2	11.4	24.6	12.8	11.8	9.2
27015	35580	6	Brown	611.1	25,819	1,567	42.3	93.5	1.0	0.5	1.0	4.9	5.4	12.7	13.5	10.3	11.9	10.3
27017	20260	2	Carlton	861.2	36,409	1,275	42.3	90.3	2.5	6.9	1.1	1.9	5.2	12.8	11.7	11.9	13.4	12.8
27019	33460	1	Carver	354.0	108,626	569	306.9	89.4	2.9	0.6	4.5	4.5	5.9	14.9	12.7	10.6	14.9	13.6
27021	14660	9	Cass	2,021.5	30,639	1,416	15.2	85.1	1.2	12.8	1.1	2.4	4.9	12.0	9.6	9.0	10.4	10.5
27023		7	Chippewa	581.2	12,357	2,252	21.3	87.0	1.5	1.8	3.2	8.2	6.2	14.5	11.0	11.3	11.9	9.9
27025	33460	1	Chisago	414.9	57,469	908	138.5	93.5	2.1	1.2	2.2	2.6	5.6	12.7	11.5	12.0	13.4	13.1
27027	22020	3	Clay	1,045.2	65,574	822	62.7	87.2	5.9	2.1	2.2	5.0	6.8	14.4	18.0	13.1	13.7	10.1
27029		8	Clearwater	998.8	8,576	2,529	8.6	87.1	1.6	11.7	1.2	2.6	6.4	14.8	11.3	10.3	11.6	10.8
27031		9	Cook	1,452.6	5,617	2,769	3.9	87.2	2.3	8.9	1.7	2.8	3.4	8.9	7.8	10.6	10.9	11.3
27033		7	Cottonwood	640.0	11,569	2,310	18.1	83.8	1.9	1.0	5.0	9.9	6.3	15.1	11.4	10.4	11.1	10.3
27035	14660	4	Crow Wing	998.4	67,270	799	67.4	96.1	1.5	1.5	0.9	1.7	5.0	12.1	10.5	10.7	12.0	10.7
27037	33460	1	Dakota	562.5	442,038	163	785.8	78.2	9.5	1.0	6.5	7.8	6.1	13.8	11.9	12.8	14.2	12.5
27039	40340	3	Dodge	439.3	20,935	1,766	47.7	93.0	1.4	0.8	1.5	5.0	6.0	14.7	12.6	12.1	13.7	12.7
27041	10820	6	Douglas	636.9	39,238	1,197	61.6	96.3	1.1	0.8	0.9	2.0	5.7	12.1	10.7	10.8	12.0	10.7
27043		6	Faribault	712.5	13,909	2,157	19.5	89.8	1.4	0.8	0.9	8.4	5.3	12.7	11.2	9.8	12.0	10.3

1. CBSA = Core Based Statistical Area. See Appendix A for explanation. See Appendix B for list of metropolitan areas with component counties. 2. County type code from the Economic Research Service of USDA Rural-Urban Continuum Codes. See Appendix A for definition. 3. Dry land or land partially or temporarily covered by water. 4. May be of any race.

STATE County	Population, 2021 (cont.)				Population change, 2000–2021							Households, 2016–2020				
	Age (percent) (cont.)				Total persons		Percent change		Components of change, 2020–2021					Percent		
	55 to 64 years	65 to 74 years	75 years and over	Percent female	2010	2020	2010–2020	2020–2021	Births	Deaths	Net Migration	Number	Persons per household	Family households	Female family householder[1]	One person
	16	17	18	19	20	21	22	23	24	25	26	27	28	29	30	31
MICHIGAN— Cont'd																
Keweenaw	15.9	22.1	14.0	49.5	2,156	2,046	-5.1	3.0	17	28	73	1,079	1.9	65.5	6.1	28.9
Lake	19.2	19.8	10.9	48.9	11,539	12,096	4.8	1.8	124	254	350	4,985	2.3	56.5	5.8	38.3
Lapeer	16.7	12.4	7.1	48.8	88,319	88,619	0.3	-0.1	953	1,373	309	34,041	2.5	71.9	8.8	23.3
Leelanau	17.4	20.2	12.9	50.6	21,708	22,301	2.7	1.4	187	352	498	9,201	2.3	68.8	7.0	26.9
Lenawee	14.2	12.1	7.6	49.2	99,892	99,423	-0.5	-0.5	1,172	1,594	-62	38,693	2.4	66.8	9.8	27.5
Livingston	16.2	11.9	6.9	49.5	180,967	193,866	7.1	0.6	2,129	2,357	1,369	72,905	2.6	71.6	6.7	23.0
Luce	14.2	12.9	9.2	40.9	6,631	5,339	-19.5	-0.6	65	120	25	2,258	2.3	65.4	8.0	28.4
Mackinac	17.3	17.8	11.1	48.9	11,113	10,834	-2.5	0.7	110	229	197	5,268	2.0	60.5	7.3	32.1
Macomb	14.5	10.8	7.1	51.0	840,978	881,217	4.8	-0.5	10,980	13,197	-2,359	349,340	2.5	64.9	12.7	29.9
Manistee	16.3	16.6	10.4	48.2	24,733	25,032	1.2	1.3	235	463	556	9,701	2.4	63.9	8.5	30.9
Marquette	13.0	12.7	7.7	49.3	67,077	66,017	-1.6	0.1	646	990	430	27,177	2.3	58.3	8.1	31.4
Mason	15.5	15.9	9.5	50.1	28,705	29,052	1.2	1.1	329	491	501	12,296	2.3	63.8	9.3	30.9
Mecosta	13.9	11.8	7.2	49.4	42,798	39,714	-7.2	0.8	486	579	410	16,276	2.5	60.3	9.8	29.9
Menominee	16.9	15.7	10.5	48.5	24,029	23,502	-2.2	-0.9	227	398	-31	10,403	2.2	59.5	6.0	34.6
Midland	14.3	11.3	8.1	50.3	83,629	83,494	-0.2	0.0	1,061	1,107	0	34,253	2.4	67.3	9.1	27.0
Missaukee	15.7	13.0	8.3	49.3	14,849	15,052	1.4	0.5	182	262	158	6,194	2.4	68.3	7.8	26.0
Monroe	15.2	11.9	7.3	50.3	152,021	154,809	1.8	0.3	1,817	2,290	934	60,804	2.4	66.6	10.1	27.3
Montcalm	14.4	11.3	7.1	47.9	63,342	66,614	5.2	0.9	784	998	827	24,143	2.5	67.9	9.2	26.3
Montmorency	19.0	21.4	12.1	48.3	9,765	9,153	-6.3	1.6	87	219	282	4,490	2.0	62.3	8.1	32.8
Muskegon	13.9	11.3	6.7	50.2	172,188	175,824	2.1	0.4	2,338	2,676	1,009	66,064	2.5	67.2	14.9	26.5
Newaygo	15.8	12.7	7.5	49.3	48,460	49,978	3.1	0.6	622	785	481	19,365	2.5	68.7	8.6	26.0
Oakland	14.3	10.9	7.0	50.6	1,202,362	1,274,395	6.0	-0.3	15,495	16,516	-3,596	509,589	2.4	62.8	9.7	30.7
Oceana	15.9	13.5	8.1	48.7	26,570	26,659	0.3	0.6	297	406	266	10,208	2.5	72.0	10.3	24.3
Ogemaw	17.9	16.6	10.5	49.9	21,699	20,770	-4.3	-0.2	222	452	189	9,314	2.2	63.6	9.8	30.0
Ontonagon	20.4	22.1	15.2	48.6	6,780	5,816	-14.2	0.9	31	142	167	2,823	2.0	61.2	7.7	33.7
Osceola	15.4	13.0	8.5	49.2	23,528	22,891	-2.7	0.9	298	390	310	9,332	2.4	69.3	10.2	26.6
Oscoda	18.4	17.7	11.0	48.9	8,640	8,219	-4.9	1.1	80	172	188	3,732	2.2	63.4	6.5	30.8
Otsego	15.5	13.6	8.2	49.8	24,164	25,091	3.8	0.8	306	435	330	9,985	2.4	67.1	11.0	26.5
Ottawa	12.1	9.6	6.3	50.3	263,801	296,200	12.3	1.0	3,928	3,168	2,154	104,586	2.7	71.7	7.4	21.9
Presque Isle	18.4	20.2	13.0	49.9	13,376	12,982	-2.9	0.9	81	280	317	5,923	2.1	66.3	6.2	29.3
Roscommon	19.0	21.1	12.5	49.5	24,449	23,459	-4.0	0.7	182	584	591	11,420	2.1	59.1	8.9	35.6
Saginaw	13.8	11.8	8.1	51.1	200,169	190,124	-5.0	-0.3	2,523	3,195	122	78,980	2.3	62.4	14.1	31.2
St. Clair	16.0	12.3	7.6	50.0	163,040	160,383	-1.6	-0.2	1,841	2,750	566	65,668	2.4	66.6	10.8	27.6
St. Joseph	14.0	11.4	7.3	49.6	61,295	60,939	-0.6	-0.3	884	972	-104	24,319	2.5	66.8	11.0	27.0
Sanilac	15.9	13.7	9.0	49.7	43,114	40,611	-5.8	-0.3	486	722	134	17,920	2.3	65.2	8.9	28.3
Schoolcraft	18.7	17.9	10.4	49.9	8,485	8,047	-5.2	-0.2	63	156	77	3,675	2.2	63.0	6.3	32.1
Shiawassee	15.3	12.1	7.3	50.2	70,648	68,094	-3.6	-0.3	819	1,109	65	27,762	2.4	67.2	10.6	26.7
Tuscola	16.0	12.8	8.7	49.3	55,729	53,323	-4.3	-0.8	603	991	-23	21,719	2.4	65.6	8.3	28.7
Van Buren	14.8	12.3	6.9	50.2	76,258	75,587	-0.9	0.1	1,046	1,167	184	29,882	2.5	70.5	11.8	24.8
Washtenaw	11.4	9.4	5.7	50.3	344,791	372,258	8.0	-0.8	4,262	3,765	-3,408	143,040	2.4	56.8	8.1	30.3
Wayne	13.1	10.0	6.2	51.6	1,820,584	1,793,561	-1.5	-1.0	26,936	27,372	-18,459	694,858	2.5	59.9	17.9	34.4
Wexford	14.8	12.4	7.7	49.7	32,735	33,673	2.9	0.7	462	514	281	13,212	2.5	68.8	12.0	25.0
MINNESOTA	13.2	10.1	6.6	49.9	5,303,925	5,706,494	7.6	0.0	79,493	66,981	-11,734	2,207,988	2.5	63.6	9.0	28.8
Aitkin	19.0	19.6	13.8	49.3	16,202	15,697	-3.1	1.2	127	353	427	7,594	2.1	63.4	7.7	31.9
Anoka	14.0	9.3	5.6	49.6	330,844	363,887	10.0	0.9	5,020	3,547	1,603	129,308	2.7	70.5	10.2	23.0
Becker	14.5	13.5	8.4	49.8	32,504	35,183	8.2	0.1	444	578	170	13,942	2.4	67.1	8.5	29.3
Beltrami	12.0	10.4	6.3	49.8	44,442	46,228	4.0	0.3	767	706	82	17,882	2.5	61.2	14.7	31.2
Benton	12.1	8.2	5.8	49.6	38,451	41,379	7.6	0.2	613	562	18	16,482	2.4	61.2	8.6	29.0
Big Stone	16.1	14.1	12.2	49.7	5,269	5,166	-2.0	-0.4	71	104	12	2,294	2.1	60.6	4.4	32.1
Blue Earth	10.3	8.8	6.0	49.6	64,013	69,112	8.0	0.2	885	689	-43	26,390	2.4	58.4	8.5	25.3
Brown	14.5	11.8	9.7	49.9	25,893	25,912	0.1	-0.4	297	408	17	10,643	2.3	64.8	6.8	30.0
Carlton	14.3	11.0	7.0	47.1	35,386	36,207	2.3	0.6	453	547	295	13,811	2.4	67.8	10.7	24.8
Carver	13.7	8.6	4.9	49.9	91,042	106,922	17.4	1.6	1,379	860	1,171	37,386	2.8	74.0	7.0	20.9
Cass	16.9	16.5	10.1	48.5	28,567	30,066	5.2	1.9	342	484	727	13,249	2.2	63.5	9.0	28.8
Chippewa	13.9	11.8	9.6	49.6	12,441	12,598	1.3	-1.9	173	203	-207	5,133	2.3	64.5	9.3	31.8
Chisago	15.2	10.0	6.4	48.0	53,887	56,621	5.1	1.5	712	622	759	20,370	2.7	74.2	7.1	20.2
Clay	10.3	8.0	5.7	50.2	58,999	65,318	10.7	0.4	1,019	707	-73	24,695	2.5	61.8	8.5	30.5
Clearwater	14.4	11.5	8.9	49.0	8,695	8,524	-2.0	0.6	134	140	58	3,452	2.5	65.3	8.0	30.8
Cook	17.2	18.9	10.9	49.7	5,176	5,600	8.2	0.3	37	70	52	2,608	2.0	63.0	5.3	29.7
Cottonwood	13.0	11.9	10.5	49.1	11,687	11,517	-1.5	0.5	163	224	115	4,915	2.2	61.7	7.9	33.7
Crow Wing	15.6	14.0	9.4	49.8	62,500	66,123	5.8	1.7	803	986	1,348	27,605	2.3	63.9	7.7	29.6
Dakota	13.5	9.4	5.8	50.4	398,552	439,882	10.4	0.5	6,208	4,238	98	163,463	2.6	69.1	10.1	24.8
Dodge	12.9	9.3	6.2	49.6	20,087	20,867	3.9	0.3	299	186	-50	7,776	2.7	74.9	7.5	21.0
Douglas	14.7	13.4	9.9	49.6	36,009	39,006	8.3	0.6	512	636	356	16,810	2.2	63.8	6.4	30.9
Faribault	15.0	13.2	10.5	49.6	14,553	13,921	-4.3	-0.1	164	242	66	6,074	2.2	62.3	6.6	33.5

1. No spouse present.

STATE County	Persons in group quarters, 2021	Daytime Population, 2016–2020		Births, 2021		Deaths, 2021		Persons under 65 with no health insurance, 2019		Medicare, 2021			COVID-19 Deaths, 2020	
		Number	Employment/ residence ratio	Total	Rate[1]	Number	Rate[1]	Number	Percent	Total beneficiaries	Enrolled in Original Medicare	Enrolled in Medicare Advantage	Number	Rate[1]
	32	33	34	35	36	37	38	39	40	41	42	43	44	45
MICHIGAN— Cont'd														
Keweenaw	9	1,945	0.8	13	6.2	22	10.6	78	6.0	794	503	290	D	D
Lake	105	10,324	0.6	94	7.7	209	17.1	734	9.2	3,971	2,229	1,742	11	0.9
Lapeer	1,414	74,279	0.7	765	8.6	1,090	12.3	5,380	7.7	19,892	9,958	9,934	101	1.1
Leelanau	262	20,212	0.9	152	6.8	284	12.6	1,315	8.9	7,614	3,947	3,667	11	0.5
Lenawee	4,912	87,074	0.7	945	9.5	1,270	12.8	5,492	7.3	23,247	13,107	10,140	83	0.8
Livingston	1,314	159,528	0.7	1,659	8.5	1,929	9.9	7,914	5.0	39,363	21,640	17,723	90	0.5
Luce	887	6,451	1.1	50	9.4	90	16.9	334	8.8	1,643	800	844	D	D
Mackinac	76	10,932	1.0	83	7.6	181	16.7	995	13.0	3,659	1,959	1,699	D	D
Macomb	7,114	804,470	0.8	8,715	9.9	10,526	12.0	52,226	7.3	179,076	97,487	81,589	1,491	1.7
Manistee	1,284	23,739	0.9	180	7.1	372	14.8	1,384	8.2	7,743	4,448	3,295	23	0.9
Marquette	3,767	66,682	1.0	505	7.6	794	12.0	3,194	6.4	15,543	9,211	6,332	47	0.7
Mason	362	29,026	1.0	257	8.8	412	14.1	1,801	8.2	8,480	4,634	3,846	23	0.8
Mecosta	2,910	43,747	1.0	381	9.5	476	11.9	2,583	8.1	9,642	4,881	4,761	18	0.5
Menominee	359	20,714	0.8	191	8.2	311	13.3	1,352	8.0	6,560	3,845	2,715	25	1.1
Midland	1,185	84,543	1.0	855	10.2	900	10.8	4,200	6.3	18,636	10,009	8,626	48	0.6
Missaukee	150	12,834	0.6	144	9.5	224	14.8	1,155	9.8	3,848	2,237	1,611	D	D
Monroe	1,405	125,773	0.7	1,453	9.4	1,834	11.8	6,706	5.5	34,146	18,656	15,490	141	0.9
Montcalm	2,983	57,816	0.8	626	9.4	786	11.8	4,111	8.3	14,604	7,290	7,313	79	1.2
Montmorency	106	8,878	0.9	75	8.1	178	19.3	550	8.9	3,932	2,313	1,620	16	1.7
Muskegon	4,568	164,482	0.9	1,874	10.6	2,180	12.4	9,617	6.9	39,501	16,484	23,017	279	1.6
Newaygo	509	43,236	0.7	491	9.8	620	12.4	3,402	8.8	12,322	5,023	7,299	35	0.7
Oakland	13,629	1,343,428	1.1	12,316	9.7	13,259	10.4	59,635	5.7	246,767	140,652	106,114	1,539	1.2
Oceana	239	24,430	0.8	231	8.6	314	11.7	2,305	11.3	6,890	3,561	3,328	43	1.6
Ogemaw	184	20,652	1.0	178	8.6	351	16.9	1,328	8.7	6,915	4,204	2,711	30	1.4
Ontonagon	75	5,342	0.8	24	4.1	114	19.5	289	8.2	2,429	1,614	816	20	3.4
Osceola	366	21,966	0.9	243	10.6	318	13.8	1,574	8.7	6,077	3,421	2,656	19	0.8
Oscoda	40	8,301	1.0	58	7.0	147	17.8	623	10.6	2,952	1,772	1,180	16	1.9
Otsego	313	25,620	1.1	240	9.5	333	13.2	1,457	7.7	6,537	4,029	2,508	20	0.8
Ottawa	8,910	279,464	0.9	3,111	10.4	2,499	8.4	14,136	5.9	52,775	17,335	35,441	248	0.8
Presque Isle	210	11,708	0.8	67	5.1	223	17.1	779	9.3	4,900	2,961	1,940	14	1.1
Roscommon	200	23,659	1.0	141	6.0	461	19.6	1,306	8.3	9,518	5,178	4,340	32	1.4
Saginaw	6,486	203,357	1.2	2,021	10.7	2,545	13.4	8,608	5.8	45,811	21,892	23,920	372	2.0
St. Clair	1,883	140,435	0.7	1,458	9.1	2,192	13.7	8,002	6.3	37,927	20,867	17,060	172	1.1
St. Joseph	669	59,047	0.9	694	11.4	779	12.8	4,767	9.7	13,108	7,944	5,164	64	1.1
Sanilac	474	38,158	0.8	380	9.4	602	14.9	2,996	9.5	10,722	6,648	4,074	71	1.8
Schoolcraft	110	7,792	0.9	48	6.0	117	14.6	612	10.6	2,625	1,560	1,065	D	D
Shiawassee	756	58,010	0.7	664	9.8	898	13.2	3,462	6.4	16,263	8,384	7,878	58	0.9
Tuscola	1,030	45,422	0.7	484	9.1	802	15.1	2,938	7.2	13,802	7,033	6,769	100	1.9
Van Buren	765	68,331	0.8	819	10.8	925	12.2	5,560	9.1	17,356	9,101	8,255	93	1.2
Washtenaw	21,007	411,980	1.2	3,367	9.1	3,020	8.2	15,815	5.3	61,158	37,272	23,886	208	0.6
Wayne	22,540	1,812,335	1.1	21,470	12.0	21,853	12.3	110,013	7.6	330,614	164,264	166,350	3,281	1.8
Wexford	315	36,010	1.2	372	11.0	408	12.1	2,084	7.8	8,388	4,852	3,536	12	0.4
MINNESOTA	123,948	5,615,574	1.0	63,065	11.0	53,578	9.4	268,829	5.8	1,045,928	539,499	506,429	5,862	1.0
Aitkin	211	14,630	0.8	95	6.0	285	18.0	810	7.9	5,765	2,139	3,626	36	2.3
Anoka	2,826	299,705	0.7	3,966	10.8	2,825	7.7	15,598	5.1	59,451	27,419	32,032	380	1.0
Becker	411	33,700	1.0	365	10.4	472	13.4	2,095	7.8	8,462	4,823	3,639	46	1.3
Beltrami	1,785	47,247	1.0	604	13.0	551	11.9	3,851	10.3	9,236	6,212	3,025	49	1.1
Benton	964	35,455	0.8	486	11.7	449	10.8	2,118	6.1	7,425	4,192	3,233	82	2.0
Big Stone	132	4,967	1.0	56	10.9	80	15.5	228	6.3	1,502	955	547	D	D
Blue Earth	4,126	71,070	1.1	684	9.9	538	7.8	3,206	5.8	11,811	7,724	4,087	36	0.5
Brown	1,109	26,925	1.1	230	8.9	335	13.0	971	5.2	6,280	4,210	2,069	32	1.2
Carlton	1,939	32,729	0.8	355	9.8	430	11.9	1,670	5.9	7,760	3,239	4,521	44	1.2
Carver	778	91,666	0.8	1,098	10.2	718	6.7	3,074	3.3	14,817	7,056	7,761	39	0.4
Cass	185	28,193	0.9	279	9.2	389	12.8	2,215	10.3	9,090	5,087	4,002	26	0.9
Chippewa	232	11,815	1.0	136	10.9	166	13.3	672	7.4	2,921	1,837	1,084	32	2.5
Chisago	1,575	45,157	0.6	551	9.7	487	8.5	2,071	4.4	10,505	4,934	5,571	32	0.6
Clay	2,877	52,296	0.7	801	12.2	587	9.0	2,724	5.1	10,239	6,690	3,549	91	1.4
Clearwater	69	8,182	0.8	96	11.2	120	14.0	683	9.9	2,062	1,139	923	11	1.3
Cook	48	5,516	1.0	28	5.0	53	9.5	378	9.9	1,754	721	1,033	D	D
Cottonwood	221	11,567	1.1	134	11.6	163	14.1	620	7.3	2,875	1,859	1,016	19	1.7
Crow Wing	668	66,063	1.0	628	9.4	795	11.9	3,190	6.5	17,798	9,537	8,261	77	1.2
Dakota	2,696	386,090	0.8	4,940	11.2	3,452	7.8	16,258	4.4	71,969	36,478	35,492	318	0.7
Dodge	100	16,089	0.6	236	11.3	137	6.6	860	4.9	3,497	2,194	1,302	D	D
Douglas	474	39,059	1.1	391	10.0	512	13.1	1,420	4.9	10,626	5,809	4,818	61	1.6
Faribault	305	12,613	0.8	132	9.5	192	13.8	711	7.0	3,696	2,369	1,327	14	1.0

1. Per 1,000 estimated resident population.

STATE County	COVID-19 Vaccinations, 2021–2022: Officers	COVID-19 Vaccinations, 2021–2022: Civilians	Education: School enrollment and attainment, 2016–2020: Enrollment[1]: Total	Enrollment[1]: Percent private	Attainment[2] (percent): High school graduate or less	Attainment[2] (percent): Bachelor's degree or more	Local government expenditures,[3] 2018–2019: Total current spending (mil dol)	Local government expenditures,[3] 2018–2019: Current spending per student (dollars)	Money income, 2016–2020: Per capita income[4]	Households: Median income (dollars)	Households: Percent with income of less than $50,000	Households: Percent with income of $200,000 or more	Income and poverty, 2020: Median household income (dollars)	Percent below poverty level: All persons	Percent below poverty level: Children under 18 years	Percent below poverty level: Children 5 to 17 years in families
	46	47	48	49	50	51	52	53	54	55	56	57	58	59	60	61
MICHIGAN— Cont'd																
Keweenaw	1,235	58.4	264	3.0	33.8	36.2	0.2	53,750	35,765	51,750	47.7	2.9	49,890	11.2	17.2	17.4
Lake	7,596	64.1	1,905	10.3	55.0	13.5	8.2	15,969	22,022	38,356	63.2	1.5	39,971	19.2	32.6	32.5
Lapeer	41,568	47.4	18,243	11.1	45.0	18.3	129.2	11,033	31,927	65,197	37.4	3.9	68,959	8.2	11.4	10.7
Leelanau	17,885	82.2	3,644	21.8	24.7	46.7	31.2	15,632	39,308	67,330	35.3	7.2	77,687	7.4	12.1	12.0
Lenawee	52,171	53.0	23,026	20.3	46.2	21.1	189.0	12,615	28,695	57,314	44.0	2.9	58,849	9.5	12.2	10.9
Livingston	115,510	60.2	43,843	14.5	30.6	36.5	303.6	11,871	41,039	84,274	27.1	9.9	87,686	5.3	5.5	5.2
Luce	2,790	44.8	1,101	12.3	45.6	19.6	6.7	11,168	24,337	50,000	50.0	1.8	48,764	19.1	29.4	27.5
Mackinac	8,085	74.9	1,625	10.6	43.7	24.0	18.2	13,362	30,872	50,058	49.9	2.7	48,480	12.5	21.6	22.0
Macomb	497,085	56.9	197,786	12.1	39.0	25.9	1,441.1	11,928	33,327	64,641	38.7	5.1	64,870	9.2	12.6	11.7
Manistee	14,734	60.0	4,369	14.1	43.0	22.3	60.4	10,889	28,365	51,658	47.6	3.5	53,488	12.4	18.9	17.7
Marquette	42,784	64.1	17,467	10.5	33.8	34.0	104.0	12,508	28,537	54,585	45.6	3.1	52,793	13.6	13.8	13.1
Mason	17,684	60.7	5,640	11.4	43.9	22.0	61.8	15,482	29,102	51,568	48.5	2.8	52,571	12.3	18.9	17.1
Mecosta	18,257	42.0	12,869	9.2	45.0	22.9	79.4	13,734	23,748	45,797	53.5	2.1	52,949	13.6	19.0	18.0
Menominee	13,024	57.2	4,038	12.2	48.8	17.6	41.1	11,830	28,517	48,548	51.5	1.5	53,031	11.4	16.5	15.9
Midland	49,124	59.1	18,805	15.2	34.7	34.8	137.4	11,552	36,338	64,078	38.8	7.4	65,249	10.1	12.1	11.2
Missaukee	7,334	48.5	2,945	14.5	50.5	15.8	22.8	10,380	25,146	47,370	52.5	1.6	51,030	12.6	17.7	16.6
Monroe	85,828	57.0	33,724	14.1	42.7	21.0	268.5	12,041	33,202	65,453	37.0	4.6	69,182	9.7	11.9	11.0
Montcalm	27,166	42.5	13,442	15.0	50.4	14.5	123.5	12,142	25,010	52,390	46.7	2.1	52,589	13.1	18.3	17.7
Montmorency	5,078	54.4	1,343	17.0	52.9	14.8	7.6	11,749	25,221	42,160	58.3	1.0	43,350	15.5	25.7	25.7
Muskegon	95,497	55.0	38,209	10.7	42.2	19.7	326.3	12,156	26,655	53,478	46.3	3.1	58,445	12.3	17.6	17.0
Newaygo	21,911	44.7	10,211	13.6	52.0	17.2	92.5	12,540	25,970	51,470	47.9	2.1	51,122	12.3	16.8	16.7
Oakland	833,986	66.3	294,192	17.0	24.0	48.0	2,297.1	12,790	46,075	81,587	30.7	12.3	82,849	7.8	7.8	7.7
Oceana	14,378	54.3	5,346	11.1	48.9	19.6	35.3	11,237	25,028	51,161	48.7	1.9	52,388	13.3	19.3	18.1
Ogemaw	9,519	45.3	3,687	9.4	50.2	12.3	23.0	10,623	24,463	41,752	58.7	1.5	46,144	15.1	24.9	23.8
Ontonagon	3,953	69.1	707	8.8	51.5	15.3	14.4	30,833	24,833	41,776	59.7	0.2	43,309	14.7	23.4	22.1
Osceola	9,879	42.1	4,461	12.5	53.1	15.0	40.1	10,330	23,238	46,969	53.7	1.4	51,474	14.2	20.1	18.9
Oscoda	3,456	41.9	1,279	15.7	54.1	12.0	9.0	10,783	25,127	43,457	56.5	1.9	43,683	15.5	26.0	26.2
Otsego	13,710	55.6	5,060	18.9	38.7	25.6	40.9	10,676	27,904	55,917	46.1	2.4	61,330	9.3	14.3	13.9
Ottawa	168,234	57.6	82,547	19.4	33.8	35.1	556.1	12,220	33,005	72,418	31.7	6.5	77,465	6.7	6.1	5.5
Presque Isle	7,542	59.9	1,927	20.0	46.3	18.8	15.0	10,977	30,068	48,734	51.4	2.6	49,713	13.1	20.2	19.3
Roscommon	13,513	56.3	3,472	17.2	46.6	16.3	40.2	14,066	27,491	41,828	58.1	2.2	43,551	15.8	28.6	26.7
Saginaw	101,154	53.1	45,707	11.0	42.5	22.1	327.9	12,347	28,628	49,565	50.4	3.6	51,893	15.9	22.1	21.0
St. Clair	79,118	49.7	33,304	10.3	42.2	19.1	307.2	11,448	31,724	58,722	43.0	4.1	59,138	12.4	18.1	17.2
St. Joseph	27,586	45.2	13,462	9.6	49.6	16.0	124.0	12,004	26,810	53,253	46.5	2.2	54,896	13.0	17.4	16.0
Sanilac	17,556	42.6	7,932	12.0	52.2	14.8	70.1	11,647	27,350	49,852	50.1	1.9	51,171	15.3	21.9	20.3
Schoolcraft	4,520	55.8	1,223	13.9	51.9	18.9	8.2	10,061	27,936	48,443	51.0	2.4	49,684	11.9	18.7	17.7
Shiawassee	35,008	51.4	14,249	9.8	43.5	17.8	130.8	12,203	29,544	56,436	44.3	2.3	59,733	11.6	16.7	15.3
Tuscola	24,057	46.0	10,623	15.3	53.0	13.5	99.7	13,779	26,905	51,891	48.1	2.0	51,940	11.4	13.8	14.0
Van Buren	43,405	57.4	16,617	9.7	44.6	20.8	200.3	12,988	28,774	56,652	44.4	3.3	56,526	14.1	18.0	16.2
Washtenaw	261,293	71.1	126,159	9.2	19.0	56.7	623.5	14,052	42,855	75,730	34.1	11.7	77,019	12.0	9.7	8.9
Wayne	949,271	54.3	428,127	11.2	42.1	25.2	3,367.9	12,217	28,403	49,359	50.5	4.6	51,777	20.0	29.4	28.0
Wexford	17,307	51.5	7,042	14.8	45.3	19.7	80.8	13,502	26,554	50,335	49.7	2.9	56,550	11.4	15.9	15.4
MINNESOTA	3,897,629	69.1	1,392,298	15.4	30.9	36.8	11,775.5	13,331	38,881	73,382	33.6	8.5	75,489	8.3	9.5	9.1
Aitkin	9,354	58.9	2,582	8.8	43.5	18.4	25.8	13,211	30,585	49,086	50.6	2.7	49,822	11.1	15.6	14.5
Anoka	212,168	59.4	84,811	11.5	33.8	30.4	809.3	12,445	37,804	84,379	26.5	7.6	84,779	7.1	7.4	6.8
Becker	18,775	54.5	7,957	10.6	36.4	25.7	57.4	12,146	34,226	60,508	40.9	6.0	60,159	11.4	15.5	14.0
Beltrami	32,035	67.9	13,565	9.3	35.5	29.9	133.0	16,127	26,563	50,525	49.5	3.5	58,138	12.1	17.5	17.0
Benton	17,867	43.7	10,223	10.2	38.1	23.1	74.5	11,263	31,515	60,564	41.6	3.2	70,143	6.9	7.6	7.9
Big Stone	3,156	63.2	930	1.9	49.4	18.2	11.6	13,689	30,588	55,909	44.3	2.8	54,796	10.9	14.0	13.7
Blue Earth	41,085	60.7	21,742	9.5	32.7	34.6	136.5	12,029	29,965	61,058	41.3	3.6	67,193	11.0	10.7	9.4
Brown	16,491	65.9	6,151	29.5	42.9	22.6	49.0	14,341	30,900	59,804	40.9	2.2	61,978	6.8	7.7	7.3
Carlton	23,159	64.6	8,342	8.8	37.6	22.6	76.3	11,792	30,619	66,201	35.4	3.6	67,695	8.7	8.9	8.2
Carver	70,884	67.5	28,138	19.3	21.0	49.1	205.2	11,831	48,492	104,011	20.0	18.1	107,932	3.5	3.2	2.9
Cass	16,982	57.0	5,706	11.9	38.9	25.0	63.1	13,933	30,979	53,845	45.6	3.2	52,271	12.6	19.4	18.0
Chippewa	6,303	53.4	2,510	7.4	43.5	19.7	29.4	13,767	30,957	57,301	43.2	2.8	63,406	9.3	11.1	10.2
Chisago	32,550	57.5	12,642	10.7	37.7	22.2	92.6	12,587	35,869	86,900	26.5	6.3	85,178	6.3	6.3	5.6
Clay	38,221	59.5	19,726	16.4	27.8	34.2	125.2	11,574	31,233	66,069	38.4	4.0	74,266	8.8	8.7	8.5
Clearwater	3,695	41.9	2,083	11.2	50.6	17.6	18.1	12,156	27,548	51,742	48.2	1.9	51,147	12.8	14.4	13.9
Cook	4,391	80.4	807	6.8	25.3	45.2	9.1	13,850	36,941	59,537	38.3	4.5	58,561	8.7	11.2	10.4
Cottonwood	6,283	56.1	2,569	10.8	44.1	20.7	26.8	13,790	27,709	51,067	49.0	1.8	53,525	11.2	14.8	14.0
Crow Wing	36,842	56.6	12,750	8.7	35.3	26.2	119.1	11,949	32,962	57,779	42.6	3.6	58,213	8.5	10.9	9.6
Dakota	298,987	69.7	106,257	13.9	24.9	42.6	980.5	13,029	42,588	88,468	26.1	10.8	90,562	4.8	5.4	5.2
Dodge	12,679	60.6	5,408	8.9	37.1	27.4	40.4	10,135	36,008	79,020	25.4	5.8	77,340	5.9	6.0	5.6
Douglas	21,937	57.5	7,897	11.3	35.0	27.2	66.5	12,043	36,559	65,430	37.1	4.6	69,848	7.4	7.8	7.8
Faribault	7,850	57.5	2,829	8.5	43.1	19.8	22.3	12,609	30,600	53,963	45.5	2.2	55,599	10.3	13.6	12.2

1. All persons 3 years old and over enrolled in nursery school through college. 2. Persons 25 years old and over. 3. Elementary and secondary education expenditures. 4. Based on population estimated by the American Community Survey, 2016–2020.

STATE County	Personal income, 2020										Earnings, 2020		
			Per capita[1]			Supplements to wages and salaries, employer contributions (mil dol)						Contributions for government social insurance (mil dol)	
	Total (mil dol)	Percent change 2019–2020	Dollars	Rank	Wages and salaries (mil dol)	Pension and insurance	Government social insurance	Proprietors' income (mil dol)	Dividends, interest, and rent (mil dol)	Personal transfer receipts (mil dol)	Total (mil dol)	From employee and self-employed	From employer
	62	63	64	65	66	67	68	69	70	71	72	73	74
MICHIGAN— Cont'd													
Keweenaw	110	8.8	51,972	938	15	3	1	4	27	41	23	3	1
Lake	458	13.3	39,507	2,501	82	16	7	18	89	229	122	13	7
Lapeer	4,333	10.0	49,441	1,204	909	170	70	216	571	1,331	1,364	108	70
Leelanau	1,592	5.8	73,238	122	265	50	21	151	555	356	487	37	21
Lenawee	4,384	8.9	44,821	1,820	1,188	226	90	209	554	1,434	1,712	134	90
Livingston	12,044	6.1	62,622	327	3,104	511	234	529	1,883	2,397	4,379	299	234
Luce	223	12.4	36,339	2,843	69	17	5	8	39	109	99	8	5
Mackinac	544	12.0	50,217	1,119	169	33	16	31	120	210	248	20	16
Macomb	45,451	9.2	52,195	920	19,439	2,937	1,459	2,629	6,051	12,677	26,464	1,787	1,459
Manistee	1,098	9.7	44,382	1,894	314	67	24	46	242	459	451	38	24
Marquette	2,926	8.9	44,445	1,883	1,221	234	95	93	492	1,024	1,643	117	95
Mason	1,322	10.1	45,326	1,749	457	88	36	67	227	512	648	49	36
Mecosta	1,650	11.8	37,579	2,730	596	131	45	60	261	598	832	61	45
Menominee	1,076	7.5	47,594	1,441	287	63	22	58	196	351	431	34	22
Midland	4,803	5.7	57,561	537	2,400	365	167	239	880	1,142	3,171	209	167
Missaukee	611	12.8	40,298	2,417	147	28	12	62	91	224	250	18	12
Monroe	7,834	7.0	52,028	933	2,107	395	155	438	1,012	2,126	3,095	226	155
Montcalm	2,540	11.0	40,018	2,456	675	141	53	159	308	896	1,028	80	53
Montmorency	394	12.4	42,154	2,173	89	18	7	16	71	206	130	15	7
Muskegon	7,651	10.8	44,000	1,947	2,786	505	211	351	1,009	2,751	3,853	281	211
Newaygo	2,078	10.8	42,117	2,179	545	104	41	130	266	735	820	62	41
Oakland	96,442	4.4	76,941	94	50,164	6,323	3,642	8,924	19,599	16,560	69,053	4,328	3,642
Oceana	1,160	12.3	43,261	2,032	274	55	22	75	182	427	427	34	22
Ogemaw	818	13.6	39,101	2,557	221	42	18	47	118	392	327	28	18
Ontonagon	259	9.6	45,761	1,690	45	12	4	9	46	127	69	8	4
Osceola	985	10.8	41,965	2,204	375	64	29	60	129	364	528	41	29
Oscoda	304	6.4	36,374	2,841	47	11	4	25	54	156	86	9	4
Otsego	1,143	11.3	46,166	1,624	479	82	38	62	188	385	661	48	38
Ottawa	15,545	7.8	52,759	873	6,608	1,144	492	1,014	2,811	3,214	9,259	594	492
Presque Isle	581	11.5	45,872	1,670	120	27	10	23	107	244	179	19	10
Roscommon	990	11.1	41,258	2,293	222	44	17	40	185	504	323	37	17
Saginaw	8,606	8.5	45,328	1,748	4,070	708	309	653	1,094	3,157	5,740	396	309
St. Clair	7,982	9.4	50,107	1,133	2,326	434	176	432	1,071	2,550	3,368	252	176
St. Joseph	2,666	12.1	43,818	1,970	935	178	71	170	371	864	1,354	94	71
Sanilac	1,797	14.7	44,093	1,932	436	82	34	178	254	715	731	53	34
Schoolcraft	367	11.2	45,281	1,755	119	26	9	11	59	167	165	13	9
Shiawassee	3,038	10.0	44,855	1,816	711	139	54	145	380	1,036	1,049	88	54
Tuscola	2,252	13.2	43,073	2,052	520	103	40	149	278	896	813	68	40
Van Buren	3,462	9.9	45,869	1,672	1,061	212	78	202	490	1,109	1,554	112	78
Washtenaw	23,328	3.7	63,655	299	13,083	2,451	925	1,413	5,125	3,973	17,871	1,060	925
Wayne	84,922	9.5	48,788	1,282	48,193	7,003	3,517	4,738	11,376	29,986	63,451	4,133	3,517
Wexford	1,402	10.3	41,545	2,264	598	120	46	80	198	533	844	61	46
MINNESOTA	350,785	6.5	61,464	X	179,144	25,780	13,174	27,449	63,624	71,410	245,547	15,336	13,174
Aitkin	735	11.5	46,390	1,591	172	34	14	35	152	297	255	25	14
Anoka	20,045	6.3	55,694	661	7,506	1,113	576	1,087	2,675	4,077	10,283	673	576
Becker	1,784	7.7	51,772	954	613	111	50	181	281	545	955	65	50
Beltrami	2,152	8.3	45,368	1,742	955	177	75	113	343	708	1,321	87	75
Benton	2,023	8.2	49,403	1,212	855	130	69	177	262	507	1,232	77	69
Big Stone	308	20.2	62,498	334	77	15	6	46	52	96	144	9	6
Blue Earth	3,363	8.7	49,288	1,218	1,961	320	153	288	578	783	2,721	166	153
Brown	1,485	10.1	59,763	439	619	114	51	184	281	382	968	60	51
Carlton	1,689	6.6	47,227	1,486	643	118	50	53	223	551	864	62	50
Carver	8,065	5.1	75,677	106	2,379	384	179	557	1,353	932	3,499	216	179
Cass	1,537	8.7	51,340	991	382	77	31	88	331	582	579	45	31
Chippewa	660	9.4	56,148	626	246	47	20	106	101	179	419	25	20
Chisago	3,018	6.3	53,140	849	791	126	64	160	402	677	1,141	84	64
Clay	3,074	9.3	47,522	1,446	973	166	81	252	409	740	1,472	96	81
Clearwater	448	14.0	49,654	1,180	120	23	10	45	76	143	199	14	10
Cook	305	4.1	56,220	621	95	20	8	29	80	92	152	11	8
Cottonwood	631	24.0	56,130	629	244	45	22	121	96	178	431	24	22
Crow Wing	3,223	7.3	49,092	1,248	1,350	223	107	249	569	1,040	1,929	141	107
Dakota	27,959	5.0	64,748	272	11,969	1,730	873	1,821	4,394	4,741	16,393	1,039	873
Dodge	1,083	11.0	51,585	973	317	55	25	91	141	228	488	31	25
Douglas	2,148	8.2	56,039	638	926	159	71	193	390	582	1,349	91	71
Faribault	684	16.6	50,321	1,110	201	37	17	96	111	221	351	23	17

1. Based on the resident population estimated as of July 1 of the year shown.

STATE County	Earnings, 2020 (cont.)									Social Security beneficiaries, December 2020		Supple-mental Security Income recipients, 2020	Housing units, 2021	
	Percent by selected industries													
	Farm	Mining, quarrying, and extractions	Construction	Manu-facturing	Information; professional, scientific, technical services	Retail trade	Finance, insurance, real estate, and leasing	Health care and social assistance	Govern-ment	Number	Rate[1]		Total	Percent change, 2010–2021
	75	76	77	78	79	80	81	82	83	84	85	86	87	88
MICHIGAN— Cont'd														
Keweenaw	0.0	0.2	D	3.8	D	5.5	D	D	29.2	815	387	24	2,287	0.7
Lake	0.9	0.2	5.4	D	2.3	4.8	4.2	21.1	24.5	4,390	357	637	13,385	0.5
Lapeer	2.0	0.6	10.1	18.8	4.4	9.0	5.7	6.6	20.4	22,380	253	1,254	36,942	0.5
Leelanau	3.5	D	12.3	5.2	D	5.0	8.5	8.7	22.3	7,550	334	110	15,567	0.7
Lenawee	2.7	D	5.6	24.0	3.8	7.4	7.3	10.5	18.7	25,195	255	1,882	43,703	0.3
Livingston	0.3	0.2	10.4	18.9	10.2	8.9	5.8	10.2	10.9	42,330	217	1,205	79,252	0.8
Luce	0.9	0.0	D	2.6	D	8.3	4.8	D	54.0	1,835	346	196	4,070	0.1
Mackinac	1.2	D	5.9	2.4	D	11.6	3.8	10.4	23.2	3,915	359	215	10,555	0.3
Macomb	0.1	0.0	7.7	20.7	14.7	6.9	5.1	10.4	13.3	188,545	215	22,813	371,226	0.4
Manistee	0.6	D	6.1	20.1	2.8	8.7	3.3	D	34.7	8,300	327	639	15,593	0.7
Marquette	0.0	8.5	5.6	5.0	6.9	7.1	4.8	20.4	22.0	17,140	259	1,054	33,523	0.2
Mason	3.1	1.2	7.1	21.0	D	8.2	4.8	11.9	18.3	9,285	316	671	17,494	0.5
Mecosta	1.4	0.1	7.4	13.9	D	10.8	3.3	9.7	34.5	10,585	264	1,132	21,011	0.5
Menominee	4.0	D	3.0	33.1	D	5.0	2.4	D	27.0	7,185	308	450	13,239	0.2
Midland	0.3	D	6.0	17.7	4.6	4.3	4.0	13.4	7.2	20,330	244	1,533	36,983	0.3
Missaukee	18.3	D	7.8	17.1	2.9	8.6	4.2	D	13.9	4,220	279	340	8,657	0.4
Monroe	1.6	D	6.0	17.8	D	6.5	3.4	8.1	12.2	36,910	238	2,473	66,249	0.5
Montcalm	5.7	D	7.9	18.6	D	8.3	4.0	14.0	21.0	16,335	243	1,813	27,952	0.2
Montmorency	2.0	D	D	19.4	D	5.6	D	14.3	16.7	4,395	473	372	8,932	0.0
Muskegon	0.7	0.2	6.3	24.6	4.3	11.1	4.2	16.5	14.2	43,545	247	5,973	74,881	0.3
Newaygo	6.3	D	7.4	18.4	5.8	11.2	9.3	7.1	17.8	13,615	271	1,336	24,735	0.6
Oakland	0.0	0.0	5.0	10.4	22.9	5.6	13.4	11.4	5.8	250,435	197	20,562	556,935	0.4
Oceana	9.0	0.6	7.2	22.4	3.0	7.4	3.6	D	22.4	7,560	282	816	15,654	0.7
Ogemaw	6.2	0.6	7.3	4.2	3.5	15.4	3.8	D	14.3	7,685	371	743	15,276	0.2
Ontonagon	1.4	0.0	4.4	1.2	D	18.2	D	13.0	31.8	2,625	447	131	5,252	0.1
Osceola	2.8	0.6	15.8	25.5	D	6.3	1.9	8.9	12.4	6,905	299	813	12,605	0.5
Oscoda	2.2	0.1	13.2	11.4	3.9	11.2	5.2	2.2	25.4	3,140	378	255	7,678	0.3
Otsego	0.4	3.5	7.9	12.1	3.8	14.0	6.3	D	14.6	7,310	289	597	14,886	0.1
Ottawa	1.8	0.1	7.2	35.3	5.7	5.2	4.7	5.5	13.0	56,205	188	2,536	116,218	1.4
Presque Isle	4.5	10.7	5.7	4.0	3.4	7.0	5.1	D	21.2	5,460	417	379	9,839	0.3
Roscommon	0.0	1.7	8.4	D	D	17.7	5.5	D	26.2	10,620	449	942	23,132	0.3
Saginaw	0.8	0.4	4.7	19.3	6.1	7.5	6.5	19.6	13.6	49,910	263	8,429	86,139	0.2
St. Clair	0.6	0.0	10.8	16.6	4.1	6.9	6.0	13.7	16.1	41,450	259	3,506	72,329	0.2
St. Joseph	4.0	0.0	4.7	40.1	3.3	7.0	2.7	9.0	13.6	14,600	240	1,268	27,191	0.3
Sanilac	15.7	0.9	5.9	23.6	2.4	8.2	4.7	D	13.2	11,755	290	963	21,719	0.2
Schoolcraft	0.7	7.8	5.0	10.3	2.8	7.2	7.5	4.5	39.2	2,740	341	235	5,967	0.2
Shiawassee	2.2	0.1	6.8	13.1	6.3	9.3	3.8	15.8	19.7	17,870	263	1,641	30,289	0.2
Tuscola	7.7	D	6.8	11.9	D	6.5	4.0	D	24.4	15,335	290	1,369	23,976	0.2
Van Buren	5.4	D	5.2	13.0	12.2	5.4	2.5	4.6	20.9	19,165	253	2,111	37,168	0.5
Washtenaw	0.1	D	2.9	6.6	19.8	3.9	4.8	10.8	33.9	61,740	167	5,232	157,985	0.6
Wayne	0.0	0.1	3.9	12.6	13.1	4.6	7.7	13.5	11.9	355,545	200	81,280	791,060	0.1
Wexford	0.4	0.4	4.3	24.0	D	7.8	4.3	12.6	18.0	9,470	279	1,119	16,493	0.4
MINNESOTA	1.7	0.3	6.2	11.9	11.3	5.2	10.2	13.6	12.8	1,069,913	187	92,761	2,517,248	1.0
Aitkin	0.3	2.0	9.0	9.3	D	8.5	3.4	D	21.4	4,985	314	250	14,120	1.1
Anoka	0.3	0.0	10.4	22.8	5.7	6.6	4.6	12.1	12.2	60,820	166	4,771	139,874	1.1
Becker	6.5	0.4	9.1	13.7	4.2	8.0	4.7	12.2	22.5	9,340	265	642	19,868	1.0
Beltrami	0.7	D	8.7	4.2	4.0	8.4	3.4	22.8	31.0	9,820	212	1,134	21,491	0.9
Benton	2.9	0.0	23.0	18.9	2.4	7.2	3.9	7.8	9.9	7,595	183	647	17,500	0.7
Big Stone	22.4	D	14.3	0.6	D	3.8	D	D	25.9	1,515	294	103	2,993	0.3
Blue Earth	2.9	D	6.4	13.2	7.6	8.0	5.8	21.6	15.3	12,085	174	1,063	29,532	1.1
Brown	8.5	D	7.2	21.4	9.0	5.5	3.7	12.7	12.1	6,530	253	253	11,809	0.2
Carlton	-0.1	D	9.2	12.8	3.2	5.8	5.7	12.9	35.4	8,330	229	566	15,818	0.6
Carver	0.7	0.0	10.2	25.6	7.3	4.8	5.8	11.4	10.8	15,180	140	580	41,177	1.6
Cass	1.2	0.0	9.7	7.0	D	7.7	5.1	D	37.9	10,190	333	586	24,176	1.1
Chippewa	10.2	D	5.1	14.7	D	13.8	6.0	D	20.2	2,770	224	147	5,630	0.1
Chisago	1.0	D	12.2	14.1	10.2	7.9	2.8	19.8	14.6	11,320	197	604	22,602	1.1
Clay	5.1	D	6.3	8.2	6.3	6.7	3.9	11.4	22.3	10,755	164	1,233	27,183	1.0
Clearwater	5.7	D	27.1	17.5	D	3.2	D	12.4	15.5	2,240	261	194	4,454	0.1
Cook	0.0	0.0	10.4	D	2.8	7.5	3.8	4.4	35.5	1,795	320	35	6,014	1.1
Cottonwood	22.1	D	6.0	24.9	D	3.7	3.0	D	12.8	3,070	265	215	5,151	0.0
Crow Wing	0.2	0.0	11.6	9.0	6.4	10.9	7.3	20.4	14.9	19,060	283	1,172	42,159	1.1
Dakota	0.3	0.1	7.8	11.6	10.7	7.1	12.7	8.0	11.5	72,565	164	4,671	176,021	1.2
Dodge	5.8	D	13.9	26.0	2.6	3.2	D	D	15.7	3,715	177	170	8,381	0.9
Douglas	1.8	0.1	9.8	21.1	4.2	8.8	5.6	10.4	18.7	11,025	281	474	22,094	1.3
Faribault	17.9	0.0	5.5	18.2	4.1	3.9	5.9	D	14.2	3,875	279	251	6,913	0.0

1. Per 1,000 resident population estimated as of July 1 of the year shown.

STATE County	Housing units, 2016–2020: Total	Occupied units: Owner-occupied: Percent	Owner-occupied: Median value[1]	Median owner cost as a percent of income: With a mortgage	Median owner cost as a percent of income: Without a mortgage[2]	Renter-occupied: Median rent[3]	Renter-occupied: Median rent as a percent of income[2]	Sub-standard units[4] (percent)	Civilian labor force, 2021: Total	Percent change, 2020–2021	Unemployment: Total	Unemployment: Rate[5]	Civilian employment[6], 2016–2020: Total	Percent: Management, business, science, and arts	Percent: Construction, production, and maintenance occupations
	89	90	91	92	93	94	95	96	97	98	99	100	101	102	103
MICHIGAN— Cont'd															
Keweenaw	1,079	88.6	141,800	17.7	11.8	562	19.5	1.7	883	-1.3	59	6.7	807	45.8	16.7
Lake	4,985	83.5	89,700	23.7	13.6	647	33.1	1.2	3,843	-2.8	316	8.2	3,932	24.4	29.1
Lapeer	34,041	85.1	179,900	20.0	10.7	797	31.6	1.6	40,133	-1.0	2,429	6.1	40,075	32.2	34.3
Leelanau	9,201	88.9	285,700	22.6	10.7	961	28.5	1.0	10,047	-1.6	523	5.2	9,754	39.9	21.1
Lenawee	38,693	77.8	143,000	20.0	11.5	796	27.2	1.2	44,522	-2.2	2,429	5.5	44,724	29.8	31.4
Livingston	72,905	85.1	256,100	18.8	10.6	1,067	27.5	0.9	101,855	1.1	4,234	4.2	97,455	42.5	20.5
Luce	2,258	80.3	97,200	18.7	10.9	739	27.6	0.3	2,119	-4.7	150	7.1	2,137	35.4	22.9
Mackinac	5,268	73.0	136,100	21.1	11.2	637	25.6	1.9	4,785	-3.0	410	8.6	4,497	32.1	23.7
Macomb	349,340	74.1	174,000	19.6	12.1	977	29.2	2.2	439,812	-0.5	26,105	5.9	426,386	36.2	24.4
Manistee	9,701	84.6	130,900	19.3	11.5	727	29.8	1.6	9,744	-4.1	710	7.3	9,682	30.9	25.3
Marquette	27,177	71.5	154,200	19.0	10.0	755	31.2	1.4	30,639	-3.2	1,644	5.4	30,641	33.5	20.3
Mason	12,296	76.0	151,400	19.9	11.4	748	30.4	1.1	13,009	-2.0	838	6.4	12,594	29.6	29.7
Mecosta	16,276	74.5	122,500	19.4	11.6	716	30.1	3.0	17,735	-3.1	1,130	6.4	18,587	30.1	30.5
Menominee	10,403	78.4	112,600	18.0	11.6	579	26.1	1.7	10,438	-1.8	472	4.5	10,651	26.0	38.4
Midland	34,253	77.3	145,900	18.0	11.1	807	28.8	1.6	38,276	-2.4	1,880	4.9	38,228	41.3	21.4
Missaukee	6,194	79.8	123,300	19.9	11.7	727	29.9	3.9	6,800	-1.4	379	5.6	6,359	26.9	39.4
Monroe	60,804	80.6	167,400	18.6	12.3	870	29.7	1.5	72,149	-2.7	4,340	6.0	70,351	32.1	32.3
Montcalm	24,143	79.7	121,800	19.2	12.2	728	28.7	2.4	27,073	-2.6	1,512	5.6	27,192	25.2	37.0
Montmorency	4,490	85.7	113,300	22.0	12.3	700	36.1	1.0	2,936	-2.5	275	9.4	3,202	26.8	32.6
Muskegon	66,064	76.2	126,400	18.9	11.7	780	29.0	2.2	75,304	-2.7	5,641	7.5	76,653	28.7	32.9
Newaygo	19,365	84.4	128,900	21.3	12.7	736	29.1	3.3	22,817	-2.0	1,284	5.6	20,702	27.7	35.7
Oakland	509,589	71.2	252,800	19.0	11.4	1,100	26.5	1.2	660,330	1.1	30,873	4.7	646,707	50.8	15.1
Oceana	10,208	83.5	121,900	20.6	11.3	725	28.0	4.4	11,581	-3.5	860	7.4	11,112	27.6	39.5
Ogemaw	9,314	81.5	103,200	22.4	12.4	686	34.9	2.4	7,874	-2.2	618	7.8	7,533	26.8	28.0
Ontonagon	2,823	88.2	74,400	20.7	11.8	550	28.2	1.6	2,012	-1.5	153	7.6	1,997	29.3	25.0
Osceola	9,332	82.3	102,800	21.0	12.1	671	28.0	2.5	11,277	-2.0	624	5.5	9,028	23.9	41.6
Oscoda	3,732	85.9	96,800	22.1	11.5	691	27.4	3.6	2,630	-5.9	239	9.1	2,788	23.3	34.5
Otsego	9,985	77.5	147,100	19.5	10.4	767	30.4	1.8	11,351	-2.2	772	6.8	11,108	31.1	25.7
Ottawa	104,586	78.4	209,400	18.4	10.0	932	28.2	2.0	156,739	-1.6	6,384	4.1	149,666	37.0	26.5
Presque Isle	5,923	88.7	111,200	20.5	10.3	552	29.7	1.5	4,796	-2.9	379	7.9	4,522	31.9	30.1
Roscommon	11,420	80.3	111,300	20.8	10.8	677	32.8	1.6	7,388	-4.5	709	9.6	7,923	30.1	25.2
Saginaw	78,980	71.5	106,200	18.7	11.9	783	31.6	1.3	81,321	-3.7	5,755	7.1	82,355	32.2	25.4
St. Clair	65,668	79.0	162,300	19.8	11.7	840	30.8	1.3	74,255	-0.5	4,393	5.9	72,946	31.2	32.0
St. Joseph	24,319	74.1	128,800	19.2	10.9	734	25.5	2.5	27,776	-4.2	1,422	5.1	28,318	25.0	44.0
Sanilac	17,920	78.4	121,500	19.8	11.2	701	26.5	2.0	18,923	-2.4	1,155	6.1	17,935	27.6	38.2
Schoolcraft	3,675	83.8	114,400	20.5	10.6	551	31.3	1.3	3,128	-3.4	251	8.0	3,067	30.6	26.1
Shiawassee	27,762	76.9	127,500	18.7	10.9	742	28.1	1.5	31,704	-3.0	1,796	5.7	31,816	28.3	31.5
Tuscola	21,719	83.7	108,200	18.9	12.4	727	26.1	1.7	22,658	-4.0	1,422	6.3	22,601	25.7	35.0
Van Buren	29,882	77.6	147,400	19.7	11.5	747	29.3	2.9	33,843	-2.4	2,049	6.1	34,827	28.8	32.6
Washtenaw	143,040	61.5	278,500	19.4	11.3	1,161	30.6	1.4	189,511	-1.9	8,161	4.3	188,718	55.4	13.3
Wayne	694,858	62.5	122,700	19.6	13.2	896	31.8	2.7	797,703	-0.5	63,563	8.0	747,847	34.5	25.2
Wexford	13,212	78.6	115,500	19.8	11.5	723	29.1	3.2	14,561	-2.1	867	6.0	14,365	29.7	35.9
MINNESOTA	2,207,988	71.9	235,700	19.6	10.5	1,010	28.2	2.6	3,021,360	-3.3	102,967	3.4	2,957,615	42.2	21.6
Aitkin	7,594	84.1	183,400	23.5	12.7	740	30.0	2.7	7,244	-3.7	340	4.7	6,372	31.7	28.9
Anoka	129,308	80.9	244,500	19.9	10.0	1,162	28.3	2.0	195,027	-3.0	6,593	3.4	192,013	37.7	25.0
Becker	13,942	78.8	202,600	21.4	10.8	737	27.4	3.0	18,683	-1.9	626	3.4	16,461	36.4	28.0
Beltrami	17,882	67.8	167,000	20.6	12.0	827	32.2	2.7	23,933	-4.3	883	3.7	21,552	37.7	19.6
Benton	16,482	65.8	187,300	20.1	10.7	780	25.0	2.9	21,312	-3.9	907	4.3	21,790	32.6	27.4
Big Stone	2,294	70.7	108,900	17.3	10.7	606	26.0	0.5	2,395	-6.3	83	3.5	2,258	38.1	27.0
Blue Earth	26,390	61.3	194,800	19.5	10.6	913	29.8	2.7	39,179	-4.0	1,198	3.1	37,919	34.7	23.8
Brown	10,643	76.6	144,000	17.9	10.2	662	24.8	1.4	13,430	-6.1	416	3.1	13,349	31.7	30.9
Carlton	13,811	79.8	179,400	19.5	11.3	847	27.0	2.0	17,106	-4.0	685	4.0	16,363	34.5	25.5
Carver	37,386	82.1	333,400	18.9	10.5	1,170	27.1	0.9	58,187	-2.7	1,581	2.7	57,269	49.5	17.1
Cass	13,249	80.3	200,700	22.5	11.4	823	24.1	3.0	15,598	7.2	689	4.4	12,904	29.5	26.2
Chippewa	5,133	67.8	118,100	18.8	10.0	659	24.4	2.7	6,462	-5.0	191	3.0	5,824	32.2	29.2
Chisago	20,370	86.4	244,600	20.8	11.9	912	27.8	1.2	29,423	-3.2	1,088	3.7	29,560	35.3	27.6
Clay	24,695	66.6	205,400	20.0	11.4	859	32.6	2.1	36,092	-1.4	984	2.7	34,058	40.1	20.6
Clearwater	3,452	80.7	139,500	21.2	12.0	666	31.0	5.1	4,409	-3.4	256	5.8	3,800	31.1	31.3
Cook	2,608	77.1	251,900	23.6	11.0	735	21.8	7.5	2,867	-4.7	129	4.5	2,815	41.1	19.1
Cottonwood	4,915	75.9	106,900	18.7	11.3	599	22.3	2.6	6,409	0.6	216	3.4	5,348	31.3	36.2
Crow Wing	27,605	76.4	208,900	21.4	10.6	806	28.8	1.7	31,834	-2.2	1,279	4.0	30,830	35.4	24.0
Dakota	163,463	75.1	280,300	19.3	10.0	1,235	28.4	2.0	237,756	-3.0	7,469	3.1	234,312	44.6	18.7
Dodge	7,776	85.3	197,100	19.1	10.0	720	21.7	1.8	11,735	-3.2	364	3.1	11,337	36.4	29.7
Douglas	16,810	73.9	226,500	19.8	11.6	710	28.1	1.6	20,894	-2.4	590	2.8	19,488	35.4	28.3
Faribault	6,074	77.0	94,100	17.7	10.0	629	23.6	1.3	6,806	-4.9	258	3.8	6,900	31.2	35.1

1. Specified owner-occupied units. 2. A value of 10.0 represents 10 percent or less; a value of 50.0 represents 50 percent or more. 3. Specified renter-occupied units. 4. Overcrowded or lacking complete plumbing facilities. 5. Percent of civilian labor force. 6. Civilian employed persons 16 years old and over.

STATE County	Private nonfarm establishments, employment and payroll, 2020									Agriculture, 2017			
		Employment						Annual payroll		Farms			Farm producers whose primary occupation is farming (percent)
											Percent with:		
	Number of establish-ments	Total	Health care and social assistance	Manufac-turing	Retail trade	Finance and insurance	Professional, scientific, and technical services	Total (mil dol)	Average per employee (dollars)	Number	Fewer than 50 acres	1000 acres or more	
	104	105	106	107	108	109	110	111	112	113	114	115	116
MICHIGAN— Cont'd													
Keweenaw	59	302	NA	30	17	NA	25	11	36,884	9	100.0	NA	NA
Lake	148	1,051	249	103	243	70	38	32	30,922	168	37.5	1.2	32.5
Lapeer	1,709	19,980	3,156	5,417	3,261	409	565	703	35,173	1,013	52.0	3.4	46.5
Leelanau	747	4,701	514	502	625	208	185	202	42,948	470	50.6	0.9	46.9
Lenawee	1,771	22,865	2,986	5,909	3,323	876	432	879	38,428	1,361	42.7	7.6	41.9
Livingston	4,373	57,870	9,198	9,907	9,160	3,926	2,592	2,262	39,079	724	61.7	2.6	41.9
Luce	160	1,465	398	184	278	52	27	55	37,544	71	56.3	1.4	35.5
Mackinac	439	2,301	421	109	357	101	37	120	52,112	101	37.6	7.9	32.0
Macomb	18,877	312,625	41,943	70,940	42,761	5,764	36,363	16,012	51,217	404	55.7	4.7	53.3
Manistee	558	5,852	921	1,037	992	151	112	217	37,072	274	37.6	1.1	41.2
Marquette	1,607	21,455	5,360	959	3,589	946	680	877	40,891	179	49.7	3.4	41.6
Mason	719	8,830	1,247	1,805	1,440	233	192	358	40,492	472	41.5	2.8	38.7
Mecosta	698	9,207	1,575	2,092	2,064	193	194	322	34,985	694	31.7	2.2	45.6
Menominee	445	5,167	275	1,897	602	119	175	196	37,885	353	29.7	3.4	42.9
Midland	1,746	35,275	7,528	5,092	3,373	1,200	3,145	2,245	63,651	530	51.3	4.2	39.2
Missaukee	299	2,378	365	398	414	43	32	87	36,606	406	35.7	6.9	46.1
Monroe	2,291	36,898	4,626	7,203	5,054	716	1,111	1,668	45,199	1,085	57.7	4.1	40.5
Montcalm	1,020	13,381	2,987	3,111	2,497	339	200	491	36,714	962	45.2	4.6	40.1
Montmorency	201	1,750	245	439	302	40	20	56	32,157	178	34.8	1.7	38.1
Muskegon	3,096	52,426	10,146	13,948	8,061	1,067	1,573	2,202	42,001	476	61.1	2.3	44.0
Newaygo	825	10,748	1,710	2,676	1,737	747	310	449	41,733	850	46.2	3.4	42.8
Oakland	39,023	723,903	121,306	53,765	74,472	48,809	104,399	44,064	60,870	514	68.9	0.6	38.1
Oceana	468	4,889	539	1,617	587	116	119	188	38,357	545	36.7	5.0	47.3
Ogemaw	554	5,439	1,226	304	1,332	141	91	188	34,549	294	34.4	4.8	50.6
Ontonagon	161	823	185	29	225	48	15	27	32,817	114	11.4	1.8	33.7
Osceola	445	6,913	1,080	2,921	502	117	67	289	41,779	625	37.4	2.2	36.9
Oscoda	189	1,575	126	331	231	35	33	51	32,468	144	54.9	0.7	21.6
Otsego	792	9,471	1,573	1,387	2,113	192	166	377	39,858	193	43.5	2.6	36.9
Ottawa	6,374	116,717	11,584	41,371	11,354	2,306	4,607	5,340	45,749	1,130	56.8	3.0	50.4
Presque Isle	314	2,136	260	183	367	93	35	79	36,828	322	25.5	3.4	40.6
Roscommon	527	4,315	575	590	1,221	150	66	140	32,381	48	43.8	2.1	32.5
Saginaw	4,126	78,468	17,710	10,667	12,371	2,954	2,505	3,324	42,360	1,250	44.2	5.8	42.1
St. Clair	3,005	39,947	7,663	8,694	6,452	1,177	1,141	1,673	41,870	1,077	52.6	3.0	42.8
St. Joseph	1,116	19,145	1,658	9,162	2,665	440	675	835	43,591	896	45.5	8.3	39.7
Sanilac	797	8,651	1,269	3,008	1,470	359	170	319	36,907	1,315	33.7	8.1	58.9
Schoolcraft	210	1,816	409	166	281	157	44	78	42,868	62	37.1	6.5	24.5
Shiawassee	1,120	13,729	2,941	1,843	2,535	300	369	520	37,908	972	51.1	4.9	41.5
Tuscola	796	9,028	2,498	1,176	1,508	270	232	366	40,583	1,241	42.4	6.5	50.3
Van Buren	1,259	16,179	2,155	3,113	2,655	302	2,260	783	48,422	953	52.2	2.3	42.4
Washtenaw	8,222	156,611	40,193	14,710	17,683	3,247	16,315	9,409	60,077	1,245	59.7	2.7	39.8
Wayne	32,586	669,584	115,274	86,350	72,956	40,089	49,508	38,391	57,335	248	79.8	NA	47.5
Wexford	882	12,921	1,837	3,391	2,064	330	241	491	38,036	304	43.1	1.6	45.3
MINNESOTA	150,819	2,738,254	480,903	315,783	303,433	168,668	185,628	155,205	56,680	68,822	28.8	9.3	45.5
Aitkin	408	3,512	987	398	679	96	32	129	36,829	462	19.3	2.4	34.9
Anoka	8,003	125,737	17,835	21,738	16,592	2,067	5,138	6,230	49,549	360	60.0	1.7	37.4
Becker	934	10,760	2,239	2,570	1,817	275	215	427	39,704	943	20.5	7.7	39.9
Beltrami	1,232	15,555	4,119	941	3,219	390	464	592	38,035	583	25.6	4.3	32.8
Benton	925	15,791	2,398	4,019	1,825	263	258	760	48,105	816	32.2	4.0	41.3
Big Stone	180	1,391	548	NA	223	68	26	57	40,868	438	17.8	19.4	47.9
Blue Earth	1,944	35,395	7,830	4,214	6,048	1,069	1,066	1,411	39,868	983	30.9	10.9	49.2
Brown	792	13,485	2,481	2,713	1,630	474	467	569	42,191	1,040	25.1	5.9	44.8
Carlton	665	7,117	2,026	1,140	990	332	156	323	45,354	529	25.7	0.9	35.4
Carver	2,534	40,614	5,304	9,857	3,887	856	3,136	2,137	52,627	689	38.3	5.2	45.0
Cass	840	6,537	1,350	315	1,064	169	158	225	34,462	432	20.8	4.4	45.8
Chippewa	379	5,099	1,242	1,226	643	220	91	191	37,527	623	26.6	15.4	52.3
Chisago	1,293	14,261	3,847	2,424	1,912	238	941	678	47,563	821	52.1	1.7	34.8
Clay	1,309	17,575	4,424	919	2,648	524	636	638	36,307	694	20.2	23.9	55.2
Clearwater	198	2,223	532	457	278	79	53	114	51,429	414	23.9	8.7	36.6
Cook	271	1,986	226	59	299	39	22	68	34,272	32	78.1	NA	20.4
Cottonwood	349	3,559	739	960	524	95	67	123	34,570	744	22.4	17.7	55.9
Crow Wing	2,192	27,290	6,250	2,890	4,811	1,048	1,068	1,114	40,814	494	29.8	2.6	34.0
Dakota	10,600	182,645	25,600	18,281	25,860	12,232	8,921	9,870	54,038	820	48.5	6.1	49.1
Dodge	403	4,793	275	1,758	451	108	100	222	46,316	611	40.9	13.3	47.9
Douglas	1,350	17,859	3,833	3,687	3,042	437	451	821	45,977	960	27.8	5.7	36.6
Faribault	389	3,527	736	890	500	180	86	139	39,459	822	28.6	14.4	55.0

STATE County	Agriculture, 2017 (cont.) Land in farms: Acreage (1,000)	Percent change, 2012–2017	Acres: Average size of farm	Acres: Total irrigated (1,000)	Acres: Total cropland (1,000)	Value of land and buildings (dollars): Average per farm	Average per acre	Value of machinery and equipment, average per farm (dollars)	Value of products sold: Total (mil dol)	Average per farm (acres)	Percent from: Crops	Livestock and poultry products	Organic farms (number)	Farms with internet access (percent)	Government payments: Total ($1,000)	Percent of farms
	117	118	119	120	121	122	123	124	125	126	127	128	129	130	131	132
MICHIGAN— Cont'd																
Keweenaw	0	-24.5	27	NA	0.1	90,000	3,375	26,667	0.0	222	100.0	NA	NA	66.7	NA	NA
Lake	22	-16.9	129	0.1	11.8	316,975	2,462	52,897	3.2	19,321	41.7	58.3	NA	69.6	49	6.5
Lapeer	165	-5.8	163	2.4	128.7	752,544	4,607	141,624	87.0	85,838	72.9	27.1	16	76.8	1,424	18.0
Leelanau	50	-15.9	106	2.3	29.9	779,662	7,321	111,622	42.4	90,302	93.7	6.3	12	87.7	376	14.0
Lenawee	386	12.0	283	9.8	345.2	1,481,398	5,226	196,185	259.9	190,951	64.7	35.3	6	81.3	11,691	53.3
Livingston	89	3.7	123	1.1	67.2	703,733	5,701	85,997	48.5	66,965	62.5	37.5	7	84.0	1,444	13.3
Luce	10	-14.7	139	D	4.0	351,299	2,521	64,881	3.8	53,113	88.4	11.6	NA	60.6	D	11.3
Mackinac	25	11.7	248	0.0	13.2	495,340	1,997	74,432	7.1	70,683	11.5	88.5	3	76.2	173	13.9
Macomb	74	8.4	182	4.3	66.6	928,906	5,095	149,403	78.8	195,111	87.2	12.8	1	81.9	800	25.0
Manistee	41	-6.6	151	1.0	19.3	435,471	2,884	81,371	10.3	37,686	75.6	24.4	7	72.6	246	15.0
Marquette	30	-1.4	169	0.1	11.3	372,759	2,206	85,310	3.7	20,536	30.8	69.2	8	83.2	46	9.5
Mason	85	8.1	181	4.2	63.0	563,138	3,111	132,221	56.7	120,097	58.1	41.9	21	75.8	943	25.8
Mecosta	115	-6.4	166	17.6	81.5	581,429	3,505	145,703	180.1	259,458	21.5	78.5	6	64.3	909	27.2
Menominee	80	-13.4	226	0.1	47.2	479,385	2,125	113,385	37.6	106,507	11.5	88.5	2	78.5	610	26.9
Midland	88	-2.1	165	0.6	69.9	916,909	5,542	121,112	46.9	88,483	57.1	42.9	5	80.2	2,366	40.0
Missaukee	114	14.2	280	8.5	88.7	1,023,840	3,658	205,707	148.7	366,276	14.8	85.2	4	77.1	759	25.6
Monroe	210	-2.2	193	4.3	194.1	1,190,516	6,156	150,143	174.5	160,833	96.2	3.8	NA	83.5	4,555	43.7
Montcalm	230	-2.9	239	59.5	191.9	955,776	3,991	170,672	180.5	187,598	71.2	28.8	9	73.5	2,732	27.4
Montmorency	26	7.2	147	0.0	16.3	314,723	2,146	110,173	9.2	51,511	39.4	60.6	NA	71.9	177	21.9
Muskegon	63	-14.9	133	3.6	45.8	852,881	6,425	112,539	74.7	156,884	58.9	41.1	5	82.8	173	11.1
Newaygo	136	8.4	160	12.0	96.7	623,318	3,889	126,490	128.3	150,958	37.6	62.4	16	78.4	296	13.3
Oakland	29	-9.0	56	0.6	17.4	652,488	11,623	67,181	22.3	43,442	88.0	12.0	9	85.0	161	4.1
Oceana	127	-0.5	233	13.1	93.6	969,750	4,159	183,666	124.7	228,791	66.2	33.8	9	81.3	699	14.9
Ogemaw	70	2.8	238	D	47.7	666,927	2,797	177,989	49.8	169,429	25.1	74.9	NA	63.9	677	41.8
Ontonagon	27	-6.7	238	D	12.5	379,699	1,597	68,540	3.1	27,167	80.5	19.5	NA	77.2	14	15.8
Osceola	104	-6.3	166	2.0	67.4	497,961	3,003	79,214	43.5	69,650	26.8	73.2	4	63.4	1,101	18.6
Oscoda	16	-3.4	112	D	6.5	307,892	2,741	39,097	5.6	38,653	23.9	76.1	7	41.7	20	4.9
Otsego	33	3.0	172	1.1	17.5	479,329	2,780	80,181	6.2	32,311	80.9	19.1	6	80.8	64	18.7
Ottawa	172	-7.7	152	23.0	145.2	1,258,057	8,271	167,813	506.7	448,373	55.7	44.3	6	85.2	2,675	19.6
Presque Isle	64	-20.9	200	1.8	41.0	469,658	2,345	93,591	18.9	58,661	68.9	31.1	1	62.1	374	26.4
Roscommon	6	-22.5	120	0.7	2.9	293,961	2,451	76,198	0.8	16,292	38.4	61.6	1	70.8	30	16.7
Saginaw	327	5.6	262	1.7	300.5	1,518,681	5,805	162,379	170.3	136,206	87.9	12.1	12	79.4	6,853	63.1
St. Clair	182	1.2	169	1.0	160.3	888,682	5,254	132,186	80.9	75,105	88.6	11.4	11	73.4	2,041	22.1
St. Joseph	245	10.5	273	123.1	212.3	1,562,992	5,717	235,762	230.7	257,450	68.8	31.2	16	64.6	5,839	39.7
Sanilac	437	-4.5	332	1.7	401.0	1,636,584	4,930	274,204	357.7	271,993	54.3	45.7	52	72.5	7,801	49.4
Schoolcraft	15	-22.6	242	0.0	5.9	441,401	1,820	65,397	2.1	34,016	48.7	51.3	NA	85.5	98	21.0
Shiawassee	210	-5.8	217	1.5	187.1	976,860	4,511	151,599	97.5	100,284	67.4	32.6	21	80.9	3,670	45.8
Tuscola	330	1.4	266	8.7	298.5	1,386,278	5,217	226,605	231.0	186,103	69.4	30.6	79	79.7	7,168	52.8
Van Buren	152	-13.3	159	35.6	118.1	921,952	5,789	150,630	205.5	215,686	81.5	18.5	7	74.5	1,602	14.4
Washtenaw	179	5.2	144	4.0	150.4	1,124,667	7,823	112,400	91.2	73,227	76.3	23.7	29	84.3	3,438	24.6
Wayne	10	-36.3	40	0.6	7.8	467,878	11,561	70,633	23.1	93,274	96.8	3.2	2	88.3	56	4.8
Wexford	40	-0.3	132	4.3	26.2	445,486	3,368	60,875	18.1	59,701	48.0	52.0	8	67.8	164	9.5
MINNESOTA	25,517	-2.0	371	611.6	21,786.8	1,799,201	4,853	223,666	18,395.4	267,289	55.4	44.6	735	79.0	394,491	59.9
Aitkin	106	-13.8	229	3.0	54.1	482,701	2,109	72,031	12.5	26,970	56.5	43.5	1	68.2	282	16.5
Anoka	39	-12.9	108	3.0	29.4	823,272	7,590	122,561	67.8	188,222	51.9	48.1	5	85.6	239	9.2
Becker	368	-15.4	390	13.4	256.0	1,133,301	2,906	151,842	174.5	185,081	59.4	40.6	4	73.6	5,253	58.4
Beltrami	169	-6.6	289	3.5	79.8	568,690	1,966	67,182	23.8	40,823	55.8	44.2	NA	81.0	775	21.1
Benton	195	3.2	239	16.7	155.8	1,048,133	4,390	181,337	207.2	253,893	30.8	69.2	5	75.4	1,702	43.5
Big Stone	269	8.0	614	4.1	246.4	2,667,748	4,348	308,736	138.8	316,790	77.1	22.9	2	78.1	3,315	75.1
Blue Earth	383	1.7	389	4.3	355.5	2,804,263	7,202	284,239	483.5	491,860	41.9	58.1	7	82.3	12,899	76.4
Brown	356	9.1	342	4.1	330.8	2,248,890	6,574	241,577	381.5	366,838	45.8	54.2	3	80.1	6,242	82.2
Carlton	93	0.9	177	D	41.3	380,506	2,155	70,143	11.0	20,766	43.5	56.5	7	80.5	196	4.3
Carver	159	2.2	230	0.6	136.1	1,552,374	6,742	218,040	111.4	161,652	61.9	38.1	7	82.0	963	47.2
Cass	134	-15.1	309	8.4	57.9	773,837	2,503	83,876	26.5	61,259	28.3	71.7	1	75.0	325	14.1
Chippewa	341	1.8	547	4.5	320.5	3,226,230	5,894	352,983	256.7	412,037	73.3	26.7	7	76.6	7,059	84.6
Chisago	116	1.5	141	4.0	82.7	643,553	4,575	94,546	52.8	64,358	74.6	25.4	6	83.3	1,379	31.5
Clay	577	-5.6	831	2.9	538.1	3,280,220	3,948	367,559	277.8	400,218	86.5	13.5	12	84.7	5,759	73.5
Clearwater	156	-6.7	376	4.9	76.1	761,920	2,026	113,597	30.1	72,609	65.7	34.3	3	77.1	417	27.1
Cook	1	-38.7	44	0.0	0.2	258,025	5,927	19,944	0.4	11,906	95.8	4.2	2	84.4	D	3.1
Cottonwood	370	-0.6	498	2.1	345.5	3,146,803	6,321	388,964	382.2	513,669	50.8	49.2	4	86.7	5,155	85.5
Crow Wing	89	-10.8	181	4.5	41.8	485,403	2,688	93,161	19.1	38,571	48.6	51.4	6	73.5	159	21.1
Dakota	227	3.3	277	62.8	205.4	1,911,437	6,902	227,421	235.4	287,091	76.3	23.7	13	78.2	2,990	43.4
Dodge	248	10.0	406	4.9	231.9	2,797,971	6,892	283,496	238.4	390,185	58.0	42.0	6	83.6	6,605	64.6
Douglas	263	-1.6	274	3.3	205.3	1,082,155	3,946	138,654	100.3	104,526	73.9	26.1	9	75.5	3,133	66.6
Faribault	408	4.5	496	D	388.9	3,372,928	6,799	352,244	337.7	410,869	68.4	31.6	5	82.8	5,464	81.8

STATE County	Water use, 2015		Wholesale Trade[1], 2017				Retail Trade[2], 2017				Real estate and rental and leasing,[2] 2017			
	Public supply water withdrawn (mil gal/ day)	Public supply gallons withdrawn per person per day	Number of establish- ments	Number of employees	Sales (mil dol)	Average payroll (mil dol)	Number of establish- ments	Number of employees	Sales (mil dol)	Average payroll (mil dol)	Number of establish- ments	Number of employees	Sales (mil dol)	Average payroll (mil dol)
	133	134	135	136	137	138	139	140	141	142	143	144	145	146
MICHIGAN— Cont'd														
Keweenaw	0.1	23.1	NA	NA	NA	NA	9	21	3.7	0.4	NA	NA	NA	NA
Lake	0.3	22.8	NA	NA	NA	NA	27	229	57.6	4.9	D	D	D	0.3
Lapeer	0.4	4.5	52	358	173.1	16.2	260	3,401	1,072.1	84.0	54	217	34.3	7.1
Leelanau	0.5	22.7	D	D	D	D	124	701	164.4	20.2	30	50	14.2	2.4
Lenawee	6.1	61.9	D	D	D	D	285	3,755	1,051.9	92.6	64	172	29.9	4.9
Livingston	6.9	36.9	175	1,649	1,921.2	132.9	603	9,428	2,808.7	240.5	156	540	171.5	23.5
Luce	0.5	77.9	D	D	D	2.2	29	274	78.5	7.2	8	69	8.3	1.6
Mackinac	1.3	118.5	D	D	D	D	99	440	130.2	12.3	12	37	6.5	1.2
Macomb	4.0	4.6	774	12,393	7,801.9	757.0	2,777	42,208	13,734.8	1,161.1	656	3,947	908.7	147.3
Manistee	1.5	63.0	15	103	173.4	6.2	104	1,126	303.9	25.3	21	46	7.7	1.4
Marquette	5.2	76.8	46	404	215.6	18.9	274	3,683	926.8	90.9	66	324	82.0	13.5
Mason	2.5	85.1	19	153	144.7	7.7	112	1,544	414.0	39.5	33	361	50.2	19.9
Mecosta	1.3	29.5	D	D	D	D	145	1,977	537.9	47.7	36	101	20.7	3.3
Menominee	1.1	45.4	17	369	189.7	15.5	68	639	134.4	12.9	11	55	5.4	0.9
Midland	0.1	1.7	50	735	2,781.2	71.8	270	3,902	1,116.0	98.0	64	338	70.3	17.3
Missaukee	0.4	25.5	19	158	87.9	6.5	35	424	147.9	13.3	5	5	1.2	0.1
Monroe	9.3	62.0	D	D	D	D	358	5,252	1,705.6	133.1	70	273	49.8	8.7
Montcalm	3.1	48.6	41	329	112.3	13.3	196	2,542	807.5	64.5	18	44	7.7	1.2
Montmorency	0.1	13.0	NA	NA	NA	NA	30	238	69.6	5.9	D	D	D	D
Muskegon	16.1	93.1	D	D	D	62.3	564	7,930	2,191.2	195.3	87	599	78.3	18.8
Newaygo	1.9	39.0	31	248	81.2	9.7	145	1,563	439.7	41.0	29	112	15.3	3.5
Oakland	19.1	15.4	2,006	33,497	35,641.4	2,461.8	4,781	75,952	24,638.8	2,243.9	1,826	16,580	3,291.9	846.6
Oceana	1.2	44.4	13	484	104.3	12.6	92	687	176.1	15.1	16	29	7.7	1.2
Ogemaw	0.4	18.1	18	487	147.9	21.3	112	1,412	401.8	36.0	D	D	D	D
Ontonagon	0.4	73.2	4	6	1.5	0.2	25	245	53.8	6.5	3	5	0.4	0.1
Osceola	1.4	59.4	10	97	86.5	4.3	65	552	149.2	12.4	D	D	D	0.5
Oscoda	0.1	8.5	D	D	D	D	34	252	58.4	5.1	D	D	D	D
Otsego	1.1	45.8	32	358	144.4	14.5	138	2,139	655.1	57.9	26	70	12.6	2.0
Ottawa	88.2	315.2	300	4,277	2,707.7	253.5	776	10,951	3,302.6	315.4	239	1,354	470.5	59.4
Presque Isle	0.5	35.8	3	3	0.8	0.1	61	371	110.6	9.0	D	D	D	0.3
Roscommon	0.3	11.7	7	23	5.9	0.5	113	1,334	404.6	35.1	D	D	D	2.2
Saginaw	0.4	2.2	160	2,070	1,307.0	111.1	826	12,804	3,233.8	309.9	123	652	139.2	20.5
St. Clair	137.9	862.5	88	1,115	622.5	63.2	505	6,823	2,030.8	173.0	94	988	78.5	24.8
St. Joseph	3.3	53.3	D	D	D	D	185	2,580	763.9	65.6	32	103	18.9	2.9
Sanilac	1.6	37.6	26	293	227.4	15.1	143	1,606	447.5	40.5	D	D	D	D
Schoolcraft	0.4	42.8	4	5	3.0	0.1	44	382	99.9	9.2	D	D	D	D
Shiawassee	2.9	42.1	44	558	204.1	24.9	196	2,577	862.2	70.3	32	112	20.9	3.3
Tuscola	1.9	35.1	40	411	282.0	22.7	153	1,608	484.6	40.6	D	D	D	1.8
Van Buren	3.6	47.3	60	524	406.4	24.0	256	2,668	753.0	66.6	38	103	17.5	2.4
Washtenaw	18.4	51.2	270	3,870	5,384.1	267.6	1,100	17,534	5,121.3	473.5	373	2,686	1,101.3	140.5
Wayne	466.6	265.2	1,434	26,754	29,897.5	1,708.7	5,927	69,229	21,293.3	1,772.1	1,162	7,082	7,908.7	332.8
Wexford	2.7	80.3	28	434	211.7	26.0	167	2,096	643.2	54.5	41	207	21.5	4.6
MINNESOTA	515.2	93.9	6,397	108,895	106,476.5	7,091.2	18,827	302,886	91,993.6	8,117.5	7,218	38,077	10,432.9	1,915.0
Aitkin	0.3	17.2	12	173	156.7	6.5	69	582	140.4	13.1	10	8	2.3	0.4
Anoka	108.2	314.5	334	5,578	3,491.1	335.3	910	16,357	4,474.3	428.4	427	1,419	330.9	51.8
Becker	1.7	49.7	31	173	121.1	8.0	129	1,812	513.6	45.8	33	74	20.0	3.1
Beltrami	1.5	31.7	40	389	132.1	17.1	214	3,089	766.6	80.6	D	D	D	D
Benton	2.1	52.4	43	1,238	827.7	68.8	119	1,869	506.8	49.5	36	81	15.5	2.2
Big Stone	0.5	97.2	9	D	172.5	D	26	178	35.1	3.6	D	D	D	0.2
Blue Earth	6.2	94.7	89	1,397	1,802.5	81.5	311	6,187	1,464.4	143.9	D	D	D	D
Brown	1.1	42.3	29	389	853.2	18.6	104	1,667	395.0	39.7	20	184	10.6	3.6
Carlton	1.5	42.5	17	304	145.0	15.2	101	1,310	268.2	33.4	13	86	8.9	1.4
Carver	8.3	84.3	116	2,167	1,652.4	201.8	207	3,596	935.2	89.0	138	745	152.6	40.5
Cass	0.5	18.8	12	306	72.2	14.6	141	1,071	260.7	26.0	D	D	D	D
Chippewa	1.2	96.6	13	433	443.3	22.9	58	716	217.9	19.5	10	99	3.4	1.7
Chisago	2.0	36.8	39	358	174.3	15.1	168	1,806	495.9	47.5	51	102	19.3	3.7
Clay	4.9	78.9	64	1,115	1,110.4	61.9	165	2,910	738.7	73.6	44	161	24.8	4.6
Clearwater	0.2	25.0	4	D	7.1	D	38	284	61.6	5.9	NA	NA	NA	NA
Cook	0.3	55.8	5	18	3.5	0.6	50	319	64.9	9.2	D	D	D	1.7
Cottonwood	1.8	152.4	23	246	306.7	13.5	50	484	92.1	10.7	8	20	2.8	1.0
Crow Wing	3.4	53.6	65	522	248.6	21.2	379	4,656	1,378.7	131.9	D	D	D	D
Dakota	40.7	98.2	528	8,246	5,546.8	586.9	1,202	25,251	7,844.3	703.4	595	2,578	706.7	117.8
Dodge	0.9	45.2	17	549	507.4	30.8	48	455	128.7	9.8	8	10	1.7	0.3
Douglas	2.2	59.3	45	983	553.3	45.4	237	3,095	828.9	80.2	45	165	34.2	9.3
Faribault	0.9	65.5	23	144	156.7	6.1	63	510	109.4	11.3	6	9	1.3	0.2

1 Merchant wholesalers, except manufacturers' sales branches and offices. 2. Employer establishments.

STATE County	Professional, scientific, and technical services, 2017				Manufacturing, 2017				Accommodation and food services, 2017			
	Number of establishments	Number of employees	Sales (mil dol)	Average payroll (mil dol)	Number of establishments	Number of employees	Sales (mil dol)	Average payroll (mil dol)	Number of establishments	Number of employees	Sales (mil dol)	Annual payroll (mil dol)
	147	148	149	150	151	152	153	154	155	156	157	158
MICHIGAN— Cont'd												
Keweenaw	D	D	D	D	4	19	1.6	0.9	18	99	8.0	2.2
Lake	D	D	7.2	D	D	78	D	D	24	D	8.8	D
Lapeer	D	D	D	D	125	5,014	1,299.4	227.3	132	2,341	112.5	33.0
Leelanau	68	210	32.9	11.3	38	392	82.6	16.4	83	820	88.1	28.6
Lenawee	117	478	44.0	17.5	119	5,356	2,303.0	289.6	179	2,856	129.0	38.9
Livingston	D	D	D	D	246	9,377	4,053.5	527.4	299	6,151	301.9	93.6
Luce	8	12	1.3	0.4	5	160	111.7	10.1	17	193	10.4	2.6
Mackinac	18	32	3.8	1.3	19	132	27.5	5.1	102	763	160.6	48.9
Macomb	D	D	D	D	1,610	68,148	29,940.0	4,232.1	1,669	31,943	1,642.4	468.6
Manistee	37	106	13.3	3.8	27	971	489.3	58.4	65	1,467	138.2	34.3
Marquette	D	D	D	D	50	889	324.2	43.2	179	3,151	140.0	44.0
Mason	44	175	18.2	6.8	36	1,928	512.4	89.2	89	1,099	59.4	18.1
Mecosta	39	225	16.7	7.0	37	2,140	795.1	90.4	74	1,269	60.4	16.2
Menominee	30	218	18.1	6.4	45	1,814	486.1	96.6	43	594	23.8	6.6
Midland	D	D	D	D	65	4,271	2,280.2	298.0	152	3,306	170.6	51.1
Missaukee	11	40	2.9	1.0	24	321	115.9	13.0	24	204	13.5	3.5
Monroe	D	D	D	D	127	6,664	2,660.6	337.7	275	4,478	216.9	60.9
Montcalm	49	164	18.0	6.1	67	2,319	613.7	115.5	82	1,244	60.7	17.5
Montmorency	D	D	1.7	D	16	408	65.2	16.7	24	159	11.8	2.6
Muskegon	D	D	D	D	267	13,190	4,003.7	712.1	351	6,148	288.0	86.0
Newaygo	48	318	49.4	22.4	40	1,925	617.2	94.9	77	1,058	53.4	15.7
Oakland	D	D	D	D	1,647	53,627	19,516.2	3,336.5	3,032	59,174	3,360.0	974.0
Oceana	28	88	8.8	3.3	39	1,870	522.8	69.3	65	644	41.1	12.1
Ogemaw	26	89	9.0	2.8	34	262	83.1	11.3	59	826	39.3	11.6
Ontonagon	D	D	D	0.3	D	D	D	0.2	D	D	D	1.7
Osceola	27	77	9.4	3.4	41	2,085	784.5	90.5	39	601	31.3	10.5
Oscoda	13	25	3.0	1.2	17	371	107.0	15.2	D	D	D	D
Otsego	D	D	D	D	30	968	241.9	39.2	78	1,586	78.9	24.8
Ottawa	D	D	D	D	575	40,564	13,878.8	2,095.7	434	9,415	466.5	148.1
Presque Isle	15	41	2.6	1.0	13	196	38.9	8.7	38	255	11.9	3.6
Roscommon	30	72	7.0	2.5	8	D	119.4	21.6	76	1,401	66.1	20.5
Saginaw	298	2,414	375.2	142.5	194	12,288	4,461.3	799.8	400	9,735	493.3	137.5
St. Clair	D	D	D	D	231	8,755	3,666.0	420.5	269	5,025	218.8	66.4
St. Joseph	70	891	42.5	20.0	134	8,797	3,887.8	440.7	110	1,606	77.4	22.8
Sanilac	51	177	16.9	5.3	64	2,724	859.2	119.7	70	709	37.0	10.1
Schoolcraft	11	50	3.7	1.7	8	162	77.5	10.9	34	258	13.5	3.9
Shiawassee	66	355	42.3	16.8	66	2,055	672.9	88.9	111	1,703	78.5	21.7
Tuscola	D	D	D	D	43	1,319	394.4	66.6	62	727	32.1	9.5
Van Buren	74	2,018	306.0	98.9	81	2,735	968.5	142.6	155	2,008	108.3	32.3
Washtenaw	1,257	15,568	2,912.8	1,205.4	337	14,480	4,603.1	850.4	860	18,272	1,027.3	310.7
Wayne	2,870	51,817	8,007.6	3,606.7	1,454	88,033	67,028.2	5,655.0	3,354	71,006	5,250.8	1,354.7
Wexford	52	231	28.3	12.4	47	3,125	981.4	154.0	86	1,395	64.4	18.6
MINNESOTA	D	D	D	D	7,198	309,097	122,013.5	17,925.8	12,022	239,194	14,234.3	4,271.9
Aitkin	D	D	D	D	28	383	83.5	17.2	51	447	23.6	7.0
Anoka	736	4,325	854.9	290.8	589	21,661	7,087.7	1,301.6	529	10,983	558.5	173.9
Becker	53	188	23.9	9.6	41	2,243	492.4	109.3	86	1,266	66.6	19.7
Beltrami	D	D	D	D	35	902	346.6	36.0	114	2,193	115.9	36.1
Benton	D	D	D	D	64	3,475	824.0	167.9	61	1,099	50.1	15.5
Big Stone	D	D	D	D	5	13	0.9	0.3	18	121	4.9	1.0
Blue Earth	D	D	D	D	91	3,775	3,284.1	213.3	168	4,190	178.2	54.4
Brown	47	441	63.3	24.0	37	4,658	1,633.8	178.6	64	962	41.3	12.2
Carlton	40	148	13.1	4.7	28	1,359	813.7	93.4	61	815	34.6	10.7
Carver	D	D	D	D	153	9,317	3,173.2	547.8	181	3,066	164.9	50.1
Cass	D	D	D	D	38	271	50.8	12.4	126	1,678	174.5	45.8
Chippewa	20	78	8.5	3.0	27	1,015	301.2	43.1	24	310	12.2	4.1
Chisago	D	D	34.0	D	87	2,049	575.0	97.5	D	D	D	18.7
Clay	91	510	75.2	24.4	39	840	368.5	38.8	102	1,789	90.1	28.0
Clearwater	D	D	D	D	D	421	D	22.2	23	188	6.5	1.5
Cook	D	D	D	D	7	41	14.1	2.2	66	768	79.3	22.4
Cottonwood	18	75	9.0	3.0	18	1,033	455.4	38.5	20	295	11.1	3.3
Crow Wing	D	D	D	D	107	2,516	463.9	117.9	203	3,255	196.1	66.4
Dakota	D	D	D	D	434	18,463	12,835.4	1,087.9	733	16,485	901.3	270.1
Dodge	D	D	8.5	D	22	1,708	1,023.0	84.8	29	314	14.9	4.5
Douglas	D	D	D	D	91	3,632	1,103.6	210.5	113	1,915	94.3	30.4
Faribault	D	D	D	D	29	886	279.4	43.5	35	300	12.6	3.5

STATE County	Health care and social assistance, 2017				Other services, 2017				Nonemployer businesses, 2019		Value of residential construction authorized by building permits, 2021	
	Number of establish-ments	Number of employees	Receipts (mil dol)	Annual payroll (mil dol)	Number of establish-ments	Number of employees	Receipts (mil dol)	Annual payroll (mil dol)	Number	Receipts (mil dol)	New construction ($1,000)	Number of housing units
	159	160	161	162	163	164	165	166	167	168	169	170
MICHIGAN— Cont'd												
Keweenaw	NA	NA	NA	NA	NA	NA	NA	NA	140	3.7	3,343	20
Lake	16	285	20.4	9.2	D	D	2.7	D	653	30.1	5,078	22
Lapeer	202	2,842	324.0	110.5	138	536	60.6	15.7	6,682	291.1	61,786	248
Leelanau	56	552	51.5	25.1	39	89	14.1	3.0	3,013	146.5	47,454	186
Lenawee	245	3,093	329.2	129.4	132	774	63.1	16.3	5,988	228.4	36,886	155
Livingston	389	6,075	502.8	216.1	317	1,795	166.2	55.6	15,432	791.3	215,474	820
Luce	17	406	43.5	17.7	D	D	D	D	328	12.2	335	2
Mackinac	17	420	57.7	19.7	16	41	7.8	1.5	877	36.0	7,908	47
Macomb	2,789	38,936	4,244.3	1,693.2	1,509	8,129	863.7	251.8	69,903	3,085.7	530,321	1,727
	65	1,069	114.3	45.1	47	175	26.3	5.1	1,744	64.7	25,003	108
Manistee												
Marquette	233	5,625	553.3	246.0	126	575	55.9	14.9	3,697	124.4	27,803	111
Mason	80	1,399	161.9	57.5	53	218	22.9	6.1	2,081	77.8	23,901	101
Mecosta	82	1,784	161.1	62.5	69	366	34.2	8.9	2,289	87.2	19,298	79
Menominee	32	251	15.9	7.3	30	103	15.6	3.0	1,256	63.3	4,455	28
Midland	282	6,998	883.2	294.3	142	980	158.5	29.7	5,243	214.6	34,601	159
Missaukee	33	434	21.1	9.2	18	58	5.2	1.4	1,096	53.7	4,168	26
Monroe	297	4,744	435.4	188.8	158	701	77.9	20.8	8,490	378.3	61,418	265
Montcalm	112	3,454	316.4	131.8	85	316	41.5	9.3	3,659	162.5	31,906	149
Montmorency	10	256	35.6	8.8	D	D	2.8	D	550	23.9	0	0
	370	10,922	1,416.0	541.0	248	1,332	132.7	35.5	9,588	398.6	73,667	328
Muskegon												
Newaygo	80	2,078	215.5	77.2	68	277	45.3	7.1	2,845	131.0	30,043	156
Oakland	5,176	107,384	12,796.2	5,033.8	2,537	19,132	2,438.7	648.2	120,182	7,113.1	784,374	3,164
Oceana	49	689	57.3	23.9	40	108	12.5	2.7	1,633	67.7	3,362	27
Ogemaw	77	1,256	132.5	45.7	D	D	13.6	D	1,321	55.3	10,086	45
Ontonagon	15	210	17.8	7.0	8	20	3.5	0.5	368	13.8	1,530	9
Osceola	46	1,202	114.7	42.2	34	165	19.1	5.9	1,425	59.7	8,102	47
Oscoda	D	D	D	3.6	15	41	5.0	0.9	649	29.1	4,161	17
Otsego	78	1,546	263.9	81.3	55	273	30.0	8.3	1,993	89.5	1,863	23
Ottawa	514	11,314	1,067.7	456.1	456	2,732	322.1	95.0	20,616	1,067.1	445,462	1,560
	24	290	23.5	10.0	22	54	5.7	1.2	926	31.1	11,505	47
Presque Isle												
Roscommon	48	570	48.1	19.0	53	135	14.9	3.7	1,571	65.6	17,061	64
Saginaw	597	17,800	2,040.7	811.3	325	1,989	183.1	49.7	10,717	435.4	45,134	195
St. Clair	400	7,724	782.4	315.4	206	837	105.7	25.5	10,579	449.8	70,562	399
St. Joseph	101	1,956	184.9	87.0	102	410	43.0	11.7	3,497	157.3	25,284	78
Sanilac	86	1,409	124.6	44.3	56	174	20.5	5.0	3,166	140.2	9,032	60
Schoolcraft	23	380	43.9	19.4	17	91	6.3	1.7	437	17.4	2,474	15
Shiawassee	130	2,830	263.2	109.3	100	415	53.8	11.8	4,196	170.8	11,709	55
Tuscola	107	2,728	229.0	110.5	46	155	14.8	3.3	3,397	135.2	8,157	34
Van Buren	111	2,268	197.3	81.7	93	369	33.7	7.6	4,845	207.8	60,225	246
	943	40,974	5,693.3	2,382.4	553	4,465	650.9	195.0	30,781	1,425.9	259,769	916
Washtenaw												
Wayne	4,118	111,962	14,321.6	5,577.6	2,725	18,581	2,525.3	643.2	137,698	4,763.5	763,416	2,240
Wexford	101	1,937	183.0	79.1	67	303	37.6	8.8	2,262	90.0	17,923	81
MINNESOTA	17,066	473,338	50,491.0	21,206.5	11,339	77,400	10,077.4	2,553.6	418,080	20,377.3	7,726,133	33,652
Aitkin	35	869	84.5	34.9	32	130	20.0	3.0	1,149	52.9	37,279	153
Anoka	774	18,582	2,155.7	866.1	614	4,087	461.9	131.9	24,387	1,105.6	568,323	2,481
Becker	83	2,186	219.3	89.5	80	351	33.9	8.3	2,904	152.4	53,129	190
Beltrami	169	3,157	368.1	131.1	86	408	61.5	14.4	2,821	122.5	32,230	315
Benton	94	2,735	159.6	64.3	68	370	36.9	10.5	2,634	120.0	24,931	92
Big Stone	19	561	54.0	17.8	17	39	5.0	0.9	408	21.3	2,410	11
Blue Earth	272	7,808	769.6	357.4	126	933	94.8	25.8	4,237	214.3	74,478	321
Brown	75	2,296	213.0	93.3	73	233	33.6	7.9	1,687	76.4	4,465	19
Carlton	92	2,148	181.6	83.3	64	282	28.0	7.5	1,906	70.4	29,036	130
Carver	246	6,261	647.3	286.9	178	1,008	107.0	30.5	8,615	459.2	335,049	1,041
Cass	70	1,275	92.8	45.4	57	226	22.5	4.6	2,596	132.7	87,750	340
Chippewa	44	1,205	83.7	37.3	33	200	23.1	5.4	827	41.8	6,191	48
Chisago	157	4,333	430.6	179.1	112	484	49.4	14.2	3,724	172.5	81,958	479
Clay	182	4,749	311.0	141.3	112	487	52.0	14.2	4,268	174.0	89,886	483
Clearwater	17	572	36.3	19.6	15	45	5.1	0.9	623	27.1	600	4
Cook	13	224	26.5	10.0	13	17	2.4	0.6	749	28.7	13,162	76
Cottonwood	31	762	55.4	22.4	26	101	10.3	2.8	794	35.0	5,370	23
Crow Wing	254	6,360	638.0	273.1	154	948	81.5	21.1	5,376	267.7	126,991	534
Dakota	1,146	23,039	2,049.6	884.9	769	5,962	688.3	209.6	30,927	1,502.8	709,655	3,484
Dodge	D	D	D	10.1	39	242	31.0	8.8	1,370	75.1	21,612	95
Douglas	147	3,662	362.4	137.2	106	456	53.1	10.9	3,455	184.9	75,213	365
Faribault	34	724	57.1	25.3	27	105	11.6	2.3	995	55.9	3,710	15

STATE County	Government employment and payroll, 2017									Local government finances, 2017				
			March payroll (percent of total)							General revenue				
												Taxes		
													Per capita[1] (dollars)	
	Full-time equivalent employees	March payroll (dollars)	Adminis-tration, judicial, and legal	Police and corrections	Fire protection	Highways and transpor-tation	Health and welfare	Natural resources and utilities	Education and libraries	Total (mil dol)	Inter-govern-mental (mil dol)	Total (mil dol)	Total	Property
	171	172	173	174	175	176	177	178	179	180	181	182	183	184
MICHIGAN— Cont'd														
Keweenaw	53	176,536	29.4	14.4	0.5	34.1	0.0	9.6	5.4	8.7	3.8	2.4	1,162	1,127
Lake	258	1,122,787	23.5	24.8	0.7	12.0	1.6	0.3	31.6	49.5	25.8	15.9	1,331	1,330
Lapeer	2,111	8,342,424	9.9	7.1	1.0	4.3	6.3	3.0	66.6	294.4	156.7	66.3	752	699
Leelanau	555	2,222,787	15.1	8.8	6.3	6.8	0.6	2.3	55.9	73.0	16.9	42.7	1,974	1,934
Lenawee	3,305	13,215,049	7.3	7.0	1.3	2.6	2.3	3.6	74.3	385.6	192.3	103.9	1,055	1,015
Livingston	3,548	16,236,810	11.0	8.2	2.8	4.1	1.4	3.1	66.3	573.2	277.0	194.9	1,026	1,013
Luce	477	1,899,175	4.8	1.2	0.1	4.7	66.6	1.3	20.3	51.3	6.0	7.0	1,103	1,101
Mackinac	616	2,469,253	9.8	5.6	0.4	6.2	46.0	4.5	25.8	52.0	14.1	26.2	2,434	2,357
Macomb	20,652	100,313,575	6.2	9.5	4.3	2.0	3.8	3.1	69.1	3,390.0	1,593.4	968.7	1,112	1,074
Manistee	1,083	4,904,556	8.7	4.0	2.3	5.4	48.5	1.3	29.4	118.7	51.7	34.0	1,392	1,378
Marquette	2,499	9,820,143	8.6	6.8	1.8	7.5	15.7	11.4	44.0	346.1	160.6	91.5	1,376	1,342
Mason	1,065	4,415,112	8.3	6.3	0.0	7.2	0.6	3.5	72.8	149.5	47.6	65.3	2,252	2,233
Mecosta	1,812	7,267,045	7.9	4.7	1.3	3.8	35.7	1.4	44.2	150.4	77.2	44.5	1,029	953
Menominee	664	2,424,168	11.7	7.1	2.7	8.0	1.5	2.1	61.6	69.9	32.3	22.0	958	951
Midland	2,197	9,909,177	10.3	8.4	3.0	5.2	3.8	5.2	62.3	319.5	151.8	114.0	1,369	1,353
Missaukee	375	1,449,856	13.9	9.0	0.1	6.1	5.1	1.8	62.3	42.6	23.1	12.7	846	844
Monroe	4,140	17,254,732	6.2	6.0	1.8	3.3	2.1	3.4	75.6	493.3	232.5	176.4	1,181	1,139
Montcalm	1,818	7,488,261	6.7	4.7	0.7	3.6	7.0	1.8	73.9	223.6	124.6	61.6	969	964
Montmorency	206	737,287	21.0	8.5	1.6	12.0	4.3	7.2	39.6	23.0	8.6	11.6	1,253	1,234
Muskegon	5,624	23,739,095	7.6	7.6	2.2	3.3	9.2	3.3	65.9	734.8	410.0	175.1	1,008	917
Newaygo	1,547	6,890,797	9.6	5.8	0.5	2.8	11.4	1.1	67.0	167.8	97.9	46.8	969	959
Oakland	31,208	151,195,089	8.7	10.5	4.4	2.7	1.8	3.3	66.6	5,319.8	2,331.1	1,974.7	1,572	1,503
Oceana	792	3,172,763	14.7	6.7	0.0	10.2	5.3	3.8	58.2	97.1	32.3	33.1	1,254	1,233
Ogemaw	479	1,957,201	15.1	8.9	0.1	9.0	9.4	2.8	51.7	52.6	24.7	18.7	894	874
Ontonagon	253	974,226	13.2	4.1	0.3	27.2	1.5	2.0	50.6	38.3	19.0	12.3	2,090	2,085
Osceola	534	2,141,546	6.0	7.7	0.8	5.0	4.3	2.1	72.7	72.8	42.3	20.8	893	875
Oscoda	269	927,896	21.0	6.8	0.7	7.0	8.5	1.9	51.5	22.2	9.4	9.7	1,177	1,161
Otsego	668	2,754,676	13.5	4.9	0.4	10.2	0.4	2.1	64.4	85.7	34.2	36.4	1,484	1,480
Ottawa	6,943	30,282,853	7.0	5.8	1.5	3.1	3.5	3.7	72.1	980.2	490.6	339.3	1,184	1,153
Presque Isle	330	1,244,727	14.7	9.5	0.0	10.6	0.3	3.2	51.8	40.1	19.9	14.9	1,170	1,166
Roscommon	893	3,337,633	8.3	8.6	2.7	7.3	1.6	1.8	66.2	101.5	35.1	44.2	1,863	1,855
Saginaw	5,450	22,845,829	8.3	7.8	1.9	2.7	12.0	4.9	60.6	801.5	464.7	162.3	845	736
St. Clair	4,506	19,039,840	9.6	10.3	2.5	5.3	2.8	4.2	63.5	646.1	334.7	190.1	1,195	1,128
St. Joseph	2,396	9,388,918	7.8	5.5	1.3	3.5	18.8	3.7	57.7	296.0	130.3	68.9	1,135	1,119
Sanilac	1,234	4,735,671	9.8	7.5	0.3	4.7	2.5	3.6	67.2	186.4	105.6	44.6	1,081	1,064
Schoolcraft	422	2,006,463	7.0	4.0	0.3	8.9	61.8	2.1	15.7	74.9	14.2	8.5	1,061	1,060
Shiawassee	2,525	10,046,356	6.3	7.3	1.1	2.6	19.5	2.6	59.0	263.6	155.5	56.3	822	804
Tuscola	1,762	6,398,509	9.0	5.9	0.4	4.2	0.2	2.3	76.6	239.0	112.8	83.0	1,571	1,554
Van Buren	2,944	11,710,625	8.0	6.9	1.1	3.2	4.0	2.3	73.6	374.7	176.5	120.1	1,595	1,576
Washtenaw	10,291	50,170,923	7.5	9.9	2.6	5.9	4.7	5.2	61.5	1,623.7	629.7	665.3	1,804	1,745
Wayne	48,307	223,215,723	8.0	14.5	4.2	6.5	1.3	6.5	55.6	9,545.1	4,481.6	2,659.3	1,513	1,151
Wexford	921	3,817,311	9.5	7.4	2.2	7.4	0.9	3.0	68.2	135.7	72.8	38.4	1,155	1,143
MINNESOTA	X	X	X	X	X	X	X	X	X	X	X	X	X	X
Aitkin	638	2,441,866	16.1	10.9	0.7	7.1	11.3	3.9	46.9	68.4	35.2	20.4	1,293	1,275
Anoka	11,869	57,343,988	6.4	9.8	1.3	2.5	5.7	3.1	69.2	1,464.4	809.1	426.1	1,217	1,159
Becker	1,242	5,527,703	9.9	7.8	0.0	6.9	16.2	7.1	50.9	152.6	77.9	45.9	1,347	1,297
Beltrami	2,161	8,819,155	5.9	10.4	0.7	2.8	8.4	1.9	67.8	239.4	154.2	48.2	1,037	880
Benton	1,284	5,492,962	6.6	8.8	0.3	12.6	8.9	2.0	60.1	156.2	90.8	46.2	1,151	1,103
Big Stone	504	1,927,996	7.7	3.0	0.1	4.8	49.4	1.7	32.3	75.8	22.2	8.4	1,688	1,636
Blue Earth	2,477	11,010,929	8.4	9.1	1.3	4.8	7.1	4.6	62.2	366.3	177.4	101.6	1,518	1,279
Brown	1,171	5,188,028	10.3	8.5	0.2	4.7	21.6	11.3	41.4	134.9	57.8	35.1	1,395	1,321
Carlton	1,695	7,460,434	6.1	5.7	4.8	3.9	24.1	3.2	51.3	198.3	93.7	49.5	1,394	1,301
Carver	3,152	15,411,363	8.3	7.6	0.4	3.4	9.0	7.5	61.6	465.7	191.7	178.0	1,743	1,625
Cass	1,263	5,156,214	11.1	11.5	0.0	5.0	13.2	1.8	55.6	157.6	85.5	45.6	1,555	1,498
Chippewa	839	3,978,680	4.7	4.2	0.4	2.8	38.0	2.0	45.3	77.3	36.6	18.8	1,574	1,536
Chisago	1,560	6,808,243	11.0	9.0	0.2	4.8	8.0	3.2	62.4	209.8	100.8	75.7	1,370	1,286
Clay	2,420	10,374,791	7.4	10.1	2.4	3.5	11.3	8.4	55.3	323.2	181.7	64.5	1,012	974
Clearwater	418	1,645,740	10.1	13.6	0.0	4.7	12.2	6.2	50.3	59.6	22.9	12.8	1,446	1,440
Cook	348	1,508,292	11.9	6.8	0.0	7.0	39.1	5.9	25.5	50.9	18.2	12.5	2,311	1,888
Cottonwood	650	2,488,355	8.3	7.2	0.7	6.0	16.5	10.0	50.2	96.9	40.8	24.5	2,179	2,158
Crow Wing	3,471	14,319,009	6.9	8.6	0.7	3.3	30.9	1.4	48.0	299.8	141.0	104.7	1,629	1,526
Dakota	15,457	71,499,309	5.4	8.3	1.2	2.4	6.6	3.6	70.4	1,873.9	938.3	608.4	1,443	1,375
Dodge	804	3,401,794	8.0	7.8	0.2	4.9	8.5	4.2	64.7	104.2	52.2	28.8	1,392	1,363
Douglas	1,485	5,931,587	8.5	9.5	0.1	4.7	7.1	6.9	61.7	164.6	77.1	60.0	1,600	1,460
Faribault	588	2,199,089	9.5	10.2	0.4	6.1	3.4	11.5	55.0	71.7	34.0	22.2	1,615	1,578

1. Based on the resident population estimated as of July 1 of the year shown.

STATE County	Local government finances, 2017 (cont.)									Government employment, 2020			Individual income tax returns, 2019		
	Direct general expenditure							Debt outstanding							
			Percent of total for:												
	Total (mil dol)	Per capita[1] (dollars)	Education	Health and hospitals	Police protection	Public welfare	Highways	Total (mil dol)	Per capita[1] (dollars)	Federal civilian	Federal military	State and local	Number of returns	Mean adjusted gross income	Mean income tax
	185	186	187	188	189	190	191	192	193	194	195	196	197	198	199
MICHIGAN— Cont'd															
Keweenaw	8.4	4,037	2.6	0.8	9.4	0.4	35.8	3.9	1,861	20	3	110	1,060	55,335	4,754
Lake	36.7	3,066	22.8	1.4	6.5	1.1	21.5	18.1	1,509	57	18	363	4,760	42,500	3,335
Lapeer	279.3	3,170	46.4	8.2	5.0	8.8	8.4	220.2	2,499	158	136	3,962	43,630	59,318	5,710
Leelanau	78.8	3,640	40.0	2.6	6.2	0.0	9.2	40.7	1,880	135	34	1,567	12,220	96,619	14,450
Lenawee	386.1	3,923	54.0	5.6	3.2	4.4	7.6	268.6	2,729	208	147	4,408	46,530	54,949	4,866
Livingston	550.3	2,898	57.9	2.3	3.5	0.6	5.0	842.9	4,439	299	303	6,395	100,080	84,545	10,487
Luce	66.3	10,410	11.1	60.2	0.7	0.3	11.6	23.9	3,753	19	8	723	2,530	46,291	3,575
Mackinac	56.2	5,219	32.0	9.5	4.0	0.1	14.2	32.6	3,025	73	63	844	6,190	46,475	3,900
Macomb	3,407.6	3,911	50.6	9.2	6.5	1.2	5.6	4,181.8	4,799	8,459	1,740	28,308	456,580	59,729	6,187
Manistee	109.8	4,499	31.2	12.4	2.7	10.0	8.0	64.4	2,640	122	79	2,197	12,100	50,257	4,459
Marquette	331.3	4,982	35.2	10.9	4.3	10.4	9.0	339.8	5,110	297	122	4,890	30,990	58,018	5,412
Mason	146.7	5,059	54.0	0.3	2.7	10.5	8.6	47.1	1,623	78	46	1,696	14,660	52,263	4,835
Mecosta	146.7	3,392	50.8	2.2	4.2	0.5	15.8	43.0	993	107	65	4,249	17,610	51,073	4,515
Menominee	69.2	3,009	46.9	0.6	7.2	0.5	11.1	20.5	891	69	35	2,006	11,290	49,042	3,967
Midland	324.6	3,896	55.6	2.2	4.0	2.1	7.2	513.6	6,165	178	130	2,922	40,620	76,847	9,478
Missaukee	43.6	2,906	53.6	1.8	2.9	1.2	15.5	51.5	3,426	33	24	504	6,960	45,576	3,323
Monroe	543.6	3,638	53.6	6.9	2.8	0.2	7.7	514.5	3,443	259	236	5,183	76,380	62,952	6,212
Montcalm	233.0	3,668	62.3	8.6	1.7	0.5	7.5	163.8	2,579	138	96	2,944	28,670	47,335	3,682
Montmorency	23.1	2,504	37.8	2.0	5.3	1.0	15.6	11.2	1,209	25	15	349	4,540	43,635	3,412
Muskegon	779.6	4,489	51.7	8.7	3.7	2.8	4.5	744.5	4,287	369	280	7,122	81,740	50,853	4,462
Newaygo	192.0	3,973	52.9	6.8	2.7	7.0	8.7	200.0	4,140	86	77	2,109	22,670	49,337	4,006
Oakland	5,621.5	4,476	49.7	6.1	5.8	0.1	7.1	4,996.7	3,978	4,762	2,000	44,253	650,790	98,410	14,817
Oceana	105.4	3,991	41.8	3.7	3.4	16.2	10.2	46.2	1,748	172	42	1,204	12,620	48,481	4,061
Ogemaw	50.6	2,421	40.5	2.6	4.2	0.0	17.8	28.6	1,370	67	34	681	9,680	43,455	3,400
Ontonagon	35.7	6,054	49.7	1.4	1.4	0.1	24.2	24.1	4,100	35	9	346	2,800	45,391	3,487
Osceola	81.4	3,497	59.5	3.3	2.8	0.3	9.5	61.2	2,632	62	36	946	10,380	45,292	3,294
Oscoda	21.7	2,631	41.9	6.2	4.4	1.9	14.8	5.9	718	54	13	297	3,700	40,637	2,785
Otsego	79.5	3,240	50.8	2.7	3.1	1.0	12.2	23.0	939	142	40	1,051	12,830	52,952	4,674
Ottawa	1,185.4	4,137	54.7	4.2	3.1	0.7	10.7	1,517.8	5,296	460	527	15,583	139,760	74,244	8,173
Presque Isle	42.6	3,341	37.8	0.6	3.4	0.5	14.0	22.4	1,756	67	20	583	6,500	48,705	4,035
Roscommon	108.8	4,587	50.2	2.1	3.8	1.8	10.3	70.5	2,970	39	38	1,294	11,650	47,629	4,337
Saginaw	842.5	4,389	39.0	18.6	4.0	0.6	8.2	484.2	2,522	1,547	292	8,884	90,750	52,217	5,027
St. Clair	671.5	4,223	44.6	9.3	4.7	1.0	10.8	620.4	3,902	738	335	5,958	80,650	57,340	5,496
St. Joseph	317.9	5,236	43.3	23.5	2.7	0.3	4.1	196.4	3,236	112	95	2,623	28,250	50,780	4,342
Sanilac	188.8	4,577	38.7	7.9	3.7	1.1	12.6	137.6	3,335	111	64	1,296	19,370	47,553	3,862
Schoolcraft	69.0	8,612	12.4	40.1	0.1	11.3	7.8	59.0	7,358	40	14	904	3,920	50,717	4,333
Shiawassee	267.9	3,916	52.5	1.4	2.4	16.5	7.6	239.9	3,507	143	106	2,971	33,360	51,983	4,442
Tuscola	218.1	4,130	55.2	2.6	2.5	9.2	12.2	142.4	2,696	131	81	2,645	25,450	47,566	3,612
Van Buren	466.6	6,196	56.1	10.6	2.5	0.5	7.7	485.0	6,440	156	118	4,424	35,600	54,657	5,122
Washtenaw	1,638.2	4,442	49.2	6.2	7.2	0.6	3.7	1,748.4	4,741	4,293	617	69,823	170,250	91,334	12,898
Wayne	9,879.6	5,622	33.7	3.2	5.7	5.6	3.5	11,792.4	6,711	14,129	3,144	71,566	817,060	55,144	6,156
Wexford	123.2	3,707	60.0	1.4	3.8	0.4	8.8	61.3	1,844	134	53	2,044	16,070	47,104	3,714
MINNESOTA	X	X	X	X	X	X	X	X	X	33,329	19,685	357,692	2,842,470	77,920	9,551
Aitkin	83.4	5,283	34.6	2.2	4.3	7.6	24.2	14.1	893	58	54	830	7,720	55,436	5,144
Anoka	1,507.4	4,304	59.0	0.6	6.5	5.1	8.1	1,631.9	4,660	435	1,230	15,357	185,600	72,583	7,804
Becker	150.9	4,429	40.4	1.2	4.8	13.1	12.6	61.2	1,795	258	117	2,853	16,550	68,842	7,462
Beltrami	255.5	5,498	51.0	1.3	4.5	10.9	9.7	275.2	5,922	408	156	5,106	20,750	54,632	5,011
Benton	133.4	3,325	54.8	1.1	5.5	8.3	9.6	128.9	3,212	60	137	1,681	20,260	58,123	5,193
Big Stone	75.0	14,987	16.5	41.7	1.8	18.4	6.7	610.7	122,043	29	16	611	2,490	51,056	4,178
Blue Earth	392.7	5,869	41.2	1.9	4.1	5.1	12.8	381.5	5,702	282	254	5,182	31,950	59,278	5,834
Brown	159.7	6,344	37.3	12.8	8.3	6.4	8.9	113.7	4,519	83	82	1,601	13,170	59,154	5,283
Carlton	251.5	7,082	53.8	12.8	3.3	6.6	9.2	296.3	8,344	78	116	4,551	17,040	58,543	4,927
Carver	529.1	5,181	52.1	0.4	5.1	4.6	8.9	818.3	8,014	230	364	4,640	52,540	108,941	15,537
Cass	176.0	6,001	52.0	1.4	3.8	6.7	12.3	106.0	3,615	268	102	3,398	14,880	61,208	6,236
Chippewa	80.1	6,708	40.4	7.6	4.3	6.5	12.5	95.9	8,030	71	40	1,192	6,070	56,207	4,598
Chisago	215.8	3,906	45.9	0.8	5.2	5.2	12.5	200.3	3,624	107	190	2,173	28,540	71,657	7,429
Clay	375.9	5,896	44.6	2.9	4.5	5.4	18.2	710.7	11,146	125	214	4,371	29,320	61,273	5,458
Clearwater	55.2	6,241	35.5	33.4	3.4	0.0	11.9	23.6	2,672	36	31	465	3,860	55,266	4,976
Cook	64.4	11,897	11.3	44.1	4.8	4.0	10.6	66.6	12,304	143	18	661	3,170	56,652	5,024
Cottonwood	107.9	9,590	25.8	23.7	3.9	11.8	12.3	66.8	5,943	62	38	813	5,550	52,252	4,090
Crow Wing	281.2	4,374	43.0	0.8	6.2	8.1	12.3	266.1	4,139	244	250	3,519	33,140	62,385	6,351
Dakota	1,912.5	4,537	55.9	0.6	5.3	4.0	10.2	1,965.7	4,663	3,259	1,483	17,867	226,030	83,919	10,211
Dodge	110.9	5,359	49.7	6.4	6.3	4.2	11.4	133.3	6,441	43	72	1,214	10,480	66,181	6,170
Douglas	173.7	4,631	40.6	0.4	6.8	5.3	17.3	301.2	8,027	151	130	3,386	19,890	67,521	6,985
Faribault	75.4	5,480	33.1	0.7	5.0	2.6	22.2	91.2	6,625	55	46	799	6,750	52,065	4,141

1. Based on the resident population estimated as of July 1 of the year shown.

State / county code	CBSA code[1]	County Type code[2]	STATE County	Land area[3] (sq. mi)	Population, 2021: Total persons 2021	Population, 2021: Rank	Population, 2021: Per square mile	Race alone or in combination, not Hispanic or Latino (percent): White	Black	American Indian, Alaska Native	Asian and Pacific Islancer	Percent Hispanic or Latino[4]	Age (percent): Under 5 years	5 to 17 years	18 to 24 years	25 to 34 years	35 to 44 years	45 to 54 years
				1	2	3	4	5	6	7	8	9	10	11	12	13	14	15
			MINNESOTA— Cont'd															
27045	40340	3	Fillmore	861.3	21,271	1,749	24.7	96.6	0.9	0.5	1.0	2.0	5.9	14.5	10.9	10.0	12.2	10.8
27047	10660	7	Freeborn	707.2	30,749	1,412	43.5	83.6	1.9	0.8	4.2	10.9	5.3	12.6	11.1	10.9	11.6	10.7
27049	39860	4	Goodhue	756.7	47,968	1,024	63.4	92.8	2.2	1.7	1.3	3.7	5.6	12.5	11.0	11.2	12.5	11.6
27051		9	Grant	547.8	6,153	2,726	11.2	95.6	1.4	1.4	0.9	2.4	5.3	13.5	10.0	11.1	12.0	10.0
27053	33460	1	Hennepin	554.0	1,267,416	34	2,287.8	70.5	15.7	1.4	8.6	7.1	5.9	12.2	11.9	16.1	14.6	11.7
27055	29100	3	Houston	552.0	18,778	1,882	34.0	96.3	1.6	0.8	1.3	1.5	5.4	12.5	10.6	9.8	12.2	11.2
27057		7	Hubbard	926.0	21,715	1,727	23.5	93.9	1.2	3.4	0.9	2.6	5.0	12.5	9.5	8.9	11.1	10.4
27059	33460	1	Isanti	435.8	41,906	1,147	96.2	94.2	1.7	1.4	2.3	2.5	5.7	13.5	11.3	12.7	13.3	12.1
27061	24330	6	Itasca	2,667.7	45,070	1,075	16.9	93.7	1.2	5.0	0.9	1.7	4.9	11.7	10.7	9.6	11.4	11.2
27063		7	Jackson	703.0	9,990	2,404	14.2	92.1	1.6	1.1	2.3	4.6	5.6	12.1	10.9	10.4	12.1	11.1
27065		6	Kanabec	521.6	16,159	2,025	31.0	95.7	1.4	1.8	1.4	1.8	5.4	12.0	11.1	10.2	11.9	12.3
27067	48820	4	Kandiyohi	797.4	43,767	1,101	54.9	78.5	6.6	0.7	1.8	13.4	6.5	13.7	12.2	12.0	11.8	10.5
27069		9	Kittson	1,099.0	4,146	2,872	3.8	95.8	1.2	0.9	0.9	2.4	5.5	13.1	11.0	9.3	9.7	11.4
27071		6	Koochiching	3,104.6	11,941	2,288	3.8	94.8	1.2	3.5	1.0	1.4	4.0	10.2	10.1	9.5	10.2	11.3
27073		9	Lac qui Parle	765.0	6,684	2,683	8.7	95.6	1.3	0.9	1.2	2.6	5.4	12.3	10.2	8.6	10.6	10.0
27075	20260	6	Lake	2,109.1	10,986	2,342	5.2	96.6	0.9	1.6	1.0	1.5	4.8	11.3	9.1	9.1	11.7	10.9
27077		9	Lake of the Woods	1,297.8	3,823	2,900	2.9	94.8	1.4	2.3	2.3	1.9	5.3	10.4	9.2	9.3	11.1	10.7
27079	33460	1	Le Sueur	448.7	28,841	1,461	64.3	91.5	1.1	0.8	1.1	6.7	5.6	13.3	11.9	11.0	12.8	12.5
27081		9	Lincoln	536.8	5,567	2,771	10.4	96.4	0.8	0.8	0.9	2.2	5.9	13.4	10.3	9.5	11.1	10.6
27083	32140	7	Lyon	714.4	25,231	1,598	35.3	83.8	3.9	0.8	5.4	7.5	7.1	15.0	13.6	11.8	12.7	10.6
27085	26780	6	McLeod	491.5	36,735	1,262	74.7	91.0	1.3	0.7	1.2	7.0	5.4	12.6	12.1	11.8	12.4	12.4
27087		8	Mahnomen	557.9	5,414	2,781	9.7	53.3	1.3	48.7	0.8	4.8	8.4	18.8	12.9	9.9	10.6	9.7
27089		8	Marshall	1,775.1	8,988	2,486	5.1	94.0	0.8	1.1	0.5	4.7	6.1	13.4	10.4	10.6	11.8	10.7
27091	21860	7	Martin	712.3	19,915	1,818	28.0	92.7	0.9	0.7	1.1	5.5	5.9	12.7	10.9	9.8	11.2	10.4
27093		6	Meeker	608.0	23,376	1,663	38.4	94.5	1.0	0.6	0.7	4.2	5.8	13.8	11.8	10.3	11.6	11.4
27095	33460	1	Mille Lacs	572.3	26,867	1,532	46.9	90.2	1.2	6.7	1.1	2.7	5.8	13.5	11.2	11.8	12.6	12.1
27097		6	Morrison	1,125.1	33,992	1,331	30.2	96.7	1.1	0.9	0.7	1.8	5.4	13.5	11.1	10.4	12.6	11.3
27099	12380	4	Mower	711.3	40,158	1,177	56.5	77.6	4.7	0.6	6.5	12.3	6.5	14.6	12.5	11.8	12.4	11.2
27101		9	Murray	704.7	8,144	2,568	11.6	92.6	0.8	0.7	2.3	4.7	5.4	12.5	10.5	8.8	11.1	10.1
27103	31860	3	Nicollet	448.6	34,332	1,320	76.5	88.8	4.8	0.7	2.3	5.0	5.2	12.8	16.8	11.8	13.9	10.8
27105	49380	7	Nobles	715.1	21,991	1,712	30.8	57.7	5.0	0.8	7.6	30.1	8.4	15.4	12.7	11.4	11.9	11.0
27107		8	Norman	872.8	6,416	2,704	7.4	90.8	1.4	3.8	1.1	5.6	5.8	13.8	11.6	9.7	11.0	11.9
27109	40340	3	Olmsted	653.5	163,436	412	250.1	80.6	8.1	0.7	7.7	5.4	6.4	13.7	12.0	14.2	13.9	11.1
27111	22260	6	Otter Tail	1,971.6	60,046	875	30.5	93.4	2.0	1.2	1.1	3.8	5.4	12.8	10.4	9.5	11.1	10.3
27113		6	Pennington	616.6	13,780	2,171	22.3	91.9	1.7	2.5	1.5	4.4	5.7	12.9	11.3	12.5	12.5	11.8
27115		6	Pine	1,411.3	29,302	1,447	20.8	90.9	2.8	4.0	1.3	3.1	4.3	11.2	10.1	10.8	12.8	12.1
27117		6	Pipestone	465.1	9,313	2,465	20.0	88.8	1.9	2.3	1.4	7.8	7.2	15.0	11.4	10.1	11.1	10.6
27119	24220	3	Polk	1,971.0	30,757	1,411	15.6	87.5	3.6	2.5	1.4	7.1	6.5	14.0	12.6	11.2	12.5	10.7
27121		8	Pope	669.5	11,403	2,320	17.0	96.6	1.0	0.8	0.9	2.0	5.4	12.8	9.5	10.3	12.0	10.1
27123	33460	1	Ramsey	152.2	543,257	129	3,569.4	62.9	14.9	1.5	16.6	7.7	6.4	13.1	13.2	16.0	13.5	10.7
27125		8	Red Lake	432.4	3,933	2,893	9.1	93.3	2.0	2.5	0.8	3.7	6.0	14.2	10.6	9.3	12.7	10.9
27127		7	Redwood	878.6	15,366	2,066	17.5	87.5	1.5	5.4	3.4	4.1	6.5	14.2	12.0	10.6	11.4	10.4
27129		8	Renville	982.9	14,608	2,108	14.9	87.4	1.2	1.5	1.2	10.0	5.9	13.3	11.4	10.4	11.6	11.1
27131	22060	4	Rice	495.8	67,262	800	135.7	81.8	7.1	0.8	3.1	9.0	5.5	12.1	18.2	11.4	12.3	11.6
27133		6	Rock	482.5	9,680	2,439	20.1	94.3	1.5	1.1	1.3	3.3	5.2	14.4	12.8	10.5	11.9	11.5
27135		7	Roseau	1,671.7	15,258	2,073	9.1	92.9	1.3	2.6	3.3	1.8	5.4	14.0	11.8	10.3	11.5	12.5
27137	20260	2	St. Louis	6,247.6	199,182	345	31.9	93.0	2.6	3.3	1.8	1.9	4.7	10.7	15.8	11.5	11.9	10.7
27139	33460	1	Scott	356.3	153,268	447	430.2	80.5	7.1	1.3	7.8	5.8	6.0	15.3	13.1	11.8	14.7	14.2
27141	33460	1	Sherburne	432.9	99,074	614	228.9	90.9	4.9	1.0	2.3	3.1	6.5	14.8	13.1	12.9	14.5	13.4
27143		1	Sibley	588.8	14,917	2,092	25.3	88.9	1.5	0.7	1.1	9.1	5.8	12.6	11.8	11.1	12.4	11.7
27145	41060	3	Stearns	1,342.8	158,947	428	118.4	84.6	9.8	0.7	3.0	3.9	6.4	13.1	18.3	11.9	11.8	10.4
27147	36940	5	Steele	429.6	37,349	1,240	86.9	86.6	4.3	0.6	1.4	8.5	5.6	14.4	12.1	11.3	12.7	12.0
27149		7	Stevens	563.6	9,700	2,436	17.2	86.7	2.2	2.7	2.5	8.5	6.3	12.1	23.1	11.4	11.3	8.5
27151		7	Swift	742.0	9,749	2,432	13.1	90.6	2.1	0.9	2.0	6.1	6.1	13.0	10.8	10.6	12.0	10.6
27153		6	Todd	945.1	25,237	1,597	26.7	90.3	1.0	1.0	1.0	7.9	6.2	14.0	10.6	9.7	10.8	10.4
27155		9	Traverse	573.9	3,286	2,941	5.7	87.6	1.8	6.2	1.1	5.1	5.8	11.7	10.3	9.3	10.7	10.2
27157	40340	3	Wabasha	522.9	21,509	1,735	41.1	95.2	1.1	0.7	0.9	3.2	5.6	12.5	10.3	10.1	11.5	11.7
27159		7	Wadena	536.3	14,177	2,136	26.4	95.4	1.8	1.6	0.9	2.2	7.0	14.9	11.5	10.6	11.2	10.8
27161		6	Waseca	423.4	19,000	1,869	44.9	89.6	2.9	1.0	1.2	6.7	5.3	13.2	12.4	11.8	13.6	11.5
27163	33460	1	Washington	384.7	272,256	257	707.7	82.1	6.6	1.0	8.2	4.8	5.6	14.1	12.2	11.4	13.9	13.0
27165		6	Watonwan	434.9	11,135	2,334	25.6	70.1	1.1	0.6	1.2	27.7	7.3	13.8	11.7	10.5	11.3	10.8
27167	47420	6	Wilkin	751.0	6,395	2,705	8.5	93.5	1.2	2.2	0.9	3.9	5.3	13.3	11.2	10.4	12.3	11.9
27169	49100	4	Winona	626.2	49,630	1,001	79.3	91.9	2.5	0.7	3.1	3.2	4.6	9.9	23.0	10.9	10.8	10.1
27171	33460	1	Wright	661.2	144,845	461	219.1	92.4	3.1	0.7	2.3	3.4	6.5	15.9	12.5	11.6	14.6	13.1
27173		9	Yellow Medicine	759.1	9,411	2,458	12.4	90.2	1.3	4.0	1.0	5.1	5.6	13.1	11.8	10.3	11.6	11.0

1. CBSA = Core Based Statistical Area. See Appendix A for explanation. See Appendix B for list of metropolitan areas with component counties. 2. County type code from the Economic Research Service of USDA Rural-Urban Continuum Codes. See Appendix A for definition. 3. Dry land or land partially or temporarily covered by water. 4. May be of any race.

STATE County	Population, 2021 (cont.): Age (percent) (cont.): 55 to 64 years	65 to 74 years	75 years and over	Percent female	Population change, 2000–2021: Total persons: 2010	2020	Percent change: 2010–2020	2020–2021	Components of change, 2020–2021: Births	Deaths	Net Migration	Households, 2016–2020: Number	Persons per household	Percent: Family house-holds	Female family house-holder[1]	One person
	16	17	18	19	20	21	22	23	24	25	26	27	28	29	30	31
MINNESOTA— Cont'd																
Fillmore	14.1	12.2	9.4	49.4	20,866	21,228	1.7	0.2	285	333	89	8,652	2.4	69.1	5.8	25.8
Freeborn	15.0	12.5	10.3	49.8	31,255	30,895	-1.2	-0.5	388	508	-27	13,005	2.3	63.5	9.4	30.8
Goodhue	15.2	12.0	8.5	50.1	46,183	47,582	3.0	0.8	600	713	502	19,623	2.3	64.4	9.0	29.5
Grant	14.3	13.2	10.4	49.4	6,018	6,074	0.9	1.3	86	90	84	2,578	2.3	66.3	7.9	31.2
Hennepin	12.5	9.3	5.8	50.3	1,152,425	1,281,565	11.2	-1.1	18,541	13,704	-18,910	513,892	2.4	57.2	9.1	32.9
Houston	15.7	13.4	9.4	49.7	19,027	18,843	-1.0	-0.3	238	289	-15	8,286	2.2	65.2	7.8	29.5
Hubbard	16.6	15.8	10.1	49.0	20,428	21,344	4.5	1.7	262	311	427	8,792	2.4	68.4	6.6	27.0
Isanti	14.8	10.1	6.7	49.3	37,816	41,135	8.8	1.9	555	478	693	15,169	2.6	68.4	8.9	23.9
Itasca	15.5	15.3	9.7	49.4	45,058	45,014	-0.1	0.1	482	724	302	19,529	2.3	64.8	8.1	28.1
Jackson	15.1	12.9	10.0	48.0	10,266	9,989	-2.7	0.0	115	142	26	4,480	2.2	63.0	5.5	28.5
Kanabec	15.6	13.3	8.1	49.4	16,239	16,032	-1.3	0.8	190	262	202	6,631	2.4	66.5	7.8	27.1
Kandiyohi	13.7	11.6	8.0	49.6	42,239	43,732	3.5	0.1	710	592	-89	16,853	2.5	67.8	10.1	25.2
Kittson	15.3	13.5	11.2	50.1	4,552	4,207	-7.6	-1.4	48	102	-7	1,834	2.2	63.7	6.8	30.0
Koochiching	17.0	16.7	11.0	49.9	13,311	12,062	-9.4	-1.0	101	197	-23	5,796	2.1	58.5	8.1	35.6
Lac qui Parle	15.3	14.5	13.2	49.5	7,259	6,719	-7.4	-0.5	90	142	18	3,048	2.1	63.5	5.4	30.3
Lake	16.3	16.0	11.0	48.8	10,866	10,905	0.4	0.7	122	208	170	5,174	2.0	64.9	7.2	30.2
Lake of the Woods	17.6	17.0	9.2	47.9	4,045	3,763	-7.0	1.6	43	58	76	1,522	2.4	57.6	5.8	39.3
Le Sueur	14.7	10.8	7.3	49.4	27,703	28,674	3.5	0.6	334	348	181	11,191	2.5	70.9	8.6	24.1
Lincoln	14.4	12.5	12.3	49.6	5,896	5,640	-4.3	-1.3	79	97	-53	2,459	2.2	61.0	5.9	34.5
Lyon	12.3	9.6	7.4	50.3	25,857	25,269	-2.3	-0.2	413	340	-115	10,067	2.4	64.0	10.3	30.2
McLeod	14.1	10.7	8.4	50.0	36,651	36,771	0.3	-0.1	467	557	49	14,736	2.4	61.3	6.5	32.7
Mahnomen	12.3	10.3	7.1	49.4	5,413	5,411	0.0	0.1	105	100	-3	1,956	2.8	64.7	16.6	30.3
Marshall	14.5	12.5	10.1	49.2	9,439	9,040	-4.2	-0.6	138	134	-56	3,952	2.3	65.9	7.0	30.3
Martin	14.6	13.5	10.9	50.5	20,840	20,025	-3.9	-0.5	275	312	-75	8,824	2.2	61.8	7.1	31.7
Meeker	14.6	12.3	8.6	49.1	23,300	23,400	0.4	-0.1	309	334	0	9,219	2.5	67.9	6.8	27.4
Mille Lacs	14.8	10.7	7.5	49.6	26,097	26,459	1.4	1.5	341	440	515	10,535	2.4	63.8	10.8	30.5
Morrison	15.0	12.3	8.4	49.3	33,198	34,010	2.4	-0.1	414	524	88	13,536	2.4	66.7	7.6	27.9
Mower	12.7	10.3	8.0	49.8	39,163	40,029	2.2	0.3	617	508	15	15,750	2.5	65.3	10.0	29.6
Murray	14.9	14.6	12.2	50.1	8,725	8,179	-6.3	-0.4	101	103	-34	3,659	2.2	64.0	5.1	31.0
Nicollet	12.0	10.1	6.7	49.8	32,727	34,454	5.3	-0.4	416	343	-197	12,821	2.4	66.0	8.4	28.2
Nobles	12.3	9.4	7.5	48.2	21,378	22,290	4.3	-1.3	456	281	-471	7,898	2.7	68.4	9.8	27.8
Norman	14.8	11.5	9.9	49.6	6,852	6,441	-6.0	-0.4	74	105	4	2,771	2.3	61.6	7.5	32.4
Olmsted	12.5	9.2	6.9	51.2	144,248	162,847	12.9	0.4	2,459	1,684	-215	63,561	2.4	64.2	8.5	27.7
Otter Tail	15.7	14.6	10.2	49.8	57,303	60,081	4.8	-0.1	739	1,084	312	24,693	2.3	66.5	6.8	28.0
Pennington	13.7	10.9	8.7	50.4	13,930	13,992	0.4	-1.5	164	173	-202	5,976	2.3	61.2	11.1	32.8
Pine	16.6	13.6	8.4	46.6	29,750	28,876	-2.9	1.5	272	445	607	11,132	2.5	62.7	7.8	31.0
Pipestone	13.5	10.9	10.3	50.8	9,596	9,424	-1.8	-1.2	150	163	-97	4,002	2.3	61.1	6.1	34.5
Polk	13.6	10.9	7.9	49.4	31,600	31,192	-1.3	-1.4	444	507	-373	12,619	2.4	61.0	7.8	34.1
Pope	15.1	14.6	10.1	48.5	10,995	11,308	2.8	0.8	144	161	113	5,010	2.2	64.5	5.2	29.0
Ramsey	11.8	9.4	5.9	50.9	508,640	552,352	8.6	-1.6	8,677	6,552	-11,132	210,424	2.5	57.4	11.4	33.8
Red Lake	14.0	12.6	9.7	48.4	4,089	3,935	-3.8	-0.1	57	43	-15	1,713	2.3	64.9	7.8	30.1
Redwood	13.6	11.5	9.8	49.7	16,059	15,425	-3.9	-0.4	243	253	-49	6,262	2.4	63.6	6.8	32.2
Renville	15.0	11.8	9.5	48.8	15,730	14,723	-6.4	-0.8	204	243	-78	6,032	2.4	62.3	6.3	32.1
Rice	12.8	9.7	6.5	48.4	64,142	67,097	4.6	0.2	824	758	84	23,183	2.5	67.7	8.3	26.2
Rock	13.5	10.9	9.3	50.2	9,687	9,704	0.2	-0.2	105	159	28	3,990	2.3	68.6	8.9	26.2
Roseau	15.7	11.2	7.6	47.9	15,629	15,331	-1.9	-0.5	188	224	-39	5,940	2.5	67.0	8.4	28.7
St. Louis	14.1	12.8	7.8	49.7	200,226	200,231	0.0	-0.5	2,250	3,157	-166	86,229	2.2	56.0	8.2	34.1
Scott	13.0	7.5	4.4	49.9	129,928	150,928	16.2	1.6	2,041	1,165	1,437	50,487	2.9	76.7	9.6	17.7
Sherburne	12.7	7.8	4.4	48.5	88,499	97,183	9.8	1.9	1,449	923	1,361	32,791	2.9	74.3	9.0	19.3
Sibley	15.7	10.6	8.2	48.9	15,226	14,836	-2.6	0.5	204	176	53	6,015	2.4	65.2	5.6	29.2
Stearns	12.3	9.4	6.5	49.4	150,642	158,292	5.1	0.4	2,479	1,713	-141	59,576	2.6	63.8	8.8	27.2
Steele	13.4	10.5	8.0	49.9	36,576	37,406	2.3	-0.2	475	465	-71	14,836	2.4	66.5	7.1	28.6
Stevens	10.1	9.6	7.8	49.5	9,726	9,671	-0.6	0.3	158	103	-27	3,683	2.6	62.2	4.9	29.6
Swift	14.3	12.2	10.3	49.0	9,783	9,838	0.6	-0.9	131	162	-58	4,243	2.2	63.1	9.0	33.8
Todd	15.5	13.2	9.5	48.0	24,895	25,262	1.5	-0.1	369	310	-86	9,888	2.5	69.1	6.1	26.0
Traverse	15.7	13.1	13.1	49.2	3,558	3,360	-5.6	-2.2	46	52	-67	1,590	2.0	58.4	5.7	37.7
Wabasha	15.7	13.1	9.5	49.7	21,676	21,387	-1.3	0.6	275	266	114	9,081	2.4	67.0	7.0	27.3
Wadena	13.0	11.6	9.4	50.3	13,843	14,065	1.6	0.8	259	233	85	5,748	2.3	62.3	10.7	29.7
Waseca	13.3	11.2	7.5	51.3	19,136	18,968	-0.9	0.2	246	215	-3	7,547	2.3	66.3	9.6	29.3
Washington	13.9	9.8	6.1	50.1	238,136	267,568	12.4	1.8	3,337	2,727	4,095	95,796	2.7	71.7	8.7	22.5
Watonwan	13.9	11.4	9.3	49.7	11,211	11,253	0.4	-1.0	210	194	-132	4,371	2.5	65.0	10.0	31.9
Wilkin	15.5	11.5	8.5	47.3	6,576	6,506	-1.1	-1.7	73	122	-62	2,799	2.2	62.0	8.9	33.8
Winona	12.5	10.9	7.3	50.1	51,461	49,671	-3.5	-0.1	563	628	16	19,466	2.4	56.8	6.5	32.4
Wright	12.5	8.2	5.1	49.2	124,700	141,337	13.3	2.5	2,114	1,311	2,713	49,097	2.8	72.8	7.2	21.8
Yellow Medicine	14.4	12.2	10.0	49.4	10,438	9,528	-8.7	-1.2	127	139	-106	4,088	2.3	69.3	8.5	27.0

1. No spouse present.

STATE County	Persons in group quarters, 2021	Daytime Population, 2016–2020		Births, 2021		Deaths, 2021		Persons under 65 with no health insurance, 2019		Medicare, 2021			COVID-19 Deaths, 2020	
		Number	Employment/ residence ratio	Total	Rate[1]	Number	Rate[1]	Number	Percent	Total beneficiaries	Enrolled in Original Medicare	Enrolled in Medicare Advantage	Number	Rate[1]
	32	33	34	35	36	37	38	39	40	41	42	43	44	45
MINNESOTA— Cont'd														
Fillmore	300	17,788	0.7	218	10.3	276	13.0	1,303	7.9	4,960	3,127	1,834	10	0.5
Freeborn	588	29,368	0.9	302	9.8	411	13.3	1,596	7.0	7,809	4,248	3,561	21	0.7
Goodhue	807	45,551	1.0	484	10.1	569	11.9	1,908	5.2	10,843	4,197	6,646	50	1.1
Grant	89	5,467	0.8	69	11.3	68	11.1	270	6.0	1,581	954	627	D	D
Hennepin	25,061	1,473,072	1.3	14,722	11.6	10,975	8.6	62,212	5.8	201,379	98,435	102,945	1,477	1.2
Houston	214	14,906	0.6	182	9.7	222	11.8	730	5.1	4,649	2,793	1,856	13	0.7
Hubbard	93	18,844	0.7	208	9.7	252	11.7	1,214	7.7	6,020	3,819	2,201	44	2.1
Isanti	373	32,318	0.6	437	10.5	387	9.3	1,956	5.8	7,940	3,883	4,057	38	0.9
Itasca	895	43,202	0.9	394	8.8	579	12.9	2,336	7.0	12,548	5,337	7,212	40	0.9
Jackson	93	9,861	1.0	95	9.5	108	10.8	445	6.0	2,443	1,750	693	13	1.3
Kanabec	167	13,405	0.6	148	9.2	210	13.0	830	6.5	3,991	1,786	2,205	24	1.5
Kandiyohi	977	44,130	1.1	550	12.6	469	10.7	2,787	8.1	9,640	5,403	4,237	72	1.6
Kittson	89	3,989	0.9	42	10.1	85	20.4	198	6.2	1,161	850	311	22	5.3
Koochiching	199	12,361	1.0	84	7.0	171	14.3	648	7.4	3,759	1,714	2,044	11	0.9
Lac qui Parle	138	6,323	0.9	63	9.4	118	17.6	331	7.0	1,899	1,227	672	19	2.8
Lake	203	10,771	1.0	101	9.2	157	14.4	409	5.3	3,153	1,360	1,793	14	1.3
Lake of the Woods	44	3,472	0.9	32	8.4	41	10.8	203	7.4	1,147	680	467	D	D
Le Sueur	213	22,791	0.6	271	9.4	284	9.9	1,543	6.5	5,758	2,238	3,520	19	0.7
Lincoln	116	4,919	0.7	66	11.8	83	14.8	277	6.6	1,511	1,062	450	D	D
Lyon	793	27,775	1.2	317	12.6	273	10.8	1,351	6.6	4,869	3,479	1,389	34	1.4
McLeod	442	35,035	1.0	386	10.5	442	12.0	1,526	5.3	7,844	2,679	5,165	46	1.3
Mahnomen	65	5,834	1.2	86	15.9	71	13.2	432	9.7	1,201	842	359	D	D
Marshall	50	8,043	0.7	112	12.4	115	12.8	478	6.7	2,219	1,358	861	16	1.8
Martin	319	19,943	1.0	221	11.1	247	12.4	953	6.5	5,368	3,612	1,755	26	1.3
Meeker	300	19,722	0.7	251	10.7	274	11.7	1,025	5.6	5,361	1,738	3,622	31	1.3
Mille Lacs	475	24,574	0.9	280	10.5	336	12.6	1,761	8.4	6,084	2,333	3,751	48	1.8
Morrison	481	29,396	0.8	323	9.5	435	12.8	1,762	6.7	7,922	4,223	3,699	48	1.4
Mower	540	37,982	0.9	474	11.8	412	10.3	2,483	7.8	8,516	5,257	3,259	32	0.8
Murray	136	7,449	0.8	78	9.6	83	10.2	422	7.0	2,325	1,679	646	D	D
Nicollet	2,797	34,270	1.0	332	9.6	270	7.8	1,280	4.9	6,195	3,973	2,221	34	1.0
Nobles	366	22,025	1.0	374	16.9	225	10.2	2,290	13.1	3,911	2,807	1,104	49	2.2
Norman	128	5,719	0.8	63	9.8	86	13.4	331	6.7	1,640	1,175	465	D	D
Olmsted	2,353	173,339	1.2	1,976	12.1	1,383	8.5	7,185	5.4	27,592	18,968	8,625	71	0.4
Otter Tail	1,118	55,094	0.9	588	9.8	856	14.3	2,979	6.8	16,458	9,141	7,317	59	1.0
Pennington	286	16,592	1.3	133	9.6	145	10.5	570	5.1	2,907	1,678	1,230	15	1.1
Pine	1,427	26,727	0.8	222	7.6	351	12.1	1,847	8.6	7,152	2,891	4,261	21	0.7
Pipestone	192	9,200	1.0	125	13.4	138	14.7	704	9.9	2,183	1,240	943	19	2.0
Polk	1,127	29,973	0.9	359	11.6	411	13.3	1,376	5.6	6,768	4,705	2,063	62	2.0
Pope	150	10,285	0.9	123	10.8	124	10.9	530	6.3	3,064	1,988	1,076	D	D
Ramsey	17,063	601,128	1.2	6,862	12.5	5,245	9.6	31,455	6.9	91,774	46,380	45,394	713	1.3
Red Lake	19	3,257	0.6	42	10.7	30	7.6	204	6.5	908	450	458	D	D
Redwood	343	15,212	1.0	189	12.3	195	12.7	973	8.3	3,511	2,255	1,256	29	1.9
Renville	309	13,768	0.9	157	10.7	191	13.0	837	7.4	3,540	2,328	1,212	36	2.5
Rice	7,188	63,728	0.9	671	10.0	610	9.1	3,647	7.4	11,816	4,585	7,231	57	0.9
Rock	251	8,329	0.8	77	7.9	134	13.8	403	5.6	2,173	1,065	1,107	13	1.3
Roseau	159	15,802	1.1	153	10.0	176	11.5	804	6.6	3,231	1,955	1,276	18	1.2
St. Louis	8,701	208,633	1.1	1,773	8.9	2,486	12.5	8,005	5.2	47,406	19,114	28,292	247	1.2
Scott	1,161	127,945	0.8	1,612	10.6	903	5.9	6,168	4.7	19,146	9,685	9,462	77	0.5
Sherburne	2,012	74,385	0.6	1,155	11.8	725	7.4	3,517	4.2	14,222	7,250	6,972	63	0.6
Sibley	196	12,105	0.7	159	10.7	146	9.8	922	7.7	3,112	1,190	1,922	D	D
Stearns	6,483	172,151	1.2	1,957	12.3	1,345	8.5	8,634	6.6	28,305	15,731	12,574	197	1.2
Steele	550	40,332	1.2	382	10.2	359	9.6	1,630	5.5	7,765	4,425	3,341	11	0.3
Stevens	882	10,992	1.2	127	13.1	77	8.0	420	5.8	1,805	1,051	755	D	D
Swift	147	8,871	0.9	107	11.0	130	13.3	538	7.6	2,313	1,507	805	18	1.8
Todd	311	21,384	0.7	293	11.6	244	9.7	1,669	8.9	5,736	2,866	2,870	33	1.3
Traverse	96	3,057	0.9	36	10.9	40	12.1	207	8.7	1,006	516	490	D	D
Wabasha	179	18,339	0.7	214	10.0	217	10.1	1,031	6.2	5,425	3,031	2,394	D	D
Wadena	450	14,603	1.2	204	14.4	183	12.9	705	6.7	3,661	2,118	1,543	12	0.9
Waseca	948	15,680	0.7	186	9.8	160	8.4	835	5.8	3,985	2,334	1,651	18	0.9
Washington	3,310	226,975	0.8	2,694	10.0	2,193	8.1	8,961	4.1	46,514	22,553	23,961	206	0.8
Watonwan	141	10,189	0.9	172	15.4	159	14.2	935	11.0	2,433	1,640	794	10	0.9
Wilkin	148	5,263	0.7	57	8.9	95	14.8	238	4.8	1,426	926	500	12	1.9
Winona	3,717	50,086	1.0	447	9.0	501	10.1	2,341	6.1	10,078	6,008	4,069	50	1.0
Wright	1,016	111,939	0.7	1,653	11.5	1,037	7.2	5,358	4.4	21,069	10,145	10,924	104	0.7
Yellow Medicine	233	9,172	0.9	104	11.0	119	12.6	488	6.4	2,261	1,144	1,117	15	1.6

1. Per 1,000 estimated resident population.

STATE County	COVID-19 Vaccinations, 2021–2022		Education						Money income, 2016–2020				Income and poverty, 2020			
			School enrollment and attainment, 2016–2020				Local government expenditures,[3] 2018–2019			Households				Percent below poverty level		
			Enrollment[1]		Attainment[2] (percent)						Percent					
	Number	Percent[5]	Total	Percent private	High school graduate or less	Bachelor's degree or more	Total current spending (mil dol)	Current spending per student (dollars)	Per capita income[4]	Median income (dollars)	with income of less than $50,000	with income of $200,000 or more	Median household income (dollars)	All persons	Children under 18 years	Children 5 to 17 years in families
	46	47	48	49	50	51	52	53	54	55	56	57	58	59	60	61
MINNESOTA— Cont'd																
Fillmore	14,469	68.7	4,615	11.6	40.8	22.5	28.5	11,421	31,083	64,375	38.5	3.3	66,204	8.2	11.2	10.4
Freeborn	17,465	57.7	6,582	5.5	46.0	17.0	59.2	13,628	30,760	54,628	45.5	2.9	62,233	10.0	13.1	12.1
Goodhue	30,887	66.7	10,095	9.5	39.3	26.2	87.9	13,262	35,767	69,334	35.3	5.1	73,474	7.2	7.4	6.8
Grant	3,291	55.1	1,282	6.2	41.1	17.9	14.8	12,596	33,407	59,246	42.4	4.2	66,740	9.3	12.7	12.0
Hennepin	939,233	74.2	310,345	16.7	22.2	51.0	2,481.8	14,575	47,618	81,169	30.6	13.2	81,772	9.3	10.5	10.5
Houston	11,025	59.3	3,938	15.8	40.8	24.1	47.7	11,228	33,546	59,514	38.6	3.3	61,117	6.4	7.3	6.9
Hubbard	10,189	47.4	4,394	12.4	35.7	28.4	30.6	11,327	30,467	58,475	42.3	2.9	62,750	9.1	13.5	13.0
Isanti	17,542	43.2	9,240	13.1	43.3	18.1	78.0	12,637	34,591	76,999	30.2	5.4	73,401	6.7	7.6	7.1
Itasca	25,558	56.6	9,470	13.2	36.6	24.6	99.2	14,400	30,504	55,744	44.7	3.0	59,365	10.5	12.8	11.9
Jackson	5,018	51.0	2,044	9.1	41.4	22.7	17.9	12,109	36,928	62,479	38.6	3.6	62,766	7.6	10.5	10.7
Kanabec	7,026	43.0	3,423	10.5	48.8	14.7	24.3	11,288	29,055	57,877	43.6	2.1	62,422	9.1	10.8	10.3
Kandiyohi	23,450	54.3	9,659	13.8	36.2	24.4	76.2	12,426	31,778	64,252	38.8	4.8	65,344	8.2	10.9	11.0
Kittson	2,563	59.6	799	6.6	42.9	26.3	9.4	15,921	29,717	55,410	43.6	2.6	51,016	10.3	11.7	11.3
Koochiching	7,189	58.8	2,440	5.7	43.1	15.1	23.3	14,354	31,453	52,297	47.7	1.7	56,870	11.6	15.4	14.5
Lac qui Parle	3,886	58.7	1,251	7.4	44.4	18.8	17.7	12,886	34,091	57,802	42.9	4.8	65,446	8.6	11.7	11.2
Lake	7,092	66.6	1,783	12.2	35.7	28.0	17.4	12,503	35,671	65,201	36.1	2.8	63,741	8.0	8.9	8.0
Lake of the Woods	2,070	55.3	626	1.3	39.5	21.3	6.3	13,189	27,833	50,669	48.5	1.3	57,302	8.8	10.2	10.3
Le Sueur	14,248	49.3	6,574	12.3	40.8	22.9	47.6	11,223	34,904	75,925	31.9	5.5	78,559	6.7	6.4	6.2
Lincoln	3,003	53.3	1,269	8.0	44.9	19.3	12.9	13,372	30,178	53,557	46.0	2.6	57,252	8.7	8.9	8.9
Lyon	14,431	56.6	7,483	8.5	38.0	26.4	91.7	19,443	30,706	57,274	44.0	3.6	63,255	8.8	10.3	10.4
McLeod	20,840	58.1	8,139	13.7	40.5	17.3	62.1	11,559	33,628	62,885	36.5	4.0	76,095	5.8	7.0	6.6
Mahnomen	3,324	60.1	1,521	7.6	49.6	12.9	21.5	14,701	21,198	45,398	55.3	2.0	48,951	15.3	24.4	22.9
Marshall	4,659	49.9	1,954	6.8	48.0	18.5	20.6	14,664	30,934	60,951	40.6	2.4	62,240	7.9	9.2	8.8
Martin	10,916	55.5	4,108	12.8	42.0	21.7	42.4	14,249	31,505	53,851	46.1	4.1	58,578	9.9	13.0	12.4
Meeker	11,181	48.1	5,175	10.4	42.4	18.2	38.6	11,470	32,412	63,841	37.7	3.7	66,861	6.2	6.8	6.6
Mille Lacs	15,226	57.9	5,537	11.4	47.1	16.0	75.4	11,887	29,149	57,173	43.0	3.2	55,547	9.2	12.4	11.0
Morrison	16,473	49.3	7,082	10.4	47.5	17.3	61.3	11,373	30,293	58,826	42.5	3.6	62,618	9.8	11.9	11.3
Mower	24,987	62.4	9,731	8.6	44.4	22.6	93.3	14,000	29,828	55,378	45.5	3.5	61,565	8.7	10.5	10.1
Murray	4,482	54.7	1,616	10.0	45.7	20.8	14.4	13,207	32,791	62,839	40.4	3.5	63,414	7.6	10.8	10.5
Nicollet	21,497	62.7	9,320	38.7	30.8	34.4	44.6	16,380	38,120	69,174	36.9	6.9	75,827	7.2	7.0	6.5
Nobles	13,279	61.4	5,521	6.1	53.6	16.3	54.2	10,913	26,290	56,000	45.8	3.0	63,011	9.4	12.2	12.4
Norman	3,848	60.4	1,523	7.8	42.5	21.4	13.5	12,884	30,915	56,081	44.8	2.8	50,573	10.5	15.4	15.1
Olmsted	121,847	77.0	40,280	16.0	24.7	46.7	311.0	12,484	42,470	80,403	29.6	9.5	82,683	6.4	6.6	6.4
Otter Tail	29,901	50.9	11,603	13.7	35.1	25.9	129.0	16,191	32,702	59,456	42.5	4.1	67,329	7.8	10.1	9.9
Pennington	7,578	53.7	2,986	7.8	37.3	19.7	75.9	33,457	31,340	60,940	40.3	2.5	64,240	8.2	8.5	8.4
Pine	14,516	49.1	5,736	11.4	49.9	15.3	45.9	12,232	27,607	55,606	45.3	2.6	58,733	10.2	12.6	12.0
Pipestone	4,989	54.7	2,148	13.2	46.5	19.3	19.3	12,243	30,084	53,688	47.8	3.9	58,662	9.2	12.5	11.9
Polk	18,217	58.1	7,370	8.6	37.3	27.3	64.2	12,269	29,828	58,682	44.0	3.3	60,068	10.6	12.0	11.5
Pope	6,465	57.5	2,121	9.1	37.1	22.3	18.7	13,417	35,244	62,878	40.1	4.3	64,306	7.9	8.3	8.0
Ramsey	395,392	71.8	142,944	22.6	30.1	43.0	1,401.2	15,163	36,598	67,238	36.9	7.7	66,123	12.6	16.4	16.1
Red Lake	2,292	56.5	898	4.5	42.3	17.0	11.1	14,377	30,190	59,698	45.1	1.9	68,683	8.3	9.0	8.6
Redwood	8,261	54.5	3,561	11.7	45.0	19.1	31.2	12,367	29,086	57,243	43.0	2.5	61,316	8.6	10.6	10.6
Renville	8,001	55.0	3,164	9.2	46.0	15.1	22.5	12,688	31,243	58,542	41.0	3.3	56,296	8.6	11.1	10.8
Rice	42,302	63.2	19,853	39.5	40.2	28.5	120.9	14,156	31,792	70,600	35.0	5.7	74,301	8.4	8.9	7.5
Rock	5,041	54.1	2,123	12.4	38.2	23.8	17.9	10,962	33,698	65,744	38.2	4.5	64,588	8.2	10.6	9.5
Roseau	7,817	51.5	3,448	10.3	43.6	19.0	34.6	12,854	31,452	62,304	37.6	3.1	61,775	7.3	9.0	8.3
St. Louis	132,772	66.7	49,049	13.4	31.5	30.1	324.3	12,978	32,890	57,480	44.3	4.1	57,972	10.1	11.5	10.5
Scott	103,856	69.7	40,087	15.2	26.1	40.9	292.3	11,413	43,890	103,261	20.9	16.2	99,924	4.3	4.9	4.5
Sherburne	44,964	46.2	24,908	7.5	34.4	25.7	229.3	11,235	36,022	88,671	24.6	7.2	92,673	4.4	5.2	4.8
Sibley	7,325	49.3	3,242	13.2	46.8	16.5	27.4	12,230	32,471	64,170	38.4	4.1	61,225	7.9	9.3	8.4
Stearns	95,216	59.1	46,712	17.6	36.3	27.8	312.4	12,371	31,574	65,244	38.2	4.8	66,317	10.6	11.0	10.5
Steele	22,344	61.0	8,896	15.2	39.2	26.8	79.3	11,767	34,648	68,172	36.6	5.0	70,532	7.3	9.5	8.4
Stevens	5,693	58.1	2,867	6.4	37.3	29.8	19.5	12,458	35,551	65,503	38.2	6.4	68,234	9.1	8.1	7.6
Swift	5,364	57.9	1,992	3.1	41.2	21.5	18.3	11,696	33,416	53,457	47.2	5.4	59,165	9.5	11.5	10.9
Todd	10,607	43.0	4,973	17.2	50.7	13.9	90.4	29,189	26,427	54,502	45.8	2.1	52,842	12.2	15.9	16.4
Traverse	2,077	63.7	598	4.2	44.3	15.8	7.6	13,524	32,983	51,216	48.9	3.7	56,085	11.6	18.2	17.3
Wabasha	15,963	73.8	4,588	11.4	39.1	24.4	47.4	10,577	35,527	67,906	35.8	4.8	74,348	6.1	7.2	7.0
Wadena	6,822	49.9	3,270	7.7	43.8	16.9	43.8	13,910	24,603	46,178	54.4	1.4	46,968	11.2	13.9	13.2
Waseca	10,671	57.3	4,156	10.3	42.8	22.1	43.9	11,949	31,563	60,450	41.2	4.7	66,523	7.6	9.4	9.3
Washington	185,232	70.6	66,857	15.4	24.3	45.6	484.6	11,822	46,842	97,584	21.1	14.6	101,409	4.4	4.3	4.0
Watonwan	6,374	58.5	2,428	8.1	53.3	17.6	23.7	12,713	28,633	53,304	47.1	2.3	60,656	9.7	12.5	12.6
Wilkin	3,349	54.0	1,315	12.2	37.0	23.7	13.5	12,339	32,868	56,829	44.2	2.5	65,769	8.3	10.9	11.0
Winona	32,888	65.1	15,735	18.3	33.3	31.3	73.3	14,323	31,384	60,020	42.5	4.0	65,302	11.0	11.1	10.4
Wright	76,107	55.0	36,025	13.4	34.6	31.0	335.0	12,071	37,416	87,772	25.3	7.1	85,855	4.6	4.4	3.8
Yellow Medicine	5,513	56.8	2,201	7.9	44.2	16.7	20.2	14,472	31,033	59,289	39.7	3.2	62,290	8.6	11.8	11.1

1. All persons 3 years old and over enrolled in nursery school through college. 2. Persons 25 years old and over. 3. Elementary and secondary education expenditures. 4. Based on population estimated by the American Community Survey, 2016–2020. 5. CDC percent based on 2019 population estimate.

STATE County	Personal income, 2020										Earnings, 2020		
			Per capita[1]			Supplements to wages and salaries, employer contributions (mil dol)						Contributions for government social insurance (mil dol)	
	Total (mil dol)	Percent change 2019–2020	Dollars	Rank	Wages and salaries (mil dol)	Pension and insurance	Government social insurance	Proprietors' income (mil dol)	Dividends, interest, and rent (mil dol)	Personal transfer reecipts (mil dol)	Total (mil dol)	From employee and self-employed	From employer
	62	63	64	65	66	67	68	69	70	71	72	73	74
MINNESOTA— Cont'd													
Fillmore	1,049	12.6	49,630	1,183	243	48	21	135	155	286	447	31	21
Freeborn	1,529	10.5	50,364	1,102	549	93	44	141	242	456	827	57	44
Goodhue	2,700	6.4	58,303	506	1,086	192	87	330	409	621	1,694	107	87
Grant	334	23.2	55,429	676	88	16	7	60	51	96	171	11	7
Hennepin	100,436	4.3	79,183	84	73,883	9,239	5,147	8,254	22,660	15,522	96,524	5,791	5,147
Houston	1,033	7.3	55,443	674	211	42	18	87	165	250	358	27	18
Hubbard	1,135	6.2	52,122	927	260	45	21	207	182	338	534	40	21
Isanti	2,033	9.4	49,082	1,249	513	93	41	107	245	527	754	54	41
Itasca	2,212	7.9	48,872	1,274	730	138	60	158	378	796	1,086	83	60
Jackson	613	17.4	62,789	323	228	46	19	125	108	139	419	21	19
Kanabec	789	11.6	48,092	1,373	180	34	15	59	103	274	287	22	15
Kandiyohi	2,464	9.7	57,122	565	1,070	179	87	366	381	625	1,702	108	87
Kittson	266	33.8	63,181	313	68	14	6	62	44	68	148	7	6
Koochiching	591	5.9	49,019	1,254	213	41	17	37	82	233	308	24	17
Lac qui Parle	393	17.5	60,286	412	93	19	8	70	65	122	189	11	8
Lake	550	5.1	51,683	964	190	35	17	34	94	188	276	21	17
Lake of the Woods	227	11.0	60,435	408	69	15	5	28	38	66	118	8	5
Le Sueur	1,562	8.2	54,361	755	426	76	36	107	248	362	644	42	36
Lincoln	298	12.8	53,464	821	63	14	5	52	45	89	134	8	5
Lyon	1,380	7.9	54,589	732	699	117	53	179	221	328	1,048	62	53
McLeod	1,934	8.7	54,149	772	774	134	60	156	326	479	1,124	76	60
Mahnomen	223	17.8	40,781	2,359	68	15	5	22	32	94	110	7	5
Marshall	588	28.4	63,090	316	121	22	10	128	78	147	281	15	10
Martin	1,129	10.0	57,955	515	408	67	30	129	237	310	634	41	30
Meeker	1,155	11.1	49,478	1,199	332	60	27	97	173	331	516	36	27
Mille Lacs	1,239	8.9	47,379	1,465	375	69	29	67	167	424	541	43	29
Morrison	1,580	12.1	47,610	1,438	458	90	38	161	237	494	747	52	38
Mower	2,029	9.6	50,537	1,085	881	136	67	137	325	558	1,221	80	67
Murray	519	20.8	63,620	301	130	26	11	125	78	127	291	15	11
Nicollet	1,830	7.4	53,083	851	730	136	57	157	326	394	1,079	66	57
Nobles	1,153	18.7	53,881	788	529	87	42	214	153	253	872	48	42
Norman	327	37.2	51,626	968	73	14	6	68	53	103	161	9	6
Olmsted	10,052	6.9	63,100	315	6,822	905	493	591	1,616	1,807	8,811	540	493
Otter Tail	3,096	9.6	52,707	878	1,026	195	83	302	561	894	1,606	111	83
Pennington	858	7.7	61,825	355	518	84	39	51	197	197	692	42	39
Pine	1,240	8.8	42,237	2,162	300	63	25	67	202	457	454	37	25
Pipestone	541	9.4	59,326	460	181	34	15	133	79	130	362	19	15
Polk	1,726	17.0	55,849	653	560	101	47	216	254	479	924	54	47
Pope	638	13.3	56,561	604	223	39	18	71	118	176	351	23	18
Ramsey	32,084	5.3	58,557	493	22,729	3,193	1,630	1,748	6,288	7,442	29,300	1,798	1,630
Red Lake	225	15.3	55,620	664	44	9	4	38	26	55	95	6	4
Redwood	931	14.7	61,772	357	277	52	22	277	129	220	628	35	22
Renville	842	19.3	58,489	496	264	47	23	159	136	222	493	27	23
Rice	3,209	6.9	47,839	1,413	1,310	207	105	217	502	769	1,839	122	105
Rock	551	16.6	59,225	468	161	29	12	138	88	125	341	17	12
Roseau	847	15.6	55,999	642	408	79	35	61	162	204	582	35	35
St. Louis	10,123	5.4	50,986	1,033	4,909	834	392	481	1,612	3,166	6,616	452	392
Scott	9,893	5.5	65,655	246	3,114	435	245	813	1,447	1,363	4,607	288	245
Sherburne	5,011	7.6	50,710	1,063	1,327	230	105	279	572	998	1,941	134	105
Sibley	790	10.8	53,677	804	162	31	15	97	125	202	305	19	15
Stearns	8,299	8.5	51,216	1,002	4,571	754	353	714	1,369	1,987	6,391	392	353
Steele	1,892	8.7	51,703	962	1,029	166	78	120	284	468	1,393	89	78
Stevens	540	17.5	55,345	679	247	45	20	106	97	127	418	22	20
Swift	514	13.6	56,060	637	156	32	13	103	70	151	304	17	13
Todd	1,165	9.3	47,123	1,499	308	57	25	183	153	364	572	41	25
Traverse	238	41.9	74,000	116	52	11	4	80	39	59	147	6	4
Wabasha	1,165	10.1	53,837	792	287	56	24	135	180	289	502	34	24
Wadena	606	10.6	43,925	1,959	242	46	19	49	92	239	356	26	19
Waseca	874	11.8	47,139	1,495	284	54	23	81	134	243	442	29	23
Washington	19,187	5.2	72,273	135	4,697	734	357	1,149	3,824	2,787	6,937	467	357
Watonwan	572	16.3	53,034	856	193	36	16	71	74	154	317	19	16
Wilkin	385	19.8	62,497	335	94	16	8	92	54	91	210	12	8
Winona	2,635	7.4	52,198	917	1,120	216	87	164	558	621	1,586	100	87
Wright	7,744	7.4	55,218	687	2,240	380	179	510	1,060	1,383	3,309	216	179
Yellow Medicine	587	11.6	61,315	374	157	32	12	124	121	155	325	20	12

1. Based on the resident population estimated as of July 1 of the year shown.

STATE County	Earnings, 2020 (cont.) — Percent by selected industries: Farm	Mining, quarrying, and extractions	Construction	Manu-facturing	Information; professional, scientific, technical services	Retail trade	Finance, insurance, real estate, and leasing	Health care and social assistance	Govern-ment	Social Security beneficiaries, December 2020: Number	Rate[1]	Supple-mental Security Income recipients, 2020	Housing units, 2021: Total	Percent change, 2010–2021
	75	76	77	78	79	80	81	82	83	84	85	86	87	88
MINNESOTA— Cont'd														
Fillmore	14.0	D	8.9	13.0	3.0	7.3	5.1	D	15.1	5,215	245	177	9,653	0.6
Freeborn	5.6	D	6.1	18.8	3.8	10.0	7.4	14.7	12.4	8,210	267	602	14,102	-0.1
Goodhue	5.0	D	6.1	24.5	D	5.6	3.4	11.2	14.7	11,190	233	506	21,056	0.7
Grant	22.6	0.0	9.9	5.3	3.2	3.2	4.3	D	15.5	1,745	284	59	3,152	-0.1
Hennepin	0.0	0.2	4.2	8.1	18.6	3.7	15.9	10.5	9.2	196,250	155	25,872	564,672	1.2
Houston	9.9	0.0	12.5	7.5	D	4.9	D	10.3	18.2	4,980	265	D	8,773	0.4
Hubbard	2.2	D	8.1	23.9	8.1	6.6	3.6	D	13.0	6,385	294	364	14,746	0.2
Isanti	0.0	0.0	10.4	12.6	D	10.9	4.1	D	17.8	8,630	206	431	16,916	1.8
Itasca	0.0	D	9.0	9.9	3.2	8.5	4.8	17.7	20.8	13,715	304	851	25,585	0.7
Jackson	20.9	0.0	3.4	26.1	2.5	2.0	5.0	D	10.0	2,440	244	110	4,896	0.1
Kanabec	1.6	D	18.4	7.8	D	7.5	6.0	9.9	31.5	4,475	277	223	7,799	0.7
Kandiyohi	3.4	D	6.8	16.4	4.1	7.2	4.5	18.6	12.8	9,895	226	732	20,137	0.8
Kittson	35.5	D	3.8	8.8	D	3.5	D	10.2	13.8	1,190	287	36	2,272	0.0
Koochiching	0.6	-0.2	6.3	D	3.7	6.8	4.0	D	21.2	4,025	337	270	7,422	0.3
Lac qui Parle	24.6	0.0	6.2	6.6	1.6	5.0	D	6.8	23.1	1,940	290	61	3,468	-0.1
Lake	0.0	D	D	19.3	3.0	5.6	4.0	D	21.3	3,250	296	114	7,385	0.8
Lake of the Woods	4.3	0.0	D	D	D	5.1	1.9	9.4	15.9	1,180	309	37	3,438	1.1
Le Sueur	7.0	D	12.2	34.1	2.8	4.5	4.2	5.3	12.5	5,650	196	306	12,962	1.0
Lincoln	31.3	0.0	6.0	2.2	D	4.8	D	D	13.0	1,490	268	46	3,058	0.2
Lyon	8.4	0.0	4.5	12.8	3.3	6.4	11.2	14.1	15.2	5,265	209	413	11,215	0.2
McLeod	2.2	D	5.7	33.5	2.6	6.4	4.8	14.3	10.8	8,240	224	380	15,913	0.5
Mahnomen	15.5	0.0	6.1	D	D	3.2	D	3.2	45.7	1,005	186	144	2,549	0.0
Marshall	28.7	D	7.6	10.0	2.8	3.6	D	D	14.9	2,265	252	80	4,421	0.1
Martin	13.3	0.0	4.4	9.8	3.4	6.4	6.4	12.8	12.3	5,655	284	387	9,751	0.0
Meeker	6.7	0.2	11.8	21.8	4.2	6.0	4.2	8.3	15.7	5,590	239	228	10,663	0.7
Mille Lacs	0.7	D	10.1	7.1	5.3	7.8	4.6	D	33.1	6,885	256	478	12,907	0.8
Morrison	10.6	0.1	7.5	8.2	5.8	7.8	3.6	D	22.2	8,355	246	619	16,190	0.6
Mower	5.3	D	4.5	19.6	D	4.6	2.9	13.4	15.1	8,945	223	747	16,945	0.0
Murray	33.9	0.7	6.2	9.5	2.3	5.4	D	D	12.8	2,275	279	83	4,407	0.4
Nicollet	4.3	0.1	3.7	21.9	D	4.3	4.4	D	23.1	6,295	183	335	13,458	0.6
Nobles	15.4	0.1	3.7	29.4	2.6	5.6	5.4	8.8	11.1	4,010	182	289	8,395	0.0
Norman	35.7	0.1	3.6	1.4	6.2	3.9	D	10.5	14.6	1,735	270	111	3,231	0.1
Olmsted	0.7	0.0	4.9	8.7	3.6	4.7	2.9	54.6	8.2	28,810	176	2,237	70,096	0.9
Otter Tail	6.1	0.1	9.2	17.8	5.1	6.5	3.9	13.6	16.2	17,090	285	710	36,641	0.3
Pennington	3.6	0.0	2.1	9.0	D	4.5	2.1	D	11.9	3,030	220	162	6,738	1.4
Pine	2.5	D	11.4	3.9	D	7.6	3.8	9.6	36.2	7,695	263	544	17,030	0.7
Pipestone	24.1	D	8.1	7.4	9.2	4.7	1.1	D	15.7	2,040	219	142	4,342	0.1
Polk	15.8	0.2	7.2	12.3	3.8	5.1	3.8	14.9	18.4	6,980	227	511	14,681	0.4
Pope	11.0	D	5.6	17.8	3.0	6.3	5.6	D	18.1	2,950	259	130	6,405	0.5
Ramsey	0.0	0.0	4.6	10.6	9.6	3.8	9.0	14.4	17.7	90,885	167	16,344	231,676	1.1
Red Lake	27.0	0.1	D	D	D	4.7	D	D	17.1	985	250	36	1,875	-0.1
Redwood	15.4	D	3.7	22.8	5.0	3.8	6.1	D	11.1	3,590	234	196	7,095	0.1
Renville	24.2	D	4.2	15.4	3.7	2.7	D	7.9	15.3	3,600	246	221	6,913	0.0
Rice	2.3	0.2	7.2	24.4	D	5.9	4.2	9.2	14.4	12,640	188	740	25,139	0.3
Rock	32.2	D	4.8	6.1	3.6	3.7	10.0	10.3	12.9	2,295	237	95	4,232	0.2
Roseau	7.2	0.0	1.4	53.5	1.3	3.6	2.4	9.3	11.7	3,550	233	114	7,167	0.4
St. Louis	0.0	6.1	6.1	5.6	6.9	7.4	5.0	26.3	17.2	49,775	250	4,761	103,972	0.2
Scott	0.4	0.1	15.5	17.2	7.4	5.6	3.8	7.6	14.3	19,830	129	1,290	55,581	1.0
Sherburne	0.8	D	13.8	15.8	3.7	8.7	3.8	10.5	16.5	15,185	153	782	36,583	1.5
Sibley	17.6	-0.4	8.6	18.6	D	2.5	2.4	6.2	14.6	3,310	222	153	6,498	0.5
Stearns	2.6	0.2	8.9	12.1	5.8	7.6	6.8	18.5	14.7	29,710	187	2,439	66,178	0.6
Steele	3.2	D	4.0	27.3	D	8.5	3.3	10.4	11.1	8,070	216	505	15,848	0.9
Stevens	19.5	D	6.1	16.6	5.7	4.7	3.5	11.1	18.6	1,780	184	110	4,211	-0.1
Swift	17.8	D	5.4	18.3	4.3	4.2	3.5	D	15.9	2,280	234	143	4,692	0.0
Todd	8.3	D	4.9	30.5	D	3.7	3.8	15.5	16.0	6,170	244	390	12,918	1.0
Traverse	48.6	0.0	2.1	1.8	D	4.1	2.4	9.1	12.2	1,005	306	68	1,879	0.1
Wabasha	12.7	D	6.4	19.9	2.7	4.9	5.0	D	14.3	5,295	246	183	10,234	0.6
Wadena	4.0	0.0	7.0	9.1	3.2	6.3	3.3	20.3	23.8	4,010	283	388	6,991	0.6
Waseca	9.9	D	7.0	18.6	D	4.9	5.5	D	22.6	4,370	230	229	7,913	0.2
Washington	0.3	D	7.1	14.3	8.6	8.5	8.8	12.9	12.3	46,995	173	2,319	107,007	2.5
Watonwan	14.2	D	7.6	23.9	2.3	3.1	5.0	9.2	14.0	2,340	210	109	4,882	0.2
Wilkin	21.5	D	3.7	1.5	D	2.3	D	10.8	11.8	1,485	232	82	2,978	0.1
Winona	4.4	D	4.1	26.0	D	5.8	4.3	9.3	15.2	10,380	209	598	21,780	0.2
Wright	0.9	D	15.1	15.2	4.0	8.4	4.6	10.3	13.4	22,300	154	850	56,061	2.4
Yellow Medicine	17.9	D	6.3	10.8	7.5	3.9	5.3	D	18.1	2,525	268	144	4,515	0.0

1. Per 1,000 resident population estimated as of July 1 of the year shown.

STATE County	Housing units, 2016–2020: Occupied units: Total	Owner-occupied: Percent	Owner-occupied: Median value[1]	Median owner cost as a percent of income: With a mortgage	Median owner cost as a percent of income: Without a mortgage[2]	Renter-occupied: Median rent[3]	Renter-occupied: Median rent as a percent of income[2]	Sub-standard units[4] (percent)	Civilian labor force, 2021: Total	Percent change, 2020–2021	Unemployment: Total	Unemployment: Rate[5]	Civilian employment[6], 2016–2020: Total	Percent: Management, business, science, and arts	Percent: Construction, production, and maintenance occupations
	89	90	91	92	93	94	95	96	97	98	99	100	101	102	103
MINNESOTA— Cont'd															
Fillmore	8,652	81.3	159,500	19.0	10.6	677	24.4	3.1	11,282	-4.0	333	3.0	10,811	35.4	29.4
Freeborn	13,005	77.2	121,600	18.7	11.2	723	28.1	1.4	15,344	-5.9	533	3.5	14,872	28.6	35.2
Goodhue	19,623	75.0	212,800	19.8	11.4	825	27.6	1.4	26,010	-3.3	834	3.2	24,312	35.1	27.6
Grant	2,578	79.2	129,400	18.9	11.3	697	27.1	1.0	3,210	-4.6	118	3.7	2,861	33.3	29.8
Hennepin	513,892	62.5	292,100	19.3	10.8	1,176	27.9	3.0	693,393	-3.1	23,706	3.4	696,368	51.8	13.9
Houston	8,286	81.5	177,000	20.5	11.8	770	24.8	1.7	10,158	-2.5	290	2.9	10,118	35.5	30.7
Hubbard	8,792	82.2	208,200	22.3	11.8	690	27.5	3.3	9,978	-0.9	407	4.1	9,716	31.7	30.0
Isanti	15,169	84.5	214,400	20.7	11.2	1,039	28.6	1.7	21,344	-2.9	868	4.1	20,563	33.0	31.4
Itasca	19,529	82.4	163,600	19.9	11.8	738	32.6	2.9	21,147	-5.1	993	4.7	19,729	32.9	27.1
Jackson	4,480	82.5	122,300	17.6	10.0	715	22.5	1.3	5,402	-7.4	170	3.1	5,226	33.3	35.6
Kanabec	6,631	83.3	168,900	21.6	13.4	760	24.6	3.0	8,885	-3.2	470	5.3	7,727	29.4	32.8
Kandiyohi	16,853	73.8	178,000	19.4	11.2	739	27.4	2.2	22,957	-7.4	815	3.6	22,201	34.8	28.3
Kittson	1,834	79.3	96,300	17.6	10.3	647	22.6	0.5	2,223	-7.6	64	2.9	2,170	34.7	30.5
Koochiching	5,796	78.8	115,500	17.8	10.0	686	31.4	1.6	5,582	-4.6	246	4.4	5,935	29.7	32.6
Lac qui Parle	3,048	82.5	97,500	18.0	10.0	544	19.1	1.0	3,303	-6.6	94	2.8	3,288	40.2	28.3
Lake	5,174	84.3	174,300	20.7	10.8	680	25.4	2.3	5,249	-2.1	189	3.6	4,827	38.6	26.8
Lake of the Woods	1,522	85.9	179,500	20.1	13.1	675	26.1	0.8	2,362	-3.6	87	3.7	1,945	18.8	48.9
Le Sueur	11,191	80.5	226,400	20.5	10.6	784	27.3	1.4	15,633	-3.6	638	4.1	15,286	32.9	33.2
Lincoln	2,459	78.7	107,800	18.1	11.2	640	26.6	1.1	2,957	-6.2	99	3.3	2,731	36.7	26.5
Lyon	10,067	68.6	152,700	18.2	10.6	687	28.4	2.3	13,966	-4.8	383	2.7	13,147	35.9	25.8
McLeod	14,736	76.3	171,200	20.9	12.2	724	24.0	1.3	18,763	-3.4	645	3.4	18,956	28.6	36.5
Mahnomen	1,956	68.8	111,400	20.5	13.1	633	24.5	4.2	2,141	-3.6	127	5.9	2,081	32.3	25.8
Marshall	3,952	83.3	121,000	18.3	10.0	625	26.2	1.6	5,173	-5.8	215	4.2	4,703	37.2	31.2
Martin	8,824	73.5	126,400	17.9	10.0	636	26.6	1.3	9,468	-6.2	304	3.2	9,721	33.7	27.8
Meeker	9,219	80.8	175,600	19.9	11.6	737	24.9	2.0	12,907	-3.5	437	3.4	11,555	30.6	36.2
Mille Lacs	10,535	75.8	170,500	23.0	12.7	763	28.4	2.4	12,462	-3.9	642	5.2	12,491	28.0	34.2
Morrison	13,536	79.1	178,100	20.9	11.7	743	24.5	1.8	17,149	-5.0	761	4.4	16,512	28.4	33.2
Mower	15,750	72.3	130,800	19.0	10.8	785	27.8	3.7	20,169	-3.8	631	3.1	19,257	28.8	36.2
Murray	3,659	80.8	132,500	17.4	10.0	577	19.8	0.7	4,599	-5.8	175	3.8	4,087	35.3	32.0
Nicollet	12,821	73.5	205,000	19.6	10.5	866	26.7	0.8	20,123	-3.9	556	2.8	19,472	37.0	24.1
Nobles	7,898	72.3	130,400	19.6	11.0	755	21.6	3.5	11,076	-5.0	316	2.9	10,538	26.9	40.2
Norman	2,771	80.5	107,600	17.5	11.0	642	27.5	3.4	3,154	-5.3	124	3.9	3,080	35.6	30.5
Olmsted	63,561	72.2	233,100	18.8	10.0	1,028	28.7	3.0	89,697	-2.3	2,524	2.8	84,169	51.9	15.3
Otter Tail	24,693	79.7	203,800	20.5	11.2	676	26.7	1.9	30,602	-3.6	1,036	3.4	28,521	34.0	28.9
Pennington	5,976	74.5	163,400	19.1	11.1	744	23.7	1.4	8,527	-2.3	316	3.7	7,442	28.8	31.2
Pine	11,132	81.8	170,700	22.4	12.8	770	31.0	2.7	13,970	-4.9	693	5.0	12,865	28.8	32.3
Pipestone	4,002	77.2	101,300	18.2	10.0	589	21.9	1.3	4,444	-5.7	127	2.9	4,353	32.9	32.9
Polk	12,619	71.5	169,100	19.1	11.0	691	28.2	2.3	15,699	-4.2	599	3.8	15,324	35.1	27.4
Pope	5,010	80.2	185,800	20.3	11.5	672	27.4	1.1	6,285	-4.5	176	2.8	5,737	37.9	27.6
Ramsey	210,424	60.0	239,000	19.8	10.9	1,060	29.4	4.6	281,343	-3.1	10,653	3.8	282,495	45.0	17.8
Red Lake	1,713	82.2	123,000	18.6	11.6	569	29.8	2.6	2,150	-4.2	85	4.0	1,950	31.1	32.6
Redwood	6,262	77.7	114,800	19.0	10.0	651	24.3	1.2	7,379	-5.5	251	3.4	7,465	33.4	30.6
Renville	6,032	77.3	112,400	18.4	10.0	652	29.7	0.9	8,153	-4.5	315	3.9	6,997	30.2	33.1
Rice	23,183	74.4	232,800	20.8	10.0	882	29.0	2.2	36,354	-3.1	1,164	3.2	33,126	35.8	26.7
Rock	3,990	74.7	160,700	18.2	10.0	691	20.4	2.1	5,801	-1.1	110	1.9	4,900	39.5	24.9
Roseau	5,940	79.2	140,800	19.5	11.1	647	24.0	2.6	7,748	-2.8	227	2.9	8,019	28.8	42.5
St. Louis	86,229	71.2	161,100	19.1	10.9	794	30.3	2.3	97,613	-4.0	3,733	3.8	97,840	37.3	22.6
Scott	50,487	83.6	317,500	20.0	10.0	1,216	28.8	2.9	82,810	-2.8	2,497	3.0	81,975	43.0	20.7
Sherburne	32,791	82.9	244,700	19.6	10.0	982	26.2	1.7	52,101	-2.7	1,807	3.5	52,213	34.9	31.2
Sibley	6,015	78.7	166,100	20.3	11.2	736	22.3	1.6	7,965	-4.6	288	3.6	7,934	29.9	39.7
Stearns	59,576	69.1	193,500	19.3	10.5	861	27.4	3.1	88,222	-3.8	3,162	3.6	85,498	35.9	26.6
Steele	14,836	76.8	173,400	18.4	10.8	802	31.3	2.4	19,944	-3.5	650	3.3	18,725	35.0	31.4
Stevens	3,683	69.3	161,000	17.1	10.0	724	27.7	2.7	5,182	-5.2	122	2.4	5,329	35.8	27.4
Swift	4,243	71.1	113,000	17.0	10.2	684	25.1	1.5	4,640	-5.4	170	3.7	4,634	36.2	28.1
Todd	9,888	84.1	151,800	20.7	12.0	691	24.8	6.1	13,158	-5.2	486	3.7	10,928	28.2	37.7
Traverse	1,590	77.9	85,700	18.8	10.0	564	25.8	2.0	1,632	-7.5	50	3.1	1,666	35.5	25.9
Wabasha	9,081	79.3	189,300	20.8	10.8	676	25.8	1.1	12,017	-3.9	361	3.0	11,316	37.5	26.4
Wadena	5,748	73.5	135,000	21.1	12.6	657	25.8	5.3	5,854	-3.3	261	4.5	6,016	26.7	37.1
Waseca	7,547	79.3	162,000	19.6	12.1	712	32.4	2.3	8,665	-5.7	342	3.9	9,460	33.0	30.3
Washington	95,796	81.6	301,000	19.5	10.0	1,329	29.8	1.5	141,988	-2.7	4,138	2.9	136,572	48.0	17.1
Watonwan	4,371	77.0	98,600	18.7	12.0	634	27.1	2.3	6,396	-4.5	192	3.0	5,309	31.9	38.3
Wilkin	2,799	80.7	138,300	19.9	10.5	539	31.5	1.0	3,323	-4.6	93	2.8	3,153	38.3	30.9
Winona	19,466	72.0	173,200	19.4	10.4	694	27.0	1.7	27,272	-4.0	778	2.9	28,638	34.4	25.3
Wright	49,097	82.9	250,800	19.8	11.0	988	27.1	1.5	75,116	-2.6	2,319	3.1	73,363	38.7	27.2
Yellow Medicine	4,088	81.2	117,900	18.7	10.6	602	23.3	2.5	4,961	-7.0	148	3.0	4,875	31.7	30.8

1. Specified owner-occupied units. 2. A value of 10.0 represents 10 percent or less; a value of 50.0 represents 50 percent or more. 3. Specified renter-occupied units. 4. Overcrowded or lacking complete plumbing facilities. 5. Percent of civilian labor force. 6. Civilian employed persons 16 years old and over.

STATE County	Private nonfarm establishments, employment and payroll, 2020: Number of establishments	Employment: Total	Employment: Health care and social assistance	Employment: Manufacturing	Employment: Retail trade	Employment: Finance and insurance	Employment: Professional, scientific, and technical services	Annual payroll: Total (mil dol)	Annual payroll: Average per employee (dollars)	Agriculture, 2017: Farms: Number	Farms: Percent with: Fewer than 50 acres	Farms: Percent with: 1000 acres or more	Farm producers whose primary occupation is farming (percent)
	104	105	106	107	108	109	110	111	112	113	114	115	116
MINNESOTA— Cont'd													
Fillmore	572	4,588	875	866	715	229	151	172	37,400	1,401	31.7	5.1	42.6
Freeborn	766	11,132	2,111	2,743	1,744	353	230	448	40,218	1,076	35.4	11.8	51.8
Goodhue	1,260	20,211	3,198	4,715	2,441	1,000	319	920	45,497	1,461	36.6	4.4	45.2
Grant	195	1,463	415	103	240	70	25	55	37,756	524	20.6	16.6	42.4
Hennepin	40,395	916,178	148,087	75,214	77,322	89,632	80,599	63,765	69,599	467	68.7	1.7	45.1
Houston	409	4,426	1,112	403	537	100	106	155	34,984	891	21.4	2.2	41.5
Hubbard	575	4,491	813	863	972	146	107	177	39,424	384	21.9	2.1	34.6
Isanti	913	9,459	2,278	1,246	2,059	232	239	366	38,684	805	46.0	3.4	34.7
Itasca	1,134	13,088	3,523	886	2,114	386	376	525	40,101	337	27.0	2.4	36.1
Jackson	301	3,948	422	1,256	329	74	80	173	43,900	799	25.4	13.0	55.1
Kanabec	302	3,141	1,200	422	507	92	60	138	43,814	624	33.2	1.6	41.2
Kandiyohi	1,383	18,862	5,300	2,512	2,898	509	612	767	40,664	1,220	32.3	9.3	39.9
Kittson	144	1,163	319	146	240	56	21	44	37,640	528	8.3	28.6	47.2
Koochiching	368	3,592	735	629	641	128	63	144	40,152	181	9.9	6.1	36.7
Lac qui Parle	194	1,685	583	192	204	85	11	61	36,491	853	20.2	14.8	44.9
Lake	305	3,214	635	662	408	104	46	124	38,568	42	54.8	NA	32.9
Lake of the Woods	154	1,413	154	232	148	23	13	56	39,693	134	14.2	14.2	35.2
Le Sueur	702	7,281	816	3,126	692	219	174	341	46,844	937	39.7	6.7	35.4
Lincoln	189	1,299	494	26	226	52	26	46	35,673	672	20.5	13.2	48.9
Lyon	818	12,460	2,419	1,982	1,905	1,159	386	552	44,270	893	19.9	12.1	50.6
McLeod	933	15,055	2,855	5,098	2,074	410	367	700	46,473	880	38.4	7.8	46.1
Mahnomen	101	1,658	328	NA	125	51	16	55	32,872	311	19.0	19.9	46.4
Marshall	255	1,619	225	364	253	124	34	72	44,548	1,086	7.2	22.4	42.9
Martin	615	7,445	1,555	1,342	1,273	379	158	347	46,627	911	23.6	16.4	56.7
Meeker	585	6,450	1,237	1,921	907	192	102	269	41,770	1,028	35.1	7.4	44.2
Mille Lacs	710	8,871	2,605	763	1,110	233	331	308	34,689	707	40.0	2.7	36.3
Morrison	890	8,131	1,841	1,028	1,645	251	174	306	37,681	1,760	25.0	2.4	46.7
Mower	816	14,292	2,890	3,534	1,789	251	220	674	47,162	1,068	34.9	12.5	47.7
Murray	268	2,471	390	585	356	174	48	92	37,314	864	24.1	14.0	53.2
Nicollet	684	14,364	2,820	4,150	1,231	196	446	678	47,181	689	22.5	7.7	51.9
Nobles	580	9,794	1,561	3,722	1,410	253	150	394	40,263	885	27.0	15.0	55.6
Norman	182	1,296	424	NA	257	86	25	57	43,735	505	13.5	35.8	55.1
Olmsted	3,628	102,619	21,426	4,501	10,956	1,577	37,768	6,109	59,531	1,139	43.2	6.2	43.2
Otter Tail	1,708	18,563	4,032	4,053	2,552	532	417	776	41,810	2,544	19.4	7.2	41.7
Pennington	365	8,804	1,156	1,041	1,026	164	84	402	45,643	409	15.4	20.8	44.6
Pine	596	7,053	1,198	381	1,116	161	273	209	29,666	823	26.6	1.8	43.7
Pipestone	315	2,951	671	441	464	106	86	119	40,231	595	32.9	8.9	49.9
Polk	737	8,991	2,283	1,681	1,390	243	197	376	41,770	1,258	14.2	25.4	56.8
Pope	382	4,146	690	915	473	126	251	180	43,468	837	25.9	12.1	42.7
Ramsey	13,417	302,612	64,392	24,463	25,822	18,986	14,624	18,299	60,470	55	96.4	NA	59.8
Red Lake	93	634	134	NA	119	47	19	22	34,043	263	11.0	19.8	48.1
Redwood	528	5,791	962	974	661	371	80	229	39,511	1,134	23.2	12.0	55.1
Renville	452	3,966	838	798	437	163	174	193	48,676	1,026	24.2	19.3	54.6
Rice	1,532	25,531	3,447	4,677	2,643	401	489	1,046	40,985	1,242	42.1	3.0	37.7
Rock	285	2,718	876	264	300	255	75	106	38,867	701	26.5	9.3	53.0
Roseau	406	6,420	777	3,204	736	174	72	273	42,531	842	14.4	16.2	39.0
St. Louis	5,309	87,923	24,392	5,145	12,192	3,087	3,503	3,979	45,258	779	27.3	1.8	36.1
Scott	3,467	52,565	5,933	8,050	6,540	639	1,773	2,573	48,941	740	50.0	2.7	32.4
Sherburne	2,165	22,727	3,254	4,200	3,424	423	710	1,018	44,805	501	47.7	5.8	40.7
Sibley	352	3,271	542	1,122	310	92	53	126	38,548	898	30.7	10.9	49.2
Stearns	4,396	84,447	17,020	11,623	11,593	4,315	2,258	4,066	48,152	2,951	24.4	2.3	49.8
Steele	1,010	19,701	2,545	5,642	2,628	2,314	303	982	49,835	746	39.9	9.9	47.4
Stevens	302	4,241	1,201	1,018	536	120	90	185	43,543	553	27.3	19.7	52.9
Swift	300	2,973	605	694	361	94	81	111	37,404	760	25.0	13.8	49.4
Todd	546	6,011	1,584	1,875	710	241	81	249	41,415	1,604	22.1	2.1	42.0
Traverse	117	712	230	33	187	45	5	31	43,170	411	22.4	30.9	59.1
Wabasha	553	5,306	977	1,185	816	153	121	202	38,020	809	22.9	4.8	50.5
Wadena	383	3,860	932	312	699	146	74	152	39,339	516	19.8	4.1	37.3
Waseca	448	4,161	838	949	548	174	193	191	45,802	729	33.2	9.1	48.8
Washington	6,075	83,874	13,529	10,655	14,711	3,813	4,520	3,784	45,120	612	64.4	3.4	44.4
Watonwan	293	3,693	522	1,317	344	172	58	139	37,657	497	27.8	15.1	52.0
Wilkin	146	1,621	351	43	174	66	477	66	40,555	391	16.9	37.9	64.5
Winona	1,141	23,508	3,319	5,448	2,716	571	337	940	40,003	1,034	25.0	4.5	49.5
Wright	3,426	40,208	5,670	6,602	7,936	730	1,202	1,822	45,319	1,338	45.1	3.3	37.2
Yellow Medicine	322	4,179	1,163	216	504	115	831	209	50,099	852	23.8	13.6	47.1

STATE County	Agriculture, 2017 (cont.)															
	Land in farms					Value of land and buildings (dollars)		Value of machinery and equipment, average per farm (dollars)	Value of products sold:				Organic farms (number)	Farms with internet access (per-cent)	Government payments	
			Acres								Percent from:					
	Acreage (1,000)	Percent change, 2012–2017	Average size of farm	Total irrigated (1,000)	Total cropland (1,000)	Average per farm	Average per acre		Total (mil dol)	Average per farm (acres)	Crops	Livestock and poultry products			Total ($1,000)	Percent of farms
	117	118	119	120	121	122	123	124	125	126	127	128	129	130	131	132
MINNESOTA— Cont'd																
Fillmore	376	-11.1	268	0.7	287.6	1,488,701	5,554	185,396	291.7	208,242	48.4	51.6	44	73.7	8,723	67.1
Freeborn	394	3.1	366	1.7	374.9	2,208,230	6,030	250,401	364.0	338,289	60.7	39.3	12	84.3	11,605	74.9
Goodhue	385	-3.4	263	6.0	325.8	1,633,399	6,204	219,974	348.6	238,596	49.9	50.1	41	83.4	11,779	59.3
Grant	324	7.0	619	5.9	303.0	2,724,030	4,403	298,988	190.3	363,141	75.6	24.4	NA	74.8	7,264	90.6
Hennepin	46	-33.4	98	0.3	36.6	1,322,909	13,464	133,330	58.6	125,418	88.7	11.3	4	77.5	193	27.0
Houston	217	-5.3	244	0.2	125.8	1,044,963	4,290	130,913	116.2	130,386	38.7	61.3	22	78.0	3,372	68.5
Hubbard	95	-19.1	246	24.5	53.4	651,843	2,646	107,044	44.2	115,221	88.6	11.4	2	82.8	495	18.5
Isanti	132	-7.0	164	4.0	96.3	639,469	3,887	100,672	48.7	60,463	74.2	25.8	10	81.7	635	12.5
Itasca	72	-14.7	213	D	36.6	604,662	2,842	67,203	8.0	23,751	64.7	35.3	NA	77.7	D	5.9
Jackson	356	-0.4	446	D	335.5	2,870,744	6,438	308,732	314.5	393,630	58.2	41.8	1	88.2	9,173	78.2
Kanabec	119	-7.8	190	2.2	66.2	504,920	2,652	89,170	29.8	47,808	60.2	39.8	7	69.2	109	19.7
Kandiyohi	456	9.8	374	26.6	402.8	1,949,625	5,218	260,271	424.1	347,605	47.0	53.0	7	76.4	10,884	81.2
Kittson	479	1.9	908	2.4	408.6	2,041,371	2,249	319,681	128.3	243,081	95.6	4.4	NA	76.3	12,450	91.5
Koochiching	56	4.5	308	D	28.2	444,918	1,443	85,478	6.9	38,050	64.6	35.4	NA	72.4	320	14.4
Lac qui Parle	420	-6.0	492	5.1	375.2	2,204,166	4,478	275,311	249.9	292,939	68.3	31.7	11	81.2	6,064	88.2
Lake	4	-4.6	85	0.0	1.4	308,042	3,629	49,065	0.4	8,524	83.0	17.0	2	92.9	41	7.1
Lake of the Woods	91	1.1	681	1.2	67.8	1,156,249	1,697	172,314	17.3	128,940	95.9	4.1	NA	67.2	772	46.3
Le Sueur	249	3.1	266	1.8	224.2	1,643,885	6,175	180,636	181.4	193,551	64.0	36.0	8	75.5	4,652	72.8
Lincoln	298	2.4	443	D	269.8	2,143,527	4,836	261,768	186.0	276,847	60.5	39.5	3	75.3	7,124	80.4
Lyon	395	-4.3	442	0.4	366.3	2,589,529	5,852	300,380	412.3	461,736	44.3	55.7	3	84.3	5,565	63.0
McLeod	269	1.8	305	0.1	248.9	1,747,482	5,724	226,601	185.6	210,928	69.3	30.7	9	78.5	4,093	66.4
Mahnomen	221	2.5	711	D	186.3	2,102,461	2,955	251,243	70.1	225,392	94.4	5.6	2	76.8	2,742	69.8
Marshall	902	10.0	831	D	824.1	2,056,182	2,474	274,618	261.5	240,750	94.2	5.8	2	71.3	18,205	85.7
Martin	449	4.8	493	0.5	434.3	3,308,478	6,712	386,978	635.5	697,610	41.8	58.2	4	86.2	8,613	79.7
Meeker	301	-0.8	293	8.8	262.1	1,521,946	5,190	204,806	265.2	257,930	44.7	55.3	7	76.7	5,200	72.9
Mille Lacs	126	-1.5	178	0.5	86.9	552,471	3,102	103,477	43.9	62,139	52.9	47.1	6	77.2	190	24.0
Morrison	382	-12.4	217	30.3	232.8	719,062	3,310	156,473	394.7	224,273	17.3	82.7	10	75.7	2,301	39.8
Mower	447	-0.6	419	5.0	420.9	2,852,833	6,813	279,549	413.2	386,915	58.7	41.3	15	84.5	10,064	74.3
Murray	395	-3.1	457	D	362.6	2,819,738	6,166	316,318	337.8	391,005	54.5	45.5	10	82.1	5,522	65.5
Nicollet	265	-3.4	384	0.0	249.5	2,691,522	7,002	299,514	339.3	492,462	40.6	59.4	1	83.5	2,277	47.8
Nobles	414	8.9	468	0.1	392.3	3,236,081	6,911	399,982	519.0	586,400	39.6	60.4	1	82.4	8,236	81.5
Norman	526	-1.2	1,041	1.4	498.9	3,437,726	3,301	410,892	218.3	432,202	94.3	5.7	4	76.0	5,243	78.4
Olmsted	286	8.1	251	0.1	239.1	1,671,227	6,657	184,486	214.4	188,248	56.7	43.3	15	83.5	9,079	61.1
Otter Tail	794	-10.0	312	75.5	576.2	927,172	2,969	150,686	349.9	137,547	57.4	42.6	33	72.9	8,675	64.2
Pennington	286	5.2	699	D	249.2	1,347,472	1,928	231,758	66.5	162,484	91.6	8.4	NA	77.0	5,293	75.3
Pine	160	-21.3	195	0.4	81.7	460,529	2,364	73,400	39.0	47,361	38.6	61.4	2	75.8	174	18.1
Pipestone	240	-0.8	403	2.2	210.6	2,352,844	5,833	343,986	326.1	547,988	30.0	70.0	5	88.1	1,582	49.2
Polk	1,023	-6.6	813	5.6	938.5	2,667,646	3,280	391,409	429.8	341,630	93.8	6.2	18	76.1	17,113	77.8
Pope	333	-0.3	398	32.0	280.3	1,648,542	4,144	254,858	199.3	238,106	63.8	36.2	8	75.7	4,173	74.8
Ramsey	1	-10.8	12	0.1	0.4	312,488	26,646	45,670	3.0	53,655	74.7	25.3	8	94.5	D	1.8
Red Lake	209	5.1	794	1.1	189.3	1,881,249	2,370	305,925	65.6	249,426	89.0	11.0	NA	80.6	2,688	81.0
Redwood	524	0.5	462	0.0	494.9	2,882,387	6,239	315,623	453.2	399,613	58.2	41.8	4	80.2	6,220	66.6
Renville	624	0.4	608	1.2	598.2	3,990,664	6,560	376,170	609.2	593,752	61.1	38.9	1	80.9	5,570	84.6
Rice	226	-4.3	182	2.8	192.6	1,249,054	6,857	145,442	205.0	165,042	49.6	50.4	13	76.9	6,228	62.0
Rock	288	2.6	411	D	266.4	3,133,759	7,631	322,110	419.1	597,825	34.2	65.8	1	89.7	2,105	73.9
Roseau	558	0.4	663	0.0	463.1	1,155,325	1,743	183,983	129.5	153,853	84.3	15.7	3	78.3	10,057	71.9
St. Louis	139	9.0	178	D	67.1	354,725	1,992	61,899	16.1	20,718	57.1	42.9	8	77.3	48	3.3
Scott	116	-18.2	156	0.0	98.0	1,184,671	7,590	120,351	75.6	102,122	58.9	41.1	15	80.4	900	38.9
Sherburne	103	-8.7	205	36.4	78.5	1,055,081	5,155	187,885	89.6	178,838	83.9	16.1	4	84.2	1,068	25.0
Sibley	350	1.1	390	0.5	326.6	2,629,735	6,746	283,199	318.7	354,924	57.2	42.8	8	82.4	4,299	62.0
Stearns	651	-14.1	221	51.8	515.9	1,135,611	5,149	185,876	748.0	253,466	23.9	76.1	57	78.0	5,926	56.4
Steele	251	5.6	337	2.0	233.5	2,088,084	6,201	251,529	251.8	337,586	60.7	39.3	11	79.5	5,216	71.0
Stevens	330	3.4	597	21.3	308.0	3,032,762	5,077	289,508	327.4	592,118	42.6	57.4	4	85.7	3,945	75.9
Swift	345	-4.4	454	26.8	316.4	2,289,023	5,043	305,866	284.2	373,895	53.0	47.0	NA	81.2	4,405	84.3
Todd	333	-15.4	208	12.9	210.5	570,580	2,745	111,342	179.5	111,884	31.6	68.4	23	70.4	1,987	45.0
Traverse	365	4.6	887	0.8	350.9	4,415,585	4,979	484,191	210.5	512,088	78.3	21.7	NA	76.6	4,735	83.5
Wabasha	231	-6.1	285	1.7	175.8	1,574,440	5,519	244,686	186.3	230,295	43.0	57.0	11	83.3	6,359	70.1
Wadena	128	-13.9	249	15.7	75.3	546,823	2,200	88,995	52.8	102,411	56.5	43.5	15	71.1	865	41.3
Waseca	247	6.6	339	D	231.0	2,243,731	6,621	279,994	275.0	377,284	48.2	51.8	9	77.9	5,793	80.9
Washington	76	-5.9	124	4.1	57.8	1,081,821	8,695	111,931	59.8	97,676	90.7	9.3	10	83.0	1,036	25.0
Watonwan	252	6.5	508	6.8	241.1	3,604,518	7,097	382,501	269.5	542,310	54.2	45.8	NA	82.3	9,171	87.3
Wilkin	428	-3.6	1,095	1.2	414.6	4,239,436	3,872	442,751	185.6	474,673	99.5	0.5	3	79.0	4,555	85.9
Winona	269	-3.1	260	0.0	180.8	1,494,722	5,753	181,789	228.2	220,662	30.6	69.4	58	78.9	3,952	60.3
Wright	241	-16.5	180	6.8	203.7	1,158,403	6,441	150,834	196.5	146,867	57.5	42.5	20	79.8	1,301	38.1
Yellow Medicine	384	-2.9	450	0.5	355.3	2,435,244	5,408	275,914	256.4	300,971	66.4	33.6	5	81.3	5,699	74.2

STATE County	Water use, 2015		Wholesale Trade[1], 2017				Retail Trade[2], 2017				Real estate and rental and leasing,[2] 2017			
	Public supply water withdrawn (mil gal/ day)	Public supply gallons withdrawn per person per day	Number of establish- ments	Number of employees	Sales (mil dol)	Average payroll (mil dol)	Number of establish- ments	Number of employees	Sales (mil dol)	Average payroll (mil dol)	Number of establish- ments	Number of employees	Sales (mil dol)	Average payroll (mil dol)
	133	134	135	136	137	138	139	140	141	142	143	144	145	146
MINNESOTA— Cont'd														
Fillmore	1.3	61.4	26	235	304.5	13.0	90	767	201.1	18.4	7	13	2.2	0.4
Freeborn	3.5	114.0	45	597	440.2	35.3	136	1,974	524.8	51.9	18	42	6.7	0.9
Goodhue	3.1	66.5	D	D	D	D	202	2,504	850.5	73.7	37	160	36.8	5.8
Grant	0.3	52.5	9	112	253.2	7.4	31	253	79.5	6.1	NA	NA	NA	NA
Hennepin	73.4	60.0	1,959	38,420	45,908.8	2,826.3	4,115	76,351	31,368.3	2,299.6	2,575	18,875	5,522.3	1,132.4
Houston	0.9	45.8	14	154	90.7	6.5	55	579	111.5	12.1	6	14	1.7	0.4
Hubbard	0.7	32.4	D	D	D	D	101	998	236.9	25.2	D	D	D	1.4
Isanti	1.3	34.3	22	127	29.1	4.7	108	1,905	577.9	49.7	33	120	17.1	2.8
Itasca	2.0	44.5	D	D	D	D	194	2,140	614.7	57.4	27	93	13.2	2.6
Jackson	0.6	55.6	13	282	171.0	11.5	43	356	82.3	7.3	4	D	1.1	D
Kanabec	0.4	24.0	6	24	8.0	0.9	47	530	135.0	11.8	3	53	2.9	1.7
Kandiyohi	4.6	107.2	68	922	1,156.7	55.6	199	2,985	865.8	81.2	45	95	18.5	3.4
Kittson	0.6	126.6	13	97	126.7	5.5	28	260	61.6	5.5	NA	NA	NA	NA
Koochiching	0.7	55.3	10	70	23.9	2.1	75	722	159.2	17.1	10	30	4.6	1.3
Lac qui Parle	0.4	54.0	D	D	D	9.2	36	240	48.9	5.1	3	7	0.5	0.1
Lake	0.8	73.4	D	D	D	1.8	46	416	149.9	11.0	6	19	1.3	0.5
Lake of the Woods	0.2	43.3	4	30	9.2	0.9	23	158	31.7	3.0	4	5	1.0	0.1
Le Sueur	2.3	83.9	25	262	123.9	12.8	82	735	138.2	12.6	23	68	8.4	1.6
Lincoln	1.0	171.5	D	D	D	D	32	216	50.9	4.5	4	9	0.3	0.1
Lyon	2.7	105.2	40	565	763.6	30.6	127	1,889	449.3	45.4	24	105	8.1	4.3
McLeod	2.7	76.3	D	D	D	D	141	2,154	513.6	49.2	28	93	13.7	2.9
Mahnomen	0.3	49.5	D	D	D	2.0	18	156	55.2	4.0	NA	NA	NA	NA
Marshall	0.5	47.8	19	141	302.2	8.0	29	263	110.7	8.4	NA	NA	NA	NA
Martin	1.6	80.4	37	668	1,165.7	60.1	92	1,341	296.5	30.5	D	D	D	D
Meeker	1.3	54.1	21	162	148.9	7.8	82	989	278.6	24.3	16	35	3.3	1.2
Mille Lacs	0.4	16.7	25	279	157.7	11.6	101	1,096	281.3	26.0	D	D	D	1.2
Morrison	2.0	59.5	18	228	81.9	9.6	125	1,547	344.6	38.1	16	56	8.1	1.2
Mower	5.9	150.1	D	D	D	D	116	1,705	352.0	38.0	D	D	D	D
Murray	0.6	65.4	13	178	299.4	8.6	44	276	57.0	5.3	D	D	D	0.7
Nicollet	4.2	126.5	31	385	268.7	21.0	81	1,103	327.3	33.8	D	D	D	D
Nobles	2.2	98.8	D	D	D	D	107	1,482	339.7	34.2	12	43	4.5	0.6
Norman	0.3	43.4	16	121	277.5	6.6	26	234	73.0	6.1	D	D	D	0.2
Olmsted	12.9	84.9	102	1,122	716.8	62.9	576	11,341	2,866.8	297.1	189	800	160.6	28.1
Otter Tail	3.4	59.6	D	D	D	D	253	2,742	793.1	69.3	44	84	29.3	3.0
Pennington	1.1	75.3	D	D	D	D	69	1,097	248.3	25.3	13	33	4.5	1.0
Pine	0.9	29.2	23	102	19.8	2.8	93	1,223	290.8	29.8	D	D	D	D
Pipestone	1.8	195.2	15	184	296.6	9.1	56	543	134.6	11.8	3	D	0.4	D
Polk	8.6	271.8	43	444	985.3	22.6	105	1,500	324.0	35.1	13	44	5.0	1.3
Pope	0.6	49.8	55	636	390.0	31.8	50	430	175.3	11.0	8	7	1.1	0.2
Ramsey	52.6	97.7	565	11,902	8,696.1	805.3	1,557	27,016	7,098.9	719.8	767	4,295	1,760.2	222.6
Red Lake	0.6	157.8	6	D	23.3	D	20	123	41.6	3.3	NA	NA	NA	NA
Redwood	1.0	62.7	28	405	439.1	24.7	55	713	178.0	17.1	D	D	D	D
Renville	1.0	68.5	30	300	509.2	18.5	62	472	123.5	10.3	4	3	0.6	0.1
Rice	5.5	84.7	55	1,237	2,046.3	73.5	194	2,636	712.2	69.0	63	224	64.8	8.4
Rock	1.5	157.3	17	173	274.6	9.5	36	397	112.5	9.6	9	21	2.2	0.7
Roseau	0.7	45.0	13	91	89.6	4.8	79	813	165.9	16.9	D	D	D	D
St. Louis	35.3	176.0	195	2,234	1,227.2	118.9	852	12,942	3,311.3	318.9	225	907	194.6	30.4
Scott	7.8	55.3	170	2,850	2,826.6	196.7	310	4,831	1,593.9	147.4	183	438	108.5	17.6
Sherburne	5.0	54.0	68	603	438.6	29.8	210	3,592	933.6	89.6	89	204	47.1	7.4
Sibley	1.5	97.5	D	D	D	D	50	332	62.5	5.9	D	D	D	D
Stearns	14.6	94.2	194	4,012	2,548.2	211.9	676	11,699	3,305.4	302.1	189	971	194.5	36.6
Steele	4.0	109.9	38	539	459.1	29.9	166	2,658	579.5	60.6	27	304	19.0	5.5
Stevens	0.8	80.6	19	139	277.5	7.3	50	564	234.9	16.6	D	D	D	D
Swift	0.8	84.6	16	206	427.2	13.3	40	340	75.9	7.4	6	64	3.4	1.6
Todd	1.2	48.6	16	123	134.7	5.0	100	729	162.5	14.7	18	30	3.3	0.5
Traverse	0.2	58.8	D	D	D	D	28	183	41.5	4.2	NA	NA	NA	NA
Wabasha	1.9	87.1	25	218	117.5	10.1	76	762	195.8	19.8	9	22	2.9	0.5
Wadena	0.9	67.0	17	546	290.1	22.7	71	725	189.1	18.7	D	D	D	D
Waseca	1.7	87.9	22	150	110.3	8.0	53	655	169.1	16.7	10	22	3.1	0.5
Washington	19.2	76.4	177	2,535	3,854.6	153.0	710	14,164	3,538.0	344.3	346	1,510	327.0	71.5
Watonwan	1.3	117.8	11	128	142.4	5.9	37	394	65.3	7.6	6	18	1.0	0.4
Wilkin	0.3	45.3	D	D	D	D	26	170	47.0	4.6	7	16	2.2	0.9
Winona	3.8	73.9	49	508	668.9	25.5	153	2,629	676.9	67.1	34	101	18.7	2.5
Wright	8.1	61.6	98	1,625	1,277.0	94.1	445	7,518	1,937.1	182.5	132	232	62.5	9.1
Yellow Medicine	2.2	226.8	12	170	731.6	8.7	48	425	120.0	10.8	D	D	D	0.1

1 Merchant wholesalers, except manufacturers' sales branches and offices. 2. Employer establishments.

STATE County	Professional, scientific, and technical services, 2017				Manufacturing, 2017				Accommodation and food services, 2017			
	Number of establish-ments	Number of employees	Sales (mil dol)	Average payroll (mil dol)	Number of establish-ments	Number of employees	Sales (mil dol)	Average payroll (mil dol)	Number of establis-hments	Number of employees	Sales (mil dol)	Annual payroll (mil dol)
	147	148	149	150	151	152	153	154	155	156	157	158
MINNESOTA— Cont'd												
Fillmore	D	D	13.8	D	43	764	248.0	35.8	68	474	20.3	5.7
Freeborn	D	D	D	D	53	2,679	962.3	123.4	68	940	41.7	12.3
Goodhue	77	836	149.2	68.4	85	4,918	1,589.3	256.5	106	2,870	373.1	81.6
Grant	D	D	D	D	9	102	20.4	3.9	10	D	2.6	D
Hennepin	6,988	86,259	17,796.1	7,221.5	1,614	76,502	23,595.6	5,056.8	3,025	73,216	4,655.1	1,492.8
Houston	19	93	9.8	3.6	28	378	83.9	17.3	34	266	9.9	2.4
Hubbard	D	D	8.0	D	29	896	369.4	38.3	81	550	36.3	10.5
Isanti	D	D	D	D	68	1,350	350.0	72.1	D	D	D	15.6
Itasca	D	D	D	D	42	1,172	564.6	72.1	109	1,319	70.0	20.7
Jackson	16	66	7.0	4.6	13	1,306	447.0	63.0	24	239	9.5	2.5
Kanabec	17	64	6.4	2.0	19	474	112.4	22.6	24	263	11.7	3.5
Kandiyohi	D	D	D	D	74	2,645	1,034.4	124.2	90	1,366	72.5	21.3
Kittson	D	D	D	D	11	204	356.6	11.3	D	D	D	0.7
Koochiching	D	D	6.0	D	D	671	D	D	43	544	26.7	7.7
Lac qui Parle	D	D	D	D	10	151	338.3	7.2	10	110	3.9	1.2
Lake	D	D	D	D	14	507	227.4	32.9	63	783	53.7	14.8
Lake of the Woods	D	D	D	D	D	204	D	15.8	39	459	32.8	8.8
Le Sueur	D	D	22.8	D	53	3,227	992.3	174.8	D	D	D	5.4
Lincoln	D	D	D	D	7	29	6.6	1.5	13	D	3.7	D
Lyon	D	D	D	D	29	1,847	1,082.0	91.0	65	1,070	44.1	13.6
McLeod	D	D	D	D	75	5,369	2,309.4	343.2	62	1,046	48.2	14.7
Mahnomen	D	D	D	0.3	NA	NA	NA	NA	D	D	D	D
Marshall	D	D	7.4	D	16	300	82.8	15.4	D	D	D	1.1
Martin	38	185	32.2	9.5	36	1,099	1,389.0	52.1	47	760	32.7	10.0
Meeker	26	110	13.5	4.6	53	1,661	933.2	83.7	41	436	16.8	4.9
Mille Lacs	D	D	39.0	D	42	764	155.0	33.7	73	1,815	197.2	38.0
Morrison	34	157	17.8	7.1	58	1,049	420.7	51.1	93	970	45.0	13.2
Mower	D	D	D	D	31	3,802	1,441.1	163.4	68	951	48.5	14.4
Murray	D	D	D	D	D	D	D	D	20	171	8.4	2.2
Nicollet	40	452	52.9	20.8	48	3,425	864.7	159.0	47	748	31.8	9.9
Nobles	D	D	D	D	27	2,538	2,082.0	164.7	40	565	28.3	8.0
Norman	D	D	D	1.1	NA	NA	NA	NA	D	D	D	0.6
Olmsted	D	D	D	D	95	4,029	2,082.4	218.5	348	8,096	496.6	152.7
Otter Tail	98	414	50.4	19.5	84	4,166	1,726.8	183.3	156	1,670	95.1	27.9
Pennington	D	D	D	D	17	1,977	918.2	89.2	33	877	56.9	14.0
Pine	D	D	15.8	D	26	325	57.7	13.8	66	2,313	268.9	48.9
Pipestone	12	102	78.5	4.5	13	473	120.6	17.9	21	310	14.1	3.7
Polk	41	187	25.3	10.2	36	1,545	1,207.3	73.8	71	1,066	44.0	14.0
Pope	D	D	D	D	25	726	195.3	44.9	29	238	13.2	3.6
Ramsey	D	D	D	D	567	23,768	6,540.7	1,464.6	1,187	24,210	1,343.3	427.7
Red Lake	D	D	D	D	NA	NA	NA	NA	D	D	D	0.6
Redwood	D	D	D	D	33	1,039	341.3	43.4	39	1,090	90.1	21.7
Renville	D	D	D	D	25	1,008	521.3	53.3	28	233	9.3	2.4
Rice	128	669	76.1	31.0	77	3,591	1,629.3	202.9	129	2,150	100.6	31.6
Rock	D	D	13.1	D	15	338	118.9	13.8	20	298	10.1	2.9
Roseau	23	73	6.9	2.4	D	3,477	D	164.5	33	545	35.2	8.9
St. Louis	372	3,177	459.1	189.6	200	4,084	1,340.3	249.0	550	10,353	544.3	168.1
Scott	D	D	D	D	177	7,532	3,252.0	499.5	220	7,164	681.3	167.3
Sherburne	173	732	82.3	32.3	158	3,732	1,106.4	215.8	125	2,379	112.9	33.8
Sibley	D	D	D	D	23	882	913.0	38.4	21	138	7.9	1.7
Stearns	D	D	D	D	249	11,838	4,314.8	609.9	374	6,985	319.0	94.4
Steele	51	205	35.8	7.0	60	4,836	1,526.4	253.9	83	1,568	66.3	20.8
Stevens	12	114	12.3	5.7	15	804	325.7	50.8	23	434	15.8	4.3
Swift	16	80	9.8	3.2	20	601	754.8	35.7	D	D	D	D
Todd	D	D	7.4	D	44	1,670	1,001.1	82.0	41	337	16.4	4.3
Traverse	D	D	D	D	5	27	5.6	1.3	D	D	D	0.2
Wabasha	D	D	13.7	D	25	1,093	511.8	56.0	65	572	25.5	7.2
Wadena	21	102	13.6	5.0	18	255	44.8	10.9	33	365	16.1	4.7
Waseca	D	D	19.2	D	25	1,674	914.9	103.8	37	373	16.0	4.4
Washington	843	3,933	639.7	263.1	203	9,111	6,677.1	606.6	443	9,926	507.1	160.3
Watonwan	8	43	4.8	1.8	15	1,401	502.1	51.2	D	D	D	D
Wilkin	D	D	20.1	D	D	49	D	D	8	90	3.2	0.8
Winona	D	D	D	D	102	5,393	1,565.7	297.3	128	2,240	88.7	25.3
Wright	319	1,096	166.5	52.0	207	6,179	1,650.5	349.1	209	3,640	161.7	51.6
Yellow Medicine	D	D	8.1	D	20	218	128.7	10.1	21	475	48.5	11.4

STATE County	Health care and social assistance, 2017				Other services, 2017				Nonemployer businesses, 2019		Value of residential construction authorized by building permits, 2021	
	Number of establish-ments	Number of employees	Receipts (mil dol)	Annual payroll (mil dol)	Number of establish-ments	Number of employees	Receipts (mil dol)	Annual payroll (mil dol)	Number	Receipts (mil dol)	New construction ($1,000)	Number of housing units
	159	160	161	162	163	164	165	166	167	168	169	170
MINNESOTA— Cont'd												
Fillmore	D	D	D	24.4	49	142	16.5	3.4	1,680	85.7	18,095	91
Freeborn	72	2,190	202.7	104.0	65	316	23.2	5.9	1,833	85.7	10,507	74
Goodhue	152	3,462	334.1	141.8	102	498	53.8	13.5	3,101	155.3	37,527	170
Grant	17	368	32.0	11.8	16	49	2.5	0.7	528	22.7	300	1
Hennepin	4,470	143,909	17,502.6	7,313.5	2,834	25,569	3,790.7	976.0	110,209	5,926.4	1,927,450	7,905
Houston	46	1,416	67.0	37.5	40	107	15.2	2.9	1,385	73.0	7,046	35
Hubbard	49	836	101.2	41.0	36	150	17.3	3.5	1,737	71.0	7,231	29
Isanti	83	2,097	155.4	95.5	68	311	25.6	6.5	2,696	127.3	96,355	468
Itasca	167	3,477	307.0	134.3	79	420	66.4	13.0	2,932	122.3	28,702	116
Jackson	27	1,344	48.8	23.2	24	106	15.6	2.8	804	33.9	4,097	17
Kanabec	35	1,064	121.2	47.0	22	85	8.1	2.1	1,059	50.1	8,368	41
Kandiyohi	198	5,779	383.9	183.2	96	493	45.3	11.0	3,131	161.7	40,798	327
Kittson	10	349	21.4	11.0	D	D	3.7	D	334	13.1	212	1
Koochiching	50	721	63.0	26.1	20	72	4.8	1.3	843	29.0	3,880	23
Lac qui Parle	17	688	54.7	22.8	13	66	7.3	1.1	592	29.6	4,143	11
Lake	35	517	41.4	15.4	20	120	11.9	4.0	871	38.3	18,824	81
Lake of the Woods	D	D	D	D	D	D	6.4	D	379	13.8	17,234	80
Le Sueur	67	902	58.2	24.3	69	216	23.4	5.3	1,952	95.2	35,186	133
Lincoln	15	464	35.7	13.4	D	D	D	0.8	503	18.6	2,810	11
Lyon	95	2,057	177.6	77.8	59	234	23.2	5.7	1,773	91.1	14,159	81
McLeod	116	3,000	263.4	115.4	79	422	62.9	11.3	2,360	121.9	25,063	115
Mahnomen	9	399	16.7	9.1	D	D	4.7	D	334	13.7	0	0
Marshall	17	344	18.2	8.2	23	77	8.1	1.3	605	23.5	535	1
Martin	81	1,546	140.2	60.1	54	128	16.6	3.4	1,482	72.3	5,311	18
Meeker	59	1,519	110.9	46.0	45	174	13.1	2.8	1,633	76.2	14,403	88
Mille Lacs	77	2,646	233.7	92.8	49	230	19.3	4.1	1,682	72.3	46,776	216
Morrison	82	1,627	146.2	63.3	85	344	44.2	9.1	2,304	116.1	17,878	131
Mower	100	2,558	248.4	97.8	83	462	77.6	11.4	1,797	90.6	11,083	41
Murray	16	423	33.2	14.8	20	44	8.8	1.2	694	40.2	7,313	30
Nicollet	92	2,577	221.5	129.9	61	406	167.5	14.8	2,184	101.4	34,693	159
Nobles	62	1,288	87.4	41.8	52	307	31.6	8.4	1,195	66.1	2,674	9
Norman	16	406	32.5	14.0	D	D	D	0.7	470	19.9	7,243	18
Olmsted	479	21,541	2,776.3	947.8	269	2,055	196.6	57.9	10,470	498.1	218,952	874
Otter Tail	178	4,329	361.6	134.7	140	544	54.9	12.8	4,915	231.8	26,129	92
Pennington	43	1,193	172.7	51.3	39	238	16.2	4.1	819	31.3	14,446	147
Pine	75	1,329	83.1	38.3	42	217	20.6	4.7	1,723	75.2	45,373	248
Pipestone	24	703	45.4	20.9	22	65	6.8	1.2	721	36.3	1,500	5
Polk	93	2,370	222.6	94.5	41	246	19.6	4.6	2,154	91.3	15,258	59
Pope	25	676	54.0	25.7	29	83	10.4	2.1	1,027	44.1	11,860	65
Ramsey	2,077	64,912	7,010.9	2,999.2	1,147	10,406	1,731.1	400.3	39,984	1,725.5	506,734	3,270
Red Lake	D	D	D	D	D	D	D	0.3	221	11.7	0	0
Redwood	53	945	76.6	28.4	52	209	24.0	5.3	1,064	47.5	5,792	22
Renville	42	911	62.8	25.9	36	86	13.1	2.9	1,032	53.1	3,429	22
Rice	176	3,430	238.1	118.8	136	633	59.4	16.0	4,271	188.4	55,287	218
Rock	16	840	60.7	22.8	19	75	5.8	1.4	758	37.2	3,087	15
Roseau	33	785	71.5	30.3	35	127	15.2	2.8	1,107	43.6	5,819	28
St. Louis	805	25,628	2,868.0	1,231.6	382	2,431	251.1	67.2	11,991	482.4	76,519	385
Scott	266	5,664	566.2	226.3	235	1,855	134.2	49.3	11,606	607.8	299,123	1,039
Sherburne	178	3,802	233.2	104.9	151	764	90.2	21.5	6,783	306.7	119,552	535
Sibley	21	481	32.6	16.3	28	59	6.7	1.0	1,051	46.0	11,926	56
Stearns	477	17,582	2,185.9	923.7	375	2,214	249.5	68.7	11,125	590.2	141,040	532
Steele	134	2,639	251.6	110.5	87	528	69.3	15.1	2,366	107.7	24,525	140
Stevens	39	1,587	97.3	45.7	17	63	3.6	0.9	627	30.3	3,315	11
Swift	23	672	50.9	20.8	D	D	D	2.8	633	24.0	1,584	7
Todd	54	1,513	159.6	69.7	46	151	19.3	2.8	1,673	83.4	41,399	182
Traverse	12	299	28.1	10.2	D	D	D	0.4	278	11.6	3,334	21
Wabasha	D	D	D	34.8	40	156	13.6	3.5	1,559	79.0	17,767	75
Wadena	45	1,045	96.3	41.7	31	120	13.3	2.3	1,008	45.2	9,219	44
Waseca	56	998	64.9	26.7	34	111	15.6	2.7	1,135	57.2	9,140	36
Washington	685	10,930	1,319.5	550.7	456	2,995	254.8	81.7	19,551	949.8	745,260	2,617
Watonwan	27	567	52.3	20.5	27	137	17.0	2.9	609	26.8	695	3
Wilkin	22	465	49.1	20.1	9	24	4.1	0.8	500	45.3	4,718	15
Winona	133	3,084	232.7	105.5	76	359	46.3	9.6	2,920	132.4	19,913	103
Wright	301	5,727	488.7	223.9	252	1,302	151.3	35.4	10,045	453.3	441,567	1,558
Yellow Medicine	32	750	53.8	24.3	30	91	10.3	2.4	820	32.4	2,550	8

STATE County	Government employment and payroll, 2017: Full-time equivalent employees	March payroll (dollars)	March payroll (percent of total): Adminis-tration, judicial, and legal	Police and corrections	Fire protection	Highways and transpor-tation	Health and welfare	Natural resources and utilities	Education and libraries	Local government finances, 2017: General revenue: Total (mil dol)	Inter-govern-mental (mil dol)	Taxes: Total (mil dol)	Per capita[1] (dollars): Total	Property
	171	172	173	174	175	176	177	178	179	180	181	182	183	184
MINNESOTA— Cont'd														
Fillmore	728	3,091,737	12.3	10.2	1.1	8.5	11.1	6.9	49.2	90.0	46.2	27.9	1,331	1,235
Freeborn	1,078	4,540,042	9.0	11.3	2.5	6.0	12.5	7.8	49.9	149.1	78.1	46.9	1,534	1,326
Goodhue	1,835	8,024,257	9.3	11.4	2.1	4.1	8.2	5.3	57.4	249.5	110.4	87.5	1,889	1,870
Grant	314	1,187,787	14.0	6.1	0.0	8.9	8.7	4.9	57.1	33.9	19.1	9.5	1,598	1,512
Hennepin	43,507	233,875,110	8.5	12.1	2.2	3.1	10.5	6.3	54.9	7,525.3	2,620.1	2,562.6	2,054	1,799
Houston	825	3,164,378	10.2	8.8	0.2	4.1	7.5	3.3	64.0	95.9	56.5	26.7	1,427	1,395
Hubbard	683	2,507,742	11.1	11.3	0.2	5.6	8.9	3.5	57.4	86.4	40.4	30.3	1,445	1,418
Isanti	1,483	6,198,777	6.0	9.7	0.4	3.9	8.0	1.9	67.5	152.5	87.2	43.2	1,093	1,066
Itasca	2,318	9,160,293	7.6	7.8	0.4	9.1	16.9	3.5	53.6	324.9	119.6	71.4	1,583	1,547
Jackson	530	2,065,186	12.7	7.5	0.0	9.4	21.8	4.2	43.0	50.9	20.7	20.4	2,044	2,006
Kanabec	1,007	4,457,414	4.2	4.9	0.0	3.5	54.8	1.0	28.3	61.7	35.2	14.8	923	907
Kandiyohi	2,747	10,664,987	4.6	8.5	0.3	2.5	41.8	2.3	35.2	338.8	108.4	60.5	1,415	1,341
Kittson	264	995,915	12.6	5.9	0.0	9.7	5.5	10.4	52.2	31.7	15.7	8.4	1,981	1,963
Koochiching	531	2,050,764	7.7	8.8	1.4	7.2	12.3	9.1	50.8	55.3	30.4	16.1	1,286	1,187
Lac qui Parle	694	2,539,449	7.4	3.2	0.0	4.8	42.9	2.8	38.5	53.6	21.5	9.2	1,379	1,291
Lake	522	2,298,915	13.7	10.6	0.2	9.8	6.7	9.7	45.9	66.2	33.9	17.6	1,679	1,537
Lake of the Woods	213	792,289	15.8	10.2	0.0	9.0	8.4	7.2	44.9	27.5	17.3	5.4	1,458	1,425
Le Sueur	924	3,572,247	9.8	7.8	0.1	3.7	11.3	2.9	63.1	117.9	61.1	37.6	1,332	1,299
Lincoln	196	669,869	20.1	10.8	1.3	15.5	1.1	11.0	35.4	28.8	13.0	10.7	1,880	1,861
Lyon	1,419	5,698,091	5.5	6.8	0.3	4.9	1.0	9.6	69.3	171.8	87.9	39.2	1,513	1,404
McLeod	1,262	5,552,383	7.8	10.1	0.2	4.5	11.7	14.1	49.1	150.0	72.5	47.4	1,320	1,268
Mahnomen	419	1,553,453	8.8	6.5	0.2	3.3	23.9	1.5	54.4	45.9	28.2	6.9	1,237	1,233
Marshall	512	1,990,991	12.5	5.7	0.1	8.0	8.9	8.8	49.4	58.0	31.7	13.6	1,454	1,441
Martin	802	3,611,946	11.8	9.0	0.2	6.7	0.3	8.2	62.0	99.5	48.9	29.6	1,488	1,475
Meeker	1,166	4,241,950	6.5	7.5	0.1	4.6	7.5	3.6	68.6	157.4	72.7	33.0	1,434	1,421
Mille Lacs	1,212	5,029,294	5.6	11.0	0.2	3.0	7.3	2.9	67.3	127.9	79.6	36.2	1,399	1,364
Morrison	1,303	5,191,373	8.1	9.7	0.2	4.1	10.9	3.7	62.3	137.9	80.8	35.2	1,064	1,036
Mower	1,561	7,559,080	5.4	8.0	0.9	3.5	7.1	9.8	64.5	199.5	112.5	43.4	1,091	1,024
Murray	482	2,062,839	7.3	6.2	0.0	5.4	35.7	4.4	36.1	54.9	19.9	13.8	1,654	1,642
Nicollet	983	4,478,601	8.5	10.5	0.6	5.4	27.8	6.8	37.6	128.4	43.7	36.5	1,071	1,011
Nobles	1,185	4,298,914	7.7	8.5	0.2	4.6	7.4	5.9	61.5	127.4	75.8	29.1	1,343	1,230
Norman	436	1,582,516	10.5	4.2	0.3	9.3	5.7	7.7	60.3	40.5	25.0	10.9	1,661	1,627
Olmsted	5,602	27,791,782	9.6	10.8	2.9	3.3	10.6	9.4	52.2	853.5	359.8	265.0	1,713	1,447
Otter Tail	2,497	9,700,961	9.3	7.8	0.3	3.9	25.8	4.7	46.1	373.3	138.4	84.8	1,457	1,359
Pennington	739	2,999,461	6.6	8.3	1.5	3.8	9.4	10.0	54.8	130.2	37.1	19.6	1,383	1,332
Pine	951	3,821,837	10.3	12.4	0.3	5.3	9.3	0.5	60.4	118.1	66.8	32.8	1,126	1,099
Pipestone	654	2,685,480	7.4	4.4	0.1	4.8	36.8	2.6	43.4	52.3	32.0	12.6	1,381	1,277
Polk	1,559	6,278,987	7.4	13.3	1.7	3.6	11.7	8.9	48.3	193.8	103.4	46.2	1,462	1,381
Pope	686	3,078,501	4.2	5.0	0.0	7.2	52.4	2.0	28.0	109.5	28.1	17.7	1,614	1,587
Ramsey	21,340	125,504,794	7.1	9.9	3.4	6.0	7.7	5.0	59.1	3,345.0	1,468.3	870.8	1,598	1,453
Red Lake	280	1,002,315	11.4	5.6	0.0	4.7	5.7	2.7	69.7	27.6	16.0	6.1	1,532	1,525
Redwood	663	2,678,050	13.3	8.7	1.3	7.2	0.9	6.8	59.5	108.4	41.5	24.5	1,606	1,577
Renville	629	2,348,964	13.9	10.4	0.3	7.8	15.8	8.5	40.4	102.9	39.6	26.5	1,801	1,777
Rice	2,171	10,959,183	5.6	7.9	0.8	2.9	41.8	3.1	36.6	354.3	125.5	78.1	1,181	1,071
Rock	404	1,645,416	11.9	4.7	1.3	7.3	1.6	10.3	57.5	53.0	26.2	14.5	1,537	1,471
Roseau	707	2,928,463	8.4	5.7	0.2	5.9	6.7	4.0	67.7	64.1	38.4	17.2	1,125	1,116
St. Louis	9,040	40,619,148	7.9	13.5	3.2	7.3	10.0	8.9	45.2	1,139.6	562.0	300.0	1,502	1,293
Scott	4,646	23,159,356	8.9	8.6	0.5	3.1	6.7	4.4	65.9	650.4	316.1	231.1	1,588	1,458
Sherburne	3,328	16,214,184	5.7	12.1	0.5	2.7	5.2	2.9	69.4	430.4	228.3	138.3	1,464	1,430
Sibley	649	2,464,239	10.7	7.3	0.6	6.1	11.4	2.3	59.5	71.9	32.5	24.8	1,666	1,646
Stearns	5,585	25,416,178	9.4	11.9	1.9	3.4	8.5	4.0	57.4	715.5	368.4	214.6	1,355	1,191
Steele	1,417	6,167,793	8.4	12.7	0.8	4.3	2.2	11.0	58.7	176.8	94.2	53.7	1,459	1,432
Stevens	657	2,641,377	7.1	4.9	0.2	5.5	5.0	2.7	72.8	56.2	29.1	15.4	1,586	1,519
Swift	744	2,886,995	6.6	5.3	0.0	4.9	41.3	2.2	35.8	83.8	29.6	18.4	1,957	1,926
Todd	1,036	4,159,879	9.1	6.8	0.4	3.4	11.5	3.3	60.2	101.2	58.7	26.0	1,059	1,024
Traverse	111	369,011	6.6	4.2	1.7	4.2	0.0	5.6	77.7	32.3	16.7	9.5	2,890	2,884
Wabasha	753	3,138,464	10.0	13.9	0.2	5.6	10.9	6.2	52.7	95.5	45.8	31.2	1,445	1,405
Wadena	789	3,019,610	8.3	6.3	0.5	5.0	12.1	4.3	60.3	83.4	46.3	16.3	1,191	1,163
Waseca	737	2,944,545	7.3	10.0	0.7	6.4	3.5	5.1	65.6	103.0	53.0	29.9	1,600	1,516
Washington	6,926	34,001,217	7.1	9.5	1.6	2.8	6.1	3.7	67.8	976.1	432.2	373.0	1,460	1,344
Watonwan	595	2,176,624	8.9	7.0	0.4	6.9	10.5	6.3	57.1	54.2	29.7	13.8	1,261	1,168
Wilkin	341	1,324,740	10.1	9.3	0.0	8.3	10.4	5.9	54.7	45.4	20.3	13.6	2,154	2,145
Winona	1,414	6,227,334	8.1	9.9	2.2	4.1	9.2	6.0	58.1	176.7	95.1	51.6	1,017	970
Wright	4,348	20,124,567	6.7	7.7	0.4	3.1	5.5	3.0	69.9	581.1	293.6	179.1	1,334	1,279
Yellow Medicine	445	2,063,297	11.2	8.1	0.4	7.2	7.6	4.9	57.1	87.1	28.5	20.2	2,053	1,995

1. Based on the resident population estimated as of July 1 of the year shown.

STATE County	Local government finances, 2017 (cont.)									Government employment, 2020			Individual income tax returns, 2019		
	Direct general expenditure							Debt outstanding							
			Percent of total for:												
	Total (mil dol)	Per capita[1] (dollars)	Education	Health and hospitals	Police protection	Public welfare	Highways	Total (mil dol)	Per capita[1] (dollars)	Federal civilian	Federal military	State and local	Number of returns	Mean adjusted gross income	Mean income tax
	185	186	187	188	189	190	191	192	193	194	195	196	197	198	199
MINNESOTA— Cont'd															
Fillmore	111.4	5,312	48.0	1.9	3.0	3.0	12.8	155.0	7,387	72	71	1,093	10,070	55,387	4,641
Freeborn	153.0	5,003	42.0	1.5	7.5	7.6	14.7	90.8	2,968	80	102	1,346	15,120	55,106	5,018
Goodhue	282.0	6,090	45.4	1.8	5.6	4.5	14.0	288.2	6,224	132	156	3,552	24,380	68,840	7,057
Grant	32.6	5,515	47.6	1.8	2.4	2.9	9.9	30.4	5,137	25	20	392	2,940	55,137	4,701
Hennepin	8,490.5	6,804	30.8	17.6	5.5	3.0	7.7	9,298.7	7,452	13,845	4,648	84,522	657,870	98,041	14,717
Houston	99.0	5,301	53.7	1.7	3.6	4.3	12.7	84.2	4,508	73	63	987	9,480	62,695	5,989
Hubbard	84.5	4,028	39.4	0.0	6.6	9.6	16.6	94.7	4,518	42	74	1,052	10,090	58,637	5,249
Isanti	165.0	4,172	51.2	1.1	7.4	8.1	9.9	161.0	4,072	83	141	1,898	20,940	62,251	5,740
Itasca	322.0	7,141	32.1	21.4	3.7	11.1	13.0	255.6	5,669	181	152	3,153	21,520	59,655	5,528
Jackson	65.2	6,546	31.4	2.3	3.7	4.3	19.6	68.5	6,878	28	33	698	5,080	54,890	4,463
Kanabec	78.4	4,884	51.1	3.2	4.8	6.6	8.1	98.2	6,113	34	56	1,261	7,790	55,036	4,865
Kandiyohi	379.7	8,877	28.7	33.2	2.4	4.3	7.1	286.8	6,704	145	145	2,926	21,620	63,229	6,339
Kittson	32.7	7,664	33.0	0.3	3.8	4.8	25.1	24.0	5,633	38	14	276	2,120	56,416	4,688
Koochiching	56.0	4,479	45.5	11.2	4.2	3.6	11.4	52.6	4,208	185	43	726	5,970	52,551	4,446
Lac qui Parle	49.8	7,449	37.1	32.1	2.0	2.1	8.2	39.2	5,868	37	23	711	3,250	60,882	5,341
Lake	63.3	6,029	29.2	5.3	7.6	5.5	13.3	92.3	8,800	31	36	846	5,480	58,750	5,060
Lake of the Woods	27.8	7,461	27.4	0.4	6.4	6.0	30.2	226.8	60,847	33	13	247	2,060	52,537	4,224
Le Sueur	118.3	4,193	42.3	2.8	4.4	6.8	14.9	130.3	4,618	78	98	1,231	14,820	66,162	6,417
Lincoln	30.9	5,459	21.5	0.3	6.3	2.9	24.5	33.3	5,878	30	19	271	2,690	56,312	4,752
Lyon	182.5	7,040	55.0	2.7	7.2	1.4	10.8	216.3	8,342	122	84	2,194	11,950	62,217	5,881
McLeod	190.7	5,314	49.0	1.6	6.0	5.8	12.6	248.0	6,913	88	121	1,694	18,960	62,652	5,818
Mahnomen	48.3	8,677	45.7	20.6	6.0	5.7	8.9	29.4	5,286	24	19	874	2,360	45,558	3,472
Marshall	65.0	6,939	34.4	0.5	3.9	6.8	20.4	21.1	2,251	45	32	579	4,440	61,315	5,607
Martin	107.0	5,387	47.4	2.8	7.8	2.8	11.4	139.9	7,045	56	66	1,229	10,060	54,883	5,012
Meeker	157.2	6,820	42.7	19.9	4.8	5.6	8.6	113.9	4,943	68	79	1,187	11,420	62,146	5,740
Mille Lacs	146.3	5,655	62.5	0.7	5.1	7.7	6.8	151.6	5,863	74	88	2,894	12,760	53,728	4,599
Morrison	159.7	4,827	56.1	2.0	3.9	6.8	11.4	136.5	4,127	466	114	1,878	16,350	54,018	4,480
Mower	209.7	5,272	48.2	3.4	4.4	5.5	9.9	994.4	25,001	140	136	2,463	19,360	59,929	5,575
Murray	54.8	6,578	27.8	30.4	4.7	2.0	16.6	15.9	1,903	45	27	554	4,080	58,395	4,953
Nicollet	159.6	4,688	47.0	19.6	2.9	5.8	7.2	126.9	3,727	38	109	3,120	16,260	69,577	7,350
Nobles	122.8	5,667	45.2	3.0	5.1	5.9	14.0	83.6	3,858	87	72	1,428	10,020	52,199	3,958
Norman	38.6	5,862	39.2	2.1	4.1	5.2	21.9	15.7	2,377	30	21	389	3,090	54,240	4,314
Olmsted	939.3	6,071	36.2	1.4	4.8	6.7	10.4	3,233.2	20,896	868	544	7,765	81,630	82,890	10,483
Otter Tail	390.0	6,699	40.5	14.5	3.1	5.0	13.1	355.6	6,108	220	198	3,683	29,130	60,278	5,659
Pennington	130.4	9,200	71.0	0.8	4.4	3.9	4.5	121.2	8,548	54	47	1,281	6,970	58,570	5,424
Pine	125.6	4,307	43.3	8.8	4.3	6.0	13.6	206.2	7,071	294	96	2,287	13,620	52,273	4,271
Pipestone	53.4	5,836	54.2	0.7	2.8	2.7	11.8	32.8	3,581	48	31	881	4,520	52,701	4,188
Polk	219.4	6,935	37.0	4.8	4.2	7.3	10.3	169.4	5,354	108	102	2,520	14,490	59,436	5,260
Pope	63.4	5,766	35.7	18.4	4.1	6.5	12.3	54.1	4,919	45	38	818	5,750	64,674	6,715
Ramsey	3,623.5	6,650	37.9	1.9	5.9	5.7	5.2	6,544.0	12,010	2,502	1,889	53,835	273,590	72,183	8,663
Red Lake	30.6	7,637	58.7	0.2	4.2	4.2	15.2	12.6	3,131	13	14	262	1,900	55,997	4,434
Redwood	113.8	7,463	30.7	27.3	4.6	2.0	12.6	79.6	5,221	58	51	1,133	7,740	55,253	4,614
Renville	119.3	8,121	20.4	21.5	3.2	5.7	18.0	86.5	5,885	61	48	1,265	7,340	56,916	4,923
Rice	342.1	5,169	33.5	30.0	4.0	5.1	8.6	272.6	4,118	150	206	3,273	30,550	67,402	6,854
Rock	52.8	5,586	36.4	0.6	4.3	8.6	12.3	88.4	9,350	30	31	709	4,540	56,768	4,492
Roseau	61.5	4,020	66.1	0.8	2.2	0.0	7.7	62.9	4,112	96	51	877	7,770	58,103	5,051
St. Louis	1,203.0	6,022	28.0	1.2	4.8	7.5	14.8	1,581.6	7,917	1,488	793	13,844	96,460	63,331	6,556
Scott	752.6	5,171	51.8	0.7	4.3	3.1	11.4	1,073.2	7,374	141	514	8,574	75,200	94,360	12,563
Sherburne	468.8	4,962	61.4	0.5	3.7	3.6	5.1	600.0	6,350	156	332	3,943	47,450	71,851	7,218
Sibley	99.5	6,678	59.7	3.0	3.8	1.6	10.7	91.0	6,107	43	50	714	7,590	57,058	4,751
Stearns	786.8	4,971	48.5	0.7	5.2	5.2	9.7	1,464.0	9,248	2,428	542	9,137	76,320	66,517	7,372
Steele	197.0	5,355	56.6	1.4	4.3	5.0	10.0	176.5	4,797	83	124	2,070	18,970	60,816	5,614
Stevens	48.4	4,988	43.0	0.3	5.4	7.3	16.0	47.0	4,847	70	30	1,259	4,630	63,922	5,786
Swift	78.4	8,354	25.1	33.9	5.2	5.9	9.5	65.0	6,926	54	31	754	4,530	53,798	4,543
Todd	126.4	5,153	53.7	2.9	5.0	9.6	14.0	62.9	2,563	86	84	1,277	11,510	49,697	4,044
Traverse	38.1	11,543	29.1	0.5	4.2	5.5	16.5	13.9	4,220	25	11	315	1,600	52,258	4,811
Wabasha	94.9	4,397	42.2	3.3	6.9	5.2	11.2	72.7	3,369	58	74	1,027	11,200	62,012	5,691
Wadena	84.0	6,154	46.2	8.0	4.3	6.0	13.9	46.9	3,437	55	46	1,383	6,450	48,828	3,730
Waseca	106.2	5,677	46.5	7.5	5.1	2.2	16.7	78.5	4,196	250	60	1,106	9,250	55,326	4,599
Washington	1,060.5	4,151	58.5	1.1	5.0	0.8	10.8	1,569.8	6,145	420	902	10,348	136,650	97,780	13,133
Watonwan	73.6	6,734	58.8	2.6	2.6	2.3	10.7	82.7	7,565	55	37	719	5,290	53,022	4,159
Wilkin	38.3	6,064	43.1	3.7	5.8	6.7	16.9	42.1	6,662	22	21	383	3,180	55,922	4,548
Winona	182.0	3,588	43.1	2.6	5.9	6.8	13.2	62.2	1,226	150	161	3,179	22,820	61,302	6,082
Wright	644.0	4,798	57.4	1.2	4.4	3.5	11.0	1,100.7	8,201	216	480	6,069	68,920	75,567	7,868
Yellow Medicine	93.9	9,545	25.0	30.1	2.8	5.2	13.8	87.3	8,875	42	32	1,061	4,960	55,922	4,737

1. Based on the resident population estimated as of July 1 of the year shown.

State / county code	CBSA code[1]	County Type code[2]	STATE County	Land area[3] (sq. mi)	Population, 2021			Population and population characteristics, 2021										
								Race alone or in combination, not Hispanic or Latino (percent)					Age (percent)					
					Total persons 2021	Rank	Per square mile	White	Black	American Indian, Alaska Native	Asian and Pacific Islancer	Percent Hispanic or Latino[4]	Under 5 years	5 to 17 years	18 to 24 years	25 to 34 years	35 to 44 years	45 to 54 years
				1	2	3	4	5	6	7	8	9	10	11	12	13	14	15
28000		0	MISSISSIPPI	46,925.5	2,949,965	X	62.9	57.1	38.3	0.9	1.5	3.5	6.0	13.3	13.6	12.9	12.5	12.1
28001	35020	5	Adams	462.3	28,742	1,466	62.2	36.5	53.3	0.8	0.9	9.7	5.5	11.0	10.9	12.3	13.4	11.8
28003	18420	7	Alcorn	400.0	34,349	1,319	85.9	82.9	13.3	0.8	0.8	3.6	5.6	12.6	12.3	12.4	12.2	12.8
28005		8	Amite	730.1	12,637	2,233	17.3	58.8	39.3	0.6	0.4	1.7	5.1	11.8	10.0	10.2	10.2	11.0
28007		6	Attala	735.0	17,742	1,933	24.1	53.1	44.2	0.6	0.7	2.3	6.3	14.5	12.4	11.5	11.5	11.6
28009		1	Benton	406.6	7,646	2,602	18.8	61.7	35.2	0.8	0.5	3.0	5.8	11.9	11.9	12.0	11.2	13.0
28011	17380	7	Bolivar	876.5	30,308	1,429	34.6	32.6	64.1	0.4	1.2	2.4	6.4	14.5	13.9	12.8	11.9	11.2
28013		9	Calhoun	586.6	13,018	2,212	22.2	65.3	28.8	0.6	0.4	6.3	5.6	12.8	12.4	10.8	11.1	13.4
28015	24900	9	Carroll	628.4	9,879	2,418	15.7	64.7	33.6	0.7	0.4	1.7	4.3	10.2	10.7	10.6	11.4	12.6
28017		7	Chickasaw	501.8	17,011	1,970	33.9	49.9	45.0	0.6	0.6	5.3	6.8	13.9	12.4	13.0	11.6	11.2
28019		9	Choctaw	418.2	8,106	2,571	19.4	68.4	29.8	0.6	0.7	1.8	5.2	12.3	11.1	11.5	11.1	12.0
28021		8	Claiborne	487.4	8,908	2,495	18.3	11.4	86.2	0.6	1.0	1.8	5.9	11.5	24.6	10.8	10.1	8.9
28023	32940	9	Clarke	691.6	15,421	2,063	22.3	63.9	34.6	0.6	0.3	1.3	6.0	11.9	11.7	11.7	10.8	12.0
28025	48500	7	Clay	410.1	18,535	1,897	45.2	38.4	59.5	0.5	0.6	1.8	6.0	12.5	12.4	12.6	11.9	11.8
28027	17260	7	Coahoma	553.1	20,810	1,770	37.6	20.2	77.6	0.3	0.6	1.9	7.3	15.6	14.1	12.1	11.1	10.6
28029	27140	2	Copiah	777.3	27,995	1,497	36.0	44.5	51.7	0.5	0.7	3.7	5.8	12.5	14.4	11.4	11.4	11.3
28031	25620	8	Covington	413.8	18,279	1,911	44.2	60.7	36.5	0.6	0.6	2.6	6.5	14.1	12.1	12.5	12.6	11.9
28033	32820	1	DeSoto	476.3	188,633	360	396.0	60.3	33.2	0.5	2.2	5.3	5.8	14.5	13.6	12.9	14.1	13.7
28035	25620	3	Forrest	466.0	77,875	729	167.1	58.2	37.9	0.6	1.4	3.3	6.4	13.3	17.6	14.5	12.2	10.6
28037		9	Franklin	564.0	7,676	2,598	13.6	63.8	35.0	0.6	0.4	1.3	5.4	13.0	12.3	10.1	11.8	11.8
28039		6	George	478.7	24,762	1,623	51.7	87.7	8.8	0.9	1.0	3.1	7.2	15.1	12.4	13.8	12.1	12.1
28041		8	Greene	712.7	13,630	2,182	19.1	72.7	25.8	0.7	0.3	1.4	5.1	10.2	12.3	16.7	14.1	14.1
28043	24980	7	Grenada	422.1	21,365	1,742	50.6	54.2	43.8	0.6	0.7	1.7	6.1	13.9	12.0	12.7	11.5	12.3
28045	25060	2	Hancock	474.0	46,055	1,059	97.2	85.9	9.3	1.5	1.5	3.9	4.9	10.9	10.7	11.7	11.4	12.7
28047	25060	2	Harrison	573.6	209,396	327	365.1	64.9	27.2	1.0	4.0	5.7	6.2	13.4	13.2	13.6	12.8	11.7
28049	27140	2	Hinds	869.8	222,679	314	256.0	24.2	73.9	0.3	1.0	1.6	6.2	13.3	14.6	13.9	12.4	11.3
28051	27140	6	Holmes	756.7	16,496	2,003	21.8	15.8	82.7	0.4	0.4	1.4	6.0	13.9	15.3	12.8	11.1	10.9
28053		6	Humphreys	418.5	7,551	2,613	18.0	20.6	75.2	0.5	0.6	3.9	6.0	14.6	13.2	10.9	11.7	11.0
28055		8	Issaquena	413.0	1,280	3,093	3.1	37.0	60.3	0.6	0.5	2.0	1.9	3.9	15.7	17.3	12.3	11.8
28057	46180	7	Itawamba	532.8	23,838	1,647	44.7	90.5	7.6	0.6	0.6	1.8	5.5	12.4	14.1	12.8	11.3	13.3
28059	25060	2	Jackson	722.8	143,987	463	199.2	68.8	22.1	0.9	3.1	7.2	5.6	13.2	12.2	12.9	13.1	12.7
28061	29860	9	Jasper	676.3	16,291	2,017	24.1	44.7	53.5	0.6	0.4	1.7	5.9	13.5	11.1	11.7	11.3	11.8
28063		8	Jefferson	519.9	7,205	2,646	13.9	14.1	85.0	0.5	0.3	0.9	5.7	12.6	11.6	12.9	12.7	11.2
28065		8	Jefferson Davis	408.4	11,134	2,335	27.3	38.1	59.7	0.6	0.4	2.0	5.1	11.5	10.4	11.5	11.2	12.0
28067	29860	4	Jones	694.8	66,744	806	96.1	64.9	29.7	0.8	0.7	4.8	6.4	14.2	13.3	11.7	12.2	11.5
28069	32940	9	Kemper	766.2	8,829	2,501	11.5	34.1	61.1	4.2	0.4	1.2	4.8	10.2	15.0	12.5	10.5	12.2
28071	37060	4	Lafayette	631.7	56,884	916	90.0	70.9	24.3	0.5	2.8	2.7	4.8	10.6	23.9	13.4	12.4	10.5
28073	25620	3	Lamar	496.6	65,353	826	131.6	73.1	22.7	0.6	1.8	3.2	6.1	14.0	12.6	14.0	14.3	12.4
28075	32940	5	Lauderdale	703.7	72,088	763	102.4	51.8	45.3	0.5	1.1	2.5	6.0	13.1	13.0	13.0	12.0	11.9
28077		8	Lawrence	430.6	11,812	2,296	27.4	64.7	32.9	0.5	0.6	2.3	6.0	14.1	11.5	11.0	12.1	11.8
28079		6	Leake	582.9	21,196	1,754	36.4	46.8	42.8	5.7	0.7	5.1	6.7	13.0	13.9	12.5	12.4	12.0
28081	46180	5	Lee	450.0	82,883	697	184.2	64.6	31.7	0.6	1.3	3.2	6.3	14.2	12.8	13.1	12.9	12.5
28083	24900	5	Leflore	594.1	27,557	1,515	46.4	21.6	74.9	0.4	0.7	3.1	7.1	15.8	15.3	12.4	11.7	10.5
28085	15020	6	Lincoln	586.2	34,943	1,304	59.6	68.0	30.4	0.5	0.7	1.4	5.6	13.2	12.1	12.0	13.0	13.1
28087	18060	5	Lowndes	505.4	58,150	903	115.1	51.2	46.0	0.6	1.3	2.1	6.8	13.4	13.0	13.8	12.1	11.3
28089	27140	2	Madison	714.4	109,813	563	153.7	55.6	38.6	0.4	3.2	3.2	6.2	13.9	13.1	12.4	13.8	13.1
28091		6	Marion	542.4	24,378	1,633	44.9	66.0	32.2	0.6	0.7	1.8	5.8	13.2	11.9	12.1	12.8	12.1
28093	32820	1	Marshall	706.2	33,725	1,339	47.8	49.2	46.2	0.7	0.5	4.5	5.6	11.4	12.7	12.8	11.4	12.7
28095		7	Monroe	765.1	33,883	1,333	44.3	67.5	30.8	0.6	0.5	1.5	5.6	12.7	11.7	12.1	11.6	12.7
28097		7	Montgomery	407.0	9,729	2,434	23.9	53.0	44.8	0.6	0.8	1.6	6.0	12.6	11.4	11.0	10.5	11.1
28099		7	Neshoba	570.1	28,993	1,457	50.9	59.1	22.6	17.1	1.0	2.2	7.3	15.5	14.0	11.9	11.9	11.4
28101		7	Newton	577.8	21,056	1,760	36.4	60.9	31.7	5.6	0.7	2.3	6.4	13.8	14.5	11.8	11.4	13.0
28103		7	Noxubee	695.2	10,123	2,398	14.6	25.8	72.5	0.5	0.4	1.5	7.3	13.5	12.6	13.4	11.1	10.9
28105	44260	5	Oktibbeha	458.2	51,842	970	113.1	56.9	38.3	0.5	3.5	1.9	4.9	9.7	32.9	13.6	9.9	7.9
28107		6	Panola	685.2	32,851	1,366	47.9	47.4	50.7	0.7	0.5	2.0	6.8	13.8	12.6	12.8	11.5	11.9
28109	38100	6	Pearl River	811.3	56,503	918	69.6	83.1	13.0	1.4	0.9	3.5	5.6	13.1	12.5	11.9	11.6	12.3
28111	25620	3	Perry	647.3	11,571	2,309	17.9	78.5	19.6	0.9	0.4	1.9	5.6	12.6	11.7	12.8	11.6	12.3
28113	32620	6	Pike	409.2	39,973	1,181	97.7	42.6	55.2	0.7	0.9	1.6	6.5	14.6	13.9	11.9	11.5	11.5
28115	46180	7	Pontotoc	497.8	31,445	1,391	63.2	76.6	16.3	0.6	0.7	7.5	6.9	14.7	12.9	12.7	12.7	12.0
28117	46180	7	Prentiss	415.0	24,996	1,611	60.2	83.4	15.4	0.5	0.6	1.4	6.0	13.0	13.1	12.8	11.9	12.2
28119		6	Quitman	405.0	5,935	2,738	14.7	25.5	72.7	0.8	0.6	1.8	5.6	13.1	12.4	12.6	10.6	12.8
28121	27140	2	Rankin	775.5	158,096	430	203.9	73.2	23.1	0.5	1.8	2.7	5.4	12.8	12.1	13.6	14.4	13.3
28123		6	Scott	609.2	27,598	1,514	45.3	49.3	38.5	0.7	0.7	12.1	8.0	15.0	12.1	12.2	11.7	12.5
28125		8	Sharkey	431.7	3,663	2,913	8.5	26.1	71.0	0.3	1.1	2.3	6.0	13.4	12.3	9.7	10.6	11.0
28127	27140	2	Simpson	589.2	25,750	1,575	43.7	62.0	35.9	0.5	0.9	1.8	6.0	13.1	12.2	12.1	11.6	12.0
28129		8	Smith	636.3	14,191	2,134	22.3	74.1	24.1	0.4	0.3	1.8	6.5	12.8	11.4	12.1	11.0	12.1
28131	25060	6	Stone	445.5	18,644	1,889	41.8	77.6	19.7	1.0	1.0	2.4	5.7	12.5	14.1	12.6	11.9	12.2

1. CBSA = Core Based Statistical Area. See Appendix A for explanation. See Appendix B for list of metropolitan areas with component counties. 2. County type code from the Economic Research Service of USDA Rural-Urban Continuum Codes. See Appendix A for definition. 3. Dry land or land partially or temporarily covered by water. 4. May be of any race.

STATE County	Population, 2021 (cont.)				Population change, 2000–2021							Households, 2016–2020				
	Age (percent) (cont.)				Total persons		Percent change		Components of change, 2020–2021					Percent		
	55 to 64 years	65 to 74 years	75 years and over	Percent female	2010	2020	2010–2020	2020–2021	Births	Deaths	Net Migration	Number	Persons per household	Family households	Female family householder[1]	One person
	16	17	18	19	20	21	22	23	24	25	26	27	28	29	30	31
MISSISSIPPI	12.9	10.3	6.5	51.3	2,967,297	2,961,279	-0.2	-0.4	43,234	47,987	-6,685	1,116,649	2.6	66.3	17.0	29.2
Adams	15.1	12.4	7.6	48.0	32,297	29,538	-8.5	-2.7	391	624	-557	11,129	2.6	60.3	22.0	35.6
Alcorn	13.3	11.0	7.8	51.1	37,057	34,740	-6.3	-1.1	477	689	-181	14,610	2.5	65.2	17.0	29.9
Amite	16.5	14.9	10.4	51.1	13,131	12,720	-3.1	-0.7	155	242	5	5,416	2.3	65.1	15.1	30.9
Attala	12.9	11.1	8.2	52.0	19,564	17,889	-8.6	-0.8	277	385	-41	6,890	2.6	70.2	20.4	27.1
Benton	15.1	11.4	7.7	50.7	8,729	7,646	-12.4	0.0	111	162	51	3,183	2.6	69.5	13.3	29.4
Bolivar	12.3	10.9	6.2	53.3	34,145	30,985	-9.3	-2.2	518	585	-607	12,114	2.5	63.7	22.5	30.8
Calhoun	13.7	11.9	8.3	51.1	14,962	13,266	-11.3	-1.9	215	257	-203	5,771	2.5	65.4	16.1	30.1
Carroll	15.0	14.5	10.7	48.8	10,597	9,998	-5.7	-1.2	111	160	-69	4,018	2.4	69.4	11.7	28.3
Chickasaw	12.6	10.6	7.7	50.7	17,392	17,106	-1.6	-0.6	279	279	-94	6,523	2.5	68.8	18.1	29.1
Choctaw	14.4	12.5	9.9	50.9	8,547	8,246	-3.5	-1.7	99	184	-56	3,353	2.4	63.0	9.1	36.0
Claiborne	11.1	10.7	6.4	52.7	9,604	9,135	-4.9	-2.5	127	176	-177	2,900	2.8	62.6	25.7	35.2
Clarke	14.3	12.9	8.7	52.7	16,732	15,615	-6.7	-1.2	202	302	-94	6,253	2.5	69.9	18.6	28.0
Clay	13.5	11.7	7.7	52.9	20,634	18,636	-9.7	-0.5	308	302	-106	7,728	2.5	62.9	17.7	33.5
Coahoma	12.8	10.2	6.1	53.3	26,151	21,390	-18.2	-2.7	397	425	-548	8,614	2.6	63.2	28.0	32.8
Copiah	14.3	11.7	7.3	51.6	29,449	28,368	-3.7	-1.3	421	464	-329	9,568	2.9	68.9	19.8	28.8
Covington	13.4	10.0	6.8	51.2	19,568	18,340	-6.3	-0.3	269	354	21	7,042	2.6	71.2	18.1	25.4
DeSoto	12.0	8.4	5.0	51.8	161,252	185,314	14.9	1.8	2,540	2,276	3,057	64,424	2.8	73.8	14.3	21.4
Forrest	11.2	8.4	5.7	52.6	74,934	78,158	4.3	-0.4	1,253	1,139	-410	28,116	2.6	62.4	18.9	30.3
Franklin	14.4	12.9	8.4	50.6	8,118	7,675	-5.5	0.0	99	143	46	3,031	2.5	73.8	17.5	22.8
George	12.7	9.4	5.3	49.2	22,578	24,350	7.8	1.7	403	414	426	8,085	2.9	73.0	9.3	24.2
Greene	11.9	9.0	6.6	42.0	14,400	13,530	-6.0	0.7	148	177	129	3,825	2.5	66.6	11.0	29.6
Grenada	13.2	11.1	7.1	52.3	21,906	21,629	-1.3	-1.2	310	421	-155	8,476	2.4	62.3	19.3	33.5
Hancock	16.3	13.2	8.1	51.0	43,929	46,053	4.8	0.0	562	775	212	21,494	2.2	69.6	13.4	25.4
Harrison	13.2	10.1	5.9	51.0	187,105	208,621	11.5	0.4	3,134	3,230	826	80,097	2.5	65.9	16.8	28.3
Hinds	12.5	9.9	5.8	53.2	245,285	227,742	-7.2	-2.2	3,556	3,383	-5,207	88,832	2.6	61.6	22.9	33.4
Holmes	13.3	9.9	6.7	51.8	19,198	17,000	-11.4	-3.0	250	336	-413	6,358	2.6	59.6	29.7	38.1
Humphreys	14.6	10.9	7.0	52.8	9,375	7,785	-17.0	-3.0	109	164	-178	3,197	2.5	66.5	35.0	30.2
Issaquena	18.8	10.6	7.7	40.2	1,406	1,338	-4.8	-4.3	10	25	-42	462	2.0	52.4	12.3	47.6
Itawamba	12.8	10.3	7.6	50.5	23,401	23,863	2.0	-0.1	296	467	143	8,525	2.6	70.3	12.3	22.7
Jackson	13.7	10.4	6.3	50.8	139,668	143,252	2.6	0.5	1,902	2,275	1,097	53,878	2.6	65.6	15.6	30.2
Jasper	13.8	12.4	8.5	51.0	17,062	16,367	-4.1	-0.5	250	293	-35	6,616	2.5	70.5	22.5	27.7
Jefferson	14.2	11.2	7.9	50.5	7,726	7,260	-6.0	-0.8	106	89	-70	2,543	2.6	66.7	29.3	33.3
Jefferson Davis	14.2	14.0	10.0	52.6	12,487	11,321	-9.3	-1.7	130	234	-83	4,615	2.4	66.1	19.2	29.3
Jones	12.9	10.9	6.9	51.3	67,761	67,246	-0.8	-0.7	1,083	1,185	-407	24,855	2.7	70.0	15.7	26.6
Kemper	12.7	12.3	9.8	49.5	10,456	8,988	-14.0	-1.8	114	160	-113	3,757	2.4	61.5	18.8	32.9
Lafayette	10.4	8.9	5.1	51.4	47,351	55,813	17.9	1.9	652	624	1,045	18,585	2.7	58.7	12.3	30.1
Lamar	11.7	9.1	5.8	52.0	55,658	64,222	15.4	1.8	894	652	887	22,467	2.8	72.8	13.4	22.1
Lauderdale	12.9	10.9	7.2	51.1	80,261	72,984	-9.1	-1.2	1,070	1,311	-663	29,718	2.4	65.8	18.8	30.7
Lawrence	14.2	11.8	7.4	50.9	12,929	12,016	-7.1	-1.7	170	222	-152	5,019	2.5	69.5	14.6	27.2
Leake	12.4	10.5	6.4	48.3	23,805	21,275	-10.6	-0.4	383	420	-47	8,113	2.7	65.8	20.1	31.6
Lee	12.7	9.3	6.0	52.0	82,910	83,343	0.5	-0.6	1,264	1,434	-306	31,866	2.7	67.2	14.7	29.1
Leflore	12.0	9.3	5.9	53.2	32,317	28,339	-12.3	-2.8	490	517	-747	9,901	2.8	60.2	27.4	36.7
Lincoln	13.3	11.0	6.8	51.8	34,869	34,907	0.1	0.1	434	587	186	13,127	2.6	67.8	14.3	28.7
Lowndes	13.0	10.3	6.5	52.0	59,779	58,879	-1.5	-1.2	919	981	-670	22,457	2.5	63.0	15.1	33.2
Madison	13.2	9.6	4.6	51.8	95,203	109,145	14.6	0.6	1,664	1,682	663	40,179	2.6	68.9	13.6	27.4
Marion	13.2	11.2	7.6	51.1	27,088	24,441	-9.8	-0.3	357	507	84	9,770	2.5	59.5	12.9	38.4
Marshall	14.9	11.7	6.8	50.2	37,144	33,752	-9.1	-0.1	470	669	171	13,311	2.5	71.7	20.5	24.7
Monroe	13.7	11.7	8.2	51.8	36,989	34,180	-7.6	-0.9	481	677	-104	13,482	2.6	68.3	15.4	28.2
Montgomery	14.8	13.1	9.5	52.1	10,925	9,822	-10.1	-0.9	144	208	-29	4,366	2.3	64.0	23.6	30.3
Neshoba	11.8	10.1	6.2	52.3	29,676	29,087	-2.0	-0.3	521	558	-62	10,495	2.8	66.7	17.5	31.1
Newton	12.1	10.2	6.8	51.7	21,720	21,291	-2.0	-1.1	321	408	-149	7,926	2.6	69.6	15.0	28.4
Noxubee	13.7	10.6	6.9	52.2	11,545	10,285	-10.9	-1.6	182	189	-155	4,015	2.6	67.0	25.9	29.5
Oktibbeha	8.9	7.2	5.0	50.0	47,671	51,788	8.6	0.1	618	516	-63	18,849	2.4	50.3	13.2	32.2
Panola	13.7	10.7	6.2	51.8	34,707	33,208	-4.3	-1.1	556	629	-288	12,354	2.7	65.1	19.2	31.2
Pearl River	13.7	11.9	7.5	50.7	55,834	56,145	0.6	0.6	743	1,033	650	21,321	2.5	73.8	13.4	23.7
Perry	13.9	11.6	7.8	51.0	12,250	11,511	-6.0	0.5	158	189	90	4,597	2.6	68.9	17.6	25.0
Pike	12.5	10.8	6.7	52.5	40,404	40,324	-0.2	-0.9	590	747	-200	14,561	2.6	56.9	16.9	41.7
Pontotoc	12.5	9.4	6.2	50.7	29,957	31,184	4.1	0.8	536	422	141	10,823	2.9	71.9	12.6	24.6
Prentiss	12.8	10.3	8.0	50.8	25,276	25,008	-1.1	0.0	318	435	103	9,255	2.6	66.9	11.0	29.7
Quitman	13.9	11.2	7.8	53.0	8,223	6,176	-24.9	-3.9	77	124	-192	3,022	2.3	56.1	27.4	39.2
Rankin	12.3	9.8	6.4	51.5	141,617	157,031	10.9	0.7	2,059	1,901	889	56,640	2.6	71.3	12.8	24.2
Scott	12.7	9.8	6.0	51.4	28,264	27,990	-1.0	-1.4	575	425	-538	10,228	2.7	71.0	16.5	26.2
Sharkey	15.5	13.2	8.3	52.5	4,916	3,800	-22.7	-3.6	54	60	-129	1,757	2.4	66.1	22.5	29.8
Simpson	14.0	11.6	7.3	51.5	27,503	25,949	-5.7	-0.8	399	462	-138	9,647	2.7	69.0	19.1	28.1
Smith	13.6	12.0	8.6	51.4	16,491	14,209	-13.8	-0.1	238	270	15	5,888	2.7	64.3	10.1	34.1
Stone	14.0	11.0	5.9	49.6	17,786	18,333	3.1	1.7	274	289	327	6,304	2.8	73.7	13.9	25.2

1. No spouse present.

STATE County	Persons in group quarters, 2021	Daytime Population, 2016–2020		Births, 2021		Deaths, 2021		Persons under 65 with no health insurance, 2019		Medicare, 2021			COVID-19 Deaths, 2020	
		Number	Employment/ residence ratio	Total	Rate[1]	Number	Rate[1]	Number	Percent	Total beneficiaries	Enrolled in Original Medicare	Enrolled in Medicare Advantage	Number	Rate[1]
	32	33	34	35	36	37	38	39	40	41	42	43	44	45
MISSISSIPPI	84,333	2,928,159	1.0	34,957	11.8	38,194	12.9	369,501	15.4	609,689	464,397	145,291	5,018	1.7
Adams	2,133	31,920	1.1	323	11.1	508	17.5	3,911	17.6	7,321	6,017	1,304	61	2.1
Alcorn	593	37,036	1.0	388	11.2	556	16.1	4,674	16.0	8,704	8,224	480	42	1.2
Amite	107	10,439	0.5	121	9.6	200	15.8	1,626	17.6	3,190	2,532	659	25	2.0
Attala	263	16,723	0.8	229	12.9	310	17.4	2,325	16.1	4,243	3,060	1,183	42	2.4
Benton	20	6,281	0.4	89	11.6	133	17.4	1,147	17.4	1,939	1,511	428	22	2.9
Bolivar	1,311	30,930	1.0	421	13.8	486	15.9	3,985	16.6	7,115	5,532	1,584	94	3.0
Calhoun	120	12,607	0.7	177	13.5	218	16.6	2,124	18.6	3,559	3,253	306	23	1.7
Carroll	354	7,796	0.4	95	9.6	128	12.9	1,164	16.2	2,681	2,247	434	21	2.1
Chickasaw	445	15,971	0.8	236	13.9	219	12.9	2,347	17.3	4,157	3,514	643	35	2.1
Choctaw	110	7,181	0.7	82	10.1	146	17.9	951	15.1	2,219	1,950	269	11	1.3
Claiborne	1,301	9,672	1.2	100	11.1	131	14.6	873	14.3	1,842	1,289	552	21	2.3
Clarke	45	12,759	0.5	170	11.0	236	15.2	1,984	16.3	4,130	3,118	1,012	58	3.7
Clay	164	18,391	0.8	247	13.3	250	13.4	2,423	15.8	4,662	4,099	563	36	1.9
Coahoma	637	22,652	1.0	332	15.8	342	16.3	2,693	15.2	5,000	3,673	1,328	61	2.9
Copiah	946	25,029	0.7	340	12.1	388	13.8	3,644	16.3	6,291	4,054	2,237	53	1.9
Covington	179	17,612	0.8	220	12.0	286	15.6	2,653	17.4	4,202	2,910	1,292	52	2.8
DeSoto	470	157,585	0.7	2,022	10.8	1,753	9.4	18,913	11.8	29,633	22,616	7,017	174	0.9
Forrest	2,838	83,189	1.2	1,009	12.9	923	11.8	9,468	15.3	13,486	9,361	4,125	101	1.3
Franklin	52	6,745	0.6	82	10.7	113	14.7	896	14.8	1,971	1,697	274	21	2.7
George	515	20,534	0.6	317	12.9	324	13.2	3,411	16.8	4,917	3,396	1,521	39	1.6
Greene	2,512	12,665	0.7	128	9.4	138	10.2	1,408	15.7	2,399	1,889	510	24	1.8
Grenada	221	23,027	1.3	247	11.5	337	15.7	2,608	15.6	5,478	4,631	847	56	2.6
Hancock	409	46,194	1.0	469	10.2	612	13.3	6,008	16.0	10,929	6,720	4,209	57	1.2
Harrison	4,884	218,872	1.1	2,551	12.2	2,523	12.1	28,528	16.7	40,535	28,796	11,740	177	0.8
Hinds	7,712	249,672	1.1	2,854	12.7	2,648	11.8	28,749	15.2	42,865	27,308	15,557	284	1.3
Holmes	804	15,739	0.7	193	11.6	266	15.9	2,059	15.5	4,047	2,730	1,317	67	4.0
Humphreys	50	7,870	0.9	89	11.7	122	16.0	1,033	16.0	1,929	1,504	424	25	3.2
Issaquena	285	1,179	0.8	7	5.4	21	16.1	136	17.7	257	195	62	D	D
Itawamba	862	19,877	0.7	237	9.9	356	14.9	2,964	16.2	5,414	5,019	396	48	2.0
Jackson	1,167	135,352	0.9	1,509	10.5	1,839	12.8	17,030	14.3	28,424	19,477	8,947	169	1.2
Jasper	70	14,205	0.6	202	12.4	231	14.2	2,130	16.7	4,113	2,861	1,252	26	1.6
Jefferson	361	6,744	0.8	88	12.2	74	10.2	880	16.4	1,753	1,362	391	19	2.6
Jefferson Davis	104	8,961	0.5	106	9.5	187	16.7	1,457	17.3	2,975	2,197	777	22	2.0
Jones	1,684	70,768	1.1	861	12.9	946	14.1	9,133	16.7	14,492	10,549	3,944	98	1.5
Kemper	660	8,934	0.8	94	10.6	136	15.3	1,265	19.0	2,173	1,609	564	22	2.4
Lafayette	4,387	55,822	1.1	522	9.3	502	8.9	6,590	15.6	8,568	7,665	903	69	1.2
Lamar	320	58,179	0.8	722	11.1	525	8.1	7,645	14.2	9,847	7,254	2,593	54	0.8
Lauderdale	3,466	80,585	1.2	861	11.9	1,036	14.3	8,366	14.5	15,283	11,856	3,428	157	2.2
Lawrence	0	10,653	0.6	135	11.3	181	15.2	1,546	15.1	2,985	2,306	679	19	1.6
Leake	1,455	19,905	0.7	303	14.3	343	16.2	3,749	21.8	4,503	3,208	1,295	67	3.2
Lee	808	98,583	1.3	1,041	12.5	1,171	14.1	11,132	15.5	17,318	15,863	1,455	139	1.7
Leflore	1,197	31,006	1.2	409	14.7	401	14.4	3,376	14.9	5,943	4,625	1,318	110	3.9
Lincoln	607	33,306	0.9	340	9.7	434	12.4	4,531	16.3	7,496	6,045	1,452	82	2.4
Lowndes	1,119	62,811	1.2	742	12.7	761	13.0	6,397	13.4	11,970	10,622	1,348	104	1.8
Madison	1,690	112,668	1.1	1,357	12.4	1,376	12.6	9,831	10.9	19,020	14,451	4,568	136	1.2
Marion	710	24,711	1.0	282	11.6	408	16.7	3,564	18.6	5,765	4,019	1,747	71	2.9
Marshall	1,562	30,595	0.7	366	10.8	543	16.1	4,185	15.5	7,867	5,621	2,246	59	1.7
Monroe	269	31,923	0.7	394	11.6	525	15.4	4,160	14.9	8,804	7,782	1,022	93	2.7
Montgomery	81	8,674	0.7	116	11.9	172	17.6	1,118	14.8	2,771	2,364	407	38	3.9
Neshoba	290	29,880	1.1	444	15.3	433	14.9	5,181	21.5	5,847	4,812	1,036	132	4.6
Newton	525	18,787	0.7	260	12.3	334	15.8	2,998	17.7	4,710	3,638	1,072	44	2.1
Noxubee	133	9,318	0.7	144	14.1	148	14.5	1,638	19.4	2,474	2,207	267	26	2.5
Oktibbeha	4,879	51,079	1.1	496	9.6	431	8.3	5,660	14.4	7,131	6,264	867	77	1.5
Panola	238	33,283	0.9	449	13.6	500	15.2	4,612	16.3	7,480	5,417	2,063	77	2.3
Pearl River	1,155	47,338	0.6	598	10.6	800	14.2	7,202	16.5	12,960	8,528	4,432	88	1.6
Perry	45	10,876	0.7	128	11.1	152	13.2	1,699	17.6	2,825	2,069	756	27	2.4
Pike	920	41,354	1.2	476	11.9	605	15.1	5,000	16.0	8,933	6,536	2,397	67	1.7
Pontotoc	151	30,816	0.9	421	13.4	324	10.3	5,023	18.6	6,569	5,961	608	44	1.4
Prentiss	657	23,521	0.8	263	10.5	315	12.6	3,353	17.0	5,786	5,379	407	53	2.1
Quitman	58	6,147	0.6	68	11.3	96	15.9	868	16.2	1,639	1,179	460	15	2.4
Rankin	6,270	150,731	1.0	1,681	10.7	1,522	9.7	16,801	13.3	28,141	21,333	6,808	164	1.0
Scott	124	29,359	1.1	456	16.4	343	12.3	5,097	21.8	5,589	3,854	1,735	50	1.8
Sharkey	35	4,082	0.8	43	11.6	51	13.7	603	17.8	1,092	790	301	15	4.0
Simpson	391	23,776	0.7	323	12.5	377	14.6	3,713	17.3	6,113	4,460	1,653	64	2.5
Smith	53	13,692	0.6	186	13.1	226	15.9	2,208	17.6	3,400	2,581	820	21	1.5
Stone	1,206	16,743	0.8	226	12.2	231	12.5	2,417	17.2	3,820	2,600	1,220	15	0.8

1. Per 1,000 estimated resident population.

STATE County	COVID-19 Vaccinations, 2021–2022		Education						Money income, 2016–2020				Income and poverty, 2020			
			School enrollment and attainment, 2016–2020				Local government expenditures,[3] 2018–2019			Households				Percent below poverty level		
			Enrollment[1]		Attainment[2] (percent)						Percent					
	Number	Percent[5]	Total	Percent private	High school graduate or less	Bachelor's degree or more	Total current spending (mil dol)	Current spending per student (dollars)	Per capita income[4]	Median income (dollars)	with income of less than $50,000	with income of $200,000 or more	Median household income (dollars)	All persons	Children under 18 years	Children 5 to 17 years in families
	46	47	48	49	50	51	52	53	54	55	56	57	58	59	60	61
MISSISSIPPI	1,541,191	51.8	754,722	14.0	44.8	22.8	4,383.2	9,300	25,444	46,511	52.9	3.4	47,368	18.7	26.0	24.7
Adams	16,866	55.0	6,738	16.3	56.2	17.8	38.8	12,163	18,551	30,633	70.1	2.1	36,519	27.2	40.1	37.8
Alcorn	14,465	39.1	8,176	9.6	51.1	17.9	50.8	8,663	22,887	40,938	59.2	1.8	46,368	17.0	22.4	20.9
Amite	4,923	40.0	2,284	20.2	59.4	12.0	15.2	16,719	22,414	30,805	65.6	2.2	42,649	21.7	25.5	25.2
Attala	9,870	54.3	4,328	10.2	52.4	15.2	33.3	9,895	22,695	35,631	60.9	3.2	40,985	18.8	27.9	27.3
Benton	4,274	51.7	1,607	1.9	58.5	10.1	11.3	10,259	21,113	39,758	61.3	1.4	38,972	19.8	29.8	30.0
Bolivar	18,075	59.0	9,364	8.0	43.7	25.4	54.4	9,806	21,420	32,412	64.6	2.6	36,034	28.1	41.3	39.7
Calhoun	6,340	44.1	3,390	5.7	57.3	11.3	20.9	8,378	20,384	40,345	60.4	0.7	42,107	17.1	25.8	24.7
Carroll	4,106	41.3	1,766	30.7	48.8	14.5	9.2	9,848	26,146	46,729	51.9	2.4	46,814	15.6	22.0	21.5
Chickasaw	8,302	48.5	4,169	7.1	59.6	12.5	26.3	9,492	19,113	35,592	63.8	1.0	40,471	24.8	31.5	31.1
Choctaw	2,974	36.2	2,081	17.8	56.1	20.3	16.0	12,063	24,353	36,648	60.3	2.7	43,449	18.7	27.4	26.5
Claiborne	4,950	55.1	3,084	7.1	49.7	20.7	17.3	12,512	17,829	32,268	68.9	1.9	34,551	34.1	42.6	44.1
Clarke	8,859	57.0	3,464	13.2	54.5	12.9	25.2	9,309	23,546	38,631	59.2	2.5	38,314	19.2	32.8	35.2
Clay	9,021	46.7	4,623	12.6	51.6	20.3	28.9	9,638	22,402	33,209	65.2	1.9	36,536	21.5	33.6	32.4
Coahoma	11,462	51.8	6,252	10.3	45.4	17.7	43.9	10,691	19,649	30,761	69.4	1.7	30,047	39.6	53.1	54.9
Copiah	15,233	54.3	6,836	12.1	50.6	16.8	35.7	8,863	24,304	44,252	55.5	2.6	41,476	22.5	31.1	31.4
Covington	9,590	51.5	3,727	20.4	52.1	14.7	27.2	9,823	19,537	32,917	63.6	0.7	42,221	20.3	31.2	30.0
DeSoto	100,864	54.5	48,712	13.6	39.1	24.8	264.5	7,690	30,573	69,990	35.3	4.4	66,532	9.5	13.1	12.0
Forrest	32,653	43.6	21,929	13.5	37.4	27.7	108.2	9,905	23,590	42,298	57.7	2.4	42,082	24.9	32.8	29.9
Franklin	3,716	48.2	1,857	6.4	52.3	12.6	13.3	10,330	22,723	39,066	66.2	2.4	41,548	21.4	26.6	24.8
George	9,886	40.4	5,743	14.3	51.8	14.1	33.7	8,180	22,333	47,044	51.2	3.1	49,995	17.8	24.3	23.3
Greene	5,065	37.3	2,445	24.2	57.6	11.0	16.9	9,028	16,548	47,033	54.5	3.1	46,493	21.4	23.0	22.9
Grenada	10,920	52.6	5,011	10.3	48.0	19.8	36.3	8,931	24,625	39,952	59.8	3.3	42,577	21.4	30.3	29.2
Hancock	21,173	44.5	9,245	13.8	37.7	26.0	57.3	9,175	32,486	54,860	46.4	5.3	55,710	15.6	20.2	20.0
Harrison	115,314	55.4	50,531	13.5	39.4	23.7	296.5	8,988	26,419	48,547	51.2	2.9	47,505	16.8	22.2	19.9
Hinds	134,468	58.0	66,248	19.2	35.6	30.2	352.9	9,665	24,463	45,380	54.1	3.0	44,671	25.9	39.6	36.8
Holmes	10,249	60.3	5,072	7.3	59.1	11.7	29.4	9,510	16,898	24,074	75.5	1.3	30,003	34.5	45.2	43.9
Humphreys	4,747	58.9	2,247	15.0	59.0	14.7	15.2	9,630	24,481	28,628	72.3	3.7	30,474	33.3	51.2	47.4
Issaquena	534	40.2	97	33.0	69.5	3.4	NA	NA	19,785	28,333	56.5	1.9	32,675	43.3	52.6	58.5
Itawamba	8,117	34.7	5,342	8.7	53.3	13.9	28.9	8,263	26,024	47,649	52.5	1.7	48,097	13.9	17.8	17.2
Jackson	68,760	47.9	34,311	12.4	40.7	22.5	238.3	10,004	28,066	53,726	46.3	4.2	55,831	13.4	17.2	16.0
Jasper	8,316	50.8	3,554	14.0	54.3	14.9	24.0	10,433	22,252	37,877	60.0	2.8	42,806	19.3	28.7	28.3
Jefferson	4,972	71.1	1,778	1.6	52.7	19.1	12.5	10,801	16,602	29,524	65.1	0.7	32,683	30.8	49.7	40.8
Jefferson Davis	5,031	45.2	1,992	22.7	53.5	14.2	15.2	10,819	21,205	32,214	62.4	1.5	35,567	25.2	45.2	41.3
Jones	29,651	43.5	16,019	16.3	44.8	20.7	97.9	8,241	23,355	43,391	54.2	2.3	49,115	18.8	26.1	26.0
Kemper	4,505	46.2	2,709	11.1	55.6	12.4	14.2	14,441	19,272	30,735	73.5	2.9	37,305	25.2	35.9	35.9
Lafayette	29,700	55.0	20,132	7.0	27.0	47.1	71.0	9,849	28,567	53,318	46.3	5.6	55,786	17.6	16.7	16.2
Lamar	37,729	59.6	16,486	18.8	36.8	33.2	90.6	8,527	32,518	61,649	40.5	6.6	62,527	12.6	16.5	15.6
Lauderdale	38,141	51.5	18,028	9.9	42.0	21.1	111.3	9,662	24,892	42,922	56.2	2.6	44,821	22.5	30.8	28.1
Lawrence	6,985	55.5	2,960	6.7	52.9	17.7	18.5	8,886	23,215	36,239	59.7	2.2	36,272	19.1	25.2	23.9
Leake	11,097	48.7	5,580	21.7	56.0	15.9	23.3	8,175	21,050	36,708	62.6	2.5	43,614	21.0	33.5	31.1
Lee	37,238	43.6	21,003	11.7	41.2	26.9	148.9	9,324	27,993	55,861	45.8	4.0	57,936	13.3	18.1	16.6
Leflore	17,556	62.3	8,326	12.3	53.7	18.8	49.1	10,123	19,672	30,077	68.4	2.2	34,818	25.3	35.9	35.0
Lincoln	13,288	38.9	8,046	13.4	51.7	15.8	51.1	8,511	23,586	41,355	56.7	2.7	44,695	18.7	24.3	23.3
Lowndes	29,948	51.1	15,007	11.3	46.3	24.0	90.5	9,687	26,439	48,170	51.4	2.9	47,860	16.5	25.8	25.2
Madison	67,657	63.7	29,147	26.2	24.9	50.0	159.9	9,579	41,224	71,621	35.2	11.9	67,151	12.6	16.5	15.0
Marion	11,368	46.3	5,431	24.6	55.9	12.9	37.0	10,025	20,769	31,629	66.3	2.6	38,727	19.2	30.0	29.5
Marshall	19,227	54.5	7,716	18.4	56.1	13.9	38.8	9,095	22,819	43,411	55.5	3.3	46,117	22.7	34.3	32.4
Monroe	17,833	50.6	7,581	10.4	55.2	16.3	47.6	9,311	23,793	45,018	54.2	1.8	49,114	17.5	21.7	20.1
Montgomery	5,456	55.8	2,200	11.5	51.8	18.9	12.2	9,642	21,912	38,022	66.2	0.8	40,300	21.2	31.2	31.1
Neshoba	12,138	41.7	7,509	9.8	51.7	13.6	34.3	8,086	20,587	40,750	59.5	2.2	49,215	18.9	28.0	26.1
Newton	11,233	53.4	5,831	7.9	46.7	16.5	34.0	9,191	24,295	42,176	55.8	3.4	49,925	16.3	23.2	22.9
Noxubee	5,765	55.3	2,366	13.7	61.1	11.9	14.5	9,707	18,206	36,958	70.2	0.5	35,880	26.2	37.1	37.4
Oktibbeha	25,450	51.3	22,254	7.3	30.9	42.9	50.7	9,975	23,827	39,490	59.0	3.9	44,234	23.5	25.5	24.8
Panola	16,329	47.8	8,523	12.0	53.9	16.3	56.1	9,814	22,357	37,232	61.5	3.2	41,060	21.0	30.7	30.2
Pearl River	26,643	48.0	12,875	17.1	45.3	14.6	80.5	9,363	25,483	51,538	48.5	3.1	50,611	15.8	21.9	21.4
Perry	4,547	38.0	2,855	4.4	59.2	10.2	17.1	10,122	24,258	47,173	56.2	1.1	47,073	18.1	27.4	27.0
Pike	19,887	50.6	9,776	11.3	52.9	16.0	63.0	9,425	18,679	32,726	69.4	1.9	37,054	26.5	37.6	38.5
Pontotoc	13,402	41.7	8,131	13.8	50.8	18.2	47.4	8,011	22,605	48,980	50.6	1.8	53,272	12.8	19.3	18.6
Prentiss	10,721	42.7	6,106	6.0	49.9	14.0	32.5	8,782	21,258	40,163	60.9	1.2	44,543	16.5	22.6	22.5
Quitman	3,673	54.1	1,526	12.7	59.1	11.1	12.9	12,645	15,852	24,233	71.7	0.3	31,077	29.9	44.9	44.4
Rankin	79,770	51.4	37,222	19.1	36.0	30.3	209.1	8,895	32,106	68,310	34.7	4.9	68,583	10.0	12.6	11.8
Scott	14,145	50.3	6,637	11.6	56.9	11.3	47.0	8,137	21,357	39,971	59.3	1.9	42,069	18.3	26.1	24.5
Sharkey	2,405	55.7	1,097	12.6	55.3	18.6	9.9	12,233	20,584	35,711	60.0	1.9	46,163	30.3	45.2	42.7
Simpson	12,048	45.2	6,151	17.8	50.0	17.4	30.8	8,545	24,170	43,403	56.9	4.1	41,988	21.2	31.3	29.9
Smith	5,451	34.2	3,161	10.2	58.7	13.0	21.9	8,228	24,423	44,714	52.9	2.0	48,968	16.1	21.3	20.9
Stone	8,456	46.1	4,366	9.5	50.5	15.2	22.2	8,767	24,093	47,683	52.4	2.7	51,493	17.4	23.6	22.5

1. All persons 3 years old and over enrolled in nursery school through college. 2. Persons 25 years old and over. 3. Elementary and secondary education expenditures. 4. Based on population estimated by the American Community Survey, 2016–2020. 5. CDC percent based on 2019 population estimate.

STATE County	Personal income, 2020										Earnings, 2020		
			Per capita[1]			Supplements to wages and salaries, employer contributions (mil dol)						Contributions for government social insurance (mil dol)	
	Total (mil dol)	Percent change 2019–2020	Dollars	Rank	Wages and salaries (mil dol)	Pension and insurance	Government social insurance	Proprietors' income (mil dol)	Dividends, interest, and rent (mil dol)	Personal transfer reecipts (mil dol)	Total (mil dol)	From employee and self-employed	From employer
	62	63	64	65	66	67	68	69	70	71	72	73	74
MISSISSIPPI	124,988	7.4	42,270	X	52,220	8,834	3,993	8,388	18,513	38,826	73,434	5,329	3,993
Adams	1,160	7.4	38,331	2,646	421	65	32	100	192	469	618	51	32
Alcorn	1,437	5.9	38,956	2,570	583	95	44	77	187	509	798	63	44
Amite	460	5.5	37,692	2,715	91	16	7	26	51	179	139	11	7
Attala	683	8.7	37,962	2,690	190	34	14	43	77	266	282	25	14
Benton	290	11.4	34,691	2,953	44	9	4	12	28	114	68	8	4
Bolivar	1,289	10.2	42,767	2,099	439	81	34	119	179	501	672	49	34
Calhoun	541	11.9	38,017	2,684	119	23	9	54	66	212	205	16	9
Carroll	405	7.1	41,624	2,251	45	9	4	13	51	142	71	8	4
Chickasaw	682	10.7	40,254	2,426	203	34	15	88	106	246	340	25	15
Choctaw	313	9.2	38,813	2,590	109	23	8	19	34	119	159	12	8
Claiborne	311	9.3	34,852	2,943	242	60	17	4	35	159	323	21	17
Clarke	646	7.6	42,207	2,165	115	22	9	26	67	243	170	17	9
Clay	816	9.5	42,187	2,170	231	37	18	58	112	287	345	27	18
Coahoma	879	7.4	40,781	2,359	312	51	23	52	125	396	438	33	23
Copiah	1,017	6.3	36,414	2,835	243	48	20	35	109	390	346	32	20
Covington	708	2.0	38,250	2,659	242	42	18	48	87	267	351	28	18
DeSoto	8,616	9.2	45,764	1,689	2,860	382	224	569	946	1,743	4,035	296	224
Forrest	3,163	7.8	42,175	2,172	1,944	337	145	193	591	994	2,619	172	145
Franklin	294	6.5	38,355	2,641	72	14	5	15	34	119	106	10	5
George	944	12.1	38,668	2,609	203	39	16	51	126	278	308	28	16
Greene	419	6.6	31,102	3,074	75	16	6	5	41	155	102	12	6
Grenada	831	9.3	40,296	2,419	422	75	32	61	93	327	590	44	32
Hancock	1,894	9.6	39,455	2,512	900	172	72	91	350	604	1,234	87	72
Harrison	8,672	9.1	41,534	2,266	4,340	846	343	525	1,565	2,688	6,054	406	343
Hinds	9,906	6.3	43,452	2,017	6,522	1,081	477	754	1,817	3,049	8,834	592	477
Holmes	561	10.0	33,567	3,000	130	25	10	4	55	315	169	17	10
Humphreys	315	12.2	40,236	2,427	76	15	6	51	36	136	148	11	6
Issaquena	47	34.1	38,921	2,575	6	1	1	18	6	12	26	1	1
Itawamba	928	7.9	39,878	2,470	248	43	19	45	99	316	354	30	19
Jackson	5,979	7.8	41,575	2,257	2,799	556	217	271	903	1,736	3,844	267	217
Jasper	685	2.9	41,967	2,203	213	37	15	62	71	248	328	26	15
Jefferson	267	7.5	38,101	2,677	46	12	4	5	24	122	67	7	4
Jefferson Davis	364	7.2	33,434	3,008	64	13	5	13	39	171	95	10	5
Jones	2,747	4.1	40,402	2,402	1,226	234	97	136	396	995	1,692	122	97
Kemper	322	10.0	33,841	2,986	78	18	6	7	37	141	110	10	6
Lafayette	2,505	5.3	46,037	1,647	1,118	193	82	209	587	561	1,603	107	82
Lamar	2,774	7.7	43,227	2,037	798	118	59	220	439	604	1,194	96	59
Lauderdale	3,147	6.8	42,673	2,105	1,607	268	123	234	501	1,009	2,233	158	123
Lawrence	457	4.3	36,649	2,806	125	22	9	28	46	196	184	17	9
Leake	733	0.6	32,239	3,053	198	35	17	46	79	289	296	25	17
Lee	3,943	7.5	46,138	1,630	2,591	368	197	306	566	1,058	3,462	242	197
Leflore	1,222	10.3	43,878	1,965	592	106	46	142	201	448	887	59	46
Lincoln	1,429	6.2	42,121	2,177	554	83	42	92	162	465	772	58	42
Lowndes	2,574	7.7	44,152	1,920	1,375	241	108	145	410	765	1,869	127	108
Madison	7,308	5.2	68,381	189	2,832	370	211	688	1,534	1,144	4,103	285	211
Marion	1,013	7.4	41,433	2,277	377	57	28	155	136	377	618	50	28
Marshall	1,325	8.5	37,543	2,734	425	55	35	69	122	472	584	50	35
Monroe	1,395	8.7	39,729	2,482	459	80	37	74	200	502	649	51	37
Montgomery	381	9.8	39,432	2,519	87	16	7	24	48	166	135	12	7
Neshoba	1,117	1.5	38,507	2,625	497	82	36	102	144	390	717	52	36
Newton	782	3.5	37,484	2,739	210	41	16	40	97	302	307	24	16
Noxubee	387	6.5	37,781	2,706	102	19	8	27	41	172	157	13	8
Oktibbeha	1,885	7.4	37,853	2,701	933	179	68	78	357	507	1,258	83	68
Panola	1,272	10.2	37,593	2,727	444	73	34	112	146	470	663	53	34
Pearl River	2,246	6.4	40,201	2,433	438	81	32	102	310	769	653	62	32
Perry	438	9.0	36,953	2,789	107	18	8	17	46	176	150	10	8
Pike	1,354	8.8	34,718	2,951	568	101	44	61	167	568	774	62	44
Pontotoc	1,212	10.6	37,342	2,756	502	75	41	86	134	370	703	52	41
Prentiss	854	8.3	34,158	2,972	293	51	23	43	98	326	409	35	23
Quitman	231	14.2	34,239	2,971	37	8	3	19	26	119	67	6	3
Rankin	7,533	6.3	48,295	1,348	3,213	458	237	444	1,122	1,704	4,352	311	237
Scott	922	3.2	32,840	3,034	534	89	45	32	90	360	700	51	45
Sharkey	178	20.2	42,775	2,095	40	8	3	30	21	80	82	5	3
Simpson	1,038	3.6	38,987	2,564	246	47	19	46	128	404	358	32	19
Smith	576	0.7	36,494	2,826	132	26	10	56	58	208	225	18	10
Stone	679	8.6	37,001	2,786	182	34	14	28	95	253	258	23	14

1. Based on the resident population estimated as of July 1 of the year shown.

STATE County	Earnings, 2020 (cont.)									Social Security beneficiaries, December 2020		Supple-mental Security Income recipients, 2020	Housing units, 2021	
	Percent by selected industries													
	Farm	Mining, quarrying, and extractions	Construction	Manu-facturing	Information; professional, scientific, technical services	Retail trade	Finance, insurance, real estate, and leasing	Health care and social assistance	Govern-ment	Number	Rate[1]		Total	Percent change, 2010–2021
	75	76	77	78	79	80	81	82	83	84	85	86	87	88
MISSISSIPPI	1.5	0.7	5.9	13.2	5.7	7.5	5.2	11.9	22.6	681,219	231	114,080	1,332,050	0.8
Adams	0.4	3.3	3.8	5.4	4.6	11.8	6.8	D	13.5	8,040	280	1,614	14,910	0.2
Alcorn	0.5	0.0	4.5	19.5	2.3	11.1	4.3	12.7	19.6	10,110	294	1,552	16,221	0.3
Amite	10.8	D	7.5	12.2	D	5.4	D	D	14.9	3,650	289	560	7,278	0.6
Attala	3.4	D	10.5	15.5	3.5	10.5	4.8	D	20.1	4,935	278	851	8,313	0.4
Benton	2.1	0.0	D	12.7	5.8	D	D	D	34.1	2,165	283	372	4,081	0.5
Bolivar	10.1	0.2	3.3	12.4	D	10.3	4.4	14.2	18.3	8,120	268	2,673	13,658	0.2
Calhoun	16.2	0.1	2.3	18.1	1.7	6.8	3.7	D	15.9	4,095	315	638	6,740	0.3
Carroll	-2.1	D	20.6	10.9	D	3.9	5.6	D	23.8	3,045	308	427	4,942	0.5
Chickasaw	18.6	0.2	4.3	32.5	2.2	7.8	2.5	D	13.4	4,705	277	916	7,826	0.4
Choctaw	5.3	D	1.4	10.1	D	3.2	D	D	29.7	1,945	240	305	4,368	0.3
Claiborne	-0.2	0.0	D	2.4	D	1.8	D	D	22.2	2,205	248	621	3,940	0.7
Clarke	6.3	5.1	10.8	11.3	D	5.7	D	D	22.2	4,585	297	708	7,618	0.5
Clay	8.7	D	4.2	18.2	D	9.8	3.4	D	13.5	5,240	283	986	9,019	0.3
Coahoma	4.7	0.0	2.4	7.7	4.8	7.0	9.3	17.2	21.7	5,595	269	1,841	10,186	0.2
Copiah	0.3	1.3	4.1	28.2	2.5	8.8	2.4	D	23.7	7,020	251	1,464	12,439	0.4
Covington	3.8	D	11.7	22.0	D	7.0	3.4	5.8	20.1	4,755	260	912	8,348	0.7
DeSoto	0.2	D	9.2	7.7	3.1	11.0	4.6	10.9	11.1	32,350	171	2,948	74,107	2.3
Forrest	0.1	0.1	4.6	9.0	3.8	5.6	4.6	17.4	28.9	15,405	198	2,634	33,652	0.4
Franklin	1.5	D	D	D	D	10.7	D	D	33.1	2,195	286	360	4,308	0.5
George	1.5	D	7.5	7.0	3.9	10.6	4.3	D	29.1	5,345	216	767	10,320	0.3
Greene	-2.3	0.5	D	D	D	6.3	D	D	44.6	2,760	202	424	5,136	0.5
Grenada	1.2	0.0	3.3	26.8	D	10.9	4.2	D	18.0	6,120	286	1,252	10,419	0.1
Hancock	-0.1	D	5.6	8.5	15.3	4.7	1.9	D	36.3	10,975	238	1,208	23,240	3.3
Harrison	0.0	0.0	5.8	3.9	4.8	7.3	4.9	8.0	37.6	45,110	215	6,489	93,503	1.9
Hinds	0.0	1.0	3.0	3.9	8.2	4.5	6.9	16.9	32.4	47,975	215	10,616	106,275	0.1
Holmes	-5.8	0.0	3.8	13.9	D	7.0	7.7	D	40.0	4,615	280	1,679	7,547	0.7
Humphreys	18.9	1.1	1.5	20.2	4.2	3.5	9.1	D	16.2	2,150	285	945	3,530	0.1
Issaquena	72.5	0.0	D	0.0	D	D	D	D	12.7	175	137	58	442	0.7
Itawamba	1.6	0.0	11.4	31.9	D	6.9	2.0	8.0	17.2	6,340	266	783	10,502	0.4
Jackson	0.1	0.1	7.0	36.7	6.0	4.8	3.2	7.2	19.5	32,560	226	3,424	62,841	0.9
Jasper	5.7	D	14.6	26.8	3.8	3.9	D	D	15.7	4,600	282	730	8,079	0.6
Jefferson	0.7	0.0	D	D	D	4.3	D	12.4	40.6	1,995	277	608	3,375	0.7
Jefferson Davis	4.5	D	19.7	6.4	D	7.4	D	D	31.7	3,040	273	523	5,662	0.5
Jones	1.0	3.9	6.1	25.5	D	6.6	3.7	5.4	22.3	15,955	239	2,431	28,677	0.7
Kemper	-0.1	D	5.8	14.7	D	2.7	D	D	29.0	2,300	261	456	3,924	0.3
Lafayette	0.1	0.3	4.5	7.3	10.4	6.3	5.8	16.2	33.8	8,990	158	866	28,412	0.5
Lamar	0.4	0.5	8.8	1.7	7.8	15.0	7.2	21.7	11.8	10,940	167	1,562	27,557	0.4
Lauderdale	0.1	0.1	3.7	6.8	3.7	8.8	4.6	20.6	20.1	17,015	236	2,894	33,524	0.1
Lawrence	5.6	D	7.7	34.4	D	5.2	3.0	5.2	18.6	3,700	313	614	5,757	0.6
Leake	7.0	0.1	D	D	D	9.2	3.6	D	14.2	5,170	244	909	9,032	0.5
Lee	0.3	0.0	3.4	19.0	7.7	8.2	6.7	20.4	9.1	19,835	239	2,897	37,528	0.6
Leflore	7.0	0.0	6.7	14.0	4.0	6.1	5.8	8.5	25.0	6,760	245	2,336	12,623	0.0
Lincoln	1.4	0.7	9.0	9.8	3.3	9.8	4.2	15.5	11.9	8,480	243	1,206	15,894	0.9
Lowndes	0.6	0.3	7.1	17.5	4.0	6.0	4.9	14.7	23.0	13,310	229	2,380	27,046	0.5
Madison	0.2	1.0	4.9	14.0	16.7	9.6	11.4	9.9	7.4	20,010	182	1,987	46,780	1.3
Marion	2.3	2.3	16.3	6.6	4.1	7.5	3.4	D	11.0	6,670	274	1,099	11,145	0.5
Marshall	1.2	0.0	13.8	16.6	D	5.3	4.4	D	12.0	8,880	263	1,676	15,247	1.5
Monroe	2.5	0.2	10.9	32.6	D	6.3	1.9	D	13.2	9,570	282	1,091	16,810	0.4
Montgomery	9.3	0.0	D	D	2.5	7.1	D	D	22.9	2,980	306	632	5,316	1.9
Neshoba	3.1	D	14.0	3.6	2.0	10.9	3.5	4.2	40.2	6,710	231	1,132	12,073	0.4
Newton	4.9	D	6.8	15.0	D	5.8	2.2	D	31.4	5,400	256	611	9,133	0.6
Noxubee	7.3	0.0	4.4	26.9	0.9	11.3	2.4	3.3	24.6	2,805	277	870	4,736	0.6
Oktibbeha	0.1	D	2.9	5.8	4.9	5.9	4.2	7.3	49.6	7,735	149	1,374	25,476	0.3
Panola	0.8	0.2	7.2	14.5	2.8	11.2	5.8	D	18.1	8,510	259	1,871	14,688	0.6
Pearl River	-0.1	D	8.8	7.0	5.6	13.5	4.6	D	27.2	15,075	267	1,880	25,097	1.5
Perry	1.6	1.4	4.4	36.9	D	5.8	D	D	17.1	3,165	274	488	5,466	0.6
Pike	-0.3	0.4	2.9	18.6	3.6	11.8	5.0	9.8	25.2	9,795	245	2,119	19,101	0.4
Pontotoc	1.0	0.1	3.5	42.3	D	6.5	3.1	D	10.4	7,250	231	839	14,052	0.7
Prentiss	1.7	0.0	8.3	21.7	D	7.4	3.7	D	19.9	6,255	250	638	11,019	0.4
Quitman	20.1	D	D	D	D	2.9	7.4	D	27.3	1,795	302	557	3,032	0.1
Rankin	0.5	D	10.8	7.1	4.7	9.6	7.3	11.8	12.3	30,840	195	2,479	64,079	0.6
Scott	0.3	D	6.3	51.8	D	6.3	2.2	D	11.7	6,365	231	1,174	11,402	0.7
Sharkey	33.0	0.3	1.2	0.3	D	5.3	5.3	D	27.6	1,275	348	352	1,687	0.4
Simpson	-0.3	0.6	8.5	2.3	3.4	8.3	6.3	D	28.0	6,540	254	1,209	11,655	0.7
Smith	9.7	D	3.2	30.3	D	2.8	D	5.3	13.8	4,050	285	475	6,676	0.7
Stone	0.3	D	7.7	12.1	3.3	10.6	3.3	D	30.2	4,340	233	642	7,584	0.9

1. Per 1,000 resident population estimated as of July 1 of the year shown.

STATE County	Housing units, 2016–2020: Occupied units: Total	Owner-occupied: Percent	Owner-occupied: Median value[1]	Median owner cost as a percent of income: With a mort-gage	Median owner cost as a percent of income: Without a mort-gage[2]	Renter-occupied: Median rent[3]	Renter-occupied: Median rent as a percent of income[2]	Sub-standard units[4] (percent)	Civilian labor force, 2021: Total	Civilian labor force, 2021: Percent change, 2020–2021	Unemployment: Total	Unemployment: Rate[5]	Civilian employment[6], 2016–2020: Total	Percent: Management, business, science, and arts	Percent: Construction, production, and maintenance occupations
	89	90	91	92	93	94	95	96	97	98	99	100	101	102	103
MISSISSIPPI	1,116,649	68.8	125,500	19.7	10.3	789	29.6	2.8	1,254,239	0.9	69,838	5.6	1,243,095	33.1	28.3
Adams	11,129	62.1	94,100	23.6	11.2	587	32.2	1.0	10,634	2.0	872	8.2	10,312	32.7	23.5
Alcorn	14,610	66.8	108,600	19.6	10.0	635	25.0	1.3	15,128	0.1	721	4.8	15,127	29.2	34.2
Amite	5,416	82.4	85,200	18.7	11.5	670	33.5	2.1	4,398	0.5	319	7.3	3,838	35.4	35.1
Attala	6,890	73.4	88,700	17.8	10.0	496	41.0	3.5	6,882	0.6	413	6.0	7,253	24.8	36.6
Benton	3,183	80.9	82,800	17.5	12.2	490	18.9	2.1	3,041	1.7	195	6.4	3,363	22.0	51.9
Bolivar	12,114	56.0	98,800	20.4	13.2	666	32.6	3.5	11,364	0.1	786	6.9	10,948	35.6	23.1
Calhoun	5,771	73.3	70,500	22.2	10.6	562	23.2	3.2	5,422	-1.7	284	5.2	5,775	19.1	47.8
Carroll	4,018	84.0	93,800	19.5	12.8	440	35.8	3.3	3,471	2.4	202	5.8	3,709	36.9	30.1
Chickasaw	6,523	70.7	70,000	19.9	13.3	641	28.6	1.7	6,870	0.0	433	6.3	6,589	19.3	42.4
Choctaw	3,353	81.0	89,700	21.6	13.0	533	34.3	1.4	3,565	0.6	171	4.8	3,105	32.2	32.4
Claiborne	2,900	70.0	69,600	22.3	13.2	533	19.5	2.7	2,980	-2.7	348	11.7	2,702	31.0	28.9
Clarke	6,253	85.1	81,100	17.0	11.7	683	31.6	2.7	5,669	-0.6	356	6.3	6,223	26.5	37.6
Clay	7,728	70.1	96,700	23.3	14.5	680	30.0	0.8	8,027	2.7	574	7.2	7,296	27.4	35.8
Coahoma	8,614	55.3	67,900	20.9	11.3	582	29.4	2.1	8,022	-2.9	706	8.8	7,740	32.5	23.5
Copiah	9,568	79.0	88,900	19.4	10.0	664	28.8	4.3	10,772	1.2	699	6.5	10,861	27.9	30.9
Covington	7,042	75.2	68,100	22.9	10.3	627	32.5	2.3	8,214	-0.1	423	5.1	7,410	25.8	35.6
DeSoto	64,424	74.8	177,800	18.7	10.0	1,073	27.4	2.3	92,926	2.0	4,092	4.4	90,778	34.1	28.1
Forrest	28,116	57.9	118,100	20.1	10.0	779	33.8	3.0	33,213	2.4	1,880	5.7	33,507	34.3	23.2
Franklin	3,031	74.4	81,200	21.9	11.5	506	24.8	1.9	2,660	-1.7	182	6.8	2,668	32.9	34.9
George	8,085	82.1	119,300	21.1	10.0	792	30.6	2.6	8,749	-1.2	613	7.0	8,139	29.1	37.3
Greene	3,825	86.1	83,100	17.1	10.0	627	28.9	3.8	4,197	-1.2	318	7.6	2,909	36.9	35.9
Grenada	8,476	67.8	107,800	20.2	10.4	678	28.9	1.6	9,083	-0.7	453	5.0	8,388	38.9	24.0
Hancock	21,494	79.8	167,700	20.4	10.7	855	29.1	3.0	19,045	2.6	1,114	5.8	21,053	40.5	23.7
Harrison	80,097	57.7	157,900	21.2	10.0	910	31.1	3.0	87,481	1.2	4,784	5.5	88,366	33.2	22.3
Hinds	88,832	57.9	121,500	20.7	10.1	875	30.8	3.0	101,911	-0.1	6,323	6.2	103,407	34.6	23.3
Holmes	6,358	59.0	58,600	24.1	15.2	508	28.9	4.0	5,208	-4.3	573	11.0	5,015	24.4	38.1
Humphreys	3,197	64.3	70,500	25.6	13.6	593	31.6	2.6	2,068	-5.2	263	12.7	2,718	24.1	36.5
Issaquena	462	49.1	87,500	19.2	10.0	350	22.5	5.8	322	-1.2	30	9.3	252	14.7	44.4
Itawamba	8,525	78.5	90,700	18.2	10.0	721	24.9	2.1	10,326	1.7	443	4.3	10,091	24.4	36.9
Jackson	53,878	71.6	143,000	20.1	10.0	902	29.7	1.8	58,667	1.7	3,528	6.0	60,976	34.1	26.9
Jasper	6,616	83.6	89,300	20.9	10.4	646	30.7	4.1	5,817	-2.6	422	7.3	6,292	24.2	38.6
Jefferson	2,543	71.3	62,000	15.5	11.9	418	38.3	2.2	1,919	-1.9	318	16.6	2,309	38.2	24.2
Jefferson Davis	4,615	80.3	82,400	27.1	11.2	605	40.5	4.4	3,897	-1.2	301	7.7	4,580	23.2	39.2
Jones	24,855	73.4	101,300	19.7	10.0	714	31.4	3.9	24,598	-2.2	1,392	5.7	28,504	30.8	32.8
Kemper	3,757	74.8	78,600	26.8	15.1	380	21.6	9.2	3,282	-0.9	244	7.4	3,674	35.1	30.7
Lafayette	18,585	60.8	217,900	18.9	10.0	968	35.5	1.7	27,635	5.1	1,137	4.1	25,566	43.3	16.0
Lamar	22,467	67.6	174,600	17.3	10.0	937	27.4	2.3	31,299	3.0	1,287	4.1	28,343	38.8	21.6
Lauderdale	29,718	64.2	103,600	20.9	11.2	736	30.2	2.0	29,077	-0.5	1,573	5.4	30,317	38.0	22.4
Lawrence	5,019	74.0	104,000	22.1	14.2	762	28.2	8.9	4,613	0.2	319	6.9	4,510	32.1	37.3
Leake	8,113	72.0	86,200	19.2	10.6	688	25.3	3.6	7,900	-0.4	443	5.6	8,446	21.8	39.9
Lee	31,866	70.0	140,600	18.3	10.0	781	27.6	3.3	41,213	1.0	1,902	4.6	39,075	33.1	29.7
Leflore	9,901	54.5	86,000	19.8	13.9	593	31.5	3.0	9,941	1.9	810	8.1	9,765	26.7	30.5
Lincoln	13,127	75.9	105,100	20.2	10.0	698	26.8	4.5	14,774	3.4	742	5.0	13,210	35.2	32.1
Lowndes	22,457	62.2	136,300	19.8	10.0	808	29.1	1.5	24,797	0.6	1,464	5.9	23,965	30.5	33.0
Madison	40,179	72.2	224,300	18.7	10.0	929	30.1	2.3	52,799	0.9	2,260	4.3	52,379	49.5	17.1
Marion	9,770	79.0	94,300	21.1	14.3	548	31.6	2.4	10,268	2.8	543	5.3	8,468	26.4	37.7
Marshall	13,311	74.3	123,700	22.4	12.7	743	27.4	2.0	14,217	1.8	826	5.8	14,877	21.4	41.7
Monroe	13,482	75.6	99,100	19.1	11.1	666	24.6	1.9	15,758	1.9	820	5.2	13,378	26.9	37.9
Montgomery	4,366	67.5	87,500	17.8	12.7	575	22.6	4.4	3,877	0.4	236	6.1	3,792	30.0	38.1
Neshoba	10,495	73.0	83,600	20.3	10.0	659	27.8	7.5	10,035	-2.1	563	5.6	11,308	27.7	28.3
Newton	7,926	79.0	86,200	16.9	10.0	632	25.7	3.6	8,146	2.6	443	5.4	8,628	34.1	38.7
Noxubee	4,015	71.8	67,100	21.4	10.0	543	28.9	5.1	3,597	-4.7	321	8.9	3,914	18.8	45.0
Oktibbeha	18,849	49.7	165,000	19.8	10.0	796	42.5	1.9	22,478	3.1	1,232	5.5	20,909	45.6	16.7
Panola	12,354	67.9	82,700	22.4	11.3	715	29.0	2.4	12,578	0.2	892	7.1	11,834	33.3	31.6
Pearl River	21,321	78.9	150,800	19.4	10.3	804	26.7	3.0	23,318	1.7	1,313	5.6	22,639	31.6	31.2
Perry	4,597	80.9	108,000	21.5	10.0	622	31.2	3.5	4,234	2.5	277	6.5	4,376	20.1	40.6
Pike	14,561	68.3	95,800	21.9	13.1	744	30.1	2.4	14,405	0.0	1,024	7.1	13,693	26.7	35.7
Pontotoc	10,823	73.3	115,300	18.6	10.2	740	23.6	4.5	15,007	1.1	666	4.4	13,767	24.4	40.8
Prentiss	9,255	73.9	95,300	21.9	11.0	540	27.3	2.8	11,272	2.1	495	4.4	10,363	25.1	40.6
Quitman	3,022	59.2	54,500	22.3	13.1	535	29.2	2.6	2,335	0.3	198	8.5	2,371	21.6	30.7
Rankin	56,640	77.7	165,200	18.2	10.0	1,044	26.7	2.0	75,393	1.5	2,724	3.6	74,969	40.0	20.4
Scott	10,228	72.6	78,500	19.4	12.2	703	25.3	3.0	12,338	-0.8	575	4.7	11,434	25.3	37.9
Sharkey	1,757	61.8	63,400	18.9	14.2	578	27.6	5.8	1,401	-3.4	131	9.4	1,792	24.7	30.0
Simpson	9,647	80.1	86,600	19.5	10.0	677	30.3	2.9	10,514	1.4	547	5.2	10,801	29.6	29.5
Smith	5,888	84.7	108,300	17.6	10.0	576	20.4	1.7	6,560	0.3	296	4.5	6,070	29.3	38.7
Stone	6,304	76.5	124,500	20.0	10.0	679	28.0	4.3	6,931	1.3	376	5.4	7,458	26.7	38.8

1. Specified owner-occupied units. 2. A value of 10.0 represents 10 percent or less; a value of 50.0 represents 50 percent or more. 3. Specified renter-occupied units. 4. Overcrowded or lacking complete plumbing facilities. 5. Percent of civilian labor force. 6. Civilian employed persons 16 years old and over.

STATE County	Private nonfarm establishments, employment and payroll, 2020									Agriculture, 2017			
		Employment						Annual payroll		Farms			Farm producers whose primary occupation is farming (percent)
											Percent with:		
	Number of establish-ments	Total	Health care and social assistance	Manufac-turing	Retail trade	Finance and insurance	Professional, scientific, and technical services	Total (mil dol)	Average per employee (dollars)	Number	Fewer than 50 acres	1000 acres or more	
	104	105	106	107	108	109	110	111	112	113	114	115	116
MISSISSIPPI	58,897	949,927	176,011	147,371	135,516	32,666	30,817	38,104	40,113	34,988	31.6	6.4	37.8
Adams	748	10,098	1,898	631	1,803	320	201	359	35,507	171	40.4	7.6	41.7
Alcorn	788	11,989	2,457	2,118	2,203	330	522	453	37,803	457	39.4	3.1	29.5
Amite	179	1,589	254	400	189	33	21	63	39,610	484	26.9	2.7	43.1
Attala	343	4,393	572	771	698	121	70	175	39,809	468	28.0	4.7	33.5
Benton	55	1,176	199	196	106	13	35	38	32,706	285	24.2	3.9	29.9
Bolivar	682	8,624	1,777	1,837	1,477	207	158	337	39,115	412	21.4	27.9	63.1
Calhoun	245	1,865	167	519	392	63	27	60	32,090	518	26.4	6.8	31.4
Carroll	117	632	84	24	94	NA	13	20	31,144	446	18.2	10.1	32.4
Chickasaw	318	5,536	371	3,307	681	105	59	164	29,570	506	22.7	7.5	33.7
Choctaw	126	1,441	391	340	148	15	7	73	50,704	227	17.6	4.8	33.7
Claiborne	101	2,157	558	91	133	30	146	162	75,257	224	17.0	8.0	35.9
Clarke	216	2,087	364	480	279	71	19	64	30,675	300	27.3	3.3	33.4
Clay	338	4,455	650	833	741	119	276	158	35,551	354	19.2	7.9	27.9
Coahoma	514	5,352	1,402	590	929	198	140	193	36,137	206	18.0	42.2	63.4
Copiah	433	5,513	917	2,103	759	124	101	206	37,439	478	28.0	3.6	40.4
Covington	321	4,448	584	1,715	641	118	50	159	35,757	523	33.7	2.1	43.6
DeSoto	3,033	57,766	6,789	4,518	9,808	1,119	995	2,045	35,399	398	51.0	9.0	39.1
Forrest	1,688	33,091	8,424	3,357	5,026	696	1,391	1,412	42,658	376	51.3	1.3	30.9
Franklin	114	1,048	354	NA	145	38	17	44	42,198	198	32.3	2.5	38.2
George	330	3,708	809	387	1,041	89	122	139	37,389	492	57.3	1.2	36.6
Greene	126	889	63	8	211	25	9	42	47,016	436	44.3	2.8	35.5
Grenada	537	8,357	1,345	2,699	1,326	214	220	309	36,944	245	24.1	6.1	28.0
Hancock	730	8,753	854	926	1,659	222	1,176	361	41,234	287	51.9	1.4	40.7
Harrison	4,217	75,059	14,948	2,713	11,248	2,686	2,083	2,927	39,001	322	72.0	NA	26.1
Hinds	5,060	97,672	32,883	3,716	9,804	4,710	4,374	4,779	48,930	872	39.8	4.8	34.1
Holmes	236	2,097	603	433	377	66	49	66	31,645	496	12.1	11.3	34.1
Humphreys	131	1,454	177	555	174	133	3	43	29,389	179	17.3	29.6	52.3
Issaquena	16	85	NA	NA	NA	NA	NA	3	34,118	119	16.8	35.3	46.7
Itawamba	377	5,411	562	2,365	544	99	31	197	36,456	364	28.0	2.2	30.1
Jackson	2,296	44,908	5,505	16,440	4,914	968	1,372	2,281	50,795	473	72.1	0.4	33.4
Jasper	197	3,443	251	1,578	364	69	65	168	48,889	507	26.4	3.0	46.8
Jefferson	60	499	202	NA	80	NA	NA	22	43,601	236	20.3	5.9	42.8
Jefferson Davis	129	1,281	288	94	249	29	10	53	41,285	355	32.1	1.7	47.7
Jones	1,285	21,924	3,388	6,572	2,997	549	443	859	39,162	882	40.4	1.5	40.0
Kemper	111	1,195	227	241	119	30	4	60	50,069	313	23.3	6.4	46.9
Lafayette	1,299	17,960	3,770	1,806	3,021	618	976	650	36,210	443	21.0	4.1	31.7
Lamar	1,454	19,059	3,714	127	4,646	1,021	949	633	33,213	491	51.5	1.8	36.5
Lauderdale	1,809	29,133	7,718	1,790	4,651	907	850	1,110	38,114	305	32.1	4.6	23.6
Lawrence	170	1,841	336	657	281	101	15	90	49,010	354	34.5	1.4	43.6
Leake	320	5,000	990	1,701	745	110	55	154	30,805	573	31.2	2.1	48.4
Lee	2,506	47,079	9,125	8,975	6,481	2,089	1,212	1,858	39,467	436	31.2	4.8	34.6
Leflore	671	11,719	2,929	1,773	1,546	298	247	435	37,097	257	11.3	35.0	51.7
Lincoln	809	11,030	1,834	1,517	1,610	320	265	424	38,403	611	32.6	1.3	35.8
Lowndes	1,431	21,376	4,039	4,240	3,041	500	437	910	42,574	444	34.5	6.3	27.6
Madison	3,230	51,305	5,132	8,776	7,202	3,300	3,243	2,275	44,343	524	29.0	8.4	34.7
Marion	549	7,558	936	479	1,100	264	270	330	43,606	511	39.1	2.0	41.5
Marshall	442	7,297	769	1,359	799	213	49	310	42,516	634	32.5	7.4	33.6
Monroe	594	7,422	1,319	2,230	978	176	66	298	40,201	644	34.6	5.6	28.7
Montgomery	197	1,951	537	181	338	98	26	62	31,699	270	26.7	3.7	31.5
Neshoba	483	11,243	1,016	410	1,193	308	482	503	44,771	652	30.8	1.8	44.9
Newton	317	3,314	573	898	563	112	33	113	34,156	527	28.3	3.2	41.4
Noxubee	181	1,667	313	528	265	60	11	59	35,126	517	19.5	8.5	39.1
Oktibbeha	918	13,273	2,129	955	2,287	384	530	423	31,907	412	27.2	3.2	28.5
Panola	561	7,904	1,302	1,616	1,550	342	70	294	37,143	627	18.7	9.7	32.4
Pearl River	830	8,138	1,553	697	2,055	306	384	275	33,820	717	47.4	2.1	37.9
Perry	137	1,824	360	642	242	25	18	88	48,384	306	43.1	1.3	41.9
Pike	922	12,970	2,029	2,892	2,524	350	256	406	31,265	508	38.8	0.2	45.2
Pontotoc	498	12,937	887	8,251	1,108	200	92	420	32,470	745	31.9	3.0	26.0
Prentiss	488	5,671	799	1,953	787	177	168	177	31,235	486	28.8	6.4	29.7
Quitman	98	570	209	NA	74	42	9	17	29,496	275	15.6	23.3	43.0
Rankin	3,780	57,207	8,809	3,957	8,599	2,740	1,587	2,511	43,892	577	38.1	3.8	37.2
Scott	466	10,205	609	5,885	1,244	171	73	408	39,935	660	34.5	2.1	39.6
Sharkey	107	749	292	NA	114	42	20	26	34,151	142	14.8	39.4	48.7
Simpson	418	5,598	2,103	430	899	288	129	176	31,528	498	25.7	2.6	47.2
Smith	156	2,048	231	955	230	47	55	94	45,966	540	25.6	1.1	48.4
Stone	274	3,260	449	534	682	102	97	107	32,971	323	46.7	1.2	44.6

Agriculture, 2017 (cont.)

STATE County	Land in farms: Acreage (1,000)	Land in farms: Percent change, 2012–2017	Land in farms: Acres: Average size of farm	Land in farms: Acres: Total irrigated (1,000)	Land in farms: Acres: Total cropland (1,000)	Value of land and buildings (dollars): Average per farm	Value of land and buildings (dollars): Average per acre	Value of machinery and equipment, average per farm (dollars)	Value of products sold: Total (mil dol)	Value of products sold: Average per farm (acres)	Value of products sold: Percent from: Crops	Value of products sold: Percent from: Livestock and poultry products	Organic farms (number)	Farms with internet access (percent)	Government payments: Total ($1,000)	Government payments: Percent of farms
	117	118	119	120	121	122	123	124	125	126	127	128	129	130	131	132
MISSISSIPPI	10,415	-4.7	298	1,814.5	4,960.6	817,041	2,745	109,875	6,196.0	177,088	37.0	63.0	37	66.0	213,785	40.8
Adams	69	5.2	406	D	21.8	1,197,343	2,950	84,618	7.6	44,363	79.9	20.1	NA	74.9	464	34.5
Alcorn	83	-11.8	181	D	39.4	385,117	2,131	65,906	19.1	41,755	78.7	21.3	NA	65.2	1,186	52.1
Amite	92	-23.9	190	0.2	19.3	607,952	3,192	69,786	85.2	176,112	2.4	97.6	NA	65.3	412	19.4
Attala	118	-5.9	252	0.3	22.1	465,417	1,846	47,727	14.3	30,585	30.4	69.6	NA	54.1	1,532	53.8
Benton	76	-7.9	267	D	25.6	513,315	1,926	75,492	11.7	41,098	65.9	34.1	NA	67.0	510	35.8
Bolivar	409	4.8	993	275.0	374.6	3,004,756	3,025	475,613	208.0	504,847	99.9	0.1	NA	78.2	17,899	76.5
Calhoun	148	-15.6	286	0.8	73.8	507,660	1,776	142,990	61.8	119,373	90.9	9.1	NA	61.0	3,916	74.3
Carroll	177	5.0	398	24.5	71.9	850,650	2,138	112,567	39.4	88,312	83.1	16.9	NA	64.3	4,063	51.3
Chickasaw	172	3.8	340	5.6	92.4	681,863	2,003	127,343	103.8	205,227	41.0	59.0	2	64.6	2,850	55.5
Choctaw	64	1.5	284	1.8	10.5	522,082	1,841	53,109	12.7	55,859	43.5	56.5	NA	65.6	858	58.1
Claiborne	72	-13.0	323	2.2	18.8	874,076	2,708	100,254	8.6	38,438	73.9	26.1	NA	56.7	1,285	52.7
Clarke	103	82.8	344	0.4	9.5	768,676	2,237	65,877	29.5	98,260	4.8	95.2	NA	61.7	373	35.0
Clay	124	-4.4	351	0.1	30.6	659,679	1,877	72,201	64.0	180,720	6.5	93.5	NA	59.0	1,977	58.2
Coahoma	267	2.2	1,294	165.8	237.5	4,279,639	3,307	617,813	156.3	758,699	91.3	8.7	NA	76.2	9,650	87.9
Copiah	122	5.3	255	0.8	22.5	654,533	2,563	76,441	92.1	192,770	3.3	96.7	1	63.0	1,412	38.1
Covington	89	-15.8	170	0.1	17.0	614,485	3,605	82,308	253.8	485,304	1.3	98.7	NA	67.5	691	22.8
DeSoto	121	1.9	304	10.7	74.2	914,718	3,009	116,103	39.4	98,912	85.9	14.1	NA	64.1	2,188	23.6
Forrest	48	12.5	128	0.4	10.7	543,054	4,244	65,447	12.4	33,016	33.5	66.5	NA	70.2	544	23.4
Franklin	41	-19.1	205	0.1	6.9	650,912	3,174	55,584	3.9	19,904	32.3	67.7	NA	68.7	240	18.2
George	55	-10.0	111	1.1	24.5	415,726	3,731	68,803	18.2	36,988	80.1	19.9	NA	77.4	425	10.8
Greene	69	0.9	159	0.1	9.0	402,646	2,528	62,767	31.2	71,502	8.9	91.1	NA	66.7	376	31.7
Grenada	73	-17.2	299	1.0	21.2	657,052	2,200	89,278	11.7	47,833	76.0	24.0	NA	64.1	1,271	50.2
Hancock	32	28.4	113	0.1	7.3	436,624	3,861	66,054	4.5	15,603	24.3	75.7	NA	79.8	66	5.2
Harrison	16	-34.3	49	0.1	4.1	412,695	8,374	52,978	3.4	10,519	70.0	30.0	3	72.4	39	4.3
Hinds	213	-15.1	244	0.5	54.1	804,312	3,292	61,962	57.4	65,807	29.1	70.9	NA	61.2	3,604	42.7
Holmes	241	1.6	487	58.4	118.6	1,180,015	2,425	120,527	66.3	133,647	96.1	3.9	NA	61.3	5,626	58.5
Humphreys	164	-15.3	917	72.1	134.1	2,998,513	3,270	419,098	95.9	535,721	75.7	24.3	NA	82.1	6,512	81.6
Issaquena	131	5.5	1,103	26.3	87.2	3,018,677	2,737	610,300	D	D	D	D	NA	63.9	2,740	71.4
Itawamba	75	-20.5	207	0.1	25.7	354,780	1,712	59,971	7.9	21,791	82.0	18.0	1	69.0	950	51.9
Jackson	36	-3.0	77	0.2	8.4	386,270	5,012	64,869	7.6	16,163	47.1	52.9	3	75.7	97	7.0
Jasper	111	14.3	219	0.1	15.1	614,597	2,805	98,483	191.2	377,083	0.9	99.1	NA	64.9	1,301	43.6
Jefferson	60	-30.4	253	0.1	11.4	636,903	2,520	51,954	30.5	129,186	9.8	90.2	NA	53.8	541	26.7
Jefferson Davis	55	-6.4	156	0.1	12.6	399,812	2,570	58,480	47.8	134,758	4.1	95.9	NA	71.3	158	14.1
Jones	123	-2.5	139	0.5	22.7	527,503	3,786	71,665	221.1	250,719	1.8	98.2	NA	68.6	1,299	17.7
Kemper	112	-9.5	358	D	15.5	723,481	2,022	59,748	19.3	61,802	5.7	94.3	NA	60.1	1,199	46.3
Lafayette	105	-3.9	236	0.6	29.0	646,938	2,740	57,637	9.4	21,176	72.0	28.0	2	69.1	1,031	42.7
Lamar	73	14.3	149	0.2	11.0	529,531	3,548	59,665	53.2	108,360	5.4	94.6	NA	81.9	510	16.7
Lauderdale	82	19.0	269	0.7	18.1	553,284	2,055	56,867	3.9	12,767	18.7	81.3	NA	73.4	312	20.7
Lawrence	56	-22.4	159	0.2	17.5	511,947	3,211	81,082	91.2	257,644	3.6	96.4	NA	68.9	490	11.0
Leake	95	-10.7	165	0.0	27.2	500,892	3,027	76,068	328.0	572,438	1.4	98.6	NA	64.2	793	43.6
Lee	123	-7.5	282	0.8	72.9	517,010	1,832	102,991	32.6	74,773	75.5	24.5	NA	70.6	2,112	37.2
Leflore	299	1.9	1,163	167.0	243.8	3,373,801	2,902	470,366	210.0	817,062	67.8	32.2	NA	67.7	13,507	85.6
Lincoln	101	-7.2	165	0.1	14.9	506,676	3,071	60,954	72.2	118,187	2.5	97.5	7	66.6	239	12.6
Lowndes	139	16.6	314	7.6	64.6	793,469	2,530	119,488	60.8	136,890	38.5	61.5	NA	75.9	2,939	50.7
Madison	157	-22.5	300	D	50.1	789,468	2,628	65,717	20.1	38,353	78.5	21.5	NA	66.2	2,653	38.7
Marion	81	-0.5	159	0.1	18.8	458,585	2,881	75,413	91.2	178,462	2.5	97.5	3	67.1	1,174	27.6
Marshall	212	4.4	335	2.3	72.4	804,766	2,403	72,214	24.7	38,882	76.2	23.8	NA	60.3	2,168	35.0
Monroe	186	-18.6	288	0.3	90.4	633,479	2,198	97,367	39.7	61,691	71.7	28.3	NA	62.4	3,401	45.7
Montgomery	68	-30.4	251	0.5	20.9	501,369	1,999	67,717	14.7	54,567	55.2	44.8	NA	62.2	840	51.1
Neshoba	112	10.8	172	0.1	25.9	459,112	2,664	77,883	248.7	381,434	1.5	98.5	2	71.0	741	29.0
Newton	105	-3.7	199	0.8	25.1	472,560	2,371	79,938	116.6	221,264	4.6	95.4	NA	71.2	1,325	37.6
Noxubee	203	-4.7	393	24.4	98.1	995,194	2,533	173,217	124.7	241,246	39.2	60.8	NA	62.7	4,890	59.8
Oktibbeha	95	-9.1	231	0.3	21.0	645,315	2,796	69,080	17.1	41,398	17.5	82.5	NA	69.4	1,124	38.6
Panola	226	-17.2	360	29.5	113.2	886,959	2,463	108,817	55.0	87,748	86.9	13.1	NA	61.7	7,916	55.2
Pearl River	105	-11.2	147	1.1	17.8	519,572	3,545	56,063	17.5	24,379	45.8	54.2	3	74.1	402	9.2
Perry	44	1.3	144	0.4	10.6	462,067	3,210	67,901	33.7	110,196	11.6	88.4	NA	60.8	209	27.5
Pike	66	-8.6	130	0.1	15.7	482,938	3,726	83,431	70.4	138,594	3.9	96.1	2	65.2	285	12.6
Pontotoc	137	-10.1	184	D	65.1	362,339	1,968	64,218	20.8	27,858	80.2	19.8	NA	52.1	2,165	51.9
Prentiss	109	16.5	223	0.5	41.5	457,174	2,046	70,477	21.2	43,621	58.6	41.4	NA	52.7	1,606	62.1
Quitman	199	-4.9	722	80.1	150.4	2,065,226	2,861	210,343	D	D	D	D	NA	61.5	9,821	93.5
Rankin	121	-3.6	210	0.1	37.3	693,646	3,300	90,066	114.0	197,615	7.7	92.3	NA	72.1	2,052	28.9
Scott	120	4.2	182	0.2	30.7	462,657	2,546	95,592	272.7	413,121	2.1	97.9	NA	65.3	884	35.9
Sharkey	172	10.9	1,214	70.6	140.8	4,016,682	3,310	476,427	86.5	608,972	93.3	6.7	NA	67.6	5,700	81.0
Simpson	95	-13.2	191	0.3	21.8	526,657	2,758	81,714	227.4	456,665	2.4	97.6	NA	63.9	535	29.7
Smith	83	-23.6	153	0.7	24.0	440,459	2,873	82,278	218.6	404,798	1.8	98.2	NA	61.5	1,135	31.5
Stone	46	-0.1	141	0.3	10.4	467,314	3,308	57,118	12.4	38,387	67.5	32.5	NA	74.3	408	11.8

Table B. States and Counties — **Water Use, Wholesale Trade, Retail Trade, and Real Estate**

STATE County	Water use, 2015		Wholesale Trade[1], 2017				Retail Trade[2], 2017				Real estate and rental and leasing,[2] 2017			
	Public supply water withdrawn (mil gal/ day)	Public supply gallons withdrawn per person per day	Number of establish- ments	Number of employees	Sales (mil dol)	Average payroll (mil dol)	Number of establish- ments	Number of employees	Sales (mil dol)	Average payroll (mil dol)	Number of establish- ments	Number of employees	Sales (mil dol)	Average payroll (mil dol)
	133	134	135	136	137	138	139	140	141	142	143	144	145	146
MISSISSIPPI	400.4	133.8	2,347	32,051	31,126.7	1,616.8	11,525	141,410	36,920.6	3,384.5	2,403	9,683	1,996.9	345.4
Adams	4.9	157.4	42	289	196.9	10.7	141	1,895	472.7	47.9	41	128	23.8	4.0
Alcorn	4.8	127.0	36	546	263.8	25.7	178	2,254	548.8	56.1	20	206	21.9	6.5
Amite	1.3	106.6	5	34	26.9	1.5	31	201	45.7	4.6	3	6	0.3	0.1
Attala	2.2	117.6	12	56	18.1	2.1	72	714	188.0	16.8	12	32	6.2	1.0
Benton	0.5	59.9	NA	NA	NA	NA	15	113	27.4	2.5	NA	NA	NA	NA
Bolivar	4.2	124.8	26	253	342.5	12.2	146	1,469	381.6	33.0	44	125	17.4	3.0
Calhoun	2.3	154.9	13	157	94.9	5.9	62	434	96.3	9.0	6	D	0.8	D
Carroll	0.9	84.0	D	D	D	D	22	106	30.6	2.0	4	6	1.1	0.1
Chickasaw	1.8	104.5	12	78	67.6	3.1	79	679	153.2	13.4	5	63	13.4	3.0
Choctaw	1.0	115.7	NA	NA	NA	NA	25	165	30.4	3.0	NA	NA	NA	NA
Claiborne	0.7	72.1	NA	NA	NA	NA	20	120	33.4	3.3	NA	NA	NA	NA
Clarke	2.0	125.0	NA	NA	NA	NA	49	296	63.4	6.0	NA	NA	NA	NA
Clay	2.5	126.2	11	164	143.4	5.8	83	773	183.5	17.0	10	23	3.9	0.5
Coahoma	3.8	155.6	28	322	491.1	15.2	101	925	236.0	21.7	38	93	20.8	2.6
Copiah	3.8	131.7	11	102	50.1	3.2	88	855	199.1	20.0	11	32	5.4	0.8
Covington	1.9	95.2	12	77	90.4	3.2	77	614	246.2	16.1	4	30	2.8	0.9
DeSoto	19.5	112.6	121	3,258	4,857.6	172.5	602	9,783	2,862.1	254.0	119	409	146.1	17.6
Forrest	12.1	159.3	76	836	664.8	38.7	342	4,033	1,155.7	106.7	95	444	84.6	16.7
Franklin	1.0	126.6	4	45	23.9	2.8	20	114	32.6	2.4	D	D	D	0.2
George	1.2	52.6	10	71	50.9	2.9	79	988	262.7	21.8	9	25	4.3	0.6
Greene	1.9	137.6	NA	NA	NA	NA	29	230	53.5	4.4	NA	NA	NA	NA
Grenada	4.0	183.5	D	D	D	6.2	118	1,390	455.1	37.7	24	77	20.4	2.9
Hancock	4.4	94.6	11	21	16.1	0.9	131	1,524	364.5	34.9	35	80	19.1	2.8
Harrison	20.8	103.5	147	1,363	716.9	66.6	807	11,916	3,124.5	286.3	221	1,007	244.8	34.8
Hinds	50.5	208.1	247	3,059	2,998.3	181.2	795	10,782	3,330.6	307.1	263	1,039	259.9	48.5
Holmes	2.2	120.0	9	53	62.3	2.5	66	422	87.2	8.7	14	33	4.0	0.5
Humphreys	0.9	106.1	6	36	59.5	1.6	27	220	48.9	4.7	D	D	D	0.2
Issaquena	0.1	89.8	NA	NA	NA	NA	NA	NA	NA	NA	NA	NA	NA	NA
Itawamba	10.4	440.1	10	216	53.0	5.7	70	682	164.4	15.8	7	18	1.9	0.3
Jackson	14.5	102.5	61	375	271.3	18.9	417	5,034	1,336.2	123.8	100	450	73.5	15.0
Jasper	3.3	198.6	8	20	25.5	1.2	39	337	74.5	8.5	NA	NA	NA	NA
Jefferson	0.7	95.9	NA	NA	NA	NA	12	81	13.6	1.4	NA	NA	NA	NA
Jefferson Davis	1.5	124.3	NA	NA	NA	NA	36	239	61.2	5.4	NA	NA	NA	NA
Jones	11.8	172.2	66	757	344.6	29.2	259	3,081	857.0	74.5	D	D	D	D
Kemper	1.8	178.6	NA	NA	NA	NA	16	134	31.8	2.8	D	D	D	D
Lafayette	5.3	99.3	28	313	229.5	11.7	230	3,165	743.7	66.9	73	251	59.8	9.1
Lamar	5.9	97.7	D	D	D	D	311	5,000	1,213.1	110.4	D	D	D	D
Lauderdale	11.0	139.4	69	1,584	1,928.8	70.1	382	4,954	1,271.5	117.2	76	355	75.2	13.3
Lawrence	1.7	136.3	NA	NA	NA	NA	31	257	53.6	5.3	NA	NA	NA	NA
Leake	2.2	97.1	3	44	12.9	1.8	85	767	179.4	17.6	6	17	1.3	0.3
Lee	4.3	50.3	152	2,135	1,232.1	99.9	505	7,338	1,759.1	169.5	100	436	91.9	14.0
Leflore	4.2	133.9	D	D	D	D	163	1,676	396.5	34.6	41	127	20.0	3.6
Lincoln	4.0	116.6	D	D	D	31.8	159	1,939	553.7	53.0	22	76	10.7	2.3
Lowndes	8.4	140.2	70	1,287	1,005.6	75.1	306	3,582	862.1	82.0	60	211	43.8	7.5
Madison	16.5	159.7	134	2,414	3,481.4	142.8	522	7,094	1,798.9	173.9	170	915	169.9	39.7
Marion	3.6	141.6	16	139	122.9	5.3	107	1,199	268.2	26.6	16	43	11.8	1.6
Marshall	2.5	70.4	20	504	210.4	19.2	108	838	214.9	19.9	7	15	2.6	0.3
Monroe	3.6	101.3	23	243	130.8	12.4	112	1,017	254.7	23.4	15	39	6.4	1.3
Montgomery	1.3	128.1	D	D	D	D	44	499	123.7	9.1	NA	NA	NA	NA
Neshoba	4.5	151.7	16	324	328.8	15.2	111	1,213	281.0	28.0	10	26	2.3	0.8
Newton	2.5	113.6	9	42	16.1	1.4	67	617	142.4	14.5	D	D	D	D
Noxubee	1.4	124.1	9	54	43.7	2.2	35	258	61.6	5.8	NA	NA	NA	NA
Oktibbeha	7.6	152.2	16	828	559.6	33.4	176	2,391	529.4	51.7	58	271	55.8	7.8
Panola	3.4	98.0	24	412	537.9	22.6	139	1,531	408.9	35.7	11	98	18.4	3.6
Pearl River	4.6	83.0	24	177	71.6	8.9	176	2,142	657.0	53.2	20	60	9.6	1.4
Perry	1.2	100.2	NA	NA	NA	NA	32	359	83.8	8.3	NA	NA	NA	NA
Pike	5.9	147.4	39	334	166.1	13.9	208	2,486	664.8	59.4	39	171	25.8	3.7
Pontotoc	3.5	111.6	18	130	74.2	4.4	95	1,071	326.8	25.3	9	30	4.4	0.5
Prentiss	3.3	128.8	8	41	5.5	0.9	97	832	185.8	17.4	16	44	5.4	1.3
Quitman	0.7	98.9	3	16	24.1	0.7	22	100	18.5	1.7	7	D	1.6	D
Rankin	17.7	118.5	208	3,908	2,633.0	222.3	613	9,859	2,676.8	231.3	185	904	183.5	32.9
Scott	8.0	283.7	14	46	81.3	1.5	124	1,195	296.1	28.1	10	44	5.1	1.0
Sharkey	0.5	113.4	13	78	106.2	4.5	19	150	30.3	3.0	7	D	2.5	D
Simpson	3.6	132.2	10	88	23.5	2.8	89	898	229.5	20.8	9	34	6.7	1.2
Smith	1.2	73.5	4	39	19.5	1.5	29	204	52.0	4.4	NA	NA	NA	NA
Stone	1.5	80.8	11	27	13.0	1.0	61	700	194.7	17.3	8	D	1.8	D

1 Merchant wholesalers, except manufacturers' sales branches and offices. 2. Employer establishments.

Table B. States and Counties — **Professional Services, Manufacturing, and Accommodation and Food Services**

STATE County	Professional, scientific, and technical services, 2017				Manufacturing, 2017				Accommodation and food services, 2017			
	Number of establish-ments	Number of employees	Sales (mil dol)	Average payroll (mil dol)	Number of establish-ments	Number of employees	Sales (mil dol)	Average payroll (mil dol)	Number of establis-hments	Number of employees	Sales (mil dol)	Annual payroll (mil dol)
	147	148	149	150	151	152	153	154	155	156	157	158
MISSISSIPPI	4,727	30,333	4,577.8	1,610.0	2,142	138,460	60,906.5	6,653.7	5,651	129,836	8,181.3	2,134.3
Adams	53	229	25.5	9.0	21	497	130.3	23.1	90	1,809	102.1	27.7
Alcorn	43	801	83.9	32.9	35	2,415	1,034.9	98.2	74	1,237	65.4	17.4
Amite	6	21	2.0	0.7	9	337	78.9	15.8	7	41	2.9	0.6
Attala	31	71	7.0	2.3	13	521	144.6	22.4	32	415	18.3	4.5
Benton	D	D	D	D	6	102	32.3	5.8	NA	NA	NA	NA
Bolivar	49	153	23.5	7.9	19	1,381	471.1	73.1	60	1,059	48.7	12.3
Calhoun	18	33	2.9	0.9	15	672	292.7	26.5	9	60	3.7	1.0
Carroll	6	8	1.6	0.4	6	20	2.7	0.7	4	10	0.7	0.1
Chickasaw	13	62	6.2	2.2	37	3,348	558.7	120.8	D	D	D	D
Choctaw	7	17	1.6	0.5	10	249	74.7	9.6	D	D	D	D
Claiborne	D	D	D	D	4	100	45.3	5.1	11	164	8.8	1.9
Clarke	8	38	1.8	0.5	10	373	125.9	14.5	14	195	9.5	2.2
Clay	D	D	D	D	16	720	384.5	47.0	39	642	26.5	7.6
Coahoma	D	D	D	D	15	569	178.0	25.2	43	1,027	76.6	17.2
Copiah	27	89	10.9	3.7	18	1,828	610.2	76.8	33	435	21.0	4.7
Covington	14	41	6.0	1.5	11	1,386	466.5	44.1	D	D	D	5.8
DeSoto	187	902	128.0	37.7	95	4,174	1,304.8	198.6	360	8,333	428.0	113.9
Forrest	D	D	D	D	68	3,493	1,003.6	151.6	D	D	D	D
Franklin	7	19	2.1	0.6	D	D	D	D	4	D	0.3	D
George	18	107	13.0	3.9	13	277	28.4	16.8	37	505	26.6	6.7
Greene	4	14	0.9	0.2	3	7	1.1	0.3	8	78	4.1	1.3
Grenada	34	191	24.8	8.3	25	2,803	896.8	123.7	60	1,055	46.6	12.6
Hancock	111	1,545	241.6	103.0	27	787	1,020.4	59.2	93	2,240	216.9	50.4
Harrison	D	D	D	D	101	2,546	1,360.8	162.7	510	21,999	1,974.3	495.4
Hinds	670	5,425	884.4	331.2	124	3,523	1,176.8	181.7	495	10,910	537.2	147.3
Holmes	12	40	9.8	1.8	5	505	207.7	14.9	18	147	6.2	1.6
Humphreys	D	D	1.5	D	D	D	D	D	5	131	4.3	1.1
Issaquena	NA	NA	NA	NA	NA	NA	NA	NA	NA	NA	NA	NA
Itawamba	11	30	8.0	2.1	34	2,204	706.7	87.0	D	D	D	D
Jackson	215	1,527	209.6	83.3	68	14,576	11,953.5	1,043.0	267	4,435	211.3	60.5
Jasper	15	49	5.2	1.5	17	1,235	369.9	53.7	11	121	6.0	1.3
Jefferson	NA	NA	NA	NA	NA	NA	NA	NA	D	D	D	0.2
Jefferson Davis	10	16	0.9	0.3	D	46	D	D	11	120	4.6	1.3
Jones	82	465	64.8	21.0	58	5,686	1,646.5	267.5	114	1,957	89.9	22.8
Kemper	5	14	0.6	0.1	7	210	26.8	6.6	12	88	3.5	0.9
Lafayette	D	D	D	D	23	1,796	259.8	81.4	199	4,000	217.2	68.0
Lamar	120	849	107.2	39.7	22	137	30.1	5.0	D	D	D	D
Lauderdale	D	D	D	D	56	1,925	659.0	81.1	175	3,990	190.1	51.6
Lawrence	11	13	2.3	0.5	D	674	D	51.0	10	D	3.7	D
Leake	19	52	6.3	1.5	D	D	D	D	24	385	16.1	4.3
Lee	184	1,071	134.1	54.1	133	8,457	3,026.1	358.0	234	4,717	235.5	65.5
Leflore	42	267	44.9	12.8	22	2,101	596.4	82.1	72	1,333	69.9	20.3
Lincoln	53	317	54.3	13.6	36	879	317.1	49.7	64	1,146	56.3	14.2
Lowndes	96	501	58.4	26.1	56	3,848	3,609.8	247.9	125	2,489	112.2	31.9
Madison	409	3,168	719.6	228.3	56	7,823	5,880.2	433.8	270	5,931	296.1	83.4
Marion	36	217	34.5	12.9	19	649	88.1	22.8	38	636	28.6	6.6
Marshall	16	61	6.8	1.9	29	748	317.0	49.4	D	D	D	D
Monroe	30	79	13.2	2.6	42	2,446	1,049.1	114.2	D	D	D	D
Montgomery	10	28	3.4	0.7	8	148	36.9	8.2	D	D	D	D
Neshoba	31	379	47.6	19.5	15	340	191.3	15.4	43	3,132	398.3	95.9
Newton	23	51	4.0	1.6	16	932	181.6	43.5	26	345	15.5	4.2
Noxubee	4	10	0.9	0.3	16	484	174.8	19.9	D	D	D	D
Oktibbeha	77	495	70.4	23.8	25	1,105	402.0	46.4	119	2,999	140.7	41.4
Panola	21	75	13.1	2.8	27	1,518	427.2	67.7	57	999	47.6	12.6
Pearl River	59	353	38.8	16.5	42	587	236.6	27.0	78	1,318	55.7	15.3
Perry	13	18	2.5	0.7	5	612	221.0	43.0	4	44	2.0	0.5
Pike	D	D	D	D	27	2,440	650.6	85.9	81	1,637	72.5	19.0
Pontotoc	22	91	11.0	4.0	61	7,262	1,634.9	267.3	D	D	D	D
Prentiss	31	162	28.4	5.7	40	1,714	873.8	67.8	35	573	26.4	6.3
Quitman	D	D	D	D	NA	NA	NA	NA	4	55	2.0	0.5
Rankin	310	1,522	219.1	74.8	120	3,691	1,553.5	202.1	326	7,005	386.2	100.4
Scott	30	83	6.6	2.1	22	6,221	1,703.9	222.9	46	731	33.3	8.3
Sharkey	8	16	1.4	0.4	NA	NA	NA	NA	D	D	D	0.6
Simpson	30	107	13.2	4.1	9	252	95.2	9.6	40	644	33.2	7.7
Smith	D	D	9.7	D	13	859	317.8	41.5	D	D	D	0.8
Stone	20	103	10.0	4.4	10	617	181.0	27.4	28	481	21.8	5.2

STATE County	Health care and social assistance, 2017				Other services, 2017				Nonemployer businesses, 2019		Value of residential construction authorized by building permits, 2021	
	Number of establish-ments	Number of employees	Receipts (mil dol)	Annual payroll (mil dol)	Number of establish-ments	Number of employees	Receipts (mil dol)	Annual payroll (mil dol)	Number	Receipts (mil dol)	New construction ($1,000)	Number of housing units
	159	160	161	162	163	164	165	166	167	168	169	170
MISSISSIPPI	6,391	169,010	18,752.3	7,533.3	3,417	18,345	2,278.6	603.2	228,123	9,530.0	1,541,523	7,988
Adams	94	1,871	198.8	66.1	37	166	16.2	4.5	2,430	97.1	585	4
Alcorn	105	2,378	288.9	85.7	47	152	17.1	4.1	2,462	136.2	2,692	15
Amite	13	210	13.1	5.3	7	26	2.3	0.6	875	39.2	0	0
Attala	29	559	57.5	18.7	D	D	D	D	1,329	54.0	1,534	25
Benton	5	139	12.8	4.4	D	D	D	D	593	24.8	0	0
Bolivar	83	1,811	172.2	65.8	50	198	17.1	4.2	2,185	79.2	3,649	26
Calhoun	25	204	16.7	7.1	D	D	4.3	D	970	39.5	0	0
Carroll	7	124	6.7	2.7	D	D	D	D	739	31.1	NA	NA
Chickasaw	23	429	24.9	13.6	18	44	3.5	0.8	1,137	44.6	160	2
Choctaw	8	377	33.5	14.4	D	D	1.9	D	685	24.9	0	0
Claiborne	12	623	36.1	16.7	6	40	2.4	0.6	363	12.4	0	0
Clarke	18	340	31.1	14.1	D	D	3.5	D	1,055	36.9	0	0
Clay	28	658	67.0	25.0	21	92	10.0	2.6	1,349	53.6	962	4
Coahoma	75	1,545	160.6	54.4	D	D	D	D	1,737	60.8	4,404	26
Copiah	52	763	55.7	21.1	D	D	D	1.9	2,127	72.9	765	5
Covington	24	507	47.2	19.4	D	D	D	D	1,548	61.4	0	0
DeSoto	290	5,553	727.1	254.4	163	1,003	99.3	28.0	15,205	676.2	326,257	1,808
Forrest	201	7,843	1,029.9	449.8	95	553	56.1	14.2	5,672	241.4	23,373	123
Franklin	11	388	30.7	12.8	NA	NA	NA	NA	598	16.3	0	0
George	32	791	80.7	34.1	D	D	D	D	1,513	55.4	2,189	19
Greene	D	D	D	D	D	D	D	1.9	710	24.9	418	2
Grenada	61	1,228	109.0	43.8	D	D	D	D	1,517	58.8	400	2
Hancock	50	986	92.5	36.5	33	235	22.7	6.3	3,635	152.8	129,933	827
Harrison	486	14,330	1,892.6	822.5	269	1,567	162.2	46.2	15,902	693.5	252,303	1,110
Hinds	719	31,975	3,912.0	1,773.7	384	2,465	334.8	99.1	20,855	795.5	52,752	264
Holmes	30	511	46.4	17.5	10	120	11.3	4.3	1,219	35.6	5,263	22
Humphreys	15	153	10.3	4.5	D	D	D	0.3	605	21.2	0	0
Issaquena	NA	NA	NA	NA	NA	NA	NA	NA	78	2.3	NA	NA
Itawamba	32	558	39.3	18.4	D	D	D	D	1,294	65.1	1,071	7
Jackson	307	5,720	653.5	280.6	134	703	97.4	19.7	9,996	379.8	123,903	770
Jasper	9	254	16.2	8.5	D	D	D	D	1,097	34.4	0	0
Jefferson	11	232	19.2	7.6	D	D	0.8	D	572	12.5	0	0
Jefferson Davis	12	265	22.7	10.0	D	D	1.5	D	850	22.9	0	0
Jones	111	3,244	290.5	140.2	D	D	D	D	4,704	204.1	9,122	81
Kemper	12	211	13.7	6.3	D	D	0.2	D	643	17.2	NA	NA
Lafayette	157	2,893	470.3	129.3	72	444	128.4	21.3	4,942	268.6	42,050	177
Lamar	D	D	D	D	D	D	D	D	5,182	267.7	4,708	30
Lauderdale	220	6,992	917.1	329.0	117	505	55.4	14.2	5,124	185.9	3,414	13
Lawrence	25	341	29.3	11.2	D	D	D	D	794	27.5	0	0
Leake	27	618	54.3	21.4	11	33	4.4	1.3	1,345	45.4	0	0
Lee	304	9,342	1,223.7	452.2	124	1,042	106.7	40.8	6,820	309.8	31,286	131
Leflore	70	2,817	203.2	96.2	D	D	D	D	1,722	73.6	3,880	10
Lincoln	78	1,791	204.0	73.0	48	303	27.8	10.2	2,709	109.4	3,090	14
Lowndes	166	3,253	417.8	129.7	89	418	46.7	12.2	4,050	138.4	10,162	100
Madison	298	8,737	539.7	223.8	159	1,269	192.8	57.5	12,281	740.4	211,790	733
Marion	45	952	63.7	29.3	32	311	34.7	9.6	1,959	74.0	0	0
Marshall	32	863	180.6	25.1	D	D	D	D	2,959	122.9	50,732	245
Monroe	73	1,408	144.4	49.0	38	162	15.6	3.6	2,092	81.6	1,476	9
Montgomery	20	738	53.0	23.9	17	61	5.7	1.4	637	20.8	3,132	118
Neshoba	37	992	92.4	38.5	D	D	D	D	1,880	63.3	0	0
Newton	31	513	44.3	15.2	18	53	5.1	1.3	1,360	52.1	0	0
Noxubee	13	307	25.4	9.0	10	15	2.0	0.4	955	30.5	0	0
Oktibbeha	91	2,026	186.6	79.8	62	374	123.0	14.4	3,294	119.0	14,397	77
Panola	65	1,694	125.5	48.5	22	57	6.9	1.7	2,795	108.3	683	7
Pearl River	98	1,516	125.2	52.6	54	220	20.0	5.2	4,278	179.7	32,408	270
Perry	D	D	D	D	D	D	D	D	738	27.8	0	0
Pike	114	2,612	233.6	100.0	51	245	24.1	6.5	3,373	123.4	407	3
Pontotoc	45	752	61.0	26.1	D	D	D	D	2,199	94.9	3,798	65
Prentiss	46	696	61.5	24.5	D	D	D	D	1,544	55.2	3,433	11
Quitman	13	159	8.6	4.3	D	D	D	0.2	515	14.9	209	1
Rankin	367	7,993	1,000.3	377.9	223	1,142	149.2	43.7	13,405	620.5	82,504	345
Scott	35	706	58.5	21.4	32	93	9.2	2.1	1,747	62.2	1,249	7
Sharkey	11	259	19.4	7.2	D	D	D	1.1	368	11.7	0	0
Simpson	51	2,201	154.7	60.2	D	D	D	D	1,915	83.2	9,361	47
Smith	7	224	15.2	6.3	D	D	D	0.8	950	35.2	350	4
Stone	25	524	47.8	18.6	D	D	D	D	1,309	59.4	9,657	62

STATE County	Government employment and payroll, 2017									Local government finances, 2017				
			March payroll (percent of total)							General revenue				
												Taxes		
													Per capita[1] (dollars)	
	Full-time equivalent employees	March payroll (dollars)	Administration, judicial, and legal	Police and corrections	Fire protection	Highways and transportation	Health and welfare	Natural resources and utilities	Education and libraries	Total (mil dol)	Intergovernmental (mil dol)	Total (mil dol)	Total	Property
	171	172	173	174	175	176	177	178	179	180	181	182	183	184
MISSISSIPPI	X	X	X	X	X	X	X	X	X	X	X	X	X	X
Adams	1,154	3,640,747	9.8	19.4	4.1	8.0	2.0	7.8	48.6	104.3	46.1	38.5	1,225	1,077
Alcorn	2,738	9,492,949	2.6	3.6	1.4	0.9	63.9	1.4	26.2	304.7	71.1	26.8	722	693
Amite	303	826,040	13.7	8.8	0.0	5.6	0.0	4.4	65.2	22.5	11.2	7.3	587	582
Attala	904	2,596,804	5.9	4.4	3.4	4.4	22.7	1.8	56.7	68.0	27.6	18.4	997	969
Benton	306	790,316	11.4	7.6	0.6	4.6	0.0	3.4	71.0	21.0	15.5	4.4	528	507
Bolivar	1,507	4,354,776	6.3	13.4	0.4	4.9	1.1	3.6	69.1	126.3	62.6	40.4	1,275	1,213
Calhoun	491	1,342,068	7.2	6.2	0.5	3.3	0.0	5.2	75.5	54.6	22.2	10.1	698	680
Carroll	342	902,475	13.2	17.6	0.2	7.6	0.0	2.8	58.5	22.4	8.6	7.5	739	720
Chickasaw	837	2,241,340	7.3	10.5	1.8	3.3	8.8	6.2	61.2	53.1	27.3	13.8	802	767
Choctaw	368	1,024,805	14.0	5.2	0.3	3.1	0.0	2.6	74.8	31.7	13.1	10.7	1,294	1,281
Claiborne	406	1,271,692	7.2	7.6	2.2	4.6	23.6	2.8	50.9	29.7	19.7	6.9	766	742
Clarke	691	1,751,565	9.6	6.4	0.9	5.3	0.1	6.5	69.8	43.5	21.9	17.5	1,105	1,078
Clay	821	2,240,934	3.8	6.5	3.8	3.1	11.0	2.3	69.1	56.3	34.3	17.6	897	870
Coahoma	1,409	4,539,054	5.6	9.0	3.4	3.0	0.9	10.0	65.6	117.7	69.5	29.2	1,258	1,188
Copiah	1,373	4,392,339	5.5	5.2	0.9	2.2	10.6	0.9	74.2	101.2	52.7	22.5	788	762
Covington	869	2,781,519	6.4	5.7	0.1	2.5	33.6	2.9	47.7	48.2	23.0	22.1	1,161	1,148
DeSoto	5,975	19,064,532	5.9	13.1	7.1	2.0	0.7	4.0	66.1	522.3	229.3	217.7	1,216	1,102
Forrest	6,730	26,043,833	2.9	4.3	2.3	1.8	61.5	2.3	24.4	795.9	114.7	102.4	1,363	1,209
Franklin	313	888,977	12.4	4.4	0.0	4.9	0.1	3.1	74.7	23.8	12.3	6.1	791	772
George	817	2,059,025	5.9	10.2	0.8	4.5	0.1	2.0	75.0	101.2	33.6	15.9	663	639
Greene	500	1,389,648	7.4	4.1	0.1	6.3	13.5	3.8	64.7	37.8	19.8	10.6	782	764
Grenada	961	3,091,225	4.2	5.0	5.1	1.1	0.0	3.5	79.3	67.7	38.5	19.6	930	851
Hancock	1,751	5,914,245	7.1	9.4	4.5	3.1	18.2	5.9	49.5	228.8	95.0	55.2	1,176	1,121
Harrison	10,056	41,422,885	3.4	6.8	4.3	3.0	41.8	1.9	37.2	1,300.8	432.3	262.2	1,279	1,086
Hinds	10,432	34,791,313	5.4	9.8	4.2	1.9	2.0	3.7	71.3	895.4	423.4	297.4	1,239	1,172
Holmes	1,303	3,991,551	5.0	7.1	0.7	1.9	0.1	2.2	82.8	87.2	55.5	14.6	820	796
Humphreys	358	907,778	4.4	7.9	1.9	2.8	0.0	5.7	77.2	33.5	19.5	10.6	1,271	1,234
Issaquena	19	55,685	43.0	24.3	0.0	24.1	0.0	7.4	0.0	6.2	0.6	1.8	1,366	1,345
Itawamba	1,021	3,695,254	3.3	3.8	0.3	1.8	0.1	3.2	87.5	114.1	56.5	27.1	1,154	1,137
Jackson	7,086	27,480,316	3.9	5.8	2.8	3.5	41.1	3.2	38.9	855.5	198.9	217.4	1,529	1,466
Jasper	820	2,360,673	7.7	4.4	0.0	4.9	31.0	4.8	46.8	56.9	21.4	21.1	1,272	1,252
Jefferson	335	714,838	1.4	0.9	0.0	0.0	37.7	1.2	58.8	46.4	12.5	6.3	873	838
Jefferson Davis	383	1,028,403	15.1	4.2	0.9	5.8	0.0	3.2	70.1	28.3	13.6	11.2	995	962
Jones	5,005	13,746,901	2.9	4.1	2.5	2.2	34.9	2.2	49.7	384.5	134.0	63.9	935	889
Kemper	716	2,651,291	4.0	7.7	0.1	2.8	0.1	1.2	83.3	69.9	42.4	12.6	1,253	1,240
Lafayette	1,446	4,445,994	5.6	13.0	4.9	4.3	1.2	7.5	61.3	148.5	58.7	65.8	1,214	1,079
Lamar	2,022	5,076,981	6.5	7.2	0.8	5.3	0.0	1.7	76.1	140.3	69.3	60.6	985	961
Lauderdale	3,125	10,374,372	9.2	5.9	4.3	6.7	2.2	3.1	67.2	252.6	127.4	83.1	1,088	1,035
Lawrence	421	1,213,411	4.9	8.4	0.7	5.6	0.0	2.7	77.7	31.5	15.7	13.1	1,039	1,019
Leake	636	1,698,494	10.7	13.6	1.9	4.7	0.4	3.0	64.2	43.8	25.3	10.9	478	460
Lee	3,894	11,602,013	6.5	9.6	3.7	3.3	2.5	7.1	66.3	267.7	136.4	96.6	1,136	1,107
Leflore	2,143	8,712,788	3.1	4.4	2.0	1.8	57.4	3.1	27.6	228.2	54.8	31.8	1,086	1,038
Lincoln	1,197	3,479,462	7.9	8.4	3.8	3.8	0.5	2.7	72.4	94.4	53.0	30.4	884	839
Lowndes	2,221	7,680,900	8.6	11.6	3.6	4.4	3.2	7.0	60.1	193.5	100.8	60.1	1,016	948
Madison	3,126	11,817,063	7.2	10.8	4.4	2.6	0.3	3.0	69.5	341.6	133.2	161.0	1,539	1,460
Marion	885	2,847,886	6.3	11.9	2.5	4.8	0.0	1.8	71.2	81.7	35.0	20.5	816	785
Marshall	1,060	3,365,642	8.7	13.3	1.5	10.5	0.3	7.2	58.2	77.1	42.9	28.8	808	780
Monroe	1,199	3,461,119	5.8	10.3	2.6	5.3	1.0	8.8	65.0	93.5	48.0	32.6	910	874
Montgomery	499	1,627,928	7.8	5.3	1.6	3.5	33.4	1.7	44.8	26.5	14.9	7.9	782	744
Neshoba	1,352	4,328,328	2.8	5.5	2.7	3.0	44.9	3.0	38.0	62.8	37.4	17.6	597	578
Newton	1,081	3,275,267	4.6	3.7	0.6	3.1	3.5	2.6	80.9	88.4	61.7	15.0	702	670
Noxubee	577	2,460,355	5.7	2.2	0.1	2.1	32.7	0.5	56.2	31.7	16.5	9.5	891	848
Oktibbeha	1,807	6,409,671	1.2	5.3	3.3	1.8	43.4	7.8	37.2	197.7	57.5	46.1	928	908
Panola	1,359	4,142,779	7.1	13.5	2.4	5.0	1.0	4.6	65.5	100.8	52.1	35.4	1,037	961
Pearl River	2,501	7,674,433	5.9	5.5	1.9	2.3	11.7	1.9	70.2	193.9	95.1	44.4	804	763
Perry	470	1,179,800	9.8	5.1	0.4	5.6	0.0	3.1	75.7	36.6	19.4	10.4	867	836
Pike	2,663	9,831,060	3.5	4.2	1.2	1.6	41.9	0.9	46.3	281.9	83.9	35.6	900	866
Pontotoc	1,054	3,276,009	5.8	7.5	1.2	2.3	0.3	5.3	76.5	86.6	48.5	19.7	621	591
Prentiss	1,300	3,958,225	4.2	5.3	2.6	2.0	1.0	1.5	83.5	87.3	56.1	17.1	678	654
Quitman	518	1,904,312	5.9	4.5	0.1	4.7	42.8	1.2	40.9	23.1	10.9	10.3	1,430	1,395
Rankin	4,216	13,330,887	5.0	11.0	6.6	3.1	0.3	3.4	70.2	405.9	174.4	155.0	1,014	972
Scott	1,023	2,718,449	6.8	10.9	1.4	3.1	0.5	5.4	71.3	70.3	43.6	19.7	692	662
Sharkey	338	985,527	10.0	6.4	0.1	3.6	29.6	3.4	46.6	18.3	9.0	6.4	1,450	1,402
Simpson	924	2,483,290	7.0	10.8	0.1	6.4	0.0	2.4	69.9	57.5	31.7	19.7	730	701
Smith	549	1,526,484	10.2	9.5	0.0	4.3	0.1	3.8	72.1	39.3	21.0	13.5	837	810
Stone	1,356	4,896,983	3.3	2.7	0.7	0.9	0.1	0.9	91.3	135.2	76.2	14.3	771	723

1. Based on the resident population estimated as of July 1 of the year shown.

STATE County	Local government finances, 2017 (cont.)									Government employment, 2020			Individual income tax returns, 2019		
	Direct general expenditure							Debt outstanding							
			Percent of total for:												
	Total (mil dol)	Per capita[1] (dollars)	Education	Health and hospitals	Police protection	Public welfare	Highways	Total (mil dol)	Per capita[1] (dollars)	Federal civilian	Federal military	State and local	Number of returns	Mean adjusted gross income	Mean income tax
	185	186	187	188	189	190	191	192	193	194	195	196	197	198	199
MISSISSIPPI	X	X	X	X	X	X	X	X	X	26,409	29,156	212,480	1,280,430	51,288	4,769
Adams	103.9	3,303	38.4	1.3	9.4	0.3	8.4	48.5	1,542	99	177	1,289	12,130	46,911	4,514
Alcorn	291.0	7,830	17.9	59.4	2.4	0.0	1.2	201.4	5,419	113	211	2,716	14,050	48,193	4,168
Amite	25.0	2,009	60.2	1.7	6.1	0.0	12.6	0.5	37	30	70	379	4,920	46,217	3,456
Attala	70.3	3,804	44.9	26.9	3.9	0.0	5.2	18.5	1,002	50	102	984	7,500	43,588	3,167
Benton	19.3	2,334	62.0	0.2	6.4	0.0	9.3	2.9	354	50	48	338	3,410	37,589	2,405
Bolivar	122.2	3,854	49.5	4.9	7.6	0.1	8.3	32.1	1,011	82	167	2,435	13,170	45,721	3,998
Calhoun	55.3	3,811	37.7	34.2	3.2	0.1	8.5	4.0	278	35	81	596	5,880	38,953	2,715
Carroll	22.8	2,263	43.2	0.4	4.8	0.0	13.1	8.9	879	21	54	328	4,200	49,977	3,986
Chickasaw	51.7	3,017	55.2	1.0	5.0	10.0	3.9	30.6	1,787	45	95	852	7,590	41,252	3,022
Choctaw	36.0	4,366	46.8	21.2	4.3	0.1	5.7	4.0	479	64	46	714	3,370	43,335	2,929
Claiborne	32.3	3,575	51.4	3.9	5.1	0.2	8.4	14.8	1,642	34	44	1,389	3,630	32,792	1,879
Clarke	43.0	2,718	60.3	0.9	6.7	0.0	10.2	10.5	665	34	88	736	6,640	45,747	3,321
Clay	56.3	2,867	58.3	0.6	7.3	0.1	7.4	33.3	1,695	56	110	826	8,770	42,395	3,441
Coahoma	125.8	5,421	59.8	0.7	4.4	0.0	4.0	164.5	7,086	64	121	1,656	9,190	37,795	3,218
Copiah	127.6	4,472	54.4	18.0	3.6	0.0	12.5	71.2	2,496	72	156	1,573	11,810	40,854	2,921
Covington	40.8	2,144	64.6	0.3	5.6	0.1	9.5	13.0	685	60	107	1,260	8,160	43,146	3,364
DeSoto	482.4	2,695	54.8	1.0	9.1	0.0	5.4	377.4	2,108	251	1,089	6,675	87,960	57,699	5,166
Forrest	759.6	10,107	14.2	66.6	2.5	0.0	2.1	403.2	5,365	728	793	10,688	31,910	49,516	4,776
Franklin	22.6	2,914	64.7	1.3	4.4	0.0	13.4	2.1	265	51	44	572	3,220	47,853	3,646
George	100.7	4,202	32.7	47.7	3.0	0.1	4.5	43.8	1,830	57	138	1,473	9,540	53,768	4,349
Greene	41.2	3,046	45.7	6.0	6.3	16.9	10.4	9.4	698	15	63	929	4,410	48,876	3,552
Grenada	69.9	3,323	51.7	0.1	10.6	0.0	4.6	22.9	1,089	224	118	1,484	9,610	44,607	3,573
Hancock	205.8	4,383	30.8	19.4	4.9	0.1	7.1	142.9	3,043	2,025	841	1,925	19,790	53,015	4,877
Harrison	1,328.7	6,483	26.3	36.6	4.1	0.2	3.5	922.8	4,502	6,104	9,229	13,799	93,350	50,824	4,773
Hinds	900.5	3,753	55.5	1.8	6.1	0.3	3.8	924.3	3,852	4,561	1,319	32,711	104,440	47,351	4,541
Holmes	92.4	5,178	81.3	0.4	3.9	0.0	4.0	33.7	1,887	61	92	1,184	7,110	29,827	1,550
Humphreys	34.0	4,077	47.2	0.9	5.7	0.1	21.0	4.1	486	23	45	503	3,300	33,858	2,619
Issaquena	6.8	5,042	0.7	5.4	10.6	0.0	13.5	1.0	772	2	5	82	400	43,650	3,453
Itawamba	106.2	4,520	81.8	0.5	2.1	0.1	4.3	32.1	1,368	50	130	1,004	9,590	48,396	3,522
Jackson	839.7	5,903	30.1	38.9	4.1	0.1	4.3	511.8	3,598	1,283	985	8,982	64,940	55,120	5,100
Jasper	53.1	3,204	46.9	14.7	5.1	0.1	12.5	15.0	905	50	94	915	7,230	44,537	3,529
Jefferson	38.7	5,356	32.7	30.5	4.4	7.3	3.3	2.4	335	23	44	505	3,210	33,179	1,926
Jefferson Davis	26.3	2,335	59.5	1.0	6.4	0.0	10.3	9.7	856	29	63	560	4,950	35,802	2,329
Jones	390.4	5,711	37.4	39.5	3.2	0.1	3.6	260.9	3,816	233	383	6,654	27,190	49,188	4,353
Kemper	82.9	8,218	81.3	0.6	1.4	0.1	3.2	58.3	5,776	34	50	566	3,970	35,226	2,152
Lafayette	132.2	2,440	52.4	0.5	8.2	0.0	7.4	110.1	2,032	328	314	8,154	21,850	72,518	8,936
Lamar	140.3	2,280	67.9	0.6	7.1	0.1	8.8	53.3	867	73	372	2,415	26,340	66,163	7,424
Lauderdale	246.7	3,233	61.3	4.3	6.3	0.0	5.1	134.7	1,766	782	1,482	4,742	31,080	55,942	6,440
Lawrence	30.1	2,382	62.8	0.9	9.6	0.0	9.1	7.5	595	41	72	631	4,990	45,798	3,219
Leake	45.6	1,998	52.5	0.3	4.9	0.0	7.7	10.8	472	60	122	731	8,540	41,581	2,822
Lee	281.3	3,306	56.4	0.7	9.6	0.2	7.2	305.5	3,591	449	518	4,794	38,840	58,061	6,152
Leflore	236.0	8,058	20.1	54.6	3.9	0.0	4.1	257.0	8,774	118	154	3,701	12,010	42,084	4,405
Lincoln	89.9	2,618	56.4	0.0	7.4	0.0	14.5	18.1	528	115	193	1,553	14,120	50,733	4,253
Lowndes	232.9	3,937	55.2	0.5	6.2	0.1	5.8	267.3	4,519	866	1,753	3,258	25,710	50,888	5,141
Madison	339.5	3,247	53.9	0.3	6.2	0.1	9.3	447.7	4,281	246	614	4,429	51,150	87,653	12,540
Marion	86.3	3,438	47.8	19.0	6.5	0.0	5.4	41.4	1,649	50	137	1,266	9,650	46,838	3,555
Marshall	80.2	2,252	50.8	1.1	7.5	0.0	11.2	46.3	1,302	90	194	1,148	15,940	40,763	3,027
Monroe	93.6	2,610	56.1	1.0	8.7	0.1	9.4	35.4	986	132	201	1,376	15,240	46,324	3,456
Montgomery	25.5	2,511	56.5	0.4	6.8	0.2	10.1	6.6	653	27	55	528	4,260	42,389	2,988
Neshoba	77.8	2,642	65.0	0.2	4.9	0.0	6.7	41.2	1,400	79	166	5,886	12,160	44,974	3,695
Newton	96.7	4,518	68.0	0.1	4.2	0.0	4.8	24.6	1,150	71	129	1,836	9,170	45,277	3,232
Noxubee	32.4	3,025	55.3	1.5	7.8	0.1	9.6	7.7	721	48	58	609	4,780	32,395	1,901
Oktibbeha	176.2	3,546	30.8	41.3	5.2	0.0	4.2	132.2	2,662	249	272	9,778	18,800	54,675	5,354
Panola	105.0	3,075	56.7	1.0	7.9	0.2	10.3	21.5	628	114	194	2,033	14,960	41,730	3,347
Pearl River	201.6	3,648	62.4	11.9	3.2	0.2	5.7	39.0	705	132	317	2,965	22,840	49,164	3,962
Perry	39.1	3,252	47.0	1.7	4.5	0.1	19.2	69.3	5,765	26	68	528	4,660	43,290	2,860
Pike	286.2	7,245	29.9	49.7	2.5	0.0	2.7	112.8	2,855	112	221	3,223	16,590	41,066	3,090
Pontotoc	78.9	2,488	63.6	1.0	5.2	0.1	7.2	26.0	821	55	187	1,237	13,460	45,536	3,184
Prentiss	95.1	3,772	79.4	0.8	3.9	0.0	3.4	26.6	1,053	49	141	1,444	9,910	42,769	2,752
Quitman	26.1	3,618	57.8	0.5	11.0	0.0	8.3	8.7	1,204	23	38	354	2,740	31,951	1,936
Rankin	414.0	2,707	56.8	0.6	7.4	0.1	5.9	590.2	3,860	609	870	8,342	68,940	63,173	6,013
Scott	75.8	2,666	66.1	0.4	5.3	0.0	7.7	36.6	1,286	188	162	1,237	11,470	40,865	2,789
Sharkey	17.8	4,039	54.9	2.5	6.1	0.0	10.7	4.3	968	26	23	422	1,770	38,984	2,997
Simpson	64.6	2,403	65.0	0.2	3.1	0.0	7.4	20.6	765	51	151	2,130	10,810	43,444	3,187
Smith	38.9	2,422	60.4	1.0	5.1	0.0	14.4	9.9	618	31	91	596	6,130	48,484	3,677
Stone	152.8	8,219	83.3	0.5	3.1	0.0	3.4	168.3	9,054	76	99	1,378	7,250	47,602	3,735

1. Based on the resident population estimated as of July 1 of the year shown.

State / county code	CBSA code[1]	County Type code[2]	STATE County	Land area[3] (sq. mi)	Population, 2021: Total persons 2021	Population, 2021: Rank	Population, 2021: Per square mile	Race alone or in combination, not Hispanic or Latino (percent): White	Black	American Indian, Alaska Native	Asian and Pacific Islancer	Percent Hispanic or Latino[4]	Age (percent): Under 5 years	5 to 17 years	18 to 24 years	25 to 34 years	35 to 44 years	45 to 54 years
				1	2	3	4	5	6	7	8	9	10	11	12	13	14	15
			MISSISSIPPI— Cont'd															
28133	26940	7	Sunflower	697.8	25,402	1,590	36.4	24.0	73.5	0.5	0.5	2.0	5.5	11.9	14.1	16.0	13.4	12.4
28135		7	Tallahatchie	645.2	12,366	2,251	19.2	35.7	55.9	0.8	1.4	7.4	5.4	10.8	12.7	17.5	13.1	12.0
28137	32820	1	Tate	404.8	28,234	1,486	69.7	65.8	31.3	0.7	0.6	2.9	6.1	12.5	15.0	12.4	11.6	12.1
28139		6	Tippah	457.8	21,635	1,729	47.3	78.2	17.6	0.5	0.5	4.8	5.8	13.7	13.6	12.1	12.0	12.5
28141		8	Tishomingo	424.3	18,750	1,885	44.2	93.1	3.2	0.6	0.5	3.6	5.2	12.3	11.4	11.9	11.0	12.7
28143	32820	1	Tunica	454.1	9,696	2,437	21.4	19.6	77.0	0.5	0.9	2.8	8.3	15.4	13.2	13.0	13.3	11.4
28145		6	Union	415.6	27,953	1,499	67.3	78.5	16.5	0.6	1.5	4.7	6.3	14.4	12.6	12.9	12.3	12.8
28147		9	Walthall	403.9	13,836	2,162	34.3	53.7	43.3	1.0	1.0	2.5	5.7	12.6	12.0	11.5	11.7	12.4
28149	46980	4	Warren	588.5	43,579	1,108	74.1	47.7	49.5	0.5	1.1	2.2	6.1	13.3	12.0	12.0	12.5	11.9
28151	24740	5	Washington	724.0	43,687	1,105	60.3	24.9	72.6	0.4	0.9	1.9	6.6	14.9	12.5	12.2	11.3	11.5
28153		7	Wayne	810.7	19,709	1,841	24.3	57.9	40.6	0.6	0.5	1.7	6.5	14.0	12.1	12.2	11.9	11.6
28155	44260	9	Webster	421.2	9,983	2,405	23.7	79.3	19.0	0.7	0.4	1.8	6.2	13.4	11.9	11.7	12.4	12.3
28157		8	Wilkinson	678.1	8,315	2,555	12.3	28.5	70.2	0.5	0.4	1.2	5.1	11.8	12.2	14.7	12.5	11.1
28159		7	Winston	607.3	17,596	1,943	29.0	50.4	47.1	1.4	0.5	1.6	5.3	12.7	12.0	11.4	12.0	12.1
28161		7	Yalobusha	467.2	12,415	2,247	26.6	59.1	39.3	0.6	0.5	1.9	5.8	11.8	11.5	11.3	11.4	12.4
28163	27140	2	Yazoo	922.3	26,373	1,550	28.6	34.8	57.4	0.6	0.9	7.4	5.3	12.3	11.8	17.1	16.5	11.6
29000		0	MISSOURI	68,745.5	6,168,187	X	89.7	80.9	12.7	1.2	3.0	4.7	5.8	12.7	13.0	13.2	12.7	11.7
29001	28860	7	Adair	567.3	25,185	1,600	44.4	90.2	4.6	0.9	3.4	2.8	5.3	9.4	31.0	10.4	8.9	9.1
29003	41140	3	Andrew	432.6	18,002	1,924	41.6	94.9	2.0	0.9	1.0	2.8	5.6	13.3	10.9	11.0	12.6	12.3
29005		9	Atchison	547.3	5,234	2,805	9.6	96.8	1.2	0.8	0.8	1.8	4.6	12.1	9.4	10.5	10.9	12.1
29007	33020	6	Audrain	692.3	24,982	1,614	36.1	89.1	7.6	0.9	1.1	3.4	6.0	12.3	12.1	12.9	12.8	11.9
29009		6	Barry	778.1	34,712	1,307	44.6	86.0	1.0	2.0	2.7	10.1	5.9	12.9	11.2	11.0	11.0	11.5
29011		6	Barton	592.0	11,658	2,303	19.7	94.1	1.4	2.5	1.1	3.4	5.9	13.2	12.1	10.8	11.6	11.2
29013	28140	1	Bates	836.7	16,105	2,029	19.2	94.8	2.2	1.7	0.8	2.8	6.2	12.9	11.7	11.5	11.7	11.4
29015		7	Benton	704.0	19,908	1,821	28.3	95.6	1.2	1.8	0.9	2.4	4.3	10.1	8.6	8.2	8.8	11.4
29017	16020	3	Bollinger	617.9	10,556	2,373	17.1	96.6	1.2	1.5	0.7	1.7	6.1	12.1	10.4	11.1	11.3	12.6
29019	17860	3	Boone	685.6	185,840	364	271.1	81.0	11.6	1.0	6.0	3.7	5.5	11.5	21.5	14.7	12.5	10.2
29021	41140	3	Buchanan	408.2	83,853	686	205.4	84.7	7.3	1.1	2.4	7.1	6.1	12.5	13.0	13.3	12.9	11.6
29023	38740	5	Butler	694.8	42,101	1,144	60.6	90.1	7.1	1.6	1.3	2.5	6.2	13.2	11.9	12.2	12.1	11.8
29025	28140	1	Caldwell	426.4	8,897	2,498	20.9	95.1	1.8	1.6	1.0	2.7	5.5	13.5	12.2	10.6	11.3	12.2
29027	27620	3	Callaway	834.6	44,638	1,083	53.5	91.6	5.7	1.4	1.2	2.3	5.5	11.5	14.0	12.9	12.7	12.3
29029		7	Camden	656.0	43,436	1,114	66.2	94.7	1.1	1.3	1.0	3.2	4.2	9.6	9.3	8.6	9.9	11.2
29031	16020	3	Cape Girardeau	578.5	82,113	702	141.9	87.5	9.2	0.7	2.3	2.6	5.6	12.1	17.4	12.6	11.9	10.8
29033		6	Carroll	694.6	8,376	2,548	12.1	95.6	2.7	0.8	0.4	2.0	5.0	12.9	11.5	10.9	11.5	12.1
29035		9	Carter	507.4	5,320	2,792	10.5	95.1	1.5	2.3	0.5	2.8	6.3	13.4	11.9	10.5	11.4	11.8
29037	28140	1	Cass	696.6	109,638	564	157.4	88.6	5.9	1.3	1.6	5.0	5.7	13.6	11.9	12.1	12.8	12.4
29039		6	Cedar	474.5	14,496	2,116	30.6	95.5	1.0	1.9	0.8	2.5	6.6	13.6	11.5	10.1	10.3	11.4
29041		9	Chariton	751.2	7,356	2,636	9.8	95.7	3.1	1.1	0.3	1.1	5.9	13.2	10.3	9.9	10.3	10.6
29043	44180	2	Christian	562.6	91,499	656	162.6	94.1	1.7	1.4	1.4	3.5	6.2	14.7	11.5	12.2	14.1	12.3
29045	22800	9	Clark	504.6	6,736	2,678	13.3	97.9	1.2	1.0	0.7	0.9	5.9	13.2	10.8	10.6	11.1	11.8
29047	28140	1	Clay	397.7	255,518	276	642.5	81.9	8.7	1.2	3.7	7.5	6.0	13.5	12.1	14.3	14.3	12.6
29049	28140	1	Clinton	418.9	21,287	1,747	50.8	94.9	2.2	1.4	0.9	2.5	5.7	12.9	11.9	11.6	12.1	12.3
29051	27620	3	Cole	391.5	77,205	734	197.2	83.2	13.0	0.8	2.0	3.2	5.5	12.6	12.6	13.0	13.2	12.3
29053	17860	6	Cooper	564.8	17,115	1,965	30.3	90.5	7.3	1.3	1.0	2.1	5.8	12.1	12.8	12.7	12.2	11.3
29055		6	Crawford	742.5	22,807	1,682	30.7	96.0	1.2	1.5	0.6	2.4	5.4	12.8	11.5	11.2	11.7	11.7
29057		8	Dade	490.0	7,599	2,608	15.5	95.4	1.4	2.6	0.9	2.5	4.9	11.8	11.0	9.0	11.6	11.7
29059	44180	2	Dallas	541.0	17,341	1,952	32.1	95.8	1.1	2.1	0.8	2.4	6.5	13.5	10.9	11.1	11.2	11.6
29061		8	Daviess	563.3	8,399	2,544	14.9	96.9	1.2	1.0	0.6	1.8	7.0	13.2	13.0	10.5	10.1	11.3
29063	41140	3	DeKalb	421.4	11,098	2,337	26.3	88.7	7.8	1.0	0.8	2.9	4.7	11.7	11.0	14.0	13.7	13.5
29065		7	Dent	752.8	14,432	2,123	19.2	95.4	1.1	2.1	1.2	2.1	5.6	13.0	10.4	10.3	11.4	11.7
29067		6	Douglas	813.6	11,732	2,300	14.4	95.9	1.3	2.5	0.9	1.7	5.4	12.6	10.3	9.3	11.0	11.1
29069	28380	7	Dunklin	541.9	27,717	1,512	51.1	80.6	12.1	0.9	1.2	7.2	6.7	15.0	12.1	11.1	11.6	11.7
29071	41180	1	Franklin	922.6	105,231	583	114.1	96.0	1.6	0.9	0.9	2.0	5.7	12.9	11.3	12.1	11.9	12.1
29073		6	Gasconade	519.0	14,791	2,098	28.5	96.6	1.2	1.0	0.8	1.9	5.3	11.6	10.7	10.5	10.6	11.9
29075		8	Gentry	491.4	6,173	2,722	12.6	96.2	1.7	0.8	0.9	2.1	6.9	15.2	10.9	11.0	11.6	11.3
29077	44180	2	Greene	675.3	300,865	233	445.5	89.3	4.8	1.5	3.2	4.2	5.5	11.7	16.9	13.9	12.3	11.0
29079		7	Grundy	435.3	9,720	2,435	22.3	94.9	1.5	1.2	1.3	2.6	6.6	14.2	11.3	12.0	10.3	10.1
29081		7	Harrison	722.5	8,164	2,564	11.3	95.5	1.2	1.0	0.9	2.9	5.6	14.5	11.6	10.1	11.2	10.4
29083		6	Henry	696.9	22,206	1,705	31.9	94.5	2.0	1.7	0.8	3.0	6.1	12.6	11.0	10.8	11.4	11.3
29085		8	Hickory	398.8	8,607	2,527	21.6	95.6	1.2	2.2	0.7	2.2	4.5	9.9	8.1	7.8	9.1	11.0
29087		8	Holt	462.7	4,226	2,869	9.1	96.0	1.3	1.8	0.6	1.7	5.6	11.2	10.2	10.1	9.8	12.2
29089	17860	6	Howard	463.8	10,168	2,396	21.9	92.1	5.8	1.4	0.8	2.1	5.3	12.7	16.0	10.1	11.2	10.5
29091	48460	7	Howell	927.2	39,975	1,180	43.1	95.4	0.9	1.8	1.1	2.4	6.1	13.9	11.7	11.8	11.6	11.8
29093		7	Iron	550.3	9,408	2,459	17.1	95.4	2.3	1.7	0.5	1.9	5.1	11.9	11.0	10.2	11.8	12.6
29095	28140	1	Jackson	604.5	716,862	93	1,185.9	64.6	24.7	1.3	3.0	9.7	6.2	13.2	12.2	15.2	13.3	11.5

1. CBSA = Core Based Statistical Area. See Appendix A for explanation. See Appendix B for list of metropolitan areas with component counties. 2. County type code from the Economic Research Service of USDA Rural-Urban Continuum Codes. See Appendix A for definition. 3. Dry land or land partially or temporarily covered by water. 4. May be of any race.

STATE County	Population, 2021 (cont.)				Population change, 2000–2021							Households, 2016–2020				
	Age (percent) (cont.)				Total persons		Percent change		Components of change, 2020–2021					Percent		
	55 to 64 years	65 to 74 years	75 years and over	Percent female	2010	2020	2010–2020	2020–2021	Births	Deaths	Net Migration	Number	Persons per household	Family house-holds	Female family house-holder[1]	One person
	16	17	18	19	20	21	22	23	24	25	26	27	28	29	30	31
MISSISSIPPI— Cont'd																
Sunflower	11.9	9.4	5.4	46.2	29,450	25,971	-11.8	-2.2	340	459	-448	8,345	2.6	61.4	27.4	32.7
Tallahatchie	12.1	9.7	6.7	43.9	15,378	12,715	-17.3	-2.7	170	216	-301	4,322	3.0	63.5	19.5	32.4
Tate	13.3	10.4	6.6	51.8	28,886	28,064	-2.8	0.6	445	445	165	10,553	2.5	75.4	17.8	20.6
Tippah	13.1	10.5	6.7	51.0	22,232	21,815	-1.9	-0.8	297	371	-110	7,842	2.8	67.6	11.9	29.4
Tishomingo	14.5	12.4	8.6	50.8	19,593	18,850	-3.8	-0.5	240	418	78	7,938	2.4	62.5	7.8	32.7
Tunica	11.6	9.2	4.6	52.9	10,778	9,782	-9.2	-0.9	179	130	-137	3,964	2.5	55.3	22.8	38.4
Union	12.1	10.0	6.6	50.9	27,134	27,777	2.4	0.6	404	447	218	9,849	2.9	68.6	12.4	28.4
Walthall	13.7	12.1	8.3	51.8	15,443	13,884	-10.1	-0.3	187	252	17	5,707	2.5	59.9	14.8	37.7
Warren	13.9	11.5	6.9	52.0	48,773	44,722	-8.3	-2.6	664	713	-1,083	18,107	2.5	61.5	17.3	34.1
Washington	13.7	11.4	6.0	53.6	51,137	44,922	-12.2	-2.7	718	896	-1,050	17,882	2.5	63.5	24.2	33.3
Wayne	13.8	10.6	7.2	51.6	20,747	19,779	-4.7	-0.4	353	317	-107	7,967	2.5	67.0	15.1	28.2
Webster	14.4	11.1	6.6	51.0	10,253	9,926	-3.2	0.6	145	206	118	3,699	2.6	70.3	13.9	24.6
Wilkinson	13.7	11.7	7.1	46.0	9,878	8,587	-13.1	-3.2	118	179	-209	3,345	2.3	57.8	26.2	38.6
Winston	13.4	12.5	8.6	50.7	19,198	17,714	-7.7	-0.7	221	322	-18	7,100	2.5	64.7	18.5	32.6
Yalobusha	14.6	13.1	8.1	51.5	12,678	12,481	-1.6	-0.5	180	276	31	5,111	2.4	63.1	16.5	34.4
Yazoo	11.4	8.5	5.6	42.4	28,065	26,743	-4.7	-1.4	350	416	-306	8,577	2.7	61.1	27.5	34.6
MISSOURI	13.4	10.5	7.0	50.6	5,988,927	6,154,913	2.8	0.2	86,276	91,907	18,604	2,440,212	2.4	63.6	11.4	29.8
Adair	10.4	8.8	6.6	51.9	25,607	25,314	-1.1	-0.5	341	294	-179	9,078	2.5	53.9	7.2	33.8
Andrew	14.3	11.9	8.0	50.2	17,291	18,135	4.9	-0.7	242	284	-93	6,799	2.6	69.5	9.3	26.5
Atchison	15.0	13.6	11.8	49.7	5,685	5,305	-6.7	-1.3	57	100	-27	2,549	2.0	60.0	9.1	34.8
Audrain	13.7	10.8	7.5	53.1	25,529	24,962	-2.2	0.1	346	454	126	9,349	2.5	65.7	12.0	30.1
Barry	14.8	12.8	8.8	49.4	35,597	34,534	-3.0	0.5	475	614	322	13,872	2.6	70.3	8.9	25.2
Barton	14.2	12.0	9.0	50.2	12,402	11,637	-6.2	0.2	171	189	39	4,830	2.4	66.4	9.5	25.9
Bates	14.9	11.5	8.4	49.8	17,049	16,042	-5.9	0.4	242	273	94	6,565	2.4	67.5	8.8	28.0
Benton	17.7	18.7	12.4	49.6	19,056	19,394	1.8	2.7	195	465	800	8,060	2.4	65.1	6.6	30.2
Bollinger	15.6	12.6	8.4	49.9	12,363	10,567	-14.5	-0.1	167	229	50	4,426	2.7	66.5	6.7	28.6
Boone	10.6	8.5	4.9	51.4	162,642	183,610	12.9	1.2	2,472	1,786	1,506	71,919	2.4	57.2	9.2	30.9
Buchanan	13.4	10.3	6.9	49.1	89,201	84,793	-4.9	-1.1	1,330	1,376	-895	33,642	2.5	60.3	12.0	32.7
Butler	13.3	11.3	8.0	51.1	42,794	42,130	-1.6	-0.1	650	832	150	16,358	2.5	64.0	13.7	28.7
Caldwell	14.4	11.6	8.5	49.1	9,424	8,815	-6.5	0.9	120	147	111	3,703	2.4	67.2	8.3	27.5
Callaway	13.8	10.9	6.3	48.2	44,332	44,283	-0.1	0.8	588	618	383	16,233	2.5	68.3	9.8	25.2
Camden	18.2	18.4	10.7	50.0	44,002	42,745	-2.9	1.6	461	864	1,116	17,300	2.6	67.8	7.4	27.1
Cape Girardeau	12.2	10.2	7.2	51.2	75,674	81,710	8.0	0.5	1,074	1,246	564	30,215	2.5	61.9	9.5	28.2
Carroll	14.1	12.7	9.4	49.6	9,295	8,495	-8.6	-1.4	105	170	-55	3,518	2.5	70.7	8.5	25.3
Carter	14.7	12.4	7.7	50.8	6,265	5,202	-17.0	2.3	96	126	151	2,334	2.6	66.4	8.1	31.1
Cass	14.0	10.2	7.3	50.9	99,478	107,824	8.4	1.7	1,378	1,446	1,893	40,397	2.6	72.7	9.5	22.7
Cedar	13.8	12.9	9.8	49.4	13,982	14,188	1.5	2.2	223	250	341	5,573	2.5	63.2	8.3	30.6
Chariton	15.1	13.2	11.4	49.5	7,831	7,408	-5.4	-0.7	102	160	6	2,723	2.7	69.9	5.3	27.3
Christian	12.5	10.0	6.3	50.8	77,422	88,842	14.8	3.0	1,260	1,086	2,506	32,487	2.7	74.0	9.3	21.0
Clark	15.4	12.2	9.0	48.5	7,139	6,634	-7.1	1.5	105	106	105	2,633	2.6	64.6	5.6	30.6
Clay	12.2	9.2	5.7	50.6	221,939	253,335	14.1	0.9	3,725	2,815	1,217	92,514	2.6	67.5	12.0	26.5
Clinton	15.1	10.7	7.6	49.5	20,743	21,184	2.1	0.5	291	376	185	8,100	2.5	70.0	10.1	24.3
Cole	12.9	10.9	7.0	49.3	75,990	77,279	1.7	-0.1	1,003	1,091	3	30,291	2.4	61.6	9.1	33.3
Cooper	13.8	11.3	7.9	48.9	17,601	17,103	-2.8	0.1	226	253	36	6,342	2.5	68.6	13.8	27.3
Crawford	15.3	12.3	8.0	50.0	24,696	23,056	-6.6	-1.1	287	435	-102	9,798	2.4	64.5	10.4	30.0
Dade	15.9	14.1	9.9	49.0	7,883	7,569	-4.0	0.4	86	152	97	3,028	2.4	70.1	11.3	25.8
Dallas	14.8	12.3	8.1	49.9	16,777	17,071	1.8	1.6	256	361	379	6,412	2.6	71.8	10.9	23.8
Daviess	13.8	12.8	8.4	49.7	8,433	8,430	0.0	-0.4	153	137	-46	3,002	2.7	70.4	8.0	25.2
DeKalb	13.0	9.9	8.6	42.6	12,892	11,029	-14.5	0.6	115	189	145	3,800	2.3	62.6	9.5	29.9
Dent	15.7	12.5	9.6	50.0	15,657	14,421	-7.9	0.1	185	323	150	6,355	2.4	65.6	9.7	31.8
Douglas	15.2	15.0	10.1	49.9	13,684	11,578	-15.4	1.3	154	248	251	5,317	2.5	71.5	7.6	25.2
Dunklin	13.2	10.6	7.9	51.9	31,953	28,283	-11.5	-2.0	450	669	-348	12,119	2.4	63.9	14.9	29.5
Franklin	15.6	11.2	7.2	49.9	101,492	104,682	3.1	0.5	1,418	1,653	776	41,127	2.5	68.4	9.7	26.2
Gasconade	16.3	13.4	9.7	49.4	15,222	14,794	-2.8	0.0	176	315	138	6,154	2.3	67.7	7.1	25.9
Gentry	13.9	10.5	8.8	51.7	6,738	6,162	-8.5	0.2	94	136	54	2,495	2.6	64.0	9.7	33.4
Greene	11.7	9.8	7.1	51.1	275,174	298,915	8.6	0.7	4,029	4,246	2,128	127,532	2.2	57.8	9.6	32.4
Grundy	13.8	11.3	10.4	50.9	10,261	9,808	-4.4	-0.9	127	190	-24	3,900	2.5	58.4	9.2	35.7
Harrison	14.2	12.3	10.1	49.8	8,957	8,157	-8.9	0.1	114	149	41	3,361	2.4	63.4	10.1	31.9
Henry	14.7	13.0	9.2	50.3	22,272	21,946	-1.5	1.2	338	450	377	9,284	2.3	63.3	12.3	31.1
Hickory	17.5	18.4	13.7	50.8	9,627	8,279	-14.0	4.0	114	199	420	4,012	2.3	57.0	5.4	40.0
Holt	15.7	13.6	11.6	51.2	4,912	4,223	-14.0	0.1	48	97	54	2,010	2.1	61.2	7.3	34.3
Howard	14.1	12.0	8.1	49.7	10,144	10,151	0.1	0.2	131	124	7	3,460	2.7	69.4	12.3	24.7
Howell	13.3	11.6	8.2	51.0	40,400	39,750	-1.6	0.6	580	774	420	15,557	2.5	67.5	10.6	28.5
Iron	15.5	13.0	9.0	50.0	10,630	9,537	-10.3	-1.4	117	245	-1	4,102	2.4	67.4	12.7	27.4
Jackson	12.7	9.5	6.2	51.4	674,158	717,204	6.4	0.0	10,783	9,759	-1,513	291,532	2.4	57.3	13.9	34.9

1. No spouse present.

STATE County	Persons in group quarters, 2021	Daytime Population, 2016–2020		Births, 2021		Deaths, 2021		Persons under 65 with no health insurance, 2019		Medicare, 2021			COVID-19 Deaths, 2020	
		Number	Employment/ residence ratio	Total	Rate[1]	Number	Rate[1]	Number	Percent	Total beneficiaries	Enrolled in Original Medicare	Enrolled in Medicare Advantage	Number	Rate[1]
	32	33	34	35	36	37	38	39	40	41	42	43	44	45
MISSISSIPPI— Cont'd														
Sunflower	4,202	25,909	1.0	286	11.2	352	13.7	2,659	15.3	5,140	4,101	1,039	62	2.4
Tallahatchie	2,178	12,913	0.8	123	9.8	176	14.1	1,474	16.0	2,722	2,158	565	33	2.6
Tate	959	22,610	0.5	360	12.8	361	12.8	3,473	15.5	5,965	4,392	1,573	66	2.3
Tippah	284	20,669	0.9	244	11.3	298	13.7	2,945	16.4	5,279	4,784	495	44	2.0
Tishomingo	200	18,513	0.9	183	9.7	329	17.5	2,626	17.3	5,159	4,847	312	49	2.6
Tunica	101	13,010	1.8	143	14.7	100	10.3	1,048	12.8	1,829	1,168	661	16	1.6
Union	171	28,965	1.0	329	11.8	356	12.8	4,106	17.3	6,192	5,557	635	49	1.8
Walthall	56	12,267	0.6	161	11.6	205	14.8	2,072	18.4	3,412	2,530	882	37	2.7
Warren	399	47,943	1.1	534	12.1	580	13.2	5,590	15.1	9,874	7,536	2,338	86	1.9
Washington	577	45,324	1.0	575	13.0	712	16.1	5,120	14.4	10,399	7,474	2,925	106	2.4
Wayne	68	18,929	0.8	303	15.3	245	12.4	2,771	16.9	4,329	3,241	1,088	30	1.5
Webster	46	8,028	0.6	116	11.7	172	17.3	1,195	15.1	2,587	2,464	123	22	2.2
Wilkinson	1,052	8,291	0.8	99	11.8	146	17.3	994	16.7	1,968	1,507	461	20	2.3
Winston	395	16,757	0.8	184	10.4	269	15.3	2,341	17.0	4,554	3,721	833	54	3.1
Yalobusha	142	10,403	0.6	141	11.3	222	17.9	1,313	13.9	3,616	3,013	604	32	2.6
Yazoo	4,314	26,314	0.7	289	10.9	319	12.0	2,911	15.4	4,973	3,720	1,253	49	1.8
MISSOURI	158,117	6,167,346	1.0	68,818	11.2	73,333	11.9	589,071	11.9	1,247,990	747,869	500,121	7,724	1.3
Adair	2,827	26,108	1.1	278	11.0	227	9.0	2,890	15.4	4,772	4,078	694	12	0.5
Andrew	175	12,011	0.3	195	10.8	220	12.2	1,562	11.0	3,805	3,253	552	19	1.1
Atchison	94	4,899	0.9	48	9.1	86	16.3	482	12.8	1,470	1,341	129	12	2.3
Audrain	1,740	24,264	0.9	284	11.4	358	14.3	2,649	14.1	5,582	4,116	1,466	47	1.9
Barry	194	35,770	1.0	356	10.3	488	14.1	5,212	18.7	8,624	4,705	3,920	53	1.5
Barton	66	10,569	0.8	140	12.0	152	13.1	1,484	16.2	2,828	1,979	849	16	1.4
Bates	244	13,704	0.6	190	11.8	211	13.1	1,902	14.9	3,778	2,514	1,264	17	1.1
Benton	180	17,129	0.7	158	8.0	370	18.8	2,163	16.4	7,019	4,665	2,354	26	1.3
Bollinger	80	9,573	0.5	143	13.6	171	16.2	1,579	16.7	2,733	2,097	636	16	1.5
Boone	8,938	186,455	1.1	1,981	10.7	1,420	7.7	16,404	11.0	27,965	17,614	10,351	95	0.5
Buchanan	3,766	97,093	1.2	1,061	12.6	1,085	12.9	9,393	13.6	17,595	13,819	3,776	125	1.5
Butler	766	44,983	1.1	519	12.3	660	15.7	5,026	15.0	11,046	8,909	2,137	58	1.4
Caldwell	161	7,435	0.6	96	10.8	110	12.4	1,016	14.5	2,077	1,505	572	D	D
Callaway	3,438	40,216	0.8	463	10.4	482	10.8	3,855	11.4	9,191	5,630	3,561	45	1.0
Camden	575	45,823	1.0	361	8.4	710	16.5	5,113	15.7	13,290	9,490	3,800	76	1.8
Cape Girardeau	3,827	82,993	1.1	846	10.3	1,003	12.2	7,199	11.6	16,386	13,699	2,687	120	1.5
Carroll	58	8,011	0.8	78	9.3	139	16.5	891	13.3	2,332	1,792	541	32	3.8
Carter	14	5,424	0.7	79	15.0	108	20.5	713	15.3	1,559	1,228	331	D	D
Cass	955	83,558	0.6	1,090	10.0	1,196	11.0	8,734	10.0	21,240	11,938	9,302	83	0.8
Cedar	111	13,051	0.8	173	12.1	199	13.9	1,761	16.3	3,969	2,228	1,741	14	1.0
Chariton	178	6,395	0.7	83	11.3	137	18.6	746	13.5	2,014	1,690	324	19	2.6
Christian	459	65,221	0.5	1,024	11.3	885	9.8	8,870	12.0	17,020	8,409	8,611	87	1.0
Clark	61	5,531	0.6	83	12.4	78	11.7	804	15.2	1,570	1,385	185	20	3.0
Clay	2,466	224,666	0.8	2,963	11.6	2,209	8.7	19,670	9.3	42,171	27,235	14,936	241	0.9
Clinton	396	16,598	0.6	216	10.2	284	13.4	1,949	11.7	4,568	3,307	1,261	47	2.2
Cole	4,185	91,113	1.4	825	10.7	853	11.0	6,153	10.4	15,352	9,483	5,869	138	1.8
Cooper	900	14,823	0.6	175	10.2	198	11.6	1,577	12.1	3,793	2,533	1,259	21	1.2
Crawford	227	21,881	0.8	231	10.1	357	15.6	2,969	15.8	5,950	3,305	2,645	31	1.3
Dade	104	7,100	0.9	62	8.2	129	17.0	966	17.1	2,154	1,133	1,020	28	3.7
Dallas	143	14,081	0.5	203	11.8	283	16.4	2,267	17.2	4,480	2,042	2,437	29	1.7
Daviess	138	7,079	0.7	121	14.4	108	12.8	1,232	19.4	1,837	1,424	413	14	1.7
DeKalb	1,823	11,423	0.9	87	7.9	154	13.9	835	11.6	2,173	1,699	473	24	2.2
Dent	122	14,586	0.9	137	9.5	274	19.0	1,977	16.6	4,072	3,269	804	28	1.9
Douglas	57	12,003	0.7	118	10.1	196	16.8	1,725	17.7	2,917	1,299	1,618	27	2.3
Dunklin	498	28,332	0.9	359	12.8	530	19.0	3,694	16.1	7,180	5,524	1,656	60	2.1
Franklin	761	94,280	0.8	1,139	10.8	1,322	12.6	10,032	11.8	23,165	9,175	13,990	149	1.4
Gasconade	213	13,518	0.8	143	9.7	242	16.4	1,589	14.1	3,893	2,285	1,608	38	2.6
Gentry	101	6,306	0.9	82	13.3	94	15.3	719	13.8	1,490	1,296	194	16	2.6
Greene	11,203	330,397	1.3	3,249	10.8	3,385	11.3	31,041	13.3	59,598	29,909	29,689	378	1.3
Grundy	325	9,646	0.9	105	10.8	138	14.2	1,145	15.4	2,457	2,174	283	36	3.7
Harrison	108	8,066	0.9	87	10.7	119	14.6	864	13.6	2,173	1,880	293	18	2.2
Henry	185	21,629	1.0	278	12.6	357	16.2	2,450	14.6	6,195	4,043	2,151	34	1.5
Hickory	38	8,437	0.6	89	10.5	163	19.3	1,098	17.5	2,775	1,388	1,387	28	3.4
Holt	77	4,018	0.8	37	8.8	82	19.5	462	14.4	1,215	1,054	161	18	4.3
Howard	704	8,425	0.7	109	10.7	95	9.4	950	12.9	2,154	1,486	668	D	D
Howell	495	41,711	1.1	470	11.8	607	15.2	5,057	16.1	10,580	6,973	3,608	89	2.2
Iron	169	9,664	0.9	98	10.4	201	21.2	1,064	13.9	2,963	2,211	752	12	1.3
Jackson	10,714	751,939	1.2	8,648	12.1	7,892	11.0	77,183	13.2	125,981	69,137	56,844	545	0.8

1. Per 1,000 estimated resident population.

STATE County	COVID-19 Vaccinations, 2021–2022: Number	COVID-19 Vaccinations, 2021–2022: Percent[5]	Education: School enrollment and attainment, 2016–2020: Enrollment[1]: Total	Enrollment[1]: Percent private	Attainment[2] (percent): High school graduate or less	Attainment[2] (percent): Bachelor's degree or more	Local government expenditures,[3] 2018–2019: Total current spending (mil dol)	Local government expenditures,[3] 2018–2019: Current spending per student (dollars)	Money income, 2016–2020: Per capita income[4]	Households: Median income (dollars)	Households: Percent with income of less than $50,000	Households: Percent with income of $200,000 or more	Income and poverty, 2020: Median household income (dollars)	Percent below poverty level: All persons	Percent below poverty level: Children under 18 years	Percent below poverty level: Children 5 to 17 years in families
	46	47	48	49	50	51	52	53	54	55	56	57	58	59	60	61
MISSISSIPPI— Cont'd																
Sunflower	13,389	53.3	5,862	12.2	57.3	16.5	36.0	10,084	16,437	31,515	66.7	2.1	35,149	34.8	41.2	39.3
Tallahatchie	5,749	41.6	2,774	8.0	56.5	11.4	19.9	11,191	17,942	30,433	68.5	0.9	35,150	32.0	39.4	40.1
Tate	12,765	45.1	7,334	11.5	47.4	17.2	36.6	9,167	25,245	55,738	45.4	3.6	61,751	14.0	19.1	19.4
Tippah	9,251	42.0	5,377	14.3	56.5	13.9	36.5	9,097	18,816	37,894	62.9	1.7	45,568	16.5	20.9	19.4
Tishomingo	7,500	38.7	4,091	8.8	57.7	11.8	28.1	9,255	21,313	38,302	60.6	1.4	48,897	14.6	20.0	19.2
Tunica	5,011	52.0	2,880	9.1	56.0	15.3	23.7	12,005	17,197	34,485	66.1	0.1	36,850	26.7	41.7	43.1
Union	11,316	39.3	6,708	7.2	54.9	14.0	43.8	8,698	23,050	47,317	52.3	3.7	50,116	13.5	17.9	17.0
Walthall	5,944	41.6	3,133	22.0	64.2	15.5	17.0	9,335	21,092	33,566	65.9	1.3	30,992	23.5	36.3	35.0
Warren	26,166	57.7	10,961	14.1	42.6	23.0	79.7	10,250	27,058	46,909	54.1	3.6	48,283	19.2	33.3	30.8
Washington	22,345	50.9	12,066	13.9	50.4	20.5	79.2	10,064	22,181	32,011	63.8	2.2	35,344	27.7	39.7	39.1
Wayne	7,900	39.1	5,257	15.6	54.2	20.6	34.5	10,384	23,892	33,612	60.6	3.5	36,193	22.1	29.8	28.8
Webster	4,658	48.1	2,266	17.2	52.8	17.9	15.5	8,646	23,773	52,382	48.6	1.3	51,351	15.7	22.1	22.1
Wilkinson	5,663	65.6	1,569	9.1	66.1	14.2	11.3	9,358	18,074	30,760	74.6	1.9	35,394	28.4	37.1	35.8
Winston	8,628	48.1	4,390	14.5	53.5	16.1	25.5	9,310	25,838	38,986	60.5	2.9	44,029	21.8	34.1	32.9
Yalobusha	7,927	65.5	2,373	16.5	59.9	12.2	15.7	9,839	21,069	41,440	58.9	0.3	42,532	21.2	30.5	29.4
Yazoo	14,626	49.3	6,921	14.8	61.4	11.8	36.7	9,360	17,341	32,729	65.5	1.3	37,367	31.0	36.2	33.7
MISSOURI	3,438,275	56.0	1,459,812	19.1	40.0	29.9	10,256.9	11,229	31,839	57,290	43.8	5.2	58,812	12.1	15.5	14.8
Adair	11,620	45.9	9,421	11.2	44.0	31.2	31.2	10,570	24,509	42,301	56.8	2.7	49,175	17.9	18.8	19.1
Andrew	6,786	38.3	3,888	7.0	43.8	26.6	27.2	9,467	29,671	58,911	41.6	2.8	69,387	9.1	10.8	10.5
Atchison	2,883	56.1	956	2.6	50.3	22.7	11.3	13,322	30,927	51,625	47.7	3.3	53,603	12.0	16.2	14.3
Audrain	9,641	38.0	5,227	12.1	56.6	14.3	32.5	9,652	23,810	44,699	58.2	2.8	48,258	17.8	27.4	28.0
Barry	15,911	44.5	7,874	10.3	57.1	15.0	65.5	9,938	26,463	45,811	52.8	2.7	47,853	16.0	23.3	22.6
Barton	3,902	33.2	2,495	14.9	53.9	18.8	18.7	10,196	26,112	44,510	55.0	2.5	46,353	16.6	22.9	21.1
Bates	6,286	38.9	3,209	11.2	59.1	14.8	26.3	10,367	27,020	46,733	52.9	2.5	52,140	14.8	19.2	18.0
Benton	9,296	47.8	3,197	18.2	53.0	14.7	23.9	10,024	27,310	41,751	59.0	1.8	44,141	16.8	27.5	26.0
Bollinger	4,022	33.1	2,521	13.4	62.8	10.8	16.9	9,127	21,813	45,140	53.8	1.2	48,198	16.3	22.7	21.9
Boone	111,680	61.9	59,526	11.6	25.9	47.7	274.3	11,393	32,050	58,740	43.4	6.7	62,673	12.8	12.5	11.7
Buchanan	33,799	38.7	20,164	10.3	48.5	21.9	118.8	9,705	26,854	51,933	48.5	3.1	53,133	13.1	17.3	16.7
Butler	14,655	34.5	9,317	6.1	54.9	13.0	62.9	9,303	22,611	42,227	59.3	2.7	42,099	21.2	26.7	26.1
Caldwell	3,544	39.3	1,953	7.8	54.4	15.0	18.4	11,330	24,934	51,451	48.2	1.2	47,870	12.4	16.2	15.8
Callaway	21,208	47.4	10,003	24.7	47.3	23.5	48.9	9,792	26,460	59,835	40.4	2.2	61,268	11.4	14.4	13.7
Camden	21,045	45.4	7,791	13.2	46.1	22.2	58.0	11,212	30,402	53,520	45.8	5.4	64,357	14.0	21.4	19.6
Cape Girardeau	38,641	49.0	21,916	15.9	39.9	31.9	102.6	9,705	27,483	53,776	46.1	3.5	57,763	11.9	13.9	13.5
Carroll	4,276	49.3	1,663	11.6	56.1	17.7	17.7	12,768	26,629	51,414	48.0	2.5	51,891	13.4	18.1	16.4
Carter	1,955	32.7	1,500	3.7	62.9	15.2	12.2	10,376	23,382	42,403	54.8	0.6	38,854	20.3	29.8	29.0
Cass	54,923	51.9	23,725	14.5	39.6	27.0	180.5	9,942	33,883	72,522	32.6	5.2	82,068	6.8	9.0	8.4
Cedar	4,596	32.0	2,730	17.3	53.6	13.7	19.9	8,946	24,397	39,408	63.6	3.3	40,130	18.5	27.9	27.0
Chariton	2,812	37.9	1,497	21.8	56.0	18.5	13.7	12,666	25,177	51,545	48.4	1.9	60,521	12.0	14.9	14.3
Christian	40,800	46.1	22,412	13.4	35.8	30.7	142.2	9,055	30,078	64,442	37.7	4.3	67,585	8.8	11.3	10.6
Clark	2,125	31.3	1,355	18.2	60.5	12.2	10.5	9,818	27,606	45,842	53.9	3.3	47,750	12.3	20.0	19.2
Clay	135,388	54.2	60,285	15.5	34.6	32.8	462.3	10,842	34,723	72,047	33.6	5.8	74,950	7.7	8.9	8.3
Clinton	9,658	47.4	4,646	14.2	50.6	22.0	40.9	10,079	28,461	62,213	37.8	2.2	66,492	9.5	11.5	10.8
Cole	40,517	52.8	17,894	27.6	36.9	35.5	115.6	8,926	31,790	61,184	39.4	3.1	63,486	9.3	10.7	10.5
Cooper	7,881	44.5	3,867	20.7	47.7	22.4	26.6	10,842	24,237	53,003	46.9	2.4	51,221	13.6	17.8	16.6
Crawford	8,040	33.6	4,944	11.5	59.1	11.9	30.7	9,420	23,082	44,380	58.7	1.5	43,785	16.3	22.3	20.9
Dade	3,269	43.2	1,481	15.9	55.6	13.8	10.5	9,714	25,237	42,117	56.4	2.6	46,535	14.1	22.2	21.2
Dallas	5,914	35.0	3,473	14.9	62.5	11.4	16.8	9,589	21,883	40,404	60.0	2.7	43,482	24.1	35.5	30.3
Daviess	2,749	33.2	1,727	16.9	53.5	20.8	14.7	11,951	24,987	52,143	45.8	2.6	49,830	14.1	22.9	23.0
DeKalb	3,520	28.1	2,289	10.8	56.3	15.8	12.6	11,726	20,810	58,433	41.9	1.5	52,868	12.8	12.5	11.6
Dent	5,323	34.2	3,499	17.2	55.2	14.9	20.3	9,239	23,254	42,714	56.8	1.8	44,057	15.1	22.2	22.5
Douglas	3,185	24.2	2,541	16.3	59.5	13.0	13.9	8,955	23,883	43,714	55.0	3.7	46,079	17.8	27.7	26.4
Dunklin	10,884	37.4	6,649	3.0	61.2	13.9	52.1	9,742	22,879	38,020	62.0	2.1	42,512	20.2	29.8	28.5
Franklin	56,500	54.3	22,858	22.1	43.3	21.3	166.5	10,416	31,133	60,129	40.8	4.3	62,781	9.1	11.1	10.6
Gasconade	7,458	50.7	2,921	12.3	50.6	21.3	25.7	9,318	29,614	56,380	44.6	3.1	54,487	11.2	14.1	13.5
Gentry	2,858	43.5	1,408	10.2	55.6	20.3	13.0	11,898	25,814	46,774	52.0	2.3	48,338	13.0	18.0	18.3
Greene	144,569	49.3	76,485	17.4	35.5	31.5	381.0	9,878	28,308	47,053	52.2	3.1	46,934	14.3	14.4	12.9
Grundy	3,507	35.6	2,275	14.2	52.7	18.2	16.5	10,900	25,928	46,885	52.7	2.2	45,363	15.1	24.2	23.1
Harrison	2,850	34.1	1,880	8.3	56.5	15.7	15.5	10,847	21,506	40,615	58.1	0.6	43,642	17.8	27.7	25.1
Henry	10,058	46.1	4,530	14.2	54.3	15.6	29.5	10,073	27,483	47,500	52.2	3.0	53,544	13.6	19.8	18.7
Hickory	3,641	38.1	1,472	16.7	60.2	8.5	16.2	10,144	19,905	33,342	73.1	0.1	36,049	19.6	28.9	30.1
Holt	1,851	42.0	785	6.8	52.5	18.2	8.6	13,677	28,497	46,442	52.0	1.8	49,531	12.2	17.4	16.9
Howard	4,334	43.3	2,719	36.8	46.8	28.7	13.1	9,053	25,159	55,000	45.4	3.3	53,190	12.7	15.6	14.4
Howell	13,355	33.3	9,280	12.5	53.9	17.3	54.0	9,806	20,375	39,482	61.6	1.3	45,808	18.4	24.7	24.1
Iron	3,946	39.0	1,937	10.4	59.1	11.9	20.0	11,423	21,769	40,082	57.6	1.0	41,744	19.5	28.6	27.7
Jackson	402,633	57.3	163,454	15.9	36.8	32.1	1,307.5	11,959	32,462	56,960	44.3	4.7	56,398	12.4	16.6	15.8

1. All persons 3 years old and over enrolled in nursery school through college. 2. Persons 25 years old and over. 3. Elementary and secondary education expenditures. 4. Based on population estimated by the American Community Survey, 2016–2020. 5. CDC percent based on 2019 population estimate.

STATE County	Personal income, 2020: Total (mil dol)	Personal income, 2020: Percent change 2019–2020	Personal income, 2020: Per capita[1]: Dollars	Personal income, 2020: Per capita[1]: Rank	Personal income, 2020: Wages and salaries (mil dol)	Personal income, 2020: Supplements to wages and salaries, employer contributions (mil dol): Pension and insurance	Personal income, 2020: Supplements to wages and salaries, employer contributions (mil dol): Government social insurance	Personal income, 2020: Proprietors' income (mil dol)	Personal income, 2020: Dividends, interest, and rent (mil dol)	Personal income, 2020: Personal transfer reecipts (mil dol)	Earnings, 2020: Total (mil dol)	Earnings, 2020: Contributions for government social insurance (mil dol): From employee and self-employed	Earnings, 2020: Contributions for government social insurance (mil dol): From employer
	62	63	64	65	66	67	68	69	70	71	72	73	74
MISSISSIPPI— Cont'd													
Sunflower	877	13.1	35,454	2,911	314	57	24	97	108	370	493	34	24
Tallahatchie	463	10.1	33,784	2,990	115	20	9	67	49	179	211	14	9
Tate	1,145	9.3	40,134	2,443	225	41	18	75	111	364	358	31	18
Tippah	915	8.6	42,051	2,186	308	62	26	50	101	306	445	34	26
Tishomingo	725	6.7	37,593	2,727	261	48	21	28	83	277	357	31	21
Tunica	385	12.8	40,994	2,336	238	31	19	42	52	148	330	22	19
Union	1,050	8.7	36,387	2,840	507	77	41	77	130	348	703	53	41
Walthall	498	7.2	34,814	2,944	89	17	7	44	59	202	158	14	7
Warren	1,992	6.5	44,422	1,887	1,010	210	79	102	298	623	1,400	96	79
Washington	1,875	13.1	43,778	1,977	678	114	52	176	229	718	1,020	76	52
Wayne	751	3.7	36,967	2,787	211	38	16	74	103	278	339	25	16
Webster	417	7.6	43,060	2,053	82	15	6	20	46	162	124	12	6
Wilkinson	290	9.3	34,759	2,947	60	12	5	11	39	130	88	9	5
Winston	695	4.9	38,970	2,566	222	37	17	35	81	279	311	26	17
Yalobusha	495	8.0	41,336	2,285	119	23	9	23	54	213	174	18	9
Yazoo	909	8.2	33,672	2,996	308	66	24	64	125	345	462	32	24
MISSOURI	318,019	5.8	51,673	X	157,350	25,727	11,309	21,818	58,605	73,998	216,205	13,894	11,309
Adair	886	5.7	34,867	2,942	399	84	30	61	157	264	574	37	30
Andrew	847	5.1	48,186	1,358	109	24	8	61	114	184	202	14	8
Atchison	275	16.0	53,958	786	66	14	5	67	37	71	152	8	5
Audrain	1,044	9.9	42,029	2,191	365	78	27	121	158	291	591	37	27
Barry	1,329	3.9	37,114	2,778	636	118	48	90	232	432	893	64	48
Barton	487	17.8	42,031	2,189	129	26	10	90	61	144	256	15	10
Bates	723	10.1	44,523	1,871	152	35	11	87	106	223	285	18	11
Benton	791	5.8	40,318	2,415	136	31	10	84	118	320	260	26	10
Bollinger	443	8.6	36,548	2,819	69	15	5	31	51	164	120	11	5
Boone	9,393	5.6	51,330	992	5,258	1,052	352	462	1,774	1,729	7,124	411	352
Buchanan	3,691	4.9	42,653	2,109	2,474	422	185	228	471	1,110	3,308	212	185
Butler	1,698	10.4	40,255	2,425	760	159	58	144	224	664	1,120	76	58
Caldwell	376	7.4	41,488	2,271	79	16	6	39	45	110	139	10	6
Callaway	1,909	8.1	42,524	2,130	778	180	57	54	286	515	1,069	70	57
Camden	1,893	5.6	40,778	2,362	681	114	52	143	396	639	991	77	52
Cape Girardeau	3,768	4.9	47,386	1,462	1,998	352	145	281	620	926	2,776	180	145
Carroll	436	7.7	50,990	1,031	103	21	8	97	58	122	229	13	8
Carter	215	8.3	35,898	2,873	53	14	4	16	28	93	87	8	4
Cass	5,410	5.4	50,654	1,070	1,217	210	91	274	747	1,185	1,792	129	91
Cedar	489	8.7	34,130	2,973	112	28	8	47	72	208	195	17	8
Chariton	365	11.4	49,650	1,181	78	16	6	64	57	104	164	9	6
Christian	3,953	6.5	43,602	1,996	749	143	57	218	521	902	1,167	93	57
Clark	279	14.7	40,825	2,350	49	12	4	39	34	81	104	7	4
Clay	13,084	6.0	51,619	970	6,124	954	453	708	1,591	2,522	8,238	527	453
Clinton	962	8.3	46,823	1,535	183	36	13	47	127	252	279	22	13
Cole	3,955	5.7	51,905	941	2,649	573	179	255	675	870	3,656	209	179
Cooper	761	8.1	44,486	1,877	203	39	16	62	103	208	320	22	16
Crawford	912	6.1	38,430	2,629	282	57	21	53	129	333	413	32	21
Dade	292	10.8	38,581	2,617	66	15	5	40	41	98	125	9	5
Dallas	617	7.2	35,840	2,880	91	20	7	61	73	230	179	16	7
Daviess	310	10.3	37,380	2,752	56	13	4	47	48	100	120	8	4
DeKalb	403	8.6	36,799	2,799	125	29	9	36	47	119	199	12	9
Dent	562	7.2	36,327	2,845	152	35	11	35	74	227	233	19	11
Douglas	414	9.2	31,031	3,075	90	20	7	23	52	173	140	13	7
Dunklin	1,121	5.8	38,821	2,588	303	62	24	70	123	491	459	35	24
Franklin	5,026	4.6	48,108	1,370	1,863	345	139	209	805	1,286	2,555	183	139
Gasconade	635	5.5	43,589	1,998	197	42	15	46	107	209	300	23	15
Gentry	301	6.4	46,483	1,579	94	17	7	35	46	94	154	10	7
Greene	13,979	3.6	47,388	1,460	8,783	1,458	639	1,339	2,360	3,419	12,218	775	639
Grundy	375	8.5	39,098	2,558	117	28	9	52	51	144	206	14	9
Harrison	343	12.5	41,238	2,297	92	21	7	57	52	116	177	11	7
Henry	989	7.8	44,780	1,829	323	72	23	85	148	342	503	36	23
Hickory	301	8.4	31,380	3,070	48	11	4	24	46	147	87	10	4
Holt	240	8.6	56,644	593	58	12	4	63	30	57	138	7	4
Howard	440	6.8	43,946	1,954	100	22	8	34	63	130	164	11	8
Howell	1,506	6.9	37,414	2,749	615	125	47	123	203	579	909	66	47
Iron	369	8.2	36,530	2,821	149	30	12	9	42	177	199	16	12
Jackson	35,444	5.5	50,209	1,124	24,726	3,768	1,737	2,581	5,440	8,528	32,813	2,039	1,737

1. Based on the resident population estimated as of July 1 of the year shown.

STATE County	Earnings, 2020 (cont.) — Percent by selected industries: Farm	Mining, quarrying, and extractions	Construction	Manu-facturing	Information; professional, scientific, technical services	Retail trade	Finance, insurance, real estate, and leasing	Health care and social assistance	Govern-ment	Social Security beneficiaries, December 2020: Number	Rate[1]	Supple-mental Security Income recipients, 2020	Housing units, 2021: Total	Percent change, 2010–2021
	75	76	77	78	79	80	81	82	83	84	85	86	87	88
MISSISSIPPI— Cont'd														
Sunflower	12.0	0.0	2.0	3.4	1.9	5.4	4.4	6.1	33.7	5,755	227	1,852	9,419	0.1
Tallahatchie	22.8	0.0	D	D	D	5.7	2.1	3.3	24.3	3,145	254	901	5,485	0.5
Tate	4.0	D	9.5	7.7	5.7	9.9	4.1	13.5	24.5	6,785	240	900	11,513	1.5
Tippah	1.6	1.4	5.9	23.4	D	6.3	2.9	D	28.2	6,015	278	990	9,941	0.6
Tishomingo	-0.7	0.1	5.4	43.8	D	6.9	3.0	D	13.1	5,775	308	697	10,553	0.3
Tunica	10.4	0.0	D	6.8	D	D	D	D	11.4	2,180	225	698	4,702	2.3
Union	0.6	0.0	5.3	38.0	1.8	5.7	2.5	D	10.7	7,255	260	753	12,187	0.5
Walthall	6.4	D	10.6	13.4	D	8.1	3.0	D	19.4	3,765	272	575	6,877	0.5
Warren	0.6	D	2.9	14.0	5.5	6.4	3.3	10.5	33.0	10,805	248	1,893	21,525	0.3
Washington	5.6	D	2.9	7.8	4.5	8.0	5.2	11.8	23.4	11,715	268	4,003	20,880	0.0
Wayne	7.3	3.6	3.2	11.5	2.8	10.9	5.0	D	20.8	4,945	251	776	9,096	0.6
Webster	5.0	0.0	8.1	8.2	D	6.3	D	D	18.4	3,215	322	633	5,088	0.4
Wilkinson	1.6	0.2	2.0	7.9	D	9.2	5.5	D	32.0	2,130	256	582	4,596	0.8
Winston	5.6	0.1	4.5	25.5	D	7.6	1.8	D	13.6	5,185	295	811	8,210	0.4
Yalobusha	2.4	D	7.7	32.2	D	4.1	4.1	D	25.0	4,450	358	849	6,461	0.7
Yazoo	10.3	D	3.0	12.8	1.7	4.9	2.4	D	36.3	5,710	217	1,533	10,464	0.3
MISSOURI	1.2	0.2	6.4	10.5	11.6	6.0	9.2	13.0	14.8	1,323,195	215	134,636	2,807,604	0.6
Adair	3.3	0.0	4.4	13.7	3.1	10.0	3.9	D	22.5	5,010	199	627	11,366	0.2
Andrew	13.9	D	10.9	1.8	D	10.4	3.5	D	19.8	3,690	205	154	7,553	0.0
Atchison	35.9	0.0	5.1	0.2	D	4.3	6.5	9.8	12.4	1,480	283	81	2,728	-0.1
Audrain	11.5	0.0	4.4	22.4	D	6.7	4.4	D	21.1	5,965	239	565	10,549	0.0
Barry	4.1	D	5.3	32.4	14.7	6.7	4.1	D	11.2	9,280	267	945	17,019	0.2
Barton	25.2	0.0	9.1	6.0	D	5.8	4.5	13.9	12.1	3,255	279	296	5,290	0.0
Bates	17.5	D	9.3	3.3	3.5	8.4	D	D	26.2	4,235	263	385	7,189	0.0
Benton	5.7	D	9.3	4.5	3.0	9.8	8.1	D	23.7	7,465	375	639	13,571	0.1
Bollinger	7.3	D	12.1	5.6	2.5	7.5	D	D	20.2	3,295	312	394	5,037	0.0
Boone	0.3	D	4.2	5.1	7.2	6.2	12.6	11.0	34.1	29,220	157	2,868	80,877	1.1
Buchanan	0.8	D	6.9	27.0	5.1	6.1	5.4	16.5	11.8	19,155	228	2,381	38,470	0.5
Butler	4.6	D	4.4	10.0	5.2	9.3	5.3	D	21.5	11,070	263	2,102	19,305	0.1
Caldwell	17.4	D	12.9	1.1	D	16.7	D	D	21.8	2,190	246	146	4,254	0.8
Callaway	0.6	0.3	5.9	14.7	4.6	4.0	2.6	D	20.6	10,160	228	858	18,619	0.4
Camden	0.4	D	12.5	3.9	4.7	12.2	7.9	20.2	10.7	13,695	315	695	39,716	0.5
Cape Girardeau	0.8	D	5.4	11.7	9.5	8.4	4.8	25.5	12.9	17,080	208	1,622	35,999	0.3
Carroll	30.7	0.0	11.4	7.6	D	3.6	4.6	D	13.3	2,355	281	200	4,372	0.2
Carter	0.3	D	10.2	13.7	D	4.9	D	12.5	27.1	1,855	349	293	2,677	0.1
Cass	2.5	0.3	12.4	6.9	4.8	10.0	5.0	10.3	17.4	21,870	199	1,059	44,657	2.5
Cedar	2.7	D	17.3	6.8	3.2	7.9	3.9	10.2	26.8	4,290	296	424	6,946	0.2
Chariton	29.5	0.0	7.4	3.1	D	6.6	7.5	D	14.1	1,975	268	160	3,791	0.0
Christian	0.4	D	16.0	7.5	6.4	10.6	6.5	6.4	17.7	18,555	203	1,099	35,921	1.8
Clark	29.2	D	6.1	6.2	2.0	8.1	D	3.3	21.9	1,645	244	116	3,225	0.3
Clay	0.1	D	7.1	15.7	12.7	7.6	5.2	8.2	15.0	44,630	175	2,704	106,639	0.8
Clinton	6.1	D	10.6	5.3	4.2	4.8	5.3	22.3	21.2	4,430	208	356	9,027	0.8
Cole	0.2	D	6.9	4.9	8.1	6.5	6.0	11.8	35.6	17,340	225	1,337	33,402	0.5
Cooper	11.7	D	11.1	6.8	3.2	9.7	5.7	8.7	19.6	4,065	238	347	7,284	0.0
Crawford	0.4	1.0	5.9	23.5	3.6	9.3	3.7	14.7	12.3	6,605	290	665	11,398	0.1
Dade	21.0	D	10.0	8.8	D	5.2	2.3	1.9	19.8	2,215	291	184	3,775	0.0
Dallas	1.5	D	20.8	3.7	2.3	10.9	6.2	D	21.0	4,680	270	522	7,605	0.1
Daviess	18.1	D	16.1	6.3	1.5	10.0	3.6	D	20.5	2,060	245	140	4,126	0.0
DeKalb	9.5	0.0	9.6	1.2	1.4	9.5	9.1	6.6	27.6	2,390	215	81	4,271	0.0
Dent	3.2	D	5.8	12.1	2.6	9.1	5.8	D	25.6	4,355	302	553	6,821	0.0
Douglas	1.0	D	9.7	D	D	9.7	3.0	D	19.1	3,875	330	326	5,351	0.1
Dunklin	7.6	0.0	4.4	3.5	3.1	10.5	5.5	D	18.9	7,810	282	1,968	13,428	0.1
Franklin	0.0	0.2	8.9	26.6	5.9	7.7	4.8	11.9	11.0	25,470	242	1,870	45,759	0.9
Gasconade	2.8	D	5.5	26.9	D	7.6	4.7	D	18.4	4,295	290	275	7,578	0.0
Gentry	15.4	0.1	5.3	9.4	D	7.5	D	21.5	15.0	1,660	269	128	2,920	0.0
Greene	0.0	0.1	4.9	8.4	10.5	8.3	6.0	20.3	11.7	62,080	206	6,461	137,847	0.9
Grundy	12.6	D	6.5	11.3	2.5	5.9	4.2	13.5	23.5	2,515	259	269	4,841	0.0
Harrison	19.3	D	3.3	1.9	2.7	18.0	5.7	5.1	25.5	2,265	277	198	4,015	-0.1
Henry	5.8	D	6.3	14.8	2.6	9.9	5.3	D	25.8	6,855	309	679	10,699	0.1
Hickory	10.3	D	8.5	0.6	D	12.8	D	13.3	20.9	3,565	414	256	5,483	0.3
Holt	34.5	D	1.6	11.7	D	5.9	3.0	7.5	11.8	1,255	297	58	2,416	0.0
Howard	12.4	D	4.1	12.0	D	4.9	D	D	14.7	2,365	233	184	4,370	0.1
Howell	2.6	0.2	3.3	13.2	5.7	7.5	5.9	21.8	14.3	11,675	292	1,580	18,077	0.1
Iron	-0.5	D	2.7	14.3	D	6.3	D	11.3	18.1	3,075	327	564	4,686	0.0
Jackson	0.0	0.0	6.3	7.0	20.0	4.6	11.7	12.0	15.5	132,885	185	17,029	333,685	1.0

1. Per 1,000 resident population estimated as of July 1 of the year shown.

STATE County	Housing units, 2016–2020: Occupied units: Total	Owner-occupied: Percent	Owner-occupied: Median value[1]	Median owner cost as a percent of income: With a mortgage	Median owner cost as a percent of income: Without a mortgage[2]	Renter-occupied: Median rent[3]	Renter-occupied: Median rent as a percent of income[2]	Sub-standard units[4] (percent)	Civilian labor force, 2021: Total	Percent change, 2020–2021	Unemployment: Total	Unemployment: Rate[5]	Civilian employment[6], 2016–2020: Total	Percent: Management, business, science, and arts	Percent: Construction, production, and maintenance occupations
	89	90	91	92	93	94	95	96	97	98	99	100	101	102	103
MISSISSIPPI— Cont'd															
Sunflower	8,345	53.3	86,300	19.8	12.2	575	30.1	3.4	7,389	-0.6	674	9.1	8,431	32.5	25.5
Tallahatchie	4,322	63.7	68,900	22.4	12.4	565	26.0	2.8	4,800	-5.7	293	6.1	4,958	26.5	41.3
Tate	10,553	77.0	139,300	22.5	10.2	747	34.5	4.5	12,106	1.4	677	5.6	12,083	29.4	33.5
Tippah	7,842	69.3	89,200	23.6	10.7	558	23.9	3.3	9,427	2.7	434	4.6	8,840	24.4	45.0
Tishomingo	7,938	73.1	97,000	18.6	10.0	546	27.4	3.7	8,317	0.9	379	4.6	7,796	26.1	40.5
Tunica	3,964	39.0	101,800	26.4	12.2	793	26.9	8.6	4,275	-3.5	379	8.9	4,044	19.1	26.7
Union	9,849	75.4	112,900	17.6	10.0	694	22.4	2.1	14,078	1.0	573	4.1	12,478	26.1	37.9
Walthall	5,707	85.2	98,100	22.4	13.5	585	23.0	6.7	4,937	0.4	340	6.9	5,139	32.4	39.3
Warren	18,107	65.9	133,100	21.1	10.0	739	28.5	2.8	19,416	-2.5	1,195	6.2	19,635	32.4	25.9
Washington	17,882	54.6	80,600	22.5	10.5	692	33.7	3.5	15,920	-1.7	1,307	8.2	17,178	29.2	28.9
Wayne	7,967	85.1	78,300	24.4	12.8	549	24.7	1.7	7,335	-0.6	493	6.7	7,631	30.2	32.3
Webster	3,699	78.5	86,600	17.6	10.0	598	34.6	1.1	3,941	2.7	212	5.4	3,988	32.7	30.2
Wilkinson	3,345	78.2	70,500	21.5	14.0	439	26.8	0.0	2,736	0.6	305	11.1	2,558	24.1	26.5
Winston	7,100	74.5	96,700	19.5	10.8	656	30.3	2.2	7,180	-1.1	445	6.2	6,832	22.0	37.2
Yalobusha	5,111	70.1	85,500	21.2	11.4	674	26.2	1.9	4,902	1.3	269	5.5	4,884	25.6	40.7
Yazoo	8,577	59.3	88,600	23.3	12.5	742	30.1	4.8	8,946	-0.2	654	7.3	8,326	26.0	30.8
MISSOURI	2,440,212	67.1	163,600	19.1	10.8	843	27.6	2.2	3,062,449	0.8	134,081	4.4	2,932,918	37.9	23.4
Adair	9,078	61.6	123,500	19.4	10.8	638	32.0	1.8	9,908	-1.4	427	4.3	10,701	38.4	23.8
Andrew	6,799	78.5	150,200	17.8	12.1	796	25.9	0.5	9,656	-0.6	292	3.0	8,492	36.6	32.0
Atchison	2,549	69.1	90,400	17.7	10.0	532	20.2	2.1	2,655	-2.2	86	3.2	2,569	29.3	30.3
Audrain	9,349	70.5	89,200	18.3	10.5	630	25.9	1.4	10,246	-0.3	376	3.7	11,092	26.1	34.3
Barry	13,872	74.1	127,400	19.3	11.3	695	28.1	6.0	15,094	-3.5	688	4.6	14,927	27.5	39.6
Barton	4,830	68.7	91,900	17.6	11.0	640	33.0	1.9	5,190	0.7	176	3.4	4,872	31.9	31.2
Bates	6,565	70.1	119,600	18.8	10.2	631	27.0	4.1	7,647	0.7	325	4.3	7,393	26.2	36.9
Benton	8,060	83.1	122,600	20.1	11.7	679	31.9	2.7	7,322	1.5	417	5.7	6,617	32.2	30.7
Bollinger	4,426	82.6	113,600	18.0	12.8	687	35.0	2.8	5,349	-0.3	222	4.2	5,032	27.1	39.7
Boone	71,919	56.0	198,700	18.8	10.0	888	29.8	2.1	99,004	3.3	2,955	3.0	94,941	46.8	15.6
Buchanan	33,642	62.1	126,000	18.6	11.2	784	27.4	2.7	43,329	-0.6	1,640	3.8	40,379	28.7	31.5
Butler	16,358	63.9	116,400	21.6	10.5	662	29.5	1.7	18,037	-0.5	850	4.7	16,912	24.1	33.1
Caldwell	3,703	76.1	109,700	18.9	12.3	620	22.6	3.6	4,298	1.5	220	5.1	3,777	23.9	37.4
Callaway	16,233	74.6	156,900	18.4	10.0	719	24.0	1.1	21,325	-0.2	727	3.4	19,972	35.7	24.4
Camden	17,300	81.5	213,200	22.8	10.0	714	26.4	1.4	19,270	2.8	955	5.0	19,026	30.0	23.9
Cape Girardeau	30,215	65.9	162,400	18.9	10.1	795	28.2	1.4	40,445	0.2	1,453	3.6	38,745	36.9	22.1
Carroll	3,518	72.5	93,400	18.4	10.6	683	26.3	0.8	4,504	-2.3	198	4.4	3,645	35.4	31.3
Carter	2,334	71.8	135,800	17.8	10.0	566	30.3	2.4	2,571	2.1	133	5.2	2,561	28.9	34.6
Cass	40,397	75.4	196,700	19.2	10.5	976	27.3	2.2	54,398	1.1	2,120	3.9	52,220	36.1	25.2
Cedar	5,573	70.0	95,200	20.9	11.6	624	28.4	3.0	5,790	1.2	212	3.7	5,177	32.8	29.0
Chariton	2,723	77.3	100,700	18.4	10.0	504	23.1	2.0	3,743	0.2	123	3.3	3,162	36.9	33.4
Christian	32,487	74.7	182,800	19.1	10.1	842	26.5	3.3	46,547	2.1	1,504	3.2	42,642	37.1	22.1
Clark	2,633	76.1	96,800	17.7	11.8	601	25.0	3.2	3,127	-1.0	145	4.6	3,090	27.5	43.1
Clay	92,514	68.4	185,700	19.3	11.3	995	27.4	1.7	138,370	1.5	6,815	4.9	130,114	38.1	23.5
Clinton	8,100	77.8	160,800	19.9	11.5	854	24.3	1.8	10,660	1.6	564	5.3	9,487	31.9	34.4
Cole	30,291	67.1	169,700	18.1	10.0	687	23.1	1.3	38,648	-0.3	1,203	3.1	37,667	39.6	21.6
Cooper	6,342	74.3	150,800	18.6	11.2	641	26.1	2.1	7,080	-1.0	256	3.6	7,533	34.2	25.9
Crawford	9,798	72.8	124,400	21.8	11.6	654	28.7	1.6	10,913	1.2	495	4.5	9,468	25.7	35.6
Dade	3,028	73.9	101,800	19.7	10.4	604	24.7	2.5	3,544	-0.1	117	3.3	3,118	23.5	44.2
Dallas	6,412	75.4	131,000	20.4	10.0	561	29.2	2.0	7,177	1.4	312	4.3	6,151	27.6	33.7
Daviess	3,002	80.0	114,600	19.3	11.0	625	28.0	3.1	4,103	0.0	155	3.8	3,566	32.3	29.2
DeKalb	3,800	69.6	125,000	18.2	10.4	700	21.5	0.6	4,167	-0.8	157	3.8	4,073	34.5	32.0
Dent	6,355	71.5	104,900	20.0	10.7	583	27.7	4.5	6,257	-0.7	270	4.3	6,552	28.7	30.4
Douglas	5,317	82.6	127,300	20.3	10.0	586	29.3	1.9	5,162	0.5	221	4.3	5,104	26.4	37.9
Dunklin	12,119	61.7	78,500	18.1	11.2	575	27.9	3.4	11,276	-2.1	686	6.1	11,591	28.6	29.3
Franklin	41,127	77.2	171,900	18.9	10.4	762	25.5	1.4	52,747	0.4	2,108	4.0	49,853	31.7	33.0
Gasconade	6,154	79.2	136,800	19.2	10.0	556	22.8	1.6	7,620	0.5	278	3.6	7,099	27.9	38.7
Gentry	2,495	76.0	86,200	17.2	11.6	581	19.3	3.9	3,334	-1.7	89	2.7	2,958	37.4	31.0
Greene	127,532	56.3	151,300	19.0	10.4	779	29.6	3.0	152,184	1.7	5,206	3.4	140,567	36.8	20.6
Grundy	3,900	67.2	101,100	19.7	11.0	593	19.1	3.1	4,178	-2.3	150	3.6	4,304	30.5	32.2
Harrison	3,361	68.8	75,300	18.2	12.5	500	30.1	2.1	3,761	-0.7	132	3.5	3,441	29.8	31.7
Henry	9,284	71.1	115,600	19.5	11.5	672	29.3	3.0	10,059	4.3	398	4.0	9,256	27.8	32.1
Hickory	4,012	83.4	81,500	27.6	12.1	646	36.1	2.9	3,963	2.5	158	4.0	2,959	23.7	33.2
Holt	2,010	76.6	88,900	17.0	12.0	527	18.5	0.5	2,479	-2.4	73	2.9	1,942	32.7	29.4
Howard	3,460	79.6	141,400	19.8	10.4	650	25.5	1.5	4,853	1.0	157	3.2	4,726	38.1	26.5
Howell	15,557	68.2	114,600	20.6	10.0	605	26.4	3.2	16,165	-0.1	778	4.8	15,778	34.1	27.3
Iron	4,102	73.2	87,100	18.2	10.5	624	35.4	2.5	3,491	0.2	202	5.8	3,871	22.7	31.0
Jackson	291,532	58.4	157,200	19.6	11.9	936	28.7	2.2	359,763	0.9	19,660	5.5	354,384	38.2	22.2

1. Specified owner-occupied units. 2. A value of 10.0 represents 10 percent or less; a value of 50.0 represents 50 percent or more. 3. Specified renter-occupied units. 4. Overcrowded or lacking complete plumbing facilities. 5. Percent of civilian labor force. 6. Civilian employed persons 16 years old and over.

STATE County	Private nonfarm establishments, employment and payroll, 2020									Agriculture, 2017			
		Employment						Annual payroll		Farms			Farm producers whose primary occupation is farming (percent)
											Percent with:		
	Number of establish-ments	Total	Health care and social assistance	Manufac-turing	Retail trade	Finance and insurance	Professional, scientific, and technical services	Total (mil dol)	Average per employee (dollars)	Number	Fewer than 50 acres	1000 acres or more	
	104	105	106	107	108	109	110	111	112	113	114	115	116
MISSISSIPPI— Cont'd													
Sunflower	411	5,554	1,651	281	939	214	56	185	33,380	311	17.7	42.1	51.3
Tallahatchie	158	1,716	540	NA	202	18	41	59	34,611	436	14.7	17.7	40.3
Tate	387	3,927	693	476	767	207	85	122	30,966	593	33.6	5.9	40.1
Tippah	366	5,969	646	2,303	1,157	139	86	210	35,262	557	25.7	3.1	33.5
Tishomingo	368	4,799	662	2,091	653	125	53	163	34,006	274	25.2	2.9	28.2
Tunica	181	5,485	227	489	226	69	17	172	31,267	91	15.4	54.9	80.5
Union	509	10,789	1,330	4,385	1,165	231	98	368	34,065	618	33.8	3.2	27.2
Walthall	209	2,163	550	366	265	58	21	72	33,184	635	33.5	1.1	46.7
Warren	978	15,353	2,410	2,785	2,345	358	373	600	39,063	160	20.0	15.6	29.7
Washington	1,069	13,135	3,238	1,054	2,198	316	311	460	34,990	273	12.8	37.7	66.7
Wayne	362	4,186	691	858	792	205	98	167	39,989	562	40.9	2.5	41.4
Webster	159	1,543	446	169	283	53	55	56	36,433	292	21.6	5.5	30.8
Wilkinson	123	1,273	310	85	237	29	17	40	31,311	163	28.2	16.6	23.4
Winston	378	5,290	709	1,770	807	76	50	205	38,838	483	32.3	3.5	36.9
Yalobusha	157	2,382	414	899	248	79	15	79	33,254	348	21.0	3.7	33.7
Yazoo	355	4,130	1,075	544	800	113	140	158	38,300	574	17.2	14.6	32.7
MISSOURI	150,761	2,566,786	424,377	276,197	310,187	141,980	167,302	128,182	49,939	95,320	29.6	6.2	38.8
Adair	565	8,133	1,828	934	1,571	191	150	266	32,765	816	27.5	6.0	33.4
Andrew	281	1,710	258	48	325	54	61	60	35,343	706	32.6	7.8	40.8
Atchison	185	1,095	289	9	242	77	33	42	38,053	401	19.0	23.7	54.7
Audrain	513	6,385	872	1,839	963	213	132	248	38,796	911	24.6	12.4	47.1
Barry	697	12,820	1,008	5,390	1,548	293	1,594	506	39,480	1,392	34.2	2.9	41.0
Barton	232	2,288	391	319	384	121	97	84	36,695	865	25.7	10.3	44.5
Bates	342	2,717	744	115	516	143	101	95	35,012	1,160	30.0	9.6	43.1
Benton	376	2,259	363	111	648	124	88	62	27,483	749	21.5	5.5	47.2
Bollinger	216	1,472	320	168	314	44	30	47	31,914	756	23.3	4.0	39.6
Boone	4,615	78,685	18,676	4,573	11,835	7,649	4,398	3,697	46,983	1,184	47.1	3.0	30.5
Buchanan	2,151	44,779	8,371	12,291	5,652	1,557	1,232	2,134	47,650	797	40.4	6.0	35.8
Butler	1,023	14,329	4,245	1,858	2,823	526	403	523	36,509	441	30.8	20.6	47.1
Caldwell	148	1,274	126	12	565	62	22	51	39,694	924	32.5	6.0	34.0
Callaway	729	11,873	2,229	1,912	1,207	272	317	562	47,361	1,438	30.0	3.5	30.9
Camden	1,435	14,215	2,720	504	3,158	457	698	529	37,195	516	20.3	2.3	40.6
Cape Girardeau	2,311	38,549	10,695	3,917	5,814	1,033	1,273	1,567	40,641	1,111	32.3	5.1	41.8
Carroll	196	1,575	408	168	225	131	25	56	35,423	1,016	18.0	10.1	39.8
Carter	156	1,119	297	245	173	53	8	27	24,413	160	31.9	11.3	37.3
Cass	2,016	22,256	3,221	1,302	4,668	612	860	828	37,185	1,477	47.1	3.7	34.9
Cedar	286	2,324	511	346	417	96	77	75	32,226	854	26.3	2.9	44.0
Chariton	195	1,290	297	97	212	85	31	43	33,490	985	21.9	9.8	41.4
Christian	1,889	15,449	1,830	1,425	2,975	593	670	534	34,562	1,169	42.2	0.8	40.4
Clark	144	923	87	84	221	88	8	27	28,989	547	19.4	9.1	37.2
Clay	5,252	109,694	14,195	14,256	12,433	2,809	20,222	6,021	54,891	552	55.6	6.0	32.4
Clinton	357	2,652	825	133	490	146	77	102	38,626	684	41.1	8.8	36.4
Cole	2,205	37,041	7,029	2,858	5,220	1,850	1,493	1,620	43,742	1,169	30.2	0.8	32.1
Cooper	376	3,772	841	198	845	116	62	135	35,786	883	22.2	8.3	34.3
Crawford	487	5,687	857	1,941	678	141	142	212	37,336	628	21.8	3.7	34.6
Dade	140	1,109	37	341	158	37	36	42	38,023	699	22.2	9.7	50.9
Dallas	288	1,824	299	162	414	131	53	52	28,373	1,176	34.3	1.8	40.2
Daviess	158	1,052	133	179	217	51	44	32	30,714	1,015	20.8	6.1	31.5
DeKalb	205	2,174	375	38	538	174	29	79	36,180	708	28.2	5.8	33.2
Dent	311	3,557	838	640	443	176	45	137	38,432	694	27.4	5.8	37.7
Douglas	201	2,051	291	620	394	58	41	59	28,542	994	22.8	3.8	46.3
Dunklin	659	6,468	1,990	264	1,367	234	112	187	28,898	283	25.1	34.3	54.8
Franklin	2,616	37,664	4,074	10,970	4,866	1,064	1,079	1,692	44,920	1,818	42.2	2.3	30.5
Gasconade	392	5,364	919	1,986	623	155	80	155	28,855	823	17.4	2.3	36.0
Gentry	181	1,712	670	263	239	72	20	53	31,113	686	22.4	7.9	40.1
Greene	8,474	163,145	32,820	12,991	19,365	7,067	7,220	7,105	43,549	1,857	51.8	1.2	34.5
Grundy	226	1,970	633	194	372	67	55	59	29,807	662	24.5	8.5	36.3
Harrison	188	1,787	492	55	547	128	18	47	26,025	974	21.0	7.8	40.1
Henry	555	6,735	2,238	1,044	1,216	211	116	261	38,800	898	24.1	11.7	45.7
Hickory	142	877	244	13	318	35	16	25	28,434	529	17.4	4.2	46.4
Holt	131	899	175	191	125	37	12	35	39,289	380	24.2	14.2	50.5
Howard	181	2,113	565	298	231	84	50	69	32,429	690	16.8	6.1	36.4
Howell	1,109	13,281	3,846	2,265	2,059	376	314	450	33,898	1,451	33.7	2.4	39.8
Iron	210	1,878	646	73	270	55	15	68	36,367	270	24.8	4.1	35.1
Jackson	18,084	349,456	57,757	27,387	36,528	25,904	28,733	19,527	55,878	706	67.1	3.5	30.1

STATE County	Agriculture, 2017 (cont.) – Land in farms: Acreage (1,000)	Land in farms: Percent change, 2012–2017	Land in farms – Acres: Average size of farm	Acres: Total irrigated (1,000)	Acres: Total cropland (1,000)	Value of land and buildings (dollars): Average per farm	Value of land and buildings (dollars): Average per acre	Value of machinery and equipment, average per farm (dollars)	Value of products sold: Total (mil dol)	Value of products sold: Average per farm (acres)	Value of products sold – Percent from: Crops	Percent from: Livestock and poultry products	Organic farms (number)	Farms with internet access (percent)	Government payments: Total ($1,000)	Government payments: Percent of farms
	117	118	119	120	121	122	123	124	125	126	127	128	129	130	131	132
MISSISSIPPI— Cont'd																
Sunflower	389	4.3	1,249	217.7	325.9	3,977,773	3,184	518,720	223.8	719,566	86.2	13.8	NA	72.3	14,647	80.7
Tallahatchie	310	-9.1	710	130.4	234.5	2,002,926	2,820	212,704	134.9	309,404	99.0	1.0	NA	61.9	7,579	72.2
Tate	158	3.0	266	4.7	67.5	751,443	2,825	93,215	40.1	67,575	71.1	28.9	NA	72.2	2,548	37.1
Tippah	109	-12.1	195	0.2	39.0	404,978	2,072	80,929	23.2	41,655	58.9	41.1	NA	62.3	1,086	64.3
Tishomingo	47	-4.7	172	0.3	19.5	325,832	1,890	55,001	7.0	25,445	90.2	9.8	NA	61.3	484	51.5
Tunica	186	-12.2	2,041	99.0	177.1	6,030,602	2,955	663,152	D	D	D	D	NA	64.8	5,159	86.8
Union	112	-7.5	181	0.0	45.4	362,278	1,999	60,172	16.3	26,299	74.7	25.3	NA	65.4	1,906	57.8
Walthall	100	-15.2	158	0.1	30.1	489,851	3,104	76,957	85.3	134,307	4.9	95.1	6	55.7	1,002	32.0
Warren	99	-20.3	621	9.3	40.4	1,508,216	2,427	174,355	18.8	117,469	95.2	4.8	NA	68.8	2,283	59.4
Washington	371	8.2	1,357	238.6	349.2	5,033,096	3,708	634,141	D	D	D	D	NA	77.3	12,792	86.1
Wayne	97	4.2	173	0.6	27.8	536,506	3,096	84,892	242.6	431,692	3.1	96.9	2	69.2	759	35.8
Webster	74	-8.0	254	0.4	29.6	464,975	1,833	90,512	19.7	67,548	76.6	23.4	NA	58.2	1,211	55.8
Wilkinson	87	-15.8	532	D	11.7	1,278,484	2,401	86,434	4.6	28,258	48.4	51.6	NA	70.6	345	26.4
Winston	108	10.2	223	0.6	17.4	507,990	2,277	66,860	80.1	165,925	3.7	96.3	NA	64.0	804	41.4
Yalobusha	81	-14.2	233	2.8	26.5	434,275	1,864	84,136	13.9	40,009	88.3	11.7	NA	56.6	741	42.5
Yazoo	308	-12.3	536	62.8	167.5	1,495,962	2,789	170,781	105.2	183,207	84.9	15.1	NA	63.1	8,817	70.9
MISSOURI	27,782	-1.7	291	1,529.2	15,599.4	986,481	3,385	104,066	10,525.9	110,427	52.0	48.0	415	72.5	323,801	32.8
Adair	268	-1.9	328	0.1	141.9	916,811	2,792	94,641	52.8	64,721	65.3	34.7	1	68.3	2,179	36.8
Andrew	205	3.2	290	1.2	158.6	1,115,611	3,843	113,518	75.0	106,218	85.2	14.8	NA	82.3	3,325	55.4
Atchison	302	15.0	754	19.9	275.1	3,698,611	4,903	367,596	147.8	368,566	97.2	2.8	NA	81.3	5,332	78.1
Audrain	405	-7.1	445	17.0	334.6	1,894,323	4,256	167,943	247.1	271,233	61.4	38.6	31	68.4	5,722	58.6
Barry	290	8.0	208	4.3	96.9	713,417	3,429	85,578	403.1	289,563	4.2	95.8	1	74.8	391	4.9
Barton	331	-0.4	383	21.7	221.5	1,053,331	2,753	167,455	132.0	152,652	61.0	39.0	NA	74.1	6,312	48.6
Bates	460	2.5	396	3.6	281.7	1,224,243	3,090	137,790	159.8	137,752	63.3	36.7	3	71.6	4,732	49.1
Benton	224	-7.0	299	0.7	77.4	817,792	2,737	78,088	82.7	110,463	19.5	80.5	2	72.9	785	21.6
Bollinger	180	-10.0	238	13.1	77.9	597,725	2,507	75,632	32.1	42,450	56.9	43.1	NA	62.7	1,470	37.0
Boone	213	-11.6	180	3.8	128.5	1,015,839	5,654	74,663	105.0	88,688	44.2	55.8	4	82.4	1,827	20.6
Buchanan	184	-2.5	231	1.2	146.3	936,040	4,053	107,515	66.9	83,923	89.3	10.7	NA	70.3	2,939	45.5
Butler	242	3.3	548	154.3	207.0	2,573,693	4,695	233,342	112.8	255,841	98.6	1.4	NA	81.2	9,945	42.0
Caldwell	250	2.1	270	D	168.1	856,166	3,170	81,607	67.2	72,720	70.9	29.1	1	71.9	5,068	57.8
Callaway	297	-6.2	206	8.8	166.6	816,689	3,960	97,888	124.5	86,602	47.6	52.4	4	81.1	3,457	27.6
Camden	123	-11.0	239	0.0	25.9	527,680	2,208	59,654	15.1	29,250	11.3	88.7	NA	66.1	243	4.1
Cape Girardeau	290	14.6	261	36.8	208.5	1,132,758	4,343	120,048	99.3	89,351	75.8	24.2	NA	69.6	4,195	48.2
Carroll	426	-1.4	419	3.9	333.2	1,500,209	3,580	151,887	144.7	142,399	87.4	12.6	4	72.1	10,429	79.1
Carter	72	-2.7	448	D	9.1	854,925	1,909	68,650	3.8	23,844	11.2	88.8	NA	81.3	73	11.9
Cass	317	-0.7	215	3.5	201.7	807,084	3,759	76,607	120.5	81,576	82.0	18.0	2	74.3	3,599	27.6
Cedar	207	9.4	243	0.8	62.2	604,805	2,489	65,465	49.5	58,000	13.4	86.6	13	69.7	665	13.8
Chariton	388	-4.5	394	1.0	273.9	1,354,347	3,439	155,013	162.8	165,317	60.4	39.6	1	67.5	5,119	54.1
Christian	154	-14.2	132	0.1	43.9	530,251	4,027	54,661	28.9	24,687	18.0	82.0	NA	72.3	105	2.5
Clark	256	6.2	468	4.3	193.8	1,673,148	3,575	177,466	99.8	182,404	77.0	23.0	NA	68.7	2,967	66.0
Clay	111	0.5	201	4.5	64.4	839,610	4,169	90,403	34.7	62,951	55.6	44.4	NA	81.3	1,272	18.7
Clinton	222	16.1	325	0.0	150.2	1,209,500	3,721	128,331	81.8	119,642	78.8	21.2	NA	77.3	2,035	33.3
Cole	186	5.3	159	0.4	70.5	578,816	3,646	69,979	36.8	31,506	36.0	64.0	6	73.7	919	26.3
Cooper	282	-8.2	319	0.2	167.3	1,043,246	3,268	121,276	97.5	110,428	64.1	35.9	9	72.6	3,451	56.6
Crawford	160	-17.6	255	0.4	37.7	658,502	2,583	58,391	14.8	23,556	25.2	74.8	1	73.1	261	8.9
Dade	266	8.2	380	3.7	113.5	1,067,218	2,807	117,152	70.2	100,418	42.2	57.8	3	66.2	1,928	25.0
Dallas	207	-5.1	176	0.2	57.9	446,303	2,538	56,030	51.3	43,648	9.5	90.5	28	66.3	425	5.4
Daviess	307	-2.7	302	0.6	192.8	985,987	3,265	98,261	131.1	129,122	36.7	63.3	9	64.5	7,048	65.2
DeKalb	202	-17.0	285	D	133.5	932,047	3,273	89,075	64.8	91,479	65.4	34.6	1	76.4	3,612	54.5
Dent	190	0.8	273	0.3	27.3	571,102	2,091	62,969	21.8	31,438	11.8	88.2	7	79.0	204	9.7
Douglas	267	5.0	268	0.1	46.6	562,982	2,100	60,494	33.8	33,970	4.4	95.6	1	72.8	220	2.7
Dunklin	283	1.1	1,000	179.3	277.9	5,087,191	5,090	465,745	196.6	694,749	98.4	1.6	NA	75.3	7,431	68.9
Franklin	266	-8.8	146	1.6	120.1	565,029	3,864	61,725	60.0	32,980	43.6	56.4	2	74.0	1,172	18.6
Gasconade	207	-0.8	252	0.1	75.4	701,975	2,787	82,115	32.3	39,273	46.3	53.7	3	72.2	1,118	31.1
Gentry	239	-5.8	348	0.0	152.0	1,077,559	3,098	118,270	120.2	175,265	31.3	68.7	22	75.7	4,896	69.2
Greene	223	6.0	120	0.5	78.3	570,292	4,745	53,364	38.7	20,854	21.2	78.8	2	74.3	807	6.1
Grundy	225	10.5	341	2.1	160.2	997,041	2,928	110,989	92.8	140,210	53.0	47.0	8	71.6	4,553	58.2
Harrison	392	-2.2	403	D	259.3	1,114,054	2,768	101,414	92.7	95,181	74.1	25.9	NA	71.4	10,309	67.0
Henry	382	6.8	425	3.3	213.4	1,143,536	2,690	129,133	98.7	109,924	59.9	40.1	3	73.7	4,645	42.0
Hickory	164	-9.7	310	D	50.9	654,352	2,108	79,880	29.9	56,609	18.8	81.2	2	67.9	301	14.6
Holt	209	4.2	550	31.9	188.3	2,688,737	4,893	253,959	108.8	286,195	96.4	3.6	4	76.3	4,386	75.0
Howard	219	-10.2	317	4.6	133.3	957,809	3,023	115,515	55.9	81,077	76.1	23.9	2	71.4	2,818	59.1
Howell	333	-5.8	230	0.6	54.7	492,355	2,144	62,506	56.9	39,193	7.8	92.2	NA	78.2	285	4.6
Iron	65	-7.4	242	D	12.9	499,202	2,065	50,579	4.3	16,052	8.7	91.3	NA	75.2	32	4.1
Jackson	106	-4.5	150	1.0	73.3	872,579	5,814	73,951	37.6	53,244	80.9	19.1	21	79.7	702	18.8

STATE County	Water use, 2015		Wholesale Trade[1], 2017				Retail Trade[2], 2017				Real estate and rental and leasing,[2] 2017			
	Public supply water withdrawn (mil gal/ day)	Public supply gallons withdrawn per person per day	Number of establish- ments	Number of employees	Sales (mil dol)	Average payroll (mil dol)	Number of establish- ments	Number of employees	Sales (mil dol)	Average payroll (mil dol)	Number of establish- ments	Number of employees	Sales (mil dol)	Average payroll (mil dol)
	133	134	135	136	137	138	139	140	141	142	143	144	145	146
MISSISSIPPI— Cont'd														
Sunflower	3.0	111.5	20	396	427.1	15.4	89	890	206.1	18.3	11	24	4.3	0.8
Tallahatchie	1.3	89.8	7	D	44.2	D	36	234	45.8	6.3	6	D	1.0	D
Tate	1.8	64.0	12	59	30.4	3.4	79	812	207.8	19.6	13	30	7.3	0.8
Tippah	2.7	121.5	18	134	287.5	9.3	74	629	143.7	14.0	6	47	2.6	0.7
Tishomingo	2.6	130.4	18	152	27.9	4.0	86	681	141.5	16.2	9	D	2.2	D
Tunica	3.1	299.7	9	95	159.8	4.9	47	253	60.8	5.6	9	21	3.5	0.5
Union	2.6	90.4	18	241	462.0	9.7	103	1,115	286.7	25.7	13	31	5.3	1.0
Walthall	2.6	180.4	D	D	D	1.6	40	325	73.0	7.1	5	D	2.6	D
Warren	8.0	168.3	37	303	354.3	14.4	189	2,486	672.1	57.1	35	137	30.2	4.6
Washington	11.6	240.0	57	692	780.8	36.6	219	2,612	591.6	55.1	41	130	22.7	4.5
Wayne	2.6	127.4	25	191	249.7	13.9	81	831	180.1	18.2	7	24	4.7	0.7
Webster	1.4	141.4	D	D	D	D	35	257	51.7	5.0	NA	NA	NA	NA
Wilkinson	1.0	111.8	7	D	27.2	D	23	245	51.1	5.4	NA	NA	NA	NA
Winston	2.0	109.2	11	140	125.6	7.0	84	859	200.7	20.2	23	81	13.0	2.3
Yalobusha	2.2	178.4	NA	NA	NA	NA	43	311	58.0	5.3	NA	NA	NA	NA
Yazoo	5.5	200.5	23	243	172.1	11.1	85	936	165.3	16.7	17	51	7.3	1.7
MISSOURI	797.1	131.0	6,293	95,156	102,651.6	5,631.7	20,694	312,616	100,394.0	8,147.5	6,644	37,144	8,975.9	1,625.7
Adair	2.5	98.5	D	D	D	D	102	1,503	307.4	31.0	18	51	12.2	1.9
Andrew	18.1	1,044.2	D	D	D	4.1	37	364	146.6	11.9	11	18	2.4	0.4
Atchison	0.5	92.3	12	139	171.2	4.9	34	374	73.4	11.0	5	D	0.8	D
Audrain	2.2	82.8	21	332	220.3	11.4	88	1,023	262.7	23.5	10	32	4.1	1.0
Barry	4.6	127.6	30	450	481.9	31.4	137	1,632	397.0	39.1	24	72	10.5	2.1
Barton	1.8	154.0	11	180	231.9	5.9	33	467	112.6	11.1	D	D	D	D
Bates	1.2	73.6	12	135	134.2	5.3	59	636	180.6	15.8	7	27	2.0	1.3
Benton	0.7	38.0	5	D	20.0	D	68	693	191.7	16.0	14	21	3.1	0.5
Bollinger	0.2	13.1	D	D	D	8.5	31	293	68.2	6.0	NA	NA	NA	NA
Boone	17.9	102.0	144	1,697	914.6	92.9	592	11,589	3,410.1	291.4	270	1,231	225.7	39.6
Buchanan	0.0	0.0	102	1,239	1,683.3	66.6	305	5,707	1,411.0	133.1	106	400	65.2	11.3
Butler	1.4	32.1	48	408	222.8	15.7	199	2,972	781.9	70.0	42	141	25.5	4.4
Caldwell	0.3	37.7	D	D	D	2.2	26	599	101.9	15.2	D	D	D	D
Callaway	3.6	80.3	22	323	151.9	14.9	120	1,244	340.0	27.2	27	105	17.7	3.2
Camden	3.9	87.5	42	297	142.0	11.6	289	3,300	791.9	81.1	89	335	63.4	10.0
Cape Girardeau	7.9	100.0	105	1,081	662.7	51.3	409	6,000	1,574.2	149.8	115	369	73.3	12.7
Carroll	0.8	90.1	12	72	120.0	3.3	37	245	52.9	5.2	D	D	D	D
Carter	0.5	73.4	5	D	17.2	D	27	163	28.7	2.8	NA	NA	NA	NA
Cass	1.6	15.3	59	545	533.3	32.6	259	4,481	1,344.4	114.0	80	244	59.7	9.3
Cedar	0.9	61.7	7	40	14.8	0.9	48	446	116.2	10.0	11	42	2.9	0.8
Chariton	0.4	48.8	15	227	389.5	10.1	35	220	57.4	5.2	6	D	0.6	D
Christian	6.6	78.7	73	700	339.4	29.9	247	2,863	752.6	70.2	80	191	43.5	5.8
Clark	0.7	101.5	12	143	116.6	6.1	30	252	80.9	4.6	3	5	0.4	0.2
Clay	124.2	527.1	287	4,540	4,081.9	273.4	612	12,795	3,927.9	350.5	255	1,060	284.6	47.5
Clinton	0.3	14.6	12	86	165.7	4.2	54	464	161.9	13.3	D	D	D	D
Cole	8.2	106.6	76	1,022	1,358.9	47.9	283	5,429	1,374.9	132.8	76	271	66.2	9.9
Cooper	1.3	75.4	13	141	99.5	5.0	58	756	277.4	18.8	12	35	4.0	0.7
Crawford	1.3	52.2	14	139	57.2	6.6	75	677	238.7	17.6	17	78	11.6	2.6
Dade	0.4	48.7	7	307	156.9	10.5	29	189	42.5	3.6	4	D	0.7	D
Dallas	0.5	28.7	8	87	80.0	2.6	47	435	115.3	10.2	10	21	1.7	0.5
Daviess	0.6	71.5	14	67	62.0	3.0	26	216	65.0	4.6	4	5	0.6	0.1
DeKalb	0.1	11.0	D	D	D	2.3	36	547	130.1	12.4	D	D	D	D
Dent	0.9	57.7	D	D	D	D	49	535	123.0	12.0	13	20	2.8	0.5
Douglas	0.6	41.9	11	36	17.1	1.1	33	448	101.5	10.1	5	5	0.7	0.1
Dunklin	3.1	99.0	D	D	D	D	131	1,462	428.1	35.5	24	601	24.0	13.5
Franklin	6.9	67.8	95	896	531.6	39.8	358	4,839	1,357.8	121.9	83	202	41.0	6.6
Gasconade	0.8	55.2	23	240	169.6	9.8	61	667	169.3	15.8	8	21	2.5	0.6
Gentry	0.6	92.6	D	D	D	4.6	31	244	54.3	6.0	4	47	1.1	0.7
Greene	33.2	115.2	386	8,467	6,884.5	426.4	1,138	19,066	5,495.5	515.1	477	3,066	501.5	103.0
Grundy	1.3	132.7	9	106	136.8	3.2	42	415	87.2	8.6	7	16	1.9	0.4
Harrison	0.9	105.6	11	136	99.6	3.6	38	560	206.9	14.8	5	4	1.5	0.1
Henry	2.0	92.0	21	165	89.1	6.5	112	1,207	347.8	29.1	27	81	9.6	1.7
Hickory	0.3	33.7	3	11	2.7	0.4	33	304	64.5	6.3	4	D	0.3	D
Holt	0.4	89.2	11	112	129.9	5.5	23	155	57.0	4.4	NA	NA	NA	NA
Howard	1.0	102.6	D	D	D	D	34	273	50.0	5.1	4	D	2.1	D
Howell	3.0	75.0	42	489	244.1	19.6	215	2,147	612.7	52.8	45	154	21.3	4.1
Iron	0.4	41.5	D	D	D	0.9	37	279	60.3	5.3	7	D	1.9	D
Jackson	26.9	39.1	804	12,327	12,797.4	739.9	2,118	35,602	10,337.7	949.9	860	5,490	1,842.2	305.3

1 Merchant wholesalers, except manufacturers' sales branches and offices. 2. Employer establishments.

Table B. States and Counties — **Professional Services, Manufacturing, and Accommodation and Food Services**

STATE County	Professional, scientific, and technical services, 2017				Manufacturing, 2017				Accommodation and food services, 2017			
	Number of establish-ments	Number of employees	Sales (mil dol)	Average payroll (mil dol)	Number of establish-ments	Number of employees	Sales (mil dol)	Average payroll (mil dol)	Number of establis-hments	Number of employees	Sales (mil dol)	Annual payroll (mil dol)
	147	148	149	150	151	152	153	154	155	156	157	158
MISSISSIPPI— Cont'd												
Sunflower	16	58	6.6	1.9	18	315	183.7	14.4	36	562	23.1	6.4
Tallahatchie	8	43	3.9	1.2	D	42	D	1.1	D	D	D	0.7
Tate	22	79	8.2	3.0	11	465	203.6	20.4	36	571	25.9	6.5
Tippah	16	73	7.8	2.9	24	1,924	443.3	73.8	D	D	D	D
Tishomingo	16	51	4.5	1.3	38	2,034	537.1	71.7	D	D	D	D
Tunica	D	D	D	D	8	479	127.6	20.5	34	5,252	605.1	157.7
Union	28	102	12.2	4.1	32	4,367	3,050.5	186.9	45	787	43.8	11.0
Walthall	10	15	2.1	0.5	12	344	66.5	13.6	17	173	9.3	2.0
Warren	D	D	D	D	35	2,913	1,824.2	148.9	119	3,726	300.6	69.1
Washington	D	D	D	D	35	1,063	748.4	55.9	88	2,239	143.8	36.8
Wayne	42	99	10.5	3.1	10	1,112	250.8	50.1	D	D	D	D
Webster	10	77	6.1	1.8	8	188	55.0	8.8	13	132	5.6	1.3
Wilkinson	6	19	1.4	0.5	3	99	36.9	4.8	D	D	D	D
Winston	26	61	6.1	1.7	18	1,894	416.4	80.8	30	451	18.9	5.2
Yalobusha	D	D	D	D	6	1,201	308.2	36.4	D	D	D	D
Yazoo	23	181	13.2	5.0	10	586	307.7	34.6	32	385	18.3	4.4
MISSOURI	14,111	160,171	29,870.1	11,490.3	5,797	259,462	118,633.7	14,216.5	12,896	263,644	15,082.4	4,274.7
Adair	D	D	D	D	12	D	333.7	34.3	63	1,238	52.5	14.5
Andrew	D	D	D	D	11	31	5.7	1.3	9	118	4.8	1.4
Atchison	D	D	D	D	D	15	D	0.4	D	D	D	D
Audrain	27	140	11.5	4.9	36	1,838	902.1	91.5	41	579	22.0	5.7
Barry	D	D	297.4	D	42	4,814	1,510.1	197.2	55	761	35.7	10.4
Barton	14	112	10.8	5.8	19	325	96.7	13.7	19	289	11.0	3.0
Bates	D	D	D	2.8	16	74	26.5	D	29	368	14.9	4.2
Benton	D	D	6.1	D	17	254	18.8	5.4	D	D	D	3.8
Bollinger	D	D	D	D	D	160	D	5.2	D	D	D	D
Boone	D	D	D	D	96	4,129	2,175.4	205.9	460	10,333	485.2	141.5
Buchanan	D	D	D	D	85	11,918	7,943.0	583.8	201	4,071	198.3	58.0
Butler	47	277	31.1	10.4	40	2,198	530.6	83.7	84	1,689	74.9	21.7
Caldwell	D	D	D	D	7	D	9.9	D	D	D	D	D
Callaway	39	349	24.0	12.8	37	1,455	498.3	82.5	69	1,014	48.0	13.6
Camden	D	D	D	49.5	40	375	143.6	18.6	163	2,672	180.9	51.3
Cape Girardeau	D	D	D	D	92	3,682	2,892.5	200.1	187	4,214	197.1	59.8
Carroll	D	D	2.2	D	11	154	137.6	7.0	D	D	D	D
Carter	D	D	0.5	D	20	143	39.8	5.7	15	120	5.9	1.6
Cass	160	677	85.5	29.8	53	2,063	503.8	89.5	156	3,038	128.7	39.3
Cedar	18	69	4.8	1.5	21	339	162.9	15.6	28	333	11.6	3.4
Chariton	D	D	D	D	7	78	14.1	3.3	D	D	D	0.8
Christian	159	674	72.8	27.9	93	1,137	291.0	50.5	117	2,000	96.3	30.1
Clark	9	10	0.7	0.3	5	29	5.7	1.4	10	113	3.8	1.3
Clay	D	D	D	D	196	15,064	14,334.3	919.7	435	11,396	824.2	210.1
Clinton	D	D	D	D	14	118	21.9	4.8	27	337	9.7	3.4
Cole	D	D	D	D	56	2,420	748.7	117.8	169	3,374	163.4	47.0
Cooper	D	D	D	D	7	196	57.0	10.4	D	D	D	13.9
Crawford	27	98	8.4	2.6	48	1,938	403.1	68.3	55	619	31.4	9.0
Dade	D	D	D	D	12	209	94.2	9.0	13	91	3.5	0.9
Dallas	20	52	4.8	1.2	12	141	57.1	5.6	24	276	12.5	3.3
Daviess	D	D	D	D	9	170	52.2	6.0	8	D	4.0	D
DeKalb	D	D	D	D	6	25	7.8	1.4	18	246	9.5	2.7
Dent	14	46	3.2	1.2	25	556	291.3	31.9	D	D	D	D
Douglas	14	40	4.9	1.3	11	D	122.1	17.1	13	225	8.9	2.3
Dunklin	29	121	13.5	4.1	10	357	100.9	14.7	46	647	30.6	8.5
Franklin	186	1,019	122.9	45.0	207	9,398	2,677.6	469.7	205	3,601	166.1	49.3
Gasconade	23	114	8.8	3.0	41	1,402	216.8	49.0	46	497	24.0	7.0
Gentry	D	D	D	D	6	172	45.6	9.7	D	D	D	0.7
Greene	D	D	D	D	288	12,379	5,020.4	635.7	785	16,133	812.7	235.6
Grundy	D	D	D	D	10	527	400.1	27.3	15	236	6.6	2.4
Harrison	D	D	1.3	D	D	31	D	1.3	16	267	11.9	3.4
Henry	32	118	14.1	3.9	19	1,003	425.6	47.7	53	667	34.4	9.4
Hickory	D	D	D	D	NA	NA	NA	NA	14	78	4.3	1.2
Holt	D	D	1.5	D	D	152	D	11.2	7	D	3.8	D
Howard	14	58	4.9	1.8	10	324	71.8	14.4	15	158	4.9	1.5
Howell	70	306	29.9	12.4	62	2,465	606.8	91.1	72	1,172	56.0	15.4
Iron	D	D	D	D	12	46	7.7	1.9	17	147	5.9	1.8
Jackson	D	D	D	D	610	24,965	9,820.8	1,497.1	1,557	37,503	2,219.3	657.1

STATE County	Health care and social assistance, 2017				Other services, 2017				Nonemployer businesses, 2019		Value of residential construction authorized by building permits, 2021	
	Number of establish-ments	Number of employees	Receipts (mil dol)	Annual payroll (mil dol)	Number of establish-ments	Number of employees	Receipts (mil dol)	Annual payroll (mil dol)	Number	Receipts (mil dol)	New construction ($1,000)	Number of housing units
	159	160	161	162	163	164	165	166	167	168	169	170
MISSISSIPPI— Cont'd												
Sunflower	46	1,339	164.8	49.4	31	191	23.5	6.8	1,615	48.9	1,594	11
Tallahatchie	17	564	45.4	20.9	11	30	4.1	0.7	754	26.1	70	2
Tate	40	634	61.0	26.3	D	D	D	D	2,144	93.4	38,506	164
Tippah	33	658	44.9	18.4	D	D	D	D	1,465	65.8	2,718	13
Tishomingo	31	543	42.1	18.9	23	99	16.2	2.6	1,115	45.6	720	6
Tunica	20	232	18.9	6.6	D	D	D	0.3	715	26.7	23,381	104
Union	53	1,149	132.8	45.7	D	D	D	D	2,212	97.3	3,521	19
Walthall	17	469	50.2	20.8	D	D	D	0.4	1,160	42.0	0	0
Warren	125	2,394	293.7	105.6	56	264	24.4	6.2	2,984	106.5	939	4
Washington	149	3,480	295.8	122.9	76	462	45.4	15.3	3,395	133.3	995	7
Wayne	17	583	41.5	23.8	D	D	D	D	1,635	61.9	150	2
Webster	15	414	42.4	18.4	D	D	D	0.7	822	33.2	1,145	9
Wilkinson	17	296	27.1	9.4	D	D	D	1.2	637	22.8	0	0
Winston	22	555	54.5	19.1	D	D	D	D	1,360	49.3	1,265	6
Yalobusha	9	352	25.8	13.1	9	19	1.8	0.4	920	33.7	609	20
Yazoo	37	1,008	71.1	28.9	D	D	5.7	D	1,700	57.9	0	0
MISSOURI	19,097	423,057	48,192.5	18,682.2	10,513	68,206	8,693.9	2,297.4	429,225	19,847.7	4,747,590	21,372
Adair	D	D	D	D	D	D	D	D	1,605	59.4	6,225	21
Andrew	26	270	15.9	7.2	25	106	12.0	2.5	1,274	51.1	400	4
Atchison	20	345	30.5	15.1	D	D	D	1.4	407	15.3	0	0
Audrain	68	1,131	100.8	46.0	43	223	20.6	7.6	1,359	62.6	1,231	14
Barry	69	1,077	106.9	38.1	53	170	16.4	3.7	2,345	97.5	4,904	30
Barton	29	426	35.3	13.1	D	D	D	D	895	38.3	0	0
Bates	36	842	70.0	28.2	D	D	D	D	1,150	47.1	430	2
Benton	35	374	22.3	9.5	31	107	9.8	1.8	1,446	70.7	1,215	5
Bollinger	D	D	D	D	D	D	D	D	778	35.3	0	0
Boone	655	19,126	2,584.4	888.4	347	2,170	255.5	69.1	12,300	615.1	267,321	1,013
Buchanan	304	9,286	1,016.9	413.5	D	D	183.4	D	4,206	163.8	21,413	98
Butler	199	4,125	580.4	177.9	62	244	24.0	5.6	2,600	135.8	555	6
Caldwell	D	D	D	D	D	D	D	D	613	26.9	7,644	28
Callaway	71	2,543	167.3	86.6	64	256	26.0	6.1	2,474	101.6	9,435	46
Camden	140	2,537	295.5	108.8	101	359	35.8	9.5	4,038	211.5	248,243	313
Cape Girardeau	332	10,265	1,317.0	480.6	D	D	D	D	5,535	255.1	51,288	177
Carroll	21	444	40.2	15.0	14	52	5.2	1.2	620	27.4	7,913	11
Carter	28	241	11.5	6.6	D	D	2.5	D	551	27.8	0	0
Cass	200	3,233	323.4	128.0	148	617	55.4	16.3	7,543	420.1	281,774	1,523
Cedar	30	606	35.6	14.8	19	43	3.9	0.8	1,205	55.4	2,014	9
Chariton	16	283	16.0	6.4	18	49	9.0	1.4	637	20.3	450	1
Christian	141	1,554	119.5	47.5	135	496	41.0	12.2	7,443	337.0	203,789	755
Clark	15	130	7.8	3.0	D	D	D	D	432	17.0	1,426	6
Clay	608	13,243	1,470.4	648.9	350	2,307	267.5	78.7	17,106	720.3	123,878	558
Clinton	44	914	123.2	39.4	D	D	D	D	1,418	54.8	17,768	68
Cole	279	6,846	793.1	310.7	221	1,332	226.1	60.8	4,934	252.3	22,200	193
Cooper	51	835	57.8	24.0	36	104	11.1	2.6	1,119	49.3	1,878	7
Crawford	51	878	88.6	33.2	33	141	13.2	3.3	1,526	63.4	11,287	20
Dade	D	D	D	0.6	D	D	D	0.4	511	19.7	0	0
Dallas	36	886	25.2	8.9	23	52	5.2	1.0	1,440	71.7	1,713	7
Daviess	11	97	7.0	2.8	D	D	2.7	D	765	38.1	0	0
DeKalb	D	D	D	D	13	88	8.6	2.3	617	30.4	596	2
Dent	31	796	50.8	20.4	17	45	4.2	0.9	928	37.4	238	1
Douglas	17	301	20.9	7.8	15	43	5.0	1.1	1,147	42.4	2,162	39
Dunklin	105	2,207	163.8	57.3	40	105	12.2	2.6	1,666	102.9	4,890	26
Franklin	245	4,651	479.5	191.9	184	931	110.8	30.5	6,921	308.3	113,880	488
Gasconade	30	897	42.6	20.6	30	93	8.9	2.2	1,239	48.3	782	13
Gentry	41	778	42.6	18.2	D	D	2.9	D	552	21.7	660	4
Greene	894	29,480	3,798.3	1,417.7	592	4,716	492.7	147.9	21,851	1,169.7	304,734	1,667
Grundy	31	617	49.9	19.4	25	62	4.6	1.5	688	31.5	474	5
Harrison	28	341	18.4	7.8	D	D	D	D	643	29.6	0	0
Henry	58	2,021	176.9	81.0	41	169	11.6	3.2	1,448	58.6	3,501	20
Hickory	9	198	13.3	5.3	D	D	D	0.3	731	29.0	NA	NA
Holt	10	151	7.3	3.6	D	D	2.4	D	402	20.7	150	1
Howard	25	605	23.3	12.5	D	D	D	D	692	30.2	1,090	9
Howell	156	4,912	473.1	181.5	73	356	44.4	9.5	3,062	124.5	12,375	68
Iron	39	628	34.4	15.2	20	56	4.6	1.1	485	19.3	0	0
Jackson	2,436	57,154	7,797.2	2,920.4	1,269	9,916	1,962.3	361.5	48,980	2,187.3	846,311	3,974

STATE County	Government employment and payroll, 2017									Local government finances, 2017				
			March payroll (percent of total)							General revenue				
												Taxes		
													Per capita[1] (dollars)	
	Full-time equivalent employees	March payroll (dollars)	Adminis-tration, judicial, and legal	Police and corrections	Fire protection	Highways and transpor-tation	Health and welfare	Natural resources and utilities	Education and libraries	Total (mil dol)	Inter-govern-mental (mil dol)	Total (mil dol)	Total	Property
	171	172	173	174	175	176	177	178	179	180	181	182	183	184
MISSISSIPPI— Cont'd														
Sunflower	2,035	7,299,191	3.4	3.6	1.2	1.7	42.9	0.9	45.9	183.1	57.3	24.4	933	902
Tallahatchie	944	2,844,137	6.0	5.5	0.0	3.5	49.3	1.2	34.5	38.5	19.7	13.7	970	944
Tate	1,245	4,687,881	2.3	3.1	1.2	1.7	0.3	2.4	88.5	114.5	68.2	24.6	860	820
Tippah	788	2,243,776	2.9	2.0	0.1	0.9	22.9	3.9	67.3	69.0	36.1	13.2	600	563
Tishomingo	648	1,867,623	9.5	8.3	1.2	2.6	0.6	5.2	71.8	50.6	27.2	18.4	941	933
Tunica	613	1,660,838	1.7	18.9	0.0	4.2	5.2	14.6	55.0	77.7	42.0	23.0	2,300	1,836
Union	983	2,922,592	4.5	7.8	2.2	2.2	0.0	10.9	72.1	71.1	43.7	19.2	675	653
Walthall	397	1,089,504	5.9	4.7	0.1	4.9	0.0	6.5	77.3	39.6	16.8	10.4	716	700
Warren	1,841	5,441,149	4.4	5.4	4.5	2.4	4.4	5.9	71.0	172.9	71.1	70.9	1,520	1,336
Washington	3,096	10,743,574	4.5	7.4	2.4	2.9	44.3	2.5	34.8	300.2	88.8	63.2	1,367	1,263
Wayne	1,072	3,496,080	4.1	3.8	0.5	2.6	38.8	2.4	46.7	76.4	30.1	11.7	571	555
Webster	360	980,701	9.8	6.2	0.2	5.1	0.1	2.1	76.2	25.3	15.3	7.0	718	689
Wilkinson	337	922,832	18.9	9.7	0.3	6.1	0.0	4.1	60.6	54.6	12.6	6.4	718	698
Winston	593	1,520,585	8.8	15.4	2.3	3.4	1.5	2.8	64.8	51.8	28.2	12.7	695	665
Yalobusha	700	2,126,577	7.3	4.0	3.3	3.0	43.4	2.8	36.1	30.5	17.7	9.0	719	703
Yazoo	862	2,505,769	6.4	7.4	3.1	6.5	2.4	8.8	61.1	75.0	40.6	24.5	856	828
MISSOURI	X	X	X	X	X	X	X	X	X	X	X	X	X	X
Adair	864	2,743,554	7.4	5.9	3.6	3.4	14.4	5.3	58.6	83.3	35.1	27.3	1,072	505
Andrew	520	1,620,539	4.8	4.2	0.9	3.0	2.9	5.9	77.7	43.9	20.2	18.0	1,032	794
Atchison	271	779,674	9.8	6.3	0.1	9.7	10.0	4.2	58.9	23.9	6.5	13.4	2,547	1,906
Audrain	811	2,619,099	7.1	10.8	0.6	4.0	16.2	4.6	55.2	71.9	23.9	31.7	1,237	777
Barry	1,414	4,405,718	4.6	5.3	1.8	2.5	2.0	5.4	77.0	122.5	53.3	55.6	1,562	1,111
Barton	658	2,128,493	3.9	3.6	0.5	2.0	38.8	6.7	44.1	55.0	15.2	13.9	1,178	816
Bates	884	2,973,990	3.7	4.8	0.2	1.7	41.9	4.6	41.4	48.2	21.3	15.6	956	670
Benton	720	1,922,673	4.4	6.6	0.1	2.2	24.0	1.7	60.9	54.2	15.5	27.2	1,424	1,156
Bollinger	370	1,005,536	5.3	5.6	0.5	3.0	0.2	2.0	83.1	27.3	13.2	11.4	926	770
Boone	6,703	23,310,166	7.9	5.7	3.5	2.7	5.2	9.4	64.0	898.3	189.1	294.5	1,654	990
Buchanan	2,957	11,239,924	4.7	9.9	5.2	3.5	2.7	5.3	67.6	318.0	107.7	156.6	1,766	917
Butler	1,652	5,253,884	6.4	6.1	2.3	4.2	1.4	2.5	73.5	133.1	64.0	51.9	1,217	639
Caldwell	475	1,404,146	6.0	8.8	0.0	2.6	7.0	3.6	71.6	31.6	16.2	9.3	1,025	773
Callaway	1,257	3,411,112	8.6	7.5	2.9	4.3	5.6	8.2	59.2	115.3	38.4	44.6	992	689
Camden	1,489	4,730,188	10.2	8.8	5.3	5.7	2.5	3.0	62.6	138.6	35.1	78.9	1,734	1,143
Cape Girardeau	2,694	7,744,192	5.5	9.3	4.7	5.2	0.1	9.1	62.5	235.5	73.5	125.8	1,608	822
Carroll	377	1,180,272	4.7	5.0	1.4	4.3	4.9	3.0	76.4	32.2	11.6	16.0	1,828	1,562
Carter	285	715,720	7.0	8.6	0.1	2.6	6.2	1.3	73.2	17.3	9.8	5.8	940	712
Cass	4,148	15,759,622	5.2	6.9	4.5	2.5	12.9	4.5	62.6	422.1	129.7	158.7	1,533	984
Cedar	621	1,672,123	5.0	5.6	0.2	2.0	24.0	9.6	52.3	52.5	15.9	11.3	805	573
Chariton	312	878,644	9.7	6.1	0.2	2.9	5.4	6.9	68.2	23.1	8.0	12.2	1,639	1,357
Christian	2,299	7,714,341	5.3	7.0	3.1	2.0	0.1	4.4	76.7	220.7	101.0	90.9	1,064	856
Clark	366	956,972	6.2	6.0	0.0	3.5	20.5	6.7	53.1	21.2	9.4	7.6	1,133	885
Clay	11,912	49,984,164	2.4	4.4	2.0	0.6	40.2	1.4	48.4	1,499.3	269.1	411.9	1,699	1,183
Clinton	680	2,252,917	6.5	9.2	1.2	4.7	3.4	7.1	67.6	57.7	24.4	25.0	1,218	868
Cole	2,381	8,477,306	7.1	8.9	3.8	4.3	4.2	5.4	63.9	228.9	70.4	118.1	1,541	818
Cooper	716	2,385,908	5.3	6.6	1.5	2.5	27.8	4.5	49.8	52.7	16.8	26.0	1,474	735
Crawford	719	1,546,090	7.8	11.9	0.0	5.2	9.0	5.2	58.5	49.3	23.0	19.2	798	588
Dade	421	1,056,840	5.1	2.7	0.0	0.4	32.0	3.6	56.2	23.5	8.9	7.4	981	831
Dallas	365	976,127	7.9	6.8	0.4	5.1	1.0	3.0	75.9	24.5	13.1	9.0	536	325
Daviess	356	1,031,668	6.2	2.8	0.0	2.5	2.4	7.8	78.1	22.6	11.1	8.4	1,008	842
DeKalb	234	777,687	18.0	0.5	0.0	2.9	3.5	5.0	69.9	18.6	8.2	7.1	569	506
Dent	697	2,121,584	7.9	2.7	0.0	3.3	36.5	3.2	45.4	75.6	16.6	11.4	736	473
Douglas	473	1,321,306	5.3	8.7	0.0	4.9	3.8	4.6	71.2	23.7	13.2	7.0	528	326
Dunklin	1,240	3,617,815	4.4	7.5	1.7	2.9	4.4	9.3	65.5	87.9	47.6	28.8	955	582
Franklin	3,447	12,044,444	4.5	9.0	2.4	3.3	7.5	3.1	69.3	307.1	113.2	149.8	1,450	921
Gasconade	769	2,577,493	4.6	4.5	0.0	3.2	35.2	3.4	48.8	78.7	16.4	20.1	1,367	996
Gentry	331	926,821	11.4	4.9	0.4	6.3	7.9	7.2	61.2	24.6	9.3	11.7	1,764	1,613
Greene	10,598	41,070,291	5.2	8.9	4.1	4.8	1.5	12.8	54.1	1,021.2	349.5	481.6	1,664	860
Grundy	728	1,939,762	3.3	5.3	0.3	2.8	14.1	7.5	65.4	61.1	28.9	13.6	1,362	837
Harrison	657	2,013,855	3.9	4.5	0.2	2.5	48.2	3.1	37.1	57.8	12.6	12.4	1,461	893
Henry	1,448	5,199,624	3.0	4.0	0.9	1.1	62.9	2.3	25.6	160.4	51.4	28.0	1,290	772
Hickory	328	963,083	6.3	6.5	0.0	2.7	0.0	1.8	82.3	22.4	12.1	7.5	799	630
Holt	212	570,842	9.4	7.1	0.0	4.4	2.4	6.9	68.3	30.5	16.9	11.0	2,498	2,075
Howard	360	1,047,325	8.1	7.4	0.3	3.5	7.8	5.6	66.3	26.2	12.5	9.1	906	626
Howell	1,574	4,372,994	5.4	5.4	1.6	3.4	6.0	7.9	68.8	107.4	52.2	35.5	885	520
Iron	495	1,426,766	5.1	5.0	0.3	6.1	8.3	1.9	72.8	31.7	12.8	14.1	1,385	1,206
Jackson	26,895	111,806,751	5.7	10.2	10.4	6.5	3.3	9.5	53.7	3,867.8	951.9	1,775.4	2,543	1,159

1. Based on the resident population estimated as of July 1 of the year shown.

STATE County	Local government finances, 2017 (cont.)									Government employment, 2020			Individual income tax returns, 2019		
	Direct general expenditure							Debt outstanding							
			Percent of total for:												
	Total (mil dol)	Per capita[1] (dollars)	Education	Health and hospitals	Police protection	Public welfare	Highways	Total (mil dol)	Per capita[1] (dollars)	Federal civilian	Federal military	State and local	Number of returns	Mean adjusted gross income	Mean income tax
	185	186	187	188	189	190	191	192	193	194	195	196	197	198	199
MISSISSIPPI— Cont'd															
Sunflower	194.3	7,431	33.7	51.8	2.7	0.0	4.3	20.5	783	59	120	2,983	9,510	38,229	3,001
Tallahatchie	40.0	2,835	50.6	1.1	4.9	0.0	7.6	11.4	807	40	65	931	4,880	35,471	2,171
Tate	139.4	4,877	81.6	0.5	3.9	0.0	3.1	38.0	1,331	81	159	1,487	12,320	48,578	3,915
Tippah	73.5	3,349	49.1	23.7	3.1	0.3	9.1	9.8	448	55	744	1,195	8,990	41,711	2,639
Tishomingo	38.4	1,966	76.9	0.1	5.0	0.0	2.0	31.2	1,598	64	110	839	7,570	46,778	3,342
Tunica	79.7	7,980	30.8	3.2	11.3	0.5	8.5	35.0	3,504	24	54	671	4,510	32,409	1,968
Union	67.1	2,355	63.4	0.4	7.5	0.0	7.6	31.4	1,103	45	166	1,209	11,980	45,815	3,380
Walthall	37.3	2,570	47.7	30.1	5.1	0.3	4.9	0.6	39	32	82	580	5,710	40,580	2,857
Warren	175.5	3,759	45.7	0.8	6.8	0.2	8.5	254.0	5,440	2,633	303	2,137	20,620	51,305	4,583
Washington	290.2	6,282	28.5	41.9	4.6	0.1	4.1	113.0	2,447	385	266	3,368	19,380	40,949	3,403
Wayne	81.2	3,972	43.6	35.0	4.3	0.0	5.7	15.2	742	43	119	1,242	8,620	44,040	3,337
Webster	24.6	2,523	63.9	1.3	5.0	0.0	8.5	5.7	585	40	56	432	4,020	47,447	3,485
Wilkinson	56.7	6,398	20.6	32.8	2.0	0.1	3.5	25.3	2,854	13	42	529	3,370	38,426	2,556
Winston	52.5	2,879	52.1	1.3	7.0	0.1	7.7	3.4	189	52	101	727	7,610	44,751	3,715
Yalobusha	29.8	2,392	51.6	1.0	6.5	0.0	10.1	12.0	962	56	69	778	5,390	40,565	2,783
Yazoo	72.7	2,536	49.5	1.3	7.4	0.3	9.7	30.0	1,047	758	130	1,366	9,560	39,705	3,146
MISSOURI	X	X	X	X	X	X	X	X	X	61,393	36,664	362,687	2,871,540	65,062	7,386
Adair	72.4	2,846	46.5	4.6	5.9	7.5	6.0	53.7	2,110	89	79	2,276	9,840	47,509	4,130
Andrew	44.6	2,550	63.0	3.5	4.0	0.2	8.1	77.0	4,404	36	61	697	8,630	61,970	6,150
Atchison	22.9	4,360	49.8	0.3	5.1	0.0	17.7	16.2	3,089	34	17	330	2,490	55,840	4,805
Audrain	76.7	2,998	53.8	2.9	4.5	7.7	6.4	85.7	3,350	81	76	1,946	10,570	47,760	3,662
Barry	108.5	3,046	64.6	2.7	4.1	0.0	9.0	71.7	2,012	129	118	1,583	14,990	47,823	4,106
Barton	55.0	4,667	37.2	38.4	2.3	0.0	4.0	50.3	4,264	43	38	571	5,080	43,944	3,167
Bates	48.3	2,966	56.3	0.0	11.6	7.0	7.7	37.9	2,326	57	159	1,084	7,220	48,506	3,791
Benton	38.6	2,025	62.3	5.4	3.0	13.6	4.5	22.4	1,176	105	95	881	8,580	42,911	3,197
Bollinger	27.1	2,206	65.9	0.9	3.7	0.3	1.7	3.2	257	31	40	426	4,820	41,917	2,630
Boone	871.1	4,893	35.9	32.4	3.4	0.2	4.3	2,544.1	14,292	2,712	601	30,535	80,760	72,425	8,748
Buchanan	310.3	3,500	48.4	1.4	6.6	0.1	6.1	804.6	9,075	480	288	5,684	39,520	54,455	5,297
Butler	133.3	3,128	70.5	0.0	7.5	0.0	5.4	63.4	1,488	841	137	2,574	17,660	44,693	3,691
Caldwell	33.5	3,699	57.4	1.9	5.1	5.7	7.6	47.0	5,190	48	29	553	3,960	49,667	3,823
Callaway	92.0	2,044	55.9	4.2	5.6	0.0	5.7	52.7	1,173	134	139	3,510	20,250	51,878	4,288
Camden	133.7	2,940	45.7	3.2	7.8	0.0	10.8	141.7	3,117	100	152	1,728	21,010	58,795	6,171
Cape Girardeau	242.7	3,101	48.2	0.4	6.1	0.0	7.2	162.3	2,074	397	284	5,988	36,070	62,116	6,518
Carroll	32.7	3,729	56.2	3.0	3.7	0.0	8.2	22.8	2,597	46	28	507	4,010	48,691	3,808
Carter	17.7	2,868	72.8	1.2	2.4	0.0	0.6	3.2	510	89	20	315	2,490	38,265	2,549
Cass	450.2	4,350	51.9	13.7	3.3	0.0	6.1	519.7	5,023	298	350	4,345	51,580	68,579	7,090
Cedar	55.5	3,944	39.4	43.9	2.7	0.0	2.4	34.6	2,459	70	47	907	5,820	37,979	2,408
Chariton	23.2	3,107	60.9	0.0	5.5	0.0	12.7	7.2	971	43	24	414	3,310	49,670	3,899
Christian	226.7	2,655	69.5	0.7	5.0	0.0	5.0	233.0	2,729	154	298	3,142	40,200	65,612	6,533
Clark	20.5	3,050	50.6	1.2	4.2	14.8	5.2	16.4	2,441	36	22	415	2,910	45,105	3,185
Clay	1,516.1	6,251	30.9	48.6	2.1	0.0	2.1	1,044.1	4,305	1,424	871	14,519	123,940	67,901	7,146
Clinton	53.8	2,618	63.9	2.4	5.4	0.0	10.8	69.2	3,367	63	67	911	10,010	58,799	5,364
Cole	226.9	2,961	49.3	3.1	9.2	0.0	6.9	191.5	2,498	641	264	18,527	37,250	63,941	6,538
Cooper	55.7	3,154	46.9	2.3	4.8	4.9	6.8	57.4	3,252	60	53	1,035	7,820	48,130	3,738
Crawford	47.0	1,951	66.1	5.6	3.2	0.0	6.3	24.4	1,013	36	78	881	10,470	44,131	3,486
Dade	24.1	3,182	58.5	0.9	2.8	22.6	5.4	14.4	1,902	30	25	496	3,230	45,512	3,867
Dallas	19.5	1,171	86.6	0.0	2.2	0.0	2.1	3.3	200	39	56	579	7,040	39,573	2,663
Daviess	22.7	2,712	70.0	2.3	3.1	0.3	9.7	9.8	1,168	39	27	456	3,590	45,092	3,378
DeKalb	16.2	1,297	74.6	2.6	0.2	0.0	6.2	9.5	759	57	30	840	4,300	48,278	3,773
Dent	54.1	3,494	40.5	40.0	4.2	0.0	4.4	8.0	518	60	51	940	6,020	40,233	2,663
Douglas	22.9	1,723	64.7	0.4	5.5	0.0	11.6	4.0	298	61	44	385	5,320	35,152	2,115
Dunklin	82.7	2,747	64.3	1.0	6.6	0.0	6.1	38.4	1,276	96	94	1,401	10,900	42,564	3,226
Franklin	293.5	2,841	57.8	3.7	6.7	0.0	7.9	325.1	3,146	238	346	4,147	51,470	62,899	6,577
Gasconade	60.8	4,139	44.9	33.0	3.5	0.6	5.0	51.4	3,501	54	50	968	7,250	46,456	3,542
Gentry	22.2	3,350	61.2	5.7	2.3	0.0	8.1	14.8	2,233	41	21	383	2,750	47,230	3,490
Greene	968.5	3,345	51.7	1.1	9.0	0.2	6.9	1,429.1	4,936	2,271	957	19,065	136,890	64,105	7,498
Grundy	59.1	5,920	56.9	0.4	4.1	9.2	7.3	23.1	2,307	56	31	857	4,090	41,973	2,820
Harrison	57.0	6,701	27.8	48.0	1.5	0.0	6.9	18.5	2,170	42	27	764	3,660	37,524	2,764
Henry	145.5	6,706	21.9	60.1	2.6	0.0	4.3	95.0	4,377	75	72	1,711	9,890	47,714	3,787
Hickory	21.9	2,334	77.2	1.7	2.9	0.0	6.4	20.8	2,213	45	32	280	3,770	38,518	2,549
Holt	15.5	3,511	54.9	0.7	4.7	0.6	6.4	6.7	1,525	35	14	267	2,020	51,449	4,691
Howard	25.2	2,505	62.6	3.1	4.2	0.3	5.8	31.6	3,139	45	31	441	4,320	49,854	4,001
Howell	106.8	2,666	67.0	3.7	5.5	0.0	4.2	17.1	426	146	131	1,999	16,520	43,827	3,732
Iron	31.7	3,117	65.6	10.1	2.3	0.0	0.6	10.7	1,055	21	33	605	4,000	40,469	2,629
Jackson	3,940.3	5,645	34.2	2.3	9.0	0.3	3.7	6,617.9	9,480	18,356	2,401	41,519	342,780	60,618	6,580

1. Based on the resident population estimated as of July 1 of the year shown.

State / county code	CBSA code[1]	County Type code[2]	STATE County	Land area[3] (sq. mi)	Population, 2021: Total persons 2021	Population, 2021: Rank	Population, 2021: Per square mile	Race alone or in combination, not Hispanic or Latino (percent): White	Black	American Indian, Alaska Native	Asian and Pacific Islancer	Percent Hispanic or Latino[4]	Age (percent): Under 5 years	5 to 17 years	18 to 24 years	25 to 34 years	35 to 44 years	45 to 54 years
				1	2	3	4	5	6	7	8	9	10	11	12	13	14	15
			MISSOURI— Cont'd															
29097	27900	3	Jasper	638.5	123,155	518	192.9	86.0	3.4	3.0	2.1	8.8	6.4	14.0	13.4	13.6	12.9	11.6
29099	41180	1	Jefferson	656.4	227,771	306	347.0	95.3	2.0	0.8	1.4	2.3	5.7	13.0	11.4	12.6	13.6	12.8
29101	47660	4	Johnson	829.3	54,150	938	65.3	87.5	5.8	1.4	3.0	5.2	6.2	12.2	22.9	14.1	11.4	9.4
29103		9	Knox	504.0	3,808	2,901	7.6	96.8	1.5	1.3	1.0	1.4	7.1	12.5	11.9	10.5	9.6	11.0
29105	30060	6	Laclede	764.6	36,133	1,280	47.3	94.7	1.8	1.6	1.3	2.8	6.6	13.8	11.8	11.6	12.1	12.1
29107	28140	1	Lafayette	628.3	32,817	1,367	52.2	93.1	3.2	1.3	1.2	3.5	6.0	13.0	11.7	11.6	11.7	12.4
29109		6	Lawrence	611.7	38,321	1,213	62.6	89.4	1.2	1.9	1.0	8.5	6.7	14.4	12.3	11.6	11.9	11.8
29111	39500	9	Lewis	505.0	10,000	2,403	19.8	94.0	4.0	0.9	0.7	2.0	5.9	12.6	16.1	10.5	10.9	10.9
29113	41180	1	Lincoln	626.6	61,586	863	98.3	94.4	3.0	1.0	0.9	2.7	6.9	14.2	11.7	14.0	13.1	11.8
29115		7	Linn	615.6	11,843	2,294	19.2	95.5	1.9	0.8	0.5	3.0	6.0	13.3	11.9	10.9	11.4	10.9
29117		6	Livingston	532.3	14,755	2,100	27.7	93.7	3.9	0.9	1.0	2.1	5.7	12.5	11.3	13.3	13.1	11.8
29119		2	McDonald	539.4	23,383	1,662	43.4	79.3	2.9	4.6	5.0	11.8	6.9	14.1	12.3	11.7	12.0	12.9
29121		7	Macon	801.2	15,183	2,079	19.0	94.5	3.4	0.8	1.2	1.7	5.8	12.8	12.0	10.6	10.8	11.9
29123		6	Madison	494.4	12,652	2,232	25.6	95.8	1.2	1.1	1.0	2.4	5.6	13.4	11.2	11.6	12.0	12.3
29125		8	Maries	527.0	8,406	2,542	16.0	96.3	1.5	1.6	0.8	1.6	5.0	11.5	11.2	10.6	11.3	12.7
29127	25300	5	Marion	436.9	28,518	1,476	65.3	92.4	6.3	0.8	1.2	1.9	6.1	13.2	13.2	11.8	12.2	11.7
29129		9	Mercer	453.8	3,488	2,924	7.7	95.2	0.6	1.3	1.0	3.0	6.5	13.2	11.5	9.3	10.1	11.2
29131		6	Miller	592.6	24,909	1,618	42.0	96.1	1.1	1.4	0.9	2.0	6.2	13.6	11.5	11.5	11.9	11.6
29133		6	Mississippi	411.6	12,538	2,240	30.5	72.9	24.9	0.8	0.5	2.5	5.8	11.9	12.0	13.5	12.9	12.9
29135	27620	3	Moniteau	415.0	15,484	2,061	37.3	90.9	3.2	1.1	0.9	5.4	6.2	14.6	12.1	12.3	13.6	12.2
29137		9	Monroe	647.6	8,712	2,510	13.5	94.7	3.9	1.1	0.8	1.6	5.8	12.5	10.7	9.6	10.8	10.7
29139		6	Montgomery	535.0	11,415	2,318	21.3	94.9	2.4	1.1	0.9	2.5	5.7	12.1	11.4	11.0	11.7	11.6
29141		8	Morgan	597.6	21,379	1,741	35.8	95.6	1.2	1.7	0.8	2.4	6.3	12.6	10.6	10.3	9.7	10.6
29143		7	New Madrid	674.9	16,035	2,032	23.8	81.3	17.0	0.8	0.7	2.1	6.2	13.4	11.1	11.2	11.2	12.5
29145	27900	3	Newton	624.8	59,386	885	95.0	88.3	1.8	4.3	3.1	5.7	6.0	13.5	12.2	12.0	11.8	12.0
29147	32340	6	Nodaway	877.0	21,160	1,755	24.1	93.6	3.1	0.6	1.9	1.8	4.4	8.4	31.9	10.4	9.7	8.5
29149		9	Oregon	789.8	8,631	2,521	10.9	95.9	0.9	2.8	0.7	1.9	5.7	13.0	10.7	10.4	10.0	11.6
29151	27620	3	Osage	606.6	13,379	2,194	22.1	98.0	0.7	0.7	0.3	1.0	5.6	12.7	13.2	11.4	11.9	12.5
29153		9	Ozark	745.0	8,782	2,505	11.8	96.8	0.7	1.9	0.6	1.9	4.5	11.2	9.2	8.2	10.3	10.9
29155		7	Pemiscot	492.6	15,236	2,074	30.9	70.2	27.5	0.9	0.7	2.9	7.3	14.6	12.1	11.3	11.6	11.5
29157		6	Perry	474.4	18,922	1,874	39.9	95.8	1.0	0.8	1.3	2.3	5.5	13.0	12.1	11.4	12.1	12.3
29159	42740	4	Pettis	682.2	43,188	1,122	63.3	86.1	4.7	1.0	1.6	9.2	7.0	14.0	12.6	12.5	12.7	11.0
29161	40620	5	Phelps	671.8	44,937	1,079	66.9	90.8	3.0	1.6	4.2	2.8	5.2	12.2	20.1	11.4	11.5	10.3
29163		6	Pike	670.4	17,761	1,931	26.5	91.1	6.8	0.7	0.8	2.3	5.9	13.0	11.5	13.2	12.4	12.0
29165	28140	1	Platte	419.8	108,569	570	258.6	81.8	8.7	1.1	4.4	6.6	5.7	13.4	12.1	13.0	14.5	12.9
29167	44180	2	Polk	635.5	32,043	1,379	50.4	94.8	1.4	1.6	1.3	2.7	6.3	12.8	16.3	11.5	11.1	11.0
29169	22780	5	Pulaski	547.1	53,816	944	98.4	72.3	13.1	1.8	5.2	11.7	6.7	12.3	24.4	17.6	12.7	8.4
29171		9	Putnam	517.3	4,712	2,841	9.1	96.1	0.7	0.9	0.9	2.8	6.9	12.1	10.9	9.9	10.5	11.3
29173	25300	9	Ralls	469.8	10,361	2,385	22.1	96.4	1.9	0.8	0.8	1.5	4.8	11.9	10.2	10.2	11.4	12.9
29175	33620	6	Randolph	482.7	24,760	1,624	51.3	91.0	7.1	1.1	1.1	2.2	5.8	12.0	12.6	14.0	13.1	12.6
29177	28140	1	Ray	569.0	23,008	1,677	40.4	94.8	2.2	1.2	0.8	2.7	5.6	13.0	11.3	11.2	12.0	12.4
29179		9	Reynolds	808.5	6,087	2,730	7.5	95.4	2.0	2.6	0.8	1.8	4.9	10.7	10.7	9.7	11.1	12.7
29181	38740	9	Ripley	629.5	10,617	2,369	16.9	96.1	1.3	1.9	0.8	1.7	6.2	13.9	10.6	11.4	11.2	11.8
29183	41180	1	St. Charles	560.5	409,981	177	731.5	87.7	6.6	0.6	3.6	3.6	5.5	13.1	12.4	12.5	14.1	12.5
29185		8	St. Clair	675.0	9,376	2,463	13.9	95.9	1.1	1.7	0.7	2.2	5.2	11.7	9.9	9.6	10.1	11.6
29186		6	Ste. Genevieve	499.2	18,588	1,892	37.2	96.8	1.3	0.8	1.1	1.1	5.9	12.4	10.6	10.9	11.5	11.4
29187	22100	4	St. Francois	451.9	67,541	797	149.5	93.0	4.9	0.9	0.7	1.8	5.3	12.0	12.0	14.2	13.8	12.8
29189	41180	1	St. Louis	507.9	997,187	50	1,963.4	66.8	26.1	0.7	5.8	3.1	5.7	12.5	12.1	12.7	12.7	11.8
29195	32180	6	Saline	755.5	23,289	1,672	30.8	80.5	6.4	1.1	3.0	11.5	5.5	12.9	15.2	11.3	11.5	11.5
29197	28860	9	Schuyler	307.3	4,025	2,887	13.1	97.7	1.1	0.7	0.6	1.5	7.9	15.0	11.5	11.9	9.9	10.6
29199		9	Scotland	436.5	4,693	2,842	10.8	98.1	0.7	0.7	0.5	1.2	8.1	16.3	12.4	11.2	10.3	9.6
29201	43460	4	Scott	420.0	37,840	1,225	90.1	84.4	13.0	1.0	0.7	2.7	6.5	13.6	11.7	12.5	11.8	11.9
29203		9	Shannon	1,003.8	7,106	2,654	7.1	95.3	1.4	2.8	0.8	2.3	5.6	12.6	10.0	10.8	10.4	11.7
29205		9	Shelby	500.9	5,976	2,736	11.9	95.9	1.9	0.7	0.5	2.5	6.1	13.8	10.6	10.5	12.1	9.9
29207		6	Stoddard	823.1	28,479	1,478	34.6	95.8	1.9	0.9	0.6	2.0	5.8	12.2	11.7	11.6	12.2	12.3
29209		6	Stone	463.8	31,548	1,390	68.0	95.5	0.9	1.8	0.7	2.6	4.1	9.3	8.9	7.8	9.2	11.3
29211		9	Sullivan	648.0	5,934	2,739	9.2	77.7	3.2	1.1	0.7	18.6	6.7	12.6	11.4	10.8	10.5	13.2
29213	14700	4	Taney	632.3	56,387	919	89.2	89.9	2.3	1.9	1.7	6.5	5.4	11.8	13.0	10.8	11.1	11.3
29215		9	Texas	1,177.3	24,987	1,613	21.2	92.7	4.1	2.1	0.7	2.4	5.5	12.2	11.4	11.5	12.1	11.6
29217		7	Vernon	826.4	19,595	1,847	23.7	95.0	1.6	1.7	1.0	2.6	6.1	13.2	12.9	11.1	11.0	11.5
29219	41180	1	Warren	428.6	36,518	1,272	85.2	93.1	3.4	0.9	0.8	3.8	5.9	13.2	11.6	12.4	11.9	11.5
29221		6	Washington	759.9	23,502	1,661	30.9	95.0	3.1	1.1	0.6	1.6	5.7	12.9	11.4	12.0	12.3	13.3
29223		9	Wayne	759.2	10,914	2,348	14.4	96.2	1.6	1.8	0.7	1.9	4.8	11.6	10.1	9.5	10.7	11.8
29225	44180	2	Webster	592.6	39,735	1,189	67.1	95.5	1.6	1.6	0.6	2.4	7.3	15.5	12.3	12.2	12.1	12.0
29227		9	Worth	266.6	1,983	3,041	7.4	96.6	1.2	0.7	0.4	1.9	5.7	10.2	10.0	10.2	10.6	9.9
29229		6	Wright	681.8	18,610	1,890	27.3	95.4	1.1	1.6	0.8	2.6	6.7	14.5	11.8	10.9	11.4	11.1
29510	41180	1	St. Louis city	61.7	293,310	242	4,753.8	47.6	45.4	1.0	4.4	4.4	5.8	9.9	11.3	19.8	14.3	11.0

1. CBSA = Core Based Statistical Area. See Appendix A for explanation. See Appendix B for list of metropolitan areas with component counties. 2. County type code from the Economic Research Service of USDA Rural-Urban Continuum Codes. See Appendix A for definition. 3. Dry land or land partially or temporarily covered by water. 4. May be of any race.

STATE County	Population, 2021 (cont.)				Population change, 2000–2021							Households, 2016–2020				
	Age (percent) (cont.)				Total persons		Percent change		Components of change, 2020–2021					Percent		
	55 to 64 years	65 to 74 years	75 years and over	Percent female	2010	2020	2010–2020	2020–2021	Births	Deaths	Net Migration	Number	Persons per household	Family house-holds	Female family house-holder[1]	One person
	16	17	18	19	20	21	22	23	24	25	26	27	28	29	30	31
MISSOURI— Cont'd																
Jasper	11.9	9.6	6.5	50.9	117,404	122,761	4.6	0.3	1,851	1,865	382	46,461	2.5	64.5	12.5	28.1
Jefferson	14.8	10.4	5.7	50.0	218,733	226,739	3.7	0.5	2,987	3,271	1,281	84,978	2.6	72.2	11.1	21.9
Johnson	11.0	7.8	5.2	48.4	52,595	54,013	2.7	0.3	825	612	-91	19,931	2.5	63.2	8.3	25.2
Knox	15.3	11.9	10.0	50.4	4,131	3,744	-9.4	1.7	64	53	54	1,400	2.8	63.0	6.6	33.4
Laclede	13.8	10.8	7.3	50.1	35,571	36,039	1.3	0.3	548	603	144	14,413	2.5	70.2	8.8	24.1
Lafayette	14.4	10.9	8.3	50.0	33,381	32,984	-1.2	-0.5	470	565	-74	12,711	2.5	68.1	11.1	25.1
Lawrence	13.3	10.2	7.9	49.7	38,634	38,001	-1.6	0.8	594	664	391	14,849	2.5	69.0	11.1	27.1
Lewis	13.8	10.7	8.6	49.7	10,211	10,032	-1.8	-0.3	122	155	0	3,597	2.5	64.7	7.6	31.4
Lincoln	13.9	9.1	5.2	49.7	52,566	59,574	13.3	3.4	947	729	1,808	19,818	2.9	73.4	10.2	21.6
Linn	14.4	12.2	9.0	50.9	12,761	11,874	-7.0	-0.3	160	231	40	5,002	2.4	68.8	11.2	27.5
Livingston	12.4	10.8	9.2	54.9	15,195	14,557	-4.2	1.4	201	245	243	5,907	2.3	63.0	8.2	30.3
McDonald	14.2	9.7	6.1	49.1	23,083	23,303	1.0	0.3	372	359	64	8,393	2.7	74.6	11.5	19.8
Macon	13.5	12.6	10.0	50.1	15,566	15,209	-2.3	-0.2	218	287	41	5,908	2.5	62.6	9.7	34.2
Madison	14.6	11.6	7.8	50.5	12,226	12,626	3.3	0.2	165	277	138	4,851	2.5	67.9	10.4	25.3
Maries	16.0	12.6	9.1	50.0	9,176	8,432	-8.1	-0.3	120	178	31	3,808	2.3	64.0	7.7	31.6
Marion	13.3	10.9	7.6	51.4	28,781	28,525	-0.9	0.0	402	455	41	11,537	2.3	66.4	10.7	28.2
Mercer	15.1	13.0	10.1	50.1	3,785	3,538	-6.5	-1.4	51	58	-42	1,333	2.7	61.6	4.7	33.1
Miller	14.1	11.9	7.7	50.1	24,748	24,722	-0.1	0.8	371	431	246	10,452	2.4	66.6	9.6	29.1
Mississippi	12.8	10.5	7.8	47.3	14,358	12,577	-12.4	-0.3	187	273	44	4,998	2.3	68.5	15.8	27.1
Moniteau	12.8	9.6	6.7	48.3	15,607	15,473	-0.9	0.1	225	259	41	5,450	2.7	70.8	8.6	25.6
Monroe	15.9	13.8	10.1	49.1	8,840	8,666	-2.0	0.5	120	151	78	3,731	2.3	64.0	9.4	32.4
Montgomery	16.1	11.6	8.8	49.7	12,236	11,322	-7.5	0.8	156	236	176	4,995	2.2	66.0	10.6	28.5
Morgan	16.1	14.0	9.7	49.5	20,565	21,006	2.1	1.8	319	446	510	7,639	2.6	67.1	9.0	29.7
New Madrid	14.5	11.9	8.0	52.4	18,956	16,434	-13.3	-2.4	253	388	-263	7,281	2.3	65.0	16.2	30.7
Newton	13.8	11.1	7.6	50.1	58,114	58,648	0.9	1.3	816	903	831	22,123	2.6	69.7	7.5	24.9
Nodaway	10.8	8.8	7.1	50.4	23,370	21,241	-9.1	-0.4	265	248	-102	8,510	2.2	54.6	7.1	31.8
Oregon	15.6	13.2	9.8	50.5	10,881	8,635	-20.6	0.0	124	197	70	4,298	2.4	69.0	10.1	25.6
Osage	14.8	10.4	7.5	48.7	13,878	13,274	-4.4	0.8	171	187	122	5,273	2.5	72.5	6.2	23.0
Ozark	17.0	17.2	11.5	49.4	9,723	8,553	-12.0	2.7	78	200	360	4,082	2.2	61.4	4.3	33.1
Pemiscot	13.7	10.5	7.4	52.7	18,296	15,661	-14.4	-2.7	286	360	-348	6,640	2.4	66.1	20.6	28.9
Perry	14.1	11.3	8.2	50.2	18,971	18,956	-0.1	-0.2	261	328	31	7,577	2.5	66.5	6.7	26.7
Pettis	13.1	10.1	7.0	50.3	42,201	42,980	1.8	0.5	731	665	136	16,193	2.6	67.2	11.1	28.4
Phelps	12.4	9.9	7.1	47.7	45,156	44,638	-1.1	0.7	499	716	516	18,213	2.3	62.3	10.3	28.6
Pike	13.4	10.8	7.9	46.7	18,516	17,587	-5.0	1.0	253	275	197	6,653	2.4	65.1	11.8	29.5
Platte	12.7	9.6	6.0	50.7	89,322	106,718	19.5	1.7	1,474	1,114	1,484	39,918	2.6	66.8	8.8	25.3
Polk	13.4	10.1	7.6	50.8	31,137	31,519	1.2	1.7	501	545	572	11,833	2.6	68.8	10.9	24.4
Pulaski	8.4	5.8	3.6	43.6	52,274	53,955	3.2	-0.3	877	480	-547	15,061	2.9	68.9	9.3	26.5
Putnam	14.3	13.7	10.4	49.4	4,979	4,681	-6.0	0.7	73	71	29	1,698	2.7	63.9	8.6	33.0
Ralls	16.0	14.0	8.8	49.7	10,167	10,355	1.8	0.1	114	174	66	4,132	2.5	69.5	6.2	26.1
Randolph	12.8	9.9	7.1	47.9	25,414	24,716	-2.7	0.2	311	381	111	8,872	2.6	65.9	12.8	30.3
Ray	15.4	11.2	7.9	49.9	23,494	23,158	-1.4	-0.6	308	446	-14	8,766	2.6	72.1	10.5	23.2
Reynolds	16.6	13.4	10.0	48.2	6,696	6,096	-9.0	-0.1	86	119	24	2,580	2.4	70.5	10.2	24.1
Ripley	14.5	11.7	8.6	50.3	14,100	10,679	-24.3	-0.6	195	284	25	4,973	2.7	66.0	11.5	28.4
St. Charles	13.7	9.9	6.4	50.5	360,485	405,262	12.4	1.2	5,180	4,774	4,277	149,472	2.6	71.3	8.9	23.1
St. Clair	15.7	14.3	11.9	49.0	9,805	9,284	-5.3	1.0	123	212	183	4,120	2.2	62.0	8.1	32.2
Ste. Genevieve	16.3	12.9	8.1	48.7	18,145	18,479	1.8	0.6	260	258	108	7,252	2.4	71.9	7.2	24.0
St. Francois	13.0	10.0	6.9	46.9	65,359	66,922	2.4	0.9	842	1,196	975	24,572	2.4	67.1	11.3	26.6
St. Louis	13.7	11.1	7.7	52.2	998,954	1,004,125	0.5	-0.7	13,310	15,378	-4,982	409,658	2.4	63.2	13.3	31.1
Saline	13.3	10.6	8.1	49.7	23,370	23,333	-0.2	-0.2	326	375	2	8,235	2.6	61.9	8.3	32.2
Schuyler	14.1	10.2	9.1	49.9	4,431	4,032	-9.0	-0.2	84	70	-21	1,440	3.1	62.8	5.8	32.4
Scotland	12.6	10.4	9.1	50.2	4,843	4,716	-2.6	-0.5	98	60	-60	1,687	2.9	68.0	6.3	30.1
Scott	13.2	11.1	7.7	51.3	39,191	38,059	-2.9	-0.6	596	704	-115	15,342	2.5	65.5	14.1	29.0
Shannon	16.1	13.4	9.5	49.7	8,441	7,031	-16.7	1.1	98	145	124	3,063	2.6	73.6	9.0	20.8
Shelby	14.7	12.2	10.1	49.4	6,373	6,103	-4.2	-2.1	83	105	-103	2,485	2.3	65.8	9.2	31.7
Stoddard	13.9	11.6	8.8	50.2	29,968	28,672	-4.3	-0.7	424	554	-66	11,545	2.5	65.7	10.7	30.1
Stone	17.6	19.7	12.1	50.5	32,202	31,076	-3.5	1.5	332	596	751	12,689	2.5	70.3	6.6	25.1
Sullivan	14.4	11.6	8.7	48.9	6,714	5,999	-10.6	-1.1	102	95	-72	2,218	2.7	60.4	6.4	36.1
Taney	13.9	13.4	9.3	51.3	51,675	56,066	8.5	0.6	752	886	455	22,390	2.4	67.8	10.8	26.8
Texas	14.4	12.2	9.0	47.2	26,008	24,487	-5.8	2.0	312	464	665	9,852	2.5	68.6	8.3	27.5
Vernon	13.8	11.7	8.7	51.0	21,159	19,707	-6.9	-0.6	310	332	-91	8,294	2.4	63.3	9.4	30.8
Warren	15.3	11.0	7.2	49.8	32,513	35,532	9.3	2.8	483	501	1,012	13,129	2.7	76.5	10.4	16.9
Washington	14.7	11.0	6.6	48.3	25,195	23,514	-6.7	-0.1	319	433	101	9,278	2.6	68.1	11.2	26.0
Wayne	17.0	14.1	10.3	50.3	13,521	10,974	-18.8	-0.5	140	276	78	5,438	2.4	63.0	8.6	30.9
Webster	12.8	9.3	6.3	48.9	36,202	39,085	8.0	1.7	704	560	507	13,697	2.8	72.3	9.0	20.8
Worth	17.0	13.7	12.7	49.8	2,171	1,973	-9.1	0.5	32	29	8	808	2.4	66.5	8.2	31.1
Wright	13.6	11.6	8.3	50.5	18,815	18,188	-3.3	2.3	276	295	447	6,977	2.6	67.7	10.1	28.3
St. Louis city	12.8	9.7	5.4	51.4	319,294	301,578	-5.5	-2.7	4,739	4,624	-8,283	143,566	2.1	45.2	15.9	45.4

1. No spouse present.

Table B. States and Counties — **Population, Vital Statistics, and Health**

STATE County	Persons in group quarters, 2021	Daytime Population, 2016–2020		Births, 2021		Deaths, 2021		Persons under 65 with no health insurance, 2019		Medicare, 2021			COVID-19 Deaths, 2020	
		Number	Employment/ residence ratio	Total	Rate[1]	Number	Rate[1]	Number	Percent	Total beneficiaries	Enrolled in Original Medicare	Enrolled in Medicare Advantage	Number	Rate[1]
	32	33	34	35	36	37	38	39	40	41	42	43	44	45
MISSOURI— Cont'd														
Jasper	2,400	124,912	1.1	1,479	12.0	1,484	12.1	16,611	16.7	23,697	15,432	8,265	191	1.6
Jefferson	1,848	169,370	0.5	2,377	10.5	2,615	11.5	21,129	11.2	44,649	20,342	24,307	221	1.0
Johnson	3,586	50,526	0.9	672	12.4	505	9.3	5,367	12.3	8,384	5,850	2,534	51	0.9
Knox	42	3,898	1.0	57	15.1	44	11.7	624	20.8	924	818	106	D	D
Laclede	286	36,710	1.1	432	12.0	480	13.3	4,117	14.2	8,376	3,850	4,525	58	1.6
Lafayette	647	28,338	0.7	382	11.6	441	13.4	2,981	11.4	7,372	4,641	2,731	46	1.4
Lawrence	454	34,076	0.7	472	12.4	534	14.0	5,462	17.7	8,399	4,106	4,292	61	1.6
Lewis	774	8,456	0.7	101	10.1	131	13.1	930	12.7	2,277	1,953	324	11	1.1
Lincoln	537	43,526	0.5	752	12.4	592	9.8	5,922	11.7	10,581	5,809	4,772	53	0.9
Linn	121	11,260	0.9	133	11.2	193	16.3	1,248	13.4	3,115	2,591	524	15	1.3
Livingston	1,196	15,898	1.1	150	10.2	208	14.2	1,370	13.1	3,485	2,864	621	35	2.4
McDonald	133	20,605	0.8	295	12.6	300	12.9	4,280	22.7	4,334	2,496	1,837	29	1.2
Macon	248	14,351	0.9	167	11.0	210	13.8	1,681	14.6	3,913	3,320	593	18	1.2
Madison	159	11,292	0.8	131	10.4	206	16.3	1,293	13.5	3,182	2,298	884	22	1.7
Maries	28	6,792	0.5	95	11.3	133	15.8	1,175	17.5	1,979	1,424	555	13	1.5
Marion	1,287	30,431	1.1	325	11.4	362	12.7	2,493	11.1	6,690	5,533	1,157	42	1.5
Mercer	40	3,507	0.9	38	10.9	40	11.4	478	17.2	809	697	112	10	2.8
Miller	181	22,012	0.7	296	11.9	331	13.3	3,203	15.7	5,578	3,674	1,904	44	1.8
Mississippi	1,314	12,354	0.8	149	11.9	208	16.6	1,299	14.5	2,959	2,421	538	24	1.9
Moniteau	815	13,404	0.6	172	11.1	202	13.1	2,073	16.9	3,020	1,999	1,022	27	1.7
Monroe	101	7,518	0.7	101	11.6	116	13.4	876	13.5	2,149	1,748	400	18	2.1
Montgomery	336	9,931	0.7	125	11.0	180	15.9	1,274	14.4	2,895	2,026	868	16	1.4
Morgan	264	19,959	0.9	246	11.6	355	16.8	3,243	21.0	5,686	4,013	1,673	37	1.8
New Madrid	243	16,463	0.9	204	12.6	314	19.4	1,870	13.9	4,170	3,302	868	40	2.4
Newton	800	58,433	1.0	672	11.4	717	12.2	7,327	15.7	12,708	8,451	4,257	87	1.5
Nodaway	3,261	21,777	1.0	205	9.7	210	9.9	2,043	13.3	4,038	3,613	425	21	1.0
Oregon	64	10,021	0.9	93	10.8	164	19.0	1,302	16.5	2,603	1,960	644	10	1.2
Osage	332	11,615	0.7	139	10.4	152	11.4	1,228	11.2	2,790	1,840	950	12	0.9
Ozark	59	7,877	0.6	68	7.9	155	17.9	1,237	19.4	2,966	1,746	1,220	12	1.4
Pemiscot	159	16,281	1.0	226	14.7	286	18.6	1,742	13.7	3,724	2,604	1,120	32	2.1
Perry	214	20,113	1.1	211	11.1	274	14.5	1,713	11.2	4,362	3,591	772	26	1.4
Pettis	789	44,951	1.1	583	13.5	518	12.0	5,348	15.6	8,713	6,190	2,524	74	1.7
Phelps	2,938	47,294	1.2	396	8.9	560	12.5	5,346	15.6	8,960	6,496	2,465	72	1.6
Pike	1,456	17,902	1.0	188	10.6	221	12.5	1,676	13.1	3,877	2,805	1,072	26	1.5
Platte	769	97,881	0.9	1,156	10.7	882	8.2	7,116	8.0	17,424	11,811	5,613	78	0.7
Polk	1,355	28,960	0.8	404	12.7	440	13.8	3,980	16.0	7,216	3,515	3,701	44	1.4
Pulaski	10,119	53,296	1.0	691	12.8	362	6.7	4,553	12.1	6,510	5,228	1,283	44	0.8
Putnam	46	4,073	0.7	62	13.2	51	10.9	552	15.8	1,301	1,105	196	D	D
Ralls	40	9,030	0.7	85	8.2	139	13.4	904	11.3	2,640	2,176	464	16	1.5
Randolph	2,222	25,154	1.0	248	10.0	305	12.3	2,330	12.7	5,381	3,934	1,446	45	1.8
Ray	267	17,783	0.5	242	10.5	343	14.9	2,259	12.2	5,067	3,245	1,821	24	1.0
Reynolds	75	6,076	0.9	66	10.9	96	15.8	745	16.0	1,621	1,195	426	D	D
Ripley	31	11,831	0.7	149	14.0	233	21.9	1,777	17.2	3,391	2,711	680	18	1.7
St. Charles	5,144	349,738	0.8	4,068	10.0	3,836	9.4	23,128	6.9	72,013	36,999	35,014	436	1.1
St. Clair	149	8,560	0.8	102	10.9	172	18.4	1,088	16.4	2,749	1,729	1,019	17	1.8
Ste. Genevieve	257	15,768	0.8	204	11.0	212	11.4	1,496	10.6	4,310	2,861	1,449	11	0.6
St. Francois	6,234	65,565	1.0	676	10.1	961	14.3	6,205	12.5	15,096	9,485	5,611	105	1.6
St. Louis	18,592	1,103,772	1.2	10,641	10.6	12,243	12.2	65,929	8.3	207,177	112,412	94,766	1,485	1.5
Saline	1,464	22,445	1.0	256	11.0	296	12.7	2,506	14.5	4,926	3,366	1,561	46	2.0
Schuyler	27	3,619	0.5	66	16.4	53	13.2	597	16.2	1,000	850	150	D	D
Scotland	49	4,708	0.9	81	17.3	47	10.0	850	21.6	917	827	90	D	D
Scott	459	39,596	1.1	466	12.3	558	14.7	4,177	13.6	9,183	7,236	1,947	59	1.6
Shannon	35	7,607	0.8	72	10.2	120	17.0	1,148	18.5	1,945	1,318	627	15	2.1
Shelby	190	5,258	0.7	65	10.8	90	14.9	667	14.7	1,558	1,309	250	D	D
Stoddard	585	29,297	1.0	327	11.4	442	15.5	3,400	14.9	7,543	5,555	1,988	52	1.8
Stone	197	28,454	0.7	262	8.4	473	15.1	3,610	16.7	10,585	5,625	4,960	47	1.5
Sullivan	82	6,615	1.2	82	13.8	67	11.3	726	15.2	1,431	1,217	215	13	2.2
Taney	1,667	59,794	1.2	589	10.5	679	12.1	7,520	18.0	14,525	7,687	6,838	75	1.3
Texas	1,556	27,451	1.2	254	10.3	355	14.4	3,492	19.4	6,402	4,932	1,470	22	0.9
Vernon	722	20,336	1.0	251	12.8	274	14.0	2,443	15.5	4,769	3,144	1,626	40	2.0
Warren	220	27,735	0.6	407	11.3	412	11.4	3,348	11.5	7,589	3,589	4,000	22	0.6
Washington	908	21,206	0.6	248	10.6	353	15.0	2,883	15.0	5,513	3,139	2,373	47	2.0
Wayne	68	11,934	0.7	113	10.4	205	18.8	1,617	16.9	3,153	2,271	881	21	1.9
Webster	650	32,974	0.6	562	14.2	452	11.5	4,792	14.8	7,818	3,396	4,423	54	1.4
Worth	47	1,650	0.6	28	14.2	23	11.7	211	14.3	534	458	76	D	D
Wright	144	17,082	0.8	220	12.0	233	12.7	2,729	19.0	4,935	2,608	2,327	31	1.7
St. Louis city	11,576	412,308	1.7	3,783	12.7	3,718	12.5	31,216	12.6	49,258	25,087	24,172	362	1.2

1. Per 1,000 estimated resident population.

STATE County	COVID-19 Vaccinations, 2021–2022		Education						Money income, 2016–2020				Income and poverty, 2020			
			School enrollment and attainment, 2016–2020				Local government expenditures,[3] 2018–2019			Households				Percent below poverty level		
			Enrollment[1]		Attainment[2] (percent)						Percent					
	Number	Percent[5]	Total	Percent private	High school graduate or less	Bachelor's degree or more	Total current spending (mil dol)	Current spending per student (dollars)	Per capita income[4]	Median income (dollars)	with income of less than $50,000	with income of $200,000 or more	Median household income (dollars)	All persons	Children under 18 years	Children 5 to 17 years in families
	46	47	48	49	50	51	52	53	54	55	56	57	58	59	60	61
MISSOURI— Cont'd																
Jasper	57,532	47.4	29,600	13.4	47.7	22.7	191.2	8,684	24,508	49,155	50.7	2.0	51,329	15.2	18.9	17.6
Jefferson	101,014	44.9	53,031	14.1	42.1	21.1	343.2	9,992	30,800	67,606	35.7	3.3	67,191	8.9	10.6	9.5
Johnson	23,495	43.5	15,854	12.3	37.5	29.5	77.4	10,283	26,327	56,440	43.2	2.2	58,373	10.8	12.5	12.3
Knox	1,578	39.9	883	22.4	58.2	15.7	5.4	11,340	20,941	37,588	62.6	0.4	41,838	14.2	29.6	29.9
Laclede	13,394	37.5	7,414	13.3	57.5	15.0	53.6	9,094	23,296	46,582	52.6	1.3	46,191	16.3	20.4	19.8
Lafayette	14,949	45.7	6,897	12.6	53.5	20.8	55.0	10,527	30,450	62,076	41.0	4.7	62,043	10.4	14.3	13.3
Lawrence	14,575	38.0	8,339	13.0	54.4	15.9	53.8	9,184	22,850	44,060	56.8	2.1	48,101	15.2	21.8	19.6
Lewis	3,330	34.1	2,488	23.4	57.4	14.4	13.9	10,177	23,054	45,118	53.9	3.3	42,710	14.4	18.1	17.1
Lincoln	23,087	39.1	13,276	15.6	50.6	17.9	87.0	9,625	28,299	70,424	36.0	2.8	70,054	9.4	11.7	11.2
Linn	5,523	46.3	2,528	7.6	56.6	18.5	23.0	10,725	26,981	51,150	49.1	1.9	47,506	14.7	19.9	18.8
Livingston	6,547	43.0	3,421	17.4	52.1	19.0	21.8	10,428	24,928	50,818	48.9	2.8	51,402	12.8	17.3	16.3
McDonald	7,544	33.0	4,974	6.1	63.4	11.4	34.9	9,193	20,964	42,876	55.1	2.3	45,446	17.6	25.0	25.8
Macon	6,128	40.5	3,424	15.6	57.3	17.5	23.2	10,550	22,876	44,696	54.1	1.4	49,013	13.0	18.3	16.8
Madison	4,803	39.7	2,741	10.6	54.5	14.1	19.3	9,334	26,063	47,984	51.8	2.3	45,002	16.3	23.6	22.0
Maries	3,820	43.9	1,749	17.2	55.4	15.8	12.1	9,928	26,756	48,276	51.6	2.6	47,698	12.9	17.6	16.7
Marion	12,006	42.1	6,440	21.5	46.2	24.8	47.7	9,681	25,708	54,277	46.5	1.8	54,230	14.3	17.5	16.5
Mercer	1,295	35.8	787	15.5	52.7	19.2	7.0	12,673	23,272	50,030	50.0	1.2	45,934	13.6	17.6	17.2
Miller	8,584	33.5	5,269	4.7	52.3	19.0	50.0	9,786	26,251	47,964	51.9	3.5	51,348	13.9	19.1	18.2
Mississippi	5,675	43.1	2,746	4.5	65.7	12.5	20.0	9,942	18,655	34,354	64.9	1.4	39,621	19.1	32.0	30.5
Moniteau	5,794	35.9	3,431	18.9	56.3	19.0	23.5	9,755	23,371	57,012	44.7	1.8	51,138	11.6	16.3	16.1
Monroe	3,840	44.4	1,562	20.9	58.2	13.8	15.8	10,831	25,180	43,422	58.1	0.8	48,661	13.0	19.9	19.4
Montgomery	5,628	48.7	2,271	10.0	58.0	16.4	16.6	10,325	25,976	52,123	47.3	1.3	56,447	13.0	16.7	15.8
Morgan	7,615	36.9	3,347	30.1	61.2	12.6	20.2	9,524	25,137	41,477	57.7	3.1	51,582	15.0	22.4	22.6
New Madrid	5,737	33.6	3,521	5.8	65.2	12.0	29.0	11,333	22,513	40,129	59.7	0.8	41,553	18.9	25.5	25.3
Newton	15,076	25.9	13,251	14.8	47.1	21.6	75.6	8,981	30,425	52,067	47.7	4.9	52,798	13.9	17.6	16.9
Nodaway	10,844	49.1	8,175	6.9	44.7	27.4	32.0	11,874	23,869	46,303	54.1	1.9	55,821	15.2	13.5	13.6
Oregon	3,295	31.3	2,207	5.3	59.7	14.9	18.5	9,690	18,775	32,766	68.9	0.6	37,835	22.0	31.3	29.0
Osage	5,410	39.7	2,956	19.2	52.3	20.4	16.4	10,275	34,195	62,087	38.3	3.9	62,679	8.5	9.1	8.5
Ozark	2,890	31.5	1,596	9.6	58.6	11.7	16.4	11,159	20,479	33,046	70.2	0.7	38,606	20.3	32.6	29.9
Pemiscot	4,973	31.5	3,763	3.7	64.8	12.0	37.3	11,947	21,634	34,709	63.4	1.8	34,498	35.3	49.9	47.7
Perry	7,595	39.7	4,564	29.7	55.2	19.1	22.8	9,706	27,294	56,861	42.7	2.7	55,605	11.7	13.9	12.9
Pettis	18,116	42.8	9,885	13.9	47.7	18.5	64.5	9,424	25,758	49,315	50.7	2.4	52,261	15.5	23.3	22.4
Phelps	19,550	43.9	14,646	11.2	40.5	29.9	67.1	10,039	25,217	44,987	53.9	2.8	50,420	17.5	17.7	16.1
Pike	6,860	37.5	3,443	9.0	64.3	15.0	26.4	10,302	22,720	44,920	55.3	1.9	51,255	14.9	19.8	19.1
Platte	59,558	57.0	25,610	17.3	26.8	43.0	207.8	11,795	41,193	82,448	28.4	10.0	86,924	5.4	6.3	5.5
Polk	12,519	38.9	8,300	26.0	49.2	20.6	51.4	9,973	23,591	47,614	52.2	1.9	50,691	15.6	21.2	21.2
Pulaski	26,955	51.2	14,621	9.9	35.5	27.7	92.1	10,214	25,098	58,426	42.3	2.3	59,126	12.5	14.3	13.8
Putnam	1,589	33.8	990	4.2	50.9	20.4	7.1	10,661	28,240	48,833	50.8	1.4	46,546	15.2	21.1	20.8
Ralls	2,940	28.5	1,956	14.3	56.6	15.4	6.6	8,976	26,913	54,194	44.4	1.0	57,061	11.4	11.5	10.7
Randolph	9,476	38.3	5,289	17.6	48.3	17.9	40.3	10,953	22,587	50,440	49.5	1.3	51,924	12.1	14.4	14.1
Ray	9,182	39.9	4,918	13.2	58.4	14.1	30.3	9,692	32,165	65,303	39.4	3.1	64,014	10.0	12.6	11.8
Reynolds	1,704	27.2	1,114	8.6	58.0	15.4	12.9	12,130	23,197	39,552	59.9	1.3	39,089	19.4	32.0	31.1
Ripley	3,912	29.4	2,995	11.9	58.6	10.8	20.2	9,233	19,106	36,066	60.4	1.1	37,771	21.3	31.6	30.4
St. Charles	246,588	61.3	101,524	26.1	28.2	40.8	700.3	11,705	40,738	87,644	25.0	9.6	90,567	5.0	5.4	5.1
St. Clair	3,239	34.5	1,692	7.2	53.0	14.5	12.8	9,712	23,158	39,000	60.3	1.1	41,486	18.7	28.4	28.1
Ste. Genevieve	8,046	45.0	3,615	26.0	46.7	17.9	23.7	12,842	33,049	61,746	40.9	3.4	58,618	9.0	11.3	10.6
St. Francois	29,309	43.6	13,740	11.9	52.4	14.0	98.6	9,288	22,577	46,307	53.4	1.9	48,476	16.2	18.8	17.5
St. Louis	637,427	64.1	243,174	29.3	27.3	44.4	2,050.5	14,458	42,682	68,661	36.1	10.5	68,964	9.1	11.6	11.5
Saline	10,639	46.7	5,838	21.0	52.1	22.5	37.2	10,085	23,692	47,585	52.3	1.6	52,850	13.1	14.8	15.0
Schuyler	1,243	26.7	987	15.9	58.0	9.2	5.9	10,162	19,482	44,420	57.2	1.5	46,191	15.2	25.8	27.1
Scotland	1,299	26.5	966	30.5	60.9	14.9	6.2	10,374	25,956	47,708	50.3	4.1	47,740	14.3	23.9	23.0
Scott	16,717	43.7	8,428	15.1	53.3	19.8	61.7	9,244	26,193	46,310	53.7	2.3	52,864	14.6	22.9	21.7
Shannon	2,499	30.6	1,554	9.0	63.2	14.5	17.7	8,901	17,782	36,229	64.8	0.4	37,599	21.8	32.5	31.4
Shelby	2,790	47.0	1,273	13.5	52.4	19.4	11.0	10,660	23,791	43,809	55.7	1.3	48,430	14.6	20.5	20.3
Stoddard	11,551	39.8	5,946	5.9	62.6	12.3	46.3	9,102	22,587	42,761	56.3	0.8	47,372	16.8	21.5	20.6
Stone	12,011	37.6	5,231	14.8	44.6	19.8	42.9	11,756	28,897	51,476	47.9	2.9	51,797	14.2	23.4	23.0
Sullivan	2,640	43.4	1,282	6.9	62.2	15.2	12.1	11,800	23,829	44,056	53.1	1.3	43,387	15.6	19.4	19.7
Taney	22,698	40.6	12,258	18.0	44.2	21.2	79.4	9,855	24,659	47,860	52.1	2.8	44,670	15.6	24.1	23.3
Texas	8,325	32.8	5,144	17.7	54.8	14.8	35.7	9,052	20,541	35,758	62.3	0.6	38,985	20.3	28.7	27.7
Vernon	7,226	35.1	4,822	19.4	52.6	17.5	29.6	9,853	23,553	43,910	54.5	1.2	45,874	15.0	21.6	20.4
Warren	14,913	41.8	7,535	21.2	47.4	19.4	51.4	10,622	31,308	64,735	39.0	6.4	69,678	9.0	12.2	11.5
Washington	7,904	32.0	5,416	7.8	59.7	11.4	36.3	10,342	23,740	42,849	56.2	2.2	42,683	19.4	25.1	23.0
Wayne	4,680	36.4	2,474	14.3	62.1	9.9	16.0	9,032	20,449	38,018	66.3	0.6	43,848	23.2	35.8	33.7
Webster	16,799	42.4	9,063	19.8	50.7	17.7	64.1	9,155	24,139	55,827	44.7	2.6	55,431	15.0	24.9	23.1
Worth	828	41.1	436	8.7	53.9	18.3	3.3	10,880	26,866	47,500	51.0	2.7	44,361	13.8	18.0	17.6
Wright	6,522	35.7	3,917	18.7	60.4	11.0	31.2	9,625	18,858	36,711	67.1	0.8	39,521	18.3	29.2	28.7
St. Louis city	176,910	58.9	67,586	35.4	35.4	37.2	474.3	14,177	31,930	45,782	53.3	4.1	45,773	20.8	28.9	28.9

1. All persons 3 years old and over enrolled in nursery school through college. 2. Persons 25 years old and over. 3. Elementary and secondary education expenditures. 4. Based on population estimated by the American Community Survey, 2016–2020. 5. CDC percent based on 2019 population estimate.

STATE County	Personal income, 2020										Earnings, 2020		
			Per capita[1]			Supplements to wages and salaries, employer contributions (mil dol)						Contributions for government social insurance (mil dol)	
	Total (mil dol)	Percent change 2019–2020	Dollars	Rank	Wages and salaries (mil dol)	Pension and insurance	Government social insurance	Proprietors' income (mil dol)	Dividends, interest, and rent (mil dol)	Personal transfer reecipts (mil dol)	Total (mil dol)	From employee and self-employed	From employer
	62	63	64	65	66	67	68	69	70	71	72	73	74
MISSOURI— Cont'd													
Jasper	5,169	3.6	42,488	2,132	2,609	464	197	387	789	1,433	3,658	246	197
Jefferson	10,427	5.4	46,027	1,650	2,245	399	170	403	1,224	2,595	3,216	245	170
Johnson	2,180	6.8	40,207	2,432	959	266	78	121	357	556	1,426	76	78
Knox	161	15.1	40,933	2,341	37	9	3	37	21	51	85	5	3
Laclede	1,378	6.1	38,403	2,635	551	119	44	119	174	484	834	59	44
Lafayette	1,512	8.3	45,825	1,679	356	75	27	126	199	453	584	41	27
Lawrence	1,403	5.8	36,746	2,801	366	73	28	92	183	474	558	42	28
Lewis	387	8.5	39,481	2,510	99	22	7	33	49	120	161	12	7
Lincoln	2,647	8.9	44,032	1,944	573	108	43	133	286	657	857	63	43
Linn	502	7.5	42,456	2,136	167	33	14	59	78	170	273	20	14
Livingston	631	6.7	43,804	1,975	260	53	19	79	99	190	410	26	19
McDonald	731	7.0	31,941	3,059	283	51	23	46	82	238	404	28	23
Macon	676	8.1	44,785	1,828	204	46	15	86	86	216	350	24	15
Madison	488	8.8	40,312	2,416	139	31	11	19	56	208	200	16	11
Maries	331	8.8	37,638	2,721	51	12	4	14	48	113	81	7	4
Marion	1,254	6.8	44,121	1,926	612	116	47	88	157	412	862	58	47
Mercer	126	9.6	35,358	2,918	39	8	3	16	18	45	66	4	3
Miller	1,015	9.7	39,349	2,531	290	58	22	62	138	315	432	30	22
Mississippi	476	13.1	37,483	2,740	131	29	10	65	62	181	236	14	10
Moniteau	653	9.2	41,930	2,212	183	40	14	63	101	165	301	19	14
Monroe	386	8.9	44,528	1,870	67	17	5	43	49	119	132	10	5
Montgomery	527	10.2	46,688	1,552	129	26	10	42	76	154	206	15	10
Morgan	888	2.9	42,880	2,081	163	34	12	87	261	306	297	26	12
New Madrid	700	9.5	41,953	2,205	325	65	26	71	68	247	486	30	26
Newton	2,442	5.4	41,771	2,233	992	183	73	152	330	683	1,401	90	73
Nodaway	790	9.0	36,315	2,847	333	79	23	98	126	214	533	32	23
Oregon	345	7.2	33,166	3,019	95	20	10	27	40	161	151	13	10
Osage	667	7.4	49,250	1,225	182	37	14	55	128	141	288	19	14
Ozark	306	7.1	33,722	2,993	50	12	4	19	45	143	85	11	4
Pemiscot	639	10.5	40,931	2,342	195	44	15	70	62	266	325	20	15
Perry	864	6.9	45,002	1,792	404	77	30	61	107	256	572	37	30
Pettis	1,741	7.3	40,971	2,337	815	155	62	148	231	558	1,181	75	62
Phelps	1,867	4.9	42,030	2,190	859	178	61	85	324	543	1,183	76	61
Pike	710	9.7	40,471	2,397	214	49	15	71	123	227	349	24	15
Platte	6,466	5.0	60,698	397	2,738	399	190	325	934	990	3,652	237	190
Polk	1,200	5.7	36,944	2,790	368	81	27	100	156	403	576	40	27
Pulaski	2,358	7.0	44,732	1,839	1,279	394	118	48	402	525	1,839	86	118
Putnam	184	9.7	39,308	2,534	41	9	3	31	31	64	85	5	3
Ralls	460	12.0	44,688	1,851	179	32	14	49	50	129	273	17	14
Randolph	1,040	6.3	42,615	2,115	428	89	33	82	126	331	631	42	33
Ray	1,055	5.8	46,047	1,644	176	42	13	73	111	297	305	22	13
Reynolds	236	6.0	38,107	2,675	81	17	7	5	39	108	109	9	7
Ripley	456	10.1	34,297	2,970	81	20	6	31	51	213	139	13	6
St. Charles	23,104	4.3	56,879	579	8,448	1,276	613	905	3,057	3,995	11,243	747	613
St. Clair	320	12.2	33,058	3,025	58	13	4	34	50	139	109	9	4
Ste. Genevieve	805	7.0	44,925	1,803	303	56	24	30	117	224	414	29	24
St. Francois	2,485	6.1	37,377	2,753	894	197	65	77	330	921	1,233	91	65
St. Louis	78,333	5.8	78,804	87	42,559	5,663	2,947	5,172	23,776	11,970	56,341	3,567	2,947
Saline	985	13.0	43,076	2,051	372	73	29	127	126	310	601	36	29
Schuyler	152	11.1	33,550	3,002	21	7	2	22	19	50	51	3	2
Scotland	203	19.0	41,576	2,256	47	12	3	52	26	53	115	6	3
Scott	1,690	6.5	44,148	1,922	719	127	57	133	237	573	1,036	72	57
Shannon	271	8.8	33,071	3,023	50	12	4	22	33	113	88	8	4
Shelby	269	13.5	45,373	1,741	68	16	5	43	37	79	131	9	5
Stoddard	1,194	9.0	41,158	2,314	439	83	35	86	137	424	642	47	35
Stone	1,363	6.1	41,975	2,201	247	45	20	79	259	472	391	38	20
Sullivan	271	14.6	44,877	1,812	140	24	12	28	29	84	204	12	12
Taney	2,180	4.7	38,859	2,584	1,009	171	79	160	314	779	1,419	103	79
Texas	823	9.5	32,774	3,036	210	56	16	77	115	321	359	27	16
Vernon	805	11.1	39,496	2,504	292	70	22	97	106	283	481	30	22
Warren	1,647	8.1	45,011	1,790	355	66	27	77	219	417	524	40	27
Washington	816	7.2	33,148	3,021	182	44	14	21	80	342	260	22	14
Wayne	434	8.3	34,018	2,978	79	19	6	17	68	204	122	11	6
Webster	1,429	6.5	35,845	2,879	330	71	25	96	182	429	522	44	25
Worth	82	9.2	41,861	2,222	12	4	1	12	13	27	29	2	1
Wright	650	8.2	35,480	2,909	152	34	11	51	79	260	249	22	11
St. Louis city	15,192	3.7	51,041	1,021	16,076	2,554	1,151	1,688	2,276	4,048	21,469	1,271	1,151

1. Based on the resident population estimated as of July 1 of the year shown.

STATE County	Earnings, 2020 (cont.) — Percent by selected industries: Farm	Mining, quarrying, and extractions	Construction	Manu-facturing	Information; professional, scientific, technical services	Retail trade	Finance, insurance, real estate, and leasing	Health care and social assistance	Govern-ment	Social Security beneficiaries, December 2020: Number	Rate[1]	Supple-mental Security Income recipients, 2020	Housing units, 2021: Total	Percent change, 2010–2021
	75	76	77	78	79	80	81	82	83	84	85	86	87	88
MISSOURI— Cont'd														
Jasper	0.9	0.2	5.2	24.3	4.8	8.1	3.9	11.9	10.8	26,025	211	3,561	53,712	1.6
Jefferson	0.0	0.3	13.1	10.0	4.7	9.2	5.4	12.4	17.4	48,825	214	2,885	93,346	0.9
Johnson	2.2	D	6.7	6.3	2.4	4.2	4.0	4.5	55.6	9,085	168	700	22,657	0.2
Knox	31.4	D	7.2	7.5	D	5.1	4.8	D	16.2	1,030	270	97	1,932	-0.1
Laclede	1.2	0.1	4.6	40.1	D	8.7	3.9	10.5	10.7	9,335	258	1,094	15,960	0.3
Lafayette	8.4	0.0	10.1	10.3	D	6.5	4.6	D	20.3	7,815	238	615	14,151	0.5
Lawrence	7.2	D	8.0	14.3	5.3	9.4	4.0	D	18.0	9,595	250	873	16,235	0.1
Lewis	9.3	D	9.0	6.6	2.4	5.1	3.9	D	18.0	2,455	246	172	4,316	0.1
Lincoln	2.2	1.5	14.9	16.3	2.9	8.3	5.2	7.9	16.1	11,990	195	876	23,642	1.0
Linn	10.6	0.1	4.8	17.9	4.5	6.5	4.9	D	15.6	3,215	271	367	5,990	-0.1
Livingston	8.2	D	7.0	7.3	3.0	11.2	5.0	12.2	19.6	3,725	252	336	6,361	0.1
McDonald	3.3	0.0	8.8	42.2	D	7.4	2.1	D	12.8	4,550	195	559	9,789	0.3
Macon	9.3	0.0	6.0	13.8	8.2	6.7	4.6	D	24.2	4,205	277	306	7,401	0.1
Madison	0.6	D	9.5	12.8	D	9.9	2.4	11.5	24.1	3,720	294	523	5,841	0.1
Maries	4.2	0.0	D	19.9	D	7.1	D	7.6	20.2	2,355	280	146	4,263	0.0
Marion	2.7	D	4.6	12.8	D	9.4	4.6	D	13.0	7,070	248	995	12,886	0.2
Mercer	29.1	D	2.0	D	D	4.0	2.6	6.5	20.3	950	272	59	1,909	-0.1
Miller	2.8	D	12.8	7.8	3.2	16.5	4.6	D	19.3	6,195	249	542	12,503	0.2
Mississippi	24.4	0.0	2.0	1.5	1.1	6.4	5.4	D	23.0	3,180	254	641	5,278	-0.1
Moniteau	7.8	D	19.9	17.0	D	5.7	D	D	18.7	3,310	214	204	6,178	0.0
Monroe	24.0	D	3.9	4.8	D	3.5	D	D	26.5	2,395	275	176	4,465	0.0
Montgomery	11.8	2.3	12.3	20.2	2.9	5.8	4.9	5.2	16.5	3,125	274	299	5,801	0.7
Morgan	5.4	D	15.9	9.1	D	15.0	4.8	D	17.5	6,435	301	621	15,147	0.2
New Madrid	9.6	D	2.0	17.8	D	10.6	2.3	D	10.1	4,040	252	790	7,878	0.1
Newton	2.1	D	7.4	14.0	3.3	7.3	3.0	28.8	10.7	13,435	226	919	24,665	0.3
Nodaway	7.9	D	6.8	17.4	3.1	6.8	3.8	12.0	25.6	4,175	197	275	9,486	0.3
Oregon	6.6	D	2.4	6.1	D	11.3	2.9	12.7	17.9	3,085	357	555	4,319	0.1
Osage	6.6	0.4	11.7	37.8	D	7.0	2.5	4.2	14.6	2,940	220	136	6,492	0.0
Ozark	2.6	0.2	9.8	6.9	D	7.4	7.4	D	25.1	3,285	374	292	5,029	0.1
Pemiscot	17.6	0.0	D	D	D	6.0	3.4	D	21.7	4,145	272	1,183	7,491	0.1
Perry	4.2	0.0	11.7	26.5	3.6	6.4	5.0	5.5	13.3	4,625	244	344	8,512	0.5
Pettis	3.3	D	5.2	24.6	5.8	7.8	3.3	7.9	17.6	9,370	217	1,352	18,553	0.0
Phelps	0.0	D	4.4	7.0	2.7	8.2	4.0	17.0	35.1	9,715	216	1,184	20,217	0.1
Pike	8.1	D	12.3	7.3	4.5	8.6	2.9	6.9	26.4	4,245	239	395	7,609	0.1
Platte	0.6	D	8.7	6.8	7.8	7.5	6.4	8.0	10.2	17,495	161	748	46,120	1.4
Polk	4.4	D	6.8	5.8	D	7.9	4.0	11.1	28.3	7,035	220	907	13,415	0.2
Pulaski	0.1	D	2.0	0.4	2.0	3.3	1.7	2.4	78.5	7,350	137	917	19,381	0.3
Putnam	27.8	0.0	D	D	D	5.3	6.6	2.3	25.1	1,315	279	123	2,832	-0.1
Ralls	9.5	0.0	6.5	47.7	D	3.5	D	D	7.9	2,670	258	123	5,034	0.1
Randolph	3.8	D	5.5	10.7	2.4	7.2	6.5	9.6	18.3	5,510	223	756	10,815	0.3
Ray	10.7	D	9.2	14.5	4.7	8.1	3.4	D	24.8	5,480	238	311	9,892	0.4
Reynolds	-2.5	D	D	12.9	D	3.7	D	10.5	16.7	2,130	350	229	3,462	0.0
Ripley	5.6	D	5.5	12.9	1.6	9.3	3.1	17.8	22.5	3,710	349	684	5,155	0.2
St. Charles	0.2	D	8.8	12.6	13.5	7.5	8.0	10.5	10.9	75,605	184	2,829	164,505	1.7
St. Clair	15.6	D	7.1	3.1	4.2	10.4	3.7	9.5	24.5	3,020	322	272	5,292	0.1
Ste. Genevieve	2.0	5.0	9.3	28.2	D	5.8	3.6	D	17.8	4,475	241	305	8,321	0.1
St. Francois	0.0	0.5	6.8	9.1	3.2	9.5	8.2	15.0	27.3	16,935	251	2,419	28,770	0.4
St. Louis	0.0	0.4	6.3	9.0	13.2	5.2	13.6	13.1	7.4	209,900	210	17,782	445,419	0.1
Saline	15.5	0.0	2.8	24.2	D	5.7	3.7	D	15.4	5,140	221	631	9,826	-0.1
Schuyler	26.9	0.0	10.8	D	D	6.2	2.0	2.0	26.8	970	241	101	1,891	0.2
Scotland	26.3	D	5.5	5.0	D	7.0	D	D	27.6	960	205	51	2,210	0.0
Scott	4.3	0.1	5.8	16.3	4.5	4.4	5.1	D	13.5	10,325	273	1,610	16,809	0.3
Shannon	3.1	D	D	25.8	D	4.3	3.3	D	18.6	2,285	322	342	3,517	0.1
Shelby	17.7	D	5.5	10.3	4.1	6.5	D	3.7	21.1	1,605	269	127	2,951	0.0
Stoddard	7.0	D	8.5	29.0	D	7.0	1.6	D	12.9	8,200	288	1,059	13,399	0.0
Stone	1.6	0.3	15.8	1.4	4.3	10.6	4.7	5.4	15.6	10,610	336	540	20,166	1.0
Sullivan	16.9	D	2.3	D	D	2.6	D	2.7	12.8	1,535	259	177	3,021	-0.1
Taney	0.3	D	3.5	2.4	3.7	11.3	6.4	13.2	11.0	15,645	277	1,227	29,750	1.0
Texas	7.0	0.3	6.5	14.2	D	7.5	3.3	5.0	30.4	6,300	252	744	11,010	0.0
Vernon	13.3	D	4.2	21.0	3.5	5.8	6.5	D	17.8	5,010	256	631	8,929	0.1
Warren	1.7	D	14.2	24.6	D	6.2	3.8	D	15.8	8,125	222	501	15,843	2.4
Washington	-0.7	1.4	5.7	10.8	2.4	7.8	4.8	D	35.9	6,070	258	1,091	10,731	0.1
Wayne	2.1	4.8	5.2	10.1	D	6.2	3.3	D	26.0	3,970	364	718	6,116	0.1
Webster	0.2	0.3	12.7	20.8	D	9.7	3.4	6.1	16.6	9,090	229	768	15,399	1.1
Worth	28.6	D	D	D	D	8.2	3.0	2.7	29.1	565	285	40	1,113	-0.1
Wright	3.0	D	8.8	13.4	D	13.4	4.4	D	20.0	5,450	293	786	8,361	0.1
St. Louis city	0.0	-0.2	D	8.5	16.9	1.5	10.5	17.6	14.1	51,860	177	14,172	173,501	0.0

1. Per 1,000 resident population estimated as of July 1 of the year shown.

STATE County	Housing units, 2016–2020: Total	Occupied units: Owner-occupied: Percent	Owner-occupied: Median value[1]	Median owner cost as a percent of income: With a mortgage	Median owner cost as a percent of income: Without a mortgage[2]	Renter-occupied: Median rent[3]	Renter-occupied: Median rent as a percent of income[2]	Sub-standard units[4] (percent)	Civilian labor force, 2021: Total	Percent change, 2020–2021	Unemployment: Total	Unemployment: Rate[5]	Civilian employment[6], 2016–2020: Total	Percent: Management, business, science, and arts	Percent: Construction, production, and maintenance occupations
	89	90	91	92	93	94	95	96	97	98	99	100	101	102	103
MISSOURI— Cont'd															
Jasper	46,461	63.6	124,200	18.4	11.3	770	28.9	2.8	56,953	2.1	2,133	3.7	56,418	31.4	28.8
Jefferson	84,978	79.5	167,700	19.0	10.5	871	25.7	1.7	117,556	0.7	4,766	4.1	112,610	33.7	27.6
Johnson	19,931	62.4	163,300	19.3	10.0	813	28.6	2.7	23,074	0.1	1,014	4.4	23,873	35.0	26.0
Knox	1,400	85.0	75,100	19.5	14.0	561	25.4	1.9	1,729	-0.9	53	3.1	1,684	26.8	33.1
Laclede	14,413	68.0	116,600	19.6	10.6	652	22.5	2.3	16,514	-1.1	712	4.3	15,709	27.5	37.5
Lafayette	12,711	70.9	154,300	17.2	10.0	711	24.0	2.1	16,674	1.1	711	4.3	15,549	28.4	35.3
Lawrence	14,849	71.3	115,300	19.3	11.2	692	25.3	3.6	17,457	-0.9	705	4.0	16,704	26.7	31.6
Lewis	3,597	76.5	88,200	15.1	12.3	575	27.0	2.9	4,826	-2.2	169	3.5	4,193	24.2	37.3
Lincoln	19,818	80.3	165,700	18.3	10.9	842	24.3	1.4	29,307	1.0	1,351	4.6	27,258	31.3	34.0
Linn	5,002	75.9	92,600	17.2	10.0	559	22.6	2.2	5,077	0.6	276	5.4	5,657	29.0	31.1
Livingston	5,907	66.7	111,800	18.4	10.2	675	21.4	2.3	7,256	-0.5	219	3.0	6,538	36.3	24.7
McDonald	8,393	68.1	102,200	19.5	11.2	674	25.2	9.0	10,608	2.8	409	3.9	9,461	20.2	43.3
Macon	5,908	74.3	100,500	18.7	12.8	545	25.2	2.8	7,365	-0.7	272	3.7	6,336	31.7	33.1
Madison	4,851	70.5	120,000	18.7	10.1	666	28.3	5.5	5,473	0.4	242	4.4	5,005	24.3	32.8
Maries	3,808	73.4	145,400	16.2	10.0	545	20.0	2.7	3,898	0.1	150	3.8	3,739	27.6	39.4
Marion	11,537	64.7	129,000	18.4	10.0	644	24.4	1.2	14,197	-0.2	492	3.5	13,055	31.8	26.2
Mercer	1,333	78.7	85,300	15.1	11.8	515	20.3	5.1	1,805	-3.1	53	2.9	1,548	38.9	33.6
Miller	10,452	73.5	140,500	20.4	10.4	672	25.4	2.5	12,593	2.6	517	4.1	11,639	28.8	27.3
Mississippi	4,998	60.6	82,900	18.9	11.3	637	34.0	0.8	5,440	-3.4	254	4.7	4,362	25.2	30.9
Moniteau	5,450	76.5	138,900	18.5	10.0	640	24.8	2.9	7,049	-0.7	239	3.4	6,619	31.6	33.0
Monroe	3,731	75.1	119,200	18.5	12.3	564	21.6	2.0	3,783	0.2	165	4.4	3,707	28.9	37.0
Montgomery	4,995	72.7	120,700	19.0	11.0	660	20.9	3.4	5,788	1.4	215	3.7	5,194	26.8	37.0
Morgan	7,639	81.2	150,100	22.6	12.9	529	23.5	2.2	8,540	4.1	403	4.7	7,372	27.1	34.8
New Madrid	7,281	62.4	77,200	15.8	10.0	676	27.6	2.8	8,326	-0.8	396	4.8	6,839	22.7	31.9
Newton	22,123	72.3	131,800	18.3	10.1	704	25.3	3.5	27,045	1.7	1,031	3.8	26,195	30.5	31.8
Nodaway	8,510	58.1	126,600	18.3	10.0	663	27.8	1.6	10,791	0.8	318	2.9	10,988	33.9	26.4
Oregon	4,298	73.0	98,600	19.5	11.9	574	34.7	3.0	3,839	-1.8	203	5.3	3,815	27.5	34.2
Osage	5,273	83.8	159,000	18.6	10.0	566	25.6	2.3	6,985	-0.4	184	2.6	6,633	32.6	33.6
Ozark	4,082	79.4	109,100	23.2	12.5	650	27.5	3.7	3,442	-0.6	188	5.5	3,099	31.4	39.4
Pemiscot	6,640	53.4	88,200	17.4	11.3	636	35.7	4.2	6,078	-2.9	445	7.3	5,656	26.0	33.2
Perry	7,577	73.6	151,900	18.7	10.0	719	27.0	1.6	9,781	-0.3	310	3.2	9,246	32.0	35.9
Pettis	16,193	69.1	128,900	18.1	10.0	727	26.6	2.5	20,298	-1.3	949	4.7	19,208	29.0	34.2
Phelps	18,213	59.8	146,200	18.6	10.0	727	29.8	2.0	20,030	1.5	746	3.7	18,642	43.6	19.2
Pike	6,653	71.4	96,600	18.7	10.0	622	24.3	3.4	7,382	-1.0	290	3.9	7,073	26.5	36.9
Platte	39,918	67.2	238,800	18.9	10.5	1,073	24.6	2.2	59,458	1.2	2,406	4.0	55,210	47.0	19.3
Polk	11,833	68.9	141,600	19.7	10.0	696	27.5	3.4	14,576	2.0	509	3.5	14,403	33.8	26.0
Pulaski	15,061	52.3	160,700	19.6	10.3	1,029	22.3	3.2	14,585	0.4	647	4.4	18,308	33.0	26.3
Putnam	1,698	78.7	89,300	18.8	10.7	613	25.7	2.7	2,233	-1.5	70	3.1	2,067	26.3	36.0
Ralls	4,132	85.4	134,700	19.0	10.9	716	27.7	1.7	5,602	-0.2	190	3.4	4,833	26.9	33.5
Randolph	8,872	71.1	108,600	18.0	10.0	677	27.9	0.8	10,273	1.5	433	4.2	10,692	27.8	32.2
Ray	8,766	77.8	139,800	17.7	10.6	725	24.4	1.9	10,983	2.1	711	6.5	11,138	24.9	38.1
Reynolds	2,580	82.0	96,000	15.9	12.9	612	25.5	2.2	2,936	0.5	121	4.1	2,534	26.2	41.6
Ripley	4,973	80.3	86,900	19.5	13.1	589	30.6	1.6	5,072	1.3	279	5.5	5,212	28.5	35.7
St. Charles	149,472	81.6	230,100	18.8	10.0	1,069	25.8	1.0	227,337	0.9	7,884	3.5	213,287	44.7	17.5
St. Clair	4,120	80.4	95,100	20.0	12.8	532	21.5	2.7	3,845	1.9	172	4.5	3,657	32.9	29.7
Ste. Genevieve	7,252	80.9	171,100	15.8	10.6	729	25.0	1.4	9,232	0.5	316	3.4	8,668	30.4	33.5
St. Francois	24,572	67.9	118,000	19.1	10.3	667	27.0	2.9	26,027	-0.8	1,255	4.8	27,081	27.2	29.4
St. Louis	409,658	68.3	206,700	19.3	11.2	985	28.0	1.2	526,087	0.9	23,679	4.5	499,911	46.7	15.4
Saline	8,235	70.8	114,600	17.3	12.6	637	28.3	1.6	10,487	-0.7	368	3.5	10,596	35.6	27.0
Schuyler	1,440	69.4	81,300	17.3	10.8	446	23.6	3.5	1,845	-2.8	80	4.3	2,014	25.3	39.9
Scotland	1,687	78.7	100,300	20.2	13.1	445	23.7	2.5	2,311	-2.7	61	2.6	2,006	35.7	35.6
Scott	15,342	66.2	113,200	18.0	10.0	719	27.0	3.1	20,195	1.7	785	3.9	17,492	31.0	28.9
Shannon	3,063	74.9	119,900	23.6	12.5	623	27.1	9.0	3,366	0.7	189	5.6	2,980	30.0	37.1
Shelby	2,485	75.7	71,700	18.5	11.6	552	21.8	0.8	2,985	-1.5	99	3.3	2,814	29.1	35.1
Stoddard	11,545	70.0	103,600	20.3	10.0	643	25.5	2.1	13,325	1.1	595	4.5	12,141	28.1	34.1
Stone	12,689	83.3	185,900	21.6	10.2	707	26.4	2.4	13,611	3.5	892	6.6	12,398	30.3	27.2
Sullivan	2,218	73.7	75,600	19.4	11.0	637	18.9	2.6	2,650	-3.7	129	4.9	2,683	29.5	45.5
Taney	22,390	65.5	149,900	20.5	11.4	795	26.2	3.7	26,276	1.2	1,970	7.5	25,910	31.4	18.2
Texas	9,852	76.2	112,600	22.6	10.0	605	28.9	3.5	9,000	0.7	410	4.6	9,456	28.3	35.4
Vernon	8,294	73.9	102,200	19.4	10.7	654	28.1	3.5	9,422	0.3	321	3.4	8,906	36.9	27.4
Warren	13,129	79.5	184,900	18.6	10.1	862	30.7	5.2	18,722	1.0	776	4.1	16,820	31.0	35.3
Washington	9,278	76.4	97,700	19.6	10.0	585	28.5	3.5	10,094	0.2	516	5.1	9,197	26.9	34.2
Wayne	5,438	74.8	93,200	22.1	11.6	561	24.6	5.2	4,838	-3.6	243	5.0	4,402	25.1	40.0
Webster	13,697	78.2	152,500	18.8	10.0	652	24.4	5.2	17,409	1.2	598	3.4	16,014	28.4	34.9
Worth	808	81.6	71,200	15.5	10.0	0	22.5	3.1	1,181	0.9	30	2.5	897	26.5	31.7
Wright	6,977	75.8	109,100	22.9	11.4	493	31.0	3.8	7,596	3.0	306	4.0	6,639	28.3	33.9
St. Louis city	143,566	44.1	143,700	19.2	12.7	840	28.8	2.6	150,531	0.3	9,583	6.4	157,422	44.2	16.0

1. Specified owner-occupied units. 2. A value of 10.0 represents 10 percent or less; a value of 50.0 represents 50 percent or more. 3. Specified renter-occupied units. 4. Overcrowded or lacking complete plumbing facilities. 5. Percent of civilian labor force. 6. Civilian employed persons 16 years old and over.

STATE County	Private nonfarm establishments, employment and payroll, 2020: Number of establishments	Employment: Total	Employment: Health care and social assistance	Employment: Manufacturing	Employment: Retail trade	Employment: Finance and insurance	Employment: Professional, scientific, and technical services	Annual payroll: Total (mil dol)	Annual payroll: Average per employee (dollars)	Agriculture, 2017: Farms: Number	Farms: Percent with: Fewer than 50 acres	Farms: Percent with: 1000 acres or more	Farm producers whose primary occupation is farming (percent)
	104	105	106	107	108	109	110	111	112	113	114	115	116
MISSOURI— Cont'd													
Jasper	2,771	51,047	6,356	10,970	7,761	1,107	1,032	2,089	40,932	1,315	42.1	3.3	38.1
Jefferson	3,870	40,698	5,694	4,300	7,211	1,169	1,203	1,592	39,127	721	43.7	1.1	37.2
Johnson	915	10,510	2,225	1,532	1,620	285	457	361	34,318	1,626	37.8	5.0	36.2
Knox	89	548	30	105	111	53	17	20	35,996	637	18.8	9.3	41.9
Laclede	746	11,978	1,225	5,239	1,841	282	179	429	35,798	1,304	27.7	2.3	36.5
Lafayette	693	6,172	1,093	1,066	814	231	181	224	36,343	1,175	38.5	7.7	39.2
Lawrence	701	6,552	979	1,121	1,291	175	142	236	35,998	1,697	41.8	3.2	40.0
Lewis	189	1,949	253	146	234	87	44	58	29,872	636	27.8	9.6	33.5
Lincoln	939	9,515	1,237	1,717	1,587	325	279	411	43,183	1,092	41.9	4.3	36.0
Linn	293	3,212	539	855	493	168	73	116	36,082	994	23.7	7.7	36.9
Livingston	398	5,019	935	577	1,092	181	115	171	34,039	784	22.1	9.3	35.9
McDonald	309	6,314	224	3,907	865	123	41	239	37,828	940	26.9	1.9	40.2
Macon	339	3,613	586	488	652	192	76	120	33,077	1,163	22.0	8.1	37.7
Madison	245	3,320	1,028	258	609	70	44	107	32,204	361	19.9	2.5	39.9
Maries	123	959	138	158	148	102	18	34	35,050	879	14.9	3.1	36.6
Marion	790	11,405	2,931	1,518	1,708	422	286	450	39,493	587	26.9	9.5	36.6
Mercer	71	396	71	16	82	26	NA	13	32,790	493	16.0	8.3	40.2
Miller	692	6,642	543	733	1,936	236	172	224	33,758	1,023	19.7	3.4	36.7
Mississippi	220	2,009	408	83	357	136	90	73	36,583	159	13.8	53.5	70.4
Moniteau	332	2,993	319	671	453	102	55	109	36,524	1,135	28.7	3.2	40.5
Monroe	178	1,299	198	302	249	72	17	41	31,554	978	23.6	7.3	35.1
Montgomery	238	2,349	287	621	349	107	50	92	39,013	698	26.8	9.5	38.8
Morgan	497	3,191	299	521	719	114	91	104	32,524	962	29.4	3.5	46.8
New Madrid	398	6,462	1,405	1,053	1,249	140	48	229	35,487	290	15.2	50.3	62.3
Newton	1,213	22,114	6,621	2,747	2,475	503	472	947	42,823	1,588	37.1	1.7	38.0
Nodaway	470	6,156	1,177	1,503	1,025	180	134	219	35,510	1,133	24.4	10.5	42.7
Oregon	178	1,489	450	133	424	46	37	41	27,465	564	19.5	8.0	44.6
Osage	271	4,556	312	2,626	482	136	32	183	40,141	1,277	15.8	3.4	33.2
Ozark	154	838	110	76	183	63	34	21	25,420	705	15.0	4.7	46.4
Pemiscot	320	3,859	1,389	526	618	145	25	128	33,193	184	14.1	49.5	63.6
Perry	511	9,511	1,113	3,707	1,022	359	174	353	37,164	921	27.3	4.3	37.4
Pettis	998	17,527	2,945	4,452	2,374	332	1,847	630	35,932	1,259	34.3	8.2	40.8
Phelps	1,029	14,606	3,618	1,287	2,551	421	332	543	37,202	728	32.1	2.6	32.0
Pike	385	4,143	806	655	587	138	87	147	35,373	926	26.0	9.1	36.0
Platte	2,450	43,782	4,782	2,974	6,379	2,055	1,823	2,014	45,995	490	41.6	8.0	30.9
Polk	593	7,469	2,294	363	1,084	308	888	343	45,863	1,562	32.8	2.9	42.0
Pulaski	652	8,751	1,708	136	1,737	333	326	295	33,702	502	25.7	1.6	36.8
Putnam	85	598	125	81	181	61	5	20	33,162	585	14.5	10.1	46.1
Ralls	215	2,804	202	1,457	238	47	34	149	53,051	672	25.0	10.1	37.3
Randolph	511	7,493	1,189	1,001	1,198	413	96	291	38,850	783	32.4	5.5	31.8
Ray	342	2,982	551	464	637	92	85	109	36,648	1,070	30.7	5.0	33.1
Reynolds	130	1,363	160	364	144	33	11	59	43,465	341	22.0	1.8	31.6
Ripley	296	2,098	923	248	398	71	13	49	23,581	438	25.1	5.3	37.4
St. Charles	8,644	139,173	17,894	14,645	23,899	10,926	6,619	6,625	47,605	604	45.0	8.1	39.1
St. Clair	164	1,149	362	72	241	69	35	34	29,719	734	18.1	7.4	43.8
Ste. Genevieve	386	4,905	1,045	1,137	464	178	77	206	42,054	660	26.4	3.6	39.4
St. Francois	1,391	18,562	5,162	1,814	3,326	1,269	376	623	33,573	688	34.9	1.9	31.7
St. Louis	30,897	620,882	93,846	43,898	63,232	40,912	50,027	37,580	60,527	184	67.4	3.8	33.7
Saline	464	6,980	1,286	2,075	939	257	78	259	37,163	882	21.5	14.9	45.2
Schuyler	71	454	14	NA	93	18	5	16	34,919	541	23.7	6.3	42.4
Scotland	135	837	241	97	189	38	21	29	34,616	713	24.1	7.0	41.1
Scott	1,024	14,161	2,903	3,264	1,331	391	365	564	39,827	450	35.1	15.6	39.9
Shannon	150	1,305	196	678	142	46	7	32	24,419	435	25.3	6.0	37.0
Shelby	152	1,078	90	161	152	90	54	36	33,218	628	20.2	13.5	31.4
Stoddard	664	8,947	1,741	3,318	1,199	312	151	345	38,578	792	31.1	22.6	46.4
Stone	687	5,151	385	101	890	130	125	159	30,828	628	35.7	1.8	34.9
Sullivan	99	2,022	199	1,287	133	51	15	85	42,052	671	11.6	10.6	46.3
Taney	1,843	24,964	2,540	517	4,678	487	470	695	27,839	395	26.6	4.8	38.1
Texas	434	4,259	846	927	809	156	78	144	33,862	1,371	25.2	4.2	43.1
Vernon	456	5,778	1,443	1,267	762	393	82	212	36,735	1,265	24.5	8.3	39.8
Warren	586	6,715	685	1,391	923	207	116	269	40,018	568	37.7	4.8	32.7
Washington	348	3,199	619	452	640	132	68	94	29,540	502	27.5	3.0	41.8
Wayne	234	1,564	399	410	276	77	22	39	25,094	340	15.9	4.7	41.6
Webster	679	6,972	654	1,679	1,236	205	251	247	35,371	1,837	37.5	1.3	39.0
Worth	48	153	21	NA	52	14	NA	5	29,510	336	17.6	9.8	35.2
Wright	398	3,338	549	442	925	175	47	104	31,208	1,115	20.4	3.9	45.0
St. Louis city	9,435	198,101	36,534	16,757	9,902	10,777	18,688	11,309	57,089	NA	NA	NA	NA

STATE County	Agriculture, 2017 (cont.) — Land in farms: Acreage (1,000)	Land in farms: Percent change, 2012–2017	Land in farms — Acres: Average size of farm	Acres: Total irrigated (1,000)	Acres: Total cropland (1,000)	Value of land and buildings (dollars): Average per farm	Value of land and buildings (dollars): Average per acre	Value of machinery and equipment, average per farm (dollars)	Value of products sold: Total (mil dol)	Value of products sold: Average per farm (acres)	Value of products sold — Percent from: Crops	Percent from: Livestock and poultry products	Organic farms (number)	Farms with internet access (percent)	Government payments: Total ($1,000)	Government payments: Percent of farms
	117	118	119	120	121	122	123	124	125	126	127	128	129	130	131	132
MISSOURI— Cont'd																
Jasper	265	7.2	201	5.3	141.2	647,953	3,221	94,672	97.2	73,947	48.1	51.9	NA	75.6	1,639	26.0
Jefferson	91	-6.5	126	0.2	34.6	531,201	4,200	50,306	12.9	17,870	58.2	41.8	NA	76.1	263	10.0
Johnson	384	-1.8	236	3.0	227.5	789,475	3,344	92,874	139.9	86,061	45.1	54.9	5	78.2	3,545	32.8
Knox	235	-16.2	370	0.4	161.7	1,124,020	3,042	140,644	97.9	153,615	52.8	47.2	8	60.8	4,645	66.4
Laclede	298	-6.8	229	0.3	75.0	575,705	2,517	64,847	45.5	34,913	11.6	88.4	NA	70.7	208	6.5
Lafayette	341	4.2	290	1.4	265.3	1,314,426	4,535	155,252	163.3	138,955	80.6	19.4	3	79.2	2,775	36.9
Lawrence	302	-2.8	178	2.9	124.1	569,764	3,198	87,304	241.0	142,032	8.9	91.1	2	69.7	1,526	12.9
Lewis	214	-24.8	336	D	153.0	1,112,669	3,312	120,524	83.6	131,465	72.2	27.8	13	68.6	3,114	58.2
Lincoln	227	-19.1	208	1.3	157.0	908,336	4,361	98,978	86.3	79,056	69.5	30.5	3	75.9	2,891	42.1
Linn	331	-1.5	333	1.3	206.7	958,778	2,883	107,802	76.4	76,814	59.7	40.3	12	68.8	7,019	56.0
Livingston	285	0.6	364	D	215.1	1,227,229	3,372	133,506	86.1	109,776	88.0	12.0	5	72.3	6,686	62.0
McDonald	191	2.6	204	0.1	44.8	546,226	2,682	77,040	197.5	210,061	2.3	97.7	7	75.7	409	7.3
Macon	393	1.7	338	0.6	236.9	1,078,661	3,194	101,249	116.9	100,521	59.9	40.1	6	69.1	4,513	50.6
Madison	94	-12.1	261	D	22.3	547,402	2,099	56,907	16.3	45,169	4.9	95.1	NA	65.9	120	8.9
Maries	248	2.9	283	0.5	64.3	557,083	1,971	69,007	32.4	36,879	14.6	85.4	NA	70.0	513	13.5
Marion	233	5.0	396	4.8	182.5	1,571,407	3,966	156,078	99.1	168,853	76.7	23.3	1	68.3	2,268	59.6
Mercer	194	-14.6	393	0.0	99.5	1,058,158	2,693	74,366	82.2	166,748	28.4	71.6	2	74.8	3,029	59.2
Miller	258	3.8	252	1.6	68.1	629,480	2,497	77,397	96.7	94,539	6.4	93.6	NA	72.5	256	10.0
Mississippi	251	2.3	1,576	116.8	243.1	9,200,783	5,837	631,538	D	D	D	D	NA	78.6	5,337	90.6
Moniteau	227	-3.6	200	0.4	104.6	713,079	3,570	84,169	144.7	127,456	21.3	78.7	7	69.2	2,023	31.4
Monroe	340	-4.4	348	1.2	226.8	1,237,626	3,559	106,640	133.8	136,833	59.6	40.4	4	69.1	5,907	61.8
Montgomery	221	-20.8	317	3.3	144.7	1,194,722	3,771	123,954	93.7	134,219	63.5	36.5	7	71.8	2,612	50.1
Morgan	210	6.2	219	0.2	85.4	839,556	3,837	87,885	199.4	207,225	9.9	90.1	9	61.9	1,243	13.7
New Madrid	418	21.4	1,443	257.3	410.5	8,066,767	5,591	659,481	231.5	798,286	100.0	0.0	NA	78.6	11,682	91.4
Newton	261	5.5	165	0.5	91.3	598,888	3,639	75,574	246.0	154,909	6.2	93.8	1	73.0	776	12.1
Nodaway	440	3.8	388	1.6	325.4	1,557,349	4,012	144,528	152.2	134,308	84.0	16.0	6	76.8	5,833	54.8
Oregon	201	-20.7	357	0.0	27.3	635,970	1,781	65,952	23.3	41,250	4.5	95.5	2	72.5	349	11.3
Osage	320	13.0	251	1.3	101.5	605,323	2,415	79,274	80.7	63,186	21.5	78.5	NA	68.8	1,009	21.1
Ozark	227	-0.8	322	1.0	30.4	686,823	2,133	68,929	25.1	35,644	6.3	93.7	1	73.3	332	6.1
Pemiscot	296	-2.9	1,610	148.1	286.7	8,426,555	5,235	614,890	159.2	865,217	100.0	0.0	1	77.2	6,158	89.1
Perry	219	-3.4	237	1.4	124.6	776,958	3,273	100,770	62.8	68,172	57.0	43.0	NA	64.7	3,033	56.8
Pettis	389	-7.2	309	0.7	240.0	1,082,193	3,500	118,802	239.1	189,934	35.5	64.5	17	69.7	5,057	42.2
Phelps	160	1.4	219	0.1	29.4	577,647	2,636	70,254	14.0	19,231	17.7	82.3	1	79.5	287	10.3
Pike	311	-14.1	336	5.0	207.8	1,179,923	3,516	141,497	133.2	143,811	59.4	40.6	2	62.7	2,795	50.2
Platte	161	5.6	330	4.5	126.9	1,459,303	4,429	144,958	60.0	122,516	88.5	11.5	1	77.8	1,255	34.1
Polk	359	6.9	230	2.4	103.4	581,099	2,525	66,217	99.4	63,609	11.1	88.9	23	71.1	613	10.7
Pulaski	111	-0.9	222	0.2	24.2	496,821	2,237	58,444	27.2	54,127	4.7	95.3	NA	73.7	60	4.8
Putnam	264	-9.7	452	D	132.6	1,138,477	2,520	103,874	93.9	160,557	23.9	76.1	NA	73.8	1,964	52.6
Ralls	243	-14.2	362	D	181.4	1,392,728	3,850	138,653	79.5	118,344	81.3	18.7	NA	73.4	3,524	68.2
Randolph	213	1.6	272	0.7	123.7	940,599	3,461	84,856	81.3	103,847	45.5	54.5	9	74.1	2,853	43.9
Ray	267	-2.4	249	4.6	179.5	876,483	3,516	98,521	79.0	73,842	80.9	19.1	3	73.2	3,613	46.2
Reynolds	87	-10.8	254	D	13.2	406,440	1,599	49,387	D	D	D	D	NA	70.7	105	8.5
Ripley	143	3.9	327	12.8	41.1	799,801	2,446	78,726	26.2	59,721	28.7	71.3	NA	73.3	1,303	20.8
St. Charles	156	-1.7	258	1.7	124.2	1,257,799	4,885	137,288	61.8	102,308	87.1	12.9	NA	77.8	1,080	37.9
St. Clair	249	4.2	339	0.0	116.0	830,734	2,453	99,643	48.4	65,917	59.5	40.5	2	67.8	1,906	20.4
Ste. Genevieve	169	3.6	255	0.2	77.1	753,601	2,951	76,204	31.8	48,171	57.3	42.7	NA	65.3	2,166	39.2
St. Francois	125	7.4	182	0.3	37.6	532,762	2,933	62,812	14.6	21,150	53.7	46.3	3	68.9	203	7.4
St. Louis	46	54.3	249	0.9	13.6	1,082,987	4,348	60,124	20.5	111,560	95.4	4.6	3	84.8	215	15.2
Saline	441	-4.3	500	7.2	355.8	2,007,141	4,010	214,564	257.4	291,841	70.4	29.6	3	74.9	4,231	68.8
Schuyler	167	4.7	309	0.0	80.8	796,550	2,581	77,623	38.4	71,002	38.8	61.2	NA	64.3	1,729	47.1
Scotland	250	2.5	351	0.0	181.5	1,182,524	3,370	135,426	156.7	219,724	36.7	63.3	19	63.5	4,814	56.1
Scott	223	-0.1	495	91.5	203.4	2,518,197	5,087	274,600	184.8	410,682	55.0	45.0	NA	70.0	8,463	65.1
Shannon	130	4.7	298	0.0	29.1	585,434	1,963	69,516	11.6	26,632	7.8	92.2	NA	71.7	233	8.3
Shelby	278	-7.2	442	1.4	204.8	1,648,469	3,729	163,179	105.5	168,002	72.4	27.6	NA	72.3	3,894	65.1
Stoddard	476	6.1	600	281.7	437.9	3,214,252	5,353	259,498	291.9	368,573	82.0	18.0	NA	69.6	17,568	63.9
Stone	106	-10.0	169	0.0	20.9	489,224	2,894	47,276	35.2	55,989	4.3	95.7	NA	78.2	145	4.1
Sullivan	310	-4.0	462	D	159.7	1,079,907	2,338	114,353	178.4	265,927	15.9	84.1	NA	70.5	5,031	57.8
Taney	108	-6.6	274	0.1	18.8	612,082	2,235	50,546	13.1	33,225	9.3	90.7	NA	73.9	235	5.3
Texas	391	-0.4	285	1.1	82.1	588,769	2,066	63,440	45.2	32,992	11.5	88.5	1	74.5	489	6.3
Vernon	436	4.1	344	12.2	272.2	978,555	2,841	126,119	215.6	170,442	38.2	61.8	10	69.6	4,835	37.4
Warren	128	-6.1	225	0.9	81.8	911,284	4,048	105,482	46.5	81,917	77.9	22.1	3	80.6	1,442	36.3
Washington	104	-16.3	207	0.1	20.4	490,458	2,372	50,335	10.0	19,859	16.3	83.7	NA	75.1	206	3.2
Wayne	98	-16.2	287	0.5	33.2	675,333	2,350	60,230	12.6	37,156	61.9	38.1	NA	70.6	637	14.1
Webster	265	-2.5	144	0.1	77.0	447,850	3,102	59,669	54.4	29,625	12.5	87.5	8	74.6	437	5.2
Worth	125	0.2	373	NA	72.8	1,061,053	2,844	106,629	41.9	124,705	37.9	62.1	NA	75.0	2,694	69.9
Wright	285	-3.1	256	0.5	67.5	551,501	2,158	59,321	44.8	40,158	7.0	93.0	1	70.9	294	5.7
St. Louis city	NA	NA	NA	NA	NA	NA	NA	NA	NA	NA	NA	NA	NA	NA	NA	NA

STATE County	Water use, 2015		Wholesale Trade[1], 2017				Retail Trade[2], 2017				Real estate and rental and leasing,[2] 2017			
	Public supply water withdrawn (mil gal/ day)	Public supply gallons withdrawn per person per day	Number of establish- ments	Number of employees	Sales (mil dol)	Average payroll (mil dol)	Number of establish- ments	Number of employees	Sales (mil dol)	Average payroll (mil dol)	Number of establish- ments	Number of employees	Sales (mil dol)	Average payroll (mil dol)
	133	134	135	136	137	138	139	140	141	142	143	144	145	146
MISSOURI— Cont'd														
Jasper	18.5	156.3	134	1,675	872.1	79.8	500	8,085	2,229.2	203.2	124	597	107.3	16.9
Jefferson	28.7	128.0	131	1,461	699.2	76.2	474	7,264	2,163.2	190.9	157	581	98.5	19.3
Johnson	5.1	95.3	30	116	59.4	5.3	129	1,687	427.7	39.8	33	83	22.1	2.5
Knox	0.0	0.0	6	D	113.3	D	14	120	30.0	2.4	NA	NA	NA	NA
Laclede	3.8	106.8	32	271	116.7	9.3	160	1,939	553.5	48.8	27	115	20.1	3.5
Lafayette	2.3	70.6	36	346	223.9	14.9	104	949	278.0	21.0	19	44	5.4	0.9
Lawrence	2.8	72.6	24	228	86.4	7.2	115	1,412	470.8	37.7	20	69	9.0	2.6
Lewis	0.7	67.6	D	D	D	D	27	321	79.1	6.6	3	5	0.6	0.1
Lincoln	2.5	45.9	D	D	D	9.8	141	1,675	604.5	47.4	31	71	17.8	2.1
Linn	2.1	170.6	D	D	D	5.6	52	515	137.3	12.7	6	12	0.9	0.2
Livingston	1.9	125.8	25	187	126.5	7.4	75	1,062	293.4	27.5	8	22	14.9	0.7
McDonald	1.9	82.1	D	D	D	D	60	957	243.2	19.6	D	D	D	D
Macon	1.9	121.3	14	158	41.4	4.1	60	623	150.2	13.4	9	33	2.8	0.6
Madison	0.6	50.0	D	D	D	D	43	533	141.7	13.3	5	18	2.2	0.4
Maries	0.3	33.5	4	D	5.1	D	17	144	41.5	2.6	3	D	1.1	D
Marion	3.7	126.7	26	449	252.2	19.8	131	1,817	496.2	41.5	27	69	9.3	2.2
Mercer	0.1	35.2	NA	NA	NA	NA	11	98	28.9	1.7	4	6	0.2	0.1
Miller	0.8	31.1	12	116	52.2	3.7	121	1,794	439.0	47.3	50	299	45.9	8.0
Mississippi	1.9	135.4	17	156	192.6	8.2	53	433	149.8	10.7	NA	NA	NA	NA
Moniteau	1.5	92.1	12	190	46.3	4.9	48	424	137.8	8.9	D	D	D	D
Monroe	4.7	548.8	6	D	76.0	D	31	270	53.8	5.5	NA	NA	NA	NA
Montgomery	0.4	37.6	13	126	216.3	6.0	42	348	100.9	9.1	4	8	1.1	0.1
Morgan	0.7	34.7	16	52	16.2	2.1	92	796	211.8	18.7	20	40	6.7	1.1
New Madrid	2.0	107.1	35	410	341.8	22.6	79	1,328	434.9	30.2	7	18	2.8	0.6
Newton	4.3	73.9	45	1,640	1,448.8	68.3	198	2,210	795.7	56.5	42	128	13.6	3.2
Nodaway	1.9	82.4	20	205	136.1	7.5	64	1,013	254.4	22.5	13	26	5.1	0.6
Oregon	0.9	80.3	D	D	D	1.8	48	461	103.8	9.8	6	D	1.5	D
Osage	0.6	40.4	5	47	23.7	1.5	51	479	152.6	11.9	D	D	D	D
Ozark	0.2	25.5	D	D	D	D	24	177	41.5	3.3	D	D	D	0.1
Pemiscot	2.1	121.8	21	182	319.1	9.9	55	569	179.1	11.6	10	33	7.4	1.6
Perry	1.5	77.2	11	301	119.5	14.9	80	1,040	279.3	26.7	15	34	6.9	0.8
Pettis	3.6	84.0	36	396	171.8	17.8	169	2,558	715.8	62.9	42	314	45.3	10.1
Phelps	2.8	63.2	37	301	108.8	12.3	184	2,464	726.4	61.9	39	161	25.8	5.1
Pike	1.1	61.6	26	362	247.2	14.4	58	683	161.5	16.4	7	27	1.7	0.3
Platte	2.4	25.2	100	1,937	8,079.7	132.8	319	6,788	3,520.2	170.7	151	1,222	308.3	62.8
Polk	1.3	41.9	18	528	59.4	8.6	100	1,141	311.5	28.7	16	62	7.1	1.6
Pulaski	5.9	109.9	D	D	D	D	139	1,760	475.7	41.4	42	170	47.1	4.7
Putnam	0.3	51.5	3	44	16.2	1.2	23	191	49.1	3.9	6	D	0.9	D
Ralls	0.0	0.0	15	166	125.1	8.0	30	221	73.9	5.3	4	6	0.2	0.0
Randolph	1.1	44.6	14	D	160.7	D	100	1,216	308.6	30.7	18	88	8.8	2.1
Ray	2.4	103.5	8	90	106.7	4.3	53	625	158.0	15.1	7	10	0.7	0.1
Reynolds	0.1	20.2	D	D	D	0.4	23	147	26.9	2.7	D	D	D	0.2
Ripley	0.6	45.6	D	D	D	1.6	43	446	112.8	8.9	6	7	0.9	0.2
St. Charles	17.9	46.5	344	4,375	8,155.1	255.6	1,124	20,236	5,882.9	536.7	415	1,932	572.9	82.8
St. Clair	0.3	33.9	3	6	1.1	0.2	35	333	80.3	6.4	3	4	0.3	0.1
Ste. Genevieve	1.4	79.8	17	148	125.4	7.6	48	479	115.3	9.4	7	31	3.9	0.6
St. Francois	5.1	76.2	D	D	D	D	241	3,344	842.1	80.1	62	210	29.5	5.6
St. Louis	226.2	225.4	1,443	27,555	35,553.3	2,077.5	3,611	66,288	29,641.9	1,909.3	1,471	11,174	3,039.4	582.9
Saline	2.9	123.8	34	356	394.0	17.0	87	941	251.0	22.5	D	D	D	D
Schuyler	0.0	0.0	NA	NA	NA	NA	18	110	30.5	2.0	NA	NA	NA	NA
Scotland	0.2	30.9	5	72	23.8	3.2	33	219	52.2	4.4	NA	NA	NA	NA
Scott	5.9	152.3	53	980	848.9	43.5	174	1,465	376.0	35.3	32	114	23.0	4.0
Shannon	0.4	53.3	4	D	36.5	D	31	150	32.4	2.6	8	6	1.3	0.3
Shelby	0.2	37.5	14	D	98.2	D	29	189	39.0	3.9	4	D	0.9	D
Stoddard	3.2	108.2	33	374	376.8	18.3	106	1,299	353.5	30.5	21	68	10.5	1.8
Stone	3.2	101.8	D	D	D	1.0	98	939	253.3	26.5	42	274	50.5	9.2
Sullivan	0.7	102.3	3	18	10.9	0.8	21	157	35.2	2.8	4	D	0.2	D
Taney	8.3	151.9	D	D	D	6.3	415	5,207	1,093.9	109.3	128	1,375	242.4	53.8
Texas	1.7	67.0	13	91	24.7	2.6	85	803	200.2	19.0	12	31	3.6	1.3
Vernon	2.0	97.0	26	202	105.0	8.0	81	936	238.6	20.5	13	40	5.5	1.1
Warren	1.6	48.6	27	475	531.3	29.7	73	915	297.6	22.2	18	93	15.0	2.4
Washington	0.7	26.6	11	79	51.6	1.8	54	569	142.9	12.8	7	16	2.0	0.5
Wayne	1.3	99.2	6	D	9.0	D	35	284	66.1	5.5	NA	NA	NA	NA
Webster	1.1	29.6	37	169	74.3	5.8	103	1,252	461.1	32.6	32	60	10.3	1.5
Worth	0.0	4.9	NA	NA	NA	NA	10	76	16.7	1.6	NA	NA	NA	NA
Wright	1.0	53.1	13	197	40.0	3.8	79	937	219.6	22.1	11	26	2.5	0.4
St. Louis city	92.7	293.6	401	6,973	6,103.3	425.4	878	9,928	2,857.2	276.4	412	2,388	632.7	108.5

1 Merchant wholesalers, except manufacturers' sales branches and offices. 2. Employer establishments.

STATE County	Professional, scientific, and technical services, 2017				Manufacturing, 2017				Accommodation and food services, 2017			
	Number of establish-ments	Number of employees	Sales (mil dol)	Average payroll (mil dol)	Number of establish-ments	Number of employees	Sales (mil dol)	Average payroll (mil dol)	Number of establis-hments	Number of employees	Sales (mil dol)	Annual payroll (mil dol)
	147	148	149	150	151	152	153	154	155	156	157	158
MISSOURI— Cont'd												
Jasper	183	1,055	143.2	47.8	159	9,995	4,135.3	477.4	264	5,076	220.8	65.4
Jefferson	275	1,212	135.3	48.6	171	4,270	1,506.2	246.1	289	6,361	288.1	86.7
Johnson	74	412	86.3	28.2	37	1,534	350.5	60.5	104	1,987	86.4	23.2
Knox	D	D	2.3	D	NA	NA	NA	NA	NA	NA	NA	NA
Laclede	D	D	D	D	54	4,231	1,561.9	174.2	74	1,165	60.1	16.5
Lafayette	D	D	27.7	D	31	918	298.5	43.4	D	D	D	D
Lawrence	40	135	11.3	3.8	41	1,139	560.2	59.4	61	913	37.7	10.7
Lewis	D	D	4.2	D	5	D	42.4	D	D	D	D	D
Lincoln	57	234	33.8	11.2	50	1,312	510.5	71.6	58	1,128	53.6	13.7
Linn	18	57	6.9	1.5	15	869	169.0	30.6	23	249	9.5	2.5
Livingston	D	D	12.7	D	20	486	135.0	21.7	29	475	20.5	6.2
McDonald	D	D	D	D	24	3,304	656.9	125.5	32	315	17.4	4.3
Macon	20	78	8.1	3.0	11	464	210.4	21.6	31	458	20.3	6.0
Madison	9	58	5.6	1.4	15	321	60.9	11.7	22	290	9.5	2.8
Maries	D	D	D	D	7	147	74.6	8.0	D	D	D	0.5
Marion	D	D	D	D	35	1,374	1,860.2	73.8	79	1,221	58.2	16.9
Mercer	NA	NA	NA	NA	NA	NA	NA	NA	4	9	0.6	0.1
Miller	44	179	18.3	7.3	24	612	190.2	25.4	52	600	31.7	10.1
Mississippi	11	91	13.3	6.5	5	78	15.5	3.2	16	247	11.2	3.3
Moniteau	17	60	5.5	1.6	D	793	D	25.4	D	D	D	D
Monroe	D	D	2.2	D	11	393	85.9	16.6	D	D	D	1.5
Montgomery	D	D	0.8	D	17	462	212.3	20.0	20	163	8.2	1.9
Morgan	22	62	5.9	1.6	21	483	143.4	19.2	53	575	31.0	8.7
New Madrid	10	53	5.3	1.8	10	934	213.1	25.4	37	509	23.7	6.7
Newton	71	424	45.2	18.4	60	2,390	854.8	110.5	93	1,848	94.3	27.3
Nodaway	29	164	18.5	6.2	19	1,231	594.8	64.5	38	833	33.6	11.7
Oregon	D	D	2.1	D	14	106	28.7	3.9	D	D	D	D
Osage	12	22	2.6	0.8	D	1,271	D	69.2	D	D	D	D
Ozark	D	D	3.0	D	8	54	13.0	1.9	15	168	6.8	2.3
Pemiscot	11	41	3.4	1.0	D	D	D	D	33	303	16.2	3.8
Perry	24	153	13.9	6.7	38	3,530	1,239.6	138.1	37	546	22.9	7.2
Pettis	63	1,482	158.0	56.3	51	4,151	1,524.0	179.5	73	1,652	75.7	22.2
Phelps	80	359	37.9	13.7	47	1,050	911.5	57.7	131	2,426	110.1	29.2
Pike	18	89	8.9	2.4	14	700	193.4	38.9	31	352	18.8	4.9
Platte	267	1,378	254.5	81.4	51	3,569	2,317.9	175.3	216	5,990	503.7	123.4
Polk	46	1,424	297.0	142.8	23	333	101.3	12.8	45	536	28.0	7.1
Pulaski	60	374	39.4	15.0	D	151	D	D	102	2,418	113.5	48.1
Putnam	D	D	0.6	D	D	74	D	2.5	4	18	1.0	0.2
Ralls	D	D	D	D	13	1,091	1,277.8	71.5	14	80	3.9	1.1
Randolph	22	95	6.8	2.0	25	959	215.9	40.2	45	660	31.2	8.0
Ray	27	94	10.5	3.9	16	401	197.2	27.9	D	D	D	D
Reynolds	D	D	D	D	22	207	41.9	7.2	D	D	D	1.5
Ripley	D	D	D	D	26	404	53.1	10.4	18	173	7.5	2.0
St. Charles	844	7,456	863.4	348.0	241	15,165	12,017.9	927.0	759	19,028	1,136.7	311.5
St. Clair	D	D	D	D	11	33	8.0	2.1	D	D	D	D
Ste. Genevieve	D	D	D	D	30	1,127	440.6	68.1	29	406	15.6	4.5
St. Francois	86	359	34.0	11.1	43	1,695	333.3	75.3	120	2,240	98.3	28.2
St. Louis	3,599	44,516	8,643.0	3,240.7	867	42,197	12,718.8	3,067.8	2,263	50,715	2,880.1	850.9
Saline	D	D	D	D	22	1,862	927.7	79.1	43	499	21.9	6.0
Schuyler	NA	NA	NA	NA	3	D	14.9	2.6	3	16	0.6	0.1
Scotland	D	D	D	D	10	84	23.2	3.3	D	D	D	D
Scott	62	353	46.5	17.0	60	2,785	1,088.5	114.7	79	1,314	65.4	19.9
Shannon	4	6	0.6	0.2	28	644	76.0	15.1	20	100	7.6	1.8
Shelby	D	D	4.4	D	D	152	D	7.8	D	D	D	0.6
Stoddard	36	171	19.4	6.6	29	2,989	939.8	142.5	47	675	32.3	8.7
Stone	36	94	8.9	3.3	21	80	11.6	3.6	100	864	87.8	20.9
Sullivan	D	D	0.9	D	D	D	D	D	5	D	0.4	D
Taney	112	483	50.6	13.9	38	312	97.4	14.9	318	6,610	556.2	153.8
Texas	24	74	6.1	1.7	42	803	223.7	34.8	36	424	14.9	4.2
Vernon	31	109	11.7	3.4	20	1,064	1,266.7	60.6	41	481	27.8	6.8
Warren	28	124	11.3	4.3	30	1,297	449.6	65.8	48	711	33.9	9.1
Washington	17	48	3.6	1.2	21	521	166.5	19.6	D	D	D	D
Wayne	D	D	2.4	D	24	395	73.7	13.9	24	197	11.3	3.2
Webster	47	206	18.9	6.2	46	921	235.3	42.7	40	753	37.1	9.9
Worth	NA	NA	NA	NA	NA	NA	NA	NA	NA	NA	NA	NA
Wright	20	54	4.4	1.0	26	373	106.9	17.2	27	357	18.3	3.7
St. Louis city	1,102	17,876	3,669.5	1,381.1	436	16,630	7,934.1	1,003.1	1,002	22,623	1,685.1	451.0

STATE County	Health care and social assistance, 2017				Other services, 2017				Nonemployer businesses, 2019		Value of residential construction authorized by building permits, 2021	
	Number of establish-ments	Number of employees	Receipts (mil dol)	Annual payroll (mil dol)	Number of establish-ments	Number of employees	Receipts (mil dol)	Annual payroll (mil dol)	Number	Receipts (mil dol)	New construction ($1,000)	Number of housing units
	159	160	161	162	163	164	165	166	167	168	169	170
MISSOURI— Cont'd												
Jasper	316	6,386	596.0	217.4	207	1,186	105.9	32.1	6,918	298.7	140,263	850
Jefferson	384	5,685	512.1	216.8	334	1,701	185.6	54.5	13,722	577.6	170,753	832
Johnson	100	2,359	217.6	94.4	67	236	21.1	5.6	3,103	120.3	14,800	94
Knox	10	46	2.6	1.1	12	34	2.6	0.7	390	22.3	100	1
Laclede	74	1,215	87.4	35.2	49	154	20.5	3.7	2,641	142.3	9,393	60
Lafayette	67	1,260	84.3	38.4	45	171	15.7	5.4	2,102	89.6	27,998	114
Lawrence	76	1,035	87.4	29.6	48	152	18.9	4.5	2,662	114.4	14,185	61
Lewis	D	D	D	4.8	D	D	4.8	D	670	30.0	410	2
Lincoln	79	1,324	93.5	42.5	D	D	D	6.7	3,717	165.8	26,048	168
Linn	26	521	38.5	17.2	22	78	8.0	2.0	877	37.1	900	1
Livingston	38	995	94.1	37.6	25	208	15.3	4.2	1,007	42.4	5,011	20
McDonald	28	206	13.8	5.8	D	D	D	1.0	1,459	58.9	1,982	19
Macon	44	598	53.1	19.5	D	D	D	D	1,093	42.3	5,303	46
Madison	37	963	48.4	23.6	16	61	5.8	1.2	745	26.6	7,702	41
Maries	13	152	8.9	3.1	D	D	3.0	D	576	24.5	0	0
Marion	119	2,967	370.2	131.2	D	D	D	D	1,677	69.3	9,589	43
Mercer	6	D	3.7	D	D	D	D	0.4	254	10.5	0	0
Miller	44	571	38.7	15.8	D	D	14.4	D	1,754	89.2	9,125	31
Mississippi	31	454	26.1	11.4	17	43	3.6	0.9	557	26.4	23	1
Moniteau	D	D	D	D	D	D	D	D	1,090	51.8	900	2
Monroe	25	230	10.0	4.3	D	D	1.3	D	557	30.0	0	0
Montgomery	17	228	19.4	5.8	17	68	11.0	2.8	800	39.9	5,386	36
Morgan	40	267	15.0	6.2	26	79	8.8	2.3	1,695	81.4	330	6
New Madrid	53	1,052	48.3	22.8	19	48	4.5	0.9	759	24.7	345	3
Newton	148	6,542	724.6	315.4	64	302	30.2	8.7	3,778	191.1	14,129	141
Nodaway	48	1,131	80.0	41.1	36	121	11.6	3.1	1,384	58.4	10,740	56
Oregon	28	349	17.0	8.0	13	32	4.5	0.7	700	26.0	475	2
Osage	D	D	D	D	D	D	D	D	994	45.9	460	5
Ozark	11	D	6.2	D	D	D	2.5	D	773	28.4	238	1
Pemiscot	70	1,278	72.7	33.2	16	61	5.9	1.3	778	28.6	480	12
Perry	63	1,137	106.3	42.4	46	512	22.5	19.3	1,231	54.0	7,153	34
Pettis	144	3,481	261.5	108.8	89	319	27.8	8.6	2,788	150.0	12,327	133
Phelps	134	3,955	392.3	136.7	70	349	35.1	10.9	2,603	107.9	8,682	56
Pike	44	826	51.5	26.0	23	41	5.8	1.1	1,130	52.1	824	9
Platte	227	3,716	492.3	181.9	170	1,071	134.5	41.2	8,274	412.6	112,792	503
Polk	67	2,358	238.6	89.2	39	116	14.1	3.0	2,443	106.1	5,189	29
Pulaski	67	1,856	243.5	90.4	59	228	24.1	5.9	2,098	77.4	9,290	61
Putnam	12	176	18.7	5.7	D	D	D	0.5	409	20.5	0	0
Ralls	14	168	11.6	5.5	D	D	D	D	724	34.4	414	9
Randolph	70	1,293	117.4	46.3	38	156	11.4	3.2	1,278	59.8	7,196	46
Ray	D	D	D	18.2	D	D	D	1.8	1,361	53.5	11,115	42
Reynolds	14	152	6.0	2.7	D	D	1.9	D	507	22.6	0	0
Ripley	84	948	34.2	17.7	D	D	1.9	D	819	33.7	65	3
St. Charles	1,055	18,396	1,912.8	702.0	660	4,692	460.7	138.6	27,862	1,249.1	676,496	3,100
St. Clair	21	410	26.4	10.7	D	D	2.6	D	790	32.1	0	0
Ste. Genevieve	46	1,027	81.0	29.9	34	136	11.7	2.7	1,189	41.6	1,597	7
St. Francois	244	5,204	428.8	187.1	108	456	39.4	10.5	3,300	134.2	20,066	105
St. Louis	4,451	93,575	11,506.2	4,645.4	2,021	18,183	2,191.6	688.0	79,507	4,064.8	430,148	1,034
Saline	64	1,508	123.8	51.4	44	138	18.6	3.6	1,217	44.1	1,420	7
Schuyler	D	D	D	D	D	D	D	D	353	17.0	1,426	6
Scotland	D	D	D	D	D	D	D	0.8	505	33.6	150	1
Scott	146	2,801	247.1	117.6	58	366	38.2	10.9	2,174	111.9	7,900	57
Shannon	19	152	11.8	4.2	4	9	1.5	0.3	786	35.5	0	0
Shelby	9	94	5.1	2.1	D	D	D	1.2	426	19.0	990	4
Stoddard	96	1,667	110.1	45.5	38	106	10.7	2.8	1,974	115.2	1,643	8
Stone	47	435	34.6	12.9	53	440	27.5	7.7	2,902	128.1	57,846	258
Sullivan	11	213	17.5	6.3	7	17	2.6	0.5	374	14.8	0	0
Taney	125	2,094	309.5	96.3	90	518	56.2	14.5	4,727	195.7	74,603	432
Texas	53	836	61.9	27.4	27	59	6.1	1.1	1,648	66.5	630	6
Vernon	64	1,330	90.5	40.6	34	156	11.0	2.6	1,345	57.5	1,337	16
Warren	52	635	42.0	18.3	35	178	20.5	5.8	2,306	101.7	81,471	381
Washington	47	693	48.5	22.6	22	78	6.4	1.6	1,049	41.5	0	0
Wayne	54	392	19.1	8.1	D	D	3.0	D	635	27.0	0	0
Webster	57	615	38.6	15.5	49	122	14.1	3.5	3,197	139.8	29,188	180
Worth	D	D	D	0.3	D	D	D	0.3	186	6.3	0	0
Wright	47	562	33.0	14.0	24	75	7.3	1.4	1,537	70.2	1,900	10
St. Louis city	1,554	39,629	4,647.7	1,753.1	625	5,377	827.8	199.1	22,012	868.5	118,427	955

STATE County	Government employment and payroll, 2017									Local government finances, 2017				
			March payroll (percent of total)							General revenue				
												Taxes		
													Per capita[1] (dollars)	
	Full-time equivalent employees	March payroll (dollars)	Adminis-tration, judicial, and legal	Police and corrections	Fire protection	Highways and transpor-tation	Health and welfare	Natural resources and utilities	Education and libraries	Total (mil dol)	Inter-govern-mental (mil dol)	Total (mil dol)	Total	Property
	171	172	173	174	175	176	177	178	179	180	181	182	183	184
MISSOURI— Cont'd														
Jasper	4,398	14,170,563	4.5	9.3	3.8	3.7	2.1	3.5	72.0	447.2	211.8	177.4	1,478	773
Jefferson	6,928	26,844,611	3.0	6.6	4.2	2.4	4.3	3.2	75.0	585.4	243.3	261.7	1,169	794
Johnson	2,338	9,601,545	3.0	3.4	1.9	2.1	42.0	2.2	45.2	347.2	52.5	62.4	1,160	701
Knox	214	535,366	8.7	3.6	0.1	6.1	21.3	5.6	54.0	11.0	3.0	4.7	1,180	864
Laclede	1,481	4,057,488	5.1	5.8	1.7	8.7	2.0	6.8	68.5	104.7	39.7	34.5	975	550
Lafayette	1,327	4,428,568	5.8	6.8	1.9	2.9	18.1	8.5	55.3	97.5	40.6	37.1	1,139	791
Lawrence	1,037	3,318,669	5.4	8.3	0.9	3.5	6.7	2.3	72.3	88.3	42.3	30.6	799	501
Lewis	449	1,201,239	7.8	5.2	0.0	3.7	21.0	4.7	57.1	28.6	12.7	11.5	1,152	844
Lincoln	1,819	5,994,734	5.2	7.4	1.4	2.6	3.9	1.2	76.6	191.5	76.6	57.3	1,023	731
Linn	601	1,786,369	6.8	6.1	0.8	3.8	6.2	7.2	68.4	47.2	22.0	18.2	1,492	1,043
Livingston	564	1,695,818	5.6	6.6	6.5	2.5	13.9	2.6	61.9	57.6	19.4	19.5	1,289	844
McDonald	773	2,253,514	5.8	6.2	0.0	3.8	3.1	3.7	77.1	60.6	30.0	24.6	1,085	922
Macon	1,075	3,112,412	4.1	3.9	1.1	4.6	42.0	8.5	35.6	47.1	17.5	18.4	1,207	770
Madison	657	2,048,596	3.0	2.5	0.2	2.0	42.6	3.5	45.3	29.9	15.9	10.2	836	554
Maries	324	876,182	6.2	6.2	0.1	7.0	8.3	3.6	67.0	19.5	8.8	8.2	935	694
Marion	1,388	4,194,523	5.8	8.1	3.7	2.6	11.7	5.9	57.6	108.5	33.5	49.1	1,718	982
Mercer	163	550,632	16.0	5.3	0.0	6.2	6.1	3.3	63.1	10.8	4.3	5.0	1,375	1,187
Miller	1,210	3,556,113	3.7	6.3	1.7	2.1	9.7	1.8	73.7	91.7	31.4	45.1	1,791	1,291
Mississippi	539	1,450,262	9.7	9.5	0.3	4.2	6.6	2.8	66.7	40.8	21.8	11.9	879	572
Moniteau	511	1,570,509	8.6	5.1	0.2	3.0	9.9	5.6	67.3	48.3	16.7	25.6	1,598	1,258
Monroe	484	1,338,886	5.2	5.3	0.5	4.7	22.5	8.8	52.2	39.1	11.5	11.6	1,347	1,045
Montgomery	416	1,286,249	8.4	10.9	0.0	5.2	6.3	5.4	60.3	30.0	9.1	15.8	1,393	982
Morgan	736	2,091,478	6.5	8.5	2.2	3.5	25.3	2.0	50.2	44.7	12.6	22.3	1,105	685
New Madrid	689	2,161,004	9.5	7.8	0.5	6.1	5.4	5.6	62.9	52.3	22.5	24.2	1,380	953
Newton	2,026	6,688,488	3.4	5.1	2.2	1.6	3.4	1.5	81.8	135.2	60.9	45.3	778	475
Nodaway	712	2,196,990	10.1	6.4	0.5	3.6	5.1	5.9	67.8	63.5	22.3	33.2	1,483	958
Oregon	437	1,150,265	5.4	4.1	0.0	3.7	5.6	3.1	77.6	24.5	13.3	7.2	686	456
Osage	395	968,305	7.4	5.2	0.0	4.2	9.0	5.9	67.8	29.4	10.7	14.9	1,091	836
Ozark	376	1,017,632	6.1	4.9	0.0	4.1	2.7	1.6	80.5	21.3	12.5	6.8	738	523
Pemiscot	816	2,452,299	4.9	7.9	0.9	2.0	5.1	7.8	70.7	56.9	30.5	17.7	1,056	642
Perry	584	2,058,654	3.6	9.8	0.0	3.2	6.4	9.4	66.6	45.5	14.9	23.5	1,220	642
Pettis	1,698	5,767,296	5.8	4.0	2.9	2.5	0.7	8.8	74.4	267.3	66.4	69.4	1,634	880
Phelps	2,566	10,173,000	2.7	3.6	1.2	1.4	54.5	4.7	30.9	315.0	57.5	44.2	992	545
Pike	642	2,385,096	2.8	2.2	0.2	0.7	29.7	2.4	61.3	43.8	17.7	19.4	1,046	681
Platte	2,890	11,780,285	5.3	7.8	3.0	1.7	2.6	2.2	77.1	343.0	102.8	180.3	1,782	1,326
Polk	2,111	8,047,769	1.7	2.2	0.5	1.6	61.1	1.5	31.0	192.9	38.3	22.5	708	485
Pulaski	1,770	5,316,782	3.6	4.2	1.3	2.5	8.1	5.1	74.2	148.8	87.8	36.6	705	470
Putnam	338	1,109,582	4.5	1.9	0.0	2.1	46.9	5.0	39.0	19.6	6.6	9.2	1,915	1,269
Ralls	179	551,668	13.1	9.4	0.7	7.6	3.5	8.4	56.0	26.7	6.3	7.5	735	481
Randolph	1,352	4,284,870	4.4	7.6	1.7	1.8	3.9	4.5	75.8	137.3	43.4	39.1	1,568	950
Ray	1,106	3,671,525	4.1	4.2	2.2	2.4	41.2	4.4	40.8	124.3	33.2	25.6	1,121	705
Reynolds	303	797,244	5.4	3.6	0.0	5.5	4.1	1.5	79.9	20.7	9.0	8.8	1,401	1,197
Ripley	589	1,595,247	4.3	3.3	1.0	2.0	27.1	2.5	59.9	44.8	22.6	16.3	1,198	828
St. Charles	13,553	52,183,204	5.5	9.1	4.6	3.1	2.7	4.8	67.6	1,402.6	398.5	775.6	1,963	1,245
St. Clair	433	1,258,079	4.9	10.0	0.0	2.7	24.9	1.4	52.8	34.6	11.9	8.0	851	733
Ste. Genevieve	491	1,927,342	7.2	15.6	0.1	2.9	4.6	6.6	62.4	45.4	16.4	22.8	1,280	789
St. Francois	2,394	8,376,327	5.2	6.7	0.6	2.6	4.1	4.3	75.5	209.1	98.5	75.7	1,135	744
St. Louis	34,807	159,175,124	4.4	10.4	7.2	2.5	1.7	2.7	69.6	4,109.3	1,101.0	2,519.9	2,529	1,593
Saline	772	2,331,088	7.0	11.6	3.9	5.1	6.4	17.5	41.0	72.4	29.3	26.6	1,162	824
Schuyler	213	500,136	7.2	1.9	0.0	4.4	28.1	4.8	53.4	13.9	7.7	4.3	953	708
Scotland	442	1,508,518	3.1	3.0	0.0	2.6	67.6	4.2	19.2	41.8	6.3	7.6	1,527	1,095
Scott	1,674	5,781,559	4.1	8.1	1.6	10.0	5.1	15.2	53.4	109.6	45.8	43.4	1,125	643
Shannon	233	602,275	8.6	8.3	0.0	6.4	6.9	5.2	64.3	12.2	7.9	3.1	379	257
Shelby	478	1,240,742	17.2	4.5	0.3	3.2	24.6	5.9	41.5	36.6	7.3	7.3	1,217	968
Stoddard	1,015	2,820,418	5.4	4.2	0.0	2.7	5.5	1.6	80.0	79.1	39.1	22.4	762	612
Stone	894	2,717,977	7.3	6.3	3.0	4.4	0.0	1.9	76.8	74.6	29.1	36.0	1,136	717
Sullivan	375	1,184,784	5.5	3.5	0.2	2.4	35.2	6.8	44.7	30.2	11.5	6.8	1,098	850
Taney	2,022	6,678,131	7.6	8.0	3.7	4.3	6.6	6.3	61.4	223.7	72.0	107.9	1,957	1,139
Texas	1,202	3,547,068	5.0	4.2	0.1	2.0	33.7	3.3	51.3	60.3	32.0	23.0	897	775
Vernon	1,130	3,728,284	3.7	4.9	1.3	1.5	34.6	3.8	48.6	50.4	22.4	20.8	1,012	576
Warren	1,085	3,585,264	5.2	9.2	4.2	1.5	5.7	3.3	69.1	86.9	36.8	38.5	1,117	787
Washington	955	3,010,693	3.5	3.1	0.3	3.0	32.9	1.0	55.7	75.2	30.8	15.0	600	434
Wayne	459	1,093,686	9.4	3.1	0.0	7.6	5.0	1.8	72.8	27.1	14.5	8.6	648	385
Webster	944	2,720,753	6.0	6.2	0.3	3.6	9.0	3.6	70.6	67.9	31.6	24.0	620	337
Worth	127	326,573	14.4	2.3	0.0	5.0	18.3	4.6	52.0	7.4	2.6	2.5	1,248	1,058
Wright	740	2,129,085	5.0	4.7	0.5	2.7	10.5	2.9	72.8	44.7	24.9	13.0	716	457
St. Louis city	14,892	75,555,604	8.0	18.8	7.9	19.5	1.4	14.2	28.0	2,003.6	463.3	889.5	2,886	1,072

1. Based on the resident population estimated as of July 1 of the year shown.

STATE County	Local government finances, 2017 (cont.)									Government employment, 2020			Individual income tax returns, 2019		
	Direct general expenditure							Debt outstanding							
			Percent of total for:												
	Total (mil dol)	Per capita[1] (dollars)	Education	Health and hospitals	Police protection	Public welfare	Highways	Total (mil dol)	Per capita[1] (dollars)	Federal civilian	Federal military	State and local	Number of returns	Mean adjusted gross income	Mean income tax
	185	186	187	188	189	190	191	192	193	194	195	196	197	198	199
MISSOURI— Cont'd															
Jasper	410.0	3,415	50.9	1.2	5.4	0.1	10.0	309.2	2,576	299	430	6,547	53,610	49,638	4,757
Jefferson	597.9	2,672	66.7	3.0	5.1	0.0	2.9	494.4	2,210	326	745	7,984	109,860	59,145	5,280
Johnson	212.6	3,956	39.8	37.7	3.1	0.0	5.4	296.1	5,510	1,286	4,107	5,616	23,200	53,151	4,337
Knox	10.8	2,730	49.6	1.3	2.8	20.1	10.6	8.5	2,147	28	14	267	1,700	37,380	2,199
Laclede	88.5	2,498	69.9	0.0	5.5	0.0	6.2	45.6	1,288	83	118	1,412	15,710	42,941	3,109
Lafayette	101.6	3,119	54.3	3.0	6.2	0.3	11.1	94.5	2,902	111	107	1,990	15,070	53,780	4,343
Lawrence	103.2	2,697	53.1	0.2	2.7	5.0	8.4	57.8	1,510	74	125	1,657	16,520	44,773	3,248
Lewis	29.7	2,988	50.2	1.9	4.5	1.5	11.9	9.1	919	50	30	493	4,250	47,482	3,520
Lincoln	220.3	3,931	43.8	19.8	3.7	0.0	4.5	929.3	16,581	125	197	1,985	28,070	57,253	4,863
Linn	46.6	3,827	51.0	1.8	5.3	0.1	16.2	34.5	2,834	60	39	758	5,490	45,426	3,453
Livingston	79.6	5,253	58.9	2.7	4.2	5.8	6.2	34.4	2,269	73	44	1,310	6,450	49,336	4,276
McDonald	46.3	2,036	79.4	3.5	3.0	0.0	1.1	35.0	1,539	81	75	783	9,410	41,138	2,713
Macon	43.5	2,852	55.4	1.6	3.9	11.3	4.6	27.1	1,775	71	49	1,372	7,100	44,184	3,075
Madison	28.0	2,293	70.2	3.0	6.1	0.0	3.8	6.9	563	42	40	787	5,180	45,557	3,504
Maries	20.1	2,287	59.6	6.1	3.9	0.0	10.3	7.4	844	13	29	305	3,870	43,481	2,969
Marion	103.5	3,619	45.0	4.2	6.5	6.5	4.2	127.2	4,450	115	90	1,728	12,910	51,742	4,457
Mercer	11.1	3,032	72.5	6.9	1.4	0.0	9.5	7.6	2,088	32	12	222	1,590	34,763	2,530
Miller	84.5	3,355	59.9	3.6	3.6	5.6	3.8	72.1	2,860	51	85	1,364	11,060	43,368	3,140
Mississippi	38.6	2,840	52.7	5.5	6.3	1.1	8.9	12.9	949	20	39	925	4,980	43,935	3,613
Moniteau	38.2	2,378	62.7	7.2	3.1	0.0	7.0	23.7	1,479	51	49	945	6,920	46,860	3,393
Monroe	31.8	3,703	49.8	2.4	4.0	17.2	11.0	48.6	5,656	71	28	567	3,920	46,459	3,354
Montgomery	32.1	2,818	51.2	4.0	5.3	0.0	7.1	25.2	2,218	50	36	556	5,280	47,070	3,483
Morgan	45.0	2,230	51.2	0.1	7.8	11.1	9.6	27.0	1,337	44	68	917	8,790	44,211	3,147
New Madrid	50.5	2,881	56.4	0.1	6.8	0.0	8.5	32.4	1,846	50	54	827	6,850	47,382	3,905
Newton	177.5	3,050	76.3	2.6	2.8	0.5	2.8	113.8	1,956	168	191	2,352	25,530	54,276	4,989
Nodaway	63.6	2,839	63.1	1.3	5.6	0.0	9.2	87.6	3,909	88	61	2,645	8,840	50,090	4,153
Oregon	23.7	2,249	75.0	5.2	2.0	0.0	4.4	3.4	320	39	34	495	3,910	36,955	2,589
Osage	29.2	2,136	58.1	11.2	3.5	0.0	6.2	13.5	986	31	44	863	6,210	53,016	4,039
Ozark	22.4	2,428	78.3	0.2	3.9	0.1	6.9	3.7	402	17	31	402	3,850	36,207	2,891
Pemiscot	59.5	3,543	64.2	0.4	5.2	0.0	3.3	13.0	776	57	51	1,215	6,110	43,922	3,722
Perry	41.4	2,151	57.6	0.3	9.0	0.2	4.5	3.6	185	51	73	1,157	9,150	51,231	3,998
Pettis	249.2	5,870	41.1	41.4	2.7	0.0	3.7	69.6	1,640	125	138	3,171	19,090	46,796	3,483
Phelps	306.6	6,881	24.1	58.1	2.1	0.3	3.1	80.4	1,804	336	146	6,065	18,500	51,035	4,554
Pike	47.2	2,543	63.3	0.9	6.6	0.6	10.9	32.3	1,741	71	53	1,493	7,370	48,220	3,851
Platte	308.4	3,049	70.7	1.1	4.9	0.0	7.5	263.9	2,609	695	436	3,910	51,720	88,116	11,225
Polk	200.6	6,318	27.9	64.3	1.2	0.0	1.0	61.5	1,939	76	103	2,200	13,110	46,147	3,499
Pulaski	149.6	2,885	67.4	1.7	3.1	0.0	4.6	41.4	798	3,471	11,963	1,954	18,950	46,972	3,056
Putnam	19.2	4,028	49.5	3.5	6.3	1.8	12.7	13.8	2,895	21	15	366	2,030	39,047	2,585
Ralls	20.8	2,033	37.9	4.6	4.1	0.0	25.3	20.5	2,006	27	34	318	4,790	56,352	4,885
Randolph	124.4	4,997	56.9	15.8	4.7	0.0	4.4	62.0	2,488	74	73	1,946	10,640	47,896	3,863
Ray	95.4	4,169	34.1	28.2	2.1	13.4	5.8	28.7	1,255	57	75	1,266	10,810	54,156	4,474
Reynolds	20.1	3,214	67.8	3.8	3.5	0.0	6.6	5.6	894	23	20	342	2,500	39,997	2,740
Ripley	41.4	3,049	50.9	2.5	5.9	0.7	14.9	11.9	876	62	44	461	4,970	35,219	2,096
St. Charles	1,357.4	3,435	55.0	2.6	6.6	0.2	6.3	1,640.9	4,153	842	1,332	15,858	202,040	79,370	9,167
St. Clair	34.3	3,661	38.4	24.7	2.3	0.0	13.7	12.9	1,374	44	31	447	3,790	40,662	2,874
Ste. Genevieve	42.9	2,410	58.5	1.1	5.8	0.8	6.7	32.9	1,850	30	58	1,055	8,490	59,433	5,295
St. Francois	220.0	3,300	60.2	4.4	5.3	0.0	7.9	174.5	2,617	155	200	5,600	27,300	48,087	3,863
St. Louis	3,942.4	3,957	54.9	1.3	7.8	1.6	5.0	4,876.3	4,895	6,033	3,294	44,615	503,980	93,892	13,994
Saline	74.3	3,245	53.5	3.3	7.4	0.0	11.0	9.8	429	81	71	1,527	9,820	45,675	3,459
Schuyler	13.1	2,892	48.0	25.0	2.0	0.7	13.9	9.5	2,113	28	15	269	1,720	35,806	2,162
Scotland	37.4	7,561	17.4	54.6	1.3	4.2	5.3	14.8	2,984	24	16	512	2,000	41,554	2,594
Scott	114.9	2,977	58.0	3.0	8.9	0.0	5.4	149.8	3,884	109	125	2,109	17,000	54,094	4,892
Shannon	11.1	1,349	69.2	1.0	3.9	0.0	11.5	0.1	6	22	27	288	3,110	35,375	2,164
Shelby	28.3	4,728	43.9	4.2	17.6	15.7	6.2	9.7	1,610	36	19	531	2,810	45,491	3,416
Stoddard	80.1	2,728	62.3	0.8	2.5	0.0	8.1	45.5	1,549	157	94	1,259	12,200	50,583	4,854
Stone	81.4	2,574	64.9	0.0	3.9	0.0	8.5	85.5	2,701	57	107	992	14,690	54,345	5,092
Sullivan	27.9	4,488	44.2	39.5	1.5	0.1	4.2	31.9	5,129	45	20	402	2,720	37,490	2,296
Taney	198.4	3,601	41.9	0.7	4.3	0.0	13.5	486.4	8,828	205	180	2,280	26,880	42,554	3,651
Texas	58.5	2,281	64.6	1.1	3.3	0.1	5.3	30.1	1,173	83	78	1,771	9,650	37,302	2,436
Vernon	51.2	2,498	57.7	2.6	4.3	0.2	7.7	49.3	2,402	93	65	1,351	8,490	42,438	3,009
Warren	86.7	2,518	59.1	7.7	5.6	0.0	6.6	68.7	1,994	53	121	1,274	17,090	59,773	5,420
Washington	72.3	2,893	52.5	31.0	2.7	0.0	3.4	15.9	637	63	78	1,436	9,270	39,176	2,368
Wayne	24.9	1,874	66.0	2.1	4.3	0.0	9.7	17.3	1,301	90	42	485	4,610	37,230	2,338
Webster	66.4	1,713	64.9	0.3	4.8	5.5	9.0	22.8	589	95	130	1,312	16,160	47,569	3,684
Worth	7.9	3,855	50.6	1.4	2.9	14.8	5.0	1.3	615	24	6	163	900	41,236	2,727
Wright	40.4	2,220	77.1	0.0	2.5	4.7	2.2	6.2	343	52	60	846	7,270	37,279	2,403
St. Louis city	2,186.0	7,092	23.5	2.6	8.7	0.0	1.4	4,818.8	15,634	14,193	1,392	17,980	143,190	57,525	7,109

1. Based on the resident population estimated as of July 1 of the year shown.

State / county code	CBSA code[1]	County Type code[2]	STATE County	Land area[3] (sq. mi)	Population, 2021: Total persons 2021	Population, 2021: Rank	Population, 2021: Per square mile	Race alone or in combination, not Hispanic or Latino (percent): White	Black	American Indian, Alaska Native	Asian and Pacific Islancer	Percent Hispanic or Latino[4]	Age (percent): Under 5 years	5 to 17 years	18 to 24 years	25 to 34 years	35 to 44 years	45 to 54 years
				1	2	3	4	5	6	7	8	9	10	11	12	13	14	15
30000		0	MONTANA	145,547.7	1,104,271	X	7.6	88.0	1.1	7.6	1.8	4.3	5.3	12.3	12.8	13.0	12.7	10.9
30001		7	Beaverhead	5,542.7	9,524	2,449	1.7	91.1	1.0	2.8	1.7	5.5	4.1	9.3	17.1	11.1	11.2	9.7
30003		6	Big Horn	4,997.8	12,957	2,216	2.6	28.8	0.8	65.9	1.3	6.2	8.1	19.6	14.3	11.9	11.1	9.6
30005		9	Blaine	4,227.5	6,980	2,664	1.7	45.4	0.9	51.8	0.7	3.9	7.2	17.6	13.6	12.2	11.7	9.2
30007		9	Broadwater	1,192.4	7,288	2,640	6.1	94.0	0.9	2.6	0.9	3.4	5.2	11.0	9.1	10.7	11.6	12.2
30009	13740	3	Carbon	2,047.8	10,847	2,356	5.3	94.4	1.1	2.0	0.8	3.0	3.7	10.1	8.7	8.9	12.2	12.1
30011		9	Carter	3,340.5	1,428	3,084	0.4	97.1	1.2	1.7	0.8	1.5	7.3	11.3	7.6	11.1	11.3	7.4
30013	24500	3	Cascade	2,698.2	84,511	681	31.3	87.7	2.4	6.4	2.2	5.2	6.1	12.9	12.6	14.0	12.1	10.1
30015		8	Chouteau	3,972.5	5,916	2,742	1.5	78.6	0.7	18.9	0.9	3.0	4.4	12.6	12.5	10.8	11.7	11.2
30017		7	Custer	3,783.3	11,916	2,290	3.1	92.4	1.2	3.6	1.2	3.7	4.9	11.3	11.9	12.0	13.2	11.4
30019		9	Daniels	1,426.3	1,686	3,068	1.2	92.8	0.9	4.0	0.5	4.3	4.6	12.8	10.0	9.8	11.7	8.7
30021		7	Dawson	2,371.9	8,904	2,497	3.8	93.1	1.0	3.1	0.8	3.6	5.4	12.5	12.4	12.1	11.8	11.1
30023		7	Deer Lodge	736.7	9,491	2,451	12.9	91.4	0.9	4.9	1.0	4.2	3.2	6.9	10.8	12.0	11.7	13.2
30025		9	Fallon	1,620.6	3,017	2,958	1.9	96.2	0.7	1.9	1.0	1.7	5.6	16.3	11.1	11.5	12.7	10.5
30027		7	Fergus	4,339.3	11,617	2,306	2.7	95.2	0.8	2.8	1.1	2.1	5.4	12.0	9.6	11.0	12.1	10.5
30029	28060	5	Flathead	5,087.2	108,454	571	21.3	94.2	0.6	2.5	1.6	3.4	5.3	12.6	10.5	12.3	13.1	11.7
30031	14580	5	Gallatin	2,605.4	122,713	520	47.1	92.5	0.8	1.7	2.6	4.5	4.8	11.2	18.8	16.6	14.3	10.6
30033		9	Garfield	4,676.6	1,209	3,099	0.3	97.4	0.7	1.6	0.3	1.1	6.1	12.7	11.2	9.3	12.7	11.1
30035		7	Glacier	2,995.1	13,785	2,169	4.6	32.8	0.6	65.2	0.7	3.8	7.9	17.7	14.6	12.8	12.3	9.7
30037		3	Golden Valley	1,174.4	831	3,114	0.7	91.6	1.0	3.6	1.3	5.1	5.2	11.1	8.3	10.7	11.3	7.8
30039		8	Granite	1,727.2	3,344	2,936	1.9	95.4	0.9	2.5	0.9	2.4	3.0	8.9	8.2	9.3	10.9	10.6
30041		7	Hill	2,899.4	16,179	2,024	5.6	70.9	0.9	25.9	1.4	4.1	8.4	15.5	13.6	13.0	12.1	9.9
30043	25740	9	Jefferson	1,657.0	12,470	2,245	7.5	94.0	0.8	3.5	1.1	3.0	4.0	11.6	10.1	9.4	11.9	13.0
30045		8	Judith Basin	1,869.7	2,044	3,038	1.1	95.5	0.3	1.5	0.7	2.9	5.1	11.4	8.5	9.0	9.9	10.0
30047		6	Lake	1,490.5	32,033	1,380	21.5	71.4	0.8	28.3	1.4	4.7	5.2	13.3	11.6	10.7	11.3	10.4
30049	25740	5	Lewis and Clark	3,458.4	72,223	760	20.9	93.0	0.9	3.4	1.5	3.8	5.3	12.4	11.3	12.3	13.3	11.4
30051		9	Liberty	1,430.0	1,946	3,046	1.4	97.3	1.2	2.0	0.9	0.9	5.8	12.5	10.1	11.5	12.3	10.4
30053		7	Lincoln	3,612.6	20,525	1,791	5.7	94.3	0.8	2.8	1.1	3.5	4.2	10.5	8.8	8.3	10.3	10.9
30055		9	McCone	2,642.2	1,718	3,063	0.7	96.3	1.5	2.0	0.6	1.9	4.9	11.9	10.0	10.5	10.1	9.5
30057		9	Madison	3,588.2	8,917	2,494	2.5	93.4	1.1	1.7	0.8	4.7	4.2	8.5	8.3	10.3	11.5	10.7
30059		9	Meagher	2,391.9	1,964	3,044	0.8	96.5	0.7	1.5	0.6	2.1	4.8	10.8	9.2	8.2	10.3	9.7
30061		8	Mineral	1,219.6	4,860	2,833	4.0	93.4	1.3	3.3	1.3	3.4	5.0	11.2	7.8	9.8	11.2	9.6
30063	33540	3	Missoula	2,593.0	119,533	529	46.1	91.2	1.1	4.0	3.1	3.8	4.5	10.5	16.5	15.7	14.0	10.7
30065		8	Musselshell	1,869.0	4,896	2,830	2.6	91.7	1.6	3.0	1.8	4.1	4.5	10.4	9.7	8.9	10.2	12.2
30067		7	Park	2,802.5	17,473	1,947	6.2	94.4	0.8	2.3	1.1	3.5	4.5	9.6	8.5	11.8	13.3	12.2
30069		9	Petroleum	1,655.6	519	3,136	0.3	95.4	0.8	2.3	0.2	2.5	3.7	8.3	7.5	9.2	9.2	11.9
30071		9	Phillips	5,140.4	4,192	2,871	0.8	86.7	1.1	11.6	1.0	3.7	5.8	14.3	10.4	9.8	10.2	9.7
30073		7	Pondera	1,624.6	5,994	2,734	3.7	82.8	1.2	14.5	1.1	2.7	6.6	13.3	11.8	11.3	11.1	10.4
30075		9	Powder River	3,298.2	1,702	3,067	0.5	94.6	0.8	3.3	0.7	3.2	5.3	8.2	8.6	10.6	8.9	9.6
30077		6	Powell	2,326.0	6,999	2,662	3.0	89.2	1.8	6.8	0.8	3.2	3.7	8.4	10.2	13.6	14.3	13.9
30079		9	Prairie	1,736.6	1,091	3,104	0.6	92.9	2.2	3.1	2.0	4.3	5.9	12.8	6.2	8.6	8.8	9.0
30081		6	Ravalli	2,391.0	45,959	1,062	19.2	93.9	0.6	2.4	1.2	3.9	4.4	10.7	9.8	9.7	11.4	11.2
30083		7	Richland	2,084.6	11,283	2,327	5.4	90.8	1.4	3.6	1.1	5.6	6.2	14.7	11.8	13.0	12.8	11.5
30085		7	Roosevelt	2,354.6	10,821	2,358	4.6	35.9	1.1	61.8	1.2	3.9	9.0	19.9	14.3	13.1	11.6	9.1
30087		9	Rosebud	5,008.1	8,124	2,570	1.6	55.5	0.9	38.9	2.4	5.0	7.3	17.2	13.1	11.7	10.4	10.2
30089		8	Sanders	2,760.4	12,959	2,215	4.7	92.1	0.8	5.2	0.9	3.7	4.0	9.8	8.4	8.2	9.2	11.0
30091		9	Sheridan	1,676.9	3,527	2,920	2.1	93.0	1.4	3.4	1.1	3.7	5.5	11.4	9.8	9.7	12.4	10.4
30093	15580	5	Silver Bow	718.0	35,411	1,296	49.3	92.0	0.9	3.2	1.4	4.7	5.0	12.0	14.1	12.8	12.0	10.7
30095	13740	8	Stillwater	1,796.7	9,044	2,484	5.0	93.7	0.7	2.5	1.2	4.2	4.4	12.1	10.7	9.0	11.3	11.9
30097		9	Sweet Grass	1,855.5	3,723	2,907	2.0	94.7	1.0	2.2	1.3	3.0	4.1	11.1	10.7	9.5	10.5	11.4
30099		8	Teton	2,271.6	6,269	2,715	2.8	94.8	0.9	3.2	1.6	1.9	6.6	13.8	11.4	10.0	11.0	10.1
30101		7	Toole	1,914.9	5,011	2,824	2.6	88.6	2.2	6.8	1.4	4.3	6.3	12.5	9.9	13.8	13.6	11.2
30103		8	Treasure	977.8	768	3,120	0.8	91.0	0.9	3.6	1.2	5.2	8.6	12.0	8.2	10.2	9.4	5.5
30105		7	Valley	4,926.1	7,537	2,616	1.5	87.2	1.0	10.0	1.6	2.7	5.5	12.7	11.5	9.8	11.5	10.4
30107		9	Wheatland	1,422.5	2,059	3,036	1.4	93.0	1.4	3.1	1.3	4.4	5.3	13.6	10.8	8.9	9.7	12.2
30109		9	Wibaux	889.6	934	3,109	1.0	93.0	1.3	2.2	1.9	3.6	4.8	11.8	10.6	8.0	11.0	11.3
30111	13740	3	Yellowstone	2,633.5	167,146	403	63.5	87.9	1.5	5.7	1.6	6.3	5.7	13.4	12.0	13.9	13.4	11.3
31000		0	NEBRASKA	76,816.5	1,963,692	X	25.6	79.3	6.1	1.4	3.4	12.0	6.4	14.0	14.0	12.9	13.0	11.1
31001	25580	4	Adams	563.3	31,027	1,401	55.1	85.1	1.6	1.0	1.6	11.8	6.2	13.1	15.0	12.0	11.4	10.6
31003		9	Antelope	857.2	6,279	2,714	7.3	95.0	0.7	0.6	0.6	3.9	7.0	13.5	10.6	9.8	10.7	9.2
31005		9	Arthur	715.2	439	3,138	0.6	95.0	0.2	1.6	0.2	3.9	4.6	15.9	14.1	10.3	12.5	10.5
31007	42420	9	Banner	746.0	692	3,127	0.9	90.5	1.7	0.9	0.3	7.2	5.6	14.9	9.4	11.0	11.1	8.5

1. CBSA = Core Based Statistical Area. See Appendix A for explanation. See Appendix B for list of metropolitan areas with component counties. 2. County type code from the Economic Research Service of USDA Rural-Urban Continuum Codes. See Appendix A for definition. 3. Dry land or land partially or temporarily covered by water. 4. May be of any race.

STATE County	Population, 2021 (cont.)				Population change, 2000–2021							Households, 2016–2020				
	Age (percent) (cont.)				Total persons		Percent change		Components of change, 2020–2021					Percent		
	55 to 64 years	65 to 74 years	75 years and over	Percent female	2010	2020	2010–2020	2020–2021	Births	Deaths	Net Migration	Number	Persons per household	Family house-holds	Female family house-holder[1]	One person
	16	17	18	19	20	21	22	23	24	25	26	27	28	29	30	31
MONTANA	13.4	12.3	7.3	49.4	989,415	1,084,225	9.6	1.8	13,285	15,072	22,062	436,048	2.4	61.3	7.7	30.8
Beaverhead	14.0	14.2	9.3	48.7	9,246	9,371	1.4	1.6	77	124	203	4,203	2.1	58.5	6.3	36.2
Big Horn	11.6	8.9	4.9	50.5	12,865	13,124	2.0	-1.3	269	236	-201	3,622	3.6	73.3	16.5	22.1
Blaine	12.8	9.3	6.3	49.6	6,491	7,044	8.5	-0.9	111	108	-68	2,399	2.8	66.2	16.2	30.6
Broadwater	16.7	14.9	8.6	48.3	5,612	6,774	20.7	7.6	70	74	527	2,436	2.5	62.1	6.1	29.5
Carbon	17.5	17.0	9.9	48.5	10,078	10,473	3.9	3.6	58	137	460	4,524	2.3	61.9	5.7	32.1
Carter	16.5	16.2	11.3	49.1	1,160	1,415	22.0	0.9	20	17	10	650	2.0	60.0	3.7	37.1
Cascade	12.9	11.3	8.0	49.2	81,327	84,414	3.8	0.1	1,216	1,295	166	34,440	2.3	60.8	10.0	33.1
Chouteau	14.5	13.7	8.6	49.3	5,813	5,895	1.4	0.4	46	80	55	2,301	2.5	68.8	7.3	29.5
Custer	14.8	12.2	8.1	49.7	11,699	11,867	1.4	0.4	129	202	123	4,837	2.3	62.6	8.6	32.2
Daniels	15.2	13.9	13.1	48.1	1,751	1,661	-5.1	1.5	14	20	32	856	2.0	55.8	3.7	41.0
Dawson	13.9	12.2	8.5	47.8	8,966	8,940	-0.3	-0.4	124	120	-40	3,892	2.2	60.8	5.1	35.7
Deer Lodge	16.6	16.4	9.2	46.3	9,298	9,421	1.3	0.7	84	172	161	4,069	2.0	57.8	11.5	39.5
Fallon	13.6	11.8	6.9	49.1	2,890	3,049	5.5	-1.0	49	38	-44	1,274	2.3	57.8	9.1	32.0
Fergus	14.6	14.8	9.9	48.9	11,586	11,446	-1.2	1.5	134	193	234	5,057	2.1	55.1	5.1	38.4
Flathead	14.1	13.4	7.1	49.9	90,928	104,357	14.8	3.9	1,277	1,455	4,337	39,925	2.5	64.2	6.4	30.2
Gallatin	10.5	8.8	4.5	47.7	89,513	118,960	32.9	3.2	1,381	929	3,318	45,287	2.4	57.9	5.7	26.7
Garfield	12.9	14.8	9.3	48.2	1,206	1,173	-2.7	3.1	14	15	39	437	2.4	68.6	6.2	27.7
Glacier	12.2	8.1	4.7	51.6	13,399	13,778	2.8	0.1	228	181	-44	4,158	3.1	63.1	17.8	32.7
Golden Valley	15.5	18.1	12.0	50.9	884	823	-6.9	1.0	16	11	2	361	2.3	65.7	5.0	31.0
Granite	18.6	18.6	11.9	48.1	3,079	3,309	7.5	1.1	26	40	51	1,355	2.4	59.4	3.0	34.2
Hill	12.1	9.7	5.8	49.2	16,096	16,309	1.3	-0.8	294	239	-186	6,471	2.5	65.3	12.9	28.5
Jefferson	16.6	16.1	7.2	49.1	11,406	12,085	6.0	3.2	107	164	449	4,445	2.7	74.7	4.9	22.5
Judith Basin	17.2	17.1	11.8	48.7	2,072	2,023	-2.4	1.0	28	22	15	915	2.2	60.1	3.7	37.4
Lake	14.1	14.3	9.1	50.7	28,746	31,134	8.3	2.9	394	466	983	11,869	2.5	68.2	11.5	24.9
Lewis and Clark	14.3	12.7	7.0	50.3	63,395	70,973	12.0	1.8	812	1,010	1,461	28,502	2.4	60.0	7.5	31.8
Liberty	14.1	12.3	11.0	51.8	2,339	1,959	-16.2	-0.7	34	15	-32	925	2.6	65.1	7.5	33.0
Lincoln	17.0	18.9	11.0	49.6	19,687	19,677	-0.1	4.3	186	395	1,078	8,622	2.3	63.5	5.5	32.1
McCone	15.0	16.5	11.6	47.6	1,734	1,729	-0.3	-0.6	29	20	-20	818	2.2	58.3	2.8	39.0
Madison	16.3	19.8	10.4	47.5	7,691	8,623	12.1	3.4	69	145	377	3,707	2.2	60.2	2.3	32.7
Meagher	16.5	19.1	11.5	47.9	1,891	1,927	1.9	1.9	17	17	37	759	2.3	61.0	4.6	36.4
Mineral	16.6	17.9	11.0	48.8	4,223	4,535	7.4	7.2	39	70	363	1,926	2.2	62.7	6.4	35.4
Missoula	11.4	10.8	6.0	49.7	109,299	117,922	7.9	1.4	1,327	1,360	1,636	49,700	2.3	55.6	7.8	31.0
Musselshell	16.1	18.5	9.6	49.3	4,538	4,730	4.2	3.5	40	83	213	2,211	2.1	63.7	4.7	30.1
Park	16.1	15.2	8.9	49.5	15,636	17,191	9.9	1.6	150	261	397	7,961	2.0	57.6	4.5	32.5
Petroleum	21.6	14.3	14.3	46.6	494	496	0.4	4.6	4	3	23	212	2.2	58.5	1.4	26.9
Phillips	16.3	14.0	9.6	49.8	4,253	4,217	-0.8	-0.6	51	78	3	1,756	2.3	60.7	5.2	35.0
Pondera	14.4	11.7	9.4	50.2	6,153	5,898	-4.1	1.6	81	90	105	2,079	2.8	67.9	7.7	28.9
Powder River	18.6	18.2	11.9	48.5	1,743	1,694	-2.8	0.5	18	26	16	748	2.1	70.2	3.2	23.7
Powell	15.6	12.4	8.0	35.8	7,027	6,946	-1.2	0.8	54	115	116	2,515	2.1	64.0	9.5	26.7
Prairie	14.3	20.5	13.8	48.3	1,179	1,088	-7.7	0.3	8	21	16	502	2.3	58.4	3.8	34.5
Ravalli	16.1	16.7	10.0	49.7	40,212	44,174	9.9	4.0	450	755	2,127	17,823	2.4	69.9	7.0	25.3
Richland	13.5	10.3	6.1	48.1	9,746	11,491	17.9	-1.8	165	131	-238	4,408	2.5	62.6	6.5	33.5
Roosevelt	11.2	7.9	3.9	49.7	10,425	10,794	3.5	0.3	236	218	7	3,248	3.3	62.5	16.5	31.1
Rosebud	13.2	11.0	5.9	49.5	9,233	8,329	-9.8	-2.5	167	133	-236	3,237	2.8	66.9	9.1	24.3
Sanders	17.4	19.7	12.3	48.7	11,413	12,400	8.6	4.5	105	211	675	5,281	2.2	58.6	4.7	35.6
Sheridan	16.0	15.0	9.8	48.1	3,384	3,539	4.6	-0.3	36	73	26	1,543	2.1	58.3	5.1	35.3
Silver Bow	14.0	11.8	7.6	49.1	34,200	35,133	2.7	0.8	382	630	529	15,026	2.2	54.9	8.9	39.4
Stillwater	16.1	15.8	8.7	48.7	9,117	8,963	-1.7	0.9	86	115	110	3,840	2.5	67.3	3.9	27.9
Sweet Grass	14.6	16.0	12.1	49.3	3,651	3,678	0.7	1.2	37	51	60	1,515	2.4	68.7	6.5	29.8
Teton	14.4	12.1	10.6	50.6	6,073	6,226	2.5	0.7	92	105	58	2,496	2.4	63.4	5.9	32.6
Toole	14.0	11.6	7.2	42.7	5,324	4,971	-6.6	0.8	82	69	26	1,827	2.3	58.3	5.3	35.8
Treasure	16.1	16.5	13.5	49.3	718	762	6.1	0.8	12	9	4	333	1.8	66.1	2.4	31.5
Valley	14.9	13.6	10.1	49.6	7,369	7,578	2.8	-0.5	77	126	7	3,324	2.2	61.2	7.4	33.1
Wheatland	13.5	15.8	10.2	48.9	2,168	2,069	-4.6	-0.5	31	30	-10	897	2.4	64.9	5.9	33.0
Wibaux	16.5	14.0	11.9	49.3	1,017	937	-7.9	-0.3	11	23	9	477	2.1	66.2	2.5	32.5
Yellowstone	12.7	10.7	6.9	50.4	147,972	164,731	11.3	1.5	2,231	2,346	2,537	68,047	2.3	62.1	8.5	30.7
NEBRASKA	12.3	9.9	6.5	49.7	1,826,341	1,961,504	7.4	0.1	29,623	24,254	-3,378	766,663	2.4	63.8	9.3	29.4
Adams	12.9	11.1	7.7	50.1	31,364	31,205	-0.5	-0.6	449	489	-142	12,786	2.3	63.2	10.1	31.1
Antelope	14.9	13.8	10.5	49.9	6,685	6,295	-5.8	-0.3	99	105	-10	2,725	2.3	60.8	6.4	35.3
Arthur	10.7	11.2	10.3	49.4	460	434	-5.7	1.2	4	4	5	192	2.3	60.4	8.9	39.6
Banner	15.6	15.9	7.9	50.1	690	674	-2.3	2.7	12	5	11	234	2.8	88.5	7.3	11.5

1. No spouse present.

STATE County	Persons in group quarters, 2021	Daytime Population, 2016–2020: Number	Daytime Population, 2016–2020: Employment/ residence ratio	Births, 2021: Total	Births, 2021: Rate[1]	Deaths, 2021: Number	Deaths, 2021: Rate[1]	Persons under 65 with no health insurance, 2019: Number	Persons under 65 with no health insurance, 2019: Percent	Medicare, 2021: Total beneficiaries	Medicare, 2021: Enrolled in Original Medicare	Medicare, 2021: Enrolled in Medicare Advantage	COVID-19 Deaths, 2020: Number	COVID-19 Deaths, 2020: Rate[1]
	32	33	34	35	36	37	38	39	40	41	42	43	44	45
MONTANA	27,250	1,058,895	1.0	10,502	9.6	12,022	11.0	86,203	10.2	237,659	188,889	48,769	1,129	1.0
Beaverhead	404	9,451	1.0	63	6.7	107	11.3	741	10.7	2,433	2,130	303	D	D
Big Horn	104	13,596	1.1	225	17.3	183	14.1	1,633	14.8	1,866	1,598	269	66	5.1
Blaine	218	6,492	0.9	84	12.0	83	11.9	838	15.4	1,155	1,141	15	24	3.4
Broadwater	50	5,149	0.6	54	7.6	65	9.2	502	10.7	1,680	1,397	283	D	D
Carbon	24	9,076	0.7	46	4.3	110	10.3	915	11.7	2,923	2,239	684	D	D
Carter	11	1,270	1.0	14	9.9	13	9.2	121	13.3	340	323	17	D	D
Cascade	2,432	81,472	1.0	961	11.4	1,024	12.1	6,236	9.7	18,068	13,056	5,012	146	1.7
Chouteau	132	5,146	0.8	33	5.6	62	10.5	615	14.1	1,325	1,078	247	D	D
Custer	428	11,514	1.0	100	8.4	173	14.6	830	9.5	2,685	2,481	204	13	1.1
Daniels	37	1,726	1.0	9	5.4	14	8.4	134	11.1	457	442	15	D	D
Dawson	494	8,882	1.0	98	11.0	99	11.1	482	7.4	1,971	1,865	105	24	2.7
Deer Lodge	845	9,160	1.0	68	7.2	135	14.3	639	10.2	2,805	2,357	448	10	1.1
Fallon	32	3,089	1.1	39	12.9	26	8.6	268	11.4	550	533	17	D	D
Fergus	451	11,212	1.0	106	9.2	152	13.2	917	11.4	3,120	2,416	704	20	1.7
Flathead	862	102,472	1.0	1,026	9.6	1,168	11.0	8,285	10.1	24,966	18,593	6,373	74	0.7
Gallatin	3,293	112,261	1.0	1,086	9.0	732	6.0	8,030	8.3	16,646	13,311	3,335	44	0.4
Garfield	0	1,061	1.0	12	10.1	13	10.9	155	16.6	303	289	14	D	D
Glacier	656	13,763	1.0	178	12.9	141	10.2	2,210	19.2	2,025	1,998	27	49	3.6
Golden Valley	89	740	0.8	13	15.7	6	7.3	76	13.0	263	201	62	D	D
Granite	27	3,447	1.1	19	5.7	32	9.6	307	13.4	930	800	130	D	D
Hill	506	16,970	1.1	239	14.7	189	11.7	1,723	12.7	2,934	2,904	30	39	2.4
Jefferson	159	9,467	0.5	82	6.7	132	10.7	843	8.9	3,159	2,599	560	D	D
Judith Basin	0	1,879	0.9	24	11.8	16	7.9	179	12.5	595	462	134	D	D
Lake	540	28,528	0.9	317	10.0	402	12.7	3,572	15.6	7,919	6,268	1,651	26	0.8
Lewis and Clark	1,895	71,633	1.1	635	8.9	805	11.2	4,363	7.9	15,792	12,271	3,521	52	0.7
Liberty	251	2,404	1.0	28	14.3	14	7.2	260	14.6	470	444	25	D	D
Lincoln	142	19,260	0.9	145	7.2	325	16.1	1,923	14.0	7,640	5,283	2,357	16	0.8
McCone	17	1,796	1.0	23	13.3	17	9.9	204	17.2	425	D	D	D	D
Madison	115	9,049	1.1	53	6.0	116	13.2	808	13.4	2,571	2,299	273	D	D
Meagher	172	1,729	0.9	12	6.2	13	6.7	125	10.0	561	532	28	D	D
Mineral	18	3,785	0.7	32	6.8	57	12.1	316	10.4	1,536	1,237	299	D	D
Missoula	3,362	122,704	1.1	1,032	8.7	1,070	9.0	8,936	9.2	23,220	18,409	4,811	68	0.6
Musselshell	49	4,416	0.9	31	6.4	74	15.3	441	13.4	1,523	1,228	295	10	2.1
Park	98	15,225	0.9	123	7.1	194	11.2	1,269	10.1	4,308	4,149	158	D	D
Petroleum	0	447	0.9	3	5.9	3	5.9	33	9.1	116	99	17	D	D
Phillips	125	3,879	0.9	44	10.5	54	12.9	481	16.2	1,035	980	55	12	2.9
Pondera	633	5,688	0.9	65	10.9	78	13.1	541	11.7	1,365	1,161	204	D	D
Powder River	33	1,643	1.0	14	8.2	23	13.5	156	13.0	405	372	33	D	D
Powell	1,702	6,789	1.0	45	6.5	94	13.5	435	11.5	1,597	1,400	196	D	D
Prairie	19	1,107	0.9	7	6.5	10	9.2	86	12.0	367	337	31	D	D
Ravalli	393	39,806	0.8	361	8.0	608	13.5	3,994	12.6	13,637	10,218	3,419	38	0.9
Richland	34	11,582	1.1	140	12.3	106	9.3	985	10.7	1,957	1,937	21	15	1.3
Roosevelt	140	11,185	1.0	180	16.7	172	15.9	1,875	20.2	1,645	1,598	47	47	4.4
Rosebud	26	9,529	1.1	132	16.1	100	12.2	946	12.9	1,698	1,521	177	40	4.8
Sanders	178	11,539	0.9	77	6.1	169	13.3	1,262	16.0	4,379	3,533	846	14	1.1
Sheridan	83	3,259	0.9	29	8.2	57	16.2	295	11.7	954	887	67	D	D
Silver Bow	930	34,899	1.0	302	8.6	509	14.4	2,514	9.2	8,114	6,697	1,416	57	1.6
Stillwater	42	9,189	0.9	68	7.5	96	10.6	586	7.9	2,477	1,878	599	10	1.1
Sweet Grass	34	3,831	1.1	28	7.6	41	11.1	293	10.9	998	860	138	D	D
Teton	438	5,797	0.9	78	12.5	86	13.7	543	11.7	1,590	1,100	490	D	D
Toole	674	5,050	1.1	59	11.8	46	9.2	432	13.3	972	941	32	D	D
Treasure	0	533	0.7	8	10.5	9	11.8	51	10.4	213	164	49	D	D
Valley	120	7,308	1.0	55	7.3	93	12.3	571	10.2	1,794	1,732	62	17	2.3
Wheatland	118	2,112	1.0	18	8.7	26	12.5	295	19.1	577	483	94	D	D
Wibaux	22	956	0.8	8	8.6	14	15.0	94	13.2	252	D	D	D	D
Yellowstone	3,593	162,943	1.0	1,771	10.7	1,866	11.2	10,839	8.3	32,355	23,991	8,364	198	1.2
NEBRASKA	48,139	1,942,595	1.0	23,524	12.0	19,213	9.8	150,342	9.5	353,641	282,431	71,210	2,116	1.1
Adams	1,188	31,803	1.0	357	11.5	371	11.9	2,320	9.6	6,739	5,819	920	52	1.7
Antelope	37	6,079	0.9	75	11.9	82	13.1	483	10.2	1,559	1,494	65	11	1.8
Arthur	0	423	0.9	4	9.2	2	4.6	44	12.4	102	D	D	D	D
Banner	0	587	0.8	7	10.2	5	7.3	39	7.0	103	D	D	D	D

1. Per 1,000 estimated resident population.

STATE County	COVID-19 Vaccinations, 2021–2022		Education						Money income, 2016–2020				Income and poverty, 2020			
			School enrollment and attainment, 2016–2020				Local government expenditures,[3] 2018–2019			Households				Percent below poverty level		
			Enrollment[1]		Attainment[2] (percent)						Percent					
	Number	Percent[5]	Total	Percent private	High school graduate or less	Bachelor's degree or more	Total current spending (mil dol)	Current spending per student (dollars)	Per capita income[4]	Median income (dollars)	with income of less than $50,000	with income of $200,000 or more	Median household income (dollars)	All persons	Children under 18 years	Children 5 to 17 years in families
	46	47	48	49	50	51	52	53	54	55	56	57	58	59	60	61
MONTANA	606,208	56.7	238,528	14.1	34.1	33.1	1,766.0	11,956	32,463	56,539	44.2	4.7	57,730	12.4	14.6	13.4
Beaverhead	5,121	54.2	2,099	19.1	35.2	32.5	14.4	12,465	28,798	45,819	52.7	4.2	52,613	13.3	15.6	15.0
Big Horn	11,908	89.4	3,937	13.9	44.3	18.6	39.5	15,262	19,109	48,273	52.1	3.4	42,823	28.9	35.6	32.0
Blaine	5,720	85.6	1,882	3.2	38.3	24.5	21.9	16,788	20,586	45,361	53.9	1.0	45,936	20.9	23.0	21.7
Broadwater	2,104	33.7	990	6.8	31.5	27.2	7.2	11,181	31,573	57,723	44.8	2.8	61,641	9.1	13.2	13.4
Carbon	5,064	47.2	1,889	12.3	35.8	31.5	19.2	13,985	34,751	61,209	40.7	5.1	62,465	11.2	13.2	12.1
Carter	390	31.2	177	41.2	38.0	21.1	2.7	17,559	27,759	42,300	53.8	2.2	48,286	14.7	18.9	21.3
Cascade	44,498	54.7	17,682	13.6	39.0	27.3	122.7	10,523	30,572	52,049	48.0	3.4	53,357	13.5	16.4	15.6
Chouteau	1,865	33.1	1,192	7.3	42.8	29.0	9.2	13,078	26,243	45,707	54.7	2.7	50,607	15.1	21.1	18.7
Custer	5,026	44.1	2,569	13.5	35.2	27.7	18.3	11,525	31,267	54,891	47.3	3.2	59,804	11.5	13.4	13.4
Daniels	714	42.2	289	7.3	39.9	23.1	3.5	12,609	33,614	56,026	45.6	4.1	50,312	11.2	13.0	12.0
Dawson	3,249	37.7	1,732	12.0	36.3	24.9	17.1	13,255	30,821	51,681	48.0	3.6	55,845	10.8	12.8	12.3
Deer Lodge	5,310	58.1	1,226	12.3	47.9	20.0	12.9	12,018	26,207	42,129	58.3	2.0	47,362	17.9	20.8	22.2
Fallon	983	34.5	625	19.0	43.1	15.6	10.4	19,252	36,409	69,792	39.4	4.5	62,597	9.4	11.0	10.8
Fergus	5,192	47.0	2,314	7.7	36.8	27.2	22.8	14,644	28,211	47,618	51.4	2.6	49,576	13.6	14.6	14.8
Flathead	44,276	42.7	20,293	19.4	34.0	32.0	155.0	10,658	32,242	57,763	43.6	4.3	58,959	10.5	12.5	11.6
Gallatin	67,812	59.3	32,684	14.3	20.8	51.6	145.7	10,598	38,885	70,124	33.9	7.9	70,029	8.8	7.1	6.3
Garfield	244	19.4	214	4.7	44.5	20.9	2.6	15,515	29,149	43,750	54.7	4.8	45,892	15.0	26.9	26.1
Glacier	11,742	85.4	3,510	2.9	47.8	23.2	41.3	14,600	18,440	37,645	64.3	3.0	40,817	24.3	25.4	24.8
Golden Valley	380	46.3	124	8.1	44.3	21.8	2.7	22,525	30,053	49,028	51.0	6.1	42,741	18.6	32.4	34.1
Granite	1,248	36.9	627	11.0	36.3	31.1	4.8	13,882	32,401	50,795	49.2	6.1	53,407	12.7	17.3	15.3
Hill	11,632	70.6	4,506	6.0	38.0	26.7	43.3	14,781	23,922	50,912	49.3	1.6	49,734	18.9	21.4	19.3
Jefferson	6,167	50.5	2,572	10.5	32.5	35.2	18.8	10,774	33,716	71,779	33.7	3.5	80,071	6.7	8.0	7.3
Judith Basin	794	39.6	385	7.3	32.0	24.5	5.4	18,497	33,720	50,329	49.7	9.9	50,610	15.7	21.0	21.0
Lake	17,272	56.7	6,805	14.7	33.1	31.4	53.7	11,892	26,889	52,169	48.3	3.9	52,493	18.3	24.1	20.5
Lewis and Clark	41,251	59.4	14,962	22.5	27.7	42.5	107.2	10,999	36,485	66,062	37.9	5.0	60,664	10.2	11.0	10.1
Liberty	797	34.1	463	1.1	47.2	21.7	3.8	13,534	46,198	46,750	52.6	6.5	53,415	19.0	22.3	21.7
Lincoln	7,052	35.3	3,018	14.3	46.0	19.7	28.1	11,691	25,169	39,820	59.3	1.7	42,501	17.9	28.2	26.3
McCone	298	17.9	307	18.2	39.9	15.9	3.3	16,302	31,242	57,045	47.1	3.7	46,755	14.5	15.6	14.5
Madison	3,835	44.6	1,278	15.4	31.2	33.8	12.9	14,745	35,668	55,892	45.1	4.5	58,201	9.9	12.9	12.4
Meagher	940	50.5	346	14.7	45.6	26.2	3.0	13,581	26,392	46,815	52.8	0.7	43,666	16.6	22.3	23.3
Mineral	2,396	54.5	725	11.6	44.0	21.9	9.0	15,432	28,644	48,672	50.9	1.2	57,169	14.9	22.2	21.8
Missoula	77,444	64.8	30,622	11.4	25.0	44.2	163.1	11,539	33,358	56,247	44.7	4.8	63,409	11.8	11.8	11.0
Musselshell	1,614	34.8	682	12.9	49.7	17.6	8.6	13,816	27,843	46,328	55.2	2.8	50,533	15.4	24.6	24.4
Park	9,762	58.8	2,797	14.1	32.5	32.1	24.9	13,411	35,446	53,082	47.5	3.5	56,657	10.9	12.0	11.6
Petroleum	150	30.8	76	0.0	39.4	26.5	1.6	23,118	28,220	40,000	55.7	2.8	38,661	15.0	29.3	27.6
Phillips	1,733	43.8	757	11.4	46.4	18.2	9.3	14,077	26,825	46,686	53.9	2.7	46,821	14.9	21.8	21.3
Pondera	3,231	54.7	1,370	9.1	36.7	24.2	10.5	12,306	27,114	54,235	45.3	3.4	49,447	18.5	23.3	22.7
Powder River	385	22.9	221	11.8	37.3	23.7	4.2	20,397	33,170	57,755	42.0	4.9	60,462	12.6	20.8	23.8
Powell	3,126	45.4	997	12.0	51.4	17.7	10.3	15,109	25,002	50,332	49.7	2.7	52,904	16.5	17.5	17.5
Prairie	409	38.0	235	26.8	40.2	27.6	2.2	16,515	28,892	42,350	54.6	4.6	48,577	12.8	20.1	21.5
Ravalli	21,366	48.8	8,068	11.8	37.6	28.4	59.0	10,610	31,545	55,090	45.3	4.5	58,781	11.3	15.9	15.1
Richland	4,300	39.8	2,607	5.0	44.0	18.5	27.5	14,325	30,330	64,158	40.5	3.0	69,169	8.0	9.5	8.8
Roosevelt	8,096	73.6	3,015	3.6	43.3	18.7	43.9	17,257	18,669	45,458	56.0	1.3	43,256	23.8	28.6	25.2
Rosebud	7,569	84.7	2,060	8.3	41.2	17.8	27.8	18,250	25,557	57,769	43.4	2.6	54,991	17.5	21.9	20.8
Sanders	4,671	38.6	1,917	10.3	48.9	19.0	20.1	14,515	26,103	42,284	58.5	2.6	45,805	16.3	24.8	24.3
Sheridan	1,603	48.4	569	18.6	43.3	25.3	9.4	18,526	37,958	54,135	44.1	5.8	50,658	11.8	15.4	14.8
Silver Bow	21,478	61.5	8,001	13.8	41.1	27.5	48.1	10,959	28,221	49,359	50.7	2.7	54,324	13.2	14.6	12.9
Stillwater	4,063	42.1	2,141	11.3	40.3	26.3	18.2	13,014	35,387	67,448	36.0	5.8	73,044	7.8	9.9	8.7
Sweet Grass	1,526	40.8	690	19.9	39.3	21.7	6.3	12,004	27,553	53,790	42.8	2.4	58,746	9.3	12.6	11.7
Teton	2,575	41.9	1,267	17.0	40.0	25.4	14.7	13,776	27,985	56,649	44.0	2.7	55,399	12.4	14.0	13.4
Toole	2,195	46.3	884	13.9	48.6	22.3	9.0	14,876	30,213	49,725	50.3	7.0	49,568	15.8	16.4	15.3
Treasure	336	48.3	60	16.7	41.2	28.2	1.6	27,525	33,685	44,671	53.8	4.5	56,919	12.5	23.0	28.1
Valley	3,431	46.4	1,475	4.9	40.6	19.3	18.1	14,983	28,440	51,087	48.8	2.0	46,766	13.4	16.3	16.2
Wheatland	763	35.9	369	1.1	48.7	19.6	5.1	17,161	21,409	35,265	66.7	2.2	39,462	20.9	24.9	23.4
Wibaux	276	28.5	239	8.4	45.2	23.1	3.3	23,085	26,405	50,972	49.3	0.0	51,368	11.7	15.0	12.5
Yellowstone	83,425	51.7	35,987	17.3	34.4	32.8	256.7	10,740	37,261	62,630	39.4	6.5	58,374	10.6	11.5	9.9
NEBRASKA	1,229,108	63.5	505,631	17.4	34.2	32.5	4,154.2	12,736	33,205	63,015	39.5	5.2	64,735	9.2	10.1	9.5
Adams	13,239	42.2	8,435	25.3	36.1	25.6	70.2	13,658	30,344	56,007	44.8	3.8	54,445	10.2	10.8	10.1
Antelope	2,344	37.2	1,269	11.1	42.4	18.0	28.4	28,798	27,217	52,569	48.5	1.8	54,136	10.4	14.5	14.3
Arthur	91	19.7	112	13.4	30.9	24.1	2.6	20,472	25,277	48,500	51.6	1.6	52,500	12.3	17.4	15.6
Banner	244	32.8	107	3.7	26.7	26.7	3.5	27,155	30,628	53,864	46.2	5.1	59,511	10.1	13.5	13.2

1. All persons 3 years old and over enrolled in nursery school through college. 2. Persons 25 years old and over. 3. Elementary and secondary education expenditures. 4. Based on population estimated by the American Community Survey, 2016–2020. 5. CDC percent based on 2019 population estimate.

STATE County	Personal income, 2020										Earnings, 2020		
	Total (mil dol)	Percent change 2019–2020	Per capita[1]		Wages and salaries (mil dol)	Supplements to wages and salaries, employer contributions (mil dol)		Proprietors' income (mil dol)	Dividends, interest, and rent (mil dol)	Personal transfer receipts (mil dol)	Total (mil dol)	Contributions for government social insurance (mil dol)	
			Dollars	Rank		Pension and insurance	Government social insurance					From employee and self-employed	From employer
	62	63	64	65	66	67	68	69	70	71	72	73	74
MONTANA	57,660	7.5	53,085	X	23,535	3,653	2,059	5,600	13,447	13,521	34,848	2,392	2,059
Beaverhead	498	9.3	52,501	889	166	30	15	61	126	131	272	17	15
Big Horn	470	12.5	35,950	2,869	200	41	17	46	68	184	304	18	17
Blaine	238	15.4	36,301	2,848	60	15	5	39	43	84	120	7	5
Broadwater	314	10.8	48,786	1,283	57	10	5	42	59	78	113	8	5
Carbon	621	7.8	56,900	576	109	19	10	69	154	143	207	15	10
Carter	66	30.9	53,760	798	14	3	1	20	14	14	38	2	1
Cascade	4,248	6.1	52,226	913	1,906	341	170	252	845	1,085	2,668	179	170
Chouteau	277	19.7	48,627	1,304	51	10	5	80	60	62	147	6	5
Custer	579	8.0	51,268	996	226	38	20	79	110	145	362	25	20
Daniels	105	29.5	64,205	286	30	5	2	28	21	23	65	3	2
Dawson	436	8.3	50,972	1,035	174	29	16	37	68	121	255	18	16
Deer Lodge	415	9.9	45,039	1,788	137	24	12	16	76	157	189	16	12
Fallon	153	7.0	54,203	766	74	11	6	21	30	31	113	7	6
Fergus	543	8.0	48,900	1,269	202	34	18	60	117	154	315	23	18
Flathead	5,583	7.2	52,740	875	2,150	295	194	530	1,455	1,362	3,169	236	194
Gallatin	7,409	7.5	63,432	302	3,293	436	282	903	2,049	979	4,914	316	282
Garfield	57	34.6	44,812	1,823	13	3	1	15	13	13	33	2	1
Glacier	568	11.9	41,773	2,232	192	41	16	60	108	196	309	17	16
Golden Valley	47	12.9	56,481	613	8	2	1	9	14	13	19	1	1
Granite	163	6.9	49,242	1,226	33	6	3	10	50	47	53	4	3
Hill	818	7.9	50,018	1,142	349	61	35	73	179	213	518	33	35
Jefferson	652	6.5	52,770	872	110	19	10	41	130	154	179	16	10
Judith Basin	114	14.2	56,953	575	23	4	2	32	24	24	62	3	2
Lake	1,365	9.3	44,068	1,938	378	66	33	90	367	450	567	44	33
Lewis and Clark	3,795	7.1	54,040	778	1,946	329	163	258	852	873	2,696	182	163
Liberty	121	12.6	51,268	996	25	5	2	44	26	24	76	3	2
Lincoln	837	10.3	41,129	2,318	223	44	21	47	186	365	335	33	21
McCone	81	24.9	48,924	1,266	26	5	2	13	21	18	46	3	2
Madison	512	9.0	57,112	566	250	28	22	67	158	114	367	25	22
Meagher	91	9.5	49,730	1,170	23	4	2	14	24	29	43	3	2
Mineral	196	11.7	43,233	2,034	40	8	4	8	37	75	60	6	4
Missoula	6,611	6.4	54,353	757	3,076	453	272	537	1,754	1,395	4,338	298	272
Musselshell	232	9.0	49,756	1,166	61	10	5	21	52	78	98	8	5
Park	925	5.2	55,213	688	260	37	24	70	302	222	390	30	24
Petroleum	21	24.5	41,080	2,325	5	1	0	6	4	5	12	1	0
Phillips	189	16.1	48,341	1,345	53	10	5	27	44	54	95	6	5
Pondera	325	11.5	56,218	623	68	12	6	88	64	80	175	10	6
Powder River	75	30.0	44,756	1,835	20	4	2	20	17	17	45	2	2
Powell	321	6.5	47,024	1,512	108	23	10	27	93	88	168	12	10
Prairie	62	22.3	57,918	518	13	3	1	14	13	16	31	2	1
Ravalli	2,244	7.6	49,860	1,158	537	88	48	169	589	648	842	74	48
Richland	704	3.0	63,761	297	308	44	26	82	132	127	461	28	26
Roosevelt	455	13.7	41,531	2,267	162	31	14	42	68	169	250	16	14
Rosebud	447	10.3	50,566	1,082	218	45	19	31	67	127	312	19	19
Sanders	503	12.8	41,398	2,279	120	24	12	45	114	216	200	19	12
Sheridan	200	19.3	61,236	377	58	11	5	39	48	45	114	7	5
Silver Bow	1,783	5.8	50,672	1,067	732	124	63	224	318	487	1,144	81	63
Stillwater	567	8.1	57,382	546	255	34	19	38	146	121	346	24	19
Sweet Grass	200	8.5	54,287	764	89	13	7	17	69	46	126	9	7
Teton	332	10.6	53,172	844	71	14	6	79	85	76	170	10	6
Toole	282	12.0	60,089	423	108	20	10	69	55	53	207	11	10
Treasure	46	17.2	66,721	221	8	2	1	17	9	9	27	1	1
Valley	401	14.3	54,556	736	149	26	14	46	86	104	236	15	14
Wheatland	91	12.6	42,348	2,147	23	5	2	18	18	31	49	3	2
Wibaux	46	17.0	48,913	1,267	11	3	1	9	8	13	24	1	1
Yellowstone	9,223	5.4	56,588	601	4,531	651	390	804	1,808	1,933	6,376	435	390
NEBRASKA	111,545	6.8	56,869	X	54,066	8,994	4,144	12,447	21,188	20,904	79,651	4,869	4,144
Adams	1,667	6.5	53,232	838	722	131	55	163	330	384	1,072	68	55
Antelope	433	24.5	69,121	176	130	23	10	123	70	79	285	13	10
Arthur	25	15.8	53,618	813	6	1	0	9	4	5	16	1	0
Banner	46	22.0	59,097	476	8	2	1	20	5	8	30	1	1

1. Based on the resident population estimated as of July 1 of the year shown.

STATE County	Earnings, 2020 (cont.) — Percent by selected industries: Farm	Mining, quarrying, and extractions	Construction	Manu-facturing	Information; professional, scientific, technical services	Retail trade	Finance, insurance, real estate, and leasing	Health care and social assistance	Govern-ment	Social Security beneficiaries, December 2020: Number	Rate[1]	Supple-mental Security Income recipients, 2020	Housing units, 2021: Total	Percent change, 2010–2021
	75	76	77	78	79	80	81	82	83	84	85	86	87	88
MONTANA	3.9	2.5	8.9	4.3	8.7	8.3	7.4	14.2	18.8	244,937	222	17,491	521,892	1.2
Beaverhead	16.1	4.4	5.9	1.2	3.2	10.7	5.7	12.8	24.3	2,480	260	142	4,959	0.8
Big Horn	13.2	15.4	D	D	1.9	4.4	2.0	D	41.0	2,235	172	301	4,525	0.1
Blaine	30.7	0.8	1.7	0.4	D	8.1	D	D	37.5	1,220	175	193	2,825	0.0
Broadwater	22.7	D	10.1	11.6	3.3	6.5	6.4	D	13.9	1,675	230	68	3,172	0.0
Carbon	16.4	1.7	11.7	D	D	D	5.8	8.0	17.9	3,000	277	110	6,401	0.6
Carter	53.4	0.2	2.9	0.0	D	4.0	D	D	14.8	330	231	D	822	0.6
Cascade	1.7	0.1	7.7	3.3	5.5	7.8	7.3	17.9	27.5	19,055	225	1,808	39,114	0.4
Chouteau	57.3	D	1.5	1.1	D	4.5	3.4	2.9	14.3	1,250	211	62	2,859	0.5
Custer	4.0	0.4	8.2	1.0	D	13.7	8.7	D	20.6	2,650	222	220	5,779	0.1
Daniels	41.5	D	1.5	D	D	D	5.3	D	10.0	445	264	10	1,043	0.0
Dawson	8.4	4.1	2.8	0.8	4.5	8.1	3.6	D	17.1	1,825	205	112	4,383	0.0
Deer Lodge	0.9	D	5.5	3.2	6.2	5.5	3.3	31.1	30.1	2,825	298	236	5,519	0.4
Fallon	9.7	25.7	8.3	0.5	2.3	5.0	2.9	6.1	15.5	575	191	11	1,570	2.3
Fergus	5.9	D	17.0	7.9	3.4	6.5	7.0	13.5	18.2	3,120	269	184	6,020	0.1
Flathead	0.4	0.6	10.6	6.5	8.2	9.3	10.5	18.2	11.6	25,985	240	1,266	50,808	1.6
Gallatin	1.3	0.4	14.5	5.3	14.9	12.4	8.0	9.0	13.4	16,840	137	503	55,263	3.8
Garfield	45.0	0.0	3.4	0.1	D	D	D	1.2	27.2	305	252	11	795	0.0
Glacier	15.9	1.7	1.3	0.3	D	5.8	1.0	D	55.1	2,195	159	593	5,344	0.0
Golden Valley	41.3	D	4.2	D	D	D	1.8	D	17.8	350	421	19	474	0.0
Granite	9.4	2.0	8.2	4.8	D	4.8	D	0.8	25.9	1,010	302	42	2,603	0.1
Hill	11.2	0.1	4.5	0.6	5.4	7.1	5.2	D	28.7	2,830	175	432	7,224	0.0
Jefferson	3.5	2.7	15.6	7.2	6.1	3.8	6.0	8.8	28.0	3,410	273	126	5,390	0.3
Judith Basin	51.9	0.2	9.0	0.0	D	3.1	D	D	15.0	595	291	24	1,248	0.0
Lake	3.3	0.8	8.6	5.3	6.7	7.8	5.0	13.9	32.7	8,075	252	669	16,441	0.3
Lewis and Clark	0.5	0.6	6.3	2.6	10.6	6.6	8.9	13.8	33.3	16,595	230	1,010	33,893	0.7
Liberty	59.3	D	1.9	0.0	0.9	2.5	D	D	9.5	440	226	47	933	0.0
Lincoln	0.4	0.3	13.6	2.4	3.8	9.4	3.3	16.4	29.0	7,655	373	565	10,982	0.2
McCone	27.7	D	3.9	0.1	D	2.9	D	D	15.3	370	215	D	1,025	0.0
Madison	8.7	D	8.9	1.4	10.1	3.9	4.3	D	9.0	2,610	293	66	6,391	0.2
Meagher	18.7	D	D	D	2.5	5.7	D	D	17.8	570	290	49	1,352	0.0
Mineral	-0.6	0.0	11.0	D	D	12.5	2.1	D	31.0	1,660	342	145	2,576	0.5
Missoula	0.2	0.1	8.4	3.2	11.6	8.9	8.2	17.4	17.7	23,455	196	1,950	55,481	1.4
Musselshell	10.5	D	7.5	0.5	D	4.4	D	8.5	13.6	1,550	317	106	2,636	0.1
Park	3.6	D	12.8	7.1	7.3	7.6	6.0	13.8	12.4	4,095	234	220	9,592	0.3
Petroleum	53.2	D	D	0.1	D	D	0.9	1.3	22.2	115	222	D	333	0.0
Phillips	24.5	D	6.8	2.2	D	8.2	4.7	9.6	23.4	1,060	253	79	2,230	0.0
Pondera	26.3	0.9	8.6	1.5	2.5	15.6	3.4	9.1	12.4	1,325	221	198	2,760	0.0
Powder River	37.5	D	D	D	D	7.5	D	0.8	22.7	410	241	D	972	0.1
Powell	7.5	D	D	D	D	5.3	1.7	9.2	46.1	1,680	240	121	2,950	1.2
Prairie	41.0	0.3	D	D	4.0	2.1	D	D	38.5	365	335	16	671	0.0
Ravalli	1.7	0.2	12.5	4.8	10.3	7.9	6.8	13.9	17.3	14,145	308	701	21,122	0.3
Richland	10.8	12.6	8.0	5.4	3.0	5.7	6.6	11.0	10.6	1,985	176	96	5,584	0.3
Roosevelt	9.5	1.8	3.4	0.5	D	8.8	2.2	D	44.5	1,785	165	370	4,065	0.0
Rosebud	9.6	16.5	7.9	0.2	D	2.3	1.3	D	32.4	1,845	227	206	3,783	0.1
Sanders	3.7	2.5	12.5	6.2	3.5	7.4	5.0	14.3	20.8	4,675	361	307	6,802	0.0
Sheridan	25.4	2.5	D	D	3.1	9.0	4.5	D	18.2	950	269	35	2,128	0.0
Silver Bow	0.1	D	D	5.4	5.7	10.1	6.3	15.8	16.4	8,660	245	952	17,397	0.8
Stillwater	6.1	D	4.3	3.4	D	3.1	1.4	D	8.2	2,595	287	79	4,660	0.0
Sweet Grass	4.7	D	9.0	3.3	3.2	3.8	4.7	D	9.8	1,010	271	18	1,951	0.1
Teton	30.1	D	9.6	0.5	D	6.6	4.2	5.2	14.2	1,580	252	116	2,935	0.0
Toole	22.1	2.4	7.0	D	D	3.0	2.7	4.4	22.1	945	189	106	2,323	0.1
Treasure	69.6	0.0	D	0.0	D	1.7	D	D	8.9	220	286	D	448	0.0
Valley	14.5	D	4.3	0.4	4.6	4.7	5.1	D	22.3	1,795	238	133	4,239	0.2
Wheatland	38.4	0.2	5.2	3.3	D	4.8	D	D	16.9	550	267	62	1,114	0.0
Wibaux	22.4	D	D	D	D	D	3.4	1.5	30.2	255	273	D	519	0.2
Yellowstone	0.7	2.5	8.0	6.2	9.2	7.3	9.0	18.3	11.6	33,705	202	2,565	73,464	1.9
NEBRASKA	5.6	0.1	6.3	9.8	8.3	5.3	9.4	11.6	15.9	357,164	182	28,920	854,328	1.0
Adams	7.8	0.0	7.1	16.4	3.5	5.3	5.9	D	14.2	6,885	222	561	13,882	0.3
Antelope	36.7	D	17.5	2.8	0.9	2.6	5.2	6.2	9.7	1,585	252	84	3,139	0.7
Arthur	55.4	0.0	D	D	D	D	D	D	15.1	115	262	D	226	0.0
Banner	60.5	0.2	1.6	2.7	0.5	1.9	D	0.0	12.1	250	361	D	326	-0.3

1. Per 1,000 resident population estimated as of July 1 of the year shown.

STATE County	Housing units, 2016–2020: Occupied units: Total	Owner-occupied: Percent	Owner-occupied: Median value[1]	Median owner cost as a percent of income: With a mortgage	Median owner cost as a percent of income: Without a mortgage[2]	Renter-occupied: Median rent[3]	Renter-occupied: Median rent as a percent of income[2]	Sub-standard units[4] (percent)	Civilian labor force, 2021: Total	Percent change, 2020–2021	Unemployment: Total	Unemployment: Rate[5]	Civilian employment[6], 2016–2020: Total	Percent: Management, business, science, and arts	Percent: Construction, production, and maintenance occupations
	89	90	91	92	93	94	95	96	97	98	99	100	101	102	103
MONTANA	436,048	68.5	244,900	22.0	10.7	836	27.7	2.4	549,743	1.3	18,541	3.4	520,043	37.5	22.8
Beaverhead	4,203	63.9	206,900	18.9	10.0	703	30.1	1.9	5,141	1.0	142	2.8	4,536	38.8	23.0
Big Horn	3,622	64.9	150,300	19.0	10.0	669	20.1	15.2	4,669	-4.1	363	7.8	4,871	38.0	21.5
Blaine	2,399	58.2	90,600	19.6	10.3	525	18.8	8.1	2,237	-1.5	86	3.8	2,532	44.1	19.5
Broadwater	2,436	84.3	238,000	23.1	11.3	697	23.7	0.2	2,667	0.6	107	4.0	2,618	36.1	29.4
Carbon	4,524	74.2	271,500	23.2	11.1	787	24.7	1.4	5,662	0.4	194	3.4	5,310	39.1	26.7
Carter	650	68.2	109,400	23.9	10.2	651	24.9	2.6	650	0.5	17	2.6	643	56.0	22.7
Cascade	34,440	66.6	184,400	21.4	10.7	778	28.6	2.1	37,812	-0.3	1,251	3.3	37,118	35.7	22.1
Chouteau	2,301	66.1	155,700	18.7	10.2	375	17.6	1.7	2,459	-0.6	67	2.7	2,533	40.3	25.2
Custer	4,837	67.2	174,500	20.0	10.0	881	24.5	1.6	6,217	-0.1	192	3.1	6,111	35.1	20.7
Daniels	856	78.4	164,700	17.8	12.7	509	18.4	1.3	875	-1.8	17	1.9	872	39.1	26.9
Dawson	3,892	65.8	152,700	20.2	11.0	751	26.0	2.3	4,511	-3.4	140	3.1	4,677	36.2	31.0
Deer Lodge	4,069	67.0	129,100	20.3	10.0	542	27.8	1.0	5,094	0.4	166	3.3	3,977	28.9	19.6
Fallon	1,274	72.1	165,900	16.8	10.0	766	19.3	2.3	1,620	-1.9	42	2.6	1,555	25.3	44.6
Fergus	5,057	70.5	138,700	20.4	11.3	720	25.3	0.9	5,822	-0.5	191	3.3	5,343	32.0	26.6
Flathead	39,925	73.8	294,600	23.1	11.6	884	29.3	3.8	51,167	2.8	2,055	4.0	49,578	35.1	21.5
Gallatin	45,287	61.1	388,000	22.6	10.0	1,131	28.9	1.7	73,887	4.2	1,771	2.4	64,341	42.7	21.7
Garfield	437	68.6	155,300	18.1	10.4	572	19.3	4.1	742	-0.5	19	2.6	562	48.8	20.5
Glacier	4,158	61.7	106,400	21.0	10.0	482	22.6	6.5	5,528	0.4	389	7.0	5,199	36.2	17.6
Golden Valley	361	80.6	107,600	26.9	11.4	827	12.5	2.8	369	1.1	13	3.5	359	35.9	32.6
Granite	1,355	79.0	252,600	27.6	10.0	564	21.0	2.1	1,620	1.2	72	4.4	1,342	37.9	24.0
Hill	6,471	63.4	153,800	19.8	10.0	633	28.0	1.4	7,543	-0.9	235	3.1	7,066	34.8	28.0
Jefferson	4,445	84.2	290,700	22.0	10.0	834	22.2	3.7	5,906	1.3	191	3.2	5,607	46.5	20.8
Judith Basin	915	76.8	154,200	24.9	10.0	547	19.4	1.0	951	-3.4	26	2.7	957	49.9	21.7
Lake	11,869	72.4	278,400	25.9	10.9	744	26.0	2.5	14,006	1.9	534	3.8	13,045	37.0	21.0
Lewis and Clark	28,502	71.8	263,900	20.3	10.8	863	26.6	1.1	37,256	1.4	1,107	3.0	35,500	47.6	16.7
Liberty	925	53.7	101,600	24.6	10.0	580	28.5	0.0	983	1.1	24	2.4	1,191	38.5	24.2
Lincoln	8,622	79.6	197,300	26.6	12.8	729	28.3	2.2	8,100	-0.2	483	6.0	7,213	29.2	30.9
McCone	818	82.6	151,300	25.0	12.0	520	15.4	4.0	968	0.9	17	1.8	917	45.8	32.7
Madison	3,707	77.0	316,900	26.1	11.3	855	27.0	2.3	4,743	1.2	151	3.2	3,996	33.3	26.8
Meagher	759	85.6	170,700	25.9	15.5	581	27.8	0.0	988	3.0	25	2.5	877	36.6	28.8
Mineral	1,926	77.7	194,800	21.8	11.0	606	19.8	2.0	1,871	4.6	99	5.3	1,739	26.6	30.1
Missoula	49,700	58.6	302,200	22.6	12.3	908	29.3	2.5	65,104	0.9	2,184	3.4	66,339	38.4	18.7
Musselshell	2,211	73.1	173,000	24.1	13.2	767	29.7	3.3	2,354	0.6	99	4.2	1,783	26.6	35.4
Park	7,961	68.6	287,800	24.8	11.2	814	25.7	2.5	9,253	2.7	327	3.5	8,675	34.3	26.2
Petroleum	212	65.6	155,700	18.8	14.8	478	26.7	1.4	271	0.0	7	2.6	249	43.4	34.9
Phillips	1,756	79.8	141,600	22.2	10.6	470	20.1	3.2	1,852	-2.3	70	3.8	1,799	30.5	36.3
Pondera	2,079	71.9	138,900	19.8	10.9	671	19.1	3.4	2,633	-1.4	84	3.2	2,564	38.5	22.0
Powder River	748	74.6	135,900	14.7	10.0	717	17.7	0.0	977	1.1	26	2.7	877	39.7	34.8
Powell	2,515	61.9	147,400	20.7	11.0	651	25.0	5.3	2,979	1.7	76	2.6	2,634	36.2	21.8
Prairie	502	79.3	101,000	14.0	12.6	733	37.8	0.0	494	4.9	18	3.6	544	48.2	22.6
Ravalli	17,823	77.4	290,400	24.6	10.0	790	29.9	2.3	21,330	2.3	766	3.6	19,020	34.9	25.8
Richland	4,408	68.6	229,100	17.6	10.0	755	21.4	2.4	5,887	-1.3	236	4.0	5,573	29.6	34.0
Roosevelt	3,248	64.2	103,800	16.2	10.0	531	18.2	4.7	4,330	-2.7	184	4.2	3,856	34.2	24.8
Rosebud	3,237	67.6	115,300	16.5	10.0	590	15.1	7.3	3,575	-4.5	143	4.0	4,014	30.7	34.8
Sanders	5,281	77.1	251,600	25.0	11.3	634	38.0	2.6	5,206	2.3	251	4.8	4,128	32.3	27.1
Sheridan	1,543	75.0	114,800	19.6	12.1	767	21.5	1.5	1,784	1.1	59	3.3	1,650	36.2	26.3
Silver Bow	15,026	69.6	155,300	21.0	11.6	680	28.4	1.2	17,489	0.7	635	3.6	16,221	32.7	22.3
Stillwater	3,840	80.8	256,600	19.9	10.0	800	22.7	1.3	5,499	2.3	159	2.9	4,453	26.7	37.2
Sweet Grass	1,515	73.9	243,300	20.9	11.6	678	21.4	0.8	1,904	2.5	45	2.4	1,781	33.9	34.6
Teton	2,496	72.0	186,300	25.1	11.0	814	29.4	2.9	2,820	1.0	88	3.1	2,729	38.2	26.9
Toole	1,827	62.0	124,600	17.4	10.0	568	24.5	2.7	2,056	-4.3	53	2.6	2,141	36.2	20.4
Treasure	333	71.5	161,800	36.8	12.8	917	27.5	0.0	346	1.5	11	3.2	319	40.4	30.1
Valley	3,324	75.1	150,500	18.9	12.1	586	23.0	0.8	4,044	-1.0	126	3.1	3,512	27.1	29.2
Wheatland	897	72.0	117,300	24.3	10.0	629	22.3	3.1	760	-0.3	40	5.3	879	35.0	31.5
Wibaux	477	79.2	107,600	16.7	11.2	924	13.7	0.6	423	-6.0	16	3.8	509	39.3	25.3
Yellowstone	68,047	68.9	238,700	21.2	10.4	910	28.4	2.3	84,311	0.8	2,657	3.2	81,609	36.3	23.5
NEBRASKA	766,663	66.2	164,000	19.3	11.4	857	26.3	2.2	1,049,033	0.4	26,371	2.5	999,772	38.8	24.1
Adams	12,786	68.1	137,700	18.1	11.7	729	27.9	2.6	16,942	-0.5	403	2.4	16,369	32.4	27.6
Antelope	2,725	75.7	82,100	17.1	10.6	617	22.8	2.5	3,693	-6.1	61	1.7	3,232	35.6	30.9
Arthur	192	70.3	129,200	31.3	11.8	758	35.5	2.1	234	0.0	6	2.6	226	47.8	26.1
Banner	234	69.2	172,900	25.4	10.9	0	31.0	2.6	389	-0.8	8	2.1	325	63.7	20.3

1. Specified owner-occupied units. 2. A value of 10.0 represents 10 percent or less; a value of 50.0 represents 50 percent or more. 3. Specified renter-occupied units. 4. Overcrowded or lacking complete plumbing facilities. 5. Percent of civilian labor force. 6. Civilian employed persons 16 years old and over.

STATE County	Private nonfarm establishments, employment and payroll, 2020									Agriculture, 2017			
		Employment						Annual payroll		Farms			Farm producers whose primary occupation is farming (percent)
											Percent with:		
	Number of establish-ments	Total	Health care and social assistance	Manufac-turing	Retail trade	Finance and insurance	Professional, scientific, and technical services	Total (mil dol)	Average per employee (dollars)	Number	Fewer than 50 acres	1000 acres or more	
	104	105	106	107	108	109	110	111	112	113	114	115	116
MONTANA	39,505	377,638	72,630	20,579	57,604	16,704	20,411	16,540	43,800	27,048	30.9	31.7	48.5
Beaverhead	384	2,579	563	81	453	104	119	90	34,716	494	40.9	30.0	54.7
Big Horn	200	1,857	603	NA	325	60	41	90	48,472	353	19.0	46.2	55.8
Blaine	129	952	250	29	202	42	32	44	46,468	491	7.5	50.7	62.0
Broadwater	175	979	46	289	167	25	38	34	34,328	296	25.3	29.7	50.9
Carbon	428	2,211	326	60	206	59	107	66	29,755	725	28.0	23.7	52.8
Carter	25	59	NA	NA	19	NA	5	3	45,373	323	4.3	71.8	66.0
Cascade	2,429	30,085	7,247	1,252	4,825	1,451	1,189	1,249	41,522	1,027	37.7	22.6	42.1
Chouteau	139	685	196	30	116	56	11	25	35,933	633	4.3	61.5	66.0
Custer	416	4,033	761	83	798	288	92	153	38,009	441	24.3	39.0	48.1
Daniels	75	536	111	NA	88	40	10	25	47,026	277	4.0	54.5	50.7
Dawson	300	2,659	642	41	425	94	69	116	43,746	487	12.3	41.9	48.7
Deer Lodge	287	2,820	1,508	109	306	66	110	135	47,805	77	15.6	22.1	32.6
Fallon	132	991	112	NA	143	31	17	52	52,891	289	13.5	55.4	60.7
Fergus	424	3,296	762	413	432	147	93	134	40,593	845	18.6	48.3	56.3
Flathead	4,464	40,494	7,407	2,868	6,488	1,929	1,728	1,704	42,079	1,146	64.7	4.3	34.3
Gallatin	6,183	51,136	6,313	3,369	8,289	1,470	3,495	2,382	46,585	1,123	57.3	10.1	36.5
Garfield	27	134	9	NA	53	NA	NA	4	30,642	260	3.1	72.7	72.7
Glacier	220	1,778	441	7	432	59	37	78	44,026	637	16.0	31.1	45.1
Golden Valley	13	71	NA	NA	NA	NA	NA	2	22,352	157	10.8	52.2	58.2
Granite	112	606	134	16	110	NA	8	20	33,789	151	17.2	41.7	50.8
Hill	495	4,741	1,309	70	867	244	137	181	38,120	698	9.3	51.0	50.3
Jefferson	309	1,744	281	258	181	42	60	80	45,893	370	37.0	16.8	32.1
Judith Basin	59	257	10	NA	82	29	17	9	34,163	357	13.7	53.5	59.6
Lake	852	6,301	1,237	316	1,129	216	394	250	39,741	1,170	55.7	6.6	43.6
Lewis and Clark	2,443	26,029	6,060	717	3,981	1,549	1,783	1,153	44,305	707	66.1	11.2	32.0
Liberty	68	302	108	NA	30	16	6	10	33,669	246	2.0	75.6	70.4
Lincoln	618	3,867	1,009	202	749	125	82	124	32,067	345	53.0	2.3	39.7
McCone	52	315	61	NA	60	33	NA	14	44,676	437	4.1	59.0	60.1
Madison	383	1,652	202	108	219	74	65	64	38,763	605	29.4	28.4	49.7
Meagher	75	300	68	NA	54	NA	10	9	30,040	145	21.4	60.7	63.5
Mineral	121	781	156	142	212	13	5	25	31,994	93	44.1	4.3	19.9
Missoula	4,610	51,367	9,669	2,404	7,976	2,241	4,215	2,092	40,726	576	66.1	3.6	32.9
Musselshell	110	898	186	11	117	21	24	45	49,671	346	14.5	34.4	54.1
Park	862	5,049	874	527	682	155	191	194	38,367	575	39.8	22.6	46.2
Petroleum	9	13	NA	NA	NA	NA	NA	0	22,615	104	12.5	64.4	68.4
Phillips	132	915	227	37	191	43	26	31	33,827	445	11.5	54.2	58.8
Pondera	172	1,139	236	93	211	67	32	41	36,259	486	14.0	39.9	54.3
Powder River	71	301	6	NA	78	NA	12	9	30,429	325	8.9	64.3	70.5
Powell	161	1,228	264	198	145	31	37	48	39,103	254	24.4	28.7	43.7
Prairie	34	154	NA	NA	24	15	6	5	30,019	179	4.5	65.9	67.0
Ravalli	1,569	9,880	1,888	974	1,700	346	313	366	37,079	1,576	74.6	3.0	39.1
Richland	503	4,691	672	428	530	133	132	234	49,980	527	13.5	50.7	53.2
Roosevelt	215	1,768	411	11	370	83	19	67	37,757	501	7.4	51.9	51.7
Rosebud	175	2,334	307	12	272	59	16	122	52,351	414	15.0	44.4	53.6
Sanders	371	2,373	616	255	346	50	58	75	31,735	521	37.2	9.6	44.3
Sheridan	158	828	216	NA	135	60	24	29	35,597	458	4.6	55.9	67.1
Silver Bow	1,140	13,108	3,104	784	2,041	313	494	540	41,234	142	45.8	11.3	24.9
Stillwater	256	3,125	247	495	288	46	66	247	79,012	562	22.8	28.8	42.0
Sweet Grass	179	1,221	116	67	144	37	18	75	61,021	301	19.3	36.9	45.6
Teton	214	1,032	224	9	133	74	43	38	36,744	686	23.6	26.2	46.5
Toole	164	1,301	236	13	158	46	35	51	38,967	362	4.4	62.7	62.4
Treasure	14	73	NA	NA	12	NA	NA	3	42,247	121	16.5	52.1	62.3
Valley	262	2,128	613	6	306	98	53	81	38,230	557	9.3	48.5	56.1
Wheatland	61	379	105	40	79	20	18	13	33,259	174	11.5	51.1	60.1
Wibaux	28	115	NA	NA	23	NA	3	4	36,817	137	10.2	56.9	54.5
Yellowstone	5,670	71,071	14,370	3,686	10,187	3,851	3,649	3,414	48,041	1,314	45.9	14.5	35.7
NEBRASKA	54,791	866,139	137,942	100,047	107,979	75,735	39,918	41,199	47,566	46,332	23.8	23.8	51.6
Adams	958	12,813	2,524	2,932	1,743	394	240	526	41,080	545	25.1	25.1	61.7
Antelope	222	1,541	295	196	240	82	135	65	42,317	704	20.7	22.2	58.5
Arthur	12	65	NA	NA	NA	NA	NA	2	32,277	95	4.2	63.2	62.9
Banner	6	34	NA	NA	NA	NA	NA	1	41,147	239	6.3	41.4	48.0

STATE County	Agriculture, 2017 (cont.) — Land in farms: Acreage (1,000)	Land in farms: Percent change, 2012–2017	Land in farms — Acres: Average size of farm	Land in farms — Acres: Total irrigated (1,000)	Land in farms — Acres: Total cropland (1,000)	Value of land and buildings (dollars): Average per farm	Value of land and buildings (dollars): Average per acre	Value of machinery and equipment, average per farm (dollars)	Value of products sold: Total (mil dol)	Value of products sold: Average per farm (acres)	Value of products sold — Percent from: Crops	Value of products sold — Percent from: Livestock and poultry products	Organic farms (number)	Farms with internet access (percent)	Government payments: Total ($1,000)	Government payments: Percent of farms
	117	118	119	120	121	122	123	124	125	126	127	128	129	130	131	132
MONTANA	58,123	-2.7	2,149	2,061.2	16,406.3	1,968,381	916	164,524	3,520.6	130,162	45.0	55.0	221	81.4	284,244	38.9
Beaverhead	1,234	-10.7	2,498	263.8	162.8	3,290,191	1,317	201,987	118.2	239,277	31.5	68.5	2	85.6	577	8.5
Big Horn	3,188	1.2	9,032	44.1	223.8	3,546,651	393	218,911	83.6	236,833	39.5	60.5	NA	76.2	2,444	36.5
Blaine	2,040	-7.4	4,155	44.2	599.0	2,460,670	592	215,403	90.0	183,253	44.0	56.0	29	79.0	10,435	63.5
Broadwater	467	-2.1	1,577	47.1	112.5	1,844,915	1,170	166,279	39.7	134,081	56.7	43.3	1	77.4	2,336	44.9
Carbon	816	3.1	1,125	98.8	135.0	1,669,647	1,484	154,004	99.0	136,585	33.4	66.6	NA	82.3	1,388	32.6
Carter	1,768	-0.6	5,473	2.3	247.5	2,943,872	538	270,868	70.6	218,663	8.5	91.5	1	79.6	7,229	68.7
Cascade	1,270	1.2	1,237	35.7	420.0	1,499,361	1,212	134,128	107.3	104,453	47.7	52.3	9	80.2	7,780	42.7
Chouteau	2,071	-0.1	3,271	14.2	1,309.7	3,053,370	933	353,122	170.7	269,733	84.1	15.9	14	84.4	21,813	83.3
Custer	2,089	-4.6	4,737	37.2	118.5	2,539,839	536	170,666	76.6	173,744	15.2	84.8	1	84.1	3,114	37.6
Daniels	770	0.2	2,779	0.6	533.7	1,762,211	634	297,586	42.2	152,300	77.3	22.7	1	78.7	7,683	85.6
Dawson	1,133	-9.9	2,326	21.2	368.1	1,554,263	668	191,646	58.2	119,485	44.0	56.0	NA	74.5	7,569	64.9
Deer Lodge	74	11.3	962	13.1	11.8	1,869,813	1,943	145,035	6.5	84,247	11.3	88.7	NA	68.8	169	14.3
Fallon	902	-7.9	3,121	1.4	191.8	1,883,893	604	196,591	45.3	156,706	15.0	85.0	NA	79.6	3,853	59.9
Fergus	2,188	11.6	2,589	16.3	623.9	2,833,620	1,094	184,680	133.6	158,135	26.9	73.1	2	84.3	12,281	51.8
Flathead	182	7.1	159	22.1	92.5	1,014,016	6,389	64,906	35.9	31,286	76.6	23.4	10	84.7	1,823	10.0
Gallatin	700	-0.3	624	81.3	208.5	1,889,690	3,030	117,382	112.1	99,825	61.6	38.4	11	88.4	3,106	15.9
Garfield	2,215	1.1	8,519	2.8	294.2	3,441,672	404	239,724	54.5	209,765	16.6	83.4	1	79.2	5,608	64.6
Glacier	1,186	-24.5	1,862	27.4	493.8	2,171,691	1,167	151,623	106.5	167,248	54.8	45.2	7	70.3	5,948	34.5
Golden Valley	683	-3.5	4,351	7.3	108.0	2,914,246	670	142,583	18.6	118,478	27.9	72.1	NA	69.4	3,049	65.0
Granite	286	0.1	1,892	31.9	28.9	3,060,313	1,618	143,069	17.9	118,530	16.5	83.5	NA	90.1	268	32.5
Hill	1,616	1.1	2,315	4.1	1,222.3	1,992,745	861	259,353	130.8	187,322	81.9	18.1	12	81.5	20,360	75.9
Jefferson	352	-5.1	952	33.5	57.9	1,619,472	1,702	88,418	20.2	54,497	20.1	79.9	NA	89.7	634	11.6
Judith Basin	860	-16.8	2,409	13.7	278.9	2,237,680	929	226,807	88.9	249,022	28.2	71.8	4	86.0	3,687	58.3
Lake	641	15.4	548	100.4	93.4	880,495	1,606	72,903	64.8	55,381	34.0	66.0	32	82.8	1,442	13.4
Lewis and Clark	801	-5.0	1,132	48.2	78.7	1,479,324	1,306	78,842	43.2	61,085	31.1	68.9	3	86.3	1,081	11.7
Liberty	914	1.7	3,714	7.0	698.8	3,329,506	897	424,336	88.3	358,911	78.2	21.8	6	83.3	10,873	90.7
Lincoln	48	1.1	139	4.9	12.5	727,103	5,250	54,620	3.1	9,017	32.5	67.5	NA	78.8	47	1.2
McCone	1,340	-2.4	3,065	7.3	592.0	1,619,356	528	237,370	61.3	140,222	49.0	51.0	NA	76.4	13,400	80.5
Madison	923	-14.9	1,526	130.3	151.2	2,610,305	1,710	149,921	83.6	138,238	27.6	72.4	NA	81.3	1,458	15.7
Meagher	882	8.6	6,084	52.1	85.2	5,524,417	908	270,602	36.8	253,586	12.1	87.9	NA	71.7	887	26.2
Mineral	18	8.0	198	0.6	5.4	989,976	5,002	42,783	0.6	6,495	37.7	62.3	2	73.1	82	12.9
Missoula	260	5.3	452	15.5	21.6	1,262,721	2,796	42,356	9.8	17,099	57.3	42.7	5	82.8	417	6.1
Musselshell	1,103	8.4	3,189	12.9	145.1	2,038,138	639	140,313	37.3	107,760	20.8	79.2	NA	78.6	2,231	30.1
Park	712	-8.0	1,238	62.0	110.7	3,230,902	2,609	98,425	33.5	58,287	28.1	71.9	1	83.5	935	15.3
Petroleum	593	-14.1	5,698	10.9	84.8	3,863,919	678	194,528	17.8	170,779	18.4	81.6	NA	86.5	861	51.9
Phillips	1,937	-6.3	4,352	31.4	508.8	2,306,077	530	224,289	74.6	167,719	34.0	66.0	17	83.1	9,471	66.1
Pondera	805	-15.9	1,656	69.8	551.1	1,998,397	1,207	272,432	111.5	229,477	68.2	31.8	1	80.7	10,629	69.5
Powder River	1,627	2.4	5,005	16.0	145.7	2,755,267	551	223,710	62.1	191,058	4.9	95.1	1	79.4	2,797	48.3
Powell	572	-2.9	2,253	51.7	58.0	2,917,797	1,295	135,021	31.8	125,370	20.5	79.5	NA	79.5	377	23.2
Prairie	747	-2.8	4,175	14.6	129.8	3,229,966	774	170,306	43.3	241,899	24.9	75.1	1	78.2	4,610	77.7
Ravalli	241	2.7	153	71.0	52.1	877,618	5,734	54,698	42.7	27,070	29.8	70.2	8	84.5	245	3.9
Richland	1,270	-1.8	2,410	53.5	479.5	2,112,650	877	242,969	100.1	189,949	55.3	44.7	8	79.5	10,227	66.6
Roosevelt	1,307	5.5	2,610	24.3	757.3	1,883,016	722	268,384	64.1	128,004	69.4	30.6	2	76.6	13,696	76.2
Rosebud	2,732	-13.0	6,600	38.7	169.8	2,835,966	430	161,371	86.6	209,271	19.6	80.4	NA	78.7	3,759	34.1
Sanders	643	89.7	1,233	21.5	43.3	1,219,226	988	65,694	16.9	32,457	30.6	69.4	8	76.4	570	8.6
Sheridan	1,064	2.1	2,323	4.6	786.1	1,611,743	694	443,294	70.6	154,083	82.8	17.2	3	86.2	11,702	80.6
Silver Bow	60	-13.5	425	2.4	3.7	956,028	2,251	52,803	2.7	19,218	20.7	79.3	NA	78.9	NA	NA
Stillwater	763	-5.8	1,357	23.2	175.7	1,823,923	1,344	103,840	51.5	91,557	30.4	69.6	NA	79.0	4,175	40.0
Sweet Grass	826	-3.5	2,745	38.8	57.2	3,117,975	1,136	121,775	25.7	85,375	12.2	87.8	NA	84.7	617	19.6
Teton	887	-9.0	1,294	93.8	460.1	1,533,701	1,186	159,196	107.2	156,277	64.1	35.9	8	82.4	8,367	57.0
Toole	1,095	-3.0	3,025	5.3	734.5	2,653,458	877	280,722	84.2	232,547	79.5	20.5	4	77.1	11,549	82.9
Treasure	614	-0.6	5,076	36.6	55.8	2,934,450	578	340,275	45.0	372,116	60.1	39.9	NA	77.7	1,197	47.1
Valley	1,630	-0.3	2,926	45.1	779.2	1,883,822	644	274,232	96.6	173,345	55.2	44.8	3	74.0	13,469	74.9
Wheatland	860	-1.6	4,944	23.0	138.8	3,425,165	693	199,401	43.1	247,718	20.3	79.7	NA	77.6	2,221	50.6
Wibaux	515	-5.5	3,762	2.9	98.3	2,321,989	617	224,104	18.0	131,467	31.0	69.0	NA	77.4	2,083	83.2
Yellowstone	1,603	-3.9	1,220	76.8	299.0	1,223,832	1,003	104,007	135.3	102,958	31.8	68.2	3	83.0	5,615	22.5
NEBRASKA	44,987	-0.8	971	8,588.4	22,242.6	2,674,492	2,754	268,968	21,983.4	474,476	42.4	57.6	292	81.3	639,975	66.6
Adams	340	-0.2	624	237.0	300.5	3,321,098	5,323	366,765	392.5	720,206	44.2	55.8	5	88.4	11,978	69.9
Antelope	492	3.6	699	255.3	364.4	3,205,709	4,588	385,363	529.5	752,134	36.3	63.7	4	86.5	10,289	72.4
Arthur	453	0.0	4,766	8.7	31.7	3,817,883	801	169,891	27.5	289,632	8.7	91.3	NA	89.5	506	25.3
Banner	423	0.2	1,770	26.1	191.2	1,543,874	872	205,818	100.5	420,540	20.7	79.3	12	83.7	4,845	80.3

STATE County	Water use, 2015		Wholesale Trade[1], 2017				Retail Trade[2], 2017				Real estate and rental and leasing,[2] 2017			
	Public supply water withdrawn (mil gal/ day)	Public supply gallons withdrawn per person per day	Number of establish-ments	Number of employees	Sales (mil dol)	Average payroll (mil dol)	Number of establish-ments	Number of employees	Sales (mil dol)	Average payroll (mil dol)	Number of establish-ments	Number of employees	Sales (mil dol)	Average payroll (mil dol)
	133	134	135	136	137	138	139	140	141	142	143	144	145	146
MONTANA	153.2	148.3	1,366	13,078	11,214.5	677.3	4,754	59,032	16,935.8	1,622.6	2,036	5,951	1,144.6	205.6
Beaverhead	1.8	195.7	13	74	41.2	2.9	48	512	146.0	10.8	19	122	14.0	4.9
Big Horn	1.2	91.4	8	35	20.3	1.6	40	372	110.3	9.1	8	15	1.6	0.4
Blaine	0.9	141.4	10	D	72.8	D	22	186	41.3	4.0	NA	NA	NA	NA
Broadwater	1.0	181.1	5	D	15.4	D	17	154	74.3	3.7	D	D	D	0.1
Carbon	1.8	169.1	15	64	22.7	2.1	D	D	D	D	16	23	2.2	0.5
Carter	0.0	33.9	NA	NA	NA	NA	5	33	17.2	0.9	NA	NA	NA	NA
Cascade	12.8	155.4	116	1,152	722.0	54.0	362	5,326	1,439.0	139.0	123	412	82.2	13.8
Chouteau	0.9	152.6	15	102	280.6	5.4	23	145	54.6	5.1	5	D	1.2	D
Custer	1.4	114.5	D	D	D	D	58	799	236.8	23.5	17	37	4.5	1.0
Daniels	0.2	119.3	5	D	28.2	D	13	97	49.1	3.3	NA	NA	NA	NA
Dawson	1.8	181.8	20	185	184.4	10.5	41	454	122.9	11.9	12	41	5.9	1.7
Deer Lodge	2.3	251.7	NA	NA	NA	NA	30	276	73.8	6.4	7	16	1.6	0.3
Fallon	0.3	87.8	8	56	42.8	3.9	15	137	30.9	3.3	D	D	D	0.1
Fergus	1.1	92.8	18	162	1,033.7	9.6	59	519	157.6	12.4	19	61	9.1	1.4
Flathead	11.4	118.9	110	956	831.0	45.0	480	6,285	1,880.1	180.8	260	834	135.9	24.2
Gallatin	11.9	118.4	149	1,422	786.5	71.1	594	7,885	2,314.2	237.4	429	1,180	248.5	40.9
Garfield	0.0	30.4	NA	NA	NA	NA	5	58	13.5	1.5	NA	NA	NA	NA
Glacier	1.8	129.0	9	44	69.6	2.1	44	447	145.3	11.9	D	D	D	0.1
Golden Valley	0.0	48.4	NA	NA	NA	NA	NA	NA	NA	NA	NA	NA	NA	NA
Granite	0.1	15.4	4	20	6.4	0.8	17	104	34.9	2.4	4	D	0.6	D
Hill	2.2	129.7	28	248	261.2	11.3	80	1,042	266.8	26.5	27	85	8.6	1.9
Jefferson	1.3	109.9	9	21	5.1	0.4	24	168	40.1	3.1	9	19	1.3	0.4
Judith Basin	0.1	46.7	6	D	21.0	D	6	28	7.1	0.6	NA	NA	NA	NA
Lake	2.4	81.1	18	123	31.9	5.6	110	1,160	288.9	31.5	D	D	D	1.2
Lewis and Clark	7.9	119.4	56	459	330.6	19.8	278	3,879	1,100.4	107.2	122	291	69.5	10.9
Liberty	0.2	91.4	9	D	112.0	D	14	83	11.0	1.3	NA	NA	NA	NA
Lincoln	2.3	119.7	D	D	D	0.8	84	676	167.5	16.7	24	47	6.7	1.0
McCone	0.1	47.5	D	D	D	D	8	62	16.7	1.6	NA	NA	NA	NA
Madison	1.1	139.0	4	14	34.4	1.0	41	213	68.3	5.4	D	D	D	D
Meagher	0.2	131.1	NA	NA	NA	NA	12	64	13.4	1.0	NA	NA	NA	NA
Mineral	0.3	77.6	NA	NA	NA	NA	17	245	51.6	4.8	3	3	0.4	0.1
Missoula	30.4	266.3	152	1,774	1,059.9	93.6	569	8,373	2,360.2	228.3	252	902	178.0	31.0
Musselshell	0.3	54.6	7	29	11.2	0.9	18	114	40.7	2.7	NA	NA	NA	NA
Park	2.4	151.5	12	57	46.1	2.4	94	744	207.6	22.7	37	39	12.3	1.5
Petroleum	0.0	21.1	NA	NA	NA	NA	D	D	D	0.1	NA	NA	NA	NA
Phillips	0.5	112.7	3	50	32.5	1.7	23	202	43.9	4.6	5	D	1.1	D
Pondera	0.8	135.8	13	144	103.1	5.7	28	252	58.2	5.5	NA	NA	NA	NA
Powder River	0.1	45.1	D	D	D	D	10	88	19.9	2.1	NA	NA	NA	NA
Powell	1.4	200.3	NA	NA	NA	NA	13	155	53.7	3.8	8	D	1.5	D
Prairie	0.0	8.6	NA	NA	NA	NA	5	D	6.9	D	NA	NA	NA	NA
Ravalli	3.3	78.6	45	169	212.8	8.3	162	1,642	368.0	37.7	65	148	20.4	3.8
Richland	1.2	98.7	21	158	370.8	8.9	54	596	164.6	16.8	21	104	26.2	6.9
Roosevelt	1.7	149.9	9	79	185.3	5.0	39	439	120.7	11.0	5	13	1.2	0.4
Rosebud	1.5	161.7	NA	NA	NA	NA	27	306	65.1	5.2	D	D	D	0.7
Sanders	0.7	62.6	10	21	20.7	0.8	50	330	80.9	7.1	13	D	2.2	D
Sheridan	0.0	10.8	6	D	86.5	D	20	165	39.7	4.4	5	D	0.2	D
Silver Bow	7.7	223.3	D	D	D	D	162	2,175	573.3	54.5	57	156	20.4	3.9
Stillwater	0.4	40.1	D	D	D	1.7	28	240	80.6	5.3	6	D	1.8	D
Sweet Grass	0.5	140.3	3	10	2.5	0.2	24	163	43.9	4.0	8	D	1.9	D
Teton	1.1	185.1	16	91	80.5	3.5	28	174	50.7	5.0	5	D	1.0	D
Toole	1.2	237.9	13	60	153.4	4.4	27	186	67.8	4.1	D	D	D	0.3
Treasure	0.1	100.4	NA	NA	NA	NA	D	D	D	D	NA	NA	NA	NA
Valley	1.6	210.2	12	188	183.1	9.9	47	333	137.6	9.1	6	12	1.7	0.4
Wheatland	0.3	151.7	NA	NA	NA	NA	8	89	14.4	1.5	NA	NA	NA	NA
Wibaux	0.1	61.9	NA	NA	NA	NA	4	22	4.5	0.5	NA	NA	NA	NA
Yellowstone	25.1	159.8	322	4,277	3,090.8	247.3	715	10,550	3,296.5	312.8	334	1,149	251.1	48.0
NEBRASKA	275.2	145.1	2,782	35,143	39,908.6	1,964.7	7,154	109,729	31,214.7	2,853.4	2,354	11,293	2,291.9	486.8
Adams	6.5	205.8	D	D	D	36.7	141	1,936	499.2	50.7	48	111	24.1	3.2
Antelope	0.7	104.5	26	276	431.4	14.2	32	243	57.3	5.0	4	D	0.5	D
Arthur	0.0	0.0	NA	NA	NA	NA	NA	NA	NA	NA	NA	NA	NA	NA
Banner	0.0	25.4	NA	NA	NA	NA	NA	NA	NA	NA	NA	NA	NA	NA

1 Merchant wholesalers, except manufacturers' sales branches and offices. 2. Employer establishments.

Table B. States and Counties — **Professional Services, Manufacturing, and Accommodation and Food Services**

STATE County	Professional, scientific, and technical services, 2017				Manufacturing, 2017				Accommodation and food services, 2017			
	Number of establish-ments	Number of employees	Sales (mil dol)	Average payroll (mil dol)	Number of establish-ments	Number of employees	Sales (mil dol)	Average payroll (mil dol)	Number of establis-hments	Number of employees	Sales (mil dol)	Annual payroll (mil dol)
	147	148	149	150	151	152	153	154	155	156	157	158
MONTANA	3,790	17,429	2,482.7	921.1	1,328	17,944	10,943.6	935.7	3,568	52,415	3,126.0	898.6
Beaverhead	D	D	D	D	14	63	10.3	2.1	51	404	22.0	6.2
Big Horn	15	59	5.3	2.0	NA	NA	NA	NA	24	196	16.4	3.8
Blaine	13	37	5.4	2.0	6	10	3.8	0.4	10	D	1.9	D
Broadwater	9	33	3.2	0.9	D	D	D	D	23	168	8.0	2.2
Carbon	D	D	D	D	12	45	7.6	1.5	60	531	35.5	9.6
Carter	D	D	0.4	D	NA	NA	NA	NA	5	D	0.9	D
Cascade	D	D	D	D	74	1,318	1,377.7	71.3	239	3,989	222.4	63.5
Chouteau	10	12	1.2	0.3	7	19	3.6	0.8	15	D	4.0	D
Custer	34	87	8.5	3.4	21	64	49.4	2.5	D	D	D	D
Daniels	4	13	1.3	0.3	NA	NA	NA	NA	8	D	1.9	D
Dawson	23	55	5.6	3.0	4	37	6.2	1.6	34	342	17.6	4.9
Deer Lodge	22	103	27.1	6.1	D	106	D	4.5	31	269	12.1	3.0
Fallon	D	D	D	0.7	NA	NA	NA	NA	16	79	5.9	1.3
Fergus	30	77	7.6	2.5	24	294	83.8	15.2	41	442	18.8	5.9
Flathead	D	D	D	D	173	2,688	726.9	145.2	380	5,398	352.9	97.6
Gallatin	765	2,962	472.6	171.5	237	3,101	728.1	136.7	470	8,695	564.7	163.7
Garfield	NA	NA	NA	NA	NA	NA	NA	NA	4	D	1.5	D
Glacier	D	D	D	D	3	5	1.1	0.2	43	638	67.2	17.7
Golden Valley	NA	NA	NA	NA	NA	NA	NA	NA	4	14	1.0	0.1
Granite	7	7	3.1	0.6	6	15	2.7	0.5	17	188	20.4	7.3
Hill	D	D	D	D	13	24	3.5	1.1	53	811	45.1	14.4
Jefferson	32	57	9.0	3.0	10	238	187.2	15.4	24	252	9.1	2.9
Judith Basin	4	11	2.1	0.4	NA	NA	NA	NA	7	D	1.7	D
Lake	D	D	D	D	37	330	60.5	11.9	87	796	46.9	14.2
Lewis and Clark	249	1,567	220.3	87.6	57	686	96.0	30.1	206	3,334	180.4	53.4
Liberty	4	7	0.4	0.2	NA	NA	NA	NA	4	34	1.0	0.3
Lincoln	36	92	8.5	2.8	23	195	27.9	5.8	68	575	35.5	10.1
McCone	NA	NA	NA	NA	NA	NA	NA	NA	5	D	2.3	D
Madison	32	54	11.7	2.7	13	78	9.4	3.0	60	281	28.4	7.2
Meagher	D	D	D	0.1	NA	NA	NA	NA	14	D	4.5	D
Mineral	6	17	0.9	0.3	7	290	78.2	12.4	18	124	7.7	1.9
Missoula	553	3,053	370.1	153.3	133	1,751	521.0	75.8	365	7,110	394.6	115.0
Musselshell	9	32	2.1	0.6	4	9	2.2	0.5	9	D	2.1	D
Park	74	176	19.1	7.1	29	441	76.3	19.5	123	1,269	107.6	30.9
Petroleum	NA	NA	NA	NA	NA	NA	NA	NA	NA	NA	NA	NA
Phillips	10	32	3.9	1.0	NA	NA	NA	NA	21	140	6.9	1.7
Pondera	12	31	2.7	1.2	10	65	63.9	3.0	15	104	3.8	0.9
Powder River	D	D	2.9	D	NA	NA	NA	NA	6	D	2.4	D
Powell	10	38	5.0	1.7	D	164	D	D	24	152	7.2	2.3
Prairie	NA	NA	NA	NA	NA	NA	NA	NA	4	D	0.4	D
Ravalli	D	D	D	D	88	872	155.1	42.7	89	943	49.6	15.3
Richland	37	133	20.9	8.3	13	335	183.9	19.8	47	580	27.6	9.4
Roosevelt	12	26	2.8	0.6	4	27	3.3	1.0	D	D	D	D
Rosebud	5	15	1.9	0.3	NA	NA	NA	NA	31	206	9.4	2.2
Sanders	25	39	2.9	1.2	21	180	44.8	8.9	45	395	21.3	6.1
Sheridan	9	30	2.9	1.2	NA	NA	NA	NA	18	117	6.3	1.6
Silver Bow	D	D	D	D	40	495	196.1	29.8	137	2,184	114.3	35.8
Stillwater	25	42	5.4	1.7	D	367	D	25.7	20	159	10.4	2.7
Sweet Grass	14	27	2.8	0.8	10	58	7.9	2.1	21	158	9.0	2.5
Teton	D	D	D	1.4	D	9	D	0.4	D	D	D	1.7
Toole	8	29	3.9	1.3	D	15	D	D	20	236	10.5	2.5
Treasure	D	D	D	D	NA	NA	NA	NA	NA	NA	NA	NA
Valley	D	D	D	D	6	36	3.6	0.9	31	372	18.8	5.5
Wheatland	4	15	2.2	0.4	4	16	0.8	0.3	9	D	1.8	D
Wibaux	D	D	1.1	D	NA	NA	NA	NA	D	D	D	0.5
Yellowstone	D	D	D	237.9	171	3,315	5,401.4	228.4	416	9,245	532.5	152.8
NEBRASKA	4,678	39,177	6,230.4	2,340.0	1,760	93,510	53,129.3	4,728.4	4,621	76,386	3,957.8	1,135.9
Adams	62	301	32.9	12.1	57	2,494	1,908.3	113.1	86	1,435	67.0	17.3
Antelope	11	25	3.9	0.8	10	209	59.9	9.5	11	49	1.9	0.5
Arthur	NA	NA	NA	NA	NA	NA	NA	NA	NA	NA	NA	NA
Banner	NA	NA	NA	NA	NA	NA	NA	NA	NA	NA	NA	NA

Table B. States and Counties — **Health Care and Social Assistance, Other Services, Nonemployer Businesses, and Residential Construction**

STATE County	Health care and social assistance, 2017				Other services, 2017				Nonemployer businesses, 2019		Value of residential construction authorized by building permits, 2021	
	Number of establish-ments	Number of employees	Receipts (mil dol)	Annual payroll (mil dol)	Number of establish-ments	Number of employees	Receipts (mil dol)	Annual payroll (mil dol)	Number	Receipts (mil dol)	New construction ($1,000)	Number of housing units
	159	160	161	162	163	164	165	166	167	168	169	170
MONTANA	3,716	73,254	8,447.9	3,303.9	2,409	12,077	1,608.6	403.0	96,566	4,708.3	0	0
Beaverhead	38	517	45.7	16.9	25	74	6.7	1.7	1,003	41.8	10,957	46
Big Horn	19	622	96.6	38.7	D	D	D	D	466	17.9	0	0
Blaine	16	273	50.0	20.0	10	41	4.6	0.8	317	8.8	308	1
Broadwater	9	D	10.0	D	D	D	3.9	D	614	33.9	0	0
Carbon	D	D	D	D	D	D	D	D	1,290	63.3	21,111	62
Carter	NA	NA	NA	NA	NA	NA	NA	NA	125	7.1	0	0
Cascade	285	6,971	802.3	322.9	155	941	105.1	29.9	4,890	220.0	55,622	272
Chouteau	9	D	6.2	D	D	D	0.7	D	391	11.4	4,755	17
Custer	49	928	95.8	34.5	20	97	12.1	3.5	879	40.0	0	0
Daniels	7	D	8.5	D	D	D	D	0.7	128	5.8	71	1
Dawson	30	647	58.1	26.1	25	92	11.7	2.7	622	24.9	0	0
Deer Lodge	47	1,551	184.8	78.1	12	43	4.6	1.3	524	18.8	6,172	21
Fallon	4	121	13.6	5.2	8	23	2.7	0.5	292	13.2	615	2
Fergus	46	1,091	85.7	40.6	35	160	16.0	2.8	1,038	42.1	1,765	4
Flathead	380	7,578	870.8	379.2	257	1,108	117.8	31.8	12,078	626.3	260,886	1,116
Gallatin	428	5,578	631.9	230.6	315	1,681	258.4	62.9	14,266	775.8	474,006	2,475
Garfield	3	6	0.4	0.1	NA	NA	NA	NA	126	5.8	0	0
Glacier	18	455	65.9	27.2	14	67	8.5	2.4	715	19.2	0	0
Golden Valley	NA	NA	NA	NA	NA	NA	NA	NA	81	3.7	NA	NA
Granite	D	D	D	D	D	D	0.6	D	379	21.0	NA	NA
Hill	56	1,342	121.8	50.0	39	155	20.2	4.1	889	29.3	475	3
Jefferson	26	287	18.2	7.2	10	35	5.4	1.2	1,155	50.8	2,170	8
Judith Basin	3	3	0.1	0.0	NA	NA	NA	NA	200	8.2	NA	NA
Lake	86	1,338	128.9	51.1	50	159	14.8	3.9	2,629	114.4	11,520	33
Lewis and Clark	288	6,098	809.4	294.9	213	1,193	163.5	50.9	5,871	292.4	43,145	212
Liberty	D	D	D	D	3	5	0.6	0.1	136	5.1	NA	NA
Lincoln	56	1,207	92.6	38.3	37	107	10.7	2.5	1,796	73.2	2,064	17
McCone	D	D	D	D	NA	NA	NA	NA	153	6.9	0	0
Madison	24	208	16.9	8.0	21	79	11.4	2.2	1,160	61.9	2,349	9
Meagher	D	D	D	D	4	4	1.4	0.1	195	7.1	NA	NA
Mineral	11	106	7.8	3.5	4	5	0.8	0.1	391	13.5	0	0
Missoula	512	10,122	1,190.9	412.7	312	2,257	362.1	79.5	11,302	554.0	264,603	1,798
Musselshell	11	D	16.1	D	D	D	1.8	D	381	16.2	308	1
Park	58	864	90.8	38.7	50	196	20.7	5.6	2,303	99.4	7,345	37
Petroleum	NA	NA	NA	NA	NA	NA	NA	NA	44	2.8	NA	NA
Phillips	10	184	13.9	5.7	15	34	3.4	0.9	382	11.7	0	0
Pondera	20	276	22.3	9.1	8	19	2.1	0.4	440	17.8	0	0
Powder River	NA	NA	NA	NA	D	D	D	1.1	180	7.3	NA	NA
Powell	18	226	23.3	9.7	D	D	D	D	493	19.2	12,301	40
Prairie	NA	NA	NA	NA	NA	NA	NA	NA	98	3.2	NA	NA
Ravalli	137	1,674	147.4	64.1	82	278	26.8	7.3	4,929	247.9	18,363	75
Richland	38	620	70.9	27.9	32	116	23.4	4.0	933	51.6	2,295	17
Roosevelt	13	D	42.2	D	15	59	5.1	1.1	463	18.5	0	0
Rosebud	12	216	12.9	7.2	D	D	5.0	D	427	13.2	0	0
Sanders	42	498	38.2	15.5	15	62	7.2	1.9	1,180	57.5	NA	NA
Sheridan	12	271	15.3	7.1	D	D	4.3	D	305	14.6	124	1
Silver Bow	169	3,114	295.5	113.6	65	277	38.2	8.1	2,293	111.2	9,057	72
Stillwater	19	269	19.2	7.7	D	D	5.5	D	894	38.0	0	0
Sweet Grass	7	D	8.9	D	D	D	3.2	D	480	21.0	100	1
Teton	18	217	14.7	5.6	7	12	1.0	0.3	638	30.1	740	4
Toole	12	225	19.5	8.7	7	23	1.5	0.3	300	13.3	88	1
Treasure	NA	NA	NA	NA	NA	NA	NA	NA	56	2.7	NA	NA
Valley	28	548	52.1	22.7	17	57	5.9	1.6	529	18.7	1,161	9
Wheatland	D	D	D	D	D	D	D	0.1	143	5.2	NA	NA
Wibaux	NA	NA	NA	NA	NA	NA	NA	NA	84	5.4	0	0
Yellowstone	582	14,657	2,069.9	808.5	397	2,244	286.8	76.5	12,490	664.4	196,725	917
NEBRASKA	5,817	135,691	16,060.4	6,116.9	4,107	21,757	3,608.2	701.0	140,567	6,531.7	2,016,001	10,723
Adams	107	2,893	323.8	136.2	52	229	26.8	5.8	2,193	98.2	9,532	37
Antelope	17	335	25.6	11.2	D	D	D	0.8	680	33.8	4,350	18
Arthur	NA	NA	NA	NA	NA	NA	NA	NA	52	2.5	NA	NA
Banner	NA	NA	NA	NA	NA	NA	NA	NA	51	2.5	NA	NA

STATE County	Government employment and payroll, 2017									Local government finances, 2017				
			March payroll (percent of total)							General revenue				
												Taxes		
													Per capita[1] (dollars)	
	Full-time equivalent employees	March payroll (dollars)	Adminis-tration, judicial, and legal	Police and corrections	Fire protection	Highways and transpor-tation	Health and welfare	Natural resources and utilities	Education and libraries	Total (mil dol)	Inter-govern-mental (mil dol)	Total (mil dol)	Total	Property
	171	172	173	174	175	176	177	178	179	180	181	182	183	184
MONTANA	X	X	X	X	X	X	X	X	X	X	X	X	X	X
Beaverhead	298	1,044,238	13.3	8.3	0.7	4.7	1.1	5.9	64.6	65.9	13.5	11.6	1,227	1,182
Big Horn	658	2,554,319	5.8	5.0	0.0	3.6	6.2	2.6	75.4	68.3	41.6	17.9	1,328	1,320
Blaine	374	1,432,727	6.6	4.4	0.5	4.9	1.1	2.9	78.7	35.4	20.8	9.9	1,461	1,451
Broadwater	168	569,372	12.7	10.2	0.6	3.2	3.1	6.0	59.1	21.3	5.2	6.6	1,119	1,111
Carbon	405	1,434,878	11.1	9.4	1.2	6.2	0.5	3.6	65.6	43.9	14.4	19.4	1,815	1,718
Carter	29	101,518	12.1	13.9	0.0	25.2	2.5	4.7	9.7	10.5	3.0	6.8	5,540	5,536
Cascade	2,747	10,563,299	7.1	12.7	4.0	6.0	4.7	5.1	59.8	271.4	111.1	93.2	1,142	1,106
Chouteau	314	1,113,787	6.9	7.2	0.0	4.8	25.8	2.9	50.2	28.6	7.6	12.0	2,090	2,083
Custer	525	2,138,175	7.1	6.8	3.3	3.5	0.5	3.5	75.1	45.3	20.3	13.7	1,170	1,142
Daniels	110	385,999	15.9	5.2	0.0	7.1	3.6	7.1	55.3	14.0	3.5	4.0	2,348	2,327
Dawson	511	1,742,612	7.8	16.9	2.1	5.5	6.3	4.8	54.3	47.8	17.5	14.7	1,646	1,638
Deer Lodge	296	1,144,779	10.6	17.9	3.7	3.5	5.4	3.0	53.8	36.1	16.0	13.6	1,494	1,484
Fallon	208	918,812	13.3	7.4	0.0	10.9	4.6	8.3	50.2	25.8	11.2	8.0	2,663	2,629
Fergus	514	1,719,722	7.8	9.1	2.4	4.8	2.2	3.7	68.7	45.2	19.7	18.5	1,638	1,624
Flathead	2,793	11,502,242	6.7	8.3	3.1	4.9	4.6	5.0	66.1	328.7	128.2	127.4	1,273	1,213
Gallatin	2,808	11,950,725	7.4	9.3	4.1	2.2	3.3	5.7	64.1	344.5	100.5	161.4	1,486	1,374
Garfield	97	242,697	18.2	4.7	0.5	7.8	20.4	2.7	44.2	7.9	2.8	2.5	1,980	1,980
Glacier	609	2,218,362	4.3	4.5	0.1	5.7	0.9	3.9	78.0	61.8	38.7	16.7	1,213	1,204
Golden Valley	62	190,453	13.6	2.8	0.2	0.5	0.0	0.2	81.9	4.4	1.8	2.0	2,471	2,471
Granite	167	611,424	10.2	4.8	0.0	4.7	32.0	4.5	41.8	11.4	4.6	5.0	1,479	1,477
Hill	748	2,806,106	4.5	7.7	2.9	4.2	2.1	5.5	72.1	80.4	46.3	24.0	1,459	1,446
Jefferson	306	1,127,486	13.8	9.7	0.2	4.3	2.6	3.7	62.4	37.0	15.1	17.2	1,440	1,430
Judith Basin	127	400,014	7.8	4.1	0.1	15.6	0.1	0.9	69.4	10.4	3.5	5.1	2,620	2,620
Lake	1,024	3,728,543	6.0	7.2	0.4	2.1	1.7	4.3	75.2	89.9	44.1	34.1	1,130	1,103
Lewis and Clark	1,948	8,463,467	8.6	10.1	2.7	3.8	6.3	5.1	60.7	226.4	92.7	82.2	1,211	1,178
Liberty	115	395,871	11.5	8.8	0.2	6.8	4.1	6.3	58.9	11.9	3.5	6.0	2,503	2,445
Lincoln	531	1,926,072	11.0	7.2	0.6	3.6	2.6	4.9	66.1	48.0	22.6	17.5	893	883
McCone	168	381,253	15.9	5.1	0.1	1.3	2.0	1.5	42.2	10.1	4.2	4.8	2,852	2,839
Madison	471	1,526,402	5.8	4.4	0.5	3.1	43.8	3.4	38.5	39.9	11.0	19.7	2,377	2,355
Meagher	85	260,367	14.8	10.8	1.5	5.0	0.5	9.6	53.5	12.1	2.8	7.1	3,826	3,816
Mineral	266	899,835	7.1	5.3	0.2	2.5	33.2	0.7	48.6	22.4	7.1	6.5	1,535	1,480
Missoula	3,480	14,645,116	8.3	11.5	6.5	6.6	8.7	4.2	51.1	389.1	154.0	168.3	1,428	1,378
Musselshell	194	610,621	8.8	9.8	0.0	5.6	1.6	3.1	67.6	15.7	7.2	6.8	1,458	1,457
Park	536	1,963,411	9.2	9.4	5.2	3.0	3.1	6.1	63.7	54.5	21.7	21.1	1,288	1,231
Petroleum	44	170,919	6.1	2.4	0.0	3.9	0.0	7.4	80.2	3.5	1.6	1.0	1,922	1,920
Phillips	229	720,323	8.7	5.9	0.1	7.5	1.3	8.7	65.4	16.2	8.3	5.7	1,395	1,381
Pondera	226	800,158	8.9	8.9	0.0	5.7	0.9	5.8	67.5	43.4	13.4	10.3	1,722	1,566
Powder River	167	522,249	10.5	5.0	0.0	11.9	34.1	2.8	31.1	15.0	7.1	3.9	2,239	2,238
Powell	235	795,317	10.1	7.0	0.4	5.1	0.2	5.3	69.4	24.6	12.6	8.1	1,189	1,179
Prairie	104	286,187	7.4	3.7	0.0	6.5	29.1	4.8	42.8	9.5	2.5	2.4	2,145	2,126
Ravalli	1,163	3,979,716	7.6	8.6	0.1	1.4	1.1	2.6	76.7	99.6	49.5	37.5	882	868
Richland	626	2,170,542	9.0	10.8	0.2	9.1	5.9	9.4	53.0	67.9	32.8	14.5	1,314	1,308
Roosevelt	689	2,517,688	5.6	5.9	0.0	3.4	10.9	3.5	68.8	71.6	48.4	14.2	1,275	1,265
Rosebud	654	2,223,967	7.1	8.0	0.1	6.4	3.7	5.9	67.7	68.5	28.9	22.8	2,471	2,468
Sanders	391	1,371,035	8.2	8.8	0.1	5.0	0.7	4.7	70.6	35.3	14.6	16.1	1,377	1,362
Sheridan	255	1,363,756	7.0	4.1	0.3	6.0	31.4	1.6	46.4	20.7	8.3	8.0	2,313	2,309
Silver Bow	1,023	4,334,062	8.0	12.4	9.6	8.2	2.6	11.0	46.5	117.4	45.0	44.7	1,285	1,255
Stillwater	356	1,292,795	8.5	9.0	0.7	5.7	0.6	5.2	69.3	34.5	15.1	15.0	1,594	1,583
Sweet Grass	150	557,685	17.8	12.6	0.1	7.8	0.2	2.5	58.4	24.1	5.7	7.2	1,963	1,961
Teton	371	1,234,432	7.8	4.2	0.2	4.1	9.7	9.2	63.9	37.4	11.4	10.3	1,697	1,680
Toole	327	1,163,779	9.9	6.7	0.1	5.3	30.1	3.9	42.4	37.3	7.8	9.0	1,843	1,837
Treasure	36	115,623	14.2	3.5	0.0	5.7	0.5	7.7	63.6	3.6	1.4	1.9	2,890	2,813
Valley	410	1,411,240	6.8	9.9	0.0	7.6	3.3	6.3	64.5	39.9	15.1	16.9	2,279	2,196
Wheatland	149	476,915	22.0	6.6	0.0	14.6	3.5	5.1	44.5	12.7	5.5	5.5	2,538	2,536
Wibaux	88	333,672	15.7	5.3	0.0	13.0	4.6	1.0	59.6	9.8	2.9	6.1	5,968	5,828
Yellowstone	4,728	21,645,773	5.8	9.5	4.6	4.1	8.5	6.5	56.2	569.1	199.2	204.1	1,282	1,191
NEBRASKA	X	X	X	X	X	X	X	X	X	X	X	X	X	X
Adams	2,059	9,251,437	3.5	4.4	1.6	2.6	0.0	16.2	65.1	371.8	61.4	104.8	3,294	2,886
Antelope	446	1,495,755	4.0	6.2	0.0	5.4	0.6	3.0	80.3	38.4	10.2	24.9	3,929	3,553
Arthur	51	187,013	5.1	1.8	0.0	3.3	0.0	25.0	64.6	9.6	1.1	8.3	18,273	11,123
Banner	70	220,174	9.5	1.8	0.0	8.0	0.0	0.0	79.2	5.8	1.6	3.9	5,427	5,222

1. Based on the resident population estimated as of July 1 of the year shown.

STATE County	Local government finances, 2017 (cont.)									Government employment, 2020			Individual income tax returns, 2019		
	Direct general expenditure							Debt outstanding							
			Percent of total for:												
	Total (mil dol)	Per capita[1] (dollars)	Education	Health and hospitals	Police protection	Public welfare	Highways	Total (mil dol)	Per capita[1] (dollars)	Federal civilian	Federal military	State and local	Number of returns	Mean adjusted gross income	Mean income tax
	185	186	187	188	189	190	191	192	193	194	195	196	197	198	199
MONTANA	X	X	X	X	X	X	X	X	X	13,682	7,998	73,775	529,690	63,924	6,970
Beaverhead	63.5	6,719	25.0	48.2	4.2	0.4	3.9	84.4	8,934	193	39	816	4,560	52,174	4,664
Big Horn	69.8	5,180	62.9	1.2	5.4	0.7	3.8	80.8	5,990	445	57	1,369	4,220	40,701	2,711
Blaine	38.5	5,705	62.1	1.8	4.1	0.0	5.2	2.9	434	187	27	458	2,650	39,826	2,849
Broadwater	22.3	3,764	35.0	3.0	10.0	0.2	4.4	3.5	589	39	27	198	3,060	58,580	5,116
Carbon	42.3	3,959	48.8	2.4	7.2	0.1	9.3	28.4	2,661	84	47	487	5,370	60,137	6,302
Carter	10.9	8,904	30.1	7.7	4.7	0.0	31.3	4.4	3,594	16	5	100	620	44,327	3,106
Cascade	276.9	3,392	49.0	2.5	10.1	1.9	4.5	235.4	2,883	1,715	3,702	3,795	40,240	56,841	5,508
Chouteau	26.3	4,585	40.1	22.4	4.1	0.0	9.6	7.3	1,269	36	24	418	2,270	46,960	3,956
Custer	53.5	4,562	61.0	3.4	8.1	0.8	6.3	16.9	1,445	199	47	883	5,500	54,801	5,270
Daniels	13.4	7,806	28.8	6.4	3.5	0.0	5.4	4.0	2,336	17	7	105	850	48,464	4,855
Dawson	45.9	5,124	54.2	3.0	5.7	0.0	4.5	39.0	4,357	40	35	754	4,160	57,457	5,027
Deer Lodge	36.8	4,039	35.8	4.9	8.2	0.2	6.7	9.9	1,085	89	36	894	4,430	49,407	4,164
Fallon	32.0	10,644	40.2	2.2	8.0	0.6	22.4	1.7	552	14	12	267	1,360	66,613	6,387
Fergus	47.4	4,201	56.5	2.4	9.7	0.1	9.8	8.1	718	135	46	800	5,580	51,091	4,414
Flathead	367.8	3,675	58.5	3.6	6.3	0.1	4.6	332.4	3,321	753	451	4,200	54,130	66,402	7,536
Gallatin	360.7	3,323	52.3	1.2	8.4	4.2	4.3	424.5	3,910	635	497	9,711	61,310	88,014	11,884
Garfield	11.6	9,084	28.4	1.4	3.5	22.4	6.7	0.6	495	26	22	134	520	35,700	2,498
Glacier	64.5	4,697	74.1	3.1	4.0	0.1	3.0	14.8	1,076	446	55	1,960	5,320	36,625	2,422
Golden Valley	4.6	5,682	64.9	0.9	3.7	0.6	8.3	0.5	625	6	3	70	420	39,036	3,052
Granite	11.6	3,457	51.2	2.2	8.5	0.0	7.8	0.9	256	38	14	201	1,470	56,859	5,567
Hill	70.9	4,305	66.6	2.1	5.6	0.0	3.8	35.0	2,126	159	68	2,058	7,450	50,850	4,181
Jefferson	38.1	3,197	49.5	1.9	7.3	0.0	4.5	18.3	1,533	40	52	551	5,980	71,481	7,411
Judith Basin	10.9	5,598	55.9	0.6	3.3	0.1	9.7	2.9	1,491	34	9	139	970	38,818	3,177
Lake	91.2	3,016	62.8	1.1	5.1	0.4	2.8	30.6	1,012	118	131	2,933	13,690	51,091	4,752
Lewis and Clark	229.3	3,379	50.3	4.8	9.3	0.5	8.4	147.3	2,171	1,996	296	8,694	35,860	66,058	6,850
Liberty	11.5	4,759	34.0	3.6	7.5	6.0	11.8	0.8	343	22	8	126	880	47,827	4,138
Lincoln	53.8	2,751	58.7	1.8	7.7	0.3	6.7	25.9	1,326	452	87	723	8,780	47,660	3,915
McCone	10.3	6,058	48.6	4.2	3.3	2.3	9.5	2.9	1,688	19	7	127	840	37,526	3,156
Madison	40.4	4,876	34.2	3.6	6.8	17.7	10.1	12.4	1,500	59	38	472	4,310	67,845	7,590
Meagher	18.2	9,843	53.0	1.2	2.1	0.1	4.2	14.8	7,964	35	7	98	1,010	40,221	3,193
Mineral	22.8	5,387	44.7	29.9	6.0	0.4	3.1	3.7	864	59	19	266	2,110	49,920	4,303
Missoula	459.0	3,895	45.7	7.4	6.3	0.6	3.3	347.1	2,946	1,461	541	9,298	61,230	66,030	7,399
Musselshell	16.2	3,494	74.0	2.4	5.0	0.0	4.3	12.6	2,710	17	20	229	2,110	47,981	4,086
Park	55.7	3,402	47.9	2.0	7.3	0.0	6.3	19.7	1,201	84	72	629	9,390	65,000	7,614
Petroleum	3.4	6,725	49.0	0.9	2.8	0.0	12.5	0.4	738	4	2	51	200	34,940	2,550
Phillips	21.8	5,289	47.8	2.0	6.0	0.0	10.4	6.7	1,624	70	17	289	1,960	42,944	3,603
Pondera	43.8	7,339	37.5	35.4	3.3	0.0	4.4	7.8	1,302	38	22	354	2,890	42,908	3,218
Powder River	14.2	8,086	34.3	1.2	5.9	28.2	8.5	0.4	225	12	7	184	820	37,490	3,487
Powell	27.4	4,033	61.4	0.9	5.0	0.5	8.1	25.5	3,759	82	22	959	2,840	50,360	4,966
Prairie	10.3	9,389	23.3	2.2	3.6	45.5	7.1	1.6	1,475	36	4	135	530	49,579	3,762
Ravalli	99.3	2,336	66.0	1.0	6.6	0.5	5.6	37.8	888	546	191	1,364	22,020	62,503	6,812
Richland	77.9	7,069	39.5	1.8	5.7	1.0	8.3	8.1	732	76	47	654	5,740	69,362	8,132
Roosevelt	73.9	6,625	64.3	9.4	6.5	0.1	5.6	28.7	2,567	163	46	1,569	3,960	44,221	3,690
Rosebud	66.5	7,227	49.8	5.3	5.5	0.2	4.0	177.6	19,289	203	38	1,458	3,790	52,977	4,462
Sanders	36.7	3,141	53.5	1.1	7.9	1.1	8.8	5.8	494	149	51	496	5,430	48,027	4,120
Sheridan	23.3	6,702	46.1	5.5	7.8	0.0	10.9	6.8	1,959	62	14	240	1,770	51,936	4,868
Silver Bow	143.1	4,111	34.8	3.3	6.1	0.2	4.6	43.9	1,261	221	158	2,278	16,930	57,305	5,676
Stillwater	34.7	3,681	57.5	0.6	5.9	0.0	12.4	8.5	907	38	42	434	4,630	67,186	6,820
Sweet Grass	25.5	6,949	29.3	0.3	5.2	38.6	8.3	0.9	243	29	16	176	1,820	64,128	6,748
Teton	40.4	6,640	39.9	21.1	0.8	6.1	4.1	17.9	2,933	51	25	435	3,050	46,869	3,557
Toole	40.6	8,360	24.1	47.4	6.5	1.3	5.5	17.8	3,659	165	17	421	2,260	46,776	4,108
Treasure	3.4	5,105	49.9	1.2	4.4	0.0	13.6	4.1	6,146	5	3	51	350	49,680	4,174
Valley	37.5	5,068	54.7	1.8	5.5	0.8	6.3	25.3	3,414	167	31	594	3,540	54,075	5,297
Wheatland	11.4	5,273	58.6	4.8	6.7	0.1	5.8	3.9	1,810	22	9	134	1,030	34,203	2,715
Wibaux	8.4	8,215	36.4	3.4	4.6	3.4	26.0	1.1	1,098	7	4	133	430	47,330	3,556
Yellowstone	644.7	4,048	45.6	8.1	5.6	0.3	7.2	557.9	3,503	1,868	724	7,403	81,220	67,899	7,582
NEBRASKA	X	X	X	X	X	X	X	X	X	17,454	12,800	142,704	932,030	67,715	7,390
Adams	385.1	12,106	40.0	43.9	1.7	0.1	2.9	192.8	6,062	107	102	2,123	14,540	59,859	5,769
Antelope	38.2	6,029	67.7	0.0	0.9	0.0	5.4	17.4	2,748	30	22	459	2,960	49,805	4,585
Arthur	9.2	20,191	29.2	0.0	0.4	0.2	5.0	22.0	48,303	2	2	46	180	21,961	1,311
Banner	5.5	7,563	67.2	0.1	1.0	0.0	17.7	0.0	0	2	3	63	300	47,893	3,447

1. Based on the resident population estimated as of July 1 of the year shown.

State / county code	CBSA code[1]	County Type code[2]	STATE County	Land area[3] (sq. mi)	Population, 2021: Total persons 2021	Population, 2021: Rank	Population, 2021: Per square mile	Race alone or in combination, not Hispanic or Latino (percent): White	Black	American Indian, Alaska Native	Asian and Pacific Islancer	Percent Hispanic or Latino[4]	Age (percent): Under 5 years	5 to 17 years	18 to 24 years	25 to 34 years	35 to 44 years	45 to 54 years
				1	2	3	4	5	6	7	8	9	10	11	12	13	14	15
			NEBRASKA— Cont'd															
31009		9	Blaine	710.7	461	3,137	0.6	96.5	1.1	1.3	0.0	2.6	6.1	12.1	8.5	13.9	7.8	11.1
31011		9	Boone	686.5	5,386	2,786	7.8	95.7	0.9	0.5	0.3	3.2	6.3	14.0	10.7	10.1	10.6	9.7
31013		7	Box Butte	1,075.4	10,604	2,370	9.9	82.2	1.8	3.7	1.1	13.4	6.1	15.0	10.9	11.4	12.4	10.4
31015		9	Boyd	539.9	1,789	3,060	3.3	94.3	0.4	1.7	1.6	2.6	4.1	11.5	9.8	8.7	9.6	9.8
31017		9	Brown	1,221.4	2,908	2,964	2.4	92.7	0.9	2.0	0.7	5.1	6.0	11.3	11.9	9.7	9.9	11.0
31019	28260	4	Buffalo	968.2	50,339	991	52.0	87.1	1.8	0.8	1.8	9.9	6.1	13.0	18.4	12.8	12.8	10.1
31021		8	Burt	491.6	6,709	2,681	13.6	92.9	1.2	2.7	1.0	3.9	5.8	13.1	10.8	9.6	11.1	10.6
31023		6	Butler	584.9	8,444	2,538	14.4	93.0	1.1	0.8	0.6	5.6	6.2	13.6	11.5	10.3	11.5	11.1
31025	36540	2	Cass	557.3	27,017	1,527	48.5	94.4	1.3	1.1	1.1	3.8	5.1	13.8	11.7	10.4	12.9	12.8
31027		9	Cedar	740.2	8,330	2,552	11.3	96.3	0.7	0.9	0.6	2.4	6.4	14.6	11.8	9.0	10.5	10.2
31029		9	Chase	894.4	3,826	2,899	4.3	83.5	0.8	0.6	0.4	15.7	6.6	14.1	11.5	9.4	11.9	11.2
31031		7	Cherry	5,960.2	5,458	2,779	0.9	88.5	1.5	7.8	1.5	4.3	6.7	13.6	10.5	9.8	12.4	11.0
31033		7	Cheyenne	1,196.0	9,529	2,448	8.0	88.8	1.3	1.4	1.4	8.6	6.1	13.3	10.9	10.7	12.0	11.2
31035		8	Clay	572.3	6,078	2,731	10.6	89.1	1.0	0.8	0.5	9.4	6.0	14.0	11.4	11.4	10.9	10.5
31037		7	Colfax	411.6	10,498	2,376	25.5	47.5	4.9	0.7	0.9	46.6	8.8	16.8	13.3	10.5	13.6	10.8
31039		7	Cuming	570.5	8,984	2,487	15.7	87.8	0.9	0.8	0.7	10.9	6.7	13.3	12.4	10.4	10.8	10.4
31041		7	Custer	2,575.6	10,460	2,379	4.1	94.6	1.3	1.0	0.5	3.8	5.9	13.9	11.1	10.8	11.1	10.4
31043	43580	3	Dakota	264.3	21,241	1,752	80.4	46.0	8.0	3.3	4.6	39.8	8.3	16.4	13.5	13.5	11.8	10.7
31045		7	Dawes	1,396.4	8,148	2,567	5.8	85.8	2.7	4.7	2.7	6.3	4.6	9.6	25.0	10.0	10.2	9.0
31047	30420	7	Dawson	1,013.1	23,898	1,644	23.6	56.7	7.2	0.7	1.6	34.6	8.0	14.6	12.8	12.6	12.0	11.3
31049		9	Deuel	439.9	1,865	3,053	4.2	90.1	0.8	1.3	0.8	8.4	4.6	12.8	9.2	8.9	8.7	11.8
31051	43580	3	Dixon	476.1	5,545	2,774	11.6	82.9	1.0	0.9	0.6	15.6	6.1	15.0	11.5	9.7	11.0	11.5
31053	23340	4	Dodge	529.1	37,103	1,250	70.1	82.1	1.5	1.0	1.1	15.6	6.2	14.0	13.7	11.2	11.8	10.9
31055	36540	2	Douglas	326.4	585,008	116	1,792.3	70.4	12.6	1.1	5.2	13.5	6.9	14.2	13.3	14.8	14.1	11.4
31057		9	Dundy	919.7	1,635	3,072	1.8	88.9	1.7	1.9	0.9	8.6	5.0	11.2	10.6	9.4	10.6	11.4
31059		8	Fillmore	575.4	5,546	2,773	9.6	93.7	1.2	0.9	0.8	4.3	5.4	10.5	10.2	11.8	12.0	10.9
31061		9	Franklin	575.8	2,903	2,965	5.0	95.9	1.1	0.9	0.7	3.1	6.3	11.6	9.5	8.9	11.2	9.5
31063		9	Frontier	974.6	2,555	2,993	2.6	95.5	1.0	0.9	0.7	3.2	4.8	11.5	14.1	9.5	9.8	11.2
31065		9	Furnas	719.1	4,604	2,848	6.4	93.1	1.3	1.1	0.6	5.0	6.3	11.5	11.7	9.4	10.4	11.0
31067	13100	6	Gage	851.5	21,616	1,731	25.4	94.7	1.3	1.3	1.0	3.1	5.3	13.3	11.0	10.5	11.9	11.4
31069		9	Garden	1,705.4	1,847	3,054	1.1	92.0	0.9	1.6	0.8	6.2	4.6	11.0	9.0	9.5	9.8	10.2
31071		9	Garfield	569.3	1,839	3,055	3.2	97.8	0.5	0.3	0.2	1.7	6.5	8.3	10.7	10.1	9.6	10.0
31073	30420	9	Gosper	458.2	1,824	3,058	4.0	92.4	1.2	1.1	1.0	5.8	5.7	11.6	9.9	9.3	11.9	10.5
31075		9	Grant	777.0	579	3,135	0.7	97.4	0.9	0.9	0.3	1.9	6.7	13.5	9.2	9.5	12.6	7.4
31077		8	Greeley	569.8	2,169	3,028	3.8	96.1	0.9	0.4	0.3	2.8	5.6	13.3	11.2	9.5	10.4	9.6
31079	24260	3	Hall	546.4	61,979	860	113.4	64.5	3.4	0.8	1.6	30.8	7.3	15.5	12.9	12.5	12.9	11.4
31081		3	Hamilton	542.1	9,386	2,462	17.3	95.0	0.9	0.7	0.7	4.0	6.1	13.8	11.5	10.8	12.0	11.5
31083		9	Harlan	553.5	3,091	2,954	5.6	96.0	1.0	0.8	0.8	2.4	5.1	12.6	9.9	8.7	9.3	11.1
31085		9	Hayes	713.1	843	3,112	1.2	91.8	1.8	0.8	0.8	6.3	6.6	13.2	8.3	9.8	10.8	5.9
31087		9	Hitchcock	709.9	2,586	2,991	3.6	94.6	0.9	1.2	0.7	3.9	5.3	13.4	10.4	8.6	12.1	10.0
31089		7	Holt	2,412.4	10,049	2,400	4.2	93.3	0.8	0.6	0.7	5.4	6.6	14.9	11.1	9.4	10.7	9.7
31091		9	Hooker	721.2	734	3,123	1.0	95.8	0.1	1.1	0.7	3.3	4.2	13.1	10.8	8.2	12.4	9.4
31093	24260	3	Howard	569.3	6,531	2,696	11.5	95.0	1.0	0.6	0.9	3.3	6.0	14.1	10.6	10.6	11.6	11.4
31095		7	Jefferson	570.2	7,176	2,649	12.6	93.2	0.9	0.9	0.6	5.4	6.0	12.6	10.6	9.5	11.3	10.8
31097		8	Johnson	376.1	5,316	2,793	14.1	79.3	7.5	1.6	1.4	11.2	4.2	10.8	11.0	15.0	13.4	13.0
31099	28260	7	Kearney	516.2	6,674	2,685	12.9	91.1	0.8	0.6	0.6	7.9	6.0	14.3	11.6	11.3	12.1	10.7
31101		7	Keith	1,061.7	8,279	2,557	7.8	89.8	1.4	1.1	0.8	8.2	5.2	11.6	10.0	9.1	10.8	10.5
31103		9	Keya Paha	773.1	787	3,118	1.0	97.5	0.0	1.7	0.6	0.8	4.1	9.7	10.7	8.4	8.6	9.4
31105		8	Kimball	951.9	3,412	2,926	3.6	87.4	1.5	2.3	1.7	9.3	5.1	12.0	9.9	10.2	10.7	10.3
31107		9	Knox	1,108.4	8,401	2,543	7.6	85.6	1.1	10.6	0.9	3.8	6.4	14.3	11.5	8.7	10.0	9.7
31109	30700	2	Lancaster	837.6	324,514	222	387.4	82.7	5.7	1.2	5.6	7.8	5.7	12.8	18.7	13.6	12.9	10.7
31111	35820	5	Lincoln	2,564.1	34,133	1,327	13.3	87.7	1.6	1.0	1.3	9.8	5.8	13.2	11.6	10.7	12.8	11.9
31113	35820	9	Logan	570.7	687	3,129	1.2	92.4	1.2	1.9	0.4	5.7	4.1	12.4	12.5	9.8	13.1	10.6
31115		9	Loup	563.5	604	3,134	1.1	94.5	1.3	0.2	0.3	3.6	4.8	11.4	9.8	9.4	8.6	10.3
31117	35820	9	McPherson	859.3	379	3,139	0.4	96.8	1.3	0.3	0.3	2.4	3.2	10.6	11.6	7.9	10.3	12.1
31119	35740	5	Madison	572.6	35,337	1,298	61.7	79.6	1.9	1.5	2.1	16.4	7.0	14.6	13.4	12.2	12.6	10.2
31121	24260	3	Merrick	487.3	7,665	2,600	15.7	92.4	1.0	1.0	1.4	5.3	5.4	12.3	11.4	11.6	11.8	11.6
31123		9	Morrill	1,424.0	4,574	2,853	3.2	81.9	1.2	1.4	0.9	16.2	5.6	12.9	11.9	10.8	11.7	11.5
31125		8	Nance	441.6	3,390	2,931	7.7	95.1	1.1	1.0	0.4	3.6	5.6	13.5	10.9	10.4	11.7	10.1
31127		7	Nemaha	407.4	7,064	2,657	17.3	94.2	2.2	0.9	1.0	3.3	5.9	13.1	16.1	10.9	11.8	9.5
31129		9	Nuckolls	575.2	4,060	2,881	7.1	94.5	0.7	0.9	1.7	3.5	5.4	11.2	10.2	9.3	10.4	9.8
31131		6	Otoe	615.7	15,930	2,036	25.9	89.3	1.7	1.0	1.2	8.3	6.0	13.7	11.3	10.8	11.9	11.8
31133		9	Pawnee	431.1	2,548	2,995	5.9	96.3	2.0	1.3	0.6	2.1	6.7	12.4	10.1	8.6	9.9	10.0
31135		9	Perkins	883.3	2,832	2,971	3.2	94.0	0.8	0.6	0.4	4.9	5.8	14.0	11.6	8.5	12.7	10.1
31137		7	Phelps	539.8	8,937	2,492	16.6	91.9	1.0	1.0	0.7	6.6	6.6	13.7	11.7	11.6	11.4	11.0
31139	35740	9	Pierce	573.2	7,313	2,639	12.8	96.4	1.0	0.6	0.5	2.4	6.5	14.4	11.9	10.2	12.2	10.9

1. CBSA = Core Based Statistical Area. See Appendix A for explanation. See Appendix B for list of metropolitan areas with component counties. 2. County type code from the Economic Research Service of USDA Rural-Urban Continuum Codes. See Appendix A for definition. 3. Dry land or land partially or temporarily covered by water. 4. May be of any race.

STATE County	Population, 2021 (cont.)				Population change, 2000–2021							Households, 2016–2020				
	Age (percent) (cont.)				Total persons		Percent change		Components of change, 2020–2021					Percent		
	55 to 64 years	65 to 74 years	75 years and over	Percent female	2010	2020	2010–2020	2020–2021	Births	Deaths	Net Migration	Number	Persons per household	Family house-holds	Female family house-holder[1]	One person
	16	17	18	19	20	21	22	23	24	25	26	27	28	29	30	31
NEBRASKA— Cont'd																
Blaine	20.2	11.9	8.5	49.0	478	431	-9.8	7.0	5	10	38	237	2.0	59.5	0.8	39.2
Boone	15.7	12.1	10.9	49.9	5,505	5,379	-2.3	0.1	78	100	31	2,261	2.3	66.1	5.6	28.0
Box Butte	13.1	13.2	7.5	50.1	11,308	10,842	-4.1	-2.2	140	178	-198	4,601	2.3	64.4	7.0	31.6
Boyd	16.5	16.6	13.3	50.3	2,099	1,810	-13.8	-1.2	19	40	0	876	2.1	66.0	3.1	30.9
Brown	14.4	13.9	12.0	50.4	3,145	2,903	-7.7	0.2	38	62	29	1,333	2.1	56.7	5.7	39.1
Buffalo	11.0	9.3	6.5	49.8	46,102	50,084	8.6	0.5	734	622	130	19,016	2.5	62.4	9.7	29.4
Burt	14.2	13.9	10.9	49.8	6,858	6,722	-2.0	-0.2	86	125	28	2,881	2.2	64.0	7.5	33.0
Butler	15.0	12.0	8.8	49.2	8,395	8,369	-0.3	0.9	125	126	78	3,387	2.3	63.7	6.1	31.2
Cass	15.1	11.5	6.7	48.9	25,241	26,598	5.4	1.6	301	388	511	10,073	2.6	70.9	6.8	23.2
Cedar	15.0	12.3	10.1	48.9	8,852	8,380	-5.3	-0.6	129	137	-42	3,479	2.4	67.7	5.1	28.4
Chase	14.1	11.3	9.9	49.8	3,966	3,893	-1.8	-1.7	66	68	-66	1,591	2.3	70.6	6.9	26.1
Cherry	13.5	12.3	10.1	48.5	5,713	5,455	-4.5	0.1	94	92	1	2,459	2.3	65.0	7.6	28.8
Cheyenne	14.0	13.3	8.5	49.7	9,998	9,468	-5.3	0.6	118	132	75	4,403	2.1	53.9	6.2	42.1
Clay	14.5	12.9	8.3	48.7	6,542	6,104	-6.7	-0.4	85	100	-10	2,575	2.4	69.2	6.9	25.7
Colfax	12.1	8.2	5.9	46.1	10,515	10,582	0.6	-0.8	238	79	-241	3,742	2.8	65.3	5.7	25.3
Cuming	13.9	11.6	10.5	49.7	9,139	9,013	-1.4	-0.3	147	140	-36	3,854	2.3	64.9	3.7	30.8
Custer	14.2	12.7	10.0	49.7	10,939	10,545	-3.6	-0.8	130	185	-32	4,828	2.2	65.4	7.6	31.4
Dakota	11.6	8.5	5.6	49.4	21,006	21,582	2.7	-1.6	419	261	-496	7,350	2.7	69.7	11.0	21.1
Dawes	12.0	10.7	8.8	50.7	9,182	8,199	-10.7	-0.6	100	127	-26	3,555	2.2	58.1	5.6	32.6
Dawson	11.6	10.0	7.1	47.5	24,326	24,111	-0.9	-0.9	460	324	-348	9,007	2.6	72.4	11.0	21.7
Deuel	16.5	16.2	11.3	48.5	1,941	1,838	-5.3	1.5	18	16	26	823	2.1	68.4	8.6	28.2
Dixon	13.8	12.8	8.6	48.9	6,000	5,606	-6.6	-1.1	67	91	-36	2,376	2.4	67.4	7.9	30.7
Dodge	13.1	10.6	8.4	49.9	36,691	37,167	1.3	-0.2	528	628	33	15,284	2.3	63.8	9.3	28.8
Douglas	11.5	8.7	5.1	50.3	517,110	584,526	13.0	0.1	9,626	6,245	-2,996	221,451	2.5	61.7	11.0	31.4
Dundy	15.5	15.4	10.8	49.1	2,008	1,654	-17.6	-1.1	17	27	-9	842	2.2	57.6	6.2	38.5
Fillmore	16.0	12.9	10.2	49.9	5,890	5,551	-5.8	-0.1	84	92	2	2,488	2.1	61.8	4.7	34.4
Franklin	15.3	15.5	12.2	49.5	3,225	2,889	-10.4	0.5	42	42	14	1,328	2.2	66.9	6.0	26.1
Frontier	14.3	13.7	11.0	48.7	2,756	2,519	-8.6	1.4	32	32	37	1,136	2.2	66.2	4.5	31.8
Furnas	13.8	14.9	10.9	50.0	4,959	4,636	-6.5	-0.7	69	83	-17	2,077	2.2	67.9	4.6	26.0
Gage	14.9	12.2	9.4	49.7	22,311	21,704	-2.7	-0.4	252	349	7	9,048	2.3	60.1	7.4	35.2
Garden	16.8	14.6	14.5	47.9	2,057	1,874	-8.9	-1.4	24	33	-17	929	2.0	57.1	6.7	38.3
Garfield	16.1	14.6	14.3	49.8	2,049	1,813	-11.5	1.4	36	34	24	906	2.2	73.0	4.0	23.1
Gosper	16.4	14.1	10.6	47.9	2,044	1,893	-7.4	-3.6	27	46	-50	940	2.1	68.6	4.9	26.4
Grant	15.0	16.2	9.8	46.8	614	611	-0.5	-5.2	9	9	-30	297	2.2	59.9	2.4	31.3
Greeley	14.6	13.3	12.4	50.0	2,538	2,188	-13.8	-0.9	27	45	0	1,045	2.2	63.9	6.5	33.4
Hall	12.2	9.2	6.3	49.2	58,607	62,895	7.3	-1.5	1,019	788	-1,142	23,496	2.6	67.9	13.2	26.2
Hamilton	13.9	11.7	8.8	49.2	9,124	9,429	3.3	-0.5	106	137	-13	3,622	2.5	74.7	6.5	22.6
Harlan	15.9	15.6	11.6	48.5	3,423	3,073	-10.2	0.6	40	55	33	1,515	2.2	59.3	3.6	33.6
Hayes	18.0	14.8	12.5	48.5	967	856	-11.5	-1.5	11	9	-14	389	2.3	60.7	1.8	38.0
Hitchcock	14.5	15.4	10.4	49.0	2,908	2,616	-10.0	-1.1	27	63	6	1,228	2.2	60.3	9.1	35.7
Holt	15.0	13.1	9.5	49.3	10,435	10,127	-3.0	-0.8	162	170	-71	4,390	2.3	62.4	5.9	31.5
Hooker	13.1	13.6	15.3	51.2	736	711	-3.4	3.2	7	10	28	316	2.2	53.8	4.7	43.0
Howard	14.3	12.3	9.1	49.0	6,274	6,475	3.2	0.9	89	95	62	2,732	2.4	69.9	7.7	25.0
Jefferson	14.9	13.8	10.4	50.1	7,547	7,240	-4.1	-0.9	109	140	-33	3,246	2.2	58.7	6.1	36.0
Johnson	14.0	10.5	8.1	39.5	5,217	5,290	1.4	0.5	51	75	51	1,847	2.2	67.5	10.5	29.5
Kearney	13.7	11.5	8.9	49.7	6,489	6,688	3.1	-0.2	100	88	-26	2,691	2.4	67.3	8.2	29.4
Keith	15.6	15.6	11.5	49.3	8,368	8,335	-0.4	-0.7	107	128	-35	3,864	2.1	57.6	6.1	36.2
Keya Paha	17.3	15.0	16.9	49.4	824	769	-6.7	2.3	7	12	25	349	2.5	64.5	5.4	31.8
Kimball	16.0	13.9	11.9	50.3	3,821	3,434	-10.1	-0.6	37	68	9	1,612	2.2	61.2	9.2	32.2
Knox	14.2	13.7	11.5	50.6	8,701	8,391	-3.6	0.1	139	176	48	3,605	2.3	64.6	6.2	31.4
Lancaster	10.8	9.3	5.5	49.6	285,407	322,608	13.0	0.6	4,500	3,287	616	126,666	2.4	60.0	9.4	29.6
Lincoln	13.3	12.3	8.3	50.2	36,288	34,676	-4.4	-1.6	451	552	-440	14,765	2.3	64.3	9.3	30.3
Logan	14.0	14.0	9.6	47.3	763	716	-6.2	-4.1	9	12	-26	319	2.8	68.7	1.6	25.4
Loup	17.7	17.2	10.8	48.3	632	607	-4.0	-0.5	8	2	-8	316	2.2	65.8	3.5	30.7
McPherson	17.7	14.2	12.4	50.1	539	399	-26.0	-5.0	3	7	-15	199	2.1	72.9	0.0	27.1
Madison	13.5	9.8	6.8	50.0	34,876	35,585	2.0	-0.7	566	492	-326	14,187	2.4	60.1	9.3	33.9
Merrick	14.8	12.0	9.2	49.0	7,845	7,668	-2.3	0.0	105	126	18	3,330	2.3	61.5	8.4	32.1
Morrill	13.6	12.5	9.6	48.3	5,042	4,555	-9.7	0.4	69	77	27	1,969	2.3	58.0	6.6	36.9
Nance	16.4	13.5	7.9	49.6	3,735	3,380	-9.5	0.3	46	58	23	1,530	2.2	66.9	8.2	27.4
Nemaha	12.5	12.1	8.1	49.9	7,248	7,074	-2.4	-0.1	94	112	8	2,912	2.2	63.2	7.0	31.6
Nuckolls	16.4	14.9	12.3	50.2	4,500	4,095	-9.0	-0.9	47	100	20	1,852	2.2	61.8	4.9	33.9
Otoe	14.2	11.5	8.8	49.9	15,740	15,912	1.1	0.1	211	243	48	6,509	2.4	68.5	10.1	25.8
Pawnee	14.1	14.8	13.5	50.2	2,773	2,544	-8.3	0.2	35	42	12	1,221	2.1	61.5	11.2	32.3
Perkins	13.0	13.5	10.7	49.3	2,970	2,858	-3.8	-0.9	36	30	-31	1,202	2.4	73.1	3.7	25.7
Phelps	13.8	10.4	9.9	49.5	9,188	8,968	-2.4	-0.3	118	141	-9	3,900	2.3	61.5	3.4	31.4
Pierce	14.0	10.9	9.0	49.1	7,266	7,317	0.7	-0.1	121	92	-34	2,990	2.4	67.5	6.8	26.4

1. No spouse present.

STATE County	Persons in group quarters, 2021	Daytime Population, 2016–2020		Births, 2021		Deaths, 2021		Persons under 65 with no health insurance, 2019		Medicare, 2021			COVID-19 Deaths, 2020	
		Number	Employment/ residence ratio	Total	Rate[1]	Number	Rate[1]	Number	Percent	Total beneficiaries	Enrolled in Original Medicare	Enrolled in Medicare Advantage	Number	Rate[1]
	32	33	34	35	36	37	38	39	40	41	42	43	44	45
NEBRASKA— Cont'd														
Blaine	0	413	0.8	4	9.0	8	17.9	67	20.1	119	D	D	D	D
Boone	94	5,332	1.0	59	11.0	77	14.3	381	9.6	1,296	1,174	121	10	1.9
Box Butte	104	11,344	1.1	107	10.0	152	14.2	887	10.3	2,408	2,279	129	D	D
Boyd	19	1,756	0.9	11	6.1	31	17.2	165	12.6	615	596	19	D	D
Brown	13	2,927	1.0	29	10.0	48	16.5	282	13.2	813	D	D	D	D
Buffalo	2,058	51,108	1.1	587	11.7	510	10.2	3,849	9.5	8,475	7,163	1,312	64	1.3
Burt	119	5,728	0.7	67	10.0	101	15.0	541	11.2	1,838	1,504	334	11	1.6
Butler	161	6,841	0.7	106	12.6	95	11.3	500	8.0	1,868	1,636	232	11	1.3
Cass	218	18,905	0.5	235	8.8	311	11.6	1,416	6.6	5,422	4,167	1,255	22	0.8
Cedar	106	7,435	0.8	105	12.6	112	13.4	617	9.5	1,958	1,611	347	21	2.5
Chase	60	3,829	1.1	48	12.5	55	14.3	422	13.8	884	D	D	D	D
Cherry	18	5,800	1.0	74	13.6	79	14.5	700	16.0	1,359	1,346	14	12	2.2
Cheyenne	66	9,641	1.0	99	10.4	103	10.8	524	7.4	2,236	2,033	203	15	1.6
Clay	42	5,708	0.8	69	11.3	83	13.6	533	10.9	1,502	1,418	83	15	2.5
Colfax	36	9,803	0.8	191	18.2	60	5.7	1,612	17.8	1,565	1,438	127	22	2.1
Cuming	75	8,308	0.9	113	12.6	105	11.7	802	11.8	2,044	1,834	209	12	1.3
Custer	82	10,803	1.0	103	9.8	150	14.3	916	11.2	2,623	2,466	157	17	1.6
Dakota	250	21,562	1.1	349	16.3	179	8.4	2,606	15.5	3,196	2,195	1,001	74	3.4
Dawes	919	8,365	0.9	81	9.9	103	12.6	660	10.6	1,731	1,531	201	16	2.0
Dawson	275	23,268	1.0	384	16.0	257	10.7	2,873	15.1	4,320	3,911	409	41	1.7
Deuel	0	1,665	0.9	17	9.2	14	7.6	145	10.7	511	497	14	D	D
Dixon	58	4,450	0.6	58	10.4	73	13.1	468	10.6	1,304	999	305	14	2.5
Dodge	1,036	36,648	1.0	412	11.1	507	13.7	2,875	10.1	8,037	6,200	1,837	62	1.7
Douglas	11,995	615,582	1.2	7,721	13.2	4,980	8.5	49,720	10.3	89,674	59,732	29,943	550	0.9
Dundy	22	1,879	1.0	15	9.1	20	12.2	249	20.0	472	D	D	D	D
Fillmore	177	5,364	0.9	62	11.2	73	13.1	354	8.7	1,466	1,359	107	14	2.5
Franklin	13	2,532	0.7	35	12.1	34	11.7	215	10.2	838	784	54	D	D
Frontier	103	2,429	0.8	23	9.1	27	10.7	207	11.1	548	533	15	D	D
Furnas	38	4,874	1.1	57	12.4	62	13.5	423	12.3	1,365	1,292	72	D	D
Gage	487	20,279	0.9	197	9.1	279	12.9	1,477	8.8	5,411	4,366	1,045	25	1.2
Garden	19	1,903	1.0	14	7.5	20	10.7	171	13.2	577	563	14	D	D
Garfield	42	2,044	1.0	30	16.5	26	14.3	133	9.7	494	464	30	D	D
Gosper	24	1,587	0.6	23	12.4	37	19.9	129	8.7	504	445	59	D	D
Grant	3	678	1.0	6	10.1	5	8.4	54	11.3	166	166	0	D	D
Greeley	35	2,193	0.9	20	9.2	40	18.4	225	12.9	592	566	26	D	D
Hall	783	65,375	1.1	805	12.9	629	10.1	6,520	12.8	10,615	8,723	1,892	114	1.8
Hamilton	106	8,409	0.8	88	9.4	112	11.9	517	7.0	2,075	1,888	187	23	2.4
Harlan	20	3,084	0.8	32	10.4	44	14.3	269	11.1	931	878	53	D	D
Hayes	0	746	0.7	11	13.0	8	9.4	126	19.4	205	205	0	D	D
Hitchcock	13	2,443	0.7	20	7.7	43	16.6	231	11.5	785	D	D	D	D
Holt	82	10,194	1.0	134	13.3	136	13.5	773	10.0	2,522	2,378	144	18	1.8
Hooker	23	763	1.1	5	6.9	8	11.1	53	11.3	232	D	D	D	D
Howard	47	5,126	0.6	70	10.7	80	12.3	469	9.4	1,474	1,354	120	15	2.3
Jefferson	85	7,482	1.1	85	11.8	114	15.8	487	9.3	1,984	1,681	303	D	D
Johnson	1,072	4,805	0.8	39	7.4	59	11.1	323	10.4	1,030	935	95	D	D
Kearney	57	5,650	0.7	73	10.9	63	9.4	380	7.4	1,427	1,280	147	D	D
Keith	28	7,965	1.0	90	10.8	107	12.9	593	10.2	2,236	2,016	220	D	D
Keya Paha	0	836	0.9	4	5.2	9	11.6	101	18.8	203	D	D	D	D
Kimball	33	3,594	1.0	31	9.1	50	14.7	330	12.3	1,002	973	29	D	D
Knox	175	7,915	0.9	102	12.2	141	16.8	767	12.5	2,299	1,929	369	14	1.7
Lancaster	15,199	326,489	1.1	3,558	11.0	2,573	7.9	21,201	8.2	51,847	41,029	10,818	173	0.5
Lincoln	448	35,576	1.0	344	10.0	436	12.7	2,331	8.5	7,943	6,809	1,134	61	1.8
Logan	0	800	0.8	4	5.7	7	10.0	64	11.1	165	152	13	D	D
Loup	0	578	0.7	7	11.6	1	1.7	53	11.0	173	160	13	D	D
McPherson	0	402	0.9	3	7.7	7	18.1	48	12.6	85	72	13	D	D
Madison	1,175	38,722	1.2	459	13.0	375	10.6	3,176	11.2	6,707	5,388	1,319	46	1.3
Merrick	139	6,830	0.7	86	11.2	101	13.2	608	10.1	1,832	1,645	187	19	2.5
Morrill	62	4,354	0.8	55	12.1	50	11.0	472	13.2	1,148	1,066	82	15	3.3
Nance	94	3,195	0.8	38	11.2	41	12.1	256	9.5	856	798	58	D	D
Nemaha	486	7,109	1.0	73	10.3	91	12.9	398	7.7	1,553	1,443	111	15	2.1
Nuckolls	31	4,135	1.0	41	10.1	80	19.7	320	10.7	1,259	1,247	12	14	3.4
Otoe	189	14,969	0.9	166	10.4	189	11.9	1,212	9.5	3,482	2,834	648	D	D
Pawnee	17	2,502	0.9	31	12.2	38	14.9	216	11.8	762	710	52	D	D
Perkins	22	2,911	1.0	31	10.9	23	8.1	251	11.4	684	650	34	11	3.9
Phelps	205	9,888	1.2	93	10.4	116	13.0	562	8.0	2,119	2,061	59	13	1.4
Pierce	95	6,100	0.7	98	13.4	76	10.4	482	8.4	1,502	1,388	114	21	2.9

1. Per 1,000 estimated resident population.

STATE County	COVID-19 Vaccinations, 2021–2022		Education						Money income, 2016–2020				Income and poverty, 2020			
			School enrollment and attainment, 2016–2020				Local government expenditures,[3] 2018–2019				Households			Percent below poverty level		
			Enrollment[1]		Attainment[2] (percent)							Percent				
	Number	Percent[5]	Total	Percent private	High school graduate or less	Bachelor's degree or more	Total current spending (mil dol)	Current spending per student (dollars)	Per capita income[4]	Median income (dollars)	with income of less than $50,000	with income of $200,000 or more	Median household income (dollars)	All persons	Children under 18 years	Children 5 to 17 years in families
	46	47	48	49	50	51	52	53	54	55	56	57	58	59	60	61
NEBRASKA— Cont'd																
Blaine	122	26.2	83	12.0	46.0	23.1	2.6	29,067	29,748	55,268	42.6	0.0	52,780	13.3	21.2	22.8
Boone	2,551	49.1	1,083	14.7	43.1	19.0	13.2	16,365	32,850	60,094	41.2	3.7	56,719	8.7	11.1	10.9
Box Butte	3,673	34.1	2,351	7.2	41.3	17.7	22.2	12,099	29,447	61,904	41.2	0.4	62,621	9.5	12.4	11.1
Boyd	674	35.1	331	9.1	47.0	18.3	5.8	16,915	31,863	53,846	47.4	3.7	51,082	12.9	18.5	17.2
Brown	1,095	37.1	570	18.1	41.1	24.2	11.4	26,597	29,420	41,979	56.9	2.7	52,962	10.8	15.0	13.4
Buffalo	20,825	41.9	14,783	9.2	33.0	33.8	99.9	11,966	30,605	63,513	40.1	3.4	68,925	9.5	9.3	8.5
Burt	3,788	58.6	1,378	9.6	44.1	22.3	18.0	14,199	31,252	51,961	47.4	3.4	51,488	11.5	13.1	12.7
Butler	4,123	51.4	1,693	26.2	43.3	23.7	17.5	18,658	33,418	59,232	41.6	3.6	63,640	7.5	8.5	7.8
Cass	16,198	61.7	6,474	14.7	34.2	29.4	48.5	12,536	34,863	73,683	32.3	5.5	70,106	5.9	6.8	5.7
Cedar	3,443	41.0	2,068	21.9	41.3	21.0	20.7	16,390	30,663	64,703	38.2	2.6	61,673	8.5	9.5	9.4
Chase	1,319	33.6	805	3.2	37.2	22.2	12.6	14,618	30,850	56,135	44.0	5.7	61,282	8.2	10.0	9.5
Cherry	1,981	34.8	1,303	14.0	35.9	23.9	13.1	16,861	30,169	55,431	45.5	4.7	53,483	11.4	14.9	13.6
Cheyenne	3,839	43.1	2,040	10.7	36.8	25.5	23.0	13,810	30,145	52,270	46.3	3.3	55,172	10.0	12.9	12.3
Clay	2,594	41.8	1,400	6.9	42.8	19.9	22.3	16,067	29,990	63,686	39.4	3.1	63,427	9.1	11.3	10.6
Colfax	5,120	47.8	2,951	5.0	57.5	14.9	33.5	12,326	24,901	64,269	37.8	3.3	63,424	8.2	9.7	9.4
Cuming	4,708	53.2	1,981	25.3	47.6	23.1	21.8	14,774	30,734	59,202	43.2	2.9	54,725	7.9	9.9	9.3
Custer	4,114	38.2	2,126	5.7	37.6	24.7	28.3	14,902	32,021	53,891	46.4	4.0	57,873	9.8	14.0	12.9
Dakota	12,943	64.6	5,501	7.7	56.5	14.7	53.0	12,456	26,416	61,227	38.3	2.9	61,220	9.9	13.1	13.1
Dawes	3,333	38.8	2,720	8.7	27.9	38.2	15.7	13,315	25,380	49,379	51.0	0.9	52,637	14.7	16.0	13.8
Dawson	11,560	49.0	5,790	4.4	51.4	16.7	68.8	12,648	31,411	56,731	41.9	2.7	61,043	8.6	10.8	10.7
Deuel	626	34.9	299	7.0	39.5	20.7	7.3	19,611	27,998	48,958	51.5	2.7	51,261	10.3	14.1	12.5
Dixon	2,471	43.8	1,315	8.3	45.7	22.5	13.7	15,601	31,967	57,243	44.1	2.8	60,437	7.9	9.2	8.6
Dodge	19,800	54.2	9,014	17.3	47.1	19.7	80.5	13,207	29,619	58,439	42.9	2.4	62,491	9.7	11.3	10.1
Douglas	381,498	66.8	152,479	23.5	30.4	40.2	1,176.9	11,718	36,303	66,600	37.3	7.4	65,788	9.8	10.2	9.8
Dundy	664	39.2	414	5.6	35.9	28.1	6.1	19,208	27,697	49,211	50.7	1.7	50,299	12.2	17.8	17.5
Fillmore	2,852	52.2	1,013	6.0	39.7	22.4	16.7	17,713	40,702	62,151	40.5	5.2	59,309	8.5	11.9	12.0
Franklin	1,152	38.7	456	1.8	43.0	18.3	5.1	18,014	27,655	50,231	49.6	1.4	49,104	10.4	16.8	17.3
Frontier	727	27.7	684	5.7	32.9	23.0	10.8	18,883	29,043	59,250	43.8	1.1	59,061	13.0	17.1	17.3
Furnas	2,092	44.7	901	3.0	43.1	19.0	16.2	15,107	27,190	53,533	45.5	2.1	50,762	10.0	13.4	13.3
Gage	9,728	45.2	4,621	10.5	44.7	20.7	46.1	14,230	29,289	51,812	47.9	2.8	61,283	8.5	9.9	8.6
Garden	835	45.5	452	8.6	37.7	23.1	4.5	17,045	33,689	42,076	60.4	2.2	41,221	13.9	20.5	18.2
Garfield	594	30.2	424	8.7	32.2	29.3	5.2	16,197	29,119	54,659	45.7	3.6	49,951	11.6	16.9	17.8
Gosper	798	40.1	373	3.2	33.9	29.1	3.6	17,085	35,290	65,086	37.7	4.4	62,698	7.9	11.5	11.4
Grant	129	20.7	159	16.4	44.8	23.0	2.9	18,270	23,806	43,625	53.9	2.0	62,487	9.2	12.2	12.5
Greeley	958	40.7	509	20.4	42.8	17.0	11.4	21,079	26,336	46,830	54.7	1.1	50,068	12.2	17.1	16.2
Hall	30,352	49.5	14,887	9.6	44.8	21.2	146.2	11,762	29,604	58,595	42.9	3.9	54,110	11.8	14.4	14.3
Hamilton	4,323	46.4	2,122	12.2	33.9	24.6	23.7	14,336	32,535	68,649	32.7	4.2	73,759	6.7	8.3	8.3
Harlan	1,360	40.2	648	6.9	33.6	23.8	5.2	14,725	31,978	51,534	49.1	6.5	55,010	9.9	13.8	12.7
Hayes	238	25.8	162	8.0	35.2	18.7	2.8	26,131	30,768	52,396	47.0	3.9	54,280	14.7	20.9	23.7
Hitchcock	940	34.0	619	9.0	37.7	15.8	6.3	20,516	29,278	46,000	53.4	4.0	48,475	12.0	13.0	10.2
Holt	4,324	43.0	2,074	22.6	37.8	24.2	27.3	15,880	31,089	60,214	39.6	2.7	56,777	10.9	13.7	13.0
Hooker	290	42.5	143	9.1	39.9	24.8	3.7	22,994	28,859	48,654	52.2	2.5	53,234	7.9	8.3	7.8
Howard	2,728	42.3	1,447	14.7	43.1	21.7	18.4	14,301	28,108	59,432	44.5	1.0	54,291	8.8	10.3	9.8
Jefferson	3,915	55.6	1,371	12.0	47.4	18.3	22.7	14,652	28,748	48,981	51.7	2.8	55,414	9.9	11.0	10.3
Johnson	2,777	54.8	987	4.1	57.2	18.7	11.3	15,245	24,145	49,382	51.2	2.7	55,062	12.3	12.2	11.7
Kearney	3,060	47.1	1,545	4.9	34.1	26.4	19.5	14,467	33,784	62,899	40.8	4.8	62,260	7.6	9.6	9.4
Keith	3,038	37.8	1,485	17.7	38.3	19.3	21.7	19,363	30,947	52,169	46.3	2.7	57,307	11.7	17.5	16.8
Keya Paha	233	28.9	192	19.8	35.0	25.5	2.2	26,128	32,202	55,250	43.8	7.2	47,053	17.3	23.3	20.8
Kimball	1,270	35.0	693	5.6	48.8	13.2	7.2	17,176	26,528	48,056	51.3	2.0	46,782	11.0	15.5	14.9
Knox	4,134	49.6	1,898	14.3	42.5	19.7	27.9	18,509	29,210	53,653	45.5	2.7	51,296	13.6	16.7	14.7
Lancaster	213,233	66.8	94,275	17.5	27.8	39.8	569.0	11,895	33,382	62,464	39.7	5.4	65,819	9.4	9.1	8.6
Lincoln	11,613	33.3	8,010	11.9	35.6	21.6	68.1	11,848	31,256	59,995	42.0	2.6	62,948	9.4	12.2	11.2
Logan	165	22.1	274	14.2	30.1	23.2	3.1	15,092	21,836	45,990	55.2	0.0	56,283	9.3	10.3	10.2
Loup	198	29.8	83	4.8	37.3	20.6	2.4	34,157	26,975	46,111	53.2	0.0	56,291	15.1	30.9	29.0
McPherson	73	14.8	71	9.9	33.4	23.8	2.0	30,308	33,001	51,932	45.7	6.0	54,876	13.1	22.7	24.1
Madison	16,097	45.9	9,094	19.6	40.2	23.7	71.7	11,957	28,735	52,334	47.6	3.3	56,970	10.6	11.5	10.3
Merrick	3,391	43.7	1,615	11.7	43.7	17.0	15.5	14,544	27,476	52,254	48.3	1.6	58,437	9.6	11.9	11.4
Morrill	1,656	35.7	1,053	11.0	44.6	22.1	14.1	16,567	25,492	46,903	53.9	1.8	54,879	12.5	16.8	15.5
Nance	1,015	28.8	740	14.1	42.2	18.4	12.7	16,755	29,841	53,147	45.2	3.0	52,534	11.4	12.9	12.1
Nemaha	3,506	50.3	1,886	9.1	38.9	28.0	22.2	17,179	28,448	50,236	49.8	3.0	55,574	11.8	11.1	10.5
Nuckolls	2,069	49.9	800	0.7	38.8	23.5	6.6	15,293	34,248	52,975	46.0	4.0	60,636	9.8	12.5	12.0
Otoe	9,022	56.3	3,468	13.6	41.7	25.4	34.9	12,444	32,165	64,755	37.7	4.3	68,443	8.4	10.0	9.3
Pawnee	1,137	43.5	463	7.8	54.5	15.6	8.2	16,786	24,870	46,063	54.0	0.7	49,089	12.7	19.5	20.9
Perkins	1,188	41.1	595	16.8	35.1	26.5	6.6	16,017	33,535	61,389	40.8	3.4	58,925	10.0	11.8	10.9
Phelps	3,626	40.1	2,030	3.4	34.8	25.6	25.2	15,866	31,259	58,105	43.2	2.4	61,442	11.3	13.0	11.2
Pierce	2,665	37.3	1,542	14.8	38.8	24.5	16.3	13,862	31,292	57,629	43.9	3.5	56,484	8.2	10.0	9.1

1. All persons 3 years old and over enrolled in nursery school through college. 2. Persons 25 years old and over. 3. Elementary and secondary education expenditures. 4. Based on population estimated by the American Community Survey, 2016–2020. 5. CDC percent based on 2019 population estimate.

STATE County	Personal income, 2020										Earnings, 2020		
			Per capita[1]			Supplements to wages and salaries, employer contributions (mil dol)						Contributions for government social insurance (mil dol)	
	Total (mil dol)	Percent change 2019–2020	Dollars	Rank	Wages and salaries (mil dol)	Pension and insurance	Government social insurance	Proprietors' income (mil dol)	Dividends, interest, and rent (mil dol)	Personal transfer reecipts (mil dol)	Total (mil dol)	From employee and self-employed	From employer
	62	63	64	65	66	67	68	69	70	71	72	73	74
NEBRASKA— Cont'd													
Blaine	32	17.0	70,372	162	6	2	1	12	8	5	20	1	1
Boone	354	16.9	69,564	170	99	20	8	107	71	65	234	10	8
Box Butte	575	8.3	53,723	803	281	46	36	71	78	168	435	29	36
Boyd	115	8.5	62,078	345	20	5	2	38	19	31	65	3	2
Brown	180	9.8	60,280	413	51	11	4	52	31	40	119	5	4
Buffalo	3,018	5.2	60,230	416	1,283	229	96	379	822	492	1,987	121	96
Burt	347	8.9	53,602	815	81	16	6	63	51	94	166	9	6
Butler	447	12.3	56,101	631	120	23	9	72	74	98	224	12	9
Cass	1,501	6.2	57,220	558	279	51	22	93	267	296	445	32	22
Cedar	491	15.8	58,373	504	115	23	9	114	86	91	261	13	9
Chase	264	15.3	68,843	181	81	15	6	88	45	49	190	8	6
Cherry	294	15.2	50,817	1,052	90	19	7	73	62	64	188	9	7
Cheyenne	459	5.5	50,334	1,106	186	34	15	47	106	118	282	18	15
Clay	355	11.7	57,104	567	117	24	9	69	56	75	219	11	9
Colfax	529	12.8	49,977	1,145	274	43	22	86	81	92	425	23	22
Cuming	630	10.6	71,653	143	179	31	14	223	98	102	447	18	14
Custer	579	11.4	54,458	747	193	41	15	112	106	135	362	20	15
Dakota	945	6.6	47,062	1,507	693	108	56	104	99	207	961	59	56
Dawes	360	9.9	43,101	2,050	125	30	10	39	61	99	203	13	10
Dawson	1,154	9.0	49,096	1,247	545	99	43	145	160	265	832	48	43
Deuel	78	6.8	43,738	1,982	21	5	2	11	16	26	38	3	2
Dixon	280	11.6	49,974	1,147	83	15	7	42	45	60	147	9	7
Dodge	1,900	5.9	52,445	895	884	146	69	226	355	453	1,326	86	69
Douglas	37,755	4.9	65,737	244	21,937	3,147	1,636	4,501	7,944	5,731	31,221	1,941	1,636
Dundy	144	20.4	86,360	53	29	6	2	59	25	26	97	3	2
Fillmore	349	11.1	63,206	312	108	22	8	74	72	77	212	12	8
Franklin	170	16.2	57,959	514	29	6	2	28	45	42	66	4	2
Frontier	120	18.3	46,216	1,618	34	8	3	23	21	28	67	4	3
Furnas	250	17.6	53,727	802	85	17	6	36	43	72	145	9	6
Gage	1,132	7.3	52,843	863	388	78	30	93	176	325	590	40	30
Garden	94	11.7	50,671	1,068	22	5	2	19	14	31	47	3	2
Garfield	94	14.3	47,856	1,411	31	7	2	18	21	26	59	4	2
Gosper	117	18.7	59,049	478	23	4	2	19	25	25	48	3	2
Grant	35	15.6	54,922	705	7	2	1	9	7	9	19	1	1
Greeley	131	18.4	56,500	609	28	6	2	34	27	28	70	3	2
Hall	2,917	6.8	47,793	1,417	1,669	286	129	223	527	663	2,306	146	129
Hamilton	566	10.4	61,230	378	187	31	14	94	109	106	326	18	14
Harlan	191	9.4	57,828	523	35	8	3	51	30	47	96	4	3
Hayes	73	23.2	79,926	80	9	2	1	38	9	9	50	1	1
Hitchcock	129	18.2	46,667	1,556	34	9	3	18	23	42	63	4	3
Holt	596	14.2	59,853	435	199	37	16	170	87	130	422	22	16
Hooker	35	10.5	54,516	740	12	2	1	9	6	10	24	2	1
Howard	330	11.7	50,857	1,046	68	15	5	51	51	73	139	8	5
Jefferson	379	11.2	53,407	824	144	27	12	50	77	102	233	14	12
Johnson	200	10.4	39,498	2,503	69	17	5	29	31	51	121	7	5
Kearney	410	11.9	61,585	364	101	20	8	88	75	83	217	10	8
Keith	407	7.2	51,040	1,022	141	26	11	61	84	107	239	15	11
Keya Paha	51	29.6	66,705	222	7	1	1	21	9	10	30	1	1
Kimball	175	9.3	50,075	1,137	65	14	5	19	40	51	103	7	5
Knox	443	13.9	53,356	830	121	26	9	82	80	112	238	14	9
Lancaster	16,958	5.4	52,887	862	9,393	1,684	710	782	3,398	3,142	12,568	797	710
Lincoln	1,856	7.3	54,043	777	818	137	80	276	256	486	1,312	82	80
Logan	44	18.7	58,616	491	7	2	1	17	4	9	26	1	1
Loup	40	15.7	61,740	358	5	1	0	17	6	8	23	1	0
McPherson	30	33.8	62,907	320	4	1	0	14	4	5	19	0	0
Madison	1,918	6.4	55,104	696	1,060	184	80	228	332	398	1,552	96	80
Merrick	397	8.4	50,870	1,043	99	19	8	63	68	96	188	11	8
Morrill	292	11.7	63,120	314	73	15	6	91	43	63	185	8	6
Nance	163	19.0	46,091	1,636	45	10	4	19	27	45	77	4	4
Nemaha	363	7.6	51,548	976	177	38	13	41	66	89	269	15	13
Nuckolls	246	14.2	59,449	456	62	13	5	52	41	68	131	7	5
Otoe	924	5.1	57,873	519	294	56	23	73	215	193	446	28	23
Pawnee	134	16.3	51,436	985	36	8	3	30	24	33	77	4	3
Perkins	204	13.0	71,191	151	61	13	5	75	30	34	154	6	5
Phelps	534	11.2	59,324	461	234	46	18	106	87	121	403	21	18
Pierce	449	10.0	62,493	336	88	18	7	118	66	77	230	11	7

1. Based on the resident population estimated as of July 1 of the year shown.

STATE County	Earnings, 2020 (cont.) — Percent by selected industries: Farm	Mining, quarrying, and extractions	Construction	Manu-facturing	Information; professional, scientific, technical services	Retail trade	Finance, insurance, real estate, and leasing	Health care and social assistance	Govern-ment	Social Security beneficiaries, December 2020: Number	Rate[1]	Supple-mental Security Income recipients, 2020	Housing units, 2021: Total	Percent change, 2010–2021
	75	76	77	78	79	80	81	82	83	84	85	86	87	88
NEBRASKA— Cont'd														
Blaine	58.8	0.0	1.6	0.2	0.2	D	D	D	24.3	110	239	D	299	0.0
Boone	40.9	0.0	4.0	5.4	D	5.4	D	4.2	17.6	1,305	242	47	2,551	-0.1
Box Butte	12.8	0.0	3.0	4.1	2.6	3.6	2.8	D	15.3	1,910	180	179	5,225	-0.1
Boyd	48.3	D	D	D	D	3.2	4.8	3.8	16.3	635	355	22	1,224	-0.1
Brown	37.8	0.0	4.5	2.9	D	5.2	D	3.8	22.0	775	267	40	1,639	-0.1
Buffalo	3.5	0.2	5.9	17.9	4.8	6.7	4.8	19.0	14.8	8,780	174	469	21,173	0.9
Burt	33.8	0.0	4.8	4.9	5.4	3.2	5.4	4.3	19.6	1,885	281	128	3,333	0.3
Butler	25.9	D	4.3	15.8	1.4	2.7	4.7	D	19.9	1,890	224	84	4,028	0.0
Cass	8.2	D	8.3	11.3	D	6.8	6.1	4.8	19.0	5,455	202	253	11,761	1.0
Cedar	32.4	D	5.8	4.8	2.5	3.8	9.4	D	16.4	1,945	233	61	3,905	0.1
Chase	37.0	-0.1	2.3	1.8	3.1	5.4	6.4	1.8	15.5	875	229	33	1,852	0.1
Cherry	34.3	0.0	5.7	2.0	D	5.7	3.7	4.8	19.6	1,295	237	70	2,992	0.3
Cheyenne	9.9	D	3.6	7.2	D	10.5	4.5	14.8	16.2	2,310	242	145	4,884	-0.1
Clay	27.0	D	7.1	9.6	D	3.0	D	3.9	23.0	1,525	251	77	2,820	0.1
Colfax	16.8	D	D	D	D	2.3	2.7	D	10.7	1,520	145	73	3,986	0.3
Cuming	43.7	D	3.9	6.8	3.9	2.8	7.1	D	9.5	2,125	237	75	4,150	0.6
Custer	24.9	0.0	6.0	15.9	3.1	5.1	6.5	D	14.7	2,550	244	138	5,324	0.2
Dakota	2.1	0.1	5.1	41.2	D	3.3	8.5	3.0	8.6	3,610	170	236	7,793	0.3
Dawes	9.6	D	3.8	D	2.9	12.5	4.2	11.7	35.6	1,715	210	97	4,005	0.1
Dawson	13.2	D	3.2	29.1	2.6	5.2	4.9	3.8	18.9	4,515	189	316	9,873	0.7
Deuel	17.1	0.1	D	0.5	D	8.5	D	2.0	27.7	525	282	30	1,048	0.0
Dixon	24.0	0.0	6.4	D	D	1.2	3.0	D	14.8	1,195	216	48	2,519	0.0
Dodge	6.2	0.1	6.7	25.0	3.0	8.4	4.6	D	11.4	8,475	228	571	16,598	2.2
Douglas	0.1	0.0	6.1	6.1	12.3	4.7	13.2	13.6	11.0	90,625	155	10,800	248,387	1.2
Dundy	50.6	0.2	4.4	1.7	D	3.4	3.6	2.1	15.2	480	294	27	1,010	0.2
Fillmore	25.0	0.1	8.7	7.7	D	3.7	D	4.5	19.1	1,520	274	52	2,721	0.1
Franklin	38.0	0.1	D	D	D	5.9	5.3	3.9	25.2	890	307	46	1,529	0.1
Frontier	27.5	0.0	7.1	4.4	D	4.3	8.8	D	26.2	570	223	28	1,396	0.1
Furnas	20.4	D	4.6	5.6	5.8	4.3	D	10.7	18.6	1,385	301	83	2,520	0.0
Gage	8.4	D	5.0	19.8	2.6	6.9	3.7	D	19.4	5,610	260	431	10,344	0.2
Garden	40.6	0.0	D	D	D	3.8	D	11.4	19.3	605	328	40	1,183	0.2
Garfield	21.9	D	3.2	12.6	D	7.2	4.2	9.6	15.7	500	272	17	1,062	0.8
Gosper	29.6	0.0	D	D	D	D	15.5	0.8	13.4	525	288	19	1,158	0.8
Grant	52.0	0.0	D	D	D	7.4	D	D	18.5	180	311	D	362	0.0
Greeley	40.6	0.0	3.6	1.8	D	3.4	6.5	0.8	19.4	600	277	38	1,198	0.7
Hall	2.5	D	6.4	21.4	3.3	8.0	7.3	11.6	15.7	11,110	179	977	25,373	0.8
Hamilton	22.5	0.0	4.3	9.8	D	5.6	4.5	D	9.5	2,205	235	65	4,115	0.5
Harlan	46.7	D	D	D	D	3.3	D	D	18.2	905	293	36	1,929	0.6
Hayes	68.3	D	D	2.0	D	D	2.6	D	9.5	195	231	D	441	-0.2
Hitchcock	20.0	6.8	4.5	16.6	D	2.5	D	0.6	25.0	810	313	46	1,570	-0.1
Holt	27.6	0.3	5.1	2.5	D	8.2	6.5	D	11.9	2,550	254	134	4,897	0.1
Hooker	12.4	0.0	D	0.9	D	7.2	D	D	18.4	225	307	D	412	0.5
Howard	32.0	D	4.1	2.0	D	5.1	D	5.1	28.2	1,510	231	59	2,884	0.5
Jefferson	17.6	D	7.3	18.6	D	5.8	2.8	10.4	14.1	1,935	270	170	3,674	0.2
Johnson	18.0	0.0	4.8	D	D	3.9	D	3.7	42.6	920	173	49	2,089	-0.1
Kearney	36.0	0.0	4.2	13.0	D	2.3	5.0	D	12.7	1,235	185	75	2,985	0.6
Keith	15.6	D	4.9	4.7	3.3	10.0	7.5	9.5	13.4	2,260	273	109	5,378	0.6
Keya Paha	57.7	0.3	D	D	D	D	D	D	11.4	270	343	D	496	0.0
Kimball	12.6	6.9	2.5	11.0	D	4.6	D	0.9	24.4	1,000	293	58	1,804	-0.1
Knox	29.1	0.0	5.9	4.3	D	4.7	4.3	D	26.0	2,330	277	117	4,515	0.2
Lancaster	0.3	D	6.7	7.7	10.7	5.7	8.2	14.0	21.7	51,980	160	5,030	137,706	1.3
Lincoln	13.2	0.0	4.4	2.3	2.9	6.0	5.1	15.9	16.2	6,745	198	713	16,549	0.1
Logan	36.6	0.0	D	D	D	7.2	4.5	D	17.2	150	218	D	367	0.0
Loup	60.0	0.1	D	5.1	0.5	D	D	D	14.3	170	281	D	424	0.7
McPherson	62.9	0.1	1.9	D	D	D	D	-0.1	9.8	75	198	D	232	0.0
Madison	4.4	D	5.5	17.7	3.5	7.1	9.8	15.6	15.7	7,320	207	524	15,485	2.2
Merrick	26.4	D	9.2	7.3	3.1	3.6	6.7	D	14.3	1,895	247	121	3,579	0.7
Morrill	42.4	D	1.1	4.1	D	3.3	3.3	2.2	21.5	970	212	86	2,268	-0.1
Nance	24.5	D	D	D	D	4.3	D	7.2	30.4	690	204	49	1,610	-0.1
Nemaha	11.5	0.0	2.2	4.6	3.2	2.7	D	4.9	59.3	1,625	230	124	3,311	0.0
Nuckolls	30.5	0.0	3.3	D	D	5.0	5.4	16.5	14.8	1,205	297	60	2,215	0.0
Otoe	8.5	0.0	7.7	22.2	D	6.2	4.6	8.2	23.8	3,620	227	189	6,962	0.2
Pawnee	27.5	D	D	15.2	D	4.0	D	3.4	20.3	650	255	46	1,405	0.2
Perkins	40.2	0.0	7.0	3.1	D	2.2	4.1	1.7	17.6	705	249	19	1,348	0.2
Phelps	23.0	D	5.2	13.4	2.4	5.8	6.0	D	11.9	2,120	237	122	4,161	0.2
Pierce	28.4	0.9	7.4	15.9	2.4	3.6	D	6.7	9.7	1,485	203	69	3,129	0.3

1. Per 1,000 resident population estimated as of July 1 of the year shown.

STATE County	Housing units, 2016–2020: Total	Occupied units: Owner-occupied: Percent	Owner-occupied: Median value[1]	Median owner cost as a percent of income: With a mortgage	Median owner cost as a percent of income: Without a mortgage[2]	Renter-occupied: Median rent[3]	Renter-occupied: Median rent as a percent of income[2]	Sub-standard units[4] (percent)	Civilian labor force, 2021: Total	Percent change, 2020–2021	Unemployment: Total	Unemployment: Rate[5]	Civilian employment[6], 2016–2020: Total	Percent: Management, business, science, and arts	Percent: Construction, production, and maintenance occupations
	89	90	91	92	93	94	95	96	97	98	99	100	101	102	103
NEBRASKA— Cont'd															
Blaine	237	67.9	77,700	29.5	10.0	788	12.5	0.8	248	-2.7	6	2.4	268	42.5	42.2
Boone	2,261	77.2	131,700	18.4	10.0	606	18.1	1.5	2,964	0.3	48	1.6	2,822	30.7	33.4
Box Butte	4,601	71.2	129,200	19.5	11.6	688	21.6	2.5	5,483	1.5	134	2.4	5,280	34.3	36.5
Boyd	876	83.8	85,000	22.1	11.3	495	27.8	1.3	1,040	-1.6	21	2.0	956	35.3	30.9
Brown	1,333	78.9	85,100	22.6	14.2	553	24.6	2.4	1,436	1.0	33	2.3	1,416	39.5	24.3
Buffalo	19,016	66.2	185,300	20.3	11.3	797	26.3	1.8	28,178	1.1	561	2.0	27,419	34.1	25.1
Burt	2,881	75.9	104,900	18.8	12.1	631	24.1	1.7	3,680	2.4	90	2.4	2,868	31.8	29.2
Butler	3,387	77.6	127,200	16.7	12.1	739	21.0	1.7	4,707	1.8	102	2.2	4,152	33.6	35.9
Cass	10,073	81.5	195,500	20.7	12.4	855	26.6	1.6	13,554	0.6	362	2.7	13,228	38.5	25.0
Cedar	3,479	80.2	121,800	17.8	10.7	674	19.6	0.5	4,665	2.2	83	1.8	4,493	35.9	28.9
Chase	1,591	77.6	139,200	20.9	10.5	688	22.2	0.4	2,263	-1.1	36	1.6	1,809	34.1	27.4
Cherry	2,459	59.6	124,900	19.9	10.0	707	24.3	1.3	3,473	2.1	55	1.6	3,362	34.6	22.8
Cheyenne	4,403	66.0	98,700	20.2	12.3	804	25.5	3.1	4,261	-0.6	119	2.8	4,841	36.5	24.1
Clay	2,575	80.6	102,500	17.8	10.0	586	23.3	3.0	3,259	-1.3	74	2.3	3,133	35.7	35.1
Colfax	3,742	72.0	92,900	20.2	10.0	692	16.2	5.4	5,728	0.9	109	1.9	5,263	25.8	52.0
Cuming	3,854	66.3	129,100	18.7	10.0	698	22.8	2.1	4,939	1.0	82	1.7	4,705	32.5	33.8
Custer	4,828	69.6	116,900	20.3	12.0	677	22.6	2.7	6,421	-0.1	102	1.6	5,443	36.1	31.2
Dakota	7,350	66.4	131,400	18.9	10.3	821	24.9	5.6	10,823	1.0	329	3.0	10,497	23.7	42.5
Dawes	3,555	63.5	125,200	21.6	11.7	745	27.2	0.8	5,020	0.7	95	1.9	4,455	37.2	20.2
Dawson	9,007	65.3	113,700	17.9	11.3	766	22.9	4.8	13,607	1.2	290	2.1	12,072	26.4	42.3
Deuel	823	78.4	89,800	22.7	11.8	639	22.1	1.6	977	1.0	21	2.1	865	38.5	26.4
Dixon	2,376	74.6	100,000	17.8	10.0	594	25.4	2.4	2,986	1.0	64	2.1	2,953	28.2	34.5
Dodge	15,284	62.2	137,100	19.2	10.7	771	24.1	2.0	20,420	0.6	480	2.4	18,229	31.7	29.2
Douglas	221,451	62.1	180,000	19.6	12.5	960	28.1	2.3	303,368	0.3	9,175	3.0	294,655	43.2	18.8
Dundy	842	77.0	76,900	18.8	10.0	491	24.7	0.4	1,171	0.3	19	1.6	1,027	41.5	24.3
Fillmore	2,488	77.8	89,200	15.8	10.0	568	21.5	0.4	3,291	2.7	64	1.9	2,941	33.7	29.4
Franklin	1,328	81.8	77,100	19.6	11.2	529	18.6	1.7	1,505	1.7	33	2.2	1,462	33.7	27.8
Frontier	1,136	69.1	111,100	19.0	10.7	607	23.9	1.8	1,576	1.3	27	1.7	1,290	42.0	28.7
Furnas	2,077	79.1	73,700	19.6	11.8	686	23.8	2.7	2,583	-1.3	49	1.9	2,338	37.1	31.0
Gage	9,048	68.0	124,100	18.7	10.5	638	27.8	1.1	10,945	-0.3	266	2.4	10,980	32.4	31.0
Garden	929	76.5	77,100	23.3	11.5	703	22.4	0.4	1,119	3.4	23	2.1	835	46.8	24.4
Garfield	906	79.0	106,000	21.2	10.0	446	20.8	1.1	1,151	-0.9	23	2.0	1,123	36.5	27.2
Gosper	940	75.5	165,500	17.7	13.3	673	19.3	0.0	1,211	8.8	20	1.7	991	41.3	29.0
Grant	297	69.0	72,500	20.0	15.7	825	21.8	2.4	428	1.9	6	1.4	343	34.4	32.4
Greeley	1,045	80.2	74,200	22.6	11.9	587	20.6	3.6	1,240	0.0	23	1.9	1,129	33.8	33.7
Hall	23,496	62.1	153,800	19.2	10.0	776	26.0	3.0	32,501	0.9	942	2.9	31,155	28.3	36.3
Hamilton	3,622	79.3	163,900	19.1	10.5	730	22.3	0.9	4,856	1.6	102	2.1	4,911	41.9	22.1
Harlan	1,515	78.4	113,900	16.8	12.4	677	23.1	6.1	1,797	2.5	34	1.9	1,681	35.4	26.1
Hayes	389	71.2	81,000	14.7	11.6	456	14.9	0.5	617	-2.7	8	1.3	454	44.5	22.0
Hitchcock	1,228	77.3	75,900	17.7	10.0	642	24.1	3.2	1,325	0.2	30	2.3	1,312	36.5	25.8
Holt	4,390	71.6	126,000	18.0	10.7	661	20.9	1.3	5,736	-0.6	100	1.7	5,520	40.3	27.3
Hooker	316	59.8	94,000	21.3	10.0	533	17.3	1.3	430	4.9	7	1.6	327	30.0	23.2
Howard	2,732	73.5	155,300	20.4	11.3	737	29.0	2.0	3,439	1.1	75	2.2	3,371	35.1	29.7
Jefferson	3,246	70.7	98,600	21.7	12.3	700	24.5	1.5	4,230	-0.1	75	1.8	3,465	35.6	33.8
Johnson	1,847	70.0	104,700	19.0	10.0	692	24.2	2.1	2,014	-3.1	58	2.9	1,976	36.3	30.8
Kearney	2,691	73.2	162,200	19.4	10.0	692	22.6	3.3	3,843	0.0	68	1.8	3,371	35.4	30.6
Keith	3,864	71.5	135,000	21.4	12.5	668	27.9	1.2	4,685	0.4	95	2.0	3,975	28.1	25.9
Keya Paha	349	73.6	65,000	14.7	13.0	786	17.5	0.3	590	0.9	10	1.7	452	47.3	25.4
Kimball	1,612	69.0	80,500	23.5	12.6	738	26.4	2.3	1,960	-1.3	44	2.2	1,799	22.0	33.2
Knox	3,605	74.1	92,300	18.0	11.0	500	19.9	2.2	4,735	1.0	97	2.0	4,229	36.9	27.7
Lancaster	126,666	59.2	190,000	19.4	10.6	873	27.0	2.5	178,631	0.1	4,359	2.4	171,589	42.0	19.3
Lincoln	14,765	67.5	153,200	18.7	11.9	763	27.1	1.4	18,596	0.3	409	2.2	17,475	32.1	32.4
Logan	319	77.1	107,900	27.5	14.2	614	32.9	2.5	471	-1.1	8	1.7	440	41.6	34.5
Loup	316	75.3	82,200	26.3	13.8	713	21.5	2.8	400	-2.2	8	2.0	365	45.5	24.7
McPherson	199	78.9	78,900	17.2	10.7	575	22.5	1.5	433	-2.3	7	1.6	233	41.6	18.5
Madison	14,187	67.8	155,200	19.3	12.1	702	25.8	2.0	20,079	1.3	481	2.4	17,919	30.1	33.0
Merrick	3,330	77.4	119,900	21.6	10.7	689	24.4	3.2	4,148	1.6	97	2.3	4,024	37.1	31.1
Morrill	1,969	75.2	103,200	19.7	14.3	684	24.7	2.5	2,641	0.1	65	2.5	2,198	36.2	29.4
Nance	1,530	87.0	78,400	19.6	10.0	654	18.6	0.9	1,972	-0.2	38	1.9	1,789	35.2	32.1
Nemaha	2,912	72.7	97,200	18.6	12.9	580	23.4	1.2	3,662	1.0	81	2.2	3,265	34.1	28.7
Nuckolls	1,852	79.8	73,900	17.9	10.0	518	26.0	1.2	2,501	0.9	46	1.8	2,222	38.8	22.0
Otoe	6,509	72.5	145,100	18.0	11.1	746	21.4	3.5	8,597	1.7	198	2.3	8,159	36.8	26.8
Pawnee	1,221	82.3	71,400	18.6	14.6	563	19.7	3.3	1,529	1.7	28	1.8	1,190	29.5	41.8
Perkins	1,202	79.3	118,400	18.2	11.2	713	21.5	0.5	1,874	0.7	26	1.4	1,463	37.0	29.5
Phelps	3,900	71.2	139,900	18.0	11.4	648	25.4	2.5	4,972	-0.8	87	1.7	4,637	35.8	32.0
Pierce	2,990	75.2	134,500	17.5	10.8	651	23.2	0.7	4,193	0.4	89	2.1	3,761	38.5	32.7

1. Specified owner-occupied units. 2. A value of 10.0 represents 10 percent or less; a value of 50.0 represents 50 percent or more. 3. Specified renter-occupied units. 4. Overcrowded or lacking complete plumbing facilities. 5. Percent of civilian labor force. 6. Civilian employed persons 16 years old and over.

STATE County	Private nonfarm establishments, employment and payroll, 2020									Agriculture, 2017			
		Employment						Annual payroll		Farms			Farm producers whose primary occupation is farming (percent)
											Percent with:		
	Number of establish-ments	Total	Health care and social assistance	Manufac-turing	Retail trade	Finance and insurance	Professional, scientific, and technical services	Total (mil dol)	Average per employee (dollars)	Number	Fewer than 50 acres	1000 acres or more	
	104	105	106	107	108	109	110	111	112	113	114	115	116
NEBRASKA— Cont'd													
Blaine	11	26	NA	NA	NA	NA	NA	1	33,192	101	5.9	72.3	70.0
Boone	192	1,426	283	90	221	95	25	61	42,607	524	15.6	23.5	57.3
Box Butte	294	2,637	495	292	366	132	101	105	39,789	431	13.7	33.4	54.1
Boyd	64	426	106	16	58	32	NA	14	31,998	286	15.7	34.3	64.6
Brown	138	932	149	51	293	51	39	31	33,606	268	21.6	40.7	51.2
Buffalo	1,695	23,086	4,228	3,615	3,814	731	738	940	40,715	953	27.7	18.4	48.0
Burt	182	1,088	186	32	185	66	68	39	36,203	521	28.0	17.5	49.4
Butler	214	1,969	391	594	226	131	40	89	45,328	723	23.9	14.9	50.1
Cass	575	4,437	441	423	798	227	145	176	39,594	766	37.9	15.7	43.2
Cedar	288	1,869	163	221	342	124	72	66	35,440	784	19.5	16.3	54.0
Chase	165	1,106	145	8	274	71	28	42	38,148	325	13.8	41.5	59.8
Cherry	211	1,368	269	26	302	48	86	46	33,663	567	10.8	61.9	63.9
Cheyenne	275	2,919	512	290	782	143	71	128	43,768	572	8.6	37.6	49.2
Clay	182	1,107	93	51	215	75	26	44	40,149	441	25.4	24.0	58.5
Colfax	251	3,955	141	NA	310	103	39	204	51,624	516	22.5	16.7	59.1
Cuming	332	2,731	385	492	362	209	141	119	43,533	804	23.9	13.2	53.0
Custer	364	3,096	621	683	599	224	106	132	42,668	1,108	18.1	36.2	55.9
Dakota	425	11,862	547	5,247	1,028	703	105	553	46,581	267	28.5	16.9	43.4
Dawes	243	1,842	404	10	567	88	64	62	33,681	491	16.7	35.0	50.4
Dawson	680	9,307	1,301	3,550	1,077	254	175	405	43,482	686	26.4	25.1	56.1
Deuel	51	267	NA	NA	95	25	NA	9	33,607	225	12.0	35.1	50.8
Dixon	114	1,120	77	NA	93	41	NA	44	39,564	567	28.7	14.3	47.1
Dodge	978	15,974	2,106	3,491	2,489	424	187	651	40,773	676	28.4	14.3	52.5
Douglas	16,028	326,958	56,095	23,146	35,688	40,504	18,972	17,627	53,913	367	61.3	6.8	32.5
Dundy	54	341	127	17	39	16	14	13	39,367	268	6.0	51.1	68.3
Fillmore	211	1,672	347	251	206	138	28	72	43,136	439	14.4	27.1	65.7
Franklin	75	352	105	NA	75	30	26	12	35,298	317	16.1	30.0	61.5
Frontier	69	419	54	NA	91	41	14	15	36,031	371	22.4	34.5	54.8
Furnas	152	1,169	304	123	209	57	23	48	41,246	377	12.7	34.2	54.1
Gage	657	6,963	1,622	1,538	1,070	212	158	266	38,207	1,188	33.2	14.8	42.3
Garden	45	211	NA	NA	61	21	NA	6	27,199	221	15.4	46.2	54.6
Garfield	98	632	127	132	125	19	19	21	32,872	202	27.7	31.7	54.4
Gosper	58	177	12	NA	26	27	NA	6	36,463	287	8.7	28.9	56.4
Grant	29	77	NA	NA	13	NA	NA	2	26,013	64	1.6	64.1	80.0
Greeley	72	336	25	14	79	34	11	11	31,777	369	8.4	28.5	59.8
Hall	1,889	33,360	4,540	8,613	4,705	1,374	596	1,337	40,082	582	28.9	18.6	54.7
Hamilton	324	2,945	433	518	362	127	102	130	44,168	586	31.2	17.9	55.4
Harlan	94	586	178	43	99	44	29	22	37,239	281	23.5	38.4	54.9
Hayes	19	54	NA	NA	12	NA	NA	2	31,630	220	9.5	43.2	53.9
Hitchcock	67	429	19	94	45	21	NA	16	38,035	288	9.0	38.9	51.7
Holt	427	3,209	802	94	515	182	97	122	37,931	1,142	15.7	33.3	55.5
Hooker	26	99	NA	NA	25	NA	NA	5	48,051	97	7.2	67.0	62.3
Howard	172	1,041	310	24	226	99	35	37	35,708	617	25.9	13.0	49.6
Jefferson	223	2,538	442	743	381	66	39	95	37,284	590	20.2	20.0	50.8
Johnson	107	859	208	183	128	56	29	30	35,425	502	24.1	11.2	41.9
Kearney	177	1,781	523	434	120	69	32	69	38,999	342	14.3	34.8	68.6
Keith	334	2,503	226	171	573	172	115	89	35,626	318	19.8	32.7	45.4
Keya Paha	16	42	NA	NA	17	NA	NA	1	30,595	237	6.3	46.0	68.9
Kimball	120	1,165	115	365	136	54	23	51	43,506	443	8.1	32.1	42.5
Knox	250	1,635	307	52	300	146	62	52	31,698	956	18.0	19.2	50.2
Lancaster	8,721	146,580	26,850	12,464	18,346	14,890	9,056	6,712	45,788	1,786	54.9	7.3	34.1
Lincoln	1,037	11,454	2,806	328	1,978	581	374	460	40,170	1,040	26.3	29.5	45.6
Logan	21	68	NA	NA	NA	NA	NA	2	31,456	117	24.8	33.3	61.6
Loup	17	40	NA	NA	10	NA	NA	1	19,675	130	19.2	37.7	62.9
McPherson	7	17	NA	NA	9	NA	NA	0	28,765	109	8.3	63.3	62.1
Madison	1,236	18,457	3,636	3,244	2,981	642	591	803	43,528	659	24.6	16.4	52.3
Merrick	232	1,662	326	208	194	97	43	69	41,747	483	28.0	16.6	52.7
Morrill	109	808	155	41	197	57	9	32	39,724	426	20.0	31.5	55.7
Nance	89	465	133	NA	103	47	15	15	31,391	375	21.1	25.1	58.7
Nemaha	176	1,348	371	180	203	95	41	48	35,771	410	24.6	21.5	49.2
Nuckolls	169	1,103	412	7	184	75	41	38	34,503	431	9.3	27.1	59.3
Otoe	456	4,673	719	1,387	695	152	78	178	38,056	815	28.6	16.6	42.5
Pawnee	72	637	106	284	83	38	12	29	44,837	460	15.2	18.7	47.0
Perkins	125	895	259	41	135	29	12	42	46,982	418	10.0	36.1	55.7
Phelps	346	3,934	740	770	468	160	159	172	43,753	371	12.4	33.7	66.6
Pierce	235	1,537	277	119	177	111	60	59	38,377	625	23.0	18.2	51.4

STATE County	Agriculture, 2017 (cont.)															
	Land in farms					Value of land and buildings (dollars)		Value of machinery and equipment, average per farm (dollars)	Value of products sold:				Organic farms (number)	Farms with internet access (percent)	Government payments	
	Acreage (1,000)	Percent change, 2012–2017	Acres								Percent from:					
			Average size of farm	Total irrigated (1,000)	Total cropland (1,000)	Average per farm	Average per acre		Total (mil dol)	Average per farm (acres)	Crops	Livestock and poultry products			Total ($1,000)	Percent of farms
	117	118	119	120	121	122	123	124	125	126	127	128	129	130	131	132
NEBRASKA— Cont'd																
Blaine	367	-8.9	3,630	8.5	28.8	3,603,549	993	173,445	32.1	317,376	6.6	93.4	NA	89.1	979	43.6
Boone	432	-0.5	825	169.8	319.2	3,669,838	4,449	399,375	473.8	904,158	34.1	65.9	1	79.6	9,212	73.3
Box Butte	677	0.3	1,571	138.5	346.6	2,096,463	1,334	311,694	176.9	410,517	60.9	39.1	2	81.0	7,657	72.2
Boyd	323	11.0	1,129	13.9	135.6	2,290,609	2,028	258,985	104.3	364,577	38.7	61.3	2	76.6	2,160	72.4
Brown	615	-15.2	2,295	40.1	108.1	2,689,620	1,172	259,836	290.7	1,084,873	7.8	92.2	NA	85.8	809	39.6
Buffalo	528	-9.0	554	214.1	324.5	2,435,697	4,393	241,065	332.7	349,120	52.1	47.9	NA	80.9	8,917	62.4
Burt	298	-3.8	572	47.5	275.2	3,524,417	6,160	318,618	263.7	506,226	55.1	44.9	6	80.4	8,438	73.5
Butler	374	1.1	517	102.3	319.1	2,946,211	5,693	273,973	259.8	359,288	62.2	37.8	10	79.4	11,674	77.3
Cass	346	0.4	452	3.9	306.4	2,534,769	5,607	202,195	164.2	214,405	92.5	7.5	9	82.4	5,164	62.9
Cedar	474	1.5	604	163.2	393.2	3,129,654	5,182	295,573	423.1	539,617	44.0	56.0	2	80.1	14,856	75.8
Chase	569	5.1	1,750	168.9	323.0	3,647,226	2,085	480,540	440.1	1,354,191	34.6	65.4	NA	88.3	10,653	72.9
Cherry	3,563	-5.2	6,284	53.0	383.7	5,862,309	933	240,960	230.9	407,279	14.6	85.4	7	85.4	3,302	22.6
Cheyenne	759	8.0	1,328	52.6	528.8	1,354,420	1,020	193,548	163.9	286,594	37.2	62.8	15	73.6	13,034	83.6
Clay	319	-3.5	723	190.6	259.5	3,508,217	4,850	345,579	356.1	807,372	44.2	55.8	2	90.0	10,804	68.3
Colfax	262	1.8	508	81.0	240.4	3,149,351	6,194	354,733	364.5	706,298	34.6	65.4	6	85.5	7,546	76.2
Cuming	364	0.2	452	53.1	330.1	2,752,249	6,087	334,881	1,132.0	1,407,956	15.7	84.3	3	76.5	9,249	76.9
Custer	1,505	0.1	1,358	258.0	481.9	3,361,912	2,475	269,342	781.2	705,014	23.5	76.5	NA	81.9	14,411	48.5
Dakota	167	5.4	624	29.2	151.1	3,527,505	5,656	268,570	85.0	318,180	91.7	8.3	NA	73.0	4,211	69.7
Dawes	750	-9.0	1,528	17.8	174.5	1,358,907	889	115,299	60.9	124,100	22.9	77.1	1	84.1	2,924	63.5
Dawson	610	-3.2	889	235.0	303.7	3,034,516	3,412	336,300	748.4	1,091,000	22.9	77.1	16	84.4	15,112	60.5
Deuel	276	-0.2	1,227	17.4	226.8	1,601,034	1,305	277,172	71.3	316,960	49.5	50.5	NA	74.7	4,297	76.9
Dixon	279	-6.6	492	28.1	221.8	2,303,075	4,676	232,241	271.6	478,968	38.0	62.0	2	83.8	8,379	68.1
Dodge	337	2.2	499	132.6	312.5	3,199,731	6,412	286,042	270.5	400,151	65.3	34.7	9	76.3	9,943	74.1
Douglas	91	5.4	247	24.6	81.6	1,891,447	7,644	169,943	55.5	151,324	93.7	6.3	NA	88.8	2,205	35.7
Dundy	540	3.7	2,016	78.4	210.5	3,082,953	1,530	404,375	161.1	601,254	37.9	62.1	NA	88.1	5,558	76.1
Fillmore	329	0.3	750	219.9	305.3	4,088,900	5,448	460,510	240.9	548,850	74.9	25.1	NA	84.5	12,680	79.5
Franklin	316	10.0	998	97.5	187.0	3,456,445	3,462	273,977	106.9	337,088	84.8	15.2	NA	82.0	5,786	75.7
Frontier	484	7.1	1,305	50.2	203.8	2,452,811	1,879	262,770	121.4	327,332	50.0	50.0	NA	84.6	4,408	57.7
Furnas	450	3.3	1,194	64.1	291.5	2,946,660	2,467	338,139	240.4	637,637	42.2	57.8	NA	75.9	5,050	79.3
Gage	539	0.9	454	90.8	449.4	2,008,444	4,427	195,339	280.2	235,836	64.4	35.6	NA	83.0	14,883	70.6
Garden	1,018	-0.8	4,608	34.6	166.3	3,992,706	866	240,357	81.2	367,416	40.8	59.2	3	86.9	1,939	61.1
Garfield	342	-1.0	1,696	15.3	66.4	2,513,876	1,483	142,181	54.7	270,891	19.7	80.3	NA	83.7	671	36.6
Gosper	282	-2.7	983	79.2	150.2	2,763,817	2,812	361,583	105.7	368,397	69.4	30.6	1	83.3	5,134	61.3
Grant	495	0.4	7,736	1.7	50.6	6,476,796	837	236,936	D	D	D	D	NA	90.6	D	3.1
Greeley	339	0.3	919	91.9	156.5	2,726,640	2,965	274,794	193.3	523,957	34.2	65.8	NA	82.1	4,895	77.8
Hall	328	-0.4	564	230.8	272.0	2,866,675	5,083	354,102	302.4	519,589	57.7	42.3	1	85.2	13,806	69.8
Hamilton	312	2.6	533	248.1	286.7	3,379,235	6,341	333,006	275.7	470,561	69.3	30.7	9	85.0	13,043	69.1
Harlan	334	6.7	1,188	86.6	220.6	3,417,433	2,878	370,997	160.3	570,374	58.6	41.4	2	83.6	5,397	69.4
Hayes	437	13.4	1,985	55.8	195.7	2,809,923	1,415	293,526	167.2	760,155	35.8	64.2	NA	84.1	2,946	83.2
Hitchcock	393	-1.7	1,363	24.3	228.3	2,145,874	1,574	230,905	59.6	207,024	76.5	23.5	1	71.9	3,038	75.3
Holt	1,393	-1.5	1,220	303.7	608.0	2,904,705	2,380	268,044	453.5	397,144	49.4	50.6	5	75.7	11,202	49.0
Hooker	427	-2.2	4,402	2.5	6.8	3,237,188	735	109,284	D	D	D	D	NA	72.2	451	24.7
Howard	281	-10.1	455	115.6	178.0	1,587,631	3,491	215,883	235.2	381,172	35.2	64.8	NA	78.3	7,045	63.5
Jefferson	359	1.9	608	105.4	283.7	2,525,053	4,151	262,657	219.6	372,158	52.0	48.0	NA	77.6	8,991	76.1
Johnson	197	-0.1	393	19.4	137.7	1,427,986	3,631	151,986	83.1	165,602	59.2	40.8	1	72.1	4,348	80.1
Kearney	291	-0.8	852	189.5	244.9	4,456,076	5,232	482,408	369.7	1,081,094	42.4	57.6	1	93.3	10,195	72.8
Keith	491	-9.2	1,546	79.9	226.7	2,513,223	1,626	294,853	161.9	508,972	48.5	51.5	9	88.4	4,957	60.4
Keya Paha	423	-9.2	1,784	25.0	95.6	2,527,270	1,416	200,328	52.3	220,810	34.8	65.2	NA	84.0	1,305	38.0
Kimball	603	1.0	1,362	33.8	410.7	1,464,107	1,075	141,161	40.0	90,237	75.9	24.1	26	65.9	9,488	81.0
Knox	601	-4.3	628	70.8	323.6	2,102,065	3,345	223,437	288.5	301,768	37.5	62.5	11	76.8	12,233	72.6
Lancaster	423	-13.5	237	21.3	362.9	1,325,789	5,598	125,910	188.8	105,730	82.3	17.7	11	85.8	9,485	53.1
Lincoln	1,357	-4.7	1,305	242.8	421.6	2,184,451	1,674	221,829	755.2	726,188	24.5	75.5	7	83.4	13,167	44.2
Logan	298	-9.7	2,547	16.2	41.9	3,055,685	1,200	227,088	28.6	244,564	35.6	64.4	NA	68.4	1,227	41.9
Loup	280	-1.1	2,152	9.4	24.0	2,502,612	1,163	167,861	30.8	236,946	14.3	85.7	NA	85.4	765	46.2
McPherson	489	3.9	4,486	8.1	22.7	3,675,404	819	168,099	28.4	260,541	7.5	92.5	NA	73.4	471	28.4
Madison	353	0.5	536	130.7	312.1	3,120,513	5,819	324,775	276.1	418,948	57.0	43.0	2	79.5	7,543	69.7
Merrick	243	3.3	503	163.8	201.5	2,551,386	5,074	278,229	240.3	497,573	47.4	52.6	5	80.7	8,619	67.1
Morrill	829	3.7	1,945	121.8	242.5	2,226,414	1,145	237,293	319.7	750,451	25.1	74.9	1	73.0	5,034	67.4
Nance	220	5.7	587	75.6	158.8	2,480,621	4,227	240,847	155.3	414,141	48.6	51.4	6	77.3	6,113	73.9
Nemaha	261	2.9	636	15.4	230.0	2,893,077	4,548	234,596	114.4	279,090	93.3	6.7	6	74.6	6,373	79.5
Nuckolls	357	2.2	829	76.7	248.7	2,975,636	3,588	321,294	147.5	342,276	79.0	21.0	9	82.6	8,084	81.9
Otoe	390	0.6	479	12.8	331.0	2,372,053	4,957	203,937	170.5	209,232	85.3	14.7	9	83.1	5,740	73.3
Pawnee	273	1.4	593	11.4	183.7	1,921,924	3,244	194,408	78.9	171,454	72.0	28.0	NA	68.7	3,568	76.5
Perkins	556	-0.1	1,330	131.9	432.1	2,847,060	2,140	350,487	196.8	470,794	74.6	25.4	2	84.9	11,277	80.4
Phelps	342	3.1	921	225.4	277.1	4,707,223	5,114	603,438	578.2	1,558,601	29.8	70.2	NA	85.7	13,067	81.7
Pierce	344	4.4	550	127.1	275.2	2,679,363	4,872	300,420	255.5	408,749	48.8	51.2	2	72.6	10,199	71.8

STATE County	Water use, 2015		Wholesale Trade[1], 2017				Retail Trade[2], 2017				Real estate and rental and leasing,[2] 2017			
	Public supply water withdrawn (mil gal/ day)	Public supply gallons withdrawn per person per day	Number of establish-ments	Number of employees	Sales (mil dol)	Average payroll (mil dol)	Number of establish-ments	Number of employees	Sales (mil dol)	Average payroll (mil dol)	Number of establish-ments	Number of employees	Sales (mil dol)	Average payroll (mil dol)
	133	134	135	136	137	138	139	140	141	142	143	144	145	146
NEBRASKA— Cont'd														
Blaine	0.0	41.1	NA	NA	NA	NA	NA	NA	NA	NA	NA	NA	NA	NA
Boone	0.6	118.5	16	205	342.9	9.2	36	272	75.8	5.4	D	D	D	D
Box Butte	1.6	139.4	20	240	164.8	10.5	39	422	101.2	9.2	D	D	D	D
Boyd	0.2	74.8	D	D	D	D	12	64	13.0	1.3	NA	NA	NA	NA
Brown	0.5	166.3	6	98	81.8	5.3	31	287	86.1	6.9	NA	NA	NA	NA
Buffalo	6.5	132.0	81	933	1,024.1	48.2	242	4,132	1,018.7	98.9	67	169	49.2	5.9
Burt	0.9	129.1	18	216	182.4	9.6	33	221	36.7	3.4	5	D	0.4	D
Butler	0.7	83.8	15	150	155.2	8.3	27	205	33.7	4.1	NA	NA	NA	NA
Cass	13.5	530.3	D	D	D	6.2	63	931	314.2	22.2	29	41	8.3	1.6
Cedar	0.7	75.9	27	185	146.5	8.6	45	339	89.8	7.6	7	D	1.3	D
Chase	0.9	230.0	22	204	458.9	10.2	31	358	113.4	10.1	4	4	0.2	0.1
Cherry	0.6	104.3	8	42	137.6	1.7	41	332	93.4	7.8	12	17	2.1	0.4
Cheyenne	2.2	212.5	16	114	68.5	6.2	48	823	646.4	24.8	8	21	2.0	0.6
Clay	1.3	198.1	18	139	153.3	6.8	27	208	71.7	5.5	3	3	0.4	0.1
Colfax	1.1	105.5	18	231	212.6	12.7	39	317	55.9	7.7	5	D	0.8	D
Cuming	1.6	176.4	23	163	139.7	8.0	48	403	128.1	9.0	4	6	0.4	0.1
Custer	1.2	109.2	11	72	36.9	3.3	76	629	169.7	15.1	5	D	0.4	D
Dakota	2.0	97.2	D	D	D	8.8	69	1,023	212.2	22.4	D	D	D	D
Dawes	1.2	130.3	5	71	11.3	1.5	46	661	174.4	17.6	5	D	0.8	D
Dawson	6.0	249.9	41	449	415.2	22.4	110	1,123	397.1	31.5	D	D	D	D
Deuel	0.5	260.3	4	D	20.5	D	14	104	79.9	2.4	NA	NA	NA	NA
Dixon	0.8	129.4	D	D	D	D	10	73	14.2	1.3	NA	NA	NA	NA
Dodge	0.7	19.1	59	874	1,121.8	49.3	144	2,415	751.5	65.4	44	174	31.5	5.6
Douglas	56.6	103.0	730	10,638	14,090.4	700.7	1,678	34,438	9,991.2	939.7	927	6,264	1,320.6	299.5
Dundy	0.3	155.6	D	D	D	D	9	29	14.9	0.8	NA	NA	NA	NA
Fillmore	0.8	138.8	23	161	165.7	7.5	32	215	54.3	4.9	4	5	0.3	0.1
Franklin	0.7	224.5	8	D	55.6	D	13	100	19.3	2.5	NA	NA	NA	NA
Frontier	0.3	102.9	D	D	D	D	13	77	17.0	1.7	NA	NA	NA	NA
Furnas	0.6	119.3	7	106	163.0	7.4	26	198	39.0	4.1	NA	NA	NA	NA
Gage	3.6	164.4	D	D	D	18.2	109	1,104	277.0	26.3	20	33	5.8	0.9
Garden	0.2	114.7	NA	NA	NA	NA	11	59	12.1	1.1	NA	NA	NA	NA
Garfield	0.2	88.8	3	60	9.5	1.0	20	142	29.8	2.7	NA	NA	NA	NA
Gosper	0.3	141.9	6	23	28.8	1.1	4	29	4.1	0.4	NA	NA	NA	NA
Grant	0.1	78.0	NA	NA	NA	NA	5	27	4.6	0.3	NA	NA	NA	NA
Greeley	0.2	94.7	7	72	47.5	2.9	14	90	36.3	2.1	NA	NA	NA	NA
Hall	11.9	193.6	95	1,251	859.6	71.2	306	5,070	1,276.3	129.7	75	313	58.1	10.5
Hamilton	1.2	134.9	23	372	651.6	25.4	40	344	131.9	8.6	9	22	1.9	0.4
Harlan	0.5	130.4	11	D	80.1	D	17	113	45.3	2.6	NA	NA	NA	NA
Hayes	0.1	96.6	NA	NA	NA	NA	4	18	1.4	0.4	NA	NA	NA	NA
Hitchcock	0.4	128.3	9	D	76.4	D	12	63	11.6	1.2	NA	NA	NA	NA
Holt	1.2	111.5	37	415	305.7	16.7	71	575	157.6	12.4	9	13	1.9	0.4
Hooker	0.2	245.9	NA	NA	NA	NA	6	27	6.1	0.6	NA	NA	NA	NA
Howard	0.6	87.4	8	55	49.3	2.4	24	241	51.8	5.3	D	D	D	D
Jefferson	1.1	152.8	19	197	212.9	9.0	27	439	161.5	10.1	7	11	1.0	0.3
Johnson	1.0	193.3	D	D	D	1.2	24	133	36.7	3.3	3	D	3.2	D
Kearney	0.9	130.6	15	158	257.0	8.6	19	133	31.4	3.3	NA	NA	NA	NA
Keith	1.1	133.9	16	163	143.7	6.5	61	690	222.1	17.7	15	30	3.0	0.7
Keya Paha	0.1	62.2	NA	NA	NA	NA	4	21	3.4	0.3	NA	NA	NA	NA
Kimball	0.5	141.0	D	D	D	D	22	171	41.2	4.1	NA	NA	NA	NA
Knox	1.0	113.5	14	137	123.0	7.0	42	342	71.8	6.4	9	D	2.0	D
Lancaster	1.5	5.0	286	4,065	4,341.6	223.6	1,010	18,415	4,810.3	477.3	415	1,999	367.7	81.7
Lincoln	5.6	157.9	D	D	D	D	190	2,257	704.5	54.4	47	158	30.9	6.0
Logan	0.1	64.4	NA	NA	NA	NA	NA	NA	NA	NA	NA	NA	NA	NA
Loup	0.0	0.0	NA	NA	NA	NA	NA	NA	NA	NA	NA	NA	NA	NA
McPherson	0.0	0.0	NA	NA	NA	NA	NA	NA	NA	NA	NA	NA	NA	NA
Madison	4.9	141.0	58	1,828	1,959.1	78.9	209	3,008	767.5	72.6	68	203	41.7	8.7
Merrick	0.8	102.7	21	162	155.2	9.1	27	208	66.7	4.8	D	D	D	D
Morrill	0.4	88.6	9	D	242.6	D	20	172	34.1	3.6	3	D	0.7	D
Nance	0.4	102.9	D	D	D	1.7	18	116	26.2	2.4	NA	NA	NA	NA
Nemaha	0.9	126.3	10	57	40.9	2.2	28	261	64.5	5.7	6	D	0.9	D
Nuckolls	0.6	127.1	15	122	106.5	5.7	25	210	61.3	5.0	NA	NA	NA	NA
Otoe	2.5	158.9	23	140	190.7	7.4	66	764	194.6	17.6	20	56	6.7	1.7
Pawnee	0.4	139.2	NA	NA	NA	NA	12	78	25.0	1.6	NA	NA	NA	NA
Perkins	0.7	231.0	15	106	238.6	6.1	18	138	71.3	4.3	NA	NA	NA	NA
Phelps	1.6	174.3	28	329	509.2	17.6	51	474	141.1	12.0	6	D	1.2	D
Pierce	0.7	95.7	D	D	D	D	30	209	46.8	3.8	D	D	D	D

1 Merchant wholesalers, except manufacturers' sales branches and offices. 2. Employer establishments.

STATE County	Professional, scientific, and technical services, 2017				Manufacturing, 2017				Accommodation and food services, 2017			
	Number of establish-ments	Number of employees	Sales (mil dol)	Average payroll (mil dol)	Number of establish-ments	Number of employees	Sales (mil dol)	Average payroll (mil dol)	Number of establis-hments	Number of employees	Sales (mil dol)	Annual payroll (mil dol)
	147	148	149	150	151	152	153	154	155	156	157	158
NEBRASKA— Cont'd												
Blaine	NA	NA	NA	NA	NA	NA	NA	NA	NA	NA	NA	NA
Boone	7	28	6.2	1.0	D	93	D	6.2	11	83	4.0	1.0
Box Butte	19	90	9.2	2.8	7	277	97.5	14.3	30	338	17.0	5.0
Boyd	NA	NA	NA	NA	4	14	1.7	0.4	3	19	0.6	0.2
Brown	8	22	2.9	0.7	D	D	D	D	11	D	4.1	D
Buffalo	115	1,088	112.2	48.1	58	3,146	1,503.2	159.0	161	3,133	154.2	45.4
Burt	9	57	13.9	3.6	6	34	21.1	1.7	13	D	3.2	D
Butler	11	40	3.9	1.8	8	490	166.6	22.0	D	D	D	D
Cass	38	126	16.5	6.5	22	376	184.8	21.0	37	401	17.1	4.8
Cedar	12	75	11.0	2.8	9	195	74.0	12.6	16	D	4.7	D
Chase	13	24	3.8	0.9	5	13	0.8	0.2	9	D	2.6	D
Cherry	23	92	10.2	2.3	7	19	4.6	1.1	27	341	22.7	7.4
Cheyenne	15	62	9.1	3.1	11	389	118.0	17.2	36	443	23.6	7.6
Clay	9	36	4.3	1.2	5	43	21.5	2.0	11	D	1.7	D
Colfax	12	46	5.9	1.6	D	D	D	D	D	D	D	D
Cuming	D	D	D	D	21	360	442.2	18.3	24	240	9.5	2.7
Custer	28	95	11.5	3.2	D	556	D	D	32	307	12.3	3.7
Dakota	D	D	D	D	36	5,462	3,633.6	234.6	43	643	37.4	10.8
Dawes	17	66	5.1	2.1	3	8	1.6	0.3	37	459	20.2	5.7
Dawson	D	D	D	D	D	D	D	D	61	651	42.4	9.2
Deuel	NA	NA	NA	NA	NA	NA	NA	NA	D	D	D	0.6
Dixon	NA	NA	NA	NA	NA	NA	NA	NA	D	D	D	D
Dodge	45	217	27.1	9.1	51	3,553	1,600.2	170.3	87	1,358	61.5	17.5
Douglas	1,845	19,367	3,257.7	1,289.7	390	20,969	11,619.9	1,047.6	1,415	28,267	1,578.4	461.6
Dundy	5	16	1.8	0.4	3	8	2.7	0.5	4	D	1.2	D
Fillmore	10	27	3.2	0.9	13	230	259.0	11.9	12	42	2.2	0.5
Franklin	4	22	2.8	0.9	NA	NA	NA	NA	6	D	1.1	D
Frontier	3	15	1.5	0.6	NA	NA	NA	NA	6	D	1.6	D
Furnas	7	23	2.6	0.8	8	129	115.3	5.5	13	68	2.7	0.6
Gage	35	146	13.9	5.6	38	1,304	669.7	71.4	49	643	29.4	7.6
Garden	NA	NA	NA	NA	NA	NA	NA	NA	6	D	0.9	D
Garfield	10	18	2.8	0.6	5	92	32.9	4.0	10	D	1.5	D
Gosper	NA	NA	NA	NA	NA	NA	NA	NA	NA	NA	NA	NA
Grant	NA	NA	NA	NA	NA	NA	NA	NA	D	D	D	0.1
Greeley	NA	NA	NA	NA	3	14	1.6	0.4	4	17	0.9	0.2
Hall	D	D	D	D	64	6,799	4,629.0	332.7	165	2,662	147.2	42.9
Hamilton	23	100	15.3	5.2	19	582	664.9	23.9	19	163	6.5	2.2
Harlan	8	30	2.9	0.8	3	31	7.1	D	17	91	5.7	1.0
Hayes	NA	NA	NA	NA	NA	NA	NA	NA	NA	NA	NA	NA
Hitchcock	NA	NA	NA	NA	3	82	127.9	6.6	4	19	0.6	0.1
Holt	24	88	12.4	4.4	19	164	91.0	7.2	29	290	12.6	3.2
Hooker	NA	NA	NA	NA	NA	NA	NA	NA	NA	NA	NA	NA
Howard	9	36	5.4	1.4	5	23	3.6	0.7	D	D	D	D
Jefferson	13	52	6.7	1.8	18	642	188.7	29.9	20	162	7.6	1.8
Johnson	6	29	2.3	0.6	D	D	D	D	D	D	D	0.5
Kearney	9	23	3.1	1.0	11	301	238.0	15.2	14	95	3.9	1.2
Keith	32	117	14.3	4.5	13	205	22.5	6.8	48	527	26.7	7.8
Keya Paha	4	4	0.3	0.1	NA	NA	NA	NA	NA	NA	NA	NA
Kimball	8	15	1.4	0.4	7	185	33.1	7.4	12	46	3.5	0.7
Knox	17	64	7.1	1.9	7	29	9.7	1.4	20	197	14.2	3.4
Lancaster	891	8,517	1,467.6	495.8	229	12,008	4,863.0	683.8	777	15,006	761.1	216.1
Lincoln	D	D	D	D	D	D	D	D	100	1,848	92.3	25.8
Logan	NA	NA	NA	NA	NA	NA	NA	NA	NA	NA	NA	NA
Loup	NA	NA	NA	NA	NA	NA	NA	NA	D	D	D	0.1
McPherson	NA	NA	NA	NA	NA	NA	NA	NA	NA	NA	NA	NA
Madison	D	D	D	D	D	3,056	D	D	93	1,634	77.8	21.5
Merrick	8	39	4.8	1.5	14	212	279.3	10.3	D	D	D	D
Morrill	4	15	1.6	0.5	NA	NA	NA	NA	8	53	2.3	0.7
Nance	D	D	D	D	NA	NA	NA	NA	10	D	2.0	D
Nemaha	11	45	3.0	1.1	D	D	D	D	21	249	9.0	3.1
Nuckolls	11	28	3.0	0.8	D	7	D	0.2	11	D	2.9	D
Otoe	28	79	8.8	2.5	16	1,474	562.1	59.7	40	434	17.1	4.7
Pawnee	D	D	D	D	D	D	D	D	6	D	0.8	D
Perkins	7	18	1.4	0.5	D	45	D	3.0	5	D	0.8	D
Phelps	23	103	12.8	4.2	D	D	D	D	18	264	9.1	2.5
Pierce	11	53	3.9	1.3	D	D	D	D	11	82	2.5	0.6

STATE County	Health care and social assistance, 2017				Other services, 2017				Nonemployer businesses, 2019		Value of residential construction authorized by building permits, 2021	
	Number of establish-ments	Number of employees	Receipts (mil dol)	Annual payroll (mil dol)	Number of establish-ments	Number of employees	Receipts (mil dol)	Annual payroll (mil dol)	Number	Receipts (mil dol)	New construction ($1,000)	Number of housing units
	159	160	161	162	163	164	165	166	167	168	169	170
NEBRASKA— Cont'd												
Blaine	NA	NA	NA	NA	NA	NA	NA	NA	41	0.9	NA	NA
Boone	18	277	19.6	7.3	15	30	4.2	1.1	525	25.1	1,500	4
Box Butte	27	548	47.9	21.0	28	83	10.8	2.5	709	29.8	0	0
Boyd	7	D	7.0	D	3	6	0.9	0.1	189	12.2	0	0
Brown	12	158	15.8	7.0	D	D	3.6	D	297	12.4	0	0
Buffalo	206	4,103	678.2	174.1	124	655	91.9	17.9	3,940	184.5	61,530	207
Burt	16	243	25.5	9.0	D	D	8.5	D	546	29.6	3,059	12
Butler	16	378	33.6	14.1	D	D	D	D	677	33.0	2,114	8
Cass	31	411	22.9	9.6	41	122	11.8	3.4	1,995	88.3	24,650	119
Cedar	14	166	8.3	4.1	D	D	D	D	780	39.7	2,136	12
Chase	D	D	D	4.7	D	D	4.9	D	445	24.4	1,000	4
Cherry	16	328	38.0	12.9	15	42	5.0	0.9	587	23.8	4,204	14
Cheyenne	20	565	75.1	25.4	21	61	7.2	1.8	739	39.3	2,073	8
Clay	14	D	5.5	D	D	D	3.6	D	523	25.1	2,423	11
Colfax	16	257	28.2	8.5	26	79	7.3	2.3	552	31.3	4,387	15
Cuming	23	379	57.4	17.8	35	136	22.9	4.8	762	46.3	3,155	11
Custer	42	648	51.0	20.8	28	50	9.3	1.5	1,158	54.0	6,167	28
Dakota	33	520	43.4	16.1	36	213	54.5	13.9	1,132	63.2	6,747	21
Dawes	34	414	45.7	16.5	20	37	3.3	0.7	637	21.3	3,514	15
Dawson	70	1,316	111.8	45.9	D	D	D	D	1,577	77.2	22,202	107
Deuel	4	D	2.5	D	NA	NA	NA	NA	183	6.1	565	3
Dixon	6	83	3.3	1.6	D	D	D	D	457	19.0	674	4
Dodge	122	2,949	268.9	109.4	87	349	38.2	9.5	2,190	102.3	32,408	130
Douglas	1,958	54,665	7,151.1	2,807.5	1,139	7,736	1,699.7	263.2	40,069	2,028.8	404,575	3,420
Dundy	4	D	11.9	D	NA	NA	NA	NA	164	7.3	560	3
Fillmore	14	314	29.5	11.2	D	D	D	2.0	500	23.2	2,568	7
Franklin	9	95	6.4	2.3	D	D	1.3	D	233	8.4	1,516	5
Frontier	8	51	1.3	0.8	D	D	2.0	D	213	10.3	2,497	9
Furnas	18	330	38.2	13.4	10	25	3.5	0.7	441	20.7	1,780	8
Gage	57	1,739	137.3	62.7	65	285	19.5	5.1	1,574	67.1	15,536	116
Garden	NA	NA	NA	NA	D	D	0.3	D	198	8.1	485	3
Garfield	8	D	6.1	D	13	33	2.9	1.0	228	9.4	1,863	10
Gosper	7	9	0.5	0.2	NA	NA	NA	NA	202	14.4	2,658	11
Grant	NA	NA	NA	NA	NA	NA	NA	NA	93	3.7	0	0
Greeley	3	21	0.4	0.2	3	10	1.6	0.3	263	14.4	2,670	13
Hall	192	4,518	514.4	196.8	152	1,067	98.0	27.3	3,930	195.6	49,813	259
Hamilton	D	D	D	D	24	68	9.2	2.5	820	30.6	8,659	26
Harlan	13	D	17.6	D	3	9	1.9	0.3	342	13.7	2,724	17
Hayes	NA	NA	NA	NA	NA	NA	NA	NA	88	4.6	0	0
Hitchcock	NA	NA	NA	NA	NA	NA	NA	NA	238	9.6	150	1
Holt	36	783	81.5	28.8	34	92	16.3	2.9	1,309	78.8	1,366	11
Hooker	NA	NA	NA	NA	D	D	D	0.1	102	3.5	1,850	3
Howard	D	D	D	D	14	42	3.5	0.9	516	22.4	3,433	14
Jefferson	19	436	33.5	14.9	15	60	6.5	1.5	474	20.8	1,750	7
Johnson	11	278	22.3	9.9	D	D	1.8	D	292	12.6	1,148	5
Kearney	10	477	31.6	16.9	14	25	3.4	0.7	566	27.0	6,003	19
Keith	22	284	31.1	11.9	24	80	10.3	2.5	812	44.7	11,093	58
Keya Paha	NA	NA	NA	NA	6	9	1.2	0.2	118	4.7	0	0
Kimball	6	95	11.1	5.4	10	25	9.1	0.8	271	11.2	195	1
Knox	19	274	19.8	8.4	D	D	3.3	D	703	28.5	4,672	22
Lancaster	1,050	24,911	2,890.7	1,102.1	727	4,334	779.5	157.9	22,493	959.6	564,793	2,546
Lincoln	D	D	D	D	D	D	D	D	2,205	95.0	14,622	88
Logan	NA	NA	NA	NA	NA	NA	NA	NA	64	2.6	NA	NA
Loup	NA	NA	NA	NA	NA	NA	NA	NA	80	2.4	3,000	14
McPherson	NA	NA	NA	NA	NA	NA	NA	NA	55	2.0	0	0
Madison	173	3,507	463.7	158.4	96	482	46.5	14.2	2,628	124.6	25,083	98
Merrick	17	311	30.3	10.7	16	64	11.5	2.2	647	29.4	7,275	32
Morrill	5	D	16.4	D	D	D	2.3	D	394	17.1	430	2
Nance	D	D	D	D	D	D	D	0.3	271	9.9	760	4
Nemaha	23	352	32.3	14.2	14	46	3.7	0.9	484	16.9	350	1
Nuckolls	17	397	43.1	13.7	D	D	3.3	D	300	12.5	450	3
Otoe	42	806	66.2	27.3	31	98	9.2	3.0	1,254	50.7	19,669	70
Pawnee	D	D	D	4.3	D	D	0.8	D	252	9.7	0	0
Perkins	7	254	23.8	9.0	D	D	D	0.7	314	17.3	2,392	7
Phelps	23	762	69.1	27.6	28	85	15.0	2.6	896	40.3	3,426	27
Pierce	D	D	D	D	D	D	2.5	D	671	34.6	4,732	16

STATE County	Government employment and payroll, 2017: Full-time equivalent employees	Government employment and payroll, 2017: March payroll (dollars)	March payroll (percent of total): Adminis-tration, judicial, and legal	March payroll (percent of total): Police and corrections	March payroll (percent of total): Fire protection	March payroll (percent of total): Highways and transpor-tation	March payroll (percent of total): Health and welfare	March payroll (percent of total): Natural resources and utilities	March payroll (percent of total): Education and libraries	Local government finances, 2017, General revenue: Total (mil dol)	Inter-govern-mental (mil dol)	Taxes: Total (mil dol)	Taxes: Per capita[1] (dollars): Total	Taxes: Per capita[1] (dollars): Property
	171	172	173	174	175	176	177	178	179	180	181	182	183	184
NEBRASKA— Cont'd														
Blaine	41	137,107	18.7	0.0	0.0	5.8	0.0	0.0	75.4	4.6	0.9	3.5	7,228	6,902
Boone	523	2,183,498	3.9	2.2	0.0	2.5	53.8	0.8	36.3	59.4	8.0	19.4	3,645	3,232
Box Butte	716	2,924,913	4.1	6.3	0.8	3.3	43.9	4.7	36.0	90.8	13.8	26.9	2,481	2,039
Boyd	132	462,199	12.1	1.6	0.0	18.9	0.8	4.6	61.1	11.3	2.6	6.2	3,154	2,951
Brown	284	1,161,041	4.2	2.5	0.0	3.9	34.1	13.1	41.7	28.6	5.0	10.2	3,415	3,091
Buffalo	1,824	7,821,914	6.4	9.3	1.3	3.5	0.9	7.1	69.3	186.1	42.4	110.0	2,230	1,747
Burt	393	1,395,814	7.7	5.6	0.0	7.6	0.7	13.2	63.7	41.3	6.6	27.1	4,150	3,805
Butler	494	1,871,938	5.2	3.6	0.0	7.7	30.0	16.4	36.9	64.3	17.4	28.7	3,577	3,263
Cass	913	3,916,978	7.5	8.9	0.1	4.2	1.0	2.7	72.4	108.9	30.9	61.5	2,370	2,118
Cedar	375	1,508,658	9.1	3.1	0.0	5.4	0.5	15.1	66.3	39.0	6.8	22.8	2,682	2,561
Chase	374	1,346,214	4.5	2.4	0.0	4.7	32.3	7.7	43.8	43.6	5.0	17.1	4,345	3,891
Cherry	356	1,368,079	5.4	5.3	0.0	5.7	37.6	5.0	39.9	52.0	7.7	19.9	3,433	2,691
Cheyenne	520	1,921,015	5.9	7.2	0.1	5.9	0.7	16.3	62.2	78.5	18.2	37.0	3,841	3,242
Clay	465	1,531,436	7.3	3.6	0.0	5.3	10.3	4.6	67.2	41.2	9.4	24.7	3,992	3,690
Colfax	523	2,018,305	5.5	5.4	0.2	3.4	0.7	6.5	76.7	70.0	16.7	35.7	3,333	3,090
Cuming	438	1,759,278	8.8	5.2	0.0	9.1	0.6	10.9	64.1	53.0	10.7	30.5	3,411	3,005
Custer	684	2,528,214	7.7	3.4	0.2	5.8	11.8	16.9	52.2	71.7	14.2	37.9	3,484	3,136
Dakota	879	3,512,617	6.8	10.0	1.2	2.6	1.1	7.0	70.7	91.5	44.5	30.7	1,534	1,197
Dawes	380	1,261,755	10.4	8.6	0.0	7.3	1.7	10.4	59.9	42.5	13.2	16.1	1,808	1,480
Dawson	1,784	7,529,079	3.1	4.5	0.0	2.3	31.6	11.1	46.4	235.4	43.1	105.2	4,449	3,676
Deuel	139	539,672	11.1	6.0	0.0	9.1	1.0	3.4	67.3	18.9	1.7	15.7	8,419	7,722
Dixon	439	1,573,949	7.5	4.4	0.0	4.0	0.0	1.2	81.9	40.5	10.4	22.1	3,849	3,635
Dodge	2,252	10,124,969	4.5	4.5	1.4	2.6	35.9	8.4	42.2	281.5	47.0	80.6	2,191	1,696
Douglas	23,705	112,709,866	3.4	9.3	4.7	3.4	5.5	21.8	50.8	2,804.7	924.4	1,317.4	2,349	1,684
Dundy	217	848,201	7.7	2.6	0.0	3.3	50.0	4.1	32.0	20.7	2.3	7.9	4,437	4,059
Fillmore	444	1,702,509	7.7	2.9	0.1	5.3	38.7	2.4	42.0	60.6	8.1	21.8	3,924	3,472
Franklin	198	688,947	18.6	3.8	0.0	6.8	28.0	3.0	37.7	20.3	3.0	10.0	3,375	3,219
Frontier	188	723,299	8.9	4.0	0.2	5.5	1.0	2.2	71.1	22.0	4.4	15.2	5,777	4,396
Furnas	428	1,519,779	6.6	2.8	0.6	3.6	19.2	15.5	51.0	35.8	9.5	19.6	4,125	3,530
Gage	954	3,899,069	7.0	7.1	4.0	5.7	0.5	20.2	55.1	99.5	25.3	55.8	2,579	2,058
Garden	125	382,534	13.3	10.0	1.8	9.2	0.8	0.4	61.5	23.8	3.5	6.5	3,428	3,124
Garfield	107	365,812	13.6	3.7	0.0	5.9	4.3	3.1	67.9	12.8	2.7	8.8	4,411	4,076
Gosper	86	342,689	12.4	6.9	0.0	15.4	0.0	15.4	46.5	15.9	2.0	9.7	4,762	4,132
Grant	63	174,460	8.4	5.0	0.0	7.4	0.0	1.3	77.4	3.8	0.6	2.9	4,516	4,276
Greeley	111	412,595	11.1	4.4	0.0	5.5	0.7	6.7	71.2	16.9	2.5	9.8	4,155	3,638
Hall	2,859	12,652,757	5.4	8.4	3.9	3.6	0.7	17.3	59.6	309.0	108.8	130.3	2,128	1,608
Hamilton	409	1,507,031	6.9	9.5	0.0	4.3	2.8	4.2	70.6	46.7	8.6	26.0	2,830	2,569
Harlan	250	843,465	7.5	3.9	0.0	4.8	38.7	7.5	36.5	21.9	1.8	10.3	3,027	2,431
Hayes	56	163,322	7.5	0.0	0.0	18.5	0.0	1.4	72.6	5.1	1.4	3.6	3,993	3,896
Hitchcock	163	655,498	14.0	4.4	0.0	3.0	0.3	27.0	51.3	21.3	8.6	8.2	2,921	2,557
Holt	498	1,700,633	8.5	5.0	0.0	10.1	0.8	4.4	70.5	61.8	12.9	36.2	3,556	3,033
Hooker	71	221,421	9.9	3.4	0.0	4.1	29.1	0.0	52.4	7.8	1.1	3.8	5,775	5,477
Howard	484	1,946,017	3.0	2.0	0.0	2.8	34.5	14.2	41.8	51.9	9.7	17.2	2,682	2,448
Jefferson	520	1,742,755	5.1	4.0	0.0	4.9	3.2	7.9	72.9	58.8	10.8	29.1	4,050	3,621
Johnson	315	1,301,494	3.7	2.6	0.0	3.6	43.0	7.0	40.0	21.2	4.5	14.5	2,800	2,472
Kearney	539	1,816,137	4.9	3.4	0.1	3.3	25.7	2.0	59.9	42.5	5.6	23.6	3,641	3,301
Keith	407	1,465,239	7.3	6.4	0.0	4.0	1.0	3.4	73.7	46.0	11.6	25.5	3,159	2,549
Keya Paha	43	135,802	8.4	2.4	0.0	9.4	0.0	0.0	78.0	4.4	1.0	3.0	3,852	3,651
Kimball	290	1,120,828	8.1	4.5	0.0	4.3	40.5	6.7	34.6	19.7	3.4	11.6	3,265	2,749
Knox	460	1,758,386	8.4	5.4	0.0	6.1	2.5	9.5	67.8	56.1	22.7	23.2	2,751	2,534
Lancaster	11,659	52,706,646	4.9	8.8	3.7	4.6	3.6	10.8	62.3	1,244.1	388.0	607.8	1,937	1,467
Lincoln	1,799	7,044,197	5.0	8.0	3.6	3.9	0.8	9.0	68.0	178.8	56.1	94.9	2,692	2,208
Logan	68	230,737	8.2	3.1	0.0	5.9	0.0	3.0	79.4	5.2	1.5	3.3	4,310	4,005
Loup	39	134,840	14.3	4.5	0.0	13.2	0.0	1.4	65.6	3.8	0.8	2.4	3,909	3,593
McPherson	54	130,557	33.7	3.6	0.0	2.6	0.0	0.0	60.0	2.8	0.6	2.1	4,207	4,030
Madison	1,901	8,282,646	4.7	6.6	2.2	2.8	0.5	7.2	75.7	203.7	47.9	113.0	3,216	2,626
Merrick	405	1,422,479	7.1	1.5	0.0	1.6	45.6	3.0	40.2	53.1	15.4	19.3	2,457	2,109
Morrill	433	1,761,898	4.7	3.9	0.1	4.2	30.9	9.3	45.8	44.4	16.8	15.8	3,299	2,839
Nance	268	991,657	10.6	5.1	0.0	6.0	24.9	1.6	50.7	31.2	4.3	14.1	3,962	3,630
Nemaha	448	1,888,679	5.1	2.3	0.0	3.8	23.9	6.9	56.2	56.1	13.2	16.6	2,381	2,171
Nuckolls	192	763,054	9.0	5.4	0.0	7.4	0.1	30.2	46.9	25.1	5.1	10.9	2,548	2,111
Otoe	813	3,087,094	5.9	5.8	1.2	3.8	19.0	11.1	49.7	89.8	17.6	39.7	2,486	2,042
Pawnee	201	759,976	7.1	2.5	0.0	4.3	36.7	4.0	44.9	26.6	11.1	9.0	3,419	3,176
Perkins	347	1,365,589	5.9	4.3	0.0	8.3	53.0	1.7	26.7	36.6	4.3	11.1	3,859	3,512
Phelps	424	1,712,705	5.9	7.4	0.0	6.4	0.9	7.6	71.4	51.6	9.2	31.8	3,510	2,976
Pierce	305	1,028,959	8.1	5.8	0.0	6.5	0.1	4.0	74.9	33.2	5.8	21.1	2,976	2,708

1. Based on the resident population estimated as of July 1 of the year shown.

STATE County	Local government finances, 2017 (cont.) — Direct general expenditure — Total (mil dol)	Per capita[1] (dollars)	Percent of total for: Education	Health and hospitals	Police protection	Public welfare	Highways	Debt outstanding — Total (mil dol)	Per capita[1] (dollars)	Government employment, 2020 — Federal civilian	Federal military	State and local	Individual income tax returns, 2019 — Number of returns	Mean adjusted gross income	Mean income tax
	185	186	187	188	189	190	191	192	193	194	195	196	197	198	199
NEBRASKA— Cont'd															
Blaine	4.5	9,359	58.2	0.0	1.3	0.1	14.7	0.9	1,967	30	2	51	210	25,433	1,538
Boone	75.3	14,158	37.9	42.7	1.1	0.1	7.1	17.1	3,216	28	17	653	2,580	57,702	5,337
Box Butte	94.3	8,700	23.5	37.8	2.4	2.0	8.2	14.4	1,333	34	36	975	5,110	56,523	4,875
Boyd	13.9	7,110	47.2	0.5	1.4	0.2	25.3	4.5	2,309	15	6	210	870	38,421	2,972
Brown	33.2	11,063	33.8	30.0	2.2	0.2	7.3	29.6	9,864	23	10	374	1,500	38,953	3,027
Buffalo	211.3	4,283	55.1	0.1	4.2	0.2	11.3	270.8	5,487	137	164	4,152	22,900	66,460	6,999
Burt	43.3	6,633	50.3	0.1	2.5	8.2	17.5	46.9	7,179	36	22	525	3,180	52,952	4,183
Butler	66.1	8,231	28.2	22.4	1.7	0.3	15.2	45.3	5,639	43	26	639	4,010	57,616	4,867
Cass	104.9	4,044	48.0	0.1	3.8	4.5	12.0	96.9	3,737	70	88	1,286	13,070	71,413	7,173
Cedar	38.5	4,520	65.5	0.1	1.1	6.6	6.1	15.7	1,843	99	29	586	4,020	55,618	4,885
Chase	46.1	11,740	34.2	40.7	1.8	0.5	8.2	18.5	4,701	26	13	469	1,700	59,219	5,541
Cherry	47.1	8,126	29.2	37.9	1.4	0.2	11.4	6.6	1,134	49	20	551	2,770	43,626	4,199
Cheyenne	56.7	5,878	42.8	0.4	3.3	0.6	12.9	94.0	9,745	37	31	699	4,530	52,758	4,454
Clay	43.9	7,104	56.7	0.8	2.9	3.4	11.0	12.0	1,941	151	21	575	2,880	61,143	5,590
Colfax	58.3	5,451	62.4	0.0	2.4	0.6	14.4	20.9	1,950	59	36	701	5,080	52,397	3,749
Cuming	57.9	6,472	46.6	0.3	2.4	4.9	15.4	26.8	2,991	36	30	695	4,380	60,178	5,485
Custer	63.8	5,869	48.1	3.5	1.7	0.2	21.4	26.8	2,465	41	36	839	5,130	46,844	3,932
Dakota	94.4	4,719	58.0	0.4	8.2	0.2	9.3	64.5	3,222	74	67	1,070	10,400	49,438	3,723
Dawes	48.1	5,408	36.7	1.4	3.4	0.4	10.5	31.9	3,592	138	25	937	3,520	45,764	3,619
Dawson	189.9	8,027	37.5	36.0	1.3	0.1	7.5	196.8	8,321	105	79	2,192	11,730	50,373	3,751
Deuel	15.3	8,222	80.3	0.0	0.7	0.1	1.9	9.9	5,341	6	6	208	830	47,093	3,428
Dixon	51.0	8,867	49.6	0.4	2.7	6.1	12.3	11.5	2,003	40	19	370	2,680	53,829	4,402
Dodge	289.3	7,865	28.4	40.5	3.0	0.0	8.2	151.1	4,108	126	124	2,042	17,770	57,315	5,050
Douglas	2,745.1	4,896	56.3	2.6	5.7	0.5	3.9	6,476.4	11,550	6,210	2,020	34,808	280,660	79,904	10,289
Dundy	21.6	12,097	28.0	42.5	2.0	0.1	8.0	4.0	2,223	12	6	225	790	46,314	4,851
Fillmore	61.0	10,972	33.0	28.5	2.0	0.6	10.5	42.7	7,685	30	18	677	2,750	61,912	5,756
Franklin	19.5	6,544	27.3	30.6	2.3	0.1	5.3	3.9	1,322	17	10	285	1,400	47,264	3,842
Frontier	23.4	8,921	48.2	0.1	2.2	0.1	11.2	1.9	712	16	8	288	1,140	37,425	3,234
Furnas	41.3	8,677	47.2	0.2	3.6	0.2	7.7	65.5	13,760	34	16	455	2,250	44,126	3,501
Gage	111.9	5,175	43.9	0.5	4.9	0.9	14.9	47.0	2,174	87	71	1,664	10,340	56,370	4,822
Garden	25.0	13,231	21.7	41.7	1.6	0.1	6.2	4.8	2,566	15	6	147	880	33,485	2,526
Garfield	15.4	7,769	48.1	0.0	1.7	0.1	13.7	12.8	6,454	12	8	151	850	38,213	3,086
Gosper	13.2	6,514	33.4	0.0	3.1	21.5	15.7	12.7	6,238	6	7	106	950	66,319	6,751
Grant	6.5	10,008	95.6	0.0	0.1	0.0	1.7	5.9	9,108	5	2	70	290	47,783	3,610
Greeley	16.9	7,139	45.8	0.4	1.6	11.0	10.2	5.5	2,314	7	8	239	1,080	33,808	3,051
Hall	347.5	5,678	51.4	0.2	5.4	0.3	3.5	300.2	4,905	686	220	4,107	30,180	55,879	5,102
Hamilton	50.2	5,459	54.2	1.7	2.9	0.3	19.9	34.2	3,724	28	31	488	4,560	69,440	6,612
Harlan	19.7	5,761	31.1	47.1	0.7	0.0	5.3	10.0	2,920	33	11	269	1,510	49,893	4,150
Hayes	5.6	6,215	54.6	0.0	1.5	0.0	19.5	1.8	2,059	11	3	81	430	21,942	2,786
Hitchcock	14.2	5,051	53.1	0.0	2.3	0.1	12.5	18.9	6,734	10	9	277	1,250	43,082	3,089
Holt	61.0	5,990	47.4	0.1	1.9	0.3	21.4	17.5	1,723	52	33	774	4,910	43,476	3,903
Hooker	8.3	12,393	44.5	0.1	4.2	20.4	7.7	1.5	2,300	3	2	103	390	38,974	2,882
Howard	52.3	8,177	37.4	33.7	1.2	0.2	8.8	36.5	5,703	32	22	566	3,080	51,116	4,062
Jefferson	53.2	7,416	48.5	1.4	3.2	0.1	15.4	22.4	3,115	34	24	557	3,420	61,036	6,011
Johnson	21.9	4,242	50.7	0.0	2.7	0.0	20.0	18.4	3,552	30	15	692	2,020	48,888	3,398
Kearney	51.6	7,943	63.5	21.9	0.7	0.2	4.0	60.2	9,269	20	22	433	3,220	64,884	6,081
Keith	45.7	5,658	49.1	0.5	3.2	0.7	11.1	39.1	4,851	39	27	487	3,910	51,382	4,505
Keya Paha	4.4	5,605	54.5	0.1	1.6	0.3	23.0	0.0	51	2	3	66	380	30,529	2,476
Kimball	19.4	5,434	39.1	1.5	3.2	0.2	10.0	11.6	3,256	18	12	424	1,670	48,521	3,923
Knox	59.1	6,999	56.4	0.1	1.7	0.1	17.5	22.1	2,613	55	27	1,060	3,890	46,475	3,698
Lancaster	1,318.5	4,202	52.8	2.9	4.1	1.2	7.2	2,458.0	7,834	3,531	1,070	30,310	151,300	68,169	7,394
Lincoln	211.7	6,003	53.0	1.0	4.3	0.2	5.4	119.7	3,395	272	115	2,558	16,520	58,143	5,486
Logan	6.7	8,729	69.2	0.1	1.9	0.1	11.5	0.1	71	6	3	78	320	38,678	2,247
Loup	3.5	5,748	59.9	0.6	2.0	0.1	8.4	0.4	707	2	2	66	300	32,273	2,373
McPherson	3.1	6,249	66.6	0.0	2.1	0.0	16.3	1.1	2,318	1	2	36	200	41,540	1,965
Madison	193.9	5,519	72.0	0.2	3.1	6.7	0.9	176.8	5,032	182	115	3,532	16,930	64,693	6,658
Merrick	48.8	6,211	34.4	27.1	2.1	0.2	12.6	14.8	1,886	26	26	445	3,630	54,307	5,188
Morrill	46.0	9,599	31.2	24.6	3.9	17.3	6.6	35.1	7,322	20	15	593	2,150	49,391	5,262
Nance	23.5	6,594	57.0	0.0	5.7	0.1	12.2	2.2	607	16	11	390	1,560	43,803	3,335
Nemaha	50.8	7,309	44.0	27.5	2.3	0.1	7.4	23.9	3,431	31	22	1,614	3,000	58,943	5,189
Nuckolls	18.5	4,323	37.2	0.3	1.8	0.5	8.5	7.2	1,685	22	14	347	2,000	50,063	3,853
Otoe	101.4	6,356	41.3	14.9	2.6	0.2	19.0	91.7	5,747	58	53	1,317	7,680	62,612	5,729
Pawnee	26.5	10,119	33.5	30.2	1.1	13.2	9.6	7.3	2,792	21	9	232	1,180	46,063	3,582
Perkins	41.2	14,292	17.0	55.0	1.6	0.3	6.1	10.2	3,545	19	10	410	1,330	53,338	4,642
Phelps	50.8	5,618	55.9	0.1	2.6	0.4	13.9	37.0	4,087	58	30	685	4,490	61,243	5,849
Pierce	35.2	4,960	51.4	0.0	2.1	13.6	12.3	11.0	1,554	26	24	375	3,460	57,610	5,245

1. Based on the resident population estimated as of July 1 of the year shown.

State / county code	CBSA code[1]	County Type code[2]	STATE County	Land area[3] (sq. mi)	Population, 2021			Population and population characteristics, 2021										
								Race alone or in combination, not Hispanic or Latino (percent)					Age (percent)					
					Total persons 2021	Rank	Per square mile	White	Black	American Indian, Alaska Native	Asian and Pacific Islancer	Percent Hispanic or Latino[4]	Under 5 years	5 to 17 years	18 to 24 years	25 to 34 years	35 to 44 years	45 to 54 years
				1	2	3	4	5	6	7	8	9	10	11	12	13	14	15
			NEBRASKA— Cont'd															
31141	18100	5	Platte	674.1	34,241	1,323	50.8	75.3	1.3	0.7	1.2	22.2	6.9	15.0	12.4	11.8	12.3	10.7
31143		9	Polk	438.7	5,174	2,808	11.8	92.6	0.7	1.0	0.5	6.3	5.7	12.7	11.7	9.6	10.4	12.0
31145		7	Red Willow	717.0	10,623	2,367	14.8	91.7	1.8	0.9	0.6	6.1	6.2	12.0	13.1	11.3	11.9	10.3
31147		7	Richardson	551.8	7,759	2,591	14.1	93.4	1.5	4.3	1.1	2.3	5.6	12.7	10.5	9.3	10.9	10.5
31149		9	Rock	1,008.3	1,264	3,095	1.3	97.3	0.3	0.8	0.4	1.6	5.0	13.4	10.5	8.5	12.2	8.2
31151		6	Saline	574.1	14,192	2,132	24.7	68.3	1.6	0.8	3.4	27.1	6.7	14.8	16.8	10.2	12.3	11.8
31153	36540	2	Sarpy	238.1	193,418	353	812.3	81.6	5.5	0.9	4.1	11.0	6.6	15.5	13.0	13.9	15.0	12.1
31155	36540	2	Saunders	748.9	22,787	1,683	30.4	95.8	1.2	0.8	1.0	2.7	6.2	14.6	11.2	10.6	12.8	11.1
31157	42420	5	Scotts Bluff	739.6	35,745	1,289	48.3	71.6	1.2	2.0	1.2	25.2	6.3	14.2	12.6	11.5	11.9	10.8
31159	30700	2	Seward	571.4	17,603	1,941	30.8	95.6	1.4	0.8	0.9	2.7	5.6	13.7	17.3	10.0	12.3	10.6
31161		9	Sheridan	2,440.9	5,095	2,815	2.1	83.2	1.6	10.8	1.6	6.2	5.9	12.1	11.1	9.5	10.6	11.1
31163		8	Sherman	565.9	2,964	2,959	5.2	96.1	0.7	0.8	0.7	2.7	5.6	11.8	10.3	9.6	9.3	10.6
31165	42420	9	Sioux	2,066.7	1,143	3,101	0.6	93.2	0.8	1.2	0.8	5.3	4.8	8.8	10.8	8.4	10.1	10.0
31167	35740	9	Stanton	427.6	5,816	2,752	13.6	91.7	1.3	1.1	0.6	6.6	6.6	13.7	11.3	10.8	12.3	11.0
31169		9	Thayer	573.8	4,913	2,827	8.6	95.5	1.1	0.9	0.5	3.3	4.7	14.1	10.9	9.2	10.2	11.3
31171		9	Thomas	712.6	673	3,130	0.9	93.9	1.8	1.8	0.6	3.0	4.9	14.6	10.8	9.2	10.4	9.8
31173		8	Thurston	393.6	6,620	2,691	16.8	36.2	1.4	55.9	1.4	7.6	9.5	20.5	16.1	12.7	10.1	8.6
31175		9	Valley	568.1	4,066	2,879	7.2	95.2	0.8	0.5	0.7	3.6	6.0	13.5	10.6	9.9	10.7	10.5
31177	36540	2	Washington	390.0	20,969	1,764	53.8	95.3	1.4	0.8	1.0	2.9	5.3	14.3	11.9	9.6	13.3	12.1
31179		6	Wayne	442.9	9,784	2,426	22.1	89.9	2.3	0.9	1.2	7.1	5.0	11.3	26.0	10.5	9.8	9.3
31181		9	Webster	574.9	3,411	2,927	5.9	92.6	1.2	1.4	1.3	5.3	5.8	13.0	10.8	11.3	9.8	11.8
31183		9	Wheeler	575.2	795	3,116	1.4	96.8	0.8	1.0	0.5	2.0	8.3	10.4	7.7	9.7	9.4	9.4
31185		6	York	572.5	14,244	2,131	24.9	91.8	2.1	1.1	1.2	5.1	5.8	13.5	13.2	11.7	11.5	10.2
32000		0	NEVADA	109,860.4	3,143,991	X	28.6	50.6	10.8	1.5	11.7	29.5	5.7	12.7	11.9	14.5	13.7	12.6
32001	21980	6	Churchill	4,950.2	25,723	1,577	5.2	75.0	3.6	5.1	5.1	15.1	6.4	13.0	11.2	14.4	12.0	10.4
32003	29820	1	Clark	7,891.7	2,292,476	12	290.5	44.2	13.6	1.1	13.7	31.8	5.8	13.0	12.0	14.6	14.1	13.0
32005	23820	4	Douglas	710.5	49,870	999	70.2	82.3	1.3	2.6	3.3	13.1	3.4	9.0	8.5	9.3	10.4	10.6
32007	21220	5	Elko	17,173.4	53,915	941	3.1	68.0	1.4	5.5	2.3	25.0	6.9	15.2	12.7	14.8	13.7	11.7
32009		9	Esmeralda	3,581.9	743	3,122	0.2	69.8	4.2	7.6	2.6	19.6	2.8	9.7	7.5	7.4	12.1	11.2
32011	21220	9	Eureka	4,175.7	1,903	3,050	0.5	80.4	1.5	3.2	2.3	14.2	3.6	14.6	9.2	11.6	12.0	14.1
32013	49080	7	Humboldt	9,640.8	17,648	1,939	1.8	66.5	1.7	4.6	2.0	27.7	7.2	15.7	11.9	13.4	12.9	11.4
32015		7	Lander	5,519.2	5,798	2,754	1.1	71.2	1.3	4.8	1.5	23.0	6.8	15.6	11.4	12.3	12.8	11.3
32017		8	Lincoln	10,633.4	4,525	2,854	0.4	86.9	3.2	2.5	1.9	7.6	5.4	10.8	10.5	11.4	12.4	11.5
32019	22280	4	Lyon	2,003.1	60,903	870	30.4	76.1	2.1	3.5	3.0	18.6	5.2	11.9	10.3	13.4	12.4	11.2
32021		7	Mineral	3,751.3	4,586	2,851	1.2	63.7	5.2	16.5	4.4	14.0	5.4	11.1	9.1	11.9	11.9	10.0
32023	37220	4	Nye	18,181.9	53,450	950	2.9	77.0	4.2	2.5	3.6	15.7	4.2	9.4	9.1	9.8	9.4	10.7
32027		9	Pershing	6,036.6	6,741	2,677	1.1	66.6	4.7	4.3	2.4	24.7	4.3	9.5	9.9	15.4	15.1	15.2
32029	39900	2	Storey	263.8	4,143	2,873	15.7	85.9	2.2	2.7	3.4	8.2	2.8	7.2	7.5	9.5	9.2	12.0
32031	39900	2	Washoe	6,315.9	493,392	147	78.1	64.5	3.3	2.0	8.2	25.4	5.4	12.1	12.2	15.1	13.1	11.9
32033		7	White Pine	8,886.7	9,182	2,474	1.0	73.8	5.0	5.0	1.8	16.7	5.3	11.3	10.9	14.5	13.7	11.7
32510	16180	3	Carson City	144.5	58,993	891	408.3	68.3	2.5	2.9	3.9	24.9	5.2	11.4	11.0	13.2	12.1	11.7
33000		0	NEW HAMPSHIRE	8,953.4	1,388,992	X	155.1	91.0	2.1	0.8	3.7	4.2	4.5	10.5	12.4	12.8	12.1	12.7
33001	29060	4	Belknap	401.8	64,460	843	160.4	96.1	1.0	0.8	1.6	1.9	4.0	10.3	10.2	10.9	11.3	12.4
33003		6	Carroll	931.9	51,500	975	55.3	96.6	1.0	1.0	1.0	1.6	3.4	8.7	8.7	9.3	9.6	11.8
33005	28300	4	Cheshire	706.7	77,329	732	109.4	95.2	1.2	0.9	2.2	2.1	4.4	10.2	13.6	12.2	11.4	11.5
33007	13620	7	Coos	1,794.6	31,289	1,393	17.4	96.0	1.2	1.3	1.0	2.0	3.9	9.3	9.7	11.0	11.2	13.1
33009	30100	5	Grafton	1,708.6	92,201	655	54.0	91.6	1.7	1.0	4.7	2.7	3.7	9.0	15.6	12.3	10.9	11.2
33011	31700	2	Hillsborough	876.5	424,079	169	483.8	84.6	3.5	0.7	5.3	7.9	5.0	11.1	11.9	14.3	12.8	13.1
33013	18180	4	Merrimack	932.9	155,238	440	166.4	93.1	2.1	0.8	2.9	2.5	4.4	10.6	12.3	12.6	12.6	12.7
33015	14460	1	Rockingham	695.4	316,947	225	455.8	93.0	1.3	0.6	3.0	3.6	4.5	10.6	10.8	12.2	12.3	13.6
33017	14460	1	Strafford	367.5	132,416	490	360.3	91.6	2.1	0.7	4.7	3.0	4.4	10.0	18.4	13.9	11.9	11.7
33019	30100	7	Sullivan	537.9	43,533	1,110	80.9	95.8	1.3	1.2	1.5	2.0	4.3	10.2	10.0	11.7	11.3	13.0
34000		0	NEW JERSEY	7,354.8	9,267,130	X	1,260.0	54.9	13.9	0.5	11.0	21.5	5.6	12.3	12.3	12.8	13.1	13.1
34001	12100	2	Atlantic	555.5	274,966	254	495.0	57.2	15.5	0.6	9.0	19.9	5.2	12.0	12.5	12.1	11.2	12.6
34003	35620	1	Bergen	232.8	953,819	56	4,097.2	54.9	6.2	0.3	18.2	22.0	5.0	12.0	11.9	11.5	13.5	13.9
34005	37980	1	Burlington	799.3	464,269	154	580.8	67.3	18.7	0.7	6.9	9.2	5.0	11.7	12.0	12.6	12.9	13.2
34007	37980	1	Camden	221.4	523,771	137	2,365.7	56.2	20.0	0.6	6.8	18.5	5.9	12.8	12.0	13.8	13.4	12.6
34009	36140	3	Cape May	251.5	95,661	635	380.4	86.3	4.9	0.5	1.6	8.4	4.3	9.9	10.0	10.3	9.7	10.7
34011	47220	3	Cumberland	483.4	153,627	445	317.8	46.0	20.1	1.3	2.0	33.0	6.1	13.9	12.4	13.7	13.1	12.5
34013	35620	1	Essex	126.1	854,917	73	6,779.7	31.0	39.1	0.6	6.8	24.3	6.3	13.5	12.4	13.5	14.1	13.7
34015	37980	1	Gloucester	322.0	304,477	232	945.6	78.3	11.9	0.5	4.1	7.4	5.0	12.4	12.7	12.6	12.9	13.3
34017	35620	1	Hudson	46.2	702,463	97	15,204.8	29.6	11.9	0.5	17.1	42.5	6.5	10.9	10.4	20.2	16.4	12.0
34019	35620	1	Hunterdon	427.8	129,924	499	303.7	84.3	3.3	0.3	5.7	7.8	4.2	10.6	12.4	9.7	11.4	14.0

1. CBSA = Core Based Statistical Area. See Appendix A for explanation. See Appendix B for list of metropolitan areas with component counties. 2. County type code from the Economic Research Service of USDA Rural-Urban Continuum Codes. See Appendix A for definition. 3. Dry land or land partially or temporarily covered by water. 4. May be of any race.

STATE County	Population, 2021 (cont.) — Age (percent) (cont.) — 55 to 64 years	65 to 74 years	75 years and over	Percent female	Population change, 2000–2021 — Total persons — 2010	2020	Percent change — 2010–2020	2020–2021	Components of change, 2020–2021 — Births	Deaths	Net Migration	Households, 2016–2020 — Number	Persons per household	Percent — Family house-holds	Female family house-holder[1]	One person
	16	17	18	19	20	21	22	23	24	25	26	27	28	29	30	31
NEBRASKA— Cont'd																
Platte	12.9	10.4	7.4	49.0	32,237	34,296	6.4	-0.2	583	430	-213	13,173	2.5	65.1	8.3	31.3
Polk	14.8	13.9	9.2	49.2	5,406	5,214	-3.6	-0.8	63	114	11	2,048	2.5	68.9	4.7	28.7
Red Willow	14.0	12.0	9.2	49.6	11,055	10,702	-3.2	-0.7	157	192	-45	4,503	2.3	56.9	8.0	38.2
Richardson	16.1	13.2	11.1	49.4	8,363	7,871	-5.9	-1.4	97	194	-14	3,706	2.1	62.2	8.7	34.7
Rock	13.6	18.6	10.0	50.2	1,526	1,262	-17.3	0.2	17	22	9	617	2.2	68.9	5.3	29.0
Saline	12.0	9.1	6.3	48.5	14,200	14,292	0.6	-0.7	237	147	-193	5,292	2.5	69.2	8.4	26.4
Sarpy	11.4	7.8	4.7	49.7	158,840	190,604	20.0	1.5	2,970	1,751	1,559	67,299	2.7	71.9	9.6	22.1
Saunders	15.1	11.0	7.4	48.9	20,780	22,278	7.2	2.3	315	339	539	8,542	2.5	68.5	6.8	26.9
Scotts Bluff	13.1	11.5	8.2	51.0	36,970	36,084	-2.4	-0.9	515	628	-228	14,657	2.4	64.0	11.1	29.8
Seward	12.9	10.3	7.4	48.4	16,750	17,609	5.1	0.0	216	219	-7	6,766	2.3	69.4	7.2	24.5
Sheridan	13.3	14.7	11.7	49.9	5,469	5,127	-6.3	-0.6	59	93	3	2,312	2.2	62.5	6.8	32.1
Sherman	15.7	15.2	11.9	49.8	3,152	2,959	-6.1	0.2	36	67	37	1,414	2.1	62.2	7.4	33.2
Sioux	16.8	17.6	12.6	46.5	1,311	1,135	-13.4	0.7	6	12	14	530	2.5	70.6	4.2	24.9
Stanton	15.1	11.8	7.4	48.3	6,129	5,842	-4.7	-0.4	80	79	-28	2,430	2.4	66.3	8.1	27.4
Thayer	14.5	14.2	10.8	50.1	5,228	5,034	-3.7	-2.4	51	84	-86	2,247	2.2	62.8	6.1	33.0
Thomas	11.3	17.8	11.1	48.7	647	669	3.4	0.6	6	6	6	276	2.1	61.6	1.8	29.0
Thurston	10.5	7.4	4.7	50.1	6,940	6,773	-2.4	-2.3	164	127	-188	2,165	3.3	76.0	23.2	21.2
Valley	13.9	13.5	11.4	49.9	4,260	4,059	-4.7	0.2	63	71	16	1,844	2.2	66.6	9.4	30.2
Washington	15.0	11.6	7.0	49.6	20,234	20,865	3.1	0.5	257	279	123	8,303	2.4	67.1	5.9	27.2
Wayne	11.4	9.2	7.5	49.4	9,595	9,697	1.1	0.9	122	87	49	3,793	2.1	57.6	1.8	28.9
Webster	14.9	12.8	9.8	50.0	3,812	3,395	-10.9	0.5	52	55	21	1,524	2.3	66.0	6.6	29.3
Wheeler	16.6	16.2	12.2	49.2	818	774	-5.4	2.7	17	7	11	353	2.0	57.8	5.9	37.4
York	13.4	11.4	9.3	50.7	13,665	14,125	3.4	0.8	176	193	137	5,685	2.2	65.5	5.1	30.8
NEVADA	12.5	10.2	6.3	49.9	2,700,551	3,104,614	15.0	1.3	42,076	39,702	36,605	1,130,011	2.7	63.7	13.0	28.2
Churchill	13.5	11.5	7.6	49.3	24,877	25,516	2.6	0.8	367	426	266	9,972	2.4	60.9	8.5	30.7
Clark	12.0	9.6	5.9	50.2	1,951,269	2,265,461	16.1	1.2	31,589	27,645	22,616	809,026	2.7	63.9	14.1	28.2
Douglas	17.5	19.0	12.3	49.7	46,997	49,488	5.3	0.8	402	839	833	21,071	2.3	70.8	9.0	22.7
Elko	12.3	8.1	4.6	48.1	48,818	53,702	10.0	0.4	854	516	-141	18,516	2.8	68.1	8.3	27.5
Esmeralda	16.7	17.1	15.5	44.0	783	729	-6.9	1.9	5	7	15	515	2.0	40.4	6.4	55.3
Eureka	16.7	11.4	6.8	45.6	1,987	1,855	-6.6	2.6	20	25	53	661	2.8	76.7	3.9	18.2
Humboldt	12.5	10.0	5.0	48.1	16,528	17,285	4.6	2.1	282	190	272	6,579	2.5	63.8	5.6	31.0
Lander	13.3	9.5	6.9	48.5	5,775	5,734	-0.7	1.1	95	61	29	2,315	2.4	70.0	9.4	27.6
Lincoln	13.9	14.1	10.0	46.6	5,345	4,499	-15.8	0.6	61	84	50	2,003	2.3	57.8	7.1	38.8
Lyon	14.3	13.7	7.7	48.7	51,980	59,235	14.0	2.8	731	984	1,946	21,726	2.6	66.3	8.4	27.3
Mineral	15.4	14.8	10.4	50.3	4,772	4,554	-4.6	0.7	50	151	135	1,938	2.3	49.3	11.5	47.4
Nye	16.9	18.7	11.9	49.0	43,946	51,591	17.4	3.6	475	1,229	2,651	19,253	2.3	60.9	8.8	31.3
Pershing	13.6	9.7	7.2	35.8	6,753	6,650	-1.5	1.4	65	76	102	2,009	2.3	67.7	8.7	29.4
Storey	18.6	21.5	11.6	48.8	4,010	4,104	2.3	1.0	28	53	67	1,704	2.4	61.5	4.6	33.9
Washoe	12.9	10.9	6.3	49.5	421,407	486,492	15.4	1.4	6,249	6,186	6,825	186,116	2.5	62.3	10.7	27.7
White Pine	13.6	10.9	8.1	42.6	10,030	9,080	-9.5	1.1	120	133	115	3,749	2.1	61.1	6.9	35.6
Carson City	14.3	12.6	8.5	49.0	55,274	58,639	6.1	0.6	683	1,097	771	22,858	2.3	62.7	12.9	31.5
NEW HAMPSHIRE	15.8	12.0	7.3	50.4	1,316,470	1,377,529	4.6	0.8	14,327	18,817	15,977	539,116	2.4	65.2	8.6	26.7
Belknap	17.7	14.7	8.5	50.6	60,088	63,705	6.0	1.2	579	1,148	1,340	25,576	2.4	66.0	9.8	28.1
Carroll	19.1	18.8	10.6	50.4	47,818	50,107	4.8	2.8	372	840	1,896	22,235	2.2	61.7	7.0	30.9
Cheshire	15.3	13.4	8.0	51.1	77,117	76,458	-0.9	1.1	756	1,091	1,221	30,513	2.4	61.1	8.0	29.5
Coos	17.1	15.3	9.5	47.6	33,055	31,268	-5.4	0.1	285	636	378	13,967	2.1	60.3	8.0	33.1
Grafton	15.2	13.5	8.6	50.4	89,118	91,118	2.2	1.2	820	1,251	1,527	35,141	2.4	60.8	8.8	30.5
Hillsborough	15.1	10.2	6.4	49.9	400,721	422,937	5.5	0.3	4,968	5,404	1,500	162,843	2.5	64.7	9.5	26.9
Merrimack	15.5	12.1	7.2	50.4	146,445	153,808	5.0	0.9	1,492	2,102	2,045	59,209	2.4	67.3	7.8	24.9
Rockingham	16.8	12.1	7.1	50.1	295,223	314,176	6.4	0.9	3,232	4,064	3,612	122,520	2.5	68.8	7.8	23.6
Strafford	13.8	10.0	6.0	50.6	123,143	130,889	6.3	1.2	1,403	1,641	1,760	49,831	2.4	63.7	7.9	26.2
Sullivan	16.5	14.4	8.6	50.0	43,742	43,063	-1.6	1.1	420	640	698	17,281	2.5	64.6	9.9	27.8
NEW JERSEY	13.8	9.9	7.0	50.8	8,791,894	9,288,994	5.7	-0.2	119,434	112,573	-29,149	3,272,054	2.7	68.7	12.8	26.0
Atlantic	15.2	11.6	7.7	51.2	274,549	274,534	0.0	0.2	3,388	3,983	994	101,103	2.6	66.3	15.2	27.9
Bergen	14.3	10.2	7.6	51.0	905,116	955,732	5.6	-0.2	10,649	10,776	-1,936	342,059	2.7	72.0	11.1	23.7
Burlington	14.9	10.4	7.3	50.5	448,734	461,860	2.9	0.5	5,272	5,798	2,909	168,195	2.6	69.5	11.9	25.6
Camden	13.3	9.8	6.5	51.5	513,657	523,485	1.9	0.1	7,139	6,942	-27	190,660	2.6	66.3	16.4	28.2
Cape May	16.8	16.9	11.4	51.1	97,265	95,263	-2.1	0.4	945	1,757	1,232	40,670	2.2	66.6	10.0	28.6
Cumberland	12.5	9.5	6.4	49.0	156,898	154,152	-1.8	-0.3	2,177	2,104	-636	50,947	2.7	67.4	17.8	26.9
Essex	12.4	8.4	5.8	51.5	783,969	863,728	10.2	-1.0	11,821	10,026	-10,666	290,680	2.7	64.7	18.6	30.6
Gloucester	14.4	10.3	6.4	51.1	288,288	302,294	4.9	0.7	3,464	3,969	2,677	106,376	2.7	70.8	12.0	24.2
Hudson	11.0	7.5	5.2	50.0	634,266	724,854	14.3	-3.1	11,687	6,763	-26,967	261,289	2.5	61.5	14.5	28.8
Hunterdon	17.5	12.2	7.9	50.3	128,349	128,947	0.5	0.8	1,219	1,421	1,194	47,647	2.5	73.6	6.8	21.6

1. No spouse present.

STATE County	Persons in group quarters, 2021	Daytime Population, 2016–2020		Births, 2021		Deaths, 2021		Persons under 65 with no health insurance, 2019		Medicare, 2021			COVID-19 Deaths, 2020	
		Number	Employment/ residence ratio	Total	Rate[1]	Number	Rate[1]	Number	Percent	Total beneficiaries	Enrolled in Original Medicare	Enrolled in Medicare Advantage	Number	Rate[1]
	32	33	34	35	36	37	38	39	40	41	42	43	44	45
NEBRASKA— Cont'd														
Platte	412	36,073	1.2	461	13.5	351	10.2	2,749	10.1	6,485	5,995	490	56	1.6
Polk	79	4,218	0.6	49	9.4	96	18.5	418	10.6	1,294	1,235	59	15	2.9
Red Willow	387	11,022	1.1	124	11.6	155	14.6	794	9.8	2,510	2,470	41	12	1.1
Richardson	105	7,326	0.8	79	10.1	146	18.7	570	9.8	2,175	2,136	39	20	2.6
Rock	12	1,428	1.0	9	7.1	17	13.4	121	12.3	385	367	18	D	D
Saline	835	14,069	1.0	184	12.9	120	8.4	1,399	12.5	2,495	2,212	283	D	D
Sarpy	1,001	161,376	0.8	2,310	12.0	1,426	7.4	9,378	5.7	26,689	19,810	6,879	132	0.7
Saunders	316	16,766	0.6	237	10.5	260	11.5	1,234	7.1	4,477	3,496	980	19	0.8
Scotts Bluff	723	36,440	1.0	409	11.4	487	13.6	3,215	11.5	8,283	7,522	762	102	2.8
Seward	1,224	15,580	0.8	168	9.5	184	10.5	886	6.7	3,424	2,971	453	25	1.4
Sheridan	118	5,093	1.0	50	9.8	75	14.7	624	16.5	1,384	1,251	133	17	3.3
Sherman	38	2,699	0.8	26	8.8	52	17.6	267	12.5	812	711	102	D	D
Sioux	0	1,179	0.8	5	4.4	12	10.5	114	14.3	289	D	D	D	D
Stanton	0	4,283	0.5	63	10.8	67	11.5	374	7.8	1,105	956	149	12	2.1
Thayer	61	5,029	1.0	42	8.5	63	12.7	340	9.2	1,424	1,336	88	D	D
Thomas	2	572	1.0	6	8.9	6	8.9	78	14.6	209	195	14	D	D
Thurston	18	7,747	1.2	117	17.5	89	13.3	984	15.9	1,078	1,031	48	10	1.5
Valley	21	4,162	1.0	54	13.3	52	12.8	342	11.2	1,102	1,027	75	D	D
Washington	97	18,696	0.8	212	10.1	222	10.6	1,134	6.7	4,326	3,136	1,190	20	1.0
Wayne	1,118	9,574	1.0	98	10.1	61	6.3	530	7.8	1,546	1,354	192	D	D
Webster	133	3,170	0.8	37	10.9	39	11.5	235	9.1	889	827	62	D	D
Wheeler	0	699	1.0	15	19.1	4	5.1	72	12.9	202	D	D	D	D
York	761	14,572	1.1	139	9.8	146	10.3	811	8.0	3,193	2,982	211	13	0.9
NEVADA	34,820	3,032,588	1.0	33,883	10.8	31,808	10.2	342,719	13.5	549,064	328,982	220,082	3,437	1.1
Churchill	290	24,190	1.0	304	11.9	326	12.7	2,662	13.4	5,885	5,011	873	46	1.8
Clark	21,145	2,233,421	1.0	25,488	11.2	22,163	9.7	260,442	13.7	371,680	203,111	168,568	2,603	1.1
Douglas	200	47,422	1.0	327	6.6	665	13.4	3,903	11.4	16,251	13,364	2,886	47	1.0
Elko	717	51,805	1.0	667	12.4	436	8.1	6,002	13.0	6,807	6,591	216	42	0.8
Esmeralda	0	1,096	1.2	4	5.4	4	5.4	103	18.2	258	244	13	D	D
Eureka	0	3,877	3.6	16	8.5	16	8.5	123	7.2	356	D	D	D	D
Humboldt	140	17,345	1.1	228	13.1	145	8.3	2,150	15.1	2,932	2,852	80	11	0.6
Lander	15	5,606	1.0	81	14.1	45	7.8	579	12.5	924	910	14	D	D
Lincoln	155	5,203	1.0	49	10.9	67	14.8	424	11.8	1,083	1,015	68	D	D
Lyon	347	45,824	0.6	578	9.6	794	13.2	5,867	13.1	14,635	10,909	3,726	65	1.1
Mineral	46	4,475	1.0	40	8.8	127	27.8	417	12.6	1,357	1,162	195	D	D
Nye	1,083	44,795	1.0	389	7.4	1,010	19.2	4,048	12.9	16,999	8,104	8,895	71	1.4
Pershing	1,701	6,743	1.1	51	7.6	56	8.4	545	14.1	1,035	1,002	32	11	1.7
Storey	2	5,219	1.7	23	5.6	43	10.4	252	9.0	1,232	919	313	D	D
Washoe	5,242	464,186	1.0	5,024	10.2	4,959	10.1	48,387	12.5	91,461	60,273	31,188	470	1.0
White Pine	1,002	10,081	1.1	99	10.8	99	10.8	684	10.4	1,921	1,848	73	D	D
Carson City	2,735	61,300	1.2	515	8.8	853	14.5	6,131	14.7	14,250	11,319	2,931	71	1.2
NEW HAMPSHIRE	39,476	1,323,455	1.0	11,414	8.3	15,158	11.0	82,733	7.7	307,453	240,053	67,400	853	0.6
Belknap	987	57,781	0.9	475	7.4	956	14.9	3,906	8.3	18,208	13,991	4,217	47	0.7
Carroll	358	47,201	1.0	301	5.9	701	13.8	3,792	11.0	16,153	12,842	3,311	D	D
Cheshire	3,862	73,743	0.9	600	7.8	883	11.5	4,263	7.5	19,031	15,127	3,904	11	0.1
Coos	2,052	30,690	0.9	220	7.0	491	15.7	1,928	8.7	10,184	8,414	1,771	21	0.7
Grafton	7,005	102,218	1.3	655	7.1	1,014	11.1	5,994	9.3	21,979	17,746	4,233	14	0.2
Hillsborough	7,451	398,104	0.9	3,990	9.4	4,325	10.2	27,581	8.0	81,114	61,914	19,200	456	1.1
Merrimack	6,436	153,460	1.0	1,167	7.5	1,678	10.9	8,643	7.3	35,120	26,020	9,100	77	0.5
Rockingham	2,274	303,376	1.0	2,575	8.2	3,284	10.4	16,057	6.4	68,220	53,985	14,235	196	0.6
Strafford	8,439	118,917	0.8	1,096	8.3	1,323	10.0	7,990	7.8	26,066	20,402	5,663	31	0.2
Sullivan	612	37,965	0.8	335	7.7	503	11.6	2,579	7.7	11,378	9,612	1,766	D	D
NEW JERSEY	182,896	8,559,123	0.9	95,254	10.3	90,557	9.8	675,782	9.3	1,636,000	1,108,201	527,799	17,927	1.9
Atlantic	6,033	264,616	1.0	2,740	10.0	3,193	11.6	22,420	10.7	58,468	40,777	17,692	338	1.2
Bergen	10,231	898,426	0.9	8,424	8.8	8,675	9.1	64,563	8.4	172,299	125,042	47,258	2,089	2.2
Burlington	11,945	428,417	0.9	4,220	9.1	4,682	10.1	21,430	6.0	90,581	59,972	30,609	629	1.4
Camden	7,389	470,528	0.9	5,760	11.0	5,579	10.7	34,449	8.2	97,175	64,494	32,681	807	1.5
Cape May	2,704	92,648	1.0	749	7.9	1,430	15.0	6,002	9.2	28,067	21,291	6,776	137	1.4
Cumberland	9,015	151,066	1.0	1,719	11.2	1,690	11.0	14,106	12.1	28,789	18,381	10,408	202	1.3
Essex	24,456	796,670	1.0	9,469	11.0	8,015	9.3	80,196	12.0	119,129	70,649	48,480	2,181	2.5
Gloucester	4,185	258,390	0.8	2,777	9.1	3,207	10.6	13,841	5.7	57,059	38,621	18,438	389	1.3
Hudson	9,852	613,736	0.8	9,337	13.1	5,412	7.6	78,318	13.5	82,089	48,000	34,089	1,603	2.2
Hunterdon	3,812	113,969	0.8	948	7.3	1,140	8.8	5,098	5.2	26,441	18,813	7,628	163	1.3

1. Per 1,000 estimated resident population.

STATE County	COVID-19 Vaccinations, 2021–2022: Number	COVID-19 Vaccinations, 2021–2022: Percent[5]	Education: School enrollment and attainment, 2016–2020: Enrollment[1]: Total	Enrollment[1]: Percent private	Attainment[2] (percent): High school graduate or less	Attainment[2] (percent): Bachelor's degree or more	Local government expenditures,[3] 2018–2019: Total current spending (mil dol)	Local government expenditures,[3] 2018–2019: Current spending per student (dollars)	Money income, 2016–2020: Per capita income[4]	Households: Median income (dollars)	Households: Percent with income of less than $50,000	Households: Percent with income of $200,000 or more	Income and poverty, 2020: Median household income (dollars)	Percent below poverty level: All persons	Percent below poverty level: Children under 18 years	Percent below poverty level: Children 5 to 17 years in families
	46	47	48	49	50	51	52	53	54	55	56	57	58	59	60	61
NEBRASKA— Cont'd																
Platte	15,753	47.1	7,946	25.1	39.6	23.4	65.9	12,621	30,822	60,878	41.1	4.2	62,776	6.6	7.5	6.9
Polk	2,173	41.7	1,293	6.9	44.5	19.2	21.6	17,383	28,978	59,837	35.5	1.7	59,159	7.3	9.0	7.8
Red Willow	3,981	37.1	2,588	7.7	36.7	23.2	21.3	12,279	28,395	48,140	51.4	2.7	55,657	9.5	12.4	12.1
Richardson	4,114	52.3	1,597	19.4	45.2	18.8	19.1	15,246	29,074	44,524	57.4	3.0	51,874	9.5	13.6	12.4
Rock	511	37.7	249	4.4	34.4	29.7	3.9	16,145	33,216	51,458	49.4	7.1	48,461	13.3	18.1	17.4
Saline	7,547	53.1	4,248	24.0	48.9	19.2	40.7	12,600	25,760	52,956	47.0	4.0	63,655	8.0	8.6	9.2
Sarpy	124,069	66.3	51,760	14.6	25.9	40.5	319.1	11,151	36,926	83,051	26.9	7.3	83,104	4.9	5.1	4.4
Saunders	11,341	52.6	5,146	18.8	35.7	27.7	39.0	12,353	34,532	70,414	33.2	3.8	72,526	5.7	6.4	5.9
Scotts Bluff	14,864	41.7	8,808	12.0	40.6	23.1	85.5	12,674	28,770	53,433	47.4	3.7	53,956	12.4	16.5	15.4
Seward	8,688	50.3	5,085	32.4	33.6	30.7	40.9	15,191	32,367	71,111	33.3	4.1	72,456	6.8	6.1	5.4
Sheridan	1,698	32.4	1,020	7.5	45.3	20.4	12.5	15,317	30,173	45,543	54.1	2.2	52,051	13.8	20.6	21.0
Sherman	1,186	39.5	593	9.9	39.6	21.6	8.2	18,026	28,344	53,158	47.0	0.8	49,684	11.4	17.6	16.4
Sioux	293	25.1	208	2.9	32.1	26.7	3.0	29,520	25,398	47,422	54.9	0.4	51,831	15.3	28.1	28.7
Stanton	1,694	28.6	1,436	9.3	36.5	19.8	6.1	15,651	30,747	64,808	36.8	1.9	64,087	6.9	8.5	8.2
Thayer	2,399	48.0	1,043	6.8	41.1	20.9	16.2	17,659	30,568	53,234	45.3	4.1	55,775	9.8	13.0	12.4
Thomas	178	24.7	108	13.0	25.1	24.6	2.5	19,609	35,694	59,000	46.0	4.0	55,599	12.3	22.0	19.8
Thurston	5,449	75.4	2,454	8.2	42.3	18.9	40.0	21,241	20,674	55,574	44.4	2.3	49,148	18.2	25.0	23.9
Valley	1,379	33.2	830	9.8	37.4	27.4	10.6	14,501	31,264	56,205	46.9	4.4	55,542	11.2	14.2	13.2
Washington	11,674	56.3	4,922	14.6	34.4	32.1	40.1	10,792	36,834	71,505	32.2	6.2	78,844	5.3	6.3	5.6
Wayne	3,901	41.6	3,474	3.7	33.5	31.9	30.6	18,179	27,460	58,894	40.2	2.8	64,569	9.5	8.4	7.8
Webster	1,342	38.5	796	17.5	37.6	22.4	9.2	15,520	32,092	51,684	47.8	3.9	52,115	10.2	11.0	10.0
Wheeler	249	31.8	104	14.4	31.1	25.1	3.1	31,455	31,775	48,438	52.1	2.8	52,154	12.4	24.4	26.4
York	7,144	52.2	3,184	26.9	32.5	27.4	26.7	13,368	34,259	63,105	39.5	5.4	63,249	9.3	11.0	10.5
NEVADA	1,871,389	60.8	697,235	11.7	41.0	25.5	4,511.6	9,157	32,629	62,043	40.3	5.9	64,608	12.5	16.7	15.2
Churchill	13,431	53.9	5,254	12.5	36.1	18.7	39.7	11,678	28,659	56,335	45.4	3.3	61,650	10.3	14.7	14.4
Clark	1,306,982	57.7	517,981	12.3	42.0	25.2	2,964.7	8,937	31,651	61,048	41.2	5.8	62,496	13.2	18.0	16.5
Douglas	25,102	51.3	8,531	12.4	29.5	31.9	61.6	10,510	41,921	71,415	31.9	7.6	84,317	8.0	11.0	9.5
Elko	22,469	42.6	13,694	7.2	46.2	16.8	115.7	11,350	34,601	79,375	32.2	4.8	73,914	11.2	13.2	11.9
Esmeralda	361	41.4	127	0.0	47.1	16.8	2.6	27,542	23,192	31,845	68.0	0.4	35,395	14.4	16.4	15.1
Eureka	560	27.6	441	14.3	49.0	11.7	8.1	25,287	30,516	67,478	34.8	7.3	68,806	10.3	13.4	10.9
Humboldt	7,123	42.3	4,057	7.0	48.4	18.8	46.1	13,115	33,258	66,123	40.2	5.1	72,907	9.8	13.2	12.1
Lander	2,242	40.5	1,440	6.9	49.0	12.3	12.6	12,616	34,911	73,797	40.3	4.9	80,894	9.4	11.4	11.0
Lincoln	2,002	38.6	983	10.2	55.3	16.4	15.2	15,348	26,805	56,537	43.0	3.0	60,180	13.2	16.7	16.8
Lyon	24,118	41.9	11,032	6.6	46.0	13.9	93.8	10,341	29,865	58,814	41.2	3.0	63,162	10.1	13.1	12.7
Mineral	2,690	59.7	699	12.4	48.2	14.6	8.7	14,960	21,746	31,500	69.0	1.6	50,069	15.4	20.7	19.5
Nye	21,681	46.6	6,369	9.1	49.6	12.4	68.5	12,768	25,622	47,308	51.9	1.0	52,783	14.2	22.0	21.5
Pershing	2,438	36.3	1,585	4.0	58.5	10.3	12.1	18,427	21,765	57,074	44.3	1.6	65,000	18.1	18.8	19.5
Storey	922	22.4	820	15.1	29.4	33.3	8.9	19,376	39,758	64,000	35.1	6.6	73,271	7.8	11.2	10.6
Washoe	303,555	64.4	110,767	11.0	34.8	31.7	646.2	9,602	37,689	68,272	35.8	7.6	75,232	10.2	11.3	9.6
White Pine	5,129	53.5	1,878	3.5	54.5	12.9	17.4	10,543	27,322	57,353	41.6	2.7	57,923	12.3	12.6	12.2
Carson City	35,984	64.4	11,577	8.3	38.5	22.9	389.5	7,718	32,819	58,305	41.8	4.9	58,382	12.5	15.9	13.9
NEW HAMPSHIRE	954,235	70.2	301,741	21.4	34.0	37.6	2,976.4	16,679	41,234	77,923	31.0	9.7	81,415	7.0	8.4	7.6
Belknap	38,257	62.4	12,102	14.0	35.6	31.7	158.3	17,989	37,766	67,328	36.8	6.0	76,105	7.4	9.8	8.6
Carroll	35,759	73.1	8,155	14.8	32.5	37.0	121.4	21,334	42,085	66,932	38.0	6.6	73,073	7.5	11.8	11.5
Cheshire	47,451	62.4	18,662	21.5	37.8	33.7	147.6	17,759	34,242	64,686	36.3	5.4	66,398	8.8	10.9	10.3
Coos	21,191	67.1	5,238	16.0	51.0	19.7	70.2	18,903	28,442	48,945	51.2	2.4	49,465	13.1	18.8	16.0
Grafton	67,769	75.4	20,750	33.1	32.7	42.1	236.2	21,148	39,669	67,476	37.6	8.6	77,022	8.6	10.6	9.1
Hillsborough	264,932	63.5	94,274	23.9	33.3	38.6	847.1	14,905	42,081	82,099	29.3	10.5	79,222	7.1	9.4	8.5
Merrimack	104,121	68.8	34,858	24.9	35.3	35.8	363.3	17,129	38,213	77,937	31.0	8.0	81,132	6.7	7.4	6.9
Rockingham	208,485	67.3	65,184	19.5	30.2	41.9	689.9	16,253	48,675	93,962	23.5	14.6	96,775	4.6	4.8	4.5
Strafford	82,959	63.5	34,802	13.2	34.2	35.2	233.7	15,781	36,659	72,682	32.7	7.4	72,817	8.2	6.7	6.6
Sullivan	26,910	62.4	7,716	16.4	45.4	29.6	108.7	19,893	33,207	63,760	39.2	5.0	65,881	8.9	11.8	10.5
NEW JERSEY	6,711,405	75.6	2,192,185	19.4	36.5	40.7	28,558.6	20,371	44,153	85,245	30.2	14.8	87,095	9.4	12.6	12.1
Atlantic	177,428	67.3	64,709	11.5	44.4	28.8	912.4	20,537	34,175	63,680	41.2	7.2	61,377	13.8	19.3	18.4
Bergen	723,473	77.6	226,202	23.4	29.1	50.7	2,981.7	21,821	52,800	104,623	24.4	21.0	107,114	6.4	6.7	6.6
Burlington	332,244	74.6	104,585	17.4	34.2	38.5	1,438.9	20,766	44,735	90,329	25.2	13.3	92,471	6.0	7.0	6.0
Camden	350,070	69.1	124,209	17.0	40.7	32.3	1,644.2	19,988	36,559	70,957	36.2	9.0	71,718	12.4	15.5	15.8
Cape May	68,201	74.1	16,739	14.7	38.7	33.6	288.9	23,315	42,987	72,385	34.9	9.1	75,829	9.6	15.6	15.9
Cumberland	78,792	52.7	36,331	7.0	58.4	16.6	541.8	18,436	28,311	55,709	45.2	4.8	60,352	13.1	17.5	16.9
Essex	579,642	72.5	207,973	16.8	41.2	36.3	2,935.9	20,289	39,695	63,959	40.7	13.1	65,528	14.3	18.4	18.3
Gloucester	182,017	62.4	72,628	14.8	38.4	33.8	907.5	19,372	40,557	89,056	27.0	11.3	87,220	7.0	8.0	7.4
Hudson	524,152	78.0	149,503	19.4	38.7	44.0	1,788.3	19,002	42,822	75,062	35.2	13.6	77,323	13.1	18.9	20.3
Hunterdon	88,378	71.1	28,902	17.5	25.0	54.0	455.9	24,768	58,795	117,858	17.9	24.0	113,611	4.1	3.9	3.7

1. All persons 3 years old and over enrolled in nursery school through college. 2. Persons 25 years old and over. 3. Elementary and secondary education expenditures. 4. Based on population estimated by the American Community Survey, 2016–2020. 5. CDC percent based on 2019 population estimate.

STATE County	Personal income, 2020: Total (mil dol)	Personal income, 2020: Percent change 2019–2020	Per capita[1]: Dollars	Per capita[1]: Rank	Wages and salaries (mil dol)	Supplements to wages and salaries, employer contributions (mil dol): Pension and insurance	Supplements to wages and salaries, employer contributions (mil dol): Government social insurance	Proprietors' income (mil dol)	Dividends, interest, and rent (mil dol)	Personal transfer reecipts (mil dol)	Earnings, 2020: Total (mil dol)	Contributions for government social insurance (mil dol): From employee and self-employed	Contributions for government social insurance (mil dol): From employer
	62	63	64	65	66	67	68	69	70	71	72	73	74
NEBRASKA— Cont'd													
Platte	1,745	8.7	52,316	908	942	188	73	181	309	347	1,384	83	73
Polk	298	8.3	57,312	552	62	13	5	69	47	63	149	7	5
Red Willow	555	11.5	52,196	918	230	43	19	61	112	152	354	22	19
Richardson	427	9.6	54,773	717	107	23	8	60	72	118	198	13	8
Rock	100	22.6	72,590	130	23	5	2	38	17	18	68	2	2
Saline	668	7.2	47,785	1,419	366	61	30	78	96	150	535	32	30
Sarpy	10,420	6.4	55,173	690	4,700	851	369	341	1,591	1,712	6,262	387	369
Saunders	1,247	8.3	56,892	577	263	51	20	115	205	239	449	29	20
Scotts Bluff	1,731	7.2	49,048	1,253	775	139	63	185	248	471	1,163	78	63
Seward	966	8.2	56,220	621	292	52	22	109	161	205	476	29	22
Sheridan	291	13.6	56,597	599	70	15	5	69	44	69	159	8	5
Sherman	151	15.0	50,461	1,095	30	6	3	31	25	40	70	4	3
Sioux	77	19.5	64,440	279	9	2	1	37	11	11	49	1	1
Stanton	309	14.1	52,621	882	91	16	6	53	51	52	166	8	6
Thayer	296	9.5	60,659	398	108	21	8	54	64	72	190	11	8
Thomas	43	11.5	57,805	526	12	2	1	13	7	8	28	2	1
Thurston	331	16.8	45,789	1,682	161	34	12	68	46	89	276	13	12
Valley	246	20.8	59,867	433	79	17	6	54	47	59	157	8	6
Washington	1,269	5.7	60,738	395	448	73	34	79	229	218	634	42	34
Wayne	466	12.0	49,143	1,239	176	40	13	79	86	93	307	16	13
Webster	184	7.2	53,815	793	41	9	3	43	28	48	95	5	3
Wheeler	56	4.5	70,710	157	10	2	1	28	10	8	41	1	1
York	763	10.5	56,457	614	361	64	28	101	144	177	554	33	28
NEVADA	168,587	6.1	54,137	X	74,242	12,024	5,517	11,865	37,331	39,268	103,648	6,306	5,517
Churchill	1,270	9.9	50,081	1,136	527	121	42	101	200	345	791	45	42
Clark	118,679	5.9	51,244	1,000	52,505	8,249	3,956	8,439	24,939	29,138	73,150	4,455	3,956
Douglas	3,849	4.4	78,416	88	1,034	159	75	276	1,425	738	1,543	111	75
Elko	2,673	5.8	50,429	1,096	1,287	207	88	104	305	466	1,687	96	88
Esmeralda	38	1.7	42,962	2,071	13	3	1	-1	7	13	16	1	1
Eureka	97	9.1	46,792	1,540	471	64	32	14	13	18	581	33	32
Humboldt	878	6.5	51,772	954	484	93	33	46	110	175	655	36	33
Lander	402	4.9	72,931	126	273	46	18	37	33	61	374	20	18
Lincoln	224	8.5	43,357	2,024	74	20	5	18	41	66	116	6	5
Lyon	2,572	10.9	44,098	1,930	608	120	46	106	377	748	881	67	46
Mineral	221	18.8	48,982	1,257	101	20	7	27	31	80	155	9	7
Nye	1,988	7.0	41,367	2,282	699	120	51	111	300	834	981	81	51
Pershing	249	12.8	37,906	2,695	131	30	8	12	34	66	180	8	8
Storey	278	13.4	65,971	242	1,354	280	108	11	47	51	1,753	95	108
Washoe	31,524	5.9	66,076	240	12,734	2,032	929	2,145	8,807	5,513	17,839	1,085	929
White Pine	479	8.6	50,653	1,071	269	59	16	33	60	124	378	20	16
Carson City	3,166	7.1	56,510	608	1,680	402	104	384	604	831	2,569	137	104
NEW HAMPSHIRE	91,673	5.6	66,534	X	41,624	6,177	2,833	9,054	14,745	17,296	59,689	3,745	2,833
Belknap	4,119	5.7	66,919	214	1,290	220	91	413	800	942	2,014	140	91
Carroll	3,117	5.1	63,403	304	864	149	63	374	839	807	1,450	105	63
Cheshire	4,275	5.9	56,088	634	1,686	290	118	255	854	1,033	2,349	168	118
Coos	1,545	9.8	49,564	1,189	517	114	38	97	246	591	765	57	38
Grafton	6,162	6.8	67,943	194	3,550	530	251	734	1,411	1,230	5,065	309	251
Hillsborough	27,866	6.3	66,548	231	15,154	2,060	1,006	2,445	3,807	4,884	20,665	1,262	1,006
Merrimack	9,743	7.2	63,839	294	4,749	805	322	962	1,434	2,150	6,839	417	322
Rockingham	24,973	3.2	80,220	78	10,131	1,353	692	3,001	3,866	3,533	15,178	940	692
Strafford	7,380	7.3	56,104	630	2,994	525	203	551	1,061	1,518	4,274	269	203
Sullivan	2,492	6.2	57,602	536	689	130	49	222	426	609	1,090	76	49
NEW JERSEY	652,499	5.4	70,314	X	287,150	42,908	20,566	62,941	105,994	120,949	413,565	24,912	20,566
Atlantic	14,673	8.6	55,802	656	6,418	1,174	519	1,192	1,963	4,565	9,302	595	519
Bergen	85,570	4.0	91,972	33	32,143	4,534	2,338	9,796	17,909	11,562	48,810	2,877	2,338
Burlington	29,991	5.8	67,154	207	14,153	2,261	1,079	2,096	4,424	5,945	19,589	1,203	1,079
Camden	29,816	7.1	58,830	484	12,617	2,062	961	1,840	3,895	7,703	17,479	1,118	961
Cape May	6,210	6.5	67,836	199	1,865	385	160	738	1,321	1,790	3,148	212	160
Cumberland	6,689	8.6	45,498	1,726	3,157	632	255	525	809	2,312	4,570	289	255
Essex	56,433	6.7	70,497	159	26,643	4,322	1,872	4,353	9,397	11,952	37,190	2,184	1,872
Gloucester	17,708	6.7	60,386	409	5,946	1,098	476	1,181	2,140	3,847	8,700	555	476
Hudson	48,146	5.7	71,682	141	23,345	3,226	1,554	6,845	4,264	8,592	34,970	1,993	1,554
Hunterdon	11,867	3.1	95,088	27	3,469	514	244	1,125	2,189	1,507	5,352	328	244

1. Based on the resident population estimated as of July 1 of the year shown.

STATE County	Earnings, 2020 (cont.)									Social Security beneficiaries, December 2020		Supple-mental Security Income recipients, 2020	Housing units, 2021	
	Percent by selected industries													
	Farm	Mining, quarrying, and extractions	Construction	Manu-facturing	Information; professional, scientific, technical services	Retail trade	Finance, insurance, real estate, and leasing	Health care and social assistance	Govern-ment	Number	Rate[1]		Total	Percent change, 2010–2021
	75	76	77	78	79	80	81	82	83	84	85	86	87	88
NEBRASKA— Cont'd														
Platte	8.4	D	5.9	32.9	2.5	6.0	5.5	8.6	14.1	6,705	196	311	14,264	0.7
Polk	39.1	D	4.5	1.4	D	4.9	D	5.7	21.0	1,315	254	45	2,526	0.1
Red Willow	10.8	0.6	4.2	8.1	3.4	7.6	6.3	14.1	18.5	2,550	240	131	5,154	0.0
Richardson	22.6	D	3.6	8.3	3.3	5.0	3.8	D	18.5	2,185	282	152	4,076	-0.1
Rock	46.3	0.1	6.4	D	D	3.6	4.9	1.0	18.6	345	273	D	794	-0.1
Saline	9.0	0.0	3.1	40.9	D	4.0	3.2	D	16.1	2,635	186	163	5,792	1.2
Sarpy	0.3	0.0	10.5	4.5	8.8	5.8	10.3	5.5	24.8	27,485	142	1,506	74,986	2.1
Saunders	15.4	D	12.1	5.7	5.2	6.2	6.6	4.4	21.9	4,360	191	186	10,149	1.3
Scotts Bluff	4.9	D	6.6	5.2	4.4	7.4	5.4	16.5	18.6	8,460	237	800	16,479	-0.1
Seward	15.4	0.0	7.6	14.1	4.2	4.4	5.8	D	15.9	3,510	199	134	7,170	0.8
Sheridan	31.3	D	D	D	1.6	4.5	D	3.9	21.5	1,360	267	71	2,698	0.0
Sherman	36.2	0.0	3.3	5.7	D	4.8	4.4	9.1	16.3	855	288	36	1,794	0.2
Sioux	72.2	0.2	1.0	1.0	D	2.1	D	D	9.2	265	232	D	704	-0.1
Stanton	21.7	D	4.1	42.8	D	0.8	3.7	1.2	10.6	1,055	181	31	2,472	0.4
Thayer	23.4	0.0	4.0	16.5	D	2.8	6.9	D	19.4	1,350	275	63	2,501	0.1
Thomas	26.4	D	D	D	D	7.5	D	D	17.4	180	267	D	381	0.5
Thurston	19.2	0.0	2.0	3.3	D	3.1	2.1	7.5	47.4	1,145	173	235	2,288	0.1
Valley	31.3	D	4.7	5.6	D	5.4	D	D	22.6	1,060	261	54	2,107	0.1
Washington	6.2	D	11.1	19.8	5.3	9.7	6.0	6.2	13.3	4,365	208	156	8,649	0.7
Wayne	19.4	0.0	2.8	14.9	1.6	4.2	9.5	8.9	24.7	1,545	158	72	3,964	0.3
Webster	34.1	D	D	D	5.3	4.2	D	5.7	18.8	920	270	72	1,786	-0.1
Wheeler	66.7	0.0	1.5	0.1	D	D	D	-0.1	9.9	165	208	D	508	1.0
York	12.5	D	4.3	13.0	D	5.5	7.7	D	14.3	3,235	227	167	6,348	0.2
NEVADA	0.3	1.7	8.9	4.9	9.5	7.2	7.2	10.1	15.6	565,671	180	56,484	1,305,509	1.5
Churchill	5.8	0.6	8.9	6.5	3.4	5.4	4.0	D	34.8	6,015	234	507	10,904	1.0
Clark	0.0	0.0	8.8	2.7	9.7	7.6	8.0	10.4	15.2	386,005	168	44,339	934,878	1.5
Douglas	0.6	D	8.1	14.5	11.7	6.1	8.6	7.6	12.7	15,960	320	400	24,546	0.8
Elko	1.5	17.0	9.7	0.8	3.9	6.9	2.3	6.7	18.0	7,150	133	537	22,009	0.9
Esmeralda	-0.9	D	D	D	D	D	0.0	0.0	33.2	265	357	22	541	0.7
Eureka	1.8	D	D	D	D	0.2	D	0.0	3.1	370	194	22	967	0.4
Humboldt	3.1	36.4	4.4	3.5	D	6.0	1.6	D	20.7	3,105	176	258	7,701	0.5
Lander	8.0	D	D	D	0.3	2.6	D	D	11.8	980	169	89	2,817	0.6
Lincoln	12.1	D	D	D	D	D	2.5	D	40.4	1,085	240	72	2,220	0.6
Lyon	2.6	5.5	9.8	19.0	4.9	8.2	3.1	D	18.9	15,410	253	929	24,824	1.4
Mineral	2.9	11.9	1.4	0.4	1.8	3.6	D	12.3	26.6	1,355	295	149	2,589	0.1
Nye	3.9	13.6	4.8	2.1	19.4	7.6	2.2	D	14.7	17,940	336	1,160	25,244	0.2
Pershing	9.2	47.0	D	D	D	3.2	0.9	D	32.4	1,065	158	92	2,287	0.3
Storey	0.0	D	4.5	72.1	D	D	0.1	D	1.4	1,225	296	13	2,007	0.9
Washoe	0.1	-0.1	11.0	6.6	11.0	6.4	6.8	11.5	14.9	91,735	186	6,713	212,930	2.1
White Pine	4.9	41.4	D	D	D	3.5	1.4	D	29.6	1,950	212	157	4,151	0.3
Carson City	0.1	D	5.4	8.0	6.9	8.0	7.0	15.1	33.3	14,055	238	1,025	24,894	1.1
NEW HAMPSHIRE	0.1	0.1	7.8	11.2	13.3	7.9	9.3	12.7	11.8	317,389	229	17,880	643,981	0.6
Belknap	0.0	0.3	12.9	7.9	8.5	11.8	5.3	12.0	14.5	18,900	293	904	38,632	0.9
Carroll	0.2	D	14.3	D	8.7	10.8	6.2	11.7	14.1	16,530	321	610	40,022	0.7
Cheshire	0.1	D	10.8	15.4	6.7	10.2	7.4	12.6	14.9	20,295	262	1,157	35,749	0.3
Coos	0.4	D	6.8	D	3.6	9.2	3.9	18.7	26.9	10,980	351	909	20,535	0.3
Grafton	0.3	0.0	4.4	7.6	12.8	6.1	5.4	26.5	10.2	22,465	244	963	51,496	1.1
Hillsborough	0.0	D	6.8	14.6	15.4	7.2	11.6	11.4	9.3	83,860	198	6,785	176,651	0.5
Merrimack	0.2	0.3	7.6	6.7	9.5	7.7	9.4	13.5	20.3	36,520	235	1,820	66,103	0.7
Rockingham	0.0	0.1	9.0	10.4	15.6	8.2	9.0	9.1	7.5	68,825	217	2,126	136,725	0.8
Strafford	0.1	D	6.5	9.0	13.4	8.1	9.9	14.1	20.2	27,270	206	1,888	56,189	0.5
Sullivan	0.5	D	9.9	22.7	6.4	10.1	4.5	8.7	14.5	11,745	270	718	21,879	0.3
NEW JERSEY	0.1	0.4	5.5	7.6	15.8	5.9	11.2	11.5	13.9	1,651,408	178	173,226	3,780,004	0.4
Atlantic	0.8	D	7.3	D	7.4	7.1	5.4	16.7	23.6	61,510	224	7,137	132,228	0.1
Bergen	0.0	0.0	5.7	6.8	14.6	6.9	11.3	14.5	9.6	166,775	175	11,985	369,209	0.4
Burlington	0.2	D	5.4	8.8	11.5	7.2	12.5	13.4	16.8	93,285	201	6,169	186,144	0.7
Camden	0.1	D	6.3	7.1	9.7	6.8	5.8	19.3	17.2	100,095	191	16,231	213,486	0.3
Cape May	0.3	0.1	11.4	D	D	10.2	9.7	9.3	26.6	29,270	306	1,670	99,494	-0.1
Cumberland	2.7	0.3	7.2	14.4	D	7.8	2.8	16.2	24.8	30,980	202	5,834	57,210	0.1
Essex	0.0	D	4.2	4.2	13.7	3.7	14.1	11.0	20.0	119,320	140	26,340	336,299	0.3
Gloucester	0.8	D	9.2	9.6	D	11.0	4.3	11.4	19.3	60,440	199	4,502	117,752	0.4
Hudson	0.0	D	2.4	2.1	16.3	5.3	29.2	6.5	11.4	82,115	117	19,340	317,046	1.1
Hunterdon	0.6	D	10.5	5.4	17.5	7.7	15.1	9.7	13.6	26,030	200	797	51,915	0.3

1. Per 1,000 resident population estimated as of July 1 of the year shown.

STATE County	Housing units, 2016–2020: Total	Occupied units: Owner-occupied: Percent	Owner-occupied: Median value[1]	Median owner cost as a percent of income: With a mortgage	Median owner cost as a percent of income: Without a mortgage[2]	Renter-occupied: Median rent[3]	Renter-occupied: Median rent as a percent of income[2]	Sub-standard units[4] (percent)	Civilian labor force, 2021: Total	Percent change, 2020–2021	Unemployment: Total	Unemployment: Rate[5]	Civilian employment[6], 2016–2020: Total	Percent: Management, business, science, and arts	Percent: Construction, production, and maintenance occupations
	89	90	91	92	93	94	95	96	97	98	99	100	101	102	103
NEBRASKA— Cont'd															
Platte	13,173	71.8	159,500	18.8	10.9	742	23.6	2.7	18,327	2.1	393	2.1	17,282	32.3	34.9
Polk	2,048	83.5	117,600	17.0	10.2	606	19.3	2.2	2,951	0.1	55	1.9	2,574	34.2	30.9
Red Willow	4,503	71.9	113,600	18.1	12.1	650	23.1	0.2	5,869	-0.3	117	2.0	5,377	31.1	27.6
Richardson	3,706	74.9	73,700	15.3	12.8	650	25.3	0.4	4,294	1.3	102	2.4	3,901	35.1	34.8
Rock	617	74.6	92,100	16.9	10.0	510	25.5	0.8	890	0.1	12	1.3	758	44.5	23.7
Saline	5,292	71.4	120,800	19.9	12.7	709	28.8	3.4	7,302	-1.0	168	2.3	7,081	28.1	40.5
Sarpy	67,299	68.9	211,400	19.1	11.2	1,050	25.7	2.0	98,538	0.6	2,343	2.4	96,086	43.8	18.5
Saunders	8,542	80.0	171,600	19.8	11.9	762	21.4	1.5	11,484	0.9	255	2.2	11,208	37.6	26.2
Scotts Bluff	14,657	66.7	130,400	20.3	12.5	805	28.6	1.5	18,154	-0.7	500	2.8	16,934	30.4	29.3
Seward	6,766	71.2	172,900	19.2	10.0	778	25.4	1.1	8,854	0.1	218	2.5	9,140	36.9	28.9
Sheridan	2,312	64.8	78,200	17.4	12.4	736	23.4	2.2	2,755	0.7	50	1.8	2,592	32.2	30.9
Sherman	1,414	73.9	91,000	20.4	12.3	609	17.3	0.0	1,701	1.4	35	2.1	1,533	37.4	29.2
Sioux	530	62.3	108,800	22.2	13.8	579	16.7	5.3	770	0.4	14	1.8	636	38.7	35.1
Stanton	2,430	78.4	129,200	17.8	10.5	779	19.8	1.9	3,620	1.8	76	2.1	3,214	31.3	32.5
Thayer	2,247	76.1	69,900	17.4	10.0	611	17.4	1.8	2,690	-3.6	46	1.7	2,522	37.0	32.3
Thomas	276	68.1	120,000	18.7	10.0	588	17.5	0.0	430	0.0	11	2.6	297	41.8	21.2
Thurston	2,165	61.3	77,700	16.3	10.0	642	18.4	11.6	3,195	2.2	107	3.3	2,882	37.7	23.0
Valley	1,844	77.6	110,500	17.3	11.6	588	23.6	2.2	2,119	-1.1	44	2.1	2,102	40.8	23.2
Washington	8,303	77.4	204,900	18.8	11.7	774	25.9	0.5	11,364	0.9	262	2.3	10,680	40.2	24.0
Wayne	3,793	67.2	144,100	17.9	12.2	709	28.6	0.4	5,737	0.4	110	1.9	5,446	34.1	22.9
Webster	1,524	81.4	74,600	14.1	10.1	537	22.3	2.3	1,660	-0.2	34	2.0	1,805	37.8	30.0
Wheeler	353	75.6	96,900	32.5	13.3	485	25.0	1.1	563	-1.1	7	1.2	374	45.7	34.5
York	5,685	73.6	135,600	18.2	10.0	741	22.7	1.7	7,338	0.2	143	1.9	6,826	36.5	26.2
NEVADA	1,130,011	57.1	290,200	22.2	10.0	1,159	30.0	4.5	1,504,761	0.1	108,822	7.2	1,425,040	30.9	21.1
Churchill	9,972	68.6	198,800	19.9	10.0	888	26.4	2.1	11,230	1.7	391	3.5	10,022	34.9	29.3
Clark	809,026	54.8	285,100	22.4	10.0	1,181	30.9	4.8	1,100,264	-0.4	91,244	8.3	1,044,351	29.8	19.4
Douglas	21,071	74.5	416,900	24.0	10.0	1,169	28.1	2.5	22,047	-0.3	1,001	4.5	21,579	37.6	20.3
Elko	18,516	69.2	225,800	18.2	10.0	961	22.0	3.1	25,803	-1.1	864	3.3	26,181	30.2	33.4
Esmeralda	515	50.5	81,100	17.5	10.0	700	35.0	0.8	426	2.2	16	3.8	394	33.0	30.2
Eureka	661	73.4	151,000	14.3	10.0	721	27.0	5.1	1,053	3.3	27	2.6	787	27.4	46.1
Humboldt	6,579	68.8	186,200	19.0	10.4	815	22.7	5.1	8,158	1.9	279	3.4	8,218	30.1	37.8
Lander	2,315	75.8	167,400	15.4	10.0	835	27.3	2.2	3,180	1.7	114	3.6	2,444	25.0	44.7
Lincoln	2,003	72.5	132,600	21.5	10.0	621	16.1	1.4	2,151	6.2	73	3.4	1,745	29.8	28.3
Lyon	21,726	73.0	238,600	21.8	10.0	1,062	27.8	2.2	23,425	3.5	1,228	5.2	23,278	27.0	32.3
Mineral	1,938	73.0	99,900	24.2	10.0	582	25.6	3.3	2,078	-1.4	79	3.8	1,512	32.1	32.1
Nye	19,253	71.5	172,300	23.2	10.6	821	27.9	3.8	17,290	-0.5	1,060	6.1	15,215	23.2	31.7
Pershing	2,009	67.8	114,400	18.4	10.0	581	25.5	2.5	2,633	2.9	94	3.6	2,177	30.2	42.9
Storey	1,704	96.5	264,000	22.1	10.0	704	13.9	0.2	2,050	2.0	95	4.6	1,500	38.6	22.6
Washoe	186,116	57.9	360,500	21.9	10.0	1,150	28.8	4.6	252,682	1.9	10,885	4.3	235,897	35.4	23.0
White Pine	3,749	72.4	157,100	15.9	10.0	788	21.5	3.7	4,628	1.9	141	3.0	3,742	27.3	32.3
Carson City	22,858	58.2	299,900	22.1	10.0	982	27.6	3.9	25,665	0.4	1,231	4.8	25,998	33.3	24.2
NEW HAMPSHIRE	539,116	71.2	272,300	22.3	14.6	1,145	28.6	2.0	755,422	-0.6	26,482	3.5	730,223	41.9	20.7
Belknap	25,576	76.6	232,000	22.6	15.6	1,039	29.8	2.5	31,024	0.3	1,142	3.7	31,475	38.3	21.4
Carroll	22,235	79.4	251,400	23.4	12.8	926	28.9	1.8	23,067	0.3	882	3.8	24,215	36.8	24.1
Cheshire	30,513	68.1	197,700	22.7	14.8	996	27.8	2.1	39,426	-0.4	1,522	3.9	39,376	39.5	23.1
Coos	13,967	72.2	132,500	20.5	15.3	724	27.5	1.7	14,322	0.7	633	4.4	14,425	31.9	26.1
Grafton	35,141	69.9	230,700	23.1	14.4	1,045	29.0	2.0	48,491	1.3	1,609	3.3	46,570	42.4	19.0
Hillsborough	162,843	65.7	287,900	22.1	13.9	1,217	29.2	2.1	237,144	-1.1	8,534	3.6	228,874	43.1	20.0
Merrimack	59,209	72.5	245,400	22.0	14.7	1,066	28.1	2.1	81,221	-1.4	2,606	3.2	79,513	41.1	21.6
Rockingham	122,520	77.8	344,000	22.0	15.0	1,274	28.2	1.6	185,013	-0.5	6,401	3.5	173,513	45.3	19.1
Strafford	49,831	66.8	243,500	22.6	15.1	1,132	27.5	2.5	72,806	-0.6	2,390	3.3	71,425	39.6	21.0
Sullivan	17,281	72.7	174,400	22.9	15.9	1,029	30.4	1.1	22,909	0.0	762	3.3	20,837	35.0	27.7
NEW JERSEY	3,272,054	64.0	343,500	23.9	15.7	1,368	30.3	3.5	4,661,087	0.4	295,690	6.3	4,426,619	44.2	18.5
Atlantic	101,103	66.9	216,600	25.2	17.9	1,129	33.9	3.5	123,181	-0.8	11,665	9.5	125,436	33.5	17.3
Bergen	342,059	64.8	477,400	24.2	15.9	1,557	29.0	2.7	493,303	-0.2	29,828	6.0	480,172	50.4	14.5
Burlington	168,195	75.1	259,600	22.7	14.8	1,388	29.3	1.6	242,242	1.2	12,813	5.3	224,384	45.5	17.4
Camden	190,660	65.6	200,400	23.1	16.1	1,107	32.2	2.7	266,839	0.8	18,025	6.8	249,407	40.1	19.9
Cape May	40,670	78.0	306,200	24.4	14.6	1,176	37.7	1.4	47,377	3.5	4,200	8.9	41,313	36.6	18.1
Cumberland	50,947	66.3	166,400	24.1	14.6	1,082	37.4	3.5	68,943	0.6	5,288	7.7	60,369	27.4	32.9
Essex	290,680	44.4	395,900	26.0	17.5	1,211	32.3	5.1	385,997	-0.3	30,894	8.0	379,534	40.2	20.0
Gloucester	106,376	80.4	224,300	22.3	15.8	1,258	31.3	1.1	158,303	0.9	9,504	6.0	150,863	43.7	19.8
Hudson	261,289	32.4	400,800	25.5	17.1	1,450	27.9	8.2	371,044	-0.5	25,372	6.8	360,200	43.8	19.8
Hunterdon	47,647	83.9	418,700	22.6	14.6	1,443	28.4	0.8	66,384	0.9	3,028	4.6	65,859	54.3	12.6

1. Specified owner-occupied units. 2. A value of 10.0 represents 10 percent or less; a value of 50.0 represents 50 percent or more. 3. Specified renter-occupied units. 4. Overcrowded or lacking complete plumbing facilities. 5. Percent of civilian labor force. 6. Civilian employed persons 16 years old and over.

STATE County	Private nonfarm establishments, employment and payroll, 2020									Agriculture, 2017			
		Employment						Annual payroll		Farms			Farm producers whose primary occupation is farming (percent)
											Percent with:		
	Number of establish-ments	Total	Health care and social assistance	Manufac-turing	Retail trade	Finance and insurance	Professional, scientific, and technical services	Total (mil dol)	Average per employee (dollars)	Number	Fewer than 50 acres	1000 acres or more	
	104	105	106	107	108	109	110	111	112	113	114	115	116
NEBRASKA— Cont'd													
Platte	1,026	16,013	1,868	5,411	2,342	521	401	701	43,758	836	26.0	12.3	52.7
Polk	145	881	251	42	143	51	14	30	34,411	432	18.5	17.8	60.7
Red Willow	391	3,335	587	297	739	182	117	133	39,756	333	34.5	32.7	48.3
Richardson	249	1,667	373	260	242	74	55	56	33,593	708	22.2	15.7	44.0
Rock	46	315	125	NA	43	14	NA	14	43,308	220	7.7	52.3	70.5
Saline	309	5,981	509	2,914	502	139	50	273	45,697	717	19.1	19.7	52.3
Sarpy	3,840	59,536	5,911	3,246	9,708	4,251	3,036	2,849	47,862	417	60.7	8.4	34.5
Saunders	546	4,005	668	522	625	216	134	151	37,612	1,118	35.1	12.6	42.7
Scotts Bluff	1,044	12,468	2,802	1,021	2,011	521	344	486	38,956	760	29.7	13.2	48.0
Seward	470	5,578	844	1,136	500	220	93	195	34,922	944	39.4	12.7	40.8
Sheridan	146	921	238	7	190	99	36	29	31,933	525	11.2	45.3	60.0
Sherman	83	481	134	NA	133	18	15	15	31,083	384	16.4	22.4	48.2
Sioux	15	34	NA	NA	7	7	NA	1	42,882	307	8.1	53.7	62.5
Stanton	104	1,052	17	NA	92	29	5	82	77,503	571	22.1	12.3	48.9
Thayer	209	1,784	323	534	196	99	19	73	40,821	414	20.3	29.0	54.6
Thomas	24	199	NA	NA	47	NA	NA	10	50,236	90	12.2	63.3	55.6
Thurston	125	2,294	567	146	203	70	574	151	65,976	309	21.7	26.5	59.7
Valley	180	1,293	371	93	279	64	83	47	36,475	362	18.0	29.0	53.1
Washington	600	6,176	673	1,002	1,020	248	290	320	51,884	747	44.4	11.5	41.2
Wayne	241	3,671	441	1,220	355	349	92	115	31,396	485	22.9	16.1	55.0
Webster	90	568	181	NA	121	28	5	22	38,519	406	16.7	26.1	49.8
Wheeler	21	93	NA	NA	NA	NA	NA	2	19,011	215	10.7	32.6	57.0
York	521	6,684	968	924	885	355	129	265	39,626	521	16.3	22.1	61.4
NEVADA	70,621	1,275,946	142,895	49,782	155,419	40,199	61,841	56,342	44,157	3,423	51.7	13.7	50.4
Churchill	469	5,327	781	373	854	130	320	247	46,366	504	59.3	5.4	53.1
Clark	49,138	922,349	101,683	23,601	114,377	29,781	42,536	38,638	41,891	179	77.1	0.6	30.5
Douglas	1,652	17,322	1,597	1,865	2,021	348	815	753	43,497	239	69.5	7.9	41.0
Elko	1,117	20,536	1,691	345	2,540	292	447	1,242	60,501	526	42.0	21.3	49.1
Esmeralda	10	135	NA	NA	NA	NA	NA	8	61,748	24	37.5	29.2	55.3
Eureka	35	1,524	NA	NA	39	NA	NA	182	119,157	86	14.0	40.7	65.6
Humboldt	416	6,502	654	214	931	69	74	411	63,172	298	33.9	24.5	59.3
Lander	93	961	203	NA	195	15	7	35	36,812	117	41.0	21.4	60.3
Lincoln	77	574	93	NA	202	32	19	17	29,134	166	36.1	9.6	48.4
Lyon	829	8,639	718	1,744	1,516	135	303	373	43,171	312	56.1	8.7	54.1
Mineral	61	1,173	162	NA	102	NA	8	53	45,029	59	71.2	1.7	51.2
Nye	758	10,297	1,149	134	1,540	152	1,352	501	48,691	211	53.6	12.8	53.3
Pershing	59	1,483	113	436	155	12	4	97	65,367	154	32.5	24.0	55.3
Storey	80	476	NA	25	67	NA	22	15	31,725	2	100.0	NA	100.0
Washoe	13,210	208,420	28,782	18,264	27,098	5,391	11,894	10,352	49,669	353	69.7	7.4	43.3
White Pine	181	2,966	303	15	455	37	41	188	63,407	176	42.0	19.9	46.4
Carson City	1,902	22,503	4,480	2,642	3,233	1,112	1,011	1,058	47,008	17	70.6	NA	53.3
NEW HAMPSHIRE	38,350	621,263	98,157	66,150	97,334	28,921	35,737	33,455	53,850	4,123	57.1	0.8	38.6
Belknap	1,859	21,449	4,232	2,332	5,034	575	629	911	42,473	256	50.8	0.4	41.5
Carroll	1,846	16,895	2,622	802	3,690	369	520	635	37,584	285	51.6	1.1	41.5
Cheshire	1,912	27,534	4,121	4,578	5,482	1,115	614	1,293	46,953	420	49.8	0.7	32.1
Coos	823	8,892	2,141	641	1,609	257	210	347	39,053	272	40.4	2.2	36.8
Grafton	2,885	51,679	13,023	5,392	7,060	829	1,727	2,874	55,610	462	39.8	1.7	42.5
Hillsborough	10,997	190,991	32,864	21,905	28,441	9,529	15,980	11,084	58,032	605	63.3	0.2	42.0
Merrimack	4,092	64,222	12,651	5,997	10,215	3,074	2,957	3,186	49,616	545	58.9	0.6	38.5
Rockingham	9,888	148,629	17,350	16,309	26,257	7,240	9,765	8,182	55,053	618	73.6	0.2	42.6
Strafford	2,687	39,918	7,713	4,979	7,139	3,676	1,327	1,967	49,286	310	65.5	0.3	32.1
Sullivan	894	11,303	1,241	3,215	2,361	347	245	544	48,123	350	61.1	1.1	32.7
NEW JERSEY	232,761	3,819,722	625,613	221,768	463,891	204,384	338,602	241,029	63,101	9,883	75.2	1.1	39.6
Atlantic	6,128	110,573	19,125	2,668	15,437	2,422	4,006	4,455	40,294	450	75.3	0.9	52.1
Bergen	31,724	442,996	79,846	30,690	52,303	16,727	31,604	27,426	61,911	74	98.6	NA	50.4
Burlington	10,502	194,483	30,975	13,757	25,064	17,959	15,714	11,072	56,932	915	72.3	2.0	47.3
Camden	11,443	192,454	49,044	12,366	24,102	5,016	13,095	9,982	51,866	197	81.2	NA	38.8
Cape May	3,729	27,000	4,245	648	5,901	1,151	1,039	1,161	43,013	164	73.8	NA	48.5
Cumberland	2,746	46,305	10,357	7,541	6,820	906	986	1,994	43,067	560	63.6	2.0	48.0
Essex	18,974	299,108	60,818	16,890	27,393	18,768	21,759	19,170	64,091	22	100.0	NA	28.9
Gloucester	6,155	104,007	16,628	8,997	21,595	1,709	3,530	4,499	43,257	580	72.6	1.2	46.5
Hudson	13,853	246,619	29,860	8,048	24,959	40,747	14,394	19,092	77,414	4	100.0	NA	50.0
Hunterdon	3,709	45,314	8,513	3,512	6,691	3,601	4,312	2,970	65,550	1,604	75.3	0.7	34.7

STATE County	Agriculture, 2017 (cont.) Land in farms Acreage (1,000)	Percent change, 2012–2017	Acres: Average size of farm	Acres: Total irrigated (1,000)	Acres: Total cropland (1,000)	Value of land and buildings (dollars): Average per farm	Value of land and buildings (dollars): Average per acre	Value of machinery and equipment, average per farm (dollars)	Value of products sold: Total (mil dol)	Average per farm (acres)	Percent from: Crops	Percent from: Livestock and poultry products	Organic farms (number)	Farms with internet access (percent)	Government payments: Total ($1,000)	Government payments: Percent of farms
	117	118	119	120	121	122	123	124	125	126	127	128	129	130	131	132
NEBRASKA— Cont'd																
Platte	384	-10.0	459	191.8	336.4	2,903,960	6,328	345,260	688.6	823,639	27.8	72.2	6	79.7	12,585	75.1
Polk	251	2.3	581	164.2	225.0	3,434,576	5,911	369,062	330.7	765,505	39.4	60.6	1	85.6	7,235	83.1
Red Willow	439	4.7	1,319	52.7	248.2	2,568,525	1,947	307,287	188.2	565,150	38.2	61.8	NA	82.6	4,049	57.1
Richardson	342	7.1	483	11.2	272.4	2,061,048	4,267	202,966	149.3	210,944	78.5	21.5	3	79.4	8,915	75.3
Rock	584	-9.4	2,655	35.2	121.4	3,019,965	1,138	221,861	108.1	491,364	20.6	79.4	1	87.3	1,581	41.4
Saline	360	-0.4	503	135.7	305.0	2,370,146	4,716	285,163	206.9	288,576	69.9	30.1	1	77.3	9,762	80.6
Sarpy	99	8.5	239	11.5	93.0	1,774,545	7,439	127,332	54.9	131,707	91.8	8.2	9	83.2	1,930	47.0
Saunders	480	2.2	429	135.6	436.2	2,420,851	5,641	235,724	360.5	322,419	62.6	37.4	7	79.2	12,010	68.5
Scotts Bluff	442	-0.8	581	170.7	218.1	1,184,110	2,038	231,435	322.7	424,641	30.6	69.4	3	84.1	5,405	54.2
Seward	363	2.4	385	138.7	310.5	2,198,064	5,710	252,569	251.0	265,841	61.5	38.5	NA	79.3	10,627	71.6
Sheridan	1,562	1.8	2,974	74.1	301.5	2,884,505	970	210,422	150.6	286,863	38.2	61.8	2	80.8	5,522	62.9
Sherman	311	10.5	809	93.3	159.0	2,165,691	2,676	223,342	139.3	362,885	58.1	41.9	NA	82.0	3,109	62.5
Sioux	1,230	0.4	4,006	41.8	97.6	3,607,478	901	175,807	133.3	434,283	13.2	86.8	NA	86.3	2,690	49.8
Stanton	266	4.6	466	34.5	203.7	2,327,041	4,991	214,703	208.4	364,956	45.4	54.6	2	79.3	7,411	79.5
Thayer	326	-0.2	787	128.4	251.0	3,083,516	3,920	360,804	227.7	550,041	56.5	43.5	2	77.5	8,364	79.0
Thomas	388	5.6	4,313	2.6	7.4	3,364,667	780	159,890	24.4	271,067	8.3	91.7	NA	94.4	D	20.0
Thurston	232	-6.3	751	14.9	206.8	3,625,111	4,827	377,357	207.3	670,731	49.1	50.9	1	76.7	6,000	79.3
Valley	351	0.4	969	111.3	172.6	2,788,775	2,878	303,059	223.9	618,483	34.7	65.3	4	82.6	4,664	68.8
Washington	248	-0.1	332	22.4	215.9	2,163,878	6,519	197,031	150.4	201,325	71.8	28.2	1	86.7	2,839	58.0
Wayne	281	0.5	580	61.6	253.6	3,196,693	5,512	310,983	223.8	461,466	57.7	42.3	1	85.8	8,593	70.9
Webster	329	8.8	810	68.1	206.2	2,219,552	2,739	254,116	347.9	856,778	22.3	77.7	2	78.3	5,547	71.9
Wheeler	357	0.0	1,662	36.9	87.8	2,539,799	1,528	258,222	283.1	1,316,963	7.4	92.6	2	88.4	2,418	54.9
York	347	2.1	665	275.4	327.3	4,575,694	6,878	498,031	340.9	654,309	59.8	40.2	NA	84.6	14,518	77.2
NEVADA	6,128	3.6	1,790	790.4	794.7	1,627,858	909	155,033	665.8	194,495	41.5	58.5	51	82.9	5,049	9.1
Churchill	250	26.7	496	45.0	47.4	949,440	1,915	106,008	90.7	179,938	21.9	78.1	3	85.1	427	11.9
Clark	D	D	D	3.7	4.0	1,439,603	3,109	76,922	12.7	70,676	90.2	9.8	1	74.9	16	2.2
Douglas	118	17.2	495	34.7	22.0	1,017,364	2,055	108,770	23.5	98,464	25.6	74.4	NA	89.5	130	4.6
Elko	2,180	2.5	4,145	199.9	215.0	2,276,052	549	136,223	72.2	137,213	15.4	84.6	1	85.0	351	3.6
Esmeralda	D	D	D	15.0	14.4	2,138,151	2,083	517,623	12.0	498,083	96.2	3.8	NA	83.3	98	45.8
Eureka	579	-9.4	6,729	50.4	59.8	3,362,856	500	423,423	40.4	470,128	73.2	26.8	1	84.9	1,066	11.6
Humboldt	990	22.4	3,323	162.6	158.3	2,945,636	887	309,287	105.7	354,534	71.2	28.8	5	89.6	747	19.5
Lander	329	4.9	2,815	37.7	46.7	2,951,893	1,049	227,081	31.8	272,043	67.1	32.9	7	74.4	144	12.8
Lincoln	66	D	399	24.2	20.6	1,028,189	2,576	237,470	22.0	132,404	58.6	41.4	2	73.5	10	3.0
Lyon	181	-50.5	581	55.8	65.1	1,328,718	2,286	147,374	102.7	329,179	28.3	71.7	13	85.3	839	9.9
Mineral	D	D	D	2.0	2.2	1,168,722	293	66,181	D	D	D	D	NA	57.6	150	27.1
Nye	93	43.4	442	21.9	22.4	766,261	1,732	128,095	65.0	307,924	8.0	92.0	3	71.6	30	1.9
Pershing	330	10.4	2,145	42.0	56.8	1,717,125	801	189,476	33.8	219,610	58.3	41.7	NA	83.8	689	26.0
Storey	D	D	D	NA	NA	D	D	D	D	D	NA	D	NA	100.0	NA	NA
Washoe	501	13.2	1,420	43.6	22.2	1,457,532	1,026	62,049	19.9	56,484	45.8	54.2	14	86.4	174	5.1
White Pine	165	-14.5	939	51.5	37.2	1,245,500	1,326	168,506	30.0	170,682	38.8	61.2	NA	79.5	177	5.7
Carson City	1	D	57	0.4	0.6	D	D	D	D	D	D	D	1	100.0	NA	NA
NEW HAMPSHIRE	425	-10.3	103	2.2	108.0	539,732	5,231	68,629	187.8	45,548	57.4	42.6	156	87.2	3,494	7.5
Belknap	25	6.4	99	0.1	5.2	487,697	4,914	62,719	7.6	29,754	56.7	43.3	5	85.9	148	9.0
Carroll	32	10.6	114	0.3	4.4	447,525	3,929	47,048	5.5	19,446	67.5	32.5	15	82.8	295	8.4
Cheshire	54	-15.3	128	0.1	10.7	484,018	3,791	72,235	14.6	34,683	47.6	52.4	23	91.7	473	7.6
Coos	47	-17.4	172	0.1	15.4	442,111	2,564	70,608	16.4	60,301	32.5	67.5	9	81.6	420	7.0
Grafton	74	-10.7	159	0.1	16.3	622,137	3,907	74,022	23.4	50,587	30.3	69.7	10	84.6	426	9.5
Hillsborough	44	-7.3	73	0.6	11.7	568,208	7,775	67,925	18.8	31,030	77.2	22.8	18	93.1	281	7.8
Merrimack	54	-16.4	100	0.4	17.5	577,576	5,798	99,615	49.3	90,541	74.1	25.9	29	87.3	492	6.6
Rockingham	32	-10.5	52	0.3	10.3	588,366	11,281	53,046	22.4	36,243	72.6	27.4	21	86.2	621	6.0
Strafford	23	-24.4	75	0.1	5.6	485,607	6,493	53,461	10.5	33,803	61.6	38.4	13	91.3	171	5.8
Sullivan	39	1.2	113	0.1	10.9	540,738	4,792	71,638	19.3	55,146	34.4	65.6	13	81.4	168	8.0
NEW JERSEY	734	2.7	74	86.8	463.0	1,000,464	13,469	86,532	1,098.0	111,095	89.7	10.3	122	80.9	7,503	7.5
Atlantic	29	306.2	64	11.6	17.8	823,031	12,764	135,393	120.7	268,162	98.7	1.3	10	85.3	198	7.8
Bergen	1	-26.6	14	0.1	0.3	1,412,811	99,475	48,545	D	D	100.0	D	1	79.7	D	1.4
Burlington	96	0.4	105	12.4	49.7	1,057,462	10,052	92,669	98.6	107,738	92.4	7.6	6	82.2	828	7.4
Camden	9	26.5	47	2.3	5.0	774,929	16,419	81,602	22.9	116,208	99.6	0.4	5	83.2	D	1.5
Cape May	8	-87.4	50	1.4	3.8	722,281	14,561	59,087	9.8	59,988	89.2	10.8	NA	81.1	D	1.2
Cumberland	66	53.1	118	20.0	49.6	1,159,637	9,801	150,219	212.6	379,730	97.5	2.5	8	77.5	665	9.6
Essex	0	49.2	9	0.0	0.1	733,010	84,431	108,943	D	D	D	100.0	NA	59.1	NA	NA
Gloucester	49	-51.5	85	8.7	35.6	1,079,229	12,676	107,289	102.5	176,645	92.6	7.4	1	78.6	1,196	12.6
Hudson	0	-100.0	7	NA	D	327,000	50,308	35,385	D	D	D	D	NA	100.0	NA	NA
Hunterdon	101	600.6	63	1.8	65.6	986,211	15,617	66,403	92.2	57,510	85.5	14.5	31	82.6	524	5.9

STATE County	Water use, 2015		Wholesale Trade[1], 2017				Retail Trade[2], 2017				Real estate and rental and leasing,[2] 2017			
	Public supply water withdrawn (mil gal/ day)	Public supply gallons withdrawn per person per day	Number of establish-ments	Number of employees	Sales (mil dol)	Average payroll (mil dol)	Number of establish-ments	Number of employees	Sales (mil dol)	Average payroll (mil dol)	Number of establish-ments	Number of employees	Sales (mil dol)	Average payroll (mil dol)
	133	134	135	136	137	138	139	140	141	142	143	144	145	146
NEBRASKA— Cont'd														
Platte	5.0	151.0	55	584	615.8	34.1	164	2,238	557.5	56.2	39	147	21.5	4.9
Polk	0.4	75.0	10	105	89.0	5.1	20	137	48.6	3.1	NA	NA	NA	NA
Red Willow	2.3	216.1	23	223	183.1	9.2	79	890	217.1	21.9	10	35	3.7	0.4
Richardson	0.7	91.4	28	140	279.6	5.7	42	296	68.7	7.0	4	9	1.3	0.2
Rock	0.2	115.9	D	D	D	D	8	47	10.2	0.8	NA	NA	NA	NA
Saline	1.4	95.2	23	196	258.1	10.9	46	533	157.8	14.2	7	16	3.4	0.4
Sarpy	30.7	174.5	195	3,329	3,359.0	195.2	432	9,545	2,762.4	263.9	187	742	204.8	30.3
Saunders	49.6	2,358.2	29	242	288.7	12.9	70	650	213.1	17.1	17	25	3.1	0.6
Scotts Bluff	5.7	156.1	D	D	D	D	163	D	571.3	D	45	139	23.8	4.6
Seward	1.4	81.2	33	284	309.3	14.4	48	516	117.7	12.3	11	16	1.9	0.5
Sheridan	0.6	113.0	13	161	51.2	4.2	45	227	55.3	4.3	NA	NA	NA	NA
Sherman	0.2	74.4	D	D	D	1.4	21	138	43.1	3.5	NA	NA	NA	NA
Sioux	0.1	63.5	NA	NA	NA	NA	3	D	2.6	D	NA	NA	NA	NA
Stanton	0.4	60.6	NA	NA	NA	NA	13	127	18.7	2.2	NA	NA	NA	NA
Thayer	0.8	156.9	25	242	348.7	13.0	35	188	35.1	3.3	D	D	D	D
Thomas	0.1	160.8	NA	NA	NA	NA	D	D	D	D	NA	NA	NA	NA
Thurston	0.6	84.9	8	85	177.1	5.3	20	179	56.9	6.1	4	10	2.9	0.2
Valley	1.3	300.9	6	D	169.4	D	29	314	98.6	8.1	NA	NA	NA	NA
Washington	12.2	601.5	D	D	D	8.1	61	1,081	771.1	41.1	22	31	4.6	0.8
Wayne	0.9	92.9	14	157	116.4	8.0	36	418	71.3	7.5	6	16	1.3	0.5
Webster	0.4	107.6	D	D	D	D	20	130	27.9	2.6	NA	NA	NA	NA
Wheeler	0.0	53.3	3	54	10.1	0.9	NA	NA	NA	NA	NA	NA	NA	NA
York	1.9	135.4	38	323	306.9	15.0	62	919	269.9	24.4	D	D	D	D
NEVADA	558.3	193.1	2,665	32,879	25,395.7	1,915.2	8,745	145,773	45,110.7	4,220.2	4,684	30,562	7,359.0	1,312.2
Churchill	3.4	139.7	24	115	86.3	3.9	58	844	249.7	25.2	28	100	15.4	3.0
Clark	432.5	204.5	1,743	19,687	15,088.0	1,212.5	6,267	107,067	32,047.7	3,038.7	3,454	24,634	6,064.6	1,085.2
Douglas	14.1	295.1	51	345	180.2	19.8	152	2,101	632.4	56.0	113	655	104.7	25.9
Elko	12.6	242.8	65	800	1,060.9	53.8	163	2,547	864.2	73.9	53	296	53.3	9.7
Esmeralda	0.1	132.7	NA	NA	NA	NA	NA	NA	NA	NA	NA	NA	NA	NA
Eureka	0.3	158.7	NA	NA	NA	NA	5	42	4.7	0.6	NA	NA	NA	NA
Humboldt	3.7	216.2	D	D	D	D	66	919	314.2	24.3	D	D	D	D
Lander	1.6	264.3	3	26	62.6	1.3	23	204	48.1	4.5	NA	NA	NA	NA
Lincoln	1.2	230.3	NA	NA	NA	NA	D	D	D	D	NA	NA	NA	NA
Lyon	9.4	178.6	48	981	364.2	30.3	105	1,306	555.1	37.3	D	D	D	D
Mineral	1.1	234.5	NA	NA	NA	NA	15	110	27.5	3.1	NA	NA	NA	NA
Nye	6.3	148.1	15	189	308.3	6.8	116	1,527	483.6	40.9	42	100	13.6	2.8
Pershing	1.3	191.4	NA	NA	NA	NA	14	131	48.1	3.1	NA	NA	NA	NA
Storey	0.5	132.9	NA	NA	NA	NA	18	48	10.8	1.4	NA	NA	NA	NA
Washoe	57.7	129.1	D	D	D	D	1,477	25,264	8,507.8	795.2	D	D	D	D
White Pine	1.2	120.3	6	54	32.9	3.5	30	345	114.9	10.4	6	D	1.5	D
Carson City	11.5	210.9	81	620	335.2	29.4	220	3,141	1,170.8	102.3	118	361	94.1	13.0
NEW HAMPSHIRE	95.5	71.8	1,509	22,314	20,328.4	1,577.3	6,032	96,591	30,039.4	2,804.6	1,523	7,920	2,000.3	381.4
Belknap	3.1	51.5	D	D	D	D	321	4,991	1,706.5	155.3	80	261	57.9	10.5
Carroll	3.5	73.0	D	D	D	D	372	3,768	948.1	103.9	93	328	53.2	12.0
Cheshire	4.1	54.3	D	D	D	D	346	5,486	1,869.5	166.7	72	247	50.7	9.6
Coos	4.2	134.6	D	D	D	D	164	1,756	545.1	46.9	27	76	15.0	3.9
Grafton	7.6	84.8	78	700	806.8	46.1	495	7,320	2,251.8	220.0	154	544	96.1	21.1
Hillsborough	38.7	95.3	531	6,897	5,718.9	498.3	1,577	28,064	9,169.1	836.6	454	2,938	616.4	142.0
Merrimack	8.3	55.8	150	3,601	4,215.3	205.6	613	9,896	3,161.9	292.3	144	950	436.7	60.0
Rockingham	15.4	50.9	476	7,641	7,418.9	616.7	1,600	26,342	7,783.6	713.6	360	1,945	522.4	98.9
Strafford	8.0	63.1	76	1,120	418.7	68.5	387	6,695	1,959.3	205.1	104	332	73.1	12.1
Sullivan	2.7	63.1	35	559	539.5	52.1	157	2,273	644.5	64.4	35	299	78.9	11.4
NEW JERSEY	1,175.4	131.2	12,289	230,006	312,405.1	18,970.9	31,200	469,615	149,171.3	13,453.1	9,622	61,052	21,184.3	3,435.2
Atlantic	30.2	110.1	172	2,049	1,304.6	115.8	1,078	16,535	4,631.1	417.9	233	1,358	356.2	56.3
Bergen	127.4	135.8	2,627	40,918	96,148.0	3,090.6	3,703	53,862	19,846.4	1,686.1	1,485	8,053	2,890.4	471.0
Burlington	54.2	120.4	480	11,758	13,279.4	753.7	1,344	26,240	8,223.1	698.2	428	4,210	1,168.0	261.4
Camden	42.8	83.8	513	8,577	6,671.1	527.9	1,694	24,257	6,810.6	637.2	425	2,450	782.0	123.8
Cape May	13.6	143.7	D	D	D	D	639	7,307	1,935.5	182.6	202	779	217.0	32.5
Cumberland	15.7	100.9	153	4,405	2,833.3	200.5	492	7,027	2,011.0	182.1	102	486	108.7	18.9
Essex	31.2	39.2	953	15,257	15,695.0	1,097.4	2,667	28,700	9,070.9	921.6	915	6,233	1,820.3	274.8
Gloucester	17.5	60.1	299	7,933	11,213.8	512.1	912	17,236	4,813.2	461.8	175	1,374	472.5	80.4
Hudson	0.0	0.0	667	17,076	19,699.7	1,121.9	2,120	27,508	7,964.9	720.1	706	4,069	1,509.0	250.7
Hunterdon	119.9	955.5	141	1,318	907.6	83.9	458	7,917	2,478.7	230.0	127	417	146.8	21.5

1 Merchant wholesalers, except manufacturers' sales branches and offices. 2. Employer establishments.

STATE County	Professional, scientific, and technical services, 2017				Manufacturing, 2017				Accommodation and food services, 2017			
	Number of establish-ments	Number of employees	Sales (mil dol)	Average payroll (mil dol)	Number of establish-ments	Number of employees	Sales (mil dol)	Average payroll (mil dol)	Number of establis-hments	Number of employees	Sales (mil dol)	Annual payroll (mil dol)
	147	148	149	150	151	152	153	154	155	156	157	158
NEBRASKA— Cont'd												
Platte	63	390	42.0	18.4	71	5,681	3,621.0	313.2	75	1,159	54.6	14.8
Polk	14	23	2.1	0.5	6	46	17.1	2.1	8	47	1.9	0.4
Red Willow	26	118	13.7	4.9	10	260	105.8	13.4	33	527	23.6	7.3
Richardson	11	65	4.1	1.7	14	264	53.9	12.1	22	178	6.6	2.0
Rock	NA	NA	NA	NA	NA	NA	NA	NA	NA	NA	NA	NA
Saline	17	44	4.8	1.4	14	2,820	1,879.5	151.4	25	286	11.3	3.0
Sarpy	D	D	D	D	91	2,991	1,176.3	178.9	279	5,693	301.5	89.4
Saunders	46	129	15.3	6.7	19	331	81.9	14.6	D	D	D	D
Scotts Bluff	D	D	D	D	34	959	280.5	39.8	107	1,511	72.8	21.3
Seward	28	118	21.0	4.2	22	1,129	397.7	55.8	31	457	19.9	6.2
Sheridan	9	20	3.2	0.6	3	5	2.9	0.3	20	84	5.7	1.6
Sherman	5	8	0.6	0.2	3	15	1.9	0.5	10	88	4.1	1.3
Sioux	NA	NA	NA	NA	NA	NA	NA	NA	NA	NA	NA	NA
Stanton	4	7	0.8	0.2	NA	NA	NA	NA	4	22	1.4	0.4
Thayer	10	28	2.1	0.7	D	D	D	D	16	D	2.7	D
Thomas	NA	NA	NA	NA	NA	NA	NA	NA	3	6	0.3	0.1
Thurston	12	192	28.9	11.0	7	295	60.6	15.7	4	26	0.9	0.2
Valley	15	65	8.0	2.6	7	70	103.5	3.7	12	D	3.4	D
Washington	56	249	35.9	12.2	26	1,302	1,549.8	86.0	39	424	16.1	5.0
Wayne	15	76	13.2	4.3	13	981	240.6	34.2	25	350	13.3	3.3
Webster	3	4	0.3	0.1	NA	NA	NA	NA	6	D	1.3	D
Wheeler	NA	NA	NA	NA	NA	NA	NA	NA	7	D	0.8	D
York	25	141	16.5	5.6	26	862	333.5	42.8	D	D	D	D
NEVADA	8,991	59,549	10,763.2	3,922.7	1,828	44,182	16,408.1	2,516.7	6,810	319,584	33,979.9	9,578.4
Churchill	37	311	48.3	18.7	16	373	223.2	27.0	D	D	D	D
Clark	6,477	45,018	8,260.8	2,991.7	992	19,985	6,795.1	974.2	4,839	268,757	30,017.1	8,468.5
Douglas	243	817	133.0	43.9	81	1,822	960.0	143.2	136	5,833	556.2	160.4
Elko	D	D	D	D	D	D	D	D	154	5,310	440.0	124.8
Esmeralda	NA	NA	NA	NA	NA	NA	NA	NA	NA	NA	NA	NA
Eureka	NA	NA	NA	NA	NA	NA	NA	NA	5	24	1.7	0.4
Humboldt	D	D	D	D	11	215	216.2	12.1	61	1,136	87.1	20.4
Lander	D	D	D	0.2	NA	NA	NA	NA	16	139	7.0	2.0
Lincoln	D	D	D	0.6	NA	NA	NA	NA	D	D	D	1.3
Lyon	D	D	D	D	79	1,830	1,004.6	100.3	70	846	56.3	13.3
Mineral	D	D	D	D	NA	NA	NA	NA	8	142	9.1	2.3
Nye	D	D	234.1	D	15	55	34.6	2.3	82	1,500	108.3	26.1
Pershing	NA	NA	NA	NA	D	D	D	D	9	99	4.3	1.4
Storey	13	21	3.8	1.4	5	69	31.3	3.6	18	118	7.4	2.4
Washoe	D	D	D	D	486	16,584	6,200.8	1,064.5	1,141	31,445	2,414.0	682.0
White Pine	D	D	D	D	D	11	D	D	36	459	31.3	9.2
Carson City	D	D	D	D	103	2,704	714.3	159.4	170	3,036	193.0	54.1
NEW HAMPSHIRE	3,638	32,034	5,537.3	2,361.0	1,790	65,211	20,304.1	3,875.2	3,784	59,531	3,722.0	1,132.7
Belknap	D	D	D	D	77	2,653	725.7	175.7	248	3,082	212.4	65.9
Carroll	D	D	D	D	69	689	181.3	37.2	296	4,103	302.2	96.3
Cheshire	D	D	D	D	124	4,316	1,135.8	231.9	185	2,547	151.1	47.0
Coos	D	D	D	D	39	590	190.1	27.2	112	2,041	95.4	37.7
Grafton	D	D	D	D	100	5,254	1,793.6	294.3	421	5,317	370.7	109.7
Hillsborough	1,334	12,550	2,564.9	1,158.2	518	21,931	7,038.6	1,432.2	922	16,755	973.2	292.3
Merrimack	D	D	D	D	203	5,681	1,752.7	327.3	325	5,425	329.7	101.3
Rockingham	D	D	D	D	429	15,793	5,506.0	891.7	902	15,041	1,001.4	296.5
Strafford	D	D	D	D	145	5,183	1,293.6	283.1	300	4,400	239.3	71.2
Sullivan	D	D	D	D	86	3,121	686.6	174.7	73	820	46.3	14.7
NEW JERSEY	28,863	323,560	66,882.0	28,572.7	7,332	219,835	95,483.0	13,908.6	21,495	318,734	23,785.1	6,431.5
Atlantic	D	D	D	D	108	2,013	474.1	98.6	830	35,488	3,550.7	1,003.8
Bergen	3,989	35,448	8,286.9	2,887.9	1,020	29,416	11,519.6	1,870.1	2,560	34,688	2,559.8	675.9
Burlington	1,297	13,902	2,507.4	963.0	319	14,429	5,853.6	1,060.9	924	15,270	902.3	251.6
Camden	1,358	13,321	2,709.2	980.5	389	11,295	3,701.2	671.3	1,055	15,647	913.3	251.8
Cape May	D	D	D	D	76	592	110.1	26.9	931	6,065	757.0	206.6
Cumberland	D	D	D	D	158	8,509	2,612.5	408.6	243	3,541	184.5	49.1
Essex	2,227	26,109	5,501.2	2,364.9	648	16,233	6,122.4	933.4	1,687	23,991	1,883.3	509.1
Gloucester	497	3,848	507.0	229.2	243	9,518	8,256.3	576.8	544	10,177	562.2	150.9
Hudson	D	D	D	D	366	8,600	2,850.2	405.5	1,564	19,766	1,579.9	413.6
Hunterdon	D	D	D	D	129	3,550	1,262.4	214.7	330	4,215	256.5	71.5

STATE County	Health care and social assistance, 2017				Other services, 2017				Nonemployer businesses, 2019		Value of residential construction authorized by building permits, 2021	
	Number of establish-ments	Number of employees	Receipts (mil dol)	Annual payroll (mil dol)	Number of establish-ments	Number of employees	Receipts (mil dol)	Annual payroll (mil dol)	Number	Receipts (mil dol)	New construction ($1,000)	Number of housing units
	159	160	161	162	163	164	165	166	167	168	169	170
NEBRASKA— Cont'd												
Platte	97	2,099	295.5	92.2	78	393	37.7	10.5	2,428	113.6	26,221	90
Polk	9	238	16.1	7.5	D	D	3.6	D	483	19.9	2,631	9
Red Willow	43	650	72.7	28.0	27	80	8.3	2.1	929	40.3	2,454	9
Richardson	23	429	41.0	15.2	23	68	6.3	1.2	596	19.0	1,843	8
Rock	D	D	D	D	D	D	0.5	D	217	10.0	250	2
Saline	27	524	47.9	19.3	27	75	10.5	1.8	838	34.4	7,944	34
Sarpy	357	5,406	495.4	190.5	250	1,633	187.5	51.4	11,606	466.9	491,173	2,406
Saunders	30	622	51.7	21.0	30	77	10.1	2.1	1,946	88.7	41,440	165
Scotts Bluff	133	3,031	385.7	135.7	D	D	D	D	2,522	117.4	2,145	9
Seward	44	869	68.3	28.2	41	141	17.0	4.2	1,346	51.6	16,919	61
Sheridan	17	244	17.1	8.8	13	41	3.1	0.6	410	16.6	212	3
Sherman	6	147	15.0	5.1	D	D	1.3	D	269	11.9	1,705	8
Sioux	NA	NA	NA	NA	NA	NA	NA	NA	106	4.7	1,895	9
Stanton	D	D	D	D	D	D	3.0	D	480	26.7	2,840	9
Thayer	11	412	32.7	14.6	D	D	D	1.5	426	23.0	1,529	7
Thomas	NA	NA	NA	NA	NA	NA	NA	NA	86	3.1	300	3
Thurston	12	325	39.3	17.2	8	34	3.4	0.6	292	14.0	3,494	10
Valley	18	387	28.7	13.1	D	D	D	1.4	437	24.2	1,663	6
Washington	34	794	57.3	26.0	43	215	15.2	6.0	1,641	77.9	24,783	92
Wayne	24	475	36.5	15.5	D	D	D	D	617	32.7	2,225	10
Webster	9	173	12.6	4.9	4	17	2.2	0.3	292	9.9	1,279	5
Wheeler	NA	NA	NA	NA	NA	NA	NA	NA	85	3.8	253	2
York	39	948	103.1	38.4	55	261	26.1	6.9	1,131	46.9	5,868	22
NEVADA	7,372	132,093	18,111.8	6,620.4	4,032	28,825	3,281.5	914.2	260,889	13,414.9	5,293,432	23,406
Churchill	43	811	80.3	34.3	41	181	13.9	4.1	1,271	58.2	24,203	104
Clark	5,349	94,935	13,080.9	4,731.3	2,784	20,781	2,256.4	638.8	203,116	9,934.6	3,761,621	16,307
Douglas	119	1,721	201.5	70.2	89	488	53.6	15.2	5,477	404.3	132,915	281
Elko	124	1,639	178.2	67.9	D	D	D	D	2,581	121.0	48,894	197
Esmeralda	NA	NA	NA	NA	NA	NA	NA	NA	64	2.1	NA	NA
Eureka	NA	NA	NA	NA	NA	NA	NA	NA	127	7.9	NA	NA
Humboldt	36	664	64.8	24.7	25	108	18.3	4.3	847	30.0	5,397	31
Lander	D	D	D	D	5	19	3.4	0.7	241	7.8	921	5
Lincoln	7	D	11.3	D	NA	NA	NA	NA	312	12.1	3,243	13
Lyon	56	597	53.7	22.1	38	196	20.3	6.1	2,851	134.5	170,349	815
Mineral	D	D	D	D	D	D	D	D	164	7.2	0	0
Nye	71	916	93.0	31.1	55	305	19.0	5.9	2,713	112.8	NA	NA
Pershing	D	D	D	D	NA	NA	NA	NA	242	7.8	0	0
Storey	NA	NA	NA	NA	D	D	D	D	332	15.1	4,724	25
Washoe	D	D	D	D	D	D	D	D	35,225	2,130.9	1,074,392	5,312
White Pine	15	285	45.4	17.7	D	D	D	D	472	17.0	2,352	9
Carson City	215	3,865	623.8	214.4	132	618	100.6	22.3	4,854	411.5	64,422	307
NEW HAMPSHIRE	3,737	94,594	11,931.6	4,741.7	3,011	17,864	2,096.2	619.2	108,655	6,541.3	1,260,568	4,892
Belknap	159	4,153	457.7	188.2	151	554	57.5	15.9	5,769	364.5	129,589	433
Carroll	152	2,498	254.0	103.8	125	505	56.3	15.8	5,875	347.6	140,083	382
Cheshire	164	4,174	471.7	185.5	141	979	96.9	28.4	5,906	326.5	42,227	177
Coos	102	2,317	224.3	97.0	59	298	29.9	10.0	2,265	103.0	19,583	99
Grafton	283	10,452	1,995.6	617.9	186	1,059	120.6	33.3	8,119	490.9	111,231	338
Hillsborough	1,167	32,354	3,938.1	1,643.7	883	6,272	746.1	231.2	29,899	1,764.4	294,881	1,342
Merrimack	415	13,052	1,428.6	640.8	406	2,245	333.0	91.0	11,546	665.9	110,298	456
Rockingham	896	16,733	2,047.9	830.7	760	4,285	466.8	139.0	27,725	1,888.5	295,218	1,148
Strafford	309	7,661	1,004.1	386.4	219	1,368	135.9	43.4	8,335	433.5	95,834	435
Sullivan	90	1,200	109.5	47.7	81	299	53.1	11.2	3,216	156.4	21,624	82
NEW JERSEY	28,005	613,406	74,723.4	30,134.1	19,162	113,846	14,025.6	3,679.3	762,163	45,639.3	5,234,056	37,094
Atlantic	801	18,708	2,202.5	951.0	540	3,437	291.1	83.9	18,523	926.7	194,034	804
Bergen	3,959	78,752	10,992.7	4,254.3	2,618	14,352	1,624.8	440.1	103,417	7,379.0	648,339	4,023
Burlington	1,283	28,853	3,281.1	1,296.8	781	4,731	413.8	134.5	30,769	1,781.9	260,838	2,119
Camden	1,559	44,197	5,497.5	2,316.9	954	6,282	641.4	190.4	34,032	1,814.8	89,505	908
Cape May	244	4,578	467.7	198.8	308	1,268	123.7	35.5	8,698	566.1	294,756	917
Cumberland	405	11,257	1,121.9	531.6	240	1,246	120.9	31.9	6,406	317.4	20,529	185
Essex	2,535	58,553	8,099.0	3,070.3	1,717	11,204	1,366.0	376.7	75,412	4,103.7	434,701	3,417
Gloucester	775	15,590	1,682.4	719.3	537	3,331	279.5	90.8	17,578	858.4	95,293	675
Hudson	1,480	28,379	3,091.1	1,210.4	1,187	5,368	608.1	150.5	62,345	3,040.2	672,704	5,257
Hunterdon	363	9,579	1,005.4	433.2	296	1,442	138.3	42.2	12,288	836.3	94,461	688

STATE County	Government employment and payroll, 2017: Full-time equivalent employees	Government employment and payroll, 2017: March payroll (dollars)	March payroll (percent of total): Administration, judicial, and legal	March payroll (percent of total): Police and corrections	March payroll (percent of total): Fire protection	March payroll (percent of total): Highways and transportation	March payroll (percent of total): Health and welfare	March payroll (percent of total): Natural resources and utilities	March payroll (percent of total): Education and libraries	Local government finances, 2017: General revenue: Total (mil dol)	General revenue: Intergovernmental (mil dol)	General revenue: Taxes: Total (mil dol)	Taxes: Per capita[1] (dollars): Total	Taxes: Per capita[1] (dollars): Property
	171	172	173	174	175	176	177	178	179	180	181	182	183	184
NEBRASKA— Cont'd														
Platte	3,283	23,192,574	1.1	2.1	0.4	1.0	0.2	81.4	13.7	155.4	32.1	72.9	2,193	1,563
Polk	404	1,568,770	5.3	1.7	0.0	3.8	15.2	12.9	61.1	45.5	9.1	25.0	4,709	4,265
Red Willow	475	1,797,139	6.3	9.7	1.5	3.3	2.9	15.2	60.5	54.7	16.7	23.2	2,160	1,694
Richardson	441	1,401,615	8.0	7.5	0.7	8.0	1.5	8.9	63.4	44.6	11.2	29.1	3,649	3,276
Rock	140	475,568	6.5	7.0	0.0	4.1	43.9	0.7	36.3	8.3	2.0	5.1	3,596	3,292
Saline	666	2,570,074	6.8	10.1	0.3	4.9	1.4	5.2	70.6	93.1	22.7	41.0	2,853	2,475
Sarpy	5,171	21,553,098	7.3	11.7	3.4	2.3	0.8	2.1	69.9	600.0	186.0	294.0	1,621	1,307
Saunders	910	3,350,353	8.1	10.1	0.4	4.8	22.4	4.5	48.3	121.0	20.6	51.6	2,452	2,149
Scotts Bluff	2,351	8,529,773	4.6	7.2	1.1	2.8	1.3	9.8	71.4	218.0	82.0	77.7	2,150	1,749
Seward	755	2,861,348	7.0	6.5	0.0	4.6	1.1	8.7	70.1	75.6	16.1	44.6	2,592	2,253
Sheridan	517	1,874,447	14.1	4.2	0.0	5.9	21.6	11.2	42.7	45.5	6.3	17.0	3,224	2,930
Sherman	163	516,043	10.1	9.1	0.0	9.7	2.3	2.0	65.5	22.9	4.0	17.7	5,757	5,464
Sioux	54	188,007	16.7	3.9	0.0	15.8	0.0	0.7	60.6	5.6	1.6	3.6	2,983	2,751
Stanton	143	596,334	11.3	7.5	0.0	13.2	1.1	19.2	47.3	24.6	5.4	9.4	1,575	1,451
Thayer	367	1,508,260	6.2	3.2	0.1	5.1	47.1	2.5	35.7	74.8	9.3	36.7	7,281	6,635
Thomas	55	117,868	27.0	4.0	0.2	6.1	0.0	14.1	43.7	4.7	1.3	3.1	4,316	4,170
Thurston	686	2,767,589	4.3	1.8	0.0	2.3	27.4	0.9	63.0	88.0	42.0	13.6	1,892	1,538
Valley	465	1,847,702	4.6	2.6	0.0	2.8	41.4	18.8	29.6	51.3	5.7	16.2	3,839	3,029
Washington	685	2,820,809	6.9	10.5	0.0	5.5	0.6	2.8	71.0	97.6	21.0	52.2	2,567	2,250
Wayne	354	1,441,303	8.7	5.3	0.0	11.1	1.0	6.5	66.7	41.6	9.7	26.2	2,848	2,511
Webster	220	736,498	10.1	4.4	0.0	6.3	25.1	7.6	45.7	23.7	4.3	11.8	3,375	3,081
Wheeler	49	157,709	14.3	0.0	0.0	15.3	0.0	0.1	70.0	4.8	1.1	3.5	4,240	4,045
York	572	2,345,805	6.0	7.1	2.7	7.9	1.9	20.4	52.2	85.2	22.1	42.6	3,092	2,375
NEVADA	X	X	X	X	X	X	X	X	X	X	X	X	X	X
Churchill	833	3,650,301	12.0	14.2	0.7	2.2	1.1	12.7	45.5	108.9	45.8	25.8	1,074	810
Clark	61,549	328,902,480	8.5	16.4	5.5	3.3	10.2	7.9	46.5	10,404.2	4,197.7	3,614.1	1,657	853
Douglas	1,529	6,567,049	11.1	16.1	7.1	2.1	1.8	11.3	45.6	208.9	82.1	89.9	1,872	1,491
Elko	1,864	8,958,548	10.3	10.4	3.2	2.5	1.9	5.6	63.0	248.3	142.4	69.9	1,336	969
Esmeralda	88	249,417	22.1	19.3	0.6	11.0	1.5	4.1	39.6	23.2	18.9	2.9	3,400	3,356
Eureka	146	809,801	15.9	10.5	0.0	8.0	5.2	10.5	48.4	32.8	9.5	21.1	10,845	10,791
Humboldt	846	4,090,004	9.3	12.5	0.2	2.8	28.7	3.7	41.0	124.2	56.8	31.0	1,852	1,636
Lander	369	1,632,378	9.8	11.5	0.0	4.7	36.0	3.3	34.2	72.3	14.9	38.4	6,882	6,615
Lincoln	303	1,433,875	8.6	12.3	0.1	3.0	19.1	12.1	42.2	29.0	18.4	5.7	1,099	1,024
Lyon	1,686	6,408,283	8.3	7.8	5.1	1.6	3.2	5.0	65.9	174.5	104.0	47.4	880	684
Mineral	299	1,163,326	7.1	6.2	0.9	2.1	42.1	7.2	33.4	31.2	11.1	5.5	1,231	1,112
Nye	1,264	5,334,954	13.8	13.8	4.4	3.3	1.1	1.5	58.9	147.7	85.1	49.6	1,127	915
Pershing	339	1,413,302	11.8	11.5	0.1	3.7	25.9	5.2	38.5	34.9	14.5	8.0	1,231	1,160
Storey	179	955,773	19.4	15.9	16.3	4.0	1.6	2.7	33.3	35.5	8.9	18.0	4,519	4,384
Washoe	13,349	63,720,984	10.1	13.5	5.8	4.3	4.5	8.7	50.6	2,074.6	935.8	702.1	1,538	979
White Pine	441	2,113,814	9.9	9.3	2.9	3.5	38.6	4.6	29.4	81.9	27.2	16.7	1,730	1,348
Carson City	1,652	7,251,836	10.3	13.8	7.8	4.2	2.8	7.3	52.0	235.3	121.5	63.2	1,159	789
NEW HAMPSHIRE	X	X	X	X	X	X	X	X	X	X	X	X	X	X
Belknap	2,697	10,844,945	5.6	10.6	5.3	4.6	5.1	2.9	65.3	367.3	76.0	240.6	3,953	3,913
Carroll	2,052	7,917,481	6.0	9.6	3.1	4.6	4.0	5.2	65.7	314.9	72.7	218.1	4,531	4,476
Cheshire	3,237	12,506,344	6.3	8.7	2.3	4.1	7.5	3.0	66.5	410.2	99.0	265.5	3,495	3,452
Coos	1,570	5,804,393	5.0	7.6	3.3	4.3	16.7	5.1	57.4	180.8	60.2	94.9	3,022	3,010
Grafton	4,302	16,931,264	6.1	9.6	4.2	5.6	4.7	3.7	65.4	503.2	112.4	343.8	3,826	3,764
Hillsborough	13,924	65,255,845	4.2	10.8	6.1	5.1	3.7	4.7	63.9	1,758.2	438.5	1,096.8	2,654	2,624
Merrimack	5,953	24,716,272	5.8	10.4	4.1	3.8	7.4	3.7	62.8	665.2	175.8	416.1	2,777	2,762
Rockingham	12,488	50,374,277	4.8	9.9	5.9	2.3	2.4	2.8	69.8	1,401.9	293.6	977.1	3,186	3,149
Strafford	4,373	18,041,005	5.8	10.9	4.8	3.3	7.5	3.4	61.8	569.7	151.1	323.8	2,494	2,423
Sullivan	1,799	7,006,104	5.7	8.6	2.3	4.8	10.4	3.8	63.1	204.5	55.2	133.8	3,110	3,068
NEW JERSEY	X	X	X	X	X	X	X	X	X	X	X	X	X	X
Atlantic	13,889	75,732,427	5.6	14.7	5.0	2.0	4.6	4.0	62.7	1,644.3	578.1	930.0	3,503	3,445
Bergen	33,707	213,265,581	3.6	14.1	1.8	2.1	2.4	3.7	71.0	5,499.1	681.6	4,069.0	4,364	4,300
Burlington	16,622	96,494,090	4.4	8.2	1.8	3.1	1.0	3.2	76.7	2,196.7	589.7	1,322.5	2,968	2,929
Camden	21,189	121,311,072	4.8	14.5	2.6	4.2	3.8	2.9	62.8	3,377.4	1,071.2	1,407.7	2,781	2,753
Cape May	6,404	30,726,844	9.5	11.4	3.5	4.4	5.6	8.4	56.0	972.3	143.8	573.0	6,152	5,996
Cumberland	7,181	38,072,311	3.2	10.2	0.7	1.1	5.7	5.9	71.6	897.5	508.3	274.3	1,812	1,776
Essex	28,131	169,331,200	5.6	20.5	6.6	1.4	6.8	5.7	51.9	4,358.2	1,295.3	2,465.0	3,095	2,947
Gloucester	12,646	66,611,744	3.4	9.5	0.7	2.0	5.3	4.7	72.2	1,513.6	427.0	878.7	3,020	2,971
Hudson	19,609	113,757,554	5.5	23.4	8.6	1.9	6.1	4.0	47.1	3,179.1	1,130.6	1,338.1	1,989	1,898
Hunterdon	4,818	27,005,860	5.0	6.0	0.3	4.2	1.0	2.2	80.1	746.8	83.6	492.1	3,946	3,905

1. Based on the resident population estimated as of July 1 of the year shown.

STATE County	Local government finances, 2017 (cont.)									Government employment, 2020			Individual income tax returns, 2019		
	Direct general expenditure							Debt outstanding							
	Total (mil dol)	Per capita[1] (dollars)	Percent of total for: Education	Health and hospitals	Police protection	Public welfare	Highways	Total (mil dol)	Per capita[1] (dollars)	Federal civilian	Federal military	State and local	Number of returns	Mean adjusted gross income	Mean income tax
	185	186	187	188	189	190	191	192	193	194	195	196	197	198	199
NEBRASKA— Cont'd															
Platte	146.8	4,417	57.2	0.1	4.2	0.0	7.0	2,579.0	77,607	95	112	2,574	17,040	61,076	5,505
Polk	48.6	9,162	59.4	13.9	1.3	0.4	10.3	51.3	9,656	23	17	503	2,640	57,437	4,667
Red Willow	62.3	5,794	35.9	0.6	3.8	13.0	6.8	35.0	3,252	76	35	988	4,950	53,682	5,147
Richardson	38.0	4,763	52.2	0.5	5.1	0.8	13.6	24.5	3,070	40	26	607	3,700	52,156	4,097
Rock	10.2	7,154	50.4	0.2	2.8	0.3	14.6	1.3	935	4	5	223	690	21,025	2,988
Saline	96.5	6,716	44.9	9.4	4.1	0.0	10.6	88.0	6,129	61	45	1,355	6,620	53,572	4,068
Sarpy	601.7	3,317	56.5	0.3	6.6	0.4	5.6	956.1	5,271	3,066	6,853	6,942	91,560	75,162	7,826
Saunders	113.7	5,405	35.6	28.3	2.4	0.1	16.2	71.1	3,379	98	73	1,532	10,670	72,706	7,496
Scotts Bluff	253.6	7,015	53.2	0.3	3.9	1.6	5.1	159.9	4,423	156	120	3,140	16,580	53,701	4,972
Seward	84.5	4,914	50.0	0.3	5.0	0.9	10.2	81.8	4,758	55	54	1,073	7,780	69,223	6,431
Sheridan	37.3	7,090	34.2	28.9	2.6	0.7	7.8	20.9	3,958	28	17	573	2,350	38,106	3,022
Sherman	12.0	3,895	68.4	0.4	1.1	0.5	6.2	2.0	656	14	10	197	1,440	38,717	2,852
Sioux	5.7	4,769	54.9	0.2	3.2	0.2	19.0	1.2	963	7	4	76	530	31,945	2,500
Stanton	24.3	4,060	25.8	0.0	7.2	0.3	41.5	18.0	3,008	20	20	268	2,780	55,445	4,760
Thayer	58.3	11,577	41.8	30.9	2.1	2.6	6.8	15.3	3,044	33	16	594	2,400	54,496	4,663
Thomas	4.4	6,097	58.5	0.0	2.4	0.0	6.5	2.2	3,112	12	2	82	330	37,082	2,873
Thurston	87.9	12,219	52.6	31.3	0.9	0.1	4.5	58.2	8,085	123	24	1,771	2,750	45,373	3,957
Valley	48.4	11,449	21.8	42.3	1.3	0.1	10.3	62.8	14,854	29	14	563	1,980	33,540	3,527
Washington	90.8	4,469	54.3	0.0	3.6	0.1	15.1	194.4	9,564	51	70	1,060	10,190	84,666	10,147
Wayne	47.1	5,114	48.3	0.3	2.9	0.7	18.3	34.9	3,791	33	28	1,187	3,780	59,196	5,371
Webster	22.1	6,300	40.7	23.8	3.0	0.2	12.2	9.7	2,766	27	11	289	1,560	48,291	3,549
Wheeler	5.2	6,368	52.0	0.0	2.1	0.0	24.6	0.4	551	3	3	68	400	26,198	2,118
York	77.7	5,642	34.4	0.3	5.0	0.6	19.8	66.9	4,863	61	43	1,062	6,630	62,156	5,896
NEVADA	X	X	X	X	X	X	X	X	X	20,985	19,762	136,245	1,540,150	70,293	9,054
Churchill	119.7	4,984	33.8	0.6	8.8	5.0	2.6	63.0	2,624	604	1,109	1,357	12,120	55,075	5,076
Clark	9,855.5	4,517	33.6	7.7	10.6	2.6	8.8	23,841.2	10,928	14,638	16,609	87,924	1,121,350	67,187	8,582
Douglas	204.7	4,261	31.9	1.1	9.3	2.3	4.8	132.4	2,756	104	124	2,154	27,710	102,623	16,006
Elko	245.5	4,689	54.6	1.7	7.5	1.5	4.4	46.0	878	358	132	3,285	24,310	72,547	7,585
Esmeralda	21.3	25,216	13.1	1.2	6.7	0.7	58.2	0.9	1,114	5	2	98	400	47,850	4,178
Eureka	22.4	11,528	38.6	5.0	7.7	0.2	10.0	0.0	0	6	5	197	790	61,390	6,265
Humboldt	141.6	8,472	31.6	39.2	7.1	1.7	4.7	2.6	158	157	49	1,398	8,080	65,426	6,467
Lander	53.4	9,574	25.3	31.9	6.3	1.5	3.7	1.6	294	82	14	476	2,450	73,904	7,187
Lincoln	29.5	5,682	48.5	1.0	7.2	2.9	8.2	7.2	1,395	50	12	569	1,770	54,510	4,199
Lyon	162.5	3,014	58.9	0.7	8.6	2.6	4.2	180.6	3,351	79	147	2,144	30,380	52,506	4,545
Mineral	32.9	7,391	24.7	39.2	6.8	0.6	3.6	6.1	1,359	56	11	467	2,090	47,682	3,687
Nye	138.8	3,155	45.1	3.5	11.5	1.5	7.5	100.6	2,287	140	119	1,775	21,530	52,119	4,641
Pershing	31.0	4,787	40.1	27.3	2.1	1.6	1.5	17.9	2,767	22	13	690	2,190	53,737	4,721
Storey	27.6	6,940	22.6	0.2	16.3	0.0	5.3	58.1	14,620	3	18	253	2,170	65,845	7,327
Washoe	1,963.3	4,300	34.4	1.4	7.5	4.8	8.6	3,086.8	6,760	3,945	1,238	23,699	249,170	86,841	12,268
White Pine	84.9	8,792	28.9	35.6	5.3	0.7	4.6	13.2	1,368	158	21	1,097	4,130	58,535	5,386
Carson City	226.4	4,152	42.3	4.1	8.4	2.9	6.4	397.7	7,292	578	139	8,662	29,630	61,253	6,641
NEW HAMPSHIRE	X	X	X	X	X	X	X	X	X	8,306	4,426	78,098	723,600	83,674	10,878
Belknap	328.1	5,390	55.5	0.2	6.2	3.4	6.7	101.8	1,672	163	196	3,811	34,820	76,483	9,561
Carroll	250.9	5,213	52.5	0.8	6.3	7.0	8.0	167.4	3,478	166	159	2,750	27,310	86,749	12,836
Cheshire	350.1	4,608	55.7	0.4	6.5	7.7	5.6	229.8	3,026	194	236	4,859	38,450	72,519	8,375
Coos	183.6	5,848	42.6	0.6	4.2	17.9	5.3	40.4	1,286	381	94	2,430	15,330	51,362	4,655
Grafton	451.7	5,027	56.9	0.4	5.6	5.5	6.8	260.7	2,902	593	276	6,388	45,420	90,457	12,586
Hillsborough	1,549.9	3,751	54.3	0.4	6.9	4.3	5.0	894.8	2,165	4,298	1,395	16,668	222,340	82,251	10,495
Merrimack	568.4	3,794	59.9	0.3	4.2	5.6	4.0	278.1	1,856	942	481	15,414	78,700	76,137	8,954
Rockingham	1,294.9	4,223	59.6	0.2	7.1	3.4	4.0	526.5	1,717	1,136	1,038	12,578	173,700	100,211	14,386
Strafford	502.8	3,873	56.6	2.1	5.7	5.4	5.7	326.5	2,514	337	413	10,945	65,470	70,541	7,879
Sullivan	174.2	4,049	51.5	0.8	4.7	12.1	6.5	73.1	1,700	96	138	2,255	22,090	69,066	7,696
NEW JERSEY	X	X	X	X	X	X	X	X	X	50,621	25,473	512,343	4,513,240	92,461	13,566
Atlantic	1,640.6	6,179	58.1	1.2	6.3	1.4	4.6	847.7	3,193	2,625	827	18,963	138,790	58,758	6,160
Bergen	5,308.8	5,694	57.7	5.9	6.5	1.0	2.9	2,273.6	2,438	2,694	1,893	43,921	473,210	118,587	20,105
Burlington	2,177.1	4,886	68.8	0.6	4.7	1.5	2.2	1,673.3	3,755	4,935	6,508	23,123	231,860	83,889	10,811
Camden	3,213.9	6,349	53.2	2.0	6.0	3.0	4.1	3,185.3	6,292	2,247	1,042	28,328	253,400	70,665	8,391
Cape May	1,325.6	14,234	23.2	1.0	3.2	2.4	6.9	959.9	10,307	457	1,158	8,163	50,760	70,669	8,452
Cumberland	984.1	6,499	63.7	2.4	3.2	1.9	4.6	340.3	2,247	667	291	11,348	67,830	51,455	4,672
Essex	4,558.1	5,724	42.1	2.9	8.1	2.4	1.6	3,386.7	4,253	9,347	1,565	59,047	387,140	93,447	14,821
Gloucester	1,615.6	5,553	60.0	0.7	4.4	1.7	1.5	958.9	3,296	540	577	18,758	146,420	76,459	8,733
Hudson	3,158.9	4,695	37.0	1.8	8.3	2.6	1.7	2,636.2	3,918	5,502	1,436	34,536	345,070	79,786	11,592
Hunterdon	827.1	6,632	53.2	1.0	2.9	1.3	4.2	380.9	3,054	287	244	7,454	65,560	128,205	20,843

1. Based on the resident population estimated as of July 1 of the year shown.

State / county code	CBSA code[1]	County Type code[2]	STATE County	Land area[3] (sq. mi)	Population, 2021: Total persons 2021	Population, 2021: Rank	Population, 2021: Per square mile	Population and population characteristics, 2021: Race alone or in combination, not Hispanic or Latino (percent): White	Black	American Indian, Alaska Native	Asian and Pacific Islancer	Percent Hispanic or Latino[4]	Age (percent): Under 5 years	5 to 17 years	18 to 24 years	25 to 34 years	35 to 44 years	45 to 54 years
				1	2	3	4	5	6	7	8	9	10	11	12	13	14	15
			NEW JERSEY— Cont'd															
34021	45940	2	Mercer	224.4	385,898	189	1,719.7	48.2	20.2	0.5	13.6	19.4	5.4	12.1	14.8	12.3	12.8	13.4
34023	35620	1	Middlesex	309.2	860,807	70	2,784.0	41.2	11.0	0.5	26.3	22.7	5.4	12.3	13.0	12.9	14.0	13.4
34025	35620	1	Monmouth	468.2	645,354	110	1,378.4	76.2	7.2	0.4	6.4	11.4	4.9	11.8	12.3	11.1	11.8	13.6
34027	35620	1	Morris	461.0	510,981	143	1,108.4	70.8	4.0	0.3	12.3	14.3	4.8	11.6	12.5	11.3	12.8	14.0
34029	35620	1	Ocean	628.3	648,998	107	1,032.9	84.7	3.8	0.3	2.6	9.8	7.2	13.6	11.3	11.1	10.3	10.6
34031	35620	1	Passaic	186.0	518,117	139	2,785.6	40.6	10.5	0.4	6.0	43.7	6.3	13.3	13.5	13.3	12.7	12.7
34033	37980	1	Salem	331.9	65,046	830	196.0	74.2	15.0	0.7	1.8	10.5	5.3	12.6	11.6	12.0	12.2	12.5
34035	35620	1	Somerset	301.9	345,647	211	1,144.9	54.3	10.3	0.4	21.0	15.8	4.8	12.1	12.4	11.3	13.0	14.5
34037	35620	1	Sussex	518.7	145,543	458	280.6	84.6	3.0	0.4	2.9	10.5	4.6	10.8	11.6	11.6	12.1	13.9
34039	35620	1	Union	102.8	572,114	122	5,565.3	39.5	21.6	0.4	6.5	33.6	6.1	13.3	12.2	12.4	14.0	13.8
34041	10900	2	Warren	356.5	110,731	559	310.6	79.5	6.6	0.4	3.6	11.4	4.7	10.7	11.9	11.7	11.8	13.5
35000		0	NEW MEXICO	121,312.2	2,115,877	X	17.4	37.3	2.5	9.5	2.3	50.1	5.4	12.9	13.4	13.3	12.7	11.1
35001	10740	2	Bernalillo	1,161.2	674,393	100	580.8	39.0	3.5	5.0	3.8	50.9	5.1	12.0	12.8	14.5	13.7	11.7
35003		9	Catron	6,924.2	3,731	2,906	0.5	75.5	1.7	4.7	0.9	19.6	2.2	7.5	7.2	7.0	6.8	8.1
35005	40740	5	Chaves	6,067.2	64,629	839	10.7	37.0	1.8	1.2	1.3	59.6	6.3	14.5	14.9	12.8	12.8	10.7
35006	24380	6	Cibola	4,540.0	27,184	1,522	6.0	19.2	1.5	40.7	1.0	39.0	5.5	13.8	12.5	14.6	13.3	11.2
35007		7	Colfax	3,758.0	12,369	2,250	3.3	48.0	1.0	2.1	1.0	49.2	4.1	10.1	9.8	10.8	10.1	10.7
35009	17580	5	Curry	1,405.5	47,999	1,021	34.2	46.9	6.6	1.4	2.7	44.9	7.9	14.4	16.1	16.8	12.3	9.1
35011		9	De Baca	2,323.1	1,680	3,069	0.7	52.5	1.4	2.3	0.6	45.1	3.8	13.6	11.1	8.2	10.2	9.0
35013	29740	3	Dona Ana	3,808.2	221,508	316	58.2	27.1	2.0	1.2	1.6	69.3	5.9	13.7	18.5	13.2	11.5	10.0
35015	16100	5	Eddy	4,176.3	60,911	869	14.6	44.5	1.8	1.6	1.1	52.2	7.0	15.2	13.0	13.9	13.6	10.8
35017	43500	7	Grant	3,961.2	27,889	1,503	7.0	47.3	1.2	1.8	1.2	49.9	4.5	11.1	11.1	9.4	10.4	10.1
35019		7	Guadalupe	3,029.8	4,449	2,860	1.5	16.6	2.2	1.9	1.6	78.6	4.6	11.4	12.4	14.9	14.0	9.8
35021		9	Harding	2,125.5	639	3,131	0.3	53.7	1.6	0.6	0.6	44.6	1.7	8.9	5.0	6.6	11.9	6.7
35023		9	Hidalgo	3,438.5	4,074	2,878	1.2	38.5	1.5	1.0	1.1	59.0	5.2	13.1	11.2	11.1	10.8	11.0
35025	26020	5	Lea	4,391.6	73,004	757	16.6	32.8	3.8	1.2	0.7	62.4	7.7	17.1	15.0	14.0	13.6	10.8
35027	40760	7	Lincoln	4,831.1	20,436	1,795	4.2	60.9	1.1	3.7	0.9	34.8	4.5	10.4	9.3	8.8	10.2	9.8
35028	31060	6	Los Alamos	109.1	19,330	1,858	177.2	72.4	1.7	1.7	7.9	18.3	4.9	12.6	10.8	13.6	13.7	12.2
35029	19700	6	Luna	2,965.2	25,532	1,583	8.6	27.8	1.4	1.1	1.3	69.5	7.4	14.7	13.3	12.2	10.7	9.9
35031	23700	5	McKinley	5,451.1	71,780	766	13.2	9.3	1.0	75.5	1.5	14.6	6.1	16.8	14.3	14.7	12.5	10.9
35033	29780	9	Mora	1,926.2	4,196	2,870	2.2	17.5	0.7	0.9	0.5	80.9	4.5	9.5	10.0	9.1	10.1	10.4
35035	10460	4	Otero	6,612.6	68,537	786	10.4	49.0	4.3	6.8	2.5	39.7	6.4	12.6	13.9	15.1	12.3	9.9
35037		7	Quay	2,874.0	8,656	2,518	3.0	49.2	2.1	1.9	1.4	46.9	5.5	12.3	10.4	9.9	10.4	10.6
35039	21580	4	Rio Arriba	5,860.9	40,179	1,176	6.9	13.3	0.6	14.7	0.7	71.3	5.3	13.5	11.9	11.3	11.4	11.5
35041	38780	7	Roosevelt	2,446.1	19,019	1,868	7.8	50.4	2.7	1.7	1.7	45.0	6.4	13.7	21.3	13.2	10.7	10.0
35043	10740	2	Sandoval	3,710.2	151,369	451	40.8	43.0	2.7	12.6	2.5	41.2	4.9	13.2	12.0	12.1	13.4	12.1
35045	22140	3	San Juan	5,517.2	120,993	524	21.9	37.9	1.1	40.4	1.1	21.8	5.8	14.9	13.4	13.0	13.2	10.8
35047	29780	6	San Miguel	4,721.5	27,150	1,523	5.8	18.6	1.8	1.5	1.4	77.6	4.2	9.4	12.8	11.8	11.1	11.4
35049	42140	3	Santa Fe	1,910.4	155,201	441	81.2	44.4	1.2	3.3	1.9	50.5	3.8	9.6	10.5	11.0	11.8	11.8
35051		6	Sierra	4,181.2	11,502	2,314	2.8	64.6	1.2	2.7	1.3	32.2	4.2	9.3	7.8	8.5	8.5	9.7
35053		6	Socorro	6,646.4	16,311	2,015	2.5	33.9	1.5	12.9	2.5	50.9	5.8	12.6	14.6	11.3	10.9	10.7
35055	45340	7	Taos	2,202.4	34,623	1,311	15.7	37.0	0.8	6.1	1.0	56.4	3.9	9.7	9.6	10.0	11.1	11.7
35057	10740	2	Torrance	3,345.2	15,307	2,070	4.6	50.7	2.1	3.3	1.1	44.8	5.2	11.3	12.1	11.7	11.7	11.5
35059		9	Union	3,825.1	4,107	2,877	1.1	51.6	2.6	2.4	1.1	43.4	5.1	11.5	10.8	14.2	13.3	11.1
35061	10740	2	Valencia	1,066.7	77,190	735	72.4	31.9	1.7	4.9	1.0	61.8	5.4	13.5	12.9	12.5	12.3	11.7
36000		0	NEW YORK	47,123.8	19,835,913	X	420.9	56.3	15.5	0.7	10.1	19.5	5.5	11.6	12.4	14.1	12.8	12.4
36001	10580	2	Albany	522.9	313,743	228	600.0	73.2	14.1	0.5	8.4	6.6	4.7	10.3	17.4	13.3	12.1	11.3
36003		7	Allegany	1,029.4	46,106	1,056	44.8	95.3	1.8	0.5	1.8	1.8	5.1	11.3	18.2	9.9	10.7	10.9
36005	35620	1	Bronx	42.2	1,424,948	28	33,766.5	9.7	29.9	0.6	4.5	56.4	6.7	13.8	13.5	15.2	12.9	12.0
36007	13780	2	Broome	705.6	197,240	346	279.5	84.6	7.3	0.6	5.6	4.8	4.9	11.0	17.5	11.4	10.8	10.6
36009	36460	4	Cattaraugus	1,308.2	76,426	739	58.4	92.0	2.6	3.9	1.3	2.4	5.4	12.6	12.9	10.7	11.3	11.8
36011	12180	4	Cayuga	691.6	75,880	740	109.7	91.4	5.6	0.8	1.3	3.3	4.8	11.0	11.4	12.3	12.3	12.2
36013	27460	4	Chautauqua	1,060.4	126,807	509	119.6	88.5	3.5	0.9	1.1	8.1	5.2	11.5	13.0	11.4	11.1	11.7
36015	21300	3	Chemung	407.3	83,045	693	203.9	88.6	8.3	0.7	2.2	3.6	5.2	12.1	11.8	12.3	12.3	12.0
36017		6	Chenango	893.6	46,537	1,045	52.1	95.8	1.5	0.8	1.0	2.4	5.1	12.0	10.8	11.1	11.3	12.1
36019	38460	5	Clinton	1,037.8	79,596	720	76.7	91.2	4.6	0.8	2.0	3.0	4.6	10.3	15.5	12.2	12.5	11.9
36021	26460	6	Columbia	634.7	61,778	862	97.3	87.6	5.6	0.6	2.7	5.5	3.9	9.0	9.8	11.0	11.3	12.7
36023	18660	4	Cortland	498.8	46,311	1,050	92.8	93.5	2.7	0.8	1.8	3.1	4.8	10.6	21.3	11.2	10.9	10.8
36025		6	Delaware	1,442.6	44,378	1,090	30.8	92.2	2.4	0.7	1.7	4.4	3.9	8.9	12.2	10.1	10.7	11.8
36027	39100	1	Dutchess	795.6	297,112	238	373.4	71.6	11.8	0.6	4.5	13.8	4.5	10.2	14.0	12.2	12.2	13.1
36029	15380	1	Erie	1,042.7	950,683	57	911.8	76.2	14.0	0.9	5.1	6.0	5.2	11.4	12.4	14.0	12.3	11.7
36031		6	Essex	1,794.1	37,268	1,243	20.8	92.9	2.9	0.9	1.2	3.4	4.0	8.5	9.7	11.9	11.7	12.5
36033	31660	7	Franklin	1,629.3	47,456	1,033	29.1	83.0	6.2	7.6	0.9	3.6	4.7	11.0	12.9	14.1	12.9	12.3
36035	24100	4	Fulton	495.5	53,116	955	107.2	92.9	2.9	0.6	1.4	3.9	4.8	11.6	10.9	11.7	12.3	12.8

1. CBSA = Core Based Statistical Area. See Appendix A for explanation. See Appendix B for list of metropolitan areas with component counties. 2. County type code from the Economic Research Service of USDA Rural-Urban Continuum Codes. See Appendix A for definition. 3. Dry land or land partially or temporarily covered by water. 4. May be of any race.

STATE County	Population, 2021 (cont.): Age (percent) (cont.): 55 to 64 years	65 to 74 years	75 years and over	Percent female	Population change, 2000–2021: Total persons: 2010	2020	Percent change: 2010–2020	2020–2021	Components of change, 2020–2021: Births	Deaths	Net Migration	Households, 2016–2020: Number	Persons per household	Percent: Family house-holds	Female family house-holder[1]	One person
	16	17	18	19	20	21	22	23	24	25	26	27	28	29	30	31
NEW JERSEY— Cont'd																
Mercer	13.3	9.4	6.6	50.8	366,513	387,340	5.7	-0.4	4,831	4,426	-1,923	131,440	2.7	66.7	13.2	28.4
Middlesex	13.2	9.5	6.4	50.2	809,858	863,162	6.6	-0.3	10,285	9,297	-3,530	287,971	2.8	72.5	11.5	22.9
Monmouth	16.0	11.2	7.5	51.0	630,380	643,615	2.1	0.3	7,015	8,427	3,121	238,235	2.6	68.3	9.1	26.1
Morris	15.2	10.1	7.6	50.4	492,276	509,285	3.5	0.3	5,590	5,789	1,847	184,162	2.6	71.0	8.8	24.2
Ocean	13.6	12.4	10.0	51.3	576,567	637,229	10.5	1.8	11,304	10,290	10,852	229,454	2.6	65.5	9.3	29.3
Passaic	12.9	9.1	6.2	50.8	501,226	524,118	4.6	-1.1	7,627	6,083	-7,550	168,681	2.9	73.1	18.7	22.3
Salem	14.7	11.3	7.9	50.7	66,083	64,837	-1.9	0.3	801	1,085	493	24,414	2.5	64.5	13.5	29.5
Somerset	15.1	9.7	7.0	50.7	323,444	345,361	6.8	0.1	3,699	3,807	335	119,721	2.7	71.6	9.7	23.8
Sussex	16.8	11.8	6.9	49.8	149,265	144,221	-3.4	0.9	1,542	1,843	1,642	54,166	2.6	71.2	8.8	23.2
Union	13.3	8.8	6.1	50.7	536,499	575,345	7.2	-0.6	7,857	6,536	-4,649	191,862	2.9	72.2	15.2	23.7
Warren	16.5	11.3	7.9	50.5	108,692	109,632	0.9	1.0	1,122	1,451	1,439	42,322	2.5	66.9	8.9	27.7
NEW MEXICO	12.7	11.3	7.3	50.2	2,059,179	2,117,522	2.8	-0.1	27,543	28,890	-364	792,755	2.6	62.7	13.7	31.0
Bernalillo	12.8	10.7	6.7	50.8	662,564	676,444	2.1	-0.3	8,308	9,162	-1,289	272,528	2.5	58.4	13.8	34.4
Catron	18.7	25.2	17.3	47.7	3,725	3,579	-3.9	4.2	17	42	181	1,546	2.2	56.5	7.4	36.6
Chaves	12.1	9.5	6.5	50.1	65,645	65,157	-0.7	-0.8	996	1,006	-525	23,641	2.7	67.2	15.7	29.8
Cibola	12.2	10.3	6.6	48.4	27,213	27,172	-0.2	0.0	371	439	78	8,408	3.0	69.1	18.0	24.5
Colfax	15.9	16.7	11.7	49.2	13,750	12,387	-9.9	-0.1	121	211	76	5,946	1.9	56.2	10.4	36.9
Curry	10.2	7.7	5.4	48.1	48,376	48,430	0.1	-0.9	997	547	-878	18,620	2.6	65.2	14.8	29.3
De Baca	14.4	15.9	13.8	49.9	2,022	1,698	-16.0	-1.1	16	40	7	554	3.6	49.3	4.0	48.9
Dona Ana	10.8	9.8	6.8	50.7	209,233	219,561	4.9	0.9	3,105	2,747	1,552	79,421	2.7	65.6	14.9	26.4
Eddy	11.7	8.9	5.9	49.0	53,829	62,314	15.8	-2.3	1,024	757	-1,652	21,548	2.7	70.2	12.5	26.5
Grant	13.9	17.2	12.3	50.4	29,514	28,185	-4.5	-1.1	306	497	-96	11,496	2.3	53.5	10.9	34.8
Guadalupe	13.0	10.9	9.1	42.0	4,687	4,452	-5.0	-0.1	45	62	14	1,345	2.6	51.2	8.0	46.8
Harding	17.8	23.2	18.2	47.9	695	657	-5.5	-2.7	1	13	-6	176	2.5	53.4	0.6	46.0
Hidalgo	14.6	13.2	9.9	49.2	4,894	4,178	-14.6	-2.5	38	72	-70	1,742	2.4	70.3	12.2	26.3
Lea	10.4	7.0	4.4	48.4	64,727	74,455	15.0	-1.9	1,404	792	-2,040	22,868	3.0	72.5	13.8	23.7
Lincoln	16.3	18.5	12.2	51.0	20,497	20,269	-1.1	0.8	204	286	254	8,478	2.3	63.2	7.2	31.1
Los Alamos	13.9	10.6	7.7	48.4	17,950	19,419	8.2	-0.5	203	171	-125	7,895	2.4	63.4	5.7	32.3
Luna	11.3	11.2	9.3	49.2	25,095	25,427	1.3	0.4	466	423	58	8,911	2.7	59.9	12.1	36.1
McKinley	11.5	8.3	4.9	51.8	71,492	72,902	2.0	-1.5	1,076	1,198	-1,006	21,247	3.4	71.0	26.4	25.0
Mora	16.8	17.7	12.0	48.7	4,881	4,189	-14.2	0.2	50	62	19	2,278	2.0	50.4	14.9	41.0
Otero	12.1	10.4	7.3	47.9	63,797	67,839	6.3	1.0	1,074	928	544	23,112	2.7	62.3	10.6	33.0
Quay	14.8	15.1	11.0	50.6	9,041	8,746	-3.3	-1.0	106	182	-14	3,182	2.6	56.0	12.1	38.4
Rio Arriba	14.2	12.3	8.5	50.8	40,246	40,363	0.3	-0.5	499	629	-58	13,035	2.9	61.1	15.1	33.7
Roosevelt	9.8	8.6	6.4	50.0	19,846	19,191	-3.3	-0.9	271	229	-217	6,785	2.6	61.4	13.9	30.7
Sandoval	13.3	12.1	7.0	50.5	131,561	148,834	13.1	1.7	1,655	1,790	2,684	52,504	2.7	71.5	12.3	21.6
San Juan	12.7	10.0	6.1	50.5	130,044	121,661	-6.4	-0.5	1,693	1,810	-576	43,582	2.8	71.1	15.8	24.5
San Miguel	15.5	14.3	9.4	50.0	29,393	27,201	-7.5	-0.2	279	403	72	11,942	2.2	55.3	15.7	39.9
Santa Fe	14.9	16.7	10.0	51.2	144,170	154,823	7.4	0.2	1,411	1,893	879	63,152	2.3	57.7	10.8	35.5
Sierra	15.0	20.4	16.6	49.6	11,988	11,576	-3.4	-0.6	98	366	199	5,402	2.0	52.4	10.3	44.0
Socorro	13.5	12.4	8.3	49.4	17,866	16,595	-7.1	-1.7	227	265	-243	5,002	3.2	57.9	10.4	35.5
Taos	15.3	17.4	11.3	50.8	32,937	34,489	4.7	0.4	289	524	378	12,592	2.6	53.9	13.3	40.1
Torrance	14.4	14.0	8.0	47.2	16,383	15,045	-8.2	1.7	190	227	302	5,957	2.6	68.6	9.3	28.7
Union	12.3	12.0	9.6	43.0	4,549	4,079	-10.3	0.7	45	59	43	1,404	2.5	53.8	10.7	42.3
Valencia	13.4	11.4	7.0	49.5	76,569	76,205	-0.5	1.3	958	1,058	1,091	26,456	2.8	68.5	13.7	25.2
NEW YORK	13.6	10.3	7.3	51.1	19,378,102	20,201,249	4.2	-1.8	264,380	238,584	-387,397	7,417,224	2.6	63.0	14.0	29.8
Albany	13.1	10.7	7.2	51.4	304,204	314,848	3.5	-0.4	3,486	3,991	-657	128,122	2.3	55.7	11.8	34.3
Allegany	13.9	12.3	7.7	48.9	48,946	46,456	-5.1	-0.8	568	696	-227	18,028	2.3	64.1	8.8	29.6
Bronx	12.0	8.0	6.0	52.6	1,385,108	1,472,654	6.3	-3.2	22,690	15,582	-54,179	510,135	2.7	64.6	29.1	31.0
Broome	14.0	11.2	8.5	50.5	200,600	198,683	-1.0	-0.7	2,373	3,117	-729	79,528	2.3	58.3	12.1	32.3
Cattaraugus	15.0	12.5	7.8	49.8	80,317	77,042	-4.1	-0.8	977	1,235	-367	31,999	2.3	63.3	11.8	30.5
Cayuga	15.4	12.5	8.1	48.3	80,026	76,248	-4.7	-0.5	902	1,093	-184	30,870	2.4	61.8	12.0	29.1
Chautauqua	15.0	12.6	8.6	50.2	134,905	127,657	-5.4	-0.7	1,575	2,124	-315	53,625	2.3	60.7	11.4	32.6
Chemung	14.4	11.9	7.9	50.1	88,830	84,148	-5.3	-1.3	1,058	1,512	-654	34,328	2.3	61.0	12.3	33.1
Chenango	16.1	12.8	8.7	49.7	50,477	47,220	-6.5	-1.4	539	820	-404	20,834	2.3	61.8	10.0	31.3
Clinton	14.7	11.2	7.1	48.3	82,128	79,843	-2.8	-0.3	859	1,140	20	31,557	2.3	60.1	10.0	29.3
Columbia	16.9	15.1	10.3	49.7	63,096	61,570	-2.4	0.3	562	1,015	670	25,323	2.3	64.0	10.2	29.2
Cortland	13.2	10.2	6.9	50.7	49,336	46,809	-5.1	-1.1	545	670	-378	17,980	2.5	64.6	12.2	24.8
Delaware	16.5	15.2	10.7	49.2	47,980	44,308	-7.7	0.2	411	818	486	18,930	2.2	61.2	8.6	31.6
Dutchess	15.4	10.9	7.6	49.9	297,488	295,911	-0.5	0.4	3,255	3,922	1,857	110,095	2.5	65.4	11.1	28.2
Erie	14.3	11.2	7.6	51.2	919,040	954,236	3.8	-0.4	11,681	14,434	-970	392,910	2.3	58.1	12.9	34.4
Essex	16.8	14.9	9.9	47.9	39,370	37,381	-5.1	-0.3	377	665	178	16,182	2.1	63.1	11.1	31.0
Franklin	14.3	10.9	6.9	44.8	51,599	47,555	-7.8	-0.2	502	726	117	18,880	2.4	62.9	10.4	30.7
Fulton	15.4	12.3	8.1	50.0	55,531	53,324	-4.0	-0.4	590	871	69	22,406	2.3	64.9	14.4	27.5

1. No spouse present.

STATE County	Persons in group quarters, 2021	Daytime Population, 2016–2020		Births, 2021		Deaths, 2021		Persons under 65 with no health insurance, 2019		Medicare, 2021			COVID-19 Deaths, 2020	
		Number	Employment/ residence ratio	Total	Rate[1]	Number	Rate[1]	Number	Percent	Total beneficiaries	Enrolled in Original Medicare	Enrolled in Medicare Advantage	Number	Rate[1]
	32	33	34	35	36	37	38	39	40	41	42	43	44	45
NEW JERSEY— Cont'd														
Mercer	20,712	421,332	1.3	3,876	10.0	3,620	9.4	28,211	9.6	65,853	40,457	25,396	663	1.7
Middlesex	23,654	816,067	1.0	8,223	9.5	7,543	8.8	61,727	9.1	138,668	94,802	43,866	1,543	1.8
Monmouth	6,578	583,882	0.9	5,525	8.6	6,747	10.5	35,682	7.1	127,486	95,653	31,833	1,016	1.6
Morris	8,602	531,776	1.2	4,412	8.7	4,702	9.2	22,979	5.7	93,105	68,701	24,404	896	1.8
Ocean	7,136	531,033	0.7	9,043	14.0	8,243	12.8	33,231	7.2	155,624	106,807	48,817	1,276	2.0
Passaic	10,343	448,454	0.8	6,060	11.6	4,821	9.3	58,912	14.2	83,228	50,967	32,261	1,438	2.7
Salem	1,222	57,240	0.8	645	9.9	877	13.5	4,229	8.5	14,278	10,216	4,062	99	1.5
Somerset	5,411	353,524	1.1	2,958	8.6	3,096	9.0	18,141	6.6	57,474	41,657	15,817	582	1.7
Sussex	1,604	111,434	0.6	1,194	8.2	1,503	10.4	6,509	5.7	29,805	21,927	7,878	233	1.6
Union	6,069	527,304	0.9	6,273	10.9	5,221	9.1	59,289	12.6	87,512	54,469	33,043	1,479	2.6
Warren	1,943	88,611	0.7	902	8.2	1,161	10.5	6,449	7.6	22,869	16,507	6,362	164	1.5
NEW MEXICO	40,898	2,088,696	1.0	21,996	10.4	23,082	10.9	202,767	12.1	432,330	261,857	170,473	2,972	1.4
Bernalillo	11,310	708,599	1.1	6,602	9.8	7,387	10.9	60,480	10.9	130,981	60,947	70,035	655	1.0
Catron	105	3,789	1.3	12	3.3	35	9.5	181	9.1	1,480	1,163	317	D	D
Chaves	1,696	62,618	0.9	792	12.2	832	12.8	6,736	12.9	11,991	8,845	3,145	120	1.8
Cibola	2,588	26,902	1.0	291	10.7	351	12.9	2,446	12.5	4,732	3,361	1,371	69	2.5
Colfax	398	12,003	1.0	97	7.9	163	13.2	841	10.1	3,693	2,720	973	31	2.5
Curry	1,366	50,399	1.0	802	16.7	422	8.8	4,520	11.0	7,576	6,141	1,436	58	1.2
De Baca	9	2,038	1.1	9	5.4	28	16.7	151	12.3	535	506	29	D	D
Dona Ana	4,170	208,597	0.9	2,506	11.4	2,175	9.9	23,882	13.5	42,625	24,542	18,084	340	1.5
Eddy	993	61,855	1.2	842	13.7	589	9.6	4,891	9.8	9,748	8,621	1,127	91	1.5
Grant	574	27,442	1.0	230	8.2	400	14.3	1,645	8.8	8,777	5,914	2,863	25	0.9
Guadalupe	574	4,725	1.3	40	9.0	51	11.5	217	7.7	1,002	879	123	D	D
Harding	0	366	0.7	0	0.0	13	20.0	37	9.7	231	208	23	D	D
Hidalgo	61	4,192	1.0	30	7.3	58	14.1	334	10.5	1,069	688	381	D	D
Lea	2,050	71,069	1.0	1,107	15.0	612	8.3	8,145	13.3	9,111	8,156	955	139	1.9
Lincoln	111	20,010	1.1	167	8.2	223	10.9	1,786	13.1	6,255	4,696	1,559	21	1.0
Los Alamos	73	27,331	1.8	161	8.3	145	7.5	458	2.8	3,520	3,151	370	D	D
Luna	546	24,020	1.0	377	14.8	324	12.7	2,524	14.2	6,642	3,512	3,130	60	2.4
McKinley	742	71,149	1.0	849	11.8	924	12.8	12,033	19.9	11,290	9,675	1,615	387	5.3
Mora	7	3,847	0.5	38	9.1	46	11.0	281	8.9	1,449	1,183	266	D	D
Otero	2,249	65,753	1.0	865	12.7	761	11.2	6,008	11.3	13,402	9,711	3,690	47	0.7
Quay	22	8,001	0.9	82	9.4	148	17.0	638	10.6	2,525	2,168	357	10	1.1
Rio Arriba	413	34,985	0.7	393	9.8	504	12.5	3,780	12.4	9,146	5,522	3,624	50	1.2
Roosevelt	1,091	17,712	0.9	224	11.7	179	9.4	1,916	13.1	3,082	2,713	369	42	2.2
Sandoval	625	123,695	0.7	1,341	8.9	1,433	9.5	10,765	9.0	31,816	16,065	15,752	158	1.1
San Juan	1,446	124,510	1.0	1,320	10.9	1,440	11.9	15,208	14.8	21,722	17,863	3,859	345	2.8
San Miguel	1,217	26,502	0.9	237	8.7	325	12.0	1,996	10.0	7,129	4,361	2,769	10	0.4
Santa Fe	2,575	152,570	1.0	1,140	7.4	1,542	9.9	15,703	14.2	41,546	26,525	15,021	92	0.6
Sierra	259	11,134	1.0	79	6.9	270	23.4	781	11.9	4,565	2,782	1,783	43	3.7
Socorro	543	16,046	0.9	181	11.0	221	13.4	1,548	12.3	3,791	2,484	1,307	48	2.9
Taos	461	32,665	1.0	234	6.8	400	11.6	3,425	14.7	9,904	6,713	3,191	45	1.3
Torrance	559	13,407	0.6	145	9.6	181	11.9	1,389	12.2	3,601	1,723	1,878	11	0.7
Union	663	4,055	1.0	34	8.3	41	10.0	330	13.1	966	914	52	D	D
Valencia	1,402	66,710	0.7	769	10.0	859	11.2	7,692	12.6	16,429	7,408	9,021	75	1.0
NEW YORK	570,005	19,921,081	1.0	210,640	10.5	192,137	9.6	973,636	6.2	3,670,152	2,067,099	1,603,054	38,646	1.9
Albany	17,061	370,570	1.4	2,795	8.9	3,197	10.2	9,639	4.0	61,754	31,905	29,848	243	0.8
Allegany	4,105	42,956	0.8	453	9.8	578	12.5	1,824	5.5	10,524	5,943	4,581	72	1.6
Bronx	45,511	1,247,918	0.7	18,196	12.6	12,645	8.7	100,053	8.5	209,336	81,615	127,720	4,631	3.2
Broome	11,342	197,702	1.1	1,892	9.6	2,454	12.4	7,520	5.2	44,220	23,108	21,112	242	1.2
Cattaraugus	2,514	73,483	0.9	790	10.3	989	12.9	4,088	6.9	18,473	8,901	9,571	57	0.7
Cayuga	3,613	68,876	0.8	720	9.5	857	11.3	2,770	4.8	17,100	10,074	7,025	31	0.4
Chautauqua	5,619	127,210	1.0	1,257	9.9	1,691	13.3	5,210	5.4	31,238	15,458	15,780	44	0.3
Chemung	3,515	85,517	1.0	839	10.1	1,193	14.3	2,636	4.1	20,120	10,557	9,563	115	1.4
Chenango	655	45,338	0.9	427	9.1	661	14.1	1,703	4.6	12,130	6,458	5,672	34	0.7
Clinton	5,940	80,590	1.0	673	8.4	880	11.0	3,018	5.0	18,510	13,287	5,224	10	0.1
Columbia	1,833	54,959	0.8	440	7.1	836	13.6	2,524	5.7	16,166	10,516	5,649	50	0.8
Cortland	3,549	45,771	0.9	427	9.2	528	11.4	1,506	4.2	9,441	6,028	3,413	32	0.7
Delaware	2,289	45,399	1.0	335	7.6	673	15.2	1,789	5.7	12,157	7,691	4,466	23	0.5
Dutchess	19,291	269,228	0.8	2,583	8.7	3,186	10.7	12,124	5.3	61,133	44,672	16,461	291	1.0
Erie	27,622	951,150	1.1	9,257	9.7	11,543	12.1	29,797	4.1	200,998	74,335	126,664	1,300	1.4
Essex	2,053	36,756	1.0	298	8.0	530	14.2	1,308	4.9	9,905	6,965	2,940	13	0.3
Franklin	5,643	50,884	1.0	389	8.2	595	12.5	2,492	7.0	11,298	7,991	3,308	12	0.3
Fulton	1,267	47,914	0.8	458	8.6	681	12.8	2,014	4.8	13,714	6,333	7,381	52	1.0

1. Per 1,000 estimated resident population.

STATE County	COVID-19 Vaccinations, 2021–2022		Education						Money income, 2016–2020				Income and poverty, 2020			
			School enrollment and attainment, 2016–2020				Local government expenditures,[3] 2018–2019			Households				Percent below poverty level		
			Enrollment[1]		Attainment[2] (percent)						Percent					
	Number	Percent[5]	Total	Percent private	High school graduate or less	Bachelor's degree or more	Total current spending (mil dol)	Current spending per student (dollars)	Per capita income[4]	Median income (dollars)	with income of less than $50,000	with income of $200,000 or more	Median household income (dollars)	All persons	Children under 18 years	Children 5 to 17 years in families
	46	47	48	49	50	51	52	53	54	55	56	57	58	59	60	61
NEW JERSEY— Cont'd																
Mercer	261,865	71.3	97,552	23.9	35.8	43.5	1,240.8	19,627	44,532	83,306	31.3	15.0	87,581	9.5	12.7	11.5
Middlesex	608,845	73.8	216,530	15.0	34.6	44.4	2,479.9	19,230	40,933	91,731	26.5	14.1	95,610	7.4	8.3	8.4
Monmouth	422,661	68.3	152,161	22.3	29.0	47.3	2,074.4	21,285	53,886	103,523	24.4	20.5	104,219	5.9	6.4	6.3
Morris	382,218	77.7	121,470	21.7	24.7	55.3	1,619.9	21,555	58,981	117,298	19.2	24.2	114,103	4.7	4.5	4.3
Ocean	331,837	54.7	149,163	38.7	41.0	31.4	1,378.8	19,641	37,041	72,679	34.9	8.7	78,181	10.5	18.2	16.5
Passaic	352,726	70.3	131,217	15.4	49.2	29.5	1,773.8	19,976	33,863	73,562	35.5	10.9	64,422	16.9	25.4	25.0
Salem	34,753	55.7	13,767	13.3	48.9	21.7	226.3	21,065	33,575	64,234	39.8	6.1	65,563	12.2	15.8	15.1
Somerset	250,815	76.3	82,455	17.9	25.3	55.6	1,118.9	20,892	58,021	116,510	20.0	25.3	115,573	4.8	5.7	5.2
Sussex	88,452	63.0	31,989	17.6	35.0	36.6	474.5	23,786	46,124	96,222	21.7	13.1	92,739	5.4	5.8	5.4
Union	397,740	71.5	139,130	14.8	41.1	37.1	1,944.6	19,592	42,606	82,644	29.7	14.9	83,189	9.2	12.0	10.8
Warren	71,922	68.3	24,970	18.7	38.0	34.5	331.2	20,480	40,626	83,497	28.9	9.5	80,412	7.3	8.9	8.3
NEW MEXICO	1,488,965	71.0	526,666	10.5	39.7	28.1	3,393.1	10,173	27,945	51,243	48.9	4.1	52,285	16.8	21.6	20.6
Bernalillo	477,046	70.2	170,556	13.1	32.9	35.3	965.3	9,913	31,229	54,308	46.3	5.0	56,632	15.3	17.0	16.5
Catron	1,624	46.0	563	0.0	49.3	16.7	6.3	20,658	21,347	36,607	68.8	0.5	27,423	22.8	36.4	33.9
Chaves	29,112	45.1	17,240	12.2	47.2	17.7	118.8	9,905	23,413	46,254	52.6	2.5	51,441	19.2	26.2	24.8
Cibola	18,863	70.7	6,429	12.5	48.9	17.3	38.8	11,139	20,507	44,731	53.8	1.2	42,705	25.1	32.4	30.6
Colfax	7,420	62.1	1,784	5.7	42.9	21.4	20.5	12,643	24,852	36,937	62.0	1.7	43,265	17.2	25.2	24.3
Curry	26,236	53.6	13,730	7.2	44.9	20.2	84.2	9,132	23,897	48,903	51.2	1.7	53,864	14.9	19.4	19.4
De Baca	884	50.6	727	12.4	45.6	13.3	4.4	13,631	15,996	31,532	60.6	0.2	42,319	17.0	29.2	27.3
Dona Ana	164,670	75.5	66,842	6.2	40.9	29.5	389.4	9,632	22,772	44,024	54.8	2.4	46,547	20.5	27.3	24.7
Eddy	27,555	47.1	13,869	8.9	48.9	17.2	119.7	9,592	31,766	65,000	39.3	4.9	66,199	12.8	14.2	13.7
Grant	18,734	69.4	5,691	11.8	40.9	25.6	47.9	12,250	25,491	37,453	60.4	2.7	43,557	20.0	26.2	23.8
Guadalupe	3,001	69.8	830	4.8	65.0	8.5	10.6	14,705	19,418	31,061	75.5	6.1	38,903	22.8	28.9	28.8
Harding	363	58.1	81	11.1	35.6	24.3	3.4	41,122	50,027	32,500	68.2	7.4	39,913	15.1	23.7	26.3
Hidalgo	2,469	58.8	700	6.4	51.0	19.9	10.0	14,590	22,472	44,722	54.6	2.0	41,858	19.8	26.3	26.1
Lea	31,584	44.4	19,509	5.8	56.5	14.6	141.4	8,951	26,551	61,867	40.1	4.3	66,780	12.6	14.2	13.7
Lincoln	11,512	58.8	3,520	15.1	42.7	25.1	33.5	11,496	27,892	44,939	54.7	2.3	49,115	16.9	28.6	28.5
Los Alamos	16,317	84.2	4,754	9.4	11.9	67.6	42.2	11,249	60,729	119,266	14.8	20.6	111,724	3.3	2.8	2.6
Luna	17,775	75.0	5,180	2.7	64.7	13.1	58.1	10,692	18,433	32,251	66.1	1.4	39,233	22.3	34.6	36.6
McKinley	63,050	88.3	19,643	3.8	58.1	11.5	162.0	12,681	16,378	36,179	61.4	2.5	35,659	32.0	39.3	36.7
Mora	2,930	64.8	673	0.3	47.6	17.6	9.9	21,103	20,662	29,458	70.0	0.0	40,618	19.8	26.1	26.6
Otero	41,219	61.1	15,740	12.8	41.2	18.9	71.1	9,307	24,777	45,032	54.8	2.1	46,735	15.5	24.7	26.1
Quay	4,131	50.1	1,865	4.4	55.1	15.4	19.0	12,399	21,594	33,962	66.1	0.5	38,389	22.0	34.9	35.9
Rio Arriba	30,738	79.0	8,574	9.5	47.0	18.5	66.9	13,408	23,819	42,264	57.1	2.8	47,400	19.7	27.1	26.2
Roosevelt	7,144	38.6	5,900	3.2	50.8	21.9	37.8	11,142	20,230	42,917	56.9	1.2	46,351	18.2	24.1	23.9
Sandoval	105,448	71.9	37,304	13.8	34.4	31.0	209.4	9,523	30,273	65,071	37.3	5.5	71,991	10.4	12.2	11.9
San Juan	92,545	74.7	32,859	8.9	43.0	15.4	231.9	9,894	22,840	47,643	51.4	2.2	44,261	21.5	29.7	27.0
San Miguel	18,468	67.7	6,838	7.4	41.9	22.0	36.4	11,945	22,678	32,310	65.7	1.3	40,804	20.9	25.5	27.4
Santa Fe	122,353	81.4	30,039	13.8	33.2	40.7	186.6	10,148	38,288	60,668	41.8	7.4	58,898	12.5	17.4	15.6
Sierra	7,184	66.6	1,625	10.2	41.2	22.1	15.1	11,555	28,014	33,873	62.7	2.1	36,823	22.1	33.5	34.1
Socorro	11,440	68.8	4,620	3.1	55.1	22.0	26.4	13,170	20,015	40,297	59.9	1.7	39,478	25.1	38.1	36.8
Taos	27,044	82.6	6,543	5.6	34.0	32.3	49.5	12,126	30,580	41,973	56.8	5.0	43,230	18.9	26.6	26.5
Torrance	7,492	48.5	3,371	9.6	50.4	15.6	47.0	10,704	21,235	38,240	56.5	2.0	47,266	21.4	27.6	26.3
Union	1,821	44.9	695	9.9	60.3	12.5	8.2	14,543	21,083	35,484	62.4	0.9	42,676	19.0	27.2	28.2
Valencia	45,686	59.6	18,372	14.4	47.7	19.9	121.3	9,343	25,106	50,801	49.0	2.7	51,564	15.5	20.4	19.1
NEW YORK	14,949,546	76.8	4,656,339	24.3	38.2	37.5	64,263.9	23,806	40,898	71,117	37.0	11.5	73,354	12.7	16.7	16.3
Albany	228,483	74.8	81,049	22.6	29.5	43.6	755.1	18,242	38,592	68,327	36.7	8.2	70,629	11.3	12.5	11.8
Allegany	20,470	44.4	13,148	26.7	43.7	22.9	148.1	22,679	26,030	51,227	48.5	2.3	53,371	15.1	21.0	20.6
Bronx	1,062,736	74.9	393,609	17.2	54.3	20.3	(6)	(6)	22,749	41,895	56.4	3.3	44,906	24.4	30.6	30.2
Broome	121,380	63.7	51,477	8.9	40.8	28.8	554.8	20,995	29,721	52,237	48.1	3.8	52,510	18.4	23.8	24.1
Cattaraugus	42,909	56.4	17,354	17.1	49.5	19.9	276.5	21,158	26,797	50,700	49.3	2.3	51,824	16.3	22.0	20.8
Cayuga	45,388	59.3	15,836	14.2	44.8	22.0	183.6	19,397	30,996	57,985	43.8	3.6	59,335	11.7	15.3	14.6
Chautauqua	75,314	59.3	27,599	8.8	45.1	23.1	384.1	19,815	27,061	48,315	51.5	2.1	50,062	14.8	19.4	19.2
Chemung	50,459	60.5	17,675	16.8	44.7	23.6	209.7	18,082	29,959	54,883	45.7	3.3	54,705	14.5	20.1	19.5
Chenango	28,891	61.2	9,457	11.4	51.8	19.0	169.9	22,632	28,780	51,756	48.2	2.7	52,545	11.5	15.7	13.8
Clinton	58,463	72.6	18,088	7.0	48.3	24.4	253.6	22,833	29,960	59,510	41.0	3.7	59,741	11.1	13.1	12.7
Columbia	44,465	74.8	10,163	16.8	38.3	33.7	175.3	25,381	40,475	68,750	36.2	7.5	66,068	10.2	16.0	14.7
Cortland	28,260	59.4	13,197	13.1	40.5	26.9	128.9	20,738	28,407	59,194	42.8	3.5	60,165	11.7	15.7	14.6
Delaware	25,343	57.4	9,139	8.0	49.8	22.1	152.7	25,339	28,139	49,945	50.0	2.7	54,440	12.8	18.7	17.9
Dutchess	206,870	70.3	70,066	27.8	35.2	36.4	932.6	23,510	42,309	81,842	31.1	11.8	79,276	8.3	8.6	8.9
Erie	642,718	70.0	213,454	17.9	34.8	35.1	2,259.0	17,767	35,050	59,464	42.5	5.6	59,584	13.2	17.8	16.2
Essex	26,435	71.7	6,290	14.7	41.4	29.8	106.2	28,066	33,906	58,109	41.8	5.1	57,129	10.2	14.9	14.8
Franklin	35,124	70.2	9,704	17.0	49.8	20.7	173.4	23,672	26,886	52,905	47.6	3.8	58,709	15.9	25.0	23.4
Fulton	29,075	54.5	10,792	9.7	47.8	18.2	153.4	19,466	29,984	51,663	48.7	3.0	55,405	13.9	20.2	18.9

1. All persons 3 years old and over enrolled in nursery school through college. 2. Persons 25 years old and over. 3. Elementary and secondary education expenditures. 4. Based on population estimated by the American Community Survey, 2016–2020. 5. CDC percent based on 2019 population estimate. 6. Bronx, Kings, Queens, and Richmond counties are included with New York county

STATE County	Personal income, 2020										Earnings, 2020		
			Per capita[1]			Supplements to wages and salaries, employer contributions (mil dol)						Contributions for government social insurance (mil dol)	
	Total (mil dol)	Percent change 2019–2020	Dollars	Rank	Wages and salaries (mil dol)	Pension and insurance	Government social insurance	Proprietors' income (mil dol)	Dividends, interest, and rent (mil dol)	Personal transfer reecipts (mil dol)	Total (mil dol)	From employee and self-employed	From employer
	62	63	64	65	66	67	68	69	70	71	72	73	74
NEW JERSEY— Cont'd													
Mercer	27,256	4.8	74,218	112	19,072	2,782	1,343	2,042	5,128	4,898	25,238	1,484	1,343
Middlesex	54,827	6.1	66,640	226	31,493	4,513	2,307	3,968	8,119	9,906	42,280	2,529	2,307
Monmouth	53,237	4.4	86,091	56	16,921	2,624	1,273	4,620	9,796	8,562	25,437	1,577	1,273
Morris	50,203	3.0	102,227	20	29,060	3,487	1,874	5,092	9,821	5,754	39,513	2,311	1,874
Ocean	35,223	8.3	57,344	550	8,761	1,642	703	2,954	5,917	9,729	14,059	1,023	703
Passaic	27,909	8.6	55,775	658	9,769	1,721	753	2,378	3,400	7,414	14,621	919	753
Salem	3,408	8.1	54,578	735	1,317	293	104	233	417	1,023	1,946	122	104
Somerset	37,157	1.9	112,825	16	19,092	2,296	1,238	7,450	6,395	3,666	30,076	1,671	1,238
Sussex	9,494	5.0	67,814	200	2,012	375	158	744	1,363	1,842	3,290	224	158
Union	40,290	5.1	72,543	131	18,141	2,634	1,219	3,387	6,453	6,912	25,381	1,518	1,219
Warren	6,393	6.4	60,525	402	1,760	333	138	382	872	1,466	2,613	179	138
NEW MEXICO	97,603	7.8	46,092	X	42,891	7,206	3,288	6,154	16,510	28,820	59,539	4,105	3,288
Bernalillo	33,186	8.1	48,683	1,297	18,777	2,965	1,429	1,754	5,585	8,727	24,925	1,664	1,429
Catron	131	16.1	36,171	2,858	26	7	2	14	28	58	50	5	2
Chaves	2,822	8.9	43,615	1,993	884	156	69	334	396	944	1,443	94	69
Cibola	863	11.6	32,755	3,037	336	67	26	38	91	379	466	35	26
Colfax	544	9.9	45,610	1,714	164	32	13	54	96	216	263	20	13
Curry	2,386	11.3	48,894	1,271	1,095	248	101	240	331	652	1,683	87	101
De Baca	95	14.0	56,603	598	19	4	2	23	17	34	48	3	2
Dona Ana	8,899	8.7	40,218	2,431	3,345	652	263	699	1,244	3,040	4,959	351	263
Eddy	3,643	2.5	62,356	338	2,164	312	157	340	597	766	2,973	191	157
Grant	1,230	7.2	45,561	1,720	405	83	30	53	193	545	572	47	30
Guadalupe	167	11.2	39,140	2,551	52	10	4	10	21	75	77	6	4
Harding	32	23.7	50,723	1,062	7	2	1	6	7	10	16	1	1
Hidalgo	198	8.6	48,166	1,363	72	18	6	22	23	76	118	7	6
Lea	3,391	-3.7	47,215	1,488	1,671	242	119	453	359	849	2,486	160	119
Lincoln	892	8.0	44,732	1,839	257	44	20	65	194	334	386	33	20
Los Alamos	1,482	4.5	76,142	100	1,747	150	132	78	239	155	2,106	136	132
Luna	909	15.9	38,022	2,683	314	68	27	74	104	420	483	37	27
McKinley	2,323	12.6	32,804	3,035	879	214	70	89	240	1,013	1,252	85	70
Mora	203	11.7	45,300	1,753	27	7	2	21	33	91	57	5	2
Otero	2,636	10.7	38,779	2,596	1,084	256	91	114	431	857	1,547	99	91
Quay	366	11.5	44,691	1,850	112	21	8	34	51	167	175	14	8
Rio Arriba	1,571	11.0	40,771	2,365	427	84	32	50	207	662	594	50	32
Roosevelt	862	12.4	46,999	1,518	234	52	18	128	102	258	433	22	18
Sandoval	7,037	8.8	47,257	1,482	1,571	240	117	290	1,133	1,796	2,219	186	117
San Juan	4,731	5.7	38,370	2,638	2,201	393	164	177	645	1,576	2,934	202	164
San Miguel	1,104	11.6	40,675	2,375	296	71	23	35	183	539	425	34	23
Santa Fe	9,573	5.2	63,004	317	3,062	495	225	609	2,977	2,082	4,392	328	225
Sierra	515	16.1	47,388	1,460	145	28	12	29	84	266	214	19	12
Socorro	646	10.9	39,055	2,561	231	54	18	42	89	261	345	24	18
Taos	1,400	11.2	42,965	2,069	397	71	32	78	316	573	578	51	32
Torrance	577	12.3	37,276	2,765	149	29	12	53	65	243	244	18	12
Union	169	16.2	41,932	2,210	54	12	4	31	23	57	101	6	4
Valencia	3,019	11.2	38,918	2,576	684	120	59	113	407	1,100	976	84	59
NEW YORK	1,440,049	5.8	71,449	X	733,269	118,448	50,213	127,354	274,799	322,884	1,029,283	55,988	50,213
Albany	20,233	7.3	66,632	227	15,174	3,463	1,183	1,454	3,596	4,717	21,274	1,101	1,183
Allegany	1,862	9.2	40,840	2,349	550	177	46	141	234	690	914	58	46
Bronx	61,537	13.9	43,919	1,960	19,708	4,577	1,609	3,012	4,291	26,511	28,906	1,726	1,609
Broome	9,341	8.4	49,314	1,216	4,191	1,032	337	466	1,359	2,972	6,026	361	337
Cattaraugus	3,429	9.4	45,200	1,770	1,212	348	100	208	433	1,250	1,868	117	100
Cayuga	3,694	8.8	48,585	1,312	1,215	306	101	248	507	1,133	1,871	112	101
Chautauqua	5,716	8.9	45,357	1,744	2,033	522	171	352	696	2,120	3,078	194	171
Chemung	4,085	7.3	49,439	1,205	1,741	407	142	182	529	1,373	2,471	151	142
Chenango	2,236	9.3	47,842	1,412	880	222	70	109	308	742	1,282	81	70
Clinton	3,853	7.3	48,292	1,349	1,608	432	135	212	480	1,234	2,386	143	135
Columbia	3,623	6.4	60,859	390	936	231	79	239	727	977	1,485	94	79
Cortland	2,159	10.0	45,776	1,687	791	221	65	128	297	668	1,205	70	65
Delaware	2,013	6.7	45,822	1,680	726	210	59	164	331	692	1,159	71	59
Dutchess	18,278	6.4	62,319	340	6,517	1,330	523	964	3,078	4,274	9,333	547	523
Erie	52,051	8.4	56,748	588	25,569	5,328	2,009	3,592	7,186	14,708	36,498	2,068	2,009
Essex	1,875	7.1	50,824	1,051	645	179	53	106	335	609	983	61	53
Franklin	2,125	7.9	42,525	2,129	848	269	69	115	291	742	1,301	79	69
Fulton	2,586	9.0	48,957	1,262	734	181	61	170	312	900	1,147	75	61

1. Based on the resident population estimated as of July 1 of the year shown.

STATE County	Earnings, 2020 (cont.)									Social Security beneficiaries, December 2020		Supple-mental Security Income recipients, 2020	Housing units, 2021	
	Percent by selected industries													
	Farm	Mining, quarrying, and extractions	Construction	Manu-facturing	Information; professional, scientific, technical services	Retail trade	Finance, insurance, real estate, and leasing	Health care and social assistance	Govern-ment	Number	Rate[1]		Total	Percent change, 2010–2021
	75	76	77	78	79	80	81	82	83	84	85	86	87	88
NEW JERSEY— Cont'd														
Mercer	0.0	D	2.8	7.1	19.8	3.2	13.2	9.0	16.3	66,295	172	9,374	150,657	0.1
Middlesex	0.0	D	4.6	8.0	19.3	4.6	7.0	9.5	13.3	137,095	159	13,362	317,113	0.4
Monmouth	0.2	D	9.2	3.3	17.1	7.7	9.5	16.9	12.9	128,875	200	7,435	269,917	0.3
Morris	0.1	0.0	4.3	7.7	24.6	4.4	11.7	9.1	8.5	88,545	173	4,218	198,761	0.4
Ocean	0.1	0.2	10.7	4.1	8.4	11.1	5.8	18.2	19.3	160,520	247	7,332	295,584	0.3
Passaic	0.0	D	8.2	11.2	7.4	8.4	7.0	14.2	19.3	86,055	166	13,292	185,497	0.0
Salem	3.1	0.1	D	11.3	4.4	4.6	2.4	10.5	18.3	15,755	242	1,727	27,735	-0.1
Somerset	0.0	2.9	3.6	20.3	20.1	3.3	7.9	5.7	5.9	55,385	160	2,817	133,263	1.0
Sussex	0.1	0.5	10.2	7.5	8.5	9.1	5.7	13.3	19.8	31,295	215	1,593	62,857	0.2
Union	0.0	D	5.7	10.3	19.7	5.4	7.1	10.1	12.8	87,845	154	10,510	211,074	0.4
Warren	1.4	0.4	D	13.1	6.7	10.1	2.4	13.4	18.0	23,925	216	1,561	46,763	0.6
NEW MEXICO	2.1	3.7	6.7	3.7	13.0	6.4	5.4	12.2	26.5	453,282	214	60,930	948,110	0.6
Bernalillo	0.0	0.1	6.8	3.4	17.3	6.1	7.4	13.5	25.5	134,915	200	17,128	300,842	0.4
Catron	21.2	D	4.2	2.9	D	D	D	6.2	40.0	1,560	418	71	3,246	0.4
Chaves	13.2	3.5	4.1	4.9	5.0	9.8	4.5	13.4	21.5	13,010	201	2,067	26,750	0.3
Cibola	1.8	D	8.3	0.9	D	6.5	1.4	16.0	38.6	5,405	199	879	11,143	0.3
Colfax	12.2	1.9	5.2	2.4	2.0	8.1	5.1	D	31.8	3,910	316	406	9,533	0.3
Curry	12.1	0.1	3.1	2.9	2.8	4.9	2.6	10.8	42.2	7,810	163	1,449	21,210	0.4
De Baca	41.8	0.5	D	D	D	5.6	D	5.0	20.2	545	324	D	1,129	0.3
Dona Ana	3.1	D	6.9	4.0	7.9	5.9	4.9	16.1	31.3	45,355	205	8,166	91,275	1.3
Eddy	1.7	31.3	11.2	4.2	4.8	5.1	4.0	5.8	11.4	10,460	172	1,118	26,821	1.8
Grant	2.6	D	3.9	0.7	3.4	7.1	4.0	10.2	34.6	9,205	330	886	14,641	0.3
Guadalupe	11.7	0.0	2.0	D	D	13.0	D	10.0	30.3	1,140	256	214	2,197	0.4
Harding	42.0	0.0	D	D	D	D	0.2	D	35.4	215	336	D	602	0.3
Hidalgo	13.5	D	D	D	D	6.9	D	D	49.7	1,155	284	167	2,202	0.5
Lea	3.7	24.4	9.9	2.9	3.0	6.7	5.2	5.5	11.4	10,020	137	1,448	28,071	0.3
Lincoln	3.4	D	7.1	1.1	D	12.3	11.1	13.6	21.1	6,570	321	380	17,744	0.5
Los Alamos	0.0	0.0	1.8	D	D	0.9	1.7	2.9	8.1	3,285	170	76	8,661	0.2
Luna	8.3	D	6.9	8.9	D	7.0	2.1	D	34.0	7,190	282	1,484	11,555	0.3
McKinley	0.4	0.2	2.8	6.8	1.7	9.1	2.8	12.8	44.6	11,950	166	4,328	25,140	0.3
Mora	29.7	0.2	D	D	D	4.2	D	D	29.0	1,640	391	264	2,878	0.3
Otero	0.9	0.3	5.2	0.3	4.1	5.1	2.6	12.0	51.8	14,220	207	1,442	32,326	0.3
Quay	12.3	0.0	5.7	D	1.8	7.7	4.0	14.8	26.4	2,680	310	378	5,491	0.3
Rio Arriba	2.9	2.4	4.7	1.0	3.4	6.5	1.7	16.5	42.5	10,470	261	1,640	19,640	0.4
Roosevelt	28.1	D	2.6	5.9	1.7	5.3	2.7	D	30.4	3,285	173	514	8,514	0.3
Sandoval	0.3	0.5	7.3	18.8	6.6	6.2	4.3	9.5	22.4	33,130	219	2,633	59,657	1.5
San Juan	1.3	14.0	8.2	2.3	D	7.1	3.3	13.4	26.7	24,190	200	3,877	47,991	0.4
San Miguel	2.8	0.1	4.6	1.1	2.5	6.8	2.8	D	49.8	7,585	279	1,692	14,832	0.4
Santa Fe	0.1	0.1	D	D	11.9	8.9	6.5	13.6	27.8	41,050	264	2,473	77,709	0.9
Sierra	8.8	D	5.2	2.8	5.3	7.8	2.4	15.5	28.4	4,770	415	573	8,119	0.7
Socorro	10.7	D	1.0	1.1	8.8	4.2	1.6	D	46.8	4,005	246	947	7,611	0.4
Taos	0.7	D	5.7	2.4	6.4	9.1	4.9	18.2	22.6	10,210	295	1,082	21,049	0.5
Torrance	14.9	D	6.0	3.0	D	9.9	D	D	24.0	3,985	260	518	7,212	0.5
Union	26.5	D	D	D	D	6.0	4.7	9.2	26.7	1,020	248	109	2,084	0.3
Valencia	1.9	0.2	17.4	5.7	5.9	9.9	2.9	8.0	25.5	17,345	225	2,439	30,235	0.9
NEW YORK	0.2	0.1	4.4	3.8	19.2	4.4	17.6	11.8	16.0	3,680,264	186	601,717	8,531,063	0.4
Albany	0.1	0.3	4.9	4.3	13.0	4.6	10.0	11.8	31.5	63,100	201	7,060	146,813	0.4
Allegany	2.3	0.3	6.5	12.5	3.0	4.5	2.1	8.4	35.6	11,485	249	1,344	23,505	0.2
Bronx	0.0	D	5.2	1.2	2.6	5.3	3.1	26.3	32.3	205,685	144	100,347	552,470	0.8
Broome	0.2	0.0	6.0	10.9	6.4	6.6	4.9	19.8	25.7	47,720	242	7,045	92,891	0.3
Cattaraugus	1.8	0.4	4.5	13.4	3.0	8.2	3.9	D	35.8	20,250	265	2,450	40,231	0.2
Cayuga	5.8	D	6.5	14.3	4.5	7.3	2.5	12.9	27.5	18,175	240	1,791	36,751	0.2
Chautauqua	2.6	0.2	5.5	20.7	3.6	8.0	2.9	13.7	25.8	34,030	268	4,374	66,338	0.1
Chemung	0.3	0.8	5.4	16.3	4.9	8.1	4.4	16.2	24.6	21,840	263	2,956	39,195	0.4
Chenango	2.6	D	4.6	32.3	3.4	5.8	8.2	6.1	23.9	13,355	287	1,632	24,421	0.7
Clinton	2.2	D	8.1	9.0	4.0	9.2	2.1	16.9	32.0	20,990	264	2,702	37,480	0.4
Columbia	2.5	D	9.9	7.4	7.3	7.3	2.3	17.5	24.8	16,335	264	1,300	33,301	0.2
Cortland	2.6	0.2	5.4	13.9	5.1	7.3	4.0	13.1	30.1	10,210	220	1,086	20,836	0.1
Delaware	1.4	1.2	5.9	27.1	8.0	4.6	2.9	8.3	28.2	12,320	278	1,049	30,014	0.2
Dutchess	0.3	0.3	6.4	10.3	7.7	7.1	4.5	17.2	22.1	63,065	212	5,179	122,641	0.4
Erie	0.1	0.2	4.6	10.5	9.8	5.9	9.7	13.5	20.6	210,450	221	26,706	440,126	0.2
Essex	0.3	0.6	7.5	7.9	4.3	7.4	4.4	10.9	34.6	10,200	274	786	25,236	0.4
Franklin	2.5	0.0	3.6	2.4	3.5	6.1	1.8	D	48.0	12,485	263	1,713	25,418	0.3
Fulton	0.5	D	6.0	8.7	3.8	13.5	3.1	17.0	24.8	14,725	277	2,019	28,133	0.1

1. Per 1,000 resident population estimated as of July 1 of the year shown.

STATE County	Housing units, 2016–2020: Occupied units: Total	Owner-occupied: Percent	Owner-occupied: Median value[1]	Median owner cost as a percent of income: With a mortgage	Median owner cost as a percent of income: Without a mortgage[2]	Renter-occupied: Median rent[3]	Renter-occupied: Median rent as a percent of income[2]	Sub-standard units[4] (percent)	Civilian labor force, 2021: Total	Percent change, 2020–2021	Unemployment: Total	Unemployment: Rate[5]	Civilian employment[6], 2016–2020: Total	Percent: Management, business, science, and arts	Percent: Construction, production, and maintenance occupations
	89	90	91	92	93	94	95	96	97	98	99	100	101	102	103
NEW JERSEY— Cont'd															
Mercer	131,440	63.5	290,100	23.2	14.6	1,311	30.6	2.7	212,752	0.6	10,997	5.2	179,189	46.6	17.5
Middlesex	287,971	63.7	351,400	24.2	15.2	1,495	28.7	4.7	453,161	1.3	25,957	5.7	408,185	47.6	19.1
Monmouth	238,235	74.3	435,300	23.3	15.3	1,437	31.8	1.7	340,535	1.1	18,823	5.5	319,494	47.8	14.7
Morris	184,162	73.8	462,100	22.9	14.4	1,622	26.6	1.7	262,719	0.6	13,058	5.0	259,034	53.9	12.7
Ocean	229,454	80.3	286,700	24.7	16.4	1,459	35.8	2.5	292,150	0.9	17,437	6.0	261,595	38.8	18.0
Passaic	168,681	52.3	352,000	26.4	17.8	1,310	31.9	7.0	250,345	-1.1	20,916	8.4	244,212	34.4	26.5
Salem	24,414	69.1	185,700	22.4	15.4	1,024	34.6	1.4	30,386	-0.3	2,228	7.3	28,725	35.9	26.3
Somerset	119,721	75.7	436,700	22.6	13.9	1,636	28.8	1.9	175,249	0.7	8,877	5.1	175,459	54.4	13.3
Sussex	54,166	83.6	271,500	23.7	14.5	1,337	29.9	0.8	76,170	0.0	4,528	5.9	75,433	41.9	20.0
Union	191,862	58.9	378,700	24.6	17.3	1,335	30.7	5.0	285,486	0.1	19,023	6.7	282,632	38.8	23.2
Warren	42,322	72.8	265,700	22.9	15.9	1,128	27.9	1.2	58,523	1.7	3,231	5.5	55,124	39.4	20.9
NEW MEXICO	792,755	68.0	175,700	21.3	10.0	857	29.3	4.2	943,356	0.8	64,027	6.8	889,193	37.8	20.8
Bernalillo	272,528	63.3	205,500	21.4	10.0	892	30.7	2.9	334,378	1.7	20,780	6.2	320,318	42.6	16.3
Catron	1,546	87.5	162,400	40.1	10.7	720	16.2	2.5	1,182	3.2	73	6.2	846	20.3	29.8
Chaves	23,641	68.2	115,400	20.4	10.0	808	25.8	3.3	27,776	0.6	1,963	7.1	27,141	27.9	28.3
Cibola	8,408	71.6	88,800	19.9	10.0	676	23.6	11.0	8,875	-1.0	825	9.3	8,860	28.3	21.1
Colfax	5,946	67.8	108,900	25.5	12.2	634	25.2	2.3	5,645	10.7	332	5.9	4,888	34.5	25.1
Curry	18,620	56.4	132,400	23.1	10.0	893	27.3	3.5	22,066	0.7	1,087	4.9	19,811	28.7	31.3
De Baca	554	62.1	130,000	22.3	10.1	616	33.8	0.7	682	-1.7	35	5.1	638	31.8	45.0
Dona Ana	79,421	64.6	153,600	21.7	10.0	765	33.3	4.6	98,170	1.3	6,522	6.6	88,633	35.2	19.8
Eddy	21,548	70.0	161,100	16.4	10.0	970	22.3	3.7	31,522	-4.6	2,021	6.4	26,292	31.6	32.5
Grant	11,496	66.4	127,100	19.5	10.0	690	29.7	5.6	11,457	-2.8	831	7.3	9,562	34.4	24.4
Guadalupe	1,345	67.7	100,500	16.5	13.3	394	28.4	1.9	1,634	9.4	114	7.0	1,496	26.4	22.8
Harding	176	57.4	87,500	25.6	13.5	717	30.7	3.4	281	1.8	13	4.6	206	37.9	18.9
Hidalgo	1,742	69.9	91,800	22.2	10.0	544	25.8	4.3	1,888	-1.3	102	5.4	1,528	31.8	27.2
Lea	22,868	68.0	138,600	17.5	10.0	911	23.7	5.4	27,957	-3.9	2,677	9.6	29,240	28.5	36.7
Lincoln	8,478	75.6	172,800	23.4	10.0	709	29.3	2.5	8,843	1.9	660	7.5	8,032	30.5	23.2
Los Alamos	7,895	73.1	322,200	14.6	10.0	1,071	16.7	0.6	10,035	2.5	298	3.0	10,139	70.5	8.6
Luna	8,911	62.3	84,700	22.4	10.0	545	29.2	1.5	9,989	-1.9	1,518	15.2	7,850	25.4	33.5
McKinley	21,247	68.0	66,700	20.0	10.0	657	22.9	20.1	23,454	-0.7	2,245	9.6	23,269	32.3	21.5
Mora	2,278	88.4	104,300	27.3	14.9	527	30.7	9.4	1,998	-1.7	124	6.2	1,340	39.5	15.7
Otero	23,112	65.9	120,800	19.6	10.0	811	28.8	4.1	25,093	-0.5	1,659	6.6	23,413	28.4	26.0
Quay	3,182	69.3	68,500	28.2	10.0	588	25.0	0.7	2,956	-2.6	209	7.1	3,123	35.5	17.5
Rio Arriba	13,035	76.7	172,900	20.2	10.0	629	27.2	4.0	16,592	0.7	1,168	7.0	14,433	38.2	19.1
Roosevelt	6,785	58.4	111,700	19.0	11.5	752	30.8	3.9	7,904	1.0	439	5.6	7,825	33.6	32.2
Sandoval	52,504	80.0	211,700	21.7	10.0	1,114	30.5	3.3	67,732	1.7	4,480	6.6	63,551	38.9	17.4
San Juan	43,582	70.8	155,000	21.1	10.0	803	27.6	8.3	49,527	-1.0	3,977	8.0	47,993	30.0	29.7
San Miguel	11,942	69.9	138,300	22.9	13.0	651	30.4	4.6	10,367	-0.6	758	7.3	10,545	33.9	23.8
Santa Fe	63,152	71.2	294,800	23.7	10.0	1,092	27.9	3.4	72,572	2.2	4,478	6.2	69,066	43.9	16.4
Sierra	5,402	73.3	120,100	22.7	10.7	561	29.4	1.2	4,074	0.1	332	8.1	3,518	42.8	19.8
Socorro	5,002	76.6	117,900	18.0	10.6	695	32.0	5.4	6,166	0.1	389	6.3	5,861	45.9	21.0
Taos	12,592	76.9	249,000	21.4	12.0	857	36.3	3.1	14,663	-0.3	1,311	8.9	13,460	38.5	14.1
Torrance	5,957	82.4	115,500	21.7	11.0	682	28.7	4.4	5,412	1.7	426	7.9	5,449	28.6	26.6
Union	1,404	62.6	93,800	19.2	10.0	496	23.5	2.6	1,572	-3.4	66	4.2	1,357	33.2	28.2
Valencia	26,456	80.6	151,600	22.3	10.0	856	27.4	3.9	30,901	2.3	2,119	6.9	29,510	32.3	27.2
NEW YORK	7,417,224	54.1	325,000	22.6	13.2	1,315	30.8	5.4	9,441,458	-1.4	655,178	6.9	9,438,639	42.6	16.8
Albany	128,122	56.1	230,300	19.5	10.5	1,057	27.9	1.7	156,527	-1.6	6,882	4.4	159,187	47.2	13.4
Allegany	18,028	79.1	78,400	18.4	11.6	659	28.4	2.4	19,042	-1.8	944	5.0	19,694	34.8	27.4
Bronx	510,135	20.1	427,900	28.6	11.5	1,247	34.8	13.0	606,729	-1.8	82,246	13.6	591,083	26.4	18.9
Broome	79,528	65.1	120,200	18.9	12.2	782	32.0	2.1	81,423	-2.3	4,262	5.2	83,285	39.5	18.9
Cattaraugus	31,999	72.2	90,200	18.7	12.0	654	28.1	3.0	32,847	-2.3	1,740	5.3	33,410	32.4	27.8
Cayuga	30,870	70.9	131,700	18.9	12.2	769	28.6	1.9	35,130	-2.5	1,657	4.7	35,795	34.2	26.1
Chautauqua	53,625	68.6	92,900	17.9	11.9	675	30.3	1.6	52,786	-1.9	2,939	5.6	55,889	32.9	27.4
Chemung	34,328	67.2	108,900	18.0	11.3	862	31.6	1.5	34,549	-3.8	1,815	5.3	37,409	34.3	23.3
Chenango	20,834	74.8	102,300	19.4	11.7	692	29.4	2.1	21,630	-2.2	952	4.4	21,628	32.7	31.4
Clinton	31,557	67.9	139,600	19.4	10.2	835	26.6	2.1	35,269	-2.3	1,630	4.6	36,323	34.1	23.9
Columbia	25,323	73.2	236,500	21.8	12.4	944	27.3	1.3	30,238	-2.0	1,153	3.8	29,352	41.0	20.5
Cortland	17,980	66.2	126,700	19.0	11.9	787	28.4	2.1	22,100	-3.0	1,122	5.1	23,678	36.5	21.2
Delaware	18,930	75.5	144,000	19.9	13.2	700	29.3	1.5	18,914	-0.2	872	4.6	19,905	31.3	29.5
Dutchess	110,095	68.2	290,700	23.0	13.8	1,237	31.5	2.1	142,246	-1.6	6,328	4.4	146,455	41.2	18.1
Erie	392,910	64.8	160,700	18.4	11.8	852	29.6	1.6	435,588	-2.1	23,765	5.5	448,836	41.4	18.0
Essex	16,182	76.4	160,400	19.6	11.6	810	29.5	1.7	16,744	-0.6	789	4.7	16,952	37.1	23.3
Franklin	18,880	72.1	110,600	18.7	11.6	706	29.2	1.9	19,114	-1.7	903	4.7	19,721	32.8	21.3
Fulton	22,406	69.7	120,100	18.2	12.7	777	29.6	1.1	22,353	-2.4	1,232	5.5	24,881	31.7	27.2

1. Specified owner-occupied units. 2. A value of 10.0 represents 10 percent or less; a value of 50.0 represents 50 percent or more. 3. Specified renter-occupied units. 4. Overcrowded or lacking complete plumbing facilities. 5. Percent of civilian labor force. 6. Civilian employed persons 16 years old and over.

STATE County	Private nonfarm establishments, employment and payroll, 2020									Agriculture, 2017			
		Employment						Annual payroll		Farms			Farm producers whose primary occupation is farming (percent)
											Percent with:		
	Number of establish-ments	Total	Health care and social assistance	Manufac-turing	Retail trade	Finance and insurance	Professional, scientific, and technical services	Total (mil dol)	Average per employee (dollars)	Number	Fewer than 50 acres	1000 acres or more	
	104	105	106	107	108	109	110	111	112	113	114	115	116
NEW JERSEY— Cont'd													
Mercer	9,669	202,228	29,320	6,572	26,035	16,730	25,194	15,031	74,326	323	72.1	0.6	35.1
Middlesex	21,651	414,357	56,393	27,352	48,904	14,083	65,090	27,479	66,317	217	82.0	0.9	38.4
Monmouth	19,194	249,614	49,579	8,238	39,731	11,712	20,923	13,456	53,908	838	85.3	0.7	46.4
Morris	16,419	302,883	39,991	15,253	29,479	18,324	46,934	25,276	83,450	418	81.6	NA	29.9
Ocean	13,765	153,423	40,054	5,832	28,285	3,425	8,236	6,242	40,683	260	87.3	NA	38.4
Passaic	11,902	144,368	28,076	16,683	22,539	4,104	7,491	7,183	49,757	89	88.8	NA	39.0
Salem	1,135	16,450	3,022	1,895	1,732	390	437	950	57,781	781	67.3	3.1	39.9
Somerset	9,773	188,791	23,530	14,037	18,665	9,227	24,456	16,648	88,183	452	76.8	2.0	31.5
Sussex	3,093	31,867	5,737	2,897	5,685	873	1,565	1,417	44,462	1,008	75.6	0.7	32.1
Union	13,934	205,090	34,622	13,922	27,105	6,232	16,429	14,249	69,476	9	100.0	NA	69.2
Warren	2,354	28,921	5,020	3,970	5,283	412	1,023	1,490	51,532	918	70.7	1.3	35.6
NEW MEXICO	43,587	651,756	128,446	27,874	91,306	25,586	60,033	28,386	43,554	25,044	52.2	18.2	42.1
Bernalillo	15,823	278,030	53,817	12,567	34,587	12,701	32,930	12,756	45,879	1,248	89.8	1.8	32.2
Catron	66	486	117	34	88	NA	79	16	32,346	341	22.9	29.0	41.3
Chaves	1,346	16,276	3,737	877	2,912	549	727	608	37,338	560	41.3	25.7	44.5
Cibola	296	5,406	1,602	57	842	99	51	199	36,764	640	47.5	18.9	44.9
Colfax	374	3,241	409	158	614	111	60	91	27,953	304	17.8	34.9	38.9
Curry	986	12,668	3,408	794	2,212	402	443	417	32,898	641	21.2	32.4	41.6
De Baca	45	209	46	NA	45	NA	NA	7	32,407	226	44.2	33.2	53.5
Dona Ana	3,675	53,960	16,014	2,729	7,811	1,851	3,741	1,902	35,254	1,946	86.7	1.8	33.1
Eddy	1,520	25,688	2,841	1,148	3,158	663	794	1,416	55,105	507	47.1	18.9	41.7
Grant	547	6,608	1,418	136	1,003	150	141	274	41,405	404	30.4	25.2	44.4
Guadalupe	92	1,045	136	NA	257	11	NA	32	31,078	297	20.2	46.5	54.7
Harding	13	40	NA	NA	11	NA	NA	1	25,000	184	4.9	54.9	49.0
Hidalgo	88	717	98	NA	245	NA	25	19	27,188	151	11.3	45.7	51.5
Lea	1,681	24,558	1,999	558	3,180	445	588	1,173	47,767	555	36.6	28.6	42.9
Lincoln	671	5,295	539	157	1,108	258	146	162	30,586	454	29.7	30.2	36.0
Los Alamos	376	16,172	936	78	470	229	11,863	1,490	92,160	2	100.0	NA	20.0
Luna	389	5,112	1,617	757	904	114	86	138	27,052	211	39.8	25.1	53.0
McKinley	954	15,940	4,378	725	3,251	503	203	554	34,777	2,441	42.4	22.6	53.1
Mora	42	265	140	NA	39	6	NA	8	30,343	700	40.4	9.1	36.0
Otero	913	11,958	2,958	94	2,281	277	423	397	33,236	473	56.0	15.4	43.7
Quay	217	1,828	417	44	379	80	52	50	27,463	613	12.6	36.2	40.7
Rio Arriba	542	5,310	1,294	115	1,110	143	83	177	33,265	1,439	61.8	11.3	36.0
Roosevelt	322	3,353	683	311	408	114	62	118	35,188	742	18.3	31.3	40.7
Sandoval	1,806	27,513	4,930	2,508	3,386	1,760	803	1,162	42,239	1,007	69.0	10.9	33.8
San Juan	2,483	35,209	7,347	1,607	5,929	828	1,171	1,495	42,449	2,965	56.5	21.0	54.9
San Miguel	430	6,194	3,003	32	883	178	95	194	31,300	1,170	35.9	18.6	38.0
Santa Fe	4,760	48,471	8,978	846	8,740	1,493	2,538	2,028	41,840	639	67.9	9.7	35.7
Sierra	213	2,167	571	112	393	58	28	68	31,371	257	38.5	25.3	56.7
Socorro	222	2,894	894	98	416	72	218	92	31,703	658	69.6	12.0	45.7
Taos	1,045	9,682	1,925	325	1,529	167	318	265	27,341	824	78.4	4.1	34.5
Torrance	202	1,771	192	91	502	28	63	56	31,487	716	18.7	22.6	43.2
Union	91	893	134	NA	133	83	13	31	34,983	369	1.1	59.9	47.8
Valencia	957	11,053	1,740	893	2,478	245	322	368	33,293	1,360	91.7	1.5	32.0
NEW YORK	537,369	8,617,513	1,789,810	407,390	917,212	547,123	677,347	601,878	69,844	33,438	36.7	3.3	48.1
Albany	9,347	179,079	38,123	7,817	21,725	11,811	17,317	9,741	54,396	440	37.7	0.9	42.6
Allegany	737	10,977	1,744	1,922	1,094	206	238	391	35,605	789	29.4	2.5	42.7
Bronx	18,183	284,865	117,196	5,648	32,885	3,962	4,999	13,534	47,510	NA	NA	NA	NA
Broome	4,056	69,271	16,740	6,743	10,406	2,019	3,651	3,063	44,217	494	37.2	1.0	41.5
Cattaraugus	1,532	20,505	3,243	2,566	3,375	728	536	787	38,403	956	31.1	1.5	42.9
Cayuga	1,534	18,602	3,848	3,268	3,247	315	398	730	39,237	842	38.7	6.7	53.5
Chautauqua	2,692	39,745	7,767	8,418	5,802	790	823	1,575	39,617	1,228	34.6	2.4	45.3
Chemung	1,691	30,929	7,083	4,903	5,076	847	744	1,275	41,234	398	29.1	1.3	37.8
Chenango	830	13,483	1,681	4,751	1,678	1,088	226	666	49,382	770	28.4	2.5	50.2
Clinton	1,756	24,904	5,730	4,262	4,643	442	562	1,007	40,435	588	27.7	5.8	46.6
Columbia	1,759	16,403	4,408	1,503	2,951	263	614	663	40,412	518	45.4	3.1	46.7
Cortland	1,019	15,065	3,128	2,317	2,264	413	881	554	36,782	536	33.2	2.8	43.6
Delaware	1,047	9,973	1,648	3,242	1,434	366	145	514	51,539	689	28.6	1.6	46.7
Dutchess	7,412	98,011	19,869	7,413	14,135	2,655	7,358	5,007	51,084	620	53.1	3.5	45.5
Erie	22,412	423,814	78,659	44,182	52,587	32,125	27,309	20,275	47,840	940	51.9	2.7	48.7
Essex	1,145	9,994	2,167	779	1,853	198	197	436	43,662	285	40.7	5.6	37.5
Franklin	928	10,556	3,662	558	1,693	180	334	398	37,697	636	25.8	3.3	52.0
Fulton	1,130	13,957	3,305	1,956	2,292	232	294	535	38,348	207	39.6	NA	39.1

STATE County	Agriculture, 2017 (cont.)															
	Land in farms					Value of land and buildings (dollars)		Value of machinery and equipment, average per farm (dollars)	Value of products sold:				Organic farms (number)	Farms with internet access (percent)	Government payments	
			Acres								Percent from:					
	Acreage (1,000)	Percent change, 2012–2017	Average size of farm	Total irrigated (1,000)	Total cropland (1,000)	Average per farm	Average per acre		Total (mil dol)	Average per farm (acres)	Crops	Livestock and poultry products			Total ($1,000)	Percent of farms
	117	118	119	120	121	122	123	124	125	126	127	128	129	130	131	132
NEW JERSEY— Cont'd																
Mercer	25	27.8	78	1.0	15.8	1,414,874	18,114	83,438	25.0	77,344	80.1	19.9	12	73.4	149	8.0
Middlesex	16	-7.2	74	2.0	11.2	1,607,661	21,773	112,644	38.4	176,770	98.0	2.0	2	77.9	92	7.8
Monmouth	39	0.6	47	3.6	23.8	981,430	20,982	79,157	80.6	96,221	83.6	16.4	3	80.5	366	3.3
Morris	15	898.2	35	1.0	6.7	743,975	21,426	68,480	24.8	59,388	93.1	6.9	11	86.4	60	3.1
Ocean	9	6.8	33	0.8	4.4	622,892	19,031	60,677	24.6	94,769	81.1	18.9	3	81.2	59	3.1
Passaic	2	-94.6	21	0.1	0.3	679,638	31,953	47,779	2.9	32,169	95.0	5.0	NA	85.4	8	3.4
Salem	98	-95.0	126	17.1	80.9	1,059,096	8,420	139,528	102.3	131,040	88.3	11.7	4	79.1	1,869	19.3
Somerset	36	-41.2	79	0.9	19.9	1,569,021	19,776	65,277	20.1	44,509	71.5	28.5	13	81.0	148	7.3
Sussex	60	62,156.3	59	0.4	25.7	683,936	11,535	47,928	18.2	18,081	59.4	40.6	9	80.0	310	3.9
Union	0	-99.9	8	0.0	D	1,303,684	156,442	118,929	D	D	D	D	NA	100.0	NA	NA
Warren	74	150.6	80	1.4	46.8	980,498	12,184	76,777	93.2	101,542	72.0	28.0	3	80.7	952	10.6
NEW MEXICO	40,660	-5.9	1,624	626.0	1,825.8	845,740	521	63,619	2,582.3	103,112	25.2	74.8	183	60.5	63,660	13.8
Bernalillo	221	-85.8	177	4.3	6.5	489,688	2,759	34,855	9.3	7,466	51.8	48.2	23	70.5	2	0.4
Catron	1,261	18.4	3,697	1.8	5.1	1,551,601	420	52,857	9.5	27,774	1.4	98.6	5	68.0	970	9.1
Chaves	2,318	251.2	4,140	42.8	62.2	1,957,270	473	164,614	404.5	722,348	10.6	89.4	NA	83.0	2,236	17.0
Cibola	1,594	9,374,482.4	2,490	0.9	5.4	789,275	317	36,619	D	D	100.0	D	4	46.6	476	9.2
Colfax	2,073	135.4	6,819	16.7	19.2	3,442,286	505	77,901	25.1	82,543	3.0	97.0	5	73.4	237	7.9
Curry	902	-15.5	1,407	58.8	428.4	977,762	695	163,697	480.6	749,735	6.6	93.4	5	78.5	14,607	69.4
De Baca	1,182	-28.1	5,231	7.6	10.1	1,962,324	375	85,317	28.1	124,487	19.5	80.5	NA	87.6	1,989	36.7
Dona Ana	528	-53.7	271	73.7	93.1	674,302	2,484	91,093	370.3	190,284	61.8	38.2	23	73.7	578	4.0
Eddy	1,088	-45.1	2,146	31.5	49.3	1,268,345	591	145,419	97.3	191,870	49.5	50.5	NA	82.4	385	9.5
Grant	894	-3.9	2,213	2.0	6.5	1,077,324	487	62,151	14.7	36,507	4.2	95.8	NA	77.7	945	8.4
Guadalupe	1,444	39.7	4,862	4.2	13.3	1,512,859	311	59,332	13.3	44,643	2.3	97.7	NA	65.0	1,851	25.3
Harding	938	20.6	5,100	0.9	14.8	1,868,529	366	D	13.4	73,054	0.3	99.7	NA	70.7	951	33.2
Hidalgo	849	54.3	5,622	18.5	25.5	D	D	157,031	23.4	155,099	55.3	44.7	NA	79.5	1,565	40.4
Lea	1,938	24.8	3,492	42.9	111.9	1,439,038	412	115,880	192.2	346,382	17.3	82.7	4	71.2	2,204	27.7
Lincoln	1,466	19.8	3,230	2.1	6.7	1,607,027	498	56,708	15.9	34,930	2.5	97.5	1	74.9	1,665	17.4
Los Alamos	D	D	D	NA	NA	D	D	D	D	D	NA	D	NA	100.0	NA	NA
Luna	576	-53.9	2,729	20.1	30.0	1,404,258	515	168,893	79.3	375,725	61.1	38.9	1	83.4	2,313	43.1
McKinley	2,570	79.3	1,053	2.5	38.7	450,977	428	26,248	8.1	3,334	7.8	92.2	NA	19.4	600	12.2
Mora	931	-38.7	1,329	11.7	21.2	734,372	552	49,430	18.2	25,931	12.7	87.3	7	52.7	548	4.6
Otero	1,019	-5.4	2,155	4.7	8.6	946,804	439	52,864	18.2	38,395	51.8	48.2	5	79.3	783	8.5
Quay	1,548	14.8	2,526	13.1	199.6	889,432	352	83,453	39.5	64,388	16.2	83.8	1	71.3	7,352	61.3
Rio Arriba	1,362	-47.2	947	26.1	41.7	812,334	858	51,633	14.6	10,172	35.7	64.3	32	60.7	1,114	7.9
Roosevelt	1,500	-36.2	2,021	44.5	317.1	923,240	457	118,420	290.6	391,699	10.4	89.6	12	74.5	10,555	56.5
Sandoval	784	9.2	778	6.9	17.5	415,220	534	33,172	12.4	12,286	63.8	36.2	6	52.2	487	4.1
San Juan	2,551	168.5	861	73.6	107.9	345,734	402	39,425	74.1	24,998	91.5	8.5	1	44.9	1,383	8.3
San Miguel	2,270	21.7	1,940	13.3	22.4	870,177	449	37,470	19.1	16,323	3.7	96.3	7	50.0	1,385	9.2
Santa Fe	D	D	D	15.6	23.7	932,062	881	65,568	25.4	39,798	54.5	45.5	14	77.0	367	5.5
Sierra	1,012	-20.4	3,939	5.8	8.5	1,422,045	361	87,711	31.9	124,093	30.8	69.2	3	75.1	316	9.7
Socorro	912	282.7	1,387	16.2	17.7	870,620	628	65,960	65.1	99,009	14.1	85.9	1	63.1	265	2.3
Taos	285	-57.4	346	15.9	16.6	565,648	1,635	45,157	7.6	9,266	55.0	45.0	17	66.3	270	3.6
Torrance	1,561	-20.7	2,180	16.1	29.8	1,038,912	477	55,855	45.9	64,096	24.7	75.3	NA	63.5	2,311	18.6
Union	1,887	438.1	5,114	15.4	48.9	2,110,381	413	89,284	83.1	225,295	9.8	90.2	NA	66.9	2,896	27.4
Valencia	518	-79.1	381	16.0	18.0	442,410	1,162	47,173	46.1	33,886	10.3	89.7	6	70.1	52	1.1
NEW YORK	6,866	-4.4	205	53.3	4,291.4	663,082	3,229	135,626	5,369.2	160,572	39.3	60.7	1,497	77.1	59,106	19.3
Albany	60	86.9	135	1.1	34.5	601,883	4,446	78,697	47.3	107,564	76.6	23.4	10	79.1	250	16.1
Allegany	162	7.5	205	0.4	88.7	412,662	2,013	85,322	69.3	87,853	37.1	62.9	45	64.6	1,280	28.4
Bronx	NA	NA	NA	NA	NA	NA	NA	NA	NA	NA	NA	NA	NA	NA	NA	NA
Broome	62	-21.6	126	0.5	33.5	390,574	3,089	72,467	32.1	64,953	32.4	67.6	10	73.9	346	14.8
Cattaraugus	166	-15.7	174	0.2	88.7	398,333	2,291	102,151	93.4	97,711	21.3	78.7	11	65.1	650	24.0
Cayuga	225	34.7	267	0.3	177.9	1,057,750	3,955	211,196	287.9	341,868	24.3	75.7	27	76.5	3,092	28.7
Chautauqua	224	-5.5	182	1.0	126.9	481,615	2,645	128,191	161.0	131,081	45.5	54.5	42	78.1	1,621	11.8
Chemung	67	15.1	168	0.1	35.0	440,268	2,619	91,732	19.0	47,771	50.6	49.4	5	78.6	384	19.1
Chenango	149	29.5	193	0.3	77.1	397,806	2,056	104,336	67.9	88,212	26.3	73.7	42	76.2	539	20.6
Clinton	162	9.8	275	0.8	85.1	727,023	2,645	179,004	167.8	285,355	26.6	73.4	8	80.4	127	7.0
Columbia	99	4.0	191	2.1	64.5	801,814	4,188	123,888	88.4	170,718	55.9	44.1	33	83.0	913	12.9
Cortland	114	-19.1	212	0.2	58.5	491,363	2,320	128,057	69.5	129,675	19.7	80.3	46	80.6	592	31.0
Delaware	140	-3.7	204	0.2	67.9	586,225	2,880	89,482	45.7	66,335	29.1	70.9	38	83.3	871	26.1
Dutchess	102	-9.4	164	0.8	40.1	1,486,434	9,040	84,120	43.9	70,818	64.8	35.2	15	88.5	242	8.4
Erie	143	0.3	152	2.0	96.4	696,510	4,576	137,967	131.0	139,333	47.3	52.7	28	81.6	1,405	19.1
Essex	58	5.1	202	0.1	22.7	481,641	2,382	84,723	13.2	46,239	51.4	48.6	12	87.0	209	12.3
Franklin	141	-3.0	221	0.5	74.8	550,272	2,487	114,437	86.4	135,822	18.6	81.4	49	68.9	446	15.9
Fulton	22	-83.1	107	0.1	12.8	299,090	2,791	84,953	10.3	49,609	42.2	57.8	4	78.7	107	11.1

STATE County	Water use, 2015: Public supply water withdrawn (mil gal/ day)	Water use, 2015: Public supply gallons withdrawn per person per day	Wholesale Trade[1], 2017: Number of establish- ments	Wholesale Trade[1], 2017: Number of employees	Wholesale Trade[1], 2017: Sales (mil dol)	Wholesale Trade[1], 2017: Average payroll (mil dol)	Retail Trade[2], 2017: Number of establish- ments	Retail Trade[2], 2017: Number of employees	Retail Trade[2], 2017: Sales (mil dol)	Retail Trade[2], 2017: Average payroll (mil dol)	Real estate and rental and leasing,[2] 2017: Number of establish- ments	Real estate and rental and leasing,[2] 2017: Number of employees	Real estate and rental and leasing,[2] 2017: Sales (mil dol)	Real estate and rental and leasing,[2] 2017: Average payroll (mil dol)
	133	134	135	136	137	138	139	140	141	142	143	144	145	146
NEW JERSEY— Cont'd														
Mercer	37.6	101.3	352	D	10,156.9	D	1,249	25,101	7,573.9	702.8	355	2,142	721.0	109.9
Middlesex	39.1	46.5	1,508	38,219	47,076.2	3,107.7	2,578	44,440	14,856.0	1,271.5	782	7,053	2,843.9	435.0
Monmouth	71.2	113.2	759	6,431	5,475.2	404.8	2,628	40,226	12,274.6	1,122.6	709	4,059	1,221.7	217.1
Morris	90.0	180.2	903	20,136	24,702.2	2,628.2	1,810	29,662	10,433.2	935.9	719	6,579	3,419.9	522.0
Ocean	52.5	89.1	446	3,997	1,839.2	200.0	2,022	28,464	8,720.1	822.7	719	2,973	813.3	128.9
Passaic	270.8	530.0	744	9,561	6,109.2	524.3	1,857	26,191	8,086.8	739.8	450	2,461	671.7	114.2
Salem	4.2	66.1	36	D	1,693.4	D	168	1,917	575.0	46.7	43	285	60.5	12.8
Somerset	2.7	8.1	479	14,123	24,434.3	1,286.6	1,059	18,630	6,750.8	597.5	350	1,905	543.5	103.7
Sussex	5.9	41.3	116	D	521.0	D	412	5,962	1,832.8	160.8	86	265	79.0	13.1
Union	141.5	254.6	788	17,565	21,882.8	2,576.7	1,936	26,666	8,666.6	761.5	548	3,675	1,275.3	177.5
Warren	7.3	67.9	D	D	D	D	374	5,767	1,616.1	153.8	63	226	63.8	9.6
NEW MEXICO	254.1	121.9	1,507	16,914	11,936.9	834.9	6,335	92,557	26,404.3	2,511.3	2,408	9,229	2,185.6	375.8
Bernalillo	87.6	129.5	723	9,958	6,130.8	510.5	1,991	34,299	10,171.3	984.3	999	4,223	1,032.8	167.9
Catron	0.2	43.4	NA	NA	NA	NA	13	75	13.1	1.4	NA	NA	NA	NA
Chaves	11.6	175.9	48	427	212.4	18.0	211	3,114	866.1	78.5	73	200	41.9	7.4
Cibola	2.4	87.1	D	D	D	D	58	826	218.6	19.7	D	D	D	D
Colfax	1.8	145.0	D	D	D	D	73	661	139.8	13.2	D	D	D	1.4
Curry	5.2	103.2	34	378	252.4	13.8	182	2,361	633.6	60.0	61	198	32.7	5.2
De Baca	0.2	131.3	NA	NA	NA	NA	11	56	16.2	1.2	NA	NA	NA	NA
Dona Ana	34.0	158.6	112	1,069	621.0	48.3	498	8,070	2,098.3	191.8	218	686	197.3	19.8
Eddy	13.5	233.6	61	538	2,063.5	32.9	183	2,764	883.8	84.6	68	369	138.0	20.2
Grant	2.5	87.0	D	D	D	D	94	1,141	260.0	28.1	34	80	10.7	2.2
Guadalupe	0.6	132.7	NA	NA	NA	NA	18	254	123.0	6.0	NA	NA	NA	NA
Harding	0.1	114.6	NA	NA	NA	NA	4	10	5.0	0.2	NA	NA	NA	NA
Hidalgo	1.7	391.1	NA	NA	NA	NA	27	251	122.0	5.1	NA	NA	NA	NA
Lea	10.2	143.2	85	1,126	575.2	57.8	218	3,264	1,076.0	95.0	88	613	161.9	37.4
Lincoln	4.4	226.1	7	28	10.5	0.8	135	1,202	291.8	32.1	54	138	20.5	3.5
Los Alamos	3.1	172.1	3	29	21.6	1.7	30	508	146.2	14.2	D	D	D	D
Luna	3.0	122.0	D	D	D	D	64	906	251.8	21.3	19	45	7.0	1.3
McKinley	3.4	44.3	D	D	D	D	216	3,438	922.8	82.9	43	211	35.0	6.3
Mora	0.3	71.8	NA	NA	NA	NA	12	43	13.9	1.0	NA	NA	NA	NA
Otero	6.7	103.9	15	73	17.4	1.8	167	2,376	585.3	57.9	44	157	23.5	4.0
Quay	1.3	149.0	D	D	D	D	33	414	185.2	8.9	11	12	0.9	0.2
Rio Arriba	1.8	46.4	6	12	8.1	0.4	86	1,119	303.4	28.1	D	D	D	D
Roosevelt	2.7	142.3	12	82	65.2	2.9	43	616	135.2	14.9	D	D	D	0.9
Sandoval	11.2	80.6	39	259	128.8	12.7	191	3,450	954.9	91.0	87	270	52.4	10.5
San Juan	18.8	158.6	129	1,053	502.9	57.5	413	5,940	1,744.6	163.8	100	560	141.0	30.8
San Miguel	2.2	78.3	6	25	8.4	1.0	79	942	219.4	21.9	17	42	7.0	1.1
Santa Fe	10.6	71.1	99	856	923.5	44.1	797	9,053	2,588.1	269.2	278	815	200.7	41.4
Sierra	1.5	135.6	NA	NA	NA	NA	43	443	109.6	10.2	8	49	2.9	0.6
Socorro	2.0	115.3	NA	NA	NA	NA	33	400	106.3	9.4	D	D	D	0.4
Taos	2.4	73.2	D	D	D	D	206	1,637	352.5	40.6	58	198	20.0	5.3
Torrance	1.8	113.7	8	30	23.0	1.0	43	490	191.5	11.8	3	4	0.4	0.2
Union	0.5	123.8	NA	NA	NA	NA	16	124	39.1	3.1	NA	NA	NA	NA
Valencia	4.9	65.2	14	61	40.3	2.3	147	2,310	636.0	59.9	41	71	10.5	1.9
NEW YORK	2,424.7	122.5	26,900	330,990	367,972.4	22,510.3	78,260	945,360	291,724.9	27,814.8	34,076	193,442	70,693.0	11,356.8
Albany	45.8	148.0	395	5,782	6,199.4	355.0	1,296	21,679	6,617.7	619.1	441	2,823	763.1	125.4
Allegany	3.1	65.7	18	141	81.5	5.3	132	1,251	247.6	26.0	18	37	5.4	1.3
Bronx	NA	NA	666	11,040	10,255.6	663.8	4,143	34,642	9,150.3	874.3	2,216	9,499	2,401.4	379.4
Broome	18.7	95.3	173	3,505	2,579.6	160.3	686	10,488	2,736.0	258.0	152	901	188.4	32.5
Cattaraugus	9.5	121.3	51	725	621.7	25.1	309	3,749	1,096.0	94.8	50	209	25.7	5.4
Cayuga	5.4	69.4	59	909	502.5	45.1	233	3,320	886.8	85.4	55	160	37.4	4.6
Chautauqua	12.6	96.2	103	1,299	609.7	58.0	469	6,221	1,508.9	150.9	90	479	103.1	17.7
Chemung	8.4	96.1	85	1,216	608.6	56.7	316	5,032	1,378.8	126.2	89	365	98.5	13.6
Chenango	2.2	45.5	23	230	72.7	8.4	157	1,719	478.7	42.9	25	97	13.6	3.4
Clinton	4.9	60.7	73	837	639.1	39.8	346	4,750	1,409.4	121.0	83	311	68.4	11.7
Columbia	3.0	48.3	47	750	345.8	37.8	275	2,915	784.6	82.7	62	168	30.2	5.9
Cortland	3.8	78.4	D	D	D	D	176	2,287	723.5	58.5	38	139	22.3	3.6
Delaware	405.5	8,805.9	28	303	133.7	13.7	189	1,568	462.3	39.2	35	113	14.0	2.6
Dutchess	19.0	64.1	201	1,839	1,146.6	120.7	1,079	15,373	3,909.6	394.9	325	1,240	330.7	49.3
Erie	171.4	185.8	950	17,608	20,991.3	1,026.6	3,269	52,962	13,619.2	1,354.7	895	6,725	1,363.4	260.1
Essex	5.5	141.6	D	D	D	D	207	1,861	502.0	49.8	39	100	20.6	2.6
Franklin	3.8	75.6	23	179	139.6	7.1	167	1,858	551.1	52.4	35	115	16.3	3.3
Fulton	5.5	101.1	41	404	174.9	18.7	202	2,291	752.5	66.0	29	155	18.9	4.2

1 Merchant wholesalers, except manufacturers' sales branches and offices. 2. Employer establishments.

STATE County	Professional, scientific, and technical services, 2017				Manufacturing, 2017				Accommodation and food services, 2017			
	Number of establish-ments	Number of employees	Sales (mil dol)	Average payroll (mil dol)	Number of establish-ments	Number of employees	Sales (mil dol)	Average payroll (mil dol)	Number of establis-hments	Number of employees	Sales (mil dol)	Annual payroll (mil dol)
	147	148	149	150	151	152	153	154	155	156	157	158
NEW JERSEY— Cont'd												
Mercer	1,614	24,223	5,681.5	2,299.6	231	6,743	2,217.8	423.3	867	14,034	912.8	260.6
Middlesex	3,964	59,695	11,905.5	5,156.7	677	27,134	12,418.8	1,771.6	1,791	24,008	1,790.5	448.9
Monmouth	2,550	21,526	4,028.7	1,561.7	404	7,829	2,558.7	461.6	1,832	26,814	1,798.7	493.1
Morris	2,531	45,725	10,267.4	4,443.1	516	15,003	7,076.0	1,038.3	1,343	21,118	1,574.7	438.9
Ocean	D	D	D	D	289	5,060	1,100.4	259.8	1,240	14,722	1,114.8	288.1
Passaic	D	D	D	D	678	16,493	4,908.8	971.3	1,039	11,792	816.9	210.1
Salem	86	577	83.9	30.9	37	2,175	723.8	157.1	100	1,565	83.8	23.5
Somerset	1,739	23,308	5,523.6	2,797.4	263	16,258	7,139.3	1,344.2	849	12,469	941.7	259.4
Sussex	D	D	D	D	109	1,839	504.8	125.7	291	4,567	274.2	77.3
Union	1,367	14,942	2,056.9	1,834.3	565	13,670	12,052.0	877.4	1,221	15,848	1,158.1	301.8
Warren	D	D	D	D	107	3,476	2,020.2	211.6	254	2,949	169.0	46.0
NEW MEXICO	D	D	9,894.7	D	1,332	23,235	13,723.6	1,286.8	4,392	91,601	5,526.0	1,583.2
Bernalillo	D	D	D	D	555	11,441	3,654.6	613.9	1,512	35,165	2,064.5	616.6
Catron	NA	NA	NA	NA	4	15	4.4	1.0	7	D	1.1	D
Chaves	D	D	D	D	32	774	629.2	38.4	127	2,398	124.5	35.3
Cibola	D	D	D	D	8	62	5.2	1.8	40	1,124	85.3	20.5
Colfax	D	D	D	D	12	103	12.0	4.0	63	1,160	78.3	25.7
Curry	D	D	D	D	25	636	979.4	30.4	82	1,796	89.7	24.7
De Baca	NA	NA	NA	NA	NA	NA	NA	NA	5	D	1.4	D
Dona Ana	D	D	D	D	139	2,065	922.8	92.7	335	7,168	361.2	106.7
Eddy	D	D	D	D	D	1,161	D	104.7	129	2,455	163.8	40.9
Grant	D	D	D	D	16	124	12.1	4.1	70	994	38.1	10.5
Guadalupe	NA	NA	NA	NA	NA	NA	NA	NA	21	359	21.1	5.1
Harding	NA	NA	NA	NA	NA	NA	NA	NA	NA	NA	NA	NA
Hidalgo	D	D	D	D	NA	NA	NA	NA	17	193	10.9	3.5
Lea	D	D	D	D	33	702	615.9	54.7	150	2,768	229.0	47.3
Lincoln	D	D	D	D	14	67	9.6	2.6	85	1,149	67.7	19.5
Los Alamos	D	D	D	D	12	78	14.9	3.2	31	513	30.6	9.8
Luna	D	D	D	D	9	402	83.4	15.0	63	803	35.5	10.1
McKinley	D	D	D	D	D	402	D	30.1	149	2,905	151.4	39.5
Mora	NA	NA	NA	NA	NA	NA	NA	NA	D	D	D	0.1
Otero	D	D	D	D	30	74	12.2	2.5	96	2,258	179.5	49.0
Quay	D	D	D	D	D	20	D	1.3	36	480	25.0	6.9
Rio Arriba	D	D	D	D	14	94	19.6	3.7	71	1,533	118.7	31.0
Roosevelt	D	D	D	D	9	218	420.3	11.9	34	559	23.6	6.6
Sandoval	D	D	D	D	59	2,006	1,327.7	141.8	168	4,574	309.5	82.3
San Juan	D	D	D	D	69	776	154.0	43.1	240	4,900	237.5	68.0
San Miguel	D	D	D	D	6	38	5.4	1.5	71	976	49.6	12.1
Santa Fe	654	2,391	386.8	146.3	120	725	165.9	32.3	429	9,749	743.9	226.0
Sierra	D	D	D	D	5	95	23.6	4.3	43	486	22.2	6.7
Socorro	D	D	D	D	9	67	19.4	3.5	35	533	26.5	7.0
Taos	D	D	D	D	35	196	42.0	6.6	160	2,479	140.4	44.6
Torrance	12	45	3.2	1.1	14	101	35.1	4.0	19	174	9.4	2.3
Union	D	D	D	D	NA	NA	NA	NA	15	134	7.1	2.0
Valencia	72	336	37.7	13.5	35	772	168.1	32.8	85	1,743	78.6	22.0
NEW YORK	61,306	633,235	167,190.7	58,010.8	15,499	411,100	155,571.9	23,751.3	54,797	824,806	66,963.5	19,792.9
Albany	1,213	14,825	2,673.3	1,101.2	234	8,444	3,864.8	504.8	1,057	16,422	1,001.2	310.1
Allegany	D	D	D	D	36	2,047	810.3	109.8	94	1,433	69.3	17.6
Bronx	D	D	D	D	312	6,037	1,600.0	249.1	1,954	18,882	1,418.7	380.3
Broome	D	D	D	D	165	7,110	2,511.7	438.5	539	8,809	448.5	139.1
Cattaraugus	D	D	D	D	72	2,790	718.0	154.3	209	4,044	337.8	75.8
Cayuga	85	432	48.4	19.5	82	2,957	1,166.0	157.6	174	1,939	112.0	30.8
Chautauqua	D	D	D	41.1	186	9,055	3,675.5	446.5	361	5,209	228.1	73.0
Chemung	D	D	D	D	82	5,229	1,296.9	286.3	210	3,073	157.5	50.4
Chenango	D	D	D	D	64	4,336	2,290.0	247.3	100	842	44.8	14.8
Clinton	108	447	56.4	20.7	91	4,135	1,585.0	214.2	200	2,797	173.6	50.7
Columbia	D	D	D	D	81	1,396	381.5	62.2	197	1,726	107.8	34.2
Cortland	D	D	D	D	56	2,125	555.4	104.5	146	3,064	150.9	44.5
Delaware	71	190	19.5	6.2	53	3,319	3,299.5	192.1	118	999	43.2	12.8
Dutchess	D	D	D	D	186	5,837	2,038.1	453.8	846	10,846	655.2	196.8
Erie	D	D	D	D	963	44,061	18,569.3	2,749.0	2,377	45,506	2,373.7	738.0
Essex	D	D	D	D	30	833	339.5	57.0	219	2,455	187.7	60.7
Franklin	D	D	D	D	26	437	322.5	19.3	110	1,774	194.4	42.6
Fulton	66	282	27.5	9.4	71	1,951	997.0	84.9	132	1,171	70.0	20.5

STATE County	Health care and social assistance, 2017				Other services, 2017				Nonemployer businesses, 2019		Value of residential construction authorized by building permits, 2021	
	Number of establish-ments	Number of employees	Receipts (mil dol)	Annual payroll (mil dol)	Number of establish-ments	Number of employees	Receipts (mil dol)	Annual payroll (mil dol)	Number	Receipts (mil dol)	New construction ($1,000)	Number of housing units
	159	160	161	162	163	164	165	166	167	168	169	170
NEW JERSEY— Cont'd												
Mercer	1,192	30,342	3,364.8	1,424.9	854	6,011	1,423.0	276.7	28,098	1,542.4	53,328	544
Middlesex	2,349	53,954	6,618.6	2,656.7	1,600	10,288	1,910.1	413.5	64,680	3,731.0	308,827	3,269
Monmouth	2,449	48,971	6,222.5	2,420.3	1,509	9,977	944.3	287.6	59,923	4,201.1	404,790	2,350
Morris	1,773	41,323	5,330.0	2,230.4	1,303	8,512	1,164.8	300.0	46,153	3,234.4	355,076	2,127
Ocean	1,693	38,798	4,219.5	1,700.7	1,120	5,885	640.5	159.4	47,098	2,941.9	704,529	3,758
Passaic	1,539	27,424	3,127.3	1,259.2	1,022	5,147	556.9	148.7	46,302	2,367.4	101,898	1,144
Salem	159	3,203	300.5	125.5	101	421	35.7	9.8	2,965	169.2	15,813	88
Somerset	1,235	23,730	2,963.2	1,216.8	728	4,733	703.4	172.5	29,016	1,998.1	140,243	1,261
Sussex	379	7,037	662.9	274.1	302	1,311	142.9	37.4	11,486	632.5	31,384	164
Union	1,526	35,061	3,951.0	1,634.5	1,214	7,816	775.5	261.8	49,467	2,806.3	287,584	3,207
Warren	307	5,117	521.9	208.3	231	1,084	120.9	35.4	7,507	390.7	25,423	189
NEW MEXICO	5,134	127,808	13,602.4	5,405.5	2,963	17,547	2,085.4	558.2	129,145	5,516.5	148,552	548
Bernalillo	1,967	52,986	6,259.9	2,466.1	1,116	7,479	868.5	246.4	43,264	1,917.6	371,819	1,924
Catron	D	D	D	2.4	3	10	2.0	0.3	361	14.2	NA	NA
Chaves	186	4,109	415.1	182.2	79	523	45.6	11.3	3,132	153.4	17,474	92
Cibola	52	1,666	150.9	64.3	17	58	7.0	1.9	1,061	33.7	NA	NA
Colfax	26	473	42.9	18.2	29	89	11.7	2.2	842	29.4	NA	NA
Curry	114	2,763	249.7	102.0	80	461	52.4	11.6	1,947	83.8	26,869	156
De Baca	D	D	D	D	NA	NA	NA	NA	117	4.9	NA	NA
Dona Ana	553	14,627	1,251.4	527.1	238	1,142	93.0	29.4	13,662	542.6	333,151	1,338
Eddy	113	2,814	291.0	122.4	85	651	93.7	21.6	2,870	171.6	32,289	129
Grant	72	1,411	134.7	56.1	43	215	14.7	4.4	1,637	51.6	0	0
Guadalupe	7	119	12.3	4.7	D	D	D	D	187	5.9	NA	NA
Harding	NA	NA	NA	NA	NA	NA	NA	NA	49	2.1	NA	NA
Hidalgo	14	185	10.0	4.6	D	D	0.3	D	198	7.5	NA	NA
Lea	116	2,422	276.1	101.7	94	643	117.5	28.4	4,202	245.4	53,033	211
Lincoln	43	566	62.7	26.2	37	151	14.6	4.5	1,979	90.7	31,341	91
Los Alamos	69	986	98.2	40.6	36	215	14.5	3.9	1,067	44.1	10,211	40
Luna	47	1,126	96.9	35.3	25	91	7.0	1.7	1,057	44.1	1,627	8
McKinley	121	5,228	518.2	196.9	68	403	38.7	10.5	2,991	74.4	615	2
Mora	6	D	6.1	D	D	D	D	0.2	261	8.9	NA	NA
Otero	112	3,083	361.9	125.4	68	334	23.7	6.8	3,505	129.6	891	3
Quay	20	369	34.8	11.9	D	D	D	2.2	383	15.8	NA	NA
Rio Arriba	80	1,736	169.7	71.0	27	179	18.7	5.6	1,785	57.7	NA	NA
Roosevelt	34	638	57.5	26.4	D	D	D	D	776	36.0	4,742	31
Sandoval	234	3,996	540.2	170.3	108	555	49.1	15.3	8,758	329.8	312,052	1,789
San Juan	282	7,628	874.3	352.8	202	1,305	207.0	44.1	5,094	217.1	25,463	97
San Miguel	73	3,090	187.3	90.0	28	74	6.2	1.6	1,277	42.0	0	0
Santa Fe	510	9,791	1,131.9	426.1	351	2,038	294.6	82.2	17,159	822.2	133,831	840
Sierra	20	720	47.9	25.2	D	D	D	2.8	771	27.7	0	0
Socorro	35	1,092	56.4	30.2	D	D	D	D	726	23.9	NA	NA
Taos	97	1,723	136.5	65.9	62	257	23.2	7.0	3,472	114.6	33,835	146
Torrance	15	168	8.5	4.2	7	13	1.5	0.4	832	31.8	NA	NA
Union	6	171	13.9	6.6	10	21	2.2	0.5	281	8.3	NA	NA
Valencia	101	1,748	97.5	42.8	64	250	22.8	6.2	3,442	133.7	84,492	308
NEW YORK	58,902	1,654,593	193,507.6	80,687.9	48,436	299,209	51,749.9	11,845.9	1,806,664	100,791.5	7,652,184	40,135
Albany	964	35,623	4,402.0	1,717.5	843	6,034	847.2	249.8	19,941	1,042.2	201,838	889
Allegany	94	1,882	133.3	63.4	73	282	23.7	5.5	2,438	96.4	3,118	34
Bronx	2,471	108,072	13,367.5	5,550.1	1,922	8,817	1,043.7	274.8	120,204	4,262.8	615,409	5,348
Broome	481	16,077	1,758.5	716.0	345	1,819	171.5	46.1	10,090	424.4	34,346	336
Cattaraugus	165	3,370	375.6	135.6	130	660	67.1	15.8	3,665	151.9	25,898	128
Cayuga	197	4,023	361.0	180.3	124	465	57.5	13.0	4,246	179.4	12,653	72
Chautauqua	269	7,795	653.3	278.3	267	1,417	117.1	27.6	7,036	281.5	25,384	88
Chemung	210	6,480	650.8	310.8	132	632	67.9	16.9	3,894	139.2	17,975	138
Chenango	112	1,890	172.0	68.0	81	271	29.2	7.9	2,702	105.1	11,033	211
Clinton	238	5,480	582.6	282.0	114	578	52.2	17.0	4,006	173.8	36,687	172
Columbia	173	4,319	378.7	172.1	105	517	56.2	14.3	6,593	319.0	36,836	101
Cortland	124	3,428	273.6	115.1	88	419	39.1	10.8	2,416	107.1	8,665	43
Delaware	121	2,325	179.0	75.4	85	365	59.0	11.8	3,728	157.3	15,818	83
Dutchess	888	20,003	2,503.7	977.5	636	2,897	317.4	86.2	23,414	1,194.3	183,521	522
Erie	2,725	79,702	9,058.2	3,756.3	1,865	12,072	1,197.5	353.9	54,312	2,501.7	413,407	1,348
Essex	157	2,046	175.2	79.4	66	284	40.6	9.9	3,055	134.1	66,567	241
Franklin	169	3,841	355.3	170.6	62	207	20.6	5.0	2,733	109.6	16,018	92
Fulton	185	4,117	316.0	147.2	85	561	49.3	15.4	2,728	107.9	12,370	70

STATE County	Government employment and payroll, 2017: Full-time equivalent employees	Government employment and payroll, 2017: March payroll (dollars)	March payroll (percent of total): Administration, judicial, and legal	March payroll (percent of total): Police and corrections	March payroll (percent of total): Fire protection	March payroll (percent of total): Highways and transportation	March payroll (percent of total): Health and welfare	March payroll (percent of total): Natural resources and utilities	March payroll (percent of total): Education and libraries	Local government finances, 2017, General revenue: Total (mil dol)	General revenue: Intergovernmental (mil dol)	Taxes: Total (mil dol)	Taxes: Per capita[1] (dollars): Total	Taxes: Per capita[1] (dollars): Property
	171	172	173	174	175	176	177	178	179	180	181	182	183	184
NEW JERSEY— Cont'd														
Mercer	14,557	89,476,151	6.3	11.2	3.5	2.2	5.1	4.7	64.1	2,186.7	669.9	1,243.6	3,378	3,332
Middlesex	28,682	174,474,309	3.9	12.8	3.1	1.5	4.1	4.0	67.9	4,052.3	1,017.5	2,417.5	2,922	2,859
Monmouth	25,418	150,306,285	5.1	13.0	0.8	3.0	1.9	4.3	70.3	3,544.9	749.5	2,385.0	3,835	3,757
Morris	20,249	117,120,799	4.5	10.0	0.7	2.8	2.9	4.7	72.3	2,941.5	383.6	2,069.1	4,189	4,143
Ocean	19,831	110,436,008	5.3	14.9	0.6	2.7	3.7	6.9	63.3	2,680.0	623.3	1,810.6	3,041	2,999
Passaic	16,364	100,071,382	4.9	16.6	4.9	1.6	7.6	4.5	58.5	2,409.2	721.9	1,497.3	2,969	2,935
Salem	3,265	17,256,254	5.4	13.2	0.1	2.6	3.8	2.7	70.7	374.1	142.8	179.1	2,848	2,819
Somerset	12,816	76,918,330	4.3	11.0	0.6	3.1	1.9	3.4	72.7	1,760.0	223.3	1,327.1	4,015	3,945
Sussex	5,872	32,546,214	6.3	9.5	0.2	4.2	1.6	1.6	75.0	809.3	168.7	564.0	3,994	3,976
Union	23,177	138,986,930	4.5	15.1	5.5	2.7	4.6	2.8	61.9	3,548.8	1,149.2	2,086.1	3,761	3,669
Warren	4,148	22,171,732	7.0	11.6	0.0	4.6	3.0	2.0	69.5	590.3	166.2	370.7	3,506	3,477
NEW MEXICO	X	X	X	X	X	X	X	X	X	X	X	X	X	X
Bernalillo	22,858	98,449,958	6.5	17.0	7.0	7.0	4.0	6.8	49.6	2,642.9	1,232.0	981.7	1,448	821
Catron	135	474,259	10.1	7.7	0.1	6.7	0.0	5.1	69.6	14.5	9.0	2.5	701	595
Chaves	2,412	8,352,745	4.6	13.6	5.0	4.0	0.5	7.3	63.8	230.8	170.6	37.7	579	502
Cibola	995	3,157,600	10.2	11.2	1.7	3.1	3.9	3.7	61.3	105.6	46.3	23.4	869	352
Colfax	675	2,163,084	8.0	10.4	4.2	4.0	9.1	12.5	45.4	67.0	29.8	23.4	1,925	1,114
Curry	2,069	7,073,175	3.3	8.6	5.0	2.7	1.0	3.6	74.1	190.0	106.4	58.3	1,170	379
De Baca	127	391,523	9.7	10.1	6.0	6.6	3.4	14.3	49.9	13.9	6.9	2.5	1,390	984
Dona Ana	8,033	28,795,832	4.8	11.2	3.2	1.7	1.5	6.9	65.2	760.4	405.6	260.8	1,206	537
Eddy	2,423	10,400,192	6.9	15.4	6.1	5.1	0.7	8.8	53.4	355.2	123.0	186.3	3,263	1,658
Grant	1,550	5,780,581	5.0	7.4	1.7	3.3	42.0	3.2	35.8	186.2	72.9	34.7	1,254	629
Guadalupe	265	783,103	12.6	8.6	0.0	5.8	1.5	7.4	60.5	23.8	14.4	6.9	1,573	779
Harding	69	216,806	19.0	3.5	0.0	11.8	4.0	3.2	56.0	9.5	5.3	2.6	3,857	3,437
Hidalgo	234	697,509	9.8	23.7	0.0	4.0	5.1	5.8	48.7	26.4	13.0	7.3	1,702	1,001
Lea	3,711	14,993,130	3.8	12.1	3.6	2.3	19.3	4.9	51.0	525.6	234.4	167.6	2,427	1,425
Lincoln	830	2,957,511	11.5	11.4	3.2	4.9	1.5	13.3	51.8	102.6	44.8	39.6	2,033	1,234
Los Alamos	1,188	4,973,128	7.7	6.7	16.3	4.1	1.5	14.0	44.1	133.5	74.3	39.6	2,112	830
Luna	1,175	3,345,403	6.3	15.3	2.2	2.9	1.2	4.4	63.7	108.0	69.2	23.7	983	523
McKinley	3,490	10,015,812	4.5	8.3	3.2	1.7	1.2	4.6	75.9	279.2	175.9	73.1	1,009	314
Mora	195	575,840	10.2	3.9	0.0	3.4	3.1	3.6	72.8	26.5	10.3	8.6	1,898	1,650
Otero	1,684	5,230,317	7.5	14.4	1.7	2.1	1.6	5.4	64.2	161.8	92.2	50.4	762	358
Quay	576	1,668,229	5.4	8.5	0.2	3.0	5.2	9.2	64.8	57.4	36.8	11.8	1,421	707
Rio Arriba	1,409	4,355,659	9.9	7.3	1.8	2.2	4.6	6.2	64.2	138.1	68.9	47.6	1,212	790
Roosevelt	732	2,561,527	6.9	10.6	3.8	2.9	0.3	3.9	70.5	71.1	41.8	16.6	879	638
Sandoval	3,840	14,507,749	7.3	12.9	5.7	2.8	1.2	3.6	64.9	441.1	223.4	150.0	1,051	647
San Juan	5,621	20,270,322	4.8	12.1	2.9	2.2	1.4	10.3	64.6	518.5	323.9	118.0	930	655
San Miguel	1,122	3,368,535	8.8	7.8	3.9	2.6	1.2	8.0	67.5	101.2	58.7	31.0	1,120	540
Santa Fe	5,045	19,287,175	8.7	13.7	6.2	5.6	3.3	12.0	47.2	639.4	266.4	264.5	1,769	1,075
Sierra	670	2,240,852	7.0	6.5	0.2	2.3	45.9	4.7	30.1	56.6	20.9	11.1	1,004	593
Socorro	649	1,830,078	8.6	12.5	4.1	3.3	3.1	11.4	56.1	56.1	35.8	12.6	751	383
Taos	1,259	3,729,730	12.2	10.7	1.4	2.3	2.3	7.3	56.9	139.1	64.1	54.2	1,654	827
Torrance	744	2,293,228	6.7	8.0	0.8	2.8	1.2	2.4	76.9	82.9	42.7	18.9	1,217	842
Union	192	631,110	13.8	11.4	3.7	9.3	2.8	4.5	50.9	21.9	11.2	5.9	1,403	528
Valencia	2,566	8,587,011	4.5	7.4	1.2	1.1	1.8	3.3	79.9	209.0	121.7	70.0	923	558
NEW YORK	X	X	X	X	X	X	X	X	X	X	X	X	X	X
Albany	12,758	68,164,060	5.4	14.9	2.8	3.5	7.9	5.2	58.9	1,876.3	544.6	1,096.3	3,563	2,264
Allegany	2,356	9,274,123	7.5	7.8	0.0	7.6	7.6	3.5	63.5	306.4	173.2	107.9	2,314	1,861
Bronx	(2)	(2)	(2)	(2)	(2)	(2)	(2)	(2)	(2)	(2)	(2)	(2)	(2)	(2)
Broome	10,984	43,183,824	4.5	8.2	2.7	4.7	8.2	3.3	66.7	1,399.3	665.2	568.2	2,943	1,998
Cattaraugus	5,125	20,920,176	4.4	6.2	1.4	6.2	10.5	2.6	67.2	585.6	318.5	198.5	2,572	1,880
Cayuga	3,718	16,218,981	6.1	8.2	2.6	4.9	6.6	2.7	68.3	455.1	195.1	195.0	2,517	1,641
Chautauqua	6,354	28,121,337	4.9	7.5	2.0	6.6	8.3	2.9	66.6	836.7	417.4	317.9	2,477	1,721
Chemung	4,253	19,683,127	4.4	7.8	2.9	4.7	9.4	3.1	66.7	507.5	228.8	195.1	2,303	1,450
Chenango	3,098	12,262,824	6.1	5.9	1.1	6.9	5.9	1.7	71.5	326.2	173.8	116.7	2,442	1,844
Clinton	3,990	18,137,505	5.8	5.8	1.7	6.5	8.6	3.5	66.9	511.2	222.1	222.8	2,766	1,838
Columbia	2,773	12,572,682	8.9	8.7	0.3	7.7	9.6	1.9	60.9	399.3	132.8	223.3	3,702	2,760
Cortland	2,079	8,544,216	7.5	10.6	3.1	5.5	7.7	3.3	57.9	297.7	132.7	133.0	2,782	1,883
Delaware	2,416	9,750,539	7.6	5.4	0.1	11.6	7.4	2.4	64.3	315.4	130.7	151.3	3,361	2,826
Dutchess	11,879	65,652,723	5.5	9.3	2.8	3.6	4.9	1.7	71.1	1,807.5	556.7	1,088.9	3,710	2,909
Erie	38,244	195,946,904	3.5	10.3	2.6	3.0	13.9	4.7	60.7	5,952.6	2,418.3	2,549.9	2,775	1,656
Essex	1,873	7,617,938	11.6	6.3	0.3	11.2	8.9	5.6	54.0	273.4	84.1	156.6	4,176	3,231
Franklin	2,753	10,599,267	6.3	5.3	1.0	6.5	6.7	3.2	69.9	343.4	188.3	114.0	2,259	1,777
Fulton	2,755	10,604,219	5.2	7.9	2.9	5.3	5.1	2.1	70.7	323.1	159.4	132.3	2,459	1,786

1. Based on the resident population estimated as of July 1 of the year shown. 2. Bronx, Kings, Queens, and Richmond counties are included with New York county.

STATE County	Local government finances, 2017 (cont.)									Government employment, 2020			Individual income tax returns, 2019		
	Direct general expenditure							Debt outstanding							
			Percent of total for:												
	Total (mil dol)	Per capita[1] (dollars)	Education	Health and hospitals	Police protection	Public welfare	Highways	Total (mil dol)	Per capita[1] (dollars)	Federal civilian	Federal military	State and local	Number of returns	Mean adjusted gross income	Mean income tax
	185	186	187	188	189	190	191	192	193	194	195	196	197	198	199
NEW JERSEY— Cont'd															
Mercer	2,256.8	6,130	55.2	1.0	5.6	3.2	1.4	1,839.7	4,997	2,348	708	36,844	180,880	97,512	14,623
Middlesex	4,151.3	5,018	58.9	0.9	6.1	2.2	1.5	3,453.9	4,175	2,570	1,627	51,272	416,670	83,996	10,687
Monmouth	3,913.5	6,292	54.7	1.1	6.0	1.6	5.0	1,993.6	3,205	2,023	1,588	31,593	327,070	115,996	18,901
Morris	2,762.3	5,593	59.0	2.0	5.9	1.8	3.1	1,620.6	3,281	5,761	1,092	25,127	257,080	137,369	23,658
Ocean	2,623.9	4,407	55.0	0.4	7.2	3.0	3.7	1,565.9	2,630	3,441	1,586	24,415	298,470	72,432	8,220
Passaic	2,543.9	5,043	48.3	2.2	6.5	3.9	1.7	2,460.6	4,878	1,118	977	26,940	257,600	63,093	7,166
Salem	414.7	6,594	64.0	0.9	4.0	1.2	1.8	181.2	2,882	163	123	4,019	30,990	62,831	6,173
Somerset	1,851.5	5,601	61.7	3.4	4.4	0.2	1.7	1,194.1	3,612	1,796	645	16,020	172,630	132,318	22,912
Sussex	769.4	5,449	63.6	1.4	3.8	2.1	4.2	334.2	2,367	358	278	6,848	73,540	84,362	10,482
Union	3,483.3	6,279	57.0	1.9	6.0	1.5	2.1	2,156.3	3,887	1,491	1,101	30,655	283,230	93,397	14,342
Warren	613.4	5,802	59.8	2.3	4.1	2.3	3.4	178.2	1,686	251	207	4,969	55,190	73,877	8,210
NEW MEXICO	X	X	X	X	X	X	X	X	X	30,187	18,074	153,403	962,820	57,598	6,007
Bernalillo	2,382.5	3,513	49.8	1.6	9.2	1.7	2.3	3,424.6	5,050	14,458	5,281	53,759	327,170	60,890	6,593
Catron	18.6	5,247	36.7	1.0	5.1	0.0	24.1	4.5	1,261	95	10	200	1,390	40,877	3,276
Chaves	230.2	3,537	54.3	0.6	7.7	1.4	5.0	75.5	1,161	261	167	4,079	26,510	49,915	5,126
Cibola	110.5	4,105	37.4	27.2	4.3	0.7	5.6	38.2	1,420	272	60	2,649	9,780	39,001	2,692
Colfax	71.1	5,848	35.6	6.1	7.0	0.7	6.5	83.0	6,833	52	29	1,131	5,610	43,446	3,524
Curry	189.8	3,812	57.8	0.0	5.1	0.8	7.3	99.8	2,004	919	4,844	2,330	21,020	43,110	3,452
De Baca	15.2	8,416	30.9	23.8	4.9	0.3	9.5	4.3	2,374	12	4	161	750	41,504	3,676
Dona Ana	708.9	3,279	60.6	1.6	7.6	2.3	2.1	452.3	2,092	3,483	884	16,404	98,100	47,140	4,238
Eddy	341.4	5,977	45.0	1.5	7.8	1.5	6.3	163.4	2,862	715	145	3,041	25,610	104,428	15,161
Grant	185.9	6,725	25.4	46.6	4.9	1.7	2.3	94.7	3,425	214	67	2,867	12,570	48,578	4,295
Guadalupe	28.2	6,395	39.1	0.5	4.9	0.6	3.1	15.0	3,405	27	9	378	1,830	32,721	2,048
Harding	8.1	11,769	42.3	0.7	1.4	0.9	21.9	6.9	10,140	13	2	80	290	33,741	2,234
Hidalgo	26.2	6,105	41.5	2.6	17.8	0.5	5.7	9.2	2,133	283	10	338	1,770	39,019	2,677
Lea	498.4	7,219	44.3	16.0	6.4	1.3	3.1	311.0	4,504	111	179	3,647	29,880	64,287	6,739
Lincoln	96.5	4,955	38.6	2.9	12.9	1.1	3.6	98.5	5,057	103	52	1,067	9,490	52,374	5,305
Los Alamos	154.5	8,245	29.4	0.0	5.9	2.5	4.9	133.1	7,099	250	52	1,588	9,740	113,299	14,983
Luna	117.9	4,892	58.7	0.9	7.4	1.6	3.1	78.7	3,266	447	59	1,503	11,010	34,452	2,118
McKinley	268.0	3,700	61.8	1.8	4.1	1.2	3.4	90.6	1,251	2,399	177	4,374	30,500	35,829	2,466
Mora	24.9	5,503	41.9	0.9	2.2	0.0	0.1	7.3	1,620	40	11	236	1,980	36,683	2,415
Otero	149.3	2,258	50.8	1.2	9.4	1.4	4.5	207.2	3,134	1,783	4,356	3,802	28,660	43,786	3,367
Quay	52.7	6,349	56.2	4.8	4.0	2.3	5.3	23.8	2,872	32	21	734	3,690	33,958	2,374
Rio Arriba	124.5	3,172	54.4	2.1	4.1	0.1	2.9	83.6	2,130	296	96	4,038	17,030	45,338	3,637
Roosevelt	68.9	3,647	58.4	0.1	6.3	2.4	4.8	43.9	2,321	54	44	2,064	7,550	38,581	3,066
Sandoval	401.6	2,814	56.4	0.1	6.3	1.6	4.9	609.9	4,275	384	374	6,981	70,750	63,707	6,416
San Juan	564.6	4,449	58.2	1.5	6.0	1.7	3.7	2,061.0	16,239	1,567	307	9,093	49,970	51,825	4,633
San Miguel	107.1	3,865	59.1	0.8	4.9	0.7	4.0	90.4	3,260	146	65	3,161	11,520	39,874	2,996
Santa Fe	553.0	3,699	43.8	0.0	7.4	1.4	2.9	844.6	5,650	979	382	14,051	79,840	80,425	10,444
Sierra	49.9	4,507	35.1	36.7	3.0	0.0	3.4	29.5	2,667	91	27	780	5,040	36,031	2,765
Socorro	59.5	3,538	49.7	0.4	6.1	0.0	6.0	33.2	1,973	187	41	2,324	6,860	39,698	2,993
Taos	136.6	4,166	40.0	2.2	3.8	1.3	4.5	126.7	3,862	287	81	1,700	16,340	43,765	4,078
Torrance	77.7	5,002	59.9	3.4	3.7	0.0	2.6	239.4	15,408	79	38	869	6,090	42,073	3,508
Union	23.6	5,647	37.2	6.5	7.1	0.0	8.0	15.7	3,755	40	8	366	1,600	37,082	3,438
Valencia	175.2	2,309	78.4	0.0	5.2	0.0	1.2	180.8	2,382	108	192	3,608	32,990	47,666	3,789
NEW YORK	X	X	X	X	X	X	X	X	X	120,546	54,755	1,288,372	9,760,440	87,620	13,677
Albany	1,840.0	5,980	45.1	4.7	5.9	11.0	3.1	1,378.3	4,479	5,482	687	55,499	155,410	90,904	13,317
Allegany	298.5	6,399	52.7	2.5	1.4	9.4	9.1	222.8	4,777	118	98	3,867	18,600	51,572	4,338
Bronx	(2)	(2)	(2)	(2)	(2)	(2)	(2)	(2)	(2)	4,450	2,275	72,299	671,360	41,648	3,331
Broome	1,443.9	7,478	45.7	3.2	2.5	14.0	4.1	970.7	5,027	534	282	16,356	88,540	58,557	6,019
Cattaraugus	607.2	7,868	45.0	6.7	2.9	12.4	9.1	354.5	4,594	257	122	8,325	34,290	50,745	4,370
Cayuga	446.9	5,770	50.3	2.8	2.8	8.9	6.7	323.2	4,172	158	120	5,313	35,520	57,086	5,468
Chautauqua	849.6	6,618	52.5	2.7	3.1	10.1	6.5	596.2	4,644	316	191	8,554	57,030	50,670	4,348
Chemung	499.8	5,899	45.2	2.9	3.2	18.4	5.7	196.0	2,313	224	126	6,054	39,040	58,489	5,843
Chenango	322.5	6,746	57.5	3.0	1.4	7.3	7.4	154.1	3,223	104	73	3,839	22,370	50,425	4,160
Clinton	512.6	6,365	50.0	5.6	1.9	11.2	5.5	255.5	3,172	727	117	7,043	37,020	57,469	5,315
Columbia	399.7	6,624	49.2	4.4	2.2	11.6	8.4	214.4	3,554	167	91	4,037	30,700	77,470	10,385
Cortland	322.6	6,748	46.6	3.8	3.5	9.2	7.6	205.1	4,289	126	70	4,048	20,800	54,153	4,614
Delaware	318.1	7,065	48.9	2.6	1.3	8.5	11.5	127.5	2,830	155	69	3,937	20,030	53,178	4,913
Dutchess	1,777.4	6,055	56.4	3.1	3.4	7.5	4.9	1,010.3	3,442	1,470	437	17,413	146,420	82,660	10,728
Erie	5,952.2	6,477	45.4	12.2	4.1	10.2	3.5	5,083.2	5,531	8,927	1,597	62,150	461,620	65,952	7,578
Essex	263.4	7,026	38.8	5.2	1.3	7.6	11.6	183.8	4,904	314	59	3,642	18,240	57,483	5,643
Franklin	357.6	7,087	56.4	3.5	1.6	9.0	6.3	213.7	4,234	177	70	6,785	20,700	52,232	4,571
Fulton	337.1	6,265	55.1	1.7	2.4	13.2	4.6	134.4	2,499	97	82	3,198	25,230	52,370	4,577

1. Based on the resident population estimated as of July 1 of the year shown. 2. Bronx, Kings, Queens, and Richmond counties are included with New York county.

State / county code	CBSA code[1]	County Type code[2]	STATE County	Land area[3] (sq. mi)	Population, 2021: Total persons 2021	Population, 2021: Rank	Population, 2021: Per square mile	Race alone or in combination, not Hispanic or Latino (percent): White	Black	American Indian, Alaska Native	Asian and Pacific Islancer	Percent Hispanic or Latino[4]	Age (percent): Under 5 years	5 to 17 years	18 to 24 years	25 to 34 years	35 to 44 years	45 to 54 years
				1	2	3	4	5	6	7	8	9	10	11	12	13	14	15
			NEW YORK— Cont'd															
36037	12860	4	Genesee	492.9	57,853	906	117.4	91.7	3.9	1.4	1.2	3.7	5.0	11.5	11.5	12.4	11.8	12.5
36039		6	Greene	647.2	48,499	1,012	74.9	86.0	6.5	0.8	1.9	6.8	4.3	8.8	11.3	12.1	11.6	12.7
36041		8	Hamilton	1,717.4	5,119	2,813	3.0	95.7	1.9	0.8	1.1	2.0	2.8	7.4	8.6	7.3	9.0	11.3
36043	46540	2	Herkimer	1,411.5	59,937	879	42.5	95.0	2.2	0.6	1.1	2.6	4.9	11.7	11.9	11.3	11.2	12.0
36045	48060	3	Jefferson	1,268.7	116,295	542	91.7	83.9	7.3	1.0	3.1	7.7	7.3	13.3	15.3	16.3	12.3	9.7
36047	35620	1	Kings	69.4	2,641,052	8	38,055.5	38.5	30.4	0.6	13.9	18.8	6.7	12.5	11.0	17.4	14.3	11.6
36049		6	Lewis	1,274.6	26,573	1,544	20.8	96.8	1.2	0.6	0.8	1.7	5.9	13.0	11.3	11.4	11.5	11.7
36051	40380	1	Livingston	631.8	61,578	864	97.5	91.6	3.2	0.6	2.0	4.1	4.2	10.0	18.3	10.5	11.3	11.5
36053	45060	2	Madison	654.9	67,658	795	103.3	94.1	2.5	0.9	1.6	2.5	4.7	10.5	15.8	10.5	11.0	11.8
36055	40380	1	Monroe	656.9	755,160	88	1,149.6	71.9	15.8	0.6	4.6	9.6	5.2	11.6	13.2	13.9	12.3	11.7
36057	11220	4	Montgomery	403.1	49,558	1,002	122.9	80.7	3.4	0.6	1.4	15.5	6.2	13.0	11.7	12.3	12.3	11.8
36059	35620	1	Nassau	284.5	1,390,907	30	4,889.0	58.6	12.3	0.4	12.7	17.6	5.3	12.2	12.3	11.8	12.4	13.1
36061	35620	1	New York	22.7	1,576,876	23	69,465.9	47.7	14.0	0.6	13.8	26.4	4.4	8.0	10.6	19.9	14.6	12.2
36063	15380	1	Niagara	522.4	211,653	323	405.2	86.8	8.7	1.5	1.9	3.7	5.1	11.3	11.4	12.3	11.8	12.2
36065	46540	2	Oneida	1,212.3	230,274	301	189.9	82.7	7.5	0.5	4.8	6.6	5.4	12.1	13.0	12.2	11.8	12.0
36067	45060	2	Onondaga	778.4	473,236	152	608.0	78.9	12.8	1.3	4.8	5.5	5.5	12.0	13.6	13.1	12.1	11.6
36069	40380	1	Ontario	644.1	112,508	548	174.7	90.6	3.3	0.5	2.1	5.2	4.6	11.3	12.4	11.2	11.8	12.1
36071	39100	1	Orange	812.3	404,525	179	498.0	63.0	12.3	0.7	3.7	22.6	6.6	14.4	14.8	11.9	12.3	12.7
36073	40380	1	Orleans	391.3	40,191	1,175	102.7	87.9	6.8	1.0	1.1	5.2	4.7	10.6	11.8	13.1	11.9	12.7
36075	45060	2	Oswego	951.6	117,387	534	123.4	94.9	1.7	0.8	1.3	2.9	5.3	11.8	13.7	12.2	11.6	12.3
36077	36580	7	Otsego	1,001.7	58,123	904	58.0	91.8	2.9	0.7	2.1	4.0	4.1	8.8	19.2	10.1	10.2	10.9
36079	35620	1	Putnam	230.2	97,936	625	425.4	76.5	3.8	0.5	3.0	17.7	4.5	10.8	11.9	11.4	12.5	14.2
36081	35620	1	Queens	108.7	2,331,143	11	21,445.7	25.8	19.0	0.9	28.5	28.1	5.7	11.1	10.4	15.0	13.6	13.2
36083	10580	2	Rensselaer	652.5	160,232	421	245.6	84.1	8.6	0.5	3.7	5.4	4.9	10.9	12.9	13.9	12.8	12.2
36085	35620	1	Richmond	57.5	493,494	146	8,582.5	59.6	10.1	0.5	12.9	18.7	5.5	12.3	12.1	13.2	12.6	13.2
36087	35620	1	Rockland	173.4	339,227	214	1,956.3	63.9	11.7	0.4	6.7	18.8	8.4	16.0	13.9	11.5	11.3	11.3
36089	36300	4	St. Lawrence	2,679.5	108,051	574	40.3	93.1	2.8	1.4	1.7	2.4	4.8	11.5	17.0	11.3	11.4	11.7
36091	10580	2	Saratoga	810.0	237,359	290	293.0	91.5	2.6	0.5	3.8	3.5	4.6	11.2	11.4	12.1	12.8	13.5
36093	10580	2	Schenectady	204.6	158,089	431	772.7	74.3	13.7	1.1	6.8	7.8	5.8	12.0	12.5	13.4	12.9	12.1
36095	10580	2	Schoharie	621.8	29,863	1,439	48.0	93.6	2.1	0.7	1.3	3.8	4.4	10.0	13.2	10.6	10.9	12.0
36097		6	Schuyler	328.3	17,752	1,932	54.1	95.9	1.8	0.8	1.2	1.9	4.7	11.0	9.7	10.8	11.5	13.0
36099	42900	6	Seneca	323.7	33,688	1,340	104.1	89.5	6.0	0.9	1.2	4.1	5.2	11.2	11.8	13.4	11.9	11.6
36101	18500	4	Steuben	1,390.5	92,948	649	66.8	94.7	2.4	0.7	2.0	1.8	5.5	12.2	11.2	11.7	11.8	12.3
36103	35620	1	Suffolk	911.2	1,526,344	25	1,675.1	67.0	8.4	0.5	5.0	20.7	5.2	11.6	12.7	12.2	11.9	13.6
36105		4	Sullivan	968.1	79,806	718	82.4	71.9	9.6	0.8	2.6	17.4	5.8	11.8	11.5	12.1	12.1	12.5
36107	13780	2	Tioga	518.8	47,980	1,022	92.5	95.7	1.5	0.6	1.3	2.1	4.7	11.8	11.1	10.8	11.8	12.0
36109	27060	3	Tompkins	474.6	105,162	584	221.6	80.3	5.2	0.8	11.6	5.5	3.6	8.1	28.4	12.3	11.1	9.8
36111	28740	3	Ulster	1,124.2	182,951	369	162.7	80.4	7.3	0.8	3.1	11.1	4.3	9.7	11.9	12.7	12.4	12.8
36113	24020	3	Warren	867.2	65,618	821	75.7	94.5	2.0	0.7	1.4	2.9	4.3	10.2	10.2	11.8	11.3	12.3
36115	24020	3	Washington	831.2	60,956	868	73.3	92.9	3.7	0.6	1.0	3.1	4.4	10.5	10.9	12.3	12.3	13.2
36117	40380	1	Wayne	603.8	90,923	661	150.6	91.3	4.1	0.6	1.3	4.8	5.4	12.0	10.8	11.6	11.5	12.6
36119	35620	1	Westchester	430.7	997,895	49	2,316.9	53.8	14.5	0.5	7.1	25.9	5.2	12.1	12.6	11.5	13.1	13.8
36121		6	Wyoming	592.8	40,491	1,171	68.3	90.2	5.8	0.6	0.8	3.5	4.5	10.5	10.5	13.6	13.1	13.2
36123	40380	1	Yates	338.1	24,613	1,629	72.8	95.8	1.5	0.5	1.0	2.2	6.2	12.3	14.5	10.6	9.9	10.1
37000		0	NORTH CAROLINA	48,620.3	10,551,162	X	217.0	63.7	22.6	1.7	4.0	10.2	5.6	12.3	13.3	13.4	12.6	12.8
37001	15500	3	Alamance	423.5	173,877	386	410.6	62.8	22.3	0.9	2.4	13.7	5.7	12.5	14.4	12.6	11.7	12.6
37003	25860	2	Alexander	260.0	36,644	1,266	140.9	87.4	7.0	0.7	1.4	5.2	4.9	11.1	11.0	12.3	11.7	13.6
37005		9	Alleghany	234.8	11,049	2,340	47.1	87.2	2.2	0.9	0.8	10.2	4.3	9.5	9.3	9.3	9.9	12.9
37007	16740	6	Anson	531.5	22,060	1,709	41.5	46.0	48.0	1.1	1.8	4.7	5.4	11.1	11.6	14.0	11.8	12.4
37009		7	Ashe	426.3	26,711	1,541	62.7	92.7	1.3	0.9	0.7	5.5	3.9	9.8	9.7	9.6	11.0	12.7
37011		8	Avery	247.3	17,864	1,927	72.2	88.8	5.2	1.0	0.9	5.2	3.8	8.0	11.6	12.5	12.7	13.9
37013	47820	6	Beaufort	832.7	44,468	1,087	53.4	67.1	24.2	0.8	0.7	8.5	4.7	11.1	10.8	10.0	10.5	12.5
37015		7	Bertie	699.2	17,505	1,945	25.0	35.5	61.2	1.2	1.0	2.4	4.3	9.6	10.9	13.0	10.4	11.6
37017		6	Bladen	875.0	29,525	1,444	33.7	56.0	33.4	3.2	0.8	8.2	5.3	11.2	11.2	10.8	10.5	12.7
37019	34820	2	Brunswick	850.1	144,215	462	169.6	84.0	10.1	1.4	1.2	5.1	3.5	8.2	7.7	9.0	9.3	10.6
37021	11700	2	Buncombe	656.5	271,534	259	413.6	84.8	7.0	1.1	2.0	7.2	4.5	10.1	10.8	13.7	13.8	12.6
37023	25860	2	Burke	506.2	87,611	670	173.1	82.4	7.5	0.9	4.2	6.9	4.6	9.9	11.5	12.3	11.0	13.7
37025	16740	1	Cabarrus	361.2	231,278	299	640.3	62.2	21.4	0.8	6.2	11.7	6.1	14.6	12.7	12.6	14.6	14.1
37027	25860	2	Caldwell	471.9	80,463	709	170.5	87.4	6.1	0.7	1.0	6.5	5.1	11.2	11.0	11.9	11.1	13.8
37029	47260	8	Camden	240.3	10,835	2,357	45.1	83.1	12.3	1.2	2.7	3.8	5.3	13.6	11.1	11.4	14.4	13.4
37031	33980	4	Carteret	507.6	68,541	785	135.0	88.3	6.0	1.2	1.9	4.7	3.8	9.9	9.6	9.7	11.2	12.3
37033		8	Caswell	425.4	22,714	1,687	53.4	62.4	32.5	1.0	1.0	4.9	4.8	10.2	10.4	11.8	10.8	13.4
37035	25860	2	Catawba	401.4	161,723	416	402.9	75.9	9.8	0.6	5.2	10.5	5.3	12.4	12.3	12.1	11.7	13.4
37037	20500	2	Chatham	681.7	77,889	728	114.3	73.7	12.2	0.8	2.8	12.2	4.4	11.1	10.2	8.8	11.4	13.5
37039		9	Cherokee	455.5	29,167	1,450	64.0	92.4	2.2	2.9	0.9	3.8	4.1	8.7	8.9	8.7	9.2	12.0

1. CBSA = Core Based Statistical Area. See Appendix A for explanation. See Appendix B for list of metropolitan areas with component counties. 2. County type code from the Economic Research Service of USDA Rural-Urban Continuum Codes. See Appendix A for definition. 3. Dry land or land partially or temporarily covered by water. 4. May be of any race.

STATE County	Population, 2021 (cont.)				Population change, 2000–2021							Households, 2016–2020				
	Age (percent) (cont.)			Percent female	Total persons		Percent change		Components of change, 2020–2021			Number	Persons per household	Percent		
	55 to 64 years	65 to 74 years	75 years and over		2010	2020	2010–2020	2020–2021	Births	Deaths	Net Migration			Family house-holds	Female family house-holder[1]	One person
	16	17	18	19	20	21	22	23	24	25	26	27	28	29	30	31
NEW YORK— Cont'd																
Genesee	15.7	11.4	8.2	49.7	60,079	58,388	-2.8	-0.9	671	974	-240	24,174	2.4	62.0	9.5	30.3
Greene	16.2	13.6	9.4	47.5	49,221	47,931	-2.6	1.2	465	800	916	17,681	2.5	60.5	8.7	32.5
Hamilton	20.5	21.3	11.8	49.5	4,836	5,107	5.6	0.2	33	92	74	1,416	3.1	66.3	5.2	26.6
Herkimer	15.5	12.9	8.6	50.1	64,519	60,139	-6.8	-0.3	714	953	34	25,093	2.4	62.9	9.7	30.3
Jefferson	11.2	8.8	5.8	47.2	116,229	116,721	0.4	-0.4	2,109	1,407	-1,148	43,046	2.4	66.0	10.4	26.8
Kings	11.3	8.9	6.2	52.4	2,504,700	2,736,074	9.2	-3.5	43,990	25,315	-112,175	972,314	2.6	61.1	17.6	29.0
Lewis	15.6	12.0	7.6	49.0	27,087	26,582	-1.9	0.0	353	436	71	10,398	2.5	68.4	8.1	25.3
Livingston	15.0	11.7	7.4	49.2	65,393	61,834	-5.4	-0.4	651	893	-20	24,496	2.3	63.4	10.6	28.1
Madison	15.8	12.1	7.7	50.2	73,442	68,016	-7.4	-0.5	753	923	-197	25,959	2.5	64.2	8.3	29.8
Monroe	13.8	10.8	7.5	51.5	744,344	759,443	2.0	-0.6	9,523	10,260	-3,637	305,210	2.4	60.0	13.7	32.1
Montgomery	13.7	11.4	7.7	50.3	50,219	49,532	-1.4	0.1	729	809	102	19,621	2.5	62.4	13.2	31.3
Nassau	14.5	10.7	7.7	50.8	1,339,532	1,395,774	4.2	-0.3	16,626	16,418	-5,269	449,967	3.0	77.0	11.6	19.6
New York	11.9	10.1	8.3	52.4	1,585,873	1,694,251	6.8	-6.9	19,755	16,457	-118,684	758,720	2.1	42.9	11.0	45.7
Niagara	15.7	12.3	7.9	50.9	216,469	212,666	-1.8	-0.5	2,487	3,561	35	90,022	2.3	61.4	11.9	32.3
Oneida	14.1	11.3	8.1	49.8	234,878	232,125	-1.2	-0.8	2,992	3,756	-1,106	90,675	2.4	63.2	12.4	31.1
Onondaga	14.1	10.8	7.3	51.4	467,026	476,516	2.0	-0.7	5,994	6,490	-2,839	187,349	2.4	60.4	12.6	31.3
Ontario	15.2	13.0	8.4	50.8	107,931	112,458	4.2	0.0	1,175	1,622	490	45,711	2.3	63.6	11.9	29.4
Orange	12.8	8.7	5.7	49.6	372,813	401,310	7.6	0.8	6,269	4,193	1,073	130,428	2.9	70.4	11.8	24.2
Orleans	15.9	12.0	7.3	49.7	42,883	40,343	-5.9	-0.4	496	631	-22	16,634	2.3	66.4	11.8	27.6
Oswego	15.5	11.0	6.5	49.7	122,109	117,525	-3.8	-0.1	1,502	1,689	28	46,597	2.4	65.0	12.9	25.3
Otsego	14.7	13.0	9.0	51.2	62,259	58,524	-6.0	-0.7	541	908	-36	23,768	2.3	61.9	8.8	30.8
Putnam	16.1	11.2	7.4	49.6	99,710	97,668	-2.0	0.3	993	1,132	401	34,915	2.8	75.5	10.0	20.3
Queens	13.7	10.2	7.2	51.1	2,230,722	2,405,464	7.8	-3.1	31,973	22,949	-82,321	783,362	2.9	67.7	15.4	25.6
Rensselaer	14.3	11.3	6.9	50.3	159,429	161,130	1.1	-0.6	1,917	2,312	-527	65,455	2.3	60.2	13.0	31.4
Richmond	14.1	10.3	6.7	51.1	468,730	495,747	5.8	-0.5	6,342	5,883	-2,794	167,160	2.8	73.6	14.8	22.8
Rockland	12.0	8.8	6.9	50.6	311,687	338,329	8.5	0.3	6,832	3,563	-2,423	101,167	3.2	74.8	10.5	21.2
St. Lawrence	14.1	11.1	7.1	48.6	111,944	108,505	-3.1	-0.4	1,182	1,616	-39	41,925	2.3	61.3	10.2	30.9
Saratoga	15.1	11.8	7.6	50.5	219,607	235,509	7.2	0.8	2,495	3,023	2,378	95,898	2.4	64.7	8.5	27.1
Schenectady	13.7	10.4	7.2	51.0	154,727	158,061	2.2	0.0	2,146	2,200	55	57,479	2.6	58.5	12.2	34.7
Schoharie	15.8	14.0	9.2	49.6	32,749	29,714	-9.3	0.5	305	477	325	12,780	2.3	63.0	10.4	29.1
Schuyler	16.8	14.2	8.3	49.7	18,343	17,898	-2.4	-0.8	181	297	-30	7,402	2.4	61.8	6.6	29.5
Seneca	14.6	12.5	7.9	47.0	35,251	33,814	-4.1	-0.4	428	488	-71	13,784	2.3	60.1	8.4	30.8
Steuben	15.1	12.2	8.1	49.9	98,990	93,584	-5.5	-0.7	1,229	1,530	-342	40,099	2.4	64.6	10.8	29.6
Suffolk	15.2	10.3	7.4	50.4	1,493,350	1,525,920	2.2	0.0	18,185	19,265	1,258	495,667	2.9	72.9	11.0	22.2
Sullivan	15.0	11.8	7.4	48.3	77,547	78,624	1.4	1.5	1,057	1,130	1,269	28,762	2.5	62.3	11.1	31.2
Tioga	16.2	12.5	9.0	49.9	51,125	48,455	-5.2	-1.0	567	730	-314	20,643	2.3	67.1	9.2	27.2
Tompkins	11.0	9.9	5.9	50.7	101,564	105,740	4.1	-0.5	852	1,019	-435	40,817	2.2	52.5	8.5	29.7
Ulster	15.5	12.4	8.3	50.1	182,493	181,851	-0.4	0.6	1,875	2,607	1,843	70,088	2.4	60.3	10.9	32.1
Warren	16.5	14.4	9.1	50.5	65,707	65,737	0.0	-0.2	638	1,062	309	29,034	2.2	59.8	9.9	32.4
Washington	15.7	12.5	8.1	47.7	63,216	61,302	-3.0	-0.6	643	998	1	24,054	2.4	63.3	11.6	27.5
Wayne	16.1	12.3	7.7	49.9	93,772	91,283	-2.7	-0.4	1,105	1,330	-146	37,281	2.4	66.2	9.5	27.8
Westchester	13.9	10.0	7.8	51.2	949,113	1,004,457	5.8	-0.7	11,890	10,974	-7,586	353,485	2.7	68.7	12.5	26.7
Wyoming	15.3	12.1	7.1	45.4	42,155	40,531	-3.9	-0.1	409	542	90	16,055	2.3	65.7	8.2	26.9
Yates	14.7	13.4	8.1	51.1	25,348	24,774	-2.3	-0.6	358	439	-81	8,901	2.7	66.2	9.3	27.8
NORTH CAROLINA	13.0	10.4	6.6	51.1	9,535,483	10,439,388	9.5	1.1	142,020	144,561	114,080	4,031,592	2.5	65.1	12.8	28.7
Alamance	13.3	10.0	7.1	52.3	151,131	171,415	13.4	1.4	2,269	2,645	2,844	65,455	2.5	64.4	13.8	29.7
Alexander	14.7	12.3	8.4	48.8	37,198	36,444	-2.0	0.5	410	619	411	14,049	2.6	72.9	12.1	23.3
Alleghany	16.3	17.2	11.3	50.2	11,155	10,888	-2.4	1.5	111	219	273	5,001	2.2	67.4	8.7	27.7
Anson	14.1	11.9	7.8	49.2	26,948	22,055	-18.2	0.0	316	407	97	9,803	2.3	58.7	18.4	33.8
Ashe	16.4	16.1	10.9	50.5	27,281	26,577	-2.6	0.5	278	565	426	11,885	2.2	67.7	10.6	28.8
Avery	14.9	13.7	8.9	45.1	17,797	17,806	0.1	0.3	168	347	240	6,569	2.1	67.2	9.3	28.1
Beaufort	15.3	15.2	9.8	52.0	47,759	44,652	-6.5	-0.4	531	896	182	20,219	2.3	65.5	13.9	28.9
Bertie	15.6	14.5	10.1	48.8	21,282	17,934	-15.7	-2.4	201	377	-250	8,008	2.2	58.9	18.7	37.7
Bladen	14.8	14.4	9.1	52.5	35,190	29,606	-15.9	-0.3	420	633	131	13,394	2.4	64.4	17.6	31.6
Brunswick	18.4	22.5	10.8	51.9	107,431	136,693	27.2	5.5	1,209	2,718	9,160	59,416	2.3	69.4	8.6	25.3
Buncombe	13.4	12.8	8.2	51.8	238,318	269,452	13.1	0.8	2,862	4,021	3,251	105,177	2.4	57.6	8.5	33.1
Burke	15.7	12.5	8.7	49.7	90,912	87,570	-3.7	0.0	1,010	1,560	587	35,664	2.5	65.8	10.7	29.7
Cabarrus	11.9	8.3	5.1	51.0	178,011	225,804	26.8	2.4	3,090	2,545	4,941	72,843	2.9	73.1	12.8	21.6
Caldwell	15.1	12.6	8.2	50.3	83,029	80,652	-2.9	-0.2	941	1,545	413	32,798	2.5	68.8	14.2	27.2
Camden	14.4	10.0	6.5	49.4	9,980	10,355	3.8	4.6	123	121	486	3,912	2.7	81.4	13.5	17.9
Carteret	17.3	16.3	10.0	50.8	66,469	67,686	1.8	1.3	608	1,366	1,642	30,060	2.3	64.1	9.0	30.8
Caswell	15.5	14.0	9.2	49.0	23,719	22,736	-4.1	-0.1	226	409	163	8,993	2.4	68.8	13.2	27.1
Catawba	14.2	11.2	7.3	50.8	154,358	160,610	4.1	0.7	1,957	2,507	1,659	62,940	2.5	68.2	12.0	26.9
Chatham	15.3	14.4	10.9	51.6	63,505	76,285	20.1	2.1	764	1,181	2,041	29,904	2.4	69.3	10.2	26.2
Cherokee	16.7	19.1	12.5	50.7	27,444	28,774	4.8	1.4	299	600	704	12,546	2.2	65.1	9.6	29.0

1. No spouse present.

STATE County	Persons in group quarters, 2021	Daytime Population, 2016–2020: Number	Daytime Population, 2016–2020: Employment/ residence ratio	Births, 2021: Total	Births, 2021: Rate[1]	Deaths, 2021: Number	Deaths, 2021: Rate[1]	Persons under 65 with no health insurance, 2019: Number	Persons under 65 with no health insurance, 2019: Percent	Medicare, 2021: Total beneficiaries	Medicare, 2021: Enrolled in Original Medicare	Medicare, 2021: Enrolled in Medicare Advantage	COVID-19 Deaths, 2020: Number	COVID-19 Deaths, 2020: Rate[1]
	32	33	34	35	36	37	38	39	40	41	42	43	44	45
NEW YORK— Cont'd														
Genesee	1,932	53,707	0.9	524	9.0	783	13.5	1,985	4.4	13,294	5,340	7,954	63	1.1
Greene	3,000	43,384	0.8	365	7.6	637	13.2	1,687	5.0	11,959	7,078	4,881	30	0.6
Hamilton	83	4,311	0.9	25	4.9	69	13.5	218	7.3	1,715	1,034	682	D	D
Herkimer	1,291	53,181	0.7	590	9.8	771	12.9	2,237	4.7	15,069	8,342	6,727	42	0.7
Jefferson	6,242	114,390	1.1	1,666	14.3	1,140	9.8	4,191	4.8	20,410	12,884	7,525	13	0.1
Kings	37,091	2,275,077	0.7	35,247	13.1	20,534	7.6	155,196	7.2	377,134	201,743	175,392	7,138	2.6
Lewis	276	23,903	0.8	273	10.3	356	13.4	1,047	5.0	6,084	3,745	2,339	10	0.4
Livingston	5,526	57,970	0.8	509	8.3	727	11.8	2,114	4.6	13,849	5,058	8,791	36	0.6
Madison	4,263	61,537	0.7	618	9.1	754	11.1	2,311	4.3	14,953	8,121	6,832	74	1.1
Monroe	26,036	770,965	1.1	7,530	9.9	8,172	10.8	24,849	4.2	160,018	48,782	111,236	729	1.0
Montgomery	820	47,656	0.9	588	11.9	642	13.0	2,044	5.2	11,567	5,483	6,084	39	0.8
Nassau	19,443	1,262,964	0.9	13,199	9.5	13,143	9.4	53,385	4.8	270,825	200,571	70,255	3,004	2.2
New York	70,934	3,249,041	2.9	15,643	9.6	13,412	8.2	73,874	5.6	286,566	169,801	116,765	3,073	1.8
Niagara	3,620	185,621	0.8	1,944	9.2	2,812	13.3	7,153	4.3	50,445	18,796	31,649	262	1.2
Oneida	12,716	236,827	1.1	2,402	10.4	2,982	12.9	9,299	5.3	52,712	29,403	23,309	272	1.2
Onondaga	16,932	491,513	1.1	4,755	10.0	5,158	10.9	17,751	4.8	96,258	47,026	49,232	527	1.1
Ontario	3,166	109,931	1.0	909	8.1	1,315	11.7	3,475	4.1	26,659	9,831	16,828	80	0.7
Orange	11,228	359,112	0.9	4,975	12.3	3,347	8.3	15,775	4.9	65,044	47,907	17,137	628	1.6
Orleans	2,420	36,559	0.8	404	10.0	505	12.6	1,817	5.9	8,968	3,539	5,429	58	1.4
Oswego	4,183	102,285	0.7	1,178	10.0	1,352	11.5	4,904	5.3	25,357	13,311	12,046	60	0.5
Otsego	5,102	60,238	1.0	426	7.3	741	12.7	2,160	5.1	14,364	10,037	4,327	21	0.4
Putnam	2,298	78,971	0.6	776	7.9	916	9.4	3,369	4.2	19,467	14,307	5,160	129	1.3
Queens	29,090	1,929,998	0.7	25,490	10.8	18,667	7.9	191,502	10.3	369,532	185,080	184,452	7,040	2.9
Rensselaer	5,620	139,982	0.8	1,510	9.4	1,913	11.9	5,339	4.2	32,469	16,904	15,565	87	0.5
Richmond	7,005	396,717	0.6	5,069	10.3	4,815	9.7	19,502	4.9	90,445	53,617	36,828	1,174	2.4
Rockland	6,443	302,505	0.8	5,458	16.1	2,863	8.5	15,161	5.6	56,999	42,833	14,166	873	2.6
St. Lawrence	10,423	105,777	0.9	937	8.7	1,315	12.2	4,451	5.7	23,789	16,157	7,632	49	0.5
Saratoga	3,365	208,730	0.8	1,966	8.3	2,472	10.5	6,612	3.6	50,456	25,423	25,034	70	0.3
Schenectady	4,439	150,139	0.9	1,729	10.9	1,751	11.1	6,032	4.8	32,026	15,060	16,965	97	0.6
Schoharie	1,109	27,974	0.8	239	8.0	388	13.0	1,160	5.1	7,604	4,898	2,705	D	D
Schuyler	170	15,353	0.7	142	8.0	244	13.7	665	4.8	4,760	2,488	2,272	12	0.7
Seneca	2,525	34,223	1.0	362	10.7	388	11.5	1,362	5.5	7,818	3,976	3,842	32	0.9
Steuben	1,470	95,548	1.0	985	10.6	1,226	13.2	3,881	5.2	22,461	11,670	10,792	132	1.4
Suffolk	29,563	1,392,429	0.9	14,600	9.6	15,459	10.1	62,909	5.2	296,308	230,315	65,993	2,991	2.0
Sullivan	3,787	70,066	0.8	850	10.7	895	11.3	3,685	6.3	17,033	12,876	4,157	71	0.9
Tioga	421	41,270	0.7	456	9.5	577	12.0	1,621	4.3	11,437	6,045	5,393	74	1.5
Tompkins	13,418	113,392	1.2	661	6.3	825	7.8	3,475	4.7	17,166	11,646	5,520	29	0.3
Ulster	11,651	164,351	0.8	1,493	8.2	2,081	11.4	7,976	5.9	41,372	28,985	12,387	161	0.9
Warren	572	69,212	1.2	508	7.7	855	13.0	2,128	4.3	17,940	9,306	8,634	47	0.7
Washington	2,970	51,716	0.7	493	8.1	786	12.9	2,344	5.1	14,650	7,423	7,228	17	0.3
Wayne	992	78,586	0.7	883	9.7	1,062	11.7	3,067	4.3	22,067	8,359	13,709	56	0.6
Westchester	28,311	951,083	1.0	9,440	9.4	8,817	8.8	45,099	5.7	178,092	123,927	54,165	2,050	2.0
Wyoming	3,340	36,701	0.8	314	7.8	413	10.2	1,289	4.4	8,898	3,677	5,221	27	0.7
Yates	1,297	23,965	0.9	280	11.4	340	13.8	1,520	8.3	5,898	2,461	3,437	17	0.7
NORTH CAROLINA	260,910	10,383,566	1.0	114,011	10.9	115,709	11.0	1,139,623	13.4	2,034,911	1,210,686	824,225	8,630	0.8
Alamance	6,081	156,295	0.9	1,795	10.4	2,076	12.0	19,822	14.8	33,912	13,974	19,938	158	0.9
Alexander	1,327	30,739	0.6	337	9.2	496	13.6	3,867	13.6	8,542	4,683	3,859	47	1.3
Alleghany	56	10,496	0.9	90	8.2	180	16.4	1,535	19.5	3,368	2,021	1,347	D	D
Anson	1,189	21,919	0.8	253	11.5	328	14.9	2,372	13.3	5,546	3,362	2,184	36	1.6
Ashe	234	25,275	0.9	203	7.6	451	16.9	3,261	16.5	8,061	5,496	2,565	40	1.5
Avery	2,439	19,183	1.3	137	7.7	263	14.7	2,135	19.2	4,707	3,091	1,615	18	1.0
Beaufort	305	45,896	0.9	412	9.2	705	15.8	5,040	14.4	13,261	9,807	3,454	68	1.5
Bertie	1,340	17,575	0.8	151	8.5	300	17.0	1,639	12.6	5,333	3,948	1,385	41	2.3
Bladen	111	34,257	1.1	345	11.7	509	17.2	3,994	16.1	8,036	4,849	3,187	28	0.9
Brunswick	563	125,850	0.8	990	7.0	2,273	16.1	12,873	13.5	50,856	36,672	14,184	88	0.6
Buncombe	7,930	282,861	1.2	2,321	8.6	3,194	11.8	29,493	14.6	61,723	40,038	21,685	195	0.7
Burke	2,809	84,543	0.9	804	9.2	1,237	14.1	10,688	15.5	21,837	11,744	10,093	97	1.1
Cabarrus	1,500	189,312	0.8	2,487	10.9	2,073	9.0	20,893	11.2	34,338	18,559	15,779	143	0.6
Caldwell	782	73,323	0.8	755	9.4	1,204	15.0	9,855	15.3	20,002	10,348	9,654	118	1.5
Camden	3	7,623	0.3	97	9.1	92	8.7	1,016	11.2	1,979	1,581	398	D	D
Carteret	798	66,888	0.9	482	7.1	1,099	16.1	6,861	13.4	19,437	15,482	3,955	35	0.5
Caswell	1,152	17,082	0.4	186	8.2	330	14.5	2,162	13.3	5,987	2,757	3,230	18	0.8
Catawba	2,400	174,485	1.2	1,557	9.7	2,007	12.4	19,832	15.4	34,663	19,456	15,207	190	1.2
Chatham	689	61,810	0.7	597	7.7	949	12.3	7,803	14.0	20,175	11,560	8,616	58	0.8
Cherokee	355	27,388	0.9	240	8.3	482	16.6	3,261	16.6	9,852	6,488	3,364	31	1.1

1. Per 1,000 estimated resident population.

STATE County	COVID-19 Vaccinations, 2021–2022: Number	COVID-19 Vaccinations, 2021–2022: Percent[5]	Education: School enrollment and attainment, 2016–2020: Enrollment[1]: Total	Enrollment[1]: Percent private	Attainment[2] (percent): High school graduate or less	Attainment[2] (percent): Bachelor's degree or more	Local government expenditures,[3] 2018–2019: Total current spending (mil dol)	Local government expenditures,[3] 2018–2019: Current spending per student (dollars)	Money income, 2016–2020: Per capita income[4]	Households: Median income (dollars)	Households: Percent with income of less than $50,000	Households: Percent with income of $200,000 or more	Income and poverty, 2020: Median household income (dollars)	Percent below poverty level: All persons	Percent below poverty level: Children under 18 years	Percent below poverty level: Children 5 to 17 years in families
	46	47	48	49	50	51	52	53	54	55	56	57	58	59	60	61
NEW YORK— Cont'd																
Genesee	34,364	60.0	11,487	12.2	45.4	21.9	168.9	20,630	30,846	60,635	41.2	3.0	62,641	10.2	12.6	12.2
Greene	29,575	62.7	7,690	11.9	50.5	23.9	140.0	23,931	30,970	56,681	44.1	4.7	60,163	11.2	16.1	15.6
Hamilton	3,671	83.1	641	18.6	48.6	19.9	19.5	45,842	28,758	60,625	39.1	2.0	56,253	8.7	14.1	12.6
Herkimer	36,324	59.2	12,783	12.0	46.1	21.1	183.6	19,599	29,540	58,438	44.4	2.5	59,893	12.1	16.2	16.0
Jefferson	80,878	73.6	24,904	10.0	43.6	22.5	318.1	17,744	28,120	54,726	45.2	2.7	57,570	13.1	17.8	17.1
Kings	1,843,544	72.0	629,036	31.2	42.0	38.8	(6)	(6)	36,295	63,973	41.6	10.6	70,390	17.8	23.5	23.5
Lewis	13,721	52.2	5,502	13.0	53.2	18.3	82.2	19,945	27,770	56,192	43.7	2.4	57,897	11.4	16.7	16.2
Livingston	37,507	59.6	16,349	14.3	40.6	27.5	157.6	20,308	30,523	60,248	40.8	3.6	60,947	10.3	12.3	10.9
Madison	43,351	61.1	17,284	26.6	42.1	26.6	192.7	20,421	32,443	61,176	40.4	4.8	64,379	10.4	13.9	13.0
Monroe	537,439	72.5	182,895	26.2	32.2	39.2	2,245.0	20,424	35,339	62,087	41.0	6.3	61,358	13.9	20.4	20.5
Montgomery	32,997	67.0	10,486	16.0	47.3	18.7	152.9	19,439	27,346	50,146	49.8	2.7	52,482	11.9	20.2	19.7
Nassau	1,111,570	81.9	335,754	26.4	30.5	46.7	5,581.8	27,270	53,363	120,036	20.1	25.1	122,730	5.7	6.3	5.7
New York	1,394,896	85.6	323,498	45.1	24.4	62.2	(6)126,897.5	(6)27,123	78,771	89,812	33.0	23.4	87,745	16.3	19.3	21.7
Niagara	139,205	66.5	44,010	18.7	40.8	25.6	539.5	18,752	31,762	57,252	44.6	3.6	54,963	11.7	14.7	15.0
Oneida	143,888	62.9	51,959	15.0	41.8	26.6	621.6	17,784	30,678	59,113	42.1	4.1	58,696	12.4	17.7	18.3
Onondaga	338,861	73.6	116,363	25.6	34.2	36.1	1,371.1	19,463	34,600	62,668	40.4	5.8	63,963	12.8	19.6	18.8
Ontario	75,055	68.4	25,659	20.9	33.0	35.8	320.1	19,986	37,044	64,795	37.6	6.1	62,777	8.8	11.0	10.1
Orange	250,301	65.0	104,879	26.2	38.7	30.8	1,430.2	24,125	35,616	80,816	32.0	10.7	78,724	10.6	15.7	15.2
Orleans	22,244	55.1	7,373	12.7	52.9	16.3	111.9	19,420	26,894	52,958	46.4	2.5	57,318	13.2	20.1	19.2
Oswego	69,693	59.5	28,027	7.3	48.4	20.1	411.2	21,384	30,026	59,070	42.6	3.6	58,439	14.2	19.2	19.1
Otsego	36,771	61.8	15,017	18.3	38.0	33.4	155.5	22,544	30,223	56,171	44.1	3.3	58,417	12.8	16.8	16.4
Putnam	72,518	73.8	21,972	17.9	33.4	40.9	399.1	28,683	47,533	107,246	20.5	16.2	104,285	5.7	5.6	5.6
Queens	1,948,903	86.5	515,092	20.0	44.3	33.5	(6)	(6)	33,626	72,028	35.5	8.7	78,847	10.3	13.0	12.7
Rensselaer	112,187	70.7	37,001	29.1	35.0	33.9	403.5	19,503	37,011	72,510	35.2	5.8	71,457	10.4	14.3	12.8
Richmond	353,097	74.2	115,846	24.0	41.3	34.7	(6)	(6)	38,096	85,381	30.4	12.4	81,003	10.6	15.0	14.7
Rockland	209,498	64.3	95,729	48.5	33.4	41.9	1,114.6	27,681	39,923	94,840	28.2	18.4	94,874	14.4	25.0	24.0
St. Lawrence	65,763	61.0	28,464	22.7	47.5	23.6	328.1	21,685	26,676	52,071	47.8	3.2	51,526	14.7	18.4	16.5
Saratoga	182,644	79.5	49,439	20.2	30.5	42.0	608.8	18,325	45,624	85,224	27.7	10.3	83,427	6.3	6.3	5.9
Schenectady	113,470	73.1	35,519	18.8	37.5	32.1	414.2	18,942	33,379	66,488	37.9	5.6	66,292	10.9	15.4	14.4
Schoharie	17,672	57.0	6,866	9.7	45.6	23.6	98.9	24,255	32,352	58,926	42.5	4.6	59,744	11.0	15.5	14.7
Schuyler	11,097	62.3	3,308	12.0	43.6	23.2	44.9	21,038	28,844	53,291	47.1	2.8	54,269	11.8	16.8	15.6
Seneca	18,258	53.7	6,648	21.9	49.4	21.3	90.7	22,424	28,703	54,865	45.1	3.8	56,929	12.1	19.1	18.4
Steuben	57,370	60.1	19,321	11.2	44.3	24.6	314.7	21,996	30,844	55,349	45.6	3.2	54,794	12.1	18.4	17.9
Suffolk	1,120,376	75.9	359,414	15.2	36.0	37.3	6,252.2	26,514	46,466	105,362	22.6	18.0	109,084	6.1	6.2	6.1
Sullivan	45,976	61.0	15,383	16.5	45.4	26.6	276.6	28,556	32,346	60,433	43.3	5.4	63,915	12.7	21.3	22.1
Tioga	29,174	60.5	10,110	10.7	44.1	26.1	146.3	19,887	32,298	61,965	40.2	3.3	62,400	9.3	12.1	11.4
Tompkins	81,277	79.5	39,884	56.4	24.0	53.1	252.3	22,750	34,194	61,361	41.7	7.8	65,308	12.4	12.4	11.5
Ulster	129,550	73.0	38,101	15.9	37.6	33.2	598.6	26,289	35,816	65,306	38.4	7.4	66,060	12.7	13.6	13.5
Warren	49,549	77.5	12,019	11.8	37.4	32.3	183.8	21,103	38,740	64,658	38.3	5.9	67,359	8.9	13.8	13.0
Washington	40,910	66.8	11,560	18.5	51.5	20.2	177.6	20,566	29,014	59,613	41.1	2.7	60,973	11.2	16.1	15.8
Wayne	56,411	62.7	19,063	13.5	42.9	23.7	302.1	21,394	32,513	62,003	39.2	3.6	62,329	9.7	12.3	11.6
Westchester	787,422	81.4	243,420	26.9	30.4	49.7	4,010.2	26,963	57,953	99,489	27.2	23.3	103,340	7.6	8.5	8.1
Wyoming	20,531	51.5	7,374	15.4	49.7	18.0	81.4	20,232	29,734	58,746	40.4	2.9	59,612	9.6	11.3	11.0
Yates	13,235	53.1	5,113	37.9	48.3	24.5	47.2	22,315	28,001	55,307	45.5	3.7	57,057	12.9	22.2	21.0
NORTH CAROLINA	6,398,376	61.0	2,521,615	15.9	36.9	32.0	15,130.1	9,746	31,993	56,642	44.4	6.0	59,616	12.9	17.9	17.0
Alamance	100,368	59.2	42,186	23.9	40.4	25.3	225.1	9,049	27,944	51,580	48.5	3.0	53,220	15.1	18.3	17.2
Alexander	17,258	46.0	7,472	14.5	56.5	14.2	48.1	9,891	27,446	51,329	48.8	4.2	53,523	11.8	16.8	15.6
Alleghany	6,690	60.1	2,074	5.8	49.0	20.8	17.1	12,081	26,026	37,158	61.8	3.7	39,916	18.1	30.7	28.8
Anson	11,350	46.4	5,404	11.8	58.5	11.1	35.6	11,227	22,483	39,799	58.6	1.1	40,818	20.7	29.3	28.8
Ashe	14,837	54.5	4,730	14.4	44.9	20.0	34.1	11,171	25,282	43,030	58.6	1.0	44,543	14.5	22.4	21.0
Avery	9,592	54.6	3,520	33.6	45.3	23.7	26.1	12,163	24,036	42,695	58.4	4.2	50,800	15.8	23.8	24.1
Beaufort	26,121	55.6	9,032	7.1	43.7	20.7	71.8	10,207	28,077	48,051	51.4	2.6	50,253	18.1	29.0	26.5
Bertie	9,892	52.2	3,547	17.7	57.9	14.5	27.6	12,058	22,245	35,042	66.1	2.2	41,889	22.8	31.5	31.2
Bladen	20,703	63.3	6,640	11.6	47.7	18.2	52.2	10,402	24,752	37,188	62.0	2.8	43,664	21.6	35.5	35.0
Brunswick	90,609	63.4	21,543	13.8	37.1	29.5	141.5	10,200	34,528	59,763	41.1	4.4	64,371	11.2	19.6	17.9
Buncombe	176,632	67.6	52,803	18.3	31.5	41.4	332.8	10,849	33,835	55,032	45.5	5.9	66,156	13.9	17.4	17.1
Burke	42,900	47.4	17,298	10.6	49.3	16.7	116.6	9,281	25,053	43,915	55.3	2.4	48,729	18.4	30.1	32.1
Cabarrus	124,298	57.4	55,507	13.6	34.8	33.5	371.9	9,030	33,548	71,177	34.3	8.2	79,736	8.0	10.5	9.9
Caldwell	38,919	47.4	16,487	11.4	51.8	15.8	116.5	10,023	24,666	46,094	53.7	1.7	50,235	13.0	19.1	17.7
Camden	6,778	62.4	2,464	5.6	44.8	19.9	19.0	10,018	28,596	63,834	43.1	2.1	72,135	7.4	8.6	7.7
Carteret	45,104	64.9	13,361	16.0	33.2	28.5	98.1	11,663	34,038	57,871	44.1	4.9	63,475	9.3	16.0	15.1
Caswell	11,319	50.1	4,447	19.4	51.6	15.8	27.6	10,921	24,121	47,938	51.8	2.0	48,070	15.4	24.0	23.6
Catawba	88,994	55.8	36,118	17.8	43.8	23.1	214.2	9,213	29,364	54,690	45.9	4.3	52,737	11.6	17.2	15.4
Chatham	47,169	63.3	14,668	18.5	30.6	43.7	110.2	10,620	45,036	69,799	36.9	12.5	74,747	9.6	13.3	11.4
Cherokee	16,453	57.5	4,331	14.5	44.6	21.9	41.2	11,907	24,024	40,793	58.9	1.5	44,449	15.1	24.9	24.4

1. All persons 3 years old and over enrolled in nursery school through college. 2. Persons 25 years old and over. 3. Elementary and secondary education expenditures. 4. Based on population estimated by the American Community Survey, 2016–2020. 5. CDC percent based on 2019 population estimate. 6. Bronx, Kings, Queens, and Richmond counties are included with New York county

STATE County	Personal income, 2020										Earnings, 2020		
			Per capita[1]			Supplements to wages and salaries, employer contributions (mil dol)						Contributions for government social insurance (mil dol)	
	Total (mil dol)	Percent change 2019–2020	Dollars	Rank	Wages and salaries (mil dol)	Pension and insurance	Government social insurance	Proprietors' income (mil dol)	Dividends, interest, and rent (mil dol)	Personal transfer reecipts (mil dol)	Total (mil dol)	From employee and self-employed	From employer
	62	63	64	65	66	67	68	69	70	71	72	73	74
NEW YORK— Cont'd													
Genesee	2,819	8.6	49,468	1,201	1,037	267	88	188	364	835	1,581	93	88
Greene	2,476	7.1	52,484	891	691	200	57	167	388	740	1,115	72	57
Hamilton	261	5.4	60,014	426	67	27	6	13	65	80	113	8	6
Herkimer	2,881	8.3	47,266	1,481	701	193	59	152	368	984	1,105	75	59
Jefferson	5,833	8.3	53,964	785	2,802	835	255	258	902	1,581	4,150	204	255
Kings	150,985	8.4	59,468	454	42,013	9,162	3,448	9,402	16,811	45,401	64,024	3,629	3,448
Lewis	1,362	9.7	51,992	935	284	93	24	125	163	366	526	30	24
Livingston	3,081	6.2	49,382	1,214	872	260	74	330	387	883	1,536	91	74
Madison	3,463	7.5	49,137	1,241	954	240	80	221	488	966	1,495	95	80
Monroe	43,194	7.4	58,299	507	21,576	4,034	1,722	2,900	6,770	11,695	30,232	1,718	1,722
Montgomery	2,278	9.9	46,332	1,603	870	181	75	126	237	841	1,252	82	75
Nassau	130,070	4.1	96,253	25	41,666	7,203	3,231	9,726	30,624	20,700	61,827	3,379	3,231
New York	308,244	0.9	191,220	2	332,772	35,253	18,591	52,984	94,003	30,733	439,599	22,551	18,591
Niagara	10,734	8.9	51,506	979	3,196	747	269	598	1,244	3,500	4,810	312	269
Oneida	11,413	7.5	50,201	1,125	4,986	1,248	404	807	1,525	3,633	7,445	436	404
Onondaga	27,057	8.0	58,919	483	13,801	2,935	1,096	2,410	3,779	7,088	20,242	1,105	1,096
Ontario	6,532	7.4	59,335	459	2,706	569	222	345	1,097	1,655	3,843	224	222
Orange	22,223	8.3	57,688	532	8,009	1,791	651	1,218	2,940	5,496	11,669	648	651
Orleans	1,778	10.7	44,477	1,878	531	168	47	141	202	599	888	53	47
Oswego	5,376	9.3	46,210	1,620	1,678	494	136	168	597	1,798	2,475	158	136
Otsego	2,893	6.7	49,275	1,221	1,099	268	89	234	427	883	1,690	102	89
Putnam	7,208	5.2	73,152	123	1,521	318	122	369	1,209	1,329	2,330	142	122
Queens	127,062	9.4	57,085	569	41,451	9,177	3,363	8,162	14,124	41,182	62,153	3,530	3,363
Rensselaer	8,656	7.9	54,748	721	3,459	775	267	337	1,168	2,275	4,838	285	267
Richmond	29,736	7.7	62,558	331	7,420	1,618	610	1,352	3,738	8,793	11,000	673	610
Rockland	21,645	6.6	66,350	235	7,245	1,434	572	1,253	3,698	4,991	10,505	598	572
St. Lawrence	4,613	8.7	43,034	2,058	1,745	502	146	214	596	1,591	2,607	160	146
Saratoga	17,825	7.5	77,398	92	5,033	961	403	804	4,257	3,008	7,201	426	403
Schenectady	9,043	7.1	58,210	508	3,732	705	291	832	1,242	2,357	5,560	326	291
Schoharie	1,447	9.2	46,469	1,583	387	114	32	84	187	454	618	38	32
Schuyler	831	9.2	46,971	1,521	208	54	18	50	105	295	331	23	18
Seneca	1,498	8.7	44,065	1,939	595	158	48	102	211	494	904	53	48
Steuben	4,764	7.0	50,331	1,107	2,201	437	170	230	669	1,476	3,038	183	170
Suffolk	113,095	6.0	76,713	95	43,701	8,239	3,284	7,362	20,551	23,233	62,585	3,471	3,284
Sullivan	3,961	8.0	52,249	912	1,302	320	109	157	621	1,338	1,887	119	109
Tioga	2,443	8.2	50,990	1,031	731	158	57	130	348	707	1,076	71	57
Tompkins	5,001	6.5	49,486	1,198	2,895	527	244	322	950	1,127	3,988	218	244
Ulster	9,965	6.6	56,071	636	2,907	728	238	608	1,739	2,806	4,481	281	238
Warren	3,794	8.5	59,509	452	1,771	362	143	281	664	1,064	2,558	152	143
Washington	2,806	8.9	46,305	1,607	739	219	62	150	371	881	1,171	78	62
Wayne	4,582	5.9	51,282	995	1,337	375	110	377	528	1,380	2,200	137	110
Westchester	111,440	2.7	115,386	14	34,579	5,399	2,410	9,485	29,021	14,431	51,873	2,763	2,410
Wyoming	1,868	9.8	47,331	1,473	641	192	56	184	228	548	1,073	59	56
Yates	1,121	8.2	45,258	1,762	277	74	24	130	205	355	504	32	24
NORTH CAROLINA	533,269	6.5	50,996	X	264,742	39,678	18,884	37,751	92,043	124,548	361,055	23,387	18,884
Alamance	7,535	8.0	43,973	1,950	3,082	445	224	384	1,166	2,018	4,134	294	224
Alexander	1,504	6.5	40,176	2,437	365	66	28	98	193	480	557	44	28
Alleghany	454	7.5	40,599	2,384	118	25	9	38	105	165	190	16	9
Anson	935	5.2	38,785	2,595	291	63	22	67	108	349	443	32	22
Ashe	1,076	7.9	39,612	2,491	318	55	24	52	215	391	448	40	24
Avery	693	7.3	39,437	2,518	269	47	21	42	158	226	379	27	21
Beaufort	2,182	5.6	46,363	1,597	701	132	51	139	379	722	1,024	79	51
Bertie	755	6.0	40,351	2,409	231	48	18	48	102	295	346	26	18
Bladen	1,292	10.4	39,264	2,539	581	101	46	109	148	490	838	56	46
Brunswick	6,979	8.2	46,829	1,533	1,588	279	118	413	1,629	2,348	2,398	225	118
Buncombe	14,046	5.5	53,309	834	6,538	1,017	491	1,292	3,354	3,336	9,337	621	491
Burke	3,521	8.1	38,946	2,572	1,270	244	95	179	510	1,186	1,788	133	95
Cabarrus	11,003	8.6	49,679	1,175	3,813	597	272	616	1,422	2,237	5,298	354	272
Caldwell	3,193	7.4	38,894	2,580	1,207	205	88	162	419	1,110	1,663	126	88
Camden	534	8.2	48,642	1,300	58	12	4	25	84	122	100	9	4
Carteret	3,706	5.5	53,276	836	1,004	179	74	232	875	1,008	1,489	118	74
Caswell	881	8.3	39,265	2,538	131	29	10	37	113	325	206	19	10
Catawba	7,886	7.1	49,193	1,230	4,329	668	321	540	1,265	2,089	5,859	387	321
Chatham	5,057	4.6	66,766	220	696	113	52	177	1,283	936	1,037	92	52
Cherokee	1,065	8.8	36,620	2,810	314	57	24	62	195	475	456	43	24

1. Based on the resident population estimated as of July 1 of the year shown.

STATE County	Earnings, 2020 (cont.) — Percent by selected industries: Farm	Mining, quarrying, and extractions	Construction	Manu-facturing	Information; professional, scientific, technical services	Retail trade	Finance, insurance, real estate, and leasing	Health care and social assistance	Govern-ment	Social Security beneficiaries, December 2020: Number	Rate[1]	Supple-mental Security Income recipients, 2020	Housing units, 2021: Total	Percent change, 2010–2021
	75	76	77	78	79	80	81	82	83	84	85	86	87	88
NEW YORK— Cont'd														
Genesee	5.4	0.4	5.7	15.4	2.8	7.3	3.2	10.7	27.6	14,430	249	1,081	26,098	0.3
Greene	0.4	0.0	5.6	7.2	5.0	8.1	3.4	5.3	34.9	12,850	265	1,248	28,993	0.2
Hamilton	0.0	0.0	7.2	1.0	D	6.9	D	D	57.2	1,705	333	59	7,880	0.6
Herkimer	2.6	0.3	8.1	12.5	2.9	11.9	2.3	10.6	29.6	15,995	267	1,532	32,408	0.2
Jefferson	2.2	0.2	4.1	3.2	2.6	6.1	2.4	10.7	57.4	23,060	198	2,733	61,726	0.2
Kings	0.0	D	5.2	1.8	11.0	6.4	4.8	24.0	24.3	347,680	132	115,619	1,086,068	0.6
Lewis	13.6	D	6.4	14.6	2.5	5.7	1.8	D	34.4	6,160	232	537	15,558	0.5
Livingston	4.9	D	7.1	8.1	2.9	6.4	1.8	8.0	32.1	14,975	243	1,253	27,163	0.1
Madison	3.3	D	6.6	13.1	5.1	8.8	2.9	D	23.3	15,650	231	1,224	30,629	0.2
Monroe	0.1	0.0	5.6	11.4	12.7	5.3	6.8	15.6	14.1	166,750	221	26,201	338,052	0.4
Montgomery	2.8	0.3	5.0	14.8	2.6	9.7	2.0	D	17.7	13,505	273	1,865	22,892	0.1
Nassau	0.0	D	6.3	2.7	12.4	6.8	10.5	21.6	16.2	264,795	190	15,460	478,163	0.2
New York	0.0	0.0	1.4	0.5	31.7	2.3	31.4	5.1	7.1	260,125	165	63,586	916,602	0.2
Niagara	1.1	0.3	5.4	19.2	5.5	7.6	2.8	13.5	24.1	54,520	258	5,645	100,304	0.1
Oneida	0.6	0.3	4.0	8.6	6.7	6.0	8.3	17.3	29.5	56,515	245	7,720	105,260	0.3
Onondaga	0.4	0.0	4.9	9.1	10.9	5.4	7.6	13.4	20.1	101,090	214	13,994	211,699	0.1
Ontario	2.0	0.1	10.7	14.2	6.4	7.8	3.7	12.5	19.7	28,210	251	1,899	52,930	0.6
Orange	0.4	0.1	6.8	5.8	8.8	7.9	4.1	15.1	27.9	68,780	170	6,752	148,237	0.7
Orleans	7.7	1.0	5.9	16.0	2.6	5.8	2.3	D	39.0	9,880	246	922	18,245	0.1
Oswego	0.7	0.2	7.1	11.9	D	7.7	2.7	10.3	30.8	28,560	243	3,280	54,819	0.6
Otsego	1.5	D	4.3	4.5	3.5	8.0	7.4	29.2	21.4	15,130	260	1,288	29,922	0.3
Putnam	0.1	D	12.0	5.4	9.8	6.1	4.1	16.6	23.6	19,705	201	806	38,359	0.1
Queens	0.0	D	9.8	2.1	5.4	5.0	5.2	16.5	26.4	348,890	150	65,076	902,824	0.6
Rensselaer	0.4	0.3	7.0	19.2	8.5	5.5	3.2	11.0	21.3	35,280	220	4,063	74,356	0.2
Richmond	0.0	0.0	10.6	0.8	5.4	6.6	4.2	21.6	26.8	92,535	188	14,598	184,162	0.2
Rockland	0.0	D	8.4	8.5	10.8	6.7	3.5	17.7	19.5	56,160	166	4,861	108,510	0.3
St. Lawrence	3.3	0.6	4.7	7.5	3.4	6.9	2.3	15.4	36.9	26,520	245	3,506	51,776	0.3
Saratoga	0.5	D	8.9	12.8	11.6	6.8	9.4	11.2	15.3	52,695	222	2,775	111,077	0.8
Schenectady	0.0	D	5.1	8.5	17.1	5.5	5.0	13.5	17.5	33,970	215	5,121	70,986	0.2
Schoharie	3.3	0.5	11.4	2.7	3.6	8.0	5.1	9.6	36.6	8,080	271	615	16,498	0.3
Schuyler	6.4	D	9.7	15.2	2.5	7.8	D	12.3	25.1	5,115	288	377	9,681	0.5
Seneca	3.9	D	4.3	23.2	D	8.3	2.0	D	30.0	8,485	252	772	16,151	0.3
Steuben	2.4	0.2	2.4	14.6	19.3	5.2	3.2	10.4	20.8	24,190	260	2,825	47,576	0.4
Suffolk	0.2	D	9.6	7.8	9.5	6.3	10.3	12.5	20.6	303,610	199	18,800	579,431	0.1
Sullivan	-0.1	0.4	6.7	5.3	3.9	6.2	3.8	19.9	30.8	18,415	231	2,612	49,565	0.8
Tioga	1.3	0.9	4.9	39.8	D	5.4	2.1	5.2	19.0	12,735	265	1,137	21,918	0.6
Tompkins	0.7	D	2.3	5.4	9.4	4.8	3.3	D	12.9	17,230	164	1,450	47,375	0.6
Ulster	0.6	0.2	6.7	5.9	7.2	8.1	4.8	13.3	29.7	43,135	236	3,909	86,168	0.3
Warren	0.1	0.7	6.8	12.0	7.9	9.2	6.2	17.7	15.0	19,345	295	1,432	40,144	0.5
Washington	4.0	0.6	8.3	17.3	D	7.4	1.9	7.1	36.6	15,280	251	1,598	29,098	0.3
Wayne	3.6	D	7.8	25.0	3.2	6.5	2.9	6.8	25.8	24,045	264	2,232	42,364	0.2
Westchester	0.0	D	5.6	3.7	19.8	4.6	13.7	13.7	15.9	172,100	172	16,594	392,186	0.7
Wyoming	12.0	D	4.7	11.2	D	6.4	1.9	D	37.1	9,710	240	632	18,275	0.2
Yates	7.7	D	10.6	14.3	D	7.7	3.8	D	19.1	6,250	254	489	13,135	0.5
NORTH CAROLINA	0.6	0.0	6.6	10.3	11.9	6.1	9.9	10.0	17.9	2,183,353	207	227,652	4,801,712	1.6
Alamance	0.0	D	7.2	14.4	4.8	9.9	7.1	18.9	10.8	36,860	212	3,638	75,276	2.2
Alexander	3.6	D	6.4	31.6	2.1	4.7	3.9	5.4	22.4	9,700	265	627	16,105	0.8
Alleghany	5.7	D	8.4	17.1	3.3	7.0	5.7	D	18.6	3,640	329	297	7,722	0.6
Anson	9.2	D	4.6	18.2	D	4.5	1.8	4.8	27.1	6,200	281	988	9,893	0.5
Ashe	-0.3	D	16.7	11.3	D	8.8	6.3	11.7	15.0	8,635	323	755	17,072	0.7
Avery	0.9	D	11.3	0.9	D	8.4	5.0	D	23.7	4,695	263	382	14,002	1.0
Beaufort	3.3	D	5.8	19.6	3.1	8.1	5.1	8.9	17.6	14,905	335	1,771	24,305	0.7
Bertie	12.3	D	D	D	D	2.5	D	D	26.1	5,970	341	1,060	8,972	0.3
Bladen	9.9	0.0	3.1	41.5	D	3.5	1.3	3.1	16.0	8,875	301	1,465	15,250	0.7
Brunswick	0.4	D	12.1	4.9	D	9.0	7.0	11.9	16.1	53,350	370	2,139	92,903	4.2
Buncombe	0.4	0.1	6.8	10.3	8.4	7.6	7.1	19.8	14.4	63,410	234	5,371	131,995	1.8
Burke	0.7	D	3.9	23.3	2.6	6.0	3.0	16.7	25.5	23,215	265	2,035	39,889	0.8
Cabarrus	0.3	D	8.1	7.2	5.9	8.4	5.0	6.6	22.3	37,545	162	3,331	90,872	3.2
Caldwell	0.9	D	5.2	24.1	D	6.3	2.7	12.5	15.4	21,560	268	2,009	37,153	0.6
Camden	7.0	0.0	10.5	1.8	4.9	4.8	6.4	6.9	29.1	2,255	208	117	4,241	2.5
Carteret	0.2	D	9.1	3.6	6.0	12.5	8.7	10.3	24.1	20,630	301	1,161	51,523	1.1
Caswell	5.3	D	12.1	7.5	3.3	3.7	3.7	D	34.8	6,705	295	649	10,472	0.2
Catawba	0.3	D	4.7	26.7	4.6	8.9	4.4	9.7	11.8	39,700	245	3,174	71,780	1.2
Chatham	0.6	D	8.0	8.8	12.0	6.8	4.5	13.1	16.8	20,100	258	910	34,803	1.8
Cherokee	1.7	D	9.2	7.5	9.1	11.2	5.9	D	21.5	10,905	374	763	18,156	1.4

1. Per 1,000 resident population estimated as of July 1 of the year shown.

STATE County	Housing units, 2016–2020: Occupied units: Total	Owner-occupied: Percent	Owner-occupied: Median value[1]	Owner-occupied: Median owner cost as a percent of income: With a mort- gage	Owner-occupied: Median owner cost as a percent of income: Without a mort- gage[2]	Renter-occupied: Median rent[3]	Renter-occupied: Median rent as a percent of income[2]	Sub- standard units[4] (percent)	Civilian labor force, 2021: Total	Civilian labor force, 2021: Percent change, 2020–2021	Unemployment: Total	Unemployment: Rate[5]	Civilian employment[6], 2016–2020: Total	Percent: Management, business, science, and arts	Percent: Construction, production, and maintenance occupations
	89	90	91	92	93	94	95	96	97	98	99	100	101	102	103
NEW YORK— Cont'd															
Genesee	24,174	72.4	125,200	18.2	11.6	786	27.2	2.5	29,268	-0.8	1,244	4.3	29,157	31.3	28.8
Greene	17,681	76.6	185,600	23.0	13.8	925	34.3	2.0	20,305	-1.3	1,003	4.9	20,869	36.5	23.5
Hamilton	1,416	85.3	170,500	20.8	11.7	841	22.9	1.2	2,210	0.8	98	4.4	2,044	30.9	27.4
Herkimer	25,093	74.3	106,600	18.0	11.0	680	24.8	1.6	27,514	-1.6	1,596	5.8	28,964	33.3	26.5
Jefferson	43,046	55.7	150,100	19.4	11.3	1,018	28.9	2.4	43,765	-0.7	2,201	5.0	42,808	33.3	23.4
Kings	972,314	30.3	734,800	28.0	13.4	1,483	31.5	10.2	1,193,447	-1.4	120,784	10.1	1,216,982	44.5	14.3
Lewis	10,398	80.9	122,800	20.2	11.2	700	25.7	1.6	11,534	-0.6	579	5.0	11,830	33.2	29.2
Livingston	24,496	76.3	134,000	19.4	12.9	793	32.1	1.2	29,821	-1.4	1,288	4.3	29,318	35.9	26.4
Madison	25,959	78.5	140,000	20.4	12.5	768	27.2	0.8	32,206	-2.2	1,457	4.5	33,627	36.9	23.7
Monroe	305,210	63.3	152,000	19.3	12.0	947	31.0	1.6	360,379	-1.5	18,619	5.2	366,871	45.7	16.1
Montgomery	19,621	67.5	110,700	19.4	13.6	759	31.6	2.1	21,900	-2.4	1,239	5.7	22,235	31.1	28.7
Nassau	449,967	81.1	524,400	25.5	16.6	1,831	32.5	3.0	708,286	-0.3	31,632	4.5	684,857	47.4	14.0
New York	758,720	24.1	1,024,500	18.6	10.0	1,787	27.6	6.3	894,457	-0.9	67,611	7.6	894,171	62.3	6.3
Niagara	90,022	71.7	131,600	18.8	12.3	714	28.3	1.3	96,212	-3.0	5,453	5.7	99,735	35.6	23.5
Oneida	90,675	68.7	133,100	18.7	11.8	777	27.5	2.4	100,177	-2.2	5,065	5.1	102,777	39.1	19.1
Onondaga	187,349	65.1	148,100	18.6	11.6	888	29.3	2.1	219,876	-1.9	10,777	4.9	220,251	43.0	16.9
Ontario	45,711	72.7	163,100	19.1	12.5	898	29.4	1.4	54,962	-1.3	2,340	4.3	54,818	42.5	19.8
Orange	130,428	67.8	278,400	24.7	15.3	1,294	32.7	3.8	183,818	-1.5	8,658	4.7	176,196	37.8	20.7
Orleans	16,634	75.1	101,400	20.0	14.3	782	27.7	1.8	16,976	-2.2	876	5.2	17,425	29.5	32.4
Oswego	46,597	72.8	109,500	18.7	11.9	806	29.5	2.9	51,853	-2.1	2,854	5.5	54,589	31.7	27.8
Otsego	23,768	72.2	150,700	19.9	11.3	827	27.8	1.8	26,786	-1.1	1,191	4.4	27,795	35.9	21.0
Putnam	34,915	82.5	366,400	25.7	15.2	1,489	30.2	1.5	50,366	-1.6	2,098	4.2	51,271	44.5	17.2
Queens	783,362	45.1	575,600	28.4	14.1	1,629	31.6	9.7	1,127,854	-2.0	108,504	9.6	1,120,366	35.9	19.5
Rensselaer	65,455	62.9	197,100	19.9	12.4	987	27.0	1.6	80,735	-1.4	3,529	4.4	81,025	43.7	18.8
Richmond	167,160	68.8	546,100	25.9	14.5	1,379	32.3	4.8	221,184	-0.8	19,219	8.7	217,404	42.1	17.2
Rockland	101,167	67.9	452,500	26.9	17.8	1,558	34.9	6.8	153,829	-1.3	6,765	4.4	146,382	46.4	14.0
St. Lawrence	41,925	72.5	97,000	18.8	11.1	715	28.6	3.5	42,919	-1.8	2,189	5.1	44,361	36.9	22.4
Saratoga	95,898	72.1	266,000	19.2	11.1	1,151	24.9	1.2	119,267	-1.7	4,513	3.8	121,132	47.7	16.6
Schenectady	57,479	64.0	172,500	20.2	11.4	964	29.0	1.3	76,733	-1.9	3,775	4.9	72,967	40.4	18.6
Schoharie	12,780	75.4	142,600	21.3	12.6	809	25.8	2.4	14,511	-1.8	659	4.5	14,564	36.2	26.6
Schuyler	7,402	74.8	127,000	19.4	14.6	765	28.5	3.3	8,046	-1.6	397	4.9	8,221	35.7	25.1
Seneca	13,784	72.6	107,500	19.0	13.1	786	26.8	1.6	15,025	-3.2	708	4.7	15,479	33.5	27.4
Steuben	40,099	73.0	104,200	18.5	11.9	714	26.4	1.6	41,448	-2.8	2,059	5.0	43,759	36.7	27.2
Suffolk	495,667	81.4	413,900	25.8	17.0	1,810	34.1	2.5	776,355	-0.3	35,366	4.6	752,725	41.4	18.3
Sullivan	28,762	69.5	175,900	22.2	15.8	886	28.6	2.0	36,118	-0.9	1,768	4.9	33,068	35.5	23.8
Tioga	20,643	77.9	119,800	19.0	11.3	782	29.3	1.2	21,974	-2.5	969	4.4	22,563	37.3	25.8
Tompkins	40,817	54.0	218,700	20.2	10.5	1,144	36.7	2.0	48,914	-1.2	1,821	3.7	51,137	54.3	12.0
Ulster	70,088	68.6	239,400	23.9	14.8	1,119	34.4	2.2	86,356	-1.2	4,024	4.7	85,866	39.3	19.8
Warren	29,034	70.7	208,600	20.3	12.0	932	29.2	1.2	31,045	-1.0	1,514	4.9	32,257	37.3	19.6
Washington	24,054	72.7	151,500	19.8	13.0	861	28.9	2.0	27,402	-0.6	1,255	4.6	28,146	31.4	28.9
Wayne	37,281	78.1	130,000	20.0	11.4	772	28.8	1.7	42,847	-1.6	1,911	4.5	44,377	33.8	27.6
Westchester	353,485	61.4	544,100	23.6	15.6	1,599	31.7	4.3	480,109	-1.2	23,100	4.8	480,956	49.3	13.6
Wyoming	16,055	76.6	118,800	18.7	11.8	681	22.4	0.9	17,916	-1.5	801	4.5	18,792	31.6	28.8
Yates	8,901	76.5	142,300	21.8	12.5	712	27.2	2.3	11,527	-2.1	438	3.8	11,019	32.8	29.1
NORTH CAROLINA	4,031,592	65.7	182,100	19.6	10.1	932	28.6	2.5	4,959,672	2.3	238,474	4.8	4,833,887	38.9	23.4
Alamance	65,455	66.5	160,900	19.1	10.0	822	29.0	2.2	81,009	2.6	3,887	4.8	77,752	34.9	27.0
Alexander	14,049	79.9	138,900	16.8	10.1	691	19.7	2.9	17,283	0.9	730	4.2	16,821	26.9	43.3
Alleghany	5,001	75.5	150,500	22.8	10.3	626	29.1	2.0	4,224	2.9	195	4.6	4,587	33.7	28.0
Anson	9,803	66.9	104,100	19.7	13.9	746	30.8	2.4	10,111	0.1	642	6.3	10,353	25.3	41.6
Ashe	11,885	79.0	158,200	21.3	10.5	657	27.8	1.6	12,614	3.0	501	4.0	12,391	28.1	29.9
Avery	6,569	77.7	151,800	23.1	10.0	759	30.3	2.0	7,380	4.0	291	3.9	6,592	31.4	21.3
Beaufort	20,219	72.2	138,000	20.3	12.6	742	29.8	1.7	19,472	3.3	935	4.8	19,680	31.9	31.4
Bertie	8,008	71.1	78,500	26.8	14.9	719	30.6	3.6	7,203	-2.4	425	5.9	6,955	22.5	39.5
Bladen	13,394	72.2	98,700	24.7	12.7	667	32.3	1.0	14,223	1.2	826	5.8	12,565	30.9	30.0
Brunswick	59,416	80.9	220,400	22.4	11.2	984	30.1	1.7	54,167	4.6	3,247	6.0	53,944	32.5	23.6
Buncombe	105,177	63.4	250,600	21.0	10.0	1,019	30.6	2.5	136,123	2.0	5,705	4.2	128,399	39.8	19.3
Burke	35,664	75.5	120,600	18.9	10.4	668	27.2	3.0	39,264	1.7	1,783	4.5	39,374	28.2	32.5
Cabarrus	72,843	73.0	219,100	18.8	10.0	966	27.0	3.5	109,654	2.3	4,809	4.4	105,370	40.8	22.5
Caldwell	32,798	73.3	125,200	18.7	10.1	647	25.8	2.9	35,073	1.4	1,733	4.9	36,303	26.8	35.2
Camden	3,912	76.9	221,000	24.2	12.8	942	24.8	1.5	4,514	1.5	178	3.9	4,483	41.2	23.3
Carteret	30,060	71.6	226,700	22.6	11.0	921	27.4	1.2	31,149	2.7	1,282	4.1	30,754	34.8	23.2
Caswell	8,993	74.2	113,600	18.3	10.0	571	32.6	0.6	9,473	0.9	503	5.3	9,381	31.7	32.0
Catawba	62,940	70.9	156,200	18.5	10.0	754	23.5	3.2	76,433	0.9	3,564	4.7	74,879	31.2	33.2
Chatham	29,904	76.9	310,000	18.9	10.1	873	29.2	1.8	36,405	4.1	1,297	3.6	33,187	46.1	19.5
Cherokee	12,546	81.5	163,900	21.0	11.6	713	27.2	1.4	10,592	-0.6	526	5.0	11,077	29.1	25.4

1. Specified owner-occupied units. 2. A value of 10.0 represents 10 percent or less; a value of 50.0 represents 50 percent or more. 3. Specified renter-occupied units. 4. Overcrowded or lacking complete plumbing facilities. 5. Percent of civilian labor force. 6. Civilian employed persons 16 years old and over.

STATE County	Private nonfarm establishments, employment and payroll, 2020									Agriculture, 2017			
		Employment						Annual payroll		Farms			Farm producers whose primary occupation is farming (percent)
											Percent with:		
	Number of establish-ments	Total	Health care and social assistance	Manufac-turing	Retail trade	Finance and insurance	Professional, scientific, and technical services	Total (mil dol)	Average per employee (dollars)	Number	Fewer than 50 acres	1000 acres or more	
	104	105	106	107	108	109	110	111	112	113	114	115	116
NEW YORK— Cont'd													
Genesee	1,245	16,611	2,889	3,463	2,611	355	320	663	39,901	485	38.8	7.8	51.5
Greene	1,135	10,313	1,223	736	2,227	338	279	383	37,180	206	35.9	2.9	50.3
Hamilton	185	899	27	NA	160	77	4	32	35,346	14	35.7	NA	33.3
Herkimer	1,080	12,350	2,125	2,588	1,908	296	156	459	37,160	596	24.3	1.2	47.4
Jefferson	2,370	28,834	6,746	2,214	5,989	766	825	1,150	39,899	792	26.5	5.6	51.5
Kings	59,985	694,127	273,988	17,270	78,277	17,328	25,080	28,753	41,423	19	100.0	NA	15.4
Lewis	518	4,661	975	1,077	856	79	120	198	42,386	625	23.8	5.0	56.6
Livingston	1,211	13,634	1,966	1,825	2,673	216	346	518	37,999	661	43.9	8.9	47.4
Madison	1,313	17,329	3,285	2,614	2,669	369	680	670	38,671	691	27.4	4.5	54.0
Monroe	17,383	354,169	74,098	36,192	40,526	12,456	25,348	17,164	48,462	527	56.4	6.1	51.8
Montgomery	1,034	16,165	4,073	2,970	3,084	264	297	644	39,814	564	28.4	2.8	62.4
Nassau	48,270	575,632	136,770	14,136	77,188	34,055	41,065	31,776	55,203	32	81.3	NA	23.1
New York	99,048	2,355,277	287,870	13,663	146,346	298,105	345,037	275,961	117,167	7	100.0	NA	50.0
Niagara	4,516	61,980	12,031	8,604	10,893	1,301	1,567	2,250	36,299	690	50.1	5.2	43.0
Oneida	4,773	87,671	20,557	9,477	11,501	6,425	4,051	3,686	42,045	967	34.1	2.5	45.5
Onondaga	11,322	222,141	44,023	16,417	27,802	9,953	15,910	10,762	48,446	623	44.6	5.1	48.9
Ontario	2,866	46,659	8,878	6,772	8,930	953	1,778	2,434	52,170	833	40.3	5.2	49.2
Orange	9,714	121,375	25,053	8,725	22,421	2,786	4,637	5,256	43,302	621	43.6	1.8	53.1
Orleans	638	7,565	1,328	1,896	1,073	390	194	290	38,341	498	43.4	5.8	56.8
Oswego	2,080	23,341	4,952	2,687	4,288	650	798	1,079	46,217	612	40.2	1.1	43.4
Otsego	1,298	18,912	6,390	963	2,839	1,195	470	806	42,608	880	27.0	1.8	45.1
Putnam	2,841	22,010	5,077	1,306	3,127	520	1,423	1,014	46,086	89	64.0	NA	32.8
Queens	49,999	603,514	165,977	17,396	59,781	18,975	17,319	29,389	48,696	4	100.0	NA	20.0
Rensselaer	3,008	45,302	8,580	4,906	5,674	1,105	3,040	2,629	58,042	470	37.0	1.9	44.6
Richmond	9,352	113,081	33,945	1,167	21,198	3,290	3,889	5,116	45,243	6	100.0	NA	6.1
Rockland	10,348	120,524	32,768	7,403	14,259	3,075	6,707	5,762	47,811	14	71.4	NA	59.5
St. Lawrence	1,827	26,318	6,846	2,156	4,416	727	639	1,139	43,295	1,253	16.7	3.9	49.0
Saratoga	5,365	75,962	12,372	8,016	11,097	3,113	5,225	3,830	50,423	591	54.0	2.0	47.3
Schenectady	2,933	53,356	12,122	4,749	6,801	2,174	5,692	2,966	55,587	185	43.8	NA	41.7
Schoharie	564	4,975	701	369	1,042	197	166	195	39,210	541	27.7	1.3	51.2
Schuyler	359	3,600	776	599	615	48	35	138	38,302	408	38.5	2.2	46.4
Seneca	706	10,032	862	1,848	2,133	204	159	361	35,997	516	39.7	3.5	55.6
Steuben	1,743	25,344	6,841	3,784	4,082	988	972	1,457	57,488	1,542	21.8	4.5	44.9
Suffolk	49,173	591,446	112,177	53,678	81,976	23,120	39,731	33,389	56,453	560	74.1	0.4	58.1
Sullivan	1,981	23,016	7,153	1,262	2,687	569	880	795	34,554	366	50.3	2.2	45.0
Tioga	745	10,365	1,091	981	1,284	199	2,809	573	55,266	535	29.0	2.2	46.4
Tompkins	2,269	48,904	6,461	2,338	4,672	1,224	2,976	2,160	44,169	523	47.6	2.9	39.6
Ulster	4,781	45,886	9,509	3,219	8,455	1,973	1,778	1,715	37,367	421	51.8	0.7	51.0
Warren	2,186	30,940	6,443	3,820	5,491	1,139	884	1,357	43,867	80	58.8	NA	40.8
Washington	1,027	10,653	1,737	2,815	1,841	200	325	460	43,174	915	37.2	2.8	43.6
Wayne	1,683	20,360	2,825	6,702	3,506	460	459	905	44,468	829	43.4	4.0	53.0
Westchester	31,014	384,010	84,815	9,647	47,425	20,486	24,403	27,526	71,679	115	81.7	1.7	49.5
Wyoming	764	8,588	1,267	1,753	1,321	359	300	354	41,174	729	41.0	6.4	51.9
Yates	525	4,990	859	935	759	89	104	166	33,328	867	30.8	1.4	60.4
NORTH CAROLINA	240,760	3,962,754	626,383	446,033	499,509	208,418	241,388	199,256	50,282	46,418	47.9	3.8	42.7
Alamance	3,406	59,474	11,312	8,383	9,530	1,381	1,616	2,397	40,299	720	45.8	0.7	40.6
Alexander	572	7,521	529	3,704	894	165	124	276	36,732	544	50.0	0.9	45.4
Alleghany	245	2,261	343	645	307	73	48	79	34,776	448	37.3	3.1	38.2
Anson	388	4,819	769	1,495	696	80	91	156	32,355	412	32.8	4.4	41.7
Ashe	534	6,055	1,109	1,226	1,104	187	96	225	37,092	864	42.0	1.9	43.5
Avery	491	4,796	717	133	906	62	73	156	32,470	351	50.4	1.7	44.7
Beaufort	1,089	12,744	2,173	2,542	2,300	383	268	506	39,730	310	38.7	15.5	46.1
Bertie	286	5,153	818	2,326	484	58	32	161	31,314	323	26.9	10.8	65.4
Bladen	519	10,581	994	5,279	806	141	127	350	33,109	512	35.9	7.4	48.6
Brunswick	2,639	28,417	4,187	1,454	5,606	653	728	1,080	38,008	231	42.0	5.2	43.9
Buncombe	9,111	124,708	26,335	13,459	18,875	2,901	5,133	5,176	41,507	1,073	67.3	0.5	38.0
Burke	1,452	24,324	5,823	7,558	3,054	365	396	870	35,780	508	56.1	0.6	38.9
Cabarrus	4,717	71,229	10,156	6,579	13,329	961	1,961	2,829	39,714	629	56.6	1.6	34.8
Caldwell	1,353	20,982	3,397	6,143	2,738	351	372	819	39,011	411	57.2	0.5	39.6
Camden	121	560	26	NA	89	16	21	17	29,934	81	48.1	24.7	59.1
Carteret	2,083	20,126	3,367	937	4,431	584	684	732	36,355	158	78.5	2.5	29.8
Caswell	234	1,754	421	92	304	46	40	57	32,433	493	28.6	3.4	44.9
Catawba	4,240	84,712	13,335	23,110	9,860	1,829	2,551	3,599	42,488	638	53.8	1.1	36.7
Chatham	1,526	15,883	2,816	3,175	2,273	293	672	581	36,576	1,116	48.7	0.4	37.8
Cherokee	583	7,228	1,107	1,352	1,473	191	112	235	32,476	277	57.4	0.7	39.0

STATE County	Agriculture, 2017 (cont.) — Land in farms: Acreage (1,000)	Land in farms: Percent change, 2012–2017	Land in farms — Acres: Average size of farm	Acres: Total irrigated (1,000)	Acres: Total cropland (1,000)	Value of land and buildings (dollars): Average per farm	Value of land and buildings (dollars): Average per acre	Value of machinery and equipment, average per farm (dollars)	Value of products sold: Total (mil dol)	Value of products sold: Average per farm (acres)	Value of products sold — Percent from: Crops	Percent from: Livestock and poultry products	Organic farms (number)	Farms with internet access (percent)	Government payments: Total ($1,000)	Government payments: Percent of farms
	117	118	119	120	121	122	123	124	125	126	127	128	129	130	131	132
NEW YORK— Cont'd																
Genesee	177	-5.5	365	3.3	148.6	1,220,292	3,345	312,434	234.9	484,402	34.4	65.6	13	77.5	2,668	44.7
Greene	35	-18.6	170	0.3	13.7	535,865	3,156	74,288	19.8	95,927	46.7	53.3	7	72.3	138	14.1
Hamilton	1	-55.1	67	D	0.1	222,415	3,341	32,734	D	D	D	NA	NA	92.9	D	14.3
Herkimer	118	-37.2	198	0.2	69.5	452,284	2,289	111,551	58.0	97,277	23.4	76.6	28	67.1	467	18.3
Jefferson	247	-14.9	312	0.4	168.8	836,501	2,677	170,553	165.1	208,404	21.6	78.4	31	74.7	1,986	22.3
Kings	0	D	1	0.0	0.0	536,994	443,604	12,004	D	D	D	D	NA	73.7	NA	NA
Lewis	182	0.4	292	0.1	105.0	586,534	2,009	171,441	153.1	244,917	13.8	86.2	12	72.8	416	22.9
Livingston	189	-2.8	287	0.2	145.9	1,064,151	3,712	196,665	183.7	277,905	30.1	69.9	5	82.8	4,427	30.7
Madison	172	-16.2	249	0.5	105.5	652,012	2,621	142,460	113.6	164,444	24.7	75.3	64	79.7	1,418	22.0
Monroe	107	8.2	203	0.6	85.7	872,523	4,306	155,561	76.6	145,433	86.9	13.1	20	88.4	2,627	17.6
Montgomery	115	29.5	204	0.1	84.5	506,591	2,485	129,396	75.0	132,906	23.8	76.2	55	70.7	404	14.9
Nassau	1	-66.1	28	0.1	0.2	493,741	17,362	39,261	D	D	D	D	2	56.3	NA	NA
New York	0	D	2	D	0.0	D	D	4,336	0.0	6,429	100.0	NA	NA	100.0	NA	NA
Niagara	140	-1.8	203	1.5	116.2	624,058	3,070	161,032	118.6	171,909	63.6	36.4	19	82.3	2,095	21.3
Oneida	193	28.3	199	0.7	119.2	530,131	2,659	118,065	100.5	103,883	29.8	70.2	15	77.4	1,066	19.6
Onondaga	161	70.6	258	1.3	113.1	1,063,488	4,122	196,839	178.4	286,371	22.2	77.8	20	86.2	1,815	25.8
Ontario	200	3.9	240	0.8	163.8	967,405	4,027	189,335	205.2	246,291	30.8	69.2	53	72.6	3,712	29.7
Orange	81	-7.8	131	2.5	49.1	906,875	6,936	113,299	87.9	141,572	75.7	24.3	17	81.3	463	11.0
Orleans	130	-4.1	260	3.2	107.7	825,545	3,173	225,733	155.3	311,811	85.8	14.2	23	71.7	3,323	39.0
Oswego	86	-52.3	141	0.8	40.3	311,560	2,213	87,168	41.2	67,369	50.7	49.3	11	80.1	126	14.4
Otsego	155	143.9	176	0.4	81.5	468,529	2,666	79,321	56.2	63,840	34.5	65.5	62	75.2	619	13.6
Putnam	7	26.5	84	0.1	2.6	503,785	6,001	55,525	3.1	35,337	91.1	8.9	3	97.8	NA	NA
Queens	D	D	D	D	D	679,231	48,517	6,091	0.1	23,500	61.7	38.3	NA	75.0	NA	NA
Rensselaer	83	5.0	176	1.0	46.8	618,709	3,513	107,314	41.0	87,255	59.2	40.8	26	81.9	1,040	22.8
Richmond	D	D	D	0.0	D	D	D	7,145	D	D	D	NA	2	66.7	NA	NA
Rockland	1	9.5	41	0.1	0.3	1,183,762	28,772	115,774	2.1	153,071	95.9	4.1	2	100.0	NA	NA
St. Lawrence	343	-4.0	273	0.4	176.7	500,868	1,832	111,812	191.1	152,496	17.6	82.4	100	77.5	1,130	12.1
Saratoga	72	260.4	121	0.7	41.6	713,614	5,890	125,743	76.8	129,968	24.8	75.2	5	88.0	369	5.1
Schenectady	17	-82.4	94	0.2	9.2	402,340	4,288	59,097	5.5	29,519	64.3	35.7	NA	78.4	21	8.1
Schoharie	100	-47.3	185	0.1	61.1	449,208	2,435	108,434	47.9	88,590	42.0	58.0	28	76.0	259	21.6
Schuyler	79	13.8	193	0.3	48.4	631,614	3,270	127,031	45.8	112,140	33.1	66.9	23	73.5	203	13.5
Seneca	119	-9.0	230	0.2	96.7	862,800	3,756	170,204	90.8	176,052	51.9	48.1	42	68.6	2,029	20.2
Steuben	397	-2.1	258	0.9	240.4	540,734	2,099	128,101	196.0	127,075	35.5	64.5	59	76.6	3,739	29.4
Suffolk	30	-16.5	54	12.1	23.1	655,303	12,219	153,042	225.6	402,818	90.4	9.6	30	86.1	76	2.1
Sullivan	60	11.3	164	0.2	26.2	689,944	4,213	78,765	28.4	77,549	19.7	80.3	15	82.0	152	7.7
Tioga	113	4.9	212	0.4	54.8	483,358	2,285	99,481	40.9	76,368	29.9	70.1	16	83.0	971	25.2
Tompkins	91	0.6	175	0.4	62.1	661,192	3,789	138,310	64.7	123,715	24.6	75.4	45	85.9	1,575	22.6
Ulster	59	-17.3	140	3.7	24.1	965,681	6,899	95,712	54.3	129,088	88.3	11.7	24	86.9	164	8.1
Warren	10	5.9	126	0.0	0.9	526,197	4,174	60,826	D	D	D	D	1	85.0	D	2.5
Washington	185	D	203	1.0	103.0	565,739	2,794	133,639	135.8	148,428	18.0	82.0	18	83.9	1,418	18.7
Wayne	159	-11.2	192	1.5	115.5	659,498	3,437	190,441	221.3	266,942	70.3	29.7	41	79.5	1,462	15.2
Westchester	7	-10.0	61	0.1	4.1	645,915	10,646	72,483	7.0	60,487	72.6	27.4	2	89.6	D	1.7
Wyoming	235	4.0	322	1.7	167.3	1,115,529	3,463	283,473	307.5	421,838	21.1	78.9	14	73.8	2,817	30.0
Yates	115	-9.5	133	0.6	83.0	692,852	5,227	138,824	114.7	132,246	41.2	58.8	119	40.0	825	9.5
NORTH CAROLINA	8,431	0.2	182	143.4	5,000.7	843,154	4,642	112,477	12,900.7	277,924	29.0	71.0	465	75.2	107,565	21.6
Alamance	80	-4.2	111	0.7	33.8	667,068	6,000	64,708	41.8	57,986	35.3	64.7	23	76.4	147	8.6
Alexander	54	-7.7	100	0.3	22.7	560,533	5,632	101,446	176.3	324,158	4.8	95.2	NA	71.1	170	5.5
Alleghany	71	-22.4	158	D	26.2	777,876	4,937	87,835	31.4	70,092	57.9	42.1	6	72.1	32	5.6
Anson	85	2.1	207	0.3	33.6	846,181	4,086	116,392	303.7	737,248	4.3	95.7	NA	69.7	817	27.2
Ashe	110	-2.4	127	0.1	36.4	668,101	5,258	71,937	57.1	66,135	76.9	23.1	6	74.1	76	1.9
Avery	29	1.6	82	0.0	11.9	530,636	6,494	63,220	20.1	57,222	96.1	3.9	6	74.1	37	3.1
Beaufort	139	-5.9	450	2.0	118.6	1,538,781	3,420	265,851	112.0	361,413	65.4	34.6	NA	73.5	4,556	58.4
Bertie	148	0.9	459	3.2	112.3	1,390,119	3,032	238,427	260.5	806,412	30.9	69.1	NA	69.0	4,249	63.2
Bladen	180	53.7	352	6.0	76.8	1,174,444	3,334	225,098	446.4	871,873	15.8	84.2	1	77.7	3,178	35.0
Brunswick	45	-1.6	193	0.5	22.8	758,353	3,920	114,405	46.1	199,437	34.2	65.8	NA	83.1	338	15.2
Buncombe	72	1.1	67	0.8	17.8	670,235	9,949	55,669	48.0	44,747	77.4	22.6	16	78.5	357	12.3
Burke	39	12.4	76	1.8	17.5	433,663	5,701	76,589	81.5	160,366	24.3	75.7	3	75.4	167	5.1
Cabarrus	64	-3.9	101	D	32.8	881,469	8,709	83,381	57.8	91,967	30.7	69.3	NA	75.2	304	10.8
Caldwell	38	18.5	92	0.6	14.4	419,469	4,538	59,705	48.1	116,922	22.9	77.1	3	77.4	152	5.6
Camden	59	20.1	731	D	53.8	2,327,456	3,182	421,303	39.9	492,988	98.3	1.7	NA	64.2	1,262	45.7
Carteret	63	-0.1	397	0.1	44.7	1,801,801	4,536	94,673	23.8	150,506	97.9	2.1	NA	75.3	137	10.1
Caswell	105	8.1	213	1.4	32.3	689,530	3,241	65,751	37.9	76,929	55.7	44.3	13	72.8	164	19.3
Catawba	64	-5.3	100	0.7	34.2	651,547	6,543	87,564	77.3	121,130	28.2	71.8	1	75.4	620	8.5
Chatham	106	-5.2	95	0.3	30.9	522,890	5,505	66,667	171.2	153,360	6.5	93.5	19	78.7	103	8.7
Cherokee	26	22.3	95	0.1	7.6	464,663	4,906	79,138	D	D	D	D	11	81.6	303	18.1

STATE County	Water use, 2015		Wholesale Trade[1], 2017				Retail Trade[2], 2017				Real estate and rental and leasing,[2] 2017			
	Public supply water withdrawn (mil gal/ day)	Public supply gallons withdrawn per person per day	Number of establish-ments	Number of employees	Sales (mil dol)	Average payroll (mil dol)	Number of establish-ments	Number of employees	Sales (mil dol)	Average payroll (mil dol)	Number of establish-ments	Number of employees	Sales (mil dol)	Average payroll (mil dol)
	133	134	135	136	137	138	139	140	141	142	143	144	145	146
NEW YORK— Cont'd														
Genesee	3.7	63.5	D	D	D	D	214	2,766	889.6	69.3	34	158	29.3	6.6
Greene	3.1	64.5	24	770	866.2	42.0	204	2,197	714.0	57.3	43	145	30.0	6.0
Hamilton	0.8	159.2	NA	NA	NA	NA	33	156	37.8	4.8	D	D	D	0.2
Herkimer	28.8	457.1	33	629	193.7	32.2	168	2,007	555.1	50.9	36	139	21.1	3.3
Jefferson	9.3	79.0	56	678	285.3	33.0	484	6,485	1,911.8	171.6	128	624	102.3	24.3
Kings	NA	NA	3,202	27,329	15,914.1	1,213.4	10,799	76,885	28,734.8	2,187.0	4,935	18,848	5,339.0	798.8
Lewis	1.8	67.1	D	D	D	D	79	874	285.5	23.6	D	D	D	D
Livingston	3.8	58.4	37	366	360.1	26.4	209	2,648	700.0	64.9	36	193	25.4	5.6
Madison	1.2	17.0	36	399	172.3	18.0	202	2,488	834.5	73.7	48	165	16.9	4.3
Monroe	53.5	71.4	753	12,126	8,925.0	717.2	2,304	40,485	10,123.1	1,018.4	865	6,191	1,319.9	278.3
Montgomery	2.6	52.6	35	343	158.9	18.7	186	2,636	705.9	72.4	20	73	12.0	2.4
Nassau	194.5	142.9	2,707	28,344	27,806.7	1,869.2	6,033	79,455	26,841.2	2,506.6	2,634	11,791	4,187.6	686.3
New York	NA	NA	6,819	86,176	141,457.7	7,023.0	11,203	161,413	54,824.9	6,029.1	9,795	84,318	40,972.3	6,325.9
Niagara	49.5	232.6	167	1,978	3,544.7	101.2	747	11,361	2,721.4	259.6	158	704	118.9	23.9
Oneida	32.8	141.2	178	2,415	1,294.4	110.3	790	11,703	3,166.5	298.1	161	610	126.0	22.1
Onondaga	58.0	123.9	550	11,142	14,738.1	646.2	1,651	28,181	7,365.6	719.8	561	3,555	739.8	162.0
Ontario	46.5	424.7	128	1,621	847.3	89.1	537	9,457	2,309.9	234.5	113	500	96.0	15.4
Orange	33.0	87.5	460	7,225	8,476.8	363.2	1,582	23,477	7,023.7	619.0	387	1,775	440.8	76.1
Orleans	1.6	39.4	17	303	170.2	12.5	87	1,092	325.4	27.3	19	59	8.0	1.1
Oswego	34.9	290.2	49	800	841.5	42.1	360	4,357	1,417.3	120.1	75	232	45.7	7.9
Otsego	3.1	51.1	37	370	143.6	15.7	272	3,008	907.9	82.9	44	179	39.3	7.2
Putnam	2.8	28.5	118	1,124	588.5	67.9	323	2,921	909.9	82.6	88	243	57.9	10.7
Queens	NA	NA	2,788	24,120	20,233.8	1,293.4	7,940	63,862	19,297.1	1,800.3	3,134	13,605	4,164.0	672.1
Rensselaer	21.6	134.8	93	1,056	1,547.3	66.7	410	5,420	1,558.4	142.5	94	452	102.3	21.8
Richmond	NA	NA	338	1,630	2,725.1	90.9	1,403	16,292	4,302.7	404.0	355	1,250	372.0	50.2
Rockland	33.2	101.8	476	4,592	4,966.3	261.5	1,335	14,543	4,732.5	425.4	596	2,527	497.7	103.8
St. Lawrence	7.0	62.6	D	D	D	D	370	4,818	1,448.8	124.1	57	169	33.3	4.9
Saratoga	26.1	115.4	178	3,698	2,952.2	228.8	739	10,803	3,289.0	299.7	240	1,138	335.4	47.6
Schenectady	23.5	152.1	80	675	508.2	40.1	444	6,692	1,938.2	184.5	121	519	129.0	19.5
Schoharie	173.8	5,548.0	14	112	83.1	7.2	100	1,138	287.0	26.9	15	39	9.5	2.1
Schuyler	0.8	45.6	NA	NA	NA	NA	48	618	152.7	16.9	11	D	3.1	D
Seneca	4.4	126.6	32	303	190.0	12.4	163	2,350	505.7	47.9	17	56	18.6	1.6
Steuben	7.5	76.8	43	319	135.4	12.5	319	4,101	1,229.7	107.5	54	204	29.8	7.5
Suffolk	246.1	163.9	2,720	40,301	34,850.1	2,609.6	6,528	82,839	27,801.1	2,544.4	1,821	7,080	2,309.2	388.2
Sullivan	89.8	1,198.9	38	781	300.6	30.0	283	2,602	872.2	76.3	109	331	48.8	10.2
Tioga	3.5	69.8	28	460	315.9	23.0	128	1,241	350.3	32.5	11	25	2.7	0.6
Tompkins	7.9	75.0	D	D	D	D	346	5,033	1,194.1	121.5	129	712	171.4	26.2
Ulster	394.2	2,188.4	153	1,565	893.5	82.5	726	8,896	2,570.5	242.2	187	611	107.7	21.8
Warren	11.6	178.7	52	566	292.7	25.6	402	5,683	1,590.4	152.4	76	256	53.4	10.9
Washington	2.6	41.6	27	210	110.1	10.8	183	1,944	603.9	52.6	22	48	7.3	1.5
Wayne	7.8	85.7	63	616	303.4	29.1	267	3,512	997.1	97.4	61	209	35.8	5.7
Westchester	65.4	67.0	1,205	16,216	23,537.3	2,457.1	3,804	50,878	16,295.6	1,589.2	2,050	9,804	2,976.5	556.3
Wyoming	3.3	79.5	21	258	188.1	13.4	126	1,378	392.4	38.3	19	111	16.7	3.6
Yates	1.1	43.9	12	74	53.7	2.7	78	699	194.6	18.1	21	90	12.6	4.1
NORTH CAROLINA	938.0	93.4	9,831	154,877	132,342.1	10,273.4	34,926	496,081	141,134.3	12,673.3	12,450	56,360	14,647.0	2,638.6
Alamance	15.4	97.0	129	2,065	814.5	115.5	642	9,115	2,313.5	206.7	134	849	213.1	38.7
Alexander	0.0	0.8	13	80	50.2	4.1	78	789	197.9	19.1	D	D	D	D
Alleghany	0.3	28.6	3	7	1.4	0.4	38	317	85.8	7.1	D	D	D	0.4
Anson	8.8	341.6	14	345	146.0	13.5	72	750	181.2	16.2	8	96	3.1	1.6
Ashe	0.7	24.8	17	83	79.8	4.5	106	1,071	291.0	25.7	27	47	10.4	1.5
Avery	1.6	88.8	9	D	39.2	D	86	938	186.6	20.8	D	D	D	4.2
Beaufort	4.3	90.4	51	515	357.1	21.6	182	2,362	637.3	57.6	39	155	25.2	4.1
Bertie	1.7	83.2	14	111	72.2	4.9	45	406	86.0	8.0	4	D	0.2	D
Bladen	37.4	1,088.4	22	136	132.2	5.4	87	851	210.3	17.3	D	D	D	D
Brunswick	2.8	22.8	47	515	252.8	24.9	421	5,221	1,414.2	133.4	169	793	123.0	27.2
Buncombe	21.1	83.4	281	3,566	1,919.2	174.0	1,276	18,500	4,594.4	465.1	550	1,936	383.0	77.2
Burke	23.0	258.9	46	840	301.2	31.9	255	3,346	836.6	75.3	D	D	D	D
Cabarrus	17.5	89.1	186	2,705	2,442.7	166.8	729	13,155	3,302.5	312.9	248	837	201.7	30.4
Caldwell	7.2	88.1	62	1,991	1,925.1	102.0	234	2,816	758.1	64.6	54	128	21.8	3.7
Camden	0.7	68.9	NA	NA	NA	NA	16	108	31.6	1.8	NA	NA	NA	NA
Carteret	7.0	101.2	52	305	120.6	12.4	376	4,371	1,158.4	109.1	133	650	79.5	18.5
Caswell	0.4	18.7	D	D	D	2.1	50	321	69.8	6.5	NA	NA	NA	NA
Catawba	4.3	27.7	233	4,158	2,525.5	222.7	675	9,939	3,015.5	261.7	203	725	179.7	28.3
Chatham	25.4	358.4	57	451	245.1	21.7	176	2,501	624.7	54.4	54	137	46.5	5.3
Cherokee	1.7	63.7	12	118	20.9	4.4	118	1,445	450.5	36.2	29	67	17.6	2.2

1 Merchant wholesalers, except manufacturers' sales branches and offices. 2. Employer establishments.

STATE County	Professional, scientific, and technical services, 2017				Manufacturing, 2017				Accommodation and food services, 2017			
	Number of establish-ments	Number of employees	Sales (mil dol)	Average payroll (mil dol)	Number of establish-ments	Number of employees	Sales (mil dol)	Average payroll (mil dol)	Number of establis-hments	Number of employees	Sales (mil dol)	Annual payroll (mil dol)
	147	148	149	150	151	152	153	154	155	156	157	158
NEW YORK— Cont'd												
Genesee	69	286	30.0	11.8	84	2,903	1,171.9	146.8	137	2,036	103.5	32.8
Greene	78	282	39.4	12.9	33	910	345.5	63.7	200	2,298	130.8	38.0
Hamilton	NA	NA	NA	NA	NA	NA	NA	NA	61	301	28.3	7.6
Herkimer	54	170	20.3	6.6	60	2,829	705.5	150.1	171	1,445	84.4	24.3
Jefferson	D	D	D	D	68	2,334	906.1	113.5	333	4,376	249.2	81.6
Kings	5,449	20,614	3,695.8	1,142.8	1,716	17,332	4,043.7	801.8	6,092	54,847	4,361.7	1,197.6
Lewis	20	101	15.2	4.1	21	1,254	629.0	65.5	62	547	26.2	7.8
Livingston	D	D	D	D	61	2,195	635.1	101.2	159	2,395	102.5	32.1
Madison	D	D	D	D	56	2,771	983.1	141.0	167	2,159	110.0	32.6
Monroe	2,013	26,170	4,338.7	1,682.9	848	35,328	12,354.4	2,124.2	1,753	28,857	1,593.4	492.3
Montgomery	D	D	D	D	57	3,272	776.0	140.7	107	1,010	57.1	15.9
Nassau	7,086	40,370	7,939.6	2,875.1	949	16,079	4,541.1	893.3	3,808	54,397	4,066.7	1,203.9
New York	17,512	345,282	116,750.4	39,074.8	1,721	17,642	4,450.8	885.4	10,453	258,047	27,902.3	8,646.6
Niagara	D	D	D	D	273	8,189	3,040.1	478.3	548	9,696	834.4	191.3
Oneida	423	3,911	656.4	224.9	229	9,037	3,009.3	475.2	602	12,179	1,007.8	258.1
Onondaga	1,191	13,590	3,097.4	946.2	417	17,753	7,228.3	1,071.4	1,187	20,088	1,137.1	354.4
Ontario	D	D	D	D	168	6,878	2,451.3	386.8	339	5,281	283.2	94.7
Orange	D	D	D	D	304	7,836	2,940.3	408.9	937	10,678	715.0	200.7
Orleans	40	148	11.8	4.0	44	2,069	688.5	104.7	67	671	35.3	11.1
Oswego	D	D	D	D	86	3,211	2,318.3	218.3	283	3,941	181.9	53.8
Otsego	D	D	D	D	63	960	233.0	41.9	217	2,293	165.5	44.5
Putnam	D	D	D	D	73	1,472	334.4	78.5	223	2,091	146.3	42.4
Queens	3,819	17,802	2,444.7	930.4	1,207	19,083	4,531.7	960.3	5,496	55,803	4,593.7	1,193.1
Rensselaer	D	D	D	D	98	4,115	1,072.5	375.8	351	4,733	274.2	83.1
Richmond	D	D	D	D	144	1,035	398.0	59.9	876	9,328	665.4	161.3
Rockland	1,345	5,933	1,767.0	398.5	230	7,442	12,887.5	529.9	830	9,332	647.4	188.2
St. Lawrence	D	D	D	D	69	2,159	993.0	133.1	244	3,149	197.4	46.9
Saratoga	D	D	D	D	126	6,899	2,336.4	562.3	571	9,672	689.0	210.3
Schenectady	D	D	D	D	101	4,134	2,483.8	261.0	337	4,487	261.4	77.2
Schoharie	D	D	D	D	29	303	46.1	12.4	65	529	34.9	8.8
Schuyler	14	46	5.0	1.7	D	D	D	D	80	659	45.3	13.1
Seneca	31	162	20.2	7.0	54	1,395	564.6	83.5	79	1,942	204.9	50.1
Steuben	125	1,067	97.9	70.2	78	3,853	1,159.2	212.7	235	2,468	139.2	40.7
Suffolk	5,668	36,027	6,471.1	2,426.0	1,893	49,115	17,177.1	2,935.6	3,910	55,011	3,936.7	1,129.8
Sullivan	157	549	60.1	21.8	54	1,017	451.2	42.7	254	1,997	207.2	51.5
Tioga	D	D	D	D	35	1,225	411.2	61.4	87	885	44.6	12.9
Tompkins	284	2,037	318.8	123.2	88	2,873	939.4	150.9	334	4,972	279.4	89.9
Ulster	D	D	D	D	187	3,298	806.4	177.2	591	7,299	479.1	155.9
Warren	147	886	118.0	44.3	78	3,481	1,005.5	181.6	430	5,120	420.9	116.8
Washington	64	282	50.3	16.9	88	2,795	1,137.0	162.6	116	694	42.3	11.4
Wayne	89	613	101.4	27.4	130	5,511	1,834.8	278.5	161	1,663	78.4	24.0
Westchester	4,088	24,562	5,440.6	2,131.8	551	13,928	4,639.6	1,002.5	2,667	33,245	2,561.6	752.5
Wyoming	D	D	D	D	47	1,728	451.0	80.4	79	728	37.1	11.3
Yates	26	108	12.0	5.5	45	893	245.2	40.4	55	466	26.1	7.3
NORTH CAROLINA	24,650	215,951	39,509.4	15,555.9	8,834	422,891	200,380.8	21,480.2	21,437	429,125	24,913.0	6,865.6
Alamance	D	D	D	D	193	8,100	2,841.6	380.2	326	7,220	365.7	103.2
Alexander	D	D	D	D	69	3,834	748.6	157.1	37	578	25.6	7.2
Alleghany	16	48	3.9	1.5	15	436	138.2	17.7	25	241	15.8	4.2
Anson	24	109	10.3	3.1	20	1,343	366.6	53.3	32	456	20.6	5.3
Ashe	23	85	6.2	2.2	22	814	213.6	31.3	D	D	D	D
Avery	33	68	9.4	2.8	17	124	11.8	3.6	58	691	46.8	16.0
Beaufort	D	D	D	D	53	2,631	1,075.9	147.8	92	1,332	65.8	17.7
Bertie	10	40	3.9	1.2	9	2,233	915.2	71.3	D	D	D	D
Bladen	34	145	20.6	5.0	26	5,321	1,725.8	203.1	49	535	31.9	8.0
Brunswick	D	D	D	D	71	1,232	393.9	75.4	295	4,144	259.6	69.1
Buncombe	1,050	4,618	634.0	254.9	318	12,371	3,995.3	658.7	846	18,664	1,177.3	349.6
Burke	D	D	D	D	121	7,288	2,515.1	312.0	127	2,788	138.6	36.9
Cabarrus	D	D	D	D	165	6,298	2,274.0	308.9	401	10,502	569.6	154.2
Caldwell	83	367	64.8	14.1	117	6,997	1,497.3	279.9	120	2,095	97.7	26.1
Camden	11	30	2.9	1.4	NA	NA	NA	NA	7	86	4.2	1.2
Carteret	134	616	90.1	29.9	63	753	221.7	28.6	245	3,728	211.9	65.1
Caswell	12	39	3.7	1.5	9	211	33.5	7.6	D	D	D	D
Catawba	334	2,219	778.9	119.6	368	22,637	6,606.2	1,008.6	361	7,310	378.0	109.6
Chatham	D	D	D	D	78	1,969	583.7	85.7	95	1,539	86.3	25.4
Cherokee	32	89	9.0	3.1	25	1,278	362.7	56.4	65	1,867	230.4	45.3

STATE County	Health care and social assistance, 2017				Other services, 2017				Nonemployer businesses, 2019		Value of residential construction authorized by building permits, 2021	
	Number of establish-ments	Number of employees	Receipts (mil dol)	Annual payroll (mil dol)	Number of establish-ments	Number of employees	Receipts (mil dol)	Annual payroll (mil dol)	Number	Receipts (mil dol)	New construction ($1,000)	Number of housing units
	159	160	161	162	163	164	165	166	167	168	169	170
NEW YORK— Cont'd												
Genesee	138	3,141	270.2	114.9	93	572	54.3	14.8	2,975	127.1	18,583	93
Greene	88	1,210	100.1	41.2	82	329	36.4	9.4	3,866	172.4	26,916	107
Hamilton	6	27	1.6	1.0	D	D	D	D	524	20.9	11,874	46
Herkimer	120	2,244	188.5	71.0	99	702	40.7	12.5	3,233	141.4	30,840	79
Jefferson	273	6,535	660.4	304.3	183	866	102.3	22.8	5,278	210.0	32,572	161
Kings	6,877	229,944	20,989.5	9,197.5	5,125	21,666	2,169.1	573.3	284,766	14,859.8	812,039	7,013
Lewis	45	922	109.6	45.0	46	186	28.9	6.3	1,622	76.0	7,930	74
Livingston	132	2,090	164.8	74.4	97	375	40.7	10.2	3,517	147.0	7,616	34
Madison	176	3,151	312.4	128.0	105	374	38.0	9.6	4,323	185.5	26,302	95
Monroe	1,992	72,084	7,179.0	3,025.4	1,297	7,911	974.8	254.5	48,243	2,221.7	220,613	1,067
Montgomery	186	4,059	414.4	173.8	88	600	63.8	17.7	2,565	111.5	19,405	110
Nassau	5,953	119,939	15,609.6	6,621.3	4,315	24,423	2,756.9	755.5	154,022	11,191.2	432,574	1,365
New York	8,474	284,981	44,469.8	17,081.4	9,976	102,738	29,591.3	5,909.8	219,769	19,230.9	362,265	3,165
Niagara	509	10,709	873.7	402.3	331	1,393	126.1	34.0	10,449	413.3	67,419	205
Oneida	599	20,938	1,934.4	903.0	424	4,958	308.9	106.9	12,392	515.7	59,201	377
Onondaga	1,288	41,752	5,179.4	2,129.3	918	5,994	675.9	189.7	30,051	1,425.1	95,010	459
Ontario	266	8,686	755.8	387.5	230	1,348	121.7	37.8	7,302	330.8	109,915	437
Orange	987	24,486	2,906.3	1,182.6	799	4,832	639.9	160.0	27,793	1,379.5	295,168	1,760
Orleans	75	1,313	92.8	41.5	61	240	25.7	5.8	1,889	77.0	5,978	31
Oswego	214	5,054	387.5	184.3	196	705	75.4	18.9	5,542	214.4	21,725	139
Otsego	154	5,925	774.1	341.8	101	484	97.6	11.9	4,277	181.2	38,917	182
Putnam	252	5,250	609.9	257.5	257	1,147	126.7	36.8	9,818	511.6	21,680	67
Queens	5,592	155,364	15,735.8	6,645.8	5,184	21,641	2,442.3	626.7	268,034	11,495.4	486,448	4,087
Rensselaer	358	8,633	870.3	361.9	245	1,379	135.8	52.4	9,347	378.3	46,000	230
Richmond	1,345	33,206	3,540.7	1,528.2	912	4,484	441.4	108.4	39,224	2,062.5	54,925	310
Rockland	1,201	28,807	2,706.3	1,207.7	781	3,325	358.9	102.6	29,485	1,870.2	95,862	486
St. Lawrence	234	6,667	708.9	315.1	171	713	73.1	16.3	4,772	189.0	40,306	253
Saratoga	620	10,603	1,149.2	456.5	358	2,056	246.5	68.1	17,512	878.7	292,966	1,086
Schenectady	429	12,036	1,179.6	535.1	D	D	214.2	D	9,259	382.0	65,887	437
Schoharie	60	887	71.9	30.2	D	D	13.3	D	1,888	77.3	11,466	55
Schuyler	27	685	55.6	26.8	D	D	D	D	1,225	44.2	12,298	80
Seneca	64	1,362	85.2	40.4	56	241	27.5	8.7	1,920	93.6	11,725	40
Steuben	237	6,707	572.6	243.0	160	831	80.7	18.6	5,068	202.6	17,840	118
Suffolk	4,915	108,385	13,050.8	5,573.8	4,251	21,465	2,416.5	664.5	141,623	8,338.2	995,962	1,459
Sullivan	233	5,033	425.8	204.1	149	456	64.1	14.0	5,952	269.2	87,860	416
Tioga	70	1,024	64.8	30.7	59	168	15.5	3.6	2,770	115.6	26,327	163
Tompkins	284	6,258	643.2	273.4	164	962	197.3	31.3	7,685	302.6	116,082	644
Ulster	525	10,035	841.2	383.2	363	1,619	149.2	40.3	17,562	798.1	98,259	342
Warren	279	6,302	774.3	305.2	150	864	101.6	30.0	4,948	244.6	77,495	280
Washington	101	1,713	105.6	56.1	75	265	32.0	8.3	3,682	156.0	25,352	104
Wayne	140	3,229	228.1	106.7	131	396	38.7	10.2	4,835	207.0	34,127	137
Westchester	3,532	80,551	10,819.9	4,784.1	2,967	16,068	2,279.4	591.9	104,393	7,262.0	556,260	2,319
Wyoming	65	1,289	130.5	45.4	68	260	28.5	7.2	2,074	86.5	10,111	39
Yates	44	904	67.7	29.7	41	136	13.5	3.2	1,989	106.3	26,541	68
NORTH CAROLINA	24,080	602,444	72,732.3	27,627.2	15,118	93,642	13,022.2	3,152.9	816,089	36,437.8	20,485,854	94,874
Alamance	366	12,073	1,705.6	651.3	199	1,292	125.7	36.1	11,225	455.3	287,458	2,294
Alexander	47	648	42.5	18.3	35	159	11.8	2.9	2,388	98.2	23,000	134
Alleghany	27	400	27.0	12.0	D	D	D	1.2	997	45.1	26,624	89
Anson	49	814	54.0	22.0	24	53	8.2	1.2	1,284	42.6	9,591	64
Ashe	48	1,167	84.1	37.9	33	134	11.3	3.1	2,512	112.7	40,840	131
Avery	41	798	58.3	23.0	23	140	18.1	4.8	1,768	75.4	133,011	204
Beaufort	119	2,049	218.4	76.3	75	364	33.2	10.2	3,683	147.7	36,281	229
Bertie	43	955	64.9	29.0	D	D	D	D	1,002	33.9	5,598	14
Bladen	55	936	47.7	23.2	25	122	11.4	3.2	1,852	67.9	8,067	30
Brunswick	220	3,902	400.5	153.0	145	654	69.2	19.1	12,612	566.5	1,191,011	5,249
Buncombe	1,003	28,143	3,678.0	1,482.0	517	2,958	326.5	96.9	29,795	1,347.7	691,470	2,793
Burke	167	5,422	644.9	259.5	90	528	58.0	14.5	5,331	225.7	59,927	402
Cabarrus	392	9,447	1,119.5	482.2	296	1,725	176.8	47.9	17,523	684.7	404,516	2,152
Caldwell	131	3,226	271.5	104.2	88	466	49.1	13.8	5,037	217.3	66,869	262
Camden	D	D	D	1.0	D	D	3.9	D	777	25.9	19,442	75
Carteret	198	3,364	372.3	148.9	142	687	70.3	18.8	7,005	348.0	242,269	684
Caswell	30	384	32.0	12.1	D	D	D	0.5	1,198	43.5	14,223	62
Catawba	419	12,285	1,390.3	534.5	247	1,556	133.6	41.1	11,049	548.9	187,036	1,082
Chatham	137	2,702	215.8	79.5	100	411	39.9	12.6	6,758	317.3	324,108	1,124
Cherokee	71	1,587	143.1	57.1	36	131	10.5	3.2	2,328	98.9	47,766	229

Table B. States and Counties — **Government Employment and Payroll, and Local Government Finances**

STATE County	Government employment and payroll, 2017: Full-time equivalent employees	Government employment and payroll, 2017: March payroll (dollars)	March payroll (percent of total): Adminis-tration, judicial, and legal	March payroll (percent of total): Police and corrections	March payroll (percent of total): Fire protection	March payroll (percent of total): Highways and transpor-tation	March payroll (percent of total): Health and welfare	March payroll (percent of total): Natural resources and utilities	March payroll (percent of total): Education and libraries	Local government finances, 2017, General revenue: Total (mil dol)	General revenue: Inter-govern-mental (mil dol)	Taxes: Total (mil dol)	Taxes: Per capita[1] (dollars): Total	Taxes: Per capita[1] (dollars): Property
	171	172	173	174	175	176	177	178	179	180	181	182	183	184
NEW YORK— Cont'd														
Genesee	4,222	19,296,881	3.9	4.9	1.2	3.4	3.5	1.1	49.5	405.7	182.5	156.1	2,700	1,663
Greene	2,298	10,115,224	7.5	6.4	0.0	7.3	10.3	2.2	65.1	316.4	105.8	172.3	3,632	2,887
Hamilton	491	2,080,685	13.7	4.2	0.7	18.1	7.9	8.2	46.0	62.5	12.4	46.3	10,356	9,408
Herkimer	2,865	11,466,437	6.7	6.1	2.3	7.7	6.3	3.6	65.4	385.8	191.0	155.9	2,507	1,851
Jefferson	5,641	24,270,939	5.8	5.5	1.8	7.2	5.7	3.2	67.8	739.1	370.0	279.4	2,469	1,419
Kings	(2)	(2)	(2)	(2)	(2)	(2)	(2)	(2)	(2)	(2)	(2)	(2)	(2)	(2)
Lewis	1,898	7,686,343	5.5	2.9	0.7	6.9	35.7	0.7	47.2	268.6	100.0	62.4	2,345	1,865
Livingston	3,484	13,651,324	6.4	7.3	0.0	5.5	15.4	1.5	62.7	406.5	171.2	146.6	2,310	1,765
Madison	2,857	12,223,460	5.5	7.3	1.1	8.0	6.4	2.9	66.0	381.6	167.1	177.9	2,507	1,913
Monroe	34,542	172,090,209	3.6	10.0	3.6	2.5	5.0	4.0	69.4	4,816.6	2,030.9	2,185.7	2,943	1,917
Montgomery	2,178	9,914,847	7.3	8.6	1.5	5.5	4.4	2.8	67.4	305.6	147.2	120.3	2,446	1,580
Nassau	61,582	417,805,788	3.4	12.5	0.8	2.1	6.7	4.4	67.9	11,881.8	2,704.9	7,683.7	5,661	4,662
New York	(2)442294	(2)80474536	(2)3.4	(2)16.2	(2)4.8	(2)16.0	(2)17.3	(2)4.8	(2)33.6	(2)111321.9	(2)37041.5	(2)55325.6	(2)6557	(2)2932
Niagara	8,142	40,535,142	5.1	9.4	3.1	4.3	6.2	3.8	66.6	1,306.8	582.1	541.3	2,567	1,656
Oneida	10,587	47,343,125	5.5	8.1	2.7	4.7	5.1	4.6	68.2	1,401.0	695.4	542.2	2,357	1,488
Onondaga	21,209	104,071,695	2.9	9.0	2.4	4.1	5.1	4.9	70.8	2,901.5	1,289.4	1,280.2	2,772	1,798
Ontario	6,340	27,805,597	6.5	7.4	1.0	4.2	3.9	2.8	73.0	690.4	243.5	361.6	3,301	2,172
Orange	16,171	90,101,768	4.4	9.8	1.4	3.8	6.2	2.4	70.9	2,752.3	998.8	1,462.4	3,851	2,871
Orleans	2,190	9,766,804	4.9	6.6	0.8	4.2	5.2	1.4	75.4	230.7	125.9	80.1	1,965	1,495
Oswego	6,356	26,849,806	3.9	5.3	2.1	5.1	4.8	2.6	73.7	798.7	378.4	284.3	2,400	1,786
Otsego	2,680	10,255,860	6.3	4.6	2.2	9.1	12.9	1.2	61.7	335.9	145.4	153.2	2,557	1,734
Putnam	3,769	22,766,685	6.7	8.5	0.0	6.3	5.8	1.9	68.8	687.0	170.1	479.8	4,854	4,138
Queens	(2)	(2)	(2)	(2)	(2)	(2)	(2)	(2)	(2)	(2)	(2)	(2)	(2)	(2)
Rensselaer	7,542	36,126,286	4.8	7.7	1.8	2.7	10.2	2.2	68.6	1,032.5	404.8	444.2	2,790	2,005
Richmond	(2)	(2)	(2)	(2)	(2)	(2)	(2)	(2)	(2)	(2)	(2)	(2)	(2)	(2)
Rockland	11,549	73,992,763	6.3	11.6	0.1	3.4	4.6	3.6	69.8	2,326.2	571.1	1,551.6	4,780	3,970
St. Lawrence	5,416	22,595,829	4.9	5.5	1.0	7.2	16.8	2.7	60.3	720.6	338.2	261.5	2,405	1,632
Saratoga	8,979	40,877,513	4.9	5.8	1.2	5.8	4.0	2.1	74.3	1,200.7	368.1	680.9	2,970	2,065
Schenectady	6,037	31,374,949	4.2	10.7	3.6	3.7	8.6	2.0	65.1	945.6	365.1	456.5	2,951	2,096
Schoharie	1,516	7,162,811	7.2	4.6	0.1	8.4	7.2	1.9	69.5	215.1	103.2	94.1	3,011	2,453
Schuyler	735	2,945,335	10.5	8.4	0.7	8.7	14.5	2.7	51.1	111.3	48.0	49.5	2,761	1,968
Seneca	1,446	5,681,942	7.9	12.0	0.0	5.7	10.9	3.0	57.3	208.6	96.4	84.9	2,480	1,633
Steuben	4,733	22,321,354	5.8	5.4	1.5	6.8	5.6	2.7	70.6	673.6	336.1	260.5	2,703	1,914
Suffolk	65,773	423,548,830	4.0	11.6	1.0	2.6	3.9	2.8	72.6	11,679.6	3,371.4	7,263.3	4,897	3,824
Sullivan	4,046	20,010,366	6.5	7.6	0.2	7.4	9.0	3.2	64.4	648.9	213.8	319.0	4,254	3,630
Tioga	2,181	8,320,257	4.4	6.8	0.1	5.4	8.9	1.3	71.1	285.2	150.5	106.5	2,191	1,651
Tompkins	4,615	22,463,397	5.1	5.9	2.8	4.9	6.6	3.9	68.1	599.8	194.0	318.4	3,102	2,262
Ulster	7,944	40,510,439	5.8	8.2	1.2	5.7	4.1	2.2	71.0	1,172.0	385.2	704.9	3,946	3,148
Warren	3,011	13,531,587	7.4	10.1	4.0	7.9	6.2	5.6	57.7	450.3	129.8	277.7	4,314	2,860
Washington	3,587	14,776,257	4.7	5.1	0.0	5.2	4.8	1.1	77.0	381.4	174.1	145.2	2,359	1,937
Wayne	4,441	18,062,784	5.4	5.5	0.1	4.7	9.8	1.9	71.2	565.1	261.1	218.6	2,417	1,816
Westchester	45,049	315,904,961	4.5	12.1	4.1	2.1	12.5	4.7	58.0	9,763.8	2,045.4	5,422.8	5,592	4,506
Wyoming	1,898	7,449,778	5.8	7.5	0.0	7.5	30.6	2.8	44.8	251.8	96.9	81.0	2,011	1,534
Yates	888	3,891,464	9.4	12.2	0.2	8.8	5.9	3.5	58.4	125.9	49.2	66.4	2,655	2,101
NORTH CAROLINA	X	X	X	X	X	X	X	X	X	X	X	X	X	X
Alamance	5,370	20,215,032	4.4	10.8	3.3	1.7	8.5	5.8	62.4	467.6	226.6	184.2	1,128	793
Alexander	1,064	3,474,220	3.9	8.7	0.4	0.0	13.8	2.3	68.4	85.9	47.0	30.6	824	595
Alleghany	370	1,198,979	4.8	10.0	0.0	1.9	10.5	3.2	65.9	33.0	16.8	12.4	1,130	847
Anson	1,234	4,221,291	2.9	6.4	2.6	0.6	7.3	4.9	73.7	61.3	48.9	4.5	180	114
Ashe	713	2,611,599	5.9	8.7	0.0	1.1	5.5	6.8	69.6	71.1	37.0	27.4	1,023	722
Avery	699	2,156,864	6.3	10.1	0.0	1.3	11.8	5.1	60.9	54.8	23.7	26.2	1,498	1,131
Beaufort	2,154	6,621,286	5.8	8.5	1.9	0.7	11.6	7.8	61.3	162.7	85.3	54.7	1,162	888
Bertie	662	2,275,555	4.1	7.4	0.2	1.1	13.7	5.1	65.4	56.1	32.5	15.6	812	619
Bladen	1,401	4,540,093	3.8	8.3	1.0	0.5	16.7	2.9	65.2	117.1	64.5	35.1	1,050	811
Brunswick	3,843	15,105,174	6.7	10.1	1.5	1.3	15.6	6.6	53.6	467.2	138.6	205.5	1,571	1,174
Buncombe	9,182	35,550,616	5.5	8.0	3.7	1.6	17.3	4.3	54.9	1,308.2	735.4	417.9	1,626	1,061
Burke	2,789	9,414,475	6.7	3.9	1.0	0.9	6.6	6.9	72.1	253.3	129.2	82.4	914	668
Cabarrus	8,191	32,543,046	3.8	7.0	4.4	1.3	19.4	5.3	55.8	737.9	293.6	313.8	1,516	1,139
Caldwell	3,080	10,733,278	3.7	6.6	2.1	0.6	9.5	3.8	72.2	238.7	137.0	77.1	941	718
Camden	377	1,104,342	26.9	0.0	0.0	0.0	0.0	0.3	71.7	29.5	17.2	10.5	995	799
Carteret	2,545	9,164,720	6.1	8.8	6.0	1.8	8.0	4.1	61.2	386.4	89.4	115.4	1,674	1,187
Caswell	726	2,304,482	3.8	7.9	0.0	0.0	12.6	2.4	63.0	50.7	29.5	16.1	712	516
Catawba	7,861	31,418,018	3.4	5.3	2.9	1.4	40.0	3.7	41.6	784.2	236.7	202.3	1,281	912
Chatham	1,925	6,848,499	4.6	9.1	0.3	0.5	8.5	5.2	66.7	198.1	76.4	96.9	1,361	1,090
Cherokee	1,138	3,665,143	3.9	7.6	0.2	0.8	8.0	8.4	63.9	91.8	51.7	29.6	1,058	695

1. Based on the resident population estimated as of July 1 of the year shown. 2. Bronx, Kings, Queens, and Richmond counties are included with New York county.

STATE County	Local government finances, 2017 (cont.)									Government employment, 2020			Individual income tax returns, 2019		
	Direct general expenditure							De(2)outstanding							
			Percent of total for:												
	Total (mil dol)	Per capita[1] (dollars)	Education	Health and hospitals	Police protection	Public welfare	Highways	Total (mil dol)	Per capita[1] (dollars)	Federal civilian	Federal military	State and local	Number of returns	Mean adjusted gross income	Mean income tax
	185	186	187	188	189	190	191	192	193	194	195	196	197	198	199
NEW YORK— Cont'd															
Genesee	432.8	7,488	57.4	2.7	2.8	10.8	5.8	219.8	3,804	570	88	4,455	28,310	54,940	4,731
Greene	312.5	6,586	47.9	6.0	2.3	8.6	8.3	163.9	3,454	107	70	4,036	23,180	61,203	6,704
Hamilton	61.6	13,781	33.2	5.1	2.1	2.4	16.4	13.4	2,996	19	7	803	2,600	57,412	5,343
Herkimer	396.9	6,384	60.9	2.1	1.8	8.2	8.4	165.2	2,658	118	94	3,927	28,410	54,399	5,003
Jefferson	718.8	6,352	52.7	3.0	2.3	8.1	6.8	408.3	3,608	3,345	15,659	7,719	50,300	52,786	4,558
Kings	(2)	(2)	(2)	(2)	(2)	(2)	(2)	(2)	(2)	8,660	4,172	116,480	1,253,070	66,681	9,173
Lewis	326.3	12,263	28.5	42.4	1.0	4.9	5.6	105.0	3,947	68	41	2,185	11,760	52,910	4,285
Livingston	396.8	6,250	44.7	6.1	4.1	16.4	7.1	214.1	3,372	141	89	5,558	28,370	60,771	5,898
Madison	378.0	5,328	52.4	3.0	2.8	7.2	8.3	213.9	3,015	148	104	3,977	31,710	66,930	7,483
Monroe	5,084.9	6,846	50.9	4.2	4.3	8.9	3.0	3,146.9	4,237	3,107	1,225	41,846	371,910	67,419	7,746
Montgomery	312.5	6,356	50.3	2.2	2.3	8.2	6.7	208.4	4,238	115	76	2,457	23,150	49,801	4,225
Nassau	12,274.7	9,043	49.2	6.4	8.7	5.1	3.4	8,617.9	6,349	5,475	2,572	71,477	725,950	119,508	20,545
New York	(2)105453.7	(2)12498	(2)30.2	(2)9.6	(2)5.4	(2)13.4	(2)2.8	(2)181077.3	(2)21461	22,409	2,566	214,413	852,720	212,534	48,722
Niagara	1,282.8	6,084	48.3	3.0	4.6	9.2	6.1	758.8	3,599	1,043	364	10,890	106,600	56,540	5,330
Oneida	1,377.7	5,990	52.7	2.2	3.2	11.1	4.5	1,087.6	4,728	2,382	405	22,291	106,870	57,819	5,754
Onondaga	3,169.5	6,864	48.3	3.1	3.4	9.2	4.6	2,019.1	4,372	4,754	905	35,257	228,360	67,680	7,763
Ontario	684.6	6,250	56.0	2.1	2.8	7.0	6.4	460.0	4,199	1,665	171	6,616	56,440	72,435	8,471
Orange	2,851.9	7,510	53.5	5.1	3.7	9.6	3.3	1,448.1	3,813	4,660	7,017	20,841	187,110	73,273	8,549
Orleans	230.2	5,645	55.2	3.3	2.3	9.3	6.8	168.1	4,121	86	60	3,589	18,780	50,188	4,199
Oswego	739.9	6,247	56.0	2.5	2.2	8.8	6.0	495.9	4,188	283	208	8,371	53,490	54,788	4,858
Otsego	320.6	5,350	51.5	3.4	1.7	8.2	9.0	174.7	2,915	152	87	4,182	26,730	57,472	5,790
Putnam	682.6	6,905	61.8	3.1	4.7	4.0	5.0	279.1	2,824	160	151	4,293	50,910	98,174	13,595
Queens	(2)	(2)	(2)	(2)	(2)	(2)	(2)	(2)	(2)	14,831	3,554	112,919	1,183,080	55,951	5,981
Rensselaer	1,043.9	6,557	50.3	4.8	3.1	13.0	3.7	826.7	5,193	385	255	10,603	79,600	65,335	6,892
Richmond	(2)	(2)	(2)	(2)	(2)	(2)	(2)	(2)	(2)	1,085	1,177	22,475	230,720	74,478	8,965
Rockland	2,466.3	7,597	46.4	9.1	4.7	6.8	3.8	1,690.8	5,209	540	505	16,437	150,200	92,366	13,956
St. Lawrence	706.2	6,497	50.1	9.6	2.0	8.6	7.5	454.1	4,178	621	172	9,441	43,680	54,549	4,766
Saratoga	1,119.3	4,882	57.3	3.1	3.4	5.5	5.8	637.4	2,780	473	759	11,148	121,680	92,052	12,613
Schenectady	1,003.0	6,483	49.7	5.2	3.7	13.1	3.5	639.6	4,134	614	261	8,904	78,440	63,498	6,660
Schoharie	203.3	6,504	49.6	3.0	1.2	8.8	9.6	106.8	3,418	77	47	2,498	14,140	56,754	5,128
Schuyler	101.3	5,655	38.5	5.1	2.0	10.2	10.3	118.6	6,620	45	28	1,019	8,690	54,520	4,884
Seneca	200.9	5,866	48.3	4.1	3.3	8.9	6.1	139.1	4,062	88	49	2,811	15,510	52,985	4,678
Steuben	661.3	6,863	57.3	3.4	1.7	8.8	8.9	424.3	4,403	1,044	170	6,225	43,620	60,215	6,182
Suffolk	11,755.1	7,925	56.1	2.6	5.6	5.2	2.7	8,810.0	5,939	11,092	2,540	93,322	800,910	95,744	14,482
Sullivan	656.9	8,759	44.5	5.6	2.3	11.2	8.5	458.7	6,116	223	114	5,617	35,400	59,128	6,256
Tioga	298.1	6,132	60.1	3.1	2.6	7.3	6.4	196.4	4,040	155	80	2,369	23,290	59,362	5,471
Tompkins	619.3	6,032	49.2	4.1	2.9	6.9	6.0	621.0	6,049	276	157	5,337	41,170	73,949	8,926
Ulster	1,209.9	6,773	55.7	1.7	3.2	9.5	6.0	668.9	3,745	471	283	12,190	89,070	69,257	8,112
Warren	420.8	6,537	46.2	4.0	3.8	7.9	7.4	212.6	3,303	209	103	4,255	34,850	63,088	6,922
Washington	372.5	6,052	60.0	3.2	2.2	8.0	7.5	156.5	2,542	134	91	4,688	28,890	52,623	4,501
Wayne	561.3	6,207	56.9	3.8	2.3	10.6	5.3	248.2	2,744	184	139	6,668	44,870	56,645	5,008
Westchester	10,234.0	10,554	40.9	15.6	4.2	5.4	1.7	6,415.1	6,616	4,572	1,480	56,204	493,560	153,510	30,383
Wyoming	251.5	6,244	32.7	23.9	2.6	7.7	11.0	124.0	3,077	94	57	4,090	18,720	54,426	4,573
Yates	120.4	4,817	43.7	3.7	4.2	7.8	11.7	85.9	3,436	63	37	1,130	10,970	56,734	5,263
NORTH CAROLINA	X	X	X	X	X	X	X	X	X	77,362	123,536	647,251	4,794,900	67,141	7,775
Alamance	439.3	2,691	53.1	4.0	9.9	6.0	1.8	147.6	904	264	359	6,559	78,110	55,894	5,187
Alexander	81.1	2,185	58.3	6.4	6.5	8.7	0.6	15.6	419	61	83	1,806	16,400	49,620	4,071
Alleghany	30.3	2,760	56.2	3.9	6.7	6.8	0.5	5.3	486	44	37	548	4,750	50,560	4,753
Anson	69.1	2,781	82.5	0.0	3.4	0.0	1.8	12.7	513	56	49	1,865	9,860	38,938	2,522
Ashe	68.1	2,542	49.7	2.5	6.8	14.9	1.1	10.5	393	65	59	1,033	11,540	50,342	4,361
Avery	54.4	3,108	46.8	4.6	9.5	8.6	4.9	9.3	533	47	33	1,376	7,470	49,574	4,383
Beaufort	157.8	3,356	53.5	4.6	8.1	8.8	0.7	88.4	1,879	141	215	2,644	21,250	52,410	4,742
Bertie	56.6	2,940	48.6	6.1	7.1	8.8	1.4	40.4	2,100	87	40	1,272	7,820	40,646	2,840
Bladen	122.6	3,665	48.5	5.8	6.2	7.9	0.8	37.9	1,133	121	70	2,031	13,100	42,826	3,246
Brunswick	434.4	3,319	33.7	12.6	10.2	4.8	2.3	433.6	3,314	564	392	4,817	70,150	69,351	7,562
Buncombe	1,366.1	5,314	27.1	31.0	6.1	6.9	1.5	691.4	2,690	3,884	652	12,522	133,150	69,023	8,272
Burke	220.9	2,450	51.5	3.6	8.3	8.4	1.6	118.9	1,319	170	188	6,801	38,960	48,512	3,942
Cabarrus	679.6	3,283	55.2	1.3	7.0	4.1	1.7	553.6	2,674	350	475	14,129	102,730	68,280	7,266
Caldwell	245.6	2,998	57.3	2.2	7.9	7.1	1.3	67.9	828	159	391	3,811	35,270	47,617	3,900
Camden	29.8	2,827	60.2	0.4	9.3	4.2	0.0	3.2	301	20	28	431	4,870	63,483	5,398
Carteret	371.1	5,384	27.4	41.5	5.5	3.5	1.5	94.8	1,376	308	429	4,547	33,460	68,899	7,704
Caswell	50.5	2,234	54.0	9.3	7.6	10.0	0.0	12.2	538	46	52	1,119	9,540	46,136	3,567
Catawba	770.5	4,881	34.1	37.0	4.5	5.1	0.9	438.2	2,776	347	341	9,351	75,440	60,434	6,493
Chatham	207.8	2,920	45.9	4.0	7.4	5.4	0.3	122.6	1,722	126	161	2,410	36,410	102,507	14,409
Cherokee	87.1	3,115	54.4	6.9	6.3	7.4	0.5	11.7	417	130	63	1,412	12,510	45,312	3,596

1. Based on the resident population estimated as of July 1 of the year shown. 2. Bronx, Kings, Queens, and Richmond counties are included with New York county.

Table B. States and Counties — **Land Area and Population**

State / county code	CBSA code[1]	County Type code[2]	STATE County	Land area[3] (sq. mi)	Population, 2021: Total persons 2021	Population, 2021: Rank	Population, 2021: Per square mile	Race alone or in combination, not Hispanic or Latino (percent): White	Black	American Indian, Alaska Native	Asian and Pacific Islancer	Percent Hispanic or Latino[4]	Age (percent): Under 5 years	5 to 17 years	18 to 24 years	25 to 34 years	35 to 44 years	45 to 54 years
				1	2	3	4	5	6	7	8	9	10	11	12	13	14	15
			NORTH CAROLINA—Cont'd															
37041		6	Chowan	172.7	13,722	2,174	79.5	61.8	34.0	0.8	1.0	3.9	4.9	11.1	10.8	10.0	11.0	10.9
37043		9	Clay	215.0	11,309	2,324	52.6	94.0	2.2	1.3	0.7	3.7	4.1	8.6	8.8	8.4	9.2	11.3
37045	43140	4	Cleveland	464.2	100,359	607	216.2	73.5	21.9	0.6	1.4	4.4	5.8	12.7	12.7	12.4	10.9	12.9
37047		6	Columbus	938.1	50,092	996	53.4	60.2	30.6	4.2	0.9	6.0	5.3	11.5	12.2	12.5	11.6	12.4
37049	35100	3	Craven	706.6	100,674	605	142.5	67.8	22.0	1.1	4.1	8.0	6.0	11.9	14.6	13.2	11.2	10.0
37051	22180	2	Cumberland	652.6	335,508	216	514.1	44.5	40.5	2.7	4.5	12.7	7.4	13.9	16.5	16.7	12.4	10.0
37053	47260	1	Currituck	261.9	29,653	1,442	113.2	87.6	6.5	1.3	1.8	5.1	5.3	13.0	10.1	12.2	13.0	13.0
37055	28620	4	Dare	383.2	37,826	1,227	98.7	88.5	3.3	1.0	1.3	7.6	4.2	10.5	9.8	9.6	12.2	13.0
37057	49180	2	Davidson	553.2	170,637	394	308.5	79.8	10.9	0.9	2.1	8.0	5.3	12.3	11.6	12.1	11.5	13.8
37059	49180	2	Davie	263.7	43,533	1,110	165.1	84.7	7.6	0.7	1.1	7.7	4.9	12.0	11.3	10.4	11.0	13.7
37061		6	Duplin	814.7	48,515	1,011	59.5	51.5	24.6	0.9	0.8	23.5	6.1	13.7	12.7	11.0	11.1	12.2
37063	20500	2	Durham	286.5	326,126	220	1,138.3	45.3	36.0	1.0	6.4	13.8	5.9	10.9	13.2	18.1	14.3	11.9
37065	40580	3	Edgecombe	505.4	48,359	1,015	95.7	36.6	57.5	0.8	0.7	5.6	5.7	12.8	11.9	12.0	10.7	11.3
37067	49180	2	Forsyth	407.9	385,523	190	945.1	56.9	27.3	0.9	3.2	13.9	5.6	13.0	13.9	13.2	12.2	12.4
37069	39580	1	Franklin	491.8	71,703	768	145.8	64.0	26.0	1.1	1.3	9.6	5.5	12.3	11.9	12.4	12.2	13.7
37071	16740	1	Gaston	355.8	230,856	300	648.8	71.0	19.7	1.0	2.2	8.3	5.7	12.8	11.9	13.5	12.5	13.8
37073	47260	1	Gates	340.6	10,366	2,384	30.4	65.8	31.8	1.6	1.1	2.4	4.5	11.3	10.5	11.0	10.6	12.7
37075		9	Graham	292.0	8,043	2,575	27.5	86.6	1.5	8.9	1.1	4.1	5.3	10.9	11.3	10.8	10.7	11.6
37077	20500	4	Granville	532.0	61,986	859	116.5	58.2	32.0	0.9	1.2	9.5	5.0	11.4	12.0	12.1	12.2	14.2
37079		8	Greene	266.7	20,417	1,796	76.6	47.1	36.0	1.0	0.7	16.3	5.1	11.4	12.1	13.9	13.6	12.7
37081	24660	2	Guilford	645.9	542,410	130	839.8	49.8	36.6	1.1	6.1	8.9	5.6	12.6	14.8	13.5	12.4	12.7
37083	40260	4	Halifax	723.7	48,272	1,017	66.7	38.9	53.7	4.3	1.2	3.4	5.5	12.1	11.4	11.5	10.9	11.6
37085	22180	4	Harnett	594.9	135,966	482	228.6	62.2	23.1	1.8	2.3	14.0	7.0	14.5	12.7	15.3	14.0	12.0
37087	11700	2	Haywood	553.6	62,476	855	112.9	92.7	1.8	1.3	1.0	4.6	4.4	10.2	9.6	11.7	11.0	12.6
37089	11700	2	Henderson	372.9	116,829	536	313.3	84.1	4.0	1.0	1.9	10.8	4.5	10.6	9.7	10.3	11.3	12.4
37091		6	Hertford	353.2	21,278	1,748	60.2	33.8	60.6	1.8	1.3	4.0	4.4	10.4	14.0	11.5	11.6	11.3
37093	22180	2	Hoke	390.2	53,114	956	136.1	40.5	36.4	9.5	2.9	15.0	7.8	15.2	12.1	17.0	14.4	11.3
37095		9	Hyde	612.3	4,508	2,856	7.4	62.0	27.2	1.0	1.1	10.2	3.4	9.7	9.7	12.0	12.8	13.4
37097	16740	1	Iredell	574.4	191,968	355	334.2	76.5	13.1	0.8	3.2	8.5	5.3	12.8	12.3	12.2	12.6	14.3
37099	19000	6	Jackson	491.1	43,410	1,115	88.4	81.8	2.9	9.2	1.6	6.6	4.2	9.4	21.2	10.8	10.5	10.7
37101	39580	1	Johnston	792.0	226,504	312	286.0	67.8	17.5	1.0	1.4	14.4	6.0	14.4	12.4	12.8	13.8	14.3
37103	35100	3	Jones	471.4	9,255	2,471	19.6	64.2	29.5	1.4	1.0	5.7	4.6	10.4	10.0	11.3	10.9	12.0
37105	41820	4	Lee	255.1	64,138	845	251.4	59.3	19.9	1.1	1.9	20.0	6.1	13.5	12.2	12.8	12.3	12.5
37107	28820	4	Lenoir	399.1	54,706	935	137.1	49.8	41.8	0.8	1.1	8.1	5.8	12.8	11.8	11.6	10.8	11.8
37109	16740	1	Lincoln	295.8	89,670	662	303.1	86.1	6.1	0.8	1.1	7.3	5.1	11.8	10.9	11.3	12.0	14.6
37111	32000	6	McDowell	440.0	44,717	1,082	101.6	88.4	4.5	0.9	1.2	6.3	4.6	11.3	10.9	12.1	11.4	13.6
37113		7	Macon	515.6	37,564	1,233	72.9	89.3	1.9	1.1	1.3	7.6	4.5	10.3	9.8	9.6	10.1	10.9
37115	11700	2	Madison	449.6	21,502	1,736	47.8	95.0	1.8	1.2	0.9	2.6	4.3	9.8	12.5	11.5	11.7	12.7
37117		6	Martin	456.4	21,754	1,725	47.7	53.1	42.2	0.7	0.9	4.4	5.3	11.6	10.7	10.5	9.8	11.8
37119	16740	1	Mecklenburg	523.6	1,122,276	41	2,143.4	47.5	32.9	0.9	7.2	13.8	6.3	12.7	12.8	17.1	14.8	13.2
37121		7	Mitchell	221.3	14,963	2,091	67.6	92.4	1.1	1.0	0.8	5.9	4.8	10.3	9.8	11.1	10.7	12.7
37123		6	Montgomery	491.5	25,798	1,570	52.5	64.2	18.8	0.9	1.8	15.7	5.2	12.0	12.3	11.2	10.6	12.6
37125	38240	4	Moore	697.7	102,763	599	147.3	78.7	12.5	1.4	2.2	7.2	5.9	12.3	9.7	11.8	12.5	11.0
37127	40580	3	Nash	540.4	95,176	638	176.1	49.4	42.4	1.2	1.3	7.4	5.6	12.3	12.7	12.2	11.2	12.8
37129	48900	2	New Hanover	192.3	229,018	302	1,190.9	79.2	13.8	1.0	2.2	6.0	4.5	10.1	15.6	12.9	12.5	12.3
37131	40260	9	Northampton	536.7	17,129	1,963	31.9	40.0	57.2	1.0	0.5	2.6	4.7	9.6	9.5	10.5	9.0	11.4
37133	27340	3	Onslow	762.1	206,160	333	270.5	69.2	16.5	1.4	4.0	13.2	7.9	13.2	24.6	17.3	11.4	7.6
37135	20500	2	Orange	397.6	148,884	454	374.5	71.7	12.2	1.0	9.1	8.6	4.0	10.9	22.2	11.6	11.4	12.2
37137	35100	3	Pamlico	336.5	12,344	2,254	36.7	75.9	19.3	1.2	1.0	4.2	3.2	8.4	8.7	9.8	10.5	11.2
37139	21020	4	Pasquotank	226.9	40,821	1,168	179.9	56.2	37.0	1.0	2.1	6.2	5.8	12.0	13.5	13.6	12.5	11.1
37141	48900	2	Pender	871.3	62,815	851	72.1	77.3	14.9	1.2	1.0	7.7	5.4	13.1	10.5	11.3	13.3	13.6
37143	21020	8	Perquimans	247.2	13,130	2,206	53.1	74.2	22.8	0.9	0.7	3.0	4.4	10.7	9.4	9.9	10.4	11.1
37145	20500	2	Person	392.3	39,127	1,200	99.7	67.7	27.7	1.1	0.7	4.8	5.2	11.5	10.9	11.6	10.8	13.3
37147	24780	3	Pitt	652.4	172,169	389	263.9	55.4	36.7	0.8	2.7	6.6	5.6	12.0	21.0	13.7	11.7	10.9
37149		8	Polk	237.7	19,656	1,844	82.7	89.0	4.6	0.9	1.1	5.9	3.8	8.8	9.3	8.5	9.0	12.2
37151	24660	2	Randolph	782.3	145,172	459	185.6	78.6	7.5	1.1	1.9	12.7	5.5	12.6	12.2	12.2	11.4	13.7
37153	40460	5	Richmond	473.7	42,724	1,129	90.2	57.3	32.7	3.6	1.5	7.3	6.2	13.2	12.6	12.4	11.2	12.8
37155	31300	4	Robeson	947.3	116,328	541	122.8	25.3	24.1	43.0	1.1	9.3	6.6	14.3	14.4	12.6	11.5	12.2
37157	24660	2	Rockingham	565.6	91,266	658	161.4	73.5	20.2	1.0	1.1	6.6	5.0	11.5	10.9	11.7	10.7	13.4
37159	16740	1	Rowan	511.6	148,150	455	289.6	71.9	17.5	0.9	1.5	10.1	5.5	12.4	12.8	12.5	11.7	12.9
37161	22580	4	Rutherford	565.4	64,586	840	114.2	84.1	11.0	0.8	1.0	5.2	5.0	11.4	11.1	11.0	10.9	13.4
37163		6	Sampson	945.9	58,990	892	62.4	51.3	25.7	2.6	1.0	21.3	6.4	13.8	12.6	11.7	11.3	12.7
37165	29900	6	Scotland	319.1	34,227	1,324	107.3	43.5	40.0	14.1	1.6	3.7	6.3	13.5	12.8	12.8	11.3	12.1
37167	10620	6	Stanly	395.1	63,425	848	160.5	81.3	12.3	0.7	2.2	4.9	5.4	12.3	11.8	12.9	11.6	12.6
37169	49180	2	Stokes	449.3	44,553	1,084	99.2	91.4	4.9	0.9	0.6	3.7	4.5	10.4	10.4	11.2	10.7	14.2
37171	34340	4	Surry	532.6	71,152	769	133.6	83.4	4.4	0.7	0.9	11.8	5.3	12.0	11.7	11.3	10.7	13.6

1. CBSA = Core Based Statistical Area. See Appendix A for explanation. See Appendix B for list of metropolitan areas with component counties. 2. County type code from the Economic Research Service of USDA Rural-Urban Continuum Codes. See Appendix A for definition. 3. Dry land or land partially or temporarily covered by water. 4. May be of any race.

STATE County	Population, 2021 (cont.): Age (percent) (cont.): 55 to 64 years	Population, 2021 (cont.): Age (percent) (cont.): 65 to 74 years	Population, 2021 (cont.): Age (percent) (cont.): 75 years and over	Population, 2021 (cont.): Percent female	Population change, 2000–2021: Total persons: 2010	Population change, 2000–2021: Total persons: 2020	Population change, 2000–2021: Percent change: 2010–2020	Population change, 2000–2021: Percent change: 2020–2021	Population change, 2000–2021: Components of change, 2020–2021: Births	Population change, 2000–2021: Components of change, 2020–2021: Deaths	Population change, 2000–2021: Components of change, 2020–2021: Net Migration	Households, 2016–2020: Number	Households, 2016–2020: Persons per household	Households, 2016–2020: Percent: Family households	Households, 2016–2020: Percent: Female family householder[1]	Households, 2016–2020: Percent: One person
	16	17	18	19	20	21	22	23	24	25	26	27	28	29	30	31
NORTH CAROLINA— Cont'd																
Chowan	15.9	15.3	10.2	52.2	14,793	13,708	-7.3	0.1	162	315	170	6,389	2.2	64.8	14.0	32.1
Clay	16.9	20.0	12.6	50.9	10,587	11,089	4.7	2.0	111	248	362	5,300	2.1	59.8	6.3	36.3
Cleveland	14.0	11.5	7.2	51.7	98,078	99,519	1.5	0.8	1,355	1,836	1,323	36,089	2.7	67.4	14.7	29.0
Columbus	14.0	12.1	8.5	50.1	58,098	50,623	-12.9	-1.0	692	1,127	-102	21,545	2.5	66.4	17.5	30.8
Craven	12.7	12.1	8.2	49.6	103,505	100,720	-2.7	0.0	1,579	1,595	-32	41,002	2.4	65.6	10.2	29.8
Cumberland	10.5	7.8	4.9	50.4	319,431	334,728	4.8	0.2	6,205	4,063	-1,453	127,532	2.5	62.0	16.6	33.2
Currituck	16.3	11.5	5.8	49.6	23,547	28,100	19.3	5.5	340	343	1,577	10,868	2.5	70.9	7.3	21.7
Dare	17.4	15.7	7.7	50.7	33,920	36,915	8.8	2.5	383	550	1,092	15,830	2.3	65.0	11.0	27.5
Davidson	14.6	11.3	7.5	50.8	162,878	168,930	3.7	1.0	2,098	2,767	2,385	67,555	2.4	69.4	12.2	25.5
Davie	15.0	12.7	8.9	51.0	41,240	42,712	3.6	1.9	487	706	1,052	16,303	2.6	70.2	10.1	25.9
Duplin	13.5	11.8	7.9	50.7	58,505	48,715	-16.7	-0.4	828	881	-150	21,437	2.7	67.6	14.4	26.6
Durham	11.4	9.1	5.2	52.2	267,587	324,833	21.4	0.4	4,966	3,388	-313	130,128	2.3	57.5	13.8	33.9
Edgecombe	14.4	12.9	8.2	53.6	56,552	48,900	-13.5	-1.1	685	979	-252	20,800	2.5	69.0	23.7	27.1
Forsyth	13.1	10.2	6.5	52.4	350,670	382,590	9.1	0.8	5,200	5,191	2,887	148,890	2.5	62.4	13.5	32.1
Franklin	14.6	11.1	6.3	50.3	60,619	68,573	13.1	4.6	927	1,000	3,237	25,729	2.6	73.1	14.1	23.1
Gaston	13.4	10.1	6.3	51.6	206,086	227,943	10.6	1.3	3,089	3,675	3,505	85,286	2.6	66.0	13.4	28.2
Gates	17.4	13.1	8.8	50.3	12,197	10,478	-14.1	-1.1	110	217	-6	4,690	2.4	65.5	11.7	30.0
Graham	14.6	14.0	10.9	49.6	8,861	8,030	-9.4	0.2	107	169	75	3,521	2.4	65.2	8.5	30.5
Granville	15.1	11.0	6.9	49.0	59,916	60,992	1.8	1.6	703	854	1,153	21,567	2.6	72.2	13.7	23.2
Greene	13.6	11.3	6.4	44.8	21,362	20,451	-4.3	-0.2	256	310	17	7,218	2.6	64.8	17.4	29.6
Guilford	12.6	9.6	6.3	52.5	488,406	541,299	10.8	0.2	7,196	7,144	942	208,234	2.5	62.4	15.5	30.8
Halifax	15.2	13.3	8.6	51.8	54,691	48,622	-11.1	-0.7	637	1,022	30	21,061	2.4	65.0	20.5	31.1
Harnett	11.3	8.4	4.9	50.3	114,678	133,568	16.5	1.8	2,262	1,630	1,752	46,525	2.8	68.2	13.1	27.3
Haywood	15.5	14.7	10.3	51.3	59,036	62,089	5.2	0.6	630	1,227	996	26,891	2.3	64.0	10.5	31.3
Henderson	14.6	15.4	11.2	51.7	106,740	116,281	8.9	0.5	1,244	2,215	1,532	49,715	2.3	67.3	9.5	27.6
Hertford	15.2	12.9	8.7	50.1	24,669	21,552	-12.6	-1.3	236	432	-80	8,903	2.4	59.5	18.6	36.6
Hoke	11.2	7.5	3.5	50.5	46,952	52,082	10.9	2.0	1,006	560	576	18,448	2.9	67.2	15.7	29.2
Hyde	15.1	15.1	8.9	45.6	5,810	4,589	-21.0	-1.8	40	85	-36	2,056	2.2	71.4	15.7	24.7
Iredell	14.3	10.1	6.1	50.5	159,437	186,693	17.1	2.8	2,354	2,532	5,497	68,374	2.6	72.9	12.8	22.5
Jackson	12.8	12.7	7.8	51.0	40,271	43,109	7.0	0.7	412	576	463	17,008	2.3	58.3	9.7	30.8
Johnston	12.6	8.9	4.9	51.1	168,878	215,999	27.9	4.9	3,041	2,605	10,172	71,332	2.8	72.7	12.3	22.8
Jones	16.3	15.3	9.2	51.3	10,153	9,172	-9.7	0.9	104	180	160	4,069	2.3	64.4	15.7	30.7
Lee	13.4	10.4	6.7	51.1	57,866	63,285	9.4	1.3	952	872	771	22,290	2.7	69.7	15.0	25.1
Lenoir	14.6	12.5	8.4	52.5	59,495	55,122	-7.4	-0.8	788	1,081	-128	23,494	2.3	59.7	16.5	35.2
Lincoln	15.5	11.8	7.0	50.5	78,265	86,810	10.9	3.3	1,066	1,359	3,187	33,621	2.5	70.7	11.5	24.1
McDowell	14.7	13.0	8.4	49.9	44,996	44,578	-0.9	0.3	491	790	441	18,275	2.4	73.0	12.8	22.9
Macon	15.6	17.0	12.1	51.8	33,922	37,014	9.1	1.5	386	652	830	16,062	2.2	61.9	8.9	32.2
Madison	14.7	13.9	8.8	50.8	20,764	21,193	2.1	1.5	215	405	506	8,373	2.5	63.5	7.1	30.8
Martin	15.2	15.2	10.0	53.0	24,505	22,031	-10.1	-1.3	278	469	-86	9,622	2.3	64.4	17.3	31.2
Mecklenburg	11.3	7.5	4.4	51.9	919,628	1,115,482	21.3	0.6	17,629	10,171	-941	421,950	2.6	60.7	13.0	31.7
Mitchell	15.3	14.8	10.5	50.9	15,579	14,903	-4.3	0.4	181	344	227	6,402	2.3	63.6	9.6	32.2
Montgomery	14.6	13.4	8.1	51.4	27,798	25,751	-7.4	0.2	337	449	160	10,265	2.6	68.4	12.3	29.8
Moore	13.2	13.1	10.6	51.5	88,247	99,727	13.0	3.0	1,419	1,767	3,427	40,575	2.4	65.2	8.9	29.8
Nash	14.1	12.0	7.2	52.2	95,840	94,970	-0.9	0.2	1,273	1,591	513	37,371	2.5	67.2	18.0	29.1
New Hanover	13.1	11.6	7.3	52.5	202,667	225,702	11.4	1.5	2,570	3,260	4,014	97,998	2.3	55.2	9.4	34.5
Northampton	17.0	16.3	12.0	51.7	22,099	17,471	-20.9	-2.0	201	385	-153	8,424	2.2	63.2	18.7	31.9
Onslow	8.1	6.2	3.7	44.1	177,772	204,576	15.1	0.8	4,485	1,791	-1,150	66,131	2.7	71.1	11.1	22.0
Orange	12.0	10.0	5.7	52.6	133,801	148,696	11.1	0.1	1,365	1,314	107	53,222	2.5	61.8	8.3	27.8
Pamlico	17.7	18.6	12.0	49.1	13,144	12,276	-6.6	0.6	98	255	231	5,506	2.2	64.2	9.1	32.2
Pasquotank	13.6	10.8	7.0	51.3	40,661	40,568	-0.2	0.6	568	650	336	14,785	2.5	66.5	12.6	29.5
Pender	14.5	11.7	6.7	50.2	52,217	60,203	15.3	4.3	733	932	2,847	22,812	2.7	66.5	9.5	28.3
Perquimans	16.2	16.3	11.6	52.5	13,453	13,005	-3.3	1.0	121	248	255	5,886	2.3	69.4	11.3	27.2
Person	15.7	12.8	8.0	51.8	39,464	39,097	-0.9	0.1	507	666	185	16,153	2.4	66.5	14.8	28.9
Pitt	10.9	9.0	5.3	53.1	168,148	170,243	1.2	1.1	2,421	2,194	1,676	70,683	2.5	60.0	16.5	28.8
Polk	16.6	17.4	14.4	52.3	20,510	19,328	-5.8	1.7	159	471	651	9,252	2.2	60.1	6.8	34.3
Randolph	14.3	11.0	7.2	50.3	141,752	144,171	1.7	0.7	1,871	2,425	1,553	56,790	2.5	68.7	12.0	26.7
Richmond	13.3	11.2	7.0	51.1	46,639	42,946	-7.9	-0.5	728	843	-115	18,201	2.4	66.1	19.0	28.5
Robeson	12.4	10.1	5.8	51.9	134,168	116,530	-13.1	-0.2	2,090	2,205	-112	45,881	2.8	66.4	19.9	29.9
Rockingham	15.6	12.7	8.4	51.5	93,643	91,096	-2.7	0.2	1,093	1,807	887	38,532	2.3	66.6	13.2	29.9
Rowan	14.2	11.0	7.0	50.5	138,428	146,875	6.1	0.9	1,896	2,412	1,787	54,137	2.5	68.0	14.0	26.6
Rutherford	15.0	13.5	8.7	51.4	67,810	64,444	-5.0	0.2	767	1,275	654	27,525	2.4	63.9	12.2	30.7
Sampson	13.0	11.1	7.3	50.6	63,431	59,036	-6.9	-0.1	898	1,024	71	23,162	2.7	69.7	14.6	27.0
Scotland	12.5	11.3	7.3	49.9	36,157	34,174	-5.5	0.2	477	614	188	12,951	2.5	63.4	21.8	32.6
Stanly	14.0	11.6	7.7	49.9	60,585	62,504	3.2	1.5	771	1,094	1,255	23,849	2.5	69.8	11.6	25.7
Stokes	16.2	13.3	9.2	50.7	47,401	44,520	-6.1	0.1	455	843	423	19,608	2.3	66.7	12.0	28.3
Surry	14.6	12.5	8.5	51.0	73,673	71,359	-3.1	-0.3	932	1,441	297	29,001	2.5	68.3	10.4	28.7

1. No spouse present.

STATE County	Persons in group quarters, 2021	Daytime Population, 2016–2020: Number	Daytime Population, 2016–2020: Employment/ residence ratio	Births, 2021: Total	Births, 2021: Rate[1]	Deaths, 2021: Number	Deaths, 2021: Rate[1]	Persons under 65 with no health insurance, 2019: Number	Persons under 65 with no health insurance, 2019: Percent	Medicare, 2021: Total beneficiaries	Medicare, 2021: Enrolled in Original Medicare	Medicare, 2021: Enrolled in Medicare Advantage	COVID-19 Deaths, 2020: Number	COVID-19 Deaths, 2020: Rate[1]
	32	33	34	35	36	37	38	39	40	41	42	43	44	45
NORTH CAROLINA—Cont'd														
Chowan	184	13,416	0.9	131	9.6	246	18.0	1,207	11.8	4,093	3,250	843	25	1.8
Clay	69	10,458	0.8	91	8.1	188	16.8	1,302	17.2	3,982	2,800	1,182	D	D
Cleveland	1,855	93,513	0.9	1,119	11.2	1,495	14.9	10,527	13.6	23,526	14,070	9,455	172	1.7
Columbus	2,377	51,003	0.8	545	10.8	907	18.0	6,779	16.6	13,244	8,783	4,461	91	1.8
Craven	4,469	106,015	1.1	1,256	12.5	1,286	12.8	9,938	12.9	24,197	20,028	4,169	105	1.0
Cumberland	15,702	360,010	1.2	4,977	14.9	3,264	9.7	34,470	12.5	54,413	35,747	18,665	158	0.5
Currituck	55	20,380	0.5	276	9.5	295	10.2	2,944	12.7	5,557	4,583	975	14	0.5
Dare	99	38,026	1.1	309	8.3	447	11.9	3,918	13.6	9,375	7,972	1,404	D	D
Davidson	1,407	141,605	0.7	1,681	9.9	2,242	13.2	19,706	14.6	37,652	14,883	22,768	148	0.9
Davie	213	38,287	0.8	396	9.2	539	12.5	4,369	13.0	10,603	4,852	5,750	35	0.8
Duplin	175	55,215	0.9	666	13.7	719	14.8	10,019	21.6	10,876	7,618	3,258	81	1.7
Durham	14,113	363,744	1.3	4,002	12.3	2,739	8.4	36,915	14.0	48,534	30,189	18,345	153	0.5
Edgecombe	638	48,588	0.8	555	11.4	758	15.6	4,790	12.1	12,603	8,550	4,053	90	1.8
Forsyth	10,524	399,980	1.1	4,160	10.8	4,106	10.7	43,632	14.2	73,690	31,607	42,083	261	0.7
Franklin	1,182	53,064	0.5	740	10.5	800	11.4	7,749	13.8	13,717	8,227	5,490	47	0.7
Gaston	3,150	199,718	0.8	2,487	10.8	2,911	12.7	25,668	13.9	45,263	23,800	21,462	249	1.1
Gates	14	8,459	0.4	86	8.3	176	16.9	1,068	11.8	2,555	1,933	622	22	2.1
Graham	46	7,755	0.8	87	10.8	129	16.1	1,200	19.0	2,264	1,452	812	11	1.4
Granville	3,476	54,611	0.8	563	9.2	687	11.2	6,156	13.2	12,012	7,209	4,803	50	0.8
Greene	2,341	16,966	0.5	207	10.1	250	12.2	3,062	20.7	3,964	2,823	1,141	28	1.4
Guilford	19,854	579,001	1.2	5,775	10.7	5,608	10.3	57,058	13.1	97,416	40,477	56,939	391	0.7
Halifax	1,051	49,530	0.9	508	10.5	816	16.9	5,633	15.0	13,461	8,838	4,623	57	1.2
Harnett	2,847	107,835	0.5	1,808	13.4	1,325	9.8	17,293	15.1	21,203	13,598	7,605	103	0.8
Haywood	584	56,124	0.8	506	8.1	961	15.4	5,782	12.4	18,400	11,217	7,183	77	1.2
Henderson	1,027	109,630	0.9	991	8.5	1,799	15.4	12,599	14.7	33,926	22,029	11,897	108	0.9
Hertford	2,115	25,063	1.2	199	9.3	353	16.5	2,196	13.6	5,363	3,880	1,483	54	2.5
Hoke	642	43,004	0.5	807	15.3	450	8.5	7,934	16.5	7,385	4,564	2,821	50	1.0
Hyde	470	5,178	1.1	31	6.8	66	14.6	562	16.8	1,186	829	357	D	D
Iredell	1,040	177,296	1.0	1,854	9.8	2,026	10.7	19,485	12.8	35,362	19,921	15,441	140	0.7
Jackson	4,024	45,235	1.1	336	7.8	450	10.4	5,921	19.2	8,866	5,891	2,975	34	0.8
Johnston	1,246	167,127	0.6	2,481	11.2	2,103	9.5	25,998	14.5	35,078	21,248	13,830	134	0.6
Jones	66	7,506	0.5	77	8.4	149	16.2	1,226	17.5	2,674	1,991	683	22	2.4
Lee	960	63,786	1.1	764	12.0	697	10.9	8,032	15.9	12,568	8,186	4,383	51	0.8
Lenoir	902	58,487	1.1	642	11.7	855	15.6	6,522	14.9	14,217	10,608	3,609	87	1.6
Lincoln	557	73,320	0.7	832	9.4	1,112	12.6	9,115	13.0	19,031	11,367	7,663	82	0.9
McDowell	1,392	44,745	1.0	394	8.8	631	14.1	5,200	14.8	11,879	6,841	5,038	70	1.6
Macon	289	35,252	1.0	313	8.4	519	13.9	4,592	18.2	11,923	8,502	3,422	22	0.6
Madison	895	17,776	0.6	169	7.9	335	15.7	2,121	13.4	5,843	3,468	2,375	14	0.7
Martin	93	20,567	0.8	219	10.0	376	17.2	2,180	13.0	6,396	4,751	1,645	34	1.5
Mecklenburg	16,646	1,246,096	1.3	14,170	12.6	8,339	7.4	127,730	13.2	142,184	82,874	59,311	683	0.6
Mitchell	146	14,225	0.9	144	9.7	274	18.4	1,604	14.6	4,465	2,744	1,722	26	1.7
Montgomery	749	26,855	1.0	274	10.6	346	13.4	3,536	17.3	6,225	3,744	2,481	41	1.6
Moore	573	97,154	1.0	1,143	11.3	1,393	13.7	9,196	12.0	26,513	17,057	9,455	112	1.1
Nash	2,066	94,461	1.0	1,036	10.9	1,245	13.1	9,344	12.6	21,835	14,831	7,003	128	1.3
New Hanover	7,499	253,550	1.2	2,075	9.1	2,558	11.2	22,453	12.2	47,592	34,589	13,003	92	0.4
Northampton	278	18,176	0.8	168	9.7	318	18.4	1,740	13.0	5,640	3,922	1,718	48	2.8
Onslow	25,150	197,878	1.0	3,599	17.5	1,397	6.8	16,678	10.6	26,277	21,220	5,057	82	0.4
Orange	10,316	158,536	1.2	1,089	7.3	1,064	7.1	12,277	10.5	23,654	13,795	9,860	58	0.4
Pamlico	623	12,056	0.9	80	6.5	200	16.2	1,191	14.6	4,100	3,332	768	D	D
Pasquotank	1,960	39,308	1.0	441	10.8	517	12.7	3,756	12.2	8,661	6,533	2,127	45	1.1
Pender	730	50,823	0.6	601	9.7	739	12.0	6,755	13.4	13,227	9,100	4,127	31	0.5
Perquimans	29	11,351	0.6	97	7.4	190	14.5	1,242	12.8	3,969	3,106	863	17	1.3
Person	308	34,128	0.7	410	10.5	529	13.5	3,972	12.7	9,612	5,305	4,306	27	0.7
Pitt	5,906	183,472	1.0	1,931	11.3	1,780	10.4	17,828	12.0	30,816	21,944	8,872	139	0.8
Polk	212	18,836	0.8	127	6.5	383	19.6	1,969	14.1	6,575	4,661	1,914	22	1.1
Randolph	1,082	130,454	0.8	1,492	10.3	1,904	13.2	20,225	17.4	31,179	11,749	19,430	148	1.0
Richmond	669	42,213	0.9	573	13.4	668	15.6	5,159	14.7	10,484	6,802	3,682	57	1.3
Robeson	3,368	128,357	0.9	1,682	14.5	1,761	15.1	19,377	18.5	24,791	14,486	10,306	202	1.7
Rockingham	891	81,186	0.8	890	9.8	1,450	15.9	9,758	13.7	23,750	9,181	14,569	115	1.3
Rowan	4,163	133,758	0.9	1,519	10.3	1,907	12.9	16,376	14.5	31,830	15,948	15,882	183	1.2
Rutherford	940	61,158	0.8	616	9.5	1,024	15.9	7,051	13.8	16,714	10,619	6,095	124	1.9
Sampson	613	58,907	0.8	707	12.0	825	14.0	10,177	20.2	13,214	7,980	5,234	62	1.1
Scotland	2,330	35,386	1.0	389	11.4	485	14.2	3,511	13.7	8,229	5,013	3,217	62	1.8
Stanly	1,979	55,955	0.8	633	10.0	875	13.9	7,153	14.6	14,288	8,377	5,912	84	1.3
Stokes	338	35,101	0.5	369	8.3	685	15.4	4,374	12.3	11,511	4,211	7,300	37	0.8
Surry	709	70,831	1.0	745	10.5	1,110	15.6	9,396	16.7	18,378	8,327	10,051	89	1.2

1. Per 1,000 estimated resident population.

STATE County	COVID-19 Vaccinations, 2021–2022: Number	COVID-19 Vaccinations, 2021–2022: Percent[5]	Education: School enrollment and attainment, 2016–2020: Enrollment[1]: Total	Enrollment[1]: Percent private	Attainment[2] (percent): High school graduate or less	Attainment[2] (percent): Bachelor's degree or more	Local government expenditures,[3] 2018–2019: Total current spending (mil dol)	Local government expenditures,[3] 2018–2019: Current spending per student (dollars)	Money income, 2016–2020: Per capita income[4]	Households: Median income (dollars)	Households: Percent with income of less than $50,000	Households: Percent with income of $200,000 or more	Income and poverty, 2020: Median household income (dollars)	Percent below poverty level: All persons	Percent below poverty level: Children under 18 years	Percent below poverty level: Children 5 to 17 years in families
	46	47	48	49	50	51	52	53	54	55	56	57	58	59	60	61
NORTH CAROLINA—Cont'd																
Chowan	7,947	57.0	2,715	11.5	48.7	21.7	24.9	12,335	27,254	44,050	55.3	2.6	45,365	17.3	28.9	26.5
Clay	6,135	54.6	1,845	11.0	39.7	27.0	15.1	11,397	32,744	42,160	56.1	4.0	44,052	16.4	24.1	23.2
Cleveland	49,155	50.2	22,511	11.8	48.5	19.5	151.5	9,656	23,061	43,512	55.6	2.4	49,041	15.0	21.7	21.5
Columbus	24,951	45.0	10,940	7.5	53.7	12.9	89.1	10,121	22,426	38,487	58.9	2.0	40,712	21.3	26.6	27.1
Craven	63,927	62.6	22,783	17.1	36.9	25.0	135.4	9,867	29,908	53,894	46.8	3.9	53,960	13.2	19.0	18.6
Cumberland	204,853	61.1	92,142	17.2	34.9	25.6	497.5	9,528	25,648	48,177	51.7	2.6	49,160	18.5	25.3	23.2
Currituck	16,626	59.9	6,439	16.0	40.4	25.2	42.5	10,219	34,726	73,741	30.4	5.5	73,433	9.6	14.8	13.8
Dare	28,183	76.2	7,332	16.0	27.5	38.3	62.9	11,900	36,532	65,420	36.4	5.8	72,962	8.8	13.2	12.5
Davidson	80,546	48.1	36,895	16.8	47.1	18.9	226.2	9,138	26,616	50,454	49.6	2.7	56,067	12.0	17.5	16.7
Davie	24,605	57.4	9,186	13.8	42.4	24.3	58.8	9,631	32,638	62,028	39.9	4.6	65,418	9.6	13.0	11.9
Duplin	26,456	45.0	14,337	7.4	52.8	14.6	95.6	9,954	21,145	43,422	55.6	1.1	49,755	18.3	26.9	24.5
Durham	230,471	71.7	81,305	27.2	28.1	49.5	488.7	10,918	36,759	62,812	39.8	7.7	65,619	11.7	16.2	14.1
Edgecombe	25,160	48.9	11,085	7.1	54.9	16.2	72.1	10,418	21,595	40,489	60.4	1.0	45,156	24.1	45.4	42.3
Forsyth	240,503	62.9	96,335	18.7	36.1	33.9	569.3	9,810	31,201	53,583	47.0	5.3	56,158	13.0	18.8	18.5
Franklin	36,408	52.2	15,019	20.2	43.2	21.2	83.2	9,449	27,588	58,172	43.4	3.5	54,868	12.0	16.4	14.7
Gaston	114,186	50.9	49,287	15.8	44.8	22.1	311.0	9,064	28,526	53,474	47.1	3.4	60,622	11.8	16.1	15.5
Gates	6,179	53.4	2,499	16.2	50.3	12.5	19.5	11,536	26,053	45,871	52.7	1.9	57,680	13.2	19.7	18.2
Graham	4,225	50.1	1,747	3.2	52.3	13.3	15.0	12,820	23,034	42,207	59.2	2.0	42,057	16.6	23.8	22.7
Granville	37,708	62.4	13,204	12.3	44.8	23.8	84.0	9,287	27,723	56,924	43.3	4.1	53,112	15.0	15.4	14.7
Greene	13,161	62.5	4,388	7.6	55.6	10.4	33.4	11,463	19,415	43,563	56.2	1.0	47,605	21.3	29.7	28.6
Guilford	335,074	62.4	143,640	16.9	33.9	36.6	797.1	9,925	31,798	54,794	46.1	5.8	55,577	13.3	19.3	17.6
Halifax	27,133	54.3	10,119	12.3	58.3	14.7	79.5	11,790	21,902	35,904	63.5	1.7	41,098	23.9	31.0	29.2
Harnett	57,657	42.4	37,851	22.2	40.8	22.1	182.1	8,749	24,693	54,565	45.3	3.0	55,586	14.4	19.5	18.1
Haywood	36,183	58.1	11,630	13.1	37.8	27.8	74.6	9,779	30,336	51,548	48.4	3.9	50,492	13.6	20.8	19.4
Henderson	69,288	59.0	22,501	19.8	34.3	31.5	129.7	9,365	32,306	58,928	42.7	4.4	60,550	11.0	17.0	15.9
Hertford	11,469	48.4	5,517	27.6	50.4	16.0	32.9	11,467	21,715	42,588	60.2	1.6	46,632	20.7	28.0	25.8
Hoke	22,626	41.0	15,427	13.2	42.0	18.4	85.8	9,503	23,066	51,140	48.8	2.6	53,728	15.0	21.3	20.9
Hyde	3,286	66.6	851	11.2	58.5	10.5	11.0	18,114	17,942	46,667	53.3	0.0	45,548	20.0	28.0	26.3
Iredell	96,442	53.0	41,079	14.7	37.2	29.7	272.3	8,686	35,261	62,551	39.3	7.5	61,892	9.7	13.6	12.1
Jackson	24,320	55.4	13,032	7.8	40.1	28.4	42.9	10,855	25,738	46,820	53.5	3.7	49,488	16.6	20.0	19.5
Johnston	111,116	53.1	52,158	12.1	39.5	24.0	347.3	9,077	29,327	61,806	39.9	4.7	63,882	11.4	13.9	12.8
Jones	5,151	54.7	1,784	19.5	53.4	14.2	15.3	13,665	22,917	38,324	57.9	0.8	44,972	18.3	29.3	28.1
Lee	35,279	57.1	14,683	12.6	42.5	20.5	96.0	9,385	25,502	52,294	47.4	3.3	57,025	15.4	22.4	21.5
Lenoir	30,592	54.7	13,116	14.8	50.9	15.5	85.9	9,743	24,894	39,923	59.3	2.0	40,586	17.2	26.1	24.3
Lincoln	42,130	48.9	17,460	11.8	41.9	23.1	114.3	8,344	33,197	59,592	42.3	7.2	56,183	11.9	13.4	12.6
McDowell	24,184	52.9	8,789	12.9	47.3	18.4	63.5	10,706	25,432	47,085	53.3	1.8	47,579	15.2	22.8	19.9
Macon	21,103	58.9	5,927	14.3	43.4	23.9	45.2	10,096	29,549	45,703	52.8	3.8	51,973	12.9	18.5	17.8
Madison	12,414	57.1	4,829	31.1	43.4	30.1	24.8	10,913	27,184	46,190	52.8	3.2	49,373	14.0	20.0	19.5
Martin	11,793	52.6	4,555	11.9	51.6	15.1	42.0	11,533	24,108	39,909	59.6	1.9	42,264	20.1	32.3	33.2
Mecklenburg	706,347	63.6	275,203	17.7	26.1	45.8	1,541.6	9,369	40,627	69,240	35.7	10.5	72,340	11.0	16.3	16.6
Mitchell	7,526	50.3	3,028	17.4	44.0	22.1	21.1	11,414	26,975	48,841	51.1	1.9	49,236	14.0	20.4	19.9
Montgomery	11,607	42.7	5,836	10.5	53.1	16.3	42.9	10,835	23,863	45,147	54.0	2.7	48,522	16.0	23.8	22.2
Moore	60,672	60.1	21,536	18.5	29.3	38.7	132.1	9,527	36,184	63,324	39.2	7.5	69,413	9.3	12.6	11.9
Nash	55,461	58.8	22,120	14.8	47.6	21.2	156.2	9,546	27,286	49,949	50.0	3.7	49,883	14.9	22.3	22.1
New Hanover	149,920	63.9	55,815	14.5	26.7	42.2	299.3	10,708	36,324	56,689	44.3	7.1	65,615	10.2	14.3	12.8
Northampton	9,414	48.3	3,706	10.9	57.6	15.1	36.3	12,855	23,946	38,969	62.6	2.6	41,630	21.7	31.8	29.5
Onslow	121,119	61.2	48,092	12.8	37.0	23.6	242.0	8,954	24,817	51,560	48.2	1.9	52,885	12.5	15.9	16.7
Orange	118,041	79.5	53,029	11.5	19.5	60.8	257.7	12,352	42,872	74,803	34.2	15.1	82,732	10.3	8.7	8.1
Pamlico	7,282	57.2	2,036	3.7	41.1	21.5	26.2	13,663	28,257	48,531	51.5	3.2	50,481	14.7	26.8	25.4
Pasquotank	21,766	54.7	9,829	13.9	42.9	23.3	61.2	10,209	26,898	54,439	45.4	2.4	56,654	14.0	23.5	24.7
Pender	33,171	52.6	14,187	13.6	38.7	29.0	88.7	9,409	30,666	60,044	40.6	5.3	59,812	12.3	16.5	14.8
Perquimans	6,576	48.8	2,601	11.6	44.2	19.6	19.1	11,548	28,160	51,036	48.0	2.7	50,813	14.4	26.0	25.2
Person	22,387	56.7	8,816	12.9	47.8	15.7	57.1	10,335	31,605	57,323	44.5	3.2	58,991	13.5	19.5	18.7
Pitt	98,509	54.5	59,528	8.3	35.2	32.1	240.4	9,715	27,599	49,337	50.5	3.7	49,955	17.1	21.5	21.2
Polk	9,106	43.9	3,476	13.8	34.3	32.7	26.8	12,050	32,327	52,125	48.9	4.0	58,607	12.0	18.7	17.7
Randolph	63,960	44.5	31,310	13.7	51.4	16.1	206.8	9,291	25,246	48,984	51.2	1.8	48,849	14.2	19.7	18.0
Richmond	21,459	47.9	10,525	9.9	47.5	17.8	72.4	9,997	22,068	39,051	60.0	1.2	42,335	21.5	34.2	34.0
Robeson	55,547	42.5	33,563	6.3	55.6	14.0	222.6	9,947	19,388	35,362	63.0	1.5	39,139	26.6	39.2	37.4
Rockingham	46,064	50.6	18,294	11.9	50.6	15.2	115.3	9,213	25,268	45,697	54.1	1.7	50,388	13.8	22.0	20.6
Rowan	63,878	45.0	33,858	18.2	46.7	19.8	187.2	9,812	26,789	51,054	48.6	3.5	55,398	14.4	22.2	20.7
Rutherford	28,171	42.0	13,056	14.4	47.0	19.2	102.4	10,329	24,308	43,183	57.9	3.4	44,004	19.1	25.5	24.9
Sampson	32,822	51.7	14,938	7.1	54.0	14.4	108.9	9,672	23,502	42,914	56.0	2.3	45,387	21.2	28.2	26.7
Scotland	16,611	47.7	7,833	9.8	52.7	15.5	67.2	11,725	20,975	35,936	63.2	1.4	33,531	29.7	45.6	40.3
Stanly	27,265	43.4	13,694	19.7	45.5	17.6	82.9	8,938	26,956	54,104	45.5	3.1	53,769	14.5	19.1	19.3
Stokes	21,419	47.0	8,425	6.0	55.5	13.4	60.9	10,279	27,979	51,668	47.6	1.7	59,068	12.1	19.0	18.3
Surry	37,322	52.0	14,953	12.6	49.3	17.9	114.2	9,922	26,074	44,979	53.3	2.8	47,114	15.4	20.0	18.2

1. All persons 3 years old and over enrolled in nursery school through college. 2. Persons 25 years old and over. 3. Elementary and secondary education expenditures. 4. Based on population estimated by the American Community Survey, 2016–2020. 5. CDC percent based on 2019 population estimate.

STATE County	Personal income, 2020: Total (mil dol)	Personal income, 2020: Percent change 2019–2020	Personal income, 2020: Per capita[1]: Dollars	Personal income, 2020: Per capita[1]: Rank	Personal income, 2020: Wages and salaries (mil dol)	Personal income, 2020: Supplements to wages and salaries, employer contributions (mil dol): Pension and insurance	Personal income, 2020: Supplements to wages and salaries, employer contributions (mil dol): Government social insurance	Personal income, 2020: Proprietors' income (mil dol)	Personal income, 2020: Dividends, interest, and rent (mil dol)	Personal income, 2020: Personal transfer reecipts (mil dol)	Earnings, 2020: Total (mil dol)	Earnings, 2020: Contributions for government social insurance (mil dol): From employee and self-employed	Earnings, 2020: Contributions for government social insurance (mil dol): From employer
	62	63	64	65	66	67	68	69	70	71	72	73	74
NORTH CAROLINA—Cont'd													
Chowan	627	6.3	45,388	1,736	204	35	15	40	139	208	294	23	15
Clay	433	10.0	37,625	2,724	78	16	6	13	100	185	113	14	6
Cleveland	4,121	8.3	41,616	2,253	1,647	278	122	193	559	1,464	2,239	165	122
Columbus	2,032	9.8	37,112	2,780	655	126	48	112	259	824	940	73	48
Craven	4,943	6.9	48,832	1,279	2,355	551	185	258	997	1,429	3,350	211	185
Cumberland	14,461	8.0	42,992	2,064	9,534	2,473	820	538	2,625	4,783	13,364	690	820
Currituck	1,428	9.0	49,152	1,237	295	47	22	71	216	313	435	34	22
Dare	2,224	6.1	59,240	467	779	123	61	277	506	471	1,239	85	61
Davidson	7,336	7.3	43,348	2,027	2,134	337	160	383	953	2,149	3,014	225	160
Davie	2,257	5.8	52,153	924	583	86	45	120	392	562	833	65	45
Duplin	2,227	7.1	37,872	2,696	775	136	61	218	341	693	1,189	75	61
Durham	17,693	6.6	54,056	776	18,685	2,279	1,256	1,311	3,161	3,238	23,531	1,410	1,256
Edgecombe	2,002	7.4	39,394	2,524	681	137	51	95	320	793	964	69	51
Forsyth	19,700	5.7	51,323	993	11,231	1,530	799	1,449	3,564	4,536	15,009	981	799
Franklin	2,838	10.4	39,490	2,507	652	112	46	143	316	773	954	73	46
Gaston	9,992	7.6	44,103	1,929	3,420	551	253	467	1,221	2,866	4,692	341	253
Gates	477	6.2	41,571	2,258	82	18	7	24	75	141	130	11	7
Graham	322	8.3	37,943	2,692	86	16	7	27	48	126	136	11	7
Granville	2,589	6.3	42,807	2,092	1,074	248	79	127	350	677	1,528	99	79
Greene	729	8.6	34,811	2,945	194	45	14	43	79	229	296	19	14
Guilford	26,948	6.6	49,856	1,159	16,162	2,271	1,146	1,997	4,732	6,200	21,576	1,380	1,146
Halifax	1,963	5.6	39,680	2,485	627	122	46	62	258	826	857	73	46
Harnett	5,247	7.4	38,280	2,652	1,136	201	85	258	769	1,509	1,680	132	85
Haywood	2,755	6.2	43,754	1,980	755	131	55	172	501	956	1,113	95	55
Henderson	5,612	4.7	47,385	1,463	1,871	293	137	403	1,297	1,641	2,704	211	137
Hertford	837	8.2	36,216	2,856	406	74	30	25	101	327	535	39	30
Hoke	1,977	9.1	35,411	2,914	371	77	28	54	262	655	530	37	28
Hyde	207	5.7	42,832	2,088	75	17	6	15	41	58	112	7	6
Iredell	10,440	7.4	56,201	624	4,553	617	317	777	1,633	2,041	6,264	412	317
Jackson	1,688	8.2	38,341	2,644	786	158	58	87	392	513	1,088	74	58
Johnston	9,534	10.0	44,087	1,935	2,559	442	185	638	1,034	2,217	3,824	259	185
Jones	400	3.4	43,254	2,033	72	15	5	26	56	152	117	8	5
Lee	2,798	6.8	44,870	1,815	1,211	202	89	135	455	832	1,637	114	89
Lenoir	2,472	7.5	44,361	1,896	1,302	237	99	134	349	862	1,772	120	99
Lincoln	4,424	7.9	50,216	1,120	1,204	193	88	219	619	1,021	1,703	128	88
McDowell	1,733	7.9	37,858	2,699	676	144	49	80	209	651	949	72	49
Macon	1,604	7.8	44,564	1,864	477	77	35	124	418	545	714	61	35
Madison	829	6.8	38,148	2,672	167	33	13	55	130	301	268	25	13
Martin	849	6.9	38,301	2,649	281	53	21	19	129	357	375	32	21
Mecklenburg	73,657	5.3	65,244	256	57,485	6,594	3,849	8,975	12,402	10,494	76,903	4,603	3,849
Mitchell	587	6.2	39,476	2,511	203	38	16	26	97	218	282	24	16
Montgomery	1,072	6.9	39,353	2,530	416	72	33	54	204	345	575	38	33
Moore	5,634	6.2	54,514	741	1,747	254	127	419	1,443	1,443	2,547	188	127
Nash	4,353	6.6	45,890	1,667	1,880	330	136	244	660	1,306	2,590	181	136
New Hanover	12,015	5.6	50,780	1,057	6,545	967	459	867	2,935	2,797	8,838	575	459
Northampton	733	4.2	38,402	2,636	239	38	18	25	106	310	321	28	18
Onslow	8,794	6.6	43,122	2,045	4,083	1,122	364	364	1,460	2,237	5,932	297	364
Orange	10,001	3.0	67,089	210	4,947	1,013	336	607	2,651	1,307	6,902	398	336
Pamlico	585	7.9	45,994	1,654	119	25	9	29	128	198	183	16	9
Pasquotank	1,717	8.7	42,529	2,126	763	159	58	97	276	525	1,078	71	58
Pender	2,670	7.5	41,292	2,290	564	98	41	172	462	785	874	68	41
Perquimans	607	8.4	44,402	1,890	91	18	7	35	112	203	150	15	7
Person	1,660	7.3	41,581	2,255	457	86	34	57	217	536	633	51	34
Pitt	8,262	6.3	45,169	1,773	4,061	797	289	608	1,316	2,067	5,755	359	289
Polk	1,012	4.7	48,125	1,366	203	37	15	55	297	309	310	29	15
Randolph	5,960	6.7	41,231	2,299	1,918	322	144	475	748	1,805	2,859	214	144
Richmond	1,709	7.8	38,554	2,619	588	116	46	87	186	691	838	66	46
Robeson	4,298	7.9	33,062	3,024	1,635	299	125	265	473	1,839	2,324	171	125
Rockingham	3,713	7.1	40,672	2,376	1,023	180	76	164	488	1,311	1,444	124	76
Rowan	6,231	7.9	43,724	1,984	2,487	429	187	355	935	1,932	3,459	240	187
Rutherford	2,463	7.8	36,714	2,802	767	140	57	124	367	937	1,088	92	57
Sampson	2,419	6.6	38,165	2,669	786	138	60	185	330	828	1,169	80	60
Scotland	1,255	6.5	36,247	2,853	504	92	38	67	162	528	700	52	38
Stanly	2,695	7.7	42,613	2,116	812	149	60	173	383	832	1,194	90	60
Stokes	1,884	6.5	41,186	2,310	307	57	23	74	228	620	461	45	23
Surry	3,020	6.1	42,133	2,174	1,223	211	90	208	451	994	1,731	128	90

1. Based on the resident population estimated as of July 1 of the year shown.

STATE County	Earnings, 2020 (cont.) Percent by selected industries: Farm	Mining, quarrying, and extractions	Construction	Manu-facturing	Information; professional, scientific, technical services	Retail trade	Finance, insurance, real estate, and leasing	Health care and social assistance	Govern-ment	Social Security beneficiaries, December 2020: Number	Rate[1]	Supple-mental Security Income recipients, 2020	Housing units, 2021: Total	Percent change, 2010–2021
	75	76	77	78	79	80	81	82	83	84	85	86	87	88
NORTH CAROLINA—Cont'd														
Chowan	4.1	0.0	4.3	11.2	7.5	8.6	5.6	D	16.0	4,430	323	498	7,160	0.4
Clay	-7.9	0.0	18.1	D	3.2	12.3	7.3	12.6	27.0	4,385	388	265	7,394	1.1
Cleveland	0.9	D	7.3	22.4	5.4	6.7	3.7	12.9	15.9	26,865	268	3,297	43,875	0.5
Columbus	5.8	0.0	4.4	15.4	D	8.0	4.8	13.0	22.8	14,760	295	2,769	23,540	0.4
Craven	0.6	0.1	3.6	8.6	5.2	6.1	4.2	9.2	47.2	25,730	256	2,491	47,473	1.2
Cumberland	0.2	D	3.4	3.4	4.4	4.6	2.8	5.4	63.7	61,760	184	11,057	142,975	0.4
Currituck	0.4	D	14.5	1.0	D	12.5	11.2	3.7	19.2	6,025	203	296	16,649	3.4
Dare	0.0	D	12.4	2.7	5.5	12.5	15.7	5.5	17.5	9,825	260	270	34,736	1.2
Davidson	0.3	D	7.9	21.7	3.2	6.5	3.1	8.8	13.1	40,820	239	3,299	75,427	1.0
Davie	0.7	D	8.7	26.3	4.7	7.5	6.4	10.1	12.0	11,280	259	648	19,058	1.3
Duplin	13.8	0.0	6.0	25.8	D	5.2	1.7	4.6	16.7	11,955	246	1,498	23,738	0.1
Durham	0.0	D	2.5	19.4	20.1	2.5	8.9	13.4	8.8	49,705	152	6,196	149,204	2.6
Edgecombe	6.3	D	3.5	18.7	3.5	10.9	2.1	D	28.7	13,310	275	2,751	23,126	0.3
Forsyth	0.1	0.1	5.2	9.2	7.6	7.5	11.6	20.7	9.1	78,150	203	8,582	173,265	1.5
Franklin	2.8	D	13.6	24.3	6.4	5.7	3.5	4.9	16.1	14,140	197	1,362	30,524	3.2
Gaston	0.2	D	7.3	20.7	4.5	8.2	4.2	16.8	14.3	49,695	215	5,521	100,040	1.6
Gates	11.2	0.0	D	D	D	5.0	D	D	32.8	2,785	269	300	4,807	0.7
Graham	0.8	D	32.7	D	D	5.6	5.4	4.5	22.5	2,425	302	231	5,230	0.3
Granville	0.9	D	5.2	22.4	2.8	4.3	1.8	D	43.1	13,195	213	1,271	24,609	1.3
Greene	8.1	0.0	8.3	5.8	1.6	3.2	3.3	8.8	42.3	4,110	201	532	7,893	0.5
Guilford	0.0	0.0	6.3	12.7	9.7	6.1	10.3	12.4	11.2	102,920	190	11,644	234,902	1.0
Halifax	1.4	0.0	5.0	16.4	2.2	9.7	4.8	11.2	27.3	15,475	321	3,459	24,796	0.2
Harnett	2.0	D	11.5	6.0	4.2	11.8	5.1	8.3	22.0	23,195	171	2,777	53,906	1.7
Haywood	0.6	D	7.0	20.5	5.2	11.4	5.4	12.9	15.6	19,720	316	1,544	35,185	0.6
Henderson	1.3	D	8.1	13.1	5.7	9.8	5.4	14.1	14.9	35,110	301	1,728	57,125	1.0
Hertford	0.6	0.0	5.5	18.4	D	9.2	3.9	D	21.9	5,835	274	1,126	9,801	0.0
Hoke	4.2	D	5.3	20.9	D	5.5	1.8	11.0	29.9	8,660	163	1,215	20,491	1.7
Hyde	9.9	0.0	9.6	9.1	D	5.8	D	D	34.1	1,225	272	133	3,153	0.2
Iredell	0.6	D	8.0	13.6	D	7.2	4.5	7.9	9.6	38,105	198	2,643	81,511	2.3
Jackson	0.2	D	5.2	2.1	D	7.1	3.8	13.7	45.1	9,390	216	673	27,643	3.0
Johnston	1.3	0.1	13.0	18.1	3.8	8.0	6.0	6.1	17.4	38,780	171	3,582	88,370	4.0
Jones	14.7	0.0	9.9	1.4	3.5	3.5	D	D	27.6	2,725	294	342	4,671	0.7
Lee	0.3	D	7.0	32.2	3.8	8.1	3.3	9.6	12.7	13,740	214	1,636	26,845	0.8
Lenoir	1.5	D	7.9	26.7	3.2	5.6	4.8	7.8	20.5	15,770	288	2,810	26,698	0.4
Lincoln	0.4	D	12.2	19.5	5.9	7.5	6.5	5.4	15.6	19,285	215	1,458	38,660	3.5
McDowell	1.5	0.6	4.7	40.8	D	8.3	3.0	7.7	16.3	12,970	290	1,380	21,407	0.6
Macon	0.8	0.1	13.6	3.4	11.6	11.6	6.1	9.5	15.3	12,550	334	731	27,036	0.3
Madison	0.0	D	11.9	9.6	D	5.6	3.1	D	20.4	6,235	290	631	11,164	0.8
Martin	1.0	0.0	4.4	22.0	4.2	9.2	4.6	D	22.0	6,935	319	1,009	11,076	0.0
Mecklenburg	0.1	D	5.7	4.6	15.3	4.5	21.0	6.0	9.5	148,495	132	17,238	492,265	2.2
Mitchell	0.0	D	6.0	D	D	7.7	4.7	16.0	18.2	4,830	323	457	8,667	0.3
Montgomery	2.6	D	6.6	31.9	2.2	8.2	3.2	D	17.0	6,305	244	668	14,872	0.6
Moore	1.1	D	7.8	4.0	D	7.3	6.6	28.3	11.4	27,875	271	1,504	49,425	2.0
Nash	1.5	D	7.8	21.9	4.7	7.3	6.6	8.7	15.3	23,415	246	3,406	43,454	0.6
New Hanover	0.2	D	9.1	5.3	16.6	8.0	8.8	10.7	19.3	49,575	216	3,966	116,984	2.6
Northampton	3.9	0.0	6.7	8.5	D	2.9	D	D	18.5	6,015	351	991	10,600	0.3
Onslow	0.8	D	3.9	0.9	3.4	5.4	3.3	3.9	65.8	30,405	147	3,271	85,916	1.7
Orange	0.3	0.0	3.6	1.8	12.4	4.4	4.7	6.1	54.4	22,910	154	1,458	61,766	0.7
Pamlico	4.1	0.0	6.8	4.8	4.1	11.7	4.0	D	29.4	4,345	352	232	7,239	1.5
Pasquotank	1.2	0.0	4.5	3.6	6.1	9.0	4.5	14.9	35.9	9,520	233	1,215	17,585	0.8
Pender	5.6	D	13.0	4.1	D	7.8	5.0	9.1	21.6	14,435	230	1,117	30,793	2.4
Perquimans	9.3	0.0	6.7	1.6	4.7	4.7	2.8	D	24.8	4,220	321	384	6,917	0.6
Person	1.6	0.0	8.4	18.0	3.7	8.7	4.5	10.8	17.1	10,530	269	1,063	18,471	0.9
Pitt	0.6	D	5.7	10.4	4.3	6.6	5.8	10.9	36.5	33,065	192	5,767	81,437	0.8
Polk	2.3	0.0	7.2	5.6	7.4	5.1	5.2	24.0	19.3	6,765	344	291	10,876	0.8
Randolph	1.5	0.1	8.9	30.7	3.4	6.5	4.3	8.0	12.8	35,020	241	3,398	62,455	0.6
Richmond	3.5	1.4	4.5	21.9	D	8.6	3.4	11.3	21.5	11,665	273	2,086	19,933	1.4
Robeson	3.1	0.0	6.3	18.5	2.6	7.5	3.4	16.4	21.7	28,490	245	7,231	48,791	0.5
Rockingham	1.1	D	7.6	21.6	D	9.3	4.2	12.0	16.1	26,065	286	3,046	43,630	0.4
Rowan	1.2	0.5	9.0	13.4	3.5	8.0	3.4	9.6	20.5	34,340	232	2,816	64,280	1.5
Rutherford	1.0	D	9.5	14.6	8.3	9.1	3.7	11.4	18.3	18,450	286	1,940	32,616	0.4
Sampson	13.0	0.0	7.1	15.4	2.4	7.5	4.0	D	21.2	14,570	247	2,030	25,654	0.5
Scotland	2.6	0.0	4.1	20.1	D	7.3	2.6	D	21.0	9,200	269	1,656	14,390	0.3
Stanly	1.5	D	10.4	18.1	3.4	10.0	4.0	6.6	23.3	15,610	246	1,393	28,027	0.9
Stokes	2.0	0.0	12.3	9.7	D	10.1	5.8	10.2	23.5	13,020	292	922	21,289	0.5
Surry	1.4	D	17.5	12.8	4.1	8.8	4.1	D	16.5	19,140	269	1,981	33,550	0.3

1. Per 1,000 resident population estimated as of July 1 of the year shown.

STATE County	Housing units, 2016–2020: Total	Occupied units, Owner-occupied: Percent	Owner-occupied: Median value[1]	Median owner cost as a percent of income: With a mortgage	Median owner cost as a percent of income: Without a mortgage[2]	Renter-occupied: Median rent[3]	Renter-occupied: Median rent as a percent of income[2]	Sub-standard units[4] (percent)	Civilian labor force, 2021: Total	Percent change, 2020–2021	Unemployment: Total	Unemployment: Rate[5]	Civilian employment[6], 2016–2020: Total	Percent: Management, business, science, and arts	Percent: Construction, production, and maintenance occupations
	89	90	91	92	93	94	95	96	97	98	99	100	101	102	103
NORTH CAROLINA—Cont'd															
Chowan	6,389	65.1	139,500	23.3	14.5	773	26.7	0.2	5,510	3.9	272	4.9	5,687	35.2	21.4
Clay	5,300	72.9	197,600	21.0	13.2	682	24.4	1.8	3,970	-0.1	195	4.9	4,452	36.3	22.7
Cleveland	36,089	68.4	130,000	19.9	10.0	694	29.9	3.5	47,667	1.2	2,535	5.3	41,423	32.2	31.5
Columbus	21,545	72.1	94,800	22.1	13.2	642	33.0	2.5	22,400	2.1	1,406	6.3	20,231	28.3	31.6
Craven	41,002	65.0	161,200	20.6	10.5	914	28.0	2.9	40,693	2.2	1,904	4.7	39,977	34.4	25.7
Cumberland	127,532	51.5	139,700	22.0	11.6	949	30.5	2.7	125,305	1.3	8,620	6.9	126,741	33.8	23.1
Currituck	10,868	83.9	263,400	22.6	10.0	1,101	28.7	1.0	14,215	1.1	583	4.1	13,311	39.4	24.7
Dare	15,830	76.2	297,200	24.0	12.4	1,137	33.3	2.8	19,631	2.8	1,169	6.0	18,492	36.6	20.1
Davidson	67,555	72.0	149,500	18.6	10.0	716	29.2	2.2	79,091	1.9	3,588	4.5	75,313	30.3	31.8
Davie	16,303	82.1	177,100	18.7	10.0	731	28.8	2.7	20,130	1.9	861	4.3	20,111	33.0	30.8
Duplin	21,437	71.9	89,500	20.8	11.8	678	27.0	5.5	24,263	0.7	1,063	4.4	25,284	25.8	39.6
Durham	130,128	55.4	241,800	18.9	10.0	1,103	29.2	3.0	174,877	3.3	7,167	4.1	164,407	51.5	15.7
Edgecombe	20,800	61.8	88,500	20.3	13.8	712	27.2	3.3	20,260	1.4	1,729	8.5	21,263	25.2	32.7
Forsyth	148,890	62.3	163,800	19.2	10.0	836	28.8	2.3	183,512	1.8	8,998	4.9	176,149	40.8	21.6
Franklin	25,729	73.2	161,500	19.1	10.9	855	26.4	3.0	32,086	4.3	1,509	4.7	31,120	33.5	27.2
Gaston	85,286	66.0	156,800	19.4	10.5	850	28.3	2.5	108,927	2.0	5,657	5.2	104,191	32.8	29.1
Gates	4,690	77.4	142,400	24.6	14.5	955	28.0	2.0	4,963	1.7	214	4.3	4,881	30.2	35.4
Graham	3,521	83.5	119,000	16.3	10.4	529	23.7	1.9	3,022	1.2	208	6.9	3,439	29.3	24.8
Granville	21,567	75.0	168,900	20.3	11.6	849	29.4	1.3	29,541	2.2	1,177	4.0	27,212	35.4	26.3
Greene	7,218	69.6	87,500	21.7	12.7	727	25.9	3.9	9,364	1.5	384	4.1	8,381	26.9	37.2
Guilford	208,234	59.0	172,900	19.4	10.0	892	29.5	2.9	254,780	1.0	14,296	5.6	257,018	39.2	22.4
Halifax	21,061	61.7	85,800	22.4	13.2	705	33.2	3.3	19,179	-1.2	1,432	7.5	18,745	25.8	35.0
Harnett	46,525	66.2	160,700	21.1	11.4	916	27.4	2.0	52,943	2.7	2,799	5.3	53,946	34.8	27.5
Haywood	26,891	72.7	185,600	19.9	10.0	811	29.6	1.6	28,887	2.8	1,225	4.2	28,027	34.6	22.6
Henderson	49,715	74.2	232,000	20.4	10.0	915	28.5	1.8	53,037	3.3	2,158	4.1	54,571	33.2	25.1
Hertford	8,903	66.6	89,800	22.2	12.5	777	31.0	1.7	8,518	-2.1	556	6.5	8,983	32.2	34.3
Hoke	18,448	68.0	146,200	21.1	10.0	863	30.4	2.7	19,848	1.9	1,280	6.4	20,120	33.1	26.8
Hyde	2,056	63.6	122,300	31.2	20.8	784	25.6	5.8	1,767	1.1	115	6.5	1,871	26.5	34.7
Iredell	68,374	71.9	200,800	19.7	10.0	913	26.4	2.3	89,608	2.2	4,131	4.6	87,514	35.9	27.1
Jackson	17,008	63.7	206,900	20.4	10.0	747	28.7	2.6	19,488	1.7	877	4.5	19,149	32.1	17.8
Johnston	71,332	74.0	180,200	19.4	10.0	835	29.9	2.6	101,800	4.3	4,273	4.2	97,838	35.2	25.7
Jones	4,069	74.2	92,200	21.7	11.9	627	35.4	2.9	4,155	2.6	176	4.2	3,702	23.7	39.5
Lee	22,290	64.8	145,600	19.7	10.8	800	26.3	3.4	25,322	0.7	1,366	5.4	27,355	30.3	33.1
Lenoir	23,494	56.9	94,000	21.7	12.3	707	28.0	3.2	26,890	0.6	1,332	5.0	23,509	30.7	32.9
Lincoln	33,621	75.8	187,000	18.8	10.0	777	28.4	2.2	43,823	2.5	1,784	4.1	40,539	34.7	27.7
McDowell	18,275	73.7	129,400	18.8	10.0	647	24.5	3.2	19,903	-0.1	897	4.5	19,226	26.5	39.1
Macon	16,062	72.9	171,700	21.6	10.0	758	28.6	1.7	15,285	2.1	644	4.2	14,256	31.8	22.8
Madison	8,373	74.9	200,700	21.4	10.0	686	31.3	2.4	9,623	3.5	411	4.3	9,574	35.3	28.2
Martin	9,622	66.2	86,400	21.9	12.3	720	30.0	1.6	8,617	-0.1	477	5.5	9,510	26.5	29.5
Mecklenburg	421,950	56.4	253,500	19.1	10.0	1,195	28.1	2.5	618,847	2.1	30,288	4.9	584,086	45.4	17.6
Mitchell	6,402	79.6	164,200	19.1	10.5	620	25.6	1.5	5,928	3.2	305	5.1	6,522	34.1	30.8
Montgomery	10,265	73.3	120,500	19.9	10.0	585	23.6	3.4	11,014	0.4	515	4.7	10,633	28.7	38.9
Moore	40,575	76.8	229,400	20.7	10.1	889	25.3	2.0	40,161	1.6	1,836	4.6	41,297	39.5	20.0
Nash	37,371	64.6	133,900	20.2	10.0	777	28.3	4.3	42,040	1.5	2,659	6.3	42,087	32.0	29.8
New Hanover	97,998	58.4	258,200	21.6	12.1	1,060	31.7	1.1	122,709	3.7	5,197	4.2	114,633	42.5	16.8
Northampton	8,424	71.2	83,600	23.9	14.2	730	32.0	1.4	7,178	-0.5	447	6.2	7,318	27.7	33.6
Onslow	66,131	54.2	162,400	22.7	10.0	1,029	29.1	2.0	65,070	3.6	3,338	5.1	65,389	31.7	24.3
Orange	53,222	63.8	331,800	19.1	10.3	1,136	30.7	2.5	79,254	3.9	2,738	3.5	72,630	57.6	11.0
Pamlico	5,506	76.8	161,600	23.6	11.6	723	28.3	1.7	5,296	2.7	227	4.3	4,534	27.1	34.8
Pasquotank	14,785	61.8	166,600	19.8	11.9	951	27.7	1.3	16,273	1.2	876	5.4	16,979	32.0	27.9
Pender	22,812	80.6	198,100	21.8	11.7	907	31.3	2.7	29,066	4.4	1,225	4.2	27,312	34.2	24.4
Perquimans	5,886	77.9	173,200	22.1	11.6	821	38.3	1.1	4,824	2.0	256	5.3	5,314	30.4	26.9
Person	16,153	78.2	134,100	19.3	10.0	709	31.8	1.9	18,428	3.2	913	5.0	19,178	33.7	28.8
Pitt	70,683	52.6	146,700	19.4	10.5	793	29.6	2.9	87,237	1.9	4,398	5.0	84,110	37.7	20.6
Polk	9,252	75.6	222,700	20.3	10.8	855	26.5	2.3	9,029	3.6	422	4.7	9,089	35.7	26.8
Randolph	56,790	73.0	128,800	18.9	10.0	707	27.5	3.4	63,631	1.3	2,976	4.7	65,916	29.0	33.7
Richmond	18,201	65.9	88,200	21.7	11.6	662	29.9	2.4	16,248	0.5	1,189	7.3	18,736	29.4	36.1
Robeson	45,881	66.3	75,600	20.7	12.6	647	29.1	4.4	48,147	-0.2	3,643	7.6	48,356	27.1	35.6
Rockingham	38,532	69.5	114,900	19.2	10.0	669	27.9	2.4	38,593	1.2	2,135	5.5	39,733	26.9	32.3
Rowan	54,137	69.7	146,600	18.8	10.0	787	26.7	2.7	64,309	2.0	3,239	5.0	63,191	30.5	33.7
Rutherford	27,525	71.6	125,100	19.0	10.0	655	29.5	3.3	24,050	1.3	1,556	6.5	26,901	28.4	33.8
Sampson	23,162	72.0	97,500	20.7	10.8	682	27.8	3.5	27,818	0.9	1,251	4.5	26,740	27.9	37.9
Scotland	12,951	59.8	87,600	19.7	12.9	662	31.3	5.4	11,096	0.8	1,055	9.5	12,396	28.1	34.4
Stanly	23,849	74.7	150,400	18.8	10.0	753	25.8	2.5	29,425	1.9	1,284	4.4	28,716	29.5	32.7
Stokes	19,608	77.9	145,000	19.9	10.0	682	27.6	3.5	20,998	2.3	886	4.2	21,073	28.0	35.4
Surry	29,001	72.7	129,700	18.6	10.0	630	27.2	3.2	32,011	0.9	1,393	4.4	31,564	31.3	32.1

1. Specified owner-occupied units. 2. A value of 10.0 represents 10 percent or less; a value of 50.0 represents 50 percent or more. 3. Specified renter-occupied units. 4. Overcrowded or lacking complete plumbing facilities. 5. Percent of civilian labor force. 6. Civilian employed persons 16 years old and over.

STATE County	Private nonfarm establishments, employment and payroll, 2020									Agriculture, 2017			
		Employment						Annual payroll		Farms			Farm producers whose primary occupation is farming (percent)
											Percent with:		
	Number of establish-ments	Total	Health care and social assistance	Manufac-turing	Retail trade	Finance and insurance	Professional, scientific, and technical services	Total (mil dol)	Average per employee (dollars)	Number	Fewer than 50 acres	1000 acres or more	
	104	105	106	107	108	109	110	111	112	113	114	115	116
NORTH CAROLINA—Cont'd													
Chowan	364	4,317	976	1,190	467	80	136	162	37,498	97	35.1	23.7	64.2
Clay	219	1,721	364	170	375	44	25	52	30,308	164	56.7	0.6	51.1
Cleveland	1,947	30,597	5,231	7,045	4,076	432	861	1,243	40,625	1,005	43.0	0.9	36.8
Columbus	950	11,478	2,572	1,722	2,397	806	212	422	36,729	514	33.9	8.4	47.7
Craven	2,172	28,676	6,968	3,428	4,577	653	1,670	1,221	42,563	245	36.3	8.6	48.1
Cumberland	5,752	93,261	19,151	6,262	17,068	1,906	6,052	3,580	38,392	336	48.5	4.5	37.7
Currituck	667	5,200	343	50	963	64	173	182	35,061	89	48.3	11.2	43.8
Dare	1,977	15,332	1,033	480	3,714	432	427	552	36,033	32	65.6	9.4	37.1
Davidson	2,839	38,606	4,318	9,583	5,308	611	917	1,503	38,944	1,003	57.2	0.9	39.0
Davie	832	10,268	1,571	1,849	1,604	174	319	366	35,637	591	46.9	2.2	41.2
Duplin	860	14,175	1,754	5,976	1,733	211	134	477	33,646	820	35.1	6.6	61.3
Durham	7,729	205,041	30,553	14,417	15,761	9,879	32,871	15,129	73,787	241	68.0	0.8	44.9
Edgecombe	709	11,227	2,428	2,330	1,565	156	150	401	35,682	249	29.3	16.1	40.9
Forsyth	8,734	189,274	44,385	17,119	22,022	11,201	7,596	9,620	50,824	557	68.6	0.4	37.1
Franklin	1,123	11,190	852	3,555	1,453	200	268	527	47,090	538	43.9	4.5	38.0
Gaston	4,289	67,003	12,054	13,752	9,727	1,196	1,339	2,666	39,790	522	58.6	0.4	32.4
Gates	118	1,026	233	143	188	35	32	37	35,900	141	40.4	11.3	46.6
Graham	163	1,754	210	19	320	61	13	68	39,046	123	65.9	NA	39.2
Granville	896	16,717	4,180	4,630	1,308	245	211	693	41,475	557	32.5	3.4	34.9
Greene	259	2,201	502	179	318	44	47	68	30,718	207	34.8	12.6	54.4
Guilford	13,730	261,286	34,941	30,624	28,115	12,760	12,100	12,327	47,179	854	58.0	0.6	39.9
Halifax	938	12,161	2,476	2,150	2,234	293	192	432	35,524	336	23.5	18.5	42.0
Harnett	1,774	22,755	3,791	1,980	4,134	548	540	790	34,732	643	54.9	3.7	40.8
Haywood	1,422	15,306	3,176	1,755	3,332	429	558	566	36,983	541	60.3	1.3	33.8
Henderson	2,839	36,374	7,336	6,195	6,006	681	965	1,462	40,182	455	70.1	1.1	43.6
Hertford	461	7,494	1,849	1,042	1,109	166	90	315	41,975	126	38.1	19.8	58.7
Hoke	483	5,810	1,425	1,832	749	71	103	188	32,353	189	45.0	7.4	32.2
Hyde	143	674	84	36	119	26	18	27	40,478	138	26.1	26.8	50.4
Iredell	5,027	74,997	9,529	13,036	9,416	1,315	3,639	3,328	44,374	1,055	47.3	1.7	42.9
Jackson	1,024	12,153	1,833	340	1,943	208	284	439	36,126	215	56.7	0.5	52.1
Johnston	3,639	45,227	6,467	7,833	8,304	866	1,171	1,789	39,553	1,063	51.3	3.7	41.2
Jones	127	812	97	25	123	12	23	27	33,739	177	39.5	9.6	51.0
Lee	1,345	24,765	2,883	9,722	3,030	354	380	1,091	44,066	250	49.6	3.2	38.3
Lenoir	1,180	23,724	4,083	6,103	2,862	498	687	898	37,867	386	37.8	8.3	53.6
Lincoln	1,805	20,584	2,965	3,630	3,529	408	560	843	40,939	614	58.6	0.8	31.9
McDowell	789	14,205	1,500	6,524	1,747	148	192	497	35,008	333	63.1	NA	41.6
Macon	1,156	9,400	1,231	431	1,877	330	271	355	37,717	340	69.7	NA	34.4
Madison	357	3,230	667	433	475	36	40	107	33,052	639	50.1	1.3	40.5
Martin	437	4,905	1,052	779	918	133	96	155	31,701	332	27.4	16.6	54.3
Mecklenburg	33,827	671,142	79,749	26,631	61,621	84,422	49,444	44,502	66,308	216	74.5	NA	36.7
Mitchell	364	3,996	769	431	653	93	64	167	41,847	250	63.6	NA	29.2
Montgomery	492	7,969	1,089	3,046	759	166	61	307	38,520	240	40.4	0.4	51.0
Moore	2,333	32,552	9,087	1,688	4,682	885	1,430	1,420	43,630	733	51.7	2.6	42.9
Nash	2,041	38,468	6,027	7,950	4,817	1,606	864	1,522	39,572	425	45.4	7.8	51.9
New Hanover	7,935	104,792	19,267	5,578	16,389	3,948	5,970	5,036	48,053	59	93.2	NA	43.9
Northampton	258	4,382	558	365	406	22	25	173	39,397	272	21.7	19.9	51.5
Onslow	2,909	35,861	5,106	1,014	8,327	1,025	1,713	1,133	31,580	340	50.3	3.5	55.9
Orange	3,316	49,105	19,899	1,490	5,515	1,094	2,670	2,389	48,641	686	51.7	0.6	44.1
Pamlico	242	2,279	305	133	584	35	37	67	29,461	100	44.0	12.0	39.3
Pasquotank	919	11,330	2,462	623	2,536	426	424	444	39,189	126	31.7	25.4	55.9
Pender	1,197	9,632	1,478	838	2,016	118	305	327	33,944	336	52.1	3.9	48.3
Perquimans	176	1,382	120	49	278	44	25	50	36,034	149	33.6	20.1	77.6
Person	705	8,352	1,116	1,802	1,482	180	110	319	38,223	393	41.7	4.8	50.9
Pitt	3,664	61,466	16,768	6,279	9,165	1,607	2,214	2,512	40,871	478	35.8	12.6	55.0
Polk	475	4,199	1,549	370	421	118	153	136	32,270	281	57.7	0.4	44.6
Randolph	2,503	39,764	4,253	14,466	4,910	764	758	1,495	37,599	1,368	45.5	0.7	41.6
Richmond	795	12,041	2,060	3,556	1,924	212	146	421	35,003	237	27.4	3.0	44.4
Robeson	1,785	32,979	6,836	9,540	4,857	1,099	681	1,152	34,931	722	43.4	11.5	46.0
Rockingham	1,600	20,373	2,305	5,584	3,387	415	384	706	34,663	844	37.3	2.5	40.1
Rowan	2,681	45,767	9,516	8,594	4,624	586	843	2,184	47,710	925	51.1	1.6	37.3
Rutherford	1,235	15,628	2,485	3,126	2,445	269	301	560	35,819	620	46.6	0.3	44.2
Sampson	975	12,582	2,281	3,127	2,174	208	213	494	39,289	960	33.2	7.1	52.2
Scotland	591	9,442	2,524	1,704	1,438	178	101	332	35,198	108	26.9	11.1	55.1
Stanly	1,357	16,756	2,782	3,622	2,882	424	259	611	36,463	672	54.0	2.8	32.6
Stokes	644	6,249	1,165	896	1,263	136	158	185	29,612	856	39.6	0.9	40.1
Surry	1,600	29,836	4,204	3,744	4,205	492	412	1,249	41,864	1,064	41.8	1.6	42.3

STATE County	Agriculture, 2017 (cont.) — Land in farms — Acreage (1,000)	Land in farms — Percent change, 2012–2017	Land in farms — Acres — Average size of farm	Land in farms — Acres — Total irrigated (1,000)	Land in farms — Acres — Total cropland (1,000)	Value of land and buildings (dollars) — Average per farm	Value of land and buildings (dollars) — Average per acre	Value of machinery and equipment, average per farm (dollars)	Value of products sold: — Total (mil dol)	Value of products sold: — Average per farm (acres)	Value of products sold: — Percent from: — Crops	Value of products sold: — Percent from: — Livestock and poultry products	Organic farms (number)	Farms with internet access (percent)	Government payments — Total ($1,000)	Government payments — Percent of farms
	117	118	119	120	121	122	123	124	125	126	127	128	129	130	131	132
NORTH CAROLINA—Cont'd																
Chowan	54	-7.9	552	4.2	43.9	1,928,100	3,494	396,748	46.6	480,258	82.7	17.3	3	79.4	2,814	66.0
Clay	13	6.6	76	0.2	4.7	479,404	6,277	42,034	2.9	17,860	69.8	30.2	NA	65.2	129	14.0
Cleveland	113	-2.8	113	0.4	45.6	526,049	4,664	66,770	133.8	133,133	11.9	88.1	6	75.4	1,076	29.3
Columbus	141	-11.4	274	2.1	113.0	895,784	3,264	156,073	162.0	315,191	36.1	63.9	1	66.9	2,708	45.3
Craven	81	15.2	332	0.9	61.9	1,307,554	3,937	175,519	71.6	292,273	51.4	48.6	2	77.1	1,461	47.8
Cumberland	66	-19.8	196	1.2	35.5	1,014,731	5,166	123,059	95.8	285,116	26.5	73.5	NA	79.8	355	25.6
Currituck	45	26.8	504	0.1	36.4	2,471,600	4,906	200,095	18.2	204,730	99.6	0.4	NA	87.6	1,247	42.7
Dare	5	D	167	0.1	4.7	702,379	4,207	83,082	1.6	48,969	64.6	35.4	NA	78.1	225	9.4
Davidson	92	5.8	92	0.4	45.5	533,839	5,797	62,547	47.1	46,929	34.5	65.5	5	76.8	523	9.3
Davie	77	29.0	130	0.3	37.5	662,441	5,089	71,003	26.9	45,569	46.0	54.0	NA	72.1	279	9.8
Duplin	243	5.3	296	8.0	165.1	1,422,426	4,798	220,716	1,261.7	1,538,648	7.8	92.2	9	79.5	3,021	30.4
Durham	19	-10.8	77	0.1	6.8	822,548	10,656	57,642	10.1	41,921	89.2	10.8	1	77.6	27	9.1
Edgecombe	149	17.6	598	2.5	106.8	1,823,586	3,049	277,862	176.2	707,614	52.5	47.5	3	61.4	3,812	61.4
Forsyth	35	-14.0	62	0.1	15.7	581,509	9,307	46,871	10.9	19,575	85.1	14.9	NA	70.7	70	5.7
Franklin	108	-7.6	201	1.8	42.8	713,579	3,556	101,007	58.5	108,669	59.4	40.6	7	72.1	575	27.0
Gaston	38	-10.1	72	0.2	15.4	443,484	6,141	50,169	23.2	44,375	24.4	75.6	8	77.8	271	14.8
Gates	58	-8.4	411	3.6	45.5	1,490,928	3,625	231,965	72.9	516,901	32.7	67.3	NA	82.3	1,997	61.7
Graham	11	60.9	89	0.0	3.0	428,116	4,788	78,974	1.4	11,089	28.5	71.5	NA	65.0	66	11.4
Granville	125	23.8	224	1.8	42.7	780,700	3,484	76,280	D	D	D	D	15	79.2	274	28.7
Greene	83	-17.7	403	1.6	69.4	1,588,126	3,945	235,131	242.5	1,171,415	28.9	71.1	NA	77.3	1,055	63.3
Guilford	76	-15.9	89	1.3	40.9	731,162	8,178	69,898	52.2	61,108	62.9	37.1	7	75.3	331	11.0
Halifax	209	6.7	622	2.5	138.1	1,596,584	2,566	245,400	133.2	396,411	62.4	37.6	10	68.8	5,417	64.3
Harnett	106	-11.3	165	2.8	69.7	921,279	5,575	128,788	204.6	318,138	35.0	65.0	5	76.5	536	25.7
Haywood	52	6.7	97	0.3	11.0	623,971	6,461	61,440	18.2	33,567	43.1	56.9	6	71.7	525	22.2
Henderson	41	15.0	90	2.5	25.0	700,622	7,756	96,176	67.2	147,780	96.1	3.9	3	71.4	385	11.9
Hertford	81	-2.6	642	2.1	60.0	2,053,706	3,199	275,035	139.3	1,105,683	32.9	67.1	NA	75.4	1,790	62.7
Hoke	54	-8.4	284	2.2	32.9	1,249,580	4,402	131,728	76.8	406,328	16.5	83.5	NA	79.9	339	31.7
Hyde	125	16.1	905	D	93.1	2,690,902	2,974	326,488	D	D	D	D	1	64.5	2,515	71.0
Iredell	133	-12.5	126	0.3	68.8	687,281	5,438	80,370	112.9	106,988	16.7	83.3	6	70.4	1,627	7.1
Jackson	16	-2.9	73	0.1	5.3	599,496	8,195	62,010	11.6	54,126	96.2	3.8	NA	75.3	86	15.8
Johnston	183	-5.9	172	2.1	129.8	817,375	4,741	117,962	267.8	251,888	55.0	45.0	12	77.0	1,938	28.2
Jones	66	10.6	371	0.5	49.2	1,503,580	4,054	228,303	213.6	1,206,910	13.8	86.2	2	87.0	1,039	45.8
Lee	35	-10.0	141	1.4	19.5	810,854	5,764	108,487	54.4	217,568	34.5	65.5	9	80.4	124	12.8
Lenoir	114	-6.9	295	2.7	85.2	1,172,512	3,980	256,044	311.4	806,666	23.5	76.5	1	77.2	1,589	50.3
Lincoln	54	-2.7	88	0.2	30.1	504,795	5,731	60,532	53.8	87,577	15.7	84.3	NA	75.2	518	16.8
McDowell	23	-7.7	69	0.3	6.2	363,086	5,258	63,862	24.6	73,880	56.6	43.4	3	73.3	73	14.7
Macon	20	-12.8	58	0.0	5.2	463,306	7,966	42,489	7.8	23,065	21.4	78.6	NA	68.2	132	20.0
Madison	57	0.9	89	0.1	11.1	440,456	4,959	34,914	D	D	D	D	12	71.0	194	17.2
Martin	141	10.8	425	D	105.4	1,137,286	2,678	206,716	92.7	279,238	84.5	15.5	NA	69.6	5,810	84.9
Mecklenburg	12	-24.4	54	0.5	5.6	1,853,146	34,288	183,007	D	D	D	100.0	NA	77.3	D	6.5
Mitchell	15	-23.4	59	0.0	4.2	344,314	5,815	50,043	2.4	9,400	74.9	25.1	NA	77.2	38	4.0
Montgomery	34	-4.4	140	1.5	9.4	662,440	4,743	110,080	143.3	597,100	5.7	94.3	2	75.0	86	8.3
Moore	89	8.4	122	2.5	29.0	621,977	5,101	82,084	150.3	205,115	12.2	87.8	11	79.1	685	9.4
Nash	129	-7.9	305	2.2	96.8	1,409,586	4,627	247,776	191.7	450,993	65.8	34.2	14	71.8	1,092	34.8
New Hanover	1	-69.5	15	0.1	0.2	507,127	34,039	106,406	D	D	D	100.0	NA	81.4	D	3.4
Northampton	170	4.6	626	2.9	110.6	1,749,629	2,797	235,146	114.4	420,706	51.4	48.6	NA	73.5	4,683	79.4
Onslow	52	-9.0	154	0.4	35.6	969,753	6,284	93,973	171.6	504,629	13.7	86.3	NA	75.0	862	25.6
Orange	70	23.4	102	0.9	32.1	681,306	6,686	68,490	37.7	54,974	67.3	32.7	28	88.3	428	18.7
Pamlico	43	-7.5	433	3.4	37.4	1,579,956	3,652	266,792	23.4	233,730	98.3	1.7	NA	86.0	1,079	64.0
Pasquotank	72	-0.1	573	0.3	68.8	2,282,057	3,984	346,522	48.8	387,452	99.1	0.9	1	76.2	2,408	59.5
Pender	64	15.6	192	1.8	41.2	1,026,573	5,349	98,925	200.3	596,140	19.2	80.8	9	78.9	583	20.2
Perquimans	80	0.3	539	D	74.5	1,919,310	3,560	300,322	70.6	473,671	57.9	42.1	3	78.5	2,646	69.8
Person	82	-13.8	209	1.6	45.6	790,145	3,778	107,022	39.3	100,000	87.6	12.4	10	72.8	345	22.4
Pitt	186	8.5	390	2.8	149.8	1,499,480	3,845	183,107	242.5	507,234	41.6	58.4	4	81.8	3,291	45.6
Polk	29	20.8	104	0.1	7.9	667,163	6,442	50,460	6.6	23,491	74.8	25.2	NA	85.4	104	13.9
Randolph	148	-5.8	108	1.2	61.7	545,745	5,052	77,013	281.9	206,035	9.9	90.1	20	75.8	360	9.3
Richmond	59	24.4	250	0.5	18.9	1,089,872	4,365	114,969	189.2	798,186	3.8	96.2	NA	72.6	473	23.6
Robeson	264	-0.7	365	11.5	212.8	1,211,105	3,315	182,661	385.8	534,294	27.0	73.0	1	72.6	3,535	43.4
Rockingham	125	11.1	148	3.0	51.3	571,868	3,873	69,782	39.1	46,294	75.1	24.9	13	71.4	580	15.5
Rowan	119	-1.8	129	0.8	67.9	752,022	5,850	103,875	81.8	88,412	58.8	41.2	NA	73.9	1,162	14.3
Rutherford	60	0.6	97	0.1	18.6	462,120	4,782	47,498	45.4	73,289	8.5	91.5	1	76.6	392	16.0
Sampson	301	3.3	314	17.9	209.6	1,534,742	4,891	269,485	1,249.1	1,301,188	16.3	83.7	18	78.1	2,424	32.5
Scotland	55	-20.4	508	D	28.6	1,828,369	3,600	196,309	112.2	1,038,500	10.3	89.7	1	72.2	500	33.3
Stanly	96	3.0	143	0.1	54.2	656,070	4,599	91,390	90.3	134,391	24.9	75.1	NA	72.9	909	20.8
Stokes	93	1.5	109	0.4	34.4	443,265	4,084	60,719	42.4	49,558	29.3	70.7	3	75.5	148	12.0
Surry	152	20.1	143	0.6	73.0	640,586	4,471	96,475	230.1	216,264	21.5	78.5	8	75.5	483	17.7

STATE County	Water use, 2015		Wholesale Trade[1], 2017				Retail Trade[2], 2017				Real estate and rental and leasing,[2] 2017			
	Public supply water withdrawn (mil gal/ day)	Public supply gallons withdrawn per person per day	Number of establish-ments	Number of employees	Sales (mil dol)	Average payroll (mil dol)	Number of establish-ments	Number of employees	Sales (mil dol)	Average payroll (mil dol)	Number of establish-ments	Number of employees	Sales (mil dol)	Average payroll (mil dol)
	133	134	135	136	137	138	139	140	141	142	143	144	145	146
NORTH CAROLINA—Cont'd														
Chowan	1.4	96.6	19	211	190.4	9.2	53	383	94.2	8.1	D	D	D	D
Clay	0.2	19.6	D	D	D	1.6	36	399	107.0	9.1	D	D	D	0.2
Cleveland	12.3	126.5	65	1,108	1,365.6	43.2	368	4,054	1,028.4	93.8	84	342	61.3	9.0
Columbus	2.0	35.6	24	306	191.2	13.7	201	2,280	570.6	57.4	31	88	16.5	2.6
Craven	10.8	104.0	58	610	933.4	30.0	372	4,539	1,285.0	114.0	118	335	55.4	10.6
Cumberland	35.9	110.7	147	2,143	952.6	79.2	1,092	17,305	4,707.6	431.1	310	1,722	414.4	63.6
Currituck	3.3	130.2	20	D	62.7	D	131	979	310.0	28.4	43	437	66.2	17.7
Dare	7.3	204.1	D	D	D	D	421	3,681	967.3	101.3	D	D	D	D
Davidson	14.9	90.5	112	1,721	1,038.0	75.0	461	5,063	1,437.9	128.7	116	425	104.5	17.6
Davie	3.6	85.7	37	330	459.2	20.6	118	1,527	396.4	37.3	D	D	D	3.3
Duplin	4.8	80.5	32	578	826.6	22.0	181	1,720	443.7	39.9	26	54	4.7	1.0
Durham	27.7	92.2	262	13,956	10,669.0	1,691.7	936	15,667	4,117.6	403.7	375	2,235	531.8	117.5
Edgecombe	3.3	60.8	18	279	104.7	11.1	117	1,415	329.9	30.6	31	105	30.6	3.5
Forsyth	48.5	131.3	367	5,651	5,370.8	308.5	1,380	22,503	6,259.9	599.1	444	1,871	709.3	84.0
Franklin	1.0	14.9	47	538	292.0	26.9	143	1,394	351.9	32.7	28	37	6.7	1.2
Gaston	25.1	117.5	197	2,697	1,811.3	120.6	637	9,596	2,511.7	236.2	190	740	187.6	24.4
Gates	0.9	74.4	D	D	D	D	19	174	30.6	3.4	NA	NA	NA	NA
Graham	0.7	77.8	NA	NA	NA	NA	31	244	54.3	6.0	6	D	1.0	D
Granville	3.0	51.0	D	D	D	D	143	1,453	389.3	33.6	40	108	27.2	3.4
Greene	1.1	50.6	D	D	D	1.1	41	283	68.6	6.5	7	11	1.9	0.3
Guilford	48.1	93.0	974	15,679	16,113.7	1,203.9	1,846	28,166	8,015.9	742.4	719	4,900	875.3	238.3
Halifax	7.6	144.9	D	D	D	D	217	2,322	627.8	55.1	32	118	15.4	2.4
Harnett	20.6	160.5	D	D	D	D	272	3,500	998.2	78.5	77	301	35.2	8.0
Haywood	5.9	98.9	41	427	198.2	14.9	236	3,214	929.4	78.5	66	201	29.6	5.7
Henderson	11.1	98.1	116	1,229	666.7	58.1	399	5,626	1,584.0	144.4	145	399	72.2	11.9
Hertford	2.1	86.4	18	152	59.3	5.6	98	1,134	261.5	25.9	D	D	D	0.9
Hoke	4.4	83.9	11	80	46.8	3.6	81	781	188.8	15.5	19	47	11.6	1.7
Hyde	1.1	195.4	11	95	44.4	3.2	40	170	29.4	3.4	9	60	6.4	3.5
Iredell	11.5	67.9	264	2,534	1,573.9	147.0	655	9,275	2,770.1	235.8	243	676	148.5	25.4
Jackson	1.9	47.0	D	D	D	D	163	1,903	449.3	47.2	D	D	D	D
Johnston	15.8	84.9	111	1,291	1,100.3	66.8	558	8,051	2,247.5	182.4	120	457	134.5	18.2
Jones	0.7	71.9	7	123	58.1	4.6	29	140	47.8	3.7	NA	NA	NA	NA
Lee	7.4	124.2	50	914	693.9	44.7	251	3,025	889.8	75.5	43	128	28.5	5.3
Lenoir	8.8	151.6	60	622	274.4	28.5	218	2,944	760.2	79.8	45	204	52.4	15.5
Lincoln	6.6	81.8	67	1,268	732.7	60.0	238	3,189	867.2	78.1	73	129	25.4	4.6
McDowell	2.0	43.3	32	277	80.6	10.6	127	1,634	473.8	39.9	23	53	8.6	1.4
Macon	2.1	60.5	21	137	82.5	8.0	218	1,962	474.9	51.7	61	116	25.8	4.3
Madison	0.9	44.0	6	19	9.5	0.6	40	451	98.2	8.5	18	20	4.1	0.6
Martin	0.6	24.0	23	186	122.0	7.6	77	966	222.4	21.3	13	35	5.7	1.0
Mecklenburg	112.2	108.5	1,889	31,210	25,783.5	2,104.7	3,608	61,937	18,367.7	1,714.1	2,389	12,728	4,500.6	766.5
Mitchell	1.1	70.2	8	23	19.4	1.0	58	743	179.7	16.9	14	79	7.2	2.0
Montgomery	2.3	81.7	22	249	109.5	10.5	76	736	202.0	17.3	15	20	3.1	0.6
Moore	6.8	71.9	60	440	245.7	21.0	361	4,797	1,439.6	116.0	113	254	57.3	9.5
Nash	9.1	97.2	112	2,462	3,704.2	115.6	393	4,931	1,309.3	115.4	81	415	61.7	14.6
New Hanover	6.3	28.4	306	3,030	1,613.6	171.5	1,082	16,087	4,908.8	447.4	501	1,820	459.9	77.9
Northampton	1.1	54.3	D	D	D	D	48	405	130.3	12.1	5	13	0.9	0.2
Onslow	17.9	95.9	55	320	144.1	13.4	547	8,416	2,334.6	206.5	200	744	146.7	24.8
Orange	8.8	62.1	80	852	580.6	53.0	346	5,825	1,618.6	177.3	188	768	146.3	29.6
Pamlico	1.3	97.8	11	75	46.4	2.5	40	622	131.4	15.2	13	38	3.2	0.8
Pasquotank	2.7	67.0	29	456	292.2	20.9	182	2,469	734.2	63.0	31	151	29.9	4.9
Pender	2.8	48.1	33	301	187.4	11.6	157	1,812	435.4	42.2	62	333	71.1	15.3
Perquimans	0.8	55.8	D	D	D	D	28	214	53.0	4.3	D	D	D	D
Person	2.5	64.4	21	206	68.9	10.0	128	1,500	384.0	35.6	25	60	13.5	2.0
Pitt	13.6	77.6	131	1,514	1,021.3	73.6	625	9,154	2,556.1	229.1	184	717	170.0	25.7
Polk	0.9	44.7	17	38	11.7	1.9	60	452	112.5	9.5	D	D	D	D
Randolph	16.8	117.4	131	1,902	858.9	98.8	395	4,659	1,269.8	115.2	77	267	43.8	9.6
Richmond	9.9	217.2	16	266	223.0	8.6	174	1,999	481.9	46.3	39	274	26.0	5.3
Robeson	21.3	158.6	65	690	630.7	30.1	404	4,898	1,414.4	118.5	59	169	34.2	4.8
Rockingham	11.4	124.3	51	1,168	607.8	42.3	299	3,611	892.2	86.1	61	154	22.9	4.0
Rowan	9.6	69.3	117	1,522	846.3	67.8	410	4,591	1,357.9	114.0	98	286	54.4	10.7
Rutherford	7.7	115.7	D	D	D	D	202	2,481	646.4	60.6	51	110	31.3	3.4
Sampson	3.7	57.6	39	675	369.8	31.0	184	2,246	621.8	50.5	29	67	14.8	2.1
Scotland	3.1	87.3	D	D	D	D	127	1,511	337.1	32.8	25	56	14.7	2.1
Stanly	6.4	105.4	D	D	D	D	228	2,768	733.6	62.4	42	186	28.7	5.2
Stokes	0.3	6.5	D	D	D	2.0	106	1,247	285.5	26.8	D	D	D	D
Surry	4.4	60.6	D	D	D	D	335	4,344	1,131.6	108.9	62	211	30.3	5.6

1 Merchant wholesalers, except manufacturers' sales branches and offices. 2. Employer establishments.

STATE County	Professional, scientific, and technical services, 2017				Manufacturing, 2017				Accommodation and food services, 2017			
	Number of establish-ments	Number of employees	Sales (mil dol)	Average payroll (mil dol)	Number of establish-ments	Number of employees	Sales (mil dol)	Average payroll (mil dol)	Number of establis-hments	Number of employees	Sales (mil dol)	Annual payroll (mil dol)
	147	148	149	150	151	152	153	154	155	156	157	158
NORTH CAROLINA—Cont'd												
Chowan	D	D	D	D	14	587	512.6	29.6	27	400	20.4	5.0
Clay	15	30	2.8	1.0	D	198	D	8.5	D	D	D	3.1
Cleveland	124	957	108.4	42.4	121	6,047	2,412.7	328.5	158	2,904	147.3	37.6
Columbus	62	208	28.0	7.6	33	1,923	761.7	117.2	87	1,128	61.9	15.4
Craven	D	D	D	D	68	3,408	1,408.6	179.4	204	3,647	199.8	52.9
Cumberland	531	6,492	795.9	325.9	95	5,745	2,570.0	329.9	703	15,036	760.9	208.5
Currituck	50	149	18.0	7.6	13	80	14.0	3.8	83	D	53.1	D
Dare	D	D	D	D	35	454	106.2	23.0	D	D	D	D
Davidson	186	821	84.4	29.1	234	9,287	2,697.4	405.4	237	3,901	192.5	53.3
Davie	D	D	D	D	42	1,402	695.7	65.9	72	1,162	56.8	14.6
Duplin	50	148	17.0	5.7	41	6,209	1,954.9	222.1	71	1,137	54.0	13.9
Durham	D	D	D	D	180	13,308	9,017.6	966.5	771	16,566	1,061.2	309.0
Edgecombe	39	118	14.0	4.5	33	2,529	779.7	100.8	57	986	45.8	12.3
Forsyth	963	6,564	1,058.6	393.8	304	16,032	26,160.4	914.9	802	17,489	934.5	265.8
Franklin	84	218	25.1	8.3	54	3,298	1,311.7	210.1	60	879	40.3	10.8
Gaston	D	D	D	D	271	12,792	5,397.7	666.0	373	7,221	394.5	105.4
Gates	D	D	D	1.0	4	150	45.6	6.6	D	D	D	D
Graham	D	D	D	0.6	7	42	8.5	1.4	D	D	D	6.3
Granville	68	273	29.0	10.9	45	4,467	4,335.3	229.8	66	1,128	54.3	13.6
Greene	8	56	5.8	2.4	13	116	37.6	5.8	19	235	11.2	3.1
Guilford	D	D	D	D	602	31,362	17,742.3	1,916.0	1,231	27,375	1,433.5	412.2
Halifax	42	195	15.7	5.2	33	1,667	599.2	74.5	D	D	D	D
Harnett	119	520	63.3	22.3	66	1,666	387.4	77.0	167	3,020	146.0	40.1
Haywood	115	442	51.9	18.8	43	1,896	993.6	116.3	152	2,383	129.6	38.1
Henderson	253	954	112.5	38.8	112	5,831	2,413.0	317.6	225	3,858	229.5	65.3
Hertford	D	D	D	D	16	1,030	1,161.7	66.0	43	685	30.6	8.2
Hoke	35	122	9.2	3.1	21	1,484	613.0	57.0	32	514	24.2	6.4
Hyde	D	D	D	0.6	4	58	12.7	2.3	30	189	17.6	4.8
Iredell	437	3,111	460.8	168.9	299	11,356	4,071.5	571.4	380	7,339	393.4	106.4
Jackson	D	D	D	D	17	270	71.9	9.8	122	4,558	715.1	131.6
Johnston	250	1,072	124.3	47.1	103	6,182	2,431.3	373.3	290	5,881	313.9	81.3
Jones	6	20	2.4	0.7	8	22	5.3	1.2	8	85	3.0	0.9
Lee	D	D	D	D	80	7,887	3,278.2	430.1	115	2,011	102.5	27.9
Lenoir	65	579	136.2	31.3	51	6,013	1,918.8	236.9	102	1,971	94.2	25.2
Lincoln	D	D	D	D	106	4,111	2,000.3	173.1	119	2,119	110.9	31.2
McDowell	38	196	15.7	6.8	47	4,651	1,638.2	224.3	80	1,277	58.1	15.5
Macon	74	214	22.6	8.5	29	385	117.5	18.8	109	1,538	122.5	32.1
Madison	24	32	4.0	1.2	14	284	107.2	14.9	38	388	21.7	6.3
Martin	18	80	7.2	2.3	18	897	641.0	38.1	D	D	D	D
Mecklenburg	D	D	D	D	760	25,616	10,022.7	1,423.5	2,758	62,105	4,016.2	1,101.5
Mitchell	17	69	6.4	2.0	23	450	76.3	21.9	38	456	23.6	6.1
Montgomery	17	64	5.7	2.2	63	2,907	1,035.8	130.2	D	D	D	D
Moore	220	1,375	245.2	84.3	73	1,415	421.5	68.8	224	5,154	309.4	91.9
Nash	135	897	123.8	37.9	88	7,157	4,144.5	339.2	188	3,846	194.3	51.4
New Hanover	D	D	D	D	185	5,596	2,092.4	449.5	771	15,249	856.2	243.6
Northampton	6	16	1.5	0.5	8	408	271.5	20.8	D	D	D	D
Onslow	D	D	D	D	47	1,040	391.8	42.3	399	7,870	435.4	117.0
Orange	D	D	D	D	75	2,233	724.5	120.7	328	6,267	349.4	110.4
Pamlico	17	44	5.3	1.7	8	96	34.6	3.7	27	526	32.8	9.2
Pasquotank	70	374	50.3	18.4	22	563	176.4	27.1	95	1,786	89.2	24.3
Pender	D	D	D	D	40	919	222.8	35.9	110	1,445	78.6	22.9
Perquimans	15	35	4.3	1.7	D	D	D	D	13	237	13.4	4.6
Person	D	D	D	3.1	29	1,368	949.5	75.2	57	940	49.7	11.9
Pitt	D	D	D	D	93	6,726	2,690.2	375.9	369	8,445	417.1	111.3
Polk	40	173	23.3	7.2	20	308	71.5	10.8	D	D	D	6.1
Randolph	139	658	69.5	22.8	281	15,975	3,568.9	581.9	207	3,883	193.9	53.6
Richmond	45	146	16.0	4.7	35	2,875	895.6	106.5	63	1,039	49.5	12.0
Robeson	D	D	D	D	57	7,537	3,487.2	301.0	184	3,678	190.5	46.5
Rockingham	D	D	D	D	82	5,998	2,177.2	270.5	146	2,264	109.4	30.0
Rowan	178	799	112.3	34.0	181	8,381	4,026.0	403.6	227	4,081	218.8	60.0
Rutherford	D	D	D	D	67	3,073	1,130.4	138.5	120	1,636	87.5	23.6
Sampson	51	268	32.3	11.6	41	3,287	955.4	132.2	88	1,323	61.3	15.7
Scotland	24	89	7.6	3.0	27	1,904	963.9	90.9	57	1,069	55.4	14.9
Stanly	63	290	35.7	11.5	91	2,713	909.3	132.3	115	1,877	88.0	23.5
Stokes	39	154	13.4	5.1	33	948	405.1	39.4	59	933	41.1	11.3
Surry	90	422	41.0	14.8	100	3,336	1,012.1	136.6	161	2,768	127.8	36.2

STATE County	Health care and social assistance, 2017				Other services, 2017				Nonemployer businesses, 2019		Value of residential construction authorized by building permits, 2021	
	Number of establish-ments	Number of employees	Receipts (mil dol)	Annual payroll (mil dol)	Number of establish-ments	Number of employees	Receipts (mil dol)	Annual payroll (mil dol)	Number	Receipts (mil dol)	New construction ($1,000)	Number of housing units
	159	160	161	162	163	164	165	166	167	168	169	170
NORTH CAROLINA—Cont'd												
Chowan	D	D	D	D	17	76	6.1	1.9	1,008	38.3	10,432	37
Clay	24	316	22.2	10.4	D	D	D	1.2	1,129	49.6	20,829	87
Cleveland	239	5,249	636.6	227.5	119	649	67.7	19.7	5,775	192.1	71,480	398
Columbus	171	2,863	262.7	98.1	D	D	D	4.4	3,545	140.2	2,834	20
Craven	264	7,776	825.0	342.0	147	603	61.9	16.8	6,534	272.6	91,753	311
Cumberland	722	20,168	2,318.6	927.1	415	2,560	254.4	74.0	19,776	747.6	159,305	852
Currituck	29	254	20.4	9.3	47	316	25.8	6.5	2,356	114.8	193,453	547
Dare	95	1,074	145.5	55.1	D	D	D	D	5,647	328.8	214,710	569
Davidson	194	4,938	398.2	165.5	197	757	82.4	22.3	11,774	488.0	244,797	878
Davie	58	1,442	133.9	50.1	66	222	22.5	5.1	3,259	151.7	57,076	267
Duplin	95	1,606	149.1	58.2	D	D	D	D	3,310	151.5	18,298	91
Durham	875	28,074	4,835.1	1,520.1	490	5,905	1,719.8	344.2	26,975	1,030.8	817,047	3,518
Edgecombe	98	2,565	231.9	77.8	40	144	12.3	3.3	2,613	82.3	17,616	145
Forsyth	830	35,474	4,304.1	1,490.1	611	3,625	631.1	116.0	28,273	1,191.8	518,771	2,695
Franklin	77	922	66.8	27.8	74	262	32.4	6.8	5,036	202.5	271,840	1,141
Gaston	473	11,894	1,321.5	524.5	308	1,520	156.6	40.6	14,802	595.5	532,940	2,184
Gates	12	99	6.9	2.8	D	D	D	D	576	18.9	1,780	10
Graham	10	264	14.8	6.7	D	D	D	0.6	748	27.6	3,000	4
Granville	103	4,059	299.4	156.1	D	D	D	D	3,614	140.1	57,938	217
Greene	38	632	39.7	17.6	D	D	D	1.9	1,059	43.1	8,083	46
Guilford	1,294	35,445	4,243.5	1,645.2	870	6,280	1,265.9	210.8	44,396	2,029.6	703,183	3,228
Halifax	122	2,808	222.9	91.4	D	D	D	D	2,704	92.6	21,383	59
Harnett	178	4,596	461.9	182.1	111	437	53.1	12.4	7,850	325.9	148,848	1,032
Haywood	138	3,171	303.1	123.8	96	467	51.6	14.4	5,279	206.9	129,873	496
Henderson	278	6,208	659.3	259.2	200	1,000	113.5	29.2	9,973	442.1	257,308	790
Hertford	78	2,037	177.1	71.3	D	D	D	D	1,071	36.2	6,489	51
Hoke	72	1,681	117.6	47.6	30	134	9.5	2.9	2,918	87.1	78,809	423
Hyde	D	D	D	D	D	D	D	D	587	24.6	4,322	20
Iredell	493	9,223	964.9	393.9	302	1,790	187.2	52.2	15,269	797.4	448,536	2,047
Jackson	91	1,772	219.2	81.6	59	219	26.6	6.4	3,174	139.6	301,827	314
Johnston	330	6,077	605.9	251.9	195	833	87.8	22.5	15,441	716.6	696,570	3,520
Jones	13	249	18.7	8.6	D	D	D	D	595	21.1	5,981	25
Lee	160	2,867	275.5	106.8	89	417	33.3	10.4	4,264	198.2	53,818	259
Lenoir	159	4,193	323.8	148.3	79	487	47.5	14.4	3,222	143.9	17,810	112
Lincoln	156	2,544	316.1	104.8	138	546	51.2	14.8	6,564	322.1	223,167	1,062
McDowell	79	1,741	157.0	57.9	39	204	24.8	6.8	2,791	107.0	63,867	194
Macon	94	1,505	165.8	60.9	81	355	48.2	10.7	3,403	147.2	53,445	149
Madison	33	544	42.2	18.2	17	62	7.4	1.9	2,055	81.3	49,705	159
Martin	55	1,094	82.4	32.2	D	D	D	D	1,299	48.4	0	0
Mecklenburg	2,950	73,197	11,317.4	4,008.5	2,043	16,834	2,629.8	581.9	106,579	5,241.8	2,406,168	14,375
Mitchell	39	817	80.2	29.5	30	81	6.6	1.7	1,169	39.5	9,172	39
Montgomery	48	1,281	67.2	32.8	34	342	23.7	10.3	1,585	61.4	22,620	104
Moore	293	9,678	1,243.4	482.7	162	880	80.0	25.5	8,686	425.8	240,854	919
Nash	227	5,927	515.3	229.8	102	562	171.1	16.6	6,210	269.0	71,187	495
New Hanover	825	18,772	2,310.5	901.7	514	3,163	320.7	94.6	22,461	1,172.3	805,210	3,401
Northampton	29	529	31.9	13.8	D	D	D	D	898	32.4	8,786	32
Onslow	263	5,331	642.5	218.9	211	1,071	104.4	28.1	11,238	421.5	295,039	1,597
Orange	406	16,410	2,030.8	876.2	216	1,930	369.8	81.9	14,058	661.3	205,056	912
Pamlico	26	333	21.4	10.1	D	D	D	D	1,045	48.4	24,854	70
Pasquotank	138	2,414	299.0	114.7	74	468	33.1	10.3	2,751	98.9	16,937	104
Pender	111	1,577	122.4	49.9	72	286	26.1	8.8	5,089	249.6	181,992	1,017
Perquimans	D	D	D	4.3	D	D	5.1	D	963	34.9	8,918	41
Person	85	1,287	106.2	40.9	47	209	24.1	8.2	2,278	87.7	37,442	129
Pitt	499	16,338	2,158.5	773.9	220	1,287	123.7	36.0	11,555	461.4	237,202	1,275
Polk	48	1,485	123.5	51.2	26	111	14.6	3.2	2,051	95.0	36,267	135
Randolph	229	4,612	383.6	165.3	157	830	91.5	24.3	10,114	433.9	115,850	487
Richmond	92	1,922	187.8	77.7	D	D	D	D	2,118	80.7	7,226	30
Robeson	267	6,823	588.2	259.1	89	330	30.2	7.6	7,843	273.1	42,903	210
Rockingham	158	3,038	326.4	109.3	110	439	40.7	12.5	5,228	204.3	66,947	249
Rowan	248	9,245	1,079.7	518.1	163	659	73.0	21.3	9,883	405.8	193,256	675
Rutherford	126	2,720	234.6	88.1	79	469	44.0	13.7	4,320	181.0	49,483	183
Sampson	121	2,485	183.5	79.0	50	305	25.2	7.5	3,799	167.6	39,775	174
Scotland	100	2,358	252.2	98.8	31	110	10.4	2.8	1,888	60.2	10,049	52
Stanly	165	2,798	282.2	108.8	88	440	38.9	12.1	4,228	194.1	61,628	366
Stokes	50	1,430	107.8	43.5	44	157	21.5	5.3	2,824	111.5	221,518	180
Surry	166	4,067	408.6	167.5	90	476	45.5	13.4	4,856	223.9	22,327	130

STATE County	Government employment and payroll, 2017									Local government finances, 2017				
			March payroll (percent of total)							General revenue				
												Taxes		
													Per capita[1] (dollars)	
	Full-time equivalent employees	March payroll (dollars)	Adminis- tration, judicial, and legal	Police and corrections	Fire protection	Highways and transpor- tation	Health and welfare	Natural resources and utilities	Education and libraries	Total (mil dol)	Inter- govern- mental (mil dol)	Total (mil dol)	Total	Property
	171	172	173	174	175	176	177	178	179	180	181	182	183	184
NORTH CAROLINA—Cont'd														
Chowan	576	1,815,508	5.8	10.4	1.7	1.1	8.0	8.4	60.0	49.3	24.8	16.5	1,176	972
Clay	406	1,175,292	5.2	11.4	0.0	0.0	22.6	3.3	52.3	32.0	17.2	11.3	1,031	783
Cleveland	3,804	13,068,896	4.1	7.9	1.7	0.9	14.1	6.5	63.0	321.2	177.3	102.0	1,050	804
Columbus	2,426	7,265,072	4.9	6.3	0.8	0.5	11.7	2.5	67.6	119.9	88.1	16.0	286	252
Craven	5,659	23,933,631	3.2	4.3	1.7	1.0	53.9	4.6	29.7	629.0	146.8	84.1	821	581
Cumberland	19,164	73,834,537	2.4	7.0	2.0	1.0	45.1	4.1	35.1	1,032.1	550.1	382.2	1,155	831
Currituck	913	3,283,009	5.3	11.2	1.6	0.3	15.3	6.0	55.9	100.2	32.3	57.8	2,198	1,182
Dare	2,036	7,931,376	10.5	14.0	4.0	1.3	15.2	10.3	40.1	238.0	56.5	160.4	4,431	2,505
Davidson	5,250	17,412,155	3.5	7.6	2.7	1.0	6.4	4.9	67.7	423.5	233.7	149.6	906	655
Davie	1,287	5,002,042	4.8	7.8	0.3	0.0	13.0	2.2	69.7	117.0	54.6	48.2	1,140	915
Duplin	2,751	9,217,556	2.6	5.4	3.6	0.6	35.9	3.4	47.1	481.5	409.3	49.9	847	601
Durham	11,409	46,922,955	5.5	11.9	5.2	1.4	14.8	6.7	49.6	1,163.6	402.7	572.6	1,834	1,377
Edgecombe	1,866	6,236,459	1.8	8.6	1.2	1.1	14.6	6.6	63.7	141.1	84.1	39.7	753	615
Forsyth	14,332	48,791,745	5.1	10.2	5.5	1.6	7.5	4.8	64.2	1,248.9	549.4	525.0	1,397	1,059
Franklin	1,901	5,975,975	4.8	9.8	0.4	0.7	15.1	4.7	60.3	91.3	62.6	21.1	319	288
Gaston	8,063	29,522,445	6.9	6.5	2.7	2.4	17.8	6.2	55.6	1,010.3	618.6	259.9	1,183	892
Gates	410	1,369,610	3.9	2.9	0.0	1.2	6.1	2.3	81.7	28.9	17.8	9.2	795	604
Graham	393	1,257,751	4.8	6.4	0.0	2.1	15.5	2.2	62.1	31.5	19.2	9.5	1,119	845
Granville	1,572	5,369,066	5.3	10.7	0.7	1.1	6.8	4.6	66.7	163.2	77.9	58.7	989	798
Greene	729	2,325,290	3.3	4.8	2.9	0.2	7.1	4.5	75.9	37.1	30.7	3.4	162	158
Guilford	18,494	73,703,685	5.2	12.0	5.0	2.6	7.8	7.1	57.5	1,905.5	821.7	783.7	1,484	1,118
Halifax	2,203	7,410,028	5.5	6.6	1.7	1.7	13.8	6.6	60.6	161.4	92.3	46.6	909	684
Harnett	4,945	15,502,659	4.3	7.0	0.1	0.7	28.1	4.4	54.8	202.1	151.6	35.5	268	248
Haywood	2,174	7,275,501	5.1	10.0	1.4	1.0	13.6	5.6	58.1	189.8	81.7	79.3	1,300	962
Henderson	4,476	17,881,311	3.7	6.4	0.8	0.4	44.1	2.7	39.8	788.6	132.8	133.4	1,158	884
Hertford	1,040	3,454,715	5.9	8.8	0.7	0.9	11.7	5.4	62.6	70.9	43.0	20.5	858	630
Hoke	1,515	4,737,322	2.7	8.5	0.5	0.0	4.0	4.8	79.2	87.5	72.4	9.7	178	160
Hyde	301	980,614	4.8	7.7	0.0	0.3	18.8	9.5	55.5	25.0	11.6	9.8	1,864	1,476
Iredell	5,860	19,989,935	5.2	8.7	4.1	0.7	9.4	6.0	63.2	559.3	232.7	227.9	1,297	1,024
Jackson	1,467	4,605,328	8.5	2.5	0.0	1.0	10.6	3.4	65.2	120.3	55.7	48.9	1,131	838
Johnston	7,829	29,315,952	2.6	4.5	1.7	0.2	28.4	3.7	57.4	860.3	309.0	204.2	1,040	792
Jones	388	1,184,828	4.7	8.2	0.0	0.0	9.6	3.4	67.2	27.8	16.5	8.8	921	725
Lee	2,729	9,721,756	4.3	8.9	2.6	1.7	6.2	4.3	68.9	230.2	121.1	80.7	1,337	997
Lenoir	2,440	8,798,545	3.3	7.7	2.2	1.9	8.1	8.8	65.6	215.8	117.4	63.5	1,122	858
Lincoln	2,379	7,944,638	3.9	9.2	1.3	1.1	14.0	6.6	59.8	209.1	92.4	90.1	1,091	792
McDowell	1,469	4,927,665	1.4	2.0	0.4	0.7	5.9	2.6	85.0	122.6	68.9	39.0	865	583
Macon	1,314	4,399,214	5.8	9.8	0.8	1.3	14.1	7.3	55.8	198.0	59.7	105.7	3,056	2,360
Madison	754	2,186,041	5.3	7.0	0.7	0.1	18.0	5.4	63.3	61.0	33.7	19.9	921	675
Martin	1,039	3,593,479	3.7	6.7	1.9	1.2	12.6	3.9	67.3	76.5	48.7	20.4	896	670
Mecklenburg	70,012	366,856,715	2.5	4.8	2.0	1.9	61.7	2.8	23.3	10,817.9	1,742.4	2,294.2	2,128	1,440
Mitchell	666	2,302,636	2.4	5.3	0.1	1.4	11.3	2.5	74.0	56.9	34.0	15.2	1,015	724
Montgomery	1,203	3,707,129	6.3	5.9	0.0	1.2	7.2	2.7	73.6	120.0	55.2	47.4	1,738	1,518
Moore	3,723	14,117,302	5.7	7.8	2.6	1.4	15.7	4.2	60.4	584.5	421.1	121.7	1,250	948
Nash	5,745	23,157,319	4.0	6.6	2.9	1.9	38.6	6.3	38.1	344.9	176.7	111.9	1,191	872
New Hanover	13,503	56,814,312	2.7	6.8	2.6	1.1	49.2	3.0	30.3	2,039.2	295.9	399.2	1,745	1,168
Northampton	786	2,459,636	5.4	9.5	0.0	1.0	19.7	3.5	46.8	37.6	28.4	6.1	306	282
Onslow	5,784	20,744,428	4.2	8.1	2.3	1.0	8.3	4.8	68.0	507.1	241.2	182.5	935	624
Orange	5,470	22,525,778	6.4	8.3	3.0	3.3	5.9	6.6	60.0	408.0	156.1	212.8	1,481	1,211
Pamlico	505	1,720,040	5.0	7.4	0.2	0.5	10.5	5.5	68.2	55.6	21.6	15.5	1,224	958
Pasquotank	1,988	6,479,973	2.8	8.3	2.4	2.4	17.0	8.3	56.5	137.9	70.4	45.3	1,150	808
Pender	1,717	6,154,687	5.5	8.1	1.1	0.4	9.6	2.4	70.5	187.7	84.5	82.2	1,354	1,065
Perquimans	417	1,644,255	5.1	7.2	0.0	0.0	11.4	3.5	70.2	35.2	19.8	11.8	875	677
Person	1,447	5,177,815	3.5	9.3	2.1	0.0	10.4	5.8	62.4	111.5	60.0	40.4	1,026	815
Pitt	7,258	24,893,380	7.1	10.4	2.2	2.4	12.6	10.0	49.6	931.3	283.9	183.1	1,025	720
Polk	687	2,236,878	10.2	8.8	0.5	2.0	8.1	4.5	62.9	53.0	24.2	22.8	1,108	869
Randolph	4,153	15,512,894	3.9	8.1	2.1	1.2	6.9	3.4	71.9	387.1	212.4	132.9	929	684
Richmond	2,035	6,946,800	8.8	3.2	1.7	1.4	9.3	5.8	67.7	159.7	98.3	42.4	945	725
Robeson	4,797	16,250,632	3.1	9.1	1.1	1.6	12.8	4.8	66.4	301.0	227.9	40.6	306	243
Rockingham	3,057	10,462,110	6.2	8.7	2.2	1.3	9.9	5.1	62.4	244.2	129.4	81.3	895	696
Rowan	5,068	16,833,762	3.8	7.1	2.5	1.3	9.6	4.1	67.9	427.9	211.7	150.7	1,074	793
Rutherford	2,441	8,181,622	4.3	7.4	1.7	1.9	10.3	4.9	66.1	187.0	95.9	67.5	1,014	744
Sampson	2,554	7,843,044	3.5	6.3	1.2	0.4	11.7	2.9	72.0	132.8	99.1	21.9	347	292
Scotland	1,491	4,808,909	4.0	7.1	0.5	1.9	13.4	4.7	64.9	114.7	67.5	35.4	1,005	763
Stanly	2,490	8,648,656	4.6	7.4	2.7	1.8	12.4	6.0	63.3	181.7	96.6	58.3	947	698
Stokes	1,540	4,795,661	5.8	6.6	2.7	0.4	12.6	2.4	67.9	108.6	58.9	39.6	866	652
Surry	3,903	13,457,582	2.7	4.5	0.8	0.2	37.8	3.5	48.8	312.3	123.3	69.5	964	589

1. Based on the resident population estimated as of July 1 of the year shown.

STATE County	Local government finances, 2017 (cont.)									Government employment, 2020			Individual income tax returns, 2019		
	Direct general expenditure							Debt outstanding							
	Total (mil dol)	Per capita[1] (dollars)	Percent of total for: Education	Health and hospitals	Police protection	Public welfare	Highways	Total (mil dol)	Per capita[1] (dollars)	Federal civilian	Federal military	State and local	Number of returns	Mean adjusted gross income	Mean income tax
	185	186	187	188	189	190	191	192	193	194	195	196	197	198	199
NORTH CAROLINA—Cont'd															
Chowan	48.8	3,480	49.3	0.3	12.8	5.8	1.0	15.1	1,076	38	29	776	6,410	54,945	5,311
Clay	29.7	2,697	48.1	7.7	11.7	8.4	0.1	8.6	784	29	24	485	4,960	53,149	5,185
Cleveland	324.2	3,337	55.9	3.8	9.7	6.8	1.2	180.7	1,860	214	211	4,991	44,190	48,093	3,864
Columbus	198.8	3,547	52.1	40.6	1.5	0.0	0.4	84.5	1,507	139	116	3,272	21,870	42,807	3,320
Craven	610.6	5,958	23.8	59.5	2.1	3.7	0.2	152.1	1,484	5,989	6,667	7,139	47,340	57,451	5,503
Cumberland	1,024.5	3,095	53.0	2.6	9.7	7.7	1.7	455.3	1,375	16,312	48,717	21,721	147,340	49,214	4,040
Currituck	96.0	3,653	41.6	7.2	9.0	5.0	0.0	24.6	935	44	63	1,217	13,790	65,211	6,368
Dare	247.1	6,827	23.9	8.4	14.8	3.7	1.4	231.0	6,382	226	188	2,722	21,310	67,225	7,627
Davidson	447.6	2,710	63.5	3.2	6.4	5.5	1.0	179.6	1,087	211	365	6,005	76,830	54,483	4,866
Davie	137.8	3,256	60.4	5.2	7.7	4.8	1.1	71.0	1,679	70	92	1,482	20,040	69,962	7,856
Duplin	532.6	9,036	28.6	60.1	2.0	2.1	0.3	78.7	1,335	147	126	3,031	21,950	43,242	2,997
Durham	1,055.8	3,382	39.1	4.6	11.1	5.9	2.1	1,049.0	3,361	6,743	706	15,214	153,160	72,507	8,733
Edgecombe	134.2	2,544	62.1	4.7	5.9	11.0	0.0	29.0	550	213	108	4,045	22,020	39,327	2,917
Forsyth	1,373.2	3,654	43.4	2.6	9.1	3.9	3.0	1,609.1	4,281	1,669	850	17,587	177,390	66,392	7,729
Franklin	90.5	1,369	84.4	0.0	3.9	0.0	1.7	14.0	211	98	151	2,139	30,320	54,946	4,665
Gaston	1,030.2	4,690	35.4	33.8	7.0	4.2	2.0	342.0	1,557	414	519	9,276	104,030	56,557	5,463
Gates	27.4	2,377	69.9	0.5	7.5	6.9	0.1	3.3	287	19	190	486	4,710	51,005	3,988
Graham	28.8	3,376	51.1	9.1	7.4	8.6	0.7	11.4	1,332	41	18	467	3,470	43,135	3,327
Granville	142.6	2,402	53.5	1.1	12.3	6.5	2.6	120.9	2,036	1,392	122	6,494	26,740	57,150	5,150
Greene	37.3	1,780	90.6	0.0	0.9	0.0	0.8	23.3	1,114	44	40	1,877	7,880	41,756	2,987
Guilford	1,923.1	3,640	46.0	3.2	7.9	4.9	3.3	2,117.4	4,008	4,024	1,160	29,056	250,190	65,052	7,651
Halifax	161.0	3,137	54.1	7.0	5.3	10.1	0.5	132.9	2,590	137	104	3,592	21,370	42,152	3,399
Harnett	207.6	1,568	84.6	0.0	3.1	0.0	1.4	246.4	1,861	162	297	5,296	54,840	52,117	4,285
Haywood	182.0	2,983	47.9	6.8	9.0	8.8	2.8	61.4	1,007	144	134	2,700	29,600	53,138	4,728
Henderson	472.0	4,096	32.5	39.7	4.9	4.3	0.9	223.1	1,937	266	252	5,407	56,210	62,072	6,112
Hertford	74.1	3,099	55.8	7.3	6.0	8.4	0.5	105.5	4,409	72	45	1,839	8,520	43,644	3,455
Hoke	86.3	1,595	91.3	0.0	1.6	0.0	1.1	57.3	1,059	75	118	2,324	21,840	44,119	2,859
Hyde	24.6	4,698	43.3	12.5	9.3	7.9	0.0	14.5	2,761	33	13	575	2,080	40,759	2,949
Iredell	533.0	3,034	51.4	1.8	9.3	4.6	1.6	506.4	2,883	317	398	8,521	88,160	76,035	9,711
Jackson	117.0	2,707	51.2	6.1	6.0	8.8	0.6	51.5	1,192	76	87	8,430	16,790	53,338	5,290
Johnston	847.8	4,318	43.5	33.2	3.6	4.1	0.6	607.7	3,095	284	462	9,557	96,380	60,649	5,652
Jones	28.1	2,937	55.3	6.5	6.7	10.1	0.2	4.5	469	25	20	506	4,270	44,250	3,466
Lee	229.5	3,799	61.9	1.4	7.8	4.4	1.4	168.5	2,789	169	132	3,101	28,120	56,158	5,306
Lenoir	215.6	3,808	50.8	3.4	7.5	6.0	0.7	161.5	2,852	204	117	5,513	24,700	45,326	4,056
Lincoln	197.1	2,387	48.9	5.9	8.0	7.0	0.8	130.1	1,576	138	189	3,711	40,110	71,520	8,040
McDowell	122.8	2,723	60.2	2.7	6.9	9.6	1.2	14.7	326	99	95	2,396	19,520	46,288	3,565
Macon	176.1	5,094	35.0	8.6	11.9	12.1	0.4	119.3	3,450	173	80	1,661	16,680	56,259	5,857
Madison	58.2	2,699	44.2	6.9	8.9	11.1	1.1	13.0	603	77	45	846	9,400	49,418	4,066
Martin	81.4	3,575	56.5	8.3	5.4	7.7	0.1	42.6	1,870	55	47	1,412	10,130	41,983	3,087
Mecklenburg	10,082.2	9,352	17.1	55.0	4.3	2.1	1.4	10,115.2	9,382	6,229	2,607	73,209	539,540	88,022	13,000
Mitchell	58.4	3,897	64.1	2.1	5.2	11.6	2.0	1.7	111	47	32	864	6,290	46,960	3,437
Montgomery	109.2	4,003	46.5	3.1	4.2	5.0	0.5	55.9	2,048	77	56	1,562	11,360	49,611	4,599
Moore	585.6	6,014	25.8	54.5	3.9	2.0	1.2	152.1	1,562	224	239	4,367	47,240	78,186	9,338
Nash	349.7	3,720	51.4	4.3	8.5	5.2	1.6	290.3	3,088	198	199	5,672	44,820	53,108	5,057
New Hanover	1,949.1	8,521	20.3	56.7	4.2	2.2	0.6	1,558.7	6,814	1,119	648	20,380	111,120	75,266	9,757
Northampton	37.8	1,898	68.0	0.1	2.0	0.0	1.8	26.9	1,351	49	40	945	7,830	43,663	3,290
Onslow	519.7	2,664	54.1	3.9	6.9	9.7	1.1	462.0	2,368	6,670	39,167	7,907	84,210	47,590	3,521
Orange	418.3	2,912	59.9	3.8	6.3	6.5	0.4	365.0	2,541	308	333	41,561	63,330	105,715	16,263
Pamlico	43.9	3,471	53.4	2.2	8.1	8.3	0.3	10.5	832	33	50	826	5,710	57,514	5,690
Pasquotank	134.2	3,408	57.1	3.8	9.7	6.4	0.9	49.7	1,263	760	931	3,491	18,310	48,180	3,840
Pender	197.0	3,244	57.1	2.6	5.2	5.1	0.3	257.9	4,247	106	174	2,547	27,820	63,070	6,239
Perquimans	35.7	2,657	52.4	4.1	8.3	6.7	1.3	29.1	2,166	37	29	609	5,970	54,511	4,631
Person	140.0	3,559	45.8	7.1	5.0	8.6	0.0	200.8	5,104	63	85	1,639	17,760	50,765	4,180
Pitt	992.6	5,557	28.8	44.4	6.0	0.0	1.4	605.9	3,392	805	421	26,377	74,930	59,715	6,533
Polk	54.3	2,641	48.8	3.2	8.7	6.8	0.5	39.9	1,939	64	86	861	9,410	62,843	6,536
Randolph	377.0	2,635	59.9	2.4	9.7	5.9	1.1	100.4	702	228	308	5,566	64,590	49,430	4,119
Richmond	160.4	3,578	58.1	3.8	7.8	6.6	0.8	46.2	1,031	112	158	2,777	18,750	40,007	2,793
Robeson	305.9	2,306	79.9	0.0	4.7	0.0	1.3	53.5	403	319	273	7,667	49,160	38,123	2,621
Rockingham	234.9	2,588	53.8	2.7	9.8	9.0	0.9	119.7	1,319	164	200	3,528	40,710	48,403	3,960
Rowan	407.9	2,906	55.6	2.9	6.9	5.6	1.6	201.9	1,439	2,739	297	6,169	65,760	52,471	4,748
Rutherford	184.9	2,779	55.8	2.3	7.2	7.8	1.7	71.5	1,074	140	142	3,236	27,370	47,379	3,837
Sampson	132.6	2,097	89.3	0.1	2.3	0.0	1.1	111.2	1,758	134	134	3,689	26,760	44,130	3,565
Scotland	113.5	3,226	57.7	4.2	6.8	8.1	1.1	10.9	311	53	69	2,205	13,990	41,941	3,176
Stanly	190.5	3,098	54.7	4.8	7.9	5.6	1.2	65.6	1,066	156	131	3,864	27,800	54,598	4,886
Stokes	105.3	2,302	57.9	5.2	7.0	7.7	0.5	42.5	929	78	114	1,662	20,000	51,664	4,179
Surry	305.9	4,242	43.9	33.1	4.0	3.8	0.6	73.3	1,016	186	152	4,479	31,100	51,211	4,539

1. Based on the resident population estimated as of July 1 of the year shown.

State / county code	CBSA code[1]	County Type code[2]	STATE County	Land area[3] (sq. mi)	Population, 2021: Total persons 2021	Population, 2021: Rank	Population, 2021: Per square mile	Race alone or in combination, not Hispanic or Latino (percent): White	Black	American Indian, Alaska Native	Asian and Pacific Islancer	Percent Hispanic or Latino[4]	Age (percent): Under 5 years	5 to 17 years	18 to 24 years	25 to 34 years	35 to 44 years	45 to 54 years
				1	2	3	4	5	6	7	8	9	10	11	12	13	14	15
			NORTH CAROLINA—Cont'd															
37173	19000	8	Swain	527.7	14,136	2,141	26.8	62.6	2.6	31.3	1.2	6.8	5.6	13.3	11.7	12.9	11.5	12.5
37175	14820	6	Transylvania	378.4	33,165	1,352	87.6	91.8	4.5	1.2	1.1	3.6	3.7	9.0	10.1	9.4	9.9	11.0
37177		9	Tyrrell	390.8	3,254	2,947	8.3	54.1	34.8	1.1	2.2	10.5	4.9	11.3	10.6	13.0	12.2	11.5
37179	16740	1	Union	632.7	243,648	286	385.1	71.5	12.9	0.8	4.7	12.0	5.3	15.2	14.7	9.7	13.3	15.9
37181	25780	4	Vance	252.4	42,185	1,142	167.1	39.0	51.9	0.7	1.2	8.7	6.3	13.2	12.6	12.3	10.7	12.0
37183	39580	1	Wake	834.6	1,150,204	39	1,378.2	60.9	21.1	0.9	9.2	10.5	5.7	13.3	13.2	14.6	15.0	14.1
37185		8	Warren	429.4	18,762	1,883	43.7	40.0	50.6	6.4	0.8	4.2	4.3	10.4	9.9	10.9	10.5	10.9
37187		7	Washington	346.5	10,892	2,352	31.4	45.6	48.5	0.9	0.6	6.2	5.2	11.3	10.3	10.2	9.2	11.5
37189	14380	5	Watauga	312.4	54,234	936	173.6	92.5	2.4	0.9	1.7	4.1	3.0	7.1	29.6	10.6	9.7	10.3
37191	24140	3	Wayne	553.9	116,835	535	210.9	53.6	32.6	1.0	2.2	13.3	6.4	13.4	13.7	13.5	11.5	11.6
37193	35900	6	Wilkes	753.7	65,806	817	87.3	87.6	5.2	0.6	0.9	7.1	4.9	11.3	11.4	11.1	10.7	13.0
37195	48980	4	Wilson	367.6	78,369	725	213.2	47.4	40.5	0.8	1.6	11.4	5.9	12.9	12.8	12.0	11.4	12.3
37197	49180	2	Yadkin	334.9	37,192	1,246	111.1	84.3	3.9	0.6	0.6	11.9	5.2	11.7	11.3	11.4	10.6	13.7
37199		8	Yancey	312.6	18,757	1,884	60.0	92.9	1.5	0.8	0.5	5.5	5.0	9.9	9.7	11.0	10.6	12.7
38000		0	NORTH DAKOTA	68,994.8	774,948	X	11.2	85.2	4.0	6.3	2.3	4.4	6.6	13.5	14.6	14.3	12.8	10.1
38001		9	Adams	987.5	2,167	3,029	2.2	91.6	2.1	2.1	3.9	2.1	5.2	11.3	9.6	9.5	10.6	8.8
38003		6	Barnes	1,491.6	10,806	2,360	7.2	93.3	2.0	2.3	1.6	2.4	4.9	11.2	13.8	10.8	10.9	10.8
38005		9	Benson	1,388.6	5,809	2,753	4.2	40.2	0.8	56.3	0.8	4.1	10.4	19.7	14.0	10.9	9.8	8.7
38007	19860	9	Billings	1,148.5	955	3,108	0.8	91.8	0.7	0.8	4.2	3.0	5.7	11.9	8.3	10.9	13.6	10.6
38009		9	Bottineau	1,668.9	6,390	2,706	3.8	91.6	1.4	5.7	1.2	2.6	5.8	12.6	11.9	10.3	10.3	9.8
38011		9	Bowman	1,161.8	2,903	2,965	2.5	92.5	0.8	2.0	0.2	5.6	5.5	14.7	10.5	9.9	12.1	9.7
38013		9	Burke	1,103.6	2,158	3,030	2.0	93.1	1.6	2.9	1.3	3.1	6.9	14.1	9.6	10.8	11.4	10.2
38015	13900	3	Burleigh	1,632.7	98,933	617	60.6	89.2	2.8	5.6	1.5	2.9	6.1	13.6	12.9	13.3	13.9	10.8
38017	22020	3	Cass	1,764.9	186,562	363	105.7	85.7	7.3	2.3	3.9	3.1	6.4	12.7	17.0	16.6	14.1	10.2
38019		9	Cavalier	1,489.1	3,662	2,914	2.5	94.6	1.0	2.2	0.8	2.5	6.6	12.1	10.0	9.2	9.9	9.8
38021		9	Dickey	1,131.5	4,897	2,829	4.3	94.1	1.1	1.5	1.2	3.6	5.8	13.8	13.2	10.0	10.8	11.0
38023		9	Divide	1,261.1	2,188	3,027	1.7	91.4	2.6	2.1	3.0	3.5	6.6	13.6	9.5	9.8	10.8	8.5
38025		9	Dunn	2,008.5	4,035	2,884	2.0	81.5	2.5	10.3	2.0	6.1	7.8	14.6	9.8	13.8	12.3	10.0
38027		9	Eddy	630.2	2,337	3,015	3.7	90.5	0.8	4.9	0.6	4.4	6.7	14.0	10.3	10.2	11.2	9.5
38029		8	Emmons	1,510.0	3,271	2,943	2.2	96.0	1.1	1.9	1.1	1.5	5.1	11.4	10.5	8.6	8.6	10.6
38031		9	Foster	634.1	3,364	2,933	5.3	95.2	1.0	2.2	0.6	2.2	5.9	12.9	9.9	11.4	10.6	11.1
38033		9	Golden Valley	1,000.9	1,770	3,061	1.8	94.0	1.3	2.0	0.5	3.8	5.1	10.2	10.1	9.9	11.9	9.8
38035	24220	3	Grand Forks	1,436.2	72,705	758	50.6	85.2	4.9	4.0	3.9	4.9	6.4	12.0	22.1	15.4	11.6	8.7
38037		8	Grant	1,659.2	2,323	3,018	1.4	96.6	1.0	2.4	0.6	1.2	5.3	12.4	8.0	8.0	9.9	10.5
38039		9	Griggs	708.7	2,281	3,020	3.2	97.6	0.6	0.8	0.2	1.2	4.7	13.0	9.2	8.6	10.2	9.6
38041		9	Hettinger	1,132.2	2,430	3,003	2.1	93.7	1.8	3.8	0.8	1.9	7.2	13.1	10.4	11.4	10.6	9.5
38043		8	Kidder	1,351.1	2,369	3,012	1.8	94.0	0.7	0.8	0.8	4.5	6.3	11.9	9.1	9.9	10.8	10.9
38045		9	LaMoure	1,146.0	4,066	2,879	3.5	96.6	0.8	1.0	0.4	2.1	5.8	11.8	10.2	8.6	9.6	10.2
38047		9	Logan	992.6	1,883	3,051	1.9	95.1	1.2	2.0	0.9	3.0	6.5	13.2	10.8	9.3	8.8	10.1
38049	33500	9	McHenry	1,873.9	5,249	2,800	2.8	95.8	1.1	1.6	0.6	2.3	5.8	14.3	9.7	9.5	13.1	11.2
38051		9	McIntosh	974.6	2,513	2,997	2.6	94.8	1.4	1.2	1.0	2.6	5.1	11.4	8.4	9.0	9.9	9.0
38053		9	McKenzie	2,760.1	13,819	2,165	5.0	77.3	2.6	10.8	1.3	11.0	8.9	18.0	13.0	16.4	13.8	9.8
38055		8	McLean	2,110.3	9,796	2,423	4.6	88.8	1.1	8.6	0.7	2.8	5.5	13.1	9.7	9.5	11.2	10.9
38057		7	Mercer	1,042.8	8,323	2,553	8.0	93.3	1.4	3.3	0.9	2.7	5.7	13.5	10.1	9.8	12.2	10.6
38059	13900	3	Morton	1,925.9	33,611	1,342	17.5	89.3	2.1	5.2	1.0	4.3	6.7	13.4	10.6	14.7	13.6	11.1
38061		9	Mountrail	1,825.2	9,576	2,445	5.2	58.6	2.2	32.2	1.2	8.9	8.4	16.0	13.1	15.1	13.2	10.9
38063		8	Nelson	981.8	3,054	2,956	3.1	92.6	1.5	2.8	0.3	4.4	4.8	12.0	9.5	10.4	10.2	9.5
38065	13900	3	Oliver	722.4	1,873	3,052	2.6	94.4	0.8	3.2	0.6	1.9	5.4	14.7	10.0	8.5	11.4	9.8
38067		9	Pembina	1,118.5	6,767	2,674	6.1	92.4	1.2	3.9	0.9	3.9	5.7	11.9	9.5	10.0	12.6	9.9
38069		7	Pierce	1,018.3	3,953	2,890	3.9	90.5	1.4	6.0	1.4	2.1	5.0	13.9	10.5	9.9	11.6	10.4
38071		7	Ramsey	1,185.4	11,572	2,308	9.8	83.0	1.5	13.7	1.3	3.5	6.8	13.8	12.0	12.0	11.0	9.9
38073		8	Ransom	862.5	5,675	2,765	6.6	94.4	1.5	1.4	1.4	2.9	5.2	13.2	11.3	10.4	11.6	12.3
38075	33500	9	Renville	877.2	2,266	3,021	2.6	95.4	1.3	1.5	0.8	2.9	4.7	13.2	10.2	10.7	11.4	11.1
38077	47420	6	Richland	1,435.7	16,560	1,998	11.5	91.5	1.7	3.8	1.1	3.9	5.9	12.5	17.0	11.5	11.0	9.4
38079		9	Rolette	903.0	12,048	2,279	13.3	18.9	0.9	80.3	0.6	2.3	8.2	20.2	14.2	11.5	11.6	10.0
38081		9	Sargent	858.5	3,829	2,898	4.5	92.5	2.5	2.2	1.2	3.4	6.2	12.4	9.8	12.2	10.8	11.0
38083		9	Sheridan	972.2	1,268	3,094	1.3	95.6	1.1	2.7	1.2	2.0	5.8	9.5	7.6	8.5	9.7	10.4
38085		3	Sioux	1,094.1	3,738	2,905	3.4	14.4	1.7	81.6	0.9	5.3	9.0	21.4	16.9	11.1	10.2	11.8
38087		9	Slope	1,215.3	690	3,128	0.6	92.0	1.2	2.8	0.1	4.8	5.8	11.3	8.7	8.0	12.0	9.6
38089	19860	7	Stark	1,334.9	33,046	1,360	24.8	87.5	3.4	2.5	2.1	6.3	8.1	15.7	11.7	15.7	13.8	9.7
38091		8	Steele	712.1	1,810	3,059	2.5	95.7	0.8	1.9	0.3	2.4	6.0	13.1	9.2	9.8	9.9	10.6
38093	27420	7	Stutsman	2,221.9	21,576	1,732	9.7	92.3	2.2	2.8	1.3	3.0	5.4	11.7	13.6	12.2	12.3	10.9
38095		9	Towner	1,025.1	2,140	3,031	2.1	90.4	0.8	6.1	1.2	3.1	5.4	13.3	8.8	8.9	9.8	9.7
38097		8	Traill	861.9	8,003	2,577	9.3	93.3	1.5	2.2	1.1	3.6	5.8	13.6	12.7	11.7	10.9	11.1
38099		6	Walsh	1,281.6	10,469	2,377	8.2	83.9	1.0	2.6	1.3	12.6	6.0	13.2	11.3	10.0	11.1	11.2

1. CBSA = Core Based Statistical Area. See Appendix A for explanation. See Appendix B for list of metropolitan areas with component counties. 2. County type code from the Economic Research Service of USDA Rural-Urban Continuum Codes. See Appendix A for definition. 3. Dry land or land partially or temporarily covered by water. 4. May be of any race.

STATE County	Population, 2021 (cont.)				Population change, 2000–2021							Households, 2016–2020				
	Age (percent) (cont.)				Total persons		Percent change		Components of change, 2020–2021					Percent		
	55 to 64 years	65 to 74 years	75 years and over	Percent female	2010	2020	2010–2020	2020–2021	Births	Deaths	Net Migration	Number	Persons per household	Family house-holds	Female family house-holder[1]	One person
	16	17	18	19	20	21	22	23	24	25	26	27	28	29	30	31
NORTH CAROLINA—Cont'd																
Swain	13.5	11.5	7.5	51.8	13,981	14,117	1.0	0.1	190	312	141	5,741	2.4	67.3	14.5	30.5
Transylvania	15.6	17.4	13.9	51.5	33,090	32,986	-0.3	0.5	283	646	553	14,648	2.2	66.9	11.5	27.9
Tyrrell	14.9	12.7	8.9	44.9	4,407	3,245	-26.4	0.3	34	57	33	1,652	1.9	65.8	11.6	30.2
Union	12.6	8.2	5.0	50.4	201,292	238,267	18.4	2.3	2,843	2,447	5,008	77,791	3.0	79.8	9.7	16.6
Vance	13.5	11.7	7.6	53.1	45,422	42,578	-6.3	-0.9	659	776	-277	16,895	2.6	64.7	21.1	30.1
Wake	11.7	7.9	4.7	51.1	900,993	1,129,410	25.4	1.8	15,331	9,505	14,775	410,552	2.6	66.0	10.6	26.3
Warren	16.4	15.9	11.0	50.3	20,972	18,642	-11.1	0.6	197	380	310	8,122	2.3	61.7	19.6	35.9
Washington	15.6	16.2	10.5	52.8	13,228	11,003	-16.8	-1.0	144	253	-2	5,237	2.2	53.8	18.9	40.6
Watauga	12.2	11.0	6.4	50.2	51,079	54,086	5.9	0.3	374	632	399	21,453	2.3	51.9	5.5	31.0
Wayne	12.9	10.5	6.6	50.9	122,623	117,333	-4.3	-0.4	1,893	2,082	-326	48,198	2.5	66.7	16.8	28.8
Wilkes	15.0	13.2	9.3	50.6	69,340	65,969	-4.9	-0.2	807	1,270	298	28,902	2.3	66.6	10.7	27.9
Wilson	13.7	11.5	7.4	52.3	81,234	78,784	-3.0	-0.5	1,143	1,376	-189	31,968	2.5	64.6	16.5	31.0
Yadkin	15.3	12.1	8.6	50.1	38,406	37,214	-3.1	-0.1	447	684	215	15,247	2.4	67.8	9.3	28.9
Yancey	14.7	15.5	10.9	50.6	17,818	18,470	3.7	1.6	216	339	416	7,466	2.4	67.7	7.6	28.5
NORTH DAKOTA	11.9	9.5	6.6	48.6	672,591	779,094	15.8	-0.5	12,436	9,704	-6,828	320,873	2.3	59.0	7.5	32.5
Adams	15.8	16.0	13.2	50.2	2,343	2,200	-6.1	-1.5	29	31	-30	1,058	2.1	58.1	2.5	39.2
Barnes	14.3	13.3	9.8	49.0	11,066	10,853	-1.9	-0.4	118	198	33	5,039	2.0	57.5	6.8	35.7
Benson	11.5	9.6	5.2	48.9	6,660	5,964	-10.5	-2.6	154	109	-198	2,265	3.0	69.4	20.1	26.0
Billings	14.7	13.6	10.8	46.6	783	945	20.7	1.1	8	8	10	366	2.3	68.3	3.8	29.5
Bottineau	14.9	14.6	9.6	48.1	6,429	6,379	-0.8	0.2	74	105	44	2,876	2.1	61.4	5.1	32.4
Bowman	14.1	12.9	10.5	48.7	3,151	2,993	-5.0	-3.0	45	51	-84	1,323	2.3	59.7	6.7	35.5
Burke	15.3	12.7	8.9	47.0	1,968	2,201	11.8	-2.0	30	29	-43	950	2.3	64.1	5.6	34.0
Burleigh	12.3	10.2	7.0	49.7	81,308	98,458	21.1	0.5	1,407	1,253	300	39,805	2.3	63.1	8.9	29.8
Cass	10.0	7.9	4.9	49.2	149,778	184,525	23.2	1.1	2,934	1,796	854	77,027	2.3	55.9	7.1	32.7
Cavalier	15.1	14.7	12.5	47.5	3,993	3,704	-7.2	-1.1	50	67	-25	1,778	2.1	59.0	2.9	33.6
Dickey	13.6	11.2	10.6	49.5	5,289	4,999	-5.5	-2.0	74	103	-72	2,127	2.2	63.0	3.9	33.2
Divide	16.2	13.8	11.2	47.7	2,071	2,195	6.0	-0.3	31	27	-10	1,060	2.1	57.9	6.5	41.3
Dunn	14.4	11.0	6.3	45.9	3,536	4,095	15.8	-1.5	101	43	-117	1,700	2.5	64.6	4.5	30.6
Eddy	15.7	12.9	9.5	49.4	2,385	2,347	-1.6	-0.4	31	47	7	1,046	2.1	58.1	6.3	36.2
Emmons	17.2	14.9	13.1	48.0	3,550	3,301	-7.0	-0.9	42	67	-4	1,546	2.1	58.5	1.7	38.6
Foster	15.2	13.0	10.1	49.6	3,343	3,397	1.6	-1.0	50	59	-24	1,483	2.1	59.9	3.8	35.9
Golden Valley	15.5	16.0	11.4	50.2	1,680	1,736	3.3	2.0	22	16	28	814	2.1	58.1	3.1	36.2
Grand Forks	10.1	8.3	5.4	48.5	66,861	73,170	9.4	-0.6	1,089	748	-813	30,779	2.1	50.9	8.4	36.7
Grant	16.1	16.4	13.6	48.6	2,394	2,301	-3.9	1.0	29	38	33	1,082	2.1	58.6	3.8	38.1
Griggs	14.6	16.6	13.5	49.5	2,420	2,306	-4.7	-1.1	21	41	-4	1,031	2.2	60.4	3.2	38.0
Hettinger	14.5	12.4	10.9	50.9	2,477	2,489	0.5	-2.4	36	48	-47	1,093	2.1	60.9	7.8	37.0
Kidder	13.9	15.6	11.6	48.0	2,435	2,394	-1.7	-1.0	34	29	-30	1,123	2.2	63.0	4.1	35.7
LaMoure	16.1	14.4	13.3	48.4	4,139	4,093	-1.1	-0.7	52	62	-17	1,869	2.2	63.0	3.4	31.3
Logan	15.1	13.0	13.2	47.8	1,990	1,876	-5.7	0.4	30	26	4	812	2.1	64.3	2.7	30.3
McHenry	15.0	12.8	8.7	47.6	5,395	5,345	-0.9	-1.8	67	106	-57	2,562	2.2	66.9	5.8	28.6
McIntosh	17.4	13.4	16.4	49.8	2,809	2,530	-9.9	-0.7	31	69	23	1,292	1.9	54.7	5.7	39.2
McKenzie	10.3	6.4	3.4	46.7	6,360	14,704	131.2	-6.0	320	133	-1,053	4,478	3.0	58.3	9.3	31.0
McLean	15.4	15.1	9.6	48.8	8,962	9,771	9.0	0.3	118	157	65	4,372	2.2	66.4	5.4	30.4
Mercer	16.3	12.9	8.9	48.4	8,424	8,350	-0.9	-0.3	102	97	-33	3,663	2.2	69.4	5.7	25.0
Morton	12.8	10.2	6.9	49.3	27,471	33,291	21.2	1.0	527	462	254	13,502	2.3	65.5	7.5	24.3
Mountrail	11.6	7.8	3.8	46.0	7,673	9,809	27.8	-2.4	206	134	-302	3,570	2.9	65.5	9.0	30.2
Nelson	17.8	14.9	10.9	48.3	3,126	3,015	-3.6	1.3	28	64	77	1,428	2.0	54.2	3.7	42.1
Oliver	16.5	14.8	8.8	47.1	1,846	1,877	1.7	-0.2	21	17	-8	743	2.6	82.8	6.9	16.8
Pembina	15.6	14.6	10.3	47.0	7,413	6,844	-7.7	-1.1	92	118	-50	3,169	2.1	59.5	6.3	35.9
Pierce	14.6	12.5	11.7	49.5	4,357	3,990	-8.4	-0.9	42	75	-3	1,843	2.1	58.6	6.5	35.8
Ramsey	14.5	11.4	8.6	48.4	11,451	11,605	1.3	-0.3	176	216	7	4,903	2.2	55.3	5.6	39.6
Ransom	14.6	11.6	9.7	47.4	5,457	5,703	4.5	-0.5	59	105	17	2,380	2.2	60.4	4.4	36.5
Renville	16.8	13.0	8.9	47.1	2,470	2,282	-7.6	-0.7	19	33	-1	931	2.5	69.6	9.3	25.5
Richland	13.3	11.1	8.3	48.3	16,321	16,529	1.3	0.2	210	191	10	6,806	2.2	61.0	9.3	30.5
Rolette	12.2	8.0	4.1	50.2	13,937	12,187	-12.6	-1.1	267	244	-162	4,402	3.2	69.3	24.7	25.0
Sargent	14.9	13.4	9.3	46.3	3,829	3,862	0.9	-0.9	50	65	-18	1,897	2.0	62.2	5.5	31.6
Sheridan	14.7	15.9	18.0	48.7	1,321	1,265	-4.2	0.2	15	20	9	684	1.9	52.8	7.0	41.8
Sioux	10.9	5.5	3.2	50.5	4,153	3,898	-6.1	-4.1	79	87	-150	1,107	3.9	74.8	27.6	21.1
Slope	18.1	15.8	10.7	46.8	727	706	-2.9	-2.3	6	5	-16	336	2.4	70.8	6.0	28.3
Stark	11.5	7.7	6.1	48.0	24,199	33,646	39.0	-1.8	677	368	-895	12,635	2.4	60.4	6.5	32.4
Steele	15.2	15.9	10.3	47.0	1,975	1,798	-9.0	0.7	25	19	7	804	2.3	65.2	0.4	30.5
Stutsman	14.2	11.6	8.2	48.5	21,100	21,593	2.3	-0.1	249	341	75	8,977	2.1	52.1	7.2	41.6
Towner	17.9	15.0	11.2	47.9	2,246	2,162	-3.7	-1.0	27	38	-9	1,104	2.0	56.3	4.4	36.1
Traill	14.1	11.2	8.8	48.3	8,121	7,997	-1.5	0.1	114	127	19	3,394	2.2	63.9	7.3	32.5
Walsh	15.6	11.9	9.6	48.3	11,119	10,563	-5.0	-0.9	129	164	-60	4,820	2.1	59.7	5.6	33.9

1. No spouse present.

STATE County	Persons in group quarters, 2021	Daytime Population, 2016–2020: Number	Daytime Population, 2016–2020: Employment/ residence ratio	Births, 2021: Total	Births, 2021: Rate[1]	Deaths, 2021: Number	Deaths, 2021: Rate[1]	Persons under 65 with no health insurance, 2019: Number	Persons under 65 with no health insurance, 2019: Percent	Medicare, 2021: Total beneficiaries	Medicare, 2021: Enrolled in Original Medicare	Medicare, 2021: Enrolled in Medicare Advantage	COVID-19 Deaths, 2020: Number	COVID-19 Deaths, 2020: Rate[1]
	32	33	34	35	36	37	38	39	40	41	42	43	44	45
NORTH CAROLINA—Cont'd														
Swain	193	14,890	1.1	156	11.1	257	18.2	2,529	22.3	3,821	2,795	1,026	10	0.7
Transylvania	829	33,009	0.9	229	6.9	518	15.7	3,625	15.9	10,444	6,704	3,741	16	0.5
Tyrrell	299	3,941	1.0	28	8.6	44	13.6	416	16.3	858	631	227	D	D
Union	2,562	205,834	0.7	2,287	9.5	1,962	8.1	23,543	11.3	34,660	21,099	13,562	128	0.5
Vance	563	43,149	0.9	553	13.1	623	14.7	5,118	14.6	10,427	5,897	4,531	78	1.8
Wake	20,986	1,141,472	1.1	12,257	10.7	7,632	6.7	97,433	10.1	150,059	91,443	58,616	504	0.4
Warren	736	17,113	0.6	151	8.1	301	16.1	2,322	17.0	5,407	3,300	2,107	15	0.8
Washington	72	11,556	0.9	118	10.8	202	18.5	1,196	14.1	3,443	2,457	986	13	1.2
Watauga	5,424	58,452	1.1	307	5.7	497	9.2	5,399	13.1	9,485	6,256	3,230	25	0.5
Wayne	2,459	122,351	1.0	1,540	13.2	1,657	14.2	15,268	15.4	24,427	16,536	7,891	165	1.4
Wilkes	747	65,077	0.9	668	10.1	1,050	15.9	8,605	16.4	17,601	8,230	9,372	88	1.3
Wilson	1,221	86,579	1.1	906	11.5	1,123	14.3	10,451	16.1	18,033	12,458	5,575	129	1.6
Yadkin	207	33,796	0.8	365	9.8	543	14.6	4,551	15.3	9,007	3,500	5,507	44	1.2
Yancey	133	16,061	0.8	167	9.0	271	14.6	2,069	15.7	5,615	3,436	2,179	22	1.2
NORTH DAKOTA	23,791	790,646	1.1	9,798	12.6	7,588	9.8	45,186	7.2	134,282	107,530	26,753	1,247	1.6
Adams	38	2,246	1.0	23	10.6	23	10.6	149	9.5	682	588	94	D	D
Barnes	528	10,096	0.9	92	8.5	148	13.7	526	6.9	2,673	2,154	519	30	2.8
Benson	3	6,830	1.0	120	20.4	93	15.8	635	11.1	1,088	1,025	63	19	3.2
Billings	9	896	1.0	7	7.4	6	6.4	64	9.0	175	153	21	D	D
Bottineau	202	6,241	0.9	59	9.2	85	13.3	383	8.4	1,672	1,659	13	22	3.4
Bowman	45	3,145	1.0	37	12.6	43	14.6	236	10.0	743	659	84	D	D
Burke	2	2,005	0.9	24	11.0	17	7.8	113	6.8	501	D	D	D	D
Burleigh	3,821	99,381	1.1	1,111	11.3	965	9.8	4,333	5.6	17,722	12,997	4,725	185	1.9
Cass	5,235	196,882	1.2	2,278	12.3	1,422	7.7	9,575	6.2	25,974	19,411	6,563	176	1.0
Cavalier	58	3,713	1.0	39	10.6	53	14.4	173	6.3	1,052	935	117	D	D
Dickey	181	4,617	0.9	60	12.2	81	16.4	295	7.9	1,135	950	185	37	7.5
Divide	39	2,294	1.0	25	11.4	17	7.8	170	10.1	520	D	D	D	D
Dunn	77	5,145	1.4	81	19.9	31	7.6	426	11.5	746	641	104	D	D
Eddy	66	2,097	0.9	21	9.0	37	15.8	144	8.3	631	546	85	D	D
Emmons	45	3,201	1.0	36	11.0	49	15.0	268	11.6	948	710	238	12	3.7
Foster	53	3,555	1.2	35	10.4	48	14.2	158	6.4	750	605	145	21	6.2
Golden Valley	52	1,630	0.8	17	9.7	14	8.0	115	9.2	418	D	D	D	D
Grand Forks	3,038	73,475	1.1	861	11.8	572	7.8	3,661	6.4	10,827	8,664	2,163	72	1.0
Grant	4	2,362	1.0	26	11.3	27	11.7	210	13.5	682	536	146	D	D
Griggs	35	2,300	1.0	20	8.7	30	13.1	118	7.7	689	559	130	D	D
Hettinger	128	2,427	0.9	26	10.6	38	15.5	213	11.7	610	515	94	D	D
Kidder	0	2,293	0.8	30	12.6	23	9.7	189	10.3	653	436	217	D	D
LaMoure	51	4,138	1.0	38	9.3	45	11.0	317	10.9	1,086	808	278	15	3.7
Logan	49	1,737	1.0	21	11.1	21	11.1	182	13.7	522	401	121	D	D
McHenry	27	5,011	0.7	49	9.3	80	15.1	385	8.5	1,337	1,123	214	14	2.6
McIntosh	88	2,552	1.0	29	11.5	53	21.1	171	10.2	857	672	186	D	D
McKenzie	102	16,118	1.3	253	17.7	104	7.3	1,220	8.9	1,178	1,148	30	15	1.0
McLean	132	9,434	1.0	97	9.9	121	12.4	651	9.1	2,430	2,003	427	28	2.9
Mercer	107	9,190	1.2	86	10.3	77	9.2	335	5.1	1,852	1,453	399	D	D
Morton	778	26,280	0.7	413	12.3	375	11.2	1,635	6.3	6,146	4,248	1,898	64	1.9
Mountrail	417	11,844	1.3	169	17.5	83	8.6	1,337	14.4	1,461	1,443	19	20	2.0
Nelson	77	2,653	0.9	23	7.6	46	15.2	169	8.1	931	841	89	12	4.0
Oliver	1	1,984	1.0	16	8.6	12	6.4	118	7.8	424	326	98	D	D
Pembina	133	7,163	1.1	71	10.4	98	14.4	426	8.3	1,794	1,560	234	11	1.6
Pierce	222	4,056	1.0	29	7.3	57	14.4	192	6.7	1,063	872	191	22	5.5
Ramsey	380	11,616	1.0	139	12.0	159	13.8	647	7.3	2,658	2,429	230	23	2.0
Ransom	137	4,968	0.9	43	7.6	89	15.6	269	6.6	1,316	1,138	179	12	2.1
Renville	46	2,116	0.8	14	6.2	27	11.9	123	6.7	550	D	D	14	6.2
Richland	890	16,776	1.1	163	9.9	165	10.0	857	6.9	3,335	2,428	907	21	1.3
Rolette	49	14,451	1.0	218	18.0	199	16.4	1,657	13.6	2,273	2,226	47	25	2.1
Sargent	23	4,842	1.5	41	10.7	50	13.0	215	7.2	936	839	97	D	D
Sheridan	1	1,203	0.9	12	9.5	17	13.5	107	12.4	422	338	83	D	D
Sioux	20	4,873	1.4	59	15.5	72	18.9	460	12.3	422	397	25	11	2.8
Slope	0	733	0.9	6	8.6	2	2.9	64	11.3	179	154	25	D	D
Stark	529	32,150	1.1	535	16.0	300	9.0	1,759	6.5	4,777	4,115	662	50	1.5
Steele	0	1,694	0.9	18	10.0	16	8.9	66	4.7	474	395	79	D	D
Stutsman	1,669	21,192	1.0	199	9.2	276	12.8	1,014	6.7	4,842	3,192	1,650	65	3.0
Towner	29	2,220	1.0	24	11.2	28	13.1	173	10.7	587	547	40	11	5.1
Traill	265	7,564	0.9	94	11.8	101	12.6	374	6.0	1,706	1,442	263	15	1.9
Walsh	296	10,759	1.0	102	9.7	129	12.3	794	9.6	2,574	2,211	363	23	2.2

1. Per 1,000 estimated resident population.

STATE County	COVID-19 Vaccinations, 2021–2022: Number	COVID-19 Vaccinations, 2021–2022: Percent[5]	Education: School enrollment and attainment, 2016–2020: Enrollment[1]: Total	Enrollment[1]: Percent private	Attainment[2] (percent): High school graduate or less	Attainment[2] (percent): Bachelor's degree or more	Local government expenditures,[3] 2018–2019: Total current spending (mil dol)	Current spending per student (dollars)	Money income, 2016–2020: Per capita income[4]	Households: Median income (dollars)	Households: Percent with income of less than $50,000	Households: Percent with income of $200,000 or more	Income and poverty, 2020: Median household income (dollars)	Percent below poverty level: All persons	Percent below poverty level: Children under 18 years	Percent below poverty level: Children 5 to 17 years in families
	46	47	48	49	50	51	52	53	54	55	56	57	58	59	60	61
NORTH CAROLINA—Cont'd																
Swain	8,264	57.9	3,060	6.0	46.6	20.6	24.9	11,193	24,234	45,554	52.8	1.2	47,559	13.9	20.9	19.2
Transylvania	19,404	56.4	6,017	21.8	33.7	33.8	43.2	11,354	30,577	51,509	48.8	4.1	56,880	12.6	20.6	19.9
Tyrrell	1,968	49.0	642	12.8	60.8	10.6	9.8	14,998	21,129	38,250	56.5	1.2	42,260	20.8	29.4	28.8
Union	133,985	55.9	67,405	17.3	34.0	36.0	417.6	9,308	37,667	82,557	28.8	12.7	90,920	7.0	8.4	7.1
Vance	25,590	57.5	10,302	14.3	51.8	17.5	81.2	10,279	23,911	41,827	58.1	1.7	41,935	21.3	30.0	24.8
Wake	821,162	73.9	292,456	18.5	21.3	54.0	1,645.2	9,314	42,721	83,567	28.9	12.3	88,763	7.4	8.3	7.9
Warren	11,018	55.8	3,665	15.0	54.5	15.3	28.0	13,101	25,340	37,476	61.4	2.8	42,808	22.8	33.3	31.4
Washington	5,846	50.5	2,689	4.9	51.7	12.8	19.2	14,127	23,249	30,941	68.4	2.2	38,704	24.3	37.8	37.2
Watauga	31,396	55.9	21,132	6.5	30.4	42.7	51.3	10,517	27,962	46,453	53.0	5.5	54,004	15.8	12.9	11.8
Wayne	60,322	49.0	30,727	13.4	44.8	19.8	185.8	9,562	26,362	47,221	52.5	3.0	52,906	14.9	23.2	23.4
Wilkes	32,257	47.2	13,604	11.6	50.0	16.0	93.3	9,700	25,634	44,980	55.2	2.5	46,830	14.4	20.1	18.1
Wilson	44,156	54.0	19,561	15.2	51.0	20.0	120.2	9,223	24,656	44,594	54.3	3.0	44,089	21.2	32.8	32.8
Yadkin	18,755	49.8	7,390	11.9	50.3	12.9	51.9	9,693	26,907	46,954	52.3	4.3	53,154	12.1	16.8	14.8
Yancey	9,340	51.7	3,104	8.9	48.4	20.3	23.8	11,094	25,767	44,554	54.0	2.3	48,662	14.9	22.2	21.7
NORTH DAKOTA	418,277	54.9	185,329	11.5	33.0	30.7	1,593.7	13,998	36,289	65,315	37.9	6.0	64,289	10.2	10.9	9.4
Adams	1,072	48.4	459	7.2	43.4	23.5	4.3	15,115	31,022	48,750	51.0	2.7	50,673	10.8	11.4	10.7
Barnes	5,948	57.1	2,369	10.2	35.6	30.4	20.8	15,442	34,334	60,472	42.5	3.8	52,327	9.9	11.2	9.8
Benson	3,532	51.7	2,015	0.9	43.5	17.2	19.9	19,222	21,629	50,329	49.7	4.8	51,189	24.2	34.5	31.4
Billings	195	21.0	176	0.0	46.0	26.2	2.5	29,800	38,113	64,896	29.2	6.6	76,478	10.0	13.6	14.3
Bottineau	3,138	50.0	1,469	7.7	34.4	25.1	15.0	16,932	37,339	65,074	36.2	5.7	61,841	9.7	11.2	10.0
Bowman	1,161	38.4	589	1.4	46.1	19.5	9.3	15,071	36,739	70,521	31.8	3.7	67,067	8.9	11.6	10.2
Burke	826	39.1	472	5.9	34.2	21.6	7.2	19,434	43,862	79,405	30.2	9.9	73,567	7.9	10.4	10.3
Burleigh	48,165	50.4	22,115	21.7	28.0	36.5	166.8	12,420	39,509	72,974	32.2	6.8	72,170	8.6	9.4	8.1
Cass	109,057	59.9	48,937	11.3	23.9	40.8	338.3	13,373	37,784	65,976	36.6	7.3	61,338	9.7	8.5	6.9
Cavalier	2,257	60.0	672	4.8	33.4	22.8	8.5	17,584	43,386	54,955	43.0	8.2	54,270	8.5	12.2	11.9
Dickey	2,569	52.7	1,032	16.3	34.2	27.7	9.5	11,405	34,263	64,521	38.0	5.7	60,682	10.2	11.6	10.0
Divide	928	41.0	407	1.5	37.7	16.2	6.0	16,634	39,464	64,650	36.9	6.4	64,594	10.7	12.1	11.2
Dunn	1,084	24.5	941	14.6	44.0	19.1	10.5	16,020	45,782	82,750	30.7	10.3	73,722	10.0	14.0	12.4
Eddy	1,173	51.3	356	3.4	40.3	22.3	6.4	19,245	34,614	52,895	48.5	4.3	54,285	11.2	14.6	13.6
Emmons	1,103	34.0	506	5.7	46.6	19.4	9.1	17,305	32,294	51,012	48.9	4.3	49,972	13.7	19.0	17.1
Foster	1,739	54.2	650	2.8	33.5	25.3	6.4	12,848	38,329	61,250	41.6	10.0	63,234	7.9	9.1	8.2
Golden Valley	532	30.2	281	9.6	34.2	24.1	5.8	18,497	37,890	72,308	36.6	4.3	57,596	11.0	15.5	15.0
Grand Forks	40,609	58.5	22,060	7.5	26.5	36.2	123.6	13,429	32,251	53,721	46.3	4.0	55,495	12.7	10.8	8.9
Grant	526	23.1	421	10.9	44.3	19.0	4.2	19,267	34,059	53,750	48.2	4.6	48,063	13.5	26.6	22.8
Griggs	1,030	46.2	389	6.9	36.3	27.5	6.6	15,214	38,386	53,917	45.0	7.6	53,751	9.6	12.1	10.6
Hettinger	975	39.0	403	6.5	45.8	15.6	7.5	14,856	35,683	59,750	44.1	5.6	53,222	11.6	18.1	17.6
Kidder	818	33.0	460	3.5	46.8	17.2	5.9	15,256	30,567	52,063	48.5	2.9	49,386	13.5	19.5	18.5
LaMoure	1,948	48.1	871	12.4	41.2	25.1	13.0	15,617	35,278	61,477	38.8	4.5	58,302	10.9	12.0	10.6
Logan	687	37.1	257	5.4	43.8	21.7	5.9	16,994	32,947	60,592	43.6	3.7	47,908	14.5	22.1	20.8
McHenry	2,392	41.6	1,217	3.3	40.8	20.4	14.6	14,950	35,125	67,039	38.4	5.6	59,052	12.0	15.7	13.0
McIntosh	1,087	43.5	367	1.6	49.4	14.9	6.4	16,348	33,281	51,136	49.2	3.0	48,839	12.2	14.6	13.4
McKenzie	3,309	22.0	3,704	11.2	39.9	26.8	30.7	12,717	36,414	75,238	29.2	8.4	84,705	7.5	8.2	7.0
McLean	4,355	46.1	1,851	4.5	41.5	21.1	24.6	14,548	37,651	70,261	34.3	4.8	70,835	8.4	10.6	9.2
Mercer	3,149	38.5	1,691	9.1	35.8	20.9	16.9	12,996	39,745	82,087	32.4	5.2	79,608	8.0	7.6	6.6
Morton	14,085	44.9	6,125	10.1	35.8	27.3	64.5	13,159	38,890	72,778	34.2	4.9	71,928	8.3	9.4	9.0
Mountrail	4,446	42.2	2,511	5.1	43.3	21.5	30.0	14,854	34,954	70,412	36.3	7.7	68,465	11.0	14.6	13.6
Nelson	2,035	70.7	468	4.9	36.8	26.2	7.7	16,923	34,189	53,063	48.5	3.8	53,008	9.8	11.8	10.0
Oliver	501	25.6	405	5.7	36.1	19.6	3.8	15,626	32,784	66,641	34.5	3.4	66,708	10.7	20.0	17.5
Pembina	3,779	55.6	1,197	15.0	41.0	21.5	19.1	15,955	35,096	60,910	40.5	3.4	61,595	7.6	8.2	7.6
Pierce	1,796	45.2	769	9.2	37.6	27.9	9.0	13,433	31,582	57,398	42.7	3.0	50,827	11.0	12.3	9.8
Ramsey	6,510	56.5	2,750	14.5	35.1	26.3	30.0	16,373	33,797	52,688	45.6	4.6	57,984	12.2	16.6	15.1
Ransom	3,078	59.0	999	4.6	44.9	20.5	11.8	12,698	34,842	62,235	39.1	2.7	65,039	9.3	10.8	9.1
Renville	897	38.5	501	5.2	40.3	22.6	8.9	14,713	34,411	69,848	31.6	2.9	67,054	7.7	7.3	6.4
Richland	8,251	51.0	4,184	5.8	33.7	22.2	34.5	15,143	32,008	60,833	43.1	4.2	65,530	9.4	10.7	9.3
Rolette	9,796	69.1	4,020	2.1	36.1	19.0	49.7	16,506	20,424	46,481	51.8	2.6	45,178	21.3	26.7	21.4
Sargent	2,281	58.5	636	3.8	42.2	18.6	10.8	17,894	38,042	64,564	34.2	3.2	68,769	7.4	10.0	9.2
Sheridan	478	36.3	148	3.4	54.3	14.9	2.5	21,368	35,335	54,250	45.2	3.5	46,424	16.6	27.7	25.9
Sioux	2,572	60.8	1,307	5.7	48.1	14.5	11.0	27,309	17,460	41,893	55.9	6.5	36,182	28.3	32.9	27.3
Slope	83	11.1	156	1.3	37.8	25.9	0.4	29,133	36,040	65,833	37.2	6.5	53,330	13.5	22.6	21.6
Stark	11,402	36.2	7,125	18.9	40.4	24.5	61.8	12,801	37,780	69,412	33.5	7.5	66,105	10.0	8.5	7.7
Steele	884	46.8	346	0.0	27.9	28.3	3.9	27,000	38,907	77,167	30.1	4.4	68,163	7.9	12.6	12.1
Stutsman	10,946	52.9	4,612	26.6	43.7	24.1	38.9	14,793	31,461	52,815	46.7	3.6	59,948	10.6	10.5	9.0
Towner	1,028	47.0	306	2.3	40.7	14.5	3.6	11,967	36,427	49,464	50.3	5.2	57,509	9.8	16.9	14.5
Traill	4,320	53.8	1,891	4.9	32.6	30.1	20.3	14,753	34,065	67,604	35.8	3.6	70,384	7.0	8.1	7.0
Walsh	6,162	57.9	2,068	3.3	46.9	17.4	26.8	15,747	34,441	55,428	43.5	5.1	57,557	10.6	12.3	9.7

1. All persons 3 years old and over enrolled in nursery school through college. 2. Persons 25 years old and over. 3. Elementary and secondary education expenditures. 4. Based on population estimated by the American Community Survey, 2016–2020. 5. CDC percent based on 2019 population estimate.

STATE County	Personal income, 2020: Total (mil dol)	Personal income, 2020: Percent change 2019–2020	Per capita[1]: Dollars	Per capita[1]: Rank	Wages and salaries (mil dol)	Supplements to wages and salaries, employer contributions (mil dol): Pension and insurance	Supplements to wages and salaries, employer contributions (mil dol): Government social insurance	Proprietors' income (mil dol)	Dividends, interest, and rent (mil dol)	Personal transfer reecipts (mil dol)	Earnings, 2020: Total (mil dol)	Contributions for government social insurance (mil dol): From employee and self-employed	Contributions for government social insurance (mil dol): From employer
	62	63	64	65	66	67	68	69	70	71	72	73	74
NORTH CAROLINA—Cont'd													
Swain	627	7.3	44,213	1,909	271	45	20	26	100	235	363	27	20
Transylvania	1,544	4.6	44,747	1,837	398	68	30	116	431	492	612	52	30
Tyrrell	142	10.5	37,638	2,721	38	9	3	19	20	48	68	4	3
Union	13,896	6.2	56,820	584	3,422	517	250	916	1,967	2,164	5,105	340	250
Vance	1,689	8.0	37,774	2,707	589	95	44	66	247	680	795	64	44
Wake	74,107	6.3	65,450	252	40,638	5,033	2,798	4,786	13,606	9,614	53,255	3,283	2,798
Warren	659	10.5	33,779	2,991	124	28	9	19	96	267	180	17	9
Washington	458	7.1	39,912	2,464	112	23	9	14	71	195	158	15	9
Watauga	2,266	4.2	40,157	2,440	1,010	186	73	202	565	535	1,471	98	73
Wayne	5,316	6.9	42,882	2,080	2,171	454	171	366	814	1,589	3,163	201	171
Wilkes	2,689	5.5	39,518	2,500	905	152	68	184	472	961	1,309	103	68
Wilson	3,534	7.3	43,111	2,048	1,876	298	134	213	460	1,166	2,521	172	134
Yadkin	1,552	5.8	41,250	2,294	404	67	30	73	210	502	574	49	30
Yancey	732	6.6	40,422	2,400	192	36	15	40	139	270	283	26	15
NORTH DAKOTA	47,089	6.0	60,451	X	23,385	3,641	1,920	6,066	9,585	8,597	35,012	2,119	1,920
Adams	130	17.9	59,255	466	42	7	4	16	22	40	69	5	4
Barnes	668	12.6	64,242	284	204	36	19	146	134	148	405	21	19
Benson	304	22.9	45,003	1,791	90	19	8	74	49	86	191	9	8
Billings	73	-4.0	82,466	67	25	5	2	15	27	8	47	2	2
Bottineau	431	10.9	68,631	184	112	21	10	103	90	91	246	13	10
Bowman	206	-0.7	68,963	179	67	10	6	41	49	40	123	8	6
Burke	164	0.2	77,237	93	40	9	3	47	37	25	99	5	3
Burleigh	6,042	3.1	62,801	321	3,123	466	252	486	1,253	1,042	4,326	282	252
Cass	11,383	5.1	61,899	352	6,787	947	545	933	2,587	1,676	9,212	581	545
Cavalier	329	37.3	88,702	44	70	12	6	144	55	53	232	8	6
Dickey	338	10.1	71,888	138	76	13	7	93	85	68	189	9	7
Divide	141	12.5	62,052	346	39	7	3	33	40	30	83	4	3
Dunn	306	3.0	68,491	186	146	22	11	47	88	48	226	14	11
Eddy	163	19.7	74,844	107	30	5	3	54	23	36	92	4	3
Emmons	205	24.0	64,430	280	40	8	4	67	42	46	119	6	4
Foster	242	21.2	76,313	97	78	12	7	100	36	39	197	11	7
Golden Valley	81	17.3	46,435	1,588	26	5	2	13	25	18	45	3	2
Grand Forks	4,006	7.7	57,659	533	2,129	387	181	410	779	726	3,107	184	181
Grant	128	24.3	57,761	528	26	5	2	38	26	34	71	3	2
Griggs	163	24.9	73,753	119	39	6	4	57	31	37	106	5	4
Hettinger	145	14.2	59,519	451	37	7	3	33	34	33	80	5	3
Kidder	160	21.1	64,918	266	30	5	3	50	31	34	88	4	3
LaMoure	284	16.5	70,351	163	56	11	5	102	62	51	174	7	5
Logan	113	17.9	59,859	434	22	4	2	33	26	28	62	3	2
McHenry	338	11.7	59,320	462	63	13	5	73	51	74	155	9	5
McIntosh	173	14.6	70,812	155	42	8	4	46	37	48	100	6	4
McKenzie	976	-4.2	64,035	290	816	106	60	109	279	125	1,091	66	60
McLean	622	7.5	66,025	241	226	45	18	119	127	138	409	26	18
Mercer	495	2.0	60,497	407	288	68	22	33	86	104	411	26	22
Morton	1,818	6.0	57,708	530	632	107	57	158	299	363	955	67	57
Mountrail	682	-1.0	64,982	263	364	50	28	99	197	112	541	34	28
Nelson	212	20.3	75,907	104	39	7	3	60	38	54	109	5	3
Oliver	100	12.2	52,076	931	59	13	5	13	18	21	90	5	5
Pembina	485	17.8	72,827	127	181	31	17	124	96	95	353	17	17
Pierce	225	16.2	57,159	562	77	13	7	49	35	62	147	9	7
Ramsey	652	13.1	57,250	556	254	45	21	115	118	160	435	26	21
Ransom	337	9.3	65,153	258	91	16	9	72	54	81	188	11	9
Renville	184	10.3	80,431	74	34	6	3	57	33	34	100	4	3
Richland	880	3.8	54,465	745	357	59	31	100	181	186	546	35	31
Rolette	593	14.0	41,884	2,219	190	51	16	65	76	230	322	18	16
Sargent	263	6.2	67,215	206	176	32	16	56	58	49	280	15	16
Sheridan	75	23.0	58,958	481	9	2	1	30	13	19	41	2	1
Sioux	141	17.0	33,675	2,995	75	19	6	17	21	59	117	6	6
Slope	45	31.9	60,039	425	10	2	1	15	11	8	28	1	1
Stark	2,044	-1.5	63,650	300	1,133	152	90	241	337	348	1,616	105	90
Steele	160	34.1	84,674	62	34	5	3	65	34	21	107	3	3
Stutsman	1,285	13.6	62,694	324	502	85	43	257	219	288	886	51	43
Towner	185	43.4	87,632	47	32	6	3	86	26	35	127	4	3
Traill	510	15.5	64,096	288	169	29	15	124	85	103	336	18	15
Walsh	666	19.8	63,790	295	223	37	21	163	117	151	445	23	21

1. Based on the resident population estimated as of July 1 of the year shown.

STATE County	Earnings, 2020 (cont.)									Social Security beneficiaries, December 2020		Supple-mental Security Income recipients, 2020	Housing units, 2021	
	Percent by selected industries													
	Farm	Mining, quarrying, and extractions	Construction	Manu-facturing	Information; professional, scientific, technical services	Retail trade	Finance, insurance, real estate, and leasing	Health care and social assistance	Govern-ment	Number	Rate[1]		Total	Percent change, 2010–2021
	75	76	77	78	79	80	81	82	83	84	85	86	87	88
NORTH CAROLINA—Cont'd														
Swain	0.7	0.0	5.4	D	1.7	5.5	2.0	D	52.4	4,455	315	344	8,447	1.0
Transylvania	1.0	D	11.5	7.9	8.0	9.8	7.9	13.7	15.9	10,660	321	584	19,039	-0.1
Tyrrell	24.8	0.0	6.0	5.4	D	5.3	D	D	34.4	940	289	122	2,004	0.2
Union	1.3	D	19.0	16.9	6.7	6.8	4.5	4.7	13.2	37,000	152	2,377	86,433	2.7
Vance	-0.1	D	3.9	12.4	4.5	10.3	5.5	14.7	17.4	11,780	279	2,217	19,363	0.4
Wake	0.1	-0.1	7.1	4.6	24.7	5.5	9.4	9.4	12.9	154,440	134	12,117	476,870	2.6
Warren	1.2	0.0	7.5	9.2	D	6.3	4.5	4.4	39.7	5,040	269	794	11,408	0.8
Washington	3.3	0.0	D	13.1	4.1	7.0	3.3	D	25.4	3,765	346	646	6,043	0.1
Watauga	0.3	0.1	6.3	1.8	6.6	9.5	8.3	17.3	28.7	9,985	184	563	32,923	0.6
Wayne	2.4	D	5.2	11.2	2.8	7.4	5.3	10.7	33.5	26,615	228	3,924	53,035	0.8
Wilkes	2.1	D	5.9	18.0	D	9.4	5.1	11.6	16.1	20,040	305	1,901	31,679	0.4
Wilson	1.8	D	10.4	23.0	6.2	6.7	6.2	9.0	12.3	21,460	274	2,947	36,634	1.0
Yadkin	1.5	0.0	13.7	24.1	D	5.9	2.5	5.6	16.7	9,890	266	763	17,113	0.9
Yancey	1.5	D	11.6	25.1	3.4	8.8	2.6	7.5	19.9	6,180	329	529	11,292	0.4
NORTH DAKOTA	8.0	6.1	7.4	6.0	6.4	5.9	7.2	12.8	17.2	138,461	179	8,304	374,447	0.9
Adams	6.9	D	7.1	7.2	D	10.4	4.7	28.4	9.6	660	305	20	1,363	-0.1
Barnes	30.0	D	5.3	9.8	3.7	4.0	3.5	11.0	16.2	2,745	254	126	5,675	0.1
Benson	35.5	0.1	6.3	D	D	0.9	D	1.1	40.2	1,225	211	162	2,546	0.2
Billings	15.3	D	D	D	D	D	0.5	D	30.4	165	173	D	571	0.7
Bottineau	31.1	9.5	5.8	2.6	3.0	4.9	4.8	D	16.2	1,695	265	43	3,945	0.3
Bowman	17.7	3.2	9.0	3.7	4.9	6.1	D	10.5	11.5	735	253	27	1,633	0.0
Burke	34.3	D	2.0	2.8	D	3.7	D	0.4	23.1	510	236	11	1,378	0.0
Burleigh	1.2	1.5	6.2	2.0	8.8	7.2	7.8	20.3	21.6	18,360	186	909	43,304	1.2
Cass	1.5	D	7.4	7.7	11.3	6.8	11.7	18.0	12.3	26,730	143	2,051	87,247	1.9
Cavalier	55.4	D	4.8	D	D	3.3	D	4.3	7.5	1,060	289	17	2,102	0.1
Dickey	40.6	0.0	2.3	6.3	D	4.2	D	9.0	8.6	1,160	237	56	2,389	0.3
Divide	28.3	D	D	D	D	2.9	D	D	17.2	520	238	15	1,397	0.0
Dunn	4.6	34.4	13.3	3.2	D	2.9	1.5	2.7	11.1	765	190	25	2,125	0.8
Eddy	52.0	D	3.9	D	D	3.7	D	9.5	9.5	620	265	33	1,239	0.0
Emmons	41.0	0.0	D	D	2.1	5.1	D	8.2	12.3	1,000	306	33	2,058	0.5
Foster	22.5	1.2	4.8	D	D	6.7	4.7	8.8	7.5	765	227	24	1,781	0.4
Golden Valley	7.4	D	D	D	D	6.5	5.0	14.6	17.0	420	237	14	903	0.4
Grand Forks	5.0	0.4	6.7	5.6	5.5	7.5	5.4	16.4	27.4	11,275	155	750	33,846	1.2
Grant	49.7	0.4	2.0	2.1	D	2.3	3.9	12.1	11.1	660	284	23	1,658	0.5
Griggs	45.9	0.2	3.4	5.2	D	4.4	D	D	8.4	660	289	26	1,376	-0.1
Hettinger	30.9	0.3	5.9	D	D	2.6	4.7	4.4	13.8	640	263	20	1,397	-0.1
Kidder	49.0	D	2.8	2.8	D	3.2	D	1.7	8.9	660	279	23	1,634	0.2
LaMoure	52.0	0.1	2.4	2.1	D	1.7	6.4	D	10.6	1,050	258	57	2,062	0.0
Logan	48.0	0.0	D	D	D	2.9	3.3	7.7	13.3	520	276	20	1,078	0.0
McHenry	32.6	2.9	D	D	D	3.1	3.5	3.0	12.9	1,320	251	36	2,822	0.1
McIntosh	33.8	0.0	4.7	2.6	D	5.2	D	15.7	9.8	860	342	26	1,701	-0.1
McKenzie	0.9	22.6	D	D	3.8	2.3	6.3	2.2	16.6	1,255	91	54	7,738	0.9
McLean	11.2	D	4.9	7.1	D	2.4	4.3	D	13.1	2,600	265	89	5,766	0.6
Mercer	2.6	21.1	6.8	0.3	3.1	3.1	2.6	D	7.4	2,075	249	44	4,659	0.0
Morton	3.1	2.1	10.8	12.0	D	6.5	6.9	8.7	12.1	6,335	188	308	15,346	1.2
Mountrail	2.9	28.2	D	D	D	4.4	D	D	11.5	1,510	158	59	5,079	1.0
Nelson	47.8	0.0	6.0	0.5	0.7	2.1	D	10.7	11.5	955	313	36	1,789	-0.1
Oliver	11.6	D	4.3	1.1	D	D	D	D	6.4	485	259	D	914	0.1
Pembina	31.7	0.2	5.7	14.0	D	2.7	D	4.1	17.1	1,860	275	45	3,502	0.1
Pierce	20.5	D	9.2	D	2.0	5.5	D	D	9.8	1,065	269	34	2,042	0.1
Ramsey	15.1	D	4.2	4.2	3.6	8.5	7.8	D	21.8	2,725	235	182	5,866	0.4
Ransom	26.1	D	3.0	8.5	D	3.8	7.3	D	14.5	1,325	233	46	2,539	0.1
Renville	52.2	2.3	D	D	2.4	3.6	D	3.3	13.2	565	249	D	1,282	0.0
Richland	8.3	D	6.5	24.5	4.3	6.1	5.7	D	19.4	3,475	210	167	7,531	0.3
Rolette	12.9	D	4.1	D	0.9	4.5	D	D	59.3	2,505	208	755	4,589	0.2
Sargent	17.6	D	4.1	D	D	1.8	D	1.2	5.7	975	255	31	2,003	0.0
Sheridan	63.0	0.4	3.1	D	D	D	D	D	11.9	410	323	23	813	0.4
Sioux	14.5	0.0	0.3	-0.1	D	D	D	D	78.4	530	142	168	1,278	0.1
Slope	32.5	26.0	D	0.6	1.4	D	0.9	0.8	7.6	155	225	D	411	0.5
Stark	1.1	18.8	12.3	9.2	4.3	6.2	5.6	7.6	10.2	4,895	148	249	15,460	0.4
Steele	58.7	0.0	7.4	5.8	D	2.8	D	D	6.2	495	273	D	1,096	0.5
Stutsman	18.7	0.0	4.4	10.5	3.5	8.2	6.3	D	15.0	4,965	230	321	10,382	0.1
Towner	62.7	0.2	D	D	D	1.7	4.1	D	6.1	635	297	14	1,288	-0.1
Traill	24.4	D	5.4	13.9	1.5	2.9	3.7	D	14.1	1,745	218	62	3,662	0.3
Walsh	30.7	D	3.4	10.0	3.2	3.1	4.4	D	14.7	2,595	248	117	5,199	0.0

1. Per 1,000 resident population estimated as of July 1 of the year shown.

STATE County	Housing units, 2016–2020								Civilian labor force, 2021				Civilian employment[6], 2016–2020		
	Occupied units										Unemployment			Percent	
		Owner-occupied				Renter-occupied									
				Median owner cost as a percent of income											
	Total	Percent	Median value[1]	With a mortgage	Without a mortgage[2]	Median rent[3]	Median rent as a percent of income[2]	Sub-standard units[4] (percent)	Total	Percent change, 2020–2021	Total	Rate[5]	Total	Management, business, science, and arts	Construction, production, and maintenance occupations
	89	90	91	92	93	94	95	96	97	98	99	100	101	102	103
NORTH CAROLINA—Cont'd															
Swain	5,741	74.8	149,300	20.1	10.0	616	24.3	4.4	6,833	1.3	308	4.5	5,898	30.2	22.4
Transylvania	14,648	75.6	231,300	21.4	10.3	731	28.3	3.1	14,101	2.5	577	4.1	14,206	34.4	22.0
Tyrrell	1,652	72.9	110,900	23.0	13.2	668	24.3	1.3	1,283	4.0	90	7.0	1,497	24.3	26.7
Union	77,791	82.7	254,100	19.3	10.0	1,078	25.8	2.4	122,890	2.9	4,802	3.9	116,497	42.4	21.5
Vance	16,895	58.0	103,700	21.1	11.2	689	29.1	2.4	16,724	1.1	1,323	7.9	19,101	27.3	31.0
Wake	410,552	63.9	301,600	18.4	10.0	1,204	27.3	2.1	594,675	3.9	23,646	4.0	579,420	53.4	13.0
Warren	8,122	71.7	89,500	23.0	12.7	634	30.3	2.6	6,437	1.8	496	7.7	7,557	27.8	34.9
Washington	5,237	63.5	86,400	24.2	15.0	621	33.1	3.2	4,273	0.6	296	6.9	4,155	20.5	35.7
Watauga	21,453	60.9	246,000	21.1	10.0	925	40.7	1.8	28,395	4.8	1,039	3.7	26,959	38.4	15.7
Wayne	48,198	62.9	125,900	19.8	10.7	784	29.0	3.0	50,451	1.5	2,535	5.0	53,058	29.6	30.0
Wilkes	28,902	75.9	129,200	19.6	10.6	642	29.7	1.6	27,164	-1.1	1,279	4.7	29,631	28.5	33.7
Wilson	31,968	60.4	127,100	20.5	11.8	744	29.2	3.3	33,434	-0.4	2,251	6.7	35,078	32.8	30.2
Yadkin	15,247	76.5	138,500	18.9	10.0	632	30.8	3.1	17,084	1.4	722	4.2	16,689	30.2	34.4
Yancey	7,466	72.9	166,900	20.0	10.0	642	24.5	2.2	7,992	0.9	343	4.3	7,343	31.6	30.9
NORTH DAKOTA	320,873	62.5	199,900	18.7	10.0	828	24.4	2.6	406,187	-1.3	14,932	3.7	401,579	38.3	24.7
Adams	1,058	72.6	95,600	20.3	10.0	587	24.5	2.3	967	-4.4	33	3.4	1,128	36.4	28.2
Barnes	5,039	70.6	138,300	16.6	10.0	732	20.0	0.4	5,273	1.2	162	3.1	5,657	34.9	27.8
Benson	2,265	72.3	79,800	14.9	10.0	443	19.8	9.8	2,300	-0.9	114	5.0	2,317	40.0	22.4
Billings	366	76.8	232,400	20.8	10.0	0	21.3	0.8	444	1.1	13	2.9	447	40.9	29.5
Bottineau	2,876	78.6	157,300	18.2	10.0	685	20.7	1.2	2,976	-0.3	142	4.8	3,166	37.2	26.7
Bowman	1,323	81.0	154,300	16.9	10.0	732	21.4	1.7	1,581	-3.3	39	2.5	1,560	36.3	30.2
Burke	950	78.6	114,100	13.3	10.0	682	15.8	2.4	1,046	0.7	45	4.3	1,070	40.1	27.4
Burleigh	39,805	69.8	266,800	19.3	10.0	880	24.8	1.7	51,696	0.8	1,616	3.1	50,509	42.5	20.4
Cass	77,027	52.5	234,100	18.9	10.0	830	25.1	2.4	107,219	0.9	3,103	2.9	105,308	42.2	19.7
Cavalier	1,778	80.3	108,600	20.2	10.0	592	28.2	2.8	1,870	-2.3	58	3.1	1,875	37.9	30.2
Dickey	2,127	75.3	129,600	14.7	10.1	640	19.9	0.9	2,265	-2.2	61	2.7	2,496	36.0	30.3
Divide	1,060	74.4	124,900	15.0	10.0	913	20.8	0.0	1,434	-0.8	35	2.4	1,061	36.3	32.3
Dunn	1,700	73.5	213,600	17.8	10.0	1,017	17.0	2.8	3,096	-2.1	102	3.3	2,068	31.6	39.8
Eddy	1,046	67.1	92,300	14.4	10.0	639	30.1	1.1	1,188	-1.5	47	4.0	1,138	43.7	20.0
Emmons	1,546	80.5	94,500	15.3	10.0	455	27.0	1.2	1,490	-0.3	69	4.6	1,515	41.7	26.3
Foster	1,483	72.6	151,200	21.1	10.0	598	26.4	1.6	1,510	-3.3	42	2.8	1,763	41.8	22.6
Golden Valley	814	75.9	113,700	16.8	10.0	689	22.8	2.7	838	-3.1	23	2.7	979	34.1	26.5
Grand Forks	30,779	48.6	208,200	19.8	10.0	828	28.1	2.8	37,114	-0.5	1,188	3.2	38,433	37.9	20.3
Grant	1,082	87.9	75,600	20.0	10.0	527	19.9	1.8	1,233	2.6	33	2.7	1,066	50.8	23.4
Griggs	1,031	79.9	100,900	18.9	10.0	565	16.5	0.5	1,026	-0.1	29	2.8	1,154	43.2	25.0
Hettinger	1,093	78.2	109,500	19.9	10.0	729	25.3	1.6	1,392	-0.4	45	3.2	1,153	35.7	31.0
Kidder	1,123	75.3	101,600	14.8	10.0	633	19.3	2.8	1,319	1.4	68	5.2	1,126	40.5	27.5
LaMoure	1,869	80.2	99,900	16.2	10.0	499	21.6	1.1	2,043	-1.4	46	2.3	2,148	42.2	25.1
Logan	812	84.2	84,500	19.0	10.0	720	26.0	1.1	863	-0.1	26	3.0	887	43.1	29.1
McHenry	2,562	83.7	119,500	18.6	10.0	541	22.6	0.8	3,135	0.4	136	4.3	2,843	37.0	28.4
McIntosh	1,292	71.4	75,700	18.5	10.0	529	19.7	0.8	1,093	-0.8	38	3.5	1,359	39.4	32.8
McKenzie	4,478	57.5	283,400	18.3	10.0	1,088	21.7	8.6	8,620	-9.6	476	5.5	6,939	34.6	34.5
McLean	4,372	80.0	184,800	19.1	10.0	707	22.4	1.2	4,698	-3.1	173	3.7	4,583	36.0	33.8
Mercer	3,663	83.4	181,100	15.1	10.0	811	22.4	2.9	3,670	0.5	172	4.7	4,124	27.7	37.5
Morton	13,502	70.9	220,900	18.8	10.0	872	24.8	0.7	17,062	0.6	653	3.8	17,633	36.8	27.2
Mountrail	3,570	64.0	171,500	16.8	10.0	778	15.6	6.0	6,486	-6.6	227	3.5	4,896	33.9	28.3
Nelson	1,428	75.1	96,100	17.8	10.5	506	20.0	1.8	1,395	-0.6	52	3.7	1,427	39.3	26.9
Oliver	743	88.8	202,400	17.9	11.0	536	33.0	1.7	873	-0.2	33	3.8	851	34.7	29.4
Pembina	3,169	72.5	92,000	14.7	10.0	629	22.1	1.0	3,327	-2.3	161	4.8	3,324	33.9	27.9
Pierce	1,843	76.6	132,300	19.1	10.8	691	44.1	0.3	1,681	-2.0	57	3.4	1,963	53.7	17.2
Ramsey	4,903	59.5	154,800	16.0	10.0	609	22.3	1.5	5,730	-0.4	187	3.3	6,120	34.2	20.5
Ransom	2,380	70.4	139,200	17.8	10.0	755	19.9	0.3	2,696	-7.0	69	2.6	2,685	34.0	39.6
Renville	931	84.3	127,900	17.3	10.0	729	22.3	1.6	1,201	-2.8	41	3.4	1,157	31.7	33.5
Richland	6,806	69.8	132,800	17.5	10.0	658	30.8	3.4	8,669	0.2	238	2.7	8,430	32.0	33.4
Rolette	4,402	71.5	85,600	15.7	10.0	423	19.4	8.1	4,780	-0.5	509	10.6	5,218	36.5	24.3
Sargent	1,897	72.6	110,900	16.3	10.0	732	18.2	1.5	2,386	-15.2	64	2.7	2,170	34.3	42.1
Sheridan	684	81.1	95,800	16.8	11.0	437	37.1	3.4	661	-3.2	35	5.3	572	42.8	24.5
Sioux	1,107	48.7	83,300	25.6	10.0	430	13.9	12.1	1,213	1.1	43	3.5	1,368	37.3	15.4
Slope	336	83.0	91,000	26.3	10.0	650	16.7	1.5	356	-9.9	10	2.8	374	60.7	23.0
Stark	12,635	63.4	240,800	19.4	10.0	915	23.0	3.4	17,518	-5.2	823	4.7	15,989	34.6	32.4
Steele	804	80.1	87,000	12.7	10.0	571	15.6	4.7	932	-3.2	28	3.0	905	46.6	27.7
Stutsman	8,977	62.5	158,900	19.0	10.0	689	24.2	2.8	10,389	-1.8	312	3.0	10,557	37.9	21.2
Towner	1,104	72.7	93,500	20.8	11.6	556	24.2	0.2	1,138	-1.8	37	3.3	1,050	36.4	27.0
Traill	3,394	72.6	152,200	18.0	10.0	643	20.5	0.4	4,439	-1.0	135	3.0	4,055	42.8	24.4
Walsh	4,820	76.7	94,100	17.9	10.0	728	21.9	2.0	5,274	1.7	242	4.6	5,411	36.3	30.7

1. Specified owner-occupied units. 2. A value of 10.0 represents 10 percent or less; a value of 50.0 represents 50 percent or more. 3. Specified renter-occupied units. 4. Overcrowded or lacking complete plumbing facilities. 5. Percent of civilian labor force. 6. Civilian employed persons 16 years old and over.

STATE County	Private nonfarm establishments, employment and payroll, 2020									Agriculture, 2017			
		Employment						Annual payroll		Farms			Farm producers whose primary occupation is farming (percent)
											Percent with:		
	Number of establish-ments	Total	Health care and social assistance	Manufac-turing	Retail trade	Finance and insurance	Professional, scientific, and technical services	Total (mil dol)	Average per employee (dollars)	Number	Fewer than 50 acres	1000 acres or more	
	104	105	106	107	108	109	110	111	112	113	114	115	116
NORTH CAROLINA—Cont'd													
Swain	376	3,677	1,135	180	607	57	69	122	33,208	99	71.7	1.0	51.4
Transylvania	903	7,925	1,285	519	1,463	217	303	275	34,672	215	69.8	0.9	39.7
Tyrrell	70	547	79	44	177	17	NA	14	25,711	68	25.0	22.1	46.5
Union	5,158	61,018	5,782	11,716	7,990	1,145	2,121	2,693	44,138	957	56.9	4.1	44.7
Vance	840	13,350	2,374	1,657	2,197	226	436	492	36,851	238	30.7	6.7	40.1
Wake	30,855	507,958	67,477	15,348	61,113	29,147	63,404	30,084	59,225	691	64.5	1.9	34.5
Warren	257	1,887	407	288	360	48	45	61	32,390	267	41.9	3.7	38.8
Washington	222	2,465	506	651	372	35	51	104	42,160	141	24.8	19.1	60.4
Watauga	1,687	18,962	4,575	748	3,713	363	574	671	35,389	520	58.1	1.0	35.3
Wayne	2,134	33,015	6,607	5,075	5,789	1,146	775	1,243	37,638	551	39.7	8.5	55.4
Wilkes	1,163	17,334	2,265	4,364	2,422	331	423	604	34,843	932	45.0	1.0	47.2
Wilson	1,773	32,464	4,624	7,464	3,859	2,845	631	1,384	42,636	276	43.8	12.3	51.2
Yadkin	607	7,954	844	2,521	863	149	221	285	35,817	818	55.4	1.8	42.5
Yancey	333	3,753	535	1,213	562	76	106	137	36,517	369	51.5	0.3	39.3
NORTH DAKOTA	24,510	355,103	65,644	27,933	48,232	18,565	18,145	17,814	50,167	26,364	11.7	40.0	54.3
Adams	93	674	294	NA	128	37	15	28	41,457	380	9.5	36.3	49.6
Barnes	353	3,557	1,028	489	572	130	62	127	35,659	749	14.4	34.3	54.3
Benson	70	842	17	NA	32	62	NA	29	34,133	473	7.6	41.0	58.1
Billings	56	288	NA	NA	12	NA	NA	19	67,333	204	7.4	53.9	58.0
Bottineau	246	1,597	267	116	282	111	70	72	44,875	684	8.6	39.5	55.6
Bowman	150	1,140	242	23	209	81	94	50	44,163	341	7.0	42.5	46.9
Burke	71	319	13	NA	105	28	22	14	43,652	356	8.7	38.5	47.5
Burleigh	3,073	48,309	11,129	2,106	7,374	1,729	3,267	2,261	46,796	785	29.9	23.7	34.4
Cass	5,634	108,470	21,026	9,256	13,389	9,270	6,026	5,726	52,789	784	20.0	46.9	61.9
Cavalier	133	1,154	228	13	210	77	16	50	43,633	523	5.9	54.7	64.6
Dickey	194	1,465	359	194	269	48	22	54	37,192	419	6.0	42.5	61.8
Divide	88	498	121	NA	37	29	8	23	46,004	416	3.4	45.4	52.0
Dunn	191	2,954	106	487	172	19	111	169	57,284	524	9.2	51.9	64.0
Eddy	78	515	199	NA	67	22	11	18	35,810	291	3.1	40.2	46.3
Emmons	126	666	197	NA	145	63	18	25	37,318	516	6.8	43.8	53.5
Foster	141	1,352	258	302	211	64	11	64	47,123	230	14.3	56.1	61.9
Golden Valley	65	370	129	NA	85	28	15	14	36,524	287	10.8	42.9	51.5
Grand Forks	1,876	33,245	7,678	3,764	5,625	865	1,321	1,479	44,498	889	14.5	24.5	48.5
Grant	74	362	168	14	57	34	8	13	37,149	412	7.5	51.7	52.4
Griggs	84	530	123	99	43	20	14	22	40,911	393	8.1	36.6	55.4
Hettinger	92	442	73	NA	82	46	36	21	46,441	482	8.9	36.7	44.1
Kidder	75	542	57	NA	95	33	27	22	39,825	476	8.2	47.5	49.8
LaMoure	149	1,002	188	75	135	129	NA	37	36,628	571	8.8	41.5	66.2
Logan	68	428	94	NA	71	29	NA	13	30,561	351	10.3	52.1	59.2
McHenry	126	1,041	113	329	115	37	21	55	52,690	750	11.2	33.9	48.5
McIntosh	114	795	325	56	111	48	23	29	36,850	363	13.5	36.1	53.7
McKenzie	576	8,410	361	NA	612	113	368	558	66,359	539	11.3	51.6	68.0
McLean	255	2,575	394	119	317	143	32	172	66,839	762	9.8	35.7	50.1
Mercer	246	3,570	499	591	471	129	41	264	73,947	317	12.0	40.7	49.3
Morton	868	10,616	1,722	1,216	1,435	381	1,561	541	51,003	781	12.0	41.5	54.7
Mountrail	383	4,374	268	116	555	81	391	234	53,540	584	6.8	49.0	54.7
Nelson	111	686	256	NA	79	57	8	26	38,370	489	8.4	30.7	48.8
Oliver	46	569	24	10	23	12	11	52	91,109	234	14.5	33.3	52.1
Pembina	254	2,511	361	790	297	142	41	104	41,331	481	10.6	38.3	66.4
Pierce	167	1,416	350	111	236	92	52	58	40,864	446	13.2	37.9	55.6
Ramsey	436	4,368	897	116	1,005	275	71	173	39,716	515	13.0	35.9	47.5
Ransom	196	1,539	379	315	194	70	66	55	35,871	507	12.4	30.6	53.0
Renville	103	507	86	NA	120	34	10	21	41,211	269	12.6	60.2	71.7
Richland	523	6,028	694	1,668	723	319	134	265	43,925	846	18.8	33.7	60.5
Rolette	194	2,146	621	60	466	123	13	85	39,464	453	8.6	35.8	58.7
Sargent	114	2,063	98	1,416	140	34	17	108	52,493	501	12.6	33.7	56.9
Sheridan	36	132	24	NA	14	9	17	4	33,697	260	2.3	54.6	60.7
Sioux	28	547	46	NA	52	NA	NA	16	28,364	187	16.0	53.5	49.5
Slope	15	73	NA	NA	NA	NA	NA	3	46,274	215	0.9	54.0	65.7
Stark	1,173	15,175	2,188	1,254	2,027	371	481	748	49,294	678	19.8	29.6	43.4
Steele	60	515	NA	112	79	45	7	25	48,596	358	16.8	37.2	56.1
Stutsman	648	8,896	2,754	757	1,263	461	239	387	43,489	939	12.6	37.7	56.7
Towner	81	497	153	NA	70	50	18	21	42,016	454	6.8	44.3	51.9
Traill	277	2,594	610	421	329	143	45	123	47,512	415	18.3	45.1	53.3
Walsh	370	3,144	659	538	448	196	97	139	44,073	763	12.1	32.2	47.6

STATE County	Agriculture, 2017 (cont.) — Land in farms: Acreage (1,000)	Land in farms: Percent change, 2012–2017	Land in farms: Acres: Average size of farm	Land in farms: Acres: Total irrigated (1,000)	Land in farms: Acres: Total cropland (1,000)	Value of land and buildings (dollars): Average per farm	Value of land and buildings (dollars): Average per acre	Value of machinery and equipment, average per farm (dollars)	Value of products sold: Total (mil dol)	Value of products sold: Average per farm (acres)	Value of products sold: Percent from: Crops	Value of products sold: Percent from: Livestock and poultry products	Organic farms (number)	Farms with internet access (percent)	Government payments: Total ($1,000)	Government payments: Percent of farms
	117	118	119	120	121	122	123	124	125	126	127	128	129	130	131	132
NORTH CAROLINA—Cont'd																
Swain	10	D	102	0.2	1.1	374,350	3,658	43,804	2.2	21,717	58.7	41.3	NA	72.7	42	12.1
Transylvania	15	-18.1	68	0.6	4.5	528,315	7,735	58,576	9.8	45,460	68.8	31.2	5	74.4	74	10.2
Tyrrell	53	-18.0	779	D	51.0	3,229,747	4,148	436,706	D	D	D	D	NA	60.3	1,312	75.0
Union	187	-7.5	195	0.2	142.3	1,040,504	5,336	130,984	482.0	503,637	17.9	82.1	4	76.0	2,529	12.6
Vance	66	20.5	278	1.2	20.6	827,874	2,978	114,092	17.2	72,315	97.6	2.4	9	78.6	164	34.5
Wake	77	-8.6	111	1.2	46.3	1,299,196	11,658	82,844	63.7	92,122	88.8	11.2	2	82.6	557	13.5
Warren	61	-7.5	228	1.2	29.2	662,147	2,909	78,681	40.1	150,176	30.7	69.3	2	69.7	428	33.0
Washington	80	-12.8	565	1.9	71.3	2,072,945	3,668	358,266	49.0	347,844	88.5	11.5	NA	78.7	3,085	68.8
Watauga	50	-11.0	95	0.0	14.4	614,311	6,439	58,217	16.7	32,162	53.4	46.6	16	76.2	351	13.3
Wayne	165	-13.5	300	4.8	130.5	1,497,288	4,990	222,201	592.1	1,074,539	18.1	81.9	13	79.9	3,611	46.1
Wilkes	107	-4.0	114	0.1	41.4	586,674	5,124	106,608	335.1	359,575	4.4	95.6	8	69.6	81	4.2
Wilson	123	10.4	445	1.1	100.3	1,685,619	3,784	304,394	210.7	763,399	77.2	22.8	6	76.4	1,129	49.6
Yadkin	88	-12.9	107	0.9	48.3	585,403	5,471	74,938	139.7	170,722	19.5	80.5	7	70.8	489	13.7
Yancey	31	-0.6	84	0.1	10.2	454,909	5,446	40,731	6.8	18,491	83.1	16.9	1	66.7	157	27.1
NORTH DAKOTA	39,342	0.2	1,492	263.9	27,951.7	2,546,783	1,707	375,872	8,234.1	312,324	81.1	18.9	129	78.9	467,034	77.8
Adams	600	-0.3	1,578	NA	388.0	1,682,952	1,067	297,071	60.4	158,937	50.4	49.6	NA	73.2	8,748	82.1
Barnes	952	1.6	1,271	2.5	819.8	2,937,290	2,311	395,596	278.7	372,143	92.4	7.6	3	80.0	8,226	78.2
Benson	751	-6.4	1,587	2.0	586.7	2,172,369	1,368	384,343	164.3	347,393	89.9	10.1	1	79.5	9,813	78.9
Billings	735	1.7	3,602	D	125.7	3,308,786	919	237,105	28.8	140,951	19.7	80.3	6	71.1	2,338	69.6
Bottineau	958	6.6	1,401	0.0	865.6	2,166,705	1,546	354,320	215.5	315,058	92.5	7.5	1	82.5	18,721	81.4
Bowman	711	-2.6	2,086	0.9	334.9	2,144,932	1,028	254,275	74.1	217,240	26.4	73.6	NA	79.2	5,354	80.1
Burke	519	-12.7	1,459	NA	393.4	1,537,171	1,054	303,368	71.6	201,062	85.4	14.6	NA	67.7	7,985	88.2
Burleigh	824	-13.3	1,050	4.0	423.4	1,994,601	1,900	200,722	134.1	170,866	48.8	51.2	NA	80.5	6,674	52.9
Cass	1,126	1.7	1,436	13.9	1,085.4	5,339,580	3,718	557,103	439.5	560,528	94.9	5.1	7	85.1	8,418	71.3
Cavalier	928	-1.3	1,775	0.3	877.2	3,691,559	2,080	546,736	280.6	536,507	98.5	1.5	2	82.8	25,654	90.4
Dickey	679	7.2	1,620	14.8	541.9	3,847,791	2,375	510,138	225.1	537,212	80.8	19.2	6	79.5	6,323	81.1
Divide	704	24.6	1,693	2.3	538.7	1,808,767	1,069	358,232	71.5	171,755	86.1	13.9	7	75.0	9,797	91.3
Dunn	1,017	-1.4	1,941	0.8	417.8	2,225,966	1,147	297,360	77.6	148,101	35.7	64.3	5	84.0	6,276	66.0
Eddy	377	-4.7	1,296	NA	285.6	1,886,332	1,455	312,599	82.2	282,584	77.3	22.7	NA	84.5	4,439	89.0
Emmons	812	9.1	1,573	10.1	500.4	2,493,059	1,585	357,337	162.1	314,151	69.0	31.0	3	79.7	7,581	81.8
Foster	394	5.3	1,713	2.8	342.9	3,438,653	2,008	609,701	118.7	516,230	76.5	23.5	2	89.1	5,532	85.7
Golden Valley	626	11.4	2,182	1.1	274.1	2,296,429	1,052	313,468	45.2	157,390	46.2	53.8	NA	79.1	5,890	76.0
Grand Forks	798	-2.2	898	27.5	744.1	3,064,078	3,411	359,812	318.4	358,112	92.6	7.4	1	74.6	14,911	87.5
Grant	959	-8.6	2,329	2.1	429.0	2,494,937	1,071	264,216	83.0	201,502	35.0	65.0	NA	76.9	8,094	87.4
Griggs	454	1.8	1,154	1.5	364.8	2,051,720	1,777	339,861	114.6	291,659	91.7	8.3	NA	75.1	7,670	88.3
Hettinger	705	-1.5	1,462	NA	586.0	2,055,386	1,405	264,427	66.6	138,077	80.1	19.9	NA	76.8	13,029	86.7
Kidder	748	-4.1	1,572	23.7	423.9	1,978,460	1,258	264,631	113.6	238,626	64.1	35.9	28	77.5	6,882	82.6
LaMoure	727	0.1	1,273	5.5	632.9	3,230,939	2,539	417,666	226.0	395,781	85.2	14.8	9	79.0	4,860	78.5
Logan	632	10.5	1,800	2.4	347.7	2,144,519	1,191	326,130	155.4	442,675	35.6	64.4	7	76.6	4,218	84.9
McHenry	1,040	-2.0	1,387	6.2	629.4	1,510,122	1,089	241,112	146.3	195,129	56.2	43.8	3	78.3	10,874	77.6
McIntosh	488	-17.3	1,343	0.7	298.3	1,832,362	1,364	275,666	94.8	261,157	56.6	43.4	6	79.6	3,200	76.6
McKenzie	1,119	5.2	2,077	26.7	433.3	2,130,024	1,026	372,024	104.7	194,230	47.9	52.1	NA	82.7	7,119	63.8
McLean	1,045	-6.0	1,372	8.1	807.3	2,448,520	1,785	327,473	176.9	232,180	85.2	14.8	NA	82.8	17,822	81.4
Mercer	518	3.0	1,635	2.4	232.8	2,236,333	1,368	291,683	57.2	180,341	43.8	56.2	2	77.6	4,684	65.3
Morton	1,226	0.5	1,570	4.7	562.8	2,203,330	1,404	275,670	146.0	186,936	43.5	56.5	3	81.8	7,594	65.7
Mountrail	1,081	12.2	1,852	0.0	697.2	2,367,371	1,278	415,245	135.7	232,435	78.0	22.0	NA	80.8	14,849	76.5
Nelson	553	-1.4	1,131	2.9	475.4	1,537,488	1,360	341,693	120.9	247,213	93.1	6.9	NA	67.5	9,416	93.5
Oliver	314	-20.5	1,340	2.7	148.5	1,932,910	1,443	292,694	47.3	202,248	46.3	53.7	NA	76.1	2,639	71.4
Pembina	691	-0.1	1,438	1.4	640.8	3,962,790	2,757	514,306	282.7	587,653	97.4	2.6	NA	78.4	11,608	78.0
Pierce	540	-9.7	1,212	0.8	435.3	1,707,184	1,409	337,405	98.8	221,466	84.3	15.7	1	80.0	8,501	86.3
Ramsey	697	-0.3	1,353	D	626.4	2,446,528	1,809	474,152	190.2	369,297	86.2	13.8	NA	77.3	12,149	84.9
Ransom	549	9.5	1,083	28.9	389.1	2,179,084	2,012	345,733	173.6	342,454	79.3	20.7	3	77.5	6,098	74.0
Renville	554	10.8	2,060	0.0	523.4	3,306,195	1,605	672,748	125.5	466,498	97.7	2.3	NA	86.2	10,660	84.0
Richland	875	0.8	1,035	6.1	823.0	3,300,158	3,189	467,825	390.8	461,935	90.8	9.2	3	78.3	6,568	77.9
Rolette	512	-4.1	1,131	1.0	373.1	1,447,711	1,280	327,186	91.5	202,079	84.3	15.7	NA	72.6	9,446	70.6
Sargent	548	6.9	1,094	16.8	489.2	3,049,460	2,787	399,455	214.1	427,433	88.1	11.9	NA	76.0	5,981	79.0
Sheridan	551	7.4	2,121	NA	397.9	2,328,439	1,098	314,736	92.0	354,015	80.2	19.8	7	78.8	5,366	80.4
Sioux	588	2.6	3,145	D	226.1	3,909,369	1,243	390,741	61.9	331,048	35.1	64.9	NA	77.0	2,912	68.4
Slope	728	7.9	3,385	NA	286.5	3,579,166	1,057	418,177	47.9	222,809	41.3	58.7	NA	77.7	4,683	83.7
Stark	736	-11.3	1,085	0.5	493.6	1,444,094	1,331	222,178	68.5	100,997	63.6	36.4	NA	77.6	7,576	59.6
Steele	421	-1.1	1,177	6.6	398.6	2,584,785	2,197	525,062	149.9	418,782	97.3	2.7	NA	77.7	5,812	80.4
Stutsman	1,316	1.0	1,401	4.2	1,048.2	2,808,671	2,005	370,108	335.6	357,428	85.2	14.8	2	79.2	10,869	74.8
Towner	631	-2.3	1,389	NA	552.4	1,923,869	1,385	399,244	166.1	365,965	84.8	15.2	NA	74.2	14,647	85.2
Traill	539	-1.6	1,298	D	526.1	4,004,597	3,084	592,272	225.9	544,410	99.0	1.0	NA	81.2	4,053	80.0
Walsh	805	0.3	1,054	1.7	720.3	2,649,975	2,513	446,123	335.6	439,840	96.4	3.6	5	76.5	13,679	86.1

STATE County	Water use, 2015		Wholesale Trade[1], 2017				Retail Trade[2], 2017				Real estate and rental and leasing,[2] 2017			
	Public supply water withdrawn (mil gal/ day)	Public supply gallons withdrawn per person per day	Number of establish- ments	Number of employees	Sales (mil dol)	Average payroll (mil dol)	Number of establish- ments	Number of employees	Sales (mil dol)	Average payroll (mil dol)	Number of establish- ments	Number of employees	Sales (mil dol)	Average payroll (mil dol)
	133	134	135	136	137	138	139	140	141	142	143	144	145	146
NORTH CAROLINA— Cont'd														
Swain	0.5	34.6	NA	NA	NA	NA	81	594	124.5	12.3	10	52	9.4	1.7
Transylvania	1.8	54.5	D	D	D	D	119	1,448	327.9	33.1	D	D	D	D
Tyrrell	0.5	117.9	NA	NA	NA	NA	21	157	35.2	2.6	D	D	D	D
Union	6.6	29.5	266	2,863	1,661.6	163.7	535	7,999	2,655.9	213.0	226	457	113.7	19.9
Vance	6.0	133.5	D	D	D	D	184	2,212	587.4	52.3	45	185	37.3	6.1
Wake	56.7	55.3	1,160	22,292	30,140.0	1,790.4	3,493	59,325	18,099.7	1,613.2	1,740	9,061	2,566.3	509.3
Warren	0.1	2.5	D	D	D	1.3	46	397	93.7	9.2	12	25	3.2	0.6
Washington	0.8	63.8	7	61	35.0	3.1	42	368	97.2	7.9	D	D	D	0.5
Watauga	3.3	62.4	32	290	169.7	15.9	323	3,658	931.8	87.1	123	435	74.0	13.5
Wayne	11.3	90.8	98	1,920	1,385.3	75.9	461	6,214	1,619.3	144.9	67	335	53.7	10.5
Wilkes	6.6	96.5	D	D	D	D	220	2,665	3,243.8	62.3	D	D	D	8.5
Wilson	9.6	117.7	104	1,120	636.4	55.5	325	3,775	1,017.7	92.4	83	276	47.4	8.0
Yadkin	1.4	36.2	D	D	D	6.9	108	839	251.6	18.0	D	D	D	D
Yancey	0.7	39.8	10	50	7.1	0.9	59	541	134.9	12.7	D	D	D	0.9
NORTH DAKOTA	84.2	111.2	1,563	20,075	23,276.8	1,203.6	3,277	49,579	19,251.1	1,453.9	1,100	5,440	1,279.6	242.3
Adams	0.0	0.0	9	70	108.0	3.0	15	126	40.3	4.2	NA	NA	NA	NA
Barnes	1.2	103.6	21	159	298.9	8.3	47	457	102.1	12.1	D	D	D	D
Benson	0.1	10.4	12	75	165.7	4.5	8	29	8.9	0.8	NA	NA	NA	NA
Billings	0.0	0.0	NA	NA	NA	NA	10	D	3.9	D	NA	NA	NA	NA
Bottineau	0.5	71.5	12	77	255.9	4.8	26	431	104.2	10.6	4	D	0.3	D
Bowman	0.2	66.8	12	140	101.8	7.0	18	221	69.2	5.4	NA	NA	NA	NA
Burke	0.3	112.7	5	41	295.4	2.7	8	116	31.1	3.5	NA	NA	NA	NA
Burleigh	11.9	128.0	140	2,507	1,943.9	158.0	402	7,654	2,109.9	216.4	163	507	125.8	19.5
Cass	14.1	82.3	353	6,399	6,183.0	386.2	681	13,234	8,502.8	410.6	331	1,843	316.6	71.2
Cavalier	0.5	130.6	13	170	592.0	11.5	26	183	91.5	5.5	NA	NA	NA	NA
Dickey	0.8	162.6	D	D	D	8.4	40	319	82.5	7.7	NA	NA	NA	NA
Divide	0.0	0.0	D	D	D	D	11	57	9.2	1.2	3	3	0.4	0.1
Dunn	0.0	0.0	13	95	115.8	7.7	15	128	39.7	4.3	D	D	D	D
Eddy	1.0	414.4	5	D	49.9	D	10	62	13.6	1.9	NA	NA	NA	NA
Emmons	0.4	126.4	13	70	125.1	3.1	23	133	27.9	3.0	NA	NA	NA	NA
Foster	0.4	128.1	19	138	332.3	9.0	24	237	66.8	6.1	5	D	1.4	D
Golden Valley	0.0	0.0	5	59	77.4	3.1	13	104	43.5	3.2	D	NA	NA	NA
Grand Forks	8.8	123.8	91	1,242	1,161.2	70.5	317	6,060	1,598.4	154.6	86	589	91.4	20.7
Grant	0.0	0.0	7	39	52.3	1.7	10	47	8.0	1.0	NA	NA	NA	NA
Griggs	0.4	164.2	6	42	29.2	1.9	11	68	18.8	1.3	NA	NA	NA	NA
Hettinger	0.0	0.0	7	D	51.0	D	15	99	52.1	3.3	NA	NA	NA	NA
Kidder	0.1	37.2	7	D	14.3	D	11	37	10.0	1.3	NA	NA	NA	NA
LaMoure	0.0	2.4	26	197	262.1	10.8	18	109	24.5	2.9	D	D	D	0.0
Logan	0.1	46.5	6	D	170.1	D	10	82	21.4	2.2	NA	NA	NA	NA
McHenry	1.0	162.5	8	184	236.1	11.1	17	148	32.1	3.4	D	D	D	D
McIntosh	0.3	94.2	13	116	169.2	4.7	17	126	48.8	3.8	NA	NA	NA	NA
McKenzie	0.8	61.6	23	290	292.3	21.2	41	479	159.9	15.3	28	231	82.2	14.3
McLean	0.6	62.6	19	161	368.0	10.4	40	326	90.0	9.6	NA	NA	NA	NA
Mercer	6.7	753.4	9	50	52.4	2.9	45	466	102.8	12.1	4	D	0.5	D
Morton	2.8	92.4	45	344	504.9	17.5	97	1,527	587.5	57.3	36	122	39.1	5.1
Mountrail	0.5	50.3	17	164	282.4	10.9	50	616	183.6	18.9	8	D	2.8	D
Nelson	1.3	448.1	12	119	271.8	7.9	18	99	22.6	1.7	3	D	0.3	D
Oliver	0.0	0.0	NA	NA	NA	NA	D	D	D	0.9	NA	NA	NA	NA
Pembina	1.1	155.1	36	322	527.8	14.7	40	323	73.1	7.5	NA	NA	NA	NA
Pierce	0.8	173.9	16	137	192.7	8.4	20	205	78.5	6.2	NA	NA	NA	NA
Ramsey	0.0	0.0	31	318	499.2	17.9	82	1,020	335.7	32.3	8	D	10.9	D
Ransom	1.0	187.2	16	128	140.0	7.3	25	206	52.9	4.7	10	D	1.4	D
Renville	0.0	0.0	14	102	211.1	5.8	16	113	35.3	3.4	NA	NA	NA	NA
Richland	2.1	126.8	D	D	D	D	69	715	215.6	18.4	11	39	5.3	0.9
Rolette	1.6	108.5	12	47	68.5	2.4	39	480	111.8	10.3	NA	NA	NA	NA
Sargent	0.3	72.2	12	108	73.0	5.3	14	160	31.0	4.1	3	6	0.2	0.0
Sheridan	0.0	7.6	NA	NA	NA	NA	D	D	D	0.2	NA	NA	NA	NA
Sioux	0.0	4.6	NA	NA	NA	NA	D	D	D	1.1	NA	NA	NA	NA
Slope	0.0	39.1	NA	NA	NA	NA	NA	NA	NA	NA	NA	NA	NA	NA
Stark	0.0	0.0	71	736	528.2	48.2	157	2,191	743.5	73.0	53	256	99.4	16.1
Steele	0.7	342.5	D	D	D	3.9	6	58	37.9	2.2	NA	NA	NA	NA
Stutsman	3.3	157.3	38	387	488.7	22.2	102	1,512	576.9	46.0	28	63	11.3	1.8
Towner	0.2	83.6	9	102	178.6	5.7	13	47	32.5	1.5	NA	NA	NA	NA
Traill	0.9	114.8	34	323	371.8	16.4	46	349	104.8	8.6	7	14	0.5	0.2
Walsh	1.1	104.6	38	371	535.6	19.7	52	465	94.6	10.6	10	27	1.4	0.4

1 Merchant wholesalers, except manufacturers' sales branches and offices. 2. Employer establishments.

STATE County	Professional, scientific, and technical services, 2017				Manufacturing, 2017				Accommodation and food services, 2017			
	Number of establish-ments	Number of employees	Sales (mil dol)	Average payroll (mil dol)	Number of establish-ments	Number of employees	Sales (mil dol)	Average payroll (mil dol)	Number of establis-hments	Number of employees	Sales (mil dol)	Annual payroll (mil dol)
	147	148	149	150	151	152	153	154	155	156	157	158
NORTH CAROLINA—Cont'd												
Swain	17	50	4.7	1.5	D	390	D	18.8	89	835	64.9	14.5
Transylvania	D	D	D	D	31	602	117.5	30.0	78	1,305	91.1	27.9
Tyrrell	NA	NA	NA	NA	4	46	8.5	3.3	D	D	D	D
Union	500	1,917	295.6	99.1	239	11,168	4,033.2	602.6	315	5,582	302.0	80.4
Vance	51	289	40.7	16.8	37	1,564	653.4	71.4	70	1,326	68.6	17.5
Wake	4,934	59,018	12,406.6	4,942.2	610	12,947	13,115.7	779.1	2,424	53,773	3,206.7	903.5
Warren	11	39	3.2	0.8	9	377	163.4	15.2	D	D	D	3.2
Washington	7	56	6.7	1.8	10	753	455.2	53.3	22	326	15.4	4.1
Watauga	154	479	50.3	19.1	34	488	78.1	17.3	184	3,943	190.4	55.1
Wayne	130	679	74.7	29.3	56	4,957	1,351.3	226.3	208	4,152	202.4	56.5
Wilkes	73	566	59.1	21.4	65	4,645	1,323.3	169.0	101	1,715	88.5	22.8
Wilson	D	D	D	D	87	7,525	7,725.8	419.7	D	D	D	D
Yadkin	34	193	22.2	9.3	47	2,480	962.7	110.4	55	855	41.1	10.7
Yancey	20	105	6.9	2.4	13	1,037	216.2	59.5	20	D	13.6	D
NORTH DAKOTA	1,804	14,780	2,411.6	942.2	701	24,214	13,604.9	1,266.4	2,080	36,648	2,118.0	619.9
Adams	4	23	3.0	0.9	NA	NA	NA	NA	8	D	2.4	D
Barnes	13	70	10.2	3.2	12	365	178.6	19.6	33	346	15.3	4.2
Benson	NA	NA	NA	NA	D	15	D	D	D	D	D	D
Billings	NA	NA	NA	NA	NA	NA	NA	NA	10	85	20.2	6.5
Bottineau	21	75	8.3	3.2	9	90	28.5	4.5	25	193	9.5	2.6
Bowman	9	50	12.1	3.9	D	27	D	1.2	17	173	5.4	1.6
Burke	4	12	1.5	0.4	NA	NA	NA	NA	8	37	4.0	0.5
Burleigh	D	D	D	D	60	1,058	375.9	64.2	210	5,516	296.9	96.8
Cass	525	5,938	924.6	382.2	186	8,334	2,870.8	412.9	457	10,766	506.0	168.8
Cavalier	7	15	1.6	0.7	6	10	3.9	0.6	10	D	3.6	D
Dickey	12	35	3.3	1.0	11	210	44.7	8.0	18	149	4.8	1.3
Divide	4	9	1.0	0.3	3	D	0.3	0.1	10	55	3.4	0.8
Dunn	D	D	D	D	D	D	D	D	9	118	27.8	4.2
Eddy	D	D	1.2	D	D	D	D	D	6	D	1.1	D
Emmons	8	12	2.0	0.5	NA	NA	NA	NA	D	D	D	0.7
Foster	4	5	0.5	0.1	D	D	D	D	9	120	4.6	1.7
Golden Valley	D	D	1.2	D	NA	NA	NA	NA	4	20	0.8	0.3
Grand Forks	130	1,376	185.3	82.0	51	2,784	797.7	136.5	202	4,267	192.2	62.0
Grant	NA	NA	NA	NA	4	11	1.5	0.4	8	D	1.1	D
Griggs	6	38	2.0	1.0	5	121	22.7	5.0	D	D	D	0.5
Hettinger	6	28	4.0	2.5	3	9	2.2	0.4	D	D	D	0.4
Kidder	7	22	6.0	0.9	NA	NA	NA	NA	9	D	2.3	D
LaMoure	NA	NA	NA	NA	6	81	21.8	3.0	D	D	D	0.6
Logan	NA	NA	NA	NA	NA	NA	NA	NA	4	45	1.5	0.3
McHenry	D	D	3.6	D	D	D	D	D	10	D	1.8	D
McIntosh	7	21	2.4	0.8	5	44	4.9	1.3	10	D	1.5	D
McKenzie	38	205	51.7	17.5	NA	NA	NA	NA	39	413	44.7	10.9
McLean	8	30	3.4	1.2	D	100	D	D	28	238	13.9	3.1
Mercer	10	51	7.4	2.3	D	D	D	D	33	287	15.2	3.9
Morton	D	D	D	D	31	856	1,559.9	63.8	D	D	D	D
Mountrail	D	D	D	D	4	D	22.2	5.3	41	337	37.5	7.8
Nelson	4	9	1.2	0.5	NA	NA	NA	NA	D	D	D	0.7
Oliver	NA	NA	NA	NA	D	D	D	D	NA	NA	NA	NA
Pembina	13	33	3.8	1.2	15	670	489.8	31.9	14	D	4.5	D
Pierce	12	68	9.6	2.8	D	D	D	2.9	16	126	5.7	1.7
Ramsey	19	80	7.8	3.3	7	171	40.2	8.6	50	742	41.3	10.5
Ransom	17	56	6.1	1.8	D	284	D	16.1	21	130	5.0	1.1
Renville	D	D	D	0.2	NA	NA	NA	NA	14	D	2.7	D
Richland	D	D	12.1	D	37	1,831	1,049.5	D	39	833	91.4	19.5
Rolette	D	D	D	0.3	D	63	D	1.7	21	569	51.9	11.7
Sargent	6	17	2.4	0.8	D	D	D	D	12	36	3.6	0.6
Sheridan	D	D	D	D	NA	NA	NA	NA	NA	NA	NA	NA
Sioux	NA	NA	NA	NA	NA	NA	NA	NA	D	D	D	D
Slope	NA	NA	NA	NA	NA	NA	NA	NA	NA	NA	NA	NA
Stark	83	552	80.0	29.9	31	1,111	1,158.8	66.8	89	1,432	88.4	28.7
Steele	NA	NA	NA	NA	8	99	18.4	3.7	D	D	D	0.2
Stutsman	35	242	26.4	10.1	21	811	406.0	44.5	62	909	43.4	14.7
Towner	6	21	1.8	0.8	3	D	1.3	0.5	8	34	2.2	0.4
Traill	15	44	4.1	1.7	D	371	D	16.3	23	157	7.4	1.8
Walsh	25	95	12.6	4.0	12	544	105.1	19.7	30	145	7.5	1.8

STATE County	Health care and social assistance, 2017				Other services, 2017				Nonemployer businesses, 2019		Value of residential construction authorized by building permits, 2021	
	Number of establish-ments	Number of employees	Receipts (mil dol)	Annual payroll (mil dol)	Number of establish-ments	Number of employees	Receipts (mil dol)	Annual payroll (mil dol)	Number	Receipts (mil dol)	New construction ($1,000)	Number of housing units
	159	160	161	162	163	164	165	166	167	168	169	170
NORTH CAROLINA—Cont'd												
Swain	27	884	109.0	38.0	D	D	D	1.1	1,346	52.3	30,170	212
Transylvania	88	1,686	182.9	61.7	52	351	31.5	9.1	3,281	147.0	101,629	195
Tyrrell	7	23	1.3	0.8	D	D	D	D	280	11.8	1,000	5
Union	333	5,911	629.4	247.1	345	1,678	161.5	50.5	20,486	1,034.0	585,677	2,773
Vance	93	2,538	222.2	95.2	D	D	D	D	2,371	105.3	27,121	166
Wake	3,040	63,396	7,715.6	3,097.5	2,004	13,651	1,716.5	518.0	98,720	4,740.7	3,550,728	16,988
Warren	19	395	23.0	11.0	D	D	D	1.2	1,105	36.6	39,795	272
Washington	35	644	39.9	18.5	8	21	4.1	1.0	590	20.8	1,729	8
Watauga	138	3,952	1,073.3	193.3	92	448	37.6	11.7	5,177	232.7	61,238	355
Wayne	259	7,604	781.9	310.8	152	810	71.4	21.2	6,691	266.7	89,592	482
Wilkes	152	3,137	239.1	86.5	62	255	29.0	7.3	4,526	208.7	42,835	169
Wilson	217	4,930	414.4	165.6	117	685	65.1	18.7	4,916	194.1	56,884	343
Yadkin	48	896	69.7	27.4	28	90	11.5	2.9	2,372	101.6	43,362	186
Yancey	31	481	33.8	13.4	25	108	12.1	3.6	1,723	69.3	17,395	79
NORTH DAKOTA	2,057	62,455	7,297.8	2,913.3	1,763	9,706	1,246.0	318.3	56,398	3,057.3	865,569	3,600
Adams	16	346	31.0	14.7	D	D	D	0.4	189	8.8	706	3
Barnes	41	1,043	69.8	32.0	24	146	11.5	3.1	870	46.4	7,758	46
Benson	5	D	0.9	D	NA	NA	NA	NA	293	12.4	200	1
Billings	NA	NA	NA	NA	4	14	3.7	0.8	111	5.3	1,153	3
Bottineau	13	269	18.9	8.7	D	D	D	0.5	638	26.9	2,828	15
Bowman	18	225	18.5	9.7	D	D	D	1.0	265	10.7	1,733	4
Burke	D	D	D	0.2	NA	NA	NA	NA	200	7.5	599	3
Burleigh	300	10,358	1,256.8	484.9	265	1,711	248.0	70.0	7,855	451.4	145,473	609
Cass	520	20,346	2,941.8	1,011.4	403	3,015	354.9	88.3	13,430	844.7	431,509	1,806
Cavalier	8	227	17.5	6.5	D	D	2.7	D	384	15.8	1,725	5
Dickey	22	371	34.6	13.4	16	49	7.3	1.8	438	20.5	1,155	6
Divide	D	D	D	D	6	18	1.5	0.2	207	8.6	400	2
Dunn	D	D	D	D	D	D	D	D	364	30.1	3,864	13
Eddy	9	190	11.6	6.2	D	D	2.0	D	190	7.8	0	0
Emmons	10	191	17.6	7.3	D	D	D	0.1	277	10.5	6,120	25
Foster	12	236	22.3	9.8	D	D	1.5	D	302	17.8	1,389	9
Golden Valley	7	D	8.2	D	D	D	D	0.2	192	7.3	1,189	5
Grand Forks	163	7,478	828.8	381.5	138	782	93.2	23.8	4,281	208.2	43,182	168
Grant	8	187	13.2	5.4	D	D	2.4	D	213	8.9	1,630	9
Griggs	5	128	9.2	3.9	D	D	D	0.2	223	9.1	245	1
Hettinger	8	97	5.9	3.1	D	D	D	0.3	220	9.7	100	1
Kidder	5	D	2.1	D	3	18	1.0	0.2	239	12.4	320	1
LaMoure	14	D	7.8	D	D	D	3.1	D	344	13.6	490	2
Logan	8	116	5.1	2.5	D	D	D	0.9	197	7.8	805	2
McHenry	D	D	D	D	D	D	2.7	D	433	19.8	295	2
McIntosh	10	316	21.5	10.6	D	D	D	0.7	236	11.9	0	0
McKenzie	14	454	28.7	13.5	25	130	13.4	4.5	983	56.6	19,058	68
McLean	19	389	24.4	11.6	D	D	D	1.3	736	29.2	13,346	49
Mercer	22	509	40.5	19.2	D	D	D	D	588	18.4	364	9
Morton	71	1,480	109.3	51.0	71	317	45.8	12.3	2,469	160.4	34,103	178
Mountrail	14	269	14.8	9.2	21	306	27.6	10.9	684	52.8	5,271	26
Nelson	12	277	15.6	7.8	D	D	2.5	D	259	8.3	0	0
Oliver	D	D	D	0.5	D	D	D	0.1	126	4.6	1,774	5
Pembina	17	338	24.3	9.4	14	30	3.6	0.8	525	20.3	238	1
Pierce	9	D	30.8	D	D	D	D	D	331	12.4	1,200	7
Ramsey	52	815	73.4	34.1	35	127	11.7	2.7	849	37.2	5,441	31
Ransom	30	386	34.5	14.1	16	68	5.4	1.2	398	18.5	1,540	8
Renville	D	D	D	D	D	D	2.1	D	170	8.8	0	0
Richland	44	551	49.9	21.3	33	122	10.2	2.7	1,167	65.0	11,543	44
Rolette	D	D	D	42.0	D	D	2.7	D	620	20.6	0	0
Sargent	8	71	5.2	2.5	D	D	D	D	271	11.9	2,009	8
Sheridan	3	23	1.0	0.6	5	8	0.9	0.2	109	3.9	805	4
Sioux	D	D	D	1.2	D	D	D	0.1	110	4.9	0	0
Slope	NA	NA	NA	NA	NA	NA	NA	NA	63	3.8	0	0
Stark	96	1,867	205.6	75.6	89	404	62.0	14.3	2,632	147.4	31,209	79
Steele	NA	NA	NA	NA	3	5	1.3	0.3	158	7.4	1,605	8
Stutsman	70	2,641	225.0	122.8	56	267	24.3	8.5	1,431	57.8	11,968	55
Towner	NA	NA	NA	NA	5	29	1.4	0.2	205	8.6	0	0
Traill	19	546	42.4	19.2	24	66	13.0	2.1	576	24.7	2,450	8
Walsh	36	692	56.7	26.5	28	71	6.2	1.9	761	41.6	1,380	6

STATE County	Government employment and payroll, 2017: Full-time equivalent employees	Government employment and payroll, 2017: March payroll (dollars)	March payroll (percent of total): Adminis-tration, judicial, and legal	March payroll (percent of total): Police and corrections	March payroll (percent of total): Fire protection	March payroll (percent of total): Highways and transpor-tation	March payroll (percent of total): Health and welfare	March payroll (percent of total): Natural resources and utilities	March payroll (percent of total): Education and libraries	Local government finances, 2017: General revenue: Total (mil dol)	General revenue: Inter-govern-mental (mil dol)	Taxes: Total (mil dol)	Taxes: Per capita[1] (dollars): Total	Taxes: Per capita[1] (dollars): Property
	171	172	173	174	175	176	177	178	179	180	181	182	183	184
NORTH CAROLINA—Cont'd														
Swain	572	1,870,157	4.2	9.9	0.0	0.6	14.5	6.1	59.2	47.2	29.2	11.6	815	461
Transylvania	1,126	3,434,915	5.9	13.1	1.2	1.0	13.6	6.1	53.3	94.8	35.7	48.2	1,428	1,112
Tyrrell	174	666,490	7.2	4.9	0.0	0.4	8.3	7.2	65.4	17.2	10.0	5.0	1,185	964
Union	7,152	25,616,934	4.2	7.2	1.5	0.7	4.5	5.3	74.2	676.5	302.7	297.0	1,284	1,005
Vance	1,972	7,360,563	2.8	6.5	2.4	2.5	10.2	2.6	70.6	157.5	92.5	42.4	958	703
Wake	33,845	151,028,554	3.7	9.2	3.9	4.1	5.6	8.0	61.0	4,021.1	1,405.6	1,881.3	1,755	1,250
Warren	558	2,079,861	3.4	9.3	0.0	0.4	11.1	4.1	69.7	57.9	27.5	23.9	1,203	1,031
Washington	542	1,589,913	7.6	11.1	0.0	0.7	16.4	4.7	57.0	42.2	23.5	12.7	1,060	752
Watauga	1,419	4,949,287	7.1	10.9	3.0	2.2	12.8	7.6	48.1	154.2	60.9	69.9	1,268	856
Wayne	4,543	14,430,137	3.0	6.6	2.3	1.5	7.8	6.9	69.4	355.9	205.6	110.1	895	614
Wilkes	3,313	11,432,319	2.1	4.8	0.3	1.2	33.7	2.3	53.3	190.7	106.8	58.6	856	619
Wilson	3,251	11,938,713	6.9	9.7	3.6	1.1	11.6	12.9	50.6	297.5	135.9	98.2	1,206	913
Yadkin	1,177	3,864,174	4.5	9.0	0.1	0.5	11.2	3.3	69.9	90.5	49.6	31.5	838	630
Yancey	753	2,341,687	2.6	6.5	0.3	1.4	7.4	4.9	64.8	66.7	25.1	36.5	2,063	1,620
NORTH DAKOTA	X	X	X	X	X	X	X	X	X	X	X	X	X	X
Adams	82	268,388	14.2	10.9	0.0	8.8	7.6	5.2	52.2	14.8	8.6	4.8	2,046	1,679
Barnes	386	1,620,424	9.9	11.1	0.5	6.9	5.9	14.8	49.9	67.4	31.8	24.2	2,262	1,953
Benson	296	1,067,230	8.8	1.6	0.6	6.7	7.6	1.5	73.1	34.6	23.8	6.3	915	899
Billings	78	365,632	15.9	12.5	1.0	27.8	8.0	2.8	29.0	23.7	18.4	4.1	4,478	3,951
Bottineau	292	1,136,510	12.0	5.6	0.4	8.1	4.3	8.7	58.7	70.5	46.1	16.6	2,545	2,304
Bowman	177	691,854	10.4	5.5	0.0	7.0	5.3	7.9	62.5	30.1	18.0	4.6	1,458	1,286
Burke	134	537,457	15.0	7.0	0.1	9.0	2.7	3.7	58.5	23.4	10.7	6.5	3,064	3,023
Burleigh	2,989	13,881,814	4.6	10.4	3.5	3.5	5.4	9.7	59.3	402.2	182.0	133.7	1,403	1,033
Cass	5,640	25,246,394	5.1	9.1	2.7	5.4	8.6	6.5	61.7	904.5	382.3	313.2	1,762	1,216
Cavalier	150	603,757	10.7	8.5	0.1	8.5	3.7	6.8	61.5	23.5	9.9	10.0	2,645	2,632
Dickey	186	725,275	10.7	6.6	0.0	5.8	9.7	5.4	58.7	39.5	15.5	15.7	3,244	3,123
Divide	124	536,408	2.6	8.4	0.0	20.0	4.9	4.7	48.5	31.8	15.2	9.6	4,192	3,941
Dunn	189	749,819	19.8	5.8	0.6	11.1	4.9	6.2	51.6	58.5	15.7	30.9	7,233	2,207
Eddy	123	378,514	7.6	5.1	0.0	5.2	2.2	5.6	73.7	12.2	6.7	3.7	1,596	1,487
Emmons	179	628,299	12.4	3.6	0.0	7.7	2.9	5.7	67.7	45.9	20.6	14.6	4,431	4,018
Foster	109	418,777	15.4	2.3	0.1	6.6	7.3	1.5	65.0	21.9	7.9	9.4	2,898	2,637
Golden Valley	110	361,391	6.1	2.6	0.0	4.0	3.0	3.4	80.3	21.0	11.9	6.6	3,689	3,581
Grand Forks	2,657	11,301,030	5.8	9.6	3.9	5.5	8.1	9.2	56.2	351.0	156.7	106.6	1,512	1,170
Grant	88	309,918	12.1	7.5	0.0	8.7	7.5	4.0	58.2	12.7	6.2	4.0	1,675	1,618
Griggs	111	405,400	8.5	2.7	0.0	8.0	8.5	3.2	68.5	18.4	6.3	10.0	4,478	4,390
Hettinger	144	556,770	12.0	4.3	0.0	6.7	4.9	3.6	68.3	20.2	10.1	6.3	2,560	2,384
Kidder	93	346,221	8.3	6.2	0.3	1.6	6.7	5.6	71.1	15.0	6.2	4.4	1,795	1,701
LaMoure	242	931,413	8.2	3.6	0.0	6.6	2.1	17.8	61.3	48.9	27.9	15.5	3,787	3,681
Logan	90	339,766	4.2	2.9	0.1	3.6	5.9	4.1	78.2	13.9	7.3	5.0	2,596	2,444
McHenry	252	947,289	11.5	3.1	0.1	5.6	3.3	3.2	71.2	30.3	15.9	10.9	1,846	1,803
McIntosh	140	501,588	11.6	4.2	0.1	12.8	4.7	7.7	58.1	18.8	7.2	8.4	3,229	3,105
McKenzie	562	2,637,964	10.0	21.9	0.0	11.4	4.4	5.8	45.8	151.2	82.1	39.7	3,126	2,613
McLean	539	2,091,520	8.1	8.9	0.0	5.5	13.1	3.0	61.0	64.4	32.2	21.7	2,250	2,117
Mercer	399	1,409,489	9.7	10.8	0.1	9.1	0.8	8.3	58.8	36.0	16.5	11.2	1,320	960
Morton	1,159	4,948,844	5.8	10.0	1.0	5.2	7.4	4.9	64.6	150.5	69.9	60.0	1,938	1,701
Mountrail	498	2,068,080	8.8	8.7	0.0	6.6	11.7	3.8	60.2	153.0	104.5	32.2	3,132	2,805
Nelson	167	597,962	16.5	3.2	0.0	9.5	5.2	7.9	57.6	22.9	12.5	7.2	2,479	2,336
Oliver	64	231,582	15.3	8.2	0.0	10.8	0.0	4.2	60.1	9.2	4.3	3.0	1,561	1,156
Pembina	335	1,313,469	12.7	7.2	0.0	4.7	7.6	7.6	59.7	43.2	15.3	16.4	2,361	2,162
Pierce	164	573,855	3.0	3.5	0.0	1.2	16.0	4.4	65.0	23.8	10.5	7.1	1,736	1,693
Ramsey	534	2,087,368	7.9	5.4	1.4	4.4	9.5	6.5	64.1	63.6	35.6	17.4	1,500	1,184
Ransom	237	824,513	8.5	4.1	0.7	4.6	5.6	4.8	70.1	29.1	16.6	8.4	1,589	1,434
Renville	147	551,394	10.1	4.8	0.0	8.7	3.1	1.8	70.5	20.6	10.8	6.3	2,571	2,376
Richland	608	2,389,542	6.1	7.8	0.1	4.7	8.5	6.6	61.8	102.7	40.0	42.1	2,585	2,368
Rolette	709	3,167,800	1.8	2.9	0.2	1.7	5.5	1.0	86.7	79.6	57.6	13.6	933	896
Sargent	179	634,102	8.5	3.5	0.1	3.2	4.2	4.5	72.3	31.5	12.0	12.3	3,192	3,094
Sheridan	63	208,074	11.4	5.7	0.1	10.8	0.0	1.8	63.7	54.4	40.0	13.3	9,861	9,784
Sioux	181	703,697	3.9	0.7	0.1	3.6	0.2	0.7	90.4	70.7	11.2	58.6	13,238	13,223
Slope	39	142,259	24.3	7.8	0.0	14.3	0.0	16.0	31.8	8.3	6.3	1.0	1,304	1,199
Stark	1,197	5,293,019	4.2	17.4	0.9	4.0	6.5	13.2	52.9	196.8	96.9	59.9	1,979	1,597
Steele	76	267,742	18.4	4.0	0.2	9.4	8.0	1.4	56.6	24.7	17.0	5.5	2,879	2,754
Stutsman	761	3,193,820	6.2	11.9	1.1	5.2	8.3	10.8	54.1	105.0	57.4	30.1	1,424	1,217
Towner	111	389,904	15.0	6.6	0.0	14.1	4.0	4.5	53.0	13.1	5.1	4.9	2,196	1,827
Traill	315	1,293,677	7.3	4.3	0.0	6.2	5.3	2.8	73.2	43.1	22.8	13.3	1,663	1,559
Walsh	566	2,218,535	6.0	4.8	0.1	3.9	4.6	5.4	72.4	68.3	40.9	18.3	1,690	1,512

1. Based on the resident population estimated as of July 1 of the year shown.

STATE County	Local government finances, 2017 (cont.)									Government employment, 2020			Individual income tax returns, 2019		
	Direct general expenditure							Debt outstanding							
			Percent of total for:												
	Total (mil dol)	Per capita[1] (dollars)	Education	Health and hospitals	Police protection	Public welfare	Highways	Total (mil dol)	Per capita[1] (dollars)	Federal civilian	Federal military	State and local	Number of returns	Mean adjusted gross income	Mean income tax
	185	186	187	188	189	190	191	192	193	194	195	196	197	198	199
NORTH CAROLINA—Cont'd															
Swain	49.6	3,475	45.6	6.2	8.2	9.6	0.4	12.6	887	124	30	2,706	8,170	43,928	3,284
Transylvania	90.9	2,691	42.6	5.6	11.0	7.6	1.3	13.8	408	153	72	1,346	15,160	65,809	6,971
Tyrrell	16.9	4,049	55.6	3.2	8.2	8.3	0.6	9.5	2,280	23	7	359	1,640	37,835	2,271
Union	665.5	2,877	55.9	1.9	8.4	4.8	1.6	531.9	2,299	318	520	9,018	106,110	89,963	12,086
Vance	158.2	3,573	62.8	5.9	7.4	7.9	0.7	41.5	937	99	94	2,222	19,240	40,909	3,069
Wake	3,797.9	3,544	50.6	3.1	6.2	3.4	2.8	8,157.5	7,612	6,094	3,009	80,514	530,030	93,967	12,736
Warren	55.0	2,773	49.1	5.7	14.8	11.3	0.5	17.7	894	37	40	1,079	7,840	43,260	3,354
Washington	40.6	3,397	48.1	5.1	7.1	10.7	0.9	5.8	490	30	24	700	5,070	40,679	2,889
Watauga	144.7	2,622	33.0	7.4	8.4	4.5	4.8	124.6	2,258	129	114	6,458	20,480	64,216	7,076
Wayne	361.9	2,941	53.6	5.6	8.1	6.3	0.9	253.1	2,057	1,244	4,901	7,758	53,150	50,518	4,177
Wilkes	186.5	2,723	63.1	5.0	5.2	9.1	0.4	63.0	920	177	144	3,335	28,320	49,745	4,267
Wilson	279.6	3,433	46.4	5.6	8.7	9.2	1.5	126.3	1,550	141	173	4,540	36,440	50,210	4,490
Yadkin	86.5	2,300	59.5	6.1	7.1	8.7	0.7	33.8	900	76	80	1,423	16,700	51,612	4,258
Yancey	49.7	2,806	51.9	11.8	6.6	8.3	0.6	15.7	890	47	39	781	7,820	49,057	3,896
NORTH DAKOTA	X	X	X	X	X	X	X	X	X	9,497	12,118	65,698	371,810	74,794	8,850
Adams	16.2	6,984	27.1	0.0	4.7	3.8	17.0	1.2	524	19	13	98	1,020	51,669	5,026
Barnes	78.8	7,375	29.3	3.3	2.6	1.7	14.9	40.8	3,819	70	60	1,040	5,200	63,094	5,946
Benson	42.4	6,137	45.8	0.8	1.8	3.7	28.7	7.9	1,135	97	41	1,221	2,350	44,650	3,575
Billings	23.9	25,963	13.0	3.9	5.0	0.0	56.0	0.6	682	32	5	173	480	70,517	9,717
Bottineau	53.0	8,130	32.1	0.0	3.7	1.9	20.7	24.9	3,813	63	37	604	3,120	66,255	6,872
Bowman	33.1	10,504	32.3	0.0	2.6	0.2	46.4	0.5	150	19	18	231	1,500	66,989	8,225
Burke	23.1	10,870	33.8	0.0	2.3	1.3	35.9	4.3	2,039	83	13	157	1,100	76,306	8,373
Burleigh	458.3	4,812	39.9	0.8	5.0	1.5	11.2	423.7	4,448	1,153	563	10,919	47,440	82,085	10,166
Cass	1,072.3	6,033	37.0	1.1	3.5	1.2	15.9	2,222.3	12,503	2,543	1,105	11,957	91,230	83,320	10,518
Cavalier	24.5	6,448	33.2	1.6	6.2	3.1	27.5	6.3	1,662	36	22	233	1,840	74,222	7,584
Dickey	40.8	8,417	26.6	3.9	3.7	0.0	20.2	34.1	7,034	25	27	283	2,380	57,190	5,465
Divide	31.0	13,490	44.8	4.9	2.8	1.6	24.5	11.8	5,153	37	13	144	1,090	61,274	6,891
Dunn	73.2	17,127	14.7	0.0	2.7	0.9	48.4	21.4	5,011	14	26	341	2,110	115,337	21,257
Eddy	14.0	6,061	49.5	2.7	4.0	0.0	21.7	2.0	873	20	13	146	1,120	49,421	4,861
Emmons	45.6	13,819	28.5	0.9	1.6	0.5	14.7	9.9	2,999	23	19	237	1,530	52,534	5,356
Foster	24.3	7,482	39.4	1.8	2.9	3.6	18.4	31.7	9,750	23	19	204	1,650	68,712	7,268
Golden Valley	27.5	15,430	21.5	5.9	3.5	2.7	15.5	0.0	14	9	10	142	770	60,718	5,787
Grand Forks	305.4	4,333	45.5	0.7	7.3	2.6	8.6	630.1	8,940	1,003	2,191	8,998	33,400	68,407	7,637
Grant	14.1	5,972	36.1	2.2	3.3	2.8	30.7	2.9	1,222	23	13	126	1,080	30,874	3,652
Griggs	13.6	6,064	51.7	7.1	1.9	0.0	7.4	5.9	2,638	22	13	144	1,120	55,327	4,562
Hettinger	18.8	7,577	55.2	0.0	0.4	0.0	24.9	5.8	2,352	21	14	175	1,130	63,642	7,390
Kidder	17.4	7,048	31.0	27.0	2.6	0.0	12.4	3.6	1,472	20	15	135	1,140	44,781	4,467
LaMoure	34.9	8,520	45.7	2.2	2.1	1.7	11.5	14.3	3,497	40	24	267	2,000	62,046	6,574
Logan	17.2	8,982	42.1	0.0	2.0	0.0	11.6	3.7	1,935	19	11	117	890	27,992	3,854
McHenry	40.8	6,924	38.4	0.0	1.6	1.2	14.7	6.5	1,108	38	34	293	2,650	56,234	5,493
McIntosh	15.0	5,760	43.7	1.6	2.8	1.8	11.1	2.1	787	20	14	163	1,270	43,424	4,532
McKenzie	281.1	22,154	12.0	0.5	3.3	0.6	31.8	274.4	21,630	80	99	2,472	5,800	121,214	19,644
McLean	73.8	7,657	37.7	1.1	5.0	4.7	19.6	59.0	6,122	118	56	719	4,640	68,066	7,214
Mercer	49.7	5,872	38.2	0.5	6.9	1.4	23.1	43.4	5,136	38	49	512	4,010	77,781	8,667
Morton	160.1	5,175	45.4	3.0	5.4	2.9	10.3	200.3	6,473	119	186	1,634	16,030	69,608	7,816
Mountrail	147.7	14,378	31.1	1.2	3.4	1.8	40.1	50.6	4,928	44	60	810	4,630	88,108	11,513
Nelson	23.0	7,909	35.8	6.7	2.2	0.0	28.3	10.6	3,663	18	16	197	1,500	59,682	5,889
Oliver	8.9	4,601	41.8	0.0	1.1	0.0	1.0	7.2	3,747	6	12	105	870	61,786	5,602
Pembina	50.3	7,228	48.5	0.6	5.2	2.6	25.2	22.8	3,277	230	68	494	3,420	66,766	6,347
Pierce	23.1	5,635	41.2	1.5	2.9	2.7	18.5	13.9	3,387	19	22	206	1,930	58,985	5,472
Ramsey	73.8	6,368	44.3	5.3	5.0	4.5	15.2	19.5	1,685	135	66	1,343	5,660	57,987	5,652
Ransom	29.2	5,512	47.9	1.9	2.9	1.5	13.4	19.3	3,640	36	30	453	2,760	60,163	5,613
Renville	20.4	8,297	49.8	1.1	2.2	1.7	16.9	4.2	1,704	25	13	194	1,150	64,880	6,017
Richland	105.5	6,479	40.6	3.8	4.3	1.5	8.9	87.4	5,368	66	97	1,696	7,870	65,167	6,272
Rolette	80.8	5,529	61.7	1.4	2.3	2.9	10.0	20.7	1,414	924	85	1,717	5,150	47,913	3,519
Sargent	33.3	8,631	32.9	0.0	3.7	0.0	14.7	20.2	5,243	32	23	237	2,060	64,207	6,112
Sheridan	6.2	4,599	39.8	1.7	3.4	0.0	13.0	1.6	1,187	9	8	107	590	43,869	3,688
Sioux	15.4	3,484	74.7	0.1	0.2	0.0	15.2	3.7	845	235	25	1,099	1,140	25,618	2,172
Slope	7.5	9,735	7.4	0.1	4.2	2.7	39.2	0.5	647	1	5	43	340	47,915	5,235
Stark	216.3	7,140	47.5	1.8	3.8	1.6	5.8	217.8	7,190	219	191	2,189	16,100	81,184	9,885
Steele	15.1	7,947	30.5	0.8	3.4	3.3	19.5	4.0	2,083	10	11	102	930	71,017	7,428
Stutsman	103.7	4,907	43.1	3.0	5.4	2.7	14.4	87.2	4,125	149	114	1,839	10,090	62,096	6,340
Towner	14.5	6,475	27.1	4.5	4.1	2.7	20.4	4.3	1,917	16	13	119	1,090	59,730	5,130
Traill	1,947.2	243,457	1.2	0.0	0.1	0.1	0.6	37.5	4,690	39	47	830	3,770	67,353	6,425
Walsh	75.6	7,000	48.3	1.7	4.3	3.3	16.1	41.7	3,865	54	61	983	5,120	61,083	5,767

1. Based on the resident population estimated as of July 1 of the year shown.

State / county code	CBSA code[1]	County Type code[2]	STATE County	Land area[3] (sq. mi)	Population, 2021: Total persons 2021	Population, 2021: Rank	Population, 2021: Per square mile	Race alone or in combination, not Hispanic or Latino (percent): White	Black	American Indian, Alaska Native	Asian and Pacific Islancer	Percent Hispanic or Latino[4]	Age (percent): Under 5 years	5 to 17 years	18 to 24 years	25 to 34 years	35 to 44 years	45 to 54 years
				1	2	3	4	5	6	7	8	9	10	11	12	13	14	15
			NORTH DAKOTA—Cont'd															
38101	33500	5	Ward	2,013.0	69,071	781	34.3	83.8	5.8	3.7	2.8	7.0	7.2	13.2	16.5	16.9	13.1	9.5
38103		9	Wells	1,270.5	3,905	2,894	3.1	97.4	0.5	1.3	0.6	1.3	5.5	12.1	8.8	8.6	9.2	10.4
38105	48780	7	Williams	2,077.6	38,484	1,209	18.5	80.3	5.3	6.6	1.8	9.5	9.4	16.8	11.7	17.8	14.0	10.2
39000		0	OHIO	40,858.8	11,780,017	X	288.3	79.8	14.3	0.8	3.2	4.3	5.7	12.5	12.8	13.2	12.4	12.1
39001		6	Adams	583.9	27,542	1,517	47.2	97.3	1.3	1.3	0.5	1.1	6.2	13.6	11.9	11.1	11.3	13.2
39003	30620	3	Allen	402.5	101,670	602	252.6	82.8	14.7	0.7	1.3	3.7	6.0	13.1	14.0	12.4	11.9	11.4
39005	11740	4	Ashland	423.0	52,316	965	123.7	96.4	1.5	0.7	1.1	1.6	5.6	12.6	14.3	11.2	11.4	11.7
39007	11780	4	Ashtabula	702.1	97,337	629	138.6	90.9	5.0	0.8	0.8	4.8	5.6	12.4	11.6	11.8	11.2	12.7
39009	11900	4	Athens	503.6	62,056	858	123.2	92.1	3.7	1.2	3.6	2.0	3.7	8.1	30.8	11.4	10.6	10.0
39011	47540	4	Auglaize	401.4	46,141	1,053	115.0	96.5	1.4	0.5	1.0	1.9	6.1	13.7	12.0	11.8	11.6	11.9
39013	48540	3	Belmont	532.1	65,849	816	123.8	93.9	5.2	0.6	0.8	1.2	4.7	10.9	10.8	12.4	12.0	12.5
39015	17140	1	Brown	489.5	43,662	1,106	89.2	97.2	1.5	0.7	0.5	1.3	5.7	13.0	11.3	11.5	11.8	12.9
39017	17140	1	Butler	466.5	390,234	185	836.5	80.7	10.9	0.6	5.0	5.4	5.8	13.3	16.4	11.7	12.4	12.0
39019	15940	2	Carroll	394.6	26,691	1,543	67.6	97.1	1.4	0.9	0.6	1.5	5.2	11.8	10.9	10.3	10.9	12.6
39021	46500	6	Champaign	429.0	38,699	1,206	90.2	95.1	3.5	1.0	0.9	1.8	5.4	12.4	12.1	12.3	11.5	13.0
39023	44220	3	Clark	396.9	135,633	484	341.7	86.2	11.0	0.9	1.3	3.8	5.8	12.7	12.9	11.7	11.3	12.0
39025	17140	1	Clermont	452.6	209,642	325	463.2	94.3	2.6	0.6	1.9	2.2	5.6	12.7	11.8	12.6	12.7	12.6
39027	48940	6	Clinton	408.7	42,004	1,146	102.8	94.8	3.5	0.9	1.0	2.0	5.7	12.9	13.5	11.7	12.0	12.2
39029	41400	4	Columbiana	531.9	101,310	603	190.5	94.9	3.4	0.7	0.6	2.1	5.0	11.7	10.8	11.5	11.8	12.7
39031	18740	6	Coshocton	564.0	36,618	1,267	64.9	96.8	2.2	0.7	0.6	1.3	6.2	13.6	11.6	11.4	11.5	11.9
39033	15340	4	Crawford	401.8	41,754	1,152	103.9	95.9	1.9	0.5	0.9	1.9	5.5	12.3	11.6	11.5	11.2	12.8
39035	17460	1	Cuyahoga	457.2	1,249,387	35	2,732.7	59.9	31.1	0.7	4.1	6.6	5.4	11.5	12.0	14.3	12.2	11.6
39037	24820	6	Darke	598.1	51,597	972	86.3	96.7	1.4	0.6	0.8	1.8	6.1	13.5	12.0	11.0	11.3	11.9
39039	19580	4	Defiance	411.5	38,144	1,219	92.7	86.6	2.5	0.6	0.7	10.8	5.5	13.0	13.0	11.5	12.4	11.8
39041	18140	1	Delaware	443.1	220,740	317	498.2	84.2	5.2	0.5	9.4	3.0	5.7	14.8	12.9	9.7	15.3	15.0
39043	41780	4	Erie	251.3	74,852	743	297.9	85.4	11.1	0.8	1.1	4.8	5.2	11.2	11.3	11.6	11.0	11.8
39045	18140	1	Fairfield	504.4	161,064	419	319.3	85.3	10.6	0.8	3.0	2.6	5.8	13.8	12.5	11.9	13.3	13.4
39047	47920	6	Fayette	406.4	28,906	1,458	71.1	93.7	3.9	0.8	1.5	2.4	5.8	13.5	12.0	11.9	12.0	12.9
39049	18140	1	Franklin	532.4	1,321,414	31	2,482.0	63.7	25.9	0.9	6.8	6.2	6.6	13.0	13.2	17.7	14.1	11.6
39051	45780	2	Fulton	405.4	42,450	1,138	104.7	89.2	1.3	0.6	0.8	9.3	5.7	13.4	12.1	11.3	11.9	12.3
39053	38580	6	Gallia	466.5	29,158	1,451	62.5	94.9	3.4	1.0	1.3	1.4	6.1	13.1	12.3	11.4	11.5	11.9
39055	17460	1	Geauga	400.3	95,565	637	238.7	96.1	1.7	0.4	1.0	1.8	5.3	12.6	12.5	9.2	10.6	12.9
39057	19430	2	Greene	413.6	168,412	401	407.2	86.1	8.8	1.0	4.3	3.2	5.3	11.8	15.2	13.1	12.2	11.1
39059	15740	6	Guernsey	522.3	38,287	1,214	73.3	96.2	2.8	0.9	0.8	1.3	5.6	12.5	11.3	12.3	11.3	12.3
39061	17140	1	Hamilton	405.4	826,139	77	2,037.8	66.6	28.0	0.7	3.7	3.9	6.3	12.9	13.1	15.0	12.7	11.1
39063	22300	4	Hancock	531.3	74,656	745	140.5	89.5	2.9	0.6	2.6	6.2	5.7	12.4	12.6	13.3	12.2	12.1
39065		6	Hardin	470.3	30,621	1,418	65.1	95.6	1.9	0.8	1.3	2.2	6.1	13.3	19.1	10.6	10.9	11.5
39067		6	Harrison	402.3	14,477	2,121	36.0	96.0	3.2	0.8	0.6	1.3	5.0	12.0	10.9	10.6	11.0	12.2
39069		6	Henry	416.0	27,538	1,518	66.2	90.5	1.2	0.7	0.7	7.9	5.8	13.1	11.8	11.4	12.1	12.2
39071		6	Highland	553.1	43,354	1,118	78.4	96.3	2.6	0.8	0.7	1.4	6.3	13.2	11.8	11.5	11.7	12.7
39073	18140	1	Hocking	421.3	28,097	1,494	66.7	97.1	1.5	1.0	0.7	1.2	5.3	12.6	11.1	11.4	11.6	13.2
39075		7	Holmes	422.6	44,271	1,092	104.8	98.2	0.7	0.3	0.5	1.0	8.4	16.7	15.3	12.9	11.0	10.6
39077	35940	4	Huron	492.2	58,367	899	118.6	91.1	2.1	0.8	0.6	7.0	6.0	13.4	12.3	12.0	11.8	12.4
39079	27160	7	Jackson	420.3	32,511	1,370	77.4	97.3	1.5	1.2	0.6	1.1	6.1	13.4	11.9	12.2	12.4	12.7
39081	48260	3	Jefferson	408.1	64,789	837	158.8	92.0	6.9	0.7	1.0	1.8	5.1	11.0	12.7	11.5	10.5	12.1
39083	34540	4	Knox	525.5	62,897	850	119.7	96.3	1.7	0.6	1.0	1.8	5.9	12.9	15.4	10.9	11.2	11.2
39085	17460	1	Lake	229.3	232,023	298	1,011.9	88.2	6.1	0.5	2.0	5.0	4.8	10.9	11.4	12.3	11.8	12.6
39087	26580	2	Lawrence	453.4	57,445	909	126.7	96.0	3.2	0.7	0.8	1.0	5.3	12.3	11.3	12.1	12.2	13.3
39089	18140	1	Licking	682.4	180,401	371	264.4	89.7	5.8	0.9	3.8	2.3	5.8	13.2	12.6	11.9	12.7	12.7
39091	13340	6	Logan	458.5	46,035	1,060	100.4	94.6	3.4	0.8	1.3	2.1	5.7	12.9	11.8	11.4	11.7	12.7
39093	17460	1	Lorain	490.5	315,595	226	643.4	79.7	9.7	0.8	1.9	10.8	5.4	12.4	12.2	11.6	12.2	12.8
39095	45780	2	Lucas	339.7	429,191	167	1,263.4	70.3	22.0	0.9	2.4	7.8	6.1	13.0	12.5	14.1	11.9	11.8
39097	18140	1	Madison	465.8	44,386	1,089	95.3	89.0	7.4	0.7	1.8	2.7	5.1	11.3	11.3	13.8	14.3	14.1
39099	49660	2	Mahoning	411.5	226,762	310	551.1	76.9	16.4	0.7	1.3	7.0	5.3	11.1	11.9	12.3	11.4	11.7
39101	32020	4	Marion	403.8	65,291	827	161.7	89.5	7.9	0.8	0.9	3.1	5.6	12.2	11.5	13.4	12.6	12.8
39103	17460	1	Medina	421.5	183,092	368	434.4	94.3	2.2	0.5	1.7	2.6	4.9	12.5	11.8	10.7	12.7	13.5
39105		6	Meigs	430.1	22,049	1,710	51.3	97.6	1.5	0.9	0.5	0.9	4.9	11.9	11.2	10.3	12.4	13.2
39107	16380	7	Mercer	462.4	42,309	1,139	91.5	95.9	1.2	0.5	1.7	1.9	7.6	14.2	12.1	11.4	11.2	10.7
39109	19430	2	Miami	406.5	109,264	565	268.8	93.3	4.1	0.6	2.2	2.0	5.7	13.2	11.3	11.7	12.7	12.5
39111		8	Monroe	455.7	13,329	2,195	29.2	98.1	1.4	0.9	0.6	0.7	4.9	12.0	10.5	10.2	11.1	12.5
39113	19430	2	Montgomery	461.4	535,840	133	1,161.3	72.2	23.3	0.9	3.2	3.6	5.9	12.4	13.0	13.8	12.0	11.4
39115		6	Morgan	416.4	13,682	2,178	32.9	95.2	5.2	1.7	1.1	1.0	4.9	11.4	11.3	10.4	11.7	12.3
39117	18140	1	Morrow	406.1	35,151	1,302	86.6	96.7	1.5	0.9	0.7	1.8	5.5	12.2	11.5	11.3	12.1	13.7
39119	49780	4	Muskingum	664.5	86,408	674	130.0	93.9	6.1	0.9	1.0	1.3	5.9	13.0	12.4	12.5	11.8	12.3
39121		7	Noble	398.0	14,176	2,137	35.6	95.3	3.8	0.9	0.5	0.8	5.0	10.8	8.7	9.2	8.6	10.3

1. CBSA = Core Based Statistical Area. See Appendix A for explanation. See Appendix B for list of metropolitan areas with component counties. 2. County type code from the Economic Research Service of USDA Rural-Urban Continuum Codes. See Appendix A for definition. 3. Dry land or land partially or temporarily covered by water. 4. May be of any race.

STATE County	Population, 2021 (cont.)				Population change, 2000–2021							Households, 2016–2020				
	Age (percent) (cont.)				Total persons		Percent change		Components of change, 2020–2021					Percent		
	55 to 64 years	65 to 74 years	75 years and over	Percent female	2010	2020	2010–2020	2020–2021	Births	Deaths	Net Migration	Number	Persons per household	Family house-holds	Female family house-holder[1]	One person
	16	17	18	19	20	21	22	23	24	25	26	27	28	29	30	31
NORTH DAKOTA—Cont'd																
Ward	10.3	7.9	5.5	47.5	61,675	69,919	13.4	-1.2	1,280	866	-1,256	28,432	2.3	58.9	6.5	32.6
Wells	17.0	14.8	13.7	49.3	4,207	3,982	-5.3	-1.9	48	72	-52	1,941	2.0	57.9	8.2	37.5
Williams	10.2	6.1	3.7	46.5	22,398	40,950	82.8	-6.0	961	310	-3,061	14,646	2.4	60.3	6.4	30.5
OHIO	13.5	10.9	7.0	50.7	11,536,504	11,799,448	2.3	-0.2	160,886	181,233	-97	4,717,226	2.4	62.6	12.3	30.9
Adams	14.2	11.5	7.0	50.1	28,550	27,477	-3.8	0.2	403	513	173	10,396	2.6	70.1	12.8	26.0
Allen	13.1	11.0	7.2	49.2	106,331	102,206	-3.9	-0.5	1,464	1,675	-341	41,025	2.4	62.4	14.2	32.5
Ashland	13.6	11.5	8.0	50.7	53,139	52,447	-1.3	-0.2	705	872	30	20,504	2.5	67.2	10.4	26.6
Ashtabula	14.7	12.2	7.8	49.2	101,497	97,574	-3.9	-0.2	1,270	1,657	139	38,614	2.4	63.5	12.5	30.7
Athens	11.3	9.3	5.0	50.1	64,757	62,431	-3.6	-0.6	572	768	-194	22,539	2.5	52.0	8.2	33.8
Auglaize	14.0	11.3	7.7	49.8	45,949	46,422	1.0	-0.6	635	776	-146	19,000	2.4	68.2	9.0	26.4
Belmont	15.0	13.3	8.4	48.6	70,400	66,497	-5.5	-1.0	758	1,273	-138	25,772	2.5	64.1	10.8	31.8
Brown	15.0	11.3	7.5	50.0	44,846	43,676	-2.6	0.0	593	808	198	17,811	2.4	68.2	10.3	26.4
Butler	12.9	9.6	5.9	50.6	368,130	390,357	6.0	0.0	5,414	5,413	-191	140,736	2.6	68.6	11.1	25.1
Carroll	16.1	13.4	8.8	49.3	28,836	26,721	-7.3	-0.1	329	479	122	11,286	2.4	66.0	7.2	29.0
Champaign	14.6	11.1	7.6	50.0	40,097	38,714	-3.4	0.0	488	653	147	15,407	2.5	69.7	11.5	25.4
Clark	13.7	11.9	7.9	51.1	138,333	136,001	-1.7	-0.3	1,896	2,575	296	54,862	2.4	64.4	14.2	29.1
Clermont	14.3	11.1	6.6	50.4	197,363	208,601	5.7	0.5	2,728	2,893	1,184	79,347	2.6	69.5	10.4	24.9
Clinton	14.1	11.0	6.9	50.4	42,040	42,018	-0.1	0.0	580	711	110	16,741	2.4	66.3	11.1	29.6
Columbiana	15.1	13.1	8.2	49.0	107,841	101,877	-5.5	-0.6	1,206	1,870	88	41,632	2.4	63.6	10.4	31.9
Coshocton	14.0	12.0	7.9	50.2	36,901	36,612	-0.8	0.0	541	610	72	14,579	2.5	68.6	10.9	26.9
Crawford	13.8	12.5	8.9	50.8	43,784	42,025	-4.0	-0.6	530	810	6	17,928	2.3	64.0	11.5	30.0
Cuyahoga	13.9	11.3	7.7	52.0	1,280,122	1,264,817	-1.2	-1.2	16,520	20,337	-11,636	547,887	2.2	55.0	15.1	38.1
Darke	14.3	11.5	8.4	50.0	52,959	51,881	-2.0	-0.5	743	897	-134	21,171	2.4	67.2	9.2	27.1
Defiance	13.2	11.8	7.7	49.9	39,037	38,286	-1.9	-0.4	511	607	-46	15,385	2.4	69.4	10.5	24.3
Delaware	12.1	9.3	5.3	50.0	174,214	214,124	22.9	3.1	2,578	2,026	6,113	71,521	2.8	76.9	7.4	19.5
Erie	15.0	13.6	9.3	50.9	77,079	75,622	-1.9	-1.0	903	1,471	-204	31,319	2.3	63.9	12.3	29.9
Fairfield	13.2	9.8	6.3	50.0	146,156	158,921	8.7	1.3	2,104	2,180	2,224	57,071	2.7	71.2	10.4	23.8
Fayette	13.6	11.0	7.2	50.8	29,030	28,951	-0.3	-0.2	383	483	54	11,737	2.4	68.5	14.3	26.3
Franklin	11.2	8.1	4.6	50.9	1,163,414	1,323,807	13.8	-0.2	21,837	15,533	-8,882	519,237	2.5	58.2	13.7	32.6
Fulton	14.3	11.6	7.4	50.0	42,698	42,713	0.0	-0.6	560	626	-201	16,582	2.5	69.6	9.6	25.7
Gallia	14.2	11.6	7.9	50.3	30,934	29,220	-5.5	-0.2	457	561	37	11,359	2.6	66.8	8.2	28.2
Geauga	15.4	12.6	8.8	49.8	93,389	95,397	2.2	0.2	1,137	1,279	313	35,303	2.6	73.2	5.8	21.2
Greene	13.3	10.9	7.0	50.3	161,573	167,966	4.0	0.3	2,027	2,339	737	65,915	2.4	65.2	9.5	27.7
Guernsey	14.4	12.3	8.0	49.9	40,087	38,438	-4.1	-0.4	530	676	-10	16,244	2.4	63.6	11.9	29.5
Hamilton	12.8	9.9	6.2	51.4	802,374	830,639	3.5	-0.5	12,886	12,062	-5,420	344,588	2.3	57.4	14.2	35.0
Hancock	13.6	10.9	7.2	50.1	74,782	74,920	0.2	-0.4	1,030	1,102	-203	32,022	2.3	59.6	8.8	33.1
Hardin	12.5	9.7	6.5	50.0	32,058	30,696	-4.2	-0.2	481	486	-74	11,777	2.5	66.4	9.5	27.2
Harrison	16.1	13.6	8.5	50.1	15,864	14,483	-8.7	0.0	208	288	76	6,221	2.4	63.7	7.6	30.9
Henry	14.2	11.5	7.9	50.1	28,215	27,662	-2.0	-0.4	370	440	-58	11,069	2.4	67.6	11.1	27.6
Highland	13.8	11.4	7.5	50.4	43,589	43,317	-0.6	0.1	615	765	183	16,747	2.5	69.6	11.6	24.1
Hocking	15.1	12.1	7.7	50.0	29,380	28,050	-4.5	0.2	359	494	182	11,533	2.4	73.0	11.4	22.6
Holmes	11.0	8.3	5.8	49.5	42,366	44,223	4.4	0.1	993	557	-396	12,351	3.5	81.2	6.9	16.6
Huron	14.0	11.2	6.9	50.1	59,626	58,565	-1.8	-0.3	809	952	-66	23,050	2.5	64.9	11.4	29.5
Jackson	13.3	11.2	6.6	50.5	33,225	32,653	-1.7	-0.4	451	601	2	12,971	2.5	70.7	11.7	24.9
Jefferson	14.9	13.5	8.8	51.0	69,709	65,249	-6.4	-0.7	806	1,310	38	27,541	2.3	63.3	11.9	31.2
Knox	13.7	11.5	7.3	50.5	60,921	62,721	3.0	0.3	845	980	304	23,027	2.5	69.9	8.9	24.8
Lake	15.2	12.6	8.5	50.9	230,041	232,603	1.1	-0.2	2,566	3,741	571	96,534	2.4	62.3	10.6	31.0
Lawrence	14.2	11.6	7.7	51.0	62,450	58,240	-6.7	-1.4	779	1,139	-438	23,208	2.6	67.0	14.1	28.5
Licking	14.0	10.5	6.6	50.5	166,492	178,519	7.2	1.1	2,338	2,521	2,064	64,466	2.7	70.3	11.5	24.1
Logan	14.8	12.0	7.1	50.2	45,858	46,150	0.6	-0.2	601	736	14	18,604	2.4	67.7	8.0	26.7
Lorain	14.1	11.7	7.5	50.4	301,356	312,964	3.9	0.8	3,984	4,630	3,278	121,669	2.5	64.4	12.3	30.4
Lucas	13.3	10.6	6.5	51.4	441,815	431,279	-2.4	-0.5	6,369	7,016	-1,513	181,472	2.3	58.6	15.1	34.2
Madison	13.9	9.8	6.3	45.4	43,435	43,824	0.9	1.3	556	595	604	15,017	2.6	66.4	12.0	26.2
Mahoning	14.3	13.1	8.7	50.5	238,823	228,614	-4.3	-0.8	2,891	4,613	-156	98,869	2.2	60.0	14.1	35.0
Marion	13.4	11.3	7.2	46.7	66,501	65,359	-1.7	-0.1	870	1,047	100	24,617	2.4	62.3	12.0	32.1
Medina	14.8	11.6	7.4	50.2	172,332	182,470	5.9	0.3	1,981	2,413	1,042	69,739	2.6	70.7	7.9	25.0
Meigs	15.1	12.9	8.0	50.1	23,770	22,210	-6.6	-0.7	225	444	58	9,090	2.5	63.8	11.0	31.4
Mercer	13.7	11.6	7.4	49.3	40,814	42,528	4.2	-0.5	769	644	-345	16,078	2.5	68.3	6.1	27.0
Miami	13.7	11.4	7.7	50.4	102,506	108,774	6.1	0.5	1,452	1,700	733	41,260	2.6	65.4	9.0	28.5
Monroe	15.2	13.8	9.9	49.2	14,642	13,385	-8.6	-0.4	168	260	36	5,854	2.3	65.9	7.7	31.5
Montgomery	13.2	10.8	7.5	51.6	535,153	537,309	0.4	-0.3	7,696	9,235	-19	227,077	2.3	58.9	14.5	34.6
Morgan	15.6	13.2	9.2	49.8	15,054	13,802	-8.3	-0.9	169	272	-19	6,076	2.4	67.2	9.8	27.6
Morrow	15.1	11.4	7.0	49.6	34,827	34,950	0.4	0.6	451	494	243	13,064	2.7	74.1	10.4	19.8
Muskingum	13.7	11.1	7.3	51.1	86,074	86,410	0.4	0.0	1,190	1,442	238	33,797	2.5	63.9	13.3	30.9
Noble	18.7	17.6	11.1	40.3	14,645	14,115	-3.6	0.4	179	226	111	4,969	2.4	60.9	6.5	35.3

1. No spouse present.

STATE County	Persons in group quarters, 2021	Daytime Population, 2016–2020: Number	Daytime Population, 2016–2020: Employment/ residence ratio	Births, 2021: Total	Births, 2021: Rate[1]	Deaths, 2021: Number	Deaths, 2021: Rate[1]	Persons under 65 with no health insurance, 2019: Number	Persons under 65 with no health insurance, 2019: Percent	Medicare, 2021: Total beneficiaries	Medicare, 2021: Enrolled in Original Medicare	Medicare, 2021: Enrolled in Medicare Advantage	COVID-19 Deaths, 2020: Number	COVID-19 Deaths, 2020: Rate[1]
	32	33	34	35	36	37	38	39	40	41	42	43	44	45
NORTH DAKOTA—Cont'd														
Ward	3,125	69,099	1.0	1,008	14.5	669	9.6	4,236	7.5	10,242	8,551	1,691	168	2.4
Wells	68	4,106	1.1	43	10.9	54	13.7	194	7.2	1,177	1,059	117	D	D
Williams	421	41,293	1.3	758	19.0	241	6.1	2,885	8.5	3,845	3,468	377	34	0.8
OHIO	301,360	11,694,379	1.0	128,595	10.9	144,406	12.3	741,409	7.9	2,380,143	1,278,219	1,101,925	15,051	1.3
Adams	265	25,297	0.8	321	11.7	408	14.8	2,132	9.6	6,518	4,021	2,497	32	1.2
Allen	5,583	107,143	1.1	1,166	11.4	1,361	13.4	5,966	7.6	22,007	13,676	8,331	189	1.9
Ashland	1,878	48,584	0.8	571	10.9	701	13.4	4,419	10.7	11,594	6,708	4,886	74	1.4
Ashtabula	3,112	88,754	0.8	1,031	10.6	1,317	13.5	7,386	9.8	23,626	15,395	8,231	144	1.5
Athens	8,994	65,200	1.0	458	7.4	629	10.1	4,271	9.1	10,618	6,907	3,711	30	0.5
Auglaize	471	44,138	0.9	504	10.9	617	13.3	2,180	5.9	9,984	7,036	2,949	80	1.7
Belmont	3,451	62,991	0.8	601	9.1	994	15.1	3,694	7.5	16,098	8,298	7,801	104	1.6
Brown	505	33,997	0.5	460	10.5	632	14.5	2,887	8.2	10,083	5,441	4,642	34	0.8
Butler	12,152	358,779	0.9	4,299	11.0	4,387	11.2	24,275	7.7	68,346	36,592	31,754	439	1.1
Carroll	333	23,720	0.7	268	10.0	393	14.7	1,763	8.4	6,729	3,160	3,570	34	1.3
Champaign	585	33,238	0.7	377	9.7	517	13.4	2,106	6.8	8,546	4,631	3,915	37	1.0
Clark	3,210	124,623	0.8	1,548	11.4	2,032	15.0	8,896	8.5	31,048	14,935	16,114	233	1.7
Clermont	1,592	170,355	0.7	2,175	10.4	2,333	11.2	12,006	7.0	41,528	20,853	20,675	156	0.7
Clinton	1,045	43,663	1.1	467	11.1	553	13.2	2,382	7.1	8,766	5,004	3,761	48	1.1
Columbiana	3,854	90,203	0.7	985	9.7	1,475	14.5	6,206	8.1	24,838	12,493	12,346	173	1.7
Coshocton	362	33,205	0.8	447	12.2	482	13.2	3,060	10.6	8,329	5,366	2,963	42	1.1
Crawford	528	37,286	0.8	432	10.3	617	14.7	2,476	7.7	10,679	7,201	3,478	85	2.0
Cuyahoga	29,995	1,367,447	1.2	13,253	10.6	16,137	12.9	71,497	7.3	259,986	133,649	126,338	1,650	1.3
Darke	549	46,384	0.8	567	11.0	711	13.7	3,321	8.2	11,825	7,889	3,936	104	2.0
Defiance	674	35,627	0.9	397	10.4	481	12.6	2,059	6.8	8,932	5,831	3,101	76	2.0
Delaware	1,767	195,607	0.9	2,065	9.5	1,654	7.6	8,122	4.5	33,303	19,375	13,927	99	0.5
Erie	1,607	75,019	1.0	709	9.4	1,151	15.3	4,258	7.5	19,557	12,498	7,059	135	1.8
Fairfield	2,535	127,532	0.6	1,715	10.7	1,746	10.9	8,893	6.8	30,051	14,622	15,429	154	1.0
Fayette	543	28,882	1.0	299	10.3	362	12.5	1,957	8.5	6,587	3,852	2,735	34	1.2
Franklin	30,222	1,409,902	1.2	17,346	13.1	12,442	9.4	100,068	8.9	185,527	94,943	90,584	1,197	0.9
Fulton	347	40,738	0.9	449	10.6	508	11.9	2,540	7.4	9,347	5,850	3,497	56	1.3
Gallia	769	29,698	1.0	367	12.6	455	15.6	2,250	9.6	6,891	4,547	2,344	34	1.2
Geauga	813	87,304	0.9	890	9.3	1,036	10.9	7,271	9.8	21,267	12,511	8,756	129	1.4
Greene	8,069	176,275	1.1	1,616	9.6	1,900	11.3	9,227	7.0	32,851	19,181	13,670	183	1.1
Guernsey	418	39,044	1.0	437	11.4	543	14.2	2,717	8.8	9,437	6,059	3,378	39	1.0
Hamilton	23,348	929,893	1.3	10,318	12.5	9,691	11.7	51,666	7.7	149,597	78,669	70,928	871	1.0
Hancock	1,208	84,653	1.2	832	11.1	884	11.8	3,916	6.4	15,373	10,344	5,029	110	1.5
Hardin	1,730	28,064	0.8	386	12.6	396	12.9	1,905	7.8	6,220	4,277	1,943	60	2.0
Harrison	155	13,997	0.8	154	10.6	237	16.4	1,015	8.7	3,800	2,272	1,527	17	1.2
Henry	315	25,219	0.9	300	10.9	355	12.9	1,517	7.0	6,204	4,352	1,852	55	2.0
Highland	401	38,477	0.8	495	11.4	611	14.1	3,374	9.8	9,842	5,948	3,894	56	1.3
Hocking	251	25,034	0.7	286	10.2	393	14.0	1,721	7.6	6,439	4,095	2,344	45	1.6
Holmes	697	47,576	1.2	792	17.9	446	10.1	8,847	23.6	5,125	3,125	2,001	81	1.8
Huron	506	54,736	0.9	653	11.2	755	12.9	4,213	8.9	12,704	8,749	3,955	88	1.5
Jackson	272	30,442	0.9	367	11.3	469	14.4	2,218	8.4	7,486	4,970	2,517	45	1.4
Jefferson	2,260	61,565	0.8	633	9.7	1,031	15.9	3,833	7.9	16,722	10,048	6,674	99	1.5
Knox	3,489	56,629	0.8	657	10.5	800	12.7	4,173	8.8	13,335	8,254	5,081	79	1.3
Lake	2,676	213,469	0.9	2,048	8.8	2,993	12.9	13,520	7.4	53,891	29,328	24,564	279	1.2
Lawrence	559	50,285	0.6	622	10.8	938	16.2	3,684	7.8	14,381	9,989	4,392	79	1.4
Licking	3,375	163,467	0.9	1,843	10.3	2,009	11.2	10,388	7.2	35,522	18,709	16,813	169	0.9
Logan	403	45,163	1.0	496	10.8	621	13.5	2,677	7.3	10,198	7,031	3,166	47	1.0
Lorain	8,218	277,694	0.8	3,157	10.0	3,749	11.9	18,632	7.6	68,250	35,937	32,312	356	1.1
Lucas	9,193	446,764	1.1	5,112	11.9	5,613	13.1	28,110	8.1	86,525	43,798	42,727	650	1.5
Madison	4,454	42,733	0.9	440	10.0	480	10.9	2,604	7.9	8,020	4,025	3,995	52	1.2
Mahoning	8,804	229,702	1.0	2,311	10.2	3,632	16.0	13,311	7.8	57,420	25,109	32,311	512	2.2
Marion	5,492	64,999	1.0	698	10.7	835	12.8	3,632	7.6	14,378	8,306	6,072	121	1.9
Medina	1,105	154,951	0.7	1,576	8.6	1,936	10.6	8,465	5.8	37,968	19,693	18,275	195	1.1
Meigs	151	19,105	0.5	183	8.3	337	15.3	1,591	8.8	5,542	3,420	2,122	27	1.2
Mercer	406	40,295	1.0	622	14.7	504	11.9	2,411	7.2	8,743	6,417	2,326	84	2.0
Miami	979	99,271	0.9	1,156	10.6	1,345	12.3	6,516	7.5	23,530	13,028	10,503	138	1.3
Monroe	116	12,570	0.8	134	10.0	209	15.7	922	9.0	3,646	1,881	1,765	28	2.1
Montgomery	15,046	551,299	1.1	6,216	11.6	7,334	13.7	37,048	8.8	112,242	53,320	58,922	764	1.4
Morgan	128	12,512	0.7	132	9.6	211	15.4	1,046	9.3	3,483	2,018	1,466	16	1.2
Morrow	277	26,649	0.5	355	10.1	401	11.4	2,483	8.6	7,264	4,345	2,919	31	0.9
Muskingum	1,471	85,291	1.0	964	11.2	1,145	13.3	5,482	7.9	20,338	12,071	8,267	96	1.1
Noble	2,593	13,318	0.8	142	10.0	178	12.6	703	8.0	2,645	1,738	907	37	2.6

1. Per 1,000 estimated resident population.

STATE County	COVID-19 Vaccinations, 2021–2022: Number	COVID-19 Vaccinations, 2021–2022: Percent[5]	Education: School enrollment and attainment, 2016–2020: Enrollment[1]: Total	Education: Enrollment[1]: Percent private	Education: Attainment[2] (percent): High school graduate or less	Education: Attainment[2] (percent): Bachelor's degree or more	Education: Local government expenditures,[3] 2018–2019: Total current spending (mil dol)	Education: Local government expenditures,[3] 2018–2019: Current spending per student (dollars)	Money income, 2016–2020: Per capita income[4]	Money income, 2016–2020: Households: Median income (dollars)	Money income, 2016–2020: Households: Percent with income of less than $50,000	Money income, 2016–2020: Households: Percent with income of $200,000 or more	Income and poverty, 2020: Median household income (dollars)	Income and poverty, 2020: Percent below poverty level: All persons	Income and poverty, 2020: Percent below poverty level: Children under 18 years	Income and poverty, 2020: Percent below poverty level: Children 5 to 17 years in families
	46	47	48	49	50	51	52	53	54	55	56	57	58	59	60	61
NORTH DAKOTA—Cont'd																
Ward	33,674	49.8	16,932	11.9	36.4	29.0	143.1	13,447	35,891	68,098	35.7	5.4	64,346	8.9	8.8	7.4
Wells	1,661	43.3	708	7.8	42.6	22.2	8.6	15,114	36,563	56,519	45.4	3.9	56,827	10.9	13.6	12.1
Williams	11,276	30.0	8,028	8.7	38.8	25.6	86.6	13,729	43,364	79,508	29.5	10.3	79,483	9.6	8.7	7.7
OHIO	6,820,544	58.3	2,771,293	18.2	42.0	28.9	22,523.6	13,294	32,465	58,116	43.3	5.2	60,360	12.6	16.6	15.3
Adams	9,675	34.9	5,926	14.6	61.2	15.5	56.6	12,384	23,294	40,067	58.1	2.7	42,342	20.6	28.7	25.8
Allen	44,745	43.7	25,233	22.4	48.6	18.7	181.1	12,549	27,231	51,892	48.6	2.5	52,558	12.9	17.9	15.7
Ashland	23,152	43.3	13,156	27.4	52.5	22.0	88.0	12,396	27,403	55,422	43.9	2.8	55,699	11.4	15.6	14.1
Ashtabula	51,357	52.8	19,712	15.3	56.7	14.9	168.9	13,014	25,556	47,925	52.0	2.2	51,252	16.5	23.6	21.8
Athens	33,586	51.4	26,526	2.5	42.0	31.8	110.4	15,656	22,287	42,414	54.6	2.4	42,215	22.0	21.0	19.3
Auglaize	18,043	39.5	10,290	7.6	50.0	19.2	91.8	11,750	32,194	66,193	35.9	3.3	69,468	5.9	7.0	6.5
Belmont	32,307	48.2	12,970	13.6	52.8	16.2	104.1	11,793	27,393	51,574	48.4	3.1	50,626	12.7	18.2	17.4
Brown	17,834	41.1	9,170	11.6	57.2	14.3	90.2	13,095	28,320	57,200	43.8	2.6	58,067	13.6	17.6	15.9
Butler	217,963	56.9	104,804	13.4	41.3	31.3	696.5	11,984	33,018	69,023	36.0	6.5	69,049	10.1	11.9	11.2
Carroll	11,846	44.0	5,262	21.8	59.8	13.2	37.0	12,634	29,915	52,574	47.2	3.4	52,065	11.6	16.4	15.9
Champaign	17,800	45.8	8,604	12.1	54.7	15.9	92.2	13,529	28,403	59,909	39.7	2.1	64,142	10.1	13.2	12.3
Clark	71,019	53.0	30,472	20.3	49.1	18.9	263.3	12,823	27,274	51,504	48.7	2.2	54,507	14.3	20.5	19.0
Clermont	117,419	56.9	46,041	17.5	42.2	28.9	313.3	11,566	35,472	69,720	35.1	6.5	72,740	9.2	10.9	9.2
Clinton	20,588	49.1	10,265	21.8	48.6	20.0	81.4	11,235	28,107	54,683	45.8	2.8	53,891	11.3	15.2	13.6
Columbiana	50,240	49.3	20,445	10.4	55.5	14.5	184.5	12,909	26,769	49,407	50.6	1.8	49,342	13.9	19.2	18.4
Coshocton	14,208	38.8	7,594	14.0	58.3	14.9	58.6	12,090	23,863	48,552	52.0	1.8	47,794	14.9	21.7	20.9
Crawford	18,736	45.2	8,420	12.8	55.7	15.3	77.7	12,399	26,286	46,391	54.0	1.4	45,952	12.1	18.0	16.5
Cuyahoga	803,130	65.0	288,506	25.7	37.2	33.5	2,699.7	16,124	34,398	51,741	48.5	5.8	55,128	15.3	19.9	18.9
Darke	20,186	39.5	11,289	9.8	56.4	15.4	98.1	11,608	28,639	54,799	46.3	2.6	57,932	10.2	12.5	11.8
Defiance	18,721	49.2	8,960	18.1	49.5	18.4	75.0	12,163	31,051	62,110	38.7	3.5	61,816	8.5	12.5	11.5
Delaware	157,174	75.1	56,959	17.1	20.7	55.5	391.6	11,776	48,312	111,411	19.8	19.7	114,423	3.7	3.3	2.9
Erie	44,031	59.3	15,385	17.8	43.0	24.9	185.6	16,739	34,352	58,408	43.2	4.3	66,252	10.9	14.5	13.2
Fairfield	90,750	57.6	37,679	15.3	39.7	29.0	303.0	12,126	33,283	70,906	35.4	6.0	74,987	7.5	8.2	7.6
Fayette	12,432	43.6	5,857	11.8	61.2	15.2	52.1	10,874	25,993	48,637	50.9	2.5	50,125	13.8	19.7	18.0
Franklin	848,041	64.4	335,029	17.2	33.3	40.4	2,737.5	13,635	34,790	62,352	40.1	6.4	62,643	15.4	20.3	19.0
Fulton	22,127	52.5	9,625	10.5	49.9	17.0	114.4	15,207	30,252	61,290	39.9	4.4	60,550	8.3	10.4	10.1
Gallia	13,990	46.8	6,572	20.4	55.5	17.4	61.0	14,314	25,567	48,975	50.8	2.5	50,642	16.1	21.8	20.8
Geauga	57,451	61.3	20,925	25.5	35.4	37.8	145.2	14,749	41,874	83,730	27.7	11.1	84,510	6.2	6.2	5.4
Greene	106,518	63.1	47,390	21.4	29.5	39.7	285.0	12,912	36,386	70,055	35.6	7.4	71,673	9.0	10.3	9.6
Guernsey	17,297	44.5	8,417	16.7	56.8	15.1	66.8	14,768	25,878	46,352	53.2	2.7	45,808	13.5	23.6	18.7
Hamilton	514,144	62.9	201,033	23.6	34.0	38.9	1,565.1	14,054	37,028	59,190	43.2	7.4	63,919	12.7	16.5	16.2
Hancock	38,458	50.7	17,788	20.9	42.9	27.6	146.4	12,131	32,829	57,384	43.2	4.6	61,473	9.3	11.0	10.3
Hardin	12,149	38.7	8,571	23.7	58.9	16.0	51.2	12,365	23,498	50,214	49.7	1.6	45,312	15.1	19.0	15.9
Harrison	6,466	43.0	2,744	16.0	61.5	12.4	19.3	12,535	25,751	49,454	50.4	2.1	49,088	13.7	18.9	17.0
Henry	14,594	54.0	6,173	14.6	50.4	17.6	70.9	16,684	30,188	60,425	41.0	3.1	64,694	8.0	10.7	9.8
Highland	16,370	37.9	9,088	13.3	59.4	13.8	84.3	11,961	24,058	47,973	51.1	1.4	57,155	14.9	21.9	19.9
Hocking	13,604	48.1	5,834	8.0	55.5	13.9	45.6	12,130	26,733	54,774	45.6	2.4	53,838	14.7	19.4	18.4
Holmes	7,927	18.0	8,777	40.0	76.2	10.4	42.9	11,528	24,751	64,453	36.5	4.9	67,967	8.4	12.1	11.4
Huron	27,832	47.8	13,029	13.4	56.2	14.7	118.6	11,818	26,766	55,041	44.7	1.6	62,143	9.8	14.6	14.0
Jackson	15,340	47.3	6,731	12.6	58.8	14.8	58.4	11,933	25,004	48,915	51.3	3.1	49,636	15.9	21.7	19.7
Jefferson	32,862	50.3	14,159	25.3	52.5	17.5	100.7	11,826	26,602	46,849	52.6	2.1	49,642	15.3	20.8	19.7
Knox	26,858	43.1	15,902	28.8	47.2	22.6	99.8	13,274	27,599	61,590	39.7	3.3	68,050	10.9	14.9	14.2
Lake	150,832	65.5	49,688	18.7	38.8	28.3	404.8	13,082	35,007	65,814	37.4	5.2	69,853	7.9	10.5	9.8
Lawrence	29,467	49.6	13,143	8.6	56.4	15.8	128.3	13,945	24,733	46,584	53.3	1.9	47,299	19.8	28.6	23.3
Licking	96,928	54.8	41,988	19.3	41.6	27.6	324.1	11,579	33,514	67,736	36.5	6.5	68,982	9.8	12.4	11.2
Logan	19,574	42.9	9,726	9.4	52.9	17.1	97.1	15,675	30,266	60,417	40.2	2.9	61,797	10.1	14.0	12.7
Lorain	197,348	63.7	72,469	21.5	40.8	25.3	536.8	12,412	31,627	58,798	42.4	4.9	59,954	11.9	16.1	13.7
Lucas	248,796	58.1	103,814	16.6	39.8	26.7	921.0	11,936	29,496	49,946	50.0	3.6	51,642	17.5	26.6	24.4
Madison	22,892	51.2	9,442	14.8	53.5	18.1	87.0	13,048	29,885	68,663	34.1	3.6	72,834	9.5	12.1	11.3
Mahoning	130,725	57.2	49,856	13.3	46.1	24.6	397.2	13,218	28,693	47,092	52.3	3.0	48,937	15.8	22.5	21.0
Marion	31,388	48.2	14,036	6.4	54.9	12.9	133.7	11,279	25,899	49,225	50.5	3.3	52,226	14.3	19.4	18.7
Medina	115,128	64.1	41,036	17.4	36.0	33.9	312.2	11,895	38,446	77,784	30.4	7.7	79,504	5.9	6.3	5.7
Meigs	10,742	46.9	4,930	6.7	60.3	12.1	40.9	12,474	24,342	43,445	57.9	1.7	44,622	18.8	23.3	21.8
Mercer	15,769	38.3	9,719	5.3	51.5	19.4	97.7	12,261	30,975	65,566	36.8	3.4	69,588	5.5	7.6	7.9
Miami	51,021	47.7	24,748	12.7	45.7	22.6	209.9	13,469	31,170	62,347	38.0	3.8	63,699	8.0	10.9	10.1
Monroe	6,376	46.7	2,578	14.4	60.4	12.1	37.2	17,843	28,521	46,241	53.3	2.6	48,944	14.6	21.0	20.3
Montgomery	300,554	56.5	129,585	24.2	37.3	28.3	1,046.5	14,121	31,146	53,064	47.3	4.0	54,692	14.7	20.5	19.2
Morgan	6,151	42.4	2,696	9.2	59.2	10.4	24.3	13,810	23,053	43,791	57.9	0.9	45,698	15.0	20.3	16.9
Morrow	14,711	41.6	7,047	8.5	56.2	14.7	54.8	10,602	30,098	61,769	34.1	3.5	68,159	9.0	13.2	12.2
Muskingum	41,855	48.5	19,681	14.4	53.6	17.5	200.6	14,194	26,376	48,350	51.7	2.9	52,457	15.0	20.9	18.5
Noble	6,297	43.7	2,859	17.0	64.4	11.0	23.1	13,839	25,776	50,070	49.9	2.2	52,583	15.0	16.0	15.2

1. All persons 3 years old and over enrolled in nursery school through college. 2. Persons 25 years old and over. 3. Elementary and secondary education expenditures. 4. Based on population estimated by the American Community Survey, 2016–2020. 5. CDC percent based on 2019 population estimate.

STATE County	Personal income, 2020										Earnings, 2020		
			Per capita[1]			Supplements to wages and salaries, employer contributions (mil dol)						Contributions for government social insurance (mil dol)	
	Total (mil dol)	Percent change 2019–2020	Dollars	Rank	Wages and salaries (mil dol)	Pension and insurance	Government social insurance	Proprietors' income (mil dol)	Dividends, interest, and rent (mil dol)	Personal transfer reecipts (mil dol)	Total (mil dol)	From employee and self-employed	From employer
	62	63	64	65	66	67	68	69	70	71	72	73	74
NORTH DAKOTA—Cont'd													
Ward	3,936	2.4	57,492	539	2,040	376	181	231	743	730	2,827	168	181
Wells	295	27.6	79,403	82	71	11	7	111	49	64	200	9	7
Williams	2,510	-4.9	64,850	268	1,863	214	138	245	515	396	2,461	154	138
OHIO	627,231	6.8	53,198	X	304,478	49,365	21,631	45,227	103,588	152,489	420,701	25,426	21,631
Adams	1,092	11.1	39,658	2,488	278	57	20	98	114	439	453	34	20
Allen	4,742	7.0	46,500	1,578	2,550	463	189	311	648	1,431	3,513	218	189
Ashland	2,297	7.6	43,041	2,055	859	157	63	161	310	664	1,241	81	63
Ashtabula	4,208	8.2	43,597	1,997	1,295	258	99	303	511	1,519	1,955	138	99
Athens	2,399	6.4	36,642	2,807	999	267	55	140	422	741	1,461	72	55
Auglaize	2,390	6.5	52,330	906	1,043	179	77	147	384	558	1,446	89	77
Belmont	2,858	2.3	43,354	2,026	913	172	67	32	473	975	1,183	90	67
Brown	1,835	8.4	42,275	2,158	315	72	22	122	199	614	530	39	22
Butler	20,284	5.8	52,598	884	9,105	1,411	644	1,795	2,942	4,466	12,956	780	644
Carroll	1,200	8.5	44,624	1,860	264	52	20	96	160	377	432	31	20
Champaign	1,816	10.0	46,605	1,561	496	95	37	134	215	497	763	49	37
Clark	6,060	8.4	45,363	1,743	2,199	387	164	316	808	1,985	3,066	206	164
Clermont	12,558	5.5	60,535	401	3,119	487	226	2,112	1,506	2,481	5,944	382	226
Clinton	2,035	7.5	48,542	1,320	1,006	187	75	285	270	552	1,554	94	75
Columbiana	4,325	7.9	42,771	2,097	1,331	255	99	260	566	1,527	1,945	142	99
Coshocton	1,445	9.0	39,640	2,490	451	92	34	129	182	528	706	49	34
Crawford	1,815	10.6	43,918	1,961	586	110	43	122	243	622	861	61	43
Cuyahoga	73,579	6.3	59,923	430	47,621	6,964	3,346	4,944	14,804	18,057	62,875	3,750	3,346
Darke	2,462	8.8	48,088	1,375	830	152	65	265	345	645	1,311	82	65
Defiance	1,715	7.7	45,385	1,737	708	122	53	131	225	524	1,015	66	53
Delaware	16,952	6.2	79,382	83	5,828	776	399	1,151	3,068	1,773	8,154	487	399
Erie	4,182	1.1	56,732	590	1,570	299	118	563	665	1,128	2,551	159	118
Fairfield	8,170	8.4	51,153	1,008	2,029	360	146	445	1,175	1,812	2,979	194	146
Fayette	1,322	15.9	46,261	1,614	474	79	36	158	159	416	747	44	36
Franklin	73,244	7.9	55,294	682	50,607	8,012	3,372	4,959	12,369	14,704	66,950	3,607	3,372
Fulton	2,109	6.1	50,349	1,105	852	149	63	200	308	521	1,264	80	63
Gallia	1,309	8.3	43,932	1,957	473	113	34	85	187	513	706	46	34
Geauga	6,898	2.7	73,958	117	1,762	281	134	699	1,556	1,062	2,876	181	134
Greene	9,296	6.3	54,645	726	5,310	1,142	400	472	1,744	1,950	7,325	417	400
Guernsey	1,753	8.1	45,218	1,769	679	133	49	93	247	606	954	64	49
Hamilton	53,197	5.7	65,035	260	36,372	5,079	2,517	3,620	12,249	10,447	47,589	2,805	2,517
Hancock	4,101	7.2	54,386	752	2,702	401	186	360	639	870	3,649	220	186
Hardin	1,149	10.1	36,506	2,824	345	74	26	90	136	375	536	35	26
Harrison	631	6.2	42,014	2,192	180	42	13	35	82	226	270	20	13
Henry	1,365	9.7	50,752	1,058	529	95	40	122	183	376	786	48	40
Highland	1,780	10.7	41,094	2,323	458	98	33	159	207	616	748	50	33
Hocking	1,189	7.3	42,337	2,149	257	58	17	62	139	416	394	29	17
Holmes	2,117	1.5	48,118	1,367	950	151	74	659	258	350	1,834	100	74
Huron	2,658	9.2	45,844	1,676	1,068	186	90	199	335	793	1,543	100	90
Jackson	1,321	10.9	40,663	2,379	443	82	32	77	156	502	634	44	32
Jefferson	2,882	8.1	44,375	1,895	952	196	71	108	362	1,108	1,327	95	71
Knox	2,994	8.4	47,964	1,397	967	177	73	260	467	837	1,477	96	73
Lake	12,875	6.1	56,085	635	4,926	851	360	630	2,001	3,056	6,767	436	360
Lawrence	2,535	8.0	42,905	2,074	578	120	42	103	269	982	844	66	42
Licking	9,049	7.5	50,810	1,053	3,381	524	257	576	1,257	2,097	4,737	297	257
Logan	2,197	9.0	48,471	1,326	928	155	74	158	263	610	1,316	85	74
Lorain	15,970	7.3	51,157	1,007	4,786	876	356	671	2,438	4,172	6,689	443	356
Lucas	21,853	6.8	51,024	1,027	11,223	1,915	824	1,955	2,984	6,263	15,916	941	824
Madison	2,080	9.7	46,679	1,554	874	154	66	205	285	488	1,300	75	66
Mahoning	10,790	7.0	47,729	1,427	4,344	779	326	765	1,756	3,573	6,214	411	326
Marion	2,687	9.0	41,449	2,274	1,171	233	87	182	327	896	1,673	105	87
Medina	10,948	5.5	60,514	405	3,075	504	221	654	1,690	2,071	4,454	294	221
Meigs	899	9.0	39,644	2,489	141	34	10	41	109	347	226	19	10
Mercer	2,251	7.1	54,527	739	907	167	68	307	341	456	1,448	82	68
Miami	5,641	7.6	52,469	893	2,035	341	150	320	865	1,317	2,846	183	150
Monroe	560	8.8	41,242	2,296	181	34	13	40	91	212	268	21	13
Montgomery	27,440	7.1	51,618	971	14,210	2,303	1,037	1,871	4,647	7,366	19,421	1,189	1,037
Morgan	552	10.3	38,583	2,616	119	26	9	30	67	208	183	14	9
Morrow	1,568	8.9	44,282	1,903	234	52	17	121	170	436	423	28	17
Muskingum	3,963	8.4	46,070	1,638	1,615	284	118	255	480	1,275	2,272	152	118
Noble	437	8.0	30,397	3,084	127	33	8	32	69	153	199	11	8

1. Based on the resident population estimated as of July 1 of the year shown.

STATE County	Earnings, 2020 (cont.) — Percent by selected industries: Farm	Mining, quarrying, and extractions	Construction	Manu-facturing	Information; professional, scientific, technical services	Retail trade	Finance, insurance, real estate, and leasing	Health care and social assistance	Govern-ment	Social Security beneficiaries, December 2020: Number	Rate[1]	Supple-mental Security Income recipients, 2020	Housing units, 2021: Total	Percent change, 2010–2021
	75	76	77	78	79	80	81	82	83	84	85	86	87	88
NORTH DAKOTA—Cont'd														
Ward	1.8	6.0	6.1	1.1	4.3	6.8	5.4	14.2	33.2	10,345	150	690	32,330	0.4
Wells	47.9	D	3.8	1.8	1.1	D	D	D	7.2	1,125	288	44	2,335	-0.1
Williams	1.1	33.7	12.8	1.4	3.5	4.5	5.9	4.7	8.1	4,075	106	195	20,318	0.3
OHIO	0.6	0.2	6.2	13.6	9.5	5.8	8.0	13.4	14.8	2,405,217	204	306,163	5,269,638	0.4
Adams	2.9	0.6	11.5	15.4	3.9	8.6	4.0	12.7	17.2	6,760	245	1,669	12,703	0.1
Allen	0.9	D	5.2	22.8	4.6	6.3	3.7	20.1	12.8	23,195	228	2,990	44,707	0.3
Ashland	1.9	D	8.6	20.4	10.3	6.9	2.9	D	13.3	12,010	230	776	22,513	0.2
Ashtabula	0.5	0.1	10.7	26.3	4.8	6.3	2.8	14.8	14.5	24,010	247	3,070	46,355	0.2
Athens	0.0	0.1	3.9	3.2	5.1	7.9	3.8	14.5	46.9	10,180	164	2,605	26,387	0.0
Auglaize	4.1	D	6.1	43.1	3.9	5.5	1.9	8.6	10.0	9,735	211	450	20,044	0.8
Belmont	-0.1	4.3	D	4.6	4.4	11.1	4.9	13.6	21.2	16,800	255	1,882	31,575	-0.1
Brown	2.8	D	11.0	8.6	D	8.5	3.6	11.6	26.4	10,530	241	1,164	19,454	0.6
Butler	0.1	D	8.8	20.3	4.9	6.9	8.9	9.7	11.7	70,320	180	7,493	154,873	0.6
Carroll	0.7	1.4	17.4	16.8	D	7.6	3.3	D	14.8	6,975	261	427	13,399	0.0
Champaign	7.4	D	5.2	37.1	4.3	5.2	3.0	7.0	16.2	8,665	224	674	16,905	0.2
Clark	1.4	0.4	4.2	15.3	3.4	6.5	7.4	14.9	15.6	31,555	233	4,003	61,040	0.1
Clermont	0.1	D	7.2	8.2	D	7.1	6.8	7.0	9.7	43,060	205	3,400	87,402	1.0
Clinton	2.2	0.1	4.1	17.0	D	4.3	5.2	D	10.0	9,420	224	1,055	17,944	0.2
Columbiana	1.0	0.6	10.7	19.3	3.5	7.9	3.2	12.9	17.4	26,315	260	2,985	46,142	0.1
Coshocton	2.6	0.5	7.8	27.9	D	6.5	3.0	11.3	14.0	8,945	244	932	16,314	0.0
Crawford	4.7	D	5.4	16.9	D	6.7	7.7	D	14.3	11,165	267	1,200	19,842	-0.1
Cuyahoga	0.0	0.1	3.7	9.0	13.9	4.1	10.6	16.0	13.3	256,335	205	48,986	615,454	0.0
Darke	7.5	D	8.2	23.9	3.7	6.3	4.5	10.1	11.0	12,155	236	797	22,645	0.2
Defiance	2.9	0.0	4.1	23.6	3.0	9.9	6.8	D	13.9	9,465	248	699	16,573	0.2
Delaware	0.4	0.1	5.7	7.1	12.7	6.5	11.8	8.7	8.8	31,610	143	1,431	84,176	2.2
Erie	1.1	D	4.2	16.7	4.6	7.8	3.9	12.5	15.1	19,365	259	1,608	38,320	0.1
Fairfield	0.7	D	10.9	10.1	5.1	8.4	4.5	17.6	17.5	30,240	188	2,542	63,340	1.2
Fayette	8.1	0.0	4.7	16.9	D	9.1	2.8	D	15.9	6,745	233	929	12,718	0.2
Franklin	0.0	0.0	5.4	5.1	12.5	4.5	11.5	12.0	19.5	181,985	138	33,206	589,008	1.2
Fulton	2.9	D	11.2	33.9	D	5.2	3.3	D	12.6	9,660	228	541	17,730	0.2
Gallia	-0.4	D	8.5	4.8	1.8	7.6	4.4	D	16.5	7,280	250	1,491	13,440	0.1
Geauga	0.3	D	16.1	18.8	6.8	7.6	3.9	9.6	8.9	20,415	214	702	37,540	0.3
Greene	0.4	D	3.0	3.1	20.7	5.4	2.9	6.8	45.1	31,660	188	2,727	71,889	0.6
Guernsey	0.1	3.2	7.4	21.3	4.2	6.1	5.1	14.9	16.2	9,865	258	1,411	19,041	0.1
Hamilton	0.0	-0.1	5.2	12.2	13.8	4.0	11.2	14.7	10.1	148,950	180	23,437	380,401	0.3
Hancock	1.1	D	2.6	23.3	4.8	4.5	2.9	10.6	6.4	15,700	210	1,063	33,908	0.7
Hardin	7.8	D	3.4	22.4	2.6	6.7	4.4	D	16.0	6,505	212	670	12,904	0.2
Harrison	0.1	D	10.5	18.9	3.8	4.0	4.5	7.6	18.0	3,985	275	518	7,378	0.0
Henry	5.0	D	10.8	31.9	2.2	5.8	3.8	8.4	15.9	6,445	234	361	12,063	0.2
Highland	4.7	0.2	10.4	15.5	D	13.1	6.3	9.7	20.2	10,250	236	1,425	18,977	0.0
Hocking	-0.4	D	12.4	13.6	D	10.1	4.2	8.6	28.3	6,860	244	1,012	12,994	0.0
Holmes	2.6	0.2	20.8	31.9	2.0	10.8	3.1	D	5.8	5,030	114	359	14,578	0.0
Huron	3.8	D	12.4	24.5	D	5.2	3.9	10.6	11.1	13,155	225	1,306	25,507	0.0
Jackson	0.4	0.1	10.9	25.0	2.4	8.4	3.2	D	16.5	7,785	239	1,428	14,512	0.7
Jefferson	-0.2	D	6.5	9.5	D	8.1	3.2	19.0	17.7	17,745	274	2,468	31,081	-0.1
Knox	1.8	0.4	12.3	24.9	3.2	6.0	3.2	13.0	12.4	13,685	218	1,105	25,920	0.4
Lake	0.6	D	6.2	27.1	6.6	7.6	4.2	10.3	12.1	54,000	233	2,985	105,937	0.5
Lawrence	-0.4	D	D	7.2	3.6	8.1	2.9	18.5	21.5	14,995	261	3,293	26,519	0.1
Licking	0.4	0.1	7.9	12.1	6.2	8.1	6.4	9.8	13.6	36,360	202	3,292	73,008	0.4
Logan	3.2	D	5.4	34.5	D	5.5	3.5	9.0	11.4	10,665	232	811	23,789	0.5
Lorain	0.6	D	6.3	21.3	4.8	7.5	3.4	12.2	18.3	69,675	221	7,304	135,686	0.8
Lucas	0.1	0.1	5.3	15.8	7.2	6.3	9.1	17.3	15.0	87,895	205	16,616	200,856	0.3
Madison	5.4	0.0	7.2	19.2	5.6	6.6	1.9	D	19.6	8,260	186	685	16,359	0.7
Mahoning	0.2	0.3	7.0	10.8	6.0	8.4	4.4	20.4	15.9	59,155	261	9,005	107,973	0.0
Marion	2.6	D	3.5	25.2	0.8	6.7	6.5	17.3	17.1	14,930	229	2,202	27,357	0.0
Medina	0.2	0.0	11.5	15.4	6.5	8.2	4.8	8.6	11.8	38,225	209	1,536	75,697	0.6
Meigs	2.1	D	9.5	3.5	D	10.8	5.2	11.5	29.3	5,715	259	1,041	10,664	0.1
Mercer	8.2	D	8.2	27.7	3.1	6.2	5.8	D	12.1	8,785	208	395	18,013	0.6
Miami	1.3	0.2	7.1	28.1	4.1	6.7	3.5	9.8	12.5	23,865	218	1,676	46,998	0.4
Monroe	-0.7	4.5	30.5	2.3	2.4	4.0	7.1	D	19.7	4,045	303	371	7,132	0.0
Montgomery	0.1	0.0	5.6	11.3	10.9	5.2	7.5	19.8	14.7	112,215	209	15,462	252,095	0.2
Morgan	1.4	0.9	8.5	16.6	2.1	5.5	2.9	D	22.8	3,445	252	542	7,286	0.6
Morrow	5.8	0.0	14.7	15.6	D	7.0	2.4	D	22.0	7,660	218	586	14,584	0.7
Muskingum	0.4	5.0	5.8	9.7	6.1	9.1	3.9	21.1	14.3	21,355	247	3,296	38,337	0.0
Noble	-0.8	3.0	5.4	6.8	5.3	5.5	3.7	6.8	37.5	2,775	196	254	5,785	0.5

1. Per 1,000 resident population estimated as of July 1 of the year shown.

Table B. States and Counties — **Housing, Labor Force, and Employment**

STATE County	Housing units, 2016–2020: Occupied units: Total	Owner-occupied: Percent	Owner-occupied: Median value[1]	Median owner cost as a percent of income: With a mortgage	Median owner cost as a percent of income: Without a mortgage[2]	Renter-occupied: Median rent[3]	Renter-occupied: Median rent as a percent of income[2]	Sub-standard units[4] (percent)	Civilian labor force, 2021: Total	Percent change, 2020–2021	Unemployment: Total	Unemployment: Rate[5]	Civilian employment[6], 2016–2020: Total	Percent: Management, business, science, and arts	Percent: Construction, production, and maintenance occupations
	89	90	91	92	93	94	95	96	97	98	99	100	101	102	103
NORTH DAKOTA—Cont'd															
Ward	28,432	59.2	217,700	19.5	10.0	939	24.7	2.7	31,812	-1.1	1,360	4.3	34,749	33.9	25.3
Wells	1,941	75.0	89,600	18.3	10.0	614	27.9	0.7	1,896	-1.1	80	4.2	1,891	35.5	24.1
Williams	14,646	53.0	254,800	17.0	10.0	1,005	21.6	5.6	20,877	-10.5	1,404	6.7	18,912	27.9	39.4
OHIO	4,717,226	66.3	151,400	18.9	11.2	825	27.5	1.7	5,736,882	0.0	295,003	5.1	5,603,630	37.6	24.4
Adams	10,396	70.3	115,000	22.0	12.7	581	29.6	3.1	10,967	1.0	692	6.3	10,397	34.8	30.0
Allen	41,025	66.7	120,300	18.1	11.8	722	28.2	1.3	47,538	-0.5	2,720	5.7	47,668	28.4	33.7
Ashland	20,504	75.2	132,200	18.2	10.0	711	24.3	2.7	26,333	0.3	1,143	4.3	25,789	29.6	33.0
Ashtabula	38,614	71.5	117,200	19.5	10.9	706	31.1	2.2	43,322	-0.7	2,378	5.5	40,733	27.0	36.2
Athens	22,539	58.9	139,100	18.7	10.6	797	33.9	1.8	25,533	-3.1	1,426	5.6	28,866	38.3	18.7
Auglaize	19,000	75.9	146,400	16.5	10.0	757	21.8	1.8	24,365	-0.6	900	3.7	23,204	31.5	35.7
Belmont	25,772	76.1	110,800	17.4	10.3	665	26.2	0.8	27,892	-2.1	1,705	6.1	28,947	28.1	30.0
Brown	17,811	73.0	138,200	18.8	10.4	741	28.7	1.8	19,366	0.7	1,035	5.3	19,364	31.0	33.0
Butler	140,736	69.1	180,200	18.7	10.0	911	27.6	1.7	195,166	0.9	8,779	4.5	185,074	38.2	22.6
Carroll	11,286	78.6	128,400	20.6	10.8	713	25.3	2.3	12,726	-0.9	720	5.7	12,006	29.7	33.3
Champaign	15,407	73.1	137,200	18.8	11.3	737	22.0	1.4	19,413	-1.9	853	4.4	18,084	29.5	37.7
Clark	54,862	67.1	120,500	18.9	10.0	757	27.0	1.6	62,458	-0.2	3,323	5.3	59,789	30.1	30.9
Clermont	79,347	73.8	178,700	18.8	10.3	868	26.3	1.7	106,976	1.1	4,630	4.3	103,007	36.9	23.8
Clinton	16,741	67.0	139,100	18.7	10.9	739	27.5	1.9	17,953	1.6	982	5.5	19,660	31.3	32.8
Columbiana	41,632	73.4	105,500	18.6	10.5	648	26.9	1.8	45,832	-2.6	2,630	5.7	45,715	27.5	33.3
Coshocton	14,579	74.4	106,300	18.5	11.2	632	24.7	2.9	13,772	-2.3	804	5.8	15,683	28.5	35.9
Crawford	17,928	70.0	93,400	18.2	10.8	646	27.3	1.2	18,066	-2.5	1,050	5.8	18,742	29.1	35.3
Cuyahoga	547,887	58.0	137,800	19.7	12.7	830	28.9	1.5	595,326	-0.3	38,716	6.5	593,905	41.5	19.0
Darke	21,171	70.8	124,700	17.7	10.3	665	22.2	1.3	25,684	0.1	1,005	3.9	24,797	27.9	38.5
Defiance	15,385	77.5	125,100	18.0	10.0	741	25.9	1.2	17,564	-0.9	825	4.7	19,043	30.0	36.9
Delaware	71,521	80.7	320,300	19.1	12.0	1,118	23.6	0.8	114,622	2.3	4,121	3.6	106,393	55.8	11.6
Erie	31,319	69.9	146,800	18.1	11.3	773	26.6	1.2	37,279	2.3	2,361	6.3	35,684	32.9	29.2
Fairfield	57,071	75.2	197,400	18.9	10.8	899	29.8	1.6	79,813	1.6	3,464	4.3	75,425	39.7	22.5
Fayette	11,737	64.7	118,200	18.4	10.5	711	26.2	1.2	13,748	-1.4	657	4.8	12,390	27.9	36.5
Franklin	519,237	53.6	185,900	19.5	11.8	1,002	27.1	2.6	709,058	1.3	35,100	5.0	683,925	44.5	18.0
Fulton	16,582	80.5	140,300	18.7	10.9	758	24.4	1.8	21,631	-0.5	1,019	4.7	20,360	30.2	33.1
Gallia	11,359	75.0	118,400	18.7	11.7	694	26.2	2.2	12,111	-0.7	684	5.6	12,333	32.8	29.2
Geauga	35,303	86.7	247,700	19.3	10.9	839	25.3	2.2	47,402	1.6	1,957	4.1	47,805	40.7	22.9
Greene	65,915	66.0	180,300	18.2	10.0	914	26.2	1.0	82,422	0.0	3,550	4.3	78,684	46.4	16.0
Guernsey	16,244	71.4	122,800	20.1	10.7	715	29.9	3.1	17,904	-1.9	998	5.6	16,861	29.7	32.6
Hamilton	344,588	58.5	163,000	19.1	11.9	831	27.9	1.9	415,153	0.6	20,176	4.9	409,604	43.8	18.2
Hancock	32,022	68.4	152,600	17.6	10.5	758	25.5	1.0	41,002	-1.0	1,691	4.1	38,044	34.2	29.5
Hardin	11,777	73.4	106,200	19.7	10.2	670	22.8	2.2	13,677	-1.7	705	5.2	14,388	26.8	38.0
Harrison	6,221	78.4	100,800	19.3	10.6	585	27.1	3.2	6,502	-2.7	406	6.2	6,005	22.9	39.3
Henry	11,069	77.2	130,800	17.8	11.2	738	22.3	0.7	12,745	-1.9	657	5.2	13,200	30.8	35.7
Highland	16,747	70.1	123,400	19.1	12.1	679	27.0	2.6	17,499	0.6	988	5.6	18,455	29.4	36.8
Hocking	11,533	77.6	139,800	18.4	11.0	625	27.3	2.9	12,874	1.3	619	4.8	12,961	27.2	31.4
Holmes	12,351	77.8	224,400	21.3	10.0	666	21.6	4.8	21,400	2.5	592	2.8	19,977	23.5	45.8
Huron	23,050	71.7	131,600	18.4	10.0	707	25.4	1.3	27,725	0.8	1,617	5.8	27,301	27.9	40.0
Jackson	12,971	72.8	105,600	20.1	12.5	693	24.7	2.8	12,672	-3.4	778	6.1	13,893	33.6	31.8
Jefferson	27,541	69.5	95,300	17.2	11.5	665	26.3	0.9	27,241	-0.7	1,766	6.5	28,200	29.5	28.6
Knox	23,027	72.2	162,700	19.8	10.6	769	25.6	1.6	31,102	0.6	1,256	4.0	29,087	32.6	28.6
Lake	96,534	73.9	160,200	19.2	11.3	912	26.3	1.1	122,641	0.6	6,243	5.1	117,003	38.4	23.5
Lawrence	23,208	72.2	107,700	19.0	12.7	726	27.8	1.3	23,226	-1.7	1,187	5.1	24,230	28.7	27.8
Licking	64,466	72.5	183,500	18.8	10.9	865	26.5	2.1	91,375	1.4	3,739	4.1	84,741	37.2	23.0
Logan	18,604	76.0	142,400	18.4	10.4	717	24.1	1.9	22,462	-1.0	930	4.1	21,254	28.3	36.6
Lorain	121,669	72.5	156,400	19.4	12.1	786	28.9	1.3	151,288	-0.3	8,701	5.8	142,606	35.9	25.0
Lucas	181,472	59.9	120,900	19.2	11.6	760	28.0	1.6	204,976	-1.5	12,762	6.2	199,822	34.5	26.7
Madison	15,017	73.6	169,200	18.5	10.7	856	23.0	1.4	20,815	1.6	801	3.8	19,547	33.4	32.0
Mahoning	98,869	69.6	108,200	19.2	11.3	684	29.1	1.2	98,659	-1.5	6,264	6.3	104,363	32.9	24.0
Marion	24,617	67.4	105,800	18.1	10.3	736	29.2	1.4	27,974	-1.0	1,315	4.7	26,507	25.8	35.2
Medina	69,739	79.6	205,800	19.1	10.0	903	26.3	1.2	95,616	0.7	4,128	4.3	94,514	41.7	21.5
Meigs	9,090	77.1	92,500	18.5	11.0	632	30.3	1.5	8,744	-2.5	580	6.6	8,555	26.7	33.2
Mercer	16,078	79.3	163,800	17.9	10.0	676	21.7	1.7	22,895	-2.1	714	3.1	21,358	28.5	40.8
Miami	41,260	72.1	155,000	18.2	10.0	783	25.1	1.0	53,518	-0.7	2,280	4.3	51,510	34.3	30.4
Monroe	5,854	78.0	109,500	16.7	10.0	627	32.3	3.3	5,312	-6.1	389	7.3	5,364	25.9	41.2
Montgomery	227,077	61.4	124,900	18.9	11.9	809	28.1	1.6	248,437	-1.0	13,831	5.6	248,019	37.5	23.2
Morgan	6,076	76.4	102,700	19.4	10.7	604	29.0	2.3	6,756	1.1	422	6.2	5,926	27.6	37.0
Morrow	13,064	82.5	154,900	19.2	10.2	773	24.8	3.1	16,911	1.2	762	4.5	17,698	28.5	31.4
Muskingum	33,797	69.8	126,400	18.8	11.1	702	29.5	1.8	40,348	0.4	2,075	5.1	38,588	29.1	32.8
Noble	4,969	81.5	106,100	20.5	10.0	623	23.7	3.5	4,628	-0.2	314	6.8	4,433	26.6	34.8

1. Specified owner-occupied units. 2. A value of 10.0 represents 10 percent or less; a value of 50.0 represents 50 percent or more. 3. Specified renter-occupied units. 4. Overcrowded or lacking complete plumbing facilities. 5. Percent of civilian labor force. 6. Civilian employed persons 16 years old and over.

STATE County	Private nonfarm establishments, employment and payroll, 2020									Agriculture, 2017			
		Employment						Annual payroll		Farms			Farm producers whose primary occupation is farming (percent)
											Percent with:		
	Number of establish-ments	Total	Health care and social assistance	Manufac-turing	Retail trade	Finance and insurance	Professional, scientific, and technical services	Total (mil dol)	Average per employee (dollars)	Number	Fewer than 50 acres	1000 acres or more	
	104	105	106	107	108	109	110	111	112	113	114	115	116
NORTH DAKOTA—Cont'd													
Ward	1,993	26,658	5,088	466	5,087	983	1,223	1,301	48,813	718	14.5	43.6	55.8
Wells	172	1,283	428	51	235	78	16	51	39,933	435	5.5	47.4	62.2
Williams	1,541	22,340	1,577	322	2,317	386	674	1,322	59,194	569	12.3	46.2	54.1
OHIO	249,857	4,978,720	872,470	673,719	561,054	253,898	262,090	246,555	49,522	77,805	47.4	3.5	37.3
Adams	385	4,572	1,357	1,001	801	158	72	167	36,620	1,194	44.0	1.3	34.2
Allen	2,286	45,012	9,711	8,917	5,719	904	1,193	1,983	44,061	855	43.5	4.1	36.5
Ashland	1,034	18,234	2,931	4,123	2,159	268	1,622	701	38,449	1,122	44.8	1.8	44.5
Ashtabula	1,806	24,464	5,153	6,887	3,506	422	830	914	37,355	1,212	51.7	1.7	36.1
Athens	1,029	13,265	3,825	440	2,451	361	501	469	35,363	687	35.1	0.9	33.0
Auglaize	975	22,072	2,617	10,129	2,031	304	681	990	44,854	976	39.3	3.7	38.8
Belmont	1,354	18,059	3,116	750	3,803	459	532	697	38,607	750	30.7	1.6	38.6
Brown	542	5,434	1,013	776	1,005	170	119	163	30,069	1,237	42.3	3.3	38.8
Butler	7,292	145,687	17,080	21,578	17,064	9,078	5,823	7,053	48,413	997	57.1	2.5	34.0
Carroll	453	5,447	948	1,308	734	68	118	190	34,896	888	44.6	1.5	40.2
Champaign	575	9,581	778	4,119	886	179	269	408	42,627	860	46.4	5.5	40.7
Clark	2,167	38,457	6,492	5,871	5,027	2,239	730	1,501	39,030	742	56.7	7.0	36.2
Clermont	3,614	51,928	6,791	5,791	9,378	2,160	3,043	2,298	44,247	928	66.4	2.2	35.3
Clinton	702	16,444	1,608	3,541	1,552	271	411	845	51,389	747	47.8	8.0	39.8
Columbiana	1,909	26,679	5,268	6,207	4,202	499	389	925	34,690	1,227	51.9	1.5	36.8
Coshocton	609	8,121	1,737	2,404	1,214	180	140	320	39,379	1,191	39.0	2.2	36.7
Crawford	767	12,093	3,005	2,966	1,307	570	592	450	37,237	719	36.7	7.9	46.1
Cuyahoga	31,708	673,763	147,022	64,436	68,638	45,431	44,865	38,514	57,163	111	92.8	NA	49.2
Darke	1,136	15,710	2,072	5,322	1,906	526	330	668	42,520	1,658	45.2	4.4	38.9
Defiance	796	13,807	1,898	3,071	2,415	814	244	576	41,727	907	39.1	6.7	33.2
Delaware	4,893	89,828	9,128	5,868	12,879	13,491	4,732	4,740	52,769	803	63.4	3.9	35.7
Erie	1,780	32,736	4,705	6,087	4,850	633	642	1,233	37,674	382	49.5	4.7	41.5
Fairfield	2,670	36,790	7,724	5,161	6,432	743	1,126	1,395	37,919	1,117	57.6	3.8	37.6
Fayette	562	9,898	1,179	1,890	2,358	126	80	367	37,054	491	46.2	12.8	45.6
Franklin	29,479	672,835	135,517	30,522	66,747	55,091	45,950	37,097	55,135	408	67.6	2.5	35.1
Fulton	938	15,762	1,909	7,183	1,667	389	231	690	43,759	785	44.6	6.5	39.8
Gallia	542	9,209	3,035	517	1,404	328	92	363	39,374	990	36.1	0.7	33.2
Geauga	2,711	29,806	5,070	6,897	4,193	591	1,364	1,294	43,426	1,049	66.7	0.6	31.2
Greene	3,255	55,902	8,262	3,016	9,549	1,520	12,404	2,731	48,845	817	59.0	6.1	38.4
Guernsey	819	13,504	3,184	3,169	1,512	220	298	520	38,475	1,103	35.7	0.9	37.5
Hamilton	20,772	493,248	91,158	46,390	42,480	34,095	40,877	30,753	62,348	318	74.2	0.3	35.1
Hancock	1,652	44,318	6,292	11,053	4,163	690	918	2,241	50,563	887	40.2	7.0	34.8
Hardin	426	6,693	860	1,597	863	206	148	230	34,414	726	36.0	8.8	45.5
Harrison	260	2,904	455	320	346	53	69	127	43,625	458	27.1	4.1	46.0
Henry	558	8,089	1,299	2,720	895	244	192	371	45,879	841	38.9	5.6	39.8
Highland	676	8,371	1,729	1,716	1,482	564	107	334	39,948	1,254	37.6	6.0	38.2
Hocking	482	5,340	934	817	891	122	76	158	29,672	377	44.8	0.3	32.9
Holmes	1,332	18,805	1,680	6,763	2,356	428	343	767	40,782	1,673	43.5	0.7	39.1
Huron	1,081	18,620	2,732	6,470	2,132	398	409	831	44,651	810	43.1	7.3	44.9
Jackson	607	8,478	1,361	2,881	1,376	239	133	296	34,970	508	38.8	1.4	36.3
Jefferson	1,188	18,549	3,977	1,649	2,648	391	312	703	37,881	599	31.6	NA	35.2
Knox	1,095	18,357	3,206	4,142	2,038	463	325	734	39,958	1,338	50.8	2.5	35.7
Lake	5,498	86,083	11,339	19,913	12,456	1,287	3,545	4,246	49,320	214	70.6	0.5	41.4
Lawrence	791	10,304	2,736	819	1,984	243	209	361	35,057	531	30.1	0.2	32.7
Licking	3,022	56,800	7,884	11,029	6,914	2,913	2,373	2,445	43,042	1,583	57.6	2.7	35.3
Logan	808	16,703	1,722	4,585	1,686	275	644	790	47,273	1,009	51.3	5.5	37.6
Lorain	5,483	85,777	16,059	15,526	13,281	1,716	3,201	3,665	42,730	1,001	63.1	2.2	34.4
Lucas	9,297	188,890	39,375	25,829	22,490	5,212	9,359	9,468	50,122	386	65.8	3.1	43.5
Madison	687	15,459	1,154	4,089	3,005	128	538	688	44,479	789	46.8	9.0	44.0
Mahoning	5,295	84,892	19,894	9,055	11,813	2,226	2,654	3,328	39,201	774	57.9	0.9	38.0
Marion	1,094	22,275	5,232	6,408	2,708	359	279	919	41,251	615	44.1	8.3	41.5
Medina	3,978	54,701	7,484	9,149	8,484	2,666	2,013	2,462	45,006	1,149	71.6	1.6	36.7
Meigs	313	2,571	622	17	610	132	66	74	28,639	515	30.7	1.0	37.5
Mercer	1,027	16,352	2,027	4,233	1,876	594	362	664	40,589	1,231	40.4	4.4	38.9
Miami	2,112	37,222	4,718	11,035	4,746	658	1,049	1,594	42,818	1,037	57.7	3.9	34.7
Monroe	263	1,820	265	147	322	147	41	61	33,482	808	27.5	0.5	35.7
Montgomery	10,960	236,680	55,507	31,028	24,016	11,370	12,870	11,711	49,480	781	63.9	2.4	38.0
Morgan	158	2,206	499	776	301	77	33	78	35,295	530	29.4	1.3	39.4
Morrow	408	4,020	857	952	468	72	237	131	32,646	865	53.8	5.0	38.2
Muskingum	1,667	27,960	6,427	2,633	4,414	734	481	1,202	42,982	1,263	39.6	1.6	32.0
Noble	219	1,903	365	274	287	87	42	55	29,121	593	32.7	1.0	36.6

STATE County	Agriculture, 2017 (cont.)															
	Land in farms					Value of land and buildings (dollars)		Value of machinery and equipment, average per farm (dollars)	Value of products sold:				Organic farms (number)	Farms with internet access (percent)	Government payments	
	Acreage (1,000)	Percent change, 2012–2017	Acres: Average size of farm	Acres: Total irrigated (1,000)	Acres: Total cropland (1,000)	Average per farm	Average per acre		Total (mil dol)	Average per farm (acres)	Percent from: Crops	Percent from: Livestock and poultry products			Total ($1,000)	Percent of farms
	117	118	119	120	121	122	123	124	125	126	127	128	129	130	131	132
NORTH DAKOTA—Cont'd																
Ward	1,153	7.5	1,607	0.5	967.5	2,623,383	1,633	373,715	206.0	286,890	91.5	8.5	2	88.9	20,719	76.3
Wells	786	6.4	1,806	1.0	664.8	3,089,877	1,711	628,953	208.2	478,733	88.8	11.2	4	80.9	10,874	80.2
Williams	999	-6.0	1,756	21.1	754.4	1,925,239	1,096	457,175	131.8	231,601	89.1	10.9	NA	75.0	9,204	58.2
OHIO	13,965	0.0	179	50.7	10,960.7	1,112,700	6,199	129,614	9,341.2	120,059	58.1	41.9	872	74.6	351,125	36.7
Adams	166	-3.7	139	0.3	89.2	539,592	3,882	76,734	40.1	33,599	62.5	37.5	6	67.5	1,814	38.1
Allen	187	1.9	218	0.4	172.7	1,583,677	7,256	163,584	139.9	163,639	61.4	38.6	2	77.8	5,704	67.7
Ashland	161	5.1	143	0.2	120.8	870,121	6,075	100,864	113.8	101,381	38.9	61.1	57	74.8	3,821	29.9
Ashtabula	154	-7.4	127	0.3	101.1	554,349	4,373	92,598	57.9	47,762	66.2	33.8	12	69.1	592	11.2
Athens	99	9.1	144	0.1	30.4	461,747	3,213	56,167	11.4	16,640	50.4	49.6	3	76.1	394	13.7
Auglaize	210	0.0	215	1.2	194.6	1,751,762	8,141	189,133	206.9	211,992	47.4	52.6	3	82.8	8,649	72.7
Belmont	129	14.2	172	0.1	41.4	660,470	3,829	94,858	25.4	33,809	23.2	76.8	4	73.1	50	3.1
Brown	208	0.7	168	0.1	154.7	741,026	4,408	124,535	71.7	57,969	88.0	12.0	8	73.2	4,162	38.1
Butler	124	-15.2	124	0.2	92.1	1,026,003	8,255	89,736	54.9	55,068	74.3	25.7	4	80.0	2,683	25.2
Carroll	111	4.2	125	0.3	64.3	587,003	4,710	97,626	48.6	54,760	39.0	61.0	4	65.9	877	14.0
Champaign	189	-0.6	220	3.8	168.7	1,575,686	7,170	159,256	119.6	139,053	82.9	17.1	4	82.0	7,634	51.2
Clark	171	-1.9	230	1.8	151.4	1,738,039	7,542	165,061	126.5	170,443	79.2	20.8	NA	80.5	6,001	43.3
Clermont	97	-19.6	105	0.1	65.5	587,976	5,605	86,038	31.8	34,234	89.5	10.5	12	79.1	2,588	12.9
Clinton	213	2.2	285	0.0	190.7	1,697,120	5,958	185,154	116.9	156,456	92.1	7.9	4	79.5	8,430	53.4
Columbiana	142	11.4	116	0.3	95.9	669,684	5,769	98,981	106.7	86,932	32.4	67.6	3	74.2	1,687	19.4
Coshocton	183	7.5	153	1.2	97.2	809,143	5,279	97,607	99.1	83,219	33.6	66.4	29	64.7	2,541	26.4
Crawford	238	-0.7	331	0.1	220.9	2,135,734	6,446	242,518	234.0	325,403	49.6	50.4	1	71.9	11,326	68.3
Cuyahoga	2	-13.8	20	0.1	0.6	330,393	16,314	57,328	6.2	56,072	98.6	1.4	4	89.2	14	3.6
Darke	344	1.1	207	0.2	316.1	1,724,791	8,319	194,900	516.2	311,335	31.3	68.7	6	77.1	8,950	60.6
Defiance	228	1.4	252	1.0	205.8	1,444,799	5,736	147,092	107.3	118,279	74.8	25.2	6	78.4	5,649	80.6
Delaware	133	-5.7	165	0.9	117.5	1,294,690	7,824	130,793	86.9	108,172	89.2	10.8	7	85.2	3,590	35.5
Erie	86	3.7	226	D	77.1	1,480,849	6,544	176,619	94.2	246,610	92.3	7.7	6	82.2	3,052	42.1
Fairfield	188	-8.8	169	0.1	153.6	1,299,166	7,702	121,720	99.8	89,303	77.6	22.4	5	83.0	7,261	41.6
Fayette	204	3.9	416	0.1	189.9	2,971,045	7,142	259,936	127.2	259,059	83.3	16.7	3	76.4	6,900	61.9
Franklin	52	-15.6	128	0.4	45.0	1,031,825	8,041	106,842	52.2	127,841	85.1	14.9	9	89.5	1,272	25.7
Fulton	196	0.5	250	0.9	182.2	1,746,704	6,985	191,817	173.1	220,513	71.0	29.0	2	78.3	7,158	59.6
Gallia	119	2.4	120	0.2	37.6	376,628	3,143	67,632	19.0	19,167	49.0	51.0	NA	62.3	511	8.8
Geauga	70	4.6	67	0.6	33.6	482,798	7,245	60,589	36.1	34,417	48.4	51.6	22	61.7	370	4.3
Greene	168	15.0	205	0.4	149.6	1,465,595	7,140	162,563	97.1	118,832	90.8	9.2	10	82.4	7,461	41.0
Guernsey	152	5.6	138	0.1	59.1	512,427	3,722	71,042	26.8	24,287	39.6	60.4	11	66.8	520	10.1
Hamilton	18	-16.9	57	0.2	8.4	751,176	13,293	54,805	23.0	72,443	60.8	39.2	3	79.2	189	3.8
Hancock	240	4.2	271	D	226.7	1,634,840	6,042	184,379	135.8	153,091	80.1	19.9	4	78.4	9,965	67.0
Hardin	262	5.6	361	0.5	244.0	2,122,858	5,888	210,499	222.9	306,978	48.1	51.9	13	77.8	7,663	65.0
Harrison	99	4.1	217	0.0	41.0	717,980	3,310	97,439	18.6	40,688	42.0	58.0	NA	71.4	397	7.2
Henry	235	-0.4	279	0.5	225.2	1,829,400	6,550	211,986	133.4	158,595	87.7	12.3	1	79.3	7,048	73.6
Highland	288	8.9	230	0.2	224.7	1,153,001	5,021	136,788	122.9	98,008	77.1	22.9	20	70.7	10,846	56.1
Hocking	38	0.7	102	0.1	14.1	460,593	4,527	55,840	5.1	13,504	80.6	19.4	NA	77.5	655	13.8
Holmes	174	-21.3	104	0.3	104.2	804,801	7,741	82,807	182.1	108,839	18.4	81.6	134	38.0	1,509	9.0
Huron	241	0.9	297	D	213.9	1,806,321	6,083	226,973	200.0	246,863	67.5	32.5	6	73.1	8,556	48.4
Jackson	67	-5.9	133	0.1	27.3	373,579	2,814	62,710	11.0	21,734	47.1	52.9	1	67.1	632	23.4
Jefferson	77	12.7	129	0.0	33.0	702,325	5,464	80,469	9.2	15,351	46.0	54.0	NA	75.6	188	8.2
Knox	194	4.5	145	0.1	140.0	878,830	6,047	110,224	135.1	101,004	46.0	54.0	37	71.1	3,456	31.1
Lake	13	-23.5	61	1.6	8.3	499,558	8,162	101,442	73.6	344,028	98.7	1.3	NA	79.9	173	7.9
Lawrence	62	-4.0	117	0.1	16.0	383,896	3,287	57,780	4.0	7,597	59.8	40.2	NA	68.7	238	10.5
Licking	220	-1.6	139	0.3	160.7	921,506	6,616	120,427	185.4	117,118	45.1	54.9	13	84.5	4,217	20.2
Logan	211	-0.8	209	0.1	183.9	1,266,978	6,051	136,955	121.7	120,638	70.7	29.3	16	76.5	6,395	45.4
Lorain	126	2.5	126	0.6	105.1	939,911	7,484	118,302	133.9	133,767	87.1	12.9	11	80.8	2,362	27.9
Lucas	66	4.0	170	1.2	61.9	1,405,729	8,277	157,847	50.7	131,288	93.1	6.9	7	81.9	2,319	42.7
Madison	252	-4.1	320	0.1	235.3	2,218,215	6,934	215,221	159.3	201,844	78.8	21.2	25	84.7	7,372	56.1
Mahoning	75	-0.5	96	0.6	56.4	638,290	6,626	101,413	68.6	88,630	35.8	64.2	7	77.8	1,277	16.9
Marion	204	7.7	331	0.2	190.3	1,935,205	5,838	231,900	135.9	221,015	63.5	36.5	7	82.9	7,767	63.6
Medina	99	4.6	86	0.9	78.6	677,096	7,833	80,359	51.5	44,842	74.1	25.9	19	78.7	1,563	14.7
Meigs	78	3.5	152	0.1	31.4	528,124	3,467	92,831	16.6	32,254	64.5	35.5	1	75.3	372	10.9
Mercer	269	-1.5	218	0.1	248.5	2,113,330	9,673	229,931	631.6	513,089	19.5	80.5	6	82.3	8,719	67.9
Miami	173	-6.0	167	1.9	158.3	1,239,097	7,421	114,326	106.7	102,889	86.2	13.8	8	83.6	4,405	53.6
Monroe	108	-3.1	133	0.1	31.1	435,691	3,268	79,164	14.0	17,280	35.0	65.0	3	66.3	69	1.2
Montgomery	113	-8.9	145	0.5	91.4	1,044,818	7,214	118,999	78.7	100,784	88.0	12.0	4	78.0	3,063	37.8
Morgan	99	4.2	187	0.1	40.3	647,339	3,458	88,037	18.0	33,972	39.8	60.2	3	73.2	244	14.5
Morrow	165	-1.5	191	0.3	139.1	1,146,537	6,002	132,894	84.2	97,334	73.1	26.9	12	79.7	3,800	35.6
Muskingum	189	9.1	150	0.4	88.1	613,803	4,101	90,918	70.1	55,482	41.1	58.9	4	70.5	2,539	16.9
Noble	80	-7.0	135	0.1	24.4	415,865	3,078	63,887	7.3	12,304	36.3	63.7	5	62.4	27	2.2

STATE County	Water use, 2015: Public supply water withdrawn (mil gal/ day)	Water use, 2015: Public supply gallons withdrawn per person per day	Wholesale Trade[1], 2017: Number of establish-ments	Wholesale Trade[1], 2017: Number of employees	Wholesale Trade[1], 2017: Sales (mil dol)	Wholesale Trade[1], 2017: Average payroll (mil dol)	Retail Trade[2], 2017: Number of establish-ments	Retail Trade[2], 2017: Number of employees	Retail Trade[2], 2017: Sales (mil dol)	Retail Trade[2], 2017: Average payroll (mil dol)	Real estate and rental and leasing,[2] 2017: Number of establish-ments	Real estate and rental and leasing,[2] 2017: Number of employees	Real estate and rental and leasing,[2] 2017: Sales (mil dol)	Real estate and rental and leasing,[2] 2017: Average payroll (mil dol)
	133	134	135	136	137	138	139	140	141	142	143	144	145	146
NORTH DAKOTA—Cont'd														
Ward	6.9	96.4	110	1,549	2,011.3	95.7	310	5,462	1,483.8	153.3	D	D	D	D
Wells	0.4	86.4	D	D	D	D	32	214	61.5	5.2	D	D	D	D
Williams	9.2	259.8	107	1,461	1,233.9	95.3	144	2,164	842.7	78.7	124	679	242.6	53.9
OHIO	1,306.3	112.5	11,430	193,412	172,949.1	11,316.0	35,500	588,060	174,299.7	14,861.4	10,782	62,902	20,524.3	2,986.2
Adams	2.1	73.2	D	D	D	4.1	88	884	262.5	22.2	12	34	5.9	0.7
Allen	18.2	174.0	123	2,106	1,905.2	104.2	388	5,898	1,678.2	140.1	84	314	64.8	9.3
Ashland	3.0	56.2	46	401	301.8	21.7	150	2,126	506.2	52.5	37	160	18.3	4.8
Ashtabula	7.2	73.0	D	D	D	D	304	3,341	1,017.4	81.3	63	210	38.0	6.8
Athens	7.5	114.0	D	D	D	D	175	2,678	742.3	65.3	57	208	37.2	5.5
Auglaize	5.3	114.9	D	D	D	D	148	2,208	502.2	47.6	31	174	12.5	7.3
Belmont	7.6	110.0	36	361	217.6	18.5	291	4,123	1,126.0	92.9	58	330	69.1	11.5
Brown	3.1	69.8	19	114	60.0	4.5	97	1,281	334.3	23.6	D	D	D	0.9
Butler	50.7	134.7	453	10,303	11,235.7	612.9	1,024	20,813	8,376.7	517.9	314	1,355	370.6	54.4
Carroll	0.8	30.2	15	160	73.9	7.6	65	739	215.7	18.4	17	108	21.0	4.1
Champaign	2.5	63.9	25	201	132.8	8.3	83	914	309.9	22.8	25	61	12.0	2.3
Clark	16.2	118.9	84	1,661	1,808.1	81.9	373	5,695	1,411.4	122.3	89	380	63.1	11.0
Clermont	18.5	91.4	144	1,411	919.4	92.1	505	10,682	3,014.6	256.7	187	797	202.6	34.7
Clinton	0.9	21.0	23	379	470.1	16.4	127	1,919	480.7	42.1	28	116	23.3	3.2
Columbiana	9.2	87.6	D	D	D	39.3	338	3,969	1,229.4	102.9	51	226	36.1	7.0
Coshocton	6.6	180.2	D	D	D	4.1	106	1,280	341.0	29.0	16	43	6.8	0.8
Crawford	2.4	57.0	28	373	243.4	16.7	121	1,334	360.3	33.2	23	93	9.4	1.6
Cuyahoga	222.5	177.1	1,824	33,298	24,854.2	2,021.8	4,125	61,527	16,920.7	1,581.5	1,607	13,273	4,519.0	735.5
Darke	3.0	57.6	52	490	412.6	25.8	164	2,075	516.6	48.3	39	101	16.1	2.9
Defiance	3.4	88.7	33	472	374.6	24.0	141	2,535	847.1	67.0	27	95	14.9	2.4
Delaware	19.7	101.9	184	2,091	2,187.9	119.6	630	12,733	4,101.9	312.2	204	1,133	310.0	58.7
Erie	12.0	158.7	54	1,853	866.9	99.8	307	4,780	1,244.0	107.8	70	287	43.7	10.4
Fairfield	9.2	60.8	D	D	D	39.5	383	6,853	1,966.6	171.0	143	546	106.8	20.6
Fayette	2.0	69.4	30	529	4,097.6	26.3	177	2,685	611.8	52.8	13	50	20.5	1.1
Franklin	155.8	124.5	1,267	28,719	32,205.0	1,767.3	3,597	70,803	25,665.4	2,065.8	1,638	11,476	3,534.9	593.4
Fulton	2.5	59.7	45	424	229.7	19.5	147	1,713	504.3	43.6	19	85	9.4	2.7
Gallia	3.5	115.1	D	D	D	D	126	1,557	392.9	35.6	17	39	9.8	1.2
Geauga	1.5	15.4	145	1,176	585.4	68.9	311	4,382	1,504.3	127.4	80	207	41.0	9.0
Greene	9.0	54.6	78	757	491.3	41.8	553	11,189	2,591.4	240.8	130	445	126.7	14.6
Guernsey	5.5	138.8	23	461	294.6	16.3	139	1,644	532.3	39.0	32	166	41.2	7.2
Hamilton	114.8	142.1	1,049	20,157	16,309.5	1,226.0	2,683	51,158	13,273.6	1,259.7	1,077	6,860	1,848.1	387.1
Hancock	11.3	149.3	74	1,054	1,095.8	59.7	257	4,444	1,244.3	110.7	61	492	76.9	18.0
Hardin	2.2	70.4	15	101	127.3	4.6	84	918	220.5	19.0	12	32	4.8	0.7
Harrison	0.6	38.8	D	D	D	D	36	311	87.1	6.6	9	112	6.5	2.5
Henry	3.0	106.4	25	193	198.1	8.8	64	857	250.8	18.5	12	57	18.3	2.0
Highland	2.3	53.5	D	D	D	4.1	132	1,720	436.2	38.3	26	63	11.4	1.7
Hocking	1.7	58.6	D	D	D	D	72	905	237.8	21.2	22	100	11.5	2.5
Holmes	1.8	41.0	70	816	478.0	35.1	178	2,385	643.4	63.4	22	133	24.3	6.2
Huron	5.5	94.8	D	D	D	D	162	2,070	687.0	49.7	43	143	23.1	4.7
Jackson	1.5	45.1	19	131	102.8	5.6	127	1,485	377.9	33.8	24	65	12.1	1.5
Jefferson	8.8	130.2	D	D	D	D	211	3,074	841.1	72.9	42	179	26.9	5.5
Knox	5.5	89.6	48	457	218.8	19.1	168	2,178	623.0	53.1	41	142	25.4	4.2
Lake	22.8	99.5	282	2,622	1,278.4	146.7	751	12,390	3,755.5	319.5	206	806	207.8	30.2
Lawrence	5.4	88.9	D	D	D	9.3	144	1,942	583.1	47.9	36	211	60.5	6.4
Licking	12.6	73.7	91	1,355	967.4	71.6	453	6,711	2,497.9	182.7	116	399	69.7	12.2
Logan	2.8	61.7	26	1,962	1,019.1	104.1	144	1,718	504.2	44.4	33	156	37.0	5.6
Lorain	42.4	139.0	242	2,599	2,315.4	162.4	807	13,044	3,875.6	330.5	215	787	141.7	28.2
Lucas	81.5	187.8	426	8,101	5,611.2	479.6	1,376	24,927	6,470.5	609.5	407	2,943	4,350.7	195.8
Madison	2.1	46.5	D	D	D	15.9	104	1,851	1,746.0	56.0	29	63	15.9	2.0
Mahoning	4.3	18.5	261	3,661	1,927.5	190.1	850	12,647	3,772.5	326.4	199	863	157.4	26.2
Marion	6.1	93.9	36	432	375.1	22.0	164	2,833	812.0	71.7	41	140	27.0	3.9
Medina	3.0	17.1	218	2,554	2,460.7	147.9	485	8,601	3,119.5	226.6	155	503	117.1	18.7
Meigs	1.8	75.2	5	D	15.4	D	66	570	186.3	15.5	8	21	2.0	0.6
Mercer	2.9	70.3	D	D	D	D	170	1,896	548.3	49.6	26	118	19.6	3.1
Miami	10.9	104.5	83	1,266	1,088.6	66.4	301	5,305	1,417.1	127.3	75	288	57.4	10.7
Monroe	1.1	74.3	NA	NA	NA	NA	38	338	75.3	9.4	D	D	D	0.4
Montgomery	81.1	152.4	500	7,607	8,384.6	487.9	1,584	28,432	8,441.2	662.9	539	3,374	610.2	143.9
Morgan	0.6	43.3	D	D	D	D	29	392	59.4	5.3	D	D	D	0.0
Morrow	0.6	15.7	D	D	D	D	50	470	174.8	10.3	12	60	18.0	1.6
Muskingum	9.9	114.6	57	844	606.1	37.5	301	4,689	1,330.2	114.0	61	290	50.4	9.1
Noble	1.0	72.6	D	D	D	D	33	261	81.1	6.6	3	3	1.7	0.1

1 Merchant wholesalers, except manufacturers' sales branches and offices. 2. Employer establishments.

STATE County	Professional, scientific, and technical services, 2017				Manufacturing, 2017				Accommodation and food services, 2017			
	Number of establish-ments	Number of employees	Sales (mil dol)	Average payroll (mil dol)	Number of establish-ments	Number of employees	Sales (mil dol)	Average payroll (mil dol)	Number of establis-hments	Number of employees	Sales (mil dol)	Annual payroll (mil dol)
	147	148	149	150	151	152	153	154	155	156	157	158
NORTH DAKOTA—Cont'd												
Ward	D	D	D	D	D	468	D	22.4	179	3,711	181.6	58.3
Wells	11	21	2.1	0.7	6	37	15.9	2.3	22	104	5.1	1.3
Williams	123	555	112.8	51.4	36	293	136.7	18.7	122	2,115	219.8	48.1
OHIO	23,745	244,541	42,661.9	16,630.8	13,922	652,462	306,222.2	36,256.8	24,346	474,616	24,560.6	7,078.1
Adams	21	86	6.4	2.2	22	1,026	183.5	47.9	33	474	21.9	6.8
Allen	D	D	D	D	119	8,261	12,616.0	536.1	213	4,452	221.9	61.2
Ashland	66	1,089	172.7	71.7	85	3,777	1,122.9	176.6	89	1,597	76.9	22.2
Ashtabula	D	D	D	D	145	6,147	2,132.3	324.5	239	2,837	153.2	40.7
Athens	D	D	D	D	D	256	D	12.9	144	2,759	119.7	36.4
Auglaize	65	475	74.7	22.2	87	9,128	3,175.5	492.7	89	1,197	57.2	16.0
Belmont	87	560	58.2	22.3	40	894	399.4	40.7	134	2,675	131.1	39.4
Brown	25	112	8.8	3.2	D	730	D	31.1	51	955	38.7	11.2
Butler	D	D	D	D	383	19,334	10,184.4	1,141.6	713	15,436	811.8	229.0
Carroll	29	151	16.6	6.5	37	1,163	360.5	52.6	47	617	29.0	7.8
Champaign	40	255	18.8	13.1	40	3,631	1,375.0	202.6	49	616	29.4	8.1
Clark	D	D	D	D	152	6,187	2,405.7	274.0	223	4,568	207.9	63.6
Clermont	357	2,798	701.7	171.5	161	5,753	1,964.6	313.1	301	6,659	334.1	100.1
Clinton	D	D	D	D	38	2,900	1,087.4	154.0	69	1,275	63.3	17.1
Columbiana	91	395	41.1	15.8	166	5,912	1,517.6	264.6	174	2,772	123.4	33.6
Coshocton	32	147	14.8	4.8	51	2,199	1,072.8	119.1	48	727	29.7	8.4
Crawford	47	650	18.7	13.8	74	2,971	1,004.4	141.2	81	1,142	50.5	13.6
Cuyahoga	D	D	D	D	1,677	65,044	23,225.4	3,932.7	3,037	56,378	3,332.7	955.0
Darke	62	305	27.9	9.5	76	5,161	2,236.9	262.0	91	1,012	44.5	12.2
Defiance	D	D	D	D	37	3,111	1,029.9	227.2	83	1,409	63.8	17.4
Delaware	D	D	D	D	124	5,311	3,096.8	318.0	469	11,025	582.9	174.2
Erie	D	D	D	D	99	5,576	2,100.9	264.9	273	5,721	344.3	92.4
Fairfield	211	993	122.9	43.2	108	3,853	1,121.6	193.1	269	5,391	252.3	75.7
Fayette	18	66	7.3	2.1	26	1,706	1,464.6	78.4	65	1,301	61.1	16.5
Franklin	D	D	D	D	821	31,316	13,796.1	1,668.7	2,950	64,725	3,728.3	1,066.4
Fulton	45	216	23.3	8.5	95	7,330	4,118.7	388.9	77	975	43.8	11.6
Gallia	27	85	6.6	1.8	19	564	161.7	25.5	51	1,032	50.3	14.1
Geauga	D	D	D	D	195	8,025	2,875.3	406.8	170	2,710	126.7	36.4
Greene	488	10,839	2,287.4	845.3	97	3,014	934.9	182.7	346	8,340	414.2	124.2
Guernsey	37	317	39.3	19.2	55	2,774	1,576.1	143.3	82	1,448	77.6	20.3
Hamilton	2,500	38,507	7,292.2	2,996.1	950	44,819	23,656.9	2,714.2	2,012	44,753	2,445.3	732.2
Hancock	D	D	D	D	97	11,347	5,114.8	569.9	188	4,540	205.9	61.2
Hardin	22	100	10.5	3.7	28	1,782	588.5	83.4	44	789	32.1	10.9
Harrison	16	44	7.1	2.3	14	300	72.4	14.2	24	199	9.0	2.4
Henry	24	159	16.9	4.8	44	3,279	3,147.4	188.4	57	686	27.5	8.2
Highland	34	122	10.9	3.2	28	1,786	833.0	86.0	56	920	44.5	12.4
Hocking	27	96	8.9	3.2	27	804	300.2	36.3	67	927	49.7	14.8
Holmes	39	298	33.3	12.2	305	6,695	1,751.9	276.9	72	1,577	76.9	24.2
Huron	69	412	46.7	16.0	95	6,183	2,455.7	286.4	121	1,585	64.0	17.3
Jackson	33	134	10.5	3.3	26	3,222	1,846.1	116.1	55	1,004	40.4	11.4
Jefferson	D	D	33.4	D	36	1,281	423.3	84.0	120	1,704	86.5	23.4
Knox	57	356	38.1	13.8	69	4,208	1,592.8	233.3	103	1,712	75.8	21.2
Lake	D	D	D	D	571	18,802	6,531.5	1,041.1	523	9,875	497.0	135.3
Lawrence	41	202	15.8	6.7	31	713	492.6	32.9	64	1,236	64.3	17.2
Licking	D	D	D	D	156	8,898	3,385.2	447.3	302	4,911	240.5	71.9
Logan	58	747	75.4	30.5	43	4,979	6,334.6	336.6	98	2,237	101.8	29.3
Lorain	D	D	D	D	355	15,443	6,058.9	939.5	522	8,874	444.4	123.5
Lucas	854	10,105	1,585.8	644.2	438	22,153	22,683.2	1,357.3	1,056	19,755	986.6	282.2
Madison	D	D	D	D	44	3,356	1,328.5	194.3	55	1,095	51.9	15.7
Mahoning	D	D	D	D	308	8,491	2,140.6	425.3	536	10,319	450.6	128.3
Marion	58	255	25.1	9.8	74	6,428	3,585.0	323.1	103	2,191	103.7	27.2
Medina	420	2,160	280.2	110.2	275	9,153	3,161.9	487.5	314	6,106	276.2	80.7
Meigs	13	62	5.6	1.7	6	13	3.7	0.7	31	427	20.2	5.9
Mercer	46	324	47.2	14.8	83	4,424	1,654.0	217.3	93	1,176	46.1	13.5
Miami	150	905	137.0	50.3	209	9,672	4,005.3	531.8	182	3,688	173.2	50.3
Monroe	13	46	4.6	1.6	8	57	13.7	3.0	D	D	D	2.5
Montgomery	1,070	12,067	1,914.0	801.9	672	29,693	9,405.7	1,776.0	1,101	23,646	1,176.5	352.2
Morgan	7	51	6.6	2.0	9	747	185.4	38.2	20	272	9.6	2.9
Morrow	27	186	18.8	6.4	28	1,047	715.5	52.9	30	353	20.2	6.1
Muskingum	104	530	79.4	24.9	75	2,800	1,012.6	143.5	193	3,395	169.6	49.4
Noble	14	61	10.8	3.0	9	89	49.6	3.4	D	D	D	D

STATE County	Health care and social assistance, 2017				Other services, 2017				Nonemployer businesses, 2019		Value of residential construction authorized by building permits, 2021	
	Number of establish-ments	Number of employees	Receipts (mil dol)	Annual payroll (mil dol)	Number of establish-ments	Number of employees	Receipts (mil dol)	Annual payroll (mil dol)	Number	Receipts (mil dol)	New construction ($1,000)	Number of housing units
	159	160	161	162	163	164	165	166	167	168	169	170
NORTH DAKOTA—Cont'd												
Ward	163	5,176	615.0	289.3	155	811	99.3	26.6	4,408	217.2	41,436	193
Wells	19	399	25.1	11.7	D	D	5.2	D	321	15.7	91	1
Williams	78	1,417	206.6	69.9	86	477	94.9	20.7	2,857	165.5	23,872	71
OHIO	29,595	856,794	97,117.4	39,468.5	18,425	126,378	15,268.0	4,043.9	817,642	38,071.3	7,339,454	30,418
Adams	49	951	71.9	30.4	D	D	D	2.4	1,758	76.7	5,854	25
Allen	289	11,913	1,427.5	561.9	176	1,150	101.6	29.0	5,492	231.4	45,789	226
Ashland	118	2,898	262.6	110.7	93	558	54.2	13.0	3,453	171.7	11,176	61
Ashtabula	196	4,910	416.9	184.3	142	575	50.3	12.2	6,189	278.8	37,055	168
Athens	172	3,332	383.7	142.1	80	371	28.9	7.2	3,438	132.5	16,174	110
Auglaize	101	2,519	198.8	76.2	87	531	41.1	12.7	2,665	123.9	33,256	156
Belmont	194	3,895	328.0	117.9	120	635	51.1	15.3	3,144	133.3	770	4
Brown	66	1,406	73.7	31.7	39	172	14.0	4.3	2,757	122.3	34,181	122
Butler	789	15,809	1,832.0	670.0	545	4,419	482.2	139.7	24,431	1,174.1	204,801	941
Carroll	46	732	49.7	21.5	37	195	18.5	4.6	1,942	97.5	502	1
Champaign	47	976	86.0	33.2	53	228	18.9	4.3	2,381	94.6	20,430	51
Clark	290	7,102	709.7	267.6	191	1,438	194.0	52.0	6,815	288.4	54,354	199
Clermont	318	6,107	640.0	222.1	276	1,709	176.4	52.5	14,051	641.2	231,090	1,224
Clinton	94	1,900	196.2	75.4	54	217	20.9	6.1	2,579	111.6	15,089	88
Columbiana	258	5,348	455.0	174.2	177	939	86.3	33.3	5,999	269.4	15,751	63
Coshocton	82	1,755	151.3	53.3	58	264	25.1	5.9	2,469	111.0	1,144	5
Crawford	89	2,732	318.3	112.7	64	300	24.2	6.0	2,208	95.1	2,280	10
Cuyahoga	3,676	147,104	17,917.0	7,895.6	2,399	18,570	2,156.6	614.4	99,039	4,596.5	279,672	784
Darke	82	2,242	185.9	80.7	98	402	27.4	6.9	3,534	163.7	23,443	63
Defiance	90	2,029	232.8	79.6	71	389	39.5	8.5	2,100	86.7	9,812	46
Delaware	531	8,103	797.8	342.6	304	2,613	499.3	107.9	18,834	1,105.6	661,025	2,359
Erie	226	5,239	536.5	225.3	126	599	57.1	14.8	5,142	210.1	56,334	289
Fairfield	355	7,396	832.7	313.7	177	1,070	117.7	32.8	11,428	519.5	219,234	875
Fayette	44	1,147	95.6	42.0	40	153	12.3	3.5	1,420	61.1	8,199	33
Franklin	3,778	117,393	14,875.9	5,676.7	1,880	16,846	2,525.6	680.7	106,978	5,099.1	1,263,587	6,652
Fulton	108	1,905	201.5	69.6	75	266	29.6	7.0	2,920	139.0	7,646	31
Gallia	78	2,894	325.8	117.0	33	217	20.3	6.6	1,683	80.0	1,529	14
Geauga	272	4,933	495.6	202.1	201	1,186	126.7	36.1	10,957	696.3	87,261	191
Greene	394	7,764	788.6	345.6	220	1,344	126.2	36.4	10,704	463.4	244,413	685
Guernsey	123	3,297	302.2	113.1	60	251	22.2	5.9	2,243	109.2	6,584	26
Hamilton	2,381	88,940	11,839.3	4,868.2	1,442	11,548	1,407.7	392.4	62,412	2,973.9	400,103	1,922
Hancock	199	5,090	579.0	216.8	141	972	132.2	32.2	4,513	218.8	31,661	121
Hardin	55	737	61.7	24.7	22	99	8.6	2.4	1,485	61.0	5,175	24
Harrison	24	492	39.4	14.6	21	73	6.0	1.5	868	48.2	0	0
Henry	53	1,284	89.6	37.6	45	227	21.4	5.2	1,647	70.0	5,932	19
Highland	103	1,683	147.8	57.7	41	153	14.0	3.5	2,935	146.9	13,442	71
Hocking	57	1,156	95.7	37.2	38	208	20.8	4.6	1,875	84.9	2,746	12
Holmes	61	1,206	163.7	37.3	59	297	45.6	10.5	5,588	363.5	2,037	4
Huron	100	2,772	293.1	118.2	100	526	41.6	12.5	3,140	141.6	19,204	142
Jackson	88	1,351	132.2	35.6	40	159	18.8	4.0	1,622	77.5	10,776	51
Jefferson	173	3,953	427.4	159.0	105	665	59.1	18.4	3,077	113.4	1,302	6
Knox	149	3,142	299.2	116.0	75	491	52.5	12.4	4,984	246.6	120,246	351
Lake	607	11,627	1,078.4	462.8	454	2,501	232.6	68.1	16,689	778.5	140,704	775
Lawrence	120	2,630	139.1	62.8	46	194	21.4	5.6	2,683	97.3	2,914	16
Licking	296	7,120	742.6	291.2	211	1,190	113.1	30.4	12,588	580.9	119,249	363
Logan	89	1,895	193.6	74.7	59	475	82.7	15.2	2,909	132.5	28,902	126
Lorain	645	15,642	1,744.5	731.8	451	2,596	239.5	67.0	19,307	794.5	285,589	1,127
Lucas	1,366	39,689	4,694.1	1,856.8	687	4,782	516.5	137.8	25,675	1,137.9	124,302	460
Madison	66	1,199	98.7	40.4	37	193	17.7	5.7	2,875	132.5	20,931	89
Mahoning	763	22,098	2,114.3	853.2	388	2,885	247.6	72.2	16,376	688.4	44,240	194
Marion	185	4,313	466.0	187.7	88	603	39.7	11.9	3,003	126.1	13,381	49
Medina	358	7,418	676.6	283.4	298	1,561	146.3	45.9	14,123	724.0	184,758	463
Meigs	45	546	46.5	15.0	23	84	7.5	1.8	1,105	38.7	695	6
Mercer	76	2,188	160.4	71.6	96	504	70.3	14.1	2,849	143.0	22,432	85
Miami	204	4,692	387.4	158.2	179	958	105.2	27.0	7,183	415.5	96,729	307
Monroe	20	253	13.2	6.4	22	121	11.5	2.5	982	36.2	100	1
Montgomery	1,511	52,281	6,622.1	2,671.1	809	6,269	676.8	236.2	34,012	1,440.9	286,395	1,047
Morgan	15	351	28.2	10.1	D	D	D	0.6	795	30.1	13,943	55
Morrow	D	D	D	31.2	25	67	7.3	1.9	2,675	151.9	37,851	150
Muskingum	180	6,227	820.3	289.3	150	968	90.8	25.3	5,150	231.5	5,264	21
Noble	22	398	15.2	7.0	18	36	4.8	0.9	768	36.3	4,742	25

STATE County	Government employment and payroll, 2017									Local government finances, 2017				
			March payroll (percent of total)							General revenue				
												Taxes		
													Per capita[1] (dollars)	
	Full-time equivalent employees	March payroll (dollars)	Adminis-tration, judicial, and legal	Police and corrections	Fire protection	Highways and transpor-tation	Health and welfare	Natural resources and utilities	Education and libraries	Total (mil dol)	Inter-govern-mental (mil dol)	Total (mil dol)	Total	Property
	171	172	173	174	175	176	177	178	179	180	181	182	183	184
NORTH DAKOTA—Cont'd														
Ward	2,226	9,838,354	5.8	8.3	3.5	5.3	6.5	6.7	61.8	387.1	207.1	119.7	1,746	1,270
Wells	163	558,834	14.4	5.1	0.1	10.2	19.1	7.9	42.3	21.1	11.7	5.7	1,438	1,313
Williams	1,323	6,301,179	5.5	12.5	4.8	8.4	5.6	12.1	45.4	373.1	180.2	153.0	4,573	3,231
OHIO	X	X	X	X	X	X	X	X	X	X	X	X	X	X
Adams	1,341	4,584,553	7.8	3.6	0.8	3.2	23.8	4.1	55.1	100.8	61.5	29.6	1,065	927
Allen	3,994	15,615,627	8.1	10.6	5.1	4.1	8.2	6.1	56.1	411.1	190.3	147.7	1,432	973
Ashland	1,575	5,738,974	8.7	8.6	4.0	5.4	11.4	4.7	55.6	157.9	63.1	70.8	1,319	851
Ashtabula	3,518	13,241,030	8.3	7.8	4.0	4.6	10.7	3.3	60.4	362.9	177.7	120.3	1,231	940
Athens	2,282	8,966,284	8.2	8.7	1.9	3.4	14.7	5.9	54.0	216.6	117.5	76.6	1,152	879
Auglaize	1,740	6,878,001	7.6	9.5	3.0	4.7	7.2	8.0	59.0	184.5	74.4	76.8	1,678	851
Belmont	2,653	8,668,632	9.8	9.2	2.2	4.7	12.0	7.1	53.2	208.2	89.1	90.3	1,328	963
Brown	1,485	5,319,265	8.7	5.5	0.6	2.8	5.3	2.5	72.2	159.0	82.0	38.4	882	675
Butler	12,961	55,036,876	7.1	10.1	5.0	2.8	5.2	5.4	63.3	1,519.8	625.6	600.2	1,577	1,137
Carroll	835	2,542,302	17.0	4.1	0.0	10.6	12.7	3.5	50.6	82.3	38.9	29.7	1,087	984
Champaign	1,612	5,783,433	8.3	8.4	2.4	3.4	9.4	1.9	64.2	152.8	75.6	56.6	1,456	918
Clark	4,730	19,251,860	8.8	10.4	4.4	2.0	9.0	3.3	60.6	483.7	238.1	185.9	1,382	876
Clermont	6,063	23,115,330	7.4	10.6	7.1	4.2	8.7	3.2	58.5	644.1	249.7	279.8	1,370	1,139
Clinton	1,761	6,201,390	9.9	8.5	1.9	3.5	7.7	5.3	62.3	158.2	72.3	62.3	1,483	991
Columbiana	3,346	11,818,467	7.6	6.7	1.5	5.1	9.3	4.7	64.1	317.6	170.9	107.9	1,047	695
Coshocton	1,432	5,411,175	10.4	5.8	11.7	4.4	13.3	2.4	50.4	126.7	61.6	44.2	1,211	975
Crawford	1,408	5,187,605	9.3	9.7	4.1	2.9	4.9	6.4	60.8	162.8	76.1	57.5	1,377	861
Cuyahoga	63,287	318,547,930	6.3	10.5	4.8	6.5	20.5	7.1	42.1	8,930.2	2,379.1	4,022.8	3,224	1,789
Darke	1,666	6,251,519	6.5	9.6	2.6	3.4	8.3	3.9	63.6	183.8	78.3	75.5	1,465	848
Defiance	1,660	6,467,187	7.0	6.1	2.2	3.5	20.3	5.1	51.5	226.9	88.5	59.5	1,559	969
Delaware	5,809	25,871,545	6.6	8.3	7.4	2.8	6.3	4.0	62.8	732.8	133.2	466.5	2,322	1,781
Erie	3,473	15,051,571	7.3	8.1	3.3	1.6	8.6	5.7	63.5	389.5	120.0	160.3	2,144	1,520
Fairfield	4,765	19,070,061	8.2	8.4	7.3	2.9	7.9	5.3	59.1	654.0	207.3	273.9	1,771	1,085
Fayette	1,435	5,512,962	6.5	6.3	2.3	3.1	34.5	3.4	40.9	164.3	55.8	48.5	1,695	1,054
Franklin	46,320	235,016,726	7.7	12.1	8.1	5.0	6.8	6.1	52.0	8,104.3	2,525.9	3,976.5	3,069	1,700
Fulton	2,019	7,317,680	8.6	6.0	2.2	4.1	4.6	4.3	68.2	183.3	75.0	79.2	1,873	1,169
Gallia	1,382	4,502,765	12.9	7.8	0.4	4.6	7.2	3.5	63.4	147.7	83.0	33.4	1,108	802
Geauga	2,969	12,687,062	8.2	10.9	1.3	5.7	8.1	5.6	58.9	360.6	92.2	201.3	2,144	1,837
Greene	5,452	22,544,757	8.6	10.6	6.8	3.2	8.4	4.5	56.6	645.2	175.7	343.7	2,064	1,596
Guernsey	1,593	5,180,768	9.3	7.2	2.0	5.2	8.3	5.5	55.7	136.6	65.7	49.1	1,257	807
Hamilton	30,891	144,061,829	7.4	12.2	8.0	5.4	8.0	8.0	48.3	4,518.2	1,287.0	2,266.3	2,784	1,645
Hancock	2,516	9,829,360	7.5	8.5	3.7	3.7	8.8	6.0	61.0	286.9	101.7	129.3	1,701	1,031
Hardin	1,232	4,171,146	9.6	4.9	1.3	4.7	9.7	2.7	65.8	110.6	44.5	49.6	1,584	985
Harrison	772	2,092,052	16.3	7.3	0.0	12.4	11.8	4.5	47.0	77.3	33.5	32.4	2,128	2,016
Henry	1,326	5,105,969	7.8	4.3	0.9	3.2	10.4	6.1	66.3	126.0	55.6	56.8	2,091	1,470
Highland	2,211	7,371,594	5.4	4.4	1.9	2.9	32.2	2.0	50.2	194.0	85.6	46.3	1,080	654
Hocking	1,068	3,400,935	10.3	8.7	1.5	4.6	7.4	2.7	62.8	124.1	42.1	33.4	1,174	914
Holmes	1,268	4,982,748	6.4	5.7	1.2	4.4	33.4	2.1	46.1	98.5	39.1	44.8	1,021	770
Huron	2,084	7,836,280	10.1	6.5	2.7	4.7	7.5	6.8	60.6	216.9	100.2	79.8	1,366	907
Jackson	984	3,483,617	5.6	5.6	2.6	2.6	0.7	7.3	73.9	108.8	65.4	26.8	826	562
Jefferson	2,663	8,769,479	7.7	11.9	2.1	4.9	12.2	5.3	54.7	256.6	117.3	91.8	1,384	902
Knox	2,409	8,636,325	6.3	6.1	4.0	4.4	10.3	3.2	63.3	200.9	85.0	84.0	1,371	1,082
Lake	9,551	42,209,385	5.8	10.3	6.2	4.8	7.5	8.7	55.6	1,067.3	322.2	549.2	2,386	1,635
Lawrence	2,243	7,789,802	6.5	5.2	0.9	2.9	7.2	3.5	72.3	242.9	124.9	51.5	857	633
Licking	6,034	23,746,451	7.2	9.4	6.0	3.1	5.8	3.3	63.1	636.5	229.8	309.8	1,784	1,231
Logan	1,974	7,287,445	6.8	5.8	2.0	4.7	15.8	3.9	59.6	196.8	79.7	74.3	1,644	1,034
Lorain	11,370	47,591,662	7.3	9.5	4.1	2.5	8.7	6.3	60.3	1,254.7	487.5	550.9	1,792	1,213
Lucas	15,869	73,046,493	8.8	13.3	7.6	4.6	8.7	5.2	50.5	2,114.5	798.6	913.5	2,119	1,237
Madison	1,539	6,248,847	8.6	7.1	5.5	3.6	5.1	3.2	62.6	153.2	53.6	74.1	1,682	1,205
Mahoning	9,303	34,495,182	6.0	12.1	3.6	3.9	8.3	6.6	58.1	884.7	358.6	384.3	1,672	1,026
Marion	2,470	9,069,451	7.1	11.2	5.6	3.0	6.4	3.0	60.7	218.9	112.9	76.0	1,168	678
Medina	5,948	25,936,956	6.5	8.5	2.4	3.4	6.6	6.5	64.9	694.1	202.7	376.2	2,111	1,618
Meigs	951	3,024,364	8.7	6.6	0.0	4.6	10.9	7.4	60.8	69.9	47.8	16.8	730	583
Mercer	2,148	8,056,550	6.7	5.5	1.1	2.6	24.0	3.3	56.0	222.2	68.8	66.2	1,620	1,030
Miami	3,665	15,185,653	8.1	8.5	2.8	3.3	4.7	6.6	64.3	432.2	151.7	198.5	1,886	1,022
Monroe	774	2,184,697	12.8	6.2	0.2	7.1	7.9	4.8	51.0	66.9	30.7	28.1	2,016	1,713
Montgomery	22,646	100,833,229	8.2	10.1	4.8	6.5	8.5	7.7	52.6	2,822.7	1,014.1	1,220.0	2,296	1,441
Morgan	430	1,395,660	13.6	4.6	0.0	4.1	2.2	2.8	71.2	55.5	33.4	12.2	834	651
Morrow	1,325	4,591,056	9.4	5.2	0.1	4.0	28.6	0.9	50.9	117.5	52.1	43.6	1,249	865
Muskingum	3,926	13,651,662	5.9	8.2	2.6	3.2	11.4	3.7	63.7	358.9	174.6	129.7	1,506	1,020
Noble	467	1,672,205	14.3	8.7	0.0	7.8	11.1	6.1	49.2	51.0	23.6	21.3	1,479	1,317

1. Based on the resident population estimated as of July 1 of the year shown.

STATE County	Local government finances, 2017 (cont.)									Government employment, 2020			Individual income tax returns, 2019		
	Direct general expenditure							Debt outstanding							
			Percent of total for:												
	Total (mil dol)	Per capita[1] (dollars)	Education	Health and hospitals	Police protection	Public welfare	Highways	Total (mil dol)	Per capita[1] (dollars)	Federal civilian	Federal military	State and local	Number of returns	Mean adjusted gross income	Mean income tax
	185	186	187	188	189	190	191	192	193	194	195	196	197	198	199
NORTH DAKOTA—Cont'd															
Ward	413.7	6,038	41.2	2.6	4.1	2.1	25.9	314.9	4,596	1,268	6,174	4,250	33,590	67,276	7,245
Wells	18.6	4,648	50.8	3.7	3.2	0.0	8.9	12.6	3,144	23	22	240	1,960	62,368	6,143
Williams	276.3	8,256	37.2	1.9	4.0	1.5	14.6	677.2	20,236	112	232	2,560	19,230	92,692	12,506
OHIO	X	X	X	X	X	X	X	X	X	81,890	35,626	669,734	5,758,240	64,191	7,217
Adams	101.9	3,671	61.5	4.6	4.3	8.4	2.3	53.0	1,911	69	68	1,140	11,210	45,492	3,227
Allen	466.4	4,524	51.6	3.1	8.5	4.4	3.7	1,857.7	18,019	340	252	5,513	48,650	55,401	5,309
Ashland	150.8	2,810	52.3	7.6	7.1	5.0	6.5	61.3	1,143	108	129	2,218	25,150	52,411	4,431
Ashtabula	396.0	4,051	49.9	8.6	4.4	5.5	5.8	154.8	1,584	201	234	4,045	45,230	47,617	3,991
Athens	229.4	3,450	53.4	2.7	3.0	13.9	3.9	123.1	1,851	263	152	9,924	22,800	51,022	4,657
Auglaize	187.4	4,097	50.8	4.3	5.7	5.2	9.3	206.8	4,521	100	113	2,035	23,820	60,905	5,699
Belmont	202.4	2,976	51.2	1.4	2.7	7.0	8.9	68.5	1,007	165	157	3,428	30,840	59,454	6,403
Brown	170.3	3,914	63.6	2.5	3.8	2.8	4.3	82.7	1,901	111	108	2,014	19,870	49,701	3,848
Butler	1,536.4	4,037	52.9	3.8	7.7	4.6	5.4	1,844.7	4,847	609	956	19,530	182,330	66,263	7,114
Carroll	72.5	2,655	54.7	8.2	3.8	6.8	9.1	91.4	3,344	52	67	969	12,690	52,947	4,514
Champaign	174.4	4,488	67.7	2.1	4.1	3.4	4.6	115.6	2,976	76	96	1,849	18,990	53,238	4,425
Clark	528.8	3,930	51.2	6.1	8.1	6.3	4.2	235.9	1,753	518	328	6,061	64,050	51,217	4,403
Clermont	732.8	3,587	55.7	5.5	5.0	5.4	4.6	495.4	2,425	416	516	7,179	102,670	68,721	7,521
Clinton	164.4	3,914	51.0	2.7	5.5	5.0	5.3	62.8	1,496	136	105	2,088	19,770	58,685	5,996
Columbiana	341.2	3,310	55.9	3.4	5.4	9.4	6.7	146.0	1,417	609	244	4,237	47,480	49,984	4,250
Coshocton	125.4	3,433	49.4	7.1	5.2	6.4	12.5	62.9	1,722	86	90	1,383	16,400	46,326	3,428
Crawford	169.2	4,057	48.4	5.1	5.0	4.8	8.3	134.8	3,232	85	103	1,672	20,770	45,718	3,333
Cuyahoga	9,303.0	7,457	35.7	15.5	6.7	3.0	2.8	13,473.2	10,799	16,806	3,506	75,732	637,840	67,384	8,665
Darke	191.6	3,716	59.8	2.2	6.6	6.0	6.6	121.3	2,353	110	127	2,020	25,230	52,081	4,418
Defiance	236.1	6,188	46.8	23.9	3.6	1.4	4.5	127.9	3,352	95	93	1,924	19,180	53,344	4,457
Delaware	804.7	4,006	51.5	3.9	4.3	1.0	11.8	938.3	4,671	271	543	8,121	103,180	112,802	16,594
Erie	408.2	5,460	48.3	2.1	5.0	4.4	5.0	267.8	3,582	242	183	4,873	40,300	57,393	5,979
Fairfield	660.8	4,272	58.9	5.0	4.6	3.7	4.5	543.9	3,516	264	418	6,520	76,320	65,190	6,503
Fayette	159.2	5,559	37.9	30.9	3.8	3.8	4.0	94.3	3,291	54	70	1,630	13,490	48,320	4,047
Franklin	8,614.7	6,650	33.2	4.8	5.9	8.1	5.2	12,166.6	9,391	13,649	3,640	124,569	655,170	66,463	7,881
Fulton	198.8	4,703	57.3	5.1	5.3	3.4	4.0	126.1	2,982	97	108	2,379	21,510	57,990	5,248
Gallia	152.7	5,063	61.8	2.1	4.5	5.1	6.9	85.7	2,840	67	73	1,978	12,090	49,967	4,100
Geauga	373.0	3,973	44.1	2.8	6.1	7.4	8.9	278.9	2,971	109	232	3,400	47,570	99,284	14,384
Greene	597.9	3,590	48.0	4.8	6.4	1.2	6.4	546.1	3,279	15,664	3,549	9,842	79,770	73,305	8,286
Guernsey	129.7	3,320	51.1	7.5	3.8	9.2	8.1	37.6	964	120	96	2,084	18,300	52,993	5,156
Hamilton	4,460.0	5,478	39.2	4.9	7.6	5.4	4.7	6,249.3	7,676	8,819	2,144	48,891	412,550	78,886	10,933
Hancock	296.8	3,907	47.3	10.5	5.6	3.0	7.0	208.6	2,746	156	186	3,100	37,760	66,925	7,752
Hardin	97.6	3,117	68.7	6.1	2.3	0.0	3.5	42.3	1,349	69	74	1,327	13,560	47,825	3,592
Harrison	67.0	4,407	44.3	2.5	3.8	10.2	3.2	45.3	2,978	50	37	742	6,730	52,847	4,657
Henry	164.0	6,034	58.6	4.7	2.2	0.3	3.9	134.8	4,958	65	67	1,791	14,070	56,384	4,860
Highland	194.9	4,542	46.9	26.4	4.8	4.4	6.4	43.4	1,013	105	111	2,145	19,200	45,763	3,274
Hocking	127.0	4,467	33.8	37.6	4.6	1.1	5.2	23.3	818	51	70	1,579	12,730	49,221	3,906
Holmes	88.6	2,018	50.3	7.4	5.5	8.0	12.8	22.2	507	62	109	1,525	18,000	58,918	5,234
Huron	209.1	3,581	57.7	4.8	4.1	3.8	5.6	201.6	3,453	140	144	2,338	29,070	50,049	4,091
Jackson	112.5	3,473	55.6	0.3	8.9	10.6	5.9	60.3	1,861	80	81	1,433	13,990	47,589	3,595
Jefferson	558.0	8,415	71.6	4.1	2.0	2.2	2.6	154.7	2,332	182	158	3,835	30,290	51,937	4,699
Knox	203.8	3,326	50.5	6.9	2.9	5.9	6.2	89.4	1,460	123	148	2,612	28,070	56,357	5,034
Lake	1,063.7	4,622	51.6	7.2	7.9	1.9	6.1	475.5	2,066	441	606	10,092	126,570	64,292	6,963
Lawrence	253.7	4,224	68.9	5.5	2.7	3.1	3.2	49.7	827	187	147	2,553	25,780	49,861	4,071
Licking	662.1	3,814	53.8	0.8	6.1	6.4	4.6	421.2	2,426	404	450	8,143	86,460	63,263	6,367
Logan	195.1	4,317	51.4	7.7	6.2	4.4	2.3	213.4	4,721	125	113	2,073	23,140	54,648	4,904
Lorain	1,327.6	4,318	52.3	2.8	6.4	6.5	3.3	1,410.0	4,586	1,145	765	14,082	156,880	62,951	6,714
Lucas	2,212.7	5,133	37.3	5.9	9.3	4.4	3.5	2,108.5	4,892	1,936	1,137	27,154	209,040	57,586	6,152
Madison	152.3	3,459	59.2	5.0	3.8	4.5	5.5	73.8	1,676	84	103	3,025	19,520	61,647	6,030
Mahoning	939.8	4,090	50.7	4.3	8.4	4.1	2.8	514.9	2,241	1,212	547	12,718	112,800	54,125	5,552
Marion	224.2	3,445	59.9	1.1	4.2	0.1	3.7	357.8	5,498	119	176	3,832	28,850	48,313	3,889
Medina	653.7	3,669	51.9	4.9	5.9	2.9	6.1	367.3	2,061	395	484	6,515	95,250	77,112	9,142
Meigs	69.7	3,020	59.7	2.5	4.4	8.8	7.3	11.7	508	66	56	979	9,410	46,918	3,484
Mercer	212.7	5,205	47.2	32.4	1.4	0.0	2.7	134.9	3,301	99	103	2,644	21,330	63,347	6,186
Miami	421.1	4,003	52.9	4.0	6.6	3.4	6.4	204.3	1,942	208	268	4,551	53,370	64,486	6,593
Monroe	72.6	5,211	46.1	4.2	6.4	8.4	14.8	49.3	3,536	55	42	763	6,180	63,023	7,080
Montgomery	2,924.6	5,503	50.5	0.5	6.1	6.5	2.9	3,132.8	5,895	4,502	3,681	25,214	263,690	57,696	5,950
Morgan	55.4	3,786	44.6	2.3	6.1	7.7	9.5	24.6	1,681	57	35	602	6,180	44,274	3,107
Morrow	166.1	4,758	34.8	39.6	2.6	5.4	4.3	83.1	2,381	50	88	1,445	16,350	53,935	4,373
Muskingum	372.0	4,320	58.2	3.7	5.6	5.8	4.5	85.8	996	237	212	4,832	40,620	50,431	4,429
Noble	47.3	3,286	52.3	3.3	4.2	6.5	11.2	4.4	307	24	29	962	5,550	52,335	4,600

1. Based on the resident population estimated as of July 1 of the year shown.

State / county code	CBSA code[1]	County Type code[2]	STATE County	Land area[3] (sq. mi)	Population, 2021: Total persons 2021	Population, 2021: Rank	Population, 2021: Per square mile	Race alone or in combination, not Hispanic or Latino (percent): White	Black	American Indian, Alaska Native	Asian and Pacific Islancer	Percent Hispanic or Latino[4]	Age (percent): Under 5 years	5 to 17 years	18 to 24 years	25 to 34 years	35 to 44 years	45 to 54 years
				1	2	3	4	5	6	7	8	9	10	11	12	13	14	15
			OHIO—Cont'd															
39123	45780	4	Ottawa	254.7	40,104	1,178	157.5	93.0	1.7	0.6	0.6	5.4	4.1	10.3	10.1	9.5	10.4	12.0
39125		6	Paulding	416.4	18,871	1,877	45.3	93.1	1.6	0.7	0.6	5.2	6.1	13.5	12.1	11.0	11.7	12.2
39127	18140	1	Perry	407.9	35,460	1,294	86.9	97.7	1.2	1.1	0.6	1.0	5.8	13.6	11.5	11.8	12.2	12.9
39129	18140	1	Pickaway	501.2	59,333	886	118.4	93.6	4.7	0.8	1.0	1.7	5.3	12.1	12.5	13.6	13.6	13.7
39131		7	Pike	440.3	27,089	1,525	61.5	96.3	2.2	1.5	0.7	1.3	6.3	13.2	12.1	11.6	11.3	12.8
39133	10420	2	Portage	487.4	162,382	414	333.2	90.5	6.1	0.7	2.7	2.2	4.4	10.5	18.9	11.6	11.0	11.8
39135		6	Preble	424.2	40,867	1,166	96.3	97.2	1.4	0.8	0.9	1.1	5.3	12.7	11.7	11.0	11.8	12.8
39137		6	Putnam	482.5	34,318	1,321	71.1	92.2	0.9	0.4	0.4	6.8	6.4	15.0	11.8	10.8	11.8	11.4
39139	31900	3	Richland	495.2	125,195	513	252.8	87.3	10.9	0.7	1.3	2.2	5.6	12.4	11.9	13.0	12.0	11.8
39141	17060	4	Ross	689.2	76,891	736	111.6	91.9	7.3	1.1	0.9	1.4	5.3	11.9	11.5	12.8	13.1	13.6
39143	23380	4	Sandusky	408.2	58,715	894	143.8	85.4	4.8	0.7	0.7	10.7	5.4	12.5	11.7	11.6	12.2	12.2
39145	39020	4	Scioto	610.1	73,346	753	120.2	94.7	3.7	1.3	0.7	1.6	5.5	12.4	12.6	12.7	12.1	12.6
39147	45660	4	Seneca	551.0	54,906	934	99.6	90.9	3.9	0.6	1.1	5.7	5.5	12.0	14.7	11.7	11.9	11.4
39149	43380	4	Shelby	407.7	47,977	1,023	117.7	94.5	4.0	0.6	1.7	1.6	6.4	13.7	12.7	11.5	11.5	12.4
39151	15940	2	Stark	575.3	373,834	196	649.8	88.3	10.0	0.8	1.4	2.4	5.5	12.1	12.2	12.1	11.8	12.1
39153	10420	2	Summit	412.8	537,633	132	1,302.4	77.8	16.8	0.8	4.9	2.5	5.4	11.7	11.8	13.4	12.2	12.3
39155	49660	2	Trumbull	618.1	201,335	341	325.7	88.5	10.1	0.7	1.0	2.1	5.2	11.6	11.4	11.9	11.0	12.2
39157	35420	4	Tuscarawas	567.4	92,500	652	163.0	94.9	1.6	0.6	0.7	3.6	6.2	12.7	11.7	11.8	11.9	11.8
39159	18140	1	Union	431.8	64,971	832	150.5	89.0	3.4	0.6	6.2	2.5	6.1	13.9	11.9	13.1	15.4	14.1
39161	46780	6	Van Wert	409.2	28,732	1,467	70.2	94.3	1.9	0.5	0.5	4.1	6.1	13.0	11.7	12.0	12.0	11.7
39163		8	Vinton	412.4	12,696	2,230	30.8	97.5	1.4	1.0	0.6	1.1	5.3	12.1	11.7	11.6	11.1	13.9
39165	17140	1	Warren	401.4	246,553	283	614.2	85.8	4.5	0.5	7.8	3.2	5.5	13.9	12.7	11.4	13.9	14.1
39167	31930	4	Washington	632.0	59,423	884	94.0	96.4	2.1	1.0	1.1	1.2	4.9	11.2	12.1	11.3	11.5	12.3
39169	49300	4	Wayne	554.8	116,710	537	210.4	95.0	2.4	0.6	1.4	2.2	6.3	13.6	13.7	11.8	11.3	11.3
39171		6	Williams	420.7	36,716	1,264	87.3	92.7	1.7	0.6	0.8	5.2	5.7	12.3	12.0	11.6	12.2	11.8
39173	45780	2	Wood	617.2	132,472	489	214.6	89.0	3.6	0.7	2.5	6.1	5.0	11.5	20.4	12.4	11.6	11.1
39175		7	Wyandot	406.9	21,708	1,728	53.3	95.4	0.9	0.6	0.8	3.3	5.2	12.8	11.5	11.0	12.2	12.4
40000		0	OKLAHOMA	68,595.9	3,986,639	X	58.1	69.3	9.1	12.8	3.4	11.7	6.2	13.8	13.8	13.5	13.0	11.4
40001		6	Adair	573.9	19,414	1,854	33.8	48.0	1.9	51.2	1.6	7.4	7.2	15.4	13.0	11.5	11.9	12.3
40003		9	Alfalfa	866.6	5,710	2,761	6.6	83.9	5.9	5.3	0.9	6.6	4.6	11.9	8.6	10.6	16.7	14.7
40005		9	Atoka	975.4	14,324	2,128	14.7	76.1	5.1	21.0	1.4	4.2	5.5	13.3	11.3	12.9	12.9	11.3
40007		9	Beaver	1,814.8	4,980	2,825	2.7	70.3	1.8	2.9	0.7	27.0	5.1	14.3	13.5	10.9	11.7	11.1
40009	21120	7	Beckham	901.7	22,046	1,711	24.4	76.0	5.1	4.4	1.3	15.7	6.5	14.6	12.4	14.5	14.0	11.3
40011		6	Blaine	928.5	8,562	2,531	9.2	74.6	5.6	10.9	1.2	13.3	6.6	14.8	12.1	10.4	11.0	11.2
40013	20460	6	Bryan	904.3	47,105	1,036	52.1	75.8	3.1	20.5	1.1	7.0	6.3	13.4	13.3	14.2	12.3	11.4
40015		6	Caddo	1,277.8	26,368	1,551	20.6	61.3	4.1	25.4	1.0	13.9	6.1	14.1	12.5	13.2	12.9	11.5
40017	36420	1	Canadian	896.6	161,737	415	180.4	78.3	4.8	7.1	4.1	10.3	6.3	14.9	12.1	14.6	15.3	12.0
40019	11620	5	Carter	822.2	48,291	1,016	58.7	74.0	8.5	14.2	1.8	8.3	6.7	14.3	12.6	12.9	12.4	11.5
40021	45140	6	Cherokee	749.1	47,627	1,029	63.6	55.0	2.3	43.2	1.4	7.6	5.6	12.4	18.3	12.1	11.8	10.4
40023		7	Choctaw	770.4	14,307	2,130	18.6	65.9	12.6	23.2	1.1	5.0	6.5	13.9	11.7	11.2	10.8	11.3
40025		9	Cimarron	1,834.8	2,248	3,023	1.2	74.1	2.2	2.2	0.9	23.7	5.3	16.3	11.2	8.2	10.6	9.8
40027	36420	1	Cleveland	538.9	297,597	237	552.2	75.6	6.9	8.0	5.9	9.5	4.9	12.1	18.3	14.1	13.6	11.2
40029		9	Coal	516.8	5,276	2,798	10.2	74.7	2.3	26.6	0.8	4.8	6.8	12.6	12.6	11.5	10.9	11.4
40031	30020	3	Comanche	1,069.3	122,063	521	114.2	60.8	19.2	8.1	5.1	13.8	6.7	13.5	15.8	16.3	13.2	10.1
40033	30020	3	Cotton	632.6	5,480	2,778	8.7	79.9	3.3	12.1	1.1	8.9	5.3	13.7	11.5	10.5	11.3	12.0
40035		6	Craig	761.3	14,115	2,143	18.5	70.3	4.6	28.9	1.5	4.0	5.5	12.9	11.9	12.5	11.8	12.4
40037	46140	2	Creek	949.9	72,029	764	75.8	81.6	3.5	16.2	1.2	4.8	5.8	13.4	12.1	12.2	12.3	12.2
40039	48220	7	Custer	988.8	28,163	1,490	28.5	70.5	3.7	8.9	1.8	18.7	6.6	14.2	20.8	12.0	12.2	9.3
40041		6	Delaware	737.8	41,000	1,163	55.6	70.8	0.9	30.6	1.5	4.0	5.0	11.4	10.8	10.4	10.3	11.7
40043		9	Dewey	999.6	4,417	2,863	4.4	84.0	2.0	8.6	1.6	7.9	6.7	15.5	11.4	11.4	11.9	10.7
40045	49260	9	Ellis	1,231.5	3,762	2,904	3.1	88.0	1.4	4.0	1.0	7.8	6.1	12.7	11.4	9.9	11.5	12.0
40047	21420	5	Garfield	1,058.5	61,926	861	58.5	75.7	4.4	4.4	6.0	13.6	6.7	14.8	13.1	13.2	13.1	10.3
40049		6	Garvin	802.1	25,804	1,569	32.2	78.6	3.3	12.8	0.9	10.1	6.2	14.6	12.1	11.7	12.9	11.8
40051	36420	1	Grady	1,100.5	55,508	929	50.4	85.3	3.0	9.3	1.0	6.2	5.3	13.7	12.6	11.5	13.5	12.4
40053		9	Grant	1,000.7	4,131	2,874	4.1	89.4	2.7	4.7	0.8	5.7	5.5	14.5	10.9	10.1	12.5	10.5
40055		7	Greer	639.3	5,487	2,777	8.6	75.8	9.4	4.9	0.6	12.4	4.7	11.3	11.7	15.5	14.4	12.7
40057		9	Harmon	537.3	2,418	3,006	4.5	57.8	9.3	3.9	1.9	30.8	6.1	14.4	11.2	10.7	11.1	11.9
40059		9	Harper	1,038.6	3,180	2,950	3.1	73.4	0.9	2.5	0.6	24.5	5.1	14.9	11.6	8.7	15.0	10.2
40061		6	Haskell	576.7	11,602	2,307	20.1	76.0	1.5	23.9	1.2	4.7	5.6	13.7	11.8	11.1	12.3	11.7
40063		7	Hughes	804.5	13,405	2,193	16.7	68.3	6.8	25.1	0.7	6.2	5.8	12.4	12.3	14.4	12.5	11.9
40065	11060	7	Jackson	802.7	24,777	1,621	30.9	64.2	8.0	3.5	2.4	25.5	7.1	14.4	13.7	14.8	12.6	10.4
40067		8	Jefferson	759.0	5,438	2,780	7.2	79.5	3.1	9.2	1.2	12.1	5.9	15.1	11.1	11.1	11.0	11.4
40069		9	Johnston	643.0	10,301	2,390	16.0	74.7	3.8	22.2	1.2	6.3	5.8	14.0	13.1	11.7	11.6	11.9
40071	38620	5	Kay	919.6	43,732	1,102	47.6	77.2	3.4	14.6	1.7	8.9	6.3	14.4	12.9	12.2	11.9	10.5
40073		6	Kingfisher	898.1	15,204	2,077	16.9	77.4	2.5	5.8	0.8	17.0	6.2	15.8	13.0	11.7	13.0	10.9

1. CBSA = Core Based Statistical Area. See Appendix A for explanation. See Appendix B for list of metropolitan areas with component counties. 2. County type code from the Economic Research Service of USDA Rural-Urban Continuum Codes. See Appendix A for definition. 3. Dry land or land partially or temporarily covered by water. 4. May be of any race.

STATE County	Population, 2021 (cont.)				Population change, 2000–2021							Households, 2016–2020				
	Age (percent) (cont.)				Total persons		Percent change		Components of change, 2020–2021					Percent		
	55 to 64 years	65 to 74 years	75 years and over	Percent female	2010	2020	2010–2020	2020–2021	Births	Deaths	Net Migration	Number	Persons per household	Family house-holds	Female family house-holder[1]	One person
	16	17	18	19	20	21	22	23	24	25	26	27	28	29	30	31
OHIO—Cont'd																
Ottawa	17.2	16.1	10.2	50.0	41,428	40,364	-2.6	-0.6	389	804	161	18,240	2.2	63.8	8.9	31.5
Paulding	14.2	11.9	7.3	50.0	19,614	18,806	-4.1	0.3	284	302	82	7,692	2.4	70.3	9.4	25.9
Perry	14.6	11.4	6.3	49.7	36,058	35,408	-1.8	0.1	516	564	96	13,216	2.7	73.3	13.5	20.6
Pickaway	13.1	9.8	6.3	47.1	55,698	58,539	5.1	1.4	767	894	925	19,808	2.7	71.3	12.2	24.1
Pike	14.3	11.0	7.4	50.2	28,709	27,088	-5.6	0.0	440	527	85	11,037	2.5	69.6	11.4	26.3
Portage	14.2	11.0	6.6	50.8	161,419	161,791	0.2	0.4	1,658	2,166	1,084	62,785	2.5	62.6	10.4	29.9
Preble	14.8	12.3	7.5	50.0	42,270	40,999	-3.0	-0.3	500	705	70	16,417	2.5	69.3	9.2	25.1
Putnam	14.4	11.2	7.2	49.6	34,499	34,451	-0.1	-0.4	494	486	-146	13,301	2.5	73.2	8.0	22.6
Richland	13.2	11.7	8.3	48.9	124,475	124,936	0.4	0.2	1,672	2,144	727	48,967	2.3	61.5	11.5	31.6
Ross	14.2	10.9	6.7	47.4	78,064	77,093	-1.2	-0.3	925	1,360	222	29,080	2.4	65.4	12.5	28.6
Sandusky	14.6	12.1	7.7	50.1	60,944	58,896	-3.4	-0.3	755	961	18	23,825	2.4	66.1	10.9	26.8
Scioto	13.5	11.2	7.6	50.4	79,499	74,008	-6.9	-0.9	927	1,517	-82	29,561	2.4	65.0	12.5	30.1
Seneca	13.9	11.6	7.3	49.7	56,745	55,069	-3.0	-0.3	713	880	-3	21,759	2.4	65.1	11.2	27.9
Shelby	14.3	10.6	6.7	49.5	49,423	48,230	-2.4	-0.5	746	769	-237	18,670	2.6	68.5	10.1	25.0
Stark	14.1	12.0	8.1	51.1	375,586	374,853	-0.2	-0.3	4,841	6,444	545	154,322	2.4	63.7	12.6	30.3
Summit	14.2	11.6	7.3	51.3	541,781	540,428	-0.2	-0.5	6,901	8,789	-990	226,721	2.3	60.8	12.6	32.2
Trumbull	14.6	13.2	8.9	50.9	210,312	201,977	-4.0	-0.3	2,472	3,863	752	85,917	2.3	61.3	13.5	33.2
Tuscarawas	14.0	11.9	8.1	50.2	92,582	93,263	0.7	-0.8	1,339	1,648	-459	36,906	2.5	66.2	8.7	28.2
Union	12.4	8.3	4.8	51.5	52,300	62,784	20.0	3.5	869	613	1,944	20,695	2.6	73.1	7.5	21.4
Van Wert	13.8	11.7	8.2	50.3	28,744	28,931	0.7	-0.7	400	479	-122	11,640	2.4	71.4	9.6	25.1
Vinton	15.6	12.0	6.7	49.7	13,435	12,800	-4.7	-0.8	146	232	-20	5,221	2.5	69.4	12.0	26.0
Warren	13.4	9.4	5.8	49.3	212,693	242,337	13.9	1.7	2,955	3,014	4,285	84,127	2.7	76.0	9.2	19.2
Washington	14.8	12.9	9.0	50.5	61,778	59,771	-3.2	-0.6	711	1,069	5	24,803	2.4	65.0	10.2	29.8
Wayne	13.3	11.2	7.5	49.9	114,520	116,894	2.1	-0.2	1,719	1,762	-158	44,238	2.5	69.0	8.9	26.7
Williams	14.4	11.6	8.4	49.9	37,642	37,102	-1.4	-1.0	485	557	-314	15,266	2.3	63.3	10.0	31.2
Wood	11.9	10.0	6.1	50.4	125,488	132,248	5.4	0.2	1,500	1,730	431	50,645	2.5	60.0	9.6	30.5
Wyandot	14.5	11.9	8.5	50.2	22,615	21,900	-3.2	-0.9	273	378	-88	9,100	2.4	66.8	8.7	28.1
OKLAHOMA	12.2	9.7	6.4	50.2	3,751,351	3,959,353	5.5	0.7	58,736	60,920	29,192	1,493,569	2.6	65.3	12.2	29.0
Adair	12.9	9.5	6.2	49.8	22,683	19,495	-14.1	-0.4	337	399	-24	7,632	2.9	70.3	15.8	25.2
Alfalfa	12.9	11.0	9.1	39.4	5,642	5,699	1.0	0.2	68	80	22	1,897	2.5	68.4	6.8	29.6
Atoka	12.9	11.5	8.5	47.5	14,182	14,143	-0.3	1.3	185	215	212	5,200	2.4	70.4	11.9	24.1
Beaver	13.7	11.5	8.2	48.6	5,636	5,049	-10.4	-1.4	60	90	-41	1,994	2.6	70.7	8.0	25.1
Beckham	11.5	9.3	5.9	46.4	22,119	22,410	1.3	-1.6	346	355	-354	7,724	2.5	63.2	10.9	32.1
Blaine	13.9	11.7	8.4	49.3	11,943	8,735	-26.9	-2.0	139	181	-130	3,940	2.1	60.8	11.3	34.5
Bryan	11.6	10.1	7.4	51.3	42,416	46,067	8.6	2.3	721	824	1,147	17,634	2.6	68.5	13.8	25.2
Caddo	12.7	9.9	7.1	47.1	29,600	26,945	-9.0	-2.1	397	571	-399	10,465	2.6	68.6	14.3	26.8
Canadian	11.2	8.5	5.0	50.5	115,541	154,405	33.6	4.7	2,120	1,738	7,023	45,724	3.1	73.6	9.9	22.7
Carter	12.6	10.1	7.0	51.3	47,557	48,003	0.9	0.6	766	886	405	18,474	2.6	62.7	12.6	32.0
Cherokee	12.1	10.5	6.7	51.3	46,987	47,078	0.2	1.2	678	759	629	17,364	2.7	64.3	11.7	30.6
Choctaw	13.8	12.3	8.6	51.9	15,205	14,204	-6.6	0.7	193	299	211	6,074	2.4	62.3	13.0	34.0
Cimarron	13.1	13.8	11.5	49.1	2,475	2,296	-7.2	-2.1	23	26	-44	952	2.3	66.6	8.3	30.7
Cleveland	11.2	8.9	5.6	50.2	255,755	295,528	15.6	0.7	3,414	3,338	1,930	108,070	2.5	64.5	10.5	26.4
Coal	13.1	12.3	8.7	50.6	5,925	5,266	-11.1	0.2	74	136	73	2,252	2.5	66.4	12.7	29.9
Comanche	11.2	8.0	5.1	48.2	124,098	121,125	-2.4	0.8	2,071	1,608	452	43,241	2.6	64.6	15.3	30.3
Cotton	15.5	12.1	8.2	50.9	6,193	5,527	-10.8	-0.9	65	107	-6	2,215	2.6	70.0	9.4	26.0
Craig	13.7	10.5	8.9	49.0	15,029	14,107	-6.1	0.1	177	333	164	5,428	2.4	64.6	10.2	29.6
Creek	13.7	10.8	7.5	50.6	69,967	71,754	2.6	0.4	1,018	1,386	640	26,393	2.7	69.9	12.1	26.7
Custer	10.6	8.1	6.2	50.1	27,469	28,513	3.8	-1.2	453	467	-340	10,697	2.6	62.2	11.3	30.1
Delaware	15.3	14.9	10.2	50.7	41,487	40,397	-2.6	1.5	517	899	1,001	16,988	2.5	67.1	12.0	28.2
Dewey	13.7	10.3	8.4	50.9	4,810	4,484	-6.8	-1.5	80	95	-51	1,715	2.8	68.0	10.4	30.6
Ellis	13.2	13.6	9.6	50.1	4,151	3,749	-9.7	0.3	65	62	11	1,581	2.5	60.2	5.9	36.0
Garfield	12.3	9.6	7.0	49.7	60,580	62,846	3.7	-1.5	976	1,015	-882	23,709	2.5	63.9	10.5	30.5
Garvin	12.7	10.5	7.4	50.5	27,576	25,656	-7.0	0.6	418	513	245	10,375	2.7	66.0	12.9	30.0
Grady	13.9	10.5	6.6	50.1	52,431	54,795	4.5	1.3	653	876	946	20,107	2.7	73.7	9.6	22.0
Grant	14.2	12.6	9.3	50.3	4,527	4,169	-7.9	-0.9	42	96	16	1,761	2.4	62.7	8.0	34.9
Greer	12.2	9.3	8.1	42.7	6,239	5,491	-12.0	-0.1	60	93	29	2,109	2.3	58.9	8.2	37.7
Harmon	13.5	12.8	8.2	51.2	2,922	2,488	-14.9	-2.8	39	47	-61	1,091	2.4	65.4	7.3	23.3
Harper	14.9	11.6	8.1	49.2	3,685	3,272	-11.2	-2.8	41	70	-62	1,236	3.0	65.5	5.4	33.2
Haskell	13.2	11.9	8.6	50.6	12,769	11,561	-9.5	0.4	175	241	107	4,935	2.6	69.5	9.8	25.5
Hughes	12.3	10.6	7.9	45.2	14,003	13,367	-4.5	0.3	191	258	105	4,106	2.9	66.1	14.5	30.9
Jackson	11.7	8.9	6.4	49.9	26,446	24,785	-6.3	0.0	427	338	-104	9,681	2.5	65.7	11.2	29.7
Jefferson	13.7	11.6	9.3	49.7	6,472	5,337	-17.5	1.9	80	104	127	2,382	2.5	61.7	11.4	34.5
Johnston	12.6	11.2	8.2	50.2	10,957	10,272	-6.3	0.3	160	231	101	4,313	2.5	67.2	12.3	29.9
Kay	12.5	11.2	8.2	50.0	46,562	43,700	-6.1	0.1	641	838	228	17,392	2.5	63.0	12.8	30.9
Kingfisher	13.0	9.6	6.8	49.7	15,034	15,184	1.0	0.1	214	214	18	5,769	2.7	70.7	10.7	25.7

1. No spouse present.

STATE County	Persons in group quarters, 2021	Daytime Population, 2016–2020		Births, 2021		Deaths, 2021		Persons under 65 with no health insurance, 2019		Medicare, 2021			COVID-19 Deaths, 2020	
		Number	Employment/ residence ratio	Total	Rate[1]	Number	Rate[1]	Number	Percent	Total beneficiaries	Enrolled in Original Medicare	Enrolled in Medicare Advantage	Number	Rate[1]
	32	33	34	35	36	37	38	39	40	41	42	43	44	45
OHIO—Cont'd														
Ottawa	421	36,532	0.8	300	7.5	628	15.6	2,098	7.1	11,858	7,254	4,605	59	1.5
Paulding	69	15,597	0.6	225	11.9	248	13.2	1,189	7.9	4,272	2,703	1,569	31	1.6
Perry	236	28,734	0.5	405	11.4	465	13.1	2,319	7.8	7,705	4,596	3,110	40	1.1
Pickaway	4,369	51,129	0.7	595	10.1	693	11.7	3,204	7.2	11,119	5,336	5,783	98	1.7
Pike	396	28,848	1.1	355	13.1	414	15.3	1,924	8.6	6,135	3,935	2,200	15	0.6
Portage	6,959	145,782	0.8	1,328	8.2	1,727	10.7	9,786	7.6	32,668	15,193	17,476	133	0.8
Preble	326	34,661	0.7	396	9.7	557	13.6	2,556	7.9	9,611	5,505	4,106	81	2.0
Putnam	271	29,676	0.8	399	11.6	392	11.4	1,938	7.0	6,963	5,068	1,895	89	2.6
Richland	6,996	123,892	1.1	1,358	10.9	1,720	13.8	7,840	8.7	28,900	18,266	10,634	159	1.3
Ross	5,269	76,382	1.0	738	9.6	1,059	13.8	4,392	7.5	16,231	9,688	6,542	116	1.5
Sandusky	824	58,430	1.0	596	10.1	777	13.2	3,395	7.3	13,578	9,153	4,425	93	1.6
Scioto	2,987	73,629	0.9	775	10.5	1,151	15.7	4,836	8.3	16,897	11,668	5,229	79	1.1
Seneca	2,366	50,127	0.8	570	10.4	683	12.4	3,089	7.2	12,375	8,994	3,381	83	1.5
Shelby	493	53,170	1.2	567	11.8	585	12.2	2,677	6.7	9,611	6,730	2,881	64	1.3
Stark	8,585	362,768	1.0	3,801	10.2	5,088	13.6	22,294	7.7	86,515	35,067	51,449	690	1.8
Summit	9,191	557,757	1.1	5,555	10.3	6,996	13.0	34,546	8.0	115,086	50,610	64,475	703	1.3
Trumbull	3,708	186,441	0.9	2,020	10.0	3,040	15.1	13,491	8.9	51,901	24,257	27,643	376	1.9
Tuscarawas	1,170	88,589	0.9	1,079	11.6	1,266	13.6	7,482	10.3	20,924	10,393	10,531	190	2.0
Union	2,482	64,426	1.2	683	10.7	483	7.5	2,867	5.8	9,093	5,128	3,964	34	0.5
Van Wert	364	26,571	0.9	326	11.3	378	13.1	1,612	7.2	6,499	4,128	2,371	61	2.1
Vinton	37	10,719	0.6	116	9.1	185	14.5	1,079	10.2	2,899	1,899	1,000	10	0.8
Warren	5,210	223,263	0.9	2,359	9.6	2,394	9.8	10,432	5.3	40,350	21,999	18,351	225	0.9
Washington	1,503	60,183	1.0	571	9.6	844	14.2	3,523	7.7	15,328	10,767	4,560	83	1.4
Wayne	3,288	116,157	1.0	1,356	11.6	1,386	11.9	11,007	12.0	23,811	12,674	11,137	175	1.5
Williams	934	37,636	1.1	395	10.7	448	12.2	2,252	7.8	8,637	5,831	2,806	54	1.5
Wood	6,392	136,444	1.1	1,201	9.1	1,388	10.5	6,482	6.2	24,433	13,918	10,515	161	1.2
Wyandot	208	20,379	0.9	226	10.4	299	13.7	1,191	6.9	5,017	3,672	1,346	38	1.7
OKLAHOMA	101,889	3,941,690	1.0	47,125	11.9	48,995	12.3	540,944	16.8	753,182	562,963	190,219	5,523	1.4
Adair	30	20,158	0.7	288	14.8	332	17.1	4,083	22.4	4,058	3,362	696	30	1.5
Alfalfa	1,029	5,585	0.9	53	9.3	65	11.4	613	17.2	1,096	1,013	83	10	1.8
Atoka	731	12,692	0.8	147	10.3	168	11.8	2,114	20.8	3,170	2,853	316	21	1.5
Beaver	24	4,835	0.8	48	9.6	66	13.2	943	22.4	971	932	40	10	2.0
Beckham	1,931	22,998	1.1	290	13.1	289	13.0	2,872	17.1	3,865	3,576	290	51	2.3
Blaine	64	9,639	1.0	109	12.6	138	16.0	1,353	18.1	2,066	1,878	189	20	2.3
Bryan	877	48,224	1.1	585	12.5	699	15.0	7,762	20.3	9,521	8,133	1,388	73	1.6
Caddo	1,626	26,486	0.8	310	11.6	461	17.3	4,348	19.9	5,957	5,226	731	90	3.4
Canadian	2,399	117,802	0.6	1,699	10.7	1,421	9.0	15,671	12.3	23,428	16,139	7,289	175	1.1
Carter	779	51,520	1.2	607	12.6	719	14.9	7,543	19.3	10,758	9,209	1,549	59	1.2
Cherokee	1,703	45,440	0.8	541	11.4	598	12.6	9,319	24.2	9,755	7,998	1,758	60	1.3
Choctaw	102	14,329	0.9	153	10.7	241	16.9	2,175	19.3	3,775	3,433	342	23	1.6
Cimarron	6	2,151	1.0	20	8.8	21	9.3	348	22.2	576	556	20	D	D
Cleveland	10,715	240,319	0.7	2,739	9.2	2,661	9.0	28,188	11.9	46,832	34,642	12,190	285	1.0
Coal	25	5,153	0.8	59	11.2	114	21.6	898	21.0	1,120	1,015	105	11	2.1
Comanche	10,020	123,138	1.0	1,630	13.4	1,316	10.8	14,125	14.9	19,551	16,854	2,697	107	0.9
Cotton	26	5,438	0.9	46	8.3	86	15.6	756	16.9	1,263	1,134	130	16	2.9
Craig	970	14,439	1.0	129	9.1	281	19.9	1,994	18.9	3,562	2,882	680	22	1.6
Creek	953	61,518	0.7	818	11.4	1,133	15.8	9,140	15.8	16,083	9,791	6,292	114	1.6
Custer	1,408	29,938	1.1	347	12.3	365	12.9	4,812	20.5	4,712	4,159	553	84	3.0
Delaware	204	39,431	0.8	410	10.1	719	17.7	7,090	22.4	11,652	8,829	2,823	102	2.5
Dewey	54	5,083	1.1	63	14.2	75	16.9	686	17.3	1,135	1,030	105	15	3.4
Ellis	32	3,705	0.9	53	14.1	55	14.7	537	18.2	946	899	48	D	D
Garfield	1,767	61,630	1.0	798	12.8	811	13.0	8,357	16.8	11,991	10,583	1,408	134	2.1
Garvin	189	27,578	1.0	347	13.5	410	15.9	4,250	19.1	6,121	4,944	1,177	53	2.1
Grady	934	47,494	0.7	518	9.4	713	12.9	6,388	14.0	10,876	8,276	2,600	101	1.8
Grant	36	4,260	1.0	33	8.0	76	18.3	542	16.2	1,067	978	88	D	D
Greer	1,046	5,310	0.8	50	9.1	77	14.0	506	14.1	1,247	1,180	67	20	3.6
Harmon	74	2,396	0.8	33	13.5	38	15.6	487	24.1	635	593	41	D	D
Harper	21	3,439	0.8	33	10.3	60	18.6	668	22.9	831	791	40	D	D
Haskell	35	11,845	0.8	138	11.9	192	16.6	2,030	20.5	2,907	2,428	479	15	1.3
Hughes	1,528	12,777	0.9	153	11.4	210	15.7	1,824	19.7	2,963	2,406	557	27	2.0
Jackson	651	25,321	1.0	337	13.6	267	10.8	3,478	17.3	4,381	4,108	273	62	2.5
Jefferson	77	5,247	0.6	67	12.4	83	15.4	896	19.7	1,512	1,343	169	10	1.9
Johnston	194	10,157	0.8	127	12.4	189	18.4	1,530	17.9	2,506	2,140	366	19	1.9
Kay	1,200	44,662	1.0	522	12.0	648	14.8	5,927	17.4	10,134	8,508	1,626	109	2.5
Kingfisher	87	16,477	1.1	165	10.9	171	11.3	2,392	18.2	2,814	2,348	466	37	2.4

1. Per 1,000 estimated resident population.

STATE County	COVID-19 Vaccinations, 2021–2022		Education						Money income, 2016–2020				Income and poverty, 2020			
			School enrollment and attainment, 2016–2020				Local government expenditures,[3] 2018–2019			Households				Percent below poverty level		
			Enrollment[1]		Attainment[2] (percent)						Percent					
	Number	Percent[5]	Total	Percent private	High school graduate or less	Bachelor's degree or more	Total current spending (mil dol)	Current spending per student (dollars)	Per capita income[4]	Median income (dollars)	with income of less than $50,000	with income of $200,000 or more	Median household income (dollars)	All persons	Children under 18 years	Children 5 to 17 years in families
	46	47	48	49	50	51	52	53	54	55	56	57	58	59	60	61
OHIO—Cont'd																
Ottawa	24,963	61.6	7,564	12.2	44.2	23.9	77.6	12,636	38,553	59,306	41.5	5.0	65,582	7.7	10.4	9.6
Paulding	7,895	42.3	4,049	11.2	55.2	15.9	43.6	14,335	28,867	56,531	44.9	1.8	62,062	9.3	13.9	12.8
Perry	14,789	40.9	7,780	11.2	59.9	13.0	73.9	12,948	24,668	52,978	47.2	2.4	56,048	13.1	17.2	15.9
Pickaway	29,613	50.7	12,760	12.5	54.9	18.6	112.4	11,877	28,017	61,629	39.2	3.2	64,412	12.5	18.3	17.0
Pike	12,286	44.2	6,235	5.7	60.1	14.2	66.9	14,513	26,006	44,115	53.5	2.0	46,413	17.4	24.5	22.5
Portage	93,213	57.4	44,020	10.5	44.5	29.9	274.9	12,814	31,658	59,485	42.1	4.4	64,250	9.9	12.3	10.4
Preble	17,648	43.2	8,325	12.6	52.6	18.2	77.0	12,724	29,769	61,339	39.8	2.6	60,856	8.8	13.0	11.9
Putnam	16,497	48.7	8,384	11.4	46.7	23.2	75.5	12,713	32,507	67,790	35.6	4.2	72,299	6.5	6.3	6.3
Richland	53,491	44.2	25,538	18.1	52.6	17.8	228.9	13,257	25,570	49,186	50.7	2.0	52,295	12.7	18.0	15.6
Ross	38,765	50.6	15,806	12.1	55.6	16.2	149.5	14,337	25,576	51,508	48.8	2.3	49,543	15.0	19.3	18.5
Sandusky	30,862	52.7	13,060	15.2	51.1	16.5	104.1	13,211	28,624	55,245	45.0	2.9	60,455	10.4	13.8	12.8
Scioto	37,356	49.6	16,475	8.6	56.8	15.6	153.3	13,312	23,512	41,866	56.8	2.3	44,297	22.8	26.6	24.1
Seneca	27,014	49.0	14,051	27.1	52.8	17.3	80.8	14,131	26,810	52,897	47.2	1.7	58,129	10.4	13.3	11.9
Shelby	17,522	36.1	11,660	10.0	51.6	19.3	91.0	11,095	30,211	64,522	38.0	3.3	67,582	9.3	12.0	11.0
Stark	202,919	54.8	83,976	16.9	46.0	23.5	677.6	12,225	30,168	55,045	45.6	3.4	57,364	13.2	18.2	17.0
Summit	342,874	63.4	122,382	17.9	37.8	32.8	981.3	13,570	34,684	59,253	42.8	5.7	60,715	12.1	15.6	14.2
Trumbull	108,652	54.9	39,382	11.1	54.6	19.2	371.5	13,925	27,255	47,799	52.3	2.4	48,929	15.8	29.4	27.1
Tuscarawas	40,868	44.4	18,742	13.3	58.1	17.9	201.0	13,042	27,208	54,451	46.0	2.2	58,256	11.6	13.6	12.0
Union	36,818	62.4	14,873	17.4	37.9	35.5	87.4	11,173	40,278	88,565	23.9	11.2	92,198	5.0	4.7	4.3
Van Wert	12,283	43.4	6,075	12.4	51.6	17.2	62.9	13,397	28,092	55,991	43.1	1.9	57,863	7.4	9.9	10.0
Vinton	5,211	39.8	2,656	5.8	62.9	12.8	26.7	13,431	22,984	45,034	54.3	0.7	49,778	16.1	24.6	23.4
Warren	150,264	64.1	58,084	19.4	31.7	43.7	448.5	11,673	43,005	89,410	24.5	13.6	90,600	5.2	5.6	5.5
Washington	33,224	55.5	12,670	17.0	49.3	18.7	94.6	12,359	30,184	51,808	48.0	2.9	53,450	13.4	19.8	17.9
Wayne	52,846	45.7	27,023	24.7	52.3	22.5	193.3	12,642	28,907	61,424	39.8	4.1	67,708	9.0	11.6	10.5
Williams	16,469	44.9	7,911	13.1	50.9	15.1	69.4	12,880	27,395	52,855	46.3	1.9	52,458	10.3	15.2	14.0
Wood	80,968	61.9	40,624	11.7	35.5	34.3	269.4	13,956	33,461	63,189	39.3	6.0	67,865	9.9	8.9	8.2
Wyandot	10,380	47.7	4,835	14.9	52.4	19.3	39.9	11,746	29,297	57,925	42.9	2.6	63,516	7.0	9.2	8.6
OKLAHOMA	2,262,941	57.2	992,436	12.2	42.6	26.1	6,402.0	9,160	29,873	53,840	46.5	4.5	54,512	14.3	18.6	17.3
Adair	8,138	36.7	5,183	7.7	64.6	10.8	49.3	11,153	17,729	34,375	63.9	1.0	36,749	22.3	31.3	29.5
Alfalfa	2,581	45.3	1,061	2.9	48.2	22.5	15.6	16,440	24,829	64,122	39.5	1.6	51,157	15.7	17.9	16.6
Atoka	4,985	36.2	2,886	5.6	56.1	16.4	26.1	11,391	22,575	42,392	56.7	2.4	42,618	18.6	22.9	21.0
Beaver	1,659	31.2	1,278	4.1	46.3	23.3	17.1	16,383	25,313	55,083	45.4	1.1	61,477	11.0	15.2	13.3
Beckham	9,051	41.4	5,378	6.0	50.2	16.7	37.7	9,195	23,299	47,095	51.7	2.3	47,625	18.8	22.1	21.3
Blaine	4,398	46.6	1,789	8.7	51.3	19.4	25.6	11,525	30,700	49,638	50.3	3.7	55,643	14.5	19.5	18.8
Bryan	20,654	43.0	11,632	8.3	46.8	22.6	77.8	9,836	25,089	47,175	52.0	2.8	45,213	15.9	19.1	17.5
Caddo	18,925	65.8	6,495	4.0	56.7	15.2	51.6	10,076	22,868	46,499	53.3	1.8	48,380	18.3	22.5	22.3
Canadian	86,464	58.3	37,685	13.3	38.4	28.4	241.2	8,221	30,970	73,591	31.3	4.9	75,452	7.6	9.1	8.4
Carter	21,269	44.2	11,560	9.3	49.0	20.2	83.6	9,477	27,211	51,148	48.9	2.7	46,781	19.0	22.6	18.9
Cherokee	23,539	48.4	13,579	8.9	43.8	27.5	76.6	10,260	22,617	43,378	55.4	2.0	49,553	19.6	25.6	24.9
Choctaw	5,214	35.5	3,323	6.4	56.7	13.5	24.4	10,148	23,194	37,121	60.6	2.1	41,622	19.5	27.5	25.9
Cimarron	704	32.9	485	9.5	48.8	26.6	5.8	14,159	30,283	47,095	54.2	1.6	50,804	15.1	24.4	21.9
Cleveland	159,633	56.2	82,434	9.9	32.2	34.3	385.1	8,320	32,489	65,412	37.9	4.9	64,011	10.8	12.0	10.6
Coal	2,242	40.8	1,194	4.2	58.7	17.3	14.4	13,571	22,611	42,277	57.9	2.2	41,162	19.3	25.5	25.2
Comanche	73,501	60.9	30,291	10.5	42.2	23.2	204.0	9,870	27,800	52,377	47.3	2.8	54,007	15.8	20.1	19.9
Cotton	2,845	50.2	1,338	6.1	58.9	15.1	9.9	9,695	25,784	49,583	50.8	2.5	46,266	17.4	24.8	22.7
Craig	7,579	53.6	2,903	8.6	52.2	14.4	27.6	10,743	22,239	43,003	58.8	1.1	43,804	17.5	22.7	20.4
Creek	31,290	43.7	15,479	10.6	51.5	16.0	110.6	8,929	26,876	52,315	48.4	3.4	49,954	12.9	17.0	16.0
Custer	14,117	48.7	9,098	4.3	42.0	26.4	51.0	9,212	28,102	51,351	48.4	3.8	55,826	12.8	16.1	15.1
Delaware	18,219	42.4	8,277	12.6	52.1	18.2	64.1	10,183	34,798	44,268	56.7	2.4	43,147	18.1	26.9	25.4
Dewey	1,240	25.4	1,214	10.8	47.8	20.9	15.3	13,747	28,634	51,169	49.2	5.1	56,711	10.6	12.3	10.8
Ellis	1,355	35.1	789	2.4	46.1	20.3	11.8	15,419	28,277	48,264	50.8	4.3	56,763	11.2	15.7	14.2
Garfield	30,781	50.4	14,278	10.3	48.6	23.3	107.7	9,417	28,755	55,435	44.2	2.8	61,501	11.8	17.3	16.1
Garvin	12,886	46.5	6,167	4.9	57.3	15.8	49.9	9,353	24,886	47,321	53.8	2.6	47,391	16.7	21.7	21.0
Grady	21,271	38.1	13,072	7.2	50.6	21.4	86.1	9,120	31,075	64,507	39.2	5.3	58,621	12.0	15.5	14.0
Grant	1,847	42.6	987	1.7	45.2	22.2	14.0	18,798	29,485	53,147	46.4	1.6	51,399	11.7	15.1	13.5
Greer	2,110	36.9	1,202	1.7	50.2	12.3	10.3	9,452	20,956	46,794	53.2	1.0	42,010	22.9	27.1	25.1
Harmon	1,312	49.5	602	4.5	48.7	18.0	5.6	10,161	28,137	53,087	45.8	5.0	40,246	23.3	34.7	31.9
Harper	1,665	45.1	821	1.9	45.0	19.5	8.0	10,277	22,148	44,318	54.5	0.6	57,833	10.5	15.4	14.2
Haskell	5,222	41.4	2,928	5.7	54.5	15.5	22.8	9,839	23,316	43,950	55.4	2.7	41,253	19.4	25.8	24.3
Hughes	6,106	46.0	2,932	3.2	57.1	14.8	24.3	11,125	20,839	38,020	59.9	1.1	39,333	21.4	26.6	25.1
Jackson	13,240	54.0	6,347	9.6	43.3	22.2	40.1	8,938	26,511	52,535	47.9	2.9	56,779	15.0	20.5	20.5
Jefferson	2,525	42.1	1,441	3.3	57.3	15.5	12.6	11,276	25,202	43,871	62.3	3.1	43,014	17.8	25.2	23.4
Johnston	4,718	42.6	2,776	1.9	48.6	22.7	18.6	9,782	21,918	44,238	58.3	1.3	45,361	18.3	23.4	21.5
Kay	18,717	43.0	10,149	12.3	43.8	19.3	73.2	9,349	26,705	47,456	51.8	2.9	50,256	15.3	22.1	20.2
Kingfisher	7,530	47.8	3,791	6.9	51.3	23.2	43.9	11,624	33,651	61,738	40.9	6.0	71,450	9.0	11.9	10.6

1. All persons 3 years old and over enrolled in nursery school through college. 2. Persons 25 years old and over. 3. Elementary and secondary education expenditures. 4. Based on population estimated by the American Community Survey, 2016–2020. 5. CDC percent based on 2019 population estimate.

STATE County	Personal income, 2020										Earnings, 2020		
			Per capita[1]			Supplements to wages and salaries, employer contributions (mil dol)						Contributions for government social insurance (mil dol)	
	Total (mil dol)	Percent change 2019–2020	Dollars	Rank	Wages and salaries (mil dol)	Pension and insurance	Government social insurance	Proprietors' income (mil dol)	Dividends, interest, and rent (mil dol)	Personal transfer reecipts (mil dol)	Total (mil dol)	From employee and self-employed	From employer
	62	63	64	65	66	67	68	69	70	71	72	73	74
OHIO—Cont'd													
Ottawa	2,312	5.6	57,446	541	662	139	50	131	432	655	981	68	50
Paulding	860	10.1	46,097	1,635	201	44	16	81	120	249	343	21	16
Perry	1,518	9.0	41,913	2,215	284	59	20	106	143	495	469	37	20
Pickaway	2,700	9.4	46,033	1,648	733	155	49	208	354	681	1,145	67	49
Pike	1,185	9.9	42,774	2,096	536	81	40	141	125	457	797	50	40
Portage	7,850	6.2	48,285	1,351	2,798	555	189	367	1,223	1,936	3,909	239	189
Preble	1,838	9.0	45,016	1,789	507	96	38	145	224	533	786	54	38
Putnam	1,839	7.2	54,646	724	529	99	41	170	296	385	838	52	41
Richland	5,311	8.5	43,928	1,958	2,216	420	164	307	773	1,696	3,106	203	164
Ross	3,236	8.3	42,348	2,147	1,453	299	108	157	392	1,086	2,017	123	108
Sandusky	2,691	8.6	46,113	1,632	1,161	230	92	141	360	806	1,624	106	92
Scioto	3,258	6.4	43,820	1,969	1,072	235	77	284	396	1,277	1,668	107	77
Seneca	2,472	10.6	44,993	1,793	849	169	64	181	323	788	1,263	86	64
Shelby	2,415	7.9	49,956	1,148	1,476	247	115	207	323	562	2,044	120	115
Stark	18,338	6.6	49,592	1,185	7,580	1,290	562	1,053	2,842	5,115	10,485	698	562
Summit	30,619	5.7	56,821	583	14,960	2,329	1,062	2,400	5,161	7,078	20,750	1,268	1,062
Trumbull	8,884	7.9	45,142	1,776	2,748	503	207	693	1,349	3,066	4,151	295	207
Tuscarawas	4,399	6.2	47,937	1,400	1,617	311	120	464	623	1,202	2,511	159	120
Union	3,850	9.0	64,147	287	2,211	341	162	257	503	527	2,971	164	162
Van Wert	1,333	9.5	47,339	1,471	525	100	38	132	162	370	794	47	38
Vinton	504	10.5	38,881	2,583	96	25	7	26	66	199	153	11	7
Warren	15,701	6.0	65,855	243	6,075	814	411	833	2,419	2,344	8,134	495	411
Washington	2,825	6.2	47,365	1,468	1,304	235	97	180	432	894	1,815	119	97
Wayne	5,773	6.2	49,901	1,151	2,486	431	181	634	997	1,316	3,732	227	181
Williams	1,683	6.6	46,040	1,645	783	148	60	134	234	491	1,126	71	60
Wood	6,706	5.3	51,147	1,010	3,514	618	264	307	1,061	1,421	4,703	274	264
Wyandot	1,098	9.4	50,573	1,081	470	86	35	96	129	280	687	41	35
OKLAHOMA	198,552	3.8	50,114	X	84,265	14,351	6,295	24,442	36,589	46,241	129,352	7,776	6,295
Adair	718	8.0	32,724	3,040	176	38	14	55	101	281	283	21	14
Alfalfa	246	6.1	43,043	2,054	70	16	5	34	71	55	125	7	5
Atoka	484	7.1	34,758	2,948	123	26	9	40	70	182	199	15	9
Beaver	298	3.1	57,190	561	62	13	5	101	44	52	181	6	5
Beckham	881	2.5	41,041	2,332	429	66	31	89	160	244	616	39	31
Blaine	420	1.2	44,435	1,886	138	26	11	44	128	115	219	14	11
Bryan	1,840	7.7	37,561	2,733	912	160	67	98	297	573	1,237	81	67
Caddo	1,138	4.8	39,673	2,487	345	78	26	84	171	371	533	37	26
Canadian	7,394	6.8	48,267	1,352	1,593	266	120	368	1,032	1,415	2,346	158	120
Carter	2,218	3.9	45,874	1,669	1,082	190	81	128	438	633	1,482	99	81
Cherokee	1,753	5.8	35,764	2,888	681	123	51	81	308	598	935	61	51
Choctaw	522	10.2	35,627	2,898	162	36	13	26	63	231	236	19	13
Cimarron	147	2.3	68,446	188	31	6	3	56	19	27	96	3	3
Cleveland	13,791	4.3	48,042	1,384	4,030	720	296	778	2,628	2,900	5,825	374	296
Coal	218	1.9	38,938	2,573	48	10	4	27	43	71	88	6	4
Comanche	5,502	6.4	45,432	1,729	2,636	649	222	200	884	1,498	3,707	203	222
Cotton	271	9.1	47,794	1,415	59	14	4	24	35	78	101	6	4
Craig	589	6.2	41,477	2,272	214	45	16	57	89	217	332	22	16
Creek	3,196	5.1	44,706	1,847	928	160	71	191	532	922	1,350	97	71
Custer	1,243	3.0	43,373	2,023	607	107	45	101	254	294	860	53	45
Delaware	1,529	5.1	35,435	2,912	357	66	27	99	298	570	550	48	27
Dewey	249	0.3	51,656	966	88	17	6	54	51	52	165	9	6
Ellis	213	2.1	55,592	668	51	11	4	48	49	46	115	6	4
Garfield	2,843	2.9	46,702	1,548	1,238	228	98	199	613	713	1,762	111	98
Garvin	1,168	5.1	42,189	2,169	505	94	38	112	202	361	749	50	38
Grady	2,432	4.2	43,506	2,011	552	99	42	155	394	613	849	59	42
Grant	232	13.8	53,075	853	78	14	6	44	50	52	142	8	6
Greer	186	9.1	32,547	3,046	37	9	3	18	32	72	66	5	3
Harmon	117	6.2	45,688	1,701	27	6	2	19	18	35	54	3	2
Harper	181	-2.5	50,223	1,118	38	9	3	49	30	39	99	4	3
Haskell	425	1.2	33,617	2,998	122	24	10	35	57	176	192	15	10
Hughes	574	3.6	43,758	1,979	110	23	9	151	81	181	293	13	9
Jackson	1,128	6.7	46,426	1,589	546	134	46	74	200	280	800	45	46
Jefferson	223	9.0	37,467	2,742	46	10	3	21	34	85	80	6	3
Johnston	422	7.3	38,971	2,565	117	24	9	32	56	153	181	14	9
Kay	1,935	6.0	44,718	1,845	845	139	62	146	317	592	1,192	82	62
Kingfisher	926	3.3	58,591	492	343	57	25	110	258	168	535	31	25

1. Based on the resident population estimated as of July 1 of the year shown.

STATE County	Earnings, 2020 (cont.) — Percent by selected industries									Social Security beneficiaries, December 2020		Supple-mental Security Income recipients, 2020	Housing units, 2021	
	Farm	Mining, quarrying, and extractions	Construction	Manu-facturing	Information; professional, scientific, technical services	Retail trade	Finance, insurance, real estate, and leasing	Health care and social assistance	Govern-ment	Number	Rate[1]		Total	Percent change, 2010–2021
	75	76	77	78	79	80	81	82	83	84	85	86	87	88
OHIO—Cont'd														
Ottawa	1.3	0.9	8.2	15.6	D	6.1	4.3	9.5	17.6	11,970	298	589	28,744	0.4
Paulding	16.0	D	6.7	20.7	D	4.4	3.0	D	19.3	4,545	241	296	8,521	0.3
Perry	1.9	2.5	21.8	11.3	2.5	5.8	3.2	9.3	20.8	8,260	233	1,248	15,006	0.3
Pickaway	5.1	0.2	11.3	17.4	2.5	5.5	2.9	D	25.6	11,570	195	1,159	22,540	0.6
Pike	1.4	D	5.5	5.0	D	4.6	2.3	D	12.0	6,670	246	1,390	12,076	0.6
Portage	0.0	0.5	7.1	20.2	6.1	7.3	2.5	7.3	24.3	32,665	201	2,512	71,037	0.4
Preble	5.9	D	7.9	34.3	D	5.8	2.8	6.5	14.1	9,605	235	700	18,120	0.1
Putnam	6.8	D	11.6	30.5	2.9	6.3	4.2	7.4	12.3	7,160	209	345	13,869	0.3
Richland	0.9	D	7.8	21.0	3.4	8.1	3.6	15.3	17.8	30,050	240	3,604	54,634	0.2
Ross	1.2	0.1	4.0	15.6	2.2	7.6	2.6	D	26.6	17,010	221	2,931	32,065	0.0
Sandusky	1.6	D	5.8	39.7	2.3	6.6	3.9	D	11.9	14,325	244	969	26,496	0.1
Scioto	0.0	D	5.4	14.5	3.2	7.0	2.6	28.3	22.0	16,580	226	5,117	33,087	0.0
Seneca	2.9	0.9	8.3	25.9	3.2	6.8	3.8	10.1	13.8	12,930	235	1,217	23,973	0.1
Shelby	2.7	0.0	8.7	49.0	2.4	3.7	3.0	5.5	8.1	10,090	210	718	20,116	0.3
Stark	0.2	D	7.1	18.0	6.7	7.2	6.5	16.3	12.7	89,105	238	10,040	167,323	0.3
Summit	0.0	0.0	7.4	10.5	9.9	7.9	7.0	15.1	11.0	114,565	213	15,384	246,735	0.1
Trumbull	0.2	0.1	9.5	14.7	2.7	9.1	6.9	14.2	15.9	54,105	269	6,299	94,373	0.0
Tuscarawas	1.1	4.9	8.6	22.2	4.2	7.9	4.7	10.4	13.8	21,400	231	1,951	40,845	0.1
Union	1.7	D	5.1	34.6	D	4.4	2.3	3.3	10.5	9,095	140	432	24,130	3.6
Van Wert	7.4	D	5.0	21.4	D	5.5	10.8	12.3	12.1	6,770	236	436	12,559	0.2
Vinton	0.6	D	5.8	19.7	D	4.0	4.7	12.7	26.9	2,845	224	587	5,933	0.2
Warren	0.2	0.0	6.7	12.9	8.1	6.8	7.0	8.6	9.7	39,975	162	1,848	95,160	1.7
Washington	0.5	1.8	8.2	18.9	3.8	6.4	5.5	21.9	11.0	15,685	264	1,858	27,969	-0.1
Wayne	2.4	0.6	8.4	33.3	2.9	6.7	4.2	7.8	12.1	23,775	204	1,860	46,830	0.5
Williams	2.8	D	4.8	36.9	D	9.7	3.3	10.1	12.0	8,860	241	552	16,571	0.1
Wood	1.0	-0.3	8.3	22.7	5.8	4.9	4.7	7.7	16.2	23,930	181	1,451	57,308	0.7
Wyandot	6.4	1.8	13.1	37.9	D	4.7	3.3	D	14.1	5,140	237	321	9,847	0.1
OKLAHOMA	1.1	7.9	6.0	8.7	7.6	6.1	5.6	10.6	19.8	811,064	203	96,502	1,762,129	0.7
Adair	6.4	D	7.3	21.0	D	9.1	3.0	D	21.1	4,955	255	901	8,096	0.4
Alfalfa	24.7	1.9	4.1	1.4	D	3.5	D	3.5	28.0	1,185	208	68	2,474	-0.1
Atoka	-0.3	3.8	5.8	3.1	D	10.3	6.0	D	33.0	3,465	242	504	5,997	0.2
Beaver	48.5	6.9	8.0	1.1	D	2.0	D	D	13.8	1,080	217	39	2,464	0.1
Beckham	1.6	24.1	11.2	1.9	3.5	9.7	5.0	D	12.1	4,380	199	533	10,129	0.0
Blaine	4.8	11.3	6.1	16.9	D	4.7	D	5.6	18.3	2,220	259	222	4,592	0.1
Bryan	0.9	0.2	4.5	8.7	3.8	6.4	3.5	9.5	42.3	10,340	220	1,547	20,522	0.6
Caddo	5.2	3.5	9.4	1.5	7.0	6.3	3.5	D	31.1	6,590	250	969	11,558	0.1
Canadian	0.7	6.1	8.9	11.4	6.6	8.1	7.7	7.0	19.3	24,465	151	1,210	61,395	1.3
Carter	-0.5	7.7	6.7	17.1	5.3	7.5	4.7	12.8	13.4	11,905	247	1,472	21,617	0.2
Cherokee	3.2	0.3	3.6	1.4	2.0	6.8	4.0	7.1	56.8	10,605	223	1,507	22,245	0.8
Choctaw	0.8	4.0	5.5	3.1	3.1	7.6	4.1	D	29.5	4,100	287	802	7,090	0.3
Cimarron	55.4	D	D	D	D	3.4	D	D	12.2	630	280	25	1,360	0.1
Cleveland	-0.1	D	9.1	4.4	7.8	8.2	5.9	9.0	30.5	49,595	167	3,831	123,297	1.2
Coal	14.9	8.5	11.9	4.2	1.6	4.3	D	14.7	21.9	1,260	239	210	2,576	0.1
Comanche	0.3	D	3.1	7.8	5.3	5.1	3.8	5.5	55.3	21,815	179	3,269	52,639	0.1
Cotton	15.5	D	3.1	1.4	D	5.1	D	3.5	48.9	1,475	269	151	2,688	0.0
Craig	8.2	D	3.1	3.1	D	8.5	4.9	D	24.9	4,120	292	691	6,375	0.1
Creek	-1.1	3.5	13.2	21.8	3.9	6.1	4.0	11.4	15.6	17,360	241	1,669	31,334	0.8
Custer	2.9	10.5	6.1	6.4	D	6.6	5.7	7.4	19.3	5,200	185	541	12,950	0.1
Delaware	8.2	D	9.0	5.6	D	9.0	4.2	D	24.2	11,795	288	1,203	24,236	0.5
Dewey	5.0	34.6	4.3	4.6	D	3.2	D	D	14.6	1,165	264	52	2,180	0.2
Ellis	29.8	5.0	1.2	0.8	D	7.1	D	D	19.4	945	251	55	2,125	-0.1
Garfield	1.8	5.3	5.5	10.3	6.7	6.8	6.5	11.7	22.1	12,805	207	1,301	27,807	-0.1
Garvin	-0.2	8.4	9.2	15.9	3.4	8.2	4.2	D	10.2	6,860	266	807	12,066	0.1
Grady	3.2	8.9	10.9	9.7	3.9	6.3	6.8	7.3	18.9	11,640	210	1,127	23,275	1.0
Grant	25.7	8.9	D	D	D	1.6	D	5.3	13.3	1,085	263	82	2,161	0.0
Greer	22.5	0.5	D	D	D	6.4	D	7.9	43.0	1,385	252	211	2,609	-0.2
Harmon	29.1	0.8	D	D	D	3.7	D	6.0	27.9	690	285	129	1,344	-0.1
Harper	42.8	D	D	D	D	3.8	D	7.7	21.2	790	248	38	1,711	-0.1
Haskell	13.1	7.3	5.6	2.9	D	7.5	2.3	D	17.8	3,525	304	501	5,669	0.3
Hughes	47.5	1.7	1.7	3.3	1.8	3.8	1.9	D	17.8	3,475	259	458	5,772	0.1
Jackson	1.3	0.2	2.2	8.1	D	6.0	3.8	3.6	51.9	4,735	191	659	12,041	0.2
Jefferson	15.3	4.3	3.1	1.0	D	5.6	D	D	29.6	1,595	293	203	2,730	0.1
Johnston	0.7	10.7	5.6	15.3	D	5.0	D	21.4	21.9	2,805	272	424	4,693	0.2
Kay	2.1	2.5	7.3	12.0	D	7.0	3.5	8.8	19.1	11,145	255	1,188	20,934	-0.1
Kingfisher	8.3	13.8	7.5	7.8	D	8.9	4.6	5.3	10.7	3,250	214	204	6,422	0.3

1. Per 1,000 resident population estimated as of July 1 of the year shown.

STATE County	Housing units, 2016–2020: Total	Occupied units: Owner-occupied: Percent	Owner-occupied: Median value[1]	Median owner cost as a percent of income: With a mortgage	Median owner cost as a percent of income: Without a mortgage[2]	Renter-occupied: Median rent[3]	Renter-occupied: Median rent as a percent of income[2]	Sub-standard units[4] (percent)	Civilian labor force, 2021: Total	Percent change, 2020–2021	Unemployment: Total	Unemployment: Rate[5]	Civilian employment[6], 2016–2020: Total	Percent: Management, business, science, and arts	Percent: Construction, production, and maintenance occupations
	89	90	91	92	93	94	95	96	97	98	99	100	101	102	103
OHIO—Cont'd															
Ottawa	18,240	79.0	154,500	18.9	10.5	752	26.4	0.9	20,630	0.3	1,259	6.1	18,768	32.1	29.6
Paulding	7,692	80.3	102,600	16.8	10.7	706	24.2	1.9	8,600	-0.9	373	4.3	8,402	28.4	39.7
Perry	13,216	75.8	120,200	19.6	10.9	623	26.5	2.2	15,922	0.9	888	5.6	15,222	26.4	37.7
Pickaway	19,808	73.6	171,400	19.7	11.5	822	26.8	2.2	26,648	1.5	1,188	4.5	24,928	33.0	28.3
Pike	11,037	66.8	119,900	17.6	12.0	726	27.0	3.0	10,912	0.5	687	6.3	10,736	33.7	32.8
Portage	62,785	70.6	160,300	18.7	12.0	870	32.4	1.0	84,767	-0.7	4,002	4.7	83,714	33.0	27.9
Preble	16,417	78.1	133,900	18.1	10.5	736	23.7	1.5	21,552	2.6	875	4.1	19,654	30.5	33.4
Putnam	13,301	82.3	154,500	17.5	10.0	718	21.0	1.1	18,877	1.9	637	3.4	17,203	35.6	33.5
Richland	48,967	66.9	115,100	18.8	10.6	677	27.6	1.7	51,520	-0.3	2,862	5.6	51,502	29.7	31.1
Ross	29,080	71.1	125,000	18.6	11.1	738	28.9	1.8	35,174	0.0	1,699	4.8	30,904	30.8	30.8
Sandusky	23,825	71.5	118,600	17.8	10.9	716	26.4	1.5	30,368	1.3	1,580	5.2	27,945	27.6	39.9
Scioto	29,561	67.4	103,400	19.2	12.4	634	29.3	2.1	29,306	0.8	1,811	6.2	27,316	32.3	28.2
Seneca	21,759	73.3	108,900	18.1	10.3	699	26.0	0.8	26,771	-1.2	1,262	4.7	26,636	27.3	38.7
Shelby	18,670	70.6	147,400	18.2	10.2	756	20.9	2.5	23,791	-0.6	994	4.2	24,493	28.3	39.8
Stark	154,322	68.1	139,000	18.3	10.5	752	27.1	1.3	182,193	-0.6	9,502	5.2	177,304	33.5	25.9
Summit	226,721	66.4	151,300	18.8	10.8	854	28.2	1.0	265,068	-1.1	14,410	5.4	268,671	38.4	20.8
Trumbull	85,917	70.4	105,500	18.4	11.3	684	29.5	1.7	83,322	-1.6	5,345	6.4	85,533	29.7	30.0
Tuscarawas	36,906	70.9	136,700	18.1	10.7	772	26.3	2.1	44,346	-0.2	2,055	4.6	43,080	27.1	37.4
Union	20,695	80.1	220,300	19.3	10.0	981	22.8	0.9	29,989	1.6	1,053	3.5	29,507	42.8	23.7
Van Wert	11,640	77.7	111,000	17.4	10.0	706	24.9	0.8	14,591	-1.0	575	3.9	13,753	30.9	36.7
Vinton	5,221	76.5	94,800	18.1	12.3	606	34.1	2.8	5,513	-1.5	341	6.2	5,518	28.9	41.8
Warren	84,127	77.6	236,400	18.5	10.3	1,076	24.3	1.0	121,173	1.3	4,838	4.0	114,556	49.1	17.9
Washington	24,803	73.7	142,100	18.7	10.0	678	28.0	1.7	26,727	-0.3	1,477	5.5	27,262	31.8	29.4
Wayne	44,238	74.4	156,300	18.8	10.0	754	23.5	2.6	60,229	-0.1	2,168	3.6	55,046	32.0	33.6
Williams	15,266	75.8	108,000	18.7	11.2	693	25.5	1.0	18,467	-1.7	795	4.3	17,602	27.0	38.5
Wood	50,645	65.3	165,400	18.4	11.4	811	25.3	0.7	69,203	0.0	2,965	4.3	69,756	38.0	23.9
Wyandot	9,100	71.3	129,900	16.8	10.0	647	21.2	0.9	12,816	-0.6	453	3.5	11,133	28.3	38.4
OKLAHOMA	1,493,569	66.1	142,400	19.2	10.0	818	27.2	3.1	1,854,234	1.0	71,154	3.8	1,779,157	35.6	25.3
Adair	7,632	68.8	92,800	19.0	10.0	534	25.5	6.2	8,467	2.5	311	3.7	7,869	26.6	40.8
Alfalfa	1,897	78.7	86,000	14.4	10.0	580	26.9	3.0	2,683	-2.3	63	2.3	2,222	35.6	29.8
Atoka	5,200	75.0	105,200	17.8	11.0	573	29.7	4.8	5,021	-1.8	237	4.7	4,794	31.6	31.4
Beaver	1,994	78.8	97,800	20.6	10.2	694	18.0	1.8	2,625	2.1	45	1.7	2,492	35.3	33.2
Beckham	7,724	67.1	127,500	19.9	14.2	749	27.1	3.7	9,706	-2.4	420	4.3	8,486	28.3	28.6
Blaine	3,940	72.7	99,600	17.9	10.0	611	19.0	2.1	4,402	0.6	130	3.0	3,503	35.6	32.5
Bryan	17,634	62.7	119,800	18.6	10.0	761	26.8	4.3	21,988	-1.5	722	3.3	20,141	31.0	27.8
Caddo	10,465	73.3	84,600	17.7	10.0	594	22.1	4.3	12,011	1.0	445	3.7	11,160	29.4	31.8
Canadian	45,724	76.3	170,700	19.4	10.0	966	24.9	2.3	78,317	1.3	2,515	3.2	71,591	38.7	21.6
Carter	18,474	67.1	117,400	18.6	10.1	787	26.3	2.6	21,388	0.7	941	4.4	21,251	29.1	32.4
Cherokee	17,364	67.3	126,400	21.4	10.0	679	26.9	2.6	19,939	2.3	823	4.1	19,976	35.8	24.8
Choctaw	6,074	67.8	99,000	20.1	11.3	573	30.2	2.3	5,940	7.0	307	5.2	5,487	31.3	31.5
Cimarron	952	73.3	62,400	21.0	10.0	579	18.1	0.3	1,503	7.6	27	1.8	966	36.7	30.1
Cleveland	108,070	64.1	170,700	19.2	10.0	935	27.1	2.7	144,386	1.6	4,642	3.2	142,912	41.0	19.9
Coal	2,252	76.9	82,000	19.0	10.0	633	24.0	3.4	2,292	0.7	104	4.5	2,100	29.4	33.8
Comanche	43,241	53.4	124,100	19.1	10.0	817	27.3	3.1	47,741	-0.2	1,939	4.1	47,776	37.5	22.4
Cotton	2,215	73.7	75,600	17.9	10.6	657	21.1	2.6	2,708	0.1	110	4.1	2,467	32.5	28.0
Craig	5,428	70.0	110,700	22.5	10.0	726	27.5	3.3	5,714	-1.2	208	3.6	5,669	29.0	27.6
Creek	26,393	74.9	130,300	19.1	11.1	790	25.0	3.8	31,131	0.7	1,319	4.2	29,936	31.2	31.1
Custer	10,697	64.1	140,100	17.9	10.0	682	28.6	2.8	15,179	1.1	493	3.2	14,494	31.6	28.4
Delaware	16,988	75.6	124,000	22.8	11.2	720	26.8	3.7	18,692	2.3	626	3.3	16,504	31.0	28.9
Dewey	1,715	73.9	99,800	16.8	10.0	802	29.2	3.4	2,728	1.9	74	2.7	2,076	26.2	33.6
Ellis	1,581	77.1	96,000	17.4	11.7	688	24.7	1.1	2,102	-1.3	59	2.8	1,691	31.8	33.3
Garfield	23,709	65.4	119,000	18.8	10.0	814	24.8	3.3	26,842	0.0	925	3.4	27,304	30.2	32.6
Garvin	10,375	67.8	103,900	17.2	10.0	665	23.3	2.3	12,682	-0.1	476	3.8	11,294	28.4	36.7
Grady	20,107	76.6	140,800	17.9	10.0	729	22.6	2.6	26,685	1.5	927	3.5	24,557	35.3	29.6
Grant	1,761	76.7	79,000	16.4	10.0	690	18.1	1.9	2,724	-1.3	69	2.5	2,030	29.9	34.5
Greer	2,109	70.7	84,600	19.1	10.2	583	24.8	1.5	1,859	-0.4	95	5.1	2,007	29.5	23.7
Harmon	1,091	69.1	72,100	14.9	10.0	705	17.0	2.2	1,184	1.4	30	2.5	1,181	38.9	31.4
Harper	1,236	80.4	83,700	18.8	12.6	669	26.2	3.6	1,789	1.5	44	2.5	1,486	29.9	34.5
Haskell	4,935	76.6	99,200	18.4	10.0	617	36.2	5.4	4,248	0.8	221	5.2	4,891	33.5	31.8
Hughes	4,106	73.2	74,200	19.5	10.6	578	28.5	2.8	5,191	-2.0	268	5.2	4,014	29.9	30.1
Jackson	9,681	61.3	99,700	18.8	10.4	722	24.6	1.9	10,785	2.1	304	2.8	10,722	30.4	30.2
Jefferson	2,382	75.3	64,800	19.0	10.0	483	28.1	1.8	2,471	-3.2	98	4.0	2,275	24.1	39.7
Johnston	4,313	73.2	85,900	17.9	10.2	600	24.7	6.2	3,684	-1.6	168	4.6	4,198	32.4	33.2
Kay	17,392	66.2	96,700	18.3	10.8	699	24.8	3.3	18,421	1.0	799	4.3	18,695	28.0	32.9
Kingfisher	5,769	79.3	152,000	18.4	10.0	834	22.0	1.4	8,647	-0.8	228	2.6	7,488	31.0	34.2

1. Specified owner-occupied units. 2. A value of 10.0 represents 10 percent or less; a value of 50.0 represents 50 percent or more. 3. Specified renter-occupied units. 4. Overcrowded or lacking complete plumbing facilities. 5. Percent of civilian labor force. 6. Civilian employed persons 16 years old and over.

STATE County	Private nonfarm establishments, employment and payroll, 2020									Agriculture, 2017			
		Employment						Annual payroll		Farms			Farm producers whose primary occupation is farming (percent)
											Percent with:		
	Number of establish-ments	Total	Health care and social assistance	Manufac-turing	Retail trade	Finance and insurance	Professional, scientific, and technical services	Total (mil dol)	Average per employee (dollars)	Number	Fewer than 50 acres	1000 acres or more	
	104	105	106	107	108	109	110	111	112	113	114	115	116
OHIO—Cont'd													
Ottawa	1,014	9,878	1,852	1,986	1,306	278	163	451	45,696	551	47.2	4.2	36.3
Paulding	298	4,045	495	1,711	417	93	66	142	35,021	622	33.3	10.6	44.5
Perry	437	4,442	943	1,050	686	118	79	150	33,837	762	44.4	1.4	29.4
Pickaway	783	10,411	1,724	2,152	1,515	261	171	426	40,914	805	43.0	10.9	49.0
Pike	402	7,184	1,339	664	989	230	1,827	352	49,024	511	31.3	2.2	29.9
Portage	2,958	47,923	6,802	10,684	8,050	605	1,603	2,049	42,758	1,118	68.4	0.9	29.9
Preble	664	9,668	1,138	3,855	1,115	188	255	445	45,994	1,055	48.6	4.8	39.9
Putnam	729	9,933	1,154	3,718	1,041	290	189	399	40,131	1,335	33.7	4.0	34.1
Richland	2,606	39,890	6,451	8,825	6,189	902	830	1,479	37,078	1,160	49.1	1.5	41.8
Ross	1,233	22,077	5,031	3,794	3,672	456	435	953	43,188	1,121	40.3	4.6	38.9
Sandusky	1,273	22,041	3,115	8,280	2,270	463	405	943	42,766	768	39.6	5.5	38.4
Scioto	1,240	19,183	7,918	1,524	3,044	390	641	722	37,622	688	42.0	0.9	36.5
Seneca	1,025	16,462	2,313	4,370	1,973	412	268	608	36,924	1,156	40.1	4.5	35.3
Shelby	964	24,765	2,091	12,532	1,917	307	406	1,287	51,984	947	39.7	3.6	36.6
Stark	8,005	143,048	29,167	24,188	20,069	5,092	4,680	5,850	40,893	1,547	67.7	1.2	32.4
Summit	13,210	246,876	43,979	27,410	30,485	9,714	13,535	12,463	50,481	392	77.6	0.8	39.6
Trumbull	3,817	55,664	9,586	7,610	11,138	1,436	1,258	2,098	37,682	1,036	52.0	1.7	33.4
Tuscarawas	2,062	30,562	5,062	8,331	4,294	646	1,277	1,241	40,593	1,155	47.3	1.6	34.4
Union	1,083	25,265	1,902	6,297	2,425	436	4,577	1,591	62,982	997	50.6	5.3	36.3
Van Wert	541	10,422	1,958	3,415	1,120	883	132	444	42,599	772	40.5	10.1	42.9
Vinton	147	1,641	400	479	167	89	25	51	30,961	227	33.5	0.9	29.3
Warren	4,456	83,544	10,848	12,749	9,484	4,943	4,626	4,529	54,209	925	73.2	2.4	29.1
Washington	1,351	22,846	5,209	3,256	2,865	691	610	1,063	46,515	1,106	32.5	0.8	34.6
Wayne	2,482	43,423	6,082	14,587	4,944	1,078	1,370	1,793	41,285	2,034	54.7	1.2	42.3
Williams	780	15,739	1,813	7,626	1,367	265	208	623	39,604	881	40.3	5.6	33.8
Wood	2,701	57,707	5,794	14,014	6,213	1,251	2,249	2,720	47,130	1,069	46.7	6.9	35.8
Wyandot	494	9,495	941	4,650	768	216	93	425	44,782	649	40.4	10.3	42.9
OKLAHOMA	93,595	1,405,824	225,482	131,269	182,871	58,421	78,909	64,020	45,539	78,531	29.6	10.3	37.5
Adair	232	2,951	506	1,010	445	104	65	106	36,001	1,031	28.9	3.1	40.7
Alfalfa	131	899	104	26	178	91	25	34	38,186	581	8.8	32.0	52.0
Atoka	257	1,852	359	132	471	141	45	56	30,042	1,057	21.6	6.4	38.1
Beaver	143	1,244	90	NA	91	52	24	51	41,269	805	5.0	31.3	37.2
Beckham	739	7,895	1,038	195	1,464	271	260	333	42,133	896	18.8	14.7	33.0
Blaine	246	2,166	350	461	301	141	42	85	39,257	731	13.5	27.4	45.4
Bryan	828	11,516	1,973	1,788	1,828	357	477	418	36,262	1,609	27.8	4.5	39.8
Caddo	439	4,692	864	70	859	187	212	177	37,696	1,396	15.5	16.1	44.2
Canadian	2,817	29,768	3,118	3,203	4,679	868	973	1,071	35,972	1,324	37.8	11.9	35.5
Carter	1,574	19,854	3,346	2,813	2,842	691	451	896	45,109	1,431	34.5	5.6	30.2
Cherokee	755	9,422	3,055	167	1,687	335	121	322	34,169	1,200	33.2	2.6	36.8
Choctaw	284	3,163	1,159	116	456	128	85	101	32,032	851	20.4	9.2	42.4
Cimarron	67	324	41	NA	88	27	7	10	31,269	447	4.7	38.3	42.0
Cleveland	5,878	76,569	14,165	3,315	15,412	2,756	3,977	2,909	37,986	1,182	59.4	1.4	31.7
Coal	84	807	210	71	164	50	11	28	35,280	590	16.8	11.2	45.9
Comanche	2,116	32,397	6,333	3,368	5,174	1,413	2,157	1,277	39,424	1,055	30.6	13.2	37.2
Cotton	75	1,383	120	NA	126	42	20	43	31,133	448	13.2	29.0	41.0
Craig	349	4,014	1,306	130	580	201	84	145	36,208	1,179	24.8	7.0	41.6
Creek	1,330	17,624	2,315	4,136	1,788	446	441	732	41,538	1,893	46.5	2.0	29.9
Custer	915	9,614	1,417	1,033	1,611	366	291	385	40,019	773	16.4	23.4	40.5
Delaware	748	8,159	1,347	635	1,434	266	299	263	32,247	1,377	33.7	3.3	43.3
Dewey	164	1,249	96	23	206	67	17	60	47,739	728	8.2	25.8	42.6
Ellis	114	820	139	NA	108	47	27	34	41,985	677	7.2	29.1	37.5
Garfield	1,566	20,986	3,780	2,596	3,369	756	592	814	38,799	936	22.1	20.6	44.8
Garvin	714	7,906	796	1,042	1,246	247	161	348	44,059	1,500	27.8	6.8	36.0
Grady	1,131	11,311	1,521	1,724	1,562	405	259	434	38,363	1,625	33.8	9.2	36.6
Grant	115	989	150	8	204	56	18	39	39,038	659	10.5	26.7	47.3
Greer	72	432	109	54	127	22	12	12	27,391	432	8.6	20.8	35.8
Harmon	47	406	135	NA	52	61	6	15	36,621	374	2.7	31.3	48.3
Harper	93	490	103	NA	134	29	33	16	33,284	438	7.5	37.4	41.1
Haskell	217	2,769	1,167	143	330	63	37	83	30,039	812	23.3	4.7	37.4
Hughes	200	2,013	683	147	301	63	32	64	31,868	928	19.4	8.1	43.9
Jackson	515	6,655	1,374	905	1,151	361	328	270	40,517	634	20.2	24.6	35.2
Jefferson	106	890	275	16	138	55	41	33	36,740	424	14.4	28.1	50.3
Johnston	163	1,996	573	323	219	27	13	79	39,335	606	21.5	8.3	35.7
Kay	1,069	14,597	2,139	2,800	1,904	385	546	588	40,302	864	28.2	18.5	46.1
Kingfisher	496	6,004	529	351	769	184	185	283	47,064	928	18.5	20.0	44.9

STATE County	Agriculture, 2017 (cont.) — Land in farms: Acreage (1,000)	Land in farms: Percent change, 2012–2017	Land in farms — Acres: Average size of farm	Land in farms — Acres: Total irrigated (1,000)	Land in farms — Acres: Total cropland (1,000)	Value of land and buildings (dollars): Average per farm	Value of land and buildings (dollars): Average per acre	Value of machinery and equipment, average per farm (dollars)	Value of products sold: Total (mil dol)	Value of products sold: Average per farm (acres)	Value of products sold — Percent from: Crops	Value of products sold — Percent from: Livestock and poultry products	Organic farms (number)	Farms with internet access (percent)	Government payments: Total ($1,000)	Government payments: Percent of farms
	117	118	119	120	121	122	123	124	125	126	127	128	129	130	131	132
OHIO—Cont'd																
Ottawa	121	7.8	221	1.2	115.1	1,192,630	5,409	173,655	59.2	107,477	92.9	7.1	2	77.3	3,064	70.8
Paulding	220	-0.6	353	0.4	208.2	2,210,654	6,260	220,491	173.5	278,860	46.3	53.7	4	76.2	4,880	83.6
Perry	101	-5.7	133	0.0	58.9	607,087	4,574	75,495	33.8	44,398	68.3	31.7	3	74.0	1,427	18.8
Pickaway	297	1.1	369	2.6	275.0	2,225,570	6,033	220,849	162.7	202,050	91.4	8.6	2	81.7	10,838	61.5
Pike	98	0.4	191	0.6	54.3	795,490	4,156	87,790	55.1	107,771	41.2	58.8	9	68.3	1,495	23.3
Portage	86	3.1	77	0.3	59.5	500,149	6,511	74,045	34.5	30,849	71.0	29.0	5	78.4	1,224	10.4
Preble	213	-4.8	202	0.3	188.3	1,294,416	6,397	133,405	146.3	138,647	67.1	32.9	7	75.3	5,681	51.3
Putnam	305	-0.2	228	0.8	291.2	1,528,572	6,694	186,197	214.5	160,661	65.0	35.0	NA	78.4	7,728	73.5
Richland	156	-3.0	134	0.2	113.1	1,008,273	7,505	108,319	135.1	116,504	37.1	62.9	20	65.4	2,687	21.0
Ross	248	11.8	221	0.7	168.2	1,013,522	4,583	105,244	77.7	69,354	85.8	14.2	8	69.8	10,095	45.2
Sandusky	179	-1.5	233	1.1	166.4	1,379,300	5,926	177,118	101.0	131,561	90.9	9.1	4	80.7	5,305	69.3
Scioto	91	-3.1	133	0.1	45.1	416,922	3,138	89,131	17.8	25,932	78.1	21.9	1	75.3	1,081	15.0
Seneca	267	-8.1	231	0.3	242.8	1,359,558	5,889	176,787	140.9	121,866	82.0	18.0	3	74.4	8,588	72.1
Shelby	215	4.2	227	D	197.3	1,745,226	7,688	179,829	178.2	188,214	52.0	48.0	5	83.7	7,162	68.0
Stark	133	-2.1	86	0.8	101.7	794,143	9,244	89,768	95.8	61,954	42.4	57.6	10	76.3	3,035	13.7
Summit	19	13.3	48	0.2	10.7	639,318	13,365	54,610	12.6	32,156	68.5	31.5	2	86.7	275	7.1
Trumbull	124	8.6	119	0.1	82.0	516,981	4,331	108,297	56.1	54,110	64.4	35.6	12	71.7	1,345	20.9
Tuscarawas	144	4.2	125	0.1	80.1	691,723	5,555	100,450	125.2	108,384	17.2	82.8	26	61.1	1,454	18.5
Union	218	-10.1	218	0.4	196.1	1,386,021	6,350	191,902	209.3	209,954	49.4	50.6	13	86.7	7,490	52.2
Van Wert	248	9.3	322	D	240.8	2,410,706	7,494	215,085	191.3	247,791	64.6	35.4	2	83.4	4,699	68.9
Vinton	31	-5.8	139	0.0	14.0	438,779	3,166	63,613	5.7	25,079	80.3	19.7	3	66.1	261	27.8
Warren	90	-15.3	98	0.5	71.2	763,996	7,824	86,177	47.7	51,536	93.8	6.2	4	81.8	2,580	15.7
Washington	144	3.9	131	0.6	57.0	416,318	3,189	70,252	42.0	38,019	55.5	44.5	NA	71.2	684	17.4
Wayne	252	-7.2	124	0.9	204.0	1,107,599	8,940	116,845	327.9	161,205	24.8	75.2	98	66.3	5,140	21.1
Williams	211	1.2	239	3.8	189.9	1,233,691	5,161	145,441	122.8	139,367	66.1	33.9	3	73.4	7,092	64.4
Wood	269	0.3	251	2.3	253.8	1,674,194	6,659	171,875	159.3	148,985	79.4	20.6	6	76.5	8,030	70.8
Wyandot	225	1.7	346	0.0	205.1	1,974,814	5,706	226,523	157.3	242,385	62.0	38.0	3	74.0	8,100	75.2
OKLAHOMA	34,156	-0.6	435	573.8	11,715.7	754,099	1,734	90,442	7,465.5	95,065	20.3	79.7	54	72.9	232,018	26.3
Adair	239	-5.3	232	0.4	47.6	554,052	2,392	76,599	163.1	158,242	2.0	98.0	1	68.1	216	8.7
Alfalfa	524	-3.9	902	1.4	343.2	1,535,433	1,703	241,428	103.0	177,248	40.3	59.7	NA	74.5	4,482	75.9
Atoka	357	1.2	338	1.5	66.8	619,842	1,834	65,617	39.0	36,901	8.6	91.4	1	67.3	743	32.0
Beaver	1,037	-7.1	1,288	21.5	296.1	1,157,188	898	104,629	155.7	193,388	12.5	87.5	NA	66.2	7,620	67.0
Beckham	498	-12.3	556	10.5	175.7	740,737	1,332	103,007	52.0	58,029	50.7	49.3	NA	70.1	4,317	41.2
Blaine	593	13.6	811	4.3	320.9	1,321,168	1,628	197,612	109.2	149,409	22.8	77.2	NA	74.3	2,599	47.2
Bryan	433	-1.9	269	6.4	104.5	610,009	2,267	69,072	61.4	38,161	33.9	66.1	NA	70.0	2,133	36.1
Caddo	756	6.8	541	37.3	326.7	937,747	1,732	122,802	132.1	94,609	37.4	62.6	5	69.8	12,419	46.6
Canadian	498	-0.5	376	5.4	255.6	884,268	2,349	129,048	135.8	102,535	20.8	79.2	NA	75.8	5,299	38.3
Carter	396	-13.2	277	1.6	64.3	562,555	2,030	59,722	39.4	27,541	16.2	83.8	NA	76.5	932	7.1
Cherokee	217	-8.0	181	0.6	41.4	449,283	2,483	66,353	67.6	56,327	44.5	55.5	2	67.8	838	24.1
Choctaw	338	2.2	397	1.6	66.2	704,003	1,774	82,113	47.0	55,197	11.3	88.7	1	75.0	1,740	15.0
Cimarron	1,097	-5.2	2,455	42.0	402.7	2,026,541	825	215,397	342.4	765,922	16.5	83.5	NA	70.0	8,980	76.1
Cleveland	123	-8.1	104	2.6	31.6	504,329	4,851	52,819	16.6	14,066	44.8	55.2	3	79.4	179	3.4
Coal	273	-0.1	463	0.5	54.4	843,799	1,821	79,114	37.9	64,205	10.6	89.4	NA	61.9	788	33.4
Comanche	467	0.9	443	D	157.7	853,568	1,928	85,581	81.0	76,787	19.0	81.0	2	75.7	3,300	33.6
Cotton	405	1.2	903	0.1	202.7	1,227,562	1,359	137,210	49.8	111,170	21.9	78.1	NA	75.2	5,750	69.9
Craig	423	-8.4	359	D	100.7	755,777	2,105	82,441	99.7	84,545	10.5	89.5	6	74.1	1,567	18.6
Creek	327	-5.7	173	0.7	62.7	379,152	2,193	54,643	18.1	9,587	16.7	83.3	3	70.5	404	3.4
Custer	638	2.5	826	7.5	253.6	1,199,008	1,452	159,557	104.5	135,208	26.5	73.5	NA	72.8	5,809	45.8
Delaware	292	2.9	212	0.1	69.4	577,810	2,729	85,609	244.0	177,207	2.6	97.4	2	73.6	453	7.3
Dewey	652	4.4	896	2.8	185.4	1,228,171	1,371	125,050	41.2	56,651	18.7	81.3	NA	76.4	2,425	56.7
Ellis	724	-4.5	1,070	8.4	127.3	1,062,853	994	79,899	115.7	170,870	4.1	95.9	NA	64.5	2,328	64.1
Garfield	675	1.3	721	3.2	442.9	1,251,739	1,736	180,572	130.4	139,318	48.1	51.9	NA	80.0	6,660	61.3
Garvin	483	4.4	322	2.0	122.1	617,731	1,917	81,615	66.9	44,607	25.3	74.7	1	70.9	2,139	25.6
Grady	593	1.7	365	12.7	200.9	766,106	2,098	116,307	152.7	93,954	14.6	85.4	NA	70.3	4,232	30.3
Grant	575	-1.3	872	1.5	414.8	1,400,015	1,605	206,900	85.3	129,398	72.2	27.8	1	75.7	6,156	78.1
Greer	328	-18.3	760	4.4	132.3	877,992	1,156	98,008	32.3	74,785	45.2	54.8	NA	74.5	4,332	63.7
Harmon	342	0.3	914	24.5	167.3	1,143,452	1,252	143,175	66.2	176,952	43.7	56.3	NA	70.1	5,079	69.0
Harper	668	8.0	1,524	4.3	180.7	1,678,361	1,101	133,044	217.1	495,710	2.8	97.2	NA	71.9	3,424	63.7
Haskell	238	-7.2	293	0.5	45.9	556,633	1,902	91,479	104.2	128,365	2.5	97.5	1	73.4	879	15.9
Hughes	414	-5.1	446	2.9	63.2	710,946	1,595	76,477	306.3	330,044	1.0	99.0	NA	67.0	1,393	19.8
Jackson	511	6.7	806	50.8	335.5	1,125,890	1,398	197,700	115.7	182,442	85.5	14.5	NA	77.4	12,582	58.8
Jefferson	472	-0.7	1,113	0.7	92.6	1,721,210	1,546	113,136	89.7	211,564	4.2	95.8	NA	70.3	3,447	49.8
Johnston	289	1.8	477	0.7	44.0	892,334	1,872	72,388	32.9	54,211	10.6	89.4	1	70.8	1,206	44.9
Kay	498	2.8	576	1.2	346.7	947,482	1,645	131,856	88.2	102,078	68.1	31.9	NA	77.2	5,685	51.7
Kingfisher	575	1.3	620	5.6	353.5	1,191,810	1,923	162,597	145.0	156,278	21.6	78.4	2	74.9	5,382	59.3

STATE County	Water use, 2015: Public supply water withdrawn (mil gal/ day)	Water use, 2015: Public supply gallons withdrawn per person per day	Wholesale Trade[1], 2017: Number of establish-ments	Wholesale Trade[1], 2017: Number of employees	Wholesale Trade[1], 2017: Sales (mil dol)	Wholesale Trade[1], 2017: Average payroll (mil dol)	Retail Trade[2], 2017: Number of establish-ments	Retail Trade[2], 2017: Number of employees	Retail Trade[2], 2017: Sales (mil dol)	Retail Trade[2], 2017: Average payroll (mil dol)	Real estate and rental and leasing,[2] 2017: Number of establish-ments	Real estate and rental and leasing,[2] 2017: Number of employees	Real estate and rental and leasing,[2] 2017: Sales (mil dol)	Real estate and rental and leasing,[2] 2017: Average payroll (mil dol)
	133	134	135	136	137	138	139	140	141	142	143	144	145	146
OHIO—Cont'd														
Ottawa	4.6	112.0	28	155	82.5	7.0	131	1,411	442.7	42.2	51	132	23.0	4.2
Paulding	1.3	69.0	15	168	119.1	7.9	51	425	136.8	9.3	5	11	2.1	0.3
Perry	1.0	26.7	15	77	52.8	3.1	68	664	191.9	14.1	12	27	8.1	0.8
Pickaway	3.7	64.2	D	D	D	30.0	128	1,583	464.7	39.2	30	115	16.7	3.8
Pike	2.6	91.4	12	105	58.2	4.8	74	998	282.4	22.7	10	73	12.2	1.8
Portage	43.9	270.2	141	2,891	2,552.6	208.4	433	8,475	2,382.7	201.9	119	502	129.3	14.1
Preble	2.6	61.9	28	189	116.4	8.0	94	1,268	387.1	28.8	20	160	14.9	6.9
Putnam	2.5	74.0	33	311	286.4	15.0	109	1,013	289.8	25.8	11	26	4.0	1.0
Richland	14.5	118.7	97	1,455	760.4	65.2	419	6,707	1,641.9	160.9	104	452	76.5	14.7
Ross	9.5	122.8	49	503	428.4	26.6	244	3,993	1,128.9	95.4	45	179	32.9	4.7
Sandusky	7.9	132.2	48	631	652.8	29.9	201	2,421	683.9	59.3	42	142	19.8	4.0
Scioto	8.6	111.9	18	168	109.2	8.4	259	3,208	930.9	80.2	46	221	31.3	6.4
Seneca	1.9	33.3	39	979	687.1	40.9	153	2,032	565.7	50.9	25	58	10.4	1.5
Shelby	3.5	71.4	32	871	458.2	38.3	140	1,914	490.6	44.4	37	84	16.3	2.4
Stark	30.4	81.1	325	4,607	3,874.9	241.4	1,214	19,873	5,377.1	488.2	270	1,379	287.8	59.2
Summit	11.1	20.4	802	13,008	9,120.2	835.4	1,655	29,860	8,582.2	830.2	532	3,044	667.8	125.9
Trumbull	33.9	166.1	148	2,275	1,791.4	123.5	668	11,479	2,584.7	269.7	137	1,546	281.1	61.0
Tuscarawas	17.7	190.2	79	927	526.5	42.0	329	4,441	1,194.7	106.9	65	348	63.9	10.9
Union	1.2	21.6	75	983	2,464.1	62.4	127	2,409	793.9	67.0	48	172	32.0	6.1
Van Wert	1.9	65.5	27	349	208.1	16.3	90	1,140	334.3	27.5	12	50	11.0	1.8
Vinton	0.2	13.8	NA	NA	NA	NA	25	135	30.3	2.7	D	D	D	0.2
Warren	15.1	67.1	182	5,568	3,800.3	409.8	516	10,913	2,934.1	258.8	214	1,068	703.4	50.4
Washington	7.6	124.9	55	755	398.6	34.7	230	3,047	882.0	76.5	42	216	40.3	6.6
Wayne	8.1	69.4	D	D	D	D	376	4,951	1,367.8	125.5	68	262	55.2	8.4
Williams	2.7	71.9	42	587	383.0	24.0	129	1,373	372.9	30.4	17	69	11.3	2.0
Wood	5.2	40.2	172	3,024	2,046.3	165.7	362	6,666	1,871.8	155.3	118	561	138.9	25.2
Wyandot	1.0	42.7	27	333	243.6	15.2	68	779	272.5	21.0	12	18	3.2	0.6
OKLAHOMA	611.2	156.3	3,859	50,233	42,221.4	2,757.0	12,963	180,451	53,382.1	4,682.9	4,461	22,135	4,696.2	941.8
Adair	6.9	314.0	9	90	47.1	2.7	46	513	124.8	10.9	7	16	2.2	0.4
Alfalfa	0.7	119.3	D	D	D	2.2	21	169	50.3	4.1	NA	NA	NA	NA
Atoka	40.4	2,930.5	D	D	D	0.7	51	490	157.4	12.3	7	20	2.9	0.7
Beaver	0.5	88.4	6	41	35.3	1.0	14	88	24.4	1.5	NA	NA	NA	NA
Beckham	3.3	136.7	33	276	165.5	12.7	118	1,511	582.0	39.8	42	311	77.4	16.4
Blaine	1.1	108.8	12	118	88.8	6.5	41	330	105.3	6.2	D	D	D	D
Bryan	5.5	123.2	31	670	496.6	25.9	128	1,640	519.8	40.9	27	79	20.9	3.1
Caddo	7.2	243.7	17	214	106.3	8.0	84	808	251.7	20.5	10	19	3.9	0.8
Canadian	4.2	31.8	96	1,228	3,082.2	80.5	293	4,278	1,469.3	116.2	164	810	211.2	40.9
Carter	5.1	104.3	71	958	1,092.6	38.0	258	2,964	874.6	69.1	73	297	55.5	12.8
Cherokee	7.4	152.7	14	771	114.3	19.9	149	1,820	426.9	40.9	35	154	23.9	3.5
Choctaw	2.7	179.4	7	71	33.6	3.0	47	450	130.8	11.7	7	12	3.3	0.2
Cimarron	0.3	153.4	6	D	33.2	D	11	85	28.1	1.6	NA	NA	NA	NA
Cleveland	23.4	85.1	146	1,495	820.2	82.2	758	12,342	3,409.8	305.6	391	1,575	331.7	62.1
Coal	0.5	81.4	D	D	D	D	17	108	26.3	2.4	NA	NA	NA	NA
Comanche	21.0	168.3	D	D	D	D	397	5,275	1,337.7	127.5	D	D	D	D
Cotton	0.5	85.1	NA	NA	NA	NA	14	96	36.5	1.9	NA	NA	NA	NA
Craig	0.1	6.7	19	176	59.4	7.3	53	583	172.8	14.8	5	15	2.3	0.3
Creek	5.9	83.1	63	1,488	573.2	76.3	148	1,783	497.6	43.6	44	125	22.0	3.6
Custer	3.7	122.7	39	408	267.6	22.2	143	1,595	508.9	39.6	45	245	50.4	14.1
Delaware	35.7	860.9	20	63	24.7	2.0	139	1,447	360.5	35.5	35	107	20.7	3.6
Dewey	0.1	22.0	8	D	7.0	D	31	224	105.1	5.2	NA	NA	NA	NA
Ellis	0.7	153.6	6	74	26.9	3.1	24	125	47.2	2.7	NA	NA	NA	NA
Garfield	2.9	45.1	D	D	D	D	268	3,780	944.3	98.8	93	383	70.4	14.3
Garvin	2.0	71.7	21	218	112.5	11.0	116	1,270	510.2	38.4	21	95	27.1	5.7
Grady	2.4	43.9	46	539	276.4	28.8	137	1,438	471.3	37.6	47	194	40.3	7.6
Grant	1.3	278.6	4	31	35.6	1.4	23	159	79.8	4.8	NA	NA	NA	NA
Greer	1.5	240.5	NA	NA	NA	NA	13	130	25.4	3.1	NA	NA	NA	NA
Harmon	0.7	261.8	NA	NA	NA	NA	11	59	13.4	1.1	NA	NA	NA	NA
Harper	0.6	159.8	NA	NA	NA	NA	19	120	19.6	2.6	6	D	1.9	D
Haskell	1.2	91.1	D	D	D	1.1	36	477	146.4	12.1	D	D	D	D
Hughes	2.6	187.1	8	50	13.9	1.4	37	392	83.3	7.6	8	23	2.2	0.7
Jackson	0.2	8.2	20	160	218.4	10.9	105	1,206	390.3	32.4	24	135	21.7	3.2
Jefferson	13.8	2,197.3	NA	NA	NA	NA	21	149	25.8	2.4	NA	NA	NA	NA
Johnston	2.0	180.3	7	32	11.8	1.3	34	235	67.1	5.4	4	D	1.0	D
Kay	18.1	399.6	48	324	142.7	15.6	174	2,180	653.6	54.9	41	113	26.3	3.2
Kingfisher	1.7	106.5	24	366	362.0	18.8	51	738	344.7	23.4	8	18	2.1	0.6

1 Merchant wholesalers, except manufacturers' sales branches and offices. 2. Employer establishments.

STATE County	Professional, scientific, and technical services, 2017				Manufacturing, 2017				Accommodation and food services, 2017			
	Number of establish-ments	Number of employees	Sales (mil dol)	Average payroll (mil dol)	Number of establish-ments	Number of employees	Sales (mil dol)	Average payroll (mil dol)	Number of establis-hments	Number of employees	Sales (mil dol)	Annual payroll (mil dol)
	147	148	149	150	151	152	153	154	155	156	157	158
OHIO—Cont'd												
Ottawa	D	D	D	D	51	2,039	633.7	123.1	175	1,734	139.3	38.3
Paulding	13	67	4.6	1.7	33	1,342	314.1	59.4	D	D	D	D
Perry	21	90	7.6	3.5	16	722	133.9	32.6	41	394	18.9	4.9
Pickaway	44	183	20.7	7.2	38	2,249	1,107.1	128.7	73	1,487	69.5	20.8
Pike	24	2,119	467.1	163.1	31	743	568.1	37.3	40	572	27.5	7.6
Portage	D	D	D	D	243	9,969	3,414.1	508.5	332	5,756	268.6	78.7
Preble	40	253	14.2	5.4	51	3,397	1,229.7	187.4	64	968	45.9	14.0
Putnam	37	199	21.7	7.3	53	3,673	2,598.1	179.8	58	832	29.9	8.3
Richland	190	844	105.7	34.3	170	8,503	3,520.3	459.3	229	4,578	214.5	63.2
Ross	59	447	31.5	14.0	30	3,683	4,320.3	258.9	123	2,929	137.3	41.4
Sandusky	81	425	53.4	16.9	100	9,365	4,040.6	424.7	125	2,076	95.2	26.1
Scioto	D	D	D	D	48	1,312	799.9	65.0	137	2,556	117.7	35.2
Seneca	51	286	29.3	10.7	68	4,355	1,367.0	209.0	103	2,011	86.6	24.4
Shelby	49	327	57.0	19.7	123	13,631	9,069.5	765.6	81	1,394	74.8	18.3
Stark	D	D	D	D	473	24,308	11,181.6	1,292.7	798	15,665	745.8	214.7
Summit	D	D	D	D	779	28,652	9,410.7	1,574.2	1,243	23,496	1,190.1	335.6
Trumbull	266	1,937	193.7	70.8	205	10,410	6,017.7	657.3	384	6,943	300.3	84.8
Tuscarawas	D	D	D	D	206	7,368	2,639.7	382.1	206	3,009	135.6	39.0
Union	101	3,224	1,079.3	300.3	53	7,285	10,397.7	505.3	79	1,624	84.7	24.3
Van Wert	28	384	34.5	13.8	40	3,186	1,387.9	144.2	45	809	31.2	8.2
Vinton	6	19	1.5	0.5	17	453	109.1	20.2	D	D	D	D
Warren	533	4,641	747.1	257.3	215	11,739	4,514.1	669.4	378	8,669	463.2	133.3
Washington	82	716	62.0	27.2	78	3,178	2,421.7	224.4	122	2,254	105.8	31.5
Wayne	142	2,044	128.4	108.7	274	12,270	4,199.4	640.1	189	3,390	157.9	47.1
Williams	32	203	12.7	8.0	109	7,349	2,215.0	344.5	71	978	46.3	12.5
Wood	D	D	D	D	181	12,099	4,609.8	729.8	318	7,038	308.1	88.2
Wyandot	29	77	10.8	2.5	35	3,464	978.2	175.1	47	426	18.4	5.0
OKLAHOMA	D	D	11,118.3	D	3,376	123,138	61,143.3	6,740.0	8,397	159,826	9,250.8	2,469.9
Adair	20	67	6.1	1.8	18	873	406.2	34.6	21	283	13.5	3.7
Alfalfa	9	30	2.7	1.0	4	30	4.9	0.9	12	D	2.7	D
Atoka	16	50	4.4	1.5	14	118	26.9	5.1	24	314	14.8	3.9
Beaver	9	29	2.7	0.9	NA	NA	NA	NA	D	D	D	0.3
Beckham	67	243	35.3	11.1	D	258	D	17.7	69	799	42.8	10.9
Blaine	14	49	6.4	1.4	9	380	220.5	28.4	21	142	8.1	1.9
Bryan	57	282	39.4	11.7	36	1,240	323.4	60.9	69	1,327	67.6	17.4
Caddo	35	519	50.5	25.8	14	79	53.2	3.4	44	402	17.8	4.9
Canadian	260	828	133.5	51.5	79	3,130	1,186.4	156.0	222	4,416	231.5	60.6
Carter	D	D	D	D	42	2,881	3,275.0	191.4	112	2,055	106.0	28.5
Cherokee	D	D	D	D	19	117	18.9	4.7	84	1,188	58.8	16.2
Choctaw	D	D	D	D	10	79	17.7	3.1	26	273	12.2	3.2
Cimarron	3	10	2.1	0.4	NA	NA	NA	NA	11	69	3.6	0.8
Cleveland	D	D	D	D	125	3,215	1,646.3	165.3	596	12,444	650.0	181.3
Coal	3	14	1.9	0.4	5	73	11.8	3.0	8	56	3.0	0.7
Comanche	D	D	D	D	D	D	D	D	D	D	D	D
Cotton	10	19	1.3	0.6	NA	NA	NA	NA	D	D	D	D
Craig	24	69	11.1	2.5	12	156	32.3	5.6	31	375	19.4	4.9
Creek	106	344	46.4	15.7	115	3,563	1,161.3	201.4	91	1,290	61.0	16.2
Custer	D	D	D	D	29	818	375.5	41.3	77	1,223	67.7	17.1
Delaware	53	335	40.5	18.3	26	468	86.7	23.1	79	1,784	198.5	42.7
Dewey	D	D	D	0.4	5	62	30.7	4.8	D	D	D	1.7
Ellis	8	27	2.1	0.7	NA	NA	NA	NA	5	88	2.6	0.9
Garfield	119	581	73.0	28.4	57	2,357	1,240.8	139.3	134	2,422	128.3	32.8
Garvin	54	149	17.3	6.0	25	1,016	1,973.1	69.4	55	729	39.6	9.8
Grady	98	343	40.9	14.1	62	1,475	697.9	57.7	80	1,102	62.7	15.9
Grant	5	16	2.0	0.7	4	9	1.6	0.3	6	28	1.1	0.3
Greer	D	D	D	2.3	D	D	D	D	4	48	1.4	0.4
Harmon	D	D	D	0.1	NA	NA	NA	NA	4	D	0.6	D
Harper	9	34	3.4	1.3	NA	NA	NA	NA	5	D	1.1	D
Haskell	18	45	3.7	1.0	D	81	D	4.1	D	D	D	D
Hughes	9	36	2.5	1.3	7	38	22.2	1.8	13	96	4.4	1.1
Jackson	D	D	D	D	11	891	388.5	42.1	55	1,123	47.0	14.5
Jefferson	7	36	6.3	1.5	4	7	1.7	0.4	13	D	4.0	D
Johnston	9	22	2.2	0.6	9	541	75.0	18.0	D	D	D	D
Kay	D	D	D	D	53	2,856	7,241.2	190.9	112	1,801	114.1	26.9
Kingfisher	29	259	24.1	10.0	14	482	131.8	21.1	36	343	19.5	4.9

STATE County	Health care and social assistance, 2017				Other services, 2017				Nonemployer businesses, 2019		Value of residential construction authorized by building permits, 2021	
	Number of establish-ments	Number of employees	Receipts (mil dol)	Annual payroll (mil dol)	Number of establish-ments	Number of employees	Receipts (mil dol)	Annual payroll (mil dol)	Number	Receipts (mil dol)	New construction ($1,000)	Number of housing units
	159	160	161	162	163	164	165	166	167	168	169	170
OHIO—Cont'd												
Ottawa	92	1,842	145.5	58.7	81	305	37.6	11.1	3,031	140.1	58,215	172
Paulding	28	552	36.6	15.3	20	74	7.1	1.6	1,049	40.8	6,947	29
Perry	D	D	D	23.3	27	127	12.9	2.2	2,049	85.9	10,486	47
Pickaway	88	1,890	193.1	72.5	45	138	17.0	4.3	3,445	143.3	69,927	262
Pike	56	1,582	146.0	52.2	18	62	8.1	1.4	1,446	67.3	6,919	29
Portage	265	6,348	508.0	215.2	229	1,520	148.1	43.4	10,744	487.9	112,597	427
Preble	62	1,413	89.0	38.6	52	248	27.6	7.3	2,471	113.3	11,791	48
Putnam	59	1,075	63.1	25.8	52	274	33.1	7.8	2,147	83.8	15,212	47
Richland	375	8,617	836.7	335.5	195	1,099	108.4	27.4	7,134	330.0	33,046	115
Ross	163	5,004	733.3	262.7	84	605	53.0	16.5	3,890	170.2	3,066	15
Sandusky	188	2,922	271.0	105.7	92	570	50.0	15.1	3,095	116.1	12,507	52
Scioto	219	7,527	765.1	287.4	75	297	32.8	7.0	3,670	125.9	380	4
Seneca	131	2,319	185.5	68.9	100	410	38.8	8.8	2,965	119.1	6,674	48
Shelby	94	2,069	210.7	74.4	60	412	41.4	11.5	2,746	125.1	23,850	75
Stark	992	28,654	2,769.8	1,151.2	648	4,677	587.5	151.3	24,956	1,091.7	199,947	952
Summit	1,518	54,081	5,512.0	2,485.6	1,098	7,441	1,546.7	242.3	39,415	1,761.8	168,363	788
Trumbull	540	11,213	1,329.6	506.7	278	1,524	124.2	37.7	13,201	604.3	20,414	120
Tuscarawas	201	5,333	416.4	167.0	175	1,080	120.2	30.0	6,245	302.0	15,979	64
Union	83	1,814	221.9	79.1	79	389	50.7	13.4	4,192	200.4	330,068	1,253
Van Wert	68	1,722	154.7	60.1	45	255	22.6	4.5	1,673	76.8	10,631	37
Vinton	17	286	14.7	6.0	8	41	4.8	1.0	609	27.8	130	2
Warren	484	10,712	1,091.4	418.9	299	2,270	221.0	69.7	18,428	948.2	397,961	1,406
Washington	141	5,211	660.8	205.8	103	465	45.9	12.2	3,731	166.6	1,063	5
Wayne	248	5,953	511.0	221.8	155	846	102.7	23.0	9,242	476.5	55,065	189
Williams	71	1,774	161.0	78.1	63	356	35.5	8.9	2,159	96.5	7,025	31
Wood	290	6,193	484.1	205.6	210	1,519	143.8	45.9	7,946	363.9	102,281	547
Wyandot	44	890	76.2	29.8	55	250	26.2	6.9	1,317	59.0	14,732	70
OKLAHOMA	11,035	226,462	27,031.0	9,952.8	5,565	31,947	4,933.6	1,083.6	296,422	14,236.8	3,454,208	14,733
Adair	21	500	50.6	18.1	D	D	D	0.3	1,361	49.7	800	7
Alfalfa	11	133	9.2	4.1	D	D	1.4	D	366	11.8	0	0
Atoka	22	374	21.3	9.0	D	D	D	1.2	966	51.6	150	1
Beaver	5	D	8.8	D	D	D	5.1	D	432	21.6	380	1
Beckham	84	1,011	103.9	38.1	35	153	27.6	5.6	1,723	99.5	1,385	5
Blaine	26	369	27.1	12.5	D	D	D	D	674	32.1	300	1
Bryan	133	2,161	268.6	80.4	36	155	18.1	4.5	3,096	160.0	18,934	140
Caddo	46	730	51.2	21.7	21	101	21.6	5.1	1,572	64.8	1,010	4
Canadian	265	2,858	256.2	104.3	170	701	79.4	21.0	12,210	563.7	125,508	533
Carter	228	3,790	356.8	167.8	92	821	153.7	34.8	3,453	171.0	10,178	54
Cherokee	109	2,974	316.8	134.5	46	227	21.6	5.4	2,930	121.6	15,935	160
Choctaw	59	1,376	103.3	39.2	D	D	D	D	1,017	45.7	1,800	15
Cimarron	D	D	D	D	D	D	0.7	D	219	12.9	0	0
Cleveland	795	12,647	1,344.1	539.9	320	1,696	307.1	50.6	22,653	1,056.1	290,674	1,147
Coal	11	191	12.3	4.9	D	D	4.3	D	426	29.2	875	11
Comanche	D	D	D	D	145	742	78.1	22.1	5,263	228.3	19,859	114
Cotton	D	D	D	D	4	10	1.4	0.4	290	9.9	666	3
Craig	67	1,005	74.5	38.5	18	88	8.1	2.7	919	41.4	14,000	7
Creek	108	2,409	185.8	71.5	78	286	33.1	8.1	4,992	218.5	30,485	215
Custer	109	1,492	127.3	48.3	48	257	32.5	9.1	2,227	113.3	5,569	16
Delaware	78	1,334	125.8	45.8	52	250	24.8	6.5	2,828	151.4	11,705	52
Dewey	7	48	3.0	1.2	D	D	D	1.4	484	24.7	NA	NA
Ellis	10	D	11.8	D	D	D	1.4	D	333	13.8	222	2
Garfield	197	3,778	386.2	141.0	108	545	63.1	15.2	4,345	174.7	11,007	35
Garvin	71	1,063	73.8	31.4	29	123	17.5	5.1	2,194	112.0	717	3
Grady	D	D	D	D	D	D	D	D	4,002	199.0	44,228	237
Grant	7	145	9.0	3.3	D	D	5.6	D	359	15.0	1,171	5
Greer	9	261	16.4	5.7	4	5	0.7	0.1	263	13.8	263	1
Harmon	6	127	11.5	4.4	NA	NA	NA	NA	146	7.3	NA	NA
Harper	8	D	6.2	D	D	D	D	0.4	308	11.8	0	0
Haskell	35	774	53.9	22.2	D	D	D	D	989	40.5	185	2
Hughes	37	754	35.6	16.1	12	22	2.6	0.6	715	30.4	725	5
Jackson	57	1,368	128.8	53.0	28	112	10.6	2.8	1,392	61.9	4,237	30
Jefferson	12	259	27.2	9.7	NA	NA	NA	NA	420	15.0	NA	NA
Johnston	21	1,818	97.7	37.3	11	32	29.4	1.7	658	23.4	0	0
Kay	132	2,119	200.0	73.0	73	409	40.7	10.6	2,445	93.1	2,048	11
Kingfisher	39	514	38.8	14.6	D	D	D	D	1,569	93.1	7,039	24

Table B. States and Counties — **Government Employment and Payroll, and Local Government Finances**

STATE County	Government employment and payroll, 2017: Full-time equivalent employees	Government employment and payroll, 2017: March payroll (dollars)	March payroll (percent of total): Administration, judicial, and legal	March payroll (percent of total): Police and corrections	March payroll (percent of total): Fire protection	March payroll (percent of total): Highways and transportation	March payroll (percent of total): Health and welfare	March payroll (percent of total): Natural resources and utilities	March payroll (percent of total): Education and libraries	Local government finances, 2017, General revenue: Total (mil dol)	General revenue: Intergovernmental (mil dol)	Taxes: Total (mil dol)	Taxes: Per capita[1] (dollars): Total	Taxes: Per capita[1] (dollars): Property
	171	172	173	174	175	176	177	178	179	180	181	182	183	184
OHIO—Cont'd														
Ottawa	1,632	6,665,839	8.6	10.0	3.8	5.6	12.8	7.7	49.7	174.1	49.1	84.7	2,085	1,662
Paulding	914	3,212,384	6.4	3.7	0.3	3.1	24.6	3.9	55.9	85.3	30.4	26.8	1,425	920
Perry	1,338	4,367,873	8.0	4.4	0.7	5.2	12.9	2.7	65.5	120.5	75.8	32.6	907	730
Pickaway	2,259	9,272,269	4.8	5.9	1.8	2.5	26.4	2.8	55.5	274.7	87.2	83.9	1,453	944
Pike	1,321	4,492,199	8.8	4.9	0.2	4.0	16.0	1.7	63.5	119.0	79.6	24.7	880	650
Portage	5,369	22,101,287	7.5	10.2	5.0	6.1	6.3	4.8	58.8	595.5	218.7	286.7	1,764	1,194
Preble	1,642	5,078,832	10.5	7.9	0.9	5.0	8.1	4.0	61.2	153.9	64.2	60.6	1,474	840
Putnam	1,518	4,779,575	8.8	15.5	0.1	2.2	3.9	2.3	67.0	131.9	57.3	52.6	1,554	959
Richland	4,967	18,600,904	8.1	8.4	4.6	2.9	15.2	4.0	55.0	485.5	220.4	191.9	1,593	961
Ross	2,881	10,938,361	7.0	6.5	2.7	2.5	14.0	2.9	62.8	277.9	141.6	90.4	1,169	719
Sandusky	2,131	8,612,401	7.2	8.7	1.6	3.4	7.0	6.9	64.5	229.5	99.4	94.0	1,591	929
Scioto	2,998	10,522,705	7.0	7.2	2.6	3.2	9.1	4.6	65.4	280.4	179.4	65.8	867	633
Seneca	2,133	7,696,532	8.3	10.3	4.6	3.7	7.2	5.1	60.2	191.2	86.9	69.1	1,250	749
Shelby	1,507	5,836,231	6.0	5.4	4.0	2.5	5.8	5.2	70.3	210.0	85.8	85.1	1,747	870
Stark	14,288	55,719,833	7.5	8.6	4.2	4.4	8.2	5.1	60.9	1,374.9	607.3	560.3	1,506	1,023
Summit	19,664	87,775,101	7.9	10.4	6.1	5.8	8.9	6.5	52.8	2,522.8	804.7	1,251.5	2,311	1,375
Trumbull	7,910	28,504,175	8.0	8.3	4.3	3.0	10.8	4.6	60.0	676.1	299.6	259.1	1,294	927
Tuscarawas	3,469	12,598,587	10.2	6.3	3.5	4.1	5.4	8.6	59.6	364.7	143.8	132.9	1,440	997
Union	2,255	10,065,693	6.6	7.3	4.4	2.7	35.0	2.7	37.0	318.8	63.0	114.5	2,016	1,294
Van Wert	1,023	3,549,200	8.2	7.5	2.7	4.2	3.3	4.5	66.2	122.6	46.9	46.0	1,627	973
Vinton	523	1,837,655	13.5	2.8	1.6	5.8	8.9	1.5	65.3	48.6	32.7	11.2	855	755
Warren	7,582	29,873,176	7.1	8.6	5.1	2.5	7.0	3.9	63.9	748.8	240.0	366.5	1,603	1,294
Washington	2,025	6,959,332	9.8	10.2	2.7	5.0	8.7	4.2	59.0	212.5	88.7	88.8	1,468	1,008
Wayne	4,842	18,900,576	5.4	5.5	2.4	3.9	26.8	4.0	51.7	506.9	149.4	168.7	1,452	1,023
Williams	1,637	5,528,317	7.9	6.3	0.8	4.7	14.3	7.2	57.0	157.8	64.6	60.9	1,660	884
Wood	4,973	20,084,911	8.8	10.6	3.6	3.4	8.9	7.2	55.6	547.3	157.2	287.3	2,202	1,393
Wyandot	1,136	4,142,231	8.0	6.9	0.5	3.1	35.5	4.6	41.1	132.0	34.3	34.5	1,563	955
OKLAHOMA	X	X	X	X	X	X	X	X	X	X	X	X	X	X
Adair	956	2,957,411	6.2	6.2	0.1	3.9	1.4	4.7	76.2	57.4	41.8	8.4	380	239
Alfalfa	317	953,473	3.7	7.2	0.0	17.5	0.0	9.0	54.7	22.4	9.8	10.2	1,726	1,334
Atoka	499	1,550,570	4.0	4.9	0.0	1.1	20.9	4.2	63.9	57.5	37.5	10.0	727	387
Beaver	364	1,311,575	7.7	3.8	0.0	10.8	15.6	2.9	57.7	25.0	11.0	11.1	2,062	1,487
Beckham	856	2,534,945	7.0	11.6	4.0	6.4	4.1	6.6	58.0	85.4	26.9	39.3	1,804	925
Blaine	526	1,516,152	9.5	7.7	1.1	8.6	17.1	3.5	51.6	43.9	14.0	18.5	1,949	1,076
Bryan	1,778	6,176,213	5.0	8.6	2.4	3.4	1.9	5.8	71.6	127.1	50.3	44.6	959	483
Caddo	1,455	4,372,847	4.8	6.8	2.4	2.9	6.0	5.0	70.6	149.5	109.6	26.7	908	529
Canadian	4,034	12,941,499	5.0	12.3	4.2	2.0	0.1	4.4	71.2	345.9	132.8	166.1	1,187	748
Carter	1,780	5,804,226	5.3	9.9	3.0	4.3	0.0	6.3	69.3	157.0	59.1	71.4	1,478	692
Cherokee	2,102	7,399,379	2.1	1.1	0.8	2.2	46.2	5.3	40.5	196.1	59.5	26.5	541	247
Choctaw	712	2,090,429	5.3	7.3	2.0	4.4	25.9	4.4	49.4	39.9	23.5	11.0	743	300
Cimarron	164	396,152	11.1	5.3	0.0	16.9	0.6	6.1	60.0	10.9	5.6	4.1	1,894	1,501
Cleveland	10,169	41,206,071	3.1	7.0	4.2	1.6	35.4	2.8	44.7	1,087.0	243.9	348.8	1,248	734
Coal	316	849,977	9.2	5.7	3.2	7.1	4.5	4.5	65.8	15.9	7.7	6.2	1,093	747
Comanche	5,989	21,027,993	3.7	6.4	3.2	2.0	36.8	3.9	43.1	591.3	144.0	113.0	928	422
Cotton	258	690,239	9.4	5.7	1.6	7.5	1.0	9.1	62.6	15.3	9.2	3.4	586	422
Craig	839	2,850,923	4.9	5.9	2.0	4.0	32.6	4.3	43.7	43.4	16.5	22.1	1,539	1,068
Creek	2,446	8,556,457	5.1	6.5	3.5	2.4	3.2	4.3	74.5	176.9	77.8	67.9	945	559
Custer	1,419	4,126,438	4.9	8.7	2.7	3.4	14.5	6.1	58.4	91.9	32.8	41.9	1,446	774
Delaware	1,352	3,655,341	6.1	7.1	1.1	3.8	0.7	4.5	74.9	89.7	46.6	34.6	812	507
Dewey	350	1,140,367	10.3	6.0	0.0	12.4	19.4	3.1	47.8	32.8	12.1	14.6	2,978	2,076
Ellis	266	870,927	9.0	6.2	0.0	13.1	2.3	2.9	65.8	24.5	12.4	8.1	2,041	1,682
Garfield	2,370	8,025,034	5.6	9.5	5.9	3.9	0.1	4.7	67.5	182.5	64.1	80.6	1,309	555
Garvin	1,447	4,063,190	5.4	6.9	1.8	4.5	28.0	6.2	46.4	103.0	34.4	29.1	1,045	582
Grady	1,930	6,362,126	4.6	5.0	2.8	3.2	30.7	2.6	49.2	130.5	49.5	58.0	1,058	604
Grant	264	792,064	10.2	6.8	0.1	18.2	1.0	10.4	52.9	20.4	4.7	12.3	2,797	1,757
Greer	246	883,154	7.5	6.3	2.0	0.8	5.3	5.9	71.3	17.9	10.2	3.9	669	382
Harmon	205	532,277	8.8	6.7	0.0	6.3	35.2	4.7	38.2	15.4	4.4	9.0	3,311	1,894
Harper	277	752,462	6.6	5.5	0.0	11.0	29.7	5.9	40.3	10.2	3.7	4.9	1,283	1,076
Haskell	442	1,327,720	5.9	10.9	0.0	6.4	1.8	1.1	70.6	44.5	27.7	11.4	899	541
Hughes	693	2,010,922	4.7	4.4	1.0	4.4	27.4	3.7	50.9	32.5	14.3	13.5	1,020	647
Jackson	1,708	6,396,652	3.3	5.1	2.1	2.0	49.1	5.3	32.4	146.1	31.4	22.9	912	353
Jefferson	365	1,102,831	5.6	3.8	0.8	3.6	16.1	12.1	56.2	23.6	11.0	4.0	656	404
Johnston	405	1,241,425	7.1	6.2	0.7	3.3	3.1	6.0	72.7	26.7	12.9	9.5	854	522
Kay	1,922	5,806,528	6.9	9.7	7.7	4.5	1.6	12.8	54.4	140.0	48.8	62.0	1,396	708
Kingfisher	723	2,133,869	8.2	7.0	3.4	5.3	0.1	5.0	69.3	70.3	19.8	40.1	2,555	2,071

1. Based on the resident population estimated as of July 1 of the year shown.

STATE County	Local government finances, 2017 (cont.)									Government employment, 2020			Individual income tax returns, 2019		
	Direct general expenditure							Debt outstanding							
			Percent of total for:												
	Total (mil dol)	Per capita[1] (dollars)	Education	Health and hospitals	Police protection	Public welfare	Highways	Total (mil dol)	Per capita[1] (dollars)	Federal civilian	Federal military	State and local	Number of returns	Mean adjusted gross income	Mean income tax
	185	186	187	188	189	190	191	192	193	194	195	196	197	198	199
OHIO—Cont'd															
Ottawa	172.4	4,243	41.1	2.9	8.1	16.3	5.8	108.3	2,667	277	144	2,004	22,040	63,435	6,654
Paulding	85.0	4,513	52.1	25.8	3.3	0.0	7.5	33.0	1,752	50	47	996	9,210	48,597	3,609
Perry	118.4	3,292	63.6	5.7	3.4	6.3	5.5	46.2	1,284	67	90	1,463	15,760	51,048	4,131
Pickaway	282.1	4,885	38.5	25.5	3.8	2.6	5.1	133.5	2,312	106	136	3,426	26,160	54,171	5,115
Pike	122.7	4,369	58.7	3.9	5.9	5.2	9.4	34.6	1,231	68	68	1,321	11,410	47,722	3,717
Portage	552.7	3,402	51.4	6.3	6.7	4.2	4.1	275.1	1,693	374	408	13,261	78,060	63,041	6,735
Preble	152.6	3,712	52.8	5.3	5.1	6.0	7.0	72.1	1,754	81	102	1,650	19,550	51,499	4,087
Putnam	124.9	3,689	60.0	0.0	4.3	0.8	13.4	72.8	2,149	70	84	1,547	17,210	63,222	5,683
Richland	493.6	4,099	50.7	9.7	5.4	5.5	6.3	175.1	1,454	652	287	6,766	58,590	49,537	4,263
Ross	286.5	3,707	62.2	0.7	4.1	5.2	4.7	290.5	3,758	1,674	180	4,774	33,640	51,152	4,392
Sandusky	256.6	4,342	49.8	5.3	7.7	5.4	5.1	232.6	3,937	121	144	2,610	30,080	50,567	4,108
Scioto	275.1	3,621	58.8	5.9	3.2	4.7	4.3	340.5	4,482	191	180	5,376	29,760	49,445	4,281
Seneca	222.1	4,018	47.9	6.8	6.7	2.1	1.9	731.9	13,242	125	132	2,508	26,940	49,308	3,912
Shelby	204.3	4,191	50.8	0.6	5.3	9.4	8.6	270.8	5,556	78	120	2,259	24,280	57,896	5,388
Stark	1,393.5	3,746	52.3	8.6	5.8	5.4	6.1	485.2	1,304	993	941	17,535	186,990	57,492	5,790
Summit	2,588.8	4,781	42.4	4.7	5.6	4.2	4.1	2,109.5	3,896	2,056	1,333	26,681	275,680	65,806	7,839
Trumbull	710.9	3,549	53.6	4.3	6.4	5.8	3.5	455.9	2,276	517	517	8,450	99,930	48,382	4,136
Tuscarawas	378.3	4,098	48.8	5.3	4.7	3.6	4.9	171.5	1,858	268	227	4,812	44,910	54,670	4,918
Union	305.1	5,372	28.6	34.6	4.0	1.6	3.4	426.6	7,511	92	145	3,771	29,070	89,465	11,521
Van Wert	113.3	4,006	58.1	3.5	4.9	0.2	6.1	68.4	2,419	51	71	1,454	14,230	53,058	4,305
Vinton	52.5	4,015	52.3	4.4	3.4	10.6	10.5	10.8	829	21	32	611	5,340	45,098	3,135
Warren	774.9	3,388	57.8	0.2	3.7	5.3	7.5	665.8	2,911	351	607	9,484	117,810	91,648	12,154
Washington	210.6	3,481	50.2	3.7	7.6	6.8	8.5	184.2	3,045	227	146	2,655	28,950	55,161	5,148
Wayne	546.5	4,704	41.1	28.9	3.6	4.3	4.3	151.6	1,305	278	282	6,396	54,440	57,670	5,164
Williams	196.3	5,349	51.3	0.7	3.8	7.4	5.7	105.7	2,879	81	89	2,001	18,540	50,128	4,086
Wood	597.0	4,577	54.2	6.8	4.1	3.3	3.2	620.7	4,759	226	333	10,664	63,200	68,858	7,628
Wyandot	136.6	6,189	33.3	32.7	5.2	5.5	1.8	45.5	2,061	55	54	1,405	11,170	54,383	4,680
OKLAHOMA	X	X	X	X	X	X	X	X	X	51,081	35,914	282,549	1,703,670	61,340	6,525
Adair	58.5	2,646	74.0	0.6	1.0	0.0	7.4	5.3	239	46	79	1,041	7,980	37,270	2,154
Alfalfa	20.3	3,433	80.6	0.0	3.6	0.0	3.9	13.0	2,203	33	18	558	2,090	55,491	5,365
Atoka	62.8	4,555	35.7	4.8	4.5	0.0	8.6	31.3	2,269	32	47	1,110	5,430	43,347	3,133
Beaver	24.1	4,489	53.5	3.1	3.7	0.0	25.2	4.5	841	31	19	450	2,180	46,375	3,759
Beckham	79.3	3,642	50.3	3.2	5.0	1.3	7.7	63.9	2,933	58	70	1,242	8,560	52,822	5,141
Blaine	42.0	4,415	47.2	15.5	5.2	0.8	10.1	13.9	1,466	51	34	677	3,880	66,696	7,927
Bryan	108.6	2,336	59.5	3.5	7.4	0.0	5.7	62.6	1,347	99	172	8,833	19,460	48,326	3,969
Caddo	98.0	3,339	54.9	1.8	5.9	0.0	10.9	27.1	922	521	96	2,207	10,770	46,895	3,796
Canadian	313.8	2,242	68.3	0.6	6.5	0.0	3.4	298.6	2,133	580	545	5,982	68,880	70,276	6,863
Carter	151.6	3,140	52.4	0.8	7.7	0.0	7.9	70.8	1,467	109	172	3,251	21,760	54,559	5,298
Cherokee	188.2	3,850	36.3	51.6	2.2	0.0	1.8	95.9	1,962	182	170	8,048	18,480	47,220	3,705
Choctaw	35.0	2,361	64.4	4.5	3.2	0.0	8.3	20.1	1,356	50	52	1,267	5,770	40,331	2,830
Cimarron	9.4	4,354	59.0	0.9	4.4	0.2	17.9	1.6	751	17	8	221	1,070	39,924	2,964
Cleveland	1,043.0	3,731	35.2	34.9	4.5	0.0	4.0	980.7	3,508	859	1,037	23,059	128,410	65,408	6,970
Coal	14.2	2,527	84.0	3.8	0.2	0.0	0.9	0.8	134	16	20	355	2,100	42,991	3,033
Comanche	594.4	4,880	30.0	43.1	3.7	0.0	4.8	298.4	2,450	3,954	13,027	9,485	48,730	49,518	4,027
Cotton	17.1	2,920	52.1	0.7	3.2	0.0	21.4	9.5	1,623	26	20	1,023	2,410	44,256	3,285
Craig	31.7	2,212	79.3	0.3	5.1	0.3	1.8	11.1	771	54	47	1,352	5,710	42,939	3,128
Creek	167.1	2,324	59.6	3.5	6.0	0.0	5.8	165.9	2,308	389	253	2,881	30,650	58,041	5,611
Custer	91.1	3,143	54.6	0.0	6.2	0.3	8.1	86.3	2,977	221	98	2,556	11,720	60,237	6,310
Delaware	86.5	2,026	72.1	0.5	6.7	0.0	2.5	53.2	1,247	88	154	2,424	16,780	50,796	4,708
Dewey	29.5	6,023	49.2	1.3	4.0	0.0	20.0	11.9	2,425	32	17	416	2,130	57,098	5,468
Ellis	41.8	10,526	29.1	3.5	3.2	0.0	31.5	7.1	1,794	22	14	384	1,640	55,171	4,717
Garfield	170.7	2,772	59.3	3.2	6.6	0.1	1.8	126.3	2,051	517	1,511	3,247	27,050	57,094	5,516
Garvin	106.6	3,825	43.2	23.8	4.4	0.0	9.0	36.6	1,315	86	98	1,287	11,150	52,482	4,591
Grady	132.1	2,410	61.2	2.8	6.0	0.0	9.7	83.3	1,520	99	197	2,677	22,820	63,924	6,081
Grant	20.4	4,656	71.7	1.2	4.7	0.0	2.5	7.0	1,601	27	15	314	1,900	50,437	5,142
Greer	19.6	3,382	42.8	5.1	7.3	0.0	20.5	8.7	1,494	27	16	476	1,830	39,324	2,683
Harmon	10.1	3,744	45.7	0.6	7.4	0.0	18.7	1.2	458	21	9	268	920	39,141	3,468
Harper	11.7	3,094	63.4	2.3	4.5	0.0	9.5	5.7	1,518	24	13	377	1,490	44,976	3,719
Haskell	31.7	2,492	64.3	0.0	4.9	0.2	3.9	17.4	1,365	53	45	546	4,550	40,305	2,844
Hughes	33.1	2,499	63.1	0.0	5.8	0.0	10.8	31.5	2,377	38	42	920	4,800	39,165	3,035
Jackson	141.2	5,622	26.1	51.0	5.2	0.0	2.3	8.0	317	1,501	1,454	2,275	10,510	52,237	4,503
Jefferson	20.4	3,315	56.8	1.9	4.5	0.0	15.6	62.7	10,169	30	21	431	2,220	36,115	2,620
Johnston	26.2	2,354	64.6	5.6	6.0	0.0	3.6	10.4	934	44	38	614	4,170	46,261	3,398
Kay	154.1	3,470	44.3	2.1	8.0	0.0	9.7	96.4	2,172	123	153	4,120	18,890	52,664	4,797
Kingfisher	69.8	4,447	58.6	0.6	5.8	0.0	16.2	26.8	1,708	45	58	983	6,950	81,584	10,446

1. Based on the resident population estimated as of July 1 of the year shown.

State / county code	CBSA code[1]	County Type code[2]	STATE County	Land area[3] (sq. mi)	Population, 2021: Total persons 2021	Population, 2021: Rank	Population, 2021: Per square mile	Race alone or in combination, not Hispanic or Latino (percent): White	Black	American Indian, Alaska Native	Asian and Pacific Islancer	Percent Hispanic or Latino[4]	Age (percent): Under 5 years	5 to 17 years	18 to 24 years	25 to 34 years	35 to 44 years	45 to 54 years
				1	2	3	4	5	6	7	8	9	10	11	12	13	14	15
			OKLAHOMA—Cont'd															
40075		6	Kiowa	1,015.1	8,410	2,540	8.3	76.4	5.7	9.3	1.0	12.2	6.3	13.8	11.9	11.0	11.2	10.5
40077		7	Latimer	722.1	9,427	2,457	13.1	69.1	2.6	30.4	1.4	4.9	5.8	12.6	13.5	11.0	11.0	10.9
40079		2	Le Flore	1,589.4	48,476	1,013	30.5	75.3	2.7	18.9	1.4	7.7	6.1	14.0	12.9	12.2	12.3	11.8
40081	36420	1	Lincoln	952.4	33,829	1,335	35.5	86.6	3.0	11.5	1.1	3.7	5.4	13.6	11.9	11.5	12.3	11.9
40083	36420	1	Logan	743.7	50,885	984	68.4	80.3	8.9	6.3	1.2	7.7	5.3	12.8	14.2	11.0	13.5	12.2
40085	11620	9	Love	513.9	10,216	2,394	19.9	72.8	3.6	9.5	1.0	17.6	5.9	14.3	12.7	12.3	12.1	11.9
40087	36420	1	McClain	570.7	43,516	1,112	76.3	82.3	1.9	11.1	1.1	9.0	5.6	15.0	12.4	11.6	14.3	12.5
40089		7	McCurtain	1,850.8	30,884	1,407	16.7	66.1	9.6	21.9	3.0	6.7	6.7	15.0	12.2	12.2	11.4	11.8
40091		6	McIntosh	618.3	19,245	1,862	31.1	73.9	4.5	25.5	1.2	3.1	4.9	11.5	10.4	10.0	10.8	11.5
40093		9	Major	955.0	7,668	2,599	8.0	85.6	1.8	3.8	1.3	10.4	6.2	15.0	11.4	9.8	12.3	10.4
40095		6	Marshall	371.5	15,594	2,053	42.0	69.3	2.9	14.4	0.9	18.7	6.1	13.0	11.6	10.5	10.8	11.5
40097		6	Mayes	655.4	39,159	1,199	59.7	72.0	1.4	31.1	1.0	3.9	5.8	13.5	12.0	12.1	12.1	12.2
40099		7	Murray	416.4	13,718	2,175	32.9	75.9	2.8	19.8	1.0	7.5	5.7	13.5	11.9	10.8	12.4	12.0
40101	34780	4	Muskogee	810.6	66,146	811	81.6	61.4	12.5	26.3	1.3	7.2	6.2	14.0	13.5	12.6	12.7	11.5
40103		6	Noble	731.7	10,933	2,345	14.9	84.0	3.1	11.9	1.1	4.6	5.7	13.5	11.6	10.8	12.2	12.1
40105		6	Nowata	565.8	9,303	2,466	16.4	74.3	4.2	26.9	1.0	3.5	5.8	13.3	10.9	11.5	11.9	12.1
40107		6	Okfuskee	618.5	11,197	2,331	18.1	65.9	8.3	26.8	1.4	4.7	6.0	12.5	12.0	12.5	13.0	13.1
40109	36420	1	Oklahoma	708.9	798,575	81	1,126.5	58.8	17.3	6.1	4.7	18.5	6.8	14.4	13.3	14.9	13.6	11.2
40111	46140	2	Okmulgee	697.4	36,843	1,258	52.8	68.9	10.0	24.1	1.3	4.8	5.8	13.7	13.5	12.3	11.6	11.4
40113	46140	2	Osage	2,246.6	45,772	1,066	20.4	69.2	12.0	20.8	0.8	4.4	4.8	12.6	11.5	11.5	11.9	11.8
40115	33060	6	Ottawa	470.8	30,340	1,427	64.4	70.6	2.1	26.9	2.3	6.2	6.5	14.8	13.8	12.3	11.0	11.3
40117	46140	2	Pawnee	568.4	15,741	2,048	27.7	81.0	2.3	18.6	1.0	3.9	5.6	13.7	11.7	11.1	11.9	12.6
40119	44660	4	Payne	684.9	81,989	704	119.7	81.4	5.2	8.8	5.3	5.0	4.8	10.7	29.9	12.9	10.8	8.6
40121	32540	5	Pittsburg	1,305.5	43,633	1,107	33.4	74.6	4.4	22.0	1.0	5.9	5.7	13.1	11.3	13.0	12.5	11.4
40123	10220	7	Pontotoc	720.4	38,163	1,218	53.0	70.3	4.0	26.2	1.7	6.2	6.6	14.0	14.9	13.3	12.3	10.5
40125	43060	4	Pottawatomie	787.8	73,019	756	92.7	76.9	4.7	18.2	1.6	5.8	5.9	13.5	13.5	12.7	12.7	12.2
40127		9	Pushmataha	1,395.5	10,815	2,359	7.7	74.7	2.2	24.1	0.8	4.5	5.2	12.4	10.8	10.9	11.4	11.1
40129		9	Roger Mills	1,141.1	3,386	2,932	3.0	84.4	1.9	6.9	0.9	8.3	5.2	13.8	11.8	10.0	12.3	10.7
40131	46140	2	Rogers	675.7	96,695	630	143.1	78.1	2.0	20.7	2.3	5.5	5.6	13.4	12.5	12.5	12.6	12.6
40133		7	Seminole	632.8	23,567	1,659	37.2	69.6	6.1	25.3	1.4	5.8	6.0	14.0	13.7	11.1	12.1	11.5
40135	22900	2	Sequoyah	673.6	39,508	1,193	58.7	69.8	2.9	30.7	1.4	5.0	6.5	13.3	12.1	12.1	11.4	12.4
40137	20340	4	Stephens	870.2	43,129	1,124	49.6	83.0	3.0	9.2	1.2	8.4	5.9	12.9	11.7	11.5	12.2	11.3
40139	25100	7	Texas	2,041.3	20,865	1,769	10.2	43.5	4.9	1.4	3.3	48.1	8.3	15.7	15.5	13.1	12.8	11.4
40141		6	Tillman	871.1	7,076	2,655	8.1	59.8	8.0	5.8	1.1	28.7	5.6	13.7	12.7	11.1	11.6	11.5
40143	46140	2	Tulsa	570.2	672,858	101	1,180.0	65.2	12.2	10.3	4.7	13.9	6.7	14.2	13.0	14.3	13.4	11.6
40145	46140	2	Wagoner	561.9	84,050	685	149.6	76.2	4.9	16.2	2.6	7.6	5.6	13.8	11.8	13.1	13.7	12.2
40147	12780	4	Washington	415.5	52,772	961	127.0	77.3	4.0	16.3	2.8	6.8	6.1	14.0	12.1	12.2	12.4	11.1
40149		7	Washita	1,003.1	10,915	2,347	10.9	84.8	2.2	4.8	0.9	10.4	6.2	14.7	11.3	11.5	12.4	10.6
40151		7	Woods	1,286.5	8,583	2,528	6.7	85.2	4.7	4.1	1.7	7.1	5.7	12.2	19.6	13.4	11.8	8.7
40153	49260	7	Woodward	1,242.8	20,205	1,806	16.3	80.1	2.5	4.3	1.1	14.2	6.2	14.0	12.4	13.6	13.7	11.7
41000		0	OREGON	95,988.0	4,246,155	X	44.2	77.4	2.9	2.4	7.0	14.0	5.0	11.7	12.0	14.1	14.0	12.2
41001		7	Baker	3,068.0	16,847	1,983	5.5	91.8	1.6	2.4	1.6	5.2	4.9	11.7	9.0	10.5	11.5	10.4
41003	18700	3	Benton	675.2	96,017	633	142.2	83.1	2.0	1.6	9.0	8.2	3.8	9.1	25.1	13.2	10.6	9.9
41005	38900	1	Clackamas	1,870.7	422,537	171	225.9	83.2	2.0	1.7	7.4	9.5	4.9	12.3	11.1	12.1	14.0	13.1
41007	11820	4	Clatsop	828.1	41,810	1,149	50.5	87.0	1.4	2.3	3.0	9.2	4.4	10.7	10.5	11.6	13.1	11.0
41009	38900	1	Columbia	658.7	53,074	957	80.6	90.3	1.4	2.9	2.8	6.2	4.9	11.8	10.6	11.9	13.1	13.0
41011	18300	5	Coos	1,596.1	64,999	831	40.7	88.2	1.1	5.1	2.6	7.2	4.5	10.5	9.4	10.8	11.3	10.9
41013	39260	6	Crook	2,978.9	25,739	1,576	8.6	89.5	0.9	2.5	1.3	8.0	5.3	11.3	9.5	10.7	11.5	11.6
41015	15060	7	Curry	1,628.4	23,683	1,655	14.5	88.3	1.0	4.5	1.8	8.0	3.6	8.3	7.0	8.7	9.2	10.1
41017	13460	3	Deschutes	3,017.6	204,801	338	67.9	88.6	1.0	1.8	2.7	8.6	4.7	11.1	10.1	13.3	14.1	12.7
41019	40700	4	Douglas	5,035.7	111,978	551	22.2	89.8	1.0	3.7	2.4	6.5	4.9	11.1	9.8	11.2	11.3	10.8
41021		9	Gilliam	1,204.7	2,005	3,040	1.7	88.9	1.3	2.7	1.7	7.9	4.3	12.6	8.6	8.5	10.9	10.4
41023		9	Grant	4,527.8	7,272	2,642	1.6	92.8	1.1	2.9	1.4	4.4	4.6	10.6	8.2	9.9	11.1	9.8
41025		7	Harney	10,134.4	7,575	2,609	0.7	88.8	1.9	5.5	1.4	5.6	4.8	11.6	10.0	11.5	11.9	10.6
41027	26220	6	Hood River	522.1	24,057	1,640	46.1	64.8	1.1	1.6	2.8	32.0	5.7	13.0	12.3	12.3	13.8	12.7
41029	32780	3	Jackson	2,783.3	223,734	313	80.4	82.0	1.5	2.4	3.1	14.3	5.0	12.0	10.6	12.5	12.7	11.3
41031		6	Jefferson	1,781.7	25,068	1,608	14.1	63.0	1.3	16.1	1.7	20.8	5.9	13.4	11.5	12.8	11.7	11.3
41033	24420	3	Josephine	1,638.6	88,346	668	53.9	88.4	1.1	3.1	2.3	8.3	4.7	11.1	9.8	11.2	11.1	10.9
41035	28900	5	Klamath	5,950.0	70,164	775	11.8	79.7	1.6	5.8	2.3	14.5	5.7	12.6	11.4	12.7	11.5	10.8
41037		7	Lake	8,138.6	8,276	2,558	1.0	86.0	1.6	3.9	1.8	10.2	4.4	11.8	9.1	10.3	11.8	12.3
41039	21660	2	Lane	4,554.1	383,189	191	84.1	84.6	2.1	2.8	5.1	9.8	4.3	10.3	15.4	13.2	12.7	11.1
41041	35440	5	Lincoln	981.0	50,862	985	51.8	84.5	1.3	5.2	2.6	10.0	3.8	9.3	8.8	9.0	10.8	11.0
41043	10540	3	Linn	2,289.3	129,839	500	56.7	86.4	1.3	2.8	2.6	10.2	5.8	12.6	11.5	13.7	12.7	11.5
41045	36620	6	Malheur	9,887.7	31,693	1,387	3.2	61.1	1.8	1.7	2.0	35.3	6.4	15.2	13.8	13.5	12.2	11.2
41047	41420	2	Marion	1,181.1	347,119	210	293.9	66.1	2.0	2.2	4.7	28.2	6.0	13.7	13.2	14.1	13.3	11.7

1. CBSA = Core Based Statistical Area. See Appendix A for explanation. See Appendix B for list of metropolitan areas with component counties. 2. County type code from the Economic Research Service of USDA Rural-Urban Continuum Codes. See Appendix A for definition. 3. Dry land or land partially or temporarily covered by water. 4. May be of any race.

STATE County	Population, 2021 (cont.): Age (percent) (cont.): 55 to 64 years	65 to 74 years	75 years and over	Percent female	Population change, 2000–2021: Total persons: 2010	2020	Percent change: 2010–2020	2020–2021	Components of change, 2020–2021: Births	Deaths	Net Migration	Households, 2016–2020: Number	Persons per household	Percent: Family house-holds	Female family house-holder[1]	One person
	16	17	18	19	20	21	22	23	24	25	26	27	28	29	30	31
OKLAHOMA—Cont'd																
Kiowa	15.4	12.1	7.8	49.9	9,446	8,509	-9.9	-1.2	116	191	-24	3,554	2.4	67.5	13.4	27.9
Latimer	13.5	11.1	10.5	48.6	11,154	9,444	-15.3	-0.2	121	182	43	4,083	2.4	71.2	12.4	25.8
Le Flore	12.9	10.8	7.1	49.5	50,384	48,129	-4.5	0.7	719	1,026	658	18,309	2.7	69.8	13.7	26.1
Lincoln	14.3	11.4	7.7	49.9	34,273	33,458	-2.4	1.1	430	543	488	13,022	2.7	69.2	10.7	27.2
Logan	13.8	10.7	6.4	50.0	41,848	49,555	18.4	2.7	607	584	1,319	15,668	2.9	72.8	9.6	22.8
Love	12.3	10.7	7.7	49.7	9,423	10,146	7.7	0.7	134	183	118	3,340	3.0	69.5	10.4	26.1
McClain	13.0	9.7	6.0	50.1	34,506	41,662	20.7	4.5	524	532	1,885	14,783	2.7	76.2	8.6	20.6
McCurtain	12.6	10.6	7.5	50.7	33,151	30,814	-7.0	0.2	535	625	159	12,651	2.6	70.9	14.1	26.5
McIntosh	15.5	14.6	10.8	50.5	20,252	18,941	-6.5	1.6	213	451	552	8,216	2.4	66.4	13.7	29.8
Major	13.5	12.1	9.2	50.3	7,527	7,782	3.4	-1.5	87	100	-101	3,064	2.5	71.2	5.6	25.5
Marshall	14.6	12.2	9.7	49.9	15,840	15,312	-3.3	1.8	247	271	308	6,384	2.6	71.8	11.7	24.7
Mayes	13.6	11.3	7.3	49.8	41,259	39,046	-5.4	0.3	537	788	364	16,071	2.5	70.7	11.5	25.2
Murray	13.7	11.5	8.4	49.4	13,488	13,904	3.1	-1.3	198	283	-102	5,207	2.6	67.2	8.8	29.3
Muskogee	12.5	10.2	6.7	51.0	70,990	66,339	-6.6	-0.3	1,005	1,376	167	26,535	2.4	64.7	15.3	31.7
Noble	13.8	11.7	8.6	50.6	11,561	10,924	-5.5	0.1	150	190	49	4,501	2.4	69.6	9.0	26.7
Nowata	15.0	11.2	8.3	50.1	10,536	9,320	-11.5	-0.2	109	200	75	4,128	2.4	69.9	11.7	27.9
Okfuskee	13.1	10.2	7.5	46.0	12,191	11,310	-7.2	-1.0	163	268	-7	4,036	2.6	71.8	12.8	24.8
Oklahoma	11.5	8.9	5.4	50.9	718,633	796,292	10.8	0.3	13,490	11,040	-362	305,780	2.5	61.2	13.6	31.7
Okmulgee	13.1	11.0	7.7	50.2	40,069	36,706	-8.4	0.4	559	780	357	14,644	2.5	65.5	15.2	29.4
Osage	14.9	12.5	8.6	49.4	47,472	45,818	-3.5	-0.1	488	778	245	18,364	2.5	71.3	11.6	25.6
Ottawa	12.2	10.5	7.5	50.7	31,848	30,285	-4.9	0.2	452	656	262	11,919	2.5	65.7	12.7	29.6
Pawnee	13.7	11.8	7.9	49.7	16,577	15,553	-6.2	1.2	217	305	280	6,260	2.6	70.8	11.5	25.6
Payne	9.1	7.8	5.4	49.1	77,350	81,646	5.6	0.4	944	957	334	31,346	2.4	53.3	8.6	33.9
Pittsburg	13.0	11.2	8.7	48.7	45,837	43,773	-4.5	-0.3	590	884	151	17,846	2.3	67.2	11.7	28.0
Pontotoc	11.8	9.4	7.1	51.4	37,492	38,065	1.5	0.3	636	680	136	14,234	2.6	65.7	13.0	28.8
Pottawatomie	12.9	10.1	6.6	51.7	69,442	72,454	4.3	0.8	1,034	1,278	807	26,066	2.7	70.0	13.5	25.8
Pushmataha	15.2	12.9	10.2	50.6	11,572	10,812	-6.6	0.0	147	235	91	4,477	2.5	67.5	10.7	29.1
Roger Mills	13.9	12.4	10.0	50.3	3,647	3,442	-5.6	-1.6	43	49	-50	1,377	2.6	70.9	11.9	24.6
Rogers	13.9	10.2	6.8	49.8	86,905	95,240	9.6	1.5	1,172	1,357	1,653	35,208	2.6	73.5	10.0	22.4
Seminole	13.4	10.6	7.7	50.7	25,482	23,556	-7.6	0.0	323	466	156	9,357	2.6	70.3	17.0	26.2
Sequoyah	13.6	10.9	7.5	50.4	42,391	39,281	-7.3	0.6	629	809	408	15,437	2.7	69.4	13.9	27.0
Stephens	14.1	12.0	8.4	51.1	45,048	42,848	-4.9	0.7	593	820	514	16,607	2.6	68.1	11.5	27.5
Texas	10.9	7.8	4.5	46.8	20,640	21,384	3.6	-2.4	421	232	-702	6,761	3.0	67.0	10.1	28.7
Tillman	14.0	11.5	8.3	48.6	7,992	6,968	-12.8	1.5	92	117	136	2,794	2.5	63.0	11.6	32.3
Tulsa	11.7	9.2	5.8	50.9	603,403	669,279	10.9	0.5	10,577	9,196	2,027	253,909	2.5	62.6	12.5	31.1
Wagoner	12.8	10.4	6.5	50.2	73,085	80,981	10.8	3.8	1,066	1,092	3,134	29,591	2.7	71.8	10.6	24.2
Washington	12.6	10.9	8.8	51.1	50,976	52,455	2.9	0.6	712	944	549	20,376	2.5	63.6	10.5	32.1
Washita	14.0	11.4	8.1	50.2	11,629	10,924	-6.1	-0.1	184	188	-6	4,296	2.5	69.8	10.5	26.9
Woods	11.1	9.7	7.9	45.7	8,878	8,624	-2.9	-0.5	99	151	9	3,140	2.6	58.4	9.8	30.4
Woodward	12.1	9.2	7.1	47.1	20,081	20,470	1.9	-1.3	289	325	-232	7,608	2.5	66.6	11.6	30.7
OREGON	12.4	11.5	7.0	50.1	3,831,074	4,237,256	10.6	0.2	50,302	55,926	14,491	1,642,579	2.5	63.0	10.1	27.4
Baker	14.9	16.2	10.7	48.7	16,134	16,668	3.3	1.1	198	315	300	7,158	2.2	61.8	8.6	31.7
Benton	10.8	11.1	6.5	49.8	85,579	95,184	11.2	0.9	814	879	892	36,051	2.4	57.8	8.0	26.1
Clackamas	13.3	11.9	7.3	50.3	375,992	421,401	12.1	0.3	4,683	5,412	1,814	159,330	2.6	68.5	8.8	23.8
Clatsop	14.6	15.9	8.3	50.2	37,039	41,072	10.9	1.8	443	610	915	16,019	2.4	58.1	8.1	33.5
Columbia	14.7	12.6	7.4	49.7	49,351	52,589	6.6	0.9	606	760	645	19,872	2.6	68.5	10.8	25.1
Coos	15.2	16.7	10.7	50.5	63,043	64,929	3.0	0.1	703	1,337	714	27,819	2.3	61.0	10.2	31.6
Crook	14.9	15.9	9.4	49.9	20,978	24,738	17.9	4.0	292	355	1,080	9,998	2.4	69.7	11.7	25.4
Curry	17.6	21.9	13.7	50.6	22,364	23,446	4.8	1.0	202	625	671	10,790	2.1	61.7	7.7	33.0
Deschutes	13.4	13.2	7.3	50.1	157,733	198,253	25.7	3.3	2,272	2,339	6,687	77,040	2.5	67.2	8.5	23.8
Douglas	14.6	15.4	10.9	50.3	107,667	111,201	3.3	0.7	1,278	2,270	1,795	46,439	2.3	65.5	10.5	27.2
Gilliam	15.9	17.4	11.5	49.2	1,871	1,995	6.6	0.5	22	33	21	905	2.1	50.4	9.1	44.8
Grant	14.4	17.3	14.1	49.4	7,445	7,233	-2.8	0.5	73	128	96	3,453	2.0	57.7	5.2	34.2
Harney	14.6	15.1	10.0	48.6	7,422	7,495	1.0	1.1	88	124	118	3,176	2.2	67.9	10.2	25.6
Hood River	13.2	10.6	6.4	49.5	22,346	23,977	7.3	0.3	287	253	44	8,892	2.5	67.1	9.9	26.5
Jackson	13.2	13.7	9.0	50.8	203,206	223,259	9.9	0.2	2,616	3,636	1,502	89,690	2.4	63.7	10.2	27.7
Jefferson	13.6	12.4	7.3	48.0	21,720	24,502	12.8	2.3	362	409	620	8,395	2.7	70.4	13.8	21.9
Josephine	14.7	15.6	10.9	51.0	82,713	88,090	6.5	0.3	943	1,831	1,160	36,606	2.4	67.3	10.1	26.2
Klamath	13.4	13.9	8.0	49.9	66,380	69,413	4.6	1.1	965	1,245	1,039	28,376	2.4	62.3	11.8	29.5
Lake	13.8	16.3	10.2	46.4	7,895	8,160	3.4	1.4	93	141	166	3,533	2.1	62.9	9.2	29.4
Lane	12.5	12.8	7.7	50.7	351,715	382,971	8.9	0.1	3,798	5,554	1,941	154,516	2.4	58.5	10.4	29.2
Lincoln	16.3	20.2	10.7	51.5	46,034	50,395	9.5	0.9	459	957	980	21,841	2.2	59.9	11.4	32.2
Linn	13.1	11.8	7.3	50.3	116,672	128,610	10.2	1.0	1,810	2,041	1,457	48,290	2.6	67.9	10.5	25.1
Malheur	10.9	9.8	6.9	45.4	31,313	31,571	0.8	0.4	503	460	72	10,059	2.7	66.1	15.3	28.3
Marion	11.7	10.0	6.3	49.8	315,335	345,920	9.7	0.3	4,925	4,405	612	120,474	2.8	68.2	13.2	24.9

1. No spouse present.

STATE County	Persons in group quarters, 2021	Daytime Population, 2016–2020: Number	Daytime Population, 2016–2020: Employment/ residence ratio	Births, 2021: Total	Births, 2021: Rate[1]	Deaths, 2021: Number	Deaths, 2021: Rate[1]	Persons under 65 with no health insurance, 2019: Number	Persons under 65 with no health insurance, 2019: Percent	Medicare, 2021: Total beneficiaries	Medicare, 2021: Enrolled in Original Medicare	Medicare, 2021: Enrolled in Medicare Advantage	COVID-19 Deaths, 2020: Number	COVID-19 Deaths, 2020: Rate[1]
	32	33	34	35	36	37	38	39	40	41	42	43	44	45
OKLAHOMA—Cont'd														
Kiowa	127	8,077	0.8	96	11.4	146	17.3	1,160	17.1	2,228	1,911	318	29	3.4
Latimer	439	10,096	1.0	95	10.1	153	16.2	1,421	19.1	2,694	2,305	389	11	1.2
Le Flore	1,354	46,290	0.8	585	12.1	837	17.3	8,727	22.4	11,131	8,621	2,510	67	1.4
Lincoln	250	29,091	0.6	354	10.5	449	13.3	4,735	16.9	7,561	5,421	2,140	53	1.6
Logan	2,139	37,036	0.5	479	9.5	467	9.3	5,823	15.0	8,946	6,307	2,639	40	0.8
Love	67	12,483	1.6	109	10.7	138	13.6	1,663	20.4	2,354	2,061	294	18	1.8
McClain	155	33,111	0.6	427	10.0	435	10.2	4,938	14.4	7,925	6,203	1,722	72	1.7
McCurtain	254	33,546	1.1	446	14.5	500	16.2	5,862	22.5	7,401	6,821	580	97	3.2
McIntosh	225	18,232	0.8	179	9.4	374	19.6	3,146	22.1	5,407	4,312	1,096	44	2.3
Major	69	7,151	0.8	76	9.9	82	10.6	1,116	18.5	1,616	1,506	110	20	2.6
Marshall	169	15,473	0.8	200	12.9	222	14.4	2,963	22.8	3,966	3,391	575	21	1.4
Mayes	384	39,794	0.9	416	10.6	654	16.7	6,257	19.1	9,458	7,037	2,421	63	1.6
Murray	258	13,312	0.9	150	10.9	220	15.9	1,944	17.6	3,203	2,846	357	19	1.4
Muskogee	3,154	72,350	1.2	807	12.2	1,095	16.6	9,746	18.5	15,479	12,260	3,219	119	1.8
Noble	192	11,903	1.1	121	11.1	147	13.5	1,314	14.8	2,594	2,324	270	13	1.2
Nowata	78	8,340	0.6	88	9.5	160	17.2	1,403	17.7	2,372	1,932	440	15	1.6
Okfuskee	1,053	10,872	0.7	130	11.6	204	18.2	1,710	19.4	2,636	2,171	465	32	2.8
Oklahoma	14,090	902,068	1.3	10,809	13.5	8,767	11.0	110,449	16.5	131,001	90,080	40,921	1,020	1.3
Okmulgee	1,112	35,305	0.8	444	12.1	645	17.5	5,495	18.5	9,107	6,710	2,397	68	1.9
Osage	1,348	38,809	0.6	381	8.3	631	13.8	5,699	15.9	10,263	7,099	3,164	50	1.1
Ottawa	827	31,187	1.0	372	12.3	545	18.0	4,801	19.7	7,216	5,528	1,688	64	2.1
Pawnee	116	13,471	0.6	171	10.9	248	15.9	2,272	17.4	3,758	3,007	751	32	2.1
Payne	7,636	83,802	1.1	757	9.3	786	9.6	11,184	17.6	12,353	10,729	1,624	58	0.7
Pittsburg	2,310	44,810	1.1	476	10.9	699	16.0	5,997	18.4	10,675	8,858	1,817	63	1.4
Pontotoc	1,553	40,213	1.1	512	13.4	550	14.4	5,708	18.7	7,967	7,024	943	47	1.2
Pottawatomie	2,852	68,283	0.9	844	11.6	1,002	13.8	9,736	16.9	15,317	10,804	4,513	87	1.2
Pushmataha	76	10,360	0.8	119	11.0	191	17.7	1,712	20.6	2,909	2,460	449	14	1.3
Roger Mills	6	3,435	0.9	36	10.6	34	10.0	567	20.5	825	776	48	11	3.2
Rogers	1,159	78,924	0.7	947	9.9	1,107	11.5	10,382	13.5	18,644	13,189	5,455	122	1.3
Seminole	432	24,039	0.9	259	11.0	364	15.5	3,962	20.7	5,499	4,141	1,359	47	2.0
Sequoyah	295	37,135	0.7	508	12.9	669	17.0	7,025	21.3	9,865	7,374	2,491	66	1.7
Stephens	448	42,652	1.0	472	11.0	632	14.7	6,170	18.2	10,389	9,141	1,248	61	1.4
Texas	583	20,437	1.0	336	15.9	178	8.4	4,085	24.1	2,607	2,471	136	40	1.9
Tillman	202	6,922	0.9	68	9.7	89	12.7	1,098	20.1	1,645	1,518	127	19	2.7
Tulsa	9,662	715,270	1.2	8,539	12.7	7,380	11.0	90,972	16.6	114,970	71,254	43,716	735	1.1
Wagoner	214	57,355	0.4	826	10.0	906	11.0	10,613	15.7	15,702	9,770	5,932	78	1.0
Washington	723	52,427	1.0	555	10.5	775	14.7	7,023	17.2	12,099	10,385	1,714	79	1.5
Washita	170	8,887	0.6	144	13.2	149	13.7	1,581	18.0	2,276	2,054	222	23	2.1
Woods	934	9,305	1.1	85	9.9	124	14.4	955	15.0	1,712	1,626	86	10	1.2
Woodward	1,227	20,823	1.1	242	11.9	273	13.5	2,885	18.3	3,578	3,369	208	31	1.5
OREGON	85,284	4,224,809	1.0	39,877	9.4	44,592	10.5	291,036	8.6	885,725	468,190	417,535	1,598	0.4
Baker	358	16,251	1.0	162	9.7	243	14.5	1,018	9.0	5,163	4,814	350	D	D
Benton	5,901	95,032	1.1	634	6.6	707	7.4	4,861	6.7	17,553	9,045	8,507	13	0.1
Clackamas	2,697	379,197	0.8	3,695	8.7	4,367	10.3	25,418	7.4	87,253	32,718	54,536	137	0.3
Clatsop	826	40,586	1.1	367	8.9	488	11.8	2,459	8.2	10,868	9,099	1,770	D	D
Columbia	369	41,762	0.6	482	9.1	597	11.3	3,069	7.3	12,258	5,944	6,314	22	0.4
Coos	1,109	63,739	1.0	557	8.6	1,042	16.0	4,164	9.1	20,840	17,491	3,349	12	0.2
Crook	158	21,992	0.8	229	9.0	286	11.3	1,817	10.1	7,304	5,250	2,054	D	D
Curry	266	22,475	1.0	160	6.8	499	21.2	1,453	10.0	9,530	8,165	1,365	D	D
Deschutes	1,207	193,263	1.0	1,789	8.9	1,913	9.5	12,432	7.9	46,658	31,826	14,832	27	0.1
Douglas	1,714	108,933	1.0	994	8.9	1,787	16.0	6,911	8.7	34,711	22,035	12,676	38	0.3
Gilliam	16	1,954	1.1	17	8.5	30	14.9	118	8.6	564	521	42	D	D
Grant	109	7,091	1.0	58	8.0	92	12.7	472	9.8	2,321	1,934	386	D	D
Harney	150	7,332	1.0	71	9.4	100	13.3	547	10.3	2,053	1,885	169	D	D
Hood River	773	25,043	1.2	232	9.7	202	8.4	2,480	12.8	4,435	3,391	1,044	14	0.6
Jackson	3,387	218,440	1.0	2,086	9.3	2,903	13.0	16,303	9.8	57,969	37,447	20,522	76	0.3
Jefferson	859	22,816	0.9	292	11.8	311	12.5	2,246	12.2	5,606	3,914	1,692	21	0.9
Josephine	1,520	86,781	1.0	748	8.5	1,443	16.4	6,416	10.3	27,027	15,450	11,577	26	0.3
Klamath	1,144	67,453	1.0	758	10.9	1,002	14.3	5,494	10.7	18,116	13,058	5,058	26	0.4
Lake	462	7,941	1.0	81	9.9	108	13.2	493	9.2	2,316	2,138	179	D	D
Lane	8,570	378,949	1.0	3,061	8.0	4,449	11.6	26,896	9.1	90,110	41,510	48,600	89	0.2
Lincoln	786	49,657	1.0	369	7.3	762	15.0	3,761	10.9	17,123	13,174	3,949	17	0.3
Linn	1,000	121,100	0.9	1,430	11.1	1,640	12.7	8,693	8.4	30,127	13,929	16,197	42	0.3
Malheur	3,294	33,463	1.3	377	11.9	328	10.4	2,633	12.2	6,316	5,132	1,184	52	1.6
Marion	10,078	346,722	1.0	3,916	11.3	3,522	10.2	29,108	10.4	66,040	26,920	39,120	214	0.6

1. Per 1,000 estimated resident population.

STATE County	COVID-19 Vaccinations, 2021–2022: Number	COVID-19 Vaccinations, 2021–2022: Percent[5]	Education: School enrollment and attainment, 2016–2020: Enrollment[1]: Total	Enrollment[1]: Percent private	Attainment[2] (percent): High school graduate or less	Attainment[2] (percent): Bachelor's degree or more	Local government expenditures,[3] 2018–2019: Total current spending (mil dol)	Local government expenditures,[3] 2018–2019: Current spending per student (dollars)	Money income, 2016–2020: Per capita income[4]	Households: Median income (dollars)	Households: Percent with income of less than $50,000	Households: Percent with income of $200,000 or more	Income and poverty, 2020: Median household income (dollars)	Percent below poverty level: All persons	Percent below poverty level: Children under 18 years	Percent below poverty level: Children 5 to 17 years in families
	46	47	48	49	50	51	52	53	54	55	56	57	58	59	60	61
OKLAHOMA—Cont'd																
Kiowa	4,467	51.3	1,789	5.8	50.8	18.1	16.9	10,699	21,855	34,747	60.3	2.4	40,112	18.0	26.7	19.2
Latimer	3,478	34.5	2,253	6.3	49.4	15.4	13.3	9,509	25,534	40,044	58.8	2.6	40,831	15.9	25.5	25.9
Le Flore	19,510	39.1	11,488	5.9	55.7	15.7	89.4	9,375	21,324	41,900	57.8	1.7	40,632	18.1	23.2	21.9
Lincoln	14,088	40.4	7,883	12.8	53.3	14.6	50.7	9,376	26,293	51,206	48.8	2.9	56,957	13.8	18.4	16.8
Logan	16,890	35.2	11,660	11.1	39.6	29.3	41.3	9,088	35,139	70,456	36.7	10.6	72,617	11.0	13.4	12.8
Love	4,332	42.3	2,492	3.1	57.4	13.4	18.1	9,937	23,266	54,423	46.4	0.9	54,219	11.7	16.3	15.9
McClain	19,528	48.2	10,138	11.4	41.8	25.4	62.9	7,903	33,810	70,005	33.7	5.7	68,563	10.4	13.4	11.9
McCurtain	11,846	36.1	7,374	5.5	59.5	14.4	68.4	10,389	20,641	39,091	59.3	1.1	45,380	18.9	24.9	24.4
McIntosh	10,641	54.3	3,529	10.5	54.2	13.1	26.4	9,279	23,467	39,588	59.2	1.8	37,535	22.5	30.2	28.1
Major	3,826	50.2	1,779	6.6	49.2	20.1	13.4	11,384	28,079	56,781	44.2	2.7	54,851	11.5	16.0	14.5
Marshall	7,596	44.9	3,559	2.6	54.8	15.2	26.9	8,734	25,375	48,573	51.8	1.8	51,072	13.7	19.9	18.3
Mayes	17,953	43.7	8,816	8.9	53.4	14.5	76.7	10,785	25,937	50,012	50.0	2.3	50,905	16.9	25.1	21.4
Murray	6,321	44.9	3,021	10.0	54.9	18.5	22.0	8,196	27,843	53,696	47.1	2.6	55,318	14.3	19.7	18.1
Muskogee	35,272	51.9	16,694	6.8	48.3	19.8	117.7	9,124	23,314	41,633	56.7	2.1	42,607	18.2	26.1	25.4
Noble	6,978	62.7	2,512	3.5	47.4	21.8	23.5	10,943	29,185	60,019	40.3	3.3	56,632	11.8	14.7	13.8
Nowata	4,424	43.9	2,134	7.8	51.8	13.5	16.5	10,020	24,532	42,051	56.2	0.7	45,719	16.5	23.0	21.8
Okfuskee	5,615	46.8	2,585	10.6	57.8	11.4	22.5	10,928	19,724	40,913	58.0	2.1	45,823	21.7	25.3	23.1
Oklahoma	520,439	65.3	203,775	15.2	36.9	33.1	1,290.9	8,395	32,165	55,519	45.0	6.2	55,332	15.2	19.9	18.8
Okmulgee	16,425	42.7	9,130	8.6	48.9	14.2	58.0	9,318	24,305	45,319	55.8	2.0	50,442	14.6	20.6	18.8
Osage	16,357	34.8	10,403	9.2	47.1	19.3	40.7	10,910	26,852	50,105	49.9	3.4	50,490	13.0	17.4	15.8
Ottawa	12,165	39.1	7,606	6.6	49.3	15.3	53.5	9,220	21,394	40,662	60.2	1.8	40,249	18.5	27.1	26.6
Pawnee	8,094	49.4	3,446	9.0	53.1	17.7	23.7	9,426	25,174	50,991	48.9	2.3	51,960	15.7	21.1	19.5
Payne	40,160	49.1	33,480	7.1	35.3	37.8	103.2	9,281	24,675	42,103	57.4	3.3	39,681	20.1	16.5	15.2
Pittsburg	19,820	45.4	9,571	9.7	49.6	18.3	78.7	10,220	25,685	47,511	52.5	2.4	50,416	16.5	22.4	20.7
Pontotoc	19,575	51.1	10,093	7.8	42.6	28.8	68.5	9,524	27,038	51,682	48.7	2.8	50,587	14.4	18.7	17.9
Pottawatomie	35,952	49.5	19,023	16.6	46.9	19.4	116.7	9,065	25,019	51,150	48.5	2.5	50,118	16.0	22.1	20.5
Pushmataha	4,013	36.2	2,279	5.1	59.1	14.7	22.8	10,321	22,812	38,325	61.9	1.8	38,912	17.4	25.3	24.4
Roger Mills	1,316	36.7	939	2.8	44.1	17.9	11.1	15,731	35,144	54,653	47.0	6.9	51,279	13.5	17.5	15.8
Rogers	43,317	46.8	21,936	13.9	40.4	24.3	117.1	8,806	33,030	66,038	35.8	5.3	67,243	8.5	10.9	10.3
Seminole	12,794	52.7	5,919	5.7	51.0	14.4	50.1	10,287	20,735	38,588	60.4	1.3	42,418	21.2	28.3	24.6
Sequoyah	16,860	40.6	9,100	6.3	57.6	13.8	72.8	9,243	21,102	41,803	58.6	1.3	47,188	16.9	23.2	19.5
Stephens	20,559	47.7	9,177	9.0	55.5	18.4	70.9	9,222	26,670	51,156	48.8	2.6	52,905	17.7	22.7	20.8
Texas	8,923	44.7	5,933	6.2	52.0	26.4	44.7	9,424	21,844	50,702	48.8	1.2	61,334	11.1	14.9	14.8
Tillman	3,630	50.1	1,614	8.9	57.0	16.5	14.0	9,917	20,984	39,975	59.4	1.3	41,610	21.9	29.9	24.8
Tulsa	403,347	61.9	165,428	19.3	35.8	32.0	1,106.8	9,192	36,303	57,024	44.3	6.4	58,863	12.8	16.7	15.5
Wagoner	38,413	47.3	19,339	13.2	41.3	23.8	53.8	8,191	30,727	64,958	36.6	3.9	66,375	10.2	15.6	14.9
Washington	22,620	43.9	12,154	11.6	43.3	28.8	76.8	8,059	31,113	53,384	45.7	5.9	48,144	14.8	18.8	17.1
Washita	4,286	39.3	2,362	7.4	50.1	20.3	20.4	10,419	28,518	52,591	44.7	2.7	51,270	14.7	22.1	20.6
Woods	3,654	41.6	2,642	4.7	41.5	29.4	20.1	15,001	25,937	51,985	49.1	2.2	52,504	15.1	16.4	15.8
Woodward	7,704	38.1	4,537	4.2	51.6	19.4	36.4	9,982	28,080	56,182	45.3	4.7	54,328	13.3	15.7	15.3
OREGON	2,934,467	69.6	948,174	15.9	31.5	34.4	7,231.4	12,432	35,393	65,667	38.1	7.2	67,832	11.0	12.2	11.3
Baker	11,325	70.2	2,920	20.8	38.2	25.0	29.3	7,007	29,615	46,250	52.9	2.7	44,872	14.5	18.8	17.9
Benton	69,642	74.8	33,437	7.9	17.6	53.3	111.1	12,314	35,305	65,142	39.0	7.8	66,378	15.7	11.3	9.9
Clackamas	288,223	68.9	94,500	17.2	27.7	38.0	691.0	11,537	42,638	82,911	28.1	11.6	82,539	6.8	6.6	6.1
Clatsop	26,783	66.6	7,729	12.6	35.1	24.0	66.2	12,678	31,631	57,466	43.5	3.2	63,238	10.5	13.0	12.3
Columbia	31,924	61.0	10,803	11.7	42.4	18.0	83.7	11,173	32,438	68,170	37.2	4.3	73,023	9.2	10.5	9.8
Coos	36,962	57.3	11,790	8.3	40.7	19.9	111.0	11,048	30,720	49,445	50.4	3.7	50,848	15.4	21.1	19.7
Crook	12,455	51.0	4,437	17.1	43.2	18.8	32.6	11,111	29,923	59,000	42.1	3.1	68,598	10.3	13.8	12.7
Curry	12,780	55.7	2,705	14.8	36.1	23.5	28.1	12,458	32,125	53,174	47.1	3.2	48,377	14.5	21.2	21.0
Deschutes	136,607	69.1	38,042	14.3	27.8	37.2	312.4	11,571	37,615	68,937	35.6	7.6	66,467	8.1	8.7	8.0
Douglas	58,542	52.8	20,543	15.5	42.0	18.5	189.0	13,141	27,484	50,031	50.0	2.5	52,355	13.3	18.5	16.5
Gilliam	862	45.1	344	8.4	39.6	21.7	7.2	23,839	26,911	41,838	57.2	2.0	63,088	10.7	14.8	13.7
Grant	3,263	45.3	1,099	11.8	45.9	20.8	15.9	18,368	29,449	48,202	51.5	2.3	50,819	13.9	19.6	18.6
Harney	3,403	46.0	1,386	19.9	44.1	16.5	22.0	12,421	26,279	43,387	55.8	3.1	48,790	12.6	21.4	21.0
Hood River	19,898	85.1	5,431	9.9	38.2	34.7	55.1	13,614	35,904	72,418	33.6	9.9	81,718	8.5	10.9	10.6
Jackson	128,628	58.2	45,718	15.2	34.8	28.8	358.6	11,790	32,044	56,327	44.1	5.3	57,334	11.9	13.1	12.6
Jefferson	15,641	63.4	5,579	8.3	42.0	21.4	52.1	14,235	26,177	55,844	45.0	3.9	63,683	12.5	17.3	16.9
Josephine	43,838	50.1	16,977	17.8	39.3	18.1	131.9	12,054	27,026	47,733	51.5	3.3	47,740	15.8	18.7	17.1
Klamath	34,595	50.7	14,890	10.8	43.9	21.2	116.7	12,033	26,508	48,560	51.1	2.3	49,675	19.7	20.6	18.1
Lake	3,105	39.5	1,209	7.4	46.2	19.4	19.3	16,131	26,299	44,237	53.0	1.9	48,669	15.7	18.6	17.4
Lane	258,141	67.6	90,303	11.2	30.6	31.9	556.9	12,044	30,911	54,942	45.9	4.5	58,818	14.5	15.2	14.4
Lincoln	35,538	71.1	8,262	13.1	32.6	27.7	65.0	11,709	30,336	50,775	49.3	3.1	53,883	14.4	20.4	19.1
Linn	72,079	55.6	26,639	13.4	39.4	19.5	237.9	10,450	27,820	59,547	42.6	2.4	65,516	11.3	14.0	11.5
Malheur	14,728	48.2	7,164	9.4	49.1	14.9	74.4	14,579	19,893	44,362	55.7	2.5	46,278	19.5	24.2	21.6
Marion	219,415	63.1	81,728	14.2	40.7	24.1	780.1	12,363	28,856	61,817	40.0	4.1	64,990	12.1	16.0	15.4

1. All persons 3 years old and over enrolled in nursery school through college. 2. Persons 25 years old and over. 3. Elementary and secondary education expenditures. 4. Based on population estimated by the American Community Survey, 2016–2020. 5. CDC percent based on 2019 population estimate.

STATE County	Personal income, 2020										Earnings, 2020		
			Per capita[1]			Supplements to wages and salaries, employer contributions (mil dol)						Contributions for government social insurance (mil dol)	
	Total (mil dol)	Percent change 2019–2020	Dollars	Rank	Wages and salaries (mil dol)	Pension and insurance	Government social insurance	Proprietors' income (mil dol)	Dividends, interest, and rent (mil dol)	Personal transfer reecipts (mil dol)	Total (mil dol)	From employee and self-employed	From employer
	62	63	64	65	66	67	68	69	70	71	72	73	74
OKLAHOMA—Cont'd													
Kiowa	356	9.0	40,736	2,367	78	18	6	50	56	118	152	10	6
Latimer	362	3.6	35,756	2,889	105	26	8	20	55	151	159	11	8
Le Flore	1,766	5.8	35,362	2,917	533	101	41	113	225	680	788	60	41
Lincoln	1,373	6.9	39,164	2,547	321	56	24	80	222	411	481	37	24
Logan	2,249	4.9	46,102	1,634	329	56	25	118	330	491	528	38	25
Love	413	6.1	40,353	2,408	260	57	19	19	65	127	355	22	19
McClain	2,054	4.1	49,683	1,174	435	71	32	170	297	456	709	50	32
McCurtain	1,164	7.5	35,511	2,905	480	89	37	68	130	447	675	48	37
McIntosh	750	6.5	38,217	2,663	148	29	12	40	120	321	228	22	12
Major	346	2.8	45,667	1,705	89	17	7	48	76	84	160	10	7
Marshall	630	8.0	36,800	2,798	195	34	16	40	99	227	285	22	16
Mayes	1,611	6.6	39,149	2,550	646	111	49	84	235	539	890	63	49
Murray	634	3.3	45,419	1,732	222	48	17	39	101	183	324	22	17
Muskogee	2,697	4.6	39,894	2,467	1,425	299	111	130	445	996	1,965	130	111
Noble	527	5.4	47,378	1,466	234	46	17	44	94	136	341	21	17
Nowata	403	6.8	39,961	2,460	84	16	6	22	62	135	128	11	6
Okfuskee	394	4.3	33,520	3,004	89	20	7	20	63	160	135	11	7
Oklahoma	45,807	2.7	56,971	574	27,606	4,485	2,025	7,767	8,758	8,759	41,883	2,366	2,025
Okmulgee	1,429	5.7	37,367	2,754	437	81	33	46	186	553	597	49	33
Osage	1,800	5.2	38,588	2,615	292	57	22	79	292	539	449	34	22
Ottawa	1,262	5.5	40,876	2,347	466	91	35	103	183	470	696	46	35
Pawnee	647	5.6	39,491	2,506	148	33	12	21	102	223	214	18	12
Payne	3,310	3.6	40,487	2,394	1,545	328	111	222	685	758	2,207	132	111
Pittsburg	1,781	2.9	40,786	2,356	745	168	57	74	315	596	1,044	71	57
Pontotoc	1,833	5.9	47,748	1,425	956	182	70	94	316	504	1,302	81	70
Pottawatomie	2,923	1.1	40,043	2,452	936	167	70	209	475	917	1,383	98	70
Pushmataha	391	8.3	35,650	2,896	102	21	8	28	53	169	159	13	8
Roger Mills	164	3.4	46,054	1,642	42	10	3	17	52	38	71	4	3
Rogers	4,712	4.2	50,583	1,079	1,371	233	104	227	749	1,067	1,935	130	104
Seminole	908	6.3	37,463	2,744	302	63	23	49	139	338	436	32	23
Sequoyah	1,518	6.5	36,537	2,820	335	69	26	65	242	576	496	43	26
Stephens	1,984	3.8	46,027	1,650	689	107	52	156	443	587	1,003	72	52
Texas	1,109	-3.1	55,434	675	412	72	33	323	124	159	841	34	33
Tillman	277	0.1	38,316	2,647	69	16	5	27	46	90	117	8	5
Tulsa	43,085	2.5	65,519	250	20,466	2,979	1,515	9,001	9,313	7,335	33,961	1,889	1,515
Wagoner	3,575	5.8	43,111	2,048	484	78	37	161	457	877	760	64	37
Washington	3,029	-1.3	58,010	511	1,092	183	80	626	515	651	1,981	115	80
Washita	412	2.9	38,017	2,684	88	18	7	41	71	130	154	11	7
Woods	410	1.8	47,226	1,487	150	31	11	53	123	87	245	14	11
Woodward	807	4.2	40,710	2,372	427	73	32	4	169	207	536	37	32
OREGON	238,847	8.0	56,311	X	115,273	18,118	9,643	20,577	44,104	56,796	163,611	10,516	9,643
Baker	754	12.2	46,277	1,611	239	54	22	53	146	271	369	27	22
Benton	4,699	5.3	50,399	1,098	2,212	449	182	349	1,122	860	3,193	196	182
Clackamas	27,316	6.4	64,791	270	10,118	1,418	856	2,083	5,516	4,720	14,475	956	856
Clatsop	1,972	7.2	48,777	1,284	831	152	75	206	341	635	1,263	86	75
Columbia	2,578	8.0	48,749	1,289	549	109	50	115	320	753	823	67	50
Coos	3,273	9.7	50,581	1,080	1,067	228	98	294	582	1,234	1,687	126	98
Crook	1,159	10.6	46,179	1,622	372	66	32	89	215	406	558	43	32
Curry	1,120	9.5	48,046	1,383	278	59	26	89	252	453	453	41	26
Deschutes	12,351	8.8	61,216	379	4,623	708	402	1,711	2,985	2,774	7,445	491	402
Douglas	5,161	11.3	46,342	1,601	1,817	359	168	317	869	1,983	2,661	205	168
Gilliam	134	23.0	67,754	201	59	11	6	31	18	29	106	5	6
Grant	342	11.9	47,569	1,443	111	33	10	18	68	123	173	12	10
Harney	347	15.2	47,009	1,513	109	31	10	52	51	117	202	12	10
Hood River	1,402	8.0	60,225	417	602	97	57	159	317	284	915	54	57
Jackson	11,497	9.1	51,824	946	4,450	768	397	1,062	2,247	3,502	6,676	469	397
Jefferson	983	12.8	39,552	2,494	315	72	29	84	145	381	501	37	29
Josephine	4,131	7.8	46,913	1,525	1,244	220	114	454	693	1,588	2,032	161	114
Klamath	3,060	10.7	44,513	1,874	1,047	215	99	266	454	1,141	1,626	114	99
Lake	377	13.5	47,402	1,459	118	35	11	52	67	120	216	13	11
Lane	18,989	8.1	49,583	1,187	7,883	1,414	695	1,597	3,425	5,531	11,589	790	695
Lincoln	2,389	6.7	47,231	1,485	785	154	71	218	459	863	1,227	98	71
Linn	6,296	10.5	48,040	1,385	2,293	399	213	473	847	2,094	3,379	238	213
Malheur	1,176	14.2	37,964	2,689	556	126	53	177	153	449	912	53	53
Marion	16,809	8.8	48,135	1,365	8,374	1,686	738	1,761	2,434	4,931	12,559	769	738

1. Based on the resident population estimated as of July 1 of the year shown.

STATE County	Earnings, 2020 (cont.)									Social Security beneficiaries, December 2020		Supple-mental Security Income recipients, 2020	Housing units, 2021	
	Percent by selected industries													
	Farm	Mining, quarrying, and extractions	Construction	Manu-facturing	Information; professional, scientific, technical services	Retail trade	Finance, insurance, real estate, and leasing	Health care and social assistance	Govern-ment	Number	Rate[1]		Total	Percent change, 2010–2021
	75	76	77	78	79	80	81	82	83	84	85	86	87	88
OKLAHOMA—Cont'd														
Kiowa	24.8	5.1	3.2	0.7	D	4.7	6.0	8.2	22.3	2,445	291	346	4,671	-0.1
Latimer	3.7	6.0	7.0	D	D	5.0	D	5.5	28.2	2,820	299	431	4,684	0.2
Le Flore	5.8	2.8	5.3	6.1	D	6.8	3.6	D	39.9	12,180	251	1,854	21,118	0.3
Lincoln	-2.4	3.4	15.0	7.1	4.7	7.7	11.4	7.4	19.6	8,610	255	772	14,505	0.3
Logan	0.2	3.8	16.8	5.0	4.9	9.8	5.4	13.4	15.0	9,405	185	621	19,357	0.2
Love	-0.5	2.0	2.4	1.5	D	3.3	1.2	D	52.8	2,525	247	223	4,717	0.3
McClain	1.1	8.7	17.1	4.5	5.4	12.3	4.6	5.7	16.5	8,590	197	619	17,140	3.5
McCurtain	3.8	D	6.3	27.6	D	8.9	3.5	D	19.4	8,200	266	1,326	13,964	0.4
McIntosh	0.1	1.3	5.9	1.5	D	20.0	6.9	11.3	25.3	6,525	339	770	11,834	0.6
Major	19.7	D	8.5	1.7	D	5.9	4.6	8.2	12.3	1,805	235	88	3,716	0.1
Marshall	-0.9	1.1	4.5	39.6	D	7.4	4.3	D	16.8	4,355	279	442	8,780	0.7
Mayes	2.2	D	13.0	24.0	D	8.7	3.3	D	21.1	10,035	256	1,175	18,340	0.4
Murray	0.5	4.0	7.3	9.2	5.0	7.3	2.8	D	42.0	3,470	253	317	6,524	0.2
Muskogee	0.4	0.1	5.7	12.4	3.0	6.3	3.8	12.4	36.5	16,965	256	2,891	29,318	0.1
Noble	4.9	1.7	3.6	D	D	3.3	D	D	20.0	2,775	254	270	5,067	0.2
Nowata	3.7	1.4	5.8	13.7	D	5.2	D	19.4	22.0	2,795	300	270	4,363	0.3
Okfuskee	-3.9	3.3	11.0	7.1	D	5.2	3.9	D	43.4	2,905	259	546	4,788	0.2
Oklahoma	0.0	10.7	4.7	4.6	10.0	5.4	6.7	12.4	19.2	138,290	173	19,786	356,767	1.0
Okmulgee	0.0	0.6	10.1	16.2	4.0	8.2	5.1	D	34.1	10,165	276	1,518	16,712	0.5
Osage	4.2	4.2	7.9	8.9	3.2	6.5	4.0	4.2	38.0	10,800	236	767	19,760	0.6
Ottawa	7.6	0.4	4.8	12.1	D	6.8	D	D	36.0	8,915	294	1,454	13,720	0.0
Pawnee	-2.7	D	6.7	2.2	12.8	8.3	D	13.3	31.0	4,505	286	412	7,302	0.3
Payne	-0.1	1.4	5.9	4.8	5.7	6.8	5.4	5.1	46.0	13,165	161	1,384	36,838	0.3
Pittsburg	0.2	5.1	4.8	6.4	D	7.0	3.8	7.5	43.6	11,015	252	1,453	22,115	0.3
Pontotoc	-0.3	2.1	4.0	6.6	5.1	5.4	4.5	10.7	45.2	8,705	228	1,206	17,508	0.6
Pottawatomie	-0.3	1.1	5.1	12.0	7.0	7.4	4.9	D	24.4	16,650	228	2,021	30,155	0.5
Pushmataha	0.2	D	13.0	9.2	4.5	8.9	4.3	15.1	29.2	3,470	321	484	5,689	0.2
Roger Mills	7.1	5.7	5.0	D	D	4.9	D	0.7	35.1	775	229	65	1,853	0.1
Rogers	-0.2	0.7	12.9	19.3	4.9	7.0	3.9	7.3	23.6	20,155	208	1,281	38,682	1.8
Seminole	-0.2	9.3	5.7	15.5	2.5	6.8	3.8	D	25.6	6,030	256	986	10,724	0.1
Sequoyah	0.5	1.0	11.4	3.9	D	10.4	4.3	D	32.2	10,920	276	1,793	18,215	0.9
Stephens	-0.2	9.6	6.8	13.6	D	6.0	6.9	D	11.9	11,545	268	1,151	20,312	0.0
Texas	34.6	1.4	D	D	4.4	3.8	2.4	2.4	10.4	2,795	134	154	8,456	0.2
Tillman	15.8	D	D	D	3.2	4.0	D	3.3	27.5	1,750	247	254	3,769	-0.2
Tulsa	0.0	10.0	5.3	11.5	9.0	5.4	5.7	11.9	7.1	120,930	180	15,549	295,350	0.8
Wagoner	1.7	D	21.2	17.6	3.7	8.7	4.0	D	15.0	16,470	196	1,222	33,482	2.5
Washington	-0.1	27.4	2.7	13.0	D	6.2	4.1	7.0	6.6	13,080	248	1,179	23,702	0.0
Washita	8.3	6.4	8.3	3.4	7.7	7.3	6.2	4.6	25.9	2,475	227	261	5,119	0.0
Woods	9.7	18.1	4.1	2.4	D	6.7	6.3	D	26.2	1,685	196	82	4,448	-0.1
Woodward	-7.2	15.8	13.6	9.4	3.3	7.5	6.1	9.0	17.0	3,935	195	276	9,392	0.1
OREGON	1.5	0.1	7.4	10.8	10.8	6.4	7.7	12.4	16.3	906,127	213	87,980	1,837,079	1.0
Baker	9.1	D	4.6	10.0	4.1	8.7	3.9	D	23.4	5,425	322	446	8,652	0.4
Benton	1.4	0.1	4.2	10.6	10.0	4.9	5.5	16.0	30.4	17,145	179	1,072	40,641	0.8
Clackamas	1.3	0.0	10.5	11.0	12.2	7.4	10.1	12.6	10.3	87,945	208	5,336	172,527	1.2
Clatsop	0.3	D	7.4	11.5	3.2	11.0	5.0	14.2	19.5	11,430	273	737	23,239	0.8
Columbia	2.1	1.2	8.9	15.6	4.7	8.2	5.8	9.5	19.8	13,060	246	1,084	21,972	1.0
Coos	1.8	0.1	6.7	7.9	3.6	8.5	5.2	11.1	27.9	22,205	342	2,370	31,701	0.8
Crook	2.9	D	17.3	7.4	14.5	4.7	4.2	8.8	19.3	7,750	301	450	11,501	2.2
Curry	2.2	D	8.5	10.1	4.2	9.4	5.0	D	23.1	10,035	424	649	13,113	0.6
Deschutes	0.0	0.1	14.7	5.3	11.8	7.8	9.9	17.0	11.3	48,020	234	2,344	96,938	2.5
Douglas	1.3	0.4	6.5	12.6	4.0	7.4	4.9	15.6	22.5	36,750	328	3,649	50,151	0.6
Gilliam	28.0	0.0	18.9	D	D	D	1.0	2.3	13.6	585	292	34	1,110	1.1
Grant	5.0	D	D	D	4.7	5.4	3.2	5.7	46.2	2,415	332	176	4,138	0.3
Harney	20.7	0.0	D	D	2.2	7.4	1.9	5.1	39.9	2,165	286	224	3,717	0.6
Hood River	6.8	0.0	6.2	12.6	13.8	7.4	4.9	13.4	11.7	4,575	190	250	10,222	0.7
Jackson	0.4	0.2	7.3	8.5	6.8	10.3	7.3	19.9	14.0	59,660	267	4,863	96,581	0.1
Jefferson	7.9	D	4.1	14.7	1.8	5.4	3.0	9.7	33.9	6,000	239	587	10,396	1.1
Josephine	0.4	D	7.4	9.9	4.5	13.3	8.8	20.0	13.1	28,460	322	2,881	39,173	0.9
Klamath	6.6	0.2	5.5	6.6	4.6	9.0	5.6	16.7	24.0	19,115	272	2,268	32,949	0.5
Lake	19.4	D	4.3	5.3	2.9	4.4	2.5	2.6	43.8	2,380	288	227	4,212	0.3
Lane	0.8	0.2	6.2	9.3	7.6	8.1	8.1	16.7	19.0	92,280	241	9,772	167,839	0.8
Lincoln	0.5	D	6.6	7.1	3.9	10.3	5.7	11.6	24.7	17,785	350	1,317	32,339	0.6
Linn	3.3	D	8.1	20.1	4.2	8.1	4.2	10.9	14.9	32,000	246	3,497	52,859	1.5
Malheur	14.7	D	2.5	7.5	3.3	9.4	3.6	D	28.8	6,785	214	1,007	11,663	0.3
Marion	3.0	0.2	9.1	5.2	5.2	6.4	7.5	14.7	29.1	69,125	199	7,585	130,365	1.1

1. Per 1,000 resident population estimated as of July 1 of the year shown.

STATE County	Housing units, 2016–2020								Civilian labor force, 2021				Civilian employment[6], 2016–2020		
		Occupied units									Unemployment			Percent	
		Owner-occupied				Renter-occupied									
				Median owner cost as a percent of income											
	Total	Percent	Median value[1]	With a mortgage	Without a mortgage[2]	Median rent[3]	Median rent as a percent of income[2]	Substandard units[4] (percent)	Total	Percent change, 2020–2021	Total	Rate[5]	Total	Management, business, science, and arts	Construction, production, and maintenance occupations
	89	90	91	92	93	94	95	96	97	98	99	100	101	102	103
OKLAHOMA—Cont'd															
Kiowa	3,554	71.9	66,200	18.4	10.0	561	28.3	2.6	3,614	3.3	121	3.3	3,711	31.8	29.2
Latimer	4,083	70.9	87,300	16.2	10.0	631	25.2	4.9	3,086	-1.7	225	7.3	3,764	31.2	32.7
Le Flore	18,309	71.7	90,900	20.4	10.0	661	27.8	2.8	19,236	1.1	896	4.7	19,156	26.4	33.1
Lincoln	13,022	80.9	116,800	19.3	10.0	624	25.7	3.2	15,810	2.3	561	3.5	14,443	32.4	29.0
Logan	15,668	84.6	176,000	17.5	10.0	765	29.1	1.9	22,737	2.3	740	3.3	21,879	33.6	26.3
Love	3,340	75.7	117,900	19.0	10.0	709	25.9	3.8	6,054	-6.8	158	2.6	4,010	26.3	30.8
McClain	14,783	78.8	183,800	20.3	10.0	784	32.2	2.4	20,387	1.9	633	3.1	19,028	36.7	25.6
McCurtain	12,651	70.8	86,100	20.0	10.0	574	26.1	5.4	15,662	4.8	693	4.4	12,895	23.4	41.7
McIntosh	8,216	77.9	115,900	20.9	10.4	658	32.4	4.3	7,106	0.0	432	6.1	6,488	26.0	35.6
Major	3,064	80.7	111,500	16.6	10.6	602	17.5	2.6	3,680	0.3	115	3.1	3,247	30.0	36.1
Marshall	6,384	76.5	107,900	18.8	10.0	681	22.5	2.3	6,987	2.7	256	3.7	6,670	27.0	36.6
Mayes	16,071	74.8	115,900	20.2	10.0	735	23.3	3.4	19,364	0.6	725	3.7	17,558	30.2	33.7
Murray	5,207	71.4	130,400	17.7	10.0	749	21.5	5.4	6,097	-0.2	237	3.9	6,092	26.4	35.5
Muskogee	26,535	65.2	109,300	19.1	11.3	678	29.7	3.6	28,881	-0.4	1,252	4.3	26,283	32.9	28.6
Noble	4,501	78.2	116,300	17.8	10.4	643	19.5	3.9	5,564	2.1	141	2.5	5,027	38.9	30.6
Nowata	4,128	73.1	91,400	20.7	10.4	664	30.0	2.2	4,637	1.1	163	3.5	4,358	28.2	34.3
Okfuskee	4,036	73.1	87,800	19.9	10.3	576	27.3	3.9	4,425	0.8	215	4.9	4,026	28.9	31.5
Oklahoma	305,780	59.5	157,500	19.8	10.2	882	28.1	2.9	389,697	1.7	15,819	4.1	376,796	38.1	21.8
Okmulgee	14,644	70.5	85,900	18.7	10.5	668	26.8	3.7	15,459	0.9	799	5.2	15,313	27.7	28.1
Osage	18,364	76.9	126,300	18.7	11.2	727	27.3	3.2	20,265	0.7	855	4.2	19,594	32.2	27.8
Ottawa	11,919	68.8	88,100	19.8	10.6	680	27.4	4.1	14,418	1.3	461	3.2	12,666	29.0	28.5
Pawnee	6,260	77.3	98,900	18.9	10.0	748	25.7	3.5	7,283	0.8	300	4.1	6,665	30.5	34.9
Payne	31,346	51.7	172,700	21.2	11.4	811	37.3	2.6	38,102	1.5	1,229	3.2	37,109	42.8	18.2
Pittsburg	17,846	72.5	109,000	18.4	10.0	719	29.8	3.0	16,392	-1.3	857	5.2	17,633	32.8	28.6
Pontotoc	14,234	65.2	134,700	17.6	10.0	730	24.6	1.8	19,191	0.4	639	3.3	16,972	37.6	25.2
Pottawatomie	26,066	71.1	123,100	18.0	10.0	727	25.8	2.9	32,707	1.7	1,263	3.9	30,162	32.5	26.3
Pushmataha	4,477	74.5	84,000	17.9	10.7	472	29.7	4.6	4,708	6.0	200	4.2	3,961	25.8	33.6
Roger Mills	1,377	80.1	131,400	22.5	10.0	683	19.1	1.7	1,802	1.6	52	2.9	1,561	31.5	28.1
Rogers	35,208	77.8	168,000	19.0	10.0	869	26.0	2.9	44,863	0.6	1,578	3.5	44,229	34.9	27.9
Seminole	9,357	67.9	75,100	21.9	10.2	631	24.9	5.0	9,125	-0.5	463	5.1	9,083	24.6	33.1
Sequoyah	15,437	72.2	99,100	19.3	11.6	691	25.6	4.8	16,550	1.1	718	4.3	16,023	24.9	30.7
Stephens	16,607	74.4	114,700	18.9	10.0	700	25.8	2.2	18,751	1.7	844	4.5	17,623	29.3	32.4
Texas	6,761	67.0	118,200	19.3	12.5	759	21.6	4.7	11,412	1.5	210	1.8	10,385	28.0	40.5
Tillman	2,794	74.1	52,800	18.1	10.0	625	23.1	6.9	2,921	-3.2	124	4.2	2,855	27.3	37.8
Tulsa	253,909	59.5	160,700	19.2	10.7	882	27.3	3.1	323,923	0.5	13,075	4.0	315,476	38.5	21.8
Wagoner	29,591	79.2	162,900	19.3	10.0	892	27.0	3.3	38,649	0.7	1,370	3.5	37,756	35.7	25.9
Washington	20,376	71.2	126,100	17.8	10.0	729	27.0	2.0	22,455	1.3	846	3.8	22,368	38.0	24.4
Washita	4,296	71.6	89,800	16.7	10.0	691	23.4	2.0	4,963	-2.3	214	4.3	4,934	33.4	31.9
Woods	3,140	68.3	114,100	17.5	10.0	726	25.1	0.5	4,733	3.3	99	2.1	4,195	35.0	29.1
Woodward	7,608	70.2	138,800	20.9	10.0	792	23.5	1.8	8,665	-2.4	365	4.2	9,458	30.0	32.1
OREGON	1,642,579	62.8	336,700	22.6	11.8	1,173	30.3	3.7	2,148,333	2.1	112,195	5.2	2,014,487	40.4	21.3
Baker	7,158	70.4	180,600	21.0	11.7	694	28.5	2.2	7,467	2.7	384	5.1	6,112	34.7	25.6
Benton	36,051	56.8	357,900	21.0	10.4	1,145	36.7	1.9	47,556	1.9	1,873	3.9	45,163	49.0	14.2
Clackamas	159,330	70.9	421,100	22.4	11.9	1,356	30.3	3.0	222,815	2.0	10,797	4.8	205,620	42.1	21.7
Clatsop	16,019	60.7	309,500	22.9	12.0	957	27.7	1.8	19,452	0.9	1,168	6.0	18,160	30.8	23.5
Columbia	19,872	75.7	282,600	22.0	10.8	985	33.5	2.3	24,640	2.1	1,418	5.8	23,394	29.5	31.3
Coos	27,819	68.3	220,400	24.0	12.8	845	29.6	3.0	27,033	1.7	1,696	6.3	25,889	32.9	24.3
Crook	9,998	73.5	265,100	22.6	11.5	913	30.3	2.3	10,941	5.5	736	6.7	9,845	27.3	29.8
Curry	10,790	73.4	285,600	23.4	13.4	896	29.3	3.4	9,158	2.2	612	6.7	7,848	33.2	17.7
Deschutes	77,040	67.9	389,300	23.8	11.9	1,306	30.9	3.4	102,553	4.4	5,429	5.3	94,505	38.8	18.9
Douglas	46,439	70.1	210,800	23.3	11.9	870	28.3	2.8	47,860	1.1	2,787	5.8	43,767	29.8	28.0
Gilliam	905	75.1	112,900	22.5	17.1	958	26.3	1.2	940	-5.2	45	4.8	800	34.3	24.6
Grant	3,453	75.4	153,900	25.3	12.1	672	24.5	2.5	3,247	1.4	217	6.7	2,929	38.6	23.9
Harney	3,176	71.9	140,300	21.6	10.0	705	27.2	2.4	3,761	3.5	193	5.1	3,167	36.4	16.9
Hood River	8,892	68.4	411,600	22.0	10.0	1,138	26.3	4.3	14,410	2.2	652	4.5	12,246	35.7	29.2
Jackson	89,690	64.3	294,500	23.4	12.4	1,057	32.0	3.9	107,706	2.5	5,843	5.4	98,551	35.9	22.0
Jefferson	8,395	68.3	242,200	21.9	10.2	819	27.8	5.2	10,459	1.3	677	6.5	9,172	33.3	29.1
Josephine	36,606	68.8	281,500	25.0	11.8	930	34.2	5.4	36,990	2.4	2,280	6.2	32,773	33.2	23.5
Klamath	28,376	64.2	188,700	21.9	10.0	781	31.1	3.4	29,770	0.9	2,008	6.7	26,586	33.8	27.0
Lake	3,533	62.2	161,000	23.3	10.0	727	23.9	5.8	3,721	1.8	204	5.5	3,203	37.7	22.4
Lane	154,516	59.1	280,000	23.3	12.0	1,037	32.0	3.1	182,197	1.7	10,055	5.5	176,797	37.1	21.3
Lincoln	21,841	67.2	265,800	25.9	12.7	945	31.0	2.4	21,119	1.7	1,439	6.8	19,457	30.7	22.0
Linn	48,290	66.4	240,200	23.0	11.6	1,037	30.2	3.0	60,636	2.6	3,401	5.6	56,332	34.4	28.1
Malheur	10,059	59.5	150,400	23.5	11.3	692	26.9	4.4	12,717	1.1	554	4.4	11,189	28.4	35.2
Marion	120,474	60.8	270,300	22.6	11.7	1,045	30.3	5.5	167,425	3.0	8,515	5.1	157,530	32.2	27.3

1. Specified owner-occupied units. 2. A value of 10.0 represents 10 percent or less; a value of 50.0 represents 50 percent or more. 3. Specified renter-occupied units. 4. Overcrowded or lacking complete plumbing facilities. 5. Percent of civilian labor force. 6. Civilian employed persons 16 years old and over.

STATE County	Private nonfarm establishments, employment and payroll, 2020									Agriculture, 2017			
		Employment						Annual payroll		Farms			Farm producers whose primary occupation is farming (percent)
											Percent with:		
	Number of establish-ments	Total	Health care and social assistance	Manufac-turing	Retail trade	Finance and insurance	Professional, scientific, and technical services	Total (mil dol)	Average per employee (dollars)	Number	Fewer than 50 acres	1000 acres or more	
	104	105	106	107	108	109	110	111	112	113	114	115	116
OKLAHOMA—Cont'd													
Kiowa	178	1,321	477	NA	241	112	33	45	34,103	579	10.7	29.5	43.8
Latimer	154	3,292	2,153	NA	222	45	60	147	44,630	707	30.8	5.4	38.0
Le Flore	801	6,719	1,665	184	1,504	421	320	209	31,158	1,672	33.4	3.8	40.4
Lincoln	560	5,849	533	719	808	499	229	240	41,006	2,231	32.9	3.5	33.0
Logan	874	7,179	995	623	1,313	187	222	258	35,870	1,262	33.4	8.0	33.6
Love	152	5,455	88	114	111	43	141	186	34,006	725	31.7	5.9	35.5
McClain	931	8,529	1,357	502	1,469	233	384	293	34,300	1,296	45.2	4.9	31.4
McCurtain	622	8,524	1,359	2,550	1,138	220	150	322	37,720	1,479	34.8	3.0	40.0
McIntosh	341	2,944	745	37	825	166	100	78	26,458	1,013	28.8	2.4	38.9
Major	253	1,726	257	48	249	71	47	71	40,857	801	18.2	17.6	35.7
Marshall	297	4,157	406	1,780	631	115	141	151	36,417	588	34.4	6.6	31.2
Mayes	786	10,720	1,409	2,885	1,602	286	434	469	43,785	1,552	41.2	2.8	35.7
Murray	280	3,656	610	482	615	106	49	132	36,071	473	34.7	9.3	34.1
Muskogee	1,371	23,369	6,350	3,681	3,242	633	430	977	41,815	1,586	39.3	3.2	40.8
Noble	203	3,844	307	2,016	310	175	36	188	48,902	835	20.1	13.9	37.2
Nowata	147	1,476	286	279	170	90	27	57	38,577	883	22.4	7.0	41.5
Okfuskee	171	1,802	887	115	238	70	18	59	32,988	934	17.8	7.1	38.3
Oklahoma	24,117	392,779	62,913	18,849	48,168	20,072	26,603	19,217	48,927	1,103	60.7	1.8	35.8
Okmulgee	626	7,015	1,899	1,094	1,294	278	231	225	32,143	1,404	36.9	4.2	33.3
Osage	592	5,798	661	438	1,045	214	204	198	34,067	1,395	31.6	12.5	36.2
Ottawa	556	9,064	1,497	1,638	981	236	155	277	30,567	947	36.4	4.1	38.5
Pawnee	248	3,308	589	187	389	88	1,150	156	47,190	818	21.5	8.7	34.8
Payne	1,803	22,837	3,686	1,540	3,907	680	1,323	782	34,242	1,541	39.1	5.1	31.9
Pittsburg	909	10,459	2,432	873	1,931	388	313	393	37,577	1,623	28.3	6.2	34.8
Pontotoc	951	13,497	3,808	1,260	1,752	490	843	541	40,071	1,438	37.0	3.9	28.9
Pottawatomie	1,264	17,283	2,904	2,396	2,770	595	749	595	34,420	1,856	40.8	3.7	35.1
Pushmataha	185	1,790	636	255	296	68	98	53	29,847	695	17.1	7.1	41.7
Roger Mills	77	474	103	NA	71	NA	NA	19	39,816	612	4.1	31.5	47.7
Rogers	1,810	29,723	2,915	6,575	2,754	881	1,857	1,515	50,984	1,776	53.9	3.3	33.8
Seminole	422	5,217	954	1,028	824	210	77	193	36,906	1,143	28.2	3.3	36.8
Sequoyah	592	6,800	2,383	246	1,156	302	154	182	26,812	1,205	40.2	3.2	36.7
Stephens	1,049	12,478	2,569	1,217	1,763	574	484	470	37,704	1,226	22.5	8.3	33.7
Texas	459	8,292	295	2,593	764	215	111	413	49,825	828	7.1	33.1	37.1
Tillman	120	1,030	162	NA	127	79	19	33	32,027	456	10.3	30.9	39.0
Tulsa	19,015	338,966	52,556	37,974	38,943	14,287	21,528	16,869	49,765	1,053	63.1	1.7	33.2
Wagoner	1,006	8,893	991	2,108	1,595	223	208	382	42,965	1,059	53.2	3.2	35.4
Washington	1,115	17,662	2,622	971	2,271	724	1,463	920	52,064	899	40.0	4.7	33.2
Washita	216	1,331	310	117	254	86	86	45	33,665	864	13.7	26.5	42.0
Woods	267	2,393	340	51	420	189	55	85	35,458	710	10.3	32.5	42.8
Woodward	758	7,318	1,078	447	1,192	278	191	317	43,294	843	17.4	25.7	35.2
OREGON	118,927	1,664,087	266,015	177,991	214,752	64,974	99,384	88,360	53,098	37,616	67.1	6.2	40.3
Baker	509	4,394	717	625	815	110	203	168	38,260	705	38.7	16.6	53.9
Benton	2,147	29,469	6,155	1,582	3,724	1,134	2,966	1,563	53,037	964	72.3	2.9	36.6
Clackamas	12,209	147,405	23,193	16,893	19,514	5,812	9,005	7,943	53,885	4,297	85.9	0.2	33.1
Clatsop	1,531	15,435	2,458	1,678	2,896	277	297	588	38,094	226	66.4	0.4	37.3
Columbia	970	9,067	1,344	1,613	1,631	367	414	355	39,122	789	75.8	0.5	30.0
Coos	1,567	18,349	4,241	1,415	2,914	460	456	750	40,848	559	45.1	4.7	48.9
Crook	566	5,241	558	1,102	673	107	150	238	45,403	620	57.1	12.1	40.2
Curry	682	5,574	1,121	735	1,045	208	135	205	36,710	200	39.5	8.5	54.1
Deschutes	7,821	74,136	11,282	5,735	11,699	2,342	4,006	3,345	45,118	1,484	85.4	0.8	34.7
Douglas	2,569	32,080	6,842	4,333	4,809	905	904	1,436	44,754	2,009	56.6	3.7	44.2
Gilliam	70	584	82	NA	58	13	30	25	43,103	153	6.5	69.9	49.2
Grant	215	1,556	414	94	237	61	63	59	37,735	383	34.5	23.8	47.0
Harney	206	1,476	363	4	344	40	83	58	39,374	532	21.4	30.8	50.6
Hood River	1,018	10,547	1,735	1,492	1,356	162	496	407	38,603	578	75.4	0.5	46.4
Jackson	6,436	79,055	16,118	6,622	12,473	2,318	2,779	3,480	44,018	2,136	78.6	1.1	39.9
Jefferson	424	4,772	670	1,545	641	82	76	183	38,370	397	45.8	12.3	51.0
Josephine	2,039	23,538	5,191	2,564	4,396	764	1,211	932	39,615	746	85.0	0.3	43.6
Klamath	1,530	17,036	3,664	1,560	3,051	481	584	715	41,973	1,005	41.9	9.0	51.5
Lake	187	1,385	389	207	213	27	64	55	39,482	381	25.7	29.4	61.9
Lane	10,001	128,420	24,251	14,332	20,241	5,097	6,038	5,639	43,914	2,646	78.2	1.1	35.9
Lincoln	1,544	14,575	1,739	990	2,978	291	259	500	34,275	384	66.4	0.3	37.2
Linn	2,713	38,205	5,723	8,048	5,442	894	1,288	1,779	46,554	2,222	71.2	3.1	41.6
Malheur	687	8,653	1,458	1,234	2,069	233	389	319	36,826	964	33.7	17.4	56.4
Marion	8,659	113,585	22,102	10,410	17,665	2,696	3,774	4,869	42,866	2,761	75.8	2.2	41.5

STATE County	Agriculture, 2017 (cont.) Land in farms: Acreage (1,000)	Land in farms: Percent change, 2012–2017	Acres: Average size of farm	Acres: Total irrigated (1,000)	Acres: Total cropland (1,000)	Value of land and buildings (dollars): Average per farm	Value of land and buildings (dollars): Average per acre	Value of machinery and equipment, average per farm (dollars)	Value of products sold: Total (mil dol)	Value of products sold: Average per farm (acres)	Percent from: Crops	Percent from: Livestock and poultry products	Organic farms (number)	Farms with internet access (percent)	Government payments: Total ($1,000)	Government payments: Percent of farms
	117	118	119	120	121	122	123	124	125	126	127	128	129	130	131	132
OKLAHOMA—Cont'd																
Kiowa	583	-1.8	1,006	0.6	302.0	1,262,052	1,254	189,899	98.2	169,539	39.3	60.7	1	76.3	7,426	57.7
Latimer	214	-3.1	302	0.3	38.8	542,932	1,796	63,905	35.4	50,122	4.7	95.3	NA	73.3	273	4.1
Le Flore	381	-3.6	228	1.8	116.2	492,429	2,162	72,515	273.6	163,654	4.2	95.8	NA	72.5	1,040	9.4
Lincoln	482	6.0	216	0.4	132.2	483,860	2,241	65,793	45.5	20,379	21.5	78.5	NA	75.9	733	9.2
Logan	393	6.9	311	0.6	154.8	696,903	2,240	77,436	44.8	35,496	36.2	63.8	NA	77.7	1,801	27.4
Love	203	-7.7	279	1.2	42.0	685,961	2,455	65,841	22.1	30,510	17.1	82.9	NA	68.0	763	14.3
McClain	286	1.2	221	0.4	85.4	582,207	2,636	67,571	42.7	32,955	24.6	75.4	NA	77.5	1,093	12.8
McCurtain	342	8.1	231	2.6	84.9	495,237	2,141	75,986	198.1	133,921	5.7	94.3	NA	70.1	1,705	8.4
McIntosh	226	-4.4	223	1.5	54.2	423,234	1,901	58,461	21.3	20,986	8.8	91.2	NA	64.8	881	14.8
Major	525	-2.2	655	17.9	218.6	972,803	1,484	137,306	107.3	133,939	24.0	76.0	1	77.2	3,562	47.8
Marshall	174	-9.1	297	1.4	31.9	718,380	2,422	59,885	12.1	20,634	16.1	83.9	NA	69.9	348	11.2
Mayes	271	-4.9	175	0.1	90.6	485,811	2,780	62,555	79.4	51,154	9.4	90.6	NA	73.8	722	8.1
Murray	209	0.6	443	0.3	28.3	946,663	2,138	84,584	16.6	35,197	9.6	90.4	NA	72.7	997	25.4
Muskogee	312	-11.0	197	8.8	95.8	443,351	2,256	60,372	47.4	29,912	28.7	71.3	1	72.5	1,872	25.7
Noble	449	1.4	538	9.1	193.6	956,821	1,779	113,383	61.4	73,519	40.7	59.3	NA	69.8	4,528	49.5
Nowata	347	18.6	392	0.1	60.5	809,467	2,063	73,048	54.0	61,142	11.1	88.9	NA	75.0	993	16.2
Okfuskee	347	8.6	372	1.6	75.1	637,122	1,713	75,997	33.3	35,617	17.2	82.8	NA	70.0	654	13.5
Oklahoma	133	-7.5	121	1.4	38.9	783,977	6,480	58,975	21.5	19,447	68.1	31.9	5	78.5	261	7.0
Okmulgee	296	-1.4	211	0.4	72.4	466,316	2,212	58,324	31.0	22,078	20.3	79.7	NA	72.4	337	5.0
Osage	1,101	-9.5	789	1.0	100.0	1,257,014	1,592	62,815	111.9	80,201	8.5	91.5	NA	72.7	3,951	13.7
Ottawa	206	6.6	217	0.2	92.8	603,803	2,776	82,877	139.7	147,558	49.8	50.2	NA	72.4	1,974	23.4
Pawnee	322	12.6	394	0.3	66.9	701,747	1,783	75,890	34.8	42,484	16.8	83.2	NA	68.1	1,780	25.2
Payne	341	-2.6	221	0.7	95.5	535,511	2,421	65,835	41.4	26,870	11.2	88.8	2	75.9	1,060	13.6
Pittsburg	519	-1.0	320	0.3	92.0	559,812	1,752	67,533	42.7	26,302	10.4	89.6	NA	68.6	573	6.8
Pontotoc	320	-1.3	223	0.4	69.3	482,701	2,168	54,476	26.1	18,182	16.5	83.5	NA	71.3	431	11.9
Pottawatomie	346	3.3	186	0.7	83.7	420,405	2,254	62,144	32.6	17,566	22.2	77.8	NA	76.8	1,272	8.9
Pushmataha	263	-11.4	379	0.6	34.0	584,413	1,542	55,456	16.4	23,535	5.7	94.3	NA	69.5	377	8.6
Roger Mills	730	1.5	1,193	3.0	123.4	1,529,868	1,282	106,486	58.5	95,533	17.8	82.2	NA	69.8	2,259	54.7
Rogers	299	-0.8	169	1.2	70.5	490,477	2,910	57,314	52.1	29,346	14.2	85.8	NA	80.0	1,091	6.6
Seminole	266	9.2	232	0.4	50.7	423,540	1,823	58,027	21.6	18,891	11.8	88.2	NA	69.9	657	20.2
Sequoyah	217	0.7	180	7.1	68.0	393,733	2,191	72,790	57.7	47,909	24.9	75.1	4	71.0	446	4.4
Stephens	462	-3.8	377	D	85.1	663,214	1,759	66,173	49.2	40,144	8.9	91.1	1	67.9	2,866	18.4
Texas	1,278	-0.7	1,544	168.8	680.0	1,563,361	1,013	210,974	1,135.7	1,371,593	11.0	89.0	NA	70.9	16,336	72.2
Tillman	557	2.9	1,221	33.0	353.5	1,621,033	1,327	240,298	138.0	302,697	57.3	42.7	NA	78.9	10,974	71.5
Tulsa	113	6.6	108	3.9	45.9	626,847	5,829	51,688	20.9	19,803	78.4	21.6	NA	77.7	178	5.3
Wagoner	194	-2.2	184	9.5	100.6	520,155	2,833	75,163	45.9	43,381	65.8	34.2	NA	75.8	1,580	24.6
Washington	219	-5.0	244	0.5	50.5	574,708	2,354	62,352	35.7	39,665	18.3	81.7	2	77.4	583	8.9
Washita	643	1.5	744	6.2	379.1	1,105,614	1,486	162,962	119.7	138,559	39.1	60.9	NA	78.0	9,041	58.1
Woods	830	2.7	1,169	3.0	285.0	1,549,585	1,326	155,030	79.8	112,376	23.3	76.7	NA	72.7	4,795	53.8
Woodward	788	10.2	935	5.5	173.6	1,136,597	1,216	95,455	70.5	83,625	8.0	92.0	5	74.1	1,892	50.5
OREGON	15,962	-2.1	424	1,664.9	4,726.1	1,032,545	2,433	100,328	5,006.8	133,103	65.6	34.4	659	85.7	92,406	10.7
Baker	755	6.2	1,070	108.5	130.5	1,337,390	1,250	146,937	79.2	112,346	41.8	58.2	4	82.0	3,466	28.1
Benton	128	2.9	132	27.2	69.0	852,300	6,438	80,922	76.5	79,401	82.6	17.4	32	86.7	1,144	6.7
Clackamas	157	-3.2	37	20.5	83.7	788,181	21,514	61,085	376.3	87,575	81.9	18.1	42	87.2	282	1.6
Clatsop	15	-8.0	67	1.9	4.4	476,979	7,153	73,613	9.7	42,743	13.5	86.5	1	85.4	11	3.5
Columbia	43	-23.5	55	2.2	12.6	475,785	8,654	47,057	D	D	D	D	3	84.0	135	1.9
Coos	138	-12.3	247	10.9	16.3	753,383	3,048	74,373	45.2	80,877	18.3	81.7	19	78.9	79	4.8
Crook	800	-2.8	1,290	67.6	49.2	1,231,591	955	98,369	44.6	71,877	27.1	72.9	NA	85.5	869	4.2
Curry	70	11.0	352	3.2	6.3	1,245,333	3,541	82,278	15.8	79,000	55.1	44.9	2	73.5	307	12.5
Deschutes	135	2.7	91	36.0	31.0	786,080	8,667	51,257	28.8	19,386	57.5	42.5	9	93.2	90	0.8
Douglas	400	4.7	199	14.7	52.3	680,086	3,414	54,494	72.5	36,092	37.8	62.2	18	82.9	866	4.4
Gilliam	612	-15.4	3,999	7.7	249.7	2,878,695	720	320,066	26.7	174,242	69.8	30.2	NA	81.0	7,680	83.7
Grant	629	-4.2	1,642	34.5	63.0	1,699,233	1,035	103,621	24.1	63,000	13.6	86.4	6	77.3	1,295	21.1
Harney	1,557	3.4	2,927	166.5	233.5	1,996,031	682	152,672	82.3	154,692	36.0	64.0	7	77.3	2,706	30.5
Hood River	28	10.2	49	16.6	19.3	685,502	13,926	95,942	126.1	218,152	99.2	0.8	25	89.6	365	5.9
Jackson	170	-20.5	80	37.5	40.7	677,191	8,494	44,300	71.0	33,262	74.7	25.3	43	86.6	55	0.8
Jefferson	793	-3.0	1,997	44.5	77.8	1,707,699	855	196,826	67.4	169,866	81.2	18.8	6	84.9	2,162	23.2
Josephine	28	-1.4	37	8.0	8.4	672,056	17,992	38,200	17.5	23,456	49.2	50.8	27	85.1	1	1.1
Klamath	483	-25.7	481	165.5	147.5	1,052,207	2,189	151,621	192.6	191,640	52.7	47.3	83	84.7	2,033	13.3
Lake	756	15.0	1,983	140.3	166.7	2,143,381	1,081	255,011	93.9	246,441	47.7	52.3	21	86.4	829	18.9
Lane	203	-7.5	77	22.3	98.0	656,860	8,556	59,094	158.4	59,873	58.0	42.0	65	83.8	659	2.9
Lincoln	29	-4.0	76	0.4	3.6	415,466	5,498	38,118	D	D	D	D	4	86.5	239	1.3
Linn	315	-4.9	142	36.9	242.6	1,005,264	7,092	100,759	243.0	109,375	74.6	25.4	39	85.8	856	4.8
Malheur	1,093	1.5	1,134	174.0	210.8	1,687,999	1,488	241,602	353.3	366,521	47.9	52.1	8	86.0	4,477	33.1
Marion	289	0.9	105	102.6	237.4	1,292,998	12,367	142,613	701.6	254,104	86.0	14.0	46	84.9	1,995	6.0

STATE County	Water use, 2015		Wholesale Trade[1], 2017				Retail Trade[2], 2017				Real estate and rental and leasing,[2] 2017			
	Public supply water withdrawn (mil gal/ day)	Public supply gallons withdrawn per person per day	Number of establish- ments	Number of employees	Sales (mil dol)	Average payroll (mil dol)	Number of establish- ments	Number of employees	Sales (mil dol)	Average payroll (mil dol)	Number of establish- ments	Number of employees	Sales (mil dol)	Average payroll (mil dol)
	133	134	135	136	137	138	139	140	141	142	143	144	145	146
OKLAHOMA—Cont'd														
Kiowa	6.4	697.7	8	46	42.5	2.6	34	266	61.4	6.5	4	D	1.1	D
Latimer	1.4	133.5	D	D	D	3.1	23	226	49.7	4.6	NA	NA	NA	NA
Le Flore	7.1	143.1	22	175	75.2	7.1	138	1,571	398.7	34.7	16	23	3.6	0.7
Lincoln	1.0	29.4	24	160	104.0	7.7	84	829	255.7	20.8	16	30	7.3	1.1
Logan	2.6	56.7	19	89	46.5	5.1	105	1,227	454.0	34.4	46	151	25.5	5.5
Love	0.8	84.1	6	21	7.2	0.7	18	97	53.0	2.5	7	13	3.7	0.3
McClain	1.4	36.3	26	144	45.9	5.4	126	1,500	485.0	43.2	37	82	12.9	2.9
McCurtain	5.6	169.5	D	D	D	4.5	103	1,234	332.9	28.6	20	80	13.5	1.7
McIntosh	4.6	229.6	6	84	18.2	1.9	70	878	295.7	22.3	12	30	5.6	1.5
Major	5.5	710.3	12	97	39.7	3.6	40	272	80.3	5.8	7	D	5.7	D
Marshall	2.3	141.1	6	79	21.8	4.5	55	615	198.0	16.1	9	25	1.9	0.5
Mayes	47.1	1,152.4	33	390	403.2	23.0	124	1,623	390.6	34.9	21	48	9.3	1.4
Murray	7.8	557.5	D	D	D	D	44	613	205.4	16.3	D	D	D	D
Muskogee	1.2	16.5	55	734	446.5	32.5	251	3,404	907.8	80.5	47	174	30.0	5.1
Noble	0.3	24.2	10	107	53.7	4.0	31	247	99.5	6.8	4	D	0.6	D
Nowata	1.2	110.1	D	D	D	1.4	23	176	60.4	3.4	4	9	1.3	0.3
Okfuskee	1.0	81.3	4	17	5.2	0.4	27	240	74.2	6.2	NA	NA	NA	NA
Oklahoma	104.3	134.3	1,141	17,335	16,731.1	995.1	2,922	45,748	14,238.3	1,288.0	1,321	6,844	1,779.5	341.7
Okmulgee	5.8	148.5	18	124	47.2	4.2	112	1,237	354.4	29.2	D	D	D	D
Osage	16.6	346.2	14	82	17.8	3.7	91	1,000	273.9	23.5	16	36	10.2	1.7
Ottawa	2.7	84.4	D	D	D	D	93	1,044	254.5	23.8	21	56	6.7	1.3
Pawnee	1.0	62.1	8	65	10.0	1.1	36	380	101.8	10.5	NA	NA	NA	NA
Payne	2.6	32.7	D	D	D	19.5	295	4,255	1,059.5	97.8	88	373	64.2	10.8
Pittsburg	5.9	132.3	D	D	D	D	163	1,978	630.1	51.0	39	148	31.3	5.1
Pontotoc	4.4	113.9	D	D	D	D	159	1,721	465.2	40.7	40	158	31.0	6.7
Pottawatomie	7.5	104.5	D	D	D	D	233	2,842	752.0	66.4	49	196	24.9	5.7
Pushmataha	0.5	47.4	D	D	D	2.2	36	348	91.0	6.9	5	11	8.0	0.9
Roger Mills	0.6	147.8	NA	NA	NA	NA	18	71	21.1	1.7	NA	NA	NA	NA
Rogers	72.7	801.0	74	907	1,731.5	54.4	219	2,954	862.8	73.2	86	248	56.1	8.1
Seminole	3.2	125.3	D	D	D	D	69	825	224.7	20.7	17	59	13.0	2.4
Sequoyah	4.5	108.4	12	69	15.6	1.4	119	1,190	343.3	28.2	14	32	6.3	0.7
Stephens	1.1	24.2	47	398	423.6	20.9	185	1,972	511.7	44.9	27	86	15.4	2.7
Texas	4.8	221.0	D	D	D	D	78	831	198.1	17.7	17	37	5.4	1.0
Tillman	1.1	147.7	10	117	94.9	5.2	20	137	25.6	2.6	NA	NA	NA	NA
Tulsa	0.0	0.0	960	14,551	10,266.0	886.2	2,301	39,982	11,878.0	1,063.2	1,016	7,058	1,264.4	288.0
Wagoner	31.3	409.0	31	204	81.3	12.0	113	1,521	417.6	37.2	27	42	7.0	1.4
Washington	1.9	35.6	26	114	48.2	4.6	173	2,385	681.7	59.2	51	342	37.0	7.4
Washita	7.1	608.9	D	D	D	D	41	267	69.9	6.4	3	D	1.7	D
Woods	0.7	79.5	21	300	118.3	9.7	44	454	119.3	11.3	11	18	4.1	0.7
Woodward	6.3	292.2	D	D	D	D	117	1,234	382.6	32.0	35	139	34.0	6.4
OREGON	567.0	140.7	4,452	67,900	58,205.2	4,306.2	14,318	211,222	61,699.3	6,066.6	6,771	29,773	6,773.7	1,263.2
Baker	3.3	204.3	13	74	22.0	2.7	82	702	182.8	18.0	15	31	5.2	1.0
Benton	12.0	136.5	41	278	176.7	16.6	266	3,935	903.3	97.0	130	493	82.4	15.3
Clackamas	134.4	334.6	563	9,140	7,174.3	608.3	1,175	19,430	5,737.7	573.5	721	3,013	767.5	139.5
Clatsop	10.0	264.3	29	183	139.5	10.4	267	2,817	766.2	78.0	83	445	206.8	16.2
Columbia	4.7	94.8	D	D	D	1.7	128	1,566	395.7	42.4	45	89	28.6	3.4
Coos	5.1	80.0	43	405	290.7	17.3	242	2,938	853.5	83.5	57	211	37.3	6.1
Crook	2.1	97.5	18	105	76.6	6.3	68	595	210.9	15.9	24	46	10.1	1.5
Curry	2.9	126.8	D	D	D	D	111	1,080	268.6	27.9	57	D	17.2	D
Deschutes	38.0	216.8	227	1,621	1,110.3	82.0	879	11,709	3,550.5	341.9	499	1,275	298.1	49.8
Douglas	14.2	131.9	D	D	D	D	390	4,761	1,268.0	121.9	122	355	61.5	9.9
Gilliam	0.6	295.9	D	D	D	1.5	13	56	18.4	1.1	NA	NA	NA	NA
Grant	1.0	135.0	7	D	11.6	D	39	272	103.2	7.2	D	D	D	0.1
Harney	1.7	238.9	6	43	23.3	1.6	30	354	160.8	9.2	7	19	2.4	0.5
Hood River	6.3	272.3	26	721	224.4	32.2	157	1,560	389.4	42.1	45	137	33.1	5.7
Jackson	39.0	183.7	230	2,127	1,280.2	104.7	889	12,331	3,796.2	363.4	377	1,201	244.5	39.4
Jefferson	4.4	193.2	17	170	91.7	8.7	57	596	178.9	15.2	22	58	8.3	1.8
Josephine	7.2	84.7	56	374	294.5	19.7	323	4,406	1,208.1	127.9	107	431	63.9	16.7
Klamath	9.5	143.1	49	447	186.9	19.3	226	2,820	824.7	72.8	75	249	41.4	7.6
Lake	1.6	199.3	D	D	D	1.4	26	203	108.6	6.2	7	16	2.1	0.5
Lane	43.7	120.4	392	5,458	2,822.2	304.4	1,313	20,047	5,373.5	585.6	613	2,395	523.8	84.9
Lincoln	8.7	183.9	D	D	D	D	294	3,167	675.8	71.9	73	367	62.2	10.9
Linn	9.6	79.4	116	1,634	1,248.8	86.5	368	5,189	1,424.8	140.2	115	428	54.7	11.1
Malheur	6.8	222.5	D	D	D	D	110	1,918	598.3	54.2	26	73	12.3	2.0
Marion	71.9	217.5	290	3,512	2,731.6	185.0	1,137	17,759	5,073.6	480.0	458	1,811	409.8	72.3

1 Merchant wholesalers, except manufacturers' sales branches and offices. 2. Employer establishments.

Table B. States and Counties — **Professional Services, Manufacturing, and Accommodation and Food Services**

STATE County	Professional, scientific, and technical services, 2017				Manufacturing, 2017				Accommodation and food services, 2017			
	Number of establish-ments	Number of employees	Sales (mil dol)	Average payroll (mil dol)	Number of establish-ments	Number of employees	Sales (mil dol)	Average payroll (mil dol)	Number of establis-hments	Number of employees	Sales (mil dol)	Annual payroll (mil dol)
	147	148	149	150	151	152	153	154	155	156	157	158
OKLAHOMA—Cont'd												
Kiowa	11	30	3.5	1.1	NA	NA	NA	NA	D	D	D	D
Latimer	18	79	28.2	4.8	D	D	D	D	7	111	5.2	1.4
Le Flore	D	D	D	D	25	215	65.2	10.2	53	740	32.1	9.0
Lincoln	41	177	31.1	8.3	30	580	201.8	28.1	47	566	26.3	8.0
Logan	76	202	29.4	8.4	31	441	123.2	25.4	57	733	39.2	10.0
Love	13	52	6.3	1.7	5	139	32.1	8.3	29	1,280	134.7	28.2
McClain	83	291	44.6	11.8	27	447	82.7	27.0	72	1,137	57.7	15.0
McCurtain	31	89	14.4	4.0	32	2,627	1,906.3	129.7	62	842	52.7	12.3
McIntosh	27	113	14.7	3.6	8	37	5.5	1.4	39	533	24.0	7.2
Major	22	39	4.6	1.2	6	46	10.3	2.6	10	110	5.8	1.4
Marshall	22	92	19.4	3.6	19	1,309	360.6	58.0	37	417	22.2	5.7
Mayes	61	364	39.3	17.7	59	2,631	1,275.4	142.5	87	1,158	53.1	14.0
Murray	25	64	6.0	2.0	17	439	126.6	27.1	38	515	32.3	9.9
Muskogee	D	D	D	D	56	3,234	1,276.8	178.5	141	2,458	113.9	31.3
Noble	12	44	5.4	1.3	D	D	D	D	26	290	15.5	4.0
Nowata	11	28	4.9	1.0	8	205	59.2	12.8	11	108	4.7	1.4
Okfuskee	9	15	2.5	0.7	8	110	16.1	3.8	13	150	7.0	1.7
Oklahoma	D	D	D	D	671	19,153	6,670.1	939.0	2,100	43,385	2,429.7	677.8
Okmulgee	47	215	23.4	9.8	32	1,228	583.7	68.1	64	1,026	42.4	13.1
Osage	44	149	19.4	9.3	30	396	99.6	24.4	54	801	59.6	14.4
Ottawa	40	245	27.1	9.8	37	1,332	432.5	57.1	63	3,002	326.2	72.0
Pawnee	23	131	44.1	5.7	11	271	50.8	13.3	21	211	10.9	2.7
Payne	D	D	D	D	68	1,409	436.4	72.3	228	4,201	194.4	52.2
Pittsburg	D	D	D	D	27	1,084	340.9	54.1	96	1,445	83.1	19.7
Pontotoc	D	D	D	D	28	1,125	319.1	50.1	73	1,299	68.4	18.4
Pottawatomie	D	D	D	D	55	2,725	806.8	131.6	140	2,831	141.2	39.3
Pushmataha	17	43	4.0	1.4	5	118	37.6	5.2	D	D	D	1.7
Roger Mills	D	D	D	0.2	NA	NA	NA	NA	6	D	0.9	D
Rogers	137	1,223	206.6	80.6	153	6,052	2,483.1	368.1	122	3,553	356.0	80.8
Seminole	27	74	9.0	2.4	23	944	237.5	48.3	42	502	24.7	6.1
Sequoyah	41	130	12.5	3.6	21	264	71.7	12.1	77	1,319	120.9	27.7
Stephens	91	427	54.2	17.4	49	1,098	1,369.6	71.1	83	1,118	54.5	14.8
Texas	D	D	D	D	D	D	D	D	52	661	34.3	8.2
Tillman	8	21	2.1	1.1	D	D	D	D	12	76	3.2	0.9
Tulsa	2,395	20,460	3,659.4	1,427.5	804	34,647	16,334.4	2,019.5	1,716	36,217	2,023.4	569.6
Wagoner	74	200	22.8	8.8	51	1,636	567.0	95.6	70	937	43.7	11.7
Washington	D	D	D	D	32	936	312.2	49.2	107	1,840	91.6	25.7
Washita	22	89	17.9	6.0	7	74	21.2	3.8	10	60	3.8	0.8
Woods	20	48	5.0	1.3	6	42	23.4	2.4	26	314	15.1	3.6
Woodward	D	D	D	D	22	505	304.9	38.3	56	757	47.1	11.6
OREGON	12,527	91,027	14,579.9	6,829.0	5,557	172,210	62,411.2	10,667.7	11,708	182,613	11,803.9	3,504.5
Baker	38	178	21.3	7.0	25	501	145.0	21.5	58	614	35.2	9.5
Benton	D	D	D	D	93	1,295	421.2	65.3	224	3,900	214.6	62.0
Clackamas	1,346	8,564	1,775.4	753.2	568	16,224	5,073.2	969.2	879	14,375	877.9	262.6
Clatsop	91	308	30.4	10.9	51	1,713	875.1	106.7	274	3,910	276.7	81.1
Columbia	D	D	D	D	51	1,453	447.4	78.4	100	1,151	63.5	19.2
Coos	D	D	D	D	58	1,435	457.3	60.4	173	2,236	157.4	43.0
Crook	42	130	15.6	5.0	32	784	154.8	34.6	43	512	36.5	10.2
Curry	33	128	13.4	4.4	20	627	234.8	37.5	111	995	62.0	17.4
Deschutes	D	D	D	D	342	4,828	1,107.8	226.0	608	10,178	707.1	224.8
Douglas	D	D	D	D	134	4,164	1,372.2	192.6	268	4,299	285.2	76.5
Gilliam	D	D	D	1.1	NA	NA	NA	NA	12	D	2.3	D
Grant	D	D	5.2	D	D	D	D	D	25	151	11.3	2.9
Harney	11	44	4.3	1.7	D	D	D	D	30	194	13.2	3.3
Hood River	D	D	D	D	65	1,561	455.1	75.7	107	1,664	100.7	34.1
Jackson	D	D	D	D	306	6,428	2,200.2	298.8	620	9,593	535.7	168.8
Jefferson	23	66	6.3	2.3	22	1,143	217.1	50.0	50	602	36.1	10.1
Josephine	D	D	D	D	109	2,528	561.2	111.2	208	2,919	169.8	49.3
Klamath	D	D	D	D	47	1,951	539.4	77.1	184	2,277	152.8	43.6
Lake	12	64	10.2	2.8	13	189	46.8	8.6	34	158	9.7	2.4
Lane	985	5,099	634.1	252.5	521	13,517	5,054.0	708.5	1,010	15,794	943.3	272.6
Lincoln	D	D	D	D	49	944	683.0	61.1	285	3,736	262.1	73.8
Linn	D	D	D	D	193	7,359	2,494.8	417.0	230	3,278	175.6	53.3
Malheur	D	D	D	D	37	907	346.5	34.5	82	1,091	63.5	16.0
Marion	671	3,652	490.5	188.7	383	10,050	3,185.2	474.2	D	D	D	D

STATE County	Health care and social assistance, 2017				Other services, 2017				Nonemployer businesses, 2019		Value of residential construction authorized by building permits, 2021	
	Number of establish-ments	Number of employees	Receipts (mil dol)	Annual payroll (mil dol)	Number of establish-ments	Number of employees	Receipts (mil dol)	Annual payroll (mil dol)	Number	Receipts (mil dol)	New construction ($1,000)	Number of housing units
	159	160	161	162	163	164	165	166	167	168	169	170
OKLAHOMA—Cont'd												
Kiowa	21	501	27.2	14.5	8	46	4.4	1.1	570	20.1	0	0
Latimer	26	2,075	213.9	90.1	10	16	2.4	0.3	777	34.4	800	10
Le Flore	96	1,664	100.4	41.3	D	D	D	D	3,126	139.6	12,649	78
Lincoln	D	D	D	D	D	D	D	D	2,499	113.1	5,030	23
Logan	D	D	D	D	61	195	25.1	5.3	4,138	200.7	5,147	36
Love	10	117	5.8	2.4	D	D	D	1.4	696	35.1	450	3
McClain	83	1,297	69.8	28.6	53	316	47.4	14.7	3,701	189.3	140,788	604
McCurtain	74	1,328	109.3	39.1	33	122	9.9	3.5	2,560	113.7	4,396	52
McIntosh	49	660	73.9	26.8	24	69	7.0	1.7	1,352	62.5	1,103	6
Major	15	261	15.6	7.7	13	87	7.0	3.2	690	27.2	218	1
Marshall	28	613	57.4	21.7	D	D	D	D	1,122	47.5	1,772	10
Mayes	67	992	105.1	38.7	44	168	12.6	3.8	2,711	125.0	5,124	37
Murray	33	528	50.6	20.7	15	62	6.1	1.6	885	36.7	2,019	15
Muskogee	228	6,010	778.7	317.8	84	557	52.9	14.7	3,889	172.7	8,864	46
Noble	19	366	18.9	8.4	D	D	D	D	770	28.4	1,882	9
Nowata	19	290	15.3	7.5	6	13	2.4	0.4	626	26.8	386	6
Okfuskee	33	1,497	106.2	49.1	5	12	0.8	0.2	718	32.1	338	5
Oklahoma	3,127	62,666	9,551.0	3,214.7	1,480	9,635	1,283.2	342.2	68,325	3,557.2	1,441,658	5,500
Okmulgee	106	1,674	125.0	52.9	D	D	D	D	2,269	96.1	1,533	11
Osage	46	762	52.6	21.5	21	315	36.5	16.3	3,186	133.1	36,312	137
Ottawa	72	1,495	122.0	49.5	33	106	10.1	2.2	1,684	69.5	899	8
Pawnee	29	509	26.0	14.1	D	D	D	D	1,029	39.1	70	1
Payne	169	3,622	336.1	149.4	119	870	253.7	30.4	5,390	240.5	49,399	215
Pittsburg	122	2,496	221.5	98.0	50	221	22.5	6.4	2,553	120.2	10,629	75
Pontotoc	128	4,198	477.0	188.2	50	256	29.3	7.5	2,789	135.6	2,627	19
Pottawatomie	178	3,144	259.8	113.8	77	349	36.2	9.8	4,532	205.8	24,690	117
Pushmataha	28	664	39.3	16.4	D	D	0.7	D	896	45.1	0	0
Roger Mills	D	D	D	D	D	D	D	0.0	339	13.8	0	0
Rogers	176	2,730	307.2	113.5	90	439	69.4	14.2	7,037	336.9	120,707	650
Seminole	46	1,112	84.0	31.2	22	67	9.0	2.0	1,384	61.8	9,500	78
Sequoyah	76	2,521	111.2	49.6	D	D	D	D	2,976	128.3	13,396	113
Stephens	120	2,035	217.2	76.8	66	332	86.8	13.1	3,083	154.6	3,598	9
Texas	39	508	44.0	19.2	31	107	13.2	2.9	1,162	63.1	822	4
Tillman	16	154	13.1	3.7	7	16	0.9	0.2	444	15.1	400	1
Tulsa	2,112	53,768	7,176.7	2,579.4	1,251	8,451	1,670.9	308.1	54,060	2,694.1	741,002	3,214
Wagoner	81	971	75.1	34.2	63	210	24.6	5.3	5,845	258.7	157,378	692
Washington	167	3,056	294.3	121.8	76	463	43.9	13.3	3,309	136.4	23,754	87
Washita	12	314	15.5	8.5	D	D	D	D	870	42.0	0	0
Woods	17	318	24.1	10.7	D	D	D	D	729	25.6	2,240	17
Woodward	77	1,102	109.7	40.5	44	218	27.4	7.9	1,462	75.7	577	3
OREGON	13,948	263,278	33,083.8	13,106.2	7,414	43,543	6,288.8	1,555.0	308,360	15,165.9	54,993	423
Baker	42	573	69.1	24.8	34	122	12.3	3.0	1,152	46.2	13,389	59
Benton	284	6,035	728.1	322.2	146	994	225.5	39.6	6,170	278.8	78,607	284
Clackamas	1,325	23,578	2,861.9	1,208.2	744	3,763	384.7	118.1	33,502	1,928.1	485,398	1,803
Clatsop	146	2,518	323.3	125.5	99	386	35.6	9.8	3,169	160.6	57,252	175
Columbia	120	1,301	77.6	32.2	D	D	D	D	2,971	120.4	68,303	291
Coos	207	4,206	493.7	195.8	76	406	51.4	13.4	3,885	181.2	10,030	46
Crook	34	540	70.8	26.5	45	184	19.8	5.2	1,693	84.4	98,998	347
Curry	94	1,187	119.0	49.1	25	117	9.3	2.6	1,967	90.1	25,807	84
Deschutes	744	12,299	1,654.6	660.7	397	2,156	261.6	70.6	20,793	1,104.5	696,237	2,737
Douglas	329	6,550	942.8	406.4	143	725	70.2	22.5	5,889	268.4	97,801	437
Gilliam	D	D	D	D	D	D	D	0.3	141	4.0	NA	NA
Grant	23	377	32.7	15.9	D	D	4.4	D	507	19.8	5,257	20
Harney	19	369	36.4	15.0	15	49	5.4	1.5	529	22.0	2,589	11
Hood River	141	1,828	179.8	79.0	50	251	24.6	7.5	2,292	114.4	20,338	66
Jackson	758	15,189	1,902.0	753.3	328	1,967	216.7	60.8	17,968	856.6	268,818	1,142
Jefferson	48	679	70.3	30.6	27	113	10.4	2.7	1,183	57.6	55,419	234
Josephine	298	5,253	525.5	221.0	107	482	40.7	12.6	6,128	289.6	67,532	333
Klamath	187	3,439	452.3	169.2	102	396	40.8	11.3	3,687	160.2	55,418	224
Lake	16	369	31.0	18.1	11	26	2.5	0.7	484	20.2	4,937	23
Lane	1,260	23,686	2,982.6	1,139.5	636	3,703	552.4	118.3	25,788	1,157.5	452,083	2,136
Lincoln	106	1,787	239.2	93.3	100	367	37.6	9.1	3,701	200.3	53,041	206
Linn	230	5,366	575.8	238.0	163	1,004	73.8	24.8	6,589	293.3	131,616	620
Malheur	92	1,645	150.4	58.4	D	D	D	D	1,425	65.0	10,079	35
Marion	1,065	20,875	2,427.5	1,028.4	509	2,535	267.2	78.0	18,553	912.9	388,512	1,838

STATE County	Government employment and payroll, 2017: Full-time equivalent employees	March payroll (dollars)	March payroll (percent of total): Administration, judicial, and legal	Police and corrections	Fire protection	Highways and transportation	Health and welfare	Natural resources and utilities	Education and libraries	Local government finances, 2017: General revenue: Total (mil dol)	Intergovernmental (mil dol)	Taxes: Total (mil dol)	Taxes: Per capita[1] (dollars): Total	Taxes: Per capita[1] (dollars): Property
	171	172	173	174	175	176	177	178	179	180	181	182	183	184
OKLAHOMA—Cont'd														
Kiowa	496	1,527,483	8.0	5.3	1.3	5.5	30.4	4.6	44.5	28.7	12.6	9.6	1,083	775
Latimer	663	2,472,658	2.7	2.0	0.0	2.8	4.2	2.6	84.1	28.8	11.6	11.4	1,106	814
Le Flore	1,741	4,832,675	6.1	7.2	0.7	4.0	4.4	6.1	70.0	134.6	72.4	37.9	757	327
Lincoln	1,029	3,037,666	8.1	7.5	1.7	5.7	2.6	5.8	66.8	116.6	34.3	65.3	1,869	1,521
Logan	861	2,505,344	6.8	10.3	5.2	4.9	1.4	5.6	64.8	73.2	29.8	21.1	450	254
Love	494	1,930,140	4.5	7.3	0.0	3.1	46.1	1.7	34.4	58.6	11.5	19.4	1,921	1,401
McClain	1,394	4,237,439	6.2	7.2	3.4	3.9	10.7	4.1	61.3	100.4	41.5	45.1	1,147	633
McCurtain	1,437	4,219,075	4.2	6.7	1.3	4.4	3.2	7.7	71.5	99.7	52.6	27.0	817	462
McIntosh	597	2,089,827	6.1	4.2	0.0	1.0	0.9	5.5	82.2	52.2	29.2	18.9	960	465
Major	362	1,187,800	9.8	4.9	1.1	10.6	24.9	5.3	42.2	24.2	9.8	10.2	1,322	732
Marshall	528	1,612,547	14.6	3.8	1.3	1.0	4.4	3.5	71.1	35.7	17.5	13.9	852	553
Mayes	1,382	4,259,809	5.2	8.3	1.6	4.1	2.7	8.1	67.5	103.3	41.3	43.8	1,068	725
Murray	509	1,611,245	7.9	8.5	3.9	2.4	36.4	13.4	26.7	50.5	14.9	15.1	1,083	532
Muskogee	3,087	9,138,742	5.5	9.0	4.7	3.9	6.3	5.8	63.2	200.2	82.4	83.5	1,209	616
Noble	594	1,743,048	5.6	6.5	3.2	7.2	21.0	7.5	48.5	61.4	13.4	33.6	2,969	2,428
Nowata	395	1,041,445	6.6	6.6	1.5	7.1	1.8	7.1	68.9	26.8	13.8	7.4	713	417
Okfuskee	426	1,153,858	7.4	5.6	0.2	6.9	0.2	3.4	75.1	29.9	16.8	9.1	755	443
Oklahoma	24,260	95,764,486	6.0	15.3	10.1	3.3	3.6	6.4	54.6	2,696.9	767.7	1,310.8	1,667	812
Okmulgee	1,412	4,000,356	7.0	5.6	3.4	3.5	3.1	6.2	69.4	87.2	48.3	25.8	664	310
Osage	1,083	3,317,455	7.8	7.3	0.9	13.9	14.5	4.6	49.8	69.9	32.9	24.3	514	334
Ottawa	1,388	4,235,686	4.8	5.3	2.4	2.7	4.4	5.2	73.4	102.5	54.6	25.3	807	346
Pawnee	612	1,823,700	5.8	5.7	2.0	3.4	22.5	5.7	53.3	44.2	18.7	20.0	1,220	857
Payne	3,794	14,869,696	3.9	7.1	3.8	2.1	42.3	6.8	32.7	214.4	59.7	114.1	1,393	772
Pittsburg	2,411	8,306,313	4.0	6.4	2.4	4.6	35.7	3.7	42.2	230.4	58.4	56.4	1,277	601
Pontotoc	1,411	4,290,560	5.4	5.8	3.2	6.4	2.1	6.5	69.2	105.6	49.3	41.8	1,088	460
Pottawatomie	2,401	7,834,203	5.0	7.2	4.5	3.7	2.2	6.5	69.5	182.2	93.4	64.3	891	369
Pushmataha	611	1,597,765	9.8	3.8	1.5	3.8	12.4	4.7	63.7	45.5	26.1	7.8	703	377
Roger Mills	235	890,831	10.5	6.0	0.0	21.3	24.0	4.2	31.9	27.1	11.1	10.0	2,718	2,132
Rogers	2,750	9,626,821	3.3	6.5	4.9	4.1	0.7	5.9	72.0	263.1	71.3	157.9	1,727	546
Seminole	1,132	3,191,815	5.7	6.0	3.6	4.2	3.0	4.6	71.1	73.5	39.9	23.9	964	436
Sequoyah	1,602	4,807,295	4.1	7.3	0.6	3.0	11.4	4.5	67.6	120.0	58.5	29.6	708	357
Stephens	1,521	4,977,785	6.4	7.8	5.0	4.2	0.6	5.3	68.4	121.1	56.4	39.8	919	565
Texas	1,006	3,006,560	5.6	8.6	3.3	6.4	15.6	1.8	57.9	70.4	31.3	27.0	1,289	668
Tillman	404	1,244,670	8.1	7.2	2.5	9.3	11.4	10.5	48.0	74.6	15.6	54.1	7,308	390
Tulsa	23,896	83,625,515	6.5	12.2	7.6	4.0	2.5	5.5	59.3	2,498.3	677.0	1,217.4	1,883	1,062
Wagoner	1,202	3,956,073	7.8	7.3	2.6	4.0	1.7	8.6	66.0	86.3	37.8	32.1	406	265
Washington	1,638	5,182,295	6.3	11.0	6.9	3.1	1.1	9.0	61.2	138.9	48.2	56.6	1,089	655
Washita	617	2,122,381	6.6	6.1	0.6	5.9	13.6	3.1	63.6	34.6	17.1	10.8	977	698
Woods	541	1,616,617	7.3	4.5	2.5	8.1	33.4	4.1	36.6	56.4	9.5	38.5	4,241	2,833
Woodward	927	3,072,031	6.0	6.9	4.0	4.7	4.1	7.5	64.5	68.9	20.5	36.2	1,765	973
OREGON	X	X	X	X	X	X	X	X	X	X	X	X	X	X
Baker	495	1,966,935	11.7	12.7	6.2	3.2	1.3	4.8	57.0	75.8	43.4	18.9	1,178	1,092
Benton	2,152	10,442,594	7.7	11.7	5.2	3.9	12.2	5.7	51.2	268.8	91.1	134.8	1,468	1,335
Clackamas	10,184	52,528,397	7.4	11.5	6.1	2.6	7.3	5.4	56.3	1,724.0	585.3	764.7	1,854	1,669
Clatsop	1,499	6,374,922	7.5	12.9	2.5	8.4	9.2	10.0	47.1	206.1	66.7	85.4	2,184	1,754
Columbia	1,430	6,651,910	7.8	8.8	9.0	2.6	0.5	14.3	52.6	190.6	77.1	73.7	1,425	1,335
Coos	3,259	15,847,439	2.8	6.0	1.6	1.6	48.7	3.0	34.9	441.9	145.1	77.2	1,212	1,098
Crook	661	2,838,257	9.1	14.2	5.0	3.7	4.4	8.8	51.0	93.4	35.0	30.1	1,306	1,078
Curry	924	4,269,627	6.4	8.7	0.3	3.9	46.4	4.3	27.9	116.0	32.9	27.0	1,194	1,051
Deschutes	5,285	26,992,573	9.1	11.0	6.1	3.2	6.3	6.9	53.4	868.5	274.6	379.2	2,031	1,737
Douglas	3,389	14,063,815	6.1	10.3	5.0	2.7	7.1	6.0	60.9	394.2	192.0	104.8	959	876
Gilliam	141	574,205	24.8	0.7	1.4	0.0	9.7	10.3	42.1	31.1	5.1	14.5	7,795	5,603
Grant	454	2,197,975	5.6	6.0	0.3	5.2	43.2	3.9	33.9	73.7	26.6	8.6	1,200	1,162
Harney	494	2,025,870	5.0	6.4	0.6	3.2	47.8	1.9	34.6	66.1	26.9	8.3	1,142	1,054
Hood River	705	3,325,908	7.9	8.0	4.5	9.5	3.3	10.1	53.3	126.6	47.8	32.7	1,396	1,167
Jackson	5,573	25,323,949	7.9	12.8	5.8	5.8	6.8	5.7	53.0	826.7	361.6	312.0	1,440	1,189
Jefferson	823	3,287,247	6.5	8.7	2.1	1.9	3.4	11.6	63.9	113.4	69.3	26.2	1,106	970
Josephine	2,126	9,641,417	6.2	10.1	2.6	3.2	1.6	2.9	71.5	273.1	137.7	81.5	941	854
Klamath	2,208	9,029,591	4.9	7.5	4.6	5.2	5.9	6.3	62.1	255.4	122.3	78.4	1,174	1,030
Lake	557	2,329,271	4.0	4.5	1.5	5.5	53.0	2.4	27.1	66.0	23.0	13.7	1,745	1,678
Lane	11,728	57,941,191	5.9	12.8	5.6	6.3	5.9	10.3	47.4	1,612.9	655.1	547.6	1,459	1,212
Lincoln	1,567	7,811,542	10.7	14.9	3.6	5.6	8.8	21.5	32.3	245.1	63.7	125.7	2,577	2,135
Linn	4,158	19,077,155	5.7	11.1	5.7	3.7	6.5	3.4	62.8	541.6	264.8	174.1	1,392	1,262
Malheur	1,506	5,538,601	4.1	7.9	1.3	2.0	7.6	5.8	69.9	152.8	89.1	28.7	945	782
Marion	11,408	59,276,335	5.9	9.2	3.6	3.3	3.9	3.1	68.5	1,610.8	867.8	467.2	1,372	1,218

1. Based on the resident population estimated as of July 1 of the year shown.

STATE County	Local government finances, 2017 (cont.)									Government employment, 2020			Individual income tax returns, 2019		
	Direct general expenditure							Debt outstanding							
			Percent of total for:												
	Total (mil dol)	Per capita[1] (dollars)	Education	Health and hospitals	Police protection	Public welfare	Highways	Total (mil dol)	Per capita[1] (dollars)	Federal civilian	Federal military	State and local	Number of returns	Mean adjusted gross income	Mean income tax
	185	186	187	188	189	190	191	192	193	194	195	196	197	198	199
OKLAHOMA—Cont'd															
Kiowa	25.6	2,894	59.5	0.8	5.4	0.0	2.4	18.1	2,041	49	31	582	3,390	41,859	3,200
Latimer	22.0	2,131	57.8	0.8	4.1	0.6	11.0	11.8	1,141	35	34	842	4,160	42,180	3,115
Le Flore	142.4	2,848	56.2	4.1	5.5	0.1	7.8	53.3	1,065	162	174	4,913	18,370	43,077	3,003
Lincoln	80.6	2,306	58.0	1.3	6.2	0.0	8.8	47.3	1,354	84	125	1,623	14,150	50,639	4,123
Logan	84.5	1,806	52.9	0.6	8.5	0.0	7.5	63.1	1,348	68	168	1,340	20,590	67,545	7,068
Love	44.5	4,420	38.3	44.6	0.6	0.0	4.5	14.2	1,412	22	36	3,100	4,540	47,096	3,762
McClain	104.6	2,660	58.9	2.3	7.7	0.0	9.1	42.7	1,087	71	148	1,797	18,630	67,740	6,677
McCurtain	95.5	2,890	62.1	3.3	2.5	0.0	8.5	47.5	1,438	125	116	2,205	12,820	42,419	3,273
McIntosh	45.4	2,305	67.1	0.7	3.5	0.0	12.2	15.7	795	44	69	1,016	7,650	44,161	3,628
Major	23.9	3,112	51.1	2.6	5.8	0.0	14.5	7.5	970	35	27	364	3,330	57,292	5,153
Marshall	35.5	2,167	68.9	3.2	4.1	0.0	2.5	7.8	475	26	60	849	6,830	49,845	4,209
Mayes	108.7	2,651	66.1	0.4	5.7	0.0	5.1	51.2	1,248	76	146	2,453	16,780	51,155	4,181
Murray	48.8	3,506	39.5	29.7	3.8	0.0	4.5	20.2	1,448	69	49	2,355	5,990	52,562	4,637
Muskogee	201.4	2,918	53.4	1.2	6.2	0.0	5.3	119.8	1,735	3,322	231	6,359	27,260	48,568	3,995
Noble	48.0	4,250	45.9	22.3	4.2	0.0	10.0	23.7	2,094	40	39	1,165	4,760	58,352	5,278
Nowata	26.4	2,555	60.6	0.0	5.3	0.0	12.1	11.2	1,085	31	36	509	4,160	47,159	3,544
Okfuskee	31.4	2,601	65.6	0.9	6.4	0.0	11.9	12.0	997	31	38	1,012	4,110	41,052	2,596
Oklahoma	2,504.7	3,186	40.9	0.4	11.7	0.0	4.7	3,658.4	4,654	28,466	9,377	55,927	355,600	67,002	8,278
Okmulgee	81.0	2,086	68.3	0.1	4.6	0.0	1.1	86.8	2,236	103	133	3,291	15,210	45,690	3,461
Osage	70.2	1,482	53.1	5.7	3.3	0.0	12.1	14.8	314	178	163	2,579	18,460	54,718	4,875
Ottawa	113.2	3,607	43.6	0.4	5.3	0.0	6.5	48.5	1,547	107	108	5,023	12,990	40,810	2,852
Pawnee	33.7	2,055	60.1	3.7	7.0	0.0	9.2	10.6	644	239	58	822	6,560	49,079	3,990
Payne	208.4	2,544	55.4	0.8	11.4	0.0	7.5	207.5	2,534	240	276	14,754	30,360	58,701	5,979
Pittsburg	226.4	5,128	29.6	38.5	4.2	0.1	6.8	92.8	2,103	2,069	149	3,802	18,110	49,931	4,236
Pontotoc	108.4	2,825	55.6	0.6	5.9	0.1	11.1	60.9	1,588	153	132	7,344	16,590	54,529	5,057
Pottawatomie	184.7	2,559	56.6	0.5	6.9	0.0	9.7	77.2	1,070	146	253	5,954	30,110	50,409	4,196
Pushmataha	42.7	3,842	49.0	18.5	3.4	0.0	9.7	9.0	809	28	39	840	4,250	42,528	3,024
Roger Mills	32.1	8,774	25.7	20.0	3.6	0.0	40.9	0.5	134	36	13	379	1,460	50,523	4,571
Rogers	203.8	2,229	53.2	1.1	5.8	0.0	3.6	154.3	1,688	545	331	5,835	42,230	70,809	7,522
Seminole	69.1	2,782	61.7	0.9	3.7	0.0	8.2	23.4	943	187	85	1,777	9,250	43,619	3,160
Sequoyah	123.4	2,956	55.5	14.9	4.7	0.0	6.3	66.9	1,603	137	163	2,793	16,260	43,015	3,058
Stephens	118.9	2,744	54.4	1.7	8.2	0.0	7.0	72.6	1,675	89	153	1,916	17,830	58,672	5,821
Texas	74.0	3,537	53.3	0.5	3.6	0.1	8.2	34.8	1,665	68	70	1,642	9,280	47,251	3,591
Tillman	51.8	6,995	24.0	8.0	2.6	0.0	8.6	14.7	1,985	31	25	571	2,800	41,051	2,563
Tulsa	2,368.1	3,663	44.4	5.6	7.3	0.9	7.1	3,702.0	5,727	3,525	2,389	30,444	298,180	72,696	8,951
Wagoner	80.3	1,017	60.3	4.2	7.4	0.0	4.6	66.4	841	77	312	1,680	35,560	63,170	5,829
Washington	139.1	2,676	49.9	1.4	7.3	0.0	4.7	130.5	2,509	98	185	2,030	22,930	67,028	7,425
Washita	41.0	3,713	45.1	1.1	4.8	0.0	17.8	18.2	1,648	47	38	640	4,530	47,622	3,833
Woods	38.0	4,187	49.6	0.9	4.5	0.0	15.6	5.4	595	29	28	1,126	3,550	57,305	6,094
Woodward	63.6	3,097	52.4	3.2	4.1	0.0	9.3	60.0	2,923	88	68	1,539	8,540	51,580	5,241
OREGON	X	X	X	X	X	X	X	X	X	29,271	11,304	245,272	2,042,980	71,183	8,331
Baker	73.9	4,598	50.6	6.7	5.2	1.4	6.8	15.0	933	199	37	894	7,440	48,164	4,015
Benton	219.5	2,391	55.4	0.0	7.5	0.0	2.7	177.8	1,937	502	249	9,628	41,670	76,252	9,012
Clackamas	1,695.2	4,110	47.2	3.7	7.4	1.2	3.7	3,247.9	7,875	1,195	1,016	14,852	209,470	89,523	11,814
Clatsop	194.8	4,981	40.8	1.8	8.1	1.7	5.1	436.7	11,168	208	536	2,311	20,500	58,007	5,553
Columbia	178.4	3,448	49.3	2.8	4.9	0.2	3.8	267.5	5,172	80	123	1,806	25,160	63,675	5,975
Coos	460.1	7,222	32.3	39.7	3.0	0.0	2.0	231.5	3,634	314	392	4,988	29,490	52,652	4,895
Crook	92.3	4,001	41.4	1.9	8.9	0.1	6.7	78.2	3,392	289	58	913	11,810	59,349	5,839
Curry	121.7	5,377	23.6	38.7	5.5	0.2	4.4	91.1	4,028	104	90	1,076	11,540	51,732	4,945
Deschutes	870.7	4,662	41.6	3.7	6.6	0.1	6.2	1,327.8	7,111	1,005	474	8,073	103,680	80,289	10,142
Douglas	411.7	3,770	51.3	7.0	5.3	0.0	5.7	200.8	1,839	1,545	295	5,691	49,610	51,812	4,606
Gilliam	44.8	24,036	16.4	1.9	2.0	0.6	7.6	39.9	21,427	13	5	210	910	52,264	4,193
Grant	63.6	8,845	26.7	37.1	3.1	0.7	13.2	14.3	1,995	266	17	731	3,240	43,619	3,751
Harney	64.0	8,818	32.4	40.2	1.6	0.5	8.1	28.3	3,895	243	17	755	3,200	41,271	3,127
Hood River	122.7	5,242	44.1	2.2	3.0	0.7	6.2	214.8	9,178	132	54	1,100	12,610	70,347	7,848
Jackson	766.8	3,538	44.2	6.2	9.3	0.0	5.4	894.6	4,127	1,905	513	8,589	107,560	60,292	6,265
Jefferson	98.6	4,169	51.9	6.6	4.1	0.0	4.4	95.0	4,015	133	56	2,127	10,770	47,693	3,769
Josephine	275.8	3,186	64.0	3.0	8.2	0.2	5.2	96.3	1,112	281	203	2,983	39,670	51,669	4,775
Klamath	267.2	4,000	56.9	1.5	3.9	0.0	6.1	123.8	1,853	857	262	3,841	30,180	49,147	4,172
Lake	71.1	9,034	24.0	50.0	2.4	0.2	5.3	39.3	4,985	255	18	877	3,400	47,501	3,964
Lane	1,560.7	4,159	48.0	5.4	6.7	1.0	3.5	1,918.9	5,114	1,973	964	22,472	180,240	62,467	6,752
Lincoln	232.0	4,759	30.4	9.6	9.1	0.1	6.7	300.5	6,163	353	194	3,238	24,480	55,506	5,325
Linn	578.9	4,630	53.2	5.0	7.4	0.3	4.8	417.7	3,341	340	306	5,966	59,850	55,974	4,824
Malheur	156.0	5,133	63.1	2.9	4.1	0.0	3.0	81.8	2,692	211	65	2,963	11,720	43,028	3,403
Marion	1,579.7	4,639	54.6	6.6	5.3	0.1	4.6	1,384.2	4,065	1,437	803	33,859	159,090	60,051	5,806

1. Based on the resident population estimated as of July 1 of the year shown.

State / county code	CBSA code[1]	County Type code[2]	STATE County	Land area[3] (sq. mi)	Population, 2021: Total persons 2021	Population, 2021: Rank	Population, 2021: Per square mile	Race alone or in combination, not Hispanic or Latino (percent): White	Black	American Indian, Alaska Native	Asian and Pacific Islancer	Percent Hispanic or Latino[4]	Age (percent): Under 5 years	5 to 17 years	18 to 24 years	25 to 34 years	35 to 44 years	45 to 54 years
				1	2	3	4	5	6	7	8	9	10	11	12	13	14	15
			OREGON—Cont'd															
41049	25840	6	Morrow	2,030.5	12,303	2,259	6.1	58.0	1.3	2.1	1.5	39.0	7.1	15.5	14.1	11.7	11.4	11.6
41051	38900	1	Multnomah	431.2	803,377	80	1,863.1	72.0	7.1	1.9	11.0	12.7	4.7	10.2	10.7	18.1	17.2	13.6
41053	41420	2	Polk	740.9	89,164	666	120.3	79.4	1.8	3.1	4.2	15.3	5.3	12.8	16.0	12.6	12.6	11.0
41055		9	Sherman	823.6	1,907	3,049	2.3	91.1	1.4	2.2	1.2	6.2	5.7	11.3	8.2	10.6	12.3	10.0
41057		6	Tillamook	1,102.4	27,748	1,508	25.2	85.9	1.1	2.4	2.3	10.9	4.4	10.5	9.2	10.7	11.4	11.0
41059	25840	4	Umatilla	3,215.4	79,988	716	24.9	66.2	1.5	4.2	1.8	28.6	6.1	14.3	13.3	14.2	12.9	11.7
41061	29260	7	Union	2,036.9	26,212	1,555	12.9	90.1	1.4	2.2	3.5	5.4	5.0	13.0	15.2	11.4	12.0	9.9
41063		9	Wallowa	3,145.9	7,545	2,614	2.4	94.3	1.1	1.6	1.4	3.9	4.6	11.7	8.0	9.3	11.8	9.8
41065	45520	6	Wasco	2,381.1	26,726	1,539	11.2	74.3	1.2	3.7	2.4	20.7	5.5	12.6	10.8	13.5	12.5	10.9
41067	38900	1	Washington	724.3	600,811	114	829.5	66.9	3.4	1.3	15.2	17.6	5.3	12.6	11.9	15.6	15.5	13.3
41069		9	Wheeler	1,716.0	1,451	3,082	0.8	90.6	1.4	3.0	2.5	6.2	3.6	7.1	8.5	7.4	8.9	9.4
41071	38900	1	Yamhill	715.9	108,239	572	151.2	78.8	1.6	2.5	3.4	16.8	5.1	12.4	13.5	12.8	13.3	12.1
42000		0	PENNSYLVANIA	44,741.7	12,964,056	X	289.8	76.5	12.1	0.5	4.5	8.4	5.3	11.7	12.4	13.1	12.4	12.1
42001	23900	3	Adams	518.7	104,127	588	200.7	89.8	2.4	0.5	1.3	7.4	4.6	11.4	12.8	11.0	10.9	12.4
42003	38300	1	Allegheny	730.0	1,238,090	36	1,696.0	79.7	14.8	0.5	5.1	2.4	5.1	10.5	11.6	15.0	13.1	11.3
42005	38300	1	Armstrong	653.3	65,093	829	99.6	97.7	1.5	0.4	0.5	0.9	4.6	11.0	10.2	10.6	11.3	12.9
42007	38300	1	Beaver	434.7	166,624	406	383.3	90.7	8.1	0.5	1.0	2.0	4.8	11.1	10.5	11.7	12.1	11.9
42009		6	Bedford	1,012.2	47,461	1,032	46.9	97.3	1.1	0.4	0.7	1.3	4.9	10.7	10.7	10.6	10.6	12.9
42011	39740	2	Berks	856.4	429,342	166	501.3	70.1	5.4	0.4	1.8	23.9	5.5	12.6	13.4	12.5	12.0	12.3
42013	11020	3	Blair	525.3	121,767	523	231.8	95.6	3.1	0.4	1.1	1.4	5.0	11.7	11.3	12.1	11.8	12.3
42015	42380	6	Bradford	1,147.5	59,892	880	52.2	96.6	1.2	0.8	1.0	1.7	5.5	12.9	10.7	11.3	10.6	11.6
42017	37980	1	Bucks	604.4	646,098	109	1,069.0	84.0	5.0	0.5	6.2	6.1	4.7	11.4	11.7	11.0	12.4	13.2
42019	38300	1	Butler	789.5	194,273	351	246.1	95.1	1.9	0.4	2.0	1.8	4.8	11.1	11.9	11.3	12.4	13.0
42021	27780	3	Cambria	687.5	132,167	492	192.2	93.5	5.1	0.4	0.9	1.9	4.7	11.0	12.6	10.5	10.7	12.2
42023		7	Cameron	396.2	4,459	2,859	11.3	96.8	1.5	0.8	0.7	1.8	3.9	10.5	8.6	9.1	9.3	11.5
42025	10900	2	Carbon	381.3	65,412	825	171.5	90.7	2.5	0.6	0.9	6.4	4.5	10.8	10.5	11.2	11.6	13.3
42027	44300	3	Centre	1,108.7	157,527	434	142.1	86.8	4.3	0.4	7.0	3.1	3.6	8.4	25.7	13.0	11.2	10.8
42029	37980	1	Chester	750.5	538,649	131	717.7	79.7	6.7	0.5	7.4	7.7	5.3	12.8	13.1	11.5	12.9	13.1
42031		6	Clarion	600.8	37,156	1,248	61.8	96.6	1.9	0.5	1.1	1.1	5.1	10.8	16.0	11.4	10.3	11.7
42033	20180	4	Clearfield	1,145.3	80,082	714	69.9	93.3	3.0	0.4	0.9	3.3	4.4	10.2	10.9	12.3	12.1	13.7
42035	30820	4	Clinton	888.0	37,465	1,237	42.2	95.5	2.2	0.5	1.1	1.9	5.3	11.2	17.3	11.7	10.5	11.4
42037	14100	3	Columbia	483.2	64,872	834	134.3	93.3	2.3	0.5	1.4	3.6	4.2	10.1	18.2	11.2	10.6	11.8
42039	32740	4	Crawford	1,012.4	83,351	692	82.3	95.6	2.7	0.5	0.9	1.6	5.3	11.6	12.4	11.1	11.1	12.2
42041	25420	2	Cumberland	545.5	262,919	270	482.0	84.9	5.8	0.5	6.2	4.8	5.2	11.7	12.8	12.9	13.2	12.3
42043	25420	2	Dauphin	524.9	287,400	247	547.5	65.5	19.3	0.7	6.9	10.7	5.9	12.8	11.7	13.9	12.6	12.0
42045	37980	1	Delaware	183.8	573,849	121	3,122.1	66.2	23.8	0.6	7.3	4.5	5.7	12.5	13.4	12.9	13.0	11.9
42047	41260	7	Elk	826.9	30,783	1,410	37.2	98.0	0.9	0.5	0.7	0.9	4.8	11.0	10.5	10.0	10.5	13.2
42049	21500	2	Erie	798.9	269,011	262	336.7	85.4	9.0	0.5	2.6	4.8	5.2	11.9	13.5	12.8	11.9	11.8
42051	38300	1	Fayette	790.8	126,931	508	160.5	93.0	6.1	0.5	0.9	1.4	5.0	10.8	10.5	12.0	11.5	13.0
42053		9	Forest	427.3	7,032	2,659	16.5	72.4	20.5	0.5	0.4	6.9	0.9	1.2	11.8	17.8	13.0	13.0
42055	16540	3	Franklin	772.3	156,289	438	202.4	88.3	4.9	0.5	1.5	6.7	5.5	12.5	11.6	11.9	11.9	12.7
42057		8	Fulton	437.6	14,523	2,114	33.2	96.5	2.1	0.7	0.5	1.5	4.9	11.1	10.9	11.0	11.1	13.8
42059		6	Greene	575.9	35,369	1,297	61.4	94.0	4.2	0.7	0.7	1.6	4.7	11.0	12.4	12.4	11.9	13.3
42061	26500	6	Huntingdon	874.7	43,889	1,099	50.2	91.2	6.3	0.4	1.1	2.1	4.3	10.1	12.7	12.5	11.8	12.9
42063	26860	4	Indiana	827.4	82,886	696	100.2	94.6	3.2	0.5	1.4	1.5	4.6	10.1	19.2	10.3	10.5	11.0
42065		7	Jefferson	652.4	44,114	1,097	67.6	97.9	1.0	0.6	0.6	1.0	5.4	12.2	10.9	11.2	11.4	12.2
42067		6	Juniata	391.4	23,297	1,670	59.5	94.4	1.3	0.4	0.7	4.1	5.6	12.1	11.7	11.1	11.5	12.3
42069	42540	2	Lackawanna	459.0	215,663	320	469.9	83.6	4.5	0.4	3.6	9.5	5.0	11.9	12.5	12.2	12.0	12.2
42071	29540	2	Lancaster	943.9	553,652	126	586.6	82.0	4.8	0.4	3.0	11.5	6.2	13.1	12.7	13.1	11.9	11.2
42073	35260	4	Lawrence	357.4	85,497	675	239.2	93.2	5.9	0.5	0.9	1.8	5.0	11.3	11.6	11.1	11.1	12.2
42075	30140	3	Lebanon	361.8	143,493	466	396.6	81.0	2.8	0.4	2.1	14.9	5.6	13.0	12.4	11.7	12.1	11.8
42077	10900	2	Lehigh	345.3	375,539	195	1,087.6	61.9	7.2	0.5	4.2	28.0	5.9	12.8	13.0	13.0	13.0	12.1
42079	42540	2	Luzerne	889.7	326,053	221	366.5	77.9	5.5	0.4	1.7	16.0	5.3	11.3	12.2	12.7	12.0	12.6
42081	48700	3	Lycoming	1,228.9	113,605	546	92.4	91.8	6.5	0.5	1.2	2.3	5.2	11.8	12.5	12.6	11.9	11.7
42083	14620	7	McKean	979.7	39,941	1,183	40.8	94.2	3.0	0.7	1.0	2.4	4.6	11.3	12.7	12.0	11.6	12.8
42085	49660	2	Mercer	672.5	109,972	562	163.5	91.4	7.1	0.5	1.1	1.7	4.8	10.5	13.1	10.8	10.9	12.3
42087	30380	4	Mifflin	411.0	46,136	1,054	112.3	96.4	1.4	0.4	0.9	1.9	6.3	12.6	11.0	11.4	10.8	12.0
42089	20700	3	Monroe	608.4	169,273	397	278.2	64.5	15.5	0.9	3.2	18.3	4.6	10.9	13.7	11.6	11.3	13.1
42091	37980	1	Montgomery	483.0	860,578	71	1,781.7	75.9	10.9	0.5	9.2	5.8	5.2	12.2	11.8	12.4	13.4	12.7
42093	14100	3	Montour	130.2	18,087	1,921	138.9	91.1	2.9	0.5	3.9	2.9	5.6	11.3	9.9	13.1	12.1	11.3
42095	10900	2	Northampton	369.8	313,628	229	848.1	75.4	7.1	0.5	3.7	15.3	4.7	11.1	13.5	12.1	12.1	12.5
42097	44980	4	Northumberland	457.7	91,266	658	199.4	92.0	3.5	0.4	0.7	4.5	5.0	11.1	10.7	12.1	12.0	12.4
42099	25420	2	Perry	551.4	45,986	1,061	83.4	95.6	1.8	0.6	0.8	2.4	5.4	11.9	10.6	11.8	12.0	13.1
42101	37980	1	Philadelphia	134.4	1,576,251	24	11,728.1	35.4	41.7	0.8	8.6	15.9	6.1	12.1	12.6	18.8	13.5	10.9
42103	35620	1	Pike	544.9	59,952	878	110.0	80.1	6.6	0.8	2.0	12.2	4.0	9.8	10.6	10.2	10.9	13.0

1. CBSA = Core Based Statistical Area. See Appendix A for explanation. See Appendix B for list of metropolitan areas with component counties. 2. County type code from the Economic Research Service of USDA Rural-Urban Continuum Codes. See Appendix A for definition. 3. Dry land or land partially or temporarily covered by water. 4. May be of any race.

STATE County	Population, 2021 (cont.): Age (percent) (cont.): 55 to 64 years	65 to 74 years	75 years and over	Percent female	Population change, 2000–2021: Total persons: 2010	2020	Percent change: 2010–2020	2020–2021	Components of change, 2020–2021: Births	Deaths	Net Migration	Households, 2016–2020: Number	Persons per household	Percent: Family house-holds	Female family house-holder[1]	One person
	16	17	18	19	20	21	22	23	24	25	26	27	28	29	30	31
OREGON—Cont'd																
Morrow	12.0	10.6	6.1	49.1	11,173	12,186	9.1	1.0	203	155	67	4,093	2.8	74.4	8.7	18.2
Multnomah	11.1	9.3	5.1	50.3	735,334	815,428	10.9	-1.5	9,514	9,094	-12,421	334,849	2.4	53.5	9.5	32.6
Polk	11.2	11.0	7.5	50.9	75,403	87,433	16.0	2.0	1,067	1,105	1,775	30,726	2.7	67.4	9.7	25.1
Sherman	15.9	13.7	12.2	48.3	1,765	1,870	5.9	2.0	24	24	37	727	2.3	59.3	9.2	33.6
Tillamook	15.3	17.8	9.6	49.3	25,250	27,390	8.5	1.3	310	488	543	11,075	2.4	64.5	9.1	27.2
Umatilla	11.5	9.7	6.4	47.3	75,889	80,075	5.5	-0.1	1,160	1,080	-184	26,823	2.7	68.8	13.5	24.1
Union	12.1	12.4	9.0	50.0	25,748	26,196	1.7	0.1	309	414	120	10,785	2.4	65.9	11.7	24.9
Wallowa	15.2	18.2	11.4	51.1	7,008	7,391	5.5	2.1	74	105	191	3,195	2.2	61.0	6.3	34.1
Wasco	13.1	12.9	8.2	49.5	25,213	26,670	5.8	0.2	341	434	150	10,333	2.4	64.1	11.0	27.9
Washington	11.4	8.8	5.5	50.1	529,710	600,372	13.3	0.1	7,568	5,456	-1,788	223,040	2.6	67.3	9.7	23.8
Wheeler	18.3	20.7	16.0	51.2	1,441	1,451	0.7	0.0	12	27	16	669	2.1	61.6	6.7	31.5
Yamhill	12.4	11.1	7.3	49.6	99,193	107,722	8.6	0.5	1,285	1,425	644	37,542	2.7	70.5	11.6	23.1
PENNSYLVANIA	14.0	11.3	7.7	50.6	12,702,379	13,002,700	2.4	-0.3	160,565	199,108	-590	5,106,601	2.4	63.7	11.7	29.8
Adams	15.4	13.0	8.5	50.5	101,407	103,852	2.4	0.3	1,063	1,513	726	39,628	2.5	70.9	9.0	24.9
Allegheny	13.8	11.8	7.9	51.2	1,223,348	1,250,578	2.2	-1.0	15,403	20,114	-7,820	545,695	2.2	55.5	10.6	36.6
Armstrong	16.2	13.8	9.3	49.8	68,941	65,558	-4.9	-0.7	760	1,276	49	28,035	2.3	67.7	9.3	27.2
Beaver	15.6	13.2	9.1	50.9	170,539	168,215	-1.4	-0.9	1,840	3,140	-303	72,086	2.3	63.2	11.6	31.1
Bedford	16.1	13.2	10.4	49.7	49,762	47,577	-4.4	-0.2	562	854	176	19,930	2.4	65.6	6.7	29.6
Berks	13.9	10.5	7.2	50.4	411,442	428,849	4.2	0.1	5,619	5,980	785	156,389	2.6	67.8	13.3	26.0
Blair	14.4	12.6	8.9	50.7	127,089	122,822	-3.4	-0.9	1,447	2,345	-170	51,647	2.3	62.7	11.9	31.2
Bradford	15.3	12.8	9.3	50.0	62,622	59,967	-4.2	-0.1	754	1,074	246	25,084	2.4	65.7	9.8	28.6
Bucks	15.9	11.9	7.9	50.5	625,249	646,538	3.4	-0.1	6,706	9,281	2,089	240,763	2.6	71.9	9.5	23.2
Butler	15.4	12.2	7.9	50.0	183,862	193,763	5.4	0.3	1,995	3,095	1,602	77,725	2.3	65.1	6.7	29.2
Cambria	14.9	14.0	9.5	50.3	143,679	133,472	-7.1	-1.0	1,459	2,680	-87	56,933	2.2	61.5	10.7	33.6
Cameron	17.7	17.7	11.7	49.4	5,085	4,547	-10.6	-1.9	27	76	-37	2,334	1.9	58.0	11.5	36.5
Carbon	16.0	13.4	8.5	49.7	65,249	64,749	-0.8	1.0	632	1,115	1,164	26,545	2.4	63.3	9.9	27.8
Centre	11.7	9.4	6.2	47.2	153,990	158,172	2.7	-0.4	1,295	1,615	-360	59,380	2.4	56.1	5.6	31.0
Chester	14.1	10.4	6.8	50.4	498,886	534,413	7.1	0.8	6,435	6,202	3,972	192,951	2.6	71.2	8.6	22.7
Clarion	14.4	12.2	8.3	50.5	39,988	37,241	-6.9	-0.2	492	620	39	15,930	2.4	63.6	7.7	28.6
Clearfield	15.2	12.4	8.8	46.8	81,642	80,562	-1.3	-0.6	879	1,460	95	31,704	2.3	65.4	10.0	28.7
Clinton	13.4	11.3	8.0	50.4	39,238	37,450	-4.6	0.0	485	614	141	15,058	2.5	64.0	8.9	27.2
Columbia	13.8	11.9	8.1	51.4	67,295	64,727	-3.8	0.2	685	1,052	514	26,482	2.3	60.5	10.3	31.8
Crawford	14.9	13.2	8.4	50.7	88,765	83,938	-5.4	-0.7	1,052	1,502	-142	35,169	2.3	65.3	10.2	28.6
Cumberland	13.1	11.0	7.8	50.0	235,406	259,469	10.2	1.3	3,117	3,609	3,963	101,176	2.4	63.7	8.9	29.7
Dauphin	13.4	10.9	6.8	51.1	268,100	286,401	6.8	0.3	3,914	3,850	892	113,759	2.4	62.2	13.2	31.0
Delaware	13.6	10.3	6.9	51.6	558,979	576,830	3.2	-0.5	7,564	8,331	-2,308	209,596	2.6	67.0	14.5	28.5
Elk	17.0	13.5	9.5	49.3	31,946	30,990	-3.0	-0.7	354	522	-38	14,215	2.1	61.1	8.3	33.4
Erie	13.8	11.7	7.4	50.2	280,566	270,876	-3.5	-0.7	3,341	4,334	-907	110,388	2.4	61.5	12.7	30.6
Fayette	15.1	13.4	8.8	49.9	136,606	128,804	-5.7	-1.5	1,470	2,694	-653	55,346	2.3	62.4	12.7	31.1
Forest	17.1	15.6	9.6	30.7	7,716	6,973	-9.6	0.8	36	130	156	2,131	1.8	54.9	6.0	39.6
Franklin	13.8	11.5	8.6	50.7	149,618	155,932	4.2	0.2	2,102	2,402	642	61,617	2.5	69.7	9.9	25.0
Fulton	15.3	12.7	9.2	48.9	14,845	14,556	-1.9	-0.2	175	228	20	6,040	2.4	69.5	9.9	26.3
Greene	14.2	12.6	7.6	47.4	38,686	35,954	-7.1	-1.6	371	642	-314	14,503	2.3	65.6	10.7	28.9
Huntingdon	14.3	12.8	8.7	46.4	45,913	44,092	-4.0	-0.5	435	736	96	16,779	2.4	68.1	8.5	27.0
Indiana	13.8	12.3	8.2	49.6	88,880	83,246	-6.3	-0.4	944	1,342	27	33,855	2.3	61.2	7.9	31.4
Jefferson	15.1	12.7	9.0	49.8	45,200	44,492	-1.6	-0.8	569	792	-158	18,400	2.3	64.1	8.4	30.0
Juniata	14.7	12.1	9.0	49.6	24,636	23,509	-4.6	-0.9	303	363	-152	9,380	2.6	69.1	7.4	26.1
Lackawanna	14.0	11.8	8.5	51.0	214,437	215,896	0.7	-0.1	2,478	3,686	967	87,737	2.3	61.1	12.4	32.9
Lancaster	13.0	10.7	8.1	50.7	519,445	552,984	6.5	0.1	8,207	7,734	103	204,003	2.6	70.1	9.3	24.1
Lawrence	14.9	13.3	9.4	51.2	91,108	86,070	-5.5	-0.7	966	1,644	100	37,300	2.3	64.4	12.3	31.2
Lebanon	13.5	11.5	8.3	50.5	133,568	143,257	7.3	0.2	1,913	2,286	591	53,857	2.5	68.3	11.0	26.0
Lehigh	13.0	10.1	7.0	50.7	349,497	374,557	7.2	0.3	5,170	5,051	792	140,072	2.6	67.4	13.6	26.2
Luzerne	14.0	11.6	8.3	50.1	320,918	325,594	1.5	0.1	3,892	5,998	2,572	130,039	2.4	62.1	13.3	32.1
Lycoming	14.2	12.0	8.1	50.8	116,111	114,188	-1.7	-0.5	1,399	1,979	-17	46,160	2.3	65.1	10.7	28.2
McKean	14.8	12.1	8.0	48.3	43,450	40,432	-6.9	-1.2	439	785	-149	17,059	2.2	63.2	9.9	31.0
Mercer	15.0	13.0	9.6	50.2	116,638	110,652	-5.1	-0.6	1,194	2,161	285	46,821	2.2	63.7	10.9	31.3
Mifflin	14.2	12.2	9.6	50.7	46,682	46,143	-1.2	0.0	656	839	175	19,075	2.4	70.4	10.7	24.8
Monroe	16.3	11.8	6.6	49.9	169,842	168,327	-0.9	0.6	1,772	2,410	1,592	59,950	2.8	71.0	11.8	22.6
Montgomery	14.0	10.7	7.7	51.0	799,874	856,553	7.1	0.5	10,219	11,801	5,539	318,648	2.5	68.2	9.4	26.3
Montour	14.8	11.9	10.1	50.8	18,267	18,136	-0.7	-0.3	286	317	-20	7,475	2.3	63.4	9.0	32.5
Northampton	14.2	11.5	8.3	50.4	297,735	312,951	5.1	0.2	3,334	4,422	1,748	115,300	2.5	68.0	11.0	25.5
Northumberland	14.9	12.8	9.1	49.2	94,528	91,647	-3.0	-0.4	1,091	1,656	179	39,048	2.2	63.9	10.4	30.4
Perry	15.4	12.6	7.1	49.0	45,969	45,842	-0.3	0.3	650	653	142	18,512	2.5	70.9	8.0	24.2
Philadelphia	11.6	8.7	5.7	52.5	1,526,006	1,603,797	5.1	-1.7	24,259	22,031	-29,581	613,125	2.5	54.0	20.0	37.2
Pike	18.0	14.1	9.4	49.0	57,369	58,535	2.0	2.4	472	761	1,742	22,717	2.4	68.7	9.0	25.9

1. No spouse present.

STATE County	Persons in group quarters, 2021	Daytime Population, 2016–2020		Births, 2021		Deaths, 2021		Persons under 65 with no health insurance, 2019		Medicare, 2021			COVID-19 Deaths, 2020	
		Number	Employment/ residence ratio	Total	Rate[1]	Number	Rate[1]	Number	Percent	Total beneficiaries	Enrolled in Original Medicare	Enrolled in Medicare Advantage	Number	Rate[1]
	32	33	34	35	36	37	38	39	40	41	42	43	44	45
OREGON—Cont'd														
Morrow	22	13,396	1.4	172	14.0	126	10.3	1,152	12.2	2,228	2,033	194	12	1.0
Multnomah	18,592	913,875	1.2	7,481	9.2	7,284	9.0	57,561	8.3	128,920	50,370	78,550	433	0.5
Polk	1,703	71,472	0.7	856	9.7	863	9.7	5,891	8.6	18,816	7,597	11,219	34	0.4
Sherman	0	1,741	1.1	19	10.1	20	10.6	100	7.6	538	445	94	D	D
Tillamook	438	26,502	1.0	229	8.3	393	14.2	1,921	10.0	8,478	6,468	2,011	D	D
Umatilla	4,142	75,275	0.9	931	11.6	852	10.7	7,074	11.7	14,760	13,608	1,152	64	0.8
Union	770	26,525	1.0	239	9.1	327	12.5	1,733	8.5	6,513	5,849	664	10	0.4
Wallowa	97	7,107	1.0	62	8.3	83	11.1	431	8.7	2,526	2,351	175	D	D
Wasco	680	25,914	1.0	267	10.0	331	12.4	2,382	11.6	6,485	5,130	1,355	30	1.1
Washington	6,938	604,506	1.0	6,035	10.0	4,377	7.3	35,674	6.9	91,679	36,500	55,179	148	0.2
Wheeler	22	1,385	0.9	10	6.9	18	12.4	92	11.2	504	414	90	D	D
Yamhill	5,127	99,139	0.9	1,011	9.4	1,097	10.2	7,763	9.3	22,019	10,636	11,383	41	0.4
PENNSYLVANIA	410,509	12,739,856	1.0	128,351	9.9	159,229	12.3	702,689	7.0	2,775,097	1,538,816	1,236,281	18,235	1.4
Adams	3,951	87,661	0.7	850	8.2	1,213	11.7	6,014	7.7	25,053	16,713	8,340	100	1.0
Allegheny	35,053	1,304,080	1.1	12,280	9.9	16,142	13.0	48,870	5.1	267,160	99,306	167,854	1,237	1.0
Armstrong	607	54,452	0.6	580	8.9	1,028	15.8	3,236	6.5	17,425	5,781	11,645	77	1.2
Beaver	3,149	145,304	0.8	1,473	8.8	2,490	14.9	7,115	5.6	42,699	14,820	27,879	278	1.7
Bedford	476	43,445	0.8	446	9.4	679	14.3	3,040	8.4	13,043	6,128	6,916	108	2.3
Berks	11,304	394,692	0.9	4,484	10.5	4,792	11.2	25,575	7.6	86,262	53,563	32,699	614	1.4
Blair	3,609	128,788	1.1	1,167	9.6	1,868	15.3	6,298	6.7	31,533	14,566	16,967	203	1.7
Bradford	573	59,860	1.0	603	10.1	841	14.0	3,815	8.2	15,125	10,242	4,882	62	1.0
Bucks	8,098	574,559	0.8	5,357	8.3	7,370	11.4	27,303	5.4	139,626	89,981	49,645	965	1.5
Butler	5,450	189,909	1.0	1,582	8.2	2,490	12.8	7,125	4.8	43,733	16,887	26,846	255	1.3
Cambria	5,985	128,163	0.9	1,154	8.7	2,076	15.7	5,487	5.8	36,760	12,543	24,217	315	2.4
Cameron	89	4,713	1.1	23	5.1	59	13.1	193	6.1	1,471	890	582	D	D
Carbon	635	50,589	0.6	501	7.7	926	14.2	3,336	6.7	16,473	11,923	4,550	95	1.5
Centre	18,682	170,818	1.1	1,006	6.4	1,328	8.4	9,766	8.2	25,121	12,256	12,864	158	1.0
Chester	13,313	517,023	1.0	5,139	9.6	5,020	9.4	25,430	5.9	97,420	71,836	25,584	602	1.1
Clarion	1,627	36,671	0.9	401	10.8	489	13.2	2,370	8.2	9,438	5,404	4,033	53	1.4
Clearfield	5,701	77,358	0.9	679	8.5	1,168	14.6	4,097	7.1	20,008	11,024	8,984	60	0.7
Clinton	1,641	36,371	0.9	375	10.0	489	13.1	2,120	7.3	8,810	4,522	4,289	30	0.8
Columbia	3,415	62,763	0.9	542	8.4	835	12.9	3,220	6.6	15,038	8,754	6,284	85	1.3
Crawford	3,592	82,579	0.9	829	9.9	1,217	14.6	5,438	8.6	21,653	12,746	8,907	105	1.3
Cumberland	11,813	263,032	1.1	2,469	9.4	2,893	11.1	13,403	6.9	54,408	31,251	23,157	337	1.3
Dauphin	7,052	324,177	1.3	3,126	10.9	3,121	10.9	17,492	7.7	57,451	27,535	29,917	370	1.3
Delaware	22,265	513,386	0.8	6,056	10.5	6,639	11.5	28,497	6.3	109,261	75,944	33,317	1,042	1.8
Elk	339	29,873	1.0	289	9.4	440	14.3	1,338	5.8	8,244	5,879	2,365	22	0.7
Erie	11,980	276,613	1.0	2,641	9.8	3,483	12.9	14,801	7.1	60,631	29,082	31,549	277	1.0
Fayette	4,114	117,336	0.8	1,138	8.9	2,127	16.7	6,712	6.8	34,560	14,403	20,157	183	1.4
Forest	2,398	7,990	1.6	29	4.1	103	14.7	217	7.2	1,754	897	857	10	1.4
Franklin	2,539	146,055	0.9	1,679	10.8	1,932	12.4	10,407	8.5	36,422	25,326	11,096	258	1.7
Fulton	100	13,108	0.8	140	9.6	183	12.6	762	6.8	3,744	2,640	1,104	15	1.0
Greene	2,909	37,610	1.1	297	8.3	505	14.2	1,682	6.4	8,647	3,572	5,075	37	1.0
Huntingdon	4,651	41,438	0.8	348	7.9	630	14.3	2,177	7.1	10,802	5,897	4,905	95	2.2
Indiana	4,795	83,316	1.0	748	9.0	1,078	13.0	5,146	8.2	19,575	7,115	12,460	131	1.6
Jefferson	724	42,244	0.9	446	10.1	635	14.3	2,619	7.8	11,277	6,064	5,212	66	1.5
Juniata	195	21,534	0.7	255	10.9	298	12.7	2,212	11.4	5,576	2,850	2,726	67	2.9
Lackawanna	7,655	210,025	1.0	1,980	9.2	2,944	13.7	11,474	7.1	52,134	35,454	16,680	289	1.3
Lancaster	12,323	535,039	1.0	6,685	12.1	6,149	11.1	48,810	11.2	113,309	64,835	48,474	793	1.4
Lawrence	2,012	78,682	0.8	773	9.0	1,284	15.0	4,250	6.6	22,779	8,581	14,198	154	1.8
Lebanon	3,563	130,763	0.9	1,530	10.7	1,843	12.9	9,080	8.2	32,434	18,032	14,402	165	1.2
Lehigh	8,737	383,680	1.1	4,155	11.1	4,025	10.7	24,067	8.1	75,248	46,884	28,364	550	1.5
Luzerne	11,750	320,165	1.0	3,125	9.6	4,729	14.5	18,116	7.4	74,635	51,262	23,373	509	1.6
Lycoming	5,194	115,620	1.0	1,117	9.8	1,544	13.6	5,753	6.7	27,227	16,621	10,606	154	1.4
McKean	2,867	39,263	0.9	357	8.9	609	15.2	1,894	6.3	10,259	7,004	3,255	35	0.9
Mercer	6,045	112,056	1.0	957	8.7	1,695	15.4	5,681	7.1	29,100	13,169	15,931	193	1.7
Mifflin	483	42,945	0.9	532	11.5	666	14.4	3,398	9.6	11,470	6,146	5,324	129	2.8
Monroe	3,913	156,058	0.8	1,427	8.5	1,945	11.5	11,267	8.3	34,769	24,520	10,249	230	1.4
Montgomery	20,831	909,313	1.2	8,173	9.5	9,482	11.0	32,798	4.9	167,387	116,708	50,679	1,246	1.5
Montour	778	26,698	2.0	233	12.9	270	14.9	868	6.2	4,395	2,091	2,303	29	1.6
Northampton	11,145	286,909	0.9	2,648	8.5	3,560	11.4	13,855	5.8	69,593	45,693	23,900	477	1.5
Northumberland	3,495	82,055	0.8	875	9.6	1,309	14.3	4,325	6.4	23,274	13,585	9,688	251	2.7
Perry	582	33,796	0.5	514	11.2	526	11.5	3,348	9.0	10,471	5,275	5,196	46	1.0
Philadelphia	55,395	1,670,636	1.1	19,463	12.3	17,769	11.2	116,921	9.0	258,677	135,925	122,752	2,679	1.7
Pike	463	43,621	0.5	378	6.4	626	10.6	3,128	7.4	14,564	11,506	3,058	51	0.9

1. Per 1,000 estimated resident population.

STATE County	COVID-19 Vaccinations, 2021–2022		Education						Money income, 2016–2020				Income and poverty, 2020			
			School enrollment and attainment, 2016–2020				Local government expenditures,[3] 2018–2019			Households				Percent below poverty level		
			Enrollment[1]		Attainment[2] (percent)						Percent					
	Number	Percent[5]	Total	Percent private	High school graduate or less	Bachelor's degree or more	Total current spending (mil dol)	Current spending per student (dollars)	Per capita income[4]	Median income (dollars)	with income of less than $50,000	with income of $200,000 or more	Median household income (dollars)	All persons	Children under 18 years	Children 5 to 17 years in families
	46	47	48	49	50	51	52	53	54	55	56	57	58	59	60	61
OREGON—Cont'd																
Morrow	6,481	55.9	2,890	2.9	56.6	9.1	34.1	13,725	24,655	56,572	44.0	3.4	59,956	11.5	13.7	12.8
Multnomah	644,115	79.2	180,840	20.4	25.2	46.5	1,290.1	13,870	41,612	71,425	35.3	10.1	74,707	11.2	11.8	11.0
Polk	54,632	63.5	21,095	12.1	32.5	30.5	80.2	11,481	31,957	65,665	37.8	5.5	66,973	11.1	12.2	10.8
Sherman	1,028	57.8	343	11.7	39.2	20.0	3.5	13,137	34,548	51,472	46.4	6.2	62,271	11.9	17.7	19.1
Tillamook	17,469	64.6	5,006	10.2	38.3	21.4	49.2	14,011	30,044	54,268	46.8	3.0	57,533	10.8	15.5	13.6
Umatilla	43,486	55.8	18,852	10.1	46.0	17.5	187.7	13,486	25,452	57,973	43.5	3.2	62,560	11.7	13.0	12.0
Union	13,211	49.2	6,259	12.9	40.0	24.2	47.1	12,056	27,748	53,940	47.5	2.7	58,779	12.6	14.8	13.7
Wallowa	4,275	59.3	1,119	7.6	35.9	26.9	16.8	19,502	34,564	53,423	47.0	2.5	51,506	11.6	16.4	15.3
Wasco	17,578	65.9	5,422	13.2	40.9	20.4	50.3	14,128	31,088	54,725	44.3	3.9	55,519	12.4	15.7	15.5
Washington	459,208	76.3	146,470	19.1	24.8	44.9	1,129.7	12,919	41,015	86,626	26.7	11.1	85,385	7.5	7.2	6.5
Wheeler	724	54.4	186	20.4	39.5	18.9	9.7	7,612	23,628	45,354	61.0	0.7	43,367	14.0	25.9	26.3
Yamhill	67,864	63.4	26,057	25.0	34.7	27.3	185.5	11,330	32,768	67,296	36.2	6.8	68,266	8.7	10.1	9.7
PENNSYLVANIA	8,745,999	68.3	2,908,512	24.0	43.2	32.3	28,492.1	16,638	35,518	63,627	39.8	7.1	64,898	10.9	14.3	13.7
Adams	57,306	55.6	22,741	25.4	50.3	22.6	293.4	21,115	32,312	68,411	35.4	4.7	70,470	8.0	11.1	10.0
Allegheny	849,510	69.9	270,329	24.6	31.6	42.5	2,688.6	18,474	39,541	62,320	40.7	7.5	64,236	10.5	13.0	12.7
Armstrong	38,884	60.1	12,099	13.0	57.4	18.1	123.5	17,656	28,824	53,545	46.0	3.2	52,958	11.7	16.1	14.4
Beaver	84,557	51.6	32,423	15.5	42.7	25.5	489.2	15,211	33,025	59,014	42.6	3.5	56,649	9.1	12.2	11.1
Bedford	18,664	39.0	8,516	13.7	60.9	15.9	90.3	14,232	26,950	51,531	48.7	1.7	52,643	11.0	14.4	13.8
Berks	255,447	60.7	101,564	17.5	49.1	25.9	1,094.9	16,106	32,781	66,154	37.4	5.7	70,057	10.9	14.0	12.6
Blair	63,936	52.5	25,616	14.6	52.6	22.3	258.8	15,001	29,336	50,856	49.2	3.0	52,177	11.6	15.2	14.2
Bradford	25,995	43.1	12,143	13.0	57.4	18.7	143.3	15,822	28,154	52,375	47.5	3.0	55,787	10.7	13.4	12.7
Bucks	457,465	72.8	138,849	24.0	33.7	42.2	1,595.3	18,766	47,266	93,181	25.3	15.3	92,441	6.0	6.1	5.3
Butler	120,810	64.3	42,027	17.4	36.3	37.5	373.8	14,665	39,906	72,642	33.5	8.4	74,721	7.4	7.8	7.3
Cambria	73,048	56.1	27,699	21.4	52.3	22.0	242.5	14,269	27,173	47,644	51.8	2.0	48,653	12.5	16.1	14.9
Cameron	2,440	54.9	721	10.3	58.3	10.8	9.4	17,618	24,379	40,342	64.0	1.1	46,151	13.5	22.0	22.1
Carbon	38,947	60.7	11,798	11.4	54.8	17.9	129.4	15,299	30,552	57,601	44.5	2.7	60,593	11.3	18.9	14.5
Centre	97,086	59.8	58,001	9.8	33.5	45.8	237.5	18,138	32,238	61,921	41.2	7.0	62,795	12.9	9.4	8.5
Chester	409,851	78.1	131,898	23.7	26.2	54.2	1,502.9	18,194	52,711	104,161	22.5	20.0	107,491	5.2	5.8	5.6
Clarion	16,879	43.9	9,109	13.9	55.4	23.0	104.3	18,885	26,595	49,695	50.3	2.1	52,642	12.8	15.2	14.3
Clearfield	39,583	49.9	13,793	15.8	60.2	16.8	174.3	16,621	25,043	50,150	49.8	1.7	48,794	14.3	19.9	17.5
Clinton	17,371	45.0	8,597	11.7	57.7	19.6	70.8	16,334	26,656	51,145	48.6	2.0	54,652	13.4	18.2	17.3
Columbia	40,264	62.0	16,637	10.0	51.9	24.3	103.1	16,988	28,051	52,219	47.9	3.3	56,176	11.7	13.2	12.3
Crawford	41,740	49.3	17,102	26.5	57.5	20.4	157.8	15,544	27,290	51,919	48.3	2.6	52,372	12.7	18.3	16.9
Cumberland	177,333	70.0	58,619	22.9	38.8	37.4	433.9	15,957	38,153	71,979	33.6	6.9	69,546	7.6	8.8	8.0
Dauphin	177,062	63.6	62,361	17.7	41.5	32.3	713.6	14,698	35,061	63,123	38.3	6.0	63,265	11.6	15.5	15.4
Delaware	423,955	74.8	142,529	31.8	36.2	39.5	1,359.0	17,859	40,740	76,238	34.0	12.0	75,174	9.3	11.4	10.0
Elk	16,764	56.0	5,748	15.8	55.8	19.2	49.7	14,755	31,333	54,961	45.0	2.6	52,952	8.3	10.7	9.8
Erie	160,949	59.7	64,113	24.9	46.3	28.7	548.0	14,503	29,001	52,863	47.5	3.7	55,181	13.4	18.0	17.1
Fayette	74,016	57.3	24,295	12.5	59.3	17.7	239.7	15,169	27,778	49,075	50.9	2.1	45,256	18.7	23.5	22.7
Forest	5,216	72.0	463	25.7	70.6	9.6	10.3	24,687	17,256	41,225	61.6	0.5	40,667	22.9	29.9	22.0
Franklin	76,753	49.5	32,650	17.1	54.7	22.2	288.9	12,580	31,887	63,420	37.6	3.4	57,812	9.4	12.2	11.2
Fulton	5,237	36.0	2,708	10.7	61.3	15.0	33.4	15,846	28,578	55,424	44.9	1.7	61,202	10.6	14.5	14.2
Greene	18,316	50.6	7,470	21.7	57.5	17.7	80.3	17,100	28,030	55,993	45.1	2.8	59,324	12.7	16.6	16.3
Huntingdon	23,173	51.3	8,975	24.8	59.2	17.8	74.7	14,062	26,454	53,597	46.6	2.2	55,282	10.7	14.2	12.7
Indiana	38,445	45.7	21,021	14.5	50.7	25.0	180.3	19,653	26,608	49,270	50.8	2.3	53,533	13.4	17.7	16.5
Jefferson	21,076	48.5	8,074	15.5	60.5	16.2	73.5	16,361	26,890	49,604	50.3	2.4	52,856	11.0	15.4	14.8
Juniata	10,096	40.8	4,564	25.0	65.6	15.2	34.6	12,737	27,221	53,502	46.2	2.3	59,591	10.0	14.6	13.6
Lackawanna	147,385	70.3	47,215	30.1	45.2	28.7	401.3	14,290	30,452	54,064	46.3	4.0	56,911	12.2	16.3	15.5
Lancaster	325,131	59.6	121,754	28.2	49.2	28.6	1,140.4	16,971	33,568	69,588	34.0	5.9	73,006	7.7	9.8	9.6
Lawrence	46,323	54.2	17,487	16.3	52.2	22.3	178.1	15,591	28,898	50,080	49.9	2.8	50,373	12.9	18.3	17.8
Lebanon	79,660	56.2	31,294	22.5	56.5	21.2	263.8	13,211	30,088	61,632	39.4	3.6	63,605	9.0	12.9	11.8
Lehigh	268,978	72.8	86,776	20.8	43.2	30.8	901.0	16,786	34,629	66,214	38.4	7.2	65,733	11.7	18.6	18.3
Luzerne	203,949	64.3	67,656	22.9	48.5	23.6	645.0	14,564	29,732	53,194	47.1	3.5	52,281	15.1	23.7	23.1
Lycoming	59,541	52.6	24,780	17.4	47.3	23.5	249.3	15,966	28,465	54,906	45.3	3.1	56,751	13.2	19.3	17.0
McKean	20,115	49.5	8,351	9.6	55.0	19.0	103.9	17,428	26,635	49,240	50.8	2.4	52,359	13.9	20.0	18.2
Mercer	58,469	53.4	23,509	23.7	52.0	22.7	257.8	17,999	27,875	50,529	49.5	2.6	51,743	12.4	20.3	18.6
Mifflin	23,059	50.0	8,547	23.3	65.2	13.2	89.5	17,035	26,432	52,641	46.7	1.8	54,517	13.2	21.0	20.4
Monroe	101,973	59.9	37,674	12.7	45.2	25.8	493.9	19,550	31,954	68,734	35.5	5.8	71,686	10.5	13.5	13.3
Montgomery	639,961	77.0	199,568	30.5	28.9	49.6	2,239.3	19,393	49,905	93,518	25.3	16.4	94,094	5.6	5.7	5.0
Montour	14,388	78.9	3,303	20.5	48.3	33.0	35.4	14,782	35,407	59,915	43.9	6.4	63,341	9.0	13.0	11.7
Northampton	208,249	68.2	72,812	26.4	42.9	31.8	780.6	17,469	37,339	73,088	33.5	7.8	73,903	7.6	10.4	10.4
Northumberland	52,577	57.9	16,103	15.7	60.2	17.9	207.5	18,428	27,365	49,273	50.6	2.4	47,825	12.1	16.9	15.9
Perry	22,706	49.1	8,866	21.5	57.1	18.5	85.0	14,074	33,473	70,660	34.3	4.8	68,991	8.5	12.1	11.3
Philadelphia	1,102,444	69.6	396,289	34.3	46.1	31.2	3,084.8	15,481	29,644	49,127	50.7	5.3	55,102	19.4	27.0	28.2
Pike	32,525	58.3	11,097	14.1	41.4	27.1	144.9	19,684	35,746	67,495	35.0	5.2	66,614	9.3	13.6	13.3

1. All persons 3 years old and over enrolled in nursery school through college. 2. Persons 25 years old and over. 3. Elementary and secondary education expenditures. 4. Based on population estimated by the American Community Survey, 2016–2020. 5. CDC percent based on 2019 population estimate.

STATE County	Personal income, 2020: Total (mil dol)	Personal income, 2020: Percent change 2019–2020	Per capita[1]: Dollars	Per capita[1]: Rank	Wages and salaries (mil dol)	Supplements to wages and salaries, employer contributions (mil dol): Pension and insurance	Supplements to wages and salaries, employer contributions (mil dol): Government social insurance	Proprietors' income (mil dol)	Dividends, interest, and rent (mil dol)	Personal transfer reecipts (mil dol)	Earnings, 2020: Total (mil dol)	Contributions for government social insurance (mil dol): From employee and self-employed	Contributions for government social insurance (mil dol): From employer
	62	63	64	65	66	67	68	69	70	71	72	73	74
OREGON—Cont'd													
Morrow	685	21.6	58,541	494	391	71	38	202	62	143	701	30	38
Multnomah	52,080	7.9	63,852	293	34,870	5,224	2,878	4,247	9,570	10,192	47,218	2,852	2,878
Polk	4,006	9.2	45,660	1,709	921	189	86	224	687	1,069	1,419	107	86
Sherman	119	16.9	66,349	236	54	12	5	33	16	30	104	5	5
Tillamook	1,319	9.0	48,060	1,382	432	86	40	138	259	449	697	50	40
Umatilla	3,593	12.0	46,209	1,621	1,449	290	140	356	449	1,062	2,234	136	140
Union	1,201	9.9	45,242	1,765	459	96	43	84	193	415	682	47	43
Wallowa	361	10.9	50,303	1,111	110	26	10	36	78	124	182	13	10
Wasco	1,284	11.5	48,643	1,299	534	96	48	107	199	408	784	51	48
Washington	40,333	5.8	66,831	218	24,262	2,845	1,774	2,996	7,884	6,230	31,876	1,983	1,774
Wheeler	57	13.8	41,366	2,283	12	3	1	3	11	24	19	2	1
Yamhill	5,494	9.0	51,028	1,023	1,730	318	164	442	969	1,407	2,654	176	164
PENNSYLVANIA	788,725	7.0	60,720	X	353,157	59,865	26,407	67,605	129,332	198,663	507,034	31,061	26,407
Adams	5,566	6.6	54,172	768	1,582	312	127	396	925	1,415	2,416	161	127
Allegheny	83,313	5.9	68,777	183	48,068	7,174	3,491	8,355	13,662	18,774	67,088	3,967	3,491
Armstrong	3,285	7.9	51,200	1,004	745	163	60	255	404	1,124	1,223	88	60
Beaver	9,015	9.1	55,449	673	3,175	594	250	499	1,044	2,946	4,517	308	250
Bedford	2,211	7.9	46,246	1,615	604	128	50	262	263	782	1,045	74	50
Berks	23,557	8.6	55,953	646	9,504	1,779	739	1,731	3,363	6,376	13,753	847	739
Blair	6,304	8.7	52,096	930	2,735	566	228	481	890	2,127	4,009	260	228
Bradford	2,769	6.4	45,979	1,655	1,159	230	90	239	451	878	1,718	113	90
Bucks	50,633	5.3	80,627	73	15,633	2,480	1,195	3,605	9,009	9,104	22,913	1,410	1,195
Butler	12,243	6.6	64,732	274	5,055	914	384	773	1,982	2,731	7,126	444	384
Cambria	6,258	7.8	48,637	1,301	2,166	473	177	319	832	2,427	3,135	226	177
Cameron	232	9.1	53,654	806	69	18	6	13	39	99	106	8	6
Carbon	3,644	7.5	56,868	580	637	142	53	645	454	1,041	1,477	94	53
Centre	8,174	5.2	50,615	1,075	4,151	1,474	306	649	1,567	1,624	6,580	343	306
Chester	48,423	4.3	91,927	34	20,768	2,901	1,423	4,815	10,118	6,364	29,906	1,702	1,423
Clarion	1,740	7.6	45,427	1,730	525	141	43	157	271	610	866	57	43
Clearfield	3,982	8.3	50,648	1,072	1,316	284	105	244	471	1,305	1,949	133	105
Clinton	1,759	7.4	46,338	1,602	602	153	47	176	223	568	978	62	47
Columbia	3,078	8.7	47,464	1,453	1,112	266	88	186	437	949	1,652	110	88
Crawford	3,880	9.1	46,356	1,599	1,274	280	102	387	499	1,387	2,043	143	102
Cumberland	15,760	8.7	61,596	363	8,139	1,352	630	1,454	2,705	3,305	11,575	697	630
Dauphin	15,895	7.9	56,792	586	11,652	2,276	873	1,260	2,195	4,202	16,062	924	873
Delaware	41,706	5.2	73,588	120	15,202	2,312	1,108	3,454	7,409	8,741	22,077	1,407	1,108
Elk	1,587	8.8	53,592	816	613	131	50	82	223	568	876	59	50
Erie	13,565	8.8	50,536	1,086	5,699	1,168	448	800	2,213	4,430	8,115	519	448
Fayette	6,151	9.2	48,007	1,394	1,738	377	141	327	733	2,379	2,583	199	141
Forest	197	10.9	28,271	3,099	104	35	8	11	49	96	158	11	8
Franklin	8,090	8.3	51,979	936	2,881	555	234	612	1,165	2,181	4,281	274	234
Fulton	710	7.7	48,976	1,258	240	54	21	74	88	245	389	25	21
Greene	1,749	8.8	49,103	1,244	760	149	62	109	282	596	1,080	70	62
Huntingdon	1,942	9.9	43,555	2,003	544	138	45	163	255	704	889	60	45
Indiana	3,721	7.6	44,472	1,880	1,457	363	112	292	521	1,260	2,225	148	112
Jefferson	2,111	7.9	48,971	1,260	649	136	54	183	320	732	1,022	73	54
Juniata	1,237	9.2	50,257	1,114	262	56	22	206	143	342	545	33	22
Lackawanna	10,989	8.2	52,580	886	4,608	871	366	650	1,606	3,493	6,496	425	366
Lancaster	31,916	7.3	58,434	499	13,041	2,191	999	4,509	4,939	7,336	20,739	1,221	999
Lawrence	4,174	8.9	49,059	1,252	1,309	258	107	237	484	1,523	1,911	144	107
Lebanon	7,472	7.7	52,743	874	2,435	519	195	604	1,139	2,058	3,753	242	195
Lehigh	21,656	8.0	58,402	502	11,910	1,890	888	1,659	3,208	5,537	16,347	994	888
Luzerne	15,973	9.5	50,391	1,099	7,041	1,348	570	763	2,286	5,229	9,723	636	570
Lycoming	5,516	8.7	48,721	1,292	2,446	522	190	312	792	1,768	3,470	227	190
McKean	1,910	6.0	47,361	1,469	633	157	52	143	297	661	986	66	52
Mercer	5,108	8.4	47,063	1,506	2,060	415	165	332	726	1,883	2,971	203	165
Mifflin	2,038	10.0	44,242	1,904	710	147	57	216	224	729	1,130	77	57
Monroe	8,237	9.7	48,409	1,338	2,711	613	214	474	1,170	2,391	4,013	261	214
Montgomery	71,996	5.5	86,340	54	41,462	5,532	2,870	521	19,899	11,604	50,384	3,243	2,870
Montour	1,130	6.7	62,658	325	1,202	189	76	69	147	269	1,536	91	76
Northampton	18,408	6.4	60,179	420	6,387	1,119	509	1,210	2,865	4,619	9,225	593	509
Northumberland	4,272	9.9	47,336	1,472	1,244	263	103	234	573	1,493	1,845	134	103
Perry	2,315	7.1	50,095	1,134	299	78	25	232	296	643	634	47	25
Philadelphia	93,038	8.4	58,941	482	52,144	8,345	3,849	16,335	10,171	29,588	80,673	4,413	3,849
Pike	2,988	5.7	53,289	835	442	107	36	191	504	841	777	58	36

1. Based on the resident population estimated as of July 1 of the year shown.

STATE County	Earnings, 2020 (cont.) — Percent by selected industries: Farm	Mining, quarrying, and extractions	Construction	Manu-facturing	Information; professional, scientific, technical services	Retail trade	Finance, insurance, real estate, and leasing	Health care and social assistance	Govern-ment	Social Security beneficiaries, December 2020: Number	Rate[1]	Supple-mental Security Income recipients, 2020	Housing units, 2021: Total	Percent change, 2010–2021
	75	76	77	78	79	80	81	82	83	84	85	86	87	88
OREGON—Cont'd														
Morrow	31.0	D	0.9	18.5	D	1.4	1.8	2.1	11.9	2,335	190	228	4,779	1.1
Multnomah	0.1	0.0	6.4	5.1	16.9	4.8	8.7	11.4	17.7	126,170	157	20,874	368,029	0.7
Polk	3.5	D	9.2	8.5	4.3	5.4	4.9	13.4	27.2	19,570	219	1,519	34,463	1.4
Sherman	24.8	0.5	9.1	D	D	5.2	D	0.6	28.1	560	294	46	932	1.2
Tillamook	7.7	0.0	8.4	15.2	3.7	6.8	3.6	11.8	21.8	9,010	325	524	19,058	0.5
Umatilla	8.5	0.2	5.6	8.4	5.0	6.6	3.9	11.4	24.8	15,285	191	1,688	31,581	1.3
Union	4.4	D	6.1	11.6	4.4	8.1	4.2	16.7	23.8	6,735	257	624	11,727	0.6
Wallowa	9.9	0.0	8.6	3.4	4.8	6.4	4.8	10.2	27.4	2,600	345	148	4,341	0.2
Wasco	7.2	D	6.4	5.0	10.3	9.4	3.9	19.9	20.2	6,740	252	694	12,096	0.8
Washington	0.4	0.1	6.3	22.8	10.1	5.3	7.5	7.9	6.7	90,565	151	7,099	240,499	1.3
Wheeler	20.8	0.0	D	D	D	D	D	D	36.9	560	386	36	949	1.2
Yamhill	5.7	0.2	7.6	19.4	6.6	6.7	6.1	12.4	13.9	22,905	212	1,675	40,627	0.9
PENNSYLVANIA	0.4	0.5	6.0	9.8	14.5	5.3	8.3	14.7	12.9	2,877,728	222	348,636	5,770,601	0.4
Adams	2.2	0.3	9.2	21.1	3.6	6.0	4.0	13.5	15.5	26,075	250	1,055	43,259	0.5
Allegheny	0.0	0.4	5.0	5.6	16.4	4.7	11.7	15.7	9.5	271,185	219	31,751	604,173	0.3
Armstrong	1.3	12.8	7.1	10.7	4.3	6.4	2.6	15.3	15.1	18,910	291	2,048	32,111	0.0
Beaver	0.1	0.1	24.0	11.7	4.8	5.6	3.1	13.4	12.6	44,850	269	4,318	79,141	0.2
Bedford	2.7	D	11.2	13.4	D	8.6	4.2	D	14.4	14,090	297	1,182	23,538	0.2
Berks	1.2	0.2	6.4	17.7	6.6	5.6	5.9	15.7	12.5	89,860	209	10,769	171,301	0.3
Blair	1.0	0.4	5.6	12.1	5.3	8.5	4.4	20.2	15.8	31,245	257	4,304	55,791	0.1
Bradford	2.4	3.8	4.7	15.6	3.0	5.5	4.6	22.9	12.7	16,530	276	1,737	29,411	0.1
Bucks	0.1	0.0	9.7	9.8	13.6	6.7	7.6	15.3	9.7	140,540	218	7,091	256,391	0.2
Butler	0.2	1.3	6.9	13.4	10.5	6.8	5.0	12.4	14.1	46,410	239	2,999	86,441	1.5
Cambria	0.3	0.2	4.5	9.3	6.6	7.6	6.2	22.8	18.0	39,035	295	4,755	64,426	0.0
Cameron	0.4	0.0	D	44.3	D	2.5	D	D	23.5	1,610	361	118	3,930	0.0
Carbon	0.2	0.0	4.3	7.3	39.5	5.6	3.1	12.0	12.8	17,850	273	1,400	34,258	0.3
Centre	0.6	0.4	4.8	5.2	8.0	4.2	4.5	10.3	50.2	25,980	165	1,374	65,855	0.5
Chester	1.1	0.0	5.6	6.8	21.7	7.0	18.4	7.4	7.7	95,625	178	4,249	210,787	1.0
Clarion	1.1	1.2	8.6	9.8	2.4	7.5	4.3	15.9	26.1	10,295	277	1,169	18,834	0.0
Clearfield	0.3	1.7	4.1	9.0	3.3	8.2	3.8	22.4	18.6	21,490	268	2,193	38,141	0.1
Clinton	1.7	2.3	6.9	31.2	1.9	6.4	2.6	D	21.6	9,440	252	986	18,625	0.1
Columbia	1.1	D	5.2	17.9	3.9	7.6	3.6	11.0	21.3	16,235	250	1,363	29,717	0.2
Crawford	1.3	1.1	6.0	23.9	4.4	6.5	3.5	17.1	14.9	23,100	277	2,706	42,110	0.1
Cumberland	0.5	0.0	4.9	5.9	12.2	5.7	10.0	14.3	14.5	55,565	211	2,880	110,182	0.7
Dauphin	0.1	0.1	4.1	8.0	8.0	3.5	8.3	17.7	22.5	59,470	207	8,440	127,150	0.4
Delaware	0.0	D	6.9	12.2	9.3	4.8	11.4	13.4	10.1	109,570	191	12,492	229,398	0.1
Elk	0.1	0.1	5.5	44.4	2.6	5.3	2.8	11.1	10.2	8,980	292	563	16,855	0.1
Erie	0.4	0.0	4.8	18.2	5.0	6.5	8.9	19.2	16.4	65,125	242	10,158	119,960	0.1
Fayette	0.3	4.5	5.2	9.4	4.3	8.2	3.5	16.4	19.3	36,690	289	7,261	61,976	0.2
Forest	0.7	D	2.1	D	D	1.3	D	11.9	63.1	1,885	268	147	6,949	0.0
Franklin	2.6	0.3	5.9	15.5	5.2	6.8	4.0	15.9	16.2	37,820	242	2,482	66,728	0.5
Fulton	4.7	D	11.7	35.3	1.4	3.6	D	D	12.4	4,045	279	329	7,126	0.3
Greene	0.4	D	7.8	2.3	3.2	5.3	3.7	D	19.2	9,125	258	1,530	16,181	0.2
Huntingdon	4.0	0.7	6.5	9.2	2.5	6.2	4.7	D	28.7	11,510	262	1,039	20,912	0.5
Indiana	0.9	5.7	6.0	6.0	3.7	7.0	7.2	12.9	24.6	21,055	254	2,348	37,632	0.0
Jefferson	0.9	3.6	5.9	24.1	5.7	5.8	2.4	13.2	12.4	12,220	277	1,236	22,038	0.2
Juniata	4.7	D	7.8	30.0	D	6.2	3.6	D	9.7	5,855	251	393	10,467	0.3
Lackawanna	0.0	0.1	5.7	10.5	6.4	7.2	9.7	19.6	13.1	54,585	253	6,993	99,970	0.1
Lancaster	1.4	0.2	11.9	14.2	7.1	7.4	7.1	13.6	8.2	116,670	211	9,138	218,063	0.6
Lawrence	0.5	0.5	12.1	14.1	4.6	6.9	6.3	15.0	13.9	24,285	284	3,273	39,553	0.1
Lebanon	1.5	D	6.6	18.2	4.1	7.8	3.3	12.3	19.3	33,965	237	2,692	59,561	0.7
Lehigh	0.2	0.1	4.8	11.1	8.5	4.6	5.9	22.5	9.1	78,730	210	9,737	150,315	0.3
Luzerne	0.1	D	5.2	11.2	5.0	6.7	5.8	16.5	15.5	79,755	245	10,124	151,050	0.2
Lycoming	0.7	2.6	5.5	16.3	5.4	6.8	5.4	18.5	18.6	29,390	259	3,186	52,662	0.1
McKean	0.3	3.3	5.8	21.3	2.8	6.2	2.1	D	18.1	11,335	284	1,538	19,438	0.1
Mercer	0.5	1.0	6.1	19.6	3.9	7.8	5.8	18.8	13.4	31,120	283	3,609	50,892	0.1
Mifflin	1.7	0.0	7.2	25.0	2.0	7.8	3.1	19.6	10.7	12,315	267	1,286	21,404	0.4
Monroe	0.1	0.1	5.1	14.9	4.5	8.0	3.4	12.9	25.2	38,240	226	3,098	79,331	0.2
Montgomery	0.0	0.1	7.2	11.4	23.9	4.9	7.8	12.4	7.0	166,050	193	8,802	348,943	0.5
Montour	0.6	D	1.0	2.2	D	1.8	9.1	57.5	7.5	4,655	257	378	8,116	0.3
Northampton	0.1	0.1	5.7	17.6	7.5	6.4	6.4	9.8	13.2	73,500	234	6,258	128,469	0.6
Northumberland	1.5	0.8	6.1	16.4	D	6.0	2.8	13.4	16.9	24,770	271	2,762	43,352	0.1
Perry	5.7	D	16.3	5.0	4.3	8.2	4.6	6.8	21.1	11,170	243	719	19,943	0.4
Philadelphia	0.0	D	2.1	2.0	28.4	2.5	8.0	15.7	14.7	258,305	164	101,178	733,058	0.7
Pike	0.1	0.7	D	D	7.1	8.5	4.9	7.7	27.1	15,870	265	734	39,804	0.3

1. Per 1,000 resident population estimated as of July 1 of the year shown.

STATE County	Housing units, 2016–2020: Total	Occupied units: Owner-occupied: Percent	Owner-occupied: Median value[1]	Median owner cost as a percent of income: With a mortgage	Median owner cost as a percent of income: Without a mortgage[2]	Renter-occupied: Median rent[3]	Renter-occupied: Median rent as a percent of income[2]	Sub-standard units[4] (percent)	Civilian labor force, 2021: Total	Percent change, 2020–2021	Unemployment: Total	Unemployment: Rate[5]	Civilian employment[6], 2016–2020: Total	Percent: Management, business, science, and arts	Percent: Construction, production, and maintenance occupations
	89	90	91	92	93	94	95	96	97	98	99	100	101	102	103
OREGON—Cont'd															
Morrow	4,093	73.0	160,600	19.8	10.0	753	22.9	7.8	5,966	3.4	272	4.6	4,830	24.6	47.4
Multnomah	334,849	54.4	410,800	22.6	13.0	1,309	30.9	4.2	461,936	1.3	25,641	5.6	446,317	47.8	16.7
Polk	30,726	65.4	290,100	21.5	10.1	1,043	29.7	2.0	42,006	3.4	2,032	4.8	38,375	36.9	21.7
Sherman	727	69.1	159,300	21.9	11.4	843	22.1	1.5	963	-1.4	41	4.3	794	34.3	36.9
Tillamook	11,075	70.0	276,700	23.0	13.1	951	28.7	4.5	12,137	2.3	668	5.5	10,756	30.7	27.8
Umatilla	26,823	65.3	183,300	19.6	10.4	776	26.4	5.8	37,687	1.9	1,969	5.2	32,369	29.1	31.9
Union	10,785	66.5	198,200	21.8	11.2	846	26.5	4.4	12,222	1.7	680	5.6	11,394	31.3	25.4
Wallowa	3,195	72.4	266,800	20.6	12.1	738	25.1	3.2	3,622	4.6	196	5.4	3,156	36.2	24.8
Wasco	10,333	64.3	230,800	22.6	11.8	821	23.7	3.2	13,684	1.7	716	5.2	11,689	33.7	26.7
Washington	223,040	61.3	413,500	21.4	10.4	1,440	28.4	3.6	327,487	2.1	14,352	4.4	314,509	47.1	17.5
Wheeler	669	75.5	178,700	26.8	15.5	715	23.3	1.2	726	4.6	24	3.3	504	43.3	19.6
Yamhill	37,542	70.2	320,900	22.8	12.6	1,103	30.4	4.3	55,328	2.2	2,624	4.7	48,759	34.2	28.0
PENNSYLVANIA	5,106,601	69.0	187,500	19.9	12.2	958	28.6	1.8	6,406,185	-1.2	406,743	6.3	6,206,839	39.9	22.3
Adams	39,628	77.8	212,300	21.8	12.4	932	27.5	1.4	54,462	-0.3	2,396	4.4	51,151	31.4	31.9
Allegheny	545,695	64.3	161,600	18.3	11.8	913	27.3	1.1	630,750	-2.1	38,469	6.1	627,514	47.7	14.7
Armstrong	28,035	77.8	112,400	19.3	10.8	686	25.8	2.1	31,268	-1.4	2,365	7.6	29,858	28.1	34.5
Beaver	72,086	73.0	148,700	18.6	13.0	729	26.4	1.3	81,745	-2.3	5,885	7.2	79,802	36.5	24.4
Bedford	19,930	79.4	141,700	19.5	11.3	684	27.9	1.6	23,723	-0.9	1,406	5.9	22,107	29.2	33.8
Berks	156,389	71.0	187,600	21.0	13.2	951	28.9	1.4	211,376	-1.7	13,889	6.6	206,343	33.6	28.9
Blair	51,647	70.3	128,200	18.1	11.6	741	29.6	1.2	59,237	-1.3	3,536	6.0	56,352	32.6	26.7
Bradford	25,084	72.7	150,900	19.2	11.8	737	25.4	2.2	27,852	-2.2	1,558	5.6	26,722	29.7	36.9
Bucks	240,763	78.1	340,500	21.7	12.7	1,252	29.5	1.4	342,596	-0.3	18,159	5.3	333,063	46.2	18.2
Butler	77,725	76.0	216,900	19.0	10.5	858	26.1	0.8	98,106	-1.3	5,490	5.6	93,626	42.8	21.5
Cambria	56,933	74.7	94,900	18.1	12.4	635	27.5	1.0	55,668	-2.3	3,908	7.0	56,969	33.3	26.9
Cameron	2,334	67.1	77,400	19.7	11.5	656	29.4	1.2	2,009	-2.7	154	7.7	1,894	21.2	40.1
Carbon	26,545	74.9	150,400	19.6	14.2	836	26.2	1.9	32,079	0.4	2,155	6.7	30,614	29.9	32.6
Centre	59,380	62.5	242,700	20.0	10.9	1,019	36.5	2.3	76,030	-2.0	3,483	4.6	77,351	49.8	14.6
Chester	192,951	75.0	369,500	20.1	11.5	1,354	27.9	1.7	286,372	0.4	12,030	4.2	273,256	53.1	14.1
Clarion	15,930	69.5	123,400	17.7	10.5	665	26.8	1.5	16,640	-2.1	1,075	6.5	17,516	32.0	28.7
Clearfield	31,704	77.4	99,400	19.0	12.2	688	29.1	2.1	35,498	-1.6	2,491	7.0	33,885	29.9	31.9
Clinton	15,058	69.6	145,700	19.0	13.0	737	25.9	1.5	17,226	-3.8	1,150	6.7	17,727	30.3	31.4
Columbia	26,482	68.2	153,900	19.3	11.8	777	26.9	1.0	33,275	-1.5	1,947	5.9	30,788	34.6	28.8
Crawford	35,169	72.8	117,400	19.0	11.5	676	24.2	2.3	37,822	-2.2	2,517	6.7	37,504	30.9	32.7
Cumberland	101,176	69.7	209,700	19.6	10.8	1,001	26.3	1.0	132,627	-0.3	6,077	4.6	126,864	44.5	20.1
Dauphin	113,759	63.4	175,700	19.7	11.7	966	26.6	1.7	145,162	-0.9	9,113	6.3	139,385	38.9	20.8
Delaware	209,596	68.7	247,900	20.9	13.4	1,109	30.5	1.9	295,824	-1.0	18,598	6.3	279,832	45.0	16.8
Elk	14,215	78.4	103,100	16.7	10.4	620	25.8	0.8	14,836	-3.8	1,022	6.9	15,276	27.3	40.9
Erie	110,388	67.0	138,500	19.3	11.9	758	29.4	1.8	126,536	-1.7	9,260	7.3	125,598	35.8	22.9
Fayette	55,346	73.4	106,200	18.5	12.4	684	27.2	1.7	55,515	-2.3	4,850	8.7	54,917	30.2	29.9
Forest	2,131	83.2	91,700	21.2	11.4	519	28.6	3.3	1,747	-3.7	145	8.3	1,413	28.3	29.6
Franklin	61,617	70.9	186,300	20.3	10.7	905	25.7	1.9	77,153	-1.7	3,957	5.1	74,316	32.2	31.2
Fulton	6,040	78.2	165,800	20.3	12.2	685	22.2	1.8	7,109	-5.3	448	6.3	6,846	25.9	38.6
Greene	14,503	75.2	122,500	17.2	11.3	699	25.1	1.5	15,723	-2.7	1,148	7.3	13,984	31.5	30.6
Huntingdon	16,779	77.0	142,800	19.1	12.0	687	24.6	1.7	19,181	-3.3	1,405	7.3	18,759	32.8	30.6
Indiana	33,855	70.1	124,100	19.0	12.3	698	31.7	2.0	37,090	-2.7	2,629	7.1	36,594	30.9	27.8
Jefferson	18,400	74.8	108,800	18.1	10.8	691	27.4	2.5	19,626	-3.6	1,280	6.5	19,617	26.4	36.6
Juniata	9,380	73.9	154,200	18.6	10.4	683	23.6	3.4	12,501	-1.9	624	5.0	11,491	26.7	40.1
Lackawanna	87,737	64.2	154,700	19.7	13.3	799	27.4	1.7	103,325	-1.6	7,100	6.9	98,930	35.4	23.7
Lancaster	204,003	69.4	218,700	21.3	11.3	1,050	28.5	2.4	284,893	-0.2	14,010	4.9	273,736	35.7	28.1
Lawrence	37,300	74.8	113,200	19.3	12.6	702	31.5	1.6	39,632	-2.8	3,020	7.6	39,513	31.4	27.8
Lebanon	53,857	70.5	176,000	20.2	11.9	879	28.7	2.7	72,636	-0.5	3,965	5.5	67,281	31.3	29.0
Lehigh	140,072	64.7	215,400	20.4	13.4	1,105	30.8	2.5	196,119	0.7	13,338	6.8	178,865	36.9	25.6
Luzerne	130,039	68.0	129,600	19.2	12.7	772	27.2	1.6	156,930	-1.6	12,948	8.3	150,945	32.2	28.1
Lycoming	46,160	68.6	161,900	20.1	12.0	797	28.9	1.7	55,322	-2.5	3,715	6.7	52,692	32.3	26.8
McKean	17,059	74.4	82,300	17.8	10.9	691	28.0	0.7	16,882	-2.5	1,171	6.9	17,648	31.0	31.6
Mercer	46,821	71.8	123,600	18.1	11.6	682	28.0	1.9	47,850	-1.8	3,415	7.1	47,844	31.7	25.8
Mifflin	19,075	73.0	115,400	18.5	13.2	692	25.5	2.5	20,860	-2.2	1,267	6.1	21,834	27.3	35.0
Monroe	59,950	77.1	173,800	23.0	14.0	1,154	29.5	2.1	81,973	-1.0	6,295	7.7	80,189	32.9	25.1
Montgomery	318,648	71.9	326,200	20.5	12.0	1,323	27.8	1.5	455,531	0.1	22,600	5.0	434,670	51.8	14.4
Montour	7,475	69.0	186,100	18.6	11.0	744	30.1	2.3	9,001	-1.0	392	4.4	8,655	41.7	22.8
Northampton	115,300	71.2	223,800	21.2	12.9	1,106	29.6	1.4	162,125	0.5	9,638	5.9	151,082	38.0	23.0
Northumberland	39,048	71.2	119,800	18.6	11.8	680	26.1	1.4	42,079	-1.7	2,855	6.8	41,462	29.2	31.8
Perry	18,512	81.1	179,400	20.1	11.0	758	23.7	2.0	24,211	-0.5	1,127	4.7	22,958	30.9	35.0
Philadelphia	613,125	52.8	171,600	21.8	13.3	1,084	31.3	3.1	721,225	-2.0	66,071	9.2	713,851	40.8	17.4
Pike	22,717	84.3	186,600	22.1	13.4	1,204	34.5	1.2	25,175	-0.9	1,848	7.3	24,968	32.7	23.9

1. Specified owner-occupied units. 2. A value of 10.0 represents 10 percent or less; a value of 50.0 represents 50 percent or more. 3. Specified renter-occupied units. 4. Overcrowded or lacking complete plumbing facilities. 5. Percent of civilian labor force. 6. Civilian employed persons 16 years old and over.

STATE County	Private nonfarm establishments, employment and payroll, 2020									Agriculture, 2017			
		Employment						Annual payroll		Farms			Farm producers whose primary occupation is farming (percent)
											Percent with:		
	Number of establish-ments	Total	Health care and social assistance	Manufac-turing	Retail trade	Finance and insurance	Professional, scientific, and technical services	Total (mil dol)	Average per employee (dollars)	Number	Fewer than 50 acres	1000 acres or more	
	104	105	106	107	108	109	110	111	112	113	114	115	116
OREGON—Cont'd													
Morrow	202	3,642	397	1,478	217	90	8	176	48,344	375	30.7	42.7	50.3
Multnomah	27,656	460,467	72,110	34,424	46,937	21,783	37,199	25,871	56,185	653	89.3	0.6	32.0
Polk	1,530	15,490	3,177	1,954	1,616	261	460	617	39,858	1,243	67.3	2.4	41.6
Sherman	65	531	9	NA	91	NA	NA	20	37,693	190	7.4	62.6	47.4
Tillamook	704	7,075	1,085	1,317	1,094	113	124	307	43,347	293	51.2	0.7	53.4
Umatilla	1,542	24,337	3,434	3,536	3,158	500	524	973	39,999	1,724	59.6	15.7	38.7
Union	756	7,671	1,437	1,289	1,566	166	361	306	39,844	820	54.6	10.2	37.6
Wallowa	362	2,024	467	112	266	50	91	78	38,632	539	40.3	21.2	42.4
Wasco	709	7,713	2,064	609	1,609	277	237	315	40,830	595	33.4	20.2	43.9
Washington	15,865	293,095	34,455	41,811	33,338	13,764	21,052	21,149	72,158	1,755	81.1	1.0	35.5
Wheeler	25	150	NA	NA	34	NA	NA	5	30,940	150	21.3	46.0	40.7
Yamhill	2,602	31,536	4,824	6,546	3,909	686	841	1,290	40,891	2,138	78.0	1.1	32.7
PENNSYLVANIA	302,018	5,574,417	1,099,559	551,201	657,825	293,254	336,793	294,187	52,775	53,157	42.1	1.4	45.7
Adams	1,948	28,891	4,796	6,238	3,510	467	640	1,085	37,552	1,146	50.2	2.2	43.4
Allegheny	33,435	701,782	140,471	33,265	70,660	54,191	56,136	39,254	55,935	389	60.7	0.5	40.2
Armstrong	1,244	14,027	3,620	1,590	1,819	545	323	506	36,094	668	28.4	4.2	43.6
Beaver	3,296	51,362	9,759	6,467	6,491	823	1,931	2,290	44,582	613	46.8	0.2	40.1
Bedford	1,031	12,647	1,733	2,207	2,209	350	210	451	35,632	1,159	29.2	3.1	50.3
Berks	8,335	161,143	31,523	30,457	20,212	5,617	6,313	7,625	47,315	1,809	49.0	0.9	52.9
Blair	3,182	54,188	13,622	6,389	8,870	1,020	1,693	2,225	41,057	496	34.9	1.6	52.7
Bradford	1,310	18,891	5,313	2,926	2,878	491	484	861	45,551	1,449	24.4	1.6	46.4
Bucks	19,389	258,419	52,562	26,596	36,892	9,093	17,465	12,489	48,328	824	72.1	1.5	43.7
Butler	4,875	86,423	14,107	11,767	11,105	2,085	6,104	4,242	49,088	955	40.4	1.4	42.2
Cambria	3,010	45,834	11,852	4,952	6,451	1,857	2,011	1,718	37,485	557	37.0	2.3	36.1
Cameron	113	1,513	187	924	120	19	10	57	37,556	37	16.2	NA	32.8
Carbon	1,138	12,653	2,884	1,371	2,125	257	307	429	33,925	200	53.0	1.0	30.3
Centre	3,303	45,062	9,445	4,027	7,266	1,064	3,101	1,838	40,786	1,023	41.3	1.4	47.0
Chester	14,784	260,642	40,051	15,790	28,151	30,322	24,905	19,825	76,061	1,646	60.6	1.2	52.3
Clarion	936	10,854	2,665	1,903	1,653	302	265	361	33,288	594	25.3	1.9	38.8
Clearfield	1,896	25,756	6,282	2,494	4,639	672	527	962	37,366	497	35.8	0.6	35.4
Clinton	765	10,771	1,593	2,972	1,755	164	144	446	41,368	267	35.6	1.9	50.9
Columbia	1,379	22,439	3,378	4,542	3,349	606	402	907	40,441	779	43.8	1.7	38.1
Crawford	1,907	26,683	5,894	7,156	3,207	543	656	969	36,318	1,091	36.8	2.1	44.3
Cumberland	6,178	127,839	17,772	8,403	20,714	8,580	8,480	6,275	49,085	1,260	45.1	1.5	51.4
Dauphin	6,911	152,895	33,982	8,968	15,576	8,594	8,522	7,892	51,620	692	52.6	1.4	46.9
Delaware	12,873	221,914	47,981	12,997	25,199	14,772	9,979	12,114	54,588	61	77.0	NA	43.0
Elk	889	13,011	1,526	6,181	1,392	220	306	518	39,784	232	43.5	NA	32.1
Erie	6,055	112,481	26,441	19,930	14,900	5,752	3,636	4,511	40,107	1,162	39.6	1.4	46.8
Fayette	2,485	33,007	7,486	3,139	5,377	495	972	1,176	35,624	834	38.6	1.8	35.6
Forest	94	1,056	441	239	60	13	12	34	32,263	36	25.0	NA	71.4
Franklin	3,084	53,967	10,712	7,911	7,632	1,164	1,755	2,181	40,410	1,581	37.3	1.6	55.5
Fulton	241	5,822	701	3,295	424	72	27	329	56,445	545	31.4	1.8	36.1
Greene	679	11,539	1,306	337	1,990	296	197	487	42,217	722	25.2	1.2	39.3
Huntingdon	828	9,825	2,256	1,065	1,412	395	341	322	32,780	714	30.5	1.4	40.4
Indiana	1,765	24,226	5,030	2,137	4,826	1,731	835	964	39,783	951	36.9	1.6	37.9
Jefferson	1,089	14,305	2,978	3,938	1,517	249	306	536	37,469	468	23.9	2.1	44.4
Juniata	484	6,135	489	2,600	697	235	59	201	32,704	670	43.9	1.2	49.3
Lackawanna	5,130	90,463	20,610	10,468	12,073	4,137	2,780	3,721	41,127	263	24.3	1.5	35.1
Lancaster	13,316	246,206	39,941	37,222	33,162	8,313	13,387	11,197	45,477	5,108	50.0	0.4	56.9
Lawrence	1,901	25,691	6,358	3,373	3,166	1,086	789	1,017	39,601	587	38.0	1.7	39.3
Lebanon	2,720	48,007	8,945	9,838	7,021	986	1,194	1,986	41,371	1,149	54.6	0.2	50.5
Lehigh	8,614	187,168	46,858	19,720	23,903	6,144	8,279	10,386	55,490	381	55.4	4.5	52.8
Luzerne	7,087	134,702	26,316	17,249	17,683	5,394	6,238	5,875	43,616	451	39.0	1.6	40.6
Lycoming	2,711	45,220	9,874	7,447	6,863	1,547	1,581	1,844	40,768	1,043	32.2	1.3	38.6
McKean	947	12,130	2,552	2,797	1,676	258	196	477	39,339	259	29.3	0.8	35.6
Mercer	2,687	43,729	9,068	9,416	6,585	1,458	843	1,663	38,019	1,168	38.5	1.5	41.5
Mifflin	977	14,551	3,673	3,675	2,077	363	163	583	40,055	711	40.4	0.6	49.7
Monroe	3,409	47,919	8,273	5,032	9,458	909	1,574	1,859	38,787	233	55.4	1.7	40.4
Montgomery	26,407	536,848	93,837	43,935	57,904	40,431	46,152	36,521	68,028	565	76.3	0.7	40.1
Montour	458	15,313	8,069	652	620	1,362	466	1,111	72,549	356	43.5	0.8	42.5
Northampton	6,382	114,513	17,615	12,449	14,892	3,574	3,987	5,272	46,040	459	64.5	2.8	43.5
Northumberland	1,614	22,861	4,176	3,906	3,309	610	588	938	41,050	728	42.7	2.9	49.3
Perry	780	6,142	703	437	1,235	229	192	170	27,748	759	38.3	1.2	45.6
Philadelphia	29,331	679,396	170,229	19,250	55,107	31,823	55,512	41,101	60,496	43	95.3	NA	25.9
Pike	935	8,679	1,067	168	1,944	140	215	258	29,697	53	56.6	1.9	22.3

STATE County	Agriculture, 2017 (cont.): Land in farms: Acreage (1,000)	Land in farms: Percent change, 2012–2017	Land in farms: Acres: Average size of farm	Land in farms: Acres: Total irrigated (1,000)	Land in farms: Acres: Total cropland (1,000)	Value of land and buildings (dollars): Average per farm	Value of land and buildings (dollars): Average per acre	Value of machinery and equipment, average per farm (dollars)	Value of products sold: Total (mil dol)	Value of products sold: Average per farm (acres)	Value of products sold: Percent from: Crops	Value of products sold: Percent from: Livestock and poultry products	Organic farms (number)	Farms with internet access (percent)	Government payments: Total ($1,000)	Government payments: Percent of farms
	117	118	119	120	121	122	123	124	125	126	127	128	129	130	131	132
OREGON—Cont'd																
Morrow	1,126	-3.3	3,003	111.5	511.9	3,385,469	1,127	416,278	596.5	1,590,632	32.0	68.0	6	86.4	11,659	57.6
Multnomah	25	-15.2	39	5.7	15.6	813,249	20,879	54,930	74.6	114,210	95.8	4.2	24	91.3	84	3.2
Polk	149	2.9	120	20.4	107.6	852,419	7,116	93,564	134.8	108,408	77.2	22.8	26	85.9	776	8.0
Sherman	525	2.2	2,762	1.1	340.9	2,349,030	850	240,036	33.8	177,879	93.7	6.3	3	77.4	9,823	86.8
Tillamook	33	-9.9	112	3.6	12.0	876,306	7,796	168,856	125.3	427,604	1.6	98.4	5	91.1	120	4.4
Umatilla	1,352	3.4	784	108.6	816.0	1,430,953	1,824	155,916	374.7	217,314	78.5	21.5	11	84.7	20,070	30.5
Union	385	-6.4	470	44.3	121.1	851,017	1,812	123,048	57.1	69,662	73.5	26.5	2	83.2	2,731	26.6
Wallowa	520	14.9	965	42.6	94.7	1,575,439	1,632	138,191	38.9	72,217	40.3	59.7	3	82.4	3,206	36.2
Wasco	1,389	-2.7	2,334	21.5	237.7	2,127,529	911	115,183	93.9	157,736	85.3	14.7	9	83.5	7,274	44.2
Washington	105	-22.9	60	18.0	75.7	1,020,247	17,099	88,896	201.6	114,874	96.2	3.8	21	89.5	1,485	9.2
Wheeler	557	-14.2	3,713	8.6	25.4	3,360,966	905	77,154	11.1	74,020	33.3	66.7	NA	80.7	921	23.3
Yamhill	169	-4.5	79	29.1	113.4	806,192	10,178	88,958	314.3	147,017	80.7	19.3	39	88.2	1,658	8.5
PENNSYLVANIA	7,279	-5.5	137	32.1	4,651.2	897,125	6,552	109,024	7,758.9	145,962	35.8	64.2	1,142	69.3	74,182	20.5
Adams	166	-3.0	145	2.2	128.4	998,833	6,886	132,547	207.6	181,122	54.2	45.8	17	77.7	1,503	18.4
Allegheny	29	-16.8	74	0.4	15.5	652,804	8,766	79,400	13.7	35,329	90.0	10.0	7	81.7	D	4.1
Armstrong	127	-1.9	190	0.2	73.7	690,965	3,644	111,565	39.8	59,533	57.8	42.2	6	77.2	654	20.7
Beaver	54	-3.5	88	0.3	30.1	531,298	6,050	80,548	23.7	38,586	61.2	38.8	3	72.6	177	8.0
Bedford	222	5.9	192	0.4	119.5	781,610	4,076	115,752	115.3	99,459	31.8	68.2	19	69.5	1,759	19.4
Berks	225	-3.9	124	1.5	184.5	1,392,373	11,209	138,139	554.7	306,609	43.8	56.2	72	68.4	3,038	22.1
Blair	79	-12.4	159	0.2	55.8	1,073,542	6,747	130,550	107.2	216,087	15.8	84.2	9	61.7	1,064	25.6
Bradford	304	-1.4	210	0.3	183.3	759,047	3,623	106,595	132.6	91,539	28.3	71.7	40	77.0	3,408	36.1
Bucks	77	20.7	94	1.0	60.0	882,088	9,408	85,710	75.8	91,938	72.5	27.5	15	84.2	635	10.1
Butler	134	-1.7	140	0.5	86.2	742,206	5,291	113,631	49.5	51,855	64.9	35.1	6	76.5	840	22.6
Cambria	79	3.2	142	0.1	50.5	659,661	4,631	100,086	30.1	53,982	60.1	39.9	2	68.8	979	30.3
Cameron	5	-15.1	143	NA	1.5	405,700	2,844	77,509	0.5	14,135	69.4	30.6	NA	59.5	61	37.8
Carbon	19	-7.9	97	0.0	13.1	645,238	6,619	106,544	13.0	65,145	87.7	12.3	1	83.5	185	25.0
Centre	150	-7.5	146	0.4	88.3	981,430	6,700	92,395	91.5	89,421	35.3	64.7	23	68.5	2,266	24.0
Chester	151	-8.5	91	1.2	105.8	1,110,075	12,140	130,513	712.5	432,848	80.1	19.9	46	74.5	1,775	10.0
Clarion	100	-13.5	169	0.0	52.5	542,206	3,210	96,875	27.7	46,582	47.9	52.1	9	74.4	835	27.6
Clearfield	61	-12.0	123	0.1	31.0	442,517	3,608	66,449	28.7	57,684	26.4	73.6	2	62.4	478	17.5
Clinton	40	-24.0	150	0.3	26.5	980,810	6,538	125,749	45.6	170,640	28.7	71.3	18	55.8	515	23.2
Columbia	107	-13.0	137	0.8	78.9	826,216	6,029	92,891	67.3	86,376	56.2	43.8	9	71.2	2,290	39.0
Crawford	194	-14.6	178	0.3	121.0	595,435	3,341	124,042	107.3	98,323	39.8	60.2	5	70.4	679	15.4
Cumberland	170	9.5	135	1.4	140.8	1,025,011	7,613	130,622	219.2	173,950	28.7	71.3	22	61.1	2,132	22.1
Dauphin	81	-37.2	117	0.4	63.4	1,032,232	8,791	106,338	93.1	134,499	29.2	70.8	43	68.4	779	21.0
Delaware	2	-49.5	39	0.1	0.7	562,808	14,395	69,987	9.5	155,656	97.7	2.3	NA	98.4	NA	NA
Elk	23	-2.2	99	0.1	9.3	415,868	4,198	65,859	4.0	17,349	50.2	49.8	4	71.1	50	9.9
Erie	153	-9.0	132	1.3	93.5	595,515	4,511	112,026	82.0	70,602	76.4	23.6	3	78.1	907	15.7
Fayette	112	-0.5	135	0.3	59.1	557,551	4,141	75,770	28.8	34,576	56.1	43.9	1	73.3	1,113	15.8
Forest	4	-49.7	116	0.0	1.7	567,562	4,900	71,350	2.1	57,194	14.7	85.3	NA	94.4	D	2.8
Franklin	270	1.9	170	2.8	213.9	1,283,405	7,528	162,878	476.5	301,372	19.2	80.8	44	59.6	3,264	23.0
Fulton	100	-10.5	184	0.0	52.9	769,540	4,175	95,703	75.8	139,110	16.2	83.8	7	72.5	686	29.2
Greene	114	1.5	158	0.0	37.5	575,776	3,644	85,505	16.4	22,763	51.3	48.7	NA	78.4	84	4.4
Huntingdon	120	-24.1	168	0.6	67.5	810,060	4,814	115,139	92.1	129,036	22.0	78.0	11	74.4	1,706	32.1
Indiana	148	-3.6	156	0.4	95.2	561,399	3,600	110,847	72.0	75,693	58.1	41.9	5	63.3	2,432	23.3
Jefferson	80	-11.9	172	0.2	46.6	569,456	3,314	82,484	22.4	47,912	50.3	49.7	3	70.7	519	19.0
Juniata	86	-5.9	128	0.2	55.7	833,587	6,522	106,123	126.8	189,194	17.5	82.5	64	63.3	904	22.8
Lackawanna	37	11.6	139	0.1	20.3	736,770	5,301	108,490	16.5	62,620	60.4	39.6	NA	77.2	119	16.7
Lancaster	394	-10.4	77	4.9	314.9	1,410,238	18,285	120,108	1,507.2	295,068	15.3	84.7	246	48.9	4,834	11.8
Lawrence	82	2.1	140	0.3	55.1	613,904	4,388	96,349	34.8	59,239	54.4	45.6	2	74.4	655	27.3
Lebanon	108	-11.4	94	0.7	86.7	1,348,192	14,400	132,813	350.8	305,312	10.6	89.4	54	71.4	1,021	13.7
Lehigh	75	-2.4	196	0.4	63.1	1,534,921	7,849	136,146	79.2	207,916	72.3	27.7	8	79.3	1,063	18.4
Luzerne	49	-19.4	109	0.3	27.6	659,902	6,063	64,776	17.8	39,452	74.7	25.3	NA	70.3	733	33.9
Lycoming	186	17.5	178	0.2	79.0	913,565	5,119	69,673	63.7	61,086	48.1	51.9	8	67.0	2,683	40.6
McKean	43	18.7	166	0.1	17.5	473,804	2,848	55,905	5.5	21,297	51.4	48.6	1	73.4	315	26.6
Mercer	156	-4.1	134	0.2	98.4	535,249	3,997	103,659	65.7	56,291	53.9	46.1	20	73.6	1,526	26.3
Mifflin	81	-10.6	114	0.1	49.9	703,683	6,179	92,455	140.0	196,896	12.0	88.0	18	65.8	818	17.0
Monroe	28	4.2	118	0.2	13.4	698,127	5,892	85,598	9.9	42,627	64.6	35.4	NA	79.4	190	9.4
Montgomery	31	0.4	55	0.6	20.5	1,058,678	19,360	62,127	35.4	62,609	73.9	26.1	2	83.5	179	4.8
Montour	39	-11.2	109	0.1	29.4	699,083	6,442	103,791	60.2	169,171	42.4	57.6	4	64.9	643	32.9
Northampton	59	-10.0	129	0.3	51.6	967,696	7,504	159,760	36.1	78,558	76.5	23.5	4	80.2	1,204	16.6
Northumberland	124	-4.1	171	0.9	92.7	1,001,321	5,872	143,349	154.6	212,339	38.0	62.0	18	67.7	2,710	35.0
Perry	115	-15.1	151	0.4	77.2	1,002,216	6,629	125,814	172.8	227,613	18.3	81.7	33	68.2	1,251	22.8
Philadelphia	0	-0.4	7	0.0	0.1	387,767	58,711	16,642	0.3	7,605	81.0	19.0	2	90.7	NA	NA
Pike	25	-12.6	466	0.0	1.4	1,037,171	2,226	74,827	0.9	16,830	50.0	50.0	NA	96.2	NA	NA

STATE County	Water use, 2015		Wholesale Trade[1], 2017				Retail Trade[2], 2017				Real estate and rental and leasing,[2] 2017			
	Public supply water withdrawn (mil gal/ day)	Public supply gallons withdrawn per person per day	Number of establish- ments	Number of employees	Sales (mil dol)	Average payroll (mil dol)	Number of establish- ments	Number of employees	Sales (mil dol)	Average payroll (mil dol)	Number of establish- ments	Number of employees	Sales (mil dol)	Average payroll (mil dol)
	133	134	135	136	137	138	139	140	141	142	143	144	145	146
OREGON—Cont'd														
Morrow	5.6	501.3	16	74	85.1	2.8	20	235	68.8	5.2	7	19	2.1	0.2
Multnomah	14.7	18.6	1,191	24,301	25,399.7	1,632.9	3,084	43,576	11,927.7	1,294.8	1,683	11,186	2,347.9	530.4
Polk	5.0	62.5	39	451	184.3	21.7	116	1,604	411.5	41.4	78	206	37.5	5.7
Sherman	0.5	279.8	6	36	71.0	1.9	7	119	59.9	2.8	NA	NA	NA	NA
Tillamook	4.6	178.1	13	132	56.8	5.0	111	1,161	274.8	27.6	42	140	20.4	4.1
Umatilla	28.2	368.1	62	839	607.0	40.7	225	3,055	885.4	81.1	71	254	44.2	9.3
Union	4.6	177.6	20	221	146.1	9.6	106	1,607	387.5	41.1	21	77	14.0	2.3
Wallowa	1.4	199.8	D	D	D	D	49	276	71.1	7.9	24	D	5.8	D
Wasco	5.3	207.2	28	435	329.5	13.3	105	1,571	470.3	44.1	42	88	9.6	2.6
Washington	50.0	87.1	745	13,135	12,095.2	980.6	1,598	33,923	11,937.5	1,033.1	1,006	4,218	1,267.8	199.5
Wheeler	0.2	125.2	NA	NA	NA	NA	7	43	11.2	1.0	NA	NA	NA	NA
Yamhill	8.8	86.0	65	465	314.7	26.4	300	3,841	1,122.2	109.5	112	273	50.0	9.5
PENNSYLVANIA	1,391.7	108.7	12,071	204,256	199,203.8	12,958.8	42,514	662,560	234,836.3	17,354.0	10,662	66,715	18,860.6	3,472.2
Adams	12.4	121.1	D	D	D	D	337	3,599	979.0	87.0	48	190	34.3	6.2
Allegheny	178.2	144.8	1,414	20,546	27,374.2	1,327.9	4,244	72,934	56,465.7	1,980.9	1,360	10,209	2,937.3	478.9
Armstrong	6.7	99.2	38	523	212.0	25.5	200	1,975	574.0	46.5	33	167	25.6	6.4
Beaver	22.1	131.1	93	1,201	817.0	64.4	504	7,120	1,626.2	156.3	83	400	86.0	16.1
Bedford	10.0	205.6	33	292	124.3	11.2	192	2,094	577.3	50.5	12	41	8.2	2.0
Berks	31.9	76.7	374	8,533	7,103.8	524.2	1,186	20,446	5,772.3	527.8	367	2,985	1,173.9	217.9
Blair	13.1	104.1	124	2,112	2,076.2	101.4	530	8,700	2,721.2	227.4	111	409	84.8	14.3
Bradford	3.0	49.3	47	410	358.5	19.9	228	2,811	857.4	69.4	35	138	29.6	5.6
Bucks	98.6	157.2	1,035	15,293	10,028.0	939.7	2,289	38,202	10,862.1	1,031.5	668	3,256	915.6	165.2
Butler	7.7	41.0	236	3,955	2,583.2	246.5	674	11,286	3,268.6	278.5	170	879	237.9	33.4
Cambria	14.9	109.4	104	988	573.3	44.9	534	6,781	1,773.7	160.2	83	460	75.9	15.1
Cameron	0.3	71.9	NA	NA	NA	NA	14	134	30.4	2.5	NA	NA	NA	NA
Carbon	23.3	364.9	D	D	D	D	179	2,145	602.5	54.5	37	107	21.6	3.4
Centre	17.9	111.3	86	703	301.3	34.9	461	7,741	2,052.5	186.4	150	957	233.2	37.5
Chester	42.2	81.7	715	13,706	17,031.5	1,271.8	1,442	28,699	14,687.9	978.2	580	3,880	1,364.2	237.1
Clarion	2.7	69.1	24	337	178.2	14.9	165	1,707	463.6	41.9	25	114	17.3	3.3
Clearfield	5.8	72.1	53	667	596.0	30.4	339	4,571	1,277.4	109.1	39	322	37.2	7.4
Clinton	4.0	101.9	D	D	D	D	131	1,753	539.7	41.4	27	148	23.8	4.9
Columbia	5.0	75.3	41	465	185.8	20.0	229	3,372	919.9	78.0	42	151	43.0	5.8
Crawford	5.7	65.6	D	D	D	D	294	3,477	991.0	91.2	51	258	34.7	6.9
Cumberland	13.4	54.2	208	3,126	2,501.8	156.9	863	19,806	6,437.1	549.1	249	1,384	343.1	77.5
Dauphin	31.5	115.3	279	6,109	7,259.1	371.7	918	15,228	4,185.3	368.5	254	1,522	391.2	64.9
Delaware	20.8	36.9	513	6,250	4,471.8	415.7	1,645	26,153	7,586.1	691.4	476	2,963	957.1	194.4
Elk	5.3	172.3	D	D	D	D	128	1,477	387.6	35.2	16	62	9.8	2.4
Erie	33.3	119.9	247	3,292	1,367.7	166.6	917	15,344	3,823.5	360.9	190	878	169.8	30.3
Fayette	45.9	343.4	83	845	531.6	36.0	449	5,798	1,691.6	136.5	72	306	49.1	9.3
Forest	0.4	55.3	NA	NA	NA	NA	18	89	19.6	1.8	NA	NA	NA	NA
Franklin	8.5	55.1	D	D	D	D	487	7,407	2,075.0	186.5	94	364	61.4	11.7
Fulton	0.4	25.3	D	D	D	D	37	370	96.9	8.4	5	D	1.5	D
Greene	7.2	191.6	19	315	240.9	14.4	125	2,007	738.6	54.4	14	88	31.9	4.4
Huntingdon	2.9	62.4	25	320	122.5	15.6	138	1,513	372.6	34.7	17	36	5.6	1.3
Indiana	4.1	47.3	56	455	720.0	24.4	280	5,146	1,587.6	135.4	48	141	23.5	3.8
Jefferson	2.1	48.2	35	480	173.3	23.1	156	1,634	492.3	38.2	24	98	20.8	3.9
Juniata	0.8	33.1	D	D	D	6.0	71	656	221.2	16.0	8	20	3.2	0.4
Lackawanna	38.7	182.6	240	4,026	5,763.9	201.7	854	12,099	3,227.7	294.3	146	696	155.5	24.4
Lancaster	54.5	101.5	562	13,388	11,432.4	742.2	1,926	31,359	8,428.8	811.5	384	2,278	524.6	101.6
Lawrence	10.1	114.3	76	983	4,066.4	50.6	272	3,260	995.3	85.9	48	290	29.1	7.0
Lebanon	3.6	25.9	103	2,211	1,915.5	105.0	416	6,740	1,694.5	168.3	75	303	54.7	10.2
Lehigh	34.6	95.9	414	10,678	10,020.2	902.0	1,282	24,146	8,467.5	669.5	346	1,799	470.9	80.7
Luzerne	22.8	71.7	284	5,482	3,359.9	273.2	1,214	18,064	5,166.5	452.7	234	1,061	280.7	47.3
Lycoming	8.8	75.7	114	1,788	1,083.6	75.3	451	7,031	1,896.4	167.4	109	731	142.6	30.4
McKean	6.8	159.6	27	349	169.0	14.5	160	1,769	466.5	43.1	10	57	5.8	1.5
Mercer	13.7	120.3	83	1,032	631.2	48.0	483	7,364	1,565.4	161.6	81	302	65.6	9.8
Mifflin	2.7	57.8	37	515	149.7	20.1	164	2,059	601.1	51.8	22	59	12.8	1.9
Monroe	11.4	68.2	107	D	525.9	D	605	9,469	2,448.5	225.8	144	539	122.4	18.8
Montgomery	63.3	77.3	1,236	21,055	19,824.7	1,626.2	3,169	57,720	18,263.6	1,657.5	1,070	8,189	2,978.2	557.9
Montour	0.0	1.6	8	98	79.4	5.5	50	639	177.6	14.7	7	16	3.7	0.5
Northampton	9.5	31.7	242	7,442	14,195.0	391.9	854	14,171	4,142.3	397.4	195	968	233.6	40.4
Northumberland	11.1	118.5	48	851	677.9	42.0	288	3,314	947.0	80.6	33	149	16.2	4.2
Perry	0.7	15.5	16	72	88.4	4.7	129	1,333	338.4	33.0	14	33	4.5	0.8
Philadelphia	249.5	159.2	1,006	17,207	16,323.4	1,169.1	4,540	53,157	14,973.0	1,305.4	1,293	10,704	3,027.6	617.0
Pike	3.1	54.5	18	D	5.3	D	141	1,916	509.6	47.4	41	352	57.0	14.5

1 Merchant wholesalers, except manufacturers' sales branches and offices. 2. Employer establishments.

STATE County	Professional, scientific, and technical services, 2017				Manufacturing, 2017				Accommodation and food services, 2017			
	Number of establish-ments	Number of employees	Sales (mil dol)	Average payroll (mil dol)	Number of establish-ments	Number of employees	Sales (mil dol)	Average payroll (mil dol)	Number of establis-hments	Number of employees	Sales (mil dol)	Annual payroll (mil dol)
	147	148	149	150	151	152	153	154	155	156	157	158
OREGON—Cont'd												
Morrow	NA	NA	NA	NA	13	1,560	1,056.5	76.5	21	126	8.5	2.5
Multnomah	4,076	36,302	6,965.0	2,822.4	1,197	33,161	10,957.3	1,823.4	3,165	52,476	3,605.4	1,094.6
Polk	117	434	51.4	16.6	73	1,448	410.5	74.1	D	D	D	D
Sherman	NA	NA	NA	NA	NA	NA	NA	NA	9	76	5.6	1.4
Tillamook	41	148	15.7	6.3	33	1,515	1,043.3	77.2	136	1,336	86.0	25.8
Umatilla	D	D	D	D	67	4,148	1,061.3	150.6	171	3,050	234.1	63.0
Union	56	242	26.6	10.1	29	1,235	339.1	59.7	69	764	37.3	10.7
Wallowa	25	88	9.0	3.3	D	84	D	D	46	184	13.1	3.5
Wasco	41	240	32.9	11.3	31	472	157.9	20.7	78	1,023	71.3	20.1
Washington	D	D	D	D	728	43,158	19,629.8	3,934.6	1,284	22,112	1,417.4	423.1
Wheeler	NA	NA	NA	NA	NA	NA	NA	NA	4	D	0.8	D
Yamhill	D	D	D	D	248	5,692	1,650.2	333.4	221	3,268	190.1	58.2
PENNSYLVANIA	29,805	329,103	63,441.9	25,746.2	13,537	536,967	227,812.0	30,392.5	28,843	481,682	28,849.4	7,931.4
Adams	D	D	D	D	112	6,561	2,010.6	314.9	227	3,958	220.6	62.9
Allegheny	D	D	10,583.7	D	1,038	34,386	15,252.8	2,094.0	3,387	62,831	3,697.0	1,069.7
Armstrong	D	D	D	D	68	1,710	348.3	77.6	111	1,156	48.4	13.0
Beaver	D	D	D	D	166	6,338	2,794.3	361.8	320	4,978	225.8	60.3
Bedford	D	D	D	D	64	1,747	575.3	86.7	96	1,739	91.7	30.0
Berks	D	D	D	D	483	31,959	10,989.4	1,674.8	770	13,389	671.4	186.8
Blair	204	1,753	261.3	87.4	130	6,802	2,282.2	344.6	286	4,683	230.9	63.2
Bradford	D	D	D	D	59	3,038	1,420.5	154.7	127	1,261	62.7	16.5
Bucks	2,392	17,522	4,433.4	1,462.6	970	25,170	9,840.0	1,422.7	1,444	23,034	1,379.3	370.4
Butler	D	D	D	D	274	13,008	4,749.4	814.9	373	7,338	384.0	105.7
Cambria	D	D	D	D	115	5,161	4,739.5	286.6	298	4,130	190.7	49.8
Cameron	D	D	D	D	22	793	210.0	41.1	10	D	2.9	D
Carbon	63	417	39.1	15.1	51	1,374	424.2	65.0	113	1,630	94.1	28.1
Centre	D	D	D	D	166	3,786	1,041.7	206.6	327	6,750	344.7	96.9
Chester	2,339	25,903	5,834.8	2,473.9	515	15,657	6,202.3	994.3	1,055	17,111	1,009.9	293.7
Clarion	D	D	19.8	D	36	1,413	620.0	62.3	94	1,439	63.4	15.9
Clearfield	D	D	D	D	97	2,304	1,037.6	102.0	179	2,590	120.5	32.4
Clinton	37	165	16.9	4.8	47	2,921	1,679.5	155.9	83	1,192	59.9	17.6
Columbia	D	D	D	D	73	4,497	1,792.7	195.8	167	2,736	137.1	39.4
Crawford	D	D	D	D	273	7,653	1,906.9	392.7	180	2,265	111.0	29.3
Cumberland	D	D	D	D	193	8,847	3,943.8	440.2	563	10,119	564.6	158.5
Dauphin	D	D	D	D	186	7,991	3,690.7	430.2	694	13,316	909.0	259.6
Delaware	D	D	D	D	348	13,365	10,442.9	1,046.8	1,145	18,599	1,080.7	302.3
Elk	43	386	27.8	11.9	134	6,499	1,734.2	342.5	79	818	36.2	9.4
Erie	408	3,267	495.3	170.6	476	20,344	6,147.9	1,215.9	627	11,662	540.9	151.4
Fayette	D	D	D	D	99	2,789	1,191.6	126.4	261	4,598	256.7	81.2
Forest	3	2	0.2	0.1	D	D	D	D	21	125	7.8	2.4
Franklin	D	D	D	D	183	7,425	2,941.8	378.9	275	4,501	217.9	62.4
Fulton	D	D	1.8	D	D	D	D	D	D	D	D	D
Greene	D	D	D	D	D	282	D	13.1	71	1,299	63.6	17.7
Huntingdon	D	D	D	D	32	1,073	355.0	52.0	77	953	52.5	14.2
Indiana	D	D	119.7	D	92	2,196	507.2	99.8	145	2,622	127.2	36.3
Jefferson	67	282	26.6	8.8	104	3,568	895.6	172.2	102	980	43.9	11.0
Juniata	D	D	D	D	61	2,215	558.5	87.8	D	D	D	D
Lackawanna	D	D	D	D	D	7,944	D	399.6	594	8,535	516.1	127.4
Lancaster	1,026	12,314	1,840.0	731.7	923	34,403	13,559.4	1,845.3	1,102	20,227	1,091.5	305.7
Lawrence	D	D	79.3	D	134	3,289	1,371.5	180.9	157	2,409	101.3	29.1
Lebanon	D	D	D	D	204	9,398	2,861.1	456.8	231	3,347	173.1	48.9
Lehigh	778	7,168	1,296.4	495.6	360	18,925	11,085.0	1,180.9	793	13,797	772.0	216.9
Luzerne	547	4,820	632.3	257.3	297	16,989	6,565.2	871.0	776	12,441	867.1	198.0
Lycoming	D	D	D	D	156	7,422	3,192.1	376.5	273	4,720	253.7	76.5
McKean	D	D	D	D	45	2,768	1,110.7	152.7	104	1,150	45.2	12.4
Mercer	D	D	D	D	177	7,455	3,156.2	384.3	270	4,393	208.6	62.9
Mifflin	D	D	D	D	82	3,168	1,085.7	177.4	85	1,289	54.1	15.5
Monroe	D	D	D	D	117	5,173	2,776.5	428.1	402	10,069	873.9	185.4
Montgomery	3,712	49,547	9,786.0	4,508.1	977	40,679	20,295.2	2,824.0	2,029	33,907	2,240.9	612.3
Montour	D	D	D	D	19	486	148.5	17.4	39	724	34.9	11.2
Northampton	D	D	D	D	327	11,922	4,534.7	690.3	698	11,807	1,163.7	247.6
Northumberland	D	D	D	D	73	3,765	1,357.2	181.8	174	1,734	84.1	22.5
Perry	47	190	18.2	6.9	37	549	88.6	24.5	64	505	24.1	6.2
Philadelphia	D	D	D	D	694	21,042	14,253.7	1,204.6	3,953	61,893	4,480.2	1,278.3
Pike	78	208	33.5	9.9	17	277	57.1	12.8	113	2,202	156.1	49.8

STATE County	Health care and social assistance, 2017				Other services, 2017				Nonemployer businesses, 2019		Value of residential construction authorized by building permits, 2021	
	Number of establish-ments	Number of employees	Receipts (mil dol)	Annual payroll (mil dol)	Number of establish-ments	Number of employees	Receipts (mil dol)	Annual payroll (mil dol)	Number	Receipts (mil dol)	New construction ($1,000)	Number of housing units
	159	160	161	162	163	164	165	166	167	168	169	170
OREGON—Cont'd												
Morrow	18	259	27.7	12.1	12	32	3.6	1.3	476	24.5	14,364	54
Multnomah	3,373	73,052	9,879.7	3,775.2	2,099	14,700	2,542.9	582.3	75,076	3,699.7	727,389	3,547
Polk	210	2,938	226.8	102.4	85	354	33.4	9.9	4,772	206.9	84,769	316
Sherman	D	D	D	0.2	NA	NA	NA	NA	126	4.7	NA	NA
Tillamook	54	930	122.3	48.8	43	148	15.7	3.7	2,206	110.7	48,363	137
Umatilla	217	3,149	383.7	143.3	107	518	63.4	17.2	3,293	172.3	63,146	330
Union	92	1,440	169.1	70.7	48	162	18.3	4.6	1,619	72.1	26,549	154
Wallowa	33	416	44.1	16.8	D	D	9.1	D	833	42.4	210	3
Wasco	83	2,138	323.6	102.7	50	224	19.0	5.9	1,486	64.5	22,399	96
Washington	1,984	34,211	4,422.1	1,712.0	915	6,476	1,136.4	286.2	41,301	2,010.5	750,589	3,096
Wheeler	D	D	D	D	NA	NA	NA	NA	131	5.1	NA	NA
Yamhill	299	4,982	531.0	208.3	140	571	53.1	15.9	6,875	316.3	188,084	609
PENNSYLVANIA	37,699	1,035,971	116,621.8	47,885.2	26,075	161,337	22,982.2	5,136.6	872,647	43,865.9	9,311,131	47,894
Adams	185	4,860	512.4	201.8	174	1,312	124.6	33.5	6,661	303.6	127,475	438
Allegheny	4,666	131,693	15,389.9	6,508.2	2,946	20,665	3,032.8	704.0	86,412	4,181.6	516,143	2,263
Armstrong	191	3,319	280.5	127.7	106	563	48.4	12.4	3,464	155.0	13,726	62
Beaver	496	9,892	976.8	406.8	316	1,484	118.1	34.8	8,971	388.0	39,703	172
Bedford	126	1,696	146.7	59.8	101	408	38.2	8.9	3,273	164.0	14,262	66
Berks	861	26,638	2,897.5	1,261.5	797	4,354	425.4	116.3	25,442	1,228.9	106,335	493
Blair	452	12,918	1,345.0	564.9	269	1,459	122.6	37.7	6,387	307.2	24,763	94
Bradford	150	5,097	681.1	286.7	124	527	43.6	11.6	3,418	159.2	22,601	82
Bucks	2,083	48,951	4,681.8	2,032.5	1,511	8,731	881.6	276.4	55,168	3,355.0	230,991	984
Butler	628	14,969	1,479.8	673.8	407	2,886	336.7	102.8	12,767	657.1	301,131	1,120
Cambria	484	11,101	1,045.2	458.7	299	1,543	145.7	35.4	6,085	259.9	15,741	62
Cameron	D	D	D	7.0	D	D	3.1	D	208	6.7	0	0
Carbon	198	3,442	263.7	117.0	90	333	31.7	7.6	3,378	153.5	36,267	144
Centre	403	9,501	1,078.6	456.8	253	1,481	145.1	41.4	10,219	473.1	161,120	654
Chester	1,508	37,117	4,068.3	1,671.6	1,155	8,779	2,769.9	353.0	44,012	2,770.4	418,399	2,056
Clarion	162	2,789	194.6	91.5	78	500	67.1	13.5	2,341	124.6	4,419	20
Clearfield	273	5,881	627.6	247.1	177	1,225	105.9	28.9	4,151	181.9	17,411	76
Clinton	73	1,290	119.1	47.1	67	305	37.7	7.4	1,912	93.2	4,058	19
Columbia	180	3,252	312.3	128.9	113	572	65.2	11.9	3,362	154.3	27,444	142
Crawford	238	5,798	524.8	223.0	163	865	86.9	20.3	5,280	239.0	12,113	73
Cumberland	720	17,881	1,949.5	869.5	555	3,877	462.9	122.0	16,975	874.7	192,641	757
Dauphin	840	34,680	4,514.9	1,909.6	681	4,405	594.4	172.6	17,604	812.0	135,763	675
Delaware	1,666	41,170	4,379.7	1,830.2	1,136	7,266	984.9	243.9	45,292	2,392.6	107,344	534
Elk	107	1,651	150.1	60.5	77	352	28.2	6.6	1,510	66.3	4,248	21
Erie	878	24,543	2,475.6	1,085.6	563	3,433	321.7	81.7	13,933	624.8	52,102	217
Fayette	419	7,612	655.4	276.9	232	1,157	123.7	33.3	6,250	269.2	59,004	235
Forest	D	D	D	D	7	13	0.8	0.2	248	9.4	714	8
Franklin	352	9,299	1,074.0	432.7	296	1,484	147.6	38.2	9,194	404.4	88,457	382
Fulton	D	D	D	30.5	30	95	7.8	2.2	922	43.9	6,639	30
Greene	105	1,257	109.1	44.6	72	309	40.9	8.8	1,488	65.5	7,553	41
Huntingdon	110	2,406	185.9	78.5	75	304	32.7	7.2	2,442	108.0	14,345	52
Indiana	263	5,086	422.9	184.9	163	1,017	122.0	32.1	4,846	219.0	6,469	26
Jefferson	138	3,305	243.0	100.9	99	405	39.3	9.1	2,901	143.8	7,729	46
Juniata	33	649	51.4	19.5	47	120	12.9	3.6	1,816	89.4	8,647	34
Lackawanna	758	20,316	2,132.9	835.6	399	2,280	228.7	68.4	12,488	652.7	62,683	254
Lancaster	1,203	38,065	4,023.2	1,637.5	1,118	7,149	772.6	212.7	43,908	2,356.1	252,158	1,039
Lawrence	277	7,083	549.7	240.6	170	794	90.6	23.3	5,064	223.6	17,916	67
Lebanon	267	8,916	993.1	417.1	252	1,209	128.9	34.2	8,655	426.1	85,328	507
Lehigh	1,135	39,656	5,451.0	2,163.2	735	4,824	515.8	152.6	24,800	1,187.4	218,125	1,024
Luzerne	930	25,920	2,958.7	1,152.4	563	2,944	355.5	83.5	18,060	891.2	86,036	365
Lycoming	302	8,805	1,146.5	415.6	225	1,591	143.2	36.9	6,323	294.6	15,123	56
McKean	143	2,827	221.4	96.5	88	371	35.7	8.3	2,049	83.4	5,951	28
Mercer	437	10,109	854.1	381.3	242	1,053	87.4	21.0	6,285	316.5	18,207	86
Mifflin	121	3,763	359.2	147.2	68	281	31.2	6.8	2,742	119.2	17,426	91
Monroe	361	7,518	784.6	317.6	304	1,564	137.4	43.4	11,174	528.7	99,404	370
Montgomery	3,136	86,556	9,664.2	3,958.8	2,015	13,020	3,667.0	445.1	74,394	4,669.9	389,500	1,498
Montour	77	7,811	1,638.3	613.1	35	230	41.4	10.5	1,015	46.2	4,320	17
Northampton	768	15,757	1,650.3	658.0	560	3,095	274.1	85.7	19,780	1,009.8	225,672	1,249
Northumberland	205	5,060	319.0	150.6	142	769	59.8	16.9	4,530	223.3	15,048	63
Perry	72	925	49.9	23.7	60	299	31.1	6.7	2,899	139.6	28,854	110
Philadelphia	3,992	161,976	21,515.8	8,284.7	2,687	20,004	2,958.1	785.8	109,486	4,321.6	4,144,779	25,257
Pike	94	1,027	74.6	29.9	106	898	82.9	24.5	4,157	206.5	73,983	377

STATE County	Government employment and payroll, 2017: Full-time equivalent employees	Government employment and payroll, 2017: March payroll (dollars)	March payroll (percent of total): Adminis-tration, judicial, and legal	March payroll (percent of total): Police and corrections	March payroll (percent of total): Fire protection	March payroll (percent of total): Highways and transpor-tation	March payroll (percent of total): Health and welfare	March payroll (percent of total): Natural resources and utilities	March payroll (percent of total): Education and libraries	Local government finances, 2017: General revenue: Total (mil dol)	General revenue: Inter-govern-mental (mil dol)	Taxes: Total (mil dol)	Taxes: Per capita[1] (dollars): Total	Taxes: Per capita[1] (dollars): Property
	171	172	173	174	175	176	177	178	179	180	181	182	183	184
OREGON—Cont'd														
Morrow	693	3,072,624	7.5	8.3	1.5	4.3	16.1	11.3	38.1	126.2	35.2	28.7	2,566	2,416
Multnomah	30,993	177,311,553	8.1	11.3	4.3	14.0	8.4	8.6	41.6	5,785.4	1,728.6	2,533.8	3,136	2,025
Polk	1,362	5,792,452	7.8	13.6	2.0	2.5	10.4	4.2	56.0	178.2	94.9	52.9	632	558
Sherman	99	409,288	28.3	12.1	0.6	12.4	7.9	5.7	29.4	34.0	5.2	8.4	4,858	4,833
Tillamook	1,173	5,111,468	9.6	7.2	1.9	6.3	5.7	22.8	43.9	147.0	47.6	60.3	2,275	2,056
Umatilla	2,801	11,651,569	6.1	9.5	3.7	2.7	2.8	4.8	68.9	352.9	185.8	100.5	1,303	1,140
Union	838	3,141,163	8.3	11.4	2.6	4.8	3.7	6.9	59.7	102.5	54.2	25.9	983	908
Wallowa	361	1,720,830	7.2	5.3	0.6	3.7	42.8	3.3	36.4	61.9	15.7	10.2	1,454	1,277
Wasco	1,045	4,438,442	11.4	5.4	4.3	3.6	6.3	12.4	54.1	126.3	56.6	42.1	1,601	1,428
Washington	15,411	80,053,640	7.4	10.5	7.2	2.4	2.2	6.6	61.1	2,448.1	840.2	1,094.6	1,851	1,608
Wheeler	95	402,914	15.6	3.7	0.0	3.9	0.0	5.9	70.3	9.9	8.5	0.8	588	560
Yamhill	3,063	14,276,675	7.6	11.3	3.2	1.5	10.5	6.7	56.3	394.2	203.7	129.8	1,233	1,079
PENNSYLVANIA	X	X	X	X	X	X	X	X	X	X	X	X	X	X
Adams	3,735	14,888,774	5.7	6.9	0.6	7.9	1.4	2.5	74.3	415.6	175.3	194.5	1,897	1,435
Allegheny	42,657	215,609,094	6.8	11.9	2.5	11.0	7.4	4.9	54.5	7,499.1	3,018.9	3,138.2	2,572	1,770
Armstrong	2,027	8,445,739	6.7	5.1	0.0	4.0	6.7	2.8	73.3	282.4	142.8	99.7	1,511	1,269
Beaver	5,157	22,428,838	6.2	9.8	0.3	4.5	7.5	5.4	65.6	764.1	361.5	270.0	1,630	1,293
Bedford	1,256	4,514,150	6.0	6.0	0.9	2.7	2.2	4.0	77.8	156.1	86.7	51.9	1,072	796
Berks	14,681	67,582,415	5.9	10.7	1.3	2.5	4.6	3.4	70.0	2,205.5	858.4	952.9	2,282	1,831
Blair	3,575	13,827,996	5.4	9.6	2.2	5.1	4.9	5.8	65.7	455.6	221.6	145.0	1,178	799
Bradford	2,218	8,868,518	8.8	4.9	0.6	6.4	10.5	4.8	63.2	286.5	154.3	88.5	1,451	1,119
Bucks	19,308	104,622,892	5.4	10.7	0.6	4.0	4.0	2.8	71.5	3,134.9	864.8	1,687.3	2,692	2,234
Butler	4,824	22,231,225	6.5	5.8	0.5	3.0	6.1	3.5	73.4	724.6	303.3	318.5	1,705	1,274
Cambria	4,432	17,315,677	6.6	9.4	1.6	6.5	5.9	4.0	62.3	581.4	337.4	163.1	1,227	939
Cameron	192	683,438	14.7	5.1	0.0	6.2	5.5	5.5	61.2	20.3	10.0	6.2	1,338	1,162
Carbon	1,897	7,011,109	9.4	10.1	0.0	3.2	3.3	4.5	67.6	242.9	87.5	123.2	1,931	1,621
Centre	3,630	14,677,666	9.0	9.2	0.0	9.4	3.5	7.0	60.1	520.6	151.4	264.0	1,626	1,174
Chester	14,012	72,047,879	6.9	8.8	0.3	2.2	3.9	2.7	73.7	2,440.8	660.1	1,450.7	2,796	2,265
Clarion	1,330	5,226,887	5.9	5.3	0.0	3.1	2.8	1.3	80.1	161.1	102.7	44.5	1,142	885
Clearfield	2,512	9,811,849	5.6	4.8	0.0	3.5	2.3	4.0	78.7	297.1	164.5	95.3	1,195	955
Clinton	1,166	4,890,713	9.0	10.2	0.3	3.1	5.2	10.5	59.7	193.6	58.2	54.5	1,404	1,074
Columbia	1,931	7,976,300	4.8	9.7	1.0	3.1	0.2	3.2	74.2	238.6	106.1	101.5	1,547	1,159
Crawford	2,132	8,652,359	9.5	9.5	1.2	5.1	12.5	3.8	57.6	272.7	130.0	99.1	1,155	955
Cumberland	7,465	31,998,627	6.0	8.7	0.0	2.1	6.9	4.1	70.7	1,183.2	382.3	605.1	2,430	1,759
Dauphin	9,952	44,975,290	6.9	13.2	1.1	5.0	2.5	4.9	64.4	1,567.1	622.8	615.1	2,231	1,547
Delaware	17,457	84,422,185	9.6	8.6	1.2	1.7	4.2	5.0	68.7	3,011.6	1,066.8	1,388.8	2,463	2,207
Elk	911	3,473,272	10.3	7.3	0.0	14.1	3.9	5.3	57.9	116.8	52.3	41.4	1,366	977
Erie	8,171	34,509,401	5.5	10.5	3.0	6.5	4.8	5.6	63.3	1,313.5	652.3	413.7	1,512	1,209
Fayette	3,795	16,108,272	5.2	4.7	0.4	3.3	5.8	3.8	76.4	473.9	298.4	125.8	958	724
Forest	170	610,591	23.1	1.9	0.0	5.2	3.7	4.3	56.8	22.7	10.9	9.2	1,255	1,055
Franklin	3,509	14,820,555	8.8	9.9	1.0	2.8	4.9	6.8	64.5	470.5	163.0	223.0	1,445	1,114
Fulton	389	1,566,148	11.7	2.7	0.0	3.3	0.0	3.7	78.2	51.5	29.6	18.9	1,303	1,093
Greene	1,326	5,053,380	10.3	5.9	0.0	4.0	6.7	6.2	65.0	168.8	81.8	67.5	1,831	1,474
Huntingdon	1,038	3,741,819	8.7	6.2	0.0	3.0	4.6	2.9	72.3	128.3	67.5	41.4	912	675
Indiana	2,464	10,033,183	5.3	6.9	0.0	5.0	3.5	4.4	71.7	318.1	164.1	110.4	1,302	1,039
Jefferson	1,243	4,369,814	8.3	6.4	0.0	6.3	2.9	4.9	70.3	138.1	78.0	42.4	968	735
Juniata	548	2,134,469	12.9	4.7	1.4	1.9	0.1	2.5	74.4	59.2	26.9	25.1	1,021	809
Lackawanna	6,002	27,420,359	6.5	10.1	3.4	4.6	7.7	4.4	61.6	919.7	346.4	409.9	1,948	1,427
Lancaster	14,385	63,875,933	5.5	10.2	1.0	3.2	2.9	4.1	71.4	2,211.0	804.0	1,004.1	1,855	1,499
Lawrence	2,411	10,328,970	7.6	9.1	1.4	5.2	1.8	2.9	71.6	329.0	177.8	114.8	1,327	1,045
Lebanon	3,630	16,331,706	5.8	8.8	0.8	3.1	4.1	5.6	70.8	524.1	174.2	233.6	1,674	1,348
Lehigh	12,126	60,052,384	6.5	9.4	1.8	5.2	8.5	3.5	63.2	1,894.9	749.7	786.2	2,151	1,697
Luzerne	9,532	40,790,805	7.2	11.4	2.3	4.2	4.9	4.1	64.1	1,218.2	524.3	533.9	1,680	1,258
Lycoming	3,735	16,093,813	7.9	7.7	1.8	4.2	1.8	6.8	69.3	504.9	219.4	183.1	1,606	1,169
McKean	1,760	6,725,097	5.7	6.4	1.5	4.2	9.4	5.8	66.5	187.5	110.4	49.0	1,185	938
Mercer	3,818	15,441,306	7.0	8.2	0.9	2.2	2.1	3.6	74.7	454.2	238.9	153.1	1,374	1,037
Mifflin	1,414	5,760,648	6.3	7.2	1.1	2.4	2.6	4.9	74.9	169.1	85.6	56.6	1,224	946
Monroe	5,561	25,725,163	5.3	5.2	0.0	3.2	1.6	1.5	82.6	816.0	272.4	464.3	2,766	2,480
Montgomery	23,842	129,438,423	5.9	12.2	0.4	2.3	3.7	4.2	69.8	4,083.5	1,074.7	2,442.2	2,963	2,386
Montour	503	1,895,714	7.7	6.5	0.0	4.7	2.6	5.0	71.3	95.5	23.9	31.8	1,743	1,111
Northampton	11,625	54,068,436	4.8	10.3	2.0	2.0	7.4	3.8	67.4	1,626.5	583.7	784.6	2,591	2,100
Northumberland	2,403	10,826,444	9.2	11.1	0.0	2.8	6.2	3.4	58.8	315.9	165.2	108.5	1,183	814
Perry	1,076	4,097,761	7.1	5.3	0.0	3.8	3.2	1.8	76.6	158.6	78.2	66.1	1,435	1,046
Philadelphia	61,107	332,698,900	9.0	20.2	5.6	19.0	8.1	8.3	27.6	12,639.4	6,005.2	4,866.1	3,079	814
Pike	1,122	4,601,891	9.2	14.0	0.0	2.4	4.5	1.7	67.8	142.5	42.4	83.5	1,507	1,406

1. Based on the resident population estimated as of July 1 of the year shown.

STATE County	Local government finances, 2017 (cont.)									Government employment, 2020			Individual income tax returns, 2019		
	Direct general expenditure							Debt outstanding							
			Percent of total for:												
	Total (mil dol)	Per capita[1] (dollars)	Education	Health and hospitals	Police protection	Public welfare	Highways	Total (mil dol)	Per capita[1] (dollars)	Federal civilian	Federal military	State and local	Number of returns	Mean adjusted gross income	Mean income tax
	185	186	187	188	189	190	191	192	193	194	195	196	197	198	199
OREGON—Cont'd															
Morrow	147.8	13,200	21.3	8.3	3.4	0.0	4.1	1,311.6	117,125	59	33	911	5,150	53,663	4,256
Multnomah	5,468.1	6,768	33.0	5.1	5.1	3.3	5.1	8,745.7	10,825	12,438	2,260	63,038	419,790	79,089	10,463
Polk	170.3	2,035	46.8	8.8	8.4	0.9	4.3	176.9	2,113	130	202	4,875	39,500	63,583	6,130
Sherman	24.7	14,212	24.6	14.4	3.7	1.3	10.5	8.2	4,733	126	4	182	900	59,178	5,093
Tillamook	131.7	4,967	42.2	6.1	4.0	0.3	5.6	136.1	5,132	134	105	1,704	13,540	56,387	5,204
Umatilla	361.1	4,682	63.0	1.9	5.2	0.1	3.4	501.4	6,502	478	173	6,305	33,950	53,572	4,614
Union	123.4	4,677	51.2	2.6	3.9	1.7	4.8	61.1	2,315	244	60	1,825	11,930	54,920	4,813
Wallowa	59.9	8,525	26.0	35.1	3.3	0.7	6.9	25.6	3,638	87	17	543	3,570	50,502	4,282
Wasco	117.8	4,478	49.6	2.6	5.0	0.5	5.1	74.2	2,820	285	60	1,499	12,410	54,924	4,964
Washington	2,578.9	4,361	48.9	2.0	6.6	0.0	5.8	3,906.3	6,606	977	1,398	20,659	294,740	85,262	10,788
Wheeler	12.6	9,335	71.3	1.2	2.4	0.0	7.0	2.0	1,488	7	3	110	560	31,638	2,525
Yamhill	411.9	3,914	50.8	8.2	5.9	0.1	4.8	518.4	4,926	466	242	3,678	49,700	68,110	7,130
PENNSYLVANIA	X	X	X	X	X	X	X	X	X	101,446	34,028	619,415	6,353,920	72,576	9,015
Adams	490.8	4,786	68.4	3.2	2.6	3.9	3.4	505.8	4,931	738	263	3,318	52,720	63,182	6,313
Allegheny	7,519.7	6,163	42.5	5.3	4.7	9.6	4.7	11,148.7	9,137	13,413	3,394	49,626	637,360	79,357	10,704
Armstrong	276.4	4,188	62.5	1.3	1.6	4.9	5.1	314.8	4,770	194	162	2,145	32,140	53,954	4,874
Beaver	763.0	4,606	53.3	3.4	3.8	8.2	4.8	1,943.2	11,730	322	408	6,735	85,540	60,150	5,890
Bedford	144.1	2,979	66.9	0.0	1.5	3.9	5.5	214.5	4,437	114	120	2,030	23,390	51,315	4,379
Berks	2,252.8	5,396	56.5	1.4	4.5	8.7	3.5	2,740.4	6,564	1,007	1,052	19,724	210,690	62,667	6,591
Blair	469.6	3,813	52.1	6.8	4.8	7.4	3.9	388.4	3,154	1,217	303	7,243	59,950	56,775	5,802
Bradford	281.8	4,622	54.6	1.8	1.7	11.8	6.8	324.7	5,327	217	152	2,651	28,650	57,303	5,541
Bucks	3,297.5	5,261	59.4	0.6	5.3	6.3	4.3	3,924.0	6,260	1,228	1,599	20,784	336,200	101,659	15,050
Butler	731.6	3,916	55.2	1.1	2.6	11.4	5.4	1,075.4	5,756	3,193	473	8,329	97,430	80,367	10,034
Cambria	626.1	4,709	54.7	2.4	2.1	9.5	3.2	513.7	3,864	987	330	6,439	63,210	52,343	4,758
Cameron	19.8	4,290	61.3	0.0	2.7	4.6	7.5	11.7	2,538	17	11	346	2,320	43,281	3,472
Carbon	287.9	4,511	66.7	0.0	2.2	2.7	3.7	325.4	5,098	124	161	2,318	32,040	54,830	5,044
Centre	539.4	3,323	57.5	1.9	3.3	3.2	5.3	421.2	2,595	591	452	47,124	60,840	74,356	8,656
Chester	2,717.6	5,237	59.7	5.5	4.2	2.9	3.4	2,431.8	4,686	2,342	1,310	22,927	260,530	120,840	19,337
Clarion	163.6	4,196	74.5	2.0	1.4	2.5	4.0	64.8	1,660	109	111	3,146	16,950	51,430	4,148
Clearfield	295.5	3,703	64.9	0.0	3.9	2.8	5.3	350.6	4,393	253	187	4,335	36,660	50,675	4,524
Clinton	150.6	3,878	50.6	0.2	2.4	2.9	3.8	104.0	2,678	152	96	2,762	17,150	51,720	4,403
Columbia	236.2	3,602	64.8	0.0	4.1	0.0	4.3	223.1	3,402	169	156	4,787	30,090	55,599	5,200
Crawford	283.8	3,309	50.2	1.4	3.3	10.8	6.7	217.6	2,537	271	205	3,549	38,440	51,103	4,386
Cumberland	1,164.4	4,676	64.6	2.4	2.8	7.1	3.3	1,003.3	4,029	4,919	1,245	11,351	130,500	74,863	8,767
Dauphin	1,721.2	6,243	44.3	4.5	3.5	10.3	4.0	2,194.0	7,958	2,703	756	37,974	147,600	62,292	6,915
Delaware	3,166.5	5,616	49.3	1.9	5.5	11.3	2.5	4,583.8	8,129	2,016	1,420	21,883	283,260	92,844	13,606
Elk	104.3	3,446	50.4	0.2	3.0	1.3	5.9	170.2	5,622	91	74	1,104	16,240	53,969	4,824
Erie	1,301.5	4,758	46.6	4.7	2.7	14.7	3.7	1,418.4	5,185	1,705	699	14,720	129,620	59,991	6,351
Fayette	480.2	3,657	58.0	2.9	1.4	9.7	3.7	964.6	7,346	380	316	5,603	61,630	51,251	4,551
Forest	21.8	2,982	53.1	4.2	1.3	4.6	11.1	16.3	2,222	83	12	971	2,260	43,311	3,339
Franklin	484.0	3,135	59.0	3.3	2.4	2.2	4.5	740.3	4,796	2,374	392	5,571	78,620	58,961	5,473
Fulton	67.7	4,682	56.5	0.0	2.9	4.8	3.9	195.8	13,529	31	37	669	7,250	53,100	4,462
Greene	175.3	4,756	54.5	1.5	1.0	4.0	9.4	166.6	4,521	124	83	2,316	15,590	67,498	7,906
Huntingdon	131.3	2,889	59.6	1.2	2.7	3.7	4.7	148.1	3,260	124	101	2,925	19,520	51,770	4,310
Indiana	321.6	3,795	65.0	0.0	1.2	6.0	4.0	340.5	4,017	220	205	6,703	36,100	55,013	5,153
Jefferson	136.0	3,103	63.5	0.0	3.6	0.0	5.9	197.1	4,497	125	108	1,618	20,970	49,281	4,160
Juniata	61.5	2,495	66.8	0.1	0.6	2.2	4.9	49.7	2,018	67	62	672	11,420	51,565	4,102
Lackawanna	931.9	4,428	47.8	0.1	4.9	5.4	3.1	1,471.7	6,993	948	523	9,143	104,710	58,539	6,197
Lancaster	2,292.0	4,234	55.6	5.9	4.6	5.2	3.2	3,717.0	6,866	1,325	1,362	19,034	273,930	67,827	7,315
Lawrence	324.9	3,754	57.3	2.2	4.4	6.0	4.9	391.2	4,520	212	236	3,059	41,870	54,125	4,955
Lebanon	520.5	3,730	57.8	1.5	3.4	10.7	3.0	583.4	4,180	3,137	352	4,744	72,040	59,882	5,667
Lehigh	1,933.2	5,288	51.6	1.2	3.6	9.3	3.8	3,232.0	8,841	971	932	15,961	190,800	67,072	7,807
Luzerne	1,252.2	3,940	57.2	0.3	3.5	6.0	5.1	1,110.8	3,495	3,488	796	13,719	161,370	54,401	5,407
Lycoming	510.6	4,479	56.7	0.0	2.8	2.6	4.3	983.6	8,627	402	277	8,168	54,910	55,739	5,352
McKean	190.7	4,610	58.9	4.7	1.5	4.7	4.1	125.1	3,025	447	95	1,814	18,970	50,612	4,267
Mercer	497.0	4,459	62.1	1.9	3.2	2.0	4.2	577.2	5,178	276	261	4,717	52,780	53,418	4,976
Mifflin	170.6	3,686	57.9	4.8	2.1	0.0	4.3	220.3	4,760	87	116	1,534	21,770	49,171	3,993
Monroe	758.0	4,515	69.4	0.1	3.3	5.4	3.0	1,152.8	6,866	3,442	455	7,866	82,370	57,702	5,811
Montgomery	4,165.1	5,053	61.2	1.9	5.0	6.1	3.3	4,473.0	5,426	2,678	2,127	31,944	430,900	113,390	17,927
Montour	89.9	4,922	45.3	0.0	2.0	1.2	4.2	2,335.8	127,851	44	45	1,449	9,000	73,201	9,110
Northampton	1,724.7	5,696	54.6	2.1	4.3	11.6	3.2	2,562.8	8,464	1,135	784	13,042	157,810	72,225	8,484
Northumberland	311.0	3,391	53.8	3.9	4.6	7.4	4.2	227.1	2,476	170	221	3,800	44,080	49,409	4,137
Perry	147.1	3,195	63.2	0.3	0.8	10.3	4.2	101.0	2,193	95	116	1,686	23,020	56,092	4,733
Philadelphia	11,840.3	7,491	36.7	14.2	5.7	1.7	1.7	14,787.8	9,356	31,409	4,522	76,588	715,080	56,085	6,502
Pike	142.7	2,576	56.4	0.5	12.9	5.1	3.4	87.7	1,584	224	142	2,268	28,460	65,008	7,145

1. Based on the resident population estimated as of July 1 of the year shown.

State / county code	CBSA code[1]	County Type code[2]	STATE County	Land area[3] (sq. mi)	Population, 2021: Total persons 2021	Rank	Per square mile	Population and population characteristics, 2021: Race alone or in combination, not Hispanic or Latino (percent): White	Black	American Indian, Alaska Native	Asian and Pacific Islancer	Percent Hispanic or Latino[4]	Age (percent): Under 5 years	5 to 17 years	18 to 24 years	25 to 34 years	35 to 44 years	45 to 54 years
				1	2	3	4	5	6	7	8	9	10	11	12	13	14	15
			PENNSYLVANIA—Cont'd															
42105		9	Potter	1,081.2	16,259	2,021	15.0	97.0	1.0	0.7	0.7	1.6	5.0	11.5	10.5	10.0	10.4	11.6
42107	39060	4	Schuylkill	778.6	143,264	468	184.0	89.3	3.8	0.4	0.9	6.7	4.8	11.4	10.9	12.0	12.2	13.3
42109	42780	7	Snyder	328.8	39,621	1,191	120.5	95.4	1.7	0.4	1.0	2.5	5.2	11.5	15.7	11.0	10.8	12.2
42111	43740	4	Somerset	1,075.0	73,627	751	68.5	94.6	3.4	0.4	0.7	1.7	4.7	10.1	10.2	11.4	11.9	13.1
42113		8	Sullivan	449.9	5,868	2,746	13.0	93.6	3.5	1.0	0.7	2.2	3.0	5.0	9.0	9.7	10.7	12.4
42115		6	Susquehanna	823.5	38,389	1,211	46.6	96.6	1.1	0.6	0.8	2.0	4.7	10.5	10.0	10.1	10.8	12.0
42117		6	Tioga	1,133.8	40,929	1,164	36.1	97.0	1.2	0.6	0.8	1.4	4.9	11.4	11.7	10.8	11.2	11.7
42119	30260	4	Union	316.0	42,568	1,136	134.7	85.2	7.0	0.6	2.3	6.3	4.6	9.7	17.0	12.5	13.4	11.9
42121	36340	4	Venango	674.3	49,938	998	74.1	96.8	2.0	0.6	0.8	1.2	4.5	10.7	10.4	10.1	11.1	12.3
42123	47620	6	Warren	884.3	38,134	1,220	43.1	97.3	1.0	0.5	0.8	1.3	5.2	11.1	10.1	10.2	10.8	12.3
42125	38300	1	Washington	857.0	209,470	326	244.4	93.4	4.6	0.5	1.6	1.9	5.0	11.2	11.5	11.3	12.0	12.5
42127		6	Wayne	725.8	51,431	978	70.9	90.4	3.8	0.6	1.1	5.2	3.8	9.3	9.7	11.4	11.6	12.7
42129	38300	1	Westmoreland	1,027.7	353,057	208	343.5	94.7	3.7	0.4	1.4	1.4	4.3	10.5	10.7	10.8	11.4	12.7
42131	42540	2	Wyoming	397.4	26,034	1,562	65.5	95.8	1.7	0.6	0.8	2.3	4.6	10.9	12.2	10.7	11.3	12.6
42133	49620	2	York	904.4	458,696	156	507.2	83.2	7.4	0.5	2.0	8.9	5.4	12.5	11.9	12.5	12.5	12.8
44000		0	RHODE ISLAND	1,033.9	1,095,610	X	1,059.7	72.3	7.5	1.0	4.4	17.1	4.9	10.7	13.6	13.9	12.4	12.2
44001	39300	1	Bristol	24.1	50,818	986	2,108.6	92.0	2.0	0.7	3.7	3.6	3.7	10.6	14.6	10.2	11.7	13.0
44003	39300	1	Kent	168.6	170,715	393	1,012.5	87.7	3.1	0.8	3.8	6.7	4.6	10.4	10.3	13.5	12.9	13.0
44005	39300	1	Newport	102.4	85,264	676	832.7	87.4	5.0	1.0	3.1	6.2	4.1	9.1	12.2	12.5	11.2	11.7
44007	39300	1	Providence	409.5	658,221	104	1,607.4	61.0	10.5	1.1	5.0	25.0	5.4	11.3	13.8	15.3	13.0	12.1
44009	39300	1	Washington	329.3	130,592	495	396.6	92.0	2.2	1.3	2.8	3.7	3.6	8.8	17.3	10.1	10.0	11.6
45000		0	SOUTH CAROLINA	30,063.7	5,190,705	X	172.7	65.1	27.2	0.9	2.5	6.4	5.5	12.3	12.7	13.0	12.3	12.2
45001		6	Abbeville	491.2	24,299	1,637	49.5	70.9	27.4	0.8	0.6	1.9	4.8	11.2	12.8	10.9	10.6	12.4
45003	12260	2	Aiken	1,070.7	170,776	392	159.5	67.2	25.9	1.1	1.7	6.3	5.4	12.1	11.6	12.6	11.9	11.8
45005		6	Allendale	408.1	7,858	2,586	19.3	23.5	72.3	0.7	1.1	3.4	4.4	10.7	11.9	13.6	11.9	12.4
45007	24860	2	Anderson	713.9	206,908	332	289.8	78.2	17.2	0.7	1.5	4.4	5.5	13.0	12.2	12.5	12.0	12.8
45009		7	Bamberg	393.4	13,189	2,201	33.5	37.8	58.9	0.9	1.0	2.6	4.8	10.2	15.5	10.7	9.5	11.3
45011		6	Barnwell	548.4	20,580	1,787	37.5	52.3	44.3	1.1	1.3	2.8	6.2	13.8	12.1	12.1	10.6	11.8
45013	25940	3	Beaufort	576.0	191,748	356	332.9	70.4	17.5	0.7	2.0	11.2	4.7	10.0	11.7	10.5	10.0	10.2
45015	16700	2	Berkeley	1,103.6	236,701	293	214.5	64.8	25.7	1.2	3.8	7.5	6.1	13.6	13.1	14.1	13.8	12.2
45017	17900	2	Calhoun	381.2	14,165	2,139	37.2	55.6	39.9	1.0	0.8	4.2	4.5	10.8	10.3	10.9	10.9	12.6
45019	16700	2	Charleston	918.0	413,024	174	449.9	67.4	25.6	0.7	2.6	5.5	5.5	10.8	11.7	15.8	14.2	11.6
45021	23500	4	Cherokee	393.0	56,052	923	142.6	73.7	21.3	0.8	0.9	5.1	5.8	13.0	12.9	13.0	11.3	13.3
45023	16740	1	Chester	580.7	32,209	1,377	55.5	60.4	37.2	1.1	0.9	2.4	5.8	12.8	11.6	12.3	11.0	12.6
45025		6	Chesterfield	799.0	43,268	1,120	54.2	61.1	33.8	1.1	1.0	5.1	5.3	12.7	11.7	12.2	11.0	13.5
45027	44940	6	Clarendon	607.2	31,024	1,402	51.1	49.8	46.1	0.8	1.0	3.4	4.3	10.5	12.0	11.0	10.6	11.4
45029		6	Colleton	1,056.5	38,462	1,210	36.4	58.9	36.7	1.4	0.8	4.0	6.0	12.8	11.3	11.8	10.9	11.9
45031	22500	3	Darlington	560.6	62,755	852	111.9	55.1	42.3	0.8	0.9	2.4	5.7	12.5	12.5	12.3	10.9	12.4
45033		6	Dillon	405.1	28,087	1,495	69.3	46.8	48.1	3.3	1.0	3.1	6.8	14.1	12.7	12.4	11.8	11.7
45035	16700	2	Dorchester	568.6	163,327	413	287.2	65.1	27.0	1.2	3.3	6.3	5.8	14.0	12.1	13.7	14.2	12.6
45037	12260	2	Edgefield	500.7	26,153	1,559	52.2	58.9	34.5	0.9	0.8	6.3	3.9	9.8	11.5	13.6	13.0	13.1
45039	17900	2	Fairfield	686.3	20,690	1,779	30.1	40.1	57.3	0.9	1.0	2.4	4.5	10.2	10.8	11.0	10.0	12.7
45041	22500	3	Florence	800.5	136,504	479	170.5	52.0	43.9	0.7	1.9	2.9	5.8	13.5	12.9	12.5	12.3	12.4
45043	23860	4	Georgetown	813.6	63,921	846	78.6	66.0	30.3	0.6	0.8	3.3	4.0	9.8	10.0	9.3	9.4	11.4
45045	24860	2	Greenville	785.9	533,834	134	679.3	69.3	18.9	0.6	3.4	9.8	5.9	13.0	12.5	13.9	13.1	12.5
45047	24940	4	Greenwood	455.6	69,241	779	152.0	60.3	32.4	0.6	1.6	6.5	5.8	13.0	13.1	12.4	11.4	12.0
45049		6	Hampton	560.0	18,180	1,914	32.5	43.7	52.7	0.7	1.0	3.2	5.3	12.4	11.8	12.1	11.8	12.5
45051	34820	2	Horry	1,133.3	365,579	203	322.6	79.4	13.4	1.0	2.1	6.2	4.3	9.9	10.0	10.8	10.9	11.9
45053	25940	3	Jasper	655.2	30,324	1,428	46.3	46.2	39.3	0.8	1.1	14.0	5.1	10.1	11.4	12.6	10.4	11.3
45055	17900	2	Kershaw	726.6	66,130	812	91.0	69.6	25.1	0.8	1.2	5.1	5.6	13.3	11.4	11.7	12.4	12.5
45057	16740	1	Lancaster	549.1	100,336	608	182.7	71.2	21.6	0.6	2.1	6.1	5.3	12.6	9.8	11.8	13.4	12.9
45059	24860	2	Laurens	712.9	67,803	793	95.1	68.8	25.6	0.7	0.9	5.6	5.8	12.5	12.5	12.3	11.3	12.7
45061		6	Lee	410.2	16,280	2,019	39.7	33.6	63.5	0.7	0.8	2.6	4.9	10.6	13.0	13.6	11.8	11.8
45063	17900	2	Lexington	699.0	300,137	234	429.4	75.3	16.5	0.9	2.9	6.4	5.5	13.2	11.7	13.2	13.3	13.0
45065		8	McCormick	358.9	9,760	2,429	27.2	54.0	44.2	0.6	0.8	1.5	2.3	6.5	6.9	10.1	9.6	11.0
45067		6	Marion	489.4	28,784	1,465	58.8	39.0	57.2	1.0	1.0	3.2	5.3	12.9	11.7	11.7	11.4	12.0
45069	13500	6	Marlboro	479.9	26,382	1,549	55.0	40.8	51.8	5.6	0.8	3.2	5.1	11.6	11.2	14.2	12.6	12.4
45071	35140	6	Newberry	630.3	37,996	1,224	60.3	61.4	30.4	0.7	0.8	8.1	5.3	12.5	13.2	11.0	10.7	12.3
45073	42860	4	Oconee	626.6	79,203	723	126.4	85.7	8.4	0.8	1.2	5.8	4.5	11.3	10.8	11.3	10.3	12.1
45075	36700	4	Orangeburg	1,106.4	82,962	694	75.0	34.3	62.3	1.1	1.3	2.4	5.4	12.6	13.8	11.3	10.6	11.1
45077	24860	2	Pickens	496.9	132,229	491	266.1	86.6	7.9	0.7	2.4	4.2	4.7	10.7	20.9	12.2	10.4	11.3
45079	17900	2	Richland	757.3	418,307	172	552.4	42.8	49.4	0.8	3.9	5.5	5.6	12.1	18.7	14.7	12.6	11.3
45081	17900	2	Saluda	452.7	18,821	1,880	41.6	60.0	24.3	0.7	0.7	15.6	5.5	12.5	10.8	10.8	11.7	12.7
45083	43900	2	Spartanburg	808.4	335,864	215	415.5	69.1	21.7	0.7	3.1	7.5	6.1	13.2	12.9	14.0	12.3	12.6

1. CBSA = Core Based Statistical Area. See Appendix A for explanation. See Appendix B for list of metropolitan areas with component counties. 2. County type code from the Economic Research Service of USDA Rural-Urban Continuum Codes. See Appendix A for definition. 3. Dry land or land partially or temporarily covered by water. 4. May be of any race.

STATE County	Population, 2021 (cont.)				Population change, 2000–2021							Households, 2016–2020				
	Age (percent) (cont.)				Total persons		Percent change		Components of change, 2020–2021					Percent		
	55 to 64 years	65 to 74 years	75 years and over	Percent female	2010	2020	2010–2020	2020–2021	Births	Deaths	Net Migration	Number	Persons per household	Family house-holds	Female family house-holder[1]	One person
	16	17	18	19	20	21	22	23	24	25	26	27	28	29	30	31
PENNSYLVANIA—Cont'd																
Potter	16.0	14.8	10.3	49.8	17,457	16,396	-6.1	-0.8	206	324	-18	6,630	2.5	66.0	9.0	28.8
Schuylkill	14.7	12.3	8.4	48.3	148,289	143,049	-3.5	0.2	1,568	2,782	1,445	58,646	2.3	64.7	13.0	29.8
Snyder	13.8	11.2	8.6	50.1	39,702	39,736	0.1	-0.3	472	583	-8	14,824	2.6	70.3	8.2	24.3
Somerset	15.5	13.6	9.5	47.2	77,742	74,129	-4.6	-0.7	736	1,415	177	29,518	2.3	67.6	8.5	27.6
Sullivan	20.7	17.7	11.8	47.8	6,428	5,840	-9.1	0.5	71	153	112	2,751	2.0	58.6	7.5	34.9
Susquehanna	17.2	14.6	10.0	49.4	43,356	38,434	-11.4	-0.1	424	670	204	17,027	2.4	66.0	9.6	28.5
Tioga	15.4	13.3	9.7	49.7	41,981	41,045	-2.2	-0.3	490	680	72	16,442	2.4	67.6	9.8	26.8
Union	12.3	10.3	8.5	45.5	44,947	42,681	-5.0	-0.3	480	576	-24	14,762	2.4	64.6	6.9	31.2
Venango	16.7	14.6	9.5	50.1	54,984	50,454	-8.2	-1.0	522	986	-55	22,103	2.3	65.0	9.7	29.0
Warren	16.3	14.2	9.9	49.6	41,815	38,587	-7.7	-1.2	456	746	-162	17,124	2.3	65.4	9.1	29.6
Washington	15.1	13.0	8.4	50.5	207,820	209,349	0.7	0.1	2,448	3,847	1,525	85,201	2.4	65.3	9.4	29.0
Wayne	16.6	15.1	9.8	46.6	52,822	51,155	-3.2	0.5	455	905	740	18,938	2.5	67.0	7.7	28.7
Westmoreland	16.0	14.1	9.5	50.6	365,169	354,663	-2.9	-0.5	3,564	6,738	1,581	153,772	2.2	64.0	9.0	31.0
Wyoming	15.2	13.6	8.9	49.6	28,276	26,069	-7.8	-0.1	277	480	171	10,887	2.4	66.3	10.3	26.6
York	14.1	11.0	7.3	50.2	434,972	456,438	4.9	0.5	5,714	6,426	2,945	174,425	2.5	68.4	11.3	25.6
RHODE ISLAND	14.2	10.8	7.3	51.0	1,052,567	1,097,379	4.3	-0.2	12,201	15,003	938	414,730	2.5	62.2	13.0	30.6
Bristol	15.6	11.9	8.7	51.5	49,875	50,793	1.8	0.0	360	737	404	18,961	2.4	65.3	8.9	30.1
Kent	15.6	11.9	7.8	51.3	166,158	170,363	2.5	0.2	1,736	2,712	1,323	70,085	2.3	62.6	10.2	29.6
Newport	15.6	13.7	9.9	50.2	82,888	85,643	3.3	-0.4	784	1,285	129	34,578	2.3	62.7	10.2	30.0
Providence	13.1	9.5	6.5	50.9	626,667	660,741	5.4	-0.4	8,335	8,368	-2,603	240,886	2.5	60.7	15.1	32.0
Washington	16.4	13.7	8.6	51.3	126,979	129,839	2.3	0.6	986	1,901	1,685	50,220	2.4	67.2	9.9	25.6
SOUTH CAROLINA	13.4	11.6	7.0	51.4	4,625,364	5,118,425	10.7	1.4	68,052	77,654	82,142	1,961,481	2.5	65.3	13.9	29.1
Abbeville	14.4	13.7	9.3	51.4	25,417	24,295	-4.4	0.0	286	433	152	9,597	2.5	65.7	11.3	29.6
Aiken	14.1	12.4	8.0	51.7	160,099	168,808	5.4	1.2	2,146	2,825	2,659	68,266	2.5	66.3	13.4	28.9
Allendale	13.3	13.7	8.1	47.6	10,419	8,039	-22.8	-2.3	69	158	-90	3,426	2.3	59.9	24.5	36.0
Anderson	13.6	11.1	7.3	51.7	187,126	203,718	8.9	1.6	2,580	3,351	3,988	78,636	2.5	68.4	13.6	27.3
Bamberg	14.6	14.1	9.4	52.3	15,987	13,311	-16.7	-0.9	171	255	-38	5,070	2.6	66.0	18.5	29.6
Barnwell	14.0	12.0	7.4	52.0	22,621	20,589	-9.0	0.0	324	384	50	8,670	2.4	60.7	19.9	35.5
Beaufort	14.4	16.8	11.7	51.1	162,233	187,117	15.3	2.5	2,236	2,680	5,143	74,231	2.5	68.5	9.4	26.3
Berkeley	12.4	9.5	5.3	50.3	177,843	229,861	29.2	3.0	3,452	2,549	5,943	79,597	2.8	70.8	14.0	23.2
Calhoun	15.9	14.5	9.6	51.6	15,175	14,119	-7.0	0.3	143	263	168	6,221	2.3	65.2	15.3	32.2
Charleston	13.1	11.0	6.4	51.5	350,209	408,235	16.6	1.2	5,964	5,433	4,241	163,411	2.4	57.4	11.0	33.7
Cherokee	13.4	10.7	6.6	50.9	55,342	56,216	1.6	-0.3	759	1,000	65	20,779	2.7	55.2	11.2	41.9
Chester	14.5	11.9	7.4	51.5	33,140	32,294	-2.6	-0.3	466	635	80	12,861	2.5	66.3	16.0	29.4
Chesterfield	14.3	12.0	7.3	51.2	46,734	43,273	-7.4	0.0	552	813	253	18,213	2.5	66.5	15.1	30.0
Clarendon	15.2	15.1	10.0	51.0	34,971	31,144	-10.9	-0.4	363	606	125	12,775	2.5	66.5	16.9	29.8
Colleton	14.9	12.8	7.8	51.8	38,892	38,604	-0.7	-0.4	546	795	107	15,281	2.4	61.3	17.4	34.9
Darlington	13.7	12.2	7.7	52.5	68,681	62,905	-8.4	-0.2	922	1,286	208	26,117	2.5	62.1	18.9	33.6
Dillon	13.1	10.8	6.7	52.7	32,062	28,292	-11.8	-0.7	501	543	-164	11,147	2.7	66.3	20.0	29.3
Dorchester	12.8	9.5	5.4	51.1	136,555	161,540	18.3	1.1	2,199	1,912	1,476	56,939	2.8	69.5	13.5	26.0
Edgefield	14.9	12.3	7.7	47.0	26,985	25,657	-4.9	1.9	224	390	671	9,171	2.7	70.0	16.5	26.7
Fairfield	17.1	15.2	8.4	52.1	23,956	20,948	-12.6	-1.2	227	455	-28	9,315	2.4	66.2	17.6	31.8
Florence	12.9	11.0	6.7	53.3	136,885	137,059	0.1	-0.4	1,891	2,469	1	52,880	2.6	65.1	18.0	30.4
Georgetown	16.3	18.5	11.4	52.8	60,158	63,404	5.4	0.8	606	1,282	1,211	25,758	2.4	68.5	13.9	28.9
Greenville	12.6	10.1	6.4	51.6	451,225	525,534	16.5	1.6	7,513	6,814	7,562	198,015	2.6	67.0	12.4	27.3
Greenwood	13.0	11.2	8.0	53.3	69,661	69,351	-0.4	-0.2	1,003	1,177	56	27,977	2.4	61.8	16.5	33.8
Hampton	13.6	12.5	8.2	51.8	21,090	18,561	-12.0	-2.1	234	381	-231	6,893	2.6	63.2	16.2	34.1
Horry	16.2	17.3	8.8	52.0	269,291	351,029	30.4	4.1	3,748	6,306	17,305	136,219	2.5	63.8	12.1	28.8
Jasper	16.4	15.4	7.3	49.7	24,777	28,791	16.2	5.3	434	444	1,556	10,724	2.7	66.2	17.6	27.4
Kershaw	14.0	11.9	7.1	51.8	61,697	65,403	6.0	1.1	867	1,149	1,013	25,293	2.6	68.1	13.3	27.9
Lancaster	12.8	12.8	8.7	51.5	76,652	96,016	25.3	4.5	1,174	1,599	4,803	35,228	2.7	70.5	13.4	25.6
Laurens	14.3	11.4	7.3	51.8	66,537	67,539	1.5	0.4	898	1,331	693	25,555	2.5	67.2	15.3	28.3
Lee	14.5	12.6	7.3	49.1	19,220	16,531	-14.0	-1.5	213	370	-94	6,455	2.4	60.4	18.6	36.7
Lexington	13.4	10.5	6.2	51.4	262,391	293,991	12.0	2.1	3,800	4,034	6,415	115,220	2.5	67.7	12.6	26.3
McCormick	17.8	21.9	13.9	46.2	10,233	9,526	-6.9	2.5	60	241	423	3,984	2.1	65.1	13.1	29.7
Marion	13.9	13.4	7.8	54.0	33,062	29,183	-11.7	-1.4	379	681	-100	11,282	2.7	64.8	25.5	32.5
Marlboro	14.0	11.7	7.2	48.4	28,933	26,667	-7.8	-1.1	346	538	-96	9,384	2.5	61.1	21.1	33.3
Newberry	14.5	12.5	8.1	51.0	37,508	37,719	0.6	0.7	511	664	431	14,976	2.5	67.3	15.4	29.4
Oconee	15.7	14.9	9.2	50.9	74,273	78,607	5.8	0.8	806	1,451	1,253	32,440	2.4	66.5	10.4	29.7
Orangeburg	14.2	12.5	8.4	53.4	92,501	84,223	-8.9	-1.5	1,120	1,705	-677	33,629	2.5	59.3	19.8	38.0
Pickens	12.7	10.1	7.0	50.3	119,224	131,404	10.2	0.6	1,535	1,921	1,196	48,522	2.5	63.3	9.1	26.3
Richland	11.4	8.7	5.0	51.9	384,504	416,147	8.2	0.5	5,817	4,755	992	155,478	2.5	59.7	18.0	32.8
Saluda	14.8	12.0	9.3	49.9	19,875	18,862	-5.1	-0.2	242	310	25	7,360	2.7	74.1	13.2	24.4
Spartanburg	12.7	10.0	6.3	51.5	284,307	327,997	15.4	2.4	4,817	4,928	8,027	118,788	2.6	67.7	13.9	27.3

1. No spouse present.

STATE County	Persons in group quarters, 2021	Daytime Population, 2016–2020: Number	Daytime Population, 2016–2020: Employment/ residence ratio	Births, 2021: Total	Births, 2021: Rate[1]	Deaths, 2021: Number	Deaths, 2021: Rate[1]	Persons under 65 with no health insurance, 2019: Number	Persons under 65 with no health insurance, 2019: Percent	Medicare, 2021: Total beneficiaries	Medicare, 2021: Enrolled in Original Medicare	Medicare, 2021: Enrolled in Medicare Advantage	COVID-19 Deaths, 2020: Number	COVID-19 Deaths, 2020: Rate[1]
	32	33	34	35	36	37	38	39	40	41	42	43	44	45
PENNSYLVANIA—Cont'd														
Potter	163	16,537	1.0	167	10.2	252	15.5	900	7.3	4,697	2,986	1,711	15	0.9
Schuylkill	6,557	132,975	0.9	1,267	8.9	2,174	15.2	6,511	6.1	35,767	23,846	11,922	265	1.9
Snyder	2,556	38,888	0.9	373	9.4	486	12.3	2,590	8.7	8,665	4,714	3,951	47	1.2
Somerset	4,848	68,549	0.8	574	7.8	1,111	15.1	3,976	7.6	19,637	7,993	11,644	116	1.6
Sullivan	325	5,601	0.8	47	8.0	123	21.0	373	8.8	1,878	1,241	637	D	D
Susquehanna	190	35,327	0.7	337	8.8	535	13.9	2,567	8.5	10,381	7,334	3,047	42	1.1
Tioga	1,277	39,385	0.9	383	9.4	540	13.2	2,516	8.3	10,793	6,828	3,965	85	2.1
Union	7,926	48,042	1.2	388	9.1	468	11.0	2,383	8.4	8,478	4,999	3,479	50	1.2
Venango	1,208	49,130	0.9	413	8.2	773	15.4	2,629	6.9	14,593	6,945	7,648	58	1.2
Warren	647	38,776	1.0	372	9.7	584	15.2	1,911	6.5	10,672	6,734	3,938	60	1.6
Washington	5,219	203,191	1.0	1,980	9.5	3,058	14.6	9,364	5.9	50,972	19,077	31,895	157	0.8
Wayne	3,657	48,923	0.9	356	6.9	711	13.9	2,672	7.6	14,133	10,666	3,468	32	0.6
Westmoreland	6,885	327,517	0.9	2,833	8.0	5,369	15.2	14,550	5.5	94,522	33,122	61,399	486	1.4
Wyoming	568	26,742	1.0	220	8.5	386	14.8	1,217	6.0	6,860	4,458	2,402	32	1.2
York	8,428	415,439	0.9	4,587	10.0	5,097	11.1	22,184	6.1	95,126	56,245	38,881	498	1.1
RHODE ISLAND	41,796	1,034,451	1.0	9,717	8.9	11,967	10.9	41,789	5.0	224,629	117,402	107,228	1,869	1.7
Bristol	2,811	41,148	0.7	283	5.6	600	11.8	1,277	3.4	11,568	6,179	5,389	73	1.4
Kent	1,090	153,511	0.9	1,362	8.0	2,135	12.5	4,944	3.7	39,962	20,303	19,659	256	1.5
Newport	4,129	87,158	1.1	635	7.4	1,024	12.0	2,537	4.2	20,202	13,069	7,132	41	0.5
Providence	26,809	630,661	1.0	6,661	10.1	6,668	10.1	29,775	5.8	121,265	59,172	62,093	1,392	2.1
Washington	6,957	121,973	0.9	776	6.0	1,540	11.8	3,256	3.5	31,633	18,678	12,954	107	0.8
SOUTH CAROLINA	121,594	5,054,289	1.0	54,713	10.6	62,520	12.1	540,230	13.2	1,105,730	737,579	368,151	5,782	1.1
Abbeville	807	20,493	0.6	232	9.6	324	13.4	2,485	13.7	6,396	3,837	2,560	35	1.4
Aiken	2,048	163,501	0.9	1,755	10.3	2,274	13.4	17,918	13.3	39,707	27,350	12,357	174	1.0
Allendale	826	8,392	0.9	53	6.7	127	16.0	618	10.8	2,079	1,139	940	14	1.8
Anderson	2,753	187,543	0.9	2,080	10.1	2,652	12.9	21,364	13.1	45,523	26,655	18,869	315	1.5
Bamberg	833	13,576	0.9	149	11.3	211	16.0	1,281	12.7	3,487	2,054	1,433	36	2.7
Barnwell	198	19,490	0.8	260	12.6	313	15.2	1,928	11.7	4,845	3,061	1,784	38	1.8
Beaufort	5,020	192,729	1.0	1,797	9.5	2,166	11.4	19,110	14.4	53,148	40,068	13,080	113	0.6
Berkeley	3,394	188,150	0.7	2,766	11.8	2,093	8.9	23,493	12.2	38,279	26,903	11,377	136	0.6
Calhoun	90	12,423	0.7	123	8.7	223	15.8	1,429	13.1	3,852	2,375	1,477	19	1.3
Charleston	10,495	474,339	1.3	4,766	11.6	4,458	10.8	43,577	13.1	76,379	56,378	20,000	305	0.7
Cherokee	975	54,754	0.9	603	10.7	797	14.2	6,303	13.7	12,645	7,125	5,520	88	1.6
Chester	163	28,678	0.7	395	12.3	507	15.7	3,169	12.4	7,882	4,856	3,027	56	1.7
Chesterfield	578	44,544	0.9	444	10.3	671	15.5	5,393	14.9	9,932	6,791	3,141	68	1.6
Clarendon	1,033	30,847	0.7	290	9.3	484	15.6	3,471	14.6	9,031	5,791	3,240	78	2.5
Colleton	349	35,637	0.9	436	11.3	647	16.8	4,497	15.4	10,006	6,385	3,621	63	1.6
Darlington	1,144	63,971	0.9	735	11.7	1,033	16.5	6,625	12.8	15,591	11,079	4,513	106	1.7
Dillon	297	29,384	0.9	407	14.4	436	15.5	4,073	16.7	6,670	4,301	2,368	49	1.7
Dorchester	1,794	131,827	0.6	1,775	10.9	1,562	9.6	16,151	11.7	28,044	19,971	8,073	116	0.7
Edgefield	2,181	23,697	0.7	180	6.9	317	12.2	2,641	13.7	5,797	3,726	2,071	30	1.2
Fairfield	217	20,364	0.8	182	8.8	355	17.1	2,044	12.1	5,682	3,429	2,253	43	2.1
Florence	2,708	147,048	1.2	1,539	11.3	1,961	14.4	13,857	12.5	29,884	22,001	7,884	256	1.9
Georgetown	473	61,747	1.0	498	7.8	1,038	16.3	6,251	14.2	20,748	14,371	6,377	97	1.5
Greenville	9,959	548,389	1.1	5,996	11.3	5,456	10.3	57,215	13.3	100,632	61,456	39,177	497	0.9
Greenwood	2,244	72,556	1.1	796	11.5	954	13.8	7,827	14.3	15,949	10,473	5,476	97	1.4
Hampton	245	18,414	0.9	185	10.1	310	16.9	1,895	13.5	4,432	2,770	1,662	35	1.9
Horry	3,346	346,949	1.0	2,985	8.3	5,123	14.2	46,935	18.0	103,809	73,489	30,320	368	1.0
Jasper	1,013	27,952	0.9	349	11.8	374	12.6	4,358	19.4	7,064	4,576	2,488	26	0.9
Kershaw	243	57,054	0.7	712	10.8	933	14.2	6,595	12.3	14,891	10,422	4,469	80	1.2
Lancaster	1,523	86,960	0.8	957	9.7	1,320	13.4	8,978	11.9	23,627	16,748	6,879	113	1.2
Laurens	2,051	62,436	0.8	716	10.6	1,029	15.2	7,470	14.2	16,604	9,896	6,708	89	1.3
Lee	1,546	14,446	0.5	166	10.1	293	17.9	1,462	12.3	4,128	2,556	1,571	56	3.4
Lexington	1,959	284,363	0.9	3,031	10.2	3,236	10.9	30,853	12.4	56,211	40,502	15,709	262	0.9
McCormick	941	8,768	0.8	47	4.9	184	19.1	613	12.0	3,857	2,303	1,554	18	1.9
Marion	121	27,770	0.7	316	10.9	543	18.8	3,199	13.5	7,765	5,054	2,711	84	2.9
Marlboro	2,493	25,150	0.9	272	10.3	388	14.7	2,578	14.1	6,326	3,960	2,366	39	1.5
Newberry	1,155	37,404	1.0	407	10.8	528	13.9	4,354	14.9	9,238	6,187	3,051	75	2.0
Oconee	627	74,499	0.9	663	8.4	1,148	14.5	8,866	14.8	22,017	14,366	7,651	84	1.1
Orangeburg	2,813	85,773	1.0	909	10.9	1,389	16.6	8,372	13.0	20,675	11,947	8,728	142	1.7
Pickens	8,460	116,206	0.8	1,215	9.2	1,531	11.6	12,827	13.2	26,692	15,503	11,188	157	1.2
Richland	28,006	450,692	1.2	4,719	11.3	3,830	9.2	37,559	11.3	68,266	48,726	19,541	338	0.8
Saluda	180	17,921	0.7	194	10.3	247	13.1	2,835	17.6	4,592	3,093	1,499	34	1.8
Spartanburg	7,562	322,421	1.1	3,878	11.7	3,957	11.9	33,742	13.0	66,614	37,418	29,195	416	1.3

1. Per 1,000 estimated resident population.

STATE County	COVID-19 Vaccinations, 2021–2022		Education						Money income, 2016–2020				Income and poverty, 2020			
			School enrollment and attainment, 2016–2020				Local government expenditures,[3] 2018–2019			Households				Percent below poverty level		
			Enrollment[1]		Attainment[2] (percent)						Percent					
	Number	Percent[5]	Total	Percent private	High school graduate or less	Bachelor's degree or more	Total current spending (mil dol)	Current spending per student (dollars)	Per capita income[4]	Median income (dollars)	with income of less than $50,000	with income of $200,000 or more	Median household income (dollars)	All persons	Children under 18 years	Children 5 to 17 years in families
	46	47	48	49	50	51	52	53	54	55	56	57	58	59	60	61
PENNSYLVANIA—Cont'd																
Potter	6,246	37.8	3,077	14.5	57.2	15.3	36.8	16,483	26,439	47,696	51.9	1.8	51,744	12.2	19.7	17.5
Schuylkill	85,514	60.5	26,950	13.4	56.5	17.0	257.9	15,239	27,749	53,703	46.7	2.4	52,307	12.7	17.4	16.4
Snyder	17,571	43.5	9,343	38.6	57.9	21.1	66.0	13,924	28,151	60,227	41.0	4.2	58,474	10.1	13.8	13.0
Somerset	35,595	48.5	12,449	14.5	59.9	16.7	132.8	15,047	27,323	51,255	48.8	2.9	51,916	11.7	16.0	14.3
Sullivan	3,257	53.7	760	21.2	56.6	18.0	13.6	21,451	31,494	49,830	50.2	2.2	52,821	12.3	16.6	18.1
Susquehanna	18,898	46.9	7,094	13.9	55.4	19.2	111.4	18,774	32,608	55,788	44.5	4.6	55,560	11.6	16.3	15.4
Tioga	18,842	46.4	8,103	12.6	53.3	19.7	79.8	14,355	26,932	51,838	48.0	2.2	47,683	11.5	16.4	16.1
Union	25,857	57.6	10,774	49.9	53.2	25.4	63.0	15,516	28,884	56,824	44.1	5.5	62,306	11.1	11.5	10.9
Venango	23,260	45.9	8,936	15.0	57.0	19.3	89.6	15,495	28,002	51,405	48.2	1.8	52,559	14.0	22.8	21.5
Warren	19,440	49.6	7,216	16.4	52.0	19.4	72.3	16,034	29,272	52,034	48.5	2.6	52,729	11.1	16.5	15.9
Washington	132,445	64.0	43,422	18.0	43.9	30.6	435.6	16,252	36,554	65,478	38.4	7.0	65,808	8.6	10.8	9.9
Wayne	31,439	61.2	8,507	17.6	52.4	20.7	90.1	20,722	28,275	55,572	44.7	3.6	55,627	10.5	14.4	14.2
Westmoreland	201,859	57.9	69,390	18.2	41.1	30.3	670.8	14,682	34,992	61,398	41.0	5.2	59,349	9.3	11.2	10.2
Wyoming	16,112	60.1	5,312	22.1	53.3	20.7	60.9	18,990	31,899	60,075	42.1	2.8	59,305	10.4	15.0	13.1
York	266,124	59.3	98,846	19.2	48.9	25.2	1,007.3	15,009	33,587	68,940	34.6	4.8	71,655	7.1	9.1	8.0
RHODE ISLAND	873,255	82.4	255,231	26.4	38.8	35.0	2,444.2	17,056	37,504	70,305	37.1	7.7	73,919	10.6	14.5	13.8
Bristol	38,225	78.8	13,145	42.9	29.4	49.2	107.6	16,358	48,321	85,413	28.4	15.9	94,591	8.2	7.6	6.7
Kent	128,877	78.4	33,793	19.3	36.4	32.7	387.0	18,016	40,969	75,857	33.5	7.9	82,413	7.5	9.8	9.2
Newport	61,727	75.2	16,855	32.3	25.5	49.7	168.2	18,134	50,514	84,282	31.1	12.1	81,218	9.5	13.9	11.1
Providence	451,381	70.6	158,459	28.1	44.3	30.3	1,502.4	16,466	32,739	62,323	41.5	5.6	67,752	12.4	17.0	16.5
Washington	98,356	78.3	32,979	15.9	27.4	46.0	279.1	18,946	44,325	86,970	28.0	11.1	83,925	7.8	9.4	8.6
SOUTH CAROLINA	2,916,467	56.6	1,187,922	14.9	40.5	29.0	8,893.1	11,390	30,727	54,864	45.8	5.1	57,216	13.8	18.7	17.8
Abbeville	9,807	40.0	5,130	19.6	52.5	18.3	33.5	11,132	25,598	43,090	55.8	2.6	47,219	15.3	20.6	20.0
Aiken	77,995	45.6	36,278	16.4	42.8	27.8	238.9	9,898	29,470	53,385	46.7	3.7	57,128	13.0	18.2	18.2
Allendale	5,062	58.3	1,707	8.4	62.9	10.4	18.8	16,779	16,985	26,074	69.0	0.3	32,701	31.6	45.1	43.8
Anderson	81,835	40.4	46,510	15.9	44.5	24.1	328.9	10,073	28,931	53,598	47.2	4.5	52,667	14.0	18.7	17.7
Bamberg	7,173	51.0	3,781	25.7	52.6	18.1	27.1	13,749	19,814	42,830	57.9	0.4	39,969	21.0	34.2	33.9
Barnwell	11,668	55.9	4,632	8.5	52.6	14.7	44.8	12,318	22,339	37,572	57.4	1.8	41,717	21.6	33.7	32.3
Beaufort	124,680	64.9	35,952	17.8	28.5	42.0	276.9	12,452	41,070	71,430	34.5	9.3	76,515	9.6	14.8	14.0
Berkeley	118,605	52.0	53,055	19.2	41.1	25.4	347.0	9,602	30,655	65,443	37.8	4.8	70,371	11.1	15.5	14.7
Calhoun	5,958	40.9	2,764	24.1	50.4	18.8	23.2	13,730	26,492	49,844	50.2	2.1	50,977	15.5	22.3	21.7
Charleston	268,985	65.4	91,214	18.0	29.2	45.3	593.0	11,914	43,141	67,182	38.0	11.1	72,451	11.9	15.0	16.3
Cherokee	19,611	34.2	13,271	14.7	54.8	14.4	94.7	10,817	21,636	37,787	61.9	1.3	45,085	14.6	20.9	20.1
Chester	14,825	46.0	6,907	9.2	57.1	13.7	62.2	12,036	22,955	43,985	55.6	1.3	45,366	18.3	27.5	28.0
Chesterfield	16,822	36.8	9,805	11.1	61.4	12.4	77.1	11,089	22,955	41,937	56.7	1.6	44,792	19.7	24.7	24.2
Clarendon	16,528	49.0	6,410	15.1	56.2	15.8	59.8	12,056	23,443	43,881	55.4	2.1	52,983	18.4	27.0	26.0
Colleton	18,229	48.4	8,545	7.8	56.6	16.3	62.5	11,287	22,218	36,748	65.7	2.2	44,399	20.1	29.1	28.7
Darlington	32,470	48.7	15,088	18.7	53.7	17.6	115.5	11,264	23,008	37,141	60.7	2.5	42,082	18.9	27.5	27.6
Dillon	13,576	44.5	7,136	8.6	59.8	12.9	57.0	9,908	19,131	36,429	63.8	1.0	40,930	22.2	31.8	29.5
Dorchester	86,706	53.3	40,994	12.1	37.1	28.2	278.7	9,777	29,856	63,501	38.0	4.2	62,928	12.1	17.9	16.1
Edgefield	16,274	59.7	5,865	14.5	53.0	18.0	39.2	11,646	27,213	52,491	48.6	3.5	55,005	16.8	21.6	20.9
Fairfield	14,372	64.3	4,378	17.5	53.3	17.8	48.2	18,299	25,698	43,861	55.6	2.4	45,648	17.6	26.0	25.8
Florence	75,897	54.9	34,820	13.6	46.5	24.2	257.3	11,384	26,636	49,645	50.3	3.1	47,429	17.1	20.8	19.4
Georgetown	34,041	54.3	11,886	9.4	38.0	29.7	106.6	11,443	34,629	52,488	47.6	6.0	57,991	15.1	26.8	26.3
Greenville	289,225	55.2	123,826	22.4	34.4	36.4	759.0	9,950	34,430	62,422	40.0	6.9	62,475	12.1	15.8	13.9
Greenwood	34,008	48.0	16,975	10.5	46.4	24.1	120.0	10,522	26,266	41,081	58.6	2.6	43,711	16.4	23.8	21.7
Hampton	12,287	63.9	3,820	15.0	60.5	11.3	38.5	13,278	19,460	38,178	63.7	0.7	43,614	19.6	29.7	28.1
Horry	199,347	56.3	67,354	8.6	41.6	24.2	492.1	10,953	29,055	51,570	48.3	3.4	55,055	12.8	19.5	19.9
Jasper	11,228	37.3	5,943	17.8	50.7	21.4	38.3	15,020	24,886	45,924	54.1	1.8	48,988	18.4	31.9	31.3
Kershaw	38,980	58.6	15,230	12.9	47.5	21.1	110.7	10,276	26,197	53,980	45.4	2.8	60,397	14.4	19.4	18.8
Lancaster	44,915	45.8	19,496	17.8	41.3	28.5	139.4	10,304	33,212	65,421	39.1	7.2	63,019	11.4	14.2	13.1
Laurens	25,997	38.5	14,456	18.5	53.0	17.2	97.9	11,060	23,482	44,374	55.6	2.0	43,766	18.4	24.0	23.8
Lee	8,057	47.9	3,613	7.8	57.9	14.9	24.3	13,361	19,510	32,851	67.4	2.7	40,400	23.0	31.6	30.4
Lexington	165,741	55.5	69,076	10.4	37.9	30.8	484.5	11,606	32,355	62,740	39.6	5.2	62,839	10.4	11.7	10.1
McCormick	5,529	58.4	1,076	16.9	50.7	21.0	13.0	18,565	26,857	47,402	51.3	2.6	50,698	17.0	32.3	29.8
Marion	14,947	48.8	6,906	10.8	64.0	13.0	51.5	11,749	18,785	30,791	68.4	0.5	38,498	21.8	32.5	31.9
Marlboro	11,422	43.7	5,310	4.3	66.9	7.7	45.7	11,519	16,092	31,528	67.6	0.3	38,877	26.0	33.9	32.8
Newberry	20,124	52.4	8,627	18.6	51.4	19.2	70.3	11,719	26,501	46,038	53.9	2.6	52,202	16.4	23.7	22.4
Oconee	35,749	44.9	16,375	12.4	43.0	27.4	124.9	11,781	31,297	49,691	50.3	4.6	58,061	11.1	18.5	16.4
Orangeburg	48,015	55.7	22,324	19.4	46.2	19.5	167.6	13,370	21,337	36,802	63.6	1.6	41,335	19.1	29.7	28.1
Pickens	59,080	46.6	38,671	10.6	42.4	26.8	149.3	9,198	28,382	51,032	48.8	3.7	54,588	15.3	14.5	14.7
Richland	245,133	59.0	115,603	12.4	30.4	39.1	1,435.5	14,548	30,990	54,441	45.8	5.2	56,993	16.0	21.4	19.7
Saluda	6,195	30.3	4,011	16.4	54.9	18.3	23.8	10,236	23,097	43,410	55.4	1.1	46,216	17.4	25.2	22.3
Spartanburg	139,841	43.7	76,469	16.9	43.5	24.8	563.2	11,471	27,788	53,757	46.5	3.9	53,485	14.2	17.8	16.9

1. All persons 3 years old and over enrolled in nursery school through college. 2. Persons 25 years old and over. 3. Elementary and secondary education expenditures. 4. Based on population estimated by the American Community Survey, 2016–2020. 5. CDC percent based on 2019 population estimate.

STATE County	Personal income, 2020										Earnings, 2020		
			Per capita[1]			Supplements to wages and salaries, employer contributions (mil dol)						Contributions for government social insurance (mil dol)	
	Total (mil dol)	Percent change 2019–2020	Dollars	Rank	Wages and salaries (mil dol)	Pension and insurance	Government social insurance	Proprietors' income (mil dol)	Dividends, interest, and rent (mil dol)	Personal transfer reecipts (mil dol)	Total (mil dol)	From employee and self-employed	From employer
	62	63	64	65	66	67	68	69	70	71	72	73	74
PENNSYLVANIA—Cont'd													
Potter	788	6.4	47,910	1,405	244	59	19	129	114	271	452	29	19
Schuylkill	6,673	8.9	47,425	1,454	2,296	472	190	353	894	2,299	3,310	232	190
Snyder	1,895	9.3	47,000	1,517	603	132	50	194	241	628	980	62	50
Somerset	3,430	9.2	47,035	1,510	1,031	238	84	293	509	1,177	1,647	115	84
Sullivan	303	5.8	51,266	999	57	16	5	25	72	103	103	8	5
Susquehanna	1,965	4.4	49,114	1,243	401	94	31	196	388	574	722	55	31
Tioga	1,830	7.3	45,319	1,751	578	139	45	152	289	625	914	64	45
Union	2,004	7.3	45,235	1,766	887	184	73	228	318	505	1,373	83	73
Venango	2,372	7.4	47,125	1,498	757	185	60	129	342	958	1,131	82	60
Warren	1,821	7.9	46,793	1,539	640	148	51	147	288	638	985	67	51
Washington	12,920	7.3	62,473	337	5,424	872	396	868	2,038	3,345	7,559	490	396
Wayne	2,516	8.0	49,172	1,232	684	155	54	221	476	818	1,114	86	54
Westmoreland	20,114	7.2	57,951	516	6,546	1,199	520	1,103	2,977	5,927	9,368	648	520
Wyoming	1,353	7.1	50,959	1,036	510	98	40	134	208	408	781	50	40
York	25,117	7.5	55,761	659	9,594	1,739	746	1,528	3,643	6,311	13,608	868	746
RHODE ISLAND	64,300	7.3	58,656	X	28,944	4,627	2,292	4,340	10,514	16,038	40,203	2,845	2,292
Bristol	4,019	3.6	83,127	66	702	122	58	247	968	642	1,128	89	58
Kent	10,751	7.0	65,299	255	4,251	652	344	591	1,604	2,540	5,839	430	344
Newport	6,237	4.2	76,214	98	2,742	544	229	563	1,624	1,220	4,079	270	229
Providence	34,274	9.2	53,844	791	18,133	2,738	1,414	2,181	4,454	9,853	24,466	1,720	1,414
Washington	9,018	4.7	71,717	140	3,116	571	247	758	1,863	1,783	4,691	336	247
SOUTH CAROLINA	250,574	6.9	48,838	X	109,988	18,572	8,080	17,149	45,915	64,276	153,788	10,457	8,080
Abbeville	928	7.7	38,033	2,681	251	55	19	48	113	362	373	30	19
Aiken	8,147	6.9	47,118	1,500	3,515	520	251	365	1,343	2,202	4,651	333	251
Allendale	325	13.7	38,991	2,563	121	29	9	17	42	137	176	13	9
Anderson	8,881	6.2	43,459	2,015	3,179	575	237	417	1,264	2,597	4,407	322	237
Bamberg	523	7.1	37,596	2,726	149	34	11	34	69	213	228	18	11
Barnwell	805	7.0	38,682	2,606	203	44	16	28	101	294	290	25	16
Beaufort	11,993	4.9	61,298	376	3,746	658	290	596	4,657	2,594	5,289	381	290
Berkeley	10,415	8.4	44,134	1,923	3,538	516	252	588	1,636	2,371	4,895	326	252
Calhoun	650	7.6	44,655	1,856	234	48	17	41	103	210	340	23	17
Charleston	27,861	4.7	66,656	225	15,584	2,552	1,139	3,425	7,350	4,586	22,699	1,374	1,139
Cherokee	2,096	8.4	36,567	2,817	854	146	64	82	271	752	1,147	85	64
Chester	1,255	9.3	38,931	2,574	483	95	35	44	172	461	656	50	35
Chesterfield	1,572	5.9	34,477	2,963	650	114	50	75	187	588	890	66	50
Clarendon	1,270	8.4	38,001	2,687	265	60	20	75	168	501	420	39	20
Colleton	1,512	8.3	40,336	2,414	450	84	34	82	230	575	650	55	34
Darlington	2,789	7.0	41,928	2,213	1,084	200	80	108	365	936	1,472	108	80
Dillon	1,003	8.5	33,030	3,028	361	62	28	37	110	419	488	40	28
Dorchester	7,071	5.9	42,662	2,106	1,683	293	125	373	1,010	1,828	2,475	207	125
Edgefield	1,117	8.9	41,178	2,312	238	52	18	65	156	331	373	32	18
Fairfield	923	8.0	41,827	2,227	333	75	24	28	134	337	460	35	24
Florence	6,432	6.4	46,749	1,543	3,413	604	247	336	981	1,898	4,600	311	247
Georgetown	3,280	5.7	51,775	952	1,172	198	85	225	852	1,038	1,680	128	85
Greenville	27,803	6.5	52,213	916	15,871	2,292	1,143	2,046	4,805	5,781	21,353	1,385	1,143
Greenwood	2,899	7.4	40,786	2,356	1,395	281	104	142	474	981	1,922	132	104
Hampton	707	8.2	39,185	2,544	225	47	16	30	90	271	317	25	16
Horry	15,389	9.6	42,110	2,180	5,471	875	410	1,161	3,078	5,245	7,917	639	410
Jasper	1,088	12.8	34,446	2,965	462	76	34	74	195	379	646	45	34
Kershaw	3,089	7.1	45,782	1,685	785	144	59	166	432	907	1,154	92	59
Lancaster	5,349	7.6	52,999	858	1,542	233	108	1,047	630	1,257	2,929	205	108
Laurens	2,587	7.1	38,108	2,673	960	176	72	102	322	990	1,310	108	72
Lee	612	8.8	36,638	2,809	166	33	13	22	66	250	233	20	13
Lexington	15,254	6.6	50,188	1,127	6,305	1,080	467	988	2,354	3,302	8,840	591	467
McCormick	400	5.8	42,422	2,142	64	16	5	18	96	176	103	13	5
Marion	1,104	7.9	36,606	2,814	280	59	21	35	127	477	396	35	21
Marlboro	914	8.0	35,748	2,890	323	66	24	34	100	375	447	35	24
Newberry	1,611	7.0	41,910	2,216	651	128	50	40	248	521	869	66	50
Oconee	3,802	5.2	47,511	1,447	1,276	259	95	153	809	1,108	1,783	139	95
Orangeburg	3,305	7.4	38,730	2,602	1,295	246	98	111	447	1,293	1,752	134	98
Pickens	5,346	5.7	41,770	2,234	1,801	355	131	250	973	1,484	2,538	191	131
Richland	20,817	6.6	49,678	1,176	12,877	2,349	940	1,744	3,353	4,817	17,910	1,080	940
Saluda	765	6.4	37,637	2,723	191	39	14	20	116	254	263	19	14
Spartanburg	15,183	7.4	46,543	1,571	7,998	1,328	586	876	2,813	3,855	10,787	719	586

1. Based on the resident population estimated as of July 1 of the year shown.

STATE County	Earnings, 2020 (cont.)									Social Security beneficiaries, December 2020		Supple-mental Security Income recipients, 2020	Housing units, 2021	
	Percent by selected industries													
	Farm	Mining, quarrying, and extractions	Construction	Manu-facturing	Information; professional, scientific, technical services	Retail trade	Finance, insurance, real estate, and leasing	Health care and social assistance	Govern-ment	Number	Rate[1]		Total	Percent change, 2010–2021
	75	76	77	78	79	80	81	82	83	84	85	86	87	88
PENNSYLVANIA—Cont'd														
Potter	3.4	0.3	5.6	9.0	23.5	3.8	1.6	D	15.0	5,110	314	472	12,361	0.1
Schuylkill	0.9	1.3	5.0	23.3	3.3	6.1	3.0	13.1	17.5	38,470	269	3,659	67,211	0.1
Snyder	2.6	D	7.3	20.4	4.2	9.4	3.0	D	16.8	9,255	234	597	16,018	0.2
Somerset	2.0	5.2	6.1	11.5	4.1	6.4	4.6	13.7	20.9	21,055	286	1,935	37,775	0.1
Sullivan	3.2	D	10.7	D	D	6.7	3.7	D	26.8	2,025	345	129	5,578	0.1
Susquehanna	2.4	9.2	10.8	4.3	7.1	7.1	2.9	7.6	18.6	11,190	291	836	21,297	0.2
Tioga	1.9	6.4	4.4	11.1	5.8	7.8	4.5	D	19.9	11,715	286	1,013	21,542	0.2
Union	1.4	D	6.1	7.6	2.9	6.1	3.8	D	19.9	8,910	209	539	16,140	0.2
Venango	0.2	0.3	4.4	23.5	2.3	7.4	3.7	16.0	21.1	15,945	319	1,917	26,172	0.0
Warren	0.9	2.8	3.7	18.7	3.1	7.7	8.1	14.0	16.1	11,570	303	885	21,599	0.1
Washington	0.1	5.6	10.8	9.2	11.5	5.3	9.0	11.5	9.6	55,265	264	4,613	97,400	0.6
Wayne	0.8	0.5	12.4	3.4	5.1	8.4	6.5	13.3	25.5	15,045	293	1,158	32,027	0.3
Westmoreland	0.3	0.9	8.0	15.1	7.2	8.5	5.1	13.1	13.0	100,650	285	7,547	168,321	0.3
Wyoming	-0.1	4.2	6.9	24.0	D	6.0	2.7	D	10.4	7,380	283	581	12,844	0.1
York	0.3	D	9.1	18.9	6.2	5.8	5.1	14.6	13.3	100,160	218	8,385	188,598	0.6
RHODE ISLAND	0.1	D	6.2	8.1	10.0	6.3	10.9	14.0	16.9	230,018	210	32,124	484,902	0.2
Bristol	0.0	-0.1	8.6	D	10.5	5.5	7.2	10.6	16.2	11,530	227	608	21,559	0.2
Kent	0.0	D	6.7	10.1	10.0	9.2	7.6	15.7	12.9	41,555	243	3,622	76,323	0.3
Newport	0.2	D	5.7	D	12.5	5.5	8.3	6.6	35.3	19,985	234	1,351	43,558	0.2
Providence	0.0	0.0	5.9	6.0	10.0	5.2	13.5	15.6	14.3	125,075	190	24,948	277,362	0.2
Washington	0.3	0.1	7.1	16.6	7.6	9.6	5.2	10.4	19.4	31,875	244	1,595	66,100	0.5
SOUTH CAROLINA	0.2	0.1	6.8	13.1	10.2	6.9	8.2	9.5	19.3	1,197,138	231	113,864	2,395,943	1.8
Abbeville	1.1	0.0	6.9	33.3	D	3.4	D	D	24.1	6,950	286	522	11,670	1.0
Aiken	-0.2	0.2	12.2	15.6	7.9	6.2	3.6	8.2	11.5	43,125	253	3,883	78,317	1.5
Allendale	5.6	0.0	1.6	29.9	D	2.5	1.3	D	33.2	2,315	295	566	4,049	0.2
Anderson	-0.1	0.3	5.8	26.3	4.5	8.1	4.1	8.5	19.8	50,255	243	4,278	90,949	1.7
Bamberg	3.7	0.0	2.2	14.3	D	6.2	7.8	11.1	20.7	3,795	288	657	6,586	0.4
Barnwell	0.0	D	6.2	27.6	D	7.9	D	D	26.3	5,120	249	1,057	9,892	0.3
Beaufort	0.1	D	8.1	1.1	10.4	8.3	8.4	9.1	28.1	53,645	280	1,891	100,918	2.3
Berkeley	0.1	D	9.8	14.7	21.2	8.7	5.0	4.5	14.5	41,970	177	3,506	97,382	3.4
Calhoun	1.8	0.0	12.5	34.0	D	1.8	D	D	12.9	4,135	292	365	7,056	0.4
Charleston	0.1	0.0	7.7	6.7	14.5	5.9	10.1	11.3	20.9	78,400	190	6,791	206,246	1.8
Cherokee	0.6	D	7.6	34.3	D	7.1	2.8	3.3	13.8	14,195	253	1,510	24,944	0.8
Chester	0.2	0.0	5.5	40.3	D	4.8	D	3.4	18.0	8,870	275	1,125	14,695	0.5
Chesterfield	0.7	0.4	3.3	35.9	D	4.8	2.7	D	13.4	11,310	261	1,553	20,635	0.9
Clarendon	3.0	0.0	4.4	5.3	5.2	12.7	4.1	8.7	33.1	9,930	320	1,420	15,975	0.8
Colleton	1.5	0.3	8.1	6.7	D	8.7	4.4	13.6	19.3	10,995	286	1,571	19,950	0.5
Darlington	0.8	0.0	7.3	26.1	2.3	5.5	2.8	10.4	13.8	17,445	278	2,740	29,599	0.6
Dillon	-0.5	0.0	2.5	19.2	2.7	9.5	3.3	D	17.4	7,480	266	1,455	12,853	0.5
Dorchester	0.1	0.2	9.8	18.7	7.5	7.6	5.4	7.3	16.9	30,675	188	2,791	66,437	2.5
Edgefield	7.1	D	7.7	15.9	D	6.1	D	D	28.6	6,300	241	846	11,290	2.1
Fairfield	0.3	D	2.4	11.0	D	3.3	1.4	6.2	18.8	6,250	302	737	10,943	0.8
Florence	0.5	0.0	3.7	12.5	6.5	7.4	12.6	12.3	21.2	32,680	239	5,468	61,485	1.1
Georgetown	0.5	D	6.5	11.8	6.6	6.8	12.0	12.5	21.6	22,135	346	1,754	36,645	1.8
Greenville	0.0	0.0	7.0	11.8	12.9	6.1	9.9	10.7	11.4	106,950	200	9,383	232,658	2.4
Greenwood	0.3	D	4.4	25.9	3.0	6.8	3.8	12.5	24.5	17,630	255	1,709	31,467	0.4
Hampton	1.9	0.0	5.3	8.0	D	6.6	D	D	30.0	5,040	277	948	8,619	0.5
Horry	0.0	0.1	8.8	2.6	7.3	12.7	11.2	12.0	15.7	113,390	310	6,007	210,311	2.7
Jasper	0.6	0.0	20.9	3.6	3.3	16.0	4.1	14.1	13.1	7,890	260	637	13,700	5.4
Kershaw	0.9	0.3	8.3	17.1	5.2	12.4	8.0	12.8	14.0	16,495	249	1,511	29,482	1.8
Lancaster	0.1	D	D	7.5	40.2	4.5	7.1	5.9	10.2	25,360	253	1,764	42,741	3.4
Laurens	0.3	D	4.8	35.6	D	4.8	2.4	7.3	18.0	18,260	269	1,880	31,620	0.9
Lee	2.5	0.0	2.4	14.7	D	7.0	D	D	24.2	4,705	289	751	7,577	0.3
Lexington	0.3	0.2	7.9	12.8	7.2	8.8	6.3	6.6	20.2	61,365	204	4,644	130,832	1.9
McCormick	2.0	D	4.4	2.7	D	4.6	D	7.9	42.7	4,040	414	298	5,521	2.3
Marion	2.0	D	4.8	8.9	D	7.7	6.3	D	25.3	8,650	301	1,529	14,386	0.7
Marlboro	2.8	D	D	38.0	1.0	7.4	3.3	D	27.0	7,175	272	1,408	12,045	0.1
Newberry	-0.2	D	7.4	38.9	D	5.7	2.0	5.1	17.3	10,155	267	924	18,392	0.8
Oconee	-0.6	D	6.3	26.1	5.3	7.8	4.7	7.4	15.4	23,675	299	1,459	41,341	1.1
Orangeburg	0.7	0.0	4.0	24.4	2.8	8.3	3.4	8.4	25.5	22,800	275	3,783	41,379	0.4
Pickens	0.0	D	5.6	16.7	5.3	8.3	4.4	7.6	35.0	28,780	218	2,232	57,406	1.5
Richland	0.0	D	3.9	5.5	12.0	5.0	13.5	11.2	28.5	74,660	178	8,555	184,378	0.9
Saluda	0.1	0.0	4.9	40.1	D	3.6	D	D	21.9	4,955	263	393	9,415	1.5
Spartanburg	0.1	D	6.8	25.5	5.4	6.0	4.9	D	16.9	72,055	215	7,185	140,821	2.3

1. Per 1,000 resident population estimated as of July 1 of the year shown.

STATE County	Housing units, 2016–2020: Occupied units: Total	Owner-occupied: Percent	Owner-occupied: Median value[1]	Owner-occupied: Median owner cost as a percent of income: With a mortgage	Owner-occupied: Median owner cost as a percent of income: Without a mortgage[2]	Renter-occupied: Median rent[3]	Renter-occupied: Median rent as a percent of income[2]	Sub-standard units[4] (percent)	Civilian labor force, 2021: Total	Percent change, 2020–2021	Unemployment: Total	Unemployment: Rate[5]	Civilian employment[6], 2016–2020: Total	Percent: Management, business, science, and arts	Percent: Construction, production, and maintenance occupations
	89	90	91	92	93	94	95	96	97	98	99	100	101	102	103
PENNSYLVANIA—Cont'd															
Potter	6,630	77.9	110,400	21.1	11.3	670	25.8	2.4	7,122	-2.3	487	6.8	6,914	31.6	32.8
Schuylkill	58,646	75.2	106,100	18.6	12.6	710	28.8	1.3	65,357	-2.4	4,421	6.8	63,687	29.1	36.1
Snyder	14,824	73.3	172,900	19.7	11.4	750	23.0	2.4	19,565	-0.4	1,008	5.2	19,806	31.2	32.7
Somerset	29,518	79.8	113,300	18.3	12.0	608	26.5	1.7	32,597	-1.7	2,198	6.7	32,820	31.7	30.8
Sullivan	2,751	82.7	160,100	20.2	11.6	649	26.0	0.8	2,569	-1.7	189	7.4	2,767	28.8	37.2
Susquehanna	17,027	77.4	173,100	21.1	11.1	761	27.8	1.6	19,956	-0.4	1,091	5.5	17,786	30.4	32.8
Tioga	16,442	74.6	151,900	19.5	12.7	728	28.8	1.4	18,887	-1.2	1,254	6.6	18,004	30.4	31.9
Union	14,762	70.6	188,400	18.7	12.5	769	29.4	0.8	19,470	-0.4	910	4.7	17,751	40.6	24.3
Venango	22,103	73.2	96,800	17.5	10.6	652	24.8	1.9	21,865	-2.4	1,495	6.8	22,320	29.7	30.1
Warren	17,124	77.6	102,000	17.4	10.4	615	24.0	2.0	18,026	-4.4	1,212	6.7	18,009	29.9	32.6
Washington	85,201	74.9	170,800	18.0	10.7	781	24.9	1.1	104,785	-1.9	6,959	6.6	100,095	37.1	23.6
Wayne	18,938	80.9	178,700	23.5	12.4	791	27.3	1.8	22,379	-0.1	1,481	6.6	21,093	30.9	29.6
Westmoreland	153,772	77.6	157,200	18.5	11.5	732	26.6	0.9	175,353	-1.9	11,081	6.3	171,082	37.9	24.6
Wyoming	10,887	75.8	172,300	20.4	12.0	789	24.9	1.0	13,216	-0.9	836	6.3	12,567	28.5	32.9
York	174,425	74.8	183,300	21.0	12.9	972	28.8	1.6	234,914	-0.6	12,733	5.4	226,081	34.8	27.8
RHODE ISLAND	414,730	61.6	276,600	22.6	13.4	1,031	29.0	2.2	571,034	0.7	32,065	5.6	535,140	40.5	19.4
Bristol	18,961	70.2	364,500	21.7	13.9	1,076	28.9	0.4	26,496	1.7	1,257	4.7	24,636	49.8	13.1
Kent	70,085	70.2	247,700	22.2	14.2	1,110	29.5	2.1	93,708	1.0	4,880	5.2	87,720	42.7	18.5
Newport	34,578	64.9	399,500	22.8	13.0	1,348	28.7	0.9	45,042	1.3	2,215	4.9	41,154	46.1	14.4
Providence	240,886	55.1	248,500	23.1	13.4	989	28.9	2.8	335,620	0.3	20,294	6.0	316,776	37.6	21.5
Washington	50,220	75.1	359,300	21.8	12.7	1,115	29.1	0.9	70,167	1.6	3,418	4.9	64,854	44.8	15.9
SOUTH CAROLINA	1,961,481	70.1	170,100	19.8	10.0	918	29.7	2.2	2,364,366	1.4	94,553	4.0	2,312,831	35.8	24.8
Abbeville	9,597	75.0	100,700	19.4	10.8	691	29.5	2.7	9,621	-1.2	437	4.5	10,117	30.8	32.4
Aiken	68,266	73.7	153,700	18.6	10.0	840	29.3	1.7	74,070	0.6	2,490	3.4	72,750	35.1	25.7
Allendale	3,426	68.5	47,100	21.5	14.5	640	29.9	3.3	2,445	-4.0	190	7.8	2,707	28.6	28.7
Anderson	78,636	72.6	153,600	18.1	10.0	791	27.9	2.9	90,029	1.8	3,343	3.7	90,974	35.7	29.3
Bamberg	5,070	77.1	78,900	22.2	12.0	664	37.1	2.5	4,691	-1.1	350	7.5	5,355	25.8	37.5
Barnwell	8,670	72.5	87,600	22.7	11.5	646	27.8	3.0	7,572	-2.3	493	6.5	8,499	27.0	31.1
Beaufort	74,231	74.8	309,600	23.7	10.7	1,229	31.0	1.6	76,131	1.9	2,629	3.5	79,205	37.2	19.6
Berkeley	79,597	72.3	197,300	19.7	10.0	1,164	28.8	2.1	107,149	3.0	3,884	3.6	103,151	33.6	25.5
Calhoun	6,221	81.4	104,500	19.8	10.0	666	46.0	3.9	6,411	1.1	289	4.5	6,584	33.6	29.3
Charleston	163,411	62.2	334,600	21.5	10.6	1,228	31.7	1.3	210,944	2.2	7,607	3.6	207,897	45.3	17.3
Cherokee	20,779	70.9	98,300	19.8	10.0	718	30.0	1.2	24,817	0.3	1,256	5.1	23,559	24.3	36.4
Chester	12,861	78.8	94,200	19.0	10.1	680	29.4	2.3	13,279	1.0	789	5.9	13,412	21.1	37.5
Chesterfield	18,213	69.9	85,600	18.9	10.5	706	26.0	4.4	21,543	1.2	973	4.5	19,515	24.6	43.0
Clarendon	12,775	77.3	105,200	19.9	10.5	617	28.7	3.3	12,307	-1.1	606	4.9	12,083	27.3	32.6
Colleton	15,281	74.1	93,500	25.6	11.0	675	28.3	1.8	16,178	-0.3	708	4.4	15,623	26.3	36.3
Darlington	26,117	69.7	102,800	18.0	11.5	689	31.8	2.8	29,869	0.2	1,348	4.5	26,208	33.4	28.2
Dillon	11,147	58.8	84,500	19.1	12.1	598	35.9	4.2	13,128	1.5	761	5.8	11,823	24.3	35.3
Dorchester	56,939	72.5	213,000	22.0	10.0	1,134	29.9	2.6	77,830	2.7	2,822	3.6	74,789	38.1	23.6
Edgefield	9,171	75.8	132,600	17.7	10.0	668	35.7	2.7	10,394	0.4	351	3.4	10,825	26.8	33.4
Fairfield	9,315	75.3	106,900	19.0	10.0	718	36.7	4.1	9,231	0.5	540	5.8	9,775	31.3	27.2
Florence	52,880	65.7	135,000	18.9	10.0	783	27.3	2.8	65,981	0.9	2,676	4.1	61,447	35.0	24.6
Georgetown	25,758	79.8	197,700	22.4	11.3	958	29.5	1.5	25,930	1.7	1,238	4.8	25,364	31.8	24.6
Greenville	198,015	68.2	197,400	18.6	10.0	954	28.5	2.1	255,544	1.8	8,715	3.4	255,580	39.8	22.8
Greenwood	27,977	62.3	128,000	18.9	10.0	746	30.3	2.3	30,333	-1.2	1,375	4.5	29,839	30.3	31.9
Hampton	6,893	76.0	76,000	20.9	11.4	605	27.3	1.6	8,019	0.6	285	3.6	7,314	27.2	30.3
Horry	136,219	73.8	187,800	22.8	10.4	975	31.1	1.4	148,763	3.1	7,538	5.1	150,783	29.8	20.1
Jasper	10,724	73.5	159,000	24.5	10.0	1,043	31.6	4.9	13,121	2.7	446	3.4	12,501	20.9	28.6
Kershaw	25,293	81.0	135,500	20.7	10.0	759	28.4	1.4	29,168	1.2	1,084	3.7	28,160	35.0	27.2
Lancaster	35,228	80.6	217,100	17.8	10.0	785	28.1	1.8	42,926	1.8	1,870	4.4	40,515	36.0	25.8
Laurens	25,555	71.6	108,100	21.5	10.0	780	29.8	2.8	29,708	1.4	1,280	4.3	28,142	27.1	32.1
Lee	6,455	77.2	79,000	21.8	12.4	709	36.6	2.9	6,595	-0.9	367	5.6	5,905	22.6	37.7
Lexington	115,220	75.3	163,200	18.7	10.0	921	28.5	2.3	149,900	1.6	4,563	3.0	143,139	38.7	23.5
McCormick	3,984	77.8	114,700	23.4	10.3	804	29.6	1.0	3,334	1.9	160	4.8	2,955	32.9	31.1
Marion	11,282	63.6	81,800	19.2	11.6	587	29.5	5.0	12,953	0.1	859	6.6	11,217	24.4	39.8
Marlboro	9,384	64.2	71,500	22.5	12.4	598	28.4	2.8	8,840	-2.3	686	7.8	8,907	28.8	35.3
Newberry	14,976	74.9	118,500	20.8	10.7	776	31.5	2.2	19,262	2.5	634	3.3	17,653	27.5	32.6
Oconee	32,440	73.2	164,000	18.8	10.0	761	34.0	2.2	34,123	-0.2	1,238	3.6	33,008	33.4	28.0
Orangeburg	33,629	67.2	91,700	23.3	11.8	699	31.9	2.1	33,801	-0.5	2,395	7.1	34,616	27.8	32.2
Pickens	48,522	68.5	159,200	18.3	10.0	786	31.3	1.8	56,837	2.3	1,971	3.5	57,456	37.9	25.4
Richland	155,478	59.8	167,500	20.0	10.0	998	31.7	1.9	196,303	1.1	8,090	4.1	197,898	41.4	18.0
Saluda	7,360	77.6	110,100	24.1	10.5	684	29.9	5.8	8,409	1.1	264	3.1	8,495	26.3	35.1
Spartanburg	118,788	71.3	153,000	19.1	10.0	825	28.6	2.8	156,109	0.3	6,174	4.0	145,469	31.4	31.1

1. Specified owner-occupied units. 2. A value of 10.0 represents 10 percent or less; a value of 50.0 represents 50 percent or more. 3. Specified renter-occupied units. 4. Overcrowded or lacking complete plumbing facilities. 5. Percent of civilian labor force. 6. Civilian employed persons 16 years old and over.

STATE County	Private nonfarm establishments, employment and payroll, 2020									Agriculture, 2017			
		Employment						Annual payroll		Farms			Farm producers whose primary occupation is farming (percent)
											Percent with:		
	Number of establish-ments	Total	Health care and social assistance	Manufac-turing	Retail trade	Finance and insurance	Professional, scientific, and technical services	Total (mil dol)	Average per employee (dollars)	Number	Fewer than 50 acres	1000 acres or more	
	104	105	106	107	108	109	110	111	112	113	114	115	116
PENNSYLVANIA—Cont'd													
Potter	367	4,586	901	598	511	81	200	203	44,374	447	25.3	4.0	43.5
Schuylkill	2,694	42,068	8,296	10,343	5,312	846	965	1,738	41,306	685	44.5	1.0	44.0
Snyder	876	14,241	1,745	3,194	2,947	257	234	437	30,714	864	49.0	0.9	49.1
Somerset	1,610	19,526	3,248	2,832	2,503	627	648	696	35,634	1,152	28.6	2.1	46.0
Sullivan	157	906	219	59	188	24	22	27	29,278	190	21.6	2.6	42.1
Susquehanna	811	6,893	1,131	609	1,195	179	257	246	35,623	909	29.6	0.8	45.7
Tioga	863	10,308	2,164	1,604	1,827	404	213	387	37,507	1,056	24.1	1.7	44.4
Union	924	16,438	3,948	1,400	1,792	472	493	661	40,235	574	38.0	0.7	53.1
Venango	1,124	15,360	3,512	3,863	2,368	346	264	567	36,923	409	40.6	2.0	36.2
Warren	871	13,447	3,100	2,895	1,967	873	254	587	43,658	452	33.0	1.3	46.1
Washington	5,185	84,165	15,018	8,859	8,727	1,733	3,636	4,812	57,176	1,760	37.7	0.1	41.8
Wayne	1,296	13,128	2,506	703	3,134	482	323	484	36,897	640	27.3	0.9	42.3
Westmoreland	8,353	130,615	20,745	18,909	18,057	2,924	6,772	5,541	42,422	1,099	42.0	2.1	38.6
Wyoming	644	10,275	616	2,173	1,112	192	274	527	51,266	410	32.0	1.2	39.7
York	8,574	167,260	25,906	30,588	22,055	4,769	6,579	7,649	45,733	2,067	62.0	2.0	39.3
RHODE ISLAND	28,586	445,846	87,110	39,321	49,616	32,300	22,980	22,497	50,459	1,043	72.5	0.4	38.6
Bristol	1,261	14,714	3,660	1,517	1,242	258	407	510	34,635	40	67.5	NA	41.7
Kent	4,645	71,352	13,045	5,877	11,823	4,372	3,070	3,474	48,683	111	72.1	1.8	29.4
Newport	2,721	32,688	4,882	1,807	4,152	1,491	3,741	1,494	45,700	196	71.4	NA	44.0
Providence	15,932	275,501	57,968	21,386	25,593	24,304	12,667	14,355	52,106	377	73.2	NA	32.5
Washington	3,690	44,437	7,418	8,734	6,803	986	1,676	2,199	49,477	319	73.0	0.6	47.0
SOUTH CAROLINA	113,383	1,986,776	256,734	248,874	254,533	79,189	101,448	86,817	43,697	24,791	49.8	3.8	36.1
Abbeville	325	4,213	448	1,803	416	79	29	167	39,701	576	39.6	1.2	30.8
Aiken	2,857	51,061	6,678	8,042	7,307	1,044	2,545	2,502	49,009	1,249	57.1	2.1	38.9
Allendale	112	1,533	351	630	150	35	33	72	46,975	165	21.8	9.1	40.7
Anderson	3,860	63,313	9,744	14,174	9,032	2,117	3,613	2,928	46,245	1,742	54.5	1.5	33.0
Bamberg	258	2,770	401	884	403	78	58	94	34,062	355	29.0	6.2	30.8
Barnwell	321	4,339	422	1,588	609	118	110	168	38,604	369	42.5	4.1	34.3
Beaufort	5,584	57,993	8,501	593	11,011	1,825	2,786	2,157	37,199	161	67.7	9.3	28.4
Berkeley	3,517	56,298	4,237	7,052	8,217	1,410	5,522	3,039	53,982	339	56.0	5.3	31.9
Calhoun	232	3,475	353	1,456	225	32	14	152	43,860	480	36.9	9.6	42.6
Charleston	14,530	212,281	27,882	15,534	29,702	7,146	16,926	9,974	46,987	403	68.2	1.0	39.3
Cherokee	916	19,370	1,258	7,137	2,814	267	184	691	35,668	415	47.0	2.2	33.0
Chester	534	8,125	615	3,624	926	136	130	334	41,094	517	40.6	4.3	38.8
Chesterfield	700	14,285	1,678	6,138	1,189	230	89	596	41,697	636	47.8	4.4	38.5
Clarendon	493	5,476	1,268	859	1,183	222	88	163	29,855	381	36.2	8.9	50.1
Colleton	735	7,357	1,268	541	1,647	240	169	257	34,990	459	44.4	7.0	32.9
Darlington	1,079	17,677	2,629	2,714	2,397	346	256	969	54,811	322	45.7	12.7	48.1
Dillon	462	6,730	1,146	1,792	1,194	152	129	234	34,836	182	22.0	14.8	54.9
Dorchester	2,529	31,353	4,376	5,817	4,676	675	1,209	1,234	39,345	358	55.3	4.2	38.7
Edgefield	324	5,473	699	959	470	43	64	189	34,459	397	43.1	4.5	35.1
Fairfield	332	5,370	540	943	530	69	1,417	331	61,688	228	25.4	8.3	27.0
Florence	3,139	65,992	24,047	7,607	8,553	2,470	2,098	2,898	43,913	540	42.4	6.7	38.1
Georgetown	1,862	19,829	3,789	2,172	3,237	519	857	840	42,378	166	36.7	8.4	32.9
Greenville	14,181	249,202	34,409	30,902	28,466	11,152	20,775	11,768	47,224	1,036	69.5	0.3	30.4
Greenwood	1,304	22,793	4,737	4,638	3,727	504	632	912	40,012	466	44.2	1.1	31.4
Hampton	312	3,017	623	333	617	115	89	128	42,507	242	24.4	12.0	42.4
Horry	9,474	117,676	14,035	3,019	25,394	3,021	3,835	3,797	32,265	767	47.3	5.7	46.6
Jasper	730	8,343	1,025	306	1,951	101	274	355	42,492	135	55.6	11.9	45.5
Kershaw	1,149	15,191	1,948	2,567	2,360	385	376	581	38,255	466	50.9	3.6	39.3
Lancaster	1,562	22,266	3,135	2,466	3,335	1,370	628	1,149	51,625	534	48.5	2.1	31.3
Laurens	913	17,653	1,779	7,250	1,818	272	440	701	39,711	840	44.9	2.1	32.6
Lee	194	2,059	281	242	353	62	34	65	31,393	334	42.2	9.6	38.4
Lexington	6,899	113,753	16,111	11,514	20,020	3,240	3,531	4,643	40,816	1,137	63.5	0.9	32.3
McCormick	91	851	171	140	129	10	10	21	24,108	92	34.8	5.4	51.4
Marion	483	5,297	1,145	777	975	294	71	160	30,159	197	43.7	6.1	41.2
Marlboro	307	5,699	1,186	2,251	851	93	106	224	39,300	201	38.8	10.0	38.8
Newberry	770	12,739	1,448	5,205	1,445	175	178	488	38,329	607	40.4	1.6	35.7
Oconee	1,608	20,426	2,315	5,427	3,351	459	503	899	44,019	815	58.9	0.2	36.7
Orangeburg	1,577	23,742	3,861	5,077	3,972	556	408	913	38,450	978	38.8	8.0	46.5
Pickens	2,102	26,655	2,964	5,353	5,423	572	821	896	33,604	740	73.6	0.1	28.6
Richland	9,185	161,794	30,217	10,373	19,416	12,634	10,955	7,379	45,607	440	62.7	1.4	42.7
Saluda	232	4,251	404	2,490	323	49	81	142	33,343	574	35.0	3.7	39.1
Spartanburg	6,725	143,354	14,860	36,294	16,433	3,139	3,765	6,670	46,529	1,433	67.9	0.3	30.0

STATE County	Agriculture, 2017 (cont.): Land in farms: Acreage (1,000)	Land in farms: Percent change, 2012–2017	Land in farms: Acres: Average size of farm	Land in farms: Acres: Total irrigated (1,000)	Land in farms: Acres: Total cropland (1,000)	Value of land and buildings (dollars): Average per farm	Value of land and buildings (dollars): Average per acre	Value of machinery and equipment, average per farm (dollars)	Value of products sold: Total (mil dol)	Value of products sold: Average per farm (acres)	Value of products sold: Percent from: Crops	Value of products sold: Percent from: Livestock and poultry products	Organic farms (number)	Farms with internet access (percent)	Government payments: Total ($1,000)	Government payments: Percent of farms
	117	118	119	120	121	122	123	124	125	126	127	128	129	130	131	132
PENNSYLVANIA—Cont'd																
Potter	98	1.1	219	0.0	45.5	750,104	3,429	110,415	39.2	87,756	27.4	72.6	7	74.3	1,139	44.7
Schuylkill	97	-8.4	141	0.4	69.7	939,868	6,645	133,965	143.4	209,400	46.5	53.5	15	74.2	1,655	42.2
Snyder	99	8.6	115	0.7	71.4	839,894	7,332	109,041	200.4	231,888	16.1	83.9	39	64.4	1,125	17.4
Somerset	219	2.1	190	0.2	136.3	612,870	3,223	111,459	115.4	100,216	31.5	68.5	40	62.6	1,265	17.5
Sullivan	43	15.9	229	0.0	20.9	934,952	4,091	109,248	12.2	64,121	31.4	68.6	NA	72.1	495	34.7
Susquehanna	154	-7.2	170	0.2	71.7	805,158	4,740	101,463	49.8	54,758	29.5	70.5	11	76.2	500	24.2
Tioga	213	3.7	202	0.5	123.2	765,228	3,797	98,872	92.3	87,363	27.9	72.1	20	71.8	1,925	39.8
Union	66	-29.5	114	0.2	49.8	1,098,979	9,599	114,872	147.4	256,829	12.7	87.3	24	52.1	800	19.2
Venango	53	-13.3	130	0.1	30.1	495,109	3,797	82,682	14.8	36,137	58.9	41.1	NA	76.3	357	14.7
Warren	68	-17.3	151	0.1	30.4	521,904	3,461	71,238	21.3	47,029	26.3	73.7	1	68.6	157	13.9
Washington	190	-7.5	108	1.0	90.9	704,588	6,511	85,650	37.0	21,022	64.3	35.7	6	74.2	399	8.5
Wayne	101	-10.9	157	0.1	46.3	675,611	4,294	82,875	29.4	45,892	31.6	68.4	4	78.4	211	10.2
Westmoreland	144	0.8	131	0.2	93.4	775,756	5,909	108,523	66.3	60,346	50.7	49.3	13	72.2	1,265	19.1
Wyoming	61	-10.8	150	0.1	29.5	619,664	4,144	78,912	13.2	32,300	49.6	50.4	1	73.9	407	23.7
York	253	-3.6	122	0.7	199.2	1,002,707	8,201	105,570	260.9	126,235	51.7	48.3	25	74.5	4,781	17.8
RHODE ISLAND	57	-18.3	55	3.0	17.7	897,835	16,468	62,786	58.0	55,607	70.5	29.5	22	84.1	1,037	7.0
Bristol	1	D	33	0.0	0.7	1,500,196	45,085	66,112	1.0	25,125	37.2	62.8	NA	75.0	D	2.5
Kent	10	D	87	0.1	1.1	1,227,510	14,155	49,665	3.1	27,856	74.9	25.1	NA	81.1	D	5.4
Newport	10	-16.0	50	0.4	5.3	1,209,495	24,407	80,755	19.3	98,367	62.7	37.3	1	81.1	158	7.1
Providence	16	D	43	0.4	4.2	617,448	14,256	46,482	12.4	32,979	72.7	27.3	7	82.5	218	6.6
Washington	20	-27.2	62	2.0	6.3	847,467	13,608	75,161	22.2	69,561	77.0	23.0	14	90.0	632	8.5
SOUTH CAROLINA	4,745	-4.6	191	210.4	2,035.3	683,873	3,573	83,077	3,008.7	121,364	36.4	63.6	75	72.6	55,192	21.4
Abbeville	89	-3.8	154	0.3	18.8	475,695	3,096	45,030	9.2	15,891	15.7	84.3	1	78.0	643	22.9
Aiken	163	5.4	130	8.5	62.9	490,520	3,767	74,216	137.4	109,990	21.2	78.8	NA	77.3	440	8.7
Allendale	87	-30.4	525	5.9	35.3	1,157,218	2,206	131,114	15.3	92,739	82.0	18.0	NA	50.9	2,259	72.1
Anderson	184	15.5	105	0.6	69.9	598,456	5,675	59,960	75.2	43,144	13.4	86.6	NA	72.1	1,896	15.6
Bamberg	103	10.9	289	9.4	53.5	847,270	2,932	106,214	36.9	104,048	62.1	37.9	NA	74.6	2,126	54.4
Barnwell	74	-15.4	201	4.9	33.3	561,132	2,785	85,317	35.3	95,745	43.2	56.8	NA	69.9	1,556	30.4
Beaufort	56	32.7	348	2.0	7.1	1,258,884	3,622	58,947	20.3	126,006	94.7	5.3	3	78.3	80	9.9
Berkeley	100	33.6	296	0.7	18.1	790,654	2,673	80,348	5.0	14,885	85.4	14.6	NA	66.1	403	12.7
Calhoun	149	25.6	310	24.5	79.9	945,231	3,051	152,649	80.8	168,329	73.0	27.0	1	80.0	3,859	40.6
Charleston	38	6.0	93	0.6	9.7	873,600	9,369	63,570	22.4	55,536	83.6	16.4	1	76.7	D	2.0
Cherokee	61	-5.0	148	D	20.9	497,342	3,364	69,235	33.4	80,407	26.8	73.2	1	66.7	504	17.1
Chester	96	0.5	186	0.2	25.0	616,832	3,323	58,274	31.1	60,077	22.4	77.6	NA	68.1	671	22.8
Chesterfield	126	-4.0	198	1.6	50.7	583,564	2,952	81,283	128.1	201,390	15.2	84.8	NA	69.5	784	21.5
Clarendon	137	-21.3	359	8.9	102.8	816,645	2,274	128,382	108.6	284,979	47.3	52.7	2	65.9	1,608	49.6
Colleton	168	-10.5	366	2.4	40.7	1,109,808	3,030	86,861	20.3	44,266	76.9	23.1	6	71.9	724	16.1
Darlington	144	-18.5	447	6.1	97.1	1,161,402	2,596	170,002	88.2	274,019	55.6	44.4	8	74.8	1,167	27.6
Dillon	91	-14.4	502	0.4	71.8	1,150,361	2,291	197,314	113.1	621,159	28.5	71.5	NA	74.2	1,230	62.6
Dorchester	74	-0.9	206	1.7	32.4	579,913	2,811	100,333	39.9	111,589	36.6	63.4	NA	68.4	901	23.7
Edgefield	79	-3.6	198	8.9	23.2	697,738	3,527	66,385	37.7	94,967	66.6	33.4	NA	76.3	689	17.4
Fairfield	73	64.2	321	0.2	10.8	918,819	2,867	54,829	16.7	73,417	10.2	89.8	NA	64.0	98	10.1
Florence	146	-6.5	270	1.3	103.5	855,509	3,166	102,599	45.3	83,848	97.6	2.4	NA	67.6	1,563	36.5
Georgetown	80	21.0	484	0.2	13.4	988,048	2,043	84,996	9.3	55,861	98.2	1.8	2	74.7	693	42.8
Greenville	59	-18.5	57	1.5	17.0	526,644	9,188	40,726	13.3	12,861	75.6	24.4	9	74.1	290	6.7
Greenwood	72	-15.5	155	0.2	15.1	529,780	3,416	53,938	9.8	20,961	17.6	82.4	NA	79.8	367	13.7
Hampton	107	-23.3	441	8.5	42.3	1,074,779	2,439	129,432	30.5	125,959	98.9	1.1	1	63.6	2,346	57.4
Horry	171	-4.0	222	2.3	117.5	1,002,891	4,510	128,399	87.8	114,536	80.9	19.1	8	71.1	2,287	37.2
Jasper	63	-8.0	468	D	11.9	1,712,283	3,661	101,313	D	D	D	D	NA	73.3	123	15.6
Kershaw	79	-4.6	170	0.4	19.8	523,961	3,089	58,053	137.5	295,155	2.3	97.7	NA	65.5	269	8.6
Lancaster	63	-3.1	118	0.5	17.2	466,819	3,952	63,920	57.1	106,919	6.1	93.9	NA	76.4	91	5.4
Laurens	122	-0.3	146	0.4	40.9	558,251	3,834	65,424	70.9	84,400	13.0	87.0	5	77.9	957	17.9
Lee	110	-22.6	330	15.6	75.2	797,300	2,416	156,323	95.3	285,278	38.4	61.6	NA	65.0	2,612	44.9
Lexington	103	-4.7	90	13.2	47.8	499,227	5,533	77,434	222.2	195,412	32.5	67.5	9	79.6	600	9.3
McCormick	41	35.5	442	D	3.9	886,483	2,004	87,978	D	D	D	D	NA	72.8	D	19.6
Marion	50	-37.2	256	0.5	27.9	596,308	2,331	120,416	22.4	113,761	55.1	44.9	1	74.1	867	46.7
Marlboro	90	-20.3	449	3.5	55.8	865,333	1,927	162,975	79.8	397,060	38.1	61.9	2	70.1	1,856	43.8
Newberry	95	-9.3	156	1.2	31.6	517,675	3,314	74,874	143.0	235,506	4.3	95.7	3	68.4	850	27.0
Oconee	62	-7.9	77	0.4	18.9	489,668	6,385	71,668	159.4	195,610	2.9	97.1	3	74.8	635	16.4
Orangeburg	294	3.8	300	38.0	165.5	906,458	3,018	139,771	213.9	218,724	50.1	49.9	NA	69.5	9,879	30.6
Pickens	39	-12.5	53	0.2	12.2	374,709	7,050	43,935	6.6	8,972	56.2	43.8	NA	75.3	194	5.7
Richland	52	-13.9	119	1.6	22.2	571,315	4,797	67,954	32.3	73,314	44.5	55.5	3	75.7	960	13.4
Saluda	119	10.7	208	5.4	33.3	643,937	3,093	108,040	159.5	277,916	11.8	88.2	1	68.5	540	18.6
Spartanburg	96	-5.9	67	1.8	34.3	550,282	8,231	45,163	30.5	21,292	70.4	29.6	NA	78.4	481	7.9

STATE County	Water use, 2015		Wholesale Trade[1], 2017				Retail Trade[2], 2017				Real estate and rental and leasing,[2] 2017			
	Public supply water withdrawn (mil gal/ day)	Public supply gallons withdrawn per person per day	Number of establish-ments	Number of employees	Sales (mil dol)	Average payroll (mil dol)	Number of establish-ments	Number of employees	Sales (mil dol)	Average payroll (mil dol)	Number of establish-ments	Number of employees	Sales (mil dol)	Average payroll (mil dol)
	133	134	135	136	137	138	139	140	141	142	143	144	145	146
PENNSYLVANIA—Cont'd														
Potter	0.9	53.2	D	D	D	0.6	71	611	164.1	14.4	D	D	D	0.3
Schuylkill	23.4	161.7	92	1,418	688.7	53.7	454	5,467	1,388.2	125.7	62	239	49.1	10.5
Snyder	1.6	39.6	31	537	227.6	26.4	186	3,035	725.1	63.8	13	71	13.4	2.8
Somerset	22.6	299.4	76	806	296.7	35.5	248	2,628	798.3	66.3	40	119	24.3	4.2
Sullivan	0.7	102.7	NA	NA	NA	NA	28	169	48.3	3.7	D	D	D	D
Susquehanna	1.4	33.8	28	268	262.2	11.4	134	1,203	440.5	31.3	16	63	15.7	3.7
Tioga	2.0	48.5	23	300	167.4	13.0	156	1,722	502.3	42.1	26	79	14.4	2.9
Union	2.9	63.8	31	329	102.6	12.6	137	1,848	540.6	43.0	22	122	19.2	3.8
Venango	4.7	88.1	D	D	D	D	193	2,430	623.8	54.7	28	96	13.7	2.0
Warren	3.1	76.0	D	D	D	D	128	2,226	597.5	53.4	19	33	5.4	0.9
Washington	39.7	190.7	221	3,334	2,325.8	209.3	642	9,024	2,763.2	230.3	174	1,282	411.7	77.7
Wayne	2.4	46.5	29	318	134.9	17.9	206	2,872	3,116.2	82.6	31	112	17.0	3.7
Westmoreland	24.2	67.6	305	6,191	8,592.3	350.3	1,206	18,468	5,515.6	488.9	271	961	211.8	33.9
Wyoming	0.7	23.7	21	466	138.5	22.1	111	1,280	425.5	31.4	16	55	13.5	3.7
York	34.8	78.6	340	7,055	6,755.3	384.1	1,212	21,792	6,119.8	538.5	291	1,983	410.2	81.0
RHODE ISLAND	97.5	92.3	1,107	16,847	13,636.5	1,042.1	3,769	48,753	13,843.5	1,444.4	1,110	5,287	1,351.1	247.7
Bristol	0.0	0.2	50	584	257.4	27.3	138	1,154	297.5	33.8	44	163	35.5	6.5
Kent	1.0	6.3	206	3,623	4,220.6	230.4	662	11,557	3,554.6	343.4	183	1,188	320.5	51.5
Newport	7.2	87.4	69	605	860.7	46.3	427	4,053	1,125.2	120.7	115	540	130.3	25.2
Providence	80.1	126.4	661	10,895	7,632.1	660.6	2,023	24,975	6,772.8	730.6	627	3,025	745.3	148.8
Washington	9.2	72.3	121	1,140	665.7	77.4	519	7,014	2,093.4	215.9	141	371	119.5	15.8
SOUTH CAROLINA	633.4	129.4	4,360	61,421	57,337.4	3,537.8	17,700	253,384	69,980.1	6,205.6	5,890	26,764	6,509.7	1,128.5
Abbeville	2.0	79.0	4	D	17.8	D	61	534	108.0	8.5	NA	NA	NA	NA
Aiken	32.0	193.0	65	629	346.3	27.3	506	7,319	2,013.6	171.6	106	358	67.8	13.1
Allendale	1.2	126.2	8	52	66.3	2.7	28	149	45.2	3.4	NA	NA	NA	NA
Anderson	19.0	97.6	170	2,971	3,006.5	177.4	701	9,535	2,445.5	227.4	159	465	122.3	16.4
Bamberg	0.9	61.8	D	D	D	D	56	492	126.1	10.4	NA	NA	NA	NA
Barnwell	1.5	70.9	D	D	D	D	68	733	154.6	14.6	7	14	2.7	0.3
Beaufort	12.8	71.1	125	695	337.2	32.5	787	10,709	2,821.7	270.2	466	1,879	444.5	85.8
Berkeley	70.3	346.9	154	2,623	4,535.4	181.8	442	7,661	2,150.7	186.5	179	690	189.7	34.2
Calhoun	1.1	75.1	D	D	D	D	34	269	86.8	6.5	D	D	D	1.0
Charleston	4.5	11.6	473	5,705	4,203.3	345.9	2,023	29,351	8,586.0	804.8	1,038	4,541	1,173.0	222.3
Cherokee	9.0	159.8	28	456	138.3	18.1	218	2,955	771.3	57.0	35	132	24.5	4.6
Chester	3.2	98.6	13	142	205.2	9.2	99	929	186.9	18.2	12	23	4.8	0.8
Chesterfield	5.8	126.7	25	474	240.6	21.5	133	1,357	325.3	27.8	15	36	35.9	1.0
Clarendon	2.3	68.4	15	91	44.3	4.2	105	1,262	344.4	27.3	14	21	3.4	0.5
Colleton	2.1	54.9	28	183	97.9	7.9	139	1,698	430.8	36.3	43	107	31.1	4.2
Darlington	6.4	94.9	55	495	731.5	24.2	219	2,408	563.2	51.9	31	91	19.9	2.7
Dillon	4.6	146.0	12	219	107.8	10.8	115	1,170	354.8	24.4	25	47	6.1	1.3
Dorchester	33.0	216.7	75	648	324.4	34.2	325	4,875	1,271.2	105.9	135	419	113.0	15.7
Edgefield	4.5	171.2	D	D	D	D	48	438	141.4	9.6	11	25	3.0	0.8
Fairfield	1.9	82.6	D	D	D	D	60	507	218.4	13.2	12	20	3.7	0.7
Florence	15.7	113.0	163	2,638	2,417.1	127.3	668	9,456	2,500.5	217.1	130	546	116.9	21.9
Georgetown	8.9	145.4	D	D	D	D	293	3,330	833.4	83.2	94	549	74.4	18.7
Greenville	45.9	93.3	776	11,331	16,046.6	730.0	1,783	27,942	7,610.7	708.7	744	3,383	937.5	144.5
Greenwood	4.9	69.4	53	D	628.1	D	281	3,951	921.8	86.1	D	D	D	D
Hampton	1.5	73.3	8	180	219.3	9.3	79	618	168.9	13.9	6	D	2.1	D
Horry	50.1	162.1	258	2,517	1,071.9	111.7	1,732	24,447	6,602.4	593.4	696	4,708	769.1	162.4
Jasper	27.3	981.2	28	708	444.2	39.3	105	2,233	911.7	63.0	23	64	20.9	3.3
Kershaw	5.3	83.8	27	124	71.4	6.4	194	2,222	686.7	55.2	35	96	15.7	2.9
Lancaster	21.0	244.5	54	1,265	975.7	67.1	242	3,071	781.9	70.7	71	148	31.0	6.4
Laurens	4.9	73.7	29	205	89.6	11.9	172	1,817	436.9	39.2	25	59	10.1	1.6
Lee	2.5	141.9	10	75	111.6	4.3	41	326	82.4	6.8	NA	NA	NA	NA
Lexington	52.2	185.3	307	6,339	4,583.1	350.8	1,098	19,592	5,858.3	481.7	308	1,280	350.1	53.3
McCormick	1.0	98.9	NA	NA	NA	NA	20	138	27.7	2.1	NA	NA	NA	NA
Marion	3.4	107.4	19	173	136.0	6.9	110	1,075	235.3	23.1	15	41	13.0	1.2
Marlboro	3.9	141.8	D	D	D	4.5	86	825	177.4	16.9	11	28	3.5	0.6
Newberry	6.6	173.1	28	270	208.8	14.3	129	1,516	431.0	34.3	23	72	19.9	2.9
Oconee	10.8	142.9	40	410	225.2	16.0	253	3,122	879.8	74.8	94	264	43.5	10.8
Orangeburg	9.0	100.4	52	771	609.2	40.1	338	3,887	1,018.7	85.7	45	146	24.6	4.9
Pickens	33.0	271.3	68	565	300.1	27.6	346	5,359	1,476.9	133.2	75	216	54.8	8.0
Richland	31.4	77.2	338	5,581	4,495.1	349.3	1,244	19,812	5,482.7	506.7	477	2,967	988.6	146.9
Saluda	0.0	1.5	9	54	16.3	1.3	47	360	117.4	8.2	D	D	D	0.7
Spartanburg	34.7	116.8	397	5,908	5,925.6	346.8	1,032	16,413	4,906.4	419.0	265	1,110	356.2	40.1

1 Merchant wholesalers, except manufacturers' sales branches and offices. 2. Employer establishments.

STATE County	Professional, scientific, and technical services, 2017				Manufacturing, 2017				Accommodation and food services, 2017			
	Number of establish-ments	Number of employees	Sales (mil dol)	Average payroll (mil dol)	Number of establish-ments	Number of employees	Sales (mil dol)	Average payroll (mil dol)	Number of establis-hments	Number of employees	Sales (mil dol)	Annual payroll (mil dol)
	147	148	149	150	151	152	153	154	155	156	157	158
PENNSYLVANIA—Cont'd												
Potter	D	D	17.7	D	19	551	122.1	22.8	43	260	13.2	3.3
Schuylkill	D	D	D	D	168	9,350	3,255.8	475.8	262	2,682	137.6	34.8
Snyder	35	211	23.6	11.0	71	4,096	814.6	160.8	84	1,863	86.7	27.1
Somerset	D	D	D	D	102	2,713	903.0	132.0	170	3,462	146.1	43.0
Sullivan	D	D	2.1	D	D	D	D	D	D	D	D	0.9
Susquehanna	57	264	27.7	10.1	60	546	116.5	23.5	83	764	47.6	11.9
Tioga	47	220	20.5	8.6	38	1,782	404.5	85.1	95	1,288	69.5	19.6
Union	D	D	D	D	40	1,304	389.9	73.1	96	2,048	102.5	30.8
Venango	D	D	D	D	83	3,787	925.5	187.4	98	1,239	52.5	15.1
Warren	D	D	D	D	56	2,952	2,121.0	151.8	73	954	42.7	12.0
Washington	D	D	D	D	216	8,571	3,060.6	500.5	422	7,014	354.9	95.4
Wayne	86	296	35.8	13.3	47	550	112.4	25.2	167	1,722	195.9	49.8
Westmoreland	D	D	1,472.8	D	519	17,333	6,427.6	975.3	773	13,585	637.3	178.0
Wyoming	D	D	D	D	D	2,376	D	152.8	63	635	36.1	9.9
York	697	6,496	884.4	397.1	517	29,074	11,501.2	1,589.0	785	14,306	706.4	195.4
RHODE ISLAND	3,011	23,479	3,990.0	1,517.2	1,340	40,221	12,416.3	2,390.2	3,167	50,642	3,617.9	1,016.4
Bristol	105	393	51.8	21.5	80	1,823	399.8	92.9	130	1,618	95.3	29.4
Kent	534	3,962	478.5	183.9	180	5,515	3,168.5	394.8	471	8,824	523.1	150.3
Newport	338	3,930	626.2	253.5	67	2,258	361.3	206.5	382	6,122	566.0	164.6
Providence	D	D	D	D	860	22,092	6,137.3	1,165.6	1,706	28,025	1,995.1	547.5
Washington	D	D	D	D	153	8,533	2,349.4	530.4	478	6,053	438.4	124.8
SOUTH CAROLINA	10,818	99,953	16,957.5	6,465.3	3,827	225,237	138,586.5	12,777.4	10,847	223,081	13,385.0	3,666.5
Abbeville	15	36	3.0	1.0	30	1,561	505.8	75.6	32	345	16.3	4.9
Aiken	228	1,927	295.2	124.2	79	7,434	3,766.6	481.1	283	5,185	271.0	74.5
Allendale	D	D	10.1	D	6	739	617.0	45.4	D	D	D	D
Anderson	D	D	D	D	192	12,576	6,161.0	627.0	388	7,170	360.9	98.3
Bamberg	D	D	7.0	D	20	946	194.9	38.4	24	202	10.1	2.5
Barnwell	24	123	13.0	5.0	16	1,172	427.6	67.8	32	502	22.0	5.7
Beaufort	650	2,544	405.8	147.6	74	505	112.3	23.7	568	13,544	984.4	287.2
Berkeley	D	D	D	D	80	5,332	5,380.9	396.4	292	5,395	289.0	77.9
Calhoun	D	D	D	D	21	1,076	1,975.4	69.2	8	70	2.8	0.7
Charleston	1,902	17,127	3,169.0	1,245.3	313	14,857	33,467.9	989.1	1,417	34,621	2,471.9	694.7
Cherokee	D	D	D	D	63	6,418	3,630.3	309.7	90	1,764	92.3	24.6
Chester	30	127	14.9	4.6	45	2,848	1,174.5	157.3	47	698	33.1	9.1
Chesterfield	D	D	9.2	D	55	5,383	1,900.0	293.9	64	1,041	46.3	14.5
Clarendon	23	74	11.0	4.6	22	590	403.9	26.9	57	692	37.8	9.3
Colleton	48	302	49.8	13.4	27	661	196.4	28.0	79	1,495	94.6	24.6
Darlington	62	291	28.4	10.6	53	2,589	1,461.6	171.3	95	1,498	74.7	18.7
Dillon	23	404	11.6	5.0	13	1,538	441.7	54.2	56	802	39.9	10.3
Dorchester	207	1,860	205.2	75.7	92	5,806	2,479.6	371.8	210	3,859	197.2	56.9
Edgefield	D	D	D	D	21	825	316.5	40.8	26	199	9.5	2.5
Fairfield	D	D	D	D	17	1,158	511.7	62.2	21	212	10.4	2.9
Florence	D	D	D	D	91	6,689	3,875.4	407.0	319	6,530	336.7	95.6
Georgetown	171	848	151.6	45.9	55	2,232	1,209.0	166.5	168	3,071	196.7	53.8
Greenville	D	D	4,663.8	D	534	28,456	11,987.3	1,713.9	1,221	24,344	1,409.4	388.2
Greenwood	D	D	D	D	60	4,839	2,774.9	283.9	121	2,644	130.5	35.3
Hampton	13	143	30.8	14.6	12	418	142.1	23.4	33	301	16.1	3.9
Horry	D	D	D	D	152	2,810	688.2	131.3	1,337	31,091	2,296.6	597.3
Jasper	40	268	31.2	11.7	22	298	61.3	11.7	64	806	53.2	13.7
Kershaw	D	D	D	D	52	3,083	1,314.0	161.4	99	1,581	78.4	20.4
Lancaster	119	3,559	478.9	166.7	47	2,266	974.6	107.8	112	2,142	118.6	31.9
Laurens	51	281	29.2	14.4	75	8,565	2,305.9	396.5	80	1,354	60.6	16.3
Lee	D	D	3.1	D	12	216	148.1	13.5	D	D	D	D
Lexington	D	D	D	D	198	7,670	3,428.8	435.1	568	11,565	594.2	162.7
McCormick	4	16	0.5	0.1	4	267	123.8	11.6	D	D	D	D
Marion	25	95	5.9	2.1	13	1,155	262.7	36.0	46	825	37.5	9.4
Marlboro	D	D	D	D	21	1,862	972.7	94.1	26	333	18.1	4.9
Newberry	50	168	18.9	6.4	44	4,594	1,874.7	189.9	67	935	48.0	12.7
Oconee	131	507	53.3	19.8	76	4,828	2,064.9	280.3	130	1,704	92.7	24.3
Orangeburg	D	D	D	D	75	5,107	2,356.6	250.1	183	3,454	175.0	43.9
Pickens	D	D	D	D	94	5,247	1,929.0	249.1	231	4,993	240.2	69.8
Richland	1,191	13,054	2,558.9	888.4	195	9,510	4,725.3	618.8	950	20,811	1,104.5	301.6
Saluda	D	D	D	D	11	2,097	630.3	71.0	13	100	6.4	1.6
Spartanburg	D	D	D	D	407	29,294	21,377.8	1,729.6	578	11,099	592.3	163.7

STATE County	Health care and social assistance, 2017				Other services, 2017				Nonemployer businesses, 2019		Value of residential construction authorized by building permits, 2021	
	Number of establish-ments	Number of employees	Receipts (mil dol)	Annual payroll (mil dol)	Number of establish-ments	Number of employees	Receipts (mil dol)	Annual payroll (mil dol)	Number	Receipts (mil dol)	New construction ($1,000)	Number of housing units
	159	160	161	162	163	164	165	166	167	168	169	170
PENNSYLVANIA—Cont'd												
Potter	38	933	113.8	39.9	D	D	9.6	D	1,133	52.8	3,221	24
Schuylkill	371	8,260	826.1	317.9	243	1,079	90.4	25.0	6,760	329.2	33,452	139
Snyder	94	1,849	141.4	56.7	73	318	32.8	7.9	2,881	150.5	11,895	57
Somerset	175	3,380	295.2	125.2	153	670	60.6	14.5	4,466	194.5	15,751	65
Sullivan	D	D	D	D	D	D	4.1	D	457	23.5	4,288	15
Susquehanna	61	1,141	79.7	34.3	70	316	37.1	7.7	3,039	162.1	14,139	59
Tioga	97	1,664	167.4	60.8	66	286	29.0	6.8	2,459	105.0	7,566	41
Union	139	3,935	416.2	189.2	73	353	33.2	7.6	2,823	147.2	26,037	55
Venango	178	3,157	276.6	123.5	109	413	41.9	8.9	2,708	111.1	6,769	31
Warren	128	3,419	257.3	133.3	77	334	25.7	6.3	2,074	89.1	3,917	27
Washington	733	14,226	1,389.6	594.5	437	2,197	252.8	66.5	13,140	683.8	192,656	692
Wayne	132	2,517	243.9	92.5	107	665	63.6	17.3	3,985	204.9	37,590	133
Westmoreland	1,178	20,721	1,835.5	795.6	811	4,592	574.7	127.0	21,856	1,004.6	149,124	679
Wyoming	63	511	44.1	20.2	55	207	21.9	5.6	1,747	77.9	8,345	25
York	988	26,954	3,178.4	1,260.7	795	5,081	513.5	146.4	26,978	1,354.1	250,114	1,316
RHODE ISLAND	3,177	87,546	9,574.0	4,092.1	2,318	13,882	1,772.9	471.0	85,116	3,983.3	328,495	1,392
Bristol	130	3,202	157.0	87.5	118	541	54.7	17.8	4,607	226.0	14,345	60
Kent	561	12,532	1,363.8	593.5	399	2,297	278.1	74.3	12,485	598.6	39,168	291
Newport	215	4,980	396.0	172.8	216	1,298	142.5	43.9	8,391	442.3	64,287	133
Providence	1,897	59,341	6,916.1	2,929.2	1,307	8,239	1,073.6	289.6	47,388	2,072.1	101,220	540
Washington	374	7,491	741.2	309.1	278	1,507	224.0	45.4	12,245	644.4	109,474	368
SOUTH CAROLINA	10,588	244,198	29,454.9	11,050.5	7,068	46,847	5,653.1	1,528.9	380,729	17,256.8	11,652,262	50,680
Abbeville	28	471	43.6	18.1	D	D	D	D	1,442	51.8	21,649	148
Aiken	337	6,219	576.6	218.3	201	1,021	114.3	27.8	11,819	454.5	412,648	1,644
Allendale	D	D	D	D	D	D	D	D	473	10.7	457	2
Anderson	361	9,714	1,123.4	413.5	233	1,189	170.1	40.4	13,486	568.3	290,885	1,425
Bamberg	37	689	44.0	18.4	D	D	D	1.2	847	25.1	1,537	6
Barnwell	24	397	32.1	12.4	27	127	17.1	3.7	1,358	38.8	527	4
Beaufort	495	8,205	947.2	359.7	329	2,696	327.8	93.6	18,406	1,012.9	943,049	2,827
Berkeley	254	3,143	262.6	117.5	214	1,159	125.3	34.2	16,118	691.7	695,610	3,121
Calhoun	D	D	D	D	D	D	D	D	933	45.5	0	0
Charleston	1,414	31,729	5,356.1	1,759.0	888	6,113	838.6	222.7	42,837	2,423.0	995,027	3,863
Cherokee	69	1,156	89.9	38.5	58	291	33.0	8.0	2,620	91.9	32,690	173
Chester	52	607	68.9	24.7	37	145	13.7	3.8	1,738	58.6	23,014	78
Chesterfield	95	1,735	127.2	54.9	37	117	9.3	2.8	2,373	78.4	28,138	134
Clarendon	37	1,259	71.6	33.9	24	158	13.6	4.3	2,271	88.9	13,455	84
Colleton	74	1,332	157.8	60.0	36	149	11.7	2.8	3,224	130.4	30,354	73
Darlington	109	2,967	221.9	100.7	62	350	33.7	8.4	3,551	127.8	25,151	143
Dillon	53	1,469	132.7	72.9	32	82	8.2	2.3	1,657	56.7	4,387	42
Dorchester	262	4,033	379.7	144.3	182	902	90.2	29.1	11,370	456.4	361,329	1,298
Edgefield	21	487	44.0	15.2	20	343	65.8	18.1	1,641	59.0	52,596	194
Fairfield	D	D	D	D	D	D	D	D	1,459	46.1	16,615	55
Florence	373	14,668	1,954.1	724.6	197	1,418	194.8	40.8	8,766	377.4	109,820	623
Georgetown	255	3,851	497.4	190.8	122	709	58.3	17.0	5,897	277.0	202,232	665
Greenville	1,223	30,021	3,252.3	1,355.8	784	6,027	846.5	210.6	44,368	2,091.1	1,539,475	7,964
Greenwood	131	4,709	555.7	203.3	D	D	D	D	4,030	150.1	51,104	282
Hampton	26	713	45.8	19.6	D	D	D	D	1,216	42.8	2,525	11
Horry	734	12,191	1,694.7	573.6	554	3,147	338.1	83.9	29,766	1,494.9	1,300,500	6,970
Jasper	46	1,117	120.2	38.4	48	244	24.2	7.6	2,264	117.2	206,351	871
Kershaw	D	D	D	D	72	372	31.2	12.4	4,693	198.4	119,449	753
Lancaster	149	2,528	283.3	107.2	113	1,082	117.3	50.6	6,562	262.5	521,219	1,445
Laurens	81	1,787	171.3	64.9	64	288	23.2	8.9	3,697	136.9	27,264	185
Lee	13	177	13.1	5.0	D	D	3.8	D	808	26.8	1,322	8
Lexington	570	13,906	1,453.7	549.0	508	3,350	371.3	116.0	21,574	956.7	700,714	2,692
McCormick	D	D	D	D	D	D	D	D	551	18.7	53,955	165
Marion	73	861	77.7	30.4	31	101	11.9	2.2	1,658	54.1	10,201	70
Marlboro	40	673	50.0	21.5	17	74	5.1	1.3	1,075	34.9	2,038	12
Newberry	66	1,473	126.1	49.9	55	229	25.2	7.2	2,213	78.7	37,113	152
Oconee	126	2,255	247.8	84.2	93	757	86.3	19.9	5,199	211.3	195,693	643
Orangeburg	213	4,281	420.0	170.7	92	410	43.1	11.1	5,235	179.5	13,121	90
Pickens	188	3,662	365.8	137.6	144	706	107.3	18.2	8,316	376.6	321,410	1,030
Richland	1,006	32,281	4,425.0	1,636.6	657	5,503	599.1	182.3	29,644	1,279.9	609,894	3,263
Saluda	D	D	D	D	D	D	D	D	1,074	41.2	23,446	118
Spartanburg	574	16,460	1,784.2	848.3	425	3,014	399.0	96.3	23,066	1,156.3	595,993	3,614

STATE County	Government employment and payroll, 2017: Full-time equivalent employees	Government employment and payroll, 2017: March payroll (dollars)	March payroll (percent of total): Administration, judicial, and legal	March payroll (percent of total): Police and corrections	March payroll (percent of total): Fire protection	March payroll (percent of total): Highways and transportation	March payroll (percent of total): Health and welfare	March payroll (percent of total): Natural resources and utilities	March payroll (percent of total): Education and libraries	Local government finances, 2017, General revenue: Total (mil dol)	General revenue: Intergovernmental (mil dol)	Taxes: Total (mil dol)	Taxes: Per capita[1] (dollars): Total	Taxes: Per capita[1] (dollars): Property
	171	172	173	174	175	176	177	178	179	180	181	182	183	184
PENNSYLVANIA—Cont'd														
Potter	578	2,313,263	12.7	5.7	0.0	3.9	9.4	3.3	64.6	74.4	41.7	24.7	1,464	1,231
Schuylkill	4,341	16,802,653	7.2	7.4	0.8	5.7	5.0	5.0	68.2	524.0	249.6	194.9	1,367	993
Snyder	953	3,640,204	6.7	8.4	0.0	3.7	3.6	2.8	73.7	127.2	47.3	58.1	1,430	970
Somerset	2,152	7,566,757	8.6	5.0	0.0	4.6	2.2	3.7	70.3	244.2	127.6	89.3	1,203	967
Sullivan	179	756,018	16.5	1.8	0.0	5.6	4.2	2.6	68.6	27.6	11.8	12.9	2,097	1,876
Susquehanna	1,356	5,322,865	6.3	4.6	0.2	3.6	1.6	1.0	80.2	176.5	96.9	59.4	1,450	1,286
Tioga	1,397	5,193,310	8.1	6.3	0.7	3.8	13.5	3.2	62.9	173.2	87.5	60.9	1,497	1,188
Union	1,435	6,048,458	5.9	5.0	0.0	2.1	3.2	3.7	78.7	179.8	76.5	60.2	1,349	952
Venango	1,804	6,783,791	8.2	6.3	2.2	4.4	6.9	3.2	67.7	223.0	128.8	62.2	1,201	949
Warren	1,355	5,345,706	8.1	7.5	1.0	4.8	15.5	3.2	59.0	151.0	67.9	48.8	1,230	921
Washington	6,306	26,355,798	6.3	7.8	1.4	3.4	8.5	3.6	67.7	903.9	421.9	346.7	1,674	1,252
Wayne	1,903	7,949,235	6.3	5.2	0.0	2.9	5.8	1.5	76.3	242.5	84.1	138.7	2,710	2,585
Westmoreland	10,133	45,166,775	5.7	8.6	0.1	3.8	7.2	7.9	65.0	1,369.5	545.8	559.0	1,588	1,235
Wyoming	897	3,100,744	17.5	6.4	0.0	3.5	1.1	1.4	67.4	125.5	55.3	48.8	1,782	1,505
York	11,962	52,520,313	6.6	13.8	1.8	2.1	5.9	3.5	63.6	1,957.2	680.8	911.8	2,047	1,668
RHODE ISLAND	X	X	X	X	X	X	X	X	X	X	X	X	X	X
Bristol	1,410	7,796,071	3.5	7.9	2.3	3.1	1.3	5.9	75.5	235.1	48.9	162.8	3,341	3,275
Kent	4,906	26,300,714	3.0	10.1	10.8	2.2	1.7	3.7	67.1	688.7	144.3	459.8	2,811	2,744
Newport	2,464	13,368,879	4.9	12.1	9.0	2.5	1.7	4.9	63.5	405.5	83.5	256.3	3,090	2,914
Providence	16,666	91,532,903	3.5	10.2	10.2	2.1	3.1	3.7	66.3	2,617.2	1,008.4	1,292.3	2,038	1,982
Washington	3,857	20,455,795	4.6	9.4	4.3	3.1	1.2	3.3	73.6	613.3	121.0	440.8	3,489	3,431
SOUTH CAROLINA	X	X	X	X	X	X	X	X	X	X	X	X	X	X
Abbeville	907	2,554,601	7.3	9.8	1.2	0.6	8.6	11.0	60.8	65.4	30.2	24.1	980	747
Aiken	4,746	16,744,243	9.9	11.0	0.6	3.4	2.4	5.7	65.3	499.8	189.7	213.4	1,268	903
Allendale	534	1,689,533	6.7	9.2	3.8	0.9	39.6	5.0	33.2	29.9	15.2	10.9	1,210	1,122
Anderson	5,811	20,434,065	6.5	10.1	1.6	1.7	0.7	6.4	71.6	563.8	243.3	204.1	1,030	811
Bamberg	591	1,801,219	12.7	10.4	1.0	2.5	0.0	2.5	69.2	48.0	25.1	18.0	1,252	1,089
Barnwell	987	3,123,982	5.2	10.1	0.5	1.1	7.1	3.9	69.8	91.9	50.2	21.1	988	836
Beaufort	6,493	28,262,745	6.2	8.9	5.4	1.4	29.7	4.0	40.7	699.5	148.1	417.4	2,238	1,855
Berkeley	6,056	20,937,267	6.4	8.5	1.8	1.7	1.6	4.8	72.8	683.5	351.4	240.3	1,120	808
Calhoun	428	1,388,007	4.8	8.4	0.9	2.1	6.0	5.1	68.3	36.7	16.2	15.1	1,026	939
Charleston	13,441	53,983,648	9.8	15.9	10.1	4.4	3.4	12.5	41.6	2,195.3	429.8	1,273.9	3,169	1,783
Cherokee	1,841	6,406,214	4.1	8.1	1.6	0.4	1.0	10.3	70.3	154.1	68.6	54.9	965	768
Chester	1,159	3,879,635	10.7	11.7	2.6	0.5	5.4	9.9	57.4	95.5	45.1	34.7	1,075	939
Chesterfield	1,463	4,604,479	6.5	8.3	0.7	0.2	0.1	4.1	75.4	113.4	56.8	46.4	1,009	807
Clarendon	1,382	4,082,937	5.3	8.7	3.1	1.1	17.1	3.6	58.0	122.1	52.9	38.7	1,137	883
Colleton	1,464	4,778,777	13.1	11.1	9.6	2.3	1.0	4.8	55.9	131.0	64.6	54.6	1,453	1,137
Darlington	2,298	7,202,642	5.6	9.7	2.3	1.6	2.3	6.0	70.8	178.3	78.7	71.1	1,062	958
Dillon	1,233	3,617,987	6.2	11.2	3.7	2.4	2.4	5.7	67.6	94.7	52.3	25.8	847	662
Dorchester	5,513	18,312,394	5.7	8.5	4.8	1.4	0.2	4.6	72.9	422.3	198.9	177.7	1,118	885
Edgefield	1,083	3,379,916	6.7	8.1	0.4	1.1	19.2	4.6	58.0	52.4	29.2	18.3	683	617
Fairfield	1,043	3,516,997	8.0	9.1	1.3	1.3	2.1	6.8	68.2	85.4	23.7	55.7	2,464	2,384
Florence	4,880	17,012,925	6.3	8.7	1.8	1.9	9.5	4.5	65.9	462.4	197.3	181.3	1,309	836
Georgetown	2,324	8,144,776	6.5	8.7	8.7	1.8	2.8	8.2	58.8	234.2	71.2	124.4	2,012	1,873
Greenville	23,509	98,678,051	3.4	5.2	3.2	1.1	43.8	5.0	37.5	3,789.4	605.6	670.7	1,323	1,132
Greenwood	4,398	18,097,146	3.9	4.2	1.1	1.6	51.5	5.2	30.7	581.3	105.6	73.7	1,045	922
Hampton	941	3,070,037	6.1	12.6	1.7	1.5	3.4	3.6	69.4	65.6	33.2	26.1	1,339	1,240
Horry	10,279	38,665,530	7.7	11.1	5.5	4.3	1.7	7.6	58.2	1,246.7	310.0	653.9	1,966	1,234
Jasper	793	2,808,151	14.0	12.5	11.3	2.2	2.3	3.1	54.6	93.1	27.2	51.3	1,797	1,441
Kershaw	2,795	11,238,632	3.9	4.6	2.0	0.6	40.9	3.8	44.1	294.0	138.1	62.9	964	827
Lancaster	2,702	9,468,935	4.5	8.3	2.5	1.0	4.0	6.4	68.7	245.0	100.0	109.8	1,188	912
Laurens	2,181	6,252,719	5.8	10.7	2.2	1.2	6.7	7.7	60.4	182.2	98.6	57.2	856	759
Lee	576	1,769,614	11.0	6.8	10.0	1.4	0.5	4.9	65.2	45.5	23.3	20.4	1,170	647
Lexington	16,001	71,004,914	2.3	3.7	1.5	0.5	42.6	2.8	45.9	2,013.7	463.0	460.9	1,588	1,386
McCormick	491	1,209,140	13.0	17.2	1.4	2.5	13.2	13.1	34.4	23.9	8.9	12.9	1,347	1,304
Marion	1,176	3,510,288	5.8	10.1	1.1	0.9	4.8	2.5	72.5	90.2	46.8	30.1	961	724
Marlboro	1,015	2,423,800	10.7	12.2	1.7	1.8	1.7	7.6	60.5	83.4	44.0	25.8	968	789
Newberry	1,694	6,050,329	5.4	6.6	1.4	2.0	27.6	8.9	46.5	182.3	50.8	54.0	1,407	1,230
Oconee	2,515	9,110,006	6.5	10.1	2.6	2.3	0.2	13.5	62.5	205.4	73.7	107.7	1,391	1,298
Orangeburg	4,783	18,322,449	3.9	5.3	0.4	1.1	41.0	4.6	40.8	521.3	120.3	110.8	1,264	1,031
Pickens	3,139	10,514,539	6.7	9.4	1.9	3.0	3.2	8.6	63.8	303.0	125.3	125.4	1,016	790
Richland	14,141	51,288,677	7.2	10.3	4.2	2.9	3.3	8.9	61.8	1,616.8	487.9	851.8	2,069	1,707
Saluda	546	1,726,702	8.0	12.3	0.6	2.6	6.1	4.1	65.1	46.2	22.1	19.1	940	878
Spartanburg	15,616	72,630,964	2.9	4.1	1.5	0.4	54.2	3.4	32.7	2,111.4	443.9	383.7	1,251	1,089

1. Based on the resident population estimated as of July 1 of the year shown.

STATE County	Local government finances, 2017 (cont.): Direct general expenditure: Total (mil dol)	Direct general expenditure: Per capita[1] (dollars)	Percent of total for: Education	Percent of total for: Health and hospitals	Percent of total for: Police protection	Percent of total for: Public welfare	Percent of total for: Highways	Debt outstanding: Total (mil dol)	Debt outstanding: Per capita[1] (dollars)	Government employment, 2020: Federal civilian	Government employment, 2020: Federal military	Government employment, 2020: State and local	Individual income tax returns, 2019: Number of returns	Individual income tax returns, 2019: Mean adjusted gross income	Individual income tax returns, 2019: Mean income tax
	185	186	187	188	189	190	191	192	193	194	195	196	197	198	199
PENNSYLVANIA—Cont'd															
Potter	72.8	4,322	56.7	1.7	1.1	10.1	6.1	46.3	2,746	49	41	954	7,530	50,235	4,299
Schuylkill	590.7	4,143	53.1	2.9	2.1	4.5	5.5	507.5	3,559	634	342	6,699	68,360	54,627	5,359
Snyder	130.0	3,203	62.3	3.5	5.9	0.1	5.4	180.8	4,455	91	97	2,040	18,380	53,315	4,468
Somerset	254.8	3,432	64.7	0.0	1.6	5.4	5.1	242.5	3,266	203	173	4,076	34,440	51,865	4,524
Sullivan	28.1	4,578	49.3	2.5	2.3	2.7	12.5	8.4	1,371	24	14	355	2,900	60,382	6,092
Susquehanna	175.4	4,285	69.8	0.8	1.2	2.2	7.2	62.4	1,525	113	101	1,666	19,470	66,250	7,656
Tioga	167.6	4,120	54.9	0.2	1.1	11.4	7.1	107.2	2,636	151	99	2,487	18,860	53,992	4,740
Union	205.1	4,595	69.6	0.7	1.9	1.2	2.9	333.5	7,471	1,428	99	1,265	17,450	66,359	7,402
Venango	225.6	4,356	57.5	2.0	1.7	7.5	5.9	145.2	2,803	131	127	2,978	24,260	49,887	4,237
Warren	155.0	3,907	54.8	0.3	2.1	12.3	5.3	178.9	4,509	180	97	1,759	18,890	53,576	4,962
Washington	970.7	4,688	56.4	1.4	2.8	11.8	5.3	1,031.6	4,982	487	538	8,598	104,890	79,551	10,178
Wayne	240.0	4,687	67.9	2.6	1.0	4.9	3.4	231.2	4,515	537	121	2,510	25,180	58,431	5,843
Westmoreland	1,371.5	3,896	58.8	1.8	3.0	6.0	4.7	2,206.0	6,267	888	886	13,170	182,870	66,713	7,292
Wyoming	121.2	4,423	54.0	0.0	3.4	4.4	9.7	50.4	1,841	66	66	956	13,260	61,339	6,422
York	1,967.7	4,417	49.6	3.5	3.5	10.0	2.9	2,310.6	5,187	4,354	1,410	14,968	230,650	65,754	6,869
RHODE ISLAND	X	X	X	X	X	X	X	X	X	11,535	7,229	54,682	551,250	71,285	8,685
Bristol	225.8	4,634	65.8	0.4	4.3	0.1	3.0	253.3	5,197	101	207	1,832	25,070	113,252	17,900
Kent	688.3	4,209	56.9	0.1	7.0	0.3	3.3	349.5	2,137	743	739	7,210	90,990	74,557	9,077
Newport	417.0	5,027	46.2	2.6	8.3	0.4	2.0	382.4	4,610	5,314	3,005	3,419	44,070	99,322	14,316
Providence	2,535.1	3,998	55.2	0.2	9.0	0.1	3.0	1,660.4	2,618	4,723	2,730	30,594	323,820	59,504	6,416
Washington	602.4	4,769	66.1	0.7	6.6	0.4	3.5	256.7	2,032	654	548	11,627	67,320	89,525	11,948
SOUTH CAROLINA	X	X	X	X	X	X	X	X	X	36,723	48,298	325,400	2,356,370	63,516	6,950
Abbeville	57.7	2,351	55.7	3.8	8.0	0.0	2.9	19.0	773	44	85	1,396	9,880	47,038	3,518
Aiken	461.5	2,742	63.7	0.2	6.8	0.0	1.0	321.4	1,909	703	619	6,936	77,300	60,684	5,976
Allendale	29.9	3,322	62.9	1.3	4.9	0.0	1.5	44.5	4,936	21	29	992	3,340	33,280	2,308
Anderson	569.6	2,874	61.7	0.4	8.2	0.3	2.3	1,356.3	6,844	409	728	11,902	90,540	56,154	5,190
Bamberg	47.3	3,291	60.7	0.3	8.2	0.0	1.8	34.2	2,375	39	47	787	5,380	40,264	3,192
Barnwell	80.1	3,753	59.7	1.5	5.9	0.0	1.9	45.7	2,141	50	74	1,321	8,630	42,280	2,987
Beaufort	644.2	3,454	45.5	2.2	7.8	0.6	4.3	928.7	4,979	2,287	9,720	8,058	91,380	91,513	12,562
Berkeley	727.0	3,389	55.2	1.0	4.0	0.3	0.3	2,699.7	12,584	863	857	8,421	107,230	63,108	6,780
Calhoun	35.3	2,404	60.7	2.5	6.5	0.1	3.7	33.1	2,250	29	52	713	6,480	52,963	4,544
Charleston	1,812.8	4,509	37.6	3.5	10.9	0.2	2.8	2,346.9	5,838	10,999	6,421	38,581	201,240	94,464	14,169
Cherokee	166.8	2,931	68.7	0.0	7.0	0.0	3.5	1,034.7	18,181	102	203	2,317	24,240	45,342	3,543
Chester	100.8	3,121	59.7	3.4	5.1	0.0	0.3	31.3	968	64	116	1,746	14,430	45,768	3,667
Chesterfield	113.8	2,474	65.5	1.6	7.9	0.0	2.3	83.0	1,804	106	161	1,931	18,420	41,825	2,911
Clarendon	118.4	3,481	52.2	12.7	5.2	0.0	4.2	61.4	1,806	74	159	2,060	13,680	41,299	3,193
Colleton	143.2	3,813	45.1	1.5	6.2	0.7	3.4	132.2	3,521	100	142	1,919	17,590	43,919	3,834
Darlington	166.9	2,491	68.7	1.7	7.0	0.1	0.9	76.9	1,148	165	236	3,127	28,420	51,968	5,123
Dillon	94.4	3,094	60.1	0.4	5.4	0.3	3.9	3.4	112	90	111	1,238	12,360	36,716	2,356
Dorchester	419.6	2,639	74.5	0.2	7.1	0.0	1.3	542.6	3,413	275	596	6,267	75,730	58,499	5,192
Edgefield	49.8	1,856	76.9	0.0	9.0	0.0	2.7	11.4	426	394	89	957	10,960	57,775	5,403
Fairfield	86.8	3,841	56.2	5.3	7.5	0.0	0.0	40.2	1,778	45	80	1,254	10,100	46,885	4,228
Florence	520.6	3,759	51.9	4.7	7.3	0.2	3.8	509.4	3,678	559	519	13,344	60,600	54,521	5,449
Georgetown	214.7	3,472	52.5	1.9	5.6	1.1	3.3	231.1	3,738	146	263	4,826	31,600	70,384	8,879
Greenville	3,512.9	6,931	22.7	57.3	2.9	0.1	1.1	2,888.8	5,700	2,340	1,944	30,917	243,950	74,407	8,275
Greenwood	510.2	7,237	23.7	58.5	2.8	0.1	1.5	391.1	5,547	145	248	6,949	29,940	50,768	4,589
Hampton	64.4	3,305	61.4	4.0	8.8	1.1	2.5	35.9	1,840	318	77	1,060	7,900	45,311	4,031
Horry	1,318.0	3,962	50.3	1.7	5.9	0.0	10.1	1,246.8	3,748	908	1,311	16,333	177,290	54,419	5,585
Jasper	85.4	2,996	43.0	1.8	7.0	0.0	7.5	74.9	2,627	62	109	1,184	13,540	51,414	4,702
Kershaw	307.5	4,715	34.7	45.3	2.4	0.1	0.6	286.8	4,398	110	242	2,428	29,850	53,685	4,603
Lancaster	301.8	3,266	50.6	2.6	24.2	0.0	3.3	373.2	4,038	131	358	4,426	44,080	65,865	6,713
Laurens	179.6	2,688	54.0	0.0	5.4	0.2	0.5	126.5	1,893	122	240	3,729	28,550	45,103	3,308
Lee	45.5	2,619	62.3	3.3	7.8	0.0	0.0	64.0	3,678	29	54	952	7,040	35,776	2,294
Lexington	2,026.2	6,979	35.5	47.4	2.6	0.0	1.1	1,986.1	6,841	728	1,088	21,368	137,540	64,485	6,794
McCormick	21.2	2,216	61.7	6.6	6.9	0.0	2.4	13.1	1,371	71	31	695	4,180	56,258	5,373
Marion	84.6	2,704	59.2	2.5	11.0	0.0	2.2	24.6	785	79	112	1,674	13,220	33,894	2,255
Marlboro	88.6	3,321	54.2	1.9	5.8	0.2	1.9	81.0	3,033	365	83	1,301	10,620	34,583	2,035
Newberry	193.0	5,030	36.5	30.3	3.5	0.1	1.2	126.9	3,305	116	138	2,261	16,930	51,144	4,382
Oconee	219.9	2,842	57.7	0.3	7.9	0.0	2.4	112.0	1,447	207	296	3,880	34,950	65,259	7,193
Orangeburg	469.5	5,355	35.6	42.3	4.4	0.0	1.1	1,175.4	13,407	263	304	6,083	37,200	41,610	3,199
Pickens	274.6	2,223	52.5	2.5	7.4	0.0	3.9	330.1	2,672	204	447	11,059	52,510	59,403	6,118
Richland	1,673.4	4,064	43.3	1.0	5.8	0.1	4.2	3,106.6	7,544	9,920	11,137	44,162	187,530	61,282	6,783
Saluda	47.8	2,354	53.4	0.4	6.5	0.4	3.6	17.3	852	37	72	951	8,240	48,053	3,781
Spartanburg	2,201.0	7,175	26.1	58.6	2.3	0.2	1.2	1,354.9	4,417	639	1,161	22,951	147,880	58,285	5,716

1. Based on the resident population estimated as of July 1 of the year shown.

State / county code	CBSA code[1]	County Type code[2]	STATE County	Land area[3] (sq. mi)	Population, 2021: Total persons 2021	Population, 2021: Rank	Population, 2021: Per square mile	Race alone or in combination, not Hispanic or Latino (percent): White	Black	American Indian, Alaska Native	Asian and Pacific Islancer	Percent Hispanic or Latino[4]	Age (percent): Under 5 years	5 to 17 years	18 to 24 years	25 to 34 years	35 to 44 years	45 to 54 years
				1	2	3	4	5	6	7	8	9	10	11	12	13	14	15
			SOUTH CAROLINA—Cont'd															
45085	44940	3	Sumter	665.1	104,758	586	157.5	46.4	48.3	0.9	2.3	4.3	6.5	13.5	13.8	14.0	11.6	10.8
45087	46420	2	Union	513.6	27,016	1,528	52.6	66.0	32.9	0.6	0.7	2.0	5.3	12.1	11.1	11.9	10.8	12.7
45089		6	Williamsburg	934.2	30,484	1,421	32.6	33.3	63.7	0.6	1.0	2.4	4.8	11.3	11.4	11.9	11.2	12.3
45091	16740	1	York	681.0	288,595	245	423.8	70.4	20.3	1.2	3.8	6.6	5.5	14.1	12.2	12.2	14.5	13.9
46000		0	SOUTH DAKOTA	75,809.7	895,376	X	11.8	83.0	3.1	9.5	2.3	4.6	6.6	13.9	13.4	12.6	12.5	10.6
46003		9	Aurora	708.5	2,748	2,981	3.9	87.8	1.0	3.7	1.1	8.0	6.4	13.6	11.6	10.6	12.7	10.1
46005	26700	7	Beadle	1,258.7	19,121	1,866	15.2	74.2	2.0	1.9	11.5	12.2	8.3	15.5	11.6	11.7	11.4	10.6
46007		9	Bennett	1,184.6	3,406	2,928	2.9	36.5	1.6	60.3	1.1	6.0	7.5	20.1	14.8	12.2	11.4	8.9
46009		9	Bon Homme	563.5	7,014	2,660	12.4	86.7	1.7	9.4	0.5	3.0	5.1	10.7	12.4	13.2	13.4	11.7
46011	15100	5	Brookings	792.2	34,639	1,309	43.7	90.5	1.9	1.8	3.4	4.0	5.8	11.8	29.0	12.2	10.8	8.1
46013	10100	5	Brown	1,713.0	38,101	1,222	22.2	86.8	2.3	4.8	4.2	4.1	6.0	13.7	13.6	12.6	12.6	10.5
46015		9	Brule	817.2	5,242	2,803	6.4	85.0	1.4	12.9	1.0	3.5	6.6	15.3	12.4	10.1	10.9	11.0
46017		9	Buffalo	471.4	1,923	3,047	4.1	17.2	1.3	77.8	0.7	5.2	8.1	22.4	18.6	11.5	11.6	9.7
46019		6	Butte	2,250.0	10,456	2,380	4.6	91.9	1.0	4.0	1.0	4.6	6.8	14.0	11.2	11.8	11.6	10.3
46021		9	Campbell	733.7	1,380	3,089	1.9	94.1	0.7	2.0	0.4	3.9	4.4	9.4	8.3	8.6	9.9	7.8
46023		9	Charles Mix	1,097.5	9,163	2,477	8.3	63.9	1.1	33.1	0.9	4.3	8.0	17.8	12.3	10.3	10.5	9.8
46025		9	Clark	957.5	3,855	2,897	4.0	93.8	2.0	1.0	0.5	3.7	9.9	15.6	8.7	11.9	10.2	8.7
46027	46820	6	Clay	412.0	15,150	2,081	36.8	88.4	2.4	5.1	3.1	3.4	4.7	10.3	33.5	13.0	9.3	7.9
46029	47980	5	Codington	687.6	28,427	1,482	41.3	92.3	1.1	3.4	1.2	3.5	5.7	13.6	12.4	12.0	12.6	11.4
46031		9	Corson	2,469.7	3,872	2,896	1.6	30.2	1.4	65.3	1.2	5.5	10.6	19.7	15.7	10.9	10.5	8.9
46033		3	Custer	1,556.9	8,609	2,526	5.5	90.1	1.1	5.1	1.2	4.5	3.6	7.3	7.9	7.5	10.3	11.4
46035	33580	7	Davison	435.6	19,878	1,824	45.6	90.5	1.5	4.5	1.4	4.1	6.2	13.2	13.4	12.3	11.8	10.2
46037		9	Day	1,028.5	5,414	2,781	5.3	86.6	1.0	10.7	1.1	2.7	5.5	13.2	10.5	9.1	10.2	9.6
46039		9	Deuel	622.7	4,272	2,868	6.9	94.5	1.3	1.5	0.5	3.7	6.2	13.8	10.6	10.7	11.2	10.7
46041		9	Dewey	2,302.4	5,246	2,802	2.3	23.0	1.2	75.3	1.0	4.4	11.1	21.5	14.3	12.1	11.3	8.8
46043		9	Douglas	431.8	2,821	2,974	6.5	94.9	1.1	3.0	0.6	2.2	7.8	14.3	11.0	9.6	10.1	9.1
46045	10100	9	Edmunds	1,126.0	4,033	2,886	3.6	95.8	0.7	1.6	0.6	2.4	6.4	12.6	10.5	10.1	10.9	10.8
46047		6	Fall River	1,739.9	7,202	2,648	4.1	86.7	1.7	8.3	2.1	4.2	3.5	9.9	9.2	8.7	9.6	11.7
46049		9	Faulk	981.7	2,137	3,032	2.2	97.6	0.7	0.8	0.6	0.9	8.5	13.7	10.9	10.1	10.1	9.3
46051		7	Grant	681.4	7,519	2,618	11.0	92.6	1.0	1.7	0.6	5.2	5.7	12.8	10.8	9.8	11.0	12.1
46053		9	Gregory	1,015.0	3,977	2,889	3.9	89.3	1.3	9.8	1.1	1.7	6.0	14.2	10.6	9.0	10.0	10.4
46055		8	Haakon	1,810.5	1,835	3,057	1.0	94.5	1.7	4.5	1.0	1.8	5.6	13.0	10.5	9.6	11.3	9.0
46057	47980	9	Hamlin	507.0	6,255	2,717	12.3	92.8	0.9	1.2	0.6	5.7	10.1	17.4	13.9	11.6	10.6	10.2
46059		9	Hand	1,436.6	3,095	2,953	2.2	97.3	0.6	1.1	0.7	1.5	5.3	12.6	10.3	9.6	10.9	9.3
46061	33580	8	Hanson	434.6	3,505	2,922	8.1	96.8	1.1	1.5	0.6	1.5	7.3	16.3	13.1	8.8	12.9	11.5
46063		9	Harding	2,671.6	1,327	3,091	0.5	92.8	1.7	3.8	0.9	2.4	6.9	12.6	10.6	12.0	11.3	10.9
46065	38180	7	Hughes	741.5	17,694	1,937	23.9	82.5	1.3	14.1	1.3	3.4	6.2	14.6	11.3	12.4	12.9	11.2
46067		8	Hutchinson	813.0	7,411	2,627	9.1	94.8	1.4	1.8	0.7	2.6	8.1	13.9	10.4	9.9	10.7	11.0
46069		9	Hyde	860.6	1,236	3,096	1.4	88.3	1.5	10.4	1.0	1.5	7.1	11.3	10.7	12.0	9.4	9.2
46071		8	Jackson	1,863.9	2,878	2,969	1.5	41.0	2.1	57.0	1.0	4.3	11.7	19.3	14.8	10.8	9.2	9.2
46073	26700	9	Jerauld	526.1	1,636	3,071	3.1	93.5	1.1	2.0	0.7	4.6	6.2	13.7	8.6	9.9	11.7	9.6
46075		9	Jones	969.7	879	3,111	0.9	90.0	1.8	8.2	0.7	3.1	5.7	13.8	8.1	9.8	9.8	11.0
46077		9	Kingsbury	832.2	5,192	2,807	6.2	94.7	0.9	1.3	0.8	3.4	6.9	13.5	10.3	10.6	11.1	9.6
46079		6	Lake	562.9	10,851	2,355	19.3	93.7	1.6	2.2	1.2	2.8	5.2	11.1	14.5	8.9	10.6	9.4
46081	43940	6	Lawrence	800.1	26,165	1,557	32.7	91.7	1.3	3.5	1.9	3.7	4.1	9.7	14.6	11.0	11.8	10.3
46083	43620	3	Lincoln	577.3	67,870	792	117.6	92.9	2.8	1.3	2.1	2.8	6.7	15.7	12.1	14.0	15.0	11.5
46085		9	Lyman	1,642.3	3,764	2,903	2.3	56.2	1.7	41.4	1.2	3.0	8.3	15.6	13.7	11.3	10.9	9.6
46087	43620	3	McCook	574.2	5,695	2,762	9.9	93.4	1.1	1.6	0.5	4.5	8.1	15.7	11.9	10.3	11.7	11.0
46089		9	McPherson	1,136.7	2,420	3,005	2.1	96.7	1.0	1.2	0.6	1.7	6.2	14.7	9.2	8.5	9.9	9.6
46091		9	Marshall	838.1	4,304	2,866	5.1	83.3	1.3	8.3	0.5	8.4	7.3	13.4	9.8	10.3	12.0	9.9
46093	39660	3	Meade	3,470.9	30,173	1,432	8.7	89.1	2.7	4.7	2.1	4.5	4.8	13.2	14.6	14.3	13.6	10.3
46095		9	Mellette	1,307.3	1,908	3,048	1.5	38.9	2.3	60.6	1.1	3.4	9.3	16.9	15.0	12.2	9.1	9.9
46097		8	Miner	570.2	2,314	3,019	4.1	95.2	1.6	1.0	0.8	3.2	6.0	13.1	12.4	10.0	9.7	9.1
46099	43620	3	Minnehaha	806.8	199,685	344	247.5	83.0	7.7	3.5	2.9	5.6	7.1	14.2	12.7	14.9	14.2	11.0
46101		8	Moody	519.4	6,315	2,709	12.2	78.5	1.8	15.5	2.5	4.9	7.0	14.9	11.9	10.0	11.8	10.7
46102		0	Oglala Lakota	2,093.6	13,586	2,186	6.5	5.9	0.6	90.2	0.4	4.3	9.4	21.8	16.7	15.0	11.5	9.4
46103	39660	3	Pennington	2,776.8	111,806	553	40.3	82.1	2.3	11.5	2.2	5.8	6.2	12.7	11.7	12.9	12.1	10.6
46105		8	Perkins	2,870.5	2,819	2,975	1.0	94.3	1.1	3.3	0.8	2.1	6.2	11.9	9.5	8.5	10.9	10.1
46107		9	Potter	861.1	2,475	3,000	2.9	92.8	1.1	3.8	1.5	2.6	4.9	13.8	10.0	9.0	9.7	9.4
46109		9	Roberts	1,101.1	10,163	2,397	9.2	57.4	1.2	39.6	0.8	4.2	8.0	17.4	12.3	10.0	9.7	9.8
46111		9	Sanborn	569.2	2,378	3,011	4.2	94.8	0.8	2.0	0.5	3.7	7.4	14.0	10.1	10.3	12.8	9.3
46115		9	Spink	1,503.5	6,269	2,715	4.2	94.0	1.1	2.4	0.5	3.3	6.8	11.5	11.3	10.2	12.1	10.2
46117	38180	9	Stanley	1,444.4	3,032	2,957	2.1	89.6	1.7	8.5	0.8	2.5	5.8	13.4	11.5	10.8	11.7	11.2
46119		9	Sully	1,006.7	1,476	3,080	1.5	93.8	1.1	3.8	0.2	2.6	6.2	11.5	10.0	8.9	10.4	10.2
46121		9	Todd	1,388.6	9,286	2,468	6.7	9.3	0.9	84.6	3.5	3.8	11.1	24.9	16.5	12.7	10.9	8.3

1. CBSA = Core Based Statistical Area. See Appendix A for explanation. See Appendix B for list of metropolitan areas with component counties. 2. County type code from the Economic Research Service of USDA Rural-Urban Continuum Codes. See Appendix A for definition. 3. Dry land or land partially or temporarily covered by water. 4. May be of any race.

STATE County	Population, 2021 (cont.)				Population change, 2000–2021							Households, 2016–2020				
	Age (percent) (cont.)				Total persons		Percent change		Components of change, 2020–2021					Percent		
	55 to 64 years	65 to 74 years	75 years and over	Percent female	2010	2020	2010–2020	2020–2021	Births	Deaths	Net Migration	Number	Persons per household	Family house-holds	Female family house-holder[1]	One person
	16	17	18	19	20	21	22	23	24	25	26	27	28	29	30	31
SOUTH CAROLINA—Cont'd																
Sumter	12.7	10.3	6.9	52.0	107,456	105,556	-1.8	-0.8	1,688	1,694	-798	41,704	2.5	65.8	17.2	30.7
Union	15.1	12.8	8.1	52.6	28,961	27,244	-5.9	-0.8	321	565	12	11,707	2.3	66.0	15.1	31.3
Williamsburg	14.2	14.2	8.7	52.4	34,423	31,026	-9.9	-1.7	344	586	-297	12,705	2.3	63.8	19.3	33.6
York	12.7	9.6	5.5	51.5	226,073	282,090	24.8	2.3	3,555	3,493	6,452	103,582	2.6	69.7	12.4	25.0
SOUTH DAKOTA	13.0	10.9	6.6	49.2	814,180	886,667	8.9	1.0	13,724	11,671	6,650	347,878	2.4	62.9	9.0	30.6
Aurora	14.0	11.9	9.1	47.6	2,710	2,747	1.4	0.0	48	41	-6	1,124	2.3	62.6	5.0	32.1
Beadle	13.3	10.2	7.3	49.7	17,398	19,149	10.1	-0.1	350	281	-97	7,684	2.3	64.8	6.3	30.6
Bennett	11.7	7.6	5.7	49.8	3,431	3,381	-1.5	0.7	56	40	8	1,036	3.3	69.6	24.9	25.3
Bon Homme	13.3	11.1	9.1	40.4	7,070	7,003	-0.9	0.2	69	120	61	2,556	2.1	60.8	5.1	33.4
Brookings	9.2	8.2	4.8	48.3	31,965	34,375	7.5	0.8	438	316	132	13,364	2.4	52.0	5.2	36.5
Brown	13.0	10.5	7.4	50.5	36,531	38,301	4.8	-0.5	512	498	-218	16,245	2.3	58.9	7.2	34.4
Brule	14.5	11.5	7.6	49.4	5,255	5,247	-0.2	-0.1	91	78	-18	2,228	2.2	62.2	5.9	34.5
Buffalo	8.8	6.3	2.9	49.8	1,912	1,948	1.9	-1.3	43	40	-27	540	3.7	67.2	24.3	28.7
Butte	14.1	12.9	7.4	49.2	10,110	10,243	1.3	2.1	141	188	262	4,179	2.4	65.5	12.6	28.2
Campbell	20.7	15.9	15.0	48.0	1,466	1,377	-6.1	0.2	10	14	7	699	2.1	63.1	2.7	35.1
Charles Mix	13.0	10.0	8.3	49.1	9,129	9,373	2.7	-2.2	167	159	-217	3,149	2.9	67.4	11.2	29.3
Clark	12.8	13.2	9.1	48.6	3,691	3,837	4.0	0.5	71	55	3	1,584	2.3	61.2	5.2	32.8
Clay	8.9	7.7	4.6	50.2	13,864	14,967	8.0	1.2	153	133	161	5,259	2.2	51.3	6.9	35.2
Codington	13.7	11.0	7.7	49.5	27,227	28,325	4.0	0.4	361	402	139	12,090	2.3	60.1	8.6	30.8
Corson	11.5	7.7	4.6	50.9	4,050	3,902	-3.7	-0.8	118	69	-78	1,205	3.4	71.7	20.0	25.5
Custer	19.7	21.3	11.0	49.7	8,216	8,318	1.2	3.5	86	145	357	3,893	2.2	70.3	4.7	24.2
Davison	12.8	11.1	8.8	50.0	19,504	19,956	2.3	-0.4	311	315	-76	8,651	2.2	58.7	6.8	37.5
Day	15.4	15.2	11.4	48.8	5,710	5,449	-4.6	-0.6	55	111	22	2,568	2.1	60.1	7.0	36.6
Deuel	14.9	13.1	8.9	48.1	4,364	4,295	-1.6	-0.5	63	65	-20	1,777	2.4	69.8	2.9	26.4
Dewey	10.7	6.4	3.8	50.7	5,301	5,239	-1.2	0.1	138	77	-55	1,731	3.3	71.0	22.4	25.2
Douglas	14.4	12.6	11.1	50.0	3,002	2,835	-5.6	-0.5	55	54	-14	1,203	2.3	72.7	1.5	25.1
Edmunds	16.0	12.5	10.1	49.3	4,071	3,986	-2.1	1.2	67	49	29	1,550	2.4	68.3	4.1	28.5
Fall River	17.2	19.0	11.2	49.5	7,094	6,973	-1.7	3.3	49	157	342	3,138	2.1	58.2	13.8	35.9
Faulk	13.2	13.1	11.1	49.4	2,364	2,125	-10.1	0.6	43	29	-2	920	2.2	63.6	3.4	34.9
Grant	16.0	13.1	8.8	47.2	7,356	7,556	2.7	-0.5	100	139	3	3,148	2.2	69.1	7.3	25.0
Gregory	14.0	14.4	11.4	48.5	4,271	3,994	-6.5	-0.4	55	71	0	1,832	2.3	61.0	7.8	34.7
Haakon	14.8	14.2	12.0	50.1	1,937	1,872	-3.4	-2.0	21	31	-26	758	2.5	64.1	3.3	33.6
Hamlin	11.4	8.7	6.2	47.9	5,903	6,164	4.4	1.5	160	104	35	2,242	2.6	73.1	5.7	20.1
Hand	15.3	13.8	12.8	49.4	3,431	3,145	-8.3	-1.6	38	39	-48	1,426	2.1	64.0	5.5	31.1
Hanson	14.4	11.9	3.9	49.1	3,331	3,461	3.9	1.3	49	24	19	1,039	3.3	71.4	6.4	26.8
Harding	14.5	13.5	7.7	46.8	1,255	1,311	4.5	1.2	20	9	6	516	2.1	62.4	2.3	32.9
Hughes	13.6	11.0	6.8	50.6	17,022	17,765	4.4	-0.4	253	285	-40	7,475	2.2	61.9	6.6	32.8
Hutchinson	13.4	11.7	10.9	50.2	7,343	7,427	1.1	-0.2	117	128	-5	2,977	2.4	68.0	7.4	29.6
Hyde	15.0	14.6	10.7	48.9	1,420	1,262	-11.1	-2.1	22	25	-22	616	2.3	71.4	7.0	26.3
Jackson	11.5	7.8	5.6	50.0	3,031	2,806	-7.4	2.6	86	28	14	815	3.9	77.4	29.2	19.9
Jerauld	13.1	15.7	11.5	50.2	2,071	1,663	-19.7	-1.6	19	40	-5	940	2.1	58.0	1.4	35.5
Jones	16.3	15.2	10.4	47.9	1,006	917	-8.8	-4.1	10	11	-35	419	2.1	56.3	4.3	40.1
Kingsbury	14.9	13.4	9.8	48.7	5,148	5,187	0.8	0.1	73	80	12	2,172	2.2	65.0	5.4	30.4
Lake	15.7	17.2	7.4	47.4	11,200	11,059	-1.3	-1.9	161	141	-226	4,712	2.6	66.7	5.5	27.8
Lawrence	14.9	15.5	8.1	49.5	24,097	25,768	6.9	1.5	266	343	478	11,250	2.2	53.5	5.9	36.3
Lincoln	10.6	9.1	5.2	50.2	44,828	65,161	45.4	4.2	973	447	2,195	20,341	2.9	74.4	8.6	20.9
Lyman	13.2	10.5	6.8	47.2	3,755	3,718	-1.0	1.2	73	40	13	1,393	2.7	67.0	12.3	25.7
McCook	12.9	10.4	8.1	49.0	5,618	5,682	1.1	0.2	95	112	29	2,206	2.4	67.7	3.5	22.5
McPherson	14.0	13.3	14.5	49.6	2,459	2,411	-2.0	0.4	31	43	21	996	2.2	58.6	2.0	39.3
Marshall	14.6	13.9	8.7	46.6	4,656	4,306	-7.5	0.0	74	57	-19	1,898	2.5	66.3	4.7	30.5
Meade	13.0	10.6	5.7	47.7	25,434	29,852	17.4	1.1	306	346	360	11,142	2.5	70.4	7.3	25.7
Mellette	12.5	10.1	5.2	49.1	2,048	1,918	-6.3	-0.5	32	27	-14	675	3.0	67.9	18.7	30.2
Miner	17.4	12.5	9.9	47.7	2,389	2,298	-3.8	0.7	33	37	20	963	2.3	61.8	3.3	36.3
Minnehaha	12.2	9.1	4.5	49.1	169,468	197,214	16.4	1.3	3,422	2,309	1,318	78,453	2.4	60.7	10.2	31.5
Moody	14.3	11.7	7.8	49.1	6,486	6,336	-2.3	-0.3	99	75	-45	2,608	2.4	68.8	7.6	26.2
Oglala Lakota	8.9	5.0	2.3	50.9	13,586	13,672	0.6	-0.6	313	221	-182	2,813	5.0	81.3	40.5	15.5
Pennington	14.4	12.9	6.4	49.3	100,948	109,222	8.2	2.4	1,773	1,512	2,340	43,947	2.5	61.3	10.5	31.3
Perkins	16.0	14.8	12.0	49.5	2,982	2,835	-4.9	-0.6	38	49	-5	1,329	2.2	65.2	7.6	30.2
Potter	15.5	14.7	13.1	50.9	2,329	2,472	6.1	0.1	28	40	17	997	2.2	63.1	4.8	35.5
Roberts	12.9	11.5	8.3	48.7	10,149	10,280	1.3	-1.1	181	169	-129	3,889	2.6	66.3	14.0	28.7
Sanborn	15.0	13.8	7.3	47.6	2,355	2,330	-1.1	2.1	37	26	37	987	2.4	65.8	8.0	28.4
Spink	15.6	12.8	9.5	49.3	6,415	6,361	-0.8	-1.4	92	100	-84	2,599	2.4	64.5	7.7	31.4
Stanley	13.1	12.8	9.7	49.3	2,966	2,980	0.5	1.7	33	25	46	1,443	2.1	69.4	7.3	27.7
Sully	16.7	15.9	10.4	46.8	1,373	1,446	5.3	2.1	20	10	19	591	2.2	62.8	6.6	34.7
Todd	8.3	5.2	2.1	51.6	9,612	9,319	-3.0	-0.4	269	174	-129	2,674	3.8	69.7	32.6	26.0

1. No spouse present.

STATE County	Persons in group quarters, 2021	Daytime Population, 2016–2020		Births, 2021		Deaths, 2021		Persons under 65 with no health insurance, 2019		Medicare, 2021			COVID-19 Deaths, 2020	
		Number	Employment/ residence ratio	Total	Rate[1]	Number	Rate[1]	Number	Percent	Total beneficiaries	Enrolled in Original Medicare	Enrolled in Medicare Advantage	Number	Rate[1]
	32	33	34	35	36	37	38	39	40	41	42	43	44	45
SOUTH CAROLINA—Cont'd														
Sumter	2,329	106,244	1.0	1,340	12.8	1,333	12.7	10,652	12.5	22,329	15,440	6,889	138	1.3
Union	393	25,193	0.8	268	9.9	443	16.4	2,642	12.5	7,397	3,956	3,441	49	1.8
Williamsburg	902	29,198	0.9	286	9.3	462	15.1	3,122	13.9	8,228	4,686	3,543	83	2.7
York	3,107	254,397	0.9	2,841	9.9	2,860	10.0	27,603	11.6	48,781	32,408	16,372	267	0.9
SOUTH DAKOTA	31,569	883,117	1.0	10,843	12.2	9,175	10.3	85,613	12.0	180,166	138,646	41,520	1,528	1.7
Aurora	91	2,476	0.8	43	15.7	33	12.0	372	17.7	599	477	122	11	4.0
Beadle	601	18,145	1.0	270	14.1	223	11.7	2,434	16.4	3,721	2,826	896	39	2.0
Bennett	28	3,285	0.9	43	12.7	27	8.0	612	21.8	514	487	27	D	D
Bon Homme	1,549	6,338	0.8	51	7.3	94	13.4	543	12.9	1,546	1,214	332	22	3.2
Brookings	3,359	35,873	1.0	352	10.2	262	7.6	2,662	9.7	5,062	3,963	1,099	33	1.0
Brown	1,217	40,184	1.1	404	10.6	395	10.4	3,796	12.2	7,602	6,672	931	62	1.6
Brule	115	5,272	1.0	66	12.6	63	12.0	728	17.5	1,128	900	229	D	D
Buffalo	2	1,904	0.8	31	16.0	30	15.5	318	18.4	225	D	D	13	6.7
Butte	71	9,455	0.8	112	10.8	139	13.4	1,297	15.9	2,447	1,669	778	19	1.9
Campbell	0	1,486	1.0	8	5.8	10	7.3	112	11.5	422	337	85	D	D
Charles Mix	502	9,600	1.1	137	14.8	122	13.2	1,397	19.3	1,774	1,605	169	16	1.7
Clark	485	3,415	0.8	54	14.0	44	11.4	375	13.0	840	543	297	D	D
Clay	2,337	13,415	0.9	118	7.8	106	7.0	1,120	11.0	2,094	1,678	416	13	0.9
Codington	320	29,350	1.1	294	10.4	318	11.2	2,321	10.2	5,837	3,553	2,284	70	2.5
Corson	1	4,083	1.0	94	24.2	53	13.7	695	20.2	570	527	43	15	3.9
Custer	192	7,692	0.7	66	7.8	111	13.1	757	12.7	3,035	2,373	663	12	1.4
Davison	713	21,335	1.1	247	12.4	261	13.1	1,567	10.2	4,355	3,389	966	53	2.7
Day	119	5,142	0.9	43	7.9	88	16.2	610	15.5	1,546	1,117	428	26	4.8
Deuel	32	3,570	0.7	46	10.7	53	12.4	414	12.3	959	614	346	D	D
Dewey	6	6,107	1.1	111	21.2	66	12.6	1,065	20.7	805	781	25	18	3.4
Douglas	141	2,936	1.0	45	15.9	38	13.5	327	15.0	768	632	136	10	3.5
Edmunds	416	3,458	0.8	49	12.2	36	9.0	340	11.4	892	802	90	10	2.5
Fall River	192	6,858	1.1	42	5.9	124	17.5	598	13.1	2,560	2,111	449	10	1.4
Faulk	355	2,244	0.9	30	14.1	23	10.8	250	14.3	561	498	63	12	5.6
Grant	101	7,241	1.0	71	9.4	113	15.0	626	11.4	1,923	1,043	879	33	4.4
Gregory	24	4,064	0.9	47	11.8	53	13.3	510	16.6	1,128	955	173	27	6.8
Haakon	32	1,971	1.1	15	8.1	25	13.5	201	14.3	518	474	44	D	D
Hamlin	195	5,547	0.8	123	19.8	88	14.2	642	12.5	1,101	739	362	30	4.9
Hand	53	3,075	1.0	31	10.0	28	9.0	260	11.0	867	781	86	D	D
Hanson	487	2,612	0.5	39	11.2	16	4.6	294	10.1	1,327	1,065	262	D	D
Harding	29	1,199	1.0	12	9.1	8	6.1	198	19.1	257	225	32	D	D
Hughes	739	18,429	1.1	195	11.0	214	12.1	1,485	10.7	3,428	3,109	320	28	1.6
Hutchinson	811	7,130	1.0	93	12.5	94	12.7	732	13.2	1,851	1,381	470	19	2.6
Hyde	25	1,595	1.2	17	13.6	20	16.0	164	16.8	345	323	22	D	D
Jackson	17	3,285	1.0	62	21.8	22	7.7	681	24.4	467	425	41	14	5.0
Jerauld	79	2,336	1.3	15	9.1	36	21.9	179	12.4	544	477	68	15	9.1
Jones	0	925	1.1	6	6.7	10	11.1	107	15.8	234	207	26	D	D
Kingsbury	199	4,566	0.9	52	10.0	65	12.5	401	10.7	1,369	1,111	258	12	2.3
Lake	671	11,977	0.9	122	11.2	120	11.0	796	8.6	2,459	1,923	536	16	1.5
Lawrence	1,001	25,675	1.0	208	8.0	267	10.3	2,283	11.9	6,600	4,788	1,812	44	1.7
Lincoln	265	50,188	0.7	746	11.2	351	5.3	3,735	6.9	9,324	6,648	2,676	71	1.1
Lyman	37	3,738	0.9	57	15.2	30	8.0	517	16.9	662	577	85	D	D
McCook	304	4,369	0.6	75	13.2	88	15.5	550	12.3	1,242	936	306	23	4.1
McPherson	343	2,226	0.9	26	10.8	30	12.5	223	13.2	705	641	65	D	D
Marshall	238	4,688	0.9	62	14.4	51	11.9	627	16.2	1,102	931	170	D	D
Meade	820	21,830	0.6	242	8.1	266	8.9	2,322	10.1	5,408	4,077	1,331	22	0.7
Mellette	38	1,961	0.8	27	14.1	17	8.9	373	22.1	335	318	16	D	D
Miner	78	1,947	0.8	26	11.3	31	13.5	206	11.9	600	525	74	D	D
Minnehaha	6,127	206,264	1.1	2,720	13.7	1,780	9.0	17,811	11.0	36,049	26,100	9,949	293	1.5
Moody	84	6,081	0.9	78	12.3	57	9.0	754	14.3	1,318	1,039	280	17	2.7
Oglala Lakota	55	14,805	1.2	241	17.7	192	14.1	2,132	17.1	1,327	1,312	14	38	2.8
Pennington	2,230	119,456	1.1	1,423	12.9	1,203	10.9	11,736	12.9	26,818	20,539	6,279	141	1.3
Perkins	59	3,057	1.0	33	11.7	38	13.5	342	16.5	788	677	110	13	4.6
Potter	64	2,361	1.1	24	9.7	31	12.5	175	11.5	663	598	65	D	D
Roberts	200	10,064	1.0	142	13.9	137	13.4	1,553	19.0	2,137	1,623	514	29	2.8
Sanborn	171	1,911	0.6	30	12.8	17	7.2	217	11.8	526	437	89	D	D
Spink	382	6,156	0.9	68	10.8	77	12.2	570	11.8	1,558	1,315	243	24	3.8
Stanley	0	2,320	0.6	26	8.7	21	7.0	276	11.1	699	621	79	D	D
Sully	0	1,317	1.1	19	13.0	6	4.1	104	10.0	339	310	29	D	D
Todd	14	10,657	1.2	219	23.5	150	16.1	1,694	19.0	925	909	16	24	2.6

1. Per 1,000 estimated resident population.

STATE County	COVID-19 Vaccinations, 2021–2022: Number	COVID-19 Vaccinations, 2021–2022: Percent[5]	Education: School enrollment and attainment, 2016–2020: Enrollment[1]: Total	Education: Enrollment[1]: Percent private	Education: Attainment[2] (percent): High school graduate or less	Education: Attainment[2] (percent): Bachelor's degree or more	Education: Local government expenditures,[3] 2018–2019: Total current spending (mil dol)	Education: Local government expenditures,[3] 2018–2019: Current spending per student (dollars)	Money income, 2016–2020: Per capita income[4]	Money income, 2016–2020: Households: Median income (dollars)	Money income, 2016–2020: Households: Percent with income of less than $50,000	Money income, 2016–2020: Households: Percent with income of $200,000 or more	Income and poverty, 2020: Median household income (dollars)	Income and poverty, 2020: Percent below poverty level: All persons	Income and poverty, 2020: Percent below poverty level: Children under 18 years	Income and poverty, 2020: Percent below poverty level: Children 5 to 17 years in families
	46	47	48	49	50	51	52	53	54	55	56	57	58	59	60	61
SOUTH CAROLINA—Cont'd																
Sumter	60,683	56.9	27,064	17.3	44.4	20.8	166.3	10,026	24,541	46,570	53.2	2.2	45,724	20.5	27.6	25.3
Union	11,384	41.7	5,583	5.6	55.8	13.5	39.7	9,971	24,142	41,117	58.5	1.0	46,567	14.9	24.3	22.8
Williamsburg	17,361	57.2	6,435	10.7	60.5	14.3	45.8	12,736	19,438	35,681	63.9	1.0	38,186	25.4	34.5	33.7
York	138,250	49.2	67,551	10.0	33.8	33.7	501.0	10,624	35,285	68,555	36.0	7.9	72,579	8.8	10.5	9.7
SOUTH DAKOTA	542,777	61.4	216,402	12.6	38.0	29.3	1,405.7	10,137	31,415	59,896	41.7	4.4	61,149	11.6	13.9	12.7
Aurora	1,513	55.0	627	6.2	47.7	20.3	6.2	12,777	35,590	65,132	33.6	5.8	54,916	10.2	15.2	15.2
Beadle	9,118	49.4	4,249	16.0	49.3	23.5	31.3	10,405	27,898	53,461	46.9	3.3	54,033	12.6	14.3	14.4
Bennett	1,997	59.3	1,249	1.0	44.3	22.4	6.5	14,297	18,632	41,887	57.7	3.2	45,478	28.3	36.4	28.9
Bon Homme	3,994	57.9	1,386	12.5	46.8	20.3	11.8	10,908	23,877	50,195	49.8	2.9	52,890	15.0	15.0	14.8
Brookings	18,275	52.1	13,583	6.4	28.7	42.2	47.5	9,746	28,867	57,471	41.6	2.6	64,542	9.9	7.7	7.2
Brown	22,119	57.0	9,459	17.8	36.3	31.7	52.2	9,380	33,535	61,816	40.0	4.9	64,993	9.1	9.5	8.9
Brule	2,956	55.8	1,114	12.5	44.1	26.5	14.0	11,640	34,517	57,181	42.1	7.7	56,691	13.7	17.9	15.6
Buffalo	1,208	61.6	664	4.7	59.9	8.1	NA	NA	12,003	35,000	68.0	0.2	22,901	32.8	43.8	39.0
Butte	4,185	40.1	2,271	9.3	49.9	21.5	16.1	9,649	28,974	49,353	51.2	3.2	52,346	12.5	17.3	16.3
Campbell	646	46.9	252	4.0	41.6	28.3	1.8	14,832	32,029	54,228	45.8	2.3	52,931	10.7	15.2	16.8
Charles Mix	5,095	54.8	2,331	7.9	48.2	20.2	22.6	12,535	23,626	52,348	48.8	3.0	44,865	24.0	31.0	28.7
Clark	1,894	50.7	703	7.0	50.0	18.9	7.2	10,581	31,096	50,709	48.7	3.5	54,164	12.3	16.8	18.7
Clay	9,594	68.2	6,127	4.2	28.1	48.9	12.0	9,267	30,300	51,447	48.6	5.2	49,834	16.2	13.8	12.8
Codington	15,411	55.0	6,730	7.3	44.3	20.0	43.5	9,255	30,157	57,885	44.9	3.6	62,123	9.0	10.5	9.2
Corson	2,263	55.4	1,251	1.2	49.7	16.1	15.2	18,133	16,521	36,705	60.0	1.8	29,860	37.1	52.1	45.8
Custer	4,551	50.7	1,241	6.4	43.2	23.2	10.5	10,827	35,677	64,556	37.1	3.3	66,654	9.7	16.5	15.6
Davison	12,220	61.8	4,784	19.0	41.3	26.0	30.7	9,339	30,006	48,267	52.5	2.9	53,664	10.7	11.2	10.4
Day	3,562	65.7	1,068	8.1	45.7	22.1	8.0	10,937	29,356	46,753	52.8	1.6	50,445	12.9	16.9	15.6
Deuel	2,023	46.5	933	7.4	42.9	22.7	5.3	9,778	30,734	67,396	33.3	1.9	58,488	9.5	12.9	12.3
Dewey	4,434	75.3	1,795	6.6	51.8	17.2	5.3	15,110	17,387	45,859	54.9	1.5	40,429	24.9	33.0	31.6
Douglas	1,521	52.1	545	18.9	42.4	18.2	5.4	11,660	30,708	61,793	41.9	2.6	59,404	11.8	13.1	13.2
Edmunds	1,768	46.2	863	13.6	40.6	25.9	8.7	12,072	34,152	64,896	38.1	4.5	56,671	12.2	13.9	13.5
Fall River	4,185	62.3	1,124	12.7	46.0	19.7	11.3	10,508	29,139	51,383	49.2	0.3	48,927	15.4	19.7	17.8
Faulk	1,266	55.1	373	4.0	35.5	28.6	3.8	11,234	26,235	49,423	50.7	0.8	50,213	18.7	27.9	31.5
Grant	3,475	49.3	1,360	12.4	46.6	22.4	11.7	10,812	32,916	65,327	40.4	6.1	59,637	9.3	11.1	11.6
Gregory	2,119	50.6	948	2.8	44.3	21.5	8.5	11,591	27,378	44,706	52.6	2.7	43,060	15.1	17.9	16.5
Haakon	798	42.0	434	2.3	49.0	16.4	3.4	11,023	23,725	40,673	61.2	6.2	50,898	11.7	17.1	15.9
Hamlin	2,893	46.9	1,589	7.8	48.2	21.8	12.9	8,888	27,863	67,626	30.4	2.1	62,651	8.9	9.2	9.2
Hand	1,563	49.0	607	9.6	38.5	22.4	5.1	11,331	34,936	58,333	44.4	4.8	59,237	9.1	11.3	10.2
Hanson	1,502	43.5	888	12.6	42.7	16.1	3.8	8,967	26,710	63,750	40.5	3.4	62,597	10.4	14.6	14.9
Harding	244	18.8	223	8.5	40.3	24.7	3.5	17,650	34,028	61,111	29.3	1.2	58,732	11.0	14.5	15.0
Hughes	12,614	72.0	3,245	8.0	32.1	36.6	23.1	8,698	34,271	69,575	36.2	3.0	70,615	9.4	10.2	9.4
Hutchinson	3,940	54.0	1,483	4.9	43.5	22.9	15.9	12,294	30,941	61,290	38.7	4.3	54,669	12.8	15.5	16.0
Hyde	705	54.2	301	3.7	42.2	22.7	3.1	12,707	33,833	59,844	38.3	2.8	55,510	11.5	16.3	15.9
Jackson	1,697	50.7	1,056	1.9	53.8	15.1	4.9	14,524	12,847	24,549	73.7	2.0	36,853	28.7	35.9	32.9
Jerauld	1,044	51.9	403	4.2	50.8	21.3	3.7	11,161	41,875	49,265	50.5	4.8	49,086	14.4	18.7	18.7
Jones	669	74.1	145	29.0	45.0	29.2	2.4	13,380	25,885	46,688	57.3	1.0	49,156	14.9	29.6	29.4
Kingsbury	3,356	67.9	971	4.0	46.5	23.4	12.4	12,667	34,711	61,316	40.6	4.1	56,758	10.2	11.1	11.3
Lake	6,442	50.3	3,146	2.0	36.9	33.1	20.0	9,259	31,971	63,165	35.0	4.5	65,643	9.9	10.6	10.2
Lawrence	14,892	57.6	6,159	7.8	32.4	35.0	33.2	10,494	34,442	52,146	47.6	4.6	56,366	11.5	11.9	10.5
Lincoln	36,227	59.3	15,480	16.8	30.1	36.7	78.2	8,882	38,307	84,260	25.9	9.2	86,972	4.5	3.4	3.2
Lyman	2,481	65.6	959	8.0	45.9	23.1	5.2	13,689	22,937	54,484	44.2	1.9	43,531	23.9	32.2	31.0
McCook	3,215	57.6	1,289	4.8	45.5	24.6	14.3	12,002	30,374	66,208	33.7	5.5	64,693	9.6	10.7	10.8
McPherson	958	40.3	385	8.1	49.4	23.5	5.4	14,440	31,765	51,379	48.4	4.5	44,625	18.4	24.1	22.7
Marshall	2,589	52.5	995	6.4	38.1	25.8	6.9	10,716	37,179	68,056	33.8	5.4	56,885	13.2	17.6	18.3
Meade	15,460	54.6	6,644	12.1	35.0	26.1	27.8	9,090	29,573	62,275	41.1	3.2	58,406	8.7	11.0	10.1
Mellette	750	36.4	558	0.2	57.5	13.2	5.9	13,660	15,298	33,882	67.1	1.0	37,844	29.9	43.5	42.4
Miner	1,212	54.7	460	3.9	51.2	20.1	4.7	12,859	28,294	53,135	47.2	2.6	49,824	12.6	14.6	13.5
Minnehaha	129,535	67.1	46,386	19.7	33.2	33.6	312.6	9,288	32,968	63,699	38.4	4.2	64,526	8.1	8.4	7.3
Moody	3,246	49.4	1,522	8.3	39.0	25.3	9.8	10,377	30,928	61,894	37.8	6.2	73,264	9.4	10.6	10.6
Oglala Lakota	11,261	79.4	5,103	10.4	51.4	11.1	25.6	18,108	11,057	31,423	66.8	3.3	32,195	38.1	41.7	37.5
Pennington	66,311	58.3	26,223	13.9	35.4	31.7	170.9	9,643	32,540	58,278	42.7	5.1	62,214	12.1	13.8	12.6
Perkins	920	32.1	620	14.7	44.4	20.8	5.6	14,381	32,369	61,815	38.1	5.2	46,786	15.4	24.6	23.9
Potter	1,313	61.0	472	9.1	44.0	23.5	5.2	14,571	30,845	57,120	46.5	2.2	57,324	9.4	12.9	11.7
Roberts	7,768	74.7	2,394	6.4	45.5	16.5	18.4	11,702	25,523	50,877	49.1	2.3	50,673	17.8	24.6	23.1
Sanborn	1,301	55.5	445	2.5	49.5	19.6	5.0	9,986	30,277	55,398	43.5	3.4	51,952	13.7	16.8	17.4
Spink	3,330	52.2	1,547	11.2	42.2	26.2	14.5	11,064	36,453	62,125	38.6	7.0	53,282	12.8	15.0	14.5
Stanley	1,840	59.4	554	8.7	41.0	28.5	4.6	10,617	44,345	71,602	36.7	9.8	76,413	7.5	11.4	11.0
Sully	619	44.5	199	3.5	40.1	21.8	4.0	15,162	40,919	60,508	43.0	5.2	59,157	7.8	6.9	6.9
Todd	7,154	70.3	3,513	5.5	54.8	13.7	28.3	13,485	10,280	24,102	77.0	1.3	31,256	42.5	49.1	43.6

1. All persons 3 years old and over enrolled in nursery school through college. 2. Persons 25 years old and over. 3. Elementary and secondary education expenditures. 4. Based on population estimated by the American Community Survey, 2016–2020. 5. CDC percent based on 2019 population estimate.

STATE County	Personal income, 2020: Total (mil dol)	Personal income, 2020: Percent change 2019–2020	Per capita[1]: Dollars	Per capita[1]: Rank	Wages and salaries (mil dol)	Supplements to wages and salaries, employer contributions (mil dol): Pension and insurance	Supplements to wages and salaries, employer contributions (mil dol): Government social insurance	Proprietors' income (mil dol)	Dividends, interest, and rent (mil dol)	Personal transfer reecipts (mil dol)	Earnings, 2020: Total (mil dol)	Contributions for government social insurance (mil dol): From employee and self-employed	Contributions for government social insurance (mil dol): From employer
	62	63	64	65	66	67	68	69	70	71	72	73	74
SOUTH CAROLINA—Cont'd													
Sumter	4,574	7.7	43,003	2,062	2,157	478	174	216	680	1,477	3,026	189	174
Union	1,013	7.5	37,515	2,737	345	64	26	29	128	424	465	39	26
Williamsburg	1,149	9.7	38,528	2,621	346	78	26	40	126	486	490	36	26
York	14,968	9.1	51,772	954	5,694	855	411	718	2,140	2,938	7,678	519	411
SOUTH DAKOTA	52,921	9.0	59,656	X	21,715	3,592	1,656	8,995	11,330	9,584	35,959	2,141	1,656
Aurora	138	23.1	50,586	1,078	30	6	3	35	26	28	73	4	3
Beadle	1,009	10.7	54,493	744	386	69	31	214	183	197	699	39	31
Bennett	142	18.3	41,856	2,223	34	9	3	29	20	42	75	3	3
Bon Homme	298	6.5	43,555	2,003	67	15	5	68	57	70	155	9	5
Brookings	1,754	6.1	49,278	1,220	881	180	69	202	394	274	1,333	76	69
Brown	2,424	11.8	62,587	329	1,017	175	79	448	538	393	1,719	99	79
Brule	286	20.1	54,352	758	77	14	6	67	61	64	164	8	6
Buffalo	52	30.1	26,748	3,106	24	7	2	3	7	26	36	2	2
Butte	435	6.3	41,250	2,294	106	20	8	52	97	115	187	14	8
Campbell	99	54.2	71,645	144	20	3	2	37	21	15	63	2	2
Charles Mix	439	16.5	47,405	1,457	138	28	11	107	82	112	284	14	11
Clark	268	57.3	70,492	160	62	10	5	104	48	37	181	6	5
Clay	620	7.2	43,533	2,007	255	55	19	72	141	126	401	23	19
Codington	1,560	7.2	55,331	680	699	122	55	191	355	303	1,066	66	55
Corson	127	15.2	31,442	3,069	36	9	3	14	18	45	62	4	3
Custer	479	5.9	53,169	845	95	19	7	36	134	125	158	13	7
Davison	1,106	4.8	55,832	654	540	88	42	156	255	218	825	52	42
Day	342	37.0	64,064	289	78	15	7	100	78	73	200	9	7
Deuel	270	23.4	62,036	348	82	15	7	82	45	47	186	8	7
Dewey	266	19.2	45,889	1,668	115	26	9	34	38	73	184	10	9
Douglas	181	6.8	62,134	344	43	9	4	61	32	33	116	5	4
Edmunds	259	24.5	67,747	202	54	11	4	86	51	39	156	6	4
Fall River	346	9.3	51,509	977	116	28	11	32	71	130	187	13	11
Faulk	155	22.3	67,007	211	28	5	2	67	28	28	102	3	2
Grant	455	16.8	65,019	261	178	32	14	109	84	87	333	18	14
Gregory	212	15.2	50,244	1,116	58	12	4	45	44	53	119	7	4
Haakon	124	33.4	66,588	228	38	7	3	40	24	21	89	4	3
Hamlin	323	20.6	51,773	953	101	16	8	77	58	56	203	10	8
Hand	217	25.3	69,452	171	54	10	5	73	43	34	141	6	5
Hanson	254	13.5	72,728	128	30	5	3	62	58	51	100	6	3
Harding	66	1.9	50,355	1,104	23	5	2	14	18	10	43	2	2
Hughes	969	1.1	55,872	650	527	95	39	62	207	181	723	47	39
Hutchinson	432	6.9	59,341	458	111	20	9	115	92	84	254	12	9
Hyde	83	34.2	64,756	271	26	5	2	26	17	14	59	2	2
Jackson	102	17.3	30,705	3,082	28	7	2	15	14	35	53	3	2
Jerauld	99	27.1	49,991	1,144	67	11	6	17	23	26	101	7	6
Jones	56	7.5	59,264	464	15	4	1	14	14	10	33	2	1
Kingsbury	350	24.4	70,268	164	77	15	6	117	58	60	215	9	6
Lake	716	9.2	57,367	549	230	45	18	140	154	137	434	24	18
Lawrence	1,463	4.5	55,779	657	514	82	40	114	428	309	749	54	40
Lincoln	4,695	6.4	74,493	111	1,422	192	103	530	1,013	450	2,247	138	103
Lyman	178	15.7	46,934	1,523	51	11	4	38	33	41	104	5	4
McCook	334	11.0	60,576	400	55	9	4	90	57	60	158	7	4
McPherson	142	41.1	60,086	424	22	4	2	61	26	27	89	3	2
Marshall	320	34.7	65,540	249	72	13	6	118	70	47	209	7	6
Meade	1,426	11.3	49,875	1,156	392	91	31	166	263	301	679	42	31
Mellette	71	17.9	33,840	2,988	10	3	1	11	9	24	25	1	1
Miner	144	31.0	65,604	248	26	5	2	51	22	34	85	3	2
Minnehaha	12,752	5.8	64,846	269	7,245	1,039	532	2,521	2,311	1,991	11,336	697	532
Moody	396	18.7	60,754	394	100	20	9	96	71	69	225	10	9
Oglala Lakota	418	15.1	29,721	3,091	203	47	16	26	39	186	292	16	16
Pennington	6,549	6.2	56,496	610	2,995	507	230	595	1,678	1,416	4,327	288	230
Perkins	138	21.5	48,591	1,311	43	10	4	26	29	33	82	5	4
Potter	190	15.8	87,915	45	38	6	3	73	46	31	120	6	3
Roberts	476	23.6	46,059	1,641	145	30	12	92	88	129	278	15	12
Sanborn	143	17.7	61,709	360	24	5	2	53	20	23	83	3	2
Spink	451	29.3	71,321	148	103	20	8	146	84	102	278	11	8
Stanley	190	0.7	60,870	389	50	8	4	16	44	32	78	5	4
Sully	140	30.8	100,301	22	48	6	4	47	25	15	106	4	4
Todd	293	11.0	28,440	3,097	129	28	10	15	34	123	181	11	10

1. Based on the resident population estimated as of July 1 of the year shown.

STATE County	Earnings, 2020 (cont.) — Percent by selected industries: Farm	Mining, quarrying, and extractions	Construction	Manu- facturing	Information; professional, scientific, technical services	Retail trade	Finance, insurance, real estate, and leasing	Health care and social assistance	Govern- ment	Social Security beneficiaries, December 2020: Number	Rate[1]	Supple- mental Security Income recipients, 2020	Housing units, 2021: Total	Percent change, 2010–2021
	75	76	77	78	79	80	81	82	83	84	85	86	87	88
SOUTH CAROLINA—Cont'd														
Sumter	0.3	0.0	7.5	15.1	3.4	5.3	3.5	11.6	35.9	24,805	237	3,961	47,216	0.8
Union	0.2	D	3.1	29.5	1.7	5.9	2.8	D	25.1	8,310	308	947	13,487	0.2
Williamsburg	2.3	0.0	7.9	19.3	D	5.8	2.4	D	27.8	8,975	294	1,689	14,829	0.5
York	0.2	0.1	6.1	12.0	11.8	7.1	9.5	8.2	11.9	53,040	184	3,781	117,804	2.2
SOUTH DAKOTA	9.4	0.3	6.9	9.2	5.9	6.3	12.6	15.0	14.6	185,752	207	14,495	400,780	1.6
Aurora	38.7	0.0	5.0	0.5	D	4.9	5.0	D	11.7	585	213	18	1,263	0.2
Beadle	17.9	D	5.7	16.9	2.7	5.3	8.3	D	13.0	3,770	197	420	8,399	0.0
Bennett	36.4	0.0	6.9	D	1.6	5.8	D	2.0	31.9	540	159	140	1,182	0.4
Bon Homme	28.1	D	6.0	4.6	1.8	4.4	7.0	10.0	20.3	1,550	221	78	2,826	0.5
Brookings	9.2	D	4.5	26.9	4.2	5.3	6.6	3.9	22.6	5,100	147	298	15,036	0.9
Brown	11.5	D	5.8	14.8	4.2	6.8	9.3	14.9	11.6	7,735	203	541	17,957	0.3
Brule	31.0	D	5.2	0.7	3.9	6.2	D	11.2	14.3	1,015	194	108	2,356	0.3
Buffalo	10.6	0.0	D	0.0	D	2.9	D	2.1	77.0	305	159	98	571	0.2
Butte	8.1	D	8.7	3.8	4.6	12.5	5.8	7.1	17.2	2,475	237	197	4,717	0.9
Campbell	57.8	0.0	1.7	5.6	D	2.9	D	1.1	5.5	380	275	11	903	0.3
Charles Mix	28.0	D	6.6	2.2	3.0	3.9	5.8	10.0	26.6	1,820	199	262	3,647	0.6
Clark	53.9	0.1	17.6	3.7	D	2.3	D	D	6.6	840	218	109	1,608	0.2
Clay	10.5	0.0	4.1	3.8	1.8	5.7	4.6	D	44.3	2,170	143	190	6,253	1.1
Codington	7.3	D	6.1	20.1	3.6	8.8	8.7	12.7	13.1	6,010	211	378	13,310	0.6
Corson	19.0	0.1	D	0.0	1.8	2.4	D	D	51.8	610	158	261	1,361	0.0
Custer	4.6	D	10.5	1.2	D	6.3	7.6	11.0	23.7	2,805	326	91	5,092	4.5
Davison	7.3	D	8.5	15.5	5.9	8.7	6.2	D	9.9	4,475	225	377	9,527	0.4
Day	46.6	0.0	3.5	6.5	1.9	4.1	5.4	6.6	10.9	1,545	285	73	3,427	0.7
Deuel	38.0	0.0	7.2	10.9	D	3.1	D	D	6.2	1,090	255	29	2,139	0.3
Dewey	13.3	D	D	D	2.0	3.8	D	D	59.9	880	168	333	1,926	0.1
Douglas	42.3	D	5.8	5.0	D	2.6	3.5	8.8	8.4	735	261	50	1,351	0.7
Edmunds	41.7	0.1	4.3	4.2	1.5	3.0	11.5	D	11.9	885	219	49	1,955	0.7
Fall River	9.7	0.5	5.5	0.4	4.1	5.1	2.7	D	40.3	2,480	344	161	4,094	0.3
Faulk	61.0	0.0	3.4	D	D	2.0	6.2	D	7.2	520	243	56	1,027	0.4
Grant	23.8	D	7.0	16.0	2.1	7.9	5.6	7.5	5.8	1,930	257	84	3,450	0.6
Gregory	27.8	D	5.8	1.9	2.9	8.3	8.3	D	11.8	1,110	279	96	2,198	0.5
Haakon	34.0	D	5.9	4.7	D	4.1	7.0	D	8.5	455	248	D	933	0.1
Hamlin	30.9	0.0	14.7	D	1.4	4.3	D	1.9	11.7	1,135	181	46	2,810	1.5
Hand	43.2	0.1	3.6	2.0	D	3.9	D	D	8.4	830	268	37	1,705	0.0
Hanson	42.1	D	12.6	10.9	D	3.1	D	D	8.8	1,305	372	48	1,284	0.2
Harding	24.8	7.2	15.6	0.1	D	5.4	D	4.4	14.2	250	188	D	722	0.3
Hughes	0.1	0.0	4.3	0.4	7.0	7.1	11.0	13.6	40.1	3,510	198	222	7,953	0.4
Hutchinson	39.2	D	3.5	7.3	D	4.0	D	D	8.7	1,850	250	96	3,230	0.3
Hyde	44.6	0.0	D	D	D	3.8	D	3.7	16.4	330	267	10	629	0.5
Jackson	24.4	0.1	D	D	D	5.7	D	D	38.6	500	174	141	1,067	0.3
Jerauld	12.1	D	1.7	D	D	2.1	D	D	6.1	630	385	23	955	0.3
Jones	30.8	0.0	D	0.0	D	9.8	5.5	D	19.5	240	273	D	510	1.0
Kingsbury	45.2	0.0	7.6	9.0	1.1	2.4	7.3	D	7.5	1,370	264	81	2,639	0.8
Lake	16.7	D	5.6	16.0	7.3	5.3	5.1	8.4	16.0	2,475	228	123	5,753	1.6
Lawrence	0.4	D	11.5	4.4	7.9	9.2	6.7	15.0	14.5	6,760	258	314	14,456	1.7
Lincoln	3.3	D	10.5	8.3	8.2	6.3	20.3	14.9	5.3	8,830	130	264	27,434	4.0
Lyman	30.1	0.0	3.2	0.8	D	5.8	D	D	34.8	720	191	69	1,554	0.5
McCook	45.8	D	8.0	D	3.7	3.7	5.2	D	8.5	1,245	219	80	2,466	0.6
McPherson	62.7	0.1	2.5	2.1	D	2.2	D	6.2	8.8	700	289	34	1,265	0.5
Marshall	55.0	D	3.9	10.4	D	2.9	D	D	9.2	1,085	252	51	2,414	0.8
Meade	7.7	D	13.0	2.5	D	6.3	5.5	6.1	36.3	6,115	203	256	12,603	1.7
Mellette	37.3	0.2	D	0.0	D	D	D	1.3	36.1	355	186	109	779	0.5
Miner	53.4	0.0	5.3	2.0	D	2.6	4.1	5.2	9.8	605	261	32	1,191	0.2
Minnehaha	0.7	D	6.8	7.9	8.0	6.8	21.5	20.4	8.2	37,990	190	2,981	86,391	2.8
Moody	37.9	0.0	9.9	8.4	D	1.8	D	5.0	17.2	1,380	219	54	2,745	0.4
Oglala Lakota	6.9	0.0	1.2	D	D	D	D	2.0	71.1	1,540	113	1,065	3,463	0.2
Pennington	0.6	0.2	7.6	4.0	7.1	7.5	8.7	21.8	19.6	28,370	254	1,924	50,391	2.3
Perkins	25.5	0.1	6.0	D	3.7	5.8	D	6.1	14.7	770	273	31	1,710	-0.1
Potter	17.3	0.0	4.7	D	D	34.2	D	D	7.3	665	269	17	1,573	0.3
Roberts	26.7	D	4.9	5.9	2.1	4.5	D	D	33.0	2,395	236	220	4,828	0.7
Sanborn	55.9	0.0	10.4	3.7	D	1.2	1.9	D	9.2	540	227	26	1,140	0.4
Spink	46.8	0.0	3.6	2.8	1.3	2.8	8.4	2.8	16.8	1,520	242	156	2,988	0.2
Stanley	10.8	D	25.0	D	D	10.9	3.4	D	14.3	765	252	11	1,446	1.1
Sully	36.8	-0.2	21.0	D	D	3.8	D	D	5.8	370	251	D	903	1.1
Todd	6.1	0.0	D	D	D	3.7	D	3.0	72.5	1,130	122	D	2,883	0.2

1. Per 1,000 resident population estimated as of July 1 of the year shown.

STATE County	Housing units, 2016–2020								Civilian labor force, 2021				Civilian employment[6], 2016–2020		
		Occupied units									Unemployment			Percent	
		Owner-occupied				Renter-occupied									
				Median owner cost as a percent of income											
	Total	Percent	Median value[1]	With a mortgage	Without a mortgage[2]	Median rent[3]	Median rent as a percent of income[2]	Sub-standard units[4] (percent)	Total	Percent change, 2020–2021	Total	Rate[5]	Total	Management, business, science, and arts	Construction, production, and maintenance occupations
	89	90	91	92	93	94	95	96	97	98	99	100	101	102	103
SOUTH CAROLINA—Cont'd															
Sumter	41,704	64.5	119,800	19.7	10.0	809	28.5	2.1	42,665	-0.5	1,960	4.6	42,736	29.4	29.1
Union	11,707	66.8	80,300	18.9	10.3	707	25.9	2.9	11,454	0.2	742	6.5	11,484	24.2	39.1
Williamsburg	12,705	72.3	73,900	22.3	13.5	660	29.8	5.0	11,170	-2.6	683	6.1	11,537	25.9	35.1
York	103,582	72.3	218,400	18.8	10.0	1,011	27.8	1.9	145,482	2.0	5,396	3.7	135,860	39.5	22.9
SOUTH DAKOTA	347,878	68.0	174,600	19.8	10.6	761	25.2	2.7	468,015	1.4	14,504	3.1	447,607	37.3	24.6
Aurora	1,124	81.6	86,600	17.9	10.0	628	16.3	2.0	1,478	1.0	35	2.4	1,486	37.1	31.0
Beadle	7,684	66.1	120,900	18.9	11.0	691	21.4	5.4	9,240	-0.7	262	2.8	8,847	32.7	35.9
Bennett	1,036	63.9	100,000	19.1	15.6	618	21.5	10.3	1,054	-1.5	45	4.3	1,250	35.8	27.0
Bon Homme	2,556	72.5	89,000	19.0	10.6	582	20.9	0.5	2,820	-0.6	80	2.8	2,699	39.6	30.7
Brookings	13,364	58.9	187,100	19.2	10.5	759	24.6	1.3	18,533	0.7	593	3.2	19,167	41.4	25.0
Brown	16,245	65.6	171,200	19.3	10.1	673	22.9	1.7	20,545	0.4	618	3.0	20,855	36.6	26.7
Brule	2,228	60.6	157,500	22.1	10.0	682	19.4	1.5	2,560	4.2	65	2.5	2,862	39.3	20.4
Buffalo	540	51.3	0	26.7	13.4	465	22.3	13.7	702	2.2	38	5.4	598	30.1	21.7
Butte	4,179	81.4	153,000	21.5	13.6	772	30.6	3.0	5,013	1.0	170	3.4	5,058	27.7	29.6
Campbell	699	82.5	63,500	14.1	11.0	661	27.5	1.7	774	-0.8	26	3.4	775	43.9	25.2
Charles Mix	3,149	70.3	127,900	20.4	10.5	568	22.5	3.1	3,804	1.3	141	3.7	3,933	35.4	21.6
Clark	1,584	79.8	108,500	21.3	12.7	601	19.1	1.1	1,925	-10.1	72	3.7	1,769	44.9	23.5
Clay	5,259	53.8	168,100	19.3	10.0	726	25.2	2.9	7,331	3.1	217	3.0	7,488	39.6	17.1
Codington	12,090	65.7	182,400	20.3	10.4	756	27.1	4.1	15,673	2.0	485	3.1	15,205	31.4	29.4
Corson	1,205	55.6	55,600	18.0	10.0	480	20.0	10.1	1,314	-0.2	62	4.7	1,277	53.6	19.8
Custer	3,893	83.5	232,000	23.1	13.4	974	24.0	3.4	4,119	2.3	165	4.0	3,902	35.8	26.9
Davison	8,651	60.0	153,600	17.6	12.1	716	24.9	1.5	10,891	0.2	302	2.8	10,453	32.1	29.7
Day	2,568	74.3	110,600	21.4	12.3	539	23.7	0.3	2,682	0.1	115	4.3	2,594	39.2	28.2
Deuel	1,777	78.4	120,300	19.4	10.0	670	18.8	2.1	2,293	-0.9	96	4.2	2,292	34.5	32.7
Dewey	1,731	59.8	65,900	16.7	11.0	586	20.8	11.4	2,288	-0.3	135	5.9	2,043	43.2	23.2
Douglas	1,203	74.3	84,100	17.9	10.0	603	29.0	2.6	1,529	-0.8	38	2.5	1,438	43.4	26.0
Edmunds	1,550	82.4	110,600	18.7	10.0	638	21.2	0.0	2,013	1.8	54	2.7	1,870	41.2	27.7
Fall River	3,138	74.5	136,800	22.7	12.8	797	40.5	1.7	3,071	2.5	124	4.0	2,931	38.0	25.5
Faulk	920	77.5	88,200	16.3	10.0	657	30.5	0.3	1,055	2.4	29	2.7	1,013	43.0	24.3
Grant	3,148	83.5	136,200	18.8	10.0	575	23.5	4.0	4,329	-0.3	148	3.4	3,668	34.4	30.5
Gregory	1,832	74.3	97,300	16.2	11.3	525	23.6	1.7	2,069	1.9	58	2.8	1,932	37.7	24.6
Haakon	758	78.8	116,200	25.7	12.2	702	25.8	0.0	1,041	-1.0	29	2.8	785	34.5	34.6
Hamlin	2,242	80.2	161,400	19.3	10.0	588	16.6	3.0	3,454	3.3	83	2.4	2,944	34.9	35.1
Hand	1,426	68.4	120,100	17.6	10.0	492	22.1	0.4	1,750	0.6	43	2.5	1,635	46.2	24.5
Hanson	1,039	87.8	139,900	18.2	11.3	715	19.6	1.4	1,757	0.5	70	4.0	1,685	37.4	27.3
Harding	516	65.5	97,400	14.3	10.0	416	10.0	2.1	718	0.3	20	2.8	682	38.0	33.0
Hughes	7,475	70.6	181,400	18.2	10.9	735	22.0	4.0	9,881	0.6	241	2.4	9,107	49.9	15.4
Hutchinson	2,977	77.9	111,600	18.9	10.0	583	21.6	3.2	3,604	0.4	112	3.1	3,736	35.8	27.4
Hyde	616	75.8	104,300	19.7	10.8	607	16.7	0.0	649	-2.6	17	2.6	778	42.7	28.9
Jackson	815	59.5	58,600	33.8	13.0	559	27.3	9.3	1,215	1.2	54	4.4	960	44.8	12.5
Jerauld	940	76.4	74,200	16.7	10.8	486	17.3	4.9	1,331	11.8	29	2.2	962	36.8	30.0
Jones	419	69.0	84,700	18.0	13.5	580	17.0	4.5	522	0.6	18	3.4	439	47.6	25.1
Kingsbury	2,172	78.4	118,700	17.5	10.2	476	24.3	1.5	2,701	1.5	78	2.9	2,548	41.2	31.5
Lake	4,712	73.9	170,300	19.2	11.2	666	24.8	1.4	6,548	1.9	199	3.0	6,845	37.6	28.3
Lawrence	11,250	64.3	224,200	21.3	12.1	785	26.6	0.8	13,789	2.2	419	3.0	13,524	32.4	23.6
Lincoln	20,341	75.9	240,200	19.7	10.1	994	26.4	1.3	36,741	2.0	900	2.4	31,766	45.6	18.2
Lyman	1,393	69.6	109,600	23.4	10.6	533	19.9	4.2	1,691	2.0	74	4.4	1,722	36.7	24.5
McCook	2,206	76.8	152,300	20.3	10.0	596	21.9	1.4	3,045	2.2	84	2.8	2,846	36.5	24.3
McPherson	996	75.9	62,600	17.8	11.4	493	23.1	0.9	962	-2.8	40	4.2	1,080	43.1	25.8
Marshall	1,898	79.1	126,300	16.9	10.0	642	18.9	1.9	2,420	0.6	85	3.5	2,618	37.9	25.7
Meade	11,142	74.1	207,700	23.1	11.3	952	26.4	1.4	14,140	2.5	428	3.0	14,641	32.9	25.3
Mellette	675	64.6	0	15.8	12.0	536	22.4	12.7	729	3.0	33	4.5	598	38.8	20.1
Miner	963	77.8	87,000	20.0	11.9	575	23.3	2.5	1,167	2.3	36	3.1	1,101	40.0	32.5
Minnehaha	78,453	62.7	201,500	19.5	10.0	814	25.4	2.4	114,373	1.5	3,265	2.9	107,499	37.0	24.2
Moody	2,608	70.9	152,700	19.7	10.0	607	21.1	1.5	4,002	0.1	112	2.8	3,312	34.7	25.3
Oglala Lakota	2,813	49.6	35,000	14.0	11.4	495	23.3	43.7	3,998	6.2	349	8.7	3,743	29.7	22.0
Pennington	43,947	68.9	197,200	21.8	12.1	859	28.8	1.6	58,416	2.4	1,870	3.2	55,404	34.8	21.7
Perkins	1,329	75.7	100,700	19.9	10.0	594	24.6	2.6	1,392	2.0	43	3.1	1,691	38.3	29.3
Potter	997	76.3	106,000	22.4	10.7	592	20.1	0.0	1,050	3.1	32	3.0	1,099	33.5	26.2
Roberts	3,889	65.3	107,000	19.9	10.4	567	24.1	3.1	4,726	-1.5	217	4.6	4,629	35.3	28.7
Sanborn	987	73.4	106,700	18.9	10.0	499	23.1	0.2	1,184	2.6	36	3.0	1,303	33.5	29.2
Spink	2,599	75.4	89,500	17.1	10.0	613	19.1	1.7	3,067	-0.3	98	3.2	3,080	39.7	25.3
Stanley	1,443	81.8	154,900	17.5	11.2	836	35.9	0.0	1,919	0.8	58	3.0	1,829	40.1	26.0
Sully	591	87.3	130,800	18.2	10.0	0	18.8	3.7	810	2.9	31	3.8	695	42.0	25.5
Todd	2,674	47.0	26,600	17.2	11.4	458	22.0	13.8	3,111	2.2	148	4.8	2,290	37.4	22.1

1. Specified owner-occupied units. 2. A value of 10.0 represents 10 percent or less; a value of 50.0 represents 50 percent or more. 3. Specified renter-occupied units. 4. Overcrowded or lacking complete plumbing facilities. 5. Percent of civilian labor force. 6. Civilian employed persons 16 years old and over.

STATE County	Private nonfarm establishments, employment and payroll, 2020									Agriculture, 2017			
		Employment						Annual payroll		Farms			Farm producers whose primary occupation is farming (percent)
											Percent with:		
	Number of establish-ments	Total	Health care and social assistance	Manufac-turing	Retail trade	Finance and insurance	Professional, scientific, and technical services	Total (mil dol)	Average per employee (dollars)	Number	Fewer than 50 acres	1000 acres or more	
	104	105	106	107	108	109	110	111	112	113	114	115	116
SOUTH CAROLINA—Cont'd													
Sumter	1,761	32,369	4,902	5,982	4,370	775	874	1,305	40,332	524	55.7	7.3	45.7
Union	392	6,069	338	1,831	871	150	46	224	36,984	241	30.3	2.5	35.3
Williamsburg	477	6,601	969	2,085	959	129	96	247	37,490	552	26.6	8.9	34.7
York	5,521	91,176	10,768	10,293	12,063	6,937	8,099	4,309	47,256	1,000	49.4	1.5	30.2
SOUTH DAKOTA	27,236	364,440	73,372	45,701	51,645	25,144	13,721	16,585	45,507	29,968	19.3	32.0	52.4
Aurora	78	632	169	57	85	27	114	22	34,823	392	17.1	24.2	46.2
Beadle	553	6,747	1,122	1,655	956	559	123	270	40,022	744	20.6	30.5	53.9
Bennett	55	628	135	NA	114	NA	8	22	35,269	213	5.6	65.3	65.1
Bon Homme	169	1,064	373	120	134	61	25	35	33,273	583	22.0	15.4	52.0
Brookings	909	14,195	2,104	4,619	1,816	741	506	621	43,738	886	31.0	14.3	38.9
Brown	1,261	18,066	3,212	3,571	2,645	939	391	791	43,802	1,034	24.3	27.4	50.5
Brule	216	2,060	472	21	274	73	53	71	34,259	394	17.3	37.8	54.4
Buffalo	11	130	18	NA	NA	NA	NA	3	21,131	68	14.7	64.7	76.6
Butte	336	2,089	256	227	471	84	80	75	35,844	565	17.7	30.4	48.8
Campbell	52	401	17	67	52	29	6	15	37,584	249	7.2	48.2	57.5
Charles Mix	275	2,326	541	100	460	106	47	75	32,087	671	12.8	32.5	53.3
Clark	123	1,018	91	116	134	24	16	67	65,985	553	10.7	33.1	52.8
Clay	303	3,863	786	241	794	97	222	111	28,789	472	26.3	16.7	50.5
Codington	1,114	13,967	1,872	3,513	2,557	799	318	547	39,151	601	34.4	19.6	44.9
Corson	35	219	10	NA	85	17	NA	5	24,776	322	5.9	67.4	73.0
Custer	289	1,392	214	24	230	34	63	59	42,325	441	24.5	22.4	43.1
Davison	714	10,775	2,313	1,320	1,654	385	1,036	421	39,030	463	30.7	16.6	43.4
Day	198	1,369	282	168	271	48	30	50	36,519	581	13.9	29.1	52.2
Deuel	134	979	146	245	93	40	21	46	46,708	634	24.8	18.3	45.4
Dewey	77	576	162	NA	86	30	NA	23	40,214	310	12.3	61.3	57.6
Douglas	102	824	193	112	122	40	8	30	36,882	392	21.7	22.7	53.4
Edmunds	120	882	189	79	200	48	28	39	44,041	348	7.8	53.2	59.0
Fall River	212	2,486	1,601	11	238	33	32	166	66,893	314	14.0	45.5	53.8
Faulk	71	418	169	NA	87	21	NA	15	36,962	291	7.2	56.4	72.2
Grant	280	3,427	700	686	478	170	47	154	44,921	554	24.5	26.2	52.9
Gregory	181	1,042	309	36	247	68	40	37	35,131	495	9.1	31.1	57.4
Haakon	83	664	161	84	100	44	8	25	37,093	293	8.2	67.2	62.1
Hamlin	181	1,362	96	399	184	57	21	62	45,509	476	27.7	18.1	47.4
Hand	132	1,019	213	57	134	66	141	38	36,993	405	12.8	50.1	70.0
Hanson	77	358	16	120	19	31	9	16	44,953	333	18.3	26.7	47.3
Harding	48	462	80	NA	51	NA	NA	23	49,626	265	6.4	79.6	70.3
Hughes	648	7,002	1,277	42	1,241	474	336	290	41,391	315	23.2	37.8	41.3
Hutchinson	218	2,112	600	332	282	96	38	83	39,200	775	20.8	19.0	49.8
Hyde	46	482	NA	NA	63	19	NA	19	40,050	174	6.9	52.9	59.5
Jackson	52	265	NA	2	102	NA	NA	7	27,400	314	4.8	65.9	70.2
Jerauld	80	1,333	128	823	58	28	27	58	43,253	244	13.1	27.9	46.1
Jones	46	224	NA	NA	64	12	NA	8	36,393	192	4.7	60.4	60.9
Kingsbury	168	1,158	236	247	161	121	15	56	48,286	518	15.3	31.9	56.0
Lake	357	3,907	635	950	513	206	214	158	40,385	463	26.8	19.4	45.8
Lawrence	1,106	10,271	1,615	438	1,400	289	324	358	34,817	275	30.2	14.5	39.6
Lincoln	1,772	22,493	3,954	2,052	2,731	2,346	1,033	1,166	51,844	756	36.1	12.0	44.1
Lyman	71	529	NA	NA	137	34	NA	15	27,955	414	5.1	43.5	51.2
McCook	183	946	250	23	140	34	29	37	39,172	512	23.0	26.2	47.6
McPherson	59	292	48	53	65	37	NA	10	34,428	382	5.0	45.0	59.8
Marshall	147	1,182	287	328	163	48	22	46	39,338	503	12.7	27.0	49.2
Meade	706	5,533	1,451	209	820	162	197	284	51,238	835	19.9	44.3	55.2
Mellette	18	154	NA	NA	NA	NA	NA	4	24,792	219	1.4	64.8	68.6
Miner	79	560	136	97	67	26	NA	24	42,320	408	15.9	26.0	39.2
Minnehaha	5,899	121,254	27,679	12,227	15,966	10,912	3,982	6,078	50,128	1,023	42.1	11.4	39.9
Moody	156	1,591	205	397	126	22	24	62	39,035	490	33.7	16.1	47.3
Oglala Lakota	71	1,933	324	NA	157	57	12	70	36,004	190	3.7	54.7	54.3
Pennington	3,819	48,811	10,639	2,595	8,071	2,267	1,898	2,127	43,568	656	24.2	28.4	42.6
Perkins	119	739	132	124	106	49	19	26	34,654	421	5.9	65.1	69.4
Potter	97	596	123	NA	102	45	11	29	48,180	221	5.4	49.3	60.4
Roberts	233	2,003	352	310	415	88	22	66	32,913	782	15.0	25.2	50.3
Sanborn	57	387	63	64	43	21	24	14	34,941	351	12.5	31.3	52.5
Spink	180	1,296	285	76	194	97	37	57	44,194	556	10.6	48.4	64.5
Stanley	121	905	24	8	181	26	49	35	39,087	172	8.7	59.3	58.1
Sully	65	337	8	47	97	22	NA	16	47,021	201	10.0	52.7	70.2
Todd	53	975	324	NA	247	16	NA	38	39,247	223	3.6	58.7	68.3

STATE County	Agriculture, 2017 (cont.) Land in farms Acreage (1,000)	Land in farms Percent change, 2012–2017	Land in farms Acres Average size of farm	Land in farms Acres Total irrigated (1,000)	Land in farms Acres Total cropland (1,000)	Value of land and buildings (dollars) Average per farm	Value of land and buildings (dollars) Average per acre	Value of machinery and equipment, average per farm (dollars)	Value of products sold: Total (mil dol)	Value of products sold: Average per farm (acres)	Value of products sold: Percent from: Crops	Value of products sold: Percent from: Livestock and poultry products	Organic farms (number)	Farms with internet access (per-cent)	Government payments Total ($1,000)	Government payments Percent of farms
	117	118	119	120	121	122	123	124	125	126	127	128	129	130	131	132
SOUTH CAROLINA—Cont'd																
Sumter	168	-4.7	320	19.1	91.4	958,464	2,995	134,000	153.4	292,763	32.6	67.4	5	79.6	1,534	30.7
Union	44	-7.5	182	0.0	7.3	460,174	2,534	64,867	10.3	42,859	10.4	89.6	NA	62.7	426	25.3
Williamsburg	209	-7.1	378	2.6	107.7	848,443	2,245	118,529	47.2	85,562	86.7	13.3	NA	60.1	2,191	55.3
York	120	-3.0	120	1.2	37.9	838,682	6,979	63,006	100.5	100,504	63.2	36.8	NA	67.7	876	17.5
SOUTH DAKOTA	43,244	0.0	1,443	492.5	19,813.5	2,984,426	2,068	282,162	9,721.5	324,397	53.1	46.9	87	81.0	419,508	72.1
Aurora	355	-19.8	904	NA	228.8	2,400,283	2,654	297,809	138.2	352,541	46.7	53.3	NA	82.1	4,879	82.9
Beadle	811	2.1	1,090	20.1	548.5	2,934,337	2,693	331,767	295.3	396,867	56.6	43.4	NA	84.9	12,672	73.7
Bennett	637	5.0	2,990	8.5	214.3	2,846,734	952	251,150	65.9	309,545	40.6	59.4	NA	72.3	3,641	71.8
Bon Homme	305	-13.3	523	8.6	228.4	2,083,627	3,984	274,056	152.9	262,182	51.0	49.0	2	79.9	6,300	86.6
Brookings	460	2.3	519	20.5	345.4	2,386,912	4,602	248,257	316.3	357,034	39.9	60.1	3	84.4	6,331	59.5
Brown	1,083	0.4	1,047	4.4	884.6	3,521,412	3,362	360,625	377.4	365,032	77.8	22.2	2	78.8	11,893	62.9
Brule	518	0.7	1,314	5.4	277.9	3,386,122	2,578	312,852	153.6	389,759	32.5	67.5	NA	78.4	5,948	77.2
Buffalo	300	1.3	4,410	9.3	85.4	6,815,539	1,545	502,785	39.5	581,059	42.2	57.8	NA	86.8	2,436	79.4
Butte	1,155	1.8	2,044	46.7	150.2	1,959,536	959	127,586	68.0	120,312	12.5	87.5	NA	78.1	5,104	52.4
Campbell	434	20.4	1,742	4.6	250.8	3,190,052	1,831	339,855	96.2	386,333	57.6	42.4	NA	73.9	3,925	87.1
Charles Mix	686	-0.9	1,022	13.4	451.0	2,850,723	2,788	350,312	262.1	390,633	45.8	54.2	1	85.5	9,733	88.5
Clark	602	-1.1	1,089	17.6	444.8	3,428,717	3,150	290,526	267.6	483,870	55.6	44.4	NA	81.7	7,415	82.3
Clay	239	-7.6	506	28.1	221.2	2,380,474	4,702	299,816	113.1	239,606	88.1	11.9	3	79.2	4,754	81.4
Codington	383	3.8	638	8.2	268.0	2,210,441	3,467	217,944	155.9	259,364	57.1	42.9	2	80.5	7,928	58.6
Corson	1,288	3.6	3,998	D	398.6	3,675,545	919	325,133	117.0	363,205	28.6	71.4	2	80.7	6,905	80.1
Custer	612	-1.8	1,387	3.9	49.4	2,213,944	1,596	86,361	26.6	60,392	7.3	92.7	NA	76.9	1,641	37.9
Davison	270	-1.8	584	2.7	212.4	1,983,497	3,398	224,120	107.7	232,538	61.4	38.6	NA	84.7	4,987	60.3
Day	611	7.1	1,051	1.3	456.5	2,779,344	2,645	275,390	184.0	316,661	82.9	17.1	NA	68.7	13,431	79.3
Deuel	335	-1.9	529	0.5	223.8	1,823,780	3,448	207,041	184.9	291,655	37.9	62.1	3	79.5	4,029	73.8
Dewey	1,137	-3.8	3,666	D	195.6	3,555,413	970	259,622	58.7	189,394	23.3	76.7	7	73.2	5,510	83.2
Douglas	275	1.9	701	1.8	214.7	2,607,726	3,721	327,367	144.6	368,954	44.4	55.6	NA	78.3	4,604	76.3
Edmunds	739	6.0	2,124	5.8	569.5	5,223,055	2,460	551,208	237.7	683,029	64.6	35.4	1	85.3	6,569	83.3
Fall River	898	-17.5	2,860	9.3	68.7	2,048,121	716	113,245	87.1	277,347	3.7	96.3	2	81.8	2,368	49.7
Faulk	627	1.9	2,155	D	408.4	5,489,770	2,547	421,205	164.0	563,416	65.9	34.1	2	86.6	12,360	82.8
Grant	426	-0.7	768	5.2	307.7	2,864,773	3,729	336,697	235.4	424,986	50.3	49.7	1	78.5	4,192	69.7
Gregory	562	-11.5	1,136	0.3	226.1	2,134,179	1,879	208,369	93.1	188,004	45.9	54.1	NA	82.6	4,617	80.6
Haakon	1,158	2.1	3,951	D	323.9	3,646,592	923	257,669	77.3	263,949	33.1	66.9	NA	87.0	7,822	84.0
Hamlin	310	-0.3	651	9.0	249.6	2,557,064	3,926	304,618	179.8	377,664	54.1	45.9	1	84.5	3,100	69.3
Hand	895	-1.1	2,211	2.6	578.0	4,545,489	2,056	456,429	224.5	554,210	63.5	36.5	1	82.0	12,357	83.5
Hanson	271	-1.1	814	5.1	226.0	3,516,095	4,322	370,625	132.8	398,778	61.8	38.2	NA	73.9	5,966	76.3
Harding	1,468	0.0	5,539	1.1	184.6	3,683,948	665	228,551	63.4	239,125	12.0	88.0	NA	86.4	6,699	67.2
Hughes	435	1.0	1,381	11.5	263.0	2,611,187	1,891	265,639	70.3	223,095	62.0	38.0	5	84.4	6,354	63.5
Hutchinson	456	-11.2	588	7.3	363.8	2,642,567	4,495	304,494	270.0	348,405	48.6	51.4	3	77.3	9,766	82.5
Hyde	506	-1.7	2,906	D	219.9	4,438,942	1,527	351,062	64.9	372,983	58.6	41.4	NA	87.4	4,401	75.9
Jackson	1,166	0.7	3,714	0.3	185.5	3,248,165	875	164,945	52.4	167,003	14.5	85.5	1	79.3	4,724	67.2
Jerauld	342	2.6	1,400	3.0	219.8	3,348,353	2,391	378,327	112.5	461,242	45.2	54.8	NA	76.6	3,271	80.3
Jones	618	1.0	3,221	D	233.8	3,680,881	1,143	323,434	57.9	301,516	55.6	44.4	NA	81.8	3,245	83.3
Kingsbury	536	2.8	1,035	2.6	391.2	3,941,833	3,810	367,554	257.9	497,790	56.0	44.0	2	82.8	3,492	70.5
Lake	273	4.1	589	8.2	225.6	3,014,550	5,121	299,337	161.9	349,624	61.4	38.6	2	84.0	2,755	76.2
Lawrence	165	3.9	600	4.4	33.6	1,073,421	1,789	103,416	13.1	47,575	14.8	85.2	NA	80.0	452	18.5
Lincoln	295	-19.4	390	2.1	267.9	2,692,014	6,906	189,954	204.8	270,886	59.8	40.2	2	77.5	6,210	70.0
Lyman	951	-7.6	2,297	D	419.2	3,792,074	1,651	300,717	97.0	234,401	56.0	44.0	1	77.1	12,929	89.6
McCook	367	1.2	717	0.0	294.3	3,131,091	4,367	271,011	195.9	382,695	62.6	37.4	NA	82.4	5,726	84.2
McPherson	723	26.2	1,893	1.3	383.9	4,077,571	2,154	363,067	140.2	367,047	45.2	54.8	6	75.7	4,087	85.3
Marshall	525	-1.3	1,045	0.7	343.4	2,939,925	2,814	321,438	270.7	538,147	39.9	60.1	2	83.7	8,489	81.3
Meade	1,999	-1.7	2,394	5.3	394.8	2,277,231	951	169,003	99.2	118,764	11.4	88.6	3	79.2	11,199	52.3
Mellette	753	7.7	3,436	0.7	131.1	3,314,464	965	216,199	45.4	207,411	18.4	81.6	5	81.7	2,321	77.6
Miner	351	-1.7	861	D	239.8	3,042,444	3,533	239,023	126.1	308,963	56.6	43.4	NA	79.7	6,404	79.2
Minnehaha	375	-8.1	366	5.2	318.0	2,362,080	6,449	232,537	253.8	248,073	58.9	41.1	2	87.4	2,507	56.0
Moody	265	4.2	541	3.3	223.5	3,147,674	5,820	296,266	216.1	440,976	47.8	52.2	2	83.9	3,759	59.0
Oglala Lakota	1,116	1.4	5,875	D	88.9	3,960,426	674	147,320	38.7	203,926	20.0	80.0	NA	82.6	3,643	55.8
Pennington	1,147	6.7	1,748	10.7	207.2	1,849,403	1,058	126,171	60.5	92,155	28.0	72.0	NA	83.1	6,415	42.7
Perkins	1,640	0.5	3,895	NA	347.7	3,236,529	831	232,943	84.9	201,646	14.6	85.4	NA	84.3	9,976	79.8
Potter	548	1.9	2,481	1.6	386.5	5,246,162	2,114	546,151	101.9	461,045	82.0	18.0	NA	79.6	7,893	92.3
Roberts	595	-4.5	761	2.4	451.7	2,288,827	3,007	260,731	204.4	261,366	78.1	21.9	7	79.7	8,289	74.9
Sanborn	364	0.9	1,036	0.0	200.4	2,959,610	2,857	265,179	112.1	319,262	46.4	53.6	NA	80.1	2,914	67.2
Spink	961	1.7	1,729	22.3	832.8	5,413,741	3,132	510,061	382.5	687,917	73.7	26.3	1	82.9	20,072	89.6
Stanley	812	2.7	4,722	NA	195.7	4,349,277	921	241,233	50.6	294,256	35.7	64.3	NA	77.9	3,863	76.7
Sully	633	0.7	3,149	23.7	505.7	6,783,106	2,154	612,046	137.2	682,781	74.2	25.8	NA	88.6	10,351	80.1
Todd	880	2.3	3,946	7.8	113.7	3,355,405	850	254,915	53.7	240,619	11.4	88.6	1	82.5	686	57.0

STATE County	Water use, 2015		Wholesale Trade[1], 2017				Retail Trade[2], 2017				Real estate and rental and leasing,[2] 2017			
	Public supply water withdrawn (mil gal/ day)	Public supply gallons withdrawn per person per day	Number of establish- ments	Number of employees	Sales (mil dol)	Average payroll (mil dol)	Number of establish- ments	Number of employees	Sales (mil dol)	Average payroll (mil dol)	Number of establish- ments	Number of employees	Sales (mil dol)	Average payroll (mil dol)
	133	134	135	136	137	138	139	140	141	142	143	144	145	146
SOUTH CAROLINA—Cont'd														
Sumter	14.6	135.8	64	634	329.7	29.9	353	4,531	1,110.3	101.7	66	300	43.6	8.4
Union	2.9	105.8	12	97	54.4	3.5	91	869	188.7	17.2	15	151	10.0	3.8
Williamsburg	3.0	92.8	17	190	117.4	6.5	114	866	216.8	17.9	13	26	4.1	0.6
York	20.6	82.1	256	4,176	3,063.4	250.7	682	11,255	3,169.3	270.2	302	1,499	329.4	72.5
SOUTH DAKOTA	72.0	81.7	1,392	16,630	17,314.3	887.0	3,884	53,134	14,673.7	1,372.0	1,143	4,330	829.0	155.0
Aurora	0.2	69.5	6	D	37.6	D	9	91	29.1	1.5	NA	NA	NA	NA
Beadle	2.3	124.6	33	454	439.5	25.7	77	1,015	260.0	24.4	31	103	9.8	1.6
Bennett	0.2	49.7	NA	NA	NA	NA	15	157	28.8	2.6	NA	NA	NA	NA
Bon Homme	0.6	80.2	D	D	D	3.9	25	151	38.8	2.9	4	D	0.7	D
Brookings	2.8	81.7	39	329	369.3	17.3	108	1,753	400.7	41.2	45	187	22.9	5.9
Brown	3.5	89.5	80	1,070	1,680.7	54.3	184	2,916	795.4	78.1	64	297	51.7	11.1
Brule	0.5	98.5	13	113	143.1	4.9	43	276	81.5	7.2	NA	NA	NA	NA
Buffalo	0.1	47.7	NA	NA	NA	NA	NA	NA	NA	NA	NA	NA	NA	NA
Butte	0.5	50.6	9	53	47.6	1.7	53	510	166.7	15.4	D	D	D	D
Campbell	0.1	57.3	6	36	43.7	1.7	7	D	6.8	D	NA	NA	NA	NA
Charles Mix	0.6	58.6	16	135	99.8	6.3	44	444	78.3	7.6	5	D	0.9	D
Clark	0.2	43.7	10	D	83.0	D	14	121	29.6	2.9	NA	NA	NA	NA
Clay	1.0	73.0	D	D	D	D	43	692	164.1	15.2	10	16	4.4	0.5
Codington	3.7	133.9	63	685	483.9	36.7	190	2,704	678.3	66.5	63	122	20.6	3.8
Corson	0.2	42.9	D	D	D	D	4	63	13.4	1.3	NA	NA	NA	NA
Custer	0.3	33.2	NA	NA	NA	NA	33	263	69.1	5.6	11	28	4.1	0.8
Davison	1.9	96.7	39	448	572.6	19.7	131	1,910	554.2	49.9	D	D	D	D
Day	0.4	79.4	12	143	191.1	7.0	33	280	82.0	6.2	D	D	D	0.0
Deuel	0.2	39.2	8	59	69.8	2.9	18	103	32.5	3.0	NA	NA	NA	NA
Dewey	0.3	58.0	4	77	36.5	2.4	10	80	23.2	1.2	3	D	0.8	D
Douglas	0.2	60.5	D	D	D	4.9	19	126	43.7	2.9	NA	NA	NA	NA
Edmunds	0.3	65.0	13	220	328.2	9.6	22	145	42.0	3.2	4	6	1.6	0.1
Fall River	0.7	96.1	NA	NA	NA	NA	35	233	62.1	5.9	8	12	1.7	0.3
Faulk	0.2	64.2	10	D	67.8	D	7	65	16.3	1.4	NA	NA	NA	NA
Grant	0.6	88.2	12	116	88.8	6.2	47	534	124.3	12.4	6	8	0.9	0.2
Gregory	0.3	61.9	7	D	32.4	D	34	215	64.3	5.3	3	8	0.5	0.2
Haakon	0.1	59.1	8	117	153.7	3.8	15	112	28.0	2.9	NA	NA	NA	NA
Hamlin	0.4	67.8	15	144	137.9	8.2	18	172	56.9	4.8	NA	NA	NA	NA
Hand	0.2	62.7	11	135	74.8	6.4	22	140	31.6	3.0	NA	NA	NA	NA
Hanson	0.1	26.6	5	29	156.1	1.5	5	37	5.9	0.6	NA	NA	NA	NA
Harding	0.0	23.7	NA	NA	NA	NA	8	46	11.6	1.0	NA	NA	NA	NA
Hughes	2.7	152.1	29	286	687.2	16.4	96	1,493	378.5	35.9	29	53	13.0	1.8
Hutchinson	0.4	53.4	25	336	436.4	15.5	36	361	83.7	7.0	NA	NA	NA	NA
Hyde	0.1	78.7	7	73	89.9	4.1	6	75	16.5	1.5	NA	NA	NA	NA
Jackson	0.1	39.1	NA	NA	NA	NA	14	113	36.0	2.0	NA	NA	NA	NA
Jerauld	0.5	270.4	6	106	48.2	4.6	9	46	12.1	1.2	NA	NA	NA	NA
Jones	0.1	54.1	NA	NA	NA	NA	9	74	38.2	2.2	NA	NA	NA	NA
Kingsbury	0.2	44.1	11	111	168.7	6.1	22	139	29.2	2.9	D	D	D	D
Lake	0.8	64.2	19	228	290.8	13.1	46	506	174.0	13.5	12	25	2.6	0.5
Lawrence	2.4	94.7	D	D	D	2.2	143	1,485	493.1	40.7	66	202	25.1	5.4
Lincoln	1.0	19.3	57	577	533.3	31.9	166	2,317	902.5	76.2	93	506	89.8	17.1
Lyman	0.2	56.8	NA	NA	NA	NA	15	185	65.2	3.6	NA	NA	NA	NA
McCook	0.7	126.8	D	D	D	D	22	177	44.7	4.0	D	D	D	D
McPherson	0.1	53.8	4	D	27.6	D	13	63	12.7	1.3	NA	NA	NA	NA
Marshall	0.2	46.1	12	75	104.7	3.6	24	184	38.7	4.5	D	D	D	D
Meade	1.4	52.6	D	D	D	D	91	837	308.7	23.6	27	69	9.2	1.8
Mellette	0.1	43.9	NA	NA	NA	NA	5	45	6.8	0.7	NA	NA	NA	NA
Miner	0.1	49.2	4	45	7.9	1.9	14	73	17.9	1.4	NA	NA	NA	NA
Minnehaha	19.7	94.7	367	5,813	4,456.2	336.2	812	15,657	4,066.9	413.3	273	1,541	313.2	70.0
Moody	0.5	76.2	D	D	D	D	18	146	34.4	2.4	D	D	D	D
Oglala Lakota	1.1	76.5	NA	NA	NA	NA	15	186	45.7	4.0	NA	NA	NA	NA
Pennington	10.6	97.7	143	1,649	1,008.4	86.2	577	9,025	2,701.1	249.3	229	681	181.3	23.1
Perkins	0.2	53.0	D	D	D	2.7	19	145	25.8	3.2	NA	NA	NA	NA
Potter	0.2	86.2	9	134	324.9	7.3	18	89	17.5	1.9	NA	NA	NA	NA
Roberts	0.6	56.3	D	D	D	D	37	382	81.5	7.7	D	D	D	D
Sanborn	0.1	55.2	4	30	38.5	1.9	D	D	D	0.5	NA	NA	NA	NA
Spink	0.5	79.7	19	179	388.2	11.4	29	213	43.5	4.7	3	D	1.0	D
Stanley	0.3	108.3	D	D	D	D	20	170	75.2	5.0	NA	NA	NA	NA
Sully	0.0	0.0	D	D	D	2.6	11	95	35.1	2.5	NA	NA	NA	NA
Todd	0.4	42.2	NA	NA	NA	NA	17	264	46.4	3.9	NA	NA	NA	NA

1 Merchant wholesalers, except manufacturers' sales branches and offices. 2. Employer establishments.

STATE County	Professional, scientific, and technical services, 2017				Manufacturing, 2017				Accommodation and food services, 2017			
	Number of establish-ments	Number of employees	Sales (mil dol)	Average payroll (mil dol)	Number of establish-ments	Number of employees	Sales (mil dol)	Average payroll (mil dol)	Number of establis-hments	Number of employees	Sales (mil dol)	Annual payroll (mil dol)
	147	148	149	150	151	152	153	154	155	156	157	158
SOUTH CAROLINA—Cont'd												
Sumter	D	D	D	D	68	5,559	1,976.3	258.4	171	3,354	164.7	44.8
Union	20	43	4.5	1.0	28	1,579	757.7	80.9	35	525	24.7	6.7
Williamsburg	20	107	13.2	6.2	29	2,177	1,486.8	101.6	32	307	14.5	3.2
York	D	D	D	D	213	10,405	4,012.9	623.7	436	9,523	492.3	136.2
SOUTH DAKOTA	1,952	12,998	1,755.9	651.6	1,051	42,935	16,779.5	2,057.4	2,495	40,704	2,315.5	659.2
Aurora	D	D	D	2.8	NA	NA	NA	NA	9	25	1.3	0.3
Beadle	26	121	12.3	4.6	33	1,595	524.4	61.5	40	514	24.2	7.3
Bennett	NA	NA	NA	NA	NA	NA	NA	NA	8	D	2.9	D
Bon Homme	6	24	2.9	1.0	10	118	30.2	5.1	8	D	1.8	D
Brookings	76	555	72.1	26.9	35	4,950	2,634.3	267.0	90	1,808	82.0	24.2
Brown	71	427	52.5	19.0	D	3,206	D	148.3	103	1,974	100.2	29.9
Brule	17	57	3.8	1.3	7	50	12.5	1.3	30	275	18.9	4.3
Buffalo	NA	NA	NA	NA	NA	NA	NA	NA	NA	NA	NA	NA
Butte	27	94	8.9	2.8	17	198	93.6	9.3	D	D	D	D
Campbell	D	D	0.8	D	3	46	37.1	2.3	7	D	0.7	D
Charles Mix	11	44	5.3	1.2	10	83	17.6	3.6	21	525	17.9	7.3
Clark	11	26	3.2	0.9	7	94	19.7	4.6	10	75	2.2	0.9
Clay	19	161	12.2	4.2	11	176	53.3	9.4	47	876	35.8	12.3
Codington	70	268	40.0	11.8	75	3,274	921.6	148.3	90	1,797	90.8	27.0
Corson	NA	NA	NA	NA	NA	NA	NA	NA	D	D	D	D
Custer	25	54	14.2	2.3	10	17	2.5	0.6	63	450	45.7	11.8
Davison	41	791	109.5	40.0	41	1,986	802.6	109.3	85	1,346	66.3	18.9
Day	9	25	3.4	0.9	10	147	36.2	7.3	20	168	7.3	2.2
Deuel	7	25	3.2	1.0	5	196	33.4	9.4	9	D	3.0	D
Dewey	NA	NA	NA	NA	NA	NA	NA	NA	4	11	0.7	0.1
Douglas	6	12	1.0	0.3	9	93	18.9	3.9	6	D	0.9	D
Edmunds	5	26	3.8	1.1	D	68	D	3.6	12	60	2.4	0.8
Fall River	12	51	4.7	1.3	5	7	1.2	0.2	40	330	18.6	4.8
Faulk	3	7	0.3	0.1	NA	NA	NA	NA	12	59	2.9	0.5
Grant	15	42	4.8	1.3	14	628	791.0	32.0	28	273	12.0	2.9
Gregory	11	34	5.7	1.1	7	31	4.9	1.7	20	99	5.8	1.2
Haakon	D	D	2.2	D	D	85	D	3.4	7	D	2.1	D
Hamlin	6	25	1.4	0.7	D	D	D	9.5	10	D	3.5	D
Hand	12	214	13.9	8.4	7	56	33.2	2.8	14	85	3.1	0.8
Hanson	7	11	0.8	0.3	4	100	23.6	4.7	7	16	1.4	0.2
Harding	NA	NA	NA	NA	NA	NA	NA	NA	4	D	1.5	D
Hughes	D	D	D	D	9	47	29.2	2.7	52	908	45.7	13.5
Hutchinson	11	32	3.0	1.3	14	242	87.5	12.2	D	D	D	0.8
Hyde	3	2	0.4	0.1	NA	NA	NA	NA	3	4	0.3	0.0
Jackson	NA	NA	NA	NA	NA	NA	NA	NA	13	48	7.1	1.7
Jerauld	5	16	2.4	0.6	D	D	D	D	9	58	3.1	0.8
Jones	NA	NA	NA	NA	NA	NA	NA	NA	18	76	5.7	1.6
Kingsbury	6	17	2.4	0.8	8	263	68.7	12.2	6	30	1.5	0.4
Lake	42	240	29.6	9.4	23	769	281.8	33.9	32	412	16.0	4.8
Lawrence	79	283	34.5	13.6	39	428	151.6	17.8	133	2,883	211.2	56.3
Lincoln	D	D	D	D	D	1,780	D	79.5	80	1,443	77.1	22.6
Lyman	D	D	D	D	NA	NA	NA	NA	15	220	13.5	4.1
McCook	12	43	5.6	1.5	5	9	1.7	0.4	19	81	3.9	0.9
McPherson	NA	NA	NA	NA	8	54	5.6	1.5	5	D	1.2	D
Marshall	9	24	2.3	0.8	6	381	206.7	20.2	13	115	4.2	1.2
Meade	D	D	D	D	36	184	37.9	9.5	69	591	50.1	11.5
Mellette	NA	NA	NA	NA	NA	NA	NA	NA	3	7	0.4	0.1
Miner	4	24	1.5	0.5	7	85	24.2	5.1	10	D	1.4	D
Minnehaha	D	D	D	D	185	12,175	3,956.3	608.8	485	11,738	637.8	185.6
Moody	12	20	1.6	0.5	10	279	70.2	12.9	12	411	42.5	8.2
Oglala Lakota	NA	NA	NA	NA	NA	NA	NA	NA	11	261	19.5	6.5
Pennington	D	D	D	D	126	2,325	579.9	103.4	382	7,075	439.8	127.6
Perkins	8	22	2.0	0.6	D	D	D	D	D	D	D	0.5
Potter	3	10	1.0	0.3	D	D	D	D	9	D	3.6	D
Roberts	D	D	D	D	12	317	85.8	11.5	D	D	D	D
Sanborn	7	19	2.5	0.5	NA	NA	NA	NA	5	D	0.9	D
Spink	7	33	4.6	1.8	7	70	122.3	4.8	18	126	6.4	1.8
Stanley	D	D	D	D	NA	NA	NA	NA	D	D	D	3.8
Sully	NA	NA	NA	NA	NA	NA	NA	NA	D	D	D	2.4
Todd	NA	NA	NA	NA	NA	NA	NA	NA	NA	NA	NA	NA

STATE County	Health care and social assistance, 2017				Other services, 2017				Nonemployer businesses, 2019		Value of residential construction authorized by building permits, 2021	
	Number of establish-ments	Number of employees	Receipts (mil dol)	Annual payroll (mil dol)	Number of establish-ments	Number of employees	Receipts (mil dol)	Annual payroll (mil dol)	Number	Receipts (mil dol)	New construction ($1,000)	Number of housing units
	159	160	161	162	163	164	165	166	167	168	169	170
SOUTH CAROLINA—Cont'd												
Sumter	189	5,237	601.9	198.2	120	991	95.0	27.6	6,339	237.9	61,745	388
Union	27	1,012	90.4	36.0	29	107	10.0	2.8	1,141	39.6	7,999	42
Williamsburg	51	894	80.8	25.8	28	165	30.2	5.3	1,651	58.4	6,569	39
York	529	10,049	1,113.4	382.8	335	2,305	269.9	81.2	20,303	841.3	981,990	3,271
SOUTH DAKOTA	2,420	71,821	8,714.4	3,458.2	1,860	8,713	1,224.4	277.6	68,801	3,396.9	1,565,480	7,917
Aurora	8	203	14.7	7.6	D	D	D	0.9	258	9.0	3,430	12
Beadle	62	1,300	97.8	43.8	44	158	18.5	4.7	1,073	50.8	21,571	132
Bennett	6	142	11.8	6.3	NA	NA	NA	NA	179	6.7	0	0
Bon Homme	17	326	23.6	10.4	D	D	4.1	D	433	19.4	3,412	19
Brookings	93	1,511	132.5	49.6	65	318	67.5	10.5	2,108	104.3	38,365	176
Brown	111	3,135	359.2	146.1	D	D	D	D	2,804	148.9	15,163	95
Brule	26	348	34.0	14.7	19	79	8.0	2.2	470	25.7	2,710	18
Buffalo	4	32	2.4	1.3	NA	NA	NA	NA	41	1.3	0	0
Butte	30	298	24.2	9.2	D	D	D	D	940	36.2	19,836	83
Campbell	5	D	1.1	D	3	5	0.6	0.1	139	6.4	0	0
Charles Mix	28	521	40.8	16.7	D	D	D	1.6	678	24.7	7,205	29
Clark	9	D	4.9	D	D	D	D	0.8	267	11.9	2,709	8
Clay	32	726	57.6	19.1	22	85	23.4	3.4	861	40.4	8,354	33
Codington	79	1,932	220.3	77.6	75	336	36.5	9.2	2,245	102.8	47,661	267
Corson	4	D	0.7	D	NA	NA	NA	NA	135	4.6	0	0
Custer	D	D	D	D	13	43	4.5	1.2	901	41.7	59,051	240
Davison	69	2,093	173.8	69.9	D	D	D	D	1,512	72.7	16,186	68
Day	17	279	25.8	8.7	16	38	2.7	0.7	490	19.7	6,767	24
Deuel	6	173	15.4	5.7	8	12	1.8	0.5	388	16.7	3,928	11
Dewey	12	151	21.0	8.2	D	D	D	D	286	15.2	218	1
Douglas	6	227	14.7	7.4	D	D	4.2	D	272	12.6	590	3
Edmunds	10	184	10.1	4.2	D	D	D	D	368	21.6	315	1
Fall River	D	D	D	D	17	61	6.3	1.4	620	26.2	1,442	13
Faulk	D	D	D	D	D	D	D	D	217	11.6	660	4
Grant	24	601	52.2	23.7	17	77	9.5	1.9	629	23.2	930	3
Gregory	16	246	21.2	8.0	17	34	3.8	0.9	526	22.5	538	2
Haakon	D	D	D	D	5	11	1.9	0.5	223	12.5	0	0
Hamlin	10	150	4.3	2.2	D	D	4.1	D	476	19.7	18,618	56
Hand	8	208	16.4	6.0	D	D	2.2	D	315	14.4	1,003	7
Hanson	3	13	0.4	0.2	D	D	D	D	323	16.1	2,667	7
Harding	6	89	2.6	1.6	NA	NA	NA	NA	175	7.0	1,210	3
Hughes	67	1,294	134.9	54.8	70	272	105.9	12.2	1,447	68.1	21,379	40
Hutchinson	16	536	45.2	16.9	D	D	D	D	566	22.3	5,307	22
Hyde	NA	NA	NA	NA	3	4	0.3	0.1	120	5.9	0	0
Jackson	NA	NA	NA	NA	NA	NA	NA	NA	183	5.9	0	0
Jerauld	6	118	10.1	4.5	D	D	2.6	D	176	6.8	0	0
Jones	NA	NA	NA	NA	NA	NA	NA	NA	110	5.0	0	4
Kingsbury	11	183	13.2	5.2	D	D	2.7	D	510	20.8	5,227	30
Lake	30	625	50.5	22.5	23	89	8.8	2.5	895	40.8	20,694	67
Lawrence	89	1,865	189.3	72.6	70	212	23.1	6.9	2,741	136.4	134,448	365
Lincoln	173	3,092	373.2	136.5	D	D	D	D	5,498	321.8	108,078	599
Lyman	NA	NA	NA	NA	4	6	0.6	0.1	229	11.6	850	3
McCook	19	241	12.4	6.1	D	D	D	D	518	25.1	5,157	22
McPherson	5	D	3.5	D	D	D	D	0.3	206	11.8	15	1
Marshall	12	182	12.0	4.5	D	D	D	0.6	346	15.3	7,592	26
Meade	D	D	D	D	50	171	24.5	5.2	2,413	107.7	44,418	175
Mellette	NA	NA	NA	NA	NA	NA	NA	NA	116	5.0	254	2
Miner	8	127	6.6	3.4	D	D	D	0.8	204	9.2	1,189	5
Minnehaha	480	27,862	3,669.3	1,509.8	374	2,704	394.8	93.7	14,613	792.2	571,911	3,340
Moody	13	196	16.4	6.1	D	D	3.4	D	413	21.7	7,042	32
Oglala Lakota	D	D	D	D	NA	NA	NA	NA	407	6.8	NA	NA
Pennington	392	10,698	1,458.5	548.1	292	1,590	188.8	52.3	9,022	433.0	233,210	1,387
Perkins	18	132	9.7	4.4	D	D	4.6	D	279	9.8	0	0
Potter	11	D	5.6	D	D	D	D	0.9	237	15.0	625	3
Roberts	21	418	31.4	13.9	13	40	4.2	1.1	638	25.4	8,971	41
Sanborn	D	D	D	D	D	D	0.7	D	201	8.6	2,756	10
Spink	16	299	19.7	8.6	14	50	5.1	1.4	513	25.1	2,078	9
Stanley	D	D	D	D	D	D	D	D	334	19.8	4,549	16
Sully	D	D	D	D	NA	NA	NA	NA	205	11.8	5,719	21
Todd	5	279	44.2	18.4	D	D	D	D	208	5.4	0	0

STATE County	Government employment and payroll, 2017									Local government finances, 2017				
			March payroll (percent of total)							General revenue				
												Taxes		
													Per capita[1] (dollars)	
	Full-time equivalent employees	March payroll (dollars)	Adminis-tration, judicial, and legal	Police and corrections	Fire protection	Highways and transpor-tation	Health and welfare	Natural resources and utilities	Education and libraries	Total (mil dol)	Inter-govern-mental (mil dol)	Total (mil dol)	Total	Property
	171	172	173	174	175	176	177	178	179	180	181	182	183	184
SOUTH CAROLINA—Cont'd														
Sumter	3,681	12,149,418	7.0	9.5	2.9	2.1	2.6	5.3	67.4	327.7	150.8	129.3	1,215	806
Union	1,044	3,525,859	8.6	11.9	0.8	1.7	2.5	8.1	64.3	81.6	37.9	27.7	1,009	872
Williamsburg	1,109	3,202,225	11.6	5.0	6.2	3.1	6.5	5.2	61.3	102.7	59.4	30.9	990	832
York	7,105	29,085,516	8.6	10.2	2.8	1.1	2.0	8.1	66.3	875.6	316.4	438.4	1,647	1,350
SOUTH DAKOTA	X	X	X	X	X	X	X	X	X	X	X	X	X	X
Aurora	124	323,894	13.4	4.1	0.1	10.2	0.8	5.3	59.6	12.4	4.8	6.6	2,386	2,099
Beadle	685	2,569,177	6.1	10.0	1.8	5.8	0.8	6.3	63.6	79.5	22.5	47.5	2,560	2,120
Bennett	152	425,079	7.7	7.9	0.0	5.4	2.5	2.0	72.0	10.8	6.2	3.7	1,077	826
Bon Homme	288	954,127	9.1	4.8	0.0	7.7	1.8	9.2	67.1	19.5	7.9	9.6	1,375	1,135
Brookings	1,453	5,999,158	4.5	6.2	0.3	3.2	23.9	11.4	37.9	206.6	27.4	67.4	1,940	1,386
Brown	1,331	5,148,388	7.0	9.9	4.2	6.0	1.4	9.3	60.3	141.8	38.5	81.3	2,069	1,460
Brule	274	866,666	6.2	6.5	0.0	4.5	1.5	7.1	71.8	30.9	12.7	13.8	2,596	1,791
Buffalo	9	28,865	51.6	20.6	0.0	22.6	5.3	0.0	0.0	1.3	0.1	1.2	586	488
Butte	431	1,270,170	6.7	7.1	0.0	4.6	0.5	16.3	61.7	38.5	13.2	18.1	1,794	1,424
Campbell	46	155,348	21.0	5.0	0.0	20.9	0.6	3.3	44.7	6.1	1.1	3.6	2,628	2,219
Charles Mix	487	1,599,649	6.0	3.2	0.0	3.9	2.5	6.5	74.2	38.7	16.2	17.6	1,876	1,548
Clark	185	518,044	11.0	3.7	0.0	13.2	2.8	3.6	65.0	15.6	4.0	10.3	2,812	2,457
Clay	335	1,243,105	9.8	11.8	0.7	5.4	1.5	15.1	50.2	37.6	9.4	19.6	1,396	1,067
Codington	1,155	4,716,648	5.0	7.0	4.1	3.6	0.4	14.3	63.4	117.4	28.0	59.6	2,120	1,698
Corson	252	860,565	4.5	2.8	0.0	4.1	0.0	3.0	84.5	19.3	14.6	3.9	934	777
Custer	245	818,492	14.0	7.1	0.0	7.3	3.5	3.3	61.6	32.4	6.1	20.0	2,287	1,865
Davison	950	3,310,784	5.3	9.6	3.8	4.4	2.6	8.0	64.9	103.0	29.5	51.8	2,608	1,903
Day	191	581,367	10.7	8.3	0.0	12.4	1.1	5.9	59.6	19.5	5.1	11.4	2,074	1,758
Deuel	129	484,861	17.3	8.1	0.0	16.2	0.2	3.0	50.5	14.0	2.8	8.7	2,021	1,711
Dewey	238	717,869	6.2	2.8	0.0	5.9	0.3	3.4	79.0	17.2	11.9	4.1	704	519
Douglas	85	312,392	30.4	6.3	0.0	14.5	0.0	5.0	36.4	12.8	2.7	8.5	2,894	2,454
Edmunds	301	888,143	7.0	3.0	0.0	8.3	35.9	0.4	41.2	29.4	4.0	13.0	3,332	2,953
Fall River	341	1,042,827	7.0	6.1	0.0	5.9	6.1	7.1	61.5	30.8	11.3	13.2	1,976	1,587
Faulk	168	625,484	9.4	4.4	0.0	6.3	60.4	0.8	18.5	19.5	1.8	7.1	3,076	2,758
Grant	271	949,862	11.8	6.8	0.0	7.1	0.6	4.5	67.0	26.1	6.4	16.3	2,272	1,783
Gregory	194	691,203	10.7	4.6	0.0	10.5	0.6	1.6	71.9	16.4	5.7	9.0	2,136	1,732
Haakon	96	297,796	10.8	4.2	0.3	10.8	1.0	4.1	47.5	12.7	3.2	7.8	4,058	3,169
Hamlin	351	1,240,059	5.0	2.0	0.0	3.3	16.4	2.3	70.7	28.2	9.0	14.7	2,457	2,210
Hand	143	416,110	11.9	7.8	0.0	13.7	2.7	9.5	53.4	14.8	4.3	8.9	2,711	2,399
Hanson	155	514,848	8.0	2.2	0.0	7.8	0.1	1.5	73.3	26.7	5.0	20.3	5,962	5,803
Harding	73	212,301	18.7	4.8	0.0	12.2	0.0	4.7	58.3	9.6	4.8	4.1	3,329	3,008
Hughes	634	2,522,234	9.3	14.5	0.4	4.4	0.6	11.0	58.5	65.3	17.5	27.0	1,528	1,444
Hutchinson	288	972,279	7.9	2.6	0.2	7.7	0.1	2.1	79.4	30.2	7.6	19.8	2,694	2,325
Hyde	72	248,598	6.6	2.3	0.0	7.3	0.1	1.4	78.4	8.8	2.4	5.6	4,286	3,770
Jackson	120	343,634	10.9	3.2	0.0	5.1	0.7	3.1	74.0	7.8	4.1	3.2	969	805
Jerauld	89	297,125	13.6	4.5	0.0	8.9	2.2	8.1	60.2	14.8	3.7	8.0	3,971	3,190
Jones	76	228,313	15.5	5.5	0.0	7.7	2.0	2.4	66.8	7.7	1.8	5.2	5,650	4,864
Kingsbury	254	773,325	10.2	2.6	0.0	7.7	0.7	4.2	74.0	25.8	5.2	17.8	3,607	3,296
Lake	467	1,748,761	6.4	7.5	2.1	5.7	2.0	14.6	59.3	51.2	13.4	30.2	2,364	1,988
Lawrence	728	2,593,722	12.2	14.1	0.9	7.1	0.1	10.7	48.4	98.7	23.6	59.9	2,333	1,610
Lincoln	1,125	3,735,403	9.9	4.3	0.0	3.7	0.4	1.7	78.1	122.3	40.1	67.6	1,193	1,074
Lyman	131	421,469	12.9	4.8	3.0	8.8	3.7	9.5	56.2	15.2	3.8	7.8	2,015	1,420
McCook	268	829,477	8.4	4.1	0.0	7.4	2.0	1.1	74.7	23.4	6.6	13.5	2,423	2,058
McPherson	134	372,207	15.1	3.2	0.0	9.1	0.4	3.2	67.1	11.8	3.1	7.6	3,150	2,856
Marshall	184	557,061	9.5	8.0	0.0	9.5	0.7	3.7	66.4	24.9	5.3	13.0	2,639	2,333
Meade	1,069	3,798,980	6.8	7.5	0.2	3.0	1.3	3.6	75.3	79.6	23.1	37.4	1,340	1,121
Mellette	116	326,678	6.0	3.9	0.0	2.1	0.6	2.5	82.1	9.5	7.1	2.0	958	893
Miner	113	403,684	10.4	6.7	0.0	14.5	1.7	6.2	59.5	11.9	1.8	8.6	3,930	3,507
Minnehaha	6,410	26,380,232	7.6	11.0	4.1	4.0	2.9	5.8	63.2	800.1	225.5	437.3	2,307	1,442
Moody	218	698,881	10.7	8.3	0.0	6.9	2.1	6.5	60.3	23.0	7.2	12.7	1,950	1,634
Oglala Lakota	373	1,141,302	1.0	0.4	0.0	1.0	0.1	0.1	97.3	31.9	29.3	1.0	73	43
Pennington	4,271	14,327,615	5.7	14.0	5.4	6.2	3.0	9.2	53.2	445.6	120.6	244.4	2,212	1,407
Perkins	158	529,501	11.0	2.8	0.2	6.4	2.5	4.7	71.7	15.8	4.5	8.5	2,879	2,428
Potter	125	368,732	10.5	4.8	0.0	10.3	0.1	2.4	67.0	14.1	2.5	10.5	4,744	4,316
Roberts	385	1,226,313	6.7	3.9	0.9	5.6	2.1	2.5	74.3	37.9	15.9	17.7	1,723	1,448
Sanborn	123	382,548	11.8	3.3	0.0	20.4	0.8	1.3	60.8	31.0	2.5	27.6	11,344	9,662
Spink	302	1,108,758	8.9	4.1	0.0	5.7	42.1	2.2	36.2	52.4	7.0	30.0	4,606	4,021
Stanley	115	415,834	11.2	5.7	0.0	10.7	0.7	9.8	60.2	14.1	3.5	8.4	2,820	2,279
Sully	83	270,364	12.6	0.0	0.0	16.1	0.0	3.8	62.1	10.0	1.4	7.9	5,629	5,167
Todd	499	1,494,157	4.2	0.8	0.0	1.9	0.0	0.7	92.4	49.5	30.8	17.7	1,719	1,656

1. Based on the resident population estimated as of July 1 of the year shown.

STATE County	Local government finances, 2017 (cont.)									Government employment, 2020			Individual income tax returns, 2019		
	Direct general expenditure							Debt outstanding							
			Percent of total for:												
	Total (mil dol)	Per capita[1] (dollars)	Education	Health and hospitals	Police protection	Public welfare	Highways	Total (mil dol)	Per capita[1] (dollars)	Federal civilian	Federal military	State and local	Number of returns	Mean adjusted gross income	Mean income tax
	185	186	187	188	189	190	191	192	193	194	195	196	197	198	199
SOUTH CAROLINA—Cont'd															
Sumter	291.8	2,741	60.7	1.4	8.0	0.3	1.1	137.3	1,290	1,386	6,306	4,923	48,020	44,697	3,483
Union	80.2	2,926	48.4	4.3	10.0	0.0	2.7	55.6	2,027	56	96	1,675	11,580	40,575	2,719
Williamsburg	99.4	3,183	60.0	2.8	4.2	0.5	1.5	93.4	2,993	382	104	1,573	12,870	36,330	2,456
York	915.4	3,439	63.0	0.4	4.8	0.1	2.0	1,416.8	5,323	541	1,033	12,773	131,510	73,339	8,218
SOUTH DAKOTA	X	X	X	X	X	X	X	X	X	11,593	8,278	64,557	436,230	65,265	7,407
Aurora	17.1	6,159	53.2	0.2	2.5	0.2	21.1	13.7	4,939	14	15	165	1,290	45,888	3,499
Beadle	69.7	3,758	51.6	0.4	4.7	0.4	11.8	40.4	2,177	303	99	989	9,030	53,176	4,750
Bennett	11.0	3,178	64.3	0.2	5.8	0.2	7.2	1.1	323	32	19	341	1,140	31,063	2,435
Bon Homme	23.4	3,367	54.9	1.1	2.9	0.3	20.3	31.8	4,581	27	29	554	3,030	45,694	3,645
Brookings	217.4	6,257	22.2	38.3	2.7	0.2	7.0	141.6	4,075	135	185	5,338	14,590	65,559	6,536
Brown	139.2	3,543	40.9	0.3	5.5	0.5	14.4	244.9	6,233	470	207	2,615	18,910	67,037	7,362
Brule	30.8	5,812	56.8	12.3	2.6	0.2	9.5	10.8	2,031	41	28	369	2,650	46,730	4,268
Buffalo	1.1	546	0.0	0.0	11.5	0.0	28.0	1.0	487	152	11	271	650	23,409	1,109
Butte	37.2	3,678	45.7	0.8	6.4	0.0	5.2	18.5	1,825	56	58	553	4,960	50,370	4,409
Campbell	9.1	6,629	18.1	0.4	2.8	0.0	14.1	1.6	1,158	3	8	78	740	56,834	4,843
Charles Mix	37.6	4,000	67.8	1.5	3.0	0.0	13.4	16.2	1,718	197	48	988	4,020	44,807	4,006
Clark	20.1	5,453	44.4	0.3	1.9	0.0	19.2	5.2	1,418	23	18	239	1,860	48,705	4,292
Clay	32.6	2,321	39.0	1.6	5.1	0.2	15.1	39.0	2,781	35	70	3,343	5,520	58,326	5,674
Codington	117.3	4,171	58.5	0.2	4.3	0.2	9.1	69.3	2,464	206	154	1,961	14,200	63,326	6,505
Corson	21.1	5,029	76.4	0.2	2.4	0.0	8.6	3.4	808	78	24	483	1,220	29,801	1,888
Custer	31.8	3,633	33.0	17.5	5.9	0.1	20.6	27.5	3,138	153	49	384	4,470	60,664	5,899
Davison	89.7	4,514	63.3	2.4	5.8	0.2	7.4	56.3	2,832	116	105	1,202	9,840	64,516	6,910
Day	21.0	3,822	38.2	0.6	3.6	0.6	22.2	11.4	2,073	58	29	359	2,700	53,829	5,854
Deuel	20.9	4,854	24.8	1.6	2.6	0.2	16.0	1.2	274	24	24	219	2,110	53,549	4,765
Dewey	16.9	2,880	79.8	0.3	3.7	0.0	7.8	0.4	71	424	32	1,226	2,410	37,805	2,929
Douglas	13.3	4,528	44.4	0.8	2.6	0.2	19.1	5.7	1,951	26	15	188	1,400	51,476	4,250
Edmunds	32.7	8,343	41.0	13.0	1.5	4.2	14.1	24.2	6,173	20	19	333	1,900	65,203	7,532
Fall River	31.1	4,646	42.1	5.3	4.9	0.1	8.3	15.8	2,355	494	36	556	3,610	51,638	4,466
Faulk	19.4	8,363	17.6	56.8	1.6	0.1	11.8	9.6	4,136	19	10	142	1,100	48,257	5,123
Grant	27.7	3,872	49.7	0.4	3.9	0.4	19.7	3.3	456	34	38	324	3,620	61,303	5,765
Gregory	17.3	4,122	52.7	0.5	2.9	0.2	18.9	7.8	1,866	31	31	215	2,010	48,707	4,582
Haakon	11.4	5,933	41.6	0.4	2.6	0.1	18.2	20.3	10,555	24	10	96	1,000	42,637	4,316
Hamlin	30.7	5,120	49.4	1.2	2.3	12.3	12.3	10.1	1,684	17	33	474	2,820	57,977	5,293
Hand	12.3	3,748	42.3	0.6	4.9	0.0	26.6	13.0	3,972	17	17	213	1,580	53,392	4,899
Hanson	23.8	6,996	62.9	0.2	1.5	0.0	9.8	72.5	21,262	5	16	184	2,240	56,992	5,314
Harding	7.7	6,184	44.7	0.4	3.1	0.0	20.6	7.9	6,310	21	7	88	590	54,720	4,773
Hughes	57.5	3,253	44.9	0.2	5.4	0.3	8.7	68.6	3,884	278	93	3,631	8,820	65,994	6,758
Hutchinson	32.2	4,380	51.3	0.4	2.6	0.2	15.0	13.8	1,879	42	36	434	3,860	48,591	4,199
Hyde	10.2	7,894	35.4	0.1	2.6	0.2	17.2	3.0	2,333	12	7	182	640	41,872	4,938
Jackson	8.5	2,598	62.5	0.6	3.9	0.1	14.4	0.1	43	94	18	226	1,100	31,163	1,969
Jerauld	13.5	6,650	31.2	4.9	4.6	0.2	36.0	14.2	6,993	12	10	126	930	37,947	2,914
Jones	5.2	5,650	47.6	2.2	5.4	0.0	18.7	0.5	528	8	5	137	500	34,576	3,264
Kingsbury	24.2	4,902	56.8	0.5	3.4	0.1	20.8	5.0	1,020	36	26	280	2,790	48,387	4,482
Lake	41.2	3,219	49.9	0.3	7.0	0.2	11.7	41.3	3,228	59	64	1,191	5,500	67,497	7,196
Lawrence	95.3	3,710	32.3	0.3	7.1	0.2	15.6	101.5	3,955	175	140	1,684	13,090	67,521	7,484
Lincoln	115.0	2,028	64.3	0.4	3.6	0.4	11.6	284.4	5,018	62	395	1,779	31,680	100,789	14,331
Lyman	14.0	3,600	40.2	15.7	3.5	0.1	20.9	2.1	542	87	21	625	1,650	40,508	3,455
McCook	25.2	4,530	52.5	1.5	3.6	0.7	14.6	14.5	2,603	24	29	238	2,940	57,787	5,343
McPherson	15.5	6,446	46.7	0.5	2.3	0.1	27.9	8.6	3,598	12	11	153	1,100	43,013	3,547
Marshall	25.2	5,099	30.1	2.0	3.9	0.1	14.1	13.5	2,734	29	25	354	2,330	46,779	4,470
Meade	82.8	2,963	52.4	0.3	5.5	0.0	12.7	85.6	3,062	1,642	158	1,305	14,720	54,829	4,682
Mellette	10.4	5,032	61.6	0.6	3.9	0.2	11.3	0.1	34	11	11	192	730	30,478	2,179
Miner	10.6	4,812	44.7	2.8	3.4	0.1	20.7	4.1	1,869	19	12	143	1,160	49,801	3,978
Minnehaha	758.7	4,003	47.4	1.5	5.5	0.6	11.8	736.9	3,888	2,721	1,080	9,287	102,970	68,258	8,514
Moody	19.8	3,051	53.8	1.9	6.8	0.0	7.9	39.2	6,039	91	35	632	3,000	54,752	5,549
Oglala Lakota	26.8	1,862	95.7	0.3	0.4	0.0	1.8	0.0	1	611	77	2,472	4,230	30,879	1,570
Pennington	381.5	3,452	44.9	1.6	7.9	0.5	8.4	357.8	3,238	1,383	4,051	6,271	59,580	65,490	7,208
Perkins	16.1	5,450	41.6	1.0	5.3	0.0	21.1	1.6	535	25	15	214	1,320	38,229	3,381
Potter	12.9	5,815	52.6	1.5	2.9	0.0	22.0	7.6	3,430	16	12	156	1,150	72,483	8,509
Roberts	37.6	3,660	59.7	0.1	3.6	0.4	11.9	15.8	1,541	203	56	1,412	4,530	51,746	4,837
Sanborn	9.1	3,724	56.3	0.8	3.9	0.0	4.7	1.4	591	11	12	155	1,240	44,776	3,752
Spink	42.5	6,529	43.1	24.5	3.0	0.2	13.8	69.4	10,662	40	33	830	3,210	52,644	5,148
Stanley	17.8	5,954	30.3	0.7	7.3	0.1	38.6	10.1	3,396	13	17	175	1,630	71,046	8,234
Sully	8.5	6,054	52.0	0.3	3.5	0.0	19.7	7.7	5,532	11	8	109	760	59,361	8,638
Todd	33.9	3,294	89.9	0.1	1.0	0.0	3.6	1.3	128	250	57	2,029	2,910	33,010	1,890

1. Based on the resident population estimated as of July 1 of the year shown.

State / county code	CBSA code[1]	County Type code[2]	STATE County	Land area[3] (sq. mi)	Population, 2021: Total persons 2021	Population, 2021: Rank	Population, 2021: Per square mile	Race alone or in combination, not Hispanic or Latino (percent): White	Black	American Indian, Alaska Native	Asian and Pacific Islancer	Percent Hispanic or Latino[4]	Age (percent): Under 5 years	5 to 17 years	18 to 24 years	25 to 34 years	35 to 44 years	45 to 54 years
				1	2	3	4	5	6	7	8	9	10	11	12	13	14	15
			SOUTH DAKOTA—Cont'd															
46123		7	Tripp	1,612.5	5,569	2,770	3.5	81.2	1.1	16.9	0.7	2.7	7.3	13.1	11.4	10.5	9.7	10.5
46125	43620	3	Turner	617.1	8,708	2,513	14.1	95.8	1.0	1.3	0.5	2.5	5.6	14.5	10.9	10.0	13.0	11.2
46127	43580	3	Union	460.8	16,872	1,981	36.6	91.8	1.8	1.6	2.1	4.3	5.7	14.0	11.6	11.7	12.7	12.1
46129		7	Walworth	708.6	5,248	2,801	7.4	80.7	0.9	17.1	2.2	2.1	6.6	12.7	11.2	10.6	10.1	10.0
46135	49460	7	Yankton	521.2	23,297	1,670	44.7	88.4	2.5	3.8	1.2	5.7	5.8	11.8	12.3	12.1	12.3	11.5
46137		8	Ziebach	1,961.2	2,380	3,010	1.2	27.1	1.4	70.8	1.1	4.0	5.7	13.9	18.7	12.9	13.4	11.1
47000		0	TENNESSEE	41,238.0	6,975,218	X	169.1	74.9	17.7	0.8	2.5	6.1	5.8	12.5	12.7	13.8	12.7	12.5
47001	28940	2	Anderson	337.2	77,576	730	230.1	90.8	5.2	1.0	1.8	3.5	5.3	11.9	11.3	12.5	11.8	12.6
47003	43180	4	Bedford	473.6	51,119	981	107.9	77.2	8.9	0.8	1.2	13.9	6.6	14.2	12.7	13.4	12.5	12.8
47005		7	Benton	394.3	15,872	2,039	40.3	93.5	3.3	1.3	0.9	2.7	5.1	11.7	9.9	10.3	10.4	13.1
47007		8	Bledsoe	406.6	15,234	2,075	37.5	88.3	8.3	1.2	0.5	3.2	3.6	7.8	9.4	13.9	15.2	15.0
47009	28940	2	Blount	558.8	137,605	474	246.3	91.8	3.7	0.9	1.4	4.0	4.9	11.3	11.2	12.0	11.7	13.1
47011	17420	3	Bradley	328.8	110,162	561	335.0	86.3	6.0	0.9	1.7	7.1	5.6	12.2	13.2	12.9	12.0	13.3
47013	28940	2	Campbell	480.2	39,578	1,192	82.4	97.0	0.9	1.0	0.6	1.7	5.6	11.3	11.1	12.2	11.1	13.9
47015	34980	1	Cannon	265.6	14,553	2,112	54.8	94.6	2.7	1.0	0.7	2.7	6.0	11.9	10.5	13.2	11.9	13.3
47017		6	Carroll	597.7	28,432	1,481	47.6	86.1	11.2	0.9	0.7	3.2	5.5	12.9	13.2	11.2	10.6	12.4
47019	27740	3	Carter	341.3	56,134	922	164.5	95.4	2.3	0.9	0.6	2.2	4.2	10.2	10.6	12.2	11.3	13.5
47021	34980	1	Cheatham	302.5	41,523	1,156	137.3	92.3	3.4	1.1	0.9	4.1	5.4	12.0	11.3	13.1	12.9	13.9
47023	27180	3	Chester	285.7	17,504	1,946	61.3	86.4	10.5	1.1	1.0	3.0	5.2	12.6	17.0	12.0	11.1	12.2
47025		6	Claiborne	434.6	32,267	1,373	74.2	95.9	1.8	1.1	1.1	1.6	5.1	10.5	12.5	12.7	11.2	13.3
47027		9	Clay	236.5	7,555	2,612	31.9	95.5	2.2	0.9	0.4	2.6	4.8	11.4	10.0	9.8	10.7	12.9
47029	35460	6	Cocke	436.1	36,418	1,274	83.5	94.0	2.8	1.1	0.7	3.0	5.1	11.5	10.5	11.3	10.8	13.2
47031	46100	4	Coffee	429.0	59,032	890	137.6	89.0	5.4	0.9	1.6	5.4	6.3	13.7	11.9	12.8	12.2	12.3
47033	27180	3	Crockett	265.5	13,979	2,152	52.7	73.8	15.0	0.8	0.5	11.7	5.9	13.9	11.9	11.9	11.7	11.9
47035	18900	4	Cumberland	681.3	62,451	856	91.7	94.8	1.1	1.1	0.9	3.3	4.3	9.8	8.8	9.6	8.9	10.6
47037	34980	1	Davidson	503.7	703,953	96	1,397.6	58.5	27.9	0.8	4.7	10.6	6.3	10.8	12.7	20.2	14.4	11.2
47039		9	Decatur	333.9	11,391	2,321	34.1	92.5	3.4	1.0	0.9	3.6	4.7	11.6	10.6	10.1	11.6	12.5
47041		6	DeKalb	304.4	20,478	1,793	67.3	88.4	2.2	1.0	1.2	8.6	5.7	12.1	10.9	12.4	12.1	13.0
47043	34980	1	Dickson	489.9	55,292	932	112.9	90.8	5.1	0.9	0.9	4.2	5.8	12.6	11.6	13.2	12.9	13.2
47045	20540	5	Dyer	512.4	36,615	1,268	71.5	80.4	16.0	0.8	0.9	3.9	6.1	13.5	12.2	12.7	11.8	12.6
47047	32820	1	Fayette	704.8	42,832	1,128	60.8	68.3	27.6	0.7	1.1	3.3	4.6	9.6	10.2	11.2	11.1	13.4
47049		9	Fentress	498.6	18,850	1,879	37.8	96.7	0.9	0.9	0.7	1.9	5.1	11.6	10.5	10.6	10.8	13.0
47051	46100	6	Franklin	554.5	43,215	1,121	77.9	89.8	5.9	1.3	1.2	3.8	5.1	10.8	15.0	11.0	11.0	12.1
47053	27180	4	Gibson	602.7	50,541	990	83.9	78.2	19.1	0.7	0.7	3.2	5.7	14.2	11.8	12.1	12.8	12.2
47055		6	Giles	610.9	30,542	1,420	50.0	85.6	11.1	1.1	0.8	3.6	5.4	11.9	11.6	11.8	11.1	12.3
47057	34100	2	Grainger	280.6	23,763	1,652	84.7	94.7	1.4	0.9	0.5	3.6	4.8	11.0	10.9	11.3	10.9	14.1
47059	24620	4	Greene	622.2	70,621	772	113.5	93.7	2.8	0.8	0.8	3.3	4.7	10.7	11.5	11.2	11.2	13.4
47061		8	Grundy	360.4	13,622	2,183	37.8	96.3	1.4	1.5	0.8	1.6	5.7	11.7	11.3	11.7	12.0	12.8
47063	34100	3	Hamblen	161.2	64,468	842	399.9	82.2	4.9	0.8	1.7	12.4	5.9	13.0	12.2	12.0	11.9	13.2
47065	16860	2	Hamilton	542.2	369,135	199	680.8	72.4	19.6	0.8	2.8	6.4	5.7	11.6	12.0	14.4	12.8	12.3
47067		8	Hancock	222.3	6,787	2,673	30.5	98.0	1.1	1.1	0.5	0.8	5.3	12.3	10.5	11.2	11.3	11.9
47069		6	Hardeman	667.8	25,426	1,588	38.1	55.1	42.5	0.8	1.1	2.1	4.7	11.0	11.8	15.0	13.2	12.3
47071		6	Hardin	577.5	26,892	1,531	46.6	92.9	4.1	1.1	0.8	2.7	4.7	11.8	10.6	10.8	10.9	12.5
47073	28700	2	Hawkins	487.1	57,288	911	117.6	95.7	2.0	0.9	0.8	1.8	4.6	11.0	11.0	11.5	11.0	14.1
47075	15140	6	Haywood	533.1	17,694	1,937	33.2	44.7	51.1	0.6	0.4	4.5	5.5	12.7	11.8	11.4	11.8	11.9
47077		6	Henderson	520.0	27,953	1,499	53.8	88.6	9.4	0.7	0.7	2.9	5.7	13.0	11.6	11.9	12.7	12.4
47079	37540	7	Henry	561.9	32,239	1,374	57.4	88.7	8.4	1.0	0.9	2.9	4.9	11.6	10.5	10.7	11.0	12.3
47081		1	Hickman	612.5	25,307	1,594	41.3	91.0	5.8	1.4	0.7	2.9	5.2	11.7	11.7	13.3	12.7	13.3
47083		8	Houston	200.3	8,317	2,554	41.5	92.7	4.4	1.0	1.0	3.1	5.3	12.2	11.1	11.2	12.2	12.7
47085		6	Humphreys	530.8	19,211	1,864	36.2	93.4	3.4	0.9	1.1	2.9	5.6	12.0	11.3	12.0	11.4	12.7
47087	18260	8	Jackson	308.8	11,750	2,299	38.1	95.7	1.5	1.3	0.5	2.4	4.3	10.5	9.9	11.5	10.3	13.7
47089	34100	3	Jefferson	275.1	55,624	928	202.2	92.9	2.6	1.0	1.0	4.0	4.6	11.0	12.1	11.7	11.0	13.5
47091		6	Johnson	298.4	18,170	1,916	60.9	94.5	3.0	0.9	0.5	2.3	4.1	9.4	10.0	12.1	11.6	14.2
47093	28940	2	Knox	508.3	486,677	148	957.5	83.6	9.9	0.8	3.1	4.9	5.4	11.8	15.3	13.9	12.8	12.1
47095		9	Lake	165.8	7,128	2,652	43.0	68.2	29.3	1.0	0.6	3.0	3.7	7.7	13.0	18.2	14.7	13.9
47097		6	Lauderdale	471.9	25,108	1,604	53.2	60.9	36.0	1.1	0.8	2.8	5.6	12.4	12.9	13.7	13.3	12.4
47099	29980	6	Lawrence	617.1	44,828	1,080	72.6	94.5	2.7	1.1	0.7	2.7	6.3	14.3	12.0	12.3	11.5	12.5
47101		6	Lewis	282.1	12,857	2,220	45.6	93.8	3.0	1.0	0.9	2.9	5.6	12.7	11.2	11.6	11.4	12.6
47103		6	Lincoln	570.3	35,433	1,295	62.1	87.9	7.8	1.4	0.9	3.9	5.4	12.6	11.7	11.2	11.6	12.6
47105	28940	2	Loudon	229.3	56,690	917	247.2	87.6	1.9	0.8	1.1	9.8	4.6	11.0	9.8	10.0	9.8	11.8
47107	11940	4	McMinn	430.1	54,059	939	125.7	90.4	4.8	1.2	1.0	4.7	5.5	11.9	11.9	12.0	11.5	13.0
47109		6	McNairy	562.8	25,860	1,565	45.9	90.6	7.1	1.0	0.6	2.5	5.4	12.0	11.9	11.2	11.6	12.9
47111	34980	1	Macon	307.1	25,699	1,578	83.7	92.0	1.8	1.0	1.1	5.5	6.7	14.0	11.9	13.5	11.7	13.0
47113	27180	3	Madison	557.2	98,775	619	177.3	56.7	38.6	0.5	1.6	4.4	6.2	12.4	14.3	12.6	11.4	11.7
47115	16860	2	Marion	498.3	28,877	1,460	58.0	92.6	4.8	1.1	0.9	2.2	5.4	11.6	11.2	11.6	11.3	13.1

1. CBSA = Core Based Statistical Area. See Appendix A for explanation. See Appendix B for list of metropolitan areas with component counties. 2. County type code from the Economic Research Service of USDA Rural-Urban Continuum Codes. See Appendix A for definition. 3. Dry land or land partially or temporarily covered by water. 4. May be of any race.

STATE County	Population, 2021 (cont.)				Population change, 2000–2021							Households, 2016–2020				
	Age (percent) (cont.)				Total persons		Percent change		Components of change, 2020–2021					Percent		
	55 to 64 years	65 to 74 years	75 years and over	Percent female	2010	2020	2010–2020	2020–2021	Births	Deaths	Net Migration	Number	Persons per household	Family house-holds	Female family house-holder[1]	One person
	16	17	18	19	20	21	22	23	24	25	26	27	28	29	30	31
SOUTH DAKOTA—Cont'd																
Tripp	15.3	12.1	10.3	49.5	5,644	5,624	-0.4	-1.0	95	107	-43	2,234	2.4	66.0	9.6	31.4
Turner	13.9	12.0	8.9	49.7	8,347	8,673	3.9	0.4	99	124	63	3,530	2.3	68.4	5.2	27.8
Union	13.4	11.8	7.0	49.1	14,399	16,811	16.8	0.4	236	202	24	6,864	2.3	65.6	7.1	28.2
Walworth	13.5	14.1	11.2	49.9	5,438	5,315	-2.3	-1.3	71	81	-57	2,263	2.2	60.5	7.6	33.6
Yankton	14.0	11.8	8.3	47.3	22,438	23,310	3.9	-0.1	316	361	30	9,558	2.2	60.5	5.4	32.1
Ziebach	13.7	6.3	4.4	49.7	2,801	2,413	-13.9	-1.4	40	43	-30	775	3.6	81.0	28.8	17.7
TENNESSEE	13.1	10.4	6.6	51.0	6,346,105	6,910,840	8.9	0.9	96,408	106,817	75,259	2,639,455	2.5	65.4	12.7	28.6
Anderson	14.3	12.1	8.3	51.0	75,129	77,123	2.7	0.6	945	1,363	873	30,886	2.4	68.1	12.8	26.6
Bedford	12.8	9.3	5.8	50.5	45,058	50,237	11.5	1.8	835	745	792	17,490	2.8	73.3	13.9	21.6
Benton	15.5	14.5	9.5	50.4	16,489	15,864	-3.8	0.1	190	405	227	6,770	2.4	60.1	12.3	35.0
Bledsoe	16.1	11.5	7.4	40.2	12,876	14,913	15.8	2.2	156	230	397	4,822	2.9	71.0	8.0	21.6
Blount	14.7	12.6	8.5	51.0	123,010	135,280	10.0	1.7	1,516	2,160	2,997	51,274	2.5	69.3	10.1	26.5
Bradley	13.3	10.4	7.1	51.3	98,963	108,620	9.8	1.4	1,418	1,739	1,871	40,730	2.5	68.4	11.7	26.0
Campbell	14.3	12.1	8.4	50.4	40,716	39,272	-3.5	0.8	558	831	583	16,461	2.4	67.0	15.1	27.4
Cannon	15.1	10.7	7.4	49.9	13,801	14,506	5.1	0.3	204	264	107	5,579	2.6	68.3	12.6	27.3
Carroll	13.9	11.9	8.3	50.5	28,522	28,440	-0.3	0.0	394	616	214	10,993	2.5	66.3	10.0	30.5
Carter	15.2	13.4	9.4	50.6	57,424	56,356	-1.9	-0.4	536	1,166	409	23,993	2.3	64.2	10.8	31.8
Cheatham	15.6	10.6	5.3	50.0	39,105	41,072	5.0	1.1	546	643	544	15,317	2.6	73.2	11.2	21.0
Chester	12.5	10.6	6.9	51.5	17,131	17,341	1.2	0.9	207	257	215	5,992	2.7	73.6	10.2	22.1
Claiborne	14.3	12.6	7.9	50.6	32,213	32,043	-0.5	0.7	382	646	493	13,561	2.3	64.5	8.1	30.2
Clay	15.2	14.5	10.7	50.4	7,861	7,581	-3.6	-0.3	89	210	97	3,176	2.4	63.9	7.1	30.9
Cocke	15.7	13.7	8.2	51.1	35,662	35,999	0.9	1.2	415	825	837	14,171	2.5	67.4	15.2	26.2
Coffee	13.5	10.3	7.0	50.8	52,796	57,889	9.6	2.0	883	1,018	1,284	22,034	2.5	66.2	9.9	29.1
Crockett	14.2	10.8	7.8	51.7	14,586	13,911	-4.6	0.5	214	296	149	5,653	2.5	69.4	13.5	24.9
Cumberland	16.0	18.9	13.1	50.9	56,053	61,145	9.1	2.1	598	1,349	2,090	26,389	2.3	69.1	9.0	26.4
Davidson	11.3	8.3	4.8	51.7	626,681	715,884	14.2	-1.7	11,905	8,515	-15,168	289,191	2.3	54.1	12.7	35.0
Decatur	15.6	13.4	10.0	50.1	11,757	11,435	-2.7	-0.4	128	290	119	4,637	2.5	68.9	8.8	28.3
DeKalb	14.9	11.7	7.2	49.8	18,723	20,080	7.2	2.0	305	399	497	7,782	2.5	71.5	8.4	24.5
Dickson	14.0	10.4	6.4	50.6	49,666	54,315	9.4	1.8	762	821	1,038	19,559	2.7	69.2	11.7	24.2
Dyer	13.3	10.7	7.1	51.4	38,335	36,801	-4.0	-0.5	559	735	-16	15,271	2.4	66.2	15.8	28.1
Fayette	17.1	14.0	8.7	50.5	38,413	41,990	9.3	2.0	475	703	1,077	16,040	2.5	73.4	11.9	23.2
Fentress	15.9	14.2	8.4	50.3	17,959	18,489	3.0	2.0	204	410	573	7,368	2.5	63.0	9.1	33.6
Franklin	14.3	12.4	8.2	50.7	41,052	42,774	4.2	1.0	495	780	733	16,497	2.4	66.4	9.7	29.7
Gibson	13.2	10.4	7.5	51.6	49,683	50,429	1.5	0.2	642	1,053	521	19,594	2.5	67.4	15.2	28.8
Giles	15.3	12.4	8.1	51.2	29,485	30,346	2.9	0.6	375	605	429	11,700	2.5	65.5	12.2	28.6
Grainger	15.5	13.6	7.9	49.3	22,657	23,527	3.8	1.0	268	494	466	9,147	2.5	70.6	8.6	26.0
Greene	15.1	13.2	9.0	50.4	68,831	70,152	1.9	0.7	765	1,420	1,131	27,515	2.4	67.0	12.7	29.2
Grundy	14.1	12.0	8.6	50.1	13,703	13,529	-1.3	0.7	206	289	178	4,944	2.7	74.4	11.1	22.1
Hamblen	13.5	10.6	7.8	50.6	62,544	64,499	3.1	0.0	883	1,236	317	24,490	2.6	65.7	11.4	29.3
Hamilton	13.1	11.0	7.2	51.5	336,463	366,207	8.8	0.8	5,177	5,561	3,272	148,296	2.4	60.3	11.4	33.4
Hancock	15.2	14.5	7.8	50.4	6,819	6,662	-2.3	1.9	76	141	194	2,731	2.3	62.1	10.7	34.7
Hardeman	13.4	11.1	7.5	44.5	27,253	25,462	-6.6	-0.1	303	446	105	9,245	2.3	64.0	16.2	32.4
Hardin	15.3	13.7	9.7	51.1	26,026	26,831	3.1	0.2	275	563	354	10,087	2.5	69.4	10.5	28.3
Hawkins	15.2	13.1	8.6	50.4	56,833	56,721	-0.2	1.0	609	1,145	1,119	23,183	2.4	69.0	11.3	27.8
Haywood	14.9	12.8	7.4	52.7	18,787	17,864	-4.9	-1.0	221	327	-65	7,148	2.4	66.5	21.6	30.4
Henderson	13.9	11.3	7.4	50.6	27,769	27,842	0.3	0.4	378	530	264	10,914	2.5	63.9	10.6	31.9
Henry	15.4	13.9	9.7	51.2	32,330	32,199	-0.4	0.1	383	728	390	13,190	2.4	64.7	11.0	30.9
Hickman	14.3	11.0	6.8	47.4	24,690	24,925	1.0	1.5	304	478	559	8,675	2.7	67.2	7.8	27.5
Houston	14.7	12.3	8.5	50.7	8,426	8,283	-1.7	0.4	97	180	116	2,919	2.7	60.9	9.4	36.0
Humphreys	14.7	12.4	8.0	49.8	18,538	18,990	2.4	1.2	253	349	321	6,869	2.7	64.8	6.6	30.3
Jackson	17.0	14.3	8.6	49.4	11,638	11,617	-0.2	1.1	105	258	290	4,525	2.6	59.6	9.8	35.6
Jefferson	15.7	12.4	8.0	50.5	51,407	54,683	6.4	1.7	613	1,047	1,390	20,038	2.6	72.3	10.2	23.2
Johnson	14.9	14.1	9.7	46.1	18,244	17,948	-1.6	1.2	181	365	411	6,979	2.3	67.4	14.9	28.6
Knox	12.4	10.0	6.4	51.1	432,226	478,971	10.8	1.6	6,258	6,942	8,402	189,536	2.4	61.5	10.9	30.2
Lake	12.7	9.5	6.7	36.4	7,832	7,005	-10.6	1.8	63	127	189	2,167	2.1	57.7	14.5	33.0
Lauderdale	13.4	10.0	6.3	48.1	27,815	25,143	-9.6	-0.1	340	421	42	9,609	2.4	69.9	20.9	26.4
Lawrence	13.4	10.5	7.2	50.4	41,869	44,159	5.5	1.5	649	844	872	16,140	2.7	67.8	12.4	28.1
Lewis	14.0	12.6	8.4	50.9	12,161	12,582	3.5	2.2	154	229	357	4,837	2.5	65.5	13.9	31.4
Lincoln	14.9	12.0	8.0	50.6	33,361	35,319	5.9	0.3	433	667	350	13,788	2.5	68.7	13.0	27.2
Loudon	15.7	16.3	11.1	50.6	48,556	54,886	13.0	3.3	641	933	2,126	20,967	2.5	70.7	7.0	26.6
McMinn	14.2	12.0	8.2	50.8	52,266	53,276	1.9	1.5	730	1,081	1,146	21,147	2.5	66.9	12.4	28.7
McNairy	14.2	12.3	8.5	50.9	26,075	25,866	-0.8	0.0	349	555	201	9,875	2.6	68.0	11.3	29.8
Macon	13.1	10.0	6.1	50.9	22,248	25,216	13.3	1.9	384	444	548	9,143	2.6	67.5	8.0	27.6
Madison	13.5	11.1	6.9	52.5	98,294	98,823	0.5	0.0	1,502	1,633	66	38,266	2.5	64.4	16.5	31.3
Marion	14.9	13.2	7.8	50.6	28,237	28,837	2.1	0.1	359	557	237	11,438	2.5	68.2	11.8	26.3

1. No spouse present.

STATE County	Persons in group quarters, 2021	Daytime Population, 2016–2020		Births, 2021		Deaths, 2021		Persons under 65 with no health insurance, 2019		Medicare, 2021			COVID-19 Deaths, 2020	
		Number	Employment/ residence ratio	Total	Rate[1]	Number	Rate[1]	Number	Percent	Total beneficiaries	Enrolled in Original Medicare	Enrolled in Medicare Advantage	Number	Rate[1]
	32	33	34	35	36	37	38	39	40	41	42	43	44	45
SOUTH DAKOTA—Cont'd														
Tripp	128	5,564	1.0	72	12.9	78	14.0	723	17.7	1,343	1,203	141	15	2.7
Turner	145	6,812	0.6	82	9.4	94	10.8	701	10.7	1,968	1,367	601	43	5.0
Union	84	17,764	1.3	195	11.6	156	9.3	1,083	8.2	3,335	2,558	778	30	1.8
Walworth	126	5,180	0.9	58	11.0	68	12.9	583	14.4	1,499	1,361	139	14	2.6
Yankton	2,270	24,590	1.2	262	11.3	272	11.7	1,852	11.1	5,060	3,862	1,198	29	1.2
Ziebach	0	2,561	0.8	26	10.9	36	15.1	485	20.0	163	152	11	D	D
TENNESSEE	150,258	6,823,070	1.0	77,353	11.1	84,944	12.2	669,850	12.1	1,384,840	796,335	588,506	7,432	1.1
Anderson	1,090	91,056	1.5	772	10.0	1,085	14.0	7,356	12.1	18,880	10,202	8,678	76	1.0
Bedford	452	44,231	0.8	675	13.3	573	11.3	6,283	15.1	9,332	5,479	3,853	71	1.4
Benton	182	14,508	0.7	157	9.9	312	19.7	1,630	13.6	4,684	3,138	1,546	36	2.3
Bledsoe	2,681	12,259	0.5	128	8.5	186	12.3	1,574	16.6	3,327	1,921	1,406	D	D
Blount	1,928	125,114	0.9	1,206	8.8	1,728	12.7	12,138	11.6	32,512	17,944	14,568	114	0.8
Bradley	2,395	106,649	1.0	1,123	10.3	1,360	12.4	12,174	14.0	23,032	12,260	10,772	79	0.7
Campbell	576	35,278	0.7	448	11.4	678	17.2	3,962	12.9	10,465	4,481	5,984	44	1.1
Cannon	93	10,935	0.4	164	11.3	202	13.9	1,473	12.5	3,305	1,998	1,308	16	1.1
Carroll	1,186	24,260	0.7	321	11.3	477	16.8	2,641	12.6	7,348	5,156	2,193	59	2.1
Carter	956	46,357	0.6	435	7.7	937	16.7	5,950	14.0	15,454	6,543	8,912	91	1.6
Cheatham	228	30,755	0.5	451	10.9	496	12.0	4,020	11.7	7,984	4,088	3,896	31	0.8
Chester	1,087	14,423	0.6	173	9.9	198	11.4	1,635	12.4	3,788	2,507	1,281	35	2.0
Claiborne	1,194	30,674	0.9	320	10.0	518	16.1	2,953	12.2	8,662	3,761	4,901	25	0.8
Clay	56	6,774	0.7	74	9.8	149	19.7	787	14.1	2,218	1,555	663	27	3.6
Cocke	322	31,282	0.7	332	9.2	669	18.5	3,544	12.9	10,438	4,763	5,675	68	1.9
Coffee	536	58,416	1.1	691	11.8	808	13.8	5,468	11.9	12,770	8,268	4,503	86	1.5
Crockett	145	11,877	0.6	167	12.0	221	15.9	1,736	15.3	3,228	2,354	874	33	2.4
Cumberland	563	59,616	1.0	486	7.9	1,074	17.4	5,862	14.3	22,785	14,381	8,405	67	1.1
Davidson	25,939	812,912	1.3	9,614	13.5	6,795	9.6	78,123	13.4	98,157	53,302	44,855	589	0.8
Decatur	166	11,082	0.9	103	9.0	215	18.9	1,105	12.7	3,287	2,152	1,135	22	1.9
DeKalb	165	19,500	0.9	245	12.1	321	15.8	2,313	14.2	4,780	2,374	2,405	31	1.5
Dickson	601	48,708	0.8	610	11.1	664	12.1	5,200	11.7	10,961	6,063	4,898	73	1.3
Dyer	426	37,311	1.0	455	12.4	565	15.4	3,440	11.5	8,331	5,781	2,551	74	2.0
Fayette	392	31,319	0.5	376	8.9	582	13.7	3,586	11.3	10,543	7,231	3,312	45	1.1
Fentress	214	16,838	0.8	160	8.6	324	17.3	1,842	13.2	5,541	3,873	1,668	35	1.9
Franklin	2,150	39,813	0.9	408	9.5	617	14.3	3,699	11.7	10,463	6,864	3,598	56	1.3
Gibson	1,092	43,836	0.7	517	10.2	823	16.3	4,596	11.7	11,715	8,054	3,661	97	1.9
Giles	632	27,213	0.8	312	10.3	456	15.0	2,994	13.1	7,400	5,062	2,337	46	1.5
Grainger	118	18,378	0.5	219	9.3	390	16.5	2,522	13.9	6,229	2,714	3,515	32	1.4
Greene	1,622	67,696	1.0	624	8.9	1,138	16.2	6,864	13.1	19,462	9,600	9,862	92	1.3
Grundy	157	11,503	0.7	162	11.9	214	15.8	1,465	14.2	3,839	2,004	1,835	19	1.4
Hamblen	868	69,161	1.2	727	11.3	947	14.7	8,105	15.6	14,936	7,579	7,357	89	1.4
Hamilton	9,485	409,171	1.3	4,114	11.2	4,456	12.1	35,273	12.0	74,659	41,303	33,357	288	0.8
Hancock	145	5,705	0.6	65	9.7	111	16.6	587	11.8	1,872	853	1,020	D	D
Hardeman	3,861	24,725	0.9	243	9.6	356	14.0	2,033	12.3	5,975	3,722	2,253	54	2.1
Hardin	360	25,504	1.0	231	8.6	458	17.1	2,370	12.2	7,474	5,312	2,162	41	1.5
Hawkins	500	49,406	0.7	488	8.6	929	16.3	5,094	11.7	16,017	5,954	10,064	61	1.1
Haywood	192	15,462	0.7	172	9.7	252	14.2	1,613	12.0	4,234	2,501	1,734	42	2.4
Henderson	311	25,492	0.8	296	10.6	399	14.3	2,834	12.7	6,791	4,111	2,679	59	2.1
Henry	430	32,526	1.0	306	9.5	578	18.0	3,121	12.9	9,148	6,482	2,666	50	1.6
Hickman	1,362	19,824	0.5	248	9.9	363	14.4	2,682	14.0	5,377	2,948	2,428	34	1.4
Houston	146	6,450	0.4	81	9.8	138	16.6	883	13.8	2,132	1,450	682	17	2.1
Humphreys	238	17,723	0.9	209	10.9	275	14.4	1,710	11.8	4,584	3,165	1,419	19	1.0
Jackson	110	9,216	0.5	81	6.9	203	17.4	1,258	14.2	3,211	2,091	1,120	25	2.2
Jefferson	1,348	47,913	0.7	476	8.6	843	15.3	5,509	13.1	13,847	6,928	6,919	69	1.3
Johnson	1,615	16,507	0.8	147	8.1	290	16.1	1,476	12.4	5,247	2,545	2,701	35	1.9
Knox	12,239	492,280	1.1	4,975	10.3	5,541	11.5	41,329	10.7	90,887	49,134	41,752	323	0.7
Lake	2,189	7,083	0.9	54	7.7	101	14.3	444	11.9	1,365	993	372	12	1.7
Lauderdale	2,030	24,490	0.9	272	10.8	340	13.5	2,374	12.5	5,373	3,405	1,969	35	1.4
Lawrence	466	40,531	0.8	515	11.6	671	15.1	4,613	13.0	10,089	7,019	3,071	67	1.5
Lewis	189	10,474	0.7	117	9.2	181	14.2	1,137	12.0	3,085	1,893	1,192	18	1.4
Lincoln	259	29,871	0.7	346	9.8	529	15.0	3,607	13.2	8,374	4,874	3,500	45	1.3
Loudon	410	49,570	0.8	509	9.1	743	13.3	5,388	13.7	17,065	9,808	7,257	50	0.9
McMinn	934	51,075	0.9	580	10.8	850	15.8	5,432	12.9	13,181	7,756	5,425	65	1.2
McNairy	271	22,866	0.7	292	11.3	428	16.6	2,295	11.5	7,016	4,897	2,120	39	1.5
Macon	306	20,008	0.6	301	11.8	344	13.5	3,011	15.0	5,177	3,148	2,030	43	1.7
Madison	4,435	115,438	1.4	1,175	11.9	1,250	12.7	8,637	11.3	21,235	14,286	6,949	170	1.7
Marion	218	25,305	0.7	279	9.7	439	15.2	2,764	12.2	7,366	3,895	3,471	38	1.3

1. Per 1,000 estimated resident population.

STATE County	COVID-19 Vaccinations, 2021–2022: Number	COVID-19 Vaccinations, 2021–2022: Percent[5]	Education: School enrollment and attainment, 2016–2020: Enrollment[1]: Total	Enrollment[1]: Percent private	Attainment[2] (percent): High school graduate or less	Attainment[2] (percent): Bachelor's degree or more	Education: Local government expenditures,[3] 2018–2019: Total current spending (mil dol)	Local government expenditures: Current spending per student (dollars)	Money income, 2016–2020: Per capita income[4]	Households: Median income (dollars)	Households: Percent with income of less than $50,000	Households: Percent with income of $200,000 or more	Income and poverty, 2020: Median household income (dollars)	Percent below poverty level: All persons	Percent below poverty level: Children under 18 years	Percent below poverty level: Children 5 to 17 years in families
	46	47	48	49	50	51	52	53	54	55	56	57	58	59	60	61
SOUTH DAKOTA—Cont'd																
Tripp	2,440	44.8	1,148	4.3	52.6	20.7	9.6	10,088	25,877	54,054	46.3	2.4	46,162	19.3	28.4	29.3
Turner	4,513	53.8	1,811	12.4	39.3	26.3	17.5	10,934	32,123	63,062	40.1	3.5	62,754	8.8	9.2	8.9
Union	8,253	51.8	3,596	5.5	35.1	30.3	28.9	9,239	44,279	74,006	34.7	9.8	82,574	5.9	5.1	4.7
Walworth	2,666	49.1	1,123	12.6	51.6	21.5	8.9	10,980	34,827	51,481	48.3	4.5	45,288	15.0	20.9	19.5
Yankton	14,761	64.7	4,632	15.9	41.8	26.7	29.5	8,977	32,804	61,878	40.0	3.9	57,075	10.4	12.3	10.2
Ziebach	938	34.0	664	5.0	54.0	16.1	13.8	18,960	18,997	36,615	60.3	8.1	31,599	43.9	52.8	41.6
TENNESSEE	3,719,940	54.5	1,560,968	18.3	43.6	28.2	9,923.8	9,862	30,869	54,833	45.7	5.1	56,962	13.6	18.4	17.4
Anderson	43,088	56.0	15,801	14.1	45.7	22.8	134.4	11,079	28,633	52,338	48.2	3.6	53,002	13.3	17.5	16.9
Bedford	21,432	43.1	11,172	10.2	57.2	18.1	70.7	8,029	26,134	52,973	45.8	3.2	58,593	13.0	20.2	19.7
Benton	7,178	44.4	3,219	12.5	63.5	12.8	22.3	10,047	23,375	39,019	59.8	2.1	44,759	16.9	24.5	23.8
Bledsoe	5,573	37.0	2,334	10.2	66.0	11.4	18.1	10,490	23,120	49,382	50.4	3.2	45,780	20.8	25.8	25.2
Blount	69,684	52.4	26,298	18.0	45.9	24.6	186.1	10,287	31,231	60,301	41.7	4.1	67,576	9.2	12.8	12.1
Bradley	45,307	41.9	25,837	24.5	45.2	23.5	144.9	9,009	26,743	51,872	48.3	2.9	49,802	13.8	17.0	15.5
Campbell	17,521	44.0	7,964	10.7	59.7	13.0	49.0	9,012	24,670	41,769	57.3	1.5	42,331	20.0	25.0	23.4
Cannon	4,742	32.3	2,862	15.1	61.8	16.3	18.5	9,352	26,971	52,518	47.1	2.7	50,628	13.3	18.3	17.3
Carroll	13,518	48.7	6,189	18.3	55.7	18.7	43.7	9,540	23,384	42,877	56.1	1.4	47,390	16.7	22.9	21.3
Carter	22,854	40.5	10,632	17.8	52.9	18.5	77.2	9,989	24,631	40,820	58.8	1.5	44,786	16.1	20.9	19.9
Cheatham	23,977	59.0	8,664	16.3	52.2	20.5	54.4	8,980	29,302	63,988	37.4	3.1	78,330	8.7	12.5	11.5
Chester	6,222	36.0	4,423	32.0	57.1	15.9	23.8	8,467	22,150	53,336	46.9	1.0	42,839	15.2	20.6	19.3
Claiborne	14,801	46.3	7,095	27.6	56.6	17.4	39.8	9,630	22,562	37,954	62.0	2.8	43,365	18.9	22.0	22.5
Clay	2,279	29.9	1,424	1.6	67.2	13.0	10.4	9,157	20,395	32,064	64.3	0.8	37,683	21.0	30.1	29.0
Cocke	17,916	49.8	6,503	6.2	66.3	11.3	49.2	9,422	22,282	38,530	61.9	1.4	41,576	19.7	30.3	27.6
Coffee	26,189	46.3	12,430	9.0	51.4	21.2	94.1	10,006	26,572	51,030	49.2	2.9	55,177	13.8	19.9	18.5
Crockett	6,940	48.8	3,384	8.3	57.1	15.2	26.1	8,479	24,769	47,581	51.3	2.1	50,046	15.2	20.4	19.1
Cumberland	28,393	46.9	9,252	11.1	52.0	17.5	64.1	8,622	26,910	49,423	50.5	2.2	52,529	12.0	20.5	19.3
Davidson	453,139	65.3	160,372	32.5	31.7	43.3	1,166.7	12,119	37,958	62,515	39.5	7.2	64,418	12.8	17.3	17.1
Decatur	4,458	38.2	2,216	7.1	58.5	14.3	14.3	8,859	24,771	40,389	60.0	1.6	47,232	17.1	24.4	22.7
DeKalb	8,500	41.5	4,101	7.7	58.7	18.9	24.6	8,350	25,135	44,389	54.2	2.5	51,002	17.5	22.5	20.7
Dickson	26,331	48.8	11,361	13.6	54.7	17.2	73.4	8,824	29,125	57,804	41.8	4.4	60,309	11.0	15.6	14.8
Dyer	15,014	40.4	8,421	10.2	50.2	18.6	64.1	9,733	29,166	45,042	54.9	4.1	50,906	16.7	22.4	21.6
Fayette	23,509	57.2	7,463	29.4	45.6	22.5	31.5	8,866	34,721	63,618	39.7	6.7	73,132	10.2	16.2	16.2
Fentress	6,300	34.0	3,621	12.5	60.5	16.6	19.4	6,993	20,295	40,203	67.4	0.7	43,931	19.4	24.4	24.7
Franklin	17,462	41.4	9,963	25.7	54.0	20.8	51.6	9,576	28,008	47,777	52.2	4.2	49,491	13.9	19.8	19.8
Gibson	22,455	45.7	10,864	12.8	52.7	17.9	82.5	9,008	23,758	45,557	53.0	2.6	47,850	13.4	18.6	16.7
Giles	11,618	39.4	5,980	20.8	57.5	17.9	36.0	9,563	26,567	49,815	50.2	1.8	51,332	12.5	19.1	18.3
Grainger	11,472	49.2	4,208	8.1	61.2	12.9	31.4	9,217	23,937	44,703	55.8	1.8	45,056	14.2	20.0	19.2
Greene	32,044	46.4	13,748	13.8	58.2	16.1	91.3	9,548	25,319	43,150	55.8	1.9	43,164	16.4	21.0	19.8
Grundy	4,115	30.6	2,835	9.1	64.4	13.4	19.1	9,448	20,702	43,116	59.2	1.1	41,133	18.2	26.2	25.1
Hamblen	27,852	42.9	13,906	9.6	55.4	18.1	95.2	9,053	23,722	43,151	55.7	1.9	48,047	15.0	21.1	19.0
Hamilton	208,088	56.6	83,701	24.8	36.0	33.3	451.6	10,023	34,707	56,606	44.3	6.2	61,478	13.3	18.6	16.6
Hancock	2,161	32.6	1,325	12.7	60.8	10.7	10.0	9,832	24,237	28,234	64.6	3.4	33,109	28.6	39.0	35.2
Hardeman	11,745	46.9	4,858	14.0	64.9	10.5	35.9	10,140	18,936	39,636	62.9	1.0	44,937	22.0	28.0	26.9
Hardin	10,461	40.8	5,108	15.2	59.2	16.5	32.6	9,130	24,664	42,285	56.8	2.6	46,776	14.8	20.4	19.3
Hawkins	25,280	44.5	10,889	13.9	55.6	16.7	71.3	9,867	25,438	45,318	54.4	1.8	52,898	15.5	23.5	22.5
Haywood	9,078	52.5	3,543	10.6	63.0	11.4	28.9	9,853	22,830	38,994	57.9	1.5	43,742	18.7	29.0	26.8
Henderson	11,649	41.4	5,971	8.9	60.7	13.6	44.8	9,243	23,097	44,534	56.0	1.4	47,599	14.6	18.9	17.2
Henry	15,458	47.8	6,130	12.8	59.5	17.7	44.4	9,460	24,731	41,037	59.4	1.4	41,598	17.8	27.2	24.6
Hickman	10,717	42.6	4,827	20.8	65.9	9.4	32.2	9,506	26,431	47,457	53.0	2.2	53,738	14.4	20.0	18.9
Houston	3,571	43.5	1,796	7.2	62.8	13.4	12.8	9,242	23,836	43,521	57.9	1.9	47,465	15.6	22.7	21.5
Humphreys	7,716	41.5	3,826	9.1	62.7	14.8	26.4	8,754	25,307	48,411	53.2	2.0	57,767	13.9	21.5	20.3
Jackson	4,114	34.9	2,066	12.7	65.8	11.6	14.9	10,056	21,148	35,880	62.1	1.7	43,115	16.8	24.7	23.2
Jefferson	27,379	50.2	11,899	19.0	52.0	17.5	64.4	8,918	25,857	51,899	47.8	2.8	57,864	12.9	18.5	16.7
Johnson	6,630	37.3	2,885	12.6	60.4	11.9	21.7	10,404	22,955	38,090	64.6	1.9	43,039	18.6	26.9	24.7
Knox	283,428	60.3	118,379	16.6	32.8	38.8	563.3	9,237	34,338	59,250	42.3	6.3	57,886	10.9	13.1	12.2
Lake	2,474	35.3	1,134	15.6	69.7	10.1	8.1	10,519	16,152	34,230	62.5	4.4	32,163	36.4	40.0	38.8
Lauderdale	9,654	37.7	5,672	12.3	66.4	9.6	40.2	10,102	19,954	41,905	58.2	0.7	43,386	19.8	26.2	25.6
Lawrence	16,263	36.8	10,269	15.9	59.7	13.9	60.9	8,741	22,826	43,734	56.7	2.3	47,353	15.2	18.7	17.4
Lewis	4,374	35.7	2,582	8.2	61.1	10.1	15.4	9,016	21,800	36,977	60.9	1.3	48,288	14.3	20.7	19.8
Lincoln	14,244	41.4	7,314	10.8	56.7	19.1	48.0	8,984	28,519	53,923	46.3	3.0	56,661	12.4	17.6	16.5
Loudon	34,574	63.9	10,006	17.6	43.6	27.3	68.3	9,431	34,158	61,664	38.8	5.8	70,292	10.6	16.7	15.2
McMinn	21,645	40.2	10,932	20.9	53.4	17.0	68.5	8,825	25,637	46,872	52.9	2.3	50,297	14.0	19.2	17.9
McNairy	12,209	47.5	5,018	13.2	61.2	13.1	37.7	8,975	21,903	40,327	58.1	2.6	44,341	15.0	18.3	19.1
Macon	8,096	32.9	5,037	11.1	67.1	9.0	34.6	8,661	22,881	38,080	58.1	1.6	47,031	16.7	23.0	22.0
Madison	53,590	54.7	23,505	29.6	45.9	25.9	119.8	9,404	26,619	48,396	51.6	3.4	47,580	22.2	32.3	33.0
Marion	13,389	46.3	5,613	9.6	59.3	12.5	39.0	8,944	25,717	50,059	49.9	2.2	50,941	14.7	21.2	20.1

1. All persons 3 years old and over enrolled in nursery school through college. 2. Persons 25 years old and over. 3. Elementary and secondary education expenditures. 4. Based on population estimated by the American Community Survey, 2016–2020. 5. CDC percent based on 2019 population estimate.

STATE County	Personal income, 2020										Earnings, 2020		
			Per capita[1]			Supplements to wages and salaries, employer contributions (mil dol)						Contributions for government social insurance (mil dol)	
	Total (mil dol)	Percent change 2019–2020	Dollars	Rank	Wages and salaries (mil dol)	Pension and insurance	Government social insurance	Proprietors' income (mil dol)	Dividends, interest, and rent (mil dol)	Personal transfer receipts (mil dol)	Total (mil dol)	From employee and self-employed	From employer
	62	63	64	65	66	67	68	69	70	71	72	73	74
SOUTH DAKOTA—Cont'd													
Tripp	305	13.5	56,765	587	88	16	7	68	60	73	179	10	7
Turner	579	10.1	69,250	175	89	17	8	217	82	92	331	16	8
Union	1,992	4.2	123,000	11	599	78	42	377	744	160	1,096	64	42
Walworth	288	13.6	54,033	780	85	17	7	46	74	72	154	10	7
Yankton	1,265	6.7	55,638	663	606	102	47	166	283	247	921	59	47
Ziebach	69	29.7	26,103	3,107	15	3	1	13	11	22	31	1	1
TENNESSEE	351,546	5.0	50,801	X	167,365	24,608	11,757	44,405	49,460	83,414	248,135	15,582	11,757
Anderson	3,585	7.3	46,225	1,616	2,627	346	185	361	473	1,040	3,519	227	185
Bedford	2,097	6.6	41,795	2,229	729	127	55	218	281	580	1,129	74	55
Benton	588	6.7	36,438	2,830	169	34	13	28	75	253	244	21	13
Bledsoe	450	9.0	29,572	3,092	74	20	5	37	48	168	137	11	5
Blount	6,549	7.1	48,601	1,307	2,617	408	187	585	1,018	1,694	3,798	257	187
Bradley	4,641	6.6	42,546	2,120	2,107	331	156	397	567	1,357	2,992	202	156
Campbell	1,483	7.2	37,229	2,767	390	78	29	82	186	607	578	48	29
Cannon	582	7.6	39,178	2,546	104	21	8	44	64	184	177	14	8
Carroll	1,068	2.2	38,461	2,628	274	57	21	62	111	430	413	36	21
Carter	2,055	5.9	36,431	2,832	483	89	35	124	276	782	730	61	35
Cheatham	1,980	3.7	48,180	1,359	449	91	34	215	213	474	790	53	34
Chester	664	11.1	38,107	2,675	157	33	12	68	72	215	269	20	12
Claiborne	1,228	6.6	38,347	2,642	364	72	28	80	139	474	544	45	28
Clay	263	8.9	34,456	2,964	58	15	4	19	35	115	96	8	4
Cocke	1,314	9.2	36,279	2,852	319	60	23	70	140	567	473	44	23
Coffee	2,478	6.9	42,990	2,065	1,345	214	95	268	300	777	1,922	126	95
Crockett	601	1.8	42,410	2,143	197	34	15	83	55	188	330	23	15
Cumberland	2,470	6.6	40,087	2,446	681	118	50	253	423	1,033	1,102	97	50
Davidson	49,744	-1.1	71,659	142	33,917	4,124	2,286	12,132	7,856	7,302	52,459	2,957	2,286
Decatur	515	5.0	44,401	1,891	144	28	10	33	60	186	215	17	10
DeKalb	880	7.0	42,229	2,164	256	49	20	95	95	270	421	29	20
Dickson	2,418	4.7	44,476	1,879	791	130	58	281	269	664	1,260	85	58
Dyer	1,642	5.4	44,761	1,834	687	133	52	180	192	511	1,053	67	52
Fayette	2,464	5.2	59,214	469	404	68	29	192	319	524	691	54	29
Fentress	684	6.8	36,398	2,839	192	40	13	83	80	295	328	27	13
Franklin	1,822	6.4	42,890	2,075	504	92	38	162	245	578	795	58	38
Gibson	2,057	6.0	41,846	2,224	630	118	47	184	198	696	980	73	47
Giles	1,213	6.3	41,074	2,328	435	77	32	77	149	426	622	46	32
Grainger	883	8.4	37,480	2,741	184	34	14	64	94	316	296	27	14
Greene	2,735	6.8	39,310	2,533	1,075	188	80	162	336	1,080	1,505	122	80
Grundy	487	9.3	36,129	2,861	76	18	6	54	54	216	154	13	6
Hamblen	2,645	6.6	40,627	2,382	1,396	249	102	265	313	867	2,013	135	102
Hamilton	20,780	6.5	55,911	648	11,897	1,799	842	2,751	3,336	4,481	17,289	1,052	842
Hancock	203	9.2	31,243	3,071	33	9	2	5	27	94	50	5	2
Hardeman	820	6.5	33,036	3,027	291	61	21	40	88	339	414	33	21
Hardin	1,104	6.5	43,171	2,039	385	70	27	92	141	407	575	43	27
Hawkins	2,127	6.8	37,460	2,745	578	118	42	103	238	812	841	70	42
Haywood	640	5.0	37,669	2,717	234	52	17	18	71	250	321	24	17
Henderson	1,121	7.3	39,940	2,462	319	59	23	111	118	362	513	37	23
Henry	1,413	3.6	44,075	1,937	473	95	34	200	195	478	801	55	34
Hickman	922	5.5	36,316	2,846	172	35	13	100	101	302	320	26	13
Houston	305	9.5	36,777	2,800	57	13	4	33	33	122	107	9	4
Humphreys	773	4.9	41,569	2,259	305	62	22	58	90	266	448	32	22
Jackson	411	8.1	34,645	2,956	63	14	5	34	49	164	116	11	5
Jefferson	2,240	8.2	40,493	2,392	652	117	50	137	294	757	956	72	50
Johnson	638	7.2	35,745	2,891	199	43	15	33	85	257	290	25	15
Knox	25,988	5.4	54,642	727	13,374	1,941	926	3,336	4,109	5,280	19,576	1,205	926
Lake	181	4.8	25,921	3,108	52	14	4	18	20	87	87	6	4
Lauderdale	898	8.1	35,267	2,922	297	61	23	89	99	329	469	33	23
Lawrence	1,685	6.9	37,918	2,694	456	87	33	181	178	585	758	59	33
Lewis	480	7.6	38,830	2,586	118	24	9	57	44	163	208	15	9
Lincoln	1,564	7.2	45,271	1,757	381	73	28	120	201	471	602	46	28
Loudon	2,939	5.4	53,519	820	842	132	62	300	548	794	1,336	101	62
McMinn	2,168	7.6	39,986	2,458	889	154	68	171	220	737	1,282	91	68
McNairy	917	6.6	35,687	2,895	214	50	16	73	92	379	353	32	16
Macon	881	7.0	35,472	2,910	201	43	15	83	93	298	343	25	15
Madison	4,581	6.9	46,574	1,566	2,844	489	203	443	590	1,338	3,979	247	203
Marion	1,228	7.0	42,471	2,133	327	61	24	85	147	400	496	40	24

1. Based on the resident population estimated as of July 1 of the year shown.

STATE County	Earnings, 2020 (cont.)									Social Security beneficiaries, December 2020		Supple-mental Security Income recipients, 2020	Housing units, 2021	
	Percent by selected industries													
	Farm	Mining, quarrying, and extractions	Construction	Manu-facturing	Information; professional, scientific, technical services	Retail trade	Finance, insurance, real estate, and leasing	Health care and social assistance	Govern-ment	Number	Rate[1]		Total	Percent change, 2010–2021
	75	76	77	78	79	80	81	82	83	84	85	86	87	88
SOUTH DAKOTA—Cont'd														
Tripp	28.6	D	3.7	1.9	6.8	6.9	D	13.0	12.8	1,345	242	129	2,765	0.1
Turner	27.4	D	6.4	27.0	D	2.0	D	D	6.1	1,930	222	78	3,890	0.3
Union	5.5	0.1	3.8	12.1	8.1	3.0	14.4	19.5	4.1	3,420	203	75	7,419	2.3
Walworth	18.3	D	4.4	0.6	D	7.3	8.9	13.0	13.8	1,525	291	99	2,940	0.4
Yankton	5.6	D	4.6	27.6	D	6.1	6.8	16.6	13.1	5,255	226	386	10,493	1.0
Ziebach	36.8	0.0	D	D	0.3	D	D	D	33.8	190	80	91	885	0.3
TENNESSEE	0.2	0.1	7.3	11.3	10.0	6.7	8.5	13.7	12.9	1,496,750	215	172,815	3,087,963	1.5
Anderson	-0.1	D	3.9	34.4	14.7	4.7	4.8	9.0	12.1	20,065	259	2,017	35,532	1.0
Bedford	0.8	D	14.8	22.1	D	7.7	3.9	D	13.6	10,415	204	1,036	20,079	1.6
Benton	-0.1	D	6.8	16.7	D	9.0	6.7	D	24.3	5,185	327	585	8,536	0.5
Bledsoe	3.9	D	15.9	1.8	D	4.6	3.0	3.9	42.1	3,550	233	402	5,892	0.3
Blount	-0.2	D	7.3	17.7	7.8	9.1	7.3	8.8	13.8	34,630	252	2,351	60,846	1.4
Bradley	0.0	D	8.4	21.4	D	7.3	4.1	11.9	10.6	25,940	235	D	45,367	1.0
Campbell	-0.2	D	8.4	14.8	D	9.7	6.4	D	20.1	11,450	289	2,037	20,336	1.7
Cannon	0.0	1.6	14.0	8.8	3.6	6.2	3.1	D	20.2	3,645	250	331	6,363	0.0
Carroll	-1.1	D	5.6	4.2	D	7.6	8.6	D	25.6	8,230	289	1,035	13,101	0.1
Carter	-0.1	D	10.9	12.8	4.5	9.6	5.5	D	19.5	16,450	293	1,707	27,957	0.6
Cheatham	-0.3	D	15.4	29.6	D	5.5	4.0	D	12.7	8,930	215	626	17,116	1.5
Chester	-1.0	0.0	D	13.7	3.3	8.3	2.9	D	23.8	4,245	243	451	7,247	0.4
Claiborne	-0.4	0.8	5.5	21.8	D	6.6	5.0	D	17.6	9,835	305	1,622	15,427	0.6
Clay	-2.5	D	5.8	14.9	D	4.9	1.4	6.2	31.9	2,315	306	258	3,974	0.7
Cocke	0.7	D	7.2	19.9	2.7	11.5	3.2	D	23.5	11,615	319	1,966	17,866	0.3
Coffee	0.7	0.0	5.8	19.4	19.5	7.4	3.4	10.4	13.4	14,200	241	1,414	25,211	0.8
Crockett	-3.1	0.0	5.4	27.3	9.3	17.7	2.8	D	14.8	3,575	256	454	6,109	0.5
Cumberland	0.7	0.8	9.7	11.8	4.9	11.6	6.1	13.8	13.2	24,210	388	D	31,016	1.4
Davidson	0.0	0.1	6.9	3.1	16.8	4.8	9.6	19.5	7.6	100,575	143	14,039	343,107	3.8
Decatur	0.4	D	7.7	15.3	D	5.8	3.4	18.7	18.8	3,880	341	468	6,573	0.2
DeKalb	2.9	0.0	5.9	32.1	10.0	5.4	2.6	D	15.2	5,240	256	616	10,010	1.2
Dickson	-0.5	D	15.1	20.5	2.9	8.9	5.0	14.6	13.5	12,030	218	1,161	23,082	2.0
Dyer	3.1	0.0	8.2	26.8	D	7.8	5.1	D	18.1	9,355	255	1,426	16,275	0.3
Fayette	-0.6	D	14.2	20.6	5.1	6.1	4.7	7.1	12.6	11,175	261	1,033	18,158	2.9
Fentress	-0.3	D	8.9	4.4	3.9	7.9	6.5	D	16.3	6,225	330	961	9,221	0.2
Franklin	1.5	1.0	7.5	16.6	D	8.8	3.7	D	14.9	11,400	264	965	19,730	1.5
Gibson	3.3	0.0	8.9	17.0	D	10.1	5.6	D	18.2	13,030	258	1,622	22,481	0.6
Giles	-0.3	D	5.7	30.8	D	8.3	4.8	D	13.9	8,200	268	762	14,054	0.8
Grainger	1.0	D	13.2	26.8	D	5.5	2.3	3.3	17.8	6,755	284	969	11,736	0.7
Greene	-0.4	D	4.5	25.7	2.8	7.8	3.8	D	16.4	21,535	305	2,312	32,402	0.7
Grundy	5.7	D	11.5	8.1	D	8.0	2.4	D	24.2	4,330	318	725	6,213	0.2
Hamblen	0.1	D	5.0	29.6	3.4	8.8	3.6	11.9	12.7	16,505	256	2,038	27,643	0.9
Hamilton	0.0	D	6.9	11.9	7.5	5.1	14.8	11.9	15.7	78,810	213	8,192	164,705	1.3
Hancock	-1.7	D	3.8	D	D	8.6	D	18.4	45.9	1,645	242	405	3,670	0.0
Hardeman	-1.4	0.0	5.0	33.5	D	5.0	D	8.6	23.0	6,570	258	1,240	10,696	0.3
Hardin	1.1	D	6.6	31.7	2.8	11.7	4.3	D	18.1	8,240	306	1,055	15,092	0.1
Hawkins	-0.4	D	5.6	37.0	D	5.6	2.0	D	18.3	17,860	312	1,981	27,252	0.6
Haywood	-3.4	0.0	3.3	33.6	D	7.1	7.5	6.5	22.3	4,760	269	871	8,249	0.1
Henderson	0.7	D	8.8	16.1	3.0	8.4	6.9	8.8	17.0	6,960	249	848	12,913	0.3
Henry	6.2	D	5.9	20.2	3.5	9.6	3.7	7.4	22.2	9,980	310	926	17,001	0.3
Hickman	-0.1	D	16.8	15.1	D	7.0	1.8	11.8	21.0	5,910	234	643	10,566	0.8
Houston	-3.6	0.0	D	9.7	D	4.6	D	23.6	24.9	2,125	256	280	3,949	0.3
Humphreys	-1.2	0.3	10.3	36.0	1.9	7.7	2.2	D	15.8	5,125	267	509	8,874	0.2
Jackson	-0.6	0.0	D	6.3	D	5.2	D	D	23.9	3,465	295	368	5,837	0.3
Jefferson	0.1	D	D	18.8	D	7.5	3.0	D	15.3	15,445	278	1,457	25,116	0.9
Johnson	-0.7	D	8.1	25.0	3.2	3.9	3.7	8.4	19.2	5,820	320	803	8,740	0.2
Knox	0.0	0.0	7.2	5.3	12.3	8.1	8.8	16.5	13.5	95,200	196	9,855	214,053	1.3
Lake	14.4	0.0	D	D	D	5.5	1.4	10.9	43.3	1,430	201	350	2,497	-0.1
Lauderdale	3.4	0.1	3.6	21.4	D	5.4	10.8	D	24.1	6,005	239	1,219	10,684	0.2
Lawrence	1.4	D	9.9	17.9	3.8	10.4	4.6	10.2	17.0	11,550	258	1,253	18,684	0.1
Lewis	0.0	0.0	5.6	18.6	D	12.4	3.0	D	19.2	3,210	250	303	5,745	0.5
Lincoln	-1.6	D	9.0	22.7	4.1	9.7	4.7	4.8	21.2	9,400	265	837	16,116	0.8
Loudon	3.3	D	8.7	26.4	5.4	9.9	3.7	7.3	11.6	17,725	313	1,024	25,120	1.9
McMinn	-0.1	D	6.3	40.5	2.3	6.8	4.6	9.4	11.1	14,520	269	1,552	23,989	0.2
McNairy	0.4	0.0	7.7	18.0	D	5.9	2.9	D	22.6	7,795	301	1,074	12,285	0.1
Macon	1.8	0.0	8.7	13.2	4.6	12.2	7.0	D	19.6	5,785	225	661	10,867	1.7
Madison	0.0	D	8.5	17.8	4.2	7.0	4.2	14.3	21.4	23,025	233	3,494	43,891	0.4
Marion	0.2	D	8.6	25.5	D	9.4	2.6	7.0	17.6	8,050	279	937	13,772	1.2

1. Per 1,000 resident population estimated as of July 1 of the year shown.

STATE County	Housing units, 2016–2020: Total	Occupied units, Owner-occupied: Percent	Owner-occupied: Median value[1]	Median owner cost as a percent of income: With a mortgage	Median owner cost as a percent of income: Without a mortgage[2]	Renter-occupied: Median rent[3]	Renter-occupied: Median rent as a percent of income[2]	Sub-standard units[4] (percent)	Civilian labor force, 2021: Total	Civilian labor force: Percent change, 2020–2021	Unemployment: Total	Unemployment: Rate[5]	Civilian employment[6], 2016–2020: Total	Percent: Management, business, science, and arts	Percent: Construction, production, and maintenance occupations
	89	90	91	92	93	94	95	96	97	98	99	100	101	102	103
SOUTH DAKOTA—Cont'd															
Tripp	2,234	73.3	100,800	19.2	11.7	608	22.9	1.1	3,004	0.7	71	2.4	2,753	40.3	28.4
Turner	3,530	79.8	137,500	19.1	10.0	624	22.7	1.3	4,643	2.0	124	2.7	4,302	34.2	29.7
Union	6,864	68.1	206,300	18.6	10.0	854	21.1	1.2	8,619	0.3	308	3.6	8,197	39.1	27.2
Walworth	2,263	72.0	96,700	18.1	10.0	719	26.9	1.9	2,159	2.0	118	5.5	2,665	45.2	19.4
Yankton	9,558	69.4	152,800	20.0	10.7	653	25.4	1.5	11,629	-0.4	316	2.7	11,733	35.6	27.8
Ziebach	775	55.6	68,800	12.2	10.7	591	28.3	12.8	952	1.1	43	4.5	976	53.0	12.9
TENNESSEE	2,639,455	66.5	177,600	19.7	10.0	897	28.8	2.1	3,327,966	0.9	142,703	4.3	3,147,330	36.3	25.4
Anderson	30,886	67.6	152,600	19.3	10.0	788	25.7	2.0	34,816	1.4	1,333	3.8	32,420	35.6	26.3
Bedford	17,490	71.0	169,800	19.6	10.6	779	27.9	3.2	21,191	0.7	871	4.1	22,517	25.0	37.5
Benton	6,770	75.8	87,700	19.4	11.4	644	27.5	1.4	6,786	0.1	324	4.8	5,645	28.5	37.5
Bledsoe	4,822	76.6	139,300	17.8	10.2	675	19.8	3.2	4,311	0.5	225	5.2	5,963	24.4	43.8
Blount	51,274	76.6	192,800	19.5	10.0	828	27.0	2.2	64,582	1.3	2,223	3.4	61,779	32.3	26.2
Bradley	40,730	66.8	167,800	19.7	10.0	796	27.4	2.1	50,805	-3.4	2,073	4.1	49,966	32.9	28.9
Campbell	16,461	66.4	121,000	18.6	11.7	621	24.1	3.0	14,796	1.4	704	4.8	15,687	29.7	34.3
Cannon	5,579	76.8	172,600	20.4	10.0	642	25.2	4.0	6,657	2.0	225	3.4	6,304	29.1	33.1
Carroll	10,993	73.6	97,200	16.8	10.9	637	27.4	1.6	11,437	0.1	522	4.6	11,544	29.5	32.2
Carter	23,993	72.0	125,100	20.6	10.4	644	24.3	1.3	24,094	1.8	1,013	4.2	23,166	30.9	28.7
Cheatham	15,317	77.4	198,900	21.5	10.0	1,008	23.1	2.5	22,015	3.0	685	3.1	20,106	33.2	28.5
Chester	5,992	77.2	118,700	18.5	10.7	643	24.4	1.1	8,507	0.4	279	3.3	6,522	26.5	31.8
Claiborne	13,561	70.9	112,000	19.4	10.1	637	28.1	2.2	12,760	-0.2	523	4.1	12,662	30.1	37.9
Clay	3,176	77.9	107,400	23.6	13.2	522	26.1	1.1	2,757	2.0	145	5.3	2,708	29.1	37.0
Cocke	14,171	69.6	112,600	21.2	10.4	676	26.8	2.8	14,771	-0.6	819	5.5	14,031	23.1	33.0
Coffee	22,034	66.8	156,200	18.7	10.0	715	26.5	3.1	25,220	-1.8	1,028	4.1	25,679	30.6	34.1
Crockett	5,653	70.1	99,100	18.4	10.6	746	31.8	2.6	6,833	0.1	244	3.6	6,221	32.3	33.2
Cumberland	26,389	79.1	159,800	19.6	10.0	693	27.9	2.0	22,618	-0.8	1,079	4.8	21,850	27.6	34.6
Davidson	289,191	54.4	267,400	20.8	10.0	1,172	29.8	2.8	404,747	1.4	16,991	4.2	383,444	44.6	18.6
Decatur	4,637	79.7	97,800	20.7	11.2	572	29.4	1.5	4,308	-3.0	247	5.7	4,377	34.0	36.0
DeKalb	7,782	68.3	157,500	19.2	10.3	645	25.7	2.7	7,758	1.1	349	4.5	8,015	33.3	37.3
Dickson	19,559	76.1	183,300	19.7	10.0	801	26.8	2.2	27,087	2.8	913	3.4	24,592	32.3	29.7
Dyer	15,271	62.3	113,800	17.2	10.9	674	27.1	1.6	16,075	1.0	742	4.6	16,376	29.0	33.6
Fayette	16,040	78.5	218,600	19.3	10.0	777	30.2	1.7	19,283	0.4	794	4.1	17,885	36.2	29.7
Fentress	7,368	76.0	106,800	20.4	10.0	529	28.0	1.1	7,526	0.1	303	4.0	7,102	26.2	33.3
Franklin	16,497	73.5	146,700	19.8	10.1	706	29.2	2.5	19,463	-2.2	745	3.8	18,315	33.2	33.2
Gibson	19,594	65.6	108,600	19.1	10.3	671	28.6	1.8	21,522	-1.3	922	4.3	20,236	28.7	31.1
Giles	11,700	70.4	136,600	18.6	10.0	679	26.4	1.9	14,638	0.0	633	4.3	12,694	28.0	35.3
Grainger	9,147	76.4	124,900	20.1	10.0	628	27.3	2.0	9,603	1.2	405	4.2	9,896	27.0	39.2
Greene	27,515	75.8	133,600	19.6	10.0	618	26.4	1.2	28,818	-0.3	1,266	4.4	28,218	28.4	33.0
Grundy	4,944	78.6	90,400	18.6	10.7	642	30.5	3.4	5,030	-1.9	273	5.4	5,385	23.9	42.2
Hamblen	24,490	66.8	139,000	19.1	10.0	720	30.5	2.8	27,883	-0.2	1,112	4.0	26,929	27.3	32.0
Hamilton	148,296	64.1	191,400	18.9	10.0	913	28.8	1.4	184,161	0.6	7,420	4.0	177,431	39.5	21.7
Hancock	2,731	77.5	99,800	22.3	11.8	472	27.9	2.5	2,253	2.6	109	4.8	2,089	29.9	28.9
Hardeman	9,245	69.4	94,100	20.9	10.0	694	29.2	1.3	8,964	-3.5	541	6.0	8,329	23.6	37.9
Hardin	10,087	75.9	120,200	19.7	10.0	612	30.7	1.7	10,193	-0.7	458	4.5	9,990	30.7	32.8
Hawkins	23,183	76.5	127,600	18.6	10.0	651	25.9	3.0	23,137	-1.1	1,025	4.4	22,001	29.0	35.5
Haywood	7,148	58.9	103,600	22.2	11.7	649	26.8	1.9	7,624	-1.9	449	5.9	7,633	19.7	38.6
Henderson	10,914	73.8	108,600	18.4	11.2	674	31.8	2.8	11,873	-0.1	517	4.4	11,238	31.1	33.3
Henry	13,190	75.2	104,500	18.7	10.8	666	27.9	2.0	14,147	0.1	562	4.0	12,493	27.7	31.4
Hickman	8,675	82.1	122,500	19.3	10.9	732	30.5	2.5	11,445	3.1	398	3.5	10,445	25.2	35.9
Houston	2,919	79.5	126,300	25.2	10.7	664	23.4	1.4	3,208	-1.2	155	4.8	3,158	18.2	44.8
Humphreys	6,869	78.5	120,000	18.9	10.0	693	26.7	1.4	8,650	-0.5	334	3.9	7,546	29.8	35.0
Jackson	4,525	80.5	115,800	21.0	10.0	601	27.8	2.6	4,773	1.2	207	4.3	4,661	22.0	39.9
Jefferson	20,038	75.7	154,800	19.0	10.7	723	23.1	2.7	24,817	-0.5	1,021	4.1	23,889	27.5	29.1
Johnson	6,979	75.5	133,700	20.1	10.2	552	29.6	3.6	7,761	1.0	273	3.5	5,725	22.7	35.4
Knox	189,536	65.0	194,200	19.0	10.0	933	28.6	1.2	247,312	1.7	8,038	3.3	233,540	42.5	17.7
Lake	2,167	51.1	91,800	21.4	10.0	435	23.7	4.4	1,659	-1.2	99	6.0	1,711	25.1	27.9
Lauderdale	9,609	56.9	90,700	19.3	10.3	644	27.6	3.2	9,621	-0.7	574	6.0	9,242	26.3	40.0
Lawrence	16,140	75.2	118,500	21.8	10.2	659	29.1	2.9	19,378	0.6	829	4.3	16,960	27.2	37.9
Lewis	4,837	78.4	98,600	21.8	11.2	608	29.3	1.6	5,555	4.0	261	4.7	4,804	27.4	35.4
Lincoln	13,788	76.9	149,400	19.4	10.1	704	28.7	2.9	16,155	1.1	655	4.1	15,536	29.6	35.8
Loudon	20,967	79.3	227,100	19.4	10.0	835	25.5	3.4	23,966	1.1	814	3.4	23,059	30.8	29.9
McMinn	21,147	74.3	140,000	19.6	10.2	724	27.7	2.4	22,540	-3.3	1,023	4.5	22,163	30.3	34.7
McNairy	9,875	76.2	101,100	19.5	11.8	615	27.1	1.7	8,335	-0.2	445	5.3	9,540	30.7	36.8
Macon	9,143	73.4	124,800	18.9	11.4	668	27.6	2.2	11,349	1.7	415	3.7	10,793	27.4	40.2
Madison	38,266	62.3	139,500	19.8	10.0	875	32.1	1.6	49,358	0.0	2,227	4.5	42,686	34.2	25.0
Marion	11,438	75.2	122,700	20.0	10.1	710	26.4	2.0	12,328	0.5	531	4.3	12,317	26.4	38.2

1. Specified owner-occupied units. 2. A value of 10.0 represents 10 percent or less; a value of 50.0 represents 50 percent or more. 3. Specified renter-occupied units. 4. Overcrowded or lacking complete plumbing facilities. 5. Percent of civilian labor force. 6. Civilian employed persons 16 years old and over.

STATE County	Private nonfarm establishments, employment and payroll, 2020									Agriculture, 2017			
		Employment						Annual payroll		Farms			Farm producers whose primary occupation is farming (percent)
											Percent with:		
	Number of establish-ments	Total	Health care and social assistance	Manufac-turing	Retail trade	Finance and insurance	Professional, scientific, and technical services	Total (mil dol)	Average per employee (dollars)	Number	Fewer than 50 acres	1000 acres or more	
	104	105	106	107	108	109	110	111	112	113	114	115	116
SOUTH DAKOTA—Cont'd													
Tripp	193	1,599	453	40	333	65	81	55	34,431	648	13.7	42.4	58.5
Turner	251	1,459	333	171	223	88	18	58	39,897	757	30.3	16.2	46.6
Union	517	9,001	1,179	2,163	501	938	260	490	54,434	557	29.1	18.3	50.7
Walworth	220	1,792	318	67	355	77	64	63	35,162	256	11.3	39.8	52.9
Yankton	718	11,756	1,868	4,068	1,599	633	213	514	43,699	610	23.8	17.4	51.7
Ziebach	44	313	69	NA	46	27	NA	11	33,674	213	1.4	74.6	70.6
TENNESSEE	140,905	2,760,605	434,848	333,095	319,918	136,009	126,003	133,052	48,197	69,983	45.2	2.3	35.8
Anderson	1,532	42,762	4,750	12,444	3,419	1,078	8,857	2,832	66,223	538	54.3	0.2	30.5
Bedford	800	14,658	1,042	4,355	1,683	578	214	616	41,999	1,430	41.9	2.4	40.3
Benton	284	3,275	559	787	589	111	47	104	31,647	399	30.8	2.0	29.2
Bledsoe	114	855	218	63	122	47	34	30	35,497	614	36.0	2.0	39.4
Blount	2,366	42,687	6,223	6,932	5,701	2,122	2,596	1,963	45,975	1,073	60.7	1.1	39.6
Bradley	1,966	41,422	5,384	9,142	6,372	1,158	747	1,711	41,305	778	52.6	0.4	42.1
Campbell	563	6,673	1,497	1,168	1,489	249	84	221	33,097	343	47.5	NA	32.2
Cannon	205	1,746	296	271	244	32	91	59	33,961	728	46.7	1.1	30.6
Carroll	423	5,405	1,444	730	817	285	77	191	35,286	662	36.3	5.6	27.8
Carter	704	8,603	1,740	1,245	1,755	319	186	289	33,551	469	58.0	NA	33.7
Cheatham	637	6,941	690	1,914	861	116	235	295	42,536	543	48.4	1.8	34.8
Chester	242	3,660	378	687	371	79	54	110	30,108	380	28.9	4.2	31.0
Claiborne	430	7,916	1,078	2,460	836	238	132	284	35,925	966	42.1	0.6	41.5
Clay	99	1,018	290	230	161	29	10	32	30,987	404	32.9	2.0	42.1
Cocke	446	5,638	874	1,363	1,375	153	83	203	35,999	645	47.6	0.5	40.7
Coffee	1,225	19,551	3,039	5,259	2,986	857	1,070	872	44,617	872	51.1	4.0	34.5
Crockett	232	2,204	459	330	336	71	56	79	35,955	322	39.8	14.9	36.8
Cumberland	1,088	14,836	2,958	2,356	2,401	514	286	504	33,988	886	48.4	1.6	30.7
Davidson	20,512	470,435	83,212	20,296	37,368	24,901	27,606	26,900	57,180	414	56.8	0.2	29.7
Decatur	208	2,907	1,081	568	281	112	54	110	37,743	374	24.1	1.9	33.0
DeKalb	300	4,594	445	2,299	565	92	59	170	36,989	654	43.3	1.5	39.8
Dickson	1,017	15,059	2,442	3,529	2,388	516	240	569	37,764	1,225	45.0	0.2	30.1
Dyer	775	12,400	1,882	3,976	1,988	467	174	529	42,626	451	35.9	21.1	39.4
Fayette	629	7,197	580	1,728	808	240	125	331	45,993	892	37.6	8.1	33.4
Fentress	266	4,207	704	346	628	197	50	128	30,421	620	41.9	2.3	37.6
Franklin	699	13,008	1,585	3,522	1,440	254	1,365	582	44,725	818	51.1	1.8	34.0
Gibson	912	11,906	1,759	2,589	1,955	316	205	443	37,187	777	49.3	10.3	37.6
Giles	529	7,850	924	2,872	1,242	283	137	312	39,694	1,599	34.8	1.7	38.0
Grainger	230	2,807	195	1,120	458	31	52	105	37,507	923	46.6	0.3	34.2
Greene	1,175	22,278	3,701	6,222	2,970	468	258	938	42,104	2,562	56.2	0.5	36.7
Grundy	157	1,284	281	250	257	92	28	38	29,652	261	38.7	1.5	41.6
Hamblen	1,295	28,159	3,798	9,850	3,908	481	264	1,091	38,733	559	61.2	0.7	40.1
Hamilton	9,296	195,251	32,623	23,863	23,360	14,568	8,906	9,035	46,276	547	56.7	0.5	37.4
Hancock	53	408	162	NA	104	11	6	13	31,081	408	21.6	2.9	46.0
Hardeman	336	5,501	1,167	1,864	576	126	41	219	39,751	613	32.0	6.9	30.2
Hardin	500	6,898	1,300	1,762	1,344	211	84	295	42,769	583	32.1	5.0	34.5
Hawkins	616	9,676	1,151	4,229	1,462	176	123	396	40,941	1,484	47.4	0.5	37.7
Haywood	289	4,672	305	2,241	538	168	98	207	44,272	361	35.7	16.3	41.5
Henderson	492	6,434	1,016	1,338	1,112	360	97	215	33,353	786	25.1	1.8	35.0
Henry	688	8,743	1,450	1,866	1,514	363	279	315	36,046	710	34.5	6.2	33.6
Hickman	301	2,611	684	397	415	47	37	93	35,794	706	32.2	1.8	38.8
Houston	100	998	282	164	140	52	36	33	32,962	326	29.4	1.2	38.1
Humphreys	329	4,445	649	1,521	666	85	65	242	54,363	657	35.5	2.3	31.1
Jackson	106	833	145	170	100	29	17	27	32,175	538	33.3	1.3	31.1
Jefferson	730	11,410	1,376	2,211	1,771	223	153	471	41,271	973	50.1	0.4	39.2
Johnson	233	3,501	555	817	375	106	69	144	41,009	517	53.2	0.4	38.6
Knox	11,785	228,802	37,522	12,128	28,836	10,864	10,973	10,349	45,232	1,037	63.6	NA	35.5
Lake	64	594	155	NA	113	16	NA	17	29,113	52	15.4	48.1	68.8
Lauderdale	288	4,747	669	1,213	605	164	32	185	39,065	404	37.4	8.7	35.5
Lawrence	755	8,822	1,363	1,959	1,536	246	209	307	34,805	1,394	40.0	2.3	35.8
Lewis	214	2,344	427	546	488	69	24	82	34,949	272	32.7	1.1	33.7
Lincoln	581	6,548	858	1,770	1,307	227	138	261	39,810	1,654	37.7	1.7	36.5
Loudon	963	14,509	1,578	3,678	1,966	318	836	616	42,441	691	55.6	0.6	36.0
McMinn	909	17,332	2,052	6,991	2,238	411	218	705	40,701	1,054	49.1	1.4	35.4
McNairy	388	4,472	602	959	520	127	68	127	28,424	654	34.9	3.1	33.0
Macon	315	3,820	711	1,108	599	296	66	118	30,801	912	38.3	2.1	35.5
Madison	2,519	54,549	13,140	9,541	7,053	1,293	1,150	2,202	40,360	549	37.9	4.9	34.3
Marion	435	5,965	686	1,752	1,244	147	90	239	40,121	308	36.4	1.9	37.7

STATE County	Agriculture, 2017 (cont.) — Land in farms — Acreage (1,000)	Land in farms — Percent change, 2012–2017	Land in farms — Acres — Average size of farm	Land in farms — Acres — Total irrigated (1,000)	Land in farms — Acres — Total cropland (1,000)	Value of land and buildings (dollars) — Average per farm	Value of land and buildings (dollars) — Average per acre	Value of machinery and equipment, average per farm (dollars)	Value of products sold — Total (mil dol)	Value of products sold — Average per farm (acres)	Value of products sold — Percent from: Crops	Value of products sold — Percent from: Livestock and poultry products	Organic farms (number)	Farms with internet access (percent)	Government payments — Total ($1,000)	Government payments — Percent of farms
	117	118	119	120	121	122	123	124	125	126	127	128	129	130	131	132
SOUTH DAKOTA—Cont'd																
Tripp	1,037	1.7	1,600	5.1	438.1	2,591,113	1,620	271,919	202.6	312,627	24.8	75.2	2	83.5	9,317	85.0
Turner	393	2.2	519	26.9	350.3	2,604,252	5,019	265,081	265.7	351,004	61.3	38.7	2	78.2	9,119	72.4
Union	290	0.5	521	40.7	266.7	3,059,199	5,875	315,383	187.0	335,772	71.8	28.2	1	83.3	4,214	81.7
Walworth	453	1.9	1,771	2.8	273.8	3,506,300	1,980	356,021	87.1	340,066	70.1	29.9	2	87.9	6,182	76.6
Yankton	330	0.6	540	38.0	252.6	2,389,517	4,422	258,025	162.4	266,193	65.2	34.8	2	80.5	7,994	76.4
Ziebach	1,099	-0.8	5,162	NA	256.8	4,412,411	855	352,110	59.9	281,272	35.4	64.6	NA	78.4	6,373	87.8
TENNESSEE	10,874	0.1	155	184.9	5,286.3	608,739	3,918	80,447	3,798.9	54,284	57.4	42.6	122	72.7	115,945	26.5
Anderson	43	21.2	81	0.1	14.7	441,499	5,465	59,863	4.3	8,015	31.4	68.6	NA	74.0	205	13.4
Bedford	238	2.4	166	1.2	92.6	693,089	4,167	86,121	151.6	106,013	14.3	85.7	NA	76.9	2,460	28.3
Benton	69	-22.0	172	D	30.3	427,822	2,489	82,014	9.5	23,797	63.2	36.8	NA	74.4	625	30.3
Bledsoe	94	-7.9	153	0.5	34.7	528,198	3,445	85,821	39.9	64,951	26.7	73.3	NA	77.7	628	32.4
Blount	95	-6.1	88	0.1	40.6	567,289	6,436	60,767	16.5	15,347	34.7	65.3	10	77.4	488	11.6
Bradley	85	-2.0	109	0.1	28.3	661,318	6,065	66,853	105.9	136,067	12.6	87.4	3	71.6	872	16.7
Campbell	28	-17.7	80	0.1	10.2	332,638	4,138	55,393	2.9	8,437	43.5	56.5	1	57.1	114	19.0
Cannon	89	-7.4	122	0.0	38.9	438,958	3,587	60,409	22.6	31,021	60.7	39.3	NA	76.6	1,013	20.2
Carroll	170	-4.7	256	4.9	106.2	700,403	2,735	101,405	52.6	79,492	94.7	5.3	NA	69.3	3,582	43.8
Carter	34	-14.9	73	0.1	12.0	379,965	5,199	57,459	7.7	16,377	33.4	66.6	3	71.9	D	2.3
Cheatham	67	28.4	124	0.1	31.8	564,719	4,557	75,846	16.3	30,072	84.6	15.4	5	76.1	313	19.2
Chester	80	31.3	210	D	42.4	534,584	2,540	79,023	16.1	42,347	89.3	10.7	NA	71.1	1,198	37.9
Claiborne	120	-1.3	124	0.0	35.4	388,110	3,128	55,041	17.4	17,971	17.9	82.1	1	58.7	1,282	42.3
Clay	75	-5.6	186	0.0	24.8	620,853	3,333	63,718	60.0	148,634	9.2	90.8	NA	69.1	438	42.1
Cocke	65	7.0	101	D	23.4	448,496	4,427	69,868	36.5	56,563	32.6	67.4	1	64.2	324	19.8
Coffee	139	-4.3	159	1.8	79.9	652,277	4,105	92,203	60.6	69,450	66.5	33.5	NA	79.2	2,149	26.4
Crockett	149	14.3	463	10.4	134.1	1,559,863	3,365	278,689	81.6	253,388	97.0	3.0	NA	64.3	2,486	61.2
Cumberland	129	0.1	146	0.0	46.3	589,663	4,043	73,047	46.7	52,746	47.0	53.0	NA	73.5	790	19.2
Davidson	34	-1.1	83	0.3	13.0	747,014	8,978	62,082	11.1	26,829	78.4	21.6	4	78.5	160	10.9
Decatur	74	-4.4	197	D	24.8	436,208	2,209	78,589	7.4	19,826	56.5	43.5	NA	67.6	583	23.0
DeKalb	88	-1.5	135	0.5	29.7	456,211	3,384	63,777	26.0	39,719	78.4	21.6	NA	72.0	633	32.9
Dickson	140	-5.6	114	0.2	46.9	480,574	4,201	64,723	18.6	15,208	56.6	43.4	2	75.7	412	15.8
Dyer	284	34.1	629	25.5	257.6	2,117,443	3,364	273,302	134.2	297,483	96.8	3.2	NA	80.3	2,700	59.6
Fayette	306	33.8	344	13.3	185.7	1,158,789	3,373	120,662	89.9	100,784	87.0	13.0	NA	71.0	3,742	39.3
Fentress	94	3.5	152	0.0	25.7	526,303	3,472	72,186	37.6	60,584	12.9	87.1	NA	74.4	549	33.4
Franklin	112	-10.4	137	1.5	61.5	563,293	4,101	83,705	72.5	88,641	44.5	55.5	1	72.1	1,795	30.6
Gibson	287	0.4	370	9.9	248.9	1,309,546	3,541	174,608	137.1	176,459	94.6	5.4	NA	73.7	6,511	51.4
Giles	251	-7.1	157	2.1	78.8	514,156	3,275	69,966	48.9	30,551	38.3	61.7	NA	74.2	4,230	37.3
Grainger	87	2.2	94	0.3	25.8	358,497	3,798	60,980	19.5	21,085	55.5	44.5	6	64.1	1,666	31.5
Greene	222	-1.9	86	D	97.2	388,623	4,493	64,414	61.5	24,014	30.8	69.2	1	67.1	1,112	15.8
Grundy	34	1.8	129	0.1	13.3	446,403	3,459	70,611	29.6	113,586	37.2	62.8	NA	68.6	258	19.2
Hamblen	50	-15.0	89	0.0	24.4	492,840	5,507	67,616	15.8	28,188	24.4	75.6	1	68.0	387	25.8
Hamilton	44	-16.5	80	0.1	14.0	786,833	9,850	59,900	20.6	37,649	12.7	87.3	3	77.7	201	12.2
Hancock	73	12.9	178	D	16.5	474,077	2,662	57,539	6.7	16,341	18.3	81.7	NA	62.5	646	40.7
Hardeman	173	12.4	282	2.3	83.9	645,321	2,289	75,727	31.5	51,408	90.7	9.3	NA	63.5	2,859	39.2
Hardin	162	28.5	278	2.2	76.2	620,402	2,232	101,400	29.7	50,871	81.5	18.5	NA	64.5	2,154	43.6
Hawkins	141	6.0	95	0.0	47.8	355,038	3,727	58,427	18.8	12,648	28.5	71.5	NA	62.9	1,252	24.7
Haywood	201	-8.5	556	21.6	178.6	1,845,293	3,319	211,930	97.8	270,925	99.2	0.8	2	71.2	3,391	63.7
Henderson	153	-5.5	195	0.0	63.7	492,153	2,522	89,292	29.2	37,104	60.2	39.8	NA	72.8	1,940	35.4
Henry	204	-0.3	287	4.1	127.5	954,925	3,324	139,412	94.1	132,530	62.2	37.8	1	81.5	2,783	42.4
Hickman	123	2.1	175	0.0	43.9	551,572	3,154	72,096	17.1	24,183	50.6	49.4	2	78.2	1,053	22.2
Houston	50	0.1	154	0.0	11.7	499,292	3,233	71,786	D	D	D	D	NA	81.9	76	10.4
Humphreys	115	-6.5	176	1.5	33.4	489,160	2,783	82,009	11.2	17,078	46.2	53.8	NA	74.0	261	6.5
Jackson	81	9.6	150	0.0	18.6	466,297	3,105	58,481	4.9	9,130	36.1	63.9	8	78.4	270	31.6
Jefferson	89	-6.9	91	0.3	37.2	470,695	5,149	61,911	24.1	24,780	21.8	78.2	NA	67.7	1,260	25.7
Johnson	47	-1.6	90	0.0	16.4	358,093	3,973	62,699	7.7	14,797	29.9	70.1	2	68.9	112	5.8
Knox	67	3.1	65	0.2	26.7	639,694	9,845	53,723	18.7	17,987	61.6	38.4	8	79.7	618	15.5
Lake	88	10.7	1,698	15.0	82.0	5,959,437	3,511	793,852	45.8	880,788	99.8	0.2	NA	84.6	2,175	76.9
Lauderdale	156	-22.5	385	6.1	134.3	1,304,233	3,385	186,207	69.6	172,260	96.0	4.0	NA	63.4	2,608	55.4
Lawrence	230	-2.3	165	D	105.7	544,725	3,296	77,410	71.1	51,024	55.6	44.4	NA	66.9	2,770	37.2
Lewis	41	32.7	150	0.0	10.4	428,585	2,859	53,189	3.0	10,996	35.2	64.8	2	72.8	161	11.4
Lincoln	271	2.0	164	3.4	102.6	600,890	3,663	90,043	124.9	75,524	30.9	69.1	NA	73.1	1,905	19.4
Loudon	59	-15.2	85	0.1	28.4	484,550	5,690	74,092	D	D	D	D	1	73.7	284	20.3
McMinn	129	5.6	123	0.1	49.9	571,882	4,666	65,080	50.1	47,555	16.2	83.8	1	69.2	1,162	24.1
McNairy	139	7.0	213	0.3	65.5	468,203	2,203	70,549	22.4	34,229	86.0	14.0	2	69.7	1,212	40.7
Macon	132	8.0	144	D	51.9	543,237	3,763	72,506	61.5	67,451	44.8	55.2	2	74.2	1,078	32.8
Madison	151	-8.9	275	6.8	107.6	898,835	3,263	136,092	49.5	90,117	93.7	6.3	NA	70.3	3,371	52.6
Marion	55	8.5	179	0.0	23.1	581,773	3,254	86,733	17.1	55,406	33.9	66.1	NA	72.7	500	11.0

STATE County	Water use, 2015		Wholesale Trade[1], 2017				Retail Trade[2], 2017				Real estate and rental and leasing,[2] 2017			
	Public supply water withdrawn (mil gal/ day)	Public supply gallons withdrawn per person per day	Number of establish-ments	Number of employees	Sales (mil dol)	Average payroll (mil dol)	Number of establish-ments	Number of employees	Sales (mil dol)	Average payroll (mil dol)	Number of establish-ments	Number of employees	Sales (mil dol)	Average payroll (mil dol)
	133	134	135	136	137	138	139	140	141	142	143	144	145	146
SOUTH DAKOTA—Cont'd														
Tripp	0.5	90.2	12	136	82.0	8.0	44	381	103.4	9.1	NA	NA	NA	NA
Turner	0.5	57.3	D	D	D	D	32	220	44.3	4.3	D	D	D	D
Union	1.6	106.6	D	D	D	D	46	432	123.6	10.5	26	55	12.0	1.9
Walworth	0.4	77.2	11	83	234.9	4.1	47	349	100.4	7.6	7	D	1.2	D
Yankton	1.1	48.9	D	D	D	D	124	1,665	419.0	40.8	28	85	11.5	2.4
Ziebach	0.0	14.3	4	D	25.0	D	8	88	20.5	1.5	NA	NA	NA	NA
TENNESSEE	849.7	128.7	5,864	100,044	111,030.0	5,824.7	22,593	322,218	101,978.3	8,574.3	6,048	36,212	10,679.1	1,759.7
Anderson	10.7	141.1	47	528	1,101.2	23.1	236	3,336	979.5	83.5	52	158	36.5	6.4
Bedford	6.0	127.8	D	D	D	D	144	1,498	423.7	41.3	33	94	19.9	2.0
Benton	1.3	77.5	D	D	D	2.0	57	671	170.4	15.6	5	D	0.6	D
Bledsoe	2.2	151.0	NA	NA	NA	NA	21	143	35.8	2.7	3	6	0.7	0.1
Blount	13.9	109.5	93	1,605	1,825.6	104.1	373	5,748	1,649.1	161.7	104	461	100.4	13.5
Bradley	13.7	132.0	63	694	807.3	48.6	347	5,857	2,087.4	159.9	D	D	D	D
Campbell	3.3	83.8	13	52	34.2	2.4	132	1,543	429.4	37.1	17	111	13.9	2.4
Cannon	5.3	381.5	D	D	D	2.5	37	252	68.9	5.7	NA	NA	NA	NA
Carroll	2.5	88.9	14	221	81.0	8.0	88	801	197.1	17.3	14	46	4.2	1.4
Carter	7.1	125.2	D	D	D	D	140	1,780	442.3	41.0	23	56	10.3	1.7
Cheatham	2.9	73.7	17	107	62.2	5.2	78	883	241.7	21.9	25	72	11.7	2.2
Chester	0.9	53.2	9	46	26.1	1.9	54	454	130.4	10.7	8	17	1.6	0.3
Claiborne	3.0	94.0	14	62	19.0	1.7	89	903	201.7	20.3	17	37	7.1	1.1
Clay	0.9	110.7	D	D	D	1.8	30	172	42.3	3.4	5	D	1.5	D
Cocke	4.7	134.2	D	D	D	D	112	1,372	396.1	32.7	17	70	4.5	1.2
Coffee	5.8	106.1	36	498	362.7	26.5	256	2,892	844.7	73.9	41	222	33.6	6.1
Crockett	1.6	106.8	21	238	231.6	10.3	34	219	67.2	4.7	7	17	6.4	0.7
Cumberland	5.7	98.1	D	D	D	D	232	2,465	774.4	62.6	34	118	25.0	3.3
Davidson	134.1	197.5	968	19,905	18,494.0	1,313.8	2,603	38,670	11,329.8	1,115.1	1,083	8,442	2,803.8	474.5
Decatur	1.4	117.5	D	D	D	3.5	47	349	90.7	8.0	NA	NA	NA	NA
DeKalb	2.2	113.1	4	40	7.0	1.4	56	564	141.4	13.5	9	21	1.8	0.7
Dickson	5.2	101.8	29	594	1,116.8	28.5	180	2,244	722.8	57.0	25	107	18.9	2.3
Dyer	2.7	71.5	42	543	858.6	23.0	170	1,943	573.6	47.9	23	82	13.3	3.2
Fayette	1.5	37.5	34	438	528.6	24.3	81	926	341.0	26.3	11	29	7.5	1.3
Fentress	1.7	92.1	D	D	D	0.5	55	674	163.3	16.3	D	D	D	D
Franklin	4.3	103.0	D	D	D	D	133	1,354	399.3	35.3	17	44	7.0	1.6
Gibson	3.8	76.9	36	464	463.9	26.1	182	1,959	502.6	46.9	25	90	37.0	4.3
Giles	3.0	103.6	19	249	328.7	13.8	123	1,435	359.5	30.9	12	41	4.3	1.2
Grainger	0.0	0.0	NA	NA	NA	NA	53	482	114.1	9.6	9	9	0.9	0.1
Greene	8.9	130.1	D	D	D	D	208	2,823	744.8	67.2	36	139	25.1	4.5
Grundy	1.6	121.3	NA	NA	NA	NA	40	244	68.8	6.1	NA	NA	NA	NA
Hamblen	9.2	144.8	50	851	785.5	39.0	273	4,148	1,175.5	108.1	51	160	36.7	4.9
Hamilton	60.0	169.5	441	6,354	4,075.0	380.6	1,367	23,791	7,171.8	652.9	401	2,072	632.3	120.4
Hancock	0.2	32.0	NA	NA	NA	NA	15	105	28.2	2.4	3	4	1.0	0.1
Hardeman	2.2	85.6	11	73	49.0	2.9	70	614	138.1	13.2	4	26	1.5	0.5
Hardin	2.6	102.1	D	D	D	4.5	111	1,368	477.4	37.2	23	46	8.1	1.7
Hawkins	3.4	60.6	D	D	D	D	113	1,428	353.0	31.4	24	108	17.2	2.8
Haywood	1.5	82.7	10	109	92.7	5.4	59	607	212.7	15.0	10	27	3.2	0.7
Henderson	0.3	11.1	17	169	61.2	6.0	108	1,109	301.7	25.5	10	20	3.2	0.6
Henry	2.1	65.6	D	D	D	D	135	1,632	620.1	49.5	24	99	24.7	2.5
Hickman	2.4	97.7	8	89	92.1	3.5	58	334	122.8	9.3	NA	NA	NA	NA
Houston	1.0	122.7	NA	NA	NA	NA	25	168	39.6	3.2	NA	NA	NA	NA
Humphreys	2.2	122.4	18	98	53.9	5.3	66	604	206.2	14.1	6	8	0.9	0.3
Jackson	0.6	48.7	D	D	D	D	18	105	28.3	2.0	NA	NA	NA	NA
Jefferson	5.3	99.2	25	200	109.9	9.1	127	1,774	580.9	46.0	27	50	9.3	1.4
Johnson	1.7	95.3	NA	NA	NA	NA	48	417	96.3	8.3	12	32	3.6	0.5
Knox	64.3	142.5	639	10,093	7,554.4	551.4	1,720	29,506	8,384.1	833.3	571	3,607	870.1	162.9
Lake	1.1	146.5	5	57	36.2	3.3	18	132	25.0	2.7	NA	NA	NA	NA
Lauderdale	2.5	93.9	24	676	1,334.8	31.0	71	653	134.5	13.5	14	94	39.4	3.7
Lawrence	4.1	95.4	D	D	D	D	178	1,649	411.3	40.1	21	52	9.5	1.4
Lewis	1.3	110.5	5	10	5.5	0.4	44	422	212.7	11.5	6	41	6.3	1.8
Lincoln	4.3	128.3	25	234	388.8	15.1	127	1,401	347.7	33.4	20	203	10.3	3.0
Loudon	13.1	257.0	38	594	669.4	26.4	143	1,954	572.6	47.8	48	165	30.0	5.7
McMinn	3.8	72.4	25	287	247.9	11.9	178	2,170	603.4	53.7	37	95	15.4	2.3
McNairy	2.5	97.4	15	139	64.1	5.2	82	577	143.4	13.6	8	27	4.5	0.8
Macon	2.1	90.2	D	D	D	1.5	62	669	174.1	17.1	10	28	3.1	0.3
Madison	15.7	161.3	148	2,383	1,331.4	103.4	483	7,147	2,071.4	181.0	117	578	118.2	21.7
Marion	3.4	120.1	17	214	100.5	13.1	98	1,244	428.5	29.7	11	28	6.3	1.0

1 Merchant wholesalers, except manufacturers' sales branches and offices. 2. Employer establishments.

STATE County	Professional, scientific, and technical services, 2017				Manufacturing, 2017				Accommodation and food services, 2017			
	Number of establish-ments	Number of employees	Sales (mil dol)	Average payroll (mil dol)	Number of establish-ments	Number of employees	Sales (mil dol)	Average payroll (mil dol)	Number of establis-hments	Number of employees	Sales (mil dol)	Annual payroll (mil dol)
	147	148	149	150	151	152	153	154	155	156	157	158
SOUTH DAKOTA—Cont'd												
Tripp	D	D	D	D	D	37	D	1.7	23	161	10.0	2.5
Turner	14	39	5.3	1.6	D	167	D	8.6	18	99	3.9	0.9
Union	41	318	54.7	16.8	D	D	D	D	34	346	21.4	4.8
Walworth	15	70	9.8	2.9	D	D	D	D	25	343	23.3	6.9
Yankton	44	221	30.4	9.6	32	3,048	875.0	147.9	76	1,018	50.8	14.9
Ziebach	NA	NA	NA	NA	NA	NA	NA	NA	4	52	3.2	0.8
TENNESSEE	11,357	110,731	17,046.5	7,102.3	5,811	321,195	155,422.4	17,021.9	13,518	287,534	17,181.8	4,839.4
Anderson	D	D	D	D	89	10,905	2,580.0	750.3	141	2,646	134.9	38.4
Bedford	47	198	22.7	6.3	52	4,501	1,488.3	199.8	66	980	51.9	13.7
Benton	15	44	4.3	1.5	21	688	92.9	21.3	29	337	17.4	4.3
Bledsoe	7	35	2.3	0.7	8	36	9.9	D	8	107	5.7	1.7
Blount	D	D	D	D	98	7,036	3,858.1	409.5	206	5,038	303.0	89.4
Bradley	135	733	86.5	29.8	108	7,425	4,214.8	366.4	198	4,126	210.6	58.5
Campbell	D	D	D	4.2	34	1,257	334.8	48.4	63	814	46.6	11.7
Cannon	16	39	3.9	1.2	15	303	43.9	11.7	14	205	9.7	2.5
Carroll	25	80	8.2	2.6	21	509	412.2	35.2	35	505	25.1	6.1
Carter	44	153	14.8	4.2	30	1,179	248.7	50.4	74	1,304	57.9	17.3
Cheatham	36	198	18.0	8.3	45	1,565	759.9	76.7	51	720	35.4	9.8
Chester	12	56	3.7	1.4	18	534	127.3	23.6	D	D	D	D
Claiborne	28	158	12.2	4.4	27	2,376	505.2	84.2	36	691	29.2	7.7
Clay	D	D	0.3	D	10	245	48.2	9.9	12	D	4.2	D
Cocke	27	83	8.3	2.9	32	1,572	592.6	76.8	68	1,056	58.4	15.0
Coffee	75	812	100.7	53.1	D	4,408	D	234.8	122	2,252	121.3	32.2
Crockett	12	46	8.9	1.9	13	200	152.6	13.4	D	D	D	D
Cumberland	70	225	30.8	9.1	50	2,515	768.4	116.8	99	1,707	123.8	33.8
Davidson	2,214	30,295	5,676.4	2,382.9	573	19,803	8,610.8	1,015.1	2,115	52,934	4,123.2	1,121.8
Decatur	13	45	3.2	1.0	18	517	147.1	18.9	24	180	8.3	2.1
DeKalb	25	81	8.0	2.3	14	2,110	680.0	92.1	30	337	19.1	5.3
Dickson	59	243	26.1	9.9	43	3,579	986.5	157.0	105	1,732	91.2	26.0
Dyer	D	D	D	D	38	3,858	1,554.2	192.3	64	1,176	59.4	15.3
Fayette	33	112	13.3	3.8	51	1,604	745.3	81.2	35	605	26.6	7.0
Fentress	17	41	3.5	0.7	21	255	49.1	12.2	20	277	11.5	3.3
Franklin	46	588	61.9	40.8	40	D	4,939.7	D	D	D	D	D
Gibson	41	220	17.1	5.8	66	2,572	940.1	151.9	75	1,070	52.9	13.8
Giles	31	153	15.0	6.5	48	4,125	1,270.6	178.9	46	611	33.4	8.4
Grainger	D	D	D	D	27	934	200.4	39.5	19	152	10.2	2.1
Greene	D	D	D	D	88	5,822	2,134.3	284.7	115	1,991	95.3	25.8
Grundy	6	22	1.6	0.5	14	213	43.2	8.3	11	D	4.0	D
Hamblen	D	D	D	D	83	10,236	3,827.1	455.0	114	2,352	110.2	32.0
Hamilton	D	D	D	D	409	22,895	11,828.3	1,270.8	929	19,999	1,194.4	333.9
Hancock	4	4	0.3	0.1	NA	NA	NA	NA	D	D	D	D
Hardeman	12	35	3.3	0.7	24	1,918	613.5	88.5	22	243	12.8	3.1
Hardin	28	77	7.8	2.8	29	1,906	950.4	122.2	49	741	35.2	8.8
Hawkins	33	104	10.5	3.8	42	4,180	1,307.2	214.9	64	1,009	42.7	11.9
Haywood	16	60	5.3	2.0	15	1,877	667.0	80.5	30	393	21.2	5.1
Henderson	28	116	10.9	3.9	27	1,307	435.9	59.5	35	758	29.8	7.9
Henry	37	306	24.6	11.8	46	1,764	386.3	64.6	63	947	42.1	11.4
Hickman	10	40	3.0	1.2	27	525	117.9	22.3	D	D	D	2.7
Houston	5	36	3.5	1.0	5	177	29.9	8.2	D	D	D	D
Humphreys	16	87	6.5	2.5	23	1,794	1,501.5	136.5	37	384	21.1	6.0
Jackson	6	52	1.3	0.7	9	190	40.9	5.6	14	88	4.0	1.4
Jefferson	40	130	14.9	4.3	38	1,729	977.1	84.9	80	1,317	64.8	18.8
Johnson	15	48	7.9	1.6	17	922	213.6	49.2	28	297	16.0	4.2
Knox	D	D	D	D	363	10,845	5,379.3	581.5	1,052	24,754	1,377.2	416.4
Lake	NA	NA	NA	NA	NA	NA	NA	NA	10	152	7.2	2.3
Lauderdale	13	34	5.1	1.3	12	1,401	296.3	50.9	D	D	D	D
Lawrence	34	248	26.5	7.9	53	1,769	485.2	77.2	62	1,039	50.3	12.3
Lewis	10	27	2.6	0.7	19	441	81.3	17.3	21	D	11.0	D
Lincoln	35	141	15.4	5.2	34	2,213	1,271.0	138.0	D	D	D	D
Loudon	54	595	59.8	39.4	48	3,004	1,321.9	170.5	91	1,591	80.7	24.1
McMinn	48	258	27.9	6.7	72	6,401	2,698.1	334.4	91	1,740	77.7	21.2
McNairy	18	71	7.2	2.4	40	1,117	385.6	54.0	D	D	D	D
Macon	21	61	5.9	2.1	31	945	216.7	35.8	24	265	14.1	3.4
Madison	D	D	D	D	93	9,691	4,880.6	483.8	229	5,306	276.1	77.9
Marion	27	85	14.3	4.9	28	1,947	829.7	91.8	52	1,006	54.8	14.3

STATE County	Health care and social assistance, 2017				Other services, 2017				Nonemployer businesses, 2019		Value of residential construction authorized by building permits, 2021	
	Number of establish-ments	Number of employees	Receipts (mil dol)	Annual payroll (mil dol)	Number of establish-ments	Number of employees	Receipts (mil dol)	Annual payroll (mil dol)	Number	Receipts (mil dol)	New construction ($1,000)	Number of housing units
	159	160	161	162	163	164	165	166	167	168	169	170
SOUTH DAKOTA—Cont'd												
Tripp	25	445	40.0	13.4	19	74	7.1	1.5	566	24.6	833	4
Turner	19	294	17.1	8.2	D	D	4.6	D	788	34.8	7,594	25
Union	66	1,135	202.2	64.8	D	D	D	D	1,514	100.4	54,032	197
Walworth	15	378	31.0	13.1	16	77	7.8	2.1	490	23.0	538	6
Yankton	72	1,847	235.4	94.0	60	238	22.4	5.2	1,668	71.1	26,476	150
Ziebach	9	D	7.3	D	NA	NA	NA	NA	75	2.6	NA	NA
TENNESSEE	15,891	414,598	52,088.8	20,219.5	8,570	61,744	8,650.0	2,149.1	555,566	27,607.7	11,477,551	57,484
Anderson	210	4,597	532.3	195.9	105	470	42.8	13.0	4,883	223.5	74,955	458
Bedford	101	1,186	116.5	42.4	45	195	16.8	5.2	3,296	162.2	51,872	390
Benton	35	706	55.4	20.9	16	83	7.6	1.7	1,081	34.5	250	4
Bledsoe	14	216	19.4	9.5	3	16	1.2	0.3	768	34.8	0	0
Blount	238	6,088	713.7	279.3	160	964	104.9	33.1	9,538	464.4	222,922	922
Bradley	241	5,172	607.7	212.3	112	926	88.9	24.3	7,702	412.3	138,594	543
Campbell	74	2,048	200.4	73.2	D	D	D	D	2,298	102.3	40,777	388
Cannon	28	367	34.8	12.7	D	D	D	1.5	1,146	45.5	2,094	28
Carroll	65	1,534	109.1	48.0	D	D	D	D	1,657	69.6	2,338	13
Carter	82	1,722	166.4	70.9	D	D	D	D	3,315	120.8	24,759	180
Cheatham	51	613	55.4	22.1	35	102	11.5	3.0	3,752	199.6	75,466	407
Chester	29	448	31.4	14.9	D	D	4.9	D	1,062	46.9	1,877	13
Claiborne	50	999	78.2	34.9	27	109	15.9	3.8	1,794	87.2	16,896	81
Clay	10	354	27.1	11.2	4	10	1.4	0.2	622	23.3	4,142	27
Cocke	37	1,031	112.3	43.4	D	D	D	D	2,165	78.2	0	0
Coffee	192	3,071	337.4	119.6	D	D	D	D	3,959	176.0	37,252	210
Crockett	23	421	29.3	11.8	D	D	D	D	912	38.1	6,640	36
Cumberland	134	2,793	259.6	95.2	64	573	45.8	16.2	4,675	222.2	135,512	477
Davidson	2,020	76,927	12,251.2	4,700.2	1,375	13,835	1,731.1	495.2	80,118	4,564.0	2,071,444	16,310
Decatur	29	991	71.8	41.8	D	D	7.8	D	857	38.2	459	3
DeKalb	39	591	57.0	20.9	D	D	D	D	1,495	75.4	22,884	147
Dickson	129	2,338	325.6	104.1	55	311	31.5	8.9	4,122	222.4	117,247	617
Dyer	106	1,993	201.6	74.1	46	186	19.6	5.5	2,412	91.2	13,372	62
Fayette	47	512	36.2	17.1	35	184	16.4	4.1	3,898	192.9	149,714	490
Fentress	33	864	66.7	30.1	D	D	D	D	1,597	89.9	0	0
Franklin	95	1,494	167.0	63.1	46	222	33.5	6.5	2,800	111.3	104,342	420
Gibson	100	1,576	120.2	48.3	57	249	24.1	6.7	2,885	127.4	45,152	194
Giles	63	947	99.4	36.4	30	101	10.9	2.6	1,939	94.4	20,830	178
Grainger	10	198	13.1	5.3	17	105	12.6	3.6	1,541	74.4	14,805	82
Greene	139	4,207	354.5	147.5	60	403	33.3	10.2	4,213	181.5	52,336	260
Grundy	16	332	19.3	8.8	4	29	1.9	0.6	1,189	52.2	1,515	5
Hamblen	173	4,263	418.4	160.1	80	468	36.2	11.9	3,546	191.0	80,740	581
Hamilton	1,132	30,166	3,795.7	1,509.9	602	4,259	597.8	148.2	29,071	1,564.5	485,713	2,804
Hancock	10	156	15.4	5.1	NA	NA	NA	NA	405	13.9	0	0
Hardeman	42	1,310	86.8	41.1	16	49	5.7	1.3	1,515	53.6	7,041	45
Hardin	63	1,154	115.4	42.9	24	157	17.1	5.7	1,755	84.6	1,716	12
Hawkins	58	1,239	139.2	48.2	38	154	17.2	4.7	3,048	110.6	20,335	172
Haywood	30	430	32.8	15.2	D	D	D	D	1,220	40.5	1,978	25
Henderson	61	1,057	79.7	32.8	35	132	14.8	3.8	1,779	75.7	3,000	20
Henry	78	1,382	153.5	56.1	46	208	16.4	4.7	2,292	104.9	1,814	22
Hickman	D	D	D	24.2	D	D	7.7	D	1,796	79.6	22,061	131
Houston	12	346	25.1	10.8	D	D	1.8	D	522	20.9	218	1
Humphreys	30	674	51.9	18.1	17	102	10.4	3.0	1,165	52.9	2,737	20
Jackson	9	116	6.8	2.6	D	D	D	D	810	34.1	0	0
Jefferson	72	1,253	130.5	46.8	46	212	20.3	6.5	3,353	156.6	93,625	330
Johnson	22	580	39.0	18.3	9	28	3.5	0.8	1,099	47.6	126	1
Knox	1,400	38,751	4,850.5	1,832.6	732	5,058	639.0	163.5	38,134	2,140.8	617,387	2,831
Lake	12	194	15.6	7.0	NA	NA	NA	NA	323	7.7	853	5
Lauderdale	33	650	77.9	21.8	D	D	D	D	1,215	52.0	6,263	32
Lawrence	82	1,315	124.1	48.1	33	107	9.9	3.2	2,961	140.9	3,687	18
Lewis	29	507	28.5	13.5	9	69	8.2	2.3	927	46.0	5,400	30
Lincoln	60	855	66.1	31.4	34	136	14.2	3.4	2,451	109.4	2,754	18
Loudon	110	1,560	151.2	57.6	62	261	35.4	8.0	3,782	198.6	253,946	1,117
McMinn	104	2,161	195.2	74.1	49	314	21.2	7.8	3,141	138.5	6,291	51
McNairy	46	734	56.0	22.5	D	D	10.8	D	1,648	80.0	598	5
Macon	37	631	45.2	17.1	D	D	D	D	1,694	84.2	17,541	110
Madison	335	13,624	1,482.7	608.6	D	D	D	D	6,756	316.0	66,647	294
Marion	43	664	57.8	22.6	29	163	24.9	5.8	1,801	76.6	53,770	244

STATE County	Government employment and payroll, 2017									Local government finances, 2017				
			March payroll (percent of total)							General revenue				
												Taxes		
													Per capita[1] (dollars)	
	Full-time equivalent employees	March payroll (dollars)	Adminis-tration, judicial, and legal	Police and corrections	Fire protection	Highways and transpor-tation	Health and welfare	Natural resources and utilities	Education and libraries	Total (mil dol)	Inter-govern-mental (mil dol)	Total (mil dol)	Total	Property
	171	172	173	174	175	176	177	178	179	180	181	182	183	184
SOUTH DAKOTA—Cont'd														
Tripp	337	1,063,765	7.8	14.4	0.0	5.8	5.5	9.1	54.0	24.8	6.4	12.5	2,288	1,811
Turner	309	1,219,605	10.1	1.5	0.0	6.4	0.3	4.3	76.7	38.9	8.2	27.7	3,333	3,044
Union	582	2,082,029	7.6	7.8	0.4	4.5	0.2	6.2	70.5	69.4	11.9	49.7	3,251	2,626
Walworth	225	798,106	6.6	13.6	0.2	5.6	0.2	4.0	69.4	24.5	7.6	12.9	2,342	1,840
Yankton	757	2,886,149	6.9	9.9	0.4	5.8	2.8	7.8	61.2	79.9	22.2	46.4	2,047	1,536
Ziebach	105	361,245	8.0	2.0	0.0	3.2	0.6	0.3	84.4	9.2	7.1	1.8	668	621
TENNESSEE	X	X	X	X	X	X	X	X	X	X	X	X	X	X
Anderson	3,008	11,222,851	7.6	9.5	3.6	1.5	3.6	10.9	62.3	244.9	97.4	97.1	1,276	830
Bedford	1,718	5,739,076	5.0	10.7	3.4	4.1	4.2	10.5	61.3	125.9	68.2	35.3	733	491
Benton	554	2,074,406	8.3	12.3	4.5	4.3	1.3	15.7	53.5	38.2	21.6	12.3	770	447
Bledsoe	606	1,567,248	5.9	7.9	0.0	2.9	3.7	5.0	60.7	34.8	28.2	3.9	263	246
Blount	5,994	22,571,498	4.7	7.3	2.0	2.5	36.4	6.0	40.0	584.7	149.1	119.7	920	825
Bradley	3,040	10,809,028	4.4	12.1	7.3	3.4	11.0	1.7	59.0	268.8	135.3	88.1	836	588
Campbell	1,680	4,210,220	6.3	9.0	2.6	4.6	9.0	20.3	48.2	108.7	54.7	31.9	802	407
Cannon	569	1,512,678	4.0	8.6	0.0	2.3	4.5	3.8	72.1	27.0	19.2	5.1	363	309
Carroll	1,097	3,230,184	5.2	10.1	1.2	4.3	1.6	12.1	60.8	77.2	43.8	20.6	740	489
Carter	2,193	6,104,153	5.5	9.0	1.8	4.0	1.6	8.8	67.9	121.5	65.9	35.6	630	350
Cheatham	1,143	3,615,388	6.8	9.8	1.3	4.3	3.9	5.3	66.6	94.6	45.4	34.8	861	583
Chester	575	1,584,780	7.8	13.0	1.3	4.6	0.0	7.8	64.3	38.5	25.2	7.2	422	317
Claiborne	1,723	5,315,708	4.8	5.0	0.0	1.7	37.7	5.4	44.3	60.5	36.0	20.7	655	434
Clay	340	942,838	7.1	9.9	0.0	5.2	5.2	9.5	60.2	20.7	14.3	3.7	477	333
Cocke	1,245	3,868,897	5.8	7.6	3.8	3.2	2.5	3.8	72.5	82.6	44.4	22.8	642	380
Coffee	2,388	7,175,942	5.6	8.1	3.2	2.8	2.8	13.9	59.7	154.0	69.1	57.0	1,037	765
Crockett	661	1,875,223	9.8	7.2	0.1	3.2	4.4	6.1	67.7	41.5	27.6	8.5	590	402
Cumberland	1,992	5,523,188	11.4	9.7	1.6	8.1	6.1	4.4	57.4	130.2	58.4	52.6	892	391
Davidson	22,221	105,597,426	6.1	14.0	6.3	2.7	7.4	14.7	46.7	3,001.9	764.0	1,611.1	2,345	1,423
Decatur	559	1,619,700	7.2	9.2	0.0	3.3	23.1	7.2	47.2	37.3	15.3	8.2	697	361
DeKalb	726	2,211,919	3.9	5.3	0.0	2.5	2.4	28.2	57.0	45.3	27.8	11.1	558	365
Dickson	1,840	6,148,534	7.8	8.3	3.3	3.2	3.6	19.6	53.6	144.1	61.8	56.9	1,078	627
Dyer	1,602	5,134,617	6.4	11.9	5.4	4.3	1.2	9.7	59.3	141.9	70.0	39.8	1,067	732
Fayette	1,026	2,893,596	9.2	16.0	2.1	4.6	4.6	7.5	55.0	60.2	31.0	20.8	518	306
Fentress	676	1,679,404	10.9	8.7	0.1	7.9	4.8	8.6	58.4	33.5	19.0	9.1	500	364
Franklin	1,291	3,957,206	3.3	9.3	1.7	3.8	1.0	9.2	70.1	101.9	46.1	35.4	851	591
Gibson	1,931	6,018,686	4.0	12.8	2.6	6.2	1.6	8.6	63.0	146.6	75.3	38.7	785	671
Giles	1,158	3,227,522	14.1	9.8	0.7	11.4	4.5	5.8	51.9	53.1	32.5	14.9	507	381
Grainger	679	1,998,640	4.1	17.0	0.0	0.6	4.4	4.2	68.8	45.1	30.6	10.7	461	369
Greene	2,263	7,462,462	5.0	11.3	2.4	4.3	4.3	13.8	58.4	156.2	75.8	52.5	763	460
Grundy	522	1,277,412	7.2	6.1	0.0	4.4	1.5	5.4	72.6	32.5	23.8	6.1	455	352
Hamblen	2,075	7,707,192	6.3	8.6	4.2	2.9	1.5	15.7	57.7	166.6	77.1	46.7	729	596
Hamilton	16,117	72,322,243	5.3	6.4	2.7	3.3	44.1	9.5	26.9	2,259.7	576.1	576.9	1,598	1,217
Hancock	420	1,149,417	9.8	6.4	0.1	5.9	16.1	2.7	58.9	19.8	13.0	2.3	344	263
Hardeman	1,046	3,010,162	5.8	9.6	1.2	4.3	4.3	12.9	61.3	60.8	36.9	14.4	563	430
Hardin	1,213	3,456,931	6.1	8.9	0.9	3.5	34.4	4.3	40.4	147.9	35.4	18.1	703	536
Hawkins	2,002	5,783,824	5.4	5.8	0.4	2.7	10.8	10.0	63.8	115.8	60.5	41.5	733	508
Haywood	950	2,822,431	8.8	9.9	3.2	2.7	3.2	9.7	56.0	62.4	32.9	18.5	1,050	784
Henderson	1,130	3,457,451	7.1	11.0	3.6	2.9	0.7	11.5	61.1	75.5	40.9	23.3	836	379
Henry	1,075	3,623,862	6.4	10.2	2.5	1.8	0.8	14.1	62.3	158.9	46.7	23.7	732	497
Hickman	1,109	2,540,582	12.3	4.4	0.0	3.6	3.4	5.3	65.7	57.6	35.0	14.5	584	411
Houston	387	1,084,439	8.3	10.7	0.5	5.6	8.2	5.8	58.1	21.9	14.7	4.3	529	336
Humphreys	608	1,876,441	12.0	11.5	0.0	5.8	0.9	10.0	58.8	43.3	26.0	11.2	607	496
Jackson	460	1,343,479	12.3	7.9	0.0	7.9	3.6	6.9	61.2	28.7	16.2	10.1	865	762
Jefferson	1,539	4,997,676	6.6	9.3	1.7	7.2	5.3	10.3	58.2	120.8	55.9	35.5	661	397
Johnson	565	1,541,974	6.9	8.1	0.0	3.6	0.9	6.0	73.3	30.1	20.6	6.3	360	253
Knox	13,331	51,598,862	5.9	12.2	3.0	3.1	3.6	16.1	54.4	1,506.5	407.3	764.3	1,656	993
Lake	320	1,046,883	15.2	14.2	0.3	4.2	2.8	9.2	54.1	17.4	11.5	3.4	451	277
Lauderdale	1,066	3,106,646	6.6	12.0	1.9	5.2	4.2	3.4	65.5	74.9	43.5	19.1	734	530
Lawrence	1,609	5,405,378	7.1	8.6	1.8	3.9	3.4	12.6	61.7	109.1	55.1	37.1	855	440
Lewis	546	1,227,740	11.9	13.0	0.6	4.8	2.6	6.3	60.7	30.7	19.5	6.3	525	308
Lincoln	1,562	4,636,209	8.8	8.2	1.9	6.1	1.5	11.4	59.9	148.7	43.6	23.3	688	362
Loudon	1,512	5,432,357	5.2	9.1	2.6	2.9	1.7	19.6	57.1	126.7	51.3	48.6	930	696
McMinn	2,143	8,077,858	5.2	5.8	1.3	2.5	27.3	8.1	48.1	103.2	60.1	24.9	471	378
McNairy	1,130	3,062,012	5.4	5.7	0.6	3.7	0.3	7.5	75.0	64.4	40.7	13.9	535	383
Macon	738	2,075,037	7.9	10.9	1.1	0.3	7.2	5.9	65.7	54.3	34.2	11.8	495	295
Madison	8,999	37,163,340	2.0	5.6	2.3	1.4	65.9	6.0	16.5	1,048.2	100.1	131.6	1,350	821
Marion	858	2,930,021	6.6	10.6	0.6	3.3	1.6	5.4	71.5	61.4	34.8	18.2	640	395

1. Based on the resident population estimated as of July 1 of the year shown.

STATE County	Local government finances, 2017 (cont.)									Government employment, 2020			Individual income tax returns, 2019		
	Direct general expenditure							Debt outstanding							
			Percent of total for:												
	Total (mil dol)	Per capita[1] (dollars)	Education	Health and hospitals	Police protection	Public welfare	Highways	Total (mil dol)	Per capita[1] (dollars)	Federal civilian	Federal military	State and local	Number of returns	Mean adjusted gross income	Mean income tax
	185	186	187	188	189	190	191	192	193	194	195	196	197	198	199
SOUTH DAKOTA—Cont'd															
Tripp	28.2	5,187	41.3	2.2	3.5	0.3	16.4	40.1	7,359	32	29	385	2,590	44,651	4,124
Turner	29.1	3,507	47.4	0.7	4.1	0.2	22.3	12.7	1,535	28	45	384	4,110	55,622	5,013
Union	65.6	4,291	53.6	0.1	4.7	0.0	12.9	42.0	2,752	52	89	766	8,030	134,045	22,118
Walworth	22.4	4,071	44.4	0.6	7.2	0.5	12.7	14.6	2,663	32	29	377	2,600	60,329	5,930
Yankton	74.0	3,262	49.0	1.7	7.7	0.3	9.3	53.9	2,375	205	113	1,590	11,340	61,440	6,079
Ziebach	9.0	3,270	68.5	0.4	2.3	0.0	18.2	1.0	368	12	15	143	530	32,168	2,004
TENNESSEE	X	X	X	X	X	X	X	X	X	52,377	21,110	377,943	3,147,310	65,367	7,646
Anderson	248.1	3,262	54.6	3.0	6.2	0.0	3.3	216.6	2,848	859	214	4,173	35,650	59,177	5,804
Bedford	131.6	2,729	52.0	2.8	7.2	0.1	4.7	83.6	1,735	137	140	2,319	22,010	51,897	4,743
Benton	38.2	2,389	57.2	2.3	7.8	0.4	10.5	16.8	1,053	63	44	882	6,850	45,127	3,492
Bledsoe	35.3	2,368	53.6	3.6	4.1	0.5	7.9	21.8	1,460	22	35	872	4,940	43,870	3,116
Blount	617.8	4,752	29.9	42.1	5.4	0.0	2.8	1,244.1	9,570	308	391	7,530	63,480	63,126	6,514
Bradley	298.6	2,832	48.0	2.8	6.4	4.9	4.5	188.4	1,787	239	297	4,554	48,100	51,097	4,420
Campbell	130.5	3,279	37.1	2.9	5.0	0.1	6.9	137.4	3,454	83	109	1,927	15,240	47,060	3,871
Cannon	27.3	1,927	66.3	2.3	9.3	0.0	0.4	9.2	647	35	41	575	6,440	49,012	3,692
Carroll	75.1	2,702	57.8	0.5	6.6	0.1	7.2	54.7	1,965	75	74	1,726	11,680	47,762	3,747
Carter	130.0	2,301	62.0	0.8	6.2	0.0	6.1	115.6	2,046	96	154	2,357	23,500	44,799	3,659
Cheatham	94.5	2,342	64.4	2.9	6.1	0.3	4.8	27.6	683	83	113	1,532	20,240	60,947	5,816
Chester	36.6	2,131	65.6	1.1	6.1	0.0	5.0	14.8	861	45	45	1,120	6,990	47,009	3,491
Claiborne	60.9	1,924	68.3	0.0	5.5	0.3	7.7	11.5	363	70	85	1,726	12,530	44,879	3,417
Clay	23.1	3,014	44.8	7.6	6.2	0.3	16.4	13.3	1,736	50	22	474	3,010	37,385	3,081
Cocke	85.3	2,401	58.0	1.3	5.6	0.0	7.7	41.7	1,173	68	99	1,766	15,710	38,855	2,617
Coffee	160.0	2,909	58.4	2.0	5.3	0.2	3.9	253.6	4,609	565	212	3,049	25,890	53,093	4,802
Crockett	40.2	2,786	62.9	3.9	4.8	1.0	7.9	16.0	1,110	34	39	818	6,240	47,274	4,334
Cumberland	132.7	2,249	48.6	9.7	5.2	0.0	5.3	112.0	1,898	144	169	2,264	28,300	52,691	4,686
Davidson	3,228.3	4,698	34.6	5.0	6.8	1.5	4.3	16,254.2	23,654	8,545	2,303	37,746	354,830	82,501	12,521
Decatur	45.7	3,899	33.7	24.1	3.2	0.2	4.5	21.2	1,810	30	33	730	4,680	46,977	3,598
DeKalb	45.9	2,309	52.6	3.3	7.6	0.1	5.0	34.9	1,756	43	60	1,050	8,600	48,726	4,360
Dickson	136.1	2,580	55.8	2.4	7.0	0.0	4.9	97.0	1,837	102	150	2,541	25,060	55,260	5,049
Dyer	131.4	3,519	50.6	0.3	8.6	0.6	8.0	53.4	1,431	104	100	2,934	15,910	51,624	4,653
Fayette	60.3	1,502	53.4	3.8	6.5	0.7	9.3	38.5	959	67	114	1,309	20,680	77,555	9,745
Fentress	37.2	2,043	61.4	4.9	6.5	0.0	1.0	10.3	563	46	51	917	7,360	41,924	3,084
Franklin	93.0	2,234	55.5	0.6	9.0	0.2	3.4	67.9	1,632	149	112	1,784	18,970	55,159	5,100
Gibson	137.7	2,796	61.8	3.1	6.4	0.6	2.0	115.6	2,346	147	133	2,769	21,620	49,676	3,998
Giles	63.9	2,174	60.2	4.5	4.0	0.1	9.2	22.1	751	71	80	1,396	13,160	49,278	4,077
Grainger	43.8	1,896	72.1	4.3	5.4	0.0	0.8	6.7	289	66	65	831	9,930	46,402	3,551
Greene	156.0	2,267	59.3	3.0	5.5	0.0	4.7	61.7	897	251	188	3,393	30,300	46,307	3,711
Grundy	30.7	2,305	66.3	0.7	3.5	0.2	7.2	18.3	1,376	29	37	685	5,820	41,491	2,875
Hamblen	186.2	2,907	50.5	0.6	6.0	0.2	4.5	290.4	4,533	201	179	3,877	27,740	48,992	4,212
Hamilton	2,102.4	5,823	20.9	45.3	5.0	0.4	2.0	1,418.9	3,930	5,315	1,071	23,860	171,870	71,113	8,651
Hancock	21.8	3,311	47.1	15.9	4.1	0.0	7.1	13.8	2,089	12	18	459	2,360	36,662	2,276
Hardeman	96.4	3,784	37.4	1.9	4.4	0.1	5.4	61.1	2,398	57	58	1,599	10,010	39,252	2,605
Hardin	144.5	5,613	26.8	52.6	2.1	0.1	4.0	77.3	3,003	115	71	1,677	11,030	50,290	4,613
Hawkins	117.7	2,079	60.6	1.7	4.3	0.2	5.6	97.2	1,716	146	156	2,266	24,120	46,811	3,740
Haywood	62.1	3,524	47.6	4.3	6.0	0.0	7.1	19.0	1,078	94	47	1,040	8,070	40,242	2,940
Henderson	69.6	2,501	66.5	0.3	7.1	0.1	5.3	68.9	2,474	59	77	1,410	11,840	46,085	3,506
Henry	186.8	5,769	27.6	55.2	2.5	0.0	3.5	68.1	2,103	119	121	2,470	14,530	48,797	4,603
Hickman	56.0	2,254	56.7	3.4	5.4	0.0	7.4	32.2	1,296	57	66	1,119	10,170	46,745	3,682
Houston	21.7	2,659	55.2	4.7	4.3	0.4	10.1	14.1	1,727	24	23	551	3,490	46,523	3,432
Humphreys	48.1	2,600	54.2	1.3	7.6	0.0	9.6	4.6	248	108	51	1,089	8,290	50,955	4,437
Jackson	26.4	2,260	58.5	2.7	3.1	0.0	8.4	23.6	2,017	27	32	512	4,800	41,564	2,933
Jefferson	153.3	2,853	42.8	3.1	5.3	7.6	3.8	126.5	2,355	136	152	2,526	24,020	51,777	4,466
Johnson	32.9	1,868	66.3	0.9	7.2	0.1	2.3	22.0	1,247	38	45	924	6,640	45,943	3,859
Knox	1,321.7	2,864	42.5	2.8	9.7	0.1	4.3	1,738.1	3,766	3,739	1,371	29,574	219,510	75,662	9,822
Lake	17.8	2,391	49.3	4.0	7.7	0.6	11.4	10.2	1,376	16	13	633	2,080	39,173	2,888
Lauderdale	69.4	2,660	57.3	2.9	8.0	0.0	7.1	19.2	734	56	65	1,904	9,650	41,389	3,081
Lawrence	100.9	2,327	60.3	2.4	6.9	0.0	7.1	84.4	1,946	121	122	1,953	17,790	46,811	3,433
Lewis	30.5	2,535	52.9	0.6	6.5	0.2	7.1	9.3	774	25	34	705	5,140	46,658	3,552
Lincoln	127.1	3,750	39.0	36.8	3.6	0.0	4.2	22.4	662	55	95	2,039	15,640	52,320	4,545
Loudon	133.1	2,547	53.7	0.6	6.7	0.2	4.6	616.9	11,804	154	151	2,066	26,530	77,828	9,349
McMinn	118.6	2,240	59.1	0.7	5.1	0.1	6.5	45.1	852	120	147	2,137	23,290	48,374	3,757
McNairy	61.1	2,350	61.9	0.3	7.8	0.0	6.1	20.5	788	88	70	1,244	10,410	45,270	3,229
Macon	57.4	2,400	60.4	4.0	6.3	0.1	7.5	22.0	919	41	68	1,191	10,100	43,576	3,246
Madison	988.3	10,138	12.8	68.5	3.8	0.0	1.8	649.4	6,661	433	263	11,876	44,950	55,567	5,711
Marion	69.6	2,450	56.6	0.8	8.2	0.0	5.2	42.0	1,480	86	79	1,304	12,820	52,128	4,473

1. Based on the resident population estimated as of July 1 of the year shown.

State / county code	CBSA code[1]	County Type code[2]	STATE County	Land area[3] (sq. mi)	Population, 2021: Total persons 2021	Population, 2021: Rank	Population, 2021: Per square mile	Race alone or in combination, not Hispanic or Latino (percent): White	Race: Black	Race: American Indian, Alaska Native	Race: Asian and Pacific Islancer	Percent Hispanic or Latino[4]	Age (percent): Under 5 years	5 to 17 years	18 to 24 years	25 to 34 years	35 to 44 years	45 to 54 years
				1	2	3	4	5	6	7	8	9	10	11	12	13	14	15
			TENNESSEE—Cont'd															
47117	30280	6	Marshall	375.5	34,984	1,303	93.2	86.5	7.3	0.9	1.0	6.3	6.0	13.3	11.7	13.2	12.7	13.1
47119	34980	1	Maury	613.1	104,760	585	170.9	80.4	12.8	0.8	1.4	6.8	6.3	12.9	11.2	14.1	13.4	12.0
47121		8	Meigs	195.1	13,049	2,210	66.9	94.5	2.8	1.4	0.7	2.4	5.4	11.8	10.9	10.6	11.4	13.9
47123		6	Monroe	635.8	46,698	1,044	73.4	92.4	2.7	1.4	0.7	4.6	5.3	11.7	10.7	11.6	10.8	12.8
47125	17300	2	Montgomery	539.2	227,900	305	422.7	64.7	23.6	1.3	4.2	11.0	7.9	15.1	14.4	18.3	14.1	10.5
47127	46100	9	Moore	129.2	6,644	2,690	51.4	93.3	3.2	1.0	1.8	2.2	5.3	10.6	10.9	10.8	11.8	13.2
47129	28940	2	Morgan	522.2	21,254	1,750	40.7	93.6	4.5	1.1	0.5	1.8	4.9	10.6	11.7	13.8	12.5	14.0
47131	46460	7	Obion	544.8	30,466	1,422	55.9	83.3	11.9	0.6	0.6	5.4	5.6	12.3	11.4	11.6	11.7	12.9
47133	18260	7	Overton	433.5	22,839	1,681	52.7	96.5	1.3	0.9	0.5	1.9	5.3	12.0	11.4	12.1	11.4	12.9
47135		8	Perry	414.8	8,472	2,537	20.4	92.8	3.8	1.6	1.3	2.6	6.3	12.4	10.6	11.7	11.4	12.4
47137		9	Pickett	163.0	5,079	2,817	31.2	96.7	0.7	0.7	0.5	2.4	4.2	9.5	10.6	8.3	9.8	12.3
47139	17420	3	Polk	434.6	17,776	1,930	40.9	96.1	1.2	1.3	0.6	2.3	4.8	10.8	10.7	10.8	11.4	14.6
47141	18260	4	Putnam	401.1	81,188	708	202.4	89.1	3.1	0.8	1.8	6.9	5.4	11.7	17.4	13.4	11.6	11.7
47143	19420	6	Rhea	315.5	33,136	1,356	105.0	91.2	3.0	1.1	0.8	5.6	5.8	12.2	13.1	11.6	11.3	12.7
47145	28940	2	Roane	360.8	53,992	940	149.6	93.7	3.5	1.2	1.0	2.3	4.4	10.6	10.7	10.9	10.9	13.3
47147	34980	1	Robertson	476.3	74,098	747	155.6	83.2	8.6	0.8	1.1	7.9	6.1	13.3	11.7	12.8	13.3	13.2
47149	34980	1	Rutherford	619.3	352,182	209	568.7	69.7	18.3	0.8	4.6	9.5	6.2	14.0	16.1	14.7	14.3	12.7
47151		6	Scott	532.3	21,917	1,720	41.2	97.7	0.7	0.8	0.6	1.2	6.0	13.2	12.5	12.3	12.5	12.8
47153	16860	2	Sequatchie	265.9	16,396	2,010	61.7	94.1	1.5	1.1	0.7	4.1	5.4	11.1	11.1	11.1	11.3	13.5
47155	42940	4	Sevier	592.5	99,517	612	168.0	89.8	1.9	1.0	1.7	7.1	5.2	11.4	11.1	12.2	11.3	13.1
47157	32820	1	Shelby	760.6	924,454	62	1,215.4	35.8	55.0	0.6	3.4	6.9	6.7	14.2	13.0	14.8	12.8	11.9
47159	34980	1	Smith	314.3	20,172	1,807	64.2	93.1	3.4	1.1	0.7	3.3	5.8	12.9	11.7	12.7	12.3	12.8
47161	17300	8	Stewart	459.8	13,855	2,161	30.1	92.5	2.8	1.7	1.4	3.8	5.4	11.6	11.3	11.2	11.6	13.0
47163	28700	2	Sullivan	413.4	159,265	427	385.3	94.2	3.1	0.8	1.1	2.3	4.7	10.8	10.9	12.2	11.3	13.4
47165	34980	1	Sumner	529.5	200,557	343	378.8	83.7	9.5	0.8	2.2	6.0	5.7	13.4	11.8	12.6	13.5	13.3
47167	32820	1	Tipton	455.6	61,004	867	133.9	77.3	19.4	1.0	1.4	3.1	5.7	13.7	12.6	12.9	13.0	12.7
47169	34980	1	Trousdale	114.3	12,035	2,280	105.3	84.5	12.8	0.8	0.6	3.1	5.0	10.5	13.4	21.5	13.6	12.6
47171	27740	3	Unicoi	186.1	17,698	1,936	95.1	92.7	1.1	0.9	0.5	6.1	4.5	10.1	10.7	10.8	11.2	13.2
47173	28940	2	Union	223.6	20,040	1,813	89.6	96.7	1.0	1.1	0.4	2.2	5.2	12.0	11.1	12.1	11.5	13.5
47175		9	Van Buren	273.4	6,324	2,708	23.1	96.3	1.5	1.0	0.5	2.2	5.6	11.5	10.1	9.8	10.7	13.7
47177	32660	6	Warren	432.7	41,523	1,156	96.0	85.7	4.3	0.9	1.1	9.7	5.9	13.0	12.0	12.3	12.4	12.9
47179	27740	3	Washington	326.5	134,236	487	411.1	89.7	5.3	0.8	2.2	4.0	4.6	10.7	15.2	12.7	11.4	12.8
47181		8	Wayne	734.1	16,409	2,007	22.4	89.8	7.5	0.8	0.5	2.4	3.9	9.1	10.9	14.4	13.4	14.2
47183	32280	7	Weakley	580.4	33,036	1,361	56.9	87.6	8.8	0.7	1.5	3.0	4.9	10.7	19.1	11.5	10.6	11.4
47185		7	White	376.7	27,650	1,513	73.4	94.0	2.7	0.9	0.8	3.0	5.5	12.4	11.1	12.0	11.5	12.7
47187	34980	1	Williamson	582.9	255,735	275	438.7	85.0	4.9	0.6	6.2	5.2	5.4	15.5	13.2	9.0	14.7	15.1
47189	34980	1	Wilson	570.9	151,917	450	266.1	84.7	8.6	0.8	2.7	5.3	5.8	13.4	11.6	12.1	14.1	13.8
48000		0	TEXAS	261,263.1	29,527,941	X	113.0	41.7	13.0	0.7	6.1	40.2	6.5	14.5	14.1	14.4	14.0	12.3
48001	37300	7	Anderson	1,062.6	58,402	897	55.0	58.5	22.2	0.8	1.2	18.8	5.1	10.5	11.1	15.9	16.6	14.4
48003	11380	6	Andrews	1,500.7	18,440	1,901	12.3	38.9	1.8	1.1	0.8	58.4	8.3	18.0	14.0	14.4	13.8	11.3
48005	31260	5	Angelina	797.9	86,506	673	108.4	60.4	15.6	0.7	1.2	23.4	6.4	14.6	13.3	12.6	12.0	11.9
48007	40530	2	Aransas	252.1	24,510	1,631	97.2	66.4	1.9	1.5	2.1	29.5	4.7	10.4	9.8	9.8	10.3	11.2
48009	48660	3	Archer	903.3	8,681	2,516	9.6	88.7	1.7	1.5	0.9	8.8	5.4	12.9	10.9	10.7	12.2	11.5
48011	11100	2	Armstrong	909.1	1,839	3,055	2.0	85.9	1.7	1.8	0.4	11.7	5.3	12.9	10.4	9.8	13.3	11.1
48013	41700	1	Atascosa	1,219.5	49,939	997	41.0	31.9	1.2	0.8	0.7	66.2	6.8	15.6	13.7	12.5	13.1	12.0
48015	26420	1	Austin	646.5	30,380	1,424	47.0	61.5	9.3	0.7	1.1	28.7	5.6	13.7	11.8	11.3	11.4	11.4
48017		7	Bailey	827.0	6,835	2,672	8.3	32.9	1.4	0.7	0.9	64.9	9.0	15.8	15.0	11.5	11.9	10.6
48019	41700	1	Bandera	791.0	21,565	1,733	27.3	77.4	1.5	1.4	0.8	20.2	4.2	9.9	8.7	8.5	10.0	11.5
48021	12420	1	Bastrop	888.2	102,058	601	114.9	51.4	7.2	1.0	1.2	40.8	6.3	14.8	13.1	12.3	12.6	11.9
48023		8	Baylor	867.5	3,477	2,925	4.0	82.3	3.4	1.0	0.8	14.7	5.5	13.6	9.9	10.7	11.4	11.0
48025	13300	6	Bee	880.2	30,924	1,404	35.1	31.1	8.6	0.6	0.8	59.7	5.0	11.9	14.7	17.1	16.0	12.4
48027	28660	2	Bell	1,053.8	379,617	193	360.2	47.1	24.7	1.1	5.3	25.9	7.7	15.6	15.3	16.0	13.7	10.4
48029	41700	1	Bexar	1,240.3	2,028,236	16	1,635.3	28.0	8.2	0.6	4.0	60.9	6.5	14.3	14.4	15.6	14.3	11.8
48031		8	Blanco	709.3	11,886	2,293	16.8	77.1	1.8	1.0	1.1	20.3	3.9	9.9	10.7	8.6	10.7	12.4
48033		8	Borden	897.4	617	3,132	0.7	80.5	1.3	1.6	0.1	17.7	5.0	12.5	10.2	8.1	11.0	16.9
48035		6	Bosque	983.0	18,503	1,898	18.8	77.8	2.5	1.0	0.7	19.3	4.7	12.2	10.7	9.7	10.9	11.7
48037	45500	3	Bowie	884.9	92,581	651	104.6	64.6	26.4	1.4	1.8	8.1	5.9	13.6	12.5	13.7	13.0	12.0
48039	26420	1	Brazoria	1,363.3	379,689	192	278.5	45.8	15.7	0.8	7.7	31.8	6.3	15.0	12.9	13.5	15.3	13.1
48041	17780	3	Brazos	586.1	237,032	292	404.4	56.3	11.4	0.6	6.8	26.5	5.6	11.7	27.8	15.0	12.0	9.1
48043		7	Brewster	6,183.8	9,450	2,455	1.5	51.2	2.2	1.2	1.9	45.0	4.7	9.8	10.6	11.8	13.4	11.7
48045		9	Briscoe	900.0	1,403	3,086	1.6	70.7	4.8	1.1	0.7	25.1	5.6	13.1	8.4	10.8	11.3	11.9
48047		7	Brooks	943.4	6,994	2,663	7.4	7.2	0.9	0.2	1.0	91.1	7.2	16.7	13.0	12.8	11.6	9.2
48049	15220	5	Brown	944.5	38,192	1,217	40.4	71.9	4.3	1.1	0.9	23.1	5.0	11.5	13.1	11.6	12.2	11.9
48051	17780	3	Burleson	659.1	18,051	1,922	27.4	65.7	12.8	0.8	0.7	21.4	5.5	12.7	10.8	11.3	11.1	11.8
48053		6	Burnet	994.8	50,954	983	51.2	74.3	2.1	1.1	1.2	22.5	4.9	11.9	11.2	10.9	11.3	11.4

1. CBSA = Core Based Statistical Area. See Appendix A for explanation. See Appendix B for list of metropolitan areas with component counties. 2. County type code from the Economic Research Service of USDA Rural-Urban Continuum Codes. See Appendix A for definition. 3. Dry land or land partially or temporarily covered by water. 4. May be of any race.

STATE County	Population, 2021 (cont.)				Population change, 2000–2021							Households, 2016–2020				
	Age (percent) (cont.)				Total persons		Percent change		Components of change, 2020–2021					Percent		
	55 to 64 years	65 to 74 years	75 years and over	Percent female	2010	2020	2010–2020	2020–2021	Births	Deaths	Net Migration	Number	Persons per household	Family house-holds	Female family house-holder[1]	One person
	16	17	18	19	20	21	22	23	24	25	26	27	28	29	30	31
TENNESSEE—Cont'd																
Marshall	13.7	10.4	6.0	50.7	30,617	34,318	12.1	1.9	497	551	722	12,436	2.7	71.1	11.9	24.5
Maury	13.4	10.8	6.0	51.5	80,956	100,974	24.7	3.7	1,565	1,479	3,727	35,163	2.7	71.1	12.2	24.1
Meigs	15.0	13.1	8.0	50.1	11,753	12,758	8.6	2.3	150	237	384	5,079	2.4	68.2	9.3	26.4
Monroe	15.2	13.5	8.5	50.2	44,519	46,250	3.9	1.0	618	887	719	18,639	2.5	69.7	11.0	26.6
Montgomery	9.7	6.4	3.4	50.1	172,331	220,069	27.7	3.6	4,287	2,262	5,817	74,606	2.7	71.2	13.9	23.1
Moore	15.2	12.4	9.7	50.0	6,362	6,461	1.6	2.8	76	106	217	2,599	2.4	71.6	5.5	23.0
Morgan	13.8	11.6	7.1	44.9	21,987	21,035	-4.3	1.0	210	346	356	7,524	2.5	71.3	10.8	24.8
Obion	13.4	12.2	8.9	51.3	31,807	30,787	-3.2	-1.0	385	640	-69	12,633	2.4	63.5	11.6	32.3
Overton	14.5	12.6	7.9	49.9	22,083	22,511	1.9	1.5	303	502	531	8,969	2.4	65.5	11.3	31.7
Perry	13.7	12.4	9.0	49.7	7,915	8,366	5.7	1.3	124	153	136	2,929	2.7	71.3	4.5	25.8
Pickett	16.9	16.7	11.8	50.3	5,077	5,001	-1.5	1.6	43	97	134	2,211	2.3	67.7	6.7	30.3
Polk	15.7	12.7	8.5	50.1	16,825	17,544	4.3	1.3	185	356	407	7,448	2.2	69.4	11.3	24.8
Putnam	12.1	10.0	6.7	50.2	72,321	79,854	10.4	1.7	1,043	1,317	1,614	31,777	2.4	63.2	13.0	29.2
Rhea	14.0	11.8	7.4	50.4	31,809	32,870	3.3	0.8	445	619	440	12,324	2.6	69.4	15.7	26.0
Roane	15.8	14.2	9.4	50.5	54,181	53,404	-1.4	1.1	563	1,116	1,155	21,596	2.4	67.6	9.4	28.4
Robertson	14.2	9.7	5.6	50.3	66,283	72,803	9.8	1.8	1,046	1,118	1,374	26,122	2.7	77.0	12.5	18.8
Rutherford	10.9	7.2	3.9	50.7	262,604	341,486	30.0	3.1	5,066	3,365	9,027	115,249	2.8	70.6	12.3	20.8
Scott	13.1	10.5	7.2	50.5	22,228	21,850	-1.7	0.3	302	374	137	8,625	2.5	68.4	14.1	26.1
Sequatchie	15.1	13.0	8.4	50.1	14,112	15,826	12.1	3.6	184	262	659	5,539	2.7	78.2	11.1	18.7
Sevier	15.2	12.8	7.7	50.4	89,889	98,380	9.4	1.2	1,256	1,601	1,491	37,993	2.6	70.3	11.0	23.5
Shelby	12.1	9.3	5.2	52.5	927,644	929,744	0.2	-0.6	15,237	13,479	-7,200	356,607	2.6	61.5	19.3	33.0
Smith	15.0	10.8	6.2	49.7	19,166	19,904	3.9	1.3	256	333	347	7,688	2.6	73.6	11.3	23.8
Stewart	15.1	12.9	7.7	49.9	13,324	13,657	2.5	1.4	182	258	278	5,226	2.6	65.7	10.0	31.3
Sullivan	14.5	12.7	9.5	51.0	156,823	158,163	0.9	0.7	1,734	3,125	2,516	66,645	2.3	64.2	11.9	30.3
Sumner	13.4	10.1	6.3	51.0	160,645	196,281	22.2	2.2	2,617	2,697	4,370	68,654	2.7	73.1	11.3	22.9
Tipton	13.9	9.8	5.6	50.6	61,081	60,970	-0.2	0.1	803	943	159	21,624	2.8	77.6	14.7	19.4
Trousdale	10.5	8.4	4.6	40.8	7,870	11,615	47.6	3.6	149	155	430	3,398	2.8	64.1	7.6	32.0
Unicoi	15.6	14.0	9.8	50.2	18,313	17,928	-2.1	-1.3	158	411	22	7,683	2.3	60.8	9.2	34.0
Union	15.7	11.8	7.1	50.3	19,109	19,802	3.6	1.2	230	384	395	7,463	2.6	76.6	13.7	19.7
Van Buren	14.7	15.2	8.8	49.5	5,548	6,168	11.2	2.5	74	103	188	2,242	2.5	73.4	9.9	22.6
Warren	13.4	10.8	7.1	50.3	39,839	40,953	2.8	1.4	573	723	724	15,515	2.6	65.6	10.9	31.1
Washington	13.3	11.6	7.7	50.9	122,979	133,001	8.1	0.9	1,473	2,199	1,962	54,603	2.3	62.0	10.6	31.0
Wayne	14.6	11.6	8.0	43.5	17,021	16,232	-4.6	1.1	173	299	307	5,737	2.5	66.9	12.0	28.0
Weakley	12.9	10.9	7.9	51.0	35,021	32,902	-6.1	0.4	395	559	298	13,563	2.3	64.3	10.6	28.4
White	14.3	12.3	8.2	50.6	25,841	27,351	5.8	1.1	368	544	478	10,219	2.6	66.3	10.3	25.4
Williamson	12.9	8.9	5.2	50.6	183,182	247,726	35.2	3.2	2,738	2,169	7,493	81,041	2.9	78.8	7.8	17.3
Wilson	13.3	10.0	6.0	50.5	113,993	147,737	29.6	2.8	2,005	1,984	4,184	51,348	2.7	75.8	8.8	20.0
TEXAS	11.2	8.2	5.0	50.1	25,145,561	29,145,505	15.9	1.3	450,827	308,742	239,792	9,906,070	2.8	69.0	13.7	25.3
Anderson	11.5	9.2	5.7	38.1	58,458	57,922	-0.9	0.8	677	962	763	16,555	2.7	70.7	13.3	25.8
Andrews	10.3	6.0	3.9	48.9	14,786	18,610	25.9	-0.9	358	154	-375	5,649	3.2	78.3	13.7	18.2
Angelina	12.3	10.0	6.9	51.0	86,771	86,395	-0.4	0.1	1,272	1,366	189	31,368	2.7	72.4	18.0	23.7
Aransas	16.3	15.7	11.7	50.2	23,158	23,830	2.9	2.9	223	537	1,012	9,917	2.4	63.6	11.0	30.7
Archer	15.9	12.2	8.4	50.4	9,054	8,560	-5.5	1.4	106	145	163	3,513	2.5	70.0	8.8	25.4
Armstrong	14.2	14.1	8.8	50.7	1,901	1,848	-2.8	-0.5	15	35	11	720	2.6	76.4	10.8	15.6
Atascosa	11.5	8.9	5.9	50.0	44,911	48,981	9.1	2.0	792	662	829	15,798	3.2	76.5	15.3	20.5
Austin	14.1	12.4	8.4	50.0	28,417	30,167	6.2	0.7	419	467	263	11,569	2.6	74.6	11.2	22.4
Bailey	10.9	8.7	6.7	49.7	7,165	6,904	-3.6	-1.0	174	74	-169	2,056	3.3	67.9	11.5	27.4
Bandera	18.3	18.1	10.8	50.5	20,485	20,851	1.8	3.4	220	399	906	8,697	2.6	69.3	10.4	23.9
Bastrop	13.4	10.2	5.4	49.1	74,171	97,216	31.1	5.0	1,311	1,117	4,709	26,173	3.2	73.4	12.7	22.9
Baylor	13.7	12.6	11.5	50.9	3,726	3,465	-7.0	0.3	53	73	32	1,621	2.2	64.3	4.3	32.1
Bee	9.9	7.7	5.2	39.2	31,861	31,047	-2.6	-0.4	371	383	-117	8,499	2.9	67.0	15.0	28.5
Bell[1]	9.8	7.2	4.3	50.3	310,235	370,647	19.5	2.4	7,276	3,711	5,358	125,747	2.7	67.8	15.6	26.9
Bexar	10.6	7.7	4.8	50.6	1,714,773	2,009,324	17.2	0.9	31,215	21,228	8,328	644,561	3.0	65.4	16.0	28.6
Blanco	18.1	16.8	9.1	50.0	10,497	11,374	8.4	4.5	120	189	588	4,665	2.5	70.0	9.6	22.9
Borden	12.6	13.1	10.5	47.7	641	631	-1.6	-2.2	8	16	-6	223	2.9	77.1	4.9	20.6
Bosque	15.1	14.3	10.7	50.9	18,212	18,235	0.1	1.5	223	388	442	7,255	2.5	72.8	11.6	24.5
Bowie	12.2	10.2	6.9	49.8	92,565	92,893	0.4	-0.3	1,226	1,525	-32	34,283	2.6	66.2	17.4	30.6
Brazoria	11.4	7.9	4.5	49.5	313,166	372,031	18.8	2.1	5,703	3,771	5,704	124,184	2.9	74.3	10.8	21.2
Brazos	8.6	6.2	3.8	49.7	194,851	233,849	20.0	1.4	3,205	1,759	1,659	81,514	2.6	56.7	12.9	29.8
Brewster	13.4	14.8	9.9	48.9	9,232	9,546	3.4	-1.0	88	129	-52	4,292	2.1	53.6	9.6	40.6
Briscoe	15.0	11.7	12.2	49.8	1,637	1,435	-12.3	-2.2	13	22	-23	588	2.3	57.7	4.1	37.9
Brooks	11.2	9.9	8.4	49.0	7,223	7,076	-2.0	-1.2	120	111	-92	2,475	2.7	57.3	18.5	40.6
Brown	14.0	12.1	8.6	50.5	38,106	38,095	0.0	0.3	457	747	388	14,614	2.5	65.7	9.4	29.2
Burleson	15.6	13.0	8.3	50.6	17,187	17,642	2.6	2.3	210	345	551	6,931	2.6	66.1	8.0	28.3
Burnet	15.4	14.1	8.9	51.1	42,750	49,130	14.9	3.7	556	806	2,101	17,384	2.7	73.4	8.9	23.0

1. No spouse present.

STATE County	Persons in group quarters, 2021	Daytime Population, 2016–2020: Number	Daytime Population, 2016–2020: Employment/ residence ratio	Births, 2021: Total	Births, 2021: Rate[1]	Deaths, 2021: Number	Deaths, 2021: Rate[1]	Persons under 65 with no health insurance, 2019: Number	Persons under 65 with no health insurance, 2019: Percent	Medicare, 2021: Total beneficiaries	Medicare, 2021: Enrolled in Original Medicare	Medicare, 2021: Enrolled in Medicare Advantage	COVID-19 Deaths, 2020: Number	COVID-19 Deaths, 2020: Rate[1]
	32	33	34	35	36	37	38	39	40	41	42	43	44	45
TENNESSEE—Cont'd														
Marshall	280	30,818	0.8	392	11.3	457	13.2	3,353	11.8	6,895	3,967	2,928	34	1.0
Maury	945	89,949	0.9	1,229	11.9	1,181	11.4	9,081	11.3	19,932	12,179	7,753	116	1.1
Meigs	130	9,990	0.5	126	9.8	180	13.9	1,249	13.1	3,404	1,921	1,482	18	1.4
Monroe	420	45,395	0.9	488	10.5	730	15.7	4,731	13.2	12,339	6,307	6,032	59	1.3
Montgomery	3,700	180,571	0.8	3,407	15.2	1,805	8.0	17,282	9.3	27,211	19,420	7,792	125	0.6
Moore	80	5,931	0.8	63	9.6	90	13.7	514	10.2	1,549	1,087	463	D	D
Morgan	2,174	18,820	0.6	171	8.1	264	12.5	1,887	12.5	5,071	2,207	2,864	13	0.6
Obion	425	30,560	1.0	323	10.6	519	17.0	2,918	12.5	8,051	5,114	2,937	80	2.6
Overton	227	19,668	0.7	239	10.5	421	18.5	2,296	13.3	5,842	3,981	1,861	48	2.1
Perry	124	8,352	1.1	102	12.1	124	14.7	901	14.5	2,155	1,292	863	20	2.4
Pickett	39	4,561	0.7	38	7.5	83	16.5	538	14.9	1,636	1,184	452	20	4.0
Polk	268	12,740	0.4	150	8.5	302	17.1	1,871	14.5	4,834	2,864	1,970	13	0.7
Putnam	2,347	86,012	1.2	862	10.7	1,034	12.8	8,504	13.3	16,871	11,543	5,328	127	1.6
Rhea	720	33,075	1.0	364	11.0	506	15.3	3,635	14.0	7,866	4,704	3,162	51	1.6
Roane	635	46,382	0.7	443	8.2	908	16.9	4,305	10.6	14,722	8,029	6,694	61	1.1
Robertson	840	61,594	0.7	859	11.7	876	11.9	6,963	11.6	13,675	7,121	6,554	83	1.1
Rutherford	5,009	303,292	0.9	4,056	11.7	2,681	7.7	30,323	10.4	43,964	25,454	18,510	250	0.7
Scott	235	20,828	0.9	246	11.2	307	14.0	2,143	12.0	5,258	2,505	2,753	30	1.4
Sequatchie	183	13,030	0.7	143	8.9	229	14.2	1,465	12.5	4,497	2,506	1,990	12	0.8
Sevier	1,053	101,888	1.1	1,004	10.1	1,294	13.1	13,557	17.6	23,956	12,400	11,556	88	0.9
Shelby	16,823	1,013,461	1.2	12,243	13.2	10,668	11.5	103,192	13.2	154,890	99,838	55,052	1,042	1.1
Smith	172	17,280	0.7	203	10.1	266	13.3	1,982	12.1	4,216	2,603	1,613	25	1.3
Stewart	116	11,423	0.6	142	10.3	194	14.1	1,353	12.6	3,379	2,411	968	22	1.6
Sullivan	2,562	166,677	1.1	1,398	8.8	2,475	15.6	14,688	12.1	42,989	16,871	26,118	205	1.3
Sumner	1,319	163,188	0.7	2,098	10.5	2,197	11.0	16,587	10.4	36,283	19,185	17,098	210	1.1
Tipton	876	46,964	0.5	657	10.8	742	12.2	5,353	10.4	11,720	8,225	3,495	65	1.1
Trousdale	2,656	8,527	0.5	119	10.0	134	11.3	933	12.9	1,865	1,049	816	13	1.1
Unicoi	405	16,185	0.8	132	7.4	337	19.0	1,752	13.0	5,291	2,404	2,887	27	1.5
Union	117	15,551	0.5	188	9.4	290	14.6	2,188	13.7	4,696	1,846	2,850	17	0.9
Van Buren	134	4,631	0.5	56	9.0	72	11.5	551	12.7	1,753	1,167	586	D	D
Warren	426	39,419	0.9	459	11.1	591	14.3	5,237	15.8	9,489	6,038	3,451	54	1.3
Washington	4,031	138,174	1.2	1,203	9.0	1,731	13.0	12,094	11.9	30,254	14,761	15,494	161	1.2
Wayne	2,127	14,965	0.7	134	8.2	236	14.5	1,497	13.4	3,871	2,443	1,428	20	1.2
Weakley	1,512	31,141	0.8	321	9.7	440	13.4	2,938	11.5	7,395	5,190	2,205	38	1.2
White	324	23,664	0.7	294	10.7	444	16.1	2,717	12.8	7,097	4,429	2,668	34	1.2
Williamson	1,086	255,585	1.2	2,202	8.7	1,791	7.1	13,215	6.3	36,396	22,768	13,628	144	0.6
Wilson	1,477	128,430	0.8	1,572	10.5	1,555	10.4	11,543	9.5	26,892	15,399	11,493	150	1.0
TEXAS	562,170	28,630,878	1.0	362,450	12.3	248,605	8.5	5,114,881	20.7	4,284,123	2,454,061	1,830,062	32,725	1.1
Anderson	14,307	58,684	1.0	532	9.2	757	13.0	7,415	20.8	10,517	6,468	4,049	95	1.6
Andrews	47	17,044	0.9	290	15.7	129	7.0	3,532	20.9	2,178	1,439	739	34	1.8
Angelina	2,401	86,672	1.0	1,023	11.8	1,085	12.6	15,329	22.0	17,696	11,041	6,655	173	2.0
Aransas	376	22,714	0.8	175	7.2	421	17.4	4,085	24.9	7,394	3,904	3,490	26	1.1
Archer	28	6,603	0.5	83	9.6	113	13.1	1,356	19.7	1,925	1,486	440	D	D
Armstrong	36	1,630	0.7	11	6.0	23	12.5	254	18.0	448	338	110	D	D
Atascosa	164	46,914	0.8	639	12.9	534	10.8	9,579	22.2	9,027	4,284	4,743	95	1.9
Austin	167	27,125	0.8	336	11.1	369	12.2	5,181	21.6	6,758	4,540	2,218	20	0.7
Bailey	88	7,002	1.0	136	19.9	50	7.3	1,635	28.1	1,087	849	239	17	2.5
Bandera	134	18,140	0.5	174	8.2	321	15.1	3,371	20.5	6,870	4,537	2,332	17	0.8
Bastrop	2,342	71,045	0.6	1,063	10.6	923	9.2	16,504	22.7	15,926	9,933	5,993	53	0.5
Baylor	48	3,493	1.0	43	12.4	62	17.9	432	16.3	983	757	226	D	D
Bee	7,303	31,755	0.9	302	9.8	303	9.8	3,847	18.6	4,905	2,460	2,445	54	1.7
Bell	10,106	357,520	1.0	5,885	15.7	2,996	8.0	51,972	16.6	53,786	33,570	20,216	221	0.6
Bexar	40,867	2,021,247	1.1	25,078	12.4	16,973	8.4	327,450	19.1	301,500	153,912	147,588	2,082	1.0
Blanco	25	10,303	0.7	94	8.1	159	13.6	1,937	21.7	3,418	2,464	953	D	D
Borden	0	751	1.4	7	11.1	12	19.1	60	12.3	132	105	27	D	D
Bosque	225	15,493	0.6	169	9.2	313	17.0	3,173	23.0	5,140	3,083	2,057	22	1.2
Bowie	5,619	99,809	1.2	988	10.7	1,208	13.0	12,418	17.3	19,661	14,079	5,582	137	1.5
Brazoria	9,916	320,105	0.7	4,541	12.1	3,017	8.0	52,277	16.4	50,792	28,373	22,419	256	0.7
Brazos	14,432	233,303	1.1	2,552	10.8	1,455	6.2	33,871	17.5	24,761	17,853	6,907	155	0.7
Brewster	42	8,962	0.9	69	7.3	108	11.4	1,462	21.2	2,233	1,517	716	12	1.3
Briscoe	0	1,343	1.0	11	7.8	21	14.9	274	24.1	399	282	117	D	D
Brooks	41	6,797	0.9	98	14.0	91	13.0	1,048	18.6	1,575	834	742	31	4.4
Brown	1,504	38,677	1.1	363	9.5	579	15.2	5,812	20.0	9,195	6,594	2,601	89	2.3
Burleson	90	15,808	0.7	168	9.4	281	15.7	2,943	20.3	4,536	2,954	1,582	22	1.2
Burnet	1,037	45,899	0.9	471	9.4	654	13.0	7,566	20.9	13,107	8,623	4,484	40	0.8

1. Per 1,000 estimated resident population.

STATE County	COVID-19 Vaccinations, 2021–2022: Number	COVID-19 Vaccinations, 2021–2022: Percent[5]	Education: School enrollment and attainment, 2016–2020: Enrollment[1]: Total	Enrollment[1]: Percent private	Attainment[2] (percent): High school graduate or less	Attainment[2] (percent): Bachelor's degree or more	Local government expenditures,[3] 2018–2019: Total current spending (mil dol)	Local government expenditures,[3] 2018–2019: Current spending per student (dollars)	Money income, 2016–2020: Per capita income[4]	Households: Median income (dollars)	Households: Percent with income of less than $50,000	Households: Percent with income of $200,000 or more	Income and poverty, 2020: Median household income (dollars)	Percent below poverty level: All persons	Percent below poverty level: Children under 18 years	Percent below poverty level: Children 5 to 17 years in families
	46	47	48	49	50	51	52	53	54	55	56	57	58	59	60	61
TENNESSEE—Cont'd																
Marshall	14,692	42.7	6,977	13.6	52.7	16.2	48.8	8,957	26,095	55,299	46.5	2.8	58,073	12.1	15.6	14.7
Maury	62,167	64.5	20,036	18.3	44.5	24.0	114.3	8,839	29,196	60,567	42.1	4.2	65,942	9.9	12.5	11.8
Meigs	8,497	68.4	2,205	12.8	60.7	10.2	16.6	9,222	24,299	50,733	49.3	1.8	49,242	16.0	22.3	21.1
Monroe	20,233	43.5	8,660	13.1	55.5	15.3	63.4	9,334	25,179	45,576	53.7	1.5	50,945	13.8	20.7	19.3
Montgomery	128,241	61.4	57,366	13.1	33.8	29.4	335.6	9,488	28,032	60,878	40.6	3.8	60,779	10.8	15.4	15.4
Moore	1,420	21.9	1,260	4.4	55.7	19.4	9.8	11,079	30,430	63,762	39.4	3.7	64,271	9.8	13.1	12.6
Morgan	11,100	51.9	3,623	7.4	64.4	11.4	28.6	9,878	20,258	41,701	59.7	1.2	48,321	18.8	22.4	21.4
Obion	12,593	41.9	6,057	7.7	61.2	15.5	47.5	9,675	23,336	39,985	61.0	1.7	45,643	15.1	22.1	20.5
Overton	7,918	35.6	4,484	7.9	66.2	12.5	26.7	8,418	22,864	36,478	60.8	2.7	43,167	16.3	22.9	21.1
Perry	3,316	41.1	1,656	18.4	67.8	8.6	11.7	11,104	26,222	48,716	51.3	4.4	46,366	16.1	24.5	24.0
Pickett	2,274	45.0	616	22.1	60.2	13.5	6.5	10,224	26,925	43,125	58.8	4.1	40,120	16.5	23.9	23.7
Polk	6,975	41.4	2,949	16.3	52.4	12.6	21.9	9,490	28,059	45,326	53.9	4.4	48,184	12.4	20.4	19.9
Putnam	41,046	51.2	20,662	9.7	49.4	26.4	105.9	9,041	25,208	45,160	55.1	3.1	47,120	17.0	22.9	22.1
Rhea	14,300	43.1	7,503	20.6	55.6	16.6	47.9	9,278	23,634	46,096	54.5	2.0	45,724	15.0	19.8	19.1
Roane	23,762	44.5	10,549	16.9	48.0	19.1	63.5	9,711	32,067	55,578	46.0	4.4	58,988	13.5	19.1	16.6
Robertson	37,698	52.5	15,255	16.4	51.8	20.4	103.0	9,045	30,620	66,088	37.0	4.2	63,918	9.2	11.7	11.6
Rutherford	180,592	54.3	88,737	12.6	35.4	32.6	507.1	9,180	31,195	68,718	34.8	4.5	73,980	8.8	9.7	8.6
Scott	8,118	36.8	4,811	8.4	66.7	9.2	39.2	9,284	19,970	37,135	62.2	0.9	39,020	19.8	25.2	23.2
Sequatchie	5,260	35.0	2,525	11.5	58.2	14.7	19.3	8,685	22,931	44,217	53.0	1.0	51,197	16.1	25.3	23.5
Sevier	49,513	50.4	18,717	15.8	50.2	18.3	152.2	10,474	26,919	51,734	48.4	4.0	54,284	13.8	19.9	19.2
Shelby	521,634	55.7	236,788	18.6	38.3	32.4	1,597.1	10,970	31,272	52,092	48.2	6.5	50,870	19.1	27.1	25.9
Smith	6,690	33.2	4,138	12.6	57.4	17.2	27.0	8,835	28,134	48,611	52.2	3.6	59,355	11.7	16.1	15.3
Stewart	6,106	44.5	2,792	4.9	56.3	18.2	19.1	9,160	25,166	49,537	50.4	2.1	55,022	13.2	21.1	20.5
Sullivan	89,587	56.6	30,257	15.8	46.7	24.5	210.1	9,860	28,790	47,438	52.0	3.5	48,968	13.6	20.7	18.8
Sumner	92,642	48.4	43,560	17.4	40.0	28.6	274.3	9,183	34,353	69,878	34.4	6.4	72,325	9.6	12.4	11.1
Tipton	25,035	40.6	14,897	10.3	48.7	17.0	92.3	8,509	28,027	62,474	40.8	3.7	61,432	12.7	20.1	17.6
Trousdale	4,170	37.0	2,419	19.9	58.9	11.6	12.1	9,501	24,036	56,981	43.8	1.4	54,970	15.4	16.0	15.0
Unicoi	9,711	54.3	3,247	12.8	51.9	16.4	22.8	9,435	23,817	44,526	58.2	1.4	45,635	16.2	22.0	20.7
Union	6,990	35.0	4,036	15.2	64.8	11.1	35.4	7,852	24,268	45,143	52.9	2.0	45,520	16.9	27.6	27.3
Van Buren	3,440	58.6	1,145	8.1	67.1	8.6	8.4	11,039	22,051	47,576	52.9	1.0	45,908	16.1	26.1	26.9
Warren	17,098	41.4	8,599	8.4	62.8	13.7	57.3	8,797	23,143	42,668	57.0	2.7	49,532	16.5	22.8	21.9
Washington	77,419	59.8	30,212	12.7	39.9	32.3	152.9	9,294	29,850	48,923	50.9	4.1	52,088	13.2	15.1	14.4
Wayne	6,844	41.0	2,813	14.4	64.2	10.6	22.1	9,834	22,231	42,206	56.8	0.9	42,754	20.2	24.2	22.6
Weakley	12,796	38.4	8,744	7.4	56.8	19.9	37.0	8,964	22,841	41,488	57.3	1.5	46,979	16.9	20.7	19.1
White	11,621	42.5	5,268	9.1	59.6	12.7	34.5	8,763	23,820	44,282	56.1	2.0	46,475	13.8	19.4	18.2
Williamson	158,071	66.3	65,284	24.0	17.8	60.5	433.8	9,844	53,320	111,196	18.9	21.2	118,257	4.1	3.6	3.3
Wilson	77,280	53.4	33,294	17.1	36.1	34.8	194.4	8,612	36,576	78,962	29.5	8.4	77,822	8.0	9.2	8.1
TEXAS	17,795,667	61.4	7,719,304	11.6	40.3	30.7	53,148.7	9,782	32,177	63,826	39.5	7.8	66,048	13.4	18.8	17.9
Anderson	22,953	39.8	12,447	4.2	56.5	11.3	84.9	10,227	19,168	45,847	53.7	2.3	50,879	20.9	27.6	27.5
Andrews	8,284	44.3	5,362	2.8	56.7	14.9	39.6	9,163	32,217	75,147	35.1	8.3	76,600	9.2	12.0	11.3
Angelina	40,818	47.1	21,216	5.7	47.7	18.2	165.6	9,623	23,878	49,684	50.3	2.6	49,943	17.0	25.1	24.2
Aransas	13,517	57.5	5,041	12.2	42.0	23.2	31.5	11,151	32,050	47,924	50.9	6.0	51,461	17.1	30.8	30.6
Archer	5,213	60.9	1,892	5.1	46.1	22.3	18.8	9,608	34,557	63,958	41.4	5.8	69,566	6.9	11.2	10.9
Armstrong	778	41.2	432	5.6	32.7	25.7	3.8	10,504	32,740	69,386	26.1	4.9	62,256	9.3	12.4	12.2
Atascosa	26,728	52.3	12,308	6.9	60.7	15.3	87.0	9,596	25,385	59,251	42.2	5.3	60,594	14.9	22.0	21.8
Austin	14,418	48.0	7,257	9.9	45.9	23.0	58.6	9,984	31,592	64,468	39.5	6.2	60,593	11.4	18.0	17.2
Bailey	2,726	38.9	1,402	0.0	62.2	17.4	15.8	11,176	23,594	55,038	46.2	2.4	48,259	14.4	23.3	22.2
Bandera	11,785	51.0	4,004	18.0	42.2	22.4	25.0	9,831	32,993	60,361	37.7	6.0	64,389	11.0	21.3	20.0
Bastrop	51,561	58.1	20,436	13.8	47.5	21.5	163.8	9,243	28,473	71,820	36.8	5.2	74,612	10.8	16.4	15.6
Baylor	1,450	41.3	673	3.7	50.5	21.0	6.9	11,866	26,220	40,946	56.9	4.1	44,392	15.3	21.8	20.2
Bee	16,450	50.5	7,624	8.2	54.4	10.8	54.2	10,170	18,568	45,287	53.8	2.4	46,316	23.1	26.1	25.0
Bell	221,807	61.1	101,037	12.9	34.8	25.3	682.3	9,053	27,171	54,987	44.7	3.7	53,639	14.7	21.4	21.2
Bexar	1,393,433	69.5	541,574	13.6	40.7	28.5	3,472.1	9,921	28,313	58,288	43.0	5.6	60,477	15.0	20.5	19.4
Blanco	6,836	57.3	1,922	10.5	35.9	28.2	18.5	11,115	40,737	70,397	37.6	5.6	66,383	9.8	14.6	13.6
Borden	230	35.2	105	21.0	27.6	45.2	5.4	25,341	33,412	83,281	22.9	4.5	69,499	7.5	8.5	7.8
Bosque	8,860	47.4	3,768	14.0	44.6	18.5	25.1	11,054	28,417	57,337	42.1	3.5	58,056	12.5	19.2	17.8
Bowie	36,865	39.5	22,610	7.4	44.4	21.9	175.3	9,822	27,572	51,796	48.2	4.3	50,326	17.4	23.4	21.1
Brazoria	217,789	58.2	98,933	9.9	36.2	31.1	709.0	9,751	35,437	83,325	28.3	10.3	83,576	8.3	10.0	9.4
Brazos	118,494	51.7	92,537	6.6	32.2	41.4	298.7	9,762	28,679	50,289	49.7	6.2	53,570	22.3	19.5	18.5
Brewster	5,451	59.2	1,944	10.3	33.4	40.8	17.2	14,517	29,696	45,296	55.8	3.7	48,537	14.0	16.6	16.3
Briscoe	694	44.9	247	1.6	50.4	17.5	4.5	10,915	24,991	37,875	61.1	1.4	50,062	13.4	22.8	21.7
Brooks	5,096	71.8	1,730	7.2	59.1	16.4	18.2	11,594	15,817	25,058	73.2	0.0	33,513	28.7	45.0	44.2
Brown	15,863	41.9	8,501	14.3	48.1	20.1	65.6	9,996	26,989	49,180	50.6	2.8	48,752	15.6	22.3	20.8
Burleson	9,095	49.3	3,862	7.9	52.8	21.3	29.0	10,337	32,382	60,058	39.2	3.4	64,836	13.1	19.9	19.0
Burnet	26,149	54.3	10,305	16.1	42.0	26.8	76.8	10,280	31,664	59,919	39.1	5.8	63,813	9.5	16.4	15.4

1. All persons 3 years old and over enrolled in nursery school through college. 2. Persons 25 years old and over. 3. Elementary and secondary education expenditures. 4. Based on population estimated by the American Community Survey, 2016–2020. 5. CDC percent based on 2019 population estimate.

STATE County	Personal income, 2020: Total (mil dol)	Personal income, 2020: Percent change 2019–2020	Per capita[1]: Dollars	Per capita[1]: Rank	Wages and salaries (mil dol)	Supplements to wages and salaries, employer contributions (mil dol): Pension and insurance	Supplements to wages and salaries, employer contributions (mil dol): Government social insurance	Proprietors' income (mil dol)	Dividends, interest, and rent (mil dol)	Personal transfer reecipts (mil dol)	Earnings, 2020: Total (mil dol)	Contributions for government social insurance (mil dol): From employee and self-employed	Contributions for government social insurance (mil dol): From employer
	62	63	64	65	66	67	68	69	70	71	72	73	74
TENNESSEE—Cont'd													
Marshall	1,486	8.1	42,427	2,141	428	80	32	123	177	425	662	46	32
Maury	4,691	8.3	47,100	1,502	1,898	306	141	420	556	1,233	2,765	185	141
Meigs	470	9.2	37,539	2,736	106	24	8	25	60	173	164	14	8
Monroe	1,784	8.2	37,822	2,704	600	118	46	127	249	667	891	69	46
Montgomery	9,828	7.7	45,871	1,671	2,581	471	185	768	1,399	2,393	4,004	250	185
Moore	284	3.9	44,085	1,936	113	28	8	15	40	82	165	10	8
Morgan	715	6.5	33,373	3,013	123	31	9	34	79	265	197	17	9
Obion	1,360	6.4	45,152	1,774	467	83	35	152	181	442	736	51	35
Overton	837	7.8	37,105	2,781	206	43	14	84	93	304	347	27	14
Perry	301	5.0	37,130	2,777	63	15	5	46	43	114	129	10	5
Pickett	207	2.8	40,804	2,352	35	8	3	36	31	80	82	6	3
Polk	617	5.7	36,639	2,808	93	20	7	33	65	226	153	16	7
Putnam	3,457	6.2	42,722	2,103	1,625	311	117	487	496	1,006	2,541	164	117
Rhea	1,284	9.4	38,408	2,633	555	118	43	64	144	467	780	56	43
Roane	2,407	6.2	44,706	1,847	1,492	175	98	123	332	784	1,886	136	98
Robertson	3,379	5.4	46,746	1,544	1,022	178	77	395	353	831	1,672	109	77
Rutherford	15,394	7.6	45,374	1,740	7,157	1,122	527	1,670	1,702	3,114	10,476	627	527
Scott	738	7.9	33,425	3,009	206	47	16	49	82	320	318	27	16
Sequatchie	638	7.8	42,009	2,193	118	25	9	33	81	231	185	16	9
Sevier	4,387	5.4	44,209	1,910	1,761	258	133	650	620	1,307	2,802	190	133
Shelby	50,409	6.6	53,855	790	31,525	4,259	2,222	4,804	7,368	11,153	42,810	2,594	2,222
Smith	861	4.4	42,452	2,137	249	49	18	82	123	239	397	27	18
Stewart	611	6.3	44,108	1,928	162	38	12	32	83	207	244	18	12
Sullivan	7,269	5.1	45,789	1,682	3,593	608	251	646	1,036	2,218	5,099	350	251
Sumner	10,248	5.0	52,403	899	2,843	443	203	1,248	1,255	2,123	4,737	304	203
Tipton	2,672	6.2	43,147	2,043	547	97	40	151	284	711	836	62	40
Trousdale	378	6.7	32,960	3,029	83	16	6	45	34	115	150	11	6
Unicoi	699	5.0	39,357	2,528	249	50	19	40	84	280	359	29	19
Union	714	7.9	35,370	2,916	109	24	8	58	80	249	199	17	8
Van Buren	203	6.6	34,084	2,975	35	9	2	14	27	88	61	5	2
Warren	1,575	7.8	37,857	2,700	552	103	40	187	175	572	881	61	40
Washington	6,250	6.6	47,940	1,399	2,944	553	205	650	940	1,699	4,352	278	205
Wayne	539	10.7	32,631	3,043	172	35	12	44	64	210	263	20	12
Weakley	1,372	6.8	41,159	2,313	550	122	40	157	171	429	869	54	40
White	999	6.0	36,062	2,864	281	56	21	95	126	386	453	37	21
Williamson	23,246	2.0	94,748	28	10,807	1,169	691	4,360	3,930	1,886	17,027	970	691
Wilson	7,944	6.4	53,628	811	2,525	343	184	829	947	1,564	3,880	251	184
TEXAS	1,618,635	4.8	55,399	X	791,107	112,255	52,865	187,412	286,568	305,577	1,143,639	62,122	52,865
Anderson	2,243	6.8	38,807	2,592	1,030	174	71	106	316	677	1,381	85	71
Andrews	949	-4.2	50,248	1,115	503	73	31	117	106	171	724	38	31
Angelina	3,692	6.2	42,536	2,123	1,552	270	109	266	620	1,221	2,197	136	109
Aransas	1,295	3.1	54,374	753	246	42	17	95	328	390	400	31	17
Archer	483	5.5	55,290	684	71	15	5	61	79	108	152	8	5
Armstrong	113	11.0	60,233	414	19	4	1	19	19	28	43	2	1
Atascosa	2,152	6.5	41,599	2,254	698	110	46	103	369	601	957	63	46
Austin	1,669	2.5	55,686	662	600	86	42	145	351	381	873	55	42
Bailey	333	9.1	49,737	1,169	94	20	7	81	45	77	202	8	7
Bandera	1,156	5.2	48,461	1,328	146	27	10	65	294	317	247	24	10
Bastrop	3,863	9.0	42,177	2,171	868	162	61	367	574	945	1,459	94	61
Baylor	190	13.8	53,984	783	58	16	4	31	31	59	109	6	4
Bee	1,035	3.9	31,834	3,063	341	75	22	54	189	368	492	29	22
Bell	17,236	7.5	46,594	1,563	8,794	1,955	705	1,091	2,698	4,408	12,545	636	705
Bexar	98,441	5.6	48,569	1,316	53,327	8,476	3,716	8,138	17,744	21,900	73,657	4,088	3,716
Blanco	721	5.7	58,805	485	197	29	14	55	230	148	295	20	14
Borden	47	-1.2	66,783	219	16	3	1	-1	18	6	20	1	1
Bosque	849	6.3	45,635	1,710	181	38	12	32	160	273	263	22	12
Bowie	4,127	6.8	44,151	1,921	1,890	368	137	275	718	1,287	2,669	160	137
Brazoria	19,716	4.8	51,812	949	7,085	1,136	478	1,064	2,662	3,720	9,763	564	478
Brazos	10,100	6.3	43,430	2,018	5,017	964	318	805	2,183	1,786	7,104	348	318
Brewster	485	6.7	52,483	892	184	38	13	34	158	112	268	16	13
Briscoe	68	-2.6	45,758	1,693	14	3	1	8	14	20	26	2	1
Brooks	289	11.4	41,529	2,268	127	32	9	13	33	138	182	11	9
Brown	1,610	5.4	42,771	2,097	631	124	44	103	235	592	903	59	44
Burleson	925	6.5	49,975	1,146	241	39	17	63	192	253	361	25	17
Burnet	2,669	6.4	53,751	799	751	123	51	270	744	652	1,195	75	51

1. Based on the resident population estimated as of July 1 of the year shown.

STATE County	Earnings, 2020 (cont.) — Percent by selected industries: Farm	Mining, quarrying, and extractions	Construction	Manu-facturing	Information; professional, scientific, technical services	Retail trade	Finance, insurance, real estate, and leasing	Health care and social assistance	Govern-ment	Social Security beneficiaries, December 2020: Number	Rate[1]	Supple-mental Security Income recipients, 2020	Housing units, 2021: Total	Percent change, 2010–2021
	75	76	77	78	79	80	81	82	83	84	85	86	87	88
TENNESSEE—Cont'd														
Marshall	0.1	D	9.9	33.7	3.7	8.2	4.0	D	17.1	7,580	217	710	14,516	1.2
Maury	-0.1	D	7.7	20.5	5.8	6.9	11.9	9.2	16.6	22,230	212	1,734	44,596	2.8
Meigs	-0.6	0.0	D	42.5	D	3.3	D	7.2	19.4	3,605	276	484	6,137	1.3
Monroe	-0.2	D	5.4	39.9	2.6	9.6	3.3	D	12.8	13,865	297	1,601	21,550	1.0
Montgomery	0.2	0.7	10.6	10.1	6.0	10.6	6.3	10.9	21.8	31,950	140	3,701	89,811	4.1
Moore	-2.0	0.0	5.4	D	D	1.5	1.3	D	30.4	1,570	236	75	2,989	0.8
Morgan	-1.0	D	D	10.9	4.0	3.9	1.6	8.4	38.4	5,830	274	850	8,534	0.3
Obion	5.6	0.0	5.3	21.5	4.4	13.3	4.0	D	14.7	8,810	289	1,084	14,312	0.0
Overton	1.1	D	10.8	16.1	3.5	7.7	5.2	12.4	18.6	6,450	282	596	10,365	0.3
Perry	0.2	D	12.8	17.6	D	8.2	D	11.8	21.2	2,290	270	228	4,830	0.5
Pickett	0.8	0.2	D	7.0	5.2	14.8	4.2	9.0	18.6	1,730	341	136	3,353	0.2
Polk	1.8	D	D	8.1	D	8.4	4.2	D	26.8	4,740	267	497	8,830	2.5
Putnam	-0.2	0.1	8.0	13.9	6.0	9.1	7.4	10.7	22.4	18,815	232	2,168	35,977	1.6
Rhea	0.0	0.4	4.3	25.3	3.3	5.3	2.1	D	41.1	8,725	263	1,248	15,323	0.7
Roane	-0.3	D	D	3.2	52.2	3.8	1.4	5.6	12.1	16,210	300	1,427	25,547	0.6
Robertson	2.4	D	14.5	22.2	3.3	7.2	4.6	4.7	13.8	14,890	201	1,184	29,129	2.0
Rutherford	-0.1	D	8.6	21.1	5.9	7.7	6.1	8.1	14.4	48,440	138	4,087	135,532	2.6
Scott	-0.2	D	11.5	18.1	1.9	9.0	2.4	D	25.0	5,880	268	1,280	9,834	0.3
Sequatchie	0.2	D	6.9	14.6	D	9.1	7.5	D	23.4	4,660	284	497	6,957	0.4
Sevier	0.0	D	9.3	5.6	3.8	12.9	9.0	5.3	12.6	26,040	262	1,856	57,786	2.0
Shelby	0.0	D	5.0	8.9	5.8	6.4	8.9	14.1	13.2	164,725	178	32,800	401,410	0.3
Smith	0.1	D	12.2	22.7	2.4	7.3	4.4	D	17.0	4,710	233	497	8,633	1.2
Stewart	0.8	0.0	D	14.5	4.8	D	2.0	3.4	43.3	3,955	285	373	6,689	0.2
Sullivan	0.0	D	6.7	24.0	6.5	8.5	4.4	16.8	9.7	46,995	295	4,648	75,937	0.5
Sumner	0.2	D	13.5	12.2	10.5	7.6	7.0	11.3	11.9	39,205	195	2,640	81,414	2.6
Tipton	0.6	D	17.2	13.8	D	8.2	4.0	D	21.1	12,855	211	1,383	24,202	0.9
Trousdale	0.2	0.1	10.7	10.4	3.9	8.8	D	D	21.0	2,015	167	238	3,852	2.1
Unicoi	0.0	D	4.5	39.2	D	5.8	2.1	D	15.6	5,440	307	551	8,720	0.2
Union	-1.3	D	D	17.4	D	6.8	D	5.6	24.3	5,355	267	745	9,703	1.1
Van Buren	-1.6	0.0	D	16.5	D	D	D	D	46.2	1,915	303	157	2,912	0.3
Warren	6.6	D	6.8	21.9	D	7.7	4.2	11.2	15.3	10,735	259	1,521	18,207	0.5
Washington	0.1	D	4.5	8.9	6.3	8.4	7.7	20.7	22.3	33,115	247	3,285	61,464	1.3
Wayne	-0.9	D	4.3	8.3	D	6.5	D	20.0	25.7	4,370	266	399	7,199	0.2
Weakley	7.0	1.2	3.2	12.5	2.1	5.7	17.4	D	25.7	8,065	244	918	15,007	0.4
White	-0.8	D	7.4	24.4	3.1	7.5	4.3	11.7	16.1	8,075	292	952	12,129	1.3
Williamson	0.0	D	8.6	2.0	18.7	5.6	14.7	13.8	5.4	36,750	144	1,056	94,657	3.1
Wilson	-0.3	D	10.2	9.4	6.6	8.1	7.1	7.8	9.7	29,030	191	1,575	60,897	3.9
TEXAS	0.4	6.8	7.6	8.2	12.6	5.5	9.4	9.3	14.1	4,421,803	150	633,515	11,869,072	2.0
Anderson	0.1	2.9	5.1	6.9	8.8	5.8	4.6	9.0	25.1	10,985	188	1,478	20,440	1.3
Andrews	1.1	31.8	19.0	1.6	2.5	4.3	3.3	D	14.6	2,360	128	257	7,099	0.5
Angelina	0.2	1.8	6.4	10.3	4.8	8.1	4.8	19.4	19.2	19,000	220	2,929	36,780	0.6
Aransas	-0.2	2.9	12.1	1.2	9.5	11.8	9.1	D	16.7	7,665	313	505	15,777	1.3
Archer	18.2	7.5	8.8	3.1	D	5.7	D	D	19.1	2,035	234	106	3,922	1.3
Armstrong	22.5	D	14.0	D	11.7	2.8	D	D	14.3	430	234	23	846	0.2
Atascosa	0.0	18.8	7.0	3.1	4.9	7.7	6.0	D	17.0	9,620	193	1,325	18,990	0.9
Austin	-0.8	1.9	14.2	14.2	9.8	10.9	8.5	4.7	11.0	6,845	225	522	14,097	2.2
Bailey	34.6	D	2.9	3.1	D	4.1	D	4.4	13.2	1,140	167	110	2,747	0.0
Bandera	-1.2	1.0	19.1	2.7	7.0	7.3	5.5	9.5	18.4	7,180	333	382	11,480	0.6
Bastrop	0.0	3.4	19.2	5.3	D	10.1	3.8	7.3	21.0	16,810	165	1,773	37,842	3.0
Baylor	14.8	D	D	D	D	3.8	D	D	12.6	1,015	292	106	2,094	0.0
Bee	0.9	3.1	5.1	2.2	3.8	9.5	5.4	D	39.8	5,045	163	902	10,616	0.4
Bell	0.0	0.2	5.2	3.8	4.9	5.5	4.4	15.0	45.1	59,325	156	9,072	151,263	2.1
Bexar	0.0	4.3	5.1	4.3	10.2	5.9	14.1	11.6	22.3	315,510	156	50,200	805,863	1.2
Blanco	-0.3	D	24.2	8.7	D	4.5	5.7	2.7	12.5	3,250	273	94	6,103	0.7
Borden	-21.7	D	D	D	D	D	D	D	43.2	130	211	D	360	0.3
Bosque	-2.6	0.2	15.1	13.6	4.6	6.3	4.0	D	29.8	5,270	285	388	9,321	0.3
Bowie	0.5	0.1	5.2	5.1	4.8	8.7	6.3	19.3	26.5	20,395	220	3,808	39,688	0.3
Brazoria	0.1	2.5	18.9	19.2	5.1	6.6	4.3	9.0	14.3	55,320	146	5,890	146,180	2.7
Brazos	0.0	1.9	6.9	4.6	9.7	6.6	5.3	10.3	35.8	24,955	105	3,429	98,955	2.0
Brewster	1.3	D	8.9	D	8.9	5.1	5.4	8.5	35.9	2,265	240	170	5,972	0.6
Briscoe	23.5	0.8	D	D	D	4.0	12.9	D	24.5	425	303	34	875	0.1
Brooks	1.6	8.3	D	0.1	D	5.1	1.4	9.3	52.1	1,720	246	434	3,100	0.1
Brown	-0.7	1.5	6.1	22.6	2.7	8.3	6.3	D	19.4	9,715	254	1,187	19,062	0.6
Burleson	1.5	13.9	14.5	7.7	5.3	9.0	5.9	D	13.9	4,600	255	466	9,471	0.9
Burnet	-1.3	3.3	17.6	8.3	6.8	8.2	6.4	13.4	14.6	13,340	262	582	24,357	3.2

1. Per 1,000 resident population estimated as of July 1 of the year shown.

STATE County	Housing units, 2016–2020: Occupied units: Total	Owner-occupied: Percent	Owner-occupied: Median value[1]	Median owner cost as a percent of income: With a mortgage	Median owner cost as a percent of income: Without a mortgage[2]	Renter-occupied: Median rent[3]	Renter-occupied: Median rent as a percent of income[2]	Sub-standard units[4] (percent)	Civilian labor force, 2021: Total	Percent change, 2020–2021	Unemployment: Total	Unemployment: Rate[5]	Civilian employment[6], 2016–2020: Total	Percent: Management, business, science, and arts	Percent: Construction, production, and maintenance occupations
	89	90	91	92	93	94	95	96	97	98	99	100	101	102	103
TENNESSEE—Cont'd															
Marshall	12,436	73.1	159,900	19.9	10.0	809	26.7	1.9	15,495	0.1	697	4.5	15,292	28.5	35.4
Maury	35,163	71.8	204,500	20.0	10.1	944	28.9	1.7	52,080	2.0	2,465	4.7	45,851	33.7	29.3
Meigs	5,079	79.9	148,700	20.7	10.0	746	31.8	3.5	5,162	-0.6	251	4.9	4,702	24.9	42.9
Monroe	18,639	74.0	146,100	21.5	10.0	635	26.4	2.8	20,635	2.4	785	3.8	17,960	24.4	38.3
Montgomery	74,606	60.9	175,000	20.2	10.0	972	26.8	2.2	87,746	0.9	3,947	4.5	85,780	33.6	25.2
Moore	2,599	83.7	200,500	22.2	10.0	647	19.5	2.4	3,577	-1.0	94	2.6	2,789	26.7	37.1
Morgan	7,524	82.4	98,000	21.2	11.1	690	31.8	2.7	7,731	2.0	334	4.3	7,197	28.2	30.2
Obion	12,633	64.2	96,600	18.1	11.5	647	26.9	1.7	12,285	1.0	575	4.7	12,613	28.1	34.8
Overton	8,969	78.0	126,300	19.9	12.3	556	29.1	1.0	9,950	2.2	356	3.6	9,545	27.4	37.3
Perry	2,929	79.4	94,100	19.7	10.6	633	22.8	1.5	2,889	-2.5	207	7.2	2,862	28.2	42.4
Pickett	2,211	80.8	135,600	19.0	10.0	523	25.6	0.4	2,200	-1.7	84	3.8	1,868	39.3	31.5
Polk	7,448	74.4	112,700	18.9	10.0	655	23.9	3.5	7,119	-3.6	293	4.1	7,351	28.4	37.7
Putnam	31,777	61.9	164,000	20.2	10.0	735	29.5	1.1	35,527	1.2	1,313	3.7	35,753	34.6	24.5
Rhea	12,324	73.7	131,100	19.1	10.0	648	26.9	1.7	13,588	3.6	652	4.8	13,031	25.0	37.1
Roane	21,596	75.6	157,900	18.5	10.5	666	25.7	1.4	23,377	1.8	926	4.0	22,969	38.0	25.1
Robertson	26,122	76.0	215,900	20.4	11.0	929	26.2	1.8	38,067	2.3	1,261	3.3	34,904	34.6	30.7
Rutherford	115,249	65.2	234,700	19.5	10.0	1,117	28.7	2.5	190,190	1.8	6,534	3.4	171,935	36.0	26.0
Scott	8,625	71.3	97,300	19.9	11.6	541	25.9	1.4	8,020	-1.6	407	5.1	8,203	26.3	42.7
Sequatchie	5,539	76.4	150,700	19.2	11.1	738	27.2	2.4	6,189	0.4	273	4.4	6,137	25.2	35.5
Sevier	37,993	71.1	189,200	21.0	10.0	810	27.3	3.3	54,854	1.4	2,149	3.9	47,086	26.4	22.1
Shelby	356,607	54.8	158,700	20.6	10.8	957	31.8	2.4	447,442	0.1	30,473	6.8	431,683	36.6	23.9
Smith	7,688	75.7	162,500	20.6	10.5	662	22.6	2.6	9,471	2.5	315	3.3	9,030	28.9	33.3
Stewart	5,226	75.6	124,600	19.9	10.0	674	26.1	2.6	5,377	-0.6	221	4.1	5,622	28.5	33.5
Sullivan	66,645	72.1	145,300	18.8	10.0	679	26.8	1.6	68,879	-0.6	2,906	4.2	67,296	35.3	24.3
Sumner	68,654	73.3	256,000	20.2	10.0	1,044	27.9	2.3	105,810	2.3	3,516	3.3	94,770	36.9	23.2
Tipton	21,624	73.6	161,300	18.7	10.0	859	27.7	2.2	27,707	0.3	1,189	4.3	27,421	30.4	32.2
Trousdale	3,398	74.5	164,300	23.4	10.0	794	20.2	0.4	5,571	2.7	204	3.7	4,747	28.0	32.7
Unicoi	7,683	72.5	136,500	19.6	10.5	629	28.4	0.7	7,062	0.6	347	4.9	7,606	29.7	36.3
Union	7,463	75.3	131,800	19.3	10.0	707	28.7	3.0	7,751	1.6	310	4.0	7,815	23.1	40.7
Van Buren	2,242	80.0	98,100	17.3	10.0	507	20.3	6.2	2,014	0.0	100	5.0	2,406	27.3	35.8
Warren	15,515	70.3	117,000	18.2	10.0	650	28.0	4.6	16,806	-2.5	787	4.7	17,790	25.2	38.7
Washington	54,603	64.1	167,400	19.1	10.0	776	29.4	1.7	61,172	1.4	2,172	3.6	60,511	40.1	20.5
Wayne	5,737	78.6	109,100	20.3	10.0	516	21.9	3.5	6,286	-1.1	255	4.1	6,151	30.5	33.8
Weakley	13,563	64.6	97,900	18.6	10.0	629	28.4	1.5	15,461	0.0	583	3.8	14,303	32.7	30.1
White	10,219	77.5	124,800	21.4	10.0	722	28.4	1.6	11,843	-1.9	464	3.9	10,914	27.4	34.9
Williamson	81,041	79.4	471,300	19.1	10.0	1,596	27.1	1.0	133,778	3.4	3,322	2.5	117,937	56.0	10.1
Wilson	51,348	76.1	283,200	19.8	10.0	1,100	27.5	1.7	79,606	2.2	2,552	3.2	70,287	40.5	21.2
TEXAS	9,906,070	62.3	187,200	20.9	11.2	1,082	29.1	5.1	14,220,446	2.5	807,410	5.7	13,461,358	37.8	23.3
Anderson	16,555	71.5	110,000	22.0	12.5	829	29.4	4.4	23,234	1.6	1,125	4.8	19,143	21.8	32.9
Andrews	5,649	74.7	153,200	17.2	10.0	1,095	24.9	3.6	8,992	-1.5	527	5.9	8,868	26.3	34.0
Angelina	31,368	65.7	110,500	19.7	10.9	826	29.2	4.6	35,754	1.6	2,323	6.5	36,535	32.3	27.6
Aransas	9,917	81.8	183,200	22.5	13.6	826	27.4	7.4	9,256	1.7	672	7.3	9,316	29.9	22.6
Archer	3,513	83.7	152,000	17.8	12.7	659	28.5	2.2	3,975	0.8	167	4.2	4,349	35.0	28.4
Armstrong	720	82.6	156,100	16.8	10.0	938	17.9	1.4	920	3.3	33	3.6	916	39.0	32.1
Atascosa	15,798	77.7	106,000	19.2	10.6	863	21.3	11.0	21,901	2.0	1,351	6.2	19,892	26.4	36.6
Austin	11,569	78.4	197,200	20.7	12.0	822	28.9	5.1	13,696	2.5	756	5.5	14,219	33.5	28.8
Bailey	2,056	77.4	75,200	19.5	10.1	543	20.1	4.7	2,411	1.8	119	4.9	2,975	18.8	49.3
Bandera	8,697	86.7	202,000	21.2	10.0	884	24.3	4.6	10,227	3.6	482	4.7	9,484	35.4	26.5
Bastrop	26,173	78.5	199,300	21.5	10.1	1,095	26.8	5.4	45,101	6.3	2,017	4.5	38,307	33.1	30.5
Baylor	1,621	73.8	69,100	24.6	10.8	481	26.5	3.7	1,816	3.4	61	3.4	1,474	33.4	30.1
Bee	8,499	64.7	88,700	22.4	10.0	860	29.0	4.7	9,293	-4.7	809	8.7	10,227	27.6	31.1
Bell	125,747	54.0	153,500	20.8	10.4	946	28.0	4.3	147,526	2.7	8,469	5.7	145,646	34.6	22.8
Bexar	644,561	58.5	171,200	21.4	11.2	1,048	30.1	4.8	945,855	2.0	50,666	5.4	923,138	35.8	20.8
Blanco	4,665	78.1	261,300	21.1	10.1	850	26.0	4.8	6,866	5.1	228	3.3	5,744	33.1	24.9
Borden	223	69.5	156,300	12.9	10.0	525	19.4	9.4	581	32.6	14	2.4	225	44.0	29.8
Bosque	7,255	76.1	135,500	19.1	10.0	760	21.6	3.5	8,429	3.0	385	4.6	7,777	29.9	29.8
Bowie	34,283	64.0	123,200	18.6	11.7	776	27.0	3.5	39,047	1.7	2,277	5.8	37,897	31.0	26.5
Brazoria	124,184	73.3	213,100	19.4	10.0	1,161	27.4	3.5	180,207	1.6	12,408	6.9	171,352	43.5	23.8
Brazos	81,514	47.0	217,700	22.6	10.0	966	36.3	3.9	121,046	4.1	4,971	4.1	109,012	43.3	18.5
Brewster	4,292	58.4	171,700	18.7	10.0	698	30.3	2.1	4,181	2.8	190	4.5	4,637	39.2	17.3
Briscoe	588	71.4	72,500	17.2	12.5	596	19.7	1.4	574	4.6	27	4.7	620	28.5	36.5
Brooks	2,475	60.1	64,200	26.4	10.0	386	24.8	3.2	2,499	-2.8	231	9.2	2,954	22.8	21.7
Brown	14,614	71.5	109,500	19.8	11.5	778	27.3	2.5	15,267	1.0	792	5.2	16,701	31.9	28.7
Burleson	6,931	77.7	126,500	19.7	10.0	800	25.2	3.3	8,396	4.0	419	5.0	7,753	33.2	35.2
Burnet	17,384	78.8	203,300	23.5	11.9	939	29.6	3.5	24,594	4.6	918	3.7	21,697	30.1	24.5

1. Specified owner-occupied units. 2. A value of 10.0 represents 10 percent or less; a value of 50.0 represents 50 percent or more. 3. Specified renter-occupied units. 4. Overcrowded or lacking complete plumbing facilities. 5. Percent of civilian labor force. 6. Civilian employed persons 16 years old and over.

STATE County	Private nonfarm establishments, employment and payroll, 2020									Agriculture, 2017			
		Employment						Annual payroll		Farms			Farm producers whose primary occupation is farming (percent)
											Percent with:		
	Number of establish-ments	Total	Health care and social assistance	Manufac-turing	Retail trade	Finance and insurance	Professional, scientific, and technical services	Total (mil dol)	Average per employee (dollars)	Number	Fewer than 50 acres	1000 acres or more	
	104	105	106	107	108	109	110	111	112	113	114	115	116
TENNESSEE—Cont'd													
Marshall	508	8,294	696	3,606	1,132	177	144	299	36,087	1,096	43.2	0.7	37.1
Maury	1,859	32,113	5,932	6,055	4,471	1,850	738	1,440	44,850	1,583	46.3	2.1	35.2
Meigs	102	1,585	135	898	228	22	NA	63	39,561	351	38.2	2.0	40.9
Monroe	717	12,165	1,358	5,571	1,674	317	177	452	37,125	838	50.6	2.6	38.8
Montgomery	3,090	46,693	8,967	6,100	8,612	1,265	1,550	1,717	36,775	787	45.0	2.3	36.2
Moore	77	1,054	124	572	110	10	30	55	51,843	375	32.0	1.1	32.7
Morgan	156	1,331	303	183	256	48	12	49	36,864	443	35.2	2.7	33.7
Obion	619	8,601	1,290	2,359	1,495	342	119	314	36,458	553	38.9	11.0	41.1
Overton	337	4,297	690	1,192	533	135	120	159	37,029	1,004	45.5	1.0	28.9
Perry	102	1,655	334	850	169	52	7	56	33,953	287	31.4	4.5	30.6
Pickett	80	617	105	121	96	47	12	18	29,008	287	38.3	1.0	30.9
Polk	233	1,418	229	153	315	57	10	43	30,540	287	52.3	1.4	36.6
Putnam	1,852	31,630	6,338	4,782	4,642	1,093	751	1,281	40,503	1,003	50.8	1.4	31.0
Rhea	480	8,729	1,214	3,367	1,161	219	93	294	33,647	498	50.4	0.4	34.1
Roane	736	9,116	2,086	1,207	1,511	195	397	331	36,284	617	54.1	0.5	32.8
Robertson	1,221	20,708	2,028	6,278	2,903	396	320	771	37,241	1,202	52.7	2.8	37.2
Rutherford	5,631	117,198	15,041	19,939	15,595	3,675	4,192	5,165	44,071	1,414	56.4	1.3	35.8
Scott	316	3,603	701	988	664	130	33	108	29,998	288	39.9	0.3	39.3
Sequatchie	188	1,947	325	154	423	208	53	60	30,983	235	48.5	1.7	34.4
Sevier	2,874	45,481	2,642	2,089	8,622	879	881	1,292	28,412	547	43.9	NA	39.7
Shelby	19,622	450,935	76,109	25,439	44,881	16,008	20,891	24,406	54,124	399	58.1	4.0	36.1
Smith	289	4,108	491	1,339	598	86	74	182	44,409	885	33.8	1.2	38.8
Stewart	164	1,610	214	571	220	58	27	63	39,142	389	28.0	3.9	33.4
Sullivan	3,334	61,966	11,416	11,934	8,647	1,988	1,536	2,968	47,894	1,183	62.3	0.3	30.0
Sumner	3,391	50,040	8,369	8,509	6,875	1,656	1,822	2,112	42,201	1,428	53.0	1.5	32.9
Tipton	720	10,231	1,456	1,512	1,638	267	175	383	37,395	527	47.1	8.5	43.6
Trousdale	115	1,394	230	167	200	49	58	52	37,283	317	40.7	NA	32.6
Unicoi	235	3,911	560	1,581	571	75	12	172	43,910	100	57.0	NA	32.9
Union	203	1,790	125	556	382	34	51	62	34,878	505	44.4	0.2	34.2
Van Buren	49	399	85	172	60	NA	1	12	28,910	329	37.7	0.6	47.9
Warren	720	9,617	1,288	2,872	1,481	358	167	387	40,258	1,133	45.3	1.9	38.9
Washington	2,964	53,739	12,899	5,201	8,134	2,662	1,409	2,276	42,355	1,428	63.5	0.6	36.8
Wayne	218	2,669	662	487	311	145	19	98	36,630	685	25.4	2.2	34.2
Weakley	551	8,439	1,449	2,138	1,123	197	102	268	31,788	788	44.8	6.3	40.0
White	407	5,536	751	2,009	838	152	86	188	33,984	971	46.9	0.4	38.4
Williamson	7,696	134,020	19,822	2,257	13,717	14,135	10,938	9,106	67,945	1,224	51.0	1.3	31.2
Wilson	2,898	45,966	4,386	4,882	7,568	1,164	2,440	1,905	41,439	1,626	44.6	0.4	34.5
TEXAS	618,272	11,210,906	1,615,065	830,260	1,333,881	582,186	783,458	613,149	54,692	248,416	44.1	8.3	35.8
Anderson	880	11,735	2,002	1,313	1,926	279	170	452	38,481	1,754	37.6	2.1	38.3
Andrews	425	5,724	517	188	565	114	138	323	56,384	156	43.6	26.9	41.8
Angelina	1,836	29,502	7,358	3,317	4,685	724	1,198	1,083	36,698	1,028	55.7	0.4	34.1
Aransas	525	4,239	335	72	1,066	177	146	141	33,171	97	68.0	4.1	35.7
Archer	211	1,100	93	66	104	23	25	42	38,092	532	19.4	24.2	34.3
Armstrong	46	277	NA	NA	22	10	NA	10	36,643	216	7.4	36.6	42.4
Atascosa	810	11,787	1,105	223	2,149	266	277	514	43,588	1,681	39.1	7.4	36.8
Austin	665	7,352	535	948	1,145	297	241	333	45,299	2,113	44.7	2.9	32.9
Bailey	142	1,341	149	144	218	51	23	48	35,594	449	11.1	31.2	44.4
Bandera	390	3,326	309	22	391	97	119	103	31,091	897	37.1	12.7	42.7
Bastrop	1,494	15,476	2,005	1,054	3,724	421	541	529	34,187	2,120	46.8	2.1	34.3
Baylor	108	728	314	32	111	39	14	22	29,871	223	17.9	35.4	38.2
Bee	467	5,417	1,542	116	1,081	159	133	169	31,222	943	35.8	8.9	35.2
Bell	5,414	98,320	23,772	6,958	14,804	3,693	3,761	4,258	43,309	2,436	61.9	2.4	28.6
Bexar	37,198	778,909	128,386	36,047	95,497	68,954	48,683	36,885	47,354	2,520	62.9	1.4	36.3
Blanco	363	2,781	203	386	275	82	122	140	50,462	1,032	36.7	8.3	38.0
Borden	6	12	NA	NA	NA	NA	NA	1	58,500	127	3.1	47.2	52.6
Bosque	303	2,638	715	437	433	63	67	102	38,606	1,305	32.0	9.2	37.5
Bowie	2,188	33,640	7,399	2,738	6,034	1,249	2,414	1,252	37,212	1,506	47.1	3.1	34.9
Brazoria	6,002	96,283	11,335	14,351	16,215	2,006	3,449	5,630	58,476	2,851	68.6	2.5	29.7
Brazos	4,594	71,917	9,956	5,790	11,688	1,909	3,465	2,848	39,600	1,363	48.1	4.4	30.8
Brewster	269	2,533	383	14	499	64	47	74	29,209	174	20.7	56.3	54.1
Briscoe	35	120	NA	NA	30	26	NA	5	44,867	249	4.4	35.7	37.0
Brooks	105	1,651	395	NA	263	62	13	37	22,653	437	25.6	7.8	31.5
Brown	846	12,143	2,232	2,864	1,703	456	159	473	38,918	1,838	41.3	6.1	37.9
Burleson	341	3,272	278	431	627	112	156	148	45,186	1,648	33.7	3.2	39.4
Burnet	1,321	13,478	2,263	1,145	2,448	376	599	580	43,045	1,623	39.4	5.9	31.8

STATE County	Agriculture, 2017 (cont.): Land in farms: Acreage (1,000)	Land in farms: Percent change, 2012–2017	Land in farms: Acres: Average size of farm	Land in farms: Acres: Total irrigated (1,000)	Land in farms: Acres: Total cropland (1,000)	Value of land and buildings (dollars): Average per farm	Value of land and buildings (dollars): Average per acre	Value of machinery and equipment, average per farm (dollars)	Value of products sold: Total (mil dol)	Value of products sold: Average per farm (acres)	Value of products sold: Percent from: Crops	Value of products sold: Percent from: Livestock and poultry products	Organic farms (number)	Farms with internet access (percent)	Government payments: Total ($1,000)	Government payments: Percent of farms
	117	118	119	120	121	122	123	124	125	126	127	128	129	130	131	132
TENNESSEE—Cont'd																
Marshall	153	-5.8	139	0.1	57.0	487,523	3,498	60,310	43.4	39,626	24.3	75.7	6	75.0	518	17.2
Maury	227	-6.3	144	0.7	80.2	579,318	4,037	62,386	45.6	28,788	48.3	51.7	2	71.4	2,408	26.0
Meigs	56	5.5	159	0.1	16.3	528,608	3,327	68,874	7.7	22,009	38.2	61.8	NA	62.4	375	28.2
Monroe	108	-2.2	129	0.0	50.4	548,896	4,252	89,599	42.1	50,186	28.6	71.4	2	67.9	1,842	23.0
Montgomery	133	-9.6	169	0.8	65.8	832,256	4,917	98,150	49.8	63,321	77.1	22.9	3	73.7	1,146	28.2
Moore	58	-0.5	156	D	17.5	563,666	3,621	97,990	20.2	53,883	5.7	94.3	NA	78.9	371	17.6
Morgan	60	7.4	135	0.0	16.9	411,449	3,058	62,700	13.1	29,596	18.1	81.9	NA	75.2	321	25.1
Obion	225	-11.1	406	17.1	186.7	1,462,228	3,599	219,944	137.4	248,488	72.1	27.9	NA	73.8	4,910	54.2
Overton	135	9.5	134	0.0	33.7	452,984	3,374	64,496	31.5	31,382	56.6	43.4	NA	77.8	1,026	35.3
Perry	62	29.7	215	0.0	15.7	477,584	2,216	52,838	4.6	16,056	68.5	31.5	NA	66.9	237	18.8
Pickett	35	-17.4	120	D	11.6	421,319	3,501	68,361	14.3	49,728	7.7	92.3	1	79.8	189	40.1
Polk	35	-0.7	123	0.1	16.6	506,140	4,113	74,965	36.5	127,087	11.8	88.2	5	74.2	451	26.8
Putnam	110	14.9	110	0.0	35.1	509,659	4,649	61,327	15.8	15,728	34.0	66.0	1	77.7	691	26.3
Rhea	46	-20.2	92	0.2	16.8	398,311	4,311	58,673	11.8	23,606	31.4	68.6	NA	70.9	308	23.3
Roane	47	0.9	77	0.0	15.2	404,495	5,266	52,781	6.1	9,877	30.2	69.8	6	79.7	259	20.4
Robertson	192	-8.1	160	1.3	132.1	844,471	5,285	123,828	138.7	115,384	83.2	16.8	3	77.2	1,397	25.6
Rutherford	153	-13.2	108	0.5	60.7	796,242	7,361	58,477	27.2	19,242	57.6	42.4	2	76.2	1,051	16.8
Scott	32	-18.1	111	0.0	10.2	297,351	2,671	48,364	1.8	6,403	45.9	54.1	2	78.8	72	19.4
Sequatchie	31	2.0	133	0.0	9.5	514,760	3,864	83,769	6.9	29,174	22.2	77.8	NA	73.2	71	9.4
Sevier	50	-10.6	91	0.0	17.0	554,793	6,114	57,122	6.1	11,168	35.9	64.1	NA	65.6	265	18.1
Shelby	75	-7.9	189	2.8	49.9	989,747	5,237	98,686	27.4	68,769	94.4	5.6	3	78.2	1,668	15.8
Smith	139	7.0	157	0.1	44.9	540,943	3,451	71,841	26.5	29,977	56.1	43.9	1	80.0	1,169	39.2
Stewart	73	20.7	188	0.0	23.0	498,744	2,650	63,795	7.8	20,149	68.1	31.9	1	78.9	265	8.5
Sullivan	84	-1.2	71	0.1	31.8	500,710	7,065	48,527	22.0	18,596	15.2	84.8	NA	77.2	250	2.3
Sumner	161	-3.8	113	0.1	70.6	598,510	5,312	66,130	44.1	30,891	55.3	44.7	1	75.5	1,402	24.1
Tipton	173	11.5	329	7.8	147.6	1,082,305	3,290	147,688	77.4	146,924	97.3	2.7	NA	77.4	2,301	27.7
Trousdale	43	3.2	134	0.1	10.8	461,107	3,432	59,710	6.4	20,256	18.8	81.2	NA	70.7	447	41.6
Unicoi	6	10.3	60	0.0	2.6	427,336	7,145	53,353	D	D	D	D	1	80.0	D	1.0
Union	44	-2.3	87	0.0	12.5	357,911	4,092	55,794	3.2	6,267	32.0	68.0	2	61.4	370	28.1
Van Buren	53	43.8	162	0.1	14.7	541,592	3,350	77,245	8.3	25,088	21.0	79.0	NA	66.0	317	30.4
Warren	154	-5.9	136	2.6	83.9	469,029	3,456	89,059	126.0	111,236	73.4	26.6	NA	80.3	1,238	30.1
Washington	106	-5.0	74	0.7	53.9	584,921	7,871	74,250	42.5	29,779	40.2	59.8	3	72.1	416	7.3
Wayne	142	6.2	207	0.0	34.7	489,765	2,367	71,722	37.9	55,288	12.8	87.2	NA	60.1	1,102	43.5
Weakley	217	-14.6	276	6.8	171.1	996,358	3,616	140,623	139.3	176,788	57.9	42.1	NA	71.1	3,829	46.7
White	119	-2.6	122	0.0	41.8	466,043	3,816	73,121	30.5	31,441	23.3	76.7	2	75.8	929	32.9
Williamson	142	2.2	116	0.5	54.8	702,557	6,061	64,432	30.9	25,239	59.2	40.8	NA	79.0	1,087	12.7
Wilson	188	0.0	116	0.0	55.7	568,298	4,911	58,928	22.2	13,631	27.4	72.6	2	74.7	1,371	25.8
TEXAS	127,036	-2.4	511	4,363.3	29,360.2	980,409	1,917	83,627	24,924.0	100,332	27.7	72.3	466	72.6	749,231	14.4
Anderson	401	6.8	228	3.1	63.8	647,610	2,836	66,640	92.9	52,989	16.7	83.3	NA	72.6	235	1.5
Andrews	887	17.9	5,684	12.8	78.3	4,473,490	787	116,341	10.6	68,045	48.3	51.7	NA	78.8	2,325	34.0
Angelina	104	-11.1	101	0.5	21.6	368,428	3,644	63,521	61.4	59,736	4.2	95.8	NA	76.1	69	1.1
Aransas	54	35.3	556	D	1.6	935,727	1,684	63,828	1.9	19,969	3.8	96.2	NA	66.0	NA	NA
Archer	560	3.5	1,053	0.2	124.1	1,564,565	1,486	96,119	72.4	136,164	8.0	92.0	NA	77.8	2,826	31.8
Armstrong	443	1.9	2,050	7.3	105.7	1,903,678	929	144,216	49.3	228,315	22.4	77.6	NA	78.2	2,848	59.7
Atascosa	746	12.1	444	25.1	107.1	1,012,562	2,283	78,838	74.3	44,192	27.6	72.4	3	66.2	1,132	4.6
Austin	330	-10.7	156	4.0	74.1	610,855	3,906	61,808	33.1	15,687	31.7	68.3	2	70.0	886	4.2
Bailey	499	5.8	1,111	54.2	332.9	947,108	852	229,500	357.0	795,140	15.4	84.6	6	75.1	11,628	83.7
Bandera	403	0.2	450	1.2	15.4	1,138,137	2,531	44,993	6.9	7,737	11.9	88.1	1	78.9	266	3.1
Bastrop	340	-12.4	160	3.4	49.9	659,245	4,114	53,044	44.7	21,061	30.6	69.4	9	73.3	347	4.6
Baylor	555	2.1	2,490	3.3	175.1	2,568,040	1,032	154,639	53.7	241,018	12.5	87.5	1	72.2	4,551	61.9
Bee	483	-10.4	512	5.5	77.2	1,047,910	2,047	58,599	37.7	39,982	65.1	34.9	2	63.9	1,511	12.0
Bell	487	15.6	200	2.3	152.6	656,224	3,282	62,850	77.0	31,622	49.4	50.6	NA	75.5	3,755	9.6
Bexar	332	-3.2	132	7.3	91.0	782,155	5,939	48,334	67.9	26,935	74.5	25.5	1	68.6	950	4.6
Blanco	337	-7.5	326	0.6	18.4	972,845	2,982	49,514	17.0	16,461	51.6	48.4	NA	76.1	190	3.9
Borden	494	6.5	3,893	2.2	90.8	3,439,101	883	194,541	28.8	226,677	59.2	40.8	1	75.6	1,211	53.5
Bosque	626	9.9	480	1.4	81.2	1,191,428	2,483	64,216	45.1	34,528	15.4	84.6	5	73.8	848	9.6
Bowie	294	7.8	196	7.8	75.1	587,246	3,003	73,633	60.1	39,921	20.8	79.2	NA	74.5	3,834	21.2
Brazoria	460	-27.1	161	20.0	131.8	755,243	4,681	63,949	79.5	27,894	53.7	46.3	NA	74.5	7,201	5.7
Brazos	291	-2.9	213	12.1	50.0	1,212,705	5,689	68,510	91.6	67,232	17.0	83.0	2	76.7	817	2.8
Brewster	2,019	5.5	11,601	4.7	57.1	7,904,621	681	90,298	16.3	93,730	6.3	93.7	NA	84.5	221	6.9
Briscoe	553	5.5	2,222	22.1	151.7	1,984,315	893	151,887	36.6	147,020	73.0	27.0	NA	64.3	5,624	84.7
Brooks	459	-19.9	1,050	0.9	11.6	1,629,772	1,552	50,945	26.2	60,048	1.0	99.0	NA	54.9	322	9.8
Brown	547	-8.2	297	4.1	76.6	717,128	2,411	54,661	46.0	25,011	20.1	79.9	1	73.8	1,071	9.0
Burleson	333	-0.6	202	17.9	67.9	693,069	3,427	66,851	58.6	35,553	38.1	61.9	NA	67.8	446	2.8
Burnet	433	-10.8	267	3.4	25.2	790,719	2,964	53,217	14.1	8,690	24.6	75.4	2	76.2	135	2.6

STATE County	Water use, 2015		Wholesale Trade[1], 2017				Retail Trade[2], 2017				Real estate and rental and leasing,[2] 2017			
	Public supply water withdrawn (mil gal/ day)	Public supply gallons withdrawn per person per day	Number of establish-ments	Number of employees	Sales (mil dol)	Average payroll (mil dol)	Number of establish-ments	Number of employees	Sales (mil dol)	Average payroll (mil dol)	Number of establish-ments	Number of employees	Sales (mil dol)	Average payroll (mil dol)
	133	134	135	136	137	138	139	140	141	142	143	144	145	146
TENNESSEE—Cont'd														
Marshall	2.7	85.3	D	D	D	D	103	1,156	314.7	27.8	15	36	3.8	0.7
Maury	12.3	140.5	65	749	377.9	38.3	324	4,093	1,291.8	111.1	77	320	96.8	11.0
Meigs	0.7	55.8	NA	NA	NA	NA	29	223	46.8	4.4	NA	NA	NA	NA
Monroe	5.6	122.8	22	140	71.1	6.2	137	1,764	480.7	43.8	24	61	9.5	1.7
Montgomery	22.4	115.8	84	1,023	460.6	47.0	530	8,734	2,261.0	220.8	175	815	177.0	26.7
Moore	0.5	85.4	NA	NA	NA	NA	17	100	19.0	1.6	NA	NA	NA	NA
Morgan	1.4	62.8	D	D	D	0.6	37	241	55.4	4.5	NA	NA	NA	NA
Obion	4.6	150.8	D	D	D	D	124	1,556	463.7	40.0	D	D	D	2.9
Overton	2.3	105.3	D	D	D	D	65	560	178.4	14.1	6	5	0.6	0.1
Perry	0.9	114.8	D	D	D	0.2	28	186	46.0	4.1	3	3	0.6	0.1
Pickett	0.8	157.4	NA	NA	NA	NA	21	94	26.9	2.2	NA	NA	NA	NA
Polk	0.9	51.9	6	35	22.8	1.2	49	289	75.0	7.3	NA	NA	NA	NA
Putnam	12.5	167.1	72	879	496.7	47.7	350	4,858	1,459.7	129.0	71	243	54.5	8.2
Rhea	3.9	120.2	D	D	D	D	109	1,209	284.5	26.6	18	43	10.8	1.5
Roane	4.9	92.1	23	157	96.9	6.2	139	1,447	396.2	35.8	24	84	15.4	2.7
Robertson	4.8	70.4	47	878	869.3	32.2	174	2,384	688.7	65.3	41	144	31.8	7.0
Rutherford	33.0	110.4	218	4,791	14,706.4	305.4	872	15,693	4,829.5	432.8	249	1,498	468.5	70.6
Scott	2.5	115.3	D	D	D	0.3	74	717	176.2	17.0	8	D	2.3	D
Sequatchie	0.8	54.7	D	D	D	D	36	434	112.0	10.4	7	16	2.7	0.4
Sevier	11.5	119.7	44	512	222.2	23.7	714	8,605	1,848.9	191.9	175	1,376	242.4	46.3
Shelby	142.3	151.7	1,097	27,087	32,209.1	1,609.8	2,992	46,337	22,284.4	1,278.1	959	8,235	2,299.9	443.3
Smith	0.6	29.5	D	D	D	D	59	641	178.0	16.9	5	17	2.6	0.6
Stewart	0.7	53.5	D	D	D	0.3	26	236	48.7	6.1	4	D	1.0	D
Sullivan	23.8	151.5	167	1,798	865.9	81.8	549	8,929	2,394.1	217.8	115	502	105.3	14.8
Sumner	24.9	141.5	119	1,304	995.7	66.2	460	6,522	1,832.5	163.9	160	1,014	293.2	61.1
Tipton	3.4	54.1	20	341	235.7	14.7	150	1,672	436.5	36.6	24	62	18.4	2.2
Trousdale	0.9	115.6	NA	NA	NA	NA	26	222	69.2	4.6	NA	NA	NA	NA
Unicoi	1.5	81.7	D	D	D	D	38	469	119.0	10.9	10	29	2.8	0.8
Union	0.8	40.8	D	D	D	D	38	354	90.4	7.6	NA	NA	NA	NA
Van Buren	0.0	0.0	NA	NA	NA	NA	8	41	8.8	0.7	NA	NA	NA	NA
Warren	4.8	118.0	22	253	85.8	11.7	157	1,546	422.2	37.3	20	57	12.2	1.5
Washington	19.1	151.1	102	1,770	1,240.9	102.9	518	8,606	2,324.0	207.4	131	783	133.2	25.6
Wayne	1.1	63.9	5	D	42.0	D	45	303	57.7	5.8	7	10	1.3	0.1
Weakley	2.3	66.5	30	320	266.2	17.8	102	1,099	283.9	24.0	22	51	7.0	1.2
White	2.8	106.0	15	110	51.4	4.8	82	829	291.1	22.5	11	25	2.6	0.7
Williamson	1.4	6.7	257	3,242	7,570.2	258.5	786	13,709	4,563.1	421.6	338	1,710	1,399.4	115.4
Wilson	15.6	120.9	107	1,608	2,274.3	95.0	437	5,976	1,724.5	150.6	118	483	142.7	21.4
TEXAS	2,885.3	105.0	28,861	435,728	779,742.5	27,818.6	80,874	1,304,540	417,231.9	36,627.8	32,290	198,712	56,443.4	10,559.8
Anderson	9.1	157.3	30	420	213.9	21.5	159	1,946	598.1	48.9	40	129	25.2	4.9
Andrews	2.4	130.4	D	D	D	D	40	752	498.6	41.4	22	150	43.5	12.3
Angelina	11.3	128.0	64	802	396.7	40.3	312	4,953	1,396.4	126.6	81	353	101.0	12.5
Aransas	0.2	8.3	7	28	11.3	0.8	74	1,010	315.7	31.9	30	88	13.2	2.1
Archer	4.6	526.7	11	44	30.5	1.7	18	102	22.2	2.1	NA	NA	NA	NA
Armstrong	0.2	118.1	D	D	D	D	NA	NA	NA	NA	NA	NA	NA	NA
Atascosa	5.3	110.3	49	336	236.0	20.5	127	1,756	590.4	49.8	41	264	77.3	16.5
Austin	2.0	68.7	21	319	809.7	17.7	97	1,099	349.8	30.9	22	57	11.5	2.6
Bailey	6.2	857.1	19	170	155.4	9.2	19	190	46.7	4.5	NA	NA	NA	NA
Bandera	0.6	29.6	3	D	5.3	D	60	360	93.7	8.5	19	47	5.8	1.2
Bastrop	10.6	131.6	35	212	118.8	11.6	209	3,416	1,198.7	92.9	47	153	28.1	5.3
Baylor	2.5	682.7	6	29	20.1	1.4	13	146	33.0	3.0	NA	NA	NA	NA
Bee	1.1	32.5	11	96	69.5	4.2	84	1,202	389.0	33.6	25	121	19.5	4.4
Bell	16.3	48.7	125	2,838	4,327.3	147.3	897	14,650	4,247.3	376.5	317	1,552	264.8	63.9
Bexar	212.3	111.9	1,457	27,152	17,631.3	1,534.5	5,114	91,714	27,360.9	2,485.1	2,118	13,354	3,513.0	692.7
Blanco	0.8	70.9	9	32	18.7	1.6	39	272	80.3	8.3	10	D	2.0	D
Borden	0.1	92.6	NA	NA	NA	NA	NA	NA	NA	NA	NA	NA	NA	NA
Bosque	2.3	130.2	9	87	13.4	2.3	58	420	106.0	9.7	7	21	2.8	0.5
Bowie	16.9	181.4	80	916	399.6	43.2	392	6,206	1,779.3	161.5	110	519	95.7	19.5
Brazoria	21.1	61.0	242	2,282	1,917.6	141.1	842	15,746	4,728.8	422.5	313	1,793	482.3	99.9
Brazos	31.5	146.3	150	2,150	1,451.0	120.2	655	10,489	3,005.1	255.9	292	1,486	337.8	53.0
Brewster	1.0	111.5	8	53	21.1	2.4	40	411	90.0	9.4	17	49	4.7	0.9
Briscoe	0.2	126.2	NA	NA	NA	NA	9	33	12.3	0.8	NA	NA	NA	NA
Brooks	1.1	152.1	3	7	1.3	0.1	14	235	71.2	6.3	5	13	1.4	0.6
Brown	0.1	1.6	32	447	342.5	23.6	167	1,961	581.5	49.1	37	115	17.8	4.1
Burleson	1.8	100.8	D	D	D	5.6	51	640	357.1	19.1	D	D	D	D
Burnet	4.1	90.0	41	234	110.0	12.1	166	2,234	749.3	67.1	64	164	38.2	7.5

1 Merchant wholesalers, except manufacturers' sales branches and offices. 2. Employer establishments.

STATE County	Professional, scientific, and technical services, 2017				Manufacturing, 2017				Accommodation and food services, 2017			
	Number of establish-ments	Number of employees	Sales (mil dol)	Average payroll (mil dol)	Number of establish-ments	Number of employees	Sales (mil dol)	Average payroll (mil dol)	Number of establis-hments	Number of employees	Sales (mil dol)	Annual payroll (mil dol)
	147	148	149	150	151	152	153	154	155	156	157	158
TENNESSEE—Cont'd												
Marshall	31	128	11.1	3.4	42	3,453	1,319.9	179.2	43	595	31.2	8.3
Maury	D	D	D	D	90	6,995	9,151.0	539.5	169	3,506	171.5	53.9
Meigs	NA	NA	NA	NA	12	878	246.1	40.1	D	D	D	D
Monroe	44	180	20.0	6.5	60	5,261	1,779.6	238.8	80	1,290	60.3	15.2
Montgomery	D	D	D	D	75	5,710	2,153.8	300.6	365	7,741	379.4	108.9
Moore	5	22	1.6	0.5	D	D	D	D	D	D	D	D
Morgan	D	D	0.9	D	16	281	152.5	10.4	D	D	D	D
Obion	23	113	14.3	4.4	37	2,560	1,095.3	94.8	D	D	D	D
Overton	25	70	11.3	3.6	33	783	192.5	33.4	32	384	20.1	5.2
Perry	5	13	1.4	0.2	D	573	D	23.1	D	D	D	0.9
Pickett	3	7	0.5	0.2	7	201	23.1	10.6	12	158	8.9	1.8
Polk	6	9	1.8	0.3	9	106	48.0	5.0	19	255	12.9	3.4
Putnam	D	D	D	D	99	5,151	1,380.1	192.5	181	4,189	210.4	61.2
Rhea	26	76	7.0	2.3	31	3,460	754.8	133.7	61	923	39.7	11.5
Roane	D	D	D	D	23	844	267.2	40.0	67	1,090	54.6	15.3
Robertson	67	421	48.8	16.7	86	6,966	1,928.5	307.6	102	2,026	101.2	27.5
Rutherford	D	D	D	D	195	17,522	15,353.1	1,024.2	575	13,307	711.2	208.0
Scott	12	34	3.3	1.3	32	937	139.4	33.4	25	438	19.3	5.0
Sequatchie	16	55	6.4	2.7	8	182	60.4	4.6	D	D	D	D
Sevier	163	719	84.1	24.2	99	1,257	382.3	61.1	565	14,592	1,124.8	323.3
Shelby	D	D	D	D	543	24,520	18,524.9	1,584.2	1,873	40,808	2,369.6	670.0
Smith	19	69	5.8	2.5	13	1,259	590.4	59.9	D	D	D	4.6
Stewart	7	29	2.1	0.7	12	449	205.5	20.5	16	174	5.6	1.8
Sullivan	237	1,820	227.1	84.5	149	13,015	5,220.9	867.1	349	7,690	376.0	106.9
Sumner	D	D	D	D	161	8,007	2,598.2	410.7	259	5,204	287.1	83.7
Tipton	D	D	D	D	26	1,302	545.7	62.5	54	951	44.7	11.5
Trousdale	6	57	4.2	1.4	5	130	30.6	8.0	9	188	8.5	2.1
Unicoi	5	10	1.3	0.3	17	1,481	394.1	98.0	38	449	21.0	5.8
Union	D	D	D	D	14	493	162.3	23.1	D	D	D	D
Van Buren	NA	NA	NA	NA	5	D	35.6	8.1	NA	NA	NA	NA
Warren	42	142	14.3	4.0	57	3,933	1,278.5	194.5	54	859	42.2	11.5
Washington	D	D	D	D	116	4,593	1,289.5	207.0	308	7,336	352.8	104.9
Wayne	8	18	1.8	0.4	20	506	104.7	19.5	18	201	9.4	2.3
Weakley	20	92	8.1	2.6	24	1,851	658.9	61.4	58	876	35.7	9.6
White	20	71	7.7	2.3	40	2,100	747.0	88.5	37	554	24.9	7.7
Williamson	978	10,699	1,916.4	819.0	128	2,263	763.8	103.5	534	12,927	808.9	226.6
Wilson	223	1,291	204.0	62.1	127	4,104	1,812.3	217.7	250	5,102	285.8	85.1
TEXAS	69,783	728,470	149,631.5	58,962.0	19,844	758,722	575,217.8	48,003.6	57,098	1,201,419	74,369.4	20,610.6
Anderson	64	178	21.3	7.9	23	1,415	442.6	46.8	80	1,241	68.5	18.7
Andrews	21	78	11.3	3.6	8	234	75.1	10.4	32	399	25.7	6.2
Angelina	144	814	106.3	37.6	61	3,803	1,377.6	158.3	155	3,198	181.5	50.6
Aransas	42	155	21.4	6.5	14	39	9.5	1.6	102	1,278	70.1	18.3
Archer	14	29	5.4	1.4	5	51	10.3	1.9	6	60	1.8	0.6
Armstrong	NA	NA	NA	NA	NA	NA	NA	NA	NA	NA	NA	NA
Atascosa	45	194	26.1	7.2	19	237	99.1	9.4	76	1,144	57.7	18.4
Austin	57	227	35.9	12.9	39	994	285.1	50.4	55	662	40.0	10.9
Bailey	8	37	5.6	1.6	9	161	63.7	6.9	15	214	10.9	3.3
Bandera	D	D	D	D	12	23	5.0	1.0	52	472	31.6	9.8
Bastrop	107	514	60.5	19.9	73	1,011	332.0	55.2	140	2,797	171.6	51.7
Baylor	8	20	2.3	0.9	D	5	D	D	9	66	3.4	0.9
Bee	D	D	D	D	14	131	35.3	6.3	54	710	41.4	10.4
Bell	369	2,983	386.8	149.8	149	5,716	1,840.9	245.5	638	13,098	663.0	180.2
Bexar	D	D	D	D	870	31,288	18,293.8	1,653.8	4,026	104,088	6,517.8	1,812.5
Blanco	32	100	18.7	5.5	27	246	50.9	9.9	38	374	20.4	5.7
Borden	3	4	0.2	0.0	NA	NA	NA	NA	NA	NA	NA	NA
Bosque	18	69	6.7	2.8	13	427	109.9	18.4	31	261	16.6	4.2
Bowie	D	D	D	D	65	2,209	724.1	109.7	197	5,006	227.7	65.5
Brazoria	D	D	D	186.3	220	13,517	24,168.0	1,409.7	622	12,865	722.7	201.0
Brazos	438	3,354	467.5	195.0	118	5,230	1,453.9	234.2	524	12,699	667.8	174.5
Brewster	D	D	D	D	7	16	6.1	1.3	53	810	52.2	13.5
Briscoe	NA	NA	NA	NA	NA	NA	NA	NA	D	D	D	D
Brooks	3	9	1.3	0.3	NA	NA	NA	NA	17	268	12.7	3.7
Brown	D	D	D	D	31	2,702	1,355.7	149.6	91	1,575	83.2	21.3
Burleson	23	144	22.0	8.1	15	336	147.5	16.1	34	404	20.0	5.2
Burnet	D	D	D	D	70	973	223.7	46.6	129	1,760	123.4	38.8

STATE County	Health care and social assistance, 2017				Other services, 2017				Nonemployer businesses, 2019		Value of residential construction authorized by building permits, 2021	
	Number of establish-ments	Number of employees	Receipts (mil dol)	Annual payroll (mil dol)	Number of establish-ments	Number of employees	Receipts (mil dol)	Annual payroll (mil dol)	Number	Receipts (mil dol)	New construction ($1,000)	Number of housing units
	159	160	161	162	163	164	165	166	167	168	169	170
TENNESSEE—Cont'd												
Marshall	56	707	66.0	23.3	24	137	20.1	4.8	2,464	116.7	44,851	236
Maury	238	5,289	579.7	232.3	108	681	77.7	21.0	8,257	375.0	307,108	2,397
Meigs	D	D	D	3.2	D	D	D	0.3	725	31.9	28,453	132
Monroe	77	1,490	125.7	50.2	42	153	14.7	4.8	2,826	136.9	61,918	215
Montgomery	351	8,502	836.5	357.2	209	1,060	114.0	30.1	12,411	583.7	536,917	4,008
Moore	4	130	7.4	4.0	D	D	D	D	479	19.8	7,279	30
Morgan	18	294	20.0	10.5	8	16	2.4	0.7	1,081	47.7	0	0
Obion	D	D	D	D	D	D	D	D	1,894	81.6	7,048	34
Overton	30	586	64.5	24.7	D	D	D	D	1,851	89.0	1,632	8
Perry	12	412	28.6	13.5	6	140	5.5	2.4	672	31.3	2,147	11
Pickett	5	D	10.4	D	D	D	D	0.3	464	25.6	NA	NA
Polk	20	319	23.6	10.4	11	25	3.0	0.5	1,063	40.6	44,715	247
Putnam	244	6,297	588.4	248.8	D	D	D	D	6,310	319.9	135,392	584
Rhea	67	1,146	84.8	35.6	D	D	8.4	D	1,803	70.9	27,595	122
Roane	99	2,040	150.2	63.8	42	166	19.9	5.2	3,134	128.1	35,596	151
Robertson	130	1,910	178.7	71.9	80	303	34.7	10.3	6,000	301.4	256,697	937
Rutherford	635	14,590	1,847.1	689.5	349	3,263	345.1	127.7	26,848	1,262.4	957,184	3,963
Scott	51	611	50.5	21.4	D	D	D	D	1,357	78.3	805	8
Sequatchie	D	D	D	D	D	D	D	D	1,075	44.7	1,615	11
Sevier	164	2,689	268.7	92.4	145	894	117.7	27.8	8,442	471.6	337,159	1,069
Shelby	2,270	71,476	9,763.1	3,674.5	1,200	10,989	2,794.3	467.1	86,195	3,268.9	429,254	2,059
Smith	D	D	D	15.4	D	D	D	D	1,475	68.6	29,467	124
Stewart	16	151	14.9	5.3	11	33	3.4	0.9	801	35.0	936	3
Sullivan	450	11,469	1,581.0	605.3	212	1,416	157.5	51.3	10,128	470.0	90,669	374
Sumner	384	7,644	985.4	396.7	237	1,477	138.2	41.7	17,538	938.2	580,942	1,842
Tipton	78	1,318	160.5	50.5	38	152	16.3	5.2	3,973	153.9	52,549	263
Trousdale	22	273	26.7	9.3	9	37	5.7	1.5	686	39.1	14,958	105
Unicoi	30	448	30.6	14.9	D	D	D	D	891	39.0	1,560	7
Union	14	130	11.6	3.9	D	D	D	D	1,264	57.5	28,491	123
Van Buren	D	D	D	D	NA	NA	NA	NA	438	20.0	290	2
Warren	100	1,430	148.5	55.2	45	158	13.3	3.8	3,072	138.4	52,272	316
Washington	386	14,110	1,792.7	794.6	198	1,048	88.2	27.3	8,867	442.6	148,718	632
Wayne	37	729	66.5	28.2	13	52	5.5	1.4	986	40.8	0	0
Weakley	72	1,480	137.8	50.6	39	183	16.9	4.9	1,805	78.3	11,431	64
White	52	989	76.3	29.6	D	D	D	D	2,037	91.7	19,741	192
Williamson	772	16,857	2,141.4	911.6	398	3,022	332.3	105.6	30,877	2,259.5	1,357,661	2,980
Wilson	304	3,911	428.3	157.9	182	1,677	186.7	66.4	13,477	731.3	657,811	2,371
TEXAS	69,952	1,581,577	186,108.7	69,899.0	37,506	285,777	39,008.3	10,468.1	2,658,054	133,580.4	52,319,224	265,955
Anderson	132	2,153	219.5	83.7	47	258	22.9	8.9	3,173	149.5	14,104	220
Andrews	18	498	61.2	27.5	D	D	D	D	1,424	92.5	4,182	20
Angelina	301	7,728	630.8	263.3	119	690	97.7	21.4	5,897	287.0	28,455	138
Aransas	46	545	55.6	15.8	47	157	16.4	4.0	2,864	140.9	47,174	214
Archer	15	54	4.6	1.5	13	37	5.0	1.2	955	49.5	8,095	44
Armstrong	D	D	D	D	D	D	D	D	199	9.4	926	8
Atascosa	85	1,190	111.3	44.0	51	228	23.9	6.3	3,828	175.2	15,923	79
Austin	49	687	57.0	24.9	37	133	21.4	5.5	3,351	156.5	4,635	22
Bailey	11	141	11.1	4.5	11	38	5.3	0.9	418	22.5	0	0
Bandera	27	363	23.9	10.9	36	122	12.8	3.5	2,683	124.0	233	1
Bastrop	136	1,837	147.6	64.1	109	428	49.8	12.7	8,032	410.9	156,954	836
Baylor	12	419	19.5	8.5	D	D	D	0.7	277	13.8	0	0
Bee	67	970	95.3	37.2	32	191	15.2	4.7	1,672	63.4	1,305	6
Bell	577	30,711	4,194.0	1,928.5	449	2,772	256.9	80.4	21,650	897.0	697,385	4,019
Bexar	4,922	123,042	14,420.4	5,248.7	2,582	19,389	1,994.8	586.9	161,301	7,453.3	2,842,768	15,294
Blanco	19	170	8.2	4.0	18	39	6.7	1.6	1,622	92.4	6,126	27
Borden	NA	NA	NA	NA	NA	NA	NA	NA	64	3.6	NA	NA
Bosque	16	523	44.7	18.1	20	58	7.7	1.7	1,673	80.8	2,430	9
Bowie	302	7,272	974.8	351.8	156	1,108	108.2	37.0	5,856	268.8	35,672	229
Brazoria	775	10,758	1,129.5	408.2	413	3,368	509.6	138.7	31,063	1,289.6	1,285,384	4,462
Brazos	443	10,581	1,445.9	506.2	289	2,158	628.2	77.4	15,378	756.0	377,512	2,212
Brewster	23	517	31.1	12.3	18	54	3.9	1.2	1,089	45.5	0	0
Briscoe	NA	NA	NA	NA	NA	NA	NA	NA	152	4.9	NA	NA
Brooks	21	471	16.4	7.8	7	25	1.7	0.6	539	13.4	110	1
Brown	129	3,266	224.0	89.1	67	328	28.7	7.5	2,670	123.2	27,920	147
Burleson	15	370	32.3	16.3	26	102	9.0	3.1	1,637	78.7	7,210	57
Burnet	129	2,257	271.0	106.1	82	367	36.2	10.3	5,825	378.4	279,704	991

STATE County	Government employment and payroll, 2017									Local government finances, 2017				
			March payroll (percent of total)							General revenue				
												Taxes		
													Per capita[1] (dollars)	
	Full-time equivalent employees	March payroll (dollars)	Adminis-tration, judicial, and legal	Police and corrections	Fire protection	Highways and transpor-tation	Health and welfare	Natural resources and utilities	Education and libraries	Total (mil dol)	Inter-govern-mental (mil dol)	Total (mil dol)	Total	Property
	171	172	173	174	175	176	177	178	179	180	181	182	183	184
TENNESSEE—Cont'd														
Marshall	1,289	4,249,144	7.9	8.8	3.5	2.9	5.1	16.0	54.0	82.7	40.8	29.5	892	634
Maury	4,902	19,380,592	3.4	6.6	3.4	1.8	45.9	7.6	30.0	580.8	89.4	88.0	954	611
Meigs	437	1,197,065	9.2	10.5	0.1	4.0	3.1	2.8	70.1	25.0	18.5	4.4	361	300
Monroe	1,560	4,538,988	7.0	12.6	1.4	3.5	5.0	6.9	61.8	112.9	56.1	37.4	812	472
Montgomery	6,642	23,037,470	4.8	10.9	3.9	3.6	3.0	6.7	65.7	611.4	250.6	238.8	1,195	744
Moore	226	636,632	3.0	19.9	0.2	12.7	1.2	13.3	49.8	18.6	8.0	8.3	1,299	1,039
Morgan	709	1,992,528	7.1	9.2	0.0	3.4	3.8	6.7	69.8	70.3	54.0	11.1	514	420
Obion	1,260	3,921,376	8.2	10.4	3.4	3.1	1.1	7.8	65.2	93.0	47.2	26.4	869	601
Overton	779	2,099,396	6.3	9.0	0.7	4.4	6.1	6.7	65.7	57.6	30.7	13.5	613	367
Perry	362	956,220	11.1	4.1	0.2	4.5	0.3	9.4	64.5	23.3	13.3	5.9	744	569
Pickett	225	724,507	14.3	5.4	0.0	17.3	6.1	6.2	50.3	10.7	6.9	3.2	625	538
Polk	548	1,472,484	11.5	17.3	0.0	7.5	1.7	10.1	51.9	30.7	17.7	11.0	658	507
Putnam	5,060	17,410,038	3.1	4.4	1.3	1.5	57.4	5.2	26.3	479.4	83.3	88.4	1,144	712
Rhea	1,366	4,219,018	5.7	6.2	1.0	2.5	17.4	7.5	55.9	101.5	42.1	30.8	943	502
Roane	1,740	8,318,872	5.8	5.8	2.1	2.4	2.6	10.6	68.6	108.8	48.6	37.5	708	556
Robertson	2,113	6,058,248	11.9	12.5	2.1	5.2	0.9	7.5	57.5	188.3	82.4	77.2	1,097	633
Rutherford	9,387	36,391,756	5.3	11.5	4.3	1.7	3.0	8.3	65.1	905.8	350.3	398.3	1,258	745
Scott	1,043	2,576,753	7.4	9.6	1.0	4.3	4.9	11.2	58.9	56.4	37.0	11.4	519	358
Sequatchie	478	1,565,295	13.9	14.6	0.0	0.5	0.7	7.9	62.1	32.5	19.9	8.3	561	398
Sevier	3,716	13,950,913	4.3	9.8	3.5	3.6	2.4	9.4	61.3	432.6	97.7	262.1	2,693	1,064
Shelby	33,448	145,003,814	8.1	15.7	7.6	3.6	11.0	15.7	37.2	4,168.4	1,264.8	1,740.2	1,861	1,311
Smith	773	2,111,612	6.5	11.2	0.1	1.6	4.6	9.4	65.3	49.9	27.0	13.1	666	359
Stewart	489	1,406,680	8.8	10.6	0.0	6.2	6.5	3.6	61.6	33.3	21.7	8.7	649	444
Sullivan	5,275	18,910,394	7.3	9.7	6.7	4.6	3.4	7.2	59.8	431.7	144.8	186.9	1,191	826
Sumner	6,120	19,778,438	6.6	10.5	5.4	1.6	3.3	8.7	61.7	516.7	205.1	197.9	1,077	790
Tipton	2,026	6,784,714	5.9	9.6	3.1	2.3	1.1	7.5	68.2	137.5	90.2	28.8	469	377
Trousdale	292	838,005	10.1	16.9	0.0	4.6	1.8	3.2	63.3	18.8	11.6	4.6	429	353
Unicoi	723	2,357,619	13.9	7.4	1.8	4.6	14.4	3.9	53.9	34.8	20.7	10.2	571	451
Union	595	1,586,119	9.0	9.8	0.0	3.2	0.8	3.5	72.9	50.5	36.3	5.9	307	244
Van Buren	305	837,106	4.2	3.7	0.6	14.7	2.8	3.4	70.5	14.0	8.8	3.2	553	365
Warren	1,333	4,289,920	6.6	10.7	2.5	2.2	5.6	12.9	58.7	93.2	53.0	27.2	669	437
Washington	4,253	14,442,914	6.2	9.6	4.0	6.0	2.3	15.3	55.7	350.1	116.8	140.1	1,098	871
Wayne	633	1,747,710	7.1	10.8	0.1	5.1	2.9	5.9	66.9	46.2	24.8	9.5	569	342
Weakley	1,240	3,792,850	5.2	11.8	2.6	5.5	9.8	13.1	51.4	62.6	36.2	12.9	388	348
White	986	2,994,200	7.1	9.2	0.6	3.8	3.1	9.8	65.5	58.5	32.8	15.6	582	308
Williamson	9,372	37,432,304	5.1	6.5	3.6	1.6	20.2	5.3	55.5	1,052.0	212.8	494.8	2,189	1,394
Wilson	4,218	15,396,898	6.6	11.8	4.7	2.3	1.3	10.5	62.0	378.6	139.6	166.1	1,215	815
TEXAS	X	X	X	X	X	X	X	X	X	X	X	X	X	X
Anderson	1,959	6,274,701	8.3	11.2	2.4	3.5	0.8	3.9	69.4	144.0	59.2	70.4	1,210	1,002
Andrews	1,209	4,076,745	6.4	8.4	0.0	2.3	22.8	6.3	53.2	158.5	19.8	91.3	5,185	4,855
Angelina	4,460	16,971,483	4.5	7.4	2.2	1.6	9.4	3.8	70.2	342.4	146.6	116.1	1,326	1,014
Aransas	951	3,138,633	9.3	14.6	0.2	5.7	0.9	6.4	59.1	89.7	14.3	61.3	2,414	2,082
Archer	450	1,359,344	10.1	6.9	0.5	2.6	3.0	3.0	73.1	31.6	12.2	16.1	1,835	1,639
Armstrong	90	279,208	12.2	3.6	0.0	8.5	0.0	0.2	73.5	10.1	2.5	4.3	2,303	2,058
Atascosa	2,465	7,902,006	6.1	7.8	0.1	2.0	15.2	3.3	64.3	283.2	180.5	84.9	1,730	1,376
Austin	1,228	4,438,530	10.8	9.9	0.0	3.1	2.6	3.5	69.6	89.4	22.5	58.0	1,952	1,731
Bailey	444	1,253,036	7.3	9.5	0.0	3.0	14.6	2.9	62.3	31.4	15.1	10.2	1,449	1,262
Bandera	600	2,038,213	10.0	12.2	0.2	4.1	3.8	3.8	64.1	51.5	6.6	37.6	1,683	1,564
Bastrop	3,277	12,419,081	5.2	12.7	0.1	2.5	1.0	2.6	75.1	290.1	125.5	135.0	1,596	1,390
Baylor	327	1,035,047	7.2	4.0	0.0	3.4	45.0	3.3	34.3	44.2	6.8	8.2	2,303	2,129
Bee	1,291	4,581,237	6.0	6.2	1.5	2.2	1.2	4.8	76.7	114.6	49.1	43.1	1,324	1,125
Bell	17,603	59,057,678	4.9	8.6	4.0	1.4	3.1	3.7	72.3	1,287.1	579.3	454.8	1,309	1,021
Bexar	83,813	366,188,878	4.7	9.0	4.3	3.7	12.4	10.8	54.0	9,214.1	2,872.9	4,100.5	2,095	1,657
Blanco	428	1,638,856	11.1	8.5	0.0	2.5	0.6	2.0	74.8	37.5	4.7	28.3	2,465	2,251
Borden	71	235,914	12.5	4.8	0.0	5.7	0.0	0.6	70.6	12.4	2.2	9.8	14,673	14,673
Bosque	680	2,178,765	9.9	8.6	0.0	2.7	0.6	3.5	71.1	69.7	16.8	44.1	2,411	2,297
Bowie	4,554	15,358,280	5.2	7.6	2.6	3.5	1.7	3.5	73.8	324.3	138.7	139.7	1,495	1,171
Brazoria	13,471	54,531,582	5.5	10.2	1.2	2.8	3.0	4.5	71.1	1,527.6	395.3	813.2	2,247	1,899
Brazos	8,278	28,154,311	9.7	13.5	6.1	3.8	2.5	6.9	55.0	699.6	163.3	429.6	1,918	1,547
Brewster	444	1,448,705	10.8	16.6	0.0	3.1	0.7	4.6	62.5	33.0	15.1	14.0	1,503	1,325
Briscoe	88	281,166	26.4	3.2	0.0	3.6	0.3	12.0	52.3	9.7	1.7	6.9	4,568	4,500
Brooks	411	1,194,673	6.9	10.7	2.7	3.9	3.1	5.4	64.3	31.2	13.3	15.5	2,173	2,055
Brown	1,813	5,801,396	6.6	10.5	2.8	2.4	9.9	8.3	56.3	136.9	57.1	60.3	1,596	1,304
Burleson	680	2,083,075	10.9	8.9	0.0	4.8	0.2	4.6	69.4	46.3	11.6	28.2	1,560	1,439
Burnet	1,905	7,169,911	10.6	15.6	4.7	2.8	2.7	6.9	54.7	167.1	20.3	121.4	2,604	2,269

1. Based on the resident population estimated as of July 1 of the year shown.

STATE County	Local government finances, 2017 (cont.) — Direct general expenditure — Total (mil dol)	Per capita[1] (dollars)	Percent of total for: Education	Health and hospitals	Police protection	Public welfare	Highways	Debt outstanding — Total (mil dol)	Per capita[1] (dollars)	Government employment, 2020 — Federal civilian	Federal military	State and local	Individual income tax returns, 2019 — Number of returns	Mean adjusted gross income	Mean income tax
	185	186	187	188	189	190	191	192	193	194	195	196	197	198	199
TENNESSEE—Cont'd															
Marshall	79.5	2,407	59.7	3.7	7.8	0.2	5.7	96.8	2,931	71	96	1,723	15,920	54,520	5,391
Maury	599.6	6,501	18.6	58.0	3.6	0.0	3.2	279.8	3,033	193	274	6,627	48,360	59,726	5,751
Meigs	26.5	2,203	65.7	2.9	6.2	0.1	8.5	5.4	452	34	34	469	5,400	50,479	4,134
Monroe	103.0	2,238	58.9	4.7	6.2	0.0	6.1	71.0	1,543	107	129	1,852	19,930	50,586	4,196
Montgomery	561.5	2,811	52.4	3.0	7.4	0.0	4.0	2,867.6	14,354	1,694	633	10,338	94,320	51,852	4,276
Moore	16.2	2,534	58.6	3.1	4.0	0.1	12.1	9.7	1,518	9	18	1,005	2,920	59,406	5,175
Morgan	47.6	2,210	60.1	4.1	4.2	0.2	6.6	36.4	1,691	38	53	1,283	7,830	47,801	3,500
Obion	92.7	3,051	53.3	0.2	6.3	4.2	7.9	28.3	932	115	82	1,659	13,740	46,281	3,595
Overton	61.3	2,789	47.6	2.5	4.0	13.0	5.2	26.9	1,224	46	63	1,145	9,450	44,569	3,184
Perry	22.6	2,836	48.7	5.6	4.6	0.0	7.8	9.3	1,175	20	22	455	3,380	45,173	3,772
Pickett	11.1	2,201	60.6	6.0	9.6	0.0	1.7	2.0	396	11	14	291	2,220	46,634	3,967
Polk	34.4	2,053	63.3	2.5	6.5	0.2	8.3	45.6	2,723	80	46	564	7,210	46,418	3,588
Putnam	479.2	6,199	21.3	59.6	3.3	0.0	1.6	281.3	3,639	280	224	8,494	34,340	61,973	7,107
Rhea	98.8	3,026	46.6	19.3	4.5	0.0	3.6	60.3	1,847	1,100	90	1,838	13,880	48,310	3,753
Roane	101.2	1,908	64.4	0.1	8.6	0.0	5.1	113.6	2,142	406	147	3,168	24,150	61,342	6,017
Robertson	178.2	2,534	55.4	2.7	8.7	0.1	5.2	169.9	2,416	98	198	3,604	34,730	57,005	5,062
Rutherford	1,008.6	3,187	52.7	1.7	10.9	1.0	3.4	1,153.4	3,644	3,014	956	17,298	158,820	59,795	5,702
Scott	55.1	2,510	67.9	0.6	5.0	0.2	6.0	63.2	2,878	102	60	1,358	8,170	41,292	2,669
Sequatchie	31.0	2,100	61.4	3.4	6.6	0.0	5.6	27.5	1,861	15	43	802	6,540	52,877	4,762
Sevier	373.6	3,840	42.4	1.7	6.5	0.0	6.2	656.8	6,749	403	272	4,693	48,420	49,647	4,816
Shelby	3,786.5	4,049	33.4	13.7	12.4	1.0	2.0	4,208.3	4,500	14,084	4,117	52,376	438,030	64,825	7,992
Smith	49.8	2,522	52.4	4.9	7.2	0.1	6.2	36.8	1,863	119	56	958	8,990	52,880	4,514
Stewart	33.8	2,516	55.3	5.1	5.6	0.2	9.9	45.7	3,402	410	38	647	5,840	48,850	3,725
Sullivan	443.2	2,825	48.9	2.1	7.1	0.0	4.6	347.3	2,213	509	434	7,067	72,500	56,525	5,685
Sumner	472.4	2,571	55.1	3.0	8.9	0.1	3.8	428.7	2,333	531	539	7,950	92,260	78,944	9,765
Tipton	147.6	2,408	63.0	0.7	7.5	0.0	5.8	48.3	788	109	169	2,647	27,470	53,648	4,388
Trousdale	23.6	2,177	63.0	2.1	5.5	0.2	8.4	0.0	0	46	25	428	4,200	48,314	3,758
Unicoi	43.6	2,449	54.4	1.1	7.8	0.4	12.2	38.6	2,170	77	48	837	7,580	46,716	3,664
Union	45.3	2,334	67.6	3.6	4.3	0.3	6.0	20.4	1,049	24	56	827	8,040	46,451	3,469
Van Buren	15.1	2,620	59.2	3.7	4.8	0.0	11.0	4.9	848	13	16	431	2,410	43,498	2,907
Warren	97.3	2,389	59.5	4.1	6.4	0.1	5.0	44.4	1,089	96	114	2,020	17,420	43,972	3,297
Washington	348.0	2,727	43.7	1.1	7.0	0.1	5.3	811.3	6,358	2,968	394	9,823	58,800	60,888	6,590
Wayne	46.6	2,799	47.5	0.4	4.7	18.6	7.0	30.1	1,812	34	40	1,196	5,900	45,303	3,556
Weakley	81.9	2,458	56.5	0.4	8.7	8.4	7.2	21.4	643	136	94	3,668	13,170	48,051	3,859
White	56.0	2,093	61.9	3.0	5.3	0.3	5.3	26.5	992	56	76	1,259	11,620	44,259	3,184
Williamson	936.4	4,142	50.4	20.2	4.4	0.2	3.0	1,048.7	4,639	1,016	678	11,645	112,230	147,973	24,898
Wilson	486.0	3,556	59.2	0.3	5.7	0.0	5.5	1,185.6	8,674	245	408	5,744	70,930	72,837	7,866
TEXAS	X	X	X	X	X	X	X	X	X	215,186	173,144	1,693,748	13,328,880	73,254	9,594
Anderson	145.1	2,494	58.0	0.0	6.1	0.6	5.2	132.2	2,273	163	114	5,064	21,000	48,113	4,112
Andrews	158.5	9,005	34.3	37.3	2.7	0.0	7.5	170.2	9,667	18	49	1,334	7,740	79,513	8,967
Angelina	318.1	3,632	58.1	9.0	5.2	0.5	3.7	341.8	3,903	362	161	6,369	37,870	51,956	5,054
Aransas	82.3	3,242	47.1	1.4	8.0	1.5	4.8	110.9	4,368	45	45	1,012	11,640	63,595	7,833
Archer	31.1	3,539	72.1	1.7	2.5	0.7	2.3	126.8	14,434	24	17	479	4,080	74,153	8,496
Armstrong	9.6	5,163	39.8	34.0	3.6	0.2	4.9	5.9	3,134	4	3	118	890	64,874	7,467
Atascosa	271.4	5,529	52.4	11.5	3.1	0.5	10.6	467.8	9,530	78	104	2,499	22,340	52,138	4,872
Austin	102.5	3,449	64.8	2.5	6.4	0.1	5.2	132.3	4,452	86	57	1,455	15,070	66,231	7,625
Bailey	28.3	4,004	55.5	14.1	9.0	0.0	5.8	43.0	6,090	24	13	423	2,740	44,917	3,947
Bandera	47.3	2,120	51.7	3.5	7.4	0.7	7.1	32.1	1,439	19	45	734	10,730	62,903	6,879
Bastrop	264.0	3,122	59.8	2.4	5.4	0.3	4.3	456.7	5,399	382	171	3,880	42,180	56,813	5,328
Baylor	41.6	11,688	23.1	65.6	2.0	0.0	2.6	9.4	2,633	20	7	222	1,480	55,909	4,695
Bee	119.4	3,664	74.3	1.7	3.6	0.1	3.0	115.7	3,549	43	118	3,108	11,540	48,670	4,532
Bell	1,345.1	3,872	61.3	2.6	5.0	0.4	3.9	1,705.4	4,909	10,654	35,218	19,932	164,190	52,026	4,593
Bexar	9,171.1	4,686	41.9	18.1	5.3	1.8	3.0	24,861.0	12,704	36,668	37,752	110,156	945,410	63,291	7,455
Blanco	35.5	3,089	58.5	0.2	8.3	0.8	4.4	30.6	2,667	53	48	515	6,030	88,643	12,296
Borden	11.0	16,416	70.4	0.0	0.0	0.0	0.0	20.2	30,221	2	20	88	280	98,882	15,454
Bosque	79.3	4,336	45.5	0.0	4.9	0.1	6.1	80.2	4,386	77	36	1,215	8,220	55,831	5,710
Bowie	316.7	3,389	63.3	0.3	5.0	0.5	5.2	292.5	3,129	3,369	184	6,302	41,430	55,174	5,492
Brazoria	1,558.9	4,308	57.4	4.1	4.5	0.2	5.0	3,476.1	9,606	610	770	19,460	166,300	75,052	8,376
Brazos	816.2	3,645	48.0	5.4	5.1	0.2	4.8	1,889.5	8,438	820	500	38,406	88,960	67,367	8,069
Brewster	33.8	3,627	50.9	7.7	5.4	0.2	4.4	18.6	1,994	288	18	1,055	4,540	55,239	5,631
Briscoe	7.0	4,631	42.8	0.0	3.2	0.1	6.6	16.8	11,109	11	3	116	640	54,261	4,803
Brooks	28.3	3,962	62.2	0.0	8.2	0.2	3.9	45.2	6,332	452	14	504	2,930	34,472	2,059
Brown	129.6	3,428	49.3	8.5	6.5	0.6	4.0	148.2	3,919	124	69	2,726	16,680	53,542	5,050
Burleson	50.4	2,790	55.5	5.9	3.6	0.1	8.5	42.8	2,370	59	35	817	8,810	59,373	6,582
Burnet	162.2	3,481	49.1	0.7	7.6	0.3	5.4	267.8	5,748	79	93	2,633	24,630	80,811	10,702

1. Based on the resident population estimated as of July 1 of the year shown.

State / county code	CBSA code[1]	County Type code[2]	STATE County	Land area[3] (sq. mi)	Population, 2021			Population and population characteristics, 2021										
								Race alone or in combination, not Hispanic or Latino (percent)					Age (percent)					
					Total persons 2021	Rank	Per square mile	White	Black	American Indian, Alaska Native	Asian and Pacific Islancer	Percent Hispanic or Latino[4]	Under 5 years	5 to 17 years	18 to 24 years	25 to 34 years	35 to 44 years	45 to 54 years
				1	2	3	4	5	6	7	8	9	10	11	12	13	14	15
			TEXAS—Cont'd															
48055	12420	1	Caldwell	544.5	46,791	1,039	85.9	38.6	6.1	0.7	1.2	54.5	5.8	12.3	15.7	13.7	13.1	11.9
48057	38920	6	Calhoun	506.9	19,727	1,837	38.9	42.1	2.7	0.6	5.7	49.8	6.2	13.5	12.7	12.0	12.0	11.0
48059	10180	3	Callahan	899.4	14,115	2,143	15.7	86.9	2.2	1.3	1.1	10.1	5.2	12.7	10.7	11.1	12.6	12.2
48061	15180	2	Cameron	891.7	423,029	170	474.4	8.7	0.5	0.2	0.8	90.1	7.3	16.8	16.1	12.7	11.7	11.6
48063	34420	6	Camp	195.8	12,616	2,235	64.4	56.6	16.9	0.8	1.4	26.4	7.1	14.6	12.8	12.1	10.9	10.6
48065	11100	2	Carson	920.2	5,746	2,757	6.2	86.6	2.1	2.0	1.1	10.3	4.5	14.2	11.5	11.1	12.7	11.6
48067		6	Cass	936.9	28,560	1,473	30.5	77.1	17.2	1.0	0.9	5.1	5.5	13.0	11.3	10.3	11.2	11.9
48069		6	Castro	894.4	7,374	2,634	8.2	30.6	2.2	0.7	0.7	66.4	7.4	16.6	14.9	11.7	11.2	10.0
48071	26420	1	Chambers	597.1	48,865	1,010	81.8	64.0	8.3	0.7	1.7	26.3	7.0	16.3	13.2	13.9	14.9	12.6
48073	27380	6	Cherokee	1,053.0	51,097	982	48.5	60.9	14.4	0.9	0.8	24.6	6.7	14.2	13.9	12.0	11.6	12.0
48075		7	Childress	696.5	6,736	2,678	9.7	55.0	11.9	1.3	1.3	32.1	4.4	10.7	16.8	20.5	13.5	9.3
48077	48660	3	Clay	1,088.8	10,263	2,392	9.4	89.7	1.7	2.1	1.2	7.3	4.2	11.6	10.7	10.0	11.5	12.0
48079		9	Cochran	775.1	2,516	2,996	3.2	34.7	4.8	1.1	0.9	59.9	6.9	14.5	13.2	12.4	12.6	11.7
48081		8	Coke	911.6	3,321	2,938	3.6	75.5	1.6	1.6	0.6	22.6	5.7	12.0	10.2	10.6	10.9	10.0
48083		6	Coleman	1,262.9	7,735	2,593	6.1	76.4	3.9	1.3	1.4	18.6	4.7	11.8	10.7	8.9	10.2	11.6
48085	19100	1	Collin	841.3	1,109,462	42	1,318.7	55.1	12.0	0.9	18.9	15.8	5.8	14.6	13.1	12.9	15.9	15.0
48087		9	Collingsworth	918.4	2,615	2,988	2.8	57.6	6.3	2.2	0.5	35.1	6.2	15.6	11.5	10.3	12.9	10.9
48089		6	Colorado	960.3	20,630	1,785	21.5	55.7	12.2	0.7	0.9	32.2	6.1	13.9	11.5	10.7	10.4	10.9
48091	41700	1	Comal	559.5	174,986	383	312.8	66.2	3.2	0.9	2.0	29.2	5.3	12.9	11.6	11.6	13.0	13.0
48093		7	Comanche	937.8	13,775	2,172	14.7	68.6	1.2	1.1	0.8	29.4	5.3	13.0	11.7	10.3	10.2	11.5
48095		8	Concho	983.8	3,341	2,937	3.4	62.0	1.5	1.0	2.2	34.1	4.5	9.1	9.8	9.5	11.4	13.0
48097	23620	6	Cooke	874.8	42,244	1,140	48.3	75.2	4.1	1.6	1.3	19.4	6.2	13.0	12.2	12.1	11.8	11.3
48099	28660	2	Coryell	1,052.2	84,232	684	80.1	59.2	18.9	1.3	4.3	20.0	6.2	12.9	15.7	18.9	15.6	11.1
48101		9	Cottle	900.6	1,381	3,087	1.5	63.8	11.6	0.8	0.7	25.1	4.7	11.3	11.5	7.7	13.0	10.1
48103		6	Crane	785.1	4,680	2,843	6.0	28.6	3.2	1.1	0.8	67.0	7.1	17.2	14.8	12.4	13.5	11.5
48105		7	Crockett	2,807.3	3,068	2,955	1.1	29.9	1.1	1.0	1.1	67.5	6.2	15.0	11.5	10.7	12.5	11.8
48107	31180	2	Crosby	900.2	5,106	2,814	5.7	38.5	3.6	0.9	0.5	57.4	6.3	14.7	13.5	11.3	12.2	10.6
48109		9	Culberson	3,812.2	2,193	3,026	0.6	23.1	2.0	1.5	2.2	72.6	6.8	12.8	11.7	12.8	11.2	10.5
48111		7	Dallam	1,503.1	7,172	2,650	4.8	48.7	2.4	1.2	1.2	47.6	10.1	17.7	13.5	13.2	11.9	11.7
48113	19100	1	Dallas	873.1	2,586,050	9	2,961.9	28.5	23.6	0.7	7.4	41.4	6.9	14.3	13.8	16.3	13.8	12.2
48115	29500	7	Dawson	900.3	12,413	2,249	13.8	33.6	6.4	0.6	1.1	59.4	7.1	14.7	14.3	16.0	13.1	10.2
48117	25820	6	Deaf Smith	1,496.8	18,329	1,908	12.2	21.8	1.3	0.6	0.7	76.2	8.6	17.4	15.2	13.2	11.7	10.8
48119		8	Delta	256.8	5,392	2,785	21.0	80.5	8.3	2.9	1.5	10.0	6.7	13.0	10.7	11.6	11.0	11.7
48121	19100	1	Denton	878.5	941,647	58	1,071.9	57.7	12.3	0.9	11.5	20.0	5.7	13.6	13.6	14.4	15.6	14.4
48123		6	DeWitt	909.0	19,918	1,816	21.9	54.5	8.6	0.6	0.6	36.7	5.7	13.1	10.8	11.6	13.1	12.1
48125		8	Dickens	901.7	1,740	3,062	1.9	61.1	5.7	1.7	1.7	31.3	4.5	8.6	12.6	13.4	11.4	11.7
48127		6	Dimmit	1,328.9	8,473	2,536	6.4	9.6	1.5	0.3	0.8	88.0	6.8	16.4	15.1	11.5	11.7	11.0
48129		8	Donley	926.9	3,268	2,945	3.5	80.1	6.2	2.1	1.1	12.5	4.7	11.6	15.6	8.9	10.5	9.8
48131	10860	7	Duval	1,793.5	9,756	2,430	5.4	8.9	1.3	0.4	0.4	89.2	7.0	15.0	14.0	12.9	11.8	10.8
48133		6	Eastland	926.5	17,864	1,927	19.3	78.6	2.7	1.3	1.1	17.8	5.7	11.8	13.8	10.8	11.1	10.6
48135	36220	3	Ector	897.9	161,091	418	179.4	29.1	4.9	0.7	1.6	64.7	8.7	17.3	14.6	15.6	13.9	10.7
48137		9	Edwards	2,117.9	1,438	3,083	0.7	42.4	1.5	1.5	0.6	55.2	5.4	12.7	10.0	8.4	9.5	11.1
48139	19100	1	Ellis	935.7	202,678	340	216.6	56.8	14.4	0.9	1.4	28.1	6.3	15.3	13.4	13.0	14.0	12.9
48141	21340	2	El Paso	1,013.2	867,947	67	856.6	12.2	3.6	0.5	1.8	82.9	6.8	15.1	15.6	15.2	12.8	11.4
48143	44500	4	Erath	1,083.2	43,378	1,117	40.0	74.1	2.4	1.1	1.3	22.3	5.7	11.9	23.3	12.6	10.9	9.8
48145	47380	2	Falls	765.5	17,313	1,953	22.6	50.8	23.0	0.8	0.9	25.7	5.9	12.0	11.8	14.2	13.0	11.5
48147	14300	6	Fannin	890.8	36,569	1,271	41.1	78.8	7.2	1.9	1.1	12.9	4.8	12.5	12.1	12.7	13.0	12.8
48149		6	Fayette	949.9	24,687	1,626	26.0	70.9	6.2	0.8	0.7	22.4	4.7	11.6	10.6	9.6	10.8	10.7
48151		8	Fisher	899.0	3,706	2,909	4.1	65.1	4.3	1.3	0.8	30.2	4.9	13.4	10.6	10.9	10.6	11.0
48153		6	Floyd	992.1	5,350	2,788	5.4	35.6	3.6	0.6	0.8	60.2	6.3	14.9	13.1	11.1	11.5	11.6
48155		9	Foard	704.4	1,080	3,105	1.5	75.0	5.6	1.1	1.1	18.7	6.2	9.9	10.2	9.1	9.4	11.9
48157	26420	1	Fort Bend	861.7	858,527	72	996.3	31.8	21.7	0.6	22.5	25.5	6.1	15.9	13.2	11.6	15.6	14.1
48159		7	Franklin	284.4	10,464	2,378	36.8	78.1	5.4	1.2	1.5	15.7	5.6	13.1	11.6	10.5	11.3	11.5
48161		7	Freestone	877.7	19,774	1,834	22.5	66.8	15.5	1.1	1.0	17.0	5.5	13.1	11.1	10.9	13.5	12.6
48163	37770	6	Frio	1,133.5	18,436	1,902	16.3	13.6	3.5	0.4	2.6	80.3	6.1	12.9	17.1	19.2	13.2	10.3
48165		7	Gaines	1,502.4	21,895	1,723	14.6	53.7	2.0	0.6	0.6	43.9	10.2	20.3	15.5	13.1	12.7	9.6
48167	26420	1	Galveston	379.3	355,062	206	936.1	57.2	13.2	0.8	4.2	26.4	5.8	13.8	12.8	12.8	13.7	12.7
48169		6	Garza	893.4	5,863	2,749	6.6	39.5	7.6	1.0	0.6	52.7	3.6	9.2	16.1	20.6	12.6	14.4
48171	23240	7	Gillespie	1,058.2	27,297	1,521	25.8	73.7	0.7	0.8	0.8	24.8	4.7	11.5	10.4	8.9	10.0	10.3
48173		8	Glasscock	900.2	1,149	3,100	1.3	58.1	3.0	0.4	0.6	38.6	7.1	14.7	12.2	15.3	12.2	11.8
48175	47020	3	Goliad	852.0	7,163	2,651	8.4	58.5	4.6	1.1	0.7	36.3	5.2	11.8	11.0	10.2	11.7	11.9
48177		6	Gonzales	1,066.7	19,641	1,846	18.4	40.7	6.2	0.7	0.8	52.6	6.7	15.0	13.5	11.6	11.6	11.5
48179	37420	6	Gray	926.0	21,030	1,762	22.7	62.4	6.1	1.6	1.0	30.8	5.8	14.7	12.1	13.3	13.5	12.4
48181	43300	3	Grayson	932.8	139,336	471	149.4	76.2	7.1	2.2	2.1	15.0	6.0	13.6	12.6	12.1	12.1	11.9
48183	30980	3	Gregg	273.4	124,201	516	454.3	57.7	21.4	0.9	1.9	20.1	6.6	14.8	13.9	13.3	12.6	11.1
48185		6	Grimes	787.5	30,287	1,430	38.5	60.0	14.8	1.0	0.8	24.8	5.5	12.7	12.0	12.7	12.6	12.4

1. CBSA = Core Based Statistical Area. See Appendix A for explanation. See Appendix B for list of metropolitan areas with component counties. 2. County type code from the Economic Research Service of USDA Rural-Urban Continuum Codes. See Appendix A for definition. 3. Dry land or land partially or temporarily covered by water. 4. May be of any race.

STATE County	Population, 2021 (cont.)				Population change, 2000–2021							Households, 2016–2020				
	Age (percent) (cont.)				Total persons		Percent change		Components of change, 2020–2021					Percent		
	55 to 64 years	65 to 74 years	75 years and over	Percent female	2010	2020	2010–2020	2020–2021	Births	Deaths	Net Migration	Number	Persons per household	Family house-holds	Female family house-holder[1]	One person
	16	17	18	19	20	21	22	23	24	25	26	27	28	29	30	31
TEXAS—Cont'd																
Caldwell	12.3	9.4	5.7	49.3	38,066	45,883	20.5	2.0	705	562	769	13,774	2.8	69.0	13.2	25.3
Calhoun	13.7	11.3	7.7	48.7	21,381	20,106	-6.0	-1.9	329	310	-393	8,027	2.6	68.5	14.2	27.4
Callahan	14.4	12.8	8.5	50.7	13,544	13,708	1.2	3.0	164	265	514	5,372	2.6	66.4	10.2	31.1
Cameron	9.8	8.1	5.9	51.1	406,220	421,017	3.6	0.5	7,260	4,266	-1,097	126,968	3.3	77.3	19.9	20.2
Camp	12.7	12.0	7.1	51.5	12,401	12,464	0.5	1.2	185	217	187	4,460	2.9	66.5	12.1	24.1
Carson	13.3	12.9	8.2	50.1	6,182	5,807	-6.1	-1.1	56	85	-30	2,332	2.5	70.5	9.2	27.7
Cass	14.4	12.7	9.7	51.6	30,464	28,454	-6.6	0.4	354	650	408	11,962	2.5	70.3	12.0	26.9
Castro	11.1	9.9	7.1	48.6	8,062	7,371	-8.6	0.0	117	77	-36	2,557	2.9	71.3	15.6	26.0
Chambers	10.4	7.7	4.1	49.4	35,096	46,571	32.7	4.9	754	412	1,970	14,266	3.0	80.7	9.7	16.7
Cherokee	11.8	10.8	7.0	48.5	50,845	50,412	-0.9	1.4	842	809	652	18,540	2.7	75.2	14.4	22.0
Childress	9.6	8.4	6.8	38.3	7,041	6,664	-5.4	1.1	80	94	85	2,308	2.5	71.3	15.3	26.2
Clay	16.2	14.4	9.5	49.7	10,752	10,218	-5.0	0.4	100	212	159	4,159	2.5	70.6	5.6	26.0
Cochran	12.2	9.1	7.2	49.7	3,127	2,547	-18.5	-1.2	48	21	-57	1,026	2.7	69.3	11.2	28.6
Coke	15.4	14.0	11.2	51.1	3,320	3,285	-1.1	1.1	48	72	60	1,625	2.0	62.2	8.6	35.7
Coleman	16.1	15.5	10.5	49.4	8,895	7,684	-13.6	0.7	80	198	170	3,492	2.4	63.1	8.2	26.5
Collin	11.5	7.1	4.2	50.4	782,341	1,064,465	36.1	4.2	14,101	7,961	39,090	353,491	2.8	74.0	9.7	21.2
Collingsworth	13.0	11.4	8.2	51.5	3,057	2,652	-13.2	-1.4	38	49	-26	1,029	2.8	70.2	11.2	24.3
Colorado	14.1	13.1	9.3	49.7	20,874	20,557	-1.5	0.4	284	377	166	7,442	2.8	69.7	12.8	26.7
Comal	14.3	11.8	6.5	50.2	108,472	161,501	48.9	8.3	2,066	2,018	13,625	54,586	2.7	73.5	8.4	22.0
Comanche	14.7	13.4	10.0	49.8	13,974	13,594	-2.7	1.3	168	287	303	5,416	2.5	65.4	8.5	30.4
Concho	15.9	15.3	11.6	45.8	4,087	3,303	-19.2	1.2	26	58	70	876	2.3	66.1	8.8	33.1
Cooke	14.2	11.6	7.5	50.2	38,437	41,668	8.4	1.4	611	666	633	15,530	2.6	71.7	11.3	23.9
Coryell	8.7	6.6	4.2	50.0	75,388	83,093	10.2	1.4	1,153	737	705	22,324	2.7	71.1	13.2	24.9
Cottle	16.1	14.0	11.6	51.6	1,505	1,380	-8.3	0.1	12	15	4	703	2.3	55.9	16.2	41.5
Crane	11.3	7.4	4.8	49.1	4,375	4,675	6.9	0.1	104	51	-49	1,500	3.1	69.9	7.1	27.6
Crockett	13.3	11.4	7.6	49.4	3,719	3,098	-16.7	-1.0	63	42	-51	1,394	2.4	71.4	3.4	28.6
Crosby	12.7	11.0	7.7	49.5	6,059	5,133	-15.3	-0.5	72	80	-20	2,107	2.7	72.0	17.9	26.2
Culberson	13.3	11.7	9.2	49.1	2,398	2,188	-8.8	0.2	35	32	2	668	3.2	59.9	19.3	40.1
Dallam	10.1	7.5	4.3	47.1	6,703	7,115	6.1	0.8	198	66	-76	2,344	3.1	70.4	10.5	24.8
Dallas	11.1	7.3	4.2	50.4	2,368,139	2,613,539	10.4	-1.1	44,732	25,273	-46,847	945,996	2.7	64.2	15.1	29.1
Dawson	10.4	7.9	6.3	44.3	13,833	12,456	-10.0	-0.3	209	178	-77	4,430	2.5	62.9	15.2	33.1
Deaf Smith	10.0	7.9	5.2	49.8	19,372	18,583	-4.1	-1.4	374	233	-395	6,053	3.0	76.6	11.4	20.0
Delta	13.6	12.6	9.2	50.9	5,231	5,230	0.0	3.1	81	69	152	2,066	2.5	66.1	8.3	31.0
Denton	11.6	7.2	3.9	50.6	662,614	906,422	36.8	3.9	12,349	6,973	29,949	300,585	2.8	70.5	9.7	23.3
DeWitt	13.7	11.1	8.8	46.9	20,097	19,824	-1.4	0.5	264	348	177	6,823	2.7	68.5	9.2	28.2
Dickens	13.0	13.7	11.0	44.1	2,444	1,770	-27.6	-1.7	16	36	-9	861	2.4	62.8	8.5	32.9
Dimmit	10.3	9.7	7.4	51.1	9,996	8,615	-13.8	-1.6	154	138	-158	3,178	3.2	76.4	25.6	21.2
Donley	14.0	14.5	10.4	51.0	3,677	3,258	-11.4	0.3	41	63	32	1,344	2.2	65.7	11.4	32.0
Duval	11.0	8.8	8.7	48.6	11,782	9,831	-16.6	-0.8	185	184	-76	3,407	3.1	68.9	18.5	27.2
Eastland	14.2	12.6	9.3	50.0	18,583	17,725	-4.6	0.8	271	413	284	7,017	2.5	63.9	7.6	34.6
Ector	9.4	6.1	3.7	48.9	137,130	165,171	20.4	-2.5	3,809	1,835	-5,980	53,602	3.0	68.9	16.6	26.1
Edwards	14.0	17.9	10.9	47.0	2,002	1,422	-29.0	1.1	22	28	21	787	2.5	62.8	13.2	37.2
Ellis	12.0	8.3	4.7	50.5	149,610	192,455	28.6	5.3	2,735	2,109	9,707	59,399	3.0	79.3	12.7	18.1
El Paso	10.4	7.6	5.2	50.2	800,647	865,657	8.1	0.3	13,776	8,489	-3,228	273,662	3.0	72.4	18.8	23.8
Erath	11.1	8.9	5.8	51.0	37,890	42,545	12.3	2.0	562	508	780	14,263	2.8	64.7	7.0	24.8
Falls	13.1	10.9	7.7	52.7	17,866	16,968	-5.0	2.0	246	258	360	5,552	2.8	61.5	11.9	37.1
Fannin	14.0	10.7	7.4	46.4	33,915	35,662	5.2	2.5	427	636	1,129	12,391	2.6	68.0	9.4	28.5
Fayette	15.5	15.3	11.3	50.4	24,554	24,435	-0.5	1.0	264	441	435	9,033	2.7	69.5	6.8	25.6
Fisher	14.2	13.8	10.5	49.5	3,974	3,672	-7.6	0.9	42	55	49	1,676	2.3	65.5	9.5	29.1
Floyd	11.9	10.4	9.1	49.7	6,446	5,402	-16.2	-1.0	83	83	-52	2,184	2.6	71.7	14.2	24.2
Foard	15.9	12.6	14.9	52.5	1,336	1,095	-18.0	-1.4	21	25	-10	509	2.3	66.2	6.9	30.6
Fort Bend	11.4	8.1	4.0	50.7	585,375	822,779	40.6	4.3	10,860	6,068	31,220	248,299	3.2	82.6	12.1	14.5
Franklin	14.4	13.2	8.7	50.2	10,605	10,359	-2.3	1.0	121	180	164	3,960	2.7	72.9	10.1	21.2
Freestone	13.1	11.8	8.4	47.9	19,816	19,435	-1.9	1.7	264	340	420	6,736	2.7	70.8	12.1	25.5
Frio	9.0	7.0	5.1	40.3	17,217	18,385	6.8	0.3	271	222	-2	4,673	3.4	70.7	19.2	27.9
Gaines	9.9	5.5	3.2	48.9	17,526	21,598	23.2	1.4	567	189	-86	5,878	3.6	78.5	10.5	19.3
Galveston	13.3	9.8	5.5	50.7	291,309	350,682	20.4	1.2	4,754	4,463	4,065	125,204	2.7	68.4	12.7	26.1
Garza	11.8	6.3	5.4	34.1	6,461	5,816	-10.0	0.8	62	57	40	1,713	2.5	74.2	14.7	21.5
Gillespie	14.9	16.3	13.1	51.3	24,837	26,725	7.6	2.1	316	513	783	10,820	2.4	68.2	8.2	29.0
Glasscock	13.0	9.1	4.6	46.0	1,226	1,116	-9.0	3.0	21	11	24	435	3.3	85.7	5.3	11.7
Goliad	14.7	14.2	9.3	50.2	7,210	7,012	-2.7	2.2	88	97	164	2,840	2.6	64.6	8.8	33.6
Gonzales	12.7	10.2	7.3	49.4	19,807	19,653	-0.8	-0.1	314	297	-31	7,465	2.8	70.4	14.5	27.4
Gray	11.7	9.2	7.3	45.5	22,535	21,227	-5.8	-0.9	320	357	-159	7,843	2.6	65.9	11.0	28.8
Grayson	13.5	11.1	7.0	50.9	120,877	135,543	12.1	2.8	1,896	2,226	4,165	49,327	2.7	68.5	12.2	26.5
Gregg	11.9	9.4	6.3	51.0	121,730	124,239	2.1	0.0	2,051	1,952	-164	46,174	2.6	66.3	15.6	27.3
Grimes	13.7	11.5	7.0	45.3	26,604	29,268	10.0	3.5	363	412	1,080	9,206	2.7	73.8	14.7	21.7

1. No spouse present.

STATE County	Persons in group quarters, 2021	Daytime Population, 2016–2020		Births, 2021		Deaths, 2021		Persons under 65 with no health insurance, 2019		Medicare, 2021			COVID-19 Deaths, 2020	
		Number	Employment/ residence ratio	Total	Rate[1]	Number	Rate[1]	Number	Percent	Total beneficiaries	Enrolled in Original Medicare	Enrolled in Medicare Advantage	Number	Rate[1]
	32	33	34	35	36	37	38	39	40	41	42	43	44	45
TEXAS—Cont'd														
Caldwell	3,401	34,382	0.6	587	12.7	476	10.3	9,102	25.7	7,696	4,700	2,996	53	1.2
Calhoun	127	25,970	1.5	256	12.9	247	12.4	3,480	20.3	4,248	3,132	1,116	12	0.6
Callahan	48	10,789	0.5	131	9.4	214	15.4	2,016	18.4	3,355	2,274	1,081	28	2.0
Cameron	3,123	416,524	1.0	5,859	13.9	3,462	8.2	109,621	30.8	65,439	29,523	35,917	1,136	2.7
Camp	29	10,900	0.6	144	11.5	183	14.6	2,279	21.8	2,802	1,784	1,018	25	2.0
Carson	14	6,062	1.0	44	7.6	70	12.1	721	15.4	1,218	852	365	15	2.6
Cass	210	27,250	0.8	294	10.3	526	18.5	3,849	16.8	8,078	5,244	2,835	64	2.3
Castro	26	7,612	1.0	96	13.1	61	8.3	1,816	29.3	1,218	897	321	24	3.3
Chambers	202	38,565	0.8	626	13.1	344	7.2	6,126	15.9	6,436	4,013	2,423	32	0.7
Cherokee	2,421	48,325	0.8	665	13.1	652	12.8	9,042	22.4	10,737	6,358	4,379	102	2.0
Childress	1,528	7,357	1.1	63	9.4	73	10.9	1,027	23.1	1,320	891	429	13	2.0
Clay	42	7,411	0.4	84	8.2	188	18.3	1,498	18.8	2,658	2,004	654	15	1.5
Cochran	36	2,486	0.7	39	15.4	14	5.5	663	28.5	559	320	239	11	4.3
Coke	25	2,831	0.7	39	11.8	57	17.2	470	19.3	943	656	287	13	4.0
Coleman	5	7,256	0.7	63	8.2	163	21.2	1,541	25.6	2,519	1,942	576	17	2.2
Collin	3,648	987,222	1.0	11,297	10.4	6,467	5.9	114,952	12.5	124,503	81,936	42,567	483	0.5
Collingsworth	23	2,837	0.9	30	11.4	35	13.3	751	32.3	642	538	104	D	D
Colorado	187	20,745	0.9	236	11.5	307	14.9	4,092	24.8	5,335	3,879	1,456	19	0.9
Comal	941	148,207	1.0	1,668	9.9	1,617	9.6	19,100	15.0	35,261	23,017	12,244	150	0.9
Comanche	96	12,972	0.9	140	10.2	224	16.4	2,462	24.1	3,589	2,618	971	37	2.7
Concho	40	3,064	1.1	19	5.7	50	15.0	442	21.9	729	482	247	D	D
Cooke	563	37,456	0.9	490	11.7	518	12.3	7,232	22.0	8,410	5,743	2,667	43	1.0
Coryell	13,691	65,015	0.7	927	11.1	580	6.9	8,941	16.0	10,736	7,179	3,557	44	0.5
Cottle	0	1,601	1.0	9	6.5	13	9.4	226	21.6	414	283	131	D	D
Crane	66	4,692	1.0	85	18.2	31	6.6	850	20.4	676	442	234	D	D
Crockett	9	3,277	0.9	48	15.5	34	11.0	593	20.9	727	527	200	11	3.5
Crosby	33	4,869	0.7	59	11.6	66	12.9	983	21.5	1,275	737	538	24	4.7
Culberson	12	2,433	1.3	25	11.4	27	12.3	405	24.3	551	398	153	D	D
Dallam	19	8,134	1.3	158	22.1	49	6.9	2,143	33.8	962	721	240	15	2.1
Dallas	29,740	2,940,958	1.3	35,991	13.9	20,305	7.8	576,926	25.1	324,978	185,210	139,769	2,481	1.0
Dawson	1,439	12,939	1.0	165	13.3	136	10.9	2,193	23.2	2,301	1,587	715	57	4.6
Deaf Smith	325	18,856	1.0	302	16.4	188	10.2	4,144	26.2	2,756	1,931	825	61	3.3
Delta	28	4,069	0.4	66	12.4	58	10.9	778	18.6	1,379	951	428	D	D
Denton	11,299	717,827	0.7	9,905	10.7	5,773	6.2	105,507	13.4	103,733	66,172	37,561	436	0.5
DeWitt	1,656	20,134	1.0	227	11.4	280	14.1	2,921	20.1	4,536	3,273	1,263	54	2.7
Dickens	222	2,139	1.0	11	6.3	31	17.7	299	22.0	541	386	155	D	D
Dimmit	29	12,968	1.8	121	14.2	101	11.9	1,676	20.5	1,952	1,056	897	13	1.5
Donley	217	3,004	0.8	33	10.1	51	15.6	476	21.3	891	646	245	D	D
Duval	464	10,371	0.8	155	15.8	149	15.2	1,857	21.9	2,376	1,294	1,082	26	2.7
Eastland	638	18,102	1.0	206	11.6	328	18.4	3,274	24.1	4,627	3,171	1,456	18	1.0
Ector	2,234	162,327	1.0	3,059	18.7	1,467	9.0	32,601	22.0	19,620	12,792	6,829	289	1.7
Edwards	1	1,964	1.0	19	13.3	18	12.6	350	25.8	539	396	143	D	D
Ellis	1,353	156,173	0.7	2,182	11.0	1,735	8.7	30,187	18.9	29,393	17,970	11,422	189	1.0
El Paso	16,799	835,333	1.0	10,986	12.7	6,772	7.8	173,169	24.3	133,285	48,379	84,906	2,173	2.5
Erath	3,361	40,876	0.9	454	10.5	422	9.8	7,823	23.7	6,923	4,881	2,042	43	1.0
Falls	1,792	15,649	0.7	200	11.7	211	12.3	2,573	21.4	3,672	2,029	1,643	24	1.4
Fannin	2,874	31,237	0.7	346	9.6	499	13.8	5,675	21.5	7,780	5,391	2,389	69	1.9
Fayette	284	26,272	1.1	226	9.2	350	14.2	4,008	21.6	7,061	5,276	1,786	40	1.6
Fisher	16	3,278	0.7	30	8.1	47	12.7	555	19.5	966	692	274	13	3.5
Floyd	17	5,276	0.8	70	13.0	68	12.7	1,191	25.9	1,244	750	493	30	5.6
Foard	25	1,162	0.9	17	15.7	16	14.8	191	22.9	344	269	76	D	D
Fort Bend	4,600	642,540	0.6	8,725	10.3	4,924	5.8	107,300	15.0	100,565	55,853	44,711	461	0.6
Franklin	26	10,125	0.9	101	9.7	147	14.1	1,434	17.3	2,388	1,605	783	15	1.4
Freestone	1,473	18,381	0.8	206	10.5	267	13.6	2,962	20.8	4,406	2,883	1,523	34	1.7
Frio	2,919	20,682	1.1	220	12.0	172	9.3	3,265	22.8	2,783	1,518	1,265	22	1.2
Gaines	29	20,726	1.0	447	20.5	144	6.6	6,949	35.8	2,025	1,460	565	33	1.5
Galveston	4,699	302,865	0.8	3,814	10.8	3,631	10.3	49,934	17.4	57,939	34,461	23,478	239	0.7
Garza	1,643	5,729	0.8	50	8.6	39	6.7	872	23.6	861	539	321	16	2.8
Gillespie	186	27,508	1.1	252	9.3	417	15.4	4,544	24.2	8,724	6,782	1,942	27	1.0
Glasscock	0	1,958	1.8	19	16.8	10	8.8	230	19.1	192	158	34	D	D
Goliad	40	6,397	0.6	80	11.3	78	11.0	982	17.0	1,765	1,202	563	D	D
Gonzales	169	20,276	0.9	254	12.9	240	12.2	4,266	25.2	4,072	2,794	1,278	29	1.5
Gray	1,829	21,849	1.0	258	12.2	292	13.8	3,922	23.9	4,091	3,108	983	43	2.0
Grayson	1,987	128,992	0.9	1,500	10.9	1,806	13.1	24,027	21.8	29,343	19,373	9,970	208	1.5
Gregg	3,761	143,149	1.4	1,667	13.4	1,551	12.5	22,634	22.4	24,746	15,437	9,309	187	1.5
Grimes	2,817	26,287	0.8	291	9.7	327	11.0	4,771	22.6	6,029	3,767	2,261	53	1.8

1. Per 1,000 estimated resident population.

STATE County	COVID-19 Vaccinations, 2021–2022		Education						Money income, 2016–2020				Income and poverty, 2020			
			School enrollment and attainment, 2016–2020				Local government expenditures,[3] 2018–2019			Households				Percent below poverty level		
			Enrollment[1]		Attainment[2] (percent)						Percent					
	Number	Percent[5]	Total	Percent private	High school graduate or less	Bachelor's degree or more	Total current spending (mil dol)	Current spending per student (dollars)	Per capita income[4]	Median income (dollars)	with income of less than $50,000	with income of $200,000 or more	Median household income (dollars)	All persons	Children under 18 years	Children 5 to 17 years in families
	46	47	48	49	50	51	52	53	54	55	56	57	58	59	60	61
TEXAS—Cont'd																
Caldwell	24,888	57.0	10,130	8.2	58.1	14.8	69.5	8,979	25,760	59,846	41.9	3.2	66,128	12.7	18.6	18.8
Calhoun	12,230	57.4	4,700	7.2	50.0	17.5	39.4	10,237	28,653	57,170	45.0	3.4	58,470	12.4	21.4	20.5
Callahan	5,874	42.1	2,914	7.1	46.2	22.4	26.1	10,378	26,546	51,955	48.1	2.4	54,862	12.2	19.0	19.5
Cameron	335,922	79.4	123,451	4.1	57.6	18.2	1,002.3	10,558	18,247	41,200	57.0	2.3	44,440	24.4	34.6	34.1
Camp	5,322	40.6	3,139	16.5	45.7	21.9	30.9	13,103	24,038	49,539	50.4	3.1	43,130	16.7	24.8	23.5
Carson	2,201	37.1	1,178	5.3	35.7	27.9	13.8	11,344	35,045	74,246	31.0	5.1	66,597	8.3	10.7	9.5
Cass	10,606	35.3	6,092	6.2	55.8	18.3	56.6	10,240	27,161	47,539	52.7	2.7	50,595	17.7	25.6	23.8
Castro	3,370	44.8	2,162	3.6	58.9	16.4	21.5	12,688	23,784	49,900	50.2	3.1	55,139	15.3	20.4	19.1
Chambers	21,107	48.1	11,598	6.9	36.8	22.5	100.4	11,715	37,276	95,989	33.0	12.6	89,991	9.3	11.0	11.1
Cherokee	20,864	39.6	12,985	8.1	50.6	17.4	105.3	9,559	23,888	50,199	49.9	2.4	45,894	16.7	24.4	23.5
Childress	3,468	47.5	914	0.0	53.5	18.8	11.0	10,038	23,373	43,564	54.7	2.0	45,473	21.4	24.1	22.0
Clay	4,890	46.7	2,159	7.7	43.9	23.6	19.9	12,055	31,217	63,125	41.4	5.1	62,763	11.1	14.6	13.9
Cochran	1,502	52.6	617	3.6	64.4	8.2	10.4	14,704	21,123	41,000	59.6	0.8	44,584	19.2	29.4	28.3
Coke	1,589	46.9	637	7.2	50.1	22.2	6.9	13,064	27,033	45,072	53.8	4.9	51,050	11.4	18.0	17.4
Coleman	3,040	37.2	1,501	9.4	49.6	16.9	14.9	11,627	29,003	46,948	52.7	4.2	43,623	16.0	28.1	26.3
Collin	696,793	67.3	283,919	12.8	20.6	53.2	2,010.6	9,327	46,240	100,541	22.4	16.3	101,560	6.2	6.7	5.8
Collingsworth	973	33.3	730	10.5	46.5	22.3	6.7	11,374	26,472	41,202	54.8	3.7	47,885	16.9	25.5	22.3
Colorado	11,400	53.0	4,844	15.8	53.8	19.1	37.5	10,393	28,868	52,663	46.6	3.9	52,726	12.7	18.4	19.6
Comal	97,300	62.3	33,226	16.3	31.8	37.9	279.5	8,455	39,942	80,781	30.4	12.3	79,290	7.5	9.4	8.4
Comanche	6,444	47.3	2,787	8.3	47.0	20.1	23.6	10,076	27,419	54,889	45.0	2.8	47,282	15.9	24.0	22.3
Concho	1,417	52.0	573	0.2	61.3	13.2	5.9	12,742	22,167	53,333	47.7	3.5	47,412	13.5	20.9	20.4
Cooke	15,658	38.0	9,264	10.0	43.4	21.8	68.1	9,914	32,078	62,733	41.0	6.4	66,323	11.3	16.1	15.7
Coryell	46,482	61.2	18,980	7.4	39.0	16.9	104.5	9,148	22,477	54,712	45.4	1.9	58,398	12.7	16.8	16.8
Cottle	454	32.5	462	13.9	46.1	18.9	2.6	12,848	23,798	40,250	59.3	5.4	44,430	17.9	31.7	28.9
Crane	1,790	37.3	1,373	5.7	59.8	13.3	14.0	12,136	26,401	54,596	41.3	4.1	67,547	9.0	12.9	12.5
Crockett	1,654	47.7	656	0.0	68.8	9.7	9.4	12,126	23,655	46,695	51.4	0.0	54,458	12.4	17.7	16.1
Crosby	2,601	45.3	1,288	8.5	56.6	14.9	16.6	14,312	24,165	42,470	56.9	3.5	42,804	19.8	30.3	28.0
Culberson	1,131	52.1	291	12.0	66.9	16.5	5.9	15,569	16,353	34,853	59.0	0.0	47,479	18.6	29.4	29.9
Dallam	3,267	44.8	1,664	17.0	60.4	17.0	18.1	9,437	29,031	58,956	40.4	3.4	55,253	11.1	16.0	15.3
Dallas	1,593,890	60.5	690,002	12.5	42.2	32.5	4,999.8	9,613	33,604	61,870	40.2	8.0	65,770	13.7	20.1	19.0
Dawson	4,356	34.2	3,547	9.0	62.1	14.5	29.8	11,886	21,109	40,469	58.9	3.6	47,233	18.7	24.4	24.1
Deaf Smith	8,063	43.5	5,350	5.8	65.1	12.0	40.3	9,475	21,588	49,790	50.2	2.0	51,412	15.5	22.6	22.0
Delta	1,909	35.8	1,192	13.8	46.5	21.6	8.1	10,000	28,197	49,868	50.0	4.7	50,456	14.3	21.5	21.5
Denton	546,437	61.6	242,400	12.7	24.8	45.8	1,411.6	9,310	42,498	90,354	25.3	13.8	90,880	6.9	7.6	6.6
DeWitt	9,167	45.5	4,236	7.8	57.2	12.2	31.9	10,992	27,359	53,815	48.3	4.2	53,899	20.5	27.6	23.7
Dickens	760	34.4	395	7.6	53.2	18.6	5.3	15,469	25,750	41,141	57.4	2.7	42,034	18.9	27.7	26.1
Dimmit	7,360	72.7	3,203	4.6	62.8	14.8	25.3	11,420	16,248	25,996	61.2	0.6	42,788	25.5	34.4	31.6
Donley	1,125	34.3	879	3.5	40.0	18.1	7.0	12,295	26,425	51,875	48.0	1.9	57,526	16.3	24.8	23.5
Duval	6,985	62.6	3,057	1.5	59.9	9.2	32.2	12,160	19,501	45,349	54.1	1.2	40,601	20.0	32.1	31.8
Eastland	6,949	37.8	4,514	7.4	45.8	19.2	29.9	10,563	26,018	41,559	57.1	4.2	50,317	17.0	23.2	23.2
Ector	71,459	43.0	44,953	6.9	53.6	16.6	293.3	8,354	29,510	63,096	39.6	4.7	62,669	13.6	17.9	17.0
Edwards	1,634	84.6	476	0.0	51.9	18.2	7.1	12,073	20,655	40,643	61.4	5.0	45,330	19.1	31.8	30.6
Ellis	100,196	54.2	48,560	11.3	40.8	25.3	388.0	9,212	33,629	79,834	28.5	7.8	79,849	7.9	11.1	10.4
El Paso	681,653	81.2	254,244	7.4	44.2	24.0	1,797.0	10,186	22,490	48,292	51.3	2.9	48,522	17.6	22.7	22.6
Erath	16,291	38.2	14,169	8.2	38.7	33.0	58.4	9,619	28,166	55,383	45.1	4.1	61,453	12.6	15.5	15.5
Falls	8,306	48.0	3,420	8.7	57.5	12.4	27.9	12,448	23,131	36,854	59.6	2.2	44,590	20.0	25.2	24.9
Fannin	15,901	44.8	7,441	11.2	50.5	17.9	60.0	10,550	28,882	57,898	43.1	5.4	59,746	15.4	17.5	16.1
Fayette	12,707	50.1	4,618	10.3	50.4	22.3	45.1	10,831	30,236	62,872	42.0	5.6	63,713	9.4	14.4	13.8
Fisher	1,398	36.5	711	8.3	46.3	20.3	6.9	12,468	30,304	52,683	46.5	2.6	52,828	13.3	17.6	16.2
Floyd	2,631	46.1	1,289	11.2	54.5	15.7	16.7	14,088	24,509	52,714	45.9	1.6	44,256	17.7	29.5	27.7
Foard	506	43.8	230	0.0	47.6	12.8	3.1	14,967	27,668	39,306	59.7	4.7	40,955	16.8	29.9	29.0
Fort Bend	582,294	71.7	236,125	13.1	27.1	46.5	1,887.9	9,456	40,607	100,189	22.7	16.0	97,210	7.4	9.4	8.7
Franklin	3,991	37.2	2,472	6.8	34.4	30.3	15.6	9,610	31,988	59,632	41.7	7.1	58,927	12.9	20.4	18.6
Freestone	7,693	39.0	4,099	6.0	50.0	14.8	39.2	10,789	25,500	52,232	48.5	4.2	54,502	13.3	16.7	15.6
Frio	13,805	68.0	4,916	9.7	68.8	8.2	34.5	11,000	20,036	48,708	51.3	2.1	47,007	22.3	28.8	27.0
Gaines	4,745	22.1	5,386	26.7	70.6	10.4	46.8	12,741	22,978	62,994	40.6	5.9	63,528	11.1	19.8	19.4
Galveston	206,014	60.2	88,393	11.4	35.0	32.1	795.6	9,574	37,530	74,633	35.1	10.6	78,465	9.9	14.1	13.0
Garza	3,288	52.8	937	4.8	66.4	12.3	12.1	12,456	17,723	58,938	47.9	1.2	50,934	20.6	23.4	22.2
Gillespie	14,555	53.9	4,940	18.9	40.3	34.1	38.4	10,308	34,689	61,445	41.6	5.9	64,365	9.2	15.2	13.6
Glasscock	638	45.3	342	7.3	53.5	25.5	7.1	23,252	30,062	74,375	40.0	10.3	85,001	7.3	9.9	9.5
Goliad	3,277	42.8	1,621	8.3	42.9	15.9	14.5	10,933	30,038	50,000	50.0	7.3	54,970	13.2	20.8	20.2
Gonzales	10,287	49.4	4,767	5.8	67.3	12.4	43.5	10,196	28,313	58,210	44.1	5.0	55,363	14.3	22.3	21.7
Gray	10,580	48.3	5,020	8.4	52.4	15.1	36.5	9,136	27,760	54,679	45.8	3.9	54,141	14.2	18.0	16.2
Grayson	61,476	45.1	31,803	11.6	40.3	20.6	235.2	9,938	29,157	58,296	42.4	4.1	59,554	13.6	20.8	18.4
Gregg	55,945	45.1	30,727	12.4	43.4	21.2	250.9	10,385	27,809	52,027	47.8	4.0	51,394	18.1	26.3	23.6
Grimes	15,440	53.5	6,309	7.4	52.9	18.3	45.9	9,917	26,734	56,086	43.9	4.8	57,795	15.3	20.6	19.9

1. All persons 3 years old and over enrolled in nursery school through college. 2. Persons 25 years old and over. 3. Elementary and secondary education expenditures. 4. Based on population estimated by the American Community Survey, 2016–2020. 5. CDC percent based on 2019 population estimate.

STATE County	Personal income, 2020										Earnings, 2020		
			Per capita[1]			Supplements to wages and salaries, employer contributions (mil dol)						Contributions for government social insurance (mil dol)	
	Total (mil dol)	Percent change 2019–2020	Dollars	Rank	Wages and salaries (mil dol)	Pension and insurance	Government social insurance	Proprietors' income (mil dol)	Dividends, interest, and rent (mil dol)	Personal transfer reecipts (mil dol)	Total (mil dol)	From employee and self-employed	From employer
	62	63	64	65	66	67	68	69	70	71	72	73	74
TEXAS—Cont'd													
Caldwell	1,703	7.9	38,734	2,599	411	74	29	141	255	503	656	44	29
Calhoun	1,096	-3.7	52,180	922	938	160	63	194	147	283	1,357	72	63
Callahan	646	7.2	45,798	1,681	122	21	8	47	94	194	198	15	8
Cameron	14,291	12.0	33,690	2,994	5,405	1,116	392	1,099	1,727	5,421	8,011	478	392
Camp	526	7.0	40,272	2,422	153	31	11	35	78	178	230	16	11
Carson	281	-3.7	48,021	1,392	457	46	31	16	40	65	550	31	31
Cass	1,233	7.8	41,275	2,291	323	68	22	82	161	503	495	36	22
Castro	530	6.6	71,612	145	100	20	8	237	54	87	366	8	8
Chambers	2,721	8.6	59,687	440	1,185	182	80	144	323	443	1,592	88	80
Cherokee	2,019	8.1	38,190	2,666	602	129	42	123	311	705	896	60	42
Childress	243	8.0	34,028	2,977	111	25	7	9	37	86	151	9	7
Clay	507	7.3	48,038	1,386	67	15	5	33	76	149	120	8	5
Cochran	130	15.6	44,903	1,808	34	7	2	21	18	40	64	3	2
Coke	152	7.5	45,856	1,675	38	7	2	5	25	55	52	4	2
Coleman	382	7.2	47,128	1,496	78	18	5	28	77	152	129	10	5
Collin	76,381	6.3	71,246	150	34,457	3,912	2,221	6,554	12,073	7,817	47,143	2,558	2,221
Collingsworth	129	4.8	44,903	1,808	38	8	3	9	21	45	59	4	3
Colorado	1,118	7.6	51,732	960	340	58	24	92	255	334	514	33	24
Comal	10,382	8.6	62,994	318	3,110	427	215	793	1,957	1,959	4,545	287	215
Comanche	659	11.3	47,959	1,398	153	32	11	103	100	211	299	17	11
Concho	117	17.3	41,219	2,303	45	8	3	15	20	47	72	4	3
Cooke	2,267	4.2	54,759	718	725	127	49	240	432	526	1,142	66	49
Coryell	2,933	7.8	38,222	2,662	759	144	46	110	529	845	1,060	66	46
Cottle	93	11.1	68,268	192	22	4	2	11	30	24	39	2	2
Crane	237	-6.2	49,749	1,167	68	13	4	25	21	52	112	6	4
Crockett	163	3.2	46,364	1,596	65	13	4	15	35	44	98	5	4
Crosby	229	2.0	41,146	2,316	54	11	4	19	31	94	88	6	4
Culberson	149	15.2	69,350	173	86	15	6	1	17	35	108	6	6
Dallam	474	3.9	65,132	259	196	28	15	176	44	73	415	17	15
Dallas	172,390	2.9	65,401	254	135,191	15,625	8,890	30,445	36,277	25,393	190,151	9,979	8,890
Dawson	553	6.0	42,595	2,117	179	36	12	100	87	167	327	15	12
Deaf Smith	1,004	5.7	54,950	704	345	58	24	338	101	207	764	27	24
Delta	233	8.7	43,628	1,990	32	9	2	28	25	84	71	5	2
Denton	58,177	8.1	63,283	310	15,435	2,128	1,050	4,079	8,083	6,992	22,692	1,266	1,050
DeWitt	1,228	-3.4	60,890	387	353	66	23	49	490	306	490	30	23
Dickens	83	8.6	38,730	2,602	22	5	2	4	17	33	33	2	2
Dimmit	445	5.0	44,874	1,813	293	49	21	72	79	152	435	24	21
Donley	150	5.0	45,336	1,747	33	8	2	11	30	50	55	4	2
Duval	469	9.1	42,410	2,143	134	32	9	9	52	217	183	13	9
Eastland	1,203	-1.2	65,416	253	321	63	22	189	428	302	595	36	22
Ector	8,366	-3.3	49,887	1,153	4,486	587	293	1,036	997	1,672	6,402	343	293
Edwards	106	17.0	55,329	681	34	6	2	8	28	30	50	3	2
Ellis	9,460	9.2	49,333	1,215	2,727	435	188	556	1,208	1,870	3,906	239	188
El Paso	35,181	8.3	41,818	2,228	15,636	3,318	1,150	2,886	5,008	9,737	22,990	1,254	1,150
Erath	1,898	6.6	43,900	1,964	663	128	45	296	361	462	1,132	57	45
Falls	689	10.8	39,865	2,471	148	37	10	58	101	249	253	15	10
Fannin	1,529	6.8	42,562	2,119	369	82	26	84	203	499	561	39	26
Fayette	1,481	3.8	57,962	513	410	69	28	82	424	390	589	41	28
Fisher	186	6.2	49,100	1,245	41	9	3	14	31	62	66	4	3
Floyd	242	-3.0	42,627	2,112	63	15	5	29	38	87	113	6	5
Foard	60	13.7	52,630	881	13	3	1	7	10	23	24	1	1
Fort Bend	51,886	4.6	61,791	356	11,104	1,528	750	4,704	8,003	6,434	18,086	998	750
Franklin	484	7.7	44,725	1,842	165	21	13	64	79	146	264	16	13
Freestone	803	4.9	40,407	2,401	221	43	17	44	138	259	324	23	17
Frio	681	8.1	33,407	3,012	379	64	27	68	118	214	538	29	27
Gaines	1,052	6.3	47,826	1,414	367	61	25	353	108	173	805	33	25
Galveston	19,995	3.4	57,941	517	6,282	1,189	408	1,298	3,503	4,028	9,177	514	408
Garza	194	0.3	31,223	3,072	76	13	5	14	43	62	108	7	5
Gillespie	1,857	3.1	68,885	180	493	77	35	150	749	406	755	52	35
Glasscock	126	-6.6	87,334	50	34	6	2	23	52	10	66	3	2
Goliad	378	3.7	49,513	1,195	62	14	4	14	87	105	94	7	4
Gonzales	990	2.9	47,272	1,478	330	60	23	139	245	266	552	29	23
Gray	977	1.4	45,091	1,782	380	68	26	87	215	266	561	32	26
Grayson	6,507	7.2	47,045	1,509	2,378	383	166	361	976	1,850	3,288	214	166
Gregg	6,106	3.7	49,152	1,237	3,710	539	265	494	1,071	1,753	5,007	303	265
Grimes	1,156	6.6	39,033	2,562	392	71	26	72	201	355	561	37	26

1. Based on the resident population estimated as of July 1 of the year shown.

STATE County	Earnings, 2020 (cont.)									Social Security beneficiaries, December 2020		Supple-mental Security Income recipients, 2020	Housing units, 2021	
	Percent by selected industries													
	Farm	Mining, quarrying, and extractions	Construction	Manu-facturing	Information; professional, scientific, technical services	Retail trade	Finance, insurance, real estate, and leasing	Health care and social assistance	Govern-ment	Number	Rate[1]		Total	Percent change, 2010–2021
	75	76	77	78	79	80	81	82	83	84	85	86	87	88
TEXAS—Cont'd														
Caldwell	-0.6	2.3	15.0	4.9	D	9.4	5.9	12.7	18.3	8,080	173	1,035	16,956	3.0
Calhoun	0.4	D	15.5	49.4	7.9	4.0	2.5	1.5	6.8	4,515	229	448	10,723	1.5
Callahan	0.3	2.6	18.6	5.2	5.4	16.2	7.7	4.9	19.9	3,550	252	301	6,530	0.6
Cameron	0.7	0.1	4.2	5.4	3.5	8.2	5.5	21.0	26.4	69,450	164	21,202	157,394	1.3
Camp	2.4	0.2	14.9	D	D	5.9	5.8	D	15.2	3,060	243	462	5,806	0.4
Carson	1.5	D	D	D	D	1.2	D	D	4.4	1,235	215	52	2,778	0.1
Cass	0.9	1.1	7.8	23.4	3.6	5.9	3.8	D	20.2	8,530	299	1,130	13,953	0.5
Castro	64.4	D	0.6	2.1	0.7	1.9	D	0.6	10.4	1,285	174	132	3,016	0.0
Chambers	1.4	0.9	21.3	25.9	D	3.2	2.5	4.0	11.7	7,060	144	498	18,108	5.7
Cherokee	5.3	0.7	7.0	14.2	D	6.1	6.0	D	27.3	11,285	221	1,295	20,938	0.4
Childress	0.2	D	D	D	9.8	8.1	4.5	D	44.3	1,365	203	147	2,819	-0.1
Clay	6.5	3.0	7.8	3.5	D	8.2	D	7.7	26.0	2,760	269	164	5,152	0.4
Cochran	32.0	D	D	0.4	1.4	2.7	2.4	1.8	27.2	575	229	94	1,241	-0.1
Coke	-1.0	D	5.3	D	D	6.5	D	1.3	30.4	980	295	64	2,147	0.7
Coleman	0.1	3.6	13.4	5.5	5.7	6.9	7.2	D	23.9	2,570	332	250	4,884	0.2
Collin	0.0	2.8	5.9	8.0	20.6	5.3	17.3	8.9	8.7	122,095	110	9,114	419,966	3.3
Collingsworth	6.7	D	5.1	2.5	4.4	5.2	D	19.4	20.8	625	239	61	1,480	-0.1
Colorado	0.9	3.6	13.6	15.8	3.9	8.7	6.3	10.2	13.3	5,585	271	435	10,052	0.5
Comal	-0.1	1.8	15.8	5.4	8.1	9.7	8.3	9.9	10.9	36,790	210	1,586	74,277	5.2
Comanche	21.6	D	4.3	3.4	D	9.5	4.7	D	14.5	3,695	268	320	6,934	0.3
Concho	16.0	D	D	D	D	2.6	4.8	10.0	20.5	760	227	59	1,411	0.2
Cooke	-0.6	7.3	5.3	24.1	4.5	6.9	13.7	D	16.5	8,600	204	570	17,822	0.5
Coryell	0.0	D	9.1	2.7	13.6	6.9	7.4	4.4	36.1	11,900	141	1,348	29,237	1.6
Cottle	25.1	0.4	12.0	2.6	D	4.2	D	D	15.9	425	308	52	889	-0.1
Crane	1.4	21.6	D	D	1.9	4.9	9.5	4.1	24.9	720	154	71	1,828	0.2
Crockett	6.7	24.0	5.1	2.0	D	4.9	3.9	D	22.9	740	241	54	1,598	0.3
Crosby	18.0	D	D	D	D	7.2	D	6.5	24.8	1,325	259	152	2,658	0.2
Culberson	0.4	7.1	D	D	D	10.4	D	D	23.7	520	237	107	1,122	4.7
Dallam	27.3	0.0	8.6	13.3	3.4	3.7	9.7	D	4.3	960	134	80	3,046	0.2
Dallas	0.0	5.0	6.2	6.6	18.2	4.6	13.6	8.7	8.7	327,995	127	60,033	1,049,372	0.7
Dawson	22.6	14.3	2.6	2.0	2.8	7.7	4.9	3.5	23.4	2,345	189	336	4,854	-0.1
Deaf Smith	40.9	0.0	3.0	15.9	1.6	5.7	2.5	1.7	10.2	2,785	152	352	6,977	0.0
Delta	26.5	0.3	D	D	D	1.1	3.1	16.2	24.0	1,410	261	182	2,434	0.5
Denton	0.0	0.3	10.1	7.2	12.3	6.9	9.8	8.9	13.5	104,050	110	7,269	362,742	3.4
DeWitt	-2.8	11.3	8.0	10.5	4.0	6.2	8.6	4.5	27.4	4,665	234	447	9,202	0.2
Dickens	3.6	D	4.6	1.1	D	D	4.4	1.0	23.8	565	325	54	1,166	0.1
Dimmit	0.5	25.2	D	D	D	3.7	4.7	D	22.3	2,100	248	510	3,998	0.4
Donley	12.8	0.9	D	D	D	7.3	D	2.6	37.8	950	291	76	1,947	0.2
Duval	-4.5	17.7	D	D	D	3.4	1.9	12.1	37.8	2,635	270	590	4,411	0.3
Eastland	-1.2	43.4	7.2	6.7	2.4	5.2	-1.3	D	15.0	4,995	280	537	9,377	0.3
Ector	0.0	20.0	13.0	6.5	4.1	6.8	5.0	5.2	12.1	20,895	130	3,088	67,692	1.8
Edwards	3.5	D	D	D	D	5.4	8.3	D	19.5	585	407	64	974	0.9
Ellis	-0.4	0.3	13.2	19.9	6.7	7.3	5.1	7.4	14.4	30,815	152	3,004	71,981	4.2
El Paso	0.0	0.0	7.1	5.1	4.7	6.8	5.2	10.3	34.1	139,060	160	28,082	320,965	0.7
Erath	11.7	1.7	10.1	10.1	D	8.0	6.3	7.4	19.4	7,115	164	566	18,515	0.5
Falls	7.4	D	8.1	2.8	5.4	8.4	D	D	36.0	3,655	211	662	7,444	0.3
Fannin	0.3	1.6	11.9	9.7	D	6.6	4.6	D	35.1	8,155	223	801	14,721	0.5
Fayette	-1.8	4.2	9.5	8.3	5.1	10.6	9.0	D	19.0	7,080	287	400	13,204	0.6
Fisher	7.5	1.2	D	D	3.8	3.6	D	3.9	28.3	970	262	97	2,110	0.0
Floyd	19.0	D	2.5	2.3	D	4.0	D	2.8	26.6	1,245	233	144	2,597	-0.2
Foard	27.7	0.5	D	D	D	4.2	D	D	22.6	315	292	30	572	0.2
Fort Bend	0.1	4.6	10.8	15.0	10.3	8.2	5.5	10.1	11.3	99,610	116	11,672	294,867	5.1
Franklin	10.6	D	5.4	2.2	D	3.9	3.8	23.3	9.8	2,485	237	161	5,107	0.3
Freestone	1.4	15.3	5.8	3.2	D	7.2	4.1	D	24.6	4,495	227	382	9,086	0.5
Frio	7.1	15.4	4.4	2.1	D	5.2	3.9	D	18.2	2,965	161	650	6,366	0.3
Gaines	15.2	12.5	23.1	2.8	2.4	3.9	3.2	1.2	11.2	2,130	97	272	7,675	0.4
Galveston	0.0	1.2	9.9	11.4	6.2	6.7	7.7	6.2	28.0	60,830	171	6,346	159,824	2.0
Garza	-2.7	30.3	D	D	D	3.9	1.7	4.4	18.7	865	148	104	2,132	0.3
Gillespie	-1.2	0.3	14.9	8.0	7.5	8.7	12.1	14.7	10.4	8,585	315	255	14,247	0.7
Glasscock	-9.8	23.2	D	D	D	8.3	6.4	1.3	13.0	210	183	D	526	0.2
Goliad	-7.2	11.2	15.4	1.5	D	4.1	6.0	D	27.1	1,775	248	173	3,517	0.3
Gonzales	14.7	8.6	6.3	12.1	3.8	5.7	3.6	D	17.1	4,215	215	472	8,970	0.5
Gray	5.8	8.4	5.3	21.7	D	6.5	4.2	8.3	15.6	4,335	206	386	9,975	-0.2
Grayson	-0.2	0.3	10.7	13.3	4.2	8.1	6.0	21.7	14.2	30,125	216	2,879	60,031	2.1
Gregg	-0.1	6.6	9.6	10.9	D	7.8	7.8	14.9	9.7	26,330	212	4,442	53,512	0.5
Grimes	-0.6	1.5	11.5	17.5	5.9	4.4	6.2	D	21.1	6,485	214	672	12,197	1.1

1. Per 1,000 resident population estimated as of July 1 of the year shown.

STATE County	Housing units, 2016–2020								Civilian labor force, 2021				Civilian employment[6], 2016–2020		
		Occupied units									Unemployment			Percent	
		Owner-occupied				Renter-occupied									
				Median owner cost as a percent of income											
	Total	Percent	Median value[1]	With a mortgage	Without a mortgage[2]	Median rent[3]	Median rent as a percent of income[2]	Substandard units[4] (percent)	Total	Percent change, 2020–2021	Total	Rate[5]	Total	Management, business, science, and arts	Construction, production, and maintenance occupations
	89	90	91	92	93	94	95	96	97	98	99	100	101	102	103
TEXAS—Cont'd															
Caldwell	13,774	68.8	147,200	18.8	10.6	946	32.9	7.4	19,988	6.2	980	4.9	19,173	28.0	31.7
Calhoun	8,027	73.7	117,400	18.3	10.0	825	23.7	7.1	12,224	3.2	599	4.9	10,210	31.3	36.7
Callahan	5,372	83.4	100,000	20.3	10.9	760	21.2	1.5	6,134	3.2	284	4.6	5,982	36.4	28.1
Cameron	126,968	66.2	89,700	21.7	11.8	746	30.8	10.6	175,073	3.4	14,287	8.2	164,139	28.3	22.9
Camp	4,460	71.9	109,400	20.8	11.6	715	34.2	2.9	5,116	3.3	304	5.9	5,234	26.0	39.3
Carson	2,332	84.2	108,700	17.6	10.0	844	18.5	2.6	2,958	3.6	114	3.9	2,972	43.0	25.0
Cass	11,962	79.7	91,100	19.0	10.6	665	28.7	4.6	12,386	2.1	830	6.7	11,367	27.8	33.5
Castro	2,557	58.4	83,300	16.8	10.0	729	23.8	4.4	3,380	4.0	117	3.5	3,557	29.9	30.6
Chambers	14,266	85.8	224,400	17.2	12.5	990	30.8	4.4	20,681	2.3	1,714	8.3	19,786	41.4	29.0
Cherokee	18,540	72.0	111,600	19.4	11.2	789	27.8	6.6	20,864	-0.6	1,337	6.4	21,156	30.4	32.6
Childress	2,308	59.1	86,800	22.5	10.0	774	26.9	0.3	3,011	0.5	108	3.6	2,930	31.2	35.8
Clay	4,159	81.4	110,000	17.6	11.7	754	19.7	3.8	4,831	1.2	238	4.9	4,783	35.1	31.2
Cochran	1,026	71.9	38,000	13.9	10.0	710	24.1	8.0	1,072	-3.0	68	6.3	1,221	25.0	42.9
Coke	1,625	66.8	74,100	18.2	10.6	629	26.8	0.8	1,365	0.9	65	4.8	1,449	34.9	30.6
Coleman	3,492	75.1	83,100	20.8	13.2	714	20.0	2.0	2,937	3.3	176	6.0	3,547	31.3	33.5
Collin	353,491	64.8	337,200	20.8	11.5	1,428	26.9	2.7	599,164	4.0	25,862	4.3	525,711	54.4	11.4
Collingsworth	1,029	75.1	57,500	16.3	10.0	568	35.9	5.3	1,090	2.7	47	4.3	1,339	30.5	27.6
Colorado	7,442	83.6	131,400	23.0	10.0	727	25.1	8.4	9,907	3.2	471	4.8	9,085	33.5	30.5
Comal	54,586	74.9	293,600	20.7	10.3	1,192	28.6	2.0	79,105	3.0	3,576	4.5	68,783	43.3	19.6
Comanche	5,416	82.1	110,900	17.9	12.3	525	25.7	4.4	6,032	8.0	276	4.6	5,927	35.6	30.7
Concho	876	81.4	107,700	19.9	10.8	633	47.3	1.9	1,350	2.2	57	4.2	798	43.6	22.3
Cooke	15,530	70.0	166,700	20.1	11.8	934	25.9	4.3	19,360	1.3	976	5.0	19,544	32.0	32.0
Coryell	22,324	60.9	120,700	19.5	10.0	894	27.9	2.9	24,346	3.0	1,378	5.7	23,646	33.8	23.8
Cottle	703	62.3	44,000	16.4	10.0	372	28.2	3.1	604	7.1	28	4.6	717	31.5	21.8
Crane	1,500	88.6	89,000	17.9	10.0	829	18.8	6.1	1,626	0.8	156	9.6	2,087	20.8	41.0
Crockett	1,394	66.2	102,200	24.5	10.0	559	23.2	4.8	1,467	-4.6	99	6.7	1,802	24.3	44.8
Crosby	2,107	72.6	61,300	19.9	11.7	620	26.1	7.2	2,376	4.3	133	5.6	2,578	27.0	29.3
Culberson	668	66.2	63,700	24.8	12.4	594	20.5	6.1	1,066	-4.8	51	4.8	930	20.5	46.0
Dallam	2,344	76.6	95,000	14.4	11.0	867	19.8	5.6	3,803	2.6	100	2.6	3,589	24.0	40.7
Dallas	945,996	50.4	193,900	22.0	12.1	1,159	28.6	6.7	1,372,277	3.8	76,579	5.6	1,315,440	36.5	25.0
Dawson	4,430	70.0	80,100	24.7	14.6	689	31.7	4.7	4,598	1.3	322	7.0	4,561	27.9	31.5
Deaf Smith	6,053	65.5	91,800	20.1	10.2	766	20.9	6.0	8,749	3.8	320	3.7	8,415	23.7	44.2
Delta	2,066	80.8	107,600	18.3	10.5	625	26.4	1.1	2,443	2.8	119	4.9	2,199	39.2	26.5
Denton	300,585	65.3	297,100	20.4	10.6	1,269	28.3	2.6	528,401	3.9	23,114	4.4	469,202	48.3	15.5
DeWitt	6,823	71.8	121,900	17.6	11.3	813	32.2	3.8	9,414	3.1	456	4.8	7,380	29.0	34.6
Dickens	861	77.6	53,100	19.4	11.9	550	27.3	2.3	693	5.6	35	5.1	814	27.4	34.9
Dimmit	3,178	70.1	61,300	50.0	12.7	694	24.8	6.6	5,830	-9.3	333	5.7	3,383	20.0	21.7
Donley	1,344	72.9	70,200	20.3	10.0	691	23.9	2.0	1,448	3.1	59	4.1	1,521	34.7	28.1
Duval	3,407	69.2	61,800	21.2	10.0	685	25.2	5.4	5,463	13.8	452	8.3	4,277	22.5	31.0
Eastland	7,017	76.8	82,600	19.4	12.4	653	25.2	4.0	7,341	0.8	423	5.8	7,201	35.7	27.0
Ector	53,602	65.5	147,900	19.6	10.1	1,073	27.1	5.8	80,507	-2.0	6,691	8.3	75,343	23.8	37.4
Edwards	787	73.8	71,800	23.0	10.5	627	18.9	2.8	1,265	3.0	55	4.3	915	10.9	38.7
Ellis	59,399	74.8	214,500	20.0	10.8	1,104	28.9	3.8	98,901	4.6	4,441	4.5	89,425	35.5	27.1
El Paso	273,662	62.3	126,500	22.5	11.5	855	30.0	6.2	363,843	1.2	22,692	6.2	354,788	31.8	23.0
Erath	14,263	64.9	166,300	19.5	10.6	951	32.7	3.3	20,529	3.6	919	4.5	20,279	34.1	24.6
Falls	5,552	75.6	76,900	19.1	11.9	552	37.0	5.8	6,576	3.6	350	5.3	5,701	25.9	37.1
Fannin	12,391	74.3	139,200	19.5	11.6	859	26.2	2.7	17,165	3.5	687	4.0	14,479	32.7	29.7
Fayette	9,033	83.4	193,200	18.0	10.5	804	23.4	2.0	11,857	1.6	507	4.3	10,894	26.3	34.8
Fisher	1,676	75.4	63,900	16.9	10.0	621	26.4	1.4	1,606	1.4	68	4.2	1,894	39.6	28.2
Floyd	2,184	74.7	70,300	17.2	10.0	710	26.0	5.0	2,503	1.0	144	5.8	2,477	28.0	30.5
Foard	509	82.5	48,500	21.9	10.0	489	19.8	2.9	589	3.2	20	3.4	541	36.4	32.0
Fort Bend	248,299	77.5	277,600	21.7	11.2	1,474	29.5	3.4	407,603	1.8	24,241	5.9	379,028	51.3	14.6
Franklin	3,960	83.0	144,300	20.1	11.8	840	24.1	3.9	5,223	9.2	229	4.4	4,939	36.6	26.3
Freestone	6,736	77.3	116,800	18.8	11.0	722	31.8	3.7	6,323	0.7	458	7.2	7,160	28.1	30.6
Frio	4,673	66.8	86,000	21.4	12.3	807	29.6	3.0	9,396	-0.7	452	4.8	6,921	23.2	30.5
Gaines	5,878	72.3	141,200	19.3	10.0	659	25.2	7.5	9,748	1.1	448	4.6	8,601	25.5	42.2
Galveston	125,204	67.5	212,600	19.9	11.2	1,106	29.5	3.4	165,052	1.3	10,987	6.7	159,363	43.1	20.9
Garza	1,713	68.4	78,200	19.1	10.0	703	27.1	2.4	1,988	-0.4	100	5.0	1,765	34.1	34.3
Gillespie	10,820	71.4	311,300	23.3	11.9	993	30.7	4.5	13,939	6.0	461	3.3	12,212	34.5	23.6
Glasscock	435	65.5	303,300	16.8	10.0	920	10.0	4.4	815	2.1	24	2.9	645	40.9	45.9
Goliad	2,840	80.4	129,000	15.7	10.0	513	34.3	1.0	3,153	1.5	207	6.6	3,055	32.5	33.2
Gonzales	7,465	70.1	113,700	19.5	10.0	773	22.9	8.6	9,594	1.6	410	4.3	8,996	21.9	43.5
Gray	7,843	72.5	79,800	17.5	10.0	740	28.4	3.8	7,681	-0.3	512	6.7	9,220	26.2	34.4
Grayson	49,327	68.2	152,400	20.4	11.4	909	28.1	2.6	65,711	3.4	2,990	4.6	62,518	30.0	27.4
Gregg	46,174	59.2	144,300	20.3	11.0	872	28.6	3.0	56,193	0.4	3,630	6.5	55,502	30.5	29.4
Grimes	9,206	76.0	163,200	19.2	10.0	693	32.0	4.4	11,133	1.1	747	6.7	10,819	30.8	31.6

1. Specified owner-occupied units. 2. A value of 10.0 represents 10 percent or less; a value of 50.0 represents 50 percent or more. 3. Specified renter-occupied units. 4. Overcrowded or lacking complete plumbing facilities. 5. Percent of civilian labor force. 6. Civilian employed persons 16 years old and over.

STATE County	Private nonfarm establishments, employment and payroll, 2020									Agriculture, 2017			
		Employment						Annual payroll		Farms			Farm producers whose primary occupation is farming (percent)
											Percent with:		
	Number of establish-ments	Total	Health care and social assistance	Manufac-turing	Retail trade	Finance and insurance	Professional, scientific, and technical services	Total (mil dol)	Average per employee (dollars)	Number	Fewer than 50 acres	1000 acres or more	
	104	105	106	107	108	109	110	111	112	113	114	115	116
TEXAS—Cont'd													
Caldwell	658	6,788	1,464	619	1,251	188	126	247	36,324	1,517	47.9	2.8	37.2
Calhoun	442	9,704	759	3,315	1,032	169	655	597	61,525	290	44.1	16.6	45.7
Callahan	222	1,704	135	160	494	67	42	70	40,914	961	37.4	10.0	38.2
Cameron	6,463	113,358	39,443	4,327	17,737	4,090	3,123	3,237	28,560	1,418	74.3	6.3	34.1
Camp	205	2,745	381	222	378	109	50	120	43,709	484	45.5	1.4	42.1
Carson	132	896	38	NA	198	44	32	44	48,927	331	19.3	34.7	45.1
Cass	529	5,808	1,206	1,289	793	183	134	215	37,089	1,081	39.1	2.0	39.7
Castro	158	1,340	260	36	143	43	55	51	37,837	411	7.3	38.9	54.1
Chambers	708	16,234	638	2,828	1,484	142	455	1,042	64,184	562	55.5	7.8	33.6
Cherokee	754	11,005	2,346	2,544	1,329	300	251	406	36,907	1,587	40.3	2.0	35.4
Childress	169	1,835	364	13	417	101	43	60	32,475	285	7.7	20.0	41.6
Clay	149	830	97	74	232	42	10	28	33,986	851	20.9	18.3	39.9
Cochran	39	196	71	NA	33	13	NA	8	39,648	286	5.6	41.6	45.9
Coke	58	250	NA	NA	95	22	NA	7	26,256	449	10.9	22.9	32.6
Coleman	191	1,547	532	148	227	63	30	50	32,371	976	14.3	16.1	40.7
Collin	26,472	463,985	61,111	19,487	54,248	64,935	51,770	31,714	68,350	2,706	74.3	1.4	28.2
Collingsworth	69	466	133	22	65	28	13	18	39,646	301	4.7	28.2	39.5
Colorado	539	6,460	798	1,647	1,075	164	201	278	43,105	1,773	37.2	5.4	32.9
Comal	4,137	57,086	8,006	3,543	8,632	1,220	2,137	2,362	41,374	1,068	54.4	5.3	32.6
Comanche	257	2,275	483	145	505	111	81	88	38,600	1,427	32.6	8.8	40.8
Concho	44	663	136	NA	63	NA	NA	27	40,802	396	9.1	32.1	44.9
Cooke	927	14,547	1,197	3,370	1,935	485	296	598	41,117	2,284	49.7	4.1	35.4
Coryell	761	9,848	1,146	377	2,019	370	514	297	30,168	1,479	38.2	5.7	36.4
Cottle	25	78	NA	NA	29	4	NA	2	22,090	154	2.6	29.9	31.9
Crane	96	1,292	250	NA	141	30	16	94	72,374	30	30.0	53.3	34.7
Crockett	117	913	21	NA	187	37	10	30	32,561	219	1.4	59.4	52.3
Crosby	89	531	144	NA	111	19	16	21	38,953	343	5.2	36.2	44.6
Culberson	56	787	83	NA	190	NA	NA	48	60,860	66	15.2	63.6	48.4
Dallam	207	2,002	44	344	221	80	69	99	49,215	340	2.4	50.9	52.0
Dallas	68,180	1,563,934	184,652	104,206	130,786	105,568	144,365	102,251	65,381	775	69.5	1.2	25.9
Dawson	270	2,628	378	254	488	115	61	108	41,158	386	11.7	34.2	50.8
Deaf Smith	362	5,947	473	2,214	805	176	177	274	46,018	562	13.5	43.4	49.0
Delta	55	232	76	NA	41	10	7	6	27,767	571	45.4	4.4	36.0
Denton	16,716	238,361	30,079	16,200	32,586	13,081	12,269	11,841	49,677	3,295	80.2	2.4	29.2
DeWitt	441	5,160	1,049	314	713	260	123	217	42,062	1,768	27.3	4.8	41.9
Dickens	40	210	19	NA	39	NA	8	9	43,067	393	11.7	23.7	28.0
Dimmit	223	4,368	615	75	461	27	104	194	44,331	328	21.0	25.9	32.9
Donley	74	396	33	NA	91	42	20	10	24,775	283	8.1	25.8	39.4
Duval	150	1,748	484	NA	241	48	29	59	33,897	1,367	11.1	11.7	29.8
Eastland	467	6,109	777	651	791	171	123	282	46,172	1,198	22.5	7.4	36.5
Ector	3,817	64,827	7,536	4,196	8,973	1,428	1,621	3,129	48,264	275	68.7	14.5	28.2
Edwards	42	297	21	NA	91	NA	NA	8	27,539	380	3.7	34.5	43.8
Ellis	3,318	47,231	5,053	10,591	6,878	988	1,112	2,087	44,177	2,551	57.5	3.7	31.8
El Paso	15,084	249,006	49,478	16,783	36,186	8,004	8,885	8,374	33,628	656	88.7	3.4	36.6
Erath	1,019	12,680	1,415	2,588	1,758	311	460	481	37,940	2,402	39.5	5.8	40.4
Falls	228	1,835	262	169	507	54	94	62	33,615	1,103	36.2	8.2	39.5
Fannin	516	5,634	1,443	678	890	219	148	225	39,930	2,255	45.8	3.3	33.0
Fayette	755	7,150	1,016	1,071	1,292	290	233	282	39,435	3,166	36.9	2.1	36.7
Fisher	66	455	100	74	48	44	17	24	52,251	486	9.7	25.7	36.1
Floyd	141	838	216	37	87	55	9	33	39,700	440	8.4	35.5	39.4
Foard	26	135	51	NA	17	NA	NA	5	36,274	172	12.2	36.0	40.8
Fort Bend	15,378	187,956	30,593	13,687	30,677	6,635	13,186	8,371	44,537	1,155	52.6	5.5	35.4
Franklin	172	6,721	4,373	79	296	73	37	136	20,197	493	32.7	2.8	34.5
Freestone	344	2,836	358	240	526	115	60	102	35,983	1,459	36.5	6.1	40.9
Frio	311	5,541	825	79	685	166	101	224	40,487	663	25.5	18.4	38.0
Gaines	489	4,860	322	264	518	115	104	232	47,799	507	11.0	43.4	51.3
Galveston	6,122	90,721	15,573	5,692	14,719	4,277	4,582	3,795	41,828	633	70.8	2.4	30.0
Garza	122	1,293	178	NA	143	23	10	48	36,892	237	13.1	31.6	34.2
Gillespie	1,099	10,383	1,706	1,019	1,678	329	291	387	37,249	2,079	38.4	8.9	32.2
Glasscock	40	439	NA	NA	25	NA	NA	40	91,572	175	6.3	54.3	57.1
Goliad	137	908	109	5	142	31	27	36	39,113	1,255	32.3	5.4	34.5
Gonzales	411	4,860	711	1,056	879	193	112	195	40,053	1,612	26.9	8.7	42.4
Gray	523	5,819	814	1,025	934	165	208	249	42,857	348	23.0	26.4	31.1
Grayson	2,650	41,151	8,422	7,708	6,154	1,719	1,046	1,696	41,223	2,845	61.4	2.4	32.3
Gregg	4,022	67,160	10,731	9,410	9,194	2,129	3,103	2,942	43,807	541	65.6	2.8	28.2
Grimes	454	5,902	282	1,706	593	143	303	294	49,776	1,771	46.6	3.1	37.6

STATE County	Agriculture, 2017 (cont.) – Land in farms – Acreage (1,000)	Land in farms – Percent change, 2012–2017	Land in farms – Acres – Average size of farm	Land in farms – Acres – Total irrigated (1,000)	Land in farms – Acres – Total cropland (1,000)	Value of land and buildings (dollars) – Average per farm	Value of land and buildings (dollars) – Average per acre	Value of machinery and equipment, average per farm (dollars)	Value of products sold: – Total (mil dol)	Value of products sold: – Average per farm (acres)	Value of products sold: – Percent from: – Crops	Value of products sold: – Percent from: – Livestock and poultry products	Organic farms (number)	Farms with internet access (per-cent)	Government payments – Total ($1,000)	Government payments – Percent of farms
	117	118	119	120	121	122	123	124	125	126	127	128	129	130	131	132
TEXAS—Cont'd																
Caldwell	285	-8.1	188	0.7	67.9	718,250	3,821	57,287	53.6	35,358	27.0	73.0	4	75.2	1,191	5.7
Calhoun	190	2.9	654	2.3	48.2	1,401,219	2,144	113,299	32.1	110,845	66.3	33.7	6	80.3	1,781	37.9
Callahan	478	-15.2	497	0.2	85.5	861,252	1,732	60,872	31.2	32,508	9.7	90.3	NA	75.0	711	20.8
Cameron	271	-12.3	191	100.9	212.5	681,492	3,560	73,661	122.6	86,428	96.2	3.8	10	64.3	6,669	26.0
Camp	77	-1.3	160	0.6	20.8	525,814	3,294	76,458	114.2	235,934	1.4	98.6	NA	73.6	235	16.3
Carson	521	7.5	1,574	64.4	322.6	2,139,551	1,359	305,633	91.8	277,426	89.5	10.5	NA	78.2	9,238	65.3
Cass	177	5.7	164	0.2	35.1	384,391	2,345	60,321	53.4	49,439	7.7	92.3	2	70.3	424	13.9
Castro	555	1.2	1,350	121.8	394.6	1,863,235	1,380	600,576	1,121.6	2,728,944	8.2	91.8	NA	76.4	15,189	84.9
Chambers	205	-19.1	365	21.0	99.0	865,025	2,367	102,607	19.3	34,256	57.5	42.5	7	71.4	5,885	16.0
Cherokee	276	-8.6	174	1.0	58.3	539,484	3,107	74,929	115.7	72,900	57.5	42.5	2	72.1	49	1.1
Childress	444	0.1	1,559	8.7	121.4	1,442,095	925	112,358	27.2	95,565	72.4	27.6	NA	65.6	2,721	72.3
Clay	648	2.4	761	0.3	100.8	1,464,315	1,924	80,343	55.7	65,394	10.7	89.3	NA	75.6	2,054	29.7
Cochran	486	8.3	1,700	113.2	373.6	1,574,348	926	320,452	87.6	306,367	94.7	5.3	2	68.2	9,199	91.3
Coke	469	-3.1	1,045	0.7	43.0	1,005,986	962	63,144	7.8	17,459	16.0	84.0	NA	65.3	644	15.8
Coleman	672	-7.4	689	0.7	146.3	1,131,892	1,643	68,996	41.2	42,215	32.4	67.6	NA	73.2	2,521	35.7
Collin	281	-10.2	104	1.0	140.3	1,032,094	9,946	57,985	66.8	24,697	44.2	55.8	NA	82.0	2,401	4.8
Collingsworth	407	-17.7	1,353	25.8	168.0	1,370,944	1,014	183,807	39.7	131,980	78.0	22.0	1	70.8	8,813	74.8
Colorado	563	16.0	317	34.1	132.3	954,840	3,009	79,375	71.0	40,040	54.7	45.3	21	64.6	8,199	11.1
Comal	206	0.7	193	0.3	23.6	660,324	3,415	45,101	9.6	8,999	9.7	90.3	2	80.0	190	3.2
Comanche	487	-5.8	341	17.4	137.6	900,640	2,639	82,769	173.3	121,419	13.5	86.5	4	73.2	2,533	16.0
Concho	561	11.8	1,417	4.3	108.5	2,089,817	1,475	123,623	28.1	71,008	47.6	52.4	NA	71.5	2,775	57.3
Cooke	492	-2.3	216	0.9	135.6	712,860	3,307	67,174	53.8	23,568	23.8	76.2	4	78.2	2,342	14.8
Coryell	457	-1.3	309	1.4	92.1	805,175	2,606	70,764	36.3	24,527	22.5	77.5	2	76.3	1,112	11.1
Cottle	579	2.5	3,759	2.3	104.4	4,174,361	1,110	133,366	27.7	180,104	35.5	64.5	NA	66.9	1,829	80.5
Crane	244	2.1	8,137	D	0.2	6,902,732	848	106,427	D	D	D	D	NA	93.3	9	10.0
Crockett	1,534	-0.8	7,005	0.0	6.3	5,686,480	812	84,106	D	D	D	D	6	73.5	208	9.1
Crosby	551	-1.4	1,605	86.5	272.9	1,556,556	970	262,721	86.9	253,364	93.4	6.6	1	69.1	5,844	79.9
Culberson	1,504	-7.0	22,791	5.7	13.5	16,763,487	736	245,880	15.9	240,864	59.5	40.5	NA	72.7	313	15.2
Dallam	895	5.1	2,633	149.9	393.6	2,986,690	1,134	451,440	634.9	1,867,426	14.6	85.4	NA	77.4	15,216	82.4
Dallas	64	-23.6	83	0.5	26.1	668,126	8,097	54,512	29.8	38,427	87.0	13.0	NA	72.0	404	3.6
Dawson	536	-4.0	1,388	54.8	408.6	1,442,556	1,040	333,933	121.3	314,236	97.6	2.4	18	73.3	11,958	79.8
Deaf Smith	967	4.8	1,722	122.4	617.3	1,942,201	1,128	349,244	1,638.8	2,916,004	5.7	94.3	4	82.6	29,893	74.9
Delta	144	9.7	252	D	80.5	495,901	1,968	78,856	36.3	63,620	69.9	30.1	NA	71.5	1,843	30.6
Denton	359	-6.3	109	2.9	144.0	1,041,728	9,550	55,272	123.2	37,393	19.7	80.3	8	82.0	1,877	6.5
DeWitt	484	-9.8	274	3.5	50.8	840,718	3,072	74,495	38.7	21,881	17.4	82.6	NA	68.3	186	1.4
Dickens	543	-5.1	1,382	8.9	166.1	1,472,068	1,065	97,078	26.9	68,336	49.5	50.5	NA	70.7	2,200	54.7
Dimmit	484	-28.5	1,476	3.5	68.0	2,080,509	1,410	95,610	28.5	86,756	8.3	91.7	NA	61.0	84	4.6
Donley	593	1.4	2,096	17.1	57.2	1,813,922	865	112,440	94.2	332,707	14.6	85.4	NA	70.7	2,234	52.7
Duval	836	-12.9	612	2.0	45.4	1,037,873	1,697	39,468	11.0	8,045	5.9	94.1	NA	47.4	1,741	17.5
Eastland	490	-2.8	409	1.9	80.1	802,949	1,964	63,040	23.5	19,632	21.1	78.9	NA	68.4	1,837	14.6
Ector	558	30.1	2,029	0.9	1.9	2,350,073	1,158	63,273	3.4	12,298	7.6	92.4	NA	75.6	57	1.5
Edwards	1,013	4.5	2,667	0.4	12.5	3,121,016	1,170	65,091	10.9	28,768	3.0	97.0	NA	66.6	1,609	22.6
Ellis	473	-0.1	186	2.4	221.5	595,894	3,211	76,740	73.1	28,673	73.1	26.9	1	75.3	5,962	17.4
El Paso	143	-31.9	217	31.6	39.9	873,269	4,015	87,385	46.7	71,248	86.4	13.6	4	76.7	286	1.5
Erath	626	3.0	260	14.3	134.3	824,386	3,166	96,022	312.3	130,007	6.1	93.9	10	77.7	1,229	3.6
Falls	392	2.4	355	4.0	203.8	893,002	2,513	124,859	157.9	143,191	26.8	73.2	NA	73.2	3,201	21.8
Fannin	482	-6.2	214	4.9	212.4	614,054	2,873	70,196	86.3	38,267	50.8	49.2	NA	74.9	7,452	24.1
Fayette	522	6.0	165	1.5	99.8	664,110	4,032	55,919	47.4	14,966	22.5	77.5	NA	70.3	446	6.3
Fisher	478	-3.4	983	10.5	248.7	1,112,312	1,131	132,231	35.7	73,537	75.5	24.5	NA	65.8	2,874	65.0
Floyd	639	9.8	1,452	120.1	437.7	1,460,850	1,006	263,008	D	D	D	D	NA	68.2	12,373	91.4
Foard	440	19.5	2,557	1.1	92.4	2,854,518	1,116	110,669	14.9	86,860	24.8	75.2	NA	65.7	2,360	64.5
Fort Bend	279	-17.6	242	9.6	140.7	750,749	3,103	102,575	85.0	73,603	82.6	17.4	1	71.7	4,623	22.3
Franklin	103	-9.2	208	0.9	28.4	645,217	3,100	87,557	134.1	272,000	2.1	97.9	NA	74.8	208	5.5
Freestone	414	-1.7	284	1.3	55.7	727,956	2,565	71,717	68.1	46,697	6.8	93.2	NA	66.2	61	1.0
Frio	678	-4.9	1,023	48.6	90.9	1,889,823	1,848	103,474	124.4	187,703	56.1	43.9	NA	69.7	1,214	11.6
Gaines	858	10.7	1,692	197.0	680.0	1,955,071	1,155	389,035	188.8	372,373	93.9	6.1	33	73.6	31,166	82.6
Galveston	73	-18.3	116	1.1	17.0	612,200	5,299	53,747	9.2	14,586	48.6	51.4	2	69.0	722	3.8
Garza	416	-8.7	1,754	8.9	68.3	1,763,789	1,005	117,857	22.1	93,338	75.6	24.4	NA	67.1	1,005	46.0
Gillespie	680	4.3	327	2.8	73.9	993,949	3,039	49,491	31.2	15,013	22.5	77.5	1	75.6	1,244	11.3
Glasscock	496	14.4	2,836	39.7	180.3	2,604,656	919	515,993	50.6	289,400	93.7	6.3	NA	85.7	1,233	60.0
Goliad	380	-23.2	303	0.1	36.2	804,567	2,658	53,417	17.7	14,072	25.9	74.1	NA	70.3	991	5.7
Gonzales	614	0.7	381	1.5	58.5	1,211,682	3,180	96,128	560.8	347,909	6.9	93.1	1	68.5	478	4.0
Gray	483	-6.2	1,389	16.9	124.8	1,588,481	1,144	111,560	154.6	444,313	15.8	84.2	10	73.9	4,042	40.8
Grayson	430	-0.3	151	2.3	207.0	1,023,106	6,770	68,105	66.2	23,259	60.8	39.2	1	81.0	4,729	9.9
Gregg	58	20.1	107	0.3	14.5	602,572	5,649	51,338	4.1	7,584	21.7	78.3	NA	73.8	D	0.4
Grimes	341	-18.3	192	4.0	54.3	740,438	3,847	68,597	47.5	26,826	29.6	70.4	NA	74.5	79	1.1

STATE County	Water use, 2015		Wholesale Trade[1], 2017				Retail Trade[2], 2017				Real estate and rental and leasing,[2] 2017			
	Public supply water withdrawn (mil gal/ day)	Public supply gallons withdrawn per person per day	Number of establish-ments	Number of employees	Sales (mil dol)	Average payroll (mil dol)	Number of establish-ments	Number of employees	Sales (mil dol)	Average payroll (mil dol)	Number of establish-ments	Number of employees	Sales (mil dol)	Average payroll (mil dol)
	133	134	135	136	137	138	139	140	141	142	143	144	145	146
TEXAS—Cont'd														
Caldwell	3.7	91.3	22	81	22.7	3.3	79	1,108	355.0	31.0	26	62	10.7	1.5
Calhoun	0.3	11.4	15	94	85.1	4.1	65	1,098	502.4	39.0	16	164	56.0	8.8
Callahan	0.3	18.4	4	29	9.2	0.9	37	385	277.1	17.8	6	25	4.2	1.0
Cameron	24.2	57.3	320	2,851	2,163.4	101.5	1,045	17,938	4,610.8	437.5	336	1,482	226.5	40.2
Camp	1.1	86.7	7	91	53.8	3.7	42	373	101.6	9.5	D	D	D	0.1
Carson	9.0	1,507.8	11	132	125.7	9.5	25	174	53.7	3.8	NA	NA	NA	NA
Cass	1.1	34.6	14	225	144.0	10.0	81	828	254.0	19.6	19	32	6.8	1.1
Castro	1.1	138.5	12	97	121.7	6.2	34	180	41.8	4.1	5	17	2.6	0.4
Chambers	1.6	40.9	39	445	240.7	25.0	104	1,089	410.6	29.5	25	158	97.5	9.0
Cherokee	6.3	122.4	21	191	79.8	8.2	127	1,855	394.8	45.4	31	52	10.3	1.5
Childress	0.0	0.0	D	D	D	D	30	380	113.7	9.7	5	11	3.0	0.4
Clay	6.3	608.1	3	5	2.2	0.1	24	190	41.8	5.8	D	D	D	D
Cochran	0.4	135.5	3	39	43.8	1.5	8	42	9.2	0.8	NA	NA	NA	NA
Coke	0.4	114.3	NA	NA	NA	NA	11	76	20.4	1.4	NA	NA	NA	NA
Coleman	1.3	157.1	5	29	19.8	1.5	33	259	69.1	5.2	8	D	1.4	D
Collin	3.0	3.3	870	13,979	40,258.4	1,243.3	2,754	55,402	19,773.5	1,669.7	1,415	8,959	2,472.4	518.4
Collingsworth	0.5	170.8	NA	NA	NA	NA	11	81	16.8	1.7	NA	NA	NA	NA
Colorado	2.9	140.9	31	324	291.0	13.6	108	928	303.5	25.6	14	21	16.5	1.5
Comal	16.7	129.4	138	2,253	2,457.0	161.4	431	7,210	2,607.6	215.9	241	879	210.7	37.2
Comanche	0.0	3.0	16	260	133.5	8.4	45	492	168.5	13.6	5	10	0.8	0.3
Concho	0.3	80.9	NA	NA	NA	NA	15	75	18.7	1.4	NA	NA	NA	NA
Cooke	4.2	106.8	49	615	278.2	34.2	149	1,865	587.3	50.1	31	86	29.2	2.9
Coryell	0.2	2.8	14	110	28.1	4.0	132	1,899	530.7	47.4	39	138	18.7	4.9
Cottle	0.2	147.3	NA	NA	NA	NA	7	52	10.9	1.1	NA	NA	NA	NA
Crane	1.4	279.3	D	D	D	0.8	12	114	34.2	3.2	D	D	D	D
Crockett	1.0	258.8	D	D	D	1.7	18	164	63.8	4.6	5	D	0.4	D
Crosby	1.5	252.6	8	128	148.4	7.7	18	132	46.7	4.3	NA	NA	NA	NA
Culberson	0.8	362.3	NA	NA	NA	NA	16	148	92.2	4.3	NA	NA	NA	NA
Dallam	2.1	287.9	18	242	190.7	13.9	32	238	94.8	7.8	D	D	D	D
Dallas	334.5	131.0	3,777	75,525	70,063.1	4,970.6	7,816	129,602	43,896.1	4,051.7	4,096	38,463	13,117.6	2,469.2
Dawson	0.5	37.7	19	113	89.9	6.0	42	632	370.7	21.4	D	D	D	D
Deaf Smith	4.3	224.3	33	429	920.6	22.7	53	838	271.8	20.0	15	60	7.9	1.3
Delta	5.4	1,029.3	3	10	10.2	0.5	12	34	16.6	0.8	NA	NA	NA	NA
Denton	31.5	40.4	664	11,758	28,775.7	813.2	1,826	31,567	10,212.3	877.8	843	4,745	1,250.9	248.1
DeWitt	2.8	135.1	15	253	88.1	7.7	65	862	243.0	22.5	15	114	47.1	4.8
Dickens	0.1	45.3	NA	NA	NA	NA	8	48	11.8	1.0	NA	NA	NA	NA
Dimmit	1.7	153.9	10	71	43.5	3.4	29	461	143.9	12.3	12	88	24.5	5.4
Donley	0.4	108.6	NA	NA	NA	NA	13	117	23.1	2.3	5	8	0.9	0.2
Duval	1.2	106.3	D	D	D	D	22	193	66.7	4.9	4	8	2.4	0.2
Eastland	0.7	37.4	14	56	56.4	2.6	76	830	273.9	20.8	15	30	4.8	0.9
Ector	0.6	4.0	301	4,598	3,087.9	298.2	460	8,193	3,004.4	270.5	188	2,007	788.5	126.2
Edwards	0.2	105.6	NA	NA	NA	NA	7	86	24.7	2.6	3	2	0.5	0.1
Ellis	15.2	93.1	115	1,165	1,197.9	71.2	391	6,063	1,812.4	158.4	135	444	115.8	14.9
El Paso	114.3	136.8	D	D	D	D	2,272	38,202	9,956.3	883.6	844	4,043	958.5	152.1
Erath	2.2	53.7	48	417	156.7	16.5	161	1,964	557.6	50.7	41	128	18.3	3.0
Falls	2.3	133.6	D	D	D	2.9	48	475	167.5	12.7	4	16	1.2	0.5
Fannin	2.6	77.2	14	132	240.9	6.3	79	912	304.4	24.6	17	55	10.1	1.2
Fayette	2.6	102.0	29	408	265.2	25.9	112	1,360	435.3	38.3	32	91	21.1	3.4
Fisher	0.0	5.2	NA	NA	NA	NA	15	59	14.8	1.6	NA	NA	NA	NA
Floyd	0.4	69.5	15	133	444.7	7.3	16	96	20.3	1.9	NA	NA	NA	NA
Foard	0.0	8.2	NA	NA	NA	NA	5	30	5.5	0.5	NA	NA	NA	NA
Fort Bend	55.9	78.0	731	8,114	11,721.4	478.6	1,769	28,190	9,259.7	773.8	670	2,150	573.0	93.5
Franklin	2.8	260.1	3	D	3.8	D	28	294	100.2	6.9	8	10	3.1	0.3
Freestone	2.1	106.6	11	128	77.6	8.9	56	474	177.5	12.0	11	32	4.6	1.2
Frio	2.7	144.7	17	193	227.5	12.4	51	612	176.9	17.2	8	22	5.6	0.9
Gaines	8.2	409.5	33	347	345.3	22.1	59	508	138.3	13.3	15	182	24.7	9.4
Galveston	0.2	0.7	218	1,952	1,445.9	107.1	944	14,163	4,498.3	384.5	338	1,920	442.9	100.9
Garza	4.7	732.7	D	D	D	D	19	188	49.6	3.9	4	D	1.0	D
Gillespie	2.1	82.0	32	290	138.5	12.5	169	1,676	402.1	44.2	47	113	24.8	4.6
Glasscock	0.0	0.0	5	25	17.4	1.2	NA	NA	NA	NA	NA	NA	NA	NA
Goliad	0.3	45.1	D	D	D	0.3	16	132	45.0	3.2	NA	NA	NA	NA
Gonzales	29.1	1,412.0	22	242	185.0	9.9	63	804	251.7	21.4	11	30	6.3	1.2
Gray	1.2	53.4	D	D	D	D	86	1,009	256.4	23.8	20	61	10.8	3.2
Grayson	21.6	172.2	97	1,024	736.7	48.3	428	6,146	1,912.7	170.4	107	329	73.4	11.1
Gregg	7.1	57.4	247	3,182	2,073.0	181.2	636	9,260	2,928.8	263.2	191	1,020	263.3	45.9
Grimes	2.2	80.7	20	188	154.2	11.5	67	565	194.9	15.6	19	74	11.0	2.7

1 Merchant wholesalers, except manufacturers' sales branches and offices. 2. Employer establishments.

STATE County	Professional, scientific, and technical services, 2017				Manufacturing, 2017				Accommodation and food services, 2017			
	Number of establish-ments	Number of employees	Sales (mil dol)	Average payroll (mil dol)	Number of establish-ments	Number of employees	Sales (mil dol)	Average payroll (mil dol)	Number of establis-hments	Number of employees	Sales (mil dol)	Annual payroll (mil dol)
	147	148	149	150	151	152	153	154	155	156	157	158
TEXAS—Cont'd												
Caldwell	30	63	8.2	2.7	21	520	178.0	25.3	66	910	59.1	15.2
Calhoun	34	615	76.7	45.1	24	3,017	7,393.0	325.9	66	765	45.7	10.1
Callahan	13	32	6.0	1.4	11	137	48.4	5.5	21	268	11.9	3.2
Cameron	D	D	D	D	188	3,983	1,301.2	161.2	735	15,258	753.2	204.0
Camp	11	38	5.2	1.5	7	192	39.8	8.6	20	190	13.5	2.7
Carson	D	D	D	D	NA	NA	NA	NA	11	139	4.3	1.5
Cass	24	100	9.9	3.6	22	1,120	731.5	118.0	53	670	28.2	7.4
Castro	10	85	7.8	3.1	5	41	61.1	1.9	14	86	6.1	1.2
Chambers	45	353	49.4	20.7	29	2,137	3,929.4	230.4	78	1,279	69.7	18.3
Cherokee	57	181	27.5	7.1	61	2,206	461.1	91.6	58	918	42.6	11.3
Childress	12	41	6.9	2.0	3	3	0.4	0.1	21	244	14.9	3.7
Clay	8	14	2.1	0.5	6	69	9.8	2.2	D	D	D	D
Cochran	NA	NA	NA	NA	NA	NA	NA	NA	D	D	D	0.1
Coke	NA	NA	NA	NA	NA	NA	NA	NA	4	31	0.8	0.3
Coleman	14	30	4.7	1.0	11	70	11.8	3.5	23	181	7.8	2.4
Collin	D	D	D	D	461	18,072	8,816.6	1,365.4	2,191	46,044	2,869.0	831.8
Collingsworth	D	D	1.6	D	4	17	1.9	0.8	8	56	2.0	0.5
Colorado	33	128	18.6	7.9	32	1,642	528.4	77.8	45	494	30.5	8.0
Comal	400	2,125	316.8	106.1	114	3,095	964.0	154.1	356	7,419	426.3	124.2
Comanche	20	73	10.2	3.5	8	113	104.9	3.5	D	D	D	D
Concho	NA	NA	NA	NA	NA	NA	NA	NA	D	D	D	0.8
Cooke	68	254	31.2	12.0	69	3,485	1,606.2	165.5	84	1,605	80.4	23.0
Coryell	52	701	93.4	34.6	22	369	108.5	21.4	91	1,430	69.9	17.5
Cottle	NA	NA	NA	NA	NA	NA	NA	NA	NA	NA	NA	NA
Crane	4	16	1.4	0.5	NA	NA	NA	NA	6	61	2.7	0.7
Crockett	4	12	0.9	0.4	NA	NA	NA	NA	24	274	13.2	3.1
Crosby	D	D	1.0	D	NA	NA	NA	NA	4	36	1.8	0.5
Culberson	NA	NA	NA	NA	NA	NA	NA	NA	14	177	12.1	2.8
Dallam	15	65	49.0	17.4	5	55	23.9	2.7	D	D	D	4.5
Dallas	D	D	D	D	2,234	92,173	36,535.0	5,961.3	6,016	134,426	9,588.6	2,677.2
Dawson	13	64	9.7	2.7	11	88	20.6	4.5	D	D	D	D
Deaf Smith	26	182	25.9	9.2	24	1,591	1,169.5	87.8	36	455	24.3	5.8
Delta	3	5	0.6	0.2	NA	NA	NA	NA	NA	NA	NA	NA
Denton	2,124	10,798	1,795.1	652.1	395	13,378	7,948.3	801.8	1,537	30,380	1,767.6	488.8
DeWitt	40	103	14.6	4.5	15	528	83.6	16.6	44	402	19.4	5.4
Dickens	D	D	D	D	NA	NA	NA	NA	4	39	1.6	0.4
Dimmit	8	45	6.8	3.0	4	40	5.7	1.9	24	281	18.2	4.6
Donley	7	19	3.5	0.6	NA	NA	NA	NA	9	95	4.5	1.3
Duval	9	27	3.8	1.1	NA	NA	NA	NA	21	153	8.8	2.7
Eastland	30	268	52.4	18.0	16	558	101.5	23.5	47	547	29.0	8.0
Ector	D	D	D	D	224	4,128	1,379.8	243.9	284	6,669	462.1	116.5
Edwards	NA	NA	NA	NA	NA	NA	NA	NA	D	D	D	0.4
Ellis	D	D	D	D	179	11,056	5,244.7	595.1	271	5,639	296.1	85.0
El Paso	D	D	D	D	D	D	D	D	1,585	34,685	1,673.4	465.1
Erath	82	384	49.1	16.9	35	2,428	1,134.2	110.9	D	D	D	D
Falls	12	52	4.3	1.8	9	130	42.2	7.0	13	D	9.3	D
Fannin	35	110	10.6	3.9	35	591	247.3	26.9	39	482	22.6	6.4
Fayette	61	214	26.8	10.0	43	1,007	271.2	42.3	84	991	55.7	15.4
Fisher	7	20	1.8	0.6	D	D	D	D	3	19	1.0	0.3
Floyd	3	5	0.5	0.2	6	34	11.9	1.6	D	D	D	D
Foard	NA	NA	NA	NA	NA	NA	NA	NA	NA	NA	NA	NA
Fort Bend	2,083	15,035	4,442.7	1,329.5	369	13,211	4,585.4	739.5	1,196	22,866	1,388.5	382.2
Franklin	13	36	3.9	1.2	D	D	D	D	D	D	D	D
Freestone	24	65	12.8	3.9	13	390	142.4	20.2	38	614	30.5	8.1
Frio	D	D	D	D	6	66	17.4	3.3	45	475	28.2	6.8
Gaines	19	72	10.9	4.0	14	184	56.4	9.9	36	406	24.1	5.9
Galveston	D	D	D	D	162	5,481	23,357.8	558.1	757	17,232	1,060.9	299.2
Garza	8	13	1.4	0.4	NA	NA	NA	NA	12	113	6.3	1.5
Gillespie	72	302	45.6	13.7	64	715	122.9	28.6	126	1,863	114.7	34.9
Glasscock	NA	NA	NA	NA	NA	NA	NA	NA	NA	NA	NA	NA
Goliad	13	25	2.5	0.7	NA	NA	NA	NA	D	D	D	D
Gonzales	34	100	10.7	4.0	18	1,081	400.5	45.5	47	425	27.4	6.4
Gray	36	239	31.6	13.1	19	724	334.1	52.4	45	681	32.4	9.6
Grayson	222	1,017	159.1	48.2	106	7,200	2,713.7	324.9	238	4,558	260.1	73.9
Gregg	D	D	D	D	176	8,399	3,283.3	500.7	376	7,023	364.7	107.9
Grimes	30	299	42.1	19.0	39	1,443	618.5	103.5	38	394	24.1	5.8

STATE County	Health care and social assistance, 2017				Other services, 2017				Nonemployer businesses, 2019		Value of residential construction authorized by building permits, 2021	
	Number of establish-ments	Number of employees	Receipts (mil dol)	Annual payroll (mil dol)	Number of establish-ments	Number of employees	Receipts (mil dol)	Annual payroll (mil dol)	Number	Receipts (mil dol)	New construction ($1,000)	Number of housing units
	159	160	161	162	163	164	165	166	167	168	169	170
TEXAS—Cont'd												
Caldwell	78	1,343	103.4	55.8	39	156	18.2	4.7	3,405	180.3	101,156	544
Calhoun	34	595	53.9	22.2	29	178	22.5	6.1	1,704	72.8	31,984	137
Callahan	10	152	8.4	4.4	12	33	2.6	0.9	1,297	56.5	0	0
Cameron	1,029	37,028	2,310.7	987.7	406	2,151	199.1	50.2	33,608	1,385.3	261,085	2,052
Camp	12	356	44.7	14.5	D	D	D	D	909	37.3	870	4
Carson	5	21	2.0	0.6	8	18	7.1	0.9	429	14.8	184	2
Cass	46	1,083	74.7	30.3	38	174	32.7	6.9	2,022	90.8	1,213	7
Castro	D	D	D	D	14	44	7.0	1.7	425	26.0	0	0
Chambers	41	783	119.5	30.9	35	194	33.7	7.5	3,421	155.8	177,069	1,052
Cherokee	75	2,570	211.2	93.9	35	183	19.7	5.6	3,483	157.3	2,431	18
Childress	19	384	40.2	17.4	8	17	1.6	0.5	405	14.4	0	0
Clay	10	105	7.8	3.9	9	37	2.9	0.6	874	39.4	500	2
Cochran	9	103	7.0	3.4	3	7	0.7	0.1	168	5.8	9,353	43
Coke	NA	NA	NA	NA	D	D	D	0.3	320	12.6	240	3
Coleman	16	469	38.2	16.3	15	41	5.7	1.1	744	42.9	1,088	5
Collin	3,599	56,314	7,848.0	2,683.8	1,299	9,562	1,458.0	340.1	109,863	6,268.2	4,309,408	17,140
Collingsworth	5	136	9.8	4.4	D	D	1.0	D	204	7.4	0	0
Colorado	47	902	90.9	31.9	37	107	12.1	2.9	2,065	103.6	3,205	15
Comal	375	6,079	685.3	260.0	258	1,628	146.5	49.4	17,629	974.5	993,815	4,459
Comanche	19	566	45.5	17.3	D	D	D	D	1,222	60.3	50	1
Concho	6	137	12.0	4.9	NA	NA	NA	NA	239	10.7	0	0
Cooke	82	1,145	104.5	45.0	54	385	38.9	11.4	3,893	227.1	15,151	51
Coryell	60	1,144	118.0	39.6	74	365	35.8	9.4	3,478	132.3	29,781	243
Cottle	NA	NA	NA	NA	NA	NA	NA	NA	127	5.0	0	0
Crane	9	181	18.7	7.2	3	11	1.4	0.4	339	15.9	435	2
Crockett	5	26	2.7	1.3	D	D	D	D	348	17.4	NA	NA
Crosby	9	172	10.1	5.0	7	12	0.8	0.2	367	11.5	0	0
Culberson	D	D	D	D	NA	NA	NA	NA	212	11.2	2,381	23
Dallam	9	40	2.8	0.9	18	62	8.3	1.9	517	40.7	1,229	6
Dallas	7,772	183,205	24,757.4	9,273.4	3,647	35,701	6,320.4	1,479.8	263,060	14,554.1	3,217,664	18,799
Dawson	13	326	33.4	11.2	24	96	8.5	2.2	676	28.4	8,188	80
Deaf Smith	21	572	43.0	19.6	36	184	35.7	7.6	1,172	70.1	390	2
Delta	5	527	9.7	5.0	4	7	0.7	0.2	397	15.8	3,045	14
Denton	1,933	28,296	3,704.7	1,385.4	942	6,019	674.3	201.2	85,626	4,380.0	2,886,956	11,575
DeWitt	34	765	68.4	32.2	39	209	29.8	7.6	1,585	77.1	2,393	11
Dickens	3	10	0.3	0.1	D	D	1.3	D	175	4.3	NA	NA
Dimmit	27	569	48.9	19.9	D	D	D	D	681	28.9	0	0
Donley	8	21	1.1	0.5	D	D	2.6	D	343	13.7	1,305	6
Duval	18	654	22.3	11.2	D	D	D	1.2	858	29.7	NA	NA
Eastland	49	841	59.5	23.3	31	134	13.7	3.5	1,401	63.5	3,122	17
Ector	285	8,075	996.1	374.9	272	2,188	331.9	88.9	13,879	881.1	330,810	1,406
Edwards	3	23	0.7	0.4	4	9	0.8	0.2	208	11.0	NA	NA
Ellis	297	4,568	482.4	172.5	201	1,134	114.3	33.2	18,044	880.5	787,927	3,895
El Paso	D	D	D	D	D	D	D	D	67,698	3,023.0	661,531	2,989
Erath	81	1,566	164.1	59.2	76	412	54.9	12.0	3,737	205.9	12,436	54
Falls	28	337	26.0	12.2	D	D	D	0.6	1,033	49.8	1,538	10
Fannin	44	1,627	157.6	65.8	29	126	12.0	2.6	2,736	121.7	10,188	59
Fayette	71	1,029	97.0	39.4	51	213	18.3	5.7	2,795	141.1	2,348	11
Fisher	3	105	9.6	5.0	5	21	1.1	0.5	269	10.1	NA	NA
Floyd	15	270	16.0	6.6	13	42	5.2	1.4	368	11.6	0	0
Foard	D	D	D	D	D	D	D	0.5	95	5.5	NA	NA
Fort Bend	2,045	27,849	2,872.2	1,064.3	778	5,073	596.3	161.2	89,072	4,431.1	2,483,299	10,762
Franklin	16	4,712	72.9	36.9	18	69	8.1	1.6	935	46.7	0	0
Freestone	27	695	63.6	21.8	32	104	13.7	3.0	1,319	57.4	657	4
Frio	31	576	44.4	16.2	D	D	D	D	1,069	41.3	1,044	10
Gaines	18	347	33.6	14.1	38	228	24.5	7.7	2,438	218.2	990	3
Galveston	648	15,736	1,487.7	627.9	463	2,828	491.3	94.9	28,841	1,328.3	605,139	2,512
Garza	12	163	14.5	5.4	4	11	2.1	0.3	381	18.0	0	0
Gillespie	100	1,795	202.1	82.8	64	308	31.3	8.3	4,152	219.1	17,416	85
Glasscock	NA	NA	NA	NA	NA	NA	NA	NA	144	12.9	NA	NA
Goliad	11	98	6.8	2.8	5	10	0.6	0.1	751	30.6	1,014	42
Gonzales	30	812	79.9	28.9	29	102	10.9	2.9	1,487	74.6	3,318	17
Gray	55	822	96.5	36.0	38	146	19.2	4.8	1,370	60.1	0	0
Grayson	360	8,454	956.3	381.4	149	689	81.7	21.5	11,537	609.8	209,723	1,048
Gregg	463	11,445	1,261.8	485.6	249	1,650	239.6	66.8	10,481	527.9	71,040	363
Grimes	18	317	29.7	13.3	D	D	D	D	2,486	109.3	14,895	92

STATE County	Government employment and payroll, 2017									Local government finances, 2017				
			March payroll (percent of total)							General revenue				
												Taxes		
													Per capita[1] (dollars)	
	Full-time equivalent employees	March payroll (dollars)	Adminis-tration, judicial, and legal	Police and corrections	Fire protection	Highways and transpor-tation	Health and welfare	Natural resources and utilities	Education and libraries	Total (mil dol)	Inter-govern-mental (mil dol)	Total (mil dol)	Total	Property
	171	172	173	174	175	176	177	178	179	180	181	182	183	184
TEXAS—Cont'd														
Caldwell	1,439	5,815,124	8.2	13.3	1.7	2.3	1.3	4.7	68.2	114.5	52.2	46.7	1,104	938
Calhoun	1,057	3,269,430	7.7	13.0	2.6	7.9	4.9	3.6	57.7	186.4	13.0	76.1	3,507	3,125
Callahan	570	1,686,820	8.1	5.9	0.0	2.4	0.7	2.8	79.6	40.1	15.7	20.3	1,456	1,333
Cameron	22,268	74,927,211	4.8	8.6	2.8	2.5	2.0	4.4	73.6	1,807.5	1,026.7	493.5	1,169	939
Camp	517	1,566,426	3.6	2.2	0.0	2.9	1.2	6.2	83.3	35.5	16.4	15.8	1,227	1,027
Carson	372	1,134,116	12.8	3.3	0.0	3.5	2.3	7.4	62.2	36.6	9.8	23.2	3,860	3,750
Cass	1,340	3,760,026	6.9	12.1	1.3	2.0	0.6	2.6	74.1	100.6	40.8	48.6	1,621	1,437
Castro	568	1,682,097	4.3	7.3	0.3	2.4	22.4	2.5	60.4	37.9	16.4	13.2	1,711	1,481
Chambers	1,835	7,504,551	8.8	8.1	0.0	2.7	6.9	6.4	65.8	240.7	57.3	143.6	3,481	3,232
Cherokee	2,101	6,902,634	7.2	9.7	2.0	2.6	5.9	2.4	69.3	146.9	73.6	53.8	1,033	830
Childress	572	2,299,505	4.4	7.0	1.9	2.1	54.9	4.4	25.0	51.0	8.1	10.3	1,419	1,294
Clay	565	1,853,596	4.8	3.2	0.0	4.1	14.0	7.6	64.0	49.1	13.8	15.8	1,503	1,390
Cochran	330	1,037,152	10.2	5.8	0.0	3.3	15.3	4.0	60.2	27.2	10.2	13.9	4,884	4,560
Coke	234	755,845	6.0	2.2	0.0	1.6	29.7	6.4	53.7	18.7	4.9	8.0	2,423	2,257
Coleman	471	1,479,173	6.2	6.2	1.2	17.8	2.3	7.5	58.5	31.4	19.0	9.7	1,159	972
Collin	36,296	160,438,595	4.3	7.4	4.6	3.4	1.2	5.8	70.8	5,103.0	674.0	2,869.6	2,953	2,582
Collingsworth	182	564,742	8.5	6.3	0.0	5.4	10.1	6.2	62.3	12.8	4.8	6.1	2,043	1,925
Colorado	903	2,990,932	10.1	10.4	0.0	6.4	0.8	4.4	66.3	72.7	17.5	44.5	2,092	1,839
Comal	5,374	20,517,352	5.6	11.0	5.4	2.6	0.9	5.1	68.0	533.0	69.6	388.3	2,759	2,299
Comanche	853	2,848,355	5.0	7.9	3.4	2.6	24.6	1.5	54.4	53.9	21.7	21.3	1,572	1,353
Concho	201	741,256	10.8	4.8	0.0	3.7	37.5	4.4	37.5	22.0	5.8	6.8	2,522	2,359
Cooke	2,234	8,897,671	3.9	7.0	2.3	1.7	20.1	3.0	60.6	211.3	65.7	84.0	2,104	1,742
Coryell	2,532	8,957,496	5.7	8.3	1.4	1.3	18.1	4.0	59.9	246.6	104.1	68.5	916	767
Cottle	82	252,144	16.8	2.7	0.0	7.4	14.6	3.6	53.8	4.2	1.3	2.7	1,940	1,940
Crane	311	1,503,929	9.0	9.2	0.0	1.5	0.7	18.2	60.8	32.9	9.7	19.8	4,236	4,049
Crockett	325	978,310	9.0	4.2	1.2	6.3	20.1	6.2	51.1	38.1	6.5	27.5	7,784	7,779
Crosby	374	1,118,291	8.0	7.8	0.0	1.9	2.9	6.2	73.1	25.2	12.7	9.7	1,666	1,370
Culberson	235	800,326	13.0	7.2	0.0	3.8	33.4	8.0	34.0	38.3	17.7	18.9	8,458	8,167
Dallam	430	1,450,727	8.7	13.7	0.6	2.7	0.1	6.2	67.0	32.1	7.6	21.3	2,930	2,522
Dallas	115,153	544,302,614	5.1	10.5	5.6	7.3	14.9	4.7	49.8	14,882.1	3,355.3	7,362.7	2,810	2,155
Dawson	1,046	3,415,451	3.6	5.2	1.3	1.8	21.9	9.8	56.2	63.1	19.1	36.3	2,851	2,544
Deaf Smith	1,062	3,811,938	4.8	8.2	0.3	2.8	19.9	3.6	59.3	149.5	24.8	32.9	1,752	1,501
Delta	310	865,259	9.3	5.4	0.1	0.3	2.0	3.8	78.8	17.9	10.0	6.3	1,200	1,047
Denton	23,475	99,570,425	6.2	9.2	5.0	1.6	2.3	7.1	66.8	2,592.9	452.5	1,737.6	2,080	1,767
DeWitt	1,593	5,458,272	4.5	4.6	0.6	3.0	26.2	3.1	56.6	168.6	31.6	106.4	5,275	5,035
Dickens	142	386,281	9.0	7.0	0.0	7.7	0.6	3.5	70.0	11.1	4.0	5.1	2,342	2,269
Dimmit	790	2,562,510	9.7	9.1	0.0	0.8	27.9	6.2	45.5	70.5	11.1	54.4	5,295	4,809
Donley	335	1,129,574	12.0	1.2	1.0	2.4	2.3	7.5	73.1	19.2	9.0	5.5	1,652	1,457
Duval	1,043	3,227,857	6.4	10.4	0.0	3.6	30.6	4.3	43.2	109.5	38.2	24.5	2,176	2,017
Eastland	1,371	4,215,159	5.5	7.8	0.9	1.8	12.4	2.4	67.9	94.1	31.4	33.0	1,804	1,489
Ector	8,000	32,951,515	4.0	7.4	3.1	1.5	28.6	2.4	51.5	876.8	185.7	341.2	2,174	1,556
Edwards	178	511,085	6.8	9.8	0.0	4.7	0.4	4.7	72.9	11.8	2.1	8.8	4,564	4,448
Ellis	6,215	23,746,559	5.9	9.9	4.5	1.8	0.8	3.9	72.0	562.2	188.5	309.1	1,783	1,570
El Paso	41,955	157,950,113	5.1	9.1	3.4	2.4	11.3	2.7	63.9	4,047.0	1,836.8	1,327.6	1,585	1,238
Erath	1,701	5,485,209	7.5	10.9	3.3	2.5	15.6	3.3	55.4	114.5	43.2	56.7	1,360	1,111
Falls	646	2,047,971	6.4	10.6	1.6	4.3	2.6	4.9	69.1	50.3	24.8	19.9	1,147	989
Fannin	1,210	3,682,491	9.3	7.3	3.9	2.9	0.4	4.0	71.2	97.7	42.6	46.0	1,331	1,134
Fayette	1,086	3,648,038	9.7	12.7	0.0	5.7	5.1	8.9	57.4	84.0	16.6	49.6	1,975	1,698
Fisher	253	842,936	10.7	1.6	0.0	3.4	46.3	1.9	35.4	18.7	4.8	5.8	1,508	1,332
Floyd	447	1,562,702	7.3	7.8	0.0	3.6	24.3	3.7	53.2	24.9	11.9	10.0	1,712	1,537
Foard	114	294,388	13.7	3.2	0.0	29.3	4.2	3.4	44.2	7.8	2.6	4.6	3,790	3,607
Fort Bend	20,284	79,790,202	6.3	9.9	2.1	1.6	1.9	2.3	74.9	2,136.7	450.1	1,352.2	1,761	1,585
Franklin	404	1,326,799	7.5	9.7	0.0	3.6	0.7	10.8	67.0	31.2	6.9	21.1	1,953	1,751
Freestone	910	2,968,110	7.1	5.4	1.2	2.4	1.8	1.2	80.8	76.4	17.0	51.1	2,600	2,509
Frio	783	2,684,048	4.5	9.6	0.0	4.4	1.1	5.5	73.9	66.4	17.3	39.9	2,007	1,858
Gaines	1,236	4,279,287	4.8	5.9	0.0	4.4	25.4	2.9	53.9	157.4	23.3	79.0	3,842	3,737
Galveston	17,131	60,202,014	6.2	10.4	2.3	3.2	4.1	4.7	68.3	1,767.6	546.8	976.9	2,919	2,529
Garza	299	979,400	9.1	13.9	0.0	2.6	2.3	2.9	68.4	22.3	7.8	11.1	1,714	1,539
Gillespie	1,146	5,013,539	6.1	8.8	0.9	2.6	2.3	20.6	54.6	85.8	7.6	64.4	2,430	1,982
Glasscock	88	338,809	4.6	1.8	0.0	6.4	0.0	3.6	78.7	29.3	0.5	26.7	19,587	19,491
Goliad	343	1,232,592	8.4	9.7	4.7	3.7	1.8	1.0	69.8	21.9	6.9	12.6	1,663	1,481
Gonzales	1,335	4,542,193	7.0	7.9	0.6	3.2	23.9	4.1	52.6	133.9	28.6	54.2	2,613	2,290
Gray	1,019	3,361,637	11.3	10.0	3.3	3.6	0.7	4.1	65.5	73.4	22.2	36.5	1,653	1,387
Grayson	5,654	19,812,399	6.1	10.4	4.1	2.3	5.3	5.8	64.9	487.4	166.5	228.8	1,745	1,467
Gregg	6,692	23,257,940	4.7	11.3	5.3	1.5	8.1	4.3	62.8	552.3	182.3	277.2	2,256	1,638
Grimes	951	3,230,359	9.7	11.2	1.0	2.5	0.3	2.2	72.5	75.8	15.6	54.0	1,932	1,788

1. Based on the resident population estimated as of July 1 of the year shown.

STATE County	Local government finances, 2017 (cont.)									Government employment, 2020			Individual income tax returns, 2019		
	Direct general expenditure							Debt outstanding							
			Percent of total for:												
	Total (mil dol)	Per capita[1] (dollars)	Education	Health and hospitals	Police protection	Public welfare	Highways	Total (mil dol)	Per capita[1] (dollars)	Federal civilian	Federal military	State and local	Number of returns	Mean adjusted gross income	Mean income tax
	185	186	187	188	189	190	191	192	193	194	195	196	197	198	199
TEXAS—Cont'd															
Caldwell	136.7	3,229	61.8	2.9	4.9	0.3	3.3	120.3	2,842	73	78	1,786	19,840	48,384	4,012
Calhoun	196.3	9,043	35.2	15.4	2.7	25.9	3.8	86.4	3,978	39	86	1,333	9,840	58,010	5,773
Callahan	45.5	3,258	73.3	0.5	5.3	0.0	2.4	39.2	2,804	45	27	618	6,310	54,521	5,045
Cameron	1,674.4	3,966	67.1	0.8	4.6	0.4	2.9	1,644.9	3,896	3,897	910	25,041	180,170	40,575	3,050
Camp	40.1	3,120	71.8	0.1	3.8	0.1	5.5	56.9	4,431	32	25	564	5,530	48,588	4,026
Carson	35.2	5,868	53.1	0.7	3.2	0.2	4.3	35.4	5,903	15	11	417	2,710	60,309	6,031
Cass	90.2	3,011	62.3	1.9	5.5	0.5	4.5	43.2	1,443	71	56	1,650	12,970	49,158	4,031
Castro	30.9	4,016	75.8	5.4	2.5	0.1	1.6	41.7	5,421	20	14	682	3,000	44,385	3,883
Chambers	244.7	5,929	50.1	8.3	4.2	5.6	5.6	444.6	10,772	63	101	2,418	21,490	87,689	10,533
Cherokee	151.1	2,899	55.7	7.7	5.4	0.2	6.6	159.0	3,050	83	106	3,913	21,840	49,004	4,283
Childress	51.8	7,127	24.0	60.4	2.5	0.1	3.1	2.4	332	22	10	1,022	2,530	48,255	4,116
Clay	40.0	3,814	51.2	15.3	6.4	0.4	9.4	24.0	2,294	27	20	521	4,760	58,936	5,227
Cochran	26.8	9,393	49.0	14.3	3.0	0.2	4.2	16.1	5,627	13	5	290	1,160	45,471	3,377
Coke	16.9	5,155	35.7	0.0	3.9	33.3	5.0	9.1	2,761	12	6	317	1,520	52,438	4,689
Coleman	24.7	2,941	66.8	7.2	2.6	0.1	4.5	15.5	1,841	39	15	509	3,630	48,352	5,461
Collin	5,153.8	5,303	51.2	1.2	3.6	0.0	4.4	20,672.9	21,271	2,269	2,154	51,745	495,250	104,105	15,087
Collingsworth	15.6	5,252	40.7	10.7	5.2	0.1	4.4	10.6	3,571	14	5	213	1,200	49,231	4,891
Colorado	69.1	3,245	51.7	7.0	6.8	0.2	6.9	68.4	3,214	57	41	1,056	10,290	64,583	7,262
Comal	595.2	4,230	60.2	1.0	5.7	0.1	4.9	1,068.5	7,593	266	314	6,628	80,240	88,755	11,586
Comanche	46.5	3,439	57.5	4.6	4.6	0.4	8.0	46.8	3,460	56	26	758	5,970	44,480	4,015
Concho	20.6	7,623	27.1	39.8	3.0	0.0	3.2	4.2	1,539	15	5	224	1,060	52,988	4,851
Cooke	233.1	5,838	55.9	17.6	4.8	0.1	2.8	224.6	5,625	77	78	2,801	19,850	71,820	8,665
Coryell	207.3	2,773	51.4	23.2	5.0	0.7	2.2	151.6	2,028	205	122	6,070	30,190	44,568	3,223
Cottle	4.0	2,907	63.6	0.0	3.2	0.3	8.2	1.3	950	11	3	106	580	38,514	2,790
Crane	30.3	6,475	66.8	0.0	6.1	0.0	3.6	6.3	1,345	6	9	382	2,100	67,449	6,305
Crockett	36.2	10,247	48.0	1.1	2.7	1.2	7.8	6.5	1,831	3	7	370	1,600	63,821	7,228
Crosby	25.4	4,337	68.5	0.0	3.9	0.3	3.5	10.9	1,866	18	11	406	2,380	43,506	3,350
Culberson	16.1	7,230	74.2	11.2	0.0	0.0	0.0	39.4	17,669	91	4	237	1,090	47,246	4,094
Dallam	24.3	3,343	78.7	0.1	2.4	0.1	2.9	20.1	2,762	20	14	281	3,320	58,032	6,574
Dallas	14,438.7	5,511	37.9	17.3	5.7	0.4	3.1	31,348.3	11,964	26,578	5,532	153,053	1,236,240	78,587	11,971
Dawson	61.4	4,818	66.0	0.2	4.9	0.8	5.0	179.9	14,120	64	22	1,173	4,930	60,773	6,670
Deaf Smith	127.0	6,773	31.2	16.6	3.4	0.1	2.8	956.2	50,987	56	34	1,189	7,950	42,438	4,059
Delta	14.4	2,736	72.5	0.0	2.0	0.2	2.0	17.6	3,340	18	10	297	2,200	44,982	3,600
Denton	2,474.3	2,962	53.4	1.6	5.4	0.1	4.2	7,148.9	8,558	2,336	1,814	35,736	430,930	91,384	12,345
DeWitt	194.6	9,641	54.7	19.2	2.1	0.2	11.4	159.5	7,906	33	35	2,213	8,570	82,538	13,403
Dickens	9.8	4,456	59.3	0.0	2.6	0.8	0.0	5.1	2,332	13	3	149	770	50,997	4,657
Dimmit	70.6	6,863	76.3	0.0	3.2	0.1	2.5	57.0	5,542	262	19	1,008	4,160	52,538	5,999
Donley	25.4	7,592	63.7	0.0	2.5	2.6	2.6	111.1	33,272	14	6	399	1,450	35,235	2,933
Duval	89.1	7,906	43.0	31.7	2.6	0.4	5.4	69.1	6,131	132	20	916	4,610	41,550	3,019
Eastland	95.8	5,235	61.3	15.8	2.9	0.2	2.8	81.7	4,468	59	123	1,444	7,760	43,860	5,554
Ector	915.0	5,830	35.1	40.8	3.5	0.0	2.5	447.1	2,849	236	317	9,895	75,890	67,148	7,428
Edwards	10.3	5,316	69.6	0.0	9.0	0.0	3.0	4.3	2,230	19	4	129	800	55,638	6,316
Ellis	600.8	3,465	64.9	0.7	5.2	0.1	1.9	1,415.4	8,162	306	364	7,949	89,330	68,967	7,288
El Paso	3,935.7	4,700	49.6	17.4	4.5	0.2	1.3	6,815.4	8,139	13,082	28,545	54,357	398,040	45,570	3,857
Erath	95.7	2,293	57.0	1.6	8.3	0.0	7.2	69.4	1,663	93	80	4,187	17,060	55,174	5,870
Falls	40.8	2,354	69.9	5.8	3.0	0.1	2.0	34.0	1,959	412	29	1,155	6,760	44,210	3,714
Fannin	98.6	2,853	61.0	0.0	4.5	0.5	6.2	107.7	3,117	780	63	1,937	14,820	55,010	5,174
Fayette	82.7	3,292	51.3	3.8	6.7	0.9	9.4	117.9	4,695	79	48	1,469	12,320	64,009	8,708
Fisher	19.6	5,059	33.1	48.0	0.9	0.1	1.1	12.1	3,129	15	7	308	1,540	58,856	5,403
Floyd	25.8	4,417	75.5	1.5	4.4	0.0	0.9	15.5	2,659	31	14	500	2,440	52,807	4,841
Foard	4.9	4,050	66.8	2.0	3.5	0.3	7.6	0.2	154	5	2	117	490	42,357	3,686
Fort Bend	2,309.2	3,008	52.8	0.8	4.4	0.2	7.8	6,319.0	8,231	1,048	1,614	24,975	372,370	94,053	12,903
Franklin	28.7	2,660	51.3	0.4	6.3	0.5	12.8	50.8	4,702	19	21	441	4,640	56,869	5,681
Freestone	69.6	3,542	64.7	3.4	6.6	0.1	6.5	68.7	3,497	45	35	1,280	8,150	54,565	4,867
Frio	79.1	3,977	62.6	6.2	4.0	0.1	4.4	125.6	6,312	196	32	1,263	6,770	45,247	4,191
Gaines	158.3	7,701	37.5	35.0	2.0	0.1	6.8	110.5	5,377	32	42	1,332	8,500	58,696	6,145
Galveston	1,688.7	5,046	53.8	4.8	5.7	0.3	2.8	2,873.3	8,586	1,143	1,023	29,127	162,500	78,716	10,012
Garza	40.1	6,175	59.6	2.2	4.7	0.0	4.0	40.1	6,179	14	17	333	1,990	53,397	5,317
Gillespie	102.2	3,859	57.7	3.1	9.3	0.3	5.6	49.1	1,852	57	51	1,167	14,340	88,990	12,533
Glasscock	32.5	23,817	95.0	0.0	0.2	0.0	0.2	16.2	11,867	6	3	134	630	158,738	31,998
Goliad	21.1	2,800	68.8	0.0	1.6	0.2	3.1	12.8	1,694	16	14	401	3,340	64,636	7,426
Gonzales	140.8	6,789	34.3	42.7	1.6	0.0	1.1	59.1	2,849	60	39	1,489	9,510	57,508	6,677
Gray	71.9	3,255	56.7	0.5	6.5	0.2	5.5	73.7	3,333	41	38	1,446	8,830	50,078	4,717
Grayson	487.5	3,717	54.3	3.7	4.9	0.5	3.7	1,071.3	8,168	381	261	6,802	63,360	61,072	6,171
Gregg	581.4	4,733	53.6	6.3	7.0	0.0	4.2	804.9	6,552	382	232	7,093	57,300	60,538	6,692
Grimes	68.9	2,463	60.4	0.4	5.2	0.1	8.6	93.4	3,339	67	51	1,783	13,070	56,441	5,748

1. Based on the resident population estimated as of July 1 of the year shown.

State / county code	CBSA code[1]	County Type code[2]	STATE County	Land area[3] (sq. mi)	Population, 2021: Total persons 2021	Population, 2021: Rank	Population, 2021: Per square mile	Race alone or in combination, not Hispanic or Latino (percent): White	Black	American Indian, Alaska Native	Asian and Pacific Islancer	Percent Hispanic or Latino[4]	Age (percent): Under 5 years	5 to 17 years	18 to 24 years	25 to 34 years	35 to 44 years	45 to 54 years
				1	2	3	4	5	6	7	8	9	10	11	12	13	14	15
			TEXAS—Cont'd															
48187	41700	1	Guadalupe	711.3	177,036	381	248.9	50.1	8.9	0.9	3.2	39.4	5.6	14.2	13.1	12.8	14.8	13.1
48189	38380	4	Hale	1,004.7	32,220	1,375	32.1	32.3	5.4	0.8	0.8	61.7	6.2	15.4	16.1	13.9	12.8	11.1
48191		9	Hall	883.5	2,845	2,970	3.2	55.4	9.4	1.4	0.5	34.8	4.0	12.9	12.8	10.2	9.8	11.2
48193		6	Hamilton	835.9	8,229	2,560	9.8	83.2	1.3	1.0	1.0	14.4	4.8	12.8	10.6	10.7	10.8	10.7
48195		7	Hansford	919.8	5,159	2,809	5.6	48.7	1.2	0.7	0.7	49.9	7.1	16.5	15.3	11.4	10.8	11.5
48197		9	Hardeman	695.1	3,552	2,919	5.1	67.1	6.9	1.5	1.2	25.6	5.1	13.0	11.9	10.7	12.2	11.8
48199	13140	2	Hardin	890.6	56,973	915	64.0	86.2	6.2	1.0	1.3	6.8	6.0	14.4	11.8	12.4	13.1	12.1
48201	26420	1	Harris	1,707.0	4,728,030	3	2,769.8	28.9	19.8	0.5	7.9	44.4	6.9	14.9	13.7	15.4	14.6	12.5
48203	30980	4	Harrison	900.1	69,150	780	76.8	64.2	21.0	1.0	1.1	14.3	5.7	14.4	13.1	11.4	12.4	11.7
48205		7	Hartley	1,462.0	5,397	2,784	3.7	62.9	7.4	0.8	0.9	28.8	6.3	11.0	10.5	15.6	15.2	15.2
48207		6	Haskell	903.1	5,411	2,783	6.0	64.7	5.4	1.2	1.6	29.0	4.0	10.7	11.8	13.3	12.9	11.1
48209	12420	1	Hays	676.9	255,397	277	377.3	53.1	4.7	0.8	2.6	40.6	5.7	13.1	19.0	14.0	14.6	11.6
48211		7	Hemphill	906.3	3,271	2,943	3.6	62.4	0.9	1.3	1.6	34.9	5.7	16.6	15.6	8.6	14.2	11.7
48213	11980	4	Henderson	873.8	83,667	688	95.8	78.1	6.9	1.4	1.0	14.3	5.4	12.2	11.6	11.0	11.1	11.7
48215	32580	2	Hidalgo	1,571.0	880,356	65	560.4	5.9	0.6	0.1	1.0	92.6	7.9	18.2	16.5	13.6	12.3	11.4
48217		6	Hill	958.9	36,471	1,273	38.0	70.3	6.8	1.0	1.0	22.5	5.7	13.4	12.2	11.3	11.6	11.4
48219	30220	6	Hockley	908.4	21,363	1,743	23.5	45.2	4.0	0.8	0.6	50.3	6.5	15.0	16.0	12.7	12.8	10.3
48221	24180	1	Hood	420.7	64,222	844	152.7	83.7	1.9	1.3	1.2	13.4	4.8	12.0	10.4	10.3	11.1	10.9
48223	44860	6	Hopkins	767.4	37,211	1,245	48.5	73.4	7.8	1.1	1.1	18.2	6.2	13.7	12.5	12.2	11.7	12.0
48225		7	Houston	1,231.0	22,241	1,703	18.1	61.8	25.0	0.8	1.0	12.7	4.9	11.3	10.3	11.3	13.2	12.8
48227	13700	4	Howard	900.8	34,128	1,328	37.9	47.0	6.7	1.2	1.5	45.0	5.8	11.8	13.3	15.6	14.0	15.2
48229	21340	2	Hudspeth	4,570.5	3,287	2,940	0.7	16.7	4.4	1.2	1.6	77.8	5.2	12.7	12.1	17.4	16.4	11.8
48231	19100	1	Hunt	840.4	103,394	593	123.0	70.3	8.6	1.5	2.0	19.5	6.1	13.7	14.0	12.8	12.2	12.1
48233	14420	6	Hutchinson	887.4	20,495	1,792	23.1	70.6	3.2	2.2	1.1	24.8	6.1	14.3	13.0	11.5	13.2	11.5
48235	41660	3	Irion	1,051.5	1,552	3,076	1.5	70.8	1.9	1.7	1.2	26.3	5.5	14.2	10.6	11.0	11.8	11.2
48237		6	Jack	911.0	8,712	2,510	9.6	76.4	4.7	0.8	0.9	18.2	4.6	13.1	13.0	14.0	13.1	12.5
48239		6	Jackson	829.4	15,121	2,085	18.2	58.4	6.5	0.8	1.4	34.1	6.9	14.2	12.6	11.6	12.7	10.4
48241		6	Jasper	938.7	32,975	1,363	35.1	75.6	16.7	1.0	1.0	7.3	5.6	13.5	11.8	11.2	11.3	11.8
48243		9	Jeff Davis	2,264.6	1,949	3,045	0.9	65.0	1.9	2.1	2.3	30.9	1.1	2.4	6.7	8.2	10.0	13.6
48245	13140	2	Jefferson	876.8	253,704	279	289.4	39.2	34.1	0.7	4.3	23.1	6.6	13.8	13.2	14.1	13.5	11.6
48247		6	Jim Hogg	1,136.2	4,801	2,837	4.2	5.4	0.9	0.6	0.6	92.8	6.1	17.9	15.5	10.7	12.4	9.7
48249	10860	4	Jim Wells	865.2	38,847	1,205	44.9	17.9	1.0	0.5	0.6	80.5	6.6	16.0	13.8	12.5	12.8	10.9
48251	19100	1	Johnson	724.8	187,280	361	258.4	69.2	5.4	1.1	2.0	24.2	6.3	15.0	13.1	13.1	13.6	12.5
48253	10180	3	Jones	928.6	19,873	1,825	21.4	58.4	12.4	0.9	0.8	28.6	4.1	10.0	13.0	16.7	15.6	13.1
48255		6	Karnes	747.8	14,754	2,101	19.7	33.9	8.3	0.4	0.6	57.3	5.5	12.4	14.1	17.3	14.8	11.1
48257	19100	1	Kaufman	780.8	157,768	433	202.1	55.4	17.5	0.9	2.1	25.9	7.0	16.5	13.1	14.1	15.0	12.2
48259	41700	1	Kendall	662.5	46,788	1,040	70.6	71.1	1.8	1.1	2.0	25.6	4.7	13.4	12.5	9.7	13.0	13.5
48261	28780	9	Kenedy	1,458.6	340	3,140	0.2	24.4	3.5	3.2	0.9	70.6	3.5	10.6	14.1	10.6	13.2	12.9
48263		9	Kent	902.5	749	3,121	0.8	77.3	1.3	2.0	0.4	20.7	4.1	15.2	10.5	8.7	11.1	9.3
48265	28500	4	Kerr	1,103.3	53,161	952	48.2	68.0	1.9	1.2	1.5	28.7	4.9	10.7	11.4	10.3	10.0	10.3
48267		7	Kimble	1,251.0	4,365	2,865	3.5	72.9	1.5	1.0	1.1	24.4	5.2	9.9	9.7	9.4	10.1	10.1
48269		9	King	910.9	258	3,141	0.3	79.1	3.1	1.9	0.8	17.8	6.2	15.1	14.0	6.2	15.1	10.9
48271		7	Kinney	1,360.5	3,130	2,951	2.3	35.2	3.0	1.5	0.6	61.6	5.1	10.8	11.9	12.3	12.7	11.8
48273	28780	4	Kleberg	881.3	30,635	1,417	34.8	20.4	3.6	0.5	2.6	73.8	6.4	13.7	23.8	13.5	11.1	9.3
48275		9	Knox	850.6	3,351	2,935	3.9	58.1	6.9	1.1	0.9	35.0	6.3	16.1	10.6	11.1	11.1	10.2
48277	37580	5	Lamar	907.3	50,098	995	55.2	75.3	14.7	2.5	1.4	9.2	6.3	13.7	12.1	12.5	11.2	12.0
48279		6	Lamb	1,016.2	12,898	2,217	12.7	38.2	4.0	0.7	0.5	57.5	6.4	16.1	13.7	11.3	12.0	10.7
48281	28660	2	Lampasas	712.5	22,252	1,702	31.2	72.9	4.9	1.7	2.5	20.5	5.0	12.5	11.3	10.3	12.0	12.6
48283		6	La Salle	1,486.7	6,670	2,687	4.5	11.4	1.5	0.7	0.4	86.5	5.2	10.9	20.0	17.5	13.5	10.6
48285		6	Lavaca	969.7	20,544	1,789	21.2	73.1	6.3	0.5	0.8	20.3	5.8	13.4	11.8	9.9	11.0	10.7
48287		6	Lee	629.0	17,706	1,935	28.1	63.8	10.6	0.8	0.9	25.3	5.6	11.3	12.0	11.3	12.4	12.0
48289		8	Leon	1,073.2	15,959	2,034	14.9	76.0	7.1	1.1	1.1	16.1	5.7	13.2	11.0	9.6	10.8	10.4
48291	26420	1	Liberty	1,158.4	97,621	627	84.3	56.0	9.2	0.8	0.9	34.3	7.2	16.9	13.6	13.9	12.8	12.1
48293		6	Limestone	905.4	22,119	1,708	24.4	58.6	17.5	0.9	1.3	23.4	5.5	12.6	12.2	12.4	12.1	11.3
48295		9	Lipscomb	932.2	2,931	2,962	3.1	61.2	2.2	2.0	1.3	35.8	6.3	14.0	12.1	10.6	13.1	9.7
48297		8	Live Oak	1,039.7	11,377	2,322	10.9	52.5	4.9	1.1	1.2	41.3	5.6	11.3	10.5	13.9	13.0	10.6
48299		7	Llano	934.1	21,978	1,716	23.5	85.4	1.6	1.2	0.9	12.2	3.9	8.5	8.2	7.8	8.0	10.1
48301	37780	9	Loving	668.8	57	3,143	0.1	75.4	3.5	0.0	0.0	21.1	3.5	29.8	10.5	14.0	8.8	10.5
48303	31180	2	Lubbock	895.6	314,451	227	351.1	52.7	7.7	0.8	2.9	37.3	6.2	13.5	20.7	14.3	12.6	9.9
48305	31180	2	Lynn	891.9	5,688	2,763	6.4	52.3	2.7	0.7	0.5	44.8	6.6	16.4	12.4	11.9	13.9	10.2
48307		7	McCulloch	1,065.6	7,533	2,617	7.1	63.7	2.8	1.0	0.9	32.8	5.3	12.1	11.4	11.0	10.9	11.0
48309	47380	2	McLennan	1,036.7	263,115	268	253.8	56.3	14.8	0.7	2.4	27.6	6.4	13.8	18.3	13.0	12.0	10.4
48311		9	McMullen	1,139.8	608	3,133	0.5	52.1	2.8	0.5	0.8	44.6	6.1	9.7	12.0	10.0	10.2	11.7
48313		6	Madison	466.1	13,718	2,175	29.4	54.7	19.8	0.8	1.5	24.8	5.9	12.0	15.5	17.7	13.1	10.6
48315		8	Marion	380.9	9,645	2,441	25.3	72.9	21.4	2.0	1.5	4.8	4.3	10.3	9.4	9.4	10.4	11.6
48317	33260	3	Martin	915.0	5,211	2,806	5.7	48.0	2.6	0.9	0.8	48.8	7.4	20.1	13.5	12.6	13.4	10.8

1. CBSA = Core Based Statistical Area. See Appendix A for explanation. See Appendix B for list of metropolitan areas with component counties. 2. County type code from the Economic Research Service of USDA Rural-Urban Continuum Codes. See Appendix A for definition. 3. Dry land or land partially or temporarily covered by water. 4. May be of any race.

STATE County	Population, 2021 (cont.)				Population change, 2000–2021							Households, 2016–2020				
	Age (percent) (cont.)				Total persons		Percent change		Components of change, 2020–2021					Percent		
	55 to 64 years	65 to 74 years	75 years and over	Percent female	2010	2020	2010–2020	2020–2021	Births	Deaths	Net Migration	Number	Persons per household	Family house-holds	Female family house-holder[1]	One person
	16	17	18	19	20	21	22	23	24	25	26	27	28	29	30	31
TEXAS—Cont'd																
Guadalupe	11.9	8.9	5.6	50.2	131,533	172,706	31.3	2.5	2,213	1,828	3,960	55,710	2.9	75.8	12.7	19.8
Hale	10.9	8.0	5.7	47.2	36,273	32,522	-10.3	-0.9	472	470	-310	10,888	2.9	69.9	14.9	27.5
Hall	14.7	12.8	11.6	49.9	3,353	2,825	-15.7	0.7	19	70	75	1,252	2.4	68.4	11.8	29.2
Hamilton	14.7	13.3	11.6	50.2	8,517	8,222	-3.5	0.1	92	182	97	3,007	2.7	66.6	9.0	32.0
Hansford	11.9	8.8	6.8	48.9	5,613	5,285	-5.8	-2.4	96	58	-163	1,859	2.9	71.4	7.8	28.3
Hardeman	13.0	12.3	10.0	49.4	4,139	3,549	-14.3	0.1	41	62	25	1,672	2.4	65.4	14.1	27.5
Hardin	13.0	10.7	6.6	50.6	54,635	56,231	2.9	1.3	805	922	864	21,188	2.7	74.5	12.4	22.5
Harris	10.8	7.3	4.1	50.2	4,092,459	4,731,145	15.6	-0.1	78,665	41,862	-40,654	1,635,749	2.8	68.1	15.2	26.3
Harrison	13.3	11.0	7.0	50.9	65,631	68,839	4.9	0.5	931	1,007	380	23,841	2.7	72.3	13.9	23.1
Hartley	10.9	8.2	7.2	39.0	6,062	5,382	-11.2	0.3	83	41	-28	1,691	2.4	71.6	7.4	26.9
Haskell	13.8	12.7	9.8	46.2	5,899	5,416	-8.2	-0.1	58	96	34	2,162	2.4	66.1	10.4	29.6
Hays	10.3	7.8	3.9	50.2	157,107	241,067	53.4	5.9	3,103	1,817	13,158	76,724	2.8	66.5	9.7	22.6
Hemphill	11.2	9.6	6.8	50.3	3,807	3,382	-11.2	-3.3	34	39	-105	1,356	2.9	69.8	5.8	27.7
Henderson	14.7	13.2	9.1	50.8	78,532	82,150	4.6	1.8	1,157	1,673	2,055	31,649	2.6	69.6	12.4	24.9
Hidalgo	8.6	6.5	4.9	50.7	774,769	870,781	12.4	1.1	16,405	7,302	164	243,878	3.5	80.2	21.8	16.9
Hill	14.0	12.0	8.5	49.8	35,089	35,874	2.2	1.7	505	668	766	13,094	2.7	70.6	11.3	25.5
Hockley	11.7	9.0	6.1	50.2	22,935	21,537	-6.1	-0.8	301	317	-162	8,071	2.8	69.1	11.2	27.6
Hood	15.1	15.0	10.3	50.9	51,182	61,598	20.4	4.3	675	1,122	3,113	23,215	2.6	73.6	7.6	23.2
Hopkins	13.2	10.9	7.6	50.6	35,161	36,787	4.6	1.2	543	626	512	13,514	2.7	72.3	11.2	24.1
Houston	13.7	12.5	10.0	46.1	23,732	22,066	-7.0	0.8	254	428	353	8,234	2.4	66.9	15.1	30.7
Howard	11.2	7.9	5.1	42.1	35,012	34,860	-0.4	-2.1	500	472	-756	11,354	2.8	63.1	11.3	32.3
Hudspeth	9.7	8.8	5.8	46.3	3,476	3,202	-7.9	2.7	53	37	70	1,127	3.4	65.9	14.6	33.1
Hunt	13.1	9.7	6.2	50.5	86,129	99,956	16.1	3.4	1,429	1,502	3,558	33,596	2.8	70.2	12.4	24.6
Hutchinson	12.7	10.9	6.9	49.2	22,150	20,617	-6.9	-0.6	323	349	-99	7,074	3.0	68.9	10.4	28.2
Irion	15.3	11.3	9.0	49.5	1,599	1,513	-5.4	2.6	29	20	29	636	2.4	66.7	7.4	31.1
Jack	12.8	9.9	6.9	43.7	9,044	8,472	-6.3	2.8	99	129	274	3,169	2.5	66.6	10.4	29.6
Jackson	12.4	11.1	8.2	50.0	14,075	14,988	6.5	0.9	248	205	88	4,924	3.0	74.1	10.3	21.5
Jasper	14.3	12.1	8.3	50.1	35,710	32,980	-7.6	0.0	468	638	164	13,725	2.5	68.0	14.6	28.3
Jeff Davis	19.0	24.4	14.7	49.6	2,342	1,996	-14.8	-2.4	14	44	-17	991	2.2	62.6	10.6	34.7
Jefferson	12.3	9.1	5.9	48.5	252,273	256,526	1.7	-1.1	3,901	3,689	-3,052	94,012	2.5	63.8	15.8	30.9
Jim Hogg	11.0	9.5	7.1	48.1	5,300	4,838	-8.7	-0.8	72	86	-24	1,545	3.3	71.9	17.5	25.2
Jim Wells	11.5	9.2	6.6	50.4	40,838	38,891	-4.8	-0.1	580	624	-10	12,924	3.1	74.1	15.6	20.5
Johnson	12.3	8.8	5.4	49.8	150,934	179,927	19.2	4.1	2,618	2,277	7,095	58,270	2.9	76.4	12.4	19.3
Jones	11.6	9.3	6.5	36.7	20,202	19,663	-2.7	1.1	186	243	265	5,646	2.3	69.8	10.5	25.6
Karnes	10.7	8.5	5.8	41.6	14,824	14,710	-0.8	0.3	201	233	74	4,552	2.6	69.3	14.3	27.5
Kaufman	10.8	7.2	3.9	50.6	103,350	145,310	40.6	8.6	2,231	1,687	12,092	39,237	3.3	77.5	13.3	18.8
Kendall	14.4	11.4	7.6	50.4	33,410	44,279	32.5	5.7	489	629	2,690	14,789	3.1	77.4	5.9	20.0
Kenedy	14.1	12.4	8.5	48.2	416	350	-15.9	-2.9	2	3	-10	129	3.0	89.1	30.2	10.9
Kent	16.7	11.6	12.7	47.4	808	753	-6.8	-0.5	3	13	7	286	2.3	62.6	5.6	34.6
Kerr	14.6	15.4	12.4	51.5	49,625	52,598	6.0	1.1	593	1,076	1,062	21,278	2.4	69.1	12.5	26.8
Kimble	15.3	17.1	13.2	50.7	4,607	4,286	-7.0	1.8	56	66	92	1,967	2.2	63.7	11.2	32.7
King	15.1	9.7	7.8	47.7	286	265	-7.3	-2.6	4	2	-9	90	3.1	73.3	11.1	21.1
Kinney	10.9	12.7	11.8	44.3	3,598	3,129	-13.0	0.0	37	57	22	1,475	2.3	53.0	7.5	43.8
Kleberg	8.7	7.6	5.9	49.2	32,061	31,040	-3.2	-1.3	475	421	-463	11,140	2.6	64.4	14.4	27.1
Knox	13.8	11.1	9.8	50.4	3,719	3,353	-9.8	-0.1	49	49	-3	1,394	2.5	71.8	10.6	27.4
Lamar	13.1	10.9	8.0	51.5	49,793	50,088	0.6	0.0	720	992	279	19,995	2.5	67.0	15.5	29.3
Lamb	12.5	9.6	7.7	50.0	13,977	13,045	-6.7	-1.1	190	204	-135	4,706	2.7	66.1	12.5	32.0
Lampasas	15.5	12.5	8.2	50.3	19,677	21,627	9.9	2.9	249	313	696	7,823	2.7	72.0	11.2	23.4
La Salle	8.7	7.4	6.3	40.5	6,886	6,664	-3.2	0.1	91	60	-27	2,142	3.1	77.5	11.4	21.3
Lavaca	13.9	13.2	10.1	50.9	19,263	20,337	5.6	1.0	288	352	275	7,904	2.5	69.9	11.2	27.6
Lee	15.5	12.2	7.7	49.1	16,612	17,478	5.2	1.3	238	213	204	6,159	2.7	75.6	12.6	21.7
Leon	15.0	14.3	10.1	49.9	16,801	15,719	-6.4	1.5	235	349	357	6,837	2.5	70.1	12.2	26.2
Liberty	11.2	7.9	4.3	50.2	75,643	91,628	21.1	6.5	1,426	1,202	5,864	27,417	2.9	71.6	11.7	25.3
Limestone	13.6	12.2	8.0	48.2	23,384	22,146	-5.3	-0.1	276	415	111	8,292	2.7	69.2	14.6	27.9
Lipscomb	14.8	11.3	8.2	48.5	3,302	3,059	-7.4	-4.2	59	35	-150	1,158	2.8	75.3	12.3	20.1
Live Oak	13.6	12.0	9.6	44.7	11,531	11,335	-1.7	0.4	148	146	41	3,854	2.8	67.7	8.6	28.7
Llano	16.8	20.8	16.0	51.3	19,301	21,243	10.1	3.5	207	534	1,086	9,031	2.4	66.3	8.6	30.1
Loving	17.5	5.3	0.0	24.6	82	64	-22.0	-10.9	2	3	-5	62	1.9	29.0	0.0	71.0
Lubbock	10.1	7.8	5.1	50.6	278,831	310,639	11.4	1.2	4,924	3,954	2,774	116,535	2.5	60.2	12.9	29.0
Lynn	12.7	8.8	7.1	47.6	5,915	5,596	-5.4	1.6	104	81	69	2,199	2.7	72.3	12.3	25.8
McCulloch	14.0	14.2	10.1	49.7	8,283	7,630	-7.9	-1.3	85	161	-21	3,151	2.5	62.8	12.8	34.2
McLennan	11.1	8.9	6.0	51.0	234,906	260,579	10.9	1.0	3,929	3,374	1,934	91,422	2.7	65.4	15.4	27.0
McMullen	15.1	11.8	13.3	47.2	707	600	-15.1	1.3	10	7	6	229	3.2	80.8	15.3	14.8
Madison	9.9	8.9	6.4	42.5	13,664	13,455	-1.5	2.0	193	184	255	4,205	2.8	71.2	14.3	27.1
Marion	17.7	15.9	11.0	51.5	10,546	9,725	-7.8	-0.8	115	221	29	4,535	2.2	58.7	11.8	38.9
Martin	10.9	7.0	4.3	49.7	4,799	5,237	9.1	-0.5	100	67	-60	1,722	3.3	78.7	6.6	19.6

1. No spouse present.

STATE County	Persons in group quarters, 2021	Daytime Population, 2016–2020		Births, 2021		Deaths, 2021		Persons under 65 with no health insurance, 2019		Medicare, 2021			COVID-19 Deaths, 2020	
		Number	Employment/ residence ratio	Total	Rate[1]	Number	Rate[1]	Number	Percent	Total beneficiaries	Enrolled in Original Medicare	Enrolled in Medicare Advantage	Number	Rate[1]
	32	33	34	35	36	37	38	39	40	41	42	43	44	45
TEXAS—Cont'd														
Guadalupe	1,767	134,190	0.6	1,799	10.3	1,474	8.4	22,560	15.9	27,825	18,063	9,762	131	0.8
Hale	2,367	32,337	0.9	362	11.2	386	11.9	6,257	24.1	5,516	3,501	2,016	134	4.1
Hall	22	2,832	0.9	17	6.0	56	19.8	668	30.2	806	582	224	D	D
Hamilton	108	8,561	1.0	74	9.0	143	17.4	1,550	24.8	2,326	1,397	929	16	1.9
Hansford	48	5,167	0.9	79	15.2	46	8.8	1,348	29.6	928	775	153	19	3.6
Hardeman	2	3,536	0.8	34	9.6	46	12.9	801	26.7	970	724	246	10	2.8
Hardin	291	46,416	0.5	659	11.6	722	12.8	7,772	16.2	11,638	6,492	5,146	59	1.0
Harris	46,039	4,985,104	1.1	63,336	13.4	33,862	7.2	998,337	24.2	562,657	278,734	283,923	3,871	0.8
Harrison	1,030	62,501	0.9	763	11.1	807	11.7	10,752	20.0	13,585	8,348	5,237	90	1.3
Hartley	1,082	5,837	1.1	62	11.5	30	5.6	837	22.9	664	506	157	12	2.2
Haskell	425	5,657	1.0	49	9.0	74	13.7	1,042	26.9	1,352	981	371	16	2.9
Hays	7,398	196,879	0.8	2,490	10.0	1,491	6.0	32,880	16.7	31,817	19,990	11,827	110	0.5
Hemphill	16	4,163	1.2	25	7.5	32	9.6	748	23.3	626	517	109	D	D
Henderson	1,029	73,719	0.7	931	11.2	1,333	16.1	14,596	23.2	21,109	12,513	8,597	110	1.3
Hidalgo	6,669	842,153	0.9	13,191	15.1	5,852	6.7	248,170	33.2	107,772	43,160	64,612	2,097	2.4
Hill	471	32,034	0.7	397	11.0	535	14.8	6,420	22.6	8,834	5,276	3,558	44	1.2
Hockley	632	21,778	0.9	245	11.4	262	12.2	4,151	22.1	3,953	2,346	1,608	93	4.3
Hood	539	54,464	0.8	553	8.8	878	13.9	8,201	17.8	17,478	10,923	6,555	86	1.4
Hopkins	313	35,113	0.9	435	11.8	510	13.8	7,026	23.5	8,016	5,758	2,257	89	2.4
Houston	2,454	21,964	0.9	198	8.9	353	15.9	3,283	21.7	5,529	3,596	1,933	29	1.3
Howard	5,388	36,774	1.0	383	11.1	378	11.0	5,082	19.1	5,323	3,792	1,531	90	2.6
Hudspeth	28	4,764	1.1	40	12.3	26	8.0	1,266	32.0	725	352	373	D	D
Hunt	2,539	89,446	0.8	1,160	11.4	1,226	12.0	15,798	19.7	18,747	12,894	5,852	101	1.0
Hutchinson	184	21,954	1.1	257	12.5	263	12.8	3,472	20.2	4,117	3,151	966	57	2.8
Irion	0	1,774	1.3	18	11.7	19	12.4	171	14.0	358	270	89	D	D
Jack	978	7,987	0.7	78	9.1	102	11.9	1,550	24.5	1,635	1,188	447	13	1.5
Jackson	186	14,389	0.9	200	13.3	166	11.0	2,632	22.1	3,141	2,240	901	24	1.6
Jasper	683	33,784	0.9	376	11.4	504	15.3	4,859	17.6	8,411	5,319	3,092	56	1.7
Jeff Davis	80	2,589	1.5	12	6.1	36	18.3	373	27.1	719	532	187	D	D
Jefferson	15,907	278,727	1.3	3,168	12.4	2,935	11.5	42,811	21.6	43,337	22,938	20,399	289	1.1
Jim Hogg	3	5,192	1.0	56	11.6	65	13.5	774	18.3	963	563	401	13	2.7
Jim Wells	221	40,268	1.0	473	12.2	503	13.0	7,341	21.8	7,898	3,633	4,265	74	1.9
Johnson	2,459	146,889	0.7	2,114	11.5	1,808	9.8	30,040	20.2	30,912	15,225	15,687	183	1.0
Jones	4,974	19,145	0.9	143	7.2	200	10.1	2,407	20.4	3,470	2,355	1,115	41	2.1
Karnes	2,399	19,675	1.8	170	11.5	178	12.1	2,028	19.5	2,706	1,817	889	24	1.6
Kaufman	1,183	106,633	0.6	1,820	11.9	1,353	8.9	20,317	17.1	21,274	12,791	8,483	143	1.0
Kendall	328	44,789	1.0	394	8.6	509	11.1	6,399	16.7	10,306	7,097	3,209	40	0.9
Kenedy	0	583	2.3	2	5.8	2	5.8	88	26.3	48	31	17	D	D
Kent	42	786	1.4	3	4.0	10	13.3	77	14.1	205	131	73	D	D
Kerr	1,765	52,355	1.0	475	9.0	872	16.5	8,656	23.8	16,530	12,512	4,017	57	1.1
Kimble	14	4,277	1.0	44	10.2	48	11.1	718	23.8	1,288	976	313	D	D
King	0	325	1.5	2	7.6	2	7.6	48	21.6	36	25	12	D	D
Kinney	257	3,967	1.2	27	8.6	47	15.0	446	18.6	917	590	327	D	D
Kleberg	1,331	30,091	1.0	380	12.3	331	10.7	4,959	19.8	5,067	2,334	2,733	67	2.2
Knox	51	3,703	1.0	36	10.7	42	12.5	717	25.0	853	624	229	12	3.6
Lamar	564	51,336	1.1	586	11.7	798	15.9	8,631	21.8	11,546	9,151	2,394	103	2.1
Lamb	163	12,126	0.8	156	12.1	161	12.4	2,810	26.9	2,636	1,699	938	70	5.4
Lampasas	166	18,667	0.7	196	8.9	250	11.4	3,143	18.5	5,390	3,602	1,788	14	0.6
La Salle	1,396	10,175	1.9	74	11.1	46	6.9	887	18.3	1,163	638	525	21	3.2
Lavaca	369	18,046	0.8	234	11.4	277	13.6	2,881	18.9	5,345	4,024	1,321	52	2.6
Lee	436	16,114	0.9	192	10.9	178	10.1	3,018	22.1	3,720	2,453	1,266	32	1.8
Leon	39	16,938	0.9	184	11.6	280	17.7	3,408	26.3	5,036	3,229	1,807	24	1.5
Liberty	4,761	76,754	0.7	1,169	12.3	968	10.2	16,352	22.8	13,937	6,958	6,979	103	1.1
Limestone	1,276	22,463	0.9	221	10.0	318	14.4	3,920	22.6	5,200	3,291	1,909	32	1.4
Lipscomb	22	3,068	0.9	46	15.4	30	10.0	759	29.2	608	486	122	10	3.3
Live Oak	963	12,580	1.1	117	10.3	112	9.9	1,932	22.4	2,539	1,536	1,003	18	1.6
Llano	77	19,534	0.8	167	7.7	419	19.4	3,176	23.3	7,529	5,022	2,508	21	1.0
Loving	0	956	12.8	1	16.1	3	48.4	17	11.4	15	D	D	NA	NA
Lubbock	11,821	312,844	1.0	3,943	12.6	3,165	10.1	45,935	17.7	47,635	27,868	19,767	664	2.1
Lynn	14	4,842	0.6	88	15.6	61	10.8	1,037	21.2	1,077	681	396	18	3.2
McCulloch	65	7,726	0.9	69	9.1	120	15.9	1,290	21.0	2,138	1,601	536	13	1.7
McLennan	8,339	261,598	1.1	3,144	12.0	2,692	10.3	38,118	18.0	45,262	26,635	18,626	340	1.3
McMullen	0	1,298	3.0	8	13.3	6	9.9	76	13.6	190	126	64	D	D
Madison	2,280	13,995	0.9	162	11.9	150	11.0	2,288	24.0	2,458	1,536	922	21	1.6
Marion	95	8,829	0.7	94	9.7	178	18.4	1,420	20.2	3,051	1,928	1,123	24	2.5
Martin	7	6,293	1.3	80	15.3	53	10.1	1,038	20.4	753	559	194	18	3.4

1. Per 1,000 estimated resident population.

STATE County	COVID-19 Vaccinations, 2021–2022: Number	COVID-19 Vaccinations, 2021–2022: Percent[5]	Education: School enrollment and attainment, 2016–2020: Enrollment[1]: Total	Enrollment[1]: Percent private	Attainment[2] (percent): High school graduate or less	Attainment[2] (percent): Bachelor's degree or more	Local government expenditures,[3] 2018–2019: Total current spending (mil dol)	Local government expenditures: Current spending per student (dollars)	Money income, 2016–2020: Per capita income[4]	Households: Median income (dollars)	Households: Percent with income of less than $50,000	Households: Percent with income of $200,000 or more	Income and poverty, 2020: Median household income (dollars)	Percent below poverty level: All persons	Percent below poverty level: Children under 18 years	Percent below poverty level: Children 5 to 17 years in families
	46	47	48	49	50	51	52	53	54	55	56	57	58	59	60	61
TEXAS—Cont'd																
Guadalupe	92,290	55.3	43,424	12.9	41.8	28.0	228.8	8,598	32,406	75,774	30.4	6.3	78,909	8.5	10.7	10.1
Hale	14,983	44.9	9,114	10.3	58.0	17.2	71.2	9,856	21,303	47,500	52.1	1.6	46,589	17.6	24.6	24.3
Hall	1,296	43.7	711	4.5	53.6	18.3	6.2	12,736	24,009	40,197	57.4	4.6	36,654	18.6	36.7	32.3
Hamilton	4,611	54.5	1,846	6.4	48.4	20.6	17.6	9,967	27,147	46,893	53.8	3.6	52,840	14.7	20.9	20.0
Hansford	2,289	42.4	1,407	4.5	56.0	23.2	17.0	11,807	22,331	46,507	50.7	0.6	61,059	10.7	15.4	14.4
Hardeman	1,824	46.4	728	4.9	48.9	16.3	10.5	15,014	26,659	47,188	51.8	2.4	63,479	15.0	23.6	21.9
Hardin	21,829	37.9	12,761	15.2	50.8	18.1	98.2	8,896	29,451	61,221	41.4	4.8	69,151	10.4	12.9	12.1
Harris	3,000,789	63.7	1,283,967	12.3	41.0	32.3	8,134.5	9,701	33,459	63,022	40.0	8.9	61,906	15.9	23.3	22.3
Harrison	27,555	41.4	16,321	13.7	45.4	20.3	150.0	8,576	26,621	54,234	45.0	3.2	55,198	15.6	21.9	19.4
Hartley	2,712	48.6	992	10.3	53.7	21.1	4.9	12,040	21,862	53,722	46.1	3.1	74,686	9.5	9.1	9.4
Haskell	2,196	38.8	1,155	8.7	59.6	16.7	11.7	14,498	27,937	48,955	51.1	3.5	44,847	20.0	25.6	23.6
Hays	144,449	62.8	69,388	9.3	32.5	38.6	343.0	9,035	32,988	68,724	35.6	8.7	77,511	9.6	9.9	8.7
Hemphill	1,610	42.2	1,075	2.0	54.3	20.6	11.0	12,086	34,702	59,605	45.6	5.3	65,718	9.5	14.5	12.9
Henderson	32,577	39.4	16,409	11.2	48.6	18.3	98.8	9,796	27,069	49,469	50.5	3.6	52,660	14.2	22.6	20.7
Hidalgo	645,066	74.3	276,588	5.2	56.9	19.3	2,672.0	10,712	17,816	41,846	56.8	2.5	46,653	23.9	32.5	31.7
Hill	15,105	41.2	8,466	6.5	49.7	17.5	72.5	10,875	26,938	55,615	45.5	4.2	56,565	14.0	20.4	19.9
Hockley	9,919	43.1	6,510	8.2	52.6	15.7	52.2	10,822	24,816	47,010	52.3	3.0	55,469	12.9	19.5	18.4
Hood	31,140	50.5	11,520	13.6	38.5	29.3	78.2	9,032	36,091	71,253	36.1	6.8	85,449	9.4	14.8	14.1
Hopkins	14,640	39.5	8,487	9.7	49.5	21.3	68.7	10,016	26,915	54,600	44.4	3.6	53,634	12.7	18.9	17.9
Houston	9,762	42.5	4,555	5.2	55.2	15.6	34.4	10,918	21,669	40,838	61.3	4.1	45,989	20.0	27.7	26.3
Howard	13,841	37.8	7,891	7.3	54.6	13.4	56.7	9,574	25,531	57,761	42.3	3.7	58,445	15.7	17.8	18.2
Hudspeth	3,645	74.6	1,012	2.0	74.8	9.9	10.3	17,684	13,267	31,505	69.3	0.0	40,666	24.2	33.1	28.6
Hunt	42,366	43.0	24,690	10.6	49.0	20.4	149.4	9,753	27,338	57,467	43.8	4.2	53,760	12.6	17.6	16.7
Hutchinson	7,351	35.1	5,324	6.1	47.5	15.4	42.5	10,038	26,387	57,921	44.1	3.0	62,536	12.1	15.4	14.4
Irion	2,142	95.0	367	3.8	44.6	20.5	4.9	18,357	29,460	53,778	46.4	3.0	73,776	6.9	7.4	6.8
Jack	3,690	41.3	1,836	13.3	57.0	14.5	18.5	11,229	25,619	54,087	46.2	3.9	56,028	13.6	18.4	16.8
Jackson	6,671	45.2	3,599	9.9	51.7	15.4	37.2	10,631	25,701	58,243	42.6	1.8	56,101	12.7	17.5	17.3
Jasper	12,922	36.4	7,656	9.5	59.9	13.3	58.7	9,965	25,690	42,756	55.9	3.2	51,153	17.3	24.9	23.5
Jeff Davis	1,217	53.5	357	15.1	34.7	29.9	4.4	16,425	23,118	0	60.1	0.2	55,718	22.2	59.7	66.7
Jefferson	128,754	51.2	59,348	8.5	48.2	19.3	422.2	10,106	27,409	50,840	49.0	4.7	48,808	18.3	25.9	25.4
Jim Hogg	2,919	56.1	1,336	0.5	66.7	13.2	15.4	13,364	16,407	35,736	61.7	0.9	41,620	20.1	30.5	30.9
Jim Wells	21,905	54.1	10,848	13.8	57.1	16.2	81.8	10,209	21,749	45,857	53.5	3.4	48,773	20.1	32.9	32.4
Johnson	81,155	46.2	35,014	12.6	50.0	19.5	337.9	9,400	28,290	65,311	35.8	4.3	67,382	9.5	11.7	11.2
Jones	8,937	44.5	3,345	13.6	59.2	11.8	31.5	11,759	17,642	52,471	48.5	1.6	47,019	19.5	21.2	20.4
Karnes	9,044	58.0	2,922	13.0	60.6	15.9	32.4	13,079	25,978	52,896	48.1	8.1	56,006	17.5	22.9	21.8
Kaufman	71,342	52.4	35,390	13.6	47.3	20.2	267.4	8,742	29,147	72,179	32.9	5.2	76,352	9.2	12.7	12.6
Kendall	29,447	62.1	11,284	17.7	25.1	45.3	90.2	8,678	47,724	98,692	23.5	19.4	103,216	6.7	8.6	7.5
Kenedy	218	54.0	67	1.5	92.6	1.5	2.2	34,500	15,058	40,083	71.3	0.0	45,980	10.8	13.8	10.9
Kent	300	39.4	198	0.0	32.2	32.8	3.3	21,816	30,835	61,706	31.8	4.2	53,472	11.3	12.3	11.2
Kerr	26,708	50.8	9,624	17.8	38.9	28.2	62.4	9,018	32,361	57,196	43.1	3.7	57,425	11.6	16.5	16.9
Kimble	1,869	43.1	642	5.1	46.9	24.7	6.7	11,056	36,406	46,602	53.4	8.6	47,894	15.7	32.7	33.7
King	63	23.2	53	0.0	73.0	13.5	3.1	29,189	17,971	39,286	60.0	1.1	78,210	12.4	21.3	20.3
Kinney	1,912	52.1	505	18.6	46.9	18.8	7.3	13,100	26,715	39,972	51.1	2.6	62,557	17.9	22.7	21.5
Kleberg	18,631	60.7	10,318	8.9	48.7	24.3	55.2	10,500	23,021	47,301	51.9	2.5	51,574	20.8	30.0	28.1
Knox	1,448	39.5	894	4.6	50.0	18.8	10.6	13,564	24,273	50,719	48.5	1.6	46,053	16.3	24.6	22.6
Lamar	19,909	39.9	10,834	7.7	47.4	18.7	85.6	10,079	24,826	48,036	52.2	1.9	44,688	19.6	26.9	26.6
Lamb	5,660	43.9	3,279	4.1	59.3	12.6	33.0	11,319	21,502	44,935	54.0	1.7	48,123	17.6	24.5	22.7
Lampasas	10,620	49.6	4,497	10.7	39.4	18.4	34.8	9,553	29,695	64,808	41.2	3.6	69,051	10.0	18.0	17.4
La Salle	4,870	64.8	1,322	28.1	79.7	6.7	18.2	13,534	17,177	47,162	53.3	1.5	45,647	24.0	28.3	29.6
Lavaca	8,356	41.5	4,674	15.2	54.5	17.9	46.3	11,422	31,241	54,211	45.5	5.2	57,999	10.6	14.5	14.9
Lee	8,152	47.3	3,937	10.9	53.6	14.0	30.3	9,950	27,216	56,696	43.0	3.3	61,444	10.6	15.0	15.5
Leon	6,267	36.0	3,463	6.9	57.1	15.0	35.2	11,172	28,976	43,392	53.5	5.1	52,878	13.8	17.9	18.2
Liberty	37,538	42.6	19,668	9.7	60.8	9.9	172.8	9,536	23,433	50,917	49.0	4.0	61,230	14.4	20.0	19.1
Limestone	8,798	37.5	4,585	6.3	52.1	16.7	40.9	10,513	22,808	45,781	54.2	1.4	53,143	16.8	19.7	19.5
Lipscomb	1,110	34.3	788	1.6	47.3	23.6	10.2	13,634	28,736	63,182	36.6	4.9	67,775	11.3	14.8	13.8
Live Oak	5,227	42.8	2,215	4.2	58.0	11.1	19.7	11,552	23,632	50,212	49.7	3.8	54,031	17.0	23.8	24.7
Llano	11,283	51.8	2,735	20.4	40.3	25.9	20.4	11,448	41,499	58,941	43.6	8.8	60,706	10.9	20.3	21.5
Loving	34	20.1	0	0.0	18.2	0.0	NA	NA	37,693	44,076	77.4	1.6	97,491	3.9	11.3	7.0
Lubbock	152,663	49.2	102,051	10.0	37.9	32.0	485.1	9,568	28,880	53,425	46.9	4.8	56,477	15.8	18.4	16.6
Lynn	2,344	39.4	1,475	13.2	50.7	20.7	18.9	12,479	25,871	46,163	54.7	3.9	51,003	14.4	19.6	18.6
McCulloch	3,084	38.6	1,544	4.3	51.0	17.7	17.5	12,503	25,567	48,618	52.3	2.9	47,617	16.2	27.1	25.1
McLennan	134,101	52.3	76,201	24.3	42.2	25.0	471.6	10,470	26,754	50,210	49.8	4.7	55,148	17.0	20.7	19.5
McMullen	342	46.0	197	4.1	56.7	14.8	5.6	19,478	31,191	67,386	31.9	8.3	45,927	9.7	12.0	13.3
Madison	5,999	42.0	2,885	10.5	57.7	13.8	27.3	9,963	22,183	60,499	39.3	4.5	58,674	17.4	21.6	21.2
Marion	4,152	42.1	1,723	11.7	53.7	16.7	13.0	9,816	25,798	39,093	63.8	1.9	42,024	20.0	31.1	28.9
Martin	1,831	31.7	1,681	2.9	55.3	19.4	16.0	11,848	32,242	70,000	33.7	7.4	73,367	11.1	17.0	15.2

1. All persons 3 years old and over enrolled in nursery school through college. 2. Persons 25 years old and over. 3. Elementary and secondary education expenditures. 4. Based on population estimated by the American Community Survey, 2016–2020. 5. CDC percent based on 2019 population estimate.

STATE County	Personal income, 2020										Earnings, 2020		
			Per capita[1]			Supplements to wages and salaries, employer contributions (mil dol)						Contributions for government social insurance (mil dol)	
	Total (mil dol)	Percent change 2019–2020	Dollars	Rank	Wages and salaries (mil dol)	Pension and insurance	Government social insurance	Proprietors' income (mil dol)	Dividends, interest, and rent (mil dol)	Personal transfer reecipts (mil dol)	Total (mil dol)	From employee and self-employed	From employer
	62	63	64	65	66	67	68	69	70	71	72	73	74
TEXAS—Cont'd													
Guadalupe	8,429	6.5	49,405	1,211	2,088	329	145	503	1,391	1,924	3,065	189	145
Hale	1,267	5.2	38,674	2,608	485	87	35	161	179	399	768	41	35
Hall	104	1.5	35,416	2,913	26	7	2	9	18	47	43	3	2
Hamilton	562	4.0	65,685	245	113	23	8	44	240	136	187	12	8
Hansford	352	-2.0	66,588	228	89	18	6	138	52	56	250	7	6
Hardeman	184	10.2	45,863	1,674	56	12	4	17	34	63	88	5	4
Hardin	2,866	4.7	49,159	1,234	635	101	45	94	339	772	875	64	45
Harris	285,161	2.3	60,183	419	177,494	22,532	11,450	46,556	53,138	45,889	258,032	13,448	11,450
Harrison	3,014	3.0	45,396	1,734	1,212	224	83	188	498	869	1,706	102	83
Hartley	414	1.8	76,005	101	107	20	8	219	50	29	355	7	8
Haskell	265	4.0	46,070	1,638	84	14	6	36	37	86	141	8	6
Hays	12,119	9.9	50,212	1,123	3,410	552	234	1,267	2,085	2,011	5,463	303	234
Hemphill	232	-1.1	61,340	370	99	19	7	49	74	36	173	8	7
Henderson	3,633	6.6	43,356	2,025	775	145	54	237	587	1,242	1,211	97	54
Hidalgo	27,265	11.9	31,153	3,073	10,200	2,119	710	2,922	2,967	9,728	15,951	892	710
Hill	1,657	7.2	44,776	1,831	431	79	29	161	227	534	701	47	29
Hockley	1,056	5.9	46,051	1,643	506	80	32	92	131	305	710	40	32
Hood	3,502	7.0	55,132	695	735	116	52	282	695	890	1,186	89	52
Hopkins	1,681	6.2	45,219	1,768	586	97	41	190	233	497	914	54	41
Houston	1,021	8.7	44,693	1,849	422	69	26	47	175	348	563	38	26
Howard	1,648	1.9	45,105	1,779	698	146	49	138	310	415	1,031	56	49
Hudspeth	132	15.9	26,835	3,105	81	20	6	17	18	45	124	6	6
Hunt	4,274	7.9	42,819	2,091	1,458	276	101	229	560	1,215	2,065	125	101
Hutchinson	969	4.9	46,860	1,530	527	106	35	31	132	263	699	42	35
Irion	113	0.9	72,353	133	50	8	3	14	35	18	76	4	3
Jack	372	3.7	41,038	2,333	136	26	9	25	80	102	196	12	9
Jackson	708	-0.2	47,642	1,435	291	51	20	45	103	200	407	24	20
Jasper	1,538	4.6	43,486	2,012	421	80	29	57	205	559	586	44	29
Jeff Davis	108	8.2	48,623	1,306	29	6	2	12	32	28	49	3	2
Jefferson	11,643	4.7	46,547	1,570	7,115	1,331	491	801	1,636	3,510	9,738	547	491
Jim Hogg	191	10.0	36,847	2,794	75	21	5	5	25	77	106	7	5
Jim Wells	1,880	9.2	46,483	1,579	656	107	44	144	216	690	950	60	44
Johnson	8,558	8.4	47,654	1,434	2,569	390	178	610	1,098	1,981	3,748	238	178
Jones	706	6.1	35,520	2,904	188	45	11	49	88	243	293	17	11
Karnes	954	-2.9	61,330	371	396	65	25	32	436	202	518	31	25
Kaufman	6,813	12.9	47,580	1,442	1,649	274	111	417	729	1,384	2,451	147	111
Kendall	4,117	3.9	84,853	61	934	133	63	495	1,202	557	1,625	94	63
Kenedy	18	6.1	46,296	1,608	31	5	2	3	4	3	41	2	2
Kent	40	8.5	51,139	1,012	13	3	1	8	7	12	24	1	1
Kerr	2,966	3.8	56,093	632	889	148	63	292	967	779	1,393	95	63
Kimble	211	7.9	48,071	1,380	50	12	3	14	52	72	78	6	3
King	23	5.0	81,541	71	4	1	0	14	2	2	19	0	0
Kinney	129	8.7	35,119	2,929	52	15	4	4	28	45	75	5	4
Kleberg	1,322	4.5	43,560	2,002	542	125	39	83	203	413	790	43	39
Knox	158	8.7	42,857	2,085	51	11	3	14	25	60	79	5	3
Lamar	2,322	7.1	46,538	1,573	1,008	170	71	184	328	766	1,433	89	71
Lamb	644	7.4	50,667	1,069	181	36	13	188	57	171	418	16	13
Lampasas	1,180	6.2	54,153	769	194	36	13	73	241	358	317	25	13
La Salle	308	1.1	41,114	2,320	198	31	13	16	111	78	259	15	13
Lavaca	1,160	1.7	57,399	544	262	45	18	116	276	319	442	31	18
Lee	936	-1.6	53,791	794	361	58	24	139	161	228	582	33	24
Leon	750	4.9	42,878	2,082	273	44	19	47	150	274	383	28	19
Liberty	3,745	9.8	40,904	2,345	903	162	61	228	431	1,077	1,354	85	61
Limestone	959	6.7	41,072	2,329	365	81	23	51	139	373	519	32	23
Lipscomb	260	-7.1	83,655	65	83	13	5	131	39	32	233	10	5
Live Oak	477	4.6	38,734	2,599	235	47	16	22	134	136	320	19	16
Llano	1,154	3.8	52,538	887	211	35	15	84	378	357	345	33	15
Loving	9	-2.5	49,072	1,250	8	1	1	0	3	1	10	1	1
Lubbock	14,637	5.0	46,502	1,577	7,013	1,170	466	1,108	2,431	3,406	9,756	535	466
Lynn	243	-8.9	40,351	2,409	83	18	5	-10	37	73	95	7	5
McCulloch	323	3.4	41,306	2,288	104	21	7	23	61	133	155	11	7
McLennan	11,888	8.3	45,772	1,688	6,097	972	425	886	1,777	3,044	8,380	487	425
McMullen	53	-3.3	73,356	121	33	5	2	-6	38	8	35	2	2
Madison	517	12.1	35,865	2,878	170	33	11	56	89	174	270	15	11
Marion	424	4.4	42,536	2,123	77	17	6	18	72	179	118	12	6
Martin	376	-2.4	64,602	278	126	22	8	61	109	61	218	10	8

1. Based on the resident population estimated as of July 1 of the year shown.

STATE County	Earnings, 2020 (cont.)									Social Security beneficiaries, December 2020		Supple-mental Security Income recipients, 2020	Housing units, 2021	
	Percent by selected industries													
	Farm	Mining, quarrying, and extractions	Construction	Manu-facturing	Information; professional, scientific, technical services	Retail trade	Finance, insurance, real estate, and leasing	Health care and social assistance	Govern-ment	Number	Rate[1]		Total	Percent change, 2010–2021
	75	76	77	78	79	80	81	82	83	84	85	86	87	88
TEXAS—Cont'd														
Guadalupe	0.0	1.1	10.0	21.3	3.3	7.6	5.6	6.5	15.2	29,500	167	1,978	67,121	3.3
Hale	14.0	1.1	6.5	5.6	3.4	5.5	5.0	D	18.5	5,760	179	875	13,393	0.0
Hall	11.5	0.8	1.8	3.8	D	10.1	7.2	6.2	31.4	810	285	86	1,741	-0.1
Hamilton	7.3	D	12.0	5.9	D	9.0	D	8.0	27.4	2,445	297	169	4,340	0.2
Hansford	49.4	3.3	2.6	1.3	D	3.4	4.4	0.3	14.9	920	178	28	2,281	0.0
Hardeman	14.7	D	D	D	D	6.5	3.2	D	28.5	1,035	291	134	1,803	-0.1
Hardin	-0.8	2.7	D	D	5.8	10.9	D	16.0	15.8	12,495	219	1,180	24,597	2.1
Harris	0.0	11.3	7.1	8.1	13.9	3.8	8.6	7.7	9.8	572,600	121	105,484	1,885,384	1.8
Harrison	-0.2	8.9	6.8	29.6	4.8	5.6	5.1	D	11.4	14,320	207	1,795	29,438	0.6
Hartley	53.1	D	8.2	0.2	D	2.3	D	D	12.7	575	107	D	1,938	0.4
Haskell	17.2	4.1	2.6	1.4	2.0	10.7	D	2.9	19.8	1,370	253	169	3,079	0.2
Hays	-0.1	0.4	14.0	8.5	7.4	8.5	6.3	7.0	18.6	32,615	128	2,304	99,332	5.2
Hemphill	16.8	30.4	11.8	2.4	3.5	2.5	3.4	D	17.8	610	186	22	1,634	0.2
Henderson	0.2	1.6	12.0	12.7	6.5	10.1	5.8	10.9	17.8	22,525	269	2,575	41,173	1.1
Hidalgo	1.0	0.7	4.9	2.7	4.4	9.2	5.3	19.9	25.7	115,215	131	39,498	301,741	1.8
Hill	0.9	3.1	19.1	11.4	D	7.4	4.1	D	18.4	9,220	253	985	16,286	0.6
Hockley	4.7	36.0	4.1	1.4	D	4.7	6.1	D	15.1	4,155	194	449	9,204	0.3
Hood	-0.3	7.8	15.1	6.3	6.4	9.4	8.3	13.0	12.1	17,830	278	885	28,811	1.5
Hopkins	9.2	0.2	8.0	14.2	D	7.7	6.0	8.1	13.3	8,510	229	894	15,726	0.2
Houston	0.3	6.9	7.4	14.0	8.7	4.8	12.6	5.3	17.7	5,725	257	787	10,814	0.4
Howard	2.0	11.1	7.2	8.9	D	6.3	4.1	10.0	27.5	5,595	164	740	14,040	0.2
Hudspeth	10.9	0.2	D	D	D	0.7	D	D	54.7	840	256	169	1,123	1.2
Hunt	-0.9	0.1	8.7	25.1	4.9	6.7	2.9	9.6	24.1	19,805	192	2,380	41,795	2.8
Hutchinson	-0.6	29.1	11.2	19.3	D	4.7	2.5	D	13.0	4,365	213	330	10,166	0.0
Irion	6.2	50.8	D	D	0.5	2.1	D	D	9.1	370	238	14	786	0.1
Jack	-2.2	22.2	8.3	2.0	D	2.8	11.3	D	20.9	1,805	207	104	3,798	0.3
Jackson	1.8	5.3	19.6	D	D	4.0	4.1	D	16.8	3,285	217	303	7,027	0.4
Jasper	-0.7	1.4	5.5	22.0	4.7	8.9	4.7	D	20.6	9,100	276	1,179	16,585	2.3
Jeff Davis	6.7	D	D	D	D	3.8	D	3.8	34.5	695	357	34	1,518	0.5
Jefferson	0.1	0.5	13.6	23.3	7.8	6.2	3.8	11.0	13.8	46,325	183	8,122	109,418	0.9
Jim Hogg	1.7	6.7	2.5	2.3	D	5.9	D	11.8	55.0	1,030	215	237	2,247	0.2
Jim Wells	3.1	26.9	3.3	3.0	2.9	6.0	4.1	D	13.5	8,740	225	1,629	16,207	0.3
Johnson	-0.2	2.7	13.9	14.5	3.9	9.1	4.8	6.8	14.5	32,450	173	3,170	68,437	3.8
Jones	2.1	6.1	7.9	2.5	1.9	5.0	4.4	D	42.6	3,610	182	333	7,051	0.2
Karnes	-1.6	24.5	1.6	5.2	D	3.8	6.0	2.3	20.3	2,815	191	372	5,889	1.3
Kaufman	-0.5	0.1	13.5	12.3	5.3	7.0	4.9	6.8	19.8	22,480	142	2,370	52,539	2.2
Kendall	-0.6	2.0	16.8	5.1	12.1	12.1	11.5	8.4	10.1	10,900	233	316	18,793	2.0
Kenedy	11.2	D	0.4	D	0.2	D	D	D	12.1	50	147	D	196	0.0
Kent	19.5	D	2.4	1.9	D	D	D	D	34.3	190	254	15	523	0.2
Kerr	-0.4	1.4	12.8	6.4	6.1	8.7	9.6	D	17.0	16,570	312	929	25,413	0.7
Kimble	0.5	1.3	12.0	6.0	D	8.0	8.1	D	28.1	1,380	316	112	2,777	0.3
King	55.5	2.2	D	0.9	D	3.3	3.2	D	18.1	30	116	D	171	0.0
Kinney	1.5	D	D	D	0.1	2.7	D	0.8	49.1	950	304	104	1,528	0.4
Kleberg	2.0	4.5	3.2	3.4	D	7.5	3.3	D	43.4	5,240	171	1,023	13,990	0.3
Knox	13.8	8.1	D	D	D	9.9	D	D	32.4	900	269	104	1,801	0.0
Lamar	1.3	0.0	9.7	28.7	2.9	7.5	3.6	15.1	12.6	12,255	245	1,816	22,718	0.2
Lamb	40.3	D	3.2	3.9	1.9	3.3	D	4.1	13.8	2,620	203	384	5,890	0.2
Lampasas	-3.1	D	18.9	9.5	6.1	15.4	9.9	D	20.0	5,840	262	444	9,794	0.8
La Salle	-1.5	39.9	D	D	D	3.1	D	2.2	26.3	1,220	183	298	2,605	0.8
Lavaca	-1.0	5.4	14.7	16.0	4.3	6.6	6.4	D	13.3	5,395	263	409	10,488	0.2
Lee	0.4	D	46.0	5.1	3.1	4.5	6.3	D	13.0	3,885	219	282	7,925	0.7
Leon	2.9	6.6	15.3	25.4	5.5	4.3	6.5	2.1	13.7	5,390	338	446	8,982	0.8
Liberty	-0.3	5.2	17.0	7.5	D	7.5	4.2	9.9	24.1	15,485	159	2,691	34,503	3.3
Limestone	1.1	12.8	3.9	3.7	6.0	6.4	3.1	8.3	34.7	5,410	245	750	10,419	0.4
Lipscomb	9.0	4.4	D	D	D	4.5	D	1.4	8.9	605	206	31	1,556	-0.1
Live Oak	-1.3	15.5	D	D	D	5.6	7.4	D	20.5	2,225	196	175	5,962	0.5
Llano	-1.3	0.6	14.8	3.9	7.4	6.9	11.0	D	16.4	7,425	338	319	15,562	1.9
Loving	3.4	D	D	D	D	0.1	0.1	D	9.5	15	263	D	35	2.9
Lubbock	0.0	1.4	7.7	3.1	7.7	8.5	7.3	15.1	24.2	49,070	156	6,147	136,444	2.8
Lynn	-20.2	D	14.9	2.5	D	2.1	16.9	D	38.1	1,100	193	128	2,526	0.0
McCulloch	-0.2	9.6	8.0	4.5	3.7	9.4	5.6	8.1	24.7	2,175	289	258	4,218	0.0
McLennan	0.0	0.2	8.5	15.9	7.1	6.8	9.7	10.7	15.1	47,760	182	7,045	107,229	1.1
McMullen	-14.5	34.4	D	D	D	3.8	D	2.1	29.4	185	304	10	407	0.5
Madison	9.8	5.0	6.1	8.2	D	12.3	3.4	D	27.4	2,645	193	254	5,089	0.6
Marion	0.2	D	3.4	21.5	D	4.7	3.0	D	20.3	3,205	332	376	5,603	1.0
Martin	4.6	15.1	16.5	3.7	D	7.7	2.3	1.5	20.1	755	145	86	2,126	0.3

1. Per 1,000 resident population estimated as of July 1 of the year shown.

STATE County	Housing units, 2016–2020: Occupied units: Total	Owner-occupied: Percent	Owner-occupied: Median value[1]	Median owner cost as a percent of income: With a mortgage	Median owner cost as a percent of income: Without a mortgage[2]	Renter-occupied: Median rent[3]	Renter-occupied: Median rent as a percent of income[2]	Sub-standard units[4] (percent)	Civilian labor force, 2021: Total	Percent change, 2020–2021	Unemployment: Total	Unemployment: Rate[5]	Civilian employment[6], 2016–2020: Total	Percent: Management, business, science, and arts	Percent: Construction, production, and maintenance occupations
	89	90	91	92	93	94	95	96	97	98	99	100	101	102	103
TEXAS—Cont'd															
Guadalupe	55,710	77.3	207,700	19.9	10.0	1,150	27.4	3.8	82,209	2.6	3,652	4.4	75,554	34.5	25.9
Hale	10,888	63.3	84,500	19.0	10.0	661	25.6	5.0	11,915	2.4	724	6.1	14,206	27.7	32.6
Hall	1,252	68.5	59,900	25.9	10.0	537	24.8	5.6	1,087	2.8	59	5.4	1,275	24.9	29.8
Hamilton	3,007	83.7	123,600	21.0	13.2	621	28.5	4.4	3,792	2.2	154	4.1	3,303	30.6	31.5
Hansford	1,859	76.8	111,300	23.7	10.0	734	29.0	2.3	2,551	3.7	77	3.0	2,257	35.2	27.8
Hardeman	1,672	69.3	53,100	16.6	11.1	472	21.8	6.3	1,722	1.8	74	4.3	1,929	31.6	30.4
Hardin	21,188	81.2	135,600	18.9	10.0	846	28.0	2.9	24,760	-1.2	1,969	8.0	24,260	32.0	29.7
Harris	1,635,749	54.9	189,400	21.2	10.7	1,115	30.1	6.2	2,283,959	0.9	147,489	6.5	2,253,218	37.4	24.8
Harrison	23,841	73.2	137,200	18.9	10.0	820	29.7	4.7	28,650	-0.6	1,893	6.6	28,314	32.0	30.9
Hartley	1,691	65.3	179,200	24.1	10.0	955	23.3	2.7	2,733	5.4	57	2.1	2,008	42.8	22.6
Haskell	2,162	71.7	60,500	17.2	11.3	686	22.3	3.3	2,740	3.4	108	3.9	2,276	33.1	29.1
Hays	76,724	62.2	258,000	22.5	11.2	1,168	33.0	4.0	129,600	5.6	5,329	4.1	114,022	39.9	19.8
Hemphill	1,356	67.5	180,300	21.0	10.0	940	21.9	4.5	1,635	-8.1	71	4.3	1,783	28.2	37.2
Henderson	31,649	76.2	120,700	21.5	12.3	803	29.7	3.5	38,202	3.8	1,962	5.1	31,848	30.1	27.8
Hidalgo	243,878	68.0	90,000	22.7	11.8	753	31.1	13.7	366,220	2.5	34,111	9.3	330,528	28.0	25.9
Hill	13,094	72.8	112,200	19.2	10.7	758	26.6	5.1	16,822	4.2	842	5.0	15,860	25.4	35.5
Hockley	8,071	73.1	92,900	18.2	12.0	691	26.7	5.2	10,657	0.7	642	6.0	10,024	30.0	33.6
Hood	23,215	79.5	208,700	19.4	10.0	1,009	29.8	3.3	28,814	3.7	1,489	5.2	25,205	34.4	31.2
Hopkins	13,514	69.2	119,600	19.8	10.0	836	22.8	3.8	17,828	2.8	773	4.3	16,859	30.4	32.4
Houston	8,234	70.4	107,500	21.4	13.4	702	34.7	4.2	10,581	5.8	513	4.8	8,086	30.8	27.3
Howard	11,354	66.4	103,500	19.0	10.0	869	26.6	2.6	13,256	-0.6	866	6.5	14,232	27.8	32.4
Hudspeth	1,127	73.5	54,500	32.1	12.3	684	31.6	13.8	1,849	0.8	107	5.8	1,383	9.8	29.5
Hunt	33,596	69.5	135,800	22.6	10.8	952	29.1	6.3	44,928	4.6	2,309	5.1	43,559	33.4	25.9
Hutchinson	7,074	80.0	81,600	16.6	10.0	817	22.1	1.2	8,498	0.7	511	6.0	9,301	26.5	36.8
Irion	636	82.5	122,000	31.1	10.0	1,014	34.3	10.5	773	2.8	38	4.9	674	28.5	36.1
Jack	3,169	77.5	95,200	19.7	12.3	666	26.1	3.9	3,398	0.8	186	5.5	3,227	27.0	34.3
Jackson	4,924	70.5	110,100	18.0	10.0	830	26.4	4.3	7,108	-1.7	356	5.0	6,157	29.8	37.0
Jasper	13,725	76.1	105,200	18.0	13.2	749	34.4	5.1	12,832	0.6	1,247	9.7	13,180	30.6	31.5
Jeff Davis	991	83.8	134,800	14.9	10.8	1,081	50.0	8.4	1,023	7.3	44	4.3	755	39.6	16.3
Jefferson	94,012	61.5	120,300	20.5	10.6	869	29.3	3.0	101,725	-2.2	10,197	10.0	103,750	28.5	30.2
Jim Hogg	1,545	71.3	77,000	20.8	11.7	496	29.2	10.9	1,859	-0.2	164	8.8	1,994	19.9	38.6
Jim Wells	12,924	71.0	76,900	20.4	10.0	779	26.0	7.3	15,607	-2.4	1,588	10.2	16,241	29.3	31.0
Johnson	58,270	73.3	168,500	19.9	10.4	1,047	27.5	4.9	85,557	3.3	4,151	4.9	79,942	28.3	38.3
Jones	5,646	78.7	80,800	18.9	10.8	773	23.4	3.3	5,730	2.6	353	6.2	5,183	34.1	23.6
Karnes	4,552	73.4	109,500	14.4	10.0	752	20.1	5.4	6,843	-1.5	356	5.2	5,013	30.3	29.5
Kaufman	39,237	76.6	195,400	21.3	12.5	1,087	31.3	4.3	71,942	4.5	3,519	4.9	61,908	33.7	26.4
Kendall	14,789	76.0	378,500	21.4	10.0	1,278	25.9	1.9	22,781	3.5	873	3.8	20,961	46.9	17.0
Kenedy	129	20.9	NA	NA	10.7	NA	NA	10.9	183	2.2	11	6.0	154	7.8	49.4
Kent	286	81.5	64,700	13.1	10.5	819	10.0	0.0	447	-2.6	13	2.9	247	42.5	20.2
Kerr	21,278	68.4	193,900	21.0	11.0	922	28.3	3.9	22,061	2.4	990	4.5	22,951	33.2	22.2
Kimble	1,967	75.6	151,700	23.2	12.2	684	24.1	3.5	1,905	4.8	79	4.1	2,091	32.0	30.5
King	90	38.9	22,800	0.0	10.0	750	50.0	0.0	448	91.5	4	0.9	97	27.8	25.8
Kinney	1,475	75.3	82,000	23.1	13.7	672	26.3	0.9	1,244	-4.3	69	5.5	1,321	30.7	26.0
Kleberg	11,140	52.2	98,500	18.4	11.3	898	31.3	9.3	13,202	0.5	941	7.1	13,063	29.9	27.4
Knox	1,394	84.6	43,300	13.4	10.0	560	33.8	2.1	1,457	1.3	68	4.7	1,614	28.4	37.6
Lamar	19,995	64.7	108,500	18.8	12.1	729	29.1	1.9	24,493	4.8	1,344	5.5	22,190	29.1	32.2
Lamb	4,706	73.1	67,900	17.4	11.6	715	29.8	4.8	5,211	0.9	260	5.0	5,423	34.7	30.9
Lampasas	7,823	79.8	166,500	20.2	11.9	782	28.6	2.9	9,291	3.7	446	4.8	8,610	33.6	24.4
La Salle	2,142	74.0	84,000	17.7	12.8	680	18.5	5.5	3,804	2.7	163	4.3	2,917	20.0	37.9
Lavaca	7,904	75.6	171,000	17.3	10.0	776	24.4	4.3	8,640	3.6	387	4.5	9,058	32.7	34.4
Lee	6,159	80.5	162,800	20.7	12.1	897	29.7	5.1	9,057	-0.3	388	4.3	8,151	29.8	28.4
Leon	6,837	78.1	120,300	17.8	10.6	772	26.6	2.6	6,184	2.3	438	7.1	6,684	27.9	31.5
Liberty	27,417	78.1	115,300	21.3	11.8	857	30.3	5.8	34,870	2.2	3,193	9.2	31,389	23.3	41.0
Limestone	8,292	74.0	115,400	21.1	12.6	678	28.0	6.2	8,528	3.4	527	6.2	8,729	25.9	34.7
Lipscomb	1,158	73.8	106,700	18.7	10.0	761	17.6	4.6	1,502	-0.7	56	3.7	1,599	25.6	35.7
Live Oak	3,854	81.9	106,200	16.5	11.6	782	23.4	4.2	4,937	-3.6	336	6.8	4,246	31.3	32.1
Llano	9,031	77.6	235,700	21.7	10.5	863	27.1	3.7	8,900	6.0	431	4.8	8,126	30.3	26.6
Loving	62	17.7	NA	NA	10.0	NA	NA	8.1	438	48.5	4	0.9	71	64.8	26.8
Lubbock	116,535	55.6	149,200	20.4	11.1	946	32.2	3.6	160,338	2.9	7,246	4.5	150,494	38.4	20.5
Lynn	2,199	69.2	89,900	23.4	12.7	825	33.1	3.5	2,798	2.8	120	4.3	2,611	36.2	28.6
McCulloch	3,151	69.8	96,300	18.9	11.6	708	24.5	3.8	3,157	-0.9	204	6.5	3,437	25.6	38.9
McLennan	91,422	59.2	152,700	20.0	12.2	886	32.0	3.2	122,192	3.2	5,945	4.9	115,898	32.9	26.4
McMullen	229	84.7	111,300	16.5	10.1	929	20.0	9.6	734	3.1	17	2.3	293	36.5	30.4
Madison	4,205	76.0	113,200	21.5	10.0	789	18.1	7.8	4,691	5.7	293	6.2	4,978	28.6	34.2
Marion	4,535	77.9	98,200	20.0	10.6	726	29.3	2.0	4,255	1.2	292	6.9	3,528	27.7	28.3
Martin	1,722	69.8	145,700	22.1	10.0	760	22.8	8.1	2,605	2.6	125	4.8	2,541	32.9	32.6

1. Specified owner-occupied units. 2. A value of 10.0 represents 10 percent or less; a value of 50.0 represents 50 percent or more. 3. Specified renter-occupied units. 4. Overcrowded or lacking complete plumbing facilities. 5. Percent of civilian labor force. 6. Civilian employed persons 16 years old and over.

STATE County	Private nonfarm establishments, employment and payroll, 2020									Agriculture, 2017			
		Employment						Annual payroll		Farms			Farm producers whose primary occupation is farming (percent)
											Percent with:		
	Number of establish-ments	Total	Health care and social assistance	Manufac-turing	Retail trade	Finance and insurance	Professional, scientific, and technical services	Total (mil dol)	Average per employee (dollars)	Number	Fewer than 50 acres	1000 acres or more	
	104	105	106	107	108	109	110	111	112	113	114	115	116
TEXAS—Cont'd													
Guadalupe	2,327	34,926	3,776	7,068	5,094	690	952	1,601	45,837	2,543	52.4	2.2	34.3
Hale	658	8,993	978	644	1,170	272	174	336	37,379	671	18.6	27.6	42.5
Hall	64	384	57	22	88	55	NA	11	29,203	327	4.3	35.8	35.6
Hamilton	218	2,042	536	205	427	46	58	75	36,894	1,163	19.4	9.7	38.9
Hansford	154	1,141	282	7	211	76	37	50	43,816	181	6.1	55.2	63.8
Hardeman	83	726	125	168	136	38	NA	28	38,669	275	6.2	24.0	38.9
Hardin	838	8,787	827	679	2,138	225	310	358	40,781	661	64.6	1.7	29.8
Harris	105,710	2,113,874	276,607	154,591	214,736	80,344	186,533	138,267	65,409	1,891	80.7	1.7	31.9
Harrison	1,297	18,992	1,594	4,655	1,953	825	807	895	47,134	1,134	51.5	2.4	32.2
Hartley	113	1,253	329	10	202	37	36	54	42,773	206	7.3	45.1	65.4
Haskell	130	990	140	NA	314	43	30	34	33,845	488	16.0	21.9	39.3
Hays	4,807	66,007	8,245	5,025	15,668	1,092	3,672	2,380	36,064	1,128	53.9	5.9	31.0
Hemphill	136	1,367	226	26	120	NA	51	79	57,584	230	7.8	38.3	49.5
Henderson	1,332	13,733	2,180	1,909	2,667	387	556	532	38,702	1,988	51.3	2.2	36.7
Hidalgo	12,446	212,954	72,655	6,849	37,424	7,354	6,165	6,260	29,395	2,436	73.6	6.4	32.0
Hill	637	7,994	915	1,894	1,322	179	135	297	37,166	2,003	40.8	4.6	39.3
Hockley	472	6,499	825	175	827	192	108	296	45,589	661	24.2	23.3	35.1
Hood	1,412	14,609	2,595	603	2,988	466	477	529	36,181	1,176	64.0	3.5	35.4
Hopkins	746	10,327	1,070	2,040	1,558	549	176	428	41,420	2,200	36.4	3.2	41.7
Houston	335	3,585	595	522	617	129	98	149	41,438	1,422	27.8	5.2	43.9
Howard	738	9,663	2,327	561	1,467	274	166	452	46,758	373	26.8	22.5	34.5
Hudspeth	32	377	NA	NA	37	NA	NA	17	46,371	134	13.4	49.3	54.1
Hunt	1,589	25,123	3,624	8,446	3,845	319	609	1,353	53,861	4,110	63.6	1.8	31.6
Hutchinson	409	5,730	545	1,583	902	155	140	362	63,091	149	26.8	37.6	45.5
Irion	57	475	NA	NA	23	NA	4	31	65,446	175	18.3	40.6	42.4
Jack	206	1,858	331	67	175	29	49	77	41,598	870	22.9	10.5	39.1
Jackson	336	5,258	321	1,495	465	153	155	233	44,273	788	30.7	12.6	37.4
Jasper	607	8,429	2,290	1,405	1,545	275	151	327	38,778	896	66.2	1.5	35.8
Jeff Davis	57	349	35	NA	73	29	17	9	25,567	77	28.6	49.4	43.2
Jefferson	5,603	101,311	17,323	13,365	14,266	2,689	5,644	5,144	50,772	729	62.3	7.5	44.6
Jim Hogg	76	1,137	671	46	201	39	NA	24	20,847	244	14.8	29.5	33.1
Jim Wells	783	13,672	5,618	345	1,713	295	152	425	31,108	1,224	42.2	6.5	36.4
Johnson	3,022	39,923	3,472	6,752	6,144	926	1,296	1,709	42,807	3,140	67.1	2.3	33.5
Jones	255	2,505	401	190	224	74	51	114	45,466	915	31.1	14.0	35.5
Karnes	335	5,928	440	200	579	100	115	315	53,209	1,213	19.5	6.8	40.6
Kaufman	2,188	29,003	3,570	4,020	4,581	720	686	1,146	39,517	2,778	64.7	2.4	35.0
Kendall	1,494	15,750	2,185	1,145	2,876	727	944	715	45,390	1,349	48.2	6.4	31.1
Kenedy	17	136	NA	NA	NA	NA	NA	12	86,596	30	3.3	56.7	67.3
Kent	12	70	NA	NA	14	NA	NA	5	76,986	164	3.0	34.1	31.4
Kerr	1,482	17,423	4,148	912	2,897	349	741	694	39,806	1,128	34.2	11.5	38.3
Kimble	143	980	130	63	277	41	10	30	31,076	670	19.3	26.0	35.6
King	NA	NA	NA	NA	NA	NA	NA	NA	NA	43	NA	39.5	21.5
Kinney	38	488	11	NA	54	NA	NA	26	54,027	236	17.4	37.7	37.4
Kleberg	530	7,207	1,579	85	1,505	274	158	252	34,976	459	60.3	3.7	29.8
Knox	87	614	174	NA	97	51	NA	27	43,801	216	17.6	22.7	43.9
Lamar	1,202	17,585	3,552	5,138	2,608	491	372	714	40,616	1,946	38.4	3.9	33.3
Lamb	234	2,095	478	206	252	120	35	93	44,490	777	13.4	22.9	42.5
Lampasas	419	4,300	362	684	747	96	137	146	33,839	1,151	42.1	8.1	41.5
La Salle	142	1,576	144	NA	247	NA	7	61	38,947	383	11.5	32.4	38.3
Lavaca	462	5,656	1,190	1,547	723	253	162	225	39,760	2,900	34.4	1.9	34.5
Lee	404	5,842	323	418	633	219	93	303	51,785	1,809	41.5	2.3	33.7
Leon	347	4,083	114	742	627	119	62	213	52,239	1,951	34.8	3.3	41.9
Liberty	1,117	14,691	1,714	1,343	2,596	354	339	612	41,663	1,538	59.5	3.0	33.8
Limestone	383	5,391	1,162	523	868	207	430	227	42,115	1,284	33.9	6.5	40.0
Lipscomb	73	890	NA	NA	90	61	21	57	63,748	299	6.7	40.5	36.9
Live Oak	272	3,077	115	336	437	88	101	173	56,227	856	21.8	12.0	37.1
Llano	485	3,833	554	75	626	184	164	131	34,293	835	30.5	15.1	37.8
Loving	9	285	NA	NA	NA	NA	NA	13	44,379	8	NA	100.0	45.8
Lubbock	7,448	118,442	25,488	5,296	18,756	5,664	4,935	4,723	39,879	1,033	48.2	14.4	37.3
Lynn	75	643	184	79	50	52	10	32	49,672	434	15.4	33.4	47.0
McCulloch	201	1,522	188	70	379	97	48	52	34,011	682	17.4	19.1	41.2
McLennan	5,418	107,642	16,728	15,790	12,947	5,112	4,400	4,420	41,066	3,366	60.2	3.2	30.5
McMullen	38	267	12	NA	62	NA	NA	14	51,873	191	6.8	45.0	46.7
Madison	260	2,513	292	37	681	72	63	83	33,080	977	35.7	4.4	42.3
Marion	155	1,619	405	343	196	41	13	59	36,329	280	39.3	5.7	27.5
Martin	123	1,356	222	NA	252	35	22	75	54,972	356	15.2	30.9	42.5

STATE County	Agriculture, 2017 (cont.): Land in farms: Acreage (1,000)	Land in farms: Percent change, 2012–2017	Land in farms: Acres: Average size of farm	Land in farms: Acres: Total irrigated (1,000)	Land in farms: Acres: Total cropland (1,000)	Value of land and buildings (dollars): Average per farm	Value of land and buildings (dollars): Average per acre	Value of machinery and equipment, average per farm (dollars)	Value of products sold: Total (mil dol)	Value of products sold: Average per farm (acres)	Value of products sold: Percent from: Crops	Value of products sold: Percent from: Livestock and poultry products	Organic farms (number)	Farms with internet access (percent)	Government payments: Total ($1,000)	Government payments: Percent of farms
	117	118	119	120	121	122	123	124	125	126	127	128	129	130	131	132
TEXAS—Cont'd																
Guadalupe	359	-6.2	141	2.2	102.5	550,283	3,893	54,175	73.6	28,937	28.1	71.9	3	73.4	1,652	6.9
Hale	584	-8.8	870	189.3	458.9	1,131,985	1,301	249,333	411.7	613,568	33.3	66.7	NA	70.6	14,493	73.0
Hall	494	-2.9	1,511	29.7	236.5	1,389,562	919	222,564	56.4	172,502	81.0	19.0	NA	67.9	5,295	77.1
Hamilton	484	8.5	416	1.5	86.1	1,044,354	2,510	67,913	62.0	53,333	10.3	89.7	1	74.6	1,045	17.5
Hansford	587	3.6	3,243	93.7	301.1	4,353,971	1,342	539,803	737.4	4,074,127	12.5	87.5	NA	71.3	7,750	73.5
Hardeman	295	-16.9	1,072	0.9	114.2	1,118,742	1,044	91,771	18.0	65,436	29.9	70.1	NA	69.8	2,537	73.8
Hardin	65	-5.0	98	1.1	13.1	307,897	3,127	74,026	4.7	7,101	50.4	49.6	1	72.9	201	1.1
Harris	219	-7.5	116	7.3	52.7	998,511	8,635	58,260	50.6	26,765	73.4	26.6	10	75.0	1,448	2.7
Harrison	190	-4.7	168	1.7	38.5	440,839	2,628	66,104	15.8	13,964	26.1	73.9	2	75.4	421	4.7
Hartley	835	-7.6	4,052	153.0	296.4	5,028,050	1,241	997,785	1,221.7	5,930,437	12.8	87.2	6	74.3	6,780	59.7
Haskell	565	-0.4	1,158	14.8	293.0	1,218,046	1,052	175,284	54.3	111,307	68.3	31.7	2	69.5	6,906	73.0
Hays	263	7.4	233	0.6	53.0	2,280,804	9,773	53,651	21.8	19,282	52.6	47.4	4	79.9	324	3.6
Hemphill	528	-8.3	2,296	2.3	32.1	2,558,235	1,114	122,556	138.9	603,870	1.7	98.3	NA	62.6	1,699	46.1
Henderson	310	-10.2	156	1.6	86.6	497,751	3,188	64,795	40.2	20,213	29.0	71.0	1	78.6	58	1.2
Hidalgo	624	-21.5	256	162.5	356.9	1,106,061	4,319	92,928	311.0	127,681	94.3	5.7	26	61.8	6,631	10.5
Hill	523	3.8	261	1.2	256.4	660,515	2,529	89,657	114.0	56,915	56.6	43.4	1	70.0	7,927	22.8
Hockley	525	8.5	794	106.4	394.1	800,066	1,008	176,801	92.0	139,215	96.6	3.4	NA	69.9	6,956	65.2
Hood	205	-8.4	175	2.7	39.7	598,809	3,428	53,816	18.9	16,109	40.6	59.4	1	83.3	25	0.9
Hopkins	395	-6.6	179	2.5	127.9	523,841	2,918	78,642	253.7	115,335	4.1	95.9	NA	73.5	1,644	14.7
Houston	395	-15.7	277	3.5	70.8	774,459	2,791	75,170	64.5	45,371	10.5	89.5	NA	68.7	358	3.0
Howard	521	4.5	1,397	6.9	148.3	1,291,868	925	132,948	26.9	72,027	75.4	24.6	NA	70.2	3,272	46.6
Hudspeth	2,276	1.1	16,985	9.7	20.5	15,341,351	903	151,528	17.4	129,881	56.4	43.6	NA	61.9	171	6.0
Hunt	483	6.2	117	3.5	155.0	363,446	3,094	54,517	55.3	13,458	46.7	53.3	5	75.8	4,192	11.5
Hutchinson	548	5.2	3,679	26.7	81.7	3,561,262	968	227,673	44.9	301,416	55.5	44.5	NA	70.5	3,068	30.9
Irion	613	23.5	3,501	0.9	4.3	3,482,288	995	81,488	9.3	53,000	3.2	96.8	NA	81.1	318	10.9
Jack	468	-11.4	537	0.8	34.2	1,253,848	2,333	62,108	23.2	26,639	6.1	93.9	1	71.7	414	5.5
Jackson	382	-13.5	485	6.4	176.9	1,411,888	2,910	146,609	85.0	107,854	79.0	21.0	1	66.6	7,988	24.0
Jasper	91	3.8	102	0.3	13.4	327,242	3,207	58,063	9.1	10,200	43.8	56.2	3	73.1	9	0.8
Jeff Davis	1,378	9.8	17,896	0.1	0.6	12,302,948	687	125,618	D	D	D	D	NA	67.5	192	10.4
Jefferson	359	1.4	492	24.9	137.3	1,159,300	2,355	96,054	32.3	44,331	54.7	45.3	9	68.7	9,154	22.8
Jim Hogg	692	7.3	2,836	0.3	10.4	4,926,365	1,737	76,129	10.4	42,816	2.0	98.0	NA	59.4	529	9.0
Jim Wells	426	-15.4	348	2.4	158.1	720,153	2,069	70,377	121.6	99,379	30.2	69.8	NA	65.8	3,855	11.0
Johnson	411	-4.2	131	3.7	136.7	517,349	3,951	57,125	57.9	18,424	29.6	70.4	1	79.3	3,814	4.1
Jones	517	-8.2	564	4.6	313.8	644,140	1,141	91,000	41.5	45,344	72.0	28.0	NA	74.5	4,470	37.4
Karnes	432	-7.1	356	0.7	75.0	870,685	2,446	81,068	29.4	24,267	37.4	62.6	NA	61.7	508	5.0
Kaufman	455	1.3	164	1.7	133.6	493,007	3,010	59,513	57.1	20,541	27.0	73.0	NA	72.4	1,551	2.2
Kendall	394	6.5	292	0.7	32.4	904,088	3,096	41,444	12.4	9,222	9.7	90.3	NA	77.8	1,207	6.6
Kenedy	869	-5.2	28,961	0.7	1.9	21,350,824	737	105,455	D	D	D	D	NA	83.3	D	6.7
Kent	578	2.6	3,522	D	45.2	3,017,965	857	73,840	9.9	60,159	10.4	89.6	NA	66.5	1,025	47.6
Kerr	518	-11.1	459	0.8	16.0	1,145,687	2,497	48,881	9.3	8,268	16.9	83.1	1	73.9	225	3.0
Kimble	746	7.5	1,114	2.2	11.3	2,218,386	1,992	49,335	10.9	16,197	8.2	91.8	NA	74.6	743	6.9
King	417	-0.1	9,700	D	10.0	6,723,919	693	95,161	13.8	320,140	0.9	99.1	NA	67.4	320	60.5
Kinney	587	1.8	2,487	2.3	15.8	3,086,936	1,241	69,026	5.0	21,377	10.3	89.7	3	60.6	386	11.4
Kleberg	483	-0.3	1,051	0.0	65.6	1,387,563	1,320	100,068	52.8	114,996	41.6	58.4	1	67.1	1,537	15.0
Knox	489	8.5	2,263	11.2	207.4	2,520,181	1,114	211,879	60.5	280,222	22.4	77.6	NA	76.9	3,982	70.8
Lamar	464	-6.6	238	5.0	170.7	597,545	2,507	80,089	73.4	37,738	34.0	66.0	NA	73.0	8,480	34.2
Lamb	569	-7.6	733	173.9	489.3	912,685	1,246	268,352	537.3	691,529	22.1	77.9	3	64.7	16,363	81.5
Lampasas	469	5.5	407	0.4	40.4	1,152,472	2,828	61,081	18.4	16,021	10.9	89.1	2	72.5	381	6.7
La Salle	533	-16.1	1,391	2.1	19.8	2,203,808	1,584	120,717	6.3	16,444	8.5	91.5	NA	58.2	165	3.1
Lavaca	507	-7.3	175	2.6	74.2	613,235	3,511	58,515	50.5	17,430	14.8	85.2	3	65.1	856	7.0
Lee	329	3.3	182	0.8	41.4	667,815	3,676	54,124	56.9	31,478	26.7	73.3	NA	67.6	608	6.1
Leon	488	-18.0	250	2.0	71.2	759,052	3,037	71,907	169.4	86,829	5.9	94.1	1	70.3	144	0.8
Liberty	252	-12.0	164	5.2	68.3	493,738	3,008	74,395	30.0	19,473	40.3	59.7	NA	75.0	3,962	4.1
Limestone	493	1.2	384	0.5	73.0	706,578	1,842	71,310	66.3	51,602	15.1	84.9	NA	68.5	678	6.2
Lipscomb	586	-0.9	1,961	23.8	115.7	2,204,190	1,124	137,377	79.3	265,204	21.5	78.5	NA	72.2	4,833	65.2
Live Oak	455	-15.9	531	2.4	47.4	1,147,237	2,159	84,738	19.5	22,723	25.8	74.2	NA	74.2	717	10.3
Llano	523	-0.9	627	0.5	21.6	1,642,693	2,620	54,170	15.7	18,832	9.5	90.5	NA	76.8	355	4.9
Loving	468	23.3	58,518	D	D	11,163,974	191	146,059	D	D	NA	D	NA	62.5	D	37.5
Lubbock	531	5.6	514	166.7	451.4	874,304	1,702	186,233	219.5	212,458	58.0	42.0	2	82.0	4,685	41.7
Lynn	499	5.7	1,150	83.1	456.3	1,158,640	1,007	318,818	111.4	256,758	95.7	4.3	10	70.5	6,493	73.3
McCulloch	563	-8.3	826	1.9	83.7	1,627,004	1,971	73,710	22.5	32,978	30.5	69.5	NA	77.9	2,261	31.5
McLennan	573	3.6	170	2.2	262.5	614,516	3,608	67,948	179.7	53,377	33.1	66.9	4	72.5	5,860	11.7
McMullen	452	-12.7	2,365	D	26.7	4,293,308	1,816	111,599	8.3	43,586	7.5	92.5	NA	77.0	360	5.8
Madison	246	-15.7	251	1.3	34.0	752,922	2,996	87,971	D	D	D	D	1	71.0	60	1.4
Marion	50	24.5	178	D	13.6	357,305	2,003	53,364	5.9	21,021	9.2	90.8	NA	71.1	151	7.1
Martin	445	-2.0	1,249	12.2	298.9	1,111,299	890	191,065	54.3	152,522	96.7	3.3	NA	79.8	5,464	68.5

STATE County	Water use, 2015		Wholesale Trade[1], 2017				Retail Trade[2], 2017				Real estate and rental and leasing,[2] 2017			
	Public supply water withdrawn (mil gal/ day)	Public supply gallons withdrawn per person per day	Number of establish- ments	Number of employees	Sales (mil dol)	Average payroll (mil dol)	Number of establish- ments	Number of employees	Sales (mil dol)	Average payroll (mil dol)	Number of establish- ments	Number of employees	Sales (mil dol)	Average payroll (mil dol)
	133	134	135	136	137	138	139	140	141	142	143	144	145	146
TEXAS—Cont'd														
Guadalupe	6.9	45.3	95	1,759	1,066.4	99.9	269	4,723	1,675.0	139.9	109	410	95.3	17.2
Hale	1.4	41.9	50	542	381.6	24.7	104	1,356	453.6	33.5	26	64	11.6	1.7
Hall	0.0	12.7	D	D	D	0.6	12	91	33.4	1.8	NA	NA	NA	NA
Hamilton	0.2	19.6	7	69	37.5	3.3	47	381	88.4	9.4	NA	NA	NA	NA
Hansford	1.0	171.1	17	110	140.2	5.3	25	218	72.9	6.8	5	D	0.7	D
Hardeman	0.1	18.2	D	D	D	1.0	14	142	60.7	2.7	NA	NA	NA	NA
Hardin	4.0	72.1	D	D	D	D	153	2,248	964.9	68.1	D	D	D	D
Harris	287.3	63.3	6,540	107,902	386,380.7	7,607.6	13,165	212,528	70,018.5	6,167.3	5,942	44,290	13,375.1	2,422.8
Harrison	8.5	127.8	D	D	D	37.7	175	1,916	604.6	52.1	66	308	75.0	19.4
Hartley	1.0	164.7	7	75	46.1	3.9	11	204	53.6	3.8	6	25	3.2	0.7
Haskell	0.1	24.4	3	3	2.7	0.1	26	346	118.6	9.4	3	2	0.4	0.0
Hays	8.2	42.2	146	1,444	1,153.9	99.2	658	15,180	4,967.7	372.5	261	1,246	289.8	48.8
Hemphill	0.5	117.3	14	275	145.6	20.8	18	149	35.6	3.6	9	18	6.0	1.0
Henderson	4.6	57.2	37	268	127.9	10.7	238	2,738	755.3	64.8	58	298	39.6	8.1
Hidalgo	64.6	76.7	871	9,035	5,467.8	353.5	2,162	37,469	9,923.4	887.1	571	2,280	490.1	68.7
Hill	3.0	85.2	23	165	76.2	6.0	133	1,413	430.6	33.4	27	67	11.9	2.0
Hockley	0.5	21.3	32	271	305.9	18.6	59	828	236.0	20.1	14	60	10.0	3.3
Hood	4.9	87.5	43	357	139.9	14.2	186	2,881	990.1	79.8	70	347	64.3	15.4
Hopkins	11.1	305.1	30	956	1,242.9	47.7	145	1,647	576.5	42.8	28	119	22.9	3.1
Houston	2.3	102.7	D	D	D	2.7	59	707	182.1	16.5	9	48	7.8	1.2
Howard	0.0	0.8	31	221	230.5	14.1	D	D	D	D	41	127	36.1	4.4
Hudspeth	0.2	71.0	NA	NA	NA	NA	8	49	8.6	0.7	NA	NA	NA	NA
Hunt	4.9	54.2	60	723	474.4	41.2	265	3,962	1,263.0	109.3	72	264	49.9	11.3
Hutchinson	5.3	243.9	20	157	93.6	7.8	68	950	244.3	22.6	11	61	13.3	2.1
Irion	0.1	51.5	NA	NA	NA	NA	5	22	5.9	0.5	NA	NA	NA	NA
Jack	0.6	62.0	8	20	42.1	1.3	26	168	51.6	4.2	9	21	3.5	0.6
Jackson	0.9	60.7	12	114	103.8	5.9	50	518	132.0	11.7	13	23	2.4	0.4
Jasper	3.0	83.6	30	215	141.1	9.6	114	1,452	434.9	34.9	19	67	14.1	2.7
Jeff Davis	1.1	519.5	NA	NA	NA	NA	11	68	10.4	1.1	NA	NA	NA	NA
Jefferson	24.0	94.2	275	3,601	2,854.6	203.9	950	13,584	4,419.5	388.2	294	2,203	541.5	103.5
Jim Hogg	0.7	128.8	4	8	2.8	0.3	18	188	66.1	4.6	NA	NA	NA	NA
Jim Wells	4.0	95.5	37	328	210.7	22.8	120	1,546	473.1	40.6	31	280	62.2	17.6
Johnson	10.3	64.6	139	1,306	798.2	63.2	404	6,006	2,255.8	182.8	141	759	159.3	38.3
Jones	8.1	404.1	15	116	166.9	5.9	37	239	192.7	9.1	7	24	2.5	0.5
Karnes	2.8	183.6	21	119	110.6	5.5	41	548	151.4	15.0	16	102	34.0	6.1
Kaufman	0.9	7.4	77	892	386.8	40.2	298	4,326	1,351.5	111.7	67	217	35.4	6.7
Kendall	1.7	41.1	56	498	314.6	25.5	174	2,754	1,381.1	95.7	78	200	40.0	7.6
Kenedy	0.1	172.0	NA	NA	NA	NA	NA	NA	NA	NA	NA	NA	NA	NA
Kent	0.1	104.7	NA	NA	NA	NA	3	15	9.2	0.4	NA	NA	NA	NA
Kerr	5.6	109.5	D	D	D	9.2	203	2,733	887.8	81.0	83	332	50.4	12.0
Kimble	0.5	102.6	NA	NA	NA	NA	34	267	123.1	6.6	4	14	1.8	0.5
King	0.2	673.8	NA	NA	NA	NA	NA	NA	NA	NA	NA	NA	NA	NA
Kinney	0.8	231.1	NA	NA	NA	NA	8	40	6.2	0.6	NA	NA	NA	NA
Kleberg	3.3	103.9	D	D	D	D	98	1,409	444.2	37.8	D	D	D	D
Knox	0.1	36.3	10	85	31.9	5.7	17	114	30.5	2.7	NA	NA	NA	NA
Lamar	14.8	300.2	55	419	160.5	16.5	212	2,629	903.1	74.8	46	173	26.0	4.5
Lamb	1.4	100.9	21	173	128.1	8.3	33	317	91.6	7.2	NA	NA	NA	NA
Lampasas	2.7	131.6	10	43	16.5	2.3	47	676	254.7	20.9	16	128	19.4	5.5
La Salle	1.4	178.2	D	D	D	D	22	303	157.3	6.5	D	D	D	D
Lavaca	1.4	72.6	19	181	97.5	12.3	82	737	177.3	18.1	11	30	5.2	0.9
Lee	4.0	234.9	22	152	53.4	6.8	63	618	158.6	16.0	11	102	44.5	5.4
Leon	1.9	111.2	15	125	82.4	7.5	62	590	182.3	12.8	16	78	16.2	4.2
Liberty	6.4	80.6	43	500	756.4	28.5	197	2,547	842.3	72.5	40	136	25.6	5.8
Limestone	2.0	83.6	D	D	D	D	86	941	270.2	22.6	12	65	6.3	1.2
Lipscomb	0.8	227.0	NA	NA	NA	NA	11	152	62.2	5.1	NA	NA	NA	NA
Live Oak	2.8	225.7	14	170	97.8	9.9	41	391	208.2	11.8	9	19	5.6	1.0
Llano	2.9	145.0	13	217	108.4	10.2	67	597	175.1	14.9	22	62	8.4	1.7
Loving	0.0	89.3	NA	NA	NA	NA	NA	NA	NA	NA	NA	NA	NA	NA
Lubbock	1.3	4.4	382	5,412	5,588.6	295.7	987	18,278	5,616.9	503.5	446	1,998	411.4	75.1
Lynn	0.2	26.2	7	49	30.9	1.8	8	72	22.5	1.6	NA	NA	NA	NA
McCulloch	2.7	322.5	4	59	25.5	1.8	47	465	152.9	13.0	7	22	1.5	0.3
McLennan	41.4	168.6	246	2,789	1,828.0	139.6	837	12,847	3,711.8	340.0	258	1,692	378.2	77.8
McMullen	0.1	122.0	NA	NA	NA	NA	5	67	26.2	2.2	NA	NA	NA	NA
Madison	2.4	168.5	D	D	D	D	37	664	299.2	21.3	12	23	5.2	1.1
Marion	0.4	34.4	NA	NA	NA	NA	27	228	60.7	4.6	6	8	1.3	0.2
Martin	1.5	262.4	8	47	45.4	2.9	13	168	115.4	7.4	D	D	D	1.0

1 Merchant wholesalers, except manufacturers' sales branches and offices. 2. Employer establishments.

STATE County	Professional, scientific, and technical services, 2017				Manufacturing, 2017				Accommodation and food services, 2017			
	Number of establish-ments	Number of employees	Sales (mil dol)	Average payroll (mil dol)	Number of establish-ments	Number of employees	Sales (mil dol)	Average payroll (mil dol)	Number of establis-hments	Number of employees	Sales (mil dol)	Annual payroll (mil dol)
	147	148	149	150	151	152	153	154	155	156	157	158
TEXAS—Cont'd												
Guadalupe	151	950	156.3	49.8	115	7,103	4,583.7	416.7	204	3,949	210.3	57.3
Hale	D	D	D	D	18	607	477.8	23.3	62	1,187	55.5	15.9
Hall	NA	NA	NA	NA	4	14	1.8	0.6	D	D	D	0.5
Hamilton	17	51	4.8	1.9	14	185	74.9	8.8	24	266	10.6	3.2
Hansford	9	39	5.0	1.9	4	16	5.6	0.9	10	70	3.7	0.9
Hardeman	NA	NA	NA	NA	NA	NA	NA	NA	D	D	D	D
Hardin	46	309	41.8	20.0	D	706	D	44.1	86	1,476	67.0	19.1
Harris	14,034	189,107	44,253.4	17,423.5	4,023	148,629	146,184.2	10,003.4	9,616	205,281	13,797.5	3,815.8
Harrison	120	672	115.2	38.1	72	3,945	2,567.2	240.6	103	1,830	93.4	27.5
Hartley	D	D	D	D	NA	NA	NA	NA	D	D	D	0.5
Haskell	9	44	2.6	0.9	NA	NA	NA	NA	16	109	5.5	1.3
Hays	450	2,200	312.6	105.6	182	4,443	1,414.8	221.6	454	10,154	541.9	156.8
Hemphill	12	51	11.8	2.9	5	21	6.6	1.0	D	D	D	D
Henderson	94	753	85.8	25.2	54	1,437	295.6	71.2	154	2,082	104.1	29.1
Hidalgo	D	D	720.2	D	280	5,703	2,136.8	225.8	1,112	23,976	1,254.7	329.5
Hill	32	143	17.2	6.9	42	953	478.6	46.1	73	1,054	60.7	15.8
Hockley	25	90	8.9	3.2	14	277	230.7	16.1	42	691	31.0	8.7
Hood	132	426	56.9	20.3	38	379	78.9	17.1	112	1,918	107.7	28.7
Hopkins	51	193	25.1	7.7	40	1,646	940.9	81.0	66	1,048	52.8	16.0
Houston	29	91	12.4	3.3	13	451	204.9	33.2	32	391	20.0	5.1
Howard	D	D	D	D	D	D	D	D	D	D	D	D
Hudspeth	NA	NA	NA	NA	NA	NA	NA	NA	6	37	1.6	0.7
Hunt	92	1,069	261.4	57.1	70	8,659	2,974.1	705.8	156	2,708	150.4	41.1
Hutchinson	27	279	39.5	19.7	19	1,673	5,756.7	166.5	51	724	32.0	8.4
Irion	6	8	0.7	0.1	NA	NA	NA	NA	D	D	D	D
Jack	10	46	5.5	2.2	6	33	16.2	2.4	D	D	D	D
Jackson	24	198	13.4	6.4	D	D	D	D	24	351	15.6	4.2
Jasper	36	152	24.5	5.0	23	1,186	672.3	93.5	53	817	40.5	11.0
Jeff Davis	D	D	D	0.2	NA	NA	NA	NA	13	117	6.8	1.9
Jefferson	D	D	D	D	185	13,150	47,196.4	1,352.0	512	10,395	583.1	155.2
Jim Hogg	NA	NA	NA	NA	5	40	24.9	1.8	11	64	3.8	0.8
Jim Wells	52	294	71.2	13.4	18	298	74.3	17.9	87	1,118	61.6	16.9
Johnson	197	716	103.1	32.8	154	5,752	1,778.9	300.7	251	4,512	238.0	60.9
Jones	11	34	3.2	1.5	8	126	57.4	8.2	17	105	5.6	1.4
Karnes	21	87	9.0	3.6	10	228	75.7	9.6	44	476	34.2	8.2
Kaufman	136	772	96.2	33.3	111	4,238	1,203.0	214.4	192	3,200	180.3	47.6
Kendall	178	801	126.6	50.4	42	950	395.3	53.8	108	1,606	99.1	31.1
Kenedy	NA	NA	NA	NA	NA	NA	NA	NA	NA	NA	NA	NA
Kent	NA	NA	NA	NA	NA	NA	NA	NA	NA	NA	NA	NA
Kerr	D	D	D	D	50	795	116.2	34.4	143	2,345	157.2	46.9
Kimble	7	11	1.2	0.4	7	57	8.2	2.1	D	D	D	D
King	NA	NA	NA	NA	NA	NA	NA	NA	NA	NA	NA	NA
Kinney	NA	NA	NA	NA	NA	NA	NA	NA	6	D	1.3	D
Kleberg	33	145	19.0	5.1	15	57	25.1	3.0	D	D	D	D
Knox	NA	NA	NA	NA	NA	NA	NA	NA	D	D	D	0.5
Lamar	D	D	D	D	56	4,769	2,631.3	236.5	116	1,933	95.3	26.2
Lamb	14	48	7.8	1.6	6	74	15.5	3.7	18	210	10.3	2.6
Lampasas	36	131	16.3	5.8	21	612	167.8	25.4	38	423	25.1	6.6
La Salle	NA	NA	NA	NA	NA	NA	NA	NA	D	D	D	D
Lavaca	35	151	22.8	9.5	33	1,415	382.0	60.6	35	385	19.1	5.7
Lee	26	101	10.3	3.4	15	440	92.8	19.2	38	373	20.7	5.1
Leon	15	55	5.9	1.7	16	650	574.3	68.3	39	403	20.2	4.8
Liberty	D	D	D	D	34	986	341.8	55.8	95	1,523	92.9	23.9
Limestone	21	117	20.5	6.3	10	539	88.0	19.0	38	434	25.1	5.7
Lipscomb	6	21	2.2	0.9	NA	NA	NA	NA	D	D	D	0.6
Live Oak	26	74	12.3	3.1	D	D	D	D	41	348	27.7	5.8
Llano	39	147	16.7	6.0	16	63	19.1	3.7	48	1,145	77.2	28.1
Loving	NA	NA	NA	NA	NA	NA	NA	NA	NA	NA	NA	NA
Lubbock	653	4,497	615.0	231.6	225	4,583	1,503.7	232.7	706	16,429	936.1	263.6
Lynn	D	D	0.4	D	D	D	D	D	6	17	0.7	0.1
McCulloch	17	57	5.0	1.7	10	204	24.3	8.9	24	276	14.7	3.7
McLennan	388	2,720	521.4	164.1	249	13,777	7,597.6	829.8	523	D	620.5	D
McMullen	NA	NA	NA	NA	NA	NA	NA	NA	3	26	2.0	0.6
Madison	16	75	8.5	2.6	7	36	7.3	1.5	44	609	29.0	7.4
Marion	11	13	2.3	0.7	8	310	203.4	18.6	24	396	14.1	5.0
Martin	D	D	D	1.4	3	11	1.3	0.3	D	D	D	D

Table B. States and Counties — **Health Care and Social Assistance, Other Services, Nonemployer Businesses, and Residential Construction**

STATE County	Health care and social assistance, 2017				Other services, 2017				Nonemployer businesses, 2019		Value of residential construction authorized by building permits, 2021	
	Number of establish-ments	Number of employees	Receipts (mil dol)	Annual payroll (mil dol)	Number of establish-ments	Number of employees	Receipts (mil dol)	Annual payroll (mil dol)	Number	Receipts (mil dol)	New construction ($1,000)	Number of housing units
	159	160	161	162	163	164	165	166	167	168	169	170
TEXAS—Cont'd												
Guadalupe	213	3,227	353.7	137.2	161	989	106.4	32.1	13,109	587.2	433,854	1,868
Hale	74	1,136	115.4	39.7	53	354	30.5	9.8	2,099	104.0	7,404	26
Hall	6	D	3.6	D	6	20	2.4	0.5	193	5.9	0	0
Hamilton	21	558	41.5	19.6	20	50	6.5	1.4	826	42.7	2,801	21
Hansford	D	D	D	D	11	45	4.6	1.6	485	25.1	0	0
Hardeman	9	138	13.7	6.0	11	47	4.4	1.1	235	9.1	0	0
Hardin	57	946	64.6	27.5	56	335	35.6	10.4	4,071	206.5	97,736	465
Harris	11,829	275,105	38,411.2	14,179.2	6,301	65,343	9,616.9	2,832.9	480,259	24,134.2	5,974,645	35,204
Harrison	116	1,799	158.7	66.8	73	821	82.3	20.2	5,103	238.8	24,034	114
Hartley	10	317	30.9	10.5	D	D	17.2	D	359	24.4	NA	NA
Haskell	8	133	11.2	5.8	17	48	3.6	0.8	435	21.4	0	0
Hays	391	7,379	854.9	332.9	267	1,531	177.7	51.0	21,437	1,062.4	1,090,037	5,439
Hemphill	7	209	12.7	7.1	D	D	D	D	420	23.4	0	0
Henderson	132	2,304	359.1	135.6	77	370	36.7	10.4	6,905	340.0	53,194	243
Hidalgo	2,193	64,956	4,371.9	1,772.6	592	3,522	322.6	90.2	81,199	3,441.6	1,065,455	6,055
Hill	48	1,094	91.9	37.0	38	140	12.1	3.5	2,728	129.6	16,839	112
Hockley	44	1,043	62.1	25.5	D	D	D	D	1,508	73.3	3,802	17
Hood	145	2,130	229.0	82.5	95	679	49.2	16.3	6,627	347.6	63,996	291
Hopkins	57	1,527	149.7	50.1	54	210	21.9	5.8	3,073	172.8	17,128	128
Houston	29	730	41.9	18.7	24	147	16.3	4.7	1,396	61.8	269	3
Howard	75	2,475	329.0	135.7	D	D	D	D	1,894	89.0	587	2
Hudspeth	NA	NA	NA	NA	NA	NA	NA	NA	284	8.6	NA	NA
Hunt	175	3,469	358.0	149.7	101	451	43.7	12.4	8,023	412.2	192,213	1,031
Hutchinson	42	586	64.2	21.7	28	197	24.2	6.8	1,018	40.5	836	4
Irion	NA	NA	NA	NA	D	D	2.3	D	197	12.3	0	0
Jack	12	258	26.2	9.4	15	36	5.1	1.1	831	45.6	13	1
Jackson	18	305	26.4	12.1	25	82	11.3	2.7	1,223	57.7	309	2
Jasper	80	2,535	139.6	54.4	35	163	14.3	3.7	2,584	97.3	24,603	161
Jeff Davis	D	D	D	2.7	D	D	D	0.6	265	9.3	NA	NA
Jefferson	900	17,612	1,945.4	675.6	372	3,569	367.8	164.9	17,390	780.1	170,196	911
Jim Hogg	10	747	15.7	10.2	NA	NA	NA	NA	394	12.0	NA	NA
Jim Wells	112	5,419	216.7	100.9	53	243	33.3	8.9	3,060	126.4	879	5
Johnson	268	3,488	361.2	130.7	216	1,549	174.3	60.7	15,570	805.5	378,099	2,218
Jones	20	548	66.5	18.7	18	44	3.0	1.0	1,344	61.6	250	1
Karnes	18	441	35.5	15.7	14	43	4.9	1.2	975	42.0	14,785	81
Kaufman	173	3,498	292.0	130.9	142	923	119.1	41.0	13,815	671.4	382,088	1,589
Kendall	158	1,912	184.5	72.5	88	518	68.4	18.3	6,240	400.8	90,429	387
Kenedy	NA	NA	NA	NA	5	85	51.1	5.6	28	0.7	NA	NA
Kent	NA	NA	NA	NA	NA	NA	NA	NA	62	2.3	NA	NA
Kerr	183	3,690	478.5	194.3	104	642	86.1	21.3	5,827	312.2	21,315	98
Kimble	7	135	9.4	4.9	9	34	3.0	0.8	646	25.8	275	1
King	NA	NA	NA	NA	NA	NA	NA	NA	33	1.0	NA	NA
Kinney	4	11	1.7	0.4	D	D	3.5	D	222	6.9	0	0
Kleberg	75	1,347	107.6	42.2	39	161	17.0	3.2	1,693	55.2	5,259	44
Knox	D	D	D	D	D	D	2.2	D	267	11.3	0	0
Lamar	196	3,655	365.0	136.5	80	408	44.2	11.7	4,171	187.3	12,120	81
Lamb	28	551	36.0	15.6	19	44	5.8	1.1	783	38.4	187	2
Lampasas	24	521	49.1	20.0	23	136	14.4	3.8	1,772	101.2	12,868	50
La Salle	13	145	13.0	4.6	D	D	D	D	560	19.0	870	4
Lavaca	39	999	94.9	34.2	40	139	13.5	3.6	1,880	86.9	1,266	10
Lee	31	288	22.1	8.5	32	124	12.2	3.1	1,611	75.4	6,525	30
Leon	12	D	5.8	D	24	95	8.7	2.3	1,540	75.9	0	0
Liberty	92	2,120	222.2	62.1	68	359	45.2	11.6	7,216	314.8	209,033	1,234
Limestone	52	1,184	101.3	39.6	21	74	7.7	2.0	1,410	59.6	1,535	8
Lipscomb	NA	NA	NA	NA	D	D	1.0	D	282	11.5	380	1
Live Oak	11	149	8.9	4.1	8	25	1.8	0.4	1,081	48.6	0	0
Llano	49	624	64.7	21.2	25	84	9.1	2.2	2,437	136.7	55,157	261
Loving	NA	NA	NA	NA	NA	NA	NA	NA	23	0.6	NA	NA
Lubbock	878	24,682	3,010.3	1,033.8	469	3,871	398.8	112.4	24,703	1,287.7	730,008	3,402
Lynn	7	170	17.4	6.7	7	34	8.8	1.5	445	23.7	478	2
McCulloch	17	198	22.9	6.7	17	65	7.5	1.5	733	31.5	0	0
McLennan	583	17,869	1,804.9	761.3	D	D	D	79.4	17,940	870.6	129,948	1,097
McMullen	NA	NA	NA	NA	NA	NA	NA	NA	129	5.6	NA	NA
Madison	21	269	25.6	12.3	14	96	9.1	3.2	1,042	49.1	1,399	6
Marion	14	475	29.5	12.7	D	D	D	0.4	741	30.6	1,378	12
Martin	8	289	28.3	12.5	8	18	4.7	0.6	530	41.0	1,343	14

STATE County	Government employment and payroll, 2017									Local government finances, 2017				
			March payroll (percent of total)							General revenue				
												Taxes		
													Per capita[1] (dollars)	
	Full-time equivalent employees	March payroll (dollars)	Adminis-tration, judicial, and legal	Police and corrections	Fire protection	Highways and transpor-tation	Health and welfare	Natural resources and utilities	Education and libraries	Total (mil dol)	Inter-govern-mental (mil dol)	Total (mil dol)	Total	Property
	171	172	173	174	175	176	177	178	179	180	181	182	183	184
TEXAS—Cont'd														
Guadalupe	5,343	21,348,342	6.0	10.3	2.7	2.1	14.7	4.2	59.0	545.4	136.7	250.0	1,566	1,310
Hale	2,228	8,615,470	4.1	5.0	2.1	1.2	5.1	2.5	79.6	133.0	56.9	54.9	1,617	1,293
Hall	229	674,102	12.4	8.3	0.3	4.7	1.5	5.9	66.3	16.2	6.5	7.9	2,592	2,131
Hamilton	605	2,098,033	6.4	6.2	0.0	0.2	45.5	1.6	39.9	52.2	9.6	14.8	1,759	1,525
Hansford	555	1,832,514	6.9	4.0	0.0	2.1	32.9	4.6	48.8	52.5	11.5	15.8	2,887	2,658
Hardeman	457	1,691,737	9.7	4.0	2.7	2.3	45.6	1.6	33.9	21.5	6.1	11.7	2,951	2,531
Hardin	2,176	7,148,427	7.0	7.5	1.1	2.3	0.8	2.7	76.7	146.0	61.5	71.7	1,256	1,094
Harris	187,579	822,114,261	4.2	10.5	3.4	4.9	8.4	2.7	64.0	24,091.5	6,040.7	12,838.7	2,756	2,295
Harrison	2,588	8,365,927	5.4	9.8	3.7	2.0	0.7	4.0	72.8	218.0	58.1	131.9	1,984	1,737
Hartley	99	347,028	17.7	2.3	0.0	0.0	0.0	1.3	72.3	9.4	1.3	7.2	1,251	1,188
Haskell	379	1,056,108	8.3	4.8	0.1	3.4	28.3	5.6	49.3	30.2	7.9	12.4	2,175	1,825
Hays	8,066	29,596,807	5.4	11.0	3.3	1.8	6.5	5.6	62.5	786.3	196.0	436.4	2,032	1,697
Hemphill	427	1,487,981	6.6	3.6	0.0	3.9	37.8	5.7	41.6	39.9	4.2	32.0	8,152	7,590
Henderson	2,869	9,571,842	6.4	10.8	1.7	2.0	0.3	3.6	74.0	237.5	74.3	131.5	1,624	1,437
Hidalgo	42,017	156,936,079	3.8	6.8	1.8	1.8	4.5	4.0	76.4	3,554.6	2,159.8	994.9	1,162	962
Hill	1,869	6,875,341	5.4	8.2	0.9	1.4	0.7	1.9	80.8	162.0	61.0	76.9	2,154	1,793
Hockley	1,854	7,035,365	3.9	4.4	0.7	1.5	0.1	2.0	86.9	151.1	58.3	62.1	2,701	2,445
Hood	1,876	6,914,567	8.5	10.6	0.3	2.1	1.3	5.1	70.1	158.3	22.0	112.6	1,942	1,644
Hopkins	1,565	4,980,595	5.3	8.6	2.9	2.8	3.1	3.6	72.6	206.5	49.2	52.0	1,427	1,145
Houston	793	2,385,024	9.6	9.3	0.5	3.0	1.7	4.2	70.8	68.3	28.7	31.6	1,370	1,129
Howard	2,197	7,472,601	5.0	7.1	4.0	2.0	12.9	7.3	61.1	153.4	51.1	67.6	1,886	1,675
Hudspeth	287	841,839	10.1	16.1	0.0	3.7	0.1	6.2	63.0	13.1	5.2	6.1	1,323	1,222
Hunt	4,521	17,022,379	4.3	6.6	2.2	1.1	27.4	8.2	49.5	428.0	126.2	142.0	1,510	1,250
Hutchinson	1,316	4,530,193	8.6	8.5	4.0	2.4	1.0	5.5	67.7	115.2	36.6	54.1	2,537	2,149
Irion	116	392,701	12.5	6.2	0.0	8.0	0.3	19.0	48.3	20.8	3.1	17.4	11,499	11,409
Jack	566	2,266,420	4.5	5.2	0.2	1.6	25.0	3.7	59.0	35.9	7.6	25.1	2,847	2,652
Jackson	1,024	3,448,643	5.4	5.9	0.0	2.4	19.3	5.6	53.2	90.6	23.0	35.6	2,403	2,135
Jasper	1,556	4,879,242	6.6	9.1	0.1	3.0	1.9	6.7	70.3	108.7	44.7	53.6	1,507	1,386
Jeff Davis	129	453,660	9.1	4.8	0.0	0.0	1.2	0.5	83.1	11.5	4.6	4.6	2,049	1,815
Jefferson	9,986	39,634,101	6.3	15.7	6.3	3.8	7.2	8.7	50.7	1,131.8	279.1	608.0	2,375	1,908
Jim Hogg	358	983,737	8.8	7.8	0.5	0.0	1.1	7.7	72.3	27.4	11.8	12.7	2,430	2,039
Jim Wells	1,870	6,179,342	7.9	10.4	2.6	5.9	1.2	3.4	66.7	136.1	63.7	55.5	1,357	989
Johnson	6,968	23,471,528	6.4	11.0	3.5	2.4	1.3	4.6	68.5	583.4	194.6	304.8	1,825	1,554
Jones	859	2,861,245	6.6	6.8	0.0	2.2	17.1	3.8	62.6	62.1	26.0	20.5	1,033	893
Karnes	889	2,965,577	6.2	10.8	0.0	5.2	17.6	3.7	55.6	111.6	25.4	76.7	4,931	4,682
Kaufman	5,273	21,071,674	4.3	8.9	1.6	2.4	8.9	2.7	69.9	457.7	192.6	211.1	1,721	1,496
Kendall	1,755	6,657,795	9.0	8.4	1.1	2.7	0.4	5.3	70.4	177.9	14.1	133.7	3,041	2,653
Kenedy	82	186,075	26.6	5.4	0.0	8.5	0.0	0.0	55.4	11.1	0.3	10.1	23,642	23,611
Kent	133	417,992	10.7	6.9	0.0	12.7	28.4	4.6	35.3	9.9	1.4	7.7	10,112	9,995
Kerr	1,814	6,748,491	8.7	14.0	6.2	2.8	0.9	5.0	60.4	136.6	26.0	93.0	1,792	1,448
Kimble	146	443,542	25.6	5.7	0.2	4.6	0.6	3.4	59.2	14.0	2.8	7.3	1,658	1,466
King	65	200,785	27.6	2.1	0.0	0.0	0.0	0.5	69.9	6.6	1.4	4.8	16,734	16,734
Kinney	204	626,114	11.9	9.4	0.0	1.2	7.5	3.6	65.5	19.1	8.1	7.9	2,137	1,826
Kleberg	1,530	6,649,322	6.9	10.2	2.4	2.5	2.7	5.1	68.3	111.7	50.8	46.3	1,506	1,211
Knox	393	1,268,571	6.4	3.3	0.0	1.4	34.3	5.1	48.8	18.7	8.9	8.2	2,220	1,968
Lamar	2,196	8,027,047	5.9	8.7	0.2	1.5	1.7	3.9	76.5	183.8	69.7	83.7	1,689	1,328
Lamb	775	2,503,676	7.2	9.8	0.3	2.9	1.9	4.6	72.7	67.4	25.3	26.1	1,985	1,733
Lampasas	929	3,077,108	22.7	4.7	1.9	2.0	0.4	3.6	63.1	55.6	19.2	30.4	1,456	1,273
La Salle	400	1,555,564	7.0	7.7	0.0	2.4	1.0	2.3	77.8	73.3	5.4	64.1	8,519	8,199
Lavaca	836	2,894,533	12.3	9.2	1.6	4.0	18.7	8.3	43.1	76.1	9.7	36.9	1,845	1,648
Lee	696	2,247,761	7.9	10.6	0.0	4.8	0.1	5.5	70.7	55.3	16.8	33.0	1,929	1,677
Leon	800	2,600,523	8.0	7.3	0.0	3.3	0.9	3.2	77.0	58.2	16.6	36.0	2,088	1,872
Liberty	3,386	11,319,873	5.7	7.6	1.0	2.2	0.5	2.6	79.2	246.8	107.9	118.3	1,415	1,254
Limestone	1,375	4,409,125	5.8	10.8	2.5	2.9	18.5	2.6	56.1	180.5	30.8	49.6	2,119	1,984
Lipscomb	264	922,493	8.4	5.8	0.0	7.0	4.1	5.5	67.1	26.1	6.9	17.0	5,059	4,644
Live Oak	632	2,424,236	6.4	10.8	0.0	3.5	1.3	4.2	70.7	45.0	6.1	35.6	2,935	2,694
Llano	659	2,053,537	13.3	14.0	0.0	4.1	0.4	9.0	57.3	66.4	3.8	57.7	2,726	2,636
Loving	12	57,878	58.1	24.4	0.0	15.4	0.0	2.1	0.0	4.3	0.0	0.0	331	233
Lubbock	14,801	59,464,737	4.6	10.4	4.5	1.0	32.6	5.5	40.2	1,628.6	432.1	515.3	1,687	1,320
Lynn	483	1,591,459	5.3	5.4	0.0	1.2	29.3	2.7	55.0	36.9	14.9	10.8	1,847	1,722
McCulloch	632	2,059,659	5.8	5.3	1.4	2.0	22.6	8.6	52.2	28.9	12.0	13.6	1,718	1,533
McLennan	11,175	42,970,259	5.7	11.5	3.1	1.8	6.0	7.2	63.7	1,119.6	400.8	470.3	1,869	1,493
McMullen	127	458,723	17.6	15.5	1.5	8.2	0.0	3.0	52.0	24.0	1.8	21.4	28,001	27,903
Madison	551	1,796,252	9.5	6.2	0.0	2.0	0.5	2.9	75.5	41.6	13.6	22.5	1,578	1,382
Marion	348	925,317	12.5	9.6	0.0	3.5	1.3	2.3	70.4	15.4	7.4	6.8	676	522
Martin	454	2,092,649	7.6	3.7	0.0	7.2	40.6	2.6	37.6	74.9	4.8	53.0	9,587	9,435

1. Based on the resident population estimated as of July 1 of the year shown.

STATE County	Local government finances, 2017 (cont.) — Direct general expenditure — Total (mil dol)	Direct general expenditure — Per capita[1] (dollars)	Direct general expenditure — Percent of total for: Education	Percent of total for: Health and hospitals	Percent of total for: Police protection	Percent of total for: Public welfare	Percent of total for: Highways	Debt outstanding — Total (mil dol)	Debt outstanding — Per capita[1] (dollars)	Government employment, 2020 — Federal civilian	Government employment, 2020 — Federal military	Government employment, 2020 — State and local	Individual income tax returns, 2019 — Number of returns	Individual income tax returns, 2019 — Mean adjusted gross income	Individual income tax returns, 2019 — Mean income tax
	185	186	187	188	189	190	191	192	193	194	195	196	197	198	199
TEXAS—Cont'd															
Guadalupe	627.3	3,929	48.1	17.7	4.3	0.6	3.4	1,494.4	9,361	249	323	6,504	81,780	63,188	6,104
Hale	123.0	3,624	55.4	7.8	8.4	0.7	4.3	84.3	2,482	81	58	2,305	13,450	42,546	3,464
Hall	15.7	5,149	52.6	1.7	5.8	0.3	6.8	5.1	1,667	18	6	252	1,260	38,889	2,913
Hamilton	48.0	5,713	31.6	47.2	2.0	0.4	2.7	21.1	2,506	36	16	775	3,920	56,191	6,490
Hansford	51.9	9,453	33.7	53.8	1.6	0.1	1.6	24.5	4,458	20	10	634	2,290	62,732	6,628
Hardeman	21.5	5,429	51.6	18.4	3.4	0.3	3.3	7.1	1,783	22	8	411	1,690	44,962	3,495
Hardin	140.0	2,451	69.5	0.5	6.5	0.6	4.0	131.0	2,293	87	111	2,352	25,460	69,576	7,197
Harris	23,989.9	5,150	47.6	12.4	5.4	0.1	3.6	57,919.7	12,435	27,317	10,151	257,451	2,141,370	77,757	11,583
Harrison	296.2	4,456	69.7	0.1	3.9	0.5	3.0	352.8	5,308	155	125	3,089	30,170	56,204	5,280
Hartley	7.4	1,298	67.9	0.0	5.8	0.0	6.7	7.9	1,376	5	8	681	1,910	50,580	6,890
Haskell	29.2	5,123	39.7	29.4	4.1	0.1	8.0	9.3	1,640	26	10	446	2,230	50,877	5,260
Hays	746.4	3,476	50.7	8.0	6.0	0.0	4.9	2,097.2	9,767	307	495	14,040	108,970	75,225	9,048
Hemphill	41.7	10,617	60.3	4.4	2.7	0.1	5.7	34.8	8,852	12	7	485	1,600	73,453	8,961
Henderson	259.9	3,211	68.3	1.2	5.0	0.0	4.0	202.0	2,495	120	159	3,330	36,650	54,247	5,542
Hidalgo	3,600.9	4,205	68.2	4.5	3.5	0.6	2.7	3,753.4	4,384	4,953	1,714	51,989	351,420	40,414	3,043
Hill	155.3	4,351	58.9	0.6	6.0	1.1	6.3	131.8	3,691	114	70	2,111	16,330	49,838	4,384
Hockley	165.8	7,216	75.2	0.5	2.5	0.3	2.9	113.4	4,936	45	42	1,782	9,670	57,672	5,408
Hood	157.6	2,718	54.1	0.5	6.5	0.1	3.4	261.3	4,507	121	120	2,090	29,790	75,355	8,960
Hopkins	217.2	5,960	36.1	42.4	3.2	0.0	3.7	179.5	4,923	82	70	1,981	16,480	53,799	5,350
Houston	65.0	2,813	50.9	2.9	8.1	0.1	6.2	69.7	3,017	82	39	1,531	8,750	46,017	4,211
Howard	142.9	3,989	56.7	15.3	5.4	0.1	4.8	399.9	11,165	1,001	59	2,625	13,790	76,473	10,470
Hudspeth	13.0	2,815	71.8	0.0	1.5	0.2	1.9	3.9	852	332	9	311	1,350	37,877	3,228
Hunt	401.0	4,263	39.3	33.9	2.7	0.2	3.7	444.7	4,728	293	273	7,512	43,530	57,927	5,564
Hutchinson	142.1	6,656	42.0	4.3	4.7	0.1	2.5	196.8	9,220	72	39	1,486	9,060	62,021	5,844
Irion	18.3	12,086	64.2	0.2	4.3	2.3	14.8	0.0	0	4	3	119	750	99,745	14,560
Jack	28.7	3,251	72.5	0.2	3.4	0.2	2.9	66.4	7,524	23	15	664	3,610	49,852	4,957
Jackson	82.7	5,589	45.9	24.1	3.9	0.1	5.1	151.9	10,262	38	28	1,106	6,890	60,268	6,204
Jasper	112.4	3,162	59.9	1.5	5.5	1.0	6.4	112.6	3,168	91	66	1,971	14,640	55,420	5,058
Jeff Davis	9.5	4,188	44.6	0.0	18.6	0.5	0.5	0.0	10	22	4	218	1,040	67,444	8,161
Jefferson	1,119.4	4,372	40.3	6.6	8.2	0.6	4.7	4,712.0	18,403	1,824	662	15,275	109,670	61,031	6,659
Jim Hogg	31.9	6,128	54.9	0.8	5.5	1.9	10.0	14.2	2,731	254	10	385	2,160	40,611	2,759
Jim Wells	135.0	3,299	56.3	0.8	8.5	0.1	4.7	113.6	2,777	96	77	2,027	17,570	47,654	4,240
Johnson	617.3	3,696	58.7	0.1	6.6	0.3	3.8	1,431.6	8,572	340	339	7,652	82,140	61,837	5,985
Jones	59.7	3,012	50.0	19.2	3.1	0.1	4.6	44.2	2,229	55	28	1,942	6,780	47,778	4,075
Karnes	127.0	8,162	75.9	0.5	1.0	0.2	4.4	133.7	8,597	85	25	1,519	6,100	99,929	19,472
Kaufman	544.2	4,438	56.4	7.3	5.9	0.0	9.0	1,055.6	8,608	233	271	7,010	66,790	61,247	5,668
Kendall	201.6	4,586	62.2	0.9	7.7	0.2	4.8	438.0	9,961	136	92	2,173	21,910	127,801	21,270
Kenedy	10.9	25,412	89.2	0.0	0.5	0.0	0.6	3.3	7,815	1	1	83	150	36,613	2,220
Kent	10.1	13,318	49.8	5.1	0.7	4.9	6.5	0.0	0	6	1	172	340	57,159	5,194
Kerr	126.7	2,442	51.1	0.9	8.9	0.1	3.7	118.8	2,289	560	98	2,656	25,960	68,929	8,225
Kimble	12.0	2,732	53.0	11.4	3.2	0.3	1.1	7.6	1,735	14	8	359	2,110	52,523	5,311
King	4.1	14,277	76.8	0.0	1.2	0.0	4.9	3.6	12,526	3	1	56	100	52,840	3,850
Kinney	21.6	5,810	42.2	3.7	9.3	0.7	4.9	5.0	1,351	142	6	274	1,350	51,208	4,141
Kleberg	100.3	3,261	61.1	1.3	8.9	1.7	3.4	121.0	3,933	855	392	3,400	13,550	50,706	4,794
Knox	20.3	5,515	69.6	3.5	4.4	0.2	2.3	16.3	4,427	27	7	427	1,530	39,863	3,369
Lamar	188.9	3,812	63.2	2.3	7.5	0.8	2.6	153.1	3,089	142	95	2,753	22,170	49,914	4,640
Lamb	70.0	5,320	50.1	20.5	5.5	0.1	5.4	23.3	1,771	40	24	950	5,600	42,384	3,509
Lampasas	61.2	2,932	57.1	0.0	7.8	0.4	4.4	60.7	2,909	53	41	1,013	10,160	58,427	5,886
La Salle	72.8	9,661	85.4	0.0	1.5	0.2	1.9	81.6	10,833	112	11	811	2,580	79,805	14,243
Lavaca	76.6	3,827	34.9	27.8	6.2	0.2	8.0	46.6	2,325	66	38	952	9,760	66,280	8,143
Lee	54.6	3,193	54.1	0.6	6.9	0.8	7.6	68.4	4,000	32	32	1,147	8,420	57,678	5,615
Leon	60.1	3,489	64.7	0.0	3.8	0.3	6.1	77.1	4,476	47	33	837	7,780	54,892	5,917
Liberty	314.6	3,763	68.8	0.0	4.2	0.4	3.2	355.0	4,247	144	166	5,023	37,260	55,324	5,007
Limestone	170.1	7,274	27.1	9.9	4.5	45.1	2.3	73.6	3,148	54	42	2,900	9,630	47,966	4,066
Lipscomb	23.1	6,857	53.2	0.3	5.3	0.4	13.5	8.2	2,431	28	6	352	1,350	58,176	6,545
Live Oak	52.5	4,319	75.1	0.0	3.6	0.2	2.6	84.9	6,992	246	21	592	5,020	69,541	9,337
Llano	71.3	3,370	61.8	0.0	7.7	0.1	4.8	59.3	2,802	49	42	788	10,080	75,490	10,190
Loving	1.0	7,361	0.0	0.0	0.6	0.0	0.7	0.0	105	0	0	15	60	88,017	8,350
Lubbock	1,662.2	5,443	32.3	35.3	6.0	0.0	2.0	2,313.0	7,573	1,465	598	29,013	138,300	63,140	7,275
Lynn	46.3	7,940	42.7	43.2	3.0	0.0	1.3	46.1	7,912	21	11	606	2,570	65,905	6,533
McCulloch	28.4	3,571	61.5	0.8	4.5	0.2	7.0	28.0	3,522	27	15	604	3,630	47,687	4,186
McLennan	977.0	3,883	52.2	6.3	6.9	0.9	2.1	1,253.1	4,980	2,947	593	14,673	114,320	58,165	6,044
McMullen	25.7	33,558	97.2	0.0	0.1	0.0	0.2	32.2	42,119	3	1	150	420	121,310	23,317
Madison	58.7	4,118	70.5	0.4	4.4	0.0	4.6	39.6	2,779	23	23	1,108	5,580	51,823	5,793
Marion	21.0	2,089	59.8	1.3	9.9	0.0	9.0	6.8	675	41	19	404	4,220	46,236	3,911
Martin	87.5	15,828	61.4	30.4	1.0	0.0	1.0	74.1	13,393	15	11	580	2,330	143,179	28,555

1. Based on the resident population estimated as of July 1 of the year shown.

State / county code	CBSA code[1]	County Type code[2]	STATE County	Land area[3] (sq. mi)	Population, 2021: Total persons 2021	Population, 2021: Rank	Population, 2021: Per square mile	Race alone or in combination, not Hispanic or Latino (percent): White	Black	American Indian, Alaska Native	Asian and Pacific Islancer	Percent Hispanic or Latino[4]	Age (percent): Under 5 years	5 to 17 years	18 to 24 years	25 to 34 years	35 to 44 years	45 to 54 years
				1	2	3	4	5	6	7	8	9	10	11	12	13	14	15
			TEXAS—Cont'd															
48319		9	Mason	928.8	3,943	2,892	4.2	73.3	1.1	0.6	0.4	25.5	4.3	11.0	10.3	8.5	10.3	10.8
48321	13060	4	Matagorda	1,092.9	36,344	1,276	33.3	42.8	10.5	0.8	2.0	45.1	7.0	14.9	12.4	12.6	11.8	10.6
48323	20580	5	Maverick	1,279.5	58,056	905	45.4	2.9	0.5	1.2	0.6	95.0	8.8	17.0	16.6	14.0	11.5	11.2
48325	41700	1	Medina	1,325.4	51,981	968	39.2	42.3	3.4	0.9	1.0	53.4	5.8	12.8	13.8	12.0	12.4	12.6
48327		9	Menard	902.0	1,982	3,042	2.2	61.2	2.2	1.2	0.5	35.8	3.8	12.0	8.9	8.2	9.3	10.6
48329	33260	3	Midland	900.4	167,969	402	186.5	42.8	7.0	0.8	2.5	48.2	8.4	16.7	12.8	16.8	15.2	10.2
48331		6	Milam	1,016.4	25,106	1,605	24.7	62.7	9.1	0.9	1.1	27.5	5.0	13.5	12.4	10.7	11.4	11.8
48333		9	Mills	748.2	4,480	2,857	6.0	78.4	1.8	0.9	0.8	19.5	4.1	12.4	11.5	8.8	9.5	10.8
48335		7	Mitchell	911.1	9,070	2,481	10.0	48.4	10.1	1.1	0.8	40.8	5.5	13.3	14.1	16.4	13.4	11.7
48337		6	Montague	930.9	20,409	1,797	21.9	85.9	1.6	1.6	0.7	11.8	5.2	13.5	11.3	10.5	11.6	11.6
48339	26420	1	Montgomery	1,042.2	648,886	108	622.6	63.7	6.7	0.8	4.2	26.4	6.3	15.0	12.9	12.6	14.1	13.2
48341	20300	7	Moore	899.7	21,118	1,757	23.5	31.3	4.5	1.0	5.1	59.1	8.6	17.5	14.4	13.4	12.9	11.0
48343		6	Morris	252.0	12,030	2,281	47.7	64.9	23.5	1.6	1.1	11.5	5.8	13.3	11.4	10.8	11.7	11.2
48345		9	Motley	989.6	1,067	3,106	1.1	75.6	3.4	1.3	0.3	20.4	5.2	10.6	10.5	10.0	9.5	10.2
48347	34860	5	Nacogdoches	946.3	64,668	838	68.3	60.3	18.3	0.9	1.6	20.7	6.0	13.3	22.3	11.6	10.4	9.8
48349	18620	4	Navarro	1,009.7	53,591	948	53.1	54.7	13.0	0.8	2.7	30.3	6.7	15.5	13.2	12.0	11.4	11.6
48351		2	Newton	933.7	12,241	2,266	13.1	75.0	20.0	1.6	0.9	4.7	4.5	11.1	11.8	12.3	11.1	12.4
48353	45020	6	Nolan	912.0	14,597	2,110	16.0	54.5	5.4	0.9	0.9	39.8	6.5	14.7	13.9	11.1	12.1	11.6
48355	18580	2	Nueces	839.1	353,079	207	420.8	28.9	3.8	0.6	2.6	65.2	6.2	13.8	14.2	13.8	13.5	11.6
48357		7	Ochiltree	917.7	9,782	2,427	10.7	41.6	1.2	0.9	0.7	56.6	7.3	17.7	15.0	12.9	12.0	11.3
48359	11100	2	Oldham	1,500.5	1,717	3,064	1.1	75.2	4.1	1.3	2.4	18.5	3.0	10.8	13.3	12.8	14.6	14.0
48361	13140	2	Orange	333.8	84,742	679	253.9	80.2	9.4	1.0	1.6	9.3	6.3	14.5	12.1	13.1	12.9	11.9
48363	33420	6	Palo Pinto	952.5	28,686	1,471	30.1	75.0	3.0	1.1	1.3	21.0	5.9	13.4	11.8	12.0	10.8	11.3
48365		6	Panola	811.4	22,675	1,689	27.9	73.9	16.0	1.1	1.0	9.5	5.8	12.9	12.7	11.3	12.3	11.6
48367	19100	1	Parker	903.7	156,764	436	173.5	82.8	2.2	1.3	1.3	14.0	5.9	14.5	11.8	11.7	13.8	12.9
48369		7	Parmer	880.8	9,813	2,421	11.1	32.2	1.3	0.5	0.9	65.6	6.9	15.9	14.2	12.4	11.8	11.5
48371		7	Pecos	4,763.8	15,118	2,086	3.2	24.0	4.7	0.7	1.4	70.0	6.5	14.4	12.5	14.7	15.5	12.4
48373		6	Polk	1,057.0	51,899	969	49.1	72.5	9.9	2.3	1.2	15.6	5.1	11.7	10.6	11.8	12.3	12.3
48375	11100	2	Potter	908.4	116,547	538	128.3	44.2	11.0	0.9	5.4	40.1	6.8	15.6	13.6	14.2	13.6	11.7
48377		7	Presidio	3,855.3	6,140	2,728	1.6	12.9	1.5	0.8	1.7	83.8	7.9	15.4	12.9	10.5	10.9	9.5
48379		8	Rains	229.5	12,509	2,243	54.5	85.2	3.3	1.9	1.5	10.0	4.7	11.6	9.8	9.4	11.3	11.7
48381	11100	2	Randall	912.7	143,854	464	157.6	69.3	4.1	1.0	2.4	24.9	5.8	14.0	14.0	14.1	14.1	11.1
48383		6	Reagan	1,175.3	3,253	2,948	2.8	23.9	3.5	0.6	0.6	72.5	8.0	16.1	14.6	12.2	14.8	11.5
48385		9	Real	699.2	2,826	2,973	4.0	67.4	2.3	1.6	1.1	29.2	4.7	9.7	8.2	9.0	9.7	11.5
48387		6	Red River	1,043.9	11,555	2,312	11.1	74.8	16.5	2.0	0.8	7.9	5.1	11.7	10.0	10.2	10.8	11.9
48389	37780	7	Reeves	2,635.4	14,487	2,120	5.5	17.9	5.2	0.6	1.6	75.4	6.2	13.0	15.3	17.0	16.2	12.1
48391		6	Refugio	770.5	6,756	2,675	8.8	41.0	6.0	1.0	1.1	52.0	5.2	13.5	11.9	10.4	11.3	11.2
48393	37420	9	Roberts	924.1	797	3,115	0.9	86.6	0.4	2.0	1.1	11.7	4.4	14.1	11.5	10.3	15.6	9.5
48395	17780	3	Robertson	855.2	16,958	1,975	19.8	57.1	19.6	0.9	1.2	22.7	6.2	13.5	11.1	11.5	12.5	11.2
48397	19100	1	Rockwall	127.2	116,381	540	914.9	67.4	9.3	1.0	4.2	20.2	5.9	15.6	13.2	11.6	15.2	14.1
48399		6	Runnels	1,051.1	9,943	2,411	9.5	60.3	2.6	1.0	1.1	35.9	6.1	13.4	12.3	10.6	12.2	11.6
48401	30980	3	Rusk	924.2	52,743	962	57.1	63.7	17.8	1.0	0.9	18.2	5.4	12.9	12.8	13.3	13.4	12.6
48403		8	Sabine	491.7	10,039	2,401	20.4	86.8	7.9	1.6	0.9	4.9	4.6	9.8	9.3	8.7	9.1	10.5
48405		9	San Augustine	530.7	7,922	2,580	14.9	69.9	21.9	1.1	0.6	8.0	4.9	11.6	9.7	10.0	9.4	11.1
48407		8	San Jacinto	569.2	27,878	1,504	49.0	74.0	9.6	1.4	1.0	15.9	5.1	12.1	11.0	11.0	10.6	11.8
48409	18580	2	San Patricio	693.4	69,699	777	100.5	38.2	2.0	0.7	1.4	58.7	6.6	15.0	13.3	13.3	13.6	11.6
48411		7	San Saba	1,135.3	5,827	2,751	5.1	63.9	4.3	1.2	1.1	30.9	5.2	11.1	13.1	14.3	10.4	9.5
48413		8	Schleicher	1,310.6	2,429	3,004	1.9	42.4	2.2	0.7	0.6	55.5	4.4	14.7	13.1	10.4	13.9	10.6
48415	43660	7	Scurry	905.4	16,824	1,984	18.6	51.8	5.5	0.7	0.9	42.2	6.2	14.2	13.9	13.4	13.7	11.6
48417		8	Shackelford	914.3	3,212	2,949	3.5	85.0	2.1	0.9	1.0	12.7	5.4	12.8	12.4	10.3	10.8	11.3
48419		7	Shelby	795.6	23,939	1,643	30.1	61.7	17.9	0.8	1.7	19.5	6.9	14.6	12.7	11.8	11.5	11.7
48421		9	Sherman	922.9	2,798	2,977	3.0	52.0	1.5	0.6	0.6	45.9	7.3	14.9	13.2	12.1	10.8	11.7
48423	46340	3	Smith	921.5	237,186	291	257.4	60.3	18.2	0.7	2.1	20.2	6.2	13.9	13.9	13.4	12.3	11.3
48425		1	Somervell	186.4	9,469	2,453	50.8	79.3	1.8	1.7	1.2	17.8	4.7	12.5	11.6	10.9	13.0	12.7
48427	40100	4	Starr	1,223.2	66,049	814	54.0	3.3	0.2	0.1	0.2	96.3	8.8	18.5	16.4	13.6	11.6	11.2
48429		7	Stephens	896.7	9,173	2,476	10.2	70.7	3.4	1.1	1.1	24.7	5.5	12.3	13.1	12.1	12.7	10.6
48431	41660	8	Sterling	923.4	1,381	3,087	1.5	58.7	3.0	1.3	0.7	38.3	6.8	16.8	13.7	10.3	15.7	10.6
48433		9	Stonewall	916.3	1,217	3,098	1.3	77.2	3.4	1.3	1.5	18.1	5.0	12.6	11.1	9.1	10.8	11.0
48435		7	Sutton	1,453.9	3,319	2,939	2.3	33.6	0.6	0.2	0.5	65.4	6.1	14.0	12.4	10.3	10.9	13.2
48437		6	Swisher	890.2	7,008	2,661	7.9	45.8	8.6	1.1	0.6	45.3	5.4	14.0	14.8	13.7	12.4	10.8
48439	19100	1	Tarrant	865.3	2,126,477	15	2,457.5	46.4	18.4	0.9	6.9	29.7	6.4	14.7	14.0	14.7	14.0	12.6
48441	10180	3	Taylor	915.5	143,326	467	156.6	64.3	8.6	0.9	3.0	25.5	6.9	14.0	17.9	14.3	12.3	9.4
48443		9	Terrell	2,358.0	724	3,125	0.3	43.3	2.1	2.1	1.9	52.6	4.8	11.3	8.3	6.9	10.5	10.5
48445		6	Terry	888.8	11,754	2,298	13.2	38.5	4.6	0.6	0.6	56.6	7.4	15.6	14.2	13.4	12.9	10.6
48447		9	Throckmorton	912.6	1,495	3,078	1.6	84.3	1.3	2.0	0.8	13.2	5.9	13.2	9.4	10.0	10.1	11.0
48449	34420	7	Titus	406.1	31,183	1,396	76.8	44.6	9.7	0.8	1.4	44.7	7.2	16.4	14.9	12.5	11.0	12.1

1. CBSA = Core Based Statistical Area. See Appendix A for explanation. See Appendix B for list of metropolitan areas with component counties. 2. County type code from the Economic Research Service of USDA Rural-Urban Continuum Codes. See Appendix A for definition. 3. Dry land or land partially or temporarily covered by water. 4. May be of any race.

STATE County	Population, 2021 (cont.)				Population change, 2000–2021							Households, 2016–2020				
	Age (percent) (cont.)				Total persons		Percent change		Components of change, 2020–2021					Percent		
	55 to 64 years	65 to 74 years	75 years and over	Percent female	2010	2020	2010–2020	2020–2021	Births	Deaths	Net Migration	Number	Persons per household	Family households	Female family householder[1]	One person
	16	17	18	19	20	21	22	23	24	25	26	27	28	29	30	31
TEXAS—Cont'd																
Mason	14.2	16.3	14.3	49.3	4,012	3,953	-1.5	-0.3	39	57	9	1,668	2.5	67.6	8.5	30.0
Matagorda	13.2	10.7	6.7	49.7	36,702	36,255	-1.2	0.2	632	554	4	13,900	2.6	66.7	11.8	31.7
Maverick	9.0	7.1	4.8	49.7	54,258	57,887	6.7	0.3	1,254	600	-499	16,647	3.5	80.5	18.6	16.4
Medina	13.4	10.5	6.7	47.9	46,006	50,748	10.3	2.4	696	719	1,267	15,978	3.0	75.2	11.9	20.2
Menard	15.6	17.0	14.6	49.3	2,242	1,962	-12.5	1.0	20	36	37	1,035	2.0	52.3	3.5	44.5
Midland	9.7	6.4	4.0	49.2	136,872	169,983	24.2	-1.2	3,568	1,704	-3,860	57,917	2.9	68.4	12.0	26.8
Milam	13.9	12.5	8.7	50.2	24,757	24,754	0.0	1.4	293	413	478	9,468	2.6	67.0	12.1	28.3
Mills	15.3	15.3	12.3	48.8	4,936	4,456	-9.7	0.5	40	115	102	1,752	2.7	69.2	6.8	29.6
Mitchell	10.6	9.0	6.1	40.6	9,403	8,990	-4.4	0.9	100	105	84	2,419	2.7	58.7	3.7	35.1
Montague	14.1	12.8	9.3	50.1	19,719	19,965	1.2	2.2	240	459	673	7,969	2.4	72.1	8.8	22.8
Montgomery	12.1	8.7	4.9	50.3	455,746	620,443	36.1	4.6	8,946	6,511	26,266	205,719	2.9	75.1	9.6	20.3
Moore	10.1	7.4	4.5	47.7	21,904	21,358	-2.5	-1.1	460	199	-501	6,659	3.2	73.9	10.3	23.4
Morris	13.8	12.9	9.1	51.7	12,934	11,973	-7.4	0.5	185	250	123	5,170	2.4	65.5	12.3	30.1
Motley	14.2	17.3	12.4	48.8	1,210	1,063	-12.1	0.4	15	30	19	496	2.8	67.7	14.7	30.2
Nacogdoches	11.1	9.5	5.9	51.9	64,524	64,653	0.2	0.0	947	934	-13	23,765	2.5	64.8	12.5	26.0
Navarro	12.7	10.2	6.7	50.6	47,735	52,624	10.2	1.8	773	812	1,013	17,509	2.8	72.6	12.2	22.8
Newton	15.1	12.9	8.8	47.9	14,445	12,217	-15.4	0.2	141	254	140	5,124	2.7	76.8	13.4	19.9
Nolan	11.7	10.7	7.8	49.4	15,216	14,738	-3.1	-1.0	232	278	-96	5,516	2.7	68.7	12.2	28.7
Nueces	11.7	9.3	6.0	50.3	340,223	353,178	3.8	0.0	5,262	4,582	-860	130,482	2.7	67.7	16.2	26.4
Ochiltree	11.4	7.9	4.6	49.6	10,223	10,015	-2.0	-2.3	156	80	-306	3,391	2.9	74.9	11.4	22.6
Oldham	15.0	10.4	6.2	47.2	2,052	1,758	-14.3	-2.3	15	15	-41	646	2.5	73.5	3.4	20.7
Orange	13.0	9.6	6.4	50.4	81,837	84,808	3.6	-0.1	1,261	1,340	0	31,570	2.6	72.5	14.2	23.9
Palo Pinto	14.6	12.0	8.1	50.8	28,111	28,409	1.1	1.0	385	539	433	10,334	2.8	68.3	12.3	24.8
Panola	13.2	12.3	7.9	50.1	23,796	22,491	-5.5	0.8	343	381	224	8,662	2.6	69.4	12.6	26.1
Parker	13.7	10.0	5.7	49.9	116,927	148,222	26.8	5.8	1,955	1,901	8,601	45,848	3.0	77.4	7.9	19.6
Parmer	12.3	8.6	6.3	48.1	10,269	9,869	-3.9	-0.6	189	91	-153	3,213	3.0	75.6	8.4	21.3
Pecos	10.6	8.0	5.4	42.8	15,507	15,193	-2.0	-0.5	243	151	-169	4,868	2.7	68.5	15.0	30.4
Polk	17.3	14.0	4.9	46.1	45,413	50,123	10.4	3.5	619	994	2,178	17,945	2.6	70.5	14.2	26.6
Potter	11.0	8.3	5.2	48.4	121,073	118,525	-2.1	-1.7	1,970	1,870	-2,073	43,957	2.5	65.2	15.2	30.1
Presidio	9.8	10.7	12.3	48.8	7,818	6,131	-21.6	0.1	125	69	-46	2,580	2.6	50.0	11.3	46.0
Rains	16.2	15.3	9.9	49.8	10,914	12,164	11.5	2.8	121	187	418	4,321	2.8	68.8	10.8	25.2
Randall	11.5	9.5	5.9	50.6	120,725	140,753	16.6	2.2	1,898	1,733	2,954	50,092	2.7	68.2	10.5	27.5
Reagan	10.8	7.7	4.3	46.3	3,367	3,385	0.5	-3.9	64	22	-171	1,117	3.3	77.3	5.0	19.8
Real	16.1	18.5	12.6	49.0	3,309	2,758	-16.7	2.5	33	69	107	1,254	2.6	67.4	14.1	30.1
Red River	15.1	14.3	11.0	51.3	12,860	11,587	-9.9	-0.3	160	305	117	5,143	2.3	64.9	11.7	34.2
Reeves	8.5	6.6	4.9	39.1	13,783	14,748	7.0	-1.8	263	170	-351	3,772	3.7	63.3	15.6	33.4
Refugio	14.1	11.9	10.6	50.7	7,383	6,741	-8.7	0.2	82	86	18	2,566	2.7	67.4	17.1	29.4
Roberts	12.2	12.7	9.8	50.3	929	827	-11.0	-3.6	8	13	-24	329	2.4	74.5	2.1	22.8
Robertson	13.6	12.3	8.2	50.7	16,622	16,757	0.8	1.2	251	279	230	6,749	2.5	69.4	15.2	28.6
Rockwall	12.0	7.9	4.6	50.2	78,337	107,819	37.6	7.9	1,334	937	8,280	34,457	2.9	81.9	8.8	14.8
Runnels	13.2	11.6	8.9	48.7	10,501	9,900	-5.7	0.4	154	199	87	3,891	2.6	66.6	10.0	29.8
Rusk	12.7	10.3	6.7	46.3	53,330	52,214	-2.1	1.0	706	778	604	18,056	2.7	72.7	13.9	23.2
Sabine	17.3	17.1	13.6	49.8	10,834	9,894	-8.7	1.5	121	219	248	4,524	2.3	70.1	11.5	27.0
San Augustine	17.1	14.3	12.0	50.4	8,865	7,918	-10.7	0.1	98	200	107	3,712	2.2	72.6	17.2	26.1
San Jacinto	15.5	14.2	8.8	49.7	26,384	27,402	3.9	1.7	356	495	621	10,143	2.8	69.0	9.2	25.7
San Patricio	11.6	9.0	6.0	49.2	64,804	68,755	6.1	1.4	1,028	901	817	23,422	2.8	71.9	17.1	23.4
San Saba	13.1	12.8	10.5	45.8	6,131	5,730	-6.5	1.7	70	89	117	2,134	2.5	65.8	6.5	30.5
Schleicher	12.1	13.0	7.8	49.6	3,461	2,451	-29.2	-0.9	30	36	-16	1,036	2.8	65.4	3.4	32.4
Scurry	11.9	8.6	6.4	45.4	16,921	16,932	0.1	-0.6	245	241	-114	6,115	2.5	65.2	7.7	32.4
Shackelford	15.7	12.6	8.7	50.3	3,378	3,105	-8.1	3.4	48	45	105	1,367	2.4	66.9	10.7	29.0
Shelby	12.9	10.6	7.3	50.0	25,448	24,022	-5.6	-0.3	391	452	-27	9,486	2.6	72.7	13.8	24.9
Sherman	13.9	8.7	7.5	47.3	3,034	2,782	-8.3	0.6	52	23	-13	1,070	2.8	76.8	9.3	20.0
Smith	11.9	10.1	7.0	51.7	209,714	233,479	11.3	1.6	3,483	3,231	3,455	77,809	2.9	69.3	12.0	25.7
Somervell	14.8	12.2	7.5	50.6	8,490	9,205	8.4	2.9	81	133	321	3,145	2.7	75.0	7.4	23.2
Starr	8.6	6.5	4.9	51.1	60,968	65,920	8.1	0.2	1,338	642	-583	16,281	3.9	78.8	25.9	20.4
Stephens	12.8	12.3	8.6	47.2	9,630	9,101	-5.5	0.8	106	151	118	3,408	2.6	66.8	15.2	30.3
Sterling	11.9	7.7	6.5	50.0	1,143	1,372	20.0	0.7	21	19	10	405	3.1	82.2	11.6	17.8
Stonewall	14.5	13.6	12.3	50.9	1,490	1,245	-16.4	-2.2	12	24	-16	529	2.6	72.6	10.2	27.4
Sutton	13.3	11.9	7.8	48.8	4,128	3,372	-18.3	-1.6	46	33	-65	1,282	2.9	74.6	11.2	25.4
Swisher	11.5	9.5	7.9	46.7	7,854	6,971	-11.2	0.5	79	93	51	2,599	2.6	62.9	11.6	33.0
Tarrant	11.6	7.6	4.4	51.1	1,809,034	2,110,640	16.7	0.8	32,493	20,978	3,615	722,446	2.8	69.3	13.9	24.9
Taylor	10.5	8.4	6.3	51.2	131,506	143,208	8.9	0.1	2,327	2,135	-103	50,396	2.6	66.4	12.9	26.2
Terrell	13.4	18.6	15.6	49.3	984	760	-22.8	-4.7	6	13	-28	419	2.2	52.0	10.5	46.3
Terry	11.2	8.6	6.2	46.9	12,651	11,831	-6.5	-0.7	227	164	-142	4,101	2.8	68.2	14.7	27.0
Throckmorton	15.1	12.4	12.8	51.8	1,641	1,440	-12.2	3.8	21	28	65	713	2.1	61.0	11.4	37.2
Titus	11.4	8.9	5.7	51.1	32,334	31,247	-3.4	-0.2	508	445	-132	11,064	2.9	75.4	12.9	20.7

1. No spouse present.

STATE County	Persons in group quarters, 2021	Daytime Population, 2016–2020		Births, 2021		Deaths, 2021		Persons under 65 with no health insurance, 2019		Medicare, 2021			COVID-19 Deaths, 2020	
		Number	Employment/ residence ratio	Total	Rate[1]	Number	Rate[1]	Number	Percent	Total beneficiaries	Enrolled in Original Medicare	Enrolled in Medicare Advantage	Number	Rate[1]
	32	33	34	35	36	37	38	39	40	41	42	43	44	45
TEXAS—Cont'd														
Mason	0	4,018	0.9	35	8.9	46	11.6	883	29.4	1,335	965	371	D	D
Matagorda	225	36,022	1.0	500	13.8	458	12.6	6,192	20.8	7,207	4,461	2,746	73	2.0
Maverick	966	54,653	0.8	1,014	17.5	472	8.1	14,265	28.5	10,385	5,580	4,805	223	3.9
Medina	2,073	42,754	0.6	553	10.7	586	11.4	7,422	18.2	9,887	5,550	4,337	61	1.2
Menard	20	1,899	0.8	16	8.1	34	17.2	407	28.5	683	487	195	D	D
Midland	1,128	197,373	1.3	2,843	16.8	1,363	8.1	29,022	18.4	19,329	13,771	5,558	211	1.2
Milam	338	21,265	0.7	240	9.6	322	12.9	3,704	19.3	6,078	3,464	2,614	24	1.0
Mills	83	4,844	1.0	33	7.4	90	20.2	908	26.9	1,410	948	462	14	3.2
Mitchell	1,502	7,785	0.8	80	8.9	70	7.8	1,085	19.9	1,432	935	497	18	2.0
Montague	167	17,318	0.7	190	9.4	358	17.7	3,321	21.7	5,264	3,975	1,289	45	2.3
Montgomery	2,823	549,980	0.9	7,178	11.3	5,310	8.3	90,482	17.3	93,040	52,535	40,504	312	0.5
Moore	139	21,778	1.1	367	17.3	162	7.6	4,996	27.2	2,563	1,998	565	67	3.1
Morris	74	10,924	0.7	155	12.9	197	16.4	1,786	18.7	3,427	2,020	1,406	15	1.3
Motley	0	1,292	0.9	14	13.2	20	18.9	189	22.7	361	256	105	D	D
Nacogdoches	4,438	64,222	1.0	757	11.7	773	12.0	10,678	21.2	11,705	7,818	3,887	110	1.7
Navarro	657	46,381	0.9	637	12.0	659	12.4	9,643	23.6	10,554	6,902	3,653	81	1.5
Newton	537	10,524	0.4	119	9.8	215	17.6	2,176	21.8	3,051	1,931	1,120	20	1.6
Nolan	349	15,735	1.1	186	12.7	229	15.6	2,383	20.5	3,267	2,213	1,054	34	2.3
Nueces	6,122	372,689	1.1	4,258	12.1	3,677	10.4	60,083	19.9	61,022	26,852	34,170	527	1.5
Ochiltree	20	10,765	1.2	127	12.9	70	7.1	2,360	27.3	1,304	1,085	219	20	2.0
Oldham	203	2,252	1.2	9	5.2	9	5.2	281	18.1	442	317	125	D	D
Orange	559	72,665	0.7	1,022	12.1	1,059	12.5	11,627	16.8	16,272	9,055	7,216	83	1.0
Palo Pinto	158	26,253	0.8	318	11.1	426	14.9	5,323	23.1	6,538	4,662	1,876	56	2.0
Panola	236	22,254	0.9	271	12.0	308	13.6	3,606	19.7	5,256	3,338	1,918	48	2.1
Parker	1,028	118,169	0.7	1,555	10.2	1,490	9.7	20,751	17.3	27,068	17,653	9,415	127	0.8
Parmer	60	10,778	1.3	147	15.0	69	7.0	2,297	28.2	1,508	1,241	267	40	4.1
Pecos	1,906	15,794	1.0	204	13.5	119	7.9	2,871	24.8	2,304	1,597	708	28	1.8
Polk	3,885	47,281	0.8	496	9.7	798	15.6	8,609	23.0	18,835	11,831	7,004	70	1.4
Potter	6,591	148,011	1.6	1,563	13.3	1,490	12.7	24,112	25.3	19,025	12,992	6,033	310	2.6
Presidio	0	6,824	1.0	104	17.0	54	8.8	1,638	32.6	1,860	1,311	549	21	3.4
Rains	27	10,077	0.6	93	7.5	155	12.5	2,071	22.1	3,202	2,101	1,100	21	1.7
Randall	2,313	104,615	0.6	1,504	10.6	1,393	9.8	15,147	13.2	23,531	16,993	6,538	217	1.5
Reagan	8	4,991	1.7	49	14.8	17	5.1	676	19.9	443	318	126	D	D
Real	24	3,445	1.0	26	9.3	53	19.0	522	22.2	1,329	948	382	12	4.4
Red River	88	10,193	0.6	134	11.6	247	21.4	1,886	21.3	3,510	2,501	1,010	30	2.6
Reeves	2,813	22,414	2.1	218	14.9	134	9.2	2,435	22.2	2,113	1,570	543	32	2.2
Refugio	78	6,309	0.8	67	9.9	69	10.2	986	18.8	1,737	1,159	578	18	2.7
Roberts	0	691	0.8	6	7.4	12	14.8	112	16.7	178	134	44	D	D
Robertson	101	15,634	0.8	198	11.8	204	12.1	2,693	20.0	3,861	2,561	1,300	23	1.4
Rockwall	491	88,216	0.7	1,070	9.5	780	6.9	13,643	14.9	15,481	10,249	5,233	67	0.6
Runnels	77	9,169	0.8	124	12.5	155	15.6	1,617	20.2	2,562	2,056	507	25	2.5
Rusk	5,742	46,176	0.6	558	10.6	638	12.2	8,119	20.7	10,270	6,189	4,081	83	1.6
Sabine	68	10,107	0.9	98	9.8	168	16.9	1,450	20.1	3,377	2,481	897	19	1.9
San Augustine	104	8,121	1.0	79	10.0	158	19.9	1,240	21.1	2,501	1,679	821	29	3.7
San Jacinto	41	21,916	0.4	298	10.8	397	14.3	5,018	22.6	6,613	3,362	3,250	25	0.9
San Patricio	444	63,395	0.9	832	12.0	711	10.3	10,456	18.7	12,963	5,482	7,481	107	1.6
San Saba	595	5,659	0.9	55	9.5	65	11.2	1,210	30.7	1,529	1,059	470	15	2.6
Schleicher	0	2,706	0.8	25	10.3	31	12.7	553	24.9	594	463	131	D	D
Scurry	1,567	17,489	1.1	193	11.4	192	11.4	2,820	22.5	2,951	2,031	920	38	2.2
Shackelford	8	3,167	0.9	36	11.4	42	13.3	578	22.5	764	541	223	D	D
Shelby	74	25,082	1.0	310	13.0	367	15.3	5,297	25.8	5,148	3,255	1,894	48	2.0
Sherman	14	2,722	0.8	45	16.1	18	6.5	720	28.3	388	310	77	13	4.7
Smith	4,879	238,031	1.1	2,801	11.9	2,589	11.0	39,717	21.1	46,779	29,978	16,801	312	1.3
Somervell	257	9,772	1.2	63	6.7	112	12.0	1,303	17.8	1,993	1,261	732	10	1.1
Starr	796	61,467	0.9	1,107	16.8	512	7.8	17,283	31.2	9,609	4,459	5,150	219	3.3
Stephens	605	9,136	0.9	86	9.4	119	13.0	1,633	24.0	2,083	1,509	574	17	1.9
Sterling	33	1,260	1.0	18	13.0	15	10.9	209	19.0	239	180	59	D	D
Stonewall	16	1,421	1.0	5	4.1	14	11.4	192	19.5	358	273	85	D	D
Sutton	5	3,795	1.0	32	9.6	23	6.9	628	20.7	781	647	133	D	D
Swisher	545	6,901	0.8	54	7.7	74	10.6	1,429	26.3	1,441	1,074	367	16	2.3
Tarrant	24,725	2,081,872	1.0	26,097	12.3	16,870	8.0	347,063	18.9	279,704	146,186	133,518	1,878	0.9
Taylor	4,891	141,595	1.1	1,834	12.8	1,719	12.0	21,168	18.5	25,111	17,179	7,932	243	1.7
Terrell	0	946	1.1	5	6.8	7	9.5	101	19.5	246	157	89	D	D
Terry	909	12,179	1.0	184	15.6	134	11.4	2,487	26.3	2,040	1,168	872	47	4.0
Throckmorton	9	1,429	0.9	18	12.3	22	15.0	257	24.3	401	310	92	D	D
Titus	299	36,514	1.3	395	12.7	347	11.1	6,864	25.1	5,613	3,679	1,935	62	2.0

1. Per 1,000 estimated resident population.

STATE County	COVID-19 Vaccinations, 2021–2022		Education						Money income, 2016–2020				Income and poverty, 2020			
			School enrollment and attainment, 2016–2020				Local government expenditures,[3] 2018–2019			Households				Percent below poverty level		
			Enrollment[1]		Attainment[2] (percent)						Percent					
	Number	Percent[5]	Total	Percent private	High school graduate or less	Bachelor's degree or more	Total current spending (mil dol)	Current spending per student (dollars)	Per capita income[4]	Median income (dollars)	with income of less than $50,000	with income of $200,000 or more	Median household income (dollars)	All persons	Children under 18 years	Children 5 to 17 years in families
	46	47	48	49	50	51	52	53	54	55	56	57	58	59	60	61
TEXAS—Cont'd																
Mason	2,045	47.8	983	2.0	33.1	35.0	8.6	11,983	34,196	61,434	41.5	4.6	63,120	9.8	20.1	18.7
Matagorda	17,200	46.9	9,257	7.7	47.8	19.5	84.5	11,641	25,206	48,733	51.3	2.9	52,241	17.3	24.0	23.4
Maverick	55,956	95.0	16,715	3.2	62.5	15.7	144.5	9,920	17,545	41,385	55.8	2.3	41,324	20.0	27.9	28.3
Medina	28,766	55.8	12,667	14.0	47.4	20.3	103.2	9,546	27,200	62,701	37.3	4.9	62,600	11.2	17.2	16.7
Menard	1,156	54.1	356	30.3	46.2	26.7	4.3	14,043	29,080	43,826	57.9	4.6	41,477	19.1	34.5	32.7
Midland	76,349	43.2	46,316	18.1	42.0	27.4	249.4	8,468	40,478	83,217	29.6	12.7	92,117	9.7	13.1	12.0
Milam	11,384	45.9	5,834	9.5	55.7	15.1	47.8	10,363	27,585	48,253	52.3	3.5	49,961	17.4	24.0	22.4
Mills	2,322	47.7	960	8.9	50.7	21.1	15.2	15,186	27,619	50,198	49.5	5.9	49,089	14.4	22.8	20.4
Mitchell	3,092	36.2	1,985	6.7	60.4	12.1	16.4	11,939	22,950	44,939	54.2	6.2	46,156	18.7	21.9	20.9
Montague	7,005	35.3	4,287	13.6	49.0	17.4	34.6	10,091	28,986	57,511	42.6	3.5	56,012	12.4	18.2	17.8
Montgomery	332,653	54.8	156,052	14.5	34.1	34.9	999.4	8,928	41,892	83,274	29.1	14.1	85,348	8.2	10.9	10.0
Moore	9,613	45.9	5,366	1.7	61.7	14.2	46.3	9,542	22,646	53,967	43.5	2.8	53,341	10.6	14.8	14.1
Morris	5,341	43.1	2,769	5.7	52.1	14.1	19.5	10,260	22,868	43,995	56.4	0.8	45,122	17.0	25.1	23.8
Motley	360	30.0	243	1.2	48.1	16.7	2.8	17,043	27,075	45,417	52.6	3.8	46,712	16.3	27.5	27.6
Nacogdoches	31,065	47.6	22,258	3.9	45.1	24.4	105.7	9,508	24,031	44,507	54.8	3.8	49,375	19.5	23.5	23.3
Navarro	22,786	45.5	12,289	8.4	50.1	17.0	99.5	9,849	24,133	47,574	51.8	4.4	50,778	14.8	21.9	20.6
Newton	3,439	25.3	2,469	3.8	61.7	8.8	22.4	11,816	21,836	40,690	57.4	1.6	45,769	21.3	27.9	23.8
Nolan	6,215	42.2	3,347	7.7	51.9	15.1	37.5	11,723	25,703	43,692	57.4	2.6	41,720	17.2	24.4	23.3
Nueces	211,544	58.4	90,841	6.6	45.4	21.7	614.2	10,011	28,078	56,784	44.0	4.7	55,727	17.5	25.9	24.4
Ochiltree	3,794	38.6	2,876	9.4	58.9	16.7	22.3	9,963	23,215	53,431	45.9	2.9	71,477	9.2	14.2	13.7
Oldham	757	35.8	720	10.8	39.2	26.8	15.9	16,183	27,166	64,250	33.7	9.0	61,013	14.0	28.8	22.3
Orange	30,408	36.5	19,589	11.1	48.4	16.0	146.4	9,701	31,260	63,488	40.1	4.8	61,323	15.1	21.1	17.2
Palo Pinto	11,326	38.8	6,313	10.3	47.7	18.1	46.5	10,247	27,473	55,986	44.7	4.9	59,450	13.9	20.9	21.0
Panola	8,878	38.3	5,212	10.4	47.1	15.6	38.6	9,593	27,267	51,297	48.9	4.9	51,936	15.3	19.5	17.4
Parker	77,159	54.0	33,201	14.8	39.1	26.7	210.1	9,410	36,420	84,189	29.7	10.4	88,617	8.0	9.8	9.5
Parmer	3,944	41.1	2,347	8.8	56.1	15.1	27.0	11,452	26,269	58,558	40.4	5.3	61,989	12.2	17.7	17.9
Pecos	9,221	58.3	3,586	1.6	63.4	11.6	35.7	11,435	23,201	53,879	46.7	4.4	52,792	16.5	19.7	19.0
Polk	24,519	47.7	9,357	9.4	55.5	14.3	74.1	10,853	24,479	50,351	49.6	3.0	47,535	15.0	22.9	21.9
Potter	53,801	45.8	30,267	5.4	55.3	15.4	338.5	9,286	23,245	43,652	55.0	3.4	45,903	20.8	29.2	27.7
Presidio	7,014	95.0	1,644	4.9	62.4	19.5	19.7	12,887	15,687	22,716	76.5	0.5	39,967	19.4	32.4	35.0
Rains	4,640	37.1	2,130	6.7	54.6	15.3	16.1	9,333	28,919	52,612	48.2	4.0	59,195	13.6	20.3	18.7
Randall	64,042	46.5	36,255	8.5	31.2	30.9	103.7	10,200	34,527	68,186	36.8	6.3	71,041	9.6	11.6	10.2
Reagan	1,500	39.0	910	1.3	60.4	11.7	12.8	14,653	25,126	61,659	43.2	3.7	66,711	8.3	10.1	10.2
Real	1,741	50.4	802	2.4	47.4	16.8	7.1	13,665	22,588	38,659	59.5	4.9	43,076	16.4	32.1	36.3
Red River	4,990	41.5	2,228	3.8	50.5	15.7	25.3	11,852	23,895	37,135	60.9	1.4	46,727	15.7	25.6	25.8
Reeves	10,129	63.4	3,400	7.3	66.8	10.6	35.1	11,783	22,670	61,543	45.7	1.7	64,863	19.0	20.5	19.5
Refugio	3,768	54.2	1,505	3.2	58.4	11.1	19.1	15,031	24,893	51,054	48.3	1.6	48,433	15.3	23.7	22.9
Roberts	293	34.3	169	4.7	40.6	23.9	2.9	13,406	29,673	61,964	40.7	4.0	69,927	6.4	9.1	9.2
Robertson	7,642	44.8	3,868	19.1	52.7	18.4	38.5	11,546	27,245	53,823	47.0	4.8	55,218	14.2	23.2	21.7
Rockwall	61,574	58.7	28,485	13.6	24.5	42.9	203.0	8,922	45,461	105,956	17.4	16.0	106,225	4.8	6.4	6.0
Runnels	4,568	44.5	2,174	11.0	54.0	16.6	23.4	11,665	24,191	48,489	52.4	2.1	50,972	14.3	21.4	20.7
Rusk	21,275	39.1	11,170	8.8	49.6	15.9	79.3	9,947	27,267	56,223	45.2	5.5	56,954	14.2	18.1	17.2
Sabine	3,903	37.0	1,755	16.6	49.5	17.4	21.9	11,498	27,345	38,917	57.1	3.5	51,046	16.0	25.4	24.1
San Augustine	3,361	40.8	1,469	3.6	59.8	14.0	13.8	11,997	23,385	41,568	59.3	1.3	45,781	19.6	29.7	28.5
San Jacinto	9,997	34.6	5,878	5.8	57.0	15.2	37.6	10,417	24,618	44,566	53.3	2.7	51,575	16.1	26.1	24.6
San Patricio	37,576	56.3	17,073	4.4	51.4	15.9	152.3	10,803	26,714	56,111	45.7	4.4	56,944	14.8	21.6	20.7
San Saba	2,402	39.7	1,261	6.9	56.2	17.4	11.5	11,476	25,201	45,169	55.0	1.5	48,349	17.4	26.1	26.5
Schleicher	1,191	42.6	695	3.7	49.0	16.1	6.2	12,000	24,030	45,250	54.1	0.0	54,471	13.2	19.0	16.5
Scurry	7,903	47.3	4,160	10.2	52.8	16.1	32.4	10,214	24,238	50,277	49.7	2.4	57,158	13.8	17.6	17.2
Shackelford	1,231	37.7	791	20.1	32.4	32.6	7.3	12,002	27,822	48,212	53.4	2.9	64,931	12.5	15.8	14.4
Shelby	9,197	36.4	6,002	5.2	56.5	14.0	57.4	10,637	22,404	41,170	56.9	2.9	41,194	18.0	24.4	24.3
Sherman	1,054	34.9	729	1.9	50.2	18.5	8.3	11,092	36,988	57,130	42.1	6.6	66,408	11.3	16.9	15.4
Smith	107,350	46.1	59,416	12.0	36.4	27.0	335.2	9,217	28,858	59,450	41.8	5.7	60,735	12.7	18.2	16.7
Somervell	4,179	45.8	1,899	6.4	42.8	28.9	23.3	11,136	32,998	64,394	37.9	6.4	67,984	8.3	12.8	12.5
Starr	64,379	95.0	20,361	2.3	68.9	10.9	193.1	11,600	14,545	30,931	70.2	2.2	35,716	25.2	35.3	34.5
Stephens	3,482	37.2	1,997	15.6	53.2	15.7	13.5	9,119	25,592	44,940	56.4	3.7	48,911	15.6	23.5	22.8
Sterling	527	40.8	303	0.0	59.6	18.4	4.7	14,468	27,551	53,194	44.9	2.7	68,435	10.2	13.5	13.5
Stonewall	547	40.5	459	2.4	58.5	12.5	2.7	12,063	23,300	58,309	45.9	1.9	59,802	14.3	22.5	21.6
Sutton	1,651	43.7	993	0.3	57.3	18.4	10.1	12,476	25,650	61,190	44.5	0.2	64,612	11.7	17.3	17.5
Swisher	3,057	41.3	2,011	1.4	59.9	15.9	18.8	11,687	18,310	36,337	69.1	1.3	39,897	19.6	27.2	25.1
Tarrant	1,189,008	56.6	567,142	13.9	37.4	32.6	3,457.0	9,622	34,045	70,306	34.5	8.3	72,064	10.5	15.4	14.9
Taylor	70,577	51.1	37,893	25.9	41.1	26.8	232.8	9,776	28,071	55,568	45.0	3.7	52,974	12.2	16.9	16.0
Terrell	412	53.1	100	0.0	37.2	22.6	2.4	19,686	26,056	42,823	68.3	0.0	42,849	14.0	13.2	12.9
Terry	5,198	42.1	2,881	7.2	60.5	11.6	25.0	10,636	21,048	44,052	56.7	1.7	47,292	18.5	27.4	26.5
Throckmorton	620	41.3	287	5.2	50.4	22.3	4.0	13,825	31,628	41,875	55.3	3.8	46,820	13.5	27.7	25.2
Titus	12,849	39.2	8,726	5.6	57.3	16.8	71.8	10,168	22,077	53,406	46.8	2.7	52,973	14.3	21.4	20.3

1. All persons 3 years old and over enrolled in nursery school through college. 2. Persons 25 years old and over. 3. Elementary and secondary education expenditures. 4. Based on population estimated by the American Community Survey, 2016–2020. 5. CDC percent based on 2019 population estimate.

STATE County	Personal income, 2020: Total (mil dol)	Percent change 2019–2020	Per capita[1]: Dollars	Per capita[1]: Rank	Wages and salaries (mil dol)	Supplements to wages and salaries, employer contributions (mil dol): Pension and insurance	Supplements to wages and salaries, employer contributions (mil dol): Government social insurance	Proprietors' income (mil dol)	Dividends, interest, and rent (mil dol)	Personal transfer reecipts (mil dol)	Earnings, 2020: Total (mil dol)	Contributions for government social insurance (mil dol): From employee and self-employed	Contributions for government social insurance (mil dol): From employer
	62	63	64	65	66	67	68	69	70	71	72	73	74
TEXAS—Cont'd													
Mason	214	3.8	49,261	1,223	43	9	3	31	68	59	86	6	3
Matagorda	1,768	3.8	48,150	1,364	642	136	43	110	295	515	931	55	43
Maverick	2,051	9.6	35,133	2,928	672	163	47	171	175	811	1,052	63	47
Medina	2,328	5.9	44,456	1,881	450	89	29	129	401	630	697	47	29
Menard	88	7.8	41,220	2,302	15	4	1	6	22	34	27	2	1
Midland	22,523	-7.6	126,631	9	7,686	939	478	10,415	3,828	1,530	19,519	831	478
Milam	1,002	8.1	40,552	2,388	238	44	17	39	165	379	338	27	17
Mills	221	11.9	45,663	1,707	54	12	4	17	55	79	87	6	4
Mitchell	304	4.6	37,113	2,779	92	23	6	15	51	110	136	8	6
Montague	894	5.6	44,790	1,826	206	39	14	75	171	315	333	25	14
Montgomery	41,036	4.1	65,516	251	12,308	1,619	806	3,111	7,628	5,801	17,844	1,027	806
Moore	1,063	6.1	51,476	982	531	102	36	204	110	188	873	38	36
Morris	533	7.4	43,036	2,056	187	35	13	38	71	228	274	19	13
Motley	47	19.8	39,505	2,502	11	3	1	11	7	17	26	1	1
Nacogdoches	2,667	4.7	41,188	2,309	970	184	66	252	432	814	1,472	86	66
Navarro	2,173	7.3	42,869	2,083	730	137	50	136	329	708	1,054	68	50
Newton	494	4.3	36,839	2,795	55	15	4	8	54	187	81	9	4
Nolan	712	5.4	48,017	1,393	311	61	21	57	100	232	450	27	21
Nueces	17,431	4.0	47,999	1,395	8,447	1,513	595	1,772	2,842	4,653	12,327	686	595
Ochiltree	575	-3.2	59,892	431	205	36	14	185	82	92	439	17	14
Oldham	120	6.7	56,033	639	47	8	4	33	15	21	93	3	4
Orange	3,992	3.9	48,173	1,360	1,307	223	89	155	439	1,212	1,774	117	89
Palo Pinto	1,322	5.8	45,095	1,781	401	72	27	82	247	402	582	38	27
Panola	1,094	0.7	47,191	1,490	390	65	26	88	202	334	569	36	26
Parker	8,881	8.4	59,929	429	1,749	269	119	628	1,473	1,529	2,766	173	119
Parmer	544	10.1	57,137	563	274	41	20	185	51	92	520	19	20
Pecos	635	0.7	40,391	2,403	296	56	19	47	94	167	418	23	19
Polk	2,270	7.6	42,830	2,089	533	96	38	101	514	985	767	72	38
Potter	5,742	3.2	49,498	1,197	4,077	695	290	1,008	923	1,490	6,070	319	290
Presidio	346	9.4	53,222	841	100	25	8	49	68	94	182	10	8
Rains	479	8.2	38,200	2,664	82	16	6	38	71	175	142	12	6
Randall	7,329	6.4	52,391	903	1,682	243	109	523	1,251	1,277	2,557	161	109
Reagan	207	0.4	54,091	774	131	22	8	23	40	39	185	9	8
Real	139	8.6	40,667	2,378	25	6	2	12	35	63	44	4	2
Red River	573	7.5	47,762	1,422	115	25	8	40	87	227	188	15	8
Reeves	705	-5.5	44,232	1,907	457	69	30	55	118	161	610	33	30
Refugio	332	2.1	48,266	1,353	97	19	7	7	66	115	129	9	7
Roberts	43	1.1	52,804	868	11	3	1	7	11	8	22	1	1
Robertson	787	5.1	45,866	1,673	225	41	16	46	132	252	328	21	16
Rockwall	7,137	8.1	64,943	265	1,616	236	113	605	1,105	932	2,570	147	113
Runnels	461	5.8	44,352	1,898	122	26	8	32	70	164	187	12	8
Rusk	2,149	3.0	39,551	2,495	618	115	42	153	322	667	928	58	42
Sabine	425	9.4	40,477	2,395	104	22	8	20	84	204	153	13	8
San Augustine	360	1.1	43,642	1,988	81	18	6	19	55	168	123	10	6
San Jacinto	1,151	5.4	39,298	2,535	94	22	6	53	184	389	176	17	6
San Patricio	3,246	3.9	48,391	1,340	1,009	166	68	167	411	942	1,410	92	68
San Saba	244	-2.9	40,340	2,413	65	16	5	15	57	87	101	7	5
Schleicher	127	6.7	46,015	1,652	40	8	3	10	19	36	61	4	3
Scurry	788	3.5	47,272	1,478	339	59	21	134	132	201	552	29	21
Shackelford	285	-3.9	86,294	55	69	11	4	106	65	46	190	9	4
Shelby	1,097	3.9	44,038	1,943	376	65	26	126	150	368	593	36	26
Sherman	278	-1.9	91,855	35	41	8	3	170	18	23	222	3	3
Smith	13,459	3.2	57,076	571	5,334	815	374	3,087	2,233	2,935	9,610	506	374
Somervell	458	5.5	50,164	1,129	228	56	14	40	70	115	338	18	14
Starr	2,066	15.1	32,146	3,054	540	156	37	120	158	900	853	53	37
Stephens	427	2.1	45,759	1,692	134	28	9	54	72	136	226	14	9
Sterling	83	2.1	63,329	307	23	5	2	10	26	15	40	2	2
Stonewall	80	3.5	59,419	457	25	5	2	10	19	25	42	2	2
Sutton	212	-10.9	56,622	594	91	15	5	26	43	52	137	8	5
Swisher	394	-2.3	53,734	801	70	17	5	155	44	88	248	7	5
Tarrant	118,091	5.3	55,615	666	58,437	8,355	4,119	9,928	21,483	20,141	80,838	4,451	4,119
Taylor	7,298	8.5	52,429	897	3,372	603	246	506	1,559	1,807	4,727	267	246
Terrell	43	13.8	61,631	362	15	4	1	2	12	13	23	1	1
Terry	507	8.0	41,634	2,249	153	29	10	102	60	160	294	13	10
Throckmorton	66	6.6	44,582	1,863	14	4	1	5	13	28	24	2	1
Titus	1,357	9.1	41,207	2,304	720	128	49	119	208	396	1,016	56	49

1. Based on the resident population estimated as of July 1 of the year shown.

STATE County	Earnings, 2020 (cont.) — Percent by selected industries: Farm	Mining, quarrying, and extractions	Construction	Manu-facturing	Information; professional, scientific, technical services	Retail trade	Finance, insurance, real estate, and leasing	Health care and social assistance	Govern-ment	Social Security beneficiaries, December 2020: Number	Rate[1]	Supple-mental Security Income recipients, 2020	Housing units, 2021: Total	Percent change, 2010–2021
	75	76	77	78	79	80	81	82	83	84	85	86	87	88
TEXAS—Cont'd														
Mason	5.1	D	15.8	2.6	D	3.6	20.3	3.8	19.6	1,300	330	77	2,476	0.3
Matagorda	4.8	2.1	10.1	2.3	D	5.2	3.0	6.4	16.3	7,665	211	1,045	18,717	1.1
Maverick	0.8	1.0	3.9	3.0	3.9	8.3	3.0	D	40.4	11,115	191	3,092	20,268	0.8
Medina	1.2	2.6	14.9	1.0	5.8	10.6	7.6	D	28.9	10,305	198	1,000	19,747	0.6
Menard	0.3	D	16.1	D	D	8.9	D	D	41.4	650	328	50	1,335	0.4
Midland	0.0	62.4	3.8	2.0	3.8	2.6	4.0	2.4	3.8	19,600	117	1,838	71,988	1.9
Milam	2.0	2.1	21.3	5.5	3.8	7.1	5.4	D	22.2	6,385	254	753	11,574	0.3
Mills	1.6	0.2	7.5	5.5	D	12.6	D	10.9	24.6	1,410	315	103	2,532	0.1
Mitchell	3.3	17.2	D	D	2.9	4.7	4.8	D	42.9	1,500	165	205	3,688	0.1
Montague	-1.9	11.4	12.5	9.2	9.6	7.9	6.1	D	20.6	5,520	270	430	10,294	0.4
Montgomery	0.0	5.1	9.7	6.3	11.7	6.6	8.7	10.1	11.6	95,465	147	7,677	251,007	4.4
Moore	18.6	1.5	D	D	D	3.7	2.2	D	13.1	2,670	126	237	8,219	0.3
Morris	3.0	D	3.3	42.5	4.3	5.7	D	3.3	13.2	3,920	326	550	5,800	0.2
Motley	28.1	1.4	D	D	D	7.0	D	6.9	21.4	345	323	23	702	-0.1
Nacogdoches	2.8	0.9	6.9	11.3	5.5	8.1	9.5	12.7	23.9	12,315	190	1,943	28,998	0.3
Navarro	-0.2	1.4	9.9	20.3	D	7.3	6.6	D	19.0	11,235	210	1,606	21,568	0.5
Newton	-4.8	1.9	D	D	D	4.8	D	5.7	40.1	2,770	226	500	6,447	0.9
Nolan	0.6	8.3	11.0	15.0	D	8.1	3.9	D	22.7	3,395	233	469	7,120	0.0
Nueces	-0.1	5.2	11.0	7.7	8.2	5.8	6.4	15.6	18.8	63,560	180	11,234	152,870	0.9
Ochiltree	24.4	27.5	6.3	0.8	2.2	3.7	3.1	D	11.5	1,365	140	91	4,337	0.1
Oldham	33.5	D	D	D	D	1.4	1.1	D	21.4	435	253	26	734	0.3
Orange	-0.3	0.4	10.3	33.4	D	7.1	3.7	4.2	14.9	18,065	213	2,139	37,689	0.8
Palo Pinto	0.0	5.3	5.7	21.8	3.0	8.6	7.0	D	21.3	6,760	236	659	15,131	0.3
Panola	2.6	12.9	17.4	10.3	D	5.5	3.3	4.9	14.2	5,650	249	568	10,821	0.7
Parker	-1.0	2.1	15.8	8.3	7.4	10.8	8.4	8.5	14.4	27,270	174	1,314	59,016	2.3
Parmer	36.6	0.0	D	D	D	1.1	1.3	1.8	9.1	1,495	152	110	3,740	0.1
Pecos	2.0	14.6	7.8	1.1	2.5	6.9	4.1	2.8	27.8	2,410	159	322	5,870	1.1
Polk	-0.7	0.7	8.3	12.8	D	8.7	6.6	10.4	23.1	20,000	385	1,685	25,390	2.7
Potter	0.1	2.4	6.0	13.5	6.2	6.3	9.4	14.5	18.2	19,800	170	2,790	49,107	0.8
Presidio	18.2	0.1	3.5	1.3	D	5.3	3.2	2.1	43.6	1,810	295	502	3,221	0.6
Rains	5.2	D	18.8	3.8	7.2	10.7	5.6	4.8	19.3	3,365	269	267	5,877	0.9
Randall	3.2	0.7	11.9	4.1	7.3	10.9	8.0	8.9	11.3	23,320	162	1,391	61,236	0.9
Reagan	3.9	45.1	D	D	D	2.8	D	D	16.6	470	144	36	1,482	0.4
Real	-5.7	D	8.0	5.9	D	13.4	D	11.8	23.1	1,315	465	103	1,673	0.8
Red River	5.6	4.4	17.0	12.6	4.1	3.0	3.2	9.1	20.7	3,735	323	469	6,167	0.5
Reeves	1.4	19.9	16.3	0.8	1.4	7.2	3.4	0.9	20.6	2,165	149	355	5,155	1.4
Refugio	1.1	11.4	15.3	1.6	D	7.0	6.7	D	29.7	1,780	263	207	3,344	2.5
Roberts	22.7	D	D	0.9	D	D	D	0.7	22.5	185	232	D	431	0.2
Robertson	4.4	7.6	10.1	2.1	3.5	4.5	2.6	D	18.6	3,975	234	583	8,592	1.8
Rockwall	0.0	0.6	12.6	6.8	9.2	10.3	8.7	14.8	11.4	15,900	137	882	41,123	6.5
Runnels	3.7	1.4	6.0	14.9	D	10.8	D	6.4	28.4	2,710	273	288	4,987	0.0
Rusk	1.6	10.8	8.3	11.9	5.1	4.9	7.6	D	16.7	11,060	210	1,104	21,202	0.4
Sabine	1.7	6.7	5.9	D	5.4	7.0	4.1	17.1	20.5	3,740	373	303	7,648	0.9
San Augustine	7.0	D	D	D	3.4	6.5	D	13.4	19.7	2,590	327	383	4,770	0.6
San Jacinto	-3.5	D	14.3	4.0	D	4.7	5.0	D	31.7	6,795	244	667	14,390	3.6
San Patricio	-0.2	6.1	25.8	8.9	6.0	7.2	4.5	D	17.8	14,090	202	2,123	29,907	1.2
San Saba	1.6	3.7	5.7	2.9	D	4.7	D	2.0	29.2	1,570	269	130	2,837	0.1
Schleicher	8.1	D	21.6	D	D	1.9	D	7.1	21.7	625	257	54	1,288	0.2
Scurry	1.2	22.6	4.3	3.2	3.0	6.0	4.1	D	19.5	3,065	182	359	6,890	0.0
Shackelford	0.0	73.6	D	D	D	1.8	5.0	D	7.2	760	237	55	1,574	0.2
Shelby	12.3	12.3	5.6	18.6	D	6.5	1.0	D	13.7	5,520	231	956	11,514	0.7
Sherman	77.1	0.1	D	D	D	2.4	1.1	0.1	7.0	375	134	16	1,165	1.0
Smith	0.1	19.7	5.9	5.0	6.9	8.8	6.3	17.6	10.6	48,220	203	5,441	98,655	1.0
Somervell	1.2	3.8	4.8	1.7	3.3	2.3	2.7	5.5	15.7	2,070	219	118	3,965	0.8
Starr	0.7	2.9	2.5	0.3	1.4	7.6	2.1	D	48.8	10,230	155	4,343	23,040	0.2
Stephens	-2.1	22.5	8.6	16.0	D	6.0	5.2	4.9	18.3	2,230	243	228	4,660	0.1
Sterling	8.9	26.5	3.9	0.8	D	2.6	D	D	24.7	255	185	17	582	0.3
Stonewall	10.4	8.3	14.5	2.0	D	7.0	D	2.9	36.1	390	320	26	842	0.2
Sutton	2.2	31.1	6.5	4.7	D	3.3	4.1	1.7	18.1	810	244	62	1,881	0.2
Swisher	58.6	D	1.9	2.3	D	2.5	1.6	D	16.9	1,490	213	154	3,031	-0.1
Tarrant	0.0	2.1	9.3	11.3	8.5	6.3	9.3	10.5	11.9	284,690	134	36,098	826,154	1.7
Taylor	-0.1	2.7	6.3	3.9	7.2	7.1	8.3	16.8	23.6	26,290	183	3,608	61,459	0.9
Terrell	9.7	0.2	3.1	D	D	2.8	D	D	55.1	205	283	23	650	0.0
Terry	28.4	8.0	3.6	3.8	D	6.1	D	4.5	21.1	2,075	177	311	4,794	0.1
Throckmorton	7.5	15.4	D	D	D	3.6	D	D	38.8	395	264	26	965	0.1
Titus	2.8	0.3	5.2	36.5	D	6.7	3.7	7.9	18.8	5,795	186	755	12,110	0.7

1. Per 1,000 resident population estimated as of July 1 of the year shown.

Table B. States and Counties — **Housing, Labor Force, and Employment**

STATE County	Housing units, 2016–2020: Occupied units: Total	Owner-occupied: Percent	Owner-occupied: Median value[1]	Median owner cost as a percent of income: With a mortgage	Median owner cost as a percent of income: Without a mortgage[2]	Renter-occupied: Median rent[3]	Renter-occupied: Median rent as a percent of income[2]	Sub-standard units[4] (percent)	Civilian labor force, 2021: Total	Percent change, 2020–2021	Unemployment: Total	Unemployment: Rate[5]	Civilian employment[6], 2016–2020: Total	Percent: Management, business, science, and arts	Percent: Construction, production, and maintenance occupations
	89	90	91	92	93	94	95	96	97	98	99	100	101	102	103
TEXAS—Cont'd															
Mason	1,668	75.1	219,900	22.3	10.7	741	28.6	0.0	1,789	4.4	84	4.7	1,928	41.4	21.9
Matagorda	13,900	70.5	128,100	18.1	11.5	851	31.2	3.8	16,489	0.7	1,375	8.3	15,505	27.2	36.6
Maverick	16,647	66.4	100,900	20.0	12.8	678	27.0	11.1	23,752	-1.5	3,013	12.7	21,843	21.0	28.2
Medina	15,978	80.0	151,600	21.2	10.0	869	29.0	3.5	21,832	3.0	1,088	5.0	22,186	32.7	31.2
Menard	1,035	61.4	87,300	25.7	12.6	691	18.6	3.4	837	-2.3	40	4.8	1,017	25.3	42.3
Midland	57,917	66.7	233,200	19.1	10.2	1,244	26.9	6.7	99,301	1.5	5,670	5.7	85,527	37.0	26.9
Milam	9,468	73.6	111,900	20.0	11.1	697	30.7	4.4	10,199	6.1	593	5.8	10,307	29.9	31.6
Mills	1,752	88.2	141,700	22.0	11.2	649	32.5	0.7	1,905	2.1	83	4.4	2,098	34.5	23.9
Mitchell	2,419	81.2	67,900	16.5	12.4	650	22.5	8.0	2,346	0.9	167	7.1	2,920	32.0	27.8
Montague	7,969	76.6	120,100	18.8	10.4	873	29.4	2.6	9,265	2.9	476	5.1	8,179	23.4	35.0
Montgomery	205,719	71.5	248,100	20.7	10.3	1,231	27.2	3.7	293,629	1.9	17,018	5.8	280,818	41.5	21.6
Moore	6,659	65.8	113,100	21.1	10.0	818	22.1	6.5	10,983	4.7	367	3.3	9,625	24.3	47.4
Morris	5,170	73.3	92,100	18.6	11.8	692	29.6	3.5	4,624	-4.1	484	10.5	5,017	24.7	34.4
Motley	496	71.0	60,000	15.5	12.7	629	14.3	3.4	453	5.6	23	5.1	602	38.4	37.9
Nacogdoches	23,765	57.7	137,300	19.6	10.0	768	34.3	5.8	28,255	2.2	1,541	5.5	28,163	30.9	28.1
Navarro	17,509	69.6	109,700	20.2	11.3	806	30.9	6.0	23,685	2.3	1,206	5.1	21,655	29.1	34.3
Newton	5,124	82.5	80,700	19.8	11.4	681	36.5	9.5	4,897	-1.0	510	10.4	5,238	24.3	37.2
Nolan	5,516	67.9	80,300	21.0	11.8	739	26.2	5.5	7,091	1.2	337	4.8	6,131	26.0	35.2
Nueces	130,482	58.7	148,100	22.0	12.2	1,048	29.0	4.7	163,825	0.3	11,340	6.9	163,776	31.8	25.4
Ochiltree	3,391	73.2	104,300	24.7	10.9	820	22.9	8.3	3,952	-1.2	180	4.6	4,544	20.9	45.2
Oldham	646	73.1	103,800	16.5	10.0	808	19.8	1.4	917	3.3	32	3.5	912	36.0	31.5
Orange	31,570	74.3	116,100	16.3	10.0	826	24.1	3.1	34,858	-1.7	3,139	9.0	37,744	31.3	32.5
Palo Pinto	10,334	74.5	115,700	21.2	11.8	832	28.5	3.2	12,902	-1.4	741	5.7	12,438	28.3	31.6
Panola	8,662	77.2	117,000	18.9	11.4	729	27.9	4.1	9,691	3.8	651	6.7	9,346	29.4	33.5
Parker	45,848	80.5	236,300	19.6	10.1	1,049	27.7	2.4	71,585	3.6	3,172	4.4	64,858	38.5	24.2
Parmer	3,213	65.5	110,000	22.0	10.0	740	23.2	7.2	4,976	3.4	142	2.9	4,591	27.3	44.5
Pecos	4,868	74.2	106,000	18.8	10.0	806	21.9	5.8	6,164	-3.1	440	7.1	5,987	23.7	39.4
Polk	17,945	77.2	125,500	21.3	10.2	789	27.2	4.8	18,571	1.9	1,492	8.0	18,855	24.3	31.2
Potter	43,957	54.7	97,000	20.2	11.4	825	29.5	5.8	54,259	2.8	2,333	4.3	50,273	24.2	33.4
Presidio	2,580	54.0	77,200	23.9	12.8	397	24.5	5.0	3,101	-2.3	327	10.5	2,828	33.9	29.8
Rains	4,321	78.4	131,100	20.3	12.6	713	23.6	4.5	6,318	6.1	245	3.9	5,108	30.9	34.2
Randall	50,092	69.6	174,100	19.8	11.2	947	25.4	2.3	74,603	2.9	2,625	3.5	70,430	38.1	22.1
Reagan	1,117	65.8	98,300	21.0	10.0	857	21.3	4.3	1,653	-7.7	127	7.7	1,710	29.8	47.8
Real	1,254	71.9	146,900	20.4	10.0	785	37.5	4.5	1,144	6.4	68	5.9	1,296	30.9	20.9
Red River	5,143	78.0	77,900	20.5	11.0	571	35.8	2.1	5,320	5.0	314	5.9	4,886	28.9	32.6
Reeves	3,772	79.6	91,600	17.5	10.4	859	35.6	5.3	8,608	-1.5	505	5.9	6,201	21.8	50.6
Refugio	2,566	72.8	85,500	17.4	10.0	637	31.6	3.8	3,037	0.5	204	6.7	2,856	25.0	25.1
Roberts	329	82.7	134,200	23.8	10.0	760	21.0	3.0	399	0.0	17	4.3	371	39.4	26.7
Robertson	6,749	73.5	121,600	18.1	10.0	752	25.7	4.0	7,557	4.1	398	5.3	7,175	28.8	28.3
Rockwall	34,457	83.4	283,000	20.9	10.8	1,472	24.3	2.2	56,678	4.5	2,438	4.3	51,166	48.5	14.9
Runnels	3,891	72.9	85,200	17.4	12.3	762	24.0	2.9	4,618	2.7	188	4.1	4,491	32.6	28.8
Rusk	18,056	79.2	131,200	19.2	10.0	813	25.2	3.7	22,047	1.1	1,326	6.0	21,871	29.9	37.2
Sabine	4,524	86.4	99,900	26.2	11.9	659	31.3	0.6	3,965	2.4	378	9.5	3,311	22.8	29.7
San Augustine	3,712	73.0	75,500	18.3	11.2	626	37.2	2.3	2,979	-0.7	245	8.2	2,960	28.8	32.3
San Jacinto	10,143	79.5	126,700	19.4	13.9	890	27.4	4.7	11,871	3.0	877	7.4	10,797	31.4	34.6
San Patricio	23,422	67.8	129,400	19.8	12.4	1,047	29.7	7.6	29,428	0.8	2,598	8.8	28,244	29.8	29.8
San Saba	2,134	70.9	119,400	25.2	12.1	777	33.2	3.8	2,203	1.3	103	4.7	2,440	32.7	33.0
Schleicher	1,036	78.0	80,900	16.5	13.2	400	24.7	2.9	1,192	-0.7	66	5.5	1,047	33.0	33.0
Scurry	6,115	78.5	87,600	19.9	11.7	757	26.3	6.1	6,086	-1.3	408	6.7	6,684	24.0	34.5
Shackelford	1,367	79.7	110,000	22.7	12.3	754	33.7	2.8	1,845	4.7	74	4.0	1,477	36.1	24.4
Shelby	9,486	75.0	81,800	18.7	10.8	631	27.1	7.7	11,484	3.1	622	5.4	9,744	27.1	35.0
Sherman	1,070	72.9	93,900	25.2	10.0	793	21.2	4.5	1,408	8.7	42	3.0	1,500	30.7	37.8
Smith	77,809	67.2	164,200	20.4	10.8	955	27.6	3.3	110,095	2.4	5,656	5.1	104,190	33.9	25.2
Somervell	3,145	83.8	205,800	21.8	10.0	715	18.6	4.5	4,398	3.7	228	5.2	3,782	42.2	26.6
Starr	16,281	74.8	76,900	26.2	11.8	572	31.0	10.6	25,381	-2.0	4,118	16.2	23,059	23.7	30.4
Stephens	3,408	74.1	81,300	23.2	12.1	710	31.1	0.9	4,190	4.9	206	4.9	3,495	24.9	39.5
Sterling	405	87.4	75,000	20.5	10.0	773	26.8	0.0	586	5.6	30	5.1	595	26.6	25.4
Stonewall	529	80.2	53,200	15.3	10.9	600	17.3	5.1	587	3.3	24	4.1	691	27.4	37.9
Sutton	1,282	68.1	101,000	18.7	11.9	648	16.5	9.8	1,149	-4.6	95	8.3	1,725	30.9	28.1
Swisher	2,599	72.4	78,600	23.4	15.7	701	28.0	4.2	2,593	3.8	128	4.9	2,756	34.8	24.4
Tarrant	722,446	60.3	209,600	20.8	11.7	1,142	29.3	4.6	1,099,856	2.8	58,300	5.3	1,037,059	37.9	23.5
Taylor	50,396	58.4	137,600	20.4	10.6	921	28.8	2.7	67,165	2.4	2,919	4.3	64,638	33.3	23.4
Terrell	419	96.4	81,400	21.0	12.5	0	0.0	0.2	411	9.0	15	3.6	332	28.9	42.5
Terry	4,101	63.2	78,500	17.9	10.0	698	28.4	3.9	4,776	0.1	292	6.1	4,975	20.2	38.2
Throckmorton	713	73.4	58,600	14.0	11.4	604	36.5	2.0	1,008	59.2	28	2.8	697	40.6	24.4
Titus	11,064	68.0	99,900	20.3	10.0	730	23.1	10.4	13,563	3.1	726	5.4	14,342	21.5	38.9

1. Specified owner-occupied units. 2. A value of 10.0 represents 10 percent or less; a value of 50.0 represents 50 percent or more. 3. Specified renter-occupied units. 4. Overcrowded or lacking complete plumbing facilities. 5. Percent of civilian labor force. 6. Civilian employed persons 16 years old and over.

STATE County	Private nonfarm establishments, employment and payroll, 2020									Agriculture, 2017			
		Employment						Annual payroll		Farms			Farm producers whose primary occupation is farming (percent)
											Percent with:		
	Number of establish-ments	Total	Health care and social assistance	Manufac-turing	Retail trade	Finance and insurance	Professional, scientific, and technical services	Total (mil dol)	Average per employee (dollars)	Number	Fewer than 50 acres	1000 acres or more	
	104	105	106	107	108	109	110	111	112	113	114	115	116
TEXAS—Cont'd													
Mason	140	746	116	27	103	40	60	25	33,047	680	15.4	22.5	39.3
Matagorda	728	7,978	1,229	809	1,471	194	222	460	57,676	858	36.2	14.8	40.4
Maverick	820	12,927	4,311	444	2,645	406	259	347	26,881	339	53.1	15.0	34.8
Medina	769	7,881	982	447	1,650	273	483	283	35,948	2,281	39.9	7.9	35.1
Menard	49	220	NA	NA	71	24	10	6	25,145	346	13.0	29.8	40.7
Midland	5,754	101,920	7,530	3,281	9,721	2,347	4,178	6,403	62,827	410	59.8	11.5	24.4
Milam	405	3,791	514	197	648	197	99	148	38,913	2,053	41.7	4.1	38.2
Mills	110	942	98	90	160	56	21	36	37,994	896	22.1	10.8	38.2
Mitchell	135	1,130	242	NA	192	55	18	46	40,332	362	23.5	18.2	27.7
Montague	418	3,334	382	338	610	189	149	132	39,573	1,615	32.1	6.3	37.4
Montgomery	12,797	180,788	25,673	9,809	27,411	6,537	11,242	10,861	60,077	1,614	69.1	1.8	30.4
Moore	446	8,676	647	4,153	996	135	76	408	47,076	250	28.4	32.4	48.1
Morris	214	2,807	148	1,508	302	129	59	124	44,053	449	39.2	2.0	35.7
Motley	21	131	NA	NA	NA	NA	NA	4	33,573	237	6.3	40.9	36.2
Nacogdoches	1,270	18,326	2,726	3,752	2,821	551	466	658	35,917	1,123	33.6	2.4	37.8
Navarro	941	13,294	2,374	3,002	2,237	361	291	470	35,384	2,471	44.7	4.0	35.9
Newton	131	834	159	82	181	17	16	26	31,604	430	58.6	0.2	34.0
Nolan	340	5,399	564	1,066	833	119	87	246	45,538	410	18.0	20.0	35.2
Nueces	7,987	140,994	29,414	6,933	18,088	4,495	6,686	5,957	42,253	646	61.8	13.3	33.4
Ochiltree	347	3,308	275	7	386	148	90	156	47,009	282	12.1	41.8	48.6
Oldham	40	546	319	NA	59	NA	NA	22	39,886	132	3.8	49.2	46.7
Orange	1,308	19,017	1,716	5,130	3,178	502	622	1,018	53,512	663	81.1	1.2	31.6
Palo Pinto	596	5,780	908	799	958	163	176	223	38,497	1,265	49.2	8.6	36.0
Panola	453	6,782	579	922	706	218	329	276	40,768	978	30.9	3.0	37.0
Parker	3,082	32,186	3,760	3,527	5,912	742	1,296	1,411	43,826	4,626	73.1	1.8	29.3
Parmer	194	3,691	173	2,125	118	78	229	203	55,027	464	10.3	36.6	52.5
Pecos	342	3,813	413	28	798	125	66	171	44,845	309	9.1	61.2	45.6
Polk	784	8,790	1,420	1,350	1,657	367	193	343	39,048	742	40.2	1.6	36.1
Potter	3,443	61,308	14,128	6,694	7,833	3,735	1,867	2,814	45,898	239	38.5	17.6	42.5
Presidio	129	958	64	13	256	63	6	23	24,318	142	5.6	58.5	53.7
Rains	186	1,485	103	89	333	50	223	51	34,358	787	57.6	2.2	34.1
Randall	2,700	34,200	3,656	4,791	6,406	1,244	1,093	1,509	44,129	781	41.4	17.4	35.2
Reagan	128	1,669	149	NA	156	18	19	79	47,473	112	10.7	56.3	50.3
Real	88	670	79	32	118	NA	47	16	23,185	198	16.2	27.8	41.7
Red River	179	1,417	219	336	254	75	25	56	39,559	1,126	26.1	8.6	41.2
Reeves	370	5,707	345	63	682	57	69	311	54,554	224	19.2	27.7	43.6
Refugio	139	1,686	207	NA	314	22	24	65	38,767	238	31.9	23.5	37.4
Roberts	20	115	NA	NA	NA	NA	10	5	46,557	104	10.6	48.1	58.2
Robertson	266	3,174	303	116	409	80	339	150	47,225	1,471	34.2	5.2	40.6
Rockwall	2,623	30,155	5,343	1,919	5,970	741	1,811	1,220	40,474	403	74.9	1.5	24.4
Runnels	219	2,170	299	475	357	95	30	81	37,167	833	18.7	17.0	38.8
Rusk	779	9,730	1,565	1,365	1,133	423	298	413	42,442	1,441	33.2	1.8	35.1
Sabine	181	1,586	433	361	335	46	27	63	39,857	200	43.5	2.5	33.5
San Augustine	133	1,394	441	65	223	38	10	51	36,876	293	30.0	1.7	40.9
San Jacinto	209	1,109	131	103	202	38	65	38	34,172	786	56.6	1.0	31.6
San Patricio	1,070	15,955	1,169	4,281	2,712	363	952	809	50,727	656	52.4	13.1	38.8
San Saba	154	823	111	55	163	23	29	25	30,840	773	16.4	22.1	43.6
Schleicher	51	460	61	NA	54	22	8	19	41,033	327	12.5	44.6	42.2
Scurry	397	4,729	492	91	648	102	162	241	50,899	560	21.8	17.5	33.5
Shackelford	116	1,058	43	128	81	57	6	58	54,974	223	15.7	30.9	37.1
Shelby	510	6,562	506	2,169	906	366	472	248	37,819	995	30.8	1.6	39.1
Sherman	59	345	NA	NA	107	24	NA	17	48,632	245	6.9	41.2	47.5
Smith	5,931	95,866	22,649	8,517	13,097	3,317	4,618	4,232	44,144	2,928	58.8	1.1	31.7
Somervell	226	3,005	484	39	200	53	79	199	66,059	352	53.7	5.1	29.5
Starr	588	9,055	5,013	42	1,742	295	142	198	21,832	1,345	31.7	8.8	34.1
Stephens	237	2,170	296	361	342	106	67	90	41,630	575	13.7	20.2	34.9
Sterling	51	285	34	NA	44	16	7	15	53,098	76	5.3	51.3	50.0
Stonewall	47	363	148	NA	29	NA	NA	14	39,799	314	5.1	29.6	33.1
Sutton	110	1,047	89	22	201	12	13	47	44,470	261	9.2	52.1	47.1
Swisher	120	885	190	115	114	36	34	32	36,634	432	4.9	34.3	46.8
Tarrant	44,319	827,789	116,878	85,939	106,457	49,857	41,858	42,663	51,538	1,173	82.5	1.8	31.1
Taylor	3,583	57,676	12,946	2,984	8,085	2,770	1,898	2,273	39,418	1,394	36.7	9.0	29.6
Terrell	10	50	NA	NA	20	NA	NA	2	33,420	85	NA	74.1	50.4
Terry	220	2,169	356	47	495	96	50	81	37,161	558	13.4	22.4	46.2
Throckmorton	45	239	NA	NA	37	13	6	8	33,502	274	4.7	27.4	38.3
Titus	642	14,374	2,108	6,731	1,659	409	98	551	38,337	812	43.2	3.0	38.4

STATE County	Agriculture, 2017 (cont.) — Land in farms — Acreage (1,000)	Land in farms — Percent change, 2012–2017	Land in farms — Acres — Average size of farm	Land in farms — Acres — Total irrigated (1,000)	Land in farms — Acres — Total cropland (1,000)	Value of land and buildings (dollars) — Average per farm	Value of land and buildings (dollars) — Average per acre	Value of machinery and equipment, average per farm (dollars)	Value of products sold: — Total (mil dol)	Value of products sold: — Average per farm (acres)	Value of products sold: — Percent from: — Crops	Value of products sold: — Percent from: — Livestock and poultry products	Organic farms (number)	Farms with internet access (percent)	Government payments — Total ($1,000)	Government payments — Percent of farms
	117	118	119	120	121	122	123	124	125	126	127	128	129	130	131	132
TEXAS—Cont'd																
Mason	539	-2.2	793	3.9	21.8	1,838,623	2,318	72,646	21.7	31,881	10.7	89.3	NA	70.3	1,416	15.0
Matagorda	551	-2.9	643	25.6	176.2	1,540,205	2,397	146,410	124.2	144,773	58.8	41.2	16	70.6	9,559	26.7
Maverick	434	-19.7	1,282	14.6	21.3	1,801,266	1,405	56,810	43.0	126,737	5.8	94.2	NA	59.3	752	8.0
Medina	782	-6.1	343	39.4	153.5	917,319	2,674	63,914	93.9	41,170	48.8	51.2	1	73.4	2,804	10.9
Menard	508	-5.4	1,467	1.2	10.5	2,174,290	1,482	68,492	9.1	26,220	6.3	93.8	NA	74.6	596	17.3
Midland	345	-14.7	841	7.4	75.8	1,353,752	1,609	99,126	16.3	39,851	79.6	20.4	NA	79.5	910	17.3
Milam	497	-5.8	242	2.7	168.0	766,554	3,163	79,326	129.5	63,087	25.7	74.3	2	70.3	3,149	8.7
Mills	441	-6.4	492	3.1	44.6	1,235,360	2,509	65,340	30.9	34,484	7.9	92.1	NA	76.9	580	14.2
Mitchell	583	1.7	1,611	3.0	153.1	1,604,910	997	96,432	21.7	60,061	62.5	37.5	NA	65.2	2,422	50.8
Montague	498	2.0	309	1.5	82.9	842,695	2,732	67,799	33.4	20,691	16.0	84.0	1	72.6	1,075	12.0
Montgomery	145	-6.8	90	0.7	25.3	1,024,558	11,414	54,308	25.8	15,963	26.5	73.5	1	82.5	201	1.4
Moore	478	-8.8	1,911	84.8	207.6	2,167,617	1,134	373,450	478.1	1,912,300	14.9	85.1	NA	71.2	8,544	58.4
Morris	74	-19.6	165	0.2	16.1	375,751	2,283	58,729	44.2	98,354	2.5	97.5	4	67.0	436	16.7
Motley	580	-2.7	2,446	4.4	100.3	2,072,503	847	112,229	15.2	64,249	15.9	84.1	NA	75.9	2,016	54.4
Nacogdoches	265	0.0	236	0.3	29.5	682,387	2,895	92,115	370.7	330,135	0.9	99.1	4	68.3	144	1.5
Navarro	559	0.2	226	1.7	178.6	531,307	2,349	68,964	73.3	29,667	45.9	54.1	4	65.9	2,195	7.2
Newton	59	0.0	137	0.1	5.5	303,605	2,221	54,042	1.6	3,691	30.6	69.4	4	63.3	24	2.8
Nolan	466	0.3	1,137	3.5	161.9	1,253,213	1,102	107,278	36.6	89,290	70.4	29.6	NA	72.4	1,351	44.1
Nueces	475	-9.4	735	1.2	332.3	2,243,539	3,052	220,795	161.0	249,260	96.2	3.8	4	63.6	8,905	27.4
Ochiltree	569	4.4	2,016	59.0	343.8	2,484,158	1,232	353,856	349.1	1,237,791	20.0	80.0	2	79.4	7,773	72.0
Oldham	945	13.8	7,157	1.8	105.3	5,834,781	815	158,947	156.0	1,181,909	3.5	96.5	NA	81.8	3,798	78.8
Orange	53	0.2	80	0.3	4.7	368,662	4,619	55,345	5.0	7,492	30.0	70.0	NA	78.4	142	0.8
Palo Pinto	573	-3.4	453	4.4	73.0	1,104,960	2,440	58,278	43.2	34,165	23.8	76.2	NA	72.4	249	3.3
Panola	206	-9.4	211	0.8	39.8	562,292	2,670	78,393	100.7	102,986	4.6	95.4	NA	70.4	96	1.6
Parker	522	5.5	113	1.7	95.1	484,457	4,296	48,756	65.0	14,060	18.7	81.3	2	81.3	250	1.0
Parmer	549	-0.9	1,183	110.1	399.2	1,330,531	1,125	346,434	893.3	1,925,302	10.3	89.7	NA	75.9	17,933	81.9
Pecos	2,868	-2.7	9,281	12.9	50.8	6,420,541	692	136,293	46.2	149,398	52.8	47.2	NA	73.1	1,560	23.6
Polk	125	-10.1	169	0.3	22.6	507,818	3,011	58,728	6.8	9,206	33.5	66.5	NA	70.1	166	0.7
Potter	424	-25.5	1,773	3.6	49.6	1,802,406	1,016	76,318	24.8	103,891	10.5	89.5	NA	67.4	1,962	20.1
Presidio	1,841	11.2	12,967	1.8	18.0	10,152,603	783	122,932	D	D	D	D	NA	77.5	644	12.0
Rains	111	-4.6	142	0.3	27.7	492,612	3,479	61,364	22.8	28,919	37.8	62.2	NA	69.4	213	3.9
Randall	560	-1.9	718	16.2	233.9	1,135,115	1,582	108,685	479.5	613,910	5.0	95.0	NA	79.9	9,464	40.1
Reagan	736	5.4	6,574	8.1	55.6	5,510,283	838	242,344	18.2	162,527	65.6	34.4	NA	76.8	768	42.0
Real	317	-1.1	1,601	0.4	1.3	3,074,966	1,921	47,687	1.3	6,379	4.9	95.1	NA	87.4	19	4.0
Red River	458	2.2	407	5.1	103.1	784,848	1,927	85,573	94.0	83,515	10.9	89.1	1	70.2	3,425	34.1
Reeves	1,064	-13.9	4,750	8.1	54.7	2,500,484	526	80,186	10.9	48,621	47.5	52.5	1	72.8	790	24.1
Refugio	489	2.9	2,053	0.5	56.3	2,565,852	1,250	170,947	35.9	150,891	69.2	30.8	NA	73.5	1,986	27.7
Roberts	553	-1.7	5,318	7.4	36.1	4,045,126	761	140,728	18.3	175,971	20.7	79.3	NA	76.0	1,450	52.9
Robertson	475	1.5	323	20.4	107.3	932,356	2,889	72,519	158.1	107,507	15.6	84.4	2	70.0	2,496	4.6
Rockwall	40	-11.0	100	0.1	21.0	554,781	5,536	52,992	7.8	19,429	79.0	21.0	3	80.4	439	3.7
Runnels	672	1.0	807	5.6	256.2	1,116,037	1,383	111,613	53.4	64,146	59.7	40.3	NA	70.9	6,275	52.1
Rusk	243	-11.5	168	0.5	46.1	431,457	2,561	71,067	100.2	69,505	5.9	94.1	NA	69.6	313	1.1
Sabine	38	31.9	192	0.1	5.6	432,114	2,256	85,329	17.7	88,575	2.5	97.5	NA	73.0	36	2.5
San Augustine	62	-15.2	211	0.0	9.2	594,832	2,820	83,472	56.7	193,433	2.3	97.7	NA	72.0	D	1.0
San Jacinto	84	-24.5	107	1.0	16.9	440,438	4,100	75,877	7.2	9,148	34.5	65.5	NA	70.2	130	0.5
San Patricio	371	-0.9	565	4.1	235.8	1,497,600	2,650	192,771	131.3	200,216	88.4	11.6	NA	78.4	6,745	25.8
San Saba	660	-1.7	854	4.8	81.3	2,091,365	2,449	87,070	35.8	46,343	18.1	81.9	2	79.8	1,777	18.2
Schleicher	811	-2.7	2,480	1.4	30.6	2,929,781	1,181	90,424	17.8	54,404	19.3	80.7	NA	74.6	1,449	22.6
Scurry	531	7.4	948	5.5	201.7	991,118	1,046	124,077	45.2	80,629	54.0	46.0	5	70.4	2,730	52.1
Shackelford	537	6.3	2,407	0.3	49.4	3,105,956	1,290	75,451	16.6	74,480	4.9	95.1	NA	76.2	610	35.4
Shelby	179	-9.2	180	0.4	28.6	631,226	3,507	88,864	467.6	469,907	0.6	99.4	NA	70.7	50	0.6
Sherman	590	1.2	2,409	184.7	355.2	3,446,896	1,431	645,756	838.1	3,420,641	17.5	82.5	3	75.9	11,501	78.0
Smith	272	-10.1	93	1.9	64.3	487,136	5,248	52,759	53.6	18,308	68.6	31.4	NA	71.8	94	1.2
Somervell	83	-9.2	236	0.3	15.7	738,349	3,133	58,179	4.1	11,648	28.1	71.9	NA	75.3	40	3.4
Starr	571	-14.5	425	3.4	74.1	779,096	1,834	49,858	47.2	35,115	19.9	80.1	NA	42.4	1,977	8.7
Stephens	470	-9.0	818	0.3	37.1	1,430,192	1,749	65,383	10.6	18,477	5.3	94.7	NA	66.8	641	21.7
Sterling	584	-0.1	7,688	0.4	9.4	5,208,932	678	107,859	D	D	D	D	NA	86.8	165	9.2
Stonewall	469	-0.8	1,493	0.8	113.4	1,365,112	914	80,900	15.5	49,500	44.3	55.7	NA	62.7	1,995	63.1
Sutton	901	-1.1	3,452	0.3	12.4	4,384,828	1,270	67,361	10.4	39,655	1.3	98.7	NA	74.3	331	9.2
Swisher	563	3.3	1,304	71.5	399.8	1,364,672	1,046	292,743	623.9	1,444,259	11.0	89.0	NA	76.4	13,019	86.1
Tarrant	191	30.9	163	1.3	43.5	992,283	6,104	53,767	29.4	25,058	59.4	40.6	NA	79.7	170	2.2
Taylor	484	-16.4	347	1.2	159.2	713,098	2,053	64,361	31.5	22,626	35.4	64.6	NA	73.7	2,520	23.2
Terrell	835	-24.1	9,825	0.6	9.4	7,373,840	751	95,965	4.2	49,306	13.1	86.9	NA	76.5	193	10.6
Terry	496	12.1	889	104.4	436.8	905,405	1,019	245,583	136.9	245,418	83.2	16.8	13	64.3	16,544	80.3
Throckmorton	507	-0.2	1,850	0.4	157.2	2,604,134	1,408	111,148	27.3	99,489	20.2	79.8	3	73.0	2,844	52.9
Titus	159	8.4	196	2.1	33.8	493,023	2,520	74,641	149.3	183,858	2.7	97.3	NA	69.2	501	17.0

Table B. States and Counties — **Water Use, Wholesale Trade, Retail Trade, and Real Estate**

STATE County	Water use, 2015		Wholesale Trade[1], 2017				Retail Trade[2], 2017				Real estate and rental and leasing,[2] 2017			
	Public supply water withdrawn (mil gal/ day)	Public supply gallons withdrawn per person per day	Number of establish- ments	Number of employees	Sales (mil dol)	Average payroll (mil dol)	Number of establish- ments	Number of employees	Sales (mil dol)	Average payroll (mil dol)	Number of establish- ments	Number of employees	Sales (mil dol)	Average payroll (mil dol)
	133	134	135	136	137	138	139	140	141	142	143	144	145	146
TEXAS—Cont'd														
Mason	0.4	109.1	7	40	10.0	1.0	24	149	39.6	3.3	6	D	3.2	D
Matagorda	4.4	120.8	26	108	104.6	5.2	129	1,349	360.0	33.3	28	148	44.6	6.6
Maverick	7.0	120.4	38	188	177.2	9.6	166	2,757	661.8	59.3	32	101	15.0	2.7
Medina	6.7	137.3	29	220	290.8	12.2	108	1,611	627.1	47.6	29	53	7.9	1.3
Menard	0.4	171.0	NA	NA	NA	NA	9	43	12.7	0.8	NA	NA	NA	NA
Midland	1.0	6.5	299	4,958	6,456.0	341.1	514	8,861	3,322.4	287.7	D	D	D	132.1
Milam	10.9	444.3	13	124	62.9	6.5	58	612	188.0	16.6	17	44	7.4	1.3
Mills	0.3	57.1	5	D	14.2	D	18	160	62.2	5.0	D	D	D	D
Mitchell	1.3	141.2	3	8	1.3	0.3	28	203	67.3	5.0	NA	NA	NA	NA
Montague	1.1	55.5	18	59	34.8	2.0	72	641	197.0	16.4	10	35	5.7	1.0
Montgomery	57.3	106.6	534	5,373	11,349.1	372.7	1,447	25,947	7,741.9	707.3	629	2,457	628.9	122.5
Moore	5.1	227.8	D	D	D	D	65	970	258.1	21.6	17	47	10.4	1.5
Morris	0.2	18.4	8	85	36.7	3.8	38	291	69.1	6.5	3	3	0.7	0.1
Motley	0.2	130.7	NA	NA	NA	NA	3	16	4.4	0.3	NA	NA	NA	NA
Nacogdoches	11.2	170.6	D	D	D	18.6	221	2,822	849.8	76.6	57	211	29.6	6.3
Navarro	2.3	48.2	35	460	386.6	22.8	161	2,203	652.7	55.0	52	133	25.3	4.1
Newton	1.0	69.4	D	D	D	D	29	172	76.4	2.7	NA	NA	NA	NA
Nolan	2.3	150.9	18	109	77.3	6.0	66	781	257.0	19.0	10	51	4.0	0.8
Nueces	72.4	201.2	395	5,963	3,789.9	315.1	1,078	18,383	5,391.2	492.6	474	3,047	777.8	154.1
Ochiltree	1.8	163.8	28	314	194.9	18.0	44	448	120.3	10.5	9	58	22.1	4.2
Oldham	0.6	270.7	NA	NA	NA	NA	D	D	D	D	NA	NA	NA	NA
Orange	8.4	99.7	35	266	204.9	14.9	255	3,081	966.0	80.9	60	243	39.0	8.8
Palo Pinto	2.0	71.0	26	208	140.3	12.8	90	986	271.7	24.2	33	115	21.5	5.7
Panola	1.2	48.4	19	103	71.3	5.9	76	846	237.8	20.9	24	113	14.0	4.0
Parker	7.5	59.6	111	1,039	603.4	52.1	356	5,446	2,292.8	176.7	128	405	108.5	18.7
Parmer	0.9	88.2	28	228	915.0	10.5	24	163	38.5	3.3	3	4	0.6	0.1
Pecos	4.3	267.2	17	128	107.7	6.4	59	704	287.6	19.2	9	44	9.2	1.6
Polk	561.8	11,960.1	17	123	78.2	6.4	132	1,764	570.5	48.4	28	80	14.9	2.5
Potter	5.5	44.8	162	2,712	2,356.5	145.5	489	7,967	2,026.7	191.1	170	804	172.2	35.3
Presidio	2.5	369.4	NA	NA	NA	NA	27	242	51.7	4.5	NA	NA	NA	NA
Rains	1.3	112.0	6	D	29.6	D	28	355	136.4	10.7	9	D	2.8	D
Randall	2.2	17.1	96	1,908	2,537.8	97.3	357	6,254	1,882.9	173.9	158	559	122.2	21.2
Reagan	0.0	0.0	13	137	177.4	9.7	10	117	64.0	3.9	NA	NA	NA	NA
Real	0.4	105.8	3	7	1.5	0.2	15	116	22.4	2.1	5	D	2.1	D
Red River	0.9	73.9	6	34	25.5	0.8	36	266	61.6	5.4	4	20	0.6	0.1
Reeves	3.7	247.8	15	144	132.7	7.6	29	448	244.6	14.3	10	158	43.7	8.4
Refugio	0.7	89.2	6	52	32.1	2.2	18	284	91.3	6.4	7	50	11.5	3.2
Roberts	0.1	141.9	NA	NA	NA	NA	NA	NA	NA	NA	NA	NA	NA	NA
Robertson	2.3	135.1	D	D	D	0.6	52	447	172.3	10.2	D	D	D	D
Rockwall	0.0	0.0	67	523	482.4	34.2	287	5,527	1,834.3	166.7	107	343	115.5	15.2
Runnels	3.8	362.1	5	19	22.0	0.7	44	428	123.9	10.4	NA	NA	NA	NA
Rusk	5.8	108.7	27	396	219.1	20.1	99	1,120	337.9	30.7	21	95	19.0	4.2
Sabine	0.8	73.3	NA	NA	NA	NA	37	316	61.1	5.9	NA	NA	NA	NA
San Augustine	0.8	95.6	4	14	3.4	0.4	25	210	60.8	5.0	NA	NA	NA	NA
San Jacinto	2.1	77.7	9	50	17.5	2.7	30	216	54.2	4.8	6	11	1.7	0.5
San Patricio	1.3	18.6	34	187	211.2	9.1	148	2,463	776.2	68.0	54	170	26.9	4.8
San Saba	1.4	242.3	8	46	9.0	2.1	32	158	40.8	3.5	NA	NA	NA	NA
Schleicher	0.4	118.3	NA	NA	NA	NA	8	56	10.7	1.1	NA	NA	NA	NA
Scurry	0.1	7.4	D	D	D	D	57	711	263.5	19.0	18	58	8.0	2.1
Shackelford	0.0	0.0	4	D	3.9	D	17	117	23.0	2.6	8	26	4.6	1.3
Shelby	4.8	188.2	13	94	79.1	6.3	81	891	233.6	22.2	18	47	7.4	1.1
Sherman	0.4	143.2	9	D	94.6	D	10	93	58.9	2.6	NA	NA	NA	NA
Smith	42.9	192.4	226	2,841	1,180.6	145.3	839	13,251	4,074.6	364.5	333	1,177	262.1	51.6
Somervell	1.2	135.0	5	26	12.4	1.2	28	192	44.5	3.6	9	22	2.0	0.4
Starr	7.8	122.4	19	110	127.5	2.7	130	1,887	474.6	41.5	13	31	3.9	0.8
Stephens	9.3	987.3	4	32	10.6	1.8	40	371	107.1	8.8	6	21	2.6	0.4
Sterling	0.2	140.5	NA	NA	NA	NA	4	35	22.4	0.9	NA	NA	NA	NA
Stonewall	0.0	0.0	3	47	34.5	2.7	8	36	9.7	0.7	NA	NA	NA	NA
Sutton	0.8	207.0	4	29	28.3	2.1	23	145	59.2	4.1	4	D	3.7	D
Swisher	0.6	78.3	12	53	26.1	1.9	17	176	57.0	3.6	NA	NA	NA	NA
Tarrant	26.5	13.4	1,960	37,008	32,115.2	2,331.4	6,078	106,920	36,282.1	2,996.0	2,171	13,084	3,580.7	637.9
Taylor	0.5	3.4	147	1,918	2,086.0	96.8	538	8,113	2,430.4	212.7	177	811	205.2	32.9
Terrell	0.1	155.3	NA	NA	NA	NA	4	18	4.9	0.6	NA	NA	NA	NA
Terry	0.2	13.3	23	344	164.8	17.7	36	339	104.8	9.2	4	8	0.8	0.2
Throckmorton	0.1	31.7	4	11	2.5	0.4	9	29	6.5	0.7	NA	NA	NA	NA
Titus	5.4	164.0	34	275	254.7	11.3	113	1,747	488.9	44.9	25	64	12.1	2.0

1 Merchant wholesalers, except manufacturers' sales branches and offices. 2. Employer establishments.

STATE County	Professional, scientific, and technical services, 2017				Manufacturing, 2017				Accommodation and food services, 2017			
	Number of establish-ments	Number of employees	Sales (mil dol)	Average payroll (mil dol)	Number of establish-ments	Number of employees	Sales (mil dol)	Average payroll (mil dol)	Number of establis-hments	Number of employees	Sales (mil dol)	Annual payroll (mil dol)
	147	148	149	150	151	152	153	154	155	156	157	158
TEXAS—Cont'd												
Mason	13	40	3.7	1.5	6	15	3.2	0.8	15	124	5.5	1.7
Matagorda	40	306	30.9	12.0	32	971	1,636.9	83.9	86	979	59.7	16.4
Maverick	D	D	D	D	14	301	72.0	13.0	78	1,460	75.4	20.3
Medina	69	395	31.9	13.4	23	319	58.6	12.9	83	1,262	57.6	16.2
Menard	D	D	0.9	D	NA	NA	NA	NA	3	25	1.0	0.3
Midland	D	D	D	D	140	2,831	1,177.2	168.1	D	D	D	D
Milam	D	D	D	D	14	147	98.1	7.8	46	466	22.0	5.6
Mills	5	15	1.9	0.5	7	36	7.4	2.4	8	79	3.6	1.1
Mitchell	10	29	4.9	1.4	NA	NA	NA	NA	16	172	7.4	2.0
Montague	47	136	15.0	5.1	17	238	96.7	9.3	35	452	18.4	5.6
Montgomery	D	D	D	D	407	10,069	3,415.5	528.5	990	22,530	1,444.1	396.6
Moore	20	94	11.5	4.3	D	D	D	201.1	47	532	31.7	8.0
Morris	17	127	16.8	7.6	17	1,786	500.6	84.1	17	204	10.3	2.5
Motley	NA	NA	NA	NA	NA	NA	NA	NA	D	D	D	0.1
Nacogdoches	D	D	D	D	62	3,417	1,333.4	140.6	119	2,275	118.8	36.3
Navarro	66	271	40.6	10.4	51	2,731	1,021.1	120.0	68	1,251	61.2	16.6
Newton	9	21	2.0	0.7	D	44	D	1.8	5	11	0.6	0.1
Nolan	31	90	8.9	3.0	9	661	371.9	47.0	42	577	31.3	7.8
Nueces	D	D	D	D	170	6,788	26,024.0	583.0	926	19,524	1,073.9	296.4
Ochiltree	18	108	13.7	5.6	7	18	4.5	0.7	18	296	15.0	4.2
Oldham	NA	NA	NA	NA	NA	NA	NA	NA	D	D	D	D
Orange	83	548	69.9	35.1	72	4,838	5,121.8	439.3	146	2,070	112.9	29.7
Palo Pinto	45	168	19.6	6.6	38	1,110	330.0	55.1	65	816	46.0	11.7
Panola	44	208	30.2	10.0	12	1,060	361.3	40.2	28	407	21.6	5.9
Parker	D	D	D	D	137	2,671	903.3	142.8	211	3,943	211.5	60.8
Parmer	12	44	4.8	1.5	D	D	D	D	8	85	4.4	1.0
Pecos	12	80	5.2	1.1	4	13	6.1	0.5	44	586	45.5	9.8
Polk	71	173	23.3	7.4	16	1,168	334.6	59.9	69	1,041	58.2	15.3
Potter	D	D	D	D	121	6,870	4,359.1	312.1	378	8,044	463.9	122.5
Presidio	NA	NA	NA	NA	D	9	D	0.5	25	320	30.2	7.4
Rains	16	194	20.0	4.3	9	67	10.7	3.8	16	176	9.6	2.4
Randall	232	993	135.2	51.7	66	4,601	1,121.1	405.4	210	4,100	221.0	61.4
Reagan	4	12	1.5	0.3	NA	NA	NA	NA	12	140	10.8	2.2
Real	D	D	2.8	D	5	25	10.8	1.1	16	165	9.7	2.0
Red River	8	23	2.3	1.0	17	336	74.3	13.7	D	D	D	D
Reeves	20	47	11.0	2.2	5	10	7.4	D	42	664	84.9	14.6
Refugio	6	24	1.9	1.1	3	9	1.2	D	18	246	13.1	3.2
Roberts	3	9	1.1	0.3	NA	NA	NA	NA	NA	NA	NA	NA
Robertson	17	58	9.8	1.9	6	127	20.1	5.1	27	486	21.0	6.4
Rockwall	D	D	D	D	63	1,639	559.5	91.0	211	4,954	263.3	76.8
Runnels	14	29	2.8	0.9	14	486	236.1	19.6	17	170	6.5	1.6
Rusk	63	285	39.3	14.4	34	1,324	398.3	59.0	68	879	45.5	12.2
Sabine	14	32	4.3	0.8	D	344	D	21.4	9	D	5.0	D
San Augustine	6	9	1.2	0.3	4	51	12.7	2.2	D	D	D	0.7
San Jacinto	24	43	5.3	1.9	9	92	23.5	5.6	D	D	D	D
San Patricio	D	D	D	D	38	3,261	2,677.3	214.4	142	2,233	126.2	30.6
San Saba	11	32	3.0	1.0	9	41	9.9	1.9	D	D	D	D
Schleicher	4	11	1.0	0.3	NA	NA	NA	NA	NA	NA	NA	NA
Scurry	19	89	12.7	2.1	10	73	81.1	4.6	48	622	27.4	8.2
Shackelford	3	7	0.7	0.2	7	149	22.5	6.8	D	D	D	0.6
Shelby	33	173	32.4	7.1	15	2,261	594.5	77.8	38	505	42.1	9.8
Sherman	NA	NA	NA	NA	NA	NA	NA	NA	NA	NA	NA	NA
Smith	624	4,570	917.0	301.9	184	6,614	4,305.0	340.6	490	10,739	596.4	182.9
Somervell	18	109	15.9	5.2	8	101	29.3	4.4	35	465	44.5	9.8
Starr	D	D	D	D	7	19	2.4	0.7	D	D	D	D
Stephens	15	37	4.0	1.3	12	252	64.3	11.5	19	164	8.9	2.3
Sterling	D	D	1.2	D	NA	NA	NA	NA	4	33	1.0	0.3
Stonewall	NA	NA	NA	NA	NA	NA	NA	NA	D	D	D	0.3
Sutton	13	25	2.0	0.5	NA	NA	NA	NA	13	195	18.4	4.1
Swisher	6	21	1.4	0.7	9	96	21.2	4.4	D	D	D	D
Tarrant	D	D	D	D	1,590	77,734	62,176.0	5,393.5	4,170	99,956	6,194.9	1,686.5
Taylor	D	D	D	D	93	2,244	1,054.7	112.3	325	7,052	363.9	106.7
Terrell	NA	NA	NA	NA	NA	NA	NA	NA	NA	NA	NA	NA
Terry	11	50	5.2	1.4	5	42	13.9	1.8	26	307	15.9	4.1
Throckmorton	NA	NA	NA	NA	NA	NA	NA	NA	3	11	0.4	0.1
Titus	22	115	12.6	4.9	37	5,757	1,703.8	222.6	68	1,104	61.3	16.2

STATE County	Health care and social assistance, 2017				Other services, 2017				Nonemployer businesses, 2019		Value of residential construction authorized by building permits, 2021	
	Number of establish-ments	Number of employees	Receipts (mil dol)	Annual payroll (mil dol)	Number of establish-ments	Number of employees	Receipts (mil dol)	Annual payroll (mil dol)	Number	Receipts (mil dol)	New construction ($1,000)	Number of housing units
	159	160	161	162	163	164	165	166	167	168	169	170
TEXAS—Cont'd												
Mason	12	109	5.6	2.6	D	D	D	0.5	731	31.1	2,900	8
Matagorda	74	1,200	146.2	46.7	65	388	54.0	15.4	3,026	122.7	52,369	506
Maverick	107	4,090	240.3	97.8	39	167	12.3	3.7	5,193	205.2	35,862	135
Medina	81	1,130	77.1	36.8	59	222	29.0	7.2	3,828	195.5	5,785	27
Menard	NA	NA	NA	NA	D	D	0.9	D	310	15.2	NA	NA
Midland	413	7,647	913.3	361.9	301	2,553	455.6	105.2	18,908	1,421.0	174,724	858
Milam	39	1,618	174.9	80.6	31	103	12.5	2.9	1,857	86.8	2,623	25
Mills	12	136	9.0	3.8	D	D	7.4	D	549	19.6	NA	NA
Mitchell	9	214	21.2	9.6	7	18	1.8	0.4	465	16.6	0	0
Montague	35	531	37.5	17.5	33	123	12.2	3.2	2,116	105.4	2,759	22
Montgomery	1,355	22,297	3,232.5	1,157.1	733	5,074	485.8	153.8	59,705	3,294.5	2,907,613	13,750
Moore	43	657	69.7	29.3	35	124	17.7	3.5	1,216	74.1	1,164	5
Morris	18	198	10.7	5.1	12	53	7.9	2.1	772	29.0	758	4
Motley	NA	NA	NA	NA	NA	NA	NA	NA	129	5.6	NA	NA
Nacogdoches	190	3,315	374.3	133.8	82	364	40.2	9.0	4,315	194.8	4,772	29
Navarro	134	2,644	186.6	76.2	59	211	22.5	5.7	3,808	177.8	101,918	478
Newton	11	180	9.0	4.3	3	8	1.5	0.2	663	23.2	NA	NA
Nolan	29	578	54.3	23.9	17	109	22.7	5.0	1,128	38.9	180	1
Nueces	1,094	30,804	2,927.6	1,159.3	540	4,227	620.3	141.6	27,576	1,222.2	454,943	1,950
Ochiltree	19	301	33.5	11.6	26	114	14.3	3.9	774	47.5	0	0
Oldham	NA	NA	NA	NA	NA	NA	NA	NA	193	8.7	0	0
Orange	128	1,462	118.6	46.4	81	699	97.6	24.2	4,951	200.2	42,507	209
Palo Pinto	51	817	109.8	36.0	39	137	16.5	4.5	2,489	130.9	2,664	13
Panola	35	568	58.0	19.3	26	127	13.7	3.9	1,810	88.4	3,000	10
Parker	261	3,345	375.3	135.5	154	789	79.4	25.1	15,591	922.9	169,405	765
Parmer	8	161	13.3	5.6	D	D	D	D	515	31.0	2,133	12
Pecos	17	390	40.2	17.5	19	91	10.6	2.9	1,082	52.5	3,273	13
Polk	78	1,368	128.7	52.0	51	256	24.1	6.4	4,641	217.5	203,128	960
Potter	469	13,427	1,850.9	655.6	239	1,956	252.3	64.0	8,512	484.8	133,003	574
Presidio	5	58	5.4	1.8	NA	NA	NA	NA	843	27.5	1,740	8
Rains	13	D	6.7	D	D	D	D	1.3	1,033	52.1	4,488	25
Randall	D	D	D	D	197	1,272	145.4	40.2	11,779	591.4	34,418	152
Reagan	D	D	D	D	7	24	4.3	1.1	354	17.3	518	3
Real	6	D	6.3	D	NA	NA	NA	NA	466	26.0	0	0
Red River	14	163	12.5	5.0	D	D	0.6	D	969	49.6	2,366	21
Reeves	19	395	32.1	13.0	D	D	D	D	892	50.8	5,984	29
Refugio	11	248	23.4	9.1	7	21	2.1	0.6	549	21.8	5,693	33
Roberts	NA	NA	NA	NA	NA	NA	NA	NA	98	4.2	NA	NA
Robertson	19	388	24.2	11.3	27	83	11.4	2.5	1,374	67.8	6,197	31
Rockwall	312	4,762	738.1	219.2	140	854	85.2	27.4	11,810	729.2	830,605	3,392
Runnels	D	D	D	D	9	27	3.3	0.7	817	39.5	1,305	6
Rusk	79	1,229	96.9	37.5	47	239	22.9	7.1	3,422	148.9	7,994	67
Sabine	23	382	21.8	10.9	11	30	3.6	0.9	716	29.6	0	0
San Augustine	20	380	24.7	11.6	3	5	0.3	0.1	540	19.4	1,305	6
San Jacinto	14	129	7.0	3.1	D	D	3.4	D	2,264	91.0	126,355	575
San Patricio	104	1,608	115.8	48.1	73	356	42.3	11.8	5,123	199.6	121,221	625
San Saba	12	126	8.7	4.1	D	D	D	D	634	25.7	0	0
Schleicher	D	D	D	D	NA	NA	NA	NA	291	11.2	0	0
Scurry	23	581	58.9	25.0	32	201	35.6	7.9	1,095	53.3	1,067	4
Shackelford	4	46	4.5	2.1	3	6	0.9	0.1	500	26.3	NA	NA
Shelby	42	609	43.8	18.2	D	D	D	D	1,728	88.5	665	1
Sherman	NA	NA	NA	NA	3	6	0.6	0.1	242	12.3	1,635	15
Smith	685	22,449	2,985.8	1,095.4	374	2,239	239.2	67.8	20,568	1,099.2	201,056	912
Somervell	19	513	54.7	19.2	16	75	9.6	3.7	927	42.4	218	1
Starr	103	5,086	169.3	88.6	D	D	D	D	7,359	208.9	310	4
Stephens	17	333	25.2	10.8	18	92	5.6	4.8	896	52.1	632	4
Sterling	NA	NA	NA	NA	NA	NA	NA	NA	172	6.8	NA	NA
Stonewall	D	D	D	D	NA	NA	NA	NA	155	7.2	NA	NA
Sutton	D	D	D	D	6	10	1.3	0.3	385	16.8	0	0
Swisher	10	183	17.4	6.4	12	37	2.9	0.7	478	18.1	0	0
Tarrant	5,412	114,635	15,432.2	5,405.9	2,743	21,725	2,796.3	684.7	194,151	9,398.2	3,463,370	18,169
Taylor	404	12,073	1,326.3	513.6	225	1,499	194.7	43.9	10,812	520.4	150,245	882
Terrell	NA	NA	NA	NA	NA	NA	NA	NA	76	2.0	NA	NA
Terry	18	431	35.5	14.2	16	68	6.7	2.0	783	35.8	150	1
Throckmorton	D	D	D	D	D	D	0.6	D	212	7.4	NA	NA
Titus	82	2,224	175.8	72.4	44	203	18.4	5.4	2,088	98.0	1,740	8

STATE County	Government employment and payroll, 2017									Local government finances, 2017				
			March payroll (percent of total)							General revenue				
												Taxes		
													Per capita[1] (dollars)	
	Full-time equivalent employees	March payroll (dollars)	Adminis-tration, judicial, and legal	Police and corrections	Fire protection	Highways and transpor-tation	Health and welfare	Natural resources and utilities	Education and libraries	Total (mil dol)	Inter-govern-mental (mil dol)	Total (mil dol)	Total	Property
	171	172	173	174	175	176	177	178	179	180	181	182	183	184
TEXAS—Cont'd														
Mason	214	674,368	11.1	7.1	0.0	4.9	4.7	9.7	59.5	13.0	4.0	7.7	1,851	1,640
Matagorda	2,161	7,462,387	5.4	8.0	0.0	2.0	22.4	4.1	56.8	319.9	47.1	103.9	2,822	2,636
Maverick	3,062	9,994,336	3.0	7.0	2.0	3.0	4.7	3.9	75.6	210.2	122.0	59.3	1,020	827
Medina	2,350	8,037,563	4.8	6.3	0.1	2.4	12.1	4.2	68.1	220.6	82.7	105.2	2,097	1,953
Menard	146	447,532	3.2	9.3	0.0	1.5	25.2	4.1	49.4	11.0	2.7	4.6	2,191	2,067
Midland	7,596	33,664,386	4.7	7.9	3.5	2.9	29.3	2.4	48.2	982.4	134.3	478.6	2,895	2,149
Milam	1,153	4,037,962	7.5	9.2	0.1	4.5	2.2	2.9	73.4	91.0	35.6	42.2	1,692	1,524
Mills	327	1,086,084	7.1	5.9	0.0	7.8	0.5	4.3	74.1	24.2	10.9	10.7	2,182	1,931
Mitchell	615	1,976,389	8.2	5.8	0.3	2.7	35.8	2.6	43.7	60.1	12.5	20.5	2,499	2,308
Montague	913	2,962,949	4.9	7.1	2.3	3.2	10.9	3.4	62.2	64.9	14.7	34.4	1,771	1,614
Montgomery	18,814	73,051,702	4.8	8.9	5.7	1.7	5.0	3.5	68.2	1,999.4	505.7	1,257.0	2,199	1,935
Moore	1,382	5,222,714	5.9	7.1	1.6	2.1	26.9	5.6	50.0	121.9	24.3	51.1	2,365	2,077
Morris	471	1,467,593	9.3	9.0	0.5	2.8	2.0	2.7	73.5	29.3	9.3	17.4	1,404	1,307
Motley	92	322,465	19.8	1.2	0.2	1.9	10.8	0.4	65.7	7.1	1.4	5.1	4,179	3,487
Nacogdoches	3,205	11,993,798	4.6	6.1	2.5	1.4	25.8	2.3	56.3	287.4	82.8	97.2	1,487	1,286
Navarro	2,758	10,157,929	4.0	8.6	3.0	2.2	2.4	3.1	75.2	243.9	94.5	98.6	2,023	1,651
Newton	539	1,594,597	9.8	5.2	0.1	2.9	0.8	5.2	73.5	53.9	18.9	21.1	1,517	1,442
Nolan	1,238	4,211,547	4.7	7.1	1.9	1.7	31.0	3.8	49.0	120.4	25.0	46.9	3,160	2,687
Nueces	15,544	60,072,732	6.2	10.0	4.7	5.8	3.7	6.7	61.5	1,684.4	456.4	789.4	2,185	1,718
Ochiltree	751	2,510,234	12.8	5.3	2.2	0.8	25.2	3.7	48.7	44.2	11.4	27.2	2,725	2,338
Oldham	256	905,109	7.0	7.6	0.0	2.0	0.0	1.6	81.3	26.4	9.5	10.4	4,924	4,456
Orange	3,505	12,384,125	7.1	12.2	2.1	3.0	0.7	9.5	63.1	283.2	90.2	136.0	1,601	1,362
Palo Pinto	1,510	5,351,012	5.9	7.2	1.7	4.5	27.8	3.8	47.0	155.5	41.7	70.8	2,479	2,211
Panola	1,165	4,316,500	6.1	7.2	0.7	4.6	0.9	2.8	76.4	121.9	28.4	77.9	3,357	3,062
Parker	4,338	17,739,986	6.5	5.7	2.6	2.4	1.7	2.9	76.3	405.5	96.8	248.8	1,863	1,652
Parmer	784	2,562,481	9.5	7.0	0.0	3.8	24.6	1.2	52.8	64.9	18.0	32.2	3,321	3,090
Pecos	1,009	3,481,520	6.7	7.0	0.0	2.3	9.8	7.2	63.1	119.0	19.3	57.7	3,692	3,367
Polk	1,551	5,222,803	6.9	11.5	0.1	3.0	1.2	3.1	73.0	121.2	44.0	64.4	1,314	1,198
Potter	9,282	35,583,891	4.3	11.7	5.5	1.9	4.3	4.3	66.5	823.0	311.6	351.6	2,922	2,008
Presidio	493	1,554,231	10.5	7.9	0.0	3.5	6.2	6.6	64.6	36.4	18.9	13.9	1,955	1,652
Rains	458	1,020,204	13.1	10.6	0.0	3.0	0.6	4.7	67.0	31.8	10.9	16.6	1,415	1,158
Randall	1,792	7,254,356	9.3	21.4	1.3	0.4	0.1	1.7	64.9	146.0	35.7	95.0	709	663
Reagan	446	1,424,626	9.8	7.8	0.4	3.9	24.6	4.0	48.3	61.8	8.3	42.2	11,361	10,348
Real	96	314,765	17.7	13.0	0.0	5.3	1.7	5.4	56.6	11.0	1.0	8.9	2,591	2,218
Red River	547	1,541,912	6.3	6.2	0.6	1.9	1.3	2.4	81.1	47.1	20.6	17.1	1,407	1,131
Reeves	1,529	5,932,035	4.9	36.3	1.3	2.5	24.7	3.5	26.3	191.7	73.5	71.1	4,685	4,282
Refugio	533	1,916,846	7.3	10.0	0.0	4.6	25.7	3.6	47.5	37.2	9.1	21.6	3,006	2,742
Roberts	89	335,619	25.8	7.4	1.8	14.2	0.0	2.8	45.8	14.8	3.3	10.6	11,283	10,394
Robertson	972	2,844,712	9.1	9.1	0.0	3.6	1.1	3.5	73.3	84.4	25.6	50.1	2,920	2,683
Rockwall	3,603	13,505,727	7.0	11.0	1.8	0.9	0.4	2.5	74.0	355.2	77.9	238.8	2,466	2,105
Runnels	642	2,056,985	7.7	6.2	0.2	3.4	26.8	2.9	52.5	50.6	19.0	16.4	1,593	1,368
Rusk	1,793	5,977,953	7.6	10.1	1.8	3.7	1.0	2.7	70.2	144.4	52.7	71.3	1,316	1,182
Sabine	406	1,368,020	9.7	7.0	0.0	2.4	7.2	7.2	64.4	26.3	11.2	11.3	1,088	930
San Augustine	334	1,098,697	12.1	7.4	0.0	2.4	5.8	5.0	66.6	32.5	7.7	17.2	2,075	1,365
San Jacinto	820	2,480,988	7.9	8.3	0.1	4.3	0.0	2.6	76.6	51.6	20.3	28.8	1,022	989
San Patricio	3,809	12,018,785	5.3	9.0	1.3	2.7	8.3	6.2	66.3	306.0	116.0	146.3	2,177	1,880
San Saba	477	1,428,900	4.4	2.8	0.0	41.1	0.7	6.3	43.2	30.0	15.0	13.1	2,192	1,809
Schleicher	254	646,199	8.2	4.4	0.0	5.4	19.0	8.3	53.6	9.9	3.5	4.4	1,487	1,418
Scurry	1,156	4,320,011	5.7	7.0	1.3	2.2	26.9	3.8	52.3	128.2	25.8	53.0	3,117	2,804
Shackelford	189	586,844	11.7	8.2	0.0	5.5	4.4	4.8	65.2	15.2	3.6	8.7	2,643	2,284
Shelby	1,300	4,370,836	5.7	6.5	0.5	2.6	0.7	3.1	80.4	83.1	43.9	31.1	1,232	1,007
Sherman	299	1,255,375	9.3	2.6	0.0	3.3	12.5	6.9	63.1	18.3	3.1	11.9	3,918	3,639
Smith	9,437	33,803,613	7.5	10.5	4.0	2.3	8.3	2.9	63.7	757.5	230.3	392.1	1,726	1,338
Somervell	468	1,782,861	7.3	10.7	0.3	6.8	1.2	5.0	61.0	83.3	6.5	49.6	5,596	5,455
Starr	4,299	14,144,787	4.3	6.2	0.6	2.1	9.0	2.3	73.7	299.5	187.5	67.0	1,044	936
Stephens	561	1,797,939	7.3	8.3	1.8	2.5	27.9	3.9	46.7	31.2	10.1	17.0	1,826	1,650
Sterling	102	428,470	17.0	5.6	0.0	2.8	0.0	2.9	70.1	14.5	2.9	8.8	6,807	6,584
Stonewall	199	660,661	7.2	2.8	0.0	10.8	56.4	1.5	20.8	19.4	4.6	6.2	4,518	4,255
Sutton	378	1,571,493	11.6	4.4	6.6	4.0	20.3	2.6	46.2	24.4	5.2	10.7	2,820	2,537
Swisher	432	1,309,586	3.0	9.1	0.0	2.8	4.8	5.4	74.7	35.5	16.3	13.8	1,856	1,513
Tarrant	79,300	343,925,258	6.3	10.6	4.7	1.5	12.2	4.7	58.8	9,084.7	2,433.2	4,733.3	2,302	1,830
Taylor	5,441	20,363,924	5.9	13.8	5.9	1.8	5.4	5.6	59.9	483.8	184.6	231.7	1,696	1,201
Terrell	101	418,512	26.1	0.0	0.0	9.1	6.2	4.9	36.1	10.3	2.1	7.3	9,012	8,631
Terry	831	2,758,686	6.4	8.9	1.3	2.9	26.0	5.4	48.2	58.0	18.9	24.2	1,947	1,776
Throckmorton	116	372,158	5.3	0.0	0.0	2.2	36.6	6.1	49.7	5.5	1.9	2.5	1,654	1,477
Titus	2,435	8,602,385	2.7	4.7	1.4	1.1	26.8	2.3	60.0	208.6	103.6	52.9	1,621	1,340

1. Based on the resident population estimated as of July 1 of the year shown.

STATE County	Local government finances, 2017 (cont.) — Direct general expenditure — Total (mil dol)	Per capita[1] (dollars)	Percent of total for: Education	Health and hospitals	Police protection	Public welfare	Highways	Debt outstanding — Total (mil dol)	Per capita[1] (dollars)	Government employment, 2020 — Federal civilian	Federal military	State and local	Individual income tax returns, 2019 — Number of returns	Mean adjusted gross income	Mean income tax
	185	186	187	188	189	190	191	192	193	194	195	196	197	198	199
TEXAS—Cont'd															
Mason	18.6	4,444	63.2	2.9	5.4	0.0	7.0	5.1	1,222	17	8	280	2,100	55,844	5,779
Matagorda	321.0	8,722	27.6	54.3	2.9	0.1	3.0	173.4	4,711	82	70	2,350	16,680	57,894	5,725
Maverick	427.0	7,349	31.0	1.8	2.3	0.1	2.6	224.9	3,871	973	110	5,126	26,970	39,337	2,363
Medina	212.0	4,224	65.5	11.8	3.1	0.4	2.6	220.7	4,397	75	96	3,143	22,600	62,523	6,301
Menard	10.7	5,091	39.6	0.0	5.6	24.8	3.0	2.7	1,267	11	4	203	950	44,424	3,731
Midland	907.5	5,490	36.5	36.3	4.2	0.0	2.2	941.9	5,698	597	338	8,587	81,290	122,202	21,266
Milam	80.1	3,212	59.8	2.2	5.7	0.8	8.0	79.5	3,188	66	46	1,241	11,100	50,017	4,538
Mills	30.4	6,183	47.8	0.2	14.2	0.4	5.5	19.6	3,987	16	9	358	2,170	48,933	4,114
Mitchell	59.6	7,252	35.7	42.1	2.8	0.1	3.9	54.9	6,680	20	13	913	2,930	58,446	5,854
Montague	67.8	3,494	53.8	13.4	5.2	0.4	5.8	40.5	2,087	59	38	1,149	9,140	59,199	6,193
Montgomery	2,275.2	3,980	59.1	4.8	5.3	0.1	4.6	5,114.7	8,948	1,324	1,197	28,538	282,160	98,412	14,785
Moore	118.6	5,492	40.2	31.6	4.3	0.1	3.1	60.4	2,798	73	39	1,624	9,530	48,817	4,076
Morris	88.7	7,169	22.5	0.0	71.9	0.2	0.3	12.5	1,011	33	23	634	5,610	44,525	3,649
Motley	6.2	5,090	43.2	2.7	7.1	0.7	7.5	1.0	794	9	4	102	480	40,996	2,758
Nacogdoches	280.6	4,295	37.1	32.9	4.6	0.2	3.0	211.3	3,234	158	122	5,051	26,400	51,744	5,081
Navarro	278.3	5,710	63.2	1.3	5.8	0.3	5.4	235.2	4,825	109	96	3,116	22,570	49,775	4,573
Newton	63.9	4,592	39.1	0.0	8.4	1.7	4.2	28.9	2,075	26	24	566	5,020	51,582	4,202
Nolan	134.5	9,058	36.0	36.3	3.8	0.1	2.8	100.5	6,764	39	28	1,586	6,600	51,617	4,820
Nueces	1,707.1	4,726	47.8	8.7	5.9	0.1	3.6	3,368.1	9,324	5,933	2,473	21,805	162,790	57,993	6,306
Ochiltree	43.4	4,342	57.4	0.7	8.1	0.0	8.2	28.6	2,859	25	18	807	4,320	60,848	5,875
Oldham	35.3	16,791	81.1	0.0	3.3	0.1	1.3	48.6	23,088	8	4	317	960	57,357	5,782
Orange	284.1	3,344	53.6	0.5	8.0	0.2	2.9	747.9	8,802	135	157	4,016	36,940	62,146	5,975
Palo Pinto	151.8	5,320	36.4	31.7	4.1	0.1	3.8	84.9	2,974	61	56	1,795	13,020	56,199	5,955
Panola	124.4	5,361	68.0	1.2	3.9	0.1	6.1	118.5	5,107	66	44	1,232	10,080	58,153	5,474
Parker	461.5	3,457	62.2	5.4	4.9	0.1	5.4	901.5	6,753	237	282	5,590	69,500	85,403	11,174
Parmer	64.7	6,666	43.6	24.0	4.2	0.6	5.8	14.2	1,463	70	18	795	4,040	43,977	3,617
Pecos	135.6	8,670	42.6	31.2	3.2	0.1	3.3	91.1	5,827	52	26	1,664	6,550	63,003	6,900
Polk	127.4	2,600	55.6	0.0	5.5	0.6	6.7	240.7	4,913	100	93	2,704	26,090	61,022	6,265
Potter	816.4	6,784	52.7	5.3	6.9	0.0	3.1	735.5	6,112	2,185	297	12,558	51,840	54,738	6,613
Presidio	33.9	4,771	56.6	1.0	3.4	0.1	6.2	22.5	3,171	342	12	539	3,740	44,881	4,126
Rains	32.9	2,808	54.8	3.3	4.5	1.0	8.7	31.4	2,675	23	24	494	5,010	53,919	4,753
Randall	149.8	1,118	56.6	0.1	7.6	0.1	2.0	225.7	1,684	220	294	4,574	65,650	72,239	8,367
Reagan	55.6	14,979	49.8	22.4	3.4	0.3	5.5	82.6	22,247	11	7	437	1,620	85,275	12,646
Real	9.7	2,852	39.0	0.5	9.5	2.1	11.1	7.8	2,272	7	6	195	1,660	51,807	4,751
Red River	44.8	3,679	53.4	10.9	4.1	0.8	6.1	17.1	1,408	43	23	680	5,360	44,015	3,685
Reeves	157.7	10,396	34.1	16.0	1.1	0.0	3.0	132.2	8,716	67	25	1,591	6,030	73,966	10,882
Refugio	52.7	7,340	69.6	8.5	2.2	0.4	2.2	58.2	8,109	22	13	668	3,320	52,491	4,646
Roberts	27.7	29,400	76.5	0.0	2.3	0.1	5.3	27.2	28,893	4	2	97	390	61,133	7,259
Robertson	75.6	4,408	66.3	0.0	5.5	1.4	4.9	36.6	2,136	42	32	973	7,900	49,570	4,442
Rockwall	388.1	4,008	59.8	0.2	5.3	0.2	5.4	1,023.9	10,574	156	209	3,943	50,010	100,529	13,804
Runnels	54.2	5,269	44.0	25.4	2.6	0.1	5.6	15.5	1,509	42	20	880	4,770	49,351	4,282
Rusk	135.6	2,501	60.5	0.3	5.9	0.4	7.4	162.0	2,989	81	92	2,464	21,530	54,589	5,009
Sabine	26.8	2,573	60.5	9.5	3.2	0.2	2.7	39.0	3,741	48	20	494	4,350	55,137	5,120
San Augustine	19.8	2,380	64.0	5.8	9.3	0.0	0.5	18.8	2,265	23	15	425	3,380	45,957	3,786
San Jacinto	43.0	1,523	82.8	0.0	0.0	0.0	0.3	32.2	1,139	37	56	930	11,580	56,479	5,671
San Patricio	335.6	4,994	58.8	6.7	4.8	0.3	8.0	450.9	6,709	106	127	3,874	32,590	56,319	5,370
San Saba	23.7	3,946	51.6	0.6	4.8	1.0	9.3	11.3	1,880	20	10	470	2,500	48,032	4,238
Schleicher	9.0	2,999	73.5	0.3	1.4	0.0	3.5	9.7	3,250	14	5	233	1,170	54,269	4,747
Scurry	125.9	7,404	45.3	30.0	2.7	0.1	4.4	126.9	7,464	38	29	1,559	6,790	64,344	6,616
Shackelford	13.9	4,213	57.8	9.8	3.9	0.4	4.7	3.8	1,163	15	6	215	1,510	66,705	8,020
Shelby	86.6	3,435	71.7	0.0	4.2	0.2	3.7	64.7	2,565	75	47	1,285	10,480	44,152	4,053
Sherman	20.0	6,559	52.1	0.0	4.5	0.3	5.9	1.1	351	9	6	264	1,160	52,602	4,077
Smith	736.2	3,240	58.0	4.9	5.9	0.1	3.6	1,714.9	7,548	751	472	13,279	106,810	65,827	7,741
Somervell	69.9	7,895	48.5	28.0	4.1	0.6	2.7	54.8	6,191	19	17	861	4,150	70,692	7,369
Starr	287.2	4,479	67.3	9.5	3.9	0.0	4.3	251.8	3,926	868	121	4,987	27,230	35,762	1,898
Stephens	34.0	3,663	47.7	2.5	5.0	0.6	4.6	36.2	3,893	20	17	683	3,850	46,372	4,170
Sterling	15.1	11,739	50.6	2.8	2.6	18.8	3.7	21.8	16,963	5	2	152	600	91,460	13,113
Stonewall	17.4	12,636	16.9	63.3	1.7	0.0	7.0	10.2	7,440	14	3	225	600	53,813	4,620
Sutton	24.2	6,383	59.1	17.9	3.1	0.3	4.4	5.5	1,448	9	7	384	1,760	66,840	9,901
Swisher	36.0	4,837	48.0	16.0	5.4	0.3	3.5	7.6	1,025	25	13	715	2,910	46,708	3,993
Tarrant	9,002.9	4,378	45.2	12.1	7.0	0.1	3.7	19,751.6	9,605	16,153	5,226	94,347	995,660	73,558	9,295
Taylor	516.1	3,777	46.7	4.4	6.8	0.5	2.4	443.1	3,243	1,201	4,811	8,843	63,870	59,217	6,257
Terrell	9.6	11,811	40.4	6.4	12.8	0.0	13.8	11.9	14,661	50	1	109	320	53,513	3,978
Terry	62.7	5,044	49.3	30.5	1.8	0.5	2.8	31.3	2,519	29	21	1,008	4,750	46,136	3,819
Throckmorton	5.0	3,309	76.2	0.0	1.7	0.1	2.0	4.1	2,741	9	3	195	670	58,319	6,476
Titus	223.9	6,864	48.4	31.9	2.7	0.1	2.4	334.1	10,242	93	62	2,915	14,300	48,349	4,031

1. Based on the resident population estimated as of July 1 of the year shown.

State / county code	CBSA code[1]	County Type code[2]	STATE County	Land area[3] (sq. mi)	Population, 2021: Total persons 2021	Population, 2021: Rank	Population, 2021: Per square mile	Race alone or in combination, not Hispanic or Latino (percent): White	Black	American Indian, Alaska Native	Asian and Pacific Islancer	Percent Hispanic or Latino[4]	Age (percent): Under 5 years	5 to 17 years	18 to 24 years	25 to 34 years	35 to 44 years	45 to 54 years
				1	2	3	4	5	6	7	8	9	10	11	12	13	14	15
			TEXAS—Cont'd															
48451	41660	3	Tom Green	1,522.0	119,411	530	78.5	53.1	4.3	0.7	2.0	41.3	6.3	13.6	15.5	14.5	12.9	9.9
48453	12420	1	Travis	994.1	1,305,154	32	1,312.9	50.6	8.9	0.7	8.6	33.3	5.6	11.6	12.3	19.5	16.8	13.1
48455		7	Trinity	693.8	13,827	2,163	19.9	78.9	9.4	1.1	0.7	11.3	4.7	11.5	10.0	9.4	10.2	11.3
48457		6	Tyler	924.4	20,077	1,811	21.7	79.8	11.0	1.2	0.8	8.6	4.7	11.2	11.8	13.4	11.4	11.1
48459	30980	3	Upshur	583.0	41,774	1,151	71.7	81.9	8.6	1.5	1.0	9.1	5.6	13.7	12.2	11.5	12.1	11.8
48461		8	Upton	1,241.3	3,265	2,946	2.6	40.8	3.3	1.6	0.5	55.1	6.7	16.4	14.0	11.7	12.9	11.5
48463	46620	6	Uvalde	1,551.9	24,729	1,625	15.9	25.6	0.9	0.4	1.2	72.5	7.5	15.3	14.9	13.5	11.4	11.0
48465	19620	5	Val Verde	3,144.8	47,564	1,030	15.1	15.1	1.7	0.5	1.1	82.4	7.8	16.1	15.5	14.7	12.1	10.6
48467		6	Van Zandt	842.6	61,275	866	72.7	83.9	3.4	1.3	0.8	12.1	5.6	13.1	11.9	10.7	11.6	12.5
48469	47020	3	Victoria	882.1	90,964	660	103.1	44.3	6.4	0.5	1.6	48.3	6.6	14.5	13.6	13.4	12.7	10.5
48471	26660	4	Walker	784.2	77,977	727	99.4	56.9	23.5	0.7	1.5	18.7	3.9	8.3	21.0	14.3	13.7	13.4
48473	26420	1	Waller	513.3	59,781	881	116.5	43.0	23.2	0.7	2.1	32.4	6.2	13.8	23.5	11.2	11.9	10.5
48475		6	Ward	835.6	11,194	2,332	13.4	37.4	5.0	1.1	0.8	57.1	8.3	16.3	13.1	13.5	13.3	10.5
48477	14780	6	Washington	604.2	35,891	1,287	59.4	64.5	16.7	0.6	1.8	17.5	5.1	12.4	14.9	9.8	10.9	10.5
48479	29700	2	Webb	3,361.5	267,945	264	79.7	3.7	0.4	0.1	0.5	95.4	8.3	18.2	16.7	13.7	12.3	11.9
48481	20900	4	Wharton	1,086.1	41,721	1,153	38.4	43.3	12.7	0.4	0.7	43.7	7.0	14.3	13.6	12.0	12.2	10.7
48483		9	Wheeler	914.5	4,927	2,826	5.4	70.5	3.3	1.3	1.0	25.5	5.1	15.0	11.3	10.7	12.2	11.5
48485	48660	3	Wichita	627.6	130,069	498	207.2	65.6	11.7	1.4	3.1	20.7	6.1	12.9	16.7	14.6	12.5	10.2
48487	46900	6	Wilbarger	970.9	12,731	2,228	13.1	56.6	8.6	1.5	4.0	31.3	5.9	11.6	13.1	12.9	13.2	11.2
48489	39700	6	Willacy	590.6	20,316	1,802	34.4	8.8	2.3	0.2	0.7	88.1	5.7	13.6	16.8	16.5	13.6	10.7
48491	12420	1	Williamson	1,115.8	643,026	111	576.3	58.2	8.0	0.8	10.3	25.4	5.9	14.3	12.2	14.1	16.9	13.6
48493	41700	1	Wilson	803.7	51,257	980	63.8	56.2	2.1	0.8	0.9	41.0	5.4	13.9	12.4	11.1	13.1	13.5
48495		6	Winkler	841.3	7,415	2,626	8.8	32.9	2.5	0.9	0.9	63.6	7.6	16.2	14.5	12.4	12.7	12.7
48497	19100	1	Wise	904.4	71,714	767	79.3	76.2	2.0	1.5	1.1	20.8	5.8	14.3	12.1	12.2	13.1	12.9
48499		6	Wood	645.2	45,875	1,063	71.1	82.7	5.6	1.2	0.9	11.0	4.5	10.8	11.7	9.5	10.0	10.6
48501		7	Yoakum	799.7	7,607	2,606	9.5	28.5	1.7	0.8	0.7	69.1	9.0	18.9	15.8	12.1	11.9	9.9
48503		7	Young	914.5	17,977	1,926	19.7	77.6	2.0	1.0	0.9	19.8	5.8	13.7	11.8	11.2	12.1	10.9
48505	49820	6	Zapata	998.4	13,908	2,158	13.9	4.3	0.3	0.2	0.2	95.1	7.6	19.7	15.7	11.9	12.0	11.0
48507		7	Zavala	1,297.4	9,534	2,447	7.3	5.0	0.9	0.3	0.2	93.7	7.2	16.4	16.6	13.7	11.4	10.8
49000		0	UTAH	82,376.9	3,337,975	X	40.5	79.4	1.8	1.4	5.1	14.8	7.1	16.2	16.4	14.6	14.0	10.7
49001		7	Beaver	2,582.9	7,249	2,643	2.8	84.9	0.7	1.4	1.7	12.7	7.1	17.9	15.5	10.2	13.0	9.7
49003	36260	2	Box Elder	5,745.6	59,688	883	10.4	88.1	0.8	1.3	1.8	9.8	7.4	18.0	14.4	12.6	13.9	10.3
49005	30860	3	Cache	1,164.7	137,417	475	118.0	84.7	1.3	1.0	3.6	11.2	7.6	16.9	23.9	13.9	11.8	8.7
49007	39220	7	Carbon	1,479.2	20,372	1,800	13.8	83.6	1.1	1.7	1.5	13.8	5.9	14.8	14.4	11.4	12.9	10.4
49009		9	Daggett	697.0	976	3,107	1.4	92.2	1.6	1.1	1.3	6.5	4.7	12.3	10.7	6.7	12.5	12.2
49011	36260	2	Davis	299.1	367,285	201	1,228.0	84.5	1.9	0.9	4.6	10.7	7.2	18.0	15.0	13.7	15.2	11.0
49013		7	Duchesne	3,235.3	19,790	1,831	6.1	86.6	0.9	4.8	1.7	8.6	8.0	19.2	13.7	11.4	14.4	10.1
49015		7	Emery	4,462.3	9,967	2,407	2.2	91.1	0.8	1.4	1.1	6.8	6.3	16.4	13.7	10.3	12.6	10.6
49017		9	Garfield	5,175.1	5,129	2,812	1.0	89.6	1.0	2.8	1.9	6.4	5.3	12.0	12.4	11.1	12.2	9.8
49019		7	Grand	3,672.7	9,663	2,440	2.6	82.2	1.4	4.5	3.0	10.8	5.2	11.9	10.2	13.9	13.8	11.3
49021	16260	4	Iron	3,296.3	60,519	873	18.4	86.5	1.0	2.4	2.3	9.7	6.9	16.0	19.9	12.9	12.1	9.2
49023	39340	2	Juab	3,391.7	12,155	2,272	3.6	92.2	1.0	1.5	1.2	5.7	8.2	19.4	15.9	12.4	13.5	10.1
49025		6	Kane	3,989.9	7,992	2,578	2.0	91.4	1.4	2.4	1.6	5.2	5.7	13.4	10.9	10.6	12.2	9.8
49027		7	Millard	6,785.5	13,164	2,203	1.9	84.3	0.9	1.7	2.1	12.5	7.4	18.1	13.8	10.3	12.4	9.7
49029	36260	2	Morgan	609.2	12,657	2,231	20.8	95.5	0.8	0.6	1.1	3.0	6.1	21.0	16.0	8.8	14.2	11.9
49031		9	Piute	758.4	1,487	3,079	2.0	90.4	1.1	0.8	1.2	7.9	4.6	12.2	13.2	9.2	9.9	10.0
49033		8	Rich	1,028.8	2,597	2,990	2.5	92.3	1.0	0.8	0.3	6.5	6.0	17.2	12.9	9.8	12.9	9.5
49035	41620	1	Salt Lake	742.1	1,186,421	37	1,598.7	71.9	2.5	1.2	7.8	19.3	6.6	14.7	14.2	16.3	15.0	11.6
49037		7	San Juan	7,819.8	14,489	2,119	1.9	46.3	0.9	47.4	1.3	6.1	6.1	17.0	14.9	12.3	11.3	11.1
49039		6	Sanpete	1,589.9	29,106	1,452	18.3	87.2	1.4	1.5	2.1	9.4	6.2	13.0	19.2	12.4	13.2	11.0
49041		7	Sevier	1,910.4	21,906	1,722	11.5	92.6	0.8	1.6	1.0	5.3	6.8	16.1	13.9	11.1	13.4	10.4
49043	25720	4	Summit	1,870.6	43,093	1,125	23.0	85.8	1.2	0.7	3.0	10.9	4.8	13.5	12.8	11.2	13.2	14.7
49045	41620	1	Tooele	6,941.9	76,640	738	11.0	82.5	1.4	1.4	2.6	14.2	7.3	18.5	14.6	13.9	15.5	11.9
49047	46860	7	Uintah	4,482.4	36,204	1,277	8.1	83.0	0.9	7.6	1.7	8.7	7.6	18.6	14.0	13.0	14.9	10.3
49049	39340	2	Utah	2,004.1	684,986	99	341.8	83.4	1.2	0.9	4.8	12.7	8.6	18.2	21.9	15.0	12.6	9.1
49051	25720	6	Wasatch	1,177.0	36,173	1,279	30.7	83.9	0.9	0.7	1.9	13.9	6.3	17.6	14.4	10.8	14.4	12.1
49053	41100	3	Washington	2,427.4	191,226	358	78.8	85.0	1.1	1.6	3.1	11.3	6.0	14.3	13.7	11.3	12.1	9.9
49055		9	Wayne	2,461.0	2,558	2,992	1.0	91.4	1.1	1.2	2.0	6.4	6.0	12.5	11.9	10.0	11.6	10.6
49057	36260	2	Weber	576.3	267,066	266	463.4	77.4	2.0	1.1	3.1	18.8	6.9	15.6	14.5	15.2	14.2	11.1
50000		0	VERMONT	9,217.9	645,570	X	70.0	94.1	2.0	1.1	2.6	2.2	4.4	10.3	13.6	12.0	12.0	12.0
50001		6	Addison	766.1	37,260	1,244	48.6	94.0	1.8	0.9	2.7	2.7	4.0	9.0	16.3	10.6	11.1	12.1
50003	13540	6	Bennington	674.8	37,312	1,242	55.3	94.6	1.8	0.9	1.7	2.6	4.4	10.6	12.9	9.6	10.7	12.0
50005		7	Caledonia	648.8	30,403	1,423	46.9	95.8	1.3	1.3	1.2	2.0	4.5	10.6	12.8	10.9	11.4	12.6

1. CBSA = Core Based Statistical Area. See Appendix A for explanation. See Appendix B for list of metropolitan areas with component counties. 2. County type code from the Economic Research Service of USDA Rural-Urban Continuum Codes. See Appendix A for definition. 3. Dry land or land partially or temporarily covered by water. 4. May be of any race.

STATE County	Population, 2021 (cont.)				Population change, 2000–2021							Households, 2016–2020				
	Age (percent) (cont.)				Total persons		Percent change		Components of change, 2020–2021					Percent		
	55 to 64 years	65 to 74 years	75 years and over	Percent female	2010	2020	2010–2020	2020–2021	Births	Deaths	Net Migration	Number	Persons per household	Family house-holds	Female family house-holder[1]	One person
	16	17	18	19	20	21	22	23	24	25	26	27	28	29	30	31
TEXAS—Cont'd																
Tom Green	11.2	9.5	6.5	50.1	110,224	120,003	8.9	-0.5	1,863	1,583	-875	42,953	2.6	64.0	11.4	29.5
Travis	10.4	7.1	3.6	49.5	1,024,266	1,290,188	26.0	1.2	18,605	9,368	5,424	491,531	2.5	57.0	9.8	30.6
Trinity	15.9	16.2	10.8	51.6	14,585	13,602	-6.7	1.7	146	325	412	6,105	2.4	70.7	8.7	23.4
Tyler	13.4	13.2	10.0	46.6	21,766	19,798	-9.0	1.4	249	381	414	7,109	2.7	66.0	12.1	30.7
Upshur	14.2	11.6	7.3	50.8	39,309	40,892	4.0	2.2	531	673	1,037	14,392	2.8	71.3	9.8	25.8
Upton	10.9	9.3	6.6	49.7	3,355	3,308	-1.4	-1.3	57	36	-63	1,344	2.7	67.6	11.8	26.7
Uvalde	10.3	9.1	7.0	50.8	26,405	24,564	-7.0	0.7	488	447	122	8,921	3.0	69.6	17.3	26.9
Val Verde	9.4	7.5	6.3	48.9	48,879	47,586	-2.6	0.0	934	584	-382	16,388	2.9	74.3	15.9	22.7
Van Zandt	14.3	12.0	8.3	51.1	52,579	59,541	13.2	2.9	747	1,039	2,056	20,494	2.7	75.0	12.0	20.5
Victoria	11.9	9.8	6.9	51.0	86,793	91,319	5.2	-0.4	1,510	1,317	-560	32,520	2.8	68.2	13.2	25.7
Walker	11.4	8.7	5.4	41.8	67,861	76,400	12.6	2.1	736	880	1,722	22,515	2.5	57.0	12.1	31.2
Waller	10.9	7.6	4.4	50.1	43,205	56,794	31.5	5.3	840	528	2,699	15,586	3.2	73.3	10.7	19.1
Ward	11.2	7.8	6.0	49.3	10,658	11,644	9.3	-3.9	241	114	-567	4,100	2.8	72.0	9.7	23.8
Washington	13.6	12.9	9.9	51.0	33,718	35,805	6.2	0.2	438	595	241	13,321	2.5	65.4	8.7	30.1
Webb	8.9	6.0	3.9	50.5	250,304	267,114	6.7	0.3	5,540	2,158	-2,607	76,382	3.6	80.3	21.4	17.3
Wharton	12.5	10.4	7.3	50.5	41,280	41,570	0.7	0.4	688	592	47	15,248	2.7	69.5	15.8	27.0
Wheeler	13.4	12.2	8.7	49.7	5,410	4,990	-7.8	-1.3	67	71	-59	2,060	2.5	69.5	15.4	27.8
Wichita	11.9	9.0	6.1	48.0	131,500	129,350	-1.6	0.6	1,961	2,033	762	48,538	2.4	63.5	13.1	30.4
Wilbarger	13.2	10.8	8.1	50.5	13,535	12,887	-4.8	-1.2	199	217	-139	5,008	2.3	59.2	12.7	36.4
Willacy	9.1	8.0	6.0	44.1	22,134	20,164	-8.9	0.8	296	269	122	5,882	3.5	74.4	22.3	22.1
Williamson	10.4	7.9	4.8	50.3	422,679	609,017	44.1	5.6	8,111	4,860	31,024	188,113	3.0	72.3	9.9	22.2
Wilson	14.1	10.4	6.1	49.6	42,918	49,753	15.9	3.0	664	659	1,513	15,975	3.1	82.8	9.4	14.7
Winkler	11.5	7.5	4.8	47.9	7,110	7,791	9.6	-4.8	163	88	-445	2,618	3.0	73.1	11.3	24.1
Wise	14.2	9.6	5.7	49.6	59,127	68,632	16.1	4.5	921	994	3,197	22,254	3.0	77.7	10.8	18.9
Wood	15.5	16.1	11.3	50.0	41,964	44,843	6.9	2.3	497	998	1,555	16,716	2.6	70.4	8.6	26.8
Yoakum	10.4	7.1	4.9	49.0	7,879	7,694	-2.3	-1.1	169	80	-175	2,601	3.3	76.0	10.4	20.6
Young	13.8	12.3	8.4	49.8	18,550	17,867	-3.7	0.6	262	356	205	7,491	2.4	68.9	11.6	27.5
Zapata	9.0	7.6	5.5	50.0	14,018	13,889	-0.9	0.1	243	150	-75	4,689	3.0	69.4	19.5	26.7
Zavala	9.6	8.7	5.6	48.8	11,677	9,670	-17.2	-1.4	200	159	-175	3,674	3.2	82.7	21.1	14.9
UTAH	9.3	7.3	4.4	49.4	2,763,885	3,271,616	18.4	2.0	56,780	27,872	37,304	1,003,345	3.1	74.4	9.0	19.5
Beaver	11.2	10.1	5.4	48.6	6,629	7,072	6.7	2.5	112	68	133	2,213	3.0	79.9	4.4	19.0
Box Elder	10.4	7.8	5.0	48.8	49,975	57,666	15.4	3.5	999	611	1,648	17,811	3.1	76.7	6.8	20.9
Cache	7.3	6.0	4.0	49.9	112,656	133,154	18.2	3.2	2,517	831	2,578	39,581	3.1	76.3	8.1	15.2
Carbon	11.7	11.8	6.8	50.0	21,403	20,412	-4.6	-0.2	290	298	-33	7,802	2.6	67.0	8.7	29.1
Daggett	15.2	16.3	9.5	44.2	1,059	935	-11.7	4.4	14	10	37	169	3.0	79.3	0.6	20.7
Davis	9.3	6.7	4.0	49.2	306,479	362,679	18.3	1.3	6,040	2,832	1,284	107,104	3.3	79.9	8.7	16.0
Duchesne	10.4	7.8	5.1	48.9	18,607	19,596	5.3	1.0	345	187	31	7,038	2.8	77.5	9.1	19.0
Emery	12.2	11.3	6.7	49.0	10,976	9,825	-10.5	1.4	139	130	134	3,732	2.7	74.4	6.6	22.7
Garfield	13.4	14.8	9.0	47.3	5,172	5,083	-1.7	0.9	66	64	44	1,851	2.6	70.9	9.2	23.9
Grand	13.4	13.1	7.2	49.8	9,225	9,669	4.8	-0.1	121	92	-34	4,442	2.2	65.9	11.8	29.0
Iron	9.3	8.7	4.9	49.9	46,163	57,289	24.1	5.6	998	518	2,781	17,381	3.0	73.8	8.5	19.3
Juab	8.8	7.4	4.4	48.2	10,246	11,786	15.0	3.1	228	119	262	3,478	3.3	81.8	10.1	15.4
Kane	13.7	14.8	8.8	49.6	7,125	7,667	7.6	4.2	104	91	317	2,847	2.6	59.2	6.3	33.6
Millard	10.8	10.3	7.2	48.3	12,503	12,975	3.8	1.5	229	174	134	4,293	3.0	81.1	7.6	17.8
Morgan	9.7	7.7	4.6	48.2	9,469	12,295	29.8	2.9	169	87	283	3,434	3.5	90.0	3.9	8.5
Piute	12.8	16.4	11.6	48.6	1,556	1,438	-7.6	3.4	20	16	47	590	3.1	64.4	3.9	34.1
Rich	12.1	11.7	7.8	46.9	2,264	2,510	10.9	3.5	38	16	67	641	3.8	81.9	6.6	16.5
Salt Lake	9.9	7.4	4.2	49.5	1,029,655	1,185,238	15.1	0.1	19,007	10,432	-7,604	383,324	3.0	69.2	10.1	23.3
San Juan	12.4	9.1	5.8	50.0	14,746	14,518	-1.5	-0.2	201	220	-14	4,577	3.3	73.7	16.3	22.2
Sanpete	10.2	9.3	5.5	46.9	27,822	28,437	2.2	2.4	454	318	536	8,887	3.1	77.0	4.5	18.8
Sevier	11.3	10.4	6.7	49.0	20,802	21,522	3.5	1.8	342	292	336	7,487	2.8	76.6	9.3	20.1
Summit	15.0	10.2	4.5	48.6	36,324	42,357	16.6	1.7	487	256	505	14,474	2.9	73.8	7.2	20.1
Tooele	9.1	6.1	3.2	49.0	58,218	72,698	24.9	5.4	1,235	540	3,281	21,147	3.3	81.2	10.5	15.1
Uintah	9.8	7.7	4.3	49.2	32,588	35,620	9.3	1.6	651	377	303	10,739	3.3	70.3	9.4	26.0
Utah	6.7	4.8	3.1	49.2	516,564	659,399	27.7	3.9	14,403	3,993	15,158	171,899	3.5	81.3	7.4	12.2
Wasatch	11.6	8.7	4.2	48.6	23,530	34,788	47.8	4.0	480	269	1,181	10,505	3.1	76.7	4.6	18.4
Washington	10.6	12.6	9.5	50.1	138,115	180,279	30.5	6.1	2,660	2,342	10,772	59,699	2.9	75.2	8.1	20.7
Wayne	14.4	14.7	8.2	48.6	2,778	2,486	-10.5	2.9	41	37	68	995	2.7	77.2	4.8	19.7
Weber	10.4	7.6	4.5	49.3	231,236	262,223	13.4	1.8	4,390	2,652	3,069	85,205	3.0	72.9	10.4	21.4
VERMONT	14.9	12.8	7.9	50.3	625,741	643,077	2.8	0.4	6,432	8,688	4,752	262,852	2.3	59.8	8.6	30.7
Addison	15.1	13.8	8.1	49.9	36,821	37,363	1.5	-0.3	345	515	62	14,700	2.3	61.6	7.6	29.9
Bennington	16.1	14.0	9.7	50.8	37,125	37,347	0.6	-0.1	346	665	288	14,585	2.3	61.6	9.7	31.8
Caledonia	15.2	14.1	8.0	49.8	31,227	30,233	-3.2	0.6	326	460	308	12,618	2.3	62.7	9.4	29.1

1. No spouse present.

STATE County	Persons in group quarters, 2021	Daytime Population, 2016–2020		Births, 2021		Deaths, 2021		Persons under 65 with no health insurance, 2019		Medicare, 2021			COVID-19 Deaths, 2020	
		Number	Employment/ residence ratio	Total	Rate[1]	Number	Rate[1]	Number	Percent	Total beneficiaries	Enrolled in Original Medicare	Enrolled in Medicare Advantage	Number	Rate[1]
	32	33	34	35	36	37	38	39	40	41	42	43	44	45
TEXAS—Cont'd														
Tom Green	4,814	118,679	1.0	1,485	12.4	1,264	10.6	16,924	17.6	22,364	14,341	8,023	202	1.7
Travis	21,743	1,386,440	1.2	14,929	11.5	7,630	5.9	185,356	16.5	140,541	91,028	49,513	617	0.5
Trinity	94	12,549	0.6	122	8.9	257	18.7	2,283	21.5	4,254	2,496	1,758	11	0.8
Tyler	1,950	20,499	0.8	211	10.6	306	15.3	2,983	20.1	5,107	3,248	1,859	20	1.0
Upshur	337	33,982	0.6	430	10.4	535	12.9	6,255	18.6	8,930	5,481	3,449	54	1.3
Upton	29	4,026	1.3	47	14.3	24	7.3	630	20.5	587	400	187	D	D
Uvalde	339	27,471	1.1	391	15.9	364	14.8	5,374	24.9	5,435	3,385	2,049	43	1.8
Val Verde	1,641	47,519	0.9	742	15.6	482	10.1	9,402	23.6	8,585	5,235	3,350	167	3.5
Van Zandt	511	48,216	0.7	607	10.0	833	13.8	10,703	23.9	13,046	7,938	5,108	78	1.3
Victoria	1,671	93,864	1.0	1,224	13.4	1,043	11.4	15,208	20.2	17,809	11,014	6,795	138	1.5
Walker	17,768	75,580	1.1	577	7.5	735	9.5	8,758	19.2	10,443	5,737	4,706	104	1.4
Waller	4,479	52,249	0.9	660	11.3	431	7.4	10,533	23.9	7,780	4,533	3,246	32	0.6
Ward	66	12,319	1.1	197	17.2	87	7.6	2,180	21.2	1,867	1,318	550	13	1.1
Washington	2,212	36,681	1.1	364	10.1	501	14.0	5,103	19.7	8,758	6,156	2,601	67	1.9
Webb	3,231	273,707	1.0	4,482	16.7	1,713	6.4	73,316	30.2	33,804	20,866	12,938	535	2.0
Wharton	365	40,227	0.9	546	13.1	471	11.3	8,663	25.6	8,499	5,594	2,905	82	2.0
Wheeler	34	5,321	1.1	56	11.3	64	12.9	1,058	26.2	1,114	892	223	11	2.2
Wichita	12,025	137,083	1.1	1,573	12.1	1,678	12.9	18,616	18.6	24,950	19,293	5,658	253	2.0
Wilbarger	618	13,204	1.1	159	12.4	177	13.8	2,192	21.8	2,811	1,937	874	40	3.1
Willacy	3,060	19,554	0.8	236	11.7	212	10.5	3,443	23.4	3,630	1,612	2,017	68	3.4
Williamson	3,829	506,219	0.8	6,557	10.4	3,961	6.3	63,856	12.4	83,220	52,941	30,279	280	0.5
Wilson	282	39,180	0.5	552	10.9	545	10.8	7,054	16.6	9,489	5,541	3,948	39	0.8
Winkler	82	9,565	1.5	141	18.6	67	8.8	1,458	21.0	1,064	765	299	18	2.3
Wise	558	60,717	0.8	746	10.6	786	11.2	12,717	21.6	12,283	7,557	4,726	83	1.2
Wood	1,506	41,453	0.8	398	8.8	825	18.2	6,987	22.2	14,805	9,448	5,357	81	1.8
Yoakum	23	9,155	1.2	138	18.1	56	7.3	2,004	26.2	1,237	861	376	23	3.0
Young	204	18,284	1.0	215	12.0	276	15.4	3,309	23.5	4,376	3,554	823	33	1.8
Zapata	16	14,128	1.0	193	13.9	130	9.4	3,521	29.3	2,007	1,275	732	22	1.6
Zavala	294	10,980	0.8	166	17.3	119	12.4	2,076	21.9	2,058	969	1,089	29	3.0
UTAH	47,057	3,153,625	1.0	45,159	13.6	22,167	6.7	298,395	10.7	414,730	248,617	166,113	1,500	0.5
Beaver	22	6,568	1.0	93	13.0	55	7.7	747	13.2	1,263	1,159	105	D	D
Box Elder	290	51,794	0.9	788	13.4	481	8.2	4,863	10.1	8,637	4,999	3,638	31	0.5
Cache	3,969	126,148	1.0	1,997	14.7	662	4.9	10,396	9.4	14,643	7,294	7,350	34	0.3
Carbon	448	20,752	1.0	233	11.4	238	11.7	1,611	10.0	4,515	3,735	780	10	0.5
Daggett	0	641	1.2	9	9.3	7	7.3	64	9.3	243	187	57	D	D
Davis	2,887	314,850	0.8	4,781	13.1	2,218	6.1	25,911	8.1	42,003	25,339	16,664	113	0.3
Duchesne	226	20,132	1.0	269	13.7	146	7.4	2,526	14.8	3,076	2,322	754	D	D
Emery	26	9,393	0.8	114	11.5	101	10.2	806	9.9	2,101	1,766	335	D	D
Garfield	171	4,931	1.0	52	10.2	53	10.4	632	17.4	1,199	1,054	144	D	D
Grand	107	10,350	1.1	93	9.6	74	7.7	1,265	16.4	1,999	1,936	63	D	D
Iron	1,107	52,029	1.0	804	13.6	403	6.8	5,683	12.3	8,754	6,273	2,481	20	0.3
Juab	65	10,719	0.8	174	14.5	98	8.2	1,158	11.1	1,703	1,412	291	D	D
Kane	226	8,266	1.2	85	10.9	67	8.6	586	10.2	1,999	1,893	105	D	D
Millard	135	12,883	1.0	184	14.1	131	10.0	1,581	15.0	2,449	2,161	288	D	D
Morgan	0	9,740	0.6	124	9.9	70	5.6	853	7.9	1,646	1,039	607	D	D
Piute	37	1,651	0.6	16	10.9	14	9.6	132	13.2	422	372	50	D	D
Rich	1	2,303	0.9	30	11.8	11	4.3	213	10.6	450	326	125	D	D
Salt Lake	14,722	1,233,747	1.2	15,156	12.8	8,357	7.0	115,752	11.4	145,655	78,066	67,589	665	0.6
San Juan	218	14,651	0.9	154	10.6	176	12.1	2,197	17.5	2,257	2,204	54	45	3.1
Sanpete	2,533	28,447	0.8	364	12.6	248	8.6	3,483	14.8	4,971	3,945	1,026	14	0.5
Sevier	248	21,871	1.1	273	12.6	232	10.7	2,073	11.8	4,292	3,566	726	D	D
Summit	80	47,108	1.2	396	9.3	218	5.1	3,728	10.1	6,332	4,243	2,090	D	D
Tooele	229	57,547	0.6	989	13.2	424	5.7	6,823	10.5	8,207	5,414	2,793	20	0.3
Uintah	214	35,361	1.0	525	14.6	283	7.9	5,076	16.2	4,759	3,477	1,283	17	0.5
Utah	14,161	603,510	0.9	11,384	16.9	3,128	4.6	53,785	9.4	58,318	31,774	26,544	266	0.4
Wasatch	179	28,104	0.7	389	10.9	219	6.2	3,419	11.5	4,571	2,700	1,871	18	0.5
Washington	2,074	173,307	1.0	2,138	11.5	1,901	10.2	20,380	15.0	40,871	27,164	13,706	123	0.7
Wayne	3	2,749	1.0	31	12.3	26	10.3	327	15.7	663	587	77	D	D
Weber	2,679	244,073	0.9	3,514	13.3	2,126	8.0	22,325	9.9	36,734	22,215	14,519	124	0.5
VERMONT	25,732	622,230	1.0	5,057	7.9	6,884	10.7	27,121	5.7	151,251	129,392	21,859	122	0.2
Addison	2,949	34,339	0.9	279	7.5	414	11.1	1,650	6.2	8,902	7,153	1,749	D	D
Bennington	1,496	37,080	1.1	285	7.6	547	14.7	1,598	6.1	10,078	8,571	1,507	D	D
Caledonia	1,151	27,879	0.9	253	8.4	363	12.0	1,320	5.9	7,780	6,804	976	D	D

1. Per 1,000 estimated resident population.

STATE County	COVID-19 Vaccinations, 2021–2022		Education								Money income, 2016–2020				Income and poverty, 2020			
			School enrollment and attainment, 2016–2020				Local government expenditures,[3] 2018–2019				Households					Percent below poverty level		
			Enrollment[1]		Attainment[2] (percent)							Percent						
	Number	Percent[5]	Total	Percent private	High school graduate or less	Bachelor's degree or more	Total current spending (mil dol)	Current spending per student (dollars)	Per capita income[4]	Median income (dollars)	with income of less than $50,000	with income of $200,000 or more	Median household income (dollars)	All persons	Children under 18 years	Children 5 to 17 years in families
	46	47	48	49	50	51	52	53	54	55	56	57	58	59	60	61
TEXAS—Cont'd																
Tom Green	60,357	50.6	31,025	10.2	42.7	25.0	201.0	9,395	29,547	57,670	44.4	3.9	55,990	12.0	16.6	15.5
Travis	893,978	70.2	311,505	14.8	25.5	51.5	1,675.0	10,337	45,453	80,668	30.2	12.6	82,605	10.2	10.9	10.7
Trinity	5,811	39.7	2,604	6.5	53.2	13.6	26.1	11,546	26,347	44,052	55.0	2.4	47,685	16.8	26.5	25.0
Tyler	7,964	36.7	3,684	4.5	60.4	14.2	38.4	10,627	21,632	47,865	51.8	2.5	48,809	18.9	27.9	27.5
Upshur	14,319	34.3	9,785	13.4	48.2	18.2	77.1	10,316	26,648	54,330	46.0	3.6	58,231	12.6	17.8	17.7
Upton	1,499	41.0	1,119	1.1	59.9	14.0	13.9	16,002	25,994	59,008	41.4	2.0	59,593	12.1	17.0	16.0
Uvalde	14,701	55.0	7,101	7.5	53.7	19.4	59.2	10,908	21,036	45,936	54.0	3.0	49,275	19.0	30.7	29.7
Val Verde	33,097	67.5	13,336	9.1	54.5	19.1	100.3	9,432	21,082	47,675	51.6	2.0	54,346	15.6	24.3	25.1
Van Zandt	21,593	38.2	12,492	12.2	47.7	15.8	93.3	9,090	30,111	57,203	43.5	5.5	57,891	12.9	17.7	17.2
Victoria	44,825	48.7	22,711	14.1	47.1	18.9	152.8	10,096	29,424	58,959	42.8	4.7	53,583	16.5	24.4	22.2
Walker	35,300	48.4	19,583	5.5	53.9	19.0	97.6	9,702	18,598	41,508	60.6	2.2	43,002	18.0	20.8	20.4
Waller	23,210	42.0	18,748	8.6	46.3	23.0	123.9	10,908	27,033	61,752	39.7	7.7	69,460	12.6	17.4	16.4
Ward	4,286	35.7	2,701	2.9	57.0	11.5	22.5	8,686	26,209	61,915	41.6	3.2	57,257	9.8	14.4	14.1
Washington	18,212	50.8	8,976	13.7	43.5	28.1	54.4	9,888	32,649	59,623	41.8	7.7	62,667	11.7	17.6	17.6
Webb	281,688	95.0	89,483	6.5	56.4	18.8	688.8	10,192	19,048	50,296	49.7	3.5	56,588	19.9	30.3	30.4
Wharton	21,091	50.8	10,019	7.3	49.0	18.8	82.2	9,878	26,724	51,770	48.8	2.5	55,887	13.8	20.6	20.7
Wheeler	2,175	43.0	1,208	5.3	50.8	15.3	14.9	14,011	27,737	49,036	51.8	3.1	49,838	13.5	20.3	18.8
Wichita	70,965	53.7	32,893	8.1	44.3	23.1	196.8	9,498	25,568	49,710	50.2	3.0	54,659	16.0	20.9	19.5
Wilbarger	6,744	52.8	2,813	6.0	54.7	14.9	22.7	9,827	23,340	45,121	54.8	0.7	51,774	14.6	21.1	21.9
Willacy	13,992	65.5	5,249	4.9	67.1	9.2	53.3	12,797	18,244	37,906	58.9	1.4	40,190	24.7	34.0	33.7
Williamson	407,181	68.9	152,401	14.4	27.0	41.9	1,117.4	8,910	38,494	90,834	23.9	10.8	91,507	5.6	6.3	6.1
Wilson	28,278	55.4	11,719	12.3	45.8	22.9	84.5	9,255	33,972	80,082	31.5	7.9	74,529	9.4	11.5	10.8
Winkler	3,106	38.8	1,849	2.8	61.5	9.5	24.0	12,365	25,141	63,585	40.3	3.0	77,960	11.8	16.9	16.5
Wise	27,455	39.2	16,279	12.7	48.1	18.8	95.6	9,886	30,693	67,726	34.4	6.2	71,636	10.0	12.4	11.6
Wood	19,652	43.2	8,947	9.2	47.4	19.2	63.3	10,118	30,587	56,749	44.1	4.3	61,886	13.5	21.4	20.3
Yoakum	3,516	40.4	2,467	1.7	60.9	11.8	24.6	11,283	25,417	69,004	34.1	8.4	67,132	10.8	14.9	14.9
Young	7,480	41.5	4,065	9.9	45.6	23.6	32.8	10,074	30,020	52,158	47.9	2.7	54,569	14.8	22.1	19.3
Zapata	8,501	60.0	4,336	1.6	65.9	12.2	36.9	10,473	18,587	32,945	64.9	3.3	39,876	24.6	39.5	36.6
Zavala	6,793	57.4	2,879	3.1	59.3	12.4	26.0	10,675	16,738	40,090	59.4	1.1	34,898	27.2	39.0	37.4
UTAH	2,057,276	64.2	992,124	14.5	29.8	34.7	5,338.2	7,885	30,986	74,197	31.4	7.0	77,785	7.3	7.5	6.7
Beaver	3,207	47.8	1,963	4.5	35.6	25.8	16.1	10,263	24,540	66,705	32.0	1.6	61,858	7.7	11.4	10.4
Box Elder	29,166	52.0	16,322	9.0	37.5	23.7	100.9	8,101	25,835	63,573	36.1	3.3	73,926	6.8	7.8	7.0
Cache	74,856	58.3	49,052	8.2	26.6	38.5	215.2	7,912	24,221	60,530	41.2	4.1	65,391	9.2	8.8	7.4
Carbon	10,188	49.8	5,297	7.7	37.2	16.8	38.0	9,354	23,613	50,328	49.4	1.4	51,902	12.8	15.3	13.9
Daggett	635	66.8	136	3.7	46.5	14.7	3.8	18,684	27,568	74,911	32.0	0.0	63,461	6.5	8.2	7.5
Davis	238,079	67.0	111,396	10.1	25.3	38.2	663.4	7,565	32,819	87,570	23.4	7.8	92,253	5.0	5.2	4.6
Duchesne	8,965	45.0	5,692	8.6	49.2	13.7	47.7	9,018	25,086	61,655	40.7	3.2	61,709	10.6	13.2	12.3
Emery	4,623	46.2	2,937	4.1	35.7	15.8	26.2	11,348	24,372	57,772	40.7	0.6	64,144	9.3	12.6	11.5
Garfield	2,889	57.2	1,080	10.1	37.0	25.4	10.8	11,108	23,926	44,279	52.9	1.8	47,638	9.7	12.8	11.8
Grand	6,605	67.7	1,799	25.4	33.2	30.7	19.1	11,361	30,948	56,639	45.5	1.7	58,852	10.4	13.5	12.2
Iron	25,181	45.9	18,206	8.3	29.7	28.9	81.1	7,451	22,409	52,045	47.8	2.2	52,942	13.7	14.5	11.7
Juab	4,414	36.7	3,504	9.4	45.4	18.7	24.6	8,637	23,467	68,333	37.7	3.6	70,086	7.7	9.6	9.0
Kane	3,954	50.1	1,582	18.0	33.4	29.7	15.8	11,663	28,142	49,486	50.6	3.1	58,352	9.0	13.1	12.2
Millard	5,991	45.4	3,545	8.3	42.7	22.4	32.6	10,579	25,479	63,221	37.1	2.9	60,316	10.7	13.7	12.6
Morgan	6,519	53.8	4,440	9.8	22.3	38.4	20.4	6,354	34,280	100,408	16.8	12.7	103,746	3.7	3.8	3.3
Piute	567	38.3	448	8.3	37.8	21.6	5.4	17,409	18,148	29,125	66.8	0.8	47,206	15.3	31.9	28.3
Rich	1,295	52.2	745	3.6	32.6	22.0	8.2	15,889	23,943	63,917	39.0	5.1	75,531	8.4	13.3	12.1
Salt Lake	812,133	70.0	328,381	13.3	30.8	36.5	1,756.5	8,038	34,640	77,128	29.7	8.5	79,294	7.0	7.2	6.3
San Juan	9,953	65.0	4,591	6.6	44.8	19.2	40.7	13,337	20,088	49,690	50.3	1.6	50,686	18.6	22.8	18.9
Sanpete	12,699	41.0	9,563	10.2	39.7	20.7	54.4	8,959	21,254	55,820	44.6	2.2	55,033	14.1	15.5	14.8
Sevier	9,507	44.0	6,225	6.1	40.2	20.9	41.0	8,576	24,041	55,361	43.6	1.8	56,318	10.0	11.6	10.7
Summit	37,248	88.4	11,006	12.8	20.8	56.1	104.1	12,346	57,308	106,973	20.4	23.0	115,756	4.5	4.8	4.1
Tooele	42,543	58.9	21,410	12.3	39.9	23.1	147.5	7,574	27,702	76,737	27.9	4.9	79,101	5.7	6.3	5.6
Uintah	15,485	43.3	10,660	14.9	49.6	16.3	66.2	8,312	24,578	59,428	42.7	3.6	63,282	10.8	12.8	12.0
Utah	366,832	57.7	242,516	23.7	21.6	41.1	1,054.1	7,139	27,365	77,057	29.7	7.1	81,804	7.8	6.5	5.7
Wasatch	20,717	60.8	10,496	15.8	25.2	43.7	73.7	9,638	38,622	85,807	26.7	12.1	87,098	4.7	6.2	5.4
Washington	92,640	52.2	46,460	11.7	28.7	29.2	258.6	7,198	29,886	61,747	38.9	5.2	71,904	6.9	9.3	8.6
Wayne	1,471	54.3	640	1.7	29.4	24.0	6.5	13,304	23,184	49,299	51.2	2.1	54,790	11.2	17.4	16.5
Weber	159,731	61.4	72,032	9.4	37.7	25.1	405.6	7,895	29,186	71,275	32.1	4.1	72,091	7.3	7.8	7.5
VERMONT	506,000	81.1	142,422	21.1	34.8	39.7	1,743.1	19,998	35,854	63,477	39.3	6.0	67,717	9.4	10.0	9.7
Addison	26,124	71.0	9,350	41.5	35.8	41.0	93.6	21,098	36,390	70,262	35.1	6.1	73,049	8.4	7.5	6.9
Bennington	15,304	43.1	7,609	31.8	35.5	37.5	104.4	18,467	34,435	58,200	43.2	5.7	65,528	10.4	13.6	12.5
Caledonia	10,931	36.4	6,575	21.6	42.0	30.7	78.5	17,199	30,902	52,481	47.9	4.0	52,203	11.0	10.7	12.1

1. All persons 3 years old and over enrolled in nursery school through college. 2. Persons 25 years old and over. 3. Elementary and secondary education expenditures. 4. Based on population estimated by the American Community Survey, 2016–2020. 5. CDC percent based on 2019 population estimate.

STATE County	Personal income, 2020										Earnings, 2020		
			Per capita[1]			Supplements to wages and salaries, employer contributions (mil dol)						Contributions for government social insurance (mil dol)	
	Total (mil dol)	Percent change 2019–2020	Dollars	Rank	Wages and salaries (mil dol)	Pension and insurance	Government social insurance	Proprietors' income (mil dol)	Dividends, interest, and rent (mil dol)	Personal transfer reecipts (mil dol)	Total (mil dol)	From employee and self-employed	From employer
	62	63	64	65	66	67	68	69	70	71	72	73	74
TEXAS—Cont'd													
Tom Green	6,354	3.1	52,947	860	2,478	449	176	774	1,380	1,478	3,877	215	176
Travis	96,279	5.5	74,032	115	62,944	7,410	3,978	12,176	21,999	10,330	86,508	4,472	3,978
Trinity	583	6.3	39,206	2,542	91	18	6	32	87	238	147	15	6
Tyler	792	9.5	36,694	2,804	172	39	12	22	104	309	246	20	12
Upshur	1,673	5.3	39,674	2,486	342	69	24	83	205	553	518	39	24
Upton	183	4.9	50,428	1,097	156	25	9	10	32	42	200	11	9
Uvalde	1,210	7.0	45,255	1,763	398	85	28	117	243	402	627	37	28
Val Verde	2,014	6.6	41,079	2,326	867	219	69	95	283	600	1,251	71	69
Van Zandt	2,454	7.9	42,656	2,108	462	85	32	181	317	772	760	57	32
Victoria	4,954	2.3	53,881	788	1,825	306	125	589	994	1,236	2,845	162	125
Walker	2,333	4.6	32,334	3,050	1,142	276	68	83	504	699	1,568	80	68
Waller	2,573	8.2	44,779	1,830	1,055	173	73	212	353	557	1,513	81	73
Ward	582	-11.1	48,109	1,369	316	45	20	20	77	136	401	24	20
Washington	2,090	1.8	58,426	500	718	125	48	165	586	547	1,057	65	48
Webb	9,893	7.5	35,626	2,899	4,163	859	292	1,132	1,344	2,881	6,445	344	292
Wharton	2,017	4.3	48,384	1,341	710	120	51	151	343	587	1,032	61	51
Wheeler	241	6.6	48,691	1,295	97	18	6	29	54	78	150	8	6
Wichita	6,170	5.5	46,322	1,604	2,719	551	201	434	1,269	1,742	3,905	223	201
Wilbarger	622	-2.2	49,537	1,192	244	57	16	34	143	194	351	20	16
Willacy	671	12.3	31,710	3,065	164	33	12	70	61	311	279	17	12
Williamson	35,028	10.2	56,693	591	12,944	1,520	805	2,219	5,026	5,017	17,488	1,026	805
Wilson	2,588	5.3	49,745	1,168	396	74	27	136	392	587	632	44	27
Winkler	491	-6.3	62,259	342	245	39	16	51	86	91	350	19	16
Wise	3,443	7.7	48,435	1,333	1,049	184	69	263	443	743	1,565	93	69
Wood	1,989	7.4	42,978	2,066	456	87	32	142	337	780	717	61	32
Yoakum	386	0.0	44,395	1,892	202	33	13	66	44	89	314	15	13
Young	953	2.5	53,227	839	308	61	21	135	203	276	525	31	21
Zapata	411	-0.4	28,981	3,095	152	31	10	13	52	170	205	13	10
Zavala	394	7.9	33,303	3,015	140	25	10	14	53	165	189	13	10
UTAH	169,656	7.8	51,698	X	89,397	13,446	6,458	14,104	34,215	25,984	123,404	7,390	6,458
Beaver	282	6.7	41,667	2,243	119	23	11	48	37	74	201	11	11
Box Elder	2,516	11.5	44,131	1,924	1,060	168	80	189	371	476	1,498	93	80
Cache	5,843	8.2	44,947	1,799	2,692	491	197	786	1,057	943	4,166	238	197
Carbon	881	7.1	42,459	2,135	419	77	31	51	130	266	577	39	31
Daggett	50	9.4	48,761	1,286	17	4	1	3	13	12	25	2	1
Davis	18,627	7.5	51,852	943	7,705	1,461	590	1,031	3,354	2,555	10,787	636	590
Duchesne	811	5.8	40,780	2,361	395	74	29	64	146	188	562	34	29
Emery	386	10.4	38,057	2,680	168	38	13	26	59	116	245	16	13
Garfield	224	13.6	44,411	1,889	92	17	7	15	43	65	131	9	7
Grand	597	4.2	60,928	386	237	40	19	96	150	120	391	24	19
Iron	2,069	9.9	36,412	2,836	861	168	64	154	358	518	1,247	79	64
Juab	516	11.0	42,531	2,125	165	31	12	47	56	114	255	16	12
Kane	357	8.9	45,074	1,785	148	25	10	31	84	90	214	15	10
Millard	558	13.5	41,843	2,225	228	49	18	81	80	128	377	20	18
Morgan	731	7.4	58,631	490	140	21	10	33	140	83	204	14	10
Piute	72	6.7	48,595	1,309	10	2	1	25	9	20	38	2	1
Rich	105	7.9	42,762	2,100	32	6	3	19	27	21	60	3	3
Salt Lake	68,855	7.1	59,077	477	47,087	6,569	3,337	6,201	14,128	9,747	63,195	3,723	3,337
San Juan	461	7.7	30,198	3,086	172	38	13	43	73	153	266	17	13
Sanpete	1,034	11.3	32,927	3,031	343	76	25	96	146	281	540	34	25
Sevier	858	8.9	39,383	2,526	394	76	29	66	149	232	564	36	29
Summit	6,653	3.8	156,537	3	1,458	170	105	455	2,985	345	2,188	129	105
Tooele	3,077	12.4	41,301	2,289	879	151	67	86	357	514	1,184	78	67
Uintah	1,185	3.5	32,945	3,030	580	101	44	69	217	288	795	50	44
Utah	30,251	9.1	46,465	1,585	14,755	2,015	1,052	2,914	5,245	4,114	20,736	1,226	1,052
Wasatch	2,176	7.3	61,653	361	536	77	38	80	594	241	732	49	38
Washington	8,096	8.7	43,782	1,976	3,171	497	235	742	2,048	1,929	4,645	324	235
Wayne	127	13.9	46,145	1,628	44	8	4	13	29	34	69	4	4
Weber	12,260	8.6	46,675	1,555	5,489	972	413	639	2,128	2,316	7,513	470	413
VERMONT	36,894	6.7	57,423	X	15,890	2,645	1,285	3,058	6,920	9,459	22,877	1,574	1,285
Addison	2,063	6.0	55,981	643	784	127	66	231	402	453	1,207	82	66
Bennington	2,090	6.4	59,131	475	797	134	66	158	480	621	1,155	85	66
Caledonia	1,429	9.3	48,094	1,372	491	89	40	124	241	463	745	56	40

1. Based on the resident population estimated as of July 1 of the year shown.

STATE County	Earnings, 2020 (cont.)									Social Security beneficiaries, December 2020		Supple-mental Security Income recipients, 2020	Housing units, 2021	
	Percent by selected industries													
	Farm	Mining, quarrying, and extractions	Construction	Manu-facturing	Information; professional, scientific, technical services	Retail trade	Finance, insurance, real estate, and leasing	Health care and social assistance	Govern-ment	Number	Rate[1]		Total	Percent change, 2010–2021
	75	76	77	78	79	80	81	82	83	84	85	86	87	88
TEXAS—Cont'd														
Tom Green	0.7	4.5	6.1	11.8	5.5	6.9	7.8	13.8	22.6	23,305	195	2,727	52,109	1.3
Travis	0.0	6.1	6.0	6.6	26.2	4.5	9.6	7.2	13.3	138,230	106	15,963	593,195	4.5
Trinity	-1.4	D	5.0	9.8	D	5.2	4.2	9.2	24.8	4,675	338	586	8,249	0.8
Tyler	-0.4	2.0	6.5	4.2	D	8.4	4.9	D	39.4	5,425	270	613	9,487	0.7
Upshur	0.0	2.6	15.6	4.8	D	5.5	4.4	D	21.3	9,710	232	1,067	17,455	0.5
Upton	-1.0	37.9	D	D	D	D	D	0.9	19.6	605	185	68	1,527	0.2
Uvalde	2.9	2.4	6.3	3.5	D	9.1	6.0	D	31.0	5,765	233	1,013	10,079	0.4
Val Verde	0.2	D	3.0	5.9	2.1	7.4	3.8	9.8	48.9	8,805	185	1,897	18,607	0.6
Van Zandt	4.6	2.0	16.4	9.5	4.9	8.5	3.9	5.6	18.1	13,750	224	1,249	25,707	0.5
Victoria	0.4	14.6	6.9	7.6	4.1	8.4	5.8	13.0	14.4	18,720	206	2,325	39,175	0.4
Walker	0.5	D	3.6	5.6	3.2	7.2	3.0	7.0	57.6	10,785	138	1,299	29,385	2.1
Waller	2.2	1.4	11.9	21.3	D	6.6	3.3	2.8	20.4	8,020	134	969	19,943	1.7
Ward	-3.6	34.6	10.6	2.6	3.7	4.5	5.4	D	14.8	1,955	175	219	5,146	0.1
Washington	-1.3	0.9	7.6	22.4	4.7	7.6	11.4	7.9	17.7	9,015	251	895	17,469	3.6
Webb	0.1	3.6	3.5	0.8	4.1	7.0	5.6	11.2	28.0	36,370	136	11,358	86,660	1.8
Wharton	8.0	5.5	7.3	8.3	2.8	9.6	5.2	11.1	16.4	8,870	213	1,073	17,495	1.0
Wheeler	8.5	24.4	4.5	1.3	D	7.4	2.9	3.3	23.5	1,130	229	72	2,599	0.0
Wichita	0.0	3.7	4.3	9.4	4.0	7.0	6.1	17.6	30.5	26,470	204	3,962	55,644	0.2
Wilbarger	2.5	0.5	2.8	17.6	D	7.0	4.7	4.0	37.5	2,890	227	391	5,831	-0.1
Willacy	14.3	D	2.1	1.9	D	4.9	3.1	9.4	25.8	3,865	190	1,136	6,832	0.8
Williamson	0.0	0.4	12.0	14.4	11.4	7.7	6.1	8.1	10.1	84,025	131	4,724	249,398	4.2
Wilson	-0.6	8.9	16.8	5.3	5.8	10.1	4.9	6.5	23.7	9,765	191	658	19,239	1.2
Winkler	-1.0	38.5	D	D	D	3.3	4.2	D	11.9	1,210	163	175	3,218	0.0
Wise	-1.6	8.9	13.1	10.9	4.4	7.9	5.4	7.1	19.9	12,805	179	761	27,120	0.8
Wood	2.7	2.8	14.9	11.9	6.1	7.9	5.6	9.6	16.4	15,295	333	1,055	22,252	0.4
Yoakum	14.5	33.4	8.4	1.5	2.8	3.2	3.9	D	15.2	1,330	175	113	3,020	0.3
Young	0.1	11.8	5.3	21.2	3.5	5.3	12.3	D	14.9	4,540	253	446	8,551	0.1
Zapata	-0.6	31.1	4.5	1.0	D	3.5	D	6.1	34.8	2,175	156	607	6,207	0.6
Zavala	1.7	5.2	D	D	2.4	3.2	D	6.7	22.3	2,225	233	710	3,940	0.4
UTAH	0.6	0.8	8.8	9.1	13.9	7.3	10.3	8.4	15.4	430,247	129	31,519	1,190,107	2.7
Beaver	26.1	D	5.3	6.0	1.0	6.0	D	2.0	22.5	1,285	177	78	2,908	1.4
Box Elder	5.5	0.1	10.6	34.1	D	5.1	4.2	5.9	11.9	9,285	156	559	20,118	2.7
Cache	1.4	0.0	6.8	20.9	10.2	6.6	11.3	8.5	17.3	15,440	112	865	45,693	3.5
Carbon	0.4	19.1	4.2	5.8	3.1	7.0	4.5	D	19.9	4,995	245	504	9,608	0.3
Daggett	6.5	-0.2	D	D	D	D	D	D	44.8	260	266	D	1,155	1.1
Davis	0.2	0.3	8.9	11.1	9.5	6.5	6.2	8.3	27.9	42,985	117	2,533	118,003	2.0
Duchesne	4.3	23.2	4.5	1.9	D	6.7	4.5	D	24.2	3,685	186	349	8,859	1.3
Emery	5.5	9.7	11.5	0.9	D	6.7	D	D	18.8	2,320	233	134	4,084	0.2
Garfield	7.1	D	3.7	1.8	D	4.3	1.9	D	25.4	1,265	247	36	3,561	1.7
Grand	0.8	D	7.1	4.0	4.8	8.1	14.3	8.3	18.5	2,150	222	120	5,335	2.1
Iron	4.5	0.4	8.7	10.4	4.2	8.5	9.1	9.4	24.3	9,540	158	780	22,699	3.8
Juab	2.6	0.3	8.1	25.7	D	3.3	3.5	D	17.1	1,835	151	123	3,940	2.8
Kane	1.7	D	5.0	3.3	D	6.5	3.4	3.8	21.5	2,130	267	73	6,260	3.9
Millard	18.8	2.5	2.2	4.9	D	5.0	3.5	D	14.9	2,620	199	122	4,979	1.2
Morgan	0.8	D	23.1	8.7	D	7.6	6.4	4.0	15.9	1,610	127	38	3,825	2.8
Piute	61.0	D	D	D	D	D	D	D	15.4	460	309	21	879	3.0
Rich	27.5	D	8.6	D	D	5.0	D	D	19.6	490	189	D	3,169	1.8
Salt Lake	0.0	0.6	7.8	7.7	15.2	7.0	12.8	7.4	13.9	148,780	125	13,151	440,493	2.3
San Juan	4.8	6.7	4.2	2.0	D	3.4	D	D	34.6	2,375	164	551	5,550	0.9
Sanpete	10.1	0.0	6.8	12.2	4.5	5.0	5.5	D	31.5	5,435	187	338	10,321	0.7
Sevier	6.7	10.6	4.2	5.0	4.2	9.4	3.5	D	19.3	4,710	215	298	8,642	1.3
Summit	0.8	0.6	9.0	4.0	14.8	7.3	15.5	5.9	8.7	6,125	142	89	26,073	1.2
Tooele	0.6	D	7.3	13.6	D	6.3	2.8	7.6	27.5	8,845	115	718	24,125	4.0
Uintah	2.4	15.8	6.5	1.3	3.4	8.8	4.3	7.0	25.0	5,135	142	429	13,736	0.5
Utah	0.3	0.1	11.7	8.1	21.9	8.6	6.9	9.1	9.6	61,615	90	4,307	201,906	3.9
Wasatch	0.4	D	26.4	4.3	8.8	8.5	2.8	8.6	16.9	4,680	129	116	15,099	3.5
Washington	0.1	0.5	12.6	4.8	6.8	10.0	11.0	16.0	12.6	42,320	221	1,575	78,974	4.7
Wayne	12.6	D	18.7	0.4	D	5.4	D	10.3	24.1	690	270	21	1,714	1.8
Weber	0.3	0.0	8.0	16.0	6.0	7.1	8.7	12.2	20.2	37,180	139	3,580	98,399	2.5
VERMONT	1.3	0.3	7.1	10.0	10.6	7.3	6.3	15.4	18.5	156,005	242	14,947	336,779	0.6
Addison	5.4	0.3	8.9	14.5	6.3	6.7	4.3	D	11.1	8,840	237	529	17,518	0.7
Bennington	0.5	0.0	6.7	12.7	D	10.2	5.2	18.1	14.2	10,410	279	1,194	20,850	0.1
Caledonia	1.9	D	8.7	12.6	D	8.9	4.3	17.5	18.2	8,160	268	862	16,076	0.4

1. Per 1,000 resident population estimated as of July 1 of the year shown.

STATE County	Housing units, 2016–2020								Civilian labor force, 2021				Civilian employment[6], 2016–2020		
	Occupied units										Unemployment			Percent	
		Owner-occupied				Renter-occupied									
				Median owner cost as a percent of income											
	Total	Percent	Median value[1]	With a mortgage	Without a mortgage[2]	Median rent[3]	Median rent as a percent of income[2]	Substandard units[4] (percent)	Total	Percent change, 2020–2021	Total	Rate[5]	Total	Management, business, science, and arts	Construction, production, and maintenance occupations
	89	90	91	92	93	94	95	96	97	98	99	100	101	102	103
TEXAS—Cont'd															
Tom Green	42,953	65.6	149,700	20.0	10.9	892	28.3	3.4	54,009	1.3	2,627	4.9	55,872	32.6	23.3
Travis	491,531	53.0	347,700	21.3	12.0	1,348	28.5	4.4	770,868	5.5	31,152	4.0	704,618	51.5	14.3
Trinity	6,105	76.3	87,500	18.6	12.0	650	30.4	5.2	5,355	1.7	393	7.3	5,256	34.6	30.3
Tyler	7,109	82.9	91,000	20.0	11.2	765	28.4	6.0	7,409	1.5	630	8.5	6,250	27.0	34.5
Upshur	14,392	77.0	153,800	18.9	11.0	798	26.2	4.2	17,555	1.0	1,099	6.3	17,130	28.6	29.5
Upton	1,344	76.9	78,900	14.9	10.0	781	18.4	2.6	1,762	-2.1	92	5.2	1,529	30.6	38.8
Uvalde	8,921	69.3	103,000	19.3	12.4	834	29.3	3.2	11,252	0.4	621	5.5	11,516	25.8	30.1
Val Verde	16,388	64.8	105,400	19.8	11.9	766	25.5	11.2	22,098	3.5	1,313	5.9	19,952	24.6	29.8
Van Zandt	20,494	79.0	152,200	20.9	11.7	865	28.4	4.2	26,780	3.5	1,265	4.7	22,595	32.7	29.2
Victoria	32,520	67.3	152,900	20.3	10.0	961	28.9	3.7	40,785	0.5	2,610	6.4	42,209	30.6	28.3
Walker	22,515	51.9	160,100	21.2	10.8	893	38.1	3.1	23,951	0.4	1,500	6.3	26,224	26.6	24.0
Waller	15,586	69.3	222,700	21.1	11.8	1,000	29.6	4.3	24,799	2.3	1,583	6.4	24,068	30.7	26.1
Ward	4,100	74.6	98,700	17.3	10.0	850	22.1	5.6	5,884	-3.7	421	7.2	5,140	28.4	36.9
Washington	13,321	73.7	193,000	21.9	11.0	922	30.5	4.2	15,187	0.6	796	5.2	15,922	37.0	27.5
Webb	76,382	63.0	135,000	24.7	11.6	851	31.9	11.4	116,373	1.0	7,340	6.3	111,451	25.5	25.5
Wharton	15,248	66.3	148,700	20.0	10.3	787	25.1	5.7	21,120	-0.2	1,206	5.7	18,093	26.3	35.8
Wheeler	2,060	70.3	83,600	20.3	10.0	800	30.7	4.1	2,066	-5.0	129	6.2	2,482	23.4	29.3
Wichita	48,538	60.9	103,200	19.9	11.8	822	29.1	2.5	55,325	0.5	2,925	5.3	56,717	31.8	25.8
Wilbarger	5,008	59.4	73,200	19.3	12.2	689	21.3	5.0	4,891	0.5	322	6.6	6,074	24.8	25.8
Willacy	5,882	67.0	62,100	18.5	11.8	687	26.8	12.4	6,976	6.5	731	10.5	8,414	21.5	36.1
Williamson	188,113	68.2	282,700	21.0	11.4	1,368	27.9	2.8	340,568	6.0	13,586	4.0	290,516	47.2	15.8
Wilson	15,975	87.3	210,600	20.8	10.0	931	28.4	6.3	24,999	3.1	1,100	4.4	22,980	32.1	26.2
Winkler	2,618	80.9	82,800	15.2	10.0	830	18.0	5.3	3,726	-5.5	287	7.7	3,476	19.1	43.1
Wise	22,254	79.6	178,200	21.8	11.0	1,030	25.6	4.0	32,980	3.3	1,600	4.9	31,930	31.0	31.4
Wood	16,716	81.4	151,400	19.9	11.2	789	28.3	2.9	17,988	1.5	1,011	5.6	16,688	30.3	33.8
Yoakum	2,601	77.3	152,900	18.3	10.0	883	26.7	5.5	3,284	-5.7	257	7.8	3,510	25.9	41.8
Young	7,491	74.0	122,100	18.8	11.1	678	26.0	2.6	8,066	4.9	365	4.5	8,135	31.0	31.1
Zapata	4,689	70.1	88,700	18.9	12.2	513	35.3	11.6	4,526	-2.5	546	12.1	5,135	20.9	38.9
Zavala	3,674	73.8	59,400	17.7	10.6	686	33.6	8.9	3,276	-2.8	415	12.7	4,905	26.7	31.8
UTAH	1,003,345	70.5	305,400	20.7	10.0	1,090	27.8	3.6	1,681,494	2.5	45,344	2.7	1,537,623	39.7	21.7
Beaver	2,213	81.6	209,000	17.5	10.0	783	19.3	2.4	2,826	-0.4	80	2.8	2,871	32.6	33.8
Box Elder	17,811	76.4	226,200	21.3	10.0	779	24.8	2.8	26,895	1.0	658	2.4	24,570	31.1	33.8
Cache	39,581	62.6	256,400	20.5	10.0	842	28.4	3.5	68,747	4.3	1,352	2.0	61,670	38.5	23.7
Carbon	7,802	72.3	148,600	20.2	10.0	681	31.3	2.8	8,424	-2.0	327	3.9	8,406	28.0	30.2
Daggett	169	71.0	152,500	13.3	10.0	0	10.0	3.0	415	0.7	15	3.6	287	28.9	31.0
Davis	107,104	77.7	320,100	19.6	10.0	1,167	25.9	2.0	179,229	1.7	4,364	2.4	169,911	42.2	20.4
Duchesne	7,038	74.0	188,300	21.5	10.0	816	24.3	5.3	7,748	-1.0	376	4.9	7,941	31.8	35.8
Emery	3,732	75.3	137,400	16.4	10.0	620	22.7	4.3	4,450	1.0	172	3.9	4,025	29.5	33.0
Garfield	1,851	78.5	182,500	23.5	10.0	715	24.2	2.1	2,778	4.7	181	6.5	2,150	33.8	19.9
Grand	4,442	65.6	287,900	21.3	10.0	1,012	28.2	9.8	6,574	5.3	289	4.4	5,582	29.2	13.9
Iron	17,381	65.2	231,300	22.1	10.0	816	28.1	2.4	26,265	3.9	746	2.8	23,642	29.5	25.7
Juab	3,478	78.3	250,900	20.3	10.0	705	21.7	5.3	6,159	5.3	123	2.0	5,071	32.7	31.1
Kane	2,847	77.1	239,900	22.7	10.0	1,018	29.0	4.6	4,002	3.3	115	2.9	3,336	36.9	13.0
Millard	4,293	73.6	166,900	18.5	10.0	754	23.5	3.1	6,018	-0.2	143	2.4	5,534	29.5	35.9
Morgan	3,434	88.5	417,600	21.0	10.0	1,230	20.7	1.2	5,779	2.0	121	2.1	4,928	48.6	21.2
Piute	590	89.0	182,400	23.7	13.2	754	26.3	1.0	479	-0.4	21	4.4	565	50.8	20.4
Rich	641	73.3	205,300	17.0	10.0	646	16.4	0.2	1,273	9.4	29	2.3	880	25.1	37.4
Salt Lake	383,324	67.5	336,100	20.8	10.0	1,176	28.1	3.5	653,817	1.6	18,161	2.8	600,270	41.3	20.7
San Juan	4,577	78.1	128,700	21.0	10.4	720	24.4	15.5	5,470	-0.4	345	6.3	5,702	32.4	28.8
Sanpete	8,887	77.2	206,800	21.2	10.0	785	26.6	5.2	13,057	2.3	366	2.8	12,599	32.6	27.6
Sevier	7,487	78.9	173,600	20.0	10.0	691	26.7	3.8	9,992	0.9	326	3.3	8,919	32.1	29.6
Summit	14,474	78.1	678,500	21.5	10.0	1,477	25.1	1.9	24,987	1.5	721	2.9	22,936	48.8	14.9
Tooele	21,147	80.7	236,600	20.3	10.0	951	26.4	3.2	36,804	2.1	1,057	2.9	32,948	33.6	29.6
Uintah	10,739	76.7	194,000	21.6	10.0	715	25.0	3.9	13,562	0.7	756	5.6	14,270	28.6	31.1
Utah	171,899	67.9	336,200	21.1	10.0	1,102	28.9	4.9	332,018	4.9	7,729	2.3	292,353	42.7	17.8
Wasatch	10,505	73.8	452,900	22.5	10.0	1,435	31.6	3.0	16,903	2.7	482	2.9	16,430	40.9	18.6
Washington	59,699	70.2	306,900	23.1	10.0	1,099	29.2	4.2	83,600	4.4	2,426	2.9	72,188	34.6	21.1
Wayne	995	73.4	228,800	29.6	10.0	680	26.2	2.5	1,506	3.9	71	4.7	1,153	34.5	27.9
Weber	85,205	74.7	249,100	20.3	10.0	958	25.9	3.3	131,718	1.3	3,792	2.9	126,486	34.3	27.5
VERMONT	262,852	71.3	230,900	22.6	14.8	999	29.8	2.1	328,216	-3.8	11,275	3.4	328,642	43.1	20.9
Addison	14,700	75.3	257,100	22.5	14.6	1,028	26.7	1.7	19,901	-3.1	549	2.8	20,062	41.5	24.9
Bennington	14,585	73.4	210,600	23.3	14.3	854	30.9	2.2	16,919	-4.6	730	4.3	16,991	40.4	19.7
Caledonia	12,618	75.1	172,700	21.9	15.4	781	29.6	2.6	14,037	-3.7	521	3.7	15,156	36.2	26.6

1. Specified owner-occupied units. 2. A value of 10.0 represents 10 percent or less; a value of 50.0 represents 50 percent or more. 3. Specified renter-occupied units. 4. Overcrowded or lacking complete plumbing facilities. 5. Percent of civilian labor force. 6. Civilian employed persons 16 years old and over.

STATE County	Private nonfarm establishments, employment and payroll, 2020									Agriculture, 2017			
		Employment						Annual payroll		Farms			Farm producers whose primary occupation is farming (percent)
											Percent with:		
	Number of establish-ments	Total	Health care and social assistance	Manufac-turing	Retail trade	Finance and insurance	Professional, scientific, and technical services	Total (mil dol)	Average per employee (dollars)	Number	Fewer than 50 acres	1000 acres or more	
	104	105	106	107	108	109	110	111	112	113	114	115	116
TEXAS—Cont'd													
Tom Green	2,788	40,252	7,228	3,100	6,587	1,817	1,716	1,669	41,462	1,303	56.3	10.3	29.4
Travis	38,547	652,191	76,209	29,161	67,890	30,486	90,197	44,203	67,777	1,099	57.0	4.7	39.5
Trinity	176	1,701	322	182	222	67	34	57	33,661	601	43.3	2.3	39.6
Tyler	269	2,186	511	119	501	78	65	74	33,694	778	61.2	2.3	35.0
Upshur	504	5,080	556	602	742	261	404	196	38,489	1,652	51.2	0.9	32.5
Upton	90	1,322	188	NA	74	23	NA	81	61,253	98	13.3	62.2	48.7
Uvalde	611	7,397	1,842	310	1,434	236	286	262	35,392	592	30.9	15.4	35.4
Val Verde	784	11,902	3,488	568	2,254	525	218	330	27,701	528	46.4	25.6	38.3
Van Zandt	928	8,935	1,087	1,039	1,490	249	290	329	36,871	3,405	56.0	1.5	35.2
Victoria	2,262	32,611	6,874	2,042	5,870	756	1,123	1,374	42,133	1,286	51.5	6.3	30.1
Walker	1,034	13,454	2,431	1,064	2,986	419	505	403	29,937	1,441	58.3	2.8	34.2
Waller	861	14,405	1,214	3,137	2,713	115	419	667	46,273	1,881	64.5	2.6	34.3
Ward	317	4,275	180	108	448	93	89	210	49,141	102	32.4	32.4	18.9
Washington	945	13,018	1,828	2,774	2,186	934	361	519	39,884	2,607	48.7	0.8	33.3
Webb	5,512	79,245	17,298	777	12,961	2,838	2,127	2,427	30,627	656	19.1	22.6	36.3
Wharton	1,005	11,501	1,790	1,556	2,265	420	278	426	37,063	1,500	42.3	10.0	37.7
Wheeler	158	1,214	285	12	267	47	68	44	35,934	510	9.6	24.9	35.4
Wichita	2,979	44,475	11,348	4,595	6,893	1,775	990	1,689	37,969	614	47.9	12.5	33.7
Wilbarger	271	4,493	1,628	826	612	140	44	174	38,666	395	18.7	23.8	39.6
Willacy	188	2,347	639	19	354	59	28	81	34,457	351	54.1	16.5	43.8
Williamson	12,467	180,325	25,896	8,630	30,170	8,826	21,529	10,404	57,698	2,634	57.3	4.6	31.4
Wilson	755	7,336	1,323	330	1,547	183	240	260	35,474	2,621	45.6	2.4	36.0
Winkler	182	3,324	97	NA	283	72	48	216	64,888	46	17.4	60.9	63.3
Wise	1,364	18,178	3,191	2,292	2,615	361	413	860	47,335	3,697	63.2	2.4	32.6
Wood	795	8,135	1,082	926	1,425	306	239	322	39,524	1,587	48.0	1.6	39.8
Yoakum	185	2,123	307	113	256	78	22	113	53,223	291	14.8	41.6	46.1
Young	563	5,753	951	1,321	772	196	191	243	42,166	853	22.2	13.7	36.2
Zapata	133	1,475	500	19	263	88	3	42	28,299	412	12.1	27.9	31.2
Zavala	96	1,386	635	NA	173	45	10	35	25,404	281	14.2	35.2	44.6
UTAH	86,927	1,405,666	153,910	132,445	160,246	73,773	99,698	72,303	51,437	18,409	62.1	6.9	32.1
Beaver	191	1,792	266	161	392	38	20	63	35,194	272	41.5	9.6	45.8
Box Elder	1,238	18,991	1,527	7,693	1,815	313	339	966	50,881	1,187	50.5	15.4	37.8
Cache	3,668	48,305	5,905	13,167	6,921	1,114	4,775	1,974	40,867	1,397	58.3	3.8	30.3
Carbon	479	5,696	1,047	514	1,005	180	126	242	42,468	309	69.9	13.3	26.4
Daggett	22	112	NA	NA	33	NA	NA	5	40,286	52	40.4	11.5	29.2
Davis	8,040	95,111	12,939	12,072	15,357	2,951	8,205	4,200	44,163	528	90.3	1.3	30.8
Duchesne	637	5,690	1,167	241	805	119	128	281	49,455	1,063	49.6	5.3	28.9
Emery	184	2,148	211	23	345	38	83	110	51,074	504	51.6	6.9	34.5
Garfield	191	1,636	179	48	157	22	27	53	32,388	286	51.7	7.0	36.5
Grand	503	4,789	437	80	843	73	165	159	33,264	102	49.0	8.8	37.4
Iron	1,651	16,183	3,144	1,917	2,428	590	603	537	33,209	486	37.9	16.7	42.1
Juab	245	2,790	482	574	275	43	309	105	37,587	292	27.7	14.7	26.4
Kane	288	3,503	234	82	412	75	48	123	35,211	182	41.2	17.0	33.3
Millard	260	3,130	265	643	592	60	175	157	50,076	654	28.0	18.3	39.0
Morgan	339	1,898	133	69	290	41	125	84	44,330	372	63.4	7.3	26.5
Piute	27	72	NA	NA	21	NA	NA	2	23,194	104	31.7	16.3	36.1
Rich	104	690	261	NA	51	NA	21	29	41,830	160	31.9	32.5	44.5
Salt Lake	33,829	643,375	67,203	56,786	66,948	48,096	49,109	36,915	57,377	592	87.2	2.0	31.6
San Juan	249	3,004	980	114	391	54	22	100	33,329	823	52.5	13.0	64.9
Sanpete	466	4,900	609	1,270	876	123	281	172	35,061	1,003	52.9	6.3	35.4
Sevier	562	6,696	940	311	1,292	142	268	270	40,356	691	67.6	2.9	30.3
Summit	2,610	30,578	1,577	730	4,316	1,150	1,165	1,226	40,091	626	67.6	5.4	26.5
Tooele	995	11,795	1,516	1,345	1,908	168	482	458	38,853	540	63.3	7.6	29.1
Uintah	1,042	9,013	797	231	1,661	194	401	380	42,141	1,114	56.7	6.3	30.3
Utah	15,535	240,915	28,323	17,652	28,293	7,081	20,873	11,989	49,763	2,589	82.2	1.9	23.6
Wasatch	1,121	7,427	882	350	1,169	180	778	369	49,701	475	82.3	1.9	23.2
Washington	5,979	58,074	10,431	3,275	9,717	1,439	2,852	2,270	39,089	537	60.5	5.8	26.8
Wayne	100	623	NA	6	148	NA	7	22	35,920	209	51.2	5.3	36.4
Weber	5,806	86,969	11,886	13,087	11,685	5,000	4,263	3,727	42,856	1,260	85.0	0.8	24.2
VERMONT	20,540	258,423	50,381	30,658	37,020	8,984	12,304	11,668	45,151	6,808	41.1	2.3	42.1
Addison	1,143	13,686	2,287	1,669	1,813	298	407	565	41,270	720	40.0	5.1	46.6
Bennington	1,296	15,586	3,399	2,314	2,700	308	366	606	38,907	250	56.4	2.4	35.4
Caledonia	900	8,894	1,845	1,263	1,594	318	214	356	39,974	585	40.9	0.5	37.8

STATE County	Agriculture, 2017 (cont.) — Land in farms — Acreage (1,000)	Land in farms — Percent change, 2012–2017	Land in farms — Acres — Average size of farm	Land in farms — Acres — Total irrigated (1,000)	Land in farms — Acres — Total cropland (1,000)	Value of land and buildings (dollars) — Average per farm	Value of land and buildings (dollars) — Average per acre	Value of machinery and equipment, average per farm (dollars)	Value of products sold: — Total (mil dol)	Value of products sold: — Average per farm (acres)	Value of products sold: — Percent from: — Crops	Value of products sold: — Percent from: — Livestock and poultry products	Organic farms (number)	Farms with internet access (percent)	Government payments — Total ($1,000)	Government payments — Percent of farms
	117	118	119	120	121	122	123	124	125	126	127	128	129	130	131	132
TEXAS—Cont'd																
Tom Green	813	-15.0	624	19.6	125.0	980,735	1,572	76,726	100.0	76,769	29.9	70.1	1	75.4	2,964	13.4
Travis	222	-12.2	202	2.0	55.1	1,263,065	6,256	62,118	28.1	25,578	71.3	28.7	8	78.3	884	11.9
Trinity	99	-11.1	165	0.3	20.1	435,080	2,644	70,677	8.2	13,691	25.6	74.4	NA	66.6	42	1.5
Tyler	91	0.5	117	0.8	18.8	399,746	3,412	61,078	14.9	19,134	64.8	35.2	NA	77.6	96	2.7
Upshur	185	-8.4	112	0.4	36.9	386,205	3,443	51,583	40.7	24,645	8.5	91.5	8	75.1	347	7.2
Upton	725	5.7	7,399	15.8	74.9	5,980,038	808	270,042	19.1	194,520	72.8	27.2	NA	79.6	568	29.6
Uvalde	987	1.0	1,668	32.6	111.3	2,165,457	1,299	108,251	87.1	147,130	43.3	56.7	NA	73.3	2,202	14.7
Val Verde	1,471	-1.7	2,787	0.7	7.2	2,808,164	1,008	52,049	9.4	17,890	1.9	98.1	NA	54.9	416	2.8
Van Zandt	380	2.5	112	2.1	99.0	409,609	3,673	55,302	104.6	30,720	40.6	59.4	3	73.5	295	1.7
Victoria	426	-2.7	331	8.1	83.2	967,562	2,920	76,948	58.4	45,392	58.6	41.4	NA	69.8	2,630	12.1
Walker	227	-19.0	158	0.6	27.5	580,115	3,679	58,302	33.8	23,452	56.7	43.3	2	75.8	143	0.9
Waller	253	-19.6	135	11.6	71.4	628,544	4,670	69,415	102.4	54,423	74.5	25.5	1	75.3	5,198	4.6
Ward	406	3.6	3,978	3.3	6.5	4,234,789	1,064	84,959	D	D	D	100.0	NA	48.0	D	20.6
Washington	320	-13.2	123	2.3	68.7	587,144	4,781	57,676	35.6	13,661	15.3	84.7	NA	64.7	417	3.2
Webb	1,845	-12.1	2,812	3.3	35.0	4,817,630	1,713	69,020	28.4	43,287	1.5	98.5	NA	47.6	525	3.2
Wharton	535	-19.0	357	56.7	325.8	1,035,627	2,902	149,677	208.5	139,027	86.0	14.0	17	67.4	14,777	36.7
Wheeler	529	1.9	1,038	12.3	121.7	1,129,454	1,089	95,512	70.6	138,424	12.0	88.0	NA	71.6	3,608	46.5
Wichita	370	1.0	603	10.2	153.0	889,018	1,474	88,165	33.8	54,992	43.3	56.7	NA	79.5	3,583	23.8
Wilbarger	620	5.7	1,571	13.7	235.1	2,009,636	1,279	187,858	51.9	131,380	68.7	31.3	NA	80.8	5,709	64.6
Willacy	318	-5.4	906	19.0	197.4	1,591,245	1,757	197,576	88.1	250,943	95.1	4.9	NA	59.0	4,971	46.2
Williamson	559	0.1	212	1.6	231.5	790,257	3,722	72,687	114.9	43,631	57.5	42.5	12	78.9	6,359	18.0
Wilson	434	-1.4	165	11.7	87.9	525,222	3,174	62,753	68.6	26,185	18.5	81.5	2	65.2	1,923	8.9
Winkler	489	-8.3	10,635	D	D	11,922,788	1,121	108,111	D	D	D	D	NA	89.1	NA	NA
Wise	514	5.5	139	4.5	110.6	541,645	3,896	58,259	46.3	12,515	25.0	75.0	4	78.1	932	5.4
Wood	210	-7.6	132	1.2	60.5	445,231	3,362	69,250	127.5	80,366	6.8	93.2	6	76.8	77	1.2
Yoakum	518	6.0	1,779	92.8	318.0	1,670,162	939	315,408	100.2	344,333	96.0	4.0	4	78.4	11,936	74.6
Young	575	9.8	674	1.9	114.5	1,139,664	1,691	59,190	21.7	25,433	12.0	88.0	6	76.1	1,277	18.2
Zapata	438	-22.2	1,063	1.5	18.9	1,500,482	1,412	68,908	6.3	15,408	6.9	93.1	NA	53.9	441	8.3
Zavala	729	5.2	2,595	43.8	76.0	4,517,368	1,741	205,052	66.6	237,103	35.2	64.8	1	61.6	1,796	14.6
UTAH	10,812	-1.5	587	1,097.2	1,654.4	1,067,323	1,817	97,789	1,838.6	99,876	30.5	69.5	95	77.7	27,868	12.0
Beaver	157	-17.4	577	40.2	44.4	1,284,918	2,226	217,327	258.0	948,559	7.8	92.2	NA	76.8	699	26.1
Box Elder	1,221	4.3	1,028	103.8	308.3	1,577,010	1,533	147,150	134.1	112,947	42.4	57.6	14	83.2	8,193	34.1
Cache	276	2.9	198	90.1	159.4	955,825	4,833	120,832	162.7	116,490	25.4	74.6	8	81.1	3,439	25.8
Carbon	231	-4.0	747	9.3	15.8	924,915	1,238	68,983	6.5	20,906	35.9	64.1	2	84.8	101	5.5
Daggett	18	D	340	7.2	6.6	943,662	2,777	98,797	2.4	46,212	14.1	85.9	NA	80.8	220	7.7
Davis	52	-5.9	98	10.0	7.7	914,737	9,325	58,022	23.8	45,074	85.0	15.0	NA	76.1	50	2.8
Duchesne	1,057	-2.9	995	96.5	77.3	970,628	976	100,563	57.9	54,461	27.9	72.1	NA	82.0	584	5.0
Emery	134	-14.4	265	32.8	36.9	557,310	2,101	74,404	15.4	30,464	31.8	68.2	2	84.5	460	14.3
Garfield	83	-9.7	289	21.2	16.3	903,654	3,127	91,968	21.8	76,175	16.5	83.5	5	72.4	D	3.8
Grand	231	D	2,268	11.5	14.6	1,868,935	824	139,177	7.2	70,294	65.5	34.5	5	81.4	D	3.9
Iron	513	-3.7	1,055	64.4	83.4	2,063,886	1,955	179,494	133.5	274,716	40.6	59.4	NA	75.7	530	12.1
Juab	265	8.9	906	23.7	56.6	1,202,491	1,327	122,499	53.7	183,832	57.3	42.7	NA	80.5	933	34.2
Kane	129	2.6	707	6.9	4.9	1,282,578	1,814	80,345	6.3	34,440	11.8	88.2	NA	83.0	56	2.7
Millard	482	-16.6	736	122.7	146.0	1,504,464	2,043	236,249	180.0	275,168	47.5	52.5	6	81.5	3,031	39.8
Morgan	243	6.1	652	9.0	16.6	1,434,803	2,200	70,446	17.1	46,046	14.4	85.6	NA	80.9	392	4.3
Piute	54	43.9	524	15.3	14.9	1,089,630	2,081	125,352	40.6	390,433	8.5	91.5	NA	81.7	68	7.7
Rich	375	-8.4	2,343	42.4	70.6	2,046,056	873	136,133	22.1	137,963	16.1	83.9	NA	76.3	633	13.1
Salt Lake	62	-20.7	105	7.4	10.9	1,013,467	9,682	52,551	19.9	33,617	85.7	14.3	10	78.7	188	2.4
San Juan	1,657	3.0	2,014	7.6	130.2	738,348	367	48,406	16.8	20,383	51.3	48.7	21	33.2	1,636	14.5
Sanpete	302	6.1	301	76.5	71.7	848,242	2,820	109,542	171.8	171,243	12.1	87.9	2	76.7	854	14.6
Sevier	109	-10.9	158	49.4	50.5	675,452	4,282	118,445	88.5	128,140	24.3	75.7	2	78.3	432	10.1
Summit	296	9.5	472	21.3	26.3	1,541,565	3,265	71,386	25.5	40,799	16.0	84.0	3	79.9	833	5.0
Tooele	349	0.6	646	21.9	21.7	888,625	1,375	89,898	40.8	75,469	15.9	84.1	1	80.6	406	2.6
Uintah	1,825	D	1,638	65.3	70.7	1,032,638	630	88,260	42.3	37,943	38.6	61.4	NA	75.9	1,402	6.4
Utah	304	-11.4	117	72.7	118.1	1,024,882	8,734	74,291	202.6	78,246	39.4	60.6	6	81.8	1,679	5.7
Wasatch	97	-34.9	204	11.3	8.8	1,135,964	5,557	62,791	8.8	18,531	21.5	78.5	NA	82.3	102	2.1
Washington	155	4.8	289	13.0	22.3	1,078,856	3,737	61,328	16.5	30,648	39.3	60.7	3	76.9	190	3.2
Wayne	43	0.9	205	16.6	14.6	928,420	4,539	89,480	12.9	61,646	15.7	84.3	NA	90.9	87	22.0
Weber	94	-19.6	75	27.2	28.3	697,872	9,319	59,112	49.4	39,240	50.0	50.0	5	75.0	497	3.1
VERMONT	1,193	-4.7	175	3.0	479.7	620,691	3,541	100,672	781.0	114,713	24.0	76.0	679	86.4	5,698	10.0
Addison	170	-18.5	236	0.4	107.8	786,959	3,335	150,113	173.4	240,889	14.7	85.3	81	92.4	1,362	17.2
Bennington	33	-20.1	132	0.5	11.0	630,681	4,766	80,601	17.6	70,200	62.2	37.8	13	88.0	63	4.8
Caledonia	87	6.3	149	0.1	31.3	474,564	3,191	77,061	42.2	72,077	16.6	83.4	46	87.4	263	6.5

STATE County	Water use, 2015		Wholesale Trade[1], 2017				Retail Trade[2], 2017				Real estate and rental and leasing,[2] 2017			
	Public supply water withdrawn (mil gal/ day)	Public supply gallons withdrawn per person per day	Number of establish- ments	Number of employees	Sales (mil dol)	Average payroll (mil dol)	Number of establish- ments	Number of employees	Sales (mil dol)	Average payroll (mil dol)	Number of establish- ments	Number of employees	Sales (mil dol)	Average payroll (mil dol)
	133	134	135	136	137	138	139	140	141	142	143	144	145	146
TEXAS—Cont'd														
Tom Green	1.2	9.8	D	D	D	D	421	6,626	1,964.8	191.3	151	627	129.5	22.4
Travis	122.1	103.8	1,266	23,554	80,511.6	1,765.7	3,815	62,409	19,457.3	1,915.0	2,409	15,454	4,406.2	934.1
Trinity	1.0	66.7	5	91	52.3	5.7	28	245	47.6	4.6	NA	NA	NA	NA
Tyler	2.8	133.0	9	57	46.3	3.1	45	519	126.4	11.4	6	D	1.5	D
Upshur	4.3	105.7	15	156	50.6	5.8	75	763	215.0	18.6	13	26	4.3	0.6
Upton	0.0	0.0	6	123	28.3	8.3	8	83	24.4	2.0	NA	NA	NA	NA
Uvalde	3.6	133.2	30	314	227.7	15.1	104	1,442	398.5	35.3	38	128	21.8	3.6
Val Verde	7.2	146.6	D	D	D	9.3	146	2,098	645.6	50.7	38	109	24.3	3.8
Van Zandt	3.4	63.1	32	417	126.9	23.9	134	1,488	507.5	38.4	29	62	7.0	1.7
Victoria	12.1	130.5	D	D	D	83.4	369	5,734	1,751.0	159.4	127	1,141	527.0	61.0
Walker	2.7	37.8	28	248	189.0	11.9	177	2,690	915.4	67.0	64	206	57.3	8.5
Waller	4.8	99.1	61	1,165	887.5	61.5	96	1,132	532.9	36.4	34	180	36.3	5.8
Ward	5.2	443.6	11	65	44.5	3.6	27	336	146.1	9.1	13	189	45.4	14.0
Washington	0.9	25.6	37	474	420.1	23.9	138	2,093	583.3	55.8	46	166	38.7	6.7
Webb	36.1	133.8	325	2,777	2,604.5	109.9	798	13,459	3,360.1	314.4	247	890	214.1	28.8
Wharton	3.7	88.9	60	608	531.0	34.2	159	2,166	634.6	59.1	44	177	38.1	6.9
Wheeler	1.1	201.5	9	51	24.7	2.2	27	228	66.5	4.6	5	D	2.0	D
Wichita	0.8	6.2	151	1,273	472.3	58.8	473	6,963	1,938.9	172.7	162	783	132.2	26.3
Wilbarger	1.9	142.0	D	D	D	D	43	652	298.7	17.5	12	73	12.7	1.7
Willacy	0.4	19.6	3	52	27.5	2.7	31	316	88.7	7.7	D	D	D	D
Williamson	35.5	69.8	343	3,263	3,249.0	345.3	1,448	26,298	9,916.0	889.9	618	2,270	684.8	112.9
Wilson	5.7	119.7	19	D	38.6	D	92	1,454	528.1	38.0	24	72	12.8	3.2
Winkler	1.5	181.1	D	D	D	D	21	215	92.2	5.0	10	D	30.1	D
Wise	2.2	35.4	61	600	517.5	37.6	170	2,346	910.7	60.1	49	232	43.6	8.9
Wood	4.2	97.1	24	144	62.1	4.1	119	1,458	503.1	42.1	40	122	17.9	4.1
Yoakum	1.0	113.5	12	102	55.9	8.0	30	269	67.7	6.7	6	60	19.7	3.1
Young	2.8	151.1	26	112	47.9	5.3	70	803	211.9	19.4	23	63	50.5	3.9
Zapata	2.2	153.1	NA	NA	NA	NA	30	269	69.7	5.3	NA	NA	NA	NA
Zavala	2.3	185.5	4	73	18.2	2.9	17	169	36.8	3.3	NA	NA	NA	NA
UTAH	785.9	262.3	3,109	46,631	41,834.1	2,880.8	9,995	153,633	50,008.3	4,445.9	5,577	19,457	5,296.5	876.9
Beaver	2.3	354.1	D	D	D	D	34	492	133.6	9.8	NA	NA	NA	NA
Box Elder	11.7	224.6	D	D	D	D	159	1,763	566.5	42.4	62	73	11.2	1.8
Cache	25.9	214.5	127	1,034	624.8	47.0	473	6,412	1,933.8	155.7	230	491	88.5	14.3
Carbon	4.4	212.4	28	131	63.1	6.0	70	986	298.1	26.3	16	49	6.1	1.3
Daggett	0.2	162.3	NA	NA	NA	NA	8	35	4.8	0.8	NA	NA	NA	NA
Davis	46.7	139.1	235	1,878	1,137.5	91.7	953	15,625	4,572.2	425.6	489	1,335	327.8	51.1
Duchesne	7.0	337.0	20	163	83.3	6.9	77	814	239.2	20.6	21	147	56.4	11.4
Emery	1.7	166.8	D	D	D	D	43	426	91.7	10.1	NA	NA	NA	NA
Garfield	1.4	283.5	NA	NA	NA	NA	21	138	31.9	2.6	5	D	0.5	D
Grand	6.1	635.8	10	96	25.5	3.1	77	841	220.2	24.8	33	129	20.9	3.7
Iron	10.6	220.0	33	282	223.9	13.5	195	2,320	676.2	56.1	102	179	40.6	6.0
Juab	4.6	433.3	7	43	32.5	1.4	33	374	91.7	5.6	NA	NA	NA	NA
Kane	2.3	326.7	D	D	D	D	38	382	72.2	7.8	17	33	5.7	1.1
Millard	3.9	309.2	14	78	250.2	3.5	56	756	181.8	13.3	D	D	D	D
Morgan	5.4	485.3	D	D	D	D	35	229	55.5	4.9	12	18	3.9	0.9
Piute	0.8	507.6	NA	NA	NA	NA	6	26	4.8	0.3	NA	NA	NA	NA
Rich	1.2	527.9	3	15	3.4	0.3	8	83	8.9	0.9	12	40	10.0	2.3
Salt Lake	394.8	356.5	1,629	28,690	27,264.8	1,904.6	3,525	63,439	23,434.7	2,041.3	2,383	10,595	3,305.3	542.9
San Juan	1.0	65.3	D	D	D	D	41	458	99.0	9.8	5	64	3.9	1.3
Sanpete	6.4	221.3	11	76	41.0	2.9	83	912	207.7	19.0	16	37	5.4	0.9
Sevier	5.2	247.3	D	D	D	5.4	89	1,339	358.8	33.6	19	92	34.7	4.5
Summit	8.8	222.0	49	450	415.6	34.7	331	3,835	1,313.1	110.5	319	1,466	310.0	60.7
Tooele	18.4	291.5	15	85	42.8	5.0	102	1,752	546.5	42.9	57	98	19.6	3.1
Uintah	4.9	130.0	47	359	247.2	19.1	135	1,709	446.3	45.9	62	244	65.3	15.2
Utah	127.7	222.0	428	7,417	4,043.4	449.7	1,915	26,903	7,988.5	744.7	D	D	D	D
Wasatch	4.3	148.8	20	82	40.9	3.8	95	999	305.1	25.7	84	185	102.3	8.2
Washington	49.4	317.3	164	1,343	1,444.0	64.5	628	9,079	2,651.3	259.4	388	849	186.0	26.7
Wayne	1.2	438.3	NA	NA	NA	NA	16	128	39.2	2.9	NA	NA	NA	NA
Weber	27.7	113.6	192	3,621	4,647.9	184.4	749	11,378	3,435.2	302.4	349	924	163.6	30.4
VERMONT	42.7	68.1	671	9,395	6,032.4	502.6	3,219	38,390	10,811.3	1,102.5	784	2,938	651.8	119.3
Addison	3.5	93.2	31	263	188.8	15.0	174	1,923	622.5	63.9	32	74	12.0	2.8
Bennington	3.3	90.9	D	D	D	D	251	2,765	801.2	79.6	49	214	35.5	7.6
Caledonia	1.8	57.5	30	321	102.5	15.0	160	1,667	524.3	47.7	D	D	D	D

1 Merchant wholesalers, except manufacturers' sales branches and offices. 2. Employer establishments.

STATE County	Professional, scientific, and technical services, 2017				Manufacturing, 2017				Accommodation and food services, 2017			
	Number of establish-ments	Number of employees	Sales (mil dol)	Average payroll (mil dol)	Number of establish-ments	Number of employees	Sales (mil dol)	Average payroll (mil dol)	Number of establis-hments	Number of employees	Sales (mil dol)	Annual payroll (mil dol)
	147	148	149	150	151	152	153	154	155	156	157	158
TEXAS—Cont'd												
Tom Green	D	D	D	D	94	3,370	1,936.4	182.0	270	5,195	279.6	78.7
Travis	D	D	D	D	796	27,003	11,868.1	1,971.1	3,254	79,884	5,781.2	1,640.7
Trinity	10	35	3.3	1.0	D	178	D	8.8	17	224	16.7	3.7
Tyler	23	67	7.9	2.4	10	170	43.5	6.6	27	269	13.5	3.5
Upshur	52	402	67.3	18.2	29	576	117.7	20.9	39	557	28.0	8.0
Upton	NA	NA	NA	NA	NA	NA	NA	NA	D	D	D	0.3
Uvalde	33	264	23.0	9.4	17	271	120.7	11.7	82	1,059	66.8	16.6
Val Verde	D	D	D	D	30	251	92.7	11.3	91	1,844	98.5	24.7
Van Zandt	82	256	27.5	9.5	34	788	179.9	45.8	84	1,254	62.9	19.2
Victoria	D	D	D	D	D	D	D	D	D	D	D	D
Walker	82	458	37.5	12.1	D	965	D	47.8	127	2,349	123.6	35.0
Waller	69	307	53.9	16.7	82	2,873	1,030.0	168.9	60	1,007	59.6	16.1
Ward	12	53	11.2	3.3	6	63	29.5	4.1	34	418	36.6	7.4
Washington	65	362	50.8	17.1	50	2,445	806.3	117.9	85	1,156	71.7	20.1
Webb	D	D	D	D	65	588	346.3	24.8	449	10,203	522.0	141.6
Wharton	55	306	54.3	13.6	42	1,386	477.6	58.9	82	1,271	61.2	16.6
Wheeler	11	48	5.7	2.0	3	3	0.3	0.1	25	263	12.0	3.6
Wichita	D	D	D	D	122	4,277	1,253.4	235.5	D	D	D	D
Wilbarger	20	67	5.9	1.7	D	D	D	D	31	394	20.4	5.2
Willacy	D	D	D	D	NA	NA	NA	NA	23	296	17.9	3.5
Williamson	D	D	D	D	328	6,872	1,816.3	376.5	985	20,762	1,214.2	354.9
Wilson	57	244	33.3	10.2	29	319	73.4	15.3	67	940	43.6	11.7
Winkler	6	6	2.0	0.4	NA	NA	NA	NA	D	D	D	D
Wise	91	377	52.6	16.7	70	1,617	469.7	82.7	109	1,662	89.8	24.3
Wood	70	592	38.9	15.5	40	935	666.8	51.3	83	1,098	67.1	15.2
Yoakum	7	18	2.1	0.5	10	132	41.6	7.5	23	147	7.8	1.9
Young	39	216	29.2	11.6	24	990	334.4	55.1	42	506	26.2	7.1
Zapata	NA	NA	NA	NA	D	8	D	D	D	D	D	D
Zavala	4	7	0.6	0.1	NA	NA	NA	NA	15	143	6.0	1.6
UTAH	10,822	91,901	15,230.7	5,581.8	3,377	121,527	55,788.0	7,171.0	5,931	118,734	7,098.2	2,003.5
Beaver	7	13	1.5	0.4	7	105	119.0	5.1	28	259	15.4	4.1
Box Elder	59	226	28.6	9.5	79	7,317	3,345.1	531.0	84	1,643	62.7	20.2
Cache	D	D	D	D	205	11,028	5,251.5	536.6	174	3,807	169.9	49.1
Carbon	33	115	16.5	6.1	24	422	133.5	22.7	34	616	28.2	7.4
Daggett	NA	NA	NA	NA	NA	NA	NA	NA	10	147	6.0	1.8
Davis	D	D	D	D	269	11,115	5,616.5	614.6	476	9,653	495.0	137.1
Duchesne	47	150	20.0	7.1	20	145	35.4	8.7	36	361	19.3	4.7
Emery	8	52	4.4	1.7	D	8	D	0.7	25	233	15.9	4.0
Garfield	D	D	D	D	7	17	3.7	0.7	67	707	90.1	23.7
Grand	27	145	51.3	6.3	12	78	30.3	4.6	94	1,811	144.3	37.7
Iron	143	477	55.4	18.8	78	1,577	845.5	72.9	119	2,022	100.7	27.1
Juab	20	286	25.6	13.6	14	562	172.9	27.5	29	293	14.5	3.6
Kane	11	38	3.2	1.1	D	103	D	3.3	58	1,022	108.3	28.7
Millard	13	114	17.9	4.2	14	540	643.0	31.7	27	288	15.2	3.9
Morgan	39	96	13.9	4.7	15	124	97.9	11.7	10	151	5.3	1.9
Piute	NA	NA	NA	NA	NA	NA	NA	NA	6	3	0.7	0.1
Rich	D	D	2.5	D	NA	NA	NA	NA	18	124	17.4	3.2
Salt Lake	D	D	D	D	1,428	53,632	26,348.7	3,415.5	2,419	50,385	3,104.8	878.5
San Juan	D	D	D	D	D	110	D	5.6	47	761	61.5	18.9
Sanpete	25	609	94.9	17.0	30	763	265.4	34.6	44	481	15.2	4.1
Sevier	41	200	27.7	10.5	21	252	64.1	11.1	57	807	39.6	10.1
Summit	D	D	D	D	51	512	159.3	30.8	210	7,276	600.8	190.3
Tooele	D	D	D	D	29	1,431	644.7	76.6	77	1,222	62.9	16.5
Uintah	97	331	48.1	16.6	38	236	41.1	10.9	70	1,050	52.5	14.8
Utah	2,142	15,278	2,474.2	976.1	548	15,909	5,758.0	885.1	839	17,217	926.5	257.9
Wasatch	144	606	72.1	31.0	35	309	60.3	13.9	58	1,253	64.2	21.2
Washington	D	D	D	D	163	2,634	620.3	119.0	363	7,354	449.3	119.5
Wayne	D	D	D	0.1	D	5	D	0.1	28	181	20.2	3.9
Weber	D	D	D	D	265	12,589	5,483.8	695.8	424	7,607	391.7	109.6
VERMONT	2,071	12,298	2,039.9	825.8	1,033	28,629	8,652.4	1,610.0	1,979	32,891	2,019.8	620.5
Addison	125	564	97.3	44.8	60	1,568	829.3	98.4	91	976	73.6	25.1
Bennington	118	362	51.3	18.0	67	2,093	488.3	91.1	141	1,757	113.4	38.3
Caledonia	D	D	D	D	52	1,172	232.4	55.7	72	792	42.2	13.1

STATE County	Health care and social assistance, 2017				Other services, 2017				Nonemployer businesses, 2019		Value of residential construction authorized by building permits, 2021	
	Number of establish-ments	Number of employees	Receipts (mil dol)	Annual payroll (mil dol)	Number of establish-ments	Number of employees	Receipts (mil dol)	Annual payroll (mil dol)	Number	Receipts (mil dol)	New construction ($1,000)	Number of housing units
	159	160	161	162	163	164	165	166	167	168	169	170
TEXAS—Cont'd												
Tom Green	D	D	D	D	D	D	170.8	D	8,980	402.9	71,863	333
Travis	3,627	76,597	9,316.7	3,583.8	2,505	21,189	3,149.1	897.6	138,601	7,944.1	4,755,409	29,052
Trinity	19	254	19.0	8.3	11	47	2.4	0.7	1,113	44.7	520	4
Tyler	32	506	38.2	17.1	D	D	D	D	1,276	57.3	1,958	9
Upshur	40	592	35.4	15.2	24	78	9.6	2.8	3,151	151.6	5,451	35
Upton	D	D	D	D	NA	NA	NA	NA	276	14.7	218	1
Uvalde	75	1,754	179.5	81.2	D	D	D	D	2,852	150.4	2,711	24
Val Verde	90	3,129	178.0	75.4	49	284	19.9	5.0	3,969	126.8	33,454	155
Van Zandt	71	1,100	79.2	31.2	58	323	35.7	9.4	5,053	243.7	9,286	82
Victoria	295	6,854	755.1	317.4	149	1,138	170.3	46.8	7,041	309.8	58,282	349
Walker	103	2,378	252.7	92.8	57	333	29.4	8.0	4,744	198.2	175,465	1,064
Waller	48	1,215	55.4	24.4	45	395	131.8	23.0	5,079	253.4	31,130	265
Ward	10	188	9.0	4.4	13	130	20.5	6.5	796	44.8	0	0
Washington	85	1,862	128.2	54.4	52	207	22.3	6.4	3,618	180.3	50,406	319
Webb	540	16,245	1,058.6	433.7	228	1,361	128.5	36.4	28,148	1,409.3	251,974	1,684
Wharton	78	1,774	109.0	46.9	72	210	23.6	5.3	3,724	154.0	54,275	261
Wheeler	9	273	23.1	9.8	D	D	6.0	D	475	22.9	0	0
Wichita	407	11,101	1,150.0	427.1	233	1,130	154.3	34.9	8,014	387.2	36,988	145
Wilbarger	33	1,153	134.7	56.6	24	86	10.0	2.0	726	25.3	435	2
Willacy	36	525	33.4	16.1	11	52	5.9	1.6	1,321	47.8	5,414	47
Williamson	1,246	22,811	2,778.7	1,129.1	804	5,282	542.7	176.1	55,704	2,570.6	2,992,519	15,036
Wilson	63	1,184	100.9	45.1	52	182	18.1	4.0	4,042	225.3	40,458	149
Winkler	7	20	7.4	3.0	D	D	D	D	689	40.7	525	2
Wise	119	3,181	452.0	152.3	78	415	44.9	12.5	6,379	371.1	34,214	132
Wood	82	1,229	115.8	43.5	48	206	22.2	5.7	3,999	208.3	4,197	22
Yoakum	9	D	30.6	D	D	D	D	1.8	657	29.1	0	0
Young	55	1,157	86.6	36.7	46	147	18.0	4.1	2,118	137.1	225	5
Zapata	16	256	8.6	4.3	D	D	D	D	1,517	51.5	NA	NA
Zavala	12	572	15.1	9.9	NA	NA	NA	NA	849	31.2	57	3
UTAH	8,254	146,365	18,708.2	6,703.4	4,763	29,903	3,526.9	957.5	256,450	12,541.4	9,188,026	39,058
Beaver	D	D	D	D	9	35	3.8	0.8	574	24.4	18,902	62
Box Elder	D	D	D	D	62	260	29.6	6.9	3,703	157.6	150,910	881
Cache	396	5,553	641.6	212.1	211	885	97.7	25.6	9,707	406.5	322,560	1,137
Carbon	73	961	104.3	38.5	42	279	29.7	9.5	1,164	42.1	12,848	42
Daggett	NA	NA	NA	NA	NA	NA	NA	NA	88	2.6	5,072	17
Davis	820	11,587	1,186.9	451.3	433	2,737	259.3	73.4	26,135	1,180.2	818,500	3,812
Duchesne	43	985	115.2	39.0	D	D	D	D	1,602	73.6	34,080	136
Emery	D	D	D	6.8	D	D	10.6	D	650	21.4	2,746	14
Garfield	D	D	D	D	NA	NA	NA	NA	480	16.6	17,371	76
Grand	D	D	D	16.9	D	D	D	D	1,131	50.1	24,764	93
Iron	157	2,435	208.6	75.6	83	276	29.2	6.9	4,371	174.7	201,754	891
Juab	22	510	47.6	14.6	D	D	D	D	843	41.3	37,855	135
Kane	D	D	D	D	D	D	126.7	D	873	36.8	65,154	338
Millard	D	D	D	D	D	D	D	D	867	36.1	10,864	53
Morgan	D	D	D	D	11	38	6.2	1.1	1,210	62.0	58,118	153
Piute	NA	NA	NA	NA	NA	NA	NA	NA	128	6.7	5,259	33
Rich	NA	NA	NA	NA	D	D	D	D	313	15.5	22,068	68
Salt Lake	3,223	67,350	9,533.4	3,510.6	2,064	14,470	1,710.4	502.3	95,332	5,030.2	2,125,291	10,649
San Juan	D	D	D	D	14	61	4.9	1.5	812	26.7	48,658	161
Sanpete	D	D	D	D	29	136	22.5	5.0	2,085	88.2	40,906	227
Sevier	66	921	92.9	31.8	27	125	21.7	4.9	1,523	72.9	40,581	188
Summit	160	1,569	206.8	70.2	119	1,173	150.5	39.0	6,800	507.3	222,251	439
Tooele	107	1,371	141.2	52.7	72	330	30.9	9.2	3,730	134.8	259,798	993
Uintah	64	709	79.1	25.2	71	352	47.7	11.7	1,970	88.2	25,615	86
Utah	1,456	25,794	2,900.9	1,042.8	D	D	D	D	54,065	2,445.5	2,733,360	11,040
Wasatch	75	698	83.9	27.4	43	203	19.5	5.5	3,817	220.9	625,260	1,179
Washington	583	9,409	1,212.8	395.3	265	1,401	138.9	37.6	16,476	864.6	721,283	3,484
Wayne	4	D	8.3	D	D	D	D	D	369	20.3	7,543	35
Weber	653	11,567	1,624.1	531.7	337	2,162	223.4	62.1	15,632	693.8	528,655	2,636
VERMONT	2,102	48,285	5,451.6	2,229.4	1,603	7,339	922.1	244.0	61,921	2,799.3	499,725	2,319
Addison	127	2,143	183.1	86.2	83	356	56.6	11.8	3,901	153.4	31,302	124
Bennington	149	3,447	358.3	156.7	95	394	36.9	9.7	3,705	176.5	31,678	77
Caledonia	107	2,144	187.1	87.8	66	217	25.5	5.6	2,965	127.9	13,907	82

STATE County	Government employment and payroll, 2017: Full-time equivalent employees	Government employment and payroll, 2017: March payroll (dollars)	March payroll (percent of total): Adminis-tration, judicial, and legal	March payroll (percent of total): Police and corrections	March payroll (percent of total): Fire protection	March payroll (percent of total): Highways and transpor-tation	March payroll (percent of total): Health and welfare	March payroll (percent of total): Natural resources and utilities	March payroll (percent of total): Education and libraries	Local government finances, 2017: General revenue: Total (mil dol)	General revenue: Inter-govern-mental (mil dol)	Taxes: Total (mil dol)	Taxes: Per capita[1] (dollars): Total	Taxes: Per capita[1] (dollars): Property
	171	172	173	174	175	176	177	178	179	180	181	182	183	184
TEXAS—Cont'd														
Tom Green	4,841	15,029,790	7.9	15.0	6.4	2.7	4.6	5.4	55.8	363.6	123.4	184.0	1,565	1,179
Travis	51,463	243,532,757	8.3	14.1	5.4	3.9	7.4	17.4	41.9	6,766.8	1,086.2	4,030.3	3,283	2,711
Trinity	688	2,230,816	4.4	4.4	0.0	1.7	19.1	3.3	65.8	41.4	23.1	15.6	1,063	985
Tyler	985	2,957,565	9.8	4.0	0.0	3.3	14.9	2.6	65.4	69.8	29.4	35.3	1,643	1,550
Upshur	1,626	4,964,608	4.4	7.9	0.6	1.9	0.6	1.7	82.4	103.6	51.1	43.2	1,051	943
Upton	440	1,729,158	8.5	8.8	0.0	4.0	37.0	4.2	35.6	55.2	5.5	41.7	11,408	11,121
Uvalde	2,248	8,364,083	3.5	5.5	0.2	2.5	23.8	2.4	61.9	362.3	67.7	59.3	2,192	1,495
Val Verde	2,377	7,983,288	13.0	5.2	4.4	2.6	3.2	4.1	66.1	203.8	115.8	59.0	1,203	925
Van Zandt	2,057	6,327,002	5.5	7.5	0.4	2.2	0.5	2.4	80.7	149.2	71.7	60.3	1,092	1,003
Victoria	5,737	20,693,284	4.2	8.5	3.5	1.7	33.2	3.0	45.1	528.8	104.2	200.0	2,173	1,705
Walker	2,264	8,416,852	12.9	13.6	0.9	2.8	0.5	20.0	47.2	188.1	64.3	76.7	1,053	811
Waller	1,917	7,261,196	7.2	9.1	0.6	2.7	0.1	3.0	76.4	171.6	59.7	99.3	1,920	1,807
Ward	596	2,124,695	13.5	14.7	0.1	4.9	3.2	7.7	54.2	76.5	11.9	45.7	4,011	3,625
Washington	2,228	8,498,259	5.2	5.3	0.9	1.8	2.5	3.5	78.9	214.8	55.6	67.9	1,947	1,537
Webb	15,338	59,020,428	5.3	11.4	5.2	2.6	3.5	3.6	67.9	1,369.4	592.0	500.1	1,827	1,480
Wharton	3,030	10,927,958	4.1	6.8	1.3	3.6	21.3	1.9	60.5	199.1	70.2	81.5	1,948	1,676
Wheeler	559	1,693,868	6.7	4.0	0.0	2.5	30.5	3.6	51.7	56.7	9.7	33.9	6,405	5,922
Wichita	5,560	21,003,333	5.3	13.4	10.2	2.6	9.6	5.3	51.9	436.1	168.9	189.5	1,439	1,160
Wilbarger	1,088	3,776,963	2.2	3.4	3.3	0.6	21.1	2.7	66.3	83.6	28.7	25.5	2,011	1,766
Willacy	1,179	3,918,839	5.7	5.1	0.0	2.2	0.7	2.6	83.4	82.4	47.9	27.1	1,261	1,095
Williamson	19,582	75,206,562	2.5	6.6	3.5	0.8	5.5	4.0	75.0	2,121.8	335.9	1,501.8	2,749	2,413
Wilson	2,173	8,547,244	4.2	4.0	0.0	1.5	13.8	5.4	70.5	170.3	65.2	62.0	1,260	1,144
Winkler	531	2,078,630	7.0	8.9	0.0	1.5	15.7	5.6	60.0	76.7	12.0	49.8	6,548	6,025
Wise	2,062	7,356,010	8.7	12.0	0.7	3.8	3.1	4.1	66.4	193.9	40.0	126.2	1,917	1,716
Wood	1,410	4,324,130	8.8	9.5	0.5	4.2	0.6	4.4	71.8	129.6	60.7	57.0	1,289	1,147
Yoakum	807	3,005,305	7.3	8.7	0.3	3.3	26.7	3.9	49.1	49.4	14.3	30.7	3,585	3,342
Young	1,100	3,752,022	5.6	7.4	1.3	1.9	28.9	3.1	50.8	66.8	24.9	29.1	1,622	1,357
Zapata	928	3,072,711	3.8	13.7	3.1	2.5	0.5	6.6	69.2	62.8	29.0	23.2	1,627	1,490
Zavala	671	2,155,340	3.1	7.7	2.2	2.3	1.9	2.4	77.4	45.8	20.6	20.7	1,730	1,624
UTAH	X	X	X	X	X	X	X	X	X	X	X	X	X	X
Beaver	450	1,782,865	9.5	17.4	0.0	2.4	23.1	7.2	38.9	312.6	14.4	15.0	2,336	1,960
Box Elder	1,838	5,661,061	7.3	10.2	2.2	2.7	1.8	7.2	67.0	188.5	75.6	81.3	1,507	1,219
Cache	3,436	12,872,862	6.9	7.2	3.0	4.3	9.8	8.2	59.0	396.3	171.3	130.4	1,049	691
Carbon	929	3,249,409	11.3	10.1	1.7	3.5	12.2	8.0	50.6	83.6	31.7	31.2	1,548	1,101
Daggett	89	336,348	16.7	26.7	0.6	4.5	0.0	1.9	48.6	8.9	3.7	3.0	2,960	2,603
Davis	9,122	35,252,166	7.4	9.0	3.2	1.9	4.6	7.7	64.9	1,098.5	460.6	377.7	1,089	785
Duchesne	1,280	4,671,224	6.5	6.4	0.4	2.5	47.0	4.3	32.0	113.7	50.8	45.2	2,276	1,684
Emery	458	1,726,217	13.3	9.6	0.1	4.9	0.4	9.8	60.5	44.5	16.8	20.3	2,027	1,742
Garfield	229	883,712	14.5	15.1	0.0	9.8	2.4	4.3	53.4	34.3	14.7	12.5	2,491	1,187
Grand	539	1,976,807	13.3	11.0	0.8	5.8	13.1	11.8	38.8	89.3	16.0	52.7	5,500	3,877
Iron	1,323	5,015,363	8.9	12.3	1.2	4.0	2.7	7.4	61.5	150.6	57.0	71.0	1,398	996
Juab	418	1,619,105	10.1	9.3	0.6	4.1	0.5	11.1	61.4	53.0	25.8	14.4	1,273	1,032
Kane	432	1,643,224	10.6	10.7	1.6	2.6	26.5	7.9	36.9	59.6	18.9	24.1	3,208	1,994
Millard	527	2,164,822	10.1	13.1	0.1	5.5	2.0	5.4	61.5	68.2	24.3	31.5	2,454	2,129
Morgan	306	1,088,010	11.5	5.4	0.8	2.0	0.0	4.7	73.3	32.5	14.1	13.4	1,132	901
Piute	86	283,969	16.6	4.3	1.2	4.6	0.9	0.5	71.3	8.6	6.2	1.5	1,060	864
Rich	134	513,182	18.1	4.3	4.7	2.9	0.0	2.6	65.7	14.7	4.7	7.9	3,286	2,590
Salt Lake	35,948	144,317,443	7.7	10.4	5.6	10.9	4.6	8.5	49.2	4,296.5	1,263.2	2,056.0	1,809	1,168
San Juan	857	3,215,493	6.8	7.4	0.3	4.4	20.8	1.6	57.3	95.2	44.8	22.0	1,438	998
Sanpete	1,296	4,137,485	6.3	7.7	0.4	2.0	20.0	4.2	58.2	132.6	56.0	23.2	776	518
Sevier	795	2,659,519	9.4	11.6	0.2	1.4	0.9	6.3	68.4	93.9	45.3	28.7	1,348	934
Summit	1,905	8,164,223	10.9	9.1	7.5	6.3	2.9	10.6	45.7	344.8	55.7	195.2	4,722	3,687
Tooele	1,952	6,924,862	7.5	9.0	0.7	2.3	7.2	3.8	67.4	206.7	96.0	74.1	1,098	820
Uintah	1,443	5,249,522	8.2	9.6	0.6	4.4	13.8	10.8	49.6	167.0	67.8	64.2	1,823	1,421
Utah	14,705	58,734,102	6.8	8.9	2.7	1.6	5.8	9.0	62.8	2,025.2	807.5	729.4	1,202	783
Wasatch	1,076	4,418,400	9.3	8.1	2.1	3.9	0.2	14.3	55.7	138.9	33.0	69.5	2,181	1,720
Washington	4,494	17,531,308	8.8	10.7	1.8	2.4	6.9	15.0	52.2	567.9	183.6	240.2	1,448	947
Wayne	122	404,320	12.0	4.6	0.0	6.1	0.0	1.9	72.1	11.8	7.6	2.6	964	652
Weber	7,190	28,603,438	6.3	11.2	4.6	1.5	8.5	8.0	57.5	814.7	285.2	337.8	1,343	864
VERMONT	X	X	X	X	X	X	X	X	X	X	X	X	X	X
Addison	991	4,172,913	6.0	3.7	0.0	6.6	0.0	4.1	79.1	150.5	96.9	37.2	1,008	977
Bennington	1,329	5,083,941	5.5	5.8	0.0	5.7	0.9	3.1	78.2	156.1	113.3	33.0	925	883
Caledonia	936	3,532,843	5.1	3.6	1.3	9.1	0.0	5.8	74.7	120.2	86.3	26.0	864	860

1. Based on the resident population estimated as of July 1 of the year shown.

STATE County	Local government finances, 2017 (cont.)									Government employment, 2020			Individual income tax returns, 2019		
	Direct general expenditure							Debt outstanding							
			Percent of total for:												
	Total (mil dol)	Per capita[1] (dollars)	Education	Health and hospitals	Police protection	Public welfare	Highways	Total (mil dol)	Per capita[1] (dollars)	Federal civilian	Federal military	State and local	Number of returns	Mean adjusted gross income	Mean income tax
	185	186	187	188	189	190	191	192	193	194	195	196	197	198	199
TEXAS—Cont'd															
Tom Green	367.7	3,128	49.6	1.1	6.8	0.1	2.8	469.7	3,996	1,243	3,775	7,576	54,990	65,966	8,073
Travis	7,070.8	5,760	38.1	9.8	6.4	0.5	11.2	17,031.6	13,874	13,417	2,809	118,140	634,500	114,369	19,028
Trinity	40.6	2,767	61.5	1.6	2.4	0.7	6.3	32.8	2,236	29	28	606	6,260	46,376	3,900
Tyler	57.3	2,664	62.3	0.2	6.7	0.4	7.3	30.0	1,392	49	37	1,580	7,930	49,245	4,118
Upshur	106.9	2,604	74.0	0.0	4.1	0.2	3.9	62.3	1,517	76	80	1,816	17,610	52,646	4,509
Upton	87.9	24,032	80.1	13.8	0.2	0.0	0.3	79.7	21,793	6	7	540	1,500	80,309	10,160
Uvalde	345.4	12,772	27.9	16.6	1.8	46.5	1.8	80.4	2,971	243	50	2,572	12,260	47,718	5,088
Val Verde	200.1	4,082	53.7	0.3	5.5	0.7	4.1	119.7	2,440	2,357	1,450	2,826	22,130	47,143	3,628
Van Zandt	158.7	2,878	73.3	0.0	3.4	0.2	5.1	119.6	2,169	106	109	2,287	24,620	56,554	5,481
Victoria	528.9	5,746	36.2	34.2	5.8	0.0	3.5	522.0	5,671	211	182	6,142	42,830	62,817	7,078
Walker	413.1	5,673	20.3	3.4	2.8	0.0	2.4	1,713.4	23,530	156	137	13,052	25,890	49,903	4,788
Waller	213.6	4,131	72.2	0.0	3.9	0.2	4.0	275.7	5,330	68	105	4,773	23,350	71,971	8,728
Ward	76.6	6,730	39.9	19.4	5.8	0.5	5.1	47.5	4,175	17	23	854	5,440	73,821	9,097
Washington	206.2	5,916	67.5	1.6	3.9	0.3	8.7	197.7	5,671	91	64	2,948	17,090	65,276	7,445
Webb	1,395.4	5,099	60.8	2.6	6.2	0.5	0.9	1,627.0	5,945	3,972	526	18,865	122,760	42,350	3,467
Wharton	242.3	5,793	51.4	26.4	4.5	0.1	4.3	109.0	2,606	92	79	2,732	20,320	54,967	5,617
Wheeler	54.5	10,287	53.2	27.9	2.4	0.2	2.3	22.7	4,283	25	9	580	2,240	51,878	4,680
Wichita	497.0	3,774	50.5	9.2	6.5	0.9	3.2	545.0	4,139	1,913	6,013	9,169	56,790	57,266	5,769
Wilbarger	83.8	6,606	52.7	25.9	3.1	0.1	3.9	19.7	1,555	44	23	2,437	5,740	48,023	3,874
Willacy	78.6	3,653	70.8	1.2	2.6	0.1	1.8	180.4	8,389	39	34	1,121	7,800	36,488	2,367
Williamson	2,269.3	4,154	57.0	3.9	4.1	0.4	5.6	5,149.2	9,426	1,060	1,213	23,869	292,530	84,701	10,154
Wilson	152.2	3,092	55.0	22.3	3.1	0.0	3.4	202.8	4,122	103	99	2,368	23,200	72,848	8,147
Winkler	71.3	9,371	49.9	17.1	4.9	0.4	2.0	73.8	9,706	9	15	590	3,450	76,530	9,531
Wise	185.5	2,817	50.9	2.4	6.3	0.5	7.0	276.0	4,192	144	134	4,311	31,730	67,401	7,071
Wood	99.7	2,253	68.4	0.3	4.7	0.0	5.8	60.6	1,370	106	85	1,809	20,330	54,639	5,129
Yoakum	65.2	7,624	80.4	1.0	2.1	0.1	2.3	113.0	13,200	13	17	804	3,730	65,772	6,527
Young	62.9	3,509	54.1	8.2	6.5	0.1	5.7	62.0	3,461	48	34	1,280	8,010	60,087	6,813
Zapata	57.6	4,044	67.2	1.5	4.3	1.2	2.5	40.6	2,848	151	27	890	5,360	34,666	2,104
Zavala	66.9	5,595	77.3	0.6	2.7	0.6	2.2	58.4	4,885	11	22	816	4,560	36,677	2,465
UTAH	X	X	X	X	X	X	X	X	X	39,375	16,784	209,037	1,430,630	74,600	8,364
Beaver	303.0	47,188	5.2	88.9	0.2	0.1	0.1	27.1	4,213	42	25	703	3,030	48,637	3,282
Box Elder	167.6	3,105	58.6	1.8	4.7	0.7	5.0	93.0	1,722	192	216	2,653	24,740	58,128	4,315
Cache	411.6	3,313	56.5	9.0	3.9	0.3	3.6	230.4	1,854	362	486	11,041	53,210	61,814	5,340
Carbon	87.5	4,345	45.5	6.5	5.0	1.4	10.2	29.4	1,459	149	76	1,913	8,630	52,110	4,095
Daggett	8.5	8,372	46.1	1.4	22.4	0.0	5.8	5.6	5,576	58	4	104	420	54,786	4,326
Davis	1,072.4	3,094	57.1	3.7	5.6	0.0	2.6	891.0	2,570	14,444	5,679	14,754	155,400	78,036	8,114
Duchesne	141.3	7,113	61.7	1.4	3.1	0.1	14.5	87.2	4,388	81	74	2,312	7,640	57,110	4,864
Emery	38.3	3,829	67.8	0.2	0.0	0.0	10.1	142.0	14,196	58	38	768	4,070	51,611	3,463
Garfield	33.0	6,564	33.9	7.7	11.5	1.0	16.1	3.9	784	152	18	373	2,280	46,987	3,388
Grand	50.7	5,286	31.3	8.3	8.3	1.0	7.8	38.0	3,966	264	36	756	5,370	53,622	4,800
Iron	139.2	2,742	58.7	0.7	7.1	0.0	5.1	43.5	858	310	212	4,454	23,070	50,737	3,807
Juab	45.2	4,006	58.6	0.9	3.6	0.3	4.6	47.3	4,186	30	45	828	4,840	57,462	4,263
Kane	52.4	6,968	32.9	18.8	4.7	0.8	4.7	47.5	6,311	86	29	642	3,460	54,169	4,555
Millard	69.7	5,435	47.5	2.0	7.1	0.2	9.9	23.6	1,841	92	51	880	5,290	52,516	3,910
Morgan	29.6	2,503	65.8	0.6	4.1	0.0	1.9	19.3	1,632	24	47	548	5,110	98,653	11,772
Piute	9.2	6,571	58.8	1.4	4.3	0.0	10.2	5.8	4,154	3	7	116	590	38,885	2,976
Rich	14.2	5,919	54.9	0.7	3.5	1.3	5.8	3.4	1,428	13	9	202	1,010	61,493	5,086
Salt Lake	4,414.0	3,883	36.6	1.3	5.8	3.4	7.4	9,978.0	8,778	11,745	4,563	96,459	552,300	74,652	8,735
San Juan	98.6	6,455	43.2	18.6	2.4	1.3	13.1	16.3	1,068	164	56	1,440	5,070	46,787	3,448
Sanpete	111.2	3,715	49.0	22.5	3.9	0.1	3.6	49.8	1,663	102	107	2,888	10,730	48,956	3,490
Sevier	91.5	4,298	46.0	8.2	6.6	0.0	13.5	53.7	2,521	188	81	1,660	8,960	56,245	4,539
Summit	336.1	8,132	28.6	0.5	2.1	0.0	2.5	277.9	6,723	67	160	2,718	24,440	177,956	35,728
Tooele	208.2	3,085	63.9	4.3	4.3	1.1	3.2	150.6	2,231	1,275	302	2,826	31,400	62,099	4,858
Uintah	173.8	4,934	38.7	11.4	4.1	0.0	10.8	89.5	2,540	383	135	2,702	13,950	55,345	4,519
Utah	1,832.7	3,021	55.9	3.8	4.3	0.3	5.4	2,304.2	3,798	1,199	2,460	30,781	259,640	83,894	9,614
Wasatch	161.6	5,066	62.0	1.0	4.2	0.0	6.0	140.3	4,401	56	132	1,833	15,450	100,357	14,692
Washington	514.8	3,103	51.2	5.2	8.3	0.1	2.6	527.3	3,178	655	692	8,465	79,920	67,821	7,284
Wayne	11.0	4,086	55.1	0.7	4.0	0.0	10.1	2.1	776	85	10	175	1,230	47,664	3,493
Weber	744.9	2,961	47.2	2.3	6.4	0.0	6.2	837.4	3,328	7,096	1,034	14,043	119,450	61,339	5,461
VERMONT	X	X	X	X	X	X	X	X	X	7,376	3,931	44,133	331,590	67,600	7,504
Addison	160.7	4,355	74.3	0.1	2.4	0.2	10.2	58.8	1,593	122	217	1,717	18,830	66,811	6,788
Bennington	191.5	5,367	76.1	0.2	3.8	0.1	7.8	45.5	1,276	214	213	2,051	18,890	67,124	8,007
Caledonia	122.4	4,061	73.7	0.2	2.0	0.0	10.4	34.3	1,139	109	179	1,873	14,990	51,951	4,554

1. Based on the resident population estimated as of July 1 of the year shown.

State / county code	CBSA code[1]	County Type code[2]	STATE County	Land area[3] (sq. mi)	Population, 2021: Total persons 2021	Population, 2021: Rank	Population, 2021: Per square mile	Population and population characteristics, 2021: Race alone or in combination, not Hispanic or Latino (percent): White	Black	American Indian, Alaska Native	Asian and Pacific Islancer	Percent Hispanic or Latino[4]	Age (percent): Under 5 years	5 to 17 years	18 to 24 years	25 to 34 years	35 to 44 years	45 to 54 years
				1	2	3	4	5	6	7	8	9	10	11	12	13	14	15
			VERMONT—Cont'd															
50007	15540	3	Chittenden	537.3	168,865	398	314.3	89.9	3.3	0.8	5.8	2.6	4.3	9.9	18.7	14.5	12.5	11.4
50009		9	Essex	662.5	5,925	2,740	8.9	96.3	1.3	1.6	1.0	1.7	3.9	9.8	9.0	8.9	10.2	13.2
50011	15540	3	Franklin	630.7	50,325	992	79.8	95.4	1.4	2.3	1.4	1.9	5.6	12.5	10.9	13.1	13.0	13.0
50013	15540	3	Grand Isle	81.8	7,421	2,625	90.7	95.0	1.7	2.7	1.5	2.0	4.2	9.7	9.5	11.3	11.3	12.7
50015		8	Lamoille	462.3	26,126	1,560	56.5	95.9	1.7	1.1	1.1	2.0	4.7	11.7	12.1	12.9	13.2	12.9
50017	30100	9	Orange	687.2	29,541	1,443	43.0	96.9	1.1	1.1	0.9	1.5	4.3	10.5	10.5	10.9	12.5	12.3
50019		7	Orleans	694.5	27,546	1,516	39.7	96.3	1.3	1.5	0.9	1.8	4.8	11.1	10.8	11.2	11.7	12.2
50021	40860	4	Rutland	929.7	60,591	872	65.2	96.4	1.2	0.9	1.2	1.8	4.1	10.0	12.2	10.9	10.9	11.9
50023	12740	4	Washington	686.6	59,969	877	87.3	95.6	1.6	1.1	1.5	2.1	4.3	10.2	13.4	11.4	12.5	12.8
50025		7	Windham	785.5	46,090	1,057	58.7	94.4	2.2	1.2	1.7	2.6	4.1	10.3	10.5	10.6	11.7	11.5
50027	30100	7	Windsor	969.8	58,196	902	60.0	95.6	1.3	1.1	1.6	2.1	4.1	10.3	9.5	11.0	12.2	11.8
51000		0	VIRGINIA	39,482.1	8,642,274	X	218.9	62.9	20.7	0.8	8.5	10.2	5.7	12.3	13.1	13.6	13.4	12.6
51001		8	Accomack	449.3	33,246	1,349	74.0	61.2	28.9	0.8	1.2	9.5	5.2	11.7	10.1	10.4	10.2	11.4
51003	16820	3	Albemarle	720.5	113,535	547	157.6	78.6	10.6	0.6	7.0	5.9	5.0	11.2	15.0	12.7	12.5	11.2
51005		6	Alleghany	446.6	14,986	2,089	33.6	92.8	5.8	0.7	0.7	1.8	4.2	10.3	10.9	10.2	10.0	12.8
51007	40060	1	Amelia	355.4	13,268	2,197	37.3	75.6	20.5	1.0	0.9	3.8	5.2	11.4	10.7	11.3	11.2	12.6
51009	31340	2	Amherst	474.0	31,273	1,394	66.0	77.0	20.3	1.4	1.2	2.7	5.1	11.3	11.3	11.5	11.1	12.7
51011	31340	2	Appomattox	334.2	16,353	2,011	48.9	79.3	19.4	0.7	0.7	2.2	6.3	12.0	10.7	12.4	11.6	11.9
51013	47900	1	Arlington	26.0	232,965	296	8,960.2	63.4	10.6	0.8	13.2	15.6	5.2	10.2	11.1	22.3	16.5	12.9
51015	44420	3	Augusta	967.1	77,563	731	80.2	90.7	5.5	0.6	1.0	3.7	4.3	10.8	11.0	11.8	12.1	12.8
51017		8	Bath	529.2	4,114	2,875	7.8	93.1	4.7	0.6	0.8	2.5	4.7	8.5	8.4	9.9	9.3	12.9
51019	31340	2	Bedford	760.1	80,131	712	105.4	88.6	7.8	0.7	1.8	2.7	4.5	11.3	11.0	10.5	10.5	13.1
51021	14140	8	Bland	357.7	6,173	2,722	17.3	94.1	4.6	0.5	0.8	1.1	3.5	8.0	9.1	12.4	12.7	15.2
51023	40220	2	Botetourt	541.3	33,866	1,334	62.6	93.6	3.8	0.7	1.3	2.1	4.2	10.8	10.6	10.0	11.1	13.5
51025		6	Brunswick	566.2	15,940	2,035	28.2	42.1	54.7	0.7	1.3	2.7	4.1	8.8	11.4	14.8	12.1	11.8
51027		9	Buchanan	502.9	19,816	1,827	39.4	94.9	3.8	0.4	0.7	1.0	4.1	9.9	9.8	11.1	11.7	13.8
51029		3	Buckingham	579.6	16,947	1,976	29.2	63.7	34.4	0.8	0.7	2.5	4.4	10.6	9.8	13.6	13.5	13.4
51031	31340	2	Campbell	503.2	55,492	930	110.3	80.2	16.4	0.8	1.6	3.1	5.2	11.2	10.9	13.1	11.6	12.6
51033		1	Caroline	527.4	31,332	1,392	59.4	65.9	28.0	1.3	1.9	6.2	5.8	13.1	10.5	13.8	13.2	12.7
51035		7	Carroll	474.7	29,048	1,454	61.2	94.2	1.5	0.5	0.5	4.3	4.2	10.2	9.7	10.1	10.3	13.5
51036	40060	1	Charles City	182.9	6,594	2,693	36.1	46.8	45.1	7.7	1.6	2.4	3.6	7.9	9.0	10.1	9.8	13.2
51037		8	Charlotte	475.3	11,448	2,316	24.1	69.7	28.0	0.9	0.6	2.6	5.3	12.0	11.3	10.5	10.1	12.0
51041	40060	1	Chesterfield	423.5	370,688	197	875.3	61.3	25.8	0.8	4.7	10.2	5.8	13.5	12.8	12.1	13.9	13.1
51043	47900	1	Clarke	175.9	14,881	2,094	84.6	86.8	5.4	1.1	2.2	7.0	4.1	11.3	11.4	9.5	11.2	13.4
51045	40220	2	Craig	328.1	4,865	2,831	14.8	97.0	1.0	0.9	0.6	1.6	3.8	10.0	10.1	11.1	9.8	13.9
51047	47900	1	Culpeper	379.2	53,596	947	141.3	71.4	15.4	0.8	2.6	13.0	6.3	14.2	12.1	11.7	13.3	12.5
51049		8	Cumberland	297.5	9,681	2,438	32.5	65.8	31.3	1.2	0.9	3.4	5.1	10.9	10.5	11.6	10.6	12.2
51051		9	Dickenson	330.5	13,787	2,168	41.7	97.9	0.9	0.5	0.4	1.0	4.3	11.2	10.2	10.9	12.5	12.9
51053	40060	1	Dinwiddie	503.9	27,912	1,502	55.4	63.8	31.6	0.8	1.5	4.1	4.6	12.0	11.0	12.9	11.8	13.5
51057		6	Essex	257.3	10,573	2,371	41.1	56.9	38.5	1.3	1.8	4.4	4.7	9.6	10.5	11.2	10.7	12.2
51059	47900	1	Fairfax	391.0	1,139,720	40	2,914.9	52.4	11.1	0.6	23.0	16.6	5.9	13.1	12.4	13.0	14.6	13.8
51061	47900	1	Fauquier	648.0	73,815	749	113.9	80.1	8.8	0.8	2.6	10.4	5.5	13.2	12.0	11.1	12.6	13.4
51063		3	Floyd	380.9	15,566	2,057	40.9	94.5	2.8	0.8	0.9	2.8	4.7	10.6	10.2	10.0	10.8	13.7
51065	16820	3	Fluvanna	287.1	27,723	1,510	96.6	79.4	16.6	0.8	1.7	4.1	4.8	10.8	10.7	12.5	13.0	12.9
51067	40220	2	Franklin	690.6	54,938	933	79.6	88.3	8.8	0.5	0.9	3.1	4.6	10.6	11.2	10.1	9.8	12.5
51069	49020	3	Frederick	413.1	93,717	645	226.9	82.4	5.9	0.6	2.7	10.6	5.5	13.1	11.8	12.0	12.9	12.7
51071	13980	3	Giles	357.2	16,562	1,997	46.4	95.6	2.4	0.6	0.9	1.9	4.6	11.4	10.9	11.3	11.1	13.5
51073	47260	1	Gloucester	217.8	39,069	1,202	179.4	86.7	8.9	1.1	1.7	4.1	4.9	11.6	10.1	11.8	12.2	12.2
51075	40060	1	Goochland	282.0	25,488	1,585	90.4	79.5	15.5	0.8	2.6	3.5	3.9	9.5	10.2	10.7	11.0	13.3
51077		9	Grayson	441.8	15,359	2,067	34.8	89.4	6.8	0.8	0.5	3.9	3.8	9.4	9.8	10.9	10.8	13.6
51079	16820	3	Greene	155.9	20,968	1,765	134.5	82.7	9.1	0.8	3.0	7.0	6.1	13.2	11.3	12.3	12.7	12.1
51081		6	Greensville	295.2	11,437	2,317	38.7	36.2	60.5	0.6	1.1	2.8	3.9	8.8	11.7	16.3	15.5	15.2
51083		6	Halifax	817.7	33,738	1,338	41.3	60.9	36.5	0.7	1.0	2.5	5.4	11.4	10.9	10.7	10.2	11.6
51085	40060	1	Hanover	467.6	111,603	555	238.7	84.6	10.2	0.8	2.9	3.5	4.8	12.5	12.6	10.5	12.6	13.3
51087	40060	1	Henrico	233.7	333,554	218	1,427.3	53.2	31.6	0.8	10.8	6.3	5.8	12.4	11.6	14.1	13.9	12.8
51089	32300	4	Henry	382.4	50,248	994	131.4	70.6	23.7	0.7	0.8	6.2	4.4	11.2	10.6	10.4	10.3	12.6
51091		8	Highland	415.2	2,226	3,025	5.4	96.5	1.1	0.3	1.0	1.5	3.6	7.6	6.3	9.3	7.9	9.2
51093	47260	1	Isle of Wight	315.7	39,278	1,196	124.4	71.6	23.6	1.0	2.1	4.2	4.9	12.5	10.7	11.1	12.6	12.3
51095	47260	1	James City	142.3	79,882	717	561.4	76.6	14.7	0.9	4.2	6.6	4.7	11.1	10.5	9.8	11.6	11.7
51097	40060	8	King and Queen	315.1	6,662	2,688	21.1	69.3	26.2	2.5	1.4	3.8	4.8	9.6	10.2	10.1	11.1	12.8
51099		6	King George	179.6	27,489	1,519	153.1	75.2	17.4	1.2	3.0	6.6	5.7	14.5	12.6	12.8	13.7	13.1
51101	40060	1	King William	273.9	18,171	1,915	66.3	79.3	16.1	2.1	2.0	3.1	5.8	12.8	11.2	13.2	13.1	12.4
51103		9	Lancaster	133.3	10,928	2,346	82.0	68.5	28.6	0.6	1.0	2.6	3.7	8.9	8.3	8.2	8.0	9.1
51105		8	Lee	435.4	21,983	1,715	50.5	93.4	4.1	0.8	0.7	2.0	4.5	10.7	10.1	12.7	11.6	13.4
51107	47900	1	Loudoun	515.7	427,592	168	829.1	56.5	8.9	0.6	24.1	13.9	6.4	15.8	12.7	11.1	17.0	15.8

1. CBSA = Core Based Statistical Area. See Appendix A for explanation. See Appendix B for list of metropolitan areas with component counties. 2. County type code from the Economic Research Service of USDA Rural-Urban Continuum Codes. See Appendix A for definition. 3. Dry land or land partially or temporarily covered by water. 4. May be of any race.

STATE County	Population, 2021 (cont.)				Population change, 2000–2021							Households, 2016–2020				
	Age (percent) (cont.)				Total persons		Percent change		Components of change, 2020–2021					Percent		
	55 to 64 years	65 to 74 years	75 years and over	Percent female	2010	2020	2010–2020	2020–2021	Births	Deaths	Net Migration	Number	Persons per household	Family house-holds	Female family house-holder[1]	One person
	16	17	18	19	20	21	22	23	24	25	26	27	28	29	30	31
VERMONT—Cont'd																
Chittenden	12.6	9.8	6.4	50.8	156,545	168,323	7.5	0.3	1,686	1,745	567	66,478	2.3	56.6	8.1	29.7
Essex	18.0	16.4	10.7	49.4	6,306	5,920	-6.1	0.1	46	111	71	2,882	2.1	64.4	11.2	31.7
Franklin	14.8	10.9	6.2	49.9	47,746	49,946	4.6	0.8	643	614	345	19,045	2.6	66.9	8.0	26.7
Grand Isle	19.0	15.3	7.1	48.9	6,970	7,293	4.6	1.8	72	87	146	2,976	2.4	68.5	6.4	24.9
Lamoille	14.3	11.2	7.0	49.8	24,475	25,945	6.0	0.7	301	312	191	10,770	2.3	60.7	8.4	27.4
Orange	16.5	14.5	8.0	49.8	28,936	29,277	1.2	0.9	286	413	395	12,670	2.2	63.7	8.2	28.7
Orleans	14.7	14.4	9.2	49.7	27,231	27,393	0.6	0.6	308	459	308	11,678	2.2	63.8	8.2	29.2
Rutland	16.4	14.7	8.9	50.2	61,642	60,572	-1.7	0.0	544	977	458	25,349	2.2	58.6	7.2	33.2
Washington	14.6	13.0	7.8	50.0	59,534	59,807	0.5	0.3	591	798	370	25,310	2.2	59.3	11.2	31.8
Windham	16.7	15.6	9.0	50.6	44,513	45,905	3.1	0.4	418	668	443	19,162	2.1	54.3	10.1	36.8
Windsor	16.5	15.0	9.7	50.6	56,670	57,753	1.9	0.8	520	864	800	24,629	2.2	59.2	7.8	32.8
VIRGINIA	13.0	9.9	6.4	50.5	8,001,024	8,631,393	7.9	0.1	116,274	105,578	210	3,184,121	2.6	66.0	11.5	27.5
Accomack	15.7	15.4	9.8	50.9	33,164	33,413	0.8	-0.5	392	694	137	13,641	2.3	65.8	10.9	30.3
Albemarle	12.7	11.6	8.2	51.8	98,970	112,395	13.6	1.0	1,229	1,311	1,220	42,381	2.4	62.6	8.1	29.3
Alleghany	15.8	14.5	11.3	51.1	16,250	15,223	-6.3	-1.6	134	342	-29	6,529	2.3	60.8	9.2	34.9
Amelia	17.1	12.5	8.1	50.1	12,690	13,265	4.5	0.0	141	244	108	5,034	2.6	69.0	6.5	25.6
Amherst	15.3	12.7	9.0	51.2	32,353	31,307	-3.2	-0.1	356	578	188	12,161	2.5	67.0	11.7	26.8
Appomattox	14.4	12.0	8.8	51.1	14,973	16,119	7.7	1.5	245	259	250	6,158	2.6	71.5	12.7	25.3
Arlington	10.2	7.1	4.5	49.6	207,627	238,643	14.9	-2.4	3,147	1,508	-7,230	108,604	2.1	45.9	5.6	39.3
Augusta	15.3	12.8	9.2	49.1	73,750	77,487	5.1	0.1	599	1,216	694	30,165	2.4	69.0	9.0	25.5
Bath	17.5	16.5	12.3	48.6	4,731	4,209	-11.0	-2.3	56	80	-69	1,831	2.2	64.1	0.1	29.8
Bedford	16.5	13.8	8.7	50.5	68,676	79,462	15.7	0.8	766	1,286	1,203	31,424	2.5	73.7	7.7	22.7
Bland	14.5	14.3	10.1	44.5	6,824	6,270	-8.1	-1.5	54	121	-30	2,326	2.3	64.7	9.2	34.6
Botetourt	16.5	14.2	9.1	50.1	33,148	33,596	1.4	0.8	280	575	574	13,171	2.5	71.8	5.4	25.3
Brunswick	15.1	13.0	8.8	45.6	17,434	15,849	-9.1	0.6	140	280	235	6,138	2.3	61.0	21.0	35.0
Buchanan	16.0	13.9	9.8	49.1	24,098	20,355	-15.5	-2.6	196	489	-244	8,270	2.5	67.2	14.4	27.7
Buckingham	14.6	12.4	7.7	44.5	17,146	16,824	-1.9	0.7	170	262	217	5,948	2.5	67.9	13.1	28.1
Campbell	14.7	12.0	8.7	51.1	54,842	55,696	1.6	-0.4	595	855	49	23,157	2.4	65.8	10.7	28.9
Caroline	14.0	10.4	6.6	50.2	28,545	30,887	8.2	1.4	391	440	496	10,978	2.6	72.1	14.7	23.1
Carroll	16.2	15.3	10.5	49.9	30,042	29,155	-3.0	-0.4	297	605	202	12,134	2.5	65.6	9.9	31.2
Charles City	20.0	16.3	10.1	51.0	7,256	6,773	-6.7	-2.6	55	161	-71	2,998	2.3	63.1	12.1	32.5
Charlotte	16.4	13.1	9.3	50.3	12,586	11,529	-8.4	-0.7	139	244	23	4,836	2.4	62.3	14.7	33.2
Chesterfield	12.9	10.1	5.6	51.7	316,236	364,548	15.3	1.7	4,714	4,139	5,575	127,230	2.7	72.6	13.0	22.5
Clarke	17.1	13.4	8.7	50.2	14,034	14,783	5.3	0.7	165	255	190	5,690	2.5	69.6	6.8	25.2
Craig	17.4	14.3	9.7	49.6	5,190	4,892	-5.7	-0.6	46	96	22	2,219	2.3	68.2	9.0	29.8
Culpeper	13.7	10.0	6.3	49.9	46,689	52,552	12.6	2.0	779	693	962	17,474	2.9	74.6	14.1	19.9
Cumberland	15.9	13.7	9.5	51.7	10,052	9,675	-3.8	0.1	102	163	67	4,112	2.4	63.4	11.5	26.8
Dickenson	14.4	13.8	9.7	48.5	15,903	14,124	-11.2	-2.4	135	332	-140	5,727	2.5	64.7	13.1	32.5
Dinwiddie	16.1	11.1	7.1	50.5	28,001	27,947	-0.2	-0.1	189	439	216	10,403	2.7	68.4	11.4	25.4
Essex	16.9	14.9	9.2	52.7	11,151	10,599	-5.0	-0.2	145	191	20	4,551	2.4	63.5	14.0	32.3
Fairfax	12.7	8.8	5.7	50.0	1,081,726	1,150,309	6.3	-0.9	15,978	8,612	-17,957	398,653	2.9	70.7	8.8	23.4
Fauquier	15.1	10.2	6.9	50.1	65,203	72,972	11.9	1.2	848	897	897	24,617	2.8	73.5	10.7	21.7
Floyd	15.8	14.6	9.7	49.8	15,279	15,476	1.3	0.6	179	219	131	6,657	2.4	66.3	9.5	29.5
Fluvanna	14.6	12.6	8.1	53.8	25,691	27,249	6.1	1.7	274	339	546	9,967	2.6	71.5	11.2	23.4
Franklin	16.7	14.9	9.6	50.4	56,159	54,477	-3.0	0.8	586	950	838	22,730	2.4	68.1	10.5	27.0
Frederick	13.9	10.9	7.3	49.9	78,305	91,419	16.7	2.5	1,101	1,179	2,397	32,094	2.7	72.3	10.7	23.0
Giles	15.0	12.9	9.2	50.4	17,286	16,787	-2.9	-1.3	178	353	-50	6,715	2.5	65.2	8.7	29.2
Gloucester	16.7	12.4	8.0	50.6	36,858	38,711	5.0	0.9	400	628	593	14,792	2.5	69.4	9.4	25.3
Goochland	18.0	14.6	8.8	50.6	21,717	24,727	13.9	3.1	227	332	875	8,711	2.6	75.8	5.6	21.7
Grayson	16.0	15.0	10.7	47.8	15,533	15,333	-1.3	0.2	131	291	190	6,388	2.3	67.8	10.1	29.0
Greene	14.1	11.3	7.0	50.5	18,403	20,552	11.7	2.0	269	262	413	7,491	2.6	71.7	10.9	23.5
Greensville	12.9	10.1	5.6	36.4	12,243	11,391	-7.0	0.4	135	172	82	3,441	2.4	62.2	16.4	32.6
Halifax	14.7	14.7	10.7	51.9	36,241	34,022	-6.1	-0.8	451	750	15	14,155	2.4	63.9	15.8	33.3
Hanover	14.9	11.3	7.3	50.6	99,863	109,979	10.1	1.5	1,108	1,443	1,976	39,226	2.7	73.5	8.4	22.1
Henrico	12.9	10.0	6.5	52.3	306,935	334,389	8.9	-0.2	4,434	4,213	-1,096	130,434	2.5	63.6	14.1	30.5
Henry	16.0	13.4	11.1	51.5	54,151	50,948	-5.9	-1.4	452	1,096	-58	21,012	2.4	58.1	11.4	37.3
Highland	19.9	22.6	13.5	50.8	2,321	2,232	-3.8	-0.3	20	47	21	987	2.2	62.9	6.6	32.1
Isle of Wight	16.2	12.2	7.6	50.8	35,270	38,606	9.5	1.7	416	582	850	14,611	2.5	70.9	11.9	24.0
James City	14.2	14.8	11.6	51.5	67,009	78,254	16.8	2.1	920	1,071	1,808	29,681	2.5	71.1	8.8	25.3
King and Queen	17.9	14.6	8.8	48.8	6,945	6,608	-4.9	0.8	84	153	126	2,816	2.5	63.5	7.1	30.2
King George	13.7	8.6	5.4	49.3	23,584	26,723	13.3	2.9	356	269	686	9,387	2.8	74.6	9.5	20.1
King William	14.6	10.3	6.4	50.8	15,935	17,810	11.8	2.0	225	236	372	6,393	2.7	77.4	12.3	21.4
Lancaster	17.2	19.9	16.9	52.0	11,391	10,919	-4.1	0.1	92	300	221	5,287	2.0	59.4	7.1	38.2
Lee	14.2	13.7	9.2	47.3	25,587	22,173	-13.3	-0.9	235	483	59	8,843	2.5	63.2	13.9	31.7
Loudoun	11.1	6.1	4.1	49.9	312,311	420,959	34.8	1.6	5,889	2,536	3,150	132,565	3.0	78.4	7.8	16.7

1. No spouse present.

STATE County	Persons in group quarters, 2021	Daytime Population, 2016–2020		Births, 2021		Deaths, 2021		Persons under 65 with no health insurance, 2019		Medicare, 2021			COVID-19 Deaths, 2020	
		Number	Employment/ residence ratio	Total	Rate[1]	Number	Rate[1]	Number	Percent	Total beneficiaries	Enrolled in Original Medicare	Enrolled in Medicare Advantage	Number	Rate[1]
	32	33	34	35	36	37	38	39	40	41	42	43	44	45
VERMONT—Cont'd														
Chittenden	10,184	176,137	1.1	1,314	7.8	1,358	8.1	6,400	4.9	30,477	25,902	4,575	69	0.4
Essex	4	4,868	0.5	37	6.3	89	15.0	289	6.5	1,854	1,612	242	D	D
Franklin	514	44,130	0.8	507	10.1	490	9.8	2,199	5.4	10,370	8,897	1,473	29	0.6
Grand Isle	0	5,265	0.5	54	7.3	65	8.8	301	5.3	2,071	1,726	345	D	D
Lamoille	725	24,735	1.0	237	9.1	250	9.6	1,392	6.9	5,512	4,799	713	D	D
Orange	633	23,314	0.6	228	7.8	319	10.9	1,371	6.3	7,480	6,640	840	D	D
Orleans	738	26,324	1.0	243	8.9	356	13.0	1,337	6.7	7,646	6,585	1,061	D	D
Rutland	2,224	57,629	1.0	413	6.8	767	12.7	2,381	5.5	16,836	14,357	2,480	D	D
Washington	2,958	62,096	1.1	464	7.8	628	10.5	2,310	5.2	14,215	12,656	1,559	13	0.2
Windham	1,415	44,365	1.1	330	7.2	548	11.9	1,927	6.2	12,113	10,311	1,802	11	0.2
Windsor	741	54,069	1.0	413	7.1	690	11.9	2,646	6.4	15,916	13,379	2,537	D	D
VIRGINIA	234,777	8,439,984	1.0	93,037	10.8	84,697	9.8	640,265	9.2	1,545,049	1,156,714	388,335	6,189	0.7
Accomack	407	32,510	1.0	318	9.6	560	16.8	3,601	15.1	9,188	7,299	1,889	39	1.2
Albemarle	6,701	115,370	1.1	991	8.8	1,068	9.5	7,182	8.7	22,137	19,186	2,951	47	0.4
Alleghany	259	14,227	0.9	112	7.4	276	18.3	1,040	9.5	4,640	3,674	967	26	1.7
Amelia	108	9,533	0.5	111	8.4	195	14.7	1,208	11.6	3,167	2,208	959	11	0.8
Amherst	1,270	25,044	0.6	291	9.3	449	14.4	2,436	10.2	7,970	5,937	2,033	19	0.6
Appomattox	40	12,394	0.5	204	12.6	200	12.3	1,485	11.9	4,054	3,072	982	D	D
Arlington	2,667	284,289	1.3	2,489	10.6	1,255	5.3	12,911	6.1	25,177	20,757	4,419	158	0.7
Augusta	2,882	67,827	0.8	476	6.1	958	12.4	5,609	10.0	18,824	15,401	3,423	50	0.6
Bath	46	4,367	1.1	39	9.4	60	14.4	310	10.5	1,280	1,124	156	D	D
Bedford	441	64,468	0.6	631	7.9	1,061	13.3	5,649	9.2	20,398	15,992	4,406	45	0.6
Bland	650	5,927	0.8	46	7.4	95	15.3	327	7.9	1,825	1,296	529	10	1.6
Botetourt	237	29,991	0.8	227	6.7	476	14.1	1,858	7.3	8,913	6,479	2,434	21	0.6
Brunswick	2,070	13,803	0.6	122	7.7	229	14.4	1,303	12.5	4,114	3,065	1,049	16	1.0
Buchanan	937	21,556	1.0	156	7.8	384	19.2	1,836	12.2	7,183	3,696	3,487	32	1.6
Buckingham	2,101	13,963	0.5	141	8.4	210	12.4	1,367	11.9	3,730	2,934	796	24	1.4
Campbell	399	51,162	0.8	471	8.5	691	12.4	4,462	10.3	13,334	10,092	3,242	48	0.9
Caroline	453	22,858	0.5	309	9.9	356	11.4	2,384	9.5	6,176	4,690	1,486	23	0.7
Carroll	230	24,598	0.6	242	8.3	485	16.7	2,677	12.2	8,603	6,839	1,763	54	1.9
Charles City	0	5,032	0.4	44	6.6	132	19.8	722	14.0	1,991	1,423	568	10	1.5
Charlotte	115	10,323	0.7	110	9.6	190	16.6	1,113	12.4	3,295	2,564	731	14	1.2
Chesterfield	4,572	310,216	0.8	3,770	10.2	3,309	9.0	26,720	9.1	63,807	46,247	17,559	196	0.5
Clarke	155	11,853	0.6	135	9.1	213	14.4	1,080	9.5	3,439	2,905	534	10	0.7
Craig	9	3,690	0.4	35	7.2	77	15.8	251	6.5	1,370	966	404	D	D
Culpeper	1,299	44,943	0.7	618	11.6	548	10.3	4,744	11.1	9,851	8,104	1,747	37	0.7
Cumberland	17	6,790	0.4	86	8.9	130	13.4	797	10.5	2,410	1,753	657	D	D
Dickenson	463	14,050	0.9	112	8.0	264	19.0	1,076	10.3	4,921	2,356	2,565	16	1.1
Dinwiddie	677	23,870	0.6	154	5.5	367	13.2	2,273	10.0	6,168	4,511	1,657	18	0.6
Essex	148	9,907	0.8	115	10.9	147	13.9	936	11.3	3,043	2,314	729	D	D
Fairfax	9,962	1,188,697	1.1	12,792	11.2	7,071	6.2	89,030	9.1	157,621	124,773	32,849	731	0.6
Fauquier	350	59,300	0.7	674	9.2	709	9.7	5,392	9.1	13,199	11,307	1,891	27	0.4
Floyd	56	12,505	0.6	147	9.5	183	11.8	1,443	12.1	4,266	3,224	1,041	15	1.0
Fluvanna	1,182	19,447	0.4	210	7.6	273	9.9	1,854	9.1	6,311	5,294	1,018	15	0.5
Franklin	975	49,113	0.7	465	8.5	776	14.2	4,259	10.3	15,395	10,475	4,920	42	0.8
Frederick	1,113	80,949	0.8	893	9.6	954	10.3	6,852	9.5	17,496	14,243	3,253	56	0.6
Giles	110	14,813	0.7	144	8.6	269	16.1	1,187	9.2	4,634	3,404	1,230	14	0.8
Gloucester	265	28,911	0.5	316	8.1	499	12.8	2,826	9.4	9,003	7,158	1,845	15	0.4
Goochland	955	29,497	1.6	188	7.5	259	10.3	1,117	6.4	6,210	4,751	1,460	13	0.5
Grayson	978	12,828	0.6	108	7.0	241	15.7	1,234	11.6	4,634	3,499	1,135	33	2.2
Greene	112	14,841	0.5	218	10.5	205	9.9	1,742	10.8	4,128	3,468	660	D	D
Greensville	3,457	11,593	1.1	106	9.3	140	12.3	527	8.6	2,135	1,426	709	21	1.8
Halifax	674	32,939	0.9	347	10.3	585	17.3	2,616	10.5	9,935	7,899	2,036	68	2.0
Hanover	1,892	97,322	0.8	869	7.8	1,140	10.3	5,789	6.7	22,402	16,402	6,000	83	0.8
Henrico	2,504	347,078	1.1	3,536	10.6	3,404	10.2	24,306	8.8	59,234	41,105	18,129	290	0.9
Henry	501	47,725	0.8	362	7.2	862	17.1	4,267	11.4	14,940	9,602	5,338	83	1.6
Highland	0	2,026	0.8	18	8.1	39	17.5	205	14.6	814	715	98	D	D
Isle of Wight	270	31,107	0.7	326	8.4	458	11.8	2,443	8.2	8,740	6,604	2,135	31	0.8
James City	1,054	71,516	0.9	727	9.2	851	10.8	3,887	6.9	21,732	18,025	3,707	38	0.5
King and Queen	0	4,600	0.3	63	9.5	121	18.3	653	12.3	1,818	1,403	415	D	D
King George	212	27,465	1.1	285	10.5	211	7.8	1,545	6.7	4,181	3,584	597	16	0.6
King William	57	13,269	0.6	187	10.4	190	10.5	1,219	8.5	3,619	2,841	779	D	D
Lancaster	165	11,443	1.2	70	6.4	241	22.1	782	11.8	4,415	3,667	748	D	D
Lee	1,313	21,044	0.6	193	8.8	403	18.3	1,807	10.9	6,442	3,002	3,440	35	1.6
Loudoun	1,463	383,175	0.9	4,654	10.9	2,046	4.8	22,946	6.1	41,134	32,457	8,677	184	0.4

1. Per 1,000 estimated resident population.

STATE County	COVID-19 Vaccinations, 2021–2022		Education						Money income, 2016–2020				Income and poverty, 2020			
			School enrollment and attainment, 2016–2020				Local government expenditures,[3] 2018–2019			Households				Percent below poverty level		
			Enrollment[1]		Attainment[2] (percent)						Percent					
	Number	Percent[5]	Total	Percent private	High school graduate or less	Bachelor's degree or more	Total current spending (mil dol)	Current spending per student (dollars)	Per capita income[4]	Median income (dollars)	with income of less than $50,000	with income of $200,000 or more	Median household income (dollars)	All persons	Children under 18 years	Children 5 to 17 years in families
	46	47	48	49	50	51	52	53	54	55	56	57	58	59	60	61
VERMONT—Cont'd																
Chittenden	121,077	73.9	46,038	19.7	23.7	52.6	436.8	19,437	40,809	76,316	33.1	9.7	80,539	8.5	6.8	6.6
Essex	2,475	40.2	1,114	21.3	55.4	18.4	8.0	17,710	27,583	47,035	53.2	1.9	50,956	12.7	18.3	17.9
Franklin	18,385	37.2	10,081	10.0	46.5	26.5	157.3	18,735	31,305	65,314	37.7	4.0	62,763	8.9	9.9	9.8
Grand Isle	5,886	81.4	1,318	14.0	34.0	42.2	13.8	22,205	41,530	81,667	30.9	6.0	79,994	7.4	10.6	10.4
Lamoille	16,063	63.3	5,734	10.9	32.0	41.0	71.6	19,323	38,794	64,179	39.6	5.9	57,909	8.1	9.4	9.1
Orange	15,347	53.1	5,614	15.9	41.8	31.9	82.6	19,753	33,384	62,737	38.0	3.5	60,624	9.6	11.5	11.7
Orleans	15,922	58.9	5,048	12.9	48.7	24.2	79.4	20,204	29,116	54,390	46.5	3.4	56,721	10.6	15.9	15.5
Rutland	40,546	69.7	11,926	15.3	39.9	32.2	151.7	19,804	31,831	57,176	44.6	3.2	62,289	12.0	12.6	12.6
Washington	27,485	47.1	13,296	26.2	31.4	43.7	163.5	21,297	36,071	64,862	37.9	5.4	70,061	8.0	8.8	8.0
Windham	28,931	68.5	8,348	29.5	36.3	39.7	126.4	23,776	34,313	54,188	46.6	5.0	59,017	11.3	13.8	13.5
Windsor	27,597	50.1	10,371	17.6	34.7	38.4	175.5	21,669	37,145	61,503	39.8	6.0	60,842	8.6	9.1	8.8
VIRGINIA	6,240,886	73.1	2,110,795	17.8	33.5	39.5	16,296.0	12,639	41,255	76,398	32.9	11.6	79,154	9.2	12.2	11.3
Accomack	23,722	73.4	6,343	15.8	54.4	19.7	56.4	11,028	27,012	46,178	52.8	2.9	44,127	17.6	24.1	21.8
Albemarle	70,953	64.9	30,625	15.9	21.9	58.7	(6)	(6)	46,241	84,643	29.5	13.2	79,708	6.3	7.0	6.5
Alleghany	5,865	39.5	2,654	10.6	53.3	14.6	25.6	12,271	28,048	48,513	51.6	2.3	52,281	11.7	17.9	16.7
Amelia	4,477	34.1	2,650	28.4	57.2	18.2	17.6	10,020	32,799	63,918	38.5	3.9	70,511	9.0	12.1	11.7
Amherst	14,738	46.6	6,745	29.3	51.3	21.3	45.5	11,167	28,866	57,368	44.9	3.4	61,111	11.2	16.1	15.1
Appomattox	5,149	32.4	3,463	19.5	49.1	21.5	23.0	10,339	27,889	55,457	45.3	3.7	55,152	12.6	18.0	15.7
Arlington	169,708	71.7	49,956	30.1	13.0	75.8	529.5	19,301	73,078	122,604	17.6	24.3	125,004	6.0	6.6	6.3
Augusta	36,937	48.9	13,948	22.4	51.5	22.3	113.9	10,946	30,493	65,076	38.2	3.0	67,698	8.3	11.5	10.0
Bath	1,796	43.3	619	24.7	51.2	17.4	10.1	18,652	34,463	55,481	44.8	5.4	56,165	11.2	15.6	16.0
Bedford	35,244	44.6	16,463	25.4	38.3	30.9	103.6	10,756	34,565	67,136	36.1	5.7	70,004	6.8	8.7	8.5
Bland	2,446	38.9	968	8.9	54.3	13.4	8.1	10,969	23,664	50,365	49.4	1.8	56,637	12.1	14.3	13.4
Botetourt	16,562	49.6	6,545	15.8	40.8	26.9	53.6	11,500	37,357	72,719	30.8	6.6	70,803	6.6	7.5	6.9
Brunswick	8,493	52.3	2,966	16.4	59.4	14.8	22.1	13,673	24,493	46,111	54.4	3.4	45,556	20.2	25.4	23.8
Buchanan	10,079	48.0	3,588	16.0	64.4	11.8	32.7	11,865	22,092	34,302	65.9	1.7	35,891	23.7	29.9	27.9
Buckingham	6,728	39.2	3,140	11.4	61.4	12.6	23.5	11,039	23,045	48,603	51.4	1.3	49,339	16.8	22.0	21.2
Campbell	21,923	39.9	11,422	22.6	44.7	23.5	83.4	10,564	28,173	52,319	47.3	2.0	59,223	8.9	12.9	11.3
Caroline	13,010	42.3	6,448	15.2	50.9	21.8	44.8	10,627	35,588	67,901	33.4	7.1	67,663	9.8	13.9	12.8
Carroll	9,831	33.0	4,946	8.6	57.0	14.8	42.2	11,228	24,476	44,518	55.9	1.3	48,555	13.2	19.2	17.4
Charles City	5,699	81.8	1,128	22.3	58.3	16.2	10.1	16,014	36,325	60,096	41.0	3.6	61,850	9.9	16.0	15.4
Charlotte	4,564	38.4	2,370	8.8	54.3	13.9	24.5	13,219	24,337	40,924	56.0	2.3	45,084	17.2	25.6	23.9
Chesterfield	200,021	56.7	88,081	15.6	30.5	40.1	624.3	10,142	42,734	84,645	26.0	9.5	83,598	6.6	8.7	8.1
Clarke	9,391	64.2	3,112	16.7	37.3	34.7	23.4	11,919	42,327	86,154	28.9	10.2	88,407	6.2	7.0	6.1
Craig	1,692	33.0	804	13.2	45.7	21.7	7.1	11,738	30,433	57,792	46.2	1.0	57,314	10.4	16.2	15.4
Culpeper	25,414	48.3	12,288	20.6	44.0	25.2	88.0	10,692	37,507	80,663	28.9	6.9	80,151	8.5	11.6	11.0
Cumberland	3,611	36.4	1,736	17.5	49.6	16.5	16.2	11,876	29,160	50,565	49.7	2.9	51,035	13.5	22.0	21.4
Dickenson	6,714	46.9	2,455	5.6	58.3	11.4	24.4	11,865	25,485	30,116	69.0	1.4	38,394	19.3	23.4	21.6
Dinwiddie	13,625	47.7	6,337	18.8	52.6	17.8	48.9	11,157	30,351	65,485	38.0	6.5	63,567	11.1	15.5	15.2
Essex	5,042	46.0	1,841	17.4	53.0	16.2	17.8	13,440	26,114	51,125	49.3	1.7	56,134	12.3	20.1	20.7
Fairfax	881,959	76.9	304,656	18.8	20.0	62.1	2,947.6	15,695	58,338	127,866	16.5	26.5	132,509	5.3	7.0	6.3
Fauquier	45,984	64.6	16,980	16.9	32.4	36.7	146.1	13,059	47,642	105,665	19.8	17.7	106,977	6.0	6.4	5.6
Floyd	5,966	37.9	2,747	14.7	47.3	21.7	22.1	11,262	27,306	51,250	48.4	1.3	54,262	10.9	14.0	13.1
Fluvanna	17,063	62.6	5,361	17.4	31.4	35.6	39.6	11,028	44,149	78,885	29.1	9.2	79,598	6.8	8.3	7.4
Franklin	24,454	43.6	12,176	23.7	45.9	22.7	83.4	11,808	32,084	56,779	44.3	4.7	61,714	11.5	17.0	14.6
Frederick	42,995	48.1	20,047	18.2	43.5	26.8	(7)	(7)	38,442	80,011	27.4	7.3	83,033	7.4	9.4	8.5
Giles	7,550	45.2	3,289	12.9	47.8	19.5	26.7	10,905	27,679	57,279	40.7	1.6	55,983	10.7	15.7	14.7
Gloucester	23,561	63.1	7,669	14.1	41.9	24.0	61.6	11,391	34,565	71,649	32.2	5.0	73,893	7.9	11.7	10.8
Goochland	15,667	66.0	4,631	26.4	30.1	43.8	32.6	12,190	52,605	97,146	22.3	18.4	101,927	5.8	7.3	6.8
Grayson	6,369	41.0	2,637	14.2	53.7	16.0	19.4	12,567	24,770	41,558	60.1	1.8	45,896	16.2	22.4	20.1
Greene	9,061	45.7	4,314	16.1	41.9	30.0	34.8	11,602	33,913	67,266	29.8	4.0	70,046	8.1	12.3	12.0
Greensville	4,116	36.3	2,146	15.1	62.3	11.3	(8)	(8)	20,011	49,756	50.2	2.3	48,578	21.5	21.8	20.1
Halifax	14,721	43.4	6,357	12.9	54.1	16.1	55.6	11,205	24,368	43,714	56.3	1.6	43,386	17.8	22.2	20.8
Hanover	63,462	58.9	27,094	18.7	31.8	40.3	186.3	10,508	43,003	91,444	25.1	11.0	97,717	5.0	5.3	4.8
Henrico	181,893	55.0	79,801	18.0	29.3	44.3	529.0	10,268	41,437	72,295	34.9	10.7	80,105	8.3	12.3	12.3
Henry	19,837	39.2	10,425	11.8	54.4	15.1	76.5	10,255	23,051	38,511	60.9	1.6	41,706	12.9	20.3	19.2
Highland	1,328	60.6	247	21.5	45.6	30.7	4.1	19,961	30,911	51,831	42.7	3.6	52,898	12.2	19.7	20.6
Isle of Wight	19,310	52.0	8,580	24.6	40.8	28.0	60.3	10,897	39,024	77,870	32.8	8.3	75,481	7.6	9.5	9.0
James City	42,897	56.1	17,230	14.9	22.3	51.0	(9)	(9)	45,862	91,675	26.4	11.1	86,501	6.5	8.0	7.1
King and Queen	3,595	51.2	1,200	13.2	45.4	25.8	10.9	13,140	34,873	65,385	39.2	4.4	60,133	11.1	15.7	14.5
King George	11,164	41.6	6,332	17.4	34.4	35.5	47.0	10,496	38,926	96,711	24.5	10.6	90,786	6.0	7.0	6.4
King William	8,902	51.9	4,094	12.7	38.8	24.1	36.5	12,020	33,261	73,284	32.0	5.8	79,313	6.2	8.8	8.5
Lancaster	6,383	60.2	1,651	5.6	40.3	33.9	16.2	14,268	48,280	59,736	44.1	8.1	55,539	10.3	21.2	21.5
Lee	11,838	50.5	4,326	5.3	56.0	9.6	38.3	11,782	19,126	35,006	63.1	1.3	38,229	26.0	34.1	32.9
Loudoun	301,712	73.0	118,862	16.5	18.5	61.6	1,227.5	14,986	57,513	147,111	12.3	31.8	155,362	3.2	3.1	2.9

1. All persons 3 years old and over enrolled in nursery school through college. 2. Persons 25 years old and over. 3. Elementary and secondary education expenditures. 4. Based on population estimated by the American Community Survey, 2016–2020. 5. CDC percent based on 2019 population estimate. 6. Albemarle county is included with Charlottesville city. 7. Frederick county is included with Winchester city. 8. Greensville county is included with Emporia city. 9. James City county is included with Williamsburg city.

STATE County	Personal income, 2020										Earnings, 2020		
	Total (mil dol)	Percent change 2019–2020	Per capita[1]		Wages and salaries (mil dol)	Supplements to wages and salaries, employer contributions (mil dol)		Proprietors' income (mil dol)	Dividends, interest, and rent (mil dol)	Personal transfer reecipts (mil dol)	Total (mil dol)	Contributions for government social insurance (mil dol)	
			Dollars	Rank		Pension and insurance	Government social insurance					From employee and self-employed	From employer
	62	63	64	65	66	67	68	69	70	71	72	73	74
VERMONT—Cont'd													
Chittenden	10,615	5.2	64,605	277	6,147	946	481	888	2,026	1,973	8,461	548	481
Essex	270	9.1	44,173	1,914	41	11	3	23	43	98	78	8	3
Franklin	2,593	7.8	52,181	921	924	186	76	203	347	633	1,389	90	76
Grand Isle	460	5.5	64,231	285	50	10	4	39	93	97	103	9	4
Lamoille	1,511	8.0	59,635	443	512	85	44	178	341	375	818	56	44
Orange	1,533	7.6	53,146	848	345	66	29	137	263	413	576	44	29
Orleans	1,345	9.6	49,998	1,143	436	85	38	120	229	489	680	50	38
Rutland	3,309	6.7	57,283	554	1,271	224	106	193	485	1,279	1,794	134	106
Washington	3,791	7.7	64,997	262	1,930	312	151	305	647	940	2,698	181	151
Windham	2,378	7.5	56,610	596	978	160	82	219	496	731	1,438	104	82
Windsor	3,507	6.7	63,786	296	1,186	211	98	240	825	893	1,735	128	98
VIRGINIA	532,256	5.9	61,661	X	268,530	40,614	18,957	30,144	100,175	95,437	358,246	22,438	18,957
Accomack	1,733	7.9	53,762	797	813	187	68	80	347	511	1,149	70	68
Albemarle	(2) 12231	(2) 2.6	(2) 77606	(2) 91	(2) 6221	(2) 1100	(2) 434	(2) 825	(2) 4421	(2) 1589	(2) 8580	(2) 510	(2) 434
Alleghany	(3) 879	(3) 7.1	(3) 43230	(3) 2036	(3) 372	(3) 66	(3) 28	(3) 25	(3) 129	(3) 344	(3) 491	(3) 38	(3) 28
Amelia	609	6.3	46,780	1,542	115	20	9	32	77	179	176	15	9
Amherst	1,276	7.2	40,293	2,420	353	65	26	34	179	434	477	40	26
Appomattox	670	7.8	41,750	2,235	130	25	9	19	87	219	184	17	9
Arlington	24,210	3.5	100,823	21	21,175	3,067	1,450	1,434	4,997	1,668	27,127	1,523	1,450
Augusta	(4) 5949	(4) 7.3	(4) 47794	(4) 1415	(4) 2362	(4) 400	(4) 176	(4) 333	(4) 1021	(4) 1578	(4) 3271	(4) 231	(4) 176
Bath	289	5.4	70,050	166	95	18	7	9	103	79	129	10	7
Bedford	3,947	6.1	49,457	1,202	855	141	62	146	706	1,021	1,204	102	62
Bland	247	6.3	39,609	2,492	99	23	8	10	34	92	140	10	8
Botetourt	1,808	5.8	53,767	796	544	89	39	58	312	434	731	55	39
Brunswick	585	9.5	36,499	2,825	148	30	11	9	79	246	197	18	11
Buchanan	803	3.9	38,969	2,567	310	58	22	44	84	385	434	35	22
Buckingham	574	10.0	33,425	3,009	149	33	11	22	72	217	215	20	11
Campbell	(5) 5616	(5) 8.6	(5) 41030	(5) 2334	(5) 3705	(5) 546	(5) 268	(5) 243	(5) 873	(5) 1901	(5) 4763	(5) 316	(5) 268
Caroline	1,441	7.2	46,682	1,553	281	60	21	40	215	366	404	31	21
Carroll	(6) 1415	(6) 9.5	(6) 38908	(6) 2579	(6) 433	(6) 81	(6) 33	(6) 63	(6) 176	(6) 587	(6) 610	(6) 54	(6) 33
Charles City	351	5.6	51,498	981	92	15	7	14	70	102	127	9	7
Charlotte	456	7.8	38,547	2,620	114	24	9	18	70	179	165	16	9
Chesterfield	20,803	6.9	58,069	509	7,759	1,167	557	883	3,411	3,884	10,366	685	557
Clarke	1,011	3.9	69,117	177	192	30	14	55	224	174	290	23	14
Craig	213	7.1	41,988	2,198	32	7	2	7	35	69	48	5	2
Culpeper	2,706	8.3	50,509	1,089	815	139	61	193	406	576	1,207	85	61
Cumberland	409	7.7	41,225	2,300	51	11	4	20	51	137	86	7	4
Dickenson	522	8.8	37,046	2,785	159	32	11	10	53	262	212	21	11
Dinwiddie	(7) 3431	(7) 10.3	(7) 44938	(7) 1802	(7) 1471	(7) 239	(7) 110	(7) 80	(7) 479	(7) 1294	(7) 1900	(7) 143	(7) 110
Essex	511	9.2	46,657	1,557	151	25	11	20	95	165	207	17	11
Fairfax	(8) 105778	(8) 3.3	(8) 88971	(8) 43	(8) 69723	(8) 7695	(8) 4566	(8) 6848	(8) 23424	(8) 9872	(8) 88832	(8) 5406	(8) 4566
Fauquier	5,338	4.1	74,801	108	1,343	202	94	358	1,160	728	1,997	132	94
Floyd	667	7.6	42,304	2,155	130	24	10	32	104	213	196	18	10
Fluvanna	1,328	6.7	48,440	1,331	216	42	16	55	255	312	328	28	16
Franklin	2,517	7.0	44,821	1,820	634	112	48	133	483	756	927	76	48
Frederick	(9) 6515	(9) 6.8	(9) 54832	(9) 713	(9) 3345	(9) 526	(9) 244	(9) 433	(9) 1066	(9) 1275	(9) 4548	(9) 289	(9) 244
Giles	726	7.5	43,561	2,001	229	44	17	23	94	251	312	26	17
Gloucester	1,998	6.0	53,341	831	406	75	30	65	348	486	576	47	30
Goochland	2,580	3.5	105,619	18	2,099	191	123	181	789	294	2,594	160	123
Grayson	544	8.9	35,093	2,932	111	27	8	13	78	226	160	16	8
Greene	978	6.8	48,573	1,315	159	27	12	59	152	230	257	21	12
Greensville	(10) 603	(10) 11.1	(10) 36450	(10) 2827	(10) 337	(10) 64	(10) 25	(10) 11	(10) 69	(10) 236	(10) 437	(10) 31	(10) 25
Halifax	1,364	7.9	40,542	2,389	511	98	39	49	196	534	697	55	39
Hanover	7,005	4.8	64,704	276	2,760	369	198	454	1,211	1,178	3,781	250	198
Henrico	23,321	3.8	69,872	168	12,490	1,574	864	3,820	3,957	3,681	18,748	1,151	864
Henry	(11) 2718	(11) 9.8	(11) 43380	(11) 2021	(11) 978	(11) 176	(11) 73	(11) 110	(11) 394	(11) 1113	(11) 1338	(11) 109	(11) 73
Highland	102	6.0	46,315	1,606	18	4	1	8	35	33	32	3	1
Isle of Wight	2,237	6.9	59,285	463	611	84	42	59	348	482	797	59	42
James City	(12) 6341	(12) 5.9	(12) 68279	(12) 190	(12) 1963	(12) 324	(12) 143	(12) 232	(12) 1754	(12) 1280	(12) 2663	(12) 194	(12) 143
King and Queen	339	8.6	48,888	1,273	53	10	4	15	48	96	83	7	4
King George	1,571	5.6	57,377	548	1,136	292	89	64	272	253	1,580	87	89
King William	899	8.9	50,951	1,038	207	32	15	30	128	204	283	22	15
Lancaster	678	5.3	63,885	292	198	31	14	42	240	197	286	22	14
Lee	768	9.9	33,056	3,026	176	46	13	21	85	366	256	25	13
Loudoun	35,672	6.8	84,374	64	13,576	1,693	911	1,640	5,018	2,737	17,820	1,064	911

1. Based on the resident population estimated as of July 1 of the year shown. 2. Charlottesville city is included with Albemarle county. 3. Covington city is included with Alleghany county. 4. Staunton and Waynesboro cities are included with Augusta county. 5. Lynchburg city is included with Campbell county. 6. Galax city is included with Carroll county. 7. Petersburg and Colonial Heights cities are included with Dinwiddie county. 8. Fairfax city and Falls Church city are included with Fairfax county. 9. Winchester city is included with Frederick county. 10. Emporia city is included with Greensville county. 11. Martinsville city is included with Henry county. 12. Williamsburg city is included with James City county.

STATE County	Earnings, 2020 (cont.)									Social Security beneficiaries, December 2020		Supple-mental Security Income recipients, 2020	Housing units, 2021	
	Percent by selected industries													
	Farm	Mining, quarrying, and extractions	Construction	Manu-facturing	Information; professional, scientific, technical services	Retail trade	Finance, insurance, real estate, and leasing	Health care and social assistance	Govern-ment	Number	Rate[1]		Total	Percent change, 2010–2021
	75	76	77	78	79	80	81	82	83	84	85	86	87	88
VERMONT—Cont'd														
Chittenden	0.3	0.1	5.6	9.6	D	6.5	7.0	16.3	17.1	31,380	186	3,079	74,100	1.2
Essex	5.6	0.0	D	9.1	D	2.8	D	D	36.0	2,095	354	206	4,913	0.9
Franklin	5.4	0.2	5.5	15.7	D	8.1	2.7	12.5	28.4	10,380	206	1,231	22,853	0.8
Grand Isle	6.5	D	D	0.3	D	6.9	7.7	D	18.8	2,100	283	131	5,294	0.4
Lamoille	1.5	D	11.1	5.7	10.7	8.2	5.1	14.6	13.8	5,590	214	450	14,046	1.0
Orange	3.7	0.2	14.1	6.2	8.1	6.3	D	17.9	21.9	7,475	253	583	15,014	0.3
Orleans	4.6	D	9.3	11.0	D	9.8	4.6	16.4	20.0	7,990	290	883	16,581	1.0
Rutland	0.4	1.9	8.0	12.5	4.8	8.5	3.5	18.9	15.2	18,115	299	1,973	33,931	0.1
Washington	0.4	0.2	5.6	6.0	7.7	6.4	12.8	13.2	24.3	14,795	247	1,345	30,818	0.5
Windham	0.6	D	8.3	12.2	D	7.8	5.3	15.3	12.5	12,325	267	1,210	30,048	0.3
Windsor	0.3	0.2	8.9	7.2	11.2	7.0	4.3	13.0	24.0	16,350	281	1,271	34,737	0.3
VIRGINIA	0.2	0.2	5.7	5.5	20.7	4.9	7.8	9.1	22.4	1,585,194	183	155,200	3,652,388	0.8
Accomack	2.5	0.0	3.0	14.7	9.1	3.7	2.2	7.8	45.5	10,065	303	1,088	21,873	0.7
Albemarle	(2) 0.0	(2) D	(2) 4.2	(2) 2.8	(2) 13.9	(2) 4.8	(2) 8.9	(2) 10.6	(2) 35.9	21,710	191	1,039	48,421	1.9
Alleghany	(3) 0.1	(3) D	(3) 7.0	(3) D	(3) D	(3) 5.9	(3) D	(3) 10.2	(3) 18.0	4,685	313	292	7,922	-0.1
Amelia	5.8	D	18.8	7.6	3.7	5.0	2.3	10.0	17.4	3,490	263	284	5,769	0.9
Amherst	0.1	0.0	9.1	24.4	3.6	8.5	2.4	11.7	20.8	8,700	278	802	14,285	0.3
Appomattox	-0.4	D	13.2	2.5	D	13.0	2.7	D	25.4	4,345	266	462	7,386	0.9
Arlington	0.0	D	1.3	D	38.3	1.5	5.2	3.2	29.2	21,455	92	2,154	119,447	0.2
Augusta	(4) 0.9	(4) 0.1	(4) D	(4) 19.3	(4) 3.8	(4) 6.6	(4) 4.8	(4) D	(4) 16.8	19,720	254	630	32,940	0.8
Bath	1.9	0.0	10.6	3.8	12.3	1.3	D	14.2	16.8	1,355	329	89	3,240	0.0
Bedford	-0.1	0.0	9.1	12.5	8.1	7.6	8.1	11.1	15.5	21,840	273	1,125	37,363	0.3
Bland	1.9	D	3.3	32.6	D	D	D	D	26.5	1,990	322	113	3,211	0.2
Botetourt	-0.1	D	8.5	18.9	4.0	4.0	4.6	D	13.5	9,020	266	767	15,020	0.7
Brunswick	0.8	D	5.7	8.0	D	4.9	3.4	D	27.0	4,470	280	589	7,918	0.3
Buchanan	0.0	26.1	3.8	5.4	4.8	5.1	3.5	10.1	19.8	8,060	407	1,507	10,331	0.1
Buckingham	1.3	D	8.2	3.9	D	5.0	1.8	11.1	36.1	3,960	234	410	7,191	0.7
Campbell	(5) 0.1	(5) D	(5) D	(5) 19.4	(5) 9.7	(5) 6.5	(5) 7.6	(5) 18.2	(5) 9.6	14,130	255	1,057	25,316	1.0
Caroline	1.8	D	7.2	5.4	D	5.7	2.0	D	31.4	6,630	212	515	12,612	1.4
Carroll	(6) 1.3	(6) D	(6) D	(6) 17.9	(6) D	(6) 10.0	(6) 3.0	(6) D	(6) 18.8	9,040	311	544	16,618	0.3
Charles City	5.1	D	27.7	11.1	D	D	D	D	16.7	2,105	319	145	3,265	0.5
Charlotte	1.0	0.1	5.2	16.8	D	5.8	2.1	8.3	27.8	3,665	320	498	5,963	0.1
Chesterfield	0.0	D	10.6	7.7	9.8	8.0	7.6	11.0	16.3	66,675	180	4,480	142,357	2.1
Clarke	1.3	D	12.8	13.2	12.3	3.9	7.0	5.1	15.2	3,535	238	D	6,474	1.0
Craig	-0.9	0.1	D	D	D	6.2	D	D	30.2	1,490	306	74	2,591	0.2
Culpeper	0.8	0.5	11.2	8.6	11.3	8.4	5.6	12.5	19.4	10,535	197	952	19,570	1.7
Cumberland	6.0	0.1	17.3	7.5	D	6.9	D	D	29.8	2,505	259	214	4,677	0.7
Dickenson	-0.1	34.6	5.2	0.7	D	5.8	D	6.1	24.0	5,405	392	842	7,344	0.0
Dinwiddie	(7) 0.0	(7) D	(7) 6.3	(7) 8.0	(7) 2.2	(7) 8.6	(7) 5.9	(7) 18.1	(7) 22.1	6,635	238	412	11,908	0.7
Essex	0.5	0.0	5.4	7.1	D	15.0	6.4	D	16.6	3,305	313	363	5,776	0.5
Fairfax	(8) 0.0	(8) 0.0	(8) 4.3	(8) 0.6	(8) 38.2	(8) 3.6	(8) 8.9	(8) 6.4	(8) 15.5	139,430	122	10,728	428,440	0.2
Fauquier	0.7	D	13.6	2.8	16.9	7.3	8.7	8.3	19.7	13,230	179	642	28,435	0.5
Floyd	1.3	D	12.5	12.5	D	6.5	4.6	15.6	19.4	4,540	292	282	7,955	0.4
Fluvanna	-0.1	0.1	19.0	3.4	D	4.6	4.2	4.4	28.3	6,480	234	238	11,299	1.3
Franklin	0.9	0.1	11.8	20.1	5.4	8.2	4.1	9.3	15.2	15,795	288	1,193	28,284	0.5
Frederick	(9) 0.0	(9) D	(9) D	(9) 13.7	(9) D	(9) 7.7	(9) 8.9	(9) 16.3	(9) 17.2	18,505	197	921	36,639	1.8
Giles	0.2	0.0	D	28.3	8.3	7.4	2.6	10.1	16.3	4,935	298	550	8,310	0.3
Gloucester	0.5	D	9.5	1.3	5.0	13.1	4.6	18.7	25.0	9,480	243	664	17,185	0.7
Goochland	0.0	0.3	4.2	1.6	D	1.5	D	1.8	3.7	6,335	249	254	10,886	2.7
Grayson	-4.3	D	5.5	11.0	D	3.2	6.7	D	36.0	5,180	337	305	8,946	0.2
Greene	0.7	D	11.8	1.3	12.1	11.9	2.5	D	20.5	4,320	206	248	8,770	3.1
Greensville	(10) 0.5	(10) D	(10) 2.4	(10) 25.9	(10) D	(10) 5.4	(10) D	(10) D	(10) 25.8	2,615	229	37	4,010	0.2
Halifax	0.2	D	7.7	19.2	2.9	6.0	2.9	D	17.0	10,740	318	1,417	17,357	0.4
Hanover	0.5	D	12.8	7.1	6.7	9.5	4.7	11.9	9.1	23,005	206	976	44,039	1.4
Henrico	0.0	0.0	4.9	3.2	14.1	5.1	15.7	12.6	7.9	61,270	184	4,999	142,776	1.2
Henry	(11) 0.9	(11) 0.2	(11) 3.3	(11) 21.6	(11) D	(11) 10.3	(11) 3.8	(11) 13.7	(11) 17.6	16,950	337	2,478	25,413	0.0
Highland	13.3	0.0	7.5	2.5	D	D	D	9.9	28.5	870	391	24	1,796	0.4
Isle of Wight	1.4	D	4.7	27.0	5.2	3.8	3.9	D	12.7	9,235	235	526	16,761	1.7
James City	(12) -0.1	(12) D	(12) 5.3	(12) D	(12) 9.9	(12) 5.9	(12) 7.2	(12) 13.5	(12) 24.8	21,155	265	667	34,407	1.0
King and Queen	5.4	D	12.0	12.1	D	2.0	D	3.2	21.3	1,950	293	131	3,481	0.6
King George	0.1	D	1.3	2.5	18.5	2.2	0.9	1.3	66.9	4,215	153	272	10,508	1.5
King William	0.8	D	8.3	25.8	D	5.3	3.7	D	16.7	3,925	216	215	7,584	2.1
Lancaster	0.4	0.0	9.1	2.2	8.2	9.0	14.7	D	11.4	4,485	410	276	7,464	0.2
Lee	-1.0	1.1	6.4	3.6	D	9.2	2.9	12.3	43.6	7,210	328	1,522	10,846	0.1
Loudoun	0.1	D	9.7	6.3	29.4	4.4	6.2	5.9	14.8	39,220	92	2,372	145,131	1.7

1. Per 1,000 resident population estimated as of July 1 of the year shown. 2. Charlottesville city is included with Albemarle county. 3. Covington city is included with Alleghany county. 4. Staunton and Waynesboro cities are included with Augusta county. 5. Lynchburg city is included with Campbell county. 6. Galax city is included with Carroll county. 7. Petersburg and Colonial Heights cities are included with Dinwiddie county. 8. Fairfax city and Falls Church city are included with Fairfax county. 9. Winchester city is included with Frederick county. 10. Emporia city is included with Greensville county. 11. Martinsville city is included with Henry county. 12. Williamsburg city is included with James City county.

STATE County	Housing units, 2016–2020: Occupied units: Total	Owner-occupied: Percent	Owner-occupied: Median value[1]	Median owner cost as a percent of income: With a mortgage	Median owner cost as a percent of income: Without a mortgage[2]	Renter-occupied: Median rent[3]	Renter-occupied: Median rent as a percent of income[2]	Sub-standard units[4] (percent)	Civilian labor force, 2021: Total	Percent change, 2020–2021	Unemployment: Total	Unemployment: Rate[5]	Civilian employment[6], 2016–2020: Total	Percent: Management, business, science, and arts	Percent: Construction, production, and maintenance occupations
	89	90	91	92	93	94	95	96	97	98	99	100	101	102	103
VERMONT—Cont'd															
Chittenden	66,478	62.9	314,200	22.0	13.7	1,293	32.3	1.5	92,865	-3.5	2,627	2.8	91,925	50.6	14.7
Essex	2,882	83.0	137,600	24.3	14.2	721	30.3	3.1	2,613	-3.7	126	4.8	2,795	32.6	28.0
Franklin	19,045	77.5	219,200	22.8	16.1	1,023	29.2	2.1	26,722	-2.4	924	3.5	25,151	37.9	28.3
Grand Isle	2,976	85.9	287,200	24.7	14.0	1,024	30.7	0.2	3,941	-3.5	155	3.9	3,554	46.0	20.5
Lamoille	10,770	72.1	228,200	23.3	13.9	941	27.5	2.6	13,380	-3.8	539	4.0	13,958	39.0	21.0
Orange	12,670	80.7	196,900	22.2	14.2	977	31.1	2.9	15,227	-4.2	490	3.2	15,491	40.7	26.8
Orleans	11,678	78.0	169,400	22.6	15.5	804	30.8	2.1	12,770	-2.7	592	4.6	13,103	35.0	26.9
Rutland	25,349	71.5	174,800	22.3	14.1	843	30.2	4.5	28,966	-4.4	1,215	4.2	29,413	35.6	23.9
Washington	25,310	70.3	230,400	22.6	15.5	938	26.6	1.3	32,392	-4.8	976	3.0	31,365	46.7	18.4
Windham	19,162	67.7	217,600	25.1	16.9	883	29.2	1.2	20,410	-5.9	904	4.4	21,900	40.9	23.3
Windsor	24,629	75.6	219,500	22.6	16.6	944	28.8	2.0	28,071	-3.2	926	3.3	27,778	43.1	20.8
VIRGINIA	3,184,121	66.7	282,800	20.9	10.0	1,257	28.8	2.2	4,267,656	-2.3	166,853	3.9	4,179,739	45.3	18.5
Accomack	13,641	65.0	173,700	21.1	11.3	825	28.6	2.7	15,176	-5.3	660	4.3	13,627	26.9	38.0
Albemarle	42,381	65.2	376,000	19.5	10.0	1,349	28.7	1.2	55,448	-1.8	1,798	3.2	53,176	55.7	11.0
Alleghany	6,529	79.2	121,100	17.8	11.1	616	28.4	0.9	6,512	-4.4	267	4.1	6,097	28.4	34.0
Amelia	5,034	83.1	215,600	22.4	10.0	846	26.4	7.3	5,984	-2.4	213	3.6	6,430	28.3	37.1
Amherst	12,161	77.4	159,900	17.9	10.0	700	27.3	2.7	14,340	-2.9	528	3.7	15,100	31.9	29.8
Appomattox	6,158	77.0	160,600	17.9	11.1	685	28.7	2.1	6,915	-2.9	267	3.9	7,299	32.2	26.1
Arlington	108,604	42.5	731,700	19.9	10.4	2,005	25.3	3.7	150,721	-1.2	4,511	3.0	148,139	70.8	6.7
Augusta	30,165	79.4	219,600	21.6	10.0	900	25.6	1.4	36,312	-2.3	1,111	3.1	35,877	34.0	29.4
Bath	1,831	81.9	168,400	19.0	10.0	656	20.9	2.0	2,219	-3.9	101	4.6	1,923	26.9	26.7
Bedford	31,424	84.2	211,600	18.9	10.0	856	25.8	1.8	37,256	-2.5	1,275	3.4	36,768	39.7	24.9
Bland	2,326	82.5	125,600	18.1	10.0	613	34.5	1.4	2,720	-3.2	93	3.4	2,281	23.0	28.7
Botetourt	13,171	85.7	230,500	20.0	10.0	807	21.3	1.0	16,976	-2.0	513	3.0	16,263	34.7	25.4
Brunswick	6,138	74.0	113,600	21.3	10.4	705	29.5	1.8	5,708	-4.1	358	6.3	6,335	21.0	37.5
Buchanan	8,270	79.8	69,500	26.0	10.6	608	25.8	1.1	6,130	-4.7	413	6.7	6,346	32.1	33.1
Buckingham	5,948	73.8	135,600	20.8	10.2	785	28.0	1.5	6,205	-1.9	326	5.3	6,619	25.4	35.7
Campbell	23,157	73.0	159,400	19.5	10.0	730	25.7	1.2	24,996	-3.0	954	3.8	26,016	34.9	27.9
Caroline	10,978	80.4	218,000	19.9	11.3	961	30.0	3.1	14,644	-2.6	632	4.3	14,401	32.9	24.3
Carroll	12,134	79.3	112,500	19.8	10.0	595	22.4	2.1	12,778	-3.2	523	4.1	12,627	27.5	35.1
Charles City	2,998	84.4	168,200	20.8	10.0	840	36.8	1.5	3,443	-2.6	151	4.4	3,322	27.1	34.0
Charlotte	4,836	68.1	121,000	19.8	10.5	640	32.9	2.9	5,206	1.8	193	3.7	4,849	27.9	32.4
Chesterfield	127,230	76.7	252,600	19.9	10.0	1,266	28.8	1.8	183,962	-2.3	6,714	3.6	177,745	44.6	18.9
Clarke	5,690	77.6	366,100	21.3	10.0	1,258	37.5	0.7	7,383	-1.3	228	3.1	7,229	45.5	19.1
Craig	2,219	71.0	147,900	18.4	10.0	611	18.2	1.2	2,222	-2.2	74	3.3	2,366	34.7	24.8
Culpeper	17,474	73.4	310,700	22.3	10.0	1,201	27.2	3.2	24,541	-1.3	796	3.2	25,008	34.5	25.3
Cumberland	4,112	76.1	159,600	21.5	11.4	705	24.4	0.2	4,537	-1.4	194	4.3	5,150	25.3	27.0
Dickenson	5,727	75.0	81,300	20.3	11.8	579	32.7	1.2	4,645	-2.1	247	5.3	4,471	32.9	21.4
Dinwiddie	10,403	77.2	185,200	18.6	10.2	1,042	28.6	2.4	13,210	-1.9	593	4.5	13,537	28.6	33.8
Essex	4,551	68.1	196,500	23.7	10.7	887	35.8	2.4	5,284	-3.7	256	4.8	4,864	28.6	31.0
Fairfax	398,653	68.6	576,700	21.1	10.0	1,898	28.3	3.1	614,999	-2.1	21,425	3.5	611,782	58.9	10.5
Fauquier	24,617	76.9	420,600	21.8	10.0	1,353	24.2	1.1	36,217	-1.5	1,079	3.0	36,115	44.5	20.1
Floyd	6,657	86.0	170,000	22.3	10.0	684	23.8	0.8	8,157	0.2	254	3.1	7,409	37.8	36.3
Fluvanna	9,967	82.4	234,500	20.5	10.0	1,235	24.7	1.7	13,572	-1.7	442	3.3	12,887	45.6	19.3
Franklin	22,730	81.6	174,600	19.6	10.0	725	30.4	1.5	25,534	-2.3	906	3.5	24,427	36.6	27.0
Frederick	32,094	77.7	265,700	19.5	10.0	1,119	26.8	1.4	49,021	-0.9	1,423	2.9	43,192	38.1	25.7
Giles	6,715	76.4	127,800	17.7	10.0	726	19.4	1.7	7,747	-0.5	268	3.5	7,468	29.5	34.5
Gloucester	14,792	80.0	230,300	21.6	10.0	1,045	27.5	0.9	18,837	-2.4	635	3.4	18,262	32.4	29.6
Goochland	8,711	85.7	379,200	18.1	10.0	1,129	26.3	2.5	11,232	-1.7	345	3.1	11,001	47.6	16.4
Grayson	6,388	84.0	109,800	19.3	10.0	538	21.9	1.3	7,841	-2.3	261	3.3	6,432	28.1	33.3
Greene	7,491	80.9	239,100	21.3	10.0	1,154	25.6	3.0	10,165	-1.9	304	3.0	10,101	39.5	21.4
Greensville	3,441	71.9	120,900	20.3	12.9	891	25.6	2.2	4,252	-0.1	207	4.9	3,670	23.5	29.0
Halifax	14,155	74.8	118,500	18.9	10.8	678	30.8	0.8	14,798	-2.5	707	4.8	13,984	32.2	35.3
Hanover	39,226	82.9	288,800	19.6	10.0	1,215	26.2	0.6	56,895	-2.0	1,687	3.0	55,809	46.6	17.2
Henrico	130,434	64.0	253,900	19.6	10.0	1,192	29.5	1.7	176,593	-2.6	7,050	4.0	174,720	44.9	15.9
Henry	21,012	72.0	97,400	19.2	10.7	600	27.8	1.9	23,520	-1.0	1,097	4.7	19,783	28.2	31.8
Highland	987	87.3	161,000	19.8	10.0	669	19.2	2.3	1,223	-0.8	35	2.9	772	36.0	26.4
Isle of Wight	14,611	76.8	280,600	20.8	12.1	1,120	28.3	1.2	19,026	-1.9	660	3.5	17,988	40.4	25.3
James City	29,681	76.5	346,100	20.5	10.0	1,243	31.0	1.9	35,844	-3.3	1,422	4.0	34,410	48.1	14.9
King and Queen	2,816	84.6	207,400	18.3	10.0	969	19.5	1.1	3,812	-1.7	120	3.1	3,544	35.6	29.8
King George	9,387	76.0	315,100	19.1	10.0	1,241	31.0	1.5	13,898	0.1	402	2.9	13,140	49.0	17.6
King William	6,393	88.4	205,800	21.4	10.0	1,076	23.2	0.6	9,114	-2.0	305	3.3	8,732	36.9	24.0
Lancaster	5,287	75.8	236,500	23.3	11.0	903	25.5	0.0	5,244	-2.2	280	5.3	3,940	35.2	22.5
Lee	8,843	69.3	85,500	19.3	10.0	551	36.0	1.9	8,030	-3.3	325	4.0	7,564	25.7	33.8
Loudoun	132,565	77.7	534,600	20.4	10.0	1,913	27.3	2.0	222,649	-2.0	6,874	3.1	220,064	59.9	9.3

1. Specified owner-occupied units. 2. A value of 10.0 represents 10 percent or less; a value of 50.0 represents 50 percent or more. 3. Specified renter-occupied units. 4. Overcrowded or lacking complete plumbing facilities. 5. Percent of civilian labor force. 6. Civilian employed persons 16 years old and over.

STATE County	Private nonfarm establishments, employment and payroll, 2020 — Number of establishments	Employment — Total	Employment — Health care and social assistance	Employment — Manufacturing	Employment — Retail trade	Employment — Finance and insurance	Employment — Professional, scientific, and technical services	Annual payroll — Total (mil dol)	Annual payroll — Average per employee (dollars)	Agriculture, 2017 — Farms — Number	Farms — Percent with: Fewer than 50 acres	Farms — Percent with: 1000 acres or more	Farm producers whose primary occupation is farming (percent)
	104	105	106	107	108	109	110	111	112	113	114	115	116
VERMONT—Cont'd													
Chittenden	5,567	88,025	16,641	9,088	12,168	2,775	6,893	4,469	50,770	585	54.4	1.0	39.7
Essex	109	543	67	156	56	9	31	18	32,565	106	31.1	3.8	50.9
Franklin	1,018	13,639	3,403	2,815	2,346	296	267	574	42,121	729	31.3	4.0	49.1
Grand Isle	179	670	55	48	143	24	32	26	38,516	119	42.0	2.5	47.4
Lamoille	966	10,894	1,748	546	1,543	265	268	384	35,293	329	39.8	1.8	35.8
Orange	679	6,287	1,859	718	845	134	305	271	43,135	569	35.5	1.4	43.6
Orleans	752	8,221	1,558	1,306	1,403	218	149	292	35,536	558	33.2	2.9	47.8
Rutland	1,967	23,466	4,691	3,393	3,563	474	544	986	42,002	614	38.8	2.0	44.6
Washington	2,153	25,801	4,423	2,922	3,823	2,538	917	1,237	47,952	553	47.2	0.9	35.6
Windham	1,664	20,391	3,544	2,367	2,217	525	491	830	40,693	414	53.6	0.2	46.4
Windsor	1,910	20,170	4,427	2,053	2,801	485	1,057	911	45,152	677	38.7	2.7	33.6
VIRGINIA	204,131	3,483,867	478,490	241,221	428,644	168,520	509,368	202,239	58,050	43,225	42.2	3.1	40.1
Accomack	712	8,957	1,120	2,963	1,354	296	424	304	33,944	239	53.6	8.8	54.9
Albemarle	2,838	42,631	9,143	2,780	6,617	2,273	4,746	2,204	51,694	913	40.7	4.3	38.6
Alleghany	247	2,452	908	210	365	46	31	75	30,767	165	35.2	3.0	40.9
Amelia	261	1,947	312	172	216	33	73	66	34,050	370	36.8	6.5	44.6
Amherst	559	6,130	667	1,319	1,143	115	192	241	39,360	369	32.5	3.8	40.3
Appomattox	287	2,371	537	97	684	91	41	68	28,574	412	28.6	2.7	34.1
Arlington	6,404	153,519	10,472	203	9,084	3,638	51,861	13,520	88,069	5	100.0	NA	NA
Augusta	1,421	21,688	3,893	5,408	2,107	274	402	1,031	47,528	1,665	45.7	2.6	44.6
Bath	119	1,914	269	102	83	NA	27	71	37,019	110	8.2	10.0	47.7
Bedford	1,708	16,954	2,387	3,980	2,668	428	901	709	41,796	1,418	38.7	2.2	36.3
Bland	72	1,308	134	516	135	NA	NA	88	67,182	339	24.2	2.7	43.5
Botetourt	749	10,655	1,037	3,015	706	236	214	480	45,030	551	35.2	1.8	38.6
Brunswick	250	2,154	158	235	239	44	40	81	37,574	242	26.0	4.1	43.3
Buchanan	356	4,620	550	227	675	149	211	206	44,577	89	52.8	NA	50.0
Buckingham	253	1,788	326	161	318	25	66	64	35,946	408	28.7	2.5	37.9
Campbell	1,157	17,454	1,276	4,462	2,178	512	698	863	49,464	702	30.6	2.1	37.1
Caroline	389	4,037	308	264	648	265	145	156	38,563	222	47.7	8.6	40.7
Carroll	402	4,366	755	1,091	748	86	139	123	28,286	900	38.9	0.9	35.0
Charles City	156	1,745	NA	393	150	5	55	82	47,225	77	49.4	15.6	40.4
Charlotte	205	1,716	296	401	283	57	27	57	32,929	460	20.9	4.1	40.3
Chesterfield	7,621	120,881	15,069	9,381	21,492	4,334	10,099	5,497	45,478	210	62.9	1.0	36.2
Clarke	362	3,217	498	595	420	84	137	132	41,074	427	47.8	3.7	43.5
Craig	59	396	67	NA	130	29	10	11	28,394	179	20.1	1.1	43.4
Culpeper	1,037	13,685	2,244	1,388	2,447	242	601	629	45,951	682	49.1	4.7	39.4
Cumberland	138	726	63	68	160	16	22	25	35,102	264	36.4	3.4	41.7
Dickenson	194	1,977	344	24	408	63	369	71	35,952	128	50.0	1.6	37.0
Dinwiddie	362	5,828	1,410	705	536	65	40	256	44,004	358	33.5	6.4	40.4
Essex	287	3,248	559	440	830	107	84	101	30,959	88	31.8	21.6	40.3
Fairfax	31,769	672,100	65,883	5,874	52,277	31,245	228,318	57,393	85,394	117	78.6	NA	31.8
Fauquier	1,898	18,969	2,259	967	2,952	819	2,223	967	50,969	1,154	50.3	4.0	39.3
Floyd	326	2,769	766	484	437	55	61	80	29,008	741	37.4	0.9	36.6
Fluvanna	405	2,678	222	136	343	35	78	105	39,257	273	44.7	0.7	42.5
Franklin	1,168	13,296	1,457	3,202	2,134	260	360	421	31,658	1,019	35.0	1.7	38.0
Frederick	1,559	29,008	1,768	5,789	5,299	2,503	825	1,328	45,784	762	55.2	2.0	34.6
Giles	285	3,393	489	791	630	77	310	146	42,976	389	40.4	3.3	32.9
Gloucester	863	7,630	1,440	152	2,205	223	308	246	32,288	166	64.5	4.8	37.7
Goochland	705	21,089	484	196	755	6,124	334	2,469	117,052	355	47.3	2.0	40.4
Grayson	155	1,300	151	363	149	108	11	41	31,464	716	39.5	1.8	38.4
Greene	367	2,833	223	60	755	59	144	99	35,094	214	39.3	0.5	39.8
Greensville	97	2,288	NA	998	249	NA	NA	77	33,535	150	27.3	8.7	40.7
Halifax	668	9,794	1,604	1,980	1,371	193	154	393	40,144	895	21.7	3.1	39.0
Hanover	3,304	50,420	6,497	3,625	6,794	1,017	1,721	2,098	41,603	567	61.7	4.6	42.5
Henrico	9,516	186,329	27,237	5,631	23,132	26,519	16,222	10,664	57,232	99	70.7	2.0	37.0
Henry	784	11,041	787	3,459	1,546	476	339	371	33,606	212	30.2	5.7	30.6
Highland	83	342	70	12	30	24	20	10	30,243	275	16.7	6.2	48.6
Isle of Wight	732	9,750	713	3,404	1,024	197	293	434	44,507	237	47.3	13.1	52.8
James City	1,754	27,990	4,064	2,511	3,858	736	1,614	1,082	38,643	72	59.7	2.8	25.8
King and Queen	113	614	18	21	71	NA	77	24	39,679	151	41.7	8.6	43.7
King George	477	5,452	356	82	974	126	2,128	312	57,310	141	36.2	4.3	33.3
King William	358	3,452	370	502	468	81	127	170	49,254	90	51.1	15.6	36.8
Lancaster	438	4,056	1,044	75	730	283	389	162	39,985	80	41.3	5.0	24.4
Lee	245	2,311	542	138	676	159	72	73	31,495	830	40.5	0.6	38.4
Loudoun	11,348	169,437	15,130	5,952	19,936	3,458	29,783	10,347	61,064	1,259	69.5	1.3	33.3

STATE County	Agriculture, 2017 (cont.) Land in farms: Acreage (1,000)	Land in farms: Percent change, 2012–2017	Land in farms: Acres: Average size of farm	Land in farms: Acres: Total irrigated (1,000)	Land in farms: Acres: Total cropland (1,000)	Value of land and buildings (dollars): Average per farm	Value of land and buildings (dollars): Average per acre	Value of machinery and equipment, average per farm (dollars)	Value of products sold: Total (mil dol)	Value of products sold: Average per farm (acres)	Value of products sold: Percent from: Crops	Value of products sold: Percent from: Livestock and poultry products	Organic farms (number)	Farms with internet access (percent)	Government payments: Total ($1,000)	Government payments: Percent of farms
	117	118	119	120	121	122	123	124	125	126	127	128	129	130	131	132
VERMONT—Cont'd																
Chittenden	64	-12.7	110	0.5	26.8	701,224	6,387	84,797	43.6	74,492	51.2	48.8	68	90.8	545	12.1
Essex	43	67.9	404	0.0	8.0	789,828	1,956	137,512	12.7	119,887	39.7	60.3	10	83.0	41	15.1
Franklin	190	1.8	260	0.3	83.2	811,688	3,119	165,431	185.6	254,615	20.8	79.2	125	84.8	965	11.7
Grand Isle	19	-1.2	158	0.0	12.6	679,940	4,304	122,915	17.9	150,723	16.9	83.1	11	88.2	354	19.3
Lamoille	53	2.0	162	0.2	14.6	563,296	3,486	72,199	27.7	84,319	36.3	63.7	48	86.6	74	9.1
Orange	86	-18.6	150	0.2	32.6	553,914	3,681	90,079	55.1	96,749	22.8	77.2	59	80.8	389	8.4
Orleans	128	-1.6	230	0.1	58.6	623,033	2,708	119,211	92.0	164,875	13.7	86.3	52	81.9	234	3.6
Rutland	99	-8.9	161	0.2	34.6	444,531	2,761	70,922	28.8	46,932	35.9	64.1	24	81.9	657	16.9
Washington	64	-4.3	117	0.1	21.6	499,088	4,283	86,311	30.7	55,566	29.8	70.2	78	86.8	153	4.0
Windham	45	-11.7	108	0.4	14.4	542,832	5,011	71,071	28.6	69,048	39.8	60.2	28	93.0	457	8.5
Windsor	113	11.1	166	0.1	22.6	643,087	3,865	74,480	25.1	37,013	34.4	65.6	36	84.8	141	8.0
VIRGINIA	7,798	-6.1	180	63.4	3,084.1	834,254	4,624	86,136	3,960.5	91,625	34.4	65.6	252	74.0	60,805	13.9
Accomack	77	-0.8	321	5.1	57.7	1,370,847	4,268	217,830	163.3	683,134	28.7	71.3	1	81.2	2,399	30.5
Albemarle	183	8.2	200	0.8	51.8	1,980,339	9,892	68,432	29.6	32,472	63.6	36.4	9	81.3	477	6.8
Alleghany	31	-16.5	187	NA	8.9	788,210	4,215	66,701	2.7	16,618	29.5	70.5	NA	81.8	16	5.5
Amelia	103	16.3	278	0.2	34.8	858,640	3,094	108,375	86.6	233,992	10.7	89.3	NA	70.5	545	34.1
Amherst	79	-20.4	214	0.2	17.3	993,967	4,654	60,527	8.1	22,068	43.2	56.8	NA	71.5	24	5.1
Appomattox	76	-21.4	184	0.0	20.9	568,840	3,094	72,238	10.0	24,218	33.3	66.7	3	66.5	329	12.1
Arlington	0	-86.1	1	NA	NA	298,000	298,000	30,686	NA	NA	NA	100.0	NA	100.0	NA	NA
Augusta	291	11.8	175	2.5	116.8	1,222,854	6,999	101,481	292.5	175,704	12.8	87.2	5	71.5	1,049	15.7
Bath	48	15.8	435	D	15.3	1,599,416	3,677	100,025	6.7	61,345	24.8	75.2	1	66.4	91	10.0
Bedford	211	2.2	149	0.1	65.9	654,822	4,399	68,521	26.5	18,667	31.9	68.1	1	76.0	658	10.4
Bland	70	-9.2	207	0.8	17.3	714,594	3,446	73,919	8.8	25,906	25.7	74.3	NA	67.3	79	11.2
Botetourt	89	-0.5	161	0.0	27.0	676,797	4,198	72,657	14.1	25,506	28.8	71.2	1	76.6	152	9.3
Brunswick	66	-26.1	274	2.1	24.4	689,842	2,514	118,499	23.1	95,438	71.7	28.3	1	69.4	378	50.8
Buchanan	11	15.5	124	D	1.2	300,008	2,418	33,157	0.4	4,876	54.8	45.2	NA	51.7	NA	NA
Buckingham	79	-5.6	194	0.1	30.5	724,596	3,731	81,081	43.4	106,480	15.7	84.3	1	73.0	555	12.7
Campbell	132	-12.6	188	0.3	42.9	578,961	3,086	78,302	25.4	36,179	25.7	74.3	NA	76.4	204	13.1
Caroline	62	9.7	279	3.4	42.4	1,029,270	3,696	134,498	22.9	103,189	95.8	4.2	4	88.3	739	19.8
Carroll	119	-15.3	132	0.6	32.2	425,568	3,219	63,111	44.5	49,488	30.7	69.3	7	65.1	113	7.9
Charles City	31	0.7	408	1.4	20.6	1,375,102	3,373	187,684	D	D	D	D	1	96.1	1,156	22.1
Charlotte	122	-18.5	264	0.5	46.1	693,206	2,621	92,833	26.0	56,470	37.8	62.2	6	67.6	950	27.6
Chesterfield	18	-9.8	86	0.1	7.2	790,553	9,216	72,007	4.5	21,481	64.3	35.7	3	81.0	122	15.7
Clarke	67	-0.5	156	0.1	24.7	1,099,589	7,046	72,761	16.4	38,375	41.2	58.8	NA	85.0	75	7.5
Craig	43	-6.9	243	0.1	12.0	725,533	2,990	80,837	4.7	26,022	18.1	81.9	5	84.4	143	14.5
Culpeper	124	-1.6	182	0.6	60.1	1,048,206	5,747	87,179	48.5	71,176	64.7	35.3	5	81.5	568	11.0
Cumberland	53	-7.9	199	0.2	15.4	758,741	3,806	71,848	39.8	150,780	10.2	89.8	NA	68.2	196	15.9
Dickenson	11	-25.8	87	NA	1.8	246,038	2,820	74,934	0.6	4,375	17.7	82.3	NA	72.7	216	10.2
Dinwiddie	93	4.0	259	1.6	42.8	795,681	3,068	105,397	25.7	71,799	85.4	14.6	NA	64.2	1,534	34.6
Essex	59	3.5	667	D	42.3	2,130,482	3,194	333,241	21.0	239,159	94.3	5.7	NA	78.4	1,341	51.1
Fairfax	6	-24.4	51	0.1	0.8	852,783	16,806	45,082	1.2	10,624	81.3	18.7	2	90.6	21	6.8
Fauquier	217	-5.1	188	0.5	83.8	1,381,646	7,359	83,383	54.8	47,497	40.0	60.0	4	85.6	403	5.6
Floyd	110	-23.8	149	0.2	32.3	565,896	3,802	62,225	33.7	45,511	48.3	51.7	11	74.8	73	3.9
Fluvanna	44	-5.7	163	0.1	13.3	702,048	4,315	66,495	6.1	22,436	63.6	36.4	2	81.3	170	11.7
Franklin	156	-5.0	153	0.4	72.8	552,387	3,602	81,393	69.2	67,909	24.6	75.4	4	66.7	705	8.0
Frederick	110	9.1	144	0.0	45.2	1,041,790	7,223	67,981	33.8	44,324	72.9	27.1	6	77.7	78	3.7
Giles	65	-0.3	168	0.0	13.0	516,470	3,073	66,106	9.7	24,871	13.7	86.3	NA	74.6	58	2.3
Gloucester	26	28.1	157	0.0	14.2	739,196	4,717	108,605	11.7	70,482	80.0	20.0	6	81.9	580	12.0
Goochland	57	13.2	160	0.1	24.0	867,877	5,430	89,076	11.7	33,070	38.6	61.4	NA	78.3	144	7.6
Grayson	119	-9.5	167	0.2	34.4	692,467	4,155	68,462	40.8	57,011	26.1	73.9	2	73.9	157	8.7
Greene	29	4.6	133	0.0	10.0	870,295	6,531	60,814	7.6	35,579	23.6	76.4	NA	78.0	211	16.4
Greensville	55	-6.4	364	D	33.5	986,245	2,712	147,447	19.4	129,653	98.1	1.9	NA	72.0	1,707	58.7
Halifax	209	-1.2	233	1.1	57.5	619,060	2,651	70,488	31.9	35,617	51.3	48.7	15	66.9	429	20.0
Hanover	89	-5.4	157	3.6	61.3	791,920	5,035	102,289	49.3	86,868	83.7	16.3	NA	81.3	768	9.3
Henrico	10	-23.8	99	D	7.3	601,700	6,066	59,847	7.3	73,606	97.5	2.5	1	75.8	36	14.1
Henry	46	6.0	215	0.0	11.7	635,840	2,961	55,004	14.1	66,618	16.1	83.9	6	72.6	34	5.2
Highland	93	-0.1	338	D	15.6	1,080,848	3,198	65,010	26.1	94,982	6.6	93.4	1	68.0	279	11.3
Isle of Wight	81	6.6	340	0.9	51.5	1,264,037	3,714	173,573	64.2	270,987	61.9	38.1	NA	89.5	2,755	36.7
James City	7	19.6	92	0.0	3.6	931,231	10,113	129,707	2.0	28,458	92.6	7.4	NA	93.1	78	15.3
King and Queen	48	14.9	320	1.2	33.6	1,078,959	3,377	158,462	18.4	121,682	75.6	24.4	NA	79.5	817	37.1
King George	26	8.4	187	D	13.0	954,694	5,111	99,089	11.9	84,546	95.1	4.9	NA	73.8	134	27.7
King William	47	-11.4	527	1.6	26.3	2,133,522	4,046	250,259	14.2	157,411	88.1	11.9	NA	87.8	713	28.9
Lancaster	16	51.8	203	0.0	11.3	860,073	4,237	123,923	5.6	69,388	91.9	8.1	3	90.0	659	37.5
Lee	95	-19.0	114	0.0	25.2	302,584	2,646	71,083	15.3	18,393	26.0	74.0	5	61.8	1,658	9.8
Loudoun	122	-9.5	97	0.4	60.2	950,622	9,816	59,142	44.0	34,940	70.2	29.8	11	88.6	190	3.9

STATE County	Water use, 2015		Wholesale Trade[1], 2017				Retail Trade[2], 2017				Real estate and rental and leasing,[2] 2017			
	Public supply water withdrawn (mil gal/ day)	Public supply gallons withdrawn per person per day	Number of establish- ments	Number of employees	Sales (mil dol)	Average payroll (mil dol)	Number of establish- ments	Number of employees	Sales (mil dol)	Average payroll (mil dol)	Number of establish- ments	Number of employees	Sales (mil dol)	Average payroll (mil dol)
	133	134	135	136	137	138	139	140	141	142	143	144	145	146
VERMONT—Cont'd														
Chittenden	13.9	86.1	242	3,834	2,709.9	232.7	813	12,376	3,361.1	357.0	253	1,083	335.9	49.9
Essex	0.3	40.6	NA	NA	NA	NA	16	71	13.9	1.3	NA	NA	NA	NA
Franklin	3.0	61.5	43	1,065	1,012.6	43.7	176	2,268	830.0	63.7	30	73	9.4	2.0
Grand Isle	0.5	72.9	D	D	D	0.4	25	156	42.8	3.9	7	9	2.0	0.2
Lamoille	1.3	51.1	D	D	D	12.8	158	1,696	390.9	43.8	39	155	35.2	7.0
Orange	2.2	74.7	21	165	61.6	6.3	82	908	225.6	24.6	20	25	6.6	1.2
Orleans	1.6	60.1	D	D	D	D	135	1,510	378.0	39.3	21	89	20.3	3.8
Rutland	4.4	73.2	D	D	D	D	375	3,858	1,124.5	106.4	63	224	34.4	8.4
Washington	1.9	31.6	D	D	D	D	347	4,159	1,112.1	124.2	58	228	43.4	8.8
Windham	2.1	48.4	39	945	568.8	46.4	232	2,296	574.1	65.3	87	280	45.6	9.3
Windsor	3.1	55.6	51	717	418.7	41.7	275	2,737	810.2	81.6	99	416	61.4	15.9
VIRGINIA	695.6	83.0	5,937	86,698	98,904.6	5,734.1	27,134	429,072	120,162.1	11,476.0	10,051	55,778	17,207.8	2,949.2
Accomack	0.9	26.7	22	112	76.9	4.7	161	1,351	366.9	29.4	37	89	13.9	2.2
Albemarle	13.3	125.7	66	480	233.9	27.1	359	6,689	1,958.6	204.8	184	939	186.3	37.3
Alleghany	0.9	58.0	5	31	7.0	1.1	45	384	101.8	9.3	5	D	3.5	D
Amelia	0.1	7.8	8	105	45.9	6.4	22	203	60.7	5.5	11	D	3.4	D
Amherst	12.0	377.0	8	153	154.5	5.7	88	1,141	302.8	25.0	15	24	2.8	0.6
Appomattox	0.0	0.0	10	63	12.1	2.2	55	701	168.0	16.0	14	39	7.5	1.0
Arlington	0.0	0.0	74	568	405.0	44.0	559	9,693	2,701.2	337.0	474	4,227	1,926.8	277.7
Augusta	7.5	100.9	52	724	307.4	36.4	193	2,161	663.4	61.7	61	165	21.6	4.3
Bath	0.3	64.9	NA	NA	NA	NA	17	75	16.5	1.5	7	38	4.4	1.4
Bedford	1.5	19.8	48	503	293.8	23.3	221	2,680	718.8	66.9	105	211	52.5	7.0
Bland	0.0	6.1	D	D	D	D	13	64	26.0	1.5	NA	NA	NA	NA
Botetourt	5.5	163.7	D	D	D	27.8	82	777	224.1	16.6	31	139	28.8	6.3
Brunswick	24.3	1,457.7	7	D	21.0	D	40	292	90.1	6.6	8	26	1.3	0.6
Buchanan	0.0	0.0	15	177	181.3	9.2	74	799	164.0	17.0	11	26	6.4	0.8
Buckingham	0.4	21.1	6	D	8.6	D	42	289	72.9	6.7	4	D	0.8	D
Campbell	4.5	81.0	39	613	339.1	34.5	189	2,072	513.4	46.4	52	125	22.3	3.7
Caroline	0.8	27.7	D	D	D	D	56	513	306.9	12.6	13	42	2.8	0.5
Carroll	1.7	57.2	17	251	45.0	4.9	81	753	237.8	15.5	15	33	5.7	1.0
Charles City	0.0	0.0	11	72	28.1	4.7	10	67	19.3	2.4	7	D	4.9	D
Charlotte	0.2	19.7	11	75	67.2	3.0	36	266	59.6	5.5	6	11	1.0	0.2
Chesterfield	39.9	118.7	285	4,108	2,653.4	255.0	963	21,672	6,746.1	596.5	358	1,511	2,021.6	70.1
Clarke	0.5	34.8	D	D	D	D	38	304	94.5	8.4	D	D	D	D
Craig	0.0	0.0	D	D	D	0.9	9	199	22.5	2.2	NA	NA	NA	NA
Culpeper	2.3	47.1	21	462	276.0	20.4	156	2,310	671.2	63.5	45	249	36.9	9.7
Cumberland	0.0	0.0	NA	NA	NA	NA	26	171	40.4	4.2	NA	NA	NA	NA
Dickenson	5.0	328.2	D	D	D	D	48	416	103.5	9.5	NA	NA	NA	NA
Dinwiddie	0.0	1.1	D	D	D	1.2	49	527	148.1	10.7	13	57	13.5	2.7
Essex	0.0	1.8	7	69	96.7	3.4	63	841	221.2	21.2	10	34	5.6	0.9
Fairfax	0.1	0.1	738	13,174	32,745.7	1,438.2	2,681	52,389	16,030.0	1,649.9	1,665	11,578	3,610.8	832.9
Fauquier	3.1	45.1	33	532	202.7	28.2	225	3,035	1,009.5	88.6	93	225	64.6	12.3
Floyd	0.1	7.0	8	27	23.0	0.7	46	365	74.8	6.9	5	14	2.1	0.3
Fluvanna	0.8	29.4	10	131	99.4	8.1	37	319	85.6	7.6	21	39	6.6	1.2
Franklin	1.8	31.3	39	438	332.7	27.0	189	1,969	515.4	50.1	D	D	D	D
Frederick	5.3	63.3	D	D	D	78.5	209	3,724	1,297.8	107.0	63	D	60.0	D
Giles	1.1	67.0	8	43	23.1	2.2	57	699	178.4	16.6	8	14	2.2	0.4
Gloucester	0.7	17.8	21	81	22.7	2.6	146	2,007	525.4	53.3	41	96	14.1	2.8
Goochland	0.1	3.6	D	D	D	23.3	58	542	190.0	15.5	18	98	32.2	6.6
Grayson	0.1	6.9	D	D	D	0.2	27	168	40.3	3.1	D	D	D	0.2
Greene	0.6	32.9	8	D	8.2	D	53	725	193.0	17.7	13	D	5.9	D
Greensville	0.0	2.5	D	D	D	1.9	23	245	152.0	6.3	5	D	2.6	D
Halifax	2.1	59.8	18	174	75.6	6.4	125	1,335	357.7	30.1	18	56	10.0	1.5
Hanover	4.1	39.5	215	3,977	2,965.1	239.6	368	7,220	2,077.0	198.7	131	549	154.7	25.5
Henrico	20.2	62.0	372	7,004	10,718.5	480.1	1,255	23,634	6,237.0	618.4	518	3,685	984.0	219.5
Henry	2.9	55.1	39	803	1,236.9	34.2	155	1,476	443.8	36.5	27	89	12.8	2.5
Highland	0.1	45.2	NA	NA	NA	NA	16	54	10.5	0.8	NA	NA	NA	NA
Isle of Wight	1.6	42.7	19	87	48.1	4.7	99	866	203.8	17.6	35	78	19.7	2.6
James City	5.4	73.3	42	366	151.3	18.6	295	4,106	749.3	79.4	92	626	153.3	28.0
King and Queen	0.0	0.0	8	D	35.3	D	10	49	19.3	1.4	D	D	D	0.1
King George	0.9	36.4	12	196	49.8	5.3	60	879	343.2	21.2	18	45	12.4	1.8
King William	0.6	34.4	D	D	D	D	50	443	141.4	11.4	12	30	3.7	1.0
Lancaster	0.1	10.9	17	87	68.1	3.6	80	781	177.0	19.4	18	33	6.5	1.1
Lee	2.3	94.6	10	51	16.5	1.6	70	728	150.0	16.3	9	D	2.1	D
Loudoun	6.9	18.3	251	3,080	1,889.7	230.9	1,039	19,612	6,080.4	555.9	435	1,676	601.4	107.7

1 Merchant wholesalers, except manufacturers' sales branches and offices. 2. Employer establishments.

Table B. Sta[illegible]sional Services, Manufacturing, and Accommodation and [illegible]Services

STATE County	[illegible]ces, 2017				Manufacturing, 2017				Accommodation and food services, 2017			
	[illegible]	[illegible]	[illegible]dol)	Average payroll (mil dol)	Number of establish-ments	Number of employees	Sales (mil dol)	Average payroll (mil dol)	Number of establis-hments	Number of employees	Sales (mil dol)	Annual payroll (mil dol)
	[illegible]	[illegible]	149	150	151	152	153	154	155	156	157	158
VERMONT—Cont'd												
Chittenden	816	7,045	1,230.9	514.5	219	9,126	2,667.1	598.8	468	9,179	611.1	182.2
Essex	4	17	4.0	1.4	8	133	26.4	5.2	14	71	4.9	1.4
Franklin	D	D	D	D	59	2,772	1,487.9	157.2	94	1,058	71.0	20.9
Grand Isle	D	D	D	D	6	50	5.4	1.6	22	89	12.6	3.0
Lamoille	82	274	35.4	12.4	45	432	225.3	23.7	124	4,155	255.6	77.8
Orange	D	D	D	D	50	721	149.7	30.8	60	613	37.9	11.8
Orleans	46	162	14.7	6.4	33	1,120	196.2	46.5	56	1,720	78.1	28.8
Rutland	D	D	D	D	101	3,111	649.9	179.3	253	2,921	169.9	49.2
Washington	D	D	D	D	128	2,411	658.9	123.0	171	2,571	135.6	44.5
Windham	D	D	D	D	90	1,968	536.5	101.9	212	3,596	179.9	54.3
Windsor	179	999	175.0	66.1	115	1,952	499.1	96.8	201	3,393	234.0	70.2
VIRGINIA	31,233	457,575	98,543.2	40,177.3	5,038	232,695	99,343.9	12,987.4	18,199	358,010	22,074.7	6,226.9
Accomack	53	503	55.3	21.5	23	3,271	470.4	99.4	100	962	66.9	16.2
Albemarle	380	3,592	589.3	263.4	81	2,278	656.0	151.9	208	5,256	326.4	100.5
Alleghany	15	34	4.4	1.1	11	276	71.7	11.9	25	414	17.9	5.6
Amelia	17	58	5.7	2.1	13	150	78.2	6.3	D	D	D	1.7
Amherst	38	214	26.0	11.0	39	1,270	731.3	78.8	47	713	33.5	8.7
Appomattox	16	48	4.6	1.3	15	106	13.9	4.0	19	259	12.3	3.0
Arlington	1,887	45,652	11,880.4	4,816.9	40	268	70.6	12.0	665	18,101	1,629.6	434.9
Augusta	D	D	D	D	69	5,052	2,249.1	256.5	94	1,429	76.9	20.5
Bath	13	177	21.9	11.9	4	D	2.6	D	20	1,072	66.8	29.3
Bedford	184	951	134.2	48.7	79	3,004	1,184.5	168.6	103	1,309	67.0	19.3
Bland	NA	NA	NA	NA	8	378	183.3	22.0	D	D	D	0.5
Botetourt	60	201	19.6	7.3	28	D	871.6	137.6	51	816	39.2	11.4
Brunswick	16	40	3.9	1.2	14	266	90.0	14.4	10	D	6.6	D
Buchanan	32	195	12.9	4.9	D	215	D	15.0	22	269	13.5	3.6
Buckingham	11	62	9.9	3.9	8	106	24.1	4.9	9	89	6.0	1.2
Campbell	95	779	89.2	57.3	56	4,349	2,135.1	317.4	77	1,241	66.5	17.7
Caroline	32	134	26.1	6.2	13	317	99.8	13.5	37	498	27.4	8.6
Carroll	35	121	13.9	4.9	24	964	245.8	32.0	38	596	27.1	7.4
Charles City	7	48	6.6	3.0	21	336	72.3	14.1	D	D	D	0.7
Charlotte	8	36	4.9	0.8	12	361	104.0	14.7	D	D	D	D
Chesterfield	900	10,207	1,152.1	492.3	169	9,481	4,049.8	658.6	599	13,435	682.9	198.3
Clarke	35	110	16.9	7.5	15	578	111.2	28.1	22	200	12.9	4.0
Craig	6	7	1.2	0.5	NA	NA	NA	NA	4	31	2.0	0.8
Culpeper	D	D	D	D	41	1,274	539.5	69.6	88	1,709	87.7	24.0
Cumberland	5	49	6.3	2.1	5	106	24.2	4.3	7	48	2.3	0.7
Dickenson	D	D	25.0	D	D	26	D	0.9	14	195	8.4	2.5
Dinwiddie	D	D	4.1	D	14	618	555.0	47.4	25	333	20.5	4.4
Essex	D	D	D	D	12	590	131.3	19.1	31	441	20.5	6.4
Fairfax	8,813	200,603	49,360.7	20,006.0	342	6,064	1,359.8	395.4	2,421	44,519	3,519.0	945.4
Fauquier	296	2,053	396.1	162.2	66	950	177.0	47.6	136	2,614	150.2	43.0
Floyd	D	D	D	D	23	399	84.2	15.7	D	D	D	D
Fluvanna	31	60	9.6	2.5	12	112	19.7	4.7	19	210	8.3	2.5
Franklin	82	296	37.5	11.9	D	3,019	D	D	72	1,087	53.7	15.5
Frederick	D	D	D	53.1	86	5,314	3,605.7	289.7	D	D	D	D
Giles	18	432	27.3	17.8	11	817	460.8	54.1	D	D	D	D
Gloucester	59	285	30.4	11.8	14	174	48.4	6.3	64	1,138	51.5	15.5
Goochland	80	348	44.7	18.9	18	192	70.0	9.0	47	573	40.0	11.1
Grayson	9	11	1.3	0.7	10	299	51.1	10.8	10	D	3.9	D
Greene	D	D	D	D	11	40	3.5	1.1	32	395	23.3	5.8
Greensville	NA	NA	NA	NA	5	909	311.4	37.1	12	207	10.1	2.3
Halifax	43	164	16.4	6.0	38	1,845	708.8	81.9	62	995	42.8	11.6
Hanover	266	1,486	231.8	76.2	134	3,574	872.5	168.7	220	4,052	209.2	59.0
Henrico	1,217	14,691	2,442.2	998.9	168	5,514	1,974.8	304.1	777	17,256	1,007.7	279.3
Henry	27	413	24.8	10.0	62	3,315	1,054.6	153.4	62	1,017	47.2	11.3
Highland	D	D	D	0.8	4	D	4.1	D	D	D	D	D
Isle of Wight	55	265	27.1	9.9	16	3,601	992.9	159.5	51	969	49.5	14.4
James City	225	1,471	223.2	95.4	35	2,446	1,613.4	141.6	148	3,812	278.7	74.8
King and Queen	12	61	10.8	3.4	6	D	6.4	D	D	D	D	0.7
King George	D	D	D	D	8	105	32.1	4.4	40	420	25.1	6.9
King William	32	156	11.4	4.3	11	506	299.1	30.8	22	309	13.9	3.7
Lancaster	52	370	41.9	20.3	9	81	24.5	3.5	32	492	25.6	10.7
Lee	20	71	4.8	1.8	D	95	D	2.5	D	D	D	D
Loudoun	D	D	D	D	183	6,523	2,123.1	494.8	777	16,541	1,310.5	365.0

STATE County	Health care and social assistance, 2017: Number of establish-ments	Number of employees	Receipts (mil dol)	Annual payroll (mil dol)	Other services, 2017: Number of establish-ments	Number of employees	Receipts (mil dol)	Annual payroll (mil dol)	[illegible]	[illegible]	[illegible]	[illegible]
	159	160	161	162	163	164	165	166	167	168	169	170
VERMONT—Cont'd												
Chittenden	599	15,593	2,123.2	714.0	439	2,422	318.2	87.4	15,601	800.4	166,284	856
Essex	D	D	D	D	12	31	4.1	0.7	451	18.3	12,378	51
Franklin	104	2,566	258.1	122.2	80	291	28.7	7.6	3,741	161.7	44,506	173
Grand Isle	13	91	3.8	2.0	14	30	3.5	1.1	764	34.5	5,250	20
Lamoille	D	D	D	D	67	297	63.7	9.5	2,863	141.0	50,139	245
Orange	87	1,505	146.3	67.2	45	144	17.0	4.5	2,953	121.1	8,933	39
Orleans	82	1,731	172.2	78.5	65	210	26.3	5.7	2,618	112.1	16,378	186
Rutland	196	4,810	546.0	210.7	156	790	68.4	19.8	4,876	193.2	14,820	61
Washington	219	4,566	460.6	204.3	219	1,025	155.9	45.0	6,157	250.9	44,752	180
Windham	165	3,317	306.3	143.3	124	469	46.7	12.7	5,184	221.8	31,187	121
Windsor	161	4,563	536.5	276.1	138	663	70.5	22.9	6,142	286.3	28,211	104
VIRGINIA	20,522	454,501	58,792.5	22,721.6	15,700	118,537	20,344.4	5,188.4	644,341	29,435.1	7,750,202	39,388
Accomack	56	1,177	71.9	33.9	59	289	32.0	7.4	2,357	90.2	41,467	206
Albemarle	356	8,120	1,278.0	534.7	169	1,455	255.1	56.1	10,068	509.4	269,728	862
Alleghany	37	829	80.5	32.7	26	116	11.9	3.6	647	22.7	1,658	5
Amelia	D	D	D	10.1	D	D	7.2	D	947	38.5	12,978	58
Amherst	47	689	41.5	19.2	52	138	11.9	3.3	1,641	57.1	17,437	70
Appomattox	26	507	24.6	11.8	23	98	9.0	2.6	938	35.3	15,043	66
Arlington	516	11,848	1,567.8	673.2	715	14,016	3,533.2	957.6	20,880	1,125.9	503,287	3,323
Augusta	117	3,940	578.9	195.6	107	445	54.6	15.1	4,682	248.8	59,574	248
Bath	5	244	23.1	11.0	8	52	2.8	1.3	348	13.9	11,587	18
Bedford	155	2,215	195.3	83.5	132	637	74.7	22.5	5,690	250.2	11,139	141
Bland	7	193	13.6	6.7	D	D	9.4	D	250	8.1	1,521	6
Botetourt	55	946	79.5	27.7	D	D	21.0	D	2,381	97.9	22,362	91
Brunswick	14	175	9.3	4.2	D	D	D	1.4	759	30.5	9,689	40
Buchanan	42	630	55.7	23.0	26	162	14.1	5.2	719	25.2	1,625	9
Buckingham	D	D	D	13.8	14	61	11.6	3.0	816	33.0	14,961	84
Campbell	89	1,092	60.7	26.6	96	378	39.4	10.4	3,084	111.0	55,280	272
Caroline	22	333	23.2	11.0	34	187	16.9	5.1	1,872	66.3	68,162	348
Carroll	34	690	48.1	19.9	D	D	D	D	1,680	66.1	16,570	79
Charles City	D	D	D	D	D	D	D	D	460	17.0	4,148	23
Charlotte	20	318	20.9	9.6	D	D	2.8	D	701	30.0	5,127	23
Chesterfield	837	14,517	1,751.9	697.6	511	3,465	318.2	103.9	26,322	1,109.1	578,605	3,831
Clarke	26	734	124.9	23.3	35	162	12.2	3.9	1,384	65.2	35,032	115
Craig	4	57	3.7	1.7	D	D	1.6	D	294	9.5	1,739	24
Culpeper	81	2,165	231.7	89.5	95	606	69.3	22.1	3,909	204.9	77,249	237
Cumberland	12	95	4.5	2.1	5	15	1.4	0.4	570	22.0	6,410	56
Dickenson	24	390	22.5	11.7	D	D	D	1.6	405	12.0	1,134	8
Dinwiddie	D	D	D	8.5	D	D	D	D	1,443	53.7	16,775	93
Essex	38	635	78.6	23.5	D	D	D	D	760	33.9	7,347	44
Fairfax	3,242	60,021	8,427.1	3,213.8	2,124	16,922	3,028.4	828.8	114,617	6,118.7	398,171	2,105
Fauquier	115	2,586	306.5	136.0	142	1,056	146.2	38.9	6,664	349.0	99,129	248
Floyd	23	499	67.7	15.6	28	92	9.8	2.5	1,281	43.2	1,441	6
Fluvanna	25	210	14.4	7.2	21	133	12.4	3.8	1,828	66.8	40,020	184
Franklin	76	1,394	126.7	48.3	101	357	36.1	9.4	3,714	161.3	58,681	169
Frederick	D	D	D	D	D	D	D	D	6,035	269.5	189,895	687
Giles	28	486	62.7	17.8	30	141	21.3	5.8	858	30.8	5,673	27
Gloucester	73	1,363	132.8	46.0	75	322	28.6	8.8	2,478	103.5	40,476	168
Goochland	30	492	44.2	19.7	48	346	61.8	20.3	2,385	147.4	106,108	353
Grayson	11	160	10.6	4.4	D	D	2.3	D	973	36.4	7,069	36
Greene	D	D	D	7.0	30	136	14.3	3.7	1,460	55.3	33,065	108
Greensville	NA	NA	NA	NA	D	D	5.9	D	381	11.3	1,352	14
Halifax	76	1,675	195.3	76.2	46	172	19.6	4.4	1,799	66.8	13,741	102
Hanover	279	6,179	868.6	289.2	271	1,712	206.0	59.8	8,671	416.4	231,400	789
Henrico	1,160	25,688	3,422.0	1,257.8	713	5,321	795.6	199.8	26,914	1,212.4	252,227	2,191
Henry	46	811	58.3	26.8	55	292	24.0	6.7	2,283	79.0	5,907	30
Highland	5	D	3.4	D	D	D	1.8	D	238	6.9	1,938	11
Isle of Wight	60	632	44.0	18.1	72	261	29.4	7.9	2,409	101.7	77,523	350
James City	159	3,957	408.3	167.9	117	901	82.3	21.7	5,824	251.1	96,482	349
King and Queen	D	D	D	0.4	D	D	1.5	D	434	15.4	6,043	23
King George	29	347	25.4	9.8	D	D	D	D	1,456	55.3	50,030	232
King William	22	327	23.7	12.0	31	103	12.4	3.1	1,117	48.0	42,326	198
Lancaster	43	948	99.7	39.5	41	188	20.4	5.8	1,123	50.2	16,731	48
Lee	30	519	40.8	16.5	D	D	D	0.7	1,041	39.3	2,241	16
Loudoun	947	14,238	1,761.1	665.5	680	4,846	657.1	202.7	38,380	2,009.3	474,627	2,099

STATE County	Government employment and payroll, 2017									Local government finances, 2017				
			March payroll (percent of total)							General revenue				
												Taxes		
	Full-time equivalent employees	March payroll (dollars)	Adminis-tration, judicial, and legal	Police and corrections	Fire protection	Highways and transpor-tation	Health and welfare	Natural resources and utilities	Education and libraries	Total (mil dol)	Inter-govern-mental (mil dol)	Total (mil dol)	Per capita[1] (dollars)	
													Total	Property
	171	172	173	174	175	176	177	178	179	180	181	182	183	184
VERMONT—Cont'd														
Chittenden	6,368	30,113,712	5.6	6.4	2.5	8.2	1.4	6.7	68.5	767.4	474.2	142.1	871	722
Essex	311	902,691	5.8	1.0	0.5	4.7	0.0	1.8	84.2	30.7	20.9	8.6	1,383	1,382
Franklin	2,134	7,474,467	4.7	2.6	0.3	4.8	1.1	3.4	82.8	183.5	136.4	33.7	689	663
Grand Isle	192	737,545	12.9	0.0	0.0	7.0	0.0	3.3	76.1	29.2	18.1	9.9	1,418	1,413
Lamoille	476	2,115,401	10.9	7.8	0.4	11.7	2.0	11.7	54.2	115.6	74.2	29.3	1,157	1,097
Orange	901	3,237,148	8.1	1.9	0.2	8.1	0.0	1.3	80.0	132.7	90.4	33.0	1,139	1,133
Orleans	1,237	4,506,161	4.2	2.5	0.4	5.7	0.0	1.9	84.2	118.6	81.3	28.5	1,064	1,058
Rutland	1,781	7,144,103	6.9	5.3	2.3	9.6	0.8	6.4	68.0	257.1	166.3	66.1	1,120	1,063
Washington	2,280	8,608,849	6.2	5.6	2.9	5.7	2.2	3.1	73.4	270.0	174.2	61.5	1,057	1,049
Windham	1,910	7,669,353	5.7	4.4	2.0	6.7	1.0	3.5	76.1	216.3	129.4	68.2	1,591	1,552
Windsor	2,876	13,142,052	3.7	4.0	1.8	4.3	0.8	3.6	81.2	267.5	171.3	70.1	1,269	1,254
VIRGINIA	X	X	X	X	X	X	X	X	X	X	X	X	X	X
Accomack	1,234	3,765,447	9.0	11.3	0.0	0.8	10.5	4.7	61.6	116.0	58.7	48.6	1,486	1,106
Albemarle	3,581	14,557,344	5.8	11.3	3.9	0.9	4.0	4.4	64.9	445.7	142.7	220.0	2,041	1,553
Alleghany	720	2,452,619	10.5	9.9	1.7	3.2	4.3	9.5	58.3	53.8	23.3	20.0	1,323	749
Amelia	338	1,180,965	9.5	7.6	0.0	0.0	0.0	3.6	75.4	31.7	16.9	10.0	772	633
Amherst	959	3,122,016	6.4	6.6	4.1	0.0	3.1	3.0	75.2	67.8	32.9	31.7	996	745
Appomattox	467	1,594,829	9.0	5.6	0.0	0.0	0.3	5.0	76.8	40.5	21.1	16.2	1,030	820
Arlington	10,302	63,767,532	6.5	9.7	4.0	22.4	7.1	5.4	41.5	3,105.9	634.0	1,107.8	4,721	3,678
Augusta	2,532	8,458,386	5.0	11.5	4.4	0.7	6.0	1.6	69.9	198.6	109.3	76.3	1,014	750
Bath	235	902,598	7.5	6.9	0.0	0.2	0.0	2.3	80.7	17.3	3.0	14.0	3,288	2,718
Bedford	2,651	9,414,798	4.7	17.8	1.8	0.7	14.7	4.8	53.8	247.4	130.8	92.5	1,180	945
Bland	217	665,699	12.9	5.5	5.6	0.0	0.0	3.7	67.8	15.6	9.0	5.0	782	725
Botetourt	1,107	3,717,883	7.9	10.8	0.4	0.1	6.0	2.2	71.0	129.4	71.4	47.8	1,434	1,181
Brunswick	498	1,647,277	10.1	8.4	0.0	2.7	5.5	4.3	65.8	36.8	18.0	16.7	1,008	898
Buchanan	731	2,092,784	7.5	7.1	1.2	2.2	0.5	6.3	71.9	100.3	55.4	26.7	1,237	1,095
Buckingham	622	1,948,843	5.1	30.4	0.0	0.0	0.3	4.8	57.7	103.3	29.6	16.8	987	889
Campbell	1,693	5,305,069	5.9	5.8	4.2	0.6	6.2	4.2	70.1	131.3	69.9	54.7	989	761
Caroline	797	2,715,160	10.0	11.1	5.4	0.0	4.7	5.1	60.7	101.2	44.1	45.9	1,509	1,234
Carroll	1,058	3,641,643	5.0	5.8	2.0	0.5	17.5	3.3	63.5	70.5	37.4	26.1	875	715
Charles City	219	739,386	13.6	7.8	0.0	0.0	2.5	3.0	64.4	17.8	5.2	12.3	1,753	1,567
Charlotte	481	1,985,592	4.7	8.7	0.0	0.4	4.5	3.0	76.9	48.6	32.8	10.8	894	741
Chesterfield	12,037	46,482,057	7.6	9.3	5.7	0.2	7.2	4.2	61.6	1,235.4	491.5	532.3	1,551	1,223
Clarke	465	1,666,629	7.8	9.5	2.9	0.8	4.2	5.2	69.2	48.3	18.1	24.7	1,706	1,480
Craig	170	506,390	11.9	9.2	0.0	0.0	6.5	3.8	68.6	10.4	5.4	4.4	875	783
Culpeper	1,925	6,793,854	8.7	9.8	2.9	1.5	3.9	5.3	64.9	180.0	81.0	80.6	1,572	1,252
Cumberland	317	998,010	10.0	7.9	0.0	0.0	0.7	2.2	74.5	27.7	16.1	10.3	1,046	935
Dickenson	516	1,599,967	7.7	7.8	0.0	0.1	0.8	14.0	67.4	72.1	44.4	17.2	1,167	1,042
Dinwiddie	883	3,272,325	6.7	7.5	2.8	0.0	5.2	4.9	67.7	82.6	42.4	36.1	1,261	1,072
Essex	374	1,318,222	9.9	9.4	3.3	2.9	0.0	4.7	64.1	36.0	15.3	18.8	1,718	1,375
Fairfax	44,022	252,473,395	7.8	8.2	5.2	0.5	6.3	5.3	59.8	6,096.2	1,439.5	3,826.5	3,331	2,737
Fauquier	2,871	11,391,634	8.6	8.4	4.3	1.0	2.2	5.0	65.2	274.9	94.7	162.2	2,332	1,984
Floyd	503	1,725,104	6.0	5.4	0.0	0.0	6.2	3.9	77.5	29.7	15.6	13.0	826	680
Fluvanna	763	2,674,700	6.2	6.9	0.0	0.0	5.7	1.9	77.1	70.0	31.6	36.8	1,390	1,248
Franklin	1,881	6,737,473	6.2	5.9	4.9	0.7	3.3	2.5	75.5	153.2	72.9	69.7	1,237	1,015
Frederick	3,242	11,189,825	5.7	12.3	4.0	0.6	0.3	3.5	72.5	251.4	83.3	148.3	1,716	1,329
Giles	773	1,953,500	12.3	10.4	0.0	2.2	0.2	6.8	60.1	73.0	44.1	21.5	1,284	997
Gloucester	1,186	4,098,264	9.4	10.0	0.0	0.0	3.7	3.6	73.1	105.7	43.6	56.3	1,508	1,155
Goochland	612	2,265,158	13.8	7.7	3.4	0.0	0.9	3.6	66.9	78.3	19.2	47.9	2,108	1,749
Grayson	552	1,507,640	7.1	8.3	0.0	0.2	1.8	4.9	77.7	33.4	16.9	12.6	804	670
Greene	752	2,411,800	6.5	4.7	0.0	2.0	3.1	5.6	71.9	65.5	28.7	24.6	1,258	1,043
Greensville	596	1,946,073	9.4	14.7	0.3	0.0	0.0	6.9	65.2	50.4	31.4	10.4	902	721
Halifax	1,241	3,464,577	7.1	7.7	1.2	1.2	0.0	1.9	80.5	113.1	54.8	41.4	1,197	847
Hanover	4,125	16,605,750	8.1	13.3	5.0	0.6	6.3	4.3	60.6	374.7	150.3	185.7	1,757	1,380
Henrico	12,233	52,050,101	7.2	15.5	7.7	3.7	4.8	5.1	53.9	1,323.7	532.3	583.6	1,782	1,227
Henry	1,715	5,150,131	7.1	8.0	2.0	0.0	8.9	1.3	68.9	151.9	90.3	36.8	716	474
Highland	93	325,265	14.2	14.3	0.0	0.0	4.1	3.6	59.9	9.3	4.5	3.9	1,761	1,510
Isle of Wight	1,032	4,780,984	7.9	7.5	1.8	1.8	1.7	3.6	69.1	183.4	73.9	68.0	1,858	1,544
James City	2,848	11,706,927	6.0	5.5	6.6	2.1	3.2	6.9	67.5	285.2	94.0	161.7	2,148	1,702
King and Queen	352	1,181,672	7.7	46.9	0.0	0.0	2.7	0.0	42.6	22.5	11.8	7.9	1,129	1,006
King George	880	2,719,706	8.1	14.3	9.7	0.0	3.5	5.1	54.9	86.6	38.3	38.1	1,447	890
King William	579	2,184,019	6.5	6.8	0.0	0.6	2.3	2.1	77.8	60.7	28.5	28.0	1,680	1,483
Lancaster	354	1,129,167	13.5	15.9	0.0	0.6	0.3	3.3	66.1	42.6	12.9	22.4	2,084	1,669
Lee	873	2,129,145	6.4	7.6	0.0	0.1	0.2	5.3	75.9	69.3	47.7	15.4	643	471
Loudoun	15,352	74,079,202	7.2	6.8	4.4	0.6	4.5	4.0	70.5	2,109.0	505.5	1,415.8	3,566	2,908

1. Based on the resident population estimated as of July 1 of the year shown.

STATE County	Local government finances, 2017 (cont.)									Government employment, 2020			Individual income tax returns, 2019		
	Direct general expenditure							Debt outstanding							
			Percent of total for:												
	Total (mil dol)	Per capita[1] (dollars)	Education	Health and hospitals	Police protection	Public welfare	Highways	Total (mil dol)	Per capita[1] (dollars)	Federal civilian	Federal military	State and local	Number of returns	Mean adjusted gross income	Mean income tax
	185	186	187	188	189	190	191	192	193	194	195	196	197	198	199
VERMONT—Cont'd															
Chittenden	783.3	4,804	61.1	0.2	5.0	0.0	5.2	562.6	3,451	2,547	1,095	13,779	86,300	83,710	10,371
Essex	29.5	4,762	74.9	0.3	1.1	0.1	13.4	4.5	735	104	38	269	2,920	44,377	3,266
Franklin	219.9	4,491	77.5	0.0	2.4	0.0	9.2	89.6	1,829	1,609	309	2,772	25,550	59,323	5,452
Grand Isle	27.2	3,903	79.1	0.0	3.0	0.0	7.1	13.8	1,977	24	45	273	4,060	80,693	10,183
Lamoille	130.7	5,154	67.3	0.9	5.7	0.1	10.6	105.1	4,146	69	155	1,506	13,940	72,371	8,955
Orange	144.3	4,984	70.7	0.8	2.0	0.1	12.6	33.7	1,165	79	177	1,841	15,050	57,714	5,343
Orleans	135.8	5,065	82.3	0.1	1.2	0.0	6.9	33.9	1,266	249	164	1,695	14,050	48,639	4,293
Rutland	277.1	4,696	64.0	0.1	5.2	0.0	9.6	93.6	1,586	308	350	3,443	31,560	56,834	5,736
Washington	292.0	5,012	67.2	1.0	3.4	0.1	8.9	103.6	1,778	257	386	7,205	31,210	65,927	6,909
Windham	234.5	5,472	68.8	0.3	4.1	0.1	7.4	106.9	2,495	163	257	2,505	23,840	56,684	5,987
Windsor	288.2	5,218	67.6	0.6	3.8	0.1	9.2	110.7	2,004	1,522	346	3,204	30,500	70,499	8,226
VIRGINIA	X	X	X	X	X	X	X	X	X	206,208	121,549	531,839	4,062,320	83,027	10,814
Accomack	109.6	3,353	56.2	1.1	3.8	5.0	0.9	48.6	1,487	670	2,065	2,129	16,000	47,517	3,989
Albemarle	398.1	3,694	55.4	1.3	4.6	5.7	0.0	449.4	4,170	(2) 1403	(2) 993	(2) 32638	51,680	114,770	17,666
Alleghany	48.9	3,235	56.9	13.4	6.8	0.5	0.8	21.2	1,402	(3) 67	(3) 74	(3) 1471	6,880	51,656	4,167
Amelia	29.7	2,285	63.4	1.6	7.0	5.6	0.7	5.5	426	27	41	441	6,260	57,789	5,126
Amherst	54.1	1,698	88.5	0.0	0.9	0.0	0.0	23.7	743	57	95	1,565	14,340	51,414	4,033
Appomattox	40.1	2,549	63.9	0.0	4.8	7.1	0.0	26.2	1,667	49	50	729	7,330	52,361	4,143
Arlington	2,334.1	9,947	24.8	2.0	2.9	3.8	4.0	9,964.4	42,465	29,153	9,412	13,117	125,170	131,528	22,596
Augusta	223.8	2,977	66.6	0.5	3.6	7.1	1.6	86.8	1,154	(4) 301	(4) 380	(4) 8087	36,180	60,039	5,444
Bath	11.5	2,695	96.0	0.0	0.0	0.0	0.0	8.9	2,087	36	19	314	2,240	51,322	4,366
Bedford	240.2	3,065	50.6	1.5	5.4	7.9	0.8	106.9	1,364	138	250	2,907	37,230	72,326	7,903
Bland	15.7	2,471	54.6	1.0	7.2	8.5	1.8	17.6	2,770	14	52	575	2,590	49,368	4,007
Botetourt	131.0	3,934	45.2	3.4	4.6	2.6	0.0	46.9	1,407	65	106	1,438	16,630	74,126	7,902
Brunswick	32.4	1,956	69.4	0.0	12.4	0.0	0.0	21.5	1,298	42	52	862	6,600	42,912	3,235
Buchanan	91.4	4,231	45.7	0.8	5.0	11.4	8.4	13.3	615	75	68	1,409	7,020	45,635	3,395
Buckingham	47.2	2,773	49.2	1.3	4.5	0.0	0.5	47.0	2,758	33	50	1,234	6,540	45,397	3,271
Campbell	122.5	2,214	67.9	2.7	5.2	7.9	0.6	43.5	786	(5) 376	(5) 442	(5) 6580	25,470	51,570	4,353
Caroline	88.4	2,906	53.8	0.8	9.7	6.6	3.6	57.4	1,887	397	183	1,197	14,680	56,539	4,861
Carroll	82.2	2,757	53.6	9.6	7.0	7.9	0.7	55.2	1,851	(6) 89	(6) 115	(6) 1829	12,490	45,068	3,211
Charles City	17.4	2,473	62.7	0.6	5.1	6.4	0.0	6.1	869	19	21	301	3,470	61,519	6,676
Charlotte	42.7	3,538	60.4	0.5	5.4	13.1	0.2	1.6	132	40	46	788	4,990	44,305	3,158
Chesterfield	1,145.0	3,336	54.4	8.7	6.6	2.4	2.3	260.2	758	3,409	1,317	17,765	176,260	77,559	8,972
Clarke	61.4	4,250	43.8	1.0	5.2	4.1	1.3	134.5	9,304	30	47	633	7,340	94,034	12,380
Craig	35.5	7,023	21.4	0.4	1.8	0.5	0.2	108.9	21,510	15	16	250	2,290	50,844	3,766
Culpeper	176.0	3,434	56.9	0.9	8.4	8.9	2.4	120.2	2,347	233	168	3,085	24,420	68,286	7,167
Cumberland	30.5	3,101	65.1	0.9	5.5	7.0	0.0	48.0	4,888	14	35	403	4,440	45,968	3,431
Dickenson	84.7	5,751	40.1	8.0	23.0	8.2	0.3	18.6	1,262	39	54	901	4,870	42,962	2,769
Dinwiddie	83.6	2,920	56.6	3.9	7.3	5.2	0.1	48.4	1,692	(7) 239	(7) 245	(7) 5675	13,160	54,690	4,549
Essex	105.3	9,597	22.5	0.0	1.9	3.2	0.1	13.5	1,231	17	43	517	5,380	54,736	5,160
Fairfax	5,705.9	4,967	52.6	5.8	4.9	4.4	0.9	5,631.9	4,903	(8) 46245	(8) 10905	(8) 60008	557,770	128,405	21,006
Fauquier	267.7	3,849	52.4	0.5	7.4	4.2	3.5	104.2	1,498	660	224	3,620	35,650	100,937	13,850
Floyd	31.3	1,986	67.7	3.5	5.7	3.5	0.0	28.7	1,824	49	49	613	6,890	52,707	4,248
Fluvanna	62.3	2,352	63.7	1.5	9.3	9.3	0.0	103.2	3,895	38	84	1,314	13,050	68,369	6,711
Franklin	151.0	2,681	64.2	0.5	3.8	7.3	0.2	33.3	591	107	175	2,186	24,510	60,668	6,165
Frederick	271.0	3,134	63.3	0.2	5.1	2.9	0.2	188.6	2,181	(9) 2454	(9) 385	(9) 6668	44,470	71,176	7,439
Giles	58.1	3,469	51.2	0.3	11.4	9.2	2.5	77.9	4,650	37	68	852	7,580	52,347	4,186
Gloucester	108.1	2,899	66.9	1.1	5.1	5.0	0.1	50.3	1,349	95	157	1,978	18,770	65,544	6,439
Goochland	63.2	2,783	50.1	1.3	5.6	6.1	0.0	99.2	4,371	47	75	1,441	12,360	151,924	25,553
Grayson	42.6	2,716	49.0	0.4	6.4	4.7	0.5	2.3	150	29	47	1,019	6,280	41,891	2,874
Greene	66.9	3,415	61.6	1.0	5.5	5.5	2.0	46.9	2,396	34	63	789	9,520	63,121	5,717
Greensville	58.8	5,079	51.4	0.3	4.9	5.5	0.4	44.0	3,806	(10) 37	(10) 40	(10) 1699	3,870	39,547	2,664
Halifax	119.6	3,459	47.9	11.3	9.0	0.0	4.5	109.8	3,174	90	104	1,921	15,050	47,449	3,587
Hanover	407.7	3,858	47.7	0.4	8.1	5.3	6.5	343.1	3,247	175	337	4,888	54,360	86,044	10,233
Henrico	1,234.1	3,768	43.6	3.0	6.3	2.7	4.1	1,040.2	3,176	2,303	1,038	17,316	168,740	80,862	10,496
Henry	162.3	3,162	56.3	13.8	3.7	5.0	0.0	66.0	1,285	(11) 141	(11) 195	(11) 3728	21,830	43,153	3,091
Highland	9.5	4,285	48.4	2.1	7.2	4.1	6.5	1.6	730	7	8	169	1,050	42,759	3,790
Isle of Wight	157.4	4,304	43.9	15.6	4.4	2.4	3.8	227.2	6,212	93	117	1,389	18,640	75,267	8,071
James City	252.4	3,353	59.7	1.5	4.9	1.8	0.0	214.4	2,848	(12) 250	(12) 873	(12) 7980	38,980	96,250	12,322
King and Queen	21.6	3,082	48.9	0.6	7.1	0.0	0.0	3.7	531	11	23	291	3,250	54,715	4,873
King George	77.9	2,956	61.2	0.9	6.5	0.0	1.4	123.6	4,693	5,512	837	1,123	12,350	79,347	8,492
King William	55.7	3,339	64.8	0.3	5.3	3.1	0.0	27.4	1,644	30	56	745	8,750	62,029	5,391
Lancaster	34.8	3,248	51.2	0.0	15.5	7.9	0.4	18.0	1,675	36	34	503	5,770	79,210	9,457
Lee	69.7	2,917	64.1	4.1	5.4	10.1	0.8	6.8	287	466	68	1,047	7,590	40,458	2,577
Loudoun	2,181.9	5,495	62.3	0.3	4.4	3.9	5.5	1,920.0	4,836	4,852	1,331	22,759	197,100	128,713	19,470

1. Based on the resident population estimated as of July 1 of the year shown. 2. Charlottesville city is included with Albemarle county. 3. Covington city is included with Alleghany county. 4. Staunton and Waynesboro cities are included with Augusta county. 5. Lynchburg city is included with Campbell county. 6. Galax city is included with Carroll county. 7. Petersburg and Colonial Heights cities are included with Dinwiddie county. 8. Fairfax city and Falls Church city are included with Fairfax county. 9. Winchester city is included with Frederick county. 10. Emporia city is included with Greensville county. 11. Martinsville city is included with Henry county. 12. Williamsburg city is included with James City county.

State / county code	CBSA code[1]	County Type code[2]	STATE County	Land area[3] (sq. mi)	Population, 2021: Total persons 2021	Population, 2021: Rank	Population, 2021: Per square mile	Race alone or in combination, not Hispanic or Latino (percent): White	Black	American Indian, Alaska Native	Asian and Pacific Islancer	Percent Hispanic or Latino[4]	Age (percent): Under 5 years	5 to 17 years	18 to 24 years	25 to 34 years	35 to 44 years	45 to 54 years
				1	2	3	4	5	6	7	8	9	10	11	12	13	14	15
			VIRGINIA—Cont'd															
51109		8	Louisa	495.0	38,848	1,204	78.5	80.3	16.4	0.9	1.4	3.6	5.1	11.3	9.8	12.1	12.1	12.2
51111		9	Lunenburg	431.7	11,926	2,289	27.6	60.8	33.6	1.0	1.1	6.0	4.8	11.2	9.9	11.5	12.8	12.3
51113	47900	8	Madison	320.6	13,942	2,154	43.5	86.9	10.0	0.9	1.2	3.5	4.9	11.4	10.6	10.7	10.9	11.7
51115	47260	1	Mathews	85.9	8,546	2,532	99.5	87.0	9.3	1.3	1.7	3.3	3.6	9.3	9.0	8.6	8.6	11.8
51117		7	Mecklenburg	625.3	30,248	1,431	48.4	62.3	34.4	0.8	1.2	3.1	5.0	10.2	10.1	10.2	10.1	11.5
51119		8	Middlesex	130.3	10,781	2,361	82.7	80.2	16.7	1.2	1.0	3.2	4.4	8.7	8.2	9.2	8.8	10.3
51121	13980	3	Montgomery	386.8	98,473	622	254.6	85.7	5.0	0.6	7.6	3.7	3.9	8.9	29.3	12.9	10.6	10.4
51125	16820	3	Nelson	470.7	14,790	2,099	31.4	83.1	11.8	1.0	1.3	4.8	4.6	9.4	9.5	9.2	10.3	11.6
51127	40060	1	New Kent	210.0	23,897	1,645	113.8	79.8	14.7	2.0	2.3	4.0	4.8	11.0	10.2	13.6	13.1	13.7
51131		8	Northampton	211.7	12,085	2,277	57.1	57.6	32.6	0.8	1.5	9.2	4.6	10.7	9.5	9.5	9.4	10.2
51133		9	Northumberland	191.4	12,029	2,282	62.8	70.3	25.4	0.8	0.9	4.3	3.8	8.2	8.1	8.0	7.9	8.9
51135		6	Nottoway	314.4	15,594	2,053	49.6	55.8	39.1	0.8	1.0	4.8	5.0	10.7	11.4	14.1	13.0	12.7
51137		6	Orange	341.1	37,188	1,247	109.0	79.1	14.4	1.0	2.1	6.3	5.6	11.9	10.7	12.2	12.0	12.4
51139		6	Page	310.0	23,807	1,649	76.8	94.4	2.9	0.7	0.8	2.5	5.3	11.0	10.5	11.4	11.5	12.9
51141		8	Patrick	483.0	17,602	1,942	36.4	90.5	5.9	0.7	0.6	3.4	3.7	10.2	9.6	8.9	9.9	13.7
51143	19260	4	Pittsylvania	969.0	59,972	876	61.9	75.2	21.7	0.6	0.8	3.0	4.2	10.4	10.9	10.2	10.8	13.0
51145	40060	1	Powhatan	260.2	31,136	1,398	119.7	87.4	9.7	0.8	1.2	2.6	4.4	10.4	10.0	11.0	13.1	15.2
51147		6	Prince Edward	349.9	21,932	1,719	62.7	63.2	32.5	0.8	1.8	3.7	4.6	8.7	28.1	11.5	9.2	9.4
51149	40060	1	Prince George	265.3	42,880	1,127	161.6	56.5	33.0	1.1	3.1	9.1	5.2	13.4	12.0	15.0	15.6	11.6
51153	47900	1	Prince William	335.3	484,472	150	1,444.9	43.6	22.5	0.9	12.0	25.4	6.8	15.2	13.5	12.9	15.1	14.0
51155	13980	3	Pulaski	319.8	33,759	1,337	105.6	91.9	6.3	0.6	1.0	2.0	4.6	10.0	10.1	12.1	10.7	14.1
51157	47900	1	Rappahannock	266.4	7,407	2,628	27.8	90.3	5.2	1.1	1.7	4.1	3.9	9.6	9.3	9.6	9.8	11.9
51159		9	Richmond	191.5	9,017	2,485	47.1	61.9	30.9	0.9	1.1	7.5	4.2	9.5	9.9	14.7	14.5	12.7
51161	40220	2	Roanoke	250.5	96,589	631	385.6	85.9	7.5	0.6	4.4	3.6	4.4	11.5	11.4	11.5	12.2	13.0
51163		6	Rockbridge	596.5	22,641	1,692	38.0	92.9	4.2	1.2	1.2	2.2	3.9	10.1	10.8	10.2	10.2	11.9
51165	25500	3	Rockingham	849.8	84,394	683	99.3	88.1	3.2	0.5	1.5	8.2	5.6	12.5	12.7	11.7	12.0	12.0
51167		7	Russell	473.5	25,550	1,582	54.0	97.0	1.3	0.5	0.5	1.5	4.9	10.7	10.3	10.8	11.4	13.3
51169	28700	2	Scott	535.8	21,419	1,739	40.0	97.0	1.3	0.6	0.4	1.6	3.8	10.6	10.2	10.6	11.5	13.0
51171		6	Shenandoah	508.1	44,752	1,081	88.1	87.8	3.7	0.8	1.5	8.1	5.5	11.9	10.7	11.7	11.4	12.3
51173		7	Smyth	451.4	29,477	1,445	65.3	94.4	3.1	0.5	0.8	2.4	4.5	10.9	11.3	11.6	10.9	13.7
51175	47260	6	Southampton	599.2	18,006	1,923	30.1	62.5	34.7	0.9	1.1	2.5	4.3	10.8	10.0	11.1	11.0	14.7
51177	47900	1	Spotsylvania	401.4	143,676	465	357.9	67.3	19.3	0.9	4.3	11.8	5.8	14.0	12.7	12.9	13.2	13.1
51179	47900	1	Stafford	269.2	160,877	420	597.6	60.1	22.1	1.1	5.7	15.5	6.0	15.1	14.3	13.0	14.8	13.7
51181		8	Surry	278.9	6,530	2,697	23.4	55.8	41.4	1.0	1.0	3.0	5.0	8.7	9.2	11.3	9.6	11.6
51183	40060	1	Sussex	490.2	10,763	2,362	22.0	40.4	55.7	0.8	0.8	3.7	3.8	8.7	11.5	18.4	13.7	12.5
51185	14140	5	Tazewell	518.8	39,925	1,185	77.0	94.4	4.1	0.5	1.1	1.1	4.7	11.0	11.1	11.1	11.8	12.8
51187	47900	1	Warren	214.6	40,925	1,165	190.7	87.0	6.2	1.0	2.2	6.4	6.2	12.0	11.7	13.0	12.3	12.4
51191	28700	2	Washington	561.2	53,635	945	95.6	96.0	2.0	0.5	0.8	1.7	4.2	10.2	11.4	10.3	11.2	13.1
51193		6	Westmoreland	229.3	18,731	1,886	81.7	66.9	26.3	1.3	1.7	6.8	5.0	10.5	9.3	11.4	10.2	11.1
51195	13720	7	Wise	403.4	35,647	1,292	88.4	91.8	6.8	0.5	0.7	1.3	4.8	11.2	12.6	13.5	12.2	13.4
51197		6	Wythe	462.0	28,178	1,489	61.0	94.8	3.7	0.6	0.9	1.5	4.8	10.9	10.3	11.2	11.6	14.0
51199	47260	1	York	104.7	70,915	771	677.3	71.8	15.2	1.0	8.4	7.5	5.3	13.8	12.6	11.6	14.3	11.8
			Independent cities															
51510	47900	1	Alexandria city	14.9	154,706	444	10,383.0	54.7	23.1	0.8	8.1	16.5	6.7	9.2	8.2	19.8	18.8	13.5
51520	28700	2	Bristol city	12.9	17,054	1,968	1,322.0	89.6	7.7	0.8	1.4	2.7	4.8	11.8	10.4	13.0	11.9	12.6
51530		6	Buena Vista city	6.4	6,601	2,692	1,031.4	89.3	6.5	1.7	1.5	3.4	6.0	11.5	18.5	12.6	10.0	10.4
51540	16820	3	Charlottesville city	10.2	45,672	1,067	4,477.6	69.2	18.7	0.6	8.6	6.0	5.3	8.5	20.8	18.4	13.4	10.0
51550	47260	1	Chesapeake city	338.5	251,269	280	742.3	58.7	31.3	1.0	5.4	7.3	6.1	13.9	12.4	13.8	14.8	12.1
51570	40060	1	Colonial Heights city	7.5	18,273	1,912	2,436.4	70.4	19.0	1.0	4.6	7.7	6.6	13.2	11.6	13.3	11.7	11.7
51580		6	Covington city	5.5	5,717	2,760	1,039.5	82.5	14.9	1.0	1.5	2.7	6.4	12.4	11.4	12.8	10.8	12.1
51590	19260	4	Danville city	42.8	42,215	1,141	986.3	41.5	52.7	0.6	1.7	5.1	5.7	12.7	12.8	12.3	10.7	10.8
51595		6	Emporia city	6.9	5,667	2,766	821.3	28.1	65.0	0.7	1.3	6.6	6.7	14.5	11.5	12.1	10.2	11.7
51600	47900	1	Fairfax city	6.2	24,276	1,638	3,915.5	55.8	7.0	0.9	21.2	18.2	8.5	11.7	12.1	14.3	13.3	12.3
51610	47900	1	Falls Church city	2.0	14,493	2,117	7,246.5	74.0	5.4	1.0	12.4	11.1	5.7	14.1	12.1	12.1	14.0	15.2
51620	47260	6	Franklin city	8.3	8,217	2,561	990.0	39.8	57.2	0.9	1.4	2.9	8.2	14.0	11.8	11.9	10.3	10.4
51630	47900	1	Fredericksburg city	10.5	28,367	1,485	2,701.6	61.0	26.0	1.0	4.9	11.6	6.2	11.9	22.1	16.3	11.3	10.5
51640		7	Galax city	8.2	6,660	2,689	812.2	75.9	7.1	0.6	1.5	17.2	6.5	14.2	12.3	12.0	11.0	13.0
51650	47260	1	Hampton city	51.5	137,746	472	2,674.7	39.3	52.8	1.5	4.0	6.7	6.0	11.9	14.9	15.6	12.3	10.0
51660	25500	3	Harrisonburg city	17.3	51,430	979	2,972.8	66.6	9.1	0.5	5.6	20.7	5.2	9.0	34.9	12.8	11.5	8.8
51670	40060	1	Hopewell city	10.4	23,140	1,673	2,225.0	45.8	44.7	1.0	2.7	9.0	7.1	14.7	12.2	14.7	12.0	11.4
51678		6	Lexington city	2.5	7,456	2,622	2,982.4	84.6	9.2	0.9	4.3	3.7	4.1	6.3	46.3	7.9	7.0	6.6
51680	31340	2	Lynchburg city	49.0	79,009	724	1,612.4	64.1	29.5	0.8	3.4	4.7	5.8	10.1	27.8	14.7	9.3	8.4
51683	47900	1	Manassas city	9.8	42,708	1,130	4,358.0	41.1	15.1	0.7	7.2	38.7	7.8	14.2	12.8	14.9	14.3	12.8
51685	47900	1	Manassas Park city	3.0	17,002	1,971	5,667.3	32.4	15.3	0.8	12.3	41.6	5.5	14.1	13.3	15.9	15.7	14.8

1. CBSA = Core Based Statistical Area. See Appendix A for explanation. See Appendix B for list of metropolitan areas with component counties. 2. County type code from the Economic Research Service of USDA Rural-Urban Continuum Codes. See Appendix A for definition. 3. Dry land or land partially or temporarily covered by water. 4. May be of any race.

STATE County	Population, 2021 (cont.)				Population change, 2000–2021							Households, 2016–2020				
	Age (percent) (cont.)				Total persons		Percent change		Components of change, 2020–2021					Percent		
	55 to 64 years	65 to 74 years	75 years and over	Percent female	2010	2020	2010–2020	2020–2021	Births	Deaths	Net Migration	Number	Persons per household	Family house-holds	Female family house-holder[1]	One person
	16	17	18	19	20	21	22	23	24	25	26	27	28	29	30	31
VIRGINIA—Cont'd																
Louisa	16.8	13.2	7.4	50.2	33,153	37,596	13.4	3.3	452	576	1,393	14,383	2.5	71.3	8.3	22.9
Lunenburg	14.4	14.2	8.9	46.6	12,914	11,936	-7.6	-0.1	127	253	117	4,472	2.5	68.0	11.3	30.1
Madison	16.6	13.9	9.2	51.5	13,308	13,837	4.0	0.8	161	197	141	5,098	2.6	72.9	9.1	21.4
Mathews	17.5	17.6	14.0	50.9	8,978	8,533	-5.0	0.2	83	187	118	3,881	2.2	57.5	4.7	33.0
Mecklenburg	16.3	15.8	10.7	51.2	32,727	30,319	-7.4	-0.2	349	704	288	12,371	2.4	62.6	11.7	33.1
Middlesex	18.0	17.9	14.7	50.2	10,959	10,625	-3.0	1.5	107	230	284	4,764	2.2	61.5	7.3	33.2
Montgomery	10.1	8.5	5.4	48.3	94,392	99,721	5.6	-1.3	875	991	-1,143	35,388	2.5	54.5	6.7	29.0
Nelson	16.5	18.2	10.6	50.9	15,020	14,775	-1.6	0.1	162	269	127	6,398	2.3	68.3	11.5	26.8
New Kent	15.5	12.3	5.8	48.5	18,429	22,945	24.5	4.1	258	301	1,005	8,117	2.7	76.6	5.9	20.0
Northampton	17.3	17.0	11.8	52.4	12,389	12,282	-0.9	-1.6	125	265	-54	5,151	2.2	64.3	14.2	31.5
Northumberland	18.5	20.7	15.9	50.7	12,330	11,839	-4.0	1.6	128	312	384	5,686	2.1	67.6	12.1	28.6
Nottoway	14.1	11.4	7.7	44.9	15,853	15,642	-1.3	-0.3	208	281	25	5,568	2.4	66.6	14.5	30.7
Orange	14.9	12.0	8.3	51.0	33,481	36,254	8.3	2.6	479	580	1,046	13,926	2.6	72.1	12.9	24.3
Page	15.6	12.9	9.0	50.3	24,042	23,709	-1.4	0.4	301	466	264	9,413	2.5	67.8	9.7	26.7
Patrick	17.0	15.4	11.7	49.8	18,490	17,608	-4.8	0.0	113	382	270	7,830	2.2	64.0	8.5	32.0
Pittsylvania	16.4	14.2	9.8	50.3	63,506	60,501	-4.7	-0.9	606	1,142	6	26,205	2.3	70.2	13.1	26.8
Powhatan	16.5	12.3	7.0	47.9	28,046	30,333	8.2	2.6	314	387	886	10,392	2.6	79.1	7.3	16.2
Prince Edward	11.7	9.8	7.0	49.5	23,368	21,849	-6.5	0.4	274	355	161	7,394	2.4	57.3	14.7	32.9
Prince George	12.2	9.2	5.8	46.1	35,725	43,010	20.4	-0.3	381	404	-116	11,763	2.9	73.8	12.1	20.1
Prince William	11.7	6.9	3.9	49.7	402,002	482,204	20.0	0.5	7,605	3,192	-2,281	144,159	3.2	77.1	11.3	18.3
Pulaski	15.3	13.8	9.3	49.4	34,872	33,800	-3.1	-0.1	368	691	285	14,666	2.3	63.3	10.2	30.9
Rappahannock	17.8	16.5	11.6	50.0	7,373	7,348	-0.3	0.8	55	110	117	2,827	2.6	70.9	8.2	24.4
Richmond	13.5	11.0	10.0	42.9	9,254	8,923	-3.6	1.1	77	153	173	2,939	2.5	68.7	10.0	25.8
Roanoke	13.9	12.8	9.3	51.6	92,376	96,929	4.9	-0.4	814	1,467	307	38,234	2.4	64.9	10.1	30.1
Rockbridge	15.9	15.6	11.5	50.4	22,307	22,650	1.5	0.0	136	370	230	9,301	2.4	68.7	11.0	27.8
Rockingham	13.7	11.5	8.3	50.5	76,314	83,757	9.8	0.8	1,012	1,135	762	31,306	2.5	69.5	9.0	25.5
Russell	15.6	13.9	9.1	50.6	28,897	25,781	-10.8	-0.9	319	549	-2	10,975	2.4	61.4	8.3	34.6
Scott	15.3	13.9	11.1	49.3	23,177	21,576	-6.9	-0.7	181	497	161	8,710	2.4	62.4	10.0	33.5
Shenandoah	14.5	12.7	9.3	50.5	41,993	44,186	5.2	1.3	581	772	765	17,541	2.5	65.2	11.5	29.6
Smyth	14.4	13.1	9.6	50.8	32,208	29,800	-7.5	-1.1	274	706	110	12,694	2.4	67.5	13.8	29.6
Southampton	16.7	12.9	8.5	47.7	18,570	17,996	-3.1	0.1	134	301	180	6,618	2.5	70.4	16.0	26.2
Spotsylvania	13.3	9.4	5.6	50.5	122,397	140,032	14.4	2.6	1,885	1,523	3,303	45,463	3.0	75.5	10.8	19.4
Stafford	12.1	7.0	3.9	49.1	128,961	156,927	21.7	2.5	2,112	1,295	3,143	48,160	3.0	78.4	11.0	17.3
Surry	19.6	15.3	9.6	49.9	7,058	6,561	-7.0	-0.5	75	103	-2	2,794	2.3	66.5	16.7	29.7
Sussex	13.3	10.9	7.3	39.5	12,087	10,829	-10.4	-0.6	93	211	51	3,792	2.4	65.6	14.0	29.3
Tazewell	14.1	14.2	9.2	50.0	45,078	40,429	-10.3	-1.2	444	966	16	16,371	2.4	67.2	12.6	29.7
Warren	15.3	10.7	6.3	49.7	37,575	40,727	8.4	0.5	619	614	186	14,641	2.7	68.6	10.5	25.5
Washington	15.3	14.5	9.9	50.5	54,876	53,935	-1.7	-0.6	538	1,082	245	22,104	2.4	65.8	9.9	29.5
Westmoreland	16.2	15.7	10.7	50.6	17,454	18,477	5.9	1.4	219	343	383	7,910	2.2	57.5	12.6	34.6
Wise	13.1	12.3	7.0	47.5	41,452	36,130	-12.8	-1.3	445	783	-148	14,916	2.3	65.5	13.5	29.7
Wythe	15.0	13.3	8.9	50.9	29,235	28,290	-3.2	-0.4	319	565	132	12,393	2.3	65.3	6.2	28.1
York	13.5	10.0	7.1	50.5	65,464	70,045	7.0	1.2	685	793	982	25,517	2.6	74.5	8.9	21.5
Independent cities																
Alexandria city	11.2	7.9	4.8	51.4	139,966	159,467	13.9	-3.0	2,932	1,250	-6,349	71,289	2.2	47.5	7.8	42.3
Bristol city	13.5	12.4	9.6	52.1	17,835	17,219	-3.5	-1.0	172	341	4	7,482	2.2	57.8	15.8	37.8
Buena Vista city	11.8	11.0	8.1	52.5	6,650	6,641	-0.1	-0.6	99	121	-18	2,509	2.4	67.6	15.9	30.3
Charlottesville city	10.3	8.7	4.5	51.6	43,475	46,553	7.1	-1.9	732	418	-1,184	18,814	2.4	47.6	11.0	33.7
Chesapeake city	12.9	8.8	5.2	50.8	222,209	249,422	12.2	0.7	3,497	3,003	1,309	86,524	2.8	74.3	13.9	21.5
Colonial Heights city	13.0	10.0	8.8	53.3	17,411	18,170	4.4	0.6	331	306	78	7,094	2.4	65.6	19.8	30.3
Covington city	14.4	11.4	8.3	51.2	5,961	5,737	-3.8	-0.3	80	103	3	2,382	2.3	64.4	7.3	33.3
Danville city	14.1	12.3	8.7	54.0	43,055	42,590	-1.1	-0.9	512	1,014	124	18,266	2.1	54.7	20.1	39.0
Emporia city	13.2	10.4	9.7	53.9	5,927	5,766	-2.7	-1.7	73	112	-60	2,076	2.5	66.2	29.0	31.8
Fairfax city	13.0	8.9	6.0	50.7	22,565	24,146	7.0	0.5	752	354	-267	8,751	2.6	64.5	5.2	24.6
Falls Church city	12.5	9.0	5.4	50.5	12,332	14,658	18.9	-1.1	228	172	-220	5,631	2.5	63.1	9.7	31.6
Franklin city	14.1	11.3	8.2	54.3	8,582	8,180	-4.7	0.5	197	151	-9	3,516	2.2	65.8	22.7	31.1
Fredericksburg city	10.1	7.1	4.5	53.5	24,286	27,982	15.2	1.4	437	354	299	11,059	2.4	51.1	8.8	37.9
Galax city	12.9	10.1	8.1	53.1	7,042	6,720	-4.6	-0.9	118	158	-21	2,614	2.3	62.3	11.7	37.3
Hampton city	13.2	9.7	6.3	51.7	137,436	137,148	-0.2	0.4	1,912	1,885	549	54,847	2.4	59.2	16.6	33.7
Harrisonburg city	7.8	6.0	4.0	51.9	48,914	51,814	5.9	-0.7	738	433	-692	16,751	2.8	55.9	12.4	28.7
Hopewell city	12.5	9.1	6.3	53.5	22,591	23,033	2.0	0.5	412	421	115	9,362	2.4	64.6	23.2	28.9
Lexington city	7.4	7.5	6.8	43.5	7,042	7,320	3.9	1.9	139	103	100	2,066	2.0	45.3	5.2	40.6
Lynchburg city	9.7	8.0	6.3	53.0	75,568	79,009	4.6	0.0	1,344	1,147	-208	28,223	2.5	59.3	16.1	29.5
Manassas city	12.2	7.4	3.6	49.7	37,821	42,772	13.1	-0.1	843	327	-583	13,066	3.1	74.4	14.3	20.9
Manassas Park city	11.8	5.6	3.3	48.7	14,273	17,219	20.6	-1.3	41	94	-170	4,596	3.8	71.5	13.3	23.8

1. No spouse present.

STATE County	Persons in group quarters, 2021	Daytime Population, 2016–2020		Births, 2021		Deaths, 2021		Persons under 65 with no health insurance, 2019		Medicare, 2021			COVID-19 Deaths, 2020	
		Number	Employment/ residence ratio	Total	Rate[1]	Number	Rate[1]	Number	Percent	Total beneficiaries	Enrolled in Original Medicare	Enrolled in Medicare Advantage	Number	Rate[1]
	32	33	34	35	36	37	38	39	40	41	42	43	44	45
VIRGINIA—Cont'd														
Louisa	126	30,933	0.7	352	9.2	465	12.1	3,614	12.1	8,801	6,752	2,049	15	0.4
Lunenburg	938	10,456	0.6	103	8.6	207	17.4	1,135	13.6	3,178	2,519	659	D	D
Madison	184	11,457	0.7	133	9.6	143	10.3	1,138	11.2	3,379	2,768	611	D	D
Mathews	55	7,018	0.5	68	8.0	151	17.7	533	8.8	2,926	2,346	580	10	1.2
Mecklenburg	796	31,739	1.1	269	8.9	565	18.7	2,628	12.0	9,422	7,211	2,212	54	1.8
Middlesex	349	9,939	0.9	86	8.0	188	17.6	794	11.5	3,717	3,025	692	11	1.0
Montgomery	9,932	104,633	1.1	686	6.9	796	8.0	6,689	8.8	14,448	11,158	3,290	55	0.6
Nelson	84	13,300	0.8	124	8.4	208	14.1	1,355	12.7	4,792	3,936	856	D	D
New Kent	462	16,514	0.5	214	9.1	239	10.2	1,593	8.6	4,953	3,884	1,070	14	0.6
Northampton	245	11,977	1.0	105	8.6	212	17.4	1,042	12.5	3,793	2,885	908	26	2.1
Northumberland	0	10,723	0.7	104	8.7	258	21.6	832	11.1	4,705	3,862	843	14	1.2
Nottoway	2,256	16,588	1.2	176	11.3	218	14.0	1,320	12.9	3,667	2,804	863	23	1.5
Orange	451	30,035	0.6	400	10.9	461	12.5	3,001	10.4	8,982	7,464	1,518	13	0.4
Page	131	19,396	0.6	237	10.0	369	15.5	2,080	11.3	6,322	5,220	1,102	37	1.6
Patrick	255	15,011	0.7	84	4.8	305	17.3	1,475	11.7	5,550	3,998	1,552	41	2.3
Pittsylvania	1,002	48,964	0.6	493	8.2	922	15.3	5,147	11.4	16,618	11,159	5,459	61	1.0
Powhatan	1,097	23,479	0.6	249	8.1	311	10.1	2,095	9.1	6,419	4,926	1,493	10	0.3
Prince Edward	3,686	25,030	1.3	224	10.2	265	12.1	1,475	9.8	4,738	3,640	1,098	18	0.8
Prince George	4,349	43,070	1.3	305	7.1	320	7.5	2,164	7.6	6,361	5,264	1,097	12	0.3
Prince William	2,932	381,402	0.7	6,080	12.6	2,597	5.4	47,465	11.3	52,016	40,110	11,906	345	0.7
Pulaski	1,008	33,491	1.0	289	8.6	539	16.0	2,074	8.3	9,226	7,031	2,194	53	1.6
Rappahannock	32	5,919	0.6	45	6.1	88	12.0	647	12.2	2,007	1,762	245	D	D
Richmond	1,579	9,058	1.0	65	7.2	129	14.4	536	9.7	1,969	1,523	447	D	D
Roanoke	2,299	85,728	0.8	652	6.7	1,157	12.0	5,400	7.5	24,209	17,555	6,655	100	1.0
Rockbridge	452	19,922	0.7	108	4.8	283	12.5	1,621	10.1	6,477	5,154	1,323	24	1.1
Rockingham	1,610	76,316	0.9	821	9.8	929	11.0	7,429	11.5	18,413	15,474	2,939	88	1.1
Russell	311	25,357	0.8	256	10.0	429	16.7	1,982	9.8	8,025	4,449	3,576	24	0.9
Scott	729	18,935	0.7	148	6.9	397	18.5	1,571	10.2	6,808	2,849	3,959	41	1.9
Shenandoah	373	37,845	0.7	475	10.7	643	14.4	3,434	10.2	10,883	8,866	2,018	69	1.6
Smyth	689	29,901	1.0	219	7.4	554	18.7	2,114	9.3	8,694	5,725	2,969	53	1.8
Southampton	1,562	14,467	0.6	103	5.7	249	13.9	1,105	8.8	4,043	3,213	830	39	2.2
Spotsylvania	449	109,825	0.6	1,541	10.8	1,242	8.7	10,348	8.9	22,558	18,277	4,282	76	0.5
Stafford	4,256	124,986	0.7	1,688	10.6	1,025	6.4	9,461	7.1	18,820	15,801	3,019	38	0.2
Surry	0	5,637	0.7	63	9.6	78	11.9	425	8.8	1,759	1,290	469	D	D
Sussex	2,515	10,734	0.9	80	7.4	160	14.9	658	10.1	2,532	1,790	742	18	1.7
Tazewell	1,675	40,534	1.0	366	9.1	793	19.8	3,072	10.4	12,021	7,409	4,612	34	0.8
Warren	627	36,297	0.8	493	12.1	507	12.4	3,338	10.1	8,084	6,749	1,335	32	0.8
Washington	1,728	53,566	1.0	417	7.8	864	16.1	4,175	10.6	15,252	8,955	6,297	68	1.3
Westmoreland	55	14,737	0.6	166	8.9	262	14.1	1,414	10.7	5,209	4,317	892	18	1.0
Wise	2,712	40,170	1.2	345	9.6	600	16.7	3,089	11.3	10,658	5,101	5,557	54	1.5
Wythe	188	28,706	1.0	252	8.9	449	15.9	2,136	9.6	7,988	5,572	2,416	43	1.5
York	599	60,095	0.8	550	7.8	646	9.2	3,923	7.0	12,615	10,531	2,084	24	0.3
Independent cities														
Alexandria city	1,655	162,684	1.0	2,336	14.9	1,046	6.7	12,663	9.1	18,444	14,858	3,586	88	0.6
Bristol city	188	20,322	1.4	141	8.2	270	15.7	1,206	9.4	4,676	2,346	2,330	22	1.3
Buena Vista city	493	5,745	0.8	75	11.3	97	14.7	375	7.9	1,499	1,144	355	10	1.5
Charlottesville city	2,244	68,003	1.9	593	12.9	329	7.1	4,204	10.7	6,364	5,362	1,002	28	0.6
Chesapeake city	4,222	225,859	0.9	2,782	11.1	2,398	9.6	16,311	7.9	40,199	29,913	10,286	146	0.6
Colonial Heights city	165	18,060	1.1	264	14.5	236	12.9	1,259	9.1	4,174	3,271	903	15	0.8
Covington city	87	5,969	1.1	64	11.2	72	12.6	345	8.0	1,579	1,236	343	D	D
Danville city	1,593	51,615	1.7	411	9.7	779	18.4	2,929	9.8	11,156	7,220	3,936	76	1.8
Emporia city	242	6,566	1.5	59	10.4	86	15.1	343	8.3	1,337	890	447	21	3.7
Fairfax city	497	42,957	2.6	602	24.9	263	10.9	1,929	9.4	3,975	3,109	866	18	0.7
Falls Church city	35	17,207	1.4	185	12.7	130	8.9	486	3.8	2,134	1,726	408	15	1.0
Franklin city	124	8,633	1.2	156	19.0	115	14.0	466	7.4	2,197	1,696	501	22	2.7
Fredericksburg city	2,377	40,835	1.8	355	12.6	285	10.1	2,393	10.4	4,269	3,387	882	11	0.4
Galax city	371	10,261	2.5	97	14.5	115	17.2	707	14.1	1,766	1,494	271	26	3.9
Hampton city	4,857	134,997	1.0	1,523	11.1	1,476	10.7	8,475	7.9	26,039	17,900	8,139	77	0.6
Harrisonburg city	7,324	66,182	1.5	593	11.5	342	6.6	5,221	13.0	5,613	4,738	874	41	0.8
Hopewell city	215	20,190	0.8	321	13.9	316	13.7	1,678	9.0	4,601	3,262	1,339	20	0.9
Lexington city	2,762	10,195	2.2	117	15.8	72	9.8	218	6.0	1,363	1,153	210	D	D
Lynchburg city	10,459	103,231	1.6	1,077	13.6	899	11.4	5,497	9.3	14,756	11,037	3,719	60	0.8
Manassas city	46	41,653	1.0	665	15.6	268	6.3	5,801	16.0	4,761	3,644	1,117	48	1.1
Manassas Park city	3	11,956	0.4	35	2.1	72	4.2	2,414	15.3	1,356	948	409	D	D

1. Per 1,000 estimated resident population.

STATE County	COVID-19 Vaccinations, 2021–2022		Education: School enrollment and attainment, 2016–2020: Enrollment[1]		Attainment[2] (percent)		Local government expenditures,[3] 2018–2019		Money income, 2016–2020	Households	Percent		Income and poverty, 2020	Percent below poverty level		
	Number	Percent[5]	Total	Percent private	High school graduate or less	Bachelor's degree or more	Total current spending (mil dol)	Current spending per student (dollars)	Per capita income[4]	Median income (dollars)	with income of less than $50,000	with income of $200,000 or more	Median household income (dollars)	All persons	Children under 18 years	Children 5 to 17 years in families
	46	47	48	49	50	51	52	53	54	55	56	57	58	59	60	61
VIRGINIA—Cont'd																
Louisa	15,528	41.3	7,050	14.2	45.4	25.2	59.8	12,194	35,894	67,027	36.3	6.0	69,907	7.9	12.3	11.5
Lunenburg	6,096	50.0	2,302	8.8	58.1	12.5	17.2	11,093	21,602	45,884	53.3	1.9	47,384	16.5	22.8	21.3
Madison	7,338	55.3	2,720	15.9	46.4	24.5	21.1	12,498	34,434	63,482	38.6	6.1	67,373	9.4	14.0	13.2
Mathews	5,446	61.6	1,297	29.4	36.0	29.1	14.0	13,170	43,918	74,489	33.0	12.6	68,946	8.5	14.6	14.1
Mecklenburg	12,950	42.3	5,623	12.1	47.3	23.1	46.5	11,036	28,048	50,224	49.7	3.1	49,542	15.4	22.9	21.9
Middlesex	6,689	63.2	1,850	13.6	42.5	26.9	16.0	13,097	33,992	57,060	43.2	4.7	60,752	11.6	19.3	18.4
Montgomery	45,695	46.4	40,393	6.4	29.3	46.0	111.8	11,265	30,581	59,126	42.6	7.0	62,418	19.3	11.9	10.7
Nelson	8,408	56.3	2,867	12.3	50.9	30.9	26.1	14,447	38,364	62,203	39.2	7.0	60,757	10.7	17.6	17.0
New Kent	11,953	51.8	4,532	17.7	37.1	32.1	33.0	9,984	40,293	97,688	22.8	10.8	107,658	4.6	6.5	6.4
Northampton	8,344	71.3	2,027	18.8	49.1	26.1	20.0	12,422	31,959	50,819	49.8	4.6	50,096	16.2	26.7	25.2
Northumberland	6,540	54.1	1,958	10.5	39.0	32.6	18.4	13,998	38,679	59,437	41.3	6.1	60,575	12.3	24.7	22.9
Nottoway	6,555	43.0	2,857	14.0	56.3	15.5	22.1	10,805	24,394	49,983	50.0	1.3	51,503	19.2	22.8	21.6
Orange	16,151	43.6	7,566	16.2	46.6	25.7	54.6	10,828	33,313	74,446	31.0	4.5	73,226	9.4	13.7	11.8
Page	9,076	38.0	4,616	18.7	62.8	14.3	36.5	10,947	26,321	51,878	48.0	1.4	52,107	11.3	17.0	16.6
Patrick	7,016	39.8	2,810	7.7	54.3	14.9	26.7	10,277	27,939	46,941	51.7	4.1	46,149	14.2	20.6	18.8
Pittsylvania	25,205	41.8	11,214	14.0	53.1	15.2	93.4	10,559	26,587	49,520	50.5	2.2	49,124	14.0	17.8	16.6
Powhatan	11,465	38.7	5,959	15.1	40.6	30.6	47.4	10,987	39,850	93,833	21.3	9.7	98,465	5.3	6.1	5.8
Prince Edward	7,002	30.7	8,123	26.6	49.0	25.5	24.6	11,853	21,051	44,253	53.0	2.1	47,968	23.6	28.0	24.7
Prince George	19,389	50.6	9,683	14.4	40.6	23.4	66.7	10,491	31,193	75,123	29.8	5.9	75,717	8.2	10.0	9.6
Prince William	342,769	72.9	132,586	15.2	30.7	41.9	1,052.0	11,580	42,298	107,707	17.8	17.7	111,117	4.9	6.7	6.2
Pulaski	14,891	43.8	6,107	9.4	44.6	19.7	47.0	11,512	28,067	53,689	44.4	1.7	50,530	12.5	15.8	14.2
Rappahannock	3,868	52.5	1,323	25.2	34.8	34.1	12.5	15,579	46,731	82,077	28.4	16.5	76,634	8.9	13.5	12.5
Richmond	3,710	41.1	1,922	11.7	55.5	18.1	15.1	11,489	24,400	53,298	44.8	3.7	55,870	16.0	17.9	16.7
Roanoke	46,336	49.2	20,096	15.8	33.9	36.0	147.9	10,475	37,859	70,076	35.0	7.4	71,613	6.0	7.2	6.7
Rockbridge	10,407	46.1	4,451	22.6	45.8	27.6	33.1	11,638	33,177	54,133	46.5	4.9	55,684	10.5	15.9	14.9
Rockingham	35,359	43.1	18,989	25.1	50.6	27.0	(7)	(7)	33,276	64,496	38.1	4.4	62,609	8.3	10.6	9.8
Russell	12,516	47.1	4,748	12.5	57.0	10.2	40.6	10,721	22,030	38,564	62.3	1.4	43,206	16.2	20.8	19.4
Scott	12,187	56.5	3,570	7.8	54.2	15.0	37.7	10,659	23,702	41,540	58.9	1.2	44,937	17.6	22.0	19.9
Shenandoah	21,537	49.4	8,908	12.6	52.9	19.7	70.1	11,628	40,163	56,114	44.7	4.4	54,294	10.1	15.1	14.1
Smyth	14,541	48.3	5,653	10.9	54.1	14.9	47.0	10,844	23,016	41,088	59.7	1.3	43,351	15.2	21.4	18.8
Southampton	6,546	37.1	3,392	19.9	44.9	19.3	32.3	11,241	27,232	63,034	41.6	2.5	60,441	12.5	17.4	15.5
Spotsylvania	60,506	44.4	34,499	16.4	37.0	32.1	265.4	11,214	38,731	90,913	24.1	10.5	94,299	6.6	9.8	9.3
Stafford	89,881	58.8	42,227	13.0	29.3	41.3	302.6	10,337	43,401	112,247	18.5	17.9	110,120	5.4	6.7	5.9
Surry	3,565	55.5	1,127	22.8	49.6	20.4	15.7	20,648	31,136	56,525	44.3	1.6	57,872	11.6	18.6	19.2
Sussex	3,940	35.3	1,907	8.8	60.2	13.3	18.7	17,367	24,391	51,701	47.4	2.0	48,040	18.9	24.9	23.6
Tazewell	17,726	43.7	8,032	14.9	53.6	15.2	53.0	9,374	25,648	42,207	58.2	2.8	45,214	16.4	20.3	19.3
Warren	14,819	36.9	8,625	17.0	48.3	20.8	58.8	11,103	32,660	70,109	33.7	5.3	63,797	10.1	15.3	16.1
Washington	30,952	57.6	10,410	23.0	46.6	24.2	77.7	10,963	28,987	50,928	49.3	4.0	53,785	13.2	17.1	15.9
Westmoreland	8,182	45.4	3,089	6.9	52.3	18.3	29.7	12,782	33,754	53,790	47.7	6.5	59,343	12.9	22.4	21.3
Wise	17,830	47.7	7,925	11.3	55.2	14.8	54.2	9,416	21,508	41,285	57.8	1.4	41,723	20.3	26.7	24.6
Wythe	11,263	39.3	5,891	7.9	51.5	19.0	43.8	10,746	31,645	51,639	48.6	3.0	54,399	12.0	17.5	16.6
York	46,097	67.5	18,466	16.1	22.2	49.5	137.5	10,787	41,994	93,356	22.1	12.8	91,711	4.7	5.7	5.1
Independent cities																
Alexandria city	101,073	63.4	31,121	29.0	17.3	65.1	289.2	18,111	64,835	102,227	21.2	19.8	99,763	8.0	12.7	13.0
Bristol city	11,531	68.8	3,110	15.6	45.1	21.8	26.4	11,640	25,979	39,679	58.2	1.7	41,444	17.2	30.7	29.3
Buena Vista city	2,399	37.0	2,145	47.6	54.0	19.1	10.5	11,478	30,647	36,634	63.7	4.7	48,837	14.0	20.4	19.2
Charlottesville city	23,912	50.6	16,046	11.8	25.6	55.7	(8)268.3	(8)14,460	39,712	59,598	43.3	9.0	70,501	15.8	15.4	15.3
Chesapeake city	129,780	53.0	63,740	18.2	30.5	34.6	481.9	11,788	37,420	81,261	28.1	8.5	80,402	7.6	9.7	8.9
Colonial Heights city	6,273	36.1	3,842	15.9	39.2	26.6	37.1	12,953	32,629	60,522	41.9	4.5	67,339	8.7	14.8	15.0
Covington city	1,877	33.9	1,403	22.0	55.0	15.1	11.1	10,383	25,287	41,024	58.8	3.0	40,683	14.8	24.0	23.6
Danville city	13,534	33.8	9,503	16.1	50.0	18.4	76.0	13,358	22,876	37,147	63.7	1.7	36,560	22.1	37.4	32.6
Emporia city	1,766	33.0	1,310	10.2	55.6	11.7	(9)27.5	(9)12,269	19,612	30,058	69.9	2.2	42,895	19.1	31.8	32.1
Fairfax city	16,272	67.7	5,840	22.9	20.8	60.3	(10)	(10)	53,488	109,708	22.8	22.8	102,828	7.2	6.2	6.6
Falls Church city	8,135	55.7	3,819	17.8	9.7	79.1	50.4	19,222	73,288	146,922	11.3	32.5	160,305	3.3	2.8	2.2
Franklin city	3,067	38.5	1,821	16.5	47.9	19.0	14.7	13,687	25,900	49,811	50.5	0.3	47,223	18.1	30.5	29.8
Fredericksburg city	11,631	40.1	9,105	12.2	31.2	42.4	48.8	13,149	36,785	69,528	34.1	7.9	72,437	12.2	19.0	19.4
Galax city	2,372	37.4	1,558	13.5	52.2	17.1	14.9	11,291	24,521	35,184	66.6	7.7	40,271	18.8	28.5	27.0
Hampton city	83,017	61.7	34,029	21.8	37.8	26.7	225.4	11,508	30,596	57,041	43.6	3.4	53,719	13.4	20.7	19.7
Harrisonburg city	20,106	37.9	23,126	8.4	42.6	35.2	224.2	12,219	23,580	49,117	51.1	3.3	52,159	22.2	16.7	16.2
Hopewell city	7,081	31.4	5,928	9.4	52.0	12.8	51.6	11,808	23,173	43,262	56.2	2.1	41,792	17.4	29.4	27.7
Lexington city	2,931	39.4	4,113	30.3	32.0	50.0	5.7	10,872	20,638	50,714	49.7	2.6	63,580	18.5	9.5	7.8
Lynchburg city	25,141	30.6	28,656	53.4	35.7	36.0	107.1	12,965	23,683	49,201	51.0	2.6	56,089	15.5	21.4	22.2
Manassas city	19,804	48.2	10,796	19.4	41.1	31.3	103.2	13,357	34,198	86,227	26.0	10.6	87,804	7.9	13.7	13.5
Manassas Park city	7,711	44.1	4,787	12.5	49.5	25.6	41.0	11,017	35,618	81,639	20.0	12.9	82,255	6.7	11.4	11.1

1. All persons 3 years old and over enrolled in nursery school through college. 2. Persons 25 years old and over. 3. Elementary and secondary education expenditures. 4. Based on population estimated by the American Community Survey, 2016–2020. 5. CDC percent based on 2019 population estimate. 7. Rockingham county is included with Harrisonburg city. 8. Albemarle county is included with Charlottesville city. 9. Greensville county is included with Emporia city. 10. Fairfax county is included with Fairfax city.

STATE County	Personal income, 2020: Total (mil dol)	Percent change 2019–2020	Per capita[1]: Dollars	Per capita[1]: Rank	Wages and salaries (mil dol)	Supplements to wages and salaries, employer contributions (mil dol): Pension and insurance	Supplements to wages and salaries, employer contributions (mil dol): Government social insurance	Proprietors' income (mil dol)	Dividends, interest, and rent (mil dol)	Personal transfer reecipts (mil dol)	Earnings, 2020: Total (mil dol)	Contributions for government social insurance (mil dol): From employee and self-employed	Contributions for government social insurance (mil dol): From employer
	62	63	64	65	66	67	68	69	70	71	72	73	74
VIRGINIA—Cont'd													
Louisa	1,756	7.4	46,040	1,645	536	105	39	83	304	461	763	55	39
Lunenburg	439	9.0	35,793	2,886	108	22	8	10	74	167	148	12	8
Madison	687	7.0	51,608	972	140	24	11	47	140	157	222	17	11
Mathews	517	4.1	59,026	480	60	12	4	30	135	138	106	12	4
Mecklenburg	1,248	9.1	40,693	2,374	481	82	35	43	210	479	641	53	35
Middlesex	586	5.1	55,466	671	136	27	10	32	163	179	205	18	10
Montgomery	(2) 4601	(2) 5.2	(2) 39442	(2) 2517	(2) 2567	(2) 556	(2) 186	(2) 198	(2) 932	(2) 1004	(2) 3507	(2) 215	(2) 186
Nelson	824	6.2	55,869	651	159	32	12	56	214	238	258	24	12
New Kent	1,844	7.7	77,957	89	254	44	18	51	237	268	368	30	18
Northampton	731	10.7	62,614	328	153	30	12	87	130	214	283	18	12
Northumberland	689	5.2	57,093	568	145	24	11	30	203	217	210	22	11
Nottoway	585	8.6	38,594	2,614	248	62	20	13	96	239	344	25	20
Orange	2,006	7.3	53,217	842	437	78	32	114	369	482	662	53	32
Page	1,013	8.3	42,307	2,154	226	44	18	48	161	333	337	29	18
Patrick	637	8.0	36,426	2,833	153	31	12	31	95	261	227	22	12
Pittsylvania	(3) 4200	(3) 9.6	(3) 42121	(3) 2177	(3) 1602	(3) 281	(3) 119	(3) 139	(3) 552	(3) 1668	(3) 2140	(3) 167	(3) 119
Powhatan	1,856	6.4	61,547	365	374	60	26	87	324	321	548	40	26
Prince Edward	779	7.9	33,868	2,984	392	76	30	30	122	285	528	38	30
Prince George	(4) 2548	(4) 7.4	(4) 41732	(4) 2237	(4) 1882	(4) 493	(4) 157	(4) 78	(4) 397	(4) 749	(4) 2611	(4) 140	(4) 157
Prince William	(5) 31964	(5) 7.2	(5) 59812	(5) 438	(5) 10330	(5) 1671	(5) 756	(5) 1661	(5) 4645	(5) 4566	(5) 14418	(5) 872	(5) 756
Pulaski	1,479	8.7	43,583	1,999	596	110	48	45	195	517	799	58	48
Rappahannock	514	2.4	70,807	156	66	11	5	49	170	89	131	10	5
Richmond	370	10.1	40,791	2,355	135	30	10	15	70	115	189	13	10
Roanoke	(6) 6589	(6) 5.7	(6) 54977	(6) 703	(6) 3086	(6) 502	(6) 222	(6) 352	(6) 1178	(6) 1548	(6) 4162	(6) 286	(6) 222
Rockbridge	(7) 1586	(7) 5.9	(7) 43534	(7) 2006	(7) 581	(7) 108	(7) 46	(7) 79	(7) 375	(7) 466	(7) 813	(7) 61	(7) 46
Rockingham	(8) 5860	(8) 7.0	(8) 43232	(8) 2035	(8) 3211	(8) 529	(8) 236	(8) 533	(8) 1007	(8) 1347	(8) 4509	(8) 285	(8) 236
Russell	971	8.3	36,423	2,834	322	57	24	32	120	422	435	38	24
Scott	776	7.5	35,882	2,874	196	38	15	26	103	320	275	28	15
Shenandoah	2,193	8.7	49,948	1,149	630	110	48	129	368	571	917	70	48
Smyth	1,210	9.0	40,220	2,430	495	102	37	36	166	469	670	52	37
Southampton	(9) 1195	(9) 7.2	(9) 46909	(9) 1526	(9) 326	(9) 68	(9) 24	(9) 33	(9) 211	(9) 386	(9) 451	(9) 35	(9) 24
Spotsylvania	(10) 9250	(10) 7.6	(10) 55077	(10) 699	(10) 3128	(10) 458	(10) 224	(10) 485	(10) 1466	(10) 1753	(10) 4296	(10) 281	(10) 224
Stafford	9,191	7.7	58,635	489	3,004	531	213	266	1,334	1,430	4,015	250	213
Surry	306	8.4	47,927	1,402	185	52	13	8	39	94	259	16	13
Sussex	383	7.6	35,062	2,935	169	35	12	13	53	145	230	16	12
Tazewell	1,613	5.7	39,795	2,478	567	113	43	58	228	662	780	67	43
Warren	2,044	7.4	50,504	1,091	612	100	46	85	290	453	844	61	46
Washington	(11) 3040	(11) 6.8	(11) 42796	(11) 2094	(11) 1199	(11) 222	(11) 91	(11) 162	(11) 567	(11) 1025	(11) 1673	(11) 127	(11) 91
Westmoreland	882	8.4	48,577	1,313	133	27	10	51	189	260	221	19	10
Wise	(12) 1480	(12) 8.1	(12) 35929	(12) 2871	(12) 620	(12) 132	(12) 46	(12) 43	(12) 170	(12) 686	(12) 841	(12) 69	(12) 46
Wythe	1,120	9.7	39,116	2,555	465	89	35	45	145	435	634	49	35
York	(13) 5103	(13) 5.4	(13) 62645	(13) 326	(13) 1141	(13) 220	(13) 87	(13) 147	(13) 1062	(13) 851	(13) 1595	(13) 105	(13) 87
Independent cities													
Alexandria city	14,894	4.2	93,835	31	7,756	1,196	563	876	3,178	1,390	10,390	610	563
Bristol city	(11)	(11)	(11)	(11)	(11)	(11)	(11)	(11)	(11)	(11)	(11)	(11)	(11)
Buena Vista city	(7)	(7)	(7)	(7)	(7)	(7)	(7)	(7)	(7)	(7)	(7)	(7)	(7)
Charlottesville city	(14)	(14)	(14)	(14)	(14)	(14)	(14)	(14)	(14)	(14)	(14)	(14)	(14)
Chesapeake city	13,245	7.9	53,622	812	5,522	831	397	454	1,997	2,706	7,204	466	397
Colonial Heights city[20]	(15)	(15)	(15)	(15)	(15)	(15)	(15)	(15)	(15)	(15)	(15)	(15)	(15)
Covington city[15]	(16)	(16)	(16)	(16)	(16)	(16)	(16)	(16)	(16)	(16)	(16)	(16)	(16)
Danville city	(3)	(3)	(3)	(3)	(3)	(3)	(3)	(3)	(3)	(3)	(3)	(3)	(3)
Emporia city[16]	(17)	(17)	(17)	(17)	(17)	(17)	(17)	(17)	(17)	(17)	(17)	(17)	(17)
Fairfax city[17]	(18)	(18)	(18)	(18)	(18)	(18)	(18)	(18)	(18)	(18)	(18)	(18)	(18)
Falls Church city	(18)	(18)	(18)	(18)	(18)	(18)	(18)	(18)	(18)	(18)	(18)	(18)	(18)
Franklin city	(9)	(9)	(9)	(9)	(9)	(9)	(9)	(9)	(9)	(9)	(9)	(9)	(9)
Fredericksburg city	(10)	(10)	(10)	(10)	(10)	(10)	(10)	(10)	(10)	(10)	(10)	(10)	(10)
Galax city[18]	(19)	(19)	(19)	(19)	(19)	(19)	(19)	(19)	(19)	(19)	(19)	(19)	(19)
Hampton city	6,254	9.5	46,165	1,625	3,475	795	276	130	979	1,844	4,676	277	276
Harrisonburg city	(8)	(8)	(8)	(8)	(8)	(8)	(8)	(8)	(8)	(8)	(8)	(8)	(8)
Hopewell city	(4)	(4)	(4)	(4)	(4)	(4)	(4)	(4)	(4)	(4)	(4)	(4)	(4)
Lexington city	(7)	(7)	(7)	(7)	(7)	(7)	(7)	(7)	(7)	(7)	(7)	(7)	(7)
Lynchburg city[19]	(20)	(20)	(20)	(20)	(20)	(20)	(20)	(20)	(20)	(20)	(20)	(20)	(20)
Manassas city	(5)	(5)	(5)	(5)	(5)	(5)	(5)	(5)	(5)	(5)	(5)	(5)	(5)
Manassas Park city	(5)	(5)	(5)	(5)	(5)	(5)	(5)	(5)	(5)	(5)	(5)	(5)	(5)

1. Based on the resident population estimated as of July 1 of the year shown. 2. Radford city is included with Montgomery county. 3. Danville city is included with Pittsylvania county. 4. Hopewell city is included with Prince George county. 5. Manassas and Manassas Park cities are included with Prince William county. 6. Salem city is included with Roanoke county. 7. Buena Vista and Lexington cities are included with Rockbridge county. 8. Harrisonburg city is included with Rockingham county. 9. Franklin city is included with Southampton county. 10. Fredericksburg city is included with Spotsylvania county. 11. Bristol city is included with Washington county. 12. Norton city is included with Wise county. 13. Poquoson city is included with York county. 14. Charlottesville city is included with Albemarle county. 15. Covington city is included with Alleghany county. 16. Emporia city is included with Greensville county. 17. Fairfax city and Falls Church city are included with Fairfax county. 18. Galax city is included with Carroll county. 19. Lynchburg city is included with Campbell county. 20. Petersburg and Colonial Heights cities are included with Dinwiddie county.

STATE County	Earnings, 2020 (cont.)									Social Security beneficiaries, December 2020		Supple-mental Security Income recipients, 2020	Housing units, 2021	
	Percent by selected industries													
	Farm	Mining, quarrying, and extractions	Construction	Manu-facturing	Information; professional, scientific, technical services	Retail trade	Finance, insurance, real estate, and leasing	Health care and social assistance	Govern-ment	Number	Rate[1]		Total	Percent change, 2010–2021
	75	76	77	78	79	80	81	82	83	84	85	86	87	88
VIRGINIA—Cont'd														
Louisa	0.3	D	11.1	11.4	4.3	5.4	3.3	3.8	13.5	9,290	239	625	17,968	2.4
Lunenburg	-0.1	0.0	9.2	13.0	2.3	4.0	D	9.5	30.7	3,330	279	355	5,881	0.2
Madison	0.7	0.1	14.6	8.8	D	19.7	2.3	D	16.6	3,305	237	187	6,090	0.5
Mathews	1.6	0.1	11.5	4.3	D	6.3	7.5	D	24.3	2,980	349	144	5,474	0.4
Mecklenburg	-0.1	D	4.4	7.0	8.8	9.5	4.2	19.6	17.1	10,235	338	1,141	19,136	0.6
Middlesex	1.0	0.0	11.6	4.3	D	6.4	6.9	D	28.0	3,920	364	283	7,131	0.4
Montgomery	(2) 0.2	(2) 0.2	(2) D	(2) 14.1	(2) D	(2) 5.6	(2) 2.8	(2) D	(2) 40.7	14,815	150	1,100	42,813	3.8
Nelson	2.3	D	8.4	10.0	D	3.6	3.1	6.1	17.4	5,045	341	388	9,940	0.6
New Kent	-0.5	D	18.9	3.1	7.6	6.9	3.1	11.5	19.2	5,335	223	237	9,410	3.4
Northampton	25.9	0.0	5.2	5.1	D	4.9	3.7	9.0	21.3	4,000	331	558	7,427	0.6
Northumberland	2.6	0.1	9.2	32.6	D	5.1	4.3	1.8	16.6	4,735	394	249	8,993	0.4
Nottoway	2.0	D	4.0	5.6	3.1	6.1	2.2	D	50.3	3,900	250	535	6,688	0.7
Orange	6.6	D	8.5	16.8	5.5	7.6	5.0	4.0	20.7	9,545	257	622	15,907	1.1
Page	4.3	0.0	7.4	10.6	6.8	8.2	5.4	D	23.5	6,920	291	545	11,822	0.5
Patrick	2.6	0.1	6.5	18.8	7.2	8.8	2.3	D	21.0	5,720	325	489	9,989	-0.1
Pittsylvania	(3) 0.9	(3) D	(3) D	(3) 19.1	(3) 4.0	(3) 8.5	(3) 4.1	(3) 16.9	(3) 18.1	18,030	301	1,408	29,408	0.1
Powhatan	0.2	D	24.8	3.0	D	6.5	6.7	4.5	20.5	6,695	215	247	11,841	1.7
Prince Edward	0.6	D	3.9	1.5	3.0	8.6	4.3	D	27.6	5,105	233	835	9,141	0.5
Prince George	(4) 0.0	(4) 0.0	(4) D	(4) 14.4	(4) D	(4) 2.5	(4) 1.3	(4) D	(4) 58.2	6,770	158	347	13,441	0.4
Prince William	(5) 0.0	(5) D	(5) D	(5) 3.7	(5) D	(5) 6.9	(5) 4.2	(5) D	(5) 26.6	51,605	107	4,358	160,111	0.8
Pulaski	0.8	D	3.5	38.7	D	7.6	2.0	D	16.2	9,865	292	844	17,022	0.2
Rappahannock	-0.4	0.2	15.7	3.8	19.1	3.6	6.1	3.1	16.6	2,105	284	71	3,842	0.3
Richmond	3.2	0.0	6.2	5.0	D	4.6	3.4	D	35.9	2,210	245	250	3,952	0.4
Roanoke	(6) 0.0	(6) 0.2	(6) D	(6) 12.3	(6) 9.6	(6) 6.2	(6) 7.9	(6) D	(6) 16.5	24,075	249	953	42,253	0.2
Rockbridge	(7) 0.6	(7) D	(7) 6.4	(7) D	(7) 4.1	(7) 7.8	(7) 3.5	(7) 8.3	(7) 21.7	6,475	286	304	11,305	0.3
Rockingham	(8) 2.1	(8) D	(8) 7.9	(8) 19.0	(8) 7.6	(8) 6.8	(8) 4.9	(8) 10.8	(8) 17.0	19,095	226	814	35,967	1.3
Russell	1.1	6.0	7.6	5.9	11.1	7.6	3.2	14.7	20.3	8,720	341	1,259	12,764	0.1
Scott	0.3	0.1	2.9	19.3	4.6	7.0	2.3	D	26.4	7,280	340	1,102	11,766	0.0
Shenandoah	1.0	D	6.5	20.9	D	7.0	4.5	9.4	14.8	11,460	256	746	21,250	0.4
Smyth	0.1	D	5.0	29.2	D	5.5	1.7	D	25.5	9,765	331	1,156	15,086	0.0
Southampton	(9) 2.5	(9) D	(9) 2.6	(9) 7.0	(9) D	(9) 8.9	(9) 5.6	(9) 15.5	(9) 29.2	4,610	256	344	7,760	0.4
Spotsylvania	(10) 0.1	(10) D	(10) 7.0	(10) D	(10) 13.4	(10) 10.9	(10) 5.4	(10) 18.6	(10) 16.6	23,590	164	1,532	53,913	2.6
Stafford	-0.1	D	6.0	1.0	13.9	5.4	D	5.6	32.5	19,280	120	1,247	53,913	1.7
Surry	1.6	0.0	3.3	D	D	1.0	D	0.4	12.4	1,885	289	161	3,426	0.6
Sussex	2.7	D	2.4	2.0	D	6.2	1.7	D	36.0	2,680	249	429	4,677	0.7
Tazewell	0.5	4.2	5.2	9.1	3.4	12.1	4.2	D	21.7	13,370	335	1,834	19,791	-0.1
Warren	-0.1	0.0	9.3	10.3	4.8	7.6	4.7	11.5	16.7	8,250	202	658	16,922	0.9
Washington	(11) 0.3	(11) D	(11) D	(11) 15.8	(11) 5.0	(11) 10.1	(11) 5.4	(11) 12.7	(11) 17.7	16,605	310	1,461	25,492	0.2
Westmoreland	14.4	0.0	6.8	13.3	D	6.5	3.5	D	24.9	5,405	289	431	11,244	0.9
Wise	(12) 0.0	(12) 2.9	(12) D	(12) 3.0	(12) 4.9	(12) 9.9	(12) 2.9	(12) D	(12) 31.3	11,905	334	2,235	16,638	0.0
Wythe	0.2	1.3	5.4	25.8	D	10.5	4.3	D	20.9	8,605	305	846	14,017	0.2
York	(13) 0.1	(13) 0.1	(13) 8.5	(13) 1.8	(13) D	(13) 9.4	(13) 4.6	(13) D	(13) 33.1	12,930	182	426	28,134	0.9
Independent cities														
Alexandria city	0.0	0.0	2.7	0.9	25.5	4.1	6.0	5.2	31.6	16,175	105	1,768	80,357	-0.1
Bristol city	(11)	(11)	(11)	(11)	(11)	(11)	(11)	(11)	(11)	5,095	299	831	8,644	-0.2
Buena Vista city	(7)	(7)	(7)	(7)	(7)	(7)	(7)	(7)	(7)	1,665	252	260	2,948	0.0
Charlottesville city	(14)	(14)	(14)	(14)	(14)	(14)	(14)	(14)	(14)	6,510	143	1,001	21,554	0.6
Chesapeake city	0.2	0.1	11.0	6.2	13.1	9.0	7.7	8.6	16.6	42,210	168	3,747	96,037	1.0
Colonial Heights city[20]	(15)	(15)	(15)	(15)	(15)	(15)	(15)	(15)	(15)	4,460	244	538	8,130	-0.2
Covington city[15]	(16)	(16)	(16)	(16)	(16)	(16)	(16)	(16)	(16)	1,900	332	447	3,043	-0.3
Danville city	(3)	(3)	(3)	(3)	(3)	(3)	(3)	(3)	(3)	12,660	300	2,962	22,186	-0.3
Emporia city[16]	(17)	(17)	(17)	(17)	(17)	(17)	(17)	(17)	(17)	1,445	255	580	2,642	-0.2
Fairfax city[17]	(18)	(18)	(18)	(18)	(18)	(18)	(18)	(18)	(18)	3,585	148	D	9,317	-0.1
Falls Church city	(18)	(18)	(18)	(18)	(18)	(18)	(18)	(18)	(18)	1,790	124	107	6,251	0.0
Franklin city	(9)	(9)	(9)	(9)	(9)	(9)	(9)	(9)	(9)	2,290	279	635	3,899	0.3
Fredericksburg city	(10)	(10)	(10)	(10)	(10)	(10)	(10)	(10)	(10)	4,370	154	597	12,310	0.6
Galax city[18]	(19)	(19)	(19)	(19)	(19)	(19)	(19)	(19)	(19)	2,145	322	596	3,154	0.0
Hampton city	0.0	0.0	3.8	3.5	10.6	4.8	1.8	8.8	50.1	27,925	203	3,451	62,531	0.1
Harrisonburg city	(8)	(8)	(8)	(8)	(8)	(8)	(8)	(8)	(8)	5,970	116	1,061	18,665	0.2
Hopewell city	(4)	(4)	(4)	(4)	(4)	(4)	(4)	(4)	(4)	5,055	218	1,113	10,467	0.5
Lexington city	(7)	(7)	(7)	(7)	(7)	(7)	(7)	(7)	(7)	1,725	231	237	2,618	0.0
Lynchburg city[19]	(20)	(20)	(20)	(20)	(20)	(20)	(20)	(20)	(20)	16,270	206	2,679	34,157	0.8
Manassas city	(5)	(5)	(5)	(5)	(5)	(5)	(5)	(5)	(5)	4,900	115	518	14,442	0.4
Manassas Park city	(5)	(5)	(5)	(5)	(5)	(5)	(5)	(5)	(5)	1,435	84	D	5,516	-0.1

1. Based on the resident population estimated as of July 1 of the year shown. 2. Radford city is included with Montgomery county. 3. Danville city is included with Pittsylvania county. 4. Hopewell city is included with Prince George county. 5. Manassas and Manassas Park cities are included with Prince William county. 6. Salem city is included with Roanoke county. 7. Buena Vista and Lexington cities are included with Rockbridge county. 8. Harrisonburg city is included with Rockingham county. 9. Franklin city is included with Southampton county. 10. Fredericksburg city is included with Spotsylvania county. 11. Bristol city is included with Washington county. 12. Norton city is included with Wise county. 13. Poquoson city is included with York county. 14. Charlottesville city is included with Albemarle county. 15. Covington city is included with Alleghany county. 16. Emporia city is included with Greensville county. 17. Fairfax city and Falls Church city are included with Fairfax county. 18. Galax city is included with Carroll county. 19. Lynchburg city is included with Campbell county. 20. Petersburg and Colonial Heights cities are included with Dinwiddie county.

STATE County	Housing units, 2016–2020: Total	Occupied units: Owner-occupied: Percent	Owner-occupied: Median value[1]	Median owner cost as a percent of income: With a mortgage	Median owner cost as a percent of income: Without a mortgage[2]	Renter-occupied: Median rent[3]	Renter-occupied: Median rent as a percent of income[2]	Substandard units[4] (percent)	Civilian labor force, 2021: Total	Civilian labor force: Percent change, 2020–2021	Unemployment: Total	Unemployment: Rate[5]	Civilian employment[6], 2016–2020: Total	Percent: Management, business, science, and arts	Percent: Construction, production, and maintenance occupations
	89	90	91	92	93	94	95	96	97	98	99	100	101	102	103
VIRGINIA—Cont'd															
Louisa	14,383	79.3	234,700	20.5	10.0	905	30.3	2.5	19,910	-0.5	671	3.4	17,333	36.4	22.1
Lunenburg	4,472	71.3	123,900	22.7	10.0	692	30.3	1.3	5,044	-4.0	192	3.8	4,692	25.8	39.0
Madison	5,098	78.5	264,100	21.6	11.5	815	35.0	3.2	7,329	-0.1	181	2.5	6,292	37.0	24.4
Mathews	3,881	83.7	265,600	15.1	10.0	931	34.9	1.6	3,936	-2.1	125	3.2	3,691	41.9	29.2
Mecklenburg	12,371	72.4	148,800	19.8	10.0	707	26.8	2.3	12,429	-1.9	587	4.7	12,692	34.7	28.5
Middlesex	4,764	78.6	265,500	22.1	12.6	888	26.8	2.2	5,085	-1.3	171	3.4	4,730	30.3	22.0
Montgomery	35,388	55.4	230,000	18.1	10.0	1,017	30.3	2.0	49,360	0.5	1,459	3.0	45,874	49.0	15.8
Nelson	6,398	75.1	233,400	18.7	10.0	834	27.9	2.3	7,106	-1.7	249	3.5	6,825	39.3	25.8
New Kent	8,117	90.0	296,700	19.1	11.2	1,066	41.1	1.9	12,555	-1.7	371	3.0	11,249	42.7	24.5
Northampton	5,151	63.0	194,000	19.3	10.8	708	23.8	1.8	5,359	-1.1	288	5.4	4,747	31.2	25.6
Northumberland	5,686	89.4	270,900	21.9	10.0	1,014	30.3	1.3	5,503	-2.8	267	4.9	4,573	36.5	28.3
Nottoway	5,568	67.3	151,000	20.0	12.2	725	23.3	1.9	7,029	-2.4	257	3.7	5,646	31.0	29.3
Orange	13,926	78.2	261,000	21.7	10.0	938	28.8	2.6	16,992	-0.9	616	3.6	17,167	32.4	26.7
Page	9,413	71.8	167,900	23.3	10.0	746	29.8	2.2	11,897	-1.0	553	4.6	11,093	23.4	31.7
Patrick	7,830	77.4	123,700	16.8	10.0	614	28.6	3.0	7,016	-3.0	315	4.5	7,809	26.8	36.3
Pittsylvania	26,205	75.8	125,200	18.9	10.0	731	26.7	2.1	29,293	-2.3	1,174	4.0	26,864	29.2	33.5
Powhatan	10,392	92.8	291,300	19.1	10.0	1,125	21.2	0.4	13,893	-2.0	401	2.9	13,938	44.8	20.0
Prince Edward	7,394	63.2	162,800	19.8	10.0	715	33.2	1.2	9,976	-1.7	478	4.8	8,549	26.2	19.6
Prince George	11,763	68.6	219,300	19.8	10.0	1,377	28.7	1.2	14,660	-2.1	662	4.5	15,111	37.9	22.0
Prince William	144,159	73.1	390,500	21.9	10.0	1,738	29.7	3.3	241,803	-2.4	9,560	4.0	240,319	45.6	17.1
Pulaski	14,666	69.4	156,600	19.8	10.0	749	23.9	0.9	15,938	-1.7	630	4.0	15,242	31.0	28.2
Rappahannock	2,827	77.1	392,600	19.7	11.3	1,107	26.7	6.2	3,584	-1.2	104	2.9	3,592	42.3	22.6
Richmond	2,939	64.2	193,700	19.1	10.0	842	24.6	1.1	3,904	-3.4	137	3.5	3,170	33.8	28.5
Roanoke	38,234	74.7	207,300	18.5	10.0	937	27.3	0.8	47,898	-2.4	1,504	3.1	45,444	44.8	19.4
Rockbridge	9,301	75.0	206,300	21.3	10.8	843	27.5	0.7	10,381	-0.5	383	3.7	10,218	35.7	28.4
Rockingham	31,306	74.4	217,600	20.3	10.0	938	24.1	2.4	41,368	-1.0	1,217	2.9	40,205	33.0	28.7
Russell	10,975	74.8	89,200	19.6	10.0	564	27.4	1.0	10,695	-4.4	462	4.3	9,271	27.6	32.1
Scott	8,710	79.4	106,900	19.0	11.3	544	24.9	2.2	8,792	-2.3	315	3.6	8,203	28.5	34.3
Shenandoah	17,541	69.7	214,900	21.9	10.0	878	27.0	1.7	21,572	-2.7	770	3.6	20,806	27.7	31.7
Smyth	12,694	70.1	99,500	19.6	10.7	615	28.3	2.0	13,524	0.7	547	4.0	12,052	24.3	35.7
Southampton	6,618	74.4	176,600	19.5	10.7	796	26.8	3.9	8,739	-3.9	304	3.5	7,666	36.6	26.3
Spotsylvania	45,463	79.0	289,200	21.1	10.0	1,462	28.8	2.1	66,679	-2.0	2,523	3.8	66,314	41.4	18.6
Stafford	48,160	77.4	356,000	19.3	10.0	1,559	29.0	1.8	72,503	-1.8	2,636	3.6	73,283	48.2	15.9
Surry	2,794	72.1	201,000	19.9	10.0	837	22.8	2.3	3,482	-3.4	133	3.8	3,021	30.6	37.2
Sussex	3,792	73.0	123,200	19.6	12.6	835	24.3	1.6	3,593	-2.6	234	6.5	4,425	28.2	33.9
Tazewell	16,371	74.7	102,600	19.0	10.0	668	25.0	1.8	14,995	-3.3	785	5.2	14,889	30.9	28.7
Warren	14,641	75.7	251,600	21.1	10.0	1,051	27.4	3.1	19,936	-2.0	705	3.5	19,282	33.8	24.9
Washington	22,104	76.1	159,000	19.8	10.0	724	25.6	0.9	25,246	-2.8	902	3.6	23,562	35.2	26.2
Westmoreland	7,910	73.9	201,000	21.8	11.8	884	31.4	1.8	9,508	-0.2	421	4.4	7,150	33.8	24.4
Wise	14,916	68.8	87,300	19.1	10.7	638	30.3	1.2	12,722	-3.1	664	5.2	13,040	33.8	20.7
Wythe	12,393	77.0	130,000	19.0	10.0	656	22.9	1.1	13,516	-2.5	544	4.0	13,574	30.9	27.6
York	25,517	72.0	338,200	20.0	10.0	1,503	29.1	1.8	31,945	-2.6	1,057	3.3	30,061	54.3	13.9
Independent cities															
Alexandria city	71,289	43.4	572,700	20.6	11.8	1,774	27.4	4.3	97,365	-2.0	3,673	3.8	96,737	60.6	11.1
Bristol city	7,482	61.5	127,900	21.3	12.3	712	27.9	1.9	7,313	-3.2	347	4.7	7,623	31.7	22.6
Buena Vista city	2,509	61.3	125,700	24.8	13.2	871	32.0	1.4	2,961	-7.5	115	3.9	3,010	28.2	23.3
Charlottesville city	18,814	40.1	329,100	19.9	10.0	1,188	32.4	1.6	24,609	-2.6	903	3.7	24,671	56.6	10.5
Chesapeake city	86,524	72.3	286,000	22.7	10.5	1,300	32.3	1.5	119,733	-2.7	4,608	3.8	112,342	42.6	20.6
Colonial Heights city	7,094	65.9	179,200	19.8	10.0	1,034	36.4	1.7	8,169	-2.5	391	4.8	8,108	35.4	25.1
Covington city	2,382	75.4	70,400	18.2	12.2	760	25.7	0.3	2,279	-5.6	132	5.8	2,235	23.8	24.9
Danville city	18,266	50.3	95,500	22.5	12.4	688	28.2	2.1	18,394	-4.4	1,204	6.5	16,159	26.1	28.7
Emporia city	2,076	41.0	121,600	22.2	13.4	756	34.5	2.1	2,336	-0.5	183	7.8	2,143	26.1	38.2
Fairfax city	8,751	69.9	587,000	22.4	11.3	1,822	29.7	1.9	12,429	-2.1	425	3.4	12,647	57.0	10.1
Falls Church city	5,631	58.8	810,900	21.4	12.2	2,044	24.3	3.0	8,196	-0.8	217	2.6	7,971	71.2	4.5
Franklin city	3,516	55.7	179,200	23.2	10.0	833	30.0	1.5	3,481	-4.6	239	6.9	3,417	23.0	26.5
Fredericksburg city	11,059	39.8	376,700	18.9	10.7	1,287	30.1	3.7	13,853	-2.3	646	4.7	15,365	49.5	14.1
Galax city	2,614	67.9	97,400	21.7	12.2	571	29.3	1.3	2,813	-2.5	115	4.1	2,639	29.0	28.7
Hampton city	54,847	56.9	188,600	22.8	10.6	1,115	31.9	1.7	62,844	-3.3	3,566	5.7	61,751	35.9	23.9
Harrisonburg city	16,751	40.5	220,100	19.9	10.0	911	28.8	3.7	23,996	-1.6	969	4.0	25,962	33.0	26.3
Hopewell city	9,362	47.1	126,100	18.1	11.3	920	28.3	3.1	9,361	-3.7	699	7.5	9,516	26.5	30.5
Lexington city	2,066	54.7	235,400	20.2	10.0	916	29.2	2.1	2,047	0.2	101	4.9	2,730	48.2	9.0
Lynchburg city	28,223	49.8	162,900	19.7	10.0	859	29.0	2.5	34,699	-3.2	1,760	5.1	37,280	37.9	18.9
Manassas city	13,066	69.3	338,100	23.1	10.2	1,549	35.2	4.8	20,983	-2.4	821	3.9	21,984	37.4	23.9
Manassas Park city	4,596	60.7	299,700	22.9	10.0	1,709	33.6	6.7	9,464	-2.6	360	3.8	10,158	38.1	24.5

1. Specified owner-occupied units. 2. A value of 10.0 represents 10 percent or less; a value of 50.0 represents 50 percent or more. 3. Specified renter-occupied units. 4. Overcrowded or lacking complete plumbing facilities. 5. Percent of civilian labor force. 6. Civilian employed persons 16 years old and over.

STATE County	Private nonfarm establishments, employment and payroll, 2020									Agriculture, 2017			
		Employment						Annual payroll		Farms			Farm producers whose primary occupation is farming (percent)
											Percent with:		
	Number of establish-ments	Total	Health care and social assistance	Manufac-turing	Retail trade	Finance and insurance	Professional, scientific, and technical services	Total (mil dol)	Average per employee (dollars)	Number	Fewer than 50 acres	1000 acres or more	
	104	105	106	107	108	109	110	111	112	113	114	115	116
VIRGINIA—Cont'd													
Louisa	618	7,638	337	1,244	1,247	93	178	382	49,980	431	38.7	1.6	38.8
Lunenburg	155	1,535	232	411	287	64	27	58	37,555	335	29.3	2.7	43.9
Madison	276	2,688	241	301	984	19	85	91	34,028	533	33.4	3.6	45.6
Mathews	185	1,118	185	53	220	20	43	30	27,191	43	65.1	2.3	31.8
Mecklenburg	773	8,849	1,819	850	1,854	234	258	296	33,433	512	25.6	4.9	42.7
Middlesex	298	2,257	397	113	389	56	89	72	31,687	79	50.6	6.3	43.5
Montgomery	1,990	30,344	4,724	5,595	4,884	751	2,306	1,292	42,580	584	41.3	2.4	39.3
Nelson	356	3,612	198	818	333	37	176	99	27,543	409	34.5	1.2	41.7
New Kent	416	4,146	617	180	630	45	130	138	33,355	138	64.5	4.3	39.5
Northampton	305	2,812	709	147	538	64	78	95	33,939	142	47.9	10.6	43.3
Northumberland	293	1,724	139	312	328	56	55	57	33,197	134	58.2	11.9	46.3
Nottoway	299	3,335	1,021	410	667	100	96	115	34,531	311	34.1	2.9	48.2
Orange	644	6,891	375	1,581	1,378	124	218	285	41,297	417	34.1	5.3	40.6
Page	418	4,102	528	520	720	127	283	142	34,585	519	47.0	1.9	46.3
Patrick	266	3,742	380	1,162	481	78	69	105	28,108	483	38.5	1.9	41.2
Pittsylvania	854	8,375	1,133	1,537	959	142	190	314	37,533	1,157	30.2	2.9	41.5
Powhatan	699	5,701	275	105	1,025	125	389	241	42,346	263	52.5	1.5	47.6
Prince Edward	521	7,367	1,932	100	1,338	151	204	246	33,398	341	27.9	2.3	37.7
Prince George	486	8,397	512	1,519	1,072	150	703	358	42,640	164	37.8	7.3	43.6
Prince William	8,726	111,563	12,896	4,449	23,156	1,861	13,180	5,433	48,695	304	75.7	1.3	38.0
Pulaski	610	10,991	1,518	4,372	1,785	145	161	444	40,418	394	40.4	3.0	31.9
Rappahannock	199	1,024	64	73	126	9	67	35	34,528	439	49.2	2.5	37.5
Richmond	179	2,157	821	171	247	39	35	65	30,021	98	38.8	9.2	64.3
Roanoke	2,015	29,195	4,371	2,956	4,061	4,099	1,320	1,258	43,095	262	52.3	0.4	43.1
Rockbridge	425	5,389	441	1,221	1,417	91	108	160	29,633	752	36.6	2.4	38.2
Rockingham	1,552	29,720	3,923	7,612	2,022	452	609	1,393	46,882	2,026	46.2	0.6	49.3
Russell	440	5,957	1,153	707	918	196	734	235	39,399	918	36.2	2.7	40.7
Scott	252	3,871	714	1,110	582	84	133	140	36,090	1,138	41.4	0.5	34.9
Shenandoah	872	12,183	1,450	3,332	1,620	257	443	466	38,290	965	49.4	1.6	42.5
Smyth	500	8,616	1,816	2,664	1,266	194	164	308	35,735	663	41.0	2.9	37.3
Southampton	223	2,042	152	528	315	13	57	97	47,643	257	23.0	20.2	51.4
Spotsylvania	2,569	32,973	4,410	1,299	7,669	537	2,570	1,350	40,936	338	57.4	2.7	40.7
Stafford	2,391	35,124	3,916	657	4,927	4,939	4,977	1,589	45,246	243	75.7	0.8	36.6
Surry	81	1,312	11	124	51	NA	27	133	101,153	111	40.5	7.2	40.0
Sussex	179	1,898	377	211	314	21	12	68	35,620	124	28.2	21.0	48.5
Tazewell	935	11,643	2,447	1,222	2,689	569	331	403	34,598	512	37.1	8.0	35.1
Warren	848	11,979	1,608	1,317	1,955	237	325	470	39,209	321	62.6	1.2	33.8
Washington	1,142	16,758	2,636	2,907	3,064	470	389	676	40,364	1,506	49.7	1.1	37.8
Westmoreland	312	2,368	187	629	484	44	70	69	29,235	183	34.4	7.7	50.5
Wise	618	7,602	1,593	189	1,706	194	301	248	32,612	147	46.3	5.4	38.1
Wythe	666	9,533	1,210	2,119	1,879	250	162	350	36,685	819	30.9	2.0	43.4
York	1,499	20,121	2,453	328	3,583	460	2,779	743	36,907	40	85.0	NA	23.1
Independent cities													
Alexandria city	4,631	81,924	7,949	1,716	7,631	3,077	16,741	5,327	65,023	NA	NA	NA	NA
Bristol city	537	8,025	977	1,078	1,576	299	167	257	32,085	NA	NA	NA	NA
Buena Vista city	104	1,993	186	676	162	23	28	66	33,065	NA	NA	NA	NA
Charlottesville city	2,012	35,451	9,887	784	3,314	940	2,808	2,223	62,698	NA	NA	NA	NA
Chesapeake city	5,632	97,895	11,547	4,616	14,822	5,048	9,240	4,413	45,080	248	76.2	5.2	33.8
Colonial Heights city	654	9,535	1,554	185	3,091	253	293	248	25,995	NA	NA	NA	NA
Covington city	197	3,446	163	1,313	560	105	35	211	61,190	NA	NA	NA	NA
Danville city	1,249	23,668	5,418	4,568	4,175	773	397	817	34,507	NA	NA	NA	NA
Emporia city	226	3,797	967	833	643	61	61	136	35,824	NA	NA	NA	NA
Fairfax city	1,977	27,442	5,084	114	4,359	1,345	5,998	1,509	54,993	NA	NA	NA	NA
Falls Church city	875	10,422	2,175	112	1,311	184	2,081	555	53,249	NA	NA	NA	NA
Franklin city	264	3,521	1,351	23	1,037	176	77	90	25,527	NA	NA	NA	NA
Fredericksburg city	1,361	21,913	6,066	406	4,213	668	1,344	960	43,805	NA	NA	NA	NA
Galax city	305	5,330	1,479	1,090	962	126	114	175	32,810	NA	NA	NA	NA
Hampton city	2,397	40,453	8,030	1,874	6,716	813	4,410	1,790	44,249	NA	NA	NA	NA
Harrisonburg city	1,636	25,719	3,067	2,925	5,537	908	1,051	888	34,532	NA	NA	NA	NA
Hopewell city	409	5,690	1,273	1,443	656	84	250	290	50,930	NA	NA	NA	NA
Lexington city	249	3,899	550	23	375	118	127	163	41,720	NA	NA	NA	NA
Lynchburg city	2,252	56,459	11,086	5,791	6,647	2,395	3,278	2,379	42,135	NA	NA	NA	NA
Manassas city	1,504	17,395	3,428	1,364	2,165	510	1,410	901	51,792	NA	NA	NA	NA
Manassas Park city	328	3,081	128	165	162	16	133	162	52,726	NA	NA	NA	NA

STATE County	Agriculture, 2017 (cont.) Land in farms Acreage (1,000)	Percent change, 2012–2017	Acres Average size of farm	Acres Total irrigated (1,000)	Acres Total cropland (1,000)	Value of land and buildings (dollars) Average per farm	Average per acre	Value of machinery and equipment, average per farm (dollars)	Value of products sold: Total (mil dol)	Average per farm (acres)	Percent from: Crops	Livestock and poultry products	Organic farms (number)	Farms with internet access (percent)	Government payments Total ($1,000)	Percent of farms
	117	118	119	120	121	122	123	124	125	126	127	128	129	130	131	132
VIRGINIA—Cont'd																
Louisa	68	-14.6	159	0.2	24.8	787,124	4,953	76,509	15.0	34,735	48.7	51.3	5	76.3	314	16.5
Lunenburg	73	-11.9	217	1.4	25.7	579,358	2,664	81,398	17.2	51,206	77.7	22.3	7	69.9	354	24.5
Madison	107	-0.1	201	0.1	45.1	1,193,189	5,949	90,957	28.4	53,263	39.6	60.4	2	74.1	1,313	17.3
Mathews	7	41.7	153	0.0	4.2	655,108	4,278	63,683	3.8	87,814	55.4	44.6	NA	81.4	31	18.6
Mecklenburg	141	-3.0	276	4.2	62.9	762,052	2,764	122,271	50.0	97,590	90.1	9.9	21	64.5	334	30.3
Middlesex	20	1.7	247	0.3	14.7	979,876	3,967	154,776	8.8	111,620	96.7	3.3	3	87.3	586	44.3
Montgomery	102	-5.2	174	0.3	28.8	842,923	4,842	78,230	24.3	41,604	30.2	69.8	2	81.8	327	8.2
Nelson	68	-15.2	166	1.0	20.2	841,397	5,073	85,319	26.7	65,328	83.0	17.0	5	72.9	118	9.0
New Kent	18	-7.0	133	0.3	11.1	711,167	5,353	85,624	5.1	37,159	93.2	6.8	NA	83.3	558	18.8
Northampton	48	-13.9	340	5.9	37.8	1,558,831	4,585	281,016	96.0	675,993	70.7	29.3	3	93.0	1,180	29.6
Northumberland	43	0.5	324	NA	33.8	975,400	3,006	226,725	20.1	149,642	85.8	14.2	NA	64.9	1,423	26.1
Nottoway	50	-18.2	162	0.0	20.1	514,211	3,174	76,270	50.5	162,486	7.9	92.1	1	71.4	405	25.7
Orange	95	-9.1	228	0.2	39.8	1,438,347	6,297	115,676	113.1	271,149	77.7	22.3	NA	79.1	292	12.7
Page	72	1.3	139	0.1	30.4	904,349	6,515	90,614	150.1	289,260	4.2	95.8	2	73.0	836	11.8
Patrick	91	15.4	189	0.2	21.6	524,237	2,775	58,469	17.3	35,762	42.5	57.5	NA	73.3	260	12.6
Pittsylvania	246	-14.3	213	1.5	83.4	603,542	2,835	93,701	72.7	62,816	41.1	58.9	6	68.3	1,441	17.2
Powhatan	35	7.8	132	0.1	11.4	696,770	5,299	47,626	11.2	42,772	22.6	77.4	1	75.3	54	9.9
Prince Edward	70	-11.9	204	0.0	20.1	580,742	2,848	65,360	23.8	69,768	11.2	88.8	NA	71.8	198	36.1
Prince George	40	8.1	242	D	22.0	920,064	3,807	88,285	9.3	56,616	94.5	5.5	NA	69.5	933	37.2
Prince William	23	-35.8	75	0.9	14.1	804,671	10,694	78,627	11.6	38,197	61.1	38.9	NA	92.1	227	5.9
Pulaski	78	-19.8	197	0.0	23.8	692,087	3,518	84,261	33.0	83,716	35.9	64.1	NA	77.4	88	7.6
Rappahannock	70	11.7	160	0.1	25.2	1,101,588	6,891	64,028	10.1	23,109	50.4	49.6	2	78.4	90	8.7
Richmond	32	-1.3	326	0.0	26.2	1,289,515	3,955	173,701	16.8	171,571	95.3	4.7	NA	48.0	823	42.9
Roanoke	26	-17.1	100	0.1	6.2	572,455	5,743	55,410	2.5	9,691	67.5	32.5	NA	66.4	D	1.9
Rockbridge	135	-19.9	179	0.1	36.5	881,466	4,918	70,368	31.0	41,201	16.9	83.1	NA	76.3	422	10.0
Rockingham	229	2.9	113	5.5	121.9	997,634	8,844	118,949	795.9	392,852	6.8	93.2	37	65.5	1,852	11.5
Russell	170	-9.2	185	D	32.7	536,112	2,890	53,598	23.2	25,277	11.4	88.6	1	61.9	269	8.8
Scott	125	-20.8	110	0.0	30.5	290,473	2,637	53,894	15.6	13,671	24.7	75.3	2	69.9	79	7.3
Shenandoah	131	-2.1	135	0.9	61.2	796,732	5,884	99,776	142.8	148,006	14.1	85.9	2	76.7	593	7.3
Smyth	123	-26.1	186	0.0	25.7	544,580	2,930	75,941	37.6	56,653	8.5	91.5	1	65.6	782	14.6
Southampton	142	-7.7	552	1.6	97.6	1,704,698	3,087	237,200	75.1	292,070	82.4	17.6	NA	76.3	6,847	72.8
Spotsylvania	42	-1.2	123	0.1	16.7	695,020	5,637	70,042	9.0	26,660	48.5	51.5	2	76.6	199	8.6
Stafford	17	13.1	71	0.0	10.1	930,372	13,104	73,999	6.1	25,206	62.6	37.4	2	85.2	68	6.2
Surry	42	-6.8	379	0.9	25.4	1,280,403	3,379	175,981	D	D	D	D	3	84.7	1,280	39.6
Sussex	66	3.1	534	0.7	44.9	1,482,681	2,775	209,543	D	D	D	D	NA	74.2	1,963	54.0
Tazewell	138	-8.1	269	D	24.7	737,125	2,736	66,474	24.6	48,117	8.5	91.5	NA	68.8	820	9.6
Warren	39	-19.4	121	0.0	13.9	909,921	7,548	68,431	5.9	18,355	36.1	63.9	2	81.0	5	1.2
Washington	176	-8.2	117	0.1	58.3	589,890	5,038	60,654	69.0	45,821	12.1	87.9	2	68.0	596	11.5
Westmoreland	53	-11.4	288	0.9	32.0	1,073,155	3,732	170,589	D	D	D	D	2	74.3	1,175	36.1
Wise	26	1.7	179	0.0	5.0	554,986	3,097	66,109	2.4	16,000	33.5	66.5	NA	66.0	15	2.7
Wythe	152	-13.0	185	0.0	49.1	725,643	3,921	87,090	65.5	80,018	8.4	91.6	NA	75.5	474	19.4
York	1	-67.5	23	0.0	0.1	276,375	12,095	39,402	1.5	37,800	75.1	24.9	NA	97.5	D	2.5
Independent cities																
Alexandria city	NA	NA	NA	NA	NA	NA	NA	NA	NA	NA	NA	NA	NA	NA	NA	NA
Bristol city	NA	NA	NA	NA	NA	NA	NA	NA	NA	NA	NA	NA	NA	NA	NA	NA
Buena Vista city	NA	NA	NA	NA	NA	NA	NA	NA	NA	NA	NA	NA	NA	NA	NA	NA
Charlottesville city	NA	NA	NA	NA	NA	NA	NA	NA	NA	NA	NA	NA	NA	NA	NA	NA
Chesapeake city	37	-18.4	148	0.1	32.3	867,657	5,848	102,911	31.1	125,552	94.8	5.2	NA	82.3	646	16.1
Colonial Heights city	NA	NA	NA	NA	NA	NA	NA	NA	NA	NA	NA	NA	NA	NA	NA	NA
Covington city	NA	NA	NA	NA	NA	NA	NA	NA	NA	NA	NA	NA	NA	NA	NA	NA
Danville city	NA	NA	NA	NA	NA	NA	NA	NA	NA	NA	NA	NA	NA	NA	NA	NA
Emporia city	NA	NA	NA	NA	NA	NA	NA	NA	NA	NA	NA	NA	NA	NA	NA	NA
Fairfax city	NA	NA	NA	NA	NA	NA	NA	NA	NA	NA	NA	NA	NA	NA	NA	NA
Falls Church city	NA	NA	NA	NA	NA	NA	NA	NA	NA	NA	NA	NA	NA	NA	NA	NA
Franklin city	NA	NA	NA	NA	NA	NA	NA	NA	NA	NA	NA	NA	NA	NA	NA	NA
Fredericksburg city	NA	NA	NA	NA	NA	NA	NA	NA	NA	NA	NA	NA	NA	NA	NA	NA
Galax city	NA	NA	NA	NA	NA	NA	NA	NA	NA	NA	NA	NA	NA	NA	NA	NA
Hampton city	NA	NA	NA	NA	NA	NA	NA	NA	NA	NA	NA	NA	NA	NA	NA	NA
Harrisonburg city	NA	NA	NA	NA	NA	NA	NA	NA	NA	NA	NA	NA	NA	NA	NA	NA
Hopewell city	NA	NA	NA	NA	NA	NA	NA	NA	NA	NA	NA	NA	NA	NA	NA	NA
Lexington city	NA	NA	NA	NA	NA	NA	NA	NA	NA	NA	NA	NA	NA	NA	NA	NA
Lynchburg city	NA	NA	NA	NA	NA	NA	NA	NA	NA	NA	NA	NA	NA	NA	NA	NA
Manassas city	NA	NA	NA	NA	NA	NA	NA	NA	NA	NA	NA	NA	NA	NA	NA	NA
Manassas Park city	NA	NA	NA	NA	NA	NA	NA	NA	NA	NA	NA	NA	NA	NA	NA	NA

STATE County	Water use, 2015		Wholesale Trade[1], 2017				Retail Trade[2], 2017				Real estate and rental and leasing,[2] 2017			
	Public supply water withdrawn (mil gal/ day)	Public supply gallons withdrawn per person per day	Number of establish- ments	Number of employees	Sales (mil dol)	Average payroll (mil dol)	Number of establish- ments	Number of employees	Sales (mil dol)	Average payroll (mil dol)	Number of establish- ments	Number of employees	Sales (mil dol)	Average payroll (mil dol)
	133	134	135	136	137	138	139	140	141	142	143	144	145	146
VIRGINIA—Cont'd														
Louisa	0.5	15.3	10	182	91.8	9.9	83	1,259	355.4	29.6	24	105	30.2	4.9
Lunenburg	0.5	39.0	8	104	84.8	4.7	37	283	60.5	6.1	NA	NA	NA	NA
Madison	0.0	0.0	7	D	11.6	D	39	703	140.3	22.0	7	11	2.1	0.2
Mathews	0.0	0.0	D	D	D	D	25	203	45.2	4.4	D	D	D	D
Mecklenburg	1.9	60.2	27	321	288.3	15.4	158	1,718	498.8	39.3	31	88	12.8	2.5
Middlesex	0.1	6.6	11	100	27.0	3.9	54	423	101.7	11.2	9	21	5.1	0.5
Montgomery	6.9	70.9	33	668	434.4	30.7	306	5,168	1,117.1	117.4	94	510	112.3	19.4
Nelson	0.2	13.5	6	D	12.8	D	48	307	201.6	8.3	10	D	2.9	D
New Kent	19.9	976.4	6	D	9.6	D	47	481	179.7	12.5	16	22	3.3	0.8
Northampton	0.4	32.9	18	125	76.1	6.6	61	454	111.5	10.4	14	D	5.5	D
Northumberland	0.1	11.4	10	D	28.9	D	46	357	71.6	7.6	18	27	5.2	1.0
Nottoway	0.5	30.6	11	89	75.6	3.8	64	636	135.1	15.2	9	23	2.3	0.9
Orange	2.1	58.8	7	151	56.1	6.6	108	1,355	407.3	37.6	23	40	6.2	1.0
Page	1.3	53.5	5	40	18.3	2.0	75	764	170.4	18.2	10	17	3.6	0.8
Patrick	0.3	16.1	6	D	20.2	D	48	485	175.1	11.9	6	D	0.6	D
Pittsylvania	1.6	26.0	26	742	386.1	28.3	121	788	260.4	17.9	23	73	12.1	2.4
Powhatan	0.1	3.9	D	D	D	9.4	78	963	332.2	27.2	27	131	12.6	4.5
Prince Edward	1.1	48.4	14	144	35.5	4.6	99	1,331	383.7	34.9	29	125	14.2	3.2
Prince George	0.1	3.7	19	605	556.0	26.1	65	806	287.3	23.8	20	91	19.9	4.4
Prince William	79.7	176.5	203	3,151	2,727.8	203.4	1,169	22,923	6,350.6	609.6	373	1,613	521.0	83.8
Pulaski	4.4	127.9	11	144	37.1	5.4	98	1,777	392.8	38.6	24	90	9.6	2.3
Rappahannock	0.0	4.1	D	D	D	D	25	154	33.6	4.9	D	D	D	D
Richmond	0.4	40.4	9	91	43.1	3.1	28	239	59.0	6.0	6	D	1.3	D
Roanoke	25.1	266.2	88	1,049	471.7	57.4	266	4,267	1,126.2	109.2	115	528	72.0	19.2
Rockbridge	1.7	77.8	13	73	28.5	2.8	72	1,563	366.3	30.9	9	D	3.6	D
Rockingham	14.8	187.7	56	1,007	1,065.8	63.0	221	1,786	455.0	42.2	41	519	116.5	24.3
Russell	1.2	42.3	10	34	15.5	1.1	78	933	276.2	22.4	D	D	D	D
Scott	1.1	50.6	D	D	D	D	69	608	168.1	11.9	5	8	0.7	0.1
Shenandoah	2.6	59.5	20	465	523.8	16.7	147	1,643	562.3	38.0	D	D	D	D
Smyth	2.2	69.6	12	172	98.0	9.5	110	1,266	272.7	26.5	12	38	4.7	1.1
Southampton	0.8	46.4	13	212	200.3	9.9	37	229	61.2	5.0	9	D	2.3	D
Spotsylvania	11.1	84.7	76	675	405.7	38.5	451	7,553	2,481.0	216.0	137	690	133.3	26.2
Stafford	22.0	154.8	49	1,100	1,467.2	62.6	281	4,609	1,362.4	118.5	104	390	101.7	15.0
Surry	0.2	22.4	NA	NA	NA	NA	12	40	12.2	0.9	4	17	1.4	0.6
Sussex	0.6	47.8	D	D	D	5.6	41	287	103.3	7.3	7	D	1.8	D
Tazewell	3.8	88.3	41	440	271.8	19.9	186	2,860	721.3	65.3	42	113	16.6	3.2
Warren	9.1	232.3	15	148	184.3	4.7	129	1,837	529.3	45.7	28	80	15.5	3.5
Washington	11.8	215.6	36	581	353.1	25.7	191	3,118	812.7	72.7	49	146	43.5	5.8
Westmoreland	0.8	44.8	11	20	39.5	0.7	51	446	116.0	10.1	8	13	2.3	0.2
Wise	4.9	123.4	28	241	144.9	12.2	150	1,820	454.5	39.7	21	59	8.5	1.8
Wythe	4.4	149.4	18	207	103.2	7.7	125	1,842	699.9	44.7	25	73	12.7	2.8
York	19.1	280.8	33	159	76.7	7.7	209	3,779	960.7	95.4	58	297	109.9	12.7
Independent cities														
Alexandria city	0.0	0.1	72	872	651.9	60.4	475	7,862	2,548.9	258.9	282	1,580	555.7	84.0
Bristol city	0.0	0.0	28	350	794.2	14.1	139	1,845	447.5	41.0	21	91	13.0	2.9
Buena Vista city	1.1	160.2	NA	NA	NA	NA	23	170	37.0	3.2	3	7	0.5	0.1
Charlottesville city	0.0	0.0	44	451	330.2	24.3	281	3,282	714.9	77.4	84	555	110.8	26.2
Chesapeake city	7.1	30.2	241	3,552	2,790.8	205.7	785	14,925	4,182.0	387.9	307	1,421	382.9	66.8
Colonial Heights city	0.0	0.0	9	58	25.6	2.3	169	3,283	738.5	69.5	35	164	41.4	6.1
Covington city	2.1	378.2	5	35	17.6	1.5	43	598	144.5	14.4	8	31	7.4	1.0
Danville city	5.4	127.4	45	560	255.9	29.6	302	4,558	1,144.0	104.0	53	237	31.6	6.9
Emporia city	0.7	125.5	D	D	D	3.3	54	626	125.7	13.5	14	45	5.2	1.1
Fairfax city	0.0	0.0	27	250	157.5	15.7	217	4,681	1,722.0	172.0	62	242	86.0	13.4
Falls Church city	0.0	0.0	16	126	51.5	6.7	103	1,304	457.8	50.0	38	176	65.1	9.3
Franklin city	0.9	102.5	4	25	14.0	1.1	58	1,039	234.8	23.8	D	D	D	D
Fredericksburg city	0.0	0.0	24	254	123.6	10.8	261	4,326	1,015.0	109.9	75	314	76.9	14.8
Galax city	1.7	251.7	D	D	D	1.4	69	1,062	242.3	24.8	15	53	10.6	1.8
Hampton city	0.0	0.0	60	921	425.1	47.0	423	6,748	1,569.0	168.8	123	784	154.5	26.7
Harrisonburg city	0.0	0.0	58	864	438.7	43.9	325	5,341	1,378.8	136.1	71	373	99.1	14.0
Hopewell city	20.6	918.3	D	D	D	5.8	72	636	162.7	15.2	19	71	22.9	3.0
Lexington city	0.0	0.0	NA	NA	NA	NA	41	377	94.7	9.1	14	34	5.6	1.4
Lynchburg city	0.0	0.0	74	898	479.1	43.2	355	6,890	2,162.9	165.3	119	458	87.4	16.6
Manassas city	0.2	5.0	47	458	227.6	23.4	176	2,153	961.8	77.1	45	226	61.4	10.7
Manassas Park city	0.0	0.0	21	257	194.1	17.4	24	143	96.2	7.8	9	51	19.4	2.4

1 Merchant wholesalers, except manufacturers' sales branches and offices. 2. Employer establishments.

STATE County	Professional, scientific, and technical services, 2017				Manufacturing, 2017				Accommodation and food services, 2017			
	Number of establish-ments	Number of employees	Sales (mil dol)	Average payroll (mil dol)	Number of establish-ments	Number of employees	Sales (mil dol)	Average payroll (mil dol)	Number of establis-hments	Number of employees	Sales (mil dol)	Annual payroll (mil dol)
	147	148	149	150	151	152	153	154	155	156	157	158
VIRGINIA—Cont'd												
Louisa	46	136	14.7	4.9	32	1,022	304.0	44.6	43	569	31.9	8.8
Lunenburg	7	33	2.6	1.3	7	483	86.1	16.1	8	90	3.0	0.8
Madison	25	75	14.0	3.5	16	312	117.3	11.9	21	247	11.2	2.9
Mathews	D	D	D	1.4	5	44	2.9	1.2	D	D	D	D
Mecklenburg	44	341	53.5	21.7	34	1,338	276.3	55.4	70	1,109	52.7	15.0
Middlesex	28	183	12.2	6.5	12	125	23.7	5.3	26	317	16.1	5.6
Montgomery	D	D	D	D	49	5,080	1,554.4	284.5	210	4,606	231.6	66.1
Nelson	42	180	19.1	7.4	27	306	82.5	15.6	22	857	62.9	20.2
New Kent	D	D	D	D	11	172	28.7	6.2	D	D	D	D
Northampton	22	62	7.2	2.6	9	435	72.8	17.1	39	487	34.3	10.0
Northumberland	21	84	9.5	3.2	15	254	119.3	17.2	19	92	5.8	2.1
Nottoway	21	76	7.2	2.4	18	385	120.2	14.7	30	340	15.6	4.4
Orange	57	236	32.3	9.9	20	1,289	232.2	67.0	62	747	44.1	12.2
Page	35	274	32.9	12.7	15	516	193.4	18.1	55	730	50.1	12.3
Patrick	22	98	6.5	2.5	29	1,212	229.5	41.7	D	D	D	D
Pittsylvania	47	190	35.6	7.9	41	1,887	645.2	76.3	48	544	26.7	7.5
Powhatan	64	393	43.3	17.9	D	118	D	6.2	31	531	24.7	7.9
Prince Edward	D	D	D	D	14	60	13.7	2.2	39	1,004	46.4	15.4
Prince George	D	D	D	D	25	1,160	950.3	64.9	47	610	39.2	11.4
Prince William	D	D	D	D	111	4,144	1,576.6	350.1	743	13,817	878.2	239.0
Pulaski	D	D	D	D	34	4,119	2,777.8	241.5	69	1,109	56.8	15.3
Rappahannock	D	D	D	D	11	87	6.5	1.5	19	415	20.0	7.2
Richmond	10	20	2.9	0.9	8	146	41.2	6.7	D	D	D	D
Roanoke	D	D	D	D	65	3,098	941.8	172.3	156	3,079	159.5	44.3
Rockbridge	25	115	19.5	5.4	22	978	321.1	38.0	53	874	57.9	15.8
Rockingham	D	D	D	D	87	6,873	3,872.0	364.0	92	2,428	102.0	44.0
Russell	D	D	D	D	14	545	136.5	20.7	30	448	22.1	6.1
Scott	20	98	11.7	4.2	9	818	415.1	32.6	25	558	21.7	5.9
Shenandoah	D	D	D	D	45	3,347	893.1	141.4	87	1,444	69.1	20.1
Smyth	D	D	D	D	33	3,081	1,169.6	144.0	44	678	31.2	9.1
Southampton	13	50	4.9	1.7	13	509	151.2	25.0	8	109	4.5	1.4
Spotsylvania	247	1,973	293.3	123.9	52	1,173	417.4	72.0	215	4,454	232.7	65.7
Stafford	D	D	D	D	38	977	252.4	42.5	202	3,841	228.4	58.3
Surry	D	D	D	0.5	4	114	36.9	4.0	4	33	0.7	0.1
Sussex	D	D	D	0.5	9	148	124.6	6.5	D	D	D	D
Tazewell	65	340	41.4	15.4	50	844	202.2	43.5	71	1,219	62.1	17.1
Warren	D	D	D	D	27	891	1,035.1	53.7	87	1,302	71.5	20.9
Washington	100	390	55.7	23.7	65	3,540	1,017.6	164.1	97	1,984	85.9	25.3
Westmoreland	23	79	10.0	4.7	10	420	125.4	19.0	31	340	15.5	5.2
Wise	61	358	55.5	13.6	15	214	46.7	10.6	56	1,079	48.6	13.5
Wythe	38	181	19.4	7.5	36	1,906	1,068.6	88.8	76	1,576	77.2	21.6
York	170	2,115	290.4	119.8	31	301	57.5	14.8	171	4,025	258.4	67.2
Independent cities												
Alexandria city	1,200	18,080	4,201.2	1,784.3	58	1,480	431.3	76.7	402	8,518	691.8	193.3
Bristol city	34	164	18.7	7.6	17	1,096	263.1	43.5	79	1,955	99.4	28.1
Buena Vista city	4	16	1.6	0.6	14	778	223.9	35.8	12	214	11.3	3.8
Charlottesville city	D	D	D	D	53	667	143.1	35.9	292	5,491	329.6	98.3
Chesapeake city	D	D	D	D	120	4,179	1,577.0	234.2	486	10,068	530.7	148.8
Colonial Heights city	45	435	60.8	25.4	D	175	D	8.0	84	2,221	112.4	30.6
Covington city	13	40	5.1	1.1	D	D	D	D	20	252	15.3	3.4
Danville city	D	D	D	D	41	5,089	1,892.3	260.1	143	2,925	148.8	41.4
Emporia city	D	D	D	D	6	1,269	282.9	58.4	28	701	31.1	9.1
Fairfax city	D	D	D	D	22	169	36.2	7.0	183	3,332	223.9	61.9
Falls Church city	164	1,847	339.8	144.5	11	60	14.9	4.0	114	1,213	94.3	24.2
Franklin city	20	107	10.6	4.9	6	D	6.3	D	D	D	D	D
Fredericksburg city	D	D	D	D	27	332	71.2	19.4	186	4,460	227.5	72.2
Galax city	23	138	9.9	4.0	15	1,297	264.2	41.4	39	701	29.6	8.4
Hampton city	285	4,393	777.9	344.4	55	2,226	597.2	125.6	256	5,902	304.4	89.2
Harrisonburg city	D	D	D	D	40	2,861	891.0	124.0	208	5,138	259.0	81.3
Hopewell city	41	293	34.8	11.6	18	1,624	1,737.4	147.3	50	771	37.5	9.7
Lexington city	D	D	D	D	4	D	1.2	0.3	50	663	43.8	14.0
Lynchburg city	D	D	D	D	76	6,377	2,415.3	366.1	270	6,023	292.1	83.4
Manassas city	D	D	D	D	40	1,319	301.5	104.0	126	1,947	117.3	32.6
Manassas Park city	19	152	26.4	9.1	13	222	31.9	7.9	14	118	6.6	2.1

STATE County	Health care and social assistance, 2017				Other services, 2017				Nonemployer businesses, 2019		Value of residential construction authorized by building permits, 2021	
	Number of establish-ments	Number of employees	Receipts (mil dol)	Annual payroll (mil dol)	Number of establish-ments	Number of employees	Receipts (mil dol)	Annual payroll (mil dol)	Number	Receipts (mil dol)	New construction ($1,000)	Number of housing units
	159	160	161	162	163	164	165	166	167	168	169	170
VIRGINIA—Cont'd												
Louisa	29	342	26.1	13.4	42	263	26.6	7.1	2,416	106.9	128,377	513
Lunenburg	16	235	18.1	7.5	D	D	D	0.5	626	26.1	7,942	42
Madison	22	324	20.1	8.4	22	55	8.4	1.7	1,273	51.7	28,486	76
Mathews	20	176	10.3	4.5	D	D	D	D	818	36.6	14,331	43
Mecklenburg	76	1,771	164.0	68.8	69	375	28.8	8.7	1,685	76.7	38,596	188
Middlesex	23	366	25.5	11.1	D	D	D	D	946	41.6	18,044	52
Montgomery	221	4,382	642.2	198.5	147	867	287.5	26.6	5,383	243.7	66,049	297
Nelson	D	D	D	8.0	21	177	15.1	5.9	1,286	54.8	23,274	82
New Kent	D	D	D	18.9	26	80	10.6	2.9	2,026	90.4	158,168	451
Northampton	36	755	80.6	28.9	20	63	4.8	1.4	1,087	42.4	36,575	106
Northumberland	11	D	6.2	D	24	63	7.0	1.9	1,094	45.4	13,960	61
Nottoway	30	927	63.6	29.5	30	96	9.1	2.5	681	22.0	7,479	57
Orange	33	393	25.9	11.2	62	434	54.5	13.1	2,616	108.8	50,840	261
Page	22	559	44.8	22.1	28	90	10.1	2.5	1,411	57.6	22,805	139
Patrick	21	559	34.1	14.9	D	D	D	1.4	1,027	33.8	10,188	32
Pittsylvania	67	1,239	81.0	36.0	67	289	27.4	7.4	3,219	116.1	17,205	71
Powhatan	33	261	24.8	11.5	63	207	28.2	8.1	2,264	106.4	57,451	213
Prince Edward	80	1,693	188.3	74.5	40	186	28.0	5.0	1,029	36.8	14,158	101
Prince George	34	469	48.8	23.6	29	149	13.8	4.8	1,643	54.7	15,502	78
Prince William	782	11,124	1,355.0	521.6	586	4,021	705.4	130.8	43,145	1,797.9	331,970	2,189
Pulaski	71	1,105	128.3	47.4	42	216	27.4	6.9	1,516	55.8	13,573	53
Rappahannock	D	D	D	1.6	D	D	D	D	976	45.0	14,344	28
Richmond	14	867	26.4	13.4	11	79	10.9	3.3	586	22.6	3,826	26
Roanoke	230	4,628	417.5	186.4	146	804	80.5	21.1	5,993	276.9	37,849	192
Rockbridge	28	409	40.1	12.9	28	134	14.3	3.8	1,527	62.6	16,750	59
Rockingham	129	4,097	635.3	215.0	105	502	53.7	17.5	5,968	269.8	184,156	619
Russell	62	877	68.3	31.8	D	D	D	D	1,149	37.0	4,091	21
Scott	34	730	49.1	22.6	19	139	17.5	7.1	873	28.3	7,656	32
Shenandoah	82	1,471	125.6	56.6	74	411	42.7	11.3	2,948	112.8	41,884	194
Smyth	63	1,841	162.1	72.6	36	169	18.8	4.8	1,416	49.3	3,672	17
Southampton	7	D	9.7	D	D	D	D	2.6	934	30.3	11,146	72
Spotsylvania	279	4,247	524.0	202.0	203	1,223	115.5	38.0	9,674	411.2	318,186	1,615
Stafford	193	3,429	354.0	130.8	232	1,590	158.6	52.4	10,705	425.4	276,793	977
Surry	D	D	D	D	NA	NA	NA	NA	388	10.8	6,210	31
Sussex	D	D	D	D	11	87	5.2	1.7	485	17.8	4,960	33
Tazewell	131	2,487	234.7	92.3	78	511	61.6	18.6	1,933	76.8	2,262	7
Warren	61	1,698	140.6	58.0	64	488	94.9	13.9	2,779	122.4	49,922	200
Washington	158	2,693	379.0	130.2	64	346	29.8	9.2	3,407	141.1	26,289	101
Westmoreland	17	214	11.8	5.7	28	91	8.0	2.0	1,201	41.8	41,882	203
Wise	92	1,627	131.7	54.2	D	D	D	D	1,523	50.0	1,000	6
Wythe	74	1,318	125.9	51.6	62	269	32.3	8.3	1,535	60.4	7,269	40
York	138	2,153	285.8	112.1	D	D	D	D	4,134	163.9	84,073	485
Independent cities												
Alexandria city	426	7,386	1,056.3	379.4	611	9,983	3,295.4	767.9	16,927	832.8	41,568	200
Bristol city	51	987	70.7	30.7	41	243	79.5	5.9	979	39.2	0	0
Buena Vista city	11	238	10.8	5.3	9	21	2.4	0.6	316	8.8	815	8
Charlottesville city	158	9,293	1,742.6	877.9	158	1,729	580.2	105.1	4,362	273.4	39,434	191
Chesapeake city	514	10,002	1,239.6	503.6	438	3,057	349.2	110.8	15,761	595.8	303,610	1,383
Colonial Heights city	91	1,616	130.8	58.3	63	517	39.7	14.9	986	38.3	1,530	13
Covington city	16	176	5.7	3.4	D	D	D	D	242	8.6	278	3
Danville city	180	5,096	489.0	210.3	89	424	59.0	11.3	2,314	78.1	21,249	244
Emporia city	41	1,170	96.8	37.8	14	83	7.8	2.2	266	12.3	861	6
Fairfax city	265	4,300	347.8	148.4	166	1,258	161.5	49.7	3,063	179.9	4,340	12
Falls Church city	123	2,335	225.3	103.0	94	573	113.9	25.4	1,447	88.5	11,005	19
Franklin city	55	1,136	101.1	39.0	26	102	11.4	3.0	490	15.9	NA	NA
Fredericksburg city	225	5,189	883.6	329.9	113	762	68.7	23.4	2,252	117.3	39,453	142
Galax city	46	1,518	187.7	59.9	22	97	9.5	2.6	410	11.8	1,127	9
Hampton city	281	7,833	1,299.2	454.5	169	953	111.9	28.0	7,812	205.7	15,095	242
Harrisonburg city	185	3,080	281.4	124.0	131	715	84.9	25.7	3,012	151.1	6,672	36
Hopewell city	45	1,183	146.7	58.7	38	231	19.6	6.9	1,091	31.5	1,013	17
Lexington city	34	554	70.8	21.8	29	221	67.3	9.1	456	17.4	2,670	11
Lynchburg city	289	10,123	1,393.7	516.1	171	1,013	107.3	31.5	4,557	160.9	28,160	143
Manassas city	177	3,231	376.1	158.6	137	902	142.6	35.8	3,866	185.2	22,829	97
Manassas Park city	D	D	D	D	D	D	D	D	1,762	75.7	3,705	13

STATE County	Government employment and payroll, 2017: Full-time equivalent employees	Government employment and payroll, 2017: March payroll (dollars)	March payroll (percent of total): Administration, judicial, and legal	March payroll (percent of total): Police and corrections	March payroll (percent of total): Fire protection	March payroll (percent of total): Highways and transportation	March payroll (percent of total): Health and welfare	March payroll (percent of total): Natural resources and utilities	March payroll (percent of total): Education and libraries	Local government finances, 2017, General revenue: Total (mil dol)	General revenue: Intergovernmental (mil dol)	Taxes: Total (mil dol)	Taxes: Per capita[1] (dollars): Total	Taxes: Per capita[1] (dollars): Property
	171	172	173	174	175	176	177	178	179	180	181	182	183	184
VIRGINIA—Cont'd														
Louisa	1,134	3,879,432	9.3	7.3	4.0	0.1	3.0	4.1	68.6	159.5	68.5	66.6	1,854	1,635
Lunenburg	366	1,243,228	3.7	15.7	0.0	0.0	0.0	6.5	71.9	37.3	22.5	12.1	981	841
Madison	397	1,613,812	7.2	7.8	0.0	0.0	4.9	0.2	77.3	39.8	18.7	18.8	1,420	1,179
Mathews	311	973,033	9.6	7.8	0.0	0.0	5.8	0.0	73.0	17.6	6.4	10.7	1,231	1,061
Mecklenburg	1,167	3,512,833	7.1	11.5	0.0	1.1	6.1	4.9	64.2	106.5	51.6	43.6	1,419	1,058
Middlesex	297	1,024,349	10.4	15.5	0.0	0.0	1.4	3.0	69.6	30.5	10.1	18.9	1,779	1,531
Montgomery	2,607	9,586,596	13.2	10.6	0.3	5.7	1.7	8.7	57.3	343.0	126.8	134.3	1,368	1,022
Nelson	470	1,633,990	8.1	5.7	0.0	0.0	1.4	2.1	77.9	51.6	18.8	28.7	1,938	1,641
New Kent	681	2,482,291	11.0	8.9	5.7	0.3	5.0	7.1	60.6	64.1	24.8	33.2	1,536	1,311
Northampton	792	3,563,409	4.6	10.9	0.0	20.9	6.3	3.0	51.4	135.6	31.0	28.4	2,394	1,899
Northumberland	392	1,439,407	7.2	8.0	0.0	0.0	0.9	1.0	78.7	33.4	10.8	21.1	1,722	1,553
Nottoway	595	1,856,153	11.6	7.7	0.0	3.4	3.6	6.4	65.2	48.9	24.1	19.4	1,257	782
Orange	1,300	4,302,812	6.5	18.0	5.2	1.2	3.8	3.0	61.8	121.3	59.6	52.8	1,473	1,167
Page	876	2,732,192	8.3	13.4	0.0	0.7	5.5	5.9	64.6	73.2	37.5	28.9	1,216	918
Patrick	643	1,910,080	5.5	14.9	0.0	0.0	4.1	1.7	71.7	40.6	23.6	14.8	834	686
Pittsylvania	1,637	5,762,439	5.8	9.1	0.1	0.1	0.3	2.3	79.3	140.2	88.8	45.4	740	605
Powhatan	817	3,614,068	6.4	6.5	0.6	0.0	2.0	1.1	80.1	75.6	31.7	41.6	1,450	1,364
Prince Edward	611	2,006,507	13.8	11.9	0.2	3.3	0.5	7.5	56.0	62.9	32.1	24.7	1,087	605
Prince George	1,469	5,634,849	6.4	27.3	1.7	0.0	3.3	1.8	58.4	134.3	79.7	42.2	1,109	891
Prince William	15,874	83,539,176	5.0	9.0	5.0	3.3	4.7	4.9	67.3	2,073.5	834.4	984.8	2,127	1,704
Pulaski	1,199	3,741,838	8.0	11.0	3.9	2.8	0.0	11.1	61.8	130.9	63.8	41.3	1,206	848
Rappahannock	202	678,379	11.1	11.5	0.0	0.0	6.8	2.6	67.4	24.7	7.6	15.8	2,137	1,790
Richmond	411	1,469,844	8.0	27.1	0.0	0.0	5.5	2.7	55.7	29.9	15.8	11.0	1,243	981
Roanoke	3,694	14,726,656	8.1	6.7	5.0	0.3	2.9	11.5	60.9	390.3	121.6	197.0	2,097	1,571
Rockbridge	721	2,265,484	8.1	7.5	0.3	0.3	4.2	4.1	72.4	68.0	25.0	34.8	1,533	1,115
Rockingham	3,116	10,412,579	7.3	8.8	3.5	0.6	5.0	5.5	68.5	248.7	107.7	96.8	1,204	1,035
Russell	990	3,567,096	5.2	8.5	0.0	0.6	0.2	3.0	76.8	81.6	41.1	25.4	938	691
Scott	812	2,547,769	8.1	6.8	0.0	0.0	7.5	3.4	71.9	81.8	40.6	37.4	1,708	1,100
Shenandoah	1,562	5,381,072	7.3	9.5	3.8	2.2	2.9	7.7	64.0	134.4	59.7	58.6	1,354	1,073
Smyth	1,327	3,913,619	7.5	10.1	2.2	2.1	11.0	5.8	59.4	103.7	63.2	26.8	871	625
Southampton	649	2,076,317	9.7	12.9	0.0	0.2	4.5	4.0	67.4	62.8	33.6	23.4	1,314	1,173
Spotsylvania	4,684	16,854,269	6.7	5.6	5.8	0.0	2.5	4.8	72.7	449.7	200.9	217.2	1,636	1,257
Stafford	4,836	19,394,927	6.6	5.2	3.1	0.2	1.7	6.4	75.2	574.8	208.6	320.7	2,185	1,663
Surry	310	1,057,019	7.8	8.0	0.0	0.0	2.6	3.0	71.5	34.9	7.3	26.1	4,016	3,829
Sussex	367	1,351,833	14.7	16.7	0.0	0.2	9.2	2.2	54.8	53.3	25.8	18.3	1,606	1,387
Tazewell	1,448	4,226,517	10.8	9.6	1.4	2.3	1.4	6.0	64.9	139.3	71.4	40.6	983	679
Warren	1,246	4,431,292	7.5	11.4	4.3	1.0	3.6	9.1	58.9	113.5	43.0	57.4	1,456	1,213
Washington	2,379	7,519,585	4.8	22.4	0.3	1.1	2.6	7.2	59.0	182.1	94.9	57.0	1,052	729
Westmoreland	584	1,969,880	12.5	10.4	0.0	0.5	4.6	2.6	68.4	66.0	27.4	26.1	1,474	1,192
Wise	1,326	4,670,621	9.1	10.2	0.1	1.7	0.2	9.1	67.7	137.5	82.3	43.6	1,130	827
Wythe	1,223	3,964,070	6.6	26.7	0.7	1.5	0.0	5.5	53.0	215.7	44.3	36.5	1,268	774
York	2,729	10,981,478	9.4	6.4	9.1	0.0	4.4	2.6	60.3	327.9	105.7	189.4	2,784	2,259
Independent cities														
Alexandria city	5,558	29,910,334	9.3	14.2	7.3	1.9	12.9	8.3	42.1	892.3	177.2	611.7	3,842	2,970
Bristol city	848	3,102,214	5.2	13.3	5.5	2.7	4.9	8.6	39.4	115.6	40.1	32.0	1,898	1,078
Buena Vista city	277	891,039	14.2	6.9	0.0	4.3	0.0	11.0	62.6	23.2	13.0	7.7	1,186	895
Charlottesville city	2,178	9,337,860	10.1	7.9	5.3	9.0	7.2	7.6	46.3	258.9	90.5	116.5	2,455	1,482
Chesapeake city	11,046	44,150,325	4.4	9.5	4.4	1.6	24.8	3.8	48.7	1,317.1	444.8	465.8	1,939	1,356
Colonial Heights city	797	3,207,146	6.7	12.4	7.5	3.8	0.5	4.2	63.0	71.9	24.0	43.5	2,496	1,284
Covington city	291	1,032,630	3.0	11.2	0.0	3.4	1.0	10.1	69.3	27.2	11.3	12.1	2,174	1,493
Danville city	2,182	7,837,955	10.7	13.4	6.7	4.0	5.6	10.5	44.5	213.5	110.0	56.2	1,369	721
Emporia city	102	426,107	28.3	33.8	6.1	5.8	0.0	25.5	0.0	24.2	6.5	12.4	2,275	1,063
Fairfax city	420	2,753,519	18.6	21.8	23.5	18.0	0.6	13.3	0.2	146.8	17.2	113.4	4,840	3,206
Falls Church city	792	4,186,167	12.4	7.6	0.1	2.9	1.8	4.4	65.2	104.9	13.2	71.9	5,046	3,822
Franklin city	605	2,117,474	4.7	35.6	5.5	2.4	2.9	6.3	38.2	46.9	26.0	12.8	1,575	890
Fredericksburg city	1,663	6,605,878	9.0	26.4	3.6	4.1	3.2	4.7	44.3	208.1	73.7	81.0	2,842	1,463
Galax city	430	1,429,941	8.2	7.1	0.3	1.0	8.6	12.5	52.9	32.1	16.9	10.6	1,632	756
Hampton city	5,451	22,010,831	7.1	11.1	7.1	0.9	5.8	7.4	58.0	596.1	268.0	244.4	1,814	1,233
Harrisonburg city	1,563	6,085,265	3.9	7.3	6.4	5.5	0.3	14.2	55.8	198.8	76.6	79.3	1,479	722
Hopewell city	1,171	4,276,913	8.5	9.1	5.4	3.0	7.9	8.2	56.0	123.7	53.6	39.2	1,743	1,273
Lexington city	270	924,775	9.0	22.4	7.1	5.2	0.0	10.9	30.7	23.8	8.2	11.1	1,545	938
Lynchburg city	3,052	10,139,414	10.4	8.6	5.8	4.9	5.9	6.5	56.7	375.9	182.2	136.8	1,699	1,007
Manassas city	2,228	11,497,197	4.1	22.2	2.9	1.8	14.3	5.6	47.6	244.2	108.0	99.7	2,423	1,844
Manassas Park city	682	3,091,611	4.9	7.1	5.1	1.0	4.3	6.2	69.9	70.9	32.9	33.8	1,973	1,638

1. Based on the resident population estimated as of July 1 of the year shown.

STATE County	Local government finances, 2017 (cont.)									Government employment, 2020			Individual income tax returns, 2019		
	Direct general expenditure							Debt outstanding							
	Total (mil dol)	Per capita[1] (dollars)	Percent of total for: Education	Health and hospitals	Police protection	Public welfare	Highways	Total (mil dol)	Per capita[1] (dollars)	Federal civilian	Federal military	State and local	Number of returns	Mean adjusted gross income	Mean income tax
	185	186	187	188	189	190	191	192	193	194	195	196	197	198	199
VIRGINIA—Cont'd															
Louisa	144.6	4,026	68.3	1.0	3.8	5.4	0.3	17.6	491	69	120	1,561	17,770	66,714	6,672
Lunenburg	48.4	3,922	52.3	0.9	4.3	5.7	1.7	13.5	1,094	21	35	758	4,770	45,279	3,352
Madison	37.9	2,872	55.7	5.0	7.8	15.2	0.3	22.7	1,718	54	41	526	6,410	64,081	6,304
Mathews	16.4	1,883	82.2	0.0	16.7	0.0	0.0	4.7	534	19	65	355	4,350	72,204	7,958
Mecklenburg	100.0	3,258	52.8	6.2	7.2	4.8	1.0	33.4	1,088	124	93	1,635	13,880	50,252	4,442
Middlesex	27.9	2,627	54.7	1.9	5.6	6.0	0.0	19.5	1,838	22	34	922	5,310	73,721	8,514
Montgomery	327.9	3,341	34.4	15.3	7.0	2.1	4.6	198.7	2,025	[2] 352	[2] 407	[2] 18128	35,630	78,545	9,768
Nelson	47.1	3,183	62.2	0.5	6.2	4.4	0.7	22.7	1,532	63	46	661	7,650	67,069	7,235
New Kent	55.7	2,575	56.6	1.0	4.8	4.4	0.0	48.0	2,217	50	73	976	12,040	112,828	19,110
Northampton	200.5	16,890	12.9	6.2	1.8	0.5	52.1	658.0	55,422	37	63	888	5,960	55,750	6,169
Northumberland	31.0	2,526	58.5	1.1	7.2	7.0	1.3	35.7	2,905	30	95	449	6,110	70,282	7,809
Nottoway	42.5	2,757	62.1	2.9	4.6	7.9	2.1	15.8	1,023	281	54	2,356	6,170	46,862	3,687
Orange	122.3	3,410	46.8	0.5	6.4	5.5	2.7	166.7	4,647	69	118	2,174	18,100	65,905	6,617
Page	88.4	3,716	42.2	1.8	21.5	4.0	1.6	82.6	3,473	194	74	1,058	11,030	48,881	3,786
Patrick	43.2	2,437	66.3	1.2	7.0	5.0	1.2	81.9	4,626	48	54	812	7,380	47,806	4,088
Pittsylvania	142.9	2,331	63.3	1.8	5.2	10.2	0.0	120.1	1,959	[3] 210	[3] 305	[3] 6084	26,790	50,484	4,233
Powhatan	67.7	2,359	67.4	0.4	7.3	3.9	0.0	187.3	6,524	59	91	1,654	14,300	97,199	12,611
Prince Edward	63.6	2,806	50.3	0.5	8.8	7.1	5.4	18.4	811	72	60	2,202	8,170	48,424	3,950
Prince George	143.1	3,766	48.5	0.5	5.3	2.5	0.0	125.8	3,309	[4] 4724	[4] 8364	[4] 3063	16,160	62,015	5,524
Prince William	2,261.8	4,884	60.4	2.3	4.9	1.9	2.2	1,817.4	3,925	[5] 7556	[5] 9571	[5] 24209	229,220	81,033	9,294
Pulaski	110.0	3,215	43.1	9.9	6.0	4.2	1.8	77.1	2,251	63	103	2,127	14,850	53,095	4,660
Rappahannock	29.4	3,980	43.5	0.0	5.4	8.6	0.0	5.4	734	18	23	317	3,620	89,057	12,637
Richmond	30.4	3,417	54.8	0.7	6.0	6.6	0.0	7.7	867	29	25	1,071	3,610	50,502	3,961
Roanoke	409.0	4,354	45.8	6.9	5.7	3.9	0.3	409.9	4,364	[6] 2152	[6] 376	[6] 6392	46,980	72,523	8,102
Rockbridge	65.4	2,883	49.7	12.0	4.2	1.8	0.0	65.6	2,892	[7] 103	[7] 153	[7] 2554	10,290	61,268	5,938
Rockingham	262.7	3,267	56.9	4.5	3.7	9.3	1.2	186.1	2,315	[8] 371	[8] 402	[8] 11332	39,050	62,964	6,061
Russell	109.9	4,064	41.3	0.5	15.0	6.5	3.8	79.5	2,941	70	83	1,398	9,850	47,429	3,475
Scott	74.5	3,404	48.9	6.1	27.8	0.0	0.7	10.6	484	57	73	1,185	8,150	45,248	3,247
Shenandoah	128.0	2,957	56.5	0.4	7.3	6.3	2.2	112.7	2,605	133	136	2,006	21,560	57,970	5,465
Smyth	101.0	3,285	56.3	0.9	7.3	10.0	0.5	84.6	2,754	86	92	2,779	12,510	42,730	2,966
Southampton	65.1	3,649	54.2	0.8	3.8	3.4	0.1	65.0	3,642	[9] 72	[9] 75	[9] 2169	7,850	52,682	4,193
Spotsylvania	443.0	3,337	65.3	0.1	4.8	4.5	0.0	425.1	3,203	[10] 588	[10] 519	[10] 9405	66,880	72,653	7,784
Stafford	457.1	3,114	69.2	0.5	4.1	2.9	2.0	739.8	5,040	4,788	479	6,444	71,530	83,838	9,413
Surry	31.6	4,867	62.5	1.3	5.0	7.6	0.0	14.2	2,186	12	20	516	3,190	54,244	4,509
Sussex	47.1	4,140	57.8	1.3	6.8	8.2	0.7	23.2	2,036	55	26	1,197	4,300	44,909	3,548
Tazewell	178.9	4,332	34.7	15.0	5.6	5.2	14.5	28.6	693	80	122	3,190	15,450	51,159	4,305
Warren	162.5	4,124	50.0	0.2	6.1	3.5	6.4	199.3	5,056	218	125	1,652	19,580	64,015	6,307
Washington	204.8	3,780	38.6	11.5	4.1	3.9	1.2	145.1	2,678	[11] 236	[11] 219	[11] 4543	22,740	57,981	5,798
Westmoreland	67.1	3,783	61.3	0.7	6.8	5.3	1.3	18.9	1,065	56	57	855	8,900	57,983	5,698
Wise	133.4	3,458	44.1	7.6	6.8	7.8	3.3	104.6	2,711	[12] 240	[12] 121	[12] 3955	13,390	44,560	3,302
Wythe	114.4	3,968	41.4	0.1	5.9	6.8	2.0	110.3	3,826	86	89	2,182	12,790	47,834	3,795
York	327.2	4,810	68.0	0.2	2.9	2.8	0.0	134.7	1,981	[13] 1073	[13] 2130	[13] 3526	32,820	85,490	9,891
Independent cities															
Alexandria city	953.5	5,989	29.3	5.1	9.9	5.1	6.3	933.6	5,864	14,062	535	8,060	85,900	114,926	18,629
Bristol city	108.0	6,400	24.7	0.6	5.7	6.3	7.1	152.4	9,026	[11]	[11]	[11]	7,280	42,504	3,331
Buena Vista city	23.2	3,575	42.3	0.0	7.5	17.8	7.3	40.9	6,315	[7]	[7]	[7]	2,770	39,175	2,398
Charlottesville city	278.5	5,868	28.6	7.9	6.5	10.5	7.0	155.8	3,283	[14]	[14]	[14]	20,500	128,526	20,204
Chesapeake city	1,271.7	5,296	38.8	26.0	4.9	1.6	4.4	652.5	2,717	1,249	1,536	14,426	117,620	68,010	6,799
Colonial Heights city[20]	70.9	4,072	52.4	0.3	5.7	1.6	3.4	53.2	3,051	[15]	[15]	[15]	9,110	51,786	4,257
Covington city[15]	24.9	4,473	47.2	0.4	10.7	7.1	5.6	41.2	7,390	[16]	[16]	[16]	2,790	41,582	2,850
Danville city	233.0	5,678	39.2	0.6	5.7	5.3	9.0	142.3	3,467	[3]	[3]	[3]	18,010	41,735	3,578
Emporia city[16]	16.3	2,986	26.6	1.6	23.5	2.2	8.3	0.0	0	[17]	[17]	[17]	2,500	36,752	2,496
Fairfax city[17]	175.1	7,470	52.0	1.6	6.8	1.9	6.1	248.3	10,597	[18]	[18]	[18]	12,870	103,974	14,868
Falls Church city	96.3	6,763	54.0	0.3	7.4	2.1	6.2	0.0	0	[18]	[18]	[18]	6,980	173,991	30,708
Franklin city	45.1	5,542	34.8	0.4	6.7	3.6	2.7	31.1	3,816	[9]	[9]	[9]	3,730	46,308	3,574
Fredericksburg city	218.8	7,677	25.1	16.5	3.8	3.1	3.4	178.8	6,274	[10]	[10]	[10]	13,460	72,000	9,432
Galax city[18]	34.2	5,270	48.1	0.6	8.7	5.7	7.0	8.0	1,229	[19]	[19]	[19]	2,930	42,405	3,305
Hampton city	589.9	4,378	38.8	1.3	5.2	5.6	3.4	309.3	2,296	7,517	7,721	7,852	66,210	49,680	4,163
Harrisonburg city	215.3	4,013	54.2	0.6	4.7	1.6	4.7	6.2	115	[8]	[8]	[8]	18,340	48,466	4,033
Hopewell city	124.8	5,543	46.0	0.5	4.6	6.2	3.5	0.0	0	[4]	[4]	[4]	10,840	39,712	2,770
Lexington city	27.2	3,809	24.6	0.3	6.5	1.7	4.5	48.2	6,732	[7]	[7]	[7]	2,360	82,043	9,544
Lynchburg city[19]	334.5	4,154	43.6	0.6	6.3	8.1	3.7	332.3	4,127	[20]	[20]	[20]	32,560	54,272	5,531
Manassas city	270.1	6,565	43.2	1.5	5.5	6.8	4.2	115.2	2,801	[5]	[5]	[5]	21,220	62,470	6,225
Manassas Park city	74.0	4,314	57.8	1.4	6.0	4.1	5.6	145.4	8,481	[5]	[5]	[5]	8,580	55,927	5,086

1. Based on the resident population estimated as of July 1 of the year shown. 2. Radford city is included with Montgomery county. 3. Danville city is included with Pittsylvania county. 4. Hopewell city is included with Prince George county. 5. Manassas and Manassas Park cities are included with Prince William county. 6. Salem city is included with Roanoke county. 7. Buena Vista and Lexington cities are included with Rockbridge county. 8. Harrisonburg city is included with Rockingham county. 9. Franklin city is included with Southampton county. 10. Fredericksburg city is included with Spotsylvania county. 11. Bristol city is included with Washington county. 12. Norton city is included with Wise county. 13. Poquoson city is included with York county. 14. Charlottesville city is included with Albemarle county. 15. Covington city is included with Alleghany county. 16. Emporia city is included with Greensville county. 17. Fairfax city and Falls Church city are included with Fairfax county. 18. Galax city is included with Carroll county. 19. Lynchburg city is included with Campbell county. 20. Petersburg and Colonial Heights cities are included with Dinwiddie county.

State / county code	CBSA code[1]	County Type code[2]	STATE County	Land area[3] (sq. mi)	Population, 2021: Total persons 2021	Population, 2021: Rank	Population, 2021: Per square mile	Race alone or in combination, not Hispanic or Latino (percent): White	Black	American Indian, Alaska Native	Asian and Pacific Islancer	Percent Hispanic or Latino[4]	Age (percent): Under 5 years	5 to 17 years	18 to 24 years	25 to 34 years	35 to 44 years	45 to 54 years
				1	2	3	4	5	6	7	8	9	10	11	12	13	14	15
			VIRGINIA—Cont'd															
51690	32300	4	Martinsville city	11.0	13,517	2,189	1,228.8	45.6	47.6	0.7	1.4	7.0	7.0	14.9	12.1	12.2	11.1	11.7
51700	47260	1	Newport News city	69.0	184,587	366	2,675.2	44.7	43.6	1.2	4.9	9.8	6.9	12.8	15.1	16.4	12.9	10.2
51710	47260	1	Norfolk city	53.3	235,089	294	4,410.7	46.0	42.3	1.3	5.4	8.9	6.2	10.4	20.1	19.3	12.2	9.1
51720	13720	7	Norton city	7.5	3,666	2,912	488.8	87.2	8.1	1.0	2.1	4.2	6.1	13.0	10.9	14.8	12.0	11.9
51730	40060	1	Petersburg city	22.7	33,429	1,344	1,472.6	16.7	77.7	1.0	1.8	5.4	7.6	12.1	11.6	16.0	11.0	10.8
51735	47260	1	Poquoson city	15.4	12,574	2,237	816.5	92.3	2.0	0.9	3.8	3.4	4.6	13.7	11.9	9.9	14.2	12.7
51740	47260	1	Portsmouth city	33.3	97,840	626	2,938.1	39.1	55.6	1.3	2.4	4.9	7.1	12.6	12.6	16.6	13.1	10.5
51750	13980	3	Radford city	9.7	16,499	2,002	1,700.9	85.1	10.8	0.7	2.7	3.2	3.4	7.0	41.1	12.4	8.9	8.9
51760	40060	1	Richmond city	59.9	226,604	311	3,783.0	44.4	46.5	0.8	3.1	7.5	5.7	9.0	13.7	21.9	13.4	10.1
51770	40220	2	Roanoke city	42.5	98,865	618	2,326.2	60.1	31.4	0.8	4.0	6.8	6.5	12.5	11.0	15.3	12.8	11.9
51775	40220	2	Salem city	14.5	25,373	1,591	1,749.9	86.0	9.3	0.7	2.3	3.9	4.6	10.7	16.8	11.4	11.7	11.7
51790	44420	3	Staunton city	19.9	25,661	1,580	1,289.5	82.9	13.8	0.9	2.1	3.8	5.9	10.2	11.1	13.8	13.2	11.7
51800	47260	1	Suffolk city	399.2	96,194	632	241.0	50.7	43.5	0.8	3.1	4.7	6.3	13.4	11.8	13.6	13.6	12.5
51810	47260	1	Virginia Beach city	244.7	457,672	157	1,870.3	63.9	21.2	1.0	9.5	8.8	5.9	12.4	12.6	15.8	14.0	11.6
51820	44420	3	Waynesboro city	15.0	22,550	1,696	1,503.3	75.9	14.5	1.0	2.3	9.6	6.6	12.8	11.2	13.9	13.5	11.5
51830	47260	1	Williamsburg city	8.9	15,590	2,055	1,751.7	71.4	16.2	1.0	7.3	7.6	3.2	6.5	36.0	11.0	8.2	7.3
51840	49020	3	Winchester city	9.2	28,136	1,491	3,058.3	68.3	12.5	0.6	3.0	18.6	6.1	12.3	14.9	14.0	12.0	11.4
53000		0	WASHINGTON	66,455.1	7,738,692	X	116.4	70.7	5.5	2.4	12.9	13.4	5.6	12.4	12.1	15.2	14.2	12.1
53001	36830	6	Adams	1,925.0	20,621	1,786	10.7	32.9	0.9	0.8	1.1	65.2	9.0	21.0	16.2	12.2	11.0	9.6
53003	30300	3	Asotin	636.1	22,397	1,699	35.2	91.8	1.5	2.7	2.2	4.5	5.2	11.4	10.3	10.9	11.7	11.1
53005	28420	2	Benton	1,700.1	210,025	324	123.5	70.3	2.3	1.6	4.5	24.0	6.4	15.3	12.8	13.6	13.5	11.1
53007	48300	3	Chelan	2,921.2	79,646	719	27.3	68.7	0.9	1.6	1.9	28.7	5.6	13.4	11.7	12.4	12.5	10.8
53009	38820	5	Clallam	1,738.7	78,209	726	45.0	84.6	1.7	6.6	3.6	7.4	4.0	9.7	8.9	10.5	11.0	9.8
53011	38900	1	Clark	628.5	511,404	142	813.7	79.7	3.6	1.8	8.3	11.0	5.6	13.2	12.2	13.7	13.7	12.8
53013		3	Columbia	868.6	4,042	2,883	4.7	85.3	2.1	2.3	4.7	8.5	4.1	10.4	9.5	10.7	10.8	10.1
53015	31020	3	Cowlitz	1,141.2	111,524	556	97.7	85.5	1.8	3.2	3.2	9.9	5.8	12.9	11.2	12.8	12.2	12.0
53017	48300	3	Douglas	1,819.2	43,696	1,104	24.0	63.8	1.1	1.8	2.0	33.4	6.1	14.6	12.6	12.4	12.5	11.4
53019		9	Ferry	2,203.2	7,273	2,641	3.3	76.9	2.1	18.0	2.6	5.3	4.0	9.4	10.1	8.3	10.3	11.8
53021	28420	2	Franklin	1,241.6	98,268	623	79.1	40.8	2.6	1.1	3.1	54.1	8.0	18.2	15.3	14.6	14.2	11.0
53023		8	Garfield	710.8	2,346	3,014	3.3	89.6	1.6	1.3	4.4	5.7	5.1	12.1	9.3	9.2	11.4	11.1
53025	34180	5	Grant	2,679.6	100,297	610	37.4	53.7	1.5	1.7	1.7	43.1	7.2	16.8	14.2	13.7	12.1	10.8
53027	10140	4	Grays Harbor	1,901.5	76,841	737	40.4	81.6	2.1	6.0	3.1	10.9	4.9	11.7	10.3	11.6	12.0	11.5
53029	36020	4	Island	208.5	87,432	671	419.3	81.8	4.2	2.1	7.8	8.7	5.1	10.0	10.8	13.7	11.4	9.4
53031		6	Jefferson	1,803.7	33,605	1,343	18.6	90.6	1.6	3.5	3.2	4.1	2.9	6.7	6.4	8.1	9.7	9.8
53033	42660	1	King	2,115.2	2,252,305	13	1,064.8	60.4	8.4	1.6	24.7	10.3	5.3	11.2	11.1	18.1	15.9	13.0
53035	14740	2	Kitsap	395.1	274,314	256	694.3	80.7	4.4	2.8	9.9	8.5	5.2	11.3	12.3	14.5	13.1	11.1
53037	21260	4	Kittitas	2,297.3	45,499	1,070	19.8	86.0	1.8	2.1	3.7	9.6	4.3	9.7	23.5	12.2	11.0	9.9
53039		6	Klickitat	1,871.6	23,118	1,674	12.4	84.3	1.1	3.2	1.8	12.0	4.6	10.7	9.4	10.5	12.0	12.1
53041	16500	4	Lewis	2,402.8	84,398	682	35.1	84.8	1.6	3.1	2.5	11.4	5.8	12.4	10.7	12.3	12.4	11.4
53043		8	Lincoln	2,310.6	11,232	2,329	4.9	92.6	1.5	3.3	1.7	3.9	5.2	12.4	10.9	8.8	11.0	10.5
53045	43220	4	Mason	959.5	67,615	796	70.5	82.1	2.3	4.9	3.5	11.3	5.1	11.0	10.1	12.1	11.8	11.0
53047		6	Okanogan	5,266.2	42,634	1,134	8.1	66.6	1.3	11.9	1.6	21.3	5.6	13.4	10.5	11.0	11.7	11.1
53049		7	Pacific	933.6	23,948	1,642	25.7	84.6	1.5	4.1	3.0	10.3	3.4	8.7	8.1	9.0	10.4	10.8
53051		2	Pend Oreille	1,400.2	13,886	2,160	9.9	89.6	1.5	5.0	2.1	4.7	4.9	11.3	9.4	9.2	10.2	11.1
53053	42660	1	Pierce	1,668.0	925,708	60	555.0	69.9	10.2	2.7	12.6	12.2	6.1	13.3	12.5	15.5	14.3	11.9
53055		9	San Juan	173.9	18,557	1,895	106.7	89.6	1.3	2.1	2.5	6.8	2.8	7.2	7.4	8.6	10.5	11.2
53057	34580	3	Skagit	1,730.2	130,696	494	75.5	75.3	1.5	2.8	3.6	19.5	5.4	12.2	10.9	12.6	12.6	11.1
53059	38900	1	Skamania	1,658.3	12,170	2,269	7.3	88.8	1.5	3.2	2.4	7.4	3.7	10.5	8.9	10.3	12.3	13.0
53061	42660	1	Snohomish	2,086.5	833,540	76	399.5	70.1	5.1	2.2	16.5	11.2	6.0	12.6	11.0	14.8	15.4	12.9
53063	44060	2	Spokane	1,764.2	546,040	128	309.5	86.8	3.4	2.6	4.8	6.6	5.6	12.5	12.8	15.0	13.3	11.5
53065	44060	2	Stevens	2,477.1	47,426	1,034	19.1	89.0	1.2	6.9	1.9	4.2	4.7	12.5	10.3	9.7	11.0	11.3
53067	36500	2	Thurston	722.5	297,977	236	412.4	77.7	5.2	2.7	10.2	10.1	5.4	12.2	11.3	14.4	14.3	11.9
53069		8	Wahkiakum	262.9	4,582	2,852	17.4	89.7	1.8	3.1	3.1	6.0	3.4	9.3	9.5	8.3	9.2	10.3
53071	47460	3	Walla Walla	1,270.0	62,682	853	49.4	72.4	2.6	1.6	3.3	22.6	5.1	12.1	16.4	12.4	12.1	10.7
53073	13380	3	Whatcom	2,107.9	228,831	304	108.6	81.0	2.1	3.7	7.1	10.3	4.6	10.9	16.5	13.8	12.8	11.1
53075	39420	4	Whitman	2,159.3	47,873	1,027	22.2	81.8	3.4	1.6	10.5	6.8	3.9	8.6	36.5	13.9	9.6	7.6
53077	49420	3	Yakima	4,294.5	256,035	274	59.6	42.4	1.4	4.5	1.9	51.8	7.3	17.1	14.6	13.4	12.1	10.7
54000		0	WEST VIRGINIA	24,041.1	1,782,959	X	74.2	93.3	4.7	0.8	1.2	1.9	5.0	11.5	12.2	11.9	12.0	12.6
54001		6	Barbour	341.1	15,468	2,062	45.3	96.6	2.0	1.6	0.5	1.1	5.1	11.2	14.5	11.1	10.8	12.8
54003	25180	2	Berkeley	321.1	126,069	510	392.6	85.4	10.0	0.8	1.9	5.4	6.0	13.0	11.4	14.4	13.6	13.1
54005	16620	3	Boone	501.5	21,312	1,746	42.5	98.2	1.3	0.5	0.3	0.7	4.8	11.7	11.4	10.1	11.6	14.4
54007		8	Braxton	510.7	12,247	2,265	24.0	97.2	1.3	1.1	0.5	1.1	4.2	11.2	9.9	11.7	11.0	13.1
54009	48260	3	Brooke	89.2	22,140	1,706	248.2	96.6	2.3	0.7	0.8	1.2	4.3	9.8	12.3	10.7	10.5	12.5
54011	26580	2	Cabell	281.0	93,418	646	332.4	92.2	6.4	0.8	1.7	1.5	5.3	11.2	16.8	12.3	11.8	11.5

1. CBSA = Core Based Statistical Area. See Appendix A for explanation. See Appendix B for list of metropolitan areas with component counties. 2. County type code from the Economic Research Service of USDA Rural-Urban Continuum Codes. See Appendix A for definition. 3. Dry land or land partially or temporarily covered by water. 4. May be of any race.

STATE County	Population, 2021 (cont.)				Population change, 2000–2021							Households, 2016–2020				
	Age (percent) (cont.)				Total persons		Percent change		Components of change, 2020–2021					Percent		
	55 to 64 years	65 to 74 years	75 years and over	Percent female	2010	2020	2010–2020	2020–2021	Births	Deaths	Net Migration	Number	Persons per household	Family house-holds	Female family house-holder[1]	One person
	16	17	18	19	20	21	22	23	24	25	26	27	28	29	30	31
VIRGINIA—Cont'd																
Martinsville city	14.0	10.5	6.5	53.3	13,821	13,485	-2.4	0.2	309	369	91	5,597	2.2	58.4	21.2	35.5
Newport News city	12.0	8.3	5.4	51.8	180,719	186,247	3.1	-0.9	3,295	2,373	-2,581	70,376	2.4	60.5	17.8	32.9
Norfolk city	10.6	7.6	4.3	47.9	242,803	238,005	-2.0	-1.2	3,999	3,042	-3,856	89,398	2.4	57.1	17.7	33.3
Norton city	12.9	10.7	7.7	52.5	3,958	3,687	-6.8	-0.6	54	63	-13	1,877	2.1	50.7	10.5	40.1
Petersburg city	13.8	10.4	6.7	54.3	32,420	33,458	3.2	-0.1	829	708	-154	13,231	2.3	47.2	21.0	46.6
Poquoson city	13.9	10.7	8.3	49.8	12,150	12,460	2.6	0.9	116	176	176	4,632	2.6	77.6	6.7	19.5
Portsmouth city	12.3	9.3	5.9	52.1	95,535	97,915	2.5	-0.1	1,760	1,459	-391	36,650	2.5	59.8	20.2	32.7
Radford city	8.7	6.3	3.4	53.0	16,408	16,070	-2.1	2.7	152	155	435	5,677	2.6	41.6	9.6	38.4
Richmond city	12.0	9.1	5.0	52.7	204,214	226,610	11.0	0.0	3,704	3,183	-538	91,005	2.4	44.2	14.5	43.1
Roanoke city	12.8	10.8	6.4	52.5	97,032	100,011	3.1	-1.1	1,765	1,732	-1,170	41,694	2.3	52.5	15.9	38.6
Salem city	13.7	11.4	8.1	52.4	24,802	25,346	2.2	0.1	342	483	166	9,876	2.3	62.7	12.5	29.6
Staunton city	13.1	12.2	8.8	53.7	23,746	25,750	8.4	-0.3	445	492	-41	10,638	2.2	58.2	15.2	36.6
Suffolk city	13.8	9.2	5.9	51.6	84,585	94,324	11.5	2.0	1,360	1,249	1,757	34,603	2.6	71.6	14.3	24.3
Virginia Beach city	12.5	9.2	6.0	51.0	437,994	459,470	4.9	-0.4	6,477	5,098	-3,234	172,452	2.6	68.8	12.9	24.0
Waynesboro city	13.0	10.2	7.4	52.3	21,006	22,196	5.7	1.6	413	392	334	9,169	2.4	53.7	12.7	39.2
Williamsburg city	10.3	9.7	7.8	54.1	14,068	15,425	9.6	1.1	95	201	270	4,485	2.4	50.0	12.6	40.6
Winchester city	12.5	10.0	6.7	50.8	26,203	28,120	7.3	0.1	432	362	-61	10,669	2.5	57.4	14.5	35.6
WASHINGTON	12.3	10.1	6.1	49.9	6,724,540	7,705,281	14.6	0.4	102,270	88,479	19,195	2,905,822	2.5	64.5	9.7	26.7
Adams	9.5	7.3	4.4	49.0	18,728	20,613	10.1	0.0	436	170	-261	6,035	3.2	76.2	16.5	19.1
Asotin	15.0	14.2	10.2	50.9	21,623	22,285	3.1	0.5	270	413	257	9,286	2.4	61.4	9.1	28.1
Benton	11.8	9.6	5.9	49.6	175,177	206,873	18.1	1.5	3,051	2,448	2,538	73,073	2.7	69.1	11.6	24.9
Chelan	13.4	12.4	7.8	49.5	72,453	79,074	9.1	0.7	1,017	1,009	563	29,383	2.6	66.9	10.1	27.6
Clallam	15.1	18.8	12.2	50.4	71,404	77,155	8.1	1.4	721	1,515	1,881	33,197	2.3	61.9	11.1	32.2
Clark	12.6	10.4	6.0	50.3	425,363	503,311	18.3	1.6	6,706	5,892	7,241	178,478	2.7	69.2	10.0	23.0
Columbia	15.7	16.4	12.2	50.6	4,078	3,952	-3.1	2.3	43	63	112	1,795	2.2	66.6	5.6	29.1
Cowlitz	13.7	11.9	7.6	50.0	102,410	110,730	8.1	0.7	1,518	1,768	1,038	42,354	2.5	66.1	11.7	28.1
Douglas	12.3	10.9	7.2	49.0	38,431	42,938	11.7	1.8	600	494	654	15,435	2.7	73.2	11.0	20.6
Ferry	16.2	20.0	9.9	49.0	7,551	7,178	-4.9	1.3	83	129	144	3,175	2.3	60.9	9.8	32.7
Franklin	8.7	6.5	3.4	48.3	78,163	96,749	23.8	1.6	1,842	738	382	27,263	3.4	77.7	14.8	18.2
Garfield	14.7	16.1	11.0	50.9	2,266	2,286	0.9	2.6	25	31	68	986	2.3	68.7	2.3	28.8
Grant	11.0	8.8	5.4	48.8	89,120	99,123	11.2	1.2	1,688	1,112	575	31,908	3.0	72.4	13.9	22.3
Grays Harbor	15.0	14.8	8.2	48.7	72,797	75,636	3.9	1.6	862	1,344	1,702	29,433	2.4	64.0	10.1	28.7
Island	13.7	16.0	10.0	49.7	78,506	86,857	10.6	0.7	993	1,142	742	35,326	2.3	68.4	7.4	24.5
Jefferson	17.2	24.5	14.6	50.9	29,872	32,977	10.4	1.9	200	581	1,031	15,051	2.1	61.2	7.0	29.3
King	11.5	8.4	5.3	49.3	1,931,249	2,269,675	17.5	-0.8	29,014	20,506	-25,890	900,061	2.4	59.4	8.1	29.9
Kitsap	13.4	12.0	7.2	48.7	251,133	275,611	9.7	-0.5	3,478	3,494	-1,290	105,758	2.5	67.5	9.5	24.4
Kittitas	12.4	10.7	6.3	49.5	40,915	44,337	8.4	2.6	477	492	1,181	19,162	2.3	56.1	6.9	25.8
Klickitat	15.5	16.1	9.1	49.0	20,318	22,735	11.9	1.7	243	323	469	9,268	2.4	60.8	6.8	29.6
Lewis	14.0	13.0	8.1	49.6	75,455	82,149	8.9	2.7	1,121	1,384	2,544	31,118	2.5	66.7	10.2	26.3
Lincoln	15.4	15.6	10.3	48.9	10,570	10,876	2.9	3.3	125	188	427	4,628	2.3	69.5	5.6	26.5
Mason	15.1	15.2	8.5	48.0	60,699	65,726	8.3	2.9	823	1,031	2,122	25,242	2.5	64.9	8.9	26.2
Okanogan	13.8	14.5	8.3	49.3	41,120	42,104	2.4	1.3	536	695	696	17,884	2.3	68.0	13.2	26.1
Pacific	16.5	21.1	11.9	50.2	20,920	23,365	11.7	2.5	200	478	875	9,714	2.3	62.3	7.6	31.2
Pend Oreille	17.3	17.6	9.1	48.7	13,001	13,401	3.1	3.6	140	251	607	5,798	2.3	69.8	9.6	24.2
Pierce	12.1	9.0	5.4	49.8	795,225	921,130	15.8	0.5	13,474	10,707	1,597	330,999	2.6	67.1	11.3	25.1
San Juan	17.2	21.9	13.2	50.9	15,769	17,788	12.8	4.3	124	212	875	8,459	2.0	61.5	6.9	30.4
Skagit	13.3	13.3	8.5	50.2	116,901	129,523	10.8	0.9	1,681	1,894	1,387	49,263	2.6	67.5	9.2	25.3
Skamania	17.1	15.9	8.3	49.0	11,066	12,036	8.8	1.1	99	150	189	4,866	2.4	71.6	9.4	19.9
Snohomish	13.0	9.2	5.1	49.5	713,335	827,957	16.1	0.7	11,533	8,931	2,795	298,815	2.7	69.1	9.8	22.7
Spokane	12.6	10.6	6.2	50.1	471,221	539,339	14.5	1.2	7,026	7,254	6,898	206,502	2.4	62.6	10.5	28.9
Stevens	15.8	15.9	8.8	49.7	43,531	46,445	6.7	2.1	492	765	1,276	17,883	2.5	68.5	9.4	25.3
Thurston	12.4	11.4	6.7	50.7	252,264	294,793	16.9	1.1	3,662	3,547	3,041	112,323	2.5	65.8	10.2	25.8
Wahkiakum	17.2	20.3	12.5	49.2	3,978	4,422	11.2	3.6	34	66	194	1,900	2.3	70.7	3.7	22.2
Walla Walla	12.1	11.2	7.9	48.8	58,781	62,584	6.5	0.2	709	883	264	22,773	2.5	65.0	10.0	27.1
Whatcom	11.9	11.5	6.9	50.4	201,140	226,847	12.8	0.9	2,445	2,599	2,120	88,978	2.5	60.4	7.9	27.0
Whitman	8.6	6.8	4.3	49.1	44,776	47,973	7.1	-0.2	444	395	-161	18,485	2.3	46.7	5.2	33.0
Yakima	10.7	8.5	5.6	49.9	243,231	256,728	5.5	-0.3	4,335	3,385	-1,688	83,765	3.0	72.0	14.5	22.7
WEST VIRGINIA	14.0	12.7	8.0	50.1	1,852,994	1,793,716	-3.2	-0.6	21,615	34,097	1,704	734,235	2.4	64.1	10.8	30.2
Barbour	13.7	12.5	8.2	50.6	16,589	15,465	-6.8	0.0	214	304	92	6,484	2.5	62.4	11.7	30.2
Berkeley	13.4	9.9	5.3	49.9	104,169	122,076	17.2	3.3	1,772	1,652	3,904	45,702	2.6	65.7	10.6	26.9
Boone	14.3	14.1	7.5	49.8	24,629	21,809	-11.4	-2.3	246	464	-276	8,691	2.5	70.0	10.9	24.2
Braxton	15.0	14.6	9.4	49.0	14,523	12,447	-14.3	-1.6	130	272	-57	5,341	2.6	71.3	12.9	24.7
Brooke	15.3	14.9	9.7	50.3	24,069	22,559	-6.3	-1.9	209	484	-143	9,792	2.2	60.2	11.7	35.0
Cabell	11.9	11.3	7.9	50.9	96,319	94,350	-2.0	-1.0	1,236	1,813	-364	39,296	2.3	55.4	11.6	35.9

1. No spouse present.

STATE County	Persons in group quarters, 2021	Daytime Population, 2016–2020		Births, 2021		Deaths, 2021		Persons under 65 with no health insurance, 2019		Medicare, 2021			COVID-19 Deaths, 2020	
		Number	Employment/ residence ratio	Total	Rate[1]	Number	Rate[1]	Number	Percent	Total beneficiaries	Enrolled in Original Medicare	Enrolled in Medicare Advantage	Number	Rate[1]
	32	33	34	35	36	37	38	39	40	41	42	43	44	45
VIRGINIA—Cont'd														
Martinsville city	376	16,393	1.8	253	18.8	262	19.5	829	8.4	3,831	2,489	1,342	33	2.5
Newport News city	8,125	205,540	1.3	2,630	14.2	1,888	10.2	13,869	9.5	29,296	20,007	9,289	98	0.5
Norfolk city	32,813	303,645	1.5	3,241	13.7	2,440	10.3	18,670	10.4	33,922	22,972	10,949	134	0.6
Norton city	31	3,980	1.0	45	12.3	49	13.3	262	8.2	1,138	613	525	D	D
Petersburg city	893	31,042	1.0	660	19.7	570	17.1	2,671	10.6	7,227	4,640	2,587	41	1.2
Poquoson city	37	8,696	0.5	97	7.8	139	11.1	569	5.7	2,657	2,260	398	D	D
Portsmouth city	2,987	103,483	1.2	1,414	14.4	1,203	12.3	6,725	8.8	18,665	12,667	5,999	99	1.0
Radford city	3,000	18,034	1.0	123	7.5	116	7.1	979	7.5	2,082	1,578	504	D	D
Richmond city	11,976	289,474	1.5	2,999	13.2	2,544	11.2	21,931	11.8	34,931	21,378	13,553	148	0.7
Roanoke city	1,986	122,103	1.5	1,425	14.3	1,391	14.0	8,929	11.1	21,433	13,816	7,617	123	1.2
Salem city	1,942	34,802	1.8	264	10.4	377	14.9	1,359	7.3	6,133	4,574	1,559	27	1.1
Staunton city	969	24,242	1.0	350	13.6	388	15.1	1,764	9.3	6,359	5,119	1,241	40	1.6
Suffolk city	899	84,583	0.9	1,096	11.5	995	10.4	6,093	7.9	17,297	12,716	4,581	92	1.0
Virginia Beach city	9,530	424,393	0.9	5,156	11.2	4,164	9.1	30,531	8.2	75,781	59,048	16,732	180	0.4
Waynesboro city	119	21,931	1.0	323	14.4	327	14.6	1,861	10.1	5,073	4,047	1,025	16	0.7
Williamsburg city	4,333	22,696	2.2	78	5.0	146	9.4	648	8.0	2,869	2,312	557	D	D
Winchester city	1,051	40,173	1.9	345	12.3	294	10.5	2,843	12.7	5,618	4,612	1,006	25	0.9
WASHINGTON	143,604	7,470,968	1.0	81,193	10.5	70,836	9.2	487,573	7.7	1,398,290	888,216	510,074	3,652	0.5
Adams	149	20,269	1.1	352	17.1	142	6.9	2,241	13.1	2,593	2,140	453	18	0.9
Asotin	112	20,215	0.7	223	10.0	325	14.5	1,253	7.4	6,428	5,443	985	26	1.2
Benton	1,285	201,390	1.0	2,447	11.7	1,926	9.2	14,210	8.3	36,807	34,143	2,665	168	0.8
Chelan	881	80,667	1.1	815	10.3	817	10.3	7,203	11.8	17,951	13,271	4,680	47	0.6
Clallam	1,668	75,117	1.0	575	7.4	1,227	15.8	5,052	9.7	27,438	25,596	1,842	D	D
Clark	3,319	436,331	0.8	5,332	10.5	4,708	9.3	29,670	7.3	92,294	36,689	55,606	144	0.3
Columbia	49	4,006	1.0	33	8.3	43	10.8	186	6.6	1,316	1,236	80	D	D
Cowlitz	1,073	106,716	1.0	1,186	10.7	1,388	12.5	6,458	7.4	26,672	12,182	14,490	28	0.3
Douglas	136	36,629	0.7	469	10.8	396	9.1	4,053	11.6	8,257	6,254	2,003	13	0.3
Ferry	194	7,543	1.0	68	9.4	91	12.6	617	11.5	2,437	2,357	80	D	D
Franklin	2,733	88,166	0.9	1,481	15.2	578	5.9	10,977	13.4	11,009	10,028	981	78	0.8
Garfield	29	2,030	0.8	18	7.8	24	10.3	96	5.8	729	709	20	D	D
Grant	1,124	98,344	1.0	1,329	13.3	885	8.9	10,953	13.4	16,505	13,261	3,244	92	0.9
Grays Harbor	2,613	71,623	0.9	694	9.1	1,077	14.1	5,377	9.7	20,827	19,232	1,595	30	0.4
Island	1,933	75,400	0.8	791	9.1	905	10.4	4,089	6.6	24,248	17,138	7,110	34	0.4
Jefferson	596	31,104	0.9	164	4.9	473	14.2	1,664	8.6	13,641	12,865	776	D	D
King	39,336	2,428,688	1.2	23,082	10.2	16,444	7.3	121,875	6.3	324,580	187,877	136,703	1,093	0.5
Kitsap	9,379	260,292	0.9	2,755	10.0	2,832	10.3	13,724	6.4	57,694	41,720	15,974	50	0.2
Kittitas	2,423	44,380	0.9	381	8.5	402	8.9	3,225	8.7	9,166	8,303	863	29	0.7
Klickitat	174	21,695	1.0	196	8.5	256	11.2	1,820	10.9	6,361	6,144	216	D	D
Lewis	821	76,048	0.9	900	10.8	1,107	13.3	5,884	9.5	21,445	13,070	8,374	32	0.4
Lincoln	68	10,247	0.9	95	8.6	160	14.4	581	7.3	3,243	3,122	120	D	D
Mason	2,335	56,934	0.7	644	9.6	832	12.5	5,117	10.6	18,112	13,302	4,810	17	0.3
Okanogan	504	42,596	1.0	422	10.0	555	13.1	4,665	14.6	11,151	9,600	1,551	38	0.9
Pacific	261	21,479	0.9	167	7.0	399	16.8	1,604	10.8	8,483	8,046	437	D	D
Pend Oreille	61	12,591	0.8	123	9.0	201	14.7	893	9.1	4,288	4,069	219	D	D
Pierce	20,421	830,921	0.9	10,690	11.6	8,582	9.3	57,627	7.6	155,500	96,843	58,657	353	0.4
San Juan	126	16,921	1.0	96	5.3	174	9.6	1,196	10.6	6,169	5,159	1,010	D	D
Skagit	1,451	128,661	1.0	1,340	10.3	1,555	11.9	9,725	9.7	32,171	21,257	10,914	47	0.4
Skamania	18	9,577	0.6	80	6.6	126	10.4	691	7.4	2,745	2,488	256	D	D
Snohomish	9,863	723,975	0.8	9,152	11.0	7,163	8.6	50,923	7.2	131,515	66,801	64,714	408	0.5
Spokane	14,355	524,331	1.1	5,509	10.1	5,802	10.7	29,350	7.0	108,154	60,411	47,743	352	0.7
Stevens	214	40,895	0.7	372	7.9	606	12.9	3,092	9.0	13,251	10,925	2,326	23	0.5
Thurston	3,898	272,194	0.9	2,904	9.8	2,818	9.5	16,174	6.9	62,181	37,557	24,625	63	0.2
Wahkiakum	14	3,950	0.7	28	6.2	55	12.2	245	8.3	1,612	1,137	475	D	D
Walla Walla	4,669	64,198	1.1	576	9.2	700	11.2	4,303	9.6	13,674	11,430	2,244	43	0.7
Whatcom	5,529	220,756	1.0	1,934	8.5	2,098	9.2	16,675	9.1	48,015	28,643	19,371	65	0.3
Whitman	6,435	52,402	1.1	329	6.9	317	6.6	2,609	6.9	6,157	5,863	294	26	0.5
Yakima	3,355	251,687	1.0	3,441	13.4	2,647	10.3	31,476	15.1	43,471	31,902	11,570	335	1.3
WEST VIRGINIA	43,973	1,787,992	1.0	17,232	9.6	27,102	15.2	112,089	8.1	442,600	275,087	167,513	1,536	0.9
Barbour	719	13,635	0.6	173	11.2	230	14.9	1,111	9.1	4,086	2,688	1,399	13	0.8
Berkeley	830	98,892	0.7	1,412	11.4	1,313	10.6	8,050	8.0	22,460	16,142	6,319	68	0.6
Boone	119	20,783	0.8	195	9.1	360	16.7	1,362	8.1	5,993	2,924	3,069	19	0.9
Braxton	273	13,332	0.9	107	8.7	217	17.6	978	9.6	3,625	2,097	1,528	D	D
Brooke	669	21,789	1.0	159	7.1	373	16.7	1,114	7.0	6,170	3,626	2,543	43	1.9
Cabell	3,826	108,289	1.4	994	10.6	1,412	15.1	5,855	8.3	21,206	12,752	8,454	104	1.1

1. Per 1,000 estimated resident population.

STATE County	COVID-19 Vaccinations, 2021–2022: Number	COVID-19 Vaccinations, 2021–2022: Percent[5]	Education: School enrollment and attainment, 2016–2020: Enrollment[1]: Total	Enrollment[1]: Percent private	Attainment[2] (percent): High school graduate or less	Attainment[2] (percent): Bachelor's degree or more	Local government expenditures,[3] 2018–2019: Total current spending (mil dol)	Local government expenditures,[3] 2018–2019: Current spending per student (dollars)	Money income, 2016–2020: Per capita income[4]	Households: Median income (dollars)	Households: Percent with income of less than $50,000	Households: Percent with income of $200,000 or more	Income and poverty, 2020: Median household income (dollars)	Percent below poverty level: All persons	Percent below poverty level: Children under 18 years	Percent below poverty level: Children 5 to 17 years in families
	46	47	48	49	50	51	52	53	54	55	56	57	58	59	60	61
VIRGINIA—Cont'd																
Martinsville city	4,932	39.3	2,740	15.1	43.9	21.7	26.1	13,456	22,855	36,166	65.5	3.2	35,715	21.3	31.2	27.8
Newport News city	93,427	52.1	48,258	13.5	36.6	28.0	335.4	11,707	33,670	54,511	45.5	3.0	60,048	14.5	20.2	19.6
Norfolk city	172,729	71.2	62,094	13.7	36.7	30.0	366.8	12,193	30,706	53,026	46.9	4.1	51,401	17.6	27.2	26.4
Norton city	1,243	31.2	809	5.4	47.9	20.2	7.7	9,163	24,808	30,518	66.4	2.8	36,004	20.5	29.4	28.0
Petersburg city	10,965	35.0	6,509	10.4	51.6	20.3	52.5	12,524	24,789	43,029	60.1	1.2	43,190	20.8	36.4	39.8
Poquoson city	5,358	43.7	3,061	12.8	27.4	42.9	23.7	11,192	42,260	100,696	22.6	12.0	99,310	4.7	5.6	4.8
Portsmouth city	47,368	50.2	22,148	15.2	41.3	20.8	166.5	11,888	27,276	53,213	47.4	2.6	52,070	15.3	24.4	23.6
Radford city	6,369	34.9	8,939	8.6	30.2	40.7	17.6	10,685	22,637	34,576	60.7	2.6	42,938	24.6	14.2	12.7
Richmond city	97,975	42.5	56,461	19.5	34.4	41.2	361.2	14,521	35,682	51,421	49.0	6.7	54,815	17.9	27.3	23.3
Roanoke city	40,727	41.1	20,530	13.7	47.6	24.8	187.8	13,661	29,585	45,664	54.5	4.0	49,313	15.9	20.8	22.4
Salem city	11,811	46.7	6,743	32.0	36.8	30.3	43.4	10,960	34,039	63,411	38.0	5.7	70,349	9.0	11.4	10.8
Staunton city	11,647	46.7	5,005	30.8	39.7	31.1	35.5	12,660	30,746	52,292	47.4	3.5	51,230	12.3	16.4	17.2
Suffolk city	49,339	53.6	23,269	21.0	35.7	29.6	157.1	11,010	38,613	79,899	31.4	7.8	72,264	9.0	13.7	12.7
Virginia Beach city	282,607	62.8	112,979	18.8	26.7	37.3	815.1	11,878	39,788	78,136	28.8	8.3	73,961	8.1	12.4	11.3
Waynesboro city	9,751	43.1	4,940	16.3	46.2	28.9	36.5	12,022	28,287	43,480	56.0	3.0	53,635	11.3	18.9	17.9
Williamsburg city	5,945	39.8	7,167	5.8	26.3	50.6	145.3	12,457	32,878	59,288	40.8	10.6	60,655	16.8	20.0	19.1
Winchester city	12,021	42.8	7,462	27.6	38.6	34.3	232.4	12,921	31,719	61,102	41.7	7.3	58,295	13.2	18.8	17.8
WASHINGTON	5,523,081	72.5	1,753,707	15.4	30.1	36.7	16,026.5	14,255	40,837	77,006	31.7	10.5	80,319	9.5	11.0	10.1
Adams	12,050	60.3	5,695	5.1	62.8	13.8	71.4	13,708	20,592	51,601	47.9	2.8	56,421	12.7	17.0	15.4
Asotin	9,401	41.6	4,234	7.9	36.5	23.4	45.3	13,543	30,397	53,941	47.0	4.0	53,377	14.1	18.5	16.2
Benton	115,960	56.7	52,527	12.7	32.6	31.6	498.9	12,903	34,287	72,046	32.9	7.6	75,882	9.1	11.5	10.3
Chelan	54,526	70.6	17,835	11.2	41.8	26.4	195.6	14,655	32,249	61,304	41.0	4.7	61,546	8.3	11.6	10.8
Clallam	52,970	68.5	12,402	13.7	33.9	28.8	146.0	13,576	31,601	55,090	45.6	3.8	54,712	13.3	18.9	17.2
Clark	316,636	64.9	115,278	12.3	31.4	31.3	1,118.4	13,998	37,009	77,184	30.0	8.0	76,929	8.7	10.0	9.0
Columbia	1,842	46.2	671	11.3	31.1	25.3	7.0	16,249	38,606	61,779	36.3	6.0	58,220	12.6	18.3	17.0
Cowlitz	65,293	59.0	24,287	12.5	40.5	17.0	235.4	13,414	30,170	58,791	43.4	4.1	64,357	11.9	14.8	13.8
Douglas	26,848	61.8	10,369	5.6	46.6	20.6	112.5	13,140	32,709	65,730	35.3	6.1	64,768	10.5	14.2	13.1
Ferry	4,305	56.4	1,179	11.3	45.2	21.2	17.0	18,655	26,983	41,685	57.1	3.7	47,722	18.4	28.0	27.1
Franklin	50,459	53.0	27,551	7.6	48.6	18.9	294.0	14,145	25,875	66,904	35.2	5.7	73,656	12.4	15.8	14.3
Garfield	872	39.2	484	7.2	32.1	25.7	5.2	13,717	28,933	56,923	45.0	1.7	56,804	11.4	15.7	14.7
Grant	56,023	57.3	25,964	7.9	48.5	18.0	286.2	13,852	25,333	59,165	42.0	3.7	54,753	13.6	18.6	16.4
Grays Harbor	45,921	61.2	14,009	7.5	45.6	16.1	161.1	14,785	27,277	50,665	49.3	2.3	54,034	15.1	19.2	16.8
Island	65,122	76.5	15,503	19.1	26.4	34.1	119.2	14,231	38,769	70,765	32.9	6.2	76,965	6.5	8.3	7.8
Jefferson	24,747	76.8	4,063	19.3	24.9	42.5	41.6	15,431	38,176	57,693	41.3	5.8	66,386	10.6	16.6	15.4
King	1,826,619	81.1	507,240	19.3	21.4	53.4	4,096.3	14,756	55,374	99,158	24.5	18.9	102,620	7.6	8.0	7.6
Kitsap	190,354	70.1	57,113	13.9	26.4	34.4	549.7	15,124	39,993	78,969	29.2	8.7	76,814	8.3	9.9	9.0
Kittitas	25,886	54.0	14,912	5.4	33.0	34.1	73.7	13,895	32,120	59,703	42.9	5.3	64,727	12.9	11.1	10.2
Klickitat	10,671	47.6	4,027	24.0	37.0	30.5	45.8	14,462	31,021	56,667	44.8	4.2	57,476	14.0	17.2	16.4
Lewis	41,546	51.5	17,136	12.6	40.3	19.1	171.5	13,882	27,941	54,970	45.9	2.6	54,578	13.3	16.1	15.3
Lincoln	6,344	58.0	2,009	9.4	34.2	25.4	35.4	16,400	31,711	58,584	42.7	3.0	61,332	11.4	14.6	14.2
Mason	40,869	61.2	12,203	10.6	41.7	18.1	139.9	13,860	30,112	60,565	40.2	3.1	63,785	12.6	17.7	15.5
Okanogan	28,580	67.7	8,986	10.9	45.1	20.2	133.5	12,752	25,216	48,528	52.0	2.3	48,979	19.8	31.1	28.1
Pacific	13,395	59.6	3,695	8.9	40.2	20.3	47.4	14,804	28,339	50,873	48.6	1.9	53,319	13.6	17.6	17.9
Pend Oreille	5,609	40.9	2,326	13.7	41.8	21.1	24.8	14,475	30,326	55,021	45.1	3.8	57,212	14.7	23.5	22.2
Pierce	594,796	65.7	210,911	16.0	34.7	27.7	1,915.7	13,755	36,548	76,438	30.8	7.4	80,236	8.7	9.0	8.3
San Juan	14,370	81.7	2,253	20.6	19.3	51.7	29.0	15,590	49,148	64,753	38.6	9.0	74,533	9.6	11.0	10.4
Skagit	86,996	67.3	27,309	14.9	35.0	27.4	314.0	16,000	35,172	71,021	34.0	6.4	78,798	9.5	12.0	10.5
Skamania	4,681	38.7	2,170	5.5	38.4	26.0	16.1	14,079	34,759	69,296	36.2	6.5	68,501	10.6	14.2	12.7
Snohomish	582,155	70.8	186,148	15.3	31.1	32.8	1,955.1	14,323	41,126	89,273	24.5	11.2	93,589	7.1	8.0	6.9
Spokane	321,372	61.5	124,533	18.5	28.8	31.6	1,089.4	14,531	32,766	60,101	41.8	5.5	60,827	13.4	15.2	13.4
Stevens	17,971	39.3	8,883	13.4	42.6	20.5	89.2	15,187	28,030	54,426	46.4	3.9	50,958	15.0	20.4	18.3
Thurston	201,668	69.4	64,435	15.0	27.9	35.7	602.2	14,239	36,256	75,867	31.9	6.3	79,769	9.7	9.9	9.5
Wahkiakum	2,201	49.0	620	27.6	35.7	20.3	6.3	12,198	28,821	54,524	41.5	3.1	62,099	10.7	18.1	16.5
Walla Walla	38,664	63.6	16,268	27.7	32.9	28.6	121.5	13,429	30,306	60,615	42.3	4.6	61,281	12.9	14.9	13.5
Whatcom	164,874	71.9	56,513	12.4	29.5	35.3	383.9	13,666	33,241	65,420	37.5	5.1	70,463	11.7	10.9	9.7
Whitman	23,466	46.8	23,877	3.5	20.3	48.2	72.1	14,510	24,396	42,288	56.0	3.9	52,066	15.7	11.0	10.0
Yakima	157,047	62.6	68,089	9.1	52.9	17.6	759.3	13,744	24,305	54,917	45.0	3.6	56,353	14.8	19.1	17.6
WEST VIRGINIA	1,031,147	57.5	378,326	10.8	52.4	21.3	3,232.8	12,064	27,346	48,037	51.6	3.1	49,202	15.8	20.3	19.0
Barbour	8,157	49.6	3,191	15.5	63.3	13.9	24.2	10,309	22,440	38,906	61.2	1.2	43,773	20.8	26.5	25.2
Berkeley	65,511	55.0	26,577	10.6	47.1	22.8	219.0	11,212	31,415	65,286	36.2	4.0	67,163	10.0	13.7	11.7
Boone	10,234	47.7	4,606	10.6	63.2	11.6	46.7	12,161	23,078	45,297	52.8	0.9	49,076	17.8	23.4	21.4
Braxton	6,276	45.0	2,423	6.5	65.3	14.0	22.5	11,156	22,409	43,819	56.2	1.8	47,959	17.8	23.0	21.1
Brooke	11,042	50.3	4,892	27.5	49.1	20.2	37.8	13,326	26,694	48,168	52.3	1.1	50,381	11.9	16.8	16.3
Cabell	55,590	60.5	23,265	7.7	44.4	27.1	151.4	12,094	26,118	41,472	57.2	3.3	44,161	19.9	21.0	20.3

1. All persons 3 years old and over enrolled in nursery school through college. 2. Persons 25 years old and over. 3. Elementary and secondary education expenditures. 4. Based on population estimated by the American Community Survey, 2016–2020. 5. CDC percent based on 2019 population estimate. 7. Williamsburg city is included with James City county. 8. Winchester city is included with Frederick county.

Table B. States and Counties — **Personal Income**

STATE County	Personal income, 2020										Earnings, 2020		
			Per capita[1]			Supplements to wages and salaries, employer contributions (mil dol)						Contributions for government social insurance (mil dol)	
	Total (mil dol)	Percent change 2019–2020	Dollars	Rank	Wages and salaries (mil dol)	Pension and insurance	Government social insurance	Proprietors' income (mil dol)	Dividends, interest, and rent (mil dol)	Personal transfer reecipts (mil dol)	Total (mil dol)	From employee and self-employed	From employer
	62	63	64	65	66	67	68	69	70	71	72	73	74
VIRGINIA—Cont'd													
Martinsville city	(2)	(2)	(2)	(2)	(2)	(2)	(2)	(2)	(2)	(2)	(2)	(2)	(2)
Newport News city	8,198	9.8	45,781	1,686	6,715	1,259	516	287	1,247	2,274	8,777	510	516
Norfolk city	10,439	8.6	42,996	2,063	10,476	2,240	816	143	2,016	2,893	13,675	761	816
Norton city	(3)	(3)	(3)	(3)	(3)	(3)	(3)	(3)	(3)	(3)	(3)	(3)	(3)
Petersburg city	(4)	(4)	(4)	(4)	(4)	(4)	(4)	(4)	(4)	(4)	(4)	(4)	(4)
Poquoson city	(5)	(5)	(5)	(5)	(5)	(5)	(5)	(5)	(5)	(5)	(5)	(5)	(5)
Portsmouth city	4,267	10.6	44,871	1,814	3,180	879	260	172	624	1,367	4,491	250	260
Radford city	(6)	(6)	(6)	(6)	(6)	(6)	(6)	(6)	(6)	(6)	(6)	(6)	(6)
Richmond city	13,736	7.7	59,148	474	11,485	1,785	787	1,184	3,188	2,991	15,240	912	787
Roanoke city	4,629	9.8	46,727	1,547	3,674	558	276	252	828	1,473	4,760	304	276
Salem city	(7)	(7)	(7)	(7)	(7)	(7)	(7)	(7)	(7)	(7)	(7)	(7)	(7)
Staunton city	(8)	(8)	(8)	(8)	(8)	(8)	(8)	(8)	(8)	(8)	(8)	(8)	(8)
Suffolk city	5,218	8.7	55,561	670	1,969	304	145	160	837	1,190	2,577	171	145
Virginia Beach city	27,433	5.8	60,796	392	10,626	1,903	802	1,448	5,756	5,113	14,779	908	802
Waynesboro city	(8)	(8)	(8)	(8)	(8)	(8)	(8)	(8)	(8)	(8)	(8)	(8)	(8)
Williamsburg city	(9)	(9)	(9)	(9)	(9)	(9)	(9)	(9)	(9)	(9)	(9)	(9)	(9)
Winchester city	(10)	(10)	(10)	(10)	(10)	(10)	(10)	(10)	(10)	(10)	(10)	(10)	(10)
WASHINGTON	516,441	7.6	66,907	X	264,145	36,185	20,375	39,554	99,518	93,183	360,258	21,070	20,375
Adams	994	18.6	49,618	1,184	347	64	35	199	166	253	645	28	35
Asotin	1,124	7.4	49,273	1,222	304	57	27	87	205	361	474	36	27
Benton	10,684	8.4	51,757	959	5,644	805	492	895	1,555	2,442	7,836	454	492
Chelan	4,695	9.7	60,518	404	1,986	356	189	592	991	1,162	3,123	179	189
Clallam	3,881	7.7	49,718	1,171	1,146	248	103	224	935	1,357	1,722	137	103
Clark	28,750	7.0	57,863	521	10,121	1,608	856	1,725	5,408	5,670	14,311	904	856
Columbia	232	4.2	57,249	557	75	17	7	46	37	74	145	8	7
Cowlitz	5,372	7.8	48,232	1,356	2,298	375	202	338	707	1,678	3,213	216	202
Douglas	1,974	11.8	45,305	1,752	533	101	53	163	347	521	851	50	53
Ferry	310	12.6	39,899	2,466	80	22	7	19	56	127	128	10	7
Franklin	4,201	12.5	43,271	2,031	1,684	307	169	569	490	999	2,729	135	169
Garfield	133	16.1	57,967	512	37	11	3	32	17	40	83	4	3
Grant	4,817	22.3	48,468	1,327	2,048	374	201	827	632	1,231	3,450	161	201
Grays Harbor	3,320	9.7	43,710	1,985	1,099	219	99	192	482	1,297	1,609	117	99
Island	5,092	6.7	59,200	470	1,414	375	134	316	1,304	1,227	2,238	141	134
Jefferson	1,850	6.4	56,585	602	434	95	38	149	590	595	716	60	38
King	219,806	6.2	96,647	24	147,896	15,434	10,129	16,820	49,019	23,828	190,278	10,848	10,129
Kitsap	16,559	6.3	60,704	396	5,979	1,390	508	835	3,588	3,407	8,712	532	508
Kittitas	2,227	9.7	45,267	1,758	750	156	69	204	461	550	1,179	72	69
Klickitat	1,180	9.6	51,973	937	409	80	41	150	240	363	680	41	41
Lewis	3,921	10.3	47,752	1,423	1,364	252	124	297	527	1,293	2,037	139	124
Lincoln	564	15.1	50,851	1,047	132	31	12	101	98	170	276	16	12
Mason	3,132	9.7	45,901	1,664	702	152	62	157	555	1,004	1,074	85	62
Okanogan	2,026	15.5	47,535	1,445	665	150	66	247	329	685	1,128	67	66
Pacific	1,006	9.2	43,749	1,981	280	62	26	61	198	441	429	37	26
Pend Oreille	659	10.3	46,571	1,567	158	36	13	35	126	249	242	19	13
Pierce	51,664	8.7	56,532	606	20,920	3,804	1,852	3,563	7,972	11,375	30,140	1,758	1,852
San Juan	1,432	4.3	81,858	70	257	45	22	135	721	274	460	34	22
Skagit	7,496	9.0	57,315	551	2,827	534	253	619	1,518	1,902	4,233	263	253
Skamania	600	6.4	49,519	1,194	93	20	9	31	122	150	153	12	9
Snohomish	51,706	8.6	62,267	341	19,576	3,003	1,634	3,650	7,172	8,918	27,863	1,662	1,634
Spokane	26,431	7.9	50,038	1,140	12,990	2,195	1,122	1,747	4,313	7,129	18,054	1,117	1,122
Stevens	1,981	8.4	42,740	2,101	508	113	46	122	306	727	789	60	46
Thurston	16,470	9.3	56,007	641	7,015	1,333	606	974	3,096	3,856	9,928	605	606
Wahkiakum	212	8.7	47,027	1,511	35	9	3	13	44	73	60	6	3
Walla Walla	3,173	11.4	51,767	957	1,395	276	129	391	593	819	2,191	119	129
Whatcom	12,195	6.9	52,787	869	4,905	899	432	1,224	2,441	2,905	7,460	451	432
Whitman	2,209	8.3	44,628	1,857	1,054	288	92	301	400	430	1,734	84	92
Yakima	12,367	12.0	49,099	1,246	4,988	889	508	1,500	1,759	3,602	7,885	404	508
WEST VIRGINIA	80,304	5.2	44,868	X	32,518	5,803	2,620	4,945	11,653	26,723	45,886	3,358	2,620
Barbour	590	6.5	35,878	2,876	175	29	14	21	74	232	240	21	14
Berkeley	5,570	9.0	45,610	1,714	1,806	352	149	214	664	1,280	2,521	177	149
Boone	832	6.7	39,493	2,505	218	39	18	17	89	372	293	27	18
Braxton	479	5.3	34,972	2,938	144	28	12	29	63	198	214	18	12
Brooke	1,075	8.6	49,579	1,188	344	62	28	100	167	336	534	39	28
Cabell	4,287	6.3	46,805	1,538	2,541	429	204	252	689	1,432	3,426	231	204

1. Based on the resident population estimated as of July 1 of the year shown. 2. Martinsville city is included with Henry county. 3. Norton city is included with Wise county. 4. Petersburg and Colonial Heights cities are included with Dinwiddie county. 5. Poquoson city is included with York county. 6. Radford city is included with Montgomery county. 7. Salem city is included with Roanoke county. 8. Staunton and Waynesboro cities are included with Augusta county. 9. Williamsburg city is included with James City county. 10. Winchester city is included with Frederick county.

STATE County	Earnings, 2020 (cont.) – Percent by selected industries: Farm	Mining, quarrying, and extractions	Construction	Manu-facturing	Information; professional, scientific, technical services	Retail trade	Finance, insurance, real estate, and leasing	Health care and social assistance	Govern-ment	Social Security beneficiaries, December 2020: Number	Rate[1]	Supple-mental Security Income recipients, 2020	Housing units, 2021: Total	Percent change, 2010–2021
	75	76	77	78	79	80	81	82	83	84	85	86	87	88
VIRGINIA—Cont'd														
Martinsville city	(2)	(2)	(2)	(2)	(2)	(2)	(2)	(2)	(2)	4,075	301	33	7,029	-0.3
Newport News city	0.0	D	3.4	31.1	7.5	4.0	3.4	11.1	23.2	31,755	172	5,038	81,920	0.0
Norfolk city	0.0	D	2.8	4.1	8.6	2.9	4.8	11.8	44.0	35,905	153	7,437	102,417	0.9
Norton city	(3)	(3)	(3)	(3)	(3)	(3)	(3)	(3)	(3)	1,405	383	345	1,930	-0.2
Petersburg city	(4)	(4)	(4)	(4)	(4)	(4)	(4)	(4)	(4)	8,150	244	2,906	18,013	0.1
Poquoson city	(5)	(5)	(5)	(5)	(5)	(5)	(5)	(5)	(5)	2,650	211	64	4,945	0.3
Portsmouth city	0.0	0.0	6.0	D	3.6	2.3	1.2	9.0	62.1	19,595	200	3,922	43,314	0.4
Radford city	(6)	(6)	(6)	(6)	(6)	(6)	(6)	(6)	(6)	2,360	143	422	6,459	0.1
Richmond city	0.0	0.2	3.3	3.3	16.2	2.2	11.5	11.9	25.3	36,180	160	8,942	112,800	0.6
Roanoke city	0.0	D	7.0	D	8.4	6.1	8.4	22.0	13.3	22,040	223	4,613	48,913	0.3
Salem city	(7)	(7)	(7)	(7)	(7)	(7)	(7)	(7)	(7)	6,565	259	608	11,101	-0.2
Staunton city	(8)	(8)	(8)	(8)	(8)	(8)	(8)	(8)	(8)	7,040	274	802	12,333	0.1
Suffolk city	1.0	D	5.2	6.4	19.8	5.4	4.3	12.7	23.3	18,515	192	2,406	39,558	2.7
Virginia Beach city	0.0	0.0	7.1	3.1	11.5	6.0	12.6	11.6	28.8	78,610	172	5,667	190,983	0.3
Waynesboro city	(8)	(8)	(8)	(8)	(8)	(8)	(8)	(8)	(8)	5,450	242	742	10,417	1.0
Williamsburg city	(9)	(9)	(9)	(9)	(9)	(9)	(9)	(9)	(9)	2,710	174	128	5,775	0.3
Winchester city	(10)	(10)	(10)	(10)	(10)	(10)	(10)	(10)	(10)	5,570	198	692	12,358	-0.1
WASHINGTON	1.6	0.1	6.8	7.9	20.8	9.4	6.6	9.6	17.0	1,401,525	181	146,666	3,257,185	1.3
Adams	30.2	0.0	1.4	11.7	1.3	4.2	4.0	D	19.3	2,745	133	349	6,857	1.5
Asotin	2.9	D	13.1	5.5	4.6	13.4	5.1	22.1	17.0	6,905	308	726	10,217	1.6
Benton	5.2	D	10.4	5.3	15.6	5.8	4.7	12.6	15.2	38,050	181	4,078	81,788	1.7
Chelan	7.3	D	11.3	3.7	4.2	6.8	5.5	17.7	19.3	18,450	232	1,384	38,085	1.8
Clallam	0.6	0.1	7.5	4.5	4.6	9.4	4.8	9.4	40.1	27,765	355	1,880	38,291	0.8
Clark	0.2	D	11.6	8.0	10.4	6.6	8.2	13.3	17.5	93,190	182	8,360	201,116	2.5
Columbia	23.3	0.9	11.5	11.3	2.6	3.4	-1.1	D	30.6	1,335	330	150	2,201	0.5
Cowlitz	0.9	D	10.9	20.3	3.9	6.9	4.8	13.2	15.8	28,570	256	3,777	45,855	0.8
Douglas	17.9	0.1	7.7	5.0	D	10.6	3.4	5.8	25.3	8,530	195	539	17,731	1.9
Ferry	6.9	D	D	D	D	3.9	1.4	D	52.9	2,600	357	237	4,096	0.7
Franklin	16.0	D	8.8	8.7	2.4	7.4	2.8	7.3	20.8	11,550	118	1,799	30,503	2.1
Garfield	33.0	0.0	D	0.4	0.6	2.9	D	D	46.1	695	296	44	1,199	0.3
Grant	24.2	D	4.9	9.8	7.4	5.1	3.6	5.1	22.4	17,390	173	2,149	39,345	1.5
Grays Harbor	2.2	D	7.4	11.6	3.7	7.3	3.6	10.4	31.8	22,320	290	3,031	36,489	1.0
Island	0.5	D	7.0	2.9	5.8	4.3	4.9	4.8	55.2	24,410	279	994	42,455	1.1
Jefferson	1.0	D	10.7	6.8	8.7	7.6	5.7	6.3	33.4	13,450	400	598	19,293	0.8
King	0.1	0.1	5.1	6.0	32.9	11.8	6.9	7.1	10.5	304,020	135	35,627	985,351	1.2
Kitsap	0.1	0.0	6.1	2.4	9.9	5.9	4.7	9.9	48.7	56,365	205	4,700	114,783	1.1
Kittitas	4.8	D	10.5	3.2	D	7.5	5.3	6.2	34.7	9,300	204	559	24,253	1.7
Klickitat	13.5	D	5.7	22.1	D	2.5	3.6	3.3	18.9	6,640	287	635	10,689	1.2
Lewis	4.0	0.7	6.5	14.8	3.2	8.5	3.5	13.8	18.7	22,925	272	2,790	35,892	1.1
Lincoln	29.7	D	8.9	D	4.3	4.0	D	D	28.8	3,400	303	257	5,805	1.0
Mason	2.1	D	6.5	4.6	D	8.7	5.0	5.9	43.4	18,915	280	1,612	33,674	1.0
Okanogan	16.4	D	5.3	1.4	3.3	8.1	2.5	8.6	33.2	11,550	271	1,243	21,967	1.0
Pacific	4.7	0.5	6.4	8.4	D	6.1	4.5	6.5	34.9	9,030	377	707	16,159	0.6
Pend Oreille	1.9	D	7.0	10.4	3.7	4.6	3.1	D	52.3	4,580	330	507	8,037	1.1
Pierce	0.2	0.1	9.2	4.7	5.1	6.5	6.4	15.9	29.8	159,290	172	18,727	365,340	1.3
San Juan	0.9	D	18.3	3.6	10.9	9.0	8.7	5.4	14.5	5,930	320	132	13,917	0.8
Skagit	5.0	0.1	11.2	14.2	6.1	8.3	6.8	7.6	22.6	32,840	251	2,267	56,423	1.0
Skamania	1.5	D	8.1	12.7	D	4.1	2.7	D	31.6	2,790	229	183	5,898	1.4
Snohomish	0.4	0.1	10.7	25.6	8.6	7.5	7.5	8.9	14.1	130,850	157	11,836	328,347	1.8
Spokane	0.6	0.2	7.0	6.7	7.9	7.2	9.9	17.8	19.6	111,290	204	14,552	227,877	1.4
Stevens	3.5	D	7.4	10.0	D	6.6	4.0	D	28.1	14,045	296	1,358	22,498	0.9
Thurston	1.1	0.0	7.2	2.5	7.7	6.2	5.4	12.8	37.8	64,335	216	5,451	123,026	1.0
Wahkiakum	6.1	0.0	10.0	5.1	7.2	6.3	D	D	30.8	1,615	352	130	2,219	1.2
Walla Walla	14.6	D	4.5	14.7	D	4.5	4.8	D	22.5	13,900	222	1,397	25,165	0.6
Whatcom	3.6	D	10.8	12.1	7.5	7.8	7.2	12.2	18.3	47,805	209	4,258	101,867	1.4
Whitman	11.1	D	2.7	16.7	3.2	4.2	3.0	5.8	42.9	6,325	132	554	21,121	0.5
Yakima	17.8	0.0	4.5	7.5	2.8	6.9	3.5	13.6	17.9	45,830	179	7,089	91,356	0.7
WEST VIRGINIA	0.1	4.7	6.1	8.3	7.7	6.7	5.0	17.5	21.8	479,303	269	69,208	858,481	0.3
Barbour	-0.2	D	D	3.9	D	4.6	2.6	D	16.7	4,300	278	686	7,117	0.0
Berkeley	0.3	D	4.9	10.9	9.4	6.0	4.4	12.7	29.7	24,535	195	2,484	52,496	2.6
Boone	0.0	D	2.4	0.7	D	7.2	D	D	32.5	6,805	319	1,223	10,152	0.2
Braxton	1.4	0.8	7.3	11.4	2.3	14.8	2.2	14.8	22.4	3,965	324	556	6,252	0.0
Brooke	0.0	D	D	20.6	D	6.8	4.1	D	9.8	6,440	291	466	10,693	-0.2
Cabell	0.0	0.5	4.6	10.1	6.1	7.3	5.2	29.1	16.8	22,510	241	4,233	46,084	-0.1

1. Per 1,000 resident population estimated as of July 1 of the year shown. 2. Martinsville city is included with Henry county. 3. Norton city is included with Wise county. 4. Petersburg and Colonial Heights cities are included with Dinwiddie county. 5. Poquoson city is included with York county. 6. Radford city is included with Montgomery county. 7. Salem city is included with Roanoke county. 8. Staunton and Waynesboro cities are included with Augusta county. 9. Williamsburg city is included with James City county. 10. Winchester city is included with Frederick county.

STATE County	Housing units, 2016–2020: Occupied units: Total	Owner-occupied: Percent	Owner-occupied: Median value[1]	Median owner cost as a percent of income: With a mortgage	Median owner cost as a percent of income: Without a mortgage[2]	Renter-occupied: Median rent[3]	Renter-occupied: Median rent as a percent of income[2]	Sub-standard units[4] (percent)	Civilian labor force, 2021: Total	Percent change, 2020–2021	Unemployment: Total	Unemployment: Rate[5]	Civilian employment[6], 2016–2020: Total	Percent: Management, business, science, and arts	Percent: Construction, production, and maintenance occupations
	89	90	91	92	93	94	95	96	97	98	99	100	101	102	103
VIRGINIA—Cont'd															
Martinsville city	5,597	55.8	79,000	25.4	11.4	664	28.0	0.0	5,531	-2.1	416	7.5	5,236	26.9	30.4
Newport News city	70,376	48.3	194,700	22.7	10.8	1,075	30.2	3.8	86,364	-3.6	4,837	5.6	81,820	35.1	24.4
Norfolk city	89,398	43.5	215,800	24.0	11.9	1,077	30.8	2.5	107,879	-3.5	6,185	5.7	104,180	35.8	21.4
Norton city	1,877	51.8	79,400	14.3	11.9	451	31.3	1.5	1,604	-3.4	79	4.9	1,630	33.1	21.7
Petersburg city	13,231	36.1	111,800	28.0	11.1	958	28.6	2.7	12,529	-4.1	1,319	10.5	13,063	28.8	28.3
Poquoson city	4,632	81.9	344,300	20.4	13.1	1,383	20.9	0.2	6,130	-1.8	170	2.8	6,008	49.9	19.9
Portsmouth city	36,650	55.3	174,200	23.4	12.8	1,083	33.4	2.0	43,482	-3.3	2,908	6.7	41,059	30.9	26.8
Radford city	5,677	48.2	171,000	19.5	15.1	839	37.7	3.1	8,551	0.1	347	4.1	8,217	38.3	17.3
Richmond city	91,005	43.7	244,200	22.5	12.3	1,070	31.8	2.1	116,270	-3.5	6,378	5.5	119,709	42.8	16.4
Roanoke city	41,694	52.3	134,900	20.6	11.7	804	29.1	1.8	47,664	-3.4	2,309	4.8	47,454	31.9	23.6
Salem city	9,876	64.4	200,000	21.0	10.0	926	24.4	1.6	12,390	-2.8	440	3.6	12,333	38.6	23.5
Staunton city	10,638	59.0	171,600	19.4	10.0	864	27.7	2.1	11,849	-3.3	452	3.8	11,989	34.6	19.7
Suffolk city	34,603	70.3	265,600	22.2	11.7	1,231	30.7	2.3	44,227	-2.5	1,944	4.4	43,622	39.6	22.7
Virginia Beach city	172,452	64.7	287,400	23.1	10.7	1,380	29.1	1.6	224,179	-2.9	8,300	3.7	223,239	42.8	17.5
Waynesboro city	9,169	59.1	183,600	22.3	12.7	790	28.7	1.5	10,298	-3.3	425	4.1	10,575	33.7	26.0
Williamsburg city	4,485	52.2	334,100	18.5	10.0	1,153	32.2	1.3	6,579	-3.7	320	4.9	6,491	40.7	8.4
Winchester city	10,669	44.7	247,800	19.1	10.0	1,096	28.2	2.3	14,437	-1.7	505	3.5	13,941	37.9	20.5
WASHINGTON	2,905,822	63.3	366,800	22.4	11.1	1,337	29.1	3.7	3,913,513	-0.4	204,775	5.2	3,660,034	42.7	21.3
Adams	6,035	61.0	159,600	22.9	10.3	824	21.4	10.6	9,611	3.7	531	5.5	7,780	21.5	48.9
Asotin	9,286	72.2	211,900	21.9	10.0	819	28.5	2.0	10,630	2.9	395	3.7	9,767	32.6	25.8
Benton	73,073	69.1	255,000	19.6	10.0	1,027	27.7	2.5	104,773	-0.7	5,858	5.6	89,438	41.4	23.8
Chelan	29,383	63.5	311,900	22.3	10.0	936	25.8	4.4	44,869	0.4	2,373	5.3	36,004	32.7	29.3
Clallam	33,197	71.3	267,900	23.8	11.3	971	30.7	2.5	29,371	1.6	1,911	6.5	29,602	33.7	22.2
Clark	178,478	67.1	355,000	21.9	10.0	1,328	29.7	3.5	246,019	0.9	13,433	5.5	231,214	38.3	23.9
Columbia	1,795	71.6	199,600	20.5	10.9	760	19.8	0.7	1,813	1.5	95	5.2	1,932	35.2	30.7
Cowlitz	42,354	66.1	245,500	22.1	12.0	895	30.3	2.9	48,443	-1.0	3,085	6.4	45,128	29.5	30.4
Douglas	15,435	68.1	284,900	21.6	10.0	956	24.2	4.9	21,948	1.7	1,203	5.5	19,859	29.9	32.4
Ferry	3,175	75.6	183,000	19.8	10.0	688	25.2	7.9	2,327	-4.3	206	8.9	2,571	38.9	22.1
Franklin	27,263	69.3	226,500	20.0	10.0	915	28.2	8.1	43,835	0.0	2,881	6.6	41,665	29.4	34.5
Garfield	986	75.9	152,400	19.2	10.0	565	14.2	1.4	821	0.7	48	5.8	1,002	36.9	23.8
Grant	31,908	64.6	191,600	20.5	10.0	813	25.1	5.9	47,490	1.1	3,133	6.6	41,801	29.0	40.6
Grays Harbor	29,433	68.8	192,600	23.0	11.2	828	28.1	3.6	29,083	1.2	2,255	7.8	28,592	31.3	27.7
Island	35,326	71.1	382,900	25.3	11.4	1,260	29.5	2.6	36,507	0.7	2,041	5.6	32,301	36.5	24.2
Jefferson	15,051	77.6	362,300	25.6	12.0	962	28.5	2.3	12,802	-0.8	794	6.2	11,449	34.9	23.3
King	900,061	56.5	601,100	22.2	12.2	1,695	28.1	4.2	1,278,003	0.0	54,571	4.3	1,225,004	54.1	14.0
Kitsap	105,758	68.1	362,700	22.5	10.9	1,349	29.4	1.9	128,186	-0.2	6,466	5.0	116,029	41.4	21.1
Kittitas	19,162	59.8	315,800	23.8	11.3	1,050	33.2	2.1	21,787	-2.4	1,381	6.3	23,140	36.8	19.5
Klickitat	9,268	70.7	281,600	22.3	11.0	868	31.2	4.0	10,105	3.8	610	6.0	9,228	37.1	28.8
													32,320	29.8	29.9
Lewis	31,118	70.4	231,900	22.9	11.5	916	29.9	3.9	34,798	0.0	2,184	6.3			
Lincoln	4,628	77.8	173,000	21.2	10.2	747	23.0	2.9	4,691	0.2	229	4.9	4,428	43.9	23.1
Mason	25,242	77.3	249,100	23.2	11.8	1,025	26.8	3.7	25,112	-1.3	1,750	7.0	25,585	31.7	28.5
Okanogan	17,884	65.5	205,300	25.1	10.0	741	26.6	5.6	19,538	0.4	1,292	6.6	17,107	30.5	29.1
Pacific	9,714	82.4	185,600	23.4	11.2	805	30.8	2.3	8,569	3.3	675	7.9	7,901	31.4	28.1
Pend Oreille	5,798	77.5	243,100	22.0	10.0	739	28.4	3.9	5,138	-0.7	391	7.6	5,016	32.8	33.3
Pierce	330,999	63.3	336,600	23.2	12.0	1,338	30.3	3.4	448,785	-1.1	27,179	6.1	422,410	35.3	25.5
San Juan	8,459	74.4	535,200	27.1	11.5	1,087	29.4	4.3	8,376	3.1	417	5.0	7,798	40.6	22.9
Skagit	49,263	70.0	341,600	23.8	11.6	1,145	29.0	4.7	61,981	-2.5	3,904	6.3	57,197	34.2	29.9
Skamania	4,866	79.0	335,600	22.3	11.6	874	28.0	3.3	5,511	1.0	350	6.4	5,387	39.4	26.8
													416,375	41.0	22.9
Snohomish	298,815	68.0	440,100	23.0	11.3	1,515	30.0	3.7	437,145	-0.4	21,791	5.0			
Spokane	206,502	63.1	245,400	21.5	10.5	950	30.1	2.2	260,902	-1.4	14,016	5.4	239,046	38.7	20.1
Stevens	17,883	79.0	219,500	22.3	10.0	709	26.0	3.9	19,010	-0.5	1,272	6.7	17,121	31.5	29.9
Thurston	112,323	66.0	315,600	22.4	10.5	1,275	31.1	2.1	145,252	-1.5	7,544	5.2	131,327	42.4	19.3
Wahkiakum	1,900	89.0	228,600	26.5	11.0	785	33.1	4.8	1,357	-2.7	90	6.6	1,356	32.1	29.9
Walla Walla	22,773	64.0	244,400	20.5	10.7	946	31.8	2.7	31,593	1.8	1,456	4.6	26,563	36.2	22.2
Whatcom	88,978	62.2	369,000	23.5	11.2	1,119	33.0	3.9	113,751	-2.8	6,822	6.0	109,687	37.0	23.8
Whitman	18,485	44.2	230,200	20.7	10.5	842	40.9	1.8	22,366	0.8	996	4.5	23,231	50.3	16.3
Yakima	83,765	62.3	191,400	22.0	10.2	868	27.8	8.5	131,217	-1.6	9,146	7.0	106,673	27.1	38.2
WEST VIRGINIA	734,235	73.7	123,200	18.1	10.0	732	28.9	1.7	788,826	0.7	39,694	5.0	744,272	34.2	25.2
Barbour	6,484	73.2	103,800	19.8	11.4	584	24.5	0.4	7,165	-0.4	379	5.3	6,629	25.1	31.4
Berkeley	45,702	74.3	187,400	20.4	10.0	1,029	27.8	2.6	60,140	3.5	2,141	3.6	58,104	34.8	28.3
Boone	8,691	78.2	76,700	17.3	10.4	657	40.8	1.2	7,259	-1.4	441	6.1	6,586	30.2	29.4
Braxton	5,341	78.6	93,700	19.4	10.0	593	14.8	2.0	5,097	-1.9	344	6.7	5,114	21.7	31.5
Brooke	9,792	72.5	97,200	17.1	10.0	546	21.8	1.6	9,939	1.9	603	6.1	9,783	31.5	25.7
Cabell	39,296	62.2	126,900	18.2	10.0	752	34.8	1.4	41,419	0.0	1,919	4.6	38,275	37.0	17.4

1. Specified owner-occupied units. 2. A value of 10.0 represents 10 percent or less; a value of 50.0 represents 50 percent or more. 3. Specified renter-occupied units. 4. Overcrowded or lacking complete plumbing facilities. 5. Percent of civilian labor force. 6. Civilian employed persons 16 years old and over.

STATE County	Private nonfarm establishments, employment and payroll, 2020									Agriculture, 2017			
		Employment						Annual payroll		Farms			Farm producers whose primary occupation is farming (percent)
											Percent with:		
	Number of establish-ments	Total	Health care and social assistance	Manufac-turing	Retail trade	Finance and insurance	Professional, scientific, and technical services	Total (mil dol)	Average per employee (dollars)	Number	Fewer than 50 acres	1000 acres or more	
	104	105	106	107	108	109	110	111	112	113	114	115	116
VIRGINIA—Cont'd													
Martinsville city	508	9,061	2,400	1,542	1,395	199	147	292	32,281	NA	NA	NA	NA
Newport News city	3,729	95,113	15,817	30,609	9,805	1,671	4,406	5,320	55,930	NA	NA	NA	NA
Norfolk city	5,357	107,435	21,441	6,901	11,486	4,158	10,808	5,579	51,925	NA	NA	NA	NA
Norton city	208	4,131	988	658	722	79	97	190	46,010	NA	NA	NA	NA
Petersburg city	694	12,029	3,674	1,203	2,635	152	156	496	41,258	NA	NA	NA	NA
Poquoson city	223	1,353	196	NA	262	51	66	39	28,656	NA	NA	NA	NA
Portsmouth city	1,635	25,842	7,454	927	3,131	379	1,399	1,120	43,341	NA	NA	NA	NA
Radford city	294	3,627	585	1,086	348	129	151	152	41,784	NA	NA	NA	NA
Richmond city	6,347	128,505	26,722	5,075	9,293	9,792	11,827	8,191	63,737	NA	NA	NA	NA
Roanoke city	3,091	66,408	16,415	3,888	8,492	3,468	2,724	3,217	48,442	NA	NA	NA	NA
Salem city	991	19,259	5,500	2,680	1,904	491	649	967	50,206	NA	NA	NA	NA
Staunton city	745	10,521	2,485	532	1,810	303	343	356	33,827	NA	NA	NA	NA
Suffolk city	1,697	24,706	4,613	1,656	3,829	890	1,135	1,075	43,527	270	57.4	11.1	38.6
Virginia Beach city	11,385	162,825	22,224	6,282	24,724	11,680	15,473	7,161	43,977	196	67.9	2.0	35.6
Waynesboro city	600	9,097	563	1,347	2,104	411	385	340	37,328	NA	NA	NA	NA
Williamsburg city	515	9,036	471	47	1,397	170	197	259	28,661	NA	NA	NA	NA
Winchester city	1,370	25,007	7,556	1,513	4,341	664	869	1,099	43,965	NA	NA	NA	NA
WASHINGTON	194,967	2,959,864	446,543	268,994	344,587	114,083	223,938	203,851	68,872	35,793	66.6	7.2	39.9
Adams	368	4,668	810	1,091	675	92	71	207	44,377	586	20.8	32.8	55.2
Asotin	443	5,030	1,321	396	1,023	143	246	216	43,026	205	42.9	35.6	37.8
Benton	4,729	73,568	12,137	4,082	10,226	1,975	7,900	4,181	56,834	1,520	81.1	4.9	34.2
Chelan	2,635	31,902	6,743	1,523	4,442	775	1,203	1,501	47,061	835	72.7	0.5	47.3
Clallam	2,050	18,018	4,208	1,024	3,602	489	686	730	40,531	528	83.9	NA	39.3
Clark	11,566	151,442	24,973	14,069	18,828	6,468	8,580	8,338	55,057	1,978	87.4	0.3	29.9
Columbia	118	951	165	220	100	16	33	41	43,084	257	27.6	17.9	43.2
Cowlitz	2,210	33,100	5,670	7,402	5,025	824	852	1,624	49,071	403	76.9	1.5	33.3
Douglas	790	8,055	856	588	1,920	165	172	307	38,173	729	41.0	25.4	49.7
Ferry	141	897	146	207	202	20	17	41	45,862	252	31.3	9.1	53.3
Franklin	1,762	23,081	2,719	3,407	3,766	398	629	1,080	46,791	772	40.2	18.0	55.9
Garfield	41	308	108	NA	54	15	NA	12	37,393	226	22.1	31.9	45.9
Grant	1,907	23,574	3,135	3,855	3,788	552	1,411	1,108	46,994	1,384	36.1	18.8	60.0
Grays Harbor	1,561	15,714	2,825	2,055	2,785	468	372	643	40,934	469	65.0	1.9	35.6
Island	1,826	13,014	2,578	804	2,273	340	743	532	40,855	390	83.6	NA	43.0
Jefferson	1,010	7,094	1,421	687	1,188	151	284	288	40,564	221	63.3	NA	39.2
King	70,304	1,310,051	159,368	86,157	111,416	52,719	131,645	118,976	90,818	1,796	93.1	0.1	35.3
Kitsap	6,016	63,101	13,364	2,212	12,008	1,719	4,947	2,708	42,921	698	96.3	NA	29.0
Kittitas	1,319	12,413	1,887	633	1,938	217	344	449	36,185	1,008	71.1	3.0	37.1
Klickitat	545	4,128	641	686	358	85	344	193	46,755	750	46.3	13.3	38.9
Lewis	1,922	21,496	3,987	2,886	3,833	368	625	956	44,461	1,723	70.3	0.6	35.9
Lincoln	259	1,745	382	33	248	58	110	81	46,538	783	15.2	43.2	53.1
Mason	1,046	9,589	1,978	869	1,969	290	211	405	42,187	324	82.1	0.6	35.5
Okanogan	1,128	8,653	1,700	424	1,852	194	209	322	37,256	1,192	55.4	8.1	44.6
Pacific	576	4,326	681	721	635	118	127	164	38,003	346	56.1	3.8	37.4
Pend Oreille	238	1,846	486	274	262	57	71	81	43,983	261	47.9	5.7	33.3
Pierce	18,783	279,552	56,652	18,416	38,700	9,067	9,954	14,297	51,143	1,607	87.4	0.2	31.8
San Juan	998	5,163	454	227	824	137	254	207	40,183	316	70.6	0.6	36.5
Skagit	3,540	45,128	7,887	6,841	7,170	1,361	1,884	2,188	48,491	1,041	75.7	1.6	40.8
Skamania	192	1,880	137	386	148	18	71	59	31,412	145	80.0	NA	24.4
Snohomish	19,344	267,802	32,783	61,457	36,420	11,077	12,926	16,034	59,874	1,558	85.2	0.4	34.3
Spokane	13,520	200,563	42,428	15,556	27,620	11,359	9,531	9,755	48,637	2,425	63.9	5.8	33.6
Stevens	916	7,769	1,906	1,153	1,263	208	233	323	41,634	1,114	44.9	5.0	41.6
Thurston	6,476	76,890	16,445	3,115	13,036	2,935	3,751	3,415	44,418	1,200	77.8	0.6	35.3
Wahkiakum	93	421	50	61	44	9	9	17	39,394	145	60.7	0.7	49.2
Walla Walla	1,405	20,686	4,585	3,687	2,456	723	558	975	47,143	903	54.2	18.4	41.7
Whatcom	6,859	78,281	10,899	9,965	10,867	2,460	3,611	3,672	46,903	1,712	79.6	0.7	35.4
Whitman	831	10,923	2,056	2,691	1,213	195	369	523	47,867	1,039	27.0	35.5	50.0
Yakima	4,760	71,520	14,373	9,134	10,330	1,520	2,323	3,115	43,550	2,952	74.1	3.8	44.3
WEST VIRGINIA	35,323	542,148	134,696	47,344	79,221	16,608	24,463	22,840	42,128	23,622	34.7	1.5	36.7
Barbour	206	2,818	934	112	289	67	67	122	43,422	594	28.1	1.3	37.7
Berkeley	1,642	28,163	6,387	4,278	4,289	538	931	1,222	43,402	946	67.2	0.5	28.8
Boone	230	3,627	1,098	NA	543	66	78	157	43,201	35	17.1	NA	34.5
Braxton	246	2,878	816	282	628	59	32	100	34,882	381	16.8	3.1	40.8
Brooke	364	6,770	2,164	1,444	923	125	72	280	41,295	89	28.1	NA	45.9
Cabell	2,334	45,691	14,832	4,210	6,051	1,016	1,939	1,941	42,487	407	36.9	NA	34.8

STATE County	Agriculture, 2017 (cont.) — Land in farms: Acreage (1,000)	Land in farms: Percent change, 2012–2017	Land in farms — Acres: Average size of farm	Acres: Total irrigated (1,000)	Acres: Total cropland (1,000)	Value of land and buildings (dollars): Average per farm	Value of land and buildings (dollars): Average per acre	Value of machinery and equipment, average per farm (dollars)	Value of products sold: Total (mil dol)	Value of products sold: Average per farm (acres)	Value of products sold — Percent from: Crops	Percent from: Livestock and poultry products	Organic farms (number)	Farms with internet access (per-cent)	Government payments: Total ($1,000)	Government payments: Percent of farms
	117	118	119	120	121	122	123	124	125	126	127	128	129	130	131	132
VIRGINIA—Cont'd																
Martinsville city	NA	NA	NA	NA	NA	NA	NA	NA	NA	NA	NA	NA	NA	NA	NA	NA
Newport News city	NA	NA	NA	NA	NA	NA	NA	NA	NA	NA	NA	NA	NA	NA	NA	NA
Norfolk city	NA	NA	NA	NA	NA	NA	NA	NA	NA	NA	NA	NA	NA	NA	NA	NA
Norton city	NA	NA	NA	NA	NA	NA	NA	NA	NA	NA	NA	NA	NA	NA	NA	NA
Petersburg city	NA	NA	NA	NA	NA	NA	NA	NA	NA	NA	NA	NA	NA	NA	NA	NA
Poquoson city	NA	NA	NA	NA	NA	NA	NA	NA	NA	NA	NA	NA	NA	NA	NA	NA
Portsmouth city	NA	NA	NA	NA	NA	NA	NA	NA	NA	NA	NA	NA	NA	NA	NA	NA
Radford city	NA	NA	NA	NA	NA	NA	NA	NA	NA	NA	NA	NA	NA	NA	NA	NA
Richmond city	NA	NA	NA	NA	NA	NA	NA	NA	NA	NA	NA	NA	NA	NA	NA	NA
Roanoke city	NA	NA	NA	NA	NA	NA	NA	NA	NA	NA	NA	NA	NA	NA	NA	NA
Salem city	NA	NA	NA	NA	NA	NA	NA	NA	NA	NA	NA	NA	NA	NA	NA	NA
Staunton city	NA	NA	NA	NA	NA	NA	NA	NA	NA	NA	NA	NA	NA	NA	NA	NA
Suffolk city	79	14.1	293	0.6	57.9	1,208,063	4,127	131,386	53.7	199,041	84.2	15.8	NA	82.6	3,185	56.3
Virginia Beach city	23	-10.8	119	0.3	18.6	1,149,351	9,648	107,202	13.7	69,796	91.1	8.9	3	82.7	382	17.3
Waynesboro city	NA	NA	NA	NA	NA	NA	NA	NA	NA	NA	NA	NA	NA	NA	NA	NA
Williamsburg city	NA	NA	NA	NA	NA	NA	NA	NA	NA	NA	NA	NA	NA	NA	NA	NA
Winchester city	NA	NA	NA	NA	NA	NA	NA	NA	NA	NA	NA	NA	NA	NA	NA	NA
WASHINGTON	14,680	-0.5	410	1,689.4	7,488.6	1,143,889	2,789	121,662	9,634.5	269,172	72.5	27.5	933	84.1	168,990	15.4
Adams	972	-6.3	1,659	127.9	745.9	2,369,294	1,428	320,442	363.9	620,947	71.4	28.6	15	80.0	16,076	67.4
Asotin	251	-4.7	1,224	0.9	79.9	1,618,697	1,323	86,684	12.9	62,961	58.5	41.5	NA	93.7	3,920	48.3
Benton	614	-12.8	404	204.3	473.1	1,573,284	3,898	188,926	1,005.3	661,374	76.5	23.5	25	84.9	6,663	7.0
Chelan	60	-21.2	72	23.8	29.1	1,102,315	15,400	78,413	258.4	309,501	98.9	1.1	54	84.7	1,087	3.6
Clallam	17	-27.3	33	3.5	7.4	415,890	12,769	40,366	12.0	22,777	42.3	57.7	20	83.5	43	3.0
Clark	91	21.4	46	4.9	24.3	410,366	8,946	42,816	47.7	24,116	41.7	58.3	32	82.9	208	1.7
Columbia	243	-18.2	947	3.0	149.5	1,541,289	1,628	155,022	30.7	119,479	86.4	13.6	NA	79.8	4,211	61.5
Cowlitz	29	-26.3	71	3.0	11.0	639,038	8,955	53,997	19.0	47,045	52.8	47.2	NA	80.9	27	1.5
Douglas	823	1.1	1,129	16.3	544.4	1,331,223	1,180	134,210	186.0	255,154	96.5	3.5	23	76.5	14,978	48.7
Ferry	789	-0.5	3,130	2.8	19.4	1,620,480	518	56,595	D	D	D	D	4	71.0	135	7.1
Franklin	615	-1.6	797	188.1	446.8	3,662,394	4,595	365,464	631.6	818,132	74.3	25.7	31	88.0	9,867	24.7
Garfield	290	-6.0	1,283	1.0	182.8	2,017,792	1,573	196,343	37.2	164,385	85.7	14.3	NA	80.1	5,997	70.8
Grant	1,042	8.1	753	448.0	800.9	2,574,272	3,421	447,392	1,938.9	1,400,936	76.3	23.7	89	84.8	13,885	29.1
Grays Harbor	105	-11.9	224	6.3	17.1	537,286	2,395	84,525	33.6	71,635	52.3	47.7	6	81.4	62	2.1
Island	16	3.9	41	1.9	6.9	446,211	10,979	42,783	12.0	30,774	24.9	75.1	19	85.6	85	4.9
Jefferson	14	-11.6	62	1.0	3.7	473,659	7,611	41,419	9.3	41,860	23.3	76.7	10	89.1	30	8.6
King	42	-10.2	23	4.1	18.7	823,790	35,248	38,650	135.5	75,425	66.9	33.1	39	87.6	760	2.6
Kitsap	9	-6.7	13	0.5	2.3	473,099	35,164	33,113	6.6	9,463	73.2	26.8	26	88.3	D	0.6
Kittitas	173	-5.8	171	66.8	71.1	706,325	4,127	90,038	83.0	82,347	76.7	23.3	7	88.1	1,257	6.7
Klickitat	574	4.1	765	24.4	229.5	1,360,462	1,778	103,084	99.2	132,212	81.4	18.6	22	81.9	4,684	33.5
Lewis	123	-7.5	71	10.0	50.5	427,935	6,001	55,899	136.3	79,132	26.1	73.9	50	83.4	442	3.6
Lincoln	1,181	5.9	1,509	29.5	817.0	1,843,885	1,222	233,510	130.2	166,331	91.5	8.5	4	78.2	24,298	79.3
Mason	18	-23.6	56	1.0	3.6	479,276	8,562	52,381	48.5	149,790	5.6	94.4	4	83.0	77	4.3
Okanogan	1,232	2.2	1,033	46.0	98.7	1,247,686	1,207	91,219	338.1	283,631	88.0	12.0	84	81.9	2,307	7.1
Pacific	52	0.4	151	3.7	15.5	524,322	3,464	81,240	38.9	112,361	18.7	81.3	15	88.2	504	5.2
Pend Oreille	58	33.1	223	1.3	19.0	593,012	2,665	48,783	4.7	18,130	47.4	52.6	NA	87.4	74	4.2
Pierce	46	-7.5	28	3.0	12.1	612,026	21,490	43,894	64.9	40,371	45.4	54.6	17	87.4	71	2.2
San Juan	18	17.4	58	0.3	5.8	550,693	9,457	28,800	4.1	13,035	58.6	41.4	12	92.1	55	2.8
Skagit	98	-8.3	94	23.5	65.7	950,360	10,130	129,653	287.1	275,789	66.6	33.4	61	83.0	407	7.8
Skamania	6	-9.3	41	0.4	2.3	489,432	12,082	41,679	5.6	38,828	29.2	70.8	1	90.3	D	2.8
Snohomish	64	-10.1	41	8.4	33.6	790,023	19,332	60,306	157.6	101,133	48.5	51.5	31	89.0	464	4.6
Spokane	549	2.1	226	12.7	378.8	843,187	3,728	78,785	117.0	48,265	83.3	16.7	4	84.6	8,095	19.6
Stevens	518	-1.7	465	7.2	77.1	729,604	1,569	60,364	30.2	27,105	39.8	60.2	47	80.2	734	7.3
Thurston	62	-18.8	52	6.4	22.1	616,274	11,880	58,420	176.1	146,742	32.0	68.0	34	86.8	107	1.9
Wahkiakum	14	44.8	95	0.1	5.1	458,501	4,805	45,757	2.6	17,959	21.4	78.6	1	91.7	52	13.1
Walla Walla	703	8.9	778	101.7	565.8	1,968,909	2,531	208,241	D	D	D	D	13	85.3	16,092	40.1
Whatcom	103	-11.5	60	36.5	75.6	1,005,681	16,794	95,376	372.9	217,786	41.3	58.7	48	83.7	1,047	12.6
Whitman	1,288	1.0	1,240	5.1	1,032.7	2,164,850	1,746	273,129	278.8	268,309	93.1	6.9	1	87.4	24,847	70.8
Yakima	1,781	0.1	603	260.0	344.0	1,662,430	2,755	174,332	1,988.0	673,451	71.3	28.7	84	79.0	5,221	6.5
WEST VIRGINIA	3,662	1.5	155	1.7	947.7	411,482	2,654	56,120	754.3	31,931	20.3	79.7	63	70.0	9,094	7.9
Barbour	95	11.7	159	0.0	26.7	371,966	2,335	56,514	6.0	10,167	33.7	66.3	3	70.9	205	5.1
Berkeley	73	4.3	77	0.1	37.6	413,514	5,349	47,415	25.9	27,387	72.2	27.8	2	68.8	857	8.4
Boone	4	61.7	103	0.0	0.5	241,209	2,339	23,954	0.1	4,114	77.1	22.9	NA	71.4	5	11.4
Braxton	90	0.8	235	0.0	17.9	482,984	2,054	51,405	4.5	11,916	28.5	71.5	NA	61.9	133	11.5
Brooke	14	-2.7	161	D	4.3	454,092	2,825	90,249	1.3	14,135	46.4	53.6	NA	78.7	4	4.5
Cabell	40	-5.0	99	0.0	7.3	352,954	3,564	42,757	2.7	6,595	64.1	35.9	NA	61.9	9	4.2

STATE County	Water use, 2015		Wholesale Trade[1], 2017				Retail Trade[2], 2017				Real estate and rental and leasing,[2] 2017			
	Public supply water withdrawn (mil gal/ day)	Public supply gallons withdrawn per person per day	Number of establish-ments	Number of employees	Sales (mil dol)	Average payroll (mil dol)	Number of establish-ments	Number of employees	Sales (mil dol)	Average payroll (mil dol)	Number of establish-ments	Number of employees	Sales (mil dol)	Average payroll (mil dol)
	133	134	135	136	137	138	139	140	141	142	143	144	145	146
VIRGINIA—Cont'd														
Martinsville city	2.0	146.6	18	154	52.9	5.5	91	1,432	301.9	32.4	22	83	16.1	2.6
Newport News city	22.2	121.7	112	1,887	1,539.2	129.7	648	10,091	2,596.7	242.7	280	1,419	348.7	59.2
Norfolk city	0.3	1.1	187	2,714	2,296.8	146.3	830	11,729	2,696.3	293.1	317	3,133	608.6	145.4
Norton city	0.5	134.6	D	D	D	D	45	768	185.2	19.7	D	D	D	D
Petersburg city	0.0	0.0	D	D	D	15.2	141	2,454	940.7	67.1	37	163	30.9	4.9
Poquoson city	0.0	0.0	NA	NA	NA	NA	27	307	57.4	6.4	8	16	3.1	0.7
Portsmouth city	60.8	632.3	43	659	226.8	33.6	261	3,060	627.3	69.4	77	388	80.4	14.0
Radford city	2.5	142.5	9	36	37.1	1.7	42	500	95.3	10.7	24	121	20.1	3.8
Richmond city	70.2	318.8	253	3,815	3,581.9	212.4	790	9,088	2,260.4	241.1	329	2,197	939.5	106.3
Roanoke city	5.0	50.0	155	2,211	1,381.3	116.4	533	8,966	2,603.5	215.5	174	938	193.3	36.6
Salem city	3.8	151.0	68	1,552	1,120.6	100.8	151	1,995	524.5	49.7	43	199	60.0	9.8
Staunton city	0.0	0.0	21	227	80.2	8.7	133	1,834	449.7	46.3	38	142	17.0	5.1
Suffolk city	44.5	504.2	36	1,117	1,443.4	78.9	238	3,997	1,160.6	99.6	74	279	53.5	12.5
Virginia Beach city	1.8	3.9	351	4,770	5,596.5	359.4	1,506	24,023	6,155.3	607.2	761	5,451	1,198.7	261.4
Waynesboro city	0.8	36.3	14	229	106.3	13.1	122	2,161	483.8	48.5	35	91	15.2	3.1
Williamsburg city	0.0	0.0	8	68	39.0	5.3	121	1,658	310.3	36.5	D	D	D	D
Winchester city	0.0	0.0	36	459	463.9	22.2	284	4,317	1,017.2	109.6	66	306	97.6	11.5
WASHINGTON	866.5	120.8	7,755	120,320	112,352.6	7,649.3	21,751	347,728	160,284.8	11,412.9	11,826	53,706	15,626.7	2,756.8
Adams	5.6	289.8	D	D	D	D	53	719	210.3	18.5	14	29	4.2	0.6
Asotin	5.2	235.7	14	106	115.4	4.8	50	1,128	325.0	34.9	20	59	4.3	1.4
Benton	34.5	181.2	131	1,248	879.7	60.6	606	10,084	2,949.8	277.4	323	1,108	264.9	39.9
Chelan	11.3	149.3	90	2,811	1,319.3	115.5	385	4,329	1,141.6	124.8	139	575	105.4	22.0
Clallam	6.2	83.8	D	D	D	D	279	3,519	945.9	103.5	92	216	40.2	7.9
Clark	46.6	101.4	449	5,314	5,654.5	300.8	1,045	18,425	5,497.0	592.5	624	2,542	579.7	114.2
Columbia	1.0	253.5	D	D	D	0.6	17	77	24.4	2.6	7	8	1.3	0.2
Cowlitz	10.3	99.6	88	1,034	755.8	55.6	333	4,985	1,485.4	143.8	133	498	83.7	18.8
Douglas	5.5	134.5	46	1,017	433.6	45.2	95	1,685	522.9	49.8	44	103	24.5	3.4
Ferry	0.6	76.5	NA	NA	NA	NA	29	200	45.3	5.2	7	24	1.9	0.5
Franklin	16.3	183.5	113	1,515	1,365.0	88.0	207	3,755	1,295.0	128.9	76	337	103.4	11.7
Garfield	0.6	256.9	D	D	D	3.3	9	54	10.7	1.1	NA	NA	NA	NA
Grant	23.5	252.2	124	1,828	974.6	87.7	287	3,492	947.0	94.5	116	286	45.0	6.5
Grays Harbor	7.6	107.3	43	813	314.8	36.3	281	2,990	780.6	80.7	76	357	38.8	9.3
Island	6.5	80.5	32	176	74.1	9.4	227	2,319	565.5	65.9	121	300	67.1	11.1
Jefferson	2.3	73.9	19	137	40.6	4.7	136	1,165	259.2	32.4	57	181	31.0	6.1
King	197.6	93.3	3,153	57,233	59,575.5	4,083.3	6,581	115,960	89,586.7	4,328.6	4,955	27,367	9,285.8	1,710.3
Kitsap	19.6	75.5	131	978	500.7	54.1	739	11,457	3,319.1	355.0	405	1,132	304.1	45.8
Kittitas	6.9	159.5	40	547	438.0	32.1	168	1,915	616.0	51.4	71	172	55.6	7.5
Klickitat	3.1	147.0	15	189	111.6	12.0	49	354	81.7	8.6	24	71	16.7	1.5
Lewis	6.0	78.4	58	413	287.1	20.4	309	4,044	1,079.4	108.4	86	312	64.8	10.2
Lincoln	2.0	196.7	29	307	321.1	21.6	35	342	73.4	7.7	8	D	3.3	D
Mason	5.0	81.3	34	440	132.7	20.4	135	1,783	504.0	57.4	51	122	24.6	5.4
Okanogan	6.1	145.7	39	338	305.5	15.8	196	1,854	499.4	52.6	49	105	12.9	2.3
Pacific	2.7	130.9	D	D	D	D	78	601	139.5	17.0	18	116	13.9	4.2
Pend Oreille	1.0	75.6	6	10	4.9	0.5	28	264	61.7	6.2	7	12	1.8	0.5
Pierce	110.4	130.8	706	11,357	9,287.7	650.9	2,169	38,808	13,775.9	1,254.5	1,170	5,276	1,357.7	230.6
San Juan	0.9	54.1	D	D	D	D	116	752	180.2	24.9	66	136	30.4	4.9
Skagit	20.3	166.7	119	1,463	832.8	76.5	538	7,589	2,272.1	235.1	171	476	120.7	16.6
Skamania	1.1	93.5	D	D	D	3.3	22	162	35.4	3.9	10	5	2.4	0.2
Snohomish	65.5	84.8	729	9,382	9,583.3	711.3	2,192	36,696	11,584.9	1,181.5	1,037	4,121	1,200.0	183.7
Spokane	138.8	282.7	616	9,651	10,302.5	520.7	1,635	26,670	7,847.0	813.2	701	3,509	748.5	129.1
Stevens	6.2	141.4	19	260	66.5	7.7	109	1,233	321.9	34.2	23	69	9.9	1.7
Thurston	22.6	83.8	176	1,902	1,320.6	102.1	796	13,008	3,958.8	386.6	340	1,133	302.6	43.6
Wahkiakum	0.3	79.2	NA	NA	NA	NA	8	34	8.1	0.9	4	D	0.7	D
Walla Walla	12.7	210.8	D	D	D	15.1	171	2,225	560.8	62.1	70	234	36.5	8.4
Whatcom	18.1	85.4	D	D	D	D	817	11,180	3,225.2	328.6	398	1,394	421.9	56.2
Whitman	6.3	129.9	52	696	906.1	43.3	91	1,456	411.3	36.5	50	281	36.1	6.8
Yakima	30.0	120.6	220	4,707	3,634.3	241.2	730	10,415	3,136.8	301.2	263	1,013	180.5	33.1
WEST VIRGINIA	185.0	100.3	1,205	14,578	12,188.8	676.7	5,963	82,985	23,057.8	2,004.1	1,432	6,061	1,368.8	228.9
Barbour	1.5	86.8	5	16	5.7	0.3	29	267	77.1	6.8	8	13	1.5	0.4
Berkeley	6.0	53.4	33	664	818.4	30.8	241	4,067	1,110.3	96.9	82	293	61.3	10.3
Boone	0.2	8.1	9	37	31.5	1.4	60	641	214.4	15.6	6	7	1.0	0.2
Braxton	1.1	75.6	7	42	8.4	1.5	51	705	200.7	16.6	8	14	2.7	0.4
Brooke	5.2	223.1	D	D	D	D	60	1,010	284.2	25.9	5	D	4.3	D
Cabell	12.2	125.7	97	1,416	902.5	70.6	417	6,509	1,478.4	140.4	105	523	149.8	23.9

1 Merchant wholesalers, except manufacturers' sales branches and offices. 2. Employer establishments.

STATE County	Professional, scientific, and technical services, 2017				Manufacturing, 2017				Accommodation and food services, 2017			
	Number of establish-ments	Number of employees	Sales (mil dol)	Average payroll (mil dol)	Number of establish-ments	Number of employees	Sales (mil dol)	Average payroll (mil dol)	Number of establis-hments	Number of employees	Sales (mil dol)	Annual payroll (mil dol)
	147	148	149	150	151	152	153	154	155	156	157	158
VIRGINIA—Cont'd												
Martinsville city	D	D	D	D	24	1,220	251.4	47.9	45	710	34.4	9.3
Newport News city	D	D	D	D	92	25,674	6,143.6	1,668.9	411	7,516	390.0	111.5
Norfolk city	D	D	D	D	133	6,747	1,601.9	362.2	612	11,326	659.3	181.7
Norton city	D	D	10.5	D	D	758	D	29.8	26	433	17.2	4.8
Petersburg city	D	D	D	D	32	1,162	482.6	60.5	94	930	50.5	13.8
Poquoson city	16	67	6.4	2.5	4	6	0.8	0.2	21	292	13.9	3.7
Portsmouth city	D	D	D	D	48	1,238	295.1	63.7	163	2,414	119.9	34.2
Radford city	25	139	14.6	6.6	17	1,346	242.5	76.3	41	993	35.5	9.3
Richmond city	897	11,297	2,503.3	1,050.3	200	4,908	16,939.3	334.1	677	14,306	793.6	258.9
Roanoke city	D	D	D	D	96	4,433	1,470.3	210.0	302	7,205	371.9	112.9
Salem city	D	D	D	D	51	3,027	971.2	173.2	97	1,885	95.9	28.0
Staunton city	64	298	40.6	15.4	18	617	106.9	28.6	84	1,333	66.2	21.8
Suffolk city	D	D	D	D	46	1,760	1,601.4	101.7	150	3,029	163.2	45.4
Virginia Beach city	1,488	21,552	4,078.6	1,607.1	215	5,584	2,279.7	304.1	1,292	25,108	1,494.1	419.4
Waynesboro city	43	320	35.0	15.6	26	1,198	380.7	67.2	77	1,678	87.2	24.8
Williamsburg city	28	129	15.9	5.7	7	37	8.6	1.2	155	3,667	242.6	72.5
Winchester city	D	D	D	D	22	1,910	1,055.4	122.1	144	3,320	160.2	48.4
WASHINGTON	D	D	D	D	7,017	263,132	140,381.5	17,943.8	17,828	289,371	21,068.6	6,395.3
Adams	10	51	9.8	2.7	12	1,194	377.5	55.8	35	428	21.0	5.8
Asotin	36	238	22.0	7.2	26	321	92.3	15.9	44	638	32.7	10.8
Benton	D	D	D	D	157	3,952	1,782.9	234.1	421	7,444	453.9	135.7
Chelan	196	994	127.6	50.7	104	1,380	308.7	59.0	325	4,189	289.6	93.4
Clallam	D	D	D	D	76	1,339	369.8	70.8	231	2,416	151.4	48.7
Clark	1,262	8,711	1,441.3	570.8	440	13,645	4,805.8	844.7	853	13,605	856.5	255.1
Columbia	9	24	1.4	0.6	D	D	D	D	13	97	5.6	1.5
Cowlitz	D	D	D	34.3	123	6,610	3,270.4	431.9	224	3,190	180.4	54.7
Douglas	46	194	17.4	7.2	22	499	112.5	26.7	60	1,091	57.2	20.8
Ferry	D	D	D	0.6	6	186	60.5	8.6	20	71	5.0	1.3
Franklin	D	D	D	D	46	2,662	1,147.4	132.3	140	2,278	133.1	37.9
Garfield	NA	NA	NA	NA	NA	NA	NA	NA	3	5	0.4	0.1
Grant	112	443	64.0	22.1	77	4,153	1,842.4	236.7	192	2,327	140.5	39.8
Grays Harbor	D	D	D	D	79	2,777	1,193.0	149.3	228	2,244	139.5	42.0
Island	183	780	101.8	39.0	59	735	195.4	41.5	162	1,829	120.5	37.1
Jefferson	D	D	D	D	74	591	233.6	34.9	100	1,064	66.8	20.5
King	10,900	134,568	29,480.6	12,159.5	2,180	86,121	47,209.2	6,181.7	6,575	116,157	9,457.2	2,930.3
Kitsap	703	4,112	617.5	247.4	150	1,996	379.0	96.4	536	9,262	640.9	191.9
Kittitas	D	D	D	D	35	460	94.4	22.4	164	2,519	137.9	48.7
Klickitat	49	365	87.8	18.7	37	689	134.1	33.7	56	345	27.4	8.0
	D	D	D	D	100	2,735	1,302.6	150.6	199	2,309	138.3	39.7
Lewis												
Lincoln	D	D	D	D	D	21	D	D	D	D	D	1.0
Mason	D	D	D	D	53	709	241.3	35.8	101	1,746	161.4	47.4
Okanogan	D	D	D	D	33	403	91.1	16.2	124	1,257	82.0	23.9
Pacific	39	126	14.7	5.5	32	603	148.2	25.3	102	897	75.0	17.1
Pend Oreille	D	D	D	D	11	252	163.0	18.2	22	163	8.2	2.5
Pierce	1,544	9,155	1,424.7	558.2	565	18,149	6,287.2	1,037.9	1,655	29,002	1,945.0	584.6
San Juan	D	D	D	D	39	186	32.5	D	103	1,036	106.8	34.2
Skagit	D	D	D	D	189	6,711	11,187.8	468.7	352	5,518	411.7	125.3
Skamania	17	62	9.7	3.9	16	404	81.6	17.3	24	568	36.7	11.7
	1,841	12,783	2,219.6	871.1	780	58,428	34,547.2	5,059.3	1,713	26,720	2,178.0	596.9
Snohomish												
Spokane	D	D	1,547.7	D	518	14,449	4,161.2	792.4	1,133	19,373	1,165.3	369.1
Stevens	D	D	D	D	53	1,131	364.2	58.6	83	557	33.8	9.8
Thurston	638	4,426	594.6	260.8	162	2,779	1,029.7	136.7	561	9,634	574.5	175.9
Wahkiakum	D	D	D	0.3	D	42	D	D	D	D	D	0.3
Walla Walla	D	D	D	D	D	D	D	D	127	2,030	120.1	36.8
Whatcom	D	D	D	D	341	11,106	11,178.0	628.0	554	8,971	609.1	191.8
Whitman	65	351	38.4	16.2	D	2,367	D	D	122	1,792	81.8	24.4
Yakima	D	D	D	D	245	9,487	3,536.6	453.2	445	6,498	418.3	118.8
WEST VIRGINIA	2,761	21,085	3,023.3	1,132.2	1,142	48,533	24,602.1	2,747.7	3,614	68,102	4,069.1	1,075.6
Barbour	12	70	6.5	2.1	11	95	28.9	3.5	21	298	12.8	3.5
Berkeley	D	D	D	D	50	2,976	1,200.4	124.5	194	3,258	164.2	47.7
Boone	D	D	D	D	D	D	D	D	20	267	12.7	3.6
Braxton	12	41	3.3	1.2	13	270	245.7	15.1	D	D	D	D
Brooke	D	D	9.4	D	18	1,671	1,280.6	95.2	48	630	35.4	10.0
Cabell	D	D	D	D	87	3,946	1,546.2	228.4	284	5,400	264.4	79.3

STATE County	Health care and social assistance, 2017				Other services, 2017				Nonemployer businesses, 2019		Value of residential construction authorized by building permits, 2021	
	Number of establish-ments	Number of employees	Receipts (mil dol)	Annual payroll (mil dol)	Number of establish-ments	Number of employees	Receipts (mil dol)	Annual payroll (mil dol)	Number	Receipts (mil dol)	New construction ($1,000)	Number of housing units
	159	160	161	162	163	164	165	166	167	168	169	170
VIRGINIA—Cont'd												
Martinsville city	107	2,190	232.6	92.5	37	178	35.2	4.4	675	30.4	446	1
Newport News city	452	15,710	1,843.3	782.2	283	1,731	186.4	49.2	10,673	351.1	16,903	106
Norfolk city	582	20,755	3,181.5	1,090.6	396	3,023	459.0	106.2	13,486	570.4	174,524	1,473
Norton city	47	1,032	139.9	46.5	D	D	D	D	198	6.4	0	0
Petersburg city	126	4,361	479.6	190.8	75	576	67.5	15.8	1,599	52.2	11,694	116
Poquoson city	16	180	13.4	5.7	D	D	D	D	825	38.6	4,591	19
Portsmouth city	227	7,627	1,142.0	385.7	143	1,143	140.7	42.2	5,346	141.2	23,737	196
Radford city	41	561	48.5	21.3	23	66	14.7	1.9	644	31.1	1,043	9
Richmond city	607	27,376	4,123.1	1,644.4	520	4,950	609.4	174.3	17,546	789.0	149,313	1,067
Roanoke city	316	13,827	2,050.3	743.0	252	1,629	154.5	48.3	6,212	320.7	55,083	393
Salem city	143	5,424	990.3	365.2	88	474	41.1	12.5	1,576	66.3	0	0
Staunton city	95	2,486	190.0	89.8	86	456	43.9	14.0	1,689	74.7	9,128	63
Suffolk city	240	4,979	593.0	226.0	137	715	65.1	19.2	6,107	212.7	228,588	1,363
Virginia Beach city	1,162	21,729	2,767.4	1,052.8	943	5,762	918.6	174.6	33,458	1,601.3	137,486	463
Waynesboro city	47	630	45.6	19.7	59	413	49.8	14.3	1,180	48.3	14,749	102
Williamsburg city	42	666	55.8	26.0	36	379	91.2	15.5	900	40.8	6,248	33
Winchester city	269	7,080	1,125.3	407.1	92	536	45.5	14.0	2,161	136.4	32,136	209
WASHINGTON	21,264	438,835	56,442.2	22,849.3	13,444	78,480	14,513.7	3,004.6	500,954	25,809.4	12,501,328	56,941
Adams	26	728	75.3	36.6	30	84	10.0	2.4	801	47.4	15,750	80
Asotin	52	1,162	138.5	53.9	26	129	8.4	2.6	1,057	46.1	7,220	31
Benton	604	12,310	1,500.4	631.5	300	1,624	160.2	50.9	9,740	452.8	446,545	1,486
Chelan	232	6,551	946.1	417.4	180	638	80.2	20.1	5,195	256.4	138,199	671
Clallam	240	4,436	421.8	195.8	160	682	62.1	18.9	5,009	200.6	81,279	314
Clark	1,224	24,118	2,833.8	1,179.0	797	4,499	567.4	144.7	35,150	1,821.1	1,531,071	5,602
Columbia	10	169	21.0	8.7	D	D	D	D	239	9.5	2,851	44
Cowlitz	236	5,617	597.1	249.1	152	816	87.2	26.6	4,848	209.1	85,157	348
Douglas	68	891	62.8	26.5	45	183	15.2	4.9	1,955	82.2	95,843	329
Ferry	13	161	13.6	6.2	D	D	1.9	D	366	12.6	6,778	34
Franklin	140	2,121	205.3	96.5	106	467	53.0	14.6	3,864	207.3	178,966	663
Garfield	D	D	D	3.7	NA	NA	NA	NA	139	4.3	680	3
Grant	171	3,139	355.4	131.1	131	456	49.4	11.6	4,156	238.7	188,361	713
Grays Harbor	186	2,881	299.6	129.3	106	537	49.5	11.8	3,468	150.1	101,302	432
Island	174	2,432	270.0	111.8	119	474	42.1	13.3	6,271	285.2	113,812	401
Jefferson	103	1,666	172.4	80.9	89	437	46.3	14.1	3,424	130.6	56,681	274
King	7,874	160,920	22,808.7	9,090.3	4,865	31,829	9,241.4	1,445.8	182,281	10,575.7	3,915,263	19,549
Kitsap	716	12,346	1,619.1	581.2	423	2,230	224.5	67.3	15,936	759.5	493,451	2,285
Kittitas	107	1,886	171.0	79.2	82	361	43.7	11.6	2,980	146.2	198,918	545
Klickitat	46	612	85.2	31.6	40	180	17.6	5.8	1,704	81.3	34,589	189
	205	3,691	390.7	164.4	124	569	50.7	15.3	3,877	179.4	66,160	454
Lewis												
Lincoln	15	395	39.8	17.3	D	D	2.4	D	728	28.6	15,192	75
Mason	105	1,771	202.0	86.2	75	317	28.8	8.5	3,142	126.9	100,577	458
Okanogan	105	1,672	197.8	75.1	74	213	21.7	5.6	2,478	104.0	59,986	277
Pacific	39	639	70.1	33.0	37	139	12.8	3.3	1,502	59.6	24,952	111
Pend Oreille	20	474	41.9	20.7	13	30	3.5	0.9	787	30.2	18,810	79
Pierce	2,003	53,231	7,449.2	3,027.9	1,440	9,304	1,109.1	338.4	49,937	2,409.0	1,339,952	6,072
San Juan	66	452	45.4	18.3	55	181	35.5	5.8	2,889	141.7	39,875	155
Skagit	355	8,148	922.3	402.4	263	1,223	139.6	41.6	8,306	425.6	167,424	914
Skamania	19	191	11.2	5.6	D	D	D	D	817	37.8	21,091	75
	1,961	33,323	3,705.0	1,555.2	1,351	7,499	760.5	252.6	52,628	2,458.5	1,197,020	5,122
Snohomish												
Spokane	1,625	41,292	4,918.3	2,010.3	893	5,164	571.7	167.7	33,213	1,614.0	640,461	3,115
Stevens	91	1,951	144.3	68.2	60	216	23.9	6.1	2,761	112.5	71,861	300
Thurston	893	15,533	1,815.9	725.3	501	3,079	430.4	129.7	16,594	761.5	324,146	2,054
Wahkiakum	D	D	D	0.8	D	D	D	0.1	381	17.7	8,068	32
Walla Walla	155	4,730	566.2	245.5	D	D	D	D	3,456	164.5	51,701	261
Whatcom	699	10,929	1,334.0	469.1	431	2,552	303.1	91.8	17,054	845.1	358,796	1,871
Whitman	100	2,076	201.9	90.9	64	225	23.5	6.7	2,188	85.7	79,056	420
Yakima	576	14,031	1,779.2	692.5	283	1,580	168.1	44.4	9,633	490.4	223,483	1,103
WEST VIRGINIA	4,869	132,627	15,236.9	5,844.2	2,524	14,894	1,896.8	465.2	86,897	3,487.1	778,004	3,692
Barbour	34	837	44.1	20.7	D	D	D	D	631	20.3	968	8
Berkeley	211	6,186	806.2	439.3	116	669	71.8	20.4	6,136	254.8	321,021	1,344
Boone	D	D	D	D	19	94	8.6	3.5	616	19.0	1,227	12
Braxton	20	843	63.6	20.1	D	D	D	D	491	17.2	0	0
Brooke	58	2,102	233.1	87.1	31	120	8.9	2.1	956	42.7	2,255	10
Cabell	369	14,250	1,889.1	688.4	142	920	144.6	33.3	4,691	192.0	12,035	56

STATE County	Government employment and payroll, 2017									Local government finances, 2017				
			March payroll (percent of total)							General revenue				
												Taxes		
													Per capita[1] (dollars)	
	Full-time equivalent employees	March payroll (dollars)	Adminis-tration, judicial, and legal	Police and corrections	Fire protection	Highways and transpor-tation	Health and welfare	Natural resources and utilities	Education and libraries	Total (mil dol)	Inter-govern-mental (mil dol)	Total (mil dol)	Total	Property
	171	172	173	174	175	176	177	178	179	180	181	182	183	184
VIRGINIA—Cont'd														
Martinsville city	727	2,553,769	10.7	14.0	4.0	3.0	0.6	10.2	55.0	74.8	39.7	18.4	1,433	806
Newport News city	7,978	33,914,885	6.2	12.4	6.1	2.4	5.3	11.0	55.6	894.8	386.1	368.0	2,051	1,455
Norfolk city	13,561	62,833,701	5.6	10.7	3.8	9.2	9.0	6.2	53.3	1,562.9	651.5	443.6	1,814	1,104
Norton city	209	683,863	7.5	14.9	0.4	4.8	6.2	11.5	53.1	27.7	13.2	11.0	2,798	1,335
Petersburg city	1,297	5,006,121	11.4	10.7	11.0	3.5	5.0	6.6	51.8	148.2	78.2	55.2	1,772	1,308
Poquoson city	420	1,601,460	7.2	7.3	8.9	3.3	0.0	3.2	66.5	44.7	17.7	21.9	1,820	1,561
Portsmouth city	4,141	17,014,076	6.0	17.8	6.2	1.6	7.7	4.5	54.3	428.9	213.4	166.4	1,755	1,255
Radford city	467	1,767,278	9.3	10.5	2.7	2.6	3.6	15.7	51.6	48.8	26.1	13.2	757	518
Richmond city	8,858	36,278,451	8.5	17.3	6.1	3.1	7.8	10.0	43.8	1,324.8	522.3	525.3	2,312	1,451
Roanoke city	3,858	15,899,140	8.6	12.8	8.0	3.5	7.4	2.3	55.4	497.7	258.5	184.9	1,868	1,142
Salem city	1,303	4,997,631	8.9	22.8	6.5	3.3	1.1	9.3	44.6	128.7	49.0	60.4	2,380	1,562
Staunton city	940	3,606,993	12.0	25.7	2.9	3.9	0.0	6.1	46.7	99.8	46.4	36.9	1,518	1,018
Suffolk city	3,408	14,357,842	10.0	8.4	10.8	3.4	3.3	7.4	55.9	389.2	167.1	168.9	1,874	1,377
Virginia Beach city	18,457	75,108,285	6.0	9.8	3.9	1.4	6.5	14.4	55.5	2,190.5	730.1	948.1	2,107	1,432
Waynesboro city	831	2,848,288	7.2	8.1	4.7	1.9	0.6	8.0	61.8	93.3	41.4	37.9	1,703	986
Williamsburg city	444	1,647,202	10.8	36.4	10.4	2.4	5.2	9.9	20.5	62.4	13.3	34.9	2,327	972
Winchester city	1,713	6,512,336	7.4	21.8	5.1	4.3	3.3	6.4	48.6	196.3	70.3	75.6	2,683	1,545
WASHINGTON	X	X	X	X	X	X	X	X	X	X	X	X	X	X
Adams	1,271	5,372,706	4.5	6.0	0.9	3.8	19.7	9.5	55.3	132.3	70.4	27.8	1,414	1,017
Asotin	773	3,356,048	6.0	7.2	6.3	4.2	3.1	7.3	64.2	79.5	42.6	23.1	1,024	732
Benton	8,892	52,858,675	4.5	5.8	2.9	3.0	17.1	28.7	36.6	1,283.4	573.7	316.0	1,595	822
Chelan	4,127	22,588,705	4.1	5.6	2.0	5.6	11.0	31.0	38.9	503.4	186.5	164.8	2,160	1,241
Clallam	3,927	21,708,301	5.8	6.9	3.6	4.0	40.7	9.5	26.6	493.0	133.6	100.7	1,332	805
Clark	14,969	81,711,108	4.7	6.7	4.3	5.4	2.5	7.1	66.6	2,115.1	967.4	754.4	1,590	1,028
Columbia	333	1,418,597	8.8	2.7	3.0	9.1	43.8	1.5	25.8	40.1	13.6	9.9	2,482	2,015
Cowlitz	3,640	18,508,063	7.2	10.5	3.3	7.0	2.9	12.2	53.9	542.9	209.0	154.7	1,448	882
Douglas	1,547	7,927,036	4.6	5.2	1.7	5.4	0.0	22.4	59.0	197.0	116.9	52.9	1,260	869
Ferry	423	1,680,561	9.9	5.7	0.4	7.7	19.8	13.2	40.6	50.8	29.8	5.8	760	553
Franklin	3,219	15,792,848	5.0	7.3	3.8	2.8	0.6	11.7	66.8	440.5	228.7	109.5	1,192	703
Garfield	202	821,892	8.3	7.3	1.4	11.0	35.7	2.0	32.7	25.5	10.4	5.9	2,673	2,318
Grant	5,811	29,561,640	3.4	5.3	1.2	2.8	20.0	23.9	41.1	712.9	266.0	151.5	1,588	1,088
Grays Harbor	3,828	18,659,149	5.3	7.1	4.0	7.5	26.2	10.7	37.2	500.1	155.7	113.0	1,558	920
Island	2,843	15,232,539	5.8	5.7	4.0	6.0	39.8	3.3	34.0	366.5	113.2	112.0	1,346	877
Jefferson	1,532	8,627,335	6.5	4.4	5.5	8.0	46.7	5.6	21.9	219.4	43.0	58.8	1,884	1,200
King	78,547	522,087,826	9.9	9.4	5.1	12.4	14.4	11.7	34.4	17,468.8	4,565.5	7,233.2	3,282	1,678
Kitsap	7,352	40,302,464	7.9	7.7	8.9	7.4	3.0	6.6	57.4	1,280.4	652.7	428.5	1,609	1,052
Kittitas	1,783	9,308,957	8.4	7.9	3.4	3.4	35.9	8.3	31.1	253.8	74.4	74.6	1,615	1,011
Klickitat	1,142	5,843,294	5.7	5.1	0.7	5.0	33.2	12.9	35.1	155.9	49.7	31.8	1,463	1,145
Lewis	2,942	14,215,448	7.6	8.5	4.0	5.9	8.7	11.5	50.3	357.0	155.8	97.5	1,245	775
Lincoln	846	3,995,893	6.1	5.0	0.9	7.1	36.8	1.1	39.9	97.0	41.2	17.0	1,607	1,334
Mason	2,574	13,523,685	5.7	5.7	4.1	5.1	29.9	10.4	37.5	333.4	116.8	87.7	1,377	1,006
Okanogan	2,321	10,618,170	5.7	6.5	0.4	6.8	25.7	9.3	45.1	282.1	136.5	52.3	1,248	802
Pacific	1,032	5,376,385	5.9	6.0	3.2	6.5	33.2	10.5	34.3	152.7	50.1	38.0	1,749	1,214
Pend Oreille	880	4,172,244	6.0	4.5	0.5	3.4	36.2	19.6	26.4	85.1	28.8	13.0	975	716
Pierce	25,902	157,612,022	8.6	7.9	8.1	8.5	2.8	11.9	50.6	4,276.7	1,618.1	1,578.9	1,795	1,196
San Juan	631	3,152,711	15.4	7.2	7.0	9.5	6.4	7.6	44.8	98.1	31.2	48.1	2,877	1,811
Skagit	6,316	34,058,435	5.1	5.3	2.2	4.5	35.2	4.8	40.1	1,108.2	363.5	253.5	2,014	1,281
Skamania	367	1,715,614	15.5	11.6	1.3	6.3	10.7	15.5	35.5	44.8	19.0	14.6	1,233	800
Snohomish	20,647	129,047,276	6.0	8.2	4.5	7.6	3.3	13.4	53.7	3,639.9	1,460.7	1,384.1	1,726	1,093
Spokane	15,579	84,768,081	8.5	11.6	6.9	6.5	2.6	7.0	54.6	2,353.2	1,115.1	775.1	1,533	925
Stevens	1,363	5,882,354	7.3	7.8	2.0	4.3	7.4	4.8	64.4	155.1	89.9	35.7	801	571
Thurston	8,635	45,715,941	9.4	8.2	6.1	6.6	2.8	6.0	58.6	1,293.7	527.4	507.6	1,811	1,121
Wahkiakum	165	754,148	15.4	9.9	0.2	7.0	13.8	15.5	32.3	85.5	75.5	4.2	995	653
Walla Walla	2,255	10,369,781	7.3	9.6	5.1	6.8	5.0	3.7	60.2	278.3	123.5	98.1	1,622	997
Whatcom	5,979	33,006,077	9.4	9.9	8.3	8.0	3.6	5.1	52.1	923.4	347.8	387.7	1,751	1,024
Whitman	1,782	8,963,685	6.9	5.9	4.3	5.4	36.0	3.8	34.2	283.9	93.9	65.2	1,321	911
Yakima	9,179	43,173,358	6.3	9.8	3.4	2.4	1.2	5.9	69.1	1,163.9	708.0	278.4	1,114	636
WEST VIRGINIA	X	X	X	X	X	X	X	X	X	X	X	X	X	X
Barbour	511	1,634,273	7.0	3.6	0.0	1.0	5.4	8.0	70.7	36.8	20.0	8.5	513	462
Berkeley	3,761	13,282,683	4.1	4.0	1.7	1.1	0.7	4.3	82.4	278.2	125.1	101.2	879	756
Boone	708	2,434,601	5.3	5.3	0.0	2.0	3.1	3.0	77.2	83.4	27.7	27.3	1,223	1,197
Braxton	476	1,356,686	8.2	3.4	5.0	1.5	1.5	4.7	75.1	28.2	15.4	8.7	609	563
Brooke	676	2,157,151	6.2	8.0	0.0	2.9	2.9	6.9	72.4	61.2	23.0	26.4	1,179	1,044
Cabell	3,013	10,461,020	4.9	7.1	3.1	4.4	7.7	3.1	67.2	294.6	99.5	124.5	1,318	1,031

1. Based on the resident population estimated as of July 1 of the year shown.

STATE County	Local government finances, 2017 (cont.) — Direct general expenditure — Total (mil dol)	Per capita[1] (dollars)	Percent of total for: Education	Health and hospitals	Police protection	Public welfare	Highways	Debt outstanding — Total (mil dol)	Per capita[1] (dollars)	Government employment, 2020 — Federal civilian	Federal military	State and local	Individual income tax returns, 2019 — Number of returns	Mean adjusted gross income	Mean income tax
	185	186	187	188	189	190	191	192	193	194	195	196	197	198	199
VIRGINIA—Cont'd															
Martinsville city	74.8	5,830	47.4	0.4	5.8	0.8	7.9	16.3	1,268	(2)	(2)	(2)	6,070	43,529	3,951
Newport News city	929.0	5,177	42.6	0.6	5.5	4.1	2.2	1,181.2	6,582	5,677	6,801	10,928	86,820	50,056	4,405
Norfolk city	1,538.8	6,293	41.6	5.5	4.8	3.0	2.4	2,033.9	8,317	21,428	18,150	18,279	105,470	53,023	5,404
Norton city	26.7	6,819	36.6	0.5	8.7	5.8	7.0	16.4	4,182	(3)	(3)	(3)	1,690	42,922	3,198
Petersburg city	151.0	4,848	38.5	0.9	8.9	11.1	4.5	35.4	1,135	(4)	(4)	(4)	16,070	34,571	2,302
Poquoson city	42.4	3,520	54.9	1.0	7.7	2.5	3.7	35.5	2,946	(5)	(5)	(5)	6,000	92,653	11,002
Portsmouth city	475.1	5,010	35.3	2.3	6.8	4.7	1.4	641.1	6,760	14,852	5,930	5,012	45,920	44,756	3,399
Radford city	57.4	3,286	44.8	0.4	7.0	5.1	4.7	26.7	1,526	(6)	(6)	(6)	5,570	52,227	4,859
Richmond city	1,274.0	5,607	29.8	6.1	8.1	5.6	3.8	2,281.4	10,040	6,309	1,096	37,491	107,030	76,009	10,832
Roanoke city	463.8	4,686	40.0	0.4	5.2	12.7	5.3	138.3	1,397	1,574	304	6,704	47,130	50,287	5,125
Salem city	142.4	5,611	44.7	0.6	4.8	1.4	4.4	112.5	4,434	(7)	(7)	(7)	11,970	62,361	6,392
Staunton city	98.7	4,057	37.1	7.3	6.0	5.9	7.2	81.3	3,342	(8)	(8)	(8)	12,400	55,088	5,029
Suffolk city	396.4	4,399	44.7	0.7	6.3	3.2	10.5	799.3	8,871	1,394	396	5,228	44,030	68,520	7,052
Virginia Beach city	2,083.8	4,632	41.1	3.2	4.7	2.8	5.2	2,366.3	5,260	6,661	20,137	21,707	225,830	74,981	9,088
Waynesboro city	84.3	3,791	47.2	0.8	5.5	5.8	8.5	64.0	2,877	(8)	(8)	(8)	11,250	50,713	4,303
Williamsburg city	65.5	4,369	13.6	0.8	7.2	3.1	2.1	14.1	943	(9)	(9)	(9)	5,780	70,188	8,499
Winchester city	176.0	6,247	43.0	1.0	4.7	4.0	2.7	298.0	10,577	(10)	(10)	(10)	13,880	61,741	7,187
WASHINGTON	X	X	X	X	X	X	X	X	X	78,622	68,608	493,152	3,757,520	92,054	12,610
Adams	133.1	6,773	49.9	12.7	3.2	0.0	7.7	144.2	7,338	39	49	1,585	9,130	46,171	3,524
Asotin	78.8	3,501	51.1	3.5	4.5	0.0	5.1	68.6	3,046	74	59	1,069	10,350	62,589	6,339
Benton	1,260.2	6,358	40.3	28.7	3.6	0.2	2.6	7,605.4	38,372	789	519	11,176	94,780	73,567	8,046
Chelan	449.5	5,892	44.2	11.0	4.4	0.3	4.8	1,051.2	13,777	610	190	6,164	40,570	68,203	7,699
Clallam	487.3	6,442	25.2	37.8	3.2	0.1	3.7	306.2	4,048	511	535	7,299	38,340	63,870	6,395
Clark	1,950.0	4,111	55.5	1.8	4.4	0.5	5.4	2,246.6	4,736	3,765	1,279	22,124	245,070	81,170	9,788
Columbia	36.9	9,221	18.7	38.0	4.0	0.1	12.2	25.6	6,401	87	10	485	1,820	58,051	5,237
Cowlitz	508.9	4,765	41.8	1.6	5.7	0.5	4.7	656.3	6,144	271	272	5,947	51,610	61,440	5,975
Douglas	169.6	4,035	51.9	15.4	5.1	0.0	10.8	330.7	7,868	297	107	2,016	20,900	61,237	6,013
Ferry	41.2	5,434	34.4	26.2	3.0	0.0	14.7	20.9	2,764	171	19	751	2,920	47,203	3,834
Franklin	427.7	4,654	58.4	1.7	4.6	0.1	2.8	416.8	4,535	499	232	6,190	42,520	56,561	4,974
Garfield	23.4	10,573	22.2	33.0	4.3	0.1	16.6	9.2	4,156	141	6	313	940	53,736	4,221
Grant	688.2	7,217	45.8	21.5	3.6	0.5	4.4	1,808.6	18,967	780	242	7,556	46,260	53,496	4,692
Grays Harbor	481.8	6,646	29.9	32.0	4.3	0.4	4.6	432.4	5,965	190	224	6,103	33,970	54,166	4,976
Island	347.5	4,174	29.0	31.2	3.6	0.2	5.2	251.7	3,023	1,344	7,577	3,267	43,620	78,184	8,703
Jefferson	198.0	6,344	21.1	45.3	3.3	0.1	4.9	311.5	9,982	437	112	2,327	17,660	73,286	8,281
King	15,016.5	6,814	30.1	13.1	4.6	0.9	5.9	27,717.5	12,577	20,089	7,075	161,940	1,156,330	135,218	22,629
Kitsap	1,207.7	4,535	41.9	5.2	3.7	0.0	5.0	880.5	3,307	21,055	5,734	12,790	133,910	85,150	10,550
Kittitas	266.5	5,771	34.2	29.8	4.3	0.1	5.6	193.9	4,199	154	122	4,424	21,170	70,565	8,119
Klickitat	136.7	6,285	33.1	32.8	3.6	0.0	9.7	227.8	10,472	87	56	1,549	11,080	68,114	7,477
Lewis	354.7	4,529	48.8	13.5	4.6	0.3	7.1	494.0	6,308	249	200	4,741	37,530	57,901	5,250
Lincoln	94.1	8,892	36.5	31.2	2.8	0.1	12.1	50.4	4,765	73	27	1,088	5,000	63,596	5,820
Mason	336.3	5,277	42.2	29.3	3.8	0.1	4.4	490.5	7,696	106	162	5,494	30,510	62,775	6,061
Okanogan	269.1	6,420	43.8	26.3	3.0	0.0	6.6	180.0	4,295	442	104	4,366	19,490	49,375	4,301
Pacific	147.9	6,804	30.4	31.5	3.9	0.0	5.4	100.1	4,606	67	164	1,675	11,050	55,163	5,188
Pend Oreille	91.6	6,859	23.1	44.5	2.9	0.1	5.8	198.6	14,866	123	46	1,431	6,070	59,123	5,714
Pierce	4,026.7	4,578	44.6	1.4	6.4	0.5	5.3	6,262.6	7,119	11,939	33,005	46,259	443,180	73,969	8,232
San Juan	106.4	6,358	30.7	6.5	3.4	0.1	11.1	92.2	5,510	63	43	762	9,840	103,111	15,666
Skagit	1,115.7	8,865	28.0	43.7	2.5	0.1	3.4	865.1	6,873	415	319	10,758	64,090	73,595	8,152
Skamania	41.9	3,544	35.2	9.3	6.1	0.0	8.9	20.1	1,705	103	30	494	5,470	80,426	10,588
Snohomish	3,438.7	4,287	45.9	8.3	5.0	0.6	4.1	4,264.5	5,317	2,303	2,830	36,250	407,680	86,407	10,502
Spokane	2,329.5	4,607	48.0	7.3	5.2	0.5	4.6	2,153.5	4,259	5,070	4,723	30,574	253,070	67,658	7,484
Stevens	150.8	3,377	54.0	6.8	4.3	0.1	11.3	88.0	1,971	342	114	2,813	20,180	57,003	5,223
Thurston	1,287.9	4,595	49.0	6.7	4.0	0.0	3.7	1,289.3	4,600	863	801	38,156	146,270	71,301	7,619
Wahkiakum	75.5	17,767	8.5	75.9	1.4	0.0	3.5	14.5	3,417	31	11	252	2,080	63,912	6,463
Walla Walla	265.3	4,384	46.0	3.5	5.4	0.1	9.6	233.0	3,850	1,983	147	4,149	27,360	64,917	6,608
Whatcom	917.9	4,146	48.9	3.2	4.9	0.0	5.6	850.4	3,841	1,538	632	13,470	111,450	72,475	7,997
Whitman	242.6	4,913	29.1	37.8	4.0	0.2	5.9	155.2	3,142	233	120	9,213	17,520	64,488	6,434
Yakima	1,133.6	4,536	60.9	0.9	4.8	0.2	4.6	803.9	3,217	1,289	711	16,132	116,870	53,353	5,008
WEST VIRGINIA	X	X	X	X	X	X	X	X	X	25,516	8,473	116,412	780,950	54,982	5,262
Barbour	42.3	2,563	64.9	3.2	4.0	0.0	1.6	20.4	1,235	46	74	633	6,510	45,074	3,225
Berkeley	309.5	2,690	73.8	0.5	4.5	0.0	0.6	333.8	2,901	3,400	589	5,006	59,430	55,973	4,888
Boone	85.9	3,838	45.2	28.3	2.5	0.4	0.9	13.3	596	71	100	1,325	7,980	48,059	3,471
Braxton	32.1	2,255	63.8	1.3	6.9	0.0	0.6	76.7	5,398	66	63	913	5,160	46,579	3,729
Brooke	70.5	3,149	70.0	0.9	7.6	0.0	2.1	56.9	2,543	35	100	926	10,640	53,275	4,720
Cabell	303.3	3,211	49.0	1.1	6.4	0.4	1.5	99.2	1,050	1,102	478	7,461	39,660	55,423	5,858

1. Based on the resident population estimated as of July 1 of the year shown. 2. Martinsville city is included with Henry county. 3. Norton city is included with Wise county. 4. Petersburg and Colonial Heights cities are included with Dinwiddie county. 5. Poquoson city is included with York county. 6. Radford city is included with Montgomery county. 7. Salem city is included with Roanoke county. 8. Staunton and Waynesboro cities are included with Augusta county. 9. Williamsburg city is included with James City county. 10. Winchester city is included with Frederick county.

State / county code	CBSA code[1]	County Type code[2]	STATE County	Land area[3] (sq. mi)	Population, 2021: Total persons 2021	Population, 2021: Rank	Population, 2021: Per square mile	Race alone or in combination, not Hispanic or Latino (percent): White	Black	American Indian, Alaska Native	Asian and Pacific Islancer	Percent Hispanic or Latino[4]	Age (percent): Under 5 years	5 to 17 years	18 to 24 years	25 to 34 years	35 to 44 years	45 to 54 years
				1	2	3	4	5	6	7	8	9	10	11	12	13	14	15
			WEST VIRGINIA—Cont'd															
54013		8	Calhoun	279.3	6,176	2,721	22.1	97.6	0.8	1.0	0.4	1.3	4.2	10.7	9.5	9.2	11.4	12.2
54015	16620	3	Clay	341.9	7,892	2,583	23.1	98.0	0.8	1.1	0.4	1.0	4.9	13.0	10.7	9.9	11.2	12.6
54017	17220	9	Doddridge	319.7	7,735	2,593	24.2	95.6	3.3	1.1	0.7	0.7	3.4	7.5	12.1	13.0	13.1	13.5
54019	13220	3	Fayette	661.6	39,927	1,184	60.3	93.8	5.2	0.9	0.5	1.4	4.8	12.1	11.1	11.0	11.9	12.8
54021		7	Gilmer	338.5	7,377	2,633	21.8	82.4	11.2	1.4	1.1	5.7	3.9	8.6	17.8	14.0	13.6	12.2
54023		7	Grant	477.4	10,983	2,343	23.0	96.9	1.3	0.7	0.4	1.7	5.4	11.0	10.0	10.7	10.5	12.9
54025		6	Greenbrier	1,019.8	32,608	1,368	32.0	94.2	3.6	1.1	1.0	2.0	4.9	11.1	10.5	10.9	11.3	12.3
54027	49020	3	Hampshire	640.4	23,302	1,668	36.4	96.5	1.8	0.7	0.6	1.6	4.6	10.0	10.1	10.4	11.0	13.5
54029	48260	3	Hancock	82.6	28,656	1,472	346.9	95.0	3.7	0.8	0.7	1.6	4.3	10.7	10.4	10.9	11.1	13.5
54031		6	Hardy	582.3	14,160	2,140	24.3	91.5	3.7	0.9	1.0	4.5	5.3	11.0	9.9	10.3	11.1	13.5
54033	17220	5	Harrison	416.0	65,158	828	156.6	95.3	2.7	0.8	1.0	1.9	5.3	12.3	11.0	11.8	12.6	12.8
54035	16620	6	Jackson	464.4	27,738	1,509	59.7	97.5	1.1	0.8	0.5	1.2	5.3	12.2	11.0	11.0	11.5	12.9
54037	47900	1	Jefferson	209.3	58,370	898	278.9	84.9	7.9	1.0	2.4	6.8	4.9	12.3	12.5	11.2	13.1	14.1
54039	16620	3	Kanawha	901.6	177,952	379	197.4	90.0	9.2	0.8	1.6	1.2	4.9	11.3	11.2	12.3	12.1	12.3
54041		7	Lewis	386.9	16,892	1,979	43.7	97.2	1.2	0.7	0.7	1.4	5.2	12.4	10.1	12.1	11.9	13.0
54043	16620	2	Lincoln	437.1	20,126	1,810	46.0	98.3	1.0	0.6	0.5	0.8	5.6	12.6	11.0	10.7	11.5	13.6
54045	34350	6	Logan	453.7	31,909	1,385	70.3	96.7	2.2	0.5	0.4	1.1	5.3	11.8	10.7	11.3	11.9	13.4
54047		7	McDowell	533.5	18,363	1,906	34.4	89.9	8.4	0.7	0.3	1.9	4.8	12.0	9.5	10.5	11.5	12.5
54049	21900	4	Marion	308.8	56,001	924	181.4	94.3	4.4	0.8	1.0	1.4	5.3	11.3	14.9	12.1	11.8	12.3
54051	48540	3	Marshall	305.4	30,115	1,436	98.6	97.3	1.5	0.7	0.7	1.0	4.4	11.0	10.2	11.6	11.1	12.9
54053	38580	6	Mason	430.8	25,157	1,602	58.4	97.4	1.8	0.8	0.6	0.8	4.8	11.9	10.7	11.2	12.1	12.4
54055	14140	4	Mercer	419.0	59,097	887	141.0	91.8	7.4	0.7	0.8	1.3	5.4	12.3	11.4	11.8	11.2	12.2
54057	19060	3	Mineral	327.9	26,857	1,534	81.9	95.1	4.2	0.7	0.9	1.1	4.9	11.5	11.7	11.4	11.0	12.8
54059		7	Mingo	423.1	23,005	1,678	54.4	96.9	2.4	0.5	0.5	0.9	5.8	12.5	10.6	10.5	12.0	13.3
54061	34060	3	Monongalia	360.1	106,387	580	295.4	90.2	5.1	0.6	4.3	2.3	4.6	9.2	22.7	16.0	13.2	10.3
54063		8	Monroe	472.8	12,332	2,257	26.1	97.1	1.5	1.2	0.6	1.3	4.6	11.6	9.8	9.9	10.9	12.6
54065	25180	8	Morgan	229.1	17,221	1,956	75.2	95.9	1.8	1.2	0.9	2.0	3.9	10.1	10.1	10.5	10.6	13.6
54067		6	Nicholas	646.8	24,300	1,636	37.6	97.6	1.1	1.0	0.6	0.9	4.5	12.0	10.0	10.5	11.4	12.8
54069	48540	3	Ohio	105.8	41,776	1,150	394.9	93.9	5.1	0.7	1.3	1.3	4.9	11.0	13.8	11.1	11.5	11.4
54071		8	Pendleton	696.1	6,142	2,727	8.8	95.8	2.8	0.9	0.6	1.4	5.1	10.5	8.8	9.5	10.5	10.9
54073		6	Pleasants	130.1	7,601	2,607	58.4	96.6	2.3	0.8	0.6	1.2	5.1	10.7	10.9	12.7	12.9	13.8
54075		9	Pocahontas	940.2	7,841	2,588	8.3	95.9	2.2	1.1	0.6	1.8	4.6	9.9	9.1	10.4	11.1	11.6
54077	34060	3	Preston	648.8	34,358	1,318	53.0	96.8	1.6	0.7	0.5	1.4	4.9	11.0	9.6	13.1	12.8	13.1
54079	26580	2	Putnam	345.7	57,260	913	165.6	96.1	2.0	0.6	1.3	1.4	4.8	12.8	11.3	11.0	13.3	13.7
54081	13220	3	Raleigh	605.4	73,771	750	121.9	89.2	9.0	0.9	1.4	1.7	5.3	12.2	11.1	12.3	12.3	12.7
54083	21180	7	Randolph	1,039.7	27,806	1,505	26.7	96.3	2.4	0.8	0.8	1.1	4.9	10.4	11.5	12.4	11.6	12.3
54085		8	Ritchie	452.0	8,383	2,546	18.5	97.9	1.2	0.7	0.5	1.0	5.2	11.0	10.3	10.1	10.9	13.0
54087		6	Roane	483.6	13,898	2,159	28.7	97.6	1.0	0.8	0.7	1.3	4.7	11.7	10.9	9.7	11.3	13.4
54089		6	Summers	360.6	11,908	2,291	33.0	93.2	5.0	1.2	0.6	1.8	3.9	8.7	9.2	10.9	12.1	12.8
54091	17220	6	Taylor	172.8	16,492	2,004	95.4	97.1	1.8	0.8	0.7	0.9	4.2	11.7	10.0	12.0	12.8	13.7
54093		8	Tucker	419.0	6,672	2,686	15.9	98.0	0.8	0.6	0.6	1.0	3.5	7.6	9.0	10.4	11.5	13.2
54095		9	Tyler	256.3	8,155	2,566	31.8	97.6	0.9	0.7	1.1	0.8	4.5	11.5	10.1	10.0	10.2	14.3
54097		7	Upshur	354.6	23,791	1,650	67.1	96.7	1.8	0.7	0.7	1.5	4.9	11.8	14.3	11.2	11.3	11.8
54099	26580	2	Wayne	506.0	38,498	1,207	76.1	97.8	1.2	0.8	0.6	0.8	4.8	11.6	11.3	11.5	11.2	13.5
54101		9	Webster	553.5	8,249	2,559	14.9	98.4	0.9	0.8	0.4	0.9	4.6	11.5	9.6	9.9	10.4	13.5
54103		6	Wetzel	358.1	14,170	2,138	39.6	97.8	1.0	0.6	0.5	1.2	5.5	11.4	10.9	10.9	10.5	12.9
54105	37620	3	Wirt	232.5	5,063	2,819	21.8	97.9	1.3	0.9	0.6	0.8	5.0	12.3	10.2	9.1	11.9	12.5
54107	37620	3	Wood	366.5	83,624	689	228.2	96.6	2.2	0.7	1.0	1.3	5.2	12.0	11.0	11.5	11.9	12.8
54109		6	Wyoming	499.5	21,051	1,761	42.1	98.1	1.2	0.7	0.4	0.9	4.8	11.7	11.0	10.6	11.4	13.4
55000		0	WISCONSIN	54,167.4	5,895,908	X	108.8	81.9	7.4	1.4	3.7	7.5	5.4	12.3	13.2	12.5	12.7	11.9
55001		8	Adams	645.6	20,875	1,767	32.3	90.6	3.5	1.5	1.1	4.6	3.1	7.9	8.0	9.5	9.8	11.2
55003		7	Ashland	1,045.0	16,107	2,028	15.4	84.5	1.3	12.7	1.1	3.5	5.5	12.2	13.3	10.6	11.4	10.8
55005		6	Barron	863.0	46,719	1,043	54.1	93.5	2.2	1.5	1.0	3.0	5.3	12.2	10.7	10.6	11.6	11.4
55007		8	Bayfield	1,477.9	16,320	2,014	11.0	86.8	1.2	11.1	1.0	2.7	4.2	9.6	8.7	8.0	10.0	11.1
55009	24580	2	Brown	530.1	269,591	260	508.6	81.2	4.1	3.2	4.1	9.7	5.8	13.3	13.3	13.3	13.2	11.9
55011		8	Buffalo	675.8	13,302	2,196	19.7	95.9	1.0	0.8	0.7	2.7	4.8	11.7	10.7	10.2	11.4	12.1
55013		8	Burnett	821.6	16,744	1,990	20.4	92.4	1.4	5.3	0.9	2.1	3.6	9.4	8.4	8.1	9.2	11.2
55015	11540	3	Calumet	318.3	52,539	964	165.1	91.3	1.5	0.9	2.9	4.9	4.9	13.2	12.1	11.1	13.4	13.7
55017	20740	3	Chippewa	1,008.4	66,865	804	66.3	94.0	2.5	1.0	1.9	2.0	5.2	12.3	11.2	12.1	13.4	12.2
55019		6	Clark	1,209.7	34,746	1,306	28.7	92.5	0.9	0.8	0.8	5.9	8.1	16.5	13.5	9.9	10.6	10.8
55021	31540	2	Columbia	765.5	58,488	896	76.4	92.6	2.5	1.0	1.3	4.0	5.1	11.7	11.0	11.9	13.1	12.8
55023		7	Crawford	570.6	16,075	2,030	28.2	94.6	2.7	0.8	1.1	2.0	4.8	11.0	11.5	9.9	11.5	11.2
55025	31540	2	Dane	1,196.5	563,951	125	471.3	80.8	6.9	0.7	7.4	6.9	5.1	11.4	16.8	15.5	14.0	11.2
55027	13180	4	Dodge	875.7	89,313	664	102.0	89.5	3.9	0.9	1.0	5.8	4.6	11.0	11.6	12.6	13.3	13.1
55029		6	Door	482.0	30,369	1,426	63.0	94.0	1.3	1.2	0.8	4.0	3.8	9.1	9.0	8.6	9.9	11.0

1. CBSA = Core Based Statistical Area. See Appendix A for explanation. See Appendix B for list of metropolitan areas with component counties. 2. County type code from the Economic Research Service of USDA Rural-Urban Continuum Codes. See Appendix A for definition. 3. Dry land or land partially or temporarily covered by water. 4. May be of any race.

STATE County	Population, 2021 (cont.): Age (percent) (cont.): 55 to 64 years	Population, 2021 (cont.): Age (percent) (cont.): 65 to 74 years	Population, 2021 (cont.): Age (percent) (cont.): 75 years and over	Population, 2021 (cont.): Percent female	Population change, 2000–2021: Total persons: 2010	Population change, 2000–2021: Total persons: 2020	Population change, 2000–2021: Percent change: 2010–2020	Population change, 2000–2021: Percent change: 2020–2021	Population change, 2000–2021: Components of change, 2020–2021: Births	Population change, 2000–2021: Components of change, 2020–2021: Deaths	Population change, 2000–2021: Components of change, 2020–2021: Net Migration	Households, 2016–2020: Number	Households, 2016–2020: Persons per household	Households, 2016–2020: Percent: Family households	Households, 2016–2020: Percent: Female family householder[1]	Households, 2016–2020: Percent: One person
	16	17	18	19	20	21	22	23	24	25	26	27	28	29	30	31
WEST VIRGINIA—Cont'd																
Calhoun	17.0	15.9	9.8	49.9	7,627	6,229	-18.3	-0.9	70	116	-5	2,814	2.6	66.1	8.4	25.9
Clay	15.3	14.0	8.4	49.1	9,386	8,051	-14.2	-2.0	100	170	-89	3,385	2.5	69.0	10.8	25.6
Doddridge	15.4	13.1	8.8	43.6	8,202	7,808	-4.8	-0.9	71	118	-25	2,623	2.9	76.0	7.2	21.5
Fayette	14.0	13.8	8.5	49.2	46,039	40,488	-12.1	-1.4	501	979	-85	17,388	2.4	66.6	10.8	30.3
Gilmer	12.1	10.1	7.7	40.2	8,693	7,408	-14.8	-0.4	70	118	17	2,516	2.6	65.0	11.2	28.5
Grant	14.7	13.9	10.9	49.0	11,937	10,976	-8.1	0.1	148	231	91	4,842	2.4	61.1	7.2	34.4
Greenbrier	15.0	14.5	9.4	50.5	35,480	32,977	-7.1	-1.1	418	807	20	15,436	2.2	59.8	9.9	35.1
Hampshire	16.6	14.8	9.1	48.7	23,964	23,093	-3.6	0.9	280	452	386	9,165	2.5	64.5	9.7	30.3
Hancock	15.2	14.5	9.4	50.9	30,676	29,095	-5.2	-1.5	312	618	-133	12,676	2.3	59.2	10.6	34.8
Hardy	16.0	13.6	9.4	49.1	14,025	14,299	2.0	-1.0	168	227	-78	5,933	2.3	68.6	8.2	25.8
Harrison	14.2	11.9	8.0	50.6	69,099	65,921	-4.6	-1.2	851	1,342	-279	27,213	2.4	63.4	11.0	30.6
Jackson	15.0	12.3	8.7	50.0	29,211	27,791	-4.9	-0.2	349	510	109	11,427	2.5	64.7	8.8	33.3
Jefferson	14.5	11.0	6.3	50.3	53,498	57,701	7.9	1.2	670	759	758	20,957	2.7	69.3	9.5	23.7
Kanawha	14.2	13.3	8.3	51.5	193,063	180,745	-6.4	-1.5	2,090	3,664	-1,224	78,137	2.3	60.4	12.3	34.1
Lewis	14.3	12.6	8.4	49.9	16,372	17,033	4.0	-0.8	205	328	-19	6,472	2.4	65.0	10.6	28.8
Lincoln	14.5	12.7	7.7	50.2	21,720	20,463	-5.8	-1.6	254	471	-121	8,295	2.5	74.1	11.1	23.4
Logan	13.7	14.2	7.6	50.5	36,743	32,567	-11.4	-2.0	431	779	-309	14,164	2.3	71.0	12.7	24.9
McDowell	15.7	14.8	8.8	50.4	22,113	19,111	-13.6	-3.9	201	462	-483	7,431	2.2	67.3	16.4	30.4
Marion	12.7	11.9	7.7	50.2	56,418	56,205	-0.4	-0.4	730	1,008	67	23,033	2.4	65.4	11.1	27.5
Marshall	15.2	14.9	8.8	49.7	33,107	30,591	-7.6	-1.6	327	603	-200	12,350	2.5	64.4	11.3	32.3
Mason	14.8	13.2	8.8	51.4	27,324	25,453	-6.8	-1.2	273	567	-3	10,593	2.5	71.8	8.2	24.6
Mercer	13.2	13.6	9.0	51.5	62,264	59,664	-4.2	-1.0	680	1,318	68	25,088	2.3	63.7	13.7	31.0
Mineral	14.3	13.5	8.9	50.0	28,212	26,938	-4.5	-0.3	307	517	129	10,810	2.4	65.1	9.7	29.3
Mingo	14.6	13.8	6.7	50.5	26,839	23,568	-12.2	-2.4	325	551	-334	10,174	2.3	68.2	12.6	29.4
Monongalia	10.5	8.6	4.9	48.4	96,189	105,822	10.0	0.5	1,291	1,084	331	40,233	2.5	53.8	7.6	32.9
Monroe	15.2	14.8	10.7	50.3	13,502	12,376	-8.3	-0.4	120	253	90	5,496	2.4	67.2	8.7	29.2
Morgan	17.1	15.2	9.1	49.1	17,541	17,063	-2.7	0.9	169	347	341	7,485	2.4	67.9	6.5	24.3
Nicholas	15.0	14.4	9.3	50.3	26,233	24,604	-6.2	-1.2	240	513	-31	10,280	2.4	70.9	9.8	26.2
Ohio	13.8	13.5	9.0	51.3	44,443	42,425	-4.5	-1.5	435	882	-206	17,254	2.3	57.8	10.9	37.0
Pendleton	16.6	15.7	12.4	49.3	7,695	6,143	-20.2	0.0	101	126	24	3,194	2.1	71.9	9.9	25.3
Pleasants	15.0	11.3	7.7	44.9	7,605	7,653	0.6	-0.7	88	141	1	2,822	2.5	70.6	9.3	21.9
Pocahontas	16.4	15.9	11.0	48.0	8,719	7,869	-9.7	-0.4	84	176	66	3,578	2.3	60.7	8.0	34.7
Preston	14.2	13.1	8.1	48.3	33,520	34,216	2.1	0.4	445	538	234	12,430	2.5	68.6	8.8	24.7
Putnam	13.8	11.7	7.5	50.3	55,486	57,440	3.5	-0.3	654	937	102	21,694	2.6	72.7	11.0	23.8
Raleigh	12.7	13.3	8.2	49.5	78,859	74,591	-5.4	-1.1	910	1,594	-142	31,116	2.3	66.9	12.8	28.8
Randolph	14.3	13.0	9.6	47.3	29,405	27,932	-5.0	-0.5	353	577	98	10,977	2.4	61.1	10.5	33.8
Ritchie	16.5	13.7	9.3	49.6	10,449	8,444	-19.2	-0.7	108	182	14	4,161	2.3	71.2	8.8	23.0
Roane	15.4	14.1	8.8	50.1	14,926	14,028	-6.0	-0.9	175	278	-26	5,599	2.5	63.4	9.7	29.5
Summers	15.5	16.4	10.5	54.3	13,927	11,959	-14.1	-0.4	119	239	71	5,617	2.1	64.5	10.5	33.2
Taylor	14.4	12.9	8.3	48.8	16,895	16,705	-1.1	-1.3	157	294	-76	6,649	2.5	65.9	11.3	28.7
Tucker	17.2	15.8	11.6	49.0	7,141	6,762	-5.3	-1.3	65	160	5	3,176	2.1	61.9	6.9	33.3
Tyler	15.5	14.5	9.5	50.0	9,208	8,313	-9.7	-1.9	77	174	-60	3,402	2.5	61.4	10.7	35.9
Upshur	13.4	12.7	8.5	50.2	24,254	23,816	-1.8	-0.1	290	403	87	9,592	2.4	63.3	12.8	31.1
Wayne	14.1	12.9	9.2	50.9	42,481	38,982	-8.2	-1.2	456	810	-131	15,228	2.6	66.3	8.3	30.5
Webster	15.7	15.6	9.2	50.2	9,154	8,378	-8.5	-1.5	85	169	-44	3,582	2.3	67.3	13.1	27.9
Wetzel	15.2	12.8	9.8	50.4	16,583	14,442	-12.9	-1.9	205	351	-127	6,022	2.5	62.4	10.0	30.5
Wirt	16.8	14.2	7.9	49.0	5,717	5,194	-9.1	-2.5	77	79	-127	2,557	2.3	64.9	5.6	30.7
Wood	14.5	12.5	8.6	51.1	86,956	84,296	-3.1	-0.8	997	1,632	-49	35,189	2.4	63.1	11.6	31.8
Wyoming	14.4	15.0	7.8	50.1	23,796	21,382	-10.1	-1.5	276	454	-155	8,674	2.4	75.2	11.0	22.0
WISCONSIN	14.1	11.0	6.9	49.9	5,686,986	5,893,718	3.6	0.0	76,033	79,179	4,881	2,377,935	2.4	62.2	9.4	30.1
Adams	19.5	19.2	11.7	46.0	20,875	20,654	-1.1	1.1	155	386	460	9,111	2.1	61.6	5.9	31.3
Ashland	15.5	13.1	7.6	49.6	16,157	16,027	-0.8	0.5	185	246	141	6,483	2.3	59.4	10.8	31.5
Barron	15.5	13.4	9.3	49.5	45,870	46,711	1.8	0.0	568	747	186	19,059	2.3	65.7	8.7	28.1
Bayfield	18.6	19.2	10.4	48.9	15,014	16,220	8.0	0.6	134	284	254	7,110	2.1	65.6	6.5	28.5
Brown	13.3	9.9	6.0	50.0	248,007	268,740	8.4	0.3	3,695	3,037	124	106,031	2.4	63.0	9.3	29.1
Buffalo	16.3	13.7	9.2	48.9	13,587	13,317	-2.0	-0.1	147	180	16	5,751	2.3	66.2	6.9	28.1
Burnett	19.3	19.5	11.3	48.5	15,457	16,526	6.9	1.3	129	244	340	7,242	2.1	64.4	7.9	28.2
Calumet	14.9	10.5	6.2	49.2	48,971	52,442	7.1	0.2	607	546	25	19,951	2.5	73.4	6.2	22.1
Chippewa	14.7	11.5	7.3	47.7	62,415	66,297	6.2	0.9	798	863	633	26,044	2.4	66.7	7.8	26.7
Clark	13.5	10.1	6.9	48.9	34,690	34,659	-0.1	0.3	699	483	-136	12,914	2.6	68.5	6.3	26.5
Columbia	15.3	11.9	7.1	48.6	56,833	58,490	2.9	0.0	702	790	76	24,336	2.3	65.4	7.7	27.5
Crawford	15.9	14.5	9.8	47.3	16,644	16,113	-3.2	-0.2	198	256	20	6,676	2.3	60.7	6.7	32.8
Dane	11.4	9.3	5.4	50.0	488,073	561,504	15.0	0.4	7,040	5,229	498	226,600	2.3	55.5	8.0	31.7
Dodge	15.5	11.0	7.4	46.8	88,759	89,396	0.7	-0.1	941	1,456	423	35,007	2.4	64.6	8.3	28.2
Door	17.6	19.4	11.7	50.0	27,785	30,066	8.2	1.0	251	523	587	13,429	2.0	65.6	7.5	29.8

1. No spouse present.

STATE County	Persons in group quarters, 2021	Daytime Population, 2016–2020		Births, 2021		Deaths, 2021		Persons under 65 with no health insurance, 2019		Medicare, 2021			COVID-19 Deaths, 2020	
		Number	Employment/ residence ratio	Total	Rate[1]	Number	Rate[1]	Number	Percent	Total beneficiaries	Enrolled in Original Medicare	Enrolled in Medicare Advantage	Number	Rate[1]
	32	33	34	35	36	37	38	39	40	41	42	43	44	45
WEST VIRGINIA—Cont'd														
Calhoun	9	6,305	0.6	51	8.2	86	13.9	474	9.0	2,000	1,328	673	D	D
Clay	37	7,744	0.7	82	10.3	140	17.6	555	8.4	2,534	1,354	1,179	D	D
Doddridge	965	7,484	0.7	62	8.0	98	12.6	475	8.6	1,691	1,020	671	D	D
Fayette	1,618	38,743	0.7	404	10.1	791	19.7	2,890	9.2	11,352	6,802	4,550	43	1.1
Gilmer	1,595	7,844	1.0	55	7.5	87	11.8	374	7.9	1,527	923	604	D	D
Grant	81	10,875	0.9	117	10.7	166	15.1	768	8.9	3,271	2,389	881	23	2.1
Greenbrier	463	36,334	1.1	326	10.0	634	19.4	2,318	8.9	9,548	6,638	2,910	47	1.4
Hampshire	357	18,865	0.5	220	9.5	357	15.4	1,795	10.4	5,932	4,354	1,578	26	1.1
Hancock	195	26,958	0.8	235	8.1	479	16.6	1,854	8.5	7,800	5,166	2,634	65	2.2
Hardy	50	14,984	1.2	134	9.4	189	13.3	1,094	10.3	3,509	2,553	956	D	D
Harrison	752	77,892	1.3	670	10.2	1,075	16.4	4,137	7.7	15,866	10,061	5,806	33	0.5
Jackson	135	26,554	0.8	276	10.0	416	15.0	1,680	7.5	7,401	4,715	2,686	31	1.1
Jefferson	1,012	47,526	0.7	532	9.2	619	10.7	3,464	7.4	11,330	8,476	2,854	36	0.6
Kanawha	3,239	203,077	1.3	1,675	9.4	2,924	16.3	11,108	8.1	46,512	26,434	20,079	217	1.2
Lewis	245	16,434	1.1	161	9.5	260	15.3	1,007	8.2	4,223	2,464	1,759	D	D
Lincoln	44	16,871	0.4	205	10.1	373	18.4	1,332	8.3	5,403	2,836	2,567	12	0.6
Logan	653	33,405	1.1	339	10.5	619	19.2	2,207	9.0	8,959	5,257	3,702	64	2.0
McDowell	139	18,831	1.2	156	8.4	365	19.6	1,580	11.8	5,587	3,414	2,173	D	D
Marion	1,331	52,277	0.8	575	10.3	800	14.3	3,426	7.8	13,134	7,854	5,280	20	0.4
Marshall	511	28,631	0.8	260	8.6	471	15.6	1,603	6.9	7,833	3,843	3,989	62	2.0
Mason	572	23,489	0.7	215	8.5	441	17.5	1,395	7.0	6,775	4,082	2,692	22	0.9
Mercer	1,078	58,373	1.0	550	9.3	1,058	17.8	3,928	8.8	16,567	10,177	6,390	54	0.9
Mineral	493	23,591	0.7	257	9.6	421	15.7	1,389	6.8	6,926	5,355	1,572	71	2.6
Mingo	69	22,739	0.8	259	11.1	448	19.3	1,797	9.7	6,713	3,795	2,918	27	1.2
Monongalia	6,237	117,301	1.2	1,002	9.4	888	8.4	5,943	6.9	14,803	8,646	6,157	35	0.3
Monroe	28	10,986	0.5	97	7.9	192	15.6	1,021	10.4	3,696	2,524	1,172	18	1.5
Morgan	75	13,212	0.4	138	8.1	264	15.4	1,336	9.8	4,757	3,516	1,242	10	0.6
Nicholas	133	23,487	0.9	198	8.1	414	17.0	1,641	8.8	7,324	4,227	3,097	11	0.4
Ohio	2,384	52,878	1.6	358	8.5	708	16.8	2,032	6.7	10,578	5,808	4,769	48	1.1
Pendleton	58	5,922	0.7	82	13.4	101	16.5	485	9.8	2,190	1,518	672	D	D
Pleasants	694	7,333	1.0	70	9.2	110	14.4	296	5.5	1,812	1,159	653	D	D
Pocahontas	239	8,301	1.0	65	8.3	140	17.8	502	8.7	2,481	1,701	780	D	D
Preston	1,811	28,290	0.6	345	10.1	414	12.1	2,095	8.5	7,841	5,033	2,808	36	1.1
Putnam	217	52,814	0.9	532	9.3	761	13.3	2,698	5.9	12,748	7,217	5,531	58	1.0
Raleigh	3,641	78,522	1.2	716	9.7	1,270	17.1	4,349	8.0	19,981	13,031	6,951	31	0.4
Randolph	2,174	29,962	1.1	291	10.5	473	17.0	1,811	9.0	7,123	4,775	2,348	D	D
Ritchie	74	10,245	1.1	83	9.9	151	18.0	668	9.1	2,626	1,705	921	D	D
Roane	89	12,944	0.8	144	10.3	222	15.9	1,059	10.1	3,991	2,408	1,583	11	0.8
Summers	910	11,643	0.7	100	8.4	182	15.3	699	8.4	3,604	2,475	1,129	12	1.0
Taylor	464	13,681	0.5	120	7.2	235	14.2	1,033	8.1	3,959	2,616	1,344	10	0.6
Tucker	153	6,327	0.8	52	7.7	137	20.4	449	9.2	2,172	1,333	839	D	D
Tyler	39	8,364	0.9	61	7.4	139	16.9	453	6.9	2,209	1,302	907	D	D
Upshur	1,151	23,038	0.9	237	10.0	328	13.8	1,732	9.7	6,013	3,429	2,584	D	D
Wayne	196	34,937	0.6	357	9.2	627	16.2	2,723	8.9	10,501	6,233	4,268	34	0.9
Webster	52	7,792	0.8	73	8.8	129	15.6	489	8.1	2,519	1,500	1,019	D	D
Wetzel	78	15,739	1.1	168	11.8	290	20.3	896	7.8	4,094	2,233	1,861	14	1.0
Wirt	0	4,550	0.4	62	12.1	70	13.7	357	7.8	1,500	962	538	D	D
Wood	943	87,903	1.1	805	9.6	1,259	15.0	4,781	7.3	22,041	14,815	7,225	81	1.0
Wyoming	54	19,275	0.7	220	10.4	376	17.7	1,421	9.0	6,106	3,404	2,703	27	1.3
WISCONSIN	138,424	5,769,960	1.0	60,404	10.2	62,985	10.7	320,719	6.8	1,200,231	645,066	555,165	6,251	1.1
Adams	1,093	17,568	0.7	133	6.4	318	15.3	1,183	9.1	7,223	4,895	2,328	18	0.9
Ashland	569	16,601	1.2	159	9.9	188	11.7	1,055	8.9	3,949	2,611	1,338	16	1.0
Barron	549	45,500	1.0	463	9.9	589	12.6	3,083	8.9	11,957	7,144	4,813	66	1.4
Bayfield	111	13,041	0.7	105	6.5	230	14.1	1,141	10.7	5,211	3,349	1,862	18	1.1
Brown	6,335	281,741	1.1	2,965	11.0	2,397	8.9	16,988	7.8	48,443	20,029	28,414	255	0.9
Buffalo	78	10,645	0.6	119	8.9	150	11.3	857	8.6	3,254	2,579	675	11	0.8
Burnett	133	14,038	0.8	92	5.5	208	12.5	978	9.2	5,465	3,467	1,998	28	1.7
Calumet	152	39,158	0.6	472	9.0	453	8.6	2,056	4.9	9,318	3,182	6,136	39	0.7
Chippewa	2,713	60,955	0.9	644	9.7	702	10.5	3,376	6.7	14,289	9,093	5,196	68	1.0
Clark	383	31,694	0.8	555	16.0	386	11.1	4,530	16.0	7,085	3,695	3,390	57	1.6
Columbia	1,309	50,696	0.8	544	9.3	629	10.8	2,700	5.9	12,779	8,453	4,326	48	0.8
Crawford	717	16,854	1.1	145	9.0	193	12.0	818	7.1	4,472	2,841	1,630	13	0.8
Dane	13,510	582,915	1.1	5,532	9.8	4,186	7.4	22,745	4.9	89,874	62,153	27,721	247	0.4
Dodge	6,323	78,143	0.8	734	8.2	1,141	12.8	4,125	6.2	18,569	10,803	7,765	156	1.7
Door	335	27,900	1.0	188	6.2	420	13.9	1,578	8.3	9,951	6,413	3,538	28	0.9

1. Per 1,000 estimated resident population.

STATE County	COVID-19 Vaccinations, 2021–2022: Number	COVID-19 Vaccinations, 2021–2022: Percent[5]	Education: School enrollment and attainment, 2016–2020: Enrollment[1]: Total	Education: Enrollment[1]: Percent private	Education: Attainment[2] (percent): High school graduate or less	Education: Attainment[2] (percent): Bachelor's degree or more	Education: Local government expenditures,[3] 2018–2019: Total current spending (mil dol)	Education: Local government expenditures,[3] 2018–2019: Current spending per student (dollars)	Money income, 2016–2020: Per capita income[4]	Money income, 2016–2020: Households: Median income (dollars)	Money income, 2016–2020: Households: Percent with income of less than $50,000	Money income, 2016–2020: Households: Percent with income of $200,000 or more	Income and poverty, 2020: Median household income (dollars)	Income and poverty, 2020: Percent below poverty level: All persons	Income and poverty, 2020: Percent below poverty level: Children under 18 years	Income and poverty, 2020: Percent below poverty level: Children 5 to 17 years in families
	46	47	48	49	50	51	52	53	54	55	56	57	58	59	60	61
WEST VIRGINIA—Cont'd																
Calhoun	2,465	34.7	1,187	9.2	62.9	12.2	11.9	12,260	23,009	38,668	62.0	1.6	41,726	20.0	25.9	24.1
Clay	4,779	56.2	1,713	6.0	74.9	10.3	23.7	12,605	18,545	35,154	69.4	1.5	36,537	23.3	33.2	31.2
Doddridge	5,047	59.7	1,373	8.2	62.3	16.6	22.6	20,118	27,040	51,300	47.5	8.2	50,445	17.0	20.7	20.1
Fayette	23,683	55.8	8,644	11.2	59.2	15.2	74.1	11,817	23,170	43,722	56.2	1.3	41,964	20.8	28.0	25.3
Gilmer	4,741	60.6	2,061	22.5	62.8	17.0	11.1	13,668	18,359	42,883	55.4	0.3	41,579	23.0	20.1	19.4
Grant	5,197	44.9	1,965	7.4	64.3	12.6	16.8	10,183	23,908	43,313	53.7	1.4	45,624	13.3	19.1	18.6
Greenbrier	19,073	55.0	6,195	13.2	52.0	20.1	60.0	12,331	26,330	39,807	60.9	2.4	40,016	17.8	25.2	23.2
Hampshire	10,704	46.2	4,237	12.4	61.0	12.3	48.7	16,090	25,409	48,528	51.5	1.1	53,333	13.7	22.8	22.6
Hancock	19,163	66.5	5,169	11.2	50.5	16.3	47.1	11,650	27,261	48,140	52.1	2.1	52,305	12.0	17.8	16.4
Hardy	7,652	55.5	2,675	4.7	66.3	13.9	23.9	10,100	27,819	46,513	52.7	2.2	47,469	13.5	19.4	19.3
Harrison	35,195	52.3	13,349	10.2	51.1	23.1	131.0	12,120	29,086	52,134	47.9	3.7	52,075	13.6	17.8	16.2
Jackson	14,947	52.3	5,503	10.6	55.0	18.0	53.9	11,756	27,591	49,115	50.5	4.1	52,123	14.2	19.1	18.0
Jefferson	36,273	63.5	13,943	17.4	40.2	31.6	107.0	11,819	36,722	82,551	29.3	9.3	85,779	7.8	9.1	8.5
Kanawha	116,758	65.5	34,703	10.9	47.3	26.4	324.9	12,612	29,981	47,122	52.1	4.1	47,830	15.7	20.3	19.0
Lewis	9,195	57.8	3,053	7.9	60.7	15.7	28.6	11,073	25,225	43,894	55.6	2.9	53,471	13.9	19.1	17.5
Lincoln	10,360	50.8	3,937	5.8	65.5	7.8	41.7	12,232	22,995	42,064	59.6	1.5	40,741	20.6	26.3	25.3
Logan	18,046	56.4	5,878	6.2	63.2	12.3	68.5	12,144	22,991	36,250	60.9	1.8	38,571	22.3	29.4	26.3
McDowell	9,164	52.0	3,042	7.9	75.4	6.8	40.0	13,070	15,150	26,072	76.6	0.6	26,582	31.8	37.8	34.5
Marion	31,997	57.1	12,410	7.4	50.3	23.1	98.9	12,422	27,763	52,856	47.0	2.8	58,878	13.2	16.4	15.7
Marshall	13,728	45.0	5,514	6.8	52.1	18.6	68.1	14,650	27,328	48,179	51.6	2.6	54,028	13.7	18.7	17.2
Mason	13,189	49.7	4,859	4.7	56.0	17.0	48.6	11,892	27,819	51,820	48.4	4.3	44,307	17.1	24.4	23.2
Mercer	31,535	53.7	12,292	12.4	54.4	20.1	101.0	11,221	23,341	40,716	60.0	1.9	42,095	15.1	24.3	22.4
Mineral	13,787	51.3	5,321	10.4	54.9	17.6	48.4	11,609	26,363	51,723	48.3	2.2	50,300	13.8	18.4	18.3
Mingo	9,480	40.5	4,915	6.8	68.3	10.0	47.8	11,356	19,400	35,454	65.3	0.6	32,955	24.9	30.3	29.0
Monongalia	62,060	58.8	35,117	7.6	33.9	43.7	140.5	12,034	33,527	54,198	46.2	7.1	55,836	15.2	12.9	12.6
Monroe	6,473	48.8	2,386	12.2	64.0	15.5	22.6	12,841	23,398	44,828	55.8	0.9	46,879	15.3	22.7	21.2
Morgan	7,240	40.5	3,509	18.4	53.9	18.6	26.6	11,425	29,803	57,116	41.9	1.7	57,432	11.0	16.1	14.8
Nicholas	12,925	52.8	4,693	7.5	60.1	17.7	43.3	11,583	22,061	40,318	60.1	0.7	42,725	19.0	24.1	22.3
Ohio	27,525	66.5	9,529	20.1	41.8	31.6	72.9	13,816	31,208	48,056	51.5	4.6	41,312	18.1	21.4	21.9
Pendleton	4,095	58.8	996	4.8	67.1	17.9	13.3	14,334	26,301	46,358	53.4	1.3	47,167	11.5	18.7	17.6
Pleasants	3,905	52.3	1,344	11.2	62.7	10.7	15.9	14,396	34,191	55,508	44.7	2.7	55,313	13.0	15.7	14.7
Pocahontas	4,351	52.8	1,384	11.1	62.6	13.6	15.1	14,894	25,811	37,642	59.9	1.8	41,173	18.1	23.4	23.1
Preston	18,711	56.0	5,785	6.0	62.5	16.2	44.8	10,157	25,331	51,992	48.7	2.4	51,757	15.7	19.1	18.0
Putnam	32,886	58.3	12,461	12.8	44.3	26.3	111.2	11,648	32,235	63,954	40.0	4.8	69,175	9.9	13.1	12.1
Raleigh	39,606	54.0	15,143	14.0	51.3	19.9	134.4	11,482	24,608	43,283	55.3	1.8	44,526	21.8	25.6	24.3
Randolph	15,663	54.6	5,147	11.5	63.5	15.7	42.2	10,679	25,414	45,206	55.6	2.2	48,306	15.2	21.1	20.7
Ritchie	4,719	49.4	1,703	15.9	63.8	11.8	17.8	13,095	25,773	44,328	55.3	2.2	45,066	16.4	23.2	22.4
Roane	6,590	48.1	2,661	7.5	62.8	13.0	22.7	10,828	21,401	38,895	61.2	1.7	42,379	20.7	30.1	27.9
Summers	7,959	63.3	2,004	11.2	57.2	16.0	15.9	10,526	22,196	37,769	61.6	1.4	38,692	21.1	29.6	29.3
Taylor	7,915	47.4	3,382	12.3	52.9	18.8	27.2	11,159	26,862	52,958	48.1	2.1	53,587	13.7	16.9	15.1
Tucker	4,156	60.8	993	16.2	57.8	19.5	12.2	12,085	26,416	47,527	52.8	0.4	44,461	13.8	19.1	19.5
Tyler	3,622	42.2	1,509	1.6	56.2	16.2	19.8	15,591	27,150	47,598	52.9	1.3	46,693	14.4	20.0	19.1
Upshur	12,160	50.3	5,129	24.2	64.4	16.2	41.1	10,801	26,401	40,802	57.9	1.6	46,171	17.1	22.8	21.1
Wayne	21,346	54.2	8,081	8.2	57.4	17.5	76.8	11,355	23,973	43,710	54.2	2.9	45,507	17.1	22.7	21.5
Webster	3,869	47.7	1,628	4.7	69.7	10.5	15.6	11,827	19,943	33,358	64.3	1.3	34,396	23.7	32.4	30.6
Wetzel	8,620	57.2	2,782	2.4	61.3	12.6	43.8	17,429	23,050	44,539	54.5	1.0	47,322	15.9	22.2	21.8
Wirt	2,821	48.5	1,037	6.9	57.0	10.6	12.7	12,586	23,776	45,315	54.4	1.5	49,504	18.0	27.7	25.9
Wood	49,171	58.9	17,267	14.2	42.9	22.0	149.1	12,001	27,983	48,711	51.1	3.0	47,019	14.4	21.0	19.3
Wyoming	10,702	52.5	3,764	1.2	68.5	11.8	45.5	11,526	23,210	44,095	57.6	1.3	39,143	21.3	25.3	23.3
WISCONSIN	3,814,685	65.5	1,393,087	16.5	37.7	30.8	10,730.9	12,496	34,450	63,293	39.4	5.2	64,901	10.0	12.4	11.3
Adams	11,503	56.9	3,022	7.8	53.8	14.8	19.3	12,938	28,386	48,906	51.0	1.7	52,060	12.3	18.1	16.9
Ashland	11,184	71.9	3,600	18.7	43.8	19.2	33.9	13,184	25,464	47,869	52.1	2.2	52,115	12.5	17.0	15.9
Barron	24,219	53.5	9,088	9.3	45.3	20.6	99.3	12,704	30,135	52,346	47.8	3.1	54,963	10.0	13.7	10.9
Bayfield	12,349	82.1	2,626	11.6	32.4	32.1	25.4	17,340	33,151	57,257	42.6	3.1	58,218	11.0	17.5	16.8
Brown	172,518	65.2	65,557	16.6	37.4	30.3	535.9	12,020	34,157	64,728	38.1	5.2	64,905	8.5	8.6	7.8
Buffalo	6,554	50.3	2,611	8.9	48.0	19.1	24.3	12,113	30,957	58,364	41.4	2.5	56,643	8.0	10.7	10.0
Burnett	8,827	57.3	2,653	8.8	43.9	21.1	31.2	11,980	30,829	53,555	45.8	2.6	57,888	10.7	13.1	16.3
Calumet	28,234	56.4	12,278	13.2	37.0	29.9	42.2	11,079	36,873	76,065	30.4	5.2	79,046	4.5	4.5	4.2
Chippewa	36,825	57.0	14,045	12.5	40.7	22.1	108.4	12,066	31,644	61,215	40.5	4.3	62,841	9.4	11.8	11.1
Clark	13,097	37.7	7,651	23.8	57.1	13.4	63.6	13,292	25,472	54,463	44.9	2.6	55,808	13.1	21.1	19.0
Columbia	38,690	67.2	11,994	10.5	39.3	24.2	102.8	12,485	35,547	69,262	34.0	4.6	74,776	6.9	7.4	6.3
Crawford	9,423	58.4	3,001	9.7	47.4	18.9	33.5	15,278	28,259	51,218	48.8	3.6	53,309	13.3	19.2	18.3
Dane	452,965	82.9	151,300	11.0	21.1	52.4	1,055.2	13,458	41,755	75,179	32.2	8.9	74,829	9.6	8.6	7.1
Dodge	45,995	52.4	17,872	18.4	49.0	18.0	124.2	11,924	31,078	62,591	39.5	2.6	65,540	7.2	7.5	6.9
Door	21,707	78.5	4,681	12.4	34.7	34.7	50.4	14,921	39,162	61,765	39.2	5.2	61,319	7.8	11.2	10.1

1. All persons 3 years old and over enrolled in nursery school through college. 2. Persons 25 years old and over. 3. Elementary and secondary education expenditures. 4. Based on population estimated by the American Community Survey, 2016–2020. 5. CDC percent based on 2019 population estimate.

STATE County	Personal income, 2020										Earnings, 2020		
			Per capita[1]			Supplements to wages and salaries, employer contributions (mil dol)						Contributions for government social insurance (mil dol)	
	Total (mil dol)	Percent change 2019–2020	Dollars	Rank	Wages and salaries (mil dol)	Pension and insurance	Government social insurance	Proprietors' income (mil dol)	Dividends, interest, and rent (mil dol)	Personal transfer reecipts (mil dol)	Total (mil dol)	From employee and self-employed	From employer
	62	63	64	65	66	67	68	69	70	71	72	73	74
WEST VIRGINIA—Cont'd													
Calhoun	241	8.5	34,734	2,950	54	10	4	6	25	120	74	8	4
Clay	298	6.6	35,702	2,892	45	10	4	13	31	126	71	9	4
Doddridge	268	3.4	32,085	3,056	97	17	7	8	54	78	131	9	7
Fayette	1,627	4.1	38,680	2,607	418	80	34	64	183	713	596	52	34
Gilmer	242	3.6	31,020	3,077	81	22	7	7	52	98	116	9	7
Grant	467	9.4	40,571	2,386	159	34	13	20	65	189	226	19	13
Greenbrier	1,399	5.1	40,759	2,366	526	90	45	64	224	565	724	59	45
Hampshire	923	5.9	39,802	2,476	146	31	12	44	136	294	233	24	12
Hancock	1,343	5.9	47,007	1,515	401	82	33	52	178	467	568	47	33
Hardy	522	7.0	38,269	2,655	225	39	20	4	80	170	287	23	20
Harrison	3,486	3.2	52,124	926	2,022	387	164	319	535	966	2,891	189	164
Jackson	1,184	5.9	41,622	2,252	418	67	34	58	131	413	577	47	34
Jefferson	3,152	5.0	54,836	712	838	155	68	129	479	662	1,191	85	68
Kanawha	9,336	5.2	52,969	859	5,201	852	403	861	1,510	2,994	7,318	498	403
Lewis	690	3.1	43,634	1,989	273	47	22	51	109	244	392	30	22
Lincoln	708	6.6	35,309	2,921	88	18	7	14	85	291	127	17	7
Logan	1,303	6.7	41,110	2,322	433	74	36	33	124	635	576	49	36
McDowell	591	5.4	34,918	2,939	201	41	16	15	61	332	273	26	16
Marion	2,557	4.4	45,684	1,703	827	142	68	151	344	816	1,188	92	68
Marshall	1,327	1.5	44,092	1,933	680	119	52	44	227	440	896	64	52
Mason	991	7.3	37,641	2,720	271	59	21	48	122	402	400	33	21
Mercer	2,410	6.0	41,372	2,281	814	145	69	120	317	1,063	1,148	94	69
Mineral	1,208	5.8	45,193	1,771	389	73	34	35	155	401	531	42	34
Mingo	806	3.1	35,115	2,930	227	40	21	25	86	430	313	30	21
Monongalia	5,213	4.6	48,802	1,281	3,353	577	254	320	957	1,109	4,505	277	254
Monroe	463	7.3	35,005	2,936	87	21	7	29	64	183	145	14	7
Morgan	703	6.9	39,311	2,532	113	22	9	34	112	259	178	17	9
Nicholas	913	6.8	37,492	2,738	288	51	24	35	130	412	398	36	24
Ohio	2,531	1.8	61,452	368	1,327	209	104	372	505	710	2,012	135	104
Pendleton	278	6.6	40,054	2,448	53	11	4	11	58	112	79	8	4
Pleasants	343	4.1	46,074	1,637	125	26	10	14	41	131	175	13	10
Pocahontas	359	7.5	43,810	1,973	113	22	10	22	60	160	167	13	10
Preston	1,354	6.4	40,563	2,387	345	78	29	71	178	451	523	42	29
Putnam	2,842	4.5	50,363	1,103	1,185	173	97	155	368	700	1,610	114	97
Raleigh	3,307	3.3	45,356	1,745	1,449	259	118	205	459	1,261	2,032	151	118
Randolph	1,169	6.6	41,194	2,307	451	84	37	70	161	467	641	49	37
Ritchie	400	4.7	42,068	2,183	146	26	12	34	68	145	218	17	12
Roane	542	8.1	40,224	2,428	131	23	10	25	60	225	189	17	10
Summers	463	5.2	37,181	2,771	91	18	9	14	61	219	133	13	9
Taylor	726	2.9	43,460	2,014	161	27	13	27	92	225	228	19	13
Tucker	322	8.4	47,175	1,492	100	20	8	16	49	118	145	11	8
Tyler	352	3.0	41,195	2,305	97	21	8	10	78	124	135	11	8
Upshur	905	4.8	37,337	2,757	317	57	27	52	126	338	453	36	27
Wayne	1,467	5.4	37,566	2,731	420	100	36	92	179	511	648	55	36
Webster	268	11.1	33,320	3,014	64	13	5	8	40	142	91	10	5
Wetzel	573	3.3	38,428	2,631	180	33	15	19	98	254	247	22	15
Wirt	201	5.7	35,205	2,926	21	5	2	6	23	76	33	4	2
Wood	4,028	3.2	48,566	1,317	1,647	315	134	474	560	1,294	2,571	182	134
Wyoming	675	6.6	33,534	3,003	190	37	16	14	66	338	257	25	16
WISCONSIN	324,252	5.2	55,030	X	156,682	28,703	11,703	22,205	58,103	68,767	219,292	14,058	11,703
Adams	905	7.6	44,159	1,918	181	46	15	60	156	328	302	22	15
Ashland	686	6.0	44,520	1,873	355	80	28	46	111	243	509	35	28
Barron	2,398	6.3	53,179	843	966	206	77	147	550	641	1,396	94	77
Bayfield	813	6.6	53,369	829	153	44	13	43	193	250	253	21	13
Brown	14,843	5.1	56,093	632	9,160	1,574	663	961	2,681	2,729	12,358	768	663
Buffalo	658	9.4	50,518	1,088	176	44	15	66	100	170	301	20	15
Burnett	756	8.1	48,574	1,314	186	47	14	52	160	267	299	25	14
Calumet	2,785	4.7	55,460	672	701	132	54	162	426	451	1,049	64	54
Chippewa	3,278	7.0	50,639	1,073	1,199	240	94	325	488	775	1,859	123	94
Clark	1,602	8.4	46,154	1,626	510	114	41	283	261	386	948	57	41
Columbia	3,237	5.1	56,134	628	1,109	236	89	267	530	668	1,700	110	89
Crawford	739	6.8	46,113	1,632	294	64	23	61	121	224	443	30	23
Dane	36,519	4.7	66,094	239	22,008	4,106	1,576	2,550	7,453	5,103	30,240	1,795	1,576
Dodge	4,240	6.0	48,547	1,319	1,809	338	140	309	627	975	2,597	168	140
Door	1,855	4.6	66,516	233	562	117	46	122	565	438	847	63	46

1. Based on the resident population estimated as of July 1 of the year shown.

STATE County	Earnings, 2020 (cont.)									Social Security beneficiaries, December 2020		Supple-mental Security Income recipients, 2020	Housing units, 2021	
	Percent by selected industries													
	Farm	Mining, quarrying, and extractions	Construction	Manu-facturing	Information; professional, scientific, technical services	Retail trade	Finance, insurance, real estate, and leasing	Health care and social assistance	Govern-ment	Number	Rate[1]		Total	Percent change, 2010–2021
	75	76	77	78	79	80	81	82	83	84	85	86	87	88
WEST VIRGINIA—Cont'd														
Calhoun	-0.2	D	22.1	D	D	D	D	D	22.2	2,235	362	471	3,182	0.0
Clay	0.2	D	8.3	D	1.7	6.3	D	19.0	36.2	2,870	364	609	3,944	0.7
Doddridge	-1.2	12.8	25.5	D	D	3.8	2.6	3.6	26.9	1,885	244	181	3,236	-0.1
Fayette	0.1	4.6	3.3	7.0	D	8.6	3.5	17.7	27.2	12,360	310	2,346	19,081	0.0
Gilmer	-0.7	D	1.7	9.7	D	5.3	D	D	58.9	1,575	214	297	3,112	0.3
Grant	-2.3	D	13.8	6.3	D	7.0	3.3	12.5	25.0	3,590	327	333	5,635	0.4
Greenbrier	0.2	4.0	5.7	5.6	4.5	9.3	4.0	20.7	19.9	10,510	322	1,325	17,863	0.3
Hampshire	0.7	D	9.4	2.6	D	7.6	6.6	D	29.9	6,545	281	626	12,530	0.8
Hancock	0.0	D	D	31.7	6.2	5.0	7.0	8.5	13.5	8,660	302	894	14,218	-0.1
Hardy	-6.6	0.0	2.8	41.8	D	7.2	4.3	D	15.4	3,910	276	400	8,198	0.7
Harrison	0.0	4.4	7.7	4.6	10.7	5.8	3.5	15.4	26.5	17,045	262	2,569	30,464	0.0
Jackson	-0.4	D	18.5	23.1	5.5	7.6	5.1	D	13.5	8,095	292	1,140	12,881	0.0
Jefferson	0.6	D	5.0	4.2	9.6	5.6	4.3	8.7	35.3	11,770	202	832	24,057	1.1
Kanawha	0.0	2.1	5.0	4.0	12.6	5.8	9.1	19.5	19.6	50,120	282	6,518	90,398	0.1
Lewis	0.7	8.6	15.3	2.9	D	7.0	1.8	D	19.5	4,720	279	803	8,204	0.0
Lincoln	-0.8	2.0	8.6	0.6	4.6	7.9	D	18.4	37.2	5,895	293	1,527	9,582	0.3
Logan	0.0	D	1.4	3.4	3.6	10.4	2.8	19.5	20.5	10,215	320	2,080	14,759	0.1
McDowell	0.0	27.6	4.7	0.6	D	3.9	2.0	7.5	36.2	6,325	344	2,400	9,353	0.1
Marion	-0.2	D	6.1	5.8	11.2	7.8	4.2	10.1	18.6	14,770	264	1,942	26,275	0.0
Marshall	-0.6	21.9	14.2	15.6	2.3	5.1	2.4	D	12.5	7,835	260	825	14,703	-0.1
Mason	4.9	D	D	12.7	3.1	5.0	2.9	12.9	20.1	7,585	302	1,177	12,164	0.1
Mercer	0.8	D	4.5	4.9	4.9	10.7	3.5	16.7	25.9	17,640	298	3,532	29,328	0.0
Mineral	-0.2	D	4.9	33.2	D	6.1	4.2	12.1	17.5	7,175	267	727	12,509	0.4
Mingo	0.0	25.0	5.1	1.7	D	4.3	2.9	D	19.7	7,660	333	2,475	11,526	0.2
Monongalia	0.0	1.0	4.3	7.4	8.3	5.1	3.3	25.3	25.1	15,245	143	1,577	49,892	0.0
Monroe	4.0	0.0	9.6	20.4	D	D	2.5	6.6	36.6	3,960	321	410	6,230	0.1
Morgan	0.9	D	7.7	6.6	4.0	8.4	6.2	19.4	21.5	5,070	294	329	9,150	0.7
Nicholas	0.1	7.9	3.4	11.7	D	12.9	2.4	D	20.8	8,020	330	1,124	12,517	0.1
Ohio	-0.1	D	4.2	3.9	16.8	6.2	8.3	20.5	11.1	11,740	281	1,224	21,145	-0.1
Pendleton	-3.7	D	4.9	6.7	D	6.2	D	D	23.7	2,380	387	152	3,685	0.4
Pleasants	-0.6	D	4.4	35.5	1.7	2.6	D	7.3	18.6	1,975	260	191	3,214	0.1
Pocahontas	1.7	D	4.4	7.3	8.8	5.9	2.7	D	28.1	2,620	334	254	6,813	0.2
Preston	0.5	0.9	13.3	6.8	3.9	6.1	3.4	D	39.8	8,575	250	1,041	15,185	0.1
Putnam	0.3	0.1	15.8	13.6	6.9	6.4	4.8	11.0	9.4	13,995	244	948	24,865	0.2
Raleigh	0.0	10.7	4.7	3.2	4.8	8.6	3.2	19.6	21.7	22,190	301	3,110	34,579	0.0
Randolph	0.6	5.3	4.8	8.6	3.9	8.9	4.5	D	18.9	7,830	282	1,121	13,043	0.0
Ritchie	-0.1	30.0	D	D	D	5.1	D	4.3	12.2	2,955	352	431	4,163	0.4
Roane	0.0	D	12.6	4.9	3.4	9.6	7.0	D	16.9	4,510	325	863	7,142	-0.1
Summers	-0.1	0.0	6.3	1.6	4.4	7.2	5.0	D	26.6	3,640	306	674	6,537	0.1
Taylor	-0.1	D	7.9	D	2.4	7.1	D	D	24.9	4,080	247	617	7,436	-0.1
Tucker	1.8	D	D	13.5	D	4.7	3.5	11.5	22.5	2,130	319	181	4,653	0.0
Tyler	-0.1	D	D	40.2	D	4.4	D	6.0	20.4	2,605	319	277	4,118	0.0
Upshur	-0.1	4.4	10.8	11.9	5.6	9.9	3.8	D	16.5	6,490	273	974	11,225	0.4
Wayne	0.1	D	6.7	11.4	3.0	4.3	D	7.0	43.4	10,680	277	1,770	18,225	0.4
Webster	0.3	D	6.4	9.6	D	5.4	D	12.7	35.9	2,815	341	616	4,389	0.2
Wetzel	-0.1	D	8.5	3.7	D	11.8	4.0	D	24.9	4,310	304	680	7,311	0.7
Wirt	-2.1	1.1	9.5	D	D	9.3	3.1	12.8	44.4	1,800	356	348	2,714	0.4
Wood	-0.1	D	4.7	9.9	4.2	8.3	6.0	16.1	21.7	23,410	280	3,158	40,301	0.0
Wyoming	0.0	28.2	3.2	1.4	D	6.2	2.1	D	23.7	6,735	320	1,461	9,953	0.0
WISCONSIN	1.6	D	6.6	17.2	8.7	5.8	8.1	12.8	14.3	1,275,932	216	116,390	2,748,940	0.7
Adams	11.0	0.0	7.2	6.7	D	5.2	5.1	D	28.1	7,755	371	375	16,828	0.7
Ashland	1.2	0.0	7.2	15.3	3.3	7.9	3.3	D	22.8	4,490	279	413	9,408	0.0
Barron	3.9	0.7	5.7	25.9	2.7	8.2	3.4	14.6	17.3	13,120	281	949	23,925	0.5
Bayfield	1.6	0.0	15.7	4.8	D	5.8	2.3	D	37.0	5,335	327	240	13,296	0.3
Brown	0.8	D	6.1	16.8	7.4	4.9	10.4	14.1	11.4	52,075	193	4,702	114,174	1.0
Buffalo	11.8	D	7.4	4.9	D	2.9	3.7	3.6	19.6	3,505	263	182	6,535	0.4
Burnett	3.9	D	6.7	23.9	2.8	6.6	2.7	9.6	27.3	5,970	357	250	15,308	0.6
Calumet	6.7	D	7.8	29.9	D	8.2	4.7	D	10.0	9,275	177	217	22,017	2.2
Chippewa	3.5	D	13.9	22.5	3.6	10.1	2.1	9.5	13.5	15,360	230	1,119	29,031	1.0
Clark	13.9	D	9.5	27.3	1.6	5.0	2.3	D	14.8	7,460	215	478	14,871	0.8
Columbia	3.1	D	6.5	26.7	2.9	6.7	3.6	11.0	15.4	13,615	233	789	26,836	0.9
Crawford	6.0	D	4.0	22.2	D	12.6	3.4	D	15.3	4,710	293	295	8,688	0.3
Dane	0.5	0.0	5.9	7.4	19.0	5.0	9.4	10.2	21.4	91,735	163	7,504	253,908	1.8
Dodge	3.4	D	11.0	27.9	2.3	4.9	2.6	9.9	13.2	19,830	222	802	38,308	0.4
Door	3.1	D	9.4	18.1	D	9.7	4.1	12.5	15.7	10,175	335	270	23,891	0.5

1. Per 1,000 resident population estimated as of July 1 of the year shown.

STATE County	Housing units, 2016–2020								Civilian labor force, 2021				Civilian employment[6], 2016–2020		
		Occupied units									Unemployment			Percent	
		Owner-occupied				Renter-occupied									
				Median owner cost as a percent of income											
	Total	Percent	Median value[1]	With a mort-gage	Without a mort-gage[2]	Median rent[3]	Median rent as a percent of income[2]	Sub-standard units[4] (percent)	Total	Percent change, 2020–2021	Total	Rate[5]	Total	Management, business, science, and arts	Construction, production, and maintenance occupations
	89	90	91	92	93	94	95	96	97	98	99	100	101	102	103
WEST VIRGINIA—Cont'd															
Calhoun	2,814	80.1	100,800	18.2	10.0	480	23.0	2.8	2,495	0.2	258	10.3	2,487	28.5	39.2
Clay	3,385	78.4	86,100	22.2	10.0	517	36.4	3.5	3,051	-1.7	236	7.7	2,503	30.2	36.6
Doddridge	2,623	91.0	124,300	17.8	10.0	378	27.2	2.6	3,867	-0.9	159	4.1	3,109	24.5	37.8
Fayette	17,388	78.4	95,100	18.7	10.9	613	31.2	2.1	15,981	-0.2	994	6.2	15,874	29.1	24.9
Gilmer	2,516	70.4	79,900	12.5	10.0	597	23.9	3.7	2,321	1.2	161	6.9	2,771	31.6	29.1
Grant	4,842	80.9	140,900	18.4	10.0	544	24.6	0.8	5,994	1.4	268	4.5	4,963	27.1	35.9
Greenbrier	15,436	72.3	123,000	20.6	10.0	709	30.4	1.7	15,744	1.3	701	4.5	14,223	30.3	25.2
Hampshire	9,165	80.5	155,300	22.3	10.0	658	25.3	3.1	11,043	3.7	373	3.4	9,648	26.7	37.6
Hancock	12,676	73.1	94,600	16.3	10.0	679	25.4	1.8	13,098	0.9	821	6.3	12,816	30.4	32.2
Hardy	5,933	75.1	141,500	18.0	11.2	813	22.0	1.2	5,672	-1.3	279	4.9	6,366	23.1	35.8
Harrison	27,213	73.7	123,000	16.5	10.0	755	28.1	2.2	33,767	0.2	1,581	4.7	30,348	35.3	23.6
Jackson	11,427	77.0	126,100	15.1	10.0	679	22.9	1.8	12,040	-3.7	684	5.7	10,719	36.4	30.7
Jefferson	20,957	78.6	261,500	19.6	10.0	1,063	28.5	2.0	30,391	2.4	940	3.1	28,162	43.3	20.7
Kanawha	78,137	70.3	115,300	17.3	10.0	749	29.2	1.4	81,818	-0.5	4,243	5.2	77,827	38.3	17.8
Lewis	6,472	73.9	108,400	17.4	10.0	642	26.1	1.5	6,196	-0.1	431	7.0	6,248	29.7	28.7
Lincoln	8,295	78.4	86,300	17.7	10.0	632	36.7	2.9	7,086	-0.3	465	6.6	7,008	22.2	28.5
Logan	14,164	72.0	97,700	19.9	11.2	703	27.7	1.9	11,111	0.4	735	6.6	10,025	29.8	28.3
McDowell	7,431	78.0	39,500	23.4	12.3	594	35.6	1.5	4,289	-2.7	353	8.2	3,614	28.7	29.2
Marion	23,033	74.4	122,700	16.3	10.0	788	28.0	1.5	25,080	0.6	1,307	5.2	25,400	35.0	25.1
Marshall	12,350	80.8	111,100	15.9	10.7	604	28.8	1.6	13,367	0.0	835	6.2	12,613	29.5	30.5
Mason	10,593	82.6	100,200	16.9	10.0	577	23.4	1.3	10,171	-0.7	562	5.5	10,196	29.3	32.7
Mercer	25,088	68.9	100,900	19.9	10.0	695	30.5	1.6	20,622	-0.6	1,245	6.0	22,194	32.1	27.3
Mineral	10,810	78.5	144,500	17.8	10.0	662	25.7	0.3	12,215	1.2	570	4.7	11,557	26.8	33.3
Mingo	10,174	71.5	78,000	19.7	11.3	522	24.7	1.8	6,220	-7.5	557	9.0	6,779	30.1	32.9
Monongalia	40,233	58.2	212,300	16.0	10.0	845	32.5	1.6	55,827	3.0	2,191	3.9	52,984	47.7	14.5
Monroe	5,496	78.1	115,300	17.9	10.0	620	24.8	1.7	6,090	1.6	221	3.6	5,027	25.5	37.8
Morgan	7,485	84.2	189,800	19.5	10.0	734	26.1	2.3	8,532	3.5	296	3.5	8,059	26.4	27.1
Nicholas	10,280	78.9	95,800	18.5	10.7	613	28.9	1.2	9,085	-2.1	544	6.0	9,168	27.5	27.8
Ohio	17,254	67.6	127,600	16.4	10.0	664	31.6	1.0	20,333	0.4	1,041	5.1	18,947	35.5	20.0
Pendleton	3,194	82.2	130,000	23.0	10.0	526	17.3	1.8	3,763	3.5	112	3.0	3,038	26.7	38.9
Pleasants	2,822	83.9	110,500	18.2	10.0	502	22.9	1.7	2,696	0.7	193	7.2	3,100	22.1	38.6
Pocahontas	3,578	84.3	119,600	20.7	10.0	639	24.3	3.8	3,920	3.2	196	5.0	3,150	26.1	32.0
Preston	12,430	81.3	121,300	16.0	10.0	662	23.7	1.9	15,649	2.7	706	4.5	13,233	28.1	33.4
Putnam	21,694	82.4	175,700	17.8	10.0	857	26.6	1.9	26,881	0.1	1,130	4.2	25,344	39.5	24.2
Raleigh	31,116	74.1	110,600	18.9	11.0	722	29.6	1.4	30,080	-0.1	1,578	5.2	28,390	32.4	20.8
Randolph	10,977	71.2	117,300	17.8	10.0	680	27.0	0.8	12,058	-1.0	672	5.6	10,704	28.9	31.9
Ritchie	4,161	80.4	96,100	16.0	10.0	556	26.3	2.2	4,330	-0.5	241	5.6	3,571	22.6	37.0
Roane	5,599	76.1	97,900	20.4	10.0	501	30.3	1.3	5,017	-1.3	425	8.5	4,536	33.8	31.8
Summers	5,617	74.4	96,000	19.2	10.0	767	26.1	4.6	4,471	3.1	210	4.7	4,077	28.8	29.0
Taylor	6,649	78.8	116,000	16.4	10.0	664	26.7	0.8	7,848	1.6	363	4.6	6,973	28.6	30.5
Tucker	3,176	79.6	126,700	18.1	10.0	581	25.8	1.5	3,427	3.7	184	5.4	3,063	32.0	31.6
Tyler	3,402	85.2	90,900	17.1	10.0	651	25.1	0.7	2,980	-1.1	238	8.0	3,049	33.3	33.9
Upshur	9,592	76.1	118,400	20.3	10.0	710	30.1	1.9	9,681	1.2	601	6.2	10,030	30.9	27.7
Wayne	15,228	75.0	103,800	17.0	10.8	702	28.9	1.7	15,573	0.0	802	5.1	13,960	34.7	24.2
Webster	3,582	74.3	74,200	24.0	10.0	465	30.5	0.6	3,241	-0.7	200	6.2	2,598	24.1	40.6
Wetzel	6,022	81.2	97,000	15.1	10.0	705	27.4	1.6	6,698	3.1	449	6.7	5,364	18.6	41.0
Wirt	2,557	82.1	93,500	18.4	10.0	437	29.9	4.7	2,271	1.7	173	7.6	2,247	28.7	30.4
Wood	35,189	72.2	126,300	17.4	10.0	715	30.2	1.4	36,539	1.2	1,931	5.3	35,481	36.1	21.9
Wyoming	8,674	84.8	72,900	16.3	10.0	669	29.6	3.3	7,183	5.2	416	5.8	6,238	32.1	34.5
WISCONSIN	2,377,935	67.1	189,200	19.8	12.0	872	27.0	2.0	3,134,439	0.9	118,400	3.8	2,983,277	37.2	26.3
Adams	9,111	82.6	140,000	23.8	13.5	673	26.6	1.9	8,020	-1.4	496	6.2	7,922	22.8	34.1
Ashland	6,483	70.7	115,300	20.1	12.8	637	29.6	2.1	7,713	0.2	389	5.0	7,281	28.1	29.9
Barron	19,059	75.9	159,300	21.6	12.6	742	28.6	2.2	24,374	0.8	940	3.9	21,921	30.4	34.0
Bayfield	7,110	81.5	176,900	20.5	11.9	626	24.3	3.8	7,606	0.5	437	5.7	7,050	36.7	23.1
Brown	106,031	64.9	181,300	18.6	10.7	820	24.6	2.4	142,598	0.5	4,841	3.4	138,713	36.4	26.0
Buffalo	5,751	76.6	164,100	22.5	12.6	771	25.7	1.6	6,371	-0.7	266	4.2	6,859	30.7	34.2
Burnett	7,242	82.7	163,200	21.4	12.4	761	25.6	2.3	7,415	2.0	391	5.3	6,544	33.3	29.5
Calumet	19,951	81.1	189,700	18.5	10.5	808	25.9	1.5	27,758	1.3	774	2.8	27,653	38.1	29.2
Chippewa	26,044	73.3	180,000	19.8	11.5	844	27.3	1.5	33,814	1.7	1,325	3.9	31,956	33.3	32.0
Clark	12,914	78.4	128,200	20.1	12.3	656	22.5	5.2	17,911	1.6	572	3.2	16,038	28.4	41.0
Columbia	24,336	74.5	202,000	20.5	12.2	834	24.0	1.9	31,978	1.4	1,081	3.4	30,458	35.0	29.0
Crawford	6,676	74.4	136,600	20.3	12.2	673	24.6	2.7	7,518	0.8	332	4.4	7,229	30.0	39.7
Dane	226,600	59.0	277,000	20.2	11.9	1,118	28.3	1.7	331,664	2.2	9,385	2.8	309,685	52.8	14.9
Dodge	35,007	69.3	169,000	20.3	11.9	830	24.0	1.6	48,501	1.3	1,530	3.2	45,842	27.9	37.5
Door	13,429	79.5	223,200	20.7	11.6	806	28.8	2.0	15,656	3.5	683	4.4	13,719	34.7	29.0

1. Specified owner-occupied units. 2. A value of 10.0 represents 10 percent or less; a value of 50.0 represents 50 percent or more. 3. Specified renter-occupied units. 4. Overcrowded or lacking complete plumbing facilities. 5. Percent of civilian labor force. 6. Civilian employed persons 16 years old and over.

STATE County	Private nonfarm establishments, employment and payroll, 2020									Agriculture, 2017			
		Employment						Annual payroll		Farms			Farm producers whose primary occupation is farming (percent)
											Percent with:		
	Number of establish-ments	Total	Health care and social assistance	Manufac-turing	Retail trade	Finance and insurance	Professional, scientific, and technical services	Total (mil dol)	Average per employee (dollars)	Number	Fewer than 50 acres	1000 acres or more	
	104	105	106	107	108	109	110	111	112	113	114	115	116
WEST VIRGINIA—Cont'd													
Calhoun	90	707	248	26	110	38	19	34	48,427	296	18.9	2.4	33.6
Clay	70	844	372	NA	105	27	NA	23	27,470	131	23.7	0.8	37.0
Doddridge	71	713	95	NA	83	44	NA	38	53,411	392	28.6	1.8	36.1
Fayette	694	7,372	1,840	544	1,247	195	187	272	36,854	253	49.8	0.4	34.2
Gilmer	101	923	173	213	156	16	38	29	31,815	264	8.3	0.4	37.1
Grant	229	2,773	978	219	360	91	42	114	40,974	522	30.5	2.9	34.9
Greenbrier	887	11,005	2,506	928	1,771	242	223	373	33,927	891	31.9	2.8	39.6
Hampshire	309	2,615	899	95	469	179	78	81	30,853	883	51.4	2.5	35.0
Hancock	549	8,085	1,165	2,249	784	243	231	292	36,062	93	43.0	1.1	35.3
Hardy	268	5,108	490	2,763	592	191	79	173	33,832	580	34.5	5.3	39.3
Harrison	1,766	29,577	7,154	1,340	4,532	889	1,811	1,394	47,141	810	33.2	1.1	35.2
Jackson	457	6,754	1,138	1,705	1,129	152	272	274	40,625	982	31.4	0.6	31.8
Jefferson	911	12,944	1,168	786	1,933	332	399	455	35,177	607	63.9	1.8	39.7
Kanawha	4,571	76,904	19,729	3,204	10,153	3,310	4,991	3,506	45,589	214	34.6	0.5	36.3
Lewis	352	3,849	723	134	932	63	70	153	39,669	481	21.2	0.8	41.8
Lincoln	157	1,588	828	NA	249	55	31	46	28,732	177	17.5	NA	42.4
Logan	560	8,042	1,950	314	1,485	186	170	335	41,686	8	50.0	NA	15.4
McDowell	199	1,692	455	5	344	100	24	57	33,942	14	100.0	NA	77.8
Marion	1,108	14,349	2,585	751	2,181	425	1,162	591	41,186	599	41.6	NA	39.5
Marshall	489	8,825	1,551	484	1,136	227	110	405	45,869	638	28.7	0.2	36.9
Mason	321	3,812	1,024	463	630	116	91	168	43,975	876	32.9	1.5	35.9
Mercer	1,182	17,161	4,661	1,197	3,031	322	474	624	36,387	410	36.3	0.7	38.4
Mineral	432	6,411	1,574	1,596	975	151	136	274	42,729	519	35.6	2.3	35.9
Mingo	335	2,959	574	43	378	128	166	94	31,792	8	62.5	NA	40.0
Monongalia	2,352	48,196	17,130	3,154	6,081	716	2,688	2,453	50,906	542	36.2	0.2	36.7
Monroe	169	1,143	193	360	119	32	55	42	36,325	929	38.2	1.6	38.4
Morgan	231	2,419	586	179	448	89	65	71	29,443	207	50.7	NA	30.1
Nicholas	559	5,730	1,328	740	1,331	126	118	198	34,572	372	43.8	1.3	36.4
Ohio	1,322	26,704	6,449	1,023	3,082	1,456	1,928	1,080	40,434	208	28.4	NA	39.1
Pendleton	138	1,116	346	155	174	61	10	33	29,563	584	19.3	5.5	42.7
Pleasants	126	2,157	232	590	92	61	34	96	44,523	208	27.9	1.0	26.5
Pocahontas	214	2,965	402	275	321	38	121	75	25,398	500	28.4	4.4	34.2
Preston	520	5,369	1,140	645	892	146	98	208	38,733	1,142	34.1	0.6	39.6
Putnam	1,192	17,163	2,457	2,290	2,275	560	722	832	48,481	514	32.9	0.4	30.5
Raleigh	1,663	24,821	6,580	594	4,542	500	1,367	933	37,601	365	50.1	1.4	35.8
Randolph	630	8,805	2,708	1,065	1,305	240	187	285	32,350	402	33.6	5.5	36.7
Ritchie	188	2,625	193	843	225	85	56	101	38,601	473	23.9	3.0	38.0
Roane	217	1,751	422	96	447	94	46	74	42,396	604	19.7	1.2	38.4
Summers	160	1,434	484	14	195	54	41	52	36,104	357	28.0	2.5	35.6
Taylor	217	2,381	686	168	364	46	54	117	49,139	413	48.4	1.2	34.7
Tucker	148	1,840	325	255	181	45	NA	61	33,386	159	28.3	1.3	40.1
Tyler	129	1,349	332	474	175	54	25	69	51,492	305	19.0	1.0	42.7
Upshur	507	5,871	1,262	809	820	93	197	237	40,286	499	37.3	1.0	36.2
Wayne	477	6,568	2,023	765	1,338	91	104	298	45,401	237	24.1	0.4	41.8
Webster	118	983	408	137	154	16	5	32	32,466	83	31.3	NA	57.2
Wetzel	320	3,941	775	842	822	112	70	178	45,219	261	13.0	0.4	35.5
Wirt	52	285	107	NA	85	13	6	8	29,014	256	28.5	1.2	37.7
Wood	1,918	28,859	6,783	2,385	5,732	834	920	1,058	36,655	881	38.4	0.2	34.5
Wyoming	261	2,418	743	55	523	51	74	80	33,133	21	52.4	NA	39.5
WISCONSIN	141,326	2,599,347	415,712	471,475	309,187	145,598	114,960	131,210	50,478	64,793	35.3	3.6	45.6
Adams	338	2,991	410	415	475	37	54	98	32,878	308	31.2	7.5	50.3
Ashland	477	6,469	1,403	1,123	993	178	168	279	43,204	263	34.6	3.0	33.9
Barron	1,317	17,512	3,025	5,611	2,786	444	246	721	41,193	1,200	31.6	4.7	45.9
Bayfield	421	2,149	281	206	384	62	35	71	33,227	427	32.6	3.3	36.4
Brown	6,545	143,640	20,361	27,764	15,533	9,278	5,302	7,558	52,621	975	52.3	3.7	45.5
Buffalo	296	3,024	293	280	290	130	60	137	45,400	966	20.5	4.9	47.8
Burnett	396	3,360	637	912	530	81	167	131	39,111	369	22.2	3.8	40.2
Calumet	892	12,655	1,088	3,921	1,750	420	218	526	41,562	684	41.5	4.7	51.4
Chippewa	1,592	21,960	3,041	5,904	3,598	402	553	979	44,594	1,409	31.3	4.7	45.3
Clark	758	8,759	834	3,584	931	157	253	385	43,991	2,095	22.5	2.2	59.5
Columbia	1,375	20,604	2,788	5,174	2,738	364	509	856	41,541	1,357	41.3	4.5	46.5
Crawford	366	5,617	810	1,870	1,025	136	156	208	37,008	1,034	24.8	2.6	39.7
Dane	14,345	303,603	53,389	27,469	32,569	25,890	29,905	17,903	58,970	2,566	44.4	3.3	43.9
Dodge	1,709	31,245	4,552	9,911	3,225	544	587	1,790	57,284	1,749	35.9	3.5	48.9
Door	1,270	10,399	1,187	2,299	1,877	194	236	415	39,942	626	41.5	2.9	43.8

STATE County	Agriculture, 2017 (cont.)															
	Land in farms					Value of land and buildings (dollars)		Value of machinery and equipment, average per farm (dollars)	Value of products sold:				Organic farms (number)	Farms with internet access (percent)	Government payments	
	Acreage (1,000)	Percent change, 2012–2017	Acres: Average size of farm	Acres: Total irrigated (1,000)	Acres: Total cropland (1,000)	Average per farm	Average per acre		Total (mil dol)	Average per farm (acres)	Percent from: Crops	Percent from: Livestock and poultry products			Total ($1,000)	Percent of farms
	117	118	119	120	121	122	123	124	125	126	127	128	129	130	131	132
WEST VIRGINIA—Cont'd																
Calhoun	61	23.3	206	0.0	12.4	375,391	1,823	62,763	2.4	8,047	39.8	60.2	NA	67.2	82	9.1
Clay	21	6.0	162	NA	3.2	279,733	1,722	39,293	0.6	4,374	45.2	54.8	NA	74.8	20	7.6
Doddridge	67	2.9	172	0.0	11.8	365,169	2,129	60,481	2.0	5,171	41.6	58.4	NA	67.3	10	1.0
Fayette	26	10.9	102	0.0	6.2	295,809	2,913	45,353	1.7	6,779	37.1	62.9	NA	81.8	48	5.5
Gilmer	65	-7.6	246	D	11.1	324,619	1,317	61,671	2.8	10,538	17.3	82.7	NA	72.7	102	5.3
Grant	120	6.7	230	0.0	26.2	601,970	2,622	74,196	57.1	109,316	3.0	97.0	NA	64.8	635	13.0
Greenbrier	192	1.2	216	0.0	44.1	562,728	2,606	76,127	69.3	77,797	6.0	94.0	2	74.9	970	18.5
Hampshire	132	-7.2	149	0.1	36.9	448,587	3,004	56,173	38.7	43,847	13.1	86.9	NA	69.4	244	12.3
Hancock	8	-6.1	90	0.0	3.4	410,404	4,574	65,960	0.5	5,667	74.0	26.0	NA	91.4	D	1.1
Hardy	155	-0.4	267	0.0	40.5	857,054	3,213	99,840	190.6	328,583	2.8	97.2	2	73.3	597	14.7
Harrison	112	-4.2	138	0.0	28.0	346,717	2,504	51,626	7.7	9,546	33.2	66.8	NA	78.0	142	5.7
Jackson	128	22.1	130	0.0	33.4	287,864	2,211	41,845	6.9	7,059	38.5	61.5	NA	71.4	162	5.3
Jefferson	66	-1.3	109	0.3	44.5	639,634	5,873	57,139	28.7	47,206	62.2	37.8	7	82.9	476	15.2
Kanawha	24	-9.0	111	0.0	4.1	429,309	3,881	38,062	1.0	4,710	39.1	60.9	1	73.8	27	8.9
Lewis	100	21.2	208	D	22.4	449,021	2,160	53,052	6.3	13,035	21.3	78.7	NA	69.6	29	4.6
Lincoln	24	-6.9	135	0.0	4.2	248,623	1,843	54,669	0.8	4,559	55.8	44.2	NA	73.4	23	15.8
Logan	1	11.7	116	D	D	287,031	2,474	22,010	0.0	5,125	82.9	17.1	NA	100.0	D	12.5
McDowell	0	-84.3	12	NA	0.1	72,143	6,196	38,104	0.3	21,214	98.7	1.3	NA	100.0	NA	NA
Marion	52	-3.4	86	0.0	13.5	255,112	2,964	40,156	2.5	4,200	45.7	54.3	1	65.9	22	2.8
Marshall	76	-11.6	119	0.0	22.6	308,256	2,587	65,533	3.8	5,966	51.1	48.9	1	66.5	95	3.9
Mason	125	-10.1	142	0.2	37.6	345,965	2,430	58,830	36.4	41,502	80.8	19.2	2	65.8	829	11.0
Mercer	53	2.6	130	0.0	12.4	326,001	2,515	57,803	6.9	16,763	21.5	78.5	NA	68.8	59	4.4
Mineral	99	30.0	191	0.1	29.6	531,811	2,788	57,610	21.6	41,667	14.8	85.2	1	66.9	134	8.1
Mingo	2	16.4	295	D	D	329,528	1,116	37,841	0.2	19,750	10.8	89.2	NA	100.0	3	50.0
Monongalia	62	7.1	115	0.0	18.6	518,881	4,530	60,065	5.0	9,273	35.1	64.9	4	71.8	68	5.7
Monroe	145	0.3	156	0.0	31.9	415,440	2,662	51,310	22.6	24,277	15.9	84.1	15	64.2	363	11.0
Morgan	17	-8.4	81	0.0	7.2	426,092	5,234	40,087	3.3	15,836	78.3	21.7	2	69.1	148	8.7
Nicholas	46	-21.6	122	0.0	11.8	319,996	2,615	47,319	3.1	8,304	33.9	66.1	NA	73.1	330	11.3
Ohio	24	-21.8	113	D	10.9	409,625	3,624	64,696	2.7	13,014	43.2	56.8	NA	78.4	24	7.2
Pendleton	176	3.5	302	0.0	29.6	678,517	2,250	84,763	99.9	171,074	2.7	97.3	2	61.1	324	12.7
Pleasants	24	11.0	115	0.0	5.3	264,777	2,308	44,817	1.1	5,524	43.4	56.6	NA	78.8	D	1.0
Pocahontas	131	10.9	263	0.0	26.4	492,444	1,875	65,758	8.6	17,128	22.7	77.3	2	67.2	372	16.4
Preston	143	-11.1	125	0.0	48.2	343,865	2,747	58,868	16.2	14,145	38.9	61.1	2	68.1	309	6.4
Putnam	52	-13.9	101	0.1	13.7	288,179	2,866	41,740	7.3	14,239	71.0	29.0	1	63.0	126	6.0
Raleigh	44	19.4	121	0.0	11.2	447,458	3,709	52,892	3.0	8,263	28.2	71.8	1	70.1	12	2.5
Randolph	98	3.6	243	0.0	26.7	588,534	2,425	65,505	7.9	19,704	32.0	68.0	4	66.7	112	8.7
Ritchie	98	9.8	206	0.0	22.6	372,079	1,805	53,870	9.6	20,334	18.4	81.6	2	72.7	148	3.0
Roane	113	1.9	187	0.0	27.8	361,187	1,930	54,938	6.4	10,675	34.7	65.3	3	72.4	118	7.0
Summers	55	-5.7	153	0.0	12.0	347,761	2,272	46,335	3.5	9,846	38.8	61.2	2	66.9	86	5.3
Taylor	46	-6.9	111	0.0	14.0	340,360	3,075	58,663	3.4	8,324	36.5	63.5	NA	71.4	28	2.9
Tucker	26	-22.1	166	D	6.5	476,151	2,863	57,473	1.9	11,937	30.4	69.6	NA	78.6	11	3.8
Tyler	56	15.4	182	0.0	12.3	348,921	1,913	51,025	2.5	8,079	40.9	59.1	NA	67.9	82	7.9
Upshur	61	-10.8	122	0.1	16.3	323,626	2,645	48,952	4.8	9,615	49.6	50.4	1	72.5	63	3.8
Wayne	39	27.5	163	0.0	5.9	326,612	2,009	46,764	1.7	7,097	44.7	55.3	NA	71.7	56	11.0
Webster	10	32.1	126	0.0	2.4	290,032	2,299	40,787	0.5	5,434	55.7	44.3	NA	65.1	D	8.4
Wetzel	41	8.5	158	0.0	8.8	305,112	1,927	45,093	1.3	4,950	54.6	45.4	NA	60.2	11	4.2
Wirt	41	9.0	162	0.0	9.3	292,717	1,808	49,820	2.3	8,949	30.2	69.8	NA	71.5	120	4.7
Wood	90	2.4	102	0.0	25.0	340,345	3,333	43,873	6.3	7,120	44.4	55.6	NA	72.3	187	3.1
Wyoming	1	-51.0	69	D	0.7	231,769	3,347	59,560	0.1	4,429	74.2	25.8	NA	76.2	20	19.0
WISCONSIN	14,319	-1.7	221	454.4	10,085.0	1,083,640	4,904	156,689	11,427.4	176,368	35.6	64.4	1,708	76.1	126,583	42.4
Adams	117	-1.0	381	50.9	84.5	1,708,212	4,489	227,089	D	D	D	D	6	80.8	637	30.2
Ashland	52	14.4	199	0.4	24.7	445,403	2,234	71,332	17.6	66,806	15.0	85.0	3	74.9	273	12.5
Barron	306	-1.3	255	15.3	208.8	870,734	3,419	170,748	266.4	222,001	28.8	71.2	6	81.7	936	36.1
Bayfield	81	12.8	190	0.2	42.6	415,918	2,191	75,186	15.9	37,302	51.6	48.4	9	78.5	100	12.6
Brown	192	6.0	197	0.5	166.6	1,672,996	8,495	205,925	292.7	300,255	13.8	86.2	17	77.7	2,847	37.4
Buffalo	293	-4.0	303	7.6	164.3	1,195,520	3,940	184,155	203.1	210,203	26.7	73.3	36	77.6	3,056	62.2
Burnett	89	6.7	242	0.3	49.0	658,630	2,723	110,503	37.9	102,835	36.0	64.0	4	71.0	360	27.6
Calumet	154	8.1	225	D	131.5	1,771,197	7,874	207,062	203.6	297,601	21.8	78.2	13	81.9	924	52.5
Chippewa	356	-7.4	253	8.6	243.0	899,774	3,559	148,239	215.3	152,830	37.5	62.5	26	74.2	2,197	42.2
Clark	451	-1.6	215	0.5	323.8	873,709	4,058	149,770	404.1	192,889	17.9	82.1	58	54.9	1,430	27.8
Columbia	304	-1.3	224	5.6	243.9	1,305,879	5,828	158,741	222.3	163,808	51.0	49.0	23	78.3	1,602	36.7
Crawford	211	-2.8	204	0.1	99.0	647,573	3,180	82,180	73.4	70,965	43.6	56.4	50	73.6	1,616	43.3
Dane	507	0.4	197	4.9	410.3	1,626,929	8,239	166,567	509.1	198,391	36.3	63.7	58	81.5	10,186	50.9
Dodge	406	1.0	232	0.2	340.5	1,356,553	5,844	210,146	345.7	197,636	42.1	57.9	18	78.0	5,238	49.7
Door	115	-13.2	183	0.6	90.1	870,229	4,757	157,612	78.7	125,786	41.5	58.5	18	77.0	795	40.7

STATE County	Water use, 2015		Wholesale Trade[1], 2017				Retail Trade[2], 2017				Real estate and rental and leasing,[2] 2017			
	Public supply water withdrawn (mil gal/ day)	Public supply gallons withdrawn per person per day	Number of establish-ments	Number of employees	Sales (mil dol)	Average payroll (mil dol)	Number of establish-ments	Number of employees	Sales (mil dol)	Average payroll (mil dol)	Number of establish-ments	Number of employees	Sales (mil dol)	Average payroll (mil dol)
	133	134	135	136	137	138	139	140	141	142	143	144	145	146
WEST VIRGINIA—Cont'd														
Calhoun	0.3	42.8	NA	NA	NA	NA	16	94	22.9	2.2	NA	NA	NA	NA
Clay	0.4	44.9	NA	NA	NA	NA	15	135	38.6	2.9	NA	NA	NA	NA
Doddridge	0.2	26.9	NA	NA	NA	NA	8	96	25.4	1.6	NA	NA	NA	NA
Fayette	5.4	119.3	14	117	135.3	6.6	128	1,393	340.4	33.3	19	72	6.9	1.2
Gilmer	0.6	75.1	D	D	D	0.7	20	149	35.1	3.4	3	8	2.2	0.2
Grant	1.0	82.4	3	5	1.6	0.1	41	390	107.0	9.7	8	D	1.2	D
Greenbrier	3.4	96.3	19	213	116.7	9.5	165	1,946	575.1	51.0	41	104	17.7	3.8
Hampshire	0.5	22.7	D	D	D	1.5	52	470	122.0	10.6	10	D	2.3	D
Hancock	1.5	49.0	10	141	74.6	5.7	83	800	184.6	16.4	19	D	11.9	D
Hardy	3.0	217.3	6	38	5.2	1.1	42	612	174.5	14.5	14	31	3.8	0.9
Harrison	7.9	115.1	75	1,020	437.4	46.7	303	4,621	1,340.9	111.1	57	D	105.5	D
Jackson	1.8	61.9	16	279	191.7	10.1	84	1,172	368.8	29.1	17	61	26.2	2.5
Jefferson	2.7	47.8	D	D	D	D	139	1,952	513.1	45.1	51	171	31.9	5.1
Kanawha	32.2	170.8	229	3,046	1,859.8	151.6	675	10,761	3,151.4	271.4	236	1,287	341.8	54.8
Lewis	1.1	65.7	15	121	88.7	5.7	63	978	271.9	24.3	9	31	5.7	0.8
Lincoln	0.3	14.0	NA	NA	NA	NA	36	297	71.9	7.0	3	D	0.6	D
Logan	4.3	123.6	27	209	105.3	8.6	116	1,662	508.5	44.5	16	60	6.2	1.6
McDowell	2.9	146.2	4	20	6.7	1.6	49	440	98.0	8.8	D	D	D	0.2
Marion	8.2	144.2	36	381	232.3	19.0	185	2,218	753.0	59.7	36	117	22.1	3.6
Marshall	4.7	146.0	15	142	72.2	5.5	77	1,199	354.9	29.6	9	35	3.7	0.7
Mason	2.3	86.2	D	D	D	D	60	647	153.9	14.4	12	38	6.1	0.9
Mercer	3.6	58.5	45	550	334.4	22.1	221	3,048	818.2	73.1	40	144	45.8	5.3
Mineral	1.6	57.2	11	97	21.2	3.3	71	948	263.5	23.7	13	38	7.2	1.0
Mingo	4.0	158.9	10	68	12.7	2.4	61	395	106.3	9.3	11	35	4.4	0.8
Monongalia	10.9	104.3	56	428	373.5	17.6	376	6,077	1,718.1	144.0	140	643	129.8	22.5
Monroe	0.5	36.3	3	15	1.8	0.3	25	123	29.9	2.8	NA	NA	NA	NA
Morgan	0.6	31.4	3	43	20.0	2.7	43	431	114.1	10.7	9	22	1.8	0.4
Nicholas	2.8	108.6	18	189	71.5	8.4	100	1,453	403.1	35.7	17	57	13.7	1.9
Ohio	7.7	178.8	66	1,224	3,905.1	54.1	193	3,148	877.0	77.4	56	328	57.0	12.5
Pendleton	0.3	42.9	4	11	1.0	0.1	26	179	38.6	3.6	3	2	0.8	0.1
Pleasants	0.6	74.3	NA	NA	NA	NA	15	128	34.2	2.6	4	D	0.7	D
Pocahontas	0.4	44.2	NA	NA	NA	NA	30	314	75.8	6.5	7	56	5.7	1.1
Preston	2.2	65.1	10	D	19.2	D	89	934	253.6	21.3	21	68	9.2	2.0
Putnam	2.6	45.9	68	1,087	676.7	56.9	160	2,350	752.4	59.6	56	215	45.2	9.4
Raleigh	9.9	127.6	89	836	394.2	39.3	332	4,861	1,503.4	121.2	72	344	69.2	15.8
Randolph	2.8	94.4	D	D	D	10.8	122	1,492	379.5	33.9	24	94	18.9	2.8
Ritchie	0.5	48.1	D	D	D	D	37	334	94.7	7.5	4	4	0.9	0.5
Roane	0.9	58.9	4	46	21.9	1.9	42	511	136.4	12.5	8	19	1.6	0.3
Summers	2.5	188.1	6	143	54.1	7.0	28	261	66.9	6.0	3	12	1.0	0.2
Taylor	1.8	107.6	D	D	D	D	32	465	122.0	11.8	NA	NA	NA	NA
Tucker	0.6	87.6	NA	NA	NA	NA	26	232	64.0	5.6	10	48	6.4	1.4
Tyler	0.6	63.5	NA	NA	NA	NA	20	148	44.7	2.9	NA	NA	NA	NA
Upshur	2.1	85.2	11	108	126.0	5.4	80	861	270.1	22.4	21	94	10.1	2.9
Wayne	2.9	71.0	17	244	119.8	11.2	101	1,464	354.9	34.3	19	D	16.1	D
Webster	0.5	56.0	NA	NA	NA	NA	25	172	43.7	3.9	NA	NA	NA	NA
Wetzel	1.8	112.5	9	79	27.5	2.5	72	893	223.1	20.7	D	D	D	0.8
Wirt	0.0	0.0	NA	NA	NA	NA	10	73	14.2	1.1	NA	NA	NA	NA
Wood	8.0	92.2	D	D	D	D	350	5,900	1,545.3	145.2	D	D	D	D
Wyoming	1.8	82.2	4	D	3.8	D	61	559	133.2	12.0	10	26	3.6	0.7
WISCONSIN	479.4	83.1	5,934	104,382	81,566.3	6,129.1	18,908	317,668	91,763.8	8,273.7	4,956	27,163	5,908.1	1,105.8
Adams	0.8	40.2	6	48	51.1	3.1	48	413	121.1	10.7	13	41	2.9	1.0
Ashland	1.0	62.5	9	84	46.0	3.6	87	952	237.2	25.6	8	25	2.3	0.5
Barron	4.5	98.3	33	284	92.5	10.9	224	2,946	840.6	78.1	36	115	19.6	3.3
Bayfield	0.4	24.7	6	54	31.9	2.8	68	391	85.9	9.6	D	D	D	0.6
Brown	19.2	74.2	331	7,479	5,440.9	414.1	854	15,612	4,385.4	407.9	219	1,448	387.9	54.7
Buffalo	0.4	30.3	9	129	56.9	6.5	41	359	84.1	6.6	8	13	2.7	0.3
Burnett	0.4	23.7	D	D	D	0.2	65	558	111.9	11.1	17	D	6.5	D
Calumet	10.9	219.6	40	455	227.7	23.6	105	1,795	454.3	40.9	18	47	5.1	1.2
Chippewa	7.0	109.6	64	808	538.2	34.2	208	3,744	1,322.1	104.1	34	162	25.4	4.6
Clark	1.2	35.7	47	469	379.0	24.6	113	974	290.6	21.9	4	D	0.5	D
Columbia	3.6	62.7	44	607	395.8	27.8	204	2,838	885.4	74.7	D	D	D	D
Crawford	1.4	87.2	9	51	68.9	1.8	70	1,165	246.3	26.8	8	43	5.0	0.9
Dane	43.5	83.1	622	12,666	9,491.3	728.3	1,671	31,714	10,139.2	894.8	744	4,834	1,068.6	215.6
Dodge	6.3	71.2	68	1,083	544.1	47.9	233	3,143	860.6	81.0	42	100	34.4	3.2
Door	1.4	49.4	21	109	53.5	5.8	251	2,016	511.4	50.5	50	221	34.2	6.3

1 Merchant wholesalers, except manufacturers' sales branches and offices. 2. Employer establishments.

STATE County	Professional, scientific, and technical services, 2017				Manufacturing, 2017				Accommodation and food services, 2017			
	Number of establish-ments	Number of employees	Sales (mil dol)	Average payroll (mil dol)	Number of establish-ments	Number of employees	Sales (mil dol)	Average payroll (mil dol)	Number of establis-hments	Number of employees	Sales (mil dol)	Annual payroll (mil dol)
	147	148	149	150	151	152	153	154	155	156	157	158
WEST VIRGINIA—Cont'd												
Calhoun	6	29	3.8	1.7	4	26	3.0	D	4	37	1.3	0.4
Clay	NA	NA	NA	NA	NA	NA	NA	NA	6	38	1.7	0.5
Doddridge	NA	NA	NA	NA	NA	NA	NA	NA	4	76	2.5	0.9
Fayette	D	D	D	D	21	422	221.8	26.5	77	1,150	89.0	26.6
Gilmer	D	D	D	0.9	4	174	51.6	6.6	12	105	5.5	1.8
Grant	D	D	3.4	D	8	294	89.3	11.0	20	188	10.0	2.2
Greenbrier	65	246	23.4	7.7	29	864	207.0	37.8	83	2,480	190.1	62.7
Hampshire	D	D	D	D	11	66	11.6	2.8	D	D	D	D
Hancock	49	341	37.6	14.0	18	2,640	1,248.0	144.9	67	1,631	178.8	31.9
Hardy	17	74	8.5	2.8	D	2,909	D	98.6	31	349	17.5	4.8
Harrison	143	1,697	292.8	101.3	D	D	D	D	169	3,408	172.4	48.3
Jackson	31	278	50.2	25.4	16	1,486	773.5	104.0	45	888	43.2	12.7
Jefferson	D	D	D	D	27	929	270.3	40.2	124	3,616	502.0	82.7
Kanawha	535	4,727	800.8	294.3	110	3,852	2,155.0	212.2	450	9,320	577.5	153.1
Lewis	14	52	8.2	1.9	13	142	15.3	5.1	34	630	35.8	11.6
Lincoln	11	47	5.9	2.6	NA	NA	NA	NA	D	D	D	D
Logan	D	D	D	D	27	470	94.4	17.4	60	821	43.7	12.0
McDowell	D	D	D	D	D	10	D	D	D	D	D	2.6
Marion	D	D	D	D	41	749	337.2	37.4	113	1,749	83.9	23.3
Marshall	D	D	D	D	19	455	325.1	23.1	54	718	34.6	9.6
Mason	16	79	11.5	3.9	11	405	792.4	27.8	26	306	13.4	3.9
Mercer	77	525	79.4	19.6	47	1,025	260.9	43.2	103	1,972	107.9	30.4
Mineral	20	109	11.0	4.1	14	1,542	520.8	117.4	51	580	22.8	6.4
Mingo	D	D	D	D	11	129	16.2	5.4	23	209	12.7	2.9
Monongalia	D	D	D	D	50	4,054	3,044.1	334.4	328	6,843	312.8	92.3
Monroe	10	52	3.8	1.2	D	589	D	D	14	D	3.3	D
Morgan	15	73	8.0	4.3	7	160	23.3	6.1	26	277	15.3	3.9
Nicholas	D	D	D	D	22	687	252.9	34.7	54	802	39.6	10.9
Ohio	D	D	D	D	46	906	262.5	42.8	139	3,334	259.1	56.2
Pendleton	D	D	D	0.4	4	139	69.0	6.8	12	102	3.8	0.9
Pleasants	6	37	6.2	2.6	10	665	266.3	42.8	10	187	8.4	2.4
Pocahontas	D	D	D	0.2	6	246	45.4	8.9	22	1,404	56.4	18.1
Preston	D	D	D	D	24	517	155.1	22.1	37	323	14.9	4.1
Putnam	93	712	106.6	38.5	39	2,262	2,213.4	143.6	101	1,830	97.9	25.6
Raleigh	D	D	D	D	49	738	192.5	31.0	144	3,180	176.8	51.2
Randolph	D	D	D	D	24	1,011	160.9	34.4	61	846	41.4	11.9
Ritchie	10	63	5.8	2.5	13	1,131	180.2	37.4	17	211	9.4	3.0
Roane	12	37	3.5	1.3	12	146	33.0	5.4	10	194	7.8	2.5
Summers	12	46	4.2	1.6	5	10	2.3	0.5	12	111	8.5	2.3
Taylor	D	D	D	D	NA	NA	NA	NA	19	242	7.1	2.2
Tucker	D	D	D	0.2	12	220	104.2	10.7	24	429	17.2	6.0
Tyler	6	21	1.9	0.4	5	886	268.0	49.3	8	103	2.7	0.9
Upshur	38	186	19.9	7.1	18	784	298.5	41.2	50	686	33.7	9.5
Wayne	20	149	20.5	6.9	19	D	483.8	D	52	D	36.5	D
Webster	D	D	D	0.1	8	206	44.3	8.3	D	D	D	D
Wetzel	D	D	D	D	11	802	682.9	72.8	D	D	D	D
Wirt	5	8	0.5	0.1	NA	NA	NA	NA	NA	NA	NA	NA
Wood	D	D	D	D	D	D	D	D	D	D	D	D
Wyoming	17	73	7.4	3.0	8	33	7.3	1.6	D	D	D	D
WISCONSIN	11,493	105,204	18,748.6	7,257.3	8,837	455,538	171,896.3	25,180.6	14,840	244,099	13,496.3	3,688.3
Adams	D	D	4.3	D	14	400	168.2	19.6	59	1,707	72.0	21.1
Ashland	28	166	15.8	6.6	21	997	196.0	51.3	56	603	32.0	8.8
Barron	62	288	29.6	12.5	87	5,333	1,829.8	227.3	153	1,767	72.2	20.2
Bayfield	D	D	D	0.9	20	154	27.6	5.9	89	490	34.2	8.9
Brown	D	D	D	D	433	24,744	10,956.1	1,401.4	620	12,417	600.5	175.7
Buffalo	18	68	5.2	1.4	14	186	95.4	10.4	49	294	14.0	3.5
Burnett	23	79	8.2	3.0	24	957	316.9	44.8	68	466	26.0	7.2
Calumet	60	216	23.3	10.0	62	3,440	1,517.3	149.7	88	1,446	61.5	16.9
Chippewa	91	577	50.9	22.8	125	5,443	1,996.0	259.6	175	1,937	87.2	22.5
Clark	32	185	15.6	5.2	72	3,269	2,473.5	157.6	60	488	16.1	4.6
Columbia	D	D	D	D	94	5,287	2,615.5	292.7	181	3,579	199.7	58.8
Crawford	20	132	22.0	5.4	24	2,088	911.2	87.5	49	610	30.1	8.3
Dane	1,904	22,044	4,791.0	1,896.8	521	26,628	9,108.6	1,556.3	1,403	27,619	1,476.7	441.3
Dodge	84	521	70.5	26.0	134	9,631	3,431.8	485.5	156	1,815	82.1	22.1
Door	66	227	29.5	10.7	66	2,576	608.9	120.9	249	2,039	180.2	51.2

STATE County	Health care and social assistance, 2017				Other services, 2017				Nonemployer businesses, 2019		Value of residential construction authorized by building permits, 2021	
	Number of establish-ments	Number of employees	Receipts (mil dol)	Annual payroll (mil dol)	Number of establish-ments	Number of employees	Receipts (mil dol)	Annual payroll (mil dol)	Number	Receipts (mil dol)	New construction ($1,000)	Number of housing units
	159	160	161	162	163	164	165	166	167	168	169	170
WEST VIRGINIA—Cont'd												
Calhoun	D	D	D	D	D	D	1.1	D	377	8.1	NA	NA
Clay	17	D	10.3	D	4	45	6.6	1.7	333	13.8	875	20
Doddridge	10	113	3.4	1.9	D	D	D	D	251	8.1	0	0
Fayette	108	2,135	182.5	70.8	53	217	31.6	7.1	1,651	61.5	3,869	32
Gilmer	13	224	13.1	6.5	D	D	3.8	D	335	8.8	1,657	10
Grant	24	820	57.7	23.5	D	D	D	1.4	693	25.1	7,483	40
Greenbrier	136	2,652	233.5	101.7	52	168	30.7	5.0	2,161	81.7	21,976	61
Hampshire	D	D	D	D	D	D	D	D	1,404	60.2	22,217	126
Hancock	66	1,256	84.5	37.5	45	232	26.9	7.0	1,230	42.2	4,822	18
Hardy	32	564	46.2	20.3	22	66	6.0	1.5	870	27.1	14,149	81
Harrison	224	6,889	888.2	356.6	131	674	63.6	16.8	3,701	168.5	27,588	141
Jackson	60	1,124	80.5	35.8	35	128	20.5	3.5	1,328	50.7	0	0
Jefferson	D	D	D	D	79	543	101.0	19.2	3,804	156.7	156,616	689
Kanawha	D	D	D	D	373	2,396	327.0	90.7	8,942	391.7	29,097	221
Lewis	34	1,169	106.8	45.1	27	88	14.4	2.9	775	32.7	0	0
Lincoln	25	923	34.0	17.2	D	D	D	D	618	17.4	1,675	7
Logan	96	1,982	210.3	79.4	43	296	32.5	9.4	1,078	43.4	100	1
McDowell	31	823	44.6	18.5	D	D	D	D	464	13.2	1,428	9
Marion	155	2,934	258.6	105.9	91	628	59.7	18.8	2,497	94.4	1,977	19
Marshall	80	1,512	98.1	46.1	42	200	17.5	4.9	1,078	38.2	0	0
Mason	43	952	110.5	40.8	27	116	12.7	3.2	928	31.2	278	2
Mercer	228	4,746	457.5	172.7	81	750	103.6	23.6	2,935	113.3	771	5
Mineral	71	1,464	89.4	36.2	34	195	15.8	4.4	1,305	45.6	8,054	33
Mingo	44	610	56.9	20.1	D	D	D	D	824	28.0	0	0
Monongalia	269	16,096	2,376.4	743.1	163	1,220	244.2	39.4	5,888	272.5	3,261	14
Monroe	20	277	16.6	7.6	D	D	D	0.5	776	26.0	20	1
Morgan	19	522	50.3	20.5	22	90	6.7	1.8	1,094	45.1	16,182	92
Nicholas	66	1,491	105.9	48.9	31	108	11.7	3.1	1,122	45.5	509	5
Ohio	230	6,200	822.1	312.2	116	1,017	119.1	35.0	2,445	117.1	14,242	92
Pendleton	17	333	18.8	9.0	D	D	4.7	D	527	17.4	4,930	26
Pleasants	D	D	D	D	D	D	D	0.4	273	8.0	2,557	11
Pocahontas	24	390	26.9	14.1	17	136	9.5	2.5	560	22.1	509	6
Preston	61	1,123	83.9	35.8	31	174	17.6	4.2	1,602	71.7	1,215	7
Putnam	127	2,134	247.1	102.0	59	339	43.3	10.5	3,133	124.8	31,735	132
Raleigh	303	7,101	764.5	307.4	112	814	96.8	24.3	3,417	141.0	15,707	71
Randolph	100	2,864	301.2	90.2	44	236	19.2	6.3	1,405	43.4	206	1
Ritchie	17	D	12.4	D	D	D	D	0.9	585	24.0	4,523	23
Roane	28	716	61.6	26.6	D	D	D	0.7	657	26.3	18	1
Summers	23	408	34.6	13.8	15	44	3.6	1.0	468	16.0	2,041	13
Taylor	32	682	44.1	20.9	D	D	D	D	711	32.2	0	0
Tucker	11	305	18.9	8.9	10	74	11.2	2.5	462	14.6	1,285	11
Tyler	15	460	24.8	12.3	D	D	1.8	D	356	10.5	0	0
Upshur	79	1,364	122.9	46.9	25	113	12.5	3.1	1,214	50.7	9,506	55
Wayne	60	2,115	312.7	125.8	32	128	11.9	3.8	1,587	51.6	5,398	71
Webster	16	437	31.9	16.0	D	D	D	D	270	12.1	0	0
Wetzel	37	753	59.4	23.5	34	129	11.8	3.1	521	14.9	1,103	5
Wirt	D	D	D	D	NA	NA	NA	NA	260	7.9	1,976	13
Wood	D	D	D	D	D	D	D	D	3,763	162.0	18,792	96
Wyoming	27	803	44.0	20.9	11	41	2.9	0.9	698	21.8	150	1
WISCONSIN	15,983	417,365	48,477.9	19,198.4	10,351	63,120	9,240.8	2,069.4	356,561	17,637.1	5,985,631	25,444
Adams	29	487	67.6	16.8	23	119	12.3	3.4	1,129	51.5	45,789	140
Ashland	63	1,368	154.6	65.1	34	131	10.4	3.2	1,101	50.3	2,856	13
Barron	132	2,430	279.6	109.4	96	331	48.1	9.6	3,153	162.4	44,847	160
Bayfield	22	360	17.7	9.7	25	71	7.7	1.9	1,549	59.5	20,585	90
Brown	724	24,177	3,453.3	1,189.1	466	3,012	317.2	88.8	14,285	757.5	259,464	1,176
Buffalo	28	315	14.1	6.1	19	69	6.9	1.6	986	47.9	4,474	36
Burnett	33	635	39.8	19.6	D	D	7.3	D	1,245	49.1	30,043	123
Calumet	90	1,168	96.3	41.6	63	275	28.8	7.3	2,557	119.5	118,976	766
Chippewa	161	2,754	230.9	94.2	101	494	60.0	16.8	4,084	229.7	88,383	348
Clark	66	913	77.9	32.9	54	163	23.5	3.9	2,331	143.5	13,979	68
Columbia	133	2,882	261.4	135.2	95	441	47.6	12.7	3,773	199.7	57,728	145
Crawford	37	1,113	99.0	47.9	25	101	10.1	2.6	1,103	45.7	13,804	59
Dane	1,364	53,120	7,128.9	2,962.3	1,165	8,810	1,477.2	353.2	38,955	2,039.6	1,362,619	6,836
Dodge	187	4,261	423.3	171.2	137	464	72.9	13.7	4,559	225.7	45,967	144
Door	77	1,310	124.2	57.7	98	444	55.9	14.2	2,992	134.3	43,530	187

STATE County	Government employment and payroll, 2017									Local government finances, 2017				
			March payroll (percent of total)							General revenue				
												Taxes		
													Per capita[1] (dollars)	
	Full-time equivalent employees	March payroll (dollars)	Administration, judicial, and legal	Police and corrections	Fire protection	Highways and transportation	Health and welfare	Natural resources and utilities	Education and libraries	Total (mil dol)	Intergovernmental (mil dol)	Total (mil dol)	Total	Property
	171	172	173	174	175	176	177	178	179	180	181	182	183	184
WEST VIRGINIA—Cont'd														
Calhoun	311	743,775	10.7	0.2	0.0	11.3	0.0	3.5	74.3	14.7	10.2	2.9	400	378
Clay	436	1,168,050	3.8	1.0	0.0	0.0	6.7	2.2	85.9	21.8	15.7	3.8	440	425
Doddridge	285	1,016,940	6.9	2.7	0.0	0.9	5.3	2.1	81.4	37.3	3.7	29.6	3,471	3,463
Fayette	1,484	4,411,432	6.4	5.3	1.4	1.4	0.6	5.7	78.6	100.1	48.7	38.6	886	748
Gilmer	169	640,640	10.2	2.8	0.0	0.5	1.4	0.4	84.3	15.1	8.0	5.7	711	629
Grant	672	2,192,767	4.3	1.3	0.0	4.1	44.1	5.4	38.9	63.8	8.6	13.2	1,134	1,080
Greenbrier	1,147	3,671,555	7.2	7.3	0.3	1.0	0.8	5.8	75.3	107.4	47.4	36.1	1,027	900
Hampshire	745	2,066,072	8.4	4.0	0.0	0.6	2.2	3.5	77.9	41.4	19.9	14.9	639	603
Hancock	1,047	3,245,725	5.6	9.1	2.7	3.1	1.9	7.8	64.2	91.2	29.3	36.9	1,256	908
Hardy	492	1,547,623	7.9	4.9	0.0	0.8	1.5	6.0	78.3	33.5	13.6	14.9	1,076	1,012
Harrison	2,649	9,379,255	8.0	7.2	4.5	3.3	1.7	7.2	66.7	212.2	62.7	113.9	1,678	1,329
Jackson	930	3,264,832	5.2	4.6	0.0	0.7	6.7	3.8	77.6	73.2	29.7	30.0	1,038	943
Jefferson	1,670	6,366,407	8.9	6.0	0.0	0.5	0.8	2.4	78.1	146.4	47.6	66.1	1,171	1,032
Kanawha	6,558	23,843,029	7.0	8.3	4.5	4.8	5.4	3.8	63.7	656.5	207.3	291.1	1,587	1,048
Lewis	621	1,475,391	10.1	6.0	1.1	0.9	6.6	1.9	68.2	39.0	16.5	18.1	1,116	1,001
Lincoln	669	2,192,499	5.7	1.7	0.0	2.1	0.7	3.1	85.0	41.6	28.1	11.0	529	521
Logan	1,246	4,074,664	7.7	5.5	0.8	0.5	0.9	4.6	77.2	77.2	38.2	30.6	927	877
McDowell	758	2,486,304	6.1	3.8	0.0	1.1	0.5	5.2	80.0	67.7	26.4	19.2	1,036	937
Marion	1,849	6,457,746	5.1	6.8	2.4	3.7	1.6	6.1	72.3	169.4	57.2	68.9	1,222	1,030
Marshall	1,147	3,794,118	11.3	6.4	0.4	1.5	2.6	6.0	69.3	117.0	13.2	80.3	2,570	2,417
Mason	830	2,893,931	5.4	4.9	0.0	0.4	1.6	4.7	81.2	61.8	27.2	23.0	858	787
Mercer	3,184	11,269,581	2.4	2.7	1.1	1.4	41.5	3.9	46.3	268.1	64.2	47.0	784	610
Mineral	904	2,717,456	6.7	3.6	0.0	1.5	2.5	3.4	80.0	63.1	31.3	21.9	805	738
Mingo	855	2,826,731	10.1	4.1	0.8	0.0	3.5	5.9	75.5	69.2	37.9	23.1	959	879
Monongalia	2,619	9,242,161	6.3	9.0	3.0	4.8	2.3	8.1	63.4	255.7	67.9	132.7	1,254	942
Monroe	333	1,060,932	5.5	1.9	0.0	0.0	0.0	3.1	87.0	24.7	14.6	5.2	392	366
Morgan	446	1,456,131	9.5	3.1	0.0	0.0	1.6	2.0	80.6	33.3	13.8	14.8	835	786
Nicholas	1,176	4,089,192	5.6	3.7	0.0	1.4	52.4	4.5	32.2	126.9	44.6	18.9	752	612
Ohio	1,975	6,700,199	4.8	7.7	5.5	6.0	3.2	20.1	50.6	208.6	43.4	95.6	2,276	1,337
Pendleton	214	780,616	8.9	1.3	0.0	0.8	1.8	4.4	80.2	13.8	7.6	4.7	667	597
Pleasants	307	1,082,025	10.8	4.0	0.0	0.4	1.5	5.1	75.4	24.5	5.0	14.2	1,909	1,902
Pocahontas	437	1,626,369	6.3	2.6	0.0	0.4	44.1	4.0	40.1	35.1	8.8	8.9	1,049	832
Preston	938	2,591,492	8.6	4.0	0.0	0.7	0.9	6.4	77.3	61.3	30.7	20.1	594	554
Putnam	1,790	6,533,244	5.1	4.4	0.1	0.5	3.0	5.1	80.6	132.5	49.7	61.3	1,081	1,013
Raleigh	2,410	8,096,096	6.7	6.5	2.2	1.6	1.9	6.0	74.1	217.5	92.2	88.0	1,172	911
Randolph	904	2,856,923	7.3	4.1	1.0	1.4	3.9	7.9	72.5	60.4	30.2	17.7	612	508
Ritchie	308	976,199	14.1	0.6	0.0	1.4	0.0	5.7	78.1	24.2	8.2	13.3	1,355	1,286
Roane	405	1,249,394	5.9	3.8	0.0	0.8	4.0	5.6	78.5	24.7	16.5	6.2	440	390
Summers	334	998,777	8.0	4.9	1.6	1.3	1.0	2.7	77.0	25.2	11.7	7.8	605	428
Taylor	483	1,437,988	4.1	2.8	0.9	1.3	6.0	5.6	76.5	57.7	14.8	17.3	1,022	939
Tucker	274	858,636	11.1	1.8	0.0	0.6	1.5	11.1	65.3	24.8	9.3	8.2	1,177	1,031
Tyler	411	1,479,004	6.2	4.3	0.0	1.6	38.5	3.2	43.1	58.2	6.6	14.8	1,677	1,625
Upshur	761	2,564,165	9.6	4.0	1.2	1.1	1.7	6.7	73.0	56.1	26.1	19.4	789	691
Wayne	1,310	4,187,944	5.2	4.6	0.0	0.4	0.5	4.8	83.8	98.1	57.5	28.9	719	663
Webster	363	1,192,118	5.2	1.8	0.0	0.6	0.9	3.3	85.3	37.2	11.3	3.7	443	402
Wetzel	860	2,975,640	7.5	4.2	0.0	0.8	27.6	7.9	49.9	98.1	10.0	51.1	3,314	3,201
Wirt	202	618,211	7.1	2.1	0.0	0.0	0.0	1.6	89.2	14.5	10.6	2.6	451	433
Wood	2,893	9,478,825	5.4	6.6	2.5	3.3	3.2	6.8	70.7	215.4	86.1	81.9	963	780
Wyoming	797	2,514,443	12.9	0.8	0.0	0.0	0.8	3.5	81.9	52.5	28.0	18.1	852	813
WISCONSIN	X	X	X	X	X	X	X	X	X	X	X	X	X	X
Adams	572	2,264,859	11.2	15.3	0.0	9.7	14.3	7.2	41.7	78.2	30.3	35.4	1,777	1,665
Ashland	817	3,164,080	7.9	9.7	4.4	8.9	9.9	3.9	51.9	85.9	47.8	23.9	1,540	1,415
Barron	1,857	7,487,952	5.9	8.2	1.4	5.3	7.0	3.0	67.9	203.3	94.8	81.4	1,803	1,672
Bayfield	753	2,902,925	10.6	8.5	0.3	11.0	26.0	3.9	37.7	80.2	32.0	33.5	2,230	2,084
Brown	9,500	46,580,783	3.8	8.7	3.4	3.2	4.7	4.9	69.5	1,229.5	575.3	401.2	1,533	1,493
Buffalo	488	1,773,496	7.8	6.9	0.2	11.1	6.9	2.4	63.9	53.2	28.9	19.6	1,495	1,414
Burnett	598	2,153,819	11.9	9.1	0.2	9.3	8.2	2.5	57.6	62.3	28.4	28.3	1,853	1,751
Calumet	1,222	4,658,317	8.3	8.1	0.0	6.1	12.7	4.2	59.9	121.8	50.5	51.9	1,039	1,016
Chippewa	2,061	8,330,286	6.0	8.1	1.7	6.8	5.9	3.9	67.0	223.5	121.6	78.8	1,236	1,108
Clark	1,408	5,217,986	8.2	6.5	0.1	5.9	27.2	3.3	47.9	149.7	75.5	40.4	1,169	1,095
Columbia	2,633	10,398,074	6.9	9.2	0.5	5.3	6.4	4.7	66.3	274.0	118.4	117.0	2,045	1,862
Crawford	597	2,205,288	7.7	9.7	0.2	10.1	7.7	3.3	60.3	68.7	37.2	25.1	1,547	1,415
Dane	20,439	91,082,709	5.3	11.5	2.7	5.4	5.8	5.5	61.6	2,723.6	999.2	1,270.9	2,365	2,183
Dodge	2,531	10,252,861	7.6	13.7	1.7	6.8	17.8	4.1	46.3	297.1	124.2	103.0	1,175	1,072
Door	1,063	4,665,555	9.3	10.6	2.2	7.9	11.5	4.4	52.9	144.6	37.5	85.7	3,123	2,876

1. Based on the resident population estimated as of July 1 of the year shown.

STATE County	Local government finances, 2017 (cont.)									Government employment, 2020			Individual income tax returns, 2019		
	Direct general expenditure							Debt outstanding							
			Percent of total for:												
	Total (mil dol)	Per capita[1] (dollars)	Education	Health and hospitals	Police protection	Public welfare	Highways	Total (mil dol)	Per capita[1] (dollars)	Federal civilian	Federal military	State and local	Number of returns	Mean adjusted gross income	Mean income tax
	185	186	187	188	189	190	191	192	193	194	195	196	197	198	199
WEST VIRGINIA—Cont'd															
Calhoun	13.6	1,859	75.1	0.0	1.4	0.0	0.1	19.4	2,658	17	33	280	2,390	46,450	3,447
Clay	25.2	2,898	79.5	7.1	3.8	0.0	0.0	4.5	516	18	39	479	3,100	43,115	2,833
Doddridge	29.2	3,429	73.0	2.5	4.7	0.0	0.1	4.6	544	18	35	578	2,830	57,581	6,122
Fayette	102.1	2,341	67.6	0.6	5.9	0.0	2.3	43.8	1,005	245	204	2,413	16,860	44,590	3,273
Gilmer	16.3	2,032	76.9	1.4	1.7	0.0	0.7	8.3	1,033	307	35	624	2,450	48,506	4,337
Grant	63.1	5,424	24.8	58.4	2.4	0.0	0.1	17.7	1,522	56	54	881	5,150	44,885	3,443
Greenbrier	101.4	2,880	53.3	0.8	7.7	0.0	1.1	95.9	2,723	122	161	2,254	15,270	48,738	4,295
Hampshire	47.1	2,015	65.5	1.1	7.5	0.5	0.6	22.4	957	56	108	1,160	10,180	47,553	3,822
Hancock	81.6	2,776	51.2	2.4	8.9	0.5	5.0	86.8	2,953	66	135	1,275	14,410	51,787	4,588
Hardy	35.2	2,539	62.0	1.3	18.8	0.0	0.3	50.1	3,615	53	65	724	6,640	43,024	3,313
Harrison	203.0	2,990	59.5	0.8	5.5	0.2	3.5	162.2	2,389	4,482	334	3,550	30,980	60,923	6,396
Jackson	84.2	2,914	62.9	3.1	6.1	0.0	0.8	55.1	1,907	89	135	1,149	12,270	52,159	4,545
Jefferson	149.8	2,655	64.6	0.6	5.4	0.1	2.0	61.8	1,096	1,590	302	2,673	27,450	70,790	7,589
Kanawha	664.1	3,621	47.5	0.9	7.2	0.2	1.9	284.4	1,551	2,237	842	18,754	83,120	58,057	6,336
Lewis	43.2	2,668	65.5	2.3	3.3	0.1	0.9	11.0	680	52	78	1,267	7,570	52,945	4,775
Lincoln	45.7	2,188	83.1	0.8	0.9	0.0	0.0	6.1	292	44	95	807	7,250	48,649	3,929
Logan	95.2	2,881	72.1	1.0	1.4	0.3	0.6	18.1	549	104	148	1,907	11,440	47,819	3,676
McDowell	67.7	3,657	58.1	0.5	4.3	0.0	1.3	20.6	1,115	358	80	1,300	5,270	37,286	2,164
Marion	172.0	3,052	55.1	0.7	5.8	1.0	2.0	222.9	3,955	213	270	3,530	25,830	53,578	4,655
Marshall	106.1	3,394	61.6	1.4	7.4	0.2	2.3	125.1	4,003	66	141	1,743	14,360	56,411	5,337
Mason	65.8	2,454	68.7	4.8	3.4	0.1	0.9	24.3	905	108	122	1,267	10,470	49,076	3,856
Mercer	276.1	4,613	35.6	43.3	4.4	0.0	1.0	90.8	1,517	183	272	4,656	24,370	45,393	3,643
Mineral	81.1	2,980	55.3	0.8	4.4	0.0	0.6	90.9	3,340	106	125	1,372	12,580	52,307	4,494
Mingo	76.5	3,167	58.9	1.0	2.2	0.1	0.0	30.9	1,279	91	109	938	7,790	43,483	2,947
Monongalia	269.4	2,547	52.2	1.5	6.8	1.0	2.6	385.7	3,646	1,165	490	15,147	43,290	73,243	9,288
Monroe	20.4	1,522	94.5	0.0	0.1	0.0	0.3	9.5	711	200	63	508	5,360	46,438	3,396
Morgan	33.1	1,869	72.6	1.0	7.9	0.0	0.3	13.4	756	36	85	683	8,360	49,943	4,146
Nicholas	125.0	4,977	47.5	40.8	4.3	0.0	0.8	47.4	1,888	112	115	1,315	10,050	46,661	3,617
Ohio	209.3	4,983	34.4	0.1	7.5	0.0	3.4	300.4	7,153	401	186	3,022	20,150	65,712	7,675
Pendleton	15.3	2,191	76.7	2.3	1.1	0.0	0.0	5.3	766	26	33	307	3,270	43,613	3,047
Pleasants	28.6	3,835	57.0	0.0	6.4	1.3	0.8	95.2	12,776	12	32	581	3,200	57,923	5,434
Pocahontas	36.1	4,245	39.6	39.5	2.3	0.3	0.4	5.7	671	68	37	775	3,900	40,837	2,901
Preston	66.3	1,959	63.3	0.7	7.0	0.0	0.7	71.2	2,105	925	150	1,666	14,070	50,498	4,077
Putnam	139.8	2,466	72.6	0.5	5.9	0.0	0.8	140.8	2,483	250	269	1,904	26,170	67,395	7,135
Raleigh	230.0	3,064	62.2	0.7	7.1	0.0	1.6	139.4	1,858	1,887	333	3,734	30,740	53,863	5,192
Randolph	68.9	2,385	54.8	0.1	6.1	0.2	1.6	98.7	3,417	168	124	1,767	12,130	47,669	3,923
Ritchie	26.4	2,677	62.9	11.1	4.0	0.0	1.1	4.5	455	35	45	437	3,960	54,200	5,335
Roane	26.7	1,910	80.1	0.0	2.9	0.1	2.2	13.2	944	32	64	532	5,220	46,209	3,622
Summers	25.8	2,007	56.6	1.0	6.8	0.1	1.3	12.6	979	53	54	716	4,380	42,487	3,055
Taylor	57.5	3,400	42.1	34.8	4.8	0.6	1.4	26.9	1,593	45	77	983	7,340	56,198	5,100
Tucker	25.3	3,622	54.2	0.9	6.3	0.0	3.3	18.3	2,620	60	32	548	3,270	45,380	3,398
Tyler	47.0	5,337	36.7	49.5	1.8	0.0	0.6	7.7	876	22	40	447	3,790	65,146	7,875
Upshur	62.4	2,541	60.5	0.6	2.8	0.3	1.7	35.3	1,439	127	110	1,143	10,020	48,365	3,907
Wayne	118.3	2,942	76.1	1.6	4.1	0.1	0.7	66.0	1,642	1,613	185	1,627	15,500	48,539	3,781
Webster	38.9	4,666	37.0	46.7	4.5	0.0	0.4	7.6	908	17	38	547	3,000	39,148	2,428
Wetzel	90.9	5,890	47.3	27.8	3.6	0.0	1.3	27.7	1,793	39	70	1,014	6,810	53,580	4,798
Wirt	15.3	2,637	83.8	0.0	0.0	0.0	0.0	1.5	263	15	27	235	2,260	45,488	3,195
Wood	225.5	2,651	60.7	0.0	6.9	0.1	4.0	256.4	3,014	2,708	392	4,011	38,620	55,407	5,452
Wyoming	57.3	2,694	74.3	0.3	5.3	0.1	0.5	41.0	1,927	99	96	918	6,930	45,981	3,201
WISCONSIN	X	X	X	X	X	X	X	X	X	30,861	15,828	373,730	2,912,730	69,415	7,972
Adams	92.4	4,642	26.0	10.7	5.7	4.2	16.6	59.7	3,001	286	50	750	9,780	49,395	4,208
Ashland	92.2	5,949	41.7	3.4	6.3	7.1	15.8	119.0	7,675	157	40	1,576	7,450	48,493	4,015
Barron	211.3	4,682	49.3	1.2	4.7	5.9	15.0	116.9	2,590	148	116	3,476	23,430	52,947	4,567
Bayfield	83.1	5,537	33.9	7.3	4.6	0.2	21.5	35.9	2,393	130	59	1,429	8,030	61,663	6,455
Brown	1,362.6	5,205	52.3	2.9	5.5	3.1	7.9	1,188.9	4,542	1,332	688	16,367	133,910	74,179	9,199
Buffalo	56.3	4,297	48.2	1.4	3.5	5.4	22.7	21.0	1,600	158	33	687	6,660	50,404	4,053
Burnett	74.9	4,897	40.9	3.7	4.0	3.3	20.4	35.2	2,302	36	40	1,411	8,070	53,910	4,764
Calumet	121.9	2,439	41.6	3.9	6.1	6.2	13.3	120.8	2,416	64	129	1,364	25,790	77,459	8,613
Chippewa	250.2	3,925	48.8	4.6	4.4	3.5	16.5	172.2	2,702	198	160	3,170	32,060	60,188	5,806
Clark	159.2	4,605	46.1	4.6	4.4	13.8	10.8	103.4	2,990	109	89	2,123	15,030	54,231	5,291
Columbia	323.7	5,656	47.4	2.0	4.3	5.3	12.0	332.2	5,804	195	146	3,500	30,810	65,812	6,871
Crawford	75.6	4,666	48.0	3.0	5.6	3.7	20.6	73.3	4,524	70	39	970	7,830	50,515	4,476
Dane	2,755.9	5,128	47.7	2.1	6.1	8.6	6.0	4,031.8	7,502	5,540	1,545	76,327	280,060	87,582	11,528
Dodge	308.0	3,512	34.0	12.6	7.6	4.1	13.4	299.5	3,415	188	211	4,549	43,600	60,204	5,807
Door	150.5	5,482	34.7	7.3	5.8	2.1	15.4	93.4	3,403	82	154	1,730	16,400	68,957	7,513

1. Based on the resident population estimated as of July 1 of the year shown.

State / county code	CBSA code[1]	County Type code[2]	STATE County	Land area[3] (sq. mi)	Population, 2021: Total persons 2021	Population, 2021: Rank	Population, 2021: Per square mile	Race alone or in combination, not Hispanic or Latino (percent): White	Black	American Indian, Alaska Native	Asian and Pacific Islancer	Percent Hispanic or Latino[4]	Age (percent): Under 5 years	5 to 17 years	18 to 24 years	25 to 34 years	35 to 44 years	45 to 54 years
				1	2	3	4	5	6	7	8	9	10	11	12	13	14	15
			WISCONSIN—Cont'd															
55031	20260	2	Douglas	1,304.3	44,203	1,094	33.9	93.7	2.4	3.3	1.7	1.9	4.7	11.2	11.9	12.4	12.7	11.9
55033	32860	6	Dunn	850.2	45,547	1,068	53.6	93.3	1.4	0.9	3.6	2.2	4.8	10.9	21.8	11.6	11.4	10.9
55035	20740	3	Eau Claire	637.9	106,452	579	166.9	90.7	2.1	1.0	5.2	2.9	5.3	11.4	19.3	13.4	12.4	10.2
55037	27020	9	Florence	488.1	4,593	2,850	9.4	96.8	1.0	1.7	1.0	1.2	3.0	8.4	6.9	8.4	10.5	11.3
55039	22540	3	Fond du Lac	719.6	104,362	587	145.0	89.4	3.1	0.8	2.1	6.0	5.1	12.0	12.5	11.6	12.7	12.1
55041		9	Forest	1,014.2	9,258	2,470	9.1	81.9	2.1	15.2	1.1	2.9	5.3	10.6	11.3	10.5	9.8	11.9
55043	38420	6	Grant	1,146.9	52,110	967	45.4	95.2	1.9	0.5	1.2	2.1	5.5	11.7	20.6	10.8	10.6	10.0
55045	31540	2	Green	584.0	36,988	1,253	63.3	94.8	1.3	0.6	1.0	3.5	5.0	12.4	11.0	10.7	12.5	12.8
55047		6	Green Lake	349.5	19,229	1,863	55.0	92.3	1.3	0.8	1.0	5.7	5.4	12.2	11.4	9.6	10.9	11.4
55049	31540	2	Iowa	762.7	23,756	1,653	31.1	95.9	1.5	0.7	1.2	2.2	5.2	12.5	10.8	10.4	12.4	12.4
55051		9	Iron	758.2	6,178	2,720	8.1	96.2	1.0	2.3	0.7	1.6	3.5	8.8	8.1	8.2	9.1	11.6
55053		6	Jackson	987.9	21,121	1,756	21.4	87.0	3.0	6.9	1.1	3.8	5.6	12.3	10.8	12.2	12.3	12.2
55055	48020	4	Jefferson	556.5	84,943	677	152.6	89.8	1.5	0.8	1.4	7.8	4.8	11.4	13.4	11.2	13.0	13.1
55057		7	Juneau	767.1	26,802	1,538	34.9	92.2	3.0	1.8	0.9	3.3	4.9	11.3	10.1	11.3	12.2	13.0
55059	16980	1	Kenosha	271.8	168,732	399	620.8	76.3	8.4	0.9	2.5	14.4	5.3	12.6	13.7	13.0	12.7	12.9
55061	24580	2	Kewaunee	342.5	20,543	1,790	60.0	94.8	1.0	0.9	0.9	3.5	5.1	11.9	10.9	10.3	12.2	12.3
55063	29100	3	La Crosse	451.8	120,433	528	266.6	90.7	2.7	0.7	5.6	2.3	4.8	11.2	19.2	12.6	11.9	10.6
55065		8	Lafayette	633.6	16,784	1,986	26.5	94.2	0.8	0.6	0.8	4.5	6.6	13.5	11.8	10.6	11.3	11.0
55067		6	Langlade	870.7	19,502	1,851	22.4	94.4	1.9	2.0	0.9	2.5	5.0	10.7	10.3	9.3	10.6	11.2
55069	48140	6	Lincoln	878.7	28,541	1,474	32.5	95.6	1.5	1.1	1.1	2.2	4.5	9.8	10.2	10.0	11.5	13.1
55071	31820	4	Manitowoc	589.3	81,505	707	138.3	90.3	1.8	1.0	3.5	4.9	5.0	11.7	11.0	10.5	11.7	12.2
55073	48140	3	Marathon	1,545.2	137,648	473	89.1	89.1	1.6	0.8	7.0	3.1	5.6	12.9	11.5	11.9	12.6	12.3
55075	31940	6	Marinette	1,399.5	41,875	1,148	29.9	95.8	1.0	1.2	0.9	2.3	4.6	10.8	9.9	9.6	11.1	11.3
55077		8	Marquette	455.7	15,792	2,043	34.7	94.0	1.2	1.1	0.9	3.9	4.6	11.1	9.5	8.8	10.5	11.5
55078	43020	8	Menominee	357.6	4,289	2,867	12.0	14.8	2.0	75.5	2.2	8.0	8.9	19.8	14.6	11.7	9.4	9.3
55079	33340	1	Milwaukee	241.5	928,059	59	3,842.9	51.3	28.2	1.2	5.6	16.4	6.6	13.4	13.3	16.1	13.3	11.2
55081		6	Monroe	900.9	46,193	1,052	51.3	90.8	2.4	1.5	1.5	5.3	6.1	14.7	11.5	10.8	13.2	11.7
55083	24580	2	Oconto	997.5	39,356	1,194	39.5	95.5	0.9	2.1	0.8	2.1	5.0	11.4	9.9	9.8	11.9	12.7
55085		7	Oneida	1,113.9	38,259	1,215	34.3	95.9	1.1	1.9	0.8	1.8	4.2	9.7	8.8	9.6	10.2	11.3
55087	11540	3	Outagamie	637.6	191,545	357	300.4	88.0	2.4	2.1	4.5	4.9	5.9	13.2	12.5	13.0	13.6	12.2
55089	33340	1	Ozaukee	233.0	92,497	653	397.0	91.6	2.5	0.6	3.4	3.5	5.1	12.1	12.6	9.7	12.3	12.4
55091		8	Pepin	232.0	7,364	2,635	31.7	96.0	0.8	0.7	0.9	2.6	5.7	12.8	10.0	10.0	11.3	10.9
55093	33460	1	Pierce	574.0	42,587	1,135	74.2	94.7	1.5	1.0	1.9	2.6	4.6	11.7	19.7	10.6	12.0	11.7
55095		6	Polk	914.3	45,431	1,071	49.7	95.9	0.9	1.5	0.9	2.0	4.6	11.5	10.8	9.9	11.7	12.4
55097	44620	4	Portage	800.9	70,468	773	88.0	91.6	1.5	0.7	3.8	3.8	4.7	10.8	19.1	11.9	11.5	10.7
55099		9	Price	1,254.1	14,050	2,148	11.2	94.7	1.0	1.4	1.9	2.3	4.0	9.7	9.6	7.7	9.7	12.4
55101	39540	3	Racine	332.6	196,896	347	592.0	72.2	13.0	0.9	1.8	14.8	5.8	13.0	12.3	12.0	12.5	12.4
55103		6	Richland	586.2	17,212	1,957	29.4	95.0	1.3	0.8	1.2	2.8	4.9	12.0	11.5	9.7	10.6	11.8
55105	27500	3	Rock	718.2	164,381	408	228.9	83.7	6.5	0.7	1.9	9.7	5.7	12.8	12.5	12.3	12.7	12.4
55107		6	Rusk	913.6	14,123	2,142	15.5	95.6	1.4	1.2	0.8	2.2	4.9	11.8	9.9	9.0	10.1	11.9
55109	33460	1	St. Croix	722.2	95,044	639	131.6	94.8	1.5	0.7	1.9	2.8	5.7	13.8	12.0	11.4	14.0	13.5
55111	12660	4	Sauk	831.5	65,697	819	79.0	91.0	1.7	1.5	1.1	5.9	5.7	12.9	11.4	11.4	12.8	12.0
55113		7	Sawyer	1,257.6	18,295	1,909	14.5	80.0	1.2	18.1	0.7	2.9	4.3	11.1	9.4	8.7	9.8	11.1
55115	43020	6	Shawano	893.2	40,859	1,167	45.7	87.6	1.0	9.2	1.0	3.3	5.4	11.9	10.9	10.4	11.1	12.4
55117	43100	3	Sheboygan	511.5	117,747	533	230.2	84.0	3.3	0.8	6.6	7.2	5.3	12.4	12.2	11.7	12.3	12.2
55119		6	Taylor	975.1	19,923	1,815	20.4	96.2	0.8	0.7	0.8	2.4	5.5	13.3	11.0	9.6	11.4	12.1
55121		6	Trempealeau	733.0	30,724	1,414	41.9	88.9	0.8	0.6	0.8	9.7	7.1	14.0	11.0	10.5	12.0	12.2
55123		6	Vernon	791.6	30,915	1,405	39.1	97.0	1.0	0.6	0.8	1.7	6.8	14.9	11.5	9.2	11.2	11.0
55125		9	Vilas	857.7	23,520	1,660	27.4	86.7	1.0	10.3	0.9	2.7	4.1	9.7	8.2	8.0	8.5	10.6
55127	48580	4	Walworth	555.4	106,799	577	192.3	86.0	1.5	0.6	1.4	11.6	4.5	11.3	16.8	10.4	11.2	11.9
55129		7	Washburn	797.1	16,752	1,989	21.0	95.4	0.7	2.5	0.9	2.1	4.2	10.6	9.3	8.2	10.2	11.6
55131	33340	1	Washington	430.6	137,175	478	318.6	92.9	2.2	0.6	2.1	3.5	4.8	12.2	11.3	10.5	12.7	13.2
55133	33340	1	Waukesha	549.7	408,756	178	743.6	88.5	2.5	0.6	4.8	5.3	5.1	12.0	11.8	10.4	13.1	12.7
55135		6	Waupaca	747.7	51,570	973	69.0	94.8	0.9	1.1	0.8	3.5	5.0	11.6	10.6	10.5	11.9	12.7
55137		6	Waushara	626.2	24,828	1,620	39.6	90.0	2.7	1.1	0.9	6.6	4.3	10.3	9.6	9.5	11.1	12.1
55139	36780	3	Winnebago	434.7	171,623	390	394.8	88.7	3.6	1.0	3.9	4.7	5.2	11.5	15.1	13.3	12.6	11.9
55141	49220	4	Wood	793.0	74,070	748	93.4	92.7	1.6	1.0	2.3	3.6	5.5	12.3	10.9	11.1	11.7	11.7
56000		0	WYOMING	97,088.7	578,803	X	6.0	85.2	1.6	2.9	1.7	10.6	5.6	13.2	13.1	12.7	13.3	11.1
56001	29660	4	Albany	4,274.3	37,608	1,232	8.8	84.2	2.0	1.5	4.6	10.2	4.4	8.9	29.5	15.5	11.2	8.5
56003		9	Big Horn	3,137.0	11,632	2,305	3.7	88.1	1.1	1.7	1.0	9.6	5.2	14.3	11.9	10.2	12.2	10.5
56005	23940	5	Campbell	4,802.1	46,401	1,047	9.7	88.7	1.0	2.1	1.3	8.8	6.6	15.7	12.8	13.5	15.0	11.2
56007		7	Carbon	7,897.8	14,649	2,105	1.9	77.7	1.6	2.2	1.3	19.0	5.7	13.1	11.5	13.5	13.8	11.1
56009		6	Converse	4,255.0	13,672	2,179	3.2	89.6	0.9	1.5	1.0	8.4	6.0	14.2	11.0	12.4	12.5	11.6
56011	23940	9	Crook	2,854.5	7,315	2,638	2.6	95.0	1.3	1.5	0.7	2.8	6.9	14.0	10.0	10.1	10.7	10.7
56013	40180	7	Fremont	9,183.6	39,336	1,195	4.3	71.8	0.9	21.2	1.1	7.8	6.2	14.7	12.2	11.1	12.3	10.7

1. CBSA = Core Based Statistical Area. See Appendix A for explanation. See Appendix B for list of metropolitan areas with component counties. 2. County type code from the Economic Research Service of USDA Rural-Urban Continuum Codes. See Appendix A for definition. 3. Dry land or land partially or temporarily covered by water. 4. May be of any race.

STATE County	Population, 2021 (cont.): Age (percent) (cont.): 55 to 64 years	Population, 2021 (cont.): Age (percent) (cont.): 65 to 74 years	Population, 2021 (cont.): Age (percent) (cont.): 75 years and over	Population, 2021 (cont.): Percent female	Population change, 2000–2021: Total persons: 2010	Population change, 2000–2021: Total persons: 2020	Population change, 2000–2021: Percent change: 2010–2020	Population change, 2000–2021: Percent change: 2020–2021	Population change, 2000–2021: Components of change, 2020–2021: Births	Population change, 2000–2021: Components of change, 2020–2021: Deaths	Population change, 2000–2021: Components of change, 2020–2021: Net Migration	Households, 2016–2020: Number	Households, 2016–2020: Persons per household	Households, 2016–2020: Percent: Family house-holds	Households, 2016–2020: Percent: Female family house-holder[1]	Households, 2016–2020: Percent: One person
	16	17	18	19	20	21	22	23	24	25	26	27	28	29	30	31
WISCONSIN—Cont'd																
Douglas	15.2	12.8	7.3	49.4	44,159	44,295	0.3	-0.2	490	690	102	18,994	2.2	60.1	10.4	32.4
Dunn	12.3	9.9	6.5	49.5	43,857	45,440	3.6	0.2	526	448	19	17,124	2.4	59.8	7.5	29.4
Eau Claire	11.6	10.2	6.2	50.3	98,736	105,710	7.1	0.7	1,381	1,241	584	41,602	2.4	57.4	7.2	30.7
Florence	22.3	18.4	10.6	48.4	4,423	4,558	3.1	0.8	31	85	91	2,038	2.1	63.7	5.6	32.0
Fond du Lac	14.7	11.6	7.7	50.4	101,633	104,154	2.5	0.2	1,240	1,456	416	41,890	2.4	65.6	6.7	28.4
Forest	17.4	14.5	8.9	48.4	9,304	9,179	-1.3	0.9	128	152	106	3,929	2.2	62.2	9.8	31.4
Grant	12.9	10.5	7.4	48.0	51,208	51,938	1.4	0.3	714	719	170	19,655	2.4	61.3	6.4	28.5
Green	15.7	12.2	7.7	49.6	36,842	37,093	0.7	-0.3	409	556	38	15,240	2.4	64.9	7.9	28.6
Green Lake	15.9	13.9	9.2	49.4	19,051	19,018	-0.2	1.1	228	329	316	8,024	2.3	65.5	7.4	28.6
Iowa	16.0	12.9	7.4	49.3	23,687	23,709	0.1	0.2	279	287	52	9,811	2.4	65.0	7.6	28.3
Iron	18.8	18.6	13.3	49.0	5,916	6,137	3.7	0.7	48	138	134	2,859	1.9	57.1	7.1	35.0
Jackson	14.9	11.8	7.8	46.2	20,449	21,145	3.4	-0.1	301	324	-5	8,246	2.3	61.0	8.6	32.1
Jefferson	14.9	11.4	6.9	49.7	83,686	84,900	1.5	0.1	980	1,127	178	33,349	2.4	66.8	8.8	27.2
Juneau	16.0	12.9	8.4	46.3	26,664	26,718	0.2	0.3	282	398	200	10,779	2.3	61.9	8.2	30.2
Kenosha	14.6	9.5	5.7	50.3	166,426	169,151	1.6	-0.2	2,169	2,172	-453	64,595	2.6	65.1	11.7	27.8
Kewaunee	15.6	12.8	8.8	49.0	20,574	20,563	-0.1	-0.1	239	310	50	8,249	2.5	71.8	5.7	24.3
La Crosse	12.3	10.4	7.0	50.9	114,638	120,784	5.4	-0.3	1,398	1,492	-274	48,105	2.4	56.8	8.2	31.4
Lafayette	15.2	12.0	8.0	49.1	16,836	16,611	-1.3	1.0	277	204	100	6,777	2.5	66.7	8.6	27.2
Langlade	17.9	14.9	10.2	49.3	19,977	19,491	-2.4	0.1	240	371	144	8,539	2.2	64.4	7.7	31.4
Lincoln	18.4	13.6	9.0	48.9	28,743	28,415	-1.1	0.4	299	517	348	12,654	2.1	61.7	6.8	31.9
Manitowoc	16.1	13.1	8.6	49.5	81,442	81,359	-0.1	0.2	917	1,286	517	34,435	2.3	62.1	7.8	31.9
Marathon	14.5	11.1	7.5	49.5	134,063	138,013	2.9	-0.3	1,793	1,815	-362	55,998	2.4	66.3	8.0	26.4
Marinette	17.8	15.0	9.8	49.1	41,749	41,872	0.3	0.0	456	753	302	18,869	2.1	59.5	7.0	34.2
Marquette	18.4	16.0	9.5	48.7	15,404	15,592	1.2	1.3	171	289	323	6,770	2.2	61.4	8.0	32.1
Menominee	13.1	8.7	4.7	51.0	4,232	4,255	0.5	0.8	105	99	28	1,400	3.2	76.0	31.6	18.1
Milwaukee	11.7	8.9	5.4	51.4	947,735	939,489	-0.9	-1.2	15,416	13,022	-13,812	383,703	2.4	55.0	15.9	36.5
Monroe	14.2	10.9	6.9	48.8	44,673	46,274	3.6	-0.2	682	625	-144	18,025	2.5	65.7	9.7	28.9
Oconto	18.0	13.8	7.6	48.2	37,660	38,965	3.5	1.0	448	577	524	16,283	2.3	67.4	6.9	25.8
Oneida	18.9	16.8	10.5	49.2	35,998	37,845	5.1	1.1	341	728	815	15,677	2.2	61.4	4.7	32.1
Outagamie	13.8	9.8	6.0	49.8	176,695	190,705	7.9	0.4	2,610	2,197	390	74,597	2.5	65.9	7.5	27.8
Ozaukee	15.1	12.2	8.6	50.4	86,395	91,503	5.9	1.1	1,016	1,242	1,233	36,166	2.4	69.1	6.6	26.3
Pepin	15.8	14.1	9.3	48.9	7,469	7,318	-2.0	0.6	103	101	45	3,127	2.3	67.4	5.9	28.2
Pierce	14.0	10.2	5.6	49.9	41,019	42,212	2.9	0.9	436	469	406	15,856	2.5	64.6	6.5	25.9
Polk	17.2	13.6	8.3	49.1	44,205	44,977	1.7	1.0	465	652	650	18,647	2.3	66.3	7.7	27.6
Portage	13.4	11.1	6.9	49.1	70,019	70,377	0.5	0.1	758	772	95	28,912	2.3	60.1	7.2	28.5
Price	18.9	17.1	10.8	48.3	14,159	14,054	-0.7	0.0	114	250	135	6,676	2.0	59.9	7.0	33.5
Racine	14.6	10.8	6.7	50.1	195,408	197,727	1.2	-0.4	2,686	2,819	-731	77,648	2.5	66.3	12.2	27.7
Richland	15.1	14.5	10.0	49.1	18,021	17,304	-4.0	-0.5	191	266	-17	7,580	2.2	61.7	8.3	32.3
Rock	14.2	10.6	6.8	50.4	160,331	163,687	2.1	0.4	2,281	2,334	728	65,237	2.5	63.7	11.7	29.6
Rusk	16.7	15.7	9.9	48.9	14,755	14,188	-3.8	-0.5	160	239	15	6,414	2.2	62.9	7.9	30.3
St. Croix	14.3	9.8	5.5	49.6	84,345	93,536	10.9	1.6	1,177	980	1,309	34,683	2.6	72.4	7.9	22.0
Sauk	14.4	11.8	7.7	49.8	61,976	65,763	6.1	-0.1	871	919	-29	26,751	2.4	64.4	8.3	29.1
Sawyer	18.4	17.6	9.7	48.5	16,557	18,074	9.2	1.2	172	329	384	7,893	2.1	62.3	9.7	31.7
Shawano	16.3	12.5	9.1	49.5	41,949	40,881	-2.5	-0.1	508	673	143	17,153	2.3	65.7	8.3	28.8
Sheboygan	14.8	11.6	7.4	49.1	115,507	118,034	2.2	-0.2	1,450	1,702	-52	47,754	2.4	63.1	7.4	30.7
Taylor	16.7	12.0	8.4	49.0	20,689	19,913	-3.8	0.1	273	271	7	8,623	2.3	67.7	6.8	27.0
Trempealeau	14.3	11.4	7.5	49.0	28,816	30,760	6.7	-0.1	509	392	-155	12,143	2.4	63.4	7.5	29.5
Vernon	15.1	12.5	7.8	49.4	29,773	30,714	3.2	0.7	525	471	146	12,146	2.5	64.5	7.0	31.0
Vilas	19.9	18.8	12.1	48.5	21,430	23,047	7.5	2.1	198	443	735	10,917	2.0	61.7	7.6	33.2
Walworth	14.8	11.9	7.2	49.7	102,228	106,478	4.2	0.3	1,095	1,524	742	41,414	2.4	65.3	8.9	27.4
Washburn	18.4	17.3	10.2	50.0	15,911	16,623	4.5	0.8	146	328	319	7,290	2.1	63.0	5.3	30.9
Washington	16.0	11.6	7.6	50.0	131,887	136,761	3.7	0.3	1,499	1,807	710	54,787	2.5	69.8	7.4	24.8
Waukesha	15.4	11.8	7.8	50.4	389,891	406,978	4.4	0.4	4,628	5,574	2,712	159,780	2.5	69.5	6.4	25.5
Waupaca	16.7	12.5	8.6	49.1	52,410	51,812	-1.1	-0.5	596	1,049	209	22,486	2.2	64.4	7.5	28.9
Waushara	17.8	15.6	9.7	46.9	24,496	24,520	0.1	1.3	249	407	475	10,053	2.3	66.3	7.1	29.4
Winnebago	13.5	10.2	6.8	49.3	166,994	171,730	2.8	-0.1	2,134	2,311	35	71,132	2.3	58.0	8.9	32.6
Wood	15.4	12.5	8.9	50.2	74,749	74,207	-0.7	-0.2	946	1,178	88	32,707	2.2	61.0	9.3	32.7
WYOMING	13.0	11.4	6.5	48.8	563,626	576,851	2.3	0.3	7,856	7,542	1,651	233,231	2.4	64.0	7.9	28.8
Albany	9.1	8.5	4.4	47.8	36,299	37,066	2.1	1.5	431	314	421	16,137	2.3	48.7	4.8	30.5
Big Horn	13.9	13.0	8.7	49.1	11,668	11,521	-1.3	1.0	124	182	171	4,408	2.6	64.6	7.6	32.5
Campbell	13.1	8.8	3.4	48.9	46,133	47,026	1.9	-1.3	747	471	-898	17,506	2.7	72.0	7.5	21.7
Carbon	13.4	11.3	6.5	45.8	15,885	14,537	-8.5	0.8	195	222	141	6,226	2.3	66.4	9.5	28.0
Converse	14.2	11.4	6.7	48.9	13,833	13,751	-0.6	-0.6	190	173	-97	5,461	2.5	67.6	5.4	25.7
Crook	15.9	14.0	7.8	49.4	7,083	7,181	1.4	1.9	138	123	120	2,826	2.6	71.3	2.7	24.5
Fremont	13.2	12.3	7.2	49.4	40,123	39,234	-2.2	0.3	577	713	236	14,834	2.6	61.3	9.8	33.0

1. No spouse present.

STATE County	Persons in group quarters, 2021	Daytime Population, 2016–2020: Number	Daytime Population, 2016–2020: Employment/ residence ratio	Births, 2021: Total	Births, 2021: Rate[1]	Deaths, 2021: Number	Deaths, 2021: Rate[1]	Persons under 65 with no health insurance, 2019: Number	Persons under 65 with no health insurance, 2019: Percent	Medicare, 2021: Total beneficiaries	Medicare, 2021: Enrolled in Original Medicare	Medicare, 2021: Enrolled in Medicare Advantage	COVID-19 Deaths, 2020: Number	COVID-19 Deaths, 2020: Rate[1]
	32	33	34	35	36	37	38	39	40	41	42	43	44	45
WISCONSIN—Cont'd														
Douglas	1,259	40,839	0.9	398	9.0	519	11.7	2,360	7.0	10,353	5,119	5,235	67	1.5
Dunn	3,205	41,741	0.9	407	8.9	358	7.9	2,357	6.7	9,271	6,255	3,016	25	0.6
Eau Claire	4,540	109,833	1.1	1,099	10.4	1,008	9.5	5,855	7.0	20,288	12,927	7,361	89	0.8
Florence	51	3,564	0.6	28	6.1	72	15.7	262	8.4	1,525	997	527	15	3.3
Fond du Lac	3,231	99,030	0.9	995	9.5	1,146	11.0	4,835	6.0	22,377	9,881	12,496	115	1.1
Forest	301	8,756	0.9	100	10.9	117	12.7	716	10.6	2,656	1,588	1,068	25	2.7
Grant	4,023	47,149	0.8	562	10.8	571	11.0	2,990	7.8	10,856	5,839	5,017	82	1.6
Green	297	33,648	0.8	325	8.8	431	11.7	1,921	6.5	8,249	6,224	2,025	17	0.5
Green Lake	143	17,135	0.8	184	9.6	255	13.3	1,372	9.5	5,111	2,207	2,905	21	1.1
Iowa	134	22,916	0.9	227	9.6	214	9.0	1,137	6.0	5,388	3,541	1,847	11	0.5
Iron	87	5,150	0.8	43	7.0	106	17.2	281	7.4	2,055	1,143	913	24	3.9
Jackson	1,281	19,784	0.9	248	11.7	256	12.1	1,524	9.9	4,610	2,889	1,721	20	0.9
Jefferson	3,071	75,653	0.8	777	9.2	902	10.6	4,281	6.3	17,584	11,441	6,143	90	1.1
Juneau	1,569	25,203	0.9	229	8.6	319	11.9	1,824	9.2	6,610	4,802	1,808	22	0.8
Kenosha	4,020	155,746	0.8	1,711	10.1	1,700	10.1	10,840	7.7	30,041	18,117	11,924	261	1.5
Kewaunee	125	17,444	0.7	193	9.4	257	12.5	1,071	6.7	4,659	2,046	2,613	33	1.6
La Crosse	5,405	127,169	1.2	1,072	8.9	1,177	9.8	4,913	5.2	23,557	13,472	10,085	76	0.6
Lafayette	67	14,289	0.7	224	13.4	167	10.0	1,536	11.6	3,509	2,150	1,359	D	D
Langlade	242	19,080	1.0	199	10.2	286	14.7	1,117	7.9	5,720	2,912	2,807	43	2.2
Lincoln	565	25,714	0.9	248	8.7	416	14.6	1,246	5.9	7,572	3,918	3,654	71	2.5
Manitowoc	940	74,300	0.9	744	9.1	987	12.1	4,101	6.6	20,073	9,657	10,415	66	0.8
Marathon	1,343	138,112	1.0	1,422	10.3	1,473	10.7	7,473	6.8	27,931	13,183	14,748	188	1.4
Marinette	562	41,021	1.0	361	8.6	597	14.3	2,033	6.8	12,077	6,242	5,835	70	1.7
Marquette	96	12,994	0.7	143	9.1	234	14.9	999	8.7	4,595	2,810	1,785	24	1.5
Menominee	23	5,175	1.4	82	19.2	81	19.0	301	8.0	871	578	293	14	3.3
Milwaukee	21,586	968,113	1.0	12,364	13.3	10,375	11.1	67,133	8.5	156,821	71,942	84,879	1,076	1.1
Monroe	1,026	47,931	1.1	527	11.4	509	11.0	3,344	8.9	9,444	6,484	2,961	29	0.6
Oconto	219	29,885	0.6	359	9.2	477	12.2	2,051	6.9	9,566	3,676	5,890	59	1.5
Oneida	592	35,754	1.0	271	7.1	577	15.2	1,821	7.1	12,133	7,276	4,858	51	1.3
Outagamie	2,781	193,396	1.1	2,060	10.8	1,754	9.2	10,565	6.7	34,192	12,246	21,946	186	1.0
Ozaukee	1,890	87,397	1.0	779	8.5	975	10.6	2,890	4.1	20,707	11,305	9,402	89	1.0
Pepin	50	6,597	0.8	78	10.6	79	10.7	419	7.6	2,076	1,632	444	D	D
Pierce	2,633	31,438	0.5	337	8.0	374	8.8	1,831	5.4	7,577	4,269	3,308	31	0.7
Polk	351	38,860	0.8	366	8.1	538	11.9	2,358	6.9	11,266	6,246	5,020	33	0.7
Portage	2,923	72,774	1.1	600	8.5	620	8.8	3,638	6.5	14,456	7,751	6,705	51	0.7
Price	153	13,554	1.0	100	7.1	206	14.7	710	7.3	4,498	2,691	1,808	D	D
Racine	4,817	181,191	0.8	2,175	11.0	2,231	11.3	11,317	7.2	41,218	20,939	20,279	288	1.5
Richland	249	16,006	0.8	156	9.0	216	12.5	1,195	9.2	4,508	3,641	868	15	0.9
Rock	2,384	152,750	0.9	1,817	11.1	1,866	11.4	9,273	7.0	33,950	20,168	13,782	154	0.9
Rusk	130	13,678	0.9	121	8.6	188	13.3	955	9.1	4,132	2,452	1,679	18	1.3
St. Croix	698	79,638	0.8	923	9.8	777	8.2	3,457	4.5	15,965	9,178	6,787	45	0.5
Sauk	669	65,953	1.1	688	10.5	718	10.9	4,315	8.3	14,415	9,394	5,020	46	0.7
Sawyer	312	16,685	1.0	131	7.2	257	14.1	1,287	10.9	5,604	3,561	2,044	19	1.0
Shawano	587	36,038	0.8	410	10.0	533	13.0	2,833	9.0	10,096	3,920	6,176	78	1.9
Sheboygan	2,769	116,208	1.0	1,158	9.8	1,353	11.5	5,748	6.3	25,354	12,529	12,825	148	1.3
Taylor	125	19,589	0.9	218	10.9	209	10.5	1,389	8.6	4,339	2,267	2,072	35	1.8
Trempealeau	426	29,191	1.0	414	13.5	324	10.5	1,937	8.1	6,312	3,899	2,413	37	1.2
Vernon	246	27,745	0.8	411	13.3	365	11.8	2,292	9.4	7,085	3,625	3,460	30	1.0
Vilas	217	21,486	1.0	163	7.0	353	15.2	1,642	10.9	8,547	5,676	2,871	32	1.4
Walworth	3,021	98,823	0.9	860	8.1	1,242	11.6	6,732	8.2	21,659	14,477	7,182	133	1.2
Washburn	197	15,532	1.0	117	7.0	259	15.5	869	7.7	5,532	3,319	2,212	17	1.0
Washington	872	122,503	0.8	1,178	8.6	1,439	10.5	5,082	4.6	28,799	14,667	14,132	127	0.9
Waukesha	5,160	438,011	1.2	3,627	8.9	4,438	10.9	13,222	4.0	88,785	45,849	42,936	477	1.2
Waupaca	1,321	46,957	0.8	485	9.4	821	15.9	2,679	6.8	13,098	5,386	7,712	125	2.4
Waushara	1,149	20,902	0.7	197	8.0	331	13.4	1,542	9.0	7,046	2,942	4,104	26	1.1
Winnebago	7,315	181,095	1.1	1,662	9.7	1,801	10.5	8,357	6.1	33,531	12,842	20,689	197	1.1
Wood	666	75,386	1.1	781	10.5	941	12.7	3,278	5.7	18,146	8,173	9,973	62	0.8
WYOMING	12,894	587,294	1.0	6,213	10.7	6,042	10.5	69,044	14.7	113,787	108,193	5,594	491	0.9
Albany	2,042	38,678	1.0	351	9.4	256	6.9	4,179	13.1	5,405	4,984	421	11	0.3
Big Horn	140	11,792	1.0	96	8.3	134	11.6	1,942	21.5	2,847	2,790	57	23	2.0
Campbell	467	49,508	1.1	583	12.5	385	8.2	5,531	13.5	6,114	6,011	103	42	0.9
Carbon	685	15,254	1.0	151	10.4	178	12.2	2,029	17.7	2,879	2,719	160	17	1.2
Converse	68	13,982	1.0	155	11.3	137	10.0	1,564	13.7	2,634	2,585	49	11	0.8
Crook	18	6,966	0.9	106	14.6	92	12.7	1,021	17.1	1,704	1,590	114	11	1.5
Fremont	969	39,297	1.0	457	11.6	567	14.4	6,931	22.3	8,754	8,116	639	69	1.8

1. Per 1,000 estimated resident population.

STATE County	COVID-19 Vaccinations, 2021–2022: Number	COVID-19 Vaccinations, 2021–2022: Percent[5]	Education: School enrollment and attainment, 2016–2020: Enrollment[1]: Total	Enrollment[1]: Percent private	Attainment[2] (percent): High school graduate or less	Attainment[2] (percent): Bachelor's degree or more	Local government expenditures,[3] 2018–2019: Total current spending (mil dol)	Local government expenditures,[3] 2018–2019: Current spending per student (dollars)	Money income, 2016–2020: Per capita income[4]	Households: Median income (dollars)	Households: Percent with income of less than $50,000	Households: Percent with income of $200,000 or more	Income and poverty, 2020: Median household income (dollars)	Percent below poverty level: All persons	Percent below poverty level: Children under 18 years	Percent below poverty level: Children 5 to 17 years in families
	46	47	48	49	50	51	52	53	54	55	56	57	58	59	60	61
WISCONSIN—Cont'd																
Douglas	19,171	44.4	9,373	11.2	34.9	25.8	86.3	13,846	30,960	56,855	44.6	2.7	60,898	10.0	11.0	10.0
Dunn	22,379	49.3	14,575	5.4	38.7	29.7	68.1	11,085	28,988	59,588	41.9	3.3	61,880	10.1	9.7	9.3
Eau Claire	64,839	62.0	29,868	8.8	30.6	33.3	174.9	12,119	33,039	62,508	39.9	4.1	67,409	9.8	10.5	9.9
Florence	2,348	54.7	662	23.1	43.3	21.3	7.0	17,869	31,961	50,821	48.9	2.4	50,420	10.6	16.8	16.0
Fond du Lac	57,756	55.9	23,353	23.1	43.4	23.9	153.5	11,737	32,508	64,147	37.2	3.3	69,280	7.6	9.4	8.2
Forest	5,469	60.7	1,763	11.0	49.3	15.2	22.6	15,075	26,863	48,394	52.4	1.8	54,555	12.0	17.2	17.0
Grant	28,349	55.1	15,343	10.0	42.8	23.2	96.6	13,716	26,534	54,144	45.8	2.4	55,779	12.0	14.5	13.8
Green	23,723	64.2	8,038	8.4	42.8	23.3	69.8	13,057	34,872	66,212	36.9	4.6	75,666	7.4	8.5	7.7
Green Lake	10,594	56.0	3,795	16.0	48.5	20.9	37.1	11,966	30,396	57,339	43.0	3.3	61,406	9.7	13.6	12.7
Iowa	16,328	69.0	5,048	9.6	38.8	25.3	58.9	17,051	36,035	68,714	35.6	5.4	75,075	7.2	8.7	8.4
Iron	3,793	66.7	846	9.7	37.2	21.8	10.3	14,569	29,146	45,588	54.7	1.5	48,614	11.2	17.6	16.5
Jackson	10,343	50.1	4,173	9.2	52.3	15.6	37.5	12,026	27,478	55,228	45.3	2.5	57,164	12.7	17.2	15.5
Jefferson	48,862	57.6	19,738	18.1	40.5	26.7	164.7	12,622	33,461	67,167	37.1	4.0	71,772	7.3	7.9	7.4
Juneau	14,302	53.6	5,053	18.3	50.5	15.0	48.1	13,101	28,288	53,928	46.1	2.7	56,025	11.9	13.4	13.0
Kenosha	102,496	60.4	42,277	14.4	39.1	27.8	363.7	12,836	33,103	66,595	37.2	5.6	70,368	11.0	12.7	11.0
Kewaunee	10,681	52.3	4,380	19.5	45.6	19.9	38.9	10,885	31,723	68,474	36.0	2.6	69,077	6.7	7.0	6.7
La Crosse	81,489	69.0	33,936	12.3	29.6	36.1	210.4	13,026	33,609	60,307	41.3	5.6	63,298	10.0	8.1	7.4
Lafayette	10,073	60.4	3,661	9.5	49.0	19.4	42.5	14,809	28,843	61,070	40.7	2.5	65,235	8.8	13.5	13.7
Langlade	10,354	54.0	3,513	17.7	52.6	16.6	36.9	13,752	28,948	52,074	48.2	2.0	55,259	10.7	17.1	16.4
Lincoln	15,321	55.5	5,019	17.3	47.0	18.7	54.7	12,119	31,609	59,183	42.1	2.4	61,066	7.7	10.5	9.9
Manitowoc	47,970	60.7	16,542	20.1	43.3	21.9	123.0	11,814	31,375	58,464	42.5	3.2	62,734	7.9	9.9	9.5
Marathon	81,860	60.3	30,525	14.1	41.5	26.2	239.4	12,185	33,608	63,029	38.9	4.5	67,074	6.7	7.8	6.9
Marinette	21,375	53.0	7,716	9.8	49.4	16.5	69.7	11,741	29,395	52,385	47.2	2.3	56,236	9.4	14.1	13.3
Marquette	8,341	53.6	2,750	14.7	51.1	14.2	21.8	12,581	28,780	53,293	46.6	1.3	52,450	10.3	14.4	13.9
Menominee	3,672	80.6	1,217	5.8	51.9	17.1	17.7	19,176	20,570	47,188	52.4	4.1	41,365	22.6	36.7	35.1
Milwaukee	610,426	64.5	244,815	24.7	40.3	31.3	1,705.6	12,668	30,159	52,260	48.0	4.0	52,281	19.0	25.5	23.9
Monroe	25,136	54.3	10,520	19.2	44.8	21.3	87.0	11,803	29,946	60,595	41.8	3.3	63,671	10.5	14.2	12.9
Oconto	20,201	53.3	7,331	8.8	50.2	17.0	49.4	12,430	31,827	64,528	38.3	2.9	65,981	7.6	9.5	9.1
Oneida	23,273	65.4	5,930	16.8	37.5	26.3	64.5	15,327	35,811	58,156	42.7	5.2	59,631	7.8	11.2	11.1
Outagamie	121,081	64.4	45,136	15.7	36.9	30.0	413.1	11,619	34,815	68,441	35.1	4.8	70,727	6.6	7.7	6.9
Ozaukee	64,116	71.9	21,938	31.4	24.0	49.6	149.3	11,840	49,070	84,394	29.2	13.3	83,274	4.3	3.4	3.2
Pepin	3,628	49.8	1,353	11.0	47.6	20.1	15.2	12,873	32,275	58,750	41.2	3.4	65,068	9.1	13.2	13.2
Pierce	18,894	44.2	12,505	7.8	35.9	29.9	88.4	11,347	34,223	73,873	31.5	5.7	80,523	7.3	5.8	5.2
Polk	22,311	51.0	8,828	9.8	41.9	22.6	88.2	12,454	31,995	61,814	40.0	2.9	65,258	8.9	11.3	10.2
Portage	44,261	62.5	19,096	8.4	37.8	33.4	113.7	12,267	32,268	60,316	40.0	4.0	67,228	8.3	8.1	8.2
Price	8,323	62.3	2,283	11.6	47.5	16.9	24.6	13,183	29,812	49,749	50.3	1.6	47,172	11.2	17.2	16.4
Racine	119,512	60.9	46,428	17.5	40.4	25.8	360.7	13,188	32,566	62,556	40.1	4.7	66,562	9.4	13.7	12.3
Richland	10,159	58.9	3,427	16.3	49.8	19.7	21.6	12,400	28,103	52,052	47.7	2.1	53,970	13.4	18.0	15.8
Rock	113,235	69.3	38,517	14.0	42.9	23.5	341.0	12,529	29,924	59,519	42.6	2.8	66,138	9.3	12.2	11.2
Rusk	5,847	41.2	2,468	17.7	51.6	16.9	25.1	13,756	27,212	48,961	51.1	1.5	50,922	11.7	19.4	18.8
St. Croix	45,697	50.4	22,517	10.3	27.9	36.8	172.9	11,749	40,285	84,985	25.9	7.8	82,797	4.9	4.5	4.0
Sauk	41,075	63.7	13,424	16.7	42.9	23.8	140.0	11,788	32,066	62,808	39.7	3.6	65,746	8.1	10.5	9.9
Sawyer	9,957	60.1	3,086	14.7	40.8	24.9	27.6	11,943	32,851	52,022	48.5	3.6	50,319	12.3	18.4	17.5
Shawano	21,976	53.7	8,183	13.7	51.8	16.3	63.7	12,160	29,682	57,322	43.2	2.8	58,088	10.3	13.0	12.7
Sheboygan	72,154	62.6	26,186	18.1	41.5	25.7	224.7	12,018	32,360	62,101	39.4	3.6	64,104	7.6	8.6	8.2
Taylor	7,232	35.6	4,337	11.7	54.4	16.2	42.6	11,992	28,102	52,860	47.3	2.9	55,370	9.6	13.5	12.9
Trempealeau	19,642	66.2	6,476	11.0	47.1	19.0	73.5	12,433	30,058	59,606	39.9	2.9	59,749	7.3	9.2	8.9
Vernon	17,026	55.2	6,357	23.1	46.8	22.9	51.6	12,781	27,192	54,549	46.4	2.7	56,561	11.9	20.1	18.4
Vilas	14,637	65.9	3,492	20.9	36.6	27.7	46.9	17,740	34,548	50,039	50.0	4.4	54,619	9.7	16.9	15.7
Walworth	56,438	54.3	26,762	10.0	39.0	29.5	203.9	13,101	34,027	66,034	36.9	5.3	67,656	8.3	9.4	8.5
Washburn	9,940	63.2	2,885	12.7	40.3	22.6	32.5	13,222	30,217	51,711	48.1	2.0	54,132	10.4	14.1	12.8
Washington	78,704	57.9	30,117	20.7	34.4	32.9	224.1	11,392	40,407	80,839	29.2	7.1	81,659	5.1	4.6	4.1
Waukesha	283,523	70.1	92,725	21.9	25.6	44.8	725.1	11,747	47,806	88,985	26.6	12.3	92,359	4.2	3.7	3.4
Waupaca	27,800	54.5	10,019	15.5	49.4	21.0	100.0	12,120	33,784	60,106	41.2	3.6	67,078	8.0	11.0	10.1
Waushara	11,007	45.0	4,087	9.4	53.8	16.6	30.8	12,105	29,296	54,320	45.8	2.4	58,929	10.5	14.5	13.6
Winnebago	105,659	61.5	41,903	11.2	39.5	29.0	271.1	11,844	33,101	59,947	41.7	4.0	64,653	8.7	8.5	7.8
Wood	45,144	61.8	14,813	12.4	45.8	20.6	148.7	12,181	32,037	55,684	44.0	3.8	54,154	9.4	11.5	10.4
WYOMING	298,297	51.5	145,076	9.0	35.0	28.2	1,528.3	16,226	34,415	65,304	38.1	5.0	67,284	9.2	10.3	9.1
Albany	21,942	56.4	16,172	7.3	17.5	55.3	61.5	15,116	29,644	51,362	48.8	3.2	59,179	15.3	10.4	9.5
Big Horn	4,669	39.6	2,704	5.8	39.1	20.1	46.3	18,462	25,587	51,237	48.9	2.5	54,684	11.5	15.0	12.4
Campbell	14,420	31.1	12,137	8.6	42.6	19.7	139.4	15,920	33,522	80,887	31.4	5.0	85,022	7.3	7.6	6.8
Carbon	6,850	46.3	3,238	9.0	47.1	20.5	43.7	18,569	30,929	62,423	40.8	4.3	66,589	10.4	12.4	11.4
Converse	4,745	34.3	3,539	13.6	43.2	19.7	40.5	17,527	34,834	73,806	34.3	4.0	79,304	8.2	11.0	9.0
Crook	2,340	30.9	1,695	3.8	37.2	24.1	21.4	18,041	29,726	66,898	37.9	3.3	67,443	7.3	9.8	9.4
Fremont	24,445	62.3	9,406	5.9	38.4	24.8	139.2	19,599	27,475	54,291	45.6	3.7	52,010	15.0	19.0	17.1

1. All persons 3 years old and over enrolled in nursery school through college. 2. Persons 25 years old and over. 3. Elementary and secondary education expenditures. 4. Based on population estimated by the American Community Survey, 2016–2020. 5. CDC percent based on 2019 population estimate.

STATE County	Personal income, 2020: Total (mil dol)	Personal income, 2020: Percent change 2019–2020	Per capita[1]: Dollars	Per capita[1]: Rank	Wages and salaries (mil dol)	Supplements to wages and salaries, employer contributions (mil dol): Pension and insurance	Supplements to wages and salaries, employer contributions (mil dol): Government social insurance	Proprietors' income (mil dol)	Dividends, interest, and rent (mil dol)	Personal transfer reecipts (mil dol)	Earnings, 2020: Total (mil dol)	Contributions for government social insurance (mil dol): From employee and self-employed	Contributions for government social insurance (mil dol): From employer
	62	63	64	65	66	67	68	69	70	71	72	73	74
WISCONSIN—Cont'd													
Douglas	2,009	4.3	45,962	1,659	821	188	73	87	296	613	1,169	84	73
Dunn	2,028	8.4	44,626	1,859	861	188	67	145	331	501	1,261	82	67
Eau Claire	5,488	5.6	52,141	925	3,130	572	231	346	1,080	1,167	4,278	272	231
Florence	243	-3.3	56,604	597	33	10	3	20	51	69	65	6	3
Fond du Lac	5,435	5.6	52,813	865	2,475	454	193	413	862	1,238	3,536	232	193
Forest	400	4.7	44,657	1,855	129	35	10	15	80	149	189	15	10
Grant	2,521	7.8	49,410	1,209	826	216	64	416	379	585	1,522	92	64
Green	2,072	5.4	56,620	595	720	147	55	175	381	416	1,098	71	55
Green Lake	906	5.0	47,898	1,406	258	58	20	76	197	245	412	31	20
Iowa	1,267	7.4	53,603	814	504	93	39	107	223	254	743	47	39
Iron	303	7.1	53,164	846	63	15	5	18	70	100	101	9	5
Jackson	1,022	8.4	49,528	1,193	384	88	31	83	183	274	587	36	31
Jefferson	4,217	5.4	49,591	1,186	1,619	330	125	224	629	957	2,298	152	125
Juneau	1,147	8.1	42,620	2,113	400	95	32	81	179	357	608	42	32
Kenosha	8,692	5.5	51,229	1,001	3,558	647	269	408	1,272	1,859	4,882	320	269
Kewaunee	1,073	8.3	52,638	880	280	62	23	140	159	227	505	29	23
La Crosse	6,462	4.8	54,532	738	3,685	702	284	491	1,234	1,354	5,163	324	284
Lafayette	814	11.9	48,891	1,272	197	47	16	125	132	178	385	22	16
Langlade	918	8.0	48,036	1,387	304	67	24	82	150	301	478	35	24
Lincoln	1,384	6.7	50,216	1,120	506	106	38	97	190	393	747	56	38
Manitowoc	4,003	6.1	50,829	1,050	1,606	333	125	285	686	1,024	2,348	159	125
Marathon	7,476	5.5	55,136	694	3,814	700	282	684	1,141	1,474	5,479	341	282
Marinette	1,995	7.0	49,557	1,190	857	187	67	119	335	639	1,230	88	67
Marquette	707	7.0	45,391	1,735	164	38	13	38	110	220	253	23	13
Menominee	159	4.0	35,082	2,933	78	32	6	7	26	66	123	7	6
Milwaukee	48,198	5.8	51,002	1,029	29,445	4,985	2,172	3,377	7,587	12,805	39,979	2,505	2,172
Monroe	2,131	8.0	45,741	1,695	1,049	250	85	170	350	541	1,554	94	85
Oconto	1,921	6.9	50,060	1,138	367	89	30	145	272	472	631	47	30
Oneida	1,961	6.1	54,861	709	763	146	58	142	416	589	1,110	80	58
Outagamie	10,356	4.7	54,862	708	5,997	1,023	450	713	1,655	1,868	8,183	517	450
Ozaukee	7,869	2.7	87,395	49	2,295	415	170	400	2,148	979	3,279	217	170
Pepin	395	9.8	54,316	761	106	23	8	49	63	102	185	13	8
Pierce	2,083	3.9	48,775	1,285	492	139	38	131	335	410	799	55	38
Polk	2,222	6.5	50,730	1,060	694	160	54	151	349	592	1,060	75	54
Portage	3,538	6.6	49,815	1,163	1,846	343	140	259	574	790	2,589	164	140
Price	660	5.4	49,837	1,162	223	52	18	55	130	226	348	26	18
Racine	10,396	4.4	53,094	850	4,068	791	307	409	1,981	2,407	5,574	384	307
Richland	837	9.5	48,516	1,321	248	59	19	77	133	243	403	27	19
Rock	7,964	6.1	48,836	1,278	3,600	659	274	347	1,313	1,975	4,881	328	274
Rusk	677	7.3	48,292	1,349	207	51	17	45	96	215	319	23	17
St. Croix	5,474	4.6	59,602	444	1,740	331	133	313	916	849	2,518	161	133
Sauk	3,555	2.5	55,166	692	1,588	300	121	492	532	768	2,501	162	121
Sawyer	840	6.4	50,276	1,113	289	66	23	56	187	282	434	33	23
Shawano	1,920	7.8	47,067	1,505	522	120	41	184	273	519	868	61	41
Sheboygan	6,409	4.5	55,616	665	3,371	581	249	444	1,157	1,299	4,645	301	249
Taylor	936	10.5	46,070	1,638	379	79	30	125	125	229	614	37	30
Trempealeau	1,434	8.0	48,324	1,347	632	130	51	114	187	372	927	60	51
Vernon	1,388	7.4	44,976	1,795	391	92	30	153	206	376	666	46	30
Vilas	1,233	5.5	55,140	693	336	74	27	152	328	374	589	50	27
Walworth	5,566	4.7	53,546	817	1,956	421	151	316	1,141	1,139	2,844	189	151
Washburn	824	7.2	52,457	894	240	56	19	72	167	287	387	32	19
Washington	8,529	4.5	62,506	332	2,977	530	223	532	1,481	1,472	4,262	286	223
Waukesha	30,852	3.2	75,958	102	15,833	2,377	1,161	1,689	6,505	4,450	21,060	1,350	1,161
Waupaca	2,519	6.0	49,711	1,172	823	186	64	174	393	712	1,247	92	64
Waushara	1,085	5.8	44,594	1,862	238	60	19	74	183	327	392	31	19
Winnebago	8,726	3.8	50,840	1,049	5,363	945	392	439	1,566	1,811	7,138	455	392
Wood	3,695	6.0	50,929	1,039	1,957	373	147	266	555	975	2,742	186	147
WYOMING	36,020	1.7	62,397	X	14,571	2,687	1,363	4,219	9,695	6,503	22,840	1,367	1,363
Albany	1,681	4.7	43,148	2,042	766	179	72	104	356	309	1,121	66	72
Big Horn	509	9.4	43,939	1,956	203	45	20	37	93	142	306	20	20
Campbell	2,517	0.2	53,932	787	1,503	236	135	257	388	419	2,131	127	135
Carbon	868	4.1	59,028	479	401	103	38	29	190	153	572	35	38
Converse	889	-2.8	64,373	281	401	73	37	103	191	172	613	36	37
Crook	363	4.2	47,752	1,423	133	26	12	29	81	83	201	13	12
Fremont	1,901	4.3	48,350	1,344	708	151	68	146	383	534	1,073	69	68

1. Based on the resident population estimated as of July 1 of the year shown.

STATE County	Earnings, 2020 (cont.)									Social Security beneficiaries, December 2020		Supple-mental Security Income recipients, 2020	Housing units, 2021	
	Percent by selected industries													
	Farm	Mining, quarrying, and extractions	Construction	Manu-facturing	Information; professional, scientific, technical services	Retail trade	Finance, insurance, real estate, and leasing	Health care and social assistance	Govern-ment	Number	Rate[1]		Total	Percent change, 2010–2021
	75	76	77	78	79	80	81	82	83	84	85	86	87	88
WISCONSIN—Cont'd														
Douglas	0.2	D	7.2	13.6	3.1	6.8	3.2	8.0	19.8	10,560	239	1,097	22,983	0.3
Dunn	4.5	D	6.7	21.4	3.2	6.3	3.8	9.6	21.8	9,655	212	725	18,811	0.5
Eau Claire	0.7	D	5.3	9.4	6.0	7.0	7.0	24.1	14.6	21,665	204	1,786	45,676	1.4
Florence	-0.6	0.0	D	16.0	D	D	4.2	-14.0	27.8	1,660	361	57	4,637	0.7
Fond du Lac	3.7	0.6	9.3	23.6	4.5	6.3	5.6	12.9	11.8	23,680	227	1,592	45,886	0.2
Forest	0.2	D	3.7	9.3	2.8	4.3	2.1	D	57.8	2,895	313	220	8,669	0.6
Grant	10.8	D	5.8	13.6	3.7	5.5	3.8	9.2	23.9	11,825	227	753	22,196	0.3
Green	6.1	D	6.0	24.0	6.0	11.7	4.3	13.1	13.0	8,750	237	405	16,392	0.6
Green Lake	6.2	1.5	10.5	11.9	D	8.0	6.2	D	18.2	5,470	284	303	10,715	0.4
Iowa	6.7	D	9.6	11.9	2.6	25.7	2.1	D	13.0	5,740	242	294	10,989	0.7
Iron	1.6	0.0	14.3	D	D	6.6	5.1	15.0	24.6	2,260	366	121	5,555	0.5
Jackson	10.3	2.1	11.8	8.8	1.5	4.6	3.1	11.4	23.6	5,025	238	360	9,662	0.4
Jefferson	1.4	D	7.9	33.4	3.6	6.3	4.3	8.7	12.3	18,580	219	978	36,699	0.8
Juneau	7.4	0.0	4.9	21.3	2.4	6.0	3.0	12.9	24.4	7,325	273	636	14,602	0.9
Kenosha	0.4	0.0	4.6	14.2	3.6	7.1	3.6	13.3	15.5	32,715	194	3,566	72,740	0.2
Kewaunee	24.7	D	7.7	21.7	3.1	4.0	3.1	D	15.4	5,020	244	222	9,301	0.3
La Crosse	0.5	0.0	5.0	13.1	5.7	5.8	7.9	21.5	14.4	24,505	203	2,048	53,154	0.5
Lafayette	23.2	D	8.0	16.3	2.2	2.9	D	D	20.0	3,720	222	190	7,176	0.2
Langlade	7.7	0.0	4.6	17.7	2.3	12.3	6.9	D	14.6	6,210	318	443	12,301	1.3
Lincoln	1.8	D	7.0	24.0	D	6.3	16.0	6.6	16.9	8,415	295	455	16,167	0.7
Manitowoc	4.7	0.3	5.7	26.5	3.4	5.5	4.0	11.0	13.0	21,770	267	1,391	37,905	0.2
Marathon	2.8	0.1	5.6	24.7	5.7	5.2	10.2	15.0	10.7	30,145	219	1,918	60,267	0.6
Marinette	3.6	D	5.1	33.8	2.1	6.4	3.3	D	13.0	13,290	317	866	29,317	0.4
Marquette	6.8	D	4.4	35.0	3.0	5.2	2.6	4.7	20.4	5,065	321	304	9,806	0.4
Menominee	0.0	0.0	D	D	D	D	D	-4.6	90.5	1,005	234	241	2,156	0.4
Milwaukee	0.0	0.0	3.4	10.9	11.4	4.3	11.1	16.0	12.9	166,195	179	42,478	424,106	0.0
Monroe	4.8	1.8	4.9	16.7	2.8	5.0	2.6	8.2	30.9	10,105	219	868	19,890	0.5
Oconto	9.2	D	9.4	22.6	D	5.8	2.5	9.7	19.5	10,470	266	550	23,964	0.7
Oneida	0.8	0.0	9.2	11.6	4.8	10.7	5.1	20.4	15.6	12,840	336	613	30,710	0.7
Outagamie	1.1	D	10.4	19.9	6.1	5.9	10.1	11.3	10.7	37,840	198	2,557	79,929	0.9
Ozaukee	0.9	D	4.9	22.9	10.4	5.8	9.9	14.5	9.2	21,015	227	596	39,531	0.9
Pepin	9.3	0.0	13.7	5.6	D	7.6	4.6	D	16.5	2,125	289	95	3,596	0.5
Pierce	5.5	0.3	7.6	15.6	4.1	4.6	4.0	4.8	33.3	8,305	195	381	17,104	1.6
Polk	3.7	0.7	7.6	24.1	D	7.1	3.3	15.0	17.2	12,235	269	605	24,374	0.8
Portage	3.3	D	4.6	12.8	5.5	6.9	20.1	9.5	14.9	15,255	216	821	31,598	1.2
Price	3.4	0.3	5.8	30.8	7.0	5.9	2.8	12.1	16.6	4,900	349	267	10,798	0.5
Racine	0.4	0.1	6.0	30.7	4.5	6.5	4.9	12.3	13.6	44,330	225	5,729	84,638	0.1
Richland	10.2	D	6.7	25.5	2.0	7.7	2.9	D	16.4	4,535	263	352	8,510	0.4
Rock	1.3	D	7.5	16.2	4.9	6.1	4.4	15.1	13.7	36,855	224	3,757	70,771	0.8
Rusk	6.9	D	6.0	24.3	D	6.2	2.1	10.8	18.2	4,565	323	345	8,640	0.8
St. Croix	2.1	D	8.9	20.1	6.2	7.6	5.7	12.5	13.6	16,750	176	587	38,293	2.1
Sauk	2.6	D	13.5	15.2	5.2	7.1	6.3	11.6	13.0	15,240	232	904	31,032	0.7
Sawyer	2.0	0.0	9.1	11.9	3.6	9.5	4.6	D	27.8	6,065	332	371	16,083	0.5
Shawano	10.6	0.0	6.6	16.7	D	7.5	3.0	9.5	20.8	10,690	262	649	20,423	0.3
Sheboygan	1.4	D	5.3	40.0	2.8	6.0	7.8	13.0	8.9	27,370	232	1,675	52,613	0.5
Taylor	10.1	D	6.4	30.7	D	5.1	3.6	9.6	11.9	4,760	239	238	9,423	0.4
Trempealeau	3.8	0.8	4.8	36.5	2.5	4.2	3.4	D	17.2	6,885	224	415	13,408	0.8
Vernon	8.7	D	8.5	9.7	4.4	6.8	4.6	14.3	17.8	7,815	253	534	13,931	0.7
Vilas	0.9	D	12.5	3.6	5.0	8.0	5.0	5.6	24.4	8,910	379	330	24,729	0.8
Walworth	1.5	D	7.0	21.6	4.2	7.1	4.3	8.4	20.2	23,190	217	1,254	53,511	0.6
Washburn	3.4	D	6.5	16.6	4.0	8.3	3.7	D	22.0	5,760	344	341	12,784	0.5
Washington	0.9	0.2	7.5	27.0	4.7	6.6	8.3	11.9	9.4	30,270	221	1,014	58,753	0.6
Waukesha	0.0	0.3	9.6	18.5	11.6	6.1	9.4	10.6	6.8	90,865	222	3,111	173,382	0.6
Waupaca	4.7	0.0	5.9	33.5	2.4	6.7	3.2	9.2	18.6	14,435	280	838	25,627	0.6
Waushara	7.7	0.1	8.0	14.7	D	7.3	3.4	D	22.6	7,540	304	404	14,777	0.4
Winnebago	0.5	D	8.7	26.2	7.6	4.5	6.5	9.7	11.8	36,415	212	2,674	76,553	0.6
Wood	2.2	0.0	6.3	13.7	6.3	5.3	5.4	25.6	12.0	20,040	271	1,481	34,673	0.2
WYOMING	2.1	9.9	8.2	4.2	6.3	5.7	5.6	7.3	24.5	118,420	205	6,992	274,371	0.8
Albany	1.3	0.6	5.7	2.9	8.5	6.0	6.4	11.8	43.3	5,340	142	331	18,731	1.1
Big Horn	9.7	11.2	10.1	7.1	D	2.8	2.9	2.5	33.8	2,835	244	148	5,353	0.5
Campbell	1.0	29.8	8.1	2.4	3.5	5.7	4.2	3.2	17.7	6,710	145	337	19,910	0.4
Carbon	3.6	D	12.3	D	2.5	5.1	-0.8	3.2	25.0	2,950	201	166	8,198	0.5
Converse	2.7	23.5	12.3	1.6	2.8	2.8	6.2	2.9	22.4	2,790	204	149	6,626	0.2
Crook	9.8	13.7	11.0	8.8	D	3.9	0.1	D	24.2	1,790	245	46	3,680	0.2
Fremont	5.8	5.5	6.6	1.5	4.3	6.8	4.0	11.2	36.2	9,485	241	886	17,429	0.1

1. Per 1,000 resident population estimated as of July 1 of the year shown.

STATE County	Housing units, 2016–2020: Occupied units: Total	Housing units, 2016–2020: Occupied units: Owner-occupied: Percent	Housing units, 2016–2020: Occupied units: Owner-occupied: Median value[1]	Housing units, 2016–2020: Occupied units: Owner-occupied: Median owner cost as a percent of income: With a mortgage	Housing units, 2016–2020: Occupied units: Owner-occupied: Median owner cost as a percent of income: Without a mortgage[2]	Housing units, 2016–2020: Occupied units: Renter-occupied: Median rent[3]	Housing units, 2016–2020: Occupied units: Renter-occupied: Median rent as a percent of income[2]	Housing units, 2016–2020: Occupied units: Sub-standard units[4] (percent)	Civilian labor force, 2021: Total	Civilian labor force, 2021: Percent change, 2020–2021	Civilian labor force, 2021: Unemployment: Total	Civilian labor force, 2021: Unemployment: Rate[5]	Civilian employment[6], 2016–2020: Total	Civilian employment[6], 2016–2020: Percent: Management, business, science, and arts	Civilian employment[6], 2016–2020: Percent: Construction, production, and maintenance occupations
	89	90	91	92	93	94	95	96	97	98	99	100	101	102	103
WISCONSIN—Cont'd															
Douglas	18,994	68.5	149,100	19.2	11.6	787	26.8	1.4	23,110	-1.5	1,010	4.4	21,849	33.0	27.2
Dunn	17,124	67.2	172,500	20.7	12.5	822	26.1	2.2	24,274	1.6	862	3.6	23,738	32.0	31.4
Eau Claire	41,602	64.2	180,000	19.0	11.7	818	26.4	2.0	60,074	1.8	1,941	3.2	56,574	36.4	23.5
Florence	2,038	87.5	130,700	20.9	14.4	478	17.7	3.2	2,244	1.6	107	4.8	1,905	31.7	32.0
Fond du Lac	41,890	70.6	162,600	19.3	11.5	786	24.2	1.5	57,149	1.4	1,838	3.2	53,458	30.2	33.7
Forest	3,929	78.2	131,600	21.5	11.5	522	23.0	2.2	3,957	0.6	265	6.7	3,709	26.5	30.3
Grant	19,655	69.3	151,600	19.1	12.2	704	26.4	2.4	27,648	0.1	831	3.0	25,940	33.1	30.6
Green	15,240	74.8	177,000	20.6	11.2	753	23.9	1.9	20,919	2.1	629	3.0	19,951	34.9	31.0
Green Lake	8,024	76.6	149,600	19.3	12.1	731	25.0	2.2	9,386	0.6	406	4.3	8,897	29.6	36.4
Iowa	9,811	74.0	194,600	19.5	12.2	784	24.7	1.3	13,712	1.1	463	3.4	12,883	33.5	29.8
Iron	2,859	79.2	130,100	22.8	13.1	534	32.7	1.6	2,580	0.1	165	6.4	2,478	30.8	31.0
Jackson	8,246	75.9	143,600	20.2	12.8	704	25.0	3.5	9,616	-4.0	496	5.2	9,389	28.0	34.9
Jefferson	33,349	71.2	194,300	20.2	12.1	869	27.0	1.9	46,726	2.4	1,554	3.3	46,230	33.6	30.1
Juneau	10,779	76.4	131,100	21.0	13.6	779	24.9	2.2	13,532	0.5	581	4.3	12,420	27.3	33.4
Kenosha	64,595	66.4	188,400	20.0	12.3	939	28.1	1.7	91,211	1.3	3,922	4.3	85,505	33.9	26.9
Kewaunee	8,249	80.7	166,900	18.5	11.7	719	23.8	1.8	10,882	1.3	310	2.8	10,794	30.6	38.1
La Crosse	48,105	62.5	184,500	20.0	11.2	854	27.4	1.4	67,244	1.8	2,037	3.0	61,864	39.3	21.3
Lafayette	6,777	77.3	143,600	19.0	13.0	722	23.7	1.9	10,241	3.2	265	2.6	8,416	32.8	34.8
Langlade	8,539	78.4	113,600	17.7	10.4	642	26.4	1.4	9,521	1.3	430	4.5	8,816	27.3	35.3
Lincoln	12,654	77.9	141,700	18.6	11.0	651	29.3	1.3	14,926	0.3	547	3.7	13,669	31.4	33.5
Manitowoc	34,435	75.9	133,200	18.4	11.2	679	22.6	1.4	41,403	1.2	1,415	3.4	40,306	30.9	34.5
Marathon	55,998	71.1	161,500	18.3	10.7	786	24.5	2.5	74,339	1.5	2,207	3.0	71,187	35.5	29.1
Marinette	18,869	75.6	125,600	19.3	11.0	686	26.7	1.8	19,634	-0.6	857	4.4	18,573	27.6	38.4
Marquette	6,770	80.6	156,500	20.8	14.8	720	24.1	1.4	7,840	1.1	347	4.4	6,965	22.8	40.3
Menominee	1,400	66.9	105,900	22.8	10.0	555	17.0	13.2	1,593	-4.4	137	8.6	1,475	21.4	26.2
Milwaukee	383,703	49.1	164,200	21.3	13.8	889	29.4	3.2	469,201	0.1	25,443	5.4	457,906	36.7	23.3
Monroe	18,025	70.7	157,600	19.5	10.7	822	25.8	3.2	23,783	0.6	770	3.2	22,063	28.9	37.1
Oconto	16,283	82.7	162,400	19.4	10.0	695	23.5	1.9	20,816	0.7	777	3.7	18,950	30.8	36.7
Oneida	15,677	82.8	179,000	19.4	12.1	789	26.8	0.4	18,205	0.7	783	4.3	16,554	33.3	27.4
Outagamie	74,597	71.3	176,900	18.5	11.6	816	23.5	1.7	105,055	0.9	3,286	3.1	100,796	36.2	29.1
Ozaukee	36,166	75.3	292,200	19.6	11.0	951	25.6	0.9	49,395	0.9	1,513	3.1	46,951	49.7	17.1
Pepin	3,127	79.9	151,200	20.9	13.3	632	22.3	1.5	4,129	-0.3	139	3.4	3,698	30.4	32.3
Pierce	15,856	72.3	224,900	20.2	12.8	880	24.1	1.5	25,048	0.2	864	3.4	23,481	34.7	28.8
Polk	18,647	79.8	177,100	20.5	13.0	770	26.1	1.6	25,025	1.0	1,040	4.2	21,770	33.6	35.0
Portage	28,912	68.9	178,600	18.5	10.7	782	27.7	1.6	38,366	1.1	1,345	3.5	37,703	36.2	27.7
Price	6,676	79.3	119,800	20.6	13.0	711	24.6	3.1	6,341	0.8	266	4.2	6,413	27.9	40.2
Racine	77,648	68.1	187,700	20.1	12.8	874	28.6	1.3	98,979	0.5	4,667	4.7	95,265	32.6	29.3
Richland	7,580	75.5	141,800	21.9	12.7	688	25.0	3.5	9,076	-0.6	318	3.5	8,153	28.0	38.2
Rock	65,237	68.4	156,800	19.8	12.4	860	27.5	1.9	86,855	1.0	3,864	4.4	80,116	31.7	32.2
Rusk	6,414	78.7	111,900	21.3	12.9	678	25.8	2.7	6,633	0.2	293	4.4	6,410	25.1	42.3
St. Croix	34,683	77.2	264,100	20.3	10.8	1,036	25.3	0.7	50,927	0.1	1,715	3.4	49,384	41.8	24.7
Sauk	26,751	70.0	185,000	20.1	12.7	812	26.6	2.0	34,936	0.5	1,414	4.0	34,197	32.9	29.1
Sawyer	7,893	73.4	174,000	21.6	11.3	600	22.5	3.2	8,109	1.0	413	5.1	7,428	29.3	28.9
Shawano	17,153	77.8	141,300	19.2	12.1	656	21.8	2.3	21,183	1.0	789	3.7	19,834	29.3	36.0
Sheboygan	47,754	70.3	165,400	18.5	11.7	744	23.6	2.0	62,287	0.3	1,937	3.1	59,448	31.8	34.2
Taylor	8,623	77.2	145,800	20.0	13.1	658	26.7	3.4	11,197	0.9	374	3.3	10,050	28.6	42.9
Trempealeau	12,143	72.2	161,500	20.8	12.8	749	24.3	1.8	15,613	-1.2	580	3.7	14,933	29.5	36.3
Vernon	12,146	77.0	161,900	21.3	13.0	718	28.0	5.2	15,531	2.9	502	3.2	13,747	33.6	31.1
Vilas	10,917	78.6	212,700	21.6	11.4	685	25.0	1.3	10,564	1.4	500	4.7	9,434	31.2	23.1
Walworth	41,414	68.7	212,900	20.0	12.9	899	26.7	2.0	58,402	2.4	2,114	3.6	54,814	31.6	28.2
Washburn	7,290	80.0	163,300	21.5	12.0	720	26.8	2.2	7,983	1.3	362	4.5	6,886	30.1	30.4
Washington	54,787	77.1	248,000	19.9	10.8	925	25.6	0.6	77,152	0.4	2,371	3.1	73,806	40.9	24.1
Waukesha	159,780	76.2	293,500	19.7	11.4	1,078	27.4	1.4	225,548	0.6	6,991	3.1	215,753	47.5	17.2
Waupaca	22,486	73.8	154,000	19.5	12.2	713	24.8	1.1	26,182	1.5	920	3.5	26,293	27.8	35.6
Waushara	10,053	82.1	149,300	21.1	11.6	690	25.1	1.4	11,394	2.5	481	4.2	10,578	25.4	37.7
Winnebago	71,132	65.7	158,400	18.7	12.2	784	25.9	1.3	93,109	0.8	2,986	3.2	88,638	33.8	27.1
Wood	32,707	71.4	133,700	18.7	10.7	726	24.4	1.1	34,769	-0.2	1,528	4.4	35,964	30.5	32.9
WYOMING	233,231	71.0	228,000	20.1	10.0	853	26.3	2.4	290,404	-1.1	13,032	4.5	287,375	35.9	27.7
Albany	16,137	52.0	243,500	21.7	10.0	818	36.3	1.5	20,767	0.9	681	3.3	21,517	49.1	18.6
Big Horn	4,408	74.6	160,000	20.5	11.1	662	22.0	2.3	5,316	0.4	235	4.4	4,898	30.0	34.3
Campbell	17,506	74.6	224,400	19.5	10.1	884	26.3	2.4	22,000	-5.0	1,158	5.3	23,570	29.0	37.6
Carbon	6,226	70.6	183,800	18.3	10.0	768	23.8	2.3	7,884	-0.5	305	3.9	7,010	27.0	37.7
Converse	5,461	76.5	224,900	18.8	10.0	738	25.5	1.7	7,496	-6.3	364	4.9	6,593	34.2	36.5
Crook	2,826	79.3	239,300	21.2	12.2	688	18.8	1.1	3,833	-0.2	129	3.4	3,562	27.1	43.0
Fremont	14,834	70.0	195,500	22.7	10.0	785	24.3	4.5	18,927	-0.5	888	4.7	17,411	35.0	24.4

1. Specified owner-occupied units. 2. A value of 10.0 represents 10 percent or less; a value of 50.0 represents 50 percent or more. 3. Specified renter-occupied units. 4. Overcrowded or lacking complete plumbing facilities. 5. Percent of civilian labor force. 6. Civilian employed persons 16 years old and over.

STATE County	Private nonfarm establishments, employment and payroll, 2020									Agriculture, 2017			
		Employment						Annual payroll		Farms			Farm producers whose primary occupation is farming (percent)
											Percent with:		
	Number of establish-ments	Total	Health care and social assistance	Manufac-turing	Retail trade	Finance and insurance	Professional, scientific, and technical services	Total (mil dol)	Average per employee (dollars)	Number	Fewer than 50 acres	1000 acres or more	
	104	105	106	107	108	109	110	111	112	113	114	115	116
WISCONSIN—Cont'd													
Douglas	1,012	13,784	1,807	1,882	2,210	362	372	578	41,899	329	24.0	2.7	35.4
Dunn	905	15,619	2,324	3,518	2,044	437	343	685	43,850	1,288	29.1	4.9	43.1
Eau Claire	2,634	52,498	11,814	5,560	7,139	2,652	1,560	2,424	46,175	1,069	33.6	1.0	37.1
Florence	104	655	53	172	121	26	16	18	27,585	101	21.8	NA	34.9
Fond du Lac	2,250	43,856	7,144	9,054	5,535	1,572	1,374	2,074	47,287	1,244	35.9	4.8	53.4
Forest	222	1,463	159	223	295	64	62	46	31,647	140	25.0	2.9	48.9
Grant	1,161	13,280	2,166	2,496	2,335	673	446	538	40,479	2,482	25.7	3.2	48.6
Green	992	12,959	1,840	3,885	2,262	398	417	571	44,093	1,428	43.8	3.4	46.3
Green Lake	446	4,828	829	819	903	258	63	196	40,662	502	29.3	5.4	53.0
Iowa	540	9,091	1,073	1,339	3,608	172	137	462	50,865	1,576	28.3	3.4	39.9
Iron	188	1,440	333	173	198	31	36	43	30,159	49	28.6	2.0	31.6
Jackson	388	5,349	917	535	794	209	73	242	45,305	855	22.3	5.4	44.5
Jefferson	2,002	30,456	4,538	8,882	4,019	630	686	1,323	43,431	1,098	41.5	3.6	41.5
Juneau	528	6,736	1,221	2,246	892	157	60	269	39,944	715	32.3	4.3	40.4
Kenosha	3,276	63,470	8,824	8,771	13,653	832	1,524	2,798	44,081	415	55.7	3.6	42.1
Kewaunee	453	4,815	464	1,890	458	162	159	199	41,426	655	33.4	4.1	51.9
La Crosse	3,102	66,632	12,276	7,451	8,448	3,149	1,991	3,055	45,845	667	29.8	2.1	46.2
Lafayette	342	3,131	266	1,053	349	136	55	132	42,160	1,327	39.5	5.0	52.8
Langlade	538	6,406	959	1,332	1,447	328	123	271	42,239	432	23.8	4.4	49.7
Lincoln	674	8,299	759	2,025	1,202	1,060	104	359	43,317	426	29.8	1.9	41.2
Manitowoc	1,726	29,725	4,030	10,102	3,553	833	567	1,318	44,356	1,171	43.2	4.1	48.4
Marathon	3,398	65,946	10,745	18,898	7,634	4,050	1,408	3,096	46,948	2,237	33.8	2.9	50.2
Marinette	1,042	15,203	2,490	5,667	2,136	400	329	641	42,161	515	32.6	5.2	47.5
Marquette	276	3,224	281	1,588	350	48	71	125	38,851	458	33.8	5.0	40.7
Menominee	24	998	NA	NA	35	NA	NA	32	32,434	3	33.3	NA	50.0
Milwaukee	19,906	447,011	93,009	46,532	41,096	34,556	22,642	25,002	55,932	86	83.7	NA	38.2
Monroe	940	16,066	3,262	3,486	2,022	358	326	756	47,046	1,555	29.2	2.3	45.2
Oconto	773	6,865	1,341	2,252	966	151	114	262	38,109	834	37.9	5.2	44.0
Oneida	1,350	13,300	2,687	1,462	3,015	312	302	577	43,349	131	39.7	3.8	38.1
Outagamie	5,135	101,377	13,454	19,343	12,719	5,130	3,865	4,991	49,232	1,130	44.8	3.6	45.8
Ozaukee	2,820	41,167	6,464	9,736	4,940	1,260	2,570	1,935	46,994	316	46.2	2.8	49.7
Pepin	216	1,732	251	168	238	48	33	80	46,333	448	27.2	4.0	41.3
Pierce	781	7,096	913	1,610	973	277	288	262	36,951	1,229	39.9	3.1	38.9
Polk	1,118	14,125	2,670	4,666	2,081	297	382	550	38,941	1,234	35.4	3.6	44.1
Portage	1,706	30,088	3,691	4,812	3,846	4,735	703	1,374	45,677	982	35.0	5.5	48.0
Price	377	4,056	778	1,614	546	94	81	161	39,650	410	25.1	2.0	41.1
Racine	4,033	68,497	11,544	16,532	9,024	1,977	1,964	3,379	49,334	611	51.7	3.8	42.6
Richland	369	4,563	994	1,445	784	156	57	174	38,102	1,103	31.1	3.0	37.0
Rock	3,338	60,856	8,934	11,645	9,247	1,342	1,528	2,845	46,746	1,587	53.7	4.7	40.6
Rusk	304	4,084	716	1,329	669	100	35	147	35,997	501	14.6	5.2	57.6
St. Croix	2,310	32,280	5,225	6,861	4,739	813	1,293	1,385	42,898	1,444	41.6	3.2	40.6
Sauk	1,794	32,097	3,897	6,209	4,144	815	1,045	1,328	41,371	1,412	31.7	2.5	43.8
Sawyer	611	5,415	990	696	1,011	149	142	212	39,072	175	22.3	4.0	45.7
Shawano	874	10,336	1,537	2,292	1,520	269	192	383	37,040	1,139	30.3	2.7	50.7
Sheboygan	2,657	52,708	6,424	18,037	6,172	2,243	1,198	2,496	47,347	958	43.6	3.9	49.6
Taylor	469	7,180	1,007	2,949	849	272	95	328	45,726	893	23.7	3.1	47.4
Trempealeau	647	15,065	1,391	8,596	994	268	263	663	44,018	1,229	24.6	4.6	40.0
Vernon	612	6,591	1,729	1,009	1,096	282	160	265	40,224	1,961	31.1	1.8	48.8
Vilas	968	6,073	520	336	1,184	172	134	208	34,265	67	64.2	1.5	23.6
Walworth	2,753	36,014	4,042	8,763	5,239	645	915	1,419	39,410	941	49.5	5.2	44.1
Washburn	510	4,385	874	1,087	764	124	168	153	34,823	372	36.0	4.3	37.2
Washington	3,270	52,834	6,122	14,816	7,048	2,161	1,500	2,446	46,292	578	40.8	3.5	53.7
Waukesha	12,624	246,809	29,546	39,588	27,082	15,248	13,828	14,000	56,723	574	56.8	4.2	39.0
Waupaca	1,175	15,786	2,329	6,387	2,177	426	206	599	37,951	1,031	33.9	3.2	44.5
Waushara	466	4,712	687	1,054	751	121	176	162	34,356	633	42.8	4.4	39.9
Winnebago	3,674	92,127	13,095	24,192	8,294	4,615	4,171	4,746	51,514	957	49.9	2.2	37.8
Wood	1,776	36,698	12,301	5,964	3,578	1,376	535	1,832	49,911	1,062	32.9	3.9	51.3
WYOMING	21,770	206,266	33,216	10,468	29,895	7,031	10,800	10,107	49,002	11,938	32.7	25.0	43.0
Albany	1,067	9,996	2,132	476	1,599	525	779	369	36,893	451	28.2	30.2	38.6
Big Horn	303	2,513	426	217	346	109	122	113	45,100	586	40.4	12.8	50.7
Campbell	1,460	19,802	1,619	607	2,442	380	664	1,142	57,658	643	25.5	45.4	44.6
Carbon	505	4,136	594	636	734	115	100	215	52,044	345	18.8	42.6	49.1
Converse	428	4,485	599	80	423	118	107	228	50,941	384	23.7	40.9	57.3
Crook	250	1,558	204	177	174	59	46	78	49,756	554	15.7	37.0	45.8
Fremont	1,243	9,889	1,847	289	1,765	320	369	384	38,881	1,152	36.3	12.1	46.1

STATE County	Agriculture, 2017 (cont.) — Land in farms: Acreage (1,000)	Land in farms: Percent change, 2012–2017	Land in farms — Acres: Average size of farm	Acres: Total irrigated (1,000)	Acres: Total cropland (1,000)	Value of land and buildings (dollars): Average per farm	Value of land and buildings (dollars): Average per acre	Value of machinery and equipment, average per farm (dollars)	Value of products sold: Total (mil dol)	Value of products sold: Average per farm (acres)	Value of products sold — Percent from: Crops	Percent from: Livestock and poultry products	Organic farms (number)	Farms with internet access (per-cent)	Government payments: Total ($1,000)	Government payments: Percent of farms
	117	118	119	120	121	122	123	124	125	126	127	128	129	130	131	132
WISCONSIN—Cont'd																
Douglas	70	-1.2	212	0.2	26.8	415,809	1,961	58,358	8.5	25,936	40.4	59.6	2	74.8	36	2.4
Dunn	348	-6.4	270	40.1	240.8	973,838	3,601	148,164	212.9	165,325	47.8	52.2	23	82.3	1,863	41.7
Eau Claire	172	-15.4	161	2.5	114.0	735,990	4,567	92,355	89.9	84,116	49.1	50.9	40	73.3	2,237	45.4
Florence	19	39.0	184	0.0	8.0	465,629	2,527	52,675	1.3	12,723	56.9	43.1	NA	67.3	18	10.9
Fond du Lac	317	0.6	255	1.9	270.4	1,855,960	7,275	227,075	396.7	318,921	24.0	76.0	33	77.7	3,762	56.5
Forest	38	25.9	272	0.4	13.1	660,064	2,426	81,548	4.9	35,064	80.6	19.4	2	75.7	24	11.4
Grant	600	2.2	242	1.0	380.0	1,140,897	4,717	168,735	447.2	180,181	32.3	67.7	71	73.2	6,383	53.8
Green	292	-3.3	205	3.0	239.5	1,111,218	5,427	158,955	221.0	154,796	41.7	58.3	18	82.8	3,648	47.4
Green Lake	127	-18.0	252	5.4	99.7	1,444,204	5,720	196,500	90.6	180,512	49.9	50.1	11	70.7	1,594	45.8
Iowa	360	2.7	229	8.6	216.4	1,111,469	4,864	141,447	206.7	131,149	38.1	61.9	41	80.8	4,969	64.4
Iron	9	-9.9	188	0.6	5.4	638,606	3,401	D	D	D	D	D	2	93.9	D	6.1
Jackson	248	3.5	290	6.3	135.6	1,103,760	3,800	161,242	154.2	180,294	52.2	47.8	41	78.1	1,034	42.6
Jefferson	221	-2.9	202	11.4	183.9	1,240,595	6,154	167,109	305.3	278,041	32.3	67.7	21	76.2	1,264	45.8
Juneau	175	-2.6	245	6.7	114.0	908,759	3,704	149,546	116.8	163,295	55.8	44.2	10	73.1	1,244	39.2
Kenosha	78	1.5	187	1.1	65.2	1,419,789	7,575	170,756	59.9	144,222	67.4	32.6	6	82.4	2,469	36.1
Kewaunee	170	-3.6	260	0.7	146.2	1,462,089	5,620	241,636	314.3	479,771	16.8	83.2	7	75.7	1,879	62.1
La Crosse	144	-9.1	216	1.1	85.9	1,079,187	4,987	124,594	74.6	111,867	37.6	62.4	27	76.8	1,955	51.4
Lafayette	343	-7.1	258	D	265.4	1,542,860	5,977	200,412	301.5	227,199	38.0	62.0	57	74.0	5,322	54.1
Langlade	116	2.2	269	18.3	75.8	881,494	3,272	208,454	102.2	236,655	58.4	41.6	16	76.4	542	32.2
Lincoln	78	1.9	184	0.3	43.0	595,649	3,241	102,719	37.0	86,838	44.7	55.3	12	74.9	206	15.0
Manitowoc	232	0.4	198	1.1	188.0	1,349,733	6,824	168,986	309.1	263,971	14.7	85.3	11	73.0	1,844	51.8
Marathon	473	-1.2	212	7.0	322.9	1,004,890	4,751	161,950	413.6	184,888	24.4	75.6	51	73.0	1,226	29.2
Marinette	133	0.8	258	1.9	88.6	1,001,818	3,877	158,953	116.0	225,266	20.6	79.4	9	79.2	1,466	36.7
Marquette	113	-5.8	247	10.7	82.0	1,031,933	4,176	145,836	71.5	156,059	51.2	48.8	7	72.3	432	25.5
Menominee	D	D	D	NA	D	143,544	1,736	D	D	D	D	D	NA	100.0	NA	NA
Milwaukee	D	D	D	0.1	D	542,871	8,928	68,761	6.8	79,047	96.2	3.8	2	72.1	64	18.6
Monroe	301	-11.0	193	4.9	165.2	767,038	3,967	138,159	202.7	130,380	34.8	65.2	134	72.0	840	34.6
Oconto	190	0.3	228	1.2	142.9	948,545	4,166	161,633	145.9	174,930	29.7	70.3	11	73.6	1,669	46.3
Oneida	35	-0.7	265	1.2	11.5	1,075,764	4,065	90,003	12.6	96,412	91.5	8.5	2	79.4	102	10.7
Outagamie	237	-5.5	210	0.8	206.2	1,511,380	7,207	198,453	263.7	233,388	27.3	72.7	6	79.2	1,606	46.3
Ozaukee	59	-8.8	188	0.4	48.3	1,229,816	6,554	158,401	75.2	238,054	25.2	74.8	7	86.1	355	44.0
Pepin	107	3.2	239	6.6	69.3	924,201	3,874	156,970	72.3	161,413	33.7	66.3	5	79.2	979	62.9
Pierce	233	-5.2	190	1.3	166.3	876,620	4,620	134,135	149.4	121,535	45.9	54.1	28	81.8	2,297	40.5
Polk	256	0.1	208	2.1	165.0	734,098	3,537	113,889	138.3	112,064	37.6	62.4	18	80.4	1,397	34.2
Portage	280	0.6	286	96.2	207.1	1,170,886	4,100	221,156	280.5	285,660	73.4	26.6	20	77.7	1,383	34.7
Price	89	-3.4	218	0.7	34.3	535,028	2,459	66,706	25.8	62,932	16.7	83.3	3	72.9	105	14.9
Racine	127	15.9	209	1.6	109.8	1,602,954	7,682	181,939	86.4	141,475	74.8	25.2	1	82.3	2,502	44.5
Richland	221	-3.1	200	0.3	118.5	671,915	3,356	108,023	136.7	123,890	22.5	77.5	37	67.6	2,493	50.7
Rock	354	-0.1	223	15.6	302.8	1,467,760	6,589	175,571	294.5	185,539	56.0	44.0	20	79.7	4,915	54.7
Rusk	136	1.8	272	0.0	70.7	674,903	2,485	130,623	53.8	107,353	24.8	75.2	12	70.9	689	24.2
St. Croix	279	4.3	193	8.7	216.5	906,467	4,688	141,360	189.1	130,944	44.0	56.0	22	79.4	1,778	49.7
Sauk	299	-10.1	212	13.2	197.7	890,636	4,207	150,164	188.5	133,470	37.2	62.8	27	73.7	2,048	45.5
Sawyer	46	5.6	263	1.5	26.0	681,805	2,593	136,876	21.9	125,091	41.6	58.4	2	72.0	152	18.3
Shawano	247	-5.3	217	0.3	186.2	1,012,006	4,662	173,988	250.4	219,851	20.9	79.1	20	72.7	1,571	50.2
Sheboygan	196	3.0	205	0.3	164.3	1,348,670	6,594	198,128	213.4	222,785	22.6	77.4	14	84.2	1,215	39.5
Taylor	226	4.1	253	0.1	133.7	742,339	2,935	119,424	113.0	126,517	24.6	75.4	20	68.6	650	27.0
Trempealeau	330	2.1	268	8.6	215.6	1,062,452	3,958	181,542	291.1	236,873	24.8	75.2	37	77.1	2,725	56.1
Vernon	337	-2.5	172	1.5	196.6	667,687	3,884	107,179	181.5	92,577	34.1	65.9	297	70.4	1,575	32.6
Vilas	6	-17.9	84	0.9	3.3	498,803	5,913	88,693	7.0	103,851	97.3	2.7	2	94.0	D	9.0
Walworth	192	2.5	204	2.1	167.7	1,417,724	6,933	162,989	167.4	177,865	46.1	53.9	15	83.2	6,423	51.4
Washburn	74	-15.6	198	2.7	34.1	620,384	3,128	85,256	30.3	81,384	32.7	67.3	2	75.5	283	18.3
Washington	126	-5.5	218	0.3	108.9	1,539,370	7,053	216,870	157.4	272,394	43.4	56.6	14	79.2	565	32.5
Waukesha	97	5.7	170	1.1	71.5	935,065	5,507	108,440	51.1	88,944	73.9	26.1	7	79.8	1,122	27.9
Waupaca	202	-6.4	196	7.7	142.6	883,093	4,516	135,842	152.1	147,516	24.8	75.2	6	74.4	1,777	48.2
Waushara	135	-6.8	214	37.6	100.2	904,427	4,231	149,181	126.7	200,161	68.4	31.6	12	75.7	1,253	25.4
Winnebago	162	4.2	169	0.5	136.2	1,180,421	6,971	140,934	122.2	127,711	40.0	60.0	7	76.6	3,326	53.1
Wood	221	-0.8	208	6.8	128.1	688,696	3,311	157,699	141.1	132,857	40.0	60.0	35	80.4	1,105	27.0
WYOMING	29,005	-4.5	2,430	1,567.6	2,587.5	1,892,340	779	126,844	1,472.1	123,313	21.6	78.4	69	80.5	30,218	17.6
Albany	1,407	-28.4	3,119	109.5	106.9	2,280,442	731	96,165	50.8	112,683	12.5	87.5	4	81.2	441	5.3
Big Horn	322	6.5	550	107.4	117.9	874,055	1,589	161,355	74.9	127,852	59.5	40.5	2	78.2	541	16.2
Campbell	2,901	0.8	4,512	5.1	184.3	2,553,745	566	134,546	69.9	108,705	3.7	96.3	NA	79.3	3,119	26.6
Carbon	2,812	18.4	8,150	187.4	143.9	4,486,393	550	145,397	73.2	212,293	8.4	91.6	1	78.6	423	6.1
Converse	2,594	6.0	6,754	65.2	106.7	3,576,045	529	159,841	56.3	146,734	12.2	87.8	NA	75.5	657	9.6
Crook	1,466	-7.6	2,646	9.4	175.5	2,590,429	979	134,976	52.9	95,552	6.8	93.2	NA	70.6	2,959	31.6
Fremont	1,165	-31.9	1,011	135.9	125.9	1,288,331	1,274	122,650	82.4	71,551	40.6	59.4	1	84.9	2,073	13.3

STATE County	Water use, 2015		Wholesale Trade[1], 2017				Retail Trade[2], 2017				Real estate and rental and leasing,[2] 2017			
	Public supply water withdrawn (mil gal/ day)	Public supply gallons withdrawn per person per day	Number of establish- ments	Number of employees	Sales (mil dol)	Average payroll (mil dol)	Number of establish- ments	Number of employees	Sales (mil dol)	Average payroll (mil dol)	Number of establish- ments	Number of employees	Sales (mil dol)	Average payroll (mil dol)
	133	134	135	136	137	138	139	140	141	142	143	144	145	146
WISCONSIN—Cont'd														
Douglas	0.0	0.7	45	694	991.0	35.4	148	2,193	630.2	60.9	35	132	22.1	4.1
Dunn	2.4	53.7	41	639	321.4	30.5	117	1,825	526.6	42.0	D	D	D	D
Eau Claire	7.4	72.5	104	1,616	1,155.8	81.1	376	7,110	1,979.2	165.4	112	585	86.6	18.5
Florence	0.1	17.9	NA	NA	NA	NA	15	131	31.1	2.5	3	6	0.4	0.1
Fond du Lac	7.9	77.8	D	D	D	D	332	6,014	1,719.9	156.8	62	344	52.3	13.7
Forest	0.4	44.2	NA	NA	NA	NA	29	264	63.8	6.2	5	20	1.3	0.4
Grant	3.4	64.9	48	395	363.7	16.9	186	2,437	658.6	56.4	50	148	21.4	5.5
Green	2.7	71.5	44	434	274.8	20.1	149	2,646	1,168.7	103.5	30	53	10.1	1.4
Green Lake	0.4	18.6	10	119	195.9	3.7	67	1,021	285.8	26.0	20	44	8.6	1.5
Iowa	1.0	42.4	28	509	533.9	32.3	75	3,810	1,513.9	149.1	D	D	D	D
Iron	0.2	36.2	12	83	25.5	3.0	27	199	45.2	4.7	5	D	1.5	D
Jackson	1.0	46.7	13	135	50.7	3.8	62	836	250.0	19.4	D	D	D	D
Jefferson	5.7	67.5	74	1,710	730.2	80.5	270	4,214	1,283.0	96.4	63	289	48.9	6.6
Juneau	1.7	64.8	16	172	158.7	6.2	88	971	301.2	22.2	D	D	D	D
Kenosha	14.9	88.2	114	1,875	2,397.1	148.1	509	13,201	5,498.6	362.4	118	528	104.5	18.5
Kewaunee	0.9	42.7	15	149	93.7	6.1	59	563	139.0	12.8	6	8	0.9	0.2
La Crosse	14.2	120.4	108	2,584	5,065.8	136.8	420	8,978	2,341.8	216.5	141	1,047	146.3	35.2
Lafayette	1.0	57.6	23	384	382.4	15.4	41	373	139.9	8.0	8	10	2.2	0.3
Langlade	1.2	60.3	24	202	187.5	9.0	90	1,398	576.0	37.9	D	D	D	D
Lincoln	1.4	49.3	16	298	146.4	10.4	111	1,345	341.0	28.8	13	35	6.1	0.9
Manitowoc	15.7	196.5	63	1,055	593.2	53.4	252	3,890	909.3	86.6	43	168	15.1	2.9
Marathon	11.0	80.8	176	2,726	1,307.9	142.3	449	10,596	3,159.3	261.3	95	508	93.4	18.1
Marinette	2.6	62.9	25	216	175.3	8.5	180	2,226	596.6	52.9	19	36	6.7	1.2
Marquette	0.2	10.6	9	95	84.0	2.3	40	303	68.2	6.0	D	D	D	0.1
Menominee	0.3	70.0	NA	NA	NA	NA	5	40	8.5	0.5	NA	NA	NA	NA
Milwaukee	114.4	119.4	795	18,826	11,531.1	1,309.5	2,629	42,827	10,997.7	1,089.3	815	5,736	1,644.5	284.9
Monroe	3.6	78.2	38	827	769.5	42.8	134	2,088	599.7	52.5	29	105	12.7	3.6
Oconto	1.4	36.3	17	100	27.6	3.5	99	979	300.2	24.7	20	37	4.9	1.1
Oneida	2.0	57.1	31	419	226.0	22.9	228	3,064	884.2	82.4	63	173	28.8	4.8
Outagamie	6.1	33.5	280	4,235	8,062.3	256.2	728	13,376	3,661.6	324.6	154	750	167.0	31.8
Ozaukee	5.1	58.2	128	1,512	979.3	92.2	314	5,169	1,418.9	130.9	D	D	D	10.7
Pepin	0.4	53.5	13	153	114.6	7.1	31	234	62.7	6.8	4	D	3.3	D
Pierce	2.0	48.9	D	D	D	D	95	989	260.1	20.7	D	D	D	D
Polk	2.0	46.5	33	366	99.0	14.0	156	1,923	516.1	47.6	34	54	9.6	1.8
Portage	8.7	123.4	71	934	678.8	49.3	225	4,065	1,099.9	98.5	57	274	49.1	9.9
Price	1.0	74.8	12	D	14.1	D	68	564	128.7	12.2	9	22	2.7	0.7
Racine	19.1	98.1	179	2,684	2,227.3	150.4	559	9,038	2,409.5	234.2	117	545	98.9	18.9
Richland	1.2	67.4	15	80	46.8	3.4	64	871	228.5	20.3	12	83	11.0	2.0
Rock	16.7	103.5	136	2,677	1,878.5	145.6	510	10,004	2,631.5	285.4	118	452	132.7	19.6
Rusk	0.5	34.0	10	58	22.7	2.2	50	602	152.2	14.6	4	14	1.4	0.3
St. Croix	4.4	50.6	101	1,468	2,505.1	78.5	260	4,684	1,669.0	144.1	73	184	35.2	6.5
Sauk	7.2	113.6	60	1,432	1,138.7	81.9	309	4,232	1,173.5	100.7	62	255	35.9	7.7
Sawyer	0.6	39.1	15	96	18.3	3.4	96	1,067	264.8	28.3	28	76	11.1	2.4
Shawano	2.4	58.6	30	1,109	582.0	71.9	115	1,435	424.8	37.7	16	54	5.0	1.1
Sheboygan	15.8	136.7	95	1,484	933.0	76.7	379	6,132	1,729.4	150.8	76	232	44.4	7.0
Taylor	0.6	29.3	11	81	31.0	3.5	69	886	245.7	20.6	16	55	8.6	1.3
Trempealeau	2.9	99.5	22	157	116.8	8.2	100	975	319.9	21.7	9	16	5.5	0.9
Vernon	1.1	35.7	30	567	735.9	28.7	92	1,147	317.2	29.1	16	31	3.7	0.8
Vilas	0.5	22.4	11	139	121.6	6.6	143	1,067	309.0	29.0	30	66	19.0	2.5
Walworth	7.4	71.5	110	1,838	1,364.5	91.0	370	4,956	1,511.8	145.3	91	427	77.7	15.1
Washburn	0.6	40.5	8	54	18.6	2.5	81	765	189.4	19.1	21	59	8.3	1.5
Washington	7.9	59.2	171	3,302	2,787.2	214.6	365	7,100	2,074.2	186.7	D	D	D	8.7
Waukesha	19.6	49.5	820	13,733	8,211.5	892.9	1,296	26,194	7,073.7	705.0	466	3,992	804.0	182.2
Waupaca	4.9	95.1	32	274	465.7	13.8	173	2,273	585.2	51.9	39	128	15.9	3.2
Waushara	1.1	47.4	18	150	92.5	7.3	71	766	263.8	17.2	8	15	3.1	0.5
Winnebago	14.0	82.5	D	D	D	114.4	487	8,865	2,335.2	214.8	129	752	198.2	29.0
Wood	4.7	64.4	57	1,042	688.3	56.1	273	4,127	1,114.7	97.5	55	195	32.5	4.7
WYOMING	101.4	172.9	696	5,967	6,061.0	342.4	2,583	29,786	9,124.4	852.8	1,199	4,777	1,216.5	220.4
Albany	6.5	169.9	20	164	140.0	7.4	125	1,670	458.6	38.7	59	155	25.4	4.1
Big Horn	2.2	183.0	D	D	D	3.1	41	356	76.0	8.1	8	D	0.9	D
Campbell	6.0	121.3	82	1,023	874.7	70.6	174	2,469	790.3	75.7	82	366	157.0	21.7
Carbon	2.9	183.2	D	D	D	1.4	79	799	270.3	22.1	31	109	17.3	4.8
Converse	2.0	143.3	9	39	21.2	1.8	53	411	106.7	10.3	23	52	7.1	1.5
Crook	6.4	865.1	D	D	D	1.7	25	181	47.8	4.3	8	D	1.3	D
Fremont	4.3	106.9	D	D	D	10.7	152	1,889	618.0	54.3	68	314	56.0	12.8

1 Merchant wholesalers, except manufacturers' sales branches and offices. 2. Employer establishments.

STATE County	Professional, scientific, and technical services, 2017: Number of establish-ments	Number of employees	Sales (mil dol)	Average payroll (mil dol)	Manufacturing, 2017: Number of establish-ments	Number of employees	Sales (mil dol)	Average payroll (mil dol)	Accommodation and food services, 2017: Number of establis-hments	Number of employees	Sales (mil dol)	Annual payroll (mil dol)
	147	148	149	150	151	152	153	154	155	156	157	158
WISCONSIN—Cont'd												
Douglas	74	389	33.1	16.2	51	1,656	1,383.9	85.5	152	1,815	77.5	22.6
Dunn	D	D	D	D	69	2,885	1,701.6	158.5	102	1,426	58.7	16.4
Eau Claire	191	1,477	199.7	80.4	97	5,285	1,809.1	262.1	274	5,158	228.5	68.6
Florence	5	7	0.6	0.2	11	174	36.2	6.0	22	142	6.6	1.4
Fond du Lac	141	1,433	156.5	104.1	146	9,480	4,108.5	486.2	222	3,542	163.0	44.3
Forest	D	D	5.6	D	14	247	56.7	11.5	D	D	D	D
Grant	D	D	D	D	67	2,680	1,132.4	125.0	130	1,378	57.5	14.5
Green	D	D	D	D	76	3,552	1,452.9	185.0	91	1,051	45.4	13.6
Green Lake	26	82	9.3	3.3	35	956	233.8	41.1	49	401	18.8	5.6
Iowa	44	159	21.8	6.4	41	1,112	1,458.0	52.8	58	582	28.4	7.5
Iron	D	D	5.4	D	12	152	46.5	6.4	D	D	D	2.4
Jackson	24	84	8.1	2.3	21	504	193.0	25.8	57	665	36.0	8.7
Jefferson	124	652	93.6	27.1	141	7,994	3,717.1	466.7	198	2,551	110.0	28.4
Juneau	14	49	5.3	2.8	48	2,130	808.0	105.2	93	754	39.7	10.3
Kenosha	239	1,303	168.3	61.6	194	7,387	3,539.6	416.0	372	6,241	305.1	88.4
Kewaunee	31	154	17.9	8.3	38	1,922	747.1	93.3	48	422	18.6	4.8
La Crosse	D	D	D	D	154	7,288	1,990.3	367.1	347	6,995	327.9	95.7
Lafayette	D	D	5.9	D	28	871	433.8	43.5	D	D	D	2.4
Langlade	24	110	9.5	4.9	44	1,512	388.0	64.5	60	591	28.2	7.6
Lincoln	36	111	12.8	4.5	45	2,358	823.7	113.4	98	839	38.8	10.8
Manitowoc	94	573	86.8	27.5	170	9,122	3,229.5	454.1	185	2,395	105.7	30.4
Marathon	D	D	D	D	240	16,995	5,596.1	855.2	312	5,290	241.8	72.0
Marinette	53	271	38.4	15.9	92	6,103	1,730.0	327.0	156	1,372	67.5	17.3
Marquette	D	D	7.9	D	21	1,977	459.7	63.6	D	D	D	3.9
Menominee	NA	NA	NA	NA	NA	NA	NA	NA	D	D	D	D
Milwaukee	1,987	24,542	4,673.1	1,923.1	966	46,242	17,269.6	2,788.9	2,102	43,834	2,811.7	743.7
Monroe	66	379	42.2	15.8	61	3,738	1,397.4	171.6	113	1,461	68.5	17.3
Oconto	33	127	13.3	4.5	60	1,979	693.7	95.4	96	657	31.8	8.5
Oneida	80	347	39.4	14.5	46	1,071	433.3	53.0	197	1,677	110.6	27.7
Outagamie	370	3,865	617.2	245.1	338	19,907	7,618.8	1,202.0	478	8,872	433.7	123.5
Ozaukee	322	2,155	388.9	137.4	200	9,331	2,936.9	554.7	207	3,616	166.0	50.5
Pepin	D	D	4.2	D	12	176	68.8	7.2	D	D	D	D
Pierce	D	D	34.2	D	51	1,711	611.3	82.4	106	1,001	47.8	13.5
Polk	D	D	D	D	102	3,889	1,473.2	181.4	119	1,201	54.1	14.7
Portage	D	D	D	D	75	4,650	1,469.3	233.7	215	3,068	138.2	41.0
Price	20	80	6.0	2.4	42	2,055	563.7	95.4	37	249	12.6	3.1
Racine	289	1,953	288.6	118.4	297	15,883	5,623.1	1,006.9	412	6,540	319.4	91.5
Richland	20	51	4.2	1.5	30	1,380	739.3	70.2	31	314	14.5	3.8
Rock	208	2,273	165.4	154.1	229	10,607	4,961.7	598.4	366	6,304	308.1	85.0
Rusk	16	38	4.2	1.5	27	1,561	480.9	65.1	31	225	12.3	2.6
St. Croix	229	1,202	241.6	72.6	173	5,925	1,561.5	326.7	208	3,763	165.5	49.3
Sauk	115	1,060	134.6	59.2	94	5,312	1,682.1	276.5	266	7,430	712.7	177.8
Sawyer	40	146	14.4	5.2	36	580	357.3	31.9	120	1,100	81.9	24.4
Shawano	D	D	17.3	D	D	D	D	D	D	D	D	D
Sheboygan	D	D	D	D	206	17,576	7,887.7	1,010.5	279	5,069	258.2	78.7
Taylor	18	108	9.9	3.9	38	3,127	957.6	155.8	39	473	15.2	5.9
Trempealeau	36	209	23.6	7.0	56	8,872	1,938.1	360.0	82	633	31.2	8.3
Vernon	33	194	17.9	7.2	37	1,106	374.8	45.0	58	647	23.8	6.9
Vilas	D	D	D	D	35	266	59.8	11.6	214	1,874	159.3	45.3
Walworth	200	1,519	175.0	65.5	202	8,638	2,704.9	435.5	296	6,180	307.0	91.2
Washburn	28	173	25.2	8.4	30	1,153	199.1	44.6	84	540	30.5	7.9
Washington	235	1,647	173.4	87.7	317	14,275	4,534.2	819.8	260	4,588	217.3	62.9
Waukesha	1,361	13,996	2,751.9	979.7	931	42,365	14,623.2	2,609.9	860	17,318	891.9	259.7
Waupaca	66	251	30.3	12.1	83	5,851	2,646.1	304.0	144	1,487	70.5	19.0
Waushara	17	194	12.8	6.5	26	808	306.5	37.8	63	493	23.6	6.0
Winnebago	D	D	D	D	291	21,965	9,101.8	1,389.8	399	6,740	296.1	87.2
Wood	100	626	82.8	27.6	111	6,046	2,555.6	327.4	182	2,211	106.0	27.5
WYOMING	2,387	9,511	1,526.6	527.7	581	9,354	7,897.7	643.3	1,839	27,248	1,946.0	556.4
Albany	D	D	D	D	39	339	143.8	22.1	109	1,758	84.7	24.1
Big Horn	D	D	6.4	D	15	235	93.0	10.3	33	D	9.2	D
Campbell	121	591	75.9	28.2	44	547	212.5	34.2	112	1,852	105.0	30.3
Carbon	36	89	14.3	3.4	D	621	D	D	80	840	60.8	19.6
Converse	34	104	15.4	5.2	D	120	D	5.6	D	D	D	D
Crook	15	29	3.6	1.0	12	137	29.0	6.7	36	173	11.6	2.8
Fremont	113	418	47.4	20.0	30	214	54.4	10.9	123	1,758	127.7	35.4

STATE County	Health care and social assistance, 2017				Other services, 2017				Nonemployer businesses, 2019		Value of residential construction authorized by building permits, 2021	
	Number of establish-ments	Number of employees	Receipts (mil dol)	Annual payroll (mil dol)	Number of establish-ments	Number of employees	Receipts (mil dol)	Annual payroll (mil dol)	Number	Receipts (mil dol)	New construction ($1,000)	Number of housing units
	159	160	161	162	163	164	165	166	167	168	169	170
WISCONSIN—Cont'd												
Douglas	114	2,033	140.1	60.0	71	549	47.2	14.7	2,227	103.3	23,980	112
Dunn	95	2,268	199.7	73.8	58	309	32.2	9.3	2,532	124.6	26,503	96
Eau Claire	341	9,985	1,153.4	422.1	202	1,356	124.4	37.2	6,190	329.0	179,922	931
Florence	D	D	D	D	6	15	1.6	0.4	314	12.5	8,343	32
Fond du Lac	295	6,619	864.7	308.7	179	975	99.3	26.0	5,239	278.3	55,758	235
Forest	D	D	D	3.5	D	D	3.2	D	699	34.2	16,570	61
Grant	110	2,233	187.8	82.9	106	363	48.5	10.6	3,352	165.9	21,424	93
Green	78	2,159	233.5	109.5	73	300	29.0	8.0	2,381	117.7	26,286	75
Green Lake	48	993	90.0	42.2	29	101	9.0	3.2	1,395	71.3	38,597	79
Iowa	56	1,155	104.7	44.7	32	103	12.6	3.2	1,907	76.9	30,439	138
Iron	13	310	14.6	8.2	D	D	D	0.2	504	24.1	11,994	49
Jackson	51	918	102.1	41.4	30	96	8.7	2.0	1,155	53.2	12,375	52
Jefferson	222	4,503	386.1	138.0	147	1,062	199.2	44.1	5,101	248.0	55,123	251
Juneau	50	1,224	110.0	53.1	45	187	24.6	4.9	1,489	69.7	47,053	162
Kenosha	447	9,354	1,030.4	406.4	235	1,407	111.2	35.1	9,138	402.7	171,154	972
Kewaunee	41	435	26.8	14.0	29	76	10.4	2.4	1,276	58.0	14,553	53
La Crosse	340	12,469	1,399.4	619.7	222	1,701	189.4	54.5	6,602	298.2	128,281	659
Lafayette	D	D	D	11.5	27	146	25.6	5.1	1,315	70.5	11,564	56
Langlade	50	858	158.4	44.6	48	167	14.7	5.0	1,201	54.8	43,990	184
Lincoln	D	D	D	D	55	254	24.1	6.3	1,717	79.3	41,585	186
Manitowoc	176	4,335	400.4	177.7	138	528	62.0	14.3	3,922	191.8	48,790	241
Marathon	390	10,447	1,418.3	529.0	215	1,253	160.7	41.3	7,786	403.2	99,349	494
Marinette	123	2,686	244.4	119.5	70	259	24.4	5.8	2,201	104.5	30,032	135
Marquette	21	468	16.3	7.8	D	D	D	D	1,079	53.4	12,540	54
Menominee	NA	NA	NA	NA	NA	NA	NA	NA	107	3.1	2,605	13
Milwaukee	3,195	97,178	11,669.2	4,374.3	1,509	11,002	3,008.8	389.1	52,074	2,253.9	89,711	371
Monroe	85	3,334	371.3	197.9	72	388	33.8	10.0	2,606	139.7	25,210	128
Oconto	110	1,612	129.1	53.3	46	142	14.9	3.7	2,287	114.6	49,710	179
Oneida	163	2,956	365.2	142.7	106	392	41.1	11.4	3,035	137.4	76,249	254
Outagamie	501	12,746	1,437.3	629.2	360	2,853	340.3	99.2	10,653	556.2	168,771	663
Ozaukee	335	7,022	772.8	315.2	196	1,191	101.6	32.0	7,124	407.9	113,225	298
Pepin	18	227	22.0	7.6	D	D	D	1.8	592	32.8	6,136	23
Pierce	70	837	51.2	21.2	61	193	24.6	5.3	2,700	117.0	64,847	269
Polk	110	2,911	339.9	116.9	73	244	24.1	6.7	3,299	160.0	57,322	247
Portage	199	4,590	449.8	178.4	124	718	79.6	20.3	4,023	188.3	40,594	139
Price	31	746	65.0	21.4	34	92	9.0	2.2	1,108	44.3	9,517	58
Racine	510	11,145	1,032.8	423.6	302	1,880	169.7	52.9	9,865	426.9	74,119	245
Richland	49	988	92.0	39.7	D	D	D	D	1,163	52.6	13,345	75
Rock	342	8,861	1,200.5	478.6	265	1,356	121.9	34.5	8,238	376.3	129,353	617
Rusk	33	748	69.5	30.5	D	D	D	D	975	44.0	24,675	102
St. Croix	238	4,882	479.1	188.8	170	843	89.2	22.7	6,652	331.1	177,024	582
Sauk	143	4,107	425.5	187.0	140	592	68.6	21.4	4,547	237.3	85,130	358
Sawyer	47	911	90.0	35.0	39	168	18.8	4.9	1,537	67.2	47,155	167
Shawano	77	1,466	107.4	56.3	D	D	D	D	2,487	126.4	20,868	80
Sheboygan	315	6,645	744.0	290.0	202	1,060	98.6	25.5	5,495	255.9	69,807	268
Taylor	46	965	108.9	38.5	D	D	D	D	1,400	84.5	8,978	41
Trempealeau	56	1,614	113.9	54.3	39	117	22.0	4.5	2,064	97.9	19,454	84
Vernon	75	1,793	147.8	67.4	41	114	10.8	2.5	2,494	124.9	19,682	83
Vilas	54	577	50.8	19.4	58	212	20.2	5.4	2,482	109.4	56,497	255
Walworth	229	4,002	453.9	160.6	220	979	96.1	27.1	7,096	362.9	148,684	405
Washburn	52	833	67.7	26.9	31	89	11.3	2.5	1,496	71.5	18,137	93
Washington	293	6,207	625.8	242.1	248	1,472	132.1	42.4	8,610	448.9	180,846	520
Waukesha	1,448	29,204	3,423.1	1,368.5	856	6,732	794.5	248.2	28,728	1,678.8	602,194	1,792
Waupaca	133	2,834	180.2	82.2	95	420	40.4	12.0	3,039	153.4	39,940	188
Waushara	37	722	44.1	21.9	D	D	D	1.9	1,551	83.8	26,578	88
Winnebago	453	12,419	1,282.3	560.5	258	2,127	240.9	72.2	8,653	415.6	169,242	948
Wood	208	8,232	1,190.2	459.1	132	791	96.1	22.8	3,857	191.6	40,781	120
WYOMING	2,001	33,540	3,871.9	1,657.4	1,368	6,245	931.2	221.4	54,304	3,039.4	1,058,126	2,706
Albany	125	2,095	227.4	81.9	76	352	94.8	10.7	2,830	117.9	31,312	138
Big Horn	28	374	32.7	14.6	17	46	3.8	1.0	927	32.2	6,702	24
Campbell	115	2,124	278.9	122.0	119	627	106.6	30.6	3,258	166.6	30,102	102
Carbon	47	583	49.7	22.7	30	121	20.2	4.1	1,148	50.5	8,472	35
Converse	24	530	74.0	33.4	36	113	12.8	3.0	1,093	51.3	4,060	27
Crook	13	209	15.4	8.3	D	D	4.2	D	763	36.3	2,095	8
Fremont	149	1,827	175.5	73.0	82	423	41.8	14.1	3,045	121.8	4,062	20

STATE County	Government employment and payroll, 2017									Local government finances, 2017				
			March payroll (percent of total)							General revenue				
												Taxes		
													Per capita[1] (dollars)	
	Full-time equivalent employees	March payroll (dollars)	Adminis-tration, judicial, and legal	Police and corrections	Fire protection	Highways and transpor-tation	Health and welfare	Natural resources and utilities	Education and libraries	Total (mil dol)	Inter-govern-mental (mil dol)	Total (mil dol)	Total	Property
	171	172	173	174	175	176	177	178	179	180	181	182	183	184
WISCONSIN—Cont'd														
Douglas	2,220	8,531,441	5.5	9.9	2.9	4.5	4.9	4.5	65.6	255.6	133.2	80.9	1,867	1,716
Dunn	1,480	5,930,390	7.5	8.9	2.6	7.0	16.3	2.8	53.6	176.2	80.7	64.3	1,439	1,336
Eau Claire	3,816	17,246,976	5.8	8.9	3.2	5.2	6.7	3.0	66.3	450.1	205.7	176.6	1,705	1,545
Florence	197	719,054	9.0	12.4	0.2	9.1	11.0	7.1	41.2	22.8	10.1	9.8	2,253	2,134
Fond du Lac	3,803	16,957,873	4.6	8.4	2.5	4.0	10.4	2.7	65.5	454.0	217.1	165.7	1,618	1,491
Forest	455	1,696,143	7.4	11.3	0.7	8.4	8.1	1.9	61.3	43.9	22.2	18.2	2,029	1,949
Grant	2,117	7,789,053	6.5	6.2	0.1	5.7	11.8	4.3	64.4	235.5	123.2	69.0	1,334	1,247
Green	1,445	5,678,043	5.5	9.0	0.5	5.6	15.1	4.9	58.5	156.5	67.7	58.5	1,586	1,480
Green Lake	751	2,789,699	8.1	11.7	0.2	5.2	10.4	5.3	55.9	85.8	35.9	40.5	2,166	2,048
Iowa	889	3,494,785	8.0	7.6	0.2	8.5	11.1	2.7	61.4	100.7	46.4	38.2	1,615	1,500
Iron	258	1,032,925	11.5	12.3	1.2	13.2	9.1	7.9	44.2	36.9	15.3	13.1	2,304	2,133
Jackson	794	2,850,058	12.2	8.9	0.3	9.2	7.9	2.6	57.6	87.8	47.0	29.7	1,448	1,346
Jefferson	2,729	11,581,146	6.6	11.2	2.0	5.3	8.2	6.0	59.7	326.6	144.4	135.1	1,595	1,475
Juneau	979	3,580,478	9.4	10.3	0.4	8.4	9.8	3.5	56.8	112.3	58.2	40.6	1,533	1,358
Kenosha	6,781	32,794,450	4.4	10.9	4.3	3.2	5.4	4.3	66.1	898.3	421.5	343.2	2,039	1,893
Kewaunee	785	3,019,472	8.3	7.9	0.5	5.4	10.7	3.9	61.9	89.5	42.3	32.1	1,573	1,542
La Crosse	4,881	21,656,178	5.9	7.4	2.8	4.0	11.4	3.3	62.5	578.4	247.7	221.8	1,879	1,699
Lafayette	881	3,297,072	6.1	6.2	0.0	5.3	26.9	3.1	51.4	94.1	41.2	23.7	1,419	1,353
Langlade	730	2,873,041	9.5	11.6	3.3	7.8	4.1	5.2	57.4	85.5	42.3	28.8	1,501	1,382
Lincoln	1,141	4,801,300	7.0	10.3	1.8	6.9	16.1	3.8	51.5	125.6	50.8	43.9	1,582	1,481
Manitowoc	2,749	11,439,956	4.7	9.1	4.0	6.2	11.1	9.1	54.6	291.0	141.7	98.4	1,245	1,208
Marathon	5,330	23,884,066	4.7	7.1	1.7	4.7	14.0	2.4	64.6	857.8	526.0	219.3	1,619	1,491
Marinette	1,553	5,534,079	7.4	11.0	2.0	6.4	10.2	6.4	55.4	164.0	80.7	62.1	1,542	1,410
Marquette	499	1,877,399	10.5	12.2	3.5	8.1	11.0	1.5	51.7	53.4	21.1	27.8	1,820	1,726
Menominee	282	1,057,076	3.5	3.6	0.6	4.6	13.0	0.7	70.4	27.9	22.3	5.0	1,093	1,074
Milwaukee	35,769	185,214,348	5.2	15.8	5.3	5.4	7.9	5.9	53.0	5,151.2	2,178.9	1,698.0	1,787	1,599
Monroe	1,704	6,405,363	6.7	9.5	0.1	5.9	11.5	3.8	61.4	183.4	94.8	60.6	1,326	1,212
Oconto	1,233	5,197,144	6.0	8.1	1.0	6.0	17.2	4.2	56.1	126.2	59.4	49.4	1,317	1,242
Oneida	1,404	5,979,000	6.9	9.8	2.3	5.9	4.7	3.0	67.3	182.1	66.2	95.9	2,723	2,544
Outagamie	7,636	35,643,735	4.2	7.1	3.3	3.0	7.0	3.3	70.2	881.1	428.0	272.2	1,465	1,401
Ozaukee	2,505	12,111,043	5.6	14.7	1.1	5.5	10.4	4.0	57.1	328.4	101.6	169.6	1,917	1,761
Pepin	308	1,151,936	9.5	9.0	0.6	10.7	9.1	3.1	57.1	33.5	16.0	13.1	1,813	1,726
Pierce	1,637	6,765,716	8.0	7.9	0.3	7.1	7.0	4.0	64.8	179.0	82.6	71.7	1,707	1,618
Polk	1,820	7,076,294	5.5	7.8	0.2	4.9	12.0	4.4	64.8	201.7	93.9	81.5	1,878	1,777
Portage	2,385	10,347,340	6.6	9.9	2.7	6.3	19.8	3.9	49.6	404.3	242.4	99.8	1,414	1,277
Price	596	2,108,423	11.0	9.6	0.1	11.8	6.8	2.4	57.3	59.8	27.9	25.3	1,890	1,799
Racine	5,884	28,010,342	3.9	12.3	5.4	3.5	5.4	4.2	63.6	810.5	394.0	295.7	1,510	1,462
Richland	714	2,572,557	8.8	8.0	0.2	7.8	21.0	9.0	44.4	69.2	35.1	18.7	1,066	974
Rock	6,384	28,667,201	5.4	9.3	3.9	4.1	10.9	3.7	61.0	783.0	426.4	256.6	1,582	1,459
Rusk	546	2,105,341	10.6	10.4	0.3	8.4	9.5	5.2	54.3	85.4	33.0	20.1	1,423	1,325
St. Croix	3,038	12,188,587	7.2	7.5	0.6	9.9	8.0	3.0	62.2	329.2	145.9	138.5	1,564	1,427
Sauk	2,827	10,650,902	6.8	14.4	0.3	4.3	11.5	4.7	56.3	505.0	327.7	136.4	2,132	1,766
Sawyer	560	2,015,604	11.0	13.9	0.2	10.5	8.7	1.9	53.6	70.4	25.3	35.6	2,174	2,010
Shawano	1,267	4,976,919	8.4	12.2	0.6	6.2	10.2	4.6	56.5	148.3	76.0	51.7	1,265	1,177
Sheboygan	4,307	19,613,015	4.3	9.6	2.4	5.4	8.1	3.7	65.1	501.1	247.2	183.3	1,593	1,516
Taylor	716	2,928,731	8.1	8.2	0.0	7.0	12.9	3.8	58.4	80.3	44.9	27.4	1,350	1,273
Trempealeau	1,638	5,929,327	7.0	6.6	0.0	5.6	17.3	4.2	55.8	169.4	81.4	44.7	1,521	1,432
Vernon	1,104	3,794,098	9.8	10.3	0.1	6.6	7.4	4.9	58.9	123.4	64.1	37.5	1,222	1,146
Vilas	703	2,972,578	11.5	12.3	0.3	9.9	4.9	3.2	57.1	100.7	34.9	57.8	2,667	2,469
Walworth	3,702	16,113,003	7.1	13.5	0.5	4.2	9.2	3.8	61.0	469.7	156.1	239.3	2,327	2,157
Washburn	727	2,631,612	10.7	9.7	0.0	8.3	7.6	5.1	57.5	77.9	28.7	39.4	2,505	2,400
Washington	3,758	15,770,528	6.0	13.1	2.1	4.2	7.9	4.3	61.3	473.3	179.5	217.3	1,610	1,465
Waukesha	11,532	58,507,193	5.5	10.2	3.5	3.5	3.8	4.7	67.3	1,577.5	513.5	811.5	2,024	1,946
Waupaca	1,945	7,657,117	6.2	11.6	0.2	5.8	6.7	4.4	63.9	219.4	101.6	88.1	1,724	1,622
Waushara	796	3,102,822	11.7	10.4	0.0	6.0	16.9	4.3	49.9	80.4	33.7	37.5	1,549	1,467
Winnebago	5,484	24,749,186	4.5	13.5	6.2	7.2	7.0	6.5	53.4	838.6	445.2	251.9	1,478	1,433
Wood	2,868	13,617,564	3.8	7.8	3.7	4.9	11.4	2.5	63.7	360.7	172.5	126.5	1,731	1,622
WYOMING	X	X	X	X	X	X	X	X	X	X	X	X	X	X
Albany	1,630	7,194,969	6.4	8.2	3.9	2.5	31.7	5.6	40.5	238.6	92.0	38.5	1,000	674
Big Horn	999	4,066,930	4.4	5.9	0.4	1.7	27.5	6.0	53.2	113.1	61.7	20.4	1,724	1,517
Campbell	3,735	18,642,479	5.3	5.7	0.9	1.5	36.3	5.3	40.8	531.7	119.8	194.4	4,189	3,769
Carbon	1,049	4,514,716	6.6	9.2	1.4	2.7	22.3	7.3	49.0	122.7	64.3	38.8	2,543	2,288
Converse	1,129	5,492,658	4.4	7.1	0.0	2.1	41.3	4.0	39.2	150.5	23.3	62.5	4,549	4,080
Crook	484	1,956,335	5.3	6.2	0.1	2.6	21.4	3.9	60.0	57.4	33.7	12.6	1,699	1,543
Fremont	2,263	9,038,694	4.6	8.6	0.6	1.7	0.5	5.9	76.1	323.9	235.7	58.1	1,460	1,195

1. Based on the resident population estimated as of July 1 of the year shown.

STATE County	Local government finances, 2017 (cont.)									Government employment, 2020			Individual income tax returns, 2019		
	Direct general expenditure							Debt outstanding							
			Percent of total for:												
	Total (mil dol)	Per capita[1] (dollars)	Education	Health and hospitals	Police protection	Public welfare	Highways	Total (mil dol)	Per capita[1] (dollars)	Federal civilian	Federal military	State and local	Number of returns	Mean adjusted gross income	Mean income tax
	185	186	187	188	189	190	191	192	193	194	195	196	197	198	199
WISCONSIN—Cont'd															
Douglas	265.0	6,115	53.4	1.5	5.1	4.0	11.4	369.4	8,526	179	110	3,167	21,440	56,721	5,129
Dunn	173.1	3,871	42.7	1.7	5.0	12.9	13.1	156.0	3,488	100	111	4,122	20,220	59,137	5,890
Eau Claire	487.0	4,702	54.9	4.8	7.0	3.6	9.1	501.6	4,842	408	263	8,124	49,530	72,203	9,014
Florence	25.9	5,972	31.7	6.1	5.4	1.3	16.3	41.1	9,473	23	11	286	2,220	57,637	5,504
Fond du Lac	502.6	4,908	51.0	5.3	5.0	8.5	11.1	445.8	4,353	211	260	5,153	51,910	64,832	6,929
Forest	46.9	5,224	50.4	2.6	6.0	5.0	16.6	4.6	517	97	22	1,497	4,350	56,735	6,006
Grant	242.8	4,694	55.1	3.3	3.9	6.5	9.9	185.0	3,576	154	121	5,442	22,750	51,300	4,398
Green	173.3	4,700	46.4	2.7	6.2	10.3	15.2	129.9	3,523	92	94	1,953	19,200	64,582	6,611
Green Lake	86.4	4,616	46.1	4.5	6.4	3.8	14.6	68.9	3,678	54	48	1,038	9,720	56,328	5,357
Iowa	113.3	4,785	55.4	0.9	4.5	7.3	12.6	91.2	3,854	83	61	1,285	12,050	64,260	6,517
Iron	35.9	6,332	31.0	10.1	7.7	0.5	16.3	26.0	4,587	24	14	330	3,180	48,287	4,364
Jackson	97.4	4,755	46.0	2.4	4.2	5.8	12.0	77.3	3,773	45	56	2,127	9,610	55,110	5,319
Jefferson	331.6	3,913	49.1	5.2	6.7	2.6	9.8	339.0	4,001	192	212	3,638	42,320	62,325	5,946
Juneau	116.1	4,389	49.7	5.2	5.2	3.8	13.0	87.3	3,301	225	65	1,792	12,840	49,605	4,176
Kenosha	905.8	5,381	53.7	3.7	6.3	6.5	5.2	892.4	5,300	291	428	9,163	84,120	63,305	6,662
Kewaunee	110.2	5,403	51.5	3.9	3.6	5.9	14.3	102.4	5,018	74	52	1,114	10,250	58,721	5,219
La Crosse	665.4	5,637	53.9	3.7	4.2	7.5	5.9	629.3	5,332	496	297	9,488	57,530	67,799	7,375
Lafayette	102.2	6,126	45.0	15.1	3.5	8.7	12.0	63.6	3,813	46	43	1,062	8,090	49,787	3,974
Langlade	90.4	4,716	48.3	3.7	5.4	3.4	15.5	69.7	3,637	55	49	963	9,710	50,533	4,392
Lincoln	144.6	5,212	39.7	5.1	5.8	11.1	14.0	78.0	2,811	65	70	1,649	14,290	53,988	4,658
Manitowoc	292.2	3,694	45.9	1.2	7.2	6.3	10.1	253.8	3,208	202	213	3,718	40,600	58,650	5,651
Marathon	920.8	6,798	37.5	9.1	3.2	28.4	7.3	469.1	3,463	401	349	7,365	69,310	68,104	7,694
Marinette	170.7	4,235	44.2	4.9	6.1	3.6	16.2	99.6	2,473	191	107	2,115	20,470	50,715	4,415
Marquette	57.1	3,736	41.9	5.4	7.2	2.6	18.9	26.3	1,724	56	40	699	7,950	48,199	4,330
Menominee	32.7	7,110	60.4	0.0	4.2	19.4	7.2	2.1	459	8	12	1,802	1,910	38,364	2,677
Milwaukee	5,309.0	5,587	40.2	8.5	9.3	1.4	5.2	6,559.5	6,903	9,819	2,749	47,599	449,450	58,908	6,493
Monroe	192.4	4,209	47.2	1.4	6.5	8.8	10.9	110.1	2,407	2,711	441	2,602	21,930	53,622	4,476
Oconto	146.6	3,907	38.5	5.4	4.4	3.7	16.1	112.8	3,007	102	99	1,730	19,180	60,190	5,476
Oneida	208.7	5,924	50.6	2.8	5.9	3.3	11.8	144.1	4,089	211	92	1,987	19,970	64,868	6,946
Outagamie	997.6	5,369	55.5	2.5	4.8	4.7	8.5	808.4	4,351	668	483	10,218	96,110	73,010	8,235
Ozaukee	389.7	4,407	48.2	2.2	6.8	5.6	13.3	322.1	3,642	169	228	3,581	46,930	121,154	19,477
Pepin	41.8	5,770	53.1	3.0	4.4	2.0	19.6	23.8	3,282	31	19	483	3,550	61,501	6,476
Pierce	202.9	4,828	53.8	2.6	6.0	2.8	13.2	267.2	6,360	87	104	4,000	19,610	71,839	7,570
Polk	216.0	4,978	51.7	4.0	4.4	5.6	11.8	134.9	3,109	141	112	2,616	22,590	59,925	5,466
Portage	467.1	6,620	24.4	2.9	3.6	47.2	7.7	126.7	1,796	175	182	5,426	34,610	63,324	6,490
Price	63.0	4,708	42.6	2.4	5.7	6.8	19.7	48.5	3,624	89	34	845	7,010	49,905	4,209
Racine	854.8	4,365	48.3	5.0	9.0	4.9	8.3	675.9	3,452	389	494	8,236	98,220	63,918	6,629
Richland	76.1	4,346	38.7	2.7	4.4	20.3	13.6	96.5	5,511	50	44	1,030	7,880	49,701	4,300
Rock	799.9	4,931	49.1	6.3	6.0	6.9	6.7	701.7	4,326	338	415	8,115	81,890	59,644	5,819
Rusk	92.3	6,525	31.2	27.2	4.1	2.6	16.3	52.6	3,721	36	36	922	6,670	45,737	3,439
St. Croix	387.5	4,376	53.8	2.9	4.8	6.6	11.5	464.3	5,243	164	235	4,560	46,280	86,223	10,534
Sauk	503.3	7,868	25.5	3.3	3.8	43.1	5.2	252.7	3,951	179	165	4,479	34,750	58,944	5,811
Sawyer	68.1	4,158	42.4	7.3	6.4	4.8	16.8	11.2	682	88	42	1,817	8,620	55,183	5,168
Shawano	190.7	4,670	40.9	4.3	4.6	3.5	14.6	90.8	2,224	117	104	2,746	20,040	53,170	4,510
Sheboygan	520.5	4,522	56.5	3.9	6.8	5.2	7.5	547.7	4,759	211	323	5,307	59,970	63,603	6,415
Taylor	84.2	4,145	47.7	4.7	4.1	8.4	15.5	27.7	1,362	62	52	1,041	9,280	51,906	4,502
Trempealeau	177.2	6,033	46.8	1.9	3.4	17.7	10.2	187.9	6,398	132	76	2,177	14,760	53,689	4,527
Vernon	123.3	4,016	45.2	2.2	3.9	12.2	14.4	89.6	2,919	117	79	1,718	13,700	52,818	4,670
Vilas	98.1	4,526	42.7	2.8	6.2	6.0	15.2	61.9	2,856	87	86	2,047	11,930	60,766	6,314
Walworth	508.3	4,943	53.4	3.5	7.7	4.4	7.1	563.2	5,476	218	261	7,823	51,770	68,972	7,897
Washburn	86.9	5,520	44.7	1.5	3.7	4.7	17.9	57.7	3,664	81	40	1,171	8,430	54,870	4,985
Washington	488.7	3,622	52.1	3.0	7.2	5.4	8.0	554.4	4,109	271	350	5,054	71,400	80,104	9,264
Waukesha	1,667.9	4,160	52.7	3.0	7.0	2.0	8.1	1,782.1	4,445	819	1,038	16,161	211,420	103,480	15,059
Waupaca	227.6	4,452	48.2	3.9	6.1	4.5	15.0	218.7	4,278	137	127	3,138	25,730	58,001	5,260
Waushara	90.5	3,739	41.6	4.7	5.7	9.6	17.4	43.9	1,815	56	60	1,267	11,720	50,915	4,391
Winnebago	872.6	5,121	34.9	2.9	4.7	26.1	6.4	874.7	5,134	448	465	10,960	85,610	66,998	7,395
Wood	394.1	5,396	50.8	7.8	4.8	5.6	10.7	285.6	3,910	193	186	4,353	37,580	58,350	5,530
WYOMING	X	X	X	X	X	X	X	X	X	7,807	6,227	59,187	280,590	83,826	10,828
Albany	245.2	6,376	38.6	29.2	3.7	0.5	3.2	79.3	2,063	212	201	6,824	16,470	63,001	6,937
Big Horn	108.4	9,138	46.8	25.8	4.0	0.2	3.4	42.7	3,598	100	60	1,365	5,120	52,165	4,590
Campbell	535.9	11,550	33.5	32.3	3.2	1.1	2.6	272.4	5,870	97	240	4,519	22,130	76,489	8,928
Carbon	133.8	8,775	58.4	3.9	4.7	0.2	2.3	39.4	2,584	189	73	1,672	6,990	67,291	8,508
Converse	178.1	12,972	26.7	35.1	4.1	0.2	6.8	1.5	106	65	71	1,511	6,580	95,062	14,351
Crook	52.6	7,105	58.0	16.3	3.1	0.2	6.4	3.0	409	75	39	607	3,370	67,409	6,945
Fremont	314.4	7,897	75.2	0.4	4.1	0.3	5.3	49.1	1,234	452	199	4,873	17,660	58,470	6,137

1. Based on the resident population estimated as of July 1 of the year shown.

State / county code	CBSA code[1]	County Type code[2]	STATE County	Land area[3] (sq. mi)	Population, 2021: Total persons 2021	Population, 2021: Rank	Population, 2021: Per square mile	Race alone or in combination, not Hispanic or Latino (percent): White	Black	American Indian, Alaska Native	Asian and Pacific Islancer	Percent Hispanic or Latino[4]	Age (percent): Under 5 years	5 to 17 years	18 to 24 years	25 to 34 years	35 to 44 years	45 to 54 years
				1	2	3	4	5	6	7	8	9	10	11	12	13	14	15
			WYOMING—Cont'd															
56015		7	Goshen	2,225.6	12,537	2,241	5.6	85.8	1.4	1.5	1.2	11.3	4.9	11.2	12.9	11.3	11.8	11.3
56017		7	Hot Springs	2,004.4	4,597	2,849	2.3	92.5	1.0	3.0	0.9	4.5	4.5	12.8	9.7	9.2	10.2	10.3
56019		7	Johnson	4,154.2	8,623	2,523	2.1	92.3	1.0	2.1	1.0	5.1	4.6	12.5	10.0	9.0	11.9	11.2
56021	16940	3	Laramie	2,685.9	100,863	604	37.6	80.4	3.2	1.4	2.2	15.4	5.8	13.0	12.9	14.1	13.3	11.1
56023		7	Lincoln	4,075.3	20,153	1,809	4.9	93.2	0.7	1.5	1.0	4.9	5.8	14.9	11.6	9.6	13.1	11.7
56025	16220	3	Natrona	5,340.5	79,555	721	14.9	88.0	1.9	1.7	1.4	9.0	6.0	13.8	12.0	13.7	14.2	11.1
56027		9	Niobrara	2,626.0	2,438	3,002	0.9	93.0	1.3	2.6	1.1	4.2	5.1	9.4	10.0	13.4	12.2	11.5
56029		7	Park	6,939.0	30,108	1,437	4.3	92.2	0.9	1.3	1.3	5.8	4.9	11.9	10.8	10.5	11.7	10.6
56031		7	Platte	2,081.5	8,699	2,514	4.2	89.4	0.9	1.5	1.3	8.6	5.1	12.0	9.6	9.8	10.7	11.0
56033	43260	7	Sheridan	2,523.4	31,646	1,389	12.5	92.6	0.9	1.8	1.4	4.7	4.9	12.2	11.5	11.3	12.7	11.6
56035		9	Sublette	4,886.5	8,697	2,515	1.8	90.2	1.2	1.6	1.3	7.3	4.3	12.8	10.2	10.4	13.5	12.7
56037	40540	5	Sweetwater	10,427.0	41,614	1,154	4.0	80.8	1.7	1.5	1.6	16.2	5.8	14.8	13.4	12.9	15.0	11.6
56039	27220	7	Teton	3,996.8	23,575	1,658	5.9	82.4	1.0	0.9	2.4	15.0	4.6	9.9	9.6	16.2	16.5	13.9
56041	21740	7	Uinta	2,081.7	20,635	1,783	9.9	88.2	0.9	1.4	1.2	9.9	6.1	16.4	12.8	11.5	13.5	11.2
56043		7	Washakie	2,238.7	7,705	2,596	3.4	84.0	1.0	1.4	1.0	14.2	4.8	11.5	11.8	9.9	12.5	11.8
56045	23940	7	Weston	2,398.0	6,745	2,676	2.8	92.2	1.4	2.7	1.9	4.1	4.5	11.8	9.9	9.9	14.1	10.8

1. CBSA = Core Based Statistical Area. See Appendix A for explanation. See Appendix B for list of metropolitan areas with component counties. 2. County type code from the Economic Research Service of USDA Rural-Urban Continuum Codes. See Appendix A for definition. 3. Dry land or land partially or temporarily covered by water. 4. May be of any race.

STATE County	Population, 2021 (cont.)				Population change, 2000–2021							Households, 2016–2020				
	Age (percent) (cont.)				Total persons		Percent change		Components of change, 2020–2021					Percent		
	55 to 64 years	65 to 74 years	75 years and over	Percent female	2010	2020	2010–2020	2020–2021	Births	Deaths	Net Migration	Number	Persons per household	Family house-holds	Female family house-holder[1]	One person
	16	17	18	19	20	21	22	23	24	25	26	27	28	29	30	31
WYOMING—Cont'd																
Goshen	13.7	13.0	10.0	46.8	13,249	12,498	-5.7	0.3	151	237	127	5,234	2.4	67.3	7.4	29.0
Hot Springs	15.2	17.0	11.1	50.1	4,812	4,621	-4.0	-0.5	48	102	31	2,187	2.0	64.9	10.1	32.3
Johnson	14.2	16.6	10.0	49.5	8,569	8,447	-1.4	2.1	94	121	206	3,961	2.1	64.8	7.6	34.0
Laramie	12.8	10.5	6.5	49.2	91,738	100,512	9.6	0.3	1,447	1,259	146	40,202	2.4	65.0	9.0	28.8
Lincoln	14.0	13.2	6.2	49.0	18,106	19,581	8.1	2.9	282	212	507	7,348	2.7	68.2	4.0	27.9
Natrona	12.8	10.6	5.9	49.5	75,450	79,955	6.0	-0.5	1,152	1,143	-414	32,896	2.4	62.7	10.5	30.4
Niobrara	13.5	14.3	10.7	54.5	2,484	2,467	-0.7	-1.2	32	38	-22	900	2.3	62.9	5.6	29.7
Park	14.7	15.0	9.9	50.3	28,205	29,624	5.0	1.6	352	433	575	12,575	2.3	66.1	6.1	29.1
Platte	15.2	15.2	11.3	49.7	8,667	8,605	-0.7	1.1	103	132	125	3,846	2.2	67.6	4.5	29.0
Sheridan	13.8	13.8	8.1	49.8	29,116	30,921	6.2	2.3	394	460	801	13,294	2.2	59.1	7.4	32.5
Sublette	14.0	14.0	8.1	46.2	10,247	8,728	-14.8	-0.4	104	100	-34	3,529	2.8	65.1	6.0	32.4
Sweetwater	12.4	9.6	4.6	48.4	43,806	42,272	-3.5	-1.6	593	516	-733	15,726	2.7	67.2	10.5	27.8
Teton	12.4	11.0	5.9	48.1	21,294	23,331	9.6	1.0	264	125	103	10,027	2.2	60.2	5.7	24.5
Uinta	12.5	10.8	5.1	49.4	21,118	20,450	-3.2	0.9	276	215	123	7,789	2.6	68.7	6.7	26.7
Washakie	14.5	13.2	9.9	49.0	8,533	7,685	-9.9	0.3	94	147	74	3,437	2.3	66.3	6.2	26.6
Weston	16.3	14.2	8.4	47.5	7,208	6,838	-5.1	-1.4	68	104	-58	2,882	2.3	68.7	7.5	27.0

1. No spouse present.

Table B. States and Counties — **Population, Vital Statistics, and Health**

STATE County	Persons in group quarters, 2021	Daytime Population, 2016–2020		Births, 2021		Deaths, 2021		Persons under 65 with no health insurance, 2019		Medicare, 2021			COVID-19 Deaths, 2020	
		Number	Employment/ residence ratio	Total	Rate[1]	Number	Rate[1]	Number	Percent	Total beneficiaries	Enrolled in Original Medicare	Enrolled in Medicare Advantage	Number	Rate[1]
	32	33	34	35	36	37	38	39	40	41	42	43	44	45
WYOMING—Cont'd														
Goshen	1,068	12,891	0.9	118	9.4	200	16.0	1,413	15.5	3,261	3,165	96	20	1.6
Hot Springs	83	4,512	1.0	39	8.5	82	17.8	476	15.2	1,437	1,381	56	D	D
Johnson	42	8,283	0.9	69	8.1	96	11.2	889	14.0	2,341	2,285	56	D	D
Laramie	1,956	101,456	1.0	1,125	11.2	996	9.9	9,645	11.8	19,635	18,748	887	71	0.7
Lincoln	36	18,924	0.9	222	11.1	186	9.3	2,607	16.1	4,004	3,837	167	11	0.6
Natrona	1,503	79,901	1.0	901	11.3	930	11.6	9,564	14.5	14,773	13,821	953	110	1.4
Niobrara	252	2,460	1.1	28	11.5	26	10.7	294	19.1	612	598	14	D	D
Park	500	29,365	1.0	276	9.2	348	11.6	3,022	14.0	8,015	7,741	274	18	0.6
Platte	83	8,618	1.0	89	10.3	104	12.0	916	15.0	2,473	2,373	100	10	1.2
Sheridan	992	29,804	1.0	307	9.8	377	12.0	3,230	13.9	7,646	7,185	460	19	0.6
Sublette	449	9,697	1.0	85	9.8	81	9.3	1,198	15.3	1,700	1,649	51	D	D
Sweetwater	720	44,480	1.1	481	11.5	400	9.5	5,044	13.9	6,523	6,393	131	26	0.6
Teton	215	27,643	1.3	220	9.4	96	4.1	3,472	17.5	3,713	3,494	219	D	D
Uinta	187	19,431	0.9	226	11.0	166	8.1	2,394	14.1	3,664	3,228	436	D	D
Washakie	119	7,864	1.0	76	9.9	115	15.0	943	15.9	1,986	1,960	26	22	2.9
Weston	300	6,488	0.8	52	7.7	90	13.3	740	14.3	1,664	1,538	126	D	D

1. Per 1,000 estimated resident population.

STATE County	COVID-19 Vaccinations, 2021–2022		Education						Money income, 2016–2020				Income and poverty, 2020			
			School enrollment and attainment, 2016–2020				Local government expenditures,[3] 2018–2019			Households			Median household income (dollars)	Percent below poverty level		
			Enrollment[1]		Attainment[2] (percent)						Percent					
	Number	Percent[5]	Total	Percent private	High school graduate or less	Bachelor's degree or more	Total current spending (mil dol)	Current spending per student (dollars)	Per capita income[4]	Median income (dollars)	with income of less than $50,000	with income of $200,000 or more		All persons	Children under 18 years	Children 5 to 17 years in families
	46	47	48	49	50	51	52	53	54	55	56	57	58	59	60	61
WYOMING—Cont'd																
Goshen	5,326	40.3	2,809	12.7	36.1	25.6	31.9	18,669	29,064	55,955	45.5	2.0	51,398	12.8	13.5	11.6
Hot Springs	2,204	49.9	899	15.4	30.9	23.5	11.2	17,470	30,170	53,398	45.3	2.1	48,864	10.9	12.9	11.6
Johnson	3,673	43.5	1,442	21.2	29.9	33.1	21.5	16,425	36,794	56,565	41.6	7.7	62,671	8.9	10.3	8.5
Laramie	56,291	56.6	24,563	10.1	31.4	30.2	239.7	15,483	36,421	69,369	34.4	5.0	69,450	7.4	8.8	7.8
Lincoln	8,695	43.8	4,643	8.4	39.8	22.3	52.6	15,028	31,672	71,898	33.0	5.0	73,062	6.9	8.5	7.5
Natrona	37,054	46.4	19,609	9.4	35.8	23.5	193.8	14,480	34,779	62,168	39.9	5.6	65,901	9.4	10.4	8.7
Niobrara	743	31.5	521	5.6	41.8	17.2	11.9	14,656	22,597	46,111	54.6	2.4	52,837	12.6	16.1	15.8
Park	13,527	46.3	6,383	9.2	29.4	34.9	64.7	16,289	34,803	63,684	36.7	3.7	63,093	8.2	11.7	10.5
Platte	3,467	41.3	1,762	11.6	46.5	19.3	25.5	20,056	36,793	57,784	43.6	4.5	60,178	9.9	13.3	12.1
Sheridan	16,166	53.0	6,900	7.3	32.3	30.6	69.7	15,004	34,495	59,380	42.4	5.0	59,947	9.5	9.6	8.3
Sublette	3,665	37.3	2,079	10.1	35.3	28.7	28.8	17,666	49,313	78,655	32.8	10.1	82,442	6.2	6.9	6.0
Sweetwater	21,186	50.0	11,559	9.8	39.7	21.2	119.4	14,960	34,282	73,384	32.9	4.4	70,583	7.6	8.4	7.3
Teton	21,730	92.6	4,694	17.4	20.9	55.1	53.3	18,452	60,331	87,053	22.6	16.7	92,488	5.2	4.3	3.8
Uinta	10,396	51.4	5,142	4.3	44.6	19.1	67.9	15,802	30,442	72,458	36.9	3.1	71,246	8.5	9.7	8.3
Washakie	3,422	43.8	1,816	3.7	36.8	23.8	25.1	18,159	30,212	57,306	41.3	3.5	58,532	9.7	10.7	11.7
Weston	2,626	37.9	1,364	1.0	44.8	17.2	19.6	19,293	26,573	53,333	47.9	2.3	58,901	10.6	12.6	11.2

1. All persons 3 years old and over enrolled in nursery school through college. 2. Persons 25 years old and over. 3. Elementary and secondary education expenditures. 4. Based on population estimated by the American Community Survey, 2016–2020. 5. CDC percent based on 2019 population estimate.

STATE County	Personal income, 2020										Earnings, 2020		
	Total (mil dol)	Percent change 2019–2020	Per capita[1]		Wages and salaries (mil dol)	Supplements to wages and salaries, employer contributions (mil dol)		Proprietors' income (mil dol)	Dividends, interest, and rent (mil dol)	Personal transfer reecipts (mil dol)	Total (mil dol)	Contributions for government social insurance (mil dol)	
			Dollars	Rank		Pension and insurance	Government social insurance					From employee and self-employed	From employer
	62	63	64	65	66	67	68	69	70	71	72	73	74
WYOMING—Cont'd													
Goshen	590	5.2	44,562	1,865	184	41	18	65	110	157	309	20	18
Hot Springs	296	4.1	67,005	212	80	18	8	88	42	75	194	11	8
Johnson	487	4.3	56,748	588	142	30	14	60	118	109	245	15	14
Laramie	5,542	3.7	55,094	697	2,774	561	268	416	1,057	1,167	4,019	242	268
Lincoln	981	7.7	48,449	1,330	360	73	32	77	243	214	542	35	32
Natrona	5,532	-1.0	68,447	187	2,010	308	187	1,522	970	920	4,027	218	187
Niobrara	126	10.1	55,291	683	39	11	4	29	27	30	84	4	4
Park	1,755	3.6	59,827	437	619	119	59	147	573	388	945	63	59
Platte	449	2.4	52,359	904	179	43	18	49	77	121	289	18	18
Sheridan	1,899	4.9	61,543	366	679	128	67	160	582	382	1,034	67	67
Sublette	537	-0.2	54,496	743	217	40	19	52	189	86	328	19	19
Sweetwater	2,304	-4.0	54,000	781	1,285	228	112	331	285	423	1,955	114	112
Teton	5,184	-0.5	220,645	1	1,232	134	112	390	3,458	218	1,869	108	112
Uinta	866	3.6	42,854	2,086	371	76	35	59	126	212	541	35	35
Washakie	422	5.4	54,361	755	168	33	17	48	96	101	266	17	17
Weston	321	0.0	47,599	1,440	116	30	11	20	60	86	177	12	11

1. Based on the resident population estimated as of July 1 of the year shown.

STATE County	Earnings, 2020 (cont.)									Social Security beneficiaries, December 2020		Supplemental Security Income recipients, 2020	Housing units, 2021	
	Percent by selected industries													
	Farm	Mining, quarrying, and extractions	Construction	Manufacturing	Information; professional, scientific, technical services	Retail trade	Finance, insurance, real estate, and leasing	Health care and social assistance	Government	Number	Rate[1]		Total	Percent change, 2010–2021
	75	76	77	78	79	80	81	82	83	84	85	86	87	88
WYOMING—Cont'd														
Goshen	10.9	0.0	5.1	2.0	D	4.7	5.4	D	30.7	3,260	260	209	5,854	0.0
Hot Springs	2.0	D	D	2.2	D	D	2.1	D	22.5	1,490	324	80	2,553	0.1
Johnson	8.7	8.5	5.5	1.5	9.9	10.7	3.9	D	30.6	2,430	282	47	4,624	0.5
Laramie	0.7	1.9	7.6	3.3	8.0	6.0	6.7	7.9	38.1	19,950	198	1,450	44,817	1.2
Lincoln	3.4	15.2	13.4	1.9	6.4	5.9	3.6	3.2	26.7	4,210	209	142	9,707	1.9
Natrona	0.3	6.0	6.6	3.6	4.3	5.2	5.0	11.2	11.3	15,715	198	1,307	37,048	0.5
Niobrara	17.9	4.7	D	D	D	D	4.2	D	37.3	620	254	25	1,322	0.0
Park	4.0	4.0	9.7	3.3	7.8	6.9	6.2	11.5	27.9	8,470	281	280	14,745	1.3
Platte	12.3	2.8	4.8	0.9	3.4	5.7	4.8	D	22.0	2,465	283	85	4,635	0.8
Sheridan	1.5	1.2	9.8	4.3	10.1	7.2	5.1	7.8	30.0	7,645	242	328	15,127	1.3
Sublette	6.8	26.4	9.8	1.2	4.5	4.5	5.5	D	24.5	1,785	205	48	5,217	0.8
Sweetwater	1.0	D	5.9	9.5	2.7	4.8	3.3	3.4	16.8	7,250	174	437	19,214	0.3
Teton	0.6	2.1	12.2	0.8	15.8	5.8	13.0	3.8	13.0	3,425	145	42	13,470	1.5
Uinta	2.1	5.2	11.6	3.5	8.6	7.3	5.3	10.7	25.4	3,950	191	294	8,851	0.5
Washakie	6.6	2.9	7.4	12.7	4.1	4.9	3.9	D	21.8	2,095	272	104	3,853	0.1
Weston	2.9	9.7	D	D	2.5	4.9	4.7	0.0	32.5	1,760	261	51	3,407	0.0

1. Per 1,000 resident population estimated as of July 1 of the year shown.

STATE County	Housing units, 2016–2020: Occupied units: Total	Owner-occupied: Percent	Owner-occupied: Median value[1]	Owner-occupied: Median owner cost as a percent of income: With a mortgage	Owner-occupied: Median owner cost as a percent of income: Without a mortgage[2]	Renter-occupied: Median rent[3]	Renter-occupied: Median rent as a percent of income[2]	Sub-standard units[4] (percent)	Civilian labor force, 2021: Total	Civilian labor force, 2021: Percent change, 2020–2021	Unemployment: Total	Unemployment: Rate[5]	Civilian employment[6], 2016–2020: Total	Percent: Management, business, science, and arts	Percent: Construction, production, and maintenance occupations
	89	90	91	92	93	94	95	96	97	98	99	100	101	102	103
WYOMING—Cont'd															
Goshen	5,234	72.4	184,500	19.9	10.6	661	25.0	1.3	6,531	0.4	227	3.5	6,049	37.3	29.3
Hot Springs	2,187	71.1	164,400	20.5	10.0	739	26.1	1.6	2,246	0.8	87	3.9	2,275	38.1	25.4
Johnson	3,961	70.9	248,200	19.9	10.7	877	24.0	1.8	4,242	1.7	174	4.1	4,080	41.6	22.9
Laramie	40,202	72.6	239,900	20.2	10.2	933	27.4	1.4	49,373	-1.5	1,976	4.0	47,402	38.0	23.4
Lincoln	7,348	80.4	253,400	19.5	10.0	710	20.3	6.1	9,514	2.4	360	3.8	9,709	30.1	35.1
Natrona	32,896	70.6	215,400	19.9	10.0	846	28.0	2.3	39,057	-2.6	2,369	6.1	41,451	34.2	25.7
Niobrara	900	75.7	141,600	23.1	10.0	823	22.5	2.4	1,259	2.1	45	3.6	996	39.2	31.2
Park	12,575	73.5	280,400	22.1	10.0	914	22.4	1.3	15,562	2.4	636	4.1	14,100	38.3	24.5
Platte	3,846	75.8	188,600	19.4	10.0	784	27.5	1.0	4,508	-1.6	181	4.0	4,110	26.6	36.5
Sheridan	13,294	67.6	284,200	23.2	10.9	859	26.7	3.1	16,018	0.1	674	4.2	14,885	40.8	24.1
Sublette	3,529	83.1	290,300	19.0	10.0	877	18.5	0.8	3,990	-0.7	224	5.6	4,815	38.0	27.8
Sweetwater	15,726	75.4	205,100	18.1	10.0	852	22.6	2.0	19,449	-5.1	1,089	5.6	21,572	31.5	35.5
Teton	10,027	55.9	850,800	22.2	10.0	1,402	24.6	4.9	15,886	4.9	511	3.2	14,909	42.2	17.3
Uinta	7,789	77.0	181,600	17.5	10.0	685	21.4	3.3	8,832	-3.0	443	5.0	9,710	30.8	32.3
Washakie	3,437	73.0	165,900	22.2	10.0	624	21.2	3.4	3,978	0.8	159	4.0	3,841	38.9	31.8
Weston	2,882	83.9	166,600	20.4	12.8	761	25.6	2.7	3,741	-1.3	119	3.2	2,910	31.4	39.2

1. Specified owner-occupied units. 2. A value of 10.0 represents 10 percent or less; a value of 50.0 represents 50 percent or more. 3. Specified renter-occupied units. 4. Overcrowded or lacking complete plumbing facilities. 5. Percent of civilian labor force. 6. Civilian employed persons 16 years old and over.

STATE County	Private nonfarm establishments, employment and payroll, 2020									Agriculture, 2017			
		Employment						Annual payroll		Farms			Farm producers whose primary occupation is farming (percent)
											Percent with:		
	Number of establish-ments	Total	Health care and social assistance	Manufac-turing	Retail trade	Finance and insurance	Professional, scientific, and technical services	Total (mil dol)	Average per employee (dollars)	Number	Fewer than 50 acres	1000 acres or more	
	104	105	106	107	108	109	110	111	112	113	114	115	116
WYOMING—Cont'd													
Goshen	327	2,884	725	404	296	113	150	104	35,899	842	19.1	24.8	48.9
Hot Springs	179	1,514	370	55	147	42	47	59	39,236	223	39.9	18.4	42.7
Johnson	517	2,405	353	62	372	173	259	100	41,417	384	21.1	42.2	46.8
Laramie	3,392	34,992	6,790	1,393	6,173	1,556	2,432	1,665	47,578	999	31.7	21.9	38.8
Lincoln	819	5,394	1,000	447	701	116	293	275	51,064	698	52.0	10.5	31.0
Natrona	2,906	32,314	5,880	1,666	4,687	943	1,761	1,593	49,290	430	40.0	25.3	39.3
Niobrara	75	368	49	NA	88	20	8	12	33,429	242	5.0	69.4	67.9
Park	1,232	9,695	2,044	457	1,654	352	358	402	41,497	1,008	45.6	9.9	40.5
Platte	270	2,157	296	97	412	129	63	98	45,210	505	24.4	33.1	45.4
Sheridan	1,612	11,718	2,928	592	1,804	358	1,015	547	46,668	833	45.7	17.5	35.1
Sublette	417	2,603	148	46	393	80	128	150	57,732	402	35.3	28.6	34.3
Sweetwater	1,185	15,109	1,434	1,892	2,214	293	512	942	62,327	219	25.6	24.7	38.3
Teton	2,257	18,350	1,475	217	1,937	414	1,053	912	49,677	142	34.5	13.4	40.6
Uinta	557	7,175	1,327	190	965	145	297	359	50,034	403	42.9	19.9	34.8
Washakie	329	2,420	612	318	334	100	110	101	41,591	246	36.2	22.8	49.6
Weston	222	1,540	340	131	231	61	34	68	44,300	247	17.8	45.7	41.8

STATE County	Agriculture, 2017 (cont.)															
	Land in farms					Value of land and buildings (dollars)		Value of machinery and equipment, average per farm (dollars)	Value of products sold:				Organic farms (number)	Farms with internet access (per-cent)	Government payments	
	Acreage (1,000)	Percent change, 2012–2017	Acres						Total (mil dol)	Average per farm (acres)	Percent from:					
			Average size of farm	Total irrigated (1,000)	Total cropland (1,000)	Average per farm	Average per acre				Crops	Livestock and poultry products			Total ($1,000)	Percent of farms
	117	118	119	120	121	122	123	124	125	126	127	128	129	130	131	132
WYOMING—Cont'd																
Goshen	1,256	-8.3	1,492	118.4	234.3	1,286,023	862	156,103	201.9	239,760	24.0	76.0	3	78.9	4,111	40.5
Hot Springs	528	2.1	2,368	14.8	22.7	1,469,992	621	90,195	15.2	68,278	6.6	93.4	1	77.6	408	13.0
Johnson	1,974	-3.0	5,142	31.7	41.0	3,020,697	588	128,544	44.1	114,966	7.0	93.0	NA	82.6	1,088	21.6
Laramie	1,630	-2.8	1,631	67.1	382.3	1,383,473	848	123,891	184.6	184,762	17.9	82.1	42	77.7	4,856	29.3
Lincoln	365	6.1	523	81.3	94.0	955,622	1,828	82,429	47.9	68,566	23.3	76.7	NA	81.2	182	5.2
Natrona	1,933	14.3	4,496	44.3	55.7	2,039,344	454	109,339	43.2	100,493	12.9	87.1	NA	76.0	318	7.9
Niobrara	1,277	-6.0	5,279	10.5	54.6	3,308,558	627	156,480	49.7	205,306	8.1	91.9	NA	71.5	1,861	37.2
Park	930	14.4	923	127.5	140.5	1,378,458	1,494	124,845	85.2	84,497	53.7	46.3	5	86.9	931	10.0
Platte	1,047	-14.5	2,073	58.9	134.8	1,820,452	878	136,932	94.2	186,598	19.7	80.3	6	82.2	2,872	27.1
Sheridan	1,214	-7.0	1,457	54.6	95.9	1,783,962	1,224	101,776	59.7	71,637	14.5	85.5	1	78.9	1,417	12.2
Sublette	546	-29.7	1,359	158.7	143.5	2,243,832	1,651	128,778	47.9	119,085	12.9	87.1	2	84.3	155	2.7
Sweetwater	1,370	-17.7	6,256	35.4	35.6	1,851,640	296	110,326	16.5	75,132	27.7	72.3	NA	82.6	201	5.9
Teton	68	68.4	476	25.5	15.8	1,929,058	4,049	103,147	17.6	123,817	22.6	77.4	NA	88.7	131	4.2
Uinta	657	1.0	1,630	76.2	84.8	1,747,715	1,072	102,095	26.7	66,159	13.6	86.4	1	80.9	130	1.5
Washakie	316	-7.4	1,285	38.5	53.4	1,502,187	1,169	211,277	43.0	174,874	37.8	62.2	NA	91.1	508	25.2
Weston	1,227	-4.9	4,968	4.2	37.5	3,321,035	669	129,296	34.3	138,761	1.8	98.2	NA	81.0	836	31.2

STATE County	Water use, 2015		Wholesale Trade[1], 2017				Retail Trade[2], 2017				Real estate and rental and leasing,[2] 2017			
	Public supply water withdrawn (mil gal/ day)	Public supply gallons withdrawn per person per day	Number of establish-ments	Number of employees	Sales (mil dol)	Average payroll (mil dol)	Number of establish-ments	Number of employees	Sales (mil dol)	Average payroll (mil dol)	Number of establish-ments	Number of employees	Sales (mil dol)	Average payroll (mil dol)
	133	134	135	136	137	138	139	140	141	142	143	144	145	146
WYOMING—Cont'd														
Goshen	1.9	138.2	19	128	178.4	5.8	42	380	94.7	9.2	D	D	D	D
Hot Springs	0.7	141.3	NA	NA	NA	NA	25	152	31.7	3.3	7	D	1.8	D
Johnson	1.6	187.5	11	23	8.8	0.8	59	370	87.3	9.8	17	37	5.2	1.1
Laramie	14.0	144.2	122	926	604.3	49.1	372	5,390	1,707.9	151.7	183	689	188.4	31.6
Lincoln	4.1	216.3	9	D	19.6	D	90	744	213.5	19.0	28	57	12.4	2.0
Natrona	12.3	149.2	164	1,812	2,888.1	115.8	344	4,766	1,386.0	139.6	181	952	285.7	54.1
Niobrara	1.0	393.4	NA	NA	NA	NA	11	99	25.6	2.0	D	D	D	0.1
Park	3.2	108.5	31	230	177.2	10.4	169	1,546	459.3	46.0	61	170	26.8	4.7
Platte	1.6	177.0	4	22	23.5	1.1	41	378	113.2	9.9	10	21	3.8	0.6
Sheridan	4.6	151.6	30	158	78.9	8.0	152	1,693	545.6	49.8	66	170	30.9	5.6
Sublette	2.2	223.3	D	D	D	1.7	43	338	100.3	10.2	26	110	16.0	4.2
Sweetwater	11.4	254.8	60	519	462.5	29.1	172	2,410	835.4	69.3	78	638	96.6	22.1
Teton	7.8	336.4	26	168	88.0	8.1	254	2,006	641.1	75.2	197	717	251.0	42.5
Uinta	3.9	187.3	14	142	123.1	8.5	86	1,117	347.2	26.9	30	101	18.7	3.8
Washakie	0.1	10.8	12	58	25.4	2.4	43	356	89.3	11.3	11	43	6.4	1.5
Weston	1.0	141.0	6	18	4.9	0.7	31	266	78.4	6.2	4	D	0.8	D

1 Merchant wholesalers, except manufacturers' sales branches and offices. 2. Employer establishments.

STATE County	Professional, scientific, and technical services, 2017				Manufacturing, 2017				Accommodation and food services, 2017			
	Number of establish-ments	Number of employees	Sales (mil dol)	Average payroll (mil dol)	Number of establish-ments	Number of employees	Sales (mil dol)	Average payroll (mil dol)	Number of establis-hments	Number of employees	Sales (mil dol)	Annual payroll (mil dol)
	147	148	149	150	151	152	153	154	155	156	157	158
WYOMING—Cont'd												
Goshen	23	153	11.8	5.0	7	261	72.2	9.2	28	257	13.5	3.1
Hot Springs	12	37	4.9	1.6	D	51	D	2.5	21	246	11.6	3.4
Johnson	74	215	34.2	11.0	D	68	D	2.7	44	347	23.1	6.5
Laramie	D	D	D	D	69	1,296	1,348.3	85.5	218	3,755	227.3	64.5
Lincoln	73	130	17.1	4.7	23	342	336.0	28.5	64	473	25.0	6.9
Natrona	266	1,440	266.6	89.1	89	1,379	1,002.2	83.6	201	3,819	211.1	65.8
Niobrara	D	D	0.3	D	NA	NA	NA	NA	D	D	D	1.2
Park	104	373	47.6	18.0	42	497	140.5	25.2	126	1,621	218.9	60.4
Platte	18	46	6.8	1.7	D	79	D	3.7	36	324	20.2	4.6
Sheridan	166	817	121.8	41.1	30	484	104.7	23.3	111	1,609	86.2	27.1
Sublette	42	111	19.7	6.0	D	D	D	1.9	43	255	24.7	7.6
Sweetwater	120	449	81.5	22.6	32	1,801	1,558.9	177.1	120	1,793	98.0	28.5
Teton	D	D	D	D	38	140	23.8	6.4	181	4,557	505.1	140.7
Uinta	48	228	45.0	18.0	17	190	186.3	10.0	54	646	33.4	9.5
Washakie	39	135	19.3	6.8	16	399	190.4	17.2	30	285	10.6	3.1
Weston	9	22	2.2	0.6	D	114	D	D	22	152	7.1	1.8

STATE County	Health care and social assistance, 2017				Other services, 2017				Nonemployer businesses, 2019		Value of residential construction authorized by building permits, 2021	
	Number of establish-ments	Number of employees	Receipts (mil dol)	Annual payroll (mil dol)	Number of establish-ments	Number of employees	Receipts (mil dol)	Annual payroll (mil dol)	Number	Receipts (mil dol)	New construction ($1,000)	Number of housing units
	159	160	161	162	163	164	165	166	167	168	169	170
WYOMING—Cont'd												
Goshen	26	734	69.2	29.5	26	86	8.9	2.2	1,013	44.2	1,045	2
Hot Springs	21	369	36.0	14.9	13	56	6.0	1.5	402	13.8	650	3
Johnson	29	386	31.9	15.4	32	151	15.0	4.8	1,388	89.3	12,804	42
Laramie	361	6,859	876.7	382.6	206	1,187	129.0	36.9	9,257	674.2	129,236	737
Lincoln	52	776	80.4	34.2	43	120	20.5	4.1	2,275	103.7	76,257	255
Natrona	333	5,588	751.8	310.6	198	976	140.4	34.5	6,310	351.5	55,177	275
Niobrara	7	55	4.5	2.3	D	D	2.5	D	243	7.7	300	1
Park	126	1,978	243.7	98.3	87	268	27.1	7.6	3,405	150.1	77,239	272
Platte	20	306	28.8	11.8	12	60	4.8	1.3	741	27.1	10,891	52
Sheridan	141	3,364	305.8	156.4	78	289	44.0	9.2	4,259	309.2	89,078	355
Sublette	20	162	12.5	5.6	27	139	27.9	7.1	1,113	52.6	15,911	52
Sweetwater	102	1,482	169.5	60.7	79	412	67.7	15.6	2,217	104.6	15,089	49
Teton	136	1,465	209.0	86.5	123	574	135.0	26.8	5,801	421.9	476,917	219
Uinta	72	1,320	117.7	57.7	28	82	8.6	2.5	1,530	68.8	10,474	36
Washakie	32	601	49.5	21.1	23	74	5.8	1.4	676	23.3	170	1
Weston	22	353	31.2	14.1	9	33	3.6	1.1	610	20.7	85	1

STATE County	Government employment and payroll, 2017									Local government finances, 2017				
			March payroll (percent of total)							General revenue				
												Taxes		
													Per capita[1] (dollars)	
	Full-time equivalent employees	March payroll (dollars)	Adminis-tration, judicial, and legal	Police and corrections	Fire protection	Highways and transpor-tation	Health and welfare	Natural resources and utilities	Education and libraries	Total (mil dol)	Inter-govern-mental (mil dol)	Total (mil dol)	Total	Property
	171	172	173	174	175	176	177	178	179	180	181	182	183	184
WYOMING—Cont'd														
Goshen	742	2,816,098	6.4	6.9	0.0	2.2	1.3	8.3	72.6	87.8	52.7	18.8	1,406	1,235
Hot Springs	390	1,487,824	7.9	6.5	0.0	2.5	32.5	3.6	45.0	25.3	13.4	8.0	1,711	1,517
Johnson	633	2,884,696	5.5	9.4	0.5	3.8	35.3	3.4	40.9	73.4	17.1	30.5	3,612	3,266
Laramie	6,340	31,230,813	2.7	5.1	1.9	1.9	39.7	2.3	45.2	848.2	316.5	110.4	1,122	833
Lincoln	1,315	5,381,730	5.6	5.7	0.0	2.7	32.4	3.7	48.9	170.8	68.3	42.1	2,185	2,003
Natrona	3,954	16,298,613	5.7	8.4	3.7	2.6	1.2	5.2	71.3	502.1	317.5	97.1	1,220	987
Niobrara	283	1,121,423	6.7	4.7	0.0	2.0	29.6	7.5	46.9	31.8	16.5	7.0	2,911	2,731
Park	2,146	9,400,479	4.0	4.8	0.5	2.1	30.6	6.7	49.6	270.3	91.0	49.2	1,686	1,501
Platte	486	1,802,664	6.5	9.8	0.3	2.9	1.1	9.7	67.4	51.0	29.4	11.7	1,367	1,089
Sheridan	1,985	9,635,803	3.5	4.2	1.0	1.5	35.0	3.6	50.8	288.8	121.4	30.8	1,022	767
Sublette	613	2,777,896	8.4	13.5	1.0	5.5	10.0	6.6	50.3	117.8	22.9	74.6	7,654	7,523
Sweetwater	3,089	14,708,500	5.2	7.2	2.2	2.5	25.5	5.9	49.7	435.4	170.1	132.0	3,037	2,666
Teton	1,853	8,974,820	6.3	5.4	1.4	7.3	41.5	6.5	31.0	287.9	60.3	78.9	3,373	2,475
Uinta	1,266	4,979,667	5.3	6.5	1.0	2.4	0.8	6.1	76.6	120.6	78.5	26.1	1,278	1,122
Washakie	447	1,611,024	6.3	8.1	0.4	3.3	0.6	8.4	72.5	48.5	33.1	9.8	1,218	1,021
Weston	523	1,956,847	11.2	3.5	0.5	0.8	32.9	5.3	45.2	63.6	29.8	15.3	2,197	1,829

1. Based on the resident population estimated as of July 1 of the year shown.

Table B. States and Counties — Local Government Finances, Government Employment, and Income Taxes

STATE County	Local government finances, 2017 (cont.)									Government employment, 2020			Individual income tax returns, 2019		
	Direct general expenditure							Debt outstanding							
			Percent of total for:												
	Total (mil dol)	Per capita[1] (dollars)	Education	Health and hospitals	Police protection	Public welfare	Highways	Total (mil dol)	Per capita[1] (dollars)	Federal civilian	Federal military	State and local	Number of returns	Mean adjusted gross income	Mean income tax
	185	186	187	188	189	190	191	192	193	194	195	196	197	198	199
WYOMING—Cont'd															
Goshen	87.3	6,536	62.3	1.0	3.8	2.9	2.3	17.6	1,320	70	62	1,317	5,690	55,602	5,278
Hot Springs	24.1	5,152	52.7	1.1	6.2	0.0	5.1	4.5	960	19	23	562	2,190	49,415	4,504
Johnson	77.0	9,114	30.7	37.5	6.0	0.8	7.4	9.3	1,107	134	44	846	4,330	70,777	8,221
Laramie	893.1	9,078	39.6	37.9	2.9	0.3	2.4	143.1	1,454	2,809	3,739	11,134	50,180	67,948	7,223
Lincoln	151.4	7,853	38.5	29.4	3.3	0.1	5.1	36.4	1,890	123	105	1,757	8,880	87,637	11,068
Natrona	518.2	6,511	62.5	0.4	4.9	0.3	4.4	110.2	1,385	713	413	4,941	39,150	76,179	9,803
Niobrara	37.8	15,799	38.2	20.8	2.3	0.0	4.5	193.9	81,050	10	12	440	1,050	54,307	5,011
Park	266.9	9,143	38.7	34.5	3.0	0.0	3.2	79.7	2,729	760	150	2,603	15,290	79,053	9,868
Platte	55.7	6,522	50.0	3.7	3.7	0.4	5.6	6.8	793	118	76	815	4,280	57,680	5,702
Sheridan	312.4	10,363	48.8	29.5	2.7	0.0	3.6	76.7	2,545	876	155	2,704	15,850	79,583	9,805
Sublette	98.7	10,129	34.2	12.7	4.3	1.5	11.7	14.1	1,445	127	49	903	4,350	83,173	10,378
Sweetwater	425.8	9,797	48.5	19.4	4.0	0.1	3.7	82.3	1,893	224	218	4,139	20,050	72,879	7,754
Teton	282.3	12,073	22.0	35.5	3.6	0.0	3.2	36.5	1,563	376	121	2,158	14,870	312,442	58,037
Uinta	122.2	5,980	64.4	0.7	4.7	0.7	3.1	9.3	456	82	104	2,045	9,370	62,855	5,915
Washakie	46.6	5,824	66.6	0.7	5.5	0.0	3.0	14.6	1,826	122	40	713	3,740	63,933	5,953
Weston	64.7	9,287	35.3	35.0	3.3	0.1	4.0	11.5	1,646	54	33	739	3,150	62,006	6,325

1. Based on the resident population estimated as of July 1 of the year shown.

Metropolitan Areas

(For explanation of symbols, see page viii)

Metropolitan Area Highlights and Rankings

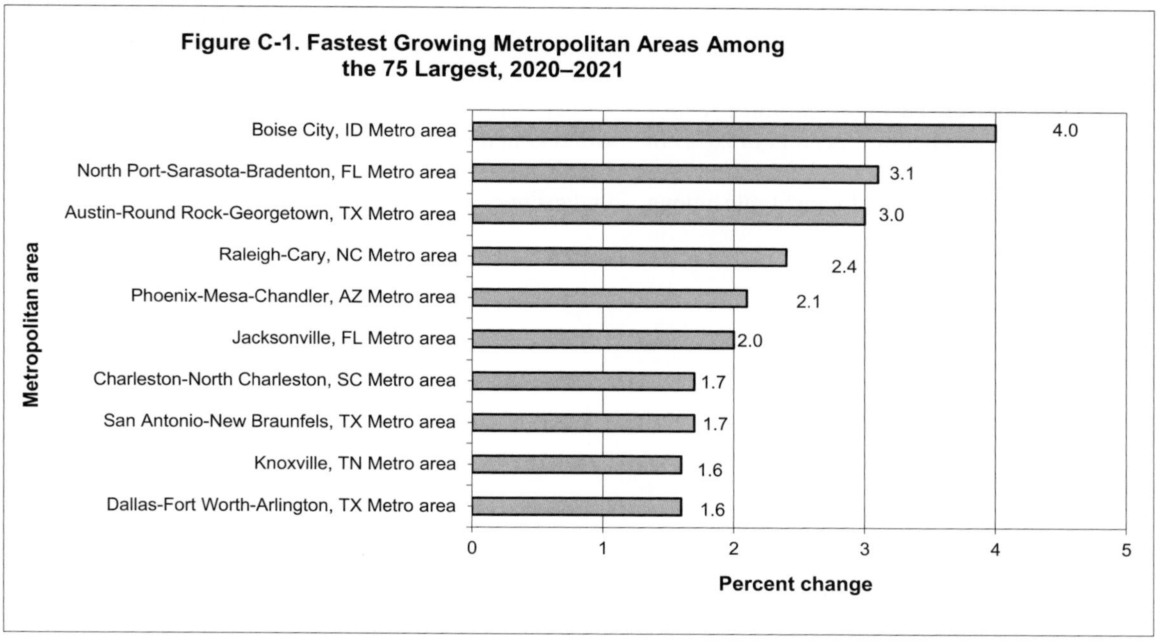

In 2021, 86.3 percent of Americans lived in metropolitan areas, but these metropolitan areas made up a mere 28 percent of the nation's land area. After nearly a decade of research and development, the Office of Management and Budget (OMB) first established new rules for defining metropolitan areas and issued a completely new list after the 2000 census. This scheme defines a variety of areas called "core-based statistical areas" (CBSAs). Along with the new definition of metropolitan areas, the OMB defined a new type of area—a micropolitan area—for the many American communities with population clusters that are too small to meet the 50,000 minimum that defines a metropolitan area. Appendix C lists these micropolitan areas as of March 2020, but because of size constraints, *County and City Extra* continues to include only metropolitan area data in Table C. In 2013, the Census Bureau released data for new metropolitan and micropolitan areas based on the 2010 census, and these were updated in 2015, 2017, 2018, and again in 2020. This edition of *County and City Extra* uses the 2018 metropolitan area delineations, unchanged in 2020, except in Appendix C which reflects the 2020 addition of one new micropolitan area.

With over 19 million people, the New York metropolitan area was the largest, followed by Los Angeles with a population of nearly 13 million. Chicago ranked third with 9.5 million people. Another 12 metropolitan areas had more than 4 million residents (Dallas, Houston, Washington, Philadelphia, Miami, Atlanta, Boston, San Francisco, Phoenix, Riverside, Detroit, and Seattle), while 41 other metropolitan areas had between 1 million and 4 million people. Nearly 57 percent of the U.S. population lived in these 56 metropolitan areas with one million or more residents.

Two hundred eleven metropolitan areas grew by 5 percent or more between 2010 and 2020. The Villages, FL, had the highest growth rate, increasing by 38.9 percent to a 2021 population of 135,638 residents. Among the 75 largest metropolitan areas, Austin-Round Rock-Georgetown, TX, had the largest increase at 33.0 percent followed by Orlando, FL, at 25.3 percent and Raleigh-Cary, NC, metro area at 25.1 percent. None of the most populous metropolitan areas lost population since 2010. While many large metropolitan areas in the Midwest lost population or increased only slightly, Columbus, Omaha, Indianapolis, Minneapolis, and Grand Rapids all grew by more than 9 percent.

Among metropolitan areas, New York and Los Angeles shared the top spots for density as well as for total population. With 2,957.4 persons per square mile, New York-Newark-Jersey City, NY-NJ-PA, was the most densely populated metropolitan area in the country. At the other extreme, ten of the largest metropolitan areas had fewer than 200 persons per square mile. These areas typically had large land areas and were located in the west and south.

In 2021, 5 metropolitan areas had unemployment rates at 10 percent or higher compared with 36 metropolitan areas in 2020. In contrast, 131 metropolitan areas had unemployment rates at 10 percent or higher in 2010 but only two had unemployment rates of over 10 percent in 2019. Topping the list are El Centro, CA (17.3 percent), and Yuma, AZ (12.9 percent), two metropolitan areas with large agricultural workforces. Six of the 10 metropolitan areas with the highest unemployment were in California. Among the 75 most populous metropolitan areas, only 7 MSAs had unemployment rates at 7 percent or above compared with 52 in 2020. In contrast, only two MSAs in 2019 had unemployment rates of 7 percent of above. Two hundred three metropolitan areas had unemployment rates below 5 percent in 2021. In contrast, only 24 MSAs had unemployment rates below 5 percent in 2020. Logan, UT-ID, had the lowest unemployment rate among all metropolitan areas at 2.0 percent followed by Provo-Orem, UT, at 2.3 percent and Lincoln, NE, at 2.4 percent . Fourteen of the 75 largest metropolitan areas had unemployment rates below 4 percent. In contrast, in 2019, 53 MSAs had unemployment rates below 4 percent but no MSA had an unemployment rate under 4 percent in 2020. Bakersfield, CA, metro area had the highest unemployment rate among the 75 largest metropolitan areas at 10.0 percent. It was the only MSA with an unemployment rate of 10 percent or higher. In 2020, MSAs with a large percentage of workers in the leisure and hospitality industry, such as Las Vegas-Henderson-Paradise, NV, and Atlantic City, NJ, had among the highest unemployment rates.

75 Largest Metropolitan Areas by 2020 Population

Selected Rankings

Population, 2021			Total land area, 2021			
Population rank	Metropolitan area	Population [col 2]	Population rank	Land area rank	Metropolitan area	Land area (square miles) [col 1]
1	New York-Newark-Jersey City, NY-NJ-PA Metro area	19,768,458	12	1	Riverside-San Bernardino-Ontario, CA Metro area	27,277.3
2	Los Angeles-Long Beach-Anaheim, CA Metro area	12,997,353	10	2	Phoenix-Mesa-Chandler, AZ Metro area	14,567.8
3	Chicago-Naperville-Elgin, IL-IN-WI Metro area	9,509,934	75	3	Boise City, ID Metro area	11,766.6
4	Dallas-Fort Worth-Arlington, TX Metro area	7,759,615	61	4	Albuquerque, NM Metro area	9,283.4
5	Houston-The Woodlands-Sugar Land, TX Metro area	7,206,841	53	5	Tucson, AZ Metro area	9,188.7
6	Washington-Arlington-Alexandria, DC-VA-MD-WV Metro area	6,356,434	8	6	Atlanta-Sandy Springs-Alpharetta, GA Metro area	8,685.7
7	Philadelphia-Camden-Wilmington, PA-NJ-DE-MD Metro area	6,228,601	4	7	Dallas-Fort Worth-Arlington, TX Metro area	8,675.2
8	Atlanta-Sandy Springs-Alpharetta, GA Metro area	6,144,050	19	8	Denver-Aurora-Lakewood, CO Metro area	8,344.7
9	Miami-Fort Lauderdale-Pompano Beach, FL Metro area	6,091,747	5	9	Houston-The Woodlands-Sugar Land, TX Metro are	8,268.7
10	Phoenix-Mesa-Chandler, AZ Metro area	4,946,145	62	10	Bakersfield, CA Metro area	8,134.6
11	Boston-Cambridge-Newton, MA-NH Metro area	4,899,932	29	11	Las Vegas-Henderson-Paradise, NV Metro area	7,891.7
12	Riverside-San Bernardino-Ontario, CA Metro area	4,653,105	21	12	St. Louis, MO-IL Metro area	7,863.7
13	San Francisco-Oakland-Berkeley, CA Metro area	4,623,264	46	13	Salt Lake City, UT Metro area	7,684.0
14	Detroit-Warren-Dearborn, MI Metro area	4,365,205	24	14	San Antonio-New Braunfels, TX Metro area	7,313.2
15	Seattle-Tacoma-Bellevue, WA Metro area	4,011,553	31	15	Kansas City, MO-KS Metro area	7,256.5
16	Minneapolis-St. Paul-Bloomington, MN Metro area	3,690,512	3	16	Chicago-Naperville-Elgin, IL-IN-WI Metro area	7,194.8
17	San Diego-Chula Vista-Carlsbad, CA Metro area	3,286,069	16	17	Minneapolis-St. Paul-Bloomington, MN Metro area	7,047.7
18	Tampa-St. Petersburg-Clearwater, FL Metro area	3,219,514	25	18	Portland-Vancouver-Hillsboro, OR-WA Metro area	6,687.5
19	Denver-Aurora-Lakewood, CO Metro area	2,972,566	1	19	New York-Newark-Jersey City, NY-NJ-PA Metro ar	6,684.3
20	Baltimore-Columbia-Towson, MD Metro area	2,838,327	6	20	Washington-Arlington-Alexandria, DC-VA-MD-WV Metro area	6,567.7
21	St. Louis, MO-IL Metro area	2,809,299	54	21	Tulsa, OK Metro area	6,270.2
22	Charlotte-Concord-Gastonia, NC-SC Metro area	2,701,046	55	22	Fresno, CA Metro area	5,958.4
23	Orlando-Kissimmee-Sanford, FL Metro area	2,691,925	15	23	Seattle-Tacoma-Bellevue, WA Metro area	5,869.7
24	San Antonio-New Braunfels, TX Metro area	2,601,788	35	24	Nashville-Davidson--Murfreesboro--Franklin, TN Metro area	5,689.4
25	Portland-Vancouver-Hillsboro, OR-WA Metro area	2,511,612	22	25	Charlotte-Concord-Gastonia, NC-SC Metro area	5,597.4
26	Sacramento-Roseville-Folsom, CA Metro area	2,411,428	67	26	El Paso, TX Metro area	5,583.8
27	Pittsburgh, PA Metro area	2,353,538	42	27	Oklahoma City, OK Metro area	5,511.7
28	Austin-Round Rock-Georgetown, TX Metro area	2,352,426	27	28	Pittsburgh, PA Metro area	5,282.9
29	Las Vegas-Henderson-Paradise, NV Metro area	2,292,476	26	29	Sacramento-Roseville-Folsom, CA Metro area	5,094.9
30	Cincinnati, OH-KY-IN Metro area	2,259,935	9	30	Miami-Fort Lauderdale-Pompano Beach, FL Metro area	5,066.9
31	Kansas City, MO-KS Metro area	2,199,490	2	31	Los Angeles-Long Beach-Anaheim, CA Metro area	4,852.1
32	Columbus, OH Metro area	2,151,017	32	32	Columbus, OH Metro area	4,796.6
33	Indianapolis-Carmel-Anderson, IN Metro area	2,126,804	7	33	Philadelphia-Camden-Wilmington, PA-NJ-DE-MD Metro area	4,603.2
34	Cleveland-Elyria, OH Metro area	2,075,662	43	34	Memphis, TN-MS-AR Metro area	4,575.2
35	Nashville-Davidson--Murfreesboro--Franklin, TN Metro area	2,012,476	30	35	Cincinnati, OH-KY-IN Metro area	4,546.4
36	San Jose-Sunnyvale-Santa Clara, CA Metro area	1,952,185	50	36	Birmingham-Hoover, AL Metro area	4,488.7
37	Virginia Beach-Norfolk-Newport News, VA-NC Metro area	1,803,328	66	37	Baton Rouge, LA Metro area	4,370.7
38	Providence-Warwick, RI-MA Metro area	1,675,774	44	38	Richmond, VA Metro area	4,364.4
39	Jacksonville, FL Metro area	1,637,666	58	39	Omaha-Council Bluffs, NE-IA Metro area	4,346.3
40	Milwaukee-Waukesha, WI Metro area	1,566,487	33	40	Indianapolis-Carmel-Anderson, IN Metro area	4,306.6
41	Raleigh-Cary, NC Metro area	1,448,411	28	41	Austin-Round Rock-Georgetown, TX Metro area	4,219.5
42	Oklahoma City, OK Metro area	1,441,647	17	42	San Diego-Chula Vista-Carlsbad, CA Metro area	4,210.2
43	Memphis, TN-MS-AR Metro area	1,336,103	14	43	Detroit-Warren-Dearborn, MI Metro area	3,892.2
44	Richmond, VA Metro area	1,324,062	72	44	Columbia, SC Metro area	3,703.1
45	Louisville/Jefferson County, KY-IN Metro area	1,284,566	37	45	Virginia Beach-Norfolk-Newport News, VA-NC Metro area	3,530.4
46	Salt Lake City, UT Metro area	1,263,061	23	46	Orlando-Kissimmee-Sanford, FL Metro area	3,490.5
47	New Orleans-Metairie, LA Metro area	1,261,726	11	47	Boston-Cambridge-Newton, MA-NH Metro area	3,486.1
48	Virginia Beach-Norfolk-Newport News, VA-NC Metro area	1,211,906	52	48	Rochester, NY Metro area	3,266.0
49	Buffalo-Cheektowaga, NY Metro area	1,162,336	45	49	Louisville/Jefferson County, KY-IN Metro area	3,237.0
50	Birmingham-Hoover, AL Metro area	1,114,262	64	50	Knoxville, TN Metro area	3,220.3
51	Grand Rapids-Kentwood, MI Metro area	1,091,620	47	51	New Orleans-Metairie, LA Metro area	3,203.5
52	Rochester, NY Metro area	1,084,973	39	52	Jacksonville, FL Metro area	3,201.8
53	Tucson, AZ Metro area	1,052,030	63	53	Albany-Schenectady-Troy, NY Metro area	2,811.7
54	Tulsa, OK Metro area	1,023,988	60	54	Greenville-Anderson, SC Metro area	2,709.6
55	Fresno, CA Metro area	1,013,581	51	55	Grand Rapids-Kentwood, MI Metro area	2,689.1
56	Urban Honolulu, HI Metro area	1,000,890	36	56	San Jose-Sunnyvale-Santa Clara, CA Metro area	2,679.7
57	Worcester, MA-CT Metro area	978,447	20	57	Baltimore-Columbia-Towson, MD Metro area	2,601.5
58	Omaha-Council Bluffs, NE-IA Metro area	971,637	74	58	Charleston-North Charleston, SC Metro area	2,590.2
59	Bridgeport-Stamford-Norwalk, CT Metro area	959,768	18	59	Tampa-St. Petersburg-Clearwater, FL Metro area	2,515.2
60	Greenville-Anderson, SC Metro area	940,774	13	60	San Francisco-Oakland-Berkeley, CA Metro area	2,470.3
61	Albuquerque, NM Metro area	918,259	41	61	Raleigh-Cary, NC Metro area	2,118.4
62	Bakersfield, CA Metro area	917,673	57	62	Worcester, MA-CT Metro area	2,023.6
63	Albany-Schenectady-Troy, NY Metro area	899,286	34	63	Cleveland-Elyria, OH Metro area	1,998.8
64	Knoxville, TN Metro area	893,412	71	64	Oxnard-Thousand Oaks-Ventura, CA Metro area	1,840.8
65	McAllen-Edinburg-Mission, TX Metro area	880,356	38	65	Providence-Warwick, RI-MA Metro area	1,587.0
66	Baton Rouge, LA Metro area	871,905	65	66	McAllen-Edinburg-Mission, TX Metro area	1,571.0
67	El Paso, TX Metro area	871,234	49	67	Buffalo-Cheektowaga, NY Metro area	1,565.1
68	Allentown-Bethlehem-Easton, PA-NJ Metro area	865,310	48	68	Virginia Beach-Norfolk-Newport News, VA-NC Metro area	1,514.6
69	New Haven-Milford, CT Metro area	863,700	40	69	Milwaukee-Waukesha, WI Metro area	1,454.9
70	North Port-Sarasota-Bradenton, FL Metro area	859,760	68	70	Allentown-Bethlehem-Easton, PA-NJ Metro area	1,453.0
71	Oxnard-Thousand Oaks-Ventura, CA Metro area	839,784	70	71	North Port-Sarasota-Bradenton, FL Metro area	1,298.8
72	Columbia, SC Metro area	838,250	73	72	Dayton-Kettering, OH Metro area	1,281.4
73	Dayton-Kettering, OH Metro area	813,516	59	73	Bridgeport-Stamford-Norwalk, CT Metro area	625.0
74	Charleston-North Charleston, SC Metro area	813,052	69	74	New Haven-Milford, CT Metro area	604.3
75	Boise City, ID Metro area	795,268	56	75	Urban Honolulu, HI Metro area	600.6

75 Largest Metropolitan Areas by 2020 Population

Selected Rankings

Population density, 2021

Population rank	Density rank	Metropolitan area	Density (per square kilometer) [col 4]
1	1	New York-Newark-Jersey City, NY-NJ-PA Metro ar	2,957.4
2	2	Los Angeles-Long Beach-Anaheim, CA Metro area	2,678.7
13	3	San Francisco-Oakland-Berkeley, CA Metro area	1,871.5
56	4	Urban Honolulu, HI Metro area	1,666.5
59	5	Bridgeport-Stamford-Norwalk, CT Metro area	1,535.6
69	6	New Haven-Milford, CT Metro area	1,429.3
11	7	Boston-Cambridge-Newton, MA-NH Metro area	1,405.6
7	8	Philadelphia-Camden-Wilmington, PA-NJ-DE-MD Metro area	1,353.1
3	9	Chicago-Naperville-Elgin, IL-IN-WI Metro area	1,321.8
18	10	Tampa-St. Petersburg-Clearwater, FL Metro area	1,280.0
9	11	Miami-Fort Lauderdale-Pompano Beach, FL Metro area	1,202.3
14	12	Detroit-Warren-Dearborn, MI Metro area	1,121.5
20	13	Baltimore-Columbia-Towson, MD Metro area	1,091.0
40	14	Milwaukee-Waukesha, WI Metro area	1,076.7
38	15	Providence-Warwick, RI-MA Metro area	1,055.9
34	16	Cleveland-Elyria, OH Metro area	1,038.5
6	17	Washington-Arlington-Alexandria, DC-VA-MD-WV Metro area	967.8
4	18	Dallas-Fort Worth-Arlington, TX Metro area	894.5
5	19	Houston-The Woodlands-Sugar Land, TX Metro are	871.6
48	20	Virginia Beach-Norfolk-Newport News, VA-NC Metro area	800.1
17	21	San Diego-Chula Vista-Carlsbad, CA Metro area	780.5
23	22	Orlando-Kissimmee-Sanford, FL Metro area	771.2
49	23	Buffalo-Cheektowaga, NY Metro area	742.7
36	24	San Jose-Sunnyvale-Santa Clara, CA Metro area	728.5
8	25	Atlanta-Sandy Springs-Alpharetta, GA Metro area	707.4
41	26	Raleigh-Cary, NC Metro area	683.7
15	27	Seattle-Tacoma-Bellevue, WA Metro area	683.4
70	28	North Port-Sarasota-Bradenton, FL Metro area	662.0
73	29	Dayton-Kettering, OH Metro area	634.9
68	30	Allentown-Bethlehem-Easton, PA-NJ Metro area	595.5
65	31	McAllen-Edinburg-Mission, TX Metro area	560.4
28	32	Austin-Round Rock-Georgetown, TX Metro area	557.5
16	33	Minneapolis-St. Paul-Bloomington, MN Metro area	523.6
39	34	Jacksonville, FL Metro area	511.5
37	35	Virginia Beach-Norfolk-Newport News, VA-NC Metro area	510.8
30	36	Cincinnati, OH-KY-IN Metro area	497.1
33	37	Indianapolis-Carmel-Anderson, IN Metro area	493.8
57	38	Worcester, MA-CT Metro area	483.5
22	39	Charlotte-Concord-Gastonia, NC-SC Metro area	482.6
26	40	Sacramento-Roseville-Folsom, CA Metro area	473.3
71	41	Oxnard-Thousand Oaks-Ventura, CA Metro area	456.2
32	42	Columbus, OH Metro area	448.4
27	43	Pittsburgh, PA Metro area	445.5
51	44	Grand Rapids-Kentwood, MI Metro area	405.9
45	45	Louisville/Jefferson County, KY-IN Metro area	396.8
47	46	New Orleans-Metairie, LA Metro area	393.9
25	47	Portland-Vancouver-Hillsboro, OR-WA Metro area	375.6
21	48	St. Louis, MO-IL Metro area	357.2
19	49	Denver-Aurora-Lakewood, CO Metro area	356.2
24	50	San Antonio-New Braunfels, TX Metro area	355.8
35	51	Nashville-Davidson--Murfreesboro--Franklin, TN Metro area	353.7
60	52	Greenville-Anderson, SC Metro area	347.2
10	53	Phoenix-Mesa-Chandler, AZ Metro area	339.5
52	54	Rochester, NY Metro area	332.2
63	55	Albany-Schenectady-Troy, NY Metro area	319.8
74	56	Charleston-North Charleston, SC Metro area	313.9
44	57	Richmond, VA Metro area	303.4
31	58	Kansas City, MO-KS Metro area	303.1
43	59	Memphis, TN-MS-AR Metro area	292.0
29	60	Las Vegas-Henderson-Paradise, NV Metro area	290.5
64	61	Knoxville, TN Metro area	277.4
42	62	Oklahoma City, OK Metro area	261.6
50	63	Birmingham-Hoover, AL Metro area	248.2
72	64	Columbia, SC Metro area	226.4
58	65	Omaha-Council Bluffs, NE-IA Metro area	223.6
66	66	Baton Rouge, LA Metro area	199.5
12	67	Riverside-San Bernardino-Ontario, CA Metro area	170.6
55	68	Fresno, CA Metro area	170.1
46	69	Salt Lake City, UT Metro area	164.4
54	70	Tulsa, OK Metro area	163.3
67	71	El Paso, TX Metro area	156.0
53	72	Tucson, AZ Metro area	114.5
62	73	Bakersfield, CA Metro area	112.8
61	74	Albuquerque, NM Metro area	98.9
75	75	Boise City, ID Metro area	67.6

Percent population change, 2010–2020

Population rank	Percent change rank	Metropolitan area	Percent change [col 22]
28	1	Austin-Round Rock-Georgetown, TX Metro area	33.0
23	2	Orlando-Kissimmee-Sanford, FL Metro area	25.3
41	3	Raleigh-Cary, NC Metro area	25.1
75	4	Boise City, ID Metro area	24.0
35	5	Nashville-Davidson--Murfreesboro--Franklin, TN	20.9
5	6	Houston-The Woodlands-Sugar Land, TX Metro area	20.3
74	6	Charleston-North Charleston, SC Metro area	20.3
4	8	Dallas-Fort Worth-Arlington, TX Metro area	20.0
24	9	San Antonio-New Braunfels, TX Metro area	19.4
39	10	Jacksonville, FL Metro area	19.3
70	11	North Port-Sarasota-Bradenton, FL Metro area	18.7
22	12	Charlotte-Concord-Gastonia, NC-SC Metro area	18.6
15	13	Seattle-Tacoma-Bellevue, WA Metro area	16.8
19	14	Denver-Aurora-Lakewood, CO Metro area	16.5
29	15	Las Vegas-Henderson-Paradise, NV Metro area	16.1
10	16	Phoenix-Mesa-Chandler, AZ Metro area	15.6
46	16	Salt Lake City, UT Metro area	15.6
8	18	Atlanta-Sandy Springs-Alpharetta, GA Metro area	15.2
18	19	Tampa-St. Petersburg-Clearwater, FL Metro area	14.1
42	20	Oklahoma City, OK Metro area	13.8
6	21	Washington-Arlington-Alexandria, DC-VA-MD-WV Metro area	13.0
25	22	Portland-Vancouver-Hillsboro, OR-WA Metro area	12.9
60	23	Greenville-Anderson, SC Metro area	12.6
32	24	Columbus, OH Metro area	12.5
65	25	McAllen-Edinburg-Mission, TX Metro area	12.4
33	26	Indianapolis-Carmel-Anderson, IN Metro area	11.8
58	26	Omaha-Council Bluffs, NE-IA Metro area	11.8
26	28	Sacramento-Roseville-Folsom, CA Metro area	11.6
44	29	Richmond, VA Metro area	10.8
16	30	Minneapolis-St. Paul-Bloomington, MN Metro are	10.7
9	31	Miami-Fort Lauderdale-Pompano Beach, FL Metro	10.3
13	32	San Francisco-Oakland-Berkeley, CA Metro area	9.5
51	32	Grand Rapids-Kentwood, MI Metro area	9.5
31	34	Kansas City, MO-KS Metro area	9.1
12	35	Riverside-San Bernardino-Ontario, CA Metro are	8.9
36	35	San Jose-Sunnyvale-Santa Clara, CA Metro area	8.9
11	37	Boston-Cambridge-Newton, MA-NH Metro area	8.5
55	38	Fresno, CA Metro area	8.4
54	39	Tulsa, OK Metro area	8.3
62	39	Bakersfield, CA Metro area	8.3
67	41	El Paso, TX Metro area	8.1
72	41	Columbia, SC Metro area	8.1
64	43	Knoxville, TN Metro area	8.0
45	44	Louisville/Jefferson County, KY-IN Metro area	6.9
47	44	New Orleans-Metairie, LA Metro area	6.9
57	46	Worcester, MA-CT Metro area	6.7
1	47	New York-Newark-Jersey City, NY-NJ-PA Metro area	6.6
17	47	San Diego-Chula Vista-Carlsbad, CA Metro area	6.6
56	47	Urban Honolulu, HI Metro area	6.6
53	50	Tucson, AZ Metro area	6.4
30	51	Cincinnati, OH-KY-IN Metro area	5.6
66	52	Baton Rouge, LA Metro area	5.4
50	53	Birmingham-Hoover, AL Metro area	5.1
37	54	Virginia Beach-Norfolk-Newport News, VA-NC Metro area	5.0
68	54	Allentown-Bethlehem-Easton, PA-NJ Metro area	5.0
20	56	Baltimore-Columbia-Towson, MD Metro area	4.9
7	57	Philadelphia-Camden-Wilmington, PA-NJ-DE-MD Metro area	4.7
38	57	Providence-Warwick, RI-MA Metro area	4.7
59	59	Bridgeport-Stamford-Norwalk, CT Metro area	4.4
61	60	Albuquerque, NM Metro area	3.3
63	60	Albany-Schenectady-Troy, NY Metro area	3.3
2	62	Los Angeles-Long Beach-Anaheim, CA Metro area	2.9
49	63	Buffalo-Cheektowaga, NY Metro area	2.8
71	64	Oxnard-Thousand Oaks-Ventura, CA Metro area	2.5
14	65	Detroit-Warren-Dearborn, MI Metro area	2.2
73	66	Dayton-Kettering, OH Metro area	1.9
3	67	Chicago-Naperville-Elgin, IL-IN-WI Metro area	1.7
43	68	Memphis, TN-MS-AR Metro area	1.6
21	69	St. Louis, MO-IL Metro area	1.2
40	69	Milwaukee-Waukesha, WI Metro area	1.2
52	71	Rochester, NY Metro area	1.0
27	72	Pittsburgh, PA Metro area	0.6
34	73	Cleveland-Elyria, OH Metro area	0.5
69	74	New Haven-Milford, CT Metro area	0.3
48	75	Hartford-East Hartford-Middletown, CT Metro area	0.1

75 Largest Metropolitan Areas by 2020 Population
Selected Rankings

Percent White, not Hispanic or Latino, alone or in combination, 2021				Percent Black, not Hispanic or Latino, alone or in combination, 2021			
Population rank	White rank	Metropolitan area	Percent White [col 5]	Population rank	Black rank	Metropolitan area	Percent Black [col 6]
64	1	Knoxville, TN Metro area	87.5	43	1	Memphis, TN-MS-AR Metro area	48.9
27	2	Pittsburgh, PA Metro area	86.4	66	2	Baton Rouge, LA Metro area	36.9
75	3	Boise City, ID Metro area	81.6	8	3	Atlanta-Sandy Springs-Alpharetta, GA Metro area	36.1
63	4	Albany-Schenectady-Troy, NY Metro area	80.8	47	4	New Orleans-Metairie, LA Metro area	35.7
30	5	Cincinnati, OH-KY-IN Metro area	80.3	72	5	Columbia, SC Metro area	35.5
51	6	Grand Rapids-Kentwood, MI Metro area	79.7	37	6	Virginia Beach-Norfolk-Newport News, VA-NC Metro area	32.3
49	7	Buffalo-Cheektowaga, NY Metro area	78.1	50	7	Birmingham-Hoover, AL Metro area	31.4
73	8	Dayton-Kettering, OH Metro area	77.9	20	8	Baltimore-Columbia-Towson, MD Metro area	31.0
70	9	North Port-Sarasota-Bradenton, FL Metro area	77.8	44	9	Richmond, VA Metro area	30.7
52	10	Rochester, NY Metro area	77.7	6	10	Washington-Arlington-Alexandria, DC-VA-MD-WV Metro area	26.8
57	11	Worcester, MA-CT Metro area	77.1	74	11	Charleston-North Charleston, SC Metro area	25.9
58	12	Omaha-Council Bluffs, NE-IA Metro area	76.9	22	12	Charlotte-Concord-Gastonia, NC-SC Metro area	24.3
16	13	Minneapolis-St. Paul-Bloomington, MN Metro area	76.3	14	13	Detroit-Warren-Dearborn, MI Metro area	23.4
45	14	Louisville/Jefferson County, KY-IN Metro area	76.2	39	14	Jacksonville, FL Metro area	22.7
38	15	Providence-Warwick, RI-MA Metro area	75.7	7	15	Philadelphia-Camden-Wilmington, PA-NJ-DE-MD Metro area	21.8
21	16	St. Louis, MO-IL Metro area	75.2	9	16	Miami-Fort Lauderdale-Pompano Beach, FL Metro area	21.1
25	17	Portland-Vancouver-Hillsboro, OR-WA Metro area	75.0	34	16	Cleveland-Elyria, OH Metro area	21.1
31	18	Kansas City, MO-KS Metro area	74.1	41	18	Raleigh-Cary, NC Metro area	20.9
60	19	Greenville-Anderson, SC Metro area	73.5	21	19	St. Louis, MO-IL Metro area	19.3
32	20	Columbus, OH Metro area	73.3	32	20	Columbus, OH Metro area	18.2
35	21	Nashville-Davidson--Murfreesboro--Franklin, TN Metro area	73.1	5	21	Houston-The Woodlands-Sugar Land, TX Metro are	18.1
46	22	Salt Lake City, UT Metro area	72.5	40	22	Milwaukee-Waukesha, WI Metro area	17.7
33	23	Indianapolis-Carmel-Anderson, IN Metro area	72.4	73	22	Dayton-Kettering, OH Metro area	17.7
68	24	Allentown-Bethlehem-Easton, PA-NJ Metro area	71.2	60	24	Greenville-Anderson, SC Metro area	17.5
34	25	Cleveland-Elyria, OH Metro area	70.8	4	25	Dallas-Fort Worth-Arlington, TX Metro area	17.4
11	26	Boston-Cambridge-Newton, MA-NH Metro area	70.6	33	26	Indianapolis-Carmel-Anderson, IN Metro area	17.3
54	27	Tulsa, OK Metro area	69.0	3	27	Chicago-Naperville-Elgin, IL-IN-WI Metro area	17.1
14	28	Detroit-Warren-Dearborn, MI Metro area	67.5	23	28	Orlando-Kissimmee-Sanford, FL Metro area	17.0
42	29	Oklahoma City, OK Metro area	67.3	45	29	Louisville/Jefferson County, KY-IN Metro area	16.9
40	30	Milwaukee-Waukesha, WI Metro area	67.1	1	30	New York-Newark-Jersey City, NY-NJ-PA Metro ar	16.8
48	31	Virginia Beach-Norfolk-Newport News, VA-NC Metro area	66.5	35	31	Nashville-Davidson--Murfreesboro--Franklin, TN Metro area	16.5
74	32	Charleston-North Charleston, SC Metro area	66.2	69	32	New Haven-Milford, CT Metro area	14.6
19	33	Denver-Aurora-Lakewood, CO Metro area	65.3	29	33	Las Vegas-Henderson-Paradise, NV Metro area	14.0
15	34	Seattle-Tacoma-Bellevue, WA Metro area	64.6	30	34	Cincinnati, OH-KY-IN Metro area	13.9
39	35	Jacksonville, FL Metro area	63.5	31	35	Kansas City, MO-KS Metro area	13.7
18	36	Tampa-St. Petersburg-Clearwater, FL Metro area	62.3	18	36	Tampa-St. Petersburg-Clearwater, FL Metro area	13.2
50	36	Birmingham-Hoover, AL Metro area	62.3	49	37	Buffalo-Cheektowaga, NY Metro area	13.0
7	38	Philadelphia-Camden-Wilmington, PA-NJ-DE-MD Metro area	62.1	48	38	Virginia Beach-Norfolk-Newport News, VA-NC Metro area	12.4
41	39	Raleigh-Cary, NC Metro area	61.9	42	39	Oklahoma City, OK Metro area	12.2
69	40	New Haven-Milford, CT Metro area	61.7	52	39	Rochester, NY Metro area	12.2
59	41	Bridgeport-Stamford-Norwalk, CT Metro area	61.1	59	39	Bridgeport-Stamford-Norwalk, CT Metro area	12.2
22	42	Charlotte-Concord-Gastonia, NC-SC Metro area	60.9	16	42	Minneapolis-St. Paul-Bloomington, MN Metro area	10.9
44	43	Richmond, VA Metro area	58.5	27	43	Pittsburgh, PA Metro area	9.9
20	44	Baltimore-Columbia-Towson, MD Metro area	57.1	54	44	Tulsa, OK Metro area	9.8
37	44	Virginia Beach-Norfolk-Newport News, VA-NC Metro area	57.1	63	45	Albany-Schenectady-Troy, NY Metro area	9.6
66	46	Baton Rouge, LA Metro area	56.7	58	46	Omaha-Council Bluffs, NE-IA Metro area	9.0
72	47	Columbia, SC Metro area	56.6	11	47	Boston-Cambridge-Newton, MA-NH Metro area	8.9
10	48	Phoenix-Mesa-Chandler, AZ Metro area	55.7	26	48	Sacramento-Roseville-Folsom, CA Metro area	8.8
26	49	Sacramento-Roseville-Folsom, CA Metro area	53.8	13	49	San Francisco-Oakland-Berkeley, CA Metro area	8.3
3	50	Chicago-Naperville-Elgin, IL-IN-WI Metro area	53.1	51	50	Grand Rapids-Kentwood, MI Metro area	8.2
28	51	Austin-Round Rock-Georgetown, TX Metro area	52.5	12	51	Riverside-San Bernardino-Ontario, CA Metro area	8.1
47	52	New Orleans-Metairie, LA Metro area	52.2	15	51	Seattle-Tacoma-Bellevue, WA Metro area	8.1
53	53	Tucson, AZ Metro area	52.1	28	51	Austin-Round Rock-Georgetown, TX Metro area	8.1
17	54	San Diego-Chula Vista-Carlsbad, CA Metro area	47.0	24	54	San Antonio-New Braunfels, TX Metro area	7.4
8	55	Atlanta-Sandy Springs-Alpharetta, GA Metro area	46.8	38	55	Providence-Warwick, RI-MA Metro area	7.3
6	56	Washington-Arlington-Alexandria, DC-VA-MD-WV Metro area	46.5	2	56	Los Angeles-Long Beach-Anaheim, CA Metro area	7.1
23	57	Orlando-Kissimmee-Sanford, FL Metro area	46.3	70	56	North Port-Sarasota-Bradenton, FL Metro area	7.1
1	58	New York-Newark-Jersey City, NY-NJ-PA Metro ar	46.2	64	58	Knoxville, TN Metro area	6.9
71	59	Oxnard-Thousand Oaks-Ventura, CA Metro area	46.0	10	59	Phoenix-Mesa-Chandler, AZ Metro area	6.8
4	60	Dallas-Fort Worth-Arlington, TX Metro area	45.5	19	60	Denver-Aurora-Lakewood, CO Metro area	6.7
29	61	Las Vegas-Henderson-Paradise, NV Metro area	43.2	68	60	Allentown-Bethlehem-Easton, PA-NJ Metro area	6.7
43	61	Memphis, TN-MS-AR Metro area	43.2	62	62	Bakersfield, CA Metro area	6.0
13	63	San Francisco-Oakland-Berkeley, CA Metro area	40.9	17	63	San Diego-Chula Vista-Carlsbad, CA Metro area	5.8
61	64	Albuquerque, NM Metro area	39.2	57	64	Worcester, MA-CT Metro area	5.7
5	65	Houston-The Woodlands-Sugar Land, TX Metro are	35.5	55	65	Fresno, CA Metro area	5.3
24	66	San Antonio-New Braunfels, TX Metro area	33.8	53	66	Tucson, AZ Metro area	4.4
62	67	Bakersfield, CA Metro area	32.8	25	67	Portland-Vancouver-Hillsboro, OR-WA Metro area	4.3
56	68	Urban Honolulu, HI Metro area	32.1	56	68	Urban Honolulu, HI Metro area	3.6
36	69	San Jose-Sunnyvale-Santa Clara, CA Metro area	31.8	67	68	El Paso, TX Metro area	3.6
12	70	Riverside-San Bernardino-Ontario, CA Metro area	31.0	61	70	Albuquerque, NM Metro area	3.2
2	71	Los Angeles-Long Beach-Anaheim, CA Metro area	30.7	36	71	San Jose-Sunnyvale-Santa Clara, CA Metro area	3.0
9	72	Miami-Fort Lauderdale-Pompano Beach, FL Metro area	30.4	46	72	Salt Lake City, UT Metro area	2.5
55	73	Fresno, CA Metro area	29.0	71	73	Oxnard-Thousand Oaks-Ventura, CA Metro area	2.4
67	74	El Paso, TX Metro area	12.2	75	74	Boise City, ID Metro area	1.6
65	75	McAllen-Edinburg-Mission, TX Metro area	5.9	65	75	McAllen-Edinburg-Mission, TX Metro area	0.6

75 Largest Metropolitan Areas by 2020 Population

Selected Rankings

Percent American Indian, Alaska Native, alone or in combination, 2021

Population rank	American Indian Alaska native rank	Metropolitan area	Percent American Indian, Alaska Native [col 7]
54	1	Tulsa, OK Metro area	13.3
42	2	Oklahoma City, OK Metro area	7.1
61	3	Albuquerque, NM Metro area	6.2
53	4	Tucson, AZ Metro area	3.1
10	5	Phoenix-Mesa-Chandler, AZ Metro area	2.5
15	6	Seattle-Tacoma-Bellevue, WA Metro area	2.0
25	7	Portland-Vancouver-Hillsboro, OR-WA Metro area	1.8
56	8	Urban Honolulu, HI Metro area	1.5
26	9	Sacramento-Roseville-Folsom, CA Metro area	1.4
16	10	Minneapolis-St. Paul-Bloomington, MN Metro area	1.3
75	10	Boise City, ID Metro area	1.3
31	12	Kansas City, MO-KS Metro area	1.2
46	12	Salt Lake City, UT Metro area	1.2
62	12	Bakersfield, CA Metro area	1.2
19	15	Denver-Aurora-Lakewood, CO Metro area	1.1
29	15	Las Vegas-Henderson-Paradise, NV Metro area	1.1
37	15	Virginia Beach-Norfolk-Newport News, VA-NC Metro area	1.1
55	15	Fresno, CA Metro area	1.1
14	19	Detroit-Warren-Dearborn, MI Metro area	1.0
49	19	Buffalo-Cheektowaga, NY Metro area	1.0
58	19	Omaha-Council Bluffs, NE-IA Metro area	1.0
74	19	Charleston-North Charleston, SC Metro area	1.0
12	23	Riverside-San Bernardino-Ontario, CA Metro area	0.9
17	23	San Diego-Chula Vista-Carlsbad, CA Metro area	0.9
22	23	Charlotte-Concord-Gastonia, NC-SC Metro area	0.9
38	23	Providence-Warwick, RI-MA Metro area	0.9
40	23	Milwaukee-Waukesha, WI Metro area	0.9
41	23	Raleigh-Cary, NC Metro area	0.9
44	23	Richmond, VA Metro area	0.9
47	23	New Orleans-Metairie, LA Metro area	0.9
51	23	Grand Rapids-Kentwood, MI Metro area	0.9
64	23	Knoxville, TN Metro area	0.9
71	23	Oxnard-Thousand Oaks-Ventura, CA Metro area	0.9
72	23	Columbia, SC Metro area	0.9
73	23	Dayton-Kettering, OH Metro area	0.9
4	36	Dallas-Fort Worth-Arlington, TX Metro area	0.8
6	36	Washington-Arlington-Alexandria, DC-VA-MD-WV Metro area	0.8
13	36	San Francisco-Oakland-Berkeley, CA Metro area	0.8
20	36	Baltimore-Columbia-Towson, MD Metro area	0.8
28	36	Austin-Round Rock-Georgetown, TX Metro area	0.8
32	36	Columbus, OH Metro area	0.8
35	36	Nashville-Davidson--Murfreesboro--Franklin, TN Metro area	0.8
39	36	Jacksonville, FL Metro area	0.8
8	44	Atlanta-Sandy Springs-Alpharetta, GA Metro area	0.7
18	44	Tampa-St. Petersburg-Clearwater, FL Metro area	0.7
21	44	St. Louis, MO-IL Metro area	0.7
24	44	San Antonio-New Braunfels, TX Metro area	0.7
33	44	Indianapolis-Carmel-Anderson, IN Metro area	0.7
34	44	Cleveland-Elyria, OH Metro area	0.7
36	44	San Jose-Sunnyvale-Santa Clara, CA Metro area	0.7
45	44	Louisville/Jefferson County, KY-IN Metro area	0.7
50	44	Birmingham-Hoover, AL Metro area	0.7
66	44	Baton Rouge, LA Metro area	0.7
2	54	Los Angeles-Long Beach-Anaheim, CA Metro area	0.6
5	54	Houston-The Woodlands-Sugar Land, TX Metro are	0.6
7	54	Philadelphia-Camden-Wilmington, PA-NJ-DE-MD Metro area	0.6
23	54	Orlando-Kissimmee-Sanford, FL Metro area	0.6
30	54	Cincinnati, OH-KY-IN Metro area	0.6
43	54	Memphis, TN-MS-AR Metro area	0.6
48	54	Virginia Beach-Norfolk-Newport News, VA-NC Metro area	0.6
52	54	Rochester, NY Metro area	0.6
57	54	Worcester, MA-CT Metro area	0.6
60	54	Greenville-Anderson, SC Metro area	0.6
63	54	Albany-Schenectady-Troy, NY Metro area	0.6
69	54	New Haven-Milford, CT Metro area	0.6
70	54	North Port-Sarasota-Bradenton, FL Metro area	0.6
1	67	New York-Newark-Jersey City, NY-NJ-PA Metro ar	0.5
3	67	Chicago-Naperville-Elgin, IL-IN-WI Metro area	0.5
11	67	Boston-Cambridge-Newton, MA-NH Metro area	0.5
27	67	Pittsburgh, PA Metro area	0.5
67	67	El Paso, TX Metro area	0.5
68	67	Allentown-Bethlehem-Easton, PA-NJ Metro area	0.5
59	73	Bridgeport-Stamford-Norwalk, CT Metro area	0.4
9	74	Miami-Fort Lauderdale-Pompano Beach, FL Metro area	0.3
65	75	McAllen-Edinburg-Mission, TX Metro area	0.1

Percent Asian and Pacific Islander, alone or in combination, 2021

Population rank	Asian and Pacific Islander rank	Metropolitan area	Percent Asian and Pacific Islander [col 8]
56	1	Urban Honolulu, HI Metro area	79.1
36	2	San Jose-Sunnyvale-Santa Clara, CA Metro area	41.7
13	3	San Francisco-Oakland-Berkeley, CA Metro area	32.2
15	4	Seattle-Tacoma-Bellevue, WA Metro area	20.2
2	5	Los Angeles-Long Beach-Anaheim, CA Metro area	18.8
26	6	Sacramento-Roseville-Folsom, CA Metro area	18.5
17	7	San Diego-Chula Vista-Carlsbad, CA Metro area	15.4
29	8	Las Vegas-Henderson-Paradise, NV Metro area	14.0
1	9	New York-Newark-Jersey City, NY-NJ-PA Metro ar	13.0
6	10	Washington-Arlington-Alexandria, DC-VA-MD-WV Metro area	12.6
55	11	Fresno, CA Metro area	12.0
25	12	Portland-Vancouver-Hillsboro, OR-WA Metro area	10.3
11	13	Boston-Cambridge-Newton, MA-NH Metro area	10.0
71	14	Oxnard-Thousand Oaks-Ventura, CA Metro area	9.5
12	15	Riverside-San Bernardino-Ontario, CA Metro area	9.0
5	16	Houston-The Woodlands-Sugar Land, TX Metro are	8.9
4	17	Dallas-Fort Worth-Arlington, TX Metro area	8.7
16	18	Minneapolis-St. Paul-Bloomington, MN Metro area	8.2
3	19	Chicago-Naperville-Elgin, IL-IN-WI Metro area	8.1
28	19	Austin-Round Rock-Georgetown, TX Metro area	8.1
41	21	Raleigh-Cary, NC Metro area	7.6
7	22	Philadelphia-Camden-Wilmington, PA-NJ-DE-MD Metro area	7.4
8	22	Atlanta-Sandy Springs-Alpharetta, GA Metro area	7.4
46	22	Salt Lake City, UT Metro area	7.4
20	25	Baltimore-Columbia-Towson, MD Metro area	7.3
59	26	Bridgeport-Stamford-Norwalk, CT Metro area	6.7
48	27	Virginia Beach-Norfolk-Newport News, VA-NC Metro area	6.3
19	28	Denver-Aurora-Lakewood, CO Metro area	6.0
32	28	Columbus, OH Metro area	6.0
62	28	Bakersfield, CA Metro area	6.0
14	31	Detroit-Warren-Dearborn, MI Metro area	5.8
37	31	Virginia Beach-Norfolk-Newport News, VA-NC Metro area	5.8
63	31	Albany-Schenectady-Troy, NY Metro area	5.8
57	34	Worcester, MA-CT Metro area	5.7
10	35	Phoenix-Mesa-Chandler, AZ Metro area	5.6
23	36	Orlando-Kissimmee-Sanford, FL Metro area	5.5
39	36	Jacksonville, FL Metro area	5.5
44	38	Richmond, VA Metro area	5.3
22	39	Charlotte-Concord-Gastonia, NC-SC Metro area	5.0
40	39	Milwaukee-Waukesha, WI Metro area	5.0
69	39	New Haven-Milford, CT Metro area	5.0
18	42	Tampa-St. Petersburg-Clearwater, FL Metro area	4.7
33	42	Indianapolis-Carmel-Anderson, IN Metro area	4.7
49	44	Buffalo-Cheektowaga, NY Metro area	4.5
42	45	Oklahoma City, OK Metro area	4.4
31	46	Kansas City, MO-KS Metro area	4.2
58	46	Omaha-Council Bluffs, NE-IA Metro area	4.2
53	48	Tucson, AZ Metro area	4.1
38	49	Providence-Warwick, RI-MA Metro area	4.0
35	50	Nashville-Davidson--Murfreesboro--Franklin, TN Metro area	3.9
75	51	Boise City, ID Metro area	3.8
21	52	St. Louis, MO-IL Metro area	3.7
30	52	Cincinnati, OH-KY-IN Metro area	3.7
52	52	Rochester, NY Metro area	3.7
54	52	Tulsa, OK Metro area	3.7
68	52	Allentown-Bethlehem-Easton, PA-NJ Metro area	3.7
24	57	San Antonio-New Braunfels, TX Metro area	3.6
47	58	New Orleans-Metairie, LA Metro area	3.5
51	58	Grand Rapids-Kentwood, MI Metro area	3.5
9	60	Miami-Fort Lauderdale-Pompano Beach, FL Metro area	3.3
27	60	Pittsburgh, PA Metro area	3.3
61	60	Albuquerque, NM Metro area	3.3
73	60	Dayton-Kettering, OH Metro area	3.3
34	64	Cleveland-Elyria, OH Metro area	3.2
72	64	Columbia, SC Metro area	3.2
74	66	Charleston-North Charleston, SC Metro area	3.1
45	67	Louisville/Jefferson County, KY-IN Metro area	3.0
43	68	Memphis, TN-MS-AR Metro area	2.8
60	69	Greenville-Anderson, SC Metro area	2.7
70	69	North Port-Sarasota-Bradenton, FL Metro area	2.7
66	71	Baton Rouge, LA Metro area	2.6
64	72	Knoxville, TN Metro area	2.3
50	73	Birmingham-Hoover, AL Metro area	2.1
67	74	El Paso, TX Metro area	1.7
65	75	McAllen-Edinburg-Mission, TX Metro area	1.0

75 Largest Metropolitan Areas by 2020 Population

Selected Rankings

Percent Hispanic or Latino[1], 2021

Population rank	Hispanic or Latino rank	Metropolitan area	Percent Hispanic or Latino [col 9]
65	1	McAllen-Edinburg-Mission, TX Metro area	92.6
67	2	El Paso, TX Metro area	82.9
24	3	San Antonio-New Braunfels, TX Metro area	56.2
62	4	Bakersfield, CA Metro area	56.1
55	5	Fresno, CA Metro area	54.7
12	6	Riverside-San Bernardino-Ontario, CA Metro area	53.6
61	7	Albuquerque, NM Metro area	50.1
9	8	Miami-Fort Lauderdale-Pompano Beach, FL Metro area	46.2
2	9	Los Angeles-Long Beach-Anaheim, CA Metro area	45.4
71	10	Oxnard-Thousand Oaks-Ventura, CA Metro area	44.1
5	11	Houston-The Woodlands-Sugar Land, TX Metro are	38.6
53	12	Tucson, AZ Metro area	38.5
17	13	San Diego-Chula Vista-Carlsbad, CA Metro area	34.8
28	14	Austin-Round Rock-Georgetown, TX Metro area	32.8
23	15	Orlando-Kissimmee-Sanford, FL Metro area	32.6
29	16	Las Vegas-Henderson-Paradise, NV Metro area	32.3
10	17	Phoenix-Mesa-Chandler, AZ Metro area	31.9
4	18	Dallas-Fort Worth-Arlington, TX Metro area	29.6
36	19	San Jose-Sunnyvale-Santa Clara, CA Metro area	26.3
1	20	New York-Newark-Jersey City, NY-NJ-PA Metro ar	25.3
19	21	Denver-Aurora-Lakewood, CO Metro area	23.6
3	22	Chicago-Naperville-Elgin, IL-IN-WI Metro area	23.1
26	23	Sacramento-Roseville-Folsom, CA Metro area	22.7
13	24	San Francisco-Oakland-Berkeley, CA Metro area	22.3
18	25	Tampa-St. Petersburg-Clearwater, FL Metro area	21.3
59	25	Bridgeport-Stamford-Norwalk, CT Metro area	21.3
69	27	New Haven-Milford, CT Metro area	20.2
68	28	Allentown-Bethlehem-Easton, PA-NJ Metro area	19.6
46	29	Salt Lake City, UT Metro area	19.0
6	30	Washington-Arlington-Alexandria, DC-VA-MD-WV Metro area	16.7
48	31	Virginia Beach-Norfolk-Newport News, VA-NC Metro area	16.2
38	32	Providence-Warwick, RI-MA Metro area	14.4
42	32	Oklahoma City, OK Metro area	14.4
75	32	Boise City, ID Metro area	14.4
70	35	North Port-Sarasota-Bradenton, FL Metro area	13.4
25	36	Portland-Vancouver-Hillsboro, OR-WA Metro area	13.0
57	37	Worcester, MA-CT Metro area	12.8
11	38	Boston-Cambridge-Newton, MA-NH Metro area	12.0
40	39	Milwaukee-Waukesha, WI Metro area	11.6
58	40	Omaha-Council Bluffs, NE-IA Metro area	11.5
8	41	Atlanta-Sandy Springs-Alpharetta, GA Metro area	11.3
22	42	Charlotte-Concord-Gastonia, NC-SC Metro area	11.1
41	42	Raleigh-Cary, NC Metro area	11.1
54	44	Tulsa, OK Metro area	11.0
15	45	Seattle-Tacoma-Bellevue, WA Metro area	10.9
7	46	Philadelphia-Camden-Wilmington, PA-NJ-DE-MD Metro area	10.4
56	46	Urban Honolulu, HI Metro area	10.4
39	48	Jacksonville, FL Metro area	10.3
51	49	Grand Rapids-Kentwood, MI Metro area	10.2
31	50	Kansas City, MO-KS Metro area	9.7
47	51	New Orleans-Metairie, LA Metro area	9.4
52	52	Rochester, NY Metro area	8.1
35	53	Nashville-Davidson--Murfreesboro--Franklin, TN Metro area	8.0
60	54	Greenville-Anderson, SC Metro area	7.7
37	55	Virginia Beach-Norfolk-Newport News, VA-NC Metro area	7.6
33	56	Indianapolis-Carmel-Anderson, IN Metro area	7.4
44	57	Richmond, VA Metro area	7.2
20	58	Baltimore-Columbia-Towson, MD Metro area	6.7
34	59	Cleveland-Elyria, OH Metro area	6.5
16	60	Minneapolis-St. Paul-Bloomington, MN Metro area	6.2
74	60	Charleston-North Charleston, SC Metro area	6.2
43	62	Memphis, TN-MS-AR Metro area	6.1
72	62	Columbia, SC Metro area	6.1
45	64	Louisville/Jefferson County, KY-IN Metro area	5.7
63	64	Albany-Schenectady-Troy, NY Metro area	5.7
49	66	Buffalo-Cheektowaga, NY Metro area	5.5
14	67	Detroit-Warren-Dearborn, MI Metro area	4.9
50	67	Birmingham-Hoover, AL Metro area	4.9
32	69	Columbus, OH Metro area	4.7
66	70	Baton Rouge, LA Metro area	4.6
64	71	Knoxville, TN Metro area	4.5
30	72	Cincinnati, OH-KY-IN Metro area	3.7
21	73	St. Louis, MO-IL Metro area	3.4
73	74	Dayton-Kettering, OH Metro area	3.3
27	75	Pittsburgh, PA Metro area	2.0

Percent under 18 years old, 2021

Population rank	Under 18 years old rank	Metropolitan area	Percent Under 18 years old [cols 10 and 11]
65	1	McAllen-Edinburg-Mission, TX Metro area	26.1
62	2	Bakersfield, CA Metro area	23.8
55	3	Fresno, CA Metro area	23.4
67	4	El Paso, TX Metro area	21.9
5	5	Houston-The Woodlands-Sugar Land, TX Metro are	21.7
46	6	Salt Lake City, UT Metro area	21.6
58	7	Omaha-Council Bluffs, NE-IA Metro area	21.0
4	8	Dallas-Fort Worth-Arlington, TX Metro area	20.9
12	9	Riverside-San Bernardino-Ontario, CA Metro area	20.7
43	10	Memphis, TN-MS-AR Metro area	20.6
24	11	San Antonio-New Braunfels, TX Metro area	20.4
54	12	Tulsa, OK Metro area	20.2
33	13	Indianapolis-Carmel-Anderson, IN Metro area	20.1
42	13	Oklahoma City, OK Metro area	20.1
31	15	Kansas City, MO-KS Metro area	19.6
32	16	Columbus, OH Metro area	19.5
75	17	Boise City, ID Metro area	19.4
8	18	Atlanta-Sandy Springs-Alpharetta, GA Metro area	19.3
16	18	Minneapolis-St. Paul-Bloomington, MN Metro area	19.3
51	18	Grand Rapids-Kentwood, MI Metro area	19.3
66	18	Baton Rouge, LA Metro area	19.3
30	22	Cincinnati, OH-KY-IN Metro area	19.1
41	22	Raleigh-Cary, NC Metro area	19.1
22	24	Charlotte-Concord-Gastonia, NC-SC Metro area	19.0
6	25	Washington-Arlington-Alexandria, DC-VA-MD-WV Metro area	18.9
50	25	Birmingham-Hoover, AL Metro area	18.9
10	27	Phoenix-Mesa-Chandler, AZ Metro area	18.8
29	27	Las Vegas-Henderson-Paradise, NV Metro area	18.8
35	27	Nashville-Davidson--Murfreesboro--Franklin, TN Metro area	18.8
40	27	Milwaukee-Waukesha, WI Metro area	18.8
26	31	Sacramento-Roseville-Folsom, CA Metro area	18.5
39	31	Jacksonville, FL Metro area	18.5
28	33	Austin-Round Rock-Georgetown, TX Metro area	18.4
47	33	New Orleans-Metairie, LA Metro area	18.4
3	35	Chicago-Naperville-Elgin, IL-IN-WI Metro area	18.3
37	35	Virginia Beach-Norfolk-Newport News, VA-NC Metro area	18.3
45	35	Louisville/Jefferson County, KY-IN Metro area	18.3
60	38	Greenville-Anderson, SC Metro area	18.2
73	38	Dayton-Kettering, OH Metro area	18.2
20	40	Baltimore-Columbia-Towson, MD Metro area	18.1
21	40	St. Louis, MO-IL Metro area	18.1
71	40	Oxnard-Thousand Oaks-Ventura, CA Metro area	18.1
72	43	Columbia, SC Metro area	18.0
14	44	Detroit-Warren-Dearborn, MI Metro area	17.9
74	44	Charleston-North Charleston, SC Metro area	17.9
56	46	Urban Honolulu, HI Metro area	17.8
1	47	New York-Newark-Jersey City, NY-NJ-PA Metro ar	17.7
7	47	Philadelphia-Camden-Wilmington, PA-NJ-DE-MD Metro area	17.7
17	47	San Diego-Chula Vista-Carlsbad, CA Metro area	17.7
23	47	Orlando-Kissimmee-Sanford, FL Metro area	17.7
59	47	Bridgeport-Stamford-Norwalk, CT Metro area	17.7
15	52	Seattle-Tacoma-Bellevue, WA Metro area	17.6
19	52	Denver-Aurora-Lakewood, CO Metro area	17.6
44	52	Richmond, VA Metro area	17.6
2	55	Los Angeles-Long Beach-Anaheim, CA Metro area	17.4
36	55	San Jose-Sunnyvale-Santa Clara, CA Metro area	17.4
61	55	Albuquerque, NM Metro area	17.4
25	58	Portland-Vancouver-Hillsboro, OR-WA Metro area	17.0
34	58	Cleveland-Elyria, OH Metro area	17.0
68	58	Allentown-Bethlehem-Easton, PA-NJ Metro area	17.0
64	61	Knoxville, TN Metro area	16.7
9	62	Miami-Fort Lauderdale-Pompano Beach, FL Metro area	16.6
49	62	Buffalo-Cheektowaga, NY Metro area	16.6
52	62	Rochester, NY Metro area	16.6
53	62	Tucson, AZ Metro area	16.6
57	62	Worcester, MA-CT Metro area	16.6
18	67	Tampa-St. Petersburg-Clearwater, FL Metro area	16.2
69	67	New Haven-Milford, CT Metro area	16.2
13	69	San Francisco-Oakland-Berkeley, CA Metro area	16.1
48	69	Virginia Beach-Norfolk-Newport News, VA-NC Metro area	16.1
38	71	Providence-Warwick, RI-MA Metro area	16.0
11	72	Boston-Cambridge-Newton, MA-NH Metro area	15.9
63	73	Albany-Schenectady-Troy, NY Metro area	15.8
27	74	Pittsburgh, PA Metro area	15.6
70	75	North Port-Sarasota-Bradenton, FL Metro area	12.8

1. Persons of Hispanic Origin

75 Largest Metropolitan Areas by 2020 Population

Selected Rankings

Percent 65 years old and over, 2021				Percent female family households, 2016-2020 (no spouse present)			
Population rank	65 years old and over rank	Metropolitan area	Percent 65 years old and over [cols 17 + 18]	Population rank	Single-parent households rank	Metropolitan area	Percent single-parent households [col 30]
70	1	North Port-Sarasota-Bradenton, FL Metro area	33.0	65	1	McAllen-Edinburg-Mission, TX Metro area	21.8
27	2	Pittsburgh, PA Metro area	20.9	67	2	El Paso, TX Metro area	18.8
53	3	Tucson, AZ Metro area	20.6	43	3	Memphis, TN-MS-AR Metro area	18.3
18	4	Tampa-St. Petersburg-Clearwater, FL Metro area	20.2	55	4	Fresno, CA Metro area	17.1
34	5	Cleveland-Elyria, OH Metro area	19.4	62	5	Bakersfield, CA Metro area	16.1
9	6	Miami-Fort Lauderdale-Pompano Beach, FL Metro area	19.0	47	6	New Orleans-Metairie, LA Metro area	15.5
49	6	Buffalo-Cheektowaga, NY Metro area	19.0	72	6	Columbia, SC Metro area	15.5
52	8	Rochester, NY Metro area	18.9	66	8	Baton Rouge, LA Metro area	15.4
64	8	Knoxville, TN Metro area	18.9	9	9	Miami-Fort Lauderdale-Pompano Beach, FL Metro area	15.3
56	10	Urban Honolulu, HI Metro area	18.8	24	10	San Antonio-New Braunfels, TX Metro area	14.8
68	11	Allentown-Bethlehem-Easton, PA-NJ Metro area	18.7	12	11	Riverside-San Bernardino-Ontario, CA Metro area	14.7
63	12	Albany-Schenectady-Troy, NY Metro area	18.4	8	12	Atlanta-Sandy Springs-Alpharetta, GA Metro area	14.5
73	13	Dayton-Kettering, OH Metro area	18.3	1	13	New York-Newark-Jersey City, NY-NJ-PA Metro ar	14.4
48	14	Virginia Beach-Norfolk-Newport News, VA-NC Metro area	18.1	37	13	Virginia Beach-Norfolk-Newport News, VA-NC Metro area	14.4
69	14	New Haven-Milford, CT Metro area	18.1	20	15	Baltimore-Columbia-Towson, MD Metro area	14.2
38	16	Providence-Warwick, RI-MA Metro area	18.0	29	16	Las Vegas-Henderson-Paradise, NV Metro area	14.1
61	17	Albuquerque, NM Metro area	17.8	50	17	Birmingham-Hoover, AL Metro area	14.0
21	18	St. Louis, MO-IL Metro area	17.5	69	17	New Haven-Milford, CT Metro area	14.0
14	19	Detroit-Warren-Dearborn, MI Metro area	17.3	2	19	Los Angeles-Long Beach-Anaheim, CA Metro area	13.9
47	20	New Orleans-Metairie, LA Metro area	17.2	5	19	Houston-The Woodlands-Sugar Land, TX Metro are	13.9
60	20	Greenville-Anderson, SC Metro area	17.2	7	19	Philadelphia-Camden-Wilmington, PA-NJ-DE-MD Metro area	13.9
7	22	Philadelphia-Camden-Wilmington, PA-NJ-DE-MD Metro area	16.8	23	22	Orlando-Kissimmee-Sanford, FL Metro area	13.6
45	22	Louisville/Jefferson County, KY-IN Metro area	16.8	38	22	Providence-Warwick, RI-MA Metro area	13.6
50	22	Birmingham-Hoover, AL Metro area	16.8	14	24	Detroit-Warren-Dearborn, MI Metro area	13.5
1	25	New York-Newark-Jersey City, NY-NJ-PA Metro ar	16.7	39	24	Jacksonville, FL Metro area	13.5
13	25	San Francisco-Oakland-Berkeley, CA Metro area	16.7	61	24	Albuquerque, NM Metro area	13.5
57	25	Worcester, MA-CT Metro area	16.7	34	27	Cleveland-Elyria, OH Metro area	13.3
71	25	Oxnard-Thousand Oaks-Ventura, CA Metro area	16.7	44	28	Richmond, VA Metro area	13.2
39	29	Jacksonville, FL Metro area	16.6	4	29	Dallas-Fort Worth-Arlington, TX Metro area	13.0
11	30	Boston-Cambridge-Newton, MA-NH Metro area	16.5	73	30	Dayton-Kettering, OH Metro area	12.9
40	30	Milwaukee-Waukesha, WI Metro area	16.5	22	31	Charlotte-Concord-Gastonia, NC-SC Metro area	12.8
44	30	Richmond, VA Metro area	16.5	52	31	Rochester, NY Metro area	12.8
59	30	Bridgeport-Stamford-Norwalk, CT Metro area	16.5	49	33	Buffalo-Cheektowaga, NY Metro area	12.7
10	34	Phoenix-Mesa-Chandler, AZ Metro area	16.3	3	34	Chicago-Naperville-Elgin, IL-IN-WI Metro area	12.6
20	34	Baltimore-Columbia-Towson, MD Metro area	16.3	45	34	Louisville/Jefferson County, KY-IN Metro area	12.6
74	36	Charleston-North Charleston, SC Metro area	16.2	48	34	Virginia Beach-Norfolk-Newport News, VA-NC Metro area	12.6
26	37	Sacramento-Roseville-Folsom, CA Metro area	16.1	21	37	St. Louis, MO-IL Metro area	12.5
30	37	Cincinnati, OH-KY-IN Metro area	16.1	32	38	Columbus, OH Metro area	12.4
54	37	Tulsa, OK Metro area	16.1	53	38	Tucson, AZ Metro area	12.4
25	40	Portland-Vancouver-Hillsboro, OR-WA Metro area	15.9	60	38	Greenville-Anderson, SC Metro area	12.4
72	41	Columbia, SC Metro area	15.8	26	41	Sacramento-Roseville-Folsom, CA Metro area	12.3
31	42	Kansas City, MO-KS Metro area	15.7	40	41	Milwaukee-Waukesha, WI Metro area	12.3
3	43	Chicago-Naperville-Elgin, IL-IN-WI Metro area	15.6	74	41	Charleston-North Charleston, SC Metro area	12.3
37	43	Virginia Beach-Norfolk-Newport News, VA-NC Metro area	15.6	42	44	Oklahoma City, OK Metro area	12.2
23	45	Orlando-Kissimmee-Sanford, FL Metro area	15.5	56	44	Urban Honolulu, HI Metro area	12.2
29	45	Las Vegas-Henderson-Paradise, NV Metro area	15.5	10	46	Phoenix-Mesa-Chandler, AZ Metro area	12.1
75	45	Boise City, ID Metro area	15.5	18	46	Tampa-St. Petersburg-Clearwater, FL Metro area	12.1
51	48	Grand Rapids-Kentwood, MI Metro area	15.2	30	46	Cincinnati, OH-KY-IN Metro area	12.1
66	48	Baton Rouge, LA Metro area	15.2	54	46	Tulsa, OK Metro area	12.1
16	50	Minneapolis-St. Paul-Bloomington, MN Metro area	15.0	57	50	Worcester, MA-CT Metro area	12.0
2	51	Los Angeles-Long Beach-Anaheim, CA Metro area	14.9	59	51	Bridgeport-Stamford-Norwalk, CT Metro area	11.9
17	52	San Diego-Chula Vista-Carlsbad, CA Metro area	14.8	68	52	Allentown-Bethlehem-Easton, PA-NJ Metro area	11.8
43	52	Memphis, TN-MS-AR Metro area	14.8	71	52	Oxnard-Thousand Oaks-Ventura, CA Metro area	11.8
42	54	Oklahoma City, OK Metro area	14.6	33	54	Indianapolis-Carmel-Anderson, IN Metro area	11.7
36	55	San Jose-Sunnyvale-Santa Clara, CA Metro area	14.5	6	55	Washington-Arlington-Alexandria, DC-VA-MD-WV Metro area	11.6
58	55	Omaha-Council Bluffs, NE-IA Metro area	14.5	17	55	San Diego-Chula Vista-Carlsbad, CA Metro area	11.6
22	57	Charlotte-Concord-Gastonia, NC-SC Metro area	14.3	35	57	Nashville-Davidson--Murfreesboro--Franklin, TN Metro area	11.5
33	57	Indianapolis-Carmel-Anderson, IN Metro area	14.3	31	58	Kansas City, MO-KS Metro area	11.4
6	59	Washington-Arlington-Alexandria, DC-VA-MD-WV Metro area	14.0	63	59	Albany-Schenectady-Troy, NY Metro area	11.2
15	59	Seattle-Tacoma-Bellevue, WA Metro area	14.0	11	60	Boston-Cambridge-Newton, MA-NH Metro area	11.1
32	59	Columbus, OH Metro area	14.0	41	61	Raleigh-Cary, NC Metro area	11.0
35	59	Nashville-Davidson--Murfreesboro--Franklin, TN Metro area	14.0	64	62	Knoxville, TN Metro area	10.9
19	63	Denver-Aurora-Lakewood, CO Metro area	13.8	58	63	Omaha-Council Bluffs, NE-IA Metro area	10.4
24	64	San Antonio-New Braunfels, TX Metro area	13.6	13	64	San Francisco-Oakland-Berkeley, CA Metro area	10.3
12	65	Riverside-San Bernardino-Ontario, CA Metro area	13.5	27	65	Pittsburgh, PA Metro area	10.1
8	66	Atlanta-Sandy Springs-Alpharetta, GA Metro area	13.2	46	65	Salt Lake City, UT Metro area	10.1
41	67	Raleigh-Cary, NC Metro area	13.0	36	67	San Jose-Sunnyvale-Santa Clara, CA Metro area	10.0
67	68	El Paso, TX Metro area	12.8	28	68	Austin-Round Rock-Georgetown, TX Metro area	9.9
55	69	Fresno, CA Metro area	12.6	51	69	Grand Rapids-Kentwood, MI Metro area	9.7
5	70	Houston-The Woodlands-Sugar Land, TX Metro are	11.9	25	70	Portland-Vancouver-Hillsboro, OR-WA Metro area	9.6
4	71	Dallas-Fort Worth-Arlington, TX Metro area	11.8	16	71	Minneapolis-St. Paul-Bloomington, MN Metro area	9.4
28	72	Austin-Round Rock-Georgetown, TX Metro area	11.7	19	72	Denver-Aurora-Lakewood, CO Metro area	9.3
46	73	Salt Lake City, UT Metro area	11.5	15	73	Seattle-Tacoma-Bellevue, WA Metro area	9.1
62	74	Bakersfield, CA Metro area	11.4	70	74	North Port-Sarasota-Bradenton, FL Metro area	9.0
65	74	McAllen-Edinburg-Mission, TX Metro area	11.4	75	75	Boise City, ID Metro area	8.9

75 Largest Metropolitan Areas by 2020 Population

Selected Rankings

Birth rate, 2021				Percent under 65 who have no health insurance, 2019			
Population rank	Birth rate rank	Metropolitan area	Births (per 1,000 population) [col 36]	Population rank	No health insurance rank	Metropolitan area	Percent with no health insurance [col 40]
65	1	McAllen-Edinburg-Mission, TX Metro area	15.1	65	1	McAllen-Edinburg-Mission, TX Metro area	33.2
55	2	Fresno, CA Metro area	13.7	67	2	El Paso, TX Metro area	24.4
62	3	Bakersfield, CA Metro area	13.5	5	3	Houston-The Woodlands-Sugar Land, TX Metro are	21.7
46	4	Salt Lake City, UT Metro area	12.8	4	4	Dallas-Fort Worth-Arlington, TX Metro area	19.5
67	5	El Paso, TX Metro area	12.7	24	5	San Antonio-New Braunfels, TX Metro area	18.6
5	6	Houston-The Woodlands-Sugar Land, TX Metro are	12.6	9	6	Miami-Fort Lauderdale-Pompano Beach, FL Metro area	18.5
43	6	Memphis, TN-MS-AR Metro area	12.6	70	7	North Port-Sarasota-Bradenton, FL Metro area	16.4
58	8	Omaha-Council Bluffs, NE-IA Metro area	12.4	54	8	Tulsa, OK Metro area	16.2
4	9	Dallas-Fort Worth-Arlington, TX Metro area	12.2	28	9	Austin-Round Rock-Georgetown, TX Metro area	15.8
32	10	Columbus, OH Metro area	12.0	18	10	Tampa-St. Petersburg-Clearwater, FL Metro area	15.2
24	11	San Antonio-New Braunfels, TX Metro area	11.9	8	11	Atlanta-Sandy Springs-Alpharetta, GA Metro area	15.1
42	11	Oklahoma City, OK Metro area	11.9	42	12	Oklahoma City, OK Metro area	14.9
54	11	Tulsa, OK Metro area	11.9	23	13	Orlando-Kissimmee-Sanford, FL Metro area	14.8
33	14	Indianapolis-Carmel-Anderson, IN Metro area	11.8	29	14	Las Vegas-Henderson-Paradise, NV Metro area	13.7
66	14	Baton Rouge, LA Metro area	11.8	39	15	Jacksonville, FL Metro area	13.3
12	16	Riverside-San Bernardino-Ontario, CA Metro are	11.7	53	15	Tucson, AZ Metro area	13.3
35	16	Nashville-Davidson--Murfreesboro--Franklin, TN	11.7	60	15	Greenville-Anderson, SC Metro area	13.3
47	18	New Orleans-Metairie, LA Metro area	11.6	10	18	Phoenix-Mesa-Chandler, AZ Metro area	13.2
6	19	Washington-Arlington-Alexandria, DC-VA-MD-WV M	11.5	43	19	Memphis, TN-MS-AR Metro area	12.8
30	19	Cincinnati, OH-KY-IN Metro area	11.5	22	20	Charlotte-Concord-Gastonia, NC-SC Metro area	12.7
31	19	Kansas City, MO-KS Metro area	11.5	74	21	Charleston-North Charleston, SC Metro area	12.6
37	19	Virginia Beach-Norfolk-Newport News, VA-NC Met	11.5	72	22	Columbia, SC Metro area	12.0
74	19	Charleston-North Charleston, SC Metro area	11.5	75	23	Boise City, ID Metro area	11.6
40	24	Milwaukee-Waukesha, WI Metro area	11.4	64	24	Knoxville, TN Metro area	11.4
50	24	Birmingham-Hoover, AL Metro area	11.4	46	25	Salt Lake City, UT Metro area	11.3
17	26	San Diego-Chula Vista-Carlsbad, CA Metro area	11.3	35	26	Nashville-Davidson--Murfreesboro--Franklin, TN Metro area	11.1
56	26	Urban Honolulu, HI Metro area	11.3	41	27	Raleigh-Cary, NC Metro area	10.9
16	28	Minneapolis-St. Paul-Bloomington, MN Metro are	11.2	61	28	Albuquerque, NM Metro area	10.8
22	28	Charlotte-Concord-Gastonia, NC-SC Metro area	11.2	47	29	New Orleans-Metairie, LA Metro area	10.7
29	28	Las Vegas-Henderson-Paradise, NV Metro area	11.2	2	30	Los Angeles-Long Beach-Anaheim, CA Metro area	10.6
45	28	Louisville/Jefferson County, KY-IN Metro area	11.2	31	30	Kansas City, MO-KS Metro area	10.6
51	28	Grand Rapids-Kentwood, MI Metro area	11.2	50	30	Birmingham-Hoover, AL Metro area	10.6
8	33	Atlanta-Sandy Springs-Alpharetta, GA Metro are	11.1	71	33	Oxnard-Thousand Oaks-Ventura, CA Metro area	10.4
10	34	Phoenix-Mesa-Chandler, AZ Metro area	11.0	12	34	Riverside-San Bernardino-Ontario, CA Metro area	9.9
28	34	Austin-Round Rock-Georgetown, TX Metro area	11.0	33	34	Indianapolis-Carmel-Anderson, IN Metro area	9.9
39	34	Jacksonville, FL Metro area	11.0	55	36	Fresno, CA Metro area	9.7
73	34	Dayton-Kettering, OH Metro area	11.0	66	36	Baton Rouge, LA Metro area	9.7
20	38	Baltimore-Columbia-Towson, MD Metro area	10.9	3	38	Chicago-Naperville-Elgin, IL-IN-WI Metro area	9.5
1	39	New York-Newark-Jersey City, NY-NJ-PA Metro ar	10.8	44	39	Richmond, VA Metro area	9.3
19	39	Denver-Aurora-Lakewood, CO Metro area	10.8	59	39	Bridgeport-Stamford-Norwalk, CT Metro area	9.3
41	39	Raleigh-Cary, NC Metro area	10.8	62	39	Bakersfield, CA Metro area	9.3
15	42	Seattle-Tacoma-Bellevue, WA Metro area	10.7	19	42	Denver-Aurora-Lakewood, CO Metro area	9.0
21	42	St. Louis, MO-IL Metro area	10.7	17	43	San Diego-Chula Vista-Carlsbad, CA Metro area	8.9
60	42	Greenville-Anderson, SC Metro area	10.7	21	44	St. Louis, MO-IL Metro area	8.6
72	42	Columbia, SC Metro area	10.7	37	44	Virginia Beach-Norfolk-Newport News, VA-NC Metro area	8.6
14	46	Detroit-Warren-Dearborn, MI Metro area	10.6	58	46	Omaha-Council Bluffs, NE-IA Metro area	8.5
44	46	Richmond, VA Metro area	10.6	73	47	Dayton-Kettering, OH Metro area	8.2
75	46	Boise City, ID Metro area	10.6	6	48	Washington-Arlington-Alexandria, DC-VA-MD-WV Metro area	8.1
3	49	Chicago-Naperville-Elgin, IL-IN-WI Metro area	10.5	32	49	Columbus, OH Metro area	8.0
26	49	Sacramento-Roseville-Folsom, CA Metro area	10.5	1	50	New York-Newark-Jersey City, NY-NJ-PA Metro ar	7.9
7	51	Philadelphia-Camden-Wilmington, PA-NJ-DE-MD Me	10.4	25	51	Portland-Vancouver-Hillsboro, OR-WA Metro area	7.6
23	51	Orlando-Kissimmee-Sanford, FL Metro area	10.4	45	52	Louisville/Jefferson County, KY-IN Metro area	7.4
36	51	San Jose-Sunnyvale-Santa Clara, CA Metro area	10.4	34	53	Cleveland-Elyria, OH Metro area	7.3
9	54	Miami-Fort Lauderdale-Pompano Beach, FL Metro	10.2	30	54	Cincinnati, OH-KY-IN Metro area	7.1
2	55	Los Angeles-Long Beach-Anaheim, CA Metro area	10.1	68	54	Allentown-Bethlehem-Easton, PA-NJ Metro area	7.1
34	55	Cleveland-Elyria, OH Metro area	10.1	51	56	Grand Rapids-Kentwood, MI Metro area	7.0
13	57	San Francisco-Oakland-Berkeley, CA Metro area	10.0	69	56	New Haven-Milford, CT Metro area	7.0
71	57	Oxnard-Thousand Oaks-Ventura, CA Metro area	10.0	7	58	Philadelphia-Camden-Wilmington, PA-NJ-DE-MD Metro area	6.8
64	59	Knoxville, TN Metro area	9.8	14	58	Detroit-Warren-Dearborn, MI Metro area	6.8
11	60	Boston-Cambridge-Newton, MA-NH Metro area	9.7	15	58	Seattle-Tacoma-Bellevue, WA Metro area	6.8
52	60	Rochester, NY Metro area	9.7	40	58	Milwaukee-Waukesha, WI Metro area	6.8
61	60	Albuquerque, NM Metro area	9.7	26	62	Sacramento-Roseville-Folsom, CA Metro area	6.5
18	63	Tampa-St. Petersburg-Clearwater, FL Metro area	9.6	20	63	Baltimore-Columbia-Towson, MD Metro area	5.9
25	63	Portland-Vancouver-Hillsboro, OR-WA Metro area	9.6	13	64	San Francisco-Oakland-Berkeley, CA Metro area	5.6
49	63	Buffalo-Cheektowaga, NY Metro area	9.6	36	64	San Jose-Sunnyvale-Santa Clara, CA Metro area	5.6
53	66	Tucson, AZ Metro area	9.5	48	64	Virginia Beach-Norfolk-Newport News, VA-NC Metro area	5.6
59	66	Bridgeport-Stamford-Norwalk, CT Metro area	9.5	16	67	Minneapolis-St. Paul-Bloomington, MN Metro area	5.4
68	66	Allentown-Bethlehem-Easton, PA-NJ Metro area	9.5	27	67	Pittsburgh, PA Metro area	5.4
27	69	Pittsburgh, PA Metro area	9.3	38	69	Providence-Warwick, RI-MA Metro area	4.6
57	69	Worcester, MA-CT Metro area	9.3	52	70	Rochester, NY Metro area	4.4
63	71	Albany-Schenectady-Troy, NY Metro area	9.2	56	70	Urban Honolulu, HI Metro area	4.4
69	71	New Haven-Milford, CT Metro area	9.2	49	72	Buffalo-Cheektowaga, NY Metro area	4.1
38	73	Providence-Warwick, RI-MA Metro area	9.0	63	72	Albany-Schenectady-Troy, NY Metro area	4.1
48	73	Hartford-East Hartford-Middletown, CT Metro ar	9.0	57	74	Worcester, MA-CT Metro area	3.9
70	75	North Port-Sarasota-Bradenton, FL Metro area	7.2	11	75	Boston-Cambridge-Newton, MA-NH Metro area	3.7

75 Largest Metropolitan Areas by 2020 Population

Selected Rankings

Percent college graduates (bachelor's degree or more), 2,016-2,020				Median household income, 2016-2020			
Population rank	Percent college graduates rank	Metropolitan area	Percent college graduates [col 51]	Population rank	Median income rank	Metropolitan area	Median income (dollars) [col 55]
36	1	San Jose-Sunnyvale-Santa Clara, CA Metro area	52.5	36	1	San Jose-Sunnyvale-Santa Clara, CA Metro area	$1,29,343
6	2	Washington-Arlington-Alexandria, DC-VA-MD-WV Metro area	51.7	13	2	San Francisco-Oakland-Berkeley, CA Metro area	$1,10,837
13	3	San Francisco-Oakland-Berkeley, CA Metro area	50.7	6	3	Washington-Arlington-Alexandria, DC-VA-MD-WV Metro area	$1,06,415
11	4	Boston-Cambridge-Newton, MA-NH Metro area	48.9	59	4	Bridgeport-Stamford-Norwalk, CT Metro area	$97,539
59	4	Bridgeport-Stamford-Norwalk, CT Metro area	48.9	11	5	Boston-Cambridge-Newton, MA-NH Metro area	$93,537
41	6	Raleigh-Cary, NC Metro area	47.8	15	6	Seattle-Tacoma-Bellevue, WA Metro area	$90,790
28	7	Austin-Round Rock-Georgetown, TX Metro area	46.0	71	7	Oxnard-Thousand Oaks-Ventura, CA Metro area	$89,295
19	8	Denver-Aurora-Lakewood, CO Metro area	44.7	56	8	Urban Honolulu, HI Metro area	$87,722
15	9	Seattle-Tacoma-Bellevue, WA Metro area	43.6	20	9	Baltimore-Columbia-Towson, MD Metro area	$83,811
16	10	Minneapolis-St. Paul-Bloomington, MN Metro area	42.7	19	10	Denver-Aurora-Lakewood, CO Metro area	$83,289
1	11	New York-Newark-Jersey City, NY-NJ-PA Metro ar	41.4	16	11	Minneapolis-St. Paul-Bloomington, MN Metro area	$82,887
20	12	Baltimore-Columbia-Towson, MD Metro area	41.0	17	12	San Diego-Chula Vista-Carlsbad, CA Metro area	$82,426
25	13	Portland-Vancouver-Hillsboro, OR-WA Metro area	40.4	1	13	New York-Newark-Jersey City, NY-NJ-PA Metro ar	$81,951
48	14	Virginia Beach-Norfolk-Newport News, VA-NC Metro area	39.6	28	14	Austin-Round Rock-Georgetown, TX Metro area	$80,852
8	15	Atlanta-Sandy Springs-Alpharetta, GA Metro area	39.5	41	15	Raleigh-Cary, NC Metro area	$78,706
17	15	San Diego-Chula Vista-Carlsbad, CA Metro area	39.5	48	16	Virginia Beach-Norfolk-Newport News, VA-NC Metro area	$78,631
3	17	Chicago-Naperville-Elgin, IL-IN-WI Metro area	39.0	25	17	Portland-Vancouver-Hillsboro, OR-WA Metro area	$77,511
7	18	Philadelphia-Camden-Wilmington, PA-NJ-DE-MD Metro area	38.7	46	18	Salt Lake City, UT Metro area	$77,102
63	19	Albany-Schenectady-Troy, NY Metro area	38.6	2	19	Los Angeles-Long Beach-Anaheim, CA Metro area	$76,399
44	20	Richmond, VA Metro area	38.0	57	20	Worcester, MA-CT Metro area	$75,705
31	21	Kansas City, MO-KS Metro area	37.5	26	21	Sacramento-Roseville-Folsom, CA Metro area	$75,533
32	22	Columbus, OH Metro area	37.3	7	22	Philadelphia-Camden-Wilmington, PA-NJ-DE-MD Metro area	$74,825
35	22	Nashville-Davidson--Murfreesboro--Franklin, TN Metro area	37.3	3	23	Chicago-Naperville-Elgin, IL-IN-WI Metro area	$74,621
58	24	Omaha-Council Bluffs, NE-IA Metro area	37.0	4	24	Dallas-Fort Worth-Arlington, TX Metro area	$72,882
74	25	Charleston-North Charleston, SC Metro area	36.5	63	25	Albany-Schenectady-Troy, NY Metro area	$72,810
40	26	Milwaukee-Waukesha, WI Metro area	36.1	69	26	New Haven-Milford, CT Metro area	$71,370
4	27	Dallas-Fort Worth-Arlington, TX Metro area	36.0	44	27	Richmond, VA Metro area	$71,223
69	27	New Haven-Milford, CT Metro area	36.0	8	28	Atlanta-Sandy Springs-Alpharetta, GA Metro area	$71,193
22	29	Charlotte-Concord-Gastonia, NC-SC Metro area	35.9	38	29	Providence-Warwick, RI-MA Metro area	$70,676
27	29	Pittsburgh, PA Metro area	35.9	68	30	Allentown-Bethlehem-Easton, PA-NJ Metro area	$69,769
46	31	Salt Lake City, UT Metro area	35.8	58	31	Omaha-Council Bluffs, NE-IA Metro area	$69,439
56	32	Urban Honolulu, HI Metro area	35.7	5	32	Houston-The Woodlands-Sugar Land, TX Metro are	$69,328
33	33	Indianapolis-Carmel-Anderson, IN Metro area	35.6	31	33	Kansas City, MO-KS Metro area	$69,240
52	33	Rochester, NY Metro area	35.6	37	34	Virginia Beach-Norfolk-Newport News, VA-NC Metro area	$68,454
2	35	Los Angeles-Long Beach-Anaheim, CA Metro area	35.4	35	35	Nashville-Davidson--Murfreesboro--Franklin, TN Metro area	$68,406
21	35	St. Louis, MO-IL Metro area	35.4	12	36	Riverside-San Bernardino-Ontario, CA Metro area	$68,331
57	35	Worcester, MA-CT Metro area	35.4	10	37	Phoenix-Mesa-Chandler, AZ Metro area	$67,068
30	38	Cincinnati, OH-KY-IN Metro area	34.5	32	38	Columbus, OH Metro area	$66,715
26	39	Sacramento-Roseville-Folsom, CA Metro area	34.3	30	39	Cincinnati, OH-KY-IN Metro area	$66,435
71	40	Oxnard-Thousand Oaks-Ventura, CA Metro area	33.9	51	40	Grand Rapids-Kentwood, MI Metro area	$66,297
51	41	Grand Rapids-Kentwood, MI Metro area	33.7	74	41	Charleston-North Charleston, SC Metro area	$65,894
5	42	Houston-The Woodlands-Sugar Land, TX Metro are	33.6	21	42	St. Louis, MO-IL Metro area	$65,725
53	42	Tucson, AZ Metro area	33.6	22	42	Charlotte-Concord-Gastonia, NC-SC Metro area	$65,725
70	44	North Port-Sarasota-Bradenton, FL Metro area	33.5	75	44	Boise City, ID Metro area	$64,717
49	45	Buffalo-Cheektowaga, NY Metro area	33.3	40	45	Milwaukee-Waukesha, WI Metro area	$63,739
75	46	Boise City, ID Metro area	33.2	33	46	Indianapolis-Carmel-Anderson, IN Metro area	$63,545
23	47	Orlando-Kissimmee-Sanford, FL Metro area	33.1	39	47	Jacksonville, FL Metro area	$63,064
9	48	Miami-Fort Lauderdale-Pompano Beach, FL Metro area	33.0	14	48	Detroit-Warren-Dearborn, MI Metro area	$62,768
38	48	Providence-Warwick, RI-MA Metro area	33.0	70	49	North Port-Sarasota-Bradenton, FL Metro area	$62,438
61	48	Albuquerque, NM Metro area	33.0	27	50	Pittsburgh, PA Metro area	$61,969
72	48	Columbia, SC Metro area	33.0	52	51	Rochester, NY Metro area	$61,747
37	52	Virginia Beach-Norfolk-Newport News, VA-NC Metro area	32.9	24	52	San Antonio-New Braunfels, TX Metro area	$61,437
50	53	Birmingham-Hoover, AL Metro area	32.3	23	53	Orlando-Kissimmee-Sanford, FL Metro area	$61,229
10	54	Phoenix-Mesa-Chandler, AZ Metro area	32.2	29	54	Las Vegas-Henderson-Paradise, NV Metro area	$61,048
14	54	Detroit-Warren-Dearborn, MI Metro area	32.2	45	55	Louisville/Jefferson County, KY-IN Metro area	$60,891
39	56	Jacksonville, FL Metro area	32.1	42	56	Oklahoma City, OK Metro area	$60,476
34	57	Cleveland-Elyria, OH Metro area	31.9	66	57	Baton Rouge, LA Metro area	$60,043
42	58	Oklahoma City, OK Metro area	31.5	50	58	Birmingham-Hoover, AL Metro area	$59,185
18	59	Tampa-St. Petersburg-Clearwater, FL Metro area	31.2	49	59	Buffalo-Cheektowaga, NY Metro area	$59,079
47	60	New Orleans-Metairie, LA Metro area	31.1	9	60	Miami-Fort Lauderdale-Pompano Beach, FL Metro area	$59,030
60	61	Greenville-Anderson, SC Metro area	30.9	73	61	Dayton-Kettering, OH Metro area	$57,631
68	62	Allentown-Bethlehem-Easton, PA-NJ Metro area	30.6	60	62	Greenville-Anderson, SC Metro area	$57,432
64	63	Knoxville, TN Metro area	30.4	54	63	Tulsa, OK Metro area	$57,341
45	64	Louisville/Jefferson County, KY-IN Metro area	30.1	34	64	Cleveland-Elyria, OH Metro area	$57,263
73	65	Dayton-Kettering, OH Metro area	29.9	55	65	Fresno, CA Metro area	$57,109
24	66	San Antonio-New Braunfels, TX Metro area	28.8	18	66	Tampa-St. Petersburg-Clearwater, FL Metro area	$57,097
43	66	Memphis, TN-MS-AR Metro area	28.8	64	67	Knoxville, TN Metro area	$56,857
66	66	Baton Rouge, LA Metro area	28.8	72	68	Columbia, SC Metro area	$56,680
54	69	Tulsa, OK Metro area	27.9	61	69	Albuquerque, NM Metro area	$55,370
29	70	Las Vegas-Henderson-Paradise, NV Metro area	25.2	53	70	Tucson, AZ Metro area	$55,023
67	71	El Paso, TX Metro area	23.9	62	71	Bakersfield, CA Metro area	$54,851
12	72	Riverside-San Bernardino-Ontario, CA Metro area	22.4	47	72	New Orleans-Metairie, LA Metro area	$54,388
55	73	Fresno, CA Metro area	22.0	43	73	Memphis, TN-MS-AR Metro area	$53,896
65	74	McAllen-Edinburg-Mission, TX Metro area	19.3	67	74	El Paso, TX Metro area	$48,193
62	75	Bakersfield, CA Metro area	17.1	65	75	McAllen-Edinburg-Mission, TX Metro area	$41,846

75 Largest Metropolitan Areas by 2020 Population

Selected Rankings

Percent of population below the poverty level, 2016-2020

Population rank	Poverty rate rank	Metropolitan area	Poverty rate [col 59]
65	1	McAllen-Edinburg-Mission, TX Metro area	28.4
55	2	Fresno, CA Metro area	20.8
62	3	Bakersfield, CA Metro area	20.4
67	4	El Paso, TX Metro area	19.5
43	5	Memphis, TN-MS-AR Metro area	17.3
47	6	New Orleans-Metairie, LA Metro area	16.9
53	7	Tucson, AZ Metro area	15.9
61	8	Albuquerque, NM Metro area	15.5
66	9	Baton Rouge, LA Metro area	15.3
72	10	Columbia, SC Metro area	14.8
24	11	San Antonio-New Braunfels, TX Metro area	14.2
34	12	Cleveland-Elyria, OH Metro area	14.0
73	12	Dayton-Kettering, OH Metro area	14.0
9	14	Miami-Fort Lauderdale-Pompano Beach, FL Metro area	13.9
14	15	Detroit-Warren-Dearborn, MI Metro area	13.8
12	16	Riverside-San Bernardino-Ontario, CA Metro area	13.7
50	17	Birmingham-Hoover, AL Metro area	13.6
54	17	Tulsa, OK Metro area	13.6
5	19	Houston-The Woodlands-Sugar Land, TX Metro are	13.5
42	19	Oklahoma City, OK Metro area	13.5
49	19	Buffalo-Cheektowaga, NY Metro area	13.5
29	22	Las Vegas-Henderson-Paradise, NV Metro area	13.4
64	22	Knoxville, TN Metro area	13.4
2	24	Los Angeles-Long Beach-Anaheim, CA Metro area	13.2
52	24	Rochester, NY Metro area	13.2
60	26	Greenville-Anderson, SC Metro area	13.1
18	27	Tampa-St. Petersburg-Clearwater, FL Metro area	13.0
40	27	Milwaukee-Waukesha, WI Metro area	13.0
23	29	Orlando-Kissimmee-Sanford, FL Metro area	12.8
10	30	Phoenix-Mesa-Chandler, AZ Metro area	12.7
26	30	Sacramento-Roseville-Folsom, CA Metro area	12.7
32	30	Columbus, OH Metro area	12.7
1	33	New York-Newark-Jersey City, NY-NJ-PA Metro ar	12.4
74	33	Charleston-North Charleston, SC Metro area	12.4
39	35	Jacksonville, FL Metro area	12.3
45	36	Louisville/Jefferson County, KY-IN Metro area	12.1
7	37	Philadelphia-Camden-Wilmington, PA-NJ-DE-MD Metro area	11.9
30	38	Cincinnati, OH-KY-IN Metro area	11.7
33	39	Indianapolis-Carmel-Anderson, IN Metro area	11.5
8	40	Atlanta-Sandy Springs-Alpharetta, GA Metro area	11.4
3	41	Chicago-Naperville-Elgin, IL-IN-WI Metro area	11.3
38	41	Providence-Warwick, RI-MA Metro area	11.3
69	43	New Haven-Milford, CT Metro area	11.2
4	44	Dallas-Fort Worth-Arlington, TX Metro area	11.1
22	44	Charlotte-Concord-Gastonia, NC-SC Metro area	11.1
35	46	Nashville-Davidson--Murfreesboro--Franklin, TN Metro area	11.0
17	47	San Diego-Chula Vista-Carlsbad, CA Metro area	10.9
21	48	St. Louis, MO-IL Metro area	10.7
27	48	Pittsburgh, PA Metro area	10.7
37	50	Virginia Beach-Norfolk-Newport News, VA-NC Metro area	10.6
68	51	Allentown-Bethlehem-Easton, PA-NJ Metro area	10.5
75	51	Boise City, ID Metro area	10.5
44	53	Richmond, VA Metro area	10.4
51	54	Grand Rapids-Kentwood, MI Metro area	10.3
28	55	Austin-Round Rock-Georgetown, TX Metro area	10.2
25	56	Portland-Vancouver-Hillsboro, OR-WA Metro area	10.1
63	56	Albany-Schenectady-Troy, NY Metro area	10.1
48	58	Virginia Beach-Norfolk-Newport News, VA-NC Metro area	10.0
31	59	Kansas City, MO-KS Metro area	9.9
57	59	Worcester, MA-CT Metro area	9.9
20	61	Baltimore-Columbia-Towson, MD Metro area	9.8
70	61	North Port-Sarasota-Bradenton, FL Metro area	9.8
58	63	Omaha-Council Bluffs, NE-IA Metro area	9.3
41	64	Raleigh-Cary, NC Metro area	9.2
11	65	Boston-Cambridge-Newton, MA-NH Metro area	9.0
59	66	Bridgeport-Stamford-Norwalk, CT Metro area	8.9
71	66	Oxnard-Thousand Oaks-Ventura, CA Metro area	8.9
13	68	San Francisco-Oakland-Berkeley, CA Metro area	8.5
15	69	Seattle-Tacoma-Bellevue, WA Metro area	8.4
46	69	Salt Lake City, UT Metro area	8.4
56	69	Urban Honolulu, HI Metro area	8.4
16	72	Minneapolis-St. Paul-Bloomington, MN Metro area	8.3
19	72	Denver-Aurora-Lakewood, CO Metro area	8.3
6	74	Washington-Arlington-Alexandria, DC-VA-MD-WV Metro area	7.6
36	75	San Jose-Sunnyvale-Santa Clara, CA Metro area	7.2

Percent of children under 18 years old below the poverty level, 2016-2020

Population rank	Poverty rate rank	Metropolitan area	Poverty rate [col 60]
65	1	McAllen-Edinburg-Mission, TX Metro area	25.5
67	2	El Paso, TX Metro area	16.9
55	3	Fresno, CA Metro area	16.7
62	3	Bakersfield, CA Metro area	16.7
43	5	Memphis, TN-MS-AR Metro area	13.1
47	6	New Orleans-Metairie, LA Metro area	12.2
61	7	Albuquerque, NM Metro area	11.4
53	8	Tucson, AZ Metro area	11.3
66	9	Baton Rouge, LA Metro area	10.9
72	10	Columbia, SC Metro area	10.8
5	11	Houston-The Woodlands-Sugar Land, TX Metro are	10.6
9	11	Miami-Fort Lauderdale-Pompano Beach, FL Metro area	10.6
12	13	Riverside-San Bernardino-Ontario, CA Metro area	10.5
24	13	San Antonio-New Braunfels, TX Metro area	10.5
54	15	Tulsa, OK Metro area	10.4
34	16	Cleveland-Elyria, OH Metro area	10.0
73	17	Dayton-Kettering, OH Metro area	9.9
14	18	Detroit-Warren-Dearborn, MI Metro area	9.8
29	18	Las Vegas-Henderson-Paradise, NV Metro area	9.8
50	20	Birmingham-Hoover, AL Metro area	9.7
2	21	Los Angeles-Long Beach-Anaheim, CA Metro area	9.6
23	22	Orlando-Kissimmee-Sanford, FL Metro area	9.5
42	22	Oklahoma City, OK Metro area	9.5
49	22	Buffalo-Cheektowaga, NY Metro area	9.5
64	25	Knoxville, TN Metro area	9.4
1	26	New York-Newark-Jersey City, NY-NJ-PA Metro ar	9.3
10	27	Phoenix-Mesa-Chandler, AZ Metro area	9.1
18	28	Tampa-St. Petersburg-Clearwater, FL Metro area	9.0
39	29	Jacksonville, FL Metro area	8.9
52	29	Rochester, NY Metro area	8.9
32	31	Columbus, OH Metro area	8.8
60	31	Greenville-Anderson, SC Metro area	8.8
40	33	Milwaukee-Waukesha, WI Metro area	8.7
26	34	Sacramento-Roseville-Folsom, CA Metro area	8.6
8	35	Atlanta-Sandy Springs-Alpharetta, GA Metro area	8.4
45	36	Louisville/Jefferson County, KY-IN Metro area	8.3
3	37	Chicago-Naperville-Elgin, IL-IN-WI Metro area	8.2
4	37	Dallas-Fort Worth-Arlington, TX Metro area	8.2
7	37	Philadelphia-Camden-Wilmington, PA-NJ-DE-MD Metro area	8.2
74	37	Charleston-North Charleston, SC Metro area	8.2
22	41	Charlotte-Concord-Gastonia, NC-SC Metro area	8.1
38	42	Providence-Warwick, RI-MA Metro area	8.0
30	43	Cincinnati, OH-KY-IN Metro area	7.9
33	43	Indianapolis-Carmel-Anderson, IN Metro area	7.9
35	43	Nashville-Davidson--Murfreesboro--Franklin, TN Metro area	7.9
69	46	New Haven-Milford, CT Metro area	7.8
37	47	Virginia Beach-Norfolk-Newport News, VA-NC Metro area	7.7
21	48	St. Louis, MO-IL Metro area	7.3
17	49	San Diego-Chula Vista-Carlsbad, CA Metro area	7.2
68	49	Allentown-Bethlehem-Easton, PA-NJ Metro area	7.2
27	51	Pittsburgh, PA Metro area	6.9
31	51	Kansas City, MO-KS Metro area	6.9
44	53	Richmond, VA Metro area	6.8
75	54	Boise City, ID Metro area	6.7
28	55	Austin-Round Rock-Georgetown, TX Metro area	6.6
48	55	Virginia Beach-Norfolk-Newport News, VA-NC Metro area	6.6
57	55	Worcester, MA-CT Metro area	6.6
20	58	Baltimore-Columbia-Towson, MD Metro area	6.4
25	58	Portland-Vancouver-Hillsboro, OR-WA Metro area	6.4
51	58	Grand Rapids-Kentwood, MI Metro area	6.4
59	61	Bridgeport-Stamford-Norwalk, CT Metro area	6.3
41	62	Raleigh-Cary, NC Metro area	6.1
58	62	Omaha-Council Bluffs, NE-IA Metro area	6.1
63	62	Albany-Schenectady-Troy, NY Metro area	6.1
70	62	North Port-Sarasota-Bradenton, FL Metro area	6.1
71	62	Oxnard-Thousand Oaks-Ventura, CA Metro area	6.1
11	67	Boston-Cambridge-Newton, MA-NH Metro area	5.8
46	68	Salt Lake City, UT Metro area	5.5
56	68	Urban Honolulu, HI Metro area	5.5
13	70	San Francisco-Oakland-Berkeley, CA Metro area	5.3
15	70	Seattle-Tacoma-Bellevue, WA Metro area	5.3
19	70	Denver-Aurora-Lakewood, CO Metro area	5.3
16	73	Minneapolis-St. Paul-Bloomington, MN Metro area	5.1
6	74	Washington-Arlington-Alexandria, DC-VA-MD-WV Metro area	5.0
36	75	San Jose-Sunnyvale-Santa Clara, CA Metro area	4.4

75 Largest Metropolitan Areas by 2020 Population
Selected Rankings

Median value of owner-occupied housing units, 2016-2020			
Population rank	Median value rank	Metropolitan area	Median value (dollars) [col 91]
36	1	San Jose-Sunnyvale-Santa Clara, CA Metro area	1,041,800
13	2	San Francisco-Oakland-Berkeley, CA Metro area	888,500
56	3	Urban Honolulu, HI Metro area	702,300
2	4	Los Angeles-Long Beach-Anaheim, CA Metro area	641,300
71	5	Oxnard-Thousand Oaks-Ventura, CA Metro area	609,200
17	6	San Diego-Chula Vista-Carlsbad, CA Metro area	595,600
15	7	Seattle-Tacoma-Bellevue, WA Metro area	471,900
1	8	New York-Newark-Jersey City, NY-NJ-PA Metro ar	465,400
11	9	Boston-Cambridge-Newton, MA-NH Metro area	461,500
6	10	Washington-Arlington-Alexandria, DC-VA-MD-WV Metro area	436,600
59	11	Bridgeport-Stamford-Norwalk, CT Metro area	433,000
26	12	Sacramento-Roseville-Folsom, CA Metro area	412,400
19	13	Denver-Aurora-Lakewood, CO Metro area	411,800
25	14	Portland-Vancouver-Hillsboro, OR-WA Metro area	392,000
12	15	Riverside-San Bernardino-Ontario, CA Metro area	360,100
46	16	Salt Lake City, UT Metro area	329,200
20	17	Baltimore-Columbia-Towson, MD Metro area	307,200
28	18	Austin-Round Rock-Georgetown, TX Metro area	303,300
9	19	Miami-Fort Lauderdale-Pompano Beach, FL Metro area	298,400
38	20	Providence-Warwick, RI-MA Metro area	290,500
29	21	Las Vegas-Henderson-Paradise, NV Metro area	285,100
57	22	Worcester, MA-CT Metro area	283,600
16	23	Minneapolis-St. Paul-Bloomington, MN Metro area	271,600
55	24	Fresno, CA Metro area	271,000
10	25	Phoenix-Mesa-Chandler, AZ Metro area	269,300
41	26	Raleigh-Cary, NC Metro area	268,900
75	27	Boise City, ID Metro area	268,500
35	28	Nashville-Davidson--Murfreesboro--Franklin, TN Metro area	262,900
70	29	North Port-Sarasota-Bradenton, FL Metro area	261,100
7	30	Philadelphia-Camden-Wilmington, PA-NJ-DE-MD Metro area	259,500
37	31	Virginia Beach-Norfolk-Newport News, VA-NC Metro area	253,800
48	32	Virginia Beach-Norfolk-Newport News, VA-NC Metro area	252,500
69	33	New Haven-Milford, CT Metro area	252,300
74	34	Charleston-North Charleston, SC Metro area	249,800
44	35	Richmond, VA Metro area	247,500
3	36	Chicago-Naperville-Elgin, IL-IN-WI Metro area	247,400
23	37	Orlando-Kissimmee-Sanford, FL Metro area	242,100
4	38	Dallas-Fort Worth-Arlington, TX Metro area	236,200
8	39	Atlanta-Sandy Springs-Alpharetta, GA Metro area	233,700
62	40	Bakersfield, CA Metro area	226,600
40	41	Milwaukee-Waukesha, WI Metro area	223,700
63	42	Albany-Schenectady-Troy, NY Metro area	221,200
39	43	Jacksonville, FL Metro area	220,000
68	44	Allentown-Bethlehem-Easton, PA-NJ Metro area	219,200
22	45	Charlotte-Concord-Gastonia, NC-SC Metro area	216,700
18	46	Tampa-St. Petersburg-Clearwater, FL Metro area	210,900
5	47	Houston-The Woodlands-Sugar Land, TX Metro are	208,100
47	48	New Orleans-Metairie, LA Metro area	205,500
61	49	Albuquerque, NM Metro area	199,700
53	50	Tucson, AZ Metro area	199,400
31	51	Kansas City, MO-KS Metro area	196,000
32	52	Columbus, OH Metro area	195,900
66	53	Baton Rouge, LA Metro area	190,000
51	54	Grand Rapids-Kentwood, MI Metro area	186,500
24	55	San Antonio-New Braunfels, TX Metro area	183,000
58	56	Omaha-Council Bluffs, NE-IA Metro area	181,200
64	57	Knoxville, TN Metro area	180,700
21	58	St. Louis, MO-IL Metro area	179,200
14	59	Detroit-Warren-Dearborn, MI Metro area	179,100
45	60	Louisville/Jefferson County, KY-IN Metro area	177,400
30	61	Cincinnati, OH-KY-IN Metro area	175,300
60	62	Greenville-Anderson, SC Metro area	172,400
33	63	Indianapolis-Carmel-Anderson, IN Metro area	172,300
50	64	Birmingham-Hoover, AL Metro area	171,400
42	65	Oklahoma City, OK Metro area	162,600
43	66	Memphis, TN-MS-AR Metro area	161,300
27	67	Pittsburgh, PA Metro area	159,800
72	68	Columbia, SC Metro area	159,700
34	69	Cleveland-Elyria, OH Metro area	156,200
49	70	Buffalo-Cheektowaga, NY Metro area	155,800
54	71	Tulsa, OK Metro area	155,000
52	72	Rochester, NY Metro area	148,000
73	73	Dayton-Kettering, OH Metro area	140,400
67	74	El Paso, TX Metro area	126,200
65	75	McAllen-Edinburg-Mission, TX Metro area	90,000

Median rent, 2016-2020			
Population rank	Median gross rent	Metropolitan area	Median rent (dollars) [col 94]
36	1	San Jose-Sunnyvale-Santa Clara, CA Metro area	$2,365
13	2	San Francisco-Oakland-Berkeley, CA Metro area	$2,021
71	3	Oxnard-Thousand Oaks-Ventura, CA Metro area	$1,854
56	4	Urban Honolulu, HI Metro area	$1,779
17	5	San Diego-Chula Vista-Carlsbad, CA Metro area	$1,732
6	6	Washington-Arlington-Alexandria, DC-VA-MD-WV M	$1,718
2	7	Los Angeles-Long Beach-Anaheim, CA Metro area	$1,624
15	8	Seattle-Tacoma-Bellevue, WA Metro area	$1,589
11	9	Boston-Cambridge-Newton, MA-NH Metro area	$1,555
59	10	Bridgeport-Stamford-Norwalk, CT Metro area	$1,511
1	11	New York-Newark-Jersey City, NY-NJ-PA Metro ar	$1,483
19	12	Denver-Aurora-Lakewood, CO Metro area	$1,446
9	13	Miami-Fort Lauderdale-Pompano Beach, FL Metro	$1,408
12	14	Riverside-San Bernardino-Ontario, CA Metro are	$1,387
26	15	Sacramento-Roseville-Folsom, CA Metro area	$1,364
25	16	Portland-Vancouver-Hillsboro, OR-WA Metro area	$1,345
28	17	Austin-Round Rock-Georgetown, TX Metro area	$1,326
20	18	Baltimore-Columbia-Towson, MD Metro area	$1,324
23	19	Orlando-Kissimmee-Sanford, FL Metro area	$1,273
70	20	North Port-Sarasota-Bradenton, FL Metro area	$1,259
8	21	Atlanta-Sandy Springs-Alpharetta, GA Metro are	$1,205
74	22	Charleston-North Charleston, SC Metro area	$1,197
4	23	Dallas-Fort Worth-Arlington, TX Metro area	$1,188
37	24	Virginia Beach-Norfolk-Newport News, VA-NC Met	$1,187
29	25	Las Vegas-Henderson-Paradise, NV Metro area	$1,181
10	26	Phoenix-Mesa-Chandler, AZ Metro area	$1,177
69	27	New Haven-Milford, CT Metro area	$1,173
7	28	Philadelphia-Camden-Wilmington, PA-NJ-DE-MD Me	$1,172
46	29	Salt Lake City, UT Metro area	$1,171
41	30	Raleigh-Cary, NC Metro area	$1,162
18	31	Tampa-St. Petersburg-Clearwater, FL Metro area	$1,160
3	32	Chicago-Naperville-Elgin, IL-IN-WI Metro area	$1,155
16	33	Minneapolis-St. Paul-Bloomington, MN Metro are	$1,144
44	34	Richmond, VA Metro area	$1,141
48	35	Hartford-East Hartford-Middletown, CT Metro ar	$1,140
5	36	Houston-The Woodlands-Sugar Land, TX Metro are	$1,136
35	37	Nashville-Davidson--Murfreesboro--Franklin, TN	$1,135
39	38	Jacksonville, FL Metro area	$1,113
68	39	Allentown-Bethlehem-Easton, PA-NJ Metro area	$1,090
22	40	Charlotte-Concord-Gastonia, NC-SC Metro area	$1,073
57	41	Worcester, MA-CT Metro area	$1,061
24	42	San Antonio-New Braunfels, TX Metro area	$1,058
63	43	Albany-Schenectady-Troy, NY Metro area	$1,039
55	44	Fresno, CA Metro area	$1,029
47	45	New Orleans-Metairie, LA Metro area	$1,017
75	46	Boise City, ID Metro area	$1,005
62	47	Bakersfield, CA Metro area	$994
38	48	Providence-Warwick, RI-MA Metro area	$993
31	49	Kansas City, MO-KS Metro area	$989
32	50	Columbus, OH Metro area	$981
14	51	Detroit-Warren-Dearborn, MI Metro area	$962
72	52	Columbia, SC Metro area	$955
58	53	Omaha-Council Bluffs, NE-IA Metro area	$952
43	54	Memphis, TN-MS-AR Metro area	$944
33	55	Indianapolis-Carmel-Anderson, IN Metro area	$936
53	56	Tucson, AZ Metro area	$931
66	57	Baton Rouge, LA Metro area	$930
50	58	Birmingham-Hoover, AL Metro area	$929
52	59	Rochester, NY Metro area	$920
40	60	Milwaukee-Waukesha, WI Metro area	$917
21	61	St. Louis, MO-IL Metro area	$913
51	62	Grand Rapids-Kentwood, MI Metro area	$910
61	63	Albuquerque, NM Metro area	$908
42	64	Oklahoma City, OK Metro area	$887
45	65	Louisville/Jefferson County, KY-IN Metro area	$882
60	65	Greenville-Anderson, SC Metro area	$882
64	67	Knoxville, TN Metro area	$864
54	68	Tulsa, OK Metro area	$863
30	69	Cincinnati, OH-KY-IN Metro area	$859
67	70	El Paso, TX Metro area	$855
27	71	Pittsburgh, PA Metro area	$850
34	72	Cleveland-Elyria, OH Metro area	$837
49	73	Buffalo-Cheektowaga, NY Metro area	$831
73	74	Dayton-Kettering, OH Metro area	$824
65	75	McAllen-Edinburg-Mission, TX Metro area	$753

75 Largest Metropolitan Areas by 2020 Population
Selected Rankings

Unemployment rate, 2021				Mean income tax, 2019			
Population rank	Unemployment rate rank	Metropolitan area	Unemployment rate [col 100]	Population rank	Mean income tax rank	Metropolitan area	Mean income tax (dollars) [col 199]
62	1	Bakersfield, CA Metro area	10.0	59	1	Bridgeport-Stamford-Norwalk, CT Metro area	32,036
65	2	McAllen-Edinburg-Mission, TX Metro area	9.3	36	2	San Jose-Sunnyvale-Santa Clara, CA Metro area	30,520
55	3	Fresno, CA Metro area	9.2	13	3	San Francisco-Oakland-Berkeley, CA Metro area	26,055
29	4	Las Vegas-Henderson-Paradise, NV Metro area	8.3	11	4	Boston-Cambridge-Newton, MA-NH Metro area	18,403
2	5	Los Angeles-Long Beach-Anaheim, CA Metro area	8.2	15	5	Seattle-Tacoma-Bellevue, WA Metro area	16,987
1	6	New York-Newark-Jersey City, NY-NJ-PA Metro ar	7.4	1	6	New York-Newark-Jersey City, NY-NJ-PA Metro ar	16,263
12	6	Riverside-San Bernardino-Ontario, CA Metro area	7.4	28	7	Austin-Round Rock-Georgetown, TX Metro area	14,876
69	8	New Haven-Milford, CT Metro area	6.6	6	8	Washington-Arlington-Alexandria, DC-VA-MD-WV Metro area	14,860
17	9	San Diego-Chula Vista-Carlsbad, CA Metro area	6.5	70	9	North Port-Sarasota-Bradenton, FL Metro area	13,271
5	10	Houston-The Woodlands-Sugar Land, TX Metro are	6.4	9	10	Miami-Fort Lauderdale-Pompano Beach, FL Metro area	12,786
26	10	Sacramento-Roseville-Folsom, CA Metro area	6.4	2	11	Los Angeles-Long Beach-Anaheim, CA Metro area	12,386
27	10	Pittsburgh, PA Metro area	6.4	19	12	Denver-Aurora-Lakewood, CO Metro area	12,261
7	13	Philadelphia-Camden-Wilmington, PA-NJ-DE-MD Metro area	6.3	3	13	Chicago-Naperville-Elgin, IL-IN-WI Metro area	11,779
47	13	New Orleans-Metairie, LA Metro area	6.3	7	14	Philadelphia-Camden-Wilmington, PA-NJ-DE-MD Metro area	11,742
61	13	Albuquerque, NM Metro area	6.3	5	15	Houston-The Woodlands-Sugar Land, TX Metro are	11,649
68	13	Allentown-Bethlehem-Easton, PA-NJ Metro area	6.3	71	16	Oxnard-Thousand Oaks-Ventura, CA Metro area	11,618
3	17	Chicago-Naperville-Elgin, IL-IN-WI Metro area	6.2	16	17	Minneapolis-St. Paul-Bloomington, MN Metro area	11,448
14	17	Detroit-Warren-Dearborn, MI Metro area	6.2	17	18	San Diego-Chula Vista-Carlsbad, CA Metro area	11,334
43	17	Memphis, TN-MS-AR Metro area	6.2	41	19	Raleigh-Cary, NC Metro area	11,323
48	17	Virginia Beach-Norfolk-Newport News, VA-NC Metro area	6.2	4	20	Dallas-Fort Worth-Arlington, TX Metro area	11,222
67	17	El Paso, TX Metro area	6.2	20	21	Baltimore-Columbia-Towson, MD Metro area	11,044
71	17	Oxnard-Thousand Oaks-Ventura, CA Metro area	6.2	35	22	Nashville-Davidson--Murfreesboro--Franklin, TN Metro area	10,993
59	23	Bridgeport-Stamford-Norwalk, CT Metro area	6.1	48	23	Virginia Beach-Norfolk-Newport News, VA-NC Metro area	10,828
34	24	Cleveland-Elyria, OH Metro area	5.9	63	24	Albany-Schenectady-Troy, NY Metro area	10,568
38	24	Providence-Warwick, RI-MA Metro area	5.9	25	25	Portland-Vancouver-Hillsboro, OR-WA Metro area	10,411
57	24	Worcester, MA-CT Metro area	5.9	74	26	Charleston-North Charleston, SC Metro area	10,337
13	27	San Francisco-Oakland-Berkeley, CA Metro area	5.6	8	27	Atlanta-Sandy Springs-Alpharetta, GA Metro area	10,104
19	28	Denver-Aurora-Lakewood, CO Metro area	5.5	22	28	Charlotte-Concord-Gastonia, NC-SC Metro area	10,075
20	28	Baltimore-Columbia-Towson, MD Metro area	5.5	40	29	Milwaukee-Waukesha, WI Metro area	9,853
49	28	Buffalo-Cheektowaga, NY Metro area	5.5	44	30	Richmond, VA Metro area	9,714
56	31	Urban Honolulu, HI Metro area	5.3	21	31	St. Louis, MO-IL Metro area	9,599
11	32	Boston-Cambridge-Newton, MA-NH Metro area	5.2	69	32	New Haven-Milford, CT Metro area	9,446
24	32	San Antonio-New Braunfels, TX Metro area	5.2	57	33	Worcester, MA-CT Metro area	9,359
4	34	Dallas-Fort Worth-Arlington, TX Metro area	5.1	27	34	Pittsburgh, PA Metro area	9,271
23	34	Orlando-Kissimmee-Sanford, FL Metro area	5.1	31	35	Kansas City, MO-KS Metro area	9,248
25	34	Portland-Vancouver-Hillsboro, OR-WA Metro area	5.1	39	36	Jacksonville, FL Metro area	9,211
73	34	Dayton-Kettering, OH Metro area	5.1	26	37	Sacramento-Roseville-Folsom, CA Metro area	9,200
53	38	Tucson, AZ Metro area	5.0	30	38	Cincinnati, OH-KY-IN Metro area	9,193
66	38	Baton Rouge, LA Metro area	5.0	10	39	Phoenix-Mesa-Chandler, AZ Metro area	9,176
6	40	Washington-Arlington-Alexandria, DC-VA-MD-WV Metro area	4.9	58	40	Omaha-Council Bluffs, NE-IA Metro area	9,089
9	40	Miami-Fort Lauderdale-Pompano Beach, FL Metro area	4.9	50	41	Birmingham-Hoover, AL Metro area	8,989
52	40	Rochester, NY Metro area	4.9	14	42	Detroit-Warren-Dearborn, MI Metro area	8,954
15	43	Seattle-Tacoma-Bellevue, WA Metro area	4.8	18	43	Tampa-St. Petersburg-Clearwater, FL Metro area	8,914
36	43	San Jose-Sunnyvale-Santa Clara, CA Metro area	4.8	29	44	Las Vegas-Henderson-Paradise, NV Metro area	8,582
21	45	St. Louis, MO-IL Metro area	4.6	46	45	Salt Lake City, UT Metro area	8,526
22	45	Charlotte-Concord-Gastonia, NC-SC Metro area	4.6	33	46	Indianapolis-Carmel-Anderson, IN Metro area	8,487
32	45	Columbus, OH Metro area	4.6	34	47	Cleveland-Elyria, OH Metro area	8,473
51	45	Grand Rapids-Kentwood, MI Metro area	4.6	38	48	Providence-Warwick, RI-MA Metro area	8,438
10	49	Phoenix-Mesa-Chandler, AZ Metro area	4.5	32	49	Columbus, OH Metro area	8,355
37	49	Virginia Beach-Norfolk-Newport News, VA-NC Metro area	4.5	75	50	Boise City, ID Metro area	8,297
30	51	Cincinnati, OH-KY-IN Metro area	4.4	64	51	Knoxville, TN Metro area	8,202
40	51	Milwaukee-Waukesha, WI Metro area	4.4	47	52	New Orleans-Metairie, LA Metro area	8,132
45	53	Louisville/Jefferson County, KY-IN Metro area	4.3	56	53	Urban Honolulu, HI Metro area	8,050
63	53	Albany-Schenectady-Troy, NY Metro area	4.3	54	54	Tulsa, OK Metro area	7,910
18	55	Tampa-St. Petersburg-Clearwater, FL Metro area	4.2	68	55	Allentown-Bethlehem-Easton, PA-NJ Metro area	7,900
31	55	Kansas City, MO-KS Metro area	4.2	66	56	Baton Rouge, LA Metro area	7,838
44	55	Richmond, VA Metro area	4.2	24	57	San Antonio-New Braunfels, TX Metro area	7,828
28	58	Austin-Round Rock-Georgetown, TX Metro area	4.1	51	57	Grand Rapids-Kentwood, MI Metro area	7,828
39	59	Jacksonville, FL Metro area	4.0	45	59	Louisville/Jefferson County, KY-IN Metro area	7,801
41	59	Raleigh-Cary, NC Metro area	4.0	23	60	Orlando-Kissimmee-Sanford, FL Metro area	7,653
54	59	Tulsa, OK Metro area	4.0	42	61	Oklahoma City, OK Metro area	7,596
8	62	Atlanta-Sandy Springs-Alpharetta, GA Metro area	3.9	52	62	Rochester, NY Metro area	7,316
70	62	North Port-Sarasota-Bradenton, FL Metro area	3.9	49	63	Buffalo-Cheektowaga, NY Metro area	7,157
42	64	Oklahoma City, OK Metro area	3.7	43	64	Memphis, TN-MS-AR Metro area	7,119
72	64	Columbia, SC Metro area	3.7	60	65	Greenville-Anderson, SC Metro area	6,989
35	66	Nashville-Davidson--Murfreesboro--Franklin, TN Metro area	3.6	37	66	Virginia Beach-Norfolk-Newport News, VA-NC Metro area	6,984
74	66	Charleston-North Charleston, SC Metro area	3.6	53	67	Tucson, AZ Metro area	6,795
33	68	Indianapolis-Carmel-Anderson, IN Metro area	3.5	73	68	Dayton-Kettering, OH Metro area	6,506
60	68	Greenville-Anderson, SC Metro area	3.5	72	69	Columbia, SC Metro area	6,444
64	68	Knoxville, TN Metro area	3.5	61	70	Albuquerque, NM Metro area	6,310
75	68	Boise City, ID Metro area	3.5	55	71	Fresno, CA Metro area	5,640
16	72	Minneapolis-St. Paul-Bloomington, MN Metro area	3.4	12	72	Riverside-San Bernardino-Ontario, CA Metro area	5,507
50	73	Birmingham-Hoover, AL Metro area	3.1	62	73	Bakersfield, CA Metro area	5,041
58	74	Omaha-Council Bluffs, NE-IA Metro area	3.0	67	74	El Paso, TX Metro area	3,855
46	75	Salt Lake City, UT Metro area	2.8	65	75	McAllen-Edinburg-Mission, TX Metro area	3,043

75 Largest Metropolitan Areas by 2020 Population

Selected Rankings

Employment in manufacturing as a percent of total nonfarm employment, 2020

Population rank	Manufacturing rank	Metropolitan area	Percent employed in manufacturing [col 107/col 105]
51	1	Grand Rapids-Kentwood, MI Metro area	22.8
60	2	Greenville-Anderson, SC Metro area	16.2
40	3	Milwaukee-Waukesha, WI Metro area	14.0
73	4	Dayton-Kettering, OH Metro area	13.7
14	5	Detroit-Warren-Dearborn, MI Metro area	12.9
45	5	Louisville/Jefferson County, KY-IN Metro area	12.9
54	7	Tulsa, OK Metro area	12.8
34	8	Cleveland-Elyria, OH Metro area	12.5
52	9	Rochester, NY Metro area	12.1
48	10	Virginia Beach-Norfolk-Newport News, VA-NC Metro area	12.0
57	11	Worcester, MA-CT Metro area	11.6
30	12	Cincinnati, OH-KY-IN Metro area	11.5
64	13	Knoxville, TN Metro area	11.0
49	14	Buffalo-Cheektowaga, NY Metro area	10.9
68	14	Allentown-Bethlehem-Easton, PA-NJ Metro area	10.9
16	16	Minneapolis-St. Paul-Bloomington, MN Metro area	10.6
25	16	Portland-Vancouver-Hillsboro, OR-WA Metro area	10.6
38	18	Providence-Warwick, RI-MA Metro area	10.3
72	19	Columbia, SC Metro area	9.7
74	20	Charleston-North Charleston, SC Metro area	9.5
71	21	Oxnard-Thousand Oaks-Ventura, CA Metro area	9.4
37	22	Virginia Beach-Norfolk-Newport News, VA-NC Metro area	9.3
55	22	Fresno, CA Metro area	9.3
75	24	Boise City, ID Metro area	9.2
3	25	Chicago-Naperville-Elgin, IL-IN-WI Metro area	9.1
15	26	Seattle-Tacoma-Bellevue, WA Metro area	8.9
21	26	St. Louis, MO-IL Metro area	8.9
22	26	Charlotte-Concord-Gastonia, NC-SC Metro area	8.9
46	26	Salt Lake City, UT Metro area	8.9
35	30	Nashville-Davidson--Murfreesboro--Franklin, TN Metro area	8.5
31	31	Kansas City, MO-KS Metro area	8.4
2	32	Los Angeles-Long Beach-Anaheim, CA Metro area	8.3
59	32	Bridgeport-Stamford-Norwalk, CT Metro area	8.3
33	34	Indianapolis-Carmel-Anderson, IN Metro area	8.2
12	35	Riverside-San Bernardino-Ontario, CA Metro area	8.0
69	35	New Haven-Milford, CT Metro area	8.0
4	37	Dallas-Fort Worth-Arlington, TX Metro area	7.9
36	37	San Jose-Sunnyvale-Santa Clara, CA Metro area	7.9
50	37	Birmingham-Hoover, AL Metro area	7.9
58	40	Omaha-Council Bluffs, NE-IA Metro area	7.8
17	41	San Diego-Chula Vista-Carlsbad, CA Metro area	7.7
5	42	Houston-The Woodlands-Sugar Land, TX Metro are	7.6
27	42	Pittsburgh, PA Metro area	7.6
32	44	Columbus, OH Metro area	7.4
66	45	Baton Rouge, LA Metro area	7.3
63	46	Albany-Schenectady-Troy, NY Metro area	7.2
43	47	Memphis, TN-MS-AR Metro area	6.7
67	47	El Paso, TX Metro area	6.7
53	49	Tucson, AZ Metro area	6.6
62	50	Bakersfield, CA Metro area	6.5
8	51	Atlanta-Sandy Springs-Alpharetta, GA Metro area	6.4
7	52	Philadelphia-Camden-Wilmington, PA-NJ-DE-MD Metro area	6.3
10	53	Phoenix-Mesa-Chandler, AZ Metro area	6.2
11	53	Boston-Cambridge-Newton, MA-NH Metro area	6.2
13	55	San Francisco-Oakland-Berkeley, CA Metro area	5.9
70	55	North Port-Sarasota-Bradenton, FL Metro area	5.9
42	57	Oklahoma City, OK Metro area	5.4
44	57	Richmond, VA Metro area	5.4
24	59	San Antonio-New Braunfels, TX Metro area	5.3
18	60	Tampa-St. Petersburg-Clearwater, FL Metro area	5.1
47	60	New Orleans-Metairie, LA Metro area	5.1
61	62	Albuquerque, NM Metro area	5.0
28	63	Austin-Round Rock-Georgetown, TX Metro area	4.8
41	64	Raleigh-Cary, NC Metro area	4.7
26	65	Sacramento-Roseville-Folsom, CA Metro area	4.6
20	66	Baltimore-Columbia-Towson, MD Metro area	4.5
39	66	Jacksonville, FL Metro area	4.5
19	68	Denver-Aurora-Lakewood, CO Metro area	4.2
1	69	New York-Newark-Jersey City, NY-NJ-PA Metro ar	3.6
23	69	Orlando-Kissimmee-Sanford, FL Metro area	3.6
9	71	Miami-Fort Lauderdale-Pompano Beach, FL Metro area	3.3
65	72	McAllen-Edinburg-Mission, TX Metro area	3.2
29	73	Las Vegas-Henderson-Paradise, NV Metro area	2.6
56	73	Urban Honolulu, HI Metro area	2.6
6	75	Washington-Arlington-Alexandria, DC-VA-MD-WV Metro area	1.8

Employment in professional, scientific, and technical services as a percent of total nonfarm employment, 2020

Population rank	Professional services rank	Metropolitan area	Percent employed in services [col 110/col 105]
6	1	Washington-Arlington-Alexandria, DC-VA-MD-WV Metro area	21.2
36	2	San Jose-Sunnyvale-Santa Clara, CA Metro area	13.6
13	3	San Francisco-Oakland-Berkeley, CA Metro area	12.7
28	4	Austin-Round Rock-Georgetown, TX Metro area	12.6
17	5	San Diego-Chula Vista-Carlsbad, CA Metro area	12.3
20	6	Baltimore-Columbia-Towson, MD Metro area	11.7
41	7	Raleigh-Cary, NC Metro area	11.5
11	8	Boston-Cambridge-Newton, MA-NH Metro area	11.1
14	9	Detroit-Warren-Dearborn, MI Metro area	10.7
61	9	Albuquerque, NM Metro area	10.7
59	11	Bridgeport-Stamford-Norwalk, CT Metro area	10.5
8	12	Atlanta-Sandy Springs-Alpharetta, GA Metro area	9.5
19	13	Denver-Aurora-Lakewood, CO Metro area	9.3
1	14	New York-Newark-Jersey City, NY-NJ-PA Metro ar	9.1
31	15	Kansas City, MO-KS Metro area	9.0
63	16	Albany-Schenectady-Troy, NY Metro area	8.8
3	17	Chicago-Naperville-Elgin, IL-IN-WI Metro area	8.5
18	18	Tampa-St. Petersburg-Clearwater, FL Metro area	8.4
15	19	Seattle-Tacoma-Bellevue, WA Metro area	8.3
71	19	Oxnard-Thousand Oaks-Ventura, CA Metro area	8.3
2	21	Los Angeles-Long Beach-Anaheim, CA Metro area	8.2
37	21	Virginia Beach-Norfolk-Newport News, VA-NC Metro area	8.2
5	23	Houston-The Woodlands-Sugar Land, TX Metro are	8.1
73	24	Dayton-Kettering, OH Metro area	8.0
9	25	Miami-Fort Lauderdale-Pompano Beach, FL Metro area	7.9
74	25	Charleston-North Charleston, SC Metro area	7.9
4	27	Dallas-Fort Worth-Arlington, TX Metro area	7.8
7	28	Philadelphia-Camden-Wilmington, PA-NJ-DE-MD Metro area	7.7
46	29	Salt Lake City, UT Metro area	7.6
66	29	Baton Rouge, LA Metro area	7.6
44	31	Richmond, VA Metro area	7.5
26	32	Sacramento-Roseville-Folsom, CA Metro area	7.4
60	33	Greenville-Anderson, SC Metro area	7.2
33	34	Indianapolis-Carmel-Anderson, IN Metro area	7.1
21	35	St. Louis, MO-IL Metro area	7.0
25	35	Portland-Vancouver-Hillsboro, OR-WA Metro area	7.0
10	37	Phoenix-Mesa-Chandler, AZ Metro area	6.9
23	37	Orlando-Kissimmee-Sanford, FL Metro area	6.9
27	37	Pittsburgh, PA Metro area	6.9
64	40	Knoxville, TN Metro area	6.8
16	41	Minneapolis-St. Paul-Bloomington, MN Metro area	6.7
32	42	Columbus, OH Metro area	6.5
39	42	Jacksonville, FL Metro area	6.5
30	44	Cincinnati, OH-KY-IN Metro area	6.4
48	45	Virginia Beach-Norfolk-Newport News, VA-NC Metro area	6.3
52	45	Rochester, NY Metro area	6.3
47	47	New Orleans-Metairie, LA Metro area	6.2
54	47	Tulsa, OK Metro area	6.2
57	47	Worcester, MA-CT Metro area	6.2
42	50	Oklahoma City, OK Metro area	6.1
22	51	Charlotte-Concord-Gastonia, NC-SC Metro area	6.0
75	51	Boise City, ID Metro area	6.0
24	53	San Antonio-New Braunfels, TX Metro area	5.9
34	53	Cleveland-Elyria, OH Metro area	5.9
49	53	Buffalo-Cheektowaga, NY Metro area	5.9
53	56	Tucson, AZ Metro area	5.8
70	56	North Port-Sarasota-Bradenton, FL Metro area	5.8
35	58	Nashville-Davidson--Murfreesboro--Franklin, TN Metro area	5.4
72	58	Columbia, SC Metro area	5.4
58	60	Omaha-Council Bluffs, NE-IA Metro area	5.3
56	61	Urban Honolulu, HI Metro area	5.2
40	62	Milwaukee-Waukesha, WI Metro area	5.1
50	62	Birmingham-Hoover, AL Metro area	5.1
45	64	Louisville/Jefferson County, KY-IN Metro area	4.8
29	65	Las Vegas-Henderson-Paradise, NV Metro area	4.6
62	66	Bakersfield, CA Metro area	4.4
69	66	New Haven-Milford, CT Metro area	4.4
38	68	Providence-Warwick, RI-MA Metro area	4.2
51	68	Grand Rapids-Kentwood, MI Metro area	4.2
43	70	Memphis, TN-MS-AR Metro area	4.1
55	71	Fresno, CA Metro area	4.0
68	71	Allentown-Bethlehem-Easton, PA-NJ Metro area	4.0
67	73	El Paso, TX Metro area	3.6
12	74	Riverside-San Bernardino-Ontario, CA Metro area	3.2
65	75	McAllen-Edinburg-Mission, TX Metro area	2.9

75 Largest Metropolitan Areas by 2020 Population

Selected Rankings

Per capita local government taxes, 2017

Population rank	Local taxes rank	Metropolitan area	Local per capita taxes (dollars) [col 183]
1	1	New York-Newark-Jersey City, NY-NJ-PA Metro ar	$5,192
6	2	Washington-Arlington-Alexandria, DC-VA-MD-WV Metro area	$3,965
59	3	Bridgeport-Stamford-Norwalk, CT Metro area	$3,926
36	4	San Jose-Sunnyvale-Santa Clara, CA Metro area	$3,517
13	5	San Francisco-Oakland-Berkeley, CA Metro area	$3,419
3	6	Chicago-Naperville-Elgin, IL-IN-WI Metro area	$3,173
63	7	Albany-Schenectady-Troy, NY Metro area	$3,142
28	8	Austin-Round Rock-Georgetown, TX Metro area	$2,907
48	9	Virginia Beach-Norfolk-Newport News, VA-NC Metro area	$2,860
52	10	Rochester, NY Metro area	$2,854
11	11	Boston-Cambridge-Newton, MA-NH Metro area	$2,821
34	12	Cleveland-Elyria, OH Metro area	$2,771
49	13	Buffalo-Cheektowaga, NY Metro area	$2,736
7	14	Philadelphia-Camden-Wilmington, PA-NJ-DE-MD Metro area	$2,726
69	15	New Haven-Milford, CT Metro area	$2,680
15	16	Seattle-Tacoma-Bellevue, WA Metro area	$2,624
19	17	Denver-Aurora-Lakewood, CO Metro area	$2,616
32	18	Columbus, OH Metro area	$2,597
5	19	Houston-The Woodlands-Sugar Land, TX Metro are	$2,559
4	20	Dallas-Fort Worth-Arlington, TX Metro area	$2,492
20	21	Baltimore-Columbia-Towson, MD Metro area	$2,488
68	22	Allentown-Bethlehem-Easton, PA-NJ Metro area	$2,464
2	23	Los Angeles-Long Beach-Anaheim, CA Metro area	$2,356
9	24	Miami-Fort Lauderdale-Pompano Beach, FL Metro area	$2,266
38	25	Providence-Warwick, RI-MA Metro area	$2,248
73	26	Dayton-Kettering, OH Metro area	$2,194
58	27	Omaha-Council Bluffs, NE-IA Metro area	$2,188
25	28	Portland-Vancouver-Hillsboro, OR-WA Metro area	$2,186
74	29	Charleston-North Charleston, SC Metro area	$2,182
47	30	New Orleans-Metairie, LA Metro area	$2,147
31	31	Kansas City, MO-KS Metro area	$2,097
24	32	San Antonio-New Braunfels, TX Metro area	$2,088
27	33	Pittsburgh, PA Metro area	$2,086
17	34	San Diego-Chula Vista-Carlsbad, CA Metro area	$2,082
66	35	Baton Rouge, LA Metro area	$2,067
21	36	St. Louis, MO-IL Metro area	$2,037
70	37	North Port-Sarasota-Bradenton, FL Metro area	$2,003
30	38	Cincinnati, OH-KY-IN Metro area	$1,975
37	39	Virginia Beach-Norfolk-Newport News, VA-NC Metro area	$1,966
57	40	Worcester, MA-CT Metro area	$1,956
71	41	Oxnard-Thousand Oaks-Ventura, CA Metro area	$1,866
40	42	Milwaukee-Waukesha, WI Metro area	$1,840
26	43	Sacramento-Roseville-Folsom, CA Metro area	$1,802
50	44	Birmingham-Hoover, AL Metro area	$1,788
72	45	Columbia, SC Metro area	$1,777
46	46	Salt Lake City, UT Metro area	$1,769
44	47	Richmond, VA Metro area	$1,766
8	48	Atlanta-Sandy Springs-Alpharetta, GA Metro area	$1,753
23	49	Orlando-Kissimmee-Sanford, FL Metro area	$1,701
35	50	Nashville-Davidson--Murfreesboro--Franklin, TN Metro area	$1,686
16	51	Minneapolis-St. Paul-Bloomington, MN Metro area	$1,670
56	52	Urban Honolulu, HI Metro area	$1,662
29	53	Las Vegas-Henderson-Paradise, NV Metro area	$1,657
22	54	Charlotte-Concord-Gastonia, NC-SC Metro area	$1,655
43	55	Memphis, TN-MS-AR Metro area	$1,604
67	56	El Paso, TX Metro area	$1,584
41	57	Raleigh-Cary, NC Metro area	$1,579
54	58	Tulsa, OK Metro area	$1,559
10	59	Phoenix-Mesa-Chandler, AZ Metro area	$1,550
45	60	Louisville/Jefferson County, KY-IN Metro area	$1,533
12	61	Riverside-San Bernardino-Ontario, CA Metro area	$1,510
53	62	Tucson, AZ Metro area	$1,500
18	63	Tampa-St. Petersburg-Clearwater, FL Metro area	$1,475
42	64	Oklahoma City, OK Metro area	$1,459
39	65	Jacksonville, FL Metro area	$1,426
14	66	Detroit-Warren-Dearborn, MI Metro area	$1,401
62	67	Bakersfield, CA Metro area	$1,378
61	68	Albuquerque, NM Metro area	$1,338
64	69	Knoxville, TN Metro area	$1,307
55	70	Fresno, CA Metro area	$1,304
51	71	Grand Rapids-Kentwood, MI Metro area	$1,235
60	72	Greenville-Anderson, SC Metro area	$1,181
33	73	Indianapolis-Carmel-Anderson, IN Metro area	$1,165
65	74	McAllen-Edinburg-Mission, TX Metro area	$1,162
75	75	Boise City, ID Metro area	$1,080

Violent crime rate, 2020 (violent crimes known to police)

Population rank	Crime rate rank	Metropolitan area	Crime rate (per 100,000 population) [col 45]
43	1	Memphis, TN-MS-AR Metro area	1,358.8
61	2	Albuquerque, NM Metro area	1,006.4
62	3	Bakersfield, CA Metro area	692.3
40	4	Milwaukee-Waukesha, WI Metro area	678.2
5	5	Houston-The Woodlands-Sugar Land, TX Metro are	631.8
47	6	New Orleans-Metairie, LA Metro area	624.3
35	7	Nashville-Davidson--Murfreesboro--Franklin, TN Metro area	616.3
55	8	Fresno, CA Metro area	596.7
54	9	Tulsa, OK Metro area	591.5
14	10	Detroit-Warren-Dearborn, MI Metro area	570.2
66	11	Baton Rouge, LA Metro area	565.9
72	12	Columbia, SC Metro area	558.0
24	13	San Antonio-New Braunfels, TX Metro area	530.6
39	14	Jacksonville, FL Metro area	499.8
21	15	St. Louis, MO-IL Metro area	497.0
19	16	Denver-Aurora-Lakewood, CO Metro area	490.4
29	17	Las Vegas-Henderson-Paradise, NV Metro area	478.7
53	18	Tucson, AZ Metro area	473.5
2	19	Los Angeles-Long Beach-Anaheim, CA Metro area	472.6
42	20	Oklahoma City, OK Metro area	470.8
10	21	Phoenix-Mesa-Chandler, AZ Metro area	464.3
74	22	Charleston-North Charleston, SC Metro area	446.2
34	23	Cleveland-Elyria, OH Metro area	440.6
13	24	San Francisco-Oakland-Berkeley, CA Metro area	440.1
12	25	Riverside-San Bernardino-Ontario, CA Metro area	431.1
58	26	Omaha-Council Bluffs, NE-IA Metro area	429.7
23	27	Orlando-Kissimmee-Sanford, FL Metro area	426.7
9	28	Miami-Fort Lauderdale-Pompano Beach, FL Metro area	417.0
46	29	Salt Lake City, UT Metro area	384.0
64	30	Knoxville, TN Metro area	381.9
26	31	Sacramento-Roseville-Folsom, CA Metro area	378.3
49	31	Buffalo-Cheektowaga, NY Metro area	378.3
37	33	Virginia Beach-Norfolk-Newport News, VA-NC Metro area	351.8
51	34	Grand Rapids-Kentwood, MI Metro area	350.1
17	35	San Diego-Chula Vista-Carlsbad, CA Metro area	345.7
15	36	Seattle-Tacoma-Bellevue, WA Metro area	339.7
70	37	North Port-Sarasota-Bradenton, FL Metro area	335.4
36	38	San Jose-Sunnyvale-Santa Clara, CA Metro area	317.2
28	39	Austin-Round Rock-Georgetown, TX Metro area	315.6
18	40	Tampa-St. Petersburg-Clearwater, FL Metro area	314.1
32	41	Columbus, OH Metro area	313.2
67	42	El Paso, TX Metro area	308.8
57	43	Worcester, MA-CT Metro area	303.7
38	44	Providence-Warwick, RI-MA Metro area	285.6
65	45	McAllen-Edinburg-Mission, TX Metro area	274.8
63	46	Albany-Schenectady-Troy, NY Metro area	272.4
75	47	Boise City, ID Metro area	262.7
52	48	Rochester, NY Metro area	262.0
69	49	New Haven-Milford, CT Metro area	256.3
11	50	Boston-Cambridge-Newton, MA-NH Metro area	253.8
30	51	Cincinnati, OH-KY-IN Metro area	235.7
41	52	Raleigh-Cary, NC Metro area	223.6
48	53	Virginia Beach-Norfolk-Newport News, VA-NC Metro area	217.9
44	54	Richmond, VA Metro area	215.7
71	55	Oxnard-Thousand Oaks-Ventura, CA Metro area	200.7
59	56	Bridgeport-Stamford-Norwalk, CT Metro area	163.9
1	NA	New York-Newark-Jersey City, NY-NJ-PA Metro ar	NA
3	NA	Chicago-Naperville-Elgin, IL-IN-WI Metro area	NA
4	NA	Dallas-Fort Worth-Arlington, TX Metro area	NA
6	NA	Washington-Arlington-Alexandria, DC-VA-MD-WV Metro area	NA
7	NA	Philadelphia-Camden-Wilmington, PA-NJ-DE-MD Metro area	NA
8	NA	Atlanta-Sandy Springs-Alpharetta, GA Metro area	NA
16	NA	Minneapolis-St. Paul-Bloomington, MN Metro area	NA
20	NA	Baltimore-Columbia-Towson, MD Metro area	NA
22	NA	Charlotte-Concord-Gastonia, NC-SC Metro area	NA
25	NA	Portland-Vancouver-Hillsboro, OR-WA Metro area	NA
27	NA	Pittsburgh, PA Metro area	NA
31	NA	Kansas City, MO-KS Metro area	NA
33	NA	Indianapolis-Carmel-Anderson, IN Metro area	NA
45	NA	Louisville/Jefferson County, KY-IN Metro area	NA
50	NA	Birmingham-Hoover, AL Metro area	NA
56	NA	Urban Honolulu, HI Metro area	NA
60	NA	Greenville-Anderson, SC Metro area	NA
68	NA	Allentown-Bethlehem-Easton, PA-NJ Metro area	NA
73	NA	Dayton-Kettering, OH Metro area	NA

75 Largest Metropolitan Areas by 2020 Population

Selected Rankings

Nonemployer businesses, 2019

Population rank	Nonemployer businesses rank	Metropolitan area	Nonemployer businesses [col 167]
1	1	New York-Newark-Jersey City, NY-NJ-PA Metro ar	1,983,082
2	2	Los Angeles-Long Beach-Anaheim, CA Metro area	1,437,599
9	3	Miami-Fort Lauderdale-Pompano Beach, FL Metro area	1,090,730
3	4	Chicago-Naperville-Elgin, IL-IN-WI Metro area	816,110
4	5	Dallas-Fort Worth-Arlington, TX Metro area	741,932
5	6	Houston-The Woodlands-Sugar Land, TX Metro are	708,007
8	7	Atlanta-Sandy Springs-Alpharetta, GA Metro area	663,253
6	8	Washington-Arlington-Alexandria, DC-VA-MD-WV Metro area	598,268
7	9	Philadelphia-Camden-Wilmington, PA-NJ-DE-MD Metro area	462,125
13	10	San Francisco-Oakland-Berkeley, CA Metro area	447,052
11	11	Boston-Cambridge-Newton, MA-NH Metro area	424,705
10	12	Phoenix-Mesa-Chandler, AZ Metro area	377,526
14	13	Detroit-Warren-Dearborn, MI Metro area	360,476
12	14	Riverside-San Bernardino-Ontario, CA Metro area	343,287
18	15	Tampa-St. Petersburg-Clearwater, FL Metro area	303,763
17	16	San Diego-Chula Vista-Carlsbad, CA Metro area	292,558
19	17	Denver-Aurora-Lakewood, CO Metro area	290,107
23	18	Orlando-Kissimmee-Sanford, FL Metro area	287,615
15	19	Seattle-Tacoma-Bellevue, WA Metro area	284,846
16	20	Minneapolis-St. Paul-Bloomington, MN Metro area	281,513
28	21	Austin-Round Rock-Georgetown, TX Metro area	227,179
20	22	Baltimore-Columbia-Towson, MD Metro area	225,741
22	23	Charlotte-Concord-Gastonia, NC-SC Metro area	220,993
24	24	San Antonio-New Braunfels, TX Metro area	212,660
29	25	Las Vegas-Henderson-Paradise, NV Metro area	203,116
35	26	Nashville-Davidson--Murfreesboro--Franklin, TN Metro area	195,990
25	27	Portland-Vancouver-Hillsboro, OR-WA Metro area	195,692
21	28	St. Louis, MO-IL Metro area	194,382
26	29	Sacramento-Roseville-Folsom, CA Metro area	181,068
32	30	Columbus, OH Metro area	166,939
34	31	Cleveland-Elyria, OH Metro area	160,115
31	32	Kansas City, MO-KS Metro area	157,185
30	33	Cincinnati, OH-KY-IN Metro area	155,143
27	34	Pittsburgh, PA Metro area	152,860
33	34	Indianapolis-Carmel-Anderson, IN Metro area	152,860
36	36	San Jose-Sunnyvale-Santa Clara, CA Metro area	147,368
39	37	Jacksonville, FL Metro area	132,101
47	38	New Orleans-Metairie, LA Metro area	130,719
38	39	Providence-Warwick, RI-MA Metro area	122,304
41	40	Raleigh-Cary, NC Metro area	119,197
43	41	Memphis, TN-MS-AR Metro area	118,850
42	42	Oklahoma City, OK Metro area	117,528
37	43	Virginia Beach-Norfolk-Newport News, VA-NC Metro area	115,164
59	44	Bridgeport-Stamford-Norwalk, CT Metro area	100,223
46	45	Salt Lake City, UT Metro area	99,062
40	46	Milwaukee-Waukesha, WI Metro area	96,536
44	47	Richmond, VA Metro area	96,333
45	48	Louisville/Jefferson County, KY-IN Metro area	92,038
70	49	North Port-Sarasota-Bradenton, FL Metro area	85,403
48	50	Virginia Beach-Norfolk-Newport News, VA-NC Metro area	85,373
50	51	Birmingham-Hoover, AL Metro area	84,839
65	52	McAllen-Edinburg-Mission, TX Metro area	81,199
54	53	Tulsa, OK Metro area	78,418
51	54	Grand Rapids-Kentwood, MI Metro area	78,000
53	55	Tucson, AZ Metro area	72,626
66	56	Baton Rouge, LA Metro area	71,506
56	57	Urban Honolulu, HI Metro area	71,327
71	58	Oxnard-Thousand Oaks-Ventura, CA Metro area	71,248
74	59	Charleston-North Charleston, SC Metro area	70,325
60	60	Greenville-Anderson, SC Metro area	69,867
67	61	El Paso, TX Metro area	67,982
52	62	Rochester, NY Metro area	67,775
57	63	Worcester, MA-CT Metro area	65,536
49	64	Buffalo-Cheektowaga, NY Metro area	64,761
69	65	New Haven-Milford, CT Metro area	64,541
58	66	Omaha-Council Bluffs, NE-IA Metro area	64,415
64	67	Knoxville, TN Metro area	64,114
75	68	Boise City, ID Metro area	62,000
72	69	Columbia, SC Metro area	59,377
63	70	Albany-Schenectady-Troy, NY Metro area	57,947
55	71	Fresno, CA Metro area	57,287
61	72	Albuquerque, NM Metro area	56,296
68	73	Allentown-Bethlehem-Easton, PA-NJ Metro area	55,465
73	74	Dayton-Kettering, OH Metro area	51,899
62	75	Bakersfield, CA Metro area	50,492

Value of residential construction authorized by building permits, 2021

Population rank	New construction rank	Metropolitan area	New construction [col 169]
4	4	Dallas-Fort Worth-Arlington, TX Metro area	16,651,948
5	5	Houston-The Woodlands-Sugar Land, TX Metro are	13,677,948
10	10	Phoenix-Mesa-Chandler, AZ Metro area	11,654,524
28	28	Austin-Round Rock-Georgetown, TX Metro area	9,096,075
8	8	Atlanta-Sandy Springs-Alpharetta, GA Metro are	8,721,861
1	1	New York-Newark-Jersey City, NY-NJ-PA Metro ar	8,691,943
2	2	Los Angeles-Long Beach-Anaheim, CA Metro area	6,964,838
9	9	Miami-Fort Lauderdale-Pompano Beach, FL Metro	6,684,442
15	15	Seattle-Tacoma-Bellevue, WA Metro area	6,452,235
35	35	Nashville-Davidson--Murfreesboro--Franklin, TN	6,445,621
22	22	Charlotte-Concord-Gastonia, NC-SC Metro area	6,330,075
23	23	Orlando-Kissimmee-Sanford, FL Metro area	6,320,024
19	19	Denver-Aurora-Lakewood, CO Metro area	6,232,227
16	16	Minneapolis-St. Paul-Bloomington, MN Metro are	6,154,859
7	7	Philadelphia-Camden-Wilmington, PA-NJ-DE-MD Me	6,037,717
18	18	Tampa-St. Petersburg-Clearwater, FL Metro area	5,801,428
6	6	Washington-Arlington-Alexandria, DC-VA-MD-WV M	5,337,620
41	41	Raleigh-Cary, NC Metro area	4,519,138
24	24	San Antonio-New Braunfels, TX Metro area	4,423,266
39	39	Jacksonville, FL Metro area	4,338,426
3	3	Chicago-Naperville-Elgin, IL-IN-WI Metro area	4,141,039
70	70	North Port-Sarasota-Bradenton, FL Metro area	3,919,519
33	33	Indianapolis-Carmel-Anderson, IN Metro area	3,799,651
13	13	San Francisco-Oakland-Berkeley, CA Metro area	3,794,520
25	25	Portland-Vancouver-Hillsboro, OR-WA Metro area	3,771,925
29	29	Las Vegas-Henderson-Paradise, NV Metro area	3,761,622
12	12	Riverside-San Bernardino-Ontario, CA Metro are	3,747,171
11	11	Boston-Cambridge-Newton, MA-NH Metro area	3,695,182
26	26	Sacramento-Roseville-Folsom, CA Metro area	3,334,568
31	31	Kansas City, MO-KS Metro area	2,760,562
32	32	Columbus, OH Metro area	2,735,106
75	75	Boise City, ID Metro area	2,665,715
14	14	Detroit-Warren-Dearborn, MI Metro area	2,425,933
46	46	Salt Lake City, UT Metro area	2,385,089
60	60	Greenville-Anderson, SC Metro area	2,179,036
17	17	San Diego-Chula Vista-Carlsbad, CA Metro area	2,092,612
42	42	Oklahoma City, OK Metro area	2,053,033
74	74	Charleston-North Charleston, SC Metro area	2,051,965
21	21	St. Louis, MO-IL Metro area	1,987,707
30	30	Cincinnati, OH-KY-IN Metro area	1,862,598
53	53	Tucson, AZ Metro area	1,753,992
44	44	Richmond, VA Metro area	1,650,238
20	20	Baltimore-Columbia-Towson, MD Metro area	1,539,647
72	72	Columbia, SC Metro area	1,470,118
37	37	Virginia Beach-Norfolk-Newport News, VA-NC Met	1,449,487
64	64	Knoxville, TN Metro area	1,274,073
27	27	Pittsburgh, PA Metro area	1,271,487
45	45	Louisville/Jefferson County, KY-IN Metro area	1,249,022
36	36	San Jose-Sunnyvale-Santa Clara, CA Metro area	1,198,432
47	47	New Orleans-Metairie, LA Metro area	1,176,024
43	43	Memphis, TN-MS-AR Metro area	1,088,408
54	54	Tulsa, OK Metro area	1,087,487
65	65	McAllen-Edinburg-Mission, TX Metro area	1,065,455
50	50	Birmingham-Hoover, AL Metro area	1,051,866
55	55	Fresno, CA Metro area	1,026,920
58	58	Omaha-Council Bluffs, NE-IA Metro area	1,026,390
66	66	Baton Rouge, LA Metro area	1,022,078
51	51	Grand Rapids-Kentwood, MI Metro area	996,567
34	34	Cleveland-Elyria, OH Metro area	977,983
40	40	Milwaukee-Waukesha, WI Metro area	969,252
61	61	Albuquerque, NM Metro area	768,363
67	67	El Paso, TX Metro area	661,530
73	73	Dayton-Kettering, OH Metro area	627,538
63	63	Albany-Schenectady-Troy, NY Metro area	618,158
59	59	Bridgeport-Stamford-Norwalk, CT Metro area	538,711
68	68	Allentown-Bethlehem-Easton, PA-NJ Metro area	505,487
38	38	Providence-Warwick, RI-MA Metro area	491,769
49	49	Buffalo-Cheektowaga, NY Metro area	480,826
56	56	Urban Honolulu, HI Metro area	468,351
62	62	Bakersfield, CA Metro area	461,217
57	57	Worcester, MA-CT Metro area	438,444
52	52	Rochester, NY Metro area	404,790
71	71	Oxnard-Thousand Oaks-Ventura, CA Metro area	343,758
48	48	Hartford-East Hartford-Middletown, CT Metro ar	293,118
69	69	New Haven-Milford, CT Metro area	149,327

75 Metropolitan Areas with Highest Agricultural Sales

Selected Rankings

Value of agricultural products sold, 2017				Number of farms, 2017		
Value of sales rank	Metropolitan area	Value of sales (millions of dollars) [col 125]	Value of sales rank	Number of farms rank	Metropolitan area	Number of farms [col 113]
55	Fresno, CA Metro area	5,742.8	55	65	Dallas-Fort Worth-Arlington, TX Metr	29,254
119	Visalia, CA Metro area	4,474.8	119	37	Kansas City, MO-KS Metro area	12,437
124	Salinas, CA Metro area	4,116.1	124	36	Portland-Vancouver-Hillsboro, OR-WA	11,755
62	Bakersfield, CA Metro area	4,076.8	62	18	Minneapolis-St. Paul-Bloomington, MN	11,525
174	Merced, CA Metro area	2,938.4	174	24	St. Louis, MO-IL Metro area	11,057
105	Modesto, CA Metro area	2,526.3	105	32	Columbus, OH Metro area	8,506
76	Stockton, CA Metro area	2,176.0	76	41	Atlanta-Sandy Springs-Alpharetta, GA	7,760
10	Phoenix-Mesa-Chandler, AZ Metro area	2,071.1	10	29	Charlotte-Concord-Gastonia, NC-SC Me	7,381
154	Greeley, CO Metro area	2,047.2	154	30	Madison, WI Metro area	6,927
190	Yakima, WA Metro area	1,988.0	190	11	Chicago-Naperville-Elgin, IL-IN-WI M	6,565
3	Chicago-Naperville-Elgin, IL-IN-WI M	1,859.9	3	25	Philadelphia-Camden-Wilmington, PA-N	6,506
241	El Centro, CA Metro area	1,859.7	241	40	Indianapolis-Carmel-Anderson, IN Met	5,999
127	Salisbury, MD-DE Metro area	1,827.9	127	72	New York-Newark-Jersey City, NY-NJ-P	5,894
9	Miami-Fort Lauderdale-Pompano Beach,	1,764.3	9	20	Omaha-Council Bluffs, NE-IA Metro ar	5,843
277	Hanford-Corcoran, CA Metro area	1,649.3	277	34	Des Moines-West Des Moines, IA Metro	5,658
166	Kennewick-Richland, WA Metro area	1,636.9	166	23	Fayetteville-Springdale-Rogers, AR M	5,444
71	Oxnard-Thousand Oaks-Ventura, CA Met	1,633.3	71	21	Lancaster, PA Metro area	5,108
16	Minneapolis-St. Paul-Bloomington, MN	1,562.8	16	35	Boise City, ID Metro area	5,108
123	Santa Maria-Santa Barbara, CA Metro	1,519.9	123	50	San Diego-Chula Vista-Carlsbad, CA M	5,082
58	Omaha-Council Bluffs, NE-IA Metro ar	1,509.8	58	1	Fresno, CA Metro area	4,774
104	Lancaster, PA Metro area	1,507.2	104	31	Sacramento-Roseville-Folsom, CA Metr	4,737
267	Madera, CA Metro area	1,492.6	267	14	Miami-Fort Lauderdale-Pompano Beach,	4,690
102	Fayetteville-Springdale-Rogers, AR M	1,382.0	102	58	Lexington-Fayette, KY Metro area	4,619
21	St. Louis, MO-IL Metro area	1,375.5	21	63	Wichita, KS Metro area	4,536
7	Philadelphia-Camden-Wilmington, PA-N	1,358.6	7	33	Peoria, IL Metro area	4,468
51	Grand Rapids-Kentwood, MI Metro area	1,332.9	51	74	Tampa-St. Petersburg-Clearwater, FL	4,325
333	Twin Falls, ID Metro area	1,319.8	333	38	Rochester, NY Metro area	4,215
12	Riverside-San Bernardino-Ontario, CA	1,305.9	12	2	Visalia, CA Metro area	4,187
22	Charlotte-Concord-Gastonia, NC-SC Me	1,305.7	22	9	Greeley, CO Metro area	4,062
89	Madison, WI Metro area	1,159.1	89	26	Grand Rapids-Kentwood, MI Metro area	4,056
26	Sacramento-Roseville-Folsom, CA Metr	1,081.4	26	62	Jackson, MS Metro area	4,019
138	Peoria, IL Metro area	1,038.7	138	49	Salem, OR Metro area	4,004
82	Des Moines-West Des Moines, IA Metro	1,026.7	82	42	Rochester, MN Metro area	3,960
75	Boise City, ID Metro area	1,021.5	75	39	St. Cloud, MN Metro area	3,767
25	Portland-Vancouver-Hillsboro, OR-WA	1,020.1	25	28	Riverside-San Bernardino-Ontario, CA	3,729
31	Kansas City, MO-KS Metro area	985.3	31	48	Cedar Rapids, IA Metro area	3,632
52	Rochester, NY Metro area	956.7	52	6	Modesto, CA Metro area	3,621
225	St. Cloud, MN Metro area	955.2	225	44	Santa Rosa-Petaluma, CA Metro area	3,594
33	Indianapolis-Carmel-Anderson, IN Met	944.4	33	46	Davenport-Moline-Rock Island, IA-IL	3,434
8	Atlanta-Sandy Springs-Alpharetta, GA	931.1	8	7	Stockton, CA Metro area	3,430
203	Rochester, MN Metro area	930.9	203	64	Columbia, SC Metro area	3,325
176	Sioux Falls, SD Metro area	920.2	176	71	Orlando-Kissimmee-Sanford, FL Metro	3,120
116	Santa Rosa-Petaluma, CA Metro area	919.1	116	43	Sioux Falls, SD Metro area	3,048
285	Sioux City, IA-NE-SD Metro area	912.3	285	10	Yakima, WA Metro area	2,952
147	Davenport-Moline-Rock Island, IA-IL	894.2	147	55	Waterloo-Cedar Falls, IA Metro area	2,691
245	Iowa City, IA Metro area	891.5	245	8	Phoenix-Mesa-Chandler, AZ Metro area	2,636
178	Cedar Rapids, IA Metro area	854.5	178	56	Green Bay, WI Metro area	2,464
125	Salem, OR Metro area	836.3	125	45	Sioux City, IA-NE-SD Metro area	2,428
17	San Diego-Chula Vista-Carlsbad, CA M	831.4	17	47	Iowa City, IA Metro area	2,386
350	Mankato, MN Metro area	822.8	350	61	San Luis Obispo-Paso Robles, CA Metr	2,349
182	Amarillo, TX Metro area	801.5	182	5	Merced, CA Metro area	2,337
302	Harrisonburg, VA Metro area	795.9	302	16	Kennewick-Richland, WA Metro area	2,292
379	Grand Island, NE Metro area	777.9	379	13	Salisbury, MD-DE Metro area	2,237
257	Waterloo-Cedar Falls, IA Metro area	757.9	257	57	Grand Forks, ND-MN Metro area	2,147
158	Green Bay, WI Metro area	752.9	158	17	Oxnard-Thousand Oaks-Ventura, CA Met	2,135
351	Grand Forks, ND-MN Metro area	748.1	351	60	Lafayette-West Lafayette, IN Metro a	2,041
109	Lexington-Fayette, KY Metro area	723.3	109	53	Harrisonburg, VA Metro area	2,026
192	Fargo, ND-MN Metro area	717.2	192	68	Yuba City, CA Metro area	1,921
205	Lafayette-West Lafayette, IN Metro a	702.5	205	69	Napa, CA Metro area	1,866
175	San Luis Obispo-Paso Robles, CA Metr	701.6	175	70	Reading, PA Metro area	1,809
99	Jackson, MS Metro area	682.5	99	4	Bakersfield, CA Metro area	1,731
93	Wichita, KS Metro area	680.7	93	52	Amarillo, TX Metro area	1,699
187	Santa Cruz-Watsonville, CA Metro are	606.5	187	27	Twin Falls, ID Metro area	1,697
334	Goldsboro, NC Metro area	592.1	334	54	Grand Island, NE Metro area	1,682
238	Yuba City, CA Metro area	591.3	238	51	Mankato, MN Metro area	1,672
301	Napa, CA Metro area	573.2	301	73	Champaign-Urbana, IL Metro area	1,636
126	Reading, PA Metro area	554.7	126	75	Athens-Clarke County, GA Metro area	1,520
23	Orlando-Kissimmee-Sanford, FL Metro	554.5	23	59	Fargo, ND-MN Metro area	1,478
1	New York-Newark-Jersey City, NY-NJ-P	545.8	1	19	Santa Maria-Santa Barbara, CA Metro	1,467
207	Champaign-Urbana, IL Metro area	540.8	207	22	Madera, CA Metro area	1,386
18	Tampa-St. Petersburg-Clearwater, FL	534.9	18	3	Salinas, CA Metro area	1,104
211	Athens-Clarke County, GA Metro area	524.8	211	15	Hanford-Corcoran, CA Metro area	963
215	Chico, CA Metro area	524.2	215	66	Santa Cruz-Watsonville, CA Metro are	625
106	Lansing-East Lansing, MI Metro area	518.9	106	67	Goldsboro, NC Metro area	551
263	Idaho Falls, ID Metro area	504.6	263	12	El Centro, CA Metro area	396

75 Metropolitan Areas with Highest Agricultural Sales

Selected Rankings

Land in farms, 2017			
Value of sales rank	Land in farms rank	Metropolitan area	Land in farms (1,000 acres) [col 117]
65	1	Dallas-Fort Worth-Arlington, TX Metro	3,793
37	2	Kansas City, MO-KS Metro area	3,126
36	3	Portland-Vancouver-Hillsboro, OR-WA	2,893
18	4	Minneapolis-St. Paul-Bloomington, MN	2,780
24	5	St. Louis, MO-IL Metro area	2,397
32	6	Columbus, OH Metro area	2,363
41	7	Atlanta-Sandy Springs-Alpharetta, GA	2,295
29	8	Charlotte-Concord-Gastonia, NC-SC Metro area	2,147
30	9	Madison, WI Metro area	2,142
11	10	Chicago-Naperville-Elgin, IL-IN-WI M	2,099
25	11	Philadelphia-Camden-Wilmington, PA-N	1,822
40	12	Indianapolis-Carmel-Anderson, IN Met	1,781
72	13	New York-Newark-Jersey City, NY-NJ-P	1,716
20	14	Omaha-Council Bluffs, NE-IA Metro area	1,703
34	15	Des Moines-West Des Moines, IA Metro	1,666
23	16	Fayetteville-Springdale-Rogers, AR Metro area	1,647
21	17	Lancaster, PA Metro area	1,617
35	18	Boise City, ID Metro area	1,603
50	19	San Diego-Chula Vista-Carlsbad, CA Metro area	1,595
1	20	Fresno, CA Metro area	1,463
31	21	Sacramento-Roseville-Folsom, CA Metro area	1,429
14	22	Miami-Fort Lauderdale-Pompano Beach, metro area	1,351
58	23	Lexington-Fayette, KY Metro area	1,340
63	24	Wichita, KS Metro area	1,258
33	25	Peoria, IL Metro area	1,250
74	26	Tampa-St. Petersburg-Clearwater, FL Metro area	1,229
38	27	Rochester, NY Metro area	1,187
2	28	Visalia, CA Metro area	1,146
9	29	Greeley, CO Metro area	1,140
26	30	Grand Rapids-Kentwood, MI Metro area	1,089
62	31	Jackson, MS Metro area	971
49	32	Salem, OR Metro area	946
42	33	Rochester, MN Metro area	931
39	34	St. Cloud, MN Metro area	929
28	35	Riverside-San Bernardino-Ontario, CA Metro area	900
48	36	Cedar Rapids, IA Metro area	885
6	37	Modesto, CA Metro area	872
44	38	Santa Rosa-Petaluma, CA Metro area	862
46	39	Davenport-Moline-Rock Island, IA-IL metro area	853
7	40	Stockton, CA Metro area	852
64	41	Columbia, SC Metro area	846
71	42	Orlando-Kissimmee-Sanford, FL Metro area	839
43	43	Sioux Falls, SD Metro area	838
10	44	Yakima, WA Metro area	794
55	45	Waterloo-Cedar Falls, IA Metro area	773
8	46	Phoenix-Mesa-Chandler, AZ Metro area	752
56	47	Green Bay, WI Metro area	723
45	48	Sioux City, IA-NE-SD Metro area	715
47	49	Iowa City, IA Metro area	656
61	50	San Luis Obispo-Paso Robles, CA Metra area	648
5	51	Merced, CA Metro area	645
16	52	Kennewick-Richland, WA Metro area	640
13	53	Salisbury, MD-DE Metro area	616
57	54	Grand Forks, ND-MN Metro area	615
17	55	Oxnard-Thousand Oaks-Ventura, CA Metro area	597
60	56	Lafayette-West Lafayette, IN Metro area	575
53	57	Harrisonburg, VA Metro area	573
68	58	Yuba City, CA Metro area	567
69	59	Napa, CA Metro area	560
70	60	Reading, PA Metro area	552
4	61	Bakersfield, CA Metro area	523
52	62	Amarillo, TX Metro area	522
27	63	Twin Falls, ID Metro area	438
54	64	Grand Island, NE Metro area	425
51	65	Mankato, MN Metro area	394
73	66	Champaign-Urbana, IL Metro area	349
75	67	Athens-Clarke County, GA Metro area	332
59	68	Fargo, ND-MN Metro area	260
19	69	Santa Maria-Santa Barbara, CA Metro	256
22	70	Madera, CA Metro area	229
3	71	Salinas, CA Metro area	225
15	72	Hanford-Corcoran, CA Metro area	222
66	73	Santa Cruz-Watsonville, CA Metro area	185
67	74	Goldsboro, NC Metro area	165
12	75	El Centro, CA Metro area	64

Average value of agricultural land and buildings per acre, 2017			
Value of sales rank	Value per Acre rank	Metropolitan area	Value per acre (1,000 acres) [col 123]
69	1	Napa, CA Metro area	44,154
17	2	Oxnard-Thousand Oaks-Ventura, CA Met	25,498
50	3	San Diego-Chula Vista-Carlsbad, CA M	23,209
44	4	Santa Rosa-Petaluma, CA Metro area	22,186
66	5	Santa Cruz-Watsonville, CA Metro are	21,352
28	6	Riverside-San Bernardino-Ontario, CA	18,504
21	7	Lancaster, PA Metro area	18,285
6	8	Modesto, CA Metro area	15,619
72	9	New York-Newark-Jersey City, NY-NJ-P	15,483
7	10	Stockton, CA Metro area	15,020
36	11	Portland-Vancouver-Hillsboro, OR-WA	14,558
5	12	Merced, CA Metro area	13,086
14	13	Miami-Fort Lauderdale-Pompano Beach,	12,654
2	14	Visalia, CA Metro area	11,726
1	15	Fresno, CA Metro area	11,359
70	16	Reading, PA Metro area	11,209
12	17	El Centro, CA Metro area	11,135
22	18	Madera, CA Metro area	10,958
15	19	Hanford-Corcoran, CA Metro area	10,815
25	20	Philadelphia-Camden-Wilmington, PA-N	10,688
49	21	Salem, OR Metro area	10,580
19	22	Santa Maria-Santa Barbara, CA Metro	10,381
74	23	Tampa-St. Petersburg-Clearwater, FL	9,761
31	24	Sacramento-Roseville-Folsom, CA Metr	9,440
73	25	Champaign-Urbana, IL Metro area	9,300
68	26	Yuba City, CA Metro area	9,107
53	27	Harrisonburg, VA Metro area	8,844
55	28	Waterloo-Cedar Falls, IA Metro area	8,630
11	29	Chicago-Naperville-Elgin, IL-IN-WI M	8,547
60	30	Lafayette-West Lafayette, IN Metro a	7,808
33	31	Peoria, IL Metro area	7,799
46	32	Davenport-Moline-Rock Island, IA-IL	7,762
61	33	San Luis Obispo-Paso Robles, CA Metr	7,547
48	34	Cedar Rapids, IA Metro area	7,533
47	35	Iowa City, IA Metro area	7,457
4	36	Bakersfield, CA Metro area	7,380
3	37	Salinas, CA Metro area	7,368
40	38	Indianapolis-Carmel-Anderson, IN Met	7,349
13	39	Salisbury, MD-DE Metro area	7,315
58	40	Lexington-Fayette, KY Metro area	7,245
51	41	Mankato, MN Metro area	7,121
34	42	Des Moines-West Des Moines, IA Metro	6,758
32	43	Columbus, OH Metro area	6,557
30	44	Madison, WI Metro area	6,346
20	45	Omaha-Council Bluffs, NE-IA Metro ar	6,243
24	46	St. Louis, MO-IL Metro area	6,158
45	47	Sioux City, IA-NE-SD Metro area	6,132
56	48	Green Bay, WI Metro area	6,120
42	49	Rochester, MN Metro area	6,115
26	50	Grand Rapids-Kentwood, MI Metro area	5,874
18	51	Minneapolis-St. Paul-Bloomington, MN	5,858
29	52	Charlotte-Concord-Gastonia, NC-SC Me	5,840
43	53	Sioux Falls, SD Metro area	5,616
75	54	Athens-Clarke County, GA Metro area	5,541
71	55	Orlando-Kissimmee-Sanford, FL Metro	5,516
41	56	Atlanta-Sandy Springs-Alpharetta, GA	5,337
67	57	Goldsboro, NC Metro area	4,990
39	58	St. Cloud, MN Metro area	4,974
27	59	Twin Falls, ID Metro area	4,868
23	60	Fayetteville-Springdale-Rogers, AR M	4,861
65	61	Dallas-Fort Worth-Arlington, TX Metr	4,846
8	62	Phoenix-Mesa-Chandler, AZ Metro area	4,689
54	63	Grand Island, NE Metro area	4,556
16	64	Kennewick-Richland, WA Metro area	4,247
38	65	Rochester, NY Metro area	3,920
59	66	Fargo, ND-MN Metro area	3,795
35	67	Boise City, ID Metro area	3,783
64	68	Columbia, SC Metro area	3,643
37	69	Kansas City, MO-KS Metro area	3,606
57	70	Grand Forks, ND-MN Metro area	3,338
62	71	Jackson, MS Metro area	2,809
10	72	Yakima, WA Metro area	2,755
9	73	Greeley, CO Metro area	2,586
63	74	Wichita, KS Metro area	2,509
52	75	Amarillo, TX Metro area	1,109

Table C. Metropolitan Areas — **Land Area and Population**

Area name	CBSA	County code[1]	Area name	Land area[2] (sq mi)	Population, 2021			Population characteristics, 2021										
					Total persons 2021	Rank	Per square mile	Race alone or in combination, not Hispanic or Latino (percent)				Percent Hispanic or Latino[3]	Age (percent)					
								White	Black	American Indian, Alaska Native	Asian and Pacific Islander		Under 5 years	5 to 17 years	18 to 24 years	25 to 34 years	35 to 44 years	45 to 54 years
				1	2	3	4	5	6	7	8	9	10	11	12	13	14	15

1. CBSA = Core Based Statistical Area. DIV = Metropolitan Division. See Appendix A for explanation. See Appendix B for list of metropolitan areas or temporarily covered by water. 2. Dry land or land partially or temporarily covered by water. 3. May be of any race.

Table C. Metropolitan Areas — **Population and Households**

Area name	Population, 2021 (cont.)				Population change and components of change, 2010-2021							Households, 2016–2020				
	Age (percent) (cont.)			Percent female	Total persons		Percent change		Components of change, 2020-2021			Number	Persons per household	Percent		
	55 to 64 years	65 to 74 years	75 years and over		2010	2020	2010-2020	2020-2021	Births	Deaths	Net migration			Family households	Female family house holds	One person
	16	17	18	19	20	21	22	23	24	25	26	27	28	29	30	31

Table C. Metropolitan Areas — **Population, Vital Statistics, Health, and Crime**

Area name	Persons in group quarters, 2021	Daytime population, 2016-2020		Births, 2021		Deaths, 2021		Persons under 65 with no health insurance 2019		Medicare, 2021			Serious crimes known to police[2], 2020	
													Violent	
		Number	Employment/ residence ratio	Total	Rate[1]	Number	Rate[1]	Number	Percent	Total Beneficiaries	Enrolled in Original Medicare	Enrolled in Medicare Advantage	Number	Rate[3]
	32	33	34	35	36	37	38	39	40	41	42	43	44	45

1. Per 1,000 estimated resident population. 2. Data for serious crimes have not been adjusted for underreporting; this may affect comparability between geographic areas and over time.
3. Per 100,000 population estimated by the FBI.

Table C. Metropolitan Areas — **Crime, Education, Money Income, and Poverty**

Area name	Serious crimes known to police[1], 2020 (cont.)		Education						Income and poverty, 2016–2020							
	Property		School enrollment and attainment, 2016-2020				Local government expenditures,[5] 2018-2019							Percent below poverty level		
			Enrollment[3]		Attainment[4] (percent)											
	Number	Rate[2]	Total	Percent private	High school graduate or less	Bachelor's degree or more	Total current spending (mil dol)	Current spending per student (dollars)	Per capita income[6] (dollars)	Mean household income (dollars)	Mean Individual income	Percent of households with income of less than $50,000	Percent of households with income of $200,000 or more	All persons	All families	families with related children under 18
	46	47	48	49	50	51	52	53	54	55	56	57	58	59	60	61

1. Data for serious crimes have not been adjusted for underreporting; this may affect comparability between geographic areas and over time. 2. Per 100,000 population estimated by the FBI. 3. All persons 3 years old and over enrolled in nursery school through college. 4. Persons 25 years old and over. 5. Elementary and secondary education expenditures. 6. Based on population estimated by the American Community Survey, 2015.

Table C. Metropolitan Areas — **Personal Income and Earnings**

Area name	Personal income, 2020										Earnings, 2020		
			Per capita[1]			Supplements to wages and salaries, employer contributions (mil dol)						Contributrions for government social insurance (mil dol)	
	Total (mil dol)	Percent change, 2019-2020	Dollars	Rank	Wages and Salaries (mil dol)	Pension and insurance	Government social insurance	Proprietors' income	Dividends, interest, and rent (mil dol)	Personal transfer receipts (mil dol)	Total (mil dol)	From employee and self-employed	From employer
	62	63	64	65	66	67	68	69	70	71	72	73	74

1. Based on the resident population estimated as of July 1 of the year shown.

Table C. Metropolitan Areas — **Earnings, Social Security, and Housing**

Area name	Earnings, 2020 (cont.)									Social Security beneficiaries, December 2020		Supplemental Security Income Recipients, December 2020	Housing units, 2021	
	Percent by selected industries													
	Farm	Mining, quarrying, and extracting	Construction	Manufacturing	Information; professional, scientific, and technical serviecs	Retail trade	Finance, insurance, real estate, rental and leasing	Health care and social assistance	Government	Number	Rate[1]		Total	Percent change, 2020-2021
	75	76	77	78	79	80	81	82	83	84	85	86	87	88

1. Per 1,000 resident population estimated as of July 1 of the year shown.

Table C. Metropolitan Areas — **Housing, Labor Force, and Employment**

Area name	Occupied housing units, 2016-2020								Civilian labor force, 2021				Civilian employment[6], 2016-2020		
	Occupied units										Unemployment			Percent	
		Owner-occupied					Renter-occupied								
				Median owner cost as a percent of income											
	Total	Percent	Median value[1]	With a mortgage	Without a mortgage[2]	Median rent[3]	Median rent as a percent of income	Substandard units[4] (percent)	Total	Percent change 2020-2021	Total	Rate[5]	Total	Management, business, science, and arts	Construction, production, and maintenance occupations
	89	90	91	92	93	94	95	96	97	98	99	100	101	102	103

1. Specified owner-occupied units. 2. A value of 10.0 represents 10 percent or less; a value of 50.0 represents 50 percent or more. 3. Specified renter-occupied units. 4. Overcrowded or lacking complete plumbing facilities. 5. Percent of civilian labor force. 6. Civilian employed persons 16 years old and over.

Table C. Metropolitan Areas — **Nonfarm Employment and Agriculture**

Area name	Private nonfarm establishments, employment and payroll, 2020									Agriculture, 2017			
		Employment						Annual payroll		Farms			Farm producers whose primary occupation is farming (percent)
											Percent with:		
	Number of establishments	Total	Health care and social assistance	Manufacturing	Retail trade	Finance and insurance	Professional, scientific, and technical services	Total (mil dol)	Average per employee (dollars)	Number	Fewer than 50 acres	1000 acres or more	
	104	105	106	107	108	109	110	111	112	113	114	115	116

Table C. Metropolitan Areas — **Agriculture**

Area name	Agriculture, 2017 (cont.)															
	Land in farms					Value of land and buildings		Value of machinery and equipmnet, average per farm (dollars)	Value of products sold:				Organic farms (number)	Farms with internet access (percent)	Government payments	
			Acres								Percent from:					
	Acreage (1,000)	Percent change, 2012-2017	Average size of farm	Total irrigated (1,000)	Total cropland (1,000)	Average per farm	Average per acre		Total (mil dol)	Average per farm (acres)	Crops	Livestock and poultry products			Total ($1,000)	Percent of farms
	117	118	119	120	121	122	123	124	125	126	127	128	129	130	131	132

Table C. Metropolitan Areas — **Water Use, Wholesale Trade, Retail Trade, and Real Estate**

Area name	Water use, 2015		Wholesale Trade[1], 2017				Retail Trade[2], 2017				Real estate and rental and leasing,[2] 2017			
	Public supply water withdrawn (mil gal/ day)	Public supply gallons withdrawn per person per day	Number of establishments	Number of employees	Sales (mil dol)	Average payroll (mil dol)	Number of establishments	Number of employees	Sales (mil dol)	Average payroll (mil dol)	Number of establishments	Number of employees	Sales (mil dol)	Average payroll (mil dol)
	133	134	135	136	137	138	139	140	141	142	143	144	145	146

1. Merchant wholesalers, except manufacturers' sales branches and offices. 2. Employer establishments.

Table C. Metropolitan Areas — **Professional Services, Manufacturing, and Accommodation and Food Services**

Area name	Professional, scientific, and technical services, 2017				Manufacturing, 2017				Accommodation and food services, 2017			
	Number of establishments	Number of employees	Sales (mil dol)	Average payroll (mil dol)	Number of establishments	Number of employees	Receipts (mil dol)	Annual payroll (mil dol)	Number of establishments	Number of employees	Receipts (mil dol)	Annual payroll (mil dol)
	147	148	149	150	151	152	153	154	155	156	157	158

Table C. Metropolitan Areas — **Health Care and Social Assistance, Other Services, Nonemployer Businesses, and Residential Construction**

Area name	Health care and social assistance, 2017				Other services, 2017				Nonemployer businesses, 2019		Value of residential construction authorized by building permits, 2021	
	Number of establishments	Number of employees	Receipts (mil dol)	Annual payroll (mil dol)	Number of establishments	Number of employees	Receipts (mil dol)	Annual payroll (mil dol)	Number	Receipts (mil dol)	New construction ($1,000)	Number of housing units
	159	160	161	162	163	164	165	166	167	168	169	170

Table C. Metropolitan Areas — **Government Employment and Payroll, and Local Government Finances**

Area name	Government employment and payroll, 2017									Local government finances, 2017				
			March payroll (percent of total)							General revenue				
												Taxes		
													Per capita[1] (dollars)	
	Full-time equivalent employees	March payroll (dollars)	Adminis-tration, judicial, and legal	Police and corrections	Fire protection	Highways and transpor-tation	Health and welfare	Natural resources and utilities	Education and libraries	Total (mil dol)	Inter-govern-mental (mil dol)	Total (mil dol)	Total	Property
	171	172	173	174	175	176	177	178	179	180	181	182	183	184

1. Based on the resident population estimated as of July 1 of the year shown

Table C. Metropolitan Areas — **Local Government Finances, Government Employment, and Income Taxes**

Area name	Local government finances, 2017 (cont.)									Government employment, 2020			Individual income tax returns, 2019		
	Direct general expenditure							Debt outstanding							
			Percent of total for:												
	Total (mil dol)	Per capita[1] (dollars)	Educa-tion	Health and hospitals	Police protection	Public welfare	Highways	Total (mil dol)	Per capita[1] (dollars)	Federal civilian	Federal military	State and local	Number of returns	Mean adjusted gross income	Mean income tax
	185	186	187	188	189	190	191	192	193	194	195	196	197	198	199

1. Based on the resident population estimated as of July 1 of the year shown.

CBSA[1]	DIV Code	Area name	Land area[2] (sq mi)	Population, 2021			Population characteristics, 2021											
							Race alone or in combination, not Hispanic or Latino (percent)					Age (percent)					
				Total persons 2021	Rank	Per square mile	White	Black	American Indian, Alaska Native	Asian and Pacific Islander	Percent Hispanic or Latino[3]	Under 5 years	5 to 17 years	18 to 24 years	25 to 34 years	35 to 44 years	45 to 54 years
			1	2	3	4	5	6	7	8	9	10	11	12	13	14	15
10180		Abilene, TX	2,743.5	177,314	244	64.6	65.0	8.6	0.9	2.6	25.1	6.4	13.4	16.7	14.3	12.7	10.1
10420		Akron, OH	900.2	700,015	85	777.6	80.8	14.3	0.8	4.4	2.4	5.1	11.4	13.4	13.0	12.0	12.2
10500		Albany, GA	1,591.0	147,773	288	92.9	41.4	54.6	0.6	1.6	3.1	6.1	13.6	14.3	13.0	12.1	11.7
10540		Albany-Lebanon, OR	2,289.3	129,839	314	56.7	86.4	1.3	2.8	2.6	10.2	5.8	12.6	11.5	13.7	12.7	11.5
10580		Albany-Schenectady-Troy, NY	2,811.7	899,286	63	319.8	80.8	9.6	0.6	5.8	5.7	4.9	10.9	14.0	13.0	12.5	12.2
10740		Albuquerque, NM	9,283.4	918,259	61	98.9	39.2	3.2	6.2	3.3	50.1	5.1	12.3	12.7	13.9	13.5	11.8
10780		Alexandria, LA	1,963.6	150,890	283	76.8	64.3	30.5	1.5	1.7	3.9	6.3	13.7	12.6	13.4	13.0	11.5
10900		Allentown-Bethlehem-Easton, PA-NJ	1,453.0	865,310	68	595.5	71.2	6.7	0.5	3.7	19.6	5.2	11.8	12.8	12.4	12.4	12.6
11020		Altoona, PA	525.3	121,767	326	231.8	95.6	3.1	0.4	1.1	1.4	5.0	11.7	11.3	12.1	11.8	12.3
11100		Amarillo, TX	5,151.0	269,703	182	52.4	59.0	7.0	1.0	3.6	31.0	6.2	14.7	13.7	14.1	13.9	11.4
11180		Ames, IA	1,143.0	126,195	319	110.4	87.1	3.2	0.6	7.0	3.7	4.4	9.8	27.8	13.1	10.9	9.2
11260		Anchorage, AK	26,413.8	398,807	137	15.1	68.8	6.0	12.1	13.0	8.5	6.5	13.9	13.1	15.8	14.3	11.6
11460		Ann Arbor, MI	706.0	369,390	148	523.2	73.2	13.7	1.0	10.7	5.2	4.7	10.3	21.3	14.1	11.8	11.3
11500		Anniston-Oxford, AL	605.9	115,972	336	191.4	73.0	22.5	1.0	1.5	4.2	5.7	12.1	13.3	12.8	12.1	12.1
11540		Appleton, WI	955.8	244,084	195	255.4	88.7	2.2	1.8	4.1	4.9	5.7	13.2	12.4	12.6	13.5	12.5
11700		Asheville, NC	2,032.6	472,341	120	232.4	86.1	5.4	1.1	1.8	7.5	4.5	10.2	10.4	12.5	12.7	12.6
12020		Athens-Clarke County, GA	1,025.0	217,759	211	212.4	67.2	20.7	0.6	4.3	9.2	5.0	11.4	21.7	13.7	12.2	11.0
12060		Atlanta-Sandy Springs-Alpharetta, GA	8,685.7	6,144,050	8	707.4	46.8	36.1	0.7	7.4	11.3	5.8	13.5	13.4	14.2	13.9	13.8
12100		Atlantic City-Hammonton, NJ	555.5	274,966	179	495.0	57.2	15.5	0.6	9.0	19.9	5.2	12.0	12.5	12.1	11.2	12.6
12220		Auburn-Opelika, AL	607.5	177,218	246	291.7	68.8	23.5	0.7	4.8	3.9	5.4	11.9	20.6	13.7	12.4	11.7
12260		Augusta-Richmond County, GA-SC	3,480.7	615,933	96	177.0	55.1	37.3	0.9	3.1	6.1	5.9	13.0	12.9	14.0	12.8	11.7
12420		Austin-Round Rock-Georgetown, TX	4,219.5	2,352,426	28	557.5	52.5	8.1	0.8	8.1	32.8	5.7	12.7	13.1	17.0	16.3	13.0
12540		Bakersfield, CA	8,134.6	917,673	62	112.8	32.8	6.0	1.2	6.0	56.1	7.2	16.6	14.8	15.4	13.4	10.9
12580		Baltimore-Columbia-Towson, MD	2,601.5	2,838,327	20	1,091.0	57.1	31.0	0.8	7.3	6.7	5.7	12.4	12.3	14.0	13.5	12.3
12620		Bangor, ME	3,397.2	152,765	279	45.0	94.8	1.5	2.1	1.7	1.7	4.3	9.9	13.8	13.0	12.0	12.4
12700		Barnstable Town, MA	394.2	232,411	201	589.6	90.6	4.2	1.1	2.3	3.6	3.5	8.1	9.7	9.3	9.2	10.7
12940		Baton Rouge, LA	4,370.7	871,905	66	199.5	56.7	36.9	0.7	2.6	4.6	6.1	13.2	14.7	13.7	13.4	11.6
12980		Battle Creek, MI	706.3	133,819	310	189.5	80.0	13.1	1.4	3.4	5.8	5.7	13.0	12.8	12.4	12.2	12.1
13020		Bay City, MI	442.4	102,985	354	232.8	91.2	2.9	1.2	0.9	5.8	4.7	11.1	11.5	12.3	11.8	12.1
13140		Beaumont-Port Arthur, TX	2,101.1	395,419	139	188.2	54.8	24.8	0.8	3.3	17.8	6.4	14.1	12.7	13.6	13.3	11.7
13220		Beckley, WV	1,267.0	113,698	340	89.7	90.8	7.7	0.9	1.1	1.6	5.1	12.1	11.1	11.8	12.2	12.7
13380		Bellingham, WA	2,107.9	228,831	202	108.6	81.0	2.1	3.7	7.1	10.3	4.6	10.9	16.5	13.8	12.8	11.1
13460		Bend, OR	3,017.6	204,801	224	67.9	88.6	1.0	1.8	2.7	8.6	4.7	11.1	10.1	13.3	14.1	12.7
13740		Billings, MT	6,478.0	187,037	232	28.9	88.5	1.4	5.3	1.6	6.0	5.5	13.2	11.8	13.3	13.2	11.4
13780		Binghamton, NY	1,224.4	245,220	194	200.3	86.7	6.2	0.6	4.8	4.3	4.9	11.1	16.3	11.2	11.0	10.9
13820		Birmingham-Hoover, AL	4,488.7	1,114,262	50	248.2	62.3	31.4	0.7	2.1	4.9	5.9	13.0	12.4	13.5	13.1	12.5
13900		Bismarck, ND	4,281.0	134,417	308	31.4	89.3	2.6	5.4	1.4	3.3	6.2	13.6	12.3	13.6	13.7	10.8
13980		Blacksburg-Christiansburg, VA	1,073.6	165,293	259	154.0	87.9	5.5	0.6	5.1	3.1	4.1	9.2	24.7	12.5	10.5	11.3
14010		Bloomington, IL	1,183.2	170,889	254	144.4	80.9	10.0	0.5	5.8	5.4	5.4	12.0	21.2	12.6	12.3	10.9
14020		Bloomington, IN	779.8	161,321	264	206.9	86.8	4.3	0.8	7.1	3.5	4.3	9.1	26.4	13.5	11.1	9.9
14100		Bloomsburg-Berwick, PA	613.5	82,959	375	135.2	92.8	2.5	0.5	1.9	3.5	4.5	10.4	16.4	11.6	10.9	11.7
14260		Boise City, ID	11,766.6	795,268	75	67.6	81.6	1.6	1.3	3.8	14.4	5.6	13.8	13.1	13.8	14.0	12.3
14460		Boston-Cambridge-Newton, MA-NH	3,486.1	4,899,932	11	1,405.6	70.6	8.9	0.5	10.0	12.0	5.0	10.9	13.3	14.8	13.2	12.6
14460	14454	Boston, MA Div	1,112.9	2,028,753	X	1,822.9	65.4	14.4	0.6	9.5	12.2	5.0	10.5	13.9	16.0	13.1	12.3
14460	15764	Cambridge-Newton-Framingham, MA Div	1,310.4	2,421,816	X	1,848.2	70.9	5.7	0.4	11.6	13.5	5.1	11.3	13.0	14.2	13.4	12.8
14460	40484	Rockingham County-Strafford County, NH Div	1,062.9	449,363	X	422.8	92.6	1.5	0.6	3.5	3.4	4.4	10.4	13.1	12.7	12.1	13.0
14500		Boulder, CO	726.4	329,543	157	453.7	79.5	1.6	0.9	6.4	14.1	4.0	10.5	17.9	13.8	12.8	12.7
14540		Bowling Green, KY	1,615.0	182,594	236	113.1	83.0	8.7	0.7	4.8	5.0	6.1	12.7	17.4	13.3	12.3	11.7
14740		Bremerton-Silverdale-Port Orchard, WA	395.1	274,314	180	694.3	80.7	4.4	2.8	9.9	8.5	5.2	11.3	12.3	14.5	13.1	11.1
14860		Bridgeport-Stamford-Norwalk, CT	625.0	959,768	59	1,535.6	61.1	12.2	0.4	6.7	21.3	5.2	12.5	13.2	11.6	12.9	13.7
15180		Brownsville-Harlingen, TX	891.7	423,029	131	474.4	8.7	0.5	0.2	0.8	90.0	7.3	16.8	16.1	12.7	11.7	11.6
15260		Brunswick, GA	1,294.2	113,963	339	88.1	69.4	23.8	0.8	1.9	5.9	5.2	11.8	11.6	11.6	11.5	12.4
15380		Buffalo-Cheektowaga, NY	1,565.1	1,162,336	49	742.7	78.1	13.0	1.0	4.5	5.5	5.2	11.4	12.2	13.7	12.2	11.8
15500		Burlington, NC	423.5	173,877	248	410.6	62.8	22.3	0.9	2.4	13.7	5.7	12.5	14.4	12.6	11.7	12.6
15540		Burlington-South Burlington, VT	1,249.7	226,611	204	181.3	91.3	2.8	1.2	4.6	2.4	4.6	10.4	16.7	14.1	12.6	11.8
15680		California-Lexington Park, MD	358.6	114,468	338	319.2	76.0	16.6	0.9	4.4	5.7	6.0	13.7	13.3	14.2	13.2	12.4
15940		Canton-Massillon, OH	969.9	400,525	136	413.0	88.9	9.4	0.8	1.4	2.4	5.4	12.1	12.1	12.0	11.7	12.1
15980		Cape Coral-Fort Myers, FL	781.0	787,976	77	1,008.9	66.0	8.9	0.5	2.3	23.8	4.4	9.7	9.8	10.7	10.6	11.3
16020		Cape Girardeau, MO-IL	1,431.8	97,699	362	68.2	87.4	9.5	0.8	2.1	2.5	5.6	12.1	16.3	12.3	11.7	11.0
16060		Carbondale-Marion, IL	1,347.5	132,907	311	98.6	84.6	10.4	0.8	2.7	3.7	5.2	11.4	16.2	12.6	12.0	11.3
16180		Carson City, NV	144.5	58,993	384	408.3	67.4	2.7	2.9	4.0	25.6	5.2	11.4	11.0	13.2	12.1	11.7
16220		Casper, WY	5,340.5	79,555	378	14.9	87.7	1.8	1.8	1.5	9.3	6.0	13.8	12.0	13.7	14.2	11.1

1. CBSA = Core Based Statistical Area. DIV = Metropolitan Division. See Appendix A for explanation. See Appendix B for list of metropolitan areas or temporarily covered by water. 2. Dry land or land partially or temporarily covered by water. 3. May be of any race.

Area name	Population, 2021 (cont.)				Population change and components of change, 2010–2021							Households, 2016–2020				
	Age (percent) (cont.)				Total persons		Percent change		Components of change, 2020–2021					Percent		
	55 to 64 years	65 to 74 years	75 years and over	Percent female	2010	2020	2010–2020	2020–2021	Births	Deaths	Net migration	Number	Persons per house-hold	Family house-holds	Female family house holds	One person
	16	17	18	19	20	21	22	23	24	25	26	27	28	29	30	31
Abilene, TX	11.0	8.9	6.5	49.4	165,252	176,579	6.9	0.4	2,677	2,643	676	61,414	2.56	66.7	12.4	26.6
Akron, OH	14.2	11.5	7.1	51.2	703,200	702,219	-0.1	-0.3	8,559	10,955	94	289,506	2.37	61.2	12.1	31.7
Albany, GA	12.5	10.4	6.4	52.5	153,857	148,922	-3.2	-0.8	2,182	2,374	-975	56,120	2.52	65.3	21.3	30.1
Albany-Lebanon, OR	13.1	11.8	7.3	50.3	116,672	128,610	10.2	1.0	1,810	2,041	1,457	48,290	2.60	67.9	10.5	25.1
Albany-Schenectady-Troy, NY	14.0	11.1	7.3	50.8	870,716	899,262	3.3	0.0	10,349	12,003	1,574	359,734	2.36	59.6	11.2	31.7
Albuquerque, NM	12.9	11.0	6.8	50.6	887,077	916,528	3.3	0.2	11,111	12,237	2,788	357,445	2.53	61.3	13.5	31.8
Alexandria, LA	12.9	10.0	6.8	50.2	153,922	152,192	-1.1	-0.9	2,243	2,507	-1,060	56,129	2.59	66.3	17.2	29.9
Allentown-Bethlehem-Easton, PA-NJ	14.1	11.0	7.7	50.5	821,173	861,889	5.0	0.4	10,258	12,039	5,143	324,239	2.52	67.2	11.8	26.3
Altoona, PA	14.4	12.6	8.9	50.7	127,089	122,822	-3.4	-0.9	1,447	2,345	-170	51,647	2.31	62.7	11.9	31.2
Amarillo, TX	11.4	9.1	5.7	49.6	251,933	268,691	6.7	0.4	3,954	3,738	821	97,747	2.60	67.0	12.5	28.5
Ames, IA	10.5	8.7	5.6	48.0	115,848	125,252	8.1	0.8	1,284	1,191	828	48,798	2.30	53.3	5.7	30.9
Anchorage, AK	12.0	8.6	4.1	48.6	380,821	398,328	4.6	0.1	6,344	3,767	-2,081	138,934	2.81	66.4	10.3	25.3
Ann Arbor, MI	11.4	9.4	5.7	50.3	344,791	372,258	8.0	-0.8	4,262	3,765	-3,408	143,040	2.43	56.8	8.1	30.3
Anniston-Oxford, AL	13.5	11.5	7.0	51.6	118,572	116,441	-1.8	-0.4	1,631	2,121	1	44,572	2.50	65.3	14.5	29.0
Appleton, WI	14.1	9.9	6.0	49.7	225,666	243,147	7.7	0.4	3,217	2,743	415	94,548	2.47	67.5	7.2	26.6
Asheville, NC	14.0	13.8	9.3	51.7	424,858	469,015	10.4	0.7	4,951	7,868	6,285	190,156	2.36	61.3	9.0	31.3
Athens-Clarke County, GA	10.7	8.7	5.5	51.7	192,541	215,415	11.9	1.1	2,609	2,219	1,953	80,156	2.48	59.1	13.2	29.0
Atlanta-Sandy Springs-Alpharetta, GA	12.3	8.4	4.8	51.5	5,286,728	6,089,815	15.2	0.9	84,897	62,346	31,328	2,152,319	2.72	67.1	14.5	26.8
Atlantic City-Hammonton, NJ	15.2	11.6	7.7	51.2	274,549	274,534	0.0	0.2	3,388	3,983	994	101,103	2.56	66.3	15.2	27.9
Auburn-Opelika, AL	11.2	8.3	4.8	50.7	140,247	174,241	24.2	1.7	2,245	1,851	2,565	60,731	2.59	62.0	12.7	28.8
Augusta-Richmond County, GA-SC	13.0	10.5	6.3	51.2	564,873	611,000	8.2	0.8	8,596	8,766	5,096	217,664	2.71	66.4	16.1	29.1
Austin-Round Rock-Georgetown, TX	10.6	7.6	4.1	49.6	1,716,289	2,283,371	33.0	3.0	31,835	17,724	55,084	796,315	2.68	62.3	9.9	27.5
Bakersfield, CA	10.3	7.1	4.3	48.6	839,631	909,235	8.3	0.9	15,385	9,696	2,506	273,556	3.15	73.8	16.1	20.9
Baltimore-Columbia-Towson, MD	13.5	9.8	6.5	51.6	2,710,489	2,844,510	4.9	-0.2	38,623	38,716	-6,398	1,062,780	2.57	64.4	14.2	29.0
Bangor, ME	15.1	12.1	7.3	50.1	153,923	152,199	-1.1	0.4	1,482	2,555	1,645	63,073	2.30	60.4	9.9	29.3
Barnstable Town, MA	18.0	18.7	13.1	51.8	215,888	228,996	6.1	1.5	1,781	4,127	5,872	95,859	2.20	62.2	8.2	31.3
Baton Rouge, LA	12.1	9.5	5.7	51.0	825,905	870,569	5.4	0.2	12,668	11,173	-202	311,169	2.68	65.9	15.4	28.0
Battle Creek, MI	13.5	11.2	7.2	50.7	136,146	134,310	-1.3	-0.4	1,745	2,203	-53	54,124	2.40	61.6	13.6	33.1
Bay City, MI	15.1	12.9	8.6	50.5	107,771	103,856	-3.6	-0.8	1,105	1,939	-47	44,627	2.29	62.2	12.1	32.4
Beaumont-Port Arthur, TX	12.6	9.4	6.1	49.2	388,745	397,565	2.3	-0.5	5,967	5,951	-2,188	146,770	2.57	67.2	15.0	28.2
Beckley, WV	13.1	13.5	8.3	49.4	124,898	115,079	-7.9	-1.2	1,411	2,573	-227	48,504	2.33	66.8	12.1	29.4
Bellingham, WA	11.9	11.5	6.9	50.4	201,140	226,847	12.8	0.9	2,445	2,599	2,120	88,978	2.47	60.4	7.9	27.0
Bend, OR	13.4	13.2	7.3	50.1	157,733	198,253	25.7	3.3	2,272	2,339	6,687	77,040	2.47	67.2	8.5	23.8
Billings, MT	13.2	11.3	7.1	50.2	167,167	184,167	10.2	1.6	2,375	2,598	3,107	76,411	2.32	62.4	8.1	30.6
Binghamton, NY	14.4	11.5	8.6	50.4	251,725	247,138	-1.8	-0.8	2,940	3,847	-1,043	100,171	2.30	60.1	11.5	31.2
Birmingham-Hoover, AL	12.8	10.4	6.4	51.8	1,061,024	1,115,289	5.1	-0.1	15,597	16,888	222	422,926	2.52	65.5	14.0	29.8
Bismarck, ND	12.5	10.2	7.0	49.6	110,625	133,626	20.8	0.6	1,955	1,732	546	54,050	2.31	64.0	8.5	28.2
Blacksburg-Christiansburg, VA	11.5	9.8	6.4	49.2	162,958	166,378	2.1	-0.7	1,573	2,190	-473	62,446	2.46	56.5	8.0	30.3
Bloomington, IL	11.4	8.7	5.5	51.2	169,572	170,954	0.8	0.0	2,129	1,847	-393	66,225	2.47	59.9	9.2	29.9
Bloomington, IN	10.9	9.2	5.7	50.1	159,549	161,039	0.9	0.2	1,560	1,839	522	65,229	2.34	54.2	9.6	32.4
Bloomsburg-Berwick, PA	14.0	11.9	8.6	51.2	85,562	82,863	-3.2	0.1	971	1,369	494	33,957	2.31	61.2	10.0	32.0
Boise City, ID	11.9	9.8	5.7	49.7	616,561	764,718	24.0	4.0	10,427	8,265	28,620	269,804	2.67	66.9	8.9	26.1
Boston-Cambridge-Newton, MA-NH	13.6	9.9	6.6	51.1	4,552,402	4,941,632	8.5	-0.8	59,909	58,065	-43,461	1,852,755	2.53	63.3	11.1	27.6
Boston, MA Div	13.1	9.6	6.5	51.5	1,887,792	2,054,736	8.8	-1.3	25,507	24,058	-27,214	771,300	2.52	60.4	12.3	29.7
Cambridge-Newton-Framingham, MA Div	13.6	9.9	6.7	50.9	2,246,244	2,441,831	8.7	-0.8	29,767	28,302	-21,619	909,104	2.55	65.0	10.8	26.5
Rockingham County-Strafford County, NH Div	15.9	11.5	6.8	50.3	418,366	445,065	6.4	1.0	4,635	5,705	5,372	172,351	2.48	67.3	7.8	24.4
Boulder, CO	12.4	10.1	5.9	49.4	294,567	330,758	12.3	-0.4	3,020	2,869	-1,416	127,365	2.46	57.5	7.2	29.3
Bowling Green, KY	11.8	9.1	5.7	50.4	158,599	179,639	13.3	1.6	2,698	2,429	2,681	67,547	2.50	64.6	12.3	27.1
Bremerton-Silverdale-Port Orchard, WA	13.4	12.0	7.2	48.7	251,133	275,611	9.7	-0.5	3,478	3,494	-1,290	105,758	2.46	67.5	9.5	24.4
Bridgeport-Stamford-Norwalk, CT	14.4	9.5	7.0	51.0	916,829	957,419	4.4	0.2	11,437	10,825	1,566	345,070	2.68	69.4	11.9	25.1
Brownsville-Harlingen, TX	9.8	8.1	5.9	50.8	406,220	421,017	3.6	0.5	7,260	4,266	-1,097	126,968	3.30	77.3	19.9	20.2
Brunswick, GA	14.4	13.0	8.5	52.4	112,370	113,495	1.0	0.4	1,388	1,969	1,045	47,297	2.46	65.8	14.1	29.8
Buffalo-Cheektowaga, NY	14.5	11.4	7.6	51.2	1,135,509	1,166,902	2.8	-0.4	14,168	17,995	-935	482,932	2.27	58.7	12.7	34.0
Burlington, NC	13.3	10.0	7.1	52.3	151,131	171,415	13.4	1.4	2,269	2,645	2,844	65,455	2.47	64.4	13.8	29.7
Burlington-South Burlington, VT	13.3	10.2	6.4	50.5	211,261	225,562	6.8	0.5	2,401	2,446	1,058	88,499	2.37	59.2	8.0	28.9
California-Lexington Park, MD	13.5	8.3	5.3	49.8	105,151	113,777	8.2	0.6	1,667	1,337	330	41,280	2.67	71.4	13.4	23.3
Canton-Massillon, OH	14.2	12.1	8.2	50.9	404,422	401,574	-0.7	-0.3	5,170	6,923	667	165,608	2.35	63.8	12.2	30.2
Cape Coral-Fort Myers, FL	14.4	15.8	13.3	50.8	618,754	760,822	23.0	3.6	8,316	12,139	31,411	288,916	2.58	65.0	9.3	28.8
Cape Girardeau, MO-IL	12.8	10.7	7.5	51.1	96,275	97,517	1.3	0.2	1,309	1,609	473	36,893	2.52	62.3	9.5	28.9
Carbondale-Marion, IL	12.6	11.0	7.7	49.3	139,157	133,435	-4.1	-0.4	1,653	2,010	-180	56,319	2.28	58.3	11.8	34.0
Carson City, NV	14.3	12.6	8.5	48.6	55,274	58,639	6.1	0.6	683	1,097	771	22,858	2.32	62.7	12.9	31.5
Casper, WY	12.8	10.6	5.9	49.4	75,450	79,955	6.0	-0.5	1,152	1,143	-414	32,896	2.38	62.7	10.5	30.4

Area name	Persons in group quarters, 2021	Daytime population, 2016–2020: Number	Daytime population, 2016–2020: Employment/residence ratio	Births, 2021: Total	Births, 2021: Rate[1]	Deaths, 2021: Number	Deaths, 2021: Rate[1]	Persons under 65 with no health insurance 2019: Number	Persons under 65 with no health insurance 2019: Percent	Medicare, 2021: Total Beneficiaries	Medicare, 2021: Enrolled in Original Medicare	Medicare, 2021: Enrolled in Medicare Advantage	Serious crimes known to police[2], 2020: Violent: Number	Serious crimes known to police[2], 2020: Violent: Rate[3]
	32	33	34	35	36	37	38	39	40	41	42	43	44	45
Abilene, TX	9,913	171,529	1.00	2,108	11.9	2,133	12.0	25,591	18.7	32,391	20,601	11,790	611	354.8
Akron, OH	16,150	703,539	1.00	6,883	9.8	8,723	12.4	44,332	7.9	150,761	63,186	87,575	2,659	378.4
Albany, GA	5,684	148,038	1.01	1,758	11.9	1,835	12.4	18,146	15.6	29,398	14,420	14,978	1,469	1,008.1
Albany-Lebanon, OR	1,000	121,100	0.89	1,430	11.1	1,640	12.7	8,693	8.4	30,520	13,278	17,242	195	149.3
Albany-Schenectady-Troy, NY	31,594	897,395	1.04	8,239	9.2	9,721	10.8	28,782	4.1	188,269	91,025	97,244	2,386	272.4
Albuquerque, NM	13,896	912,411	0.99	8,857	9.7	9,860	10.7	80,326	10.8	176,671	85,427	91,244	9,296	1,006.4
Alexandria, LA	7,242	153,580	1.01	1,820	12.0	2,021	13.4	12,881	10.7	32,380	21,991	10,389	1,464	967.8
Allentown-Bethlehem-Easton, PA-NJ	22,460	809,789	0.92	8,206	9.5	9,672	11.2	47,707	7.1	188,231	119,187	69,044	NA	NA
Altoona, PA	3,609	128,788	1.11	1,167	9.6	1,868	15.3	6,298	6.7	31,759	13,881	17,878	NA	NA
Amarillo, TX	9,157	262,570	0.99	3,131	11.6	2,985	11.1	40,515	18.6	45,573	29,961	15,612	1,787	672.6
Ames, IA	11,194	125,857	1.03	1,013	8.1	972	7.7	5,733	6.0	20,551	15,976	4,575	228	183.8
Anchorage, AK	9,640	397,582	0.99	5,048	12.7	2,997	7.5	39,677	11.6	58,286	56,949	1,337	3,576	1,171.5
Ann Arbor, MI	21,007	411,980	1.24	3,367	9.1	3,020	8.2	15,815	5.3	62,986	36,519	26,467	1,521	412.3
Anniston-Oxford, AL	3,251	114,402	1.00	1,320	11.4	1,712	14.7	10,767	11.9	26,940	15,228	11,712	NA	NA
Appleton, WI	2,933	232,554	0.97	2,532	10.4	2,207	9.1	12,621	6.3	44,901	14,731	30,170	408	170.6
Asheville, NC	10,436	466,391	1.03	3,987	8.5	6,289	13.4	49,995	14.3	122,363	73,613	48,750	1,481	317.1
Athens-Clarke County, GA	10,837	215,463	1.05	2,063	9.5	1,802	8.3	27,418	15.8	35,439	19,506	15,933	834	386.4
Atlanta-Sandy Springs-Alpharetta, GA	83,624	5,970,393	1.01	68,252	11.1	50,454	8.2	780,294	15.1	799,930	408,084	391,846	NA	NA
Atlantic City-Hammonton, NJ	6,033	264,616	1.00	2,740	10.0	3,193	11.6	22,420	10.7	60,104	39,021	21,083	665	253.6
Auburn-Opelika, AL	5,120	153,313	0.86	1,813	10.3	1,483	8.4	14,928	10.7	26,382	13,973	12,409	NA	NA
Augusta-Richmond County, GA-SC	18,288	606,967	1.01	6,953	11.3	7,081	11.5	66,418	13.6	122,827	70,119	52,708	NA	NA
Austin-Round Rock-Georgetown, TX	38,713	2,194,965	1.02	25,626	11.0	14,481	6.2	307,698	15.8	291,830	176,126	115,704	7,207	315.6
Bakersfield, CA	30,494	894,422	1.01	12,371	13.5	7,682	8.4	70,588	9.3	123,171	70,299	52,872	6,216	692.3
Baltimore-Columbia-Towson, MD	69,602	2,783,684	0.99	30,824	10.9	30,933	10.9	134,580	5.9	511,407	414,169	97,238	NA	NA
Bangor, ME	7,170	155,295	1.05	1,164	7.6	2,029	13.3	13,631	11.7	38,150	20,858	17,292	88	57.7
Barnstable Town, MA	4,238	208,803	0.95	1,419	6.2	3,360	14.6	5,496	3.8	80,551	64,663	15,888	635	300.2
Baton Rouge, LA	25,124	861,922	1.01	10,236	11.8	8,970	10.3	68,183	9.7	150,935	61,696	89,239	4,839	565.9
Battle Creek, MI	4,121	139,348	1.09	1,419	10.6	1,769	13.2	7,646	7.2	30,712	17,536	13,176	886	663.6
Bay City, MI	1,347	94,291	0.80	875	8.5	1,521	14.7	5,631	7.0	27,086	13,850	13,236	384	375.4
Beaumont-Port Arthur, TX	16,757	397,808	1.02	4,849	12.2	4,716	11.9	62,210	19.7	71,779	34,668	37,111	2,372	605.7
Beckley, WV	5,259	117,265	0.99	1,120	9.8	2,061	18.0	7,239	8.4	31,103	17,754	13,349	433	377.4
Bellingham, WA	5,529	220,756	0.96	1,934	8.5	2,098	9.2	16,675	9.1	49,645	27,920	21,725	428	184.7
Bend, OR	1,207	193,263	1.02	1,789	8.9	1,913	9.5	12,432	7.9	48,455	31,816	16,639	360	178.5
Billings, MT	3,659	181,208	1.01	1,885	10.1	2,072	11.2	12,340	8.4	39,106	27,681	11,425	1,152	627.1
Binghamton, NY	11,763	238,972	0.99	2,348	9.5	3,031	12.3	9,141	5.0	56,170	27,134	29,036	673	285.4
Birmingham-Hoover, AL	23,442	1,095,946	1.02	12,663	11.4	13,439	12.1	94,223	10.6	220,174	88,602	131,572	NA	NA
Bismarck, ND	4,600	127,645	0.99	1,540	11.5	1,352	10.1	6,086	5.8	25,106	17,147	7,959	433	333.9
Blacksburg-Christiansburg, VA	14,050	170,971	1.05	1,242	7.5	1,720	10.4	10,929	8.6	30,624	21,947	8,677	313	186.4
Bloomington, IL	10,311	176,020	1.05	1,663	9.7	1,474	8.6	7,970	5.8	27,998	17,745	10,253	483	282.8
Bloomington, IN	14,118	172,878	1.06	1,251	7.8	1,488	9.2	12,824	9.8	27,335	18,084	9,251	586	344.4
Bloomsburg-Berwick, PA	4,193	89,461	1.15	775	9.4	1,105	13.3	4,088	6.5	19,785	10,747	9,038	NA	NA
Boise City, ID	14,650	727,526	0.99	8,299	10.6	6,602	8.4	72,805	11.6	141,412	64,051	77,361	2,026	262.7
Boston-Cambridge-Newton, MA-NH	165,271	5,034,808	1.07	47,684	9.7	46,648	9.5	147,365	3.7	907,554	647,358	260,196	12,399	253.8
Boston, MA Div	80,151	2,213,838	1.18	20,279	9.9	19,430	9.5	57,356	3.5	363,258	260,008	103,250	7,590	372.6
Cambridge-Newton-Framingham, MA Div	74,407	2,398,677	1.00	23,734	9.8	22,611	9.3	65,962	3.4	445,733	313,621	132,112	4,421	183.8
Rockingham County-Strafford County, NH Div	10,713	422,293	0.93	3,671	8.2	4,607	10.3	24,047	6.8	98,563	73,729	24,834	388	87.5
Boulder, CO	10,435	361,024	1.21	2,415	7.3	2,319	7.0	20,712	7.7	56,000	30,243	25,757	961	293.2
Bowling Green, KY	6,954	178,432	1.02	2,194	12.1	1,951	10.8	13,022	9.0	32,329	18,828	13,501	341	188.0
Bremerton-Silverdale-Port Orchard, WA	9,379	260,292	0.93	2,755	10.0	2,832	10.3	13,724	6.4	60,032	41,089	18,943	597	218.8
Bridgeport-Stamford-Norwalk, CT	19,219	941,120	0.99	9,146	9.5	8,696	9.1	72,442	9.3	162,836	99,137	63,699	1,522	163.9
Brownsville-Harlingen, TX	3,123	416,524	0.97	5,859	13.9	3,462	8.2	109,621	30.8	66,446	26,415	40,031	1,528	360.8
Brunswick, GA	1,375	117,051	0.98	1,140	10.0	1,603	14.1	16,784	18.3	26,941	15,738	11,203	NA	NA
Buffalo-Cheektowaga, NY	31,242	1,136,771	1.01	11,201	9.6	14,355	12.3	36,950	4.1	254,940	88,935	166,005	4,237	378.3
Burlington, NC	6,081	156,295	0.87	1,795	10.4	2,076	12.0	19,822	14.8	34,518	13,191	21,327	820	477.7
Burlington-South Burlington, VT	10,698	225,532	1.05	1,875	8.3	1,913	8.5	8,900	5.0	44,865	34,795	10,070	439	198.4
California-Lexington Park, MD	2,561	108,735	0.92	1,337	11.7	1,067	9.3	4,997	5.2	17,584	17,054	530	224	196.4
Canton-Massillon, OH	8,918	386,488	0.93	4,069	10.2	5,481	13.7	24,057	7.7	94,261	36,421	57,840	1,451	366.2
Cape Coral-Fort Myers, FL	7,712	741,221	0.95	6,677	8.6	9,861	12.7	96,245	17.9	211,793	121,117	90,676	2,100	266.8
Cape Girardeau, MO-IL	3,976	97,634	1.01	1,043	10.7	1,280	13.1	9,114	12.0	20,978	16,148	4,830	532	549.7
Carbondale-Marion, IL	6,390	139,989	1.06	1,292	9.7	1,619	12.2	7,812	7.5	28,889	19,052	9,837	NA	NA
Carson City, NV	2,735	61,300	1.24	515	8.8	853	14.5	6,131	14.7	14,479	10,691	3,788	225	400.0
Casper, WY	1,503	79,901	1.00	901	11.3	930	11.6	9,564	14.5	15,367	14,229	1,138	183	227.0

1. Per 1,000 estimated resident population. 2. Data for serious crimes have not been adjusted for underreporting; this may affect comparability between geographic areas and over time. 3. Per 100,000 population estimated by the FBI.

Area name	Serious crimes known to police[1], 2020 (cont.): Property: Number	Property: Rate[2]	Education: School enrollment and attainment, 2016–2020: Enrollment[3]: Total	Enrollment[3]: Percent private	Attainment[4] (percent): High school graduate or less	Attainment[4] (percent): Bachelor's degree or more	Local government expenditures,[5] 2018–2019: Total current spending (mil dol)	Local government expenditures: Current spending per student (dollars)	Income and poverty, 2016–2020: Per capita income[6] (dollars)	Mean household income (dollars)	Mean Individual income	Percent of households with income of less than $50,000	Percent of households with income of $200,000 or more	Percent below poverty level: All persons	Percent below poverty level: All families	Percent below poverty level: Age 65 years and older
	46	47	48	49	50	51	52	53	54	55	56	57	58	59	60	61
Abilene, TX	3,088	1,793.1	44,152	23.7	44.0	24.4	290.4	10,012	26,737	54,857	68,388	45.6	3.4	13.3	8.6	13.9
Akron, OH	15,032	2,139.4	166,402	15.9	39.3	32.1	1,256.2	13,397	33,985	59,313	76,842	42.7	5.4	12.5	8.6	15.1
Albany, GA	4,281	2,937.9	41,499	10.3	46.1	20.7	285.1	11,332	24,385	46,323	56,166	53.5	2.4	23.3	18.6	28.3
Albany-Lebanon, OR	2,821	2,159.8	26,639	13.4	39.4	19.5	237.9	10,450	27,820	59,547	68,860	42.6	2.4	12.3	7.6	13.0
Albany-Schenectady-Troy, NY	14,552	1,661.5	209,874	22.1	32.8	38.6	2,280.5	18,808	38,998	72,810	95,438	34.4	7.8	10.1	6.1	10.7
Albuquerque, NM	33,754	3,654.1	229,603	13.3	34.7	33.0	1,343.1	9,821	30,397	55,370	68,660	45.3	4.8	15.5	11.4	17.7
Alexandria, LA	6,079	4,018.7	37,668	16.7	51.3	19.9	280.2	10,696	26,843	48,294	59,394	51.7	4.2	18.4	14.6	21.4
Allentown-Bethlehem-Easton, PA-NJ	NA	NA	196,356	22.1	43.3	30.6	2,142.2	17,417	36,053	69,769	84,676	35.9	7.4	10.5	7.2	12.5
Altoona, PA	NA	NA	25,616	14.6	52.6	22.3	258.8	15,001	29,336	50,856	67,495	49.2	3.0	13.8	9.8	17.8
Amarillo, TX	8,083	3,042.5	68,852	7.1	41.9	24.0	475.7	9,672	29,417	56,055	69,716	44.7	5.0	14.4	10.9	16.3
Ames, IA	D	D	47,654	4.8	25.1	44.9	170.9	10,860	31,672	60,442	90,464	41.9	5.2	17.0	4.4	6.2
Anchorage, AK	10,393	3,404.7	99,615	13.6	32.6	32.7	1,003.1	15,320	38,664	82,890	98,403	27.3	10.2	9.2	6.1	9.1
Ann Arbor, MI	4,670	1,266.0	126,159	9.2	19.0	56.7	623.5	14,052	42,855	75,730	105,224	34.1	11.7	13.9	6.3	9.2
Anniston-Oxford, AL	NA	NA	27,122	11.3	49.4	18.9	178.7	10,300	26,238	50,128	59,609	49.8	2.6	15.8	10.7	17.5
Appleton, WI	2,798	1,170.0	57,414	15.2	36.9	30.0	455.4	11,567	35,249	70,261	86,686	34.1	4.9	6.8	4.9	7.9
Asheville, NC	12,301	2,633.6	91,763	18.7	33.6	36.5	561.9	10,324	32,664	54,992	71,595	45.5	5.1	11.5	7.3	13.5
Athens-Clarke County, GA	4,719	2,186.5	70,823	9.9	34.7	40.1	374.3	12,350	29,718	49,503	71,301	50.3	5.5	20.5	11.0	17.4
Atlanta-Sandy Springs-Alpharetta, GA	NA	NA	1,587,762	16.6	33.5	39.5	11,493.9	11,290	36,867	71,193	84,791	34.9	9.6	11.4	8.4	12.2
Atlantic City-Hammonton, NJ	5,054	1,927.5	64,709	11.5	44.4	28.8	912.4	20,537	34,175	63,680	78,974	41.2	7.2	13.5	10.1	16.8
Auburn-Opelika, AL	NA	NA	56,398	12.6	31.9	36.4	230.1	10,106	28,804	52,930	75,091	48.0	4.9	19.4	10.5	14.1
Augusta-Richmond County, GA-SC	NA	NA	145,466	14.5	42.7	26.7	991.5	10,275	28,499	55,049	67,596	45.5	4.4	15.5	11.7	20.3
Austin-Round Rock-Georgetown, TX	54,045	2,366.6	563,860	13.9	28.0	46.0	3,368.7	9,601	41,283	80,852	100,215	29.7	11.4	10.2	6.6	9.3
Bakersfield, CA	27,890	3,106.0	261,742	9.4	52.2	17.1	2,657.0	13,842	23,855	54,851	61,044	45.9	4.7	20.4	16.7	22.2
Baltimore-Columbia-Towson, MD	NA	NA	700,679	21.2	33.1	41.0	5,999.0	14,794	42,782	83,811	104,637	30.1	12.5	9.8	6.4	9.9
Bangor, ME	2,339	1,534.7	36,421	14.9	40.5	28.6	298.4	13,745	29,603	52,128	67,988	48.4	3.4	13.4	7.8	15.0
Barnstable Town, MA	1,730	817.8	37,386	16.4	26.9	45.0	490.5	20,040	47,315	76,863	99,410	31.7	10.7	6.7	4.3	8.1
Baton Rouge, LA	26,433	3,091.0	227,062	19.6	43.6	28.8	1,647.2	12,345	32,252	60,043	77,948	42.0	6.3	15.3	10.9	17.3
Battle Creek, MI	3,170	2,374.4	31,066	12.8	45.0	21.5	273.9	14,172	27,939	50,219	64,670	49.8	3.4	16.7	11.7	20.6
Bay City, MI	1,084	1,059.8	21,763	12.6	43.9	19.7	166.9	12,191	28,331	48,290	62,204	51.6	2.5	16.1	11.9	22.2
Beaumont-Port Arthur, TX	8,036	2,052.0	91,698	10.0	48.6	18.4	666.8	9,819	28,525	54,256	68,971	46.0	4.8	15.8	12.1	20.2
Beckley, WV	2,269	1,977.9	23,787	13.0	54.2	18.2	208.4	11,599	24,081	43,444	56,860	55.6	1.6	21.0	16.3	26.4
Bellingham, WA	5,459	2,355.2	56,513	12.4	29.5	35.3	383.9	13,666	33,241	65,420	83,751	37.5	5.1	13.9	7.3	11.2
Bend, OR	3,664	1,816.5	38,042	14.3	27.8	37.2	312.4	11,571	37,615	68,937	81,822	35.6	7.6	9.8	6.4	10.4
Billings, MT	6,378	3,471.9	40,017	16.7	34.9	32.4	294.1	11,027	37,013	62,722	80,720	39.3	6.4	9.5	6.6	11.2
Binghamton, NY	4,857	2,059.8	61,587	9.2	41.5	28.2	701.1	20,753	30,240	54,695	71,132	46.5	3.7	16.7	10.6	20.1
Birmingham-Hoover, AL	NA	NA	262,344	16.6	37.5	32.3	1,757.8	10,533	33,226	59,185	75,287	42.7	6.5	13.6	9.7	15.4
Bismarck, ND	3,692	2,847.1	28,645	19.0	30.0	34.0	235.1	12,657	39,256	72,886	93,359	32.7	6.3	7.6	4.3	6.8
Blacksburg-Christiansburg, VA	2,476	1,474.6	58,728	7.4	35.4	35.9	203.0	11,219	28,930	55,475	74,841	44.5	4.8	21.4	7.9	13.6
Bloomington, IL	D	D	56,942	11.9	27.9	44.6	348.4	13,866	34,496	68,037	93,882	38.5	7.0	15.2	8.0	9.6
Bloomington, IN	3,072	1,805.7	61,591	7.3	33.2	40.7	183.4	10,789	29,170	52,226	74,499	48.1	4.6	21.5	10.3	17.2
Bloomsburg-Berwick, PA	NA	NA	19,940	11.8	51.1	26.3	138.5	16,364	29,651	53,546	70,725	47.0	3.9	13.2	7.9	14.1
Boise City, ID	8,958	1,161.7	190,730	14.7	32.3	33.2	991.0	7,705	32,704	64,717	77,090	37.0	6.5	10.5	6.7	9.7
Boston-Cambridge-Newton, MA-NH	48,653	995.9	1,214,195	30.4	29.6	48.9	11,913.9	18,063	49,528	93,537	116,181	27.9	17.1	9.0	5.8	9.0
Boston, MA Div	24,457	1,200.6	519,644	34.0	31.0	47.6	5,017.0	18,756	48,764	90,063	112,607	29.9	16.3	10.6	6.9	10.5
Cambridge-Newton-Framingham, MA Div	19,930	828.7	594,565	29.4	28.1	51.7	5,973.2	17,840	50,984	97,956	121,481	26.6	18.7	8.2	5.4	8.4
Rockingham County-Strafford County, NH Div	4,266	962.0	99,986	17.3	31.3	40.0	923.6	16,131	45,107	87,124	107,377	26.2	12.5	5.8	3.4	5.7
Boulder, CO	9,046	2,760.1	97,287	10.9	15.8	63.0	743.4	11,651	48,776	87,476	118,307	29.7	15.6	11.2	4.2	5.9
Bowling Green, KY	4,163	2,294.5	47,807	9.7	44.6	27.1	280.6	10,075	28,280	51,591	62,888	48.5	3.8	17.5	13.0	21.0
Bremerton-Silverdale-Port Orchard, WA	4,887	1,791.0	57,113	13.9	26.4	34.4	549.7	15,124	39,993	78,969	93,126	29.2	8.7	8.2	5.7	9.9
Bridgeport-Stamford-Norwalk, CT	D	D	248,483	24.6	30.6	48.9	3,029.1	21,004	58,851	97,539	120,156	27.3	22.2	8.9	6.3	9.6
Brownsville-Harlingen, TX	8,261	1,950.8	123,451	4.1	57.6	18.2	1,002.3	10,558	18,247	41,200	47,332	57.0	2.3	26.7	23.6	31.2
Brunswick, GA	NA	NA	25,897	14.8	44.3	24.5	199.5	11,044	30,881	53,541	68,432	47.0	4.2	17.1	13.2	23.9
Buffalo-Cheektowaga, NY	21,574	1,926.3	257,464	18.1	35.9	33.3	2,798.5	17,948	34,438	59,079	79,486	42.9	5.2	13.5	9.5	16.3
Burlington, NC	4,070	2,370.9	42,186	23.9	40.4	25.3	225.1	9,049	27,944	51,580	66,737	48.5	3.0	15.4	11.6	18.4
Burlington-South Burlington, VT	3,561	1,609.5	57,437	17.9	29.4	46.2	607.9	19,304	38,701	73,447	95,011	34.0	8.4	10.7	5.2	8.1
California-Lexington Park, MD	1,556	1,364.5	29,775	16.9	40.2	32.0	241.9	13,438	41,430	95,864	110,946	24.4	11.9	8.0	6.7	10.6
Canton-Massillon, OH	8,546	2,156.5	89,238	17.2	47.0	22.8	714.6	12,245	30,150	54,854	70,028	45.7	3.4	13.3	9.6	18.0
Cape Coral-Fort Myers, FL	8,118	1,031.5	144,206	14.0	41.9	28.5	911.7	9,657	34,818	59,608	71,043	41.4	6.4	11.8	7.9	14.6
Cape Girardeau, MO-IL	1,811	1,871.2	25,752	15.1	43.9	27.6	133.2	10,129	26,335	51,428	67,914	48.3	3.1	16.5	9.2	15.5
Carbondale-Marion, IL	NA	NA	36,737	8.2	36.6	28.4	261.8	13,806	27,566	46,563	67,046	52.8	3.5	18.1	11.8	20.9
Carson City, NV	643	1,143.1	11,577	8.3	38.5	22.9	389.5	7,718	32,819	58,305	69,727	41.8	4.9	10.0	6.3	9.5
Casper, WY	1,954	2,423.6	19,609	9.4	35.8	23.5	193.8	14,480	34,779	62,168	78,926	39.9	5.6	9.6	6.4	11.3

1. Data for serious crimes have not been adjusted for underreporting; this may affect comparability between geographic areas and over time. 2. Per 100,000 population estimated by the FBI. 3. All persons 3 years old and over enrolled in nursery school through college. 4. Persons 25 years old and over. 5. Elementary and secondary education expenditures. 6. Based on population estimated by the American Community Survey, 2015.

Area name	Personal income, 2020: Total (mil dol)	Personal income, 2020: Percent change, 2019–2020	Personal income, 2020: Per capita[1]: Dollars	Personal income, 2020: Per capita[1]: Rank	Personal income, 2020: Wages and Salaries (mil dol)	Personal income, 2020: Supplements to wages and salaries, employer contributions (mil dol): Pension and insurance	Personal income, 2020: Supplements to wages and salaries, employer contributions (mil dol): Government social insurance	Personal income, 2020: Proprietors' income	Personal income, 2020: Dividends, interest, and rent (mil dol)	Personal income, 2020: Personal transfer receipts (mil dol)	Earnings, 2020: Total (mil dol)	Earnings, 2020: Contributrions for government social insurance (mil dol): From employee and self-employed	Earnings, 2020: Contributrions for government social insurance (mil dol): From employer
	62	63	64	65	66	67	68	69	70	71	72	73	74
Abilene, TX	8,650	8.2	49,948	202	3,682	668	265	602	1,741	2,245	5,217	299	265
Akron, OH	38,469	5.8	54,843	123	17,758	2,884	1,250	2,766	6,384	9,014	24,659	1,507	1,250
Albany, GA	6,207	9.2	42,744	343	2,847	524	198	281	871	2,031	3,850	242	198
Albany-Lebanon, OR	6,296	10.5	48,040	242	2,293	399	213	473	847	2,094	3,379	238	213
Albany-Schenectady-Troy, NY	57,204	7.4	65,112	34	27,786	6,018	2,175	3,512	10,450	12,811	39,491	2,176	2,175
Albuquerque, NM	43,819	8.4	47,442	257	21,182	3,354	1,617	2,211	7,189	11,866	28,364	1,952	1,617
Alexandria, LA	7,233	6.9	47,961	245	2,883	572	193	762	1,077	2,352	4,410	263	193
Allentown-Bethlehem-Easton, PA-NJ	50,101	7.2	59,193	72	20,694	3,484	1,588	3,896	7,400	12,663	29,662	1,861	1,588
Altoona, PA	6,304	8.7	52,096	159	2,735	566	228	481	890	2,127	4,009	260	228
Amarillo, TX	13,585	4.8	51,116	179	6,282	996	435	1,599	2,247	2,881	9,313	516	435
Ames, IA	5,881	5.2	47,233	261	2,942	682	223	386	1,254	1,128	4,233	262	223
Anchorage, AK	25,787	2.7	64,904	36	11,744	2,795	881	1,942	4,735	4,909	17,363	944	881
Ann Arbor, MI	23,328	3.7	63,655	40	13,083	2,451	925	1,413	5,125	3,973	17,871	1,060	925
Anniston-Oxford, AL	4,561	6.0	40,195	370	2,000	415	150	189	715	1,536	2,754	198	150
Appleton, WI	13,141	4.7	54,988	122	6,698	1,155	503	875	2,081	2,319	9,232	581	503
Asheville, NC	23,243	5.4	49,809	208	9,331	1,474	696	1,922	5,282	6,234	13,422	953	696
Athens-Clarke County, GA	9,528	5.2	44,364	318	4,634	914	298	671	1,911	2,150	6,517	367	298
Atlanta-Sandy Springs-Alpharetta, GA	357,796	6.6	58,773	74	188,668	24,683	12,408	36,805	62,245	60,984	262,564	15,286	12,408
Atlantic City-Hammonton, NJ	14,673	8.6	55,802	107	6,418	1,174	519	1,192	1,963	4,565	9,302	595	519
Auburn-Opelika, AL	7,085	6.2	42,468	345	2,800	500	206	321	1,431	1,522	3,826	252	206
Augusta-Richmond County, GA-SC	28,623	7.8	46,594	274	13,700	2,584	978	1,557	4,574	7,714	18,819	1,152	978
Austin-Round Rock-Georgetown, TX	148,994	7.1	64,913	35	80,577	9,719	5,107	16,171	29,939	18,806	111,574	5,938	5,107
Bakersfield, CA	40,310	13.4	44,721	309	18,026	4,024	1,359	4,347	4,554	11,326	27,756	1,494	1,359
Baltimore-Columbia-Towson, MD	186,760	6.2	66,695	30	99,023	15,706	7,086	12,478	30,860	36,927	134,292	8,052	7,086
Bangor, ME	7,176	9.7	47,315	258	3,524	658	256	316	974	2,237	4,754	321	256
Barnstable Town, MA	17,143	6.9	80,420	10	5,085	932	378	1,601	4,279	4,323	7,996	497	378
Baton Rouge, LA	45,486	6.1	52,978	143	22,576	3,825	1,441	3,632	7,373	10,652	31,473	1,786	1,441
Battle Creek, MI	5,975	10.5	44,729	308	3,092	520	232	231	899	2,114	4,074	277	232
Bay City, MI	4,893	9.1	47,786	249	1,724	315	130	233	701	1,764	2,402	177	130
Beaumont-Port Arthur, TX	18,501	4.6	47,281	259	9,057	1,655	625	1,050	2,414	5,493	12,387	728	625
Beckley, WV	4,934	3.5	42,914	340	1,867	339	153	269	642	1,974	2,628	204	153
Bellingham, WA	12,195	6.9	52,787	145	4,905	899	432	1,224	2,441	2,905	7,460	451	432
Bend, OR	12,351	8.8	61,216	56	4,623	708	402	1,711	2,985	2,774	7,445	491	402
Billings, MT	10,412	5.7	56,649	97	4,895	704	420	910	2,108	2,197	6,929	474	420
Binghamton, NY	11,784	8.4	49,652	210	4,922	1,189	394	596	1,707	3,679	7,101	432	394
Birmingham-Hoover, AL	60,136	3.6	55,074	119	29,879	4,315	2,117	5,087	11,316	12,744	41,398	2,734	2,117
Bismarck, ND	7,960	3.9	61,404	55	3,814	586	314	657	1,569	1,426	5,371	354	314
Blacksburg-Christiansburg, VA	6,806	6.2	40,692	368	3,392	710	250	266	1,220	1,772	4,618	299	250
Bloomington, IL	9,357	9.8	54,639	127	5,553	913	343	730	1,423	1,613	7,539	417	343
Bloomington, IN	7,861	6.4	46,502	276	3,715	824	273	530	1,592	1,653	5,341	324	273
Bloomsburg-Berwick, PA	4,208	8.1	50,771	185	2,314	455	164	255	584	1,218	3,188	201	164
Boise City, ID	38,882	8.7	50,474	192	19,084	2,720	1,569	3,502	7,440	7,614	26,874	1,794	1,569
Boston-Cambridge-Newton, MA-NH	418,178	5.9	85,724	6	239,358	30,851	15,352	37,030	79,478	68,509	322,591	17,456	15,352
Boston, MA Div	180,910	6.5	88,911	X	114,729	15,045	7,143	18,101	35,126	31,310	155,019	8,174	7,143
Cambridge-Newton-Framingham, MA Div	204,915	5.7	85,358	X	111,504	13,927	7,313	15,376	39,424	32,149	148,121	8,073	7,313
Rockingham County-Strafford County, NH Div	32,353	4.1	73,057	X	13,125	1,879	895	3,552	4,927	5,051	19,451	1,209	895
Boulder, CO	26,059	3.4	79,649	12	14,939	1,729	978	1,931	7,302	3,094	19,576	1,115	978
Bowling Green, KY	7,182	8.2	39,734	376	3,343	620	260	477	942	2,206	4,700	315	260
Bremerton-Silverdale-Port Orchard, WA	16,559	6.3	60,704	64	5,979	1,390	508	835	3,588	3,407	8,712	532	508
Bridgeport-Stamford-Norwalk, CT	113,322	1.2	120,244	3	39,482	4,918	2,404	12,439	32,949	11,496	59,242	3,283	2,404
Brownsville-Harlingen, TX	14,291	12.0	33,690	383	5,405	1,116	392	1,099	1,727	5,421	8,011	478	392
Brunswick, GA	5,392	6.6	45,251	300	2,030	377	142	294	1,336	1,527	2,843	189	142
Buffalo-Cheektowaga, NY	62,785	8.5	55,777	108	28,765	6,075	2,278	4,190	8,430	18,207	41,308	2,380	2,278
Burlington, NC	7,535	8.0	43,973	326	3,082	445	224	384	1,166	2,018	4,134	294	224
Burlington-South Burlington, VT	13,668	5.7	61,802	51	7,120	1,141	561	1,130	2,466	2,703	9,953	647	561
California-Lexington Park, MD	7,012	6.5	61,144	59	3,945	816	301	263	1,123	1,222	5,325	303	301
Canton-Massillon, OH	19,538	6.8	49,255	217	7,844	1,342	582	1,149	3,002	5,492	10,917	729	582
Cape Coral-Fort Myers, FL	43,261	6.0	54,707	125	14,566	2,021	1,003	2,847	15,722	10,388	20,437	1,526	1,003
Cape Girardeau, MO-IL	4,448	5.5	45,802	287	2,117	381	153	328	699	1,212	2,979	196	153
Carbondale-Marion, IL	6,005	7.2	44,335	320	2,712	676	180	316	911	1,761	3,883	221	180
Carson City, NV	3,166	7.1	56,510	98	1,680	402	104	384	604	831	2,569	137	104
Casper, WY	5,532	-1.0	68,447	22	2,010	308	187	1,522	970	920	4,027	218	187

1. Based on the resident population estimated as of July 1 of the year shown.

Area name	Earnings, 2020 (cont.) — Percent by selected industries: Farm	Mining, quarrying, and extracting	Construction	Manufacturing	Information; professional, scientific, and technical services	Retail trade	Finance, insurance, real estate, rental and leasing	Health care and social assistance	Government	Social Security beneficiaries, December 2020: Number	Rate[1]	Supplemental Security Income Recipients, December 2020	Housing units, 2021: Total	Percent change, 2020–2021
	75	76	77	78	79	80	81	82	83	84	85	86	87	88
Abilene, TX	0.0	2.9	6.9	3.9	6.9	7.3	8.1	D	24.5	33,450	189	4,242	75,040	0.8
Akron, OH	0.0	0.1	7.4	12.0	9.3	7.8	6.3	13.8	13.1	147,230	210	17,896	317,772	0.2
Albany, GA	2.7	D	4.9	8.9	4.8	7.2	D	16.8	22.3	31,775	215	6,586	67,131	0.4
Albany-Lebanon, OR	3.3	D	8.1	20.1	4.2	8.1	4.2	10.9	14.9	32,000	246	3,497	52,859	1.5
Albany-Schenectady-Troy, NY	0.2	D	6.0	8.2	12.6	5.3	8.3	11.8	25.4	193,125	215	19,634	419,730	0.4
Albuquerque, NM	0.2	D	7.2	4.7	D	6.2	D	D	25.3	189,375	206	22,718	397,946	0.6
Alexandria, LA	1.4	D	6.7	7.7	D	10.0	D	D	23.2	33,675	223	7,266	67,331	0.5
Allentown-Bethlehem-Easton, PA-NJ	0.2	0.1	4.6	13.1	9.6	5.7	5.6	17.2	11.3	194,005	224	18,956	359,805	0.4
Altoona, PA	1.0	0.4	5.6	12.1	5.3	8.5	4.4	20.2	15.8	31,245	257	4,304	55,791	0.1
Amarillo, TX	1.5	1.8	D	14.7	D	7.2	D	12.1	15.5	45,220	168	4,282	114,701	0.8
Ames, IA	1.4	D	6.6	11.6	8.2	5.4	4.3	7.8	36.0	20,215	160	1,060	53,619	0.4
Anchorage, AK	0.1	3.1	8.4	D	9.0	6.1	5.4	15.2	28.4	56,665	142	7,449	170,953	0.6
Ann Arbor, MI	0.1	D	2.9	6.6	19.8	3.9	4.8	10.8	33.9	61,740	167	5,232	157,985	0.6
Anniston-Oxford, AL	0.1	D	3.7	16.0	4.4	8.1	4.0	8.8	33.5	30,370	262	4,354	53,205	0.2
Appleton, WI	1.8	0.2	10.1	21.1	D	6.2	9.5	D	10.6	47,115	193	2,774	101,946	1.2
Asheville, NC	0.6	0.1	7.2	11.7	D	8.3	6.6	D	14.7	124,475	264	9,274	235,469	1.4
Athens-Clarke County, GA	0.7	0.2	5.2	7.7	D	6.6	8.6	15.7	29.1	37,085	170	4,597	90,765	1.3
Atlanta-Sandy Springs-Alpharetta, GA	0.0	D	D	5.7	20.9	5.4	11.8	8.9	10.6	921,005	150	116,611	2,451,423	1.2
Atlantic City-Hammonton, NJ	0.8	D	7.3	D	7.4	7.1	5.4	16.7	23.6	61,510	224	7,137	132,228	0.1
Auburn-Opelika, AL	0.5	D	7.4	10.8	5.4	7.0	3.9	6.1	33.1	27,700	156	3,166	77,656	3.0
Augusta-Richmond County, GA-SC	0.4	D	D	10.0	D	5.8	D	10.6	27.1	131,185	213	16,842	267,702	1.3
Austin-Round Rock-Georgetown, TX	0.0	4.8	7.6	7.9	D	5.3	8.8	7.4	13.2	279,760	119	25,799	996,723	4.4
Bakersfield, CA	8.4	4.8	5.8	4.0	4.6	6.5	3.5	9.8	24.9	128,525	140	33,197	303,888	0.8
Baltimore-Columbia-Towson, MD	0.1	0.0	6.4	4.8	16.7	4.4	9.2	12.2	22.1	498,500	176	68,420	1,196,227	0.4
Bangor, ME	0.3	D	6.2	4.2	5.2	8.7	4.7	24.4	19.6	38,945	255	5,379	75,281	0.5
Barnstable Town, MA	0.1	D	12.7	2.5	8.8	9.7	8.1	15.7	18.2	74,660	321	3,046	165,524	0.3
Baton Rouge, LA	0.2	D	13.2	D	D	5.5	D	11.0	17.1	152,105	174	24,760	380,176	1.0
Battle Creek, MI	0.7	0.1	4.1	20.6	9.5	5.5	2.5	14.2	21.2	33,385	249	4,707	59,558	0.1
Bay City, MI	1.3	0.1	4.9	19.3	8.4	8.1	4.5	15.4	16.1	29,570	287	3,080	48,652	0.2
Beaumont-Port Arthur, TX	0.0	0.7	D	D	D	6.7	D	10.4	14.1	76,885	194	11,441	171,704	1.0
Beckley, WV	0.0	9.3	4.4	4.1	D	8.6	3.2	19.2	23.0	34,550	304	5,456	53,660	0.0
Bellingham, WA	3.6	D	10.8	12.1	7.5	7.8	7.2	12.2	18.3	47,805	209	4,258	101,867	1.4
Bend, OR	0.0	0.1	14.7	5.3	11.8	7.8	9.9	17.0	11.3	48,020	234	2,344	96,938	2.5
Billings, MT	1.4	D	8.0	D	8.7	D	8.5	D	11.6	39,300	210	2,754	84,525	1.7
Binghamton, NY	0.4	0.2	5.9	15.3	D	6.4	4.5	17.6	24.7	60,455	247	8,182	114,809	0.3
Birmingham-Hoover, AL	0.1	0.8	7.9	7.0	D	5.6	12.0	D	14.4	236,355	212	29,936	492,054	0.7
Bismarck, ND	1.7	D	7.0	3.8	D	D	7.5	17.9	19.6	25,180	187	1,217	59,564	1.2
Blacksburg-Christiansburg, VA	0.3	D	4.4	19.3	8.5	6.1	2.6	8.9	34.8	31,975	193	2,916	74,604	2.2
Bloomington, IL	2.3	D	3.3	3.7	D	5.5	38.3	D	14.5	28,265	165	1,931	75,077	0.3
Bloomington, IN	0.2	0.6	4.9	14.5	9.6	4.8	4.9	13.4	30.7	28,435	176	2,198	74,207	0.9
Bloomsburg-Berwick, PA	0.8	D	3.1	10.3	D	4.8	6.2	33.4	14.7	20,890	252	1,741	37,833	0.2
Boise City, ID	1.8	0.1	9.4	11.2	D	8.1	D	12.7	13.0	142,555	179	11,904	307,886	3.2
Boston-Cambridge-Newton, MA-NH	0.0	D	5.7	6.8	25.4	4.1	13.3	11.6	10.0	837,680	171	101,241	2,048,740	0.6
Boston, MA Div 14,454	0.0	D	5.2	3.0	22.1	3.9	20.5	13.6	10.7	334,825	165	51,663	863,555	0.7
Cambridge-Newton-Framingham, MA Div 15,754	0.1	0.0	5.8	10.4	30.3	3.7	6.3	9.6	9.2	406,760	168	45,564	992,271	0.5
Rockingham County-Strafford County, NH Div 40,484	0.0	D	8.4	10.1	15.1	8.2	9.2	10.2	10.3	96,095	214	4,014	192,914	0.7
Boulder, CO	0.1	0.2	3.7	11.7	33.4	4.5	6.2	9.1	14.2	49,545	150	2,163	143,154	1.3
Bowling Green, KY	1.6	D	7.7	17.4	5.1	7.2	D	14.0	14.3	34,100	187	5,033	79,045	1.3
Bremerton-Silverdale-Port Orchard, WA	0.1	0.0	6.1	2.4	9.9	5.9	4.7	9.9	48.7	56,365	205	4,700	114,783	1.1
Bridgeport-Stamford-Norwalk, CT	0.0	-0.1	4.8	7.3	16.8	5.1	24.3	9.6	7.8	155,430	162	12,672	380,686	0.4
Brownsville-Harlingen, TX	0.7	0.1	4.2	5.4	3.5	8.2	5.5	21.0	26.4	69,450	164	21,202	157,394	1.3
Brunswick, GA	0.1	D	5.6	D	D	7.7	D	15.0	25.2	28,055	246	2,803	57,566	0.9
Buffalo-Cheektowaga, NY	0.2	0.2	4.7	11.5	9.3	6.1	8.9	13.5	21.0	264,970	228	32,351	540,430	0.2
Burlington, NC	0.0	D	7.2	14.4	4.8	9.9	7.1	18.9	10.8	36,860	212	3,638	75,276	2.2
Burlington-South Burlington, VT	1.0	D	5.5	10.3	D	6.7	6.4	D	18.7	43,860	194	4,441	102,247	1.0
California-Lexington Park, MD	0.1	0.0	4.4	1.2	25.8	3.7	1.8	6.5	46.0	17,475	153	1,695	46,196	1.1
Canton-Massillon, OH	0.2	D	7.5	17.9	D	7.3	6.4	D	12.8	96,080	240	10,467	180,722	0.2
Cape Coral-Fort Myers, FL	0.4	0.1	12.2	2.4	11.5	9.2	8.3	11.8	16.9	208,320	264	12,961	428,910	2.5
Cape Girardeau, MO-IL	1.4	0.6	5.5	11.4	D	8.2	4.6	24.3	13.7	21,990	225	2,326	43,980	0.3
Carbondale-Marion, IL	0.7	1.7	4.6	7.0	D	6.7	5.2	18.7	34.4	29,610	223	3,503	65,268	0.2
Carson City, NV	0.1	D	5.4	8.0	6.9	8.0	7.0	15.1	33.3	14,055	238	1,025	24,894	1.1
Casper, WY	0.3	6.0	6.6	3.6	4.3	5.2	5.0	11.2	11.3	15,715	198	1,307	37,048	0.5

1. Per 1,000 resident population estimated as of July 1 of the year shown.

Area name	Occupied housing units, 2016-2020: Occupied units: Total	Owner-occupied: Percent	Owner-occupied: Median value[1]	Owner-occupied: Median owner cost as a percent of income: With a mortgage	Owner-occupied: Median owner cost as a percent of income: Without a mortgage[2]	Renter-occupied: Median rent[3]	Renter-occupied: Median rent as a percent of income	Renter-occupied: Substandard units[4] (percent)	Civilian labor force, 2021: Total	Civilian labor force, 2021: Percent change 2020-2021	Unemployment: Total	Unemployment: Rate[5]	Civilian employment[6], 2016-2020: Total	Percent: Management, business, science, and arts	Percent: Construction, production, and maintenance occupations
	89	90	91	92	93	94	95	96	97	98	99	100	101	102	103
Abilene, TX	61,414	62.4	124,900	20.2	10.7	908	28.1	2.7	79,029	2.5	3,556	4.5	75,803	33.6	23.8
Akron, OH	289,506	67.3	153,600	18.8	11.2	857	28.8	1.0	349,835	-1.0	18,412	5.3	352,385	37.1	22.5
Albany, GA	56,120	55.6	120,200	20.7	11.0	779	30.6	1.9	65,123	0.4	3,423	5.3	61,515	31.3	27.1
Albany-Lebanon, OR	48,290	66.4	240,200	23.0	11.6	1,037	30.2	3.0	60,636	2.6	3,401	5.6	56,332	34.4	28.1
Albany-Schenectady-Troy, NY	359,734	63.5	221,200	19.6	11.3	1,039	27.3	1.5	447,773	-1.7	19,358	4.3	448,875	45.3	16.5
Albuquerque, NM	357,445	67.4	199,700	21.5	10.0	908	30.4	3.1	438,423	1.8	27,805	6.3	418,828	41.1	17.4
Alexandria, LA	56,129	65.7	144,500	18.5	10.0	814	32.6	2.5	63,632	1.3	2,558	4.0	63,036	33.3	24.7
Allentown-Bethlehem-Easton, PA-NJ	324,239	68.9	219,200	21.1	13.7	1,090	29.7	1.9	448,846	0.7	28,362	6.3	415,685	37.1	24.5
Altoona, PA	51,647	70.3	128,200	18.1	11.6	741	29.6	1.2	59,237	-1.3	3,536	6.0	56,352	32.6	26.7
Amarillo, TX	97,747	63.4	147,600	19.8	11.1	878	27.7	3.9	133,657	2.8	5,137	3.8	125,503	32.6	26.9
Ames, IA	48,798	59.7	179,700	18.8	11.0	909	31.5	0.9	71,947	0.4	2,208	3.1	65,574	43.2	19.4
Anchorage, AK	138,934	65.6	301,100	22.5	10.7	1,277	28.7	5.8	199,763	2.1	12,094	6.1	189,260	39.5	21.5
Ann Arbor, MI	143,040	61.5	278,500	19.4	11.3	1,161	30.6	1.4	189,511	-1.9	8,161	4.3	188,718	55.4	13.3
Anniston-Oxford, AL	44,572	70.4	121,600	18.9	10.0	720	26.0	1.5	46,118	-1.9	1,906	4.1	47,905	30.4	30.5
Appleton, WI	94,548	73.4	180,300	18.5	11.3	815	23.7	1.6	132,813	1.0	4,060	3.1	128,449	36.6	29.2
Asheville, NC	190,156	68.0	232,400	20.7	10.0	953	30.0	2.2	227,670	2.4	9,499	4.2	220,571	37.3	21.5
Athens-Clarke County, GA	80,156	54.6	193,700	19.4	10.0	869	32.8	2.2	100,078	2.5	3,304	3.3	101,079	42.7	20.5
Atlanta-Sandy Springs-Alpharetta, GA	2,152,319	64.2	233,700	19.9	10.0	1,205	29.8	2.3	3,132,224	2.3	122,955	3.9	2,962,178	42.7	20.1
Atlantic City-Hammonton, NJ	101,103	66.9	216,600	25.2	17.9	1,129	33.9	3.5	123,181	-0.8	11,665	9.5	125,436	33.5	17.3
Auburn-Opelika, AL	60,731	63.4	173,700	19.0	10.0	856	31.6	3.7	76,658	0.2	2,180	2.8	75,428	43.7	20.3
Augusta-Richmond County, GA-SC	217,664	67.5	153,300	19.2	10.0	899	30.9	1.7	266,626	0.8	10,539	4.0	258,561	34.9	24.3
Austin-Round Rock-Georgetown, TX	796,315	58.6	303,300	21.3	11.6	1,326	28.7	4.0	1,306,125	5.7	53,064	4.1	1,166,636	48.3	16.0
Bakersfield, CA	273,556	58.9	226,600	23.6	11.6	994	32.5	9.6	383,987	-0.5	38,555	10.0	346,787	28.2	33.9
Baltimore-Columbia-Towson, MD	1,062,780	66.6	307,200	20.8	10.6	1,324	29.4	1.9	1,482,507	-1.5	81,177	5.5	1,411,981	48.3	15.8
Bangor, ME	63,073	70.1	148,300	19.4	11.8	823	29.3	2.1	74,855	0.9	3,543	4.7	73,848	36.5	21.2
Barnstable Town, MA	95,859	79.6	414,000	24.8	13.6	1,362	32.8	1.4	112,478	1.8	7,553	6.7	105,798	40.6	18.0
Baton Rouge, LA	311,169	69.7	190,000	18.9	10.0	930	31.1	2.6	424,075	0.7	21,004	5.0	398,991	38.0	23.3
Battle Creek, MI	54,124	69.5	115,500	18.8	12.0	776	29.5	1.6	59,357	-3.9	3,898	6.6	59,819	31.1	30.3
Bay City, MI	44,627	76.1	106,400	19.5	12.1	679	27.8	1.3	47,921	-2.9	2,918	6.1	46,970	31.3	26.8
Beaumont-Port Arthur, TX	146,770	67.1	120,900	19.0	10.0	860	28.5	3.0	161,343	-2.0	15,305	9.5	165,754	29.6	30.6
Beckley, WV	48,504	75.7	104,100	18.9	10.9	691	30.1	1.6	46,061	-0.2	2,572	5.6	44,264	31.2	22.3
Bellingham, WA	88,978	62.2	369,000	23.5	11.2	1,119	33.0	3.9	113,751	-2.8	6,822	6.0	109,687	37.0	23.8
Bend, OR	77,040	67.9	389,300	23.8	11.9	1,306	30.9	3.4	102,553	4.4	5,429	5.3	94,505	38.8	18.9
Billings, MT	76,411	69.8	240,700	21.2	10.4	901	28.1	2.2	95,472	0.9	3,010	3.2	91,372	36.0	24.4
Binghamton, NY	100,171	67.7	120,100	18.9	12.0	782	31.6	1.9	103,397	-2.3	5,231	5.1	105,848	39.0	20.3
Birmingham-Hoover, AL	422,926	69.2	171,400	19.2	10.0	929	28.9	1.8	530,264	-0.6	16,654	3.1	498,583	39.7	22.2
Bismarck, ND	54,050	70.4	254,900	19.1	10.0	877	24.9	1.5	69,631	0.7	2,302	3.3	68,993	41.0	22.3
Blacksburg-Christiansburg, VA	62,446	60.3	189,300	18.7	10.0	905	29.2	1.8	81,596	0.0	2,704	3.3	76,801	42.4	20.2
Bloomington, IL	66,225	64.9	166,400	18.2	10.0	842	26.2	1.6	85,656	1.0	3,910	4.6	86,450	43.7	15.8
Bloomington, IN	65,229	58.3	177,700	18.4	10.0	931	34.2	1.7	78,337	1.8	2,341	3.0	83,450	44.0	18.2
Bloomsburg-Berwick, PA	33,957	68.4	160,800	19.2	11.6	772	27.4	1.3	42,276	-1.4	2,339	5.5	39,443	36.1	27.5
Boise City, ID	269,804	71.0	268,500	20.3	10.0	1,005	27.7	2.5	395,257	2.8	13,859	3.5	359,376	39.5	21.8
Boston-Cambridge-Newton, MA-NH	1,852,755	61.7	461,500	22.3	13.9	1,555	29.3	2.5	2,715,680	0.1	142,203	5.2	2,632,548	51.0	14.2
Boston, MA Div 14,454	771,300	57.7	465,600	22.6	13.6	1,612	29.8	2.8	1,127,428	-0.2	64,497	5.7	1,089,275	49.5	13.5
Cambridge-Newton-Framingham, MA Div 15,754	909,104	62.7	495,200	22.1	13.7	1,561	29.0	2.5	1,330,433	0.4	68,915	5.2	1,298,335	53.6	13.7
Rockingham County-Strafford County, NH Div 40,484	172,351	74.6	316,600	22.2	15.0	1,209	27.9	1.9	257,819	-0.5	8,791	3.4	244,938	43.6	19.7
Boulder, CO	127,365	63.6	539,100	20.7	10.0	1,582	33.7	1.7	195,616	2.6	8,522	4.4	175,556	54.9	13.0
Bowling Green, KY	67,547	62.7	161,500	19.0	10.0	798	28.0	3.7	83,011	1.8	3,572	4.3	85,431	32.3	28.2
Bremerton-Silverdale-Port Orchard, WA	105,758	68.1	362,700	22.5	10.9	1,349	29.4	1.9	128,186	-0.2	6,466	5.0	116,029	41.4	21.1
Bridgeport-Stamford-Norwalk, CT	345,070	66.7	433,000	23.7	15.0	1,511	32.2	3.0	465,448	-1.6	28,397	6.1	476,757	47.2	14.5
Brownsville-Harlingen, TX	126,968	66.2	89,700	21.7	11.8	746	30.8	10.6	175,073	3.4	14,287	8.2	164,139	28.3	22.9
Brunswick, GA	47,297	69.3	167,100	20.6	11.1	853	28.3	1.7	52,626	2.7	1,965	3.7	51,893	32.2	24.6
Buffalo-Cheektowaga, NY	482,932	66.1	155,800	18.5	11.9	831	29.4	1.6	531,800	-2.3	29,218	5.5	548,571	40.4	19.0
Burlington, NC	65,455	66.5	160,900	19.1	10.0	822	29.0	2.2	81,009	2.6	3,887	4.8	77,752	34.9	27.0
Burlington-South Burlington, VT	88,499	66.8	285,200	22.3	14.2	1,248	31.7	1.6	123,528	-3.2	3,706	3.0	120,630	47.8	17.7
California-Lexington Park, MD	41,280	70.3	318,500	20.3	10.0	1,436	26.5	1.9	57,574	-1.6	2,579	4.5	55,942	46.2	21.4
Canton-Massillon, OH	165,608	68.8	138,300	18.4	10.5	750	27.0	1.3	194,919	-0.6	10,222	5.2	189,310	33.3	26.3
Cape Coral-Fort Myers, FL	288,916	72.7	235,300	23.4	12.3	1,225	31.9	2.7	357,018	3.4	14,901	4.2	323,278	32.1	22.2
Cape Girardeau, MO-IL	36,893	68.5	152,300	19.0	11.3	776	28.3	1.5	47,625	0.1	1,824	3.8	45,720	35.3	24.3
Carbondale-Marion, IL	56,319	62.8	118,300	18.6	10.8	696	31.1	1.2	62,434	-0.2	3,442	5.5	58,067	36.5	21.6
Carson City, NV	22,858	58.2	299,900	22.1	10.0	982	27.6	3.9	25,665	0.4	1,231	4.8	25,998	33.3	24.2
Casper, WY	32,896	70.6	215,400	19.9	10.0	846	28.0	2.3	39,057	-2.6	2,369	6.1	41,451	34.2	25.7

1. Specified owner-occupied units. 2. A value of 10.0 represents 10 percent or less; a value of 50.0 represents 50 percent or more. 3. Specified renter-occupied units. 4. Overcrowded or lacking complete plumbing facilities. 5. Percent of civilian labor force. 6. Civilian employed persons 16 years old and over.

Area name	Private nonfarm establishments, employment and payroll, 2020									Agriculture, 2017			
		Employment						Annual payroll		Farms			
											Percent with:		
	Number of establish-ments	Total	Health care and social assistance	Manufactur-ing	Retail trade	Finance and insurance	Professional, scientific, and technical services	Total (mil dol)	Average per employee (dollars)	Number	Fewer than 50 acres	1000 acres or more	Farm producers whose primary occupation is farming (percent)
	104	105	106	107	108	109	110	111	112	113	114	115	116
Abilene, TX	4,060	61,885	13,482	3,334	8,803	2,911	1,991	2,457	39,704	3,270	35.4	10.7	33.8
Akron, OH	16,168	294,799	50,781	38,094	38,535	10,319	15,138	14,512	49,226	1,510	70.8	0.9	32.4
Albany, GA	3,079	46,150	9,696	4,343	7,312	1,298	2,169	1,861	40,326	1,041	32.2	14.7	41.2
Albany-Lebanon, OR	2,713	38,205	5,723	8,048	5,442	894	1,288	1,779	46,554	2,222	71.2	3.1	41.6
Albany-Schenectady-Troy, NY	21,217	358,674	71,898	25,857	46,339	18,400	31,440	19,362	53,982	2,227	40.0	1.4	46.4
Albuquerque, NM	18,788	318,367	60,679	16,059	40,953	14,734	34,118	14,342	45,048	4,331	73.8	7.3	34.3
Alexandria, LA	3,326	47,938	14,534	3,199	7,749	1,403	1,874	2,023	42,203	1,063	48.1	6.6	41.9
Allentown-Bethlehem-Easton, PA-NJ	18,488	343,255	72,377	37,510	46,203	10,387	13,596	17,578	51,209	1,958	64.5	2.2	40.4
Altoona, PA	3,182	54,188	13,622	6,389	8,870	1,020	1,693	2,225	41,057	496	34.9	1.6	52.7
Amarillo, TX	6,361	97,227	18,141	11,485	14,518	5,033	2,992	4,399	45,244	1,699	29.4	25.7	40.1
Ames, IA	2,687	39,387	7,257	6,057	6,012	823	1,270	1,836	46,619	1,922	46.0	10.5	37.2
Anchorage, AK	11,122	166,580	32,194	3,145	18,979	5,124	15,502	10,305	61,860	350	64.3	0.9	44.4
Ann Arbor, MI	8,222	156,611	40,193	14,710	17,683	3,247	16,315	9,409	60,077	1,245	59.7	2.7	39.8
Anniston-Oxford, AL	2,234	35,684	6,081	6,923	6,238	918	931	1,278	35,819	643	43.4	1.4	34.5
Appleton, WI	6,027	114,032	14,542	23,264	14,469	5,550	4,083	5,517	48,381	1,814	43.6	4.0	47.9
Asheville, NC	13,729	179,618	37,514	21,842	28,688	4,047	6,696	7,311	40,701	2,708	62.3	0.9	38.7
Athens-Clarke County, GA	4,936	67,140	13,468	7,417	10,941	1,770	2,878	2,732	40,687	1,520	47.8	1.6	38.8
Atlanta-Sandy Springs-Alpharetta, GA	152,690	2,478,931	303,159	158,055	281,393	122,004	236,248	147,845	59,640	7,760	55.7	1.0	39.4
Atlantic City-Hammonton, NJ	6,128	110,573	19,125	2,668	15,437	2,422	4,006	4,455	40,294	450	75.3	0.9	52.1
Auburn-Opelika, AL	2,979	47,269	6,756	7,204	7,274	1,074	1,810	1,704	36,055	314	43.9	5.7	35.5
Augusta-Richmond County, GA-SC	11,005	194,902	39,089	20,123	27,422	3,545	8,592	9,003	46,192	2,787	48.4	4.6	37.0
Austin-Round Rock-Georgetown, TX	57,973	920,787	113,819	44,489	118,703	41,013	116,065	57,764	62,733	8,498	52.5	3.8	34.1
Bakersfield, CA	13,447	203,389	32,910	13,226	30,855	5,091	9,040	9,684	47,611	1,731	40.3	17.6	51.1
Baltimore-Columbia-Towson, MD	67,391	1,211,106	215,974	54,158	143,737	52,921	141,944	72,244	59,651	3,704	61.7	2.6	40.3
Bangor, ME	4,073	57,767	14,866	2,827	10,594	1,912	1,849	2,623	45,404	601	41.3	3.2	44.6
Barnstable Town, MA	8,560	76,154	15,945	2,075	15,051	1,961	4,747	3,652	47,961	321	93.5	0.0	46.5
Baton Rouge, LA	18,904	352,078	46,744	25,552	41,850	14,480	26,720	17,886	50,801	2,866	53.4	8.1	40.4
Battle Creek, MI	2,409	50,383	9,313	13,446	5,918	1,027	1,822	2,580	51,199	958	42.6	5.8	44.2
Bay City, MI	2,040	29,293	6,412	4,323	5,065	863	1,176	1,240	42,330	726	36.8	8.8	48.8
Beaumont-Port Arthur, TX	7,749	129,115	19,866	19,174	19,582	3,416	6,576	6,520	50,495	2,053	69.1	3.6	35.5
Beckley, WV	2,357	32,193	8,420	1,138	5,789	695	1,554	1,205	37,430	618	50.0	1.0	35.1
Bellingham, WA	6,859	78,281	10,899	9,965	10,867	2,460	3,611	3,672	46,903	1,712	79.6	0.7	35.4
Bend, OR	7,821	74,136	11,282	5,735	11,699	2,342	4,006	3,345	45,118	1,484	85.4	0.8	34.7
Billings, MT	6,354	76,407	14,943	4,241	10,681	3,956	3,822	3,727	48,779	2,601	35.9	20.2	41.8
Binghamton, NY	4,801	79,636	17,831	7,724	11,690	2,218	6,460	3,636	45,655	1,029	32.9	1.7	44.1
Birmingham-Hoover, AL	24,941	464,362	82,560	36,472	54,222	32,507	23,708	24,559	52,887	3,138	45.0	1.6	36.8
Bismarck, ND	3,987	59,494	12,875	3,332	8,832	2,122	4,839	2,854	47,971	1,800	20.2	32.7	45.6
Blacksburg-Christiansburg, VA	3,179	48,355	7,316	11,844	7,647	1,102	2,928	2,034	42,056	1,367	40.7	2.9	35.4
Bloomington, IL	3,461	72,607	8,488	3,494	8,770	18,750	2,530	4,092	56,357	1,416	33.9	13.8	46.4
Bloomington, IN	3,395	56,880	11,646	9,658	6,878	1,801	1,977	2,363	41,548	1,139	47.5	2.4	31.0
Bloomsburg-Berwick, PA	1,837	37,752	11,447	5,194	3,969	1,968	868	2,018	53,465	1,135	43.7	1.4	39.5
Boise City, ID	21,105	288,704	49,736	26,504	36,149	11,450	17,372	14,509	50,255	5,108	76.4	4.1	37.5
Boston-Cambridge-Newton, MA-NH	131,172	2,608,456	447,470	161,560	268,816	157,465	289,119	202,842	77,763	2,943	74.4	0.4	43.1
Boston, MA Div 14,454	54,914	1,186,802	234,211	37,134	113,070	106,091	122,332	95,212	80,226	976	76.6	0.7	46.1
Cambridge-Newton-Framingham, MA Div 15,754	63,683	1,233,107	188,196	103,138	122,350	40,458	155,695	97,480	79,052	1,039	75.6	0.2	43.8
Rockingham County-Strafford County, NH Div 40,484	12,575	188,547	25,063	21,288	33,396	10,916	11,092	10,150	53,832	928	70.9	0.2	39.1
Boulder, CO	13,013	157,780	21,664	14,700	18,673	3,959	26,954	10,802	68,460	1,012	79.0	2.2	33.1
Bowling Green, KY	3,379	62,283	9,496	11,626	8,501	1,627	3,478	2,628	42,196	4,102	41.2	2.2	33.9
Bremerton-Silverdale-Port Orchard, WA	6,016	63,101	13,364	2,212	12,008	1,719	4,947	2,708	42,921	698	96.3	0.0	29.0
Bridgeport-Stamford-Norwalk, CT	26,625	426,426	74,303	35,401	49,271	30,392	44,933	35,375	82,957	402	81.8	2.2	49.3
Brownsville-Harlingen, TX	6,463	113,358	39,443	4,327	17,737	4,090	3,123	3,237	28,560	1,418	74.3	6.3	34.1
Brunswick, GA	2,971	34,273	5,742	2,116	5,789	803	1,065	1,279	37,319	320	55.0	0.6	32.2
Buffalo-Cheektowaga, NY	26,928	485,794	90,690	52,786	63,480	33,426	28,876	22,525	46,368	1,630	51.2	3.7	46.3
Burlington, NC	3,406	59,474	11,312	8,383	9,530	1,381	1,616	2,397	40,299	720	45.8	0.7	40.6
Burlington-South Burlington, VT	6,764	102,334	20,099	11,951	14,657	3,095	7,192	5,069	49,537	1,433	41.6	2.7	45.0
California-Lexington Park, MD	2,006	34,465	4,638	504	5,003	460	11,543	1,956	56,764	615	57.2	1.5	43.7
Canton-Massillon, OH	8,458	148,495	30,115	25,496	20,803	5,160	4,798	6,040	40,673	2,435	59.3	1.3	35.1
Cape Coral-Fort Myers, FL	20,054	235,798	38,416	5,385	41,511	6,061	13,990	10,277	43,584	800	81.6	2.4	38.5
Cape Girardeau, MO-IL	2,610	40,916	11,193	4,231	6,189	1,090	1,312	1,651	40,353	1,993	28.8	5.1	40.6
Carbondale-Marion, IL	2,930	40,793	10,678	4,160	7,041	2,013	1,296	1,588	38,933	2,035	37.8	4.8	35.6
Carson City, NV	1,902	22,503	4,480	2,642	3,233	1,112	1,011	1,058	47,008	17	70.6	D	53.3
Casper, WY	2,906	32,314	5,880	1,666	4,687	943	1,761	1,593	49,290	430	40.0	25.3	39.3

Area name	Agriculture, 2017 (cont.)															
	Land in farms					Value of land and buildings		Value of machinery and equipmnet, average per farm (dollars)	Value of products sold:				Organic farms (number)	Farms with internet access (percent)	Government payments	
	Acreage (1,000)	Percent change, 2012–2017	Acres			Average per farm	Average per acre		Total (mil dol)	Average per farm (acres)	Percent from:				Total ($1,000)	Percent of farms
			Average size of farm	Total irrigated (1,000)	Total cropland (1,000)						Crops	Livestock and poultry products				
	117	118	119	120	121	122	123	124	125	126	127	128	129	130	131	132
Abilene, TX	1,479	-13.3	452	6.0	558.5	737,343	1,631	70,790	104.3	31,887	42.2	57.8	0	74.3	7,701	26.5
Akron, OH	105	4.8	69	0.5	70.1	536,277	7,740	69,000	47.1	31,188	70.3	29.7	7	80.5	1,499	9.5
Albany, GA	537	3.0	515	118.7	302.2	1,619,933	3,143	230,125	258.1	247,927	85.1	14.9	0	76.9	21,748	55.8
Albany-Lebanon, OR	315	-4.9	142	36.9	242.6	1,005,264	7,092	100,759	243.0	109,375	74.6	25.4	39	85.8	856	4.8
Albany-Schenectady-Troy, NY	331	-5.2	149	3.1	193.3	581,420	3,911	102,818	218.5	98,131	47.2	52.8	69	81.2	1,939	15.3
Albuquerque, NM	3,084	-19.6	712	43.1	71.8	548,325	770	41,738	113.7	26,245	25.3	74.7	35	65.0	2,852	4.5
Alexandria, LA	254	-1.9	239	26.3	148.7	847,287	3,545	122,673	155.3	146,070	90.5	9.5	1	73.1	3,988	23.4
Allentown-Bethlehem-Easton, PA-NJ	227	-3.6	116	2.1	174.6	1,051,135	9,064	110,824	221.5	113,135	73.7	26.3	16	80.6	3,404	15.0
Altoona, PA	79	-12.4	159	0.2	55.8	1,073,542	6,747	130,550	107.2	216,087	15.8	84.2	9	61.7	1,064	25.6
Amarillo, TX	2,893	0.1	1,703	93.3	817.1	1,887,508	1,109	150,924	801.5	471,719	15.6	84.4	0	77.8	27,310	47.7
Ames, IA	619	0.0	322	0.6	572.9	2,803,265	8,703	202,624	443.3	230,632	73.4	26.6	16	84.8	10,626	61.2
Anchorage, AK	34	-5.5	98	1.1	15.6	809,797	8,242	D	37.5	107,246	45.6	54.4	4	87.7	262	20.6
Ann Arbor, MI	179	5.2	144	4.0	150.4	1,124,667	7,823	112,400	91.2	73,227	76.3	23.7	29	84.3	3,438	24.6
Anniston-Oxford, AL	89	9.5	138	1.1	28.5	587,726	4,246	74,079	86.8	135,003	15.0	85.0	0	77.1	913	28.8
Appleton, WI	391	-0.6	215	0.8	337.7	1,609,348	7,470	201,699	467.3	257,601	24.9	75.1	19	80.2	2,530	48.6
Asheville, NC	222	4.7	82	3.7	65.0	611,878	7,451	58,730	133.4	49,267	82.2	17.8	37	74.2	1,461	15.4
Athens-Clarke County, GA	185	-10.2	122	2.6	50.4	675,115	5,541	76,858	524.8	345,272	7.0	93.0	6	80.7	1,945	24.5
Atlanta-Sandy Springs-Alpharetta, GA	872	1.9	112	7.9	208.4	599,404	5,337	63,245	931.1	119,985	10.6	89.4	31	79.1	5,463	12.9
Atlantic City-Hammonton, NJ	29	-1.6	64	11.6	17.8	823,031	12,764	135,393	120.7	268,162	98.7	1.3	10	85.3	198	7.8
Auburn-Opelika, AL	68	14.8	216	0.2	9.0	895,685	4,150	95,631	D	D	D	D	4	79.9	432	26.8
Augusta-Richmond County, GA-SC	562	15.8	202	61.4	231.2	668,247	3,312	101,967	302.2	108,416	41.7	58.3	8	76.7	8,683	17.4
Austin-Round Rock-Georgetown, TX	1,669	-4.8	196	8.2	457.4	1,003,716	5,110	61,144	263.1	30,957	47.8	52.2	37	76.9	9,105	9.8
Bakersfield, CA	2,295	-1.5	1,326	730.7	954.1	9,787,244	7,380	406,230	4,076.8	2,355,161	84.3	15.7	30	82.7	5,101	13.8
Baltimore-Columbia-Towson, MD	520	5.8	140	20.2	379.8	1,325,778	9,451	114,805	449.8	121,442	65.2	34.8	33	83.6	11,036	26.3
Bangor, ME	105	-6.6	175	1.6	41.1	432,699	2,466	93,820	50.9	84,717	35.6	64.4	33	79.0	603	9.2
Barnstable Town, MA	7	40.4	20	1.1	1.6	624,807	30,555	60,763	23.1	72,019	40.4	59.6	11	90.0	197	4.7
Baton Rouge, LA	876	4.2	306	6.9	433.0	985,685	3,226	136,025	275.0	95,941	73.2	26.8	5	74.7	6,462	14.1
Battle Creek, MI	214	-4.9	223	13.3	174.6	1,185,546	5,309	138,963	113.9	118,861	61.1	38.9	20	71.5	4,522	36.7
Bay City, MI	210	8.3	289	5.2	197.1	1,460,329	5,052	242,521	116.5	160,519	88.3	11.7	0	69.3	4,501	67.8
Beaumont-Port Arthur, TX	477	0.3	232	26.3	155.1	629,846	2,711	75,815	42.0	20,447	51.3	48.7	10	73.2	9,497	8.7
Beckley, WV	70	16.1	113	0.0	17.3	385,375	3,416	49,804	4.7	7,655	31.4	68.6	1	74.9	60	3.7
Bellingham, WA	103	-11.5	60	36.5	75.6	1,005,680	16,794	95,376	372.9	217,786	41.3	58.7	48	83.7	1,047	12.6
Bend, OR	135	2.7	91	36.0	31.0	786,080	8,667	51,257	28.8	19,386	57.5	42.5	9	93.2	90	0.8
Billings, MT	3,181	-2.7	1,223	198.8	609.7	1,477,760	1,208	117,787	285.8	109,868	32.1	67.9	3	81.9	11,178	29.1
Binghamton, NY	176	-6.3	171	0.8	88.3	438,814	2,571	86,513	72.9	70,888	31.0	69.0	26	78.6	1,317	20.2
Birmingham-Hoover, AL	445	-3.1	142	4.9	129.3	524,825	3,704	76,246	341.3	108,757	13.2	86.8	9	76.7	5,506	23.7
Bismarck, ND	2,364	-7.9	1,313	11.4	1,134.7	2,077,147	1,582	245,198	327.5	181,918	46.1	53.9	3	80.5	16,907	60.8
Blacksburg-Christiansburg, VA	245	-9.2	179	0.4	65.5	706,552	3,949	76,518	67.0	48,980	30.6	69.4	2	78.5	473	6.4
Bloomington, IL	620	-10.4	438	3.2	599.9	4,310,555	9,844	280,498	457.1	322,784	85.0	15.0	3	81.1	9,368	73.0
Bloomington, IN	160	7.7	140	0.3	95.8	721,922	5,149	68,376	43.5	38,219	82.3	17.7	19	76.3	2,350	27.6
Bloomsburg-Berwick, PA	145	-12.5	128	0.9	108.3	786,339	6,139	96,310	127.5	112,345	49.7	50.3	13	69.3	2,933	37.1
Boise City, ID	1,351	-1.8	264	420.9	450.1	1,000,490	3,783	131,482	1,021.5	199,985	42.7	57.3	35	86.1	6,139	9.0
Boston-Cambridge-Newton, MA-NH	171	-10.3	58	15.3	61.1	687,073	11,814	62,502	201.5	68,484	84.2	15.8	97	87.7	1,398	5.0
Boston, MA Div 14,454	68	-7.9	69	12.4	21.3	727,928	10,497	69,057	72.5	74,237	86.5	13.5	31	88.7	380	5.4
Cambridge-Newton-Framingham, MA Div 15,754	48	-5.1	46	2.5	23.9	767,516	16,593	64,666	96.2	92,604	87.6	12.4	32	86.6	226	3.8
Rockingham County-Strafford County, NH Div 40,484	55	-16.9	60	0.4	15.8	554,039	9,278	53,184	32.9	35,428	69.1	30.9	34	87.9	792	5.9
Boulder, CO	107	-19.5	106	27.2	38.1	1,329,691	12,571	67,039	43.9	43,378	87.4	12.6	29	90.7	501	5.6
Bowling Green, KY	659	4.7	161	0.6	344.6	641,344	3,990	78,685	275.9	67,255	44.4	55.6	8	71.8	11,581	25.2
Bremerton-Silverdale-Port Orchard, WA	9	-6.7	13	0.5	2.3	473,099	35,164	33,113	6.6	9,463	73.2	26.8	26	88.3	0	0.6
Bridgeport-Stamford-Norwalk, CT	52	-3.2	130	0.2	4.6	1,402,826	10,794	57,697	42.1	104,649	52.7	47.3	9	87.1	33	3.5
Brownsville-Harlingen, TX	271	-12.3	191	100.9	212.5	681,492	3,560	73,661	122.6	86,428	96.2	3.8	10	64.3	6,669	26.0
Brunswick, GA	36	-18.0	113	1.0	7.0	388,278	3,436	54,650	0.3	975	26.0	74.0	2	75.6	135	14.4
Buffalo-Cheektowaga, NY	283	-0.8	174	3.5	212.6	665,840	3,830	147,731	249.6	153,123	55.1	44.9	47	81.9	3,500	20.1
Burlington, NC	80	-4.2	111	0.7	33.8	667,068	6,000	64,708	41.8	57,986	35.3	64.7	23	76.4	147	8.6
Burlington-South Burlington, VT	273	-2.2	190	0.8	122.6	755,652	3,970	128,983	247.1	172,455	25.9	74.1	204	87.5	1,864	12.5
California-Lexington Park, MD	62	-7.9	100	0.7	37.0	999,805	9,949	75,424	26.0	42,203	78.8	21.2	2	58.0	970	19.5
Canton-Massillon, OH	244	0.6	100	1.1	166.0	718,603	7,184	92,634	144.5	59,331	41.2	58.8	14	72.5	3,912	13.8
Cape Coral-Fort Myers, FL	87	0.1	109	10.5	22.2	1,330,329	12,206	53,238	104.4	130,449	93.8	6.2	7	76.0	163	1.8
Cape Girardeau, MO-IL	521	1.0	261	52.5	329.5	944,908	3,618	104,757	148.0	74,249	74.2	25.8	0	67.7	6,795	44.9
Carbondale-Marion, IL	431	5.8	212	2.2	305.8	980,108	4,628	106,433	140.1	68,824	82.3	17.7	3	68.5	9,107	44.5
Carson City, NV	D	D	57	0.4	0.6	D	D	D	D	D	D	D	D	D	D	D
Casper, WY	1,933	14.3	4,496	44.3	55.7	2,039,344	454	109,340	43.2	100,493	12.9	87.1	0	76.0	318	7.9

Area name	Water use, 2015		Wholesale Trade[1], 2017				Retail Trade[2], 2017				Real estate and rental and leasing,[2] 2017			
	Public supply water withdrawn (mil gal/ day)	Public supply gallons withdrawn per person per day	Number of establish- ments	Number of employees	Sales (mil dol)	Average payroll (mil dol)	Number of establish- ments	Number of employees	Sales (mil dol)	Average payroll (mil dol)	Number of establish- ments	Number of employees	Sales (mil dol)	Average payroll (mil dol)
	133	134	135	136	137	138	139	140	141	142	143	144	145	146
Abilene, TX	8.78	51.8	166	2,063	2,262.1	103.7	612	8,737	2,900.3	239.5	190	860	211.9	34.4
Akron, OH	54.93	78.0	943	15,899	11,672.8	1,043.8	2,088	38,335	10,964.9	1,032.1	651	3,546	797.1	140.0
Albany, GA	15.89	105.7	166	2,545	2,519.0	139.2	596	7,620	2,031.2	176.3	142	548	123.7	19.2
Albany-Lebanon, OR	9.57	79.4	116	1,634	1,248.8	86.5	368	5,189	1,424.8	140.2	115	428	54.7	11.1
Albany-Schenectady-Troy, NY	290.84	329.8	760	11,323	11,290.2	697.8	2,989	45,732	13,690.3	1,272.7	911	4,971	1,339.3	216.3
Albuquerque, NM	105.54	116.3	784	10,308	6,322.8	526.5	2,372	40,549	11,953.7	1,146.9	1,130	4,568	1,096.1	180.6
Alexandria, LA	23.45	151.8	D	D	D	D	579	7,730	2,189.4	201.3	D	D	D	D
Allentown-Bethlehem-Easton, PA-NJ	74.71	89.8	656	18,120	24,215.1	1,293.9	2,689	46,229	14,828.4	1,275.2	641	3,100	789.9	134.1
Altoona, PA	13.07	104.1	124	2,112	2,076.2	101.4	530	8,700	2,721.2	227.4	111	409	84.8	14.3
Amarillo, TX	17.48	66.7	269	4,752	5,019.9	252.3	871	14,395	3,963.3	368.8	328	1,363	294.4	56.5
Ames, IA	10.81	88.1	78	1,444	1,083.4	56.5	345	6,110	1,454.8	145.9	135	575	96.0	24.3
Anchorage, AK	47.18	118.0	380	5,363	3,898.7	325.5	1,106	19,354	6,158.7	632.2	518	2,774	730.4	132.1
Ann Arbor, MI	18.36	51.2	270	3,870	5,384.1	267.6	1,100	17,534	5,121.3	473.5	373	2,686	1,101.3	140.5
Anniston-Oxford, AL	25.25	218.4	90	1,614	1,347.9	69.2	466	6,380	1,652.3	151.6	76	307	58.6	10.8
Appleton, WI	17.06	73.2	320	4,690	8,290.0	279.8	833	15,171	4,115.9	365.5	172	797	172.1	33.1
Asheville, NC	39.02	87.3	444	5,241	2,793.6	247.6	1,951	27,791	7,206.1	696.5	779	2,556	488.9	95.4
Athens-Clarke County, GA	12.62	62.1	123	2,257	3,090.5	114.9	706	11,026	2,696.2	258.9	290	1,871	339.4	83.7
Atlanta-Sandy Springs-Alpharetta, GA	480.18	84.1	7,129	116,733	144,514.3	8,174.5	17,594	279,506	91,665.8	7,549.3	8,378	47,617	19,335.1	3,187.4
Atlantic City-Hammonton, NJ	30.20	110.1	172	2,049	1,304.6	115.8	1,078	16,535	4,631.1	417.9	233	1,358	356.2	56.3
Auburn-Opelika, AL	15.83	100.8	83	999	465.5	48.1	478	7,212	1,901.9	169.0	157	678	139.6	25.1
Augusta-Richmond County, GA-SC	95.09	161.1	352	4,208	2,389.7	207.2	1,810	27,390	7,706.9	688.7	465	1,798	462.6	75.1
Austin-Round Rock-Georgetown, TX	180.10	90.0	1,812	28,554	85,056.1	2,225.0	6,209	108,411	35,894.7	3,301.2	3,361	19,185	5,419.7	1,102.5
Bakersfield, CA	168.87	191.4	561	8,010	6,451.9	443.1	1,960	31,869	9,382.8	860.7	670	3,474	759.1	147.4
Baltimore-Columbia-Towson, MD	267.62	95.7	2,513	43,748	38,700.5	2,908.6	8,821	142,444	41,386.1	3,968.6	3,244	22,667	8,672.8	1,301.6
Bangor, ME	4.79	31.4	156	1,816	1,056.4	93.9	697	10,573	3,261.5	276.5	184	924	270.0	29.3
Barnstable Town, MA	31.84	148.6	D	D	D	D	1,450	16,168	4,537.5	500.4	386	1,533	361.5	66.0
Baton Rouge, LA	108.01	126.6	834	12,108	8,984.2	721.0	2,914	45,152	12,723.3	1,179.3	926	4,856	1,312.1	234.8
Battle Creek, MI	12.53	93.3	83	808	1,385.5	43.5	467	6,105	1,855.4	157.7	82	387	59.1	12.5
Bay City, MI	8.97	84.9	80	1,168	691.9	50.3	385	5,258	1,465.6	139.5	60	182	26.3	4.4
Beaumont-Port Arthur, TX	36.38	92.2	310	3,867	3,059.6	218.8	1,358	18,913	6,350.4	537.2	354	2,446	580.5	112.3
Beckley, WV	15.26	124.6	103	953	529.6	45.9	460	6,254	1,843.7	154.5	91	416	76.1	17.0
Bellingham, WA	18.13	85.4	D	D	D	D	817	11,180	3,225.2	328.6	398	1,394	421.9	56.2
Bend, OR	38.00	216.8	227	1,621	1,110.3	82.0	879	11,709	3,550.5	341.9	499	1,275	298.1	49.8
Billings, MT	27.23	153.9	337	4,341	3,113.5	251.1	743	10,790	3,377.2	318.1	356	1,172	255.1	48.5
Binghamton, NY	22.18	90.2	201	3,965	2,895.4	183.2	814	11,729	3,086.3	290.5	163	926	191.1	33.1
Birmingham-Hoover, AL	138.56	128.3	1,377	22,432	26,930.5	1,355.0	3,923	54,812	15,738.7	1,451.9	1,100	7,208	2,558.5	399.4
Bismarck, ND	14.70	117.5	185	2,851	2,448.9	175.6	499	9,181	2,697.4	274.6	199	629	164.9	24.6
Blacksburg-Christiansburg, VA	14.91	89.8	61	891	531.7	39.9	503	8,144	1,783.6	183.3	150	735	144.2	25.9
Bloomington, IL	10.50	60.6	165	2,108	7,165.7	150.4	523	9,562	2,301.8	211.7	154	754	151.1	26.2
Bloomington, IN	17.18	103.8	D	D	D	D	483	7,038	1,982.4	169.8	199	1,049	194.9	37.0
Bloomsburg-Berwick, PA	5.05	59.3	49	563	265.2	25.5	279	4,011	1,097.5	92.7	49	167	46.7	6.3
Boise City, ID	90.70	134.0	753	10,976	11,072.9	649.3	2,100	33,223	10,352.6	995.5	1,167	3,818	860.7	152.7
Boston-Cambridge-Newton, MA-NH	274.73	57.5	4,846	94,229	112,588.5	8,625.3	16,524	264,474	81,036.0	8,038.1	5,711	43,513	15,985.5	3,009.6
Boston, MA Div 14,454	103.97	52.4	1,923	36,261	38,799.9	3,222.8	6,851	110,079	34,986.3	3,436.8	2,713	23,752	8,255.2	1,773.6
Cambridge-Newton-Framingham, MA Div 15,754	147.41	62.4	2,371	49,207	65,951.0	4,717.3	7,686	121,358	36,306.9	3,682.6	2,534	17,484	7,134.8	1,125.0
Rockingham County-Strafford County, NH Div 40,484	23.35	54.5	552	8,761	7,837.7	685.2	1,987	33,037	9,742.8	918.7	464	2,277	595.5	111.0
Boulder, CO	48.30	151.2	428	6,066	4,884.6	516.0	1,187	19,230	5,635.2	602.1	775	2,894	754.0	161.8
Bowling Green, KY	21.30	126.5	153	2,252	2,539.9	115.3	605	8,751	2,192.4	209.2	154	648	124.9	20.2
Bremerton-Silverdale-Port Orchard, WA	19.63	75.5	131	978	500.7	54.1	739	11,457	3,319.1	355.0	405	1,132	304.1	45.8
Bridgeport-Stamford-Norwalk, CT	87.98	92.8	1,131	19,293	66,731.7	1,916.5	3,368	51,210	16,458.8	1,717.6	1,165	7,605	2,604.5	536.9
Brownsville-Harlingen, TX	24.18	57.3	320	2,851	2,163.4	101.5	1,045	17,938	4,610.8	437.5	336	1,482	226.5	40.2
Brunswick, GA	10.59	91.3	93	857	784.5	33.7	551	6,183	1,660.7	144.5	165	510	98.0	18.0
Buffalo-Cheektowaga, NY	220.89	194.6	1,117	19,586	24,536.0	1,127.8	4,016	64,323	16,340.6	1,614.3	1,053	7,429	1,482.3	284.0
Burlington, NC	15.35	97.0	129	2,065	814.5	115.5	642	9,115	2,313.5	206.7	134	849	213.1	38.7
Burlington-South Burlington, VT	17.39	80.1	285	4,899	3,722.5	276.8	1,014	14,800	4,233.9	424.6	290	1,165	347.2	52.1
California-Lexington Park, MD	4.15	37.2	37	D	131.0	D	306	4,740	1,370.3	125.0	88	274	95.6	11.5
Canton-Massillon, OH	31.28	77.6	340	4,767	3,948.8	249.0	1,279	20,612	5,592.8	506.6	287	1,487	308.8	63.3
Cape Coral-Fort Myers, FL	64.55	92.0	638	5,832	3,164.5	278.6	2,651	39,847	12,227.8	1,071.9	1,562	6,205	1,535.0	384.0
Cape Girardeau, MO-IL	9.63	98.7	105	1,081	662.7	60.5	458	6,380	1,661.0	157.4	115	369	73.3	12.7
Carbondale-Marion, IL	8.04	57.6	89	924	434.2	40.3	498	7,434	2,171.0	181.5	141	547	98.9	14.0
Carson City, NV	11.50	210.9	81	620	335.2	29.4	220	3,141	1,170.8	102.3	118	361	94.1	13.0
Casper, WY	12.26	149.2	164	1,812	2,888.1	115.8	344	4,766	1,386.0	139.6	181	952	285.7	54.1

1. Merchant wholesalers, except manufacturers' sales branches and offices. 2. Employer establishments.

Table C. Metropolitan Areas — **Professional Services, Manufacturing, and Accommodation and Food Services**

Area name	Professional, scientific, and technical services, 2017				Manufacturing, 2017				Accommodation and food services, 2017			
	Number of establish-ments	Number of employees	Sales (mil dol)	Average payroll (mil dol)	Number of establish-ments	Number of employees	Receipts (mil dol)	Annual payroll (mil dol)	Number of establish-ments	Number of employees	Receipts (mil dol)	Annual payroll (mil dol)
	147	148	149	150	151	152	153	154	155	156	157	158
Abilene, TX	24	66	9.2	2.9	112	2,507	1,160.5	125.9	363	7,425	381.4	111.3
Akron, OH	D	D	D	D	1,022	38,621	12,824.8	2,082.7	1,575	29,252	1,458.6	414.3
Albany, GA	270	2,368	295.6	114.1	91	4,240	3,307.4	228.9	246	4,753	255.2	68.2
Albany-Lebanon, OR	D	D	D	D	193	7,359	2,494.8	417.0	230	3,278	175.6	53.3
Albany-Schenectady-Troy, NY	1,213	14,825	2,673.3	1,101.2	588	23,895	9,803.5	1,716.4	2,381	35,843	2,260.6	689.5
Albuquerque, NM	84	381	40.8	14.6	663	14,320	5,185.5	792.5	1,784	41,656	2,461.9	723.2
Alexandria, LA	277	1,826	242.1	86.4	D	D	D	D	250	5,012	271.7	74.8
Allentown-Bethlehem-Easton, PA-NJ	841	7,585	1,335.5	510.7	845	35,697	18,064.1	2,147.8	1,858	30,183	2,198.8	538.7
Altoona, PA	204	1,753	261.3	87.4	130	6,802	2,282.2	344.6	286	4,683	230.9	63.2
Amarillo, TX	232	993	135.2	51.7	187	11,471	5,480.2	717.4	599	12,283	689.2	185.4
Ames, IA	38	134	16.5	6.3	110	5,075	3,409.2	297.1	290	5,605	267.3	76.3
Anchorage, AK	1,342	14,840	2,671.2	1,080.8	228	2,021	476.5	106.2	1,034	18,108	1,440.2	438.0
Ann Arbor, MI	1,257	15,568	2,912.8	1,205.4	337	14,480	4,603.1	850.4	860	18,272	1,027.3	310.7
Anniston-Oxford, AL	D	D	D	D	106	5,986	2,699.2	308.1	225	4,642	247.0	66.2
Appleton, WI	430	4,081	640.5	255.1	400	23,347	9,136.1	1,351.7	566	10,318	495.2	140.4
Asheville, NC	1,442	6,046	802.3	313.7	487	20,382	7,509.1	1,107.5	1,261	25,293	1,558.1	459.3
Athens-Clarke County, GA	525	2,544	325.2	118.9	151	8,203	2,993.2	389.1	468	9,915	488.3	136.4
Atlanta-Sandy Springs-Alpharetta, GA	21,301	210,839	47,674.2	17,302.2	3,850	145,460	65,430.9	7,923.9	12,324	255,597	16,419.7	4,456.4
Atlantic City-Hammonton, NJ	D	D	D	D	108	2,013	474.1	98.6	830	35,488	3,550.7	1,003.8
Auburn-Opelika, AL	254	1,277	163.5	56.6	118	7,008	2,707.0	317.6	363	7,591	371.4	100.0
Augusta-Richmond County, GA-SC	908	8,086	1,387.9	473.4	303	21,290	11,520.5	1,255.5	1,077	21,741	1,145.8	306.4
Austin-Round Rock-Georgetown, TX	587	2,777	381.3	128.3	1,400	39,849	15,609.2	2,649.7	4,899	114,507	7,768.0	2,219.4
Bakersfield, CA	1,189	9,602	1,542.5	569.4	376	13,484	6,938.0	678.5	1,467	23,929	1,507.6	410.3
Baltimore-Columbia-Towson, MD	4,101	59,850	13,762.4	5,751.0	1,538	53,613	23,685.5	3,651.5	5,935	117,407	8,180.4	2,212.2
Bangor, ME	D	D	D	D	147	2,881	686.3	142.8	332	6,001	365.7	102.4
Barnstable Town, MA	D	D	D	D	188	2,046	645.3	129.0	1,112	14,179	1,266.5	386.3
Baton Rouge, LA	376	3,476	465.2	228.9	577	D	55,851.9	D	1,624	35,832	2,060.9	562.0
Battle Creek, MI	D	D	D	D	149	14,437	6,760.7	781.4	272	6,655	567.1	126.1
Bay City, MI	143	1,201	100.4	51.5	116	3,824	1,209.0	242.1	225	3,858	176.3	50.1
Beaumont-Port Arthur, TX	129	857	111.7	55.1	D	18,694	D	1,835.3	744	13,941	763.1	204.1
Beckley, WV	D	D	D	D	70	1,160	414.4	57.5	221	4,330	265.9	77.8
Bellingham, WA	D	D	D	D	341	11,106	11,178.0	628.0	554	8,971	609.1	191.8
Bend, OR	D	D	D	D	342	4,828	1,107.8	226.0	608	10,178	707.1	224.8
Billings, MT	25	42	5.4	239.6	D	3,727	D	255.6	496	9,935	578.4	165.0
Binghamton, NY	D	D	D	D	200	8,335	2,922.9	499.8	626	9,694	493.1	152.0
Birmingham-Hoover, AL	190	1,023	130.0	357.8	868	34,725	12,516.6	1,901.6	2,131	44,349	2,481.8	707.6
Bismarck, ND	D	D	D	D	D	D	D	D	210	5,516	296.9	96.8
Blacksburg-Christiansburg, VA	43	571	41.8	24.4	111	11,362	5,035.5	656.4	320	6,708	323.9	90.8
Bloomington, IL	D	D	D	D	81	4,592	993.1	185.3	417	8,518	413.1	123.6
Bloomington, IN	298	1,937	250.6	98.4	125	8,487	1,619.3	422.7	417	8,381	437.1	123.0
Bloomsburg-Berwick, PA	D	D	D	D	92	4,983	1,941.2	213.1	206	3,460	172.0	50.6
Boise City, ID	1,922	13,849	2,195.9	819.9	D	D	D	1,810.3	1,355	26,863	1,411.2	412.8
Boston-Cambridge-Newton, MA-NH	16,402	256,642	67,699.7	28,023.6	4,313	158,541	57,287.4	11,097.6	12,560	235,954	17,957.0	5,356.5
Boston, MA Div 14,454	7,420	116,086	31,414.4	12,268.2	1,333	39,241	14,957.4	2,429.6	5,501	115,221	9,622.9	2,833.5
Cambridge-Newton-Framingham, MA Div 15,754	8,982	140,556	36,285.2	15,755.4	2,406	98,324	35,530.4	7,493.2	5,857	101,292	7,093.4	2,155.3
Rockingham County-Strafford County, NH Div 40,484	D	D	D	D	574	20,976	6,799.6	1,174.8	1,202	19,441	1,240.7	367.7
Boulder, CO	D	D	D	D	561	14,472	5,400.1	939.4	939	19,279	1,157.9	360.1
Bowling Green, KY	26	122	10.1	3.2	D	D	D	D	316	7,217	372.6	113.3
Bremerton-Silverdale-Port Orchard, WA	703	4,112	617.5	247.4	150	1,996	379.0	96.4	536	9,262	640.9	191.9
Bridgeport-Stamford-Norwalk, CT	3,519	47,964	10,735.9	4,661.4	779	34,375	12,255.6	2,634.2	2,438	35,172	2,597.3	767.7
Brownsville-Harlingen, TX	D	D	6.0	D	188	3,983	1,301.2	161.2	735	15,258	753.2	204.0
Brunswick, GA	23	56	6.0	2.0	63	2,125	1,025.6	146.6	331	8,159	622.8	173.0
Buffalo-Cheektowaga, NY	D	D	D	D	1,236	52,250	21,609.3	3,227.4	2,925	55,202	3,208.1	929.3
Burlington, NC	D	D	D	D	193	8,100	2,841.6	380.2	326	7,220	365.7	103.2
Burlington-South Burlington, VT	816	7,045	1,230.9	514.5	284	11,948	4,160.3	757.5	584	10,326	694.7	206.1
California-Lexington Park, MD	D	D	D	D	27	409	117.5	24.1	190	3,797	215.6	60.3
Canton-Massillon, OH	29	151	16.6	6.5	510	25,471	11,542.1	1,345.2	845	16,282	774.8	222.5
Cape Coral-Fort Myers, FL	D	D	2,197.4	D	366	5,117	1,176.3	249.1	1,432	31,343	1,925.7	566.6
Cape Girardeau, MO-IL	D	D	D	D	D	3,984	D	212.2	187	4,214	197.1	59.8
Carbondale-Marion, IL	10	160	4.7	1.3	98	4,156	1,430.5	182.6	308	5,619	251.8	71.7
Carson City, NV	D	D	D	D	103	2,704	714.3	159.4	170	3,036	193.0	54.1
Casper, WY	266	1,440	266.6	89.1	89	1,379	1,002.2	83.6	201	3,819	211.1	65.8

Area name	Health care and social assistance, 2017				Other services, 2017				Nonemployer businesses, 2019		Value of residential construction authorized by building permits, 2021	
	Number of establish-ments	Number of employees	Receipts (mil dol)	Annual payroll (mil dol)	Number of establish-ments	Number of employees	Receipts (mil dol)	Annual payroll (mil dol)	Number	Receipts (mil dol)	New construc-tion ($1,000)	Number of housing units
	159	160	161	162	163	164	165	166	167	168	169	170
Abilene, TX	434	12,773	1,401.2	536.7	255	1,576	200.3	45.7	13,453	638.5	150,496	883
Akron, OH	1,783	60,429	6,020.0	2,700.8	1,327	8,961	1,694.9	285.7	50,159	2,249.7	280,960	1,215
Albany, GA	354	8,868	1,191.3	471.6	184	1,209	118.2	35.8	11,000	389.6	32,292	224
Albany-Lebanon, OR	230	5,366	575.8	238.0	163	1,004	73.8	24.8	6,589	293.3	131,617	620
Albany-Schenectady-Troy, NY	2,431	67,782	7,672.9	3,101.2	1,446	9,469	1,456.9	370.3	57,947	2,758.4	618,158	2,697
Albuquerque, NM	2,317	58,898	6,906.1	2,683.5	1,295	8,297	941.9	268.3	56,296	2,412.8	768,363	4,021
Alexandria, LA	561	13,947	1,731.7	634.7	189	1,068	128.8	34.0	9,342	421.0	70,754	289
Allentown-Bethlehem-Easton, PA-NJ	2,408	63,972	7,886.8	3,146.6	1,616	9,336	942.5	281.3	55,465	2,741.4	505,487	2,606
Altoona, PA	452	12,918	1,345.0	564.9	269	1,459	122.6	37.7	6,387	307.2	24,763	94
Amarillo, TX	474	13,448	1,852.9	656.2	444	3,246	404.8	105.2	21,112	1,109.1	168,532	736
Ames, IA	270	7,715	816.3	337.6	206	1,310	294.2	42.0	7,418	303.8	94,018	394
Anchorage, AK	1,622	31,851	5,052.0	1,892.6	716	4,523	987.7	171.2	29,141	1,462.6	324,796	1,183
Ann Arbor, MI	943	40,974	5,693.3	2,382.4	553	4,465	650.9	195.0	30,781	1,425.9	259,769	916
Anniston-Oxford, AL	275	6,358	622.7	249.8	166	718	79.2	19.7	6,721	264.2	10,515	68
Appleton, WI	591	13,914	1,533.6	670.8	423	3,128	369.1	106.4	13,210	675.6	287,748	1,429
Asheville, NC	1,452	38,066	4,682.5	1,883.1	830	4,487	499.1	142.5	47,102	2,078.0	1,128,357	4,238
Athens-Clarke County, GA	650	12,411	1,876.0	711.5	251	1,848	341.3	68.0	17,538	725.4	375,304	1,848
Atlanta-Sandy Springs-Alpharetta, GA	14,829	284,534	40,118.3	15,093.9	9,366	65,573	10,639.4	2,358.3	663,253	28,261.2	8,721,861	39,466
Atlantic City-Hammonton, NJ	801	18,708	2,202.5	951.0	540	3,437	291.1	83.9	18,523	926.7	194,034	804
Auburn-Opelika, AL	258	6,926	697.5	276.4	177	1,068	91.5	26.2	11,110	527.6	461,414	1,851
Augusta-Richmond County, GA-SC	1,322	37,218	5,008.1	1,818.1	697	4,260	533.6	139.6	42,895	1,595.3	925,681	4,280
Austin-Round Rock-Georgetown, TX	5,478	109,967	13,201.3	5,165.8	3,724	28,586	3,937.5	1,142.1	227,179	12,168.4	9,096,075	50,907
Bakersfield, CA	1,684	30,531	4,574.8	1,580.8	865	6,057	671.3	199.2	50,492	2,637.4	461,217	2,293
Baltimore-Columbia-Towson, MD	7,848	209,638	27,814.0	10,620.7	5,042	38,293	4,950.8	1,427.7	225,741	10,502.0	1,539,647	7,834
Bangor, ME	541	15,666	1,719.6	776.9	274	1,425	189.9	44.6	9,498	403.5	77,353	368
Barnstable Town, MA	795	17,032	2,064.8	858.8	627	3,498	395.6	125.5	27,736	1,543.0	0	672
Baton Rouge, LA	1,940	49,816	5,740.8	2,076.4	1,306	9,608	1,465.9	397.9	71,506	3,107.8	1,022,078	4,460
Battle Creek, MI	321	9,318	1,138.8	443.5	215	1,304	519.5	57.0	6,648	259.3	20,922	108
Bay City, MI	339	6,674	706.0	257.4	168	900	81.1	23.0	5,670	234.8	20,613	74
Beaumont-Port Arthur, TX	1,085	20,020	2,128.6	749.5	509	4,603	501.1	199.5	26,412	1,186.7	310,438	1,585
Beckley, WV	411	9,236	947.0	378.2	165	1,031	128.4	31.4	5,068	202.5	19,576	103
Bellingham, WA	699	10,929	1,334.0	469.1	431	2,552	303.1	91.8	17,054	845.1	358,796	1,871
Bend, OR	744	12,299	1,654.6	660.7	397	2,156	261.6	70.6	20,793	1,104.5	696,238	2,737
Billings, MT	601	14,926	2,089.2	816.2	397	2,244	292.2	76.5	14,674	765.7	217,836	979
Binghamton, NY	551	17,101	1,823.3	746.7	404	1,987	187.0	49.7	12,860	540.0	60,673	499
Birmingham-Hoover, AL	2,512	73,121	11,087.9	4,016.8	1,452	11,679	2,664.2	469.8	84,839	4,013.7	1,051,866	3,984
Bismarck, ND	371	11,838	1,366.2	536.3	336	2,028	293.8	82.4	10,450	616.4	181,349	792
Blacksburg-Christiansburg, VA	361	6,534	881.7	285.1	242	1,290	350.9	41.1	8,401	361.4	86,337	386
Bloomington, IL	377	8,713	1,061.4	402.1	272	2,436	262.9	85.3	9,674	409.1	56,741	283
Bloomington, IN	453	11,112	1,013.8	435.5	239	1,599	436.1	56.7	10,856	437.0	271,538	2,086
Bloomsburg-Berwick, PA	257	11,063	1,950.6	742.1	148	802	106.6	22.4	4,377	200.5	31,764	159
Boise City, ID	2,026	44,022	4,952.3	2,118.5	1,101	6,319	726.8	209.3	62,000	2,940.4	2,665,715	12,196
Boston-Cambridge-Newton, MA-NH	13,841	461,435	54,542.1	23,902.5	10,971	77,747	10,647.7	2,909.4	424,705	24,396.3	3,695,182	16,602
Boston, MA Div 14,454	5,650	251,894	31,442.8	13,903.8	4,718	38,377	5,688.8	1,464.4	169,470	9,794.8	1,982,408	8,645
Cambridge-Newton-Framingham, MA Div 15,754	6,986	185,147	20,047.2	8,781.6	5,274	33,717	4,356.2	1,262.6	219,175	12,279.4	1,321,723	6,374
Rockingham County-Strafford County, NH Div 40,484	1,205	24,394	3,052.0	1,217.1	979	5,653	602.7	182.4	36,060	2,322.0	391,052	1,583
Boulder, CO	1,432	21,332	2,566.9	1,012.1	823	5,173	671.5	202.2	41,219	2,223.4	401,187	1,237
Bowling Green, KY	400	9,097	1,196.9	438.1	256	1,415	130.0	36.4	13,679	760.7	336,499	2,137
Bremerton-Silverdale-Port Orchard, WA	716	12,346	1,619.1	581.2	423	2,230	224.5	67.3	15,936	759.5	493,451	2,285
Bridgeport-Stamford-Norwalk, CT	3,071	72,290	10,942.1	3,753.5	2,180	14,442	2,103.2	530.8	100,223	7,174.6	538,711	1,292
Brownsville-Harlingen, TX	1,029	37,028	2,310.7	987.7	406	2,151	199.1	50.2	33,608	1,385.3	261,085	2,052
Brunswick, GA	257	5,461	670.2	260.3	172	1,012	107.9	25.4	9,652	440.9	245,866	723
Buffalo-Cheektowaga, NY	3,234	90,411	9,931.9	4,158.6	2,196	13,465	1,323.5	387.9	64,761	2,915.0	480,826	1,553
Burlington, NC	366	12,073	1,705.6	651.3	199	1,292	125.7	36.1	11,225	455.3	287,457	2,294
Burlington-South Burlington, VT	716	18,250	2,385.0	838.2	533	2,743	350.3	96.2	20,106	996.7	216,040	1,049
California-Lexington Park, MD	181	4,735	528.0	201.5	140	816	83.4	29.8	7,211	305.9	114,067	359
Canton-Massillon, OH	1,038	29,386	2,819.5	1,172.8	685	4,872	606.1	155.9	26,898	1,189.2	200,450	953
Cape Coral-Fort Myers, FL	1,700	38,678	5,215.6	2,158.8	1,425	7,305	834.2	222.8	79,000	3,950.3	2,671,616	13,394
Cape Girardeau, MO-IL	332	10,265	1,317.0	480.6	D	D	D	D	6,558	297.9	51,288	177
Carbondale-Marion, IL	384	11,627	1,592.0	501.9	189	1,035	111.9	24.4	7,892	299.6	16,666	99
Carson City, NV	215	3,865	623.8	214.4	132	618	100.6	22.3	4,854	411.5	64,422	307
Casper, WY	333	5,588	751.8	310.6	198	976	140.4	34.5	6,310	351.5	55,177	275

Area name	Government employment and payroll, 2017: Full-time equivalent employees	Government employment and payroll, 2017: March payroll (dollars)	March payroll (percent of total): Adminis-tration, judicial, and legal	March payroll (percent of total): Police and corrections	March payroll (percent of total): Fire protection	March payroll (percent of total): Highways and transpor-tation	March payroll (percent of total): Health and welfare	March payroll (percent of total): Natural resources and utilities	March payroll (percent of total): Education and libraries	Local government finances, 2017, General revenue: Total (mil dol)	General revenue: Inter-govern-mental (mil dol)	Taxes: Total (mil dol)	Taxes: Per capita[1] (dollars): Total	Taxes: Per capita[1] (dollars): Property
	171	172	173	174	175	176	177	178	179	180	181	182	183	184
Abilene, TX	6,870	24,911,989	6.2	12.5	4.8	1.9	6.4	5.2	61.5	586.0	226.3	272.6	1,599	1,176
Akron, OH	25,033	109,876,388	7.8	10.3	5.9	5.9	8.4	6.2	54.0	3,118.4	1,023.5	1,538.2	2,185	1,333
Albany, GA	6,840	22,227,686	6.2	10.6	4.3	2.9	5.8	7.0	60.8	545.2	222.5	209.5	1,415	922
Albany-Lebanon, OR	4,158	19,077,155	5.7	11.1	5.7	3.7	6.5	3.4	62.8	541.6	264.8	174.1	1,392	1,262
Albany-Schenectady-Troy, NY	36,832	183,705,619	5.0	10.3	2.3	4.1	7.6	3.3	65.7	5,270.2	1,785.9	2,772.0	3,142	2,143
Albuquerque, NM	30,008	123,837,946	6.5	15.7	6.3	6.0	3.4	6.1	54.0	3,375.9	1,619.8	1,220.7	1,338	773
Alexandria, LA	6,161	19,052,868	8.9	13.7	5.2	3.3	1.0	6.7	59.7	477.1	215.2	209.2	1,362	526
Allentown-Bethlehem-Easton, PA-NJ	29,796	143,303,661	6.1	10.1	1.5	3.8	7.0	3.4	66.0	4,354.7	1,587.0	2,064.7	2,464	2,061
Altoona, PA	3,575	13,827,996	5.4	9.6	2.2	5.1	4.9	5.8	65.7	455.6	221.6	145.0	1,178	799
Amarillo, TX	11,792	45,156,680	5.4	12.9	4.5	1.7	3.5	3.9	66.4	1,042.0	369.2	484.4	1,833	1,386
Ames, IA	4,009	17,651,859	6.0	6.9	2.2	6.9	15.5	8.7	51.4	655.4	150.8	196.9	1,591	1,355
Anchorage, AK	12,481	69,716,457	5.1	7.5	5.7	4.0	3.5	8.2	64.0	1,936.6	906.2	770.4	1,923	1,635
Ann Arbor, MI	10,291	50,170,923	7.5	9.9	2.6	5.9	4.7	5.2	61.5	1,623.7	629.7	665.3	1,804	1,745
Anniston-Oxford, AL	5,653	18,814,816	3.4	5.0	2.7	2.5	37.3	5.5	41.1	531.6	161.2	130.2	1,135	389
Appleton, WI	8,858	40,302,052	4.7	7.2	2.9	3.4	7.7	3.4	69.0	1,002.8	478.6	324.2	1,375	1,319
Asheville, NC	16,586	62,893,469	4.9	7.8	2.5	1.1	24.5	4.0	51.2	2,347.6	983.6	650.5	1,430	984
Athens-Clarke County, GA	7,302	25,954,698	6.9	11.1	3.3	2.5	5.5	7.0	59.7	1,093.4	240.8	282.0	1,349	938
Atlanta-Sandy Springs-Alpharetta, GA	205,101	883,124,518	6.8	8.9	4.1	3.8	6.3	4.9	63.9	22,444.9	6,968.5	10,292.2	1,753	1,210
Atlantic City-Hammonton, NJ	13,889	75,732,427	5.6	14.7	5.0	2.0	4.6	4.0	62.7	1,644.3	578.1	930.0	3,503	3,445
Auburn-Opelika, AL	7,104	27,907,786	2.7	6.0	2.4	1.6	44.2	5.5	36.9	792.6	189.0	215.4	1,334	592
Augusta-Richmond County, GA-SC	21,283	71,438,497	7.4	10.3	3.9	2.7	3.7	5.7	65.0	1,927.0	741.1	809.4	1,348	909
Austin-Round Rock-Georgetown, TX	83,827	366,570,331	6.8	12.3	4.6	3.0	6.6	13.0	51.9	10,079.5	1,795.8	6,150.2	2,907	2,443
Bakersfield, CA	34,360	176,954,893	4.6	10.6	4.2	2.3	11.2	4.9	61.3	5,452.6	3,333.2	1,223.1	1,378	1,104
Baltimore-Columbia-Towson, MD	101,382	520,866,759	5.2	11.8	5.3	2.5	3.8	4.9	64.6	13,262.2	4,436.6	6,962.9	2,488	1,365
Bangor, ME	4,862	18,469,574	6.5	8.5	5.4	7.2	2.8	5.2	62.9	493.2	177.7	234.2	1,544	1,531
Barnstable Town, MA	8,286	44,597,245	6.6	11.6	9.9	4.4	3.2	6.7	55.0	1,119.8	177.1	766.0	3,587	3,359
Baton Rouge, LA	29,467	126,557,979	20.1	10.1	3.6	4.5	6.3	4.3	50.5	3,364.3	1,045.8	1,765.8	2,067	882
Battle Creek, MI	3,902	17,403,464	10.1	10.3	3.5	2.2	6.9	4.6	59.9	615.2	302.7	179.7	1,339	1,163
Bay City, MI	4,219	17,395,958	6.6	5.0	2.0	4.1	15.6	3.4	61.1	526.0	268.5	126.8	1,219	1,193
Beaumont-Port Arthur, TX	15,667	59,166,653	6.6	14.0	4.8	3.5	5.0	8.1	56.5	1,561.0	430.8	815.8	2,049	1,675
Beckley, WV	3,894	12,507,528	6.6	6.1	1.9	1.5	1.4	5.9	75.7	317.6	140.9	126.6	1,067	851
Bellingham, WA	5,979	33,006,077	9.4	9.9	8.3	8.0	3.6	5.1	52.1	923.4	347.8	387.7	1,751	1,024
Bend, OR	5,285	26,992,573	9.1	11.0	6.1	3.2	6.3	6.9	53.4	868.5	274.6	379.2	2,031	1,737
Billings, MT	5,489	24,373,446	6.3	9.4	4.2	4.3	7.6	6.2	57.5	647.5	228.7	238.5	1,330	1,243
Binghamton, NY	13,165	51,504,081	4.4	8.0	2.3	4.8	8.3	3.0	67.4	1,684.4	815.7	674.7	2,792	1,928
Birmingham-Hoover, AL	36,849	143,090,750	7.4	13.9	6.9	4.1	4.4	9.6	51.3	4,111.4	1,412.9	1,940.9	1,788	756
Bismarck, ND	4,212	19,062,240	5.0	10.3	2.8	4.0	5.9	8.4	60.7	562.0	256.2	196.7	1,535	1,196
Blacksburg-Christiansburg, VA	5,046	17,049,212	11.5	10.7	1.3	4.3	1.3	9.8	58.0	595.8	260.8	210.3	1,262	931
Bloomington, IL	6,093	27,474,898	6.9	11.6	5.5	5.0	3.2	7.0	58.0	710.8	161.0	421.6	2,440	1,942
Bloomington, IN	4,258	15,173,384	10.8	13.2	5.3	5.1	2.3	6.5	54.9	442.2	174.4	186.9	1,116	1,060
Bloomsburg-Berwick, PA	2,434	9,872,014	5.4	9.1	0.8	3.4	0.6	3.6	73.7	334.1	130.1	133.3	1,590	1,148
Boise City, ID	21,065	76,002,008	9.9	12.9	5.2	3.8	2.9	5.1	57.5	2,172.4	928.1	766.6	1,080	999
Boston-Cambridge-Newton, MA-NH	162,731	880,588,530	3.8	10.8	7.4	2.5	5.6	4.2	63.6	23,609.0	6,718.1	13,659.8	2,821	2,688
Boston, MA Div 14,454	65,674	377,921,263	3.5	13.1	8.4	2.3	4.8	4.6	61.5	10,120.6	2,945.9	5,898.3	2,925	2,741
Cambridge-Newton-Framingham, MA Div 15,754	80,196	434,251,985	3.8	9.0	6.9	2.7	6.6	4.0	64.8	11,516.7	3,327.5	6,460.6	2,705	2,599
Rockingham County-Strafford County, NH Div 40,484	16,861	68,415,282	5.0	10.2	5.6	2.5	3.8	2.9	67.7	1,971.7	444.7	1,300.9	2,980	2,933
Boulder, CO	12,053	61,752,806	8.2	10.5	5.2	2.6	6.2	8.9	54.2	1,954.8	451.4	1,117.5	3,466	2,375
Bowling Green, KY	5,736	18,566,807	2.6	8.9	3.6	2.0	5.1	8.4	65.8	420.8	177.6	188.4	1,077	536
Bremerton-Silverdale-Port Orchard, WA	7,352	40,302,464	7.9	7.7	8.9	7.4	3.0	6.6	57.4	1,280.4	652.7	428.5	1,609	1,052
Bridgeport-Stamford-Norwalk, CT	32,456	194,415,331	3.6	10.0	5.5	3.2	3.2	2.7	70.4	5,258.8	1,080.1	3,702.6	3,926	3,839
Brownsville-Harlingen, TX	22,268	74,927,211	4.8	8.6	2.8	2.5	2.0	4.4	73.6	1,807.5	1,026.7	493.5	1,169	939
Brunswick, GA	6,632	26,982,644	4.2	6.4	2.7	1.6	45.3	2.7	35.8	732.1	136.7	198.7	1,690	1,104
Buffalo-Cheektowaga, NY	46,386	236,482,046	3.8	10.1	2.7	3.2	12.6	4.5	61.7	7,259.4	3,000.4	3,091.2	2,736	1,656
Burlington, NC	5,370	20,215,032	4.4	10.8	3.3	1.7	8.5	5.8	62.4	467.6	226.6	184.2	1,128	793
Burlington-South Burlington, VT	8,694	38,325,724	5.6	5.5	2.0	7.5	1.3	6.0	71.4	980.1	628.7	185.7	848	731
California-Lexington Park, MD	3,228	15,729,729	6.4	10.5	0.0	2.2	1.2	4.4	72.5	423.1	139.9	222.2	1,975	1,009
Canton-Massillon, OH	15,123	58,262,135	7.9	8.4	4.0	4.7	8.4	5.0	60.4	1,457.2	646.2	590.0	1,477	1,020
Cape Coral-Fort Myers, FL	33,112	154,572,301	3.8	7.4	4.9	3.0	47.3	4.2	28.2	4,646.6	703.6	1,284.1	1,735	1,464
Cape Girardeau, MO-IL	3,369	9,729,545	5.8	9.1	3.8	5.8	0.8	7.7	63.8	284.6	100.5	142.3	1,470	810
Carbondale-Marion, IL	5,097	18,208,421	5.7	9.3	3.3	4.1	4.6	6.0	65.8	476.1	217.3	186.0	1,354	1,134
Carson City, NV	1,652	7,251,836	10.3	13.8	7.8	4.2	2.8	7.3	52.0	235.3	121.5	63.2	1,159	789
Casper, WY	3,954	16,298,613	5.7	8.4	3.7	2.6	1.2	5.2	71.3	502.1	317.5	97.1	1,220	987

1. Based on the resident population estimated as of July 1 of the year shown

Area name	Local government finances, 2017 (cont.) — Direct general expenditure: Total (mil dol)	Per capita[1] (dollars)	Percent of total for: Educa-tion	Health and hospitals	Police protection	Public welfare	Highways	Debt outstanding: Total (mil dol)	Per capita[1] (dollars)	Government employment, 2020: Federal civilian	Federal military	State and local	Individual income tax returns, 2019: Number of returns	Mean adjusted gross income	Mean income tax
	185	186	187	188	189	190	191	192	193	194	195	196	197	198	199
Abilene, TX	621.4	3,646	49.0	5.5	6.3	0.5	2.6	526.5	3,089	1,301	4,866	11,403	76,960	57,825	5,966
Akron, OH	3,141.4	4,462	44.0	5.0	5.8	4.2	4.1	2,384.6	3,387	2,430	1,741	39,942	353,740	65,196	7,596
Albany, GA	579.7	3,915	52.9	2.5	7.3	0.0	3.6	270.3	1,825	2,763	684	8,949	61,790	47,918	4,348
Albany-Lebanon, OR	578.9	4,630	53.2	5.0	7.4	0.3	4.8	417.7	3,341	340	306	5,966	59,850	55,974	4,824
Albany-Schenectady-Troy, NY	5,209.6	5,905	49.8	4.4	4.2	10.6	4.2	3,588.7	4,068	7,031	2,009	88,652	449,270	80,825	10,568
Albuquerque, NM	3,037.0	3,329	52.6	1.3	8.4	1.6	2.6	4,454.7	4,883	15,029	5,885	65,217	437,000	60,086	6,310
Alexandria, LA	527.6	3,436	52.8	0.0	10.0	0.0	2.6	473.5	3,084	2,790	558	10,642	64,070	54,898	5,289
Allentown-Bethlehem-Easton, PA-NJ	4,559.2	5,441	54.8	1.6	3.8	8.8	3.5	6,298.5	7,517	2,481	2,084	36,290	435,840	68,900	7,900
Altoona, PA	469.6	3,813	52.1	6.8	4.8	7.4	3.9	388.4	3,154	1,217	303	7,243	59,950	56,775	5,802
Amarillo, TX	1,046.4	3,959	54.1	4.5	6.8	0.0	2.9	1,051.0	3,976	2,432	609	17,984	122,050	64,370	7,543
Ames, IA	636.9	5,148	31.6	40.8	3.5	0.6	4.2	657.1	5,311	1,062	437	20,574	51,310	70,376	7,418
Anchorage, AK	1,915.0	4,781	50.9	1.9	7.5	0.1	7.9	2,063.7	5,152	8,887	13,348	22,959	197,270	78,991	10,060
Ann Arbor, MI	1,638.2	4,442	49.2	6.2	7.2	0.6	3.7	1,748.4	4,741	4,293	617	69,823	170,250	91,334	12,898
Anniston-Oxford, AL	618.0	5,387	32.3	36.7	5.3	0.0	3.4	461.6	4,024	4,276	500	8,363	48,800	48,885	4,049
Appleton, WI	1,119.5	4,747	54.0	2.6	5.0	4.8	9.0	929.2	3,941	732	612	11,582	121,900	73,952	8,315
Asheville, NC	2,078.3	4,569	30.6	30.2	6.2	6.6	1.5	989.0	2,174	4,371	1,083	21,475	228,360	64,446	7,108
Athens-Clarke County, GA	1,124.7	5,378	31.4	40.4	3.6	0.1	2.4	844.9	4,041	1,067	598	26,864	86,860	68,102	8,165
Atlanta-Sandy Springs-Alpharetta, GA	22,633.7	3,854	50.6	5.7	6.0	0.2	4.1	36,598.7	6,232	50,904	16,633	282,071	2,820,060	76,515	10,104
Atlantic City-Hammonton, NJ	1,640.6	6,179	58.1	1.2	6.3	1.4	4.6	847.7	3,193	2,625	827	18,963	138,790	58,758	6,160
Auburn-Opelika, AL	790.2	4,895	32.9	41.4	3.9	0.0	2.8	800.7	4,960	331	726	17,874	66,930	65,264	6,901
Augusta-Richmond County, GA-SC	1,915.1	3,190	56.9	2.7	5.6	0.1	4.2	2,056.1	3,425	9,670	13,786	40,737	268,120	58,841	5,816
Austin-Round Rock-Georgetown, TX	10,487.2	4,957	43.9	8.1	5.9	0.5	9.3	24,855.1	11,749	15,239	4,766	161,715	1,098,020	99,177	14,876
Bakersfield, CA	7,088.4	7,988	40.8	3.7	3.6	5.7	1.6	4,158.1	4,686	11,487	3,956	53,810	360,880	54,635	5,041
Baltimore-Columbia-Towson, MD	13,725.1	4,904	49.9	1.9	7.9	0.3	3.0	12,275.1	4,386	80,568	23,946	161,579	1,387,490	84,278	11,044
Bangor, ME	508.2	3,352	50.2	1.4	5.1	0.3	5.1	383.0	2,526	1,195	444	12,541	69,830	56,281	5,463
Barnstable Town, MA	1,227.3	5,746	47.1	1.0	5.2	0.4	3.7	916.3	4,290	1,670	1,219	12,671	129,610	86,539	11,530
Baton Rouge, LA	3,604.4	4,219	46.3	5.9	6.3	0.2	7.0	2,994.4	3,505	3,120	3,345	68,162	385,520	66,820	7,838
Battle Creek, MI	634.2	4,727	46.9	2.5	5.8	5.4	12.5	651.6	4,856	2,984	255	7,450	62,180	52,720	4,689
Bay City, MI	486.0	4,671	50.5	10.2	3.8	5.7	5.8	292.8	2,814	268	224	5,250	53,240	53,444	5,081
Beaumont-Port Arthur, TX	1,543.5	3,877	45.4	5.0	8.0	0.6	4.3	5,591.0	14,043	2,046	930	21,643	172,070	62,535	6,591
Beckley, WV	332.1	2,799	63.9	0.6	6.7	0.0	1.8	183.3	1,544	2,132	537	6,147	47,600	50,579	4,513
Bellingham, WA	917.9	4,146	48.9	3.2	4.9	0.0	5.6	850.4	3,841	1,538	632	13,470	111,450	72,475	7,997
Bend, OR	870.7	4,662	41.6	3.7	6.6	0.1	6.2	1,327.8	7,111	1,005	474	8,073	103,680	80,289	10,142
Billings, MT	721.6	4,023	46.4	7.4	5.7	0.3	7.6	594.9	3,317	1,990	813	8,324	91,220	67,406	7,468
Binghamton, NY	1,742.0	7,207	48.2	3.2	2.5	12.8	4.5	1,167.1	4,829	689	362	18,725	111,830	58,725	5,905
Birmingham-Hoover, AL	4,024.4	3,707	45.6	2.6	7.5	0.0	4.8	8,542.9	7,869	9,219	4,745	69,956	486,980	73,267	8,989
Bismarck, ND	627.3	4,896	41.3	1.3	5.0	1.9	10.8	631.2	4,927	1,278	761	12,658	64,340	78,702	9,519
Blacksburg-Christiansburg, VA	553.5	3,322	39.0	11.1	7.3	3.6	3.8	380.3	2,283	452	578	21,107	63,630	67,181	7,481
Bloomington, IL	716.1	4,145	43.6	1.2	7.8	1.4	6.3	932.9	5,400	440	331	14,317	77,550	76,828	9,045
Bloomington, IN	545.5	3,258	32.0	0.6	3.0	0.1	3.5	627.5	3,748	387	472	24,780	68,170	63,828	7,197
Bloomsburg-Berwick, PA	326.1	3,889	59.4	0.0	3.5	0.3	4.3	2,558.9	30,518	213	201	6,236	39,090	59,652	6,100
Boise City, ID	1,985.4	2,798	43.6	2.2	8.4	0.6	6.2	1,064.8	1,500	6,862	2,392	41,260	353,830	72,351	8,297
Boston-Cambridge-Newton, MA-NH	23,814.8	4,919	51.4	4.1	5.6	0.5	3.3	14,786.3	3,054	37,096	14,096	258,764	2,481,690	113,831	18,403
Boston, MA Div 14,454	10,347.4	5,130	48.7	3.0	6.7	0.2	3.2	6,658.0	3,301	19,983	5,876	123,206	1,023,940	113,082	18,747
Cambridge-Newton-Framingham, MA Div 15,754	11,669.6	4,886	52.7	5.5	4.4	0.2	3.3	7,275.2	3,046	15,640	6,769	112,035	1,218,580	118,729	19,251
Rockingham County-Strafford County, NH Div 40,484	1,797.7	4,118	58.8	0.7	6.7	4.0	4.4	853.0	1,954	1,473	1,451	23,523	239,170	92,089	12,605
Boulder, CO	2,018.9	6,261	43.6	1.9	5.4	2.4	6.8	2,807.4	8,707	2,172	845	33,151	164,710	114,568	18,225
Bowling Green, KY	374.1	2,138	58.5	1.8	5.2	0.1	4.8	781.6	4,467	677	529	10,671	75,090	54,451	5,245
Bremerton-Silverdale-Port Orchard, WA	1,207.7	4,535	41.9	5.2	3.7	0.0	5.0	880.5	3,307	21,055	5,734	12,790	133,910	85,150	10,550
Bridgeport-Stamford-Norwalk, CT	4,968.1	5,268	53.4	1.0	6.9	0.9	3.8	3,859.8	4,093	3,072	1,868	41,667	467,180	160,632	32,036
Brownsville-Harlingen, TX	1,674.4	3,966	67.1	0.8	4.6	0.4	2.9	1,644.9	3,896	3,897	910	25,041	180,170	40,575	3,050
Brunswick, GA	745.2	6,338	29.1	46.1	3.3	0.0	3.8	398.2	3,386	2,092	377	6,489	51,150	63,778	7,204
Buffalo-Cheektowaga, NY	7,235.0	6,403	45.9	10.5	4.2	10.0	3.9	5,842.0	5,170	9,970	1,961	73,040	568,220	64,186	7,157
Burlington, NC	439.3	2,691	53.1	4.0	9.9	6.0	1.8	147.6	904	264	359	6,559	78,110	55,894	5,187
Burlington-South Burlington, VT	1,030.4	4,706	65.1	0.2	4.4	0.0	6.1	665.9	3,041	4,180	1,449	16,824	115,910	78,229	9,280
California-Lexington Park, MD	391.5	3,481	59.9	2.0	7.1	0.0	4.1	366.3	3,256	10,457	2,706	4,689	54,070	83,972	9,763
Canton-Massillon, OH	1,466.0	3,671	52.4	8.5	5.7	5.5	6.3	576.6	1,444	1,045	1,008	18,504	199,680	57,204	5,709
Cape Coral-Fort Myers, FL	4,462.4	6,030	24.7	37.4	5.2	0.2	2.4	4,561.8	6,165	2,633	1,410	40,843	375,900	84,490	11,941
Cape Girardeau, MO-IL	294.5	3,042	49.9	0.5	6.0	0.0	6.7	169.9	1,755	454	339	6,726	43,180	58,746	5,888
Carbondale-Marion, IL	479.4	3,490	53.2	1.9	7.1	0.1	6.1	458.6	3,339	1,930	269	15,639	57,830	56,367	5,542
Carson City, NV	226.4	4,152	42.3	4.1	8.4	2.9	6.4	397.7	7,292	578	139	8,662	29,630	61,253	6,641
Casper, WY	518.2	6,511	62.5	0.4	4.9	0.3	4.4	110.2	1,385	713	413	4,941	39,150	76,179	9,803

1. Based on the resident population estimated as of July 1 of the year shown.

CBSA[1]	DIV Code	Area name	Land area[2] (sq mi)	Population, 2021: Total persons 2021	Population, 2021: Rank	Population, 2021: Per square mile	Race alone or in combination, not Hispanic or Latino (percent): White	Black	American Indian, Alaska Native	Asian and Pacific Islander	Percent Hispanic or Latino[3]	Age (percent): Under 5 years	5 to 17 years	18 to 24 years	25 to 34 years	35 to 44 years	45 to 54 years
			1	2	3	4	5	6	7	8	9	10	11	12	13	14	15
16300		Cedar Rapids, IA	2,008.8	275,435	178	137.1	88.4	7.1	0.6	3.1	3.4	5.8	12.8	12.7	12.8	13.3	12.1
16540		Chambersburg-Waynesboro, PA	772.3	156,289	273	202.4	88.3	4.9	0.5	1.5	6.7	5.5	12.5	11.6	11.9	11.9	12.7
16580		Champaign-Urbana, IL	1,435.3	222,696	207	155.2	70.6	14.4	0.5	11.3	6.3	5.3	10.8	24.6	13.3	11.7	9.8
16620		Charleston, WV	2,646.6	255,020	191	96.4	92.4	6.7	0.7	1.2	1.1	5.0	11.6	11.2	11.8	11.9	12.7
16700		Charleston-North Charleston, SC	2,590.2	813,052	74	313.9	66.2	25.9	1.0	3.1	6.2	5.7	12.2	12.2	14.9	14.1	12.0
16740		Charlotte-Concord-Gastonia, NC-SC	5,597.4	2,701,046	22	482.6	60.9	24.3	0.9	5.0	11.1	5.8	13.2	12.6	14.1	13.9	13.7
16820		Charlottesville, VA	1,644.5	222,688	208	135.4	77.5	13.0	0.7	5.9	5.7	5.1	10.7	14.9	13.6	12.6	11.3
16860		Chattanooga, TN-GA	2,088.8	567,641	101	271.8	79.3	14.2	0.9	2.3	5.3	5.5	11.8	11.9	13.6	12.6	12.6
16940		Cheyenne, WY	2,685.9	100,863	357	37.6	80.3	3.2	1.4	2.3	15.5	5.8	13.0	12.9	14.1	13.3	11.1
16980		Chicago-Naperville-Elgin, IL-IN-WI	7,194.8	9,509,934	3	1,321.8	53.1	17.1	0.5	8.1	23.1	5.6	12.7	12.9	14.0	13.7	12.8
16980	16984	Chicago-Naperville-Evanston, IL Div 16,984	3,130.1	7,159,394	X	2,287.3	49.8	19.2	0.5	9.0	23.3	5.6	12.4	12.5	14.7	13.8	12.7
16980	20994	Elgin, IL Div 20,994	1,470.9	750,869	X	510.5	61.5	7.0	0.4	4.6	28.1	5.9	14.0	15.0	12.1	13.6	13.3
16980	23844	Gary, IN Div 23,844	1,878.3	719,700	X	383.2	63.7	18.1	0.7	2.0	17.2	5.6	13.0	12.9	12.1	13.1	12.4
16980	29404	Lake County-Kenosha County, IL-WI Div 29,404	715.5	879,971	X	1,229.9	63.9	7.8	0.6	8.3	21.4	5.4	13.3	14.5	11.6	12.8	13.2
17020		Chico, CA	1,636.5	208,309	215	127.3	72.8	3.0	2.8	7.2	18.4	5.3	11.5	18.1	13.0	11.8	10.2
17140		Cincinnati, OH-KY-IN	4,546.4	2,259,935	30	497.1	80.3	13.9	0.6	3.7	3.7	6.0	13.1	13.3	13.3	12.8	12.1
17300		Clarksville, TN-KY	2,158.0	328,304	159	152.1	67.7	22.0	1.2	3.6	9.8	8.0	14.7	15.2	17.4	13.0	10.3
17420		Cleveland, TN	763.4	127,938	316	167.6	87.7	5.4	1.0	1.5	6.4	5.5	12.0	12.9	12.6	11.9	13.4
17460		Cleveland-Elyria, OH	1,998.8	2,075,662	34	1,038.5	70.8	21.1	0.7	3.2	6.5	5.3	11.7	12.0	13.1	12.1	12.2
17660		Coeur d'Alene, ID	1,237.8	179,789	242	145.2	92.0	0.8	2.2	2.1	5.4	5.6	13.1	11.2	12.8	12.9	11.7
17780		College Station-Bryan, TX	2,100.4	272,041	181	129.5	56.7	12.1	0.7	5.9	26.4	5.7	11.9	25.6	14.6	12.0	9.4
17820		Colorado Springs, CO	2,683.5	762,793	79	284.3	71.9	7.6	1.5	5.3	18.1	6.1	13.1	14.4	15.9	13.6	11.2
17860		Columbia, MO	1,714.1	213,123	213	124.3	82.3	11.0	1.1	5.4	3.5	5.5	11.6	20.5	14.4	12.4	10.3
17900		Columbia, SC	3,703.1	838,250	72	226.4	56.6	35.5	0.9	3.2	6.1	5.5	12.5	15.1	13.7	12.7	12.1
17980		Columbus, GA-AL	2,786.1	327,536	160	117.6	46.9	43.5	1.0	3.4	8.0	6.5	13.5	13.3	15.4	12.9	11.3
18020		Columbus, IN	406.9	82,475	377	202.7	81.4	3.0	0.7	8.5	8.0	6.2	13.7	12.0	14.1	12.8	12.3
18140		Columbus, OH	4,796.6	2,151,017	32	448.4	73.3	18.2	0.8	6.0	4.7	6.3	13.2	12.9	15.3	14.0	12.4
18580		Corpus Christi, TX	1,532.5	422,778	132	275.9	30.4	3.5	0.6	2.4	64.1	6.2	14.0	14.0	13.7	13.5	11.6
18700		Corvallis, OR	675.2	96,017	364	142.2	83.1	2.0	1.6	9.0	8.2	3.8	9.1	25.1	13.2	10.6	9.9
18880		Crestview-Fort Walton Beach-Destin, FL	1,968.5	293,324	169	149.0	78.6	10.0	1.3	4.6	9.3	6.0	12.4	11.7	14.3	13.1	11.1
19060		Cumberland, MD-WV	750.1	94,586	367	126.1	90.1	8.3	0.6	1.4	1.8	4.7	10.2	14.3	12.4	11.7	12.2
19100		Dallas-Fort Worth-Arlington, TX	8,675.2	7,759,615	4	894.5	45.5	17.4	0.8	8.7	29.6	6.4	14.5	13.6	14.7	14.4	13.0
19100	19124	Dallas-Plano-Irving, TX Div 19,124	5,277.0	5,217,380	X	988.7	43.0	17.9	0.8	10.0	30.2	6.4	14.4	13.6	14.9	14.6	13.3
19100	23104	Fort Worth-Arlington-Grapevine, TX Div 23,104	3,398.2	2,542,235	X	748.1	50.5	16.2	0.9	6.0	28.5	6.4	14.7	13.8	14.3	13.9	12.6
19140		Dalton, GA	634.9	142,799	295	224.9	64.2	3.5	0.6	1.5	31.3	6.1	14.1	14.0	13.0	12.6	13.1
19180		Danville, IL	898.3	73,095	380	81.4	79.5	15.4	0.5	1.3	5.6	6.0	13.3	11.8	11.7	11.9	11.5
19300		Daphne-Fairhope-Foley, AL	1,589.8	239,294	197	150.5	84.9	9.2	1.4	1.6	4.8	5.1	12.2	10.9	11.0	12.1	12.7
19340		Davenport-Moline-Rock Island, IA-IL	2,269.9	381,568	147	168.1	79.7	9.8	0.7	3.1	9.4	5.7	13.0	12.3	12.1	12.9	11.9
19430		Dayton-Kettering, OH	1,281.4	813,516	73	634.9	77.9	17.7	0.9	3.3	3.3	5.8	12.4	13.2	13.4	12.1	11.5
19460		Decatur, AL	1,270.4	156,758	272	123.4	77.4	13.4	3.3	1.0	7.6	5.8	12.9	11.8	12.1	12.1	12.8
19500		Decatur, IL	580.6	102,432	355	176.4	77.8	20.6	0.5	1.8	2.6	6.0	12.6	12.5	11.8	11.6	11.3
19660		Deltona-Daytona Beach-Ormond Beach, FL	1,587.5	685,344	88	431.7	71.8	11.4	0.8	2.7	15.3	4.3	9.9	10.6	11.2	10.7	11.7
19740		Denver-Aurora-Lakewood, CO	8,344.7	2,972,566	19	356.2	65.3	6.7	1.1	6.0	23.6	5.5	12.1	11.9	16.9	15.4	12.8
19780		Des Moines-West Des Moines, IA	3,612.4	719,146	82	199.1	81.7	7.0	0.6	5.2	7.8	6.4	14.0	12.6	14.4	14.4	12.2
19820		Detroit-Warren-Dearborn, MI	3,892.2	4,365,205	14	1,121.5	67.5	23.4	1.0	5.8	4.9	5.6	12.3	12.0	13.7	12.2	12.9
19820	19804	Detroit-Dearborn-Livonia, MI Div 19,804	611.8	1,774,816	X	2,901.0	51.4	39.4	1.1	4.5	6.5	6.3	13.3	12.3	14.4	11.9	12.4
19820	47664	Warren-Troy-Farmington Hills, MI Div 47,664	3,280.4	2,590,389	X	789.7	78.6	12.4	0.9	6.7	3.9	5.2	11.6	11.7	13.2	12.4	13.3
20020		Dothan, AL	1,716.1	151,618	281	88.4	70.7	25.0	1.2	1.4	3.7	5.9	12.6	11.5	12.2	12.3	12.5
20100		Dover, DE	586.1	184,149	234	314.2	61.8	29.4	1.3	3.6	7.8	5.9	13.0	13.6	13.2	12.2	11.1
20220		Dubuque, IA	608.3	98,718	360	162.3	91.2	4.7	0.5	2.5	2.9	6.0	12.9	13.7	12.8	11.8	10.8
20260		Duluth, MN-WI	10,522.1	290,780	171	27.6	92.9	2.5	3.7	1.7	1.9	4.8	11.0	14.5	11.6	12.2	11.1
20500		Durham-Chapel Hill, NC	2,290.1	654,012	92	285.6	57.2	26.9	1.0	5.7	11.5	5.1	11.0	14.6	14.6	12.9	12.5
20700		East Stroudsburg, PA	608.4	169,273	256	278.2	64.5	15.5	0.9	3.2	18.3	4.6	10.9	13.7	11.6	11.3	13.1
20740		Eau Claire, WI	1,646.3	173,317	249	105.3	92.0	2.3	1.0	4.0	2.6	5.3	11.8	16.2	12.9	12.8	11.0
20940		El Centro, CA	4,175.5	179,851	241	43.1	9.7	2.6	0.9	1.5	85.8	7.1	16.6	14.6	14.7	12.7	10.7
21060		Elizabethtown-Fort Knox, KY	1,190.4	156,766	271	131.7	82.5	11.2	1.1	3.2	5.5	6.1	13.8	12.7	13.1	13.6	12.3
21140		Elkhart-Goshen, IN	463.2	206,921	219	446.7	75.3	7.1	0.7	1.7	17.6	7.3	15.3	13.9	12.8	12.1	11.7
21300		Elmira, NY	407.3	83,045	374	203.9	88.6	8.3	0.7	2.2	3.6	5.2	12.1	11.8	12.3	12.3	12.0
21340		El Paso, TX	5,583.8	871,234	67	156.0	12.2	3.6	0.5	1.7	82.9	6.8	15.1	15.6	15.2	12.8	11.4
21420		Enid, OK	1,058.5	61,926	383	58.5	74.9	4.5	4.5	6.0	14.2	6.7	14.8	13.1	13.2	13.1	10.3
21500		Erie, PA	798.9	269,011	183	336.7	85.4	9.0	0.5	2.6	4.8	5.2	11.9	13.5	12.8	11.9	11.8
21660		Eugene-Springfield, OR	4,554.1	383,189	146	84.1	84.6	2.1	2.8	5.1	9.8	4.3	10.3	15.4	13.2	12.7	11.1

1. CBSA = Core Based Statistical Area. DIV = Metropolitan Division. See Appendix A for explanation. See Appendix B for list of metropolitan areas or temporarily covered by water. 2. Dry land or land partially or temporarily covered by water. 3. May be of any race.

Area name	Population, 2021 (cont.)				Population change and components of change, 2010–2021							Households, 2016–2020				
	Age (percent) (cont.)				Total persons		Percent change		Components of change, 2020–2021					Percent		
	55 to 64 years	65 to 74 years	75 years and over	Percent female	2010	2020	2010–2020	2020–2021	Births	Deaths	Net migration	Number	Persons per house-hold	Family house-holds	Female family house holds	One person
	16	17	18	19	20	21	22	23	24	25	26	27	28	29	30	31
Cedar Rapids, IA	13.2	10.2	7.0	50.2	257,940	276,520	7.2	-0.4	3,843	3,605	-1,333	109,796	2.42	63.4	9.1	29.0
Chambersburg-Waynesboro, PA	13.8	11.5	8.6	50.7	149,618	155,932	4.2	0.2	2,102	2,402	642	61,617	2.48	69.7	9.9	25.0
Champaign-Urbana, IL	10.3	8.7	5.5	50.2	217,810	222,538	2.2	0.1	2,905	2,403	-403	89,814	2.35	52.8	9.4	35.5
Charleston, WV	14.4	13.3	8.3	51.1	278,009	258,859	-6.9	-1.5	3,039	5,279	-1,601	109,935	2.34	62.9	11.7	32.2
Charleston-North Charleston, SC	12.8	10.3	5.9	51.1	664,607	799,636	20.3	1.7	11,615	9,894	11,660	299,947	2.58	63.3	12.3	29.4
Charlotte-Concord-Gastonia, NC-SC	12.4	8.9	5.4	51.2	2,243,960	2,660,329	18.6	1.5	37,478	31,275	34,416	975,476	2.62	66.6	12.8	27.3
Charlottesville, VA	12.8	11.5	7.5	51.8	201,559	221,524	9.9	0.5	2,666	2,599	1,122	85,051	2.42	61.5	9.6	28.9
Chattanooga, TN-GA	13.4	11.2	7.4	51.2	528,143	562,647	6.5	0.9	7,601	8,913	6,287	222,885	2.45	64.0	11.5	30.5
Cheyenne, WY	12.8	10.5	6.5	49.2	91,738	100,512	9.6	0.3	1,447	1,259	146	40,202	2.42	65.0	9.0	28.8
Chicago-Naperville-Elgin, IL-IN-WI	12.8	9.5	6.1	50.7	9,461,105	9,618,502	1.7	-1.1	125,780	110,901	-123,457	3,548,735	2.63	64.5	12.6	29.1
Chicago-Naperville-Evanston, IL Div 16,984	12.7	9.4	6.2	50.9	7,147,982	7,267,535	1.7	-1.5	95,472	83,259	-119,992	2,701,523	2.60	62.8	12.9	30.4
Elgin, IL Div 20,994	12.3	8.6	5.3	50.0	735,165	748,811	1.9	0.3	10,393	7,259	-1,207	261,859	2.88	72.1	11.4	22.3
Gary, IN Div 23,844	13.5	10.7	6.7	50.9	708,070	718,663	1.5	0.1	9,341	10,959	2,562	272,074	2.54	66.2	13.9	28.4
Lake County-Kenosha County, IL-WI Div 29,404	13.9	9.4	5.9	49.8	869,888	883,493	1.6	-0.4	10,574	9,424	-4,820	313,279	2.70	71.0	10.3	23.8
Chico, CA	11.8	11.1	7.2	50.3	220,000	211,632	-3.8	-1.6	2,526	2,990	-2,888	83,879	2.59	60.6	11.9	27.5
Cincinnati, OH-KY-IN	13.3	10.0	6.1	50.6	2,137,667	2,256,884	5.6	0.1	32,552	31,328	1,576	870,103	2.49	64.6	12.1	28.8
Clarksville, TN-KY	10.0	7.2	4.3	49.3	273,949	320,535	17.0	2.4	6,531	3,806	5,066	111,845	2.63	69.7	13.6	24.7
Cleveland, TN	13.7	10.7	7.3	51.1	115,788	126,164	9.0	1.4	1,603	2,095	2,278	48,178	2.49	68.5	11.6	25.8
Cleveland-Elyria, OH	14.2	11.6	7.8	51.4	2,077,240	2,088,251	0.5	-0.6	26,188	32,400	-6,432	871,132	2.31	59.1	13.3	34.5
Coeur d'Alene, ID	13.4	12.2	7.3	50.2	138,494	171,362	23.7	4.9	2,269	2,278	8,543	64,475	2.48	69.6	8.4	23.8
College Station-Bryan, TX	9.4	7.1	4.4	49.8	228,660	268,248	17.3	1.4	3,666	2,383	2,440	95,194	2.58	58.3	12.7	29.6
Colorado Springs, CO	11.8	8.9	5.0	49.2	645,613	755,105	17.0	1.0	11,235	7,754	4,055	273,240	2.62	68.0	9.6	24.9
Columbia, MO	11.0	8.9	5.3	51.2	190,387	210,864	10.8	1.1	2,829	2,163	1,549	81,721	2.40	58.6	9.7	30.4
Columbia, SC	12.6	9.9	5.9	51.4	767,598	829,470	8.1	1.1	11,096	10,966	8,585	318,887	2.50	63.9	15.5	29.8
Columbus, GA-AL	12.1	9.3	5.7	50.5	307,788	328,883	6.9	-0.4	5,161	4,591	-1,914	120,480	2.54	64.2	17.2	31.8
Columbus, IN	12.1	9.8	6.8	49.5	76,794	82,208	7.1	0.3	1,234	1,139	161	31,772	2.59	65.6	10.0	28.4
Columbus, OH	12.0	8.8	5.2	50.5	1,901,974	2,138,926	12.5	0.6	32,375	25,914	5,513	805,628	2.54	63.3	12.4	29.0
Corpus Christi, TX	11.7	9.2	6.0	50.1	405,027	421,933	4.2	0.2	6,290	5,483	-43	153,904	2.73	68.3	16.3	25.9
Corvallis, OR	10.8	11.1	6.5	49.8	85,579	95,184	11.2	0.9	814	879	892	36,051	2.39	57.8	8.0	26.1
Crestview-Fort Walton Beach-Destin, FL	14.1	10.8	6.6	49.1	235,865	286,973	21.7	2.2	4,219	4,026	6,198	107,870	2.51	66.5	9.8	27.2
Cumberland, MD-WV	13.5	12.0	8.9	48.2	103,299	95,044	-8.0	-0.5	1,086	1,857	308	38,179	2.33	61.9	10.8	31.2
Dallas-Fort Worth-Arlington, TX	11.5	7.5	4.3	50.5	6,366,542	7,637,387	20.0	1.6	116,898	72,592	78,337	2,615,579	2.82	69.1	13.0	25.1
Dallas-Plano-Irving, TX Div 19,124	11.4	7.3	4.2	50.4	4,230,520	5,129,966	21.3	1.7	78,911	46,442	55,829	1,766,761	2.80	68.5	12.8	25.6
Fort Worth-Arlington-Grapevine, TX Div 23,104	11.8	7.9	4.6	50.7	2,136,022	2,507,421	17.4	1.4	37,987	26,150	22,508	848,818	2.86	70.5	13.4	24.0
Dalton, GA	12.3	8.8	6.0	50.1	142,227	142,837	0.4	0.0	2,038	1,883	-231	50,932	2.79	72.6	14.0	22.9
Danville, IL	13.7	11.7	8.3	49.8	81,625	74,188	-9.1	-1.5	1,050	1,385	-757	31,013	2.39	61.4	14.5	33.3
Daphne-Fairhope-Foley, AL	14.6	13.2	8.2	51.3	182,265	231,767	27.2	3.2	2,787	3,528	8,358	84,047	2.56	66.7	8.7	29.0
Davenport-Moline-Rock Island, IA-IL	13.2	11.3	7.7	50.4	379,690	384,324	1.2	-0.7	5,201	5,678	-2,314	154,517	2.40	63.4	11.1	31.0
Dayton-Kettering, OH	13.3	10.9	7.4	51.2	799,232	814,049	1.9	-0.1	11,175	13,274	1,451	334,252	2.33	61.0	12.9	32.5
Decatur, AL	14.2	10.9	7.3	50.6	153,829	156,494	1.7	0.2	2,142	2,709	818	58,939	2.55	67.2	11.7	29.2
Decatur, IL	13.4	12.1	8.6	51.9	110,768	103,998	-6.1	-1.5	1,476	1,805	-1,232	43,810	2.31	59.7	11.8	34.9
Deltona-Daytona Beach-Ormond Beach, FL	15.5	15.2	10.9	51.1	590,289	668,921	13.3	2.5	6,789	12,792	22,733	264,426	2.45	63.6	10.5	29.1
Denver-Aurora-Lakewood, CO	11.7	8.8	5.0	49.6	2,543,482	2,963,821	16.5	0.3	40,265	29,412	-2,438	1,097,674	2.64	62.6	9.3	28.4
Des Moines-West Des Moines, IA	11.7	8.8	5.4	50.1	606,475	709,466	17.0	1.4	10,889	8,156	6,888	271,569	2.50	63.3	10.2	28.9
Detroit-Warren-Dearborn, MI	14.0	10.6	6.7	51.0	4,296,250	4,392,041	2.2	-0.6	58,334	63,565	-22,170	1,726,401	2.47	62.8	13.5	31.4
Detroit-Dearborn-Livonia, MI Div 19,804	13.1	10.0	6.2	51.6	1,820,584	1,793,561	-1.5	-1.0	26,936	27,372	-18,459	694,858	2.49	59.9	17.9	34.4
Warren-Troy-Farmington Hills, MI Div 47,664	14.7	11.1	7.0	50.6	2,475,666	2,598,480	5.0	-0.3	31,398	36,193	-3,711	1,031,543	2.46	64.7	10.5	29.4
Dothan, AL	13.6	11.6	7.9	51.7	145,639	151,007	3.7	0.4	2,120	2,578	1,060	56,912	2.59	66.7	13.3	29.7
Dover, DE	13.0	10.7	7.2	51.7	162,310	181,851	12.0	1.3	2,495	2,598	2,394	67,299	2.59	67.6	15.7	25.8
Dubuque, IA	13.4	11.0	7.7	50.4	93,653	99,266	6.0	-0.6	1,368	1,341	-579	38,655	2.41	65.2	8.5	28.7
Duluth, MN-WI	14.4	12.7	7.8	49.3	290,637	291,638	0.3	-0.3	3,315	4,602	401	124,208	2.22	58.3	8.8	32.6
Durham-Chapel Hill, NC	12.6	10.3	6.3	51.8	564,273	649,903	15.2	0.6	8,305	7,403	3,173	250,974	2.41	61.6	12.3	30.4
East Stroudsburg, PA	16.3	11.8	6.6	49.9	169,842	168,327	-0.9	0.6	1,772	2,410	1,592	59,950	2.78	71.0	11.8	22.6
Eau Claire, WI	12.8	10.7	6.6	49.3	161,151	172,007	6.7	0.8	2,179	2,104	1,217	67,646	2.39	61.0	7.4	29.1
El Centro, CA	10.1	7.8	5.6	48.5	174,528	179,702	3.0	0.1	2,851	2,034	-722	45,768	3.73	74.7	19.0	22.1
Elizabethtown-Fort Knox, KY	13.3	9.4	5.7	49.8	148,338	155,572	4.9	0.8	2,220	2,146	1,111	58,528	2.55	68.4	11.4	25.8
Elkhart-Goshen, IN	11.7	9.0	6.2	50.3	197,559	207,047	4.8	-0.1	3,657	2,551	-1,269	72,362	2.79	69.4	12.8	25.7
Elmira, NY	14.4	11.9	7.9	50.1	88,830	84,148	-5.3	-1.3	1,058	1,512	-654	34,328	2.32	61.0	12.3	33.1
El Paso, TX	10.4	7.6	5.2	50.2	804,123	868,859	8.1	0.3	13,829	8,526	-3,158	274,789	3.01	72.4	18.8	23.8
Enid, OK	12.3	9.6	7.0	49.6	60,580	62,846	3.7	-1.5	976	1,015	-882	23,709	2.53	63.9	10.5	30.5
Erie, PA	13.8	11.7	7.4	50.2	280,566	270,876	-3.5	-0.7	3,341	4,334	-907	110,388	2.35	61.5	12.7	30.6
Eugene-Springfield, OR	12.5	12.8	7.7	50.7	351,715	382,971	8.9	0.1	3,798	5,554	1,941	154,516	2.39	58.5	10.4	29.2

Area name	Persons in group quarters, 2021	Daytime population, 2016–2020: Number	Daytime population, 2016–2020: Employ-ment/ residence ratio	Births, 2021: Total	Births, 2021: Rate[1]	Deaths, 2021: Number	Deaths, 2021: Rate[1]	Persons under 65 with no health insurance 2019: Number	Persons under 65 with no health insurance 2019: Percent	Medicare, 2021: Total Ben-eficiaries	Medicare, 2021: Enrolled in Original Medicare	Medicare, 2021: Enrolled in Medicare Advantage	Serious crimes known to police[2], 2020: Violent: Number	Serious crimes known to police[2], 2020: Violent: Rate[3]
	32	33	34	35	36	37	38	39	40	41	42	43	44	45
Cedar Rapids, IA	6,425	273,239	1.01	3,051	11.1	2,914	10.6	10,657	4.8	53,757	33,897	19,860	691	251.9
Chambersburg-Waynesboro, PA	2,539	146,055	0.88	1,679	10.8	1,932	12.4	10,407	8.5	36,925	24,294	12,631	NA	NA
Champaign-Urbana, IL	15,976	231,681	1.05	2,317	10.4	1,903	8.6	12,559	7.0	34,649	16,097	18,552	D	D
Charleston, WV	3,574	275,029	1.14	2,433	9.5	4,213	16.4	16,037	8.0	67,559	34,644	32,915	1,366	536.3
Charleston-North Charleston, SC	15,683	794,316	1.01	9,307	11.5	8,113	10.0	83,221	12.6	148,475	102,022	46,453	3,657	446.2
Charlotte-Concord-Gastonia, NC-SC	35,600	2,617,288	1.02	30,082	11.2	25,345	9.4	284,932	12.7	441,538	239,486	202,052	NA	NA
Charlottesville, VA	10,323	230,961	1.13	2,136	9.6	2,083	9.4	16,337	9.7	45,444	36,933	8,511	415	188.3
Chattanooga, TN-GA	12,385	571,899	1.04	6,041	10.7	7,172	12.7	56,829	12.6	121,977	65,153	56,824	3,487	612.7
Cheyenne, WY	1,956	101,456	1.04	1,125	11.2	996	9.9	9,645	11.8	20,134	19,249	885	330	327.8
Chicago-Naperville-Elgin, IL-IN-WI	160,440	9,518,274	1.01	100,116	10.5	88,978	9.3	750,044	9.5	1,421,300	926,786	494,514	NA	NA
Chicago-Naperville-Evanston, IL Div 16,984	115,380	7,294,959	1.04	76,016	10.5	66,871	9.3	577,789	9.7	1,177,873	765,214	412,659	NA	NA
Elgin, IL Div 20,994	11,490	689,972	0.81	8,214	11.0	5,885	7.8	59,930	9.2	117,666	79,042	38,624	NA	NA
Gary, IN Div 23,844	10,657	665,450	0.88	7,494	10.4	8,713	12.1	54,083	9.4	70,054	46,636	23,418	NA	NA
Lake County-Kenosha County, IL-WI Div 29,404	22,913	867,893	1.00	8,392	9.5	7,509	8.5	58,242	8.1	55,707	35,894	19,813	NA	NA
Chico, CA	5,112	223,257	1.00	2,022	9.7	2,383	11.4	13,710	7.8	45,836	41,104	4,732	1,069	492.8
Cincinnati, OH-KY-IN	50,482	2,211,991	1.00	25,985	11.5	25,266	11.2	130,813	7.1	416,324	210,588	205,736	5,250	235.7
Clarksville, TN-KY	10,013	296,094	0.94	5,200	16.0	3,050	9.4	24,317	9.3	47,572	31,661	15,911	1,321	423.6
Cleveland, TN	2,663	119,389	0.92	1,273	10.0	1,662	13.1	14,045	14.1	28,161	14,340	13,821	710	563.5
Cleveland-Elyria, OH	42,807	2,100,865	1.05	20,924	10.1	25,851	12.4	119,385	7.3	448,294	221,482	226,812	9,002	440.6
Coeur d'Alene, ID	1,384	155,624	0.92	1,782	10.1	1,815	10.3	16,442	12.4	42,029	26,148	15,881	343	201.5
College Station-Bryan, TX	14,623	264,745	1.03	2,918	10.8	1,940	7.2	39,507	17.9	34,840	22,735	12,105	799	298.0
Colorado Springs, CO	19,507	726,791	0.98	8,997	11.8	6,143	8.1	55,987	9.0	12,402	6,934	5,468	3,661	486.6
Columbia, MO	10,542	209,703	1.02	2,265	10.7	1,713	8.1	18,931	11.2	35,081	20,851	14,230	769	366.0
Columbia, SC	30,695	842,817	1.02	8,961	10.7	8,824	10.6	81,315	12.0	158,805	105,624	53,181	4,729	558.0
Columbus, GA-AL	11,445	329,810	1.07	4,145	12.6	3,779	11.5	33,486	12.8	60,408	32,398	28,010	NA	NA
Columbus, IN	935	93,567	1.26	975	11.8	898	10.9	6,827	9.8	16,025	10,874	5,151	NA	NA
Columbus, OH	49,968	2,135,213	1.03	25,733	12.0	20,766	9.7	142,669	8.0	342,129	169,813	172,316	6,718	313.2
Corpus Christi, TX	6,566	436,084	1.04	5,090	12.1	4,388	10.4	70,539	19.7	75,352	30,912	44,440	3,176	738.0
Corvallis, OR	5,901	95,032	1.06	634	6.6	707	7.4	4,861	6.7	18,278	9,061	9,217	NA	NA
Crestview-Fort Walton Beach-Destin, FL	6,860	290,033	1.09	3,432	11.8	3,172	10.9	34,378	15.0	60,288	42,509	17,779	780	268.9
Cumberland, MD-WV	7,691	98,235	1.00	866	9.1	1,491	15.7	4,231	6.1	23,892	20,618	3,274	NA	NA
Dallas-Fort Worth-Arlington, TX	79,023	7,494,122	1.01	93,937	12.2	58,593	7.6	1,287,901	19.5	1,020,570	520,053	500,517	NA	NA
Dallas-Plano-Irving, TX Div 19,124	50,253	5,086,475	1.04	63,425	12.2	37,639	7.3	877,330	19.7	658,820	339,258	319,562	NA	NA
Fort Worth-Arlington-Grapevine, TX Div 23,104	28,770	2,407,647	0.96	30,512	12.1	20,954	8.3	410,571	19.0	361,750	180,795	180,955	NA	NA
Dalton, GA	1,163	147,675	1.06	1,639	11.5	1,485	10.4	26,967	22.2	25,370	17,141	8,229	NA	NA
Danville, IL	2,701	76,202	0.98	863	11.7	1,093	14.9	3,829	6.6	17,452	9,326	8,126	785	1,050.3
Daphne-Fairhope-Foley, AL	2,177	204,552	0.86	2,260	9.6	2,867	12.1	19,085	10.9	57,826	28,140	29,686	NA	NA
Davenport-Moline-Rock Island, IA-IL	8,627	383,649	1.02	4,134	10.8	4,515	11.8	19,970	6.6	81,066	46,575	34,491	1,798	475.9
Dayton-Kettering, OH	24,094	826,845	1.06	8,988	11.0	10,579	13.0	52,791	8.2	170,276	81,758	88,518	NA	NA
Decatur, AL	2,142	146,955	0.92	1,740	11.1	2,131	13.6	16,285	13.2	34,387	19,647	14,740	NA	NA
Decatur, IL	3,859	110,904	1.14	1,191	11.6	1,430	13.9	4,788	6.0	24,422	18,074	6,348	540	525.6
Deltona-Daytona Beach-Ormond Beach, FL	14,363	619,611	0.86	5,446	8.0	10,147	15.0	79,310	16.5	198,032	90,819	107,213	2,280	337.5
Denver-Aurora-Lakewood, CO	32,177	2,925,683	1.00	32,211	10.8	23,680	8.0	229,794	9.0	554,357	260,863	293,494	14,701	490.4
Des Moines-West Des Moines, IA	12,996	695,810	1.01	8,677	12.1	6,508	9.1	31,630	5.3	118,480	79,343	39,137	2,402	338.6
Detroit-Warren-Dearborn, MI	47,894	4,334,475	1.01	46,383	10.6	50,849	11.6	243,170	6.8	868,458	429,257	439,201	24,568	570.2
Detroit-Dearborn-Livonia, MI Div 19,804	22,540	1,812,335	1.08	21,470	12.0	21,853	12.3	110,013	7.6	333,381	150,355	183,026	18,894	1,088.2
Warren-Troy-Farmington Hills, MI Div 47,664	25,354	2,522,140	0.97	24,913	9.6	28,996	11.2	133,157	6.3	535,077	278,902	256,175	5,674	220.6
Dothan, AL	1,642	148,719	1.00	1,719	11.4	2,060	13.6	15,970	13.4	36,554	18,117	18,437	NA	NA
Dover, DE	4,360	170,776	0.90	2,049	11.2	2,119	11.6	13,058	9.0	39,654	30,262	9,392	813	442.6
Dubuque, IA	4,071	105,429	1.17	1,112	11.2	1,100	11.1	3,726	4.9	21,198	9,776	11,422	262	268.6
Duluth, MN-WI	12,102	292,972	1.03	2,627	9.0	3,592	12.3	12,444	5.6	70,651	27,688	42,963	607	211.1
Durham-Chapel Hill, NC	28,902	672,829	1.12	6,661	10.2	5,968	9.1	67,123	13.0	118,460	66,280	52,180	3,272	500.4
East Stroudsburg, PA	3,913	156,058	0.84	1,427	8.5	1,945	11.5	11,267	8.3	35,764	23,892	11,872	NA	NA
Eau Claire, WI	7,253	170,788	1.03	1,743	10.1	1,710	9.9	9,231	6.9	35,570	21,827	13,743	326	191.7
El Centro, CA	8,296	177,918	0.95	2,289	12.7	1,567	8.7	14,070	9.6	33,055	23,432	9,623	609	338.1
Elizabethtown-Fort Knox, KY	3,501	145,999	0.91	1,760	11.3	1,673	10.7	8,334	6.5	30,099	19,277	10,822	155	100.5
Elkhart-Goshen, IN	3,489	234,476	1.30	2,927	14.1	1,999	9.7	25,976	15.1	35,454	20,549	14,905	NA	NA
Elmira, NY	3,515	85,517	1.04	839	10.1	1,193	14.3	2,636	4.1	20,172	9,620	10,552	173	210.1
El Paso, TX	16,827	840,097	1.00	11,026	12.7	6,798	7.8	174,435	24.4	31,725	18,071	13,654	2,611	308.8
Enid, OK	1,767	61,630	1.00	798	12.8	811	13.0	8,357	16.8	12,113	9,902	2,211	254	415.8
Erie, PA	11,980	276,613	1.04	2,641	9.8	3,483	12.9	14,801	7.1	61,572	27,769	33,803	NA	NA
Eugene-Springfield, OR	8,570	378,949	1.01	3,061	8.0	4,449	11.6	26,896	9.1	92,107	39,879	52,228	NA	NA

1. Per 1,000 estimated resident population. 2. Data for serious crimes have not been adjusted for underreporting; this may affect comparability between geographic areas and over time. 3. Per 100,000 population estimated by the FBI.

Area name	Serious crimes known to police[1], 2020 (cont.) — Property — Number	Property — Rate[2]	Education — School enrollment and attainment, 2016–2020 — Enrollment[3] — Total	Enrollment[3] — Percent private	Attainment[4] (percent) — High school graduate or less	Attainment[4] (percent) — Bachelor's degree or more	Local government expenditures,[5] 2018–2019 — Total current spending (mil dol)	Local government expenditures — Current spending per student (dollars)	Income and poverty, 2016–2020 — Per capita income[6] (dollars)	Mean household income (dollars)	Mean Individual income	Percent of households with income of less than $50,000	Percent of households with income of $200,000 or more	Percent below poverty level — All persons	Percent below poverty level — All families	Percent below poverty level — Age 65 years and older
	46	47	48	49	50	51	52	53	54	55	56	57	58	59	60	61
Cedar Rapids, IA	5,803	2,115.5	65,475	17.5	34.0	31.6	558.9	12,453	35,423	66,620	85,854	36.8	6.0	9.3	6.3	10.3
Chambersburg-Waynesboro, PA	NA	NA	32,650	17.1	54.7	22.2	288.9	12,580	31,887	63,420	75,297	37.6	3.4	8.9	5.7	10.6
Champaign-Urbana, IL	D	D	81,577	8.8	28.1	43.7	433.0	15,583	31,502	54,897	83,169	46.0	5.8	18.1	8.3	13.0
Charleston, WV	5,873	2,305.7	50,462	10.3	51.8	22.3	491.0	12,436	28,209	46,099	60,682	53.1	3.6	18.1	13.5	22.6
Charleston-North Charleston, SC	20,333	2,480.6	185,263	17.0	34.0	36.5	1,218.6	10,651	36,925	65,894	82,122	37.9	8.1	12.4	8.2	13.9
Charlotte-Concord-Gastonia, NC-SC	NA	NA	639,157	15.9	33.7	35.9	3,954.3	9,458	36,155	65,725	80,486	37.9	8.5	11.1	8.1	12.5
Charlottesville, VA	2,849	1,292.7	59,213	14.8	27.9	50.3	368.8	13,684	42,909	75,176	95,708	33.3	10.5	11.1	5.4	8.5
Chattanooga, TN-GA	17,474	3,070.2	126,850	20.8	41.1	28.2	770.1	10,330	31,733	54,425	70,533	46.1	5.2	12.9	8.9	14.8
Cheyenne, WY	2,617	2,599.8	24,563	10.1	31.4	30.2	239.7	15,483	36,421	69,369	82,325	34.4	5.0	8.9	5.8	9.2
Chicago-Naperville-Elgin, IL-IN-WI	NA	NA	2,386,200	20.4	34.4	39.0	24,745.0	16,634	39,625	74,621	92,668	34.2	10.7	11.3	8.2	12.5
Chicago-Naperville-Evanston, IL Div 16,984	NA	NA	1,772,925	22.1	33.6	40.5	18,588.6	17,291	40,217	74,236	92,622	34.6	10.8	11.7	8.4	12.8
Elgin, IL Div 20,994	NA	NA	217,214	14.1	35.7	34.6	2,050.6	14,591	36,310	82,139	97,326	28.7	9.8	8.8	6.2	9.5
Gary, IN Div 23,844	NA	NA	166,569	15.3	45.7	23.8	1,158.3	10,229	31,215	61,276	75,625	41.4	4.7	13.6	10.5	17.4
Lake County-Kenosha County, IL-WI Div 29,404	NA	NA	229,492	16.7	31.3	42.4	2,947.6	18,555	44,476	85,927	105,876	29.0	15.2	8.4	5.8	9.0
Chico, CA	4,328	1,995.0	62,563	8.4	32.9	28.3	465.0	14,600	30,700	54,972	71,089	46.3	6.3	18.2	10.8	16.6
Cincinnati, OH-KY-IN	36,953	1,658.8	548,650	19.2	37.9	34.5	4,006.2	12,374	35,861	66,435	84,990	37.9	7.3	11.7	7.9	12.9
Clarksville, TN-KY	5,777	1,852.5	80,601	14.1	37.6	26.0	464.4	9,638	27,022	54,911	65,849	45.2	3.5	13.8	10.7	15.5
Cleveland, TN	3,398	2,696.8	28,786	23.7	46.2	21.9	166.9	9,069	26,921	51,015	63,243	49.1	3.1	15.1	10.8	16.3
Cleveland-Elyria, OH	34,823	1,704.5	472,624	23.6	37.7	31.9	4,098.7	14,759	34,743	57,263	76,766	44.2	6.0	14.0	10.0	16.9
Coeur d'Alene, ID	1,807	1,061.5	35,337	17.9	32.9	26.6	180.3	7,742	30,912	60,903	72,376	40.1	3.7	10.3	7.4	13.1
College Station-Bryan, TX	4,970	1,853.9	100,267	7.1	35.7	37.8	366.2	9,968	28,843	51,261	71,727	48.7	5.9	22.3	12.6	17.3
Colorado Springs, CO	19,960	2,653.0	193,954	14.4	25.6	38.6	1,271.7	10,240	35,155	71,171	83,751	34.0	7.3	9.8	6.5	9.9
Columbia, MO	4,635	2,206.1	66,112	13.1	29.1	44.3	313.9	11,224	31,056	57,980	78,168	43.8	6.2	16.3	7.7	11.9
Columbia, SC	27,730	3,272.0	211,062	12.1	36.3	33.0	2,125.9	13,468	30,681	56,680	71,993	44.1	4.8	14.8	10.8	17.0
Columbus, GA-AL	NA	NA	82,886	12.9	40.3	25.1	540.4	10,582	27,061	48,903	62,459	50.9	4.0	18.6	13.9	21.3
Columbus, IN	NA	NA	19,130	17.1	41.0	33.9	130.0	10,459	32,371	66,978	79,194	37.9	5.4	12.7	8.8	16.3
Columbus, OH	47,407	2,209.9	529,391	16.8	35.7	37.3	4,217.4	12,953	35,394	66,715	84,088	37.2	7.4	12.7	8.8	13.8
Corpus Christi, TX	12,668	2,943.6	107,914	6.2	46.4	20.8	766.5	10,159	27,865	56,714	67,685	44.3	4.7	16.0	12.4	19.6
Corvallis, OR	NA	NA	33,437	7.9	17.6	53.3	111.1	12,314	35,305	65,142	89,816	39.0	7.8	18.6	7.9	14.4
Crestview-Fort Walton Beach-Destin, FL	3,927	1,354.0	61,228	14.0	34.4	31.6	396.3	9,508	34,775	65,075	79,490	37.9	6.5	10.9	7.3	13.5
Cumberland, MD-WV	NA	NA	21,733	8.2	51.9	18.9	169.9	13,371	25,214	50,188	63,095	49.8	2.1	14.9	10.2	17.2
Dallas-Fort Worth-Arlington, TX	NA	NA	2,005,082	13.0	36.0	36.0	13,530.5	9,493	36,368	72,882	86,296	33.5	9.8	11.1	8.2	11.9
Dallas-Plano-Irving, TX Div 19,124	NA	NA	1,353,446	12.6	34.6	38.4	9,429.8	9,448	37,687	74,251	88,315	33.2	10.7	11.1	8.2	11.8
Fort Worth-Arlington-Grapevine, TX Div 23,104	NA	NA	651,636	13.9	38.7	30.9	4,100.7	9,598	33,684	70,491	82,649	34.3	8.1	11.1	8.2	12.3
Dalton, GA	NA	NA	35,875	3.7	60.1	14.8	294.6	10,464	24,042	50,322	58,145	49.7	3.5	16.2	11.5	18.6
Danville, IL	D	D	17,411	6.7	51.7	15.5	185.7	14,983	25,484	46,842	60,958	52.8	2.1	19.0	14.7	25.5
Daphne-Fairhope-Foley, AL	NA	NA	46,076	20.4	36.7	31.9	324.2	10,046	33,751	61,756	79,907	41.6	6.6	9.2	6.3	9.6
Davenport-Moline-Rock Island, IA-IL	D	D	88,664	16.3	38.5	27.5	799.0	13,056	32,570	59,876	76,902	41.4	4.8	12.6	9.1	15.5
Dayton-Kettering, OH	NA	NA	201,723	22.1	36.8	29.9	1,541.4	13,791	32,241	57,631	75,125	43.8	4.7	14.0	9.9	17.1
Decatur, AL	NA	NA	34,072	10.5	50.1	20.1	256.8	10,522	27,674	51,842	65,097	48.7	3.7	15.3	12.4	20.8
Decatur, IL	D	D	22,817	17.5	43.0	23.6	205.5	12,798	30,681	53,725	71,270	47.4	4.2	15.2	11.3	20.4
Deltona-Daytona Beach-Ormond Beach, FL	9,815	1,452.7	132,590	19.5	40.8	24.6	677.2	8,887	30,350	53,339	65,794	46.7	4.2	12.8	8.1	14.5
Denver-Aurora-Lakewood, CO	99,017	3,302.7	695,051	14.3	28.3	44.7	5,246.2	11,103	43,427	83,289	103,157	28.1	11.8	8.3	5.3	8.2
Des Moines-West Des Moines, IA	14,354	2,023.5	170,285	16.8	32.7	37.1	1,445.3	11,924	37,089	71,734	89,538	33.7	7.2	9.2	6.3	9.6
Detroit-Warren-Dearborn, MI	57,445	1,333.3	1,015,495	13.2	35.6	32.2	7,846.0	12,256	35,288	62,768	81,609	40.7	7.2	13.8	9.8	16.2
Detroit-Dearborn-Livonia, MI Div 19,804	35,699	2,056.1	428,127	11.2	42.1	25.2	3,367.9	12,217	28,403	49,359	63,896	50.5	4.6	21.3	16.0	25.8
Warren-Troy-Farmington Hills, MI Div 47,664	21,746	845.4	587,368	14.6	31.4	36.8	4,478.1	12,285	39,994	73,198	92,419	34.1	8.9	8.7	5.9	9.5
Dothan, AL	NA	NA	33,819	16.3	47.2	20.1	212.9	9,745	26,636	47,608	61,627	51.8	3.5	18.1	13.1	22.2
Dover, DE	3,404	1,853.3	44,836	13.6	45.3	24.5	390.1	14,188	28,911	60,117	70,383	42.2	3.0	13.2	10.3	17.5
Dubuque, IA	1,363	1,397.2	24,422	29.3	39.4	31.4	173.8	11,847	34,275	64,493	82,099	38.4	5.4	9.9	5.7	10.5
Duluth, MN-WI	6,924	2,407.5	68,547	12.5	32.9	28.4	504.4	12,903	32,421	58,729	77,796	43.0	3.8	12.9	6.7	12.0
Durham-Chapel Hill, NC	16,350	2,500.5	171,022	19.7	29.5	46.4	997.7	11,016	37,943	64,745	84,764	38.9	9.2	13.2	8.8	14.3
East Stroudsburg, PA	NA	NA	37,674	12.7	45.2	25.8	493.9	19,550	31,954	68,734	79,538	35.5	5.8	10.7	8.2	14.1
Eau Claire, WI	2,951	1,735.6	43,913	10.0	34.7	28.7	283.3	12,099	32,507	62,031	79,795	40.1	4.2	11.9	5.8	9.7
El Centro, CA	3,526	1,957.5	55,676	4.4	55.3	15.4	583.1	15,466	18,064	46,222	53,558	53.4	2.9	22.5	19.4	26.7
Elizabethtown-Fort Knox, KY	1,286	833.8	36,224	12.7	41.1	20.7	254.7	10,349	29,866	56,680	71,446	44.0	3.3	12.1	9.1	13.3
Elkhart-Goshen, IN	NA	NA	49,053	17.0	53.4	19.5	374.4	10,330	26,806	58,509	70,610	42.3	3.5	11.7	8.8	14.7
Elmira, NY	1,329	1,613.9	17,675	16.8	44.7	23.6	209.7	18,082	29,959	54,883	70,617	45.7	3.3	14.7	10.2	17.9
El Paso, TX	9,708	1,148.2	255,256	7.4	44.4	23.9	1,807.3	10,211	22,439	48,193	53,920	51.4	2.9	19.5	16.9	23.0
Enid, OK	1,576	2,579.7	14,278	10.3	48.6	23.3	107.7	9,417	28,755	55,435	65,663	44.2	2.8	13.7	12.2	16.4
Erie, PA	NA	NA	64,113	24.9	46.3	28.7	548.0	14,503	29,001	52,863	68,789	47.5	3.7	15.5	10.4	18.4
Eugene-Springfield, OR	NA	NA	90,303	11.2	30.6	31.9	556.9	12,044	30,911	54,942	72,092	45.9	4.5	17.2	9.3	16.1

1. Data for serious crimes have not been adjusted for underreporting; this may affect comparability between geographic areas and over time. 2. Per 100,000 population estimated by the FBI. 3. All persons 3 years old and over enrolled in nursery school through college. 4. Persons 25 years old and over. 5. Elementary and secondary education expenditures. 6. Based on population estimated by the American Community Survey, 2015.

Table C. Metropolitan Areas — **Personal Income and Earnings**

Area name	Personal income, 2020: Total (mil dol)	Personal income, 2020: Percent change, 2019–2020	Personal income, 2020: Per capita[1]: Dollars	Personal income, 2020: Per capita[1]: Rank	Personal income, 2020: Wages and Salaries (mil dol)	Personal income, 2020: Supplements to wages and salaries, employer contributions (mil dol): Pension and insurance	Personal income, 2020: Supplements to wages and salaries, employer contributions (mil dol): Government social insurance	Personal income, 2020: Proprietors' income	Personal income, 2020: Dividends, interest, and rent (mil dol)	Personal income, 2020: Personal transfer receipts (mil dol)	Earnings, 2020: Total (mil dol)	Earnings, 2020: Contributrions for government social insurance (mil dol): From employee and self-employed	Earnings, 2020: Contributrions for government social insurance (mil dol): From employer
	62	63	64	65	66	67	68	69	70	71	72	73	74
Cedar Rapids, IA	15,330	6.0	55,971	104	7,994	1,263	628	843	2,879	3,208	10,727	716	628
Chambersburg-Waynesboro, PA	8,090	8.3	51,979	162	2,881	555	234	612	1,165	2,181	4,281	274	234
Champaign-Urbana, IL	11,270	7.9	49,967	201	5,730	1,360	352	781	2,104	2,072	8,224	400	352
Charleston, WV	12,357	5.5	48,623	230	5,970	986	466	963	1,845	4,196	8,386	598	466
Charleston-North Charleston, SC	45,347	5.7	55,321	113	20,805	3,362	1,516	4,386	9,996	8,786	30,069	1,906	1,516
Charlotte-Concord-Gastonia, NC-SC	152,149	6.6	56,682	96	84,392	10,745	5,792	14,200	23,249	27,761	115,129	7,224	5,792
Charlottesville, VA	15,361	3.4	69,853	18	6,754	1,201	473	994	5,042	2,369	9,423	584	473
Chattanooga, TN-GA	28,420	6.8	49,865	205	13,726	2,157	974	3,184	4,239	6,953	20,041	1,266	974
Cheyenne, WY	5,542	3.7	55,094	118	2,774	561	268	416	1,057	1,167	4,019	242	268
Chicago-Naperville-Elgin, IL-IN-WI	636,555	5.1	67,671	25	326,294	48,546	21,782	49,112	127,101	115,163	445,734	25,570	21,782
Chicago-Naperville-Evanston, IL Div 16,984	491,120	5.1	69,452	X	264,346	38,167	17,544	40,662	99,801	89,277	360,719	20,541	17,544
Elgin, IL Div 20,994	41,538	6.6	54,217	X	15,146	2,835	1,031	2,139	6,404	7,466	21,152	1,196	1,031
Gary, IN Div 23,844	36,139	7.0	51,199	X	13,709	2,274	1,045	2,093	4,883	9,397	19,121	1,293	1,045
Lake County-Kenosha County, IL-WI Div 29,404	67,758	3.0	78,490	X	33,093	5,270	2,161	4,218	16,014	9,023	44,742	2,540	2,161
Chico, CA	10,697	8.3	50,279	195	4,020	862	297	986	1,633	3,421	6,165	384	297
Cincinnati, OH-KY-IN	133,098	6.0	59,607	71	67,288	9,811	4,750	10,235	24,272	26,630	92,085	5,622	4,750
Clarksville, TN-KY	14,118	8.0	44,908	305	6,159	1,470	519	1,122	2,072	3,729	9,270	500	519
Cleveland, TN	5,257	6.5	41,756	355	2,200	351	163	430	633	1,583	3,145	217	163
Cleveland-Elyria, OH	120,270	6.2	58,846	73	62,170	9,476	4,417	7,598	22,489	28,419	83,661	5,104	4,417
Coeur d'Alene, ID	8,353	7.8	48,953	222	3,130	496	276	615	1,715	2,036	4,517	333	276
College Station-Bryan, TX	11,812	6.2	44,037	323	5,483	1,044	351	915	2,507	2,292	7,792	394	351
Colorado Springs, CO	40,832	7.4	54,166	132	19,694	3,287	1,487	2,457	7,302	8,862	26,925	1,512	1,487
Columbia, MO	10,593	5.8	50,421	193	5,561	1,113	376	558	1,940	2,066	7,608	444	376
Columbia, SC	41,498	6.7	48,971	220	20,725	3,734	1,522	2,986	6,491	9,825	28,966	1,840	1,522
Columbus, GA-AL	14,442	7.4	44,760	307	7,353	1,539	554	502	3,084	4,225	9,948	576	554
Columbus, IN	4,713	5.2	55,804	106	3,012	458	226	350	749	947	4,045	253	226
Columbus, OH	120,321	7.8	56,252	100	66,437	10,493	4,506	8,088	19,464	23,429	89,524	4,984	4,506
Corpus Christi, TX	20,676	4.0	48,060	241	9,456	1,678	664	1,939	3,253	5,595	13,736	779	664
Corvallis, OR	4,699	5.3	50,399	194	2,212	449	182	349	1,122	860	3,193	196	182
Crestview-Fort Walton Beach-Destin, FL	16,981	7.8	58,663	77	7,729	1,467	597	1,229	4,743	3,536	11,022	671	597
Cumberland, MD-WV	4,288	6.9	44,308	321	1,797	366	147	158	568	1,605	2,468	174	147
Dallas-Fort Worth-Arlington, TX	473,604	5.2	61,554	53	256,339	32,085	17,158	54,312	84,533	69,997	359,893	19,419	17,158
Dallas-Plano-Irving, TX Div 19,124	334,632	5.0	64,701	X	192,534	22,886	12,673	42,884	60,037	45,603	270,977	14,463	12,673
Fort Worth-Arlington-Grapevine, TX Div 23,104	138,972	5.7	55,100	X	63,805	9,198	4,485	11,428	24,497	24,394	88,917	4,956	4,485
Dalton, GA	5,867	7.0	40,781	367	3,102	481	219	493	1,060	1,615	4,296	267	219
Danville, IL	3,334	10.9	44,533	311	1,333	293	94	250	438	1,102	1,970	121	94
Daphne-Fairhope-Foley, AL	11,683	8.3	50,953	181	3,359	496	251	696	2,482	2,818	4,802	368	251
Davenport-Moline-Rock Island, IA-IL	20,256	7.6	53,620	135	10,168	1,732	730	1,175	3,588	4,797	13,804	879	730
Dayton-Kettering, OH	42,378	7.0	52,367	155	21,555	3,786	1,587	2,663	7,257	10,632	29,592	1,789	1,587
Decatur, AL	6,608	7.0	43,264	335	2,893	484	216	309	975	1,887	3,902	280	216
Decatur, IL	5,377	7.4	52,196	158	2,786	492	199	369	822	1,531	3,846	236	199
Deltona-Daytona Beach-Ormond Beach, FL	32,089	6.1	47,194	262	9,497	1,415	667	1,533	7,283	9,935	13,111	1,094	667
Denver-Aurora-Lakewood, CO	208,853	5.0	69,822	19	114,561	13,595	7,795	23,054	38,861	29,887	159,004	9,099	7,795
Des Moines-West Des Moines, IA	41,113	6.6	58,076	83	23,349	3,334	1,759	2,403	6,995	7,356	30,845	2,008	1,759
Detroit-Warren-Dearborn, MI	251,173	7.3	58,356	81	124,135	17,379	9,098	17,467	40,551	65,501	168,079	10,906	9,098
Detroit-Dearborn-Livonia, MI Div 19,804	84,922	9.5	48,788	X	48,193	7,003	3,517	4,738	11,376	29,986	63,451	4,133	3,517
Warren-Troy-Farmington Hills, MI Div 47,664	166,252	6.1	64,853	X	75,942	10,376	5,581	12,729	29,175	35,515	104,628	6,773	5,581
Dothan, AL	6,812	6.2	45,349	297	2,744	460	203	443	1,078	2,025	3,849	275	203
Dover, DE	8,558	7.7	46,600	273	3,647	885	290	505	1,370	2,522	5,328	325	290
Dubuque, IA	5,343	6.8	54,751	124	2,907	466	230	365	1,129	1,214	3,968	267	230
Duluth, MN-WI	14,370	5.4	49,785	209	6,564	1,174	533	655	2,225	4,518	8,926	619	533
Durham-Chapel Hill, NC	37,001	5.3	56,703	95	25,858	3,739	1,756	2,278	7,662	6,694	33,632	2,050	1,756
East Stroudsburg, PA	8,237	9.7	48,409	233	2,711	613	214	474	1,170	2,391	4,013	261	214
Eau Claire, WI	8,767	6.1	51,569	171	4,329	812	325	670	1,567	1,942	6,137	395	325
El Centro, CA	8,022	19.5	44,500	315	2,973	831	229	980	699	2,984	5,014	258	229
Elizabethtown-Fort Knox, KY	7,219	8.2	46,770	269	2,915	703	242	456	1,083	2,089	4,316	262	242
Elkhart-Goshen, IN	10,282	6.4	49,875	204	7,156	1,131	567	962	1,628	2,285	9,816	602	567
Elmira, NY	4,085	7.3	49,439	215	1,741	407	142	182	529	1,373	2,471	151	142
El Paso, TX	35,313	8.4	41,732	356	15,717	3,338	1,156	2,903	5,026	9,782	23,115	1,261	1,156
Enid, OK	2,843	2.9	46,702	270	1,238	228	98	199	613	713	1,762	111	98
Erie, PA	13,565	8.8	50,536	190	5,699	1,168	448	800	2,213	4,430	8,115	519	448
Eugene-Springfield, OR	18,989	8.1	49,583	211	7,883	1,414	695	1,597	3,425	5,531	11,589	790	695

1. Based on the resident population estimated as of July 1 of the year shown.

Area name	Earnings, 2020 (cont.)									Social Security beneficiaries, December 2020		Supple-mental Security Income Recipi-ents, December 2020	Housing units, 2021	
	Percent by selected industries													
	Farm	Mining, quarrying, and extracting	Construc-tion	Manufac-turing	Informa-tion; pro-fessional, scientific, and technical serviecs	Retail trade	Finance, insur-ance, real estate, rental and leasing	Health care and social assistance	Govern-ment	Number	Rate[1]		Total	Percent change, 2020–2021
	75	76	77	78	79	80	81	82	83	84	85	86	87	88
Cedar Rapids, IA	1.3	0.1	7.4	20.7	D	5.5	9.9	D	11.3	55,275	201	4,599	121,871	0.4
Chambersburg-Waynesboro, PA	2.6	0.3	5.9	15.5	5.2	6.8	4.0	15.9	16.2	37,820	242	2,482	66,728	0.5
Champaign-Urbana, IL	2.7	D	4.7	6.0	6.9	5.2	5.1	D	37.2	32,635	147	3,381	102,133	1.4
Charleston, WV	0.0	2.7	5.9	D	D	6.0	D	D	20.1	73,785	289	11,017	126,957	0.1
Charleston-North Charleston, SC	0.1	D	8.2	9.0	15.0	6.5	8.9	9.9	19.6	151,045	186	13,088	370,065	2.3
Charlotte-Concord-Gastonia, NC-SC	0.3	D	D	7.7	D	5.4	D	6.7	11.2	457,935	170	43,042	1,139,194	2.3
Charlottesville, VA	0.1	0.1	5.1	3.0	13.5	5.0	8.4	D	34.7	44,065	198	2,914	99,984	1.5
Chattanooga, TN-GA	0.1	D	D	13.2	D	5.8	D	11.3	16.1	127,555	225	12,877	250,532	1.1
Cheyenne, WY	0.7	1.9	7.6	3.3	8.0	6.0	6.7	7.9	38.1	19,950	198	1,450	44,817	1.2
Chicago-Naperville-Elgin, IL-IN-WI	0.1	0.1	4.7	9.6	D	4.8	12.8	10.0	11.9	1,543,855	162	193,201	3,956,349	0.2
Chicago-Naperville-Evanston, IL Div 16,984	0.0	0.1	4.4	7.4	18.6	4.4	14.3	10.1	11.2	1,133,450	158	159,257	3,028,621	0.2
Elgin, IL Div 20,994	0.7	D	8.3	15.7	7.7	6.2	5.8	9.8	19.6	114,905	153	7,063	276,883	0.6
Gary, IN Div 23,844	1.0	0.1	8.8	18.0	5.1	6.7	4.9	16.0	10.6	151,355	210	15,135	308,086	0.6
Lake County-Kenosha County, IL-WI Div 29,404	0.1	0.0	4.0	21.4	9.0	6.7	6.7	7.0	14.1	144,145	164	11,746	342,759	0.2
Chico, CA	4.1	0.1	7.6	4.9	5.3	9.3	6.2	19.6	21.5	46,535	223	9,420	90,314	0.0
Cincinnati, OH-KY-IN	0.1	0.0	6.4	13.2	D	5.3	D	12.3	10.7	418,435	185	47,245	964,737	0.6
Clarksville, TN-KY	1.1	D	5.8	9.1	D	6.1	3.8	D	45.4	52,920	161	6,738	133,431	2.8
Cleveland, TN	0.1	D	D	20.8	D	7.3	4.1	D	11.4	30,680	240	497	54,197	1.3
Cleveland-Elyria, OH	0.1	0.1	4.9	12.1	11.9	5.0	8.9	14.6	13.4	438,650	211	61,513	970,314	0.2
Coeur d'Alene, ID	0.2	0.6	10.4	8.1	8.2	9.7	7.9	12.8	19.0	42,655	237	2,538	78,262	3.9
College Station-Bryan, TX	0.3	2.7	7.4	4.6	9.3	6.7	5.2	9.8	34.1	33,530	123	4,478	117,018	1.9
Colorado Springs, CO	0.1	D	8.0	D	15.4	5.9	8.0	10.2	30.5	120,635	158	9,367	308,836	2.2
Columbia, MO	1.0	D	4.5	5.4	6.9	6.4	12.1	10.7	33.1	35,650	167	3,399	92,531	0.9
Columbia, SC	0.2	0.1	5.4	8.9	9.9	6.4	10.6	9.6	25.0	167,860	200	16,205	372,106	1.3
Columbus, GA-AL	0.1	D	3.5	8.2	6.2	4.6	D	10.7	36.5	66,860	204	11,145	145,536	1.1
Columbus, IN	1.0	D	3.9	44.4	5.2	4.8	4.0	7.4	9.1	16,800	204	1,215	35,500	0.4
Columbus, OH	0.3	0.1	6.0	7.2	11.6	5.1	10.4	11.3	18.0	331,900	154	45,593	915,145	1.3
Corpus Christi, TX	-0.1	5.3	12.5	7.8	8.0	5.9	6.2	D	18.7	77,650	184	13,357	182,777	0.9
Corvallis, OR	1.4	0.1	4.2	10.6	10.0	4.9	5.5	16.0	30.4	17,145	179	1,072	40,641	0.8
Crestview-Fort Walton Beach-Destin, FL	0.2	0.0	6.2	3.1	14.5	7.7	7.1	7.2	35.4	62,500	213	4,386	160,841	1.6
Cumberland, MD-WV	0.0	0.1	4.6	11.5	D	7.3	4.4	19.3	29.2	24,710	261	3,057	45,312	-0.1
Dallas-Fort Worth-Arlington, TX	0.0	3.6	7.5	8.3	15.3	5.4	12.5	9.1	10.1	1,000,355	129	126,395	3,020,245	2.0
Dallas-Plano-Irving, TX Div 19,124	0.0	4.1	6.7	7.3	17.7	5.1	13.6	8.7	9.4	643,140	123	85,052	2,039,518	2.0
Fort Worth-Arlington-Grapevine, TX Div 23,104	-0.1	2.2	9.8	11.4	8.2	6.6	9.0	10.3	12.2	357,215	141	41,343	980,727	1.9
Dalton, GA	0.1	0.3	2.8	31.4	D	6.1	6.6	D	10.9	27,975	196	3,681	55,433	0.8
Danville, IL	5.9	D	3.2	19.9	2.0	5.6	4.6	9.3	22.7	18,495	253	2,603	34,356	-0.1
Daphne-Fairhope-Foley, AL	0.8	0.3	9.6	5.7	6.4	11.8	8.6	12.8	13.7	60,305	252	3,434	128,519	2.9
Davenport-Moline-Rock Island, IA-IL	1.7	0.1	7.1	13.0	D	6.4	5.0	D	15.8	83,185	218	7,534	174,453	0.2
Dayton-Kettering, OH	0.3	D	5.1	10.9	12.7	5.4	6.0	15.6	22.1	167,740	206	19,865	370,982	0.3
Decatur, AL	-0.3	D	10.0	31.1	D	6.4	4.8	D	13.5	38,115	243	4,502	68,836	0.4
Decatur, IL	1.8	0.0	7.2	29.4	4.4	5.2	5.2	12.9	11.0	24,990	244	3,183	49,678	-0.1
Deltona-Daytona Beach-Ormond Beach, FL	0.9	D	8.1	6.5	8.1	9.9	7.0	17.7	13.4	203,475	297	14,545	335,104	1.9
Denver-Aurora-Lakewood, CO	0.1	6.2	7.5	D	D	4.4	D	D	12.1	413,555	139	35,465	1,265,931	1.5
Des Moines-West Des Moines, IA	0.5	D	7.6	5.9	10.5	5.6	D	D	12.7	119,440	166	9,934	308,354	2.0
Detroit-Warren-Dearborn, MI	0.1	0.1	5.3	13.2	17.1	5.6	9.5	12.0	9.7	900,685	206	130,620	1,907,744	0.3
Detroit-Dearborn-Livonia, MI Div 19,804	0.0	0.1	3.9	12.6	13.1	4.6	7.7	13.5	11.9	355,545	200	81,280	791,060	0.1
Warren-Troy-Farmington Hills, MI Div 47,664	0.1	0.0	6.2	13.6	19.5	6.2	10.7	11.1	8.4	545,140	210	49,340	1,116,684	0.4
Dothan, AL	2.1	0.1	5.4	7.9	D	10.0	4.8	15.5	18.5	39,700	262	5,677	71,423	0.7
Dover, DE	1.9	D	6.2	D	4.6	7.3	4.5	12.4	38.2	40,520	220	3,570	75,086	2.8
Dubuque, IA	1.9	D	5.8	20.2	7.2	6.0	11.5	13.8	8.3	21,985	223	1,654	42,899	0.5
Duluth, MN-WI	0.0	4.9	6.4	7.7	5.9	7.1	4.8	21.8	19.4	71,915	247	6,538	150,158	0.3
Durham-Chapel Hill, NC	0.2	0.0	3.1	15.6	17.2	3.2	7.5	11.2	20.1	116,440	178	10,898	288,853	1.9
East Stroudsburg, PA	0.1	0.1	5.1	14.9	4.5	8.0	3.4	12.9	25.2	38,240	226	3,098	79,331	0.2
Eau Claire, WI	1.5	0.1	7.9	13.3	5.3	7.9	5.5	19.7	14.3	37,025	214	2,905	74,707	1.2
El Centro, CA	13.8	D	2.7	2.7	2.4	7.1	2.5	7.3	37.0	34,750	193	9,816	57,106	0.7
Elizabethtown-Fort Knox, KY	0.9	D	4.1	13.9	D	6.2	4.7	6.8	40.5	32,890	210	4,325	65,948	1.2
Elkhart-Goshen, IN	1.0	D	4.1	48.6	2.2	4.3	3.4	7.5	5.5	37,085	179	2,969	80,101	0.6
Elmira, NY	0.3	0.8	5.4	16.3	4.9	8.1	4.4	16.2	24.6	21,840	263	2,956	39,195	0.4
El Paso, TX	0.1	0.0	D	D	D	6.7	D	D	34.2	139,900	161	28,251	322,088	0.7
Enid, OK	1.8	5.3	5.5	10.3	6.7	6.8	6.5	11.7	22.1	12,805	207	1,301	27,807	-0.1
Erie, PA	0.4	0.0	4.8	18.2	5.0	6.5	8.9	19.2	16.4	65,125	242	10,158	119,960	0.1
Eugene-Springfield, OR	0.8	0.2	6.2	9.3	7.6	8.1	8.1	16.7	19.0	92,280	241	9,772	167,839	0.8

1. Per 1,000 resident population estimated as of July 1 of the year shown.

Area name	Occupied housing units, 2016-2020								Civilian labor force, 2021				Civilian employment[6], 2016-2020		
		Occupied units									Unemployment			Percent	
		Owner-occupied					Renter-occupied								
				Median owner cost as a percent of income											
	Total	Percent	Median value[1]	With a mortgage	Without a mortgage[2]	Median rent[3]	Median rent as a percent of income	Substandard units[4] (percent)	Total	Percent change 2020-2021	Total	Rate[5]	Total	Management, business, science, and arts	Construction, production, and maintenance occupations
	89	90	91	92	93	94	95	96	97	98	99	100	101	102	103
Cedar Rapids, IA	109,796	75.3	159,800	19.2	11.4	768	26.8	1.5	141,837	-1.2	7,010	4.9	143,108	38.2	24.6
Chambersburg-Waynesboro, PA	61,617	70.9	186,300	20.3	10.7	905	25.7	1.9	77,153	-1.7	3,957	5.1	74,316	32.2	31.2
Champaign-Urbana, IL	89,814	55.3	163,900	18.8	10.7	873	31.5	3.5	116,984	1.6	5,601	4.8	111,074	46.8	17.5
Charleston, WV	109,935	72.5	110,100	17.2	10.0	728	29.5	1.6	111,254	-1.0	6,069	5.5	104,643	36.3	21.0
Charleston-North Charleston, SC	299,947	66.8	249,800	21.1	10.2	1,197	30.7	1.8	395,923	2.5	14,313	3.6	385,837	40.8	20.7
Charlotte-Concord-Gastonia, NC-SC	975,476	66.0	216,700	19.0	10.0	1,073	27.8	2.4	1,369,856	2.1	63,407	4.6	1,301,528	40.7	22.2
Charlottesville, VA	85,051	63.8	304,700	19.8	10.0	1,260	29.4	1.6	110,900	-2.0	3,696	3.3	107,660	52.1	13.8
Chattanooga, TN-GA	222,885	67.4	169,600	19.1	10.2	859	28.3	1.8	275,488	1.1	10,317	3.7	265,416	36.3	25.1
Cheyenne, WY	40,202	72.6	239,900	20.2	10.2	933	27.4	1.4	49,373	-1.5	1,976	4.0	47,402	38.0	23.4
Chicago-Naperville-Elgin, IL-IN-WI	3,548,735	64.8	247,400	22.0	13.3	1,155	28.9	3.0	4,804,093	-0.9	296,740	6.2	4,741,241	41.2	20.8
Chicago-Naperville-Evanston, IL Div 16,984	2,701,523	62.4	260,300	22.6	13.7	1,181	28.9	3.2	3,636,737	-1.1	234,450	6.4	3,593,129	42.3	19.8
Elgin, IL Div 20,994	261,859	73.5	237,000	22.1	13.0	1,142	29.8	2.9	382,448	-0.5	21,597	5.6	390,832	36.4	24.3
Gary, IN Div 23,844	272,074	71.8	164,400	18.6	10.7	893	29.1	2.1	327,881	-1.4	17,515	5.3	321,312	32.5	28.8
Lake County-Kenosha County, IL-WI Div 29,404	313,279	72.1	249,600	21.0	13.2	1,134	28.4	2.3	457,027	0.7	23,178	5.1	435,968	42.7	20.1
Chico, CA	83,879	59.5	304,700	23.2	12.7	1,087	34.3	3.9	92,031	-1.1	6,311	6.9	96,056	38.0	20.2
Cincinnati, OH-KY-IN	870,103	67.1	175,300	18.7	10.6	859	27.2	1.7	1,136,061	0.9	50,209	4.4	1,101,373	41.0	21.4
Clarksville, TN-KY	111,845	59.3	165,100	20.1	10.0	920	27.4	2.1	123,980	1.0	5,919	4.8	120,694	32.1	26.9
Cleveland, TN	48,178	68.0	161,600	19.6	10.0	776	27.1	2.4	57,924	-3.4	2,366	4.1	57,317	32.4	30.0
Cleveland-Elyria, OH	871,132	64.6	156,200	19.5	12.2	837	28.5	1.4	1,012,273	0.0	59,745	5.9	995,833	40.3	20.8
Coeur d'Alene, ID	64,475	71.3	294,100	22.3	10.0	1,037	29.3	2.1	82,719	1.0	3,540	4.3	75,049	34.5	23.2
College Station-Bryan, TX	95,194	51.1	201,900	22.1	10.0	954	35.2	3.8	136,999	4.1	5,788	4.2	123,940	41.9	20.1
Colorado Springs, CO	273,240	65.8	300,400	21.5	10.0	1,232	31.4	3.0	363,751	2.5	20,406	5.6	340,763	42.8	18.0
Columbia, MO	81,721	58.4	189,900	18.9	10.0	875	29.6	2.1	110,937	2.9	3,368	3.0	107,200	45.5	16.8
Columbia, SC	318,887	68.4	159,700	19.5	10.0	955	30.7	2.2	399,422	1.3	14,830	3.7	394,051	39.2	21.4
Columbus, GA-AL	120,480	56.7	146,300	21.0	10.4	898	29.4	2.3	127,297	-0.8	5,703	4.5	127,183	33.5	24.5
Columbus, IN	31,772	70.9	163,400	18.1	10.0	940	23.5	2.4	42,821	-2.0	1,227	2.9	40,240	41.4	27.0
Columbus, OH	805,628	61.8	195,900	19.3	11.4	981	26.9	2.2	1,118,027	1.4	51,735	4.6	1,070,347	43.5	19.4
Corpus Christi, TX	153,904	60.1	145,100	21.6	12.2	1,048	29.1	5.1	193,253	0.4	13,938	7.2	192,020	31.5	26.0
Corvallis, OR	36,051	56.8	357,900	21.0	10.4	1,145	36.7	1.9	47,556	1.9	1,873	3.9	45,163	49.0	14.2
Crestview-Fort Walton Beach-Destin, FL	107,870	68.6	236,800	21.8	10.0	1,141	31.1	2.2	133,209	4.4	4,510	3.4	123,724	38.6	18.5
Cumberland, MD-WV	38,179	71.7	131,300	18.4	10.3	708	29.0	0.8	42,719	-1.7	2,536	5.9	39,048	30.1	26.3
Dallas-Fort Worth-Arlington, TX	2,615,579	59.7	236,200	21.0	11.6	1,188	28.6	4.8	4,062,269	3.6	205,485	5.1	3,770,200	40.7	21.8
Dallas-Plano-Irving, TX Div 19,124	1,766,761	58.2	254,300	21.2	11.7	1,211	28.3	5.0	2,772,291	3.9	138,262	5.0	2,556,411	42.4	20.4
Fort Worth-Arlington-Grapevine, TX Div 23,104	848,818	62.8	206,600	20.6	11.4	1,134	29.1	4.5	1,289,978	2.9	67,223	5.2	1,213,789	37.1	24.7
Dalton, GA	50,932	67.2	136,800	19.1	10.3	721	24.7	5.0	58,838	0.6	2,362	4.0	65,175	23.6	42.8
Danville, IL	31,013	70.8	80,900	17.4	11.1	683	27.0	1.7	31,753	-1.7	2,064	6.5	31,356	28.2	31.5
Daphne-Fairhope-Foley, AL	84,047	77.0	211,600	19.9	10.0	1,032	28.2	1.7	99,427	0.5	2,946	3.0	98,768	36.8	22.3
Davenport-Moline-Rock Island, IA-IL	154,517	70.7	141,600	18.4	11.6	773	27.6	1.6	186,024	-0.6	10,043	5.4	182,143	35.5	26.4
Dayton-Kettering, OH	334,252	63.6	140,400	18.7	11.1	824	27.5	1.4	384,377	-0.8	19,661	5.1	378,213	38.9	22.7
Decatur, AL	58,939	73.5	137,600	18.1	10.0	666	27.2	2.2	73,634	-0.8	1,962	2.7	64,708	30.6	32.9
Decatur, IL	43,810	69.1	103,100	17.9	10.0	690	28.2	1.4	46,552	-1.1	3,563	7.7	46,000	33.4	27.3
Deltona-Daytona Beach-Ormond Beach, FL	264,426	72.1	203,000	22.7	12.3	1,127	33.4	1.2	303,402	2.6	14,032	4.6	279,455	33.0	21.1
Denver-Aurora-Lakewood, CO	1,097,674	64.8	411,800	21.1	10.0	1,446	30.1	2.9	1,683,499	2.0	92,159	5.5	1,597,531	45.6	17.6
Des Moines-West Des Moines, IA	271,569	69.6	193,100	19.0	11.5	935	26.3	2.4	381,121	0.7	16,050	4.2	366,010	43.2	20.2
Detroit-Warren-Dearborn, MI	1,726,401	69.5	179,100	19.4	12.3	962	29.5	2.0	2,114,088	0.1	131,597	6.2	2,031,416	40.3	22.0
Detroit-Dearborn-Livonia, MI Div 19,804	694,858	62.5	122,700	19.6	13.2	896	31.8	2.7	797,703	-0.5	63,563	8.0	747,847	34.5	25.2
Warren-Troy-Farmington Hills, MI Div 47,664	1,031,543	74.1	214,600	19.2	11.6	1,031	27.8	1.5	1,316,385	0.4	68,034	5.2	1,283,569	43.7	20.1
Dothan, AL	56,912	69.7	131,600	18.9	10.0	744	27.6	1.4	64,754	-0.6	2,122	3.3	62,212	32.1	27.0
Dover, DE	67,299	68.8	226,600	22.7	10.0	1,110	32.0	1.9	81,389	2.0	5,069	6.2	79,624	34.0	24.8
Dubuque, IA	38,655	73.4	175,300	19.1	11.3	802	26.6	1.7	54,963	-0.9	2,432	4.4	50,479	37.3	25.0
Duluth, MN-WI	124,208	72.3	162,700	19.2	11.1	794	29.2	2.2	143,078	-3.5	5,617	3.9	140,879	36.4	23.8
Durham-Chapel Hill, NC	250,974	62.9	245,100	19.1	10.0	1,068	29.6	2.5	338,505	3.4	13,292	3.9	316,614	49.9	16.7
East Stroudsburg, PA	59,950	77.1	173,800	23.0	14.0	1,154	29.5	2.1	81,973	-1.0	6,295	7.7	80,189	32.9	25.1
Eau Claire, WI	67,646	67.7	180,000	19.2	11.6	828	26.7	1.8	93,888	1.7	3,266	3.5	88,530	35.3	26.6
El Centro, CA	45,768	58.1	206,700	24.1	11.6	847	32.1	10.2	69,075	-3.4	11,981	17.3	59,490	25.0	26.6
Elizabethtown-Fort Knox, KY	58,528	65.0	153,700	18.5	10.0	806	23.4	2.3	64,560	-1.1	3,137	4.9	66,919	33.8	30.0
Elkhart-Goshen, IN	72,362	70.4	149,300	17.7	10.0	820	27.1	2.7	115,907	4.9	2,900	2.5	98,737	28.0	37.0
Elmira, NY	34,328	67.2	108,900	18.0	11.3	862	31.6	1.5	34,549	-3.8	1,815	5.3	37,409	34.3	23.3
El Paso, TX	274,789	62.3	126,200	22.5	11.5	855	30.0	6.2	365,692	1.2	22,799	6.2	356,171	31.7	23.0
Enid, OK	23,709	65.4	119,000	18.8	10.0	814	24.8	3.3	26,842	0.0	925	3.4	27,304	30.2	32.6
Erie, PA	110,388	67.0	138,500	19.3	11.9	758	29.4	1.8	126,536	-1.7	9,260	7.3	125,598	35.8	22.9
Eugene-Springfield, OR	154,516	59.1	280,000	23.3	12.0	1,037	32.0	3.1	182,197	1.7	10,055	5.5	176,797	37.1	21.3

1. Specified owner-occupied units. 2. A value of 10.0 represents 10 percent or less; a value of 50.0 represents 50 percent or more. 3. Specified renter-occupied units. 4. Overcrowded or lacking complete plumbing facilities. 5. Percent of civilian labor force. 6. Civilian employed persons 16 years old and over.

Area name	Private nonfarm establishments, employment and payroll, 2020									Agriculture, 2017			
		Employment						Annual payroll		Farms			Farm producers whose primary occupation is farming (percent)
											Percent with:		
	Number of establish-ments	Total	Health care and social assistance	Manufactur-ing	Retail trade	Finance and insurance	Professional, scientific, and technical services	Total (mil dol)	Average per employee (dollars)	Number	Fewer than 50 acres	1000 acres or more	
	104	105	106	107	108	109	110	111	112	113	114	115	116
Cedar Rapids, IA	6,735	129,509	17,915	18,594	17,414	9,336	7,978	6,733	51,987	3,632	37.7	8.6	43.7
Chambersburg-Waynesboro, PA	3,084	53,967	10,712	7,911	7,632	1,164	1,755	2,181	40,410	1,581	37.3	1.6	55.5
Champaign-Urbana, IL	4,545	72,292	15,164	6,357	9,938	3,386	2,711	3,318	45,903	1,636	33.9	17.3	50.9
Charleston, WV	5,485	89,717	23,165	4,909	12,179	3,610	5,372	4,006	44,650	1,539	29.2	0.5	34.0
Charleston-North Charleston, SC	20,576	299,932	36,495	28,403	42,595	9,231	23,657	14,247	47,501	1,100	60.3	3.4	36.9
Charlotte-Concord-Gastonia, NC-SC	65,509	1,138,126	145,038	101,816	127,256	98,556	68,855	64,992	57,105	7,381	51.5	2.1	36.9
Charlottesville, VA	5,978	87,205	19,673	4,578	11,362	3,344	7,952	4,731	54,246	1,809	39.7	2.6	40.0
Chattanooga, TN-GA	11,771	230,248	36,292	33,165	30,301	15,682	9,569	10,257	44,549	2,162	47.2	1.2	37.1
Cheyenne, WY	3,392	34,992	6,790	1,393	6,173	1,556	2,432	1,665	47,578	999	31.7	21.9	38.8
Chicago-Naperville-Elgin, IL-IN-WI	247,829	4,251,206	623,183	386,102	445,421	267,686	362,676	269,952	63,500	6,565	49.3	9.5	46.8
Chicago-Naperville-Evanston, IL Div 16,984	192,902	3,385,445	498,557	266,898	328,287	237,253	308,674	219,804	64,926	2,353	55.1	8.3	46.1
Elgin, IL Div 20,994	17,215	243,319	32,028	36,967	33,867	9,013	11,930	11,552	47,477	1,697	42.5	11.9	51.4
Gary, IN Div 23,844	14,667	238,818	46,258	34,698	33,523	5,691	8,548	11,027	46,173	1,798	42.0	11.2	45.7
Lake County-Kenosha County, IL-WI Div 29,404	23,045	383,624	46,340	47,539	49,744	15,729	33,524	27,569	71,866	717	65.0	3.2	41.5
Chico, CA	4,646	64,614	15,377	4,437	10,822	2,555	2,561	2,712	41,972	1,912	65.2	2.9	51.3
Cincinnati, OH-KY-IN	46,895	981,071	151,664	112,669	104,901	60,556	62,658	54,356	55,405	10,403	48.6	1.8	32.8
Clarksville, TN-KY	4,738	74,633	13,303	13,988	12,346	1,974	2,575	2,794	37,438	2,718	36.1	4.8	39.0
Cleveland, TN	2,199	42,840	5,613	9,295	6,687	1,215	757	1,754	40,948	1,065	52.5	0.7	40.7
Cleveland-Elyria, OH	49,378	930,130	186,974	115,921	107,052	51,691	54,988	50,182	53,951	3,524	68.4	1.3	35.0
Coeur d'Alene, ID	5,372	57,834	10,949	5,161	8,913	2,354	2,897	2,506	43,334	1,073	68.7	2.1	32.1
College Station-Bryan, TX	5,201	78,363	10,537	6,337	12,724	2,101	3,960	3,146	40,142	4,482	38.3	4.2	37.2
Colorado Springs, CO	18,944	263,694	41,962	12,304	32,665	12,956	25,601	12,970	49,187	1,504	46.1	10.5	35.4
Columbia, MO	5,172	84,570	20,082	5,069	12,911	7,849	4,510	3,900	46,120	2,757	31.6	5.4	33.1
Columbia, SC	18,029	303,834	49,573	29,343	42,874	16,409	16,374	13,229	43,539	3,325	50.3	3.6	37.0
Columbus, GA-AL	6,000	103,033	17,996	10,638	13,648	13,468	3,465	4,540	44,061	1,062	33.1	6.3	36.5
Columbus, IN	1,889	46,272	5,229	12,677	4,918	958	2,835	2,417	52,232	564	47.0	8.7	36.6
Columbus, OH	43,944	921,190	167,767	67,937	101,962	73,375	59,859	48,822	52,999	8,506	53.3	4.6	37.5
Corpus Christi, TX	9,057	156,949	30,583	11,214	20,800	4,858	7,638	6,767	43,114	1,302	57.1	13.2	36.0
Corvallis, OR	2,147	29,469	6,155	1,582	3,724	1,134	2,966	1,563	53,037	964	72.3	2.9	36.6
Crestview-Fort Walton Beach-Destin, FL	8,341	86,347	11,164	2,641	17,420	2,305	7,832	3,612	41,828	1,079	56.4	2.3	38.5
Cumberland, MD-WV	1,893	28,843	7,428	3,637	4,940	976	678	1,080	37,439	809	38.6	1.6	35.7
Dallas-Fort Worth-Arlington, TX	172,873	3,315,868	420,733	263,379	360,022	238,238	257,485	198,255	59,790	29,254	68.9	2.2	31.1
Dallas-Plano-Irving, TX Div 19,124	121,086	2,397,792	293,432	164,869	238,894	186,352	212,622	151,612	63,230	16,618	68.4	2.2	30.7
Fort Worth-Arlington-Grapevine, TX Div 23,104	51,787	918,076	127,301	98,510	121,128	51,886	44,863	46,643	50,805	12,636	69.6	2.1	31.5
Dalton, GA	2,607	61,581	5,990	22,796	5,776	748	2,020	2,522	40,947	664	49.2	0.9	37.3
Danville, IL	1,338	23,491	5,046	4,536	3,356	1,127	367	1,038	44,184	1,049	38.9	14.1	47.8
Daphne-Fairhope-Foley, AL	5,726	66,943	8,578	4,508	13,655	1,695	2,140	2,474	36,951	842	53.8	4.5	45.0
Davenport-Moline-Rock Island, IA-IL	8,787	162,507	25,371	23,037	21,947	6,095	6,131	8,001	49,238	3,434	36.1	9.5	45.3
Dayton-Kettering, OH	16,327	329,804	68,487	45,079	38,311	13,548	26,323	16,035	48,621	2,635	59.9	4.1	36.8
Decatur, AL	3,014	50,085	6,837	13,730	6,103	1,428	2,501	2,380	47,521	2,416	49.0	1.8	36.1
Decatur, IL	2,353	45,126	8,123	8,234	4,890	1,547	1,318	2,398	53,139	589	41.8	16.0	49.9
Deltona-Daytona Beach-Ormond Beach, FL	15,736	178,466	31,511	9,801	32,276	6,294	9,348	6,908	38,709	1,691	81.3	2.5	39.9
Denver-Aurora-Lakewood, CO	88,394	1,352,957	174,267	56,496	147,501	84,995	126,443	84,686	62,594	5,606	59.6	7.3	28.6
Des Moines-West Des Moines, IA	18,169	346,752	46,701	22,171	43,851	47,962	23,171	19,092	55,059	5,658	40.6	8.4	36.9
Detroit-Warren-Dearborn, MI	99,573	1,823,909	298,540	235,073	209,062	100,174	194,568	103,104	56,529	3,980	58.2	2.7	44.3
Detroit-Dearborn-Livonia, MI Div 19,804	32,586	669,584	115,274	86,350	72,956	40,089	49,508	38,391	57,335	248	79.8	0.0	47.5
Warren-Troy-Farmington Hills, MI Div 47,664	66,987	1,154,325	183,266	148,723	136,106	60,085	145,060	64,713	56,061	3,732	56.8	2.9	44.0
Dothan, AL	3,398	51,822	10,389	5,407	8,386	1,464	1,382	2,160	41,681	1,973	35.0	6.0	38.4
Dover, DE	4,163	56,012	12,301	4,483	9,628	1,503	2,948	2,496	44,557	822	53.4	6.3	48.5
Dubuque, IA	2,747	55,313	8,464	9,473	7,183	4,320	1,700	2,542	45,962	1,402	30.5	3.4	42.8
Duluth, MN-WI	7,291	112,038	28,860	8,829	15,800	3,885	4,077	5,003	44,659	1,679	26.9	1.7	35.7
Durham-Chapel Hill, NC	14,172	295,098	58,564	25,514	26,339	11,691	36,534	19,111	64,763	2,993	47.0	1.6	41.1
East Stroudsburg, PA	3,409	47,919	8,273	5,032	9,458	909	1,574	1,859	38,787	233	55.4	1.7	40.4
Eau Claire, WI	4,226	74,458	14,855	11,464	10,737	3,054	2,113	3,403	45,709	2,478	32.3	3.1	41.7
El Centro, CA	2,558	32,636	6,308	1,960	8,210	732	859	1,219	37,342	396	24.7	35.1	73.7
Elizabethtown-Fort Knox, KY	2,703	44,947	9,457	7,610	7,167	1,799	1,584	1,765	39,267	2,804	49.8	2.8	34.4
Elkhart-Goshen, IN	4,989	133,932	11,511	73,473	10,323	1,931	1,935	6,408	47,844	1,667	64.1	1.9	34.8
Elmira, NY	1,691	30,929	7,083	4,903	5,076	847	744	1,275	41,234	398	29.1	1.3	37.8
El Paso, TX	15,116	249,383	49,478	16,783	36,223	8,004	8,885	8,391	33,647	790	75.9	11.1	39.6
Enid, OK	1,566	20,986	3,780	2,596	3,369	756	592	814	38,799	936	22.1	20.6	44.8
Erie, PA	6,055	112,481	26,441	19,930	14,900	5,752	3,636	4,511	40,107	1,162	39.6	1.4	46.8
Eugene-Springfield, OR	10,001	128,420	24,251	14,332	20,241	5,097	6,038	5,639	43,914	2,646	78.2	1.1	35.9

Area name	Agriculture, 2017 (cont.) — Land in farms: Acreage (1,000)	Land in farms: Percent change, 2012–2017	Land in farms — Acres: Average size of farm	Acres: Total irrigated (1,000)	Acres: Total cropland (1,000)	Value of land and buildings: Average per farm	Value of land and buildings: Average per acre	Value of machinery and equipmnet, average per farm (dollars)	Value of products sold: Total (mil dol)	Value of products sold: Average per farm (acres)	Value of products sold — Percent from: Crops	Percent from: Livestock and poultry products	Organic farms (number)	Farms with internet access (percent)	Government payments: Total ($1,000)	Government payments: Percent of farms
	117	118	119	120	121	122	123	124	125	126	127	128	129	130	131	132
Cedar Rapids, IA	1,089	1.2	300	1.0	954.7	2,258,419	7,533	212,260	854.5	235,265	62.8	37.2	14	82.0	23,487	71.1
Chambersburg-Waynesboro, PA	270	1.9	170	2.8	213.9	1,283,405	7,528	162,879	476.5	301,372	19.2	80.8	44	59.6	3,264	23.0
Champaign-Urbana, IL	839	-4.2	513	15.3	817.6	4,767,532	9,300	327,703	540.8	330,584	97.2	2.8	7	81.7	9,705	78.6
Charleston, WV	200	12.1	130	0.0	45.4	301,266	2,315	42,169	9.5	6,149	41.0	59.0	1	72.3	237	7.3
Charleston-North Charleston, SC	212	14.4	192	3.1	60.1	752,456	3,909	80,705	67.4	61,251	55.9	44.1	1	70.7	1,304	12.4
Charlotte-Concord-Gastonia, NC-SC	971	-5.1	131	4.4	476.5	767,934	5,840	86,273	1,305.7	176,897	20.9	79.1	18	73.0	8,866	13.9
Charlottesville, VA	324	0.1	179	1.9	95.2	1,398,609	7,820	71,057	70.1	38,753	66.7	33.3	16	79.0	976	9.2
Chattanooga, TN-GA	274	2.8	127	0.4	85.0	630,797	4,977	70,938	248.7	115,034	8.0	92.0	7	76.6	2,430	18.9
Cheyenne, WY	1,630	-2.8	1,631	67.1	382.3	1,383,473	848	123,891	184.6	184,762	17.9	82.1	42	77.7	4,856	29.3
Chicago-Naperville-Elgin, IL-IN-WI	2,147	-3.8	327	59.4	2,016.0	2,794,684	8,547	216,405	1,859.9	283,303	71.1	28.9	53	82.4	36,682	45.6
Chicago-Naperville-Evanston, IL Div 16,984	672	-4.1	286	10.2	635.2	2,661,483	9,317	188,605	456.3	193,918	87.7	12.3	14	82.7	6,760	32.2
Elgin, IL Div 20,994	680	-2.3	401	1.8	658.1	3,859,110	9,632	267,239	667.1	393,094	72.2	27.8	24	85.6	14,683	60.3
Gary, IN Div 23,844	686	-5.8	382	45.8	633.6	2,544,392	6,668	234,527	637.6	354,611	57.6	42.4	1	79.9	12,347	57.1
Lake County-Kenosha County, IL-WI Div 29,404	108	1.6	151	1.6	89.1	1,340,176	8,866	141,879	98.9	137,964	74.4	25.6	14	80.5	2,892	25.5
Chico, CA	348	-8.6	182	192.5	214.2	2,193,552	12,042	163,066	524.2	274,140	96.8	3.2	100	80.4	6,677	6.1
Cincinnati, OH-KY-IN	1,331	-0.7	128	2.1	784.7	671,715	5,249	79,548	420.7	40,443	79.8	20.2	35	75.4	19,347	19.0
Clarksville, TN-KY	674	-3.3	248	8.2	410.5	1,109,600	4,473	120,824	321.7	118,376	79.0	21.0	22	65.3	10,373	32.7
Cleveland, TN	120	-1.6	113	0.2	44.8	619,500	5,491	69,039	142.3	133,647	12.4	87.6	8	72.3	1,323	19.4
Cleveland-Elyria, OH	310	2.0	88	3.9	226.3	672,210	7,634	85,806	301.4	85,520	83.3	16.7	56	74.6	4,482	14.6
Coeur d'Alene, ID	140	12.4	130	13.7	62.2	719,382	5,525	49,847	21.5	20,057	81.0	19.0	3	81.7	1,211	9.9
College Station-Bryan, TX	1,099	-0.3	245	50.4	225.2	929,627	3,792	69,216	308.4	68,802	20.3	79.7	4	71.2	3,759	3.4
Colorado Springs, CO	701	-2.6	466	9.8	57.1	685,392	1,470	45,681	33.1	22,035	42.1	57.9	8	81.1	1,300	6.7
Columbia, MO	713	-9.9	259	8.7	429.1	1,010,094	3,904	99,816	258.5	93,746	58.6	41.4	15	76.5	8,096	41.8
Columbia, SC	575	10.2	173	45.3	213.9	630,372	3,643	88,055	649.0	195,201	26.1	73.9	14	74.2	6,326	15.9
Columbus, GA-AL	297	-0.6	279	6.0	73.2	775,478	2,775	77,092	58.1	54,683	39.3	60.7	1	70.9	4,287	31.5
Columbus, IN	160	-6.5	284	15.5	142.2	1,902,512	6,688	159,738	93.0	164,929	88.3	11.7	0	79.3	3,919	55.7
Columbus, OH	1,666	-4.6	196	5.1	1,395.2	1,284,052	6,557	141,978	1,078.5	126,795	69.5	30.5	89	82.9	47,922	36.9
Corpus Christi, TX	846	-5.8	649	5.3	568.2	1,867,705	2,876	206,676	292.4	224,550	92.7	7.3	4	71.0	15,650	26.6
Corvallis, OR	128	2.9	132	27.2	69.0	852,301	6,438	80,922	76.5	79,401	82.6	17.4	32	86.7	1,144	6.7
Crestview-Fort Walton Beach-Destin, FL	136	-35.2	126	1.6	36.8	517,386	4,111	42,599	38.9	36,088	30.4	69.6	0	76.5	1,999	15.7
Cumberland, MD-WV	134	19.4	166	0.1	42.8	585,037	3,525	56,221	25.8	31,879	24.2	75.8	2	64.9	379	13.3
Dallas-Fort Worth-Arlington, TX	3,793	0.9	130	23.3	1,227.2	628,364	4,846	57,126	611.7	20,911	39.0	61.0	24	78.4	21,992	6.0
Dallas-Plano-Irving, TX Div 19,124	2,156	-2.1	130	12.1	841.4	683,005	5,265	59,441	413.2	24,863	43.7	56.3	17	77.3	16,826	8.2
Fort Worth-Arlington-Grapevine, TX Div 23,104	1,637	5.2	130	11.2	385.8	556,504	4,294	54,081	198.6	15,713	29.4	70.6	7	79.7	5,166	3.2
Dalton, GA	84	-2.7	126	0.9	21.0	700,661	5,556	81,532	259.5	390,855	2.3	97.7	0	77.9	1,035	32.8
Danville, IL	471	8.5	449	0.8	443.7	3,686,595	8,203	261,347	283.0	269,783	95.2	4.8	6	77.8	5,125	56.7
Daphne-Fairhope-Foley, AL	175	-9.1	208	7.4	110.4	1,208,663	5,822	136,496	120.4	142,973	84.4	15.6	0	78.1	6,316	27.3
Davenport-Moline-Rock Island, IA-IL	1,146	4.1	334	21.9	1,022.2	2,590,577	7,762	218,339	894.2	260,397	71.4	28.6	18	79.9	29,119	71.3
Dayton-Kettering, OH	454	0.0	172	2.8	399.3	1,251,741	7,266	130,667	282.5	107,208	88.3	11.7	22	81.6	14,929	45.0
Decatur, AL	349	-12.1	144	6.7	166.7	581,656	4,031	89,976	312.6	129,400	22.3	77.7	2	74.0	5,769	32.8
Decatur, IL	277	-17.6	471	0.1	268.0	4,356,859	9,250	281,637	180.0	305,610	97.7	2.3	5	84.6	4,815	69.4
Deltona-Daytona Beach-Ormond Beach, FL	194	29.3	114	12.6	30.9	957,517	8,366	53,386	210.7	124,603	93.2	6.8	9	76.1	1,194	6.0
Denver-Aurora-Lakewood, CO	2,489	-0.1	444	46.4	965.9	1,006,299	2,267	66,978	222.6	39,705	68.1	31.9	27	85.3	10,661	11.3
Des Moines-West Des Moines, IA	1,716	-1.7	303	2.7	1,380.8	2,049,378	6,758	177,961	1,026.7	181,462	66.5	33.5	33	80.6	30,378	52.1
Detroit-Warren-Dearborn, MI	550	-1.4	138	9.9	448.1	767,746	5,560	115,703	340.6	85,581	81.1	18.9	46	79.5	5,926	16.3
Detroit-Dearborn-Livonia, MI Div 19,804	10	-36.3	40	0.6	7.8	467,879	11,561	70,633	23.1	93,274	96.8	3.2	2	88.3	56	4.8
Warren-Troy-Farmington Hills, MI Div 47,664	540	-0.3	145	9.4	440.3	787,673	5,448	118,698	317.5	85,069	79.9	20.1	44	78.9	5,870	17.1
Dothan, AL	506	-13.8	256	28.3	241.8	723,587	2,822	111,553	330.2	167,361	33.3	66.7	1	72.8	16,021	53.2
Dover, DE	182	5.9	222	57.8	155.7	1,758,029	7,923	179,332	391.3	476,038	27.9	72.1	4	76.6	4,531	34.3
Dubuque, IA	313	7.6	224	0.4	258.5	1,930,243	8,633	188,850	440.1	313,898	29.2	70.8	15	82.0	5,667	73.5
Duluth, MN-WI	305	3.9	182	0.2	136.6	373,649	2,054	63,481	36.0	21,450	49.2	50.8	19	78.2	321	3.6
Durham-Chapel Hill, NC	402	4.2	134	4.6	158.0	666,399	4,968	73,446	258.3	86,290	31.0	69.0	73	80.1	1,177	16.5
East Stroudsburg, PA	28	4.2	118	0.2	13.4	698,129	5,892	85,597	9.9	42,627	64.6	35.4	0	79.4	190	9.4
Eau Claire, WI	528	-10.2	213	11.0	357.0	829,118	3,888	124,131	305.3	123,187	40.9	59.1	66	73.8	4,434	43.6
El Centro, CA	522	1.2	1,317	456.1	504.0	14,670,311	11,135	884,987	1,859.7	4,696,157	65.7	34.3	45	90.7	3,640	27.5
Elizabethtown-Fort Knox, KY	451	3.7	161	0.0	257.6	683,751	4,255	88,940	146.1	52,121	69.8	30.2	1	78.4	4,561	24.4
Elkhart-Goshen, IN	175	1.2	105	25.0	146.5	1,173,020	11,178	98,422	298.3	178,936	23.4	76.6	86	45.5	3,082	16.3
Elmira, NY	67	15.1	168	0.1	35.0	440,269	2,619	91,731	19.0	47,771	50.6	49.4	5	78.6	384	19.1
El Paso, TX	2,419	-1.7	3,062	41.3	60.4	3,327,349	1,087	98,266	64.1	81,194	78.3	21.7	4	74.2	457	2.3
Enid, OK	675	1.3	721	3.2	442.9	1,251,739	1,736	180,573	130.4	139,318	48.1	51.9	0	80.0	6,660	61.3
Erie, PA	153	-9.0	132	1.3	93.5	595,515	4,511	112,026	82.0	70,602	76.4	23.6	3	78.1	907	15.7
Eugene-Springfield, OR	203	-7.5	77	22.3	98.0	656,860	8,556	59,094	158.4	59,873	58.0	42.0	65	83.8	659	2.9

Area name	Water use, 2015		Wholesale Trade[1], 2017				Retail Trade[2], 2017				Real estate and rental and leasing,[2] 2017			
	Public supply water withdrawn (mil gal/ day)	Public supply gallons withdrawn per person per day	Number of establish-ments	Number of employees	Sales (mil dol)	Average payroll (mil dol)	Number of establish-ments	Number of employees	Sales (mil dol)	Average payroll (mil dol)	Number of establish-ments	Number of employees	Sales (mil dol)	Average payroll (mil dol)
	133	134	135	136	137	138	139	140	141	142	143	144	145	146
Cedar Rapids, IA	44.04	165.5	364	5,819	3,988.4	358.6	834	16,751	6,868.5	414.3	251	1,123	256.0	47.3
Chambersburg-Waynesboro, PA	8.47	55.1	D	D	D	D	487	7,407	2,075.0	186.5	94	364	61.4	11.7
Champaign-Urbana, IL	25.54	113.4	189	3,221	2,719.7	150.5	655	10,285	2,601.7	243.9	231	2,083	388.5	85.4
Charleston, WV	34.86	128.5	254	3,362	2,083.1	163.1	870	13,006	3,845.2	326.1	262	1,355	369.5	57.4
Charleston-North Charleston, SC	107.90	144.9	702	8,976	9,063.0	561.8	2,790	41,887	12,008.0	1,097.2	1,352	5,650	1,475.6	272.3
Charlotte-Concord-Gastonia, NC-SC	242.84	99.0	3,323	50,727	39,242.1	3,171.2	7,907	125,747	36,152.5	3,279.3	3,860	17,619	5,600.4	963.1
Charlottesville, VA	14.89	70.1	134	1,062	684.4	59.5	778	11,322	3,153.7	315.9	312	1,533	312.5	64.6
Chattanooga, TN-GA	77.58	141.6	537	7,284	4,711.6	427.1	1,895	30,420	9,150.1	815.8	476	2,299	674.0	127.1
Cheyenne, WY	14.00	144.2	122	926	604.3	49.1	372	5,390	1,707.9	151.7	183	689	188.4	31.6
Chicago-Naperville-Elgin, IL-IN-WI	1,142.97	119.7	11,933	220,423	254,367.4	16,507.1	27,260	480,326	137,141.2	12,646.6	11,120	71,483	30,181.7	4,429.9
Chicago-Naperville-Evanston, IL Div 16,984	898.05	124.4	9,300	168,581	197,635.3	12,332.7	20,399	358,052	99,423.8	9,515.5	8,928	61,271	26,228.9	3,906.8
Elgin, IL Div 20,994	77.05	101.6	878	13,769	16,835.4	864.3	1,987	35,868	9,164.7	864.7	634	3,148	1,386.3	156.7
Gary, IN Div 23,844	93.36	132.8	570	6,589	6,202.9	375.0	2,161	34,698	10,237.1	856.1	603	2,800	580.1	107.8
Lake County-Kenosha County, IL-WI Div 29,404	74.51	85.4	1,185	31,484	33,693.8	2,935.1	2,713	51,708	18,315.5	1,410.3	955	4,264	1,986.3	258.5
Chico, CA	28.81	127.8	144	2,073	975.0	102.1	693	10,652	3,137.5	307.3	262	1,136	207.2	36.2
Cincinnati, OH-KY-IN	240.45	110.3	2,253	48,234	73,070.1	3,157.6	6,287	125,116	36,913.2	3,042.0	2,229	12,476	3,702.4	646.4
Clarksville, TN-KY	37.39	127.1	154	1,804	1,277.6	83.9	849	12,496	3,340.8	313.1	249	1,184	240.9	43.6
Cleveland, TN	14.61	120.9	69	729	830.1	49.8	396	6,146	2,162.4	167.2	D	D	D	D
Cleveland-Elyria, OH	292.15	141.8	2,711	42,249	31,494.2	2,547.8	6,479	99,944	29,175.5	2,585.5	2,263	15,576	5,026.6	821.7
Coeur d'Alene, ID	34.69	230.7	135	1,540	1,066.9	77.1	600	8,570	2,942.5	255.1	301	731	181.1	28.7
College Station-Bryan, TX	35.47	142.4	150	2,150	1,451.0	126.4	758	11,576	3,534.5	285.2	292	1,486	337.8	53.0
Colorado Springs, CO	94.52	135.4	470	4,871	3,019.3	321.6	2,166	32,833	9,962.3	949.6	1,380	4,548	1,033.2	191.4
Columbia, MO	20.22	99.7	157	1,838	1,014.0	97.9	684	12,618	3,737.5	315.3	286	1,266	231.8	40.3
Columbia, SC	92.00	113.6	681	12,098	9,165.9	707.8	2,677	42,762	12,450.4	1,071.6	832	4,363	1,358.1	205.4
Columbus, GA-AL	55.31	169.7	152	1,978	1,683.1	112.5	1,062	14,281	3,646.7	327.1	242	1,314	342.8	54.5
Columbus, IN	9.49	116.9	D	D	D	D	315	5,106	1,311.6	112.8	75	355	91.4	12.4
Columbus, OH	207.31	102.5	1,632	33,225	37,877.3	2,109.5	5,612	104,982	37,840.9	2,939.5	2,254	14,091	4,123.8	701.7
Corpus Christi, TX	73.63	172.4	429	6,150	4,001.0	324.3	1,226	20,846	6,167.4	560.6	528	3,217	804.7	158.9
Corvallis, OR	11.95	136.5	41	278	176.7	16.6	266	3,935	903.3	97.0	130	493	82.4	15.3
Crestview-Fort Walton Beach-Destin, FL	32.98	125.8	180	1,275	670.3	58.2	1,287	17,111	4,731.8	437.0	718	3,111	701.9	125.6
Cumberland, MD-WV	2.24	22.4	54	546	162.1	22.9	341	4,804	1,281.6	114.2	74	230	43.0	7.8
Dallas-Fort Worth-Arlington, TX	436.65	62.0	7,901	144,518	175,673.0	9,698.2	20,645	357,167	121,884.6	10,560.9	9,224	67,915	21,049.7	3,987.6
Dallas-Plano-Irving, TX Div 19,124	390.06	82.9	5,630	104,565	141,638.8	7,213.9	13,637	236,449	80,143.2	7,145.3	6,735	53,435	17,157.7	3,283.8
Fort Worth-Arlington-Grapevine, TX Div 23,104	46.59	20.0	2,271	39,953	34,034.3	2,484.3	7,008	120,718	41,741.4	3,415.6	2,489	14,480	3,892.0	703.8
Dalton, GA	25.85	179.8	245	4,074	1,534.2	189.1	488	5,545	1,603.4	136.2	0	0	0.0	15.9
Danville, IL	8.95	112.9	D	D	D	91.7	247	3,709	934.8	84.3	46	153	38.3	5.9
Daphne-Fairhope-Foley, AL	23.67	116.2	194	2,404	1,447.4	124.6	989	13,735	3,703.4	340.2	365	1,842	369.7	65.2
Davenport-Moline-Rock Island, IA-IL	40.06	104.4	393	6,467	4,788.4	359.0	1,249	21,925	5,758.7	561.0	352	1,412	305.6	50.2
Dayton-Kettering, OH	101.01	126.1	661	9,630	9,964.5	596.1	2,438	44,926	12,449.7	1,031.0	744	4,107	794.4	169.3
Decatur, AL	33.33	218.3	16	107	62.3	98.9	546	6,313	1,977.8	162.7	100	422	108.9	18.3
Decatur, IL	20.02	186.6	95	1,303	1,363.5	74.8	395	5,594	1,515.3	143.5	88	484	78.7	14.9
Deltona-Daytona Beach-Ormond Beach, FL	64.62	103.7	455	3,123	1,564.8	151.3	2,242	30,781	8,827.0	804.5	922	3,178	689.9	113.4
Denver-Aurora-Lakewood, CO	453.79	161.2	3,395	53,171	62,554.5	3,584.1	8,815	142,779	44,500.0	4,400.0	6,036	25,091	7,859.5	1,425.8
Des Moines-West Des Moines, IA	64.73	98.1	838	15,078	17,616.8	927.4	2,067	40,570	11,501.8	1,082.5	847	4,805	1,067.6	231.0
Detroit-Warren-Dearborn, MI	634.84	147.6	4,529	75,766	76,057.4	5,139.7	14,853	207,041	65,578.4	5,674.6	3,948	29,354	12,393.7	1,382.1
Detroit-Dearborn-Livonia, MI Div 19,804	466.55	265.2	1,434	26,754	29,897.5	1,708.7	5,927	69,229	21,293.3	1,772.1	1,162	7,082	7,908.7	332.8
Warren-Troy-Farmington Hills, MI Div 47,664	168.29	66.2	3,095	49,012	46,159.9	3,431.0	8,926	137,812	44,285.1	3,902.5	2,786	22,272	4,485.0	1,049.3
Dothan, AL	22.38	151.0	188	3,531	11,757.4	194.9	673	8,868	2,466.7	225.8	108	510	103.8	20.5
Dover, DE	11.81	68.1	D	D	D	D	600	9,606	3,059.7	263.9	161	697	225.2	26.9
Dubuque, IA	7.71	79.4	156	2,348	2,185.6	122.0	424	7,233	1,763.9	175.4	121	400	94.9	14.4
Duluth, MN-WI	37.60	129.6	257	3,232	2,363.2	171.3	1,147	16,861	4,359.7	424.1	279	1,144	226.9	36.5
Durham-Chapel Hill, NC	67.46	110.4	420	15,465	11,563.5	1,776.3	1,729	26,946	7,134.2	704.5	682	3,308	765.3	157.8
East Stroudsburg, PA	11.35	68.2	107	D	525.9	D	605	9,469	2,448.5	225.8	144	539	122.4	18.8
Eau Claire, WI	14.36	86.7	168	2,424	1,694.0	115.4	584	10,854	3,301.3	269.5	146	747	112.0	23.0
El Centro, CA	24.47	135.8	202	1,837	1,656.4	87.4	473	8,444	1,815.1	199.7	161	736	136.0	22.6
Elizabethtown-Fort Knox, KY	15.75	106.0	77	681	605.5	31.5	480	7,186	2,027.1	178.9	116	556	86.8	15.3
Elkhart-Goshen, IN	12.95	63.6	317	6,495	4,827.8	332.6	705	9,603	2,889.9	262.5	181	767	167.3	28.7
Elmira, NY	8.37	96.1	85	1,216	608.6	56.7	316	5,032	1,378.8	126.2	89	365	98.5	13.6
El Paso, TX	114.57	136.6	D	D	D	D	2,280	38,251	9,964.9	884.3	844	4,043	958.5	152.1
Enid, OK	2.87	45.1	D	D	D	D	268	3,780	944.3	98.8	93	383	70.4	14.3
Erie, PA	33.34	119.9	247	3,292	1,367.7	166.6	917	15,344	3,823.5	360.9	190	878	169.8	30.3
Eugene-Springfield, OR	43.68	120.4	392	5,458	2,822.2	304.4	1,313	20,047	5,373.5	585.6	613	2,395	523.8	84.9

1. Merchant wholesalers, except manufacturers' sales branches and offices. 2. Employer establishments.

Area name	Professional, scientific, and technical services, 2017				Manufacturing, 2017				Accommodation and food services, 2017			
	Number of establish-ments	Number of employees	Sales (mil dol)	Average payroll (mil dol)	Number of establish-ments	Number of employees	Receipts (mil dol)	Annual payroll (mil dol)	Number of establish-ments	Number of employees	Receipts (mil dol)	Annual payroll (mil dol)
	147	148	149	150	151	152	153	154	155	156	157	158
Cedar Rapids, IA	577	6,694	1,060.7	475.0	255	18,227	10,947.2	1,511.9	612	10,427	511.8	157.7
Chambersburg-Waynesboro, PA	D	D	D	D	183	7,425	2,941.8	378.9	275	4,501	217.9	62.4
Champaign-Urbana, IL	24	114	10.3	4.8	135	6,526	2,615.7	322.4	607	11,535	587.6	173.5
Charleston, WV	577	5,052	856.9	322.3	D	D	D	D	521	10,513	635.0	169.8
Charleston-North Charleston, SC	2,109	18,987	3,374.2	1,321.0	485	25,995	41,328.4	1,757.4	1,919	43,875	2,958.0	829.5
Charlotte-Concord-Gastonia, NC-SC	1,288	9,622	1,372.7	476.4	2,346	96,584	38,354.0	5,091.2	5,200	111,768	6,670.0	1,821.5
Charlottesville, VA	453	3,832	618.1	273.2	184	3,403	904.8	209.2	573	12,209	750.5	227.2
Chattanooga, TN-GA	101	360	45.7	16.6	544	30,926	14,901.7	1,620.1	1,138	23,933	1,403.9	389.3
Cheyenne, WY	D	D	D	D	69	1,296	1,348.3	85.5	218	3,755	227.3	64.5
Chicago-Naperville-Elgin, IL-IN-WI	20,041	249,957	61,495.6	23,322.9	10,004	378,300	174,495.9	22,707.0	21,395	417,084	29,679.8	8,554.5
Chicago-Naperville-Evanston, IL Div 16,984	19,413	246,675	61,025.3	23,166.0	7,476	271,214	115,192.8	15,802.4	16,671	329,866	24,695.4	7,141.5
Elgin, IL Div 20,994	375	1,929	297.5	93.7	968	36,788	14,286.3	2,065.9	1,356	25,268	1,414.1	405.5
Gary, IN Div 23,844	14	50	4.5	1.6	549	34,555	30,613.4	2,671.3	1,433	27,566	1,587.6	429.7
Lake County-Kenosha County, IL-WI Div 29,404	239	1,303	168.3	61.6	1,011	35,743	14,403.5	2,167.4	1,935	34,384	1,982.8	577.8
Chico, CA	D	D	D	D	180	4,287	1,340.8	207.0	452	8,241	498.3	138.1
Cincinnati, OH-KY-IN	3,783	48,350	9,135.3	3,544.3	2,128	104,052	49,352.9	6,130.9	4,345	95,734	5,175.7	1,514.1
Clarksville, TN-KY	18	64	6.2	2.2	181	12,975	4,942.2	640.5	522	10,732	524.2	150.4
Cleveland, TN	141	742	88.3	30.0	117	7,531	4,262.8	371.3	217	4,381	223.5	62.0
Cleveland-Elyria, OH	420	2,160	280.2	110.2	3,073	116,467	41,853.0	6,807.6	4,566	83,943	4,677.0	1,331.0
Coeur d'Alene, ID	499	2,576	388.7	138.5	262	4,995	1,241.2	238.2	416	7,789	502.1	141.2
College Station-Bryan, TX	478	3,556	499.3	204.9	139	5,693	1,621.5	255.4	585	13,589	708.8	186.1
Colorado Springs, CO	2,754	23,029	4,532.5	1,779.2	464	11,082	3,345.4	676.3	1,442	32,703	2,039.0	591.1
Columbia, MO	14	58	4.9	1.8	113	4,649	2,304.2	230.8	475	10,491	490.1	156.9
Columbia, SC	1,191	13,054	2,558.9	888.4	494	24,594	12,585.4	1,417.7	1,659	34,339	1,796.7	489.8
Columbus, GA-AL	87	301	33.7	10.3	D	D	D	D	571	12,555	668.0	194.3
Columbus, IN	D	D	D	D	140	12,239	5,531.9	637.4	176	4,414	216.3	62.5
Columbus, OH	431	4,772	1,258.1	363.8	1,415	64,841	35,382.7	3,577.2	4,335	91,932	5,099.0	1,474.7
Corpus Christi, TX	D	D	D	D	208	10,049	28,701.3	797.4	1,068	21,757	1,200.0	327.0
Corvallis, OR	D	D	D	D	93	1,295	421.2	65.3	224	3,900	214.6	62.0
Crestview-Fort Walton Beach-Destin, FL	265	655	114.8	32.6	133	1,767	545.8	89.8	757	17,576	1,221.6	346.4
Cumberland, MD-WV	20	109	11.0	4.1	65	4,233	1,713.3	236.5	51	580	22.8	61.7
Dallas-Fort Worth-Arlington, TX	2,640	13,732	2,308.3	792.0	5,464	236,989	128,609.1	15,654.5	15,315	337,424	21,849.5	6,080.9
Dallas-Plano-Irving, TX Div 19,124	2,352	12,639	2,152.6	742.6	3,513	149,215	63,281.2	9,734.7	10,574	227,351	15,115.3	4,248.4
Fort Worth-Arlington-Grapevine, TX Div 23,104	288	1,093	155.8	49.4	1,951	87,774	65,327.8	5,919.8	4,741	110,073	6,734.3	1,832.6
Dalton, GA	16	76	17.8	6.6	303	20,955	7,829.6	868.3	221	4,155	241.7	63.2
Danville, IL	76	385	57.8	17.6	80	4,496	1,881.2	244.5	152	2,338	101.6	28.0
Daphne-Fairhope-Foley, AL	D	D	D	D	165	4,505	2,616.0	215.9	572	12,977	794.1	228.8
Davenport-Moline-Rock Island, IA-IL	65	309	24.7	9.1	354	24,961	12,055.6	1,280.8	918	17,365	972.8	262.4
Dayton-Kettering, OH	1,708	23,811	4,338.5	1,697.5	978	42,379	14,345.9	2,490.5	1,629	35,674	1,763.9	526.7
Decatur, AL	224	2,560	550.0	151.9	181	12,080	10,392.2	748.4	D	D	D	D
Decatur, IL	142	1,099	146.8	54.3	101	6,731	6,948.0	460.3	255	4,345	206.4	62.5
Deltona-Daytona Beach-Ormond Beach, FL	223	591	86.7	31.9	416	9,656	2,527.1	464.2	1,367	26,056	1,544.0	427.2
Denver-Aurora-Lakewood, CO	5,335	50,197	12,676.7	4,755.6	D	57,130	D	D	6,716	146,316	10,463.0	3,073.9
Des Moines-West Des Moines, IA	2,021	18,985	3,583.9	1,311.1	472	21,989	9,986.6	1,151.6	1,502	29,033	1,755.0	505.1
Detroit-Warren-Dearborn, MI	2,870	51,817	8,007.6	3,606.7	5,313	232,954	125,503.3	14,398.8	8,755	175,640	10,886.5	2,990.4
Detroit-Dearborn-Livonia, MI Div 19,804	2,870	51,817	8,007.6	3,606.7	1,454	88,033	67,028.2	5,655.0	3,354	71,006	5,250.8	1,354.7
Warren-Troy-Farmington Hills, MI Div 47,664	D	D	D	D	3,859	144,921	58,475.1	8,743.8	5,401	104,634	5,635.7	1,635.6
Dothan, AL	54	238	28.0	9.9	139	5,672	1,709.6	229.7	256	5,206	280.2	73.1
Dover, DE	D	D	D	D	70	4,635	2,139.3	210.0	285	6,916	476.3	115.0
Dubuque, IA	D	D	D	D	148	9,356	4,987.4	463.1	251	4,953	270.8	78.0
Duluth, MN-WI	486	3,714	505.2	210.5	293	7,606	3,765.4	460.8	826	13,766	710.1	216.3
Durham-Chapel Hill, NC	68	273	29.0	13.9	407	23,345	15,610.5	1,477.9	1,317	26,440	1,600.9	470.3
East Stroudsburg, PA	D	D	D	D	117	5,173	2,776.5	428.1	402	10,069	873.9	185.4
Eau Claire, WI	282	2,054	250.6	103.3	222	10,728	3,805.1	521.7	449	7,095	315.7	91.1
El Centro, CA	178	826	87.9	34.7	65	2,679	1,291.9	121.7	281	4,212	246.3	69.9
Elizabethtown-Fort Knox, KY	193	1,361	199.3	71.6	D	7,200	D	D	235	5,422	261.3	74.4
Elkhart-Goshen, IN	D	D	D	D	819	70,059	24,520.9	3,763.1	378	7,145	369.0	97.5
Elmira, NY	D	D	D	D	82	5,229	1,296.9	286.3	210	3,073	157.5	50.4
El Paso, TX	D	D	D	D	D	D	D	D	1,591	34,722	1,675.0	465.8
Enid, OK	119	581	73.0	28.4	57	2,357	1,240.8	139.3	134	2,422	128.3	32.8
Erie, PA	408	3,267	495.3	170.6	476	20,344	6,147.9	1,215.9	627	11,662	540.9	151.4
Eugene-Springfield, OR	985	5,099	634.1	252.5	521	13,517	5,054.0	708.5	1,010	15,794	943.3	272.6

Area name	Health care and social assistance, 2017: Number of establishments	Health care and social assistance, 2017: Number of employees	Health care and social assistance, 2017: Receipts (mil dol)	Health care and social assistance, 2017: Annual payroll (mil dol)	Other services, 2017: Number of establishments	Other services, 2017: Number of employees	Other services, 2017: Receipts (mil dol)	Other services, 2017: Annual payroll (mil dol)	Nonemployer businesses, 2019: Number	Nonemployer businesses, 2019: Receipts (mil dol)	Value of residential construction authorized by building permits, 2021: New construction ($1,000)	Value of residential construction authorized by building permits, 2021: Number of housing units
	159	160	161	162	163	164	165	166	167	168	169	170
Cedar Rapids, IA	753	17,246	1,973.8	761.6	383	2,815	303.6	98.3	16,842	767.7	136,453	898
Chambersburg-Waynesboro, PA	352	9,299	1,074.0	432.7	296	1,484	147.6	38.2	9,194	404.4	88,457	382
Champaign-Urbana, IL	D	D	D	D	321	2,236	755.6	86.0	13,634	545.2	124,026	616
Charleston, WV	102	2,047	124.8	53.0	431	2,663	362.8	99.4	11,837	492.6	32,874	260
Charleston-North Charleston, SC	1,930	38,905	5,998.4	2,020.7	1,284	8,174	1,054.0	285.9	70,325	3,571.1	2,051,965	8,282
Charlotte-Concord-Gastonia, NC-SC	5,824	135,459	18,268.2	6,815.7	4,104	28,337	3,845.2	946.1	220,993	10,286.3	6,330,075	30,126
Charlottesville, VA	539	17,623	3,035.0	1,434.8	399	3,630	877.0	174.6	19,004	959.7	405,521	1,427
Chattanooga, TN-GA	1,335	34,077	4,151.6	1,635.1	720	4,937	674.5	168.6	41,829	2,144.3	647,072	3,673
Cheyenne, WY	361	6,859	876.7	382.6	206	1,187	129.0	36.9	9,257	674.2	129,236	737
Chicago-Naperville-Elgin, IL-IN-WI	27,004	611,322	75,246.9	29,310.3	18,638	140,089	25,431.0	6,121.7	816,110	38,719.5	4,141,039	18,511
Chicago-Naperville-Evanston, IL Div 16,984	21,098	490,490	59,148.1	23,565.3	14,607	114,300	22,650.3	5,278.5	655,740	31,044.8	2,424,180	11,765
Elgin, IL Div 20,994	1,625	30,648	4,006.1	1,491.4	1,244	7,904	869.1	255.9	51,676	2,233.3	490,440	2,257
Gary, IN Div 23,844	1,757	44,036	5,703.1	2,028.3	1,149	8,451	882.2	280.9	43,146	1,813.2	760,372	2,615
Lake County-Kenosha County, IL-WI Div 29,404	2,524	46,148	6,389.6	2,225.3	1,638	9,434	1,029.4	306.3	65,548	3,628.2	466,046	1,874
Chico, CA	720	15,210	1,977.3	749.0	334	3,579	221.1	71.1	12,745	674.2	336,724	2,050
Cincinnati, OH-KY-IN	5,128	149,459	18,734.5	7,481.8	3,248	25,080	2,805.3	809.6	155,143	7,341.0	1,862,598	8,429
Clarksville, TN-KY	547	12,467	1,256.9	512.9	329	1,662	168.0	45.8	17,979	829.3	550,114	4,112
Cleveland, TN	261	5,491	631.3	222.7	123	951	91.9	24.8	8,765	452.9	183,309	790
Cleveland-Elyria, OH	5,558	186,724	21,912.0	9,575.8	3,803	26,414	2,901.6	831.5	160,115	7,589.9	977,983	3,340
Coeur d'Alene, ID	528	10,600	1,069.8	492.9	284	1,450	139.3	41.4	14,546	698.2	538,557	2,426
College Station-Bryan, TX	477	11,339	1,502.4	533.8	342	2,343	648.7	82.9	18,389	902.5	390,918	2,300
Colorado Springs, CO	2,188	39,863	4,543.4	1,867.6	1,315	10,802	2,394.5	457.6	59,366	2,540.5	2,622,384	9,335
Columbia, MO	731	20,566	2,665.5	924.9	383	2,274	266.6	71.8	14,111	694.6	270,290	1,029
Columbia, SC	1,576	46,187	5,878.7	2,185.6	1,237	9,225	1,001.6	310.6	59,377	2,567.7	1,470,118	6,881
Columbus, GA-AL	708	16,170	1,854.9	708.9	58	271	29.1	71.6	20,961	746.0	216,388	1,133
Columbus, IN	217	5,146	608.5	229.4	112	729	87.2	21.5	4,356	184.6	63,407	231
Columbus, OH	5,254	146,071	17,858.5	6,907.9	2,823	22,841	3,382.2	884.0	166,939	8,104.1	2,735,106	12,062
Corpus Christi, TX	1,198	32,412	3,043.4	1,207.3	613	4,583	662.7	153.5	32,699	1,421.8	576,164	2,575
Corvallis, OR	284	6,035	728.1	322.2	146	994	225.5	39.6	6,170	278.8	78,608	284
Crestview-Fort Walton Beach-Destin, FL	725	10,454	1,392.0	494.9	483	2,021	216.3	59.7	27,989	1,583.9	1,519,259	3,892
Cumberland, MD-WV	306	7,278	755.2	286.8	167	944	82.2	24.1	4,260	160.8	16,840	69
Dallas-Fort Worth-Arlington, TX	20,321	408,761	54,801.2	19,839.4	9,663	79,122	11,909.8	2,918.1	741,932	39,393.4	16,651,948	78,705
Dallas-Plano-Irving, TX Div 19,124	14,261	284,112	38,180.5	14,014.9	6,472	54,644	8,815.0	2,135.1	510,241	27,895.6	12,606,861	57,421
Fort Worth-Arlington-Grapevine, TX Div 23,104	6,060	124,649	16,620.6	5,824.4	3,191	24,478	3,094.8	783.0	231,691	11,497.7	4,045,088	21,284
Dalton, GA	D	D	D	D	152	966	127.7	34.4	8,108	401.0	102,386	732
Danville, IL	146	5,046	578.9	265.4	112	509	53.0	14.3	3,910	137.0	1,103	6
Daphne-Fairhope-Foley, AL	503	8,049	848.4	327.8	323	1,544	187.4	46.3	20,803	1,060.6	844,324	3,705
Davenport-Moline-Rock Island, IA-IL	1,039	24,097	2,457.5	994.2	629	4,007	393.5	118.7	21,232	924.8	138,806	629
Dayton-Kettering, OH	2,109	64,737	7,798.1	3,174.9	1,208	8,571	908.2	299.6	51,899	2,319.9	627,538	2,039
Decatur, AL	382	6,364	564.2	239.4	D	D	D	D	9,711	402.9	59,185	226
Decatur, IL	287	8,451	1,014.4	362.8	172	1,030	293.2	35.5	5,047	177.4	9,057	33
Deltona-Daytona Beach-Ormond Beach, FL	1,682	32,361	3,965.7	1,440.2	1,211	5,345	759.1	166.6	58,481	2,504.6	2,146,653	8,214
Denver-Aurora-Lakewood, CO	8,296	171,590	22,532.7	8,718.4	6,017	40,996	5,794.6	1,567.2	290,107	14,922.9	6,232,227	30,006
Des Moines-West Des Moines, IA	1,712	43,242	4,985.7	2,144.5	1,356	9,065	1,354.1	359.3	50,064	2,443.6	1,744,930	6,969
Detroit-Warren-Dearborn, MI	13,074	274,923	32,971.4	12,946.6	7,432	49,010	6,160.3	1,640.0	360,476	16,494.6	2,425,933	8,598
Detroit-Dearborn-Livonia, MI Div 19,804	4,118	111,962	14,321.6	5,577.6	2,725	18,581	2,525.3	643.2	137,698	4,763.5	763,416	2,240
Warren-Troy-Farmington Hills, MI Div 47,664	8,956	162,961	18,649.8	7,368.9	4,707	30,429	3,635.0	996.8	222,778	11,731.1	1,662,517	6,358
Dothan, AL	375	10,572	1,236.4	517.5	206	974	116.0	27.5	10,528	485.5	129,999	494
Dover, DE	433	10,827	1,248.9	497.3	248	1,249	124.2	37.3	12,047	883.3	270,500	1,873
Dubuque, IA	283	8,469	943.9	405.4	205	1,118	135.7	31.4	6,472	303.4	109,497	537
Duluth, MN-WI	1,046	30,326	3,231.1	1,390.3	537	3,382	338.3	93.3	16,995	694.3	148,359	708
Durham-Chapel Hill, NC	1,606	52,532	7,487.2	2,672.7	853	8,455	2,153.6	446.9	53,683	2,237.3	1,441,591	5,900
East Stroudsburg, PA	361	7,518	784.6	317.6	304	1,564	137.4	43.4	11,174	528.7	99,404	370
Eau Claire, WI	502	12,739	1,384.2	516.3	303	1,850	184.4	54.0	10,274	558.8	268,304	1,279
El Centro, CA	288	5,327	652.5	237.9	143	695	73.4	20.1	10,075	387.3	79,993	555
Elizabethtown-Fort Knox, KY	303	8,248	860.6	383.9	180	1,006	98.6	27.8	8,621	354.2	111,186	526
Elkhart-Goshen, IN	373	11,322	1,394.3	488.3	345	2,646	334.3	98.6	13,076	603.8	114,735	458
Elmira, NY	210	6,480	650.8	310.8	132	632	67.9	16.9	3,894	139.2	17,975	138
El Paso, TX	D	D	D	D	D	D	D	D	67,982	3,031.6	661,530	2,989
Enid, OK	197	3,778	386.2	141.0	108	545	63.1	15.2	4,345	174.7	11,007	35
Erie, PA	878	24,543	2,475.6	1,085.6	563	3,433	321.7	81.7	13,933	624.8	52,102	217
Eugene-Springfield, OR	1,260	23,686	2,982.6	1,139.5	636	3,703	552.4	118.3	25,788	1,157.5	452,083	2,136

Area name	Government employment and payroll, 2017									Local government finances, 2017				
			March payroll (percent of total)							General revenue				
												Taxes		
													Per capita[1] (dollars)	
	Full-time equivalent employees	March payroll (dollars)	Adminis-tration, judicial, and legal	Police and corrections	Fire protection	Highways and transpor-tation	Health and welfare	Natural resources and utilities	Education and libraries	Total (mil dol)	Inter-govern-mental (mil dol)	Total (mil dol)	Total	Property
	171	172	173	174	175	176	177	178	179	180	181	182	183	184
Cedar Rapids, IA	10,938	48,372,538	3.8	8.4	2.4	4.7	2.5	5.7	71.2	1,393.4	561.3	544.4	2,011	1,680
Chambersburg-Waynesboro, PA	3,509	14,820,555	8.8	9.9	1.0	2.8	4.9	6.8	64.5	470.5	163.0	223.0	1,445	1,114
Champaign-Urbana, IL	8,074	34,122,603	6.8	10.0	4.1	6.7	6.9	5.2	58.0	869.4	294.0	436.8	1,926	1,626
Charleston, WV	9,301	32,903,011	6.5	7.1	3.3	3.8	5.1	3.7	68.3	876.6	308.4	363.3	1,375	987
Charleston-North Charleston, SC	25,010	93,233,309	8.2	12.8	7.2	3.2	2.4	9.2	54.8	3,301.1	980.0	1,692.0	2,182	1,329
Charlotte-Concord-Gastonia, NC-SC	118,925	545,962,852	3.5	5.8	2.3	1.7	44.9	3.9	36.5	15,716.3	4,004.6	4,221.0	1,655	1,196
Charlottesville, VA	7,744	30,615,694	7.3	9.0	3.5	3.3	4.9	5.1	61.5	891.8	312.3	426.7	1,974	1,460
Chattanooga, TN-GA	22,494	94,289,741	5.5	6.6	2.6	2.9	34.8	8.4	37.6	2,932.2	835.2	721.4	1,298	952
Cheyenne, WY	6,340	31,230,813	2.7	5.1	1.9	1.9	39.7	2.3	45.2	848.2	316.5	110.4	1,122	833
Chicago-Naperville-Elgin, IL-IN-WI	370,392	2,008,221,393	5.4	12.9	5.1	7.1	4.1	6.3	56.7	57,261.7	17,993.2	30,192.9	3,173	2,491
Chicago-Naperville-Evanston, IL Div 16,984	277,815	1,578,142,028	5.2	13.9	5.3	8.3	4.5	6.4	53.7	45,457.1	14,062.4	23,950.3	3,336	2,492
Elgin, IL Div 20,994	31,708	155,550,255	5.1	9.1	4.7	2.0	1.9	5.6	70.6	4,100.3	1,237.4	2,348.8	3,079	2,814
Gary, IN Div 23,844	24,510	89,508,611	9.6	11.0	4.5	5.0	2.3	7.7	58.5	2,741.2	1,223.0	995.3	1,421	1,351
Lake County-Kenosha County, IL-WI Div 29,404	36,359	185,020,499	4.7	8.9	4.1	2.4	3.6	5.6	69.4	4,963.1	1,470.3	2,898.4	3,328	3,117
Chico, CA	8,504	42,774,851	6.8	10.0	1.8	1.9	13.8	4.8	59.1	1,192.9	763.9	283.0	1,237	929
Cincinnati, OH-KY-IN	76,381	322,830,314	6.7	10.9	6.5	4.9	6.3	6.2	56.5	9,540.7	3,097.8	4,351.1	1,975	1,295
Clarksville, TN-KY	9,239	32,080,174	4.6	10.5	4.0	3.3	5.0	7.6	62.2	821.7	361.4	321.0	1,075	642
Cleveland, TN	3,588	12,281,512	5.2	12.8	6.4	3.9	9.9	2.7	58.2	299.5	153.0	99.1	811	577
Cleveland-Elyria, OH	93,125	446,972,995	6.5	10.2	4.6	5.7	16.8	7.1	47.1	12,306.8	3,483.7	5,700.4	2,771	1,673
Coeur d'Alene, ID	7,757	33,973,530	5.6	7.5	3.1	2.0	43.3	3.4	34.7	903.2	235.7	172.7	1,098	1,032
College Station-Bryan, TX	9,930	33,082,098	9.7	12.9	5.2	3.9	2.3	6.5	57.5	830.2	200.5	507.8	1,960	1,614
Colorado Springs, CO	22,053	95,494,427	5.6	12.6	5.0	2.9	4.0	16.1	51.8	2,613.9	1,070.5	1,080.0	1,490	765
Columbia, MO	7,779	26,743,399	7.7	5.9	3.2	2.8	7.3	8.8	62.8	977.2	218.3	329.6	1,602	950
Columbia, SC	34,954	140,163,929	4.4	6.5	2.5	1.5	26.3	5.2	52.6	4,092.9	1,151.1	1,465.5	1,777	1,509
Columbus, GA-AL	13,049	43,882,975	4.8	11.7	4.2	2.7	7.9	6.9	58.6	1,059.9	422.9	410.0	1,298	833
Columbus, IN	4,111	16,129,167	3.8	7.4	3.0	1.4	41.3	4.3	37.9	614.4	104.8	80.3	977	940
Columbus, OH	72,712	341,651,456	7.6	10.8	7.3	4.4	8.5	5.3	54.1	11,236.4	3,470.0	5,408.7	2,597	1,539
Corpus Christi, TX	19,353	72,091,517	6.0	9.9	4.1	5.3	4.5	6.6	62.3	1,990.5	572.5	935.7	2,184	1,743
Corvallis, OR	2,152	10,442,594	7.7	11.7	5.2	3.9	12.2	5.7	51.2	268.8	91.1	134.8	1,468	1,335
Crestview-Fort Walton Beach-Destin, FL	9,679	34,202,616	6.6	12.1	7.5	3.9	1.9	6.2	57.7	994.3	308.4	462.7	1,704	1,306
Cumberland, MD-WV	3,350	15,234,499	4.1	6.8	1.6	3.4	1.5	4.9	75.5	370.5	190.4	114.9	1,165	795
Dallas-Fort Worth-Arlington, TX	287,204	1,272,150,755	5.5	9.9	4.9	4.3	10.6	5.0	58.0	34,648.7	7,831.5	18,284.1	2,492	2,012
Dallas-Plano-Irving, TX Div 19,124	194,536	879,657,973	5.1	9.7	5.1	5.4	10.5	5.2	57.0	24,381.2	5,066.9	12,871.0	2,619	2,118
Fort Worth-Arlington-Grapevine, TX Div 23,104	92,668	392,492,782	6.4	10.4	4.5	1.7	10.9	4.6	60.4	10,267.5	2,764.6	5,413.1	2,234	1,798
Dalton, GA	5,308	19,803,932	3.7	7.4	4.6	3.0	4.5	5.2	66.0	538.3	246.2	176.3	1,224	744
Danville, IL	3,100	11,926,933	8.2	8.8	2.8	3.9	4.1	4.3	64.0	364.0	228.8	92.7	1,193	1,097
Daphne-Fairhope-Foley, AL	7,998	27,159,727	6.9	8.8	3.3	4.6	13.2	8.1	51.4	778.0	221.7	271.7	1,278	507
Davenport-Moline-Rock Island, IA-IL	14,893	64,255,844	5.5	9.4	3.6	4.8	5.7	5.5	63.6	1,734.2	674.9	734.3	1,927	1,687
Dayton-Kettering, OH	31,763	138,563,639	8.2	10.0	4.9	5.6	8.1	7.1	54.6	3,900.2	1,341.5	1,762.2	2,194	1,418
Decatur, AL	5,002	17,822,978	4.1	9.2	3.3	2.7	3.9	10.8	63.5	492.4	208.3	179.9	1,184	515
Decatur, IL	3,903	16,584,624	6.5	13.5	5.1	3.4	3.3	7.1	58.7	459.7	187.3	179.9	1,707	1,439
Deltona-Daytona Beach-Ormond Beach, FL	19,007	72,712,023	9.0	15.4	5.7	3.5	3.4	8.9	51.0	2,858.7	704.4	979.1	1,511	1,155
Denver-Aurora-Lakewood, CO	102,997	507,857,612	6.9	13.2	5.3	6.4	13.1	8.2	45.3	16,649.8	4,070.6	7,563.9	2,616	1,550
Des Moines-West Des Moines, IA	25,500	121,156,720	5.2	7.7	3.1	4.3	8.8	5.4	64.2	3,514.5	1,322.1	1,400.9	2,056	1,870
Detroit-Warren-Dearborn, MI	110,332	518,343,461	8.1	11.9	4.1	4.4	2.1	4.7	62.2	19,768.6	9,174.4	6,054.0	1,401	1,222
Detroit-Dearborn-Livonia, MI Div 19,804	48,307	223,215,723	8.0	14.5	4.2	6.5	1.3	6.5	55.6	9,545.1	4,481.6	2,659.3	1,513	1,151
Warren-Troy-Farmington Hills, MI Div 47,664	62,025	295,127,738	8.1	9.9	4.0	2.8	2.6	3.3	67.2	10,223.5	4,692.8	3,394.6	1,324	1,270
Dothan, AL	7,279	37,160,101	2.8	5.0	2.2	1.9	30.3	4.9	51.8	807.7	190.4	151.3	1,023	361
Dover, DE	4,452	19,533,638	5.1	6.3	0.1	0.8	1.8	5.1	79.4	513.1	312.8	109.2	619	544
Dubuque, IA	3,536	14,203,131	6.2	8.7	3.8	7.3	5.2	4.6	62.8	432.9	186.4	173.0	1,782	1,463
Duluth, MN-WI	13,477	58,909,938	7.5	11.9	3.2	6.6	10.9	7.6	48.9	1,659.7	822.9	448.0	1,550	1,366
Durham-Chapel Hill, NC	21,823	86,844,113	5.5	10.5	3.8	1.7	11.2	6.4	55.5	2,044.4	773.2	981.3	1,568	1,216
East Stroudsburg, PA	5,561	25,725,163	5.3	5.2	0.0	3.2	1.6	1.5	82.6	816.0	272.4	464.3	2,766	2,480
Eau Claire, WI	5,877	25,577,262	5.8	8.6	2.7	5.8	6.4	3.3	66.5	673.6	327.2	255.4	1,526	1,379
El Centro, CA	11,605	61,911,631	3.6	5.2	1.6	1.1	22.1	13.1	47.5	1,462.1	823.5	203.7	1,121	778
Elizabethtown-Fort Knox, KY	6,955	26,839,479	1.7	3.8	1.4	1.2	44.4	4.0	42.3	678.7	181.8	132.9	884	529
Elkhart-Goshen, IN	7,096	28,545,949	5.0	8.8	4.0	2.1	1.6	3.1	72.4	664.7	333.5	219.8	1,077	1,000
Elmira, NY	4,253	19,683,127	4.4	7.8	2.9	4.7	9.4	3.1	66.7	507.5	228.8	195.1	2,303	1,450
El Paso, TX	42,242	158,791,952	5.1	9.2	3.4	2.4	11.2	2.7	63.8	4,060.0	1,842.0	1,333.7	1,584	1,238
Enid, OK	2,370	8,025,034	5.6	9.5	5.9	3.9	0.1	4.7	67.5	182.5	64.1	80.6	1,309	555
Erie, PA	8,171	34,509,401	5.5	10.5	3.0	6.5	4.8	5.6	63.3	1,313.5	652.3	413.7	1,512	1,209
Eugene-Springfield, OR	11,728	57,941,191	5.9	12.8	5.6	6.3	5.9	10.3	47.4	1,612.9	655.1	547.6	1,459	1,212

1. Based on the resident population estimated as of July 1 of the year shown

Area name	Local government finances, 2017 (cont.) — Direct general expenditure: Total (mil dol)	Per capita[1] (dollars)	Percent of total for: Education	Health and hospitals	Police protection	Public welfare	Highways	Debt outstanding: Total (mil dol)	Per capita[1] (dollars)	Government employment, 2020: Federal civilian	Federal military	State and local	Individual income tax returns, 2019: Number of returns	Mean adjusted gross income	Mean income tax
	185	186	187	188	189	190	191	192	193	194	195	196	197	198	199
Cedar Rapids, IA	1,437.2	5,310	51.2	2.0	5.1	0.8	4.6	1,507.2	5,569	1,183	965	14,790	131,900	69,412	7,282
Chambersburg-Waynesboro, PA	484.0	3,135	59.0	3.3	2.4	2.2	4.5	740.3	4,796	2,374	392	5,571	78,620	58,961	5,473
Champaign-Urbana, IL	862.4	3,802	49.8	3.6	6.1	2.4	5.9	745.8	3,288	1,354	456	36,303	94,770	68,790	7,789
Charleston, WV	905.0	3,425	51.4	3.9	6.3	0.2	1.6	363.5	1,376	2,459	1,211	22,514	113,720	55,712	5,693
Charleston-North Charleston, SC	2,959.4	3,816	47.2	2.4	8.6	0.2	2.0	5,589.2	7,207	12,137	7,874	53,269	384,200	78,624	10,337
Charlotte-Concord-Gastonia, NC-SC	14,982.5	5,875	28.5	39.8	5.5	2.5	1.5	14,215.1	5,574	11,297	6,561	144,843	1,246,320	77,469	10,075
Charlottesville, VA	852.9	3,947	48.1	3.4	5.7	7.4	2.5	777.9	3,600	1,538	1,186	35,402	102,400	103,245	14,888
Chattanooga, TN-GA	2,697.8	4,853	28.3	38.8	4.9	0.4	2.4	1,763.9	3,173	5,647	1,592	31,945	253,410	64,638	7,223
Cheyenne, WY	893.1	9,078	39.6	37.9	2.9	0.3	2.4	143.1	1,454	2,809	3,739	11,134	50,180	67,948	7,223
Chicago-Naperville-Elgin, IL-IN-WI	53,454.9	5,618	44.2	4.2	7.3	0.9	4.4	93,411.1	9,818	56,599	36,022	480,187	4,686,990	83,763	11,779
Chicago-Naperville-Evanston, IL Div 16,984	42,203.6	5,878	41.4	4.9	7.6	1.0	4.3	79,270.9	11,041	46,589	14,616	360,742	3,549,150	84,134	12,015
Elgin, IL Div 20,994	3,928.9	5,151	56.8	0.9	7.0	0.6	4.7	6,422.2	8,420	2,074	1,527	45,119	363,100	75,438	8,824
Gary, IN Div 23,844	2,375.8	3,391	47.1	0.6	5.8	0.1	3.6	3,383.7	4,830	2,180	2,060	30,165	344,600	62,407	6,566
Lake County-Kenosha County, IL-WI Div 29,404	4,946.6	5,680	56.3	2.3	6.0	1.3	5.1	4,334.1	4,977	5,756	17,819	44,161	430,140	104,833	16,505
Chico, CA	1,303.8	5,701	50.9	7.0	4.3	9.8	3.6	710.4	3,106	738	310	14,955	90,090	60,805	6,198
Cincinnati, OH-KY-IN	9,442.0	4,287	45.6	5.6	6.5	4.2	5.0	13,555.8	6,155	14,915	5,941	111,402	1,093,480	74,276	9,193
Clarksville, TN-KY	756.6	2,534	53.3	3.2	6.8	0.0	4.4	3,381.5	11,323	5,595	29,248	14,714	136,450	50,010	4,064
Cleveland, TN	333.0	2,725	49.6	2.7	6.4	4.4	4.9	234.0	1,915	319	343	5,118	55,310	50,487	4,312
Cleveland-Elyria, OH	12,721.0	6,184	39.8	12.5	6.7	3.4	3.5	16,005.0	7,780	18,896	5,593	109,821	1,064,110	68,659	8,473
Coeur d'Alene, ID	909.8	5,783	24.0	51.5	3.8	0.2	2.5	282.6	1,796	699	514	11,010	84,360	66,780	7,083
College Station-Bryan, TX	942.2	3,636	49.9	5.0	5.1	0.3	5.0	1,968.9	7,598	921	567	40,196	105,670	65,370	7,673
Colorado Springs, CO	2,444.4	3,373	51.0	1.4	7.5	3.0	8.3	4,656.7	6,425	12,661	40,265	42,173	360,480	69,778	7,569
Columbia, MO	951.9	4,627	37.3	29.9	3.5	0.4	4.5	2,633.1	12,799	2,817	685	32,011	92,900	69,331	8,105
Columbia, SC	4,176.9	5,063	39.4	26.9	4.1	0.1	2.3	5,470.1	6,631	10,869	12,671	70,876	379,740	61,033	6,444
Columbus, GA-AL	1,129.5	3,575	50.2	6.6	6.2	3.3	3.9	954.3	3,020	6,841	23,239	17,476	135,000	53,924	5,371
Columbus, IN	629.6	7,658	19.8	63.2	2.4	0.1	2.0	281.4	3,422	201	245	6,001	40,160	69,987	7,647
Columbus, OH	11,893.4	5,711	37.7	6.6	5.5	6.8	5.5	14,856.5	7,134	15,038	5,683	162,062	1,040,720	70,300	8,355
Corpus Christi, TX	2,042.7	4,768	49.6	8.4	5.7	0.1	4.3	3,819.1	8,914	6,039	2,600	25,679	195,380	57,713	6,150
Corvallis, OR	219.5	2,391	55.4	0.0	7.5	0.0	2.7	177.8	1,937	502	249	9,628	41,670	76,252	9,012
Crestview-Fort Walton Beach-Destin, FL	1,007.1	3,709	44.4	3.0	8.7	0.3	5.1	558.7	2,058	9,482	18,949	11,441	143,950	79,305	10,904
Cumberland, MD-WV	389.1	3,947	55.8	0.8	5.3	0.0	4.4	305.6	3,100	619	1,396	6,692	41,490	51,260	4,399
Dallas-Fort Worth-Arlington, TX	34,267.9	4,671	44.8	11.4	5.7	0.2	3.7	85,470.2	11,649	49,045	16,598	378,848	3,591,110	81,391	11,222
Dallas-Plano-Irving, TX Div 19,124	24,000.8	4,884	43.9	11.6	5.1	0.3	3.6	63,109.5	12,842	32,171	10,617	266,948	2,412,080	85,359	12,252
Fort Worth-Arlington-Grapevine, TX Div 23,104	10,267.2	4,238	46.9	10.9	6.8	0.1	3.9	22,360.7	9,229	16,874	5,981	111,900	1,179,030	73,274	9,115
Dalton, GA	533.3	3,703	57.3	10.8	4.0	0.0	4.4	130.3	904	273	375	6,678	59,830	50,436	4,514
Danville, IL	307.4	3,957	52.9	0.9	5.4	0.1	7.9	108.9	1,402	1,390	145	4,298	33,090	49,246	4,217
Daphne-Fairhope-Foley, AL	833.5	3,922	37.7	18.0	5.7	0.1	8.0	1,143.7	5,382	405	988	9,778	105,840	68,887	7,830
Davenport-Moline-Rock Island, IA-IL	1,798.5	4,719	50.9	4.7	6.4	0.5	4.7	1,622.1	4,256	5,939	1,380	19,264	185,200	64,425	6,814
Dayton-Kettering, OH	3,943.7	4,910	50.4	1.5	6.2	5.4	3.8	3,883.2	4,834	20,374	7,498	39,607	396,830	61,747	6,506
Decatur, AL	558.0	3,671	53.7	1.9	6.7	0.4	2.8	762.5	5,017	373	628	7,877	67,540	56,954	5,370
Decatur, IL	452.0	4,288	47.3	1.2	10.4	1.1	5.4	425.2	4,034	313	202	5,110	48,200	60,818	6,389
Deltona-Daytona Beach-Ormond Beach, FL	2,713.1	4,188	29.8	23.7	6.9	0.3	4.6	2,857.4	4,410	1,628	1,254	23,126	333,810	59,941	6,761
Denver-Aurora-Lakewood, CO	15,273.3	5,282	34.2	7.9	5.5	2.5	4.8	30,580.8	10,575	29,013	10,194	183,045	1,521,390	89,195	12,261
Des Moines-West Des Moines, IA	3,513.1	5,156	51.1	8.4	4.6	0.9	4.4	3,930.5	5,768	6,537	2,615	39,731	339,950	77,820	9,267
Detroit-Warren-Dearborn, MI	20,409.8	4,723	42.1	5.2	5.8	3.1	5.2	22,654.5	5,242	28,545	7,658	160,442	2,148,790	70,759	8,954
Detroit-Dearborn-Livonia, MI Div 19,804	9,879.6	5,622	33.7	3.2	5.7	5.6	3.5	11,792.4	6,711	14,129	3,144	71,566	817,060	55,144	6,156
Warren-Troy-Farmington Hills, MI Div 47,664	10,530.2	4,106	50.0	7.2	5.8	0.8	6.7	10,862.0	4,236	14,416	4,514	88,876	1,331,730	80,339	10,670
Dothan, AL	863.8	5,842	24.6	48.1	3.6	0.1	3.6	578.5	3,912	441	666	10,352	64,150	55,732	5,870
Dover, DE	520.7	2,950	74.0	1.3	5.4	0.0	1.4	371.1	2,103	1,775	4,572	17,448	86,400	55,363	4,985
Dubuque, IA	417.0	4,296	46.7	1.8	5.2	0.3	5.1	473.0	4,873	286	356	4,373	47,890	68,985	7,641
Duluth, MN-WI	1,782.7	6,166	35.5	3.0	4.8	6.8	13.5	2,339.7	8,093	1,776	1,055	22,408	140,420	61,562	6,082
Durham-Chapel Hill, NC	1,964.6	3,140	45.8	4.3	9.3	6.2	1.5	1,858.3	2,970	8,632	1,407	67,318	297,400	80,572	10,437
East Stroudsburg, PA	758.0	4,515	69.4	0.1	3.3	5.4	3.0	1,152.8	6,866	3,442	455	7,866	82,370	57,702	5,811
Eau Claire, WI	737.3	4,406	52.8	4.8	6.1	3.5	11.6	673.8	4,027	606	423	11,294	81,590	67,481	7,753
El Centro, CA	1,512.6	8,327	43.0	24.1	3.4	7.9	2.3	1,540.3	8,480	2,342	500	16,158	86,310	42,938	3,170
Elizabethtown-Fort Knox, KY	676.0	4,495	32.9	48.2	1.4	0.0	2.3	558.9	3,716	5,318	5,558	9,085	70,410	53,614	4,487
Elkhart-Goshen, IN	693.5	3,396	57.5	1.1	4.4	0.0	4.3	677.6	3,318	300	597	8,180	97,630	59,097	5,964
Elmira, NY	499.8	5,899	45.2	2.9	3.2	18.4	5.7	196.0	2,313	224	126	6,054	39,040	58,489	5,843
El Paso, TX	3,948.7	4,690	49.7	17.3	4.5	0.2	1.3	6,819.3	8,099	13,414	28,554	54,668	399,390	45,544	3,855
Enid, OK	170.7	2,772	59.3	3.2	6.6	0.1	1.8	126.3	2,051	517	1,511	3,247	27,050	57,094	5,516
Erie, PA	1,301.5	4,758	46.6	4.7	2.7	14.7	3.7	1,418.4	5,185	1,705	699	14,720	129,620	59,991	6,351
Eugene-Springfield, OR	1,560.7	4,159	48.0	5.4	6.7	1.0	3.5	1,918.9	5,114	1,973	964	22,472	180,240	62,467	6,752

1. Based on the resident population estimated as of July 1 of the year shown.

Table C. Metropolitan Areas — **Land Area and Population**

CBSA[1]	DIV Code	Area name	Land area[2] (sq mi)	Population, 2021: Total persons 2021	Population, 2021: Rank	Population, 2021: Per square mile	Population characteristics, 2021: Race alone or in combination, not Hispanic or Latino (percent): White	Black	American Indian, Alaska Native	Asian and Pacific Islander	Percent Hispanic or Latino[3]	Age (percent): Under 5 years	5 to 17 years	18 to 24 years	25 to 34 years	35 to 44 years	45 to 54 years
			1	2	3	4	5	6	7	8	9	10	11	12	13	14	15
21780		Evansville, IN-KY	1,464.0	313,946	164	214.4	87.9	9.0	0.6	2.2	2.8	5.6	12.7	12.6	13.0	12.6	11.8
21820		Fairbanks, AK	7,334.8	95,593	366	13.0	74.9	6.3	11.2	6.3	8.4	6.9	13.2	16.0	18.2	13.6	9.7
22020		Fargo, ND-MN	2,810.1	252,136	192	89.7	86.1	6.9	2.3	3.5	3.6	6.5	13.2	17.3	15.7	14.0	10.2
22140		Farmington, NM	5,517.2	120,993	328	21.9	37.9	1.1	40.4	1.1	21.8	5.8	14.9	13.4	13.0	13.2	10.8
22180		Fayetteville, NC	1,637.6	524,588	108	320.3	48.7	35.6	3.1	3.7	13.2	7.3	14.2	15.1	16.4	13.0	10.7
22220		Fayetteville-Springdale-Rogers, AR	2,623.4	560,709	102	213.7	73.6	3.4	2.5	6.0	17.2	6.5	14.1	15.1	14.7	14.2	11.6
22380		Flagstaff, AZ	18,616.4	145,052	291	7.8	55.8	2.0	26.6	3.4	14.9	4.9	11.5	23.3	13.9	11.4	9.9
22420		Flint, MI	636.9	404,208	135	634.6	74.4	21.8	1.3	1.6	3.9	5.7	12.6	12.4	12.8	11.7	12.5
22500		Florence, SC	1,361.1	199,259	226	146.4	52.7	43.6	0.7	1.7	2.9	5.8	13.2	12.8	12.4	11.9	12.4
22520		Florence-Muscle Shoals, AL	1,261.0	151,517	282	120.2	83.3	13.2	1.1	1.1	3.2	5.3	11.5	13.4	12.4	11.3	12.1
22540		Fond du Lac, WI	719.6	104,362	348	145.0	89.4	3.1	0.8	2.1	6.0	5.1	12.0	12.5	11.6	12.7	12.1
22660		Fort Collins, CO	2,595.8	362,533	150	139.7	83.6	1.8	1.1	3.5	12.4	4.4	10.8	17.3	14.8	13.0	11.0
22900		Fort Smith, AR-OK	2,409.0	245,459	193	101.9	76.0	5.4	8.0	3.7	11.3	6.2	13.4	12.6	12.7	12.2	12.2
23060		Fort Wayne, IN	992.9	423,038	130	426.1	76.6	12.6	0.8	5.4	7.7	6.7	14.3	13.2	14.0	12.6	11.7
23420		Fresno, CA	5,958.4	1,013,581	55	170.1	29.0	5.3	1.1	12.0	54.7	7.1	16.3	14.4	15.0	13.3	11.0
23460		Gadsden, AL	535.1	103,162	353	192.8	78.5	16.4	1.1	1.1	4.6	5.8	12.1	11.8	12.3	11.9	13.3
23540		Gainesville, FL	2,343.6	341,756	153	145.8	65.9	19.1	0.7	6.3	10.6	4.9	10.5	20.7	14.1	11.5	10.0
23580		Gainesville, GA	393.0	207,369	217	527.7	60.6	8.2	0.6	2.6	29.5	6.1	13.5	13.8	12.9	12.4	13.1
23900		Gettysburg, PA	518.7	104,127	349	200.7	89.8	2.4	0.5	1.3	7.4	4.6	11.4	12.8	11.0	10.9	12.4
24020		Glens Falls, NY	1,698.4	126,574	318	74.5	93.7	2.8	0.6	1.2	3.0	4.3	10.4	10.5	12.0	11.8	12.7
24140		Goldsboro, NC	553.9	116,835	334	210.9	53.6	32.6	1.0	2.2	13.3	6.4	13.4	13.7	13.5	11.5	11.6
24220		Grand Forks, ND-MN	3,407.2	103,462	351	30.4	85.9	4.5	3.5	3.2	5.5	6.4	12.6	19.3	14.1	11.9	9.3
24260		Grand Island, NE	1,603.0	76,175	379	47.5	69.9	2.9	0.8	1.5	25.8	7.0	15.1	12.5	12.2	12.6	11.4
24300		Grand Junction, CO	3,328.7	157,335	270	47.3	82.1	1.4	1.4	1.8	15.3	5.1	12.0	12.4	12.9	13.0	10.7
24340		Grand Rapids-Kentwood, MI	2,689.1	1,091,620	51	405.9	79.7	8.2	0.9	3.5	10.2	6.0	13.3	14.2	14.5	13.0	11.5
24420		Grants Pass, OR	1,638.6	88,346	369	53.9	88.4	1.1	3.1	2.3	8.3	4.7	11.1	9.8	11.2	11.1	10.9
24500		Great Falls, MT	2,698.2	84,511	371	31.3	87.7	2.4	6.4	2.2	5.2	6.1	12.9	12.6	14.0	12.1	10.1
24540		Greeley, CO	3,984.9	340,036	154	85.3	65.5	1.8	1.2	2.6	30.6	6.8	14.5	13.3	15.1	14.7	12.0
24580		Green Bay, WI	1,870.0	329,490	158	176.2	83.8	3.5	3.0	3.5	8.4	5.7	13.0	12.7	12.7	13.0	12.0
24660		Greensboro-High Point, NC	1,993.9	778,848	78	390.6	58.0	29.2	1.1	4.8	9.3	5.5	12.5	13.9	13.0	12.0	12.9
24780		Greenville, NC	652.4	172,169	252	263.9	54.8	37.1	0.8	2.7	6.9	5.6	12.0	21.0	13.7	11.7	10.9
24860		Greenville-Anderson, SC	2,709.6	940,774	60	347.2	73.5	17.5	0.6	2.7	7.7	5.6	12.6	13.6	13.2	12.4	12.4
25060		Gulfport-Biloxi, MS	2,215.9	418,082	133	188.7	69.1	23.2	1.0	3.3	5.9	5.8	13.0	12.6	13.1	12.7	12.2
25180		Hagerstown-Martinsburg, MD-WV	1,008.0	298,227	167	295.9	82.5	12.0	0.7	2.2	5.8	5.6	12.4	11.7	13.4	13.0	13.1
25220		Hammond, LA	791.2	135,217	306	170.9	63.8	31.0	0.9	1.1	4.7	6.8	13.8	13.5	14.4	12.9	11.2
25260		Hanford-Corcoran, CA	1,391.0	153,443	277	110.3	32.0	7.1	1.4	5.3	56.6	7.2	15.4	15.0	16.6	14.6	11.1
25420		Harrisburg-Carlisle, PA	1,621.8	596,305	97	367.7	76.4	12.0	0.6	6.1	7.5	5.6	12.3	12.1	13.3	12.8	12.2
25500		Harrisonburg, VA	867.1	135,824	302	156.6	79.8	5.5	0.6	3.0	13.0	5.5	11.2	21.1	12.1	11.8	10.8
25540		Hartford-East Hartford-Middletown, CT	1,514.6	1,211,906	48	800.1	66.5	12.4	0.6	6.3	16.2	4.9	11.2	13.7	12.9	12.7	12.4
25620		Hattiesburg, MS	2,023.7	173,078	251	85.5	65.4	30.8	0.6	1.4	3.1	6.3	13.6	14.7	14.0	13.0	11.5
25860		Hickory-Lenoir-Morganton, NC	1,639.5	366,441	149	223.5	81.1	8.1	0.7	3.6	8.2	5.1	11.4	11.7	12.1	11.4	13.6
25940		Hilton Head Island-Bluffton, SC	1,231.2	222,072	209	180.4	67.3	20.3	0.7	1.9	11.6	4.8	10.0	11.6	10.8	10.0	10.4
25980		Hinesville, GA	916.9	82,863	376	90.4	44.5	42.6	1.2	3.7	12.4	9.4	15.2	15.7	18.5	12.4	9.1
26140		Homosassa Springs, FL	581.9	158,083	268	271.7	88.2	3.7	1.0	2.2	6.7	3.6	8.5	7.9	8.7	8.4	10.2
26300		Hot Springs, AR	677.6	100,330	358	148.1	83.4	9.8	1.6	1.4	6.4	5.2	11.1	10.7	11.2	11.3	11.8
26380		Houma-Thibodaux, LA	2,297.6	206,212	221	89.8	72.9	17.8	5.3	1.4	5.1	6.2	13.8	12.3	13.3	13.2	11.8
26420		Houston-The Woodlands-Sugar Land, TX	8,268.7	7,206,841	5	871.6	35.5	18.1	0.6	8.9	38.6	6.7	15.0	13.5	14.4	14.6	12.8
26580		Huntington-Ashland, WV-KY-OH	2,499.9	356,581	151	142.6	95.2	3.3	0.8	1.1	1.4	5.2	12.0	12.7	11.7	12.1	12.8
26620		Huntsville, AL	1,361.6	502,728	113	369.2	68.8	23.3	1.5	3.4	5.7	5.5	12.4	12.6	14.0	13.1	12.6
26820		Idaho Falls, ID	5,196.2	162,786	263	31.3	84.5	0.9	1.2	1.8	13.2	7.5	18.0	13.6	13.1	13.7	10.3
26900		Indianapolis-Carmel-Anderson, IN	4,306.6	2,126,804	33	493.8	72.4	17.3	0.7	4.7	7.4	6.2	13.9	12.9	14.3	13.7	12.3
26980		Iowa City, IA	1,181.8	177,239	245	150.0	80.7	8.1	0.6	6.7	6.2	5.6	11.4	22.1	14.6	12.4	10.1
27060		Ithaca, NY	474.6	105,162	347	221.6	80.3	5.2	0.8	11.6	5.5	3.6	8.1	28.4	12.3	11.1	9.8
27100		Jackson, MI	701.9	160,050	266	228.0	86.9	10.0	1.0	1.4	3.9	5.4	12.1	12.1	12.9	11.9	12.5
27140		Jackson, MS	5,405.2	587,202	99	108.6	46.1	50.4	0.4	1.6	2.6	5.9	13.2	13.4	13.5	13.3	12.2
27180		Jackson, TN	1,711.2	180,799	240	105.7	66.9	28.6	0.6	1.2	4.5	5.9	13.0	13.6	12.4	11.8	11.9
27260		Jacksonville, FL	3,201.8	1,637,666	39	511.5	63.5	22.7	0.8	5.5	10.3	5.8	12.7	11.8	14.0	13.3	12.4
27340		Jacksonville, NC	762.1	206,160	222	270.5	69.0	16.6	1.5	4.0	13.4	7.9	13.2	24.6	17.3	11.4	7.6
27500		Janesville-Beloit, WI	718.2	164,381	260	228.9	83.7	6.5	0.7	1.9	9.7	5.7	12.8	12.5	12.3	12.7	12.4
27620		Jefferson City, MO	2,247.7	150,706	284	67.0	87.7	8.8	1.0	1.5	3.0	5.6	12.5	13.0	12.8	12.9	12.3
27740		Johnson City, TN	853.8	208,068	216	243.7	91.5	4.2	0.9	1.6	3.7	4.5	10.5	13.6	12.4	11.3	13.0
27780		Johnstown, PA	687.5	132,167	312	192.2	93.5	5.1	0.4	0.9	1.9	4.7	11.0	12.6	10.5	10.7	12.2

1. CBSA = Core Based Statistical Area. DIV = Metropolitan Division. See Appendix A for explanation. See Appendix B for list of metropolitan areas or temporarily covered by water. 2. Dry land or land partially or temporarily covered by water. 3. May be of any race.

Table C. Metropolitan Areas — **Population and Households**

Area name	Population, 2020 (cont.): Age (percent) (cont.): 55 to 64 years	Population, 2020 (cont.): Age (percent) (cont.): 65 to 74 years	Population, 2020 (cont.): Age (percent) (cont.): 75 years and over	Population, 2020 (cont.): Percent female	Population change and components of change, 2000–2020: Total persons: 2000	Population change and components of change, 2000–2020: Total persons: 2010	Population change and components of change, 2000–2020: Percent change: 2000–2010	Population change and components of change, 2000–2020: Percent change: 2010–2019	Population change and components of change, 2000–2020: Components of change, 2010–2020: Births	Population change and components of change, 2000–2020: Components of change, 2010–2020: Deaths	Population change and components of change, 2000–2020: Components of change, 2010–2020: Net migration	Households, 2016–2020: Number	Households, 2016–2020: Persons per household	Households, 2016–2020: Percent: Family households	Households, 2016–2020: Percent: Single parent households	Households, 2016–2020: Percent: One person
	16	17	18	19	20	21	22	23	24	25	26	27	28	29	30	31
Evansville, IN-KY	13.7	11.0	7.0	50.9	311,552	314,049	0.8	0.0	4,242	5,163	786	129,824	2.4	64.4	11.8	29.2
Fairbanks, AK	10.4	8.2	3.7	45.9	97,581	95,655	-2.0	-0.1	1,628	778	-928	36,199	2.6	65.9	7.9	25.1
Fargo, ND-MN	10.1	7.9	5.1	49.5	208,777	249,843	19.7	0.9	3,953	2,503	781	101,722	2.3	57.3	7.5	32.2
Farmington, NM	12.7	10.0	6.1	50.5	130,044	121,661	-6.4	-0.5	1,693	1,810	-576	43,582	2.8	71.1	15.8	24.5
Fayetteville, NC	10.8	7.9	4.7	50.4	481,061	520,378	8.2	0.8	9,473	6,253	875	192,505	2.6	64.0	15.7	31.4
Fayetteville-Springdale-Rogers, AR	10.7	8.1	5.1	49.8	440,121	546,725	24.2	2.6	8,351	5,751	11,364	194,800	2.7	68.4	10.4	24.0
Flagstaff, AZ	11.1	9.3	4.8	50.6	134,421	145,101	7.9	0.0	1,651	1,430	-306	49,016	2.6	59.4	12.0	26.9
Flint, MI	14.1	11.1	7.1	51.5	425,790	406,211	-4.6	-0.5	5,458	7,058	-477	170,581	2.4	63.6	15.6	30.4
Florence, SC	13.1	11.4	7.0	52.9	205,566	199,964	-2.7	-0.4	2,813	3,755	209	78,997	2.5	64.1	18.3	31.5
Florence-Muscle Shoals, AL	13.7	12.1	8.3	51.7	147,137	150,791	2.5	0.5	1,883	2,819	1,667	60,310	2.4	63.9	12.1	30.1
Fond du Lac, WI	14.7	11.6	7.7	50.4	101,633	104,154	2.5	0.2	1,240	1,456	416	41,890	2.4	65.6	6.7	28.4
Fort Collins, CO	11.8	10.7	6.2	50.0	299,630	359,066	19.8	1.0	3,691	3,454	3,185	134,185	2.5	62.5	7.0	24.6
Fort Smith, AR-OK	13.2	10.5	7.0	50.6	248,208	244,310	-1.6	0.5	3,784	4,037	1,372	98,199	2.5	67.1	12.6	27.8
Fort Wayne, IN	12.0	9.6	5.9	50.7	388,621	419,601	8.0	0.8	6,820	5,494	2,033	160,865	2.5	63.9	11.9	29.6
Fresno, CA	10.3	7.6	5.0	49.8	930,450	1,008,654	8.4	0.5	17,245	11,142	-1,499	310,097	3.1	72.3	17.1	22.2
Gadsden, AL	13.6	12.0	7.3	51.3	104,430	103,436	-1.0	-0.3	1,487	2,157	385	38,765	2.6	65.5	15.1	30.8
Gainesville, FL	11.3	10.2	6.6	51.4	305,076	339,247	11.2	0.7	3,940	4,206	2,731	125,651	2.5	52.5	10.9	35.6
Gainesville, GA	12.3	9.5	6.4	50.0	179,684	203,136	13.1	2.1	3,117	2,544	3,662	65,555	3.1	74.7	12.9	20.5
Gettysburg, PA	15.4	13.0	8.5	50.5	101,407	103,852	2.4	0.3	1,063	1,513	726	39,628	2.5	70.9	9.0	24.9
Glens Falls, NY	16.1	13.5	8.6	49.2	128,923	127,039	-1.5	-0.4	1,281	2,060	310	53,088	2.3	61.4	10.7	30.2
Goldsboro, NC	12.9	10.5	6.6	50.9	122,623	117,333	-4.3	-0.4	1,893	2,082	-326	48,198	2.5	66.7	16.8	28.8
Grand Forks, ND-MN	11.2	9.1	6.2	48.8	98,461	104,362	6.0	-0.9	1,533	1,255	-1,186	43,398	2.2	53.8	8.3	35.9
Grand Island, NE	12.6	9.7	6.8	49.2	72,726	77,038	5.9	-1.1	1,213	1,009	-1,062	29,558	2.5	67.3	12.2	26.8
Grand Junction, CO	13.4	12.6	7.9	50.3	146,723	155,703	6.1	1.0	1,911	2,298	2,019	59,750	2.5	62.8	9.7	29.7
Grand Rapids-Kentwood, MI	12.3	9.4	5.8	49.9	993,670	1,087,592	9.5	0.4	15,451	12,334	740	396,595	2.6	68.2	9.7	24.8
Grants Pass, OR	14.7	15.6	10.9	51.0	82,713	88,090	6.5	0.3	943	1,831	1,160	36,606	2.4	67.3	10.1	26.2
Great Falls, MT	12.9	11.3	8.0	49.2	81,327	84,414	3.8	0.1	1,216	1,295	166	34,440	2.3	60.8	10.0	33.1
Greeley, CO	11.0	8.1	4.6	49.2	252,825	328,981	30.1	3.4	5,467	2,898	8,503	102,046	3.0	73.6	10.1	20.8
Green Bay, WI	14.0	10.6	6.3	49.8	306,241	328,268	7.2	0.4	4,382	3,924	698	130,563	2.4	64.1	8.8	28.4
Greensboro-High Point, NC	13.2	10.2	6.7	52.0	723,801	776,566	7.3	0.3	10,160	11,376	3,382	303,556	2.5	64.1	14.5	29.9
Greenville, NC	10.9	9.0	5.3	53.0	168,148	170,243	1.2	1.1	2,421	2,194	1,676	70,683	2.5	60.0	16.5	28.8
Greenville-Anderson, SC	13.0	10.4	6.8	51.2	824,112	928,195	12.6	1.4	12,526	13,417	13,439	350,728	2.5	66.8	12.4	27.3
Gulfport-Biloxi, MS	13.7	10.6	6.2	50.9	388,488	416,259	7.1	0.4	5,872	6,569	2,462	161,773	2.5	66.6	15.8	28.4
Hagerstown-Martinsburg, MD-WV	13.8	10.4	6.6	49.3	269,140	293,844	9.2	1.5	3,902	4,419	4,918	109,554	2.5	66.7	11.1	27.1
Hammond, LA	12.2	9.8	5.4	51.3	121,097	133,157	10.0	1.5	2,259	1,986	1,774	48,548	2.7	66.3	17.2	28.0
Hanford-Corcoran, CA	9.4	6.4	4.3	44.7	152,982	152,486	-0.3	0.6	2,718	1,345	-466	43,604	3.1	78.3	16.7	17.1
Harrisburg-Carlisle, PA	13.4	11.1	7.3	50.5	549,475	591,712	7.7	0.8	7,681	8,112	4,997	233,447	2.4	63.5	11.0	29.9
Harrisonburg, VA	11.5	9.4	6.6	50.9	125,228	135,571	8.3	0.2	1,750	1,568	70	48,057	2.6	64.8	10.2	26.6
Hartford-East Hartford-Middletown, CT	14.2	10.5	7.6	50.9	1,212,381	1,213,531	0.1	-0.1	13,674	16,270	792	477,495	2.4	63.9	12.6	29.3
Hattiesburg, MS	11.8	9.1	6.0	52.1	162,410	172,231	6.0	0.5	2,574	2,334	588	62,222	2.6	67.6	16.7	26.4
Hickory-Lenoir-Morganton, NC	14.8	12.0	7.9	50.2	365,497	365,276	-0.1	0.3	4,318	6,231	3,070	145,451	2.5	68.2	12.2	27.3
Hilton Head Island-Bluffton, SC	14.7	16.6	11.1	50.9	187,010	215,908	15.5	2.9	2,670	3,124	6,699	84,955	2.5	68.2	10.4	26.5
Hinesville, GA	9.4	6.7	3.5	49.3	77,917	81,424	4.5	1.8	2,084	731	88	30,059	2.6	69.6	17.8	25.4
Homosassa Springs, FL	16.4	20.0	16.3	51.2	141,236	153,843	8.9	2.8	1,298	4,115	7,185	64,621	2.3	62.0	9.0	32.2
Hot Springs, AR	14.3	14.3	10.1	51.5	96,024	100,180	4.3	0.1	1,282	2,094	969	40,906	2.4	63.7	13.2	31.1
Houma-Thibodaux, LA	13.7	9.6	6.2	50.6	208,178	207,137	-0.5	-0.4	2,973	3,019	-920	77,019	2.7	68.4	14.5	24.9
Houston-The Woodlands-Sugar Land, TX	11.1	7.7	4.2	50.2	5,920,416	7,122,240	20.3	1.2	112,367	65,284	37,397	2,407,993	2.9	70.7	13.9	24.1
Huntington-Ashland, WV-KY-OH	13.4	11.9	8.1	50.7	370,908	359,862	-3.0	-0.9	4,486	6,821	-973	141,577	2.5	64.7	11.7	30.1
Huntsville, AL	14.2	9.4	6.1	50.4	417,593	491,723	17.8	2.2	6,365	6,471	11,145	184,353	2.5	64.7	12.1	30.1
Idaho Falls, ID	10.3	8.4	5.0	49.6	133,265	157,429	18.1	3.4	2,810	1,670	4,248	50,737	2.9	71.9	9.8	23.6
Indianapolis-Carmel-Anderson, IN	12.3	8.9	5.4	50.8	1,887,877	2,111,040	11.8	0.7	31,254	25,984	10,494	790,050	2.6	63.8	11.7	29.5
Iowa City, IA	10.1	8.6	5.2	50.3	152,586	175,419	15.0	1.0	2,441	1,530	867	69,306	2.4	56.2	7.5	28.6
Ithaca, NY	11.0	9.9	5.9	50.7	101,564	105,740	4.1	-0.5	852	1,019	-435	40,817	2.2	52.5	8.5	29.7
Jackson, MI	14.4	11.5	7.2	48.7	160,248	160,366	0.1	-0.2	2,012	2,502	148	62,216	2.4	64.1	12.0	30.8
Jackson, MS	12.7	9.9	5.9	51.8	586,320	591,978	1.0	-0.8	8,699	8,644	-4,841	219,801	2.6	66.0	18.7	29.7
Jackson, TN	13.4	10.8	7.1	52.1	179,694	180,504	0.5	0.2	2,565	3,239	951	69,505	2.5	66.5	15.3	29.3
Jacksonville, FL	13.3	10.4	6.2	51.0	1,345,596	1,605,848	19.3	2.0	22,270	21,452	31,186	578,620	2.6	65.8	13.5	27.7
Jacksonville, NC	8.1	6.2	3.7	44.3	177,772	204,576	15.1	0.8	4,485	1,791	-1,150	66,131	2.7	71.1	11.1	22.0
Janesville-Beloit, WI	14.2	10.6	6.8	50.4	160,331	163,687	2.1	0.4	2,281	2,334	728	65,237	2.5	63.7	11.7	29.6
Jefferson City, MO	13.4	10.7	6.8	48.8	149,807	150,309	0.3	0.3	1,987	2,155	549	57,247	2.5	65.4	9.0	29.3
Johnson City, TN	14.0	12.3	8.4	50.7	198,716	207,285	4.3	0.4	2,167	3,776	2,393	86,279	2.3	62.5	10.5	31.5
Johnstown, PA	14.9	14.0	9.5	50.3	143,679	133,472	-7.1	-1.0	1,459	2,680	-87	56,933	2.2	61.5	10.7	33.6

Area name	Persons in group quarters, 2020	Daytime population, 2019		Births, 2020		Deaths, 2020		Persons under 65 with no health insurance 2019		Medicare, 2020			Serious crimes known to police[2], 2019	
													Violent	
		Number	Employ-ment/ residence ratio	Total	Rate[1]	Number	Rate[1]	Number	Percent	Total Ben-eficiaries	Enrolled in Original Medicare	Enrolled in Medicare Advantage	Number	Rate[3]
	32	33	34	35	36	37	38	39	40	41	42	43	44	45
Evansville, IN-KY	8,583	321,777	1.04	3,437	10.9	4,100	13.1	23,268	9.2	67,872	40,759	27,113	1,601	508.0
Fairbanks, AK	4,562	97,481	0.98	1,276	13.4	641	6.7	9,282	11.3	12,466	12,320	146	277	841.4
Fargo, ND-MN	8,112	249,178	1.04	3,079	12.3	2,009	8.0	12,299	5.9	37,724	25,727	11,997	871	350.7
Farmington, NM	1,446	124,510	0.98	1,320	10.9	1,440	11.9	15,208	14.8	7,197	4,017	3,180	817	661.0
Fayetteville, NC	19,191	510,849	0.95	7,592	14.5	5,039	9.6	59,697	13.6	85,295	50,024	35,271	2,938	553.2
Fayetteville-Springdale-Rogers, AR	9,837	533,097	1.03	6,693	12.1	4,655	8.4	57,369	12.5	86,896	52,495	34,401	NA	NA
Flagstaff, AZ	11,896	142,573	1.00	1,304	9.0	1,182	8.1	17,084	15.2	22,304	16,596	5,708	NA	NA
Flint, MI	5,412	387,756	0.89	4,387	10.8	5,581	13.8	21,718	6.6	91,694	39,225	52,469	2,324	577.6
Florence, SC	3,852	211,019	1.07	2,274	11.4	2,994	15.0	20,482	12.6	45,762	29,738	16,024	1,764	860.2
Florence-Muscle Shoals, AL	2,747	145,672	0.97	1,496	9.9	2,284	15.1	13,292	11.5	36,915	21,113	15,802	NA	NA
Fond du Lac, WI	3,231	99,030	0.93	995	9.5	1,146	11.0	4,835	6.0	22,918	9,300	13,618	181	174.9
Fort Collins, CO	9,675	348,546	0.99	2,960	8.2	2,759	7.6	22,447	7.7	68,337	38,830	29,507	NA	NA
Fort Smith, AR-OK	3,019	251,704	1.01	3,031	12.4	3,248	13.3	29,262	14.3	55,509	32,760	22,749	1,541	614.9
Fort Wayne, IN	6,268	416,730	1.04	5,469	13.0	4,387	10.4	35,922	10.4	77,196	33,652	43,544	1,392	334.9
Fresno, CA	17,384	992,126	1.00	13,817	13.7	8,865	8.8	82,348	9.7	147,639	90,904	56,735	5,948	596.7
Gadsden, AL	1,975	97,391	0.87	1,200	11.6	1,751	17.0	10,281	12.7	25,984	12,020	13,964	NA	NA
Gainesville, FL	16,248	335,149	1.05	3,170	9.3	3,421	10.0	35,108	13.5	64,471	41,282	23,189	2,516	760.3
Gainesville, GA	2,663	203,563	1.02	2,503	12.2	2,022	9.8	36,780	21.6	37,067	20,843	16,224	479	231.4
Gettysburg, PA	3,951	87,661	0.70	850	8.2	1,213	11.7	6,014	7.7	25,867	16,476	9,391	NA	NA
Glens Falls, NY	3,542	120,928	0.92	1,001	7.9	1,641	13.0	4,472	4.7	33,294	15,950	17,344	156	125.9
Goldsboro, NC	2,459	122,351	0.97	1,540	13.2	1,657	14.2	15,268	15.4	24,709	14,815	9,894	593	481.4
Grand Forks, ND-MN	4,165	103,448	1.03	1,220	11.8	983	9.5	5,037	6.1	18,012	13,073	4,939	233	232.6
Grand Island, NE	969	77,331	1.05	961	12.6	810	10.6	7,597	12.2	14,240	10,779	3,461	257	340.5
Grand Junction, CO	4,310	151,697	0.98	1,529	9.8	1,877	12.0	13,094	10.9	36,942	23,090	13,852	565	366.6
Grand Rapids-Kentwood, MI	27,946	1,100,777	1.06	12,211	11.2	9,773	9.0	63,094	7.0	194,399	66,634	127,765	3,793	350.1
Grants Pass, OR	1,520	86,781	0.99	748	8.5	1,443	16.4	6,416	10.3	27,122	14,358	12,764	252	287.7
Great Falls, MT	2,432	81,472	1.00	961	11.4	1,024	12.1	6,236	9.7	18,446	12,850	5,596	359	440.3
Greeley, CO	5,434	285,728	0.81	4,333	12.9	2,340	7.0	30,273	10.9	48,333	25,242	23,091	1,074	324.2
Green Bay, WI	6,679	329,070	1.05	3,517	10.7	3,131	9.5	20,110	7.6	64,983	24,544	40,439	730	225.0
Greensboro-High Point, NC	21,827	790,641	1.07	8,157	10.5	8,962	11.5	87,041	14.0	155,056	56,999	98,057	4,479	576.2
Greenville, NC	5,906	183,472	1.04	1,931	11.3	1,780	10.4	17,828	12.0	31,751	19,837	11,914	664	364.6
Greenville-Anderson, SC	23,223	914,574	1.01	10,007	10.7	10,668	11.4	98,876	13.3	193,863	109,618	84,245	NA	NA
Gulfport-Biloxi, MS	7,666	417,161	1.01	4,755	11.4	5,205	12.5	53,983	15.8	85,676	53,742	31,934	NA	NA
Hagerstown-Martinsburg, MD-WV	9,279	264,801	0.84	3,105	10.5	3,490	11.8	17,292	7.5	60,136	46,339	13,797	NA	NA
Hammond, LA	3,350	123,993	0.82	1,863	13.9	1,617	12.0	11,986	10.8	24,667	11,848	12,819	NA	NA
Hanford-Corcoran, CA	15,702	151,242	1.00	2,176	14.2	1,083	7.1	11,212	9.4	18,117	12,973	5,144	777	513.0
Harrisburg-Carlisle, PA	19,447	621,005	1.16	6,109	10.3	6,540	11.0	34,243	7.5	125,311	62,718	62,593	NA	NA
Harrisonburg, VA	8,934	142,498	1.12	1,414	10.4	1,271	9.4	12,650	12.1	24,466	19,560	4,906	207	152.2
Hartford-East Hartford-Middletown, CT	43,955	1,238,174	1.05	10,895	9.0	12,980	10.7	54,047	5.6	245,577	108,608	136,969	2,211	217.9
Hattiesburg, MS	3,382	169,856	1.02	2,079	12.0	1,886	10.9	21,465	15.3	30,967	19,863	11,104	422	249.8
Hickory-Lenoir-Morganton, NC	7,318	363,090	0.97	3,453	9.4	4,944	13.5	44,242	15.2	85,878	42,497	43,381	NA	NA
Hilton Head Island-Bluffton, SC	6,033	220,681	1.01	2,146	9.8	2,540	11.6	23,468	15.1	63,549	45,150	18,399	741	326.9
Hinesville, GA	2,552	81,320	1.00	1,690	20.6	564	6.9	9,527	13.5	10,187	6,020	4,167	NA	NA
Homosassa Springs, FL	2,146	141,956	0.87	1,038	6.6	3,242	20.7	15,868	17.1	61,673	32,462	29,211	405	269.7
Hot Springs, AR	2,036	100,739	1.04	1,030	10.3	1,657	16.5	8,848	12.0	29,251	18,344	10,907	582	583.4
Houma-Thibodaux, LA	2,791	210,445	1.01	2,391	11.6	2,435	11.8	21,772	12.6	63,091	40,415	22,676	NA	NA
Houston-The Woodlands-Sugar Land, TX	77,686	6,995,287	1.00	90,385	12.6	52,856	7.4	1,336,522	21.7	937,441	447,932	489,509	45,368	631.8
Huntington-Ashland, WV-KY-OH	7,656	354,343	0.96	3,611	10.1	5,428	15.2	21,141	7.6	86,828	48,246	38,582	850	240.2
Huntsville, AL	10,899	485,972	1.10	5,109	10.3	5,179	10.4	37,772	9.7	89,316	55,505	33,811	NA	NA
Idaho Falls, ID	1,391	153,082	1.06	2,243	14.0	1,322	8.2	14,856	11.4	25,333	17,135	8,198	439	283.6
Indianapolis-Carmel-Anderson, IN	39,406	2,066,534	1.02	25,108	11.8	20,801	9.8	172,296	9.9	354,717	197,612	157,105	NA	NA
Iowa City, IA	8,472	178,846	1.06	1,942	11.0	1,239	7.0	8,528	6.0	27,459	20,585	6,874	475	271.0
Ithaca, NY	13,418	113,392	1.22	661	6.3	825	7.8	3,475	4.7	17,639	10,802	6,837	163	160.5
Jackson, MI	7,734	152,195	0.91	1,575	9.8	2,025	12.6	8,320	6.9	35,653	19,394	16,259	881	558.3
Jackson, MS	22,127	603,929	1.03	7,037	11.9	6,896	11.7	67,708	14.1	113,399	73,885	39,514	NA	NA
Jackson, TN	6,759	185,574	1.09	2,032	11.3	2,492	13.8	16,604	11.8	40,137	25,642	14,495	1,115	624.6
Jacksonville, FL	27,740	1,540,789	1.01	17,934	11.0	17,313	10.7	170,529	13.3	313,533	183,925	129,608	7,901	499.8
Jacksonville, NC	25,150	197,878	1.00	3,599	17.5	1,397	6.8	16,678	10.6	27,673	21,116	6,557	419	210.3
Janesville-Beloit, WI	2,384	152,750	0.88	1,817	11.1	1,866	11.4	9,273	7.0	34,699	19,738	14,961	381	232.9
Jefferson City, MO	8,770	156,348	1.07	1,599	10.6	1,689	11.2	13,309	11.5	31,039	17,827	13,212	251	165.9
Johnson City, TN	5,392	200,716	0.97	1,770	8.5	3,005	14.5	19,796	12.5	51,639	22,444	29,195	625	306.1
Johnstown, PA	5,985	128,163	0.94	1,154	8.7	2,076	15.7	5,487	5.8	37,017	11,434	25,583	NA	NA

1. Per 1,000 estimated resident population. 2. Data for serious crimes have not been adjusted for underreporting; this may affect comparability between geographic areas and over time. 3. Per 100,000 population estimated by the FBI.

Area name	Serious crimes known to police[1], 2019 (cont.) — Property — Number	Serious crimes known to police[1], 2019 (cont.) — Property — Rate[2]	Education — School enrollment and attainment, 2019 — Enrollment[3] — Total	Education — School enrollment and attainment, 2019 — Enrollment[3] — Percent private	Education — School enrollment and attainment, 2019 — Attainment[4] — High school gradu-ate or less	Education — School enrollment and attainment, 2019 — Attainment[4] — Bach-elor's degree or more	Education — Local government expenditures,[5] 2017–2018 — Total current expendi-tures (mil dol)	Education — Local government expenditures,[5] 2017–2018 — Current expen-ditures per student (dollars)	Income and poverty, 2016–2020 — Per capita income[6] (dollars)	Income and poverty, 2016–2020 — Median house-hold income (dollars)	Income and poverty, 2016–2020 — Median family income	Income and poverty, 2016–2020 — Percent of house-holds with income less than $50,000	Income and poverty, 2016–2020 — Percent of house-holds with income of $200,000 or more	Percent below poverty level — All persons	Percent below poverty level — All fami-lies	Percent below poverty level — Age 65 years and older
	46	47	48	49	50	51	52	53	54	55	56	57	58	59	60	61
Evansville, IN-KY	6,557	2,080.5	73,817	19.1	41.4	26.5	470.1	10,609	31,696	55,553	72,963	44.6	4.0	13.8	9.6	16.7
Fairbanks, AK	1,367	4,152.2	25,500	15.2	29.6	32.3	260.6	17,079	38,031	76,464	89,208	28.8	8.4	6.5	3.7	5.2
Fargo, ND-MN	7,027	2,829.3	68,663	12.7	24.9	39.1	463.5	12,834	36,064	65,995	90,450	37.1	6.5	11.2	6.2	10.0
Farmington, NM	2,026	1,639.1	32,859	8.9	43.0	15.4	231.9	9,894	22,840	47,643	55,199	51.4	2.2	21.7	17.1	26.9
Fayetteville, NC	12,396	2,334.0	145,420	18.1	37.2	23.9	765.4	9,328	25,134	50,133	61,027	49.9	2.7	18.0	14.1	20.6
Fayetteville-Springdale-Rogers, AR	NA	NA	141,436	11.9	40.9	33.2	925.0	9,937	32,942	61,761	75,899	40.0	7.4	12.1	8.6	12.2
Flagstaff, AZ	NA	NA	48,201	7.3	30.7	37.6	185.5	10,419	27,631	59,000	74,357	42.1	5.2	17.1	9.4	14.1
Flint, MI	5,823	1,447.2	94,933	10.6	41.0	21.5	768.8	12,208	28,696	50,269	62,084	49.7	3.6	18.0	12.9	22.4
Florence, SC	7,384	3,600.8	49,908	15.1	48.9	22.0	372.8	11,346	25,454	45,037	58,215	53.7	2.9	18.7	14.5	22.1
Florence-Muscle Shoals, AL	NA	NA	32,846	11.0	48.2	22.2	223.5	10,870	27,524	48,244	65,316	51.3	2.4	14.0	9.9	16.1
Fond du Lac, WI	1,187	1,146.7	23,353	23.1	43.4	23.9	153.5	11,737	32,508	64,147	81,968	37.2	3.3	8.2	5.5	10.4
Fort Collins, CO	NA	NA	96,273	11.7	22.4	47.7	512.9	10,737	38,142	76,366	96,221	32.6	8.5	11.1	4.7	7.4
Fort Smith, AR-OK	7,224	2,882.6	58,108	9.4	49.5	19.5	416.6	9,910	26,005	46,424	56,536	53.3	2.7	17.8	12.1	20.9
Fort Wayne, IN	7,266	1,748.2	103,305	24.1	39.3	28.4	608.2	9,929	30,123	57,693	71,896	43.0	4.0	12.4	9.0	15.2
Fresno, CA	24,724	2,480.5	296,119	7.9	45.3	22.0	2,865.1	14,128	25,757	57,109	64,036	44.6	5.7	20.8	16.7	24.4
Gadsden, AL	NA	NA	21,923	8.2	48.1	17.7	145.5	9,566	25,094	44,934	59,713	54.6	2.1	16.0	12.7	22.0
Gainesville, FL	7,414	2,240.5	104,413	10.8	33.3	37.8	371.9	9,474	28,546	47,848	67,742	51.6	4.8	20.1	10.4	15.9
Gainesville, GA	2,631	1,270.9	50,271	10.8	48.9	24.0	369.1	10,516	30,459	63,651	74,139	38.1	6.3	14.0	10.3	17.1
Gettysburg, PA	NA	NA	22,741	25.4	50.3	22.6	293.4	21,115	32,312	68,411	84,709	35.4	4.7	7.9	5.3	10.5
Glens Falls, NY	914	737.5	23,579	15.1	44.2	26.4	361.5	20,835	33,989	62,284	77,435	39.6	4.5	9.7	5.9	10.7
Goldsboro, NC	3,094	2,512.0	30,727	13.4	44.8	19.8	185.8	9,562	26,362	47,221	59,689	52.5	3.0	18.7	15.0	24.7
Grand Forks, ND-MN	1,762	1,758.7	29,430	7.8	30.1	33.2	187.8	13,009	31,503	55,122	82,257	45.6	3.8	14.3	7.5	11.1
Grand Island, NE	1,383	1,832.2	17,949	10.2	44.5	20.8	180.1	12,184	29,256	57,938	70,828	43.7	3.3	10.9	8.0	14.2
Grand Junction, CO	4,594	2,980.7	35,695	11.5	37.7	27.4	253.0	11,142	29,783	57,157	72,740	44.7	3.7	13.0	8.5	16.1
Grand Rapids-Kentwood, MI	13,853	1,278.7	276,224	19.2	35.1	33.7	2,084.1	12,242	32,489	66,297	80,705	36.9	5.8	10.3	6.4	10.3
Grants Pass, OR	1,500	1,712.8	16,977	17.8	39.3	18.1	131.9	12,054	27,026	47,733	57,003	51.5	3.3	16.0	11.6	18.1
Great Falls, MT	3,261	3,999.8	17,682	13.6	39.0	27.3	122.7	10,523	30,572	52,049	67,789	48.0	3.4	13.5	8.8	15.4
Greeley, CO	7,165	2,162.8	85,420	9.4	39.8	27.6	459.3	10,253	32,399	74,332	85,167	32.2	6.4	10.3	6.8	9.7
Green Bay, WI	3,216	991.1	77,268	16.0	39.6	27.9	624.2	11,974	33,727	64,951	81,870	38.0	4.7	9.4	6.6	11.0
Greensboro-High Point, NC	20,792	2,674.6	193,244	15.9	39.4	30.0	1,119.2	9,725	29,798	52,233	65,831	48.0	4.5	15.5	11.6	18.7
Greenville, NC	3,665	2,012.3	59,528	8.3	35.2	32.1	240.4	9,715	27,599	49,337	63,272	50.5	3.7	20.8	12.9	21.0
Greenville-Anderson, SC	NA	NA	223,463	18.7	39.1	30.9	1,335.1	9,962	31,577	57,432	71,958	44.0	5.6	13.1	8.8	14.4
Gulfport-Biloxi, MS	NA	NA	98,453	13.0	40.1	23.2	614.4	9,366	27,577	51,058	62,967	49.0	3.6	16.6	13.8	21.4
Hagerstown-Martinsburg, MD-WV	NA	NA	63,617	13.0	47.9	22.3	559.9	12,571	31,372	64,118	77,963	38.7	4.6	11.2	8.0	13.0
Hammond, LA	NA	NA	33,222	18.0	53.0	22.0	202.6	10,334	25,628	48,745	62,373	50.7	3.1	20.2	15.8	24.1
Hanford-Corcoran, CA	2,506	1,654.4	44,433	13.6	52.3	15.0	393.3	14,786	22,919	61,556	64,353	40.9	4.1	16.0	13.1	18.2
Harrisburg-Carlisle, PA	NA	NA	129,846	20.3	41.6	33.4	1,232.4	15,070	36,286	67,219	84,347	35.9	6.3	9.6	6.5	11.7
Harrisonburg, VA	1,335	981.9	42,115	15.9	47.9	29.7	224.2	12,219	29,421	59,261	72,527	42.7	4.0	14.4	7.3	10.5
Hartford-East Hartford-Middletown, CT	21,196	2,088.9	301,853	15.9	34.8	39.6	3,580.8	20,231	42,203	78,631	101,543	32.5	11.1	10.0	6.6	10.6
Hattiesburg, MS	3,743	2,215.6	44,997	15.4	40.5	27.1	243.2	9,348	26,504	48,231	58,430	52.1	3.6	22.1	16.9	25.0
Hickory-Lenoir-Morganton, NC	NA	NA	77,375	14.5	48.3	18.9	495.4	9,473	27,066	49,706	60,878	50.3	3.2	14.2	10.3	17.1
Hilton Head Island-Bluffton, SC	3,354	1,479.8	41,895	17.8	31.4	39.3	315.2	12,716	38,888	67,723	79,770	37.0	8.3	10.6	7.3	14.3
Hinesville, GA	NA	NA	21,393	11.6	42.1	18.1	147.6	10,615	23,750	50,588	54,993	49.4	1.8	16.1	14.0	20.0
Homosassa Springs, FL	1,928	1,283.7	22,302	16.4	48.5	18.9	145.7	9,416	28,174	45,689	57,253	54.8	2.7	15.0	10.1	23.3
Hot Springs, AR	3,575	3,583.5	19,650	8.8	41.8	22.8	151.9	9,933	27,274	48,150	60,892	51.2	2.5	17.0	11.2	22.0
Houma-Thibodaux, LA	NA	NA	48,564	19.2	59.8	16.3	325.8	10,253	27,834	53,267	65,137	48.0	4.0	18.1	14.0	21.9
Houston-The Woodlands-Sugar Land, TX	187,935	2,617.4	1,920,741	12.3	38.5	33.6	12,982.1	9,617	35,125	69,328	81,859	36.5	10.2	13.5	10.6	15.2
Huntington-Ashland, WV-KY-OH	5,213	1,472.9	80,599	9.0	49.5	21.0	662.1	11,845	26,330	48,085	61,976	51.6	3.1	18.6	13.6	21.2
Huntsville, AL	NA	NA	117,688	18.4	31.2	39.8	662.4	9,562	36,211	66,450	85,279	39.0	7.5	11.7	8.5	14.4
Idaho Falls, ID	1,994	1,288.2	42,994	15.7	33.1	29.5	233.1	6,995	27,734	61,877	73,934	38.8	5.1	9.7	7.5	11.4
Indianapolis-Carmel-Anderson, IN	NA	NA	510,478	17.3	37.3	35.6	3,638.9	10,263	34,755	63,545	80,981	39.0	6.9	11.5	7.9	12.6
Iowa City, IA	2,623	1,496.7	59,685	8.2	24.1	49.7	269.0	11,659	35,174	63,131	93,237	40.9	7.3	16.0	6.6	10.6
Ithaca, NY	1,924	1,894.1	39,884	56.4	24.0	53.1	252.3	22,750	34,194	61,361	87,977	41.7	7.8	17.5	5.5	10.3
Jackson, MI	2,641	1,673.7	35,772	13.7	41.4	22.5	303.4	13,202	29,141	54,511	67,657	45.8	3.4	12.4	8.6	16.2
Jackson, MS	NA	NA	157,597	19.5	37.1	31.1	854.4	9,353	28,821	53,639	67,202	46.9	5.0	16.7	12.1	18.9
Jackson, TN	3,840	2,151.0	42,176	23.8	49.8	21.9	252.2	9,076	25,251	48,146	58,697	51.5	2.9	17.6	13.6	22.6
Jacksonville, FL	34,037	2,153.1	366,013	19.0	36.6	32.1	2,029.7	8,898	34,228	63,064	76,537	39.1	6.6	12.3	8.9	13.9
Jacksonville, NC	3,151	1,581.6	48,092	12.8	37.0	23.6	242.0	8,954	24,817	51,560	57,756	48.2	1.9	12.4	10.3	15.0
Janesville-Beloit, WI	2,916	1,782.9	38,517	14.0	42.9	23.5	341.0	12,529	29,924	59,519	72,372	42.6	2.8	12.2	8.8	14.2
Jefferson City, MO	2,465	1,629.2	34,284	25.1	43.3	28.9	204.4	9,312	29,535	60,586	75,505	40.1	2.8	9.6	7.3	12.5
Johnson City, TN	4,371	2,140.7	44,091	13.9	44.8	26.8	252.9	9,509	27,870	45,970	60,890	53.7	3.1	16.5	11.5	18.9
Johnstown, PA	NA	NA	27,699	21.4	52.3	22.0	242.5	14,269	27,173	47,644	65,560	51.8	2.0	14.5	9.3	18.4

1. Data for serious crimes have not been adjusted for underreporting; this may affect comparability between geographic areas and over time. 2. Per 100,000 population estimated by the FBI. 3. All persons 3 years old and over enrolled in nursery school through college. 4. Persons 25 years old and over. 5. Elementary and secondary education expenditures. 6. Based on population estimated by the American Community Survey, 2015.

Area name	Personal income, 2019: Total (mil dol)	Personal income, 2019: Percent change, 2018–2019	Personal income, 2019: Per capita[1]: Dollars	Personal income, 2019: Per capita[1]: Rank	Personal income, 2019: Wages and Salaries (mil dol)	Personal income, 2019: Supplements to wages and salaries, employer contributions (mil dol): Pension and insurance	Personal income, 2019: Supplements to wages and salaries, employer contributions (mil dol): Government social insurance	Personal income, 2019: Proprietors' income	Personal income, 2019: Dividends, interest, and rent (mil dol)	Personal income, 2019: Personal transfer receipts (mil dol)	Earnings, 2019: Contributions for government social insurance (mil dol): Total (mil dol)	Earnings, 2019: Contributions for government social insurance (mil dol): From employee and self-employed	Earnings, 2019: Contributions for government social insurance (mil dol): From employer
	62	63	64	65	66	67	68	69	70	71	72	73	74
Evansville, IN-KY	16,322	5.4	51,695	169	7,929	1,303	596	1,040	2,699	4,193	10,869	717	596
Fairbanks, AK	5,955	3.6	62,254	46	2,781	826	221	216	1,107	1,160	4,043	197	221
Fargo, ND-MN	14,458	6.0	58,158	82	7,760	1,113	626	1,185	2,997	2,417	10,685	677	626
Farmington, NM	4,731	5.7	38,370	377	2,201	393	164	177	645	1,576	2,934	202	164
Fayetteville, NC	21,684	7.9	40,972	363	11,041	2,751	933	849	3,655	6,947	15,574	859	933
Fayetteville-Springdale-Rogers, AR	38,451	4.3	70,085	17	15,342	1,781	1,077	1,182	16,931	5,011	19,383	1,337	1,077
Flagstaff, AZ	7,557	7.5	53,036	142	2,961	591	222	560	1,669	1,837	4,335	266	222
Flint, MI	18,682	9.8	46,152	284	6,625	1,095	505	931	2,551	6,800	9,156	678	505
Florence, SC	9,221	6.6	45,178	301	4,498	803	327	444	1,347	2,833	6,072	419	327
Florence-Muscle Shoals, AL	6,127	7.6	41,181	361	2,435	421	185	298	1,022	1,921	3,338	251	185
Fond du Lac, WI	5,435	5.6	52,813	144	2,475	454	193	413	862	1,238	3,536	232	193
Fort Collins, CO	21,166	5.9	58,725	75	9,930	1,394	674	1,462	4,660	3,662	13,460	776	674
Fort Smith, AR-OK	10,218	5.5	40,801	365	4,589	681	358	694	1,582	3,217	6,322	469	358
Fort Wayne, IN	20,928	6.1	50,238	196	10,937	1,699	831	1,590	3,404	4,892	15,057	966	831
Fresno, CA	48,539	13.1	48,495	231	20,364	4,388	1,542	5,018	5,955	14,865	31,312	1,746	1,542
Gadsden, AL	4,080	5.6	39,852	374	1,433	236	111	245	518	1,515	2,024	161	111
Gainesville, FL	15,861	7.5	47,729	251	8,206	1,477	570	637	3,118	3,790	10,890	686	570
Gainesville, GA	10,073	6.2	48,759	225	5,116	764	339	716	1,849	2,190	6,936	425	339
Gettysburg, PA	5,566	6.6	54,172	131	1,582	312	127	396	925	1,415	2,416	161	127
Glens Falls, NY	6,600	8.7	53,074	140	2,510	581	205	432	1,035	1,945	3,728	229	205
Goldsboro, NC	5,316	6.9	42,882	341	2,171	454	171	366	814	1,589	3,163	201	171
Grand Forks, ND-MN	5,732	10.4	57,102	92	2,689	488	228	626	1,033	1,205	4,031	239	228
Grand Island, NE	3,644	7.4	48,375	234	1,835	319	141	337	646	832	2,633	165	141
Grand Junction, CO	7,537	6.2	48,435	232	3,174	478	236	578	1,311	2,053	4,467	288	236
Grand Rapids-Kentwood, MI	58,434	7.5	54,037	133	30,184	4,769	2,233	4,377	11,056	12,682	41,562	2,618	2,233
Grants Pass, OR	4,131	7.8	46,913	267	1,244	220	114	454	693	1,588	2,032	161	114
Great Falls, MT	4,248	6.1	52,226	157	1,906	341	170	252	845	1,085	2,668	179	170
Greeley, CO	17,385	9.4	52,054	160	6,476	873	463	1,744	2,383	3,048	9,556	542	463
Green Bay, WI	17,837	5.5	55,159	115	9,807	1,725	716	1,247	3,111	3,428	13,494	844	716
Greensboro-High Point, NC	36,622	6.6	47,171	263	19,103	2,773	1,366	2,636	5,968	9,316	25,879	1,719	1,366
Greenville, NC	8,262	6.3	45,169	302	4,061	797	289	608	1,316	2,067	5,755	359	289
Greenville-Anderson, SC	44,617	6.4	47,836	246	21,812	3,398	1,583	2,815	7,364	10,851	29,608	2,006	1,583
Gulfport-Biloxi, MS	17,224	8.7	41,111	362	8,221	1,608	646	915	2,913	5,281	11,391	783	646
Hagerstown-Martinsburg, MD-WV	13,905	8.0	47,759	250	5,188	903	404	732	1,777	3,626	7,227	490	404
Hammond, LA	5,716	8.8	41,792	353	1,976	408	123	305	715	1,932	2,812	170	123
Hanford-Corcoran, CA	6,387	14.8	41,829	351	2,957	808	232	578	808	1,801	4,575	210	232
Harrisburg-Carlisle, PA	33,969	8.2	58,372	80	20,091	3,706	1,528	2,947	5,197	8,149	28,271	1,668	1,528
Harrisonburg, VA	5,860	7.0	43,232	336	3,211	529	236	533	1,007	1,347	4,509	285	236
Hartford-East Hartford-Middletown, CT	80,911	4.8	67,343	27	44,634	6,986	3,160	7,944	11,167	16,304	62,725	3,535	3,160
Hattiesburg, MS	7,084	7.2	41,779	354	3,090	516	230	477	1,163	2,041	4,314	306	230
Hickory-Lenoir-Morganton, NC	16,105	7.3	43,496	333	7,171	1,184	532	979	2,387	4,865	9,867	691	532
Hilton Head Island-Bluffton, SC	13,081	5.5	57,565	89	4,208	734	324	669	4,852	2,973	5,936	426	324
Hinesville, GA	3,126	8.8	37,578	379	1,938	584	172	46	550	930	2,740	123	172
Homosassa Springs, FL	6,416	7.6	41,933	350	1,443	234	102	307	1,515	2,758	2,085	235	102
Hot Springs, AR	4,426	7.2	44,358	319	1,636	227	126	318	835	1,583	2,308	198	126
Houma-Thibodaux, LA	9,804	6.7	47,259	260	4,629	738	305	917	1,621	2,735	6,589	405	305
Houston-The Woodlands-Sugar Land, TX	428,501	3.0	59,893	68	218,016	28,607	14,147	57,463	76,393	68,330	318,233	16,859	14,147
Huntington-Ashland, WV-KY-OH	15,730	6.9	44,423	317	6,550	1,190	522	793	2,019	5,457	9,055	655	522
Huntsville, AL	26,553	7.8	55,126	116	16,301	2,486	1,195	1,250	4,559	5,107	21,232	1,342	1,195
Idaho Falls, ID	8,037	6.8	51,729	168	3,719	516	313	1,480	1,525	1,496	6,027	377	313
Indianapolis-Carmel-Anderson, IN	126,362	5.8	60,431	66	63,477	9,154	4,664	18,325	19,166	22,869	95,621	5,735	4,664
Iowa City, IA	10,007	3.3	56,947	94	5,008	1,300	377	779	2,201	1,588	7,465	432	377
Ithaca, NY	5,001	6.5	49,486	213	2,895	527	244	322	950	1,127	3,988	218	244
Jackson, MI	7,044	10.1	44,889	306	2,976	583	223	380	1,020	2,329	4,162	287	223
Jackson, MS	28,272	6.0	47,992	243	13,495	2,097	997	2,035	4,890	7,351	18,624	1,301	997
Jackson, TN	7,904	6.6	44,123	322	3,828	675	277	779	916	2,437	5,558	362	277
Jacksonville, FL	87,532	7.4	55,125	117	43,891	6,087	3,064	5,139	17,593	18,723	58,181	3,786	3,064
Jacksonville, NC	8,794	6.6	43,122	338	4,083	1,122	364	364	1,460	2,237	5,932	297	364
Janesville-Beloit, WI	7,964	6.1	48,836	224	3,600	659	274	347	1,313	1,975	4,881	328	274
Jefferson City, MO	7,184	6.8	47,827	247	3,793	830	263	428	1,190	1,690	5,314	317	263
Johnson City, TN	9,004	6.3	44,020	324	3,676	692	260	813	1,300	2,761	5,441	367	260
Johnstown, PA	6,258	7.8	48,637	229	2,166	473	177	319	832	2,427	3,135	226	177

1. Based on the resident population estimated as of July 1 of the year shown.

Area name	Earnings, 2019 (cont.)									Social Security beneficiaries, December 2019		Supple-mental Security Income Recipi-ents, December 2019	Housing units, 2020	
	Percent by selected industries													
	Farm	Mining, quarrying, and extracting	Construc-tion	Manufac-turing	Informa-tion; pro-fessional, scientific, and technical serviecs	Retail trade	Finance, insur-ance, real estate, rental and leasing	Health care and social assistance	Govern-ment	Number	Rate[1]		Total	Percent change, 2010–2020
	75	76	77	78	79	80	81	82	83	84	85	86	87	88
Evansville, IN-KY	1.0	0.2	7.5	17.9	6.8	6.2	5.6	18.1	9.5	71,805	229	7,006	142,396	0.7
Fairbanks, AK	0.1	2.6	8.0	0.9	4.0	5.8	2.9	10.5	48.8	12,375	129	1,117	42,668	0.0
Fargo, ND-MN	2.0	D	7.3	7.8	10.6	6.8	10.6	17.1	13.7	37,485	149	3,284	114,430	1.7
Farmington, NM	1.3	14.0	8.2	2.3	D	7.1	3.3	13.4	26.7	24,190	200	3,877	47,991	0.4
Fayetteville, NC	0.5	D	4.3	4.3	D	5.4	3.0	5.9	58.1	93,615	178	15,049	217,372	0.8
Fayetteville-Springdale-Rogers, AR	-0.5	D	6.4	9.0	D	5.5	4.6	9.2	11.2	91,265	163	8,008	229,031	2.8
Flagstaff, AZ	0.7	0.0	5.0	8.5	5.1	7.0	5.3	16.7	29.4	22,250	153	2,321	70,056	0.9
Flint, MI	0.2	0.0	6.4	12.0	5.1	9.0	6.6	19.1	15.9	101,520	251	16,108	183,563	0.2
Florence, SC	0.6	0.0	4.6	15.8	5.4	7.0	10.2	11.8	19.4	50,125	252	8,208	91,084	0.9
Florence-Muscle Shoals, AL	0.2	0.3	9.1	17.2	3.9	9.6	5.1	12.7	20.4	40,310	266	4,323	72,608	0.4
Fond du Lac, WI	3.7	0.6	9.3	23.6	4.5	6.3	5.6	12.9	11.8	23,680	227	1,592	45,886	0.2
Fort Collins, CO	0.4	0.3	9.2	12.9	13.0	6.4	6.4	9.1	21.5	62,495	172	2,537	162,052	1.6
Fort Smith, AR-OK	-0.4	0.8	5.3	16.7	4.4	7.2	9.1	14.8	13.7	61,220	249	8,526	108,566	0.6
Fort Wayne, IN	0.5	D	7.9	17.8	D	6.6	8.3	19.2	9.2	81,145	192	8,388	179,307	0.9
Fresno, CA	6.6	0.2	6.4	6.0	5.4	6.4	5.8	14.6	21.5	145,435	143	42,645	341,686	0.7
Gadsden, AL	0.0	D	5.3	14.9	3.5	9.2	4.9	D	15.4	28,955	281	4,245	47,418	0.2
Gainesville, FL	1.7	0.1	4.3	4.1	8.5	5.5	5.5	D	34.9	66,165	194	8,722	154,308	1.3
Gainesville, GA	-0.1	D	7.4	18.9	5.0	7.0	7.2	17.0	10.5	39,155	189	3,151	79,005	2.3
Gettysburg, PA	2.2	0.3	9.2	21.1	3.6	6.0	4.0	13.5	15.5	26,075	250	1,055	43,259	0.5
Glens Falls, NY	1.3	0.7	7.3	13.7	D	8.7	4.8	14.4	21.8	34,625	274	3,030	69,242	0.4
Goldsboro, NC	2.4	D	5.2	11.2	2.8	7.4	5.3	10.7	33.5	26,615	228	3,924	53,035	0.8
Grand Forks, ND-MN	7.5	0.4	6.8	7.1	5.1	6.9	5.1	16.1	25.3	18,255	176	1,261	48,527	0.9
Grand Island, NE	5.7	0.2	6.5	19.3	3.3	7.5	D	10.4	16.2	14,515	191	1,157	31,836	0.7
Grand Junction, CO	0.8	3.7	10.6	4.4	5.9	8.5	8.1	18.5	16.9	35,830	228	2,645	68,652	1.5
Grand Rapids-Kentwood, MI	0.9	D	6.3	22.4	D	5.6	7.6	13.8	9.2	201,300	184	18,377	435,930	0.7
Grants Pass, OR	0.4	D	7.4	9.9	4.5	13.3	8.8	20.0	13.1	28,460	322	2,881	39,173	0.9
Great Falls, MT	1.7	0.1	7.7	3.3	5.5	7.8	7.3	17.9	27.5	19,055	225	1,808	39,114	0.4
Greeley, CO	5.8	7.8	14.0	12.1	4.9	6.3	5.2	7.1	11.7	46,630	137	3,553	124,909	3.3
Green Bay, WI	2.1	0.1	6.3	17.2	D	5.0	9.8	D	11.9	67,565	205	5,474	147,439	0.9
Greensboro-High Point, NC	0.3	D	6.7	15.2	D	6.3	9.3	11.9	11.6	164,005	211	18,088	340,987	0.8
Greenville, NC	0.6	D	5.7	10.4	4.3	6.6	5.8	10.9	36.5	33,065	192	5,767	81,437	0.8
Greenville-Anderson, SC	0.0	0.1	6.6	15.4	D	6.5	8.2	10.0	15.0	204,245	217	17,773	412,633	2.0
Gulfport-Biloxi, MS	0.0	D	6.2	15.7	6.3	6.2	3.9	D	31.1	92,985	222	11,763	187,168	1.7
Hagerstown-Martinsburg, MD-WV	1.0	D	5.7	11.2	6.6	8.2	7.2	14.9	20.3	63,385	213	6,569	125,581	1.2
Hammond, LA	0.3	0.7	6.2	6.2	4.5	10.4	6.2	11.5	28.3	25,320	187	4,890	58,591	2.9
Hanford-Corcoran, CA	13.1	D	2.0	7.5	1.7	4.3	1.8	8.2	45.5	19,365	126	4,610	46,758	0.8
Harrisburg-Carlisle, PA	0.4	D	4.7	7.1	9.6	4.5	8.9	16.1	19.2	126,205	212	12,039	257,275	0.5
Harrisonburg, VA	2.1	D	7.9	19.0	7.6	6.8	4.9	10.8	17.0	25,065	185	1,875	54,632	0.9
Hartford-East Hartford-Middletown, CT	0.1	D	5.2	12.0	11.6	4.7	18.1	12.2	14.8	242,110	200	24,608	523,895	0.2
Hattiesburg, MS	0.5	D	6.4	9.0	D	8.3	D	D	23.1	34,265	198	5,596	75,023	0.4
Hickory-Lenoir-Morganton, NC	0.6	0.1	4.7	25.9	D	7.7	3.8	11.2	15.5	94,175	257	7,845	164,927	0.9
Hilton Head Island-Bluffton, SC	0.2	D	9.5	1.3	9.6	9.1	8.0	9.6	26.5	61,535	277	2,528	114,618	2.7
Hinesville, GA	0.1	D	1.1	D	D	3.2	D	D	73.5	11,425	138	1,722	33,716	2.2
Homosassa Springs, FL	0.1	0.3	12.1	1.7	5.8	12.0	5.9	22.1	12.9	64,195	406	3,676	82,832	1.1
Hot Springs, AR	0.1	0.3	10.3	7.3	4.9	11.2	5.6	23.1	12.8	31,020	309	3,743	52,471	0.2
Houma-Thibodaux, LA	0.5	10.3	6.5	10.1	4.8	6.1	5.0	11.7	11.2	43,945	213	7,637	88,964	0.7
Houston-The Woodlands-Sugar Land, TX	0.0	9.8	8.0	9.0	D	4.5	8.2	7.9	10.8	921,235	128	141,749	2,823,913	2.5
Huntington-Ashland, WV-KY-OH	0.0	0.6	D	11.5	6.0	7.1	D	21.0	17.1	91,400	256	15,416	165,950	0.1
Huntsville, AL	0.1	D	4.4	11.7	27.6	5.3	3.8	6.8	26.4	91,395	182	8,665	217,514	2.0
Idaho Falls, ID	3.5	D	D	D	D	17.7	D	D	8.8	26,375	162	2,839	58,063	2.0
Indianapolis-Carmel-Anderson, IN	0.3	0.1	6.4	10.4	D	4.8	D	12.4	10.9	369,920	174	37,371	905,740	1.1
Iowa City, IA	1.3	D	5.3	7.2	4.6	5.3	4.3	7.1	45.5	26,635	150	2,138	76,710	1.3
Ithaca, NY	0.7	D	2.3	5.4	9.4	4.8	3.3	D	12.9	17,230	164	1,450	47,375	0.6
Jackson, MI	0.3	0.2	5.0	17.4	4.7	6.6	5.5	15.6	13.8	38,345	240	4,496	69,210	0.2
Jackson, MS	0.4	1.1	5.4	7.6	8.9	7.0	7.8	14.0	22.1	122,710	209	20,967	259,239	0.5
Jackson, TN	0.3	D	D	18.0	3.9	8.2	4.3	12.4	20.5	43,875	243	6,021	79,728	0.5
Jacksonville, FL	0.1	D	6.8	D	D	6.5	13.7	13.2	13.7	317,615	194	34,745	710,325	2.4
Jacksonville, NC	0.8	D	3.9	0.9	3.4	5.4	3.3	3.9	65.8	30,405	147	3,271	85,916	1.7
Janesville-Beloit, WI	1.3	D	7.5	16.2	4.9	6.1	4.4	15.1	13.7	36,855	224	3,757	70,771	0.8
Jefferson City, MO	1.0	0.2	7.7	9.3	D	6.0	D	9.4	30.5	33,750	224	2,535	64,691	0.3
Johnson City, TN	0.1	D	5.3	11.5	D	8.4	7.0	19.2	21.5	55,005	264	5,543	98,141	1.0
Johnstown, PA	0.3	0.2	4.5	9.3	6.6	7.6	6.2	22.8	18.0	39,035	295	4,755	64,426	0.0

1. Per 1,000 resident population estimated as of July 1 of the year shown.

Area name	Occupied housing units, 2016-2020: Occupied units: Total	Owner-occupied: Percent	Owner-occupied: Median value[1]	Median owner cost as a percent of income: With a mortgage	Median owner cost as a percent of income: Without a mortgage[2]	Renter-occupied: Median rent[3]	Renter-occupied: Median rent as a percent of income	Sub-standard units[4] (percent)	Civilian labor force, 2021: Total	Percent change 2020-2021	Unemployment: Total	Unemployment: Rate[5]	Civilian employment[6], 2016-2020: Total	Percent: Management, business, science, and arts	Percent: Construction, production, and maintenance occupations
	89	90	91	92	93	94	95	96	97	98	99	100	101	102	103
Evansville, IN-KY	129,824	69.0	146,000	18.3	10.6	797	28.3	1.3	156,856	-0.4	5,406	3.4	152,338	35.3	26.2
Fairbanks, AK	36,199	58.9	240,300	21.2	10.0	1,297	27.3	9.5	45,375	1.7	2,276	5.0	44,303	37.2	24.3
Fargo, ND-MN	101,722	55.9	225,600	19.2	10.0	835	26.5	2.3	143,311	0.3	4,087	2.9	139,366	41.7	19.9
Farmington, NM	43,582	70.8	155,000	21.1	10.0	803	27.6	8.3	49,527	-1.0	3,977	8.0	47,993	30.0	29.7
Fayetteville, NC	192,505	56.6	146,800	21.6	11.3	940	29.8	2.6	198,096	1.8	12,699	6.4	200,807	34.0	24.6
Fayetteville-Springdale-Rogers, AR	194,800	60.7	186,500	17.9	10.0	868	24.9	4.4	275,092	0.3	7,905	2.9	253,798	39.3	24.6
Flagstaff, AZ	49,016	60.8	299,100	22.0	10.0	1,185	31.5	9.2	72,223	0.3	4,366	6.0	65,975	37.9	18.0
Flint, MI	170,581	70.0	119,500	19.8	12.7	781	30.9	1.6	174,492	-2.8	13,251	7.6	171,063	33.0	26.8
Florence, SC	78,997	67.0	125,100	18.6	10.5	754	28.4	2.8	95,850	0.7	4,024	4.2	87,655	34.5	25.7
Florence-Muscle Shoals, AL	60,310	69.3	140,000	19.1	10.0	683	27.4	1.0	65,540	-1.5	2,271	3.5	64,767	30.5	29.2
Fond du Lac, WI	41,890	70.6	162,600	19.3	11.5	786	24.2	1.5	57,149	1.4	1,838	3.2	53,458	30.2	33.7
Fort Collins, CO	134,185	66.3	390,600	21.2	10.0	1,340	32.4	1.5	206,492	2.6	9,617	4.7	185,199	45.2	17.6
Fort Smith, AR-OK	98,199	66.2	119,500	18.7	10.0	701	27.1	3.6	103,883	-2.4	3,926	3.8	107,341	30.9	29.7
Fort Wayne, IN	160,865	69.7	138,200	17.7	10.0	788	26.7	1.6	201,350	-0.7	7,231	3.6	200,648	34.7	27.5
Fresno, CA	310,097	53.7	271,000	22.9	10.0	1,029	33.1	10.0	443,383	-0.4	40,741	9.2	408,625	31.2	28.3
Gadsden, AL	38,765	73.0	124,400	18.7	10.5	676	28.2	1.5	39,262	-5.2	1,604	4.1	43,002	28.1	31.2
Gainesville, FL	125,651	59.5	181,700	20.4	10.7	978	36.0	2.4	162,533	2.9	6,166	3.8	150,026	44.1	15.0
Gainesville, GA	65,555	68.9	212,700	20.2	10.0	987	29.0	5.3	104,792	2.4	2,792	2.7	95,737	31.1	33.1
Gettysburg, PA	39,628	77.8	212,300	21.8	12.4	932	27.5	1.4	54,462	-0.3	2,396	4.4	51,151	31.4	31.9
Glens Falls, NY	53,088	71.6	177,000	20.1	12.5	898	29.0	1.6	58,447	-0.9	2,769	4.7	60,403	34.5	23.9
Goldsboro, NC	48,198	62.9	125,900	19.8	10.7	784	29.0	3.0	50,451	1.5	2,535	5.0	53,058	29.6	30.0
Grand Forks, ND-MN	43,398	55.2	195,500	19.6	10.0	804	28.2	2.6	52,813	-1.6	1,787	3.4	53,757	37.1	22.3
Grand Island, NE	29,558	64.9	150,600	19.5	10.2	766	26.0	3.0	40,088	1.0	1,114	2.8	38,550	29.8	35.2
Grand Junction, CO	59,750	69.1	245,000	22.1	10.0	963	30.0	2.4	77,219	3.3	4,421	5.7	71,273	35.6	24.8
Grand Rapids-Kentwood, MI	396,595	73.4	186,500	18.5	10.2	910	28.6	2.2	562,492	-1.8	25,733	4.6	542,588	37.0	26.2
Grants Pass, OR	36,606	68.8	281,500	25.0	11.8	930	34.2	5.4	36,990	2.4	2,280	6.2	32,773	33.2	23.5
Great Falls, MT	34,440	66.6	184,400	21.4	10.7	778	28.6	2.1	37,812	-0.3	1,251	3.3	37,118	35.7	22.1
Greeley, CO	102,046	74.5	326,100	22.5	10.0	1,143	30.6	3.6	165,660	0.5	9,478	5.7	156,119	33.7	29.2
Green Bay, WI	130,563	68.1	176,800	18.7	10.7	807	24.5	2.3	174,296	0.6	5,928	3.4	168,457	35.4	28.0
Greensboro-High Point, NC	303,556	63.0	155,200	19.3	10.0	846	29.1	2.9	357,004	1.1	19,407	5.4	362,667	36.0	25.5
Greenville, NC	70,683	52.6	146,700	19.4	10.5	793	29.6	2.9	87,237	1.9	4,398	5.0	84,110	37.7	20.6
Greenville-Anderson, SC	350,728	69.5	172,400	18.6	10.0	882	28.8	2.3	432,118	1.8	15,309	3.5	432,152	37.8	25.1
Gulfport-Biloxi, MS	161,773	66.0	153,600	20.7	10.0	897	30.3	2.6	172,124	1.5	9,802	5.7	177,853	34.1	24.7
Hagerstown-Martinsburg, MD-WV	109,554	71.0	203,800	20.2	10.0	963	28.1	2.0	141,130	1.3	6,321	4.5	135,016	34.7	26.2
Hammond, LA	48,548	70.3	167,900	19.1	10.0	828	32.3	3.3	56,131	0.0	3,607	6.4	55,975	33.7	26.9
Hanford-Corcoran, CA	43,604	53.6	227,400	21.8	10.0	1,030	27.8	8.5	55,930	-1.7	5,386	9.6	53,687	25.2	35.6
Harrisburg-Carlisle, PA	233,447	67.5	190,700	19.6	11.2	970	26.3	1.4	302,000	-0.6	16,317	5.4	289,207	40.7	21.6
Harrisonburg, VA	48,057	62.6	218,400	20.3	10.0	926	26.8	2.8	65,364	-1.2	2,186	3.3	66,167	33.0	27.8
Hartford-East Hartford-Middletown, CT	477,495	66.4	252,500	21.4	14.1	1,140	30.3	1.8	643,808	-2.7	39,669	6.2	614,992	45.3	17.2
Hattiesburg, MS	62,222	65.1	135,600	19.1	10.0	815	31.2	2.7	76,960	2.4	3,867	5.0	73,636	34.3	24.9
Hickory-Lenoir-Morganton, NC	145,451	73.4	139,100	18.5	10.0	708	24.7	3.0	168,053	1.2	7,810	4.6	167,377	29.1	34.5
Hilton Head Island-Bluffton, SC	84,955	74.6	295,000	23.8	10.6	1,203	31.1	2.0	89,252	2.0	3,075	3.4	91,706	35.0	20.8
Hinesville, GA	30,059	49.3	133,000	19.4	10.4	1,034	29.9	2.5	34,816	2.7	1,302	3.7	29,487	29.9	30.5
Homosassa Springs, FL	64,621	83.5	144,100	21.4	10.0	847	32.5	1.1	47,343	1.6	2,687	5.7	47,389	31.2	23.6
Hot Springs, AR	40,906	67.1	142,100	19.8	10.0	791	27.3	3.1	40,528	-1.9	2,028	5.0	40,787	31.9	20.8
Houma-Thibodaux, LA	77,019	73.9	157,000	19.6	10.0	842	30.1	3.0	85,672	-1.3	4,449	5.2	88,668	29.8	30.4
Houston-The Woodlands-Sugar Land, TX	2,407,993	60.9	208,100	21.0	10.8	1,136	29.7	5.4	3,424,496	1.2	219,389	6.4	3,333,241	39.7	23.3
Huntington-Ashland, WV-KY-OH	141,577	71.7	123,900	18.4	10.2	736	29.9	1.6	147,098	-0.3	7,759	5.3	142,949	35.6	23.3
Huntsville, AL	184,353	69.3	186,100	17.6	10.0	869	26.9	1.7	238,776	1.4	6,246	2.6	224,318	46.1	19.7
Idaho Falls, ID	50,737	71.9	204,800	19.7	10.0	820	25.3	3.9	76,591	3.4	2,203	2.9	67,564	36.9	24.6
Indianapolis-Carmel-Anderson, IN	790,050	65.7	172,300	18.1	10.0	936	28.8	1.7	1,082,050	1.3	37,435	3.5	1,025,444	40.9	22.2
Iowa City, IA	69,306	59.9	228,600	19.7	10.0	957	33.2	2.2	95,756	-1.0	3,580	3.7	95,007	46.6	17.8
Ithaca, NY	40,817	54.0	218,700	20.2	10.5	1,144	36.7	2.0	48,914	-1.2	1,821	3.7	51,137	54.3	12.0
Jackson, MI	62,216	74.3	138,900	19.8	10.7	800	28.8	1.5	71,993	-3.1	4,130	5.7	69,089	33.3	27.6
Jackson, MS	219,801	67.6	148,300	19.3	10.0	884	29.7	2.8	265,543	0.6	13,780	5.2	265,758	38.1	22.3
Jackson, TN	69,505	65.1	123,300	19.3	10.0	797	30.7	1.7	86,220	-0.3	3,672	4.3	75,665	31.9	27.9
Jacksonville, FL	578,620	65.3	220,000	20.9	10.0	1,113	30.1	2.1	797,001	2.7	31,981	4.0	724,227	38.6	19.8
Jacksonville, NC	66,131	54.2	162,400	22.7	10.0	1,029	29.1	2.0	65,070	3.6	3,338	5.1	65,389	31.7	24.3
Janesville-Beloit, WI	65,237	68.4	156,800	19.8	12.4	860	27.5	1.9	86,855	1.0	3,864	4.4	80,116	31.7	32.2
Jefferson City, MO	57,247	71.7	162,100	18.3	10.0	686	23.5	1.5	74,007	-0.3	2,353	3.2	70,891	37.1	24.6
Johnson City, TN	86,279	67.0	152,600	19.5	10.0	734	28.3	1.5	92,328	1.4	3,532	3.8	91,283	36.9	23.9
Johnstown, PA	56,933	74.7	94,900	18.1	12.4	635	27.5	1.0	55,668	-2.3	3,908	7.0	56,969	33.3	26.9

1. Specified owner-occupied units. 2. A value of 10.0 represents 10 percent or less; a value of 50.0 represents 50 percent or more. 3. Specified renter-occupied units. 4. Overcrowded or lacking complete plumbing facilities. 5. Percent of civilian labor force. 6. Civilian employed persons 16 years old and over.

Area name	Private nonfarm establishments, employment and payroll, 2019										Agriculture, 2017			
		Employment							Annual payroll		Farms			Farm producers whose primary occupation is farming (percent)
												Percent with:		
	Number of establish-ments	Total	Health care and social assistance	Manufactur-ing	Retail trade	Finance and insurance	Professional, scientific, and technical services	Total (mil dol)	Average per employee (dollars)	Number	Fewer than 50 acres	1000 acres or more	
	104	105	106	107	108	109	110	111	112	113	114	115	116
Evansville, IN-KY	7,743	147,285	27,518	23,264	16,774	5,811	7,007	6,958	47,241	1,564	45.7	11.1	43.6
Fairbanks, AK	2,485	26,391	6,520	503	4,428	615	1,306	1,517	57,491	274	49.6	8.0	45.0
Fargo, ND-MN	6,943	126,045	25,450	10,175	16,037	9,794	6,662	6,364	50,491	1,478	20.1	36.1	58.8
Farmington, NM	2,483	35,209	7,347	1,607	5,929	828	1,171	1,495	42,449	2,965	56.5	21.0	54.9
Fayetteville, NC	8,009	121,826	24,367	10,074	21,951	2,525	6,695	4,559	37,420	1,168	51.5	4.5	38.3
Fayetteville-Springdale-Rogers, AR	13,017	224,948	27,328	27,142	25,565	6,186	13,776	12,350	54,900	5,444	39.8	1.7	39.8
Flagstaff, AZ	3,773	55,308	9,441	5,943	7,905	875	1,795	2,383	43,084	2,142	77.8	11.6	55.7
Flint, MI	7,528	119,084	26,264	11,698	18,665	3,892	4,010	5,138	43,144	820	59.4	3.4	46.2
Florence, SC	4,218	83,669	26,676	10,321	10,950	2,816	2,354	3,867	46,216	862	43.6	8.9	42.1
Florence-Muscle Shoals, AL	3,178	49,696	8,308	9,456	7,769	1,717	1,010	1,823	36,690	1,900	45.6	4.9	36.6
Fond du Lac, WI	2,250	43,856	7,144	9,054	5,535	1,572	1,374	2,074	47,287	1,244	35.9	4.8	53.4
Fort Collins, CO	11,342	133,524	21,170	12,842	19,658	3,544	10,103	6,635	49,692	2,043	71.0	4.4	31.6
Fort Smith, AR-OK	5,278	86,559	15,778	19,522	11,453	2,674	2,152	3,447	39,824	3,462	38.7	3.2	37.2
Fort Wayne, IN	10,036	194,740	38,113	32,299	24,586	9,077	6,533	9,005	46,241	2,244	55.1	5.5	32.6
Fresno, CA	17,653	284,131	51,046	26,540	37,141	9,190	11,271	13,042	45,902	4,774	54.1	6.6	57.1
Gadsden, AL	1,911	29,096	7,137	4,695	4,821	1,012	672	1,007	34,596	817	55.2	0.5	38.2
Gainesville, FL	7,417	110,844	31,511	4,802	15,894	4,198	6,313	4,882	44,048	3,234	69.4	2.9	41.3
Gainesville, GA	4,602	86,434	15,109	23,841	9,379	2,090	2,223	4,179	48,351	551	63.5	0.4	38.1
Gettysburg, PA	1,948	28,891	4,796	6,238	3,510	467	640	1,085	37,552	1,146	50.2	2.2	43.4
Glens Falls, NY	3,213	41,593	8,180	6,635	7,332	1,339	1,209	1,817	43,689	995	38.9	2.6	43.4
Goldsboro, NC	2,134	33,015	6,607	5,075	5,789	1,146	775	1,243	37,638	551	39.7	8.5	55.4
Grand Forks, ND-MN	2,613	42,236	9,961	5,445	7,015	1,108	1,518	1,855	43,917	2,147	14.3	25.0	53.5
Grand Island, NE	2,293	36,063	5,176	8,845	5,125	1,570	674	1,444	40,032	1,682	27.5	15.9	52.1
Grand Junction, CO	4,549	55,267	12,410	3,177	8,283	1,679	2,600	2,404	43,497	2,465	80.1	2.6	32.1
Grand Rapids-Kentwood, MI	25,214	517,305	70,248	118,155	52,606	19,239	21,920	25,064	48,451	4,056	50.4	4.1	45.3
Grants Pass, OR	2,039	23,538	5,191	2,564	4,396	764	1,211	932	39,615	746	85.0	0.3	43.6
Great Falls, MT	2,429	30,085	7,247	1,252	4,825	1,451	1,189	1,249	41,522	1,027	37.7	22.6	42.1
Greeley, CO	6,703	96,024	9,210	15,122	10,732	3,051	3,242	4,944	51,491	4,062	46.3	10.2	38.1
Green Bay, WI	7,771	155,320	22,166	31,906	16,957	9,591	5,575	8,020	51,632	2,464	42.4	4.3	46.7
Greensboro-High Point, NC	17,833	321,423	41,499	50,674	36,412	13,939	13,242	14,529	45,201	3,066	46.7	1.1	40.7
Greenville, NC	3,664	61,466	16,768	6,279	9,165	1,607	2,214	2,512	40,871	478	35.8	12.6	55.0
Greenville-Anderson, SC	21,056	356,823	48,896	57,679	44,739	14,113	25,649	16,293	45,661	4,358	59.5	1.1	31.5
Gulfport-Biloxi, MS	7,517	131,980	21,756	20,613	18,503	3,978	4,728	5,677	43,013	1,405	62.1	0.7	35.7
Hagerstown-Martinsburg, MD-WV	5,315	91,616	17,656	11,214	14,414	5,533	2,674	3,892	42,478	2,030	58.2	0.7	36.4
Hammond, LA	2,506	37,878	9,058	2,493	6,747	1,210	1,173	1,389	36,677	967	55.0	1.1	37.4
Hanford-Corcoran, CA	1,707	25,988	5,028	4,457	4,137	502	945	1,095	42,129	963	48.9	9.2	54.1
Harrisburg-Carlisle, PA	13,869	286,876	52,457	17,808	37,525	17,403	17,194	14,338	49,979	2,711	45.1	1.4	48.6
Harrisonburg, VA	3,188	55,439	6,990	10,537	7,559	1,360	1,660	2,281	41,153	2,026	46.2	0.6	49.3
Hartford-East Hartford-Middletown, CT	29,138	560,409	109,885	67,292	62,960	60,718	35,384	34,598	61,736	1,747	72.9	0.5	38.6
Hattiesburg, MS	3,600	58,422	13,082	5,841	10,555	1,860	2,408	2,292	39,230	1,696	44.5	1.7	38.3
Hickory-Lenoir-Morganton, NC	7,617	137,539	23,084	40,515	16,546	2,710	3,443	5,564	40,457	2,101	54.0	0.8	40.1
Hilton Head Island-Bluffton, SC	6,314	66,336	9,526	899	12,962	1,926	3,060	2,512	37,865	296	62.2	10.5	35.4
Hinesville, GA	955	14,418	2,278	2,792	2,343	367	436	608	42,163	154	53.2	0.6	26.3
Homosassa Springs, FL	2,813	30,516	10,551	345	5,684	679	808	1,147	37,585	609	75.2	2.1	43.4
Hot Springs, AR	2,785	34,517	8,197	2,647	5,893	1,020	1,075	1,205	34,901	357	47.6	0.3	38.5
Houma-Thibodaux, LA	4,379	70,885	12,038	4,987	10,038	1,865	3,218	3,463	48,848	592	54.1	7.4	33.2
Houston-The Woodlands-Sugar Land, TX	149,360	2,722,304	363,882	206,386	311,696	100,707	220,446	169,578	62,292	14,238	63.5	2.9	32.2
Huntington-Ashland, WV-KY-OH	6,854	111,942	30,659	11,439	16,961	2,809	3,971	4,816	43,018	3,194	32.7	0.4	34.9
Huntsville, AL	10,136	200,013	30,336	22,214	23,873	4,193	48,009	11,414	57,066	2,177	54.2	4.0	35.9
Idaho Falls, ID	4,396	62,049	11,702	4,285	8,362	1,620	9,915	3,047	49,111	2,048	60.5	10.7	37.5
Indianapolis-Carmel-Anderson, IN	48,356	935,504	152,942	76,907	105,660	50,396	66,106	49,336	52,737	5,999	55.1	7.4	37.4
Iowa City, IA	4,030	73,393	20,251	5,423	10,979	3,012	2,943	3,247	44,238	2,386	34.7	4.9	46.3
Ithaca, NY	2,269	48,904	6,461	2,338	4,672	1,224	2,976	2,160	44,169	523	47.6	2.9	39.6
Jackson, MI	2,994	52,350	10,880	9,595	7,106	1,665	2,749	2,559	48,881	923	52.1	3.9	41.5
Jackson, MS	13,512	223,522	51,522	19,959	28,440	11,341	9,623	10,172	45,510	4,019	28.4	6.9	36.7
Jackson, TN	3,905	72,319	15,736	13,147	9,715	1,759	1,465	2,834	39,184	2,028	40.9	8.4	35.3
Jacksonville, FL	40,255	616,525	91,422	27,908	78,462	49,762	40,376	30,043	48,729	1,681	75.1	2.0	40.6
Jacksonville, NC	2,909	35,861	5,106	1,014	8,327	1,025	1,713	1,133	31,580	340	50.3	3.5	55.9
Janesville-Beloit, WI	3,338	60,856	8,934	11,645	9,247	1,342	1,528	2,845	46,746	1,587	53.7	4.7	40.6
Jefferson City, MO	3,537	56,463	9,889	8,067	7,362	2,360	1,897	2,475	43,830	5,019	26.2	2.8	33.9
Johnson City, TN	3,903	66,253	15,199	8,027	10,460	3,056	1,607	2,737	41,304	1,997	61.9	0.4	35.9
Johnstown, PA	3,010	45,834	11,852	4,952	6,451	1,857	2,011	1,718	37,485	557	37.0	2.3	36.1

Agriculture, 2017 (cont.)

Area name	Land in farms: Acreage (1,000)	Land in farms: Percent change, 2012–2017	Land in farms: Acres: Average size of farm	Land in farms: Acres: Total irrigated (1,000)	Land in farms: Acres: Total cropland (1,000)	Value of land and buildings (dollars): Average per farm	Value of land and buildings (dollars): Average per acre	Value of machinery and equipmnet, average per farm (dollars)	Value of products sold: Total (mil dol)	Value of products sold: Average per farm (acres)	Value of products sold: Percent from: Crops	Value of products sold: Percent from: Livestock and poultry products	Organic farms (number)	Farms with internet access (percent)	Government payments: Total ($1,000)	Government payments: Percent of farms
	117	118	119	120	121	122	123	124	125	126	127	128	129	130	131	132
Evansville, IN-KY	544	-6.4	348.0	23.5	479.4	2,029,390	5,839	213,324	304.3	194,577	92.2	7.8	2	77.8	16,227	57.6
Fairbanks, AK	102	2.4	372.0	1.1	63.2	610,606	1,640	D	10.4	37,927	81.6	18.4	5	86.9	1,124	21.9
Fargo, ND-MN	1,703	-0.9	1,152.0	16.8	1,623.6	4,372,599	3,795	467,605	717.2	485,254	91.7	8.3	19	84.9	14,177	72.3
Farmington, NM	2,551	-1.1	861.0	73.6	107.9	345,734	402	39,306	74.1	24,998	91.5	8.5	1	44.9	1,383	8.3
Fayetteville, NC	226	-13.3	193.0	6.2	138.1	1,001,288	5,177	127,616	377.2	322,909	29.1	70.9	5	78.0	1,230	26.6
Fayetteville-Springdale-Rogers, AR	838	-5.4	154.0	1.2	218.7	748,454	4,861	75,575	1,382.0	253,852	1.5	98.5	18	76.2	1,982	6.5
Flagstaff, AZ	6,139	5.6	2,866.0	1.3	6.9	607,822	212	34,544	23.9	11,162	4.1	95.9	2	43.9	807	0.8
Flint, MI	124	0.5	151.0	1.5	104.3	795,230	5,262	103,909	70.4	85,871	86.5	13.5	11	84.8	2,561	25.0
Florence, SC	290	-12.9	336.0	7.4	200.6	969,775	2,883	127,777	133.5	154,886	69.8	30.2	8	70.3	2,730	33.2
Florence-Muscle Shoals, AL	361	-1.0	190.0	0.9	194.8	612,645	3,226	91,579	132.5	69,754	58.9	41.1	0	70.7	7,434	40.9
Fond du Lac, WI	317	0.6	255.0	1.9	270.4	1,855,960	7,275	227,075	396.7	318,921	24.0	76.0	33	77.7	3,762	56.5
Fort Collins, CO	482	7.1	236.0	60.2	98.6	1,095,047	4,637	76,905	150.7	73,772	45.7	54.3	20	85.1	633	5.5
Fort Smith, AR-OK	623	0.7	180.0	11.3	205.6	478,884	2,659	72,249	411.2	118,784	9.4	90.6	9	73.6	1,456	4.6
Fort Wayne, IN	458	11.4	204.0	2.0	403.6	1,496,008	7,332	136,852	296.8	132,251	68.7	31.3	19	69.6	8,492	48.4
Fresno, CA	1,647	-4.3	345.0	972.6	1,142.7	3,917,829	11,359	234,782	5,742.8	1,202,926	71.1	28.9	183	75.6	8,894	7.7
Gadsden, AL	89	3.7	109.0	0.6	24.8	419,479	3,836	78,982	93.4	114,356	6.7	93.3	0	73.8	804	21.5
Gainesville, FL	448	2.0	138.0	42.1	177.0	833,888	6,021	72,751	320.7	99,151	48.7	51.3	25	79.7	3,694	6.6
Gainesville, GA	41	-21.7	74.0	0.1	13.8	689,172	9,332	79,541	128.5	233,156	2.3	97.7	1	80.9	789	20.3
Gettysburg, PA	166	-3.0	145.0	2.2	128.4	998,832	6,886	132,547	207.6	181,122	54.2	45.8	17	77.7	1,503	18.4
Glens Falls, NY	195	-1.8	196.0	1.0	103.9	562,560	2,865	127,784	135.8	136,494	18.0	82.0	19	84.0	1,418	17.4
Goldsboro, NC	165	-13.5	300.0	4.8	130.5	1,497,289	4,990	222,201	592.1	1,074,539	18.1	81.9	13	79.9	3,611	46.1
Grand Forks, ND-MN	1,822	-4.7	848.0	33.1	1,682.6	2,831,795	3,338	378,326	748.1	348,455	93.3	6.7	19	75.5	32,024	81.8
Grand Island, NE	852	-2.9	506.0	510.2	651.5	2,306,951	4,556	281,613	777.9	462,492	47.7	52.3	6	81.4	29,470	66.7
Grand Junction, CO	343	-11.5	139.0	76.2	79.8	767,492	5,523	57,249	94.2	38,209	48.7	51.3	12	86.2	730	3.9
Grand Rapids-Kentwood, MI	794	-4.3	196.0	102.9	662.0	1,149,541	5,874	169,142	1,332.9	328,622	52.3	47.7	42	81.0	12,659	27.3
Grants Pass, OR	28	-1.4	37.0	8.0	8.4	672,056	17,992	38,200	17.5	23,456	49.2	50.8	27	85.1	1	1.1
Great Falls, MT	1,270	1.2	1,237.0	35.7	420.0	1,499,360	1,212	134,128	107.3	104,453	47.7	52.3	9	80.2	7,780	42.7
Greeley, CO	2,099	7.3	517.0	323.4	923.0	1,335,953	2,586	159,663	2,047.2	503,982	17.0	83.0	42	82.9	19,375	26.0
Green Bay, WI	552	0.9	224.0	2.4	455.7	1,371,723	6,120	200,427	752.9	305,556	18.1	81.9	35	75.8	6,395	47.0
Greensboro-High Point, NC	349	-3.1	114.0	5.4	153.8	604,582	5,315	73,041	373.1	121,694	24.2	75.8	40	74.5	1,271	11.5
Greenville, NC	186	8.5	390.0	2.8	149.8	1,499,479	3,845	183,107	242.5	507,234	41.6	58.4	4	81.8	3,291	45.6
Greenville-Anderson, SC	405	1.3	93.0	2.7	140.1	535,642	5,767	53,720	166.0	38,095	19.9	80.1	14	74.2	3,337	12.2
Gulfport-Biloxi, MS	130	-1.7	93.0	0.7	30.2	421,243	4,539	60,528	27.9	19,864	55.3	44.7	6	75.4	610	7.1
Hagerstown-Martinsburg, MD-WV	209	-4.1	103.0	0.7	127.0	709,469	6,883	78,595	182.9	90,104	32.4	67.6	16	69.0	2,000	12.5
Hammond, LA	98	-8.1	101.0	1.2	29.6	513,368	5,061	63,007	42.4	43,845	47.3	52.7	5	67.6	208	5.0
Hanford-Corcoran, CA	616	-8.6	640.0	371.7	488.5	6,917,469	10,815	349,654	1,649.3	1,712,640	50.1	49.9	25	80.4	5,849	29.8
Harrisburg-Carlisle, PA	366	-12.8	135.0	2.1	281.4	1,020,473	7,566	123,077	485.0	178,904	25.1	74.9	98	65.0	4,162	22.0
Harrisonburg, VA	229	2.9	113.0	5.5	121.9	997,634	8,844	118,949	795.9	392,852	6.8	93.2	37	65.5	1,852	11.5
Hartford-East Hartford-Middletown, CT	100	-20.6	57.0	4.3	48.9	779,882	13,635	64,238	204.4	117,004	87.0	13.0	22	81.2	731	3.9
Hattiesburg, MS	255	-0.6	150.0	1.2	49.3	546,554	3,641	69,415	353.2	208,227	4.0	96.0	0	71.0	1,954	22.0
Hickory-Lenoir-Morganton, NC	194	1.1	92.0	3.5	88.8	529,900	5,730	83,055	383.1	182,363	15.9	84.1	7	74.7	1,109	6.3
Hilton Head Island-Bluffton, SC	119	7.5	402.0	2.0	19.0	1,465,669	3,643	78,267	20.3	68,537	94.7	5.3	3	76.0	203	12.5
Hinesville, GA	17	0.4	107.0	0.2	4.0	441,065	4,103	55,760	7.8	50,331	12.1	87.9	0	81.2	82	10.4
Homosassa Springs, FL	56	37.5	92.0	0.9	9.6	726,031	7,929	49,552	13.5	22,118	67.3	32.7	0	81.0	197	2.6
Hot Springs, AR	34	-4.9	95.0	0.1	8.2	496,952	5,226	46,232	10.0	27,972	30.5	69.5	0	74.5	93	5.9
Houma-Thibodaux, LA	236	-6.1	398.0	0.3	94.4	1,316,841	3,306	143,334	69.1	116,730	62.4	37.6	0	73.6	255	3.4
Houston-The Woodlands-Sugar Land, TX	2,218	-17.2	156.0	80.6	680.3	749,277	4,810	67,839	434.9	30,543	62.4	37.6	24	74.4	30,126	5.9
Huntington-Ashland, WV-KY-OH	378	-6.4	118.0	0.4	88.8	306,815	2,594	50,542	29.6	9,260	52.9	47.1	7	69.1	719	6.0
Huntsville, AL	410	-10.2	188.0	21.1	282.6	877,456	4,662	110,397	201.8	92,678	71.0	29.0	2	76.4	6,048	30.9
Idaho Falls, ID	883	3.0	431.0	399.3	567.5	1,300,466	3,017	187,303	504.6	246,386	63.3	36.7	14	85.2	13,659	25.9
Indianapolis-Carmel-Anderson, IN	1,603	-5.1	267.0	10.0	1,440.5	1,963,457	7,349	158,827	944.4	157,420	89.0	11.0	23	82.3	39,946	42.9
Iowa City, IA	615	-4.4	258.0	1.2	528.6	1,921,071	7,457	191,325	891.5	373,645	31.5	68.5	132	75.6	20,966	68.6
Ithaca, NY	91	0.6	175.0	0.4	62.1	661,191	3,789	138,310	64.7	123,715	24.6	75.4	45	85.9	1,575	22.6
Jackson, MI	160	-12.4	174.0	4.7	125.8	866,522	4,986	116,065	70.8	76,714	61.6	38.4	6	78.2	3,526	25.9
Jackson, MS	1,258	-9.7	313.0	122.9	472.0	879,420	2,809	93,282	682.5	169,823	29.7	70.3	1	64.2	24,699	44.0
Jackson, TN	668	3.8	329.0	27.1	533.0	1,092,897	3,319	162,797	284.3	140,171	94.8	5.2	0	70.8	13,566	50.7
Jacksonville, FL	152	-18.0	91.0	17.4	36.3	599,377	6,617	58,273	101.9	60,642	69.5	30.5	6	75.4	466	5.1
Jacksonville, NC	52	-9.0	154.0	0.4	35.6	969,753	6,284	93,974	171.6	504,629	13.7	86.3	0	75.0	862	25.6
Janesville-Beloit, WI	354	-0.1	223.0	15.6	302.8	1,467,761	6,589	175,570	294.5	185,539	56.0	44.0	20	79.7	4,915	54.7
Jefferson City, MO	1,029	1.8	205.0	10.8	443.2	684,076	3,337	83,549	386.7	77,050	31.2	68.8	17	73.6	7,408	26.5
Johnson City, TN	146	-7.0	73.0	0.8	68.4	528,895	7,215	69,260	50.2	25,140	39.2	60.8	7	72.5	416	5.8
Johnstown, PA	79	3.2	142.0	0.1	50.5	659,661	4,631	100,086	30.1	53,982	60.1	39.9	2	68.8	979	30.3

Table C. Metropolitan Areas — **Water Use, Wholesale Trade, Retail Trade, and Real Estate**

Area name	Water use, 2015		Wholesale Trade[1], 2017				Retail Trade[2], 2017				Real estate and rental and leasing,[2] 2017			
	Public supply water withdrawn (mil gal/ day)	Public supply gallons withdrawn per person per day	Number of establish- ments	Number of employees	Sales (mil dol)	Average payroll (mil dol)	Number of establish- ments	Number of employees	Sales (mil dol)	Average payroll (mil dol)	Number of establish- ments	Number of employees	Sales (mil dol)	Average payroll (mil dol)
	133	134	135	136	137	138	139	140	141	142	143	144	145	146
Evansville, IN-KY	29.8	94.3	343	4,794	3,531.5	257.4	1,096	17,298	5,002.5	438.1	337	1,695	365.6	61.1
Fairbanks, AK	14.1	141.7	70	693	470.6	38.4	294	4,749	1,484.8	159.0	158	764	188.3	42.1
Fargo, ND-MN	19.0	81.4	417	7,514	7,293.4	448.1	846	16,144	9,241.6	484.2	375	2,004	341.5	75.8
Farmington, NM	18.8	158.6	129	1,053	502.9	57.5	413	5,940	1,744.6	163.8	100	560	141.0	30.8
Fayetteville, NC	60.8	120.6	158	2,223	999.4	82.8	1,445	21,586	5,894.6	525.1	406	2,070	461.2	73.3
Fayetteville-Springdale-Rogers, AR	64.9	132.3	482	5,529	4,789.3	325.8	1,574	25,929	7,401.1	691.9	622	2,374	622.0	93.6
Flagstaff, AZ	19.9	142.8	96	832	365.3	37.9	580	8,004	2,197.1	207.2	224	884	201.3	30.5
Flint, MI	4.2	10.3	269	4,989	3,403.5	270.6	1,355	19,591	8,429.7	497.7	328	2,107	338.1	73.5
Florence, SC	22.1	107.1	218	3,133	3,148.6	151.5	887	11,864	3,063.7	269.0	161	637	136.9	24.6
Florence-Muscle Shoals, AL	20.7	140.5	147	1,877	1,075.9	89.6	629	8,289	2,121.0	207.6	143	528	96.2	17.4
Fond du Lac, WI	7.9	77.8	D	D	D	D	332	6,014	1,719.9	156.8	62	344	52.3	13.7
Fort Collins, CO	30.6	91.7	336	4,724	3,723.5	349.3	1,266	19,902	5,893.8	574.0	766	2,404	663.9	109.9
Fort Smith, AR-OK	36.5	146.8	264	3,769	2,238.4	189.1	904	12,227	3,297.9	300.9	225	1,404	227.6	53.9
Fort Wayne, IN	37.1	92.3	497	8,411	8,761.7	445.3	1,373	24,329	7,369.0	671.8	464	2,302	569.1	94.5
Fresno, CA	157.1	161.1	827	14,164	10,890.9	780.4	2,438	38,243	11,347.0	1,066.6	852	4,904	1,097.9	207.2
Gadsden, AL	16.9	163.5	70	758	497.3	32.4	393	4,777	1,319.8	114.3	61	232	64.4	7.8
Gainesville, FL	25.1	79.1	230	2,191	1,827.9	122.5	1,096	15,974	4,200.4	376.8	399	2,096	357.5	75.6
Gainesville, GA	88.2	455.6	261	4,205	7,901.5	236.0	619	9,240	2,948.9	268.3	220	549	180.7	25.3
Gettysburg, PA	12.4	121.1	D	D	D	D	337	3,599	979.0	87.0	48	190	34.3	6.2
Glens Falls, NY	14.2	111.5	79	776	402.8	36.4	585	7,627	2,194.3	205.0	98	304	60.7	12.5
Goldsboro, NC	11.3	90.8	98	1,920	1,385.3	75.9	461	6,214	1,619.3	144.9	67	335	53.7	10.5
Grand Forks, ND-MN	17.4	169.4	134	1,686	2,146.5	93.1	422	7,560	1,922.4	189.7	99	633	96.4	22.0
Grand Island, NE	13.3	175.3	124	1,468	1,064.1	82.7	357	5,519	1,394.8	139.7	75	313	58.1	10.5
Grand Junction, CO	17.5	117.9	200	1,731	942.8	90.2	572	8,305	2,463.2	237.0	303	936	208.8	39.0
Grand Rapids-Kentwood, MI	105.3	100.9	1,347	29,171	22,290.1	1,708.2	3,334	51,077	15,659.9	1,404.9	968	5,609	1,452.3	245.2
Grants Pass, OR	7.2	84.7	56	374	294.5	19.7	323	4,406	1,208.1	127.9	107	431	63.9	16.7
Great Falls, MT	12.8	155.4	116	1,152	722.0	54.0	362	5,326	1,439.0	139.0	123	412	82.2	13.8
Greeley, CO	28.3	99.2	274	3,365	3,733.5	201.6	668	10,289	3,768.8	327.5	314	1,616	358.6	79.6
Green Bay, WI	21.4	67.7	363	7,728	5,562.2	423.7	1,012	17,154	4,824.6	445.4	245	1,493	393.8	56.0
Greensboro-High Point, NC	76.3	101.4	1,156	18,749	17,580.4	1,345.0	2,540	36,436	10,177.9	943.8	857	5,321	942.0	251.9
Greenville, NC	13.6	77.6	131	1,514	1,021.3	73.6	625	9,154	2,556.1	229.1	184	717	170.0	25.7
Greenville-Anderson, SC	102.8	117.5	1,043	15,072	19,442.8	946.9	3,002	44,653	11,970.0	1,108.6	1,003	4,123	1,124.8	170.5
Gulfport-Biloxi, MS	41.2	101.1	230	1,786	1,017.3	87.4	1,416	19,174	5,019.8	462.4	364	1,537	339.1	52.6
Hagerstown-Martinsburg, MD-WV	23.8	85.3	172	2,772	3,118.1	142.6	886	14,706	3,843.0	346.6	237	1,208	273.6	44.3
Hammond, LA	15.1	117.0	89	2,288	1,747.3	111.0	454	6,671	1,984.3	168.0	113	541	86.5	20.8
Hanford-Corcoran, CA	29.1	192.6	61	704	969.0	42.0	292	4,155	1,272.1	117.0	112	436	95.6	14.5
Harrisburg-Carlisle, PA	45.5	80.6	503	9,307	9,849.3	533.3	1,910	36,367	10,960.8	950.7	517	2,939	738.8	143.3
Harrisonburg, VA	14.8	112.5	114	1,871	1,504.5	106.9	546	7,127	1,833.8	178.3	112	892	215.6	38.3
Hartford-East Hartford-Middletown, CT	71.5	59.0	1,144	22,088	20,949.8	1,464.5	4,130	63,828	18,188.9	1,786.0	1,124	6,434	1,750.6	313.3
Hattiesburg, MS	21.1	125.4	88	913	755.2	41.9	762	10,006	2,698.8	241.5	99	474	87.4	17.6
Hickory-Lenoir-Morganton, NC	34.5	95.1	354	7,069	4,801.9	360.6	1,242	16,890	4,808.2	420.7	257	853	201.6	32.1
Hilton Head Island-Bluffton, SC	40.1	193.1	153	1,403	781.4	71.7	892	12,942	3,733.4	333.2	489	1,943	465.3	89.1
Hinesville, GA	6.9	86.4	D	D	D	D	199	2,196	617.7	53.6	0	0	0.0	5.6
Homosassa Springs, FL	14.2	100.3	74	527	272.7	24.8	431	5,633	1,864.0	157.5	163	1,014	94.7	21.7
Hot Springs, AR	16.1	165.4	75	659	460.1	39.1	496	6,194	1,684.3	157.7	130	490	77.5	17.1
Houma-Thibodaux, LA	27.5	129.7	195	1,750	824.5	87.2	770	10,780	2,902.6	273.2	222	1,711	519.7	110.9
Houston-The Woodlands-Sugar Land, TX	436.7	65.6	8,429	128,052	415,508.9	8,839.8	18,661	302,441	98,382.8	8,624.7	8,013	53,141	15,673.0	2,862.9
Huntington-Ashland, WV-KY-OH	42.1	114.6	254	3,709	2,328.7	185.6	1,232	17,655	4,552.1	396.7	290	1,269	340.9	53.3
Huntsville, AL	78.7	176.9	346	5,403	5,362.0	327.2	1,564	22,337	6,222.2	600.9	477	1,987	595.5	78.6
Idaho Falls, ID	39.1	279.9	216	2,305	4,476.6	112.5	586	8,543	2,476.3	221.7	151	477	124.9	19.4
Indianapolis-Carmel-Anderson, IN	202.5	101.8	2,107	41,088	37,575.1	2,632.4	5,868	108,446	35,674.9	2,962.2	2,644	17,003	4,928.0	888.9
Iowa City, IA	11.9	71.2	144	1,982	1,756.8	108.6	557	10,148	2,465.8	260.6	158	715	149.8	31.8
Ithaca, NY	7.9	75.0	D	D	D	D	346	5,033	1,194.1	121.5	129	712	171.4	26.2
Jackson, MI	10.8	68.0	128	1,327	1,023.5	78.3	497	7,174	2,031.9	187.5	109	573	104.9	19.7
Jackson, MS	99.8	167.1	642	9,867	9,420.6	565.9	2,258	30,846	8,487.3	778.5	669	3,008	636.7	125.4
Jackson, TN	22.0	123.0	214	3,131	2,053.1	141.7	753	9,779	2,771.5	243.2	157	702	163.2	27.0
Jacksonville, FL	147.3	101.6	1,338	24,247	22,172.0	1,556.0	5,167	77,260	23,699.5	2,066.5	2,317	11,376	3,719.8	586.3
Jacksonville, NC	17.9	95.9	55	320	144.1	13.4	547	8,416	2,334.6	206.5	200	744	146.7	24.8
Janesville-Beloit, WI	16.7	103.5	136	2,677	1,878.5	145.6	510	10,004	2,631.5	285.4	118	452	132.7	19.6
Jefferson City, MO	13.8	91.3	115	1,582	1,580.8	69.2	502	7,576	2,005.3	180.7	103	376	83.9	13.0
Johnson City, TN	27.6	137.6	102	1,770	1,240.9	102.9	696	10,855	2,885.3	259.4	164	868	146.2	28.1
Johnstown, PA	14.9	109.4	104	988	573.3	44.9	534	6,781	1,773.7	160.2	83	460	75.9	15.1

1. Merchant wholesalers, except manufacturers' sales branches and offices. 2. Employer establishments.

Table C. Metropolitan Areas — **Professional Services, Manufacturing, and Accommodation and Food Services**

Area name	Professional, scientific, and technical services, 2017				Manufacturing, 2017				Accommodation and food services, 2017			
	Number of establish-ments	Number of employees	Sales (mil dol)	Average payroll (mil dol)	Number of establish-ments	Number of employees	Receipts (mil dol)	Annual payroll (mil dol)	Number of establish-ments	Number of employees	Receipts (mil dol)	Annual payroll (mil dol)
	147	148	149	150	151	152	153	154	155	156	157	158
Evansville, IN-KY	215	1,157	144.2	52.8	387	22,435	11,651.4	1,241.5	654	14,431	789.7	215.4
Fairbanks, AK	212	1,356	313.2	91.0	69	454	226.6	24.4	233	3,306	250.7	70.7
Fargo, ND-MN	616	6,448	999.8	406.5	225	9,174	3,239.3	451.7	559	12,555	596.1	196.8
Farmington, NM	D	D	D	D	69	776	154.0	43.1	240	4,900	237.5	68.0
Fayetteville, NC	685	7,134	868.4	351.3	182	8,895	3,570.3	464.0	902	18,570	931.2	255.0
Fayetteville-Springdale-Rogers, AR	D	D	D	D	399	25,666	8,082.6	1,070.6	1,100	22,361	1,201.9	349.4
Flagstaff, AZ	349	1,471	190.8	68.8	88	4,893	2,250.3	425.7	601	15,061	1,200.0	323.8
Flint, MI	D	D	D	D	279	11,516	13,080.7	738.1	730	14,666	707.3	209.7
Florence, SC	62	291	28.4	10.6	144	9,278	5,337.0	578.4	414	8,028	411.4	114.3
Florence-Muscle Shoals, AL	217	992	106.2	38.4	176	9,012	4,634.2	458.7	291	6,313	285.6	82.3
Fond du Lac, WI	141	1,433	156.5	104.1	146	9,480	4,108.5	486.2	222	3,542	163.0	44.3
Fort Collins, CO	1,642	9,285	1,637.8	668.0	444	9,931	3,909.8	646.2	949	18,194	1,087.4	338.0
Fort Smith, AR-OK	146	488	54.9	17.7	251	19,204	5,983.8	788.8	491	9,213	511.7	143.6
Fort Wayne, IN	858	5,855	892.8	314.7	531	31,277	21,098.4	1,815.6	806	17,815	860.0	254.9
Fresno, CA	1,581	10,913	1,576.6	610.6	579	22,774	9,073.4	1,091.3	1,647	30,013	1,783.4	501.2
Gadsden, AL	127	656	80.8	28.2	89	5,358	1,607.9	231.1	187	3,587	187.6	50.4
Gainesville, FL	933	5,714	809.1	320.3	198	4,479	1,299.9	277.3	677	14,133	739.7	216.8
Gainesville, GA	410	1,919	331.0	107.0	223	20,766	8,353.0	932.3	312	5,862	338.5	93.2
Gettysburg, PA	D	D	D	D	112	6,561	2,010.6	314.9	227	3,958	220.6	62.9
Glens Falls, NY	211	1,168	168.3	61.2	166	6,276	2,142.4	344.2	546	5,814	463.2	128.1
Goldsboro, NC	130	679	74.7	29.3	56	4,957	1,351.3	226.3	208	4,152	202.4	56.5
Grand Forks, ND-MN	171	1,563	210.6	92.2	87	4,329	2,005.0	210.3	273	5,333	236.3	76.0
Grand Island, NE	17	75	10.2	2.9	83	7,034	4,911.9	343.6	165	2,662	147.2	42.9
Grand Junction, CO	497	3,416	527.2	209.4	150	2,740	552.2	124.2	335	6,462	356.5	117.5
Grand Rapids-Kentwood, MI	95	326	35.5	13.2	1,818	112,568	34,055.6	6,015.4	1,921	42,291	2,119.3	669.4
Grants Pass, OR	D	D	D	D	109	2,528	561.2	111.2	208	2,919	169.8	49.3
Great Falls, MT	D	D	D	D	74	1,318	1,377.7	71.3	239	3,989	222.4	63.5
Greeley, CO	D	D	D	D	305	11,968	5,959.4	657.2	472	7,843	406.0	117.9
Green Bay, WI	64	281	31.3	12.7	531	28,645	12,397.0	1,590.0	764	13,496	651.0	189.0
Greensboro-High Point, NC	139	658	69.5	22.8	965	53,335	23,488.4	2,768.4	1,584	33,522	1,736.9	495.7
Greenville, NC	D	D	D	D	93	6,726	2,690.2	375.9	369	8,445	417.1	111.3
Greenville-Anderson, SC	51	281	4,693.0	14.4	895	54,844	22,383.1	2,986.5	1,920	37,861	2,071.2	572.7
Gulfport-Biloxi, MS	346	3,175	461.2	190.7	206	18,526	14,515.7	1,292.4	898	29,155	2,424.4	611.4
Hagerstown-Martinsburg, MD-WV	15	73	8.0	4.3	188	8,884	5,133.7	477.2	539	9,342	493.4	141.7
Hammond, LA	209	1,142	174.4	60.4	77	2,023	625.2	87.3	252	4,913	238.7	67.2
Hanford-Corcoran, CA	105	965	109.9	44.9	60	4,514	2,819.7	215.2	196	4,210	460.0	97.9
Harrisburg-Carlisle, PA	47	190	18.2	6.9	416	17,387	7,723.1	894.9	1,321	23,940	1,497.7	424.3
Harrisonburg, VA	D	D	D	D	127	9,734	4,763.0	488.0	300	7,566	361.0	125.3
Hartford-East Hartford-Middletown, CT	D	D	D	D	1,498	64,785	23,826.9	4,667.5	2,840	47,390	2,999.0	888.5
Hattiesburg, MS	147	908	115.7	41.9	106	5,628	1,721.3	243.7	4	44	2.0	6.3
Hickory-Lenoir-Morganton, NC	417	2,586	843.7	133.6	675	40,756	11,367.2	1,757.5	645	12,771	639.9	179.8
Hilton Head Island-Bluffton, SC	690	2,812	437.0	159.3	96	803	173.6	35.4	632	14,350	1,037.6	300.8
Hinesville, GA	D	D	D	D	19	1,904	1,276.2	123.5	114	2,078	104.3	26.4
Homosassa Springs, FL	D	D	D	D	55	338	75.1	13.6	235	3,513	175.3	50.8
Hot Springs, AR	D	D	D	D	88	2,427	694.6	115.8	306	5,510	291.2	85.8
Houma-Thibodaux, LA	426	4,166	522.2	245.0	182	6,023	1,614.3	342.7	405	7,171	388.7	110.1
Houston-The Woodlands-Sugar Land, TX	16,288	205,029	48,835.2	18,989.6	5,365	197,897	207,297.1	13,744.8	13,469	285,245	18,675.9	5,164.0
Huntington-Ashland, WV-KY-OH	205	1,326	165.3	60.3	D	D	D	D	671	12,309	643.4	172.8
Huntsville, AL	1,469	37,711	10,167.3	3,380.3	331	19,339	8,186.3	1,165.6	898	19,126	992.7	281.2
Idaho Falls, ID	39	125	15.1	3.9	D	D	D	D	237	5,065	257.2	77.1
Indianapolis-Carmel-Anderson, IN	4,017	57,436	12,082.6	4,973.8	1,704	78,199	35,336.4	4,903.2	4,398	99,434	5,604.7	1,630.1
Iowa City, IA	344	3,072	386.2	151.8	117	5,690	7,070.3	285.6	D	D	D	D
Ithaca, NY	284	2,037	318.8	123.2	88	2,873	939.4	150.9	334	4,972	279.4	89.9
Jackson, MI	D	D	D	D	248	9,000	3,017.6	486.8	272	4,870	243.9	69.4
Jackson, MS	1,481	10,532	1,870.3	648.9	342	18,208	9,831.2	953.6	1,214	25,457	1,298.2	349.4
Jackson, TN	65	322	29.7	9.1	190	12,997	6,100.6	672.7	304	6,376	328.9	91.7
Jacksonville, FL	3,635	38,234	6,827.2	2,705.8	829	27,062	13,053.4	1,581.3	3,297	70,314	4,264.6	1,209.7
Jacksonville, NC	D	D	D	D	47	1,040	391.8	42.3	399	7,870	435.4	117.0
Janesville-Beloit, WI	208	2,273	165.4	154.1	229	10,607	4,961.7	598.4	366	6,304	308.1	85.0
Jefferson City, MO	68	431	32.1	15.2	D	5,939	D	295.0	238	4,388	211.4	60.5
Johnson City, TN	49	163	16.1	4.5	163	7,253	1,932.3	355.4	420	9,089	431.6	127.9
Johnstown, PA	D	D	D	D	115	5,161	4,739.5	286.6	298	4,130	190.7	49.8

Area name	Health care and social assistance, 2017				Other services, 2017				Nonemployer businesses, 2018		Value of residential construction authorized by building permits, 2020	
	Number of establish-ments	Number of employees	Receipts (mil dol)	Annual payroll (mil dol)	Number of establish-ments	Number of employees	Receipts (mil dol)	Annual payroll (mil dol)	Number	Receipts (mil dol)	New construc-tion ($1,000)	Number of housing units
	159	160	161	162	163	164	165	166	167	168	169	170
Evansville, IN-KY	957	26,880	3,219.3	1,154.0	566	4,016	489.9	126.8	17,771	742.5	331,024	1,349
Fairbanks, AK	313	6,507	890.8	371.6	178	896	121.0	32.9	6,035	245.0	8,034	36
Fargo, ND-MN	702	25,095	3,252.9	1,152.7	515	3,502	406.9	102.4	17,698	1,018.6	521,395	2,289
Farmington, NM	282	7,628	874.3	352.8	202	1,305	207.0	44.1	5,094	217.1	25,463	97
Fayetteville, NC	972	26,445	2,898.1	1,156.8	556	3,131	316.9	89.2	30,544	1,160.6	386,963	2,307
Fayetteville-Springdale-Rogers, AR	1,202	25,981	3,024.6	1,265.3	628	3,936	776.3	131.5	41,247	1,926.6	1,698,570	7,120
Flagstaff, AZ	422	8,994	1,229.8	448.2	249	1,422	143.0	43.3	10,011	429.6	234,809	1,051
Flint, MI	1,286	27,955	3,165.7	1,254.4	569	3,886	606.1	116.9	28,457	1,065.0	125,172	510
Florence, SC	482	17,635	2,176.1	825.3	259	1,768	228.5	49.3	12,317	505.2	134,972	766
Florence-Muscle Shoals, AL	359	8,212	912.1	336.5	D	D	D	33.3	10,415	486.4	42,567	359
Fond du Lac, WI	295	6,619	864.7	308.7	179	975	99.3	26.0	5,239	278.3	55,758	235
Fort Collins, CO	1,147	19,461	2,304.6	932.0	734	4,247	640.0	141.2	34,654	1,652.3	834,591	3,221
Fort Smith, AR-OK	649	16,059	1,709.5	677.0	276	1,231	124.3	34.2	17,080	829.9	95,634	662
Fort Wayne, IN	1,105	37,370	4,622.5	1,744.1	734	5,454	593.7	179.0	27,095	1,163.0	528,573	1,978
Fresno, CA	2,398	47,713	6,660.5	2,612.0	1,035	8,607	994.0	274.0	57,287	3,096.1	1,026,920	3,902
Gadsden, AL	300	7,233	761.6	303.7	114	779	125.7	24.3	7,632	354.2	28,773	188
Gainesville, FL	891	27,359	4,031.2	1,509.1	478	4,073	589.2	131.2	24,926	983.4	439,778	2,743
Gainesville, GA	488	13,913	1,965.5	721.0	282	1,514	177.5	51.0	17,795	852.5	432,874	2,249
Gettysburg, PA	185	4,860	512.4	201.8	174	1,312	124.6	33.5	6,661	303.6	127,475	438
Glens Falls, NY	380	8,015	879.9	361.3	225	1,129	133.6	38.3	8,630	400.7	102,847	384
Goldsboro, NC	259	7,604	781.9	310.8	152	810	71.4	21.2	6,691	266.7	89,592	482
Grand Forks, ND-MN	256	9,848	1,051.4	476.0	179	1,028	112.8	28.4	6,435	299.5	58,441	227
Grand Island, NE	209	4,829	544.8	207.4	182	1,173	113.0	30.3	5,093	247.3	60,521	305
Grand Junction, CO	438	11,405	1,429.2	530.6	315	1,662	188.0	55.8	12,670	591.6	194,945	1,231
Grand Rapids-Kentwood, MI	2,374	71,291	8,496.1	3,249.0	1,812	13,259	1,397.1	405.1	78,000	3,906.9	996,567	3,705
Grants Pass, OR	298	5,253	525.5	221.0	107	482	40.7	12.6	6,128	289.6	67,531	333
Great Falls, MT	285	6,971	802.3	322.9	155	941	105.1	29.9	4,890	220.0	55,622	272
Greeley, CO	551	8,971	1,127.3	446.2	418	2,212	278.9	74.4	25,419	1,268.5	1,249,558	5,268
Green Bay, WI	875	26,224	3,609.2	1,256.5	541	3,230	342.5	94.9	17,848	930.1	323,728	1,408
Greensboro-High Point, NC	1,681	43,095	4,953.5	1,919.8	1,137	7,549	1,398.0	247.6	59,738	2,667.8	885,980	3,964
Greenville, NC	499	16,338	2,158.5	773.9	220	1,287	123.7	36.0	11,555	461.4	237,203	1,275
Greenville-Anderson, SC	1,853	45,184	4,912.9	1,971.8	1,225	8,210	1,147.1	278.1	69,867	3,172.9	2,179,036	10,604
Gulfport-Biloxi, MS	868	21,560	2,686.4	1,158.3	436	2,505	282.3	72.2	30,842	1,285.5	515,796	2,769
Hagerstown-Martinsburg, MD-WV	669	16,247	1,944.6	902.2	394	2,465	227.0	74.4	16,375	707.8	422,275	1,768
Hammond, LA	321	8,978	880.7	357.3	160	1,207	127.0	37.2	11,167	416.4	229,452	1,508
Hanford-Corcoran, CA	213	4,803	631.8	221.0	116	501	59.1	14.2	5,183	233.0	138,978	508
Harrisburg-Carlisle, PA	1,632	53,486	6,514.3	2,802.8	1,296	8,581	1,088.4	301.4	37,478	1,826.3	357,258	1,542
Harrisonburg, VA	314	7,177	916.6	339.0	236	1,217	138.7	43.1	8,980	420.8	190,828	655
Hartford-East Hartford-Middletown, CT	3,820	111,796	11,858.2	5,222.4	2,522	16,629	2,127.3	625.0	85,373	4,648.0	293,118	1,508
Hattiesburg, MS	225	8,350	1,077.1	469.3	95	553	56.1	14.2	13,140	598.2	28,081	153
Hickory-Lenoir-Morganton, NC	764	21,581	2,349.2	916.4	460	2,709	252.6	72.4	23,805	1,090.2	336,831	1,880
Hilton Head Island-Bluffton, SC	541	9,322	1,067.4	398.1	377	2,940	352.1	101.2	20,670	1,130.1	1,149,400	3,698
Hinesville, GA	96	2,182	262.4	105.0	D	D	D	D	4,226	122.0	187,718	837
Homosassa Springs, FL	393	9,117	940.2	381.0	225	964	70.3	19.9	10,763	446.0	434,456	1,983
Hot Springs, AR	343	8,736	1,069.9	380.5	186	762	67.3	19.5	8,362	365.8	37,597	330
Houma-Thibodaux, LA	464	11,491	1,219.8	503.8	264	1,811	264.9	84.4	15,489	688.3	131,642	587
Houston-The Woodlands-Sugar Land, TX	16,882	356,550	47,587.1	17,579.0	8,873	82,767	11,931.9	3,429.0	708,007	35,358.2	1,3,677,948	69,263
Huntington-Ashland, WV-KY-OH	982	29,947	3,545.2	1,392.1	392	2,346	295.1	80.0	17,969	703.5	61,826	305
Huntsville, AL	1,161	27,578	3,656.9	1,322.4	578	4,408	556.9	154.4	33,343	1,439.6	1,069,708	6,172
Idaho Falls, ID	578	9,005	1,077.5	377.8	D	D	D	D	12,135	605.2	289,998	1,478
Indianapolis-Carmel-Anderson, IN	5,475	146,136	18,863.1	7,337.2	3,285	28,490	5,226.1	1,094.4	152,860	7,008.6	3,799,651	13,451
Iowa City, IA	503	19,840	2,733.7	1,016.9	273	1,530	321.0	55.3	12,231	581.5	277,040	1,167
Ithaca, NY	284	6,258	643.2	273.4	164	962	197.3	31.3	7,685	302.6	116,081	644
Jackson, MI	361	9,998	1,123.1	492.2	211	1,210	152.8	37.1	8,844	366.5	41,766	176
Jackson, MS	1,554	53,188	5,779.9	2,503.1	776	4,996	693.8	206.5	53,502	2,406.0	362,435	1,416
Jackson, TN	487	16,069	1,663.6	683.6	57	249	29.0	6.7	11,615	528.4	120,316	537
Jacksonville, FL	4,256	94,242	12,989.2	4,792.7	2,341	17,350	3,486.9	659.6	132,101	5,694.8	4,338,426	22,738
Jacksonville, NC	263	5,331	642.5	218.9	211	1,071	104.4	28.1	11,238	421.5	295,039	1,597
Janesville-Beloit, WI	342	8,861	1,200.5	478.6	265	1,356	121.9	34.5	8,238	376.3	129,353	617
Jefferson City, MO	350	9,389	960.4	397.3	285	1,588	252.1	66.9	9,492	451.5	32,996	246
Johnson City, TN	498	16,280	1,989.8	880.4	198	1,048	88.2	27.3	13,073	602.4	175,038	819
Johnstown, PA	484	11,101	1,045.2	458.7	299	1,543	145.7	35.4	6,085	259.9	15,741	62

Area name	Government employment and payroll, 2017									Local government finances, 2017				
			March payroll (percent of total)							General revenue				
												Taxes		
													Per capita[1] (dollars)	
	Full-time equivalent employees	March payroll (dollars)	Administration, judicial, and legal	Police and corrections	Fire protection	Highways and transportation	Health and welfare	Natural resources and utilities	Education and libraries	Total (mil dol)	Intergovernmental (mil dol)	Total (mil dol)	Total	Property
	171	172	173	174	175	176	177	178	179	180	181	182	183	184
Evansville, IN-KY	9,902	3,6,941,786	6.8	12.1	4.7	4.4	2.1	7.5	60.6	1,018.5	468.6	334.9	1,064	950
Fairbanks, AK	3,002	1,6,676,902	7.1	2.7	3.0	4.7	1.3	2.3	77.7	420.1	226.7	155.1	1,556	1,370
Fargo, ND-MN	8,060	3,5,621,185	5.8	9.4	2.6	4.8	9.4	7.1	59.9	1,227.7	564.0	377.7	1,564	1,152
Farmington, NM	5,621	2,0,270,322	4.8	12.1	2.9	2.2	1.4	10.3	64.6	518.5	323.9	118.0	930	655
Fayetteville, NC	25,624	9,4,074,518	2.7	7.1	1.6	0.9	40.2	4.2	40.6	1,321.7	774.1	427.4	826	611
Fayetteville-Springdale-Rogers, AR	16,064	5,4,460,063	5.9	10.4	4.9	3.6	0.6	6.3	66.6	1,638.8	908.6	471.7	915	358
Flagstaff, AZ	4,429	1,9,039,894	12.5	13.9	10.9	3.0	3.7	6.5	46.5	547.2	192.8	256.6	1,820	982
Flint, MI	14,500	6,4,991,149	5.0	5.5	1.6	4.1	26.9	2.5	53.4	2,164.1	1,125.9	370.3	909	840
Florence, SC	7,178	2,4,215,567	6.1	9.0	2.0	1.8	7.3	4.9	67.3	640.7	276.0	252.4	1,228	875
Florence-Muscle Shoals, AL	5,046	1,7,607,090	3.5	8.3	4.4	3.9	4.2	18.5	54.5	407.5	182.7	142.8	970	437
Fond du Lac, WI	3,803	1,6,957,873	4.6	8.4	2.5	4.0	10.4	2.7	65.5	454.0	217.1	165.7	1,618	1,491
Fort Collins, CO	11,808	5,4,787,902	10.2	11.8	1.5	3.1	9.4	17.5	42.7	1,540.8	372.6	770.7	2,240	1,405
Fort Smith, AR-OK	8,795	3,0,475,057	5.0	8.0	3.5	3.2	2.9	6.9	70.1	815.3	441.4	224.3	896	351
Fort Wayne, IN	12,071	4,7,809,113	6.4	13.4	4.1	4.5	2.2	5.2	63.0	1,257.3	594.2	493.3	1,217	942
Fresno, CA	36,934	19,7,609,273	3.7	9.8	2.2	3.1	10.2	4.8	65.2	7,476.9	5,082.5	1,284.5	1,304	863
Gadsden, AL	3,617	1,3,009,490	5.6	11.4	6.0	3.8	7.4	7.0	56.2	298.2	139.3	104.1	1,011	317
Gainesville, FL	11,373	4,2,019,036	10.7	15.7	4.5	5.0	3.9	10.6	46.7	1,136.1	422.9	408.1	1,258	1,002
Gainesville, GA	6,731	2,5,935,061	6.3	9.9	7.4	1.6	4.5	5.5	63.2	690.5	254.6	301.9	1,518	931
Gettysburg, PA	3,735	1,4,888,774	5.7	6.9	0.6	7.9	1.4	2.5	74.3	415.6	175.3	194.5	1,897	1,435
Glens Falls, NY	6,598	2,8,307,844	6.0	7.5	1.9	6.5	5.4	3.3	67.7	831.7	303.9	422.9	3,359	2,409
Goldsboro, NC	4,543	1,4,430,137	3.0	6.6	2.3	1.5	7.8	6.9	69.4	355.9	205.6	110.1	895	614
Grand Forks, ND-MN	4,216	1,7,580,017	6.4	10.9	3.1	4.9	9.4	9.1	53.4	544.8	260.1	152.8	1,497	1,235
Grand Island, NE	3,748	1,6,021,253	5.3	7.0	3.1	3.3	8.8	15.7	55.7	414.0	133.9	166.7	2,210	1,731
Grand Junction, CO	5,190	2,2,403,036	4.9	11.8	4.6	3.6	5.4	9.0	57.7	577.7	216.3	242.8	1,606	965
Grand Rapids-Kentwood, MI	27,958	12,4,940,548	6.9	8.4	2.2	4.4	2.8	3.5	69.2	4,226.9	2,171.7	1,313.6	1,235	1,096
Grants Pass, OR	2,126	9,641,417	6.2	10.1	2.6	3.2	1.6	2.9	71.5	273.1	137.7	81.5	941	854
Great Falls, MT	2,747	1,0,563,299	7.1	12.7	4.0	6.0	4.7	5.1	59.8	271.4	111.1	93.2	1,142	1,106
Greeley, CO	9,283	3,8,633,927	9.4	12.0	4.9	4.5	6.1	8.0	51.9	1,519.5	370.2	817.7	2,673	1,807
Green Bay, WI	11,518	5,4,797,399	4.3	8.6	3.0	3.6	6.2	4.8	67.9	1,445.2	677.0	482.8	1,510	1,467
Greensboro-High Point, NC	25,704	9,9,678,689	5.1	11.0	4.2	2.2	7.9	6.3	60.2	2,536.8	1,163.5	997.8	1,309	986
Greenville, NC	7,258	2,4,893,380	7.1	10.4	2.2	2.4	12.6	10.0	49.6	931.3	283.9	183.1	1,025	720
Greenville-Anderson, SC	34,640	13,5,879,374	4.2	6.5	2.8	1.3	32.5	5.6	45.7	4,838.4	1,072.7	1,057.5	1,181	986
Gulfport-Biloxi, MS	20,249	7,9,714,429	3.9	6.4	3.6	3.1	37.3	2.6	42.1	2,520.3	802.4	549.2	1,331	1,205
Hagerstown-Martinsburg, MD-WV	9,772	3,8,973,336	4.3	5.3	1.7	2.3	1.8	4.8	77.2	902.5	390.0	372.8	1,318	896
Hammond, LA	6,779	2,5,167,545	4.7	6.0	1.3	2.0	46.1	2.3	36.2	779.7	229.4	257.9	1,949	370
Hanford-Corcoran, CA	5,524	2,8,583,504	5.7	10.6	2.5	2.1	9.0	5.0	62.4	740.6	510.5	136.2	910	697
Harrisburg-Carlisle, PA	18,493	8,1,071,678	6.6	11.0	0.6	3.8	4.3	4.5	67.5	2,908.8	1,083.3	1,286.3	2,253	1,599
Harrisonburg, VA	4,679	1,6,497,844	6.1	8.2	4.6	2.4	3.2	8.7	63.8	447.5	184.3	176.1	1,314	909
Hartford-East Hartford-Middletown, CT	44,055	24,1,342,339	3.5	7.5	3.4	2.8	2.8	4.2	73.5	5,985.9	2,042.5	3,451.9	2,860	2,833
Hattiesburg, MS	10,091	3,5,082,133	3.9	4.9	1.9	2.5	48.3	2.3	35.5	1,021.0	226.4	195.5	1,166	1,085
Hickory-Lenoir-Morganton, NC	14,794	5,5,039,991	4.1	5.5	2.3	1.1	26.7	4.2	54.5	1,362.2	549.8	392.4	1,069	777
Hilton Head Island-Bluffton, SC	7,286	3,1,070,896	6.9	9.2	5.9	1.5	27.2	3.9	41.9	792.7	175.3	468.7	2,180	1,800
Hinesville, GA	3,184	1,0,476,566	5.6	9.1	2.0	1.1	16.5	1.8	60.7	286.2	127.4	77.1	959	680
Homosassa Springs, FL	3,578	1,1,361,255	9.3	10.8	0.3	3.5	2.1	4.9	64.4	336.2	116.8	150.9	1,038	922
Hot Springs, AR	2,866	1,0,381,906	5.0	10.8	3.8	3.3	1.5	7.3	67.5	304.8	156.1	87.2	886	270
Houma-Thibodaux, LA	10,191	3,7,994,926	5.6	9.2	0.6	2.5	34.4	4.0	42.7	1,294.7	400.9	370.4	1,764	974
Houston-The Woodlands-Sugar Land, TX	265,645	1,12,0,213,911	4.6	10.3	3.2	4.2	7.1	3.0	65.9	32,271.5	8,186.0	17,657.1	2,559	2,163
Huntington-Ashland, WV-KY-OH	12,791	4,2,889,437	4.7	6.3	2.3	2.8	5.3	5.1	71.4	1,066.5	485.9	374.4	1,034	787
Huntsville, AL	21,033	9,6,058,347	3.1	5.7	2.8	2.6	46.2	5.7	30.7	2,857.7	1,135.9	565.7	1,241	536
Idaho Falls, ID	5,031	1,6,371,062	6.9	10.2	5.3	4.4	6.0	9.2	56.8	433.4	230.5	117.9	810	773
Indianapolis-Carmel-Anderson, IN	71,926	29,4,569,457	4.6	7.4	6.2	2.3	19.6	5.7	53.1	9,945.1	3,484.9	2,361.5	1,165	958
Iowa City, IA	5,447	2,3,291,400	6.2	7.7	1.8	5.3	10.0	5.9	60.3	714.3	236.8	330.7	1,928	1,720
Ithaca, NY	4,615	2,2,463,397	5.1	5.9	2.8	4.9	6.6	3.9	68.1	599.8	194.0	318.4	3,102	2,262
Jackson, MI	4,580	1,9,841,345	6.9	7.2	1.5	4.1	4.5	2.4	72.5	658.3	378.1	159.5	1,006	930
Jackson, MS	22,236	7,3,312,212	5.7	9.7	4.1	2.5	1.8	3.4	71.2	1,963.8	911.6	694.6	1,159	1,103
Jackson, TN	12,166	4,6,642,029	2.8	6.8	2.2	2.2	52.9	6.4	26.2	1,274.8	228.3	186.1	1,043	697
Jacksonville, FL	41,501	15,8,263,187	5.8	13.1	6.6	2.5	1.2	7.2	58.8	5,424.0	1,860.7	2,146.8	1,426	1,035
Jacksonville, NC	5,784	2,0,744,428	4.2	8.1	2.3	1.0	8.3	4.8	68.0	507.1	241.2	182.5	935	624
Janesville-Beloit, WI	6,384	2,8,667,201	5.4	9.3	3.9	4.1	10.9	3.7	61.0	783.0	426.4	256.6	1,582	1,459
Jefferson City, MO	4,544	1,4,427,232	7.6	7.9	2.9	4.2	5.5	6.1	63.4	422.0	136.3	203.3	1,343	828
Johnson City, TN	7,169	2,2,904,686	6.8	9.2	3.2	5.3	3.4	12.4	58.8	506.4	203.4	185.9	921	688
Johnstown, PA	4,432	1,7,315,677	6.6	9.4	1.6	6.5	5.9	4.0	62.3	581.4	337.4	163.1	1,227	939

1. Based on the resident population estimated as of July 1 of the year shown

Area name	Local government finances, 2017 (cont.)									Government employment, 2019			Individual income tax returns, 2018		
	Direct general expenditure							Debt outstanding							
			Percent of total for:												
	Total (mil dol)	Per capita[1] (dollars)	Educa-tion	Health and hospitals	Police protection	Public welfare	Highways	Total (mil dol)	Per capita[1] (dollars)	Federal civilian	Federal military	State and local	Number of returns	Mean adjusted gross income	Mean income tax
	185	186	187	188	189	190	191	192	193	194	195	196	197	198	199
Evansville, IN-KY	921.8	2,928	48.4	1.2	6.4	0.2	3.1	2,100.1	6,672	1,442	957	14,775	150,880	63,836	6,991
Fairbanks, AK	387.5	3,888	55.4	1.1	1.9	0.0	6.2	171.3	1,719	3,295	9,656	6,975	46,560	70,844	7,908
Fargo, ND-MN	1,448.2	5,996	38.9	1.6	3.8	2.3	16.5	2,933.0	12,145	2,668	1,319	16,328	120,550	77,958	9,287
Farmington, NM	564.6	4,449	58.2	1.5	6.0	1.7	3.7	2,061.0	16,239	1,567	307	9,093	49,970	51,825	4,633
Fayetteville, NC	1,318.4	2,548	60.5	2.0	8.1	6.0	1.6	759.0	1,467	16,549	49,132	29,341	224,020	49,428	3,985
Fayetteville-Springdale-Rogers, AR	1,568.8	3,043	57.0	0.5	5.6	0.0	7.5	2,367.6	4,592	2,850	2,085	29,060	240,260	81,977	10,175
Flagstaff, AZ	510.3	3,619	36.3	2.7	7.6	0.9	8.5	201.0	1,426	2,727	289	14,651	63,540	62,499	6,681
Flint, MI	2,110.3	5,179	40.0	28.9	4.1	1.6	3.9	912.4	2,239	1,132	634	17,955	195,710	53,368	5,197
Florence, SC	687.4	3,346	56.0	4.0	7.2	0.2	3.1	586.2	2,853	724	755	16,471	89,020	53,706	5,345
Florence-Muscle Shoals, AL	410.9	2,791	54.8	3.7	5.8	0.1	6.6	411.2	2,792	939	613	8,957	64,070	56,910	5,576
Fond du Lac, WI	502.6	4,908	51.0	5.3	5.0	8.5	11.1	445.8	4,353	211	260	5,153	51,910	64,832	6,929
Fort Collins, CO	1,367.1	3,973	34.9	5.0	7.1	3.4	10.2	1,497.6	4,352	2,657	859	36,926	179,310	81,897	10,513
Fort Smith, AR-OK	805.4	3,218	54.6	2.7	5.0	0.1	8.1	1,523.2	6,087	1,377	997	12,402	103,450	51,392	4,662
Fort Wayne, IN	1,159.3	2,859	50.9	1.2	8.0	0.0	6.4	1,227.2	3,027	2,286	1,252	17,949	204,100	62,318	6,716
Fresno, CA	7,002.6	7,108	41.9	23.6	5.5	6.2	2.3	5,206.5	5,285	11,020	1,543	61,888	424,470	56,374	5,640
Gadsden, AL	302.7	2,939	49.8	2.2	10.0	0.2	4.2	235.4	2,285	315	418	4,878	42,940	49,180	4,204
Gainesville, FL	1,164.2	3,588	39.3	3.4	7.8	1.6	4.6	2,461.5	7,586	5,006	667	40,041	145,800	63,652	7,591
Gainesville, GA	705.1	3,544	54.9	6.3	5.7	0.3	3.3	1,794.7	9,021	535	536	10,478	94,240	66,181	7,438
Gettysburg, PA	490.8	4,786	68.4	3.2	2.6	3.9	3.4	505.8	4,931	738	263	3,318	52,720	63,182	6,313
Glens Falls, NY	793.3	6,300	52.7	3.6	3.0	8.0	7.5	369.1	2,931	343	194	8,943	63,740	58,345	5,825
Goldsboro, NC	361.9	2,941	53.6	5.6	8.1	6.3	0.9	253.1	2,057	1,244	4,901	7,758	53,150	50,518	4,177
Grand Forks, ND-MN	524.8	5,139	41.9	2.4	6.0	4.5	9.3	799.5	7,829	1,111	2,293	11,518	47,890	65,692	6,917
Grand Island, NE	448.6	5,946	47.9	7.0	4.5	0.3	5.1	351.5	4,658	744	268	5,118	36,890	55,327	5,024
Grand Junction, CO	590.7	3,907	38.0	2.0	11.7	5.4	9.0	401.0	2,653	1,774	378	8,703	74,150	61,497	6,191
Grand Rapids-Kentwood, MI	4,654.2	4,376	53.2	5.5	3.8	0.8	8.5	5,701.5	5,360	3,686	1,792	45,498	519,270	70,022	7,828
Grants Pass, OR	275.8	3,186	64.0	3.0	8.2	0.2	5.2	96.3	1,112	281	203	2,983	39,670	51,669	4,775
Great Falls, MT	276.9	3,392	49.0	2.5	10.1	1.9	4.5	235.4	2,883	1,715	3,702	3,795	40,240	56,841	5,508
Greeley, CO	1,346.8	4,403	41.0	1.2	6.1	2.3	8.2	1,730.4	5,657	649	787	16,493	153,010	72,572	7,940
Green Bay, WI	1,619.4	5,066	51.0	3.2	5.3	3.3	9.1	1,404.1	4,392	1,508	839	19,211	163,340	71,567	8,512
Greensboro-High Point, NC	2,535.0	3,326	48.8	3.1	8.3	5.4	2.7	2,337.5	3,067	4,416	1,668	38,150	355,490	60,307	6,587
Greenville, NC	992.6	5,557	28.8	44.4	6.0	0.0	1.4	605.9	3,392	805	421	26,377	74,930	59,715	6,533
Greenville-Anderson, SC	4,536.7	5,067	30.6	44.6	4.0	0.1	1.4	4,701.6	5,251	3,075	3,359	57,607	415,550	66,521	6,989
Gulfport-Biloxi, MS	2,527.0	6,122	31.4	33.8	4.1	0.2	4.1	1,745.8	4,230	9,488	11,154	26,084	185,330	52,437	4,858
Hagerstown-Martinsburg, MD-WV	926.2	3,273	63.3	0.6	4.8	0.0	3.3	774.5	2,737	3,931	1,142	13,223	139,910	57,435	5,323
Hammond, LA	688.6	5,203	29.1	46.7	3.7	0.0	2.2	306.9	2,318	409	504	10,633	55,840	51,607	4,881
Hanford-Corcoran, CA	800.5	5,349	48.0	4.4	4.9	9.9	2.5	315.7	2,110	1,281	6,976	13,492	58,520	50,579	4,118
Harrisburg-Carlisle, PA	3,032.8	5,313	53.0	3.5	3.1	9.1	3.7	3,298.3	5,779	7,717	2,117	51,011	301,120	67,266	7,551
Harrisonburg, VA	477.9	3,566	55.7	2.7	4.2	5.9	2.8	192.3	1,435	371	402	11,332	57,390	58,331	5,413
Hartford-East Hartford-Middletown, CT	5,753.0	4,766	58.7	0.8	4.7	0.6	3.6	4,272.8	3,540	6,577	2,456	88,675	611,700	82,564	10,828
Hattiesburg, MS	979.8	5,842	25.3	51.8	3.3	0.0	4.1	538.8	3,213	887	1,340	14,891	71,070	54,546	5,470
Hickory-Lenoir-Morganton, NC	1,318.2	3,591	42.8	23.1	5.9	6.2	1.1	640.5	1,745	737	1,003	21,769	166,070	53,847	5,104
Hilton Head Island-Bluffton, SC	729.6	3,393	45.2	2.2	7.7	0.6	4.7	1,003.6	4,667	2,349	9,829	9,242	104,920	86,338	11,548
Hinesville, GA	299.4	3,724	51.9	17.4	5.4	0.1	1.9	137.1	1,705	3,770	15,907	3,906	34,550	41,289	2,585
Homosassa Springs, FL	372.5	2,562	41.6	6.4	9.6	0.6	8.5	478.1	3,288	236	257	4,084	71,910	53,896	5,436
Hot Springs, AR	292.2	2,972	52.9	0.3	5.9	0.1	3.2	550.8	5,602	510	376	3,793	45,410	54,377	5,514
Houma-Thibodaux, LA	1,181.3	5,627	29.3	37.5	4.0	0.7	4.0	345.0	1,643	445	885	10,109	88,270	42,722	6,081
Houston-The Woodlands-Sugar Land, TX	32,697.3	4,739	50.0	10.0	5.3	0.2	4.0	76,910.3	11,146	31,803	15,184	373,220	3,221,870	81,069	11,649
Huntington-Ashland, WV-KY-OH	1,094.8	3,025	62.5	3.0	4.6	0.9	2.7	807.4	2,230	3,684	1,393	19,036	151,720	55,097	5,231
Huntsville, AL	2,934.3	6,436	25.9	49.6	3.1	0.0	2.5	3,356.5	7,363	20,315	2,676	31,876	224,480	76,017	8,915
Idaho Falls, ID	391.7	2,692	49.1	5.2	7.2	0.3	4.0	275.2	1,891	858	490	7,448	66,190	64,572	5,807
Indianapolis-Carmel-Anderson, IN	9,316.1	4,595	35.9	31.9	4.2	0.0	1.6	13,571.8	6,694	17,820	6,693	118,672	1,014,550	70,819	8,487
Iowa City, IA	745.7	4,347	46.1	7.6	5.2	0.4	8.0	872.2	5,085	2,155	649	38,743	78,280	76,408	9,052
Ithaca, NY	619.3	6,032	49.2	4.1	2.9	6.9	6.0	621.0	6,049	276	157	5,337	41,170	73,949	8,926
Jackson, MI	668.6	4,217	50.5	11.8	4.6	3.8	6.7	543.5	3,428	344	238	7,242	72,880	56,281	5,409
Jackson, MS	2,011.3	3,356	56.7	2.2	6.1	0.2	6.0	2,117.6	3,533	6,358	3,332	51,735	263,820	58,099	6,217
Jackson, TN	1,202.8	6,745	21.7	56.8	4.2	0.1	2.2	795.7	4,462	659	480	16,583	79,800	52,573	4,945
Jacksonville, FL	5,156.1	3,426	44.6	2.6	10.3	0.5	2.7	11,861.3	7,881	19,680	16,553	59,376	785,430	72,467	9,211
Jacksonville, NC	519.7	2,664	54.1	3.9	6.9	9.7	1.1	462.0	2,368	6,670	39,167	7,907	84,210	47,590	3,521
Janesville-Beloit, WI	799.9	4,931	49.1	6.3	6.0	6.9	6.7	701.7	4,326	338	415	8,115	81,890	59,644	5,819
Jefferson City, MO	386.2	2,552	52.9	4.4	7.3	0.0	6.6	281.4	1,860	857	496	23,845	70,630	57,848	5,365
Johnson City, TN	521.6	2,583	49.2	1.0	6.9	0.1	6.1	965.5	4,782	3,141	596	13,017	89,880	55,486	5,577
Johnstown, PA	626.1	4,709	54.7	2.4	2.1	9.5	3.2	513.7	3,864	987	330	6,439	63,210	52,343	4,758

1. Based on the resident population estimated as of July 1 of the year shown.

CBSA[1]	DIV Code	Area name	Land area[2] (sq mi)	Population, 2021: Total persons 2021	Population, 2021: Rank	Population, 2021: Per square mile	Population characteristics, 2021: Race alone or in combination, not Hispanic or Latino (percent): White	Black	American Indian, Alaska Native	Asian and Pacific Islander	Percent Hispanic or Latino[3]	Age (percent): Under 5 years	5 to 17 years	18 to 24 years	25 to 34 years	35 to 44 years	45 to 54 years
			1	2	3	4	5	6	7	8	9	10	11	12	13	14	15
27860		Jonesboro, AR	1,465.5	134,878	307	92.0	77.4	16.8	0.8	1.5	5.2	6.5	14.1	14.5	14.6	12.9	11.4
27900		Joplin, MO	1,263.3	182,541	237	144.5	86.6	2.9	3.4	2.5	7.9	6.3	13.9	13.1	13.1	12.5	11.7
27980		Kahului-Wailuku-Lahaina, HI	1,161.5	164,221	261	141.4	44.4	1.6	1.7	67.5	12.1	5.6	12.4	10.2	11.5	13.8	12.7
28020		Kalamazoo-Portage, MI	562.0	261,108	189	464.6	79.7	13.6	1.2	3.6	5.6	5.7	12.1	18.7	13.7	12.1	10.7
28100		Kankakee, IL	676.5	106,601	346	157.6	72.3	16.0	0.5	1.5	11.6	5.8	12.6	15.2	12.2	12.0	12.0
28140		Kansas City, MO-KS	7,256.5	2,199,490	31	303.1	74.1	13.7	1.2	4.2	9.7	6.1	13.5	12.2	14.0	13.8	12.1
28420		Kennewick-Richland, WA	2,941.7	308,293	166	104.8	60.9	2.4	1.4	4.1	33.6	6.9	16.2	13.6	13.9	13.7	11.0
28660		Killeen-Temple, TX	2,818.6	486,101	115	172.5	50.0	22.7	1.1	5.0	25.1	7.4	15.0	15.2	16.3	13.9	10.6
28700		Kingsport-Bristol, TN-VA	2,010.4	308,661	165	153.5	94.7	2.9	0.8	1.0	2.1	4.5	10.7	11.0	11.7	11.3	13.4
28740		Kingston, NY	1,124.2	182,951	235	162.7	80.4	7.3	0.8	3.1	11.1	4.3	9.7	11.9	12.7	12.4	12.8
28940		Knoxville, TN	3,220.3	893,412	64	277.4	87.5	6.9	0.9	2.3	4.5	5.2	11.5	13.3	12.9	12.1	12.5
29020		Kokomo, IN	293.1	83,687	372	285.5	86.4	9.8	0.9	1.9	3.9	6.1	12.9	12.0	12.4	11.4	11.8
29100		La Crosse-Onalaska, WI-MN	1,003.8	139,211	299	138.7	91.4	2.5	0.7	5.0	2.2	4.9	11.3	18.1	12.2	11.9	10.7
29180		Lafayette, LA	3,408.9	479,212	118	140.6	68.1	26.4	0.7	2.2	4.2	6.4	13.9	12.6	13.9	13.4	11.5
29200		Lafayette-West Lafayette, IN	1,642.2	224,709	205	136.8	79.3	6.1	0.6	7.6	8.4	5.5	11.6	24.4	13.7	11.0	10.1
29340		Lake Charles, LA	2,348.7	210,362	214	89.6	69.4	25.4	1.1	1.9	4.2	6.8	13.8	12.3	13.8	12.9	11.4
29420		Lake Havasu City-Kingman, AZ	13,332.1	217,692	212	16.3	77.4	1.7	3.0	2.2	17.7	4.1	9.4	8.8	10.2	9.4	10.2
29460		Lakeland-Winter Haven, FL	1,797.8	753,520	80	419.1	55.5	15.9	0.7	2.4	27.4	5.6	12.6	12.2	13.3	12.6	11.7
29540		Lancaster, PA	943.9	553,652	104	586.6	82.0	4.8	0.4	3.0	11.5	6.2	13.1	12.7	13.1	11.9	11.2
29620		Lansing-East Lansing, MI	2,228.6	540,281	106	242.4	80.6	9.8	1.2	5.0	6.6	5.2	11.4	17.2	13.4	12.1	11.4
29700		Laredo, TX	3,361.5	267,945	186	79.7	3.7	0.4	0.1	0.5	95.4	8.3	18.2	16.7	13.7	12.3	11.9
29740		Las Cruces, NM	3,808.2	221,508	210	58.2	27.1	2.0	1.2	1.6	69.3	5.9	13.7	18.5	13.2	11.5	10.0
29820		Las Vegas-Henderson-Paradise, NV	7,891.7	2,292,476	29	290.5	43.2	14.0	1.1	14.0	32.3	5.8	13.0	12.0	14.6	14.1	13.0
29940		Lawrence, KS	455.8	119,363	331	261.9	81.8	6.2	3.5	6.1	6.7	4.5	10.2	26.0	13.8	12.4	9.7
30020		Lawton, OK	1,702.0	127,543	317	74.9	61.3	18.2	8.5	5.0	14.1	6.7	13.5	15.6	16.0	13.1	10.2
30140		Lebanon, PA	361.8	143,493	294	396.6	81.0	2.8	0.4	2.1	14.9	5.6	13.0	12.4	11.7	12.1	11.8
30300		Lewiston, ID-WA	1,484.4	64,851	381	43.7	89.5	1.2	5.2	2.0	4.6	5.4	11.8	11.5	12.1	11.8	11.4
30340		Lewiston-Auburn, ME	468.0	111,034	345	237.3	91.8	5.9	1.0	1.7	2.1	5.4	12.2	12.3	12.5	12.4	12.3
30460		Lexington-Fayette, KY	1,469.9	517,846	109	352.3	78.7	13.0	0.7	3.8	6.5	5.7	12.3	15.7	14.1	13.0	12.1
30620		Lima, OH	402.5	101,670	356	252.6	82.8	14.7	0.7	1.3	3.7	6.0	13.1	14.0	12.4	11.9	11.4
30700		Lincoln, NE	1,409.0	342,117	152	242.8	83.3	5.5	1.2	5.3	7.5	5.7	12.8	18.6	13.4	12.8	10.7
30780		Little Rock-North Little Rock-Conway, AR	4,083.8	750,936	81	183.9	67.4	25.5	1.1	2.4	5.8	6.0	13.3	13.2	13.8	13.2	12.0
30860		Logan, UT-ID	1,827.7	152,083	280	83.2	85.4	1.2	1.0	3.3	10.8	7.5	17.0	23.1	13.6	11.8	8.9
30980		Longview, TX	2,680.6	287,868	173	107.4	63.8	18.8	1.0	1.4	16.8	6.0	14.2	13.3	12.6	12.6	11.6
31020		Longview, WA	1,141.2	111,524	344	97.7	85.5	1.8	3.2	3.2	9.9	5.8	12.9	11.2	12.8	12.2	12.0
31080		Los Angeles-Long Beach-Anaheim, CA	4,852.1	12,997,353	2	2,678.7	30.7	7.1	0.6	18.8	45.4	5.3	12.1	12.6	15.5	13.8	13.3
31080	11244	Anaheim-Santa Ana-Irvine, CA Div 11,244	792.8	3,167,809	X	3,995.7	41.2	2.3	0.6	24.9	34.1	5.5	12.1	12.6	14.3	13.1	13.5
31080	31084	Los Angeles-Long Beach-Glendale, CA Div 31,084	4,059.3	9,829,544	X	2,421.5	27.3	8.7	0.6	16.8	49.1	5.3	12.0	12.6	15.9	14.0	13.2
31140		Louisville/Jefferson County, KY-IN	3,237.0	1,284,566	45	396.8	76.2	16.9	0.7	3.0	5.7	5.8	12.5	12.1	13.8	13.1	12.5
31180		Lubbock, TX	2,687.7	325,245	161	121.0	52.5	7.5	0.8	2.8	37.8	6.2	13.5	20.4	14.2	12.6	9.9
31340		Lynchburg, VA	2,120.5	262,258	188	123.7	77.5	18.3	0.8	2.1	3.4	5.2	10.9	16.1	12.6	10.5	11.4
31420		Macon-Bibb County, GA	1,723.6	233,883	199	135.7	48.7	46.6	0.6	2.2	3.5	5.8	13.3	13.5	13.1	12.0	11.8
31460		Madera, CA	2,136.9	159,410	267	74.6	33.1	3.6	1.7	3.0	60.2	6.8	15.9	13.9	13.8	13.2	11.3
31540		Madison, WI	3,308.8	683,183	89	206.5	83.1	6.0	0.8	6.4	6.3	5.1	11.5	15.8	14.7	13.8	11.5
31700		Manchester-Nashua, NH	876.5	424,079	129	483.8	84.6	3.5	0.7	5.3	7.9	5.0	11.1	11.9	14.3	12.8	13.1
31740		Manhattan, KS	1,835.1	133,932	309	73.0	76.8	9.9	1.5	5.4	10.3	7.2	12.5	25.2	16.7	12.0	7.5
31860		Mankato, MN	1,196.4	103,612	350	86.6	88.2	5.6	0.7	2.9	4.6	5.2	11.9	22.0	12.4	12.5	9.7
31900		Mansfield, OH	495.2	125,195	322	252.8	87.3	10.9	0.7	1.3	2.2	5.6	12.4	11.9	13.0	12.0	11.8
32580		McAllen-Edinburg-Mission, TX	1,571.0	880,356	65	560.4	5.9	0.6	0.1	1.0	92.6	7.9	18.2	16.5	13.6	12.3	11.4
32780		Medford, OR	2,783.3	223,734	206	80.4	82.0	1.5	2.4	3.1	14.3	5.0	12.0	10.6	12.5	12.7	11.3
32820		Memphis, TN-MS-AR	4,575.2	1,336,103	43	292.0	43.2	48.9	0.6	2.8	6.1	6.5	14.1	13.0	14.2	12.8	12.2
32900		Merced, CA	1,938.0	286,461	174	147.8	26.5	3.7	0.9	8.5	62.5	7.2	16.7	16.3	14.5	12.8	10.9
33100		Miami-Fort Lauderdale-Pompano Beach, FL	5,066.9	6,091,747	9	1,202.3	30.4	21.1	0.3	3.3	46.2	5.3	11.3	11.2	12.8	13.2	13.6
33100	22744	Fort Lauderdale-Pompano Beach-Sunrise, FL Div 22,744	1,202.7	1,930,983	X	1,605.5	34.7	29.9	0.5	4.8	32.0	5.5	11.8	11.2	13.0	13.7	13.5
33100	33124	Miami-Miami Beach-Kendall, FL Div 33,124	1,899.9	2,662,777	X	1,401.5	14.1	15.5	0.2	1.9	69.1	5.5	11.2	11.5	13.5	13.8	14.3
33100	48424	West Palm Beach-Boca Raton-Boynton Beach, FL Div 48,424	1,964.3	1,497,987	X	762.6	53.8	19.7	0.4	3.7	23.9	4.9	10.6	10.7	11.6	11.8	12.3
33140		Michigan City-La Porte, IN	598.3	112,390	342	187.8	80.3	13.0	0.7	1.1	7.3	5.6	12.2	11.6	13.4	12.4	12.3
33220		Midland, MI	517.5	83,457	373	161.3	92.5	2.1	1.0	2.8	3.3	5.4	11.8	12.2	12.4	12.4	12.1
33260		Midland, TX	1,815.3	173,180	250	95.4	42.9	6.9	0.8	2.5	48.2	8.3	16.8	12.8	16.7	15.1	10.2
33340		Milwaukee-Waukesha, WI	1,454.9	1,566,487	40	1,076.7	67.1	17.7	0.9	5.0	11.6	5.9	12.9	12.7	13.7	13.2	11.9
33460		Minneapolis-St. Paul-Bloomington, MN	7,047.7	3,690,512	16	523.6	76.3	10.9	1.3	8.2	6.2	6.0	13.3	12.3	14.1	14.2	12.2
33540		Missoula, MT	2,593.0	119,533	330	46.1	91.2	1.1	4.0	3.1	3.8	4.5	10.5	16.5	15.7	14.0	10.7

1. CBSA = Core Based Statistical Area. DIV = Metropolitan Division. See Appendix A for explanation. See Appendix B for list of metropolitan areas or temporarily covered by water. 2. Dry land or land partially or temporarily covered by water. 3. May be of any race.

Area name	Population, 2020 (cont.): Age (percent) (cont.): 55 to 64 years	65 to 74 years	75 years and over	Percent female	Population change and components of change, 2000–2020: Total persons: 2000	2010	Percent change: 2000–2010	2010–2019	Components of change, 2010–2020: Births	Deaths	Net migration	Households, 2016–2020: Number	Persons per house-hold	Percent: Family house-holds	Single parent house holds	One person
	16	17	18	19	20	21	22	23	24	25	26	27	28	29	30	31
Jonesboro, AR	11.3	8.8	5.9	51.2	121,026	134,196	10.9	0.5	2,061	2,002	596	51,770	2.5	66.1	14.7	26.8
Joplin, MO	12.5	10.0	6.9	50.6	175,518	181,409	3.4	0.6	2,667	2,768	1,213	68,584	2.6	66.1	10.8	27.1
Kahului-Wailuku-Lahaina, HI	14.0	12.3	7.5	50.2	154,834	164,754	6.4	-0.3	2,193	2,059	-678	55,620	3.0	71.3	13.2	21.6
Kalamazoo-Portage, MI	11.3	9.6	6.2	50.9	250,331	261,670	4.5	-0.2	3,647	3,349	-902	104,278	2.5	60.1	10.8	29.9
Kankakee, IL	13.0	10.2	7.1	50.4	113,449	107,502	-5.2	-0.8	1,498	1,696	-719	40,297	2.6	65.7	11.7	29.0
Kansas City, MO-KS	12.7	9.6	6.1	50.6	2,009,342	2,192,035	9.1	0.3	31,771	27,168	2,503	843,359	2.5	64.4	11.4	29.1
Kennewick-Richland, WA	10.8	8.7	5.1	49.2	253,340	303,622	19.8	1.5	4,893	3,186	2,920	100,336	2.9	71.4	12.5	23.1
Killeen-Temple, TX	9.9	7.3	4.5	50.0	405,300	475,367	17.3	2.3	8,678	4,761	6,759	155,894	2.7	68.5	15.0	26.5
Kingsport-Bristol, TN-VA	14.8	13.2	9.5	50.7	309,544	307,614	-0.6	0.3	3,234	6,190	4,045	128,124	2.4	64.8	11.6	30.4
Kingston, NY	15.5	12.4	8.3	50.1	182,493	181,851	-0.4	0.6	1,875	2,607	1,843	70,088	2.4	60.3	10.9	32.1
Knoxville, TN	13.5	11.4	7.5	50.8	814,914	879,773	8.0	1.6	10,921	14,075	16,887	345,707	2.4	65.0	10.9	28.5
Kokomo, IN	13.6	11.4	8.3	51.3	82,752	83,658	1.1	0.0	1,217	1,562	369	34,632	2.4	63.6	14.3	32.0
La Crosse-Onalaska, WI-MN	12.8	10.8	7.3	50.7	133,665	139,627	4.5	-0.3	1,636	1,781	-289	56,391	2.3	58.0	8.1	31.1
Lafayette, LA	13.0	9.6	5.7	51.1	466,750	478,384	2.5	0.2	7,451	6,701	5	183,685	2.6	67.2	13.8	26.7
Lafayette-West Lafayette, IN	10.4	8.1	5.3	48.9	210,297	223,716	6.4	0.4	2,949	2,344	331	86,627	2.5	58.4	9.4	30.2
Lake Charles, LA	12.8	10.0	6.1	50.7	199,607	222,402	11.4	-5.4	3,610	3,177	-12,266	81,329	2.5	66.6	15.0	26.8
Lake Havasu City-Kingman, AZ	16.2	18.5	13.3	49.2	200,186	213,267	6.5	2.1	2,077	5,051	7,504	90,413	2.3	62.5	10.0	30.6
Lakeland-Winter Haven, FL	12.1	11.3	8.6	50.7	602,095	725,046	20.4	3.9	9,964	11,253	30,129	240,879	2.9	68.6	13.4	25.2
Lancaster, PA	13.0	10.7	8.1	50.7	519,445	552,984	6.5	0.1	8,207	7,734	103	204,003	2.6	70.1	9.3	24.1
Lansing-East Lansing, MI	12.7	10.4	6.2	50.8	534,684	541,297	1.2	-0.2	6,764	7,064	-812	216,659	2.4	59.9	10.5	30.9
Laredo, TX	8.9	6.0	3.9	50.5	250,304	267,114	6.7	0.3	5,540	2,158	-2,607	76,382	3.6	80.3	21.4	17.3
Las Cruces, NM	10.8	9.8	6.8	50.7	209,233	219,561	4.9	0.9	3,105	2,747	1,552	79,421	2.7	65.6	14.9	26.4
Las Vegas-Henderson-Paradise, NV	12.0	9.6	5.9	49.9	1,951,269	2,265,461	16.1	1.2	31,589	27,645	22,616	809,026	2.7	63.9	14.1	28.2
Lawrence, KS	9.9	8.6	4.9	50.2	110,826	118,785	7.2	0.5	1,303	1,044	282	47,972	2.4	54.8	6.7	28.9
Lawton, OK	11.4	8.2	5.3	48.1	130,291	126,652	-2.8	0.7	2,136	1,715	446	45,456	2.6	64.9	15.0	30.1
Lebanon, PA	13.5	11.5	8.3	50.5	133,568	143,257	7.3	0.2	1,913	2,286	591	53,857	2.5	68.3	11.0	26.0
Lewiston, ID-WA	14.0	12.8	9.2	50.7	60,888	64,375	5.7	0.7	821	1,101	759	25,834	2.4	63.9	9.3	28.7
Lewiston-Auburn, ME	14.5	11.2	7.1	50.8	107,702	111,139	3.2	-0.1	1,364	1,749	268	45,906	2.3	60.5	10.3	29.8
Lexington-Fayette, KY	12.0	9.5	5.7	50.9	472,099	516,811	9.5	0.2	7,183	6,383	164	203,965	2.4	61.9	11.8	29.1
Lima, OH	13.1	11.0	7.2	49.2	106,331	102,206	-3.9	-0.5	1,464	1,675	-341	41,025	2.4	62.4	14.2	32.5
Lincoln, NE	10.9	9.4	5.6	49.5	302,157	340,217	12.6	0.6	4,716	3,506	609	133,432	2.4	60.5	9.3	29.4
Little Rock-North Little Rock-Conway, AR	12.4	10.0	6.2	51.6	699,757	748,031	6.9	0.4	11,044	10,763	2,550	289,808	2.5	63.4	14.2	30.7
Logan, UT-ID	7.7	6.2	4.1	49.8	125,442	147,348	17.5	3.2	2,778	951	2,911	44,013	3.1	76.6	8.0	15.4
Longview, TX	12.7	10.3	6.7	50.1	280,000	286,184	2.2	0.6	4,219	4,410	1,857	102,463	2.7	69.6	14.1	25.4
Longview, WA	13.7	11.9	7.6	50.0	102,410	110,730	8.1	0.7	1,518	1,768	1,038	42,354	2.5	66.1	11.7	28.1
Los Angeles-Long Beach-Anaheim, CA	12.5	8.8	6.1	50.4	12,828,837	13,200,998	2.9	-1.5	163,963	134,220	-232,818	4,372,505	3.0	67.5	13.9	24.7
Anaheim-Santa Ana-Irvine, CA Div 11,244	13.1	9.2	6.6	50.4	3,010,232	3,186,989	5.9	-0.6	40,070	31,088	-28,481	1,040,001	3.0	71.4	11.5	21.2
Los Angeles-Long Beach-Glendale, CA Div 31,084	12.4	8.7	6.0	50.4	9,818,605	10,014,009	2.0	-1.8	123,893	103,132	-204,337	3,332,504	3.0	66.4	14.7	25.8
Louisville/Jefferson County, KY-IN	13.4	10.5	6.3	50.9	1,202,718	1,285,439	6.9	-0.1	17,873	19,238	386	497,106	2.5	63.4	12.6	30.5
Lubbock, TX	10.1	7.9	5.1	50.5	290,805	321,368	10.5	1.2	5,100	4,115	2,823	120,841	2.5	60.7	13.0	28.9
Lynchburg, VA	13.8	11.4	8.0	51.4	246,412	261,593	6.2	0.3	3,306	4,125	1,482	101,123	2.5	66.9	11.5	26.7
Macon-Bibb County, GA	13.2	10.6	6.7	52.2	232,293	233,802	0.6	0.0	3,213	3,921	774	86,898	2.6	63.0	17.1	32.4
Madera, CA	10.8	8.8	5.4	51.4	150,865	156,255	3.6	2.0	2,603	1,638	2,196	44,479	3.3	78.6	13.5	16.6
Madison, WI	12.1	9.8	5.7	49.9	605,435	680,796	12.4	0.4	8,430	6,862	664	275,987	2.3	57.3	7.9	31.1
Manchester-Nashua, NH	15.1	10.2	6.4	49.9	400,721	422,937	5.5	0.3	4,968	5,404	1,500	162,843	2.5	64.7	9.5	26.9
Manhattan, KS	7.9	6.6	4.3	47.9	127,081	134,046	5.5	-0.1	2,442	1,126	-1,422	48,627	2.5	61.2	8.8	28.3
Mankato, MN	10.8	9.2	6.2	49.5	96,740	103,566	7.1	0.0	1,301	1,032	-240	39,211	2.4	60.9	8.5	26.2
Mansfield, OH	13.2	11.7	8.3	48.9	124,475	124,936	0.4	0.2	1,672	2,144	727	48,967	2.3	61.5	11.5	31.6
McAllen-Edinburg-Mission, TX	8.6	6.5	4.9	50.7	774,769	870,781	12.4	1.1	16,405	7,302	164	243,878	3.5	80.2	21.8	16.9
Medford, OR	13.2	13.7	9.0	50.8	203,206	223,259	9.9	0.2	2,616	3,636	1,502	89,690	2.4	63.7	10.2	27.7
Memphis, TN-MS-AR	12.4	9.4	5.4	52.2	1,316,100	1,337,779	1.6	-0.1	20,970	19,450	-3,364	505,544	2.6	64.7	18.3	30.1
Merced, CA	10.1	7.0	4.5	49.2	255,793	281,202	9.9	1.9	4,713	2,812	3,339	81,306	3.3	76.3	16.9	19.0
Miami-Fort Lauderdale-Pompano Beach, FL	13.6	10.3	8.7	51.0	5,564,635	6,138,333	10.3	-0.8	77,291	80,705	-42,960	2,172,740	2.8	65.3	15.3	28.4
Fort Lauderdale-Pompano Beach-Sunrise, FL Div 22,744	13.9	10.1	7.4	50.9	1,748,066	1,944,375	11.2	-0.7	25,061	24,055	-14,462	704,942	2.7	63.5	14.9	29.8
Miami-Miami Beach-Kendall, FL Div 33,124	13.4	9.3	7.6	51.0	2,496,435	2,701,767	8.2	-1.4	34,623	33,451	-39,861	902,200	3.0	68.7	17.8	25.6
West Palm Beach-Boca Raton-Boynton Beach, FL Div 48,424	13.6	12.3	12.3	51.2	1,320,134	1,492,191	13.0	0.4	17,607	23,199	11,363	565,598	2.6	62.2	11.6	31.0
Michigan City-La Porte, IN	13.9	11.6	7.1	48.0	111,467	112,417	0.9	0.0	1,413	1,838	386	42,725	2.4	64.7	12.9	28.3
Midland, MI	14.3	11.3	8.1	50.3	83,629	83,494	-0.2	0.0	1,061	1,107	0	34,253	2.4	67.3	9.1	27.0
Midland, TX	9.7	6.4	4.0	49.2	141,671	175,220	23.7	-1.2	3,668	1,771	-3,920	59,639	2.9	68.7	11.8	26.6
Milwaukee-Waukesha, WI	13.2	10.1	6.4	51.0	1,555,908	1,574,731	1.2	-0.5	22,559	21,645	-9,157	634,436	2.4	60.7	12.3	32.1
Minneapolis-St. Paul-Bloomington, MN	13.0	9.3	5.7	50.1	3,333,633	3,690,261	10.7	0.0	52,321	38,364	-13,701	1,390,448	2.6	64.0	9.4	28.1
Missoula, MT	11.4	10.8	6.0	49.7	109,299	117,922	7.9	1.4	1,327	1,360	1,636	49,700	2.3	55.6	7.8	31.0

Area name	Persons in group quarters, 2020	Daytime population, 2019: Number	Daytime population, 2019: Employment/ residence ratio	Births, 2020: Total	Births, 2020: Rate[1]	Deaths, 2020: Number	Deaths, 2020: Rate[1]	Persons under 65 with no health insurance 2019: Number	Persons under 65 with no health insurance 2019: Percent	Medicare, 2020: Total Beneficiaries	Medicare, 2020: Enrolled in Original Medicare	Medicare, 2020: Enrolled in Medicare Advantage	Serious crimes known to police[2], 2019: Violent: Number	Serious crimes known to police[2], 2019: Violent: Rate[3]
	32	33	34	35	36	37	38	39	40	41	42	43	44	45
Jonesboro, AR	3,991	135,036	1.04	1,633	12.1	1,636	12.1	11,357	10.3	24,915	16,590	8,325	893	659.6
Joplin, MO	3,200	183,345	1.06	2,151	11.8	2,201	12.1	23,938	16.4	36,946	22,553	14,393	655	364.1
Kahului-Wailuku-Lahaina, HI	2,313	166,802	1.00	1,766	10.7	1,628	9.9	7,904	5.9	33,039	15,155	17,884	379	226.7
Kalamazoo-Portage, MI	7,704	270,943	1.05	2,901	11.1	2,650	10.1	14,695	6.8	50,755	21,612	29,143	1,763	663.3
Kankakee, IL	5,940	106,091	0.92	1,207	11.3	1,366	12.8	6,322	7.4	22,146	15,363	6,783	387	355.4
Kansas City, MO-KS	29,640	2,161,825	1.02	25,348	11.5	21,689	9.9	191,651	10.6	387,339	224,166	163,173	NA	NA
Kennewick-Richland, WA	4,018	289,556	0.96	3,928	12.8	2,504	8.2	25,187	10.0	49,398	42,116	7,282	718	236.2
Killeen-Temple, TX	23,963	441,202	0.94	7,008	14.6	3,826	7.9	64,056	16.6	72,888	42,086	30,802	1,754	377.2
Kingsport-Bristol, TN-VA	5,707	308,906	1.01	2,592	8.4	4,935	16.0	26,734	11.5	86,340	34,883	51,457	1,116	363.6
Kingston, NY	11,651	164,351	0.83	1,493	8.2	2,081	11.4	7,976	5.9	42,323	28,262	14,061	246	139.8
Knoxville, TN	19,169	874,051	1.03	8,712	9.8	11,237	12.7	78,553	11.4	197,817	99,759	98,058	3,343	381.9
Kokomo, IN	1,196	85,929	1.09	953	11.4	1,250	14.9	6,419	9.9	19,648	11,487	8,161	498	604.0
La Crosse-Onalaska, WI-MN	5,619	142,075	1.07	1,254	9.0	1,399	10.0	5,643	5.2	29,070	15,831	13,239	213	155.8
Lafayette, LA	7,280	491,216	1.00	6,068	12.7	5,392	11.3	41,568	10.1	52,688	34,417	18,271	2,205	450.0
Lafayette-West Lafayette, IN	15,750	236,348	1.06	2,342	10.4	1,861	8.3	18,853	10.1	34,486	22,766	11,720	NA	NA
Lake Charles, LA	3,892	224,931	1.16	2,897	13.4	2,535	11.7	16,742	9.6	37,251	24,782	12,469	1,663	788.7
Lake Havasu City-Kingman, AZ	3,945	200,206	0.85	1,671	7.7	4,021	18.6	19,205	13.6	70,508	41,293	29,215	490	228.3
Lakeland-Winter Haven, FL	13,115	674,420	0.89	8,086	10.9	8,962	12.1	95,885	17.1	164,936	64,343	100,593	2,115	286.8
Lancaster, PA	12,323	535,039	0.97	6,685	12.1	6,149	11.1	48,810	11.2	115,700	63,525	52,175	NA	NA
Lansing-East Lansing, MI	19,661	549,491	1.01	5,367	9.9	5,660	10.5	30,067	6.8	106,869	43,805	63,064	2,741	498.1
Laredo, TX	3,231	273,707	0.99	4,482	16.7	1,713	6.4	73,316	30.2	34,660	18,933	15,727	936	335.9
Las Cruces, NM	4,170	208,597	0.90	2,506	11.4	2,175	9.9	23,882	13.5	43,732	23,894	19,838	NA	NA
Las Vegas-Henderson-Paradise, NV	21,145	2,233,421	1.00	25,488	11.2	22,163	9.7	260,442	13.7	382,062	193,542	188,520	11,077	478.7
Lawrence, KS	8,352	113,441	0.88	1,009	8.5	854	7.2	9,568	9.7	18,998	14,367	4,631	NA	NA
Lawton, OK	10,046	128,576	1.02	1,676	13.2	1,402	11.0	14,881	15.0	21,246	17,105	4,141	759	603.0
Lebanon, PA	3,563	130,763	0.85	1,530	10.7	1,843	12.9	9,080	8.2	32,825	17,326	15,499	NA	NA
Lewiston, ID-WA	1,138	63,444	1.01	661	10.2	849	13.1	5,104	10.5	17,195	13,036	4,159	117	184.4
Lewiston-Auburn, ME	3,135	104,825	0.94	1,094	9.9	1,384	12.5	8,323	9.7	25,512	11,046	14,466	193	177.6
Lexington-Fayette, KY	16,264	542,758	1.11	5,721	11.1	5,008	9.7	35,235	8.3	89,930	47,156	42,774	1,308	250.8
Lima, OH	5,583	107,143	1.09	1,166	11.4	1,361	13.4	5,966	7.6	22,212	13,058	9,154	NA	NA
Lincoln, NE	16,423	342,069	1.05	3,726	10.9	2,757	8.1	22,087	8.1	57,244	42,923	14,321	NA	NA
Little Rock-North Little Rock-Conway, AR	14,113	753,462	1.04	8,865	11.8	8,595	11.5	57,492	9.4	149,285	102,950	46,335	7,014	938.8
Logan, UT-ID	4,048	137,401	0.96	2,212	14.8	754	5.0	11,942	9.7	17,886	9,130	8,756	170	118.2
Longview, TX	10,870	285,808	1.00	3,418	11.9	3,531	12.3	47,760	21.0	58,304	32,969	25,335	893	311.8
Longview, WA	1,073	106,716	0.96	1,186	10.7	1,388	12.5	6,458	7.4	27,045	11,272	15,773	208	187.1
Los Angeles-Long Beach-Anaheim, CA	221,638	13,435,940	1.04	132,063	10.1	107,458	8.2	1,175,754	10.6	2,087,868	970,186	1,117,682	62,030	472.6
Anaheim-Santa Ana-Irvine, CA Div 11,244	42,899	3,269,032	1.06	32,347	10.2	25,108	7.9	235,378	8.8	535,774	249,101	286,673	7,340	232.1
Los Angeles-Long Beach-Glendale, CA Div 31,084	178,739	10,166,908	1.03	99,716	10.1	82,350	8.3	940,376	11.1	1,552,094	721,085	831,009	54,690	549.0
Louisville/Jefferson County, KY-IN	26,313	1,287,258	1.04	14,387	11.2	15,256	11.9	76,564	7.4	252,481	148,700	103,781	NA	NA
Lubbock, TX	11,868	322,555	1.02	4,090	12.6	3,292	10.2	47,955	17.8	51,124	27,774	23,350	2,985	919.4
Lynchburg, VA	12,609	256,299	0.94	2,674	10.2	3,300	12.6	19,529	9.7	61,538	42,994	18,544	646	244.2
Macon-Bibb County, GA	8,217	236,564	1.07	2,596	11.1	3,112	13.3	26,577	14.6	48,655	23,866	24,789	1,624	707.9
Madera, CA	6,862	149,254	0.88	2,069	13.1	1,302	8.2	13,807	11.0	25,362	15,049	10,313	578	369.4
Madison, WI	15,250	690,175	1.08	6,628	9.7	5,460	8.0	28,503	5.1	120,900	80,009	40,891	1,354	201.7
Manchester-Nashua, NH	7,451	398,104	0.92	3,990	9.4	4,325	10.2	27,581	8.0	83,777	60,573	23,204	913	217.7
Manhattan, KS	10,097	134,766	1.05	1,941	14.5	886	6.6	9,940	9.4	17,036	14,766	2,270	490	376.1
Mankato, MN	6,923	105,340	1.07	1,016	9.8	808	7.8	4,486	5.5	18,444	11,422	7,022	191	187.0
Mansfield, OH	6,996	123,892	1.06	1,358	10.9	1,720	13.8	7,840	8.7	29,097	17,237	11,860	NA	NA
McAllen-Edinburg-Mission, TX	6,669	842,153	0.94	13,191	15.1	5,852	6.7	248,170	33.2	110,015	38,031	71,984	2,408	274.8
Medford, OR	3,387	218,440	1.00	2,086	9.3	2,903	13.0	16,303	9.8	58,458	35,542	22,916	663	298.8
Memphis, TN-MS-AR	22,104	1,361,087	1.03	16,824	12.6	15,392	11.5	143,397	12.8	235,193	148,533	86,660	18,324	1,358.8
Merced, CA	6,763	256,593	0.83	3,737	13.2	2,224	7.8	26,939	11.4	38,536	31,035	7,501	1,660	598.6
Miami-Fort Lauderdale-Pompano Beach, FL	77,913	6,146,770	1.01	62,222	10.2	64,333	10.5	910,265	18.5	1,167,025	453,066	713,959	25,920	417.0
Fort Lauderdale-Pompano Beach-Sunrise, FL Div 22,744	15,538	1,860,056	0.91	20,130	10.4	19,099	9.9	282,874	17.7	341,166	131,685	209,481	7,058	358.2
Miami-Miami Beach-Kendall, FL Div 33,124	41,295	2,783,378	1.06	27,851	10.4	26,611	9.9	428,190	19.4	485,276	130,834	354,442	13,301	486.6
West Palm Beach-Boca Raton-Boynton Beach, FL Div 48,424	21,080	1,503,336	1.03	14,241	9.5	18,623	12.5	199,201	17.9	340,583	190,547	150,036	5,561	367.6
Michigan City-La Porte, IN	6,488	104,018	0.87	1,137	10.1	1,464	13.0	8,550	10.3	96,739	59,238	37,501	NA	NA
Midland, MI	1,185	84,543	1.03	855	10.2	900	10.8	4,200	6.3	19,219	9,599	9,620	120	144.9
Midland, TX	1,135	203,666	1.31	2,923	16.8	1,416	8.1	30,060	18.4	20,669	13,582	7,087	700	374.0
Milwaukee-Waukesha, WI	29,508	1,616,024	1.05	17,948	11.4	17,227	11.0	88,327	6.8	301,880	134,390	167,490	10,688	678.2
Minneapolis-St. Paul-Bloomington, MN	61,890	3,628,821	1.01	41,501	11.2	30,718	8.3	165,220	5.4	613,382	269,875	343,507	NA	NA
Missoula, MT	3,362	122,704	1.06	1,032	8.7	1,070	9.0	8,936	9.2	23,993	18,475	5,518	489	404.0

1. Per 1,000 estimated resident population. 2. Data for serious crimes have not been adjusted for underreporting; this may affect comparability between geographic areas and over time. 3. Per 100,000 population estimated by the FBI.

Area name	Serious crimes known to police[1], 2019 (cont.)		Education						Income and poverty, 2016–2020							
	Property		School enrollment and attainment, 2019				Local government expenditures,[5] 2017–2018							Percent below poverty level		
			Enrollment[3]		Attainment[4]											
	Number	Rate[2]	Total	Percent private	High school gradu- ate or less	Bach- elor's degree or more	Total current expendi- tures (mil dol)	Current expen- ditures per student (dollars)	Per capita income[6] (dollars)	Median house- hold income (dol- lars)	Median family income	Percent of house- holds with income less than $50,000	Percent of house- holds with income of $200,000 or more	All persons	All fami- lies	Age 65 years and older
	46	47	48	49	50	51	52	53	54	55	56	57	58	59	60	61
Jonesboro, AR	3,964	2,928.1	35,425	6.5	47.9	24.2	237.2	9,902	27,110	47,610	60,922	51.8	3.7	18.2	12.8	20.1
Joplin, MO	6,354	3,531.9	42,851	13.8	47.5	22.3	266.8	8,766	26,437	50,244	61,218	49.7	3.0	16.4	11.3	18.9
Kahului-Wailuku-Lahaina, HI	3,537	2,115.7	32,725	18.7	38.9	28.3	NA	NA	36,872	84,363	92,627	28.5	10.7	9.0	6.3	8.4
Kalamazoo-Portage, MI	8,789	3,306.6	76,631	12.1	28.7	39.8	459.5	13,221	33,450	58,836	80,439	42.4	5.9	14.4	8.3	14.7
Kankakee, IL	D	D	27,114	21.1	46.4	20.6	257.1	14,731	28,445	59,370	73,857	42.5	3.8	13.0	9.3	14.8
Kansas City, MO-KS	NA	NA	521,438	15.9	32.9	37.5	4,009.9	11,276	36,728	69,240	86,562	36.2	7.4	9.9	6.9	11.1
Kennewick-Richland, WA	6,869	2,259.8	80,078	10.9	37.3	27.9	792.9	13,337	31,610	70,545	80,918	33.5	7.0	11.5	8.5	12.7
Killeen-Temple, TX	D	D	124,514	12.0	35.8	23.5	821.5	9,085	26,504	55,306	66,430	44.7	3.4	13.7	10.2	15.6
Kingsport-Bristol, TN-VA	6,466	2,106.9	58,236	16.2	48.7	22.2	423.2	10,216	27,689	46,685	60,792	52.8	3.0	15.9	11.6	21.6
Kingston, NY	1,846	1,049.4	38,101	15.9	37.6	33.2	598.6	26,289	35,816	65,306	87,034	38.4	7.4	13.7	7.5	13.2
Knoxville, TN	17,024	1,945.0	196,656	16.2	40.6	30.4	1,128.6	9,578	32,177	56,857	72,608	44.1	5.1	13.4	9.4	15.1
Kokomo, IN	1,313	1,592.6	18,626	8.8	46.6	21.1	137.0	9,859	29,647	56,387	69,896	44.5	3.0	12.0	9.6	17.3
La Crosse-Onalaska, WI-MN	3,421	2,501.6	37,874	12.7	31.3	34.3	258.0	12,652	33,600	60,165	81,684	40.9	5.2	11.5	4.2	7.1
Lafayette, LA	12,188	2,487.4	120,019	18.5	51.0	24.3	740.7	10,130	29,448	52,827	66,741	47.5	4.6	18.5	14.6	22.4
Lafayette-West Lafayette, IN	NA	NA	81,797	8.4	38.2	35.3	305.8	10,313	28,016	52,826	73,007	47.6	4.0	17.4	8.3	14.4
Lake Charles, LA	8,041	3,813.6	50,560	15.9	46.5	21.7	440.1	12,437	29,816	52,986	65,881	47.0	4.7	16.5	12.7	20.7
Lake Havasu City-Kingman, AZ	4,643	2,163.3	34,836	16.0	47.9	13.4	192.9	8,127	27,968	47,686	57,058	52.2	2.5	16.2	10.6	18.4
Lakeland-Winter Haven, FL	10,002	1,356.1	160,280	18.8	48.3	20.6	1,004.0	9,503	25,820	51,535	59,623	48.5	3.7	15.1	11.5	19.1
Lancaster, PA	NA	NA	121,754	28.2	49.2	28.6	1,140.4	16,971	33,568	69,588	82,568	34.0	5.9	9.1	5.7	9.6
Lansing-East Lansing, MI	9,020	1,639.1	154,798	10.0	31.8	33.1	993.3	12,376	32,267	60,278	78,657	41.6	4.7	13.9	7.8	13.6
Laredo, TX	4,175	1,498.2	89,483	6.5	56.4	18.8	688.8	10,192	19,048	50,296	54,078	49.7	3.5	24.6	22.2	28.5
Las Cruces, NM	NA	NA	66,842	6.2	40.9	29.5	389.4	9,632	22,772	44,024	51,928	54.8	2.4	24.8	20.7	30.8
Las Vegas-Henderson-Paradise, NV	47,356	2,046.5	517,981	12.3	42.0	25.2	2,964.7	8,937	31,651	61,048	71,896	41.2	5.8	13.4	9.8	15.2
Lawrence, KS	NA	NA	42,844	10.3	23.2	51.2	168.8	11,108	32,776	61,020	90,062	42.0	6.3	16.5	6.8	9.3
Lawton, OK	2,343	1,861.6	31,629	10.3	43.0	22.8	213.9	9,862	27,708	52,219	65,335	47.5	2.8	16.0	12.0	18.8
Lebanon, PA	NA	NA	31,294	22.5	56.5	21.2	263.8	13,211	30,088	61,632	76,282	39.4	3.6	10.7	8.0	13.7
Lewiston, ID-WA	1,307	2,060.3	13,076	10.1	37.5	23.8	101.6	11,605	30,208	55,657	74,144	45.5	3.7	13.1	7.5	13.7
Lewiston-Auburn, ME	1,449	1,333.5	24,710	19.8	44.3	22.7	233.8	13,546	29,947	55,002	70,817	46.1	3.1	11.3	7.0	11.8
Lexington-Fayette, KY	13,357	2,560.7	136,204	17.3	32.9	38.6	857.0	11,749	34,203	60,769	78,944	41.8	6.3	14.5	9.5	15.6
Lima, OH	NA	NA	25,233	22.4	48.6	18.7	181.1	12,549	27,231	51,892	64,913	48.6	2.5	12.9	9.5	15.8
Lincoln, NE	NA	NA	99,360	18.2	28.1	39.3	609.9	12,070	33,329	62,883	82,381	39.4	5.4	11.6	6.6	10.9
Little Rock-North Little Rock-Conway, AR	23,746	3,178.5	184,039	15.1	38.0	31.4	1,195.6	10,139	31,654	55,983	72,289	45.3	5.1	14.1	10.2	16.1
Logan, UT-ID	1,148	798.2	53,156	8.3	29.4	36.1	237.0	7,790	24,379	60,466	69,237	40.9	4.1	14.1	9.3	12.6
Longview, TX	5,930	2,070.7	68,003	12.3	45.8	19.5	557.2	9,761	27,261	53,524	64,818	46.5	4.0	15.9	11.7	18.7
Longview, WA	2,224	2,000.3	24,287	12.5	40.5	17.0	235.4	13,414	30,170	58,791	72,234	43.4	4.1	13.3	8.8	13.8
Los Angeles-Long Beach-Anaheim, CA	274,976	2,095.1	3,430,386	15.7	38.3	35.4	26,993.7	13,930	37,452	76,399	86,317	33.8	12.4	13.2	9.6	14.4
Anaheim-Santa Ana-Irvine, CA Div 11,244	61,066	1,931.2	844,632	15.8	31.2	41.2	6,147.0	12,838	43,049	94,441	106,451	26.0	16.7	10.1	6.9	10.0
Los Angeles-Long Beach-Glendale, CA Div 31,084	213,910	2,147.1	2,585,754	15.7	40.6	33.5	20,846.7	14,288	35,685	71,358	80,317	36.2	11.1	14.2	10.5	15.8
Louisville/Jefferson County, KY-IN	NA	NA	289,193	21.6	38.9	30.1	2,179.8	12,310	33,589	60,891	77,584	40.9	5.7	12.1	8.3	13.7
Lubbock, TX	11,956	3,682.4	104,814	10.0	38.6	31.4	520.6	9,753	28,740	53,003	70,036	47.2	4.8	18.5	11.4	17.6
Lynchburg, VA	3,103	1,172.8	66,749	37.0	41.4	28.7	362.6	11,301	28,777	56,983	70,981	44.4	3.6	11.9	7.6	12.8
Macon-Bibb County, GA	6,299	2,745.9	57,185	21.9	46.7	23.5	416.3	11,475	26,696	46,083	62,540	52.7	4.2	21.4	16.4	24.7
Madera, CA	2,132	1,362.6	44,234	9.1	51.4	15.2	431.6	13,520	23,212	61,924	65,627	41.6	4.2	19.0	14.2	22.0
Madison, WI	12,117	1,805.4	176,380	10.8	24.7	47.1	1,286.8	13,482	40,627	73,807	97,334	32.7	8.1	10.4	4.9	7.8
Manchester-Nashua, NH	4,772	1,138.0	94,274	23.9	33.3	38.6	847.1	14,905	42,081	82,099	103,238	29.3	10.5	7.4	5.0	8.5
Manhattan, KS	D	D	45,473	7.5	25.6	38.3	220.8	11,316	27,526	54,488	70,357	46.0	3.4	17.8	11.0	17.4
Mankato, MN	1,479	1,448.1	31,062	18.2	32.0	34.5	181.1	12,871	32,710	63,288	83,590	39.9	4.7	13.8	6.8	10.0
Mansfield, OH	NA	NA	25,538	18.1	52.6	17.8	228.9	13,257	25,570	49,186	63,284	50.7	2.0	13.7	10.0	17.7
McAllen-Edinburg-Mission, TX	15,851	1,808.9	276,588	5.2	56.9	19.3	2,672.0	10,712	17,816	41,846	46,609	56.8	2.5	28.4	25.5	33.0
Medford, OR	6,289	2,834.4	45,718	15.2	34.8	28.8	358.6	11,790	32,044	56,327	70,436	44.1	5.3	13.7	8.5	15.9
Memphis, TN-MS-AR	50,144	3,718.5	338,268	17.1	40.3	28.8	2,184.0	10,183	30,423	53,896	68,008	46.5	5.7	17.3	13.1	20.6
Merced, CA	5,951	2,146.0	87,116	5.1	55.7	14.1	817.6	13,820	23,677	56,330	61,162	44.8	4.7	18.8	15.4	22.5
Miami-Fort Lauderdale-Pompano Beach, FL	136,292	2,192.4	1,451,311	20.7	40.2	33.0	8,120.8	9,907	33,759	59,030	69,172	43.0	8.0	13.9	10.6	15.3
Fort Lauderdale-Pompano Beach-Sunrise, FL Div 22,744	40,341	2,047.3	472,306	21.1	37.6	33.1	2,659.9	9,760	34,063	60,922	73,430	41.5	7.7	12.7	9.7	13.5
Miami-Miami Beach-Kendall, FL Div 33,124	67,793	2,480.4	657,474	20.9	44.9	30.7	3,465.0	9,888	29,598	53,975	60,666	46.6	6.7	16.0	12.7	17.6
West Palm Beach-Boca Raton-Boynton Beach, FL Div 48,424	28,158	1,861.3	321,531	19.6	35.2	37.1	1,995.9	10,145	40,957	65,015	79,785	39.1	10.4	11.6	8.0	13.0
Michigan City-La Porte, IN	NA	NA	21,559	13.3	50.1	19.1	183.6	10,550	27,706	57,010	70,726	44.2	2.9	15.5	11.1	22.5
Midland, MI	580	700.3	18,805	15.2	34.7	34.8	137.4	11,552	36,338	64,078	79,062	38.8	7.4	10.1	7.2	11.5
Midland, TX	4,058	2,167.9	47,997	17.6	42.4	27.2	265.4	8,617	40,214	82,768	97,494	29.7	12.5	9.8	7.9	11.4
Milwaukee-Waukesha, WI	30,821	1,955.8	389,595	24.1	34.9	36.1	2,804.1	12,264	36,617	63,739	84,829	39.9	6.9	13.0	8.7	14.4
Minneapolis-St. Paul-Bloomington, MN	NA	NA	909,387	15.9	27.0	42.7	7,774.1	13,364	42,614	82,887	103,977	29.0	11.0	8.3	5.1	8.0
Missoula, MT	3,080	2,544.5	30,622	11.4	25.0	44.2	163.1	11,539	33,358	56,247	76,923	44.7	4.8	13.3	6.1	9.7

1. Data for serious crimes have not been adjusted for underreporting; this may affect comparability between geographic areas and over time. 2. Per 100,000 population estimated by the FBI. 3. All persons 3 years old and over enrolled in nursery school through college. 4. Persons 25 years old and over. 5. Elementary and secondary education expenditures. 6. Based on population estimated by the American Community Survey, 2015.

Table C. Metropolitan Areas — **Personal Income and Earnings**

Area name	Personal income, 2019: Total (mil dol)	Personal income, 2019: Percent change, 2018–2019	Per capita[1]: Dollars	Per capita[1]: Rank	Wages and Salaries (mil dol)	Supplements to wages and salaries, employer contributions (mil dol): Pension and insurance	Supplements to wages and salaries, employer contributions (mil dol): Government social insurance	Proprietors' income	Dividends, interest, and rent (mil dol)	Personal transfer receipts (mil dol)	Earnings, 2019: Total (mil dol)	Contributrions for government social insurance (mil dol): From employee and self-employed	Contributrions for government social insurance (mil dol): From employer
	62	63	64	65	66	67	68	69	70	71	72	73	74
Jonesboro, AR	5,440	7.4	40,140	371	2,746	397	212	414	654	1,649	3,768	263	212
Joplin, MO	7,610	4.2	42,255	347	3,601	647	271	540	1,119	2,116	5,059	335	271
Kahului-Wailuku-Lahaina, HI	8,708	2.7	51,838	164	3,320	629	265	1,001	1,615	2,455	5,215	341	265
Kalamazoo-Portage, MI	13,939	6.5	52,403	151	6,896	1,167	510	925	2,537	3,345	9,498	602	510
Kankakee, IL	5,103	8.7	46,988	265	2,199	450	155	236	693	1,495	3,041	184	155
Kansas City, MO-KS	126,169	4.8	58,057	85	67,123	9,510	4,891	11,776	20,696	23,280	93,300	5,800	4,891
Kennewick-Richland, WA	14,884	9.5	49,042	219	7,328	1,111	661	1,464	2,044	3,441	10,565	589	661
Killeen-Temple, TX	21,349	7.5	45,574	291	9,747	2,135	765	1,275	3,468	5,611	13,922	727	765
Kingsport-Bristol, TN-VA	13,212	5.9	42,869	342	5,566	987	398	936	1,944	4,375	7,887	576	398
Kingston, NY	9,965	6.6	56,071	102	2,907	728	238	608	1,739	2,806	4,481	281	238
Knoxville, TN	44,380	6.0	50,540	189	21,573	3,133	1,503	4,879	6,825	10,712	31,089	2,007	1,503
Kokomo, IN	3,718	6.1	44,945	304	1,933	324	159	157	506	1,244	2,574	179	159
La Crosse-Onalaska, WI-MN	7,495	5.2	54,656	126	3,897	745	301	578	1,398	1,604	5,520	350	301
Lafayette, LA	23,289	6.7	47,553	254	9,924	1,552	663	2,019	4,038	6,295	14,158	863	663
Lafayette-West Lafayette, IN	9,907	6.4	42,467	346	5,135	975	389	697	1,681	2,124	7,196	434	389
Lake Charles, LA	10,712	2.5	50,935	182	5,873	1,042	386	741	1,560	2,905	8,041	470	386
Lake Havasu City-Kingman, AZ	7,934	8.3	36,529	381	2,344	388	175	454	1,277	3,378	3,361	315	175
Lakeland-Winter Haven, FL	29,604	9.8	39,760	375	12,370	1,800	863	1,372	5,622	9,377	16,405	1,214	863
Lancaster, PA	31,916	7.3	58,434	79	13,041	2,191	999	4,509	4,939	7,336	20,739	1,221	999
Lansing-East Lansing, MI	25,397	8.7	46,323	281	12,139	2,168	889	1,300	3,983	7,049	16,496	1,081	889
Laredo, TX	9,893	7.5	35,626	382	4,163	859	292	1,132	1,344	2,881	6,445	344	292
Las Cruces, NM	8,899	8.7	40,218	369	3,345	652	263	699	1,244	3,040	4,959	351	263
Las Vegas-Henderson-Paradise, NV	118,679	5.9	51,244	175	52,505	8,249	3,956	8,439	24,939	29,138	73,150	4,455	3,956
Lawrence, KS	5,819	5.4	47,494	255	2,299	428	173	438	1,152	1,073	3,337	208	173
Lawton, OK	5,773	6.6	45,538	292	2,695	663	226	224	919	1,576	3,808	210	226
Lebanon, PA	7,472	7.7	52,743	147	2,435	519	195	604	1,139	2,058	3,753	242	195
Lewiston, ID-WA	3,185	8.8	50,092	199	1,334	230	119	285	593	902	1,967	138	119
Lewiston-Auburn, ME	5,032	8.8	46,357	279	2,512	412	189	267	591	1,578	3,381	235	189
Lexington-Fayette, KY	27,351	6.1	52,559	150	14,309	2,540	1,087	2,108	5,533	5,732	20,044	1,198	1,087
Lima, OH	4,742	7.0	46,500	277	2,550	463	189	311	648	1,431	3,513	218	189
Lincoln, NE	17,924	5.6	53,057	141	9,685	1,736	732	891	3,559	3,347	13,044	826	732
Little Rock-North Little Rock-Conway, AR	37,207	6.5	49,837	207	19,095	2,758	1,430	2,192	6,373	9,356	25,475	1,738	1,430
Logan, UT-ID	6,419	8.7	44,508	314	2,832	520	209	862	1,132	1,069	4,424	253	209
Longview, TX	12,941	3.6	45,075	303	5,882	947	413	917	2,095	3,841	8,159	502	413
Longview, WA	5,372	7.8	48,232	236	2,298	375	202	338	707	1,678	3,213	216	202
Los Angeles-Long Beach-Anaheim, CA	915,133	7.3	69,805	20	444,009	69,068	30,493	92,374	168,937	198,332	635,944	36,542	30,493
Anaheim-Santa Ana-Irvine, CA Div 11,244	236,303	6.5	74,618	X	117,750	17,050	8,298	23,029	50,081	38,574	166,127	9,672	8,298
Los Angeles-Long Beach-Glendale, CA Div 31,084	678,829	7.6	68,272	X	326,259	52,017	22,196	69,345	118,855	159,758	469,817	26,871	22,196
Louisville/Jefferson County, KY-IN	70,652	6.7	55,676	110	36,484	5,515	2,770	4,813	12,052	16,256	49,582	3,218	2,770
Lubbock, TX	15,110	4.7	46,297	282	7,150	1,198	476	1,116	2,499	3,573	9,940	548	476
Lynchburg, VA	11,509	7.5	43,529	332	5,043	776	366	442	1,846	3,574	6,627	476	366
Macon-Bibb County, GA	10,235	7.5	44,520	313	4,947	819	336	522	1,651	3,191	6,625	424	336
Madera, CA	7,025	15.7	44,532	312	2,613	610	198	1,177	844	1,973	4,598	231	198
Madison, WI	43,096	4.9	64,280	37	24,342	4,582	1,758	3,100	8,587	6,442	33,781	2,024	1,758
Manchester-Nashua, NH	27,866	6.3	66,548	31	15,154	2,060	1,006	2,445	3,807	4,884	20,665	1,262	1,006
Manhattan, KS	6,490	6.2	49,865	206	3,452	851	292	316	1,271	1,146	4,911	255	292
Mankato, MN	5,194	8.3	50,562	188	2,690	456	210	444	905	1,176	3,800	233	210
Mansfield, OH	5,311	8.5	43,928	327	2,216	420	164	307	773	1,696	3,106	203	164
McAllen-Edinburg-Mission, TX	27,265	11.9	31,153	384	10,200	2,119	710	2,922	2,967	9,728	15,951	892	710
Medford, OR	11,497	9.1	51,824	165	4,450	768	397	1,062	2,247	3,502	6,676	469	397
Memphis, TN-MS-AR	68,992	7.0	51,155	178	36,913	5,040	2,641	6,090	9,398	15,784	50,684	3,182	2,641
Merced, CA	12,263	16.6	43,914	328	3,958	928	309	1,429	1,323	3,955	6,625	338	309
Miami-Fort Lauderdale-Pompano Beach, FL	396,247	4.7	64,190	38	167,024	21,486	11,152	29,054	123,580	73,840	228,715	15,009	11,152
Fort Lauderdale-Pompano Beach-Sunrise, FL Div 22,744	109,474	5.9	55,908	X	51,901	6,587	3,474	6,231	25,833	21,752	68,193	4,451	3,474
Miami-Miami Beach-Kendall, FL Div 33,124	154,892	5.2	57,213	X	74,381	9,975	5,011	14,547	38,053	32,876	103,914	6,720	5,011
West Palm Beach-Boca Raton-Boynton Beach, FL Div 48,424	131,881	3.3	87,478	X	40,742	4,924	2,668	8,276	59,694	19,212	56,609	3,839	2,668
Michigan City-La Porte, IN	5,075	7.1	46,274	283	1,894	329	147	279	740	1,466	2,648	187	147
Midland, MI	4,803	5.7	57,561	90	2,400	365	167	239	880	1,142	3,171	209	167
Midland, TX	22,899	-7.5	124,667	1	7,813	962	487	10,476	3,938	1,591	19,737	841	487
Milwaukee-Waukesha, WI	95,448	4.6	60,499	65	50,550	8,307	3,726	5,997	17,721	19,707	68,580	4,358	3,726
Minneapolis-St. Paul-Bloomington, MN	245,833	5.1	67,214	28	134,182	18,271	9,632	17,104	46,586	42,496	179,189	11,061	9,632
Missoula, MT	6,611	6.4	54,353	129	3,076	453	272	537	1,754	1,395	4,338	298	272

1. Based on the resident population estimated as of July 1 of the year shown.

Area name	Earnings, 2019 (cont.)									Social Security beneficiaries, December 2019		Supplemental Security Income Recipients, December 2019	Housing units, 2020	
	Percent by selected industries													
	Farm	Mining, quarrying, and extracting	Construction	Manufacturing	Information; professional, scientific, and technical serviecs	Retail trade	Finance, insurance, real estate, rental and leasing	Health care and social assistance	Government	Number	Rate[1]		Total	Percent change, 2010–2020
	75	76	77	78	79	80	81	82	83	84	85	86	87	88
Jonesboro, AR	1.9	0.1	6.0	14.2	D	7.4	5.4	22.3	14.7	27,495	204	5,469	58,283	1.8
Joplin, MO	1.2	D	5.8	21.5	4.4	7.9	3.6	16.6	10.8	39,460	216	4,480	78,377	1.2
Kahului-Wailuku-Lahaina, HI	0.5	D	10.8	1.4	5.7	8.3	7.5	12.2	15.9	32,905	200	1,960	72,086	0.7
Kalamazoo-Portage, MI	1.0	D	6.8	23.1	6.7	6.1	8.5	16.6	11.3	53,115	203	6,350	114,532	0.3
Kankakee, IL	2.4	D	4.2	24.3	D	6.5	4.3	16.0	15.3	23,025	216	2,596	45,332	0.1
Kansas City, MO-KS	0.3	0.1	6.4	7.8	D	5.1	13.6	11.4	13.1	390,990	178	33,655	950,172	1.0
Kennewick-Richland, WA	8.0	D	10.0	6.2	12.2	6.2	4.2	11.2	16.7	49,600	161	5,877	112,291	1.8
Killeen-Temple, TX	-0.1	0.2	5.8	3.9	5.6	5.9	4.8	D	43.9	77,065	159	10,864	190,294	1.9
Kingsport-Bristol, TN-VA	0.0	D	D	23.5	D	8.5	4.3	14.9	12.9	93,835	304	10,023	149,091	0.4
Kingston, NY	0.6	0.2	6.7	5.9	7.2	8.1	4.8	13.3	29.7	43,135	236	3,909	86,168	0.3
Knoxville, TN	0.1	0.1	6.7	11.2	D	7.7	D	D	13.5	206,465	231	20,306	399,671	1.3
Kokomo, IN	1.0	D	4.0	41.1	2.7	6.6	4.4	13.5	10.5	21,610	258	2,252	39,768	0.3
La Crosse-Onalaska, WI-MN	1.1	0.0	5.5	12.8	D	5.7	D	20.8	14.6	29,485	212	2,048	61,927	0.5
Lafayette, LA	1.3	9.6	6.6	8.4	9.0	7.4	6.9	D	12.7	94,680	198	15,330	215,972	1.2
Lafayette-West Lafayette, IN	2.6	D	5.0	D	5.6	5.0	D	D	25.3	36,285	161	2,848	96,329	1.4
Lake Charles, LA	0.1	0.4	19.8	19.8	D	D	D	10.9	12.7	40,815	194	5,707	98,386	0.7
Lake Havasu City-Kingman, AZ	1.6	0.5	8.3	6.1	4.8	12.7	6.4	18.6	16.9	74,085	340	4,642	119,461	1.2
Lakeland-Winter Haven, FL	0.8	0.5	6.9	9.1	5.3	7.9	8.4	13.3	11.9	174,055	231	23,328	327,799	2.9
Lancaster, PA	1.4	0.2	11.9	14.2	7.1	7.4	7.1	13.6	8.2	116,670	211	9,138	218,063	0.6
Lansing-East Lansing, MI	0.8	0.1	5.4	10.0	8.9	5.7	10.1	12.7	25.5	113,700	210	11,765	236,885	0.4
Laredo, TX	0.1	3.6	3.5	0.8	4.1	7.0	5.6	11.2	28.0	36,370	136	11,358	86,660	1.8
Las Cruces, NM	3.1	D	6.9	4.0	7.9	5.9	4.9	16.1	31.3	45,355	205	8,166	91,275	1.3
Las Vegas-Henderson-Paradise, NV	0.0	0.0	8.8	2.7	9.7	7.6	8.0	10.4	15.2	386,005	168	44,339	934,878	1.5
Lawrence, KS	0.5	0.0	5.5	9.5	11.2	6.9	7.5	7.6	32.0	18,825	158	1,371	53,310	0.7
Lawton, OK	0.7	D	3.1	7.6	D	5.1	D	5.5	55.1	23,290	183	3,420	55,327	0.1
Lebanon, PA	1.5	D	6.6	18.2	4.1	7.8	3.3	12.3	19.3	33,965	237	2,692	59,561	0.7
Lewiston, ID-WA	2.5	D	7.5	17.2	4.6	8.8	8.3	16.9	17.2	17,920	276	1,699	28,708	0.9
Lewiston-Auburn, ME	0.9	D	8.0	10.7	7.1	8.1	5.8	20.2	11.2	26,620	240	4,052	50,149	0.5
Lexington-Fayette, KY	2.7	0.2	6.7	12.9	9.1	6.0	5.1	11.2	21.3	91,720	177	11,097	228,714	0.9
Lima, OH	0.9	D	5.2	22.8	4.6	6.3	3.7	20.1	12.8	23,195	228	2,990	44,707	0.3
Lincoln, NE	0.9	D	6.7	7.9	10.5	5.6	8.1	D	21.5	55,490	162	5,164	144,876	1.3
Little Rock-North Little Rock-Conway, AR	0.2	0.4	6.3	5.6	9.3	6.3	D	14.3	22.2	157,075	209	24,035	340,578	0.9
Logan, UT-ID	2.4	0.1	6.9	20.1	D	6.6	10.9	D	17.5	18,050	119	1,027	50,789	3.3
Longview, TX	0.1	7.3	9.2	14.5	D	6.9	7.0	11.7	11.6	61,420	213	8,408	121,607	0.5
Longview, WA	0.9	D	10.9	20.3	3.9	6.9	4.8	13.2	15.8	28,570	256	3,777	45,855	0.8
Los Angeles-Long Beach-Anaheim, CA	0.0	0.1	4.9	7.9	19.0	5.1	11.6	10.2	13.7	1,888,200	145	450,217	4,759,274	0.6
Anaheim-Santa Ana-Irvine, CA Div 11,244	0.1	0.0	7.5	10.4	15.2	5.3	14.7	9.1	10.4	479,160	151	71,953	1,138,966	0.6
Los Angeles-Long Beach-Glendale, CA Div 31,084	0.0	0.1	4.0	7.0	20.3	5.0	10.5	10.5	14.9	1,409,040	143	378,264	3,620,308	0.6
Louisville/Jefferson County, KY-IN	0.3	0.1	5.8	13.3	D	5.4	12.0	13.3	10.8	261,070	203	32,172	565,488	0.6
Lubbock, TX	0.0	1.4	D	D	D	8.4	D	D	24.3	51,495	158	6,427	141,628	2.7
Lynchburg, VA	0.0	D	D	18.1	D	7.1	7.2	D	11.9	65,285	249	6,125	118,507	0.6
Macon-Bibb County, GA	0.2	0.7	D	D	D	D	D	20.3	14.0	51,995	222	9,500	104,222	0.4
Madera, CA	17.8	D	4.4	5.9	2.3	5.0	2.9	15.2	21.0	26,480	166	4,464	49,982	0.7
Madison, WI	1.0	0.1	6.0	9.1	17.4	5.8	8.8	D	20.6	119,840	175	8,992	308,125	1.6
Manchester-Nashua, NH	0.0	D	6.8	14.6	15.4	7.2	11.6	11.4	9.3	83,860	198	6,785	176,651	0.5
Manhattan, KS	0.7	D	4.1	5.7	D	4.6	5.4	D	54.8	17,460	130	1,410	56,717	0.7
Mankato, MN	3.3	D	5.6	15.6	D	6.9	5.4	D	17.5	18,380	177	1,398	42,990	1.0
Mansfield, OH	0.9	D	7.8	21.0	3.4	8.1	3.6	15.3	17.8	30,050	240	3,604	54,634	0.2
McAllen-Edinburg-Mission, TX	1.0	0.7	4.9	2.7	4.4	9.2	5.3	19.9	25.7	115,215	131	39,498	301,741	1.8
Medford, OR	0.4	0.2	7.3	8.5	6.8	10.3	7.3	19.9	14.0	59,660	267	4,863	96,581	0.1
Memphis, TN-MS-AR	0.2	D	D	9.2	5.4	D	D	13.5	13.2	249,660	187	44,496	570,692	0.7
Merced, CA	17.2	D	4.1	10.3	1.8	6.1	4.0	9.5	24.4	39,985	140	10,561	89,320	1.5
Miami-Fort Lauderdale-Pompano Beach, FL	0.3	0.0	6.6	3.1	14.7	6.9	11.7	11.3	12.5	1,110,660	182	225,961	2,662,576	0.7
Fort Lauderdale-Pompano Beach-Sunrise, FL Div 22,744	0.0	0.0	7.1	3.4	14.7	8.0	10.5	10.2	13.3	337,650	175	45,595	864,436	0.4
Miami-Miami Beach-Kendall, FL Div 33,124	0.4	0.1	6.6	2.8	14.8	6.5	12.0	11.5	13.2	438,835	165	156,825	1,084,353	0.7
West Palm Beach-Boca Raton-Boynton Beach, FL Div 48,424	0.6	0.1	6.0	3.4	14.5	6.5	12.8	12.2	10.2	334,175	223	23,541	713,787	0.9
Michigan City-La Porte, IN	2.3	0.1	8.5	21.4	3.5	6.8	4.7	13.8	15.0	25,640	228	2,166	49,860	0.1
Midland, MI	0.3	D	6.0	17.7	4.6	4.3	4.0	13.4	7.2	20,330	244	1,533	36,983	0.3
Midland, TX	0.1	61.9	3.9	2.0	D	2.6	4.0	2.4	4.0	20,355	118	1,924	74,114	1.9
Milwaukee-Waukesha, WI	0.1	D	5.6	14.8	11.0	5.1	10.4	14.0	10.6	308,345	197	47,199	695,772	0.2
Minneapolis-St. Paul-Bloomington, MN	0.2	0.1	6.0	11.0	13.9	4.7	12.3	11.1	11.7	597,550	162	60,266	1,529,436	1.4
Missoula, MT	0.2	0.1	8.4	3.2	11.6	8.9	8.2	17.4	17.7	23,455	196	1,950	55,481	1.4

1. Per 1,000 resident population estimated as of July 1 of the year shown.

Area name	Occupied housing units, 2016-2020: Occupied units: Total	Owner-occupied: Percent	Owner-occupied: Median value[1]	Owner-occupied: Median owner cost as a percent of income: With a mortgage	Owner-occupied: Median owner cost as a percent of income: Without a mortgage[2]	Renter-occupied: Median rent[3]	Renter-occupied: Median rent as a percent of income	Renter-occupied: Substandard units[4] (percent)	Civilian labor force, 2021: Total	Civilian labor force, 2021: Percent change 2020-2021	Unemployment: Total	Unemployment: Rate[5]	Civilian employment[6], 2016-2020: Total	Percent: Management, business, science, and arts	Percent: Construction, production, and maintenance occupations
	89	90	91	92	93	94	95	96	97	98	99	100	101	102	103
Jonesboro, AR	51,770	58.1	136,000	17.1	10.0	761	27.7	2.4	65,358	-1.1	2,198	3.4	60,597	33.9	26.8
Joplin, MO	68,584	66.4	126,200	18.4	10.9	748	27.8	3.0	83,998	2.0	3,164	3.8	82,613	31.1	29.7
Kahului-Wailuku-Lahaina, HI	55,620	62.5	657,400	26.3	10.0	1,543	30.6	9.8	86,954	2.2	6,379	7.3	83,846	31.2	18.7
Kalamazoo-Portage, MI	104,278	64.5	168,500	18.5	11.3	846	28.9	1.5	128,630	-2.3	6,441	5.0	132,109	40.9	20.5
Kankakee, IL	40,297	67.1	152,800	19.9	13.5	906	30.3	2.2	52,515	-2.5	3,415	6.5	50,893	30.7	30.0
Kansas City, MO-KS	843,359	65.2	196,000	19.3	11.3	989	27.4	2.2	1,142,697	0.9	48,322	4.2	1,099,476	41.6	21.1
Kennewick-Richland, WA	100,336	69.1	246,700	19.7	10.0	994	27.8	4.0	148,608	-0.5	8,739	5.9	131,103	37.6	27.2
Killeen-Temple, TX	155,894	56.3	150,300	20.6	10.5	937	28.0	4.0	181,163	2.8	10,293	5.7	177,902	34.4	23.0
Kingsport-Bristol, TN-VA	128,124	73.5	140,800	19.1	10.0	678	26.6	1.8	133,367	-1.3	5,495	4.1	128,685	33.6	27.1
Kingston, NY	70,088	68.6	239,400	23.9	14.8	1,119	34.4	2.2	86,356	-1.2	4,024	4.7	85,866	39.3	19.8
Knoxville, TN	345,707	69.2	180,700	19.1	10.0	864	27.7	1.8	424,331	1.6	14,682	3.5	404,466	38.3	22.1
Kokomo, IN	34,632	72.1	113,900	17.0	10.0	743	25.9	1.4	34,727	-6.5	2,136	6.2	37,368	30.6	32.4
La Crosse-Onalaska, WI-MN	56,391	65.3	183,200	20.0	11.3	847	27.2	1.4	77,402	1.2	2,327	3.0	71,982	38.8	22.6
Lafayette, LA	183,685	69.4	162,600	18.7	10.0	823	30.3	3.3	212,057	0.8	10,676	5.0	219,530	33.6	25.3
Lafayette-West Lafayette, IN	86,627	59.2	152,500	17.5	10.0	868	32.2	1.7	110,877	1.4	3,532	3.2	112,833	39.8	25.8
Lake Charles, LA	81,329	69.2	159,600	18.2	10.0	851	29.5	2.6	99,437	-1.4	5,515	5.5	93,397	32.4	27.4
Lake Havasu City-Kingman, AZ	90,413	70.4	172,100	22.0	10.0	839	27.5	4.1	87,215	1.5	4,833	5.5	74,114	26.8	23.8
Lakeland-Winter Haven, FL	240,879	69.5	162,400	22.0	11.3	1,014	30.2	3.5	328,590	2.8	17,585	5.4	296,493	29.9	25.6
Lancaster, PA	204,003	69.4	218,700	21.3	11.3	1,050	28.5	2.4	284,893	-0.2	14,010	4.9	273,736	35.7	28.1
Lansing-East Lansing, MI	216,659	67.3	153,300	18.7	11.4	884	28.8	1.7	266,370	-3.2	14,309	5.4	269,560	38.8	21.6
Laredo, TX	76,382	63.0	135,000	24.7	11.6	851	31.9	11.4	116,373	1.0	7,340	6.3	111,451	25.5	25.5
Las Cruces, NM	79,421	64.6	153,600	21.7	10.0	765	33.3	4.6	98,170	1.3	6,522	6.6	88,633	35.2	19.8
Las Vegas-Henderson-Paradise, NV	809,026	54.8	285,100	22.4	10.0	1,181	30.9	4.8	1,100,264	-0.4	91,244	8.3	1,044,351	29.8	19.4
Lawrence, KS	47,972	50.7	212,400	19.2	10.7	952	29.4	2.0	64,611	1.0	2,030	3.1	68,255	45.5	16.9
Lawton, OK	45,456	54.4	121,500	19.0	10.0	810	27.1	3.0	50,449	-0.1	2,049	4.1	50,243	37.3	22.6
Lebanon, PA	53,857	70.5	176,000	20.2	11.9	879	28.7	2.7	72,636	-0.5	3,965	5.5	67,281	31.3	29.0
Lewiston, ID-WA	25,834	72.7	207,200	20.4	10.0	762	30.2	2.3	31,548	1.0	1,078	3.4	28,849	32.4	27.5
Lewiston-Auburn, ME	45,906	64.9	166,600	20.1	13.4	771	28.1	2.0	54,219	-0.1	2,643	4.9	54,139	34.9	23.9
Lexington-Fayette, KY	203,965	59.8	193,700	18.5	10.0	887	27.8	2.2	271,054	0.8	10,576	3.9	260,830	41.6	20.6
Lima, OH	41,025	66.7	120,300	18.1	11.8	722	28.2	1.3	47,538	-0.5	2,720	5.7	47,668	28.4	33.7
Lincoln, NE	133,432	59.8	188,700	19.4	10.5	870	27.0	2.4	187,485	0.1	4,577	2.4	180,729	41.8	19.8
Little Rock-North Little Rock-Conway, AR	289,808	63.9	157,900	18.6	10.0	853	28.3	2.5	349,208	-1.9	14,566	4.2	345,991	40.6	20.8
Logan, UT-ID	44,013	64.7	252,800	20.5	10.0	839	28.7	3.7	76,116	4.1	1,534	2.0	67,911	37.5	25.2
Longview, TX	102,463	68.5	141,700	19.5	10.5	850	28.2	3.7	124,445	0.4	7,948	6.4	122,817	30.5	31.2
Longview, WA	42,354	66.1	245,500	22.1	12.0	895	30.3	2.9	48,443	-1.0	3,085	6.4	45,128	29.5	30.4
Los Angeles-Long Beach-Anaheim, CA	4,372,505	48.7	641,300	26.6	10.7	1,624	33.6	11.0	6,547,954	0.3	537,948	8.2	6,501,703	39.9	19.8
Anaheim-Santa Ana-Irvine, CA Div 11,244	1,040,001	57.2	703,800	25.3	10.0	1,928	33.0	9.0	1,553,897	-0.5	92,743	6.0	1,592,877	43.6	16.8
Los Angeles-Long Beach-Glendale, CA Div 31,084	3,332,504	46.0	615,500	27.2	11.1	1,534	33.8	11.6	4,994,057	0.5	445,205	8.9	4,908,826	38.7	20.8
Louisville/Jefferson County, KY-IN	497,106	67.4	177,400	19.0	10.6	882	27.0	2.1	651,007	1.0	27,944	4.3	626,540	37.0	26.2
Lubbock, TX	120,841	56.2	146,400	20.4	11.2	942	32.1	3.7	165,512	2.9	7,499	4.5	155,683	38.2	20.8
Lynchburg, VA	101,123	70.8	173,900	19.0	10.0	815	27.6	2.0	118,206	-2.9	4,784	4.0	122,463	36.7	24.4
Macon-Bibb County, GA	86,898	61.4	132,700	19.6	10.8	816	33.0	2.3	102,968	1.3	4,579	4.4	95,838	33.3	23.0
Madera, CA	44,479	65.8	268,500	23.7	10.0	1,068	30.3	11.1	61,944	0.1	5,476	8.8	58,917	25.8	36.1
Madison, WI	275,987	61.8	260,600	20.2	11.9	1,080	27.8	1.7	398,273	2.1	11,558	2.9	372,977	49.7	17.4
Manchester-Nashua, NH	162,843	65.7	287,900	22.1	13.9	1,217	29.2	2.1	237,144	-1.1	8,534	3.6	228,874	43.1	20.0
Manhattan, KS	48,627	49.1	180,500	20.3	11.0	944	29.4	3.0	57,375	0.1	1,735	3.0	60,832	40.8	19.9
Mankato, MN	39,211	65.3	198,100	19.6	10.6	898	29.2	2.1	59,302	-4.0	1,754	3.0	57,391	35.5	23.9
Mansfield, OH	48,967	66.9	115,100	18.8	10.6	677	27.6	1.7	51,520	-0.3	2,862	5.6	51,502	29.7	31.1
McAllen-Edinburg-Mission, TX	243,878	68.0	90,000	22.7	11.8	753	31.1	13.7	366,220	2.5	34,111	9.3	330,528	28.0	25.9
Medford, OR	89,690	64.3	294,500	23.4	12.4	1,057	32.0	3.9	107,706	2.5	5,843	5.4	98,551	35.9	22.0
Memphis, TN-MS-AR	505,544	59.8	161,300	20.0	10.4	944	31.0	2.5	638,458	0.3	39,538	6.2	619,412	35.1	25.9
Merced, CA	81,306	52.2	268,800	23.2	11.0	1,054	29.3	8.9	115,158	-0.2	11,935	10.4	107,059	23.7	38.8
Miami-Fort Lauderdale-Pompano Beach, FL	2,172,740	59.8	298,400	25.9	14.4	1,408	36.8	5.0	3,071,324	2.1	150,400	4.9	2,987,330	35.8	19.4
Fort Lauderdale-Pompano Beach-Sunrise, FL Div 22,744	704,942	62.8	282,400	25.7	14.8	1,433	36.2	4.4	1,029,454	0.8	50,390	4.9	974,826	37.0	18.1
Miami-Miami Beach-Kendall, FL Div 33,124	902,200	51.6	310,700	27.1	14.1	1,373	37.6	6.6	1,307,815	2.8	68,341	5.2	1,326,437	33.8	21.5
West Palm Beach-Boca Raton-Boynton Beach, FL Div 48,424	565,598	69.2	301,000	24.5	14.2	1,452	35.6	3.3	734,055	2.6	31,669	4.3	686,067	37.7	17.4
Michigan City-La Porte, IN	42,725	73.3	139,900	17.9	10.0	763	28.4	2.8	46,208	-2.4	2,335	5.1	48,248	28.1	30.2
Midland, MI	34,253	77.3	145,900	18.0	11.1	807	28.8	1.6	38,276	-2.4	1,880	4.9	38,228	41.3	21.4
Midland, TX	59,639	66.8	231,100	19.1	10.1	1,239	26.8	6.7	101,906	1.5	5,795	5.7	88,068	36.8	27.1
Milwaukee-Waukesha, WI	634,436	59.8	223,700	20.4	12.6	917	28.8	2.4	821,296	0.3	36,318	4.4	794,416	40.8	21.4
Minneapolis-St. Paul-Bloomington, MN	1,390,448	70.4	271,600	19.6	10.2	1,144	28.2	2.7	1,972,558	-2.9	66,578	3.4	1,957,345	45.7	18.8
Missoula, MT	49,700	58.6	302,200	22.6	12.3	908	29.3	2.5	65,104	0.9	2,184	3.4	66,339	38.4	18.7

1. Specified owner-occupied units. 2. A value of 10.0 represents 10 percent or less; a value of 50.0 represents 50 percent or more. 3. Specified renter-occupied units. 4. Overcrowded or lacking complete plumbing facilities. 5. Percent of civilian labor force. 6. Civilian employed persons 16 years old and over.

Weirton-Steubenville, WV-OH	Private nonfarm establishments, employment and payroll, 2019									Agriculture, 2017			
		Employment						Annual payroll		Farms			Farm producers whose primary occupation is farming (percent)
											Percent with:		
	Number of establish-ments	Total	Health care and social assistance	Manufactur-ing	Retail trade	Finance and insurance	Professional, scientific, and technical services	Total (mil dol)	Average per employee (dollars)	Number	Fewer than 50 acres	1000 acres or more	
	104	105	106	107	108	109	110	111	112	113	114	115	116
Jonesboro, AR	2,916	49,734	12,091	8,321	7,452	1,389	1,249	2,038	40,981	886	28.6	24.9	50.4
Joplin, MO	3,984	73,161	12,977	13,717	10,236	1,610	1,504	3,036	41,504	2,903	39.3	2.4	38.0
Kahului-Wailuku-Lahaina, HI	4,798	67,107	7,042	1,028	9,579	914	1,931	2,403	35,813	1,408	89.6	2.3	43.8
Kalamazoo-Portage, MI	5,574	111,428	20,231	17,730	14,130	4,872	4,483	5,520	49,541	707	61.8	5.1	43.2
Kankakee, IL	2,277	37,296	8,082	6,131	5,672	1,024	685	1,643	44,056	756	36.6	12.3	46.9
Kansas City, MO-KS	53,022	980,924	145,932	82,444	111,915	66,040	88,488	54,288	55,343	12,437	42.0	5.7	34.5
Kennewick-Richland, WA	6,491	96,649	14,856	7,489	13,992	2,373	8,529	5,261	54,435	2,292	67.3	9.3	41.6
Killeen-Temple, TX	6,594	112,468	25,280	8,019	17,570	4,159	4,412	4,701	41,796	5,066	50.5	4.7	33.8
Kingsport-Bristol, TN-VA	5,881	100,296	16,894	21,258	15,331	3,017	2,348	4,438	44,245	5,311	50.1	0.6	35.4
Kingston, NY	4,781	45,886	9,509	3,219	8,455	1,973	1,778	1,715	37,367	421	51.8	0.7	51.0
Knoxville, TN	18,304	347,670	54,084	38,296	43,560	14,908	23,806	16,422	47,236	5,247	54.6	0.6	35.1
Kokomo, IN	1,774	30,733	5,293	8,559	4,641	787	717	1,281	41,689	422	36.3	10.0	49.1
La Crosse-Onalaska, WI-MN	3,511	71,058	13,388	7,854	8,985	3,249	2,097	3,210	45,168	1,558	25.0	2.2	43.6
Lafayette, LA	13,087	183,629	35,325	13,789	26,257	5,808	10,361	8,351	45,476	3,511	54.1	7.7	36.4
Lafayette-West Lafayette, IN	4,342	79,537	13,366	21,388	9,892	1,959	3,346	3,430	43,121	2,041	43.6	13.4	40.5
Lake Charles, LA	4,795	82,457	13,824	9,142	10,964	2,136	5,656	3,863	46,845	1,225	44.1	9.4	29.0
Lake Havasu City-Kingman, AZ	3,949	45,156	8,967	3,242	10,467	1,000	1,305	1,702	37,684	317	60.6	17.4	40.7
Lakeland-Winter Haven, FL	12,491	203,461	30,981	17,148	31,020	10,930	7,115	8,889	43,687	2,080	63.2	4.8	37.6
Lancaster, PA	13,316	246,206	39,941	37,222	33,162	8,313	13,387	11,197	45,477	5,108	50.0	0.4	56.9
Lansing-East Lansing, MI	10,687	185,499	31,901	20,067	24,003	15,284	9,285	8,599	46,354	3,863	49.7	5.1	41.2
Laredo, TX	5,512	79,245	17,298	777	12,961	2,838	2,127	2,427	30,627	656	19.1	22.6	36.3
Las Cruces, NM	3,675	53,960	16,014	2,729	7,811	1,851	3,741	1,902	35,254	1,946	86.7	1.8	33.1
Las Vegas-Henderson-Paradise, NV	49,138	922,349	101,683	23,601	114,377	29,781	42,536	38,638	41,891	179	77.1	0.6	30.5
Lawrence, KS	2,724	37,380	6,479	4,261	6,178	1,272	2,480	1,409	37,694	998	44.7	5.6	33.5
Lawton, OK	2,191	33,780	6,453	3,368	5,300	1,455	2,177	1,320	39,084	1,503	25.4	17.9	38.3
Lebanon, PA	2,720	48,007	8,945	9,838	7,021	986	1,194	1,986	41,371	1,149	54.6	0.2	50.5
Lewiston, ID-WA	1,581	21,785	4,259	3,796	3,464	1,294	734	949	43,578	651	45.9	27.8	41.0
Lewiston-Auburn, ME	2,808	44,668	9,829	5,421	5,978	3,352	1,561	1,989	44,525	496	58.7	1.0	61.0
Lexington-Fayette, KY	12,667	233,561	39,797	27,824	29,374	6,131	15,906	10,686	45,754	4,619	46.2	2.3	40.6
Lima, OH	2,286	45,012	9,711	8,917	5,719	904	1,193	1,983	44,061	855	43.5	4.1	36.5
Lincoln, NE	9,191	152,158	27,694	13,600	18,846	15,110	9,149	6,906	45,389	2,730	49.5	9.2	36.3
Little Rock-North Little Rock-Conway, AR	18,575	289,075	61,108	20,604	38,065	17,936	13,420	13,873	47,992	3,353	42.8	4.8	37.6
Logan, UT-ID	4,000	50,775	6,361	13,526	7,497	1,183	4,825	2,061	40,584	2,184	53.4	5.2	31.6
Longview, TX	6,602	100,962	14,446	16,032	13,022	3,638	4,612	4,446	44,034	4,768	47.5	1.7	32.7
Longview, WA	2,210	33,100	5,670	7,402	5,025	824	852	1,624	49,071	403	76.9	1.5	33.3
Los Angeles-Long Beach-Anaheim, CA	393,514	5,465,998	782,740	455,478	564,931	250,644	447,635	341,826	62,537	1,228	88.8	1.1	45.6
Anaheim-Santa Ana-Irvine, CA Div 11,244	101,681	1,551,280	183,483	143,595	149,379	92,755	136,474	97,481	62,839	193	83.4	1.6	42.6
Los Angeles-Long Beach-Glendale, CA Div 31,084	291,833	3,914,718	599,257	311,883	415,552	157,889	311,161	244,345	62,417	1,035	89.9	1.0	46.1
Louisville/Jefferson County, KY-IN	29,324	607,720	90,896	78,381	71,923	37,421	28,978	30,888	50,826	6,851	49.8	2.5	35.2
Lubbock, TX	7,612	119,616	25,816	5,375	18,917	5,735	4,961	4,776	39,928	1,810	32.2	23.1	40.8
Lynchburg, VA	5,963	99,368	15,953	15,649	13,320	3,541	5,110	4,260	42,870	2,901	34.5	2.4	36.7
Macon-Bibb County, GA	5,210	88,298	17,810	6,308	13,356	10,088	2,681	3,842	43,514	790	39.5	5.1	35.1
Madera, CA	2,095	27,969	6,743	3,848	3,705	444	499	1,374	49,127	1,386	41.6	8.7	52.7
Madison, WI	17,252	346,257	59,090	37,867	41,177	26,824	30,968	19,793	57,163	6,927	40.0	3.6	44.0
Manchester-Nashua, NH	10,997	190,991	32,864	21,905	28,441	9,529	15,980	11,084	58,032	605	63.3	0.2	42.0
Manhattan, KS	2,823	38,169	6,520	3,068	6,766	1,354	1,562	1,368	35,851	1,491	27.7	15.4	34.9
Mankato, MN	2,628	49,759	10,650	8,364	7,279	1,265	1,512	2,089	41,979	1,672	27.5	9.6	50.3
Mansfield, OH	2,606	39,890	6,451	8,825	6,189	902	830	1,479	37,078	1,160	49.1	1.5	41.8
McAllen-Edinburg-Mission, TX	12,446	212,954	72,655	6,849	37,424	7,354	6,165	6,260	29,395	2,436	73.6	6.4	32.0
Medford, OR	6,436	79,055	16,118	6,622	12,473	2,318	2,779	3,480	44,018	2,136	78.6	1.1	39.9
Memphis, TN-MS-AR	25,858	556,672	88,449	37,555	60,855	18,350	22,559	28,255	50,758	3,796	39.7	10.3	39.4
Merced, CA	3,273	47,847	7,532	9,719	8,345	1,182	828	2,005	41,913	2,337	53.5	7.4	56.3
Miami-Fort Lauderdale-Pompano Beach, FL	206,705	2,300,443	346,271	75,031	332,468	104,533	182,035	117,350	51,012	4,690	92.6	1.0	46.7
Fort Lauderdale-Pompano Beach-Sunrise, FL Div 22,744	64,660	736,561	105,097	23,900	108,416	34,094	59,404	37,388	50,760	640	97.2	0.2	41.5
Miami-Miami Beach-Kendall, FL Div 33,124	90,482	1,009,024	148,685	36,305	143,447	48,434	77,725	51,382	50,922	2,752	93.2	0.3	47.1
West Palm Beach-Boca Raton-Boynton Beach, FL Div 48,424	51,563	554,858	92,489	14,826	80,605	22,005	44,906	28,581	51,510	1,298	89.1	3.0	48.3
Michigan City-La Porte, IN	2,207	35,745	5,474	7,839	5,532	829	780	1,438	40,218	740	42.4	9.5	45.4
Midland, MI	1,746	35,275	7,528	5,092	3,373	1,200	3,145	2,245	63,651	530	51.3	4.2	39.2
Midland, TX	5,877	103,276	7,752	3,281	9,973	2,382	4,200	6,478	62,724	766	39.0	20.5	32.4
Milwaukee-Waukesha, WI	38,620	787,821	135,141	110,672	80,166	53,225	40,540	43,382	55,066	1,554	50.2	3.4	46.8
Minneapolis-St. Paul-Bloomington, MN	96,791	1,846,408	305,288	195,090	193,579	131,390	123,889	112,839	61,113	11,525	46.9	3.7	39.3
Missoula, MT	4,610	51,367	9,669	2,404	7,976	2,241	4,215	2,092	40,726	576	66.1	3.6	32.9

Area name	Agriculture, 2017 (cont.)															
	Land in farms					Value of land and buildings (dollars)		Value of machinery and equipmnet, average per farm (dollars)	Value of products sold:				Organic farms (number)	Farms with internet access (percent)	Government payments	
	Acreage (1,000)	Percent change, 2012–2017	Acres: Average size of farm	Acres: Total irrigated (1,000)	Acres: Total cropland (1,000)	Average per farm	Average per acre		Total (mil dol)	Average per farm (acres)	Percent from: Crops	Percent from: Livestock and poultry products			Total ($1,000)	Percent of farms
	117	118	119	120	121	122	123	124	125	126	127	128	129	130	131	132
Jonesboro, AR	638	-11.8	720.0	510.0	592.3	3,038,718	4,220	385,903	381.0	430,029	98.8	1.2	0	75.4	31,077	63.2
Joplin, MO	526	6.4	181.0	5.8	232.4	621,114	3,429	84,225	343.2	118,235	18.1	81.9	1	74.2	2,415	18.4
Kahului-Wailuku-Lahaina, HI	249	8.6	177.0	4.8	56.6	2,027,298	11,466	51,466	82.2	58,385	90.3	9.7	40	83.5	2,174	9.4
Kalamazoo-Portage, MI	139	-3.5	196.0	43.0	111.8	1,382,696	7,055	206,187	236.9	335,109	74.5	25.5	2	83.7	2,664	21.6
Kankakee, IL	313	-8.7	414.0	18.4	300.4	3,237,466	7,822	285,392	221.1	292,508	91.3	8.7	3	75.5	2,346	45.4
Kansas City, MO-KS	3,126	0.1	251.0	26.0	2,026.9	906,374	3,606	99,443	985.3	79,220	75.1	24.9	39	76.7	29,916	34.7
Kennewick-Richland, WA	1,229	-7.5	536.0	392.4	919.9	2,276,946	4,247	248,388	1,636.9	714,174	75.7	24.3	56	86.0	16,530	13.0
Killeen-Temple, TX	1,413	6.3	279.0	4.1	285.1	812,458	2,913	64,759	131.7	26,006	36.6	63.4	4	75.0	5,248	9.4
Kingsport-Bristol, TN-VA	527	-7.3	99.0	0.2	168.3	440,247	4,437	55,882	125.3	23,599	16.7	83.3	4	69.0	2,177	12.2
Kingston, NY	59	-17.3	140.0	3.7	24.1	965,682	6,899	95,713	54.3	129,088	88.3	11.7	24	86.9	164	8.1
Knoxville, TN	443	-2.1	84.0	0.7	165.1	490,013	5,804	59,431	64.7	12,330	38.7	61.3	28	74.2	2,659	18.0
Kokomo, IN	146	1.1	345.0	0.0	138.0	2,681,235	7,765	219,981	97.1	230,078	83.1	16.9	3	79.9	4,286	68.2
La Crosse-Onalaska, WI-MN	361	-6.8	232.0	1.3	211.6	1,059,615	4,568	128,124	190.8	122,458	38.2	61.8	49	77.5	5,327	61.2
Lafayette, LA	923	21.4	263.0	165.7	606.7	793,548	3,018	142,157	336.8	95,939	77.2	22.8	2	64.8	31,262	40.4
Lafayette-West Lafayette, IN	885	3.6	434.0	20.0	824.7	3,386,478	7,808	254,098	702.5	344,214	73.4	26.6	11	79.4	16,217	61.6
Lake Charles, LA	542	-5.4	442.0	18.9	128.4	1,386,167	3,133	80,170	37.7	30,793	49.9	50.1	0	75.0	5,190	22.4
Lake Havasu City-Kingman, AZ	745	-40.1	2,351.0	20.9	30.7	1,972,874	839	96,073	32.3	101,871	71.1	28.9	0	87.4	390	2.8
Lakeland-Winter Haven, FL	487	-6.5	234.0	88.6	131.0	1,420,064	6,064	69,094	297.7	143,136	81.0	19.0	5	71.5	2,242	11.5
Lancaster, PA	394	-10.4	77.0	4.9	314.9	1,410,238	18,285	120,108	1,507.2	295,068	15.3	84.7	246	48.9	4,834	11.8
Lansing-East Lansing, MI	829	-7.0	214.0	6.6	717.4	1,054,915	4,918	156,236	518.9	134,316	55.0	45.0	73	80.0	16,175	36.5
Laredo, TX	1,845	-12.1	2,812.0	3.3	35.0	4,817,630	1,713	69,020	28.4	43,287	1.5	98.5	0	47.6	525	3.2
Las Cruces, NM	528	-20.0	271.0	73.7	93.1	674,302	2,484	91,092	370.3	190,284	61.8	38.2	23	73.7	578	4.0
Las Vegas-Henderson-Paradise, NV	D	D	D	3.7	4.0	1,439,603	D	76,922	12.7	70,676	90.2	9.8	1	74.9	16	2.2
Lawrence, KS	230	9.3	231.0	3.5	159.3	939,826	4,072	94,196	65.9	65,999	76.7	23.3	11	78.3	1,316	38.8
Lawton, OK	872	1.0	580.0	0.1	360.4	965,045	1,664	100,970	130.8	87,035	20.1	79.9	2	75.6	9,050	44.4
Lebanon, PA	108	-11.4	94.0	0.7	86.7	1,348,192	14,400	132,813	350.8	305,312	10.6	89.4	54	71.4	1,021	13.7
Lewiston, ID-WA	632	8.0	972.0	2.0	313.7	1,728,575	1,779	185,061	87.2	133,986	78.0	22.0	1	87.1	11,239	44.7
Lewiston-Auburn, ME	56	-6.4	112.0	1.0	24.6	395,349	3,526	68,417	40.5	81,726	37.6	62.4	18	85.1	481	10.5
Lexington-Fayette, KY	752	-1.0	163.0	1.3	305.4	1,179,163	7,245	87,936	723.3	156,582	15.0	85.0	15	82.1	2,574	10.6
Lima, OH	187	1.9	218.0	0.4	172.7	1,583,677	7,256	163,585	139.9	163,639	61.4	38.6	2	77.8	5,704	67.7
Lincoln, NE	786	-6.8	288.0	160.0	673.4	1,627,411	5,650	169,707	439.8	161,095	70.4	29.6	11	83.6	20,112	59.5
Little Rock-North Little Rock-Conway, AR	816	3.5	243.0	258.9	451.5	885,319	3,640	104,215	302.1	90,088	66.2	33.8	18	76.8	19,878	16.2
Logan, UT-ID	505	-5.0	231.0	155.4	291.4	854,536	3,698	123,635	245.5	112,417	27.4	72.6	34	82.0	6,169	30.8
Longview, TX	676	-6.7	142.0	2.9	136.0	437,425	3,085	60,897	160.8	33,727	9.0	91.0	10	73.4	1,081	4.0
Longview, WA	29	-26.3	71.0	3.0	11.0	639,037	8,955	53,998	19.0	47,045	52.8	47.2	0	80.9	27	1.5
Los Angeles-Long Beach-Anaheim, CA	90	-40.7	73.0	18.0	39.2	1,378,476	18,765	72,823	237.1	193,090	91.0	9.0	48	78.9	529	2.3
Anaheim-Santa Ana-Irvine, CA Div 11,244	32	-46.4	168.0	4.2	9.6	3,205,503	19,094	162,435	82.5	427,497	99.5	0.5	7	79.8	6	3.1
Los Angeles-Long Beach-Glendale, CA Div 31,084	58	-37.0	56.0	13.8	29.6	1,037,785	18,580	56,113	154.6	149,380	86.5	13.5	41	78.7	523	2.1
Louisville/Jefferson County, KY-IN	1,002	4.2	146.0	2.7	602.9	756,977	5,177	83,594	450.1	65,699	56.2	43.8	13	74.8	11,063	17.6
Lubbock, TX	1,580	3.1	873.0	336.3	1,180.5	1,071,771	1,228	232,519	417.8	230,832	75.4	24.6	13	76.8	17,022	56.5
Lynchburg, VA	497	-10.0	171.0	0.6	147.0	667,392	3,893	70,399	70.0	24,126	31.1	68.9	4	74.1	1,215	10.6
Macon-Bibb County, GA	169	16.4	213.0	6.3	41.5	677,035	3,172	83,004	129.7	164,133	16.2	83.8	7	81.1	974	17.1
Madera, CA	645	-1.3	466.0	300.2	346.1	5,102,429	10,958	229,882	1,492.6	1,076,903	77.4	22.6	74	77.1	2,192	8.4
Madison, WI	1,463	-0.2	211.0	22.0	1,110.1	1,340,446	6,346	157,750	1,159.1	167,331	40.5	59.5	140	81.0	20,405	50.5
Manchester-Nashua, NH	44	-7.3	73.0	0.6	11.7	568,208	7,775	67,926	18.8	31,030	77.2	22.8	18	93.1	281	7.8
Manhattan, KS	775	0.3	520.0	26.2	329.9	1,344,062	2,584	132,384	184.4	123,655	48.4	51.6	3	79.9	4,561	52.8
Mankato, MN	648	-0.5	387.0	4.3	605.0	2,757,805	7,121	290,184	822.8	492,108	41.4	58.6	8	82.8	15,176	64.6
Mansfield, OH	156	-3.0	134.0	0.2	113.1	1,008,272	7,505	108,319	135.1	116,504	37.1	62.9	20	65.4	2,687	21.0
McAllen-Edinburg-Mission, TX	624	-21.5	256.0	162.5	356.9	1,106,061	4,319	92,928	311.0	127,681	94.3	5.7	26	61.8	6,631	10.5
Medford, OR	170	-20.5	80.0	37.5	40.7	677,191	8,494	44,300	71.0	33,262	74.7	25.3	43	86.6	55	0.8
Memphis, TN-MS-AR	1,547	3.7	407.0	327.8	1,067.0	1,338,096	3,284	141,950	464.1	122,263	91.6	8.4	4	70.1	32,022	36.6
Merced, CA	946	-3.3	405.0	493.7	546.5	5,299,308	13,086	334,860	2,938.4	1,257,337	43.9	56.1	68	78.5	8,726	12.5
Miami-Fort Lauderdale-Pompano Beach, FL	573	-6.0	122.0	408.2	495.8	1,546,374	12,654	84,442	1,764.3	376,191	98.5	1.5	45	76.4	1,865	1.4
Fort Lauderdale-Pompano Beach-Sunrise, FL Div 22,744	7	-53.5	11.0	0.7	1.6	348,906	33,140	31,889	24.9	38,883	94.2	5.8	0	85.5	18	0.6
Miami-Miami Beach-Kendall, FL Div 33,124	79	-3.4	29.0	36.8	55.2	1,068,826	37,450	51,638	837.7	304,409	98.8	1.2	35	70.6	1,733	1.8
West Palm Beach-Boca Raton-Boynton Beach, FL Div 48,424	488	-5.1	376.0	370.7	438.9	3,149,297	8,379	179,904	901.7	694,699	98.3	1.7	10	84.2	114	1.1
Michigan City-La Porte, IN	249	9.2	336.0	68.5	230.0	2,473,619	7,355	210,853	166.4	224,842	82.2	17.8	7	79.6	8,644	58.4
Midland, MI	88	-2.1	165.0	0.6	69.9	916,909	5,542	121,113	46.9	88,483	57.1	42.9	5	80.2	2,366	40.0
Midland, TX	790	-8.0	1,031.0	19.6	374.7	1,241,070	1,204	141,855	70.6	92,215	92.7	7.3	0	79.6	6,374	41.1
Milwaukee-Waukesha, WI	283	-4.2	182.0	1.9	228.7	1,198,064	6,581	156,733	290.5	186,950	45.3	54.7	30	80.4	2,106	32.4
Minneapolis-St. Paul-Bloomington, MN	2,142	-4.9	186.0	134.4	1,718.7	1,088,585	5,858	144,831	1,562.8	135,599	63.4	36.6	166	80.4	19,621	37.7
Missoula, MT	260	5.3	452.0	15.5	21.6	1,262,722	2,796	42,356	9.8	17,099	57.3	42.7	5	82.8	417	6.1

Area name	Water use, 2015		Wholesale Trade[1], 2017				Retail Trade[2], 2017				Real estate and rental and leasing,[2] 2017			
	Public supply water withdrawn (mil gal/ day)	Public supply gallons withdrawn per person per day	Number of establish- ments	Number of employees	Sales (mil dol)	Average payroll (mil dol)	Number of establish- ments	Number of employees	Sales (mil dol)	Average payroll (mil dol)	Number of establish- ments	Number of employees	Sales (mil dol)	Average payroll (mil dol)
	133	134	135	136	137	138	139	140	141	142	143	144	145	146
Jonesboro, AR	16.3	127.0	151	2,133	1,782.1	90.7	528	7,340	1,995.1	178.5	132	531	122.9	19.8
Joplin, MO	22.9	129.1	179	3,315	2,321.0	148.2	698	10,295	3,024.9	259.7	166	725	120.8	20.1
Kahului-Wailuku-Lahaina, HI	42.1	255.7	146	1,354	828.7	63.7	D	D	D	D	343	1,984	651.4	87.5
Kalamazoo-Portage, MI	24.4	93.6	243	4,193	2,158.4	235.8	876	13,882	3,706.7	350.7	224	2,412	297.0	86.6
Kankakee, IL	13.3	119.6	116	2,199	1,384.6	110.9	366	5,932	1,516.0	134.1	89	331	68.4	12.2
Kansas City, MO-KS	270.8	129.7	2,482	43,045	60,613.7	2,832.2	6,159	111,632	33,514.8	3,012.7	2,663	14,229	4,703.0	728.0
Kennewick-Richland, WA	50.8	181.9	244	2,763	2,244.7	148.6	813	13,839	4,244.8	406.3	399	1,445	368.3	51.6
Killeen-Temple, TX	19.2	44.6	149	2,991	4,371.8	153.7	1,076	17,225	5,032.7	444.8	372	1,818	302.9	74.3
Kingsport-Bristol, TN-VA	40.1	130.5	231	2,729	2,013.2	121.7	1,061	15,928	4,175.4	374.9	214	855	179.7	26.4
Kingston, NY	394.2	2,188.4	153	1,565	893.5	82.5	726	8,896	2,570.5	242.2	187	611	107.7	21.8
Knoxville, TN	112.4	134.1	853	13,029	11,281.7	714.2	2,818	44,129	12,556.7	1,211.3	816	4,586	1,066.4	193.6
Kokomo, IN	8.5	102.6	D	D	D	D	341	5,141	1,382.5	117.8	78	300	62.9	9.9
La Crosse-Onalaska, WI-MN	15.1	110.2	122	2,738	5,156.5	143.3	475	9,557	2,453.3	228.6	147	1,061	148.0	35.6
Lafayette, LA	51.4	104.9	684	9,448	5,391.5	495.1	1,882	26,943	7,197.4	686.4	706	5,258	1,427.2	304.0
Lafayette-West Lafayette, IN	15.0	67.3	156	1,957	1,744.1	97.7	648	10,324	2,871.0	247.9	226	1,244	213.0	45.8
Lake Charles, LA	29.0	141.1	D	D	D	115.9	808	11,384	3,659.9	291.5	0	0	0.0	0.0
Lake Havasu City-Kingman, AZ	47.9	233.8	101	1,217	455.1	53.7	626	9,435	3,063.4	262.1	241	736	150.2	20.1
Lakeland-Winter Haven, FL	67.5	103.9	528	7,950	13,505.1	402.1	1,793	27,302	8,333.4	726.9	727	3,332	734.1	127.7
Lancaster, PA	54.5	101.5	562	13,388	11,432.4	742.2	1,926	31,359	8,428.8	811.5	384	2,278	524.6	101.6
Lansing-East Lansing, MI	32.8	60.6	368	6,050	11,183.6	301.2	1,626	24,711	7,077.9	619.6	459	2,988	487.5	125.8
Laredo, TX	36.1	133.8	325	2,777	2,604.5	109.9	798	13,459	3,360.1	314.4	247	890	214.1	28.8
Las Cruces, NM	34.0	158.6	112	1,069	621.0	48.3	498	8,070	2,098.3	191.8	218	686	197.3	19.8
Las Vegas-Henderson-Paradise, NV	432.5	204.5	1,743	19,687	15,088.0	1,212.5	6,267	107,067	32,047.7	3,038.7	3,454	24,634	6,064.6	1,085.2
Lawrence, KS	12.7	107.3	78	619	464.2	29.0	371	6,373	1,529.3	146.7	156	711	114.2	24.2
Lawton, OK	21.5	164.5	D	D	D	D	411	5,371	1,374.2	129.4	D	D	D	D
Lebanon, PA	3.6	25.9	103	2,211	1,915.5	105.0	416	6,740	1,694.5	168.3	75	303	54.7	10.2
Lewiston, ID-WA	15.3	245.8	62	666	602.9	30.3	255	3,685	1,042.5	106.1	65	198	31.5	6.0
Lewiston-Auburn, ME	7.9	73.9	104	1,274	559.5	64.1	431	5,933	1,816.8	162.8	130	466	86.1	17.1
Lexington-Fayette, KY	55.6	111.0	456	7,339	7,628.3	408.8	1,735	31,208	9,108.1	812.1	643	2,709	675.9	102.1
Lima, OH	18.2	174.0	123	2,106	1,905.2	104.2	388	5,898	1,678.2	140.1	84	314	64.8	9.3
Lincoln, NE	2.9	9.0	319	4,349	4,651.0	238.0	1,058	18,931	4,928.0	489.6	426	2,015	369.6	82.2
Little Rock-North Little Rock-Conway, AR	76.5	104.5	821	13,648	10,537.2	761.5	2,719	39,385	11,877.5	1,062.9	982	4,273	967.1	180.8
Logan, UT-ID	37.5	280.4	139	1,176	918.5	54.5	518	6,987	2,070.6	167.0	243	508	90.4	14.5
Longview, TX	25.7	90.4	289	3,734	2,342.8	244.9	985	13,059	4,086.3	364.6	291	1,449	361.7	70.2
Longview, WA	10.3	99.6	88	1,034	755.8	55.6	333	4,985	1,485.4	143.8	133	498	83.7	18.8
Los Angeles-Long Beach-Anaheim, CA	1,714.0	128.5	27,788	328,151	316,422.3	20,186.7	39,063	590,548	202,708.1	18,534.1	23,461	142,715	53,009.7	8,801.4
Anaheim-Santa Ana-Irvine, CA Div 11,244	457.5	144.3	6,681	86,779	107,972.6	6,183.7	9,707	156,535	52,345.3	4,927.0	6,589	45,719	15,227.2	3,118.6
Los Angeles-Long Beach-Glendale, CA Div 31,084	1,256.4	123.5	21,107	241,372	208,449.7	14,003.0	29,356	434,013	150,362.8	13,607.1	16,872	96,996	37,782.5	5,682.8
Louisville/Jefferson County, KY-IN	169.0	135.7	1,266	19,589	14,209.4	1,178.3	3,996	70,621	20,612.1	1,863.8	1,458	7,065	2,935.8	338.2
Lubbock, TX	3.0	9.6	397	5,589	5,767.9	305.3	1,013	18,482	5,686.1	509.4	446	1,998	411.4	75.1
Lynchburg, VA	18.0	69.4	179	2,230	1,278.6	108.9	908	13,484	3,865.8	319.7	305	857	172.4	28.8
Macon-Bibb County, GA	29.3	127.3	178	2,913	1,943.5	154.2	917	11,911	3,062.2	293.3	224	1,089	216.2	41.5
Madera, CA	15.6	100.8	87	1,032	709.1	59.7	315	3,648	1,157.5	101.3	103	390	68.6	12.7
Madison, WI	50.7	79.1	738	14,216	10,695.8	808.5	2,099	41,008	13,707.2	1,222.1	774	4,887	1,078.7	217.0
Manchester-Nashua, NH	38.7	95.3	531	6,897	5,718.9	498.3	1,577	28,064	9,169.1	836.6	454	2,938	616.4	142.0
Manhattan, KS	13.7	101.3	64	894	348.0	38.7	414	7,135	1,575.4	170.7	204	969	175.2	32.6
Mankato, MN	10.5	105.4	120	1,782	2,071.2	102.4	392	7,290	1,791.6	177.7	0	0	0.0	0.0
Mansfield, OH	14.5	118.7	97	1,455	760.4	65.2	419	6,707	1,641.9	160.9	104	452	76.5	14.7
McAllen-Edinburg-Mission, TX	64.6	76.7	871	9,035	5,467.8	353.5	2,162	37,469	9,923.4	887.1	571	2,280	490.1	68.7
Medford, OR	39.0	183.7	230	2,127	1,280.2	104.7	889	12,331	3,796.2	363.4	377	1,201	244.5	39.4
Memphis, TN-MS-AR	181.2	135.7	1,363	32,824	39,701.4	1,895.1	4,201	62,746	27,072.7	1,689.4	1,185	9,022	2,521.1	472.8
Merced, CA	50.2	186.9	105	1,759	1,948.0	87.1	544	8,453	2,366.8	214.4	156	569	116.3	18.4
Miami-Fort Lauderdale-Pompano Beach, FL	824.3	137.1	14,028	124,740	142,034.7	6,991.0	23,580	329,398	104,587.7	9,458.6	13,264	59,852	18,206.1	2,898.0
Fort Lauderdale-Pompano Beach-Sunrise, FL Div 22,744	233.7	123.2	3,886	38,460	43,614.1	2,218.3	7,220	107,986	35,031.3	3,159.0	4,042	19,924	6,193.7	936.6
Miami-Miami Beach-Kendall, FL Div 33,124	351.9	130.7	8,150	67,693	80,939.0	3,590.8	10,680	141,982	45,110.7	3,964.1	6,073	25,412	8,315.8	1,227.9
West Palm Beach-Boca Raton-Boynton Beach, FL Div 48,424	238.7	167.8	1,992	18,587	17,481.6	1,181.9	5,680	79,430	24,445.7	2,335.5	3,149	14,516	3,696.6	733.4
Michigan City-La Porte, IN	9.4	84.3	92	1,254	756.2	53.1	428	5,969	1,507.0	131.8	84	343	67.0	13.6
Midland, MI	0.1	1.7	50	735	2,781.2	71.8	270	3,902	1,116.0	98.0	64	338	70.3	17.3
Midland, TX	2.5	15.1	307	5,005	6,501.5	344.0	527	9,029	3,437.8	295.1	0	0	0.0	133.1
Milwaukee-Waukesha, WI	147.0	93.3	1,914	37,373	23,509.1	2,509.1	4,604	81,290	21,564.4	2,111.8	1,281	9,728	2,448.5	486.5
Minneapolis-St. Paul-Bloomington, MN	335.8	95.7	4,227	76,420	76,682.1	5,351.9	10,480	189,891	63,145.8	5,304.7	5,432	30,770	9,098.0	1,686.5
Missoula, MT	30.4	266.3	152	1,774	1,059.9	93.6	569	8,373	2,360.2	228.3	252	902	178.0	31.0

1. Merchant wholesalers, except manufacturers' sales branches and offices. 2. Employer establishments.

Area name	Professional, scientific, and technical services, 2017: Number of establishments	Number of employees	Sales (mil dol)	Average payroll (mil dol)	Manufacturing, 2017: Number of establishments	Number of employees	Receipts (mil dol)	Annual payroll (mil dol)	Accommodation and food services, 2017: Number of establishments	Number of employees	Receipts (mil dol)	Annual payroll (mil dol)
	147	148	149	150	151	152	153	154	155	156	157	158
Jonesboro, AR	14	56	4.0	1.3	111	6,989	2,800.9	328.4	280	5,514	271.5	78.6
Joplin, MO	254	1,479	188.4	66.2	219	12,385	4,990.2	587.9	357	6,924	315.1	92.7
Kahului-Wailuku-Lahaina, HI	D	D	D	D	120	845	220.4	40.8	546	21,971	2,929.7	812.5
Kalamazoo-Portage, MI	543	4,855	723.1	282.0	294	17,105	8,166.0	1,137.7	598	13,151	622.3	198.8
Kankakee, IL	143	767	89.4	35.3	109	5,400	5,619.1	331.0	243	4,101	187.0	56.8
Kansas City, MO-KS	3,231	32,619	6,506.5	2,464.8	1,689	D	44,995.8	4,869.3	4,091	97,190	5,812.6	1,684.0
Kennewick-Richland, WA	D	D	D	D	203	6,614	2,930.2	366.4	561	9,722	587.0	173.6
Killeen-Temple, TX	457	3,815	496.5	190.1	192	6,697	2,117.2	292.3	767	14,951	758.0	204.3
Kingsport-Bristol, TN-VA	424	2,576	323.7	123.8	282	22,649	8,223.9	1,322.3	614	13,196	625.7	178.2
Kingston, NY	D	D	D	D	187	3,298	806.4	177.2	591	7,299	479.1	155.9
Knoxville, TN	54	595	60.7	43.6	685	34,665	14,056.1	2,033.7	1,620	35,933	1,997.1	595.5
Kokomo, IN	118	714	93.0	29.8	62	9,251	4,005.0	629.8	195	4,095	185.4	54.0
La Crosse-Onalaska, WI-MN	19	93	9.8	3.6	182	7,666	2,074.2	384.4	381	7,261	337.9	98.1
Lafayette, LA	1,735	9,966	1,758.0	616.4	529	12,515	4,092.1	664.4	1,093	21,263	1,271.3	332.0
Lafayette-West Lafayette, IN	362	3,048	452.3	177.7	D	D	D	D	492	9,618	503.2	137.0
Lake Charles, LA	489	4,700	721.4	323.6	D	D	D	D	457	14,160	1,377.0	296.5
Lake Havasu City-Kingman, AZ	D	D	D	D	141	2,855	1,027.6	130.0	401	6,670	397.4	110.7
Lakeland-Winter Haven, FL	1,077	6,200	780.3	299.4	408	14,431	8,312.3	772.9	893	18,045	1,019.0	272.7
Lancaster, PA	1,026	12,314	1,840.0	731.7	923	34,403	13,559.4	1,845.3	1,102	20,227	1,091.5	305.7
Lansing-East Lansing, MI	1,065	8,874	1,414.3	534.3	405	20,165	15,671.7	1,139.6	1,092	20,714	990.9	299.6
Laredo, TX	D	D	D	D	65	588	346.3	24.8	449	10,203	522.0	141.6
Las Cruces, NM	D	D	D	D	139	2,065	922.8	92.7	335	7,168	361.2	106.7
Las Vegas-Henderson-Paradise, NV	6,477	45,018	8,260.8	2,991.7	992	19,985	6,795.1	974.2	4,839	268,757	30,017.1	8,468.5
Lawrence, KS	304	4,993	331.9	131.3	65	3,723	1,499.1	183.9	327	7,255	326.0	96.0
Lawton, OK	10	19	1.3	0.6	D	D	D	D	D	D	D	D
Lebanon, PA	D	D	D	D	204	9,398	2,861.1	456.8	231	3,347	173.1	48.9
Lewiston, ID-WA	36	238	22.0	7.2	65	4,159	1,575.5	235.4	152	2,573	132.9	39.7
Lewiston-Auburn, ME	D	D	D	D	152	5,665	1,693.9	263.2	238	3,455	207.1	61.3
Lexington-Fayette, KY	1,502	14,219	2,475.7	835.7	426	27,995	17,021.1	1,652.8	1,102	25,726	1,382.0	403.3
Lima, OH	D	D	D	D	119	8,261	12,616.0	536.1	213	4,452	221.9	61.2
Lincoln, NE	919	8,635	1,488.7	500.0	251	13,137	5,260.7	739.7	808	15,463	781.1	222.3
Little Rock-North Little Rock-Conway, AR	280	1,389	204.8	69.3	D	D	D	D	1,540	30,382	1,613.6	473.9
Logan, UT-ID	24	50	5.4	1.7	226	11,375	5,307.9	553.1	193	4,071	177.1	51.4
Longview, TX	235	1,359	221.8	70.8	311	14,244	6,366.5	821.2	586	10,289	531.5	155.7
Longview, WA	D	D	D	34.3	123	6,610	3,270.4	431.9	224	3,190	180.4	54.7
Los Angeles-Long Beach-Anaheim, CA	51,845	442,517	97,482.8	36,524.9	16,366	463,171	196,848.6	28,752.6	31,822	633,379	48,019.3	13,582.4
Anaheim-Santa Ana-Irvine, CA Div 11,244	15,867	136,767	27,614.5	10,958.5	4,572	146,707	46,800.8	9,553.6	8,230	176,590	13,293.4	3,749.0
Los Angeles-Long Beach-Glendale, CA Div 31,084	35,978	305,750	69,868.3	25,566.5	11,794	316,464	150,047.8	19,199.0	23,592	456,789	34,725.9	9,833.4
Louisville/Jefferson County, KY-IN	2,712	26,032	4,390.3	1,616.3	D	D	D	D	2,474	59,121	3,481.6	968.1
Lubbock, TX	653	4,497	616.5	231.6	D	D	D	D	716	16,482	938.6	264.2
Lynchburg, VA	333	1,992	253.9	118.3	265	15,106	6,480.1	934.8	516	9,545	471.5	132.0
Macon-Bibb County, GA	60	276	32.1	12.8	D	5,831	D	320.2	492	9,174	485.4	131.8
Madera, CA	107	401	45.2	15.7	104	3,517	1,490.1	192.4	210	2,882	200.0	52.1
Madison, WI	1,948	22,203	4,812.8	1,903.2	732	36,579	14,635.0	2,086.7	1,733	32,831	1,750.1	521.3
Manchester-Nashua, NH	1,334	12,550	2,564.9	1,158.2	518	21,931	7,038.6	1,432.2	922	16,755	973.2	292.3
Manhattan, KS	D	D	D	D	67	2,614	826.0	142.0	297	6,579	275.4	81.9
Mankato, MN	40	452	52.9	20.8	139	7,200	4,148.9	372.2	215	4,938	210.0	64.2
Mansfield, OH	190	844	105.7	34.3	170	8,503	3,520.3	459.3	229	4,578	214.5	63.2
McAllen-Edinburg-Mission, TX	D	D	720.2	D	280	5,703	2,136.8	225.8	1,112	23,976	1,254.7	329.5
Medford, OR	D	D	D	D	306	6,428	2,200.2	298.8	620	9,593	535.7	168.8
Memphis, TN-MS-AR	258	1,154	156.4	46.4	798	34,966	22,426.2	2,093.3	2,485	58,133	3,590.0	991.1
Merced, CA	157	800	87.6	30.4	116	9,822	5,969.6	459.9	340	5,365	320.4	81.5
Miami-Fort Lauderdale-Pompano Beach, FL	32,927	169,474	33,208.7	11,967.0	4,555	67,769	18,515.9	3,481.8	12,870	283,919	22,189.4	6,011.4
Fort Lauderdale-Pompano Beach-Sunrise, FL Div 22,744	10,546	54,062	9,519.6	3,632.7	1,432	22,969	6,516.5	1,183.8	4,113	83,312	6,473.1	1,691.1
Miami-Miami Beach-Kendall, FL Div 33,124	14,033	71,986	15,104.0	5,282.6	2,157	31,558	7,916.7	1,515.7	5,693	131,647	11,060.0	2,971.1
West Palm Beach-Boca Raton-Boynton Beach, FL Div 48,424	8,348	43,426	8,585.1	3,051.8	966	13,242	4,082.6	782.3	3,064	68,960	4,656.3	1,349.2
Michigan City-La Porte, IN	145	706	89.6	32.7	166	7,181	2,445.0	373.8	228	5,006	367.7	88.1
Midland, MI	D	D	D	D	65	4,271	2,280.2	298.0	152	3,306	170.6	51.1
Midland, TX	D	D	D	1.4	143	2,842	1,178.5	168.4	D	D	D	D
Milwaukee-Waukesha, WI	3,905	42,340	7,987.3	3,127.9	2,414	112,213	39,363.7	6,773.3	3,429	69,356	4,086.9	1,116.7
Minneapolis-St. Paul-Bloomington, MN	9,288	97,547	19,911.1	7,932.3	4,576	191,291	70,163.5	11,916.8	7,039	157,648	9,496.6	2,968.0
Missoula, MT	553	3,053	370.1	153.3	133	1,751	521.0	75.8	365	7,110	394.6	115.0

Area name	Health care and social assistance, 2017: Number of establish-ments	Health care and social assistance, 2017: Number of employees	Health care and social assistance, 2017: Receipts (mil dol)	Health care and social assistance, 2017: Annual payroll (mil dol)	Other services, 2017: Number of establish-ments	Other services, 2017: Number of employees	Other services, 2017: Receipts (mil dol)	Other services, 2017: Annual payroll (mil dol)	Nonemployer businesses, 2018: Number	Nonemployer businesses, 2018: Receipts (mil dol)	Value of residential construction authorized by building permits, 2020: New construc-tion ($1,000)	Value of residential construction authorized by building permits, 2020: Number of housing units
	159	160	161	162	163	164	165	166	167	168	169	170
Jonesboro, AR	397	10,829	1,234.0	497.1	125	776	81.1	20.5	10,234	491.5	148,206	1,147
Joplin, MO	464	12,928	1,320.5	532.7	271	1,488	136.1	40.8	10,696	489.8	154,393	991
Kahului-Wailuku-Lahaina, HI	431	7,778	932.7	403.9	409	2,392	299.4	79.2	18,667	951.0	396,206	880
Kalamazoo-Portage, MI	685	21,274	2,818.2	1,154.6	421	3,340	410.2	101.4	16,903	744.9	123,085	419
Kankakee, IL	290	7,298	720.7	336.0	175	846	92.4	27.1	5,773	216.4	34,567	140
Kansas City, MO-KS	6,027	141,853	18,567.6	7,081.7	3,330	23,648	3,739.6	846.1	157,185	7,636.7	2,760,562	11,254
Kennewick-Richland, WA	744	14,431	1,705.7	728.0	406	2,091	213.2	65.5	13,604	660.1	625,511	2,149
Killeen-Temple, TX	661	32,376	4,361.2	1,988.1	546	3,273	307.2	93.6	26,900	1,130.6	740,033	4,312
Kingsport-Bristol, TN-VA	751	17,118	2,219.0	837.0	374	2,298	301.5	78.2	18,435	789.2	144,949	679
Kingston, NY	525	10,035	841.2	383.2	363	1,619	149.2	40.3	17,562	798.1	98,259	342
Knoxville, TN	2,163	55,508	6,629.8	2,516.7	1,109	6,935	844.4	223.5	64,114	3,362.9	1,274,073	5,990
Kokomo, IN	233	5,323	589.4	222.2	126	705	88.2	17.4	4,168	148.0	46,559	190
La Crosse-Onalaska, WI-MN	386	13,885	1,466.5	657.2	262	1,808	204.6	57.4	7,987	371.2	135,327	694
Lafayette, LA	1,716	34,628	3,764.1	1,358.4	727	4,575	550.8	152.8	44,976	2,055.2	625,006	3,044
Lafayette-West Lafayette, IN	537	13,337	1,679.3	633.4	249	2,110	497.0	74.0	12,142	537.0	235,757	1,212
Lake Charles, LA	556	13,893	1,437.4	557.3	D	D	D	D	14,231	621.3	189,433	1,064
Lake Havasu City-Kingman, AZ	500	8,679	1,115.4	403.1	293	1,375	133.7	35.5	12,342	595.7	345,167	1,637
Lakeland-Winter Haven, FL	1,148	27,693	3,505.9	1,282.2	717	3,805	460.2	122.5	54,665	2,109.1	2,708,544	13,071
Lancaster, PA	1,203	38,065	4,023.2	1,637.5	1,118	7,149	772.6	212.7	43,908	2,356.1	252,158	1,039
Lansing-East Lansing, MI	1,260	31,458	3,499.7	1,411.6	931	7,128	1,026.8	288.6	36,485	1,627.0	213,783	1,016
Laredo, TX	540	16,245	1,058.6	433.7	228	1,361	128.5	36.4	28,148	1,409.3	251,973	1,684
Las Cruces, NM	553	14,627	1,251.4	527.1	238	1,142	93.0	29.4	13,662	542.6	333,151	1,338
Las Vegas-Henderson-Paradise, NV	5,349	94,935	13,080.9	4,731.3	2,784	20,781	2,256.4	638.8	203,116	9,934.6	3,761,622	16,307
Lawrence, KS	316	6,533	649.4	260.4	197	1,251	226.5	42.9	8,669	358.5	106,087	518
Lawton, OK	D	D	D	D	149	752	79.4	22.4	5,553	238.2	20,525	117
Lebanon, PA	267	8,916	993.1	417.1	252	1,209	128.9	34.2	8,655	426.1	85,328	507
Lewiston, ID-WA	191	4,450	447.9	178.4	97	602	48.3	15.8	3,223	134.6	47,763	127
Lewiston-Auburn, ME	380	10,347	1,145.9	488.6	212	1,029	103.3	30.8	6,579	299.4	47,003	221
Lexington-Fayette, KY	1,638	39,216	5,298.1	1,941.5	847	5,999	1,067.6	193.8	39,199	1,904.1	542,307	2,943
Lima, OH	289	11,913	1,427.5	561.9	176	1,150	101.6	29.0	5,492	231.4	45,790	226
Lincoln, NE	1,094	25,780	2,959.0	1,130.4	768	4,475	796.5	162.1	23,839	1,011.2	581,712	2,607
Little Rock-North Little Rock-Conway, AR	2,228	58,812	7,733.5	3,050.6	1,161	7,742	1,171.4	271.0	55,370	2,545.2	675,182	3,635
Logan, UT-ID	423	5,990	674.7	227.1	211	885	97.7	25.6	10,867	457.9	365,733	1,309
Longview, TX	698	15,065	1,552.8	605.1	393	2,788	354.4	96.9	22,157	1,067.3	108,518	579
Longview, WA	236	5,617	597.1	249.1	152	816	87.2	26.6	4,848	209.1	85,157	348
Los Angeles-Long Beach-Anaheim, CA	45,199	745,534	110,035.8	40,512.0	22,793	159,460	22,673.3	5,462.3	1,437,599	82,809.4	6,964,838	31,151
Anaheim-Santa Ana-Irvine, CA Div 11,244	12,231	176,838	25,663.6	9,314.5	5,568	39,646	4,742.0	1,311.0	324,958	19,853.1	1,873,932	7,867
Los Angeles-Long Beach-Glendale, CA Div 31,084	32,968	568,696	84,372.2	31,197.5	17,225	119,814	17,931.3	4,151.3	1,112,641	62,956.3	5,090,906	23,284
Louisville/Jefferson County, KY-IN	3,497	91,220	11,561.3	4,441.2	1,930	15,460	1,915.0	515.1	92,038	4,300.8	1,249,022	5,508
Lubbock, TX	894	25,024	3,037.8	1,045.6	483	3,917	408.4	114.1	25,515	1,322.8	730,487	3,404
Lynchburg, VA	606	14,626	1,715.8	657.1	474	2,264	242.3	70.3	15,910	614.4	127,060	692
Macon-Bibb County, GA	657	17,340	2,156.4	769.5	317	1,886	253.4	67.7	19,715	688.9	114,159	563
Madera, CA	210	6,171	999.5	387.3	117	576	59.2	16.5	7,775	412.0	274,438	1,066
Madison, WI	1,631	59,316	7,728.5	3,251.6	1,365	9,654	1,566.4	377.0	47,016	2,433.8	1,477,072	7,194
Manchester-Nashua, NH	1,167	32,354	3,938.1	1,643.7	883	6,272	746.1	231.2	29,899	1,764.4	294,881	1,342
Manhattan, KS	315	6,688	661.5	248.3	217	1,545	331.0	59.5	6,774	288.0	83,475	278
Mankato, MN	364	10,385	991.1	487.3	187	1,339	262.3	40.6	6,421	315.7	109,171	480
Mansfield, OH	375	8,617	836.7	335.5	195	1,099	108.4	27.4	7,134	330.0	33,046	115
McAllen-Edinburg-Mission, TX	2,193	64,956	4,371.9	1,772.6	592	3,522	322.6	90.2	81,199	3,441.6	1,065,455	6,055
Medford, OR	758	15,189	1,902.0	753.3	328	1,967	216.7	60.8	17,968	856.6	268,818	1,142
Memphis, TN-MS-AR	2,903	82,332	11,076.9	4,107.6	1,484	12,661	2,957.3	513.5	118,850	4,674.3	1,088,408	5,205
Merced, CA	444	7,595	944.4	372.0	188	944	95.5	25.1	12,261	648.7	307,754	1,017
Miami-Fort Lauderdale-Pompano Beach, FL	21,676	327,305	46,754.6	16,274.5	13,598	74,945	9,492.6	2,336.0	1,090,730	50,258.0	6,684,442	25,313
Fort Lauderdale-Pompano Beach-Sunrise, FL Div 22,744	6,614	95,619	13,231.2	4,736.4	4,538	22,941	2,920.0	750.2	308,930	13,592.7	786,842	4,069
Miami-Miami Beach-Kendall, FL Div 33,124	9,159	144,441	21,236.1	7,238.0	5,335	31,051	3,952.6	909.2	576,770	25,840.3	3,373,741	13,393
West Palm Beach-Boca Raton-Boynton Beach, FL Div 48,424	5,903	87,245	12,287.3	4,300.0	3,725	20,953	2,620.0	676.6	205,030	10,825.1	2,523,859	7,851
Michigan City-La Porte, IN	229	5,904	777.2	299.5	198	1,031	133.0	29.0	6,072	225.0	47,719	138
Midland, MI	282	6,998	883.2	294.3	142	980	158.5	29.7	5,243	214.6	34,600	159
Midland, TX	421	7,936	941.6	374.5	309	2,571	460.3	105.8	19,438	1,461.9	176,067	872
Milwaukee-Waukesha, WI	5,271	139,611	16,490.9	6,300.2	2,809	20,397	4,037.0	711.8	96,536	4,789.5	969,252	2,929
Minneapolis-St. Paul-Bloomington, MN	10,835	298,523	33,382.1	14,058.1	7,165	56,225	7,641.0	1,994.2	281,513	13,952.3	6,154,859	26,077
Missoula, MT	512	10,122	1,190.9	412.7	312	2,257	362.1	79.5	11,302	554.0	264,603	1,798

Area name	Government employment and payroll, 2017: Full-time equivalent employees	Government employment and payroll, 2017: March payroll (dollars)	March payroll (percent of total): Administration, judicial, and legal	March payroll (percent of total): Police and corrections	March payroll (percent of total): Fire protection	March payroll (percent of total): Highways and transportation	March payroll (percent of total): Health and welfare	March payroll (percent of total): Natural resources and utilities	March payroll (percent of total): Education and libraries	Local government finances, 2017, General revenue: Total (mil dol)	General revenue: Intergovernmental (mil dol)	General revenue, Taxes: Total (mil dol)	Taxes, Per capita[1] (dollars): Total	Taxes, Per capita[1] (dollars): Property
	171	172	173	174	175	176	177	178	179	180	181	182	183	184
Jonesboro, AR	4,583	15,309,542	5.3	9.0	2.4	3.6	1.6	9.1	68.7	402.4	245.6	97.0	739	361
Joplin, MO	6,424	20,859,051	4.2	8.0	3.3	3.0	2.5	2.9	75.1	582.4	272.6	222.7	1,249	676
Kahului-Wailuku-Lahaina, HI	2,489	15,157,755	20.1	26.1	17.0	6.5	3.3	24.9	0.0	479.7	60.6	331.2	1,994	1,641
Kalamazoo-Portage, MI	7,505	31,550,062	7.4	11.7	2.4	2.8	2.4	2.9	69.1	1,031.0	525.6	328.5	1,249	1,210
Kankakee, IL	4,432	18,124,649	7.1	11.6	4.2	3.3	1.1	3.4	67.9	414.1	162.1	176.4	1,596	1,513
Kansas City, MO-KS	86,246	354,737,276	5.4	8.9	6.1	3.5	10.2	7.1	57.5	10,706.1	3,047.2	4,460.6	2,097	1,211
Kennewick-Richland, WA	12,111	68,651,523	4.6	6.2	3.1	2.9	13.3	24.8	43.6	1,723.9	802.4	425.5	1,467	784
Killeen-Temple, TX	21,064	71,092,282	5.8	8.4	3.6	1.4	4.9	3.7	70.4	1,589.3	702.6	553.7	1,250	990
Kingsport-Bristol, TN-VA	11,316	37,863,786	6.4	11.8	3.9	3.1	4.8	7.5	59.4	927.0	381.0	354.8	1,158	783
Kingston, NY	7,944	40,510,439	5.8	8.2	1.2	5.7	4.1	2.2	71.0	1,172.0	385.2	704.9	3,946	3,148
Knoxville, TN	28,569	106,933,307	5.8	10.0	2.6	2.8	10.5	13.0	53.7	2,801.1	898.6	1,116.1	1,307	849
Kokomo, IN	3,042	10,199,579	6.3	12.7	4.2	3.2	3.2	3.4	65.3	262.2	141.0	92.8	1,129	1,108
La Crosse-Onalaska, WI-MN	5,706	24,820,556	6.4	7.6	2.5	4.0	10.9	3.3	62.7	674.3	304.2	248.4	1,817	1,657
Lafayette, LA	18,074	56,271,873	6.4	11.6	3.3	3.2	9.8	6.9	57.9	1,680.6	564.9	791.9	1,615	696
Lafayette-West Lafayette, IN	6,189	23,040,680	7.9	11.4	4.4	4.8	1.9	5.5	62.7	704.6	321.1	233.5	1,024	956
Lake Charles, LA	10,222	33,914,186	5.9	12.3	3.6	5.6	9.5	4.9	55.7	1,141.6	290.2	622.2	2,971	1,106
Lake Havasu City-Kingman, AZ	5,008	18,841,384	14.4	15.1	13.1	5.0	2.0	7.1	41.4	586.3	225.7	230.7	1,114	793
Lakeland-Winter Haven, FL	24,085	82,688,018	8.2	12.8	5.3	2.2	2.2	10.4	55.7	2,121.7	833.2	708.7	1,034	683
Lancaster, PA	14,385	63,875,933	5.5	10.2	1.0	3.2	2.9	4.1	71.4	2,211.0	804.0	1,004.1	1,855	1,499
Lansing-East Lansing, MI	17,747	80,130,669	7.7	7.3	2.8	4.1	10.5	7.3	55.7	2,203.5	1,041.7	696.6	1,270	1,172
Laredo, TX	15,338	59,020,428	5.3	11.4	5.2	2.6	3.5	3.6	67.9	1,369.4	592.0	500.1	1,827	1,480
Las Cruces, NM	8,033	28,795,832	4.8	11.2	3.2	1.7	1.5	6.9	65.2	760.4	405.6	260.8	1,206	537
Las Vegas-Henderson-Paradise, NV	61,549	328,902,480	8.5	16.4	5.5	3.3	10.2	7.9	46.5	10,404.2	4,197.7	3,614.1	1,657	853
Lawrence, KS	5,231	23,730,724	5.5	10.3	4.9	3.3	33.9	8.7	31.5	655.6	134.8	204.1	1,697	1,155
Lawton, OK	6,247	21,718,232	3.9	6.4	3.1	2.2	35.7	4.1	43.7	606.6	153.2	116.4	912	422
Lebanon, PA	3,630	16,331,706	5.8	8.8	0.8	3.1	4.1	5.6	70.8	524.1	174.2	233.6	1,674	1,348
Lewiston, ID-WA	2,193	9,109,038	7.7	10.6	6.5	4.0	3.6	7.3	56.4	225.8	105.0	75.8	1,207	1,061
Lewiston-Auburn, ME	4,097	15,739,689	4.1	8.0	5.5	4.7	2.1	5.4	68.8	419.1	171.6	196.9	1,833	1,822
Lexington-Fayette, KY	16,450	62,470,924	4.6	12.2	8.2	2.5	4.1	5.6	59.8	1,659.9	436.1	943.0	1,840	886
Lima, OH	3,994	15,615,627	8.1	10.6	5.1	4.1	8.2	6.1	56.1	411.1	190.3	147.7	1,432	973
Lincoln, NE	12,414	55,567,994	5.0	8.7	3.5	4.6	3.5	10.7	62.7	1,319.6	404.1	652.4	1,971	1,508
Little Rock-North Little Rock-Conway, AR	24,453	89,371,093	5.8	11.4	5.6	4.3	2.7	8.7	59.7	2,435.9	1,217.0	733.7	995	471
Logan, UT-ID	4,086	14,948,932	6.6	6.9	2.6	4.1	13.3	7.5	57.6	431.8	195.2	137.7	1,000	674
Longview, TX	12,699	42,566,428	5.2	10.4	3.9	2.0	4.8	3.7	68.1	1,018.2	344.2	523.5	1,839	1,474
Longview, WA	3,640	18,508,063	7.2	10.5	3.3	7.0	2.9	12.2	53.9	542.9	209.0	154.7	1,448	882
Los Angeles-Long Beach-Anaheim, CA	493,015	3,243,212,859	8.7	12.2	4.2	5.5	14.1	8.2	44.5	93,808.2	40,622.1	31,283.0	2,356	1,576
Anaheim-Santa Ana-Irvine, CA Div 11,244	92,158	640,816,778	6.4	12.9	4.5	3.4	7.1	5.6	58.9	17,778.6	6,803.8	7,027.1	2,214	1,642
Los Angeles-Long Beach-Glendale, CA Div 31,084	400,857	2,602,396,081	9.3	12.0	4.1	6.0	15.8	8.9	41.0	76,029.6	33,818.3	24,255.9	2,401	1,555
Louisville/Jefferson County, KY-IN	41,775	174,583,976	3.6	9.3	3.8	3.3	9.4	7.0	62.4	4,227.8	1,442.5	1,931.4	1,533	903
Lubbock, TX	15,658	62,174,487	4.7	10.2	4.3	1.0	32.0	5.4	41.2	1,690.7	459.7	535.8	1,690	1,328
Lynchburg, VA	8,822	29,576,126	7.3	10.6	3.7	2.0	8.2	5.1	61.2	863.0	437.0	331.9	1,268	893
Macon-Bibb County, GA	8,443	29,792,058	6.9	10.9	5.0	2.5	5.2	5.2	61.7	687.6	317.1	227.5	994	718
Madera, CA	5,262	26,791,038	8.4	9.4	1.2	1.9	12.2	3.1	62.3	765.1	488.6	169.1	1,088	800
Madison, WI	25,406	110,653,611	5.5	11.1	2.3	5.5	6.5	5.3	61.9	3,254.7	1,231.7	1,484.7	2,266	2,091
Manchester-Nashua, NH	13,924	65,255,845	4.2	10.8	6.1	5.1	3.7	4.7	63.9	1,758.2	438.5	1,096.8	2,654	2,624
Manhattan, KS	5,712	19,755,413	6.6	10.0	4.2	3.6	9.4	5.3	59.6	561.7	214.3	222.3	1,688	1,111
Mankato, MN	3,460	15,489,530	8.4	9.5	1.1	5.0	13.1	5.2	55.1	494.7	221.1	138.0	1,367	1,189
Mansfield, OH	4,967	18,600,904	8.1	8.4	4.6	2.9	15.2	4.0	55.0	485.5	220.4	191.9	1,593	961
McAllen-Edinburg-Mission, TX	42,017	156,936,079	3.8	6.8	1.8	1.8	4.5	4.0	76.4	3,554.6	2,159.8	994.9	1,162	962
Medford, OR	5,573	25,323,949	7.9	12.8	5.8	5.8	6.8	5.7	53.0	826.7	361.6	312.0	1,440	1,189
Memphis, TN-MS-AR	47,599	190,916,078	7.5	14.7	6.9	3.4	8.6	13.3	44.3	5,371.3	1,888.9	2,147.3	1,604	1,161
Merced, CA	11,500	58,776,936	5.1	7.4	1.2	0.8	9.4	5.9	67.6	1,626.6	1,064.3	295.0	1,088	823
Miami-Fort Lauderdale-Pompano Beach, FL	222,781	1,085,361,286	6.6	15.5	6.8	5.4	18.7	8.2	36.0	34,184.6	7,177.3	13,866.2	2,266	1,783
Fort Lauderdale-Pompano Beach-Sunrise, FL Div 22,744	78,792	389,220,424	5.0	13.2	5.4	3.7	32.3	6.1	32.6	12,006.7	2,460.8	3,819.2	1,974	1,586
Miami-Miami Beach-Kendall, FL Div 33,124	93,991	469,157,165	7.3	16.4	6.7	8.4	14.5	8.1	35.3	14,969.4	3,265.1	6,118.7	2,255	1,664
West Palm Beach-Boca Raton-Boynton Beach, FL Div 48,424	49,998	226,983,697	8.2	17.4	9.4	2.1	4.2	12.1	43.4	7,208.5	1,451.4	3,928.2	2,672	2,261
Michigan City-La Porte, IN	4,410	14,500,631	6.4	12.0	4.0	3.7	2.8	6.2	63.3	390.5	185.2	125.9	1,146	1,100
Midland, MI	2,197	9,909,177	10.3	8.4	3.0	5.2	3.8	5.2	62.3	319.5	151.8	114.0	1,369	1,353
Midland, TX	8,050	35,757,035	4.9	7.6	3.3	3.1	30.0	2.5	47.6	1,057.4	139.1	531.6	3,112	2,385
Milwaukee-Waukesha, WI	53,564	271,603,112	5.3	14.4	4.5	4.9	7.1	5.5	56.7	7,530.4	2,973.5	2,896.3	1,840	1,685
Minneapolis-St. Paul-Bloomington, MN	124,427	637,696,752	7.4	10.3	1.9	3.7	8.2	4.9	61.4	18,428.7	7,855.1	5,970.2	1,670	1,519
Missoula, MT	3,480	14,645,116	8.3	11.5	6.5	6.6	8.7	4.2	51.1	389.1	154.0	168.3	1,428	1,378

1. Based on the resident population estimated as of July 1 of the year shown

Area name	Local government finances, 2017 (cont.)									Government employment, 2019			Individual income tax returns, 2018		
	Direct general expenditure							Debt outstanding							
			Percent of total for:												
	Total (mil dol)	Per capita[1] (dollars)	Educa-tion	Health and hospitals	Police protection	Public welfare	Highways	Total (mil dol)	Per capita[1] (dollars)	Federal civilian	Federal military	State and local	Number of returns	Mean adjusted gross income	Mean income tax
	185	186	187	188	189	190	191	192	193	194	195	196	197	198	199
Jonesboro, AR	392.9	2,993	61.3	0.4	5.4	0.1	5.3	536.0	4,083	431	509	8,997	54,930	56,066	5,802
Joplin, MO	587.5	3,296	58.6	1.6	4.7	0.2	7.8	423.1	2,374	467	621	8,899	79,140	51,134	4,832
Kahului-Wailuku-Lahaina, HI	467.9	2,816	0.0	0.0	11.5	13.0	10.1	336.6	2,026	881	1,213	7,852	86,620	64,950	7,015
Kalamazoo-Portage, MI	1,030.7	3,919	55.8	9.5	3.4	0.4	5.5	1,217.5	4,629	743	420	13,038	124,330	70,072	8,249
Kankakee, IL	447.3	4,046	52.8	0.5	6.7	0.1	5.4	491.0	4,442	250	211	5,770	50,670	58,281	5,460
Kansas City, MO-KS	10,573.0	4,970	40.6	9.6	6.9	0.5	5.3	18,038.5	8,480	29,887	11,215	119,044	1,047,120	75,573	9,248
Kennewick-Richland, WA	1,687.9	5,819	44.9	21.8	3.9	0.1	2.7	8,022.2	27,653	1,288	751	17,366	137,300	68,300	7,095
Killeen-Temple, TX	1,613.6	3,642	59.9	5.1	5.1	0.4	3.7	1,917.7	4,329	10,912	35,381	27,015	204,540	51,244	4,455
Kingsport-Bristol, TN-VA	948.3	3,094	45.3	4.2	7.6	1.6	3.9	752.5	2,455	948	882	15,061	134,790	53,593	5,081
Kingston, NY	1,209.9	6,773	55.7	1.7	3.2	9.5	6.0	668.9	3,745	471	283	12,190	89,070	69,257	8,112
Knoxville, TN	2,645.2	3,099	42.6	11.8	7.8	0.1	4.1	4,123.5	4,830	5,611	2,492	50,548	400,430	69,267	8,202
Kokomo, IN	263.3	3,202	53.5	0.4	6.4	0.1	2.3	246.6	2,999	186	241	4,739	41,260	54,695	4,915
La Crosse-Onalaska, WI-MN	764.4	5,591	53.9	3.4	4.1	7.1	6.8	713.5	5,219	569	360	10,475	67,010	67,077	7,179
Lafayette, LA	1,734.3	3,537	46.5	9.3	9.5	0.4	5.4	1,495.9	3,051	1,530	1,955	23,781	217,070	59,258	6,466
Lafayette-West Lafayette, IN	619.1	2,714	49.7	0.7	4.6	0.6	7.1	537.2	2,355	568	715	25,637	96,270	61,634	6,279
Lake Charles, LA	1,052.5	5,026	39.4	8.7	7.7	0.4	7.5	1,112.3	5,311	593	859	13,453	91,170	62,411	6,705
Lake Havasu City-Kingman, AZ	532.1	2,570	33.3	4.1	9.9	0.1	6.2	543.6	2,626	551	448	7,482	91,950	48,316	4,402
Lakeland-Winter Haven, FL	2,193.4	3,200	47.9	2.6	8.2	1.4	4.0	2,340.3	3,415	1,411	1,259	27,660	336,020	52,426	4,872
Lancaster, PA	2,292.0	4,234	55.6	5.9	4.6	5.2	3.2	3,717.0	6,866	1,325	1,362	19,034	273,930	67,827	7,315
Lansing-East Lansing, MI	2,344.8	4,276	48.7	8.2	5.3	4.5	5.7	2,585.8	4,715	2,192	1,046	48,918	254,740	61,948	6,489
Laredo, TX	1,395.4	5,099	60.8	2.6	6.2	0.5	0.9	1,627.0	5,945	3,972	526	18,865	122,760	42,350	3,467
Las Cruces, NM	708.9	3,279	60.6	1.6	7.6	2.3	2.1	452.3	2,092	3,483	884	16,404	98,100	47,140	4,238
Las Vegas-Henderson-Paradise, NV	9,855.5	4,517	33.6	7.7	10.6	2.6	8.8	23,841.2	10,928	14,638	16,609	87,924	1,121,350	67,187	8,582
Lawrence, KS	638.1	5,305	25.4	35.8	4.3	0.0	3.0	783.8	6,517	471	463	17,576	53,160	68,458	7,814
Lawton, OK	611.5	4,790	30.6	41.9	3.7	0.0	5.2	307.9	2,412	3,980	13,047	10,508	51,140	49,270	3,992
Lebanon, PA	520.5	3,730	57.8	1.5	3.4	10.7	3.0	583.4	4,180	3,137	352	4,744	72,040	59,882	5,667
Lewiston, ID-WA	222.1	3,537	42.1	5.2	7.0	0.1	6.7	183.9	2,929	285	181	4,963	29,550	59,359	5,538
Lewiston-Auburn, ME	392.1	3,651	53.5	0.3	3.8	0.3	4.7	282.6	2,631	393	320	5,123	52,160	53,237	4,692
Lexington-Fayette, KY	1,545.1	3,015	46.0	3.0	5.5	0.7	2.0	2,665.5	5,202	4,721	1,579	48,915	234,480	67,083	7,902
Lima, OH	466.4	4,524	51.6	3.1	8.5	4.4	3.7	1,857.7	18,019	340	252	5,513	48,650	55,401	5,309
Lincoln, NE	1,403.0	4,239	52.6	2.7	4.2	1.2	7.4	2,539.9	7,674	3,586	1,124	31,383	159,080	68,221	7,347
Little Rock-North Little Rock-Conway, AR	2,494.1	3,382	47.7	1.8	6.7	0.0	5.9	3,867.0	5,243	9,928	6,609	57,442	336,140	63,789	7,114
Logan, UT-ID	445.9	3,238	57.0	8.4	4.2	0.3	3.9	237.0	1,721	399	529	12,083	59,000	60,872	5,179
Longview, TX	1,120.1	3,936	60.6	3.3	5.8	0.2	4.2	1,382.1	4,856	694	529	14,462	126,610	57,396	5,766
Longview, WA	508.9	4,765	41.8	1.6	5.7	0.5	4.7	656.3	6,144	271	272	5,947	51,610	61,440	5,975
Los Angeles-Long Beach-Anaheim, CA	87,198.5	6,567	37.0	10.4	8.6	7.8	2.8	126,596.1	9,534	62,611	22,096	682,905	6,368,030	83,556	12,386
Anaheim-Santa Ana-Irvine, CA Div 11,244	16,921.3	5,331	45.3	3.6	8.0	5.5	3.9	24,733.3	7,792	11,759	5,066	144,402	1,562,000	95,004	14,128
Los Angeles-Long Beach-Glendale, CA Div 31,084	70,277.2	6,956	35.1	12.0	8.8	8.4	2.5	101,862.8	10,082	50,852	17,030	538,503	4,806,030	79,836	11,820
Louisville/Jefferson County, KY-IN	4,149.0	3,294	47.0	3.3	6.2	0.5	3.3	7,772.8	6,171	10,522	3,940	59,008	620,320	67,829	7,801
Lubbock, TX	1,733.9	5,468	33.1	35.0	5.8	0.0	2.0	2,370.1	7,474	1,504	620	30,025	143,250	62,863	7,196
Lynchburg, VA	791.4	3,023	53.6	1.1	5.4	7.4	1.9	532.6	2,034	620	837	11,781	116,930	58,962	5,759
Macon-Bibb County, GA	750.8	3,279	56.0	7.1	5.7	0.0	2.0	436.3	1,905	1,143	615	13,014	99,870	54,661	5,539
Madera, CA	839.1	5,399	50.1	4.5	3.8	8.2	6.4	657.0	4,227	362	221	10,416	63,010	52,568	4,619
Madison, WI	3,366.3	5,137	47.9	2.1	5.9	8.3	7.2	4,585.2	6,998	5,910	1,846	83,065	342,120	83,509	10,656
Manchester-Nashua, NH	1,549.9	3,751	54.3	0.4	6.9	4.3	5.0	894.8	2,165	4,298	1,395	16,668	222,340	82,251	10,495
Manhattan, KS	517.2	3,928	43.3	10.9	10.1	0.1	6.0	961.1	7,300	3,892	16,280	16,872	55,470	57,611	5,179
Mankato, MN	552.3	5,470	42.9	7.0	3.7	5.3	11.2	508.5	5,036	320	363	8,302	48,210	62,752	6,345
Mansfield, OH	493.6	4,099	50.7	9.7	5.4	5.5	6.3	175.1	1,454	652	287	6,766	58,590	49,537	4,263
McAllen-Edinburg-Mission, TX	3,600.9	4,205	68.2	4.5	3.5	0.6	2.7	3,753.4	4,384	4,953	1,714	51,989	351,420	40,414	3,043
Medford, OR	766.8	3,538	44.2	6.2	9.3	0.0	5.4	894.6	4,127	1,905	513	8,589	107,560	60,292	6,265
Memphis, TN-MS-AR	4,991.9	3,729	39.3	10.7	11.3	0.8	2.9	5,027.1	3,756	14,807	6,075	68,790	627,950	62,001	7,119
Merced, CA	1,616.8	5,964	57.0	4.2	4.0	8.9	3.7	974.0	3,593	833	404	16,484	112,450	48,593	3,969
Miami-Fort Lauderdale-Pompano Beach, FL	33,348.0	5,451	27.5	16.7	9.7	2.3	1.6	45,314.7	7,407	36,987	13,482	270,798	3,138,780	80,796	12,786
Fort Lauderdale-Pompano Beach-Sunrise, FL Div 22,744	11,894.2	6,148	25.1	28.0	9.9	1.2	1.3	11,449.4	5,919	7,601	3,764	96,778	996,250	71,681	10,181
Miami-Miami Beach-Kendall, FL Div 33,124	14,469.2	5,333	28.2	13.3	9.2	3.4	1.6	28,281.1	10,423	21,994	7,052	119,512	1,387,160	68,290	10,487
West Palm Beach-Boca Raton-Boynton Beach, FL Div 48,424	6,984.6	4,750	30.3	4.6	10.4	1.7	2.1	5,584.1	3,798	7,392	2,666	54,508	755,370	115,786	20,444
Michigan City-La Porte, IN	385.7	3,511	46.8	0.7	5.0	0.1	3.5	349.2	3,179	192	324	6,186	52,840	55,101	5,339
Midland, MI	324.6	3,896	55.6	2.2	4.0	2.1	7.2	513.6	6,165	178	130	2,922	40,620	76,847	9,478
Midland, TX	995.1	5,824	38.7	35.8	3.9	0.0	2.1	1,016.0	5,947	612	349	9,167	83,620	122,786	21,469
Milwaukee-Waukesha, WI	7,855.3	4,989	44.0	6.7	8.6	2.0	6.4	9,218.1	5,855	11,078	4,365	72,395	779,200	76,693	9,853
Minneapolis-St. Paul-Bloomington, MN	20,224.7	5,656	42.2	8.1	5.4	3.9	8.1	25,977.0	7,265	21,797	12,698	221,911	1,866,800	86,725	11,448
Missoula, MT	459.0	3,895	45.7	7.4	6.3	0.6	3.3	347.1	2,946	1,461	541	9,298	61,230	66,030	7,399

1. Based on the resident population estimated as of July 1 of the year shown.

Table C. Metropolitan Areas — **Land Area and Population**

CBSA[1]	DIV Code	Area name	Land area[2] (sq mi)	Population, 2021: Total persons 2021	Population, 2021: Rank	Population, 2021: Per square mile	Race alone or in combination, not Hispanic or Latino (percent): White	Black	American Indian, Alaska Native	Asian and Pacific Islander	Percent Hispanic or Latino[3]	Age (percent): Under 5 years	5 to 17 years	18 to 24 years	25 to 34 years	35 to 44 years	45 to 54 years
			1	2	3	4	5	6	7	8	9	10	11	12	13	14	15
33660		Mobile, AL	2,309.6	428,220	128	185.4	57.7	36.7	1.7	2.6	3.1	6.3	13.0	12.6	13.7	12.3	11.7
33700		Modesto, CA	1,496.0	552,999	105	369.7	40.6	3.6	1.2	8.2	49.5	6.8	15.4	14.1	14.3	13.3	11.6
33740		Monroe, LA	2,282.2	204,884	223	89.8	58.5	38.3	0.6	1.2	2.6	6.3	13.7	13.3	13.1	12.5	11.7
33780		Monroe, MI	549.4	155,274	274	282.6	92.2	3.7	0.9	1.1	4.0	5.1	12.1	11.6	12.0	11.9	12.9
33860		Montgomery, AL	2,714.4	385,798	144	142.1	48.2	46.2	0.7	2.9	3.6	6.3	13.0	12.9	13.8	12.8	12.2
34060		Morgantown, WV	1,008.9	140,745	297	139.5	91.8	4.2	0.6	3.4	2.1	4.7	9.7	19.5	15.3	13.1	11.0
34100		Morristown, TN	716.8	143,855	292	200.7	88.4	3.4	0.9	1.2	7.7	5.2	11.9	11.9	11.8	11.4	13.5
34580		Mount Vernon-Anacortes, WA	1,730.2	130,696	313	75.5	75.3	1.5	2.8	3.6	19.5	5.4	12.2	10.9	12.6	12.6	11.1
34620		Muncie, IN	392.1	111,871	343	285.3	88.4	8.5	0.7	2.1	2.8	4.6	10.2	22.7	11.7	10.4	11.0
34740		Muskegon, MI	503.9	176,511	247	350.3	78.9	15.3	1.6	1.2	6.2	5.8	13.0	11.9	13.1	12.5	11.7
34820		Myrtle Beach-Conway-North Myrtle Beach, SC-NC	1,983.4	509,794	111	257.0	80.7	12.4	1.1	1.8	6.0	4.0	9.4	9.3	10.3	10.4	11.5
34900		Napa, CA	748.3	136,207	301	182.0	52.7	2.9	1.0	10.6	35.6	4.5	11.3	12.3	12.2	13.0	12.9
34940		Naples-Marco Island, FL	1,997.0	385,980	141	193.3	62.5	7.1	0.4	2.1	29.0	4.1	9.4	9.3	9.3	9.8	10.9
34980		Nashville-Davidson--Murfreesboro--Franklin, TN	5,689.4	2,012,476	35	353.7	73.1	16.5	0.8	3.9	8.0	6.0	12.8	13.0	15.3	14.1	12.6
35100		New Bern, NC	1,514.5	122,273	325	80.7	68.3	22.3	1.2	3.5	7.5	5.7	11.4	13.7	12.7	11.1	10.3
35300		New Haven-Milford, CT	604.3	863,700	69	1,429.3	61.7	14.6	0.6	5.0	20.2	5.0	11.2	13.4	13.3	12.5	12.4
35380		New Orleans-Metairie, LA	3,203.5	1,261,726	47	393.9	52.2	35.7	0.9	3.5	9.4	5.9	12.5	11.5	13.7	13.8	11.9
35620		New York-Newark-Jersey City, NY-NJ-PA	6,684.3	19,768,458	1	2,957.4	46.2	16.8	0.5	13.0	25.3	5.7	12.0	11.9	14.2	13.3	12.9
35620	35004	Nassau County-Suffolk County, NY Div 35,004	1,195.7	2,917,251	X	2,439.8	63.0	10.3	0.5	8.6	19.2	5.2	11.9	12.5	12.0	12.1	13.4
35620	35084	Newark, NJ-PA Div 35,084	2,181.2	2,273,431	X	1,042.3	49.8	21.6	0.4	7.5	22.2	5.6	12.6	12.3	12.3	13.4	13.8
35620	35154	New Brunswick-Lakewood, NJ Div 35,154	1,707.6	2,500,806	X	1,464.5	63.3	8.0	0.4	14.3	15.5	5.6	12.5	12.3	11.7	12.3	12.9
35620	35614	New York-Jersey City-White Plains, NY-NJ Div 35,614	1,599.8	12,076,970	X	7,549.0	37.9	19.3	0.6	14.9	29.3	5.9	11.7	11.6	15.6	13.8	12.5
35660		Niles, MI	567.8	153,101	278	269.6	77.1	15.5	1.2	2.8	6.1	5.4	12.2	12.0	11.5	11.8	12.0
35840		North Port-Sarasota-Bradenton, FL	1,298.8	859,760	70	662.0	77.8	7.1	0.6	2.7	13.4	3.8	9.0	8.9	9.3	9.6	11.0
35980		Norwich-New London, CT	665.1	268,805	184	404.2	76.9	7.4	1.8	5.4	12.0	4.7	10.8	13.3	13.2	11.8	11.9
36100		Ocala, FL	1,588.4	385,915	142	243.0	69.6	13.6	0.8	2.3	15.5	4.8	10.7	9.9	11.0	10.4	10.8
36140		Ocean City, NJ	251.5	95,661	365	380.4	86.3	4.9	0.5	1.6	8.4	4.3	9.9	10.0	10.3	9.7	10.7
36220		Odessa, TX	897.9	161,091	265	179.4	29.1	4.9	0.7	1.6	64.7	8.7	17.3	14.6	15.6	13.9	10.7
36260		Ogden-Clearfield, UT	7,230.1	706,696	83	97.7	82.4	1.8	1.0	3.7	13.6	7.1	17.1	14.8	14.1	14.7	11.0
36420		Oklahoma City, OK	5,511.7	1,441,647	42	261.6	67.3	12.2	7.1	4.4	14.4	6.2	13.9	14.1	14.3	13.8	11.4
36500		Olympia-Lacey-Tumwater, WA	722.5	297,977	168	412.4	77.7	5.2	2.7	10.2	10.1	5.4	12.2	11.3	14.4	14.3	11.9
36540		Omaha-Council Bluffs, NE-IA	4,346.3	971,637	58	223.6	76.9	9.0	1.0	4.2	11.5	6.6	14.4	13.0	13.9	14.0	11.6
36740		Orlando-Kissimmee-Sanford, FL	3,490.5	2,691,925	23	771.2	46.3	17.0	0.6	5.5	32.6	5.5	12.2	12.7	14.8	14.2	12.9
36780		Oshkosh-Neenah, WI	434.7	171,623	253	394.8	88.7	3.6	1.0	3.9	4.7	5.2	11.5	15.1	13.3	12.6	11.9
36980		Owensboro, KY	898.6	121,227	327	134.9	90.3	5.9	0.5	2.2	3.3	6.2	13.8	12.4	12.5	12.2	11.9
37100		Oxnard-Thousand Oaks-Ventura, CA	1,840.8	839,784	71	456.2	46.0	2.4	0.9	9.5	44.1	5.3	12.8	13.0	13.4	12.8	12.7
37340		Palm Bay-Melbourne-Titusville, FL	1,015.0	616,628	95	607.5	75.1	11.3	0.8	3.8	11.6	4.4	10.5	10.3	11.4	11.2	11.7
37460		Panama City, FL	758.6	179,168	243	236.2	78.2	12.4	1.4	3.9	7.4	5.5	11.7	11.0	13.2	12.7	12.5
37620		Parkersburg-Vienna, WV	599.0	88,687	368	148.1	96.7	2.2	0.7	0.9	1.3	5.2	12.0	11.0	11.3	11.9	12.8
37860		Pensacola-Ferry Pass-Brent, FL	1,669.4	516,388	110	309.3	73.2	17.8	1.5	4.7	6.4	5.6	12.1	13.4	14.2	12.5	11.6
37900		Peoria, IL	3,333.3	398,224	138	119.5	84.1	10.7	0.6	2.9	3.9	5.8	13.0	12.1	12.2	12.7	12.0
37980		Philadelphia-Camden-Wilmington, PA-NJ-DE-MD	4,603.2	6,228,601	7	1,353.1	62.1	21.8	0.6	7.4	10.4	5.5	12.2	12.4	14.1	13.1	12.3
37980	15804	Camden, NJ Div 15,804	1,342.7	1,292,517	X	962.6	65.4	17.6	0.6	6.2	12.6	5.4	12.3	12.2	13.1	13.1	13.0
37980	33874	Montgomery-Bucks-Chester Counties, PA Div 33,874	1,837.9	2,045,325	X	1,112.9	79.4	7.9	0.5	7.8	6.4	5.1	12.1	12.1	11.7	12.9	13.0
37980	37964	Philadelphia, PA Div 37,964	318.2	2,150,100	X	6,757.1	43.6	37.0	0.8	8.2	12.8	6.0	12.2	12.8	17.2	13.4	11.2
37980	48864	Wilmington, DE-MD-NJ Div 48,864	1,104.5	740,659	X	670.6	62.4	23.6	0.7	5.6	10.1	5.4	12.2	12.6	13.7	12.8	12.5
38060		Phoenix-Mesa-Chandler, AZ	14,567.8	4,946,145	10	339.5	55.7	6.8	2.5	5.6	31.9	5.7	13.1	13.2	14.4	13.3	12.2
38220		Pine Bluff, AR	2,029.7	86,412	370	42.6	46.9	49.6	0.9	1.1	2.9	5.4	11.6	13.5	13.1	12.4	12.1
38300		Pittsburgh, PA	5,282.9	2,353,538	27	445.5	86.4	9.9	0.5	3.3	2.0	4.9	10.7	11.3	13.2	12.4	11.9
38340		Pittsfield, MA	926.9	128,657	315	138.8	89.1	4.6	0.6	2.5	5.5	3.9	9.1	12.3	10.9	11.2	11.8
38540		Pocatello, ID	2,516.3	96,213	363	38.2	82.8	1.4	3.6	2.8	11.7	6.4	15.0	14.6	13.8	13.5	10.5
38860		Portland-South Portland, ME	2,081.4	556,893	103	267.6	93.2	2.9	0.9	2.7	2.2	4.6	10.2	11.1	13.1	12.7	12.5
38900		Portland-Vancouver-Hillsboro, OR-WA	6,687.5	2,511,612	25	375.6	75.0	4.3	1.8	10.3	13.0	5.1	11.9	11.5	15.2	15.3	13.2
38940		Port St. Lucie, FL	1,115.5	503,521	112	451.4	62.8	16.9	0.6	2.5	19.1	4.6	10.6	10.1	10.7	10.9	11.6
39100		Poughkeepsie-Newburgh-Middletown, NY	1,608.0	701,637	84	436.3	66.6	12.1	0.6	4.1	18.9	5.7	12.6	14.4	12.0	12.3	12.8
39150		Prescott Valley-Prescott, AZ	8,122.9	242,253	196	29.8	81.0	1.2	2.4	2.0	15.3	3.8	9.0	9.1	9.0	9.0	10.0
39300		Providence-Warwick, RI-MA	1,587.0	1,675,774	38	1,055.9	75.7	7.3	0.9	4.0	14.4	5.0	11.0	13.2	13.6	12.5	12.5
39340		Provo-Orem, UT	5,395.8	697,141	86	129.2	83.5	1.2	0.9	4.7	12.6	8.6	18.2	21.8	14.9	12.6	9.2
39380		Pueblo, CO	2,386.6	169,622	255	71.1	52.6	2.5	1.5	1.6	43.7	5.5	12.7	12.6	13.2	12.7	11.4
39460		Punta Gorda, FL	681.1	194,843	229	286.1	84.5	6.2	0.7	2.0	8.2	2.8	6.8	7.1	7.8	7.8	9.8
39540		Racine, WI	332.6	196,896	227	592.0	72.2	13.0	0.9	1.8	14.8	5.8	13.0	12.3	12.0	12.5	12.4
39580		Raleigh-Cary, NC	2,118.4	1,448,411	41	683.7	61.9	20.9	0.9	7.6	11.1	5.7	13.4	13.0	14.2	14.6	14.1
39660		Rapid City, SD	6,247.7	141,979	296	22.7	83.6	2.3	10.1	2.2	5.5	5.9	12.8	12.3	13.2	12.4	10.5

1. CBSA = Core Based Statistical Area. DIV = Metropolitan Division. See Appendix A for explanation. See Appendix B for list of metropolitan areas or temporarily covered by water. 2. Dry land or land partially or temporarily covered by water. 3. May be of any race.

Area name	Population, 2020 (cont.): Age (percent) (cont.): 55 to 64 years	65 to 74 years	75 years and over	Percent female	Population change and components of change, 2000–2020: Total persons: 2000	2010	Percent change: 2000–2010	2010–2019	Components of change, 2010–2020: Births	Deaths	Net migration	Households, 2016–2020: Number	Persons per house-hold	Percent: Family house-holds	Single parent house holds	One person
	16	17	18	19	20	21	22	23	24	25	26	27	28	29	30	31
Mobile, AL	13.2	10.5	6.6	52.2	430,573	430,197	-0.1	-0.5	6,509	7,197	-1,364	163,387	2.6	65.4	15.9	30.4
Modesto, CA	11.1	8.1	5.3	50.1	514,453	552,878	7.5	0.0	8,935	6,440	-2,524	174,826	3.1	74.4	14.8	20.5
Monroe, LA	12.6	10.3	6.6	51.7	204,420	207,104	1.3	-1.1	3,046	3,425	-1,859	75,093	2.6	61.7	15.7	33.9
Monroe, MI	15.2	11.9	7.3	50.3	152,021	154,809	1.8	0.3	1,817	2,290	934	60,804	2.4	66.6	10.1	27.3
Montgomery, AL	12.9	9.9	6.3	52.2	374,536	386,047	3.1	-0.1	5,857	5,483	-651	145,077	2.5	64.7	17.5	31.2
Morgantown, WV	11.4	9.7	5.7	48.4	129,709	140,038	8.0	0.5	1,736	1,622	565	52,663	2.5	57.3	7.9	31.0
Morristown, TN	14.7	11.8	7.9	50.4	136,608	142,709	4.5	0.8	1,764	2,777	2,173	53,675	2.6	69.0	10.5	26.4
Mount Vernon-Anacortes, WA	13.3	13.3	8.5	50.2	116,901	129,523	10.8	0.9	1,681	1,894	1,387	49,263	2.6	67.5	9.2	25.3
Muncie, IN	12.1	10.0	7.3	51.7	117,671	111,903	-4.9	0.0	1,258	1,935	636	46,632	2.3	58.4	12.5	31.1
Muskegon, MI	13.9	11.3	6.7	50.2	172,188	175,824	2.1	0.4	2,338	2,676	1,009	66,064	2.5	67.2	14.9	26.5
Myrtle Beach-Conway-North Myrtle Beach, SC-NC	16.9	18.8	9.3	51.8	376,722	487,722	29.5	4.5	4,957	9,024	26,465	195,635	2.4	65.5	11.0	27.8
Napa, CA	13.6	11.6	8.6	49.8	136,484	138,019	1.1	-1.3	1,503	1,706	-1,610	48,484	2.8	68.4	10.2	25.2
Naples-Marco Island, FL	14.1	16.3	16.8	50.4	321,520	375,752	16.9	2.7	3,813	5,795	12,384	147,977	2.5	66.3	8.6	28.7
Nashville-Davidson--Murfreesboro--Franklin, TN	12.2	8.9	5.1	51.0	1,646,200	1,989,519	20.9	1.2	29,243	23,987	18,021	727,452	2.6	65.8	11.5	26.6
New Bern, NC	13.5	13.0	8.7	49.6	126,802	122,168	-3.7	0.1	1,781	2,030	359	50,577	2.3	65.4	10.5	30.1
New Haven-Milford, CT	14.1	10.6	7.5	51.6	862,477	864,835	0.3	-0.1	9,991	11,956	677	332,765	2.5	62.6	14.0	31.0
New Orleans-Metairie, LA	13.6	10.8	6.4	51.7	1,189,866	1,271,845	6.9	-0.8	18,140	18,058	-10,033	486,509	2.6	59.8	15.5	34.4
New York-Newark-Jersey City, NY-NJ-PA	13.3	9.7	7.0	51.3	18,897,109	20,140,470	6.6	-1.8	270,043	219,357	-418,337	7,065,536	2.7	65.7	14.4	27.9
Nassau County-Suffolk County, NY Div 35,004	14.9	10.5	7.5	50.6	2,832,882	2,921,694	3.1	-0.2	34,811	35,683	-4,011	945,634	3.0	74.8	11.3	21.0
Newark, NJ-PA Div 35,084	14.0	9.5	6.6	50.8	2,147,727	2,280,061	6.2	-0.3	28,501	26,376	-8,890	791,234	2.7	69.1	13.8	26.3
New Brunswick-Lakewood, NJ Div 35,154	14.3	10.7	7.7	50.8	2,340,249	2,489,367	6.4	0.5	32,303	31,821	10,778	875,381	2.7	69.4	10.0	25.6
New York-Jersey City-White Plains, NY-NJ Div 35,614	12.6	9.4	6.9	51.6	11,576,251	12,449,348	7.5	-3.0	174,428	125,477	-416,214	4,453,287	2.6	62.4	16.0	30.2
Niles, MI	14.4	12.4	8.3	50.7	156,813	154,316	-1.6	-0.8	1,941	2,536	-626	63,136	2.4	64.4	12.8	29.4
North Port-Sarasota-Bradenton, FL	15.4	17.5	15.5	51.7	702,281	833,716	18.7	3.1	7,607	15,878	34,865	339,573	2.4	63.8	9.0	29.9
Norwich-New London, CT	14.9	11.4	7.9	49.6	274,055	268,555	-2.0	0.1	2,948	3,647	920	109,616	2.3	65.2	11.9	28.1
Ocala, FL	13.8	15.7	13.0	51.8	331,298	375,908	13.5	2.7	4,237	7,861	13,826	145,863	2.4	64.9	11.4	30.0
Ocean City, NJ	16.8	16.9	11.4	51.1	97,265	95,263	-2.1	0.4	945	1,757	1,232	40,670	2.2	66.6	10.0	28.6
Odessa, TX	9.4	6.1	3.7	48.9	137,130	165,171	20.4	-2.5	3,809	1,835	-5,980	53,602	3.0	68.9	16.6	26.1
Ogden-Clearfield, UT	9.8	7.1	4.3	49.2	597,159	694,863	16.4	1.7	11,598	6,182	6,284	213,554	3.1	77.0	9.1	18.5
Oklahoma City, OK	11.7	9.1	5.5	50.5	1,252,987	1,425,695	13.8	1.1	21,238	18,651	13,229	523,154	2.6	64.5	12.2	28.8
Olympia-Lacey-Tumwater, WA	12.4	11.4	6.7	50.7	252,264	294,793	16.9	1.1	3,662	3,547	3,041	112,323	2.5	65.8	10.2	25.8
Omaha-Council Bluffs, NE-IA	12.1	9.1	5.4	50.1	865,350	967,604	11.8	0.4	15,155	11,011	-250	364,079	2.5	64.6	10.4	28.9
Orlando-Kissimmee-Sanford, FL	12.1	9.2	6.3	50.8	2,134,411	2,673,376	25.3	0.7	34,807	29,364	13,241	893,257	2.8	67.7	13.6	24.4
Oshkosh-Neenah, WI	13.5	10.2	6.8	49.3	166,994	171,730	2.8	-0.1	2,134	2,311	35	71,132	2.3	58.0	8.9	32.6
Owensboro, KY	13.3	10.6	7.1	50.7	114,752	121,559	5.9	-0.3	1,706	1,892	-165	47,340	2.4	67.5	11.5	27.0
Oxnard-Thousand Oaks-Ventura, CA	13.3	9.9	6.8	50.2	823,318	843,843	2.5	-0.5	10,447	8,931	-5,692	271,639	3.1	72.3	11.8	21.7
Palm Bay-Melbourne-Titusville, FL	16.3	13.8	10.4	50.7	543,376	606,612	11.6	1.7	6,156	10,911	14,952	236,005	2.5	63.1	9.8	30.7
Panama City, FL	15.0	11.2	7.3	50.2	168,852	175,216	3.8	2.3	2,353	2,763	4,434	73,536	2.4	64.5	12.1	29.0
Parkersburg-Vienna, WV	14.7	12.6	8.5	51.0	92,673	89,490	-3.4	-0.9	1,074	1,711	-176	37,746	2.4	63.2	11.2	31.7
Pensacola-Ferry Pass-Brent, FL	13.7	10.6	6.4	49.8	448,991	509,905	13.6	1.3	6,925	7,870	7,431	187,866	2.5	64.9	13.5	27.5
Peoria, IL	13.1	11.2	7.8	50.5	416,255	402,391	-3.3	-1.0	5,473	6,332	-3,332	163,466	2.4	62.9	10.7	31.8
Philadelphia-Camden-Wilmington, PA-NJ-DE-MD	13.6	10.1	6.7	51.3	5,965,343	6,245,051	4.7	-0.3	80,582	84,350	-13,023	2,311,452	2.6	64.6	13.9	29.1
Camden, NJ Div 15,804	14.1	10.1	6.8	51.0	1,250,679	1,287,639	3.0	0.4	15,875	16,709	5,559	465,231	2.6	68.5	13.8	26.3
Montgomery-Bucks-Chester Counties, PA Div 33,874	14.6	11.0	7.5	50.7	1,924,009	2,037,504	5.9	0.4	23,360	27,284	11,600	752,362	2.6	70.1	9.2	24.4
Philadelphia, PA Div 37,964	12.1	9.1	6.0	52.2	2,084,985	2,180,627	4.6	-1.4	31,823	30,362	-31,889	822,721	2.5	57.3	18.6	35.0
Wilmington, DE-MD-NJ Div 48,864	14.0	10.3	6.6	51.1	705,670	739,281	4.8	0.2	9,524	9,995	1,707	271,138	2.6	64.6	12.7	28.8
Phoenix-Mesa-Chandler, AZ	11.7	9.6	6.7	50.1	4,192,887	4,845,832	15.6	2.1	66,390	56,674	90,467	1,745,219	2.7	66.1	12.1	26.3
Pine Bluff, AR	13.4	11.2	7.2	48.3	100,258	87,751	-12.5	-1.5	1,130	1,517	-950	33,398	2.3	63.7	17.4	31.8
Pittsburgh, PA	14.6	12.5	8.4	50.8	2,356,285	2,370,930	0.6	-0.7	27,480	40,904	-4,019	1,017,860	2.2	59.6	10.1	33.6
Pittsfield, MA	16.3	14.5	10.2	51.3	131,219	129,026	-1.7	-0.3	1,116	2,086	603	54,786	2.2	58.0	11.4	34.3
Pocatello, ID	11.0	9.8	5.4	50.0	90,656	94,896	4.7	1.4	1,450	1,195	1,055	34,362	2.6	64.1	9.1	29.2
Portland-South Portland, ME	15.1	12.6	8.0	51.0	514,098	551,740	7.3	0.9	5,920	7,962	7,213	226,327	2.3	61.5	8.2	29.0
Portland-Vancouver-Hillsboro, OR-WA	12.0	10.0	5.9	50.2	2,226,009	2,512,859	12.9	0.0	30,461	28,189	-3,676	957,977	2.5	63.2	9.6	26.7
Port St. Lucie, FL	14.7	14.5	12.3	50.7	424,107	487,657	15.0	3.3	5,256	8,559	19,452	183,397	2.6	66.4	11.0	27.5
Poughkeepsie-Newburgh-Middletown, NY	13.9	9.7	6.5	49.7	670,301	697,221	4.0	0.6	9,524	8,115	2,930	240,523	2.7	68.1	11.5	26.0
Prescott Valley-Prescott, AZ	16.5	20.4	13.2	50.8	211,033	236,209	11.9	2.6	2,128	4,646	8,700	101,245	2.2	61.4	7.9	31.8
Providence-Warwick, RI-MA	14.2	10.7	7.3	51.1	1,600,852	1,676,579	4.7	0.0	19,001	23,201	3,218	635,095	2.5	63.4	13.6	29.8
Provo-Orem, UT	6.8	4.9	3.1	49.2	526,810	671,185	27.4	3.9	14,631	4,112	15,420	175,377	3.5	81.3	7.4	12.3
Pueblo, CO	12.8	11.6	7.5	50.4	159,063	168,162	5.7	0.9	2,154	2,873	2,182	65,206	2.5	61.7	13.0	32.6
Punta Gorda, FL	17.5	22.1	18.4	50.9	159,978	186,847	16.8	4.3	1,261	4,331	11,260	79,789	2.3	63.9	7.5	30.1
Racine, WI	14.6	10.8	6.7	50.1	195,408	197,727	1.2	-0.4	2,686	2,819	-731	77,648	2.5	66.3	12.2	27.7
Raleigh-Cary, NC	12.0	8.2	4.8	51.0	1,130,490	1,413,982	25.1	2.4	19,299	13,110	28,184	507,613	2.6	67.3	11.0	25.6
Rapid City, SD	14.1	12.4	6.3	48.9	126,382	139,074	10.0	2.1	2,079	1,858	2,700	55,089	2.5	63.1	9.9	30.2

Area name	Persons in group quarters, 2020	Daytime population, 2019		Births, 2020		Deaths, 2020		Persons under 65 with no health insurance 2019		Medicare, 2020			Serious crimes known to police[2], 2019 Violent	
		Number	Employ-ment/ residence ratio	Total	Rate[1]	Number	Rate[1]	Number	Percent	Total Ben-eficiaries	Enrolled in Original Medicare	Enrolled in Medicare Advantage	Number	Rate[3]
	32	33	34	35	36	37	38	39	40	41	42	43	44	45
Mobile, AL	7,230	438,482	1.05	5,232	12.2	5,695	13.3	44,548	12.7	90,151	33,843	56,308	NA	NA
Modesto, CA	6,164	520,724	0.89	7,180	13.0	5,094	9.2	39,386	8.4	89,349	43,744	45,605	2,823	514.0
Monroe, LA	6,792	203,972	1.02	2,446	11.9	2,727	13.3	15,264	9.5	40,844	24,598	16,246	2,605	1,308.5
Monroe, MI	1,405	125,773	0.65	1,453	9.4	1,834	11.8	6,706	5.5	34,927	17,637	17,290	NA	NA
Montgomery, AL	13,674	380,498	1.04	4,727	12.3	4,404	11.4	32,096	10.7	76,417	34,852	41,565	NA	NA
Morgantown, WV	8,048	145,591	1.09	1,347	9.6	1,302	9.3	8,038	7.3	23,144	12,901	10,243	NA	NA
Morristown, TN	2,334	135,452	0.89	1,422	9.9	2,180	15.2	16,136	14.4	35,148	16,195	18,953	519	361.9
Mount Vernon-Anacortes, WA	1,451	128,661	1.02	1,340	10.3	1,555	11.9	9,725	9.7	33,105	20,583	12,522	192	147.5
Muncie, IN	8,316	113,950	0.99	1,003	9.0	1,502	13.4	8,911	10.3	23,905	14,357	9,548	NA	NA
Muskegon, MI	4,568	164,482	0.88	1,874	10.6	2,180	12.4	9,617	6.9	40,233	14,546	25,687	714	412.3
Myrtle Beach-Conway-North Myrtle Beach, SC-NC	3,909	472,799	0.96	3,975	7.9	7,396	14.8	59,808	16.8	164,865	109,352	55,513	NA	NA
Napa, CA	4,960	148,717	1.15	1,214	8.9	1,399	10.2	9,391	8.7	30,283	17,342	12,941	539	394.9
Naples-Marco Island, FL	3,956	390,555	1.07	3,036	8.0	4,761	12.5	54,372	21.3	109,971	74,342	35,629	876	223.8
Nashville-Davidson--Murfreesboro--Franklin, TN	40,671	1,951,163	1.05	23,478	11.7	19,182	9.6	182,454	11.1	318,178	171,962	146,216	12,137	616.3
New Bern, NC	5,158	125,577	1.02	1,413	11.6	1,635	13.4	12,355	13.4	31,861	24,603	7,258	451	363.8
New Haven-Milford, CT	28,367	825,058	0.93	7,980	9.2	9,516	11.0	47,465	7.0	170,622	83,021	87,601	2,049	256.3
New Orleans-Metairie, LA	18,646	1,298,226	1.05	14,626	11.6	14,530	11.5	111,904	10.7	244,039	91,483	152,556	7,960	624.3
New York-Newark-Jersey City, NY-NJ-PA	393,900	19,456,599	1.02	215,362	10.8	177,015	8.9	1,247,823	7.9	3,398,765	2,046,473	1,352,292	NA	NA
Nassau County-Suffolk County, NY Div 35,004	49,006	2,655,393	0.87	27,799	9.5	28,602	9.8	116,294	5.0	578,613	426,182	152,431	NA	NA
Newark, NJ-PA Div 35,084	45,006	2,124,774	0.96	22,674	10.0	21,207	9.3	177,199	9.9	377,725	239,706	138,019	NA	NA
New Brunswick-Lakewood, NJ Div 35,154	42,779	2,284,506	0.92	25,749	10.3	25,629	10.3	148,781	7.7	490,174	333,613	156,561	NA	NA
New York-Jersey City-White Plains, NY-NJ Div 35,614	257,109	12,391,926	1.09	139,140	11.4	101,577	8.3	805,549	8.2	1,952,253	1,046,972	905,281	NA	NA
Niles, MI	3,335	151,528	0.97	1,564	10.2	2,027	13.2	10,145	8.5	36,908	20,272	16,636	1,013	664.2
North Port-Sarasota-Bradenton, FL	9,830	821,380	1.00	6,144	7.2	12,787	15.1	91,412	16.4	264,761	159,364	105,397	2,854	335.4
Norwich-New London, CT	10,719	265,511	0.99	2,325	8.7	2,938	10.9	12,556	6.1	58,803	31,853	26,950	313	180.1
Ocala, FL	9,187	351,545	0.93	3,442	9.0	6,192	16.2	42,094	16.9	122,698	57,676	65,022	1,557	422.5
Ocean City, NJ	2,704	92,648	1.00	749	7.9	1,430	15.0	6,002	9.2	28,978	21,193	7,785	154	168.5
Odessa, TX	2,234	162,327	1.00	3,059	18.7	1,467	9.0	32,601	22.0	19,830	11,447	8,383	1,180	697.1
Ogden-Clearfield, UT	5,856	620,457	0.84	9,207	13.1	4,895	7.0	53,952	8.9	92,100	51,595	40,505	1,197	172.9
Oklahoma City, OK	30,682	1,406,921	1.01	17,025	11.9	14,913	10.4	176,192	14.9	242,961	159,640	83,321	6,719	470.8
Olympia-Lacey-Tumwater, WA	3,898	272,194	0.91	2,904	9.8	2,818	9.5	16,174	6.9	64,191	36,739	27,452	657	223.4
Omaha-Council Bluffs, NE-IA	16,206	941,213	1.00	12,052	12.4	8,787	9.1	68,515	8.5	161,969	106,525	55,444	4,103	429.7
Orlando-Kissimmee-Sanford, FL	46,040	2,622,556	1.05	28,048	10.4	23,571	8.8	321,710	14.8	460,766	208,682	252,084	11,347	426.7
Oshkosh-Neenah, WI	7,315	181,095	1.12	1,662	9.7	1,801	10.5	8,357	6.1	34,755	12,351	22,404	332	192.7
Owensboro, KY	2,801	120,285	1.03	1,392	11.5	1,486	12.2	7,014	7.3	26,962	16,350	10,612	197	164.4
Oxnard-Thousand Oaks-Ventura, CA	10,900	804,318	0.90	8,380	10.0	7,178	8.5	72,745	10.4	158,828	97,555	61,273	1,686	200.7
Palm Bay-Melbourne-Titusville, FL	6,418	584,944	0.96	4,938	8.1	8,659	14.1	62,753	13.9	164,093	89,793	74,300	2,288	377.0
Panama City, FL	3,540	182,394	1.03	1,908	10.8	2,238	12.7	20,640	14.8	38,113	25,181	12,932	847	484.4
Parkersburg-Vienna, WV	943	92,453	1.06	867	9.7	1,329	14.9	5,138	7.3	23,674	14,683	8,991	257	289.0
Pensacola-Ferry Pass-Brent, FL	23,776	483,252	0.94	5,545	10.8	6,283	12.2	52,551	13.3	110,218	65,451	44,767	2,180	429.7
Peoria, IL	10,986	402,840	0.99	4,353	10.9	5,024	12.6	20,767	6.6	86,843	54,241	32,602	1,689	425.7
Philadelphia-Camden-Wilmington, PA-NJ-DE-MD	163,371	6,061,913	0.99	64,631	10.4	67,816	10.9	340,601	6.8	1,175,534	744,931	430,603	NA	NA
Camden, NJ Div 15,804	23,519	1,157,335	0.86	12,757	9.9	13,468	10.4	69,720	6.8	249,458	157,615	91,843	NA	NA
Montgomery-Bucks-Chester Counties, PA Div 33,874	42,242	2,000,895	1.02	18,669	9.1	21,872	10.7	85,531	5.3	416,774	279,201	137,573	NA	NA
Philadelphia, PA Div 37,964	77,660	2,184,022	1.04	25,519	11.8	24,408	11.3	145,418	8.3	369,490	201,340	168,150	NA	NA
Wilmington, DE-MD-NJ Div 48,864	19,950	719,661	0.99	7,686	10.4	8,068	10.9	39,932	6.8	139,812	106,775	33,037	NA	NA
Phoenix-Mesa-Chandler, AZ	82,632	4,849,628	1.00	53,798	11.0	45,656	9.3	537,313	13.2	828,714	436,131	392,583	23,512	464.3
Pine Bluff, AR	8,856	88,573	0.97	920	10.6	1,201	13.8	5,222	8.3	19,776	12,778	6,998	950	1,097.8
Pittsburgh, PA	60,477	2,341,789	1.02	21,866	9.3	32,704	13.9	96,972	5.4	558,180	199,128	359,052	NA	NA
Pittsfield, MA	5,846	127,419	1.02	865	6.7	1,663	12.9	3,482	3.9	36,012	31,522	4,490	533	431.2
Pocatello, ID	1,826	93,213	0.97	1,163	12.2	938	9.8	9,981	12.6	17,640	10,485	7,155	260	268.8
Portland-South Portland, ME	12,985	534,987	1.00	4,707	8.5	6,349	11.5	34,757	8.2	133,742	66,817	66,925	516	95.0
Portland-Vancouver-Hillsboro, OR-WA	37,060	2,484,387	1.01	24,116	9.6	22,556	9.0	159,846	7.6	449,764	171,221	278,543	D	D
Port St. Lucie, FL	6,601	453,026	0.86	4,232	8.5	6,930	14.0	61,549	17.5	135,117	75,509	59,608	1,170	236.1
Poughkeepsie-Newburgh-Middletown, NY	30,519	628,340	0.85	7,558	10.8	6,533	9.3	27,899	5.1	129,056	90,111	38,945	NA	NA
Prescott Valley-Prescott, AZ	3,740	228,890	0.96	1,740	7.3	3,729	15.6	23,125	14.8	88,058	56,748	31,310	581	242.9
Providence-Warwick, RI-MA	56,717	1,544,565	0.90	15,127	9.0	18,481	11.0	59,370	4.6	354,694	202,524	152,170	4,630	285.6
Provo-Orem, UT	14,226	614,229	0.94	11,558	16.8	3,226	4.7	54,943	9.4	62,692	32,492	30,200	NA	NA
Pueblo, CO	3,791	165,514	0.97	1,723	10.2	2,283	13.5	12,543	9.6	39,225	18,531	20,694	1,216	722.2
Punta Gorda, FL	2,536	177,938	0.87	1,002	5.2	3,500	18.3	19,097	17.4	74,843	41,729	33,114	292	152.2
Racine, WI	4,817	181,191	0.84	2,175	11.0	2,231	11.3	11,317	7.2	42,139	19,679	22,460	540	275.2
Raleigh-Cary, NC	23,414	1,361,663	1.00	15,478	10.8	10,535	7.3	131,180	10.9	208,756	119,017	89,739	3,180	223.6
Rapid City, SD	3,050	141,286	1.01	1,665	11.8	1,469	10.4	14,058	12.3	33,801	24,340	9,461	957	665.1

1. Per 1,000 estimated resident population. 2. Data for serious crimes have not been adjusted for underreporting; this may affect comparability between geographic areas and over time. 3. Per 100,000 population estimated by the FBI.

Area name	Serious crimes known to police[1], 2019 (cont.) — Property — Number	Property — Rate[2]	Education — School enrollment and attainment, 2019 — Enrollment[3] — Total	Enrollment[3] — Percent private	Attainment[4] — High school graduate or less	Attainment[4] — Bachelor's degree or more	Local government expenditures,[5] 2017–2018 — Total current expenditures (mil dol)	Current expenditures per student (dollars)	Income and poverty, 2016–2020 — Per capita income[6] (dollars)	Median household income (dollars)	Median family income	Percent of households with income less than $50,000	Percent of households with income of $200,000 or more	Percent below poverty level — All persons	Percent below poverty level — All families	Percent below poverty level — Age 65 years and older
	46	47	48	49	50	51	52	53	54	55	56	57	58	59	60	61
Mobile, AL	NA	NA	100,954	18.6	46.7	24.0	621.4	9,905	26,915	49,370	61,626	50.5	3.5	17.8	13.1	21.9
Modesto, CA	10,843	1,974.3	152,621	8.5	50.1	17.7	1,497.5	13,627	27,225	62,873	69,654	39.7	5.8	13.5	10.4	14.9
Monroe, LA	7,275	3,654.3	49,290	15.1	49.9	22.5	383.7	11,138	25,392	43,212	56,295	56.2	3.2	23.5	18.2	28.3
Monroe, MI	NA	NA	33,724	14.1	42.7	21.0	268.5	12,041	33,202	65,453	80,507	37.0	4.6	11.2	7.6	13.8
Montgomery, AL	NA	NA	91,358	21.3	40.2	30.6	513.5	9,442	29,372	54,250	68,115	46.4	4.3	16.6	13.1	21.0
Morgantown, WV	NA	NA	40,902	7.4	41.7	36.1	185.4	11,519	31,557	53,681	77,584	46.8	6.0	19.1	9.1	13.0
Morristown, TN	2,686	1,872.9	30,013	13.1	55.1	17.0	191.0	9,033	24,572	46,798	58,448	52.8	2.2	15.5	11.5	18.7
Mount Vernon-Anacortes, WA	3,153	2,421.4	27,309	14.9	35.0	27.4	314.0	16,000	35,172	71,021	82,149	34.0	6.4	10.7	6.9	12.6
Muncie, IN	NA	NA	34,215	7.0	44.1	24.9	156.0	9,845	25,718	45,910	61,415	53.5	2.9	21.4	12.3	21.6
Muskegon, MI	3,581	2,068.0	38,209	10.7	42.2	19.7	326.3	12,156	26,655	53,478	64,668	46.3	3.1	14.1	10.3	17.5
Myrtle Beach-Conway-North Myrtle Beach, SC-NC	NA	NA	88,897	9.9	40.2	25.7	633.6	10,775	30,616	53,832	65,152	46.1	3.7	13.4	9.0	17.9
Napa, CA	2,306	1,689.7	32,863	18.6	32.0	37.2	308.9	15,282	46,912	92,219	107,995	26.8	16.4	7.5	4.9	7.1
Naples-Marco Island, FL	3,806	972.5	67,847	18.6	38.0	35.9	534.5	11,268	46,785	70,217	84,784	35.5	12.2	11.0	7.1	13.1
Nashville-Davidson--Murfreesboro--Franklin, TN	46,329	2,352.5	461,019	22.4	35.5	37.3	3,013.6	10,146	36,626	68,406	83,085	35.8	7.8	11.0	7.9	12.4
New Bern, NC	2,666	2,150.8	26,603	16.3	38.8	23.6	176.9	10,556	29,209	52,345	65,462	48.2	3.5	15.2	11.3	18.9
New Haven-Milford, CT	17,342	2,169.2	212,715	23.7	39.7	36.0	2,432.4	20,464	39,134	71,370	92,508	35.9	9.7	11.2	7.8	13.0
New Orleans-Metairie, LA	35,121	2,754.6	307,578	28.0	40.0	31.1	2,214.5	12,886	32,727	54,388	72,053	46.2	5.9	16.9	12.2	19.9
New York-Newark-Jersey City, NY-NJ-PA	NA	NA	4,681,162	24.2	37.2	41.4	65,426.8	23,737	45,049	81,951	99,148	32.8	15.4	12.4	9.3	13.7
Nassau County-Suffolk County, NY Div 35,004	NA	NA	695,168	20.6	33.4	41.8	11,834.0	26,865	49,762	111,542	130,301	21.4	21.4	6.0	4.0	5.9
Newark, NJ-PA Div 35,084	NA	NA	540,561	17.4	36.0	41.7	7,575.7	20,765	46,241	85,504	107,333	30.2	16.6	9.8	7.3	11.1
New Brunswick-Lakewood, NJ Div 35,154	NA	NA	600,309	23.1	33.4	43.5	7,051.9	20,138	45,702	91,851	113,495	27.2	16.0	7.9	5.4	8.0
New York-Jersey City-White Plains, NY-NJ Div 35,614	NA	NA	2,845,124	26.7	39.0	40.9	38,965.2	24,340	43,574	73,561	85,483	36.8	13.9	15.3	11.9	17.3
Niles, MI	2,882	1,889.6	34,183	19.0	38.0	27.6	317.7	12,527	30,839	52,500	67,533	48.0	4.6	16.3	11.7	21.9
North Port-Sarasota-Bradenton, FL	12,831	1,507.9	138,818	17.4	37.2	33.5	1,005.1	10,877	39,965	62,438	77,172	39.8	7.7	9.8	6.1	12.2
Norwich-New London, CT	2,210	1,271.6	59,892	18.6	35.7	34.4	721.7	20,553	40,995	75,831	94,894	32.0	9.1	8.5	6.1	10.5
Ocala, FL	6,012	1,631.5	67,411	18.4	48.5	20.7	418.8	9,760	26,990	46,587	56,181	53.4	3.0	15.5	10.7	21.3
Ocean City, NJ	1,856	2,031.0	16,739	14.7	38.7	33.6	288.9	23,315	42,987	72,385	87,716	34.9	9.1	9.9	7.5	14.1
Odessa, TX	5,005	2,956.8	44,953	6.9	53.6	16.6	293.3	8,354	29,510	63,096	74,327	39.6	4.7	13.0	10.2	14.7
Ogden-Clearfield, UT	11,454	1,654.9	204,190	9.8	31.1	31.9	1,190.3	7,692	30,897	78,680	88,021	27.8	6.0	6.7	4.9	7.0
Oklahoma City, OK	41,616	2,916.2	366,647	13.3	37.3	31.5	2,158.2	8,406	32,065	60,476	75,170	41.6	5.8	13.5	9.5	14.6
Olympia-Lacey-Tumwater, WA	5,636	1,916.6	64,435	15.0	27.9	35.7	602.2	14,239	36,256	75,867	91,125	31.9	6.3	9.8	6.3	10.0
Omaha-Council Bluffs, NE-IA	21,780	2,280.9	249,286	19.7	31.6	37.0	1,898.7	11,793	35,722	69,439	87,733	35.4	6.8	9.3	6.1	9.4
Orlando-Kissimmee-Sanford, FL	49,514	1,862.1	649,644	18.4	35.7	33.1	3,706.6	9,381	30,941	61,229	70,774	40.7	6.3	12.8	9.5	14.1
Oshkosh-Neenah, WI	2,283	1,325.0	41,903	11.2	39.5	29.0	271.1	11,844	33,101	59,947	79,200	41.7	4.0	11.0	5.6	9.2
Owensboro, KY	2,793	2,330.6	28,314	15.0	44.7	22.8	220.5	11,037	29,690	54,946	68,358	45.7	3.3	15.8	12.8	20.5
Oxnard-Thousand Oaks-Ventura, CA	13,083	1,557.8	219,446	14.0	33.8	33.9	1,912.3	12,832	39,403	89,295	101,160	27.0	14.1	8.9	6.1	9.1
Palm Bay-Melbourne-Titusville, FL	10,662	1,756.6	124,375	20.5	34.5	30.9	673.2	9,130	33,662	59,359	73,440	41.9	6.0	11.2	7.7	13.3
Panama City, FL	4,626	2,645.6	39,584	15.6	38.6	24.5	241.6	8,589	30,774	56,483	68,575	43.6	3.9	13.0	8.9	14.0
Parkersburg-Vienna, WV	2,013	2,263.9	18,304	13.8	43.9	21.2	161.8	12,045	27,714	48,369	61,708	51.3	2.9	16.0	11.8	21.7
Pensacola-Ferry Pass-Brent, FL	9,849	1,941.4	115,183	20.6	36.2	27.2	620.6	9,067	30,308	58,759	71,094	42.7	4.8	12.5	8.9	15.0
Peoria, IL	D	D	95,150	18.3	38.6	27.9	861.7	14,053	33,028	60,094	77,873	41.4	5.2	12.1	8.1	12.9
Philadelphia-Camden-Wilmington, PA-NJ-DE-MD	NA	NA	1,487,241	26.1	37.4	38.7	15,563.2	18,067	40,420	74,825	95,369	34.5	11.3	11.9	8.2	12.6
Camden, NJ Div 15,804	NA	NA	301,422	16.6	37.8	34.9	3,990.7	20,114	40,427	81,817	100,987	30.1	11.1	8.8	6.0	9.5
Montgomery-Bucks-Chester Counties, PA Div 33,874	NA	NA	470,315	26.6	29.8	48.4	5,337.4	18,855	49,808	95,985	117,345	24.6	17.0	5.9	3.7	5.7
Philadelphia, PA Div 37,964	NA	NA	538,818	33.6	43.5	33.4	4,443.8	16,138	32,566	54,520	68,458	46.4	7.0	19.6	15.0	22.0
Wilmington, DE-MD-NJ Div 48,864	NA	NA	176,686	17.7	40.2	33.7	1,791.3	17,127	38,060	74,820	93,347	33.7	8.9	10.8	7.0	11.7
Phoenix-Mesa-Chandler, AZ	112,293	2,217.4	1,205,583	13.1	34.9	32.2	6,806.3	8,510	34,378	67,068	78,930	36.6	7.7	12.7	9.1	14.1
Pine Bluff, AR	2,638	3,048.3	20,796	13.3	55.6	16.3	148.3	11,158	20,975	41,856	53,908	57.6	2.3	20.0	16.8	26.5
Pittsburgh, PA	NA	NA	493,985	21.0	37.6	35.9	5,021.0	16,823	37,195	61,969	82,642	40.8	6.5	10.7	6.9	12.1
Pittsfield, MA	1,401	1,133.5	26,213	21.9	37.0	35.3	298.0	19,079	37,025	62,166	82,207	40.7	6.5	9.7	5.9	10.7
Pocatello, ID	1,747	1,806.1	27,059	9.4	36.4	26.1	124.1	7,419	25,022	51,914	66,208	48.2	2.6	13.8	9.3	15.4
Portland-South Portland, ME	5,524	1,017.5	112,186	21.4	30.7	41.2	1,093.3	15,544	39,534	72,552	89,988	33.7	7.3	8.1	4.9	7.9
Portland-Vancouver-Hillsboro, OR-WA	67,267	2,678.4	576,118	17.9	27.5	40.4	4,514.4	13,076	40,138	77,511	94,727	31.2	9.9	10.1	6.4	9.8
Port St. Lucie, FL	5,459	1,101.6	96,321	17.6	41.2	26.3	577.1	9,613	33,536	58,039	68,546	43.1	5.9	12.2	8.2	14.6
Poughkeepsie-Newburgh-Middletown, NY	NA	NA	174,945	26.8	37.1	33.4	2,362.8	23,879	38,524	81,331	100,123	31.6	11.2	10.3	6.9	10.9
Prescott Valley-Prescott, AZ	2,910	1,216.8	43,985	21.3	34.3	26.3	209.5	8,797	31,779	53,329	66,999	46.9	4.1	12.6	7.4	13.5
Providence-Warwick, RI-MA	18,808	1,160.2	384,808	23.0	40.6	33.0	3,698.9	16,606	37,294	70,676	89,555	37.0	7.8	11.3	8.0	13.0
Provo-Orem, UT	NA	NA	246,020	23.4	22.1	40.7	1,078.8	7,167	27,293	76,864	83,669	29.9	7.1	10.1	6.9	8.0
Pueblo, CO	D	D	39,754	7.8	39.3	22.9	258.6	9,777	26,504	49,979	62,959	50.0	3.2	17.6	13.0	21.4
Punta Gorda, FL	1,651	860.4	24,026	15.9	42.6	23.8	154.5	9,650	33,275	52,724	63,887	47.1	4.2	10.6	7.4	16.5
Racine, WI	2,437	1,241.9	46,428	17.5	40.4	25.8	360.7	13,188	32,566	62,556	77,503	40.1	4.7	12.3	8.6	15.4
Raleigh-Cary, NC	21,397	1,504.3	359,633	17.7	25.1	47.8	2,075.7	9,279	39,968	78,706	96,929	31.2	10.8	9.2	6.1	9.4
Rapid City, SD	4,275	2,971.1	32,867	13.5	35.3	30.6	198.7	9,562	31,947	59,076	74,413	42.4	4.7	12.5	7.4	13.5

1. Data for serious crimes have not been adjusted for underreporting; this may affect comparability between geographic areas and over time. 2. Per 100,000 population estimated by the FBI. 3. All persons 3 years old and over enrolled in nursery school through college. 4. Persons 25 years old and over. 5. Elementary and secondary education expenditures. 6. Based on population estimated by the American Community Survey, 2015.

Area name	Personal income, 2019										Earnings, 2019		
			Per capita[1]			Supplements to wages and salaries, employer contributions (mil dol)						Contributrions for government social insurance (mil dol)	
	Total (mil dol)	Percent change, 2018–2019	Dollars	Rank	Wages and Salaries (mil dol)	Pension and insurance	Government social insurance	Proprietors' income	Dividends, interest, and rent (mil dol)	Personal transfer receipts (mil dol)	Total (mil dol)	From employee and self-employed	From employer
	62	63	64	65	66	67	68	69	70	71	72	73	74
Mobile, AL	18,319	6.8	42,731	344	9,626	1,504	708	1,368	2,712	5,575	13,206	898	708
Modesto, CA	26,929	12.9	48,954	221	10,635	2,038	807	2,355	3,265	7,650	15,835	922	807
Monroe, LA	8,998	7.7	45,252	299	3,629	643	242	743	1,273	3,051	5,257	325	242
Monroe, MI	7,834	7.0	52,028	161	2,107	395	155	438	1,012	2,126	3,095	226	155
Montgomery, AL	17,677	6.5	47,446	256	8,626	1,549	649	990	3,169	4,758	11,814	773	649
Morgantown, WV	6,567	5.0	46,841	268	3,698	655	283	391	1,135	1,560	5,028	319	283
Morristown, TN	5,768	7.5	40,061	372	2,232	400	166	466	702	1,940	3,265	234	166
Mount Vernon-Anacortes, WA	7,496	9.0	57,315	91	2,827	534	253	619	1,518	1,902	4,233	263	253
Muncie, IN	4,646	7.0	40,948	364	2,180	402	165	226	673	1,618	2,973	204	165
Muskegon, MI	7,651	10.8	44,000	325	2,786	505	211	351	1,009	2,751	3,853	281	211
Myrtle Beach-Conway-North Myrtle Beach, SC-NC	22,368	9.1	43,477	334	7,059	1,154	528	1,574	4,707	7,593	10,314	863	528
Napa, CA	11,205	10.1	82,408	8	4,722	875	349	1,394	2,564	1,979	7,342	411	349
Naples-Marco Island, FL	40,816	2.5	103,865	5	8,936	1,075	602	2,234	23,112	5,020	12,847	929	602
Nashville-Davidson--Murfreesboro--Franklin, TN	121,745	2.4	62,076	47	62,046	8,035	4,247	21,803	17,395	20,028	96,131	5,617	4,247
New Bern, NC	5,928	6.8	48,121	240	2,546	591	200	313	1,181	1,779	3,650	236	200
New Haven-Milford, CT	51,195	5.7	60,092	67	23,492	3,857	1,811	4,452	7,227	12,417	33,611	1,953	1,811
New Orleans-Metairie, LA	73,652	5.8	57,891	87	32,077	5,189	2,109	9,381	13,351	17,407	48,756	2,855	2,109
New York-Newark-Jersey City, NY-NJ-PA	1,574,365	5.1	82,322	9	793,365	114,376	52,806	156,010	303,597	305,544	1,116,557	61,675	52,806
Nassau County-Suffolk County, NY Div 35,004	243,165	5.0	86,058	X	85,367	15,442	6,515	17,088	51,175	43,933	124,412	6,850	6,515
Newark, NJ-PA Div 35,084	171,274	4.9	79,007	X	79,766	11,440	5,403	14,892	29,726	28,808	111,502	6,624	5,403
New Brunswick-Lakewood, NJ Div 35,154	180,444	5.1	75,668	X	76,266	11,075	5,520	18,992	30,227	31,863	111,852	6,800	5,520
New York-Jersey City-White Plains, NY-NJ Div 35,614	979,481	5.1	83,387	X	551,966	76,419	35,368	105,038	192,469	200,939	768,791	41,401	35,368
Niles, MI	8,018	8.4	52,395	152	3,258	623	246	472	1,366	2,338	4,599	313	246
North Port-Sarasota-Bradenton, FL	52,980	5.5	61,988	48	16,347	2,144	1,123	3,476	19,709	12,327	23,090	1,787	1,123
Norwich-New London, CT	16,216	5.0	61,191	57	7,455	1,489	552	1,172	2,540	3,782	10,668	605	552
Ocala, FL	15,520	9.4	41,553	358	5,048	783	356	637	3,393	5,842	6,825	597	356
Ocean City, NJ	6,210	6.5	67,836	24	1,865	385	160	738	1,321	1,790	3,148	212	160
Odessa, TX	8,366	-3.3	49,887	203	4,486	587	293	1,036	997	1,672	6,402	343	293
Ogden-Clearfield, UT	34,133	8.2	49,371	216	14,394	2,623	1,094	1,891	5,993	5,430	20,002	1,212	1,094
Oklahoma City, OK	75,100	3.6	52,688	149	34,866	5,754	2,564	9,436	13,661	15,045	52,621	3,083	2,564
Olympia-Lacey-Tumwater, WA	16,470	9.3	56,007	103	7,015	1,333	606	974	3,096	3,856	9,928	605	606
Omaha-Council Bluffs, NE-IA	58,248	5.2	61,040	60	29,847	4,571	2,264	5,547	11,106	9,772	42,228	2,661	2,264
Orlando-Kissimmee-Sanford, FL	127,278	6.7	48,223	237	70,639	9,015	4,818	7,352	21,265	29,919	91,825	5,966	4,818
Oshkosh-Neenah, WI	8,726	3.8	50,840	184	5,363	945	392	439	1,566	1,811	7,138	455	392
Owensboro, KY	5,473	8.1	45,684	289	2,496	441	190	329	827	1,702	3,456	234	190
Oxnard-Thousand Oaks-Ventura, CA	56,728	6.3	67,422	26	21,609	3,693	1,550	4,767	10,925	10,794	31,618	1,856	1,550
Palm Bay-Melbourne-Titusville, FL	31,340	7.4	51,507	172	13,590	1,957	945	1,365	6,531	8,624	17,856	1,290	945
Panama City, FL	8,685	6.7	50,696	186	3,919	657	286	477	1,800	2,324	5,339	357	286
Parkersburg-Vienna, WV	4,229	3.3	47,706	252	1,668	320	136	480	582	1,370	2,604	187	136
Pensacola-Ferry Pass-Brent, FL	24,631	8.0	48,154	238	10,391	1,837	766	1,150	4,497	6,504	14,144	944	766
Peoria, IL	20,927	7.2	52,742	148	10,228	1,741	696	1,218	3,389	5,161	13,882	843	696
Philadelphia-Camden-Wilmington, PA-NJ-DE-MD	425,749	6.1	69,705	21	201,614	30,851	14,676	35,991	74,152	92,585	283,132	17,030	14,676
Camden, NJ Div 15,804	77,514	6.5	62,178	X	32,716	5,421	2,516	5,117	10,460	17,495	45,769	2,876	2,516
Montgomery-Bucks-Chester Counties, PA Div 33,874	171,052	5.1	86,016	X	77,863	10,912	5,487	8,941	39,026	27,072	103,203	6,355	5,487
Philadelphia, PA Div 37,964	134,745	7.4	62,811	X	67,347	10,657	4,957	19,789	17,580	38,328	102,750	5,820	4,957
Wilmington, DE-MD-NJ Div 48,864	42,437	5.2	58,341	X	23,689	3,861	1,717	2,144	7,086	9,690	31,411	1,979	1,717
Phoenix-Mesa-Chandler, AZ	262,363	10.1	51,851	163	136,171	18,010	9,533	18,618	44,938	55,696	182,333	11,712	9,533
Pine Bluff, AR	3,275	5.8	37,962	378	1,501	268	120	123	428	1,267	2,012	147	120
Pittsburgh, PA	147,041	6.6	63,675	39	70,751	11,293	5,241	12,179	22,840	37,226	99,463	6,144	5,241
Pittsfield, MA	7,707	7.4	61,872	49	3,070	559	227	532	1,431	2,429	4,388	262	227
Pocatello, ID	4,068	9.6	42,186	348	1,728	320	153	291	584	1,062	2,492	165	153
Portland-South Portland, ME	34,493	6.9	63,497	41	16,472	2,615	1,212	2,565	6,474	7,171	22,865	1,541	1,212
Portland-Vancouver-Hillsboro, OR-WA	157,150	7.0	62,603	44	81,743	11,542	6,586	11,638	29,789	29,123	111,510	6,949	6,586
Port St. Lucie, FL	29,282	5.7	58,649	78	7,631	1,130	534	1,231	9,832	6,921	10,526	826	534
Poughkeepsie-Newburgh-Middletown, NY	40,501	7.5	59,690	70	14,526	3,121	1,174	2,182	6,017	9,770	21,001	1,195	1,174
Prescott Valley-Prescott, AZ	10,688	10.2	44,490	316	3,059	507	227	685	2,633	3,922	4,477	408	227
Providence-Warwick, RI-MA	98,890	8.4	60,897	61	41,516	6,922	3,216	6,934	14,334	25,862	58,589	3,892	3,216
Provo-Orem, UT	30,767	9.2	46,393	278	14,920	2,045	1,064	2,961	5,301	4,228	20,990	1,242	1,064
Pueblo, CO	7,336	10.2	43,196	337	3,208	491	241	352	1,027	2,548	4,291	286	241
Punta Gorda, FL	8,880	7.5	45,606	290	2,338	339	165	429	2,495	3,309	3,270	322	165
Racine, WI	10,396	4.4	53,094	139	4,068	791	307	409	1,981	2,407	5,574	384	307
Raleigh-Cary, NC	86,479	6.8	60,884	62	43,848	5,588	3,030	5,567	14,956	12,604	58,033	3,615	3,030
Rapid City, SD	7,975	7.1	55,187	114	3,387	597	261	761	1,941	1,717	5,006	330	261

1. Based on the resident population estimated as of July 1 of the year shown.

Area name	Earnings, 2019 (cont.) — Percent by selected industries: Farm	Mining, quarrying, and extracting	Construction	Manufacturing	Information; professional, scientific, and technical serviecs	Retail trade	Finance, insurance, real estate, rental and leasing	Health care and social assistance	Government	Social Security beneficiaries, December 2019: Number	Rate[1]	Supplemental Security Income Recipients, December 2019	Housing units, 2020: Total	Percent change, 2010–2020
	75	76	77	78	79	80	81	82	83	84	85	86	87	88
Mobile, AL	0.4	0.2	8.2	14.8	8.5	6.4	7.1	12.9	14.5	99,110	231	15,575	193,056	0.4
Modesto, CA	7.0	0.0	6.4	11.6	4.0	7.4	4.9	17.7	17.6	91,355	165	19,915	183,898	0.3
Monroe, LA	1.9	D	6.0	9.7	D	8.8	6.4	17.1	15.8	43,025	210	9,544	92,886	0.6
Monroe, MI	1.6	D	6.0	17.8	D	6.5	3.4	8.1	12.2	36,910	238	2,473	66,249	0.5
Montgomery, AL	0.5	D	5.5	10.9	D	6.4	5.7	D	28.9	83,385	216	13,874	172,384	0.6
Morgantown, WV	0.1	1.0	5.3	7.3	7.8	5.2	3.3	D	26.7	23,820	169	2,618	65,077	0.0
Morristown, TN	0.2	D	D	26.2	D	8.1	3.3	D	13.9	38,705	269	4,464	64,495	0.8
Mount Vernon-Anacortes, WA	5.0	0.1	11.2	14.2	6.1	8.3	6.8	7.6	22.6	32,840	251	2,267	56,423	1.0
Muncie, IN	0.8	D	4.5	8.1	6.4	8.0	6.8	22.4	21.4	25,825	231	2,946	51,578	0.2
Muskegon, MI	0.7	0.2	6.3	24.6	4.3	11.1	4.2	16.5	14.2	43,545	247	5,973	74,881	0.3
Myrtle Beach-Conway-North Myrtle Beach, SC-NC	0.1	D	9.6	3.1	D	11.8	10.2	12.0	15.8	166,740	327	8,146	303,214	3.1
Napa, CA	3.4	D	7.6	20.5	6.6	5.0	6.0	9.8	15.7	28,025	206	2,026	55,318	-0.3
Naples-Marco Island, FL	0.9	0.0	11.7	3.7	12.3	8.6	11.9	14.0	8.5	104,050	270	4,079	233,658	1.9
Nashville-Davidson--Murfreesboro--Franklin, TN	0.0	0.1	8.3	7.0	14.2	5.8	D	15.5	8.9	328,235	163	29,829	859,245	3.1
New Bern, NC	1.2	0.1	4.0	8.2	5.1	6.3	D	9.6	45.7	32,800	268	3,065	59,383	1.2
New Haven-Milford, CT	0.1	0.0	6.5	8.5	9.9	6.0	6.3	16.3	14.0	169,565	196	21,088	370,802	0.3
New Orleans-Metairie, LA	0.0	7.2	5.8	7.5	D	5.4	7.4	D	14.0	246,130	195	42,328	575,959	0.6
New York-Newark-Jersey City, NY-NJ-PA	0.0	D	4.4	3.5	20.7	4.4	18.3	11.1	13.4	3,257,010	165	535,502	8,027,114	0.4
Nassau County-Suffolk County, NY Div 35,004	0.1	D	7.9	5.2	11.0	6.5	10.4	17.0	18.4	568,405	195	34,260	1,057,594	0.1
Newark, NJ-PA Div 35,084	0.1	0.4	5.0	7.0	18.9	4.7	11.4	10.1	14.0	368,905	162	44,192	900,710	0.3
New Brunswick-Lakewood, NJ Div 35,154	0.1	0.8	6.2	9.7	17.7	5.8	7.7	11.3	12.0	481,875	193	30,946	1,015,877	0.4
New York-Jersey City-White Plains, NY-NJ Div 35,614	0.0	0.1	3.5	1.8	22.9	3.8	22.1	10.3	12.7	1,837,825	152	426,104	5,052,933	0.5
Niles, MI	2.1	0.2	4.5	28.9	3.9	5.7	5.9	12.4	13.0	38,475	251	4,468	77,040	0.3
North Port-Sarasota-Bradenton, FL	0.8	D	10.5	5.5	11.9	8.8	9.4	16.0	9.6	259,790	302	10,855	471,309	2.0
Norwich-New London, CT	0.6	0.1	5.4	21.4	8.5	5.9	3.1	11.8	23.7	59,005	220	4,572	123,392	0.3
Ocala, FL	0.6	0.1	8.5	9.4	6.0	10.6	5.4	17.7	14.6	125,085	324	10,638	181,756	2.1
Ocean City, NJ	0.3	0.1	11.4	D	D	10.2	9.7	9.3	26.6	29,270	306	1,670	99,494	-0.1
Odessa, TX	0.0	20.0	13.0	6.5	4.1	6.8	5.0	5.2	12.1	20,895	130	3,088	67,692	1.8
Ogden-Clearfield, UT	0.6	D	8.8	14.6	D	6.6	7.0	9.6	23.6	91,060	129	6,710	240,345	2.3
Oklahoma City, OK	0.1	9.1	5.9	5.0	9.4	6.0	6.7	11.6	20.3	250,595	174	27,966	615,736	1.1
Olympia-Lacey-Tumwater, WA	1.1	0.0	7.2	2.5	7.7	6.2	5.4	12.8	37.8	64,335	216	5,451	123,026	1.0
Omaha-Council Bluffs, NE-IA	0.6	0.1	7.1	6.6	10.9	5.3	11.8	12.0	13.8	159,580	164	15,559	406,762	1.2
Orlando-Kissimmee-Sanford, FL	0.3	0.0	8.0	4.9	14.5	7.2	9.0	11.2	10.4	473,810	176	60,309	1,117,137	2.1
Oshkosh-Neenah, WI	0.5	D	8.7	26.2	7.6	4.5	6.5	9.7	11.8	36,415	212	2,674	76,553	0.6
Owensboro, KY	3.2	D	4.7	22.8	D	6.5	D	D	10.9	28,925	239	3,729	52,268	0.6
Oxnard-Thousand Oaks-Ventura, CA	3.8	0.6	6.1	8.5	11.2	6.7	9.0	9.7	17.2	148,010	176	15,555	294,681	0.4
Palm Bay-Melbourne-Titusville, FL	0.1	0.0	7.1	19.4	12.1	6.8	5.1	12.3	14.5	169,725	275	12,015	294,224	1.5
Panama City, FL	0.1	D	9.6	5.0	8.3	9.6	7.7	D	23.7	40,385	225	4,025	106,152	2.7
Parkersburg-Vienna, WV	-0.1	D	4.7	D	D	8.3	5.9	16.1	22.0	25,210	284	3,506	43,015	0.0
Pensacola-Ferry Pass-Brent, FL	0.2	0.1	6.6	4.4	8.1	7.1	10.1	14.8	25.9	115,750	224	12,618	226,078	1.9
Peoria, IL	2.5	D	6.0	20.1	D	5.8	D	16.0	12.1	90,415	227	7,962	183,594	0.0
Philadelphia-Camden-Wilmington, PA-NJ-DE-MD	0.2	D	D	D	D	5.0	10.9	13.7	12.3	1,166,680	187	174,605	2,603,131	0.5
Camden, NJ Div 15,804	0.3	D	6.5	8.3	D	7.8	8.4	15.3	17.4	253,820	196	26,902	517,382	0.4
Montgomery-Bucks-Chester Counties, PA Div 33,874	0.4	0.0	7.3	9.7	21.0	5.9	10.8	11.6	7.8	402,215	197	20,142	816,121	0.6
Philadelphia, PA Div 37,964	0.0	D	3.1	4.2	24.3	3.0	8.8	15.2	13.7	367,875	171	113,670	962,456	0.6
Wilmington, DE-MD-NJ Div 48,864	0.4	0.3	D	D	12.8	5.0	22.2	13.3	14.6	142,770	193	13,891	307,172	0.5
Phoenix-Mesa-Chandler, AZ	0.5	0.4	7.4	7.6	D	6.7	13.6	12.4	11.7	846,085	171	67,204	2,028,469	1.8
Pine Bluff, AR	3.0	D	3.4	19.0	D	5.6	D	14.0	29.1	21,030	243	4,752	38,602	0.2
Pittsburgh, PA	0.1	1.2	6.8	7.8	13.7	5.4	9.7	14.8	10.6	573,960	244	60,537	1,129,563	0.4
Pittsfield, MA	0.0	0.1	8.4	6.9	11.3	7.5	6.3	20.0	14.8	35,070	273	3,778	69,984	0.2
Pocatello, ID	6.0	D	5.3	9.8	D	6.8	D	13.9	21.6	17,550	182	2,147	38,690	2.0
Portland-South Portland, ME	0.1	D	7.0	D	11.9	6.6	10.6	15.0	14.5	128,630	231	9,238	284,007	1.0
Portland-Vancouver-Hillsboro, OR-WA	0.5	0.1	7.6	11.7	D	5.6	8.4	D	13.5	436,625	174	44,611	1,050,668	1.3
Port St. Lucie, FL	0.9	D	8.8	5.1	8.5	8.6	6.9	17.0	13.9	136,830	272	8,851	235,330	2.2
Poughkeepsie-Newburgh-Middletown, NY	0.3	0.2	6.6	7.8	8.3	7.5	4.3	16.0	25.3	131,845	188	11,931	270,878	0.6
Prescott Valley-Prescott, AZ	0.7	2.5	10.2	5.8	6.6	9.8	5.8	15.5	18.9	87,965	363	3,533	123,885	1.8
Providence-Warwick, RI-MA	0.1	D	6.7	D	9.1	6.8	8.9	14.3	16.2	354,305	211	50,184	729,133	0.2
Provo-Orem, UT	0.3	0.1	11.7	8.3	D	8.5	6.9	D	9.7	63,450	91	4,430	205,846	3.9
Pueblo, CO	0.5	D	8.9	8.4	7.5	8.4	3.8	20.6	20.1	38,455	227	6,018	72,976	1.2
Punta Gorda, FL	0.8	0.2	10.1	1.6	8.6	12.4	7.0	21.7	13.8	75,025	385	2,948	113,474	2.6
Racine, WI	0.4	0.1	6.0	30.7	4.5	6.5	4.9	12.3	13.6	44,330	225	5,729	84,638	0.1
Raleigh-Cary, NC	0.2	D	7.6	5.8	23.0	5.7	9.1	9.2	13.3	207,360	143	17,061	595,764	2.8
Rapid City, SD	1.6	0.1	8.4	3.8	D	7.4	8.2	19.7	21.9	34,485	243	2,180	62,994	2.1

1. Per 1,000 resident population estimated as of July 1 of the year shown.

Table C. Metropolitan Areas — **Housing, Labor Force, and Employment**

Area name	Occupied housing units, 2016-2020								Civilian labor force, 2021				Civilian employment[6], 2016-2020		
	Occupied units										Unemployment			Percent	
		Owner-occupied				Renter-occupied									
				Median owner cost as a percent of income											
	Total	Percent	Median value[1]	With a mortgage	Without a mortgage[2]	Median rent[3]	Median rent as a percent of income	Substandard units[4] (percent)	Total	Percent change 2020-2021	Total	Rate[5]	Total	Management, business, science, and arts	Construction, production, and maintenance occupations
	89	90	91	92	93	94	95	96	97	98	99	100	101	102	103
Mobile, AL	163,387	65.0	137,200	19.9	10.0	866	31.6	2.0	198,249	-1.8	9,344	4.7	181,159	33.8	26.6
Modesto, CA	174,826	58.7	314,100	23.8	11.5	1,210	31.2	7.4	239,538	-0.9	20,042	8.4	231,043	29.1	32.1
Monroe, LA	75,093	63.2	134,500	18.6	10.0	739	33.6	3.0	88,339	0.0	4,644	5.3	82,865	33.1	24.4
Monroe, MI	60,804	80.6	167,400	18.6	12.3	870	29.7	1.5	72,149	-2.7	4,340	6.0	70,351	32.1	32.3
Montgomery, AL	145,077	64.3	144,800	18.9	10.0	917	30.0	2.1	174,164	-1.1	7,271	4.2	162,730	37.6	23.0
Morgantown, WV	52,663	63.6	181,600	16.0	10.0	831	31.4	1.6	71,476	2.9	2,897	4.1	66,217	43.8	18.3
Morristown, TN	53,675	71.8	142,800	19.2	10.0	715	27.4	2.6	62,303	-0.1	2,538	4.1	60,714	27.4	32.0
Mount Vernon-Anacortes, WA	49,263	70.0	341,600	23.8	11.6	1,145	29.0	4.7	61,981	-2.5	3,904	6.3	57,197	34.2	29.9
Muncie, IN	46,632	64.5	96,600	17.1	10.6	725	32.3	1.7	51,868	-1.1	2,026	3.9	52,838	35.0	22.7
Muskegon, MI	66,064	76.2	126,400	18.9	11.7	780	29.0	2.2	75,304	-2.7	5,641	7.5	76,653	28.7	32.9
Myrtle Beach-Conway-North Myrtle Beach, SC-NC	195,635	76.0	195,700	22.7	10.7	976	30.9	1.5	202,930	3.5	10,785	5.3	204,727	30.5	21.0
Napa, CA	48,484	64.8	666,900	24.6	10.6	1,775	31.4	6.3	68,437	-0.5	4,132	6.0	70,752	37.6	20.9
Naples-Marco Island, FL	147,977	74.4	366,600	24.4	12.6	1,374	33.9	4.0	180,891	2.6	6,617	3.7	159,715	32.8	21.2
Nashville-Davidson--Murfreesboro--Franklin, TN	727,452	65.6	262,900	20.0	10.0	1,135	28.8	2.3	1,086,428	2.0	39,398	3.6	994,700	41.5	21.4
New Bern, NC	50,577	67.0	155,900	20.9	10.7	883	28.4	2.8	50,144	2.3	2,307	4.6	48,213	32.9	27.6
New Haven-Milford, CT	332,765	62.1	252,300	22.9	15.0	1,173	31.1	2.3	453,791	-1.9	29,734	6.6	429,416	43.1	18.8
New Orleans-Metairie, LA	486,509	63.7	205,500	21.5	10.1	1,017	33.5	2.2	584,853	-0.5	37,012	6.3	587,292	38.8	20.5
New York-Newark-Jersey City, NY-NJ-PA	7,065,536	51.6	465,400	24.9	14.9	1,483	31.0	6.3	9,690,334	-0.7	716,914	7.4	9,492,974	44.4	16.1
Nassau County-Suffolk County, NY Div 35,004	945,634	81.3	463,100	25.7	16.8	1,819	33.4	2.7	1,484,641	-0.3	66,998	4.5	1,437,582	44.2	16.2
Newark, NJ-PA Div 35,084	791,234	61.0	388,400	24.1	15.7	1,307	30.7	3.6	1,101,931	0.1	72,379	6.6	1,087,460	43.9	18.7
New Brunswick-Lakewood, NJ Div 35,154	875,381	72.6	361,900	23.8	15.3	1,490	30.6	2.9	1,261,095	1.1	71,094	5.6	1,164,733	46.7	16.8
New York-Jersey City-White Plains, NY-NJ Div 35,614	4,453,287	39.5	553,200	25.5	14.0	1,487	30.9	8.1	5,842,667	-1.3	506,443	8.7	5,803,199	44.1	15.5
Niles, MI	63,136	71.2	157,500	19.6	10.9	757	29.6	1.7	69,898	-3.5	4,055	5.8	71,218	35.2	25.8
North Port-Sarasota-Bradenton, FL	339,573	75.1	261,100	23.2	11.7	1,259	32.4	2.1	373,938	4.0	14,540	3.9	340,181	35.8	19.1
Norwich-New London, CT	109,616	67.1	246,800	21.8	13.9	1,144	28.5	1.7	129,504	-3.2	8,873	6.9	132,072	42.1	18.0
Ocala, FL	145,863	74.8	151,700	21.8	11.1	929	29.7	2.6	141,992	2.2	6,983	4.9	132,240	30.6	22.5
Ocean City, NJ	40,670	78.0	306,200	24.4	14.6	1,176	37.7	1.4	47,377	3.5	4,200	8.9	41,313	36.6	18.1
Odessa, TX	53,602	65.5	147,900	19.6	10.1	1,073	27.1	5.8	80,507	-2.0	6,691	8.3	75,343	23.8	37.4
Ogden-Clearfield, UT	213,554	76.6	284,500	19.9	10.0	1,038	25.7	2.6	343,621	1.5	8,935	2.6	325,895	38.4	24.2
Oklahoma City, OK	523,154	64.4	162,600	19.5	10.0	887	27.6	2.8	698,019	1.7	25,837	3.7	671,206	38.4	22.1
Olympia-Lacey-Tumwater, WA	112,323	66.0	315,600	22.4	10.5	1,275	31.1	2.1	145,252	-1.5	7,544	5.2	131,327	42.4	19.3
Omaha-Council Bluffs, NE-IA	364,079	65.8	181,200	19.4	12.0	952	27.4	2.1	499,367	0.3	14,916	3.0	487,173	41.8	20.2
Orlando-Kissimmee-Sanford, FL	893,257	61.9	242,100	22.5	10.8	1,273	32.6	3.2	1,330,880	0.3	67,401	5.1	1,260,022	37.6	18.4
Oshkosh-Neenah, WI	71,132	65.7	158,400	18.7	12.2	784	25.9	1.3	93,109	0.8	2,986	3.2	88,638	33.8	27.1
Owensboro, KY	47,340	68.5	139,300	19.3	10.0	795	26.4	2.8	54,166	1.0	2,347	4.3	53,770	32.3	30.7
Oxnard-Thousand Oaks-Ventura, CA	271,639	63.3	609,200	25.8	10.2	1,854	34.2	6.5	404,923	-1.1	24,928	6.2	411,295	38.4	22.4
Palm Bay-Melbourne-Titusville, FL	236,005	75.6	220,000	22.3	10.5	1,111	30.7	1.7	289,653	2.9	11,702	4.0	260,668	40.5	19.1
Panama City, FL	73,536	67.3	195,000	22.8	10.5	1,099	31.3	2.8	85,937	3.9	3,333	3.9	82,380	34.0	22.2
Parkersburg-Vienna, WV	37,746	72.8	123,800	17.5	10.0	710	30.1	1.6	38,810	1.2	2,104	5.4	37,728	35.7	22.4
Pensacola-Ferry Pass-Brent, FL	187,866	67.8	176,600	20.7	10.0	1,046	29.5	2.0	230,913	1.9	9,551	4.1	212,436	35.9	20.0
Peoria, IL	163,466	72.1	133,600	18.9	11.4	776	27.1	1.5	183,959	-0.7	10,961	6.0	183,678	37.8	22.5
Philadelphia-Camden-Wilmington, PA-NJ-DE-MD	2,311,452	67.2	259,500	21.4	13.1	1,172	30.0	2.1	3,155,083	-0.2	198,900	6.3	3,015,064	45.2	17.4
Camden, NJ Div 15,804	465,231	72.4	227,300	22.7	15.5	1,212	31.1	1.9	667,384	1.0	40,342	6.0	624,654	42.9	19.0
Montgomery-Bucks-Chester Counties, PA Div 33,874	752,362	74.7	341,400	20.8	12.1	1,310	28.3	1.5	1,084,499	0.1	52,789	4.9	1,040,989	50.3	15.5
Philadelphia, PA Div 37,964	822,721	56.9	189,700	21.4	13.4	1,089	31.1	2.8	1,017,049	-1.7	84,669	8.3	993,683	42.0	17.3
Wilmington, DE-MD-NJ Div 48,864	271,138	68.9	256,400	20.5	10.0	1,165	29.1	1.7	386,151	0.9	21,100	5.5	355,738	42.7	20.1
Phoenix-Mesa-Chandler, AZ	1,745,219	64.4	269,300	20.6	10.0	1,177	29.0	4.7	2,504,295	2.4	112,103	4.5	2,296,475	38.8	19.4
Pine Bluff, AR	33,398	65.2	85,700	17.9	10.2	726	28.5	2.6	32,965	-4.2	2,009	6.1	31,756	29.9	31.7
Pittsburgh, PA	1,017,860	69.6	159,800	18.4	11.6	850	26.9	1.1	1,177,522	-2.0	75,099	6.4	1,156,894	42.8	19.4
Pittsfield, MA	54,786	70.0	221,000	21.7	13.6	894	29.9	0.6	62,666	0.5	4,175	6.7	62,805	41.6	19.0
Pocatello, ID	34,362	68.3	165,800	19.2	10.0	702	26.8	2.6	46,894	0.9	1,680	3.6	40,230	36.6	23.4
Portland-South Portland, ME	226,327	72.1	273,100	21.5	12.9	1,115	28.7	1.8	293,838	1.1	12,251	4.2	292,949	43.6	19.4
Portland-Vancouver-Hillsboro, OR-WA	957,977	62.3	392,000	22.1	11.5	1,345	29.9	3.7	1,343,736	1.6	68,615	5.1	1,275,200	44.1	19.8
Port St. Lucie, FL	183,397	76.6	227,800	24.2	12.3	1,194	33.1	2.3	223,858	2.6	9,978	4.5	204,833	32.7	21.3
Poughkeepsie-Newburgh-Middletown, NY	240,523	68.0	284,300	23.9	14.5	1,267	32.2	3.1	326,064	-1.5	14,986	4.6	322,651	39.3	19.5
Prescott Valley-Prescott, AZ	101,245	72.6	273,300	23.6	11.1	982	29.0	2.3	105,108	1.6	4,337	4.1	90,114	32.4	20.8
Providence-Warwick, RI-MA	635,095	62.0	290,500	22.3	13.5	993	28.9	2.1	870,580	0.4	51,671	5.9	818,887	39.7	20.4
Provo-Orem, UT	175,377	68.1	334,500	21.0	10.0	1,095	28.8	4.9	338,177	4.9	7,852	2.3	297,424	42.5	18.0
Pueblo, CO	65,206	65.1	172,500	21.6	11.0	853	31.3	2.7	77,498	1.8	6,151	7.9	69,867	32.2	23.1
Punta Gorda, FL	79,789	81.6	209,500	23.7	12.7	1,042	35.0	1.6	73,248	2.6	3,188	4.4	64,605	30.6	20.4
Racine, WI	77,648	68.1	187,700	20.1	12.8	874	28.6	1.3	98,979	0.5	4,667	4.7	95,265	32.6	29.3
Raleigh-Cary, NC	507,613	65.8	268,900	18.6	10.0	1,162	27.5	2.2	728,561	4.0	29,428	4.0	708,378	50.0	15.4
Rapid City, SD	55,089	70.0	199,100	22.1	11.9	870	28.3	1.5	72,556	2.4	2,298	3.2	70,045	34.5	22.4

1. Specified owner-occupied units. 2. A value of 10.0 represents 10 percent or less; a value of 50.0 represents 50 percent or more. 3. Specified renter-occupied units. 4. Overcrowded or lacking complete plumbing facilities. 5. Percent of civilian labor force. 6. Civilian employed persons 16 years old and over.

Area name	Private nonfarm establishments, employment and payroll, 2019									Agriculture, 2017			
		Employment						Annual payroll		Farms			Farm producers whose primary occupation is farming (percent)
											Percent with:		
	Number of establish-ments	Total	Health care and social assistance	Manufactur-ing	Retail trade	Finance and insurance	Professional, scientific, and technical services	Total (mil dol)	Average per employee (dollars)	Number	Fewer than 50 acres	1000 acres or more	
	104	105	106	107	108	109	110	111	112	113	114	115	116
Mobile, AL	8,970	158,797	22,081	18,570	20,559	5,194	9,673	7,546	47,517	1,088	51.2	4.0	37.3
Modesto, CA	9,345	145,654	26,759	19,375	23,665	3,484	6,256	7,194	49,393	3,621	65.3	3.5	51.3
Monroe, LA	4,961	69,867	16,055	6,246	10,268	3,716	2,825	2,706	38,733	1,323	40.1	8.1	39.9
Monroe, MI	2,291	36,898	4,626	7,203	5,054	716	1,111	1,668	45,199	1,085	57.7	4.1	40.5
Montgomery, AL	7,708	132,419	22,072	16,813	17,388	4,917	6,686	5,606	42,337	1,996	35.3	7.6	37.5
Morgantown, WV	2,872	53,565	18,270	3,799	6,973	862	2,786	2,661	49,686	1,684	34.7	0.5	38.6
Morristown, TN	2,255	42,376	5,369	13,181	6,137	735	469	1,667	39,335	2,455	51.3	0.4	37.5
Mount Vernon-Anacortes, WA	3,540	45,128	7,887	6,841	7,170	1,361	1,884	2,188	48,491	1,041	75.7	1.6	40.8
Muncie, IN	2,356	40,708	10,619	3,740	5,801	2,154	1,275	1,592	39,108	546	52.9	8.1	45.0
Muskegon, MI	3,096	52,426	10,146	13,948	8,061	1,067	1,573	2,202	42,001	476	61.1	2.3	44.0
Myrtle Beach-Conway-North Myrtle Beach, SC-NC	12,113	146,093	18,222	4,473	31,000	3,674	4,563	4,877	33,382	998	46.1	5.6	45.9
Napa, CA	4,350	64,556	10,000	11,961	6,663	1,404	2,026	3,515	54,456	1,866	74.9	2.8	32.2
Naples-Marco Island, FL	12,935	140,574	21,640	4,233	24,335	4,189	5,468	6,423	45,693	322	77.3	7.1	36.2
Nashville-Davidson--Murfreesboro--Franklin, TN	45,786	903,548	143,650	76,544	93,387	48,872	48,820	48,674	53,870	13,501	47.7	1.4	34.0
New Bern, NC	2,541	31,767	7,370	3,586	5,284	700	1,730	1,315	41,398	522	38.9	9.6	47.2
New Haven-Milford, CT	19,176	344,442	77,498	27,467	41,872	12,142	15,124	18,588	53,965	686	81.9	0.3	38.3
New Orleans-Metairie, LA	31,418	501,058	80,355	25,327	60,840	20,309	31,251	24,859	49,613	1,376	72.6	3.6	34.6
New York-Newark-Jersey City, NY-NJ-PA	557,139	8,477,595	1,708,669	304,836	896,145	570,879	773,061	633,086	74,678	5,894	78.6	0.7	38.1
Nassau County-Suffolk County, NY Div 35,004	97,443	1,167,078	248,947	67,814	159,164	57,175	80,796	65,165	55,836	592	74.5	0.3	56.1
Newark, NJ-PA Div 35,084	57,064	892,941	150,748	52,642	98,297	47,938	91,214	63,339	70,933	3,114	76.2	0.6	33.0
New Brunswick-Lakewood, NJ Div 35,154	64,383	1,006,185	169,556	55,459	135,585	38,447	118,705	63,825	63,433	1,767	83.0	1.0	40.5
New York-Jersey City-White Plains, NY-NJ Div 35,614	338,249	5,411,391	1,139,418	128,921	503,099	427,319	482,346	440,757	81,450	421	83.8	0.5	37.6
Niles, MI	3,453	52,675	9,394	9,099	6,921	1,264	2,590	2,593	49,226	872	57.8	3.3	48.8
North Port-Sarasota-Bradenton, FL	24,240	261,427	45,529	15,368	45,870	8,335	15,255	11,410	43,646	1,045	67.7	6.7	44.6
Norwich-New London, CT	5,780	105,420	17,460	14,990	14,745	1,941	7,549	5,596	53,086	823	63.1	0.6	43.3
Ocala, FL	7,471	90,111	16,556	8,881	17,910	1,993	3,285	3,443	38,204	3,985	81.2	1.2	43.8
Ocean City, NJ	3,729	27,000	4,245	648	5,901	1,151	1,039	1,161	43,013	164	73.8	0.0	48.5
Odessa, TX	3,817	64,827	7,536	4,196	8,973	1,428	1,621	3,129	48,264	275	68.7	14.5	28.2
Ogden-Clearfield, UT	15,423	202,969	26,485	32,921	29,147	8,305	12,932	8,978	44,233	3,347	71.2	6.8	30.5
Oklahoma City, OK	36,308	531,984	84,602	28,935	73,411	25,020	32,647	24,421	45,905	10,023	41.5	5.9	33.9
Olympia-Lacey-Tumwater, WA	6,476	76,890	16,445	3,115	13,036	2,935	3,751	3,415	44,418	1,200	77.8	0.6	35.3
Omaha-Council Bluffs, NE-IA	24,176	437,479	69,764	34,290	54,213	46,289	23,380	22,628	51,725	5,843	38.9	13.3	43.7
Orlando-Kissimmee-Sanford, FL	70,454	1,159,102	140,344	41,534	153,148	46,334	80,386	52,991	45,717	3,120	77.0	3.2	40.8
Oshkosh-Neenah, WI	3,674	92,127	13,095	24,192	8,294	4,615	4,171	4,746	51,514	957	49.9	2.2	37.8
Owensboro, KY	2,587	46,444	8,168	8,574	5,598	2,938	935	2,056	44,272	1,679	46.8	6.6	37.2
Oxnard-Thousand Oaks-Ventura, CA	21,762	264,604	41,482	24,835	38,844	11,488	21,977	15,045	56,859	2,135	78.4	2.2	43.0
Palm Bay-Melbourne-Titusville, FL	14,646	191,581	31,839	15,688	28,940	5,178	21,218	9,155	47,787	522	81.0	3.1	43.5
Panama City, FL	4,813	60,002	10,383	3,458	11,754	1,590	3,714	2,404	40,059	190	69.5	4.2	23.2
Parkersburg-Vienna, WV	1,970	29,144	6,890	2,385	5,817	847	926	1,066	36,580	1,137	36.1	0.4	35.3
Pensacola-Ferry Pass-Brent, FL	10,107	145,311	27,194	5,374	22,067	11,785	9,399	6,229	42,865	1,348	67.8	2.5	37.5
Peoria, IL	8,677	159,511	33,705	15,332	19,703	6,211	6,647	8,599	53,906	4,468	32.5	10.6	43.5
Philadelphia-Camden-Wilmington, PA-NJ-DE-MD	150,631	2,775,565	558,663	174,161	311,781	188,350	213,354	169,046	60,905	6,506	67.9	1.8	45.3
Camden, NJ Div 15,804	28,100	490,944	96,647	35,120	70,761	24,684	32,339	25,553	52,049	1,692	73.5	1.5	46.0
Montgomery-Bucks-Chester Counties, PA Div 33,874	60,580	1,055,909	186,450	86,321	122,947	79,846	88,522	68,835	65,190	3,035	66.6	1.2	47.7
Philadelphia, PA Div 37,964	42,204	901,310	218,210	32,247	80,306	46,595	65,491	53,214	59,041	104	84.6	0.0	31.8
Wilmington, DE-MD-NJ Div 48,864	19,747	327,402	57,356	20,473	37,767	37,225	27,002	21,444	65,498	1,675	63.5	3.2	41.4
Phoenix-Mesa-Chandler, AZ	104,297	1,883,457	270,047	116,728	229,544	151,887	129,913	100,883	53,563	2,636	74.3	8.0	47.6
Pine Bluff, AR	1,473	21,533	4,583	4,740	3,076	767	290	871	40,440	1,010	33.7	13.7	46.8
Pittsburgh, PA	58,873	1,101,381	211,206	83,996	122,236	62,796	75,874	57,822	52,499	6,318	40.3	1.3	40.4
Pittsfield, MA	3,728	51,747	11,593	4,837	7,836	1,676	2,755	2,419	46,752	475	50.9	1.3	42.6
Pocatello, ID	2,379	28,058	5,859	3,146	4,723	2,642	956	1,078	38,413	1,052	45.5	17.5	40.4
Portland-South Portland, ME	18,322	246,685	48,438	24,987	34,369	16,555	14,032	12,670	51,362	1,612	61.0	0.7	44.3
Portland-Vancouver-Hillsboro, OR-WA	71,060	1,094,892	161,036	115,742	124,305	48,898	77,162	65,005	59,371	11,755	83.4	0.5	32.5
Port St. Lucie, FL	12,215	130,765	27,250	6,632	22,856	3,180	5,584	5,168	39,521	1,009	69.4	8.9	44.3
Poughkeepsie-Newburgh-Middletown, NY	17,126	219,386	44,922	16,138	36,556	5,441	11,995	10,263	46,779	1,241	48.3	2.7	49.1
Prescott Valley-Prescott, AZ	6,106	61,828	13,577	3,231	10,398	1,154	2,030	2,407	38,935	850	73.2	8.5	46.2
Providence-Warwick, RI-MA	41,066	644,260	129,548	66,606	83,496	35,712	27,096	32,137	49,882	1,731	73.8	0.2	43.5
Provo-Orem, UT	15,780	243,705	28,805	18,226	28,568	7,124	21,182	12,094	49,624	2,881	76.7	3.2	23.9
Pueblo, CO	3,178	53,924	13,644	5,025	8,395	1,171	2,377	2,240	41,541	839	41.7	14.2	37.6
Punta Gorda, FL	4,125	39,684	8,793	412	9,876	1,053	1,528	1,496	37,709	306	66.3	6.2	37.2
Racine, WI	4,033	68,497	11,544	16,532	9,024	1,977	1,964	3,379	49,334	611	51.7	3.8	42.6
Raleigh-Cary, NC	35,617	564,375	74,796	26,736	70,870	30,213	64,843	32,400	57,408	2,292	53.5	3.3	38.3
Rapid City, SD	4,525	54,344	12,090	2,804	8,891	2,429	2,095	2,410	44,349	1,491	21.8	37.3	49.7

Area name	Agriculture, 2017 (cont.)															
	Land in farms					Value of land and buildings (dollars)		Value of machinery and equipmnet, average per farm (dollars)	Value of products sold:				Organic farms (number)	Farms with internet access (percent)	Government payments	
	Acreage (1,000)	Percent change, 2012–2017	Acres: Average size of farm	Acres: Total irrigated (1,000)	Acres: Total cropland (1,000)	Average per farm	Average per acre		Total (mil dol)	Average per farm (acres)	Percent from: Crops	Percent from: Livestock and poultry products			Total ($1,000)	Percent of farms
	117	118	119	120	121	122	123	124	125	126	127	128	129	130	131	132
Mobile, AL	215	16.4	197.0	3.1	60.0	636,089	3,226	79,393	121.8	111,994	72.0	28.0	0	72.2	3,276	23.0
Modesto, CA	723	-5.9	200.0	380.6	404.7	3,116,617	15,619	182,695	2,526.3	697,690	53.0	47.0	35	82.2	5,006	7.5
Monroe, LA	425	-2.2	321.0	160.7	264.5	1,090,082	3,393	139,435	295.9	223,632	51.1	48.9	3	74.9	12,544	29.2
Monroe, MI	210	-2.2	193.0	4.3	194.1	1,190,516	6,156	150,143	174.5	160,833	96.2	3.8	0	83.5	4,555	43.7
Montgomery, AL	643	0.5	322.0	10.3	175.2	769,306	2,388	88,952	176.8	88,562	32.3	67.7	3	70.8	7,305	38.3
Morgantown, WV	205	-6.2	122.0	0.1	66.8	400,195	3,287	59,253	21.2	12,577	38.0	62.0	6	69.3	377	6.2
Morristown, TN	226	-5.6	92.0	0.7	87.3	433,554	4,708	62,859	59.3	24,167	33.5	66.5	7	66.4	3,313	27.9
Mount Vernon-Anacortes, WA	98	-8.3	94.0	23.5	65.7	950,360	10,130	129,653	287.1	275,789	66.6	33.4	61	83.0	407	7.8
Muncie, IN	168	-4.3	307.0	0.6	157.6	2,038,397	6,633	188,658	92.2	168,773	92.9	7.1	0	83.5	4,044	56.4
Muskegon, MI	63	-14.9	133.0	3.6	45.8	852,880	6,425	112,540	74.7	156,884	58.9	41.1	5	82.8	173	11.1
Myrtle Beach-Conway-North Myrtle Beach, SC-NC	215	-3.5	216.0	2.8	140.3	946,291	4,388	125,160	133.9	134,187	64.9	35.1	8	73.8	2,625	32.1
Napa, CA	256	1.0	137.0	60.9	67.7	6,052,361	44,154	94,303	573.2	307,198	97.7	2.3	117	84.7	924	2.1
Naples-Marco Island, FL	148	20.1	461.0	37.3	82.7	2,189,705	4,749	121,438	189.7	588,994	96.8	3.2	2	83.5	141	5.3
Nashville-Davidson--Murfreesboro--Franklin, TN	1,707	-2.3	126.0	3.9	692.4	617,818	4,886	69,490	471.8	34,942	62.0	38.0	24	75.7	13,308	23.3
New Bern, NC	190	7.6	365.0	4.8	148.5	1,426,209	3,913	210,902	308.6	591,193	28.9	71.1	4	82.2	3,579	50.2
New Haven-Milford, CT	27	-36.3	39.0	1.3	11.4	922,401	23,490	67,525	111.6	162,720	95.9	4.1	26	78.4	323	5.2
New Orleans-Metairie, LA	263	14.5	191.0	0.5	85.0	690,802	3,613	78,734	61.3	44,569	74.0	26.0	2	76.3	68	1.2
New York-Newark-Jersey City, NY-NJ-PA	349	-1.7	59.0	23.3	189.6	917,081	15,483	74,162	545.8	92,603	86.9	13.1	114	82.4	1,643	4.2
Nassau County-Suffolk County, NY Div 35,004	31	-20.0	52.0	12.2	23.3	646,571	12,371	146,890	225.6	381,044	90.4	9.6	32	84.5	76	2.0
Newark, NJ-PA Div 35,084	201	0.3	64.0	3.3	99.4	855,845	13,290	61,297	136.3	43,757	83.1	16.9	51	82.4	894	4.7
New Brunswick-Lakewood, NJ Div 35,154	100	0.7	56.0	7.2	59.3	1,155,886	20,508	77,000	163.8	92,671	85.1	14.9	21	80.4	665	4.9
New York-Jersey City-White Plains, NY-NJ Div 35,614	18	2.9	43.0	0.5	7.7	748,109	17,469	55,131	20.2	48,024	87.9	12.1	10	88.1	8	1.4
Niles, MI	145	-7.6	166.0	20.0	123.5	1,068,560	6,445	142,166	171.3	196,501	91.4	8.6	15	76.4	2,594	20.6
North Port-Sarasota-Bradenton, FL	264	-1.0	252.0	61.8	82.2	2,060,967	8,164	101,807	383.2	366,712	88.5	11.5	4	76.4	499	4.0
Norwich-New London, CT	60	-7.7	73.0	0.6	23.9	837,723	11,467	67,605	135.8	164,989	55.5	44.5	22	88.0	267	6.1
Ocala, FL	331	2.9	83.0	13.2	79.3	922,892	11,114	47,624	145.5	36,501	41.1	58.9	5	82.3	813	1.4
Ocean City, NJ	8	10.7	50.0	1.4	3.8	722,280	14,561	59,085	9.8	59,988	89.2	10.8	0	81.1	0	1.2
Odessa, TX	558	30.1	2,029.0	0.9	1.9	2,350,073	1,158	63,273	3.4	12,298	7.6	92.4	0	75.6	57	1.5
Ogden-Clearfield, UT	1,610	2.4	481.0	150.0	360.9	1,125,771	2,341	91,422	224.4	67,057	46.5	53.5	19	78.8	9,132	14.2
Oklahoma City, OK	2,509	1.7	250.0	23.5	899.4	657,494	2,627	81,754	459.5	45,842	23.8	76.2	8	76.1	13,598	18.3
Olympia-Lacey-Tumwater, WA	62	-18.8	52.0	6.4	22.1	616,274	11,880	58,420	176.1	146,742	32.0	68.0	34	86.8	107	1.9
Omaha-Council Bluffs, NE-IA	2,363	-0.4	404.0	245.9	2,123.4	2,524,750	6,243	228,075	1,509.8	258,390	75.9	24.1	37	82.4	39,142	60.7
Orlando-Kissimmee-Sanford, FL	853	0.0	273.0	65.4	106.4	1,508,463	5,516	67,498	554.5	177,714	87.4	12.6	31	79.6	2,279	5.7
Oshkosh-Neenah, WI	162	4.2	169.0	0.5	136.2	1,180,421	6,971	140,933	122.2	127,711	40.0	60.0	7	76.6	3,326	53.1
Owensboro, KY	415	0.3	247.0	10.9	320.3	1,135,275	4,593	152,676	388.3	231,278	47.6	52.4	0	76.4	7,178	46.9
Oxnard-Thousand Oaks-Ventura, CA	260	-7.5	122.0	98.1	123.4	3,106,351	25,498	127,982	1,633.3	765,008	99.2	0.8	128	80.6	830	2.5
Palm Bay-Melbourne-Titusville, FL	157	6.9	300.0	10.5	21.0	1,507,864	5,027	62,406	59.0	112,977	76.9	23.1	1	78.7	186	3.6
Panama City, FL	74	601.5	387.0	1.7	4.6	794,316	2,051	41,295	2.9	15,274	69.6	30.4	0	73.2	23	3.2
Parkersburg-Vienna, WV	131	4.4	116.0	0.0	34.3	329,622	2,852	45,212	8.6	7,532	40.6	59.4	0	72.1	307	3.4
Pensacola-Ferry Pass-Brent, FL	144	-16.4	107.0	3.2	85.9	609,257	5,707	67,962	65.5	48,565	89.9	10.1	4	78.1	6,506	17.7
Peoria, IL	1,617	-1.6	362.0	47.0	1,412.8	2,823,086	7,799	212,486	1,038.7	232,469	84.1	15.9	53	78.0	22,120	67.1
Philadelphia-Camden-Wilmington, PA-NJ-DE-MD	656	0.4	101.0	50.1	466.6	1,077,298	10,688	111,066	1,358.6	208,822	79.0	21.0	91	79.9	9,299	12.0
Camden, NJ Div 15,804	155	5.9	92.0	23.5	90.4	1,032,028	11,270	96,392	223.9	132,345	93.2	6.8	12	81.1	2,024	8.5
Montgomery-Bucks-Chester Counties, PA Div 33,874	259	-0.2	85.0	2.8	186.2	1,038,608	12,186	105,618	823.6	271,367	79.2	20.8	63	78.8	2,589	9.0
Philadelphia, PA Div 37,964	3	-46.7	26.0	0.1	0.9	490,433	19,110	47,933	9.8	94,442	97.2	2.8	2	95.2	0	0.0
Wilmington, DE-MD-NJ Div 48,864	239	-1.3	143.0	23.8	189.2	1,229,570	8,600	139,681	301.3	179,851	67.3	32.7	14	79.6	4,686	21.8
Phoenix-Mesa-Chandler, AZ	1,595	-3.4	605.0	412.4	551.3	2,837,548	4,689	203,720	2,071.1	785,687	37.8	62.2	22	85.1	9,253	12.7
Pine Bluff, AR	533	2.7	527.0	348.4	421.5	1,715,145	3,252	258,302	477.5	472,780	49.9	50.1	0	67.1	21,923	47.0
Pittsburgh, PA	790	-3.3	125.0	2.8	448.9	681,802	5,450	94,414	258.8	40,969	60.1	39.9	42	74.7	4,448	14.4
Pittsfield, MA	59	-4.9	123.0	0.3	19.1	943,836	7,644	72,648	23.5	49,453	42.8	57.2	16	85.5	447	7.8
Pocatello, ID	801	5.1	762.0	187.7	562.9	1,725,773	2,265	192,883	273.2	259,742	85.0	15.0	4	82.9	16,223	41.1
Portland-South Portland, ME	129	-12.6	80.0	2.6	38.8	451,159	5,649	59,199	54.2	33,620	72.3	27.7	106	86.8	1,496	5.6
Portland-Vancouver-Hillsboro, OR-WA	597	-7.3	51.0	80.8	327.7	739,269	14,558	65,709	1,020.1	86,784	83.2	16.8	162	87.1	3,852	4.1
Port St. Lucie, FL	380	13.5	376.0	77.0	118.3	2,008,239	5,337	96,887	252.2	249,942	90.2	9.8	5	76.3	1,434	8.4
Poughkeepsie-Newburgh-Middletown, NY	183	-8.7	148.0	3.2	89.3	1,196,421	8,107	98,721	131.8	106,223	72.1	27.9	32	84.9	705	9.7
Prescott Valley-Prescott, AZ	822	-0.3	967.0	7.5	8.0	1,596,867	1,651	63,906	35.7	42,036	40.1	59.9	4	86.4	115	1.5
Providence-Warwick, RI-MA	89	20.6	51.0	4.9	30.7	877,440	17,087	65,103	93.0	53,738	73.7	26.3	40	80.6	1,437	9.2
Provo-Orem, UT	568	-3.0	197.0	96.4	174.7	1,042,883	5,286	79,177	256.3	88,948	43.1	56.9	6	81.7	2,612	8.6
Pueblo, CO	896	0.0	1,067.0	18.1	72.0	1,097,156	1,028	75,875	52.0	62,033	41.0	59.0	7	77.5	2,117	13.9
Punta Gorda, FL	113	-48.1	368.0	11.6	18.5	2,644,176	7,176	66,706	43.9	143,402	91.8	8.2	2	73.9	329	5.2
Racine, WI	127	15.9	209.0	1.6	109.8	1,602,954	7,682	181,939	86.4	141,475	74.8	25.2	1	82.3	2,502	44.5
Raleigh-Cary, NC	368	-7.0	161.0	5.1	218.9	938,272	5,840	103,395	389.9	170,103	61.2	38.8	21	77.6	3,070	23.5
Rapid City, SD	3,145	1.2	2,110.0	16.0	602.0	2,088,998	990	150,158	159.6	107,057	17.7	82.3	3	80.9	17,614	48.1

Area name	Water use, 2015		Wholesale Trade[1], 2017				Retail Trade[2], 2017				Real estate and rental and leasing,[2] 2017			
	Public supply water withdrawn (mil gal/ day)	Public supply gallons withdrawn per person per day	Number of establish- ments	Number of employees	Sales (mil dol)	Average payroll (mil dol)	Number of establish- ments	Number of employees	Sales (mil dol)	Average payroll (mil dol)	Number of establish- ments	Number of employees	Sales (mil dol)	Average payroll (mil dol)
	133	134	135	136	137	138	139	140	141	142	143	144	145	146
Mobile, AL	68.9	159.4	515	6,179	3,524.8	321.7	1,525	20,598	5,678.4	533.3	438	2,424	565.7	98.4
Modesto, CA	80.5	149.5	406	6,921	6,198.1	401.0	1,462	24,398	7,486.4	680.1	481	2,047	505.1	85.9
Monroe, LA	32.1	155.9	210	2,458	1,920.9	116.4	813	10,905	2,782.3	265.7	254	1,380	279.2	51.6
Monroe, MI	9.3	62.0	D	D	D	D	358	5,252	1,705.6	133.1	70	273	49.8	8.7
Montgomery, AL	44.8	119.8	298	5,857	4,544.7	322.1	1,319	18,404	4,965.9	460.5	366	1,825	390.6	76.0
Morgantown, WV	13.1	94.7	66	428	392.7	17.6	465	7,011	1,971.6	165.3	161	711	139.0	24.4
Morristown, TN	14.5	103.7	75	1,051	895.4	48.1	453	6,404	1,870.6	163.7	87	219	46.9	6.4
Mount Vernon-Anacortes, WA	20.3	166.7	119	1,463	832.8	76.5	538	7,589	2,272.1	235.1	171	476	120.7	16.6
Muncie, IN	9.6	82.0	89	829	520.8	35.7	430	5,983	1,662.1	144.3	104	430	91.5	16.7
Muskegon, MI	16.1	93.1	D	D	D	62.3	564	7,930	2,191.2	195.3	87	599	78.3	18.8
Myrtle Beach-Conway-North Myrtle Beach, SC-NC	52.9	122.5	305	3,032	1,324.8	136.7	2,153	29,668	8,016.6	726.8	865	5,501	892.1	189.6
Napa, CA	15.3	107.3	D	D	D	D	497	6,742	2,005.4	219.8	219	1,041	256.2	50.0
Naples-Marco Island, FL	51.8	145.0	309	3,273	3,862.1	269.5	1,499	22,521	7,302.9	693.1	1,189	3,758	863.4	184.6
Nashville-Davidson--Murfreesboro--Franklin, TN	243.2	134.7	1,827	33,178	46,467.0	2,147.2	6,098	91,958	27,714.6	2,583.6	2,131	13,835	5,272.6	766.4
New Bern, NC	12.7	100.8	76	808	1,038.0	37.1	441	5,301	1,464.2	133.0	131	373	58.6	11.3
New Haven-Milford, CT	54.5	63.4	880	16,151	12,689.6	1,516.0	2,870	42,459	12,606.7	1,225.2	753	4,825	1,990.9	210.9
New Orleans-Metairie, LA	261.2	206.8	1,362	18,990	22,368.7	1,122.3	4,483	64,251	17,973.8	1,690.2	1,483	8,358	2,132.0	383.6
New York-Newark-Jersey City, NY-NJ-PA	1,497.3	76.7	31,188	425,473	546,830.9	33,671.9	76,902	923,874	304,381.5	28,460.3	35,261	207,059	80,569.3	12,715.6
Nassau County-Suffolk County, NY Div 35,004	440.6	153.9	5,427	68,645	62,656.8	4,478.8	12,561	162,294	54,642.3	5,051.1	4,455	18,871	6,496.7	1,074.5
Newark, NJ-PA Div 35,084	391.7	179.8	2,919	54,276	63,713.9	6,386.2	7,424	100,823	32,991.9	3,057.2	2,436	17,521	6,798.3	1,023.4
New Brunswick-Lakewood, NJ Div 35,154	165.4	69.2	3,192	62,770	78,824.9	4,999.1	8,287	131,760	42,601.5	3,814.3	2,560	15,990	5,422.4	884.7
New York-Jersey City-White Plains, NY-NJ Div 35,614	499.6	41.4	19,650	239,782	341,635.3	17,807.7	48,630	528,997	174,145.8	16,537.7	25,810	154,677	61,851.9	9,733.0
Niles, MI	12.4	80.3	D	D	D	78.1	553	7,053	1,781.5	171.4	156	656	277.4	23.3
North Port-Sarasota-Bradenton, FL	63.0	81.9	760	7,355	4,958.3	398.9	3,054	43,108	12,819.2	1,188.8	1,663	5,459	1,257.7	233.8
Norwich-New London, CT	8.1	29.8	149	2,638	1,679.6	176.0	1,015	15,140	4,030.8	422.3	228	818	236.0	32.3
Ocala, FL	27.7	80.7	280	3,742	2,243.1	188.1	1,152	16,765	5,080.9	454.7	416	1,614	301.9	47.7
Ocean City, NJ	13.6	143.7	D	D	D	D	639	7,307	1,935.5	182.6	202	779	217.0	32.5
Odessa, TX	0.6	4.0	301	4,598	3,087.9	298.2	460	8,193	3,004.4	270.5	188	2,007	788.5	126.2
Ogden-Clearfield, UT	91.5	142.3	427	5,499	5,785.4	276.1	1,896	28,995	8,629.4	775.4	912	2,350	506.5	84.2
Oklahoma City, OK	139.3	102.6	1,498	20,990	21,106.3	1,204.7	4,425	67,362	20,783.3	1,845.8	2,022	9,686	2,408.4	461.7
Olympia-Lacey-Tumwater, WA	22.6	83.8	176	1,902	1,320.6	102.1	796	13,008	3,958.8	386.6	340	1,133	302.6	43.6
Omaha-Council Bluffs, NE-IA	179.4	196.0	1,048	15,694	19,179.8	1,041.2	2,648	53,252	15,986.5	1,444.1	1,296	7,543	1,621.1	348.3
Orlando-Kissimmee-Sanford, FL	371.0	155.4	2,688	35,041	40,665.2	2,278.9	8,756	145,107	45,062.7	3,814.5	4,807	34,984	11,083.6	1,796.1
Oshkosh-Neenah, WI	14.0	82.5	D	D	D	114.4	487	8,865	2,335.2	214.8	129	752	198.2	29.0
Owensboro, KY	14.6	124.1	97	1,267	1,008.3	65.5	448	5,876	1,618.5	141.3	97	549	90.2	15.7
Oxnard-Thousand Oaks-Ventura, CA	130.0	152.9	1,028	15,216	24,894.7	1,221.6	2,569	40,494	13,115.6	1,238.4	1,204	4,751	1,300.4	235.6
Palm Bay-Melbourne-Titusville, FL	31.5	55.4	454	3,798	2,494.8	207.9	2,026	29,154	7,884.4	747.1	860	2,623	512.5	92.3
Panama City, FL	47.6	262.2	155	1,728	746.4	81.2	826	11,802	3,219.3	305.2	313	1,138	272.3	37.7
Parkersburg-Vienna, WV	8.0	86.3	D	D	D	D	360	5,973	1,559.5	146.3	D	D	D	D
Pensacola-Ferry Pass-Brent, FL	52.5	109.8	337	3,078	1,974.5	156.9	1,454	21,088	6,042.6	549.9	576	2,120	504.8	74.0
Peoria, IL	50.8	122.7	329	5,263	3,644.3	321.5	1,316	21,262	5,542.0	538.7	314	1,452	259.6	54.2
Philadelphia-Camden-Wilmington, PA-NJ-DE-MD	657.4	108.3	5,833	101,779	100,537.2	7,216.1	19,413	312,616	98,646.8	8,549.0	6,066	41,640	16,396.5	2,469.1
Camden, NJ Div 15,804	114.6	91.4	1,292	28,268	31,164.3	1,793.7	3,950	67,733	19,847.0	1,797.2	1,028	8,034	2,422.4	465.7
Montgomery-Bucks-Chester Counties, PA Div 33,874	204.1	104.0	2,986	50,054	46,884.2	3,837.7	6,900	124,621	43,813.6	3,667.3	2,318	15,325	5,257.9	960.2
Philadelphia, PA Div 37,964	270.3	126.8	1,519	23,457	20,795.2	1,584.8	6,185	79,310	22,559.1	1,996.8	1,769	13,667	3,984.8	811.4
Wilmington, DE-MD-NJ Div 48,864	68.5	94.6	36	D	1,693.4	D	2,378	40,952	12,427.2	1,087.7	951	4,614	4,731.3	231.8
Phoenix-Mesa-Chandler, AZ	839.8	183.6	4,065	65,234	62,385.0	4,121.9	11,378	224,360	76,911.2	6,833.3	7,158	37,383	10,784.1	1,874.9
Pine Bluff, AR	12.9	137.6	57	465	314.3	21.8	326	3,399	859.8	82.5	56	202	34.5	6.5
Pittsburgh, PA	324.4	137.9	2,390	36,595	42,436.1	2,259.8	7,919	126,605	71,904.9	3,317.9	2,163	14,204	3,959.2	655.7
Pittsfield, MA	14.3	112.1	98	1,276	491.8	66.1	653	8,151	2,049.7	221.0	116	496	92.7	18.7
Pocatello, ID	19.1	208.6	96	1,079	817.7	46.9	338	4,776	1,322.1	117.7	108	270	57.0	7.6
Portland-South Portland, ME	42.1	80.0	590	6,995	6,307.0	404.8	2,451	34,119	10,265.6	962.7	942	3,733	799.0	171.2
Portland-Vancouver-Hillsboro, OR-WA	260.3	108.9	3,013	52,355	50,638.4	3,554.0	7,352	120,923	36,653.3	3,649.8	4,201	21,326	5,043.9	996.7
Port St. Lucie, FL	45.0	98.9	381	2,848	1,432.5	140.8	1,514	22,235	6,884.6	607.2	662	3,122	670.2	112.0
Poughkeepsie-Newburgh-Middletown, NY	52.0	77.2	661	9,064	9,623.4	483.9	2,661	38,850	10,933.3	1,013.9	712	3,015	771.5	125.4
Prescott Valley-Prescott, AZ	21.1	95.1	141	1,447	952.8	72.9	815	10,820	2,952.7	294.1	414	1,075	245.0	42.3
Providence-Warwick, RI-MA	124.1	76.9	1,617	29,125	26,968.7	1,832.2	5,870	82,444	23,459.9	2,387.6	1,563	7,413	1,790.9	323.6
Provo-Orem, UT	132.3	225.8	435	7,460	4,075.9	451.1	1,948	27,277	8,080.2	750.3	D	D	D	D
Pueblo, CO	41.3	252.4	94	1,037	684.5	57.8	506	8,124	2,144.4	214.1	148	658	116.3	19.4
Punta Gorda, FL	7.5	43.4	102	1,037	578.8	53.3	599	9,574	2,757.2	254.8	304	963	208.8	29.7
Racine, WI	19.1	98.1	179	2,684	2,227.3	150.4	559	9,038	2,409.5	234.2	117	545	98.9	18.9
Raleigh-Cary, NC	73.4	57.6	1,318	24,121	31,532.3	1,884.1	4,194	68,770	20,699.1	1,828.2	1,888	9,555	2,707.5	528.6
Rapid City, SD	12.0	88.7	143	1,649	1,008.4	86.2	668	9,862	3,009.8	273.0	256	750	190.6	24.9

1. Merchant wholesalers, except manufacturers' sales branches and offices. 2. Employer establishments.

Table C. Metropolitan Areas — **Professional Services, Manufacturing, and Accommodation and Food Services**

Area name	Professional, scientific, and technical services, 2017				Manufacturing, 2017				Accommodation and food services, 2017			
	Number of establish-ments	Number of employees	Sales (mil dol)	Average payroll (mil dol)	Number of establish-ments	Number of employees	Receipts (mil dol)	Annual payroll (mil dol)	Number of establish-ments	Number of employees	Receipts (mil dol)	Annual payroll (mil dol)
	147	148	149	150	151	152	153	154	155	156	157	158
Mobile, AL	10	29	7.4	2.2	337	19,403	16,284.0	1,343.2	705	15,002	791.9	218.0
Modesto, CA	682	5,805	761.7	314.5	406	19,982	12,685.7	1,202.1	926	16,562	971.6	273.6
Monroe, LA	463	2,813	425.1	144.6	D	D	D	323.3	30	D	24.0	D
Monroe, MI	D	D	D	D	127	6,664	2,660.6	337.7	275	4,478	216.9	60.9
Montgomery, AL	155	717	121.8	32.7	260	17,272	14,003.8	939.7	620	14,446	1,316.5	245.5
Morgantown, WV	D	D	D	D	74	4,571	3,199.2	356.5	365	7,166	327.8	96.5
Morristown, TN	40	130	14.9	4.3	148	12,899	5,004.6	579.3	213	3,821	185.2	52.9
Mount Vernon-Anacortes, WA	D	D	D	D	189	6,711	11,187.8	468.7	352	5,518	411.7	125.3
Muncie, IN	D	D	D	D	118	4,234	1,723.0	219.5	220	5,143	225.4	66.9
Muskegon, MI	D	D	D	D	267	13,190	4,003.7	712.1	351	6,148	288.0	86.0
Myrtle Beach-Conway-North Myrtle Beach, SC-NC	D	D	D	D	223	4,042	1,082.1	206.8	1,632	35,235	2,556.2	666.4
Napa, CA	430	2,044	363.0	130.9	492	13,127	5,873.9	890.0	408	11,705	1,068.5	339.4
Naples-Marco Island, FL	1,602	5,768	1,103.6	381.5	209	3,397	797.0	173.7	881	24,719	1,957.8	527.6
Nashville-Davidson--Murfreesboro--Franklin, TN	3,639	43,373	7,909.5	3,306.1	1,512	73,441	42,845.7	3,967.3	4,207	98,116	6,648.0	1,854.8
New Bern, NC	23	64	7.7	2.3	84	3,526	1,448.4	184.2	239	4,258	235.6	62.9
New Haven-Milford, CT	1,814	14,470	2,620.3	1,218.0	1,048	29,004	10,764.2	1,792.6	2,047	29,719	1,854.2	534.1
New Orleans-Metairie, LA	147	1,723	239.9	108.1	D	25,628	D	2,117.0	3,572	80,244	6,016.3	1,643.3
New York-Newark-Jersey City, NY-NJ-PA	63,412	717,551	192,112.8	70,035.3	14,477	310,527	124,174.4	18,682.7	52,169	767,183	66,206.2	19,133.1
Nassau County-Suffolk County, NY Div 35,004	12,754	76,397	14,410.7	5,301.1	2,842	65,194	21,718.2	3,828.9	7,718	109,408	8,003.4	2,333.7
Newark, NJ-PA Div 35,084	6,203	86,984	17,858.9	8,652.1	1,984	50,572	27,074.7	3,202.3	4,985	71,941	5,302.9	1,448.3
New Brunswick-Lakewood, NJ Div 35,154	8,253	104,529	21,457.8	9,515.9	1,633	56,281	23,217.2	3,837.1	5,712	78,013	5,645.8	1,489.5
New York-Jersey City-White Plains, NY-NJ Div 35,614	36,202	449,641	138,385.4	46,566.2	8,018	138,480	52,164.2	7,814.3	33,754	507,821	47,254.0	13,861.6
Niles, MI	D	D	D	D	281	8,819	2,277.9	455.5	379	6,404	331.2	101.2
North Port-Sarasota-Bradenton, FL	D	D	D	D	628	14,185	3,777.6	756.7	1,636	32,440	1,917.9	578.5
Norwich-New London, CT	527	8,313	973.2	972.2	175	14,024	6,228.6	1,105.9	750	25,852	2,816.6	722.2
Ocala, FL	D	D	D	D	188	7,109	3,330.8	337.8	516	9,478	531.8	146.7
Ocean City, NJ	D	D	D	D	76	592	110.1	26.9	931	6,065	757.0	206.6
Odessa, TX	D	D	D	D	224	4,128	1,379.8	243.9	284	6,669	462.1	116.5
Ogden-Clearfield, UT	98	322	42.5	14.2	628	31,145	14,543.3	1,853.1	994	19,054	954.7	268.8
Oklahoma City, OK	558	1,841	279.6	94.1	1,025	28,441	10,608.4	1,398.6	3,174	63,783	3,497.1	968.8
Olympia-Lacey-Tumwater, WA	638	4,426	594.6	260.8	162	2,779	1,029.7	136.7	561	9,634	574.5	175.9
Omaha-Council Bluffs, NE-IA	2,035	20,039	3,345.9	1,322.3	634	31,207	18,159.4	1,586.5	2,008	40,812	2,529.1	680.7
Orlando-Kissimmee-Sanford, FL	8,881	67,714	10,861.4	4,613.2	1,469	36,717	11,560.5	2,144.5	5,334	172,151	14,317.5	3,685.7
Oshkosh-Neenah, WI	D	D	D	D	291	21,965	9,101.8	1,389.8	399	6,740	296.1	87.2
Owensboro, KY	16	73	6.6	2.7	121	7,538	5,441.0	470.0	13	72	3.4	0.9
Oxnard-Thousand Oaks-Ventura, CA	2,816	23,034	3,556.9	2,558.7	872	25,626	9,751.9	1,585.0	1,718	32,483	2,147.4	629.8
Palm Bay-Melbourne-Titusville, FL	1,920	19,218	3,795.1	1,440.5	447	19,579	5,939.2	1,622.5	1,202	23,254	1,343.2	384.3
Panama City, FL	D	D	D	D	106	3,728	1,488.1	208.0	515	11,608	757.4	215.8
Parkersburg-Vienna, WV	5	8	0.5	0.1	D	D	D	D	D	D	D	D
Pensacola-Ferry Pass-Brent, FL	324	1,687	258.9	101.6	211	4,320	3,414.7	297.0	807	18,949	1,044.2	288.9
Peoria, IL	293	1,974	223.2	97.3	322	D	6,068.2	863.6	951	16,034	833.1	240.0
Philadelphia-Camden-Wilmington, PA-NJ-DE-MD	11,681	124,620	25,861.8	10,648.2	4,897	170,097	92,492.1	11,186.0	13,637	223,664	14,234.5	3,978.5
Camden, NJ Div 15,804	3,152	31,071	5,723.6	2,172.7	951	35,242	17,811.1	2,309.0	2,523	41,094	2,377.8	654.3
Montgomery-Bucks-Chester Counties, PA Div 33,874	8,443	92,972	20,054.3	8,444.6	2,462	81,506	36,337.5	5,241.0	4,528	74,052	4,630.1	1,276.4
Philadelphia, PA Div 37,964	D	D	D	D	1,042	34,407	24,696.6	2,251.4	5,098	80,492	5,560.9	1,580.6
Wilmington, DE-MD-NJ Div 48,864	86	577	83.9	30.9	442	18,942	13,646.9	1,384.6	1,488	28,026	1,665.8	467.2
Phoenix-Mesa-Chandler, AZ	D	D	D	D	3,065	103,689	41,122.9	6,269.0	8,373	202,441	13,558.4	3,860.7
Pine Bluff, AR	D	D	D	D	65	5,207	1,679.3	252.2	D	D	D	23.9
Pittsburgh, PA	D	D	12,056.5	D	2,380	84,135	33,824.7	4,950.3	5,647	101,500	5,604.1	1,603.2
Pittsfield, MA	D	D	D	D	142	5,115	1,554.7	324.2	516	7,311	487.9	156.4
Pocatello, ID	10	28	3.4	1.1	D	D	D	D	215	3,523	179.6	48.0
Portland-South Portland, ME	424	1,756	260.5	96.4	D	D	D	D	1,989	27,304	2,026.3	612.1
Portland-Vancouver-Hillsboro, OR-WA	6,701	53,639	10,191.4	4,150.3	3,248	113,737	42,645.4	8,000.8	6,526	107,555	7,047.3	2,124.4
Port St. Lucie, FL	1,312	6,156	829.0	287.6	345	5,658	1,566.2	284.0	828	15,683	896.4	254.2
Poughkeepsie-Newburgh-Middletown, NY	D	D	D	D	490	13,673	4,978.4	862.7	1,783	21,524	1,370.2	397.5
Prescott Valley-Prescott, AZ	565	1,909	235.6	87.9	190	3,261	716.3	160.0	575	9,695	563.9	187.5
Providence-Warwick, RI-MA	2,016	14,277	2,015.2	797.7	1,957	67,080	21,326.0	4,033.2	4,433	72,327	4,816.3	1,386.6
Provo-Orem, UT	2,162	15,564	2,499.7	989.7	562	16,471	5,930.8	912.7	868	17,510	941.0	261.5
Pueblo, CO	D	D	D	D	94	4,380	2,103.4	256.3	336	5,761	289.7	84.7
Punta Gorda, FL	D	D	D	D	78	512	101.9	21.2	294	6,067	336.5	96.2
Racine, WI	289	1,953	288.6	118.4	297	15,883	5,623.1	1,006.9	412	6,540	319.4	91.5
Raleigh-Cary, NC	5,268	60,308	12,556.0	4,997.6	767	22,427	16,858.7	1,362.5	2,774	60,533	3,560.9	995.6
Rapid City, SD	D	D	D	D	162	2,509	617.9	112.9	451	7,666	490.0	139.1

Area name	Health care and social assistance, 2017				Other services, 2017				Nonemployer businesses, 2018		Value of residential construction authorized by building permits, 2020	
	Number of establish-ments	Number of employees	Receipts (mil dol)	Annual payroll (mil dol)	Number of establish-ments	Number of employees	Receipts (mil dol)	Annual payroll (mil dol)	Number	Receipts (mil dol)	New construc-tion ($1,000)	Number of housing units
	159	160	161	162	163	164	165	166	167	168	169	170
Mobile, AL	809	21,605	2,670.4	996.8	547	4,061	453.1	121.2	31,893	1,246.9	227,029	1,022
Modesto, CA	1,150	26,140	4,257.6	1,674.9	691	4,587	592.0	171.6	30,847	1,594.0	164,257	811
Monroe, LA	774	17,038	1,679.2	618.0	33	116	8.5	2.2	15,824	655.4	125,320	620
Monroe, MI	297	4,744	435.4	188.8	158	701	77.9	20.8	8,490	378.3	61,418	265
Montgomery, AL	788	20,474	2,300.3	956.2	498	2,991	440.7	116.9	25,608	1,136.9	246,900	1,014
Morgantown, WV	330	17,219	2,460.3	778.9	194	1,394	261.8	43.6	7,490	344.2	4,476	21
Morristown, TN	255	5,714	561.9	212.2	143	785	69.1	22.0	8,440	422.0	189,170	993
Mount Vernon-Anacortes, WA	355	8,148	922.3	402.4	263	1,223	139.6	41.6	8,306	425.6	167,425	914
Muncie, IN	379	10,377	1,061.6	418.1	169	1,102	133.5	31.5	5,714	214.2	30,192	113
Muskegon, MI	370	10,922	1,416.0	541.0	248	1,332	132.7	35.5	9,588	398.6	73,667	328
Myrtle Beach-Conway-North Myrtle Beach, SC-NC	954	16,093	2,095.2	726.6	699	3,801	407.3	103.0	42,378	2,061.4	2,491,512	12,219
Napa, CA	433	10,558	1,653.4	671.2	264	1,645	203.6	54.3	12,337	800.9	216,261	1,204
Naples-Marco Island, FL	1,143	20,535	2,704.8	980.5	1,011	6,309	662.8	191.7	46,683	3,037.2	1,990,453	6,766
Nashville-Davidson--Murfrees-boro--Franklin, TN	4,750	131,350	18,899.5	7,340.7	2,828	24,708	2,894.5	882.9	195,990	11,091.2	6,445,621	32,191
New Bern, NC	303	8,358	865.1	360.7	147	603	61.9	16.8	8,174	342.1	122,588	406
New Haven-Milford, CT	2,585	76,203	9,164.6	3,610.4	1,772	10,522	1,229.8	347.7	64,541	3,410.6	149,327	983
New Orleans-Metairie, LA	3,493	78,207	10,146.2	3,813.7	1,951	12,853	1,714.6	448.7	130,719	6,181.5	1,176,024	5,282
New York-Newark-Jersey City, NY-NJ-PA	61,986	1,607,087	197,257.4	80,838.4	50,412	312,707	54,284.9	12,459.1	1,983,082	118,562.8	8,691,943	56,661
Nassau County-Suffolk County, NY Div 35,004	10,868	228,324	28,660.4	12,195.2	8,566	45,888	5,173.4	1,419.9	295,645	19,529.4	1,428,536	2,824
Newark, NJ-PA Div 35,084	6,670	152,580	19,122.8	7,672.3	4,938	31,183	3,670.4	1,042.5	198,963	11,819.6	1,277,189	9,980
New Brunswick-Lakewood, NJ Div 35,154	7,726	165,453	20,023.8	7,994.6	4,957	30,883	4,198.4	1,033.0	200,717	12,872.1	1,558,389	10,638
New York-Jersey City-White Plains, NY-NJ Div 35,614	36,722	1,060,730	129,450.4	52,976.3	31,951	204,753	41,242.7	8,963.6	1,287,757	74,341.8	4,427,829	33,219
Niles, MI	387	9,499	987.6	414.4	258	1,325	158.5	40.3	10,233	442.3	123,871	331
North Port-Sarasota-Braden-ton, FL	2,552	44,802	5,709.9	2,026.0	1,671	8,063	1,018.2	242.5	85,403	4,540.3	3,919,519	15,924
Norwich-New London, CT	798	17,766	1,817.6	795.5	483	2,577	312.5	70.6	17,537	871.6	113,504	456
Ocala, FL	909	15,902	2,033.6	716.2	516	2,545	263.3	71.9	28,673	1,293.6	1,208,547	6,229
Ocean City, NJ	244	4,578	467.7	198.8	308	1,268	123.7	35.5	8,698	566.1	294,756	917
Odessa, TX	285	8,075	996.1	374.9	272	2,188	331.9	88.9	13,879	881.1	330,811	1,406
Ogden-Clearfield, UT	1,473	23,154	2,811.0	983.0	843	5,197	518.5	143.4	46,680	2,093.6	1,556,183	7,482
Oklahoma City, OK	4,270	79,468	11,221.1	3,887.6	2,084	12,543	1,742.2	433.8	117,528	5,879.1	2,053,033	8,080
Olympia-Lacey-Tumwater, WA	893	15,533	1,815.9	725.3	501	3,079	430.4	129.7	16,594	761.5	324,145	2,054
Omaha-Council Bluffs, NE-IA	2,712	68,611	8,457.0	3,319.1	1,686	10,564	2,044.7	349.6	64,415	3,080.4	1,026,390	6,382
Orlando-Kissimmee-Sanford, FL	6,613	127,510	18,014.7	6,236.4	4,184	28,846	4,749.8	931.5	287,615	11,925.9	6,320,024	30,618
Oshkosh-Neenah, WI	453	12,419	1,282.3	560.5	258	2,127	240.9	72.2	8,653	415.6	169,242	948
Owensboro, KY	362	9,931	1,100.6	481.7	146	1,072	87.9	31.2	6,922	310.8	38,136	398
Oxnard-Thousand Oaks-Ventura, CA	2,785	39,199	5,017.7	1,883.6	1,319	6,955	794.9	205.1	71,248	4,033.1	343,758	1,477
Palm Bay-Melbourne-Titus-ville, FL	1,600	32,031	3,775.1	1,369.8	1,023	4,793	466.5	135.2	48,279	1,957.3	1,537,334	5,174
Panama City, FL	549	10,448	1,288.9	495.7	319	1,922	176.4	47.3	15,550	826.2	683,169	2,610
Parkersburg-Vienna, WV	D	D	D	D	D	D	D	D	4,023	169.9	20,768	109
Pensacola-Ferry Pass-Brent, FL	1,119	25,833	3,481.5	1,315.0	618	3,828	375.8	103.0	37,549	1,638.3	757,534	4,051
Peoria, IL	933	33,858	4,018.6	1,667.9	610	5,909	629.9	256.3	20,914	831.9	74,366	379
Philadelphia-Camden-Wilm-ington, PA-NJ-DE-MD	18,016	518,895	61,725.7	25,143.8	12,061	80,754	13,637.2	2,805.5	462,125	25,319.7	6,037,717	36,307
Camden, NJ Div 15,804	3,617	88,640	10,461.0	4,333.1	2,272	14,344	1,334.6	415.7	82,379	4,455.1	445,636	3,702
Montgomery-Bucks-Chester Counties, PA Div 33,874	6,727	172,624	18,414.2	7,662.8	4,681	30,530	7,318.5	1,074.5	173,574	10,795.3	1,038,890	4,538
Philadelphia, PA Div 37,964	5,658	203,146	25,895.5	10,114.9	3,823	27,270	3,943.0	1,029.7	154,778	6,714.2	4,252,123	25,791
Wilmington, DE-MD-NJ Div 48,864	2,014	54,485	6,955.0	3,033.0	1,285	8,610	1,041.1	285.7	51,394	3,355.1	301,068	2,276
Phoenix-Mesa-Chandler, AZ	12,900	258,648	33,804.6	12,851.6	6,178	49,883	6,731.3	1,786.8	377,526	19,076.1	11,654,524	50,581
Pine Bluff, AR	226	4,363	428.2	179.5	87	435	47.1	12.2	4,712	172.5	19,347	46
Pittsburgh, PA	8,311	202,432	22,007.5	9,383.5	5,255	33,544	4,487.3	1,080.8	152,860	7,339.3	1,271,487	5,223
Pittsfield, MA	436	11,773	1,277.1	569.5	267	1,591	166.8	44.2	10,512	498.3	78,486	193
Pocatello, ID	401	5,751	634.9	219.9	125	547	75.4	17.1	6,025	246.7	96,778	510
Portland-South Portland, ME	2,082	45,765	5,157.5	2,069.0	1,256	6,794	863.2	232.4	52,053	2,726.0	940,558	3,712
Portland-Vancouver-Hillsboro, OR-WA	8,344	161,433	20,617.4	8,120.5	4,695	30,009	4,684.5	1,147.2	195,692	9,933.9	3,771,925	15,023
Port St. Lucie, FL	1,373	24,465	3,110.2	1,134.0	851	3,897	405.0	116.5	48,907	2,172.7	1,821,567	8,403
Poughkeepsie-Newburgh-Middletown, NY	1,875	44,489	5,409.9	2,160.1	1,435	7,729	957.2	246.2	51,207	2,573.8	478,690	2,282
Prescott Valley-Prescott, AZ	790	13,844	1,568.4	579.8	390	1,672	178.9	49.5	21,462	935.1	682,636	2,481
Providence-Warwick, RI-MA	4,611	129,505	13,976.1	6,005.0	3,430	19,761	2,333.9	641.0	122,304	5,747.5	491,769	2,258
Provo-Orem, UT	1,478	26,304	2,948.5	1,057.3	D	D	D	D	54,908	2,486.7	2,771,216	11,175
Pueblo, CO	407	13,427	1,403.4	602.5	235	1,348	125.1	36.1	9,224	394.4	120,065	742
Punta Gorda, FL	514	8,529	1,259.5	400.0	335	1,418	146.7	39.7	15,697	730.0	1,246,157	4,830
Racine, WI	510	11,145	1,032.8	423.6	302	1,880	169.7	52.9	9,865	426.9	74,118	245
Raleigh-Cary, NC	3,447	70,395	8,388.3	3,377.3	2,273	14,746	1,836.7	547.3	119,197	5,659.8	4,519,138	21,649
Rapid City, SD	392	10,698	1,458.5	548.1	342	1,761	213.3	57.5	11,435	540.7	277,628	1,562

Table C. Metropolitan Areas — **Government Employment and Payroll, and Local Government Finances**

Area name	Government employment and payroll, 2017									Local government finances, 2017				
			March payroll (percent of total)							General revenue				
												Taxes		
													Per capita[1] (dollars)	
	Full-time equivalent employees	March payroll (dollars)	Adminis-tration, judicial, and legal	Police and corrections	Fire protection	Highways and trans-portation	Health and welfare	Natural resources and utilities	Education and libraries	Total (mil dol)	Inter-govern-mental (mil dol)	Total (mil dol)	Total	Property
	171	172	173	174	175	176	177	178	179	180	181	182	183	184
Mobile, AL	16,158	54,780,612	6.0	12.7	4.5	4.1	11.9	6.8	51.3	1,551.5	657.6	627.2	1,457	578
Modesto, CA	21,814	11,742,0075	5.4	8.3	2.5	1.5	10.8	8.8	60.3	3,252.8	1,916.6	608.7	1,117	790
Monroe, LA	8,813	27,842,880	7.1	11.6	5.5	2.1	7.9	4.6	60.3	824.1	331.2	365.3	1,792	669
Monroe, MI	4,140	17,254,732	6.2	6.0	1.8	3.3	2.1	3.4	75.6	493.3	232.5	176.4	1,181	1,139
Montgomery, AL	11,956	42,267,586	4.9	13.6	6.0	3.2	2.5	9.8	54.3	1,678.9	484.6	412.4	1,102	331
Morgantown, WV	3,557	11,833,653	6.8	7.9	2.3	3.9	2.0	7.7	66.4	317.0	98.5	152.8	1,094	848
Morristown, TN	4,293	14,703,508	6.1	10.0	2.8	4.1	3.2	12.3	59.4	332.5	163.6	92.9	659	483
Mount Vernon-Anacortes, WA	6,316	34,058,435	5.1	5.3	2.2	4.5	35.2	4.8	40.1	1,108.2	363.5	253.5	2,014	1,281
Muncie, IN	3,844	13,695,351	5.6	8.5	3.6	3.7	3.0	4.5	69.0	411.1	185.8	88.7	769	723
Muskegon, MI	5,624	23,739,095	7.6	7.6	2.2	3.3	9.2	3.3	65.9	734.8	410.0	175.1	1,008	917
Myrtle Beach-Conway-North Myrtle Beach, SC-NC	14,122	53,770,704	7.4	10.8	4.4	3.5	5.6	7.3	56.9	1,713.9	448.5	859.4	1,854	1,217
Napa, CA	5,188	34,539,364	11.5	13.0	3.1	2.6	10.1	4.7	51.6	1,003.8	286.8	481.0	3,439	2,612
Naples-Marco Island, FL	10,447	46,883,097	6.7	17.1	7.6	3.2	5.8	8.0	48.7	1,526.6	242.6	884.1	2,372	2,131
Nashville-Davidson--Murfreesboro--Franklin, TN	63,688	25,633,6916	5.9	11.3	4.8	2.3	10.5	10.7	52.6	7,012.9	2,042.9	3,159.8	1,686	1,048
New Bern, NC	6,552	26,838,499	3.4	4.7	1.5	0.9	49.2	4.6	33.8	712.4	184.9	108.4	869	630
New Haven-Milford, CT	29,926	15,337,6297	3.4	10.0	6.1	3.3	3.0	4.9	68.4	4,281.3	1,605.5	2,298.8	2,680	2,641
New Orleans-Metairie, LA	40,736	17,511,3122	8.3	17.9	3.2	3.0	17.7	7.5	39.7	6,351.8	1,654.9	2,727.8	2,147	1,070
New York-Newark-Jersey City, NY-NJ-PA	869,812	5,46,331,5906	3.9	14.9	3.7	9.3	11.5	4.4	49.4	183,331.7	54,175.1	100,331.4	5,192	3,360
Nassau County-Suffolk County, NY Div 35,004	127,355	84,135,4618	3.7	12.1	0.9	2.4	5.3	3.6	70.3	23,561.4	6,076.3	14,946.9	5,262	4,224
Newark, NJ-PA Div 35,084	83,369	48,959,2894	5.1	14.9	4.0	2.5	4.6	4.1	62.9	12,547.0	3,122.9	7,759.8	3,582	3,487
New Brunswick-Lakewood, NJ Div 35,154	86,747	51,213,4932	4.6	13.0	1.5	2.5	3.0	4.6	68.4	12,037.1	2,613.6	7,940.3	3,343	3,281
New York-Jersey City-White Plains, NY-NJ Div 35,614	572,341	3,62,023,3462	3.7	15.8	4.6	12.8	15.0	4.7	40.0	135,186.2	42,362.3	69,684.4	5,836	3,147
Niles, MI	4,916	20,205,038	9.5	10.0	1.7	2.9	2.8	4.4	66.9	642.6	301.4	220.9	1,433	1,406
North Port-Sarasota-Bradenton, FL	29,030	12,256,2501	7.4	11.3	5.8	3.5	24.8	5.8	38.2	4,037.1	655.0	1,612.5	2,003	1,617
Norwich-New London, CT	9,464	49,779,946	3.9	7.1	3.6	3.2	2.1	5.2	70.6	1,247.5	411.9	703.0	2,629	2,606
Ocala, FL	10,693	35,122,480	4.8	11.0	9.8	2.1	0.8	6.7	62.3	962.8	383.9	311.7	882	738
Ocean City, NJ	6,404	30,726,844	9.5	11.4	3.5	4.4	5.6	8.4	56.0	972.3	143.8	573.0	6,152	5,996
Odessa, TX	8,000	32,951,515	4.0	7.4	3.1	1.5	28.6	2.4	51.5	876.8	185.7	341.2	2,174	1,556
Ogden-Clearfield, UT	18,456	70,604,675	7.0	9.9	3.7	1.8	5.9	7.7	62.2	2,134.2	835.5	810.2	1,220	852
Oklahoma City, OK	43,677	16,605,4631	5.2	12.2	7.5	2.9	12.4	5.1	53.7	4,550.6	1,299.4	2,015.2	1,459	776
Olympia-Lacey-Tumwater, WA	8,635	45,715,941	9.4	8.2	6.1	6.6	2.8	6.0	58.6	1,293.7	527.4	507.6	1,811	1,121
Omaha-Council Bluffs, NE-IA	36,806	16,677,9572	4.4	9.9	4.0	3.5	4.6	15.6	56.8	4,360.8	1,458.3	2,039.2	2,188	1,659
Orlando-Kissimmee-Sanford, FL	83,077	31,732,6498	6.6	13.4	7.4	4.2	1.8	8.5	53.8	10,685.0	3,163.6	4,281.5	1,701	1,189
Oshkosh-Neenah, WI	5,484	24,749,186	4.5	13.5	6.2	7.2	7.0	6.5	53.4	838.6	445.2	251.9	1,478	1,433
Owensboro, KY	4,973	16,279,975	4.4	6.6	3.5	3.6	4.4	12.0	60.9	391.0	149.9	140.1	1,183	693
Oxnard-Thousand Oaks-Ventura, CA	30,149	19,558,3899	9.7	10.1	4.8	2.6	14.9	6.1	50.1	5,323.1	2,073.3	1,584.4	1,866	1,524
Palm Bay-Melbourne-Titusville, FL	19,876	71,754,734	7.2	12.8	6.8	4.6	7.5	8.1	51.1	2,102.4	685.7	749.1	1,275	944
Panama City, FL	8,252	28,582,062	5.1	9.8	2.7	3.8	24.7	5.2	47.3	727.1	246.4	300.1	1,625	1,070
Parkersburg-Vienna, WV	3,095	10,097,036	5.5	6.3	2.4	3.1	3.0	6.5	71.8	229.9	96.7	84.5	930	758
Pensacola-Ferry Pass-Brent, FL	14,655	50,092,302	6.8	14.7	2.9	2.4	2.0	8.3	60.5	1,634.1	623.5	525.4	1,078	723
Peoria, IL	15,588	63,363,344	5.6	10.9	4.0	4.2	3.5	5.9	64.5	1,680.0	589.9	776.3	1,908	1,667
Philadelphia-Camden-Wilmington, PA-NJ-DE-MD	206,721	1,10,921,2623	6.6	13.5	2.5	7.8	4.9	5.0	57.7	35,204.3	12,957.9	16,568.5	2,726	1,901
Camden, NJ Div 15,804	50,457	28,441,6906	4.4	11.2	1.9	3.3	3.2	3.4	69.7	7,087.7	2,087.8	3,608.9	2,904	2,867
Montgomery-Bucks-Chester Counties, PA Div 33,874	57,162	30,610,9194	5.9	10.9	0.5	2.9	3.9	3.4	71.3	9,659.2	2,599.5	5,580.1	2,833	2,306
Philadelphia, PA Div 37,964	78,564	41,712,1085	9.1	17.8	4.7	15.5	7.3	7.7	35.9	15,651.0	7,071.9	6,254.9	2,917	1,180
Wilmington, DE-MD-NJ Div 48,864	20,538	10,156,5438	5.1	10.3	1.1	3.2	2.7	3.7	72.2	2,806.4	1,198.6	1,124.6	1,559	1,270
Phoenix-Mesa-Chandler, AZ	133,626	64,496,3932	9.1	15.0	6.5	3.1	6.2	13.9	45.1	17,176.8	6,049.9	7,375.5	1,550	954
Pine Bluff, AR	3,046	9,287,297	6.2	10.9	3.1	3.8	1.7	1.8	72.2	270.4	165.4	72.9	802	374
Pittsburgh, PA	74,899	35,634,5741	6.5	10.2	1.7	8.1	7.3	5.0	60.1	12,017.4	5,092.7	4,857.9	2,086	1,496
Pittsfield, MA	4,678	20,287,892	4.8	7.3	3.1	4.6	2.3	4.1	72.2	589.6	246.5	294.0	2,326	2,238
Pocatello, ID	3,290	11,919,347	7.3	13.8	4.9	5.5	6.4	7.4	51.8	298.4	130.5	103.5	1,111	1,075
Portland-South Portland, ME	19,499	81,364,976	5.7	8.9	5.2	5.0	3.1	6.4	63.1	2,114.7	477.8	1,314.0	2,470	2,433
Portland-Vancouver-Hillsboro, OR-WA	76,417	41,424,8897	7.2	10.2	5.1	8.0	5.8	7.6	52.8	12,702.3	4,421.2	5,365.6	2,186	1,611
Port St. Lucie, FL	14,593	56,559,821	6.7	13.4	9.8	2.0	1.7	7.6	54.0	1,823.7	468.3	835.6	1,767	1,539
Poughkeepsie-Newburgh-Middletown, NY	28,050	15,575,4491	4.9	9.6	2.0	3.7	5.6	2.1	71.0	4,559.8	1,555.6	2,551.3	3,789	2,887
Prescott Valley-Prescott, AZ	6,183	24,573,588	10.4	15.0	8.4	6.0	4.2	5.0	41.7	671.5	233.0	333.0	1,460	889
Providence-Warwick, RI-MA	47,406	24,988,8612	3.5	10.2	8.2	2.3	2.8	3.8	67.9	6,852.7	2,374.3	3,634.5	2,248	2,177
Provo-Orem, UT	15,123	60,353,207	6.9	8.9	2.6	1.6	5.6	9.1	62.8	2,078.2	833.2	743.8	1,203	788
Pueblo, CO	5,844	27,151,176	5.3	12.1	10.8	2.9	7.3	6.0	53.1	632.0	278.7	262.3	1,578	1,002
Punta Gorda, FL	4,751	17,974,279	14.2	16.9	10.5	6.1	1.4	9.3	39.5	618.7	101.2	291.7	1,607	1,248
Racine, WI	5,884	28,010,342	3.9	12.3	5.4	3.5	5.4	4.2	63.6	810.5	394.0	295.7	1,510	1,462
Raleigh-Cary, NC	43,575	18,632,0481	3.6	8.5	3.4	3.4	9.5	7.2	60.4	4,972.7	1,777.3	2,106.6	1,579	1,135
Rapid City, SD	5,340	18,126,595	5.9	12.7	4.3	5.5	2.6	8.0	57.8	525.2	143.7	281.9	2,036	1,350

1. Based on the resident population estimated as of July 1 of the year shown

Area name	Local government finances, 2017 (cont.)									Government employment, 2019			Individual income tax returns, 2018		
	Direct general expenditure							Debt outstanding							
			Percent of total for:												
	Total (mil dol)	Per capita[1] (dollars)	Educa-tion	Health and hospitals	Police protection	Public welfare	Highways	Total (mil dol)	Per capita[1] (dollars)	Federal civilian	Federal military	State and local	Number of returns	Mean adjusted gross income	Mean income tax
	185	186	187	188	189	190	191	192	193	194	195	196	197	198	199
Mobile, AL	1,587.7	3,688	40.6	11.1	7.2	0.2	5.1	1,496.5	3,476	2,844	2,681	22,769	186,110	53,295	5,293
Modesto, CA	3,266.2	5,996	49.6	7.6	5.3	9.3	2.5	6,781.2	12,449	897	804	28,526	238,950	58,426	5,750
Monroe, LA	816.3	4,003	54.2	6.0	6.6	0.2	3.2	766.3	3,759	616	731	11,540	86,290	52,562	5,144
Monroe, MI	543.6	3,638	53.6	6.9	2.8	0.2	7.7	514.5	3,443	259	236	5,183	76,380	62,952	6,212
Montgomery, AL	1,652.3	4,416	32.0	39.6	5.1	0.2	2.9	1,290.9	3,450	6,772	4,395	32,661	166,960	57,100	5,672
Morgantown, WV	335.7	2,405	54.4	1.4	6.9	0.8	2.2	456.9	3,272	2,090	640	16,813	57,360	67,664	8,010
Morristown, TN	383.3	2,721	49.9	2.0	5.7	3.1	3.8	423.6	3,007	403	396	7,234	61,690	49,660	4,205
Mount Vernon-Anacortes, WA	1,115.7	8,865	28.0	43.7	2.5	0.1	3.4	865.1	6,873	415	319	10,758	64,090	73,595	8,152
Muncie, IN	644.3	5,590	24.6	0.6	2.4	0.0	1.8	330.8	2,870	327	316	10,525	48,720	50,679	4,706
Muskegon, MI	779.6	4,489	51.7	8.7	3.7	2.8	4.5	744.5	4,287	369	280	7,122	81,740	50,853	4,462
Myrtle Beach-Conway-North Myrtle Beach, SC-NC	1,752.4	3,781	46.2	4.4	7.0	1.2	8.1	1,680.4	3,625	1,472	1,703	21,150	247,440	58,652	6,145
Napa, CA	964.8	6,897	37.4	6.8	8.1	4.4	5.0	1,190.6	8,512	252	192	10,156	69,200	100,314	15,186
Naples-Marco Island, FL	1,422.5	3,817	38.1	3.4	12.7	0.5	5.2	1,944.8	5,219	813	663	12,388	198,250	161,646	30,328
Nashville-Davidson--Murfreesboro--Franklin, TN	7,298.3	3,893	42.6	10.3	6.9	0.9	4.0	20,712.8	11,050	14,068	5,809	97,839	947,190	81,027	10,993
New Bern, NC	682.6	5,474	27.0	53.7	2.7	4.2	0.2	167.1	1,340	6,047	6,737	8,471	57,320	56,473	5,370
New Haven-Milford, CT	4,329.0	5,047	54.3	0.8	5.3	0.3	3.3	3,393.1	3,956	5,815	1,918	41,558	424,220	75,800	9,446
New Orleans-Metairie, LA	6,044.5	4,758	33.8	12.6	7.1	0.8	4.3	8,601.4	6,771	13,635	6,771	64,159	590,360	65,022	8,132
New York-Newark-Jersey City, NY-NJ-PA	178,961.0	9,262	38.8	7.8	5.8	9.4	2.8	230,434.8	11,926	109,886	35,166	1,140,415	9,798,210	98,580	16,263
Nassau County-Suffolk County, NY Div 35,004	24,029.7	8,459	52.6	4.5	7.2	5.2	3.1	17,428.0	6,135	16,567	5,112	164,799	1,526,860	107,043	17,365
Newark, NJ-PA Div 35,084	12,542.8	5,790	52.2	2.2	6.5	2.0	2.4	7,966.5	3,677	17,468	4,422	131,399	1,095,010	104,478	16,642
New Brunswick-Lakewood, NJ Div 35,154	12,540.2	5,279	57.2	1.2	6.0	1.9	3.1	8,207.6	3,455	9,830	5,446	123,300	1,214,840	96,637	14,029
New York-Jersey City-White Plains, NY-NJ Div 35,614	129,848.3	10,875	33.2	9.5	5.4	11.6	2.7	196,832.8	16,485	66,021	20,186	720,917	5,961,500	95,725	16,366
Niles, MI	712.3	4,622	50.9	8.7	3.9	1.3	5.1	534.7	3,469	362	258	8,385	75,010	62,385	7,184
North Port-Sarasota-Bradenton, FL	3,730.1	4,633	31.1	21.9	6.7	0.2	4.2	3,396.5	4,218	2,170	1,525	25,973	423,930	90,106	13,271
Norwich-New London, CT	1,142.3	4,271	59.0	0.8	6.3	0.5	6.0	611.7	2,288	2,973	5,024	21,395	138,450	74,413	8,864
Ocala, FL	965.7	2,733	49.5	3.7	7.4	0.9	5.5	629.5	1,782	885	625	14,472	176,180	53,122	5,519
Ocean City, NJ	1,325.6	14,234	23.2	1.0	3.2	2.4	6.9	959.9	10,307	457	1,158	8,163	50,760	70,669	8,452
Odessa, TX	915.0	5,830	35.1	40.8	3.5	0.0	2.5	447.1	2,849	236	317	9,895	75,890	67,148	7,428
Ogden-Clearfield, UT	2,014.5	3,034	53.7	3.0	5.8	0.1	4.1	1,840.6	2,772	21,756	6,976	31,998	304,700	70,220	6,827
Oklahoma City, OK	4,263.3	3,086	43.2	9.0	9.1	0.0	4.8	5,174.1	3,745	30,227	11,597	92,405	629,080	66,595	7,596
Olympia-Lacey-Tumwater, WA	1,287.9	4,595	49.0	6.7	4.0	0.0	3.7	1,289.3	4,600	863	801	38,156	146,270	71,301	7,619
Omaha-Council Bluffs, NE-IA	4,264.8	4,576	55.8	2.7	5.6	0.6	5.3	8,245.8	8,848	9,826	9,533	53,175	463,640	76,349	9,089
Orlando-Kissimmee-Sanford, FL	10,770.3	4,278	40.8	1.8	7.5	0.5	4.0	14,561.9	5,784	15,366	4,732	109,082	1,309,230	63,593	7,653
Oshkosh-Neenah, WI	872.6	5,121	34.9	2.9	4.7	26.1	6.4	874.7	5,134	448	465	10,960	85,610	66,998	7,395
Owensboro, KY	375.0	3,165	48.1	6.2	3.0	0.2	4.2	2,274.1	19,198	335	373	5,817	54,390	57,593	5,418
Oxnard-Thousand Oaks-Ventura, CA	5,425.7	6,390	40.7	12.5	7.4	4.4	2.7	4,701.3	5,537	7,875	5,898	36,169	415,730	85,387	11,618
Palm Bay-Melbourne-Titusville, FL	2,232.0	3,797	35.9	9.2	7.0	0.2	4.6	1,844.7	3,138	6,900	2,952	22,000	305,340	66,971	8,078
Panama City, FL	718.8	3,891	43.3	2.6	8.1	0.0	4.5	596.2	3,227	3,971	2,747	8,596	85,660	60,706	6,903
Parkersburg-Vienna, WV	240.7	2,650	62.2	0.0	6.4	0.1	3.7	257.9	2,839	2,723	419	4,246	40,880	54,859	5,327
Pensacola-Ferry Pass-Brent, FL	1,706.2	3,501	42.6	1.7	7.4	0.0	3.7	4,496.6	9,228	6,983	14,573	21,135	239,970	62,218	6,804
Peoria, IL	1,660.1	4,080	50.8	1.5	6.6	1.0	6.9	1,282.1	3,151	2,258	850	19,912	192,040	68,360	7,694
Philadelphia-Camden-Wilmington, PA-NJ-DE-MD	35,039.2	5,764	51.2	6.0	5.5	3.6	2.8	38,405.9	6,318	53,290	22,475	286,169	3,015,270	84,860	11,742
Camden, NJ Div 15,804	7,006.6	5,638	59.6	1.3	5.2	2.3	2.9	5,817.5	4,681	7,722	8,127	70,209	631,680	76,862	9,359
Montgomery-Bucks-Chester Counties, PA Div 33,874	10,180.1	5,168	60.2	2.5	4.9	5.3	3.7	10,828.7	5,497	6,248	5,036	75,655	1,027,630	111,441	17,343
Philadelphia, PA Div 37,964	15,006.8	6,998	39.4	11.6	5.6	3.7	1.9	19,371.5	9,033	33,425	5,942	98,471	998,340	66,514	8,518
Wilmington, DE-MD-NJ Div 48,864	2,845.7	3,945	60.5	0.9	7.5	0.2	4.2	2,388.2	3,311	5,895	3,370	41,834	357,620	73,820	8,856
Phoenix-Mesa-Chandler, AZ	16,004.3	3,363	40.1	5.0	9.4	1.6	3.8	28,954.9	6,085	24,227	15,847	215,818	2,243,680	73,682	9,176
Pine Bluff, AR	255.1	2,808	56.7	0.1	8.7	0.2	4.8	216.6	2,384	1,439	322	7,795	35,820	44,625	3,556
Pittsburgh, PA	12,113.1	5,201	47.9	4.1	4.0	9.3	4.7	18,684.2	8,022	18,877	6,177	94,206	1,201,860	74,044	9,271
Pittsfield, MA	681.9	5,397	58.0	0.3	3.3	0.4	6.4	435.0	3,443	414	287	7,439	64,700	68,577	8,070
Pocatello, ID	272.4	2,927	41.5	4.8	8.0	0.5	7.2	71.6	769	616	289	8,506	40,800	53,844	4,426
Portland-South Portland, ME	2,149.5	4,041	50.8	0.8	5.0	1.9	5.4	1,864.2	3,505	10,263	2,523	27,828	292,420	76,075	9,086
Portland-Vancouver-Hillsboro, OR-WA	12,324.2	5,020	42.7	3.8	5.6	1.7	5.1	18,952.7	7,721	19,024	6,348	126,651	1,249,400	81,962	10,411
Port St. Lucie, FL	1,815.4	3,839	38.4	2.7	8.7	1.4	7.6	2,383.6	5,041	1,121	914	18,156	242,320	78,985	10,653
Poughkeepsie-Newburgh-Middletown, NY	4,629.3	6,876	54.6	4.3	3.6	8.8	3.9	2,458.4	3,651	6,130	7,454	38,254	333,530	77,394	9,506
Prescott Valley-Prescott, AZ	710.2	3,114	35.4	3.3	9.4	0.1	10.8	559.6	2,454	1,692	509	8,996	117,170	60,993	6,518
Providence-Warwick, RI-MA	6,766.0	4,185	57.5	0.6	7.2	0.4	3.1	4,172.2	2,581	12,813	8,524	81,507	834,940	70,746	8,438
Provo-Orem, UT	1,877.9	3,039	55.9	3.8	4.2	0.3	5.3	2,351.5	3,805	1,229	2,505	31,609	264,480	83,410	9,516
Pueblo, CO	625.0	3,759	39.5	1.4	7.3	4.1	4.1	578.0	3,476	1,069	413	11,326	75,510	53,068	4,770
Punta Gorda, FL	621.4	3,423	26.1	3.8	10.9	1.3	15.4	578.0	3,184	380	332	5,698	93,520	65,185	7,368
Racine, WI	854.8	4,365	48.3	5.0	9.0	4.9	8.3	675.9	3,452	389	494	8,236	98,220	63,918	6,629
Raleigh-Cary, NC	4,736.3	3,550	50.0	8.4	5.7	3.5	2.4	8,779.2	6,580	6,476	3,622	92,210	656,730	87,276	11,323
Rapid City, SD	464.3	3,353	46.2	1.4	7.5	0.4	9.2	443.4	3,202	3,025	4,209	7,576	74,300	63,377	6,708

1. Based on the resident population estimated as of July 1 of the year shown.

Table C. Metropolitan Areas — **Land Area and Population**

CBSA[1]	DIV Code	Area name	Land area[2] (sq mi)	Population, 2021: Total persons 2021	Population, 2021: Rank	Population, 2021: Per square mile	Population characteristics, 2020: Race alone or in combination, not Hispanic or Latino (percent): White	Black	American Indian, Alaska Native	Asian and Pacific Islander	Percent Hispanic or Latino[3]	Age (percent): Under 5 years	5 to 17 years	18 to 24 years	25 to 34 years	35 to 44 years	45 to 54 years
			1	2	3	4	5	6	7	8	9	10	11	12	13	14	15
39740		Reading, PA	856.4	4,29,342	126	501.3	70.1	5.4	0.4	1.8	23.9	5.5	12.6	13.4	12.5	12.0	12.3
39820		Redding, CA	3,775.5	1,82,139	239	48.2	81.6	2.3	3.8	5.2	11.4	5.5	12.5	11.2	12.7	12.4	10.8
39900		Reno, NV	6,579.7	4,97,535	114	75.6	64.0	3.4	1.9	8.3	25.8	5.4	12.0	12.2	15.1	13.1	11.9
40060		Richmond, VA	4,364.4	13,24,062	44	303.4	58.5	30.7	0.9	5.3	7.2	5.6	12.0	12.3	14.4	13.4	12.4
40140		Riverside-San Bernardino-Ontario, CA	27,277.3	46,53,105	12	170.6	31.0	8.1	0.9	9.0	53.6	6.2	14.5	14.1	14.6	13.5	12.1
40220		Roanoke, VA	1,867.6	3,14,496	163	168.4	79.1	15.0	0.7	3.1	4.4	5.0	11.5	11.6	12.3	11.8	12.6
40340		Rochester, MN	2,477.0	2,27,151	203	91.7	84.3	6.4	0.7	5.9	4.9	6.2	13.8	11.8	13.3	13.5	11.3
40380		Rochester, NY	3,266.0	10,84,973	52	332.2	77.7	12.2	0.6	3.7	8.1	5.1	11.5	13.2	13.1	12.0	11.8
40420		Rockford, IL	793.8	3,36,278	155	423.6	69.3	13.4	0.6	3.3	15.9	6.0	13.3	12.6	12.3	12.0	12.4
40580		Rocky Mount, NC	1,045.9	1,43,535	293	137.2	44.7	47.6	1.1	1.2	7.0	5.7	12.5	12.4	12.1	11.1	12.3
40660		Rome, GA	509.8	98,771	359	193.7	71.6	15.6	0.7	1.9	12.1	5.7	13.0	14.2	13.0	12.1	12.4
40900		Sacramento-Roseville-Folsom, CA	5,094.9	24,11,428	26	473.3	53.8	8.8	1.4	18.5	22.7	5.6	12.9	12.9	14.1	13.8	12.2
40980		Saginaw, MI	800.8	1,89,591	231	236.8	70.6	20.0	0.9	1.7	9.2	5.7	12.0	13.1	12.7	11.2	11.6
41060		St. Cloud, MN	1,751.1	2,00,406	225	114.4	85.6	9.2	0.8	2.8	3.8	6.4	13.4	17.0	12.4	12.3	10.7
41100		St. George, UT	2,427.4	1,91,226	230	78.8	85.0	1.1	1.6	3.1	11.3	6.0	14.3	13.7	11.3	12.1	9.9
41140		St. Joseph, MO-KS	1,655.7	1,20,424	329	72.7	87.1	6.4	1.1	2.0	5.9	5.8	12.5	12.6	12.9	12.8	11.9
41180		St. Louis, MO-IL	7,863.7	28,09,299	21	357.2	75.2	19.3	0.7	3.7	3.4	5.7	12.4	11.9	13.3	13.2	12.0
41420		Salem, OR	1,922.0	4,36,283	125	227.0	68.8	2.0	2.4	4.6	25.6	5.9	13.5	13.8	13.8	13.1	11.6
41500		Salinas, CA	3,281.7	4,37,325	124	133.3	30.4	3.1	0.9	7.8	60.4	6.6	14.9	14.1	13.7	13.4	11.7
41540		Salisbury, MD-DE	2,098.7	4,29,223	127	204.5	73.2	18.3	0.9	2.3	7.7	4.9	10.6	12.0	10.5	10.2	10.6
41620		Salt Lake City, UT	7,684.0	12,63,061	46	164.4	72.5	2.5	1.2	7.4	19.0	6.6	15.0	14.2	16.2	15.0	11.7
41660		San Angelo, TX	3,497.0	1,22,344	324	35.0	52.8	4.3	0.8	2.0	41.8	6.3	13.7	15.4	14.4	12.9	10.0
41700		San Antonio-New Braunfels, TX	7,313.2	26,01,788	24	355.8	33.8	7.4	0.7	3.6	56.2	6.3	14.1	14.0	14.7	14.1	12.1
41740		San Diego-Chula Vista-Carlsbad, CA	4,210.2	32,86,069	17	780.5	47.0	5.8	0.9	15.4	34.8	5.7	12.0	13.4	16.1	14.1	12.1
41860		San Francisco-Oakland-Berkeley, CA	2,470.3	46,23,264	13	1,871.5	40.9	8.3	0.8	32.2	22.3	5.1	11.0	10.8	15.1	15.0	13.5
41860	36084	Oakland-Berkeley-Livermore, CA Div 36,084	1,454.4	28,09,969	X	1,932.0	37.7	10.8	0.9	31.2	24.2	5.3	11.9	11.6	14.3	15.1	13.4
41860	41884	San Francisco-San Mateo-Redwood City, CA Div 41,884	495.5	15,53,089	X	3,134.4	41.2	4.7	0.7	38.0	19.6	4.7	9.3	9.5	17.4	15.5	13.4
41860	42034	San Rafael, CA Div 42,034	520.4	2,60,206	X	500.0	73.3	3.4	0.8	9.3	16.8	4.2	11.0	10.8	8.7	11.8	14.8
41940		San Jose-Sunnyvale-Santa Clara, CA	2,679.7	19,52,185	36	728.5	31.8	3.0	0.7	41.7	26.3	5.4	12.0	12.1	15.7	14.6	13.5
42020		San Luis Obispo-Paso Robles, CA	3,300.9	2,83,159	175	85.8	69.9	2.5	1.1	5.5	23.8	4.3	10.0	18.0	11.2	11.8	10.5
42100		Santa Cruz-Watsonville, CA	445.1	2,67,792	187	601.6	59.1	1.8	1.1	7.0	34.4	4.4	10.7	18.0	11.9	11.9	11.9
42140		Santa Fe, NM	1,910.4	1,55,201	275	81.2	44.4	1.2	3.3	1.9	50.5	3.8	9.6	10.5	11.0	11.8	11.8
42200		Santa Maria-Santa Barbara, CA	2,733.9	4,46,475	123	163.3	45.0	2.4	1.0	7.1	47.2	6.0	12.5	19.0	13.4	11.7	10.4
42220		Santa Rosa-Petaluma, CA	1,575.6	4,85,887	116	308.4	64.3	2.5	1.6	6.6	28.3	4.6	10.9	11.5	12.4	13.2	12.3
42340		Savannah, GA	1,349.5	4,10,008	134	303.8	56.5	34.6	0.8	3.5	6.9	6.0	12.8	13.7	15.1	13.7	11.6
42540		Scranton--Wilkes-Barre, PA	1,746.1	5,67,750	100	325.2	80.9	5.0	0.4	2.4	12.9	5.2	11.5	12.3	12.4	12.0	12.4
42660		Seattle-Tacoma-Bellevue, WA	5,869.7	40,11,553	15	683.4	64.6	8.1	2.0	20.2	10.9	5.6	12.0	11.4	16.8	15.4	12.7
42660	42644	Seattle-Bellevue-Kent, WA Div 42,644	4,201.8	30,85,845	X	734.4	63.0	7.5	1.8	22.5	10.5	5.5	11.6	11.1	17.2	15.8	13.0
42660	45104	Tacoma-Lakewood, WA Div 45,104	1,668.0	9,25,708	X	555.0	69.9	10.2	2.7	12.6	12.2	6.1	13.3	12.5	15.5	14.3	11.9
42680		Sebastian-Vero Beach, FL	502.8	1,63,662	262	325.5	75.7	9.7	0.6	2.1	13.3	3.9	8.5	8.8	9.3	9.0	10.4
42700		Sebring-Avon Park, FL	1,017.7	1,03,296	352	101.5	66.1	10.4	0.9	1.9	22.1	4.1	9.9	8.8	9.6	9.2	9.4
43100		Sheboygan, WI	511.5	1,17,747	332	230.2	84.0	3.3	0.8	6.6	7.2	5.3	12.4	12.2	11.7	12.3	12.2
43300		Sherman-Denison, TX	932.8	1,39,336	298	149.4	76.2	7.1	2.2	2.1	15.0	6.0	13.6	12.6	12.1	12.1	11.9
43340		Shreveport-Bossier City, LA	2,595.4	3,89,155	140	149.9	53.3	41.1	1.0	2.1	4.4	6.2	13.7	12.5	13.3	13.2	11.3
43420		Sierra Vista-Douglas, AZ	6,209.8	1,26,050	320	20.3	56.7	4.9	1.7	3.7	35.9	5.3	12.1	12.0	12.3	11.6	10.0
43580		Sioux City, IA-NE-SD	2,074.0	1,49,265	285	72.0	70.5	5.9	2.3	3.9	19.9	6.9	14.9	13.9	12.6	12.6	11.4
43620		Sioux Falls, SD	2,575.4	2,81,958	176	109.5	86.0	6.1	2.9	2.6	4.8	7.0	14.6	12.5	14.5	14.3	11.1
43780		South Bend-Mishawaka, IN-MI	947.9	3,23,695	162	341.5	76.2	13.8	1.1	3.2	8.9	6.0	12.9	14.5	12.9	12.1	11.6
43900		Spartanburg, SC	808.4	3,35,864	156	415.5	68.7	21.7	0.7	3.1	7.9	6.1	13.2	12.9	14.0	12.3	12.6
44060		Spokane-Spokane Valley, WA	4,241.3	5,93,466	98	139.9	87.0	3.2	3.0	4.6	6.4	5.5	12.5	12.6	14.5	13.1	11.5
44100		Springfield, IL	1,182.6	2,06,898	220	175.0	82.4	14.3	0.6	2.8	2.6	5.6	12.4	12.0	12.1	12.8	12.1
44140		Springfield, MA	1,843.4	6,95,305	87	377.2	70.1	7.2	0.7	3.9	20.2	4.6	10.9	16.2	12.5	11.8	11.7
44180		Springfield, MO	3,007.0	4,81,483	117	160.1	91.3	3.6	1.5	2.4	3.8	5.9	12.7	15.3	13.2	12.5	11.3
44220		Springfield, OH	396.9	1,35,633	305	341.7	86.2	11.0	0.9	1.3	3.8	5.8	12.7	12.9	11.7	11.3	12.0
44300		State College, PA	1,108.7	1,57,527	269	142.1	86.8	4.3	0.4	7.0	3.1	3.6	8.4	25.7	13.0	11.2	10.8
44420		Staunton, VA	1,002.0	1,25,774	321	125.5	86.3	8.8	0.8	1.5	4.9	5.1	11.0	11.1	12.6	12.6	12.3
44700		Stockton, CA	1,392.4	7,89,410	76	566.9	31.4	8.3	1.2	20.2	43.0	6.6	15.3	14.2	14.0	13.7	12.0
44940		Sumter, SC	1,272.3	1,35,782	303	106.7	47.0	47.9	0.9	2.0	4.2	6.0	12.8	13.4	13.3	11.4	10.9
45060		Syracuse, NY	2,384.9	6,58,281	91	276.0	83.3	9.7	1.2	3.8	4.7	5.4	11.8	13.8	12.7	11.9	11.7
45220		Tallahassee, FL	2,389.3	3,85,776	145	161.5	56.7	33.7	0.8	3.7	7.2	5.0	10.8	20.9	13.6	11.8	10.9
45300		Tampa-St. Petersburg-Clearwater, FL	2,515.2	32,19,514	18	1,280.0	62.3	13.2	0.7	4.7	21.3	5.0	11.2	10.9	13.2	12.9	12.8
45460		Terre Haute, IN	1,910.0	1,84,910	233	96.8	90.6	6.3	0.8	1.8	2.5	5.4	11.7	15.4	12.9	12.1	11.8

1. CBSA = Core Based Statistical Area. DIV = Metropolitan Division. See Appendix A for explanation. See Appendix B for list of metropolitan areas or temporarily covered by water. 2. Dry land or land partially or temporarily covered by water. 3. May be of any race.

Area name	Population, 2021 (cont.)				Population change and components of change, 2010–2021							Households, 2016–2020				
	Age (percent) (cont.)				Total persons		Percent change		Components of change, 2020–2021					Percent		
	55 to 64 years	65 to 74 years	75 years and over	Percent female	2010	2020	2010–2020	2020–2021	Births	Deaths	Net migration	Number	Persons per house-hold	Family house-holds	Female family house holds	One person
	16	17	18	19	20	21	22	23	24	25	26	27	28	29	30	31
Reading, PA	13.9	10.5	7.2	50.4	4,11,442	4,28,849	4.2	0.1	5,619	5,980	785	1,56,389	2.6	67.8	13.3	26.0
Redding, CA	13.8	12.6	8.4	50.6	1,77,223	1,82,155	2.8	0.0	2,291	3,113	806	70,845	2.5	66.3	11.5	27.1
Reno, NV	13.0	11.0	6.3	49.3	4,25,417	4,90,596	15.3	1.4	6,277	6,239	6,892	1,87,820	2.5	62.3	10.7	27.7
Richmond, VA	13.3	10.3	6.2	51.5	11,86,501	13,14,434	10.8	0.7	17,499	17,281	9,408	4,88,001	2.6	64.1	13.2	29.3
Riverside-San Bernardino-Ontario, CA	11.5	8.2	5.3	49.9	42,24,851	45,99,839	8.9	1.2	67,389	51,821	37,100	13,76,503	3.3	74.8	14.7	19.9
Roanoke, VA	14.4	12.6	8.3	51.4	3,08,707	3,15,251	2.1	-0.2	3,833	5,303	737	1,27,924	2.4	62.0	11.8	31.8
Rochester, MN	13.0	9.9	7.3	50.6	2,06,877	2,26,329	9.4	0.4	3,318	2,469	-62	89,070	2.4	65.9	8.0	26.9
Rochester, NY	14.3	11.3	7.6	51.1	10,79,671	10,90,135	1.0	-0.5	13,308	15,175	-3,416	4,38,233	2.4	61.4	12.8	31.0
Rockford, IL	13.4	10.7	7.3	50.8	3,49,431	3,38,798	-3.0	-0.7	4,795	4,911	-2,445	1,34,567	2.5	65.3	14.0	28.9
Rocky Mount, NC	14.2	12.3	7.5	52.4	1,52,392	1,43,870	-5.6	-0.2	1,958	2,570	261	58,171	2.5	67.8	20.1	28.4
Rome, GA	12.6	10.1	6.9	51.1	96,317	98,584	2.4	0.2	1,324	1,669	515	36,192	2.6	70.2	16.0	25.4
Sacramento-Roseville-Folsom, CA	12.4	9.8	6.3	50.8	21,49,127	23,97,382	11.6	0.6	31,542	27,011	9,195	8,40,925	2.7	67.1	12.3	24.9
Saginaw, MI	13.8	11.8	8.1	51.1	2,00,169	1,90,124	-5.0	-0.3	2,523	3,195	122	78,980	2.3	62.4	14.1	31.2
St. Cloud, MN	12.2	9.1	6.3	49.5	1,89,093	1,99,671	5.6	0.4	3,092	2,275	-123	76,058	2.5	63.3	8.8	27.6
St. George, UT	10.6	12.6	9.5	50.1	1,38,115	1,80,279	30.5	6.1	2,660	2,342	10,772	59,699	2.9	75.2	8.1	20.7
St. Joseph, MO-KS	13.5	10.6	7.3	48.7	1,27,329	1,21,467	-4.6	-0.9	1,773	1,972	-846	47,244	2.5	62.1	11.1	31.4
St. Louis, MO-IL	13.9	10.6	6.9	51.2	27,87,701	28,20,253	1.2	-0.4	37,714	41,796	-7,038	11,37,735	2.4	63.7	12.5	30.2
Salem, OR	11.6	10.2	6.6	50.0	3,90,738	4,33,353	10.9	0.7	5,992	5,510	2,387	1,51,200	2.8	68.0	12.5	24.9
Salinas, CA	11.0	8.7	5.8	48.9	4,15,057	4,39,035	5.8	-0.4	7,031	3,898	-4,901	1,28,003	3.3	72.6	12.5	21.4
Salisbury, MD-DE	15.5	16.0	9.6	51.3	3,73,802	4,18,046	11.8	2.7	5,136	7,342	13,537	1,63,535	2.4	66.6	12.2	27.2
Salt Lake City, UT	9.9	7.3	4.2	49.5	10,87,873	12,57,936	15.6	0.4	20,242	10,972	-4,323	4,04,471	3.0	69.9	10.1	22.9
San Angelo, TX	11.3	9.6	6.6	50.0	1,12,966	1,22,888	8.8	-0.4	1,913	1,622	-836	43,994	2.6	64.2	11.4	29.4
San Antonio-New Braunfels, TX	11.2	8.4	5.2	50.3	21,42,508	25,58,143	19.4	1.7	38,355	28,142	33,118	8,26,094	3.0	67.6	14.8	26.8
San Diego-Chula Vista-Carlsbad, CA	11.8	8.9	5.9	49.3	30,95,313	32,98,634	6.6	-0.4	46,391	32,777	-26,554	11,30,703	2.9	67.2	11.6	23.9
San Francisco-Oakland-Berkeley, CA	12.8	9.8	6.9	50.2	43,35,391	47,49,008	9.5	-2.6	58,634	46,261	-1,36,602	17,01,865	2.7	63.9	10.3	26.3
Oakland-Berkeley-Livermore, CA Div 36,084	12.7	9.4	6.3	50.6	25,59,296	28,48,280	11.3	-1.3	36,309	27,578	-46,862	9,71,473	2.9	68.7	11.6	23.4
San Francisco-San Mateo-Redwood City, CA Div 41,884	12.7	10.1	7.4	49.5	15,23,686	16,38,407	7.5	-5.2	19,759	15,829	-87,910	6,25,492	2.6	56.7	8.8	30.4
San Rafael, CA Div 42,034	15.1	13.3	10.1	50.6	2,52,409	2,62,321	3.9	-0.8	2,566	2,854	-1,830	1,04,900	2.4	63.0	8.3	29.3
San Jose-Sunnyvale-Santa Clara, CA	12.2	8.3	6.2	49.1	18,36,911	20,00,468	8.9	-2.4	25,836	16,375	-57,128	6,53,703	3.0	71.7	10.0	20.2
San Luis Obispo-Paso Robles, CA	12.9	13.1	8.3	49.2	2,69,637	2,82,424	4.7	0.3	2,983	3,358	1,099	1,06,244	2.5	63.2	8.7	26.6
Santa Cruz-Watsonville, CA	12.8	11.7	6.6	50.3	2,62,382	2,70,861	3.2	-1.1	2,848	2,691	-3,230	96,275	2.7	63.2	10.1	25.1
Santa Fe, NM	14.9	16.7	10.0	51.2	1,44,170	1,54,823	7.4	0.2	1,411	1,893	879	63,152	2.3	57.7	10.8	35.5
Santa Maria-Santa Barbara, CA	11.1	9.2	6.8	49.8	4,23,895	4,48,229	5.7	-0.4	6,722	4,541	-3,973	1,48,309	2.9	65.7	11.0	23.9
Santa Rosa-Petaluma, CA	14.0	13.0	8.1	50.8	4,83,878	4,88,863	1.0	-0.6	5,430	6,077	-2,361	1,88,958	2.6	63.6	9.6	27.0
Savannah, GA	12.0	9.4	5.8	51.4	3,47,611	4,04,798	16.5	1.3	5,957	4,896	4,162	1,45,199	2.6	64.2	15.3	28.3
Scranton--Wilkes-Barre, PA	14.1	11.7	8.4	50.4	5,63,631	5,67,559	0.7	0.0	6,647	10,164	3,710	2,28,663	2.3	61.9	12.8	32.1
Seattle-Tacoma-Bellevue, WA	12.0	8.7	5.3	49.5	34,39,809	40,18,762	16.8	-0.2	54,021	40,144	-21,498	15,29,875	2.5	63.0	9.1	27.4
Seattle-Bellevue-Kent, WA Div 42,644	11.9	8.7	5.3	49.4	26,44,584	30,97,632	17.1	-0.4	40,547	29,437	-23,095	11,98,876	2.5	61.8	8.5	28.1
Tacoma-Lakewood, WA Div 45,104	12.1	9.0	5.4	49.8	7,95,225	9,21,130	15.8	0.5	13,474	10,707	1,597	3,30,999	2.6	67.1	11.3	25.1
Sebastian-Vero Beach, FL	15.7	18.4	15.9	51.7	1,38,028	1,59,788	15.8	2.4	1,517	3,196	5,637	60,959	2.6	61.8	6.7	33.2
Sebring-Avon Park, FL	13.3	17.4	18.3	50.9	98,786	1,01,235	2.5	2.0	961	2,404	3,573	42,721	2.4	63.6	10.0	31.5
Sheboygan, WI	14.8	11.6	7.4	49.1	1,15,507	1,18,034	2.2	-0.2	1,450	1,702	-52	47,754	2.4	63.1	7.4	30.7
Sherman-Denison, TX	13.5	11.1	7.0	50.9	1,20,877	1,35,543	12.1	2.8	1,896	2,226	4,165	49,327	2.7	68.5	12.2	26.5
Shreveport-Bossier City, LA	12.5	10.5	6.8	51.7	3,98,604	3,93,406	-1.3	-1.1	6,059	6,246	-4,063	1,56,594	2.5	62.1	16.8	32.8
Sierra Vista-Douglas, AZ	13.0	13.8	9.9	48.8	1,31,346	1,25,447	-4.5	0.5	1,574	1,986	1,016	50,917	2.3	62.2	10.2	32.9
Sioux City, IA-NE-SD	12.1	9.7	6.0	49.7	1,43,577	1,49,940	4.4	-0.5	2,486	2,032	-1,148	56,113	2.5	66.0	12.3	27.1
Sioux Falls, SD	11.9	9.2	4.9	49.4	2,28,261	2,76,730	21.2	1.9	4,589	2,992	3,605	1,04,530	2.5	63.8	9.5	29.1
South Bend-Mishawaka, IN-MI	12.7	10.7	6.7	50.7	3,19,224	3,24,501	1.7	-0.2	4,716	4,806	-768	1,25,606	2.5	62.4	12.1	31.7
Spartanburg, SC	12.7	10.0	6.3	51.2	2,84,307	3,27,997	15.4	2.4	4,817	4,928	8,027	1,18,788	2.6	67.7	13.9	27.3
Spokane-Spokane Valley, WA	12.8	11.0	6.4	50.0	5,14,752	5,85,784	13.8	1.3	7,518	8,019	8,174	2,24,385	2.4	63.1	10.4	28.6
Springfield, IL	14.1	11.6	7.3	51.7	2,10,170	2,08,640	-0.7	-0.8	2,640	3,224	-1,184	89,304	2.3	60.3	13.2	33.2
Springfield, MA	13.7	11.4	7.2	51.8	6,92,942	6,99,162	0.9	-0.6	7,623	10,030	-1,537	2,70,889	2.4	62.4	15.1	30.2
Springfield, MO	12.2	9.9	7.0	50.8	4,36,712	4,75,432	8.9	1.3	6,750	6,798	6,092	1,91,961	2.4	62.7	9.6	28.9
Springfield, OH	13.7	11.9	7.9	51.1	1,38,333	1,36,001	-1.7	-0.3	1,896	2,575	296	54,862	2.4	64.4	14.2	29.1
State College, PA	11.7	9.4	6.2	47.2	1,53,990	1,58,172	2.7	-0.4	1,295	1,615	-360	59,380	2.4	56.1	5.6	31.0
Staunton, VA	14.4	12.2	8.8	50.5	1,18,502	1,25,433	5.8	0.3	1,457	2,100	987	49,972	2.3	63.9	11.0	30.4
Stockton, CA	11.2	7.9	5.1	49.8	6,85,306	7,79,233	13.7	1.3	12,218	8,939	6,798	2,31,092	3.2	74.7	15.1	20.2
Sumter, SC	13.3	11.4	7.6	51.6	1,42,427	1,36,700	-4.0	-0.7	2,051	2,300	-673	54,479	2.5	65.9	17.1	30.5
Syracuse, NY	14.5	11.0	7.2	51.0	6,62,577	6,62,057	-0.1	-0.6	8,249	9,102	-3,008	2,59,905	2.4	61.6	12.2	30.1
Tallahassee, FL	11.4	9.8	5.8	51.8	3,67,413	3,84,298	4.6	0.4	4,675	4,625	1,368	1,50,862	2.4	56.6	13.6	31.0
Tampa-St. Petersburg-Clearwater, FL	13.8	11.6	8.6	51.2	27,83,243	31,75,275	14.1	1.4	38,023	49,708	56,245	12,39,349	2.5	61.5	12.1	30.8
Terre Haute, IN	12.7	10.7	7.1	49.3	1,89,764	1,85,031	-2.5	-0.1	2,406	3,015	463	73,479	2.4	63.8	11.8	29.3

Area name	Persons in group quarters, 2021	Daytime population, 2016–2020: Number	Daytime population, 2016–2020: Employment/residence ratio	Births, 2021: Total	Births, 2021: Rate[1]	Deaths, 2021: Number	Deaths, 2021: Rate[1]	Persons under 65 with no health insurance 2019: Number	Persons under 65 with no health insurance 2019: Percent	Medicare, 2021: Total Beneficiaries	Medicare, 2021: Enrolled in Original Medicare	Medicare, 2021: Enrolled in Medicare Advantage	Serious crimes known to police[2], 2020: Violent: Number	Serious crimes known to police[2], 2020: Violent: Rate[3]
	32	33	34	35	36	37	38	39	40	41	42	43	44	45
Reading, PA	11,304	3,94,692	0.88	4,484	10.5	4,792	11.2	25,575	7.6	87,761	52,756	35,005	NA	NA
Redding, CA	2,851	1,79,516	1.00	1,826	10.0	2,480	13.6	11,387	8.1	47,810	43,541	4,269	977	547.1
Reno, NV	5,244	4,69,405	1.00	5,047	10.2	5,002	10.1	48,639	12.4	95,631	58,979	36,652	2,238	462.9
Richmond, VA	32,437	12,92,980	1.02	14,014	10.6	13,813	10.5	98,056	9.3	2,46,451	1,63,438	83,013	2,811	215.7
Riverside-San Bernardino-Ontario, CA	69,959	43,61,549	0.88	54,288	11.7	41,108	8.9	3,88,520	9.9	7,11,183	2,72,633	4,38,550	20,054	431.1
Roanoke, VA	7,448	3,25,427	1.08	3,068	9.7	4,254	13.5	22,056	9.1	78,251	51,142	27,109	821	261.9
Rochester, MN	2,932	2,25,555	1.05	2,644	11.7	2,013	8.9	10,379	5.7	43,083	27,340	15,743	418	187.6
Rochester, NY	39,437	10,77,976	1.01	10,515	9.7	12,121	11.2	36,842	4.4	2,41,882	73,703	1,68,179	2,782	262.0
Rockford, IL	4,823	3,33,849	0.98	3,786	11.2	3,907	11.6	22,270	8.2	69,981	36,727	33,254	2,566	770.7
Rocky Mount, NC	2,704	1,43,049	0.95	1,591	11.1	2,003	13.9	14,134	12.4	34,947	20,848	14,099	NA	NA
Rome, GA	3,551	99,919	1.05	1,076	10.9	1,349	13.7	14,101	18.1	20,865	11,299	9,566	NA	NA
Sacramento-Roseville-Folsom, CA	37,948	23,30,207	0.99	25,248	10.5	21,822	9.1	1,26,618	6.5	4,40,638	2,10,967	2,29,671	8,945	378.3
Saginaw, MI	6,486	2,03,357	1.15	2,021	10.7	2,545	13.4	8,608	5.8	46,087	20,488	25,599	1,501	794.6
St. Cloud, MN	7,447	2,07,606	1.07	2,443	12.2	1,794	9.0	10,752	6.5	36,800	18,957	17,843	NA	NA
St. George, UT	2,074	1,73,307	1.02	2,138	11.5	1,901	10.2	20,380	15.0	42,652	26,246	16,406	294	161.5
St. Joseph, MO-KS	6,165	1,27,073	1.04	1,417	11.7	1,555	12.9	12,364	12.9	25,679	19,416	6,263	521	417.0
St. Louis, MO-IL	52,061	28,19,953	1.01	30,080	10.7	33,414	11.9	1,97,062	8.6	5,66,492	2,80,374	2,86,118	13,925	497.0
Salem, OR	11,781	4,18,194	0.95	4,772	11.0	4,385	10.1	34,999	10.0	86,579	33,675	52,904	1,177	269.5
Salinas, CA	17,194	4,25,939	0.96	5,595	12.8	3,128	7.1	42,273	11.9	68,391	60,621	7,770	1,480	342.8
Salisbury, MD-DE	12,837	4,03,748	0.96	4,175	9.8	5,978	14.1	28,033	9.3	1,20,653	1,00,422	20,231	NA	NA
Salt Lake City, UT	14,951	12,91,294	1.12	16,145	12.8	8,781	7.0	1,22,575	11.3	1,58,629	80,561	78,068	4,785	384.0
San Angelo, TX	4,847	1,21,713	1.00	1,521	12.4	1,298	10.6	17,304	17.6	23,190	13,819	9,371	397	323.8
San Antonio-New Braunfels, TX	46,556	24,95,421	0.99	30,857	11.9	22,559	8.7	4,02,935	18.6	4,23,650	2,17,291	2,06,359	13,749	530.6
San Diego-Chula Vista-Carlsbad, CA	1,07,528	33,61,529	1.02	37,107	11.3	26,463	8.0	2,47,271	8.9	5,60,299	2,71,058	2,89,241	11,517	345.7
San Francisco-Oakland-Berkeley, CA	88,930	47,96,847	1.04	46,755	10.0	37,703	8.1	2,20,183	5.6	8,03,551	4,17,301	3,86,250	20,814	440.1
Oakland-Berkeley-Livermore, CA Div 36,084	46,272	26,50,967	0.88	28,949	10.2	22,509	8.0	1,34,869	5.7	4,60,396	2,33,161	2,27,235	13,515	478.1
San Francisco-San Mateo-Redwood City, CA Div 41,884	34,262	18,87,022	1.27	15,772	9.9	12,889	8.1	74,908	5.4	2,82,498	1,50,006	1,32,492	6,676	405.6
San Rafael, CA Div 42,034	8,396	2,58,858	1.00	2,034	7.8	2,305	8.8	10,406	5.3	60,657	34,134	26,523	623	242.5
San Jose-Sunnyvale-Santa Clara, CA	30,477	21,12,907	1.13	20,609	10.4	13,405	6.8	96,132	5.6	2,89,142	1,53,611	1,35,531	6,306	317.2
San Luis Obispo-Paso Robles, CA	16,055	2,83,153	1.00	2,357	8.3	2,671	9.4	14,763	7.0	67,930	54,208	13,722	816	289.6
Santa Cruz-Watsonville, CA	13,456	2,61,860	0.91	2,258	8.4	2,226	8.3	17,026	7.9	53,921	43,440	10,481	970	357.1
Santa Fe, NM	2,575	1,52,570	1.03	1,140	7.4	1,542	9.9	15,703	14.2	43,102	26,613	16,489	NA	NA
Santa Maria-Santa Barbara, CA	19,813	4,56,042	1.05	5,303	11.9	3,632	8.1	43,058	12.0	79,698	65,137	14,561	1,824	410.3
Santa Rosa-Petaluma, CA	10,061	4,81,971	0.94	4,290	8.8	4,933	10.1	30,207	7.8	1,10,504	54,784	55,720	2,212	451.0
Savannah, GA	15,464	4,01,148	1.06	4,800	11.8	3,955	9.7	49,440	15.4	69,463	36,417	33,046	NA	NA
Scranton--Wilkes-Barre, PA	19,973	5,56,932	1.01	5,325	9.4	8,059	14.2	30,807	7.2	1,34,613	87,858	46,755	NA	NA
Seattle-Tacoma-Bellevue, WA	69,620	39,83,584	1.03	42,924	10.7	32,189	8.0	2,30,425	6.8	6,29,821	3,39,664	2,90,157	13,692	339.7
Seattle-Bellevue-Kent, WA Div 42,644	49,199	31,52,663	1.07	32,234	10.4	23,607	7.6	1,72,798	6.5	4,69,793	2,46,195	2,23,598	9,720	312.0
Tacoma-Lakewood, WA Div 45,104	20,421	8,30,921	0.86	10,690	11.6	8,582	9.3	57,627	7.6	1,60,028	93,469	66,559	3,972	434.1
Sebastian-Vero Beach, FL	1,147	1,58,529	1.03	1,237	7.6	2,563	15.8	19,417	18.6	57,037	36,620	20,417	219	135.1
Sebring-Avon Park, FL	1,354	1,03,606	0.97	784	7.7	1,880	18.4	13,536	20.4	34,950	18,133	16,817	296	277.2
Sheboygan, WI	2,769	1,16,208	1.02	1,158	9.8	1,353	11.5	5,748	6.3	26,222	12,171	14,051	209	181.4
Sherman-Denison, TX	1,987	1,28,992	0.93	1,500	10.9	1,806	13.1	24,027	21.8	30,024	18,469	11,555	392	285.0
Shreveport-Bossier City, LA	8,512	4,02,174	1.03	4,893	12.5	5,082	13.0	31,250	9.8	79,148	49,320	29,828	2,683	683.0
Sierra Vista-Douglas, AZ	5,063	1,25,360	0.98	1,291	10.3	1,582	12.6	10,599	11.5	34,290	21,232	13,058	310	246.2
Sioux City, IA-NE-SD	2,888	1,45,141	1.01	1,978	13.2	1,549	10.4	10,631	8.9	27,025	17,778	9,247	619	428.3
Sioux Falls, SD	6,841	2,67,633	1.02	3,623	13.0	2,313	8.3	22,797	10.0	50,579	34,630	15,949	1,304	477.7
South Bend-Mishawaka, IN-MI	11,861	3,15,199	0.95	3,740	11.5	3,850	11.9	25,282	9.8	64,276	35,836	28,440	2,121	655.2
Spartanburg, SC	7,562	3,22,421	1.06	3,878	11.7	3,957	11.9	33,742	13.0	67,628	35,793	31,835	1,643	506.6
Spokane-Spokane Valley, WA	14,569	5,65,226	1.03	5,881	10.0	6,408	10.9	32,442	7.1	1,24,905	68,400	56,505	2,005	350.0
Springfield, IL	3,975	2,18,489	1.10	2,103	10.1	2,607	12.6	10,719	6.5	45,390	23,883	21,507	1,369	666.5
Springfield, MA	38,558	6,86,690	0.96	6,115	8.8	8,025	11.5	21,121	3.9	1,59,880	1,04,439	55,441	3,216	463.4
Springfield, MO	13,810	4,71,633	1.02	5,442	11.4	5,445	11.4	50,950	13.5	98,086	45,264	52,822	2,993	631.6
Springfield, OH	3,210	1,24,623	0.83	1,548	11.4	2,032	15.0	8,896	8.5	31,050	14,019	17,031	401	300.5
State College, PA	18,682	1,70,818	1.11	1,006	6.4	1,328	8.4	9,766	8.2	25,748	11,912	13,836	NA	NA
Staunton, VA	3,970	1,14,000	0.85	1,149	9.1	1,673	13.3	9,234	9.9	30,785	23,552	7,233	231	186.9
Stockton, CA	15,767	7,15,967	0.88	9,682	12.3	7,059	9.0	53,036	8.2	1,16,686	61,645	55,041	5,517	722.8
Sumter, SC	3,362	1,37,091	0.94	1,630	12.0	1,817	13.3	14,123	12.9	31,683	19,482	12,201	1,140	812.0
Syracuse, NY	25,378	6,55,335	1.02	6,551	9.9	7,264	11.0	24,966	4.9	1,38,960	64,790	74,170	1,953	303.8
Tallahassee, FL	21,958	3,90,622	1.03	3,747	9.7	3,667	9.5	38,627	12.6	69,435	31,036	38,399	2,157	555.7
Tampa-St. Petersburg-Clearwater, FL	48,115	31,39,034	0.99	30,692	9.6	39,983	12.5	3,82,967	15.2	7,05,277	2,99,452	4,05,825	10,159	314.1
Terre Haute, IN	13,564	1,84,434	0.97	1,928	10.4	2,436	13.2	14,045	10.0	40,650	26,840	13,810	NA	NA

1. Per 1,000 estimated resident population. 2. Data for serious crimes have not been adjusted for underreporting; this may affect comparability between geographic areas and over time. 3. Per 100,000 population estimated by the FBI.

Area name	Serious crimes known to police[2], 2020 (cont.): Property: Number	Property: Rate	Education: School enrollment and attainment, 2016–2020: Enrollment[3]: Total	Enrollment[3]: Percent private	Attainment[4] (percent): High school graduate or less	Attainment[4] (percent): Bachelor's degree or more	Local government expenditures,[5] 2018–2019: Total current spending (mil dol)	Current spending per student (dollars)	Income and poverty, 2016–2020: Per capita income[6] (dollars)	Mean household income (dollars)	Mean Individual income	Percent of households with income of less than $50,000	Percent of households with income of $200,000 or more	Percent below poverty level: All persons	All families	Age 65 years and older
	46	47	48	49	50	51	52	53	54	55	56	57	58	59	60	61
Reading, PA	NA	NA	1,01,564	17.5	49.1	25.9	1,094.9	16,106	32,781	66,154	81,425	37.4	5.7	11.7	8.3	14.4
Redding, CA	3,430	1,920.6	40,910	15.1	34.5	22.1	370.2	13,422	31,049	57,139	69,052	44.5	5.2	15.1	9.8	16.1
Reno, NV	8,842	1,828.9	1,11,587	11.0	34.8	31.7	655.1	9,668	37,707	68,214	84,215	35.8	7.6	10.9	6.5	10.5
Richmond, VA	23,905	1,834.5	3,09,837	17.2	34.1	38.0	2,164.5	11,073	39,237	71,223	91,165	35.0	8.8	10.4	6.8	11.3
Riverside-San Bernardino-Ontario, CA	92,307	1,984.5	12,89,108	11.7	44.7	22.4	11,186.0	13,450	28,263	68,331	76,686	36.7	7.4	13.7	10.5	15.1
Roanoke, VA	6,607	2,107.6	66,894	18.2	41.5	28.4	523.2	11,849	33,722	57,642	73,561	43.0	5.5	12.5	8.8	16.4
Rochester, MN	3,041	1,364.8	54,891	14.6	28.9	40.3	427.2	11,911	40,088	76,787	94,698	30.7	8.1	7.8	4.7	7.8
Rochester, NY	17,338	1,633.0	2,56,452	23.8	34.9	35.6	3,184.0	20,450	34,501	61,747	80,423	40.8	5.7	13.2	8.9	16.0
Rockford, IL	D	D	80,225	18.6	43.4	23.2	798.1	14,599	30,331	56,899	69,881	43.9	4.4	14.6	10.8	18.4
Rocky Mount, NC	NA	NA	33,205	12.3	50.2	19.4	228.3	9,805	25,261	46,482	57,013	53.7	2.8	18.1	14.2	24.8
Rome, GA	NA	NA	24,112	20.7	49.7	21.4	193.5	11,915	27,418	50,657	61,841	49.5	3.8	18.6	14.0	24.1
Sacramento-Roseville-Folsom, CA	47,650	2,015.3	6,17,938	11.1	31.2	34.3	4,852.8	12,941	37,122	75,533	90,500	33.2	10.2	12.7	8.6	13.0
Saginaw, MI	2,410	1,275.9	45,707	11.0	42.5	22.1	327.9	12,347	28,628	49,565	64,094	50.4	3.6	17.6	12.1	21.2
St. Cloud, MN	NA	NA	56,935	16.3	36.7	26.8	386.9	12,141	31,562	64,118	80,403	38.9	4.5	11.3	6.2	10.4
St. George, UT	2,118	1,163.3	46,460	11.7	28.7	29.2	258.6	7,198	29,886	61,747	72,683	38.9	5.2	10.0	7.2	11.8
St. Joseph, MO-KS	4,424	3,541.3	28,294	9.5	48.2	21.8	176.4	10,067	26,679	53,298	66,409	47.0	2.9	14.0	9.9	16.3
St. Louis, MO-IL	D	D	6,75,362	24.4	33.3	35.4	5,288.9	13,129	36,995	65,725	84,758	38.1	7.3	10.7	7.3	12.1
Salem, OR	12,462	2,853.6	1,02,823	13.8	39.1	25.4	860.3	12,275	29,469	62,539	73,679	39.6	4.4	13.1	8.9	14.7
Salinas, CA	7,728	1,790.1	1,22,217	9.4	47.1	26.2	1,094.4	14,275	32,122	76,943	83,052	31.3	11.1	12.0	8.8	13.4
Salisbury, MD-DE	NA	NA	88,022	11.8	42.8	28.3	860.3	15,078	34,277	62,799	76,095	40.0	5.8	12.8	8.1	15.9
Salt Lake City, UT	47,566	3,816.8	3,49,791	13.3	31.3	35.8	1,904.0	8,000	34,242	77,102	90,360	29.6	8.3	8.4	5.5	8.1
San Angelo, TX	3,259	2,658.1	31,695	10.0	42.9	24.9	210.6	9,579	29,525	57,431	71,287	44.4	3.9	12.1	8.0	13.7
San Antonio-New Braunfels, TX	72,783	2,808.9	6,70,206	13.7	40.5	28.8	4,370.4	9,678	29,695	61,437	74,284	40.6	6.4	14.2	10.5	15.7
San Diego-Chula Vista-Carlsbad, CA	49,471	1,484.8	8,60,261	14.5	30.2	39.5	6,777.1	13,075	39,737	82,426	95,623	30.1	12.9	10.9	7.2	10.7
San Francisco-Oakland-Berkeley, CA	1,42,267	3,008.2	11,03,721	20.0	25.7	50.7	8,573.5	14,445	57,778	1,10,837	1,31,087	23.3	24.8	8.5	5.3	7.6
Oakland-Berkeley-Livermore, CA Div 36,084	81,991	2,900.6	7,05,032	15.8	27.8	46.5	5,429.6	13,418	49,979	1,04,504	1,23,312	24.0	21.2	8.8	5.8	8.2
San Francisco-San Mateo-Redwood City, CA Div 41,884	55,003	3,342.1	3,39,566	28.2	23.7	55.8	2,584.5	16,625	68,498	1,22,826	1,43,526	22.5	29.5	8.3	4.6	6.6
San Rafael, CA Div 42,034	5,273	2,052.6	59,123	23.3	16.6	60.2	559.4	16,728	74,446	1,21,671	1,59,898	21.3	29.8	6.9	3.9	5.3
San Jose-Sunnyvale-Santa Clara, CA	44,263	2,226.6	5,19,431	21.8	25.8	52.5	4,122.9	14,913	58,508	1,29,343	1,45,548	19.3	29.7	7.2	4.4	5.7
San Luis Obispo-Paso Robles, CA	4,610	1,636.0	76,579	8.1	28.1	36.1	450.9	13,062	38,686	77,948	97,590	31.9	10.2	11.1	5.3	7.6
Santa Cruz-Watsonville, CA	6,155	2,266.1	80,697	13.1	27.3	41.8	587.0	14,372	44,278	89,986	1,09,931	28.5	16.8	11.9	6.6	9.4
Santa Fe, NM	NA	NA	30,039	13.8	33.2	40.7	186.6	10,148	38,288	60,668	73,862	41.8	7.4	13.0	9.0	18.2
Santa Maria-Santa Barbara, CA	8,827	1,985.6	1,35,871	9.6	35.1	35.0	972.7	14,031	38,141	78,925	89,549	31.5	13.2	12.9	7.1	11.2
Santa Rosa-Petaluma, CA	6,412	1,307.4	1,14,484	12.0	29.1	36.4	976.4	13,970	44,071	86,173	1,02,411	27.9	12.3	8.8	5.1	8.5
Savannah, GA	NA	NA	1,05,106	23.6	36.2	32.6	653.0	10,893	32,999	60,851	75,128	40.9	5.9	12.8	9.0	14.7
Scranton--Wilkes-Barre, PA	NA	NA	1,20,183	25.7	47.5	25.3	1,107.2	14,650	30,111	53,853	70,003	46.6	3.6	14.1	10.3	18.9
Seattle-Tacoma-Bellevue, WA	1,27,233	3,156.9	9,04,299	17.7	26.3	43.6	7,967.0	14,397	48,157	90,790	1,09,109	25.8	14.9	8.4	5.3	8.0
Seattle-Bellevue-Kent, WA Div 42,644	97,577	3,132.2	6,93,388	18.2	24.0	48.0	6,051.4	14,613	51,566	96,148	1,16,853	24.5	17.0	8.1	5.0	7.3
Tacoma-Lakewood, WA Div 45,104	29,656	3,241.0	2,10,911	16.0	34.7	27.7	1,915.7	13,755	36,548	76,438	88,892	30.8	7.4	9.5	6.4	10.2
Sebastian-Vero Beach, FL	1,880	1,160.2	28,747	19.6	38.7	30.6	175.3	9,817	38,274	57,945	72,001	44.3	7.1	10.3	5.8	11.8
Sebring-Avon Park, FL	1,889	1,769.0	17,405	13.8	51.8	17.5	116.2	9,424	27,979	43,708	52,793	55.8	2.7	16.0	12.0	21.8
Sheboygan, WI	1,364	1,183.8	26,186	18.1	41.5	25.7	224.7	12,018	32,360	62,101	76,845	39.4	3.6	7.0	3.8	6.3
Sherman-Denison, TX	2,064	1,500.6	31,803	11.6	40.3	20.6	235.2	9,938	29,157	58,296	71,649	42.4	4.1	12.0	8.6	14.2
Shreveport-Bossier City, LA	14,095	3,588.1	96,369	12.4	43.5	24.1	792.3	12,037	32,415	46,610	59,467	52.7	4.6	20.9	16.2	25.5
Sierra Vista-Douglas, AZ	2,598	2,063.2	28,273	11.9	35.3	25.6	169.9	9,150	28,021	51,505	64,128	48.2	2.8	15.2	10.9	19.5
Sioux City, IA-NE-SD	3,326	2,301.4	37,185	13.3	44.7	23.1	333.1	12,219	30,358	61,399	74,387	39.9	4.5	12.1	9.3	14.8
Sioux Falls, SD	6,891	2,524.2	64,966	18.5	33.0	33.9	422.7	9,339	34,076	67,713	84,874	35.9	5.2	8.2	5.3	7.1
South Bend-Mishawaka, IN-MI	7,031	2,172.1	84,192	31.8	40.9	29.2	460.9	10,130	30,148	55,101	70,437	45.7	4.4	14.3	10.4	17.2
Spartanburg, SC	7,935	2,446.7	76,469	16.9	43.5	24.8	563.2	11,471	27,788	53,757	65,214	46.5	3.9	14.4	10.7	16.5
Spokane-Spokane Valley, WA	19,927	3,478.6	1,33,416	18.1	30.0	30.7	1,178.6	14,578	32,382	59,656	76,280	42.1	5.3	12.9	8.0	13.2
Springfield, IL	D	D	49,436	15.9	35.3	33.5	423.2	13,459	35,765	62,590	83,948	40.4	5.4	13.6	9.4	16.8
Springfield, MA	10,788	1,554.5	1,84,160	19.0	39.6	33.2	1,776.2	17,931	33,113	61,360	79,907	41.9	6.5	14.1	9.7	15.9
Springfield, MO	15,647	3,301.7	1,19,733	17.3	38.7	28.7	655.5	9,614	27,734	50,496	64,545	49.4	3.2	14.5	9.1	14.0
Springfield, OH	3,872	2,901.3	30,472	20.3	49.1	18.9	263.3	12,823	27,274	51,504	63,361	48.7	2.2	15.3	11.1	18.4
State College, PA	NA	NA	58,001	9.8	33.5	45.8	237.5	18,138	32,238	61,921	90,415	41.2	7.0	17.8	4.6	7.0
Staunton, VA	1,812	1,466.4	23,893	22.9	48.2	25.2	185.9	11,443	30,143	58,166	73,822	43.5	3.1	10.7	7.4	12.9
Stockton, CA	17,805	2,332.8	2,10,914	12.1	48.3	19.2	2,001.3	13,581	28,928	68,628	76,536	36.1	7.7	13.7	10.8	15.3
Sumter, SC	3,852	2,743.6	33,474	16.8	47.5	19.5	226.1	10,493	24,276	45,854	57,134	53.7	2.2	19.0	14.4	24.7
Syracuse, NY	10,985	1,708.7	1,61,674	22.5	37.6	32.2	1,975.0	19,927	33,537	61,890	79,766	40.8	5.3	13.8	10.0	17.5
Tallahassee, FL	8,643	2,226.7	1,21,777	12.8	32.9	39.0	436.5	9,074	29,989	53,423	72,943	47.3	5.2	18.7	10.2	16.8
Tampa-St. Petersburg-Clearwater, FL	44,114	1,363.9	6,97,709	18.8	38.8	31.2	3,868.3	9,231	33,448	57,097	71,769	43.9	6.2	13.0	9.0	14.2
Terre Haute, IN	NA	NA	45,608	12.6	47.4	20.2	283.3	10,610	26,286	50,418	63,958	49.6	2.5	16.3	11.5	19.1

1. Data for serious crimes have not been adjusted for underreporting; this may affect comparability between geographic areas and over time. 2. Per 100,000 population estimated by the FBI. 3. All persons 3 years old and over enrolled in nursery school through college. 4. Persons 25 years old and over. 5. Elementary and secondary education expenditures. 6. Based on population estimated by the American Community Survey, 2015.

Area name	Personal income, 2020										Earnings, 2020		
			Per capita[1]			Supplements to wages and salaries, employer contributions (mil dol)						Contributrions for government social insurance (mil dol)	
	Total (mil dol)	Percent change, 2019–2020	Dollars	Rank	Wages and Salaries (mil dol)	Pension and insurance	Government social insurance	Proprietors' income	Dividends, interest, and rent (mil dol)	Personal transfer receipts (mil dol)	Total (mil dol)	From employee and self-employed	From employer
	62	63	64	65	66	67	68	69	70	71	72	73	74
Reading, PA	23,557	8.6	55,953	105	9,504	1,779	739	1,731	3,363	6,376	13,753	847	739
Redding, CA	9,247	10.9	51,649	170	3,523	731	263	696	1,333	3,297	5,213	348	263
Reno, NV	31,801	6.0	66,075	33	14,088	2,311	1,037	2,156	8,854	5,564	19,592	1,180	1,037
Richmond, VA	79,704	6.0	61,148	58	41,210	6,035	2,888	6,922	14,370	15,387	57,054	3,581	2,888
Riverside-San Bernardino-Ontario, CA	2,12,234	11.5	45,365	295	84,997	16,400	6,323	14,110	26,544	58,384	1,21,829	7,463	6,323
Roanoke, VA	15,757	7.1	50,215	197	7,970	1,269	587	802	2,836	4,280	10,628	726	587
Rochester, MN	13,348	7.9	59,842	69	7,670	1,064	562	951	2,091	2,610	10,248	637	562
Rochester, NY	60,289	7.3	56,477	99	27,301	5,481	2,199	4,224	9,189	16,568	39,204	2,254	2,199
Rockford, IL	16,030	7.0	47,982	244	7,418	1,360	532	729	2,221	4,469	10,039	621	532
Rocky Mount, NC	6,355	6.9	43,623	331	2,560	468	187	339	980	2,099	3,554	250	187
Rome, GA	4,066	7.1	41,238	360	1,905	321	135	290	589	1,338	2,651	170	135
Sacramento-Roseville-Folsom, CA	1,46,882	9.0	61,852	50	70,672	14,407	4,737	10,577	22,381	33,657	1,00,393	5,587	4,737
Saginaw, MI	8,606	8.5	45,328	298	4,070	708	309	653	1,094	3,157	5,740	396	309
St. Cloud, MN	10,322	8.4	50,850	183	5,425	884	422	891	1,631	2,494	7,623	469	422
St. George, UT	8,096	8.7	43,782	329	3,171	497	235	742	2,048	1,929	4,645	324	235
St. Joseph, MO-KS	5,277	5.1	43,061	339	2,808	494	210	364	680	1,505	3,875	249	210
St. Louis, MO-IL	1,70,697	5.6	60,844	63	84,270	12,939	5,977	10,414	36,702	34,129	1,13,600	7,189	5,977
Salem, OR	20,816	8.9	47,638	253	9,294	1,875	824	1,985	3,121	6,000	13,978	876	824
Salinas, CA	26,505	8.2	61,510	54	10,711	2,364	859	3,655	5,001	5,671	17,589	883	859
Salisbury, MD-DE	21,694	6.0	51,228	176	7,482	1,375	576	1,960	4,106	6,774	11,394	781	576
Salt Lake City, UT	71,932	7.3	58,008	86	47,967	6,721	3,404	6,287	14,485	10,261	64,379	3,801	3,404
San Angelo, TX	6,551	3.0	53,305	138	2,551	463	181	799	1,441	1,512	3,993	221	181
San Antonio-New Braunfels, TX	1,29,593	5.8	50,022	200	61,148	9,665	4,252	10,361	23,748	28,475	85,426	4,835	4,252
San Diego-Chula Vista-Carlsbad, CA	2,20,826	9.0	66,266	32	1,11,843	19,314	7,960	14,921	41,911	44,237	1,54,038	8,831	7,960
San Francisco-Oakland-Berkeley, CA	5,21,590	7.8	1,11,050	4	2,85,443	33,028	15,775	45,015	1,12,966	64,322	3,79,261	21,372	15,775
Oakland-Berkeley-Livermore, CA Div 36,084	2,51,070	9.6	89,201	X	98,746	14,938	6,594	19,748	43,528	38,471	1,40,026	7,971	6,594
San Francisco-San Mateo-Redwood City, CA Div 41,884	2,33,059	6.6	1,43,428	X	1,77,187	16,700	8,575	20,803	57,702	22,363	2,23,265	12,490	8,575
San Rafael, CA Div 42,034	37,461	4.1	1,45,575	X	9,511	1,389	605	4,464	11,736	3,488	15,969	911	605
San Jose-Sunnyvale-Santa Clara, CA	2,39,730	7.2	1,21,619	2	1,81,334	15,043	8,449	16,704	44,269	22,804	2,21,530	12,679	8,449
San Luis Obispo-Paso Robles, CA	17,596	6.0	62,342	45	6,549	1,395	458	1,978	3,967	3,618	10,380	623	458
Santa Cruz-Watsonville, CA	20,503	8.9	75,957	14	6,311	1,197	448	2,042	4,039	3,645	9,998	575	448
Santa Fe, NM	9,573	5.2	63,004	42	3,062	495	225	609	2,977	2,082	4,392	328	225
Santa Maria-Santa Barbara, CA	30,190	8.1	67,879	23	13,015	2,426	961	3,469	7,951	5,375	19,872	1,097	961
Santa Rosa-Petaluma, CA	34,966	9.5	71,386	16	13,316	2,214	964	3,784	7,408	6,980	20,277	1,227	964
Savannah, GA	20,268	7.2	51,184	177	9,737	1,635	697	1,180	3,708	4,670	13,248	786	697
Scranton--Wilkes-Barre, PA	28,315	8.9	51,246	174	12,159	2,317	977	1,547	4,101	9,130	17,000	1,110	977
Seattle-Tacoma-Bellevue, WA	3,23,176	6.9	80,420	11	1,88,392	22,241	13,615	24,033	64,163	44,121	2,48,281	14,268	13,615
Seattle-Bellevue-Kent, WA Div 42,644	2,71,512	6.6	87,452	X	1,67,472	18,437	11,763	20,470	56,191	32,746	2,18,142	12,510	11,763
Tacoma-Lakewood, WA Div 45,104	51,664	8.7	56,532	X	20,920	3,804	1,852	3,563	7,972	11,375	30,140	1,758	1,852
Sebastian-Vero Beach, FL	13,750	3.4	84,607	7	2,748	375	190	761	6,361	2,579	4,074	334	190
Sebring-Avon Park, FL	3,962	8.7	37,158	380	1,157	202	84	169	773	1,702	1,612	150	84
Sheboygan, WI	6,409	4.5	55,616	111	3,371	581	249	444	1,157	1,299	4,645	301	249
Sherman-Denison, TX	6,507	7.2	47,045	264	2,378	383	166	361	976	1,850	3,288	214	166
Shreveport-Bossier City, LA	20,558	7.8	52,391	153	8,520	1,588	587	1,558	4,244	5,710	12,253	722	587
Sierra Vista-Douglas, AZ	5,835	13.1	45,786	288	2,243	501	176	264	957	2,181	3,185	221	176
Sioux City, IA-NE-SD	8,139	6.3	56,131	101	3,756	614	301	910	1,587	1,651	5,581	358	301
Sioux Falls, SD	18,361	6.2	67,117	29	8,811	1,257	647	3,358	3,463	2,593	14,073	858	647
South Bend-Mishawaka, IN-MI	16,482	6.7	51,017	180	6,888	1,082	528	1,401	2,741	4,112	9,900	648	528
Spartanburg, SC	15,183	7.4	46,543	275	7,998	1,328	586	876	2,813	3,855	10,787	719	586
Spokane-Spokane Valley, WA	28,413	7.9	49,449	214	13,497	2,308	1,168	1,870	4,620	7,856	18,843	1,177	1,168
Springfield, IL	10,870	6.7	52,782	146	5,423	1,076	358	749	1,881	2,632	7,605	431	358
Springfield, MA	40,238	8.0	57,843	88	15,941	3,278	1,139	2,482	5,365	12,809	22,840	1,269	1,139
Springfield, MO	21,178	4.5	44,565	310	10,321	1,773	754	1,813	3,291	5,382	14,661	968	754
Springfield, OH	6,060	8.4	45,363	296	2,199	387	164	316	808	1,985	3,066	206	164
State College, PA	8,174	5.2	50,615	187	4,151	1,474	306	649	1,567	1,624	6,580	343	306
Staunton, VA	5,949	7.3	47,794	248	2,362	400	176	333	1,021	1,578	3,271	231	176
Stockton, CA	39,793	15.9	51,816	166	14,617	2,823	1,109	3,096	4,484	11,403	21,644	1,263	1,109
Sumter, SC	5,844	7.9	41,807	352	2,423	538	194	291	848	1,978	3,446	229	194
Syracuse, NY	35,896	8.1	55,563	112	16,432	3,669	1,312	2,799	4,864	9,852	24,212	1,359	1,312
Tallahassee, FL	18,188	6.7	46,685	271	9,196	1,630	634	987	3,325	4,124	12,447	778	634
Tampa-St. Petersburg-Clearwater, FL	1,69,629	7.8	52,291	156	82,925	11,118	5,611	8,260	32,265	41,585	1,07,915	7,319	5,611
Terre Haute, IN	7,733	7.8	41,658	357	3,178	606	246	451	1,117	2,601	4,480	309	246

1. Based on the resident population estimated as of July 1 of the year shown.

Area name	Earnings, 2020 (cont.): Percent by selected industries: Farm	Mining, quarrying, and extracting	Construction	Manufacturing	Information; professional, scientific, and technical services	Retail trade	Finance, insurance, real estate, rental and leasing	Health care and social assistance	Government	Social Security beneficiaries, December 2020: Number	Rate[1]	Supplemental Security Income Recipients, December 2020	Housing units, 2021: Total	Percent change, 2020–2021
	75	76	77	78	79	80	81	82	83	84	85	86	87	88
Reading, PA	1.2	0.2	6.4	17.7	6.6	5.6	5.9	15.7	12.5	89,860	209	10,769	1,71,301	0.3
Redding, CA	0.9	0.3	8.2	3.7	6.1	10.1	6.3	19.3	22.1	49,110	270	8,928	79,711	0.4
Reno, NV	0.1	D	10.4	12.4	D	D	6.2	D	13.7	92,960	187	6,726	2,14,937	2.1
Richmond, VA	0.1	D	D	5.1	11.7	D	D	11.3	17.2	2,50,715	189	26,655	5,60,844	1.3
Riverside-San Bernardino-Ontario, CA	0.6	0.2	9.1	6.4	5.0	7.6	4.8	12.4	22.0	7,17,200	154	1,32,172	15,94,692	0.7
Roanoke, VA	0.1	0.3	6.6	10.5	D	6.2	D	17.2	14.8	78,985	251	8,208	1,48,162	0.3
Rochester, MN	2.1	0.1	5.6	10.3	3.5	4.7	D	48.0	9.2	43,035	189	2,767	98,364	0.8
Rochester, NY	0.9	0.5	6.4	12.5	D	5.7	5.9	14.3	16.6	2,50,110	231	32,996	4,91,889	0.4
Rockford, IL	0.4	D	5.7	23.3	4.3	6.1	5.1	18.5	13.2	73,155	218	8,012	1,45,181	0.0
Rocky Mount, NC	2.8	0.1	6.6	21.0	4.4	8.3	5.3	D	18.9	36,725	256	6,157	66,580	0.5
Rome, GA	0.3	D	3.0	17.4	D	6.5	5.6	25.8	13.8	22,795	231	3,217	40,751	0.6
Sacramento-Roseville-Folsom, CA	0.4	D	8.2	3.4	D	5.4	8.4	12.7	30.2	4,19,275	174	76,783	9,43,659	0.9
Saginaw, MI	0.8	0.4	4.7	19.3	6.1	7.5	6.5	19.6	13.6	49,910	263	8,429	86,139	0.2
St. Cloud, MN	2.7	0.2	11.2	13.2	5.2	7.5	6.3	16.8	13.9	37,305	186	3,086	83,678	0.6
St. George, UT	0.1	0.5	12.6	4.8	6.8	10.0	11.0	16.0	12.6	42,320	221	1,575	78,974	4.7
St. Joseph, MO-KS	2.6	D	7.3	23.9	D	6.3	5.5	D	13.6	26,965	224	2,711	53,666	0.4
St. Louis, MO-IL	0.3	0.2	D	D	D	5.2	10.5	13.3	11.8	5,78,610	206	56,033	12,66,580	0.5
Salem, OR	3.1	D	9.1	5.6	5.1	6.3	7.2	14.6	28.9	88,695	203	9,104	1,64,828	1.2
Salinas, CA	11.5	0.3	4.3	2.3	5.1	5.3	5.7	7.9	24.7	66,445	152	7,849	1,44,403	0.4
Salisbury, MD-DE	1.8	0.0	9.6	7.8	5.8	8.9	8.0	16.1	16.5	1,21,110	282	7,818	2,58,860	1.9
Salt Lake City, UT	0.0	D	7.8	7.8	D	7.0	12.6	7.4	14.1	1,57,625	125	13,869	4,64,618	2.4
San Angelo, TX	0.9	5.6	D	D	5.4	6.8	D	D	22.4	23,930	196	2,758	53,477	1.2
San Antonio-New Braunfels, TX	0.0	4.2	6.3	5.0	9.7	6.3	13.2	11.1	21.2	4,29,570	165	57,445	10,35,510	1.6
San Diego-Chula Vista-Carlsbad, CA	0.4	0.0	5.6	9.2	19.5	4.9	8.1	9.0	22.4	5,25,345	160	79,491	12,37,638	0.6
San Francisco-Oakland-Berkeley, CA	0.1	0.0	4.9	6.3	32.6	3.7	12.3	7.5	11.1	7,14,145	154	1,22,611	18,65,101	0.8
Oakland-Berkeley-Livermore, CA Div 36,084	0.1	0.1	7.4	10.5	19.3	4.9	8.2	11.5	14.4	4,15,780	148	71,344	10,55,474	0.8
San Francisco-San Mateo-Redwood City, CA Div 41,884	0.0	D	3.2	3.6	41.8	2.8	14.7	4.9	9.0	2,44,550	157	48,253	6,97,883	0.9
San Rafael, CA Div 42,034	0.3	D	7.6	7.3	19.3	6.4	14.1	10.2	11.5	53,815	207	3,014	1,11,744	0.1
San Jose-Sunnyvale-Santa Clara, CA	0.1	D	3.2	23.0	D	2.6	5.5	5.8	5.7	2,50,505	128	43,053	7,14,200	0.7
San Luis Obispo-Paso Robles, CA	2.5	0.1	10.8	6.1	9.7	8.4	6.7	10.6	20.7	63,625	225	4,182	1,24,740	0.7
Santa Cruz-Watsonville, CA	4.2	0.0	7.2	6.4	10.6	6.9	8.0	13.1	20.2	50,150	187	5,308	1,06,543	0.1
Santa Fe, NM	0.1	0.1	D	D	11.9	8.9	6.5	13.6	27.8	41,050	264	2,473	77,709	0.9
Santa Maria-Santa Barbara, CA	4.9	0.8	5.1	6.7	13.2	5.4	8.6	10.8	19.5	75,965	170	8,176	1,59,798	0.8
Santa Rosa-Petaluma, CA	1.5	0.1	11.0	13.0	9.7	6.8	7.5	13.6	13.3	1,03,190	212	8,094	2,05,903	0.4
Savannah, GA	0.1	D	5.1	14.7	6.0	7.1	6.0	D	17.9	72,400	177	8,408	1,78,520	1.6
Scranton--Wilkes-Barre, PA	0.0	D	5.4	11.5	D	6.8	7.2	D	14.4	1,41,720	250	17,698	2,63,864	0.2
Seattle-Tacoma-Bellevue, WA	0.1	0.1	6.2	8.1	26.8	10.7	6.9	8.4	13.3	5,94,160	148	66,190	16,79,038	1.4
Seattle-Bellevue-Kent, WA Div 42,644	0.1	0.1	5.8	8.5	29.8	11.3	6.9	7.3	11.0	4,34,870	141	47,463	13,13,698	1.4
Tacoma-Lakewood, WA Div 45,104	0.2	0.1	9.2	4.7	5.1	6.5	6.4	15.9	29.8	1,59,290	172	18,727	3,65,340	1.3
Sebastian-Vero Beach, FL	1.2	D	7.6	5.8	11.9	8.8	10.1	16.7	9.5	57,015	348	2,689	84,973	1.3
Sebring-Avon Park, FL	5.5	D	6.0	2.5	4.5	11.2	4.3	23.5	16.1	36,165	350	3,076	57,930	0.7
Sheboygan, WI	1.4	D	5.3	40.0	2.8	6.0	7.8	13.0	8.9	27,370	232	1,675	52,613	0.5
Sherman-Denison, TX	-0.2	0.3	10.7	13.3	4.2	8.1	6.0	21.7	14.2	30,125	216	2,879	60,031	2.1
Shreveport-Bossier City, LA	-0.1	5.0	4.8	6.1	6.2	7.4	6.0	17.6	23.6	81,010	208	17,548	1,81,093	0.5
Sierra Vista-Douglas, AZ	2.1	0.4	8.5	1.3	9.6	6.1	2.6	8.5	45.3	35,400	281	3,158	59,157	0.6
Sioux City, IA-NE-SD	2.9	D	7.7	D	4.5	5.9	7.0	D	11.5	28,175	189	2,321	61,010	1.1
Sioux Falls, SD	2.3	D	7.4	D	7.8	6.5	D	19.1	7.7	49,995	177	3,403	1,20,181	2.9
South Bend-Mishawaka, IN-MI	0.7	D	5.6	13.6	9.6	6.5	D	D	9.9	66,970	207	6,617	1,43,864	0.3
Spartanburg, SC	0.1	D	6.8	25.5	5.4	6.0	4.9	D	16.9	72,055	215	7,185	1,40,821	2.3
Spokane-Spokane Valley, WA	0.7	D	7.1	6.8	D	7.2	9.6	D	20.0	1,25,335	211	15,910	2,50,375	1.3
Springfield, IL	2.0	D	4.4	2.9	10.1	6.0	D	D	24.2	47,340	229	4,698	98,856	0.2
Springfield, MA	0.1	D	D	8.8	5.9	6.3	8.3	18.7	21.2	1,54,570	222	35,035	2,98,378	0.2
Springfield, MO	0.2	0.1	6.3	8.6	9.6	8.6	5.9	D	13.1	1,01,440	211	9,757	2,10,187	1.0
Springfield, OH	1.4	0.4	4.2	15.3	3.4	6.5	7.4	14.9	15.6	31,555	233	4,003	61,040	0.1
State College, PA	0.6	0.4	4.8	5.2	8.0	4.2	4.5	10.3	50.2	25,980	165	1,374	65,855	0.5
Staunton, VA	0.9	0.1	D	19.3	3.8	6.6	4.8	D	16.8	32,210	256	2,174	55,690	0.7
Stockton, CA	4.5	0.1	6.8	7.6	3.2	6.5	5.2	11.2	20.0	1,16,600	148	26,768	2,55,171	1.2
Sumter, SC	0.7	0.0	7.1	13.9	3.6	6.2	3.5	11.3	35.5	34,735	256	5,381	63,191	0.8
Syracuse, NY	0.6	D	5.2	9.6	D	5.9	6.8	D	21.4	1,45,300	221	18,498	2,97,147	0.2
Tallahassee, FL	1.2	D	D	D	D	5.7	6.2	D	34.0	71,945	186	10,313	1,75,591	1.3
Tampa-St. Petersburg-Clearwater, FL	0.3	0.0	6.4	5.5	D	7.1	12.5	13.2	12.0	7,22,575	224	80,151	14,89,351	1.3
Terre Haute, IN	2.2	2.0	7.3	16.2	D	7.4	D	16.1	18.7	43,680	236	4,888	82,252	0.1

1. Per 1,000 resident population estimated as of July 1 of the year shown.

Area name	Occupied housing units, 2016-2020: Occupied units: Total	Owner-occupied: Percent	Owner-occupied: Median value[1]	Median owner cost as a percent of income: With a mortgage	Median owner cost as a percent of income: Without a mortgage[2]	Renter-occupied: Median rent[3]	Renter-occupied: Median rent as a percent of income	Renter-occupied: Substandard units[4] (percent)	Civilian labor force, 2021: Total	Civilian labor force, 2021: Percent change 2020-2021	Unemployment: Total	Unemployment: Rate[5]	Civilian employment[6], 2016-2020: Total	Percent: Management, business, science, and arts	Percent: Construction, production, and maintenance occupations
	89	90	91	92	93	94	95	96	97	98	99	100	101	102	103
Reading, PA	1,56,389	71.0	1,87,600	21.0	13.2	951	28.9	1.4	2,11,376	-1.7	13,889	6.6	2,06,343	33.6	28.9
Redding, CA	70,845	65.3	2,61,000	24.1	13.3	1,075	31.3	3.7	72,809	-0.4	4,975	6.8	73,991	35.1	21.2
Reno, NV	1,87,820	58.2	3,59,500	21.9	10.0	1,149	28.8	4.6	2,54,732	1.9	10,980	4.3	2,37,397	35.4	23.0
Richmond, VA	4,88,001	66.6	2,47,500	20.0	10.0	1,141	29.8	1.8	6,55,275	-2.6	27,633	4.2	6,49,959	42.9	18.9
Riverside-San Bernardino-Ontario, CA	13,76,503	64.1	3,60,100	25.2	11.7	1,387	33.9	8.1	21,18,166	1.4	1,56,354	7.4	19,77,374	30.7	27.2
Roanoke, VA	1,27,924	68.9	1,83,800	19.5	10.0	833	27.7	1.3	1,52,684	-2.7	5,746	3.8	1,48,287	37.5	23.1
Rochester, MN	89,070	75.0	2,18,500	19.0	10.0	952	27.8	2.7	1,24,731	-2.7	3,582	2.9	1,17,633	47.5	19.1
Rochester, NY	4,38,233	67.0	1,48,000	19.4	12.2	920	30.6	1.6	5,16,512	-1.5	25,472	4.9	5,23,828	43.0	18.9
Rockford, IL	1,34,567	67.9	1,26,700	19.4	11.9	826	28.3	2.3	1,58,399	-1.5	13,389	8.5	1,57,305	30.9	30.3
Rocky Mount, NC	58,171	63.6	1,15,400	20.2	11.4	753	27.9	4.0	62,300	1.5	4,388	7.0	63,350	29.7	30.8
Rome, GA	36,192	62.5	1,37,600	19.4	10.0	786	29.3	3.3	43,891	1.8	1,614	3.7	42,403	29.2	31.9
Sacramento-Roseville-Folsom, CA	8,40,925	61.2	4,12,400	23.6	10.8	1,364	32.0	4.7	10,99,341	0.7	70,495	6.4	10,84,293	42.1	17.9
Saginaw, MI	78,980	71.5	1,06,200	18.7	11.9	783	31.6	1.3	81,321	-3.7	5,755	7.1	82,355	32.2	25.4
St. Cloud, MN	76,058	68.4	1,92,100	19.5	10.5	838	26.9	3.1	1,09,534	-3.8	4,069	3.7	1,07,288	35.2	26.7
St. George, UT	59,699	70.2	3,06,900	23.1	10.0	1,099	29.2	4.2	83,600	4.4	2,426	2.9	72,188	34.6	21.1
St. Joseph, MO-KS	47,244	66.0	1,26,500	18.4	11.5	775	26.7	2.2	61,276	-0.6	2,202	3.6	56,813	30.4	31.7
St. Louis, MO-IL	11,37,735	69.3	1,79,200	19.0	11.1	913	28.1	1.5	14,57,232	0.6	67,282	4.6	14,04,619	41.6	20.0
Salem, OR	1,51,200	61.7	2,74,600	22.4	11.4	1,045	30.1	4.8	2,09,431	3.1	10,547	5.0	1,95,905	33.1	26.2
Salinas, CA	1,28,003	51.8	5,59,400	25.3	10.0	1,600	32.5	13.8	2,11,858	-0.9	17,548	8.3	1,88,734	30.4	31.2
Salisbury, MD-DE	1,63,535	74.3	2,43,900	21.3	11.0	1,032	32.0	2.4	1,95,350	2.2	11,146	5.7	1,84,103	34.8	22.0
Salt Lake City, UT	4,04,471	68.2	3,29,200	20.7	10.0	1,171	28.0	3.5	6,90,621	1.6	19,218	2.8	6,33,218	40.9	21.2
San Angelo, TX	43,994	66.0	1,48,600	20.0	10.8	892	28.3	3.4	55,368	1.4	2,695	4.9	57,141	32.5	23.5
San Antonio-New Braunfels, TX	8,26,094	62.8	1,83,000	21.2	10.8	1,058	29.7	4.6	12,08,909	2.2	62,788	5.2	11,62,978	36.1	21.6
San Diego-Chula Vista-Carlsbad, CA	11,30,703	53.9	5,95,600	25.7	10.7	1,732	33.3	7.1	15,43,678	0.1	99,863	6.5	15,89,275	43.4	16.9
San Francisco-Oakland-Berkeley, CA	17,01,865	55.0	8,88,500	24.2	10.3	2,021	28.1	7.3	24,58,394	-1.2	1,36,571	5.6	24,96,926	51.9	13.7
Oakland-Berkeley-Livermore, CA Div 36,084	9,71,473	59.0	7,42,700	24.0	10.3	1,913	29.9	7.0	13,52,316	-0.7	83,583	6.2	14,31,736	49.1	16.0
San Francisco-San Mateo-Redwood City, CA Div 41,884	6,25,492	47.2	11,57,600	24.4	10.0	2,192	25.6	8.1	9,77,158	-1.9	47,240	4.8	9,35,152	55.6	10.8
San Rafael, CA Div 42,034	1,04,900	63.6	10,53,600	25.0	12.6	2,170	30.3	4.8	1,28,920	-1.1	5,748	4.5	1,30,038	56.7	10.1
San Jose-Sunnyvale-Santa Clara, CA	6,53,703	56.6	10,41,800	24.0	10.0	2,365	28.0	8.3	10,45,590	-0.8	49,923	4.8	10,32,879	54.8	14.2
San Luis Obispo-Paso Robles, CA	1,06,244	62.7	6,05,200	26.5	11.4	1,535	32.5	3.2	1,35,268	1.0	7,082	5.2	1,31,426	39.6	19.0
Santa Cruz-Watsonville, CA	96,275	60.3	7,87,000	25.6	11.7	1,843	33.3	7.1	1,33,351	-0.9	9,185	6.9	1,37,107	44.2	19.1
Santa Fe, NM	63,152	71.2	2,94,800	23.7	10.0	1,092	27.9	3.4	72,572	2.2	4,478	6.2	69,066	43.9	16.4
Santa Maria-Santa Barbara, CA	1,48,309	52.3	6,10,300	24.9	10.5	1,697	32.8	10.6	2,17,988	-0.1	12,565	5.8	2,12,400	37.1	22.4
Santa Rosa-Petaluma, CA	1,88,958	61.3	6,40,000	25.8	11.6	1,743	32.3	5.5	2,42,752	-1.0	13,313	5.5	2,53,919	39.6	19.9
Savannah, GA	1,45,199	60.2	2,00,000	21.4	10.9	1,114	29.2	2.0	1,97,037	3.3	7,780	3.9	1,84,629	37.5	22.8
Scranton--Wilkes-Barre, PA	2,28,663	66.9	1,42,500	19.4	12.9	788	27.2	1.6	2,73,471	-1.6	20,884	7.6	2,62,442	33.2	26.7
Seattle-Tacoma-Bellevue, WA	15,29,875	60.2	4,71,900	22.6	12.0	1,589	28.8	3.9	21,63,933	-0.3	1,03,541	4.8	20,63,789	47.6	18.2
Seattle-Bellevue-Kent, WA Div 42,644	11,98,876	59.4	5,37,400	22.5	12.0	1,659	28.5	4.1	17,15,148	-0.1	76,362	4.5	16,41,379	50.8	16.3
Tacoma-Lakewood, WA Div 45,104	3,30,999	63.3	3,36,600	23.2	12.0	1,338	30.3	3.4	4,48,785	-1.1	27,179	6.1	4,22,410	35.3	25.5
Sebastian-Vero Beach, FL	60,959	80.0	2,20,700	22.6	11.6	994	33.1	1.4	65,119	1.5	3,076	4.7	60,128	35.3	20.1
Sebring-Avon Park, FL	42,721	77.0	1,20,500	20.2	10.7	801	29.9	2.3	34,977	1.0	2,058	5.9	34,339	29.8	25.8
Sheboygan, WI	47,754	70.3	1,65,400	18.5	11.7	744	23.6	2.0	62,287	0.3	1,937	3.1	59,448	31.8	34.2
Sherman-Denison, TX	49,327	68.2	1,52,400	20.4	11.4	909	28.1	2.6	65,711	3.4	2,990	4.6	62,518	30.0	27.4
Shreveport-Bossier City, LA	1,56,594	62.9	1,56,900	21.0	10.0	850	33.5	2.2	1,69,279	0.2	9,022	5.3	1,65,959	35.9	22.3
Sierra Vista-Douglas, AZ	50,917	69.1	1,50,100	19.8	10.0	803	27.0	2.7	49,027	-2.1	2,360	4.8	44,219	35.7	18.7
Sioux City, IA-NE-SD	56,113	67.7	1,37,300	18.1	10.0	806	25.1	2.8	77,217	0.1	3,059	4.0	73,486	30.6	32.7
Sioux Falls, SD	1,04,530	66.2	2,08,400	19.5	10.0	836	25.5	2.1	1,58,802	1.6	4,373	2.8	1,46,413	38.8	23.0
South Bend-Mishawaka, IN-MI	1,25,606	70.2	1,38,200	17.8	10.0	816	28.4	2.1	1,54,101	-2.4	6,667	4.3	1,53,248	36.5	26.4
Spartanburg, SC	1,18,788	71.3	1,53,000	19.1	10.0	825	28.6	2.8	1,56,109	0.3	6,174	4.0	1,45,469	31.4	31.1
Spokane-Spokane Valley, WA	2,24,385	64.4	2,43,000	21.5	10.4	941	29.9	2.4	2,79,912	-1.3	15,288	5.5	2,56,167	38.2	20.8
Springfield, IL	89,304	70.5	1,44,600	18.7	10.3	826	28.5	1.6	1,03,989	1.4	5,673	5.5	99,312	43.2	17.0
Springfield, MA	2,70,889	63.9	2,36,200	22.0	13.8	952	31.5	1.9	3,57,259	0.8	23,354	6.5	3,35,815	40.3	20.0
Springfield, MO	1,91,961	62.4	1,56,400	19.1	10.0	773	28.8	3.2	2,37,893	1.8	8,129	3.4	2,19,777	35.8	22.6
Springfield, OH	54,862	67.1	1,20,500	18.9	10.0	757	27.0	1.6	62,458	-0.2	3,323	5.3	59,789	30.1	30.9
State College, PA	59,380	62.5	2,42,700	20.0	10.9	1,019	36.5	2.3	76,030	-2.0	3,483	4.6	77,351	49.8	14.6
Staunton, VA	49,972	71.3	2,03,300	21.3	10.0	870	27.3	1.6	58,459	-2.7	1,988	3.4	58,441	34.1	26.8
Stockton, CA	2,31,092	57.7	3,67,900	23.9	10.9	1,286	31.9	8.3	3,34,250	0.0	28,972	8.7	3,19,808	29.5	31.8
Sumter, SC	54,479	67.5	1,16,000	19.8	10.0	773	28.5	2.4	54,972	-0.6	2,566	4.7	54,819	29.0	29.9
Syracuse, NY	2,59,905	67.8	1,40,900	18.8	11.7	869	29.2	2.1	3,03,935	-2.0	15,088	5.0	3,08,467	40.3	19.6
Tallahassee, FL	1,50,862	58.2	1,87,400	20.7	10.0	990	33.5	2.6	1,94,623	2.8	8,226	4.2	1,85,914	44.4	14.5
Tampa-St. Petersburg-Clearwater, FL	12,39,349	65.8	2,10,900	21.9	11.7	1,160	31.7	2.6	15,75,096	2.1	66,771	4.2	14,70,542	39.5	18.1
Terre Haute, IN	73,479	69.2	99,700	17.7	10.0	740	31.1	3.1	78,186	-1.3	3,128	4.0	82,808	30.8	29.5

1. Specified owner-occupied units. 2. A value of 10.0 represents 10 percent or less; a value of 50.0 represents 50 percent or more. 3. Specified renter-occupied units. 4. Overcrowded or lacking complete plumbing facilities. 5. Percent of civilian labor force. 6. Civilian employed persons 16 years old and over.

Area name	Private nonfarm establishments, employment and payroll, 2020									Agriculture, 2017			
		Employment						Annual payroll		Farms			Farm producers whose primary occupation is farming (percent)
											Percent with:		
	Number of establish-ments	Total	Health care and social assistance	Manufactur-ing	Retail trade	Finance and insurance	Professional, scientific, and technical services	Total (mil dol)	Average per employee (dollars)	Number	Fewer than 50 acres	1000 acres or more	
	104	105	106	107	108	109	110	111	112	113	114	115	116
Reading, PA	8,335	1,61,143	31,523	30,457	20,212	5,617	6,313	7,625	47,315	1,809	49.0	0.9	52.9
Redding, CA	4,407	51,288	10,826	2,154	9,527	2,074	2,214	2,342	45,660	1,337	71.4	4.6	31.5
Reno, NV	13,290	2,08,896	28,782	18,289	27,165	5,391	11,916	10,367	49,629	355	69.9	7.3	43.5
Richmond, VA	32,280	5,68,206	86,401	30,547	72,330	48,800	42,508	31,357	55,186	2,966	48.8	5.8	42.0
Riverside-San Bernardino-Ontario, CA	79,813	12,63,658	1,92,968	1,01,409	1,91,166	27,638	40,123	57,024	45,126	3,729	86.4	1.9	41.2
Roanoke, VA	8,073	1,39,209	28,847	15,741	17,427	8,583	5,277	6,354	45,644	2,011	36.0	1.5	39.3
Rochester, MN	5,156	1,17,306	23,553	8,310	12,938	2,067	38,140	6,704	57,152	3,960	34.6	6.6	45.2
Rochester, NY	24,306	4,47,377	89,954	54,322	57,467	14,564	28,229	21,478	48,008	4,215	41.9	4.9	53.2
Rockford, IL	7,030	1,32,583	21,355	32,657	15,783	3,516	4,777	6,101	46,020	1,193	52.1	6.1	42.6
Rocky Mount, NC	2,750	49,695	8,455	10,280	6,382	1,762	1,014	1,923	38,693	674	39.5	10.8	47.6
Rome, GA	2,023	36,680	8,718	6,749	4,165	718	768	1,505	41,038	547	51.7	2.0	35.2
Sacramento-Roseville-Folsom, CA	51,723	7,97,263	1,30,298	36,443	1,00,563	44,093	59,023	46,316	58,094	4,737	73.0	3.9	43.9
Saginaw, MI	4,126	78,468	17,710	10,667	12,371	2,954	2,505	3,324	42,360	1,250	44.2	5.8	42.1
St. Cloud, MN	5,321	1,00,238	19,418	15,642	13,418	4,578	2,516	4,826	48,145	3,767	26.1	2.7	48.0
St. George, UT	5,979	58,074	10,431	3,275	9,717	1,439	2,852	2,270	39,089	537	60.5	5.8	26.8
St. Joseph, MO-KS	2,788	50,311	9,158	12,853	6,665	1,830	1,336	2,340	46,504	2,641	32.3	7.6	37.9
St. Louis, MO-IL	70,849	12,47,757	1,93,781	1,11,365	1,41,712	71,671	87,307	67,684	54,244	11,057	40.9	6.3	37.1
Salem, OR	10,189	1,29,075	25,279	12,364	19,281	2,957	4,234	5,486	42,505	4,004	73.2	2.3	41.5
Salinas, CA	8,883	1,18,088	17,256	8,484	17,589	2,492	8,218	5,667	47,986	1,104	45.6	20.2	44.3
Salisbury, MD-DE	11,016	1,34,266	25,358	14,452	23,822	3,767	4,626	5,456	40,633	2,237	51.7	6.6	54.3
Salt Lake City, UT	34,824	6,55,170	68,719	58,131	68,856	48,264	49,591	37,373	57,044	1,132	75.8	4.7	30.5
San Angelo, TX	2,896	41,012	7,262	3,100	6,654	1,833	1,727	1,715	41,821	1,554	49.5	15.7	31.8
San Antonio-New Braunfels, TX	47,880	9,17,001	1,46,072	48,825	1,17,836	72,410	53,835	42,723	46,590	14,960	48.4	4.8	35.4
San Diego-Chula Vista-Carlsbad, CA	88,654	13,33,731	1,92,379	1,03,352	1,47,339	58,951	1,64,689	84,083	63,043	5,082	90.8	0.8	36.2
San Francisco-Oakland-Berkeley, CA	1,32,274	23,24,751	2,94,717	1,37,758	2,17,597	1,32,133	2,94,466	2,46,245	1,05,923	1,499	63.4	8.5	42.6
Oakland-Berkeley-Livermore, CA Div 36,084	66,080	10,65,958	1,64,849	1,00,528	1,15,527	45,115	1,04,769	82,886	77,758	905	69.2	7.1	41.1
San Francisco-San Mateo-Redwood City, CA Div 41,884	56,169	11,54,803	1,12,848	34,514	87,292	83,356	1,80,857	1,55,570	1,34,715	251	67.7	6.0	47.7
San Rafael, CA Div 42,034	10,025	1,03,990	17,020	2,716	14,778	3,662	8,840	7,789	74,903	343	44.9	14.0	42.6
San Jose-Sunnyvale-Santa Clara, CA	50,047	11,42,518	1,20,507	89,910	82,747	27,420	1,54,816	1,65,737	1,45,063	1,500	70.7	7.5	45.2
San Luis Obispo-Paso Robles, CA	8,600	97,529	15,983	7,042	14,350	2,093	5,638	4,626	47,427	2,349	56.4	7.8	40.8
Santa Cruz-Watsonville, CA	6,985	82,173	14,221	5,351	12,510	2,447	4,701	4,211	51,240	625	80.5	2.1	43.2
Santa Fe, NM	4,760	48,471	8,978	846	8,740	1,493	2,538	2,028	41,840	639	67.9	9.7	35.7
Santa Maria-Santa Barbara, CA	11,977	1,56,499	23,832	13,731	18,824	4,463	12,124	8,996	57,484	1,467	60.7	9.5	44.0
Santa Rosa-Petaluma, CA	14,242	1,77,333	27,671	21,999	24,885	6,197	8,681	10,242	57,756	3,594	73.7	3.5	40.6
Savannah, GA	9,745	1,61,869	21,958	18,470	22,290	2,849	5,958	7,084	43,764	416	59.1	6.0	36.9
Scranton--Wilkes-Barre, PA	12,861	2,35,440	47,542	29,890	30,868	9,723	9,292	10,122	42,994	1,124	33.0	1.4	38.9
Seattle-Tacoma-Bellevue, WA	1,08,431	18,57,405	2,48,803	1,66,030	1,86,536	72,863	1,54,525	1,49,308	80,385	4,961	88.8	0.2	33.9
Seattle-Bellevue-Kent, WA Div 42,644	89,648	15,77,853	1,92,151	1,47,614	1,47,836	63,796	1,44,571	1,35,011	85,566	3,354	89.4	0.3	34.9
Tacoma-Lakewood, WA Div 45,104	18,783	2,79,552	56,652	18,416	38,700	9,067	9,954	14,297	51,143	1,607	87.4	0.2	31.8
Sebastian-Vero Beach, FL	4,449	48,131	9,539	2,206	8,985	1,563	2,643	1,972	40,970	450	76.2	5.1	42.6
Sebring-Avon Park, FL	1,994	20,582	5,879	839	4,687	511	679	713	34,644	989	66.4	6.1	45.7
Sheboygan, WI	2,657	52,708	6,424	18,037	6,172	2,243	1,198	2,496	47,347	958	43.6	3.9	49.6
Sherman-Denison, TX	2,650	41,151	8,422	7,708	6,154	1,719	1,046	1,696	41,223	2,845	61.4	2.4	32.3
Shreveport-Bossier City, LA	9,026	1,37,950	31,636	8,270	19,717	4,016	6,008	5,954	43,163	1,824	49.9	7.0	39.5
Sierra Vista-Douglas, AZ	2,120	25,545	4,905	340	5,068	479	3,272	1,032	40,402	1,083	39.6	17.7	47.4
Sioux City, IA-NE-SD	3,653	69,923	11,616	15,060	8,942	2,816	1,479	3,091	44,213	2,428	29.7	15.0	45.4
Sioux Falls, SD	8,105	1,46,152	32,216	14,473	19,060	13,380	5,062	7,340	50,219	3,048	34.5	15.3	44.0
South Bend-Mishawaka, IN-MI	6,609	1,30,444	20,713	17,249	17,041	4,090	5,236	5,723	43,876	1,376	53.3	5.5	42.2
Spartanburg, SC	6,725	1,43,354	14,860	36,294	16,433	3,139	3,765	6,670	46,529	1,433	67.9	0.3	30.0
Spokane-Spokane Valley, WA	14,436	2,08,332	44,334	16,709	28,883	11,567	9,764	10,078	48,376	3,539	57.9	5.6	36.0
Springfield, IL	5,015	82,232	22,604	2,473	11,938	5,438	4,208	3,711	45,129	1,469	42.7	12.9	45.0
Springfield, MA	14,390	2,45,055	58,281	25,640	31,442	10,672	9,050	11,134	45,434	2,045	55.4	0.3	40.3
Springfield, MO	11,923	1,94,859	37,897	16,620	25,074	8,304	9,082	8,280	42,490	7,601	40.2	1.6	38.9
Springfield, OH	2,167	38,457	6,492	5,871	5,027	2,239	730	1,501	39,030	742	56.7	7.0	36.2
State College, PA	3,303	45,062	9,445	4,027	7,266	1,064	3,101	1,838	40,786	1,023	41.3	1.4	47.0
Staunton, VA	2,766	41,306	6,941	7,287	6,021	988	1,130	1,726	41,792	1,665	45.7	2.6	44.6
Stockton, CA	12,226	2,00,637	30,473	18,605	27,547	6,178	5,451	9,644	48,066	3,430	62.1	5.4	55.0
Sumter, SC	2,254	37,845	6,170	6,841	5,553	997	962	1,469	38,816	905	47.5	8.0	47.4
Syracuse, NY	14,715	2,62,811	52,260	21,718	34,759	10,972	17,388	12,511	47,603	1,926	37.0	3.6	49.1
Tallahassee, FL	9,211	1,17,047	21,265	3,098	18,821	5,079	10,446	5,227	44,653	1,648	62.1	2.7	34.3
Tampa-St. Petersburg-Clearwater, FL	83,611	11,96,047	2,06,106	60,659	1,61,848	89,765	1,01,059	60,506	50,588	4,325	80.3	1.8	39.7
Terre Haute, IN	3,677	58,900	11,990	10,225	9,123	1,424	1,332	2,374	40,306	2,392	42.6	9.2	41.5

Area name	Agriculture, 2017 (cont.) — Land in farms: Acreage (1,000)	Land in farms: Percent change, 2012–2017	Land in farms: Acres: Average size of farm	Land in farms: Acres: Total irrigated (1,000)	Land in farms: Acres: Total cropland (1,000)	Value of land and buildings: Average per farm	Value of land and buildings: Average per acre	Value of machinery and equipmnet, average per farm (dollars)	Value of products sold: Total (mil dol)	Value of products sold: Average per farm (acres)	Value of products sold: Percent from: Crops	Value of products sold: Percent from: Livestock and poultry products	Organic farms (number)	Farms with internet access (percent)	Government payments: Total ($1,000)	Government payments: Percent of farms
	117	118	119	120	121	122	123	124	125	126	127	128	129	130	131	132
Reading, PA	225	-3.9	124.0	1.5	184.5	13,92,374	11,209	1,38,139	554.7	3,06,609	43.8	56.2	72	68.4	3,038	22.1
Redding, CA	410	8.9	307.0	48.8	38.9	8,95,229	2,919	51,324	62.2	46,546	35.0	65.0	16	81.5	547	2.0
Reno, NV	501	13.2	1,412.0	43.6	22.2	14,49,321	1,026	61,699	19.9	56,166	45.8	54.2	14	86.5	174	5.1
Richmond, VA	655	3.3	221.0	10.8	347.3	8,97,575	4,063	1,05,935	243.3	82,022	53.2	46.8	6	76.4	9,343	22.1
Riverside-San Bernardino-Ontario, CA	332	-21.2	89.0	148.4	209.0	16,47,577	18,504	95,567	1,305.9	3,50,203	61.4	38.6	253	79.1	2,268	2.4
Roanoke, VA	315	-5.2	156.0	0.6	117.9	6,04,500	3,864	75,565	90.5	44,978	26.1	73.9	10	71.0	1,000	8.2
Rochester, MN	1,140	-1.5	288.0	7.5	934.5	17,60,727	6,115	2,12,289	930.9	2,35,069	51.7	48.3	76	80.0	30,766	65.6
Rochester, NY	900	-3.0	214.0	7.0	701.5	8,36,920	3,920	1,80,390	956.7	2,26,983	54.5	45.5	261	70.7	16,376	22.4
Rockford, IL	292	-8.0	245.0	2.5	267.0	18,11,732	7,399	1,55,547	185.6	1,55,583	77.0	23.0	15	82.6	10,252	48.6
Rocky Mount, NC	278	4.2	413.0	4.7	203.6	15,62,533	3,783	2,58,892	367.9	5,45,798	59.4	40.6	17	68.0	4,904	44.7
Rome, GA	75	6.7	137.0	0.7	21.7	6,65,898	4,866	88,750	53.4	97,700	10.2	89.8	0	77.3	442	13.5
Sacramento-Roseville-Folsom, CA	929	0.2	196.0	360.9	468.5	18,52,189	9,440	1,03,724	1,081.4	2,28,294	84.7	15.3	178	86.4	5,225	7.3
Saginaw, MI	327	5.6	262.0	1.7	300.5	15,18,681	5,805	1,62,378	170.3	1,36,206	87.9	12.1	12	79.4	6,853	63.1
St. Cloud, MN	846	-10.6	224.0	68.5	671.7	11,16,661	4,974	1,84,892	955.2	2,53,558	25.4	74.6	62	77.4	7,628	53.6
St. George, UT	155	4.8	289.0	13.0	22.3	10,78,857	3,737	61,328	16.5	30,648	39.3	60.7	3	76.9	190	3.2
St. Joseph, MO-KS	768	-5.1	291.0	4.2	583.3	10,61,151	3,648	1,21,612	287.9	1,09,001	84.3	15.7	1	75.9	14,004	54.8
St. Louis, MO-IL	2,780	-4.6	251.0	12.2	2,129.8	15,47,992	6,158	1,44,778	1,375.5	1,24,397	74.7	25.3	24	76.0	44,123	46.8
Salem, OR	438	1.5	109.0	123.0	345.0	11,56,225	10,580	1,27,386	836.3	2,08,874	84.6	15.4	72	85.2	2,771	6.6
Salinas, CA	1,340	5.7	1,214.0	294.6	366.7	89,44,364	7,368	8,05,557	4,116.1	37,28,396	99.1	0.9	191	75.5	1,269	7.4
Salisbury, MD-DE	523	0.4	234.0	117.5	418.0	17,09,210	7,315	2,00,515	1,827.9	8,17,121	17.0	83.0	13	77.0	17,204	43.7
Salt Lake City, UT	411	-3.4	363.0	29.3	32.6	9,53,913	2,628	70,367	60.7	53,581	38.8	61.2	11	79.6	594	2.5
San Angelo, TX	2,010	-1.4	1,293.0	20.9	138.8	14,69,225	1,136	78,784	109.3	70,338	27.6	72.4	1	76.6	3,447	12.9
San Antonio-New Braunfels, TX	3,657	0.4	244.0	87.8	613.5	7,67,866	3,141	56,604	407.3	27,225	37.6	62.4	13	71.5	10,124	6.7
San Diego-Chula Vista-Carlsbad, CA	222	0.3	44.0	42.7	64.1	10,14,281	23,209	43,529	831.4	1,63,601	93.5	6.5	419	84.2	558	1.1
San Francisco-Oakland-Berkeley, CA	525	0.1	350.0	38.1	79.4	24,39,344	6,965	81,559	304.2	2,02,908	62.2	37.8	109	85.7	1,416	6.9
Oakland-Berkeley-Livermore, CA Div 36,084	339	10.9	374.0	30.1	58.8	26,29,149	7,022	76,063	129.4	1,42,977	77.4	22.6	22	84.5	704	6.2
San Francisco-San Mateo-Redwood City, CA Div 41,884	46	-4.4	184.0	3.0	6.9	18,17,211	9,902	73,187	79.4	3,16,430	98.2	1.8	20	88.0	0	0.8
San Rafael, CA Div 42,034	140	-18.0	408.0	5.0	13.7	23,93,810	5,862	1,02,187	95.3	2,77,962	11.6	88.4	67	86.9	712	13.1
San Jose-Sunnyvale-Santa Clara, CA	808	-3.1	539.0	37.3	69.9	28,00,069	5,197	93,026	473.1	3,15,395	89.6	10.4	109	84.2	1,093	6.1
San Luis Obispo-Paso Robles, CA	931	-30.4	396.0	75.8	246.4	29,91,940	7,547	87,783	701.6	2,98,676	95.2	4.8	132	84.4	4,285	9.4
Santa Cruz-Watsonville, CA	64	-36.1	102.0	20.1	23.5	21,83,024	21,352	1,16,842	606.5	9,70,464	98.7	1.3	130	85.1	37	1.9
Santa Fe, NM	D	D	D	15.6	23.7	9,32,061	D	65,568	25.4	39,798	54.5	45.5	14	77.0	367	5.5
Santa Maria-Santa Barbara, CA	715	2.0	487.0	119.9	146.3	50,60,151	10,381	1,83,019	1,519.9	10,36,090	98.0	2.0	163	87.7	854	5.2
Santa Rosa-Petaluma, CA	567	-3.8	158.0	86.4	129.9	35,01,852	22,186	77,693	919.1	2,55,719	66.9	33.1	332	87.7	2,410	3.8
Savannah, GA	81	36.2	195.0	3.5	33.7	6,42,800	3,300	1,00,149	31.5	75,671	87.9	12.1	5	81.3	402	15.1
Scranton--Wilkes-Barre, PA	147	-9.5	131.0	0.5	77.4	6,63,210	5,073	80,161	47.5	42,264	62.7	37.3	1	73.2	1,259	26.2
Seattle-Tacoma-Bellevue, WA	151	-9.4	31.0	15.5	64.3	7,44,589	24,396	47,150	357.9	72,144	54.9	45.1	87	88.0	1,295	3.1
Seattle-Bellevue-Kent, WA Div 42,644	106	-10.1	31.0	12.5	52.3	8,08,104	25,655	48,710	293.0	87,367	57.0	43.0	70	88.3	1,224	3.5
Tacoma-Lakewood, WA Div 45,104	46	-7.5	28.0	3.0	12.1	6,12,026	21,490	43,894	64.9	40,371	45.4	54.6	17	87.4	71	2.2
Sebastian-Vero Beach, FL	183	12.4	406.0	52.9	55.5	23,30,718	5,745	90,644	106.5	2,36,611	89.3	10.7	9	68.2	426	7.1
Sebring-Avon Park, FL	376	-23.3	380.0	73.3	87.6	14,84,269	3,906	92,897	196.7	1,98,865	72.5	27.5	2	71.1	2,471	11.0
Sheboygan, WI	196	3.0	205.0	0.3	164.3	13,48,670	6,594	1,98,127	213.4	2,22,785	22.6	77.4	14	84.2	1,215	39.5
Sherman-Denison, TX	430	-0.3	151.0	2.3	207.0	10,23,105	6,770	68,105	66.2	23,259	60.8	39.2	1	81.0	4,729	9.9
Shreveport-Bossier City, LA	443	14.8	243.0	24.8	147.1	7,30,792	3,011	95,830	96.1	52,671	52.4	47.6	0	74.0	2,725	8.9
Sierra Vista-Douglas, AZ	973	6.2	899.0	86.0	152.9	18,02,553	2,005	99,038	144.7	1,33,648	56.9	43.1	4	78.9	3,119	10.6
Sioux City, IA-NE-SD	1,187	-0.4	489.0	102.6	1,035.2	29,96,651	6,132	2,65,159	912.3	3,75,747	56.4	43.6	4	81.5	29,267	74.0
Sioux Falls, SD	1,429	-6.0	469.0	34.3	1,230.4	26,33,238	5,616	2,36,521	920.2	3,01,909	60.6	39.4	6	81.8	23,562	68.3
South Bend-Mishawaka, IN-MI	348	2.3	253.0	99.4	297.5	15,48,314	6,113	1,78,869	257.3	1,87,018	71.1	28.9	13	77.3	8,438	43.5
Spartanburg, SC	96	-5.9	67.0	1.8	34.3	5,50,283	8,231	45,163	30.5	21,292	70.4	29.6	0	78.4	481	7.9
Spokane-Spokane Valley, WA	1,066	0.2	301.0	19.9	455.9	8,07,433	2,679	72,986	147.2	41,604	74.4	25.6	51	83.2	8,829	15.7
Springfield, IL	699	4.1	476.0	4.6	635.8	41,23,080	8,661	2,59,955	442.3	3,01,075	92.6	7.4	3	79.2	10,299	65.3
Springfield, MA	175	-4.1	86.0	3.6	56.8	6,48,777	7,586	66,977	140.8	68,855	76.2	23.8	67	83.5	1,311	8.1
Springfield, MO	1,209	-0.6	159.0	3.3	360.6	5,17,580	3,255	58,141	272.7	35,876	13.2	86.8	61	72.1	2,387	6.2
Springfield, OH	171	-1.9	230.0	1.8	151.4	17,38,039	7,542	1,65,062	126.5	1,70,443	79.2	20.8	0	80.5	6,001	43.3
State College, PA	150	-7.5	146.0	0.4	88.3	9,81,430	6,700	92,395	91.5	89,421	35.3	64.7	23	68.5	2,266	24.0
Staunton, VA	291	11.8	175.0	2.5	116.8	12,22,854	6,999	1,01,481	292.5	1,75,704	12.8	87.2	5	71.5	1,049	15.7
Stockton, CA	773	-1.8	225.0	487.1	524.4	33,84,002	15,020	1,89,084	2,176.0	6,34,404	74.8	25.2	35	81.7	5,788	6.9
Sumter, SC	305	-13.0	336.0	28.0	194.2	8,98,759	2,671	1,31,634	262.0	2,89,486	38.7	61.3	7	73.8	3,142	38.7
Syracuse, NY	419	-3.1	217.0	2.5	258.9	6,76,931	3,113	1,42,481	333.3	1,73,037	26.6	73.4	95	81.9	3,359	20.8
Tallahassee, FL	350	19.5	212.0	9.3	64.5	8,11,049	3,823	54,877	134.5	81,627	64.7	35.3	12	76.2	1,600	8.5
Tampa-St. Petersburg-Clearwater, FL	425	-5.6	98.0	31.5	111.1	9,58,142	9,761	57,092	534.9	1,23,682	82.5	17.5	30	76.9	1,773	5.7
Terre Haute, IN	746	0.0	312.0	13.4	623.9	16,83,833	5,400	1,68,563	390.0	1,63,056	88.7	11.3	28	72.2	14,469	57.9

Area name	Water use, 2015		Wholesale Trade[1], 2017				Retail Trade[2], 2017				Real estate and rental and leasing,[2] 2017			
	Public supply water withdrawn (mil gal/ day)	Public supply gallons withdrawn per person per day	Number of establish-ments	Number of employees	Sales (mil dol)	Average payroll (mil dol)	Number of establish-ments	Number of employees	Sales (mil dol)	Average payroll (mil dol)	Number of establish-ments	Number of employees	Sales (mil dol)	Average payroll (mil dol)
	133	134	135	136	137	138	139	140	141	142	143	144	145	146
Reading, PA	31.9	76.7	374	8,533	7,103.8	524.2	1,186	20,446	5,772.3	527.8	367	2,985	1,173.9	217.9
Redding, CA	33.5	186.4	157	1,664	1,056.6	85.1	634	9,391	2,847.7	274.5	220	887	188.2	32.5
Reno, NV	58.2	129.1	D	D	D	D	1,495	25,312	8,518.6	796.6	D	D	D	D
Richmond, VA	176.4	141.3	1,186	19,744	20,619.6	1,287.0	4,188	72,355	20,643.9	1,924.2	1,558	8,769	4,290.4	455.4
Riverside-San Bernardino-Ontario, CA	778.4	173.4	4,508	66,395	67,695.8	3,619.0	10,203	1,91,153	64,394.3	5,603.5	4,227	19,656	5,332.5	877.0
Roanoke, VA	41.2	130.9	350	5,250	3,306.2	330.3	1,230	18,173	5,016.1	443.3	363	1,804	354.1	71.8
Rochester, MN	16.9	79.1	170	2,124	1,646.2	116.8	790	13,325	3,392.5	345.0	213	845	167.5	29.3
Rochester, NY	114.4	105.8	1,010	15,106	10,659.6	877.0	3,482	57,893	14,650.1	1,460.6	1,115	7,242	1,497.7	310.2
Rockford, IL	32.8	96.3	337	4,561	2,920.9	244.4	1,026	15,411	4,342.0	384.2	256	1,376	293.4	59.1
Rocky Mount, NC	12.4	83.9	130	2,741	3,808.9	126.7	510	6,346	1,639.2	146.0	112	520	92.3	18.1
Rome, GA	11.8	122.3	67	1,010	655.3	50.1	389	4,269	1,214.8	106.6	83	260	56.2	9.3
Sacramento-Roseville-Folsom, CA	340.1	149.5	1,769	28,073	39,577.8	1,721.5	5,845	1,00,416	31,776.5	3,056.7	3,121	15,546	4,049.3	761.1
Saginaw, MI	0.4	2.2	160	2,070	1,307.0	111.1	826	12,804	3,233.8	309.9	123	652	139.2	20.5
St. Cloud, MN	16.7	85.7	237	5,250	3,376.0	280.7	795	13,568	3,812.2	351.6	225	1,052	210.1	38.8
St. George, UT	49.4	317.3	164	1,343	1,444.0	64.5	628	9,079	2,651.3	259.4	388	849	186.0	26.7
St. Joseph, MO-KS	18.4	145.1	102	1,239	1,683.3	77.9	399	6,762	1,734.7	161.0	117	418	67.6	11.7
St. Louis, MO-IL	459.4	163.4	2,955	48,659	58,992.5	3,282.5	8,758	1,42,553	51,349.8	3,910.1	3,142	18,794	4,935.3	894.6
Salem, OR	76.9	187.5	329	3,963	2,915.8	206.7	1,253	19,363	5,485.1	521.4	536	2,017	447.3	77.9
Salinas, CA	38.2	88.1	349	5,528	8,040.7	353.6	1,292	17,597	5,629.5	529.7	474	1,987	587.0	90.9
Salisbury, MD-DE	29.6	74.8	102	1,051	1,110.8	59.1	1,886	24,042	6,750.0	610.2	617	2,531	536.8	93.1
Salt Lake City, UT	413.2	353.0	1,644	28,775	27,307.6	1,909.6	3,627	65,191	23,981.2	2,084.2	2,440	10,693	3,324.9	546.0
San Angelo, TX	1.4	11.8	D	D	D	D	430	6,683	1,993.1	192.7	151	627	129.5	22.4
San Antonio-New Braunfels, TX	255.9	107.3	1,846	32,218	22,040.0	1,854.0	6,375	1,11,582	34,864.0	3,080.4	2,659	15,279	3,962.9	777.0
San Diego-Chula Vista-Carlsbad, CA	408.8	123.9	3,905	46,390	38,374.0	3,219.4	9,455	1,52,542	46,665.9	4,557.3	6,381	29,423	11,062.2	1,670.4
San Francisco-Oakland-Berkeley, CA	472.8	101.5	5,322	83,209	96,647.3	6,810.7	13,232	2,21,632	86,926.9	8,134.4	7,706	48,614	21,031.2	3,357.6
Oakland-Berkeley-Livermore, CA Div 36,084	308.7	111.7	3,073	51,058	53,727.0	3,814.2	6,807	1,18,589	41,875.1	4,015.7	3,667	18,584	6,389.5	1,079.1
San Francisco-San Mateo-Redwood City, CA Div 41,884	135.9	83.4	1,932	29,819	41,089.6	2,833.3	5,414	87,494	39,426.6	3,473.5	3,397	27,061	12,767.2	2,048.6
San Rafael, CA Div 42,034	28.2	107.9	317	2,332	1,830.8	163.2	1,011	15,549	5,625.2	645.1	642	2,969	1,874.6	229.9
San Jose-Sunnyvale-Santa Clara, CA	199.8	101.1	2,287	74,875	1,37,070.7	13,096.3	4,784	87,843	47,932.7	3,400.1	2,831	15,891	6,399.3	1,028.2
San Luis Obispo-Paso Robles, CA	29.1	103.4	276	2,519	1,282.1	131.0	1,130	14,708	4,372.0	442.0	494	2,024	420.2	80.3
Santa Cruz-Watsonville, CA	18.5	67.3	D	D	D	D	893	12,885	4,650.4	364.9	370	1,539	351.3	69.8
Santa Fe, NM	10.6	71.1	99	856	923.5	44.1	797	9,053	2,588.1	269.2	278	815	200.7	41.4
Santa Maria-Santa Barbara, CA	49.9	112.3	405	5,968	5,075.3	490.4	1,479	18,889	5,267.8	547.6	747	3,072	712.4	130.7
Santa Rosa-Petaluma, CA	40.5	80.6	560	8,903	6,419.4	684.6	1,815	25,679	7,760.5	843.1	712	3,334	817.5	152.7
Savannah, GA	66.5	175.3	369	5,323	6,526.0	316.1	1,528	21,949	5,824.1	534.5	535	2,567	632.0	98.9
Scranton--Wilkes-Barre, PA	62.2	111.4	545	9,974	9,262.4	497.0	2,179	31,443	8,819.8	778.3	396	1,812	449.7	75.3
Seattle-Tacoma-Bellevue, WA	373.6	100.1	4,588	77,972	78,446.5	5,445.5	10,942	1,91,464	1,14,947.5	6,764.6	7,162	36,764	11,843.6	2,124.6
Seattle-Bellevue-Kent, WA Div 42,644	263.1	91.1	3,882	66,615	69,158.8	4,794.6	8,773	1,52,656	1,01,171.6	5,510.2	5,992	31,488	10,485.9	1,894.0
Tacoma-Lakewood, WA Div 45,104	110.4	130.8	706	11,357	9,287.7	650.9	2,169	38,808	13,775.9	1,254.5	1,170	5,276	1,357.7	230.6
Sebastian-Vero Beach, FL	16.9	114.5	133	856	5,125.0	96.6	684	9,009	2,267.7	222.7	276	1,569	257.8	52.5
Sebring-Avon Park, FL	7.5	75.3	53	434	200.2	20.7	329	4,589	1,261.2	109.9	98	302	60.5	8.3
Sheboygan, WI	15.8	136.7	95	1,484	933.0	76.7	379	6,132	1,729.4	150.8	76	232	44.4	7.0
Sherman-Denison, TX	21.6	172.2	97	1,024	736.7	48.3	428	6,146	1,912.7	170.4	107	329	73.4	11.1
Shreveport-Bossier City, LA	59.2	146.7	441	6,716	8,809.0	363.9	1,399	21,366	6,200.1	553.4	486	2,480	534.3	98.2
Sierra Vista-Douglas, AZ	16.2	127.7	D	D	D	11.4	386	5,160	1,324.4	126.6	107	391	57.8	10.8
Sioux City, IA-NE-SD	18.3	127.1	163	2,368	2,167.6	132.3	532	8,901	2,359.5	210.3	121	552	92.9	17.5
Sioux Falls, SD	21.9	79.7	424	6,390	4,989.5	368.1	1,032	18,371	5,058.4	497.7	366	2,047	402.9	87.1
South Bend-Mishawaka, IN-MI	22.9	71.6	323	4,677	4,091.3	267.9	1,035	17,248	5,671.1	462.3	265	1,657	295.6	62.2
Spartanburg, SC	34.7	116.8	397	5,908	5,925.6	346.8	1,032	16,413	4,906.4	419.0	265	1,110	356.2	40.1
Spokane-Spokane Valley, WA	145.0	271.2	635	9,911	10,369.1	528.4	1,744	27,903	8,169.0	847.4	724	3,578	758.4	130.8
Springfield, IL	24.0	113.8	185	2,517	3,179.5	133.1	750	12,390	3,089.5	295.1	246	895	228.1	29.8
Springfield, MA	67.2	95.6	450	8,122	9,053.6	474.3	2,297	32,820	8,634.4	900.4	556	3,232	685.8	123.4
Springfield, MO	42.6	93.4	522	9,951	7,437.6	473.4	1,635	24,757	7,136.1	656.8	615	3,400	564.1	112.4
Springfield, OH	16.2	118.9	84	1,661	1,808.1	81.9	373	5,695	1,411.4	122.3	89	380	63.1	11.0
State College, PA	17.9	111.3	86	703	301.3	34.9	461	7,741	2,052.5	186.4	150	957	233.2	37.5
Staunton, VA	8.3	68.9	87	1,180	493.8	58.2	448	6,156	1,597.0	156.5	134	398	53.9	12.6
Stockton, CA	93.4	128.6	528	11,280	14,265.8	728.0	1,635	27,256	8,856.3	789.3	566	2,832	634.9	119.8
Sumter, SC	16.9	119.7	79	725	374.0	34.1	458	5,793	1,454.8	129.0	80	321	47.0	9.0
Syracuse, NY	94.1	142.5	635	12,341	15,751.9	706.2	2,213	35,026	9,617.4	913.6	684	3,952	802.4	174.2
Tallahassee, FL	35.5	94.0	247	3,191	2,417.8	199.1	1,257	18,840	4,773.6	450.6	486	2,922	465.0	99.4
Tampa-St. Petersburg-Clearwater, FL	299.6	100.7	3,259	42,190	33,298.6	2,400.0	10,377	1,58,678	50,609.6	4,447.7	5,057	23,347	6,130.6	996.3
Terre Haute, IN	16.1	85.5	143	1,551	833.9	65.0	633	9,040	2,433.8	209.4	108	611	107.1	19.0

1. Merchant wholesalers, except manufacturers' sales branches and offices. 2. Employer establishments.

Area name	Professional, scientific, and technical services, 2017				Manufacturing, 2017				Accommodation and food services, 2017			
	Number of establish-ments	Number of employees	Sales (mil dol)	Average payroll (mil dol)	Number of establish-ments	Number of employees	Receipts (mil dol)	Annual payroll (mil dol)	Number of establish-ments	Number of employees	Receipts (mil dol)	Annual payroll (mil dol)
	147	148	149	150	151	152	153	154	155	156	157	158
Reading, PA	D	D	D	D	483	31,959	10,989.4	1,674.8	770	13,389	671.4	186.8
Redding, CA	357	2,043	272.7	116.7	130	2,158	656.3	106.5	373	6,351	428.5	118.5
Reno, NV	13	21	3.8	1.4	491	16,653	6,232.1	1,068.1	1,159	31,563	2,421.4	684.4
Richmond, VA	3,578	39,473	6,551.6	2,705.0	D	D	D	D	2,673	55,327	3,032.1	891.2
Riverside-San Bernardino-Ontario, CA	6,359	39,530	5,689.0	2,054.1	3,342	93,958	36,097.3	4,948.4	7,586	1,58,600	11,100.0	3,111.0
Roanoke, VA	148	504	58.3	19.7	D	D	D	D	682	14,103	722.2	212.9
Rochester, MN	D	D	36.0	D	185	7,594	3,865.1	395.1	510	9,456	557.3	170.2
Rochester, NY	2,168	27,039	4,463.9	1,719.8	1,296	52,874	18,209.3	3,035.9	2,534	39,333	2,118.9	661.6
Rockford, IL	577	5,044	817.5	286.8	643	31,314	13,918.0	2,065.5	643	12,291	633.7	183.0
Rocky Mount, NC	174	1,015	137.8	42.3	121	9,686	4,924.3	440.0	245	4,832	240.1	63.7
Rome, GA	178	808	123.2	31.6	98	6,153	3,872.4	358.9	202	4,241	227.3	64.8
Sacramento-Roseville-Folsom, CA	5,225	52,037	9,468.0	4,711.8	1,362	32,814	12,106.9	1,928.3	4,804	95,400	6,944.8	1,865.9
Saginaw, MI	298	2,414	375.2	142.5	194	12,288	4,461.3	799.8	400	9,735	493.3	137.5
St. Cloud, MN	D	D	D	D	313	15,313	5,138.8	777.8	435	8,084	369.1	109.8
St. George, UT	D	D	D	D	163	2,634	620.3	119.0	363	7,354	449.3	119.5
St. Joseph, MO-KS	D	D	D	D	112	12,344	8,051.1	606.3	235	4,481	214.7	62.8
St. Louis, MO-IL	6,245	73,385	13,619.6	5,137.3	2,451	1,07,501	53,307.7	6,867.3	6,011	1,29,726	7,542.4	2,140.9
Salem, OR	788	4,086	541.9	205.3	456	11,498	3,595.6	548.3	D	D	D	D
Salinas, CA	D	D	D	D	280	9,070	4,346.2	429.1	1,095	22,103	1,894.5	524.6
Salisbury, MD-DE	169	820	99.9	39.6	258	14,136	5,151.3	621.5	1,338	20,757	1,633.1	472.6
Salt Lake City, UT	D	D	D	D	1,457	55,063	26,993.4	3,492.0	2,496	51,607	3,167.7	895.0
San Angelo, TX	6	8	1.9	0.1	94	3,370	1,936.4	182.0	274	5,228	280.6	79.0
San Antonio-New Braunfels, TX	900	4,709	691.0	237.1	1,224	43,334	24,472.8	2,317.0	4,972	1,20,880	7,444.0	2,081.3
San Diego-Chula Vista-Carlsbad, CA	14,150	1,43,999	37,220.4	14,266.1	2,972	1,00,773	31,443.8	7,335.4	7,810	1,84,771	14,854.7	4,139.0
San Francisco-Oakland-Berkeley, CA	21,738	2,59,352	79,228.5	30,551.3	3,898	1,39,885	89,194.6	12,056.5	13,754	2,44,786	21,854.4	6,260.6
Oakland-Berkeley-Livermore, CA Div 36,084	9,586	92,928	22,371.4	9,198.5	2,351	96,246	56,672.8	8,022.8	6,265	1,00,517	7,490.7	2,115.1
San Francisco-San Mateo-Redwood City, CA Div 41,884	10,356	1,58,424	55,077.6	20,680.8	1,315	40,677	31,740.9	3,866.3	6,726	1,30,584	13,338.0	3,824.2
San Rafael, CA Div 42,034	1,796	8,000	1,779.5	671.9	232	2,962	780.9	167.4	763	13,685	1,025.8	321.3
San Jose-Sunnyvale-Santa Clara, CA	8,834	1,44,293	42,491.3	18,201.6	2,258	95,476	37,428.3	8,281.7	5,203	92,242	7,351.8	2,169.9
San Luis Obispo-Paso Robles, CA	929	4,853	797.0	298.6	453	6,433	2,341.3	343.5	985	17,024	1,148.8	331.1
Santa Cruz-Watsonville, CA	878	4,262	648.4	315.9	314	5,049	1,707.6	301.1	711	12,032	831.9	251.5
Santa Fe, NM	654	2,391	386.8	146.3	120	725	165.9	32.3	429	9,749	743.9	226.0
Santa Maria-Santa Barbara, CA	1,389	10,005	2,285.7	777.4	495	12,939	4,208.2	916.0	1,215	25,145	2,149.9	607.0
Santa Rosa-Petaluma, CA	1,585	8,289	1,357.1	544.3	891	21,445	7,370.0	1,344.2	1,306	24,035	2,085.6	534.8
Savannah, GA	74	262	40.1	12.4	218	18,300	11,185.5	1,530.7	1,158	24,242	1,597.6	410.2
Scranton--Wilkes-Barre, PA	547	4,820	632.3	257.3	D	27,309	D	1,423.4	1,433	21,611	1,419.3	335.3
Seattle-Tacoma-Bellevue, WA	14,285	1,56,506	33,125.0	13,588.8	3,525	1,62,698	88,043.6	12,278.9	9,943	1,71,879	13,580.2	4,111.8
Seattle-Bellevue-Kent, WA Div 42,644	12,741	1,47,351	31,700.2	13,030.7	2,960	1,44,549	81,756.4	11,241.0	8,288	1,42,877	11,635.2	3,527.2
Tacoma-Lakewood, WA Div 45,104	1,544	9,155	1,424.7	558.2	565	18,149	6,287.2	1,037.9	1,655	29,002	1,945.0	584.6
Sebastian-Vero Beach, FL	518	2,076	286.9	116.0	87	1,538	362.3	82.6	282	5,660	334.0	97.0
Sebring-Avon Park, FL	D	D	D	D	46	707	284.3	33.2	143	2,450	125.6	35.8
Sheboygan, WI	D	D	D	D	206	17,576	7,887.7	1,010.5	279	5,069	258.2	78.7
Sherman-Denison, TX	222	1,017	159.1	48.2	106	7,200	2,713.7	324.9	238	4,558	260.1	73.9
Shreveport-Bossier City, LA	28	127	14.1	4.7	D	D	D	D	802	21,392	1,571.1	370.9
Sierra Vista-Douglas, AZ	223	3,433	501.8	227.8	41	268	118.0	13.6	261	3,522	183.7	55.3
Sioux City, IA-NE-SD	41	318	54.7	16.8	D	D	D	D	343	6,697	437.4	106.4
Sioux Falls, SD	26	82	11.0	3.1	D	14,131	D	697.3	602	13,361	722.7	210.0
South Bend-Mishawaka, IN-MI	553	4,962	1,586.6	303.2	404	17,830	7,055.2	969.1	632	12,192	625.7	176.2
Spartanburg, SC	D	D	D	D	407	29,294	21,377.8	1,729.6	578	11,099	592.3	163.7
Spokane-Spokane Valley, WA	D	D	1,547.7	D	571	15,580	4,525.4	851.0	1,216	19,930	1,199.1	378.9
Springfield, IL	512	5,360	764.8	324.2	97	2,742	854.6	140.3	572	10,167	497.4	150.1
Springfield, MA	1,142	8,091	1,209.6	481.1	788	25,166	8,695.7	1,440.3	1,458	22,607	1,248.6	387.4
Springfield, MO	272	2,356	393.7	178.0	462	14,911	5,705.2	747.2	1,011	19,698	986.7	286.0
Springfield, OH	D	D	D	D	152	6,187	2,405.7	274.0	223	4,568	207.9	63.6
State College, PA	D	D	D	D	166	3,786	1,041.7	206.6	327	6,750	344.7	96.9
Staunton, VA	107	618	75.6	31.0	113	6,867	2,736.7	352.3	255	4,440	230.3	67.1
Stockton, CA	808	4,858	616.0	259.4	533	19,833	9,574.9	1,001.7	1,185	19,118	1,206.4	332.1
Sumter, SC	23	74	11.0	4.6	90	6,149	2,380.2	285.3	228	4,046	202.6	54.1
Syracuse, NY	1,191	13,590	3,097.4	946.2	559	23,735	10,529.8	1,430.8	1,637	26,188	1,429.1	440.8
Tallahassee, FL	21	135	12.9	5.0	D	D	D	D	837	17,137	918.2	251.2
Tampa-St. Petersburg-Clearwater, FL	6,139	63,153	11,602.0	4,758.1	2,145	52,836	21,574.8	2,884.3	5,726	1,21,393	8,280.6	2,213.3
Terre Haute, IN	64	292	37.3	15.1	188	10,704	5,228.3	564.5	387	7,113	344.1	100.3

Area name	Health care and social assistance, 2017				Other services, 2017				Nonemployer businesses, 2019		Value of residential construction authorized by building permits, 2021	
	Number of establish-ments	Number of employees	Receipts (mil dol)	Annual payroll (mil dol)	Number of establish-ments	Number of employees	Receipts (mil dol)	Annual payroll (mil dol)	Number	Receipts (mil dol)	New construc-tion ($1,000)	Number of housing units
	159	160	161	162	163	164	165	166	167	168	169	170
Reading, PA	861	26,638	2,897.5	1,261.5	797	4,354	425.4	116.3	25,442	1,228.9	1,06,335	493
Redding, CA	670	11,319	1,553.8	575.1	300	1,659	211.8	51.1	12,028	587.4	1,06,969	368
Reno, NV	D	D	D	D	D	D	D	D	35,557	2,145.9	10,79,115	5,337
Richmond, VA	3,264	82,469	11,064.2	4,301.5	2,399	17,744	2,196.6	616.3	96,333	4,238.4	16,50,238	9,547
Riverside-San Bernardino-Ontario, CA	9,041	1,78,897	25,064.1	9,349.5	5,187	33,554	3,491.7	1,003.4	3,43,287	15,724.0	37,47,171	15,606
Roanoke, VA	824	26,276	3,667.9	1,372.3	587	3,264	334.8	91.2	20,170	932.5	1,75,714	869
Rochester, MN	479	21,541	2,776.3	1,017.1	397	2,595	257.7	73.6	15,079	737.9	2,76,426	1,135
Rochester, NY	2,649	88,306	8,488.1	3,665.2	1,857	10,406	1,215.0	321.7	67,775	3,089.9	4,04,790	1,774
Rockford, IL	719	21,226	2,723.0	1,047.1	570	3,435	382.1	100.3	20,359	784.2	46,339	280
Rocky Mount, NC	325	8,492	747.3	307.6	142	706	183.4	19.9	8,823	351.3	88,803	640
Rome, GA	322	8,395	1,147.7	397.0	115	808	79.6	23.5	7,095	290.8	61,657	204
Sacramento-Roseville-Folsom, CA	5,763	1,26,716	21,303.3	8,492.8	3,658	25,778	3,335.3	992.6	1,81,068	9,428.2	33,34,568	12,434
Saginaw, MI	597	17,800	2,040.7	811.3	325	1,989	183.1	49.7	10,717	435.4	45,134	195
St. Cloud, MN	571	20,317	2,345.5	988.0	443	2,584	286.5	79.2	13,759	710.2	1,65,970	624
St. George, UT	583	9,409	1,212.8	395.3	265	1,401	138.9	37.6	16,476	864.6	7,21,283	3,484
St. Joseph, MO-KS	330	9,556	1,032.8	420.7	38	194	207.0	4.8	6,561	263.7	23,493	108
St. Louis, MO-IL	9,408	1,98,887	22,481.5	8,907.1	4,985	37,262	4,418.9	1,309.9	1,94,382	8,800.6	19,87,707	8,326
Salem, OR	1,275	23,813	2,654.2	1,130.8	594	2,889	300.5	87.8	23,325	1,119.8	4,73,280	2,154
Salinas, CA	999	17,169	2,803.9	1,072.6	607	4,058	573.0	128.9	26,100	1,521.3	1,87,665	882
Salisbury, MD-DE	1,099	24,107	2,852.2	1,143.7	706	4,073	435.1	124.9	33,045	1,819.2	8,56,170	5,552
Salt Lake City, UT	3,330	68,721	9,674.6	3,563.4	2,136	14,800	1,741.3	511.5	99,062	5,165.0	23,85,089	11,642
San Angelo, TX	D	D	D	D	D	D	173.2	D	9,349	422.0	71,863	333
San Antonio-New Braunfels, TX	5,924	1,38,127	15,957.1	5,855.3	3,287	23,278	2,400.0	707.5	2,12,660	10,135.8	44,23,266	22,264
San Diego-Chula Vista-Carlsbad, CA	9,592	1,75,430	26,431.3	10,143.4	5,823	42,595	4,888.7	1,379.5	2,92,558	15,195.6	20,92,612	10,048
San Francisco-Oakland-Berkeley, CA	15,015	2,83,893	47,686.4	19,336.5	9,486	76,980	14,303.7	3,342.9	4,47,052	27,814.3	37,94,520	13,606
Oakland-Berkeley-Livermore, CA Div 36,084	8,045	1,58,335	26,234.4	10,497.3	4,815	34,868	5,125.8	1,431.2	2,47,074	13,806.1	20,93,179	8,926
San Francisco-San Mateo-Redwood City, CA Div 41,884	5,812	1,08,759	19,101.3	7,774.4	3,968	37,222	8,330.6	1,708.3	1,62,829	10,996.7	15,90,519	4,415
San Rafael, CA Div 42,034	1,158	16,799	2,350.7	1,064.8	703	4,890	847.4	203.5	37,149	3,011.5	1,10,822	265
San Jose-Sunnyvale-Santa Clara, CA	5,993	1,16,645	22,363.4	9,137.7	3,380	22,818	5,506.3	983.0	1,47,368	9,125.0	11,98,432	4,529
San Luis Obispo-Paso Robles, CA	1,055	15,066	1,912.6	788.2	450	2,986	265.6	78.7	26,134	1,457.5	2,49,800	1,120
Santa Cruz-Watsonville, CA	940	15,312	2,175.2	831.2	473	3,232	413.6	127.6	24,733	1,320.0	1,10,222	598
Santa Fe, NM	510	9,791	1,131.9	426.1	351	2,038	294.6	82.2	17,159	822.2	1,33,832	840
Santa Maria-Santa Barbara, CA	1,428	23,163	3,662.0	1,207.5	785	5,846	1,759.0	211.2	35,300	2,156.0	1,70,755	1,152
Santa Rosa-Petaluma, CA	1,537	26,382	3,737.9	1,632.2	959	5,810	684.6	206.7	45,633	2,534.5	7,09,704	2,618
Savannah, GA	893	22,833	2,694.6	1,037.6	571	4,578	536.3	162.5	31,663	1,434.4	7,44,715	3,227
Scranton--Wilkes-Barre, PA	1,751	46,747	5,135.6	2,008.2	1,017	5,431	606.0	157.5	32,295	1,621.8	1,57,064	644
Seattle-Tacoma-Bellevue, WA	11,838	2,47,474	33,962.9	13,673.4	7,656	48,632	11,111.0	2,036.8	2,84,846	15,443.1	64,52,235	30,743
Seattle-Bellevue-Kent, WA Div 42,644	9,835	1,94,243	26,513.7	10,645.5	6,216	39,328	10,001.9	1,698.4	2,34,909	13,034.2	51,12,283	24,671
Tacoma-Lakewood, WA Div 45,104	2,003	53,231	7,449.2	3,027.9	1,440	9,304	1,109.1	338.4	49,937	2,409.0	13,39,952	6,072
Sebastian-Vero Beach, FL	495	9,718	1,155.2	454.1	313	1,726	167.0	51.2	15,714	861.7	6,14,020	1,592
Sebring-Avon Park, FL	309	6,442	729.3	284.6	125	403	39.6	9.5	6,638	284.3	1,37,252	644
Sheboygan, WI	315	6,645	744.0	290.0	202	1,060	98.6	25.5	5,495	255.9	69,807	268
Sherman-Denison, TX	360	8,454	956.3	381.4	149	689	81.7	21.5	11,537	609.8	2,09,723	1,048
Shreveport-Bossier City, LA	1,118	33,275	4,640.4	1,691.0	130	1,055	107.0	31.0	32,900	1,418.1	2,75,788	1,136
Sierra Vista-Douglas, AZ	283	4,921	454.5	188.2	160	661	66.2	16.9	7,191	231.1	58,058	434
Sioux City, IA-NE-SD	441	11,199	1,300.2	494.3	209	1,323	170.4	44.1	8,568	443.6	1,09,577	457
Sioux Falls, SD	691	31,489	4,072.0	1,660.6	374	2,704	399.4	93.7	21,417	1,173.9	6,92,740	3,986
South Bend-Mishawaka, IN-MI	728	20,510	2,480.6	865.6	487	3,316	384.2	108.7	19,265	819.0	1,71,745	492
Spartanburg, SC	574	16,460	1,784.2	848.3	425	3,014	399.0	96.3	23,066	1,156.3	5,95,993	3,614
Spokane-Spokane Valley, WA	1,716	43,243	5,062.6	2,078.5	953	5,380	595.6	173.8	35,974	1,726.5	7,12,322	3,415
Springfield, IL	478	22,613	3,039.2	1,054.0	483	3,317	412.8	133.4	12,725	503.3	66,281	332
Springfield, MA	1,832	57,305	6,096.0	2,644.7	1,232	8,090	939.2	253.5	46,790	2,121.1	1,72,008	745
Springfield, MO	1,195	34,893	4,220.1	1,578.9	838	5,502	567.0	167.7	36,374	1,824.4	5,44,615	2,638
Springfield, OH	290	7,102	709.7	267.6	191	1,438	194.0	52.0	6,815	288.4	54,354	199
State College, PA	403	9,501	1,078.6	456.8	253	1,481	145.1	41.4	10,219	473.1	1,61,121	654
Staunton, VA	259	7,056	814.5	305.1	252	1,314	148.3	43.4	7,551	371.8	83,452	413
Stockton, CA	1,513	32,650	4,236.8	1,600.6	890	5,434	565.0	163.8	44,792	2,502.2	12,77,507	4,389
Sumter, SC	226	6,496	673.6	232.1	144	1,149	108.6	31.9	8,610	326.8	75,200	472
Syracuse, NY	1,678	49,957	5,879.3	2,441.7	1,219	7,073	789.2	218.2	39,916	1,825.1	1,43,037	693
Tallahassee, FL	839	21,217	2,577.5	1,050.1	701	4,744	754.7	201.7	29,933	1,182.9	4,91,047	2,905
Tampa-St. Petersburg-Clearwater, FL	9,483	1,85,514	27,593.2	9,516.2	5,435	32,574	3,896.7	969.6	3,03,763	13,628.1	58,01,428	24,831
Terre Haute, IN	491	11,401	1,467.2	512.8	284	1,487	172.4	40.8	9,135	351.3	26,593	170

Table C. Metropolitan Areas — Government Employment and Payroll, and Local Government Finances

Area name	Government employment and payroll, 2017									Local government finances, 2017				
			March payroll (percent of total)							General revenue				
												Taxes		
													Per capita[1] (dollars)	
	Full-time equivalent employees	March payroll (dollars)	Adminis-tration, judicial, and legal	Police and corrections	Fire protection	Highways and transpor-tation	Health and welfare	Natural resources and utilities	Education and libraries	Total (mil dol)	Inter-govern-mental (mil dol)	Total (mil dol)	Total	Property
	171	172	173	174	175	176	177	178	179	180	181	182	183	184
Reading, PA	14,681	6,75,82,415	5.9	10.7	1.3	2.5	4.6	3.4	70.0	2,205.5	858.4	952.9	2,282	1,831
Redding, CA	7,243	3,62,94,479	6.8	9.0	2.6	3.2	14.4	8.3	53.1	1,172.7	746.1	233.3	1,300	1,022
Reno, NV	13,528	6,46,76,757	10.2	13.6	5.9	4.3	4.4	8.6	50.3	2,110.0	944.7	720.1	1,563	1,008
Richmond, VA	46,835	18,78,13,105	7.9	13.7	5.9	2.0	5.9	5.6	56.1	5,223.5	2,138.2	2,242.3	1,766	1,282
Riverside-San Bernardino-Ontario, CA	1,52,935	94,85,66,442	7.2	10.6	2.8	2.2	13.3	5.0	57.0	31,726.1	18,092.8	6,892.7	1,510	1,066
Roanoke, VA	12,013	4,65,85,173	8.1	10.7	5.7	1.8	4.6	6.0	60.3	1,309.7	578.8	564.1	1,802	1,280
Rochester, MN	7,887	3,74,23,777	9.7	10.7	2.3	4.1	10.5	8.5	53.2	1,143.3	504.0	353.0	1,619	1,414
Rochester, NY	51,885	24,52,68,182	4.4	9.1	2.7	3.2	5.9	3.4	69.6	6,835.2	2,881.7	3,059.1	2,854	1,914
Rockford, IL	11,726	5,24,83,712	5.2	12.4	5.9	3.5	4.0	6.7	61.2	1,493.1	646.9	638.3	1,887	1,647
Rocky Mount, NC	7,611	2,93,93,778	3.6	7.0	2.6	1.7	33.5	6.4	43.6	486.0	260.9	151.7	1,033	780
Rome, GA	3,978	1,31,44,682	5.5	10.4	4.8	3.7	2.2	6.5	65.2	377.8	154.9	149.8	1,537	984
Sacramento-Roseville-Folsom, CA	79,610	49,50,84,789	6.2	12.4	4.7	3.6	8.0	11.9	49.8	14,635.7	6,526.1	4,180.6	1,802	1,283
Saginaw, MI	5,450	2,28,45,829	8.3	7.8	1.9	2.7	12.0	4.9	60.6	801.5	464.7	162.3	845	736
St. Cloud, MN	6,869	3,09,09,140	8.9	11.4	1.7	5.1	8.6	3.7	57.9	871.7	459.2	260.8	1,314	1,173
St. George, UT	4,494	1,75,31,308	8.8	10.7	1.8	2.4	6.9	15.0	52.2	567.9	183.6	240.2	1,448	947
St. Joseph, MO-KS	4,416	1,59,72,895	5.2	7.9	3.8	3.4	2.7	5.1	71.0	429.0	161.1	194.6	1,541	892
St. Louis, MO-IL	99,482	43,11,49,817	5.7	11.4	5.6	5.8	2.8	5.5	61.4	11,390.1	3,644.6	5,715.4	2,037	1,313
Salem, OR	12,770	6,50,68,787	6.1	9.6	3.4	3.3	4.5	3.2	67.4	1,788.9	962.8	520.1	1,226	1,088
Salinas, CA	19,396	12,47,81,670	5.0	7.7	2.4	3.5	27.9	4.3	45.9	3,511.6	1,416.5	905.1	2,083	1,363
Salisbury, MD-DE	13,385	5,94,86,106	5.7	9.7	0.8	1.9	2.5	6.0	71.4	1,674.0	704.5	666.7	1,650	1,143
Salt Lake City, UT	37,900	15,12,42,305	7.7	10.3	5.4	10.5	4.7	8.3	50.0	4,503.2	1,359.2	2,130.1	1,769	1,148
San Angelo, TX	5,059	1,58,50,961	8.3	14.6	6.1	2.9	4.4	5.7	56.0	399.0	129.4	210.1	1,746	1,365
San Antonio-New Braunfels, TX	1,03,873	44,12,37,393	4.9	9.0	4.0	3.5	11.8	9.8	55.9	11,196.0	3,428.2	5,162.2	2,088	1,678
San Diego-Chula Vista-Carlsbad, CA	1,06,292	62,98,93,092	7.5	10.0	3.7	3.2	10.6	6.2	54.8	19,787.8	7,386.6	6,914.4	2,082	1,537
San Francisco-Oakland-Berkeley, CA	1,74,248	1,25,10,34,774	6.7	12.0	5.3	11.3	17.0	8.3	37.1	40,739.7	12,173.0	16,112.4	3,419	2,252
Oakland-Berkeley-Livermore, CA Div 36,084	96,003	68,63,38,466	5.2	11.7	4.6	9.3	16.9	8.1	42.1	22,204.3	7,557.6	7,786.2	2,775	1,845
San Francisco-San Mateo-Redwood City, CA Div 41,884	69,282	50,01,63,023	8.6	12.7	6.1	15.0	18.1	8.2	29.0	16,691.3	4,186.1	7,333.8	4,453	2,880
San Rafael, CA Div 42,034	8,963	6,45,33,285	8.9	10.4	7.2	3.3	9.5	10.9	46.6	1,844.1	429.4	992.4	3,820	2,667
San Jose-Sunnyvale-Santa Clara, CA	66,718	51,37,79,027	7.3	9.0	2.9	4.9	24.0	5.0	45.1	17,165.3	4,145.0	7,008.9	3,517	2,571
San Luis Obispo-Paso Robles, CA	8,813	5,06,53,491	7.9	12.7	2.9	2.9	9.1	5.7	55.0	1,483.1	506.8	703.3	2,490	1,941
Santa Cruz-Watsonville, CA	9,852	6,10,97,077	8.1	9.9	4.0	7.1	13.0	8.3	47.4	1,679.8	750.9	583.8	2,124	1,525
Santa Fe, NM	5,045	1,92,87,175	8.7	13.7	6.2	5.6	3.3	12.0	47.2	639.4	266.4	264.5	1,769	1,075
Santa Maria-Santa Barbara, CA	21,940	14,45,99,650	4.5	8.3	4.1	2.5	11.8	5.0	62.2	3,756.5	1,907.2	1,050.1	2,358	1,793
Santa Rosa-Petaluma, CA	17,488	11,12,65,857	7.9	11.7	4.0	2.5	14.7	6.4	51.1	3,029.9	1,128.7	1,172.0	2,332	1,749
Savannah, GA	14,092	5,38,03,266	8.5	13.4	4.5	4.6	5.5	6.7	53.1	2,227.7	466.9	798.8	2,067	1,318
Scranton--Wilkes-Barre, PA	16,431	7,13,11,908	7.4	10.7	2.7	4.3	5.8	4.1	63.3	2,263.4	925.9	992.6	1,786	1,334
Seattle-Tacoma-Bellevue, WA	1,25,096	80,87,47,124	9.0	8.9	5.6	10.9	10.4	12.0	40.6	25,385.5	7,644.3	10,196.2	2,624	1,448
Seattle-Bellevue-Kent, WA Div 42,644	99,194	65,11,35,102	9.2	9.1	5.0	11.5	12.2	12.1	38.2	21,108.8	6,026.2	8,617.3	2,867	1,522
Tacoma-Lakewood, WA Div 45,104	25,902	15,76,12,022	8.6	7.9	8.1	8.5	2.8	11.9	50.6	4,276.7	1,618.1	1,578.9	1,795	1,196
Sebastian-Vero Beach, FL	4,114	1,62,29,719	5.2	17.3	4.8	4.9	3.8	12.9	48.2	515.4	108.8	297.9	1,931	1,523
Sebring-Avon Park, FL	3,221	1,01,34,596	7.5	15.0	2.0	3.4	1.9	4.9	63.1	302.8	127.4	101.8	980	722
Sheboygan, WI	4,307	1,96,13,015	4.3	9.6	2.4	5.4	8.1	3.7	65.1	501.1	247.2	183.3	1,593	1,516
Sherman-Denison, TX	5,654	1,98,12,399	6.1	10.4	4.1	2.3	5.3	5.8	64.9	487.4	166.5	228.8	1,745	1,467
Shreveport-Bossier City, LA	16,212	5,65,14,633	7.0	16.1	6.7	2.8	2.1	4.4	58.7	1,693.0	520.1	892.5	2,230	1,159
Sierra Vista-Douglas, AZ	4,703	1,73,32,719	11.3	11.0	5.9	3.1	2.2	4.0	60.1	436.0	208.8	154.2	1,235	895
Sioux City, IA-NE-SD	6,257	2,73,60,833	5.0	8.7	3.0	4.6	2.0	5.0	70.4	722.1	322.4	284.6	1,988	1,584
Sioux Falls, SD	8,112	3,21,64,717	8.0	9.6	3.4	4.2	2.5	5.1	65.8	984.8	280.4	546.1	2,100	1,426
South Bend-Mishawaka, IN-MI	9,840	3,66,84,987	6.6	12.2	7.1	4.6	2.3	6.3	59.5	1,239.0	544.8	448.7	1,395	1,137
Spartanburg, SC	15,616	7,26,30,964	2.9	4.1	1.5	0.4	54.2	3.4	32.7	2,111.4	443.9	383.7	1,251	1,089
Spokane-Spokane Valley, WA	16,942	9,06,50,435	8.4	11.3	6.6	6.3	2.9	6.8	55.3	2,508.2	1,205.1	810.8	1,474	896
Springfield, IL	8,706	4,00,71,271	4.7	9.8	4.4	5.2	3.0	14.5	58.2	886.8	320.6	409.9	1,958	1,668
Springfield, MA	28,210	13,38,72,927	3.7	9.3	6.2	2.8	2.7	6.2	66.3	2,963.2	1,322.4	1,284.0	1,836	1,777
Springfield, MO	16,317	6,05,29,281	4.8	7.6	3.3	4.0	9.6	9.6	55.0	1,527.1	533.6	627.9	1,359	770
Springfield, OH	4,730	1,92,51,860	8.8	10.4	4.4	2.0	9.0	3.3	60.6	483.7	238.1	185.9	1,382	876
State College, PA	3,630	1,46,77,666	9.0	9.2	0.0	9.4	3.5	7.0	60.1	520.6	151.4	264.0	1,626	1,174
Staunton, VA	4,303	1,49,13,667	7.1	14.3	4.1	1.7	3.5	3.9	62.8	391.8	197.1	151.1	1,241	847
Stockton, CA	26,849	15,56,24,972	5.8	10.0	3.2	3.1	16.7	4.3	55.8	4,670.9	2,331.8	1,193.2	1,605	1,058
Sumter, SC	5,063	1,62,32,355	6.6	9.3	3.0	1.8	6.2	4.9	65.0	449.8	203.6	168.0	1,196	824
Syracuse, NY	30,422	14,31,44,961	3.3	8.1	2.3	4.6	5.2	4.3	71.0	4,081.7	1,834.9	1,742.3	2,676	1,808
Tallahassee, FL	13,633	5,15,57,334	10.9	11.8	4.0	4.6	3.3	14.7	46.9	1,365.6	504.8	465.8	1,216	834
Tampa-St. Petersburg-Clearwater, FL	98,460	38,98,54,339	7.4	14.8	6.3	4.3	2.9	9.0	52.3	11,723.1	4,167.1	4,583.4	1,475	1,105
Terre Haute, IN	5,972	2,11,53,016	7.9	9.9	4.6	4.2	6.6	3.7	61.9	617.0	277.0	195.0	1,044	917

1. Based on the resident population estimated as of July 1 of the year shown

Area name	Local government finances, 2017 (cont.)									Government employment, 2020			Individual income tax returns, 2019		
	Direct general expenditure							Debt outstanding							
			Percent of total for:												
	Total (mil dol)	Per capita[1] (dollars)	Educa-tion	Health and hospitals	Police protection	Public welfare	Highways	Total (mil dol)	Per capita[1] (dollars)	Federal civilian	Federal military	State and local	Number of returns	Mean adjusted gross income	Mean income tax
	185	186	187	188	189	190	191	192	193	194	195	196	197	198	199
Reading, PA	2,252.8	5,396	56.5	1.4	4.5	8.7	3.5	2,740.4	6,564	1,007	1,052	19,724	2,10,690	62,667	6,591
Redding, CA	1,007.3	5,615	46.0	8.4	6.0	11.3	2.6	573.9	3,199	1,345	302	11,305	80,280	59,517	5,921
Reno, NV	1,990.9	4,322	34.2	1.4	7.6	4.8	8.5	3,144.9	6,828	3,948	1,256	23,952	2,51,340	86,660	12,226
Richmond, VA	4,992.3	3,932	44.4	4.5	7.0	4.1	3.3	4,588.2	3,614	17,457	12,803	93,244	6,36,460	77,652	9,714
Riverside-San Bernardino-Ontario, CA	32,108.9	7,032	38.0	19.7	6.0	6.4	3.5	29,154.1	6,385	22,455	21,183	2,30,599	20,56,090	57,931	5,507
Roanoke, VA	1,332.7	4,258	45.0	2.7	5.0	6.9	2.4	849.8	2,715	3,913	977	16,970	1,49,510	62,603	6,620
Rochester, MN	1,256.6	5,764	38.9	2.0	4.9	6.1	10.8	3,594.2	16,488	1,041	761	11,099	1,13,380	76,841	9,092
Rochester, NY	7,078.3	6,603	51.5	4.0	3.9	9.3	4.0	4,323.1	4,033	5,246	1,721	65,407	5,31,340	65,857	7,316
Rockford, IL	1,552.6	4,591	52.1	0.9	9.2	2.4	6.4	1,090.1	3,223	964	697	14,838	1,63,190	58,060	5,826
Rocky Mount, NC	483.9	3,297	54.4	4.4	7.7	6.8	1.2	319.3	2,175	411	307	9,717	66,840	48,568	4,352
Rome, GA	407.1	4,176	48.2	8.6	5.5	0.1	2.8	185.7	1,904	226	253	5,367	41,560	57,662	5,750
Sacramento-Roseville-Folsom, CA	13,996.0	6,034	40.1	5.8	5.9	6.5	3.7	26,562.1	11,451	15,009	4,297	2,35,041	11,17,300	76,352	9,200
Saginaw, MI	842.5	4,389	39.0	18.6	4.0	0.6	8.2	484.2	2,522	1,547	292	8,884	90,750	52,217	5,027
St. Cloud, MN	920.3	4,638	49.4	0.8	5.2	5.6	9.7	1,592.9	8,027	2,488	679	10,818	96,580	64,756	6,915
St. George, UT	514.8	3,103	51.2	5.2	8.3	0.1	2.6	527.3	3,178	655	692	8,465	79,920	67,821	7,284
St. Joseph, MO-KS	417.0	3,301	53.9	1.8	5.7	0.1	6.3	902.3	7,142	603	405	8,116	55,760	55,084	5,254
St. Louis, MO-IL	11,216.3	3,998	48.1	2.8	7.6	0.9	4.6	15,335.4	5,466	28,546	13,460	1,29,212	13,80,660	75,988	9,599
Salem, OR	1,750.1	4,125	53.9	6.8	5.6	0.1	4.6	1,561.0	3,680	1,567	1,005	38,734	1,98,590	60,753	5,870
Salinas, CA	3,623.3	8,338	38.0	22.1	4.4	5.0	2.3	2,222.3	5,114	5,722	5,734	28,381	2,01,650	70,766	8,328
Salisbury, MD-DE	1,709.1	4,229	56.0	1.6	5.5	0.6	3.0	1,053.4	2,606	1,270	1,921	21,243	2,07,610	65,300	7,236
Salt Lake City, UT	4,622.2	3,838	37.8	1.4	5.8	3.3	7.2	10,128.6	8,411	13,020	4,865	99,285	5,83,700	73,977	8,526
San Angelo, TX	401.1	3,333	50.3	1.2	6.5	0.9	3.4	491.6	4,084	1,252	3,780	7,847	56,340	66,687	8,213
San Antonio-New Braunfels, TX	11,278.0	4,562	44.4	16.6	5.2	1.5	3.4	28,785.3	11,644	37,594	38,825	1,34,205	12,08,210	66,105	7,828
San Diego-Chula Vista-Carlsbad, CA	20,668.2	6,223	39.3	9.4	5.6	4.4	3.1	41,671.1	12,547	49,309	88,491	1,92,464	16,46,850	83,984	11,334
San Francisco-Oakland-Berkeley, CA	40,686.9	8,634	25.3	18.9	5.7	6.8	4.4	68,469.0	14,529	32,353	9,370	2,80,468	23,54,990	1,43,907	26,055
Oakland-Berkeley-Livermore, CA Div 36,084	21,848.4	7,787	28.9	17.0	5.9	4.9	6.6	35,862.7	12,782	14,357	5,935	1,44,622	13,71,520	1,15,540	18,142
San Francisco-San Mateo-Redwood City, CA Div 41,884	17,017.5	10,333	19.8	22.7	5.4	9.6	1.6	29,692.6	18,029	17,240	2,952	1,21,946	8,51,290	1,81,512	36,751
San Rafael, CA Div 42,034	1,820.9	7,010	33.9	7.4	6.6	3.6	3.4	2,913.7	11,217	756	483	13,900	1,32,180	1,96,050	39,280
San Jose-Sunnyvale-Santa Clara, CA	15,971.7	8,015	31.1	24.9	4.9	5.6	1.9	20,746.3	10,411	10,782	3,308	87,321	9,69,620	1,63,636	30,520
San Luis Obispo-Paso Robles, CA	1,449.8	5,132	41.1	6.4	6.0	7.8	4.0	1,526.6	5,404	634	554	21,596	1,35,180	80,955	10,233
Santa Cruz-Watsonville, CA	1,650.8	6,006	38.1	7.8	5.8	7.8	3.0	1,276.1	4,643	603	377	19,601	1,31,880	96,749	14,138
Santa Fe, NM	553.0	3,699	43.8	0.0	7.4	1.4	2.9	844.6	5,650	979	382	14,051	79,840	80,425	10,444
Santa Maria-Santa Barbara, CA	3,448.8	7,745	33.0	26.8	4.7	4.2	1.9	1,732.6	3,891	3,604	3,189	32,334	2,07,530	83,790	11,795
Santa Rosa-Petaluma, CA	3,042.2	6,054	40.6	9.0	6.5	6.9	3.8	3,352.6	6,672	1,534	1,479	24,505	2,49,160	86,214	11,364
Savannah, GA	2,217.1	5,738	32.4	28.2	6.2	0.7	5.0	844.0	2,184	3,037	5,859	21,249	1,80,250	65,203	7,229
Scranton--Wilkes-Barre, PA	2,305.3	4,149	53.2	0.2	4.1	5.7	4.5	2,632.9	4,738	4,502	1,385	23,818	2,79,340	56,281	5,751
Seattle-Tacoma-Bellevue, WA	22,482.0	5,786	35.1	10.2	5.0	0.7	5.5	38,244.6	9,843	34,331	42,910	2,44,449	20,07,190	1,11,780	16,987
Seattle-Bellevue-Kent, WA Div 42,644	18,455.2	6,140	33.1	12.2	4.7	0.8	5.6	31,982.0	10,640	22,392	9,905	1,98,190	15,64,010	1,22,494	19,468
Tacoma-Lakewood, WA Div 45,104	4,026.7	4,578	44.6	1.4	6.4	0.5	5.3	6,262.6	7,119	11,939	33,005	46,259	4,43,180	73,969	8,232
Sebastian-Vero Beach, FL	533.9	3,462	35.9	4.1	7.3	0.9	7.3	253.7	1,645	406	275	4,514	81,830	1,16,349	18,779
Sebring-Avon Park, FL	317.5	3,058	44.6	3.2	10.1	0.6	5.4	109.0	1,050	313	180	3,816	44,520	47,026	4,185
Sheboygan, WI	520.5	4,522	56.5	3.9	6.8	5.2	7.5	547.7	4,759	211	323	5,307	59,970	63,603	6,415
Sherman-Denison, TX	487.5	3,717	54.3	3.7	4.9	0.5	3.7	1,071.3	8,168	381	261	6,802	63,360	61,072	6,171
Shreveport-Bossier City, LA	1,664.9	4,161	51.3	2.4	7.2	0.2	2.6	1,377.2	3,442	5,003	6,743	22,366	1,77,980	58,477	6,502
Sierra Vista-Douglas, AZ	399.0	3,196	48.4	1.3	10.9	2.7	7.5	162.4	1,301	4,956	4,457	5,830	55,370	50,721	4,347
Sioux City, IA-NE-SD	741.3	5,178	55.9	1.4	5.3	0.9	6.0	552.4	3,858	802	538	8,024	69,930	63,979	6,848
Sioux Falls, SD	928.0	3,568	49.6	1.3	5.1	0.5	12.2	1,048.6	4,032	2,835	1,549	11,688	1,41,700	74,947	9,647
South Bend-Mishawaka, IN-MI	1,068.9	3,324	44.6	2.4	5.8	0.9	4.9	859.3	2,672	986	932	14,516	1,53,030	60,168	6,396
Spartanburg, SC	2,201.0	7,175	26.1	58.6	2.3	0.2	1.2	1,354.9	4,417	639	1,161	22,951	1,47,880	58,285	5,716
Spokane-Spokane Valley, WA	2,480.3	4,507	48.4	7.2	5.2	0.5	5.0	2,241.5	4,073	5,412	4,837	33,387	2,73,250	66,871	7,317
Springfield, IL	929.9	4,442	45.6	2.4	8.8	0.2	8.3	3,149.4	15,042	1,817	469	18,371	1,05,260	71,069	8,223
Springfield, MA	3,054.5	4,367	57.5	0.6	4.6	0.3	3.7	1,705.7	2,439	5,491	1,724	50,393	3,32,380	64,530	6,973
Springfield, MO	1,481.7	3,207	52.3	9.5	7.1	0.4	5.9	1,749.8	3,787	2,635	1,544	26,298	2,13,400	61,224	6,622
Springfield, OH	528.8	3,930	51.2	6.1	8.1	6.3	4.2	235.9	1,753	518	328	6,061	64,050	51,217	4,403
State College, PA	539.4	3,323	57.5	1.9	3.3	3.2	5.3	421.2	2,595	591	452	47,124	60,840	74,356	8,656
Staunton, VA	406.8	3,341	55.4	2.2	4.6	6.6	4.4	232.1	1,906	301	380	8,087	59,830	57,259	5,143
Stockton, CA	4,399.2	5,918	46.3	10.7	6.0	7.0	4.7	5,064.4	6,813	3,336	1,171	39,287	3,38,510	63,048	6,316
Sumter, SC	410.2	2,921	58.3	4.6	7.2	0.2	2.0	198.7	1,415	1,460	6,465	6,983	61,700	43,944	3,418
Syracuse, NY	4,287.4	6,584	50.0	3.0	3.1	9.0	5.2	2,729.0	4,191	5,185	1,217	47,605	3,13,560	65,405	7,239
Tallahassee, FL	1,356.5	3,540	41.1	2.8	8.8	0.4	7.2	4,923.4	12,849	2,197	673	56,555	1,76,510	61,192	6,922
Tampa-St. Petersburg-Clearwater, FL	11,968.6	3,852	37.8	3.6	8.6	0.9	3.1	11,598.0	3,733	25,781	12,577	1,21,893	15,73,720	69,720	8,914
Terre Haute, IN	646.1	3,458	42.3	5.7	4.8	0.0	4.3	541.1	2,896	1,301	525	12,320	82,130	50,911	4,454

1. Based on the resident population estimated as of July 1 of the year shown.

Table C. Metropolitan Areas — **Land Area and Population**

CBSA[1]	DIV Code	Area name	Land area[2] (sq mi)	Population, 2021: Total persons 2021	Population, 2021: Rank	Population, 2021: Per square mile	Race alone or in combination, not Hispanic or Latino (percent): White	Black	American Indian, Alaska Native	Asian and Pacific Islander	Percent Hispanic or Latino[3]	Age (percent): Under 5 years	5 to 17 years	18 to 24 years	25 to 34 years	35 to 44 years	45 to 54 years
			1	2	3	4	5	6	7	8	9	10	11	12	13	14	15
45500		Texarkana, TX-AR	2,040.2	147,174	289	72.1	66.3	26.2	1.5	1.5	6.7	6.0	13.5	12.3	13.3	12.8	12.2
45540		The Villages, FL	557.1	135,638	304	243.5	85.6	7.0	0.7	1.4	6.2	1.7	4.1	4.0	5.8	6.1	6.4
45780		Toledo, OH	1,617.0	644,217	94	398.4	76.8	15.6	0.8	2.2	7.4	5.7	12.6	14.0	13.3	11.8	11.7
45820		Topeka, KS	3,232.7	232,670	200	72.0	80.0	8.0	2.5	1.9	11.2	5.8	13.2	12.5	11.6	12.3	11.4
45940		Trenton-Princeton, NJ	224.4	385,898	143	1,719.7	48.2	20.2	0.5	13.6	19.4	5.4	12.1	14.8	12.3	12.8	13.4
46060		Tucson, AZ	9,188.7	1,052,030	53	114.5	52.1	4.4	3.1	4.1	38.5	5.0	11.6	15.1	13.0	11.7	10.8
46140		Tulsa, OK	6,270.2	1,023,988	54	163.3	69.0	9.8	13.3	3.7	11.0	6.3	13.9	12.7	13.6	13.1	11.8
46220		Tuscaloosa, AL	3,493.3	268,191	185	76.8	58.3	36.5	0.6	1.9	4.1	5.7	12.0	18.1	13.9	12.1	11.3
46300		Twin Falls, ID	2,519.3	116,905	333	46.4	74.9	1.0	1.3	2.2	22.1	6.7	16.0	13.1	13.4	13.5	10.5
46340		Tyler, TX	921.5	237,186	198	257.4	59.9	18.2	0.7	2.1	20.7	6.2	13.9	13.9	13.4	12.3	11.3
46520		Urban Honolulu, HI	600.6	1,000,890	56	1,666.5	32.1	3.6	1.5	79.1	10.4	5.9	11.9	12.1	14.4	13.3	11.7
46540		Utica-Rome, NY	2,623.9	290,211	172	110.6	85.2	6.4	0.6	4.1	5.8	5.3	12.0	12.8	12.0	11.7	12.0
46660		Valdosta, GA	1,607.4	149,152	286	92.8	55.5	36.3	0.8	2.7	7.0	6.5	13.7	18.4	14.1	11.9	10.4
46700		Vallejo, CA	821.8	451,716	122	549.7	39.9	15.9	1.3	20.6	28.6	5.7	12.5	12.1	14.2	13.6	12.0
47020		Victoria, TX	1,734.1	98,127	361	56.6	44.7	6.2	0.6	1.5	48.2	6.5	14.3	13.4	13.2	12.6	10.6
47220		Vineland-Bridgeton, NJ	483.4	153,627	276	317.8	46.0	20.1	1.3	2.0	33.0	6.1	13.9	12.4	13.7	13.1	12.5
47260		Virginia Beach-Norfolk-Newport News, VA-NC	3,530.4	1,803,328	37	510.8	57.1	32.3	1.1	5.8	7.6	6.0	12.3	13.8	15.0	13.3	11.1
47300		Visalia, CA	4,823.9	477,054	119	98.9	27.7	1.8	1.2	4.3	66.7	7.3	17.6	15.4	14.1	13.1	10.9
47380		Waco, TX	1,802.2	280,428	177	155.6	56.0	15.4	0.7	2.3	27.5	6.4	13.7	17.9	13.1	12.0	10.5
47460		Walla Walla, WA	1,270.0	62,682	382	49.4	72.4	2.6	1.6	3.3	22.6	5.1	12.1	16.4	12.4	12.1	10.7
47580		Warner Robins, GA	526.3	195,246	228	371.0	54.8	36.3	0.8	4.0	7.1	6.2	14.5	13.7	13.9	13.6	11.6
47900		Washington-Arlington-Alexandria, DC-VA-MD-WV	6,567.7	6,356,434	6	967.8	46.5	26.8	0.8	12.6	16.7	6.0	12.9	12.4	14.2	14.7	13.3
47900	23224	Frederick-Gaithersburg-Rockville, MD Div 23,224	1,153.7	1,334,662	X	1,156.9	50.4	18.6	0.7	15.2	18.2	5.8	13.1	11.9	12.2	14.0	13.5
47900	47894	Washington-Arlington-Alexandria, DC-VA-MD-WV Div 47,894	5,414.0	5,021,772	X	927.6	45.4	28.9	0.8	11.9	16.3	6.1	12.9	12.5	14.8	14.9	13.3
47940		Waterloo-Cedar Falls, IA	1,503.1	167,796	257	111.6	85.2	9.1	0.6	3.3	4.2	5.9	12.5	17.1	12.3	12.0	10.4
48060		Watertown-Fort Drum, NY	1,268.7	116,295	335	91.7	83.9	7.3	1.0	3.1	7.7	7.3	13.3	15.3	16.3	12.3	9.7
48140		Wausau-Weston, WI	2,423.9	166,189	258	68.6	90.2	1.6	0.9	6.0	3.0	5.4	12.4	11.3	11.6	12.4	12.5
48260		Weirton-Steubenville, WV-OH	579.9	115,585	337	199.3	93.6	5.2	0.7	0.9	1.7	4.7	10.7	12.0	11.2	10.7	12.5
48300		Wenatchee, WA	4,740.4	123,342	323	26.0	67.0	1.0	1.7	1.9	30.4	5.8	13.8	12.0	12.4	12.5	11.0
48540		Wheeling, WV-OH	943.4	137,740	300	146.0	94.6	4.4	0.7	0.9	1.2	4.7	11.0	11.6	11.9	11.6	12.3
48620		Wichita, KS	4,148.1	647,919	93	156.2	73.6	9.1	1.9	4.7	14.1	6.2	14.5	13.5	13.5	12.9	11.1
48660		Wichita Falls, TX	2,619.6	149,013	287	56.9	68.6	10.4	1.4	2.8	19.1	5.9	12.8	15.9	14.1	12.4	10.4
48700		Williamsport, PA	1,228.9	113,605	341	92.4	91.8	6.5	0.5	1.2	2.3	5.2	11.8	12.5	12.6	11.9	11.7
48900		Wilmington, NC	1,063.6	291,833	170	274.4	78.7	13.8	1.1	2.0	6.6	4.7	10.7	14.5	12.6	12.7	12.6
49020		Winchester, VA-WV	1,062.7	145,155	290	136.6	81.8	6.5	0.7	2.4	10.8	5.5	12.4	12.1	12.1	12.4	12.6
49180		Winston-Salem, NC	2,009.0	681,438	90	339.2	68.1	19.2	0.9	2.5	11.3	5.4	12.5	12.8	12.5	11.8	13.0
49340		Worcester, MA-CT	2,023.6	978,447	57	483.5	77.1	5.7	0.6	5.7	12.8	5.0	11.6	13.2	13.0	12.7	13.2
49420		Yakima, WA	4,294.5	256,035	190	59.6	42.4	1.4	4.5	1.9	51.8	7.3	17.1	14.6	13.4	12.1	10.7
49620		York-Hanover, PA	904.4	458,696	121	507.2	83.2	7.4	0.5	2.0	8.9	5.4	12.5	11.9	12.5	12.5	12.8
49660		Youngstown-Warren-Boardman, OH-PA	1,702.1	538,069	107	316.1	84.2	12.1	0.7	1.2	4.1	5.2	11.2	11.9	11.8	11.2	12.0
49700		Yuba City, CA	1,234.7	182,484	238	147.8	50.9	4.4	2.5	15.1	31.8	6.9	15.1	13.2	14.5	13.2	10.8
49740		Yuma, AZ	5,513.8	206,990	218	37.5	30.3	2.3	1.4	1.8	65.5	6.9	14.0	14.9	14.0	11.4	9.6

1. CBSA = Core Based Statistical Area. DIV = Metropolitan Division. See Appendix A for explanation. See Appendix B for list of metropolitan areas or temporarily covered by water. 2. Dry land or land partially or temporarily covered by water. 3. May be of any race.

Area name	Population, 2020 (cont.)				Population change and components of change, 2000–2020							Households, 2016–2020				
	Age (percent) (cont.)				Total persons		Percent change		Components of change, 2010–2020					Percent		
	55 to 64 years	65 to 74 years	75 years and over	Percent female	2000	2010	2000–2010	2010–2019	Births	Deaths	Net migration	Number	Persons per house-hold	Family house-holds	Single parent house holds	One person
	16	17	18	19	20	21	22	23	24	25	26	27	28	29	30	31
Texarkana, TX-AR	12.5	10.4	7.1	50.0	149,198	147,519	-1.1	-0.2	2,043	2,511	98	55,812	2.6	66.1	16.8	30.0
The Villages, FL	13.8	31.4	26.8	50.1	93,420	129,752	38.9	4.5	549	3,338	8,846	59,076	2.0	67.0	4.8	28.9
Toledo, OH	13.3	10.9	6.7	51.0	651,429	646,604	-0.7	-0.4	8,818	10,176	-1,122	266,939	2.4	59.9	13.3	32.8
Topeka, KS	13.8	11.7	7.7	50.8	233,870	233,152	-0.3	-0.2	3,200	3,622	-92	95,356	2.4	63.9	10.5	30.7
Trenton-Princeton, NJ	13.3	9.4	6.6	50.8	366,513	387,340	5.7	-0.4	4,831	4,426	-1,923	131,440	2.7	66.7	13.2	28.4
Tucson, AZ	12.1	11.9	8.7	50.5	980,263	1,043,433	6.4	0.8	12,339	15,387	11,592	410,942	2.5	61.0	12.4	31.0
Tulsa, OK	12.4	9.8	6.3	50.6	937,478	1,015,331	8.3	0.9	15,097	14,894	8,336	384,369	2.6	65.5	12.1	29.0
Tuscaloosa, AL	11.7	9.6	5.6	51.7	239,207	268,674	12.3	-0.2	3,690	3,580	-649	91,112	2.6	63.8	14.9	29.9
Twin Falls, ID	11.3	9.4	6.1	50.0	99,604	114,283	14.7	2.3	1,807	1,508	2,329	39,762	2.7	70.3	9.3	23.4
Tyler, TX	11.9	10.1	7.0	51.5	209,714	233,479	11.3	1.6	3,483	3,231	3,455	77,809	2.9	69.3	12.0	25.7
Urban Honolulu, HI	12.0	10.3	8.5	49.4	953,207	1,016,508	6.6	-1.5	14,250	12,457	-17,266	316,928	3.0	69.4	12.2	24.5
Utica-Rome, NY	14.4	11.6	8.2	49.9	299,397	292,264	-2.4	-0.7	3,706	4,709	-1,072	115,768	2.4	63.1	11.8	30.9
Valdosta, GA	11.0	8.6	5.3	51.5	139,588	148,126	6.1	0.7	2,365	1,950	578	54,469	2.6	63.6	15.1	29.3
Vallejo, CA	13.1	10.5	6.4	49.8	413,344	453,491	9.7	-0.4	6,217	5,133	-2,921	151,191	2.9	72.3	13.8	21.8
Victoria, TX	12.1	10.2	7.1	50.7	94,003	98,331	4.6	-0.2	1,598	1,414	-396	35,360	2.8	67.9	12.8	26.4
Vineland-Bridgeton, NJ	12.5	9.5	6.4	49.0	156,898	154,152	-1.8	-0.3	2,177	2,104	-636	50,947	2.7	67.4	17.8	26.9
Virginia Beach-Norfolk-Newport News, VA-NC	12.8	9.5	6.1	50.6	1,713,954	1,799,674	5.0	0.2	25,919	22,880	578	672,053	2.5	66.3	14.4	27.3
Visalia, CA	9.9	7.1	4.6	49.9	442,179	473,117	7.0	0.8	8,226	4,866	434	139,044	3.3	77.9	17.2	17.7
Waco, TX	11.2	9.1	6.1	51.1	252,772	277,547	9.8	1.0	4,175	3,632	2,294	96,974	2.7	65.2	15.2	27.6
Walla Walla, WA	12.1	11.2	7.9	48.8	58,781	62,584	6.5	0.2	709	883	264	22,773	2.5	65.0	10.0	27.1
Warner Robins, GA	12.6	8.7	5.1	51.6	167,595	191,614	14.3	1.9	2,810	2,388	3,208	68,257	2.6	69.4	14.3	26.0
Washington-Arlington-Alexandria, DC-VA-MD-WV	12.5	8.5	5.5	50.8	5,649,540	6,385,162	13.0	-0.4	91,297	58,348	-61,338	2,244,311	2.7	65.4	11.6	27.5
Frederick-Gaithersburg-Rockville, MD Div 23,224	13.3	9.5	6.7	51.1	1,205,162	1,333,778	10.7	0.1	17,879	12,415	-4,524	467,124	2.8	70.4	11.0	24.0
Washington-Arlington-Alexandria, DC-VA-MD-WV Div 47,894	12.3	8.2	5.1	50.7	4,444,378	5,051,384	13.7	-0.6	73,418	45,933	-56,814	1,777,187	2.7	64.1	11.7	28.5
Waterloo-Cedar Falls, IA	11.8	10.7	7.3	50.6	167,819	168,461	0.4	-0.4	2,476	2,466	-684	68,165	2.4	61.1	9.2	30.6
Watertown-Fort Drum, NY	11.2	8.8	5.8	47.2	116,229	116,721	0.4	-0.4	2,109	1,407	-1,148	43,046	2.4	66.0	10.4	26.8
Wausau-Weston, WI	15.1	11.5	7.8	49.4	162,806	166,428	2.2	-0.1	2,092	2,332	-14	68,652	2.3	65.5	7.8	27.4
Weirton-Steubenville, WV-OH	15.1	14.0	9.1	50.9	124,454	116,903	-6.1	-1.1	1,327	2,412	-238	50,009	2.3	61.6	11.5	32.8
Wenatchee, WA	13.0	11.9	7.6	49.3	110,884	122,012	10.0	1.1	1,617	1,503	1,217	44,818	2.6	69.1	10.4	25.2
Wheeling, WV-OH	14.7	13.7	8.7	49.7	147,950	139,513	-5.7	-1.3	1,520	2,758	-544	55,376	2.4	62.2	11.0	33.5
Wichita, KS	12.4	9.8	6.1	50.2	623,061	647,610	3.9	0.0	9,680	8,859	-613	247,011	2.6	64.6	11.5	29.7
Wichita Falls, TX	12.4	9.6	6.5	48.2	151,306	148,128	-2.1	0.6	2,167	2,390	1,084	56,210	2.4	64.4	12.3	29.8
Williamsport, PA	14.2	12.0	8.1	50.8	116,111	114,188	-1.7	-0.5	1,399	1,979	-17	46,160	2.3	65.1	10.7	28.2
Wilmington, NC	13.4	11.6	7.2	51.7	254,884	285,905	12.2	2.1	3,303	4,192	6,861	120,810	2.4	57.3	9.4	33.3
Winchester, VA-WV	14.1	11.3	7.5	49.9	128,472	142,632	11.0	1.8	1,813	1,993	2,722	51,928	2.6	67.8	11.3	26.9
Winston-Salem, NC	13.9	10.9	7.2	51.7	640,595	675,966	5.5	0.8	8,687	10,191	6,962	267,603	2.5	65.3	12.6	29.6
Worcester, MA-CT	14.6	10.2	6.5	50.3	916,980	978,529	6.7	0.0	11,371	12,257	591	359,670	2.5	65.4	12.0	27.3
Yakima, WA	10.7	8.5	5.6	49.9	243,231	256,728	5.5	-0.3	4,335	3,385	-1,688	83,765	3.0	72.0	14.5	22.7
York-Hanover, PA	14.1	11.0	7.3	50.2	434,972	456,438	4.9	0.5	5,714	6,426	2,945	174,425	2.5	68.4	11.3	25.6
Youngstown-Warren-Boardman, OH-PA	14.6	13.1	9.0	50.6	565,773	541,243	-4.3	-0.6	6,557	10,637	881	231,607	2.3	61.2	13.3	33.6
Yuba City, CA	11.5	8.9	5.8	49.6	166,892	181,208	8.6	0.7	2,945	2,034	347	59,020	2.9	71.1	12.8	23.0
Yuma, AZ	9.7	9.8	9.8	48.2	195,751	203,881	4.2	1.5	3,527	2,926	2,490	74,624	2.8	72.8	14.1	21.9

Area name	Persons in group quarters, 2020	Daytime population, 2019		Births, 2020		Deaths, 2020		Persons under 65 with no health insurance 2019		Medicare, 2020			Serious crimes known to police[2], 2019	
													Violent	
		Number	Employ-ment/ residence ratio	Total	Rate[1]	Number	Rate[1]	Number	Percent	Total Ben-eficiaries	Enrolled in Original Medicare	Enrolled in Medicare Advantage	Number	Rate[3]
	32	33	34	35	36	37	38	39	40	41	42	43	44	45
Texarkana, TX-AR	6,853	150,881	1.02	1,651	11.2	2,016	13.7	16,567	14.3	31,778	21,806	9,972	NA	NA
The Villages, FL	7,704	140,663	1.42	434	3.3	2,687	20.2	5,957	12.5	78,690	39,916	38,774	279	203.5
Toledo, OH	16,353	660,478	1.06	7,062	10.9	8,137	12.6	39,230	7.6	134,120	67,175	66,945	3,108	485.6
Topeka, KS	4,771	232,827	1.01	2,560	11.0	2,894	12.4	16,747	9.1	52,751	40,387	12,364	NA	NA
Trenton-Princeton, NJ	20,712	421,332	1.31	3,876	10.0	3,620	9.4	28,211	9.6	66,614	39,251	27,363	1,316	358.6
Tucson, AZ	23,601	1,038,679	1.00	9,925	9.5	12,448	11.9	107,748	13.3	242,122	116,145	125,977	5,020	473.5
Tulsa, OK	14,564	1,000,652	1.01	12,126	11.9	12,050	11.8	134,573	16.2	192,309	111,955	80,354	5,947	591.5
Tuscaloosa, AL	13,228	255,081	1.03	2,958	11.0	2,931	10.9	21,043	10.4	48,596	24,686	23,910	NA	NA
Twin Falls, ID	1,004	110,996	1.01	1,430	12.4	1,162	10.0	14,528	15.7	21,259	11,883	9,376	435	383.4
Tyler, TX	4,879	238,031	1.08	2,801	11.9	2,589	11.0	39,717	21.1	47,477	28,276	19,201	869	370.5
Urban Honolulu, HI	35,294	980,834	1.00	11,366	11.3	9,898	9.8	33,662	4.4	192,240	92,591	99,649	NA	NA
Utica-Rome, NY	14,007	290,008	0.99	2,992	10.3	3,753	12.9	11,536	5.2	68,224	35,991	32,233	644	224.3
Valdosta, GA	6,103	147,390	1.01	1,935	13.0	1,543	10.4	21,010	17.5	25,479	15,538	9,941	472	319.1
Vallejo, CA	11,840	393,918	0.76	4,957	11.0	4,157	9.2	21,935	6.0	83,836	42,134	41,702	2,350	525.7
Victoria, TX	1,711	100,261	1.01	1,304	13.3	1,121	11.4	16,190	20.0	19,943	11,188	8,755	449	448.8
Vineland-Bridgeton, NJ	9,015	151,066	1.02	1,719	11.2	1,690	11.0	14,106	12.1	28,816	16,753	12,063	669	450.2
Virginia Beach-Norfolk-Newport News, VA-NC	71,804	1,772,101	1.00	20,722	11.5	18,381	10.2	122,102	8.6	327,267	229,741	97,526	6,239	351.8
Visalia, CA	4,746	454,584	0.95	6,584	13.8	3,890	8.2	38,062	9.5	65,185	47,412	17,773	1,699	366.0
Waco, TX	10,131	277,247	1.05	3,344	12.0	2,903	10.4	40,691	18.2	49,894	26,725	23,169	1,274	462.7
Walla Walla, WA	4,669	64,198	1.13	576	9.2	700	11.2	4,303	9.6	13,983	11,112	2,871	129	212.3
Warner Robins, GA	2,896	182,053	0.99	2,255	11.6	1,898	9.8	21,654	13.8	32,655	20,910	11,745	NA	NA
Washington-Arlington-Alexandria, DC-VA-MD-WV	102,506	6,389,498	1.04	72,970	11.5	47,450	7.4	431,946	8.1	917,044	721,601	195,443	NA	NA
Frederick-Gaithersburg-Rockville, MD Div 23,224	12,667	1,256,192	0.93	14,150	10.6	10,077	7.6	82,692	7.6	221,417	187,380	34,037	NA	NA
Washington-Arlington-Alexandria, DC-VA-MD-WV Div 47,894	89,839	5,133,306	1.07	58,820	11.7	37,373	7.4	349,254	8.2	695,627	534,221	161,406	NA	NA
Waterloo-Cedar Falls, IA	5,727	174,404	1.06	1,961	11.7	1,967	11.7	7,043	5.3	35,673	21,948	13,725	NA	NA
Watertown-Fort Drum, NY	6,242	114,390	1.06	1,666	14.3	1,140	9.8	4,191	4.8	20,913	12,354	8,559	271	249.9
Wausau-Weston, WI	1,908	163,826	1.01	1,670	10.0	1,889	11.4	8,719	6.6	36,634	16,361	20,273	399	244.5
Weirton-Steubenville, WV-OH	3,124	110,312	0.86	1,027	8.8	1,883	16.2	6,801	7.8	30,538	17,595	12,943	NA	NA
Wenatchee, WA	1,017	117,296	0.97	1,284	10.5	1,213	9.9	11,256	11.8	27,088	19,115	7,973	141	116.2
Wheeling, WV-OH	6,346	144,500	1.07	1,219	8.8	2,173	15.7	7,329	7.1	34,497	17,071	17,426	585	424.3
Wichita, KS	10,692	641,110	1.00	7,804	12.0	7,092	10.9	62,582	11.8	119,315	79,874	39,441	NA	NA
Wichita Falls, TX	12,095	151,097	1.00	1,740	11.7	1,979	13.3	21,470	18.7	29,921	22,049	7,872	544	361.0
Williamsport, PA	5,194	115,620	1.03	1,117	9.8	1,544	13.6	5,753	6.7	27,483	15,677	11,806	NA	NA
Wilmington, NC	8,229	304,373	1.08	2,676	9.3	3,297	11.4	29,208	12.4	63,041	42,044	20,997	1,126	372.1
Winchester, VA-WV	2,521	139,987	1.01	1,458	10.1	1,605	11.1	11,490	10.3	29,827	22,458	7,369	214	150.8
Winston-Salem, NC	12,689	648,769	0.93	6,971	10.3	8,115	12.0	76,632	14.1	145,825	56,226	89,599	NA	NA
Worcester, MA-CT	32,906	877,224	0.86	9,057	9.3	9,841	10.1	29,695	3.9	188,933	112,648	76,285	2,648	303.7
Yakima, WA	3,355	251,687	1.01	3,441	13.4	2,647	10.3	31,476	15.1	44,001	29,988	14,013	966	385.2
York-Hanover, PA	8,428	415,439	0.85	4,587	10.0	5,097	11.1	22,184	6.1	96,972	53,921	43,051	NA	NA
Youngstown-Warren-Boardman, OH-PA	18,557	528,199	0.96	5,288	9.8	8,367	15.5	32,483	8.1	139,236	59,460	79,776	NA	NA
Yuba City, CA	1,849	161,312	0.82	2,369	13.0	1,638	9.0	12,637	8.6	31,310	27,262	4,048	715	408.9
Yuma, AZ	8,490	209,133	0.97	2,895	14.1	2,350	11.4	28,673	17.7	39,301	24,577	14,724	717	330.7

1. Per 1,000 estimated resident population. 2. Data for serious crimes have not been adjusted for underreporting; this may affect comparability between geographic areas and over time. 3. Per 100,000 population estimated by the FBI.

Area name	Serious crimes known to police[1], 2019 (cont.): Property: Number	Property: Rate[2]	Education: School enrollment and attainment, 2019: Enrollment[3]: Total	Enrollment[3]: Percent private	Attainment[4]: High school graduate or less	Attainment[4]: Bachelor's degree or more	Local government expenditures,[5] 2017–2018: Total current expenditures (mil dol)	Current expenditures per student (dollars)	Income and poverty, 2016–2020: Per capita income[6] (dollars)	Median household income (dollars)	Median family income	Percent of households with income less than $50,000	Percent of households with income of $200,000 or more	Percent below poverty level: All persons	Percent below poverty level: All families	Percent below poverty level: Age 65 years and older
	46	47	48	49	50	51	52	53	54	55	56	57	58	59	60	61
Texarkana, TX-AR	NA	NA	35,009	7.8	46.5	20.1	264.6	10,034	26,439	49,496	63,851	50.4	3.5	16.9	13.4	21.6
The Villages, FL	967	705.3	9,736	17.6	38.3	32.0	87.7	9,925	35,879	59,618	72,792	40.5	3.3	8.8	5.6	28.5
Toledo, OH	12,956	2,024.4	161,627	14.8	40.0	27.3	1,382.4	12,553	30,921	53,600	70,917	46.8	4.2	16.3	11.2	19.6
Topeka, KS	NA	NA	52,985	11.8	40.6	29.1	470.8	12,500	31,347	59,815	75,758	41.9	3.8	10.7	7.1	11.5
Trenton-Princeton, NJ	4,910	1,337.9	97,552	23.9	35.8	43.5	1,240.8	19,627	44,532	83,306	108,756	31.3	15.0	11.1	7.7	11.6
Tucson, AZ	29,948	2,824.8	261,541	11.3	32.4	33.6	1,260.6	8,732	30,747	55,023	69,466	45.6	5.0	15.9	11.3	18.5
Tulsa, OK	31,267	3,109.7	245,161	16.8	39.2	27.9	1,510.9	9,149	33,780	57,341	72,203	44.0	5.6	13.6	10.4	16.8
Tuscaloosa, AL	NA	NA	69,855	9.8	42.7	27.9	370.6	10,495	26,507	50,871	68,505	49.3	3.7	18.9	12.7	19.7
Twin Falls, ID	D	D	29,176	13.2	42.1	21.5	161.7	7,537	26,232	53,944	62,242	45.3	3.1	14.5	10.0	16.5
Tyler, TX	5,092	2,170.8	59,416	12.0	36.4	27.0	335.2	9,217	28,858	59,450	73,199	41.8	5.7	14.0	9.9	15.8
Urban Honolulu, HI	NA	NA	228,611	24.5	33.3	35.7	2,924.3	16,132	38,288	87,722	103,845	26.7	12.7	8.4	5.5	8.5
Utica-Rome, NY	4,684	1,631.2	64,742	14.4	42.7	25.5	805.3	18,167	30,436	58,983	75,037	42.6	3.8	14.1	9.9	16.6
Valdosta, GA	3,380	2,285.3	41,077	8.6	46.5	24.0	249.9	10,237	24,304	43,859	59,281	54.0	3.0	23.1	17.7	24.7
Vallejo, CA	10,689	2,391.1	106,977	13.7	34.9	27.1	804.6	12,360	36,685	84,638	95,438	27.3	10.2	9.1	6.5	10.3
Victoria, TX	2,205	2,203.9	24,332	13.8	46.8	18.7	167.4	10,163	29,471	58,629	71,697	43.4	4.9	15.4	11.1	17.6
Vineland-Bridgeton, NJ	3,192	2,148.1	36,331	7.0	58.4	16.6	541.8	18,436	28,311	55,709	67,467	45.2	4.8	16.0	12.0	18.0
Virginia Beach-Norfolk-Newport News, VA-NC	34,571	1,949.2	446,602	17.0	32.7	32.9	3,118.6	11,710	35,927	68,454	83,421	35.6	6.5	10.6	7.7	12.9
Visalia, CA	9,400	2,025.2	140,503	7.6	54.6	14.5	1,480.1	14,241	22,092	52,534	55,395	47.4	4.1	21.8	18.4	24.5
Waco, TX	7,078	2,570.8	79,621	23.6	43.4	24.1	499.6	10,564	26,523	49,534	66,852	50.4	4.5	18.9	13.3	20.6
Walla Walla, WA	1,267	2,085.0	16,268	27.7	32.9	28.6	121.5	13,429	30,306	60,615	75,853	42.3	4.6	11.4	6.0	10.7
Warner Robins, GA	NA	NA	52,251	12.8	36.2	29.6	360.7	10,815	29,911	63,074	77,307	40.1	4.4	12.9	9.9	14.8
Washington-Arlington-Alexandria, DC-VA-MD-WV	NA	NA	1,613,737	20.9	26.6	51.7	15,249.7	15,522	51,515	106,415	126,840	21.4	20.0	7.6	5.0	7.4
Frederick-Gaithersburg-Rockville, MD Div 23,224	NA	NA	335,429	21.1	23.8	55.8	3,256.4	15,855	53,410	109,034	129,092	20.9	21.5	6.6	4.4	6.4
Washington-Arlington-Alexandria, DC-VA-MD-WV Div 47,894	NA	NA	1,278,308	20.8	27.3	50.6	11,993.3	15,434	51,015	105,701	126,224	21.6	19.6	7.8	5.2	7.7
Waterloo-Cedar Falls, IA	NA	NA	46,614	14.0	37.4	29.6	352.2	12,874	32,103	58,996	76,924	42.4	4.4	13.5	8.4	14.2
Watertown-Fort Drum, NY	1,749	1,613.1	24,904	10.0	43.6	22.5	318.1	17,744	28,120	54,726	66,711	45.2	2.7	14.4	9.4	15.9
Wausau-Weston, WI	1,487	911.2	35,544	14.6	42.5	24.9	294.1	12,172	33,269	62,237	77,632	39.5	4.1	8.9	5.4	8.5
Weirton-Steubenville, WV-OH	NA	NA	24,220	22.7	51.4	17.7	185.5	12,056	26,783	47,525	61,496	52.4	1.9	15.3	10.8	20.0
Wenatchee, WA	1,392	1,147.4	28,204	9.1	43.5	24.4	308.1	14,063	32,413	62,894	72,924	39.0	5.2	10.8	7.7	12.1
Wheeling, WV-OH	1,423	1,032.2	28,013	14.5	49.5	21.1	245.1	13,070	28,518	49,928	65,607	50.1	3.4	13.4	9.3	17.4
Wichita, KS	NA	NA	169,177	16.4	36.3	31.0	1,256.7	11,051	30,212	58,333	74,120	43.2	4.3	12.7	8.7	13.5
Wichita Falls, TX	3,864	2,564.0	36,944	7.9	44.4	23.1	235.4	9,680	26,478	51,099	66,634	49.0	3.3	16.6	11.4	17.9
Williamsport, PA	NA	NA	24,780	17.4	47.3	23.5	249.3	15,966	28,465	54,906	66,824	45.3	3.1	13.6	9.3	17.0
Wilmington, NC	6,058	2,001.9	70,002	14.4	29.3	39.4	388.0	10,381	35,130	57,488	78,711	43.6	6.8	14.5	8.5	14.5
Winchester, VA-WV	1,629	1,148.2	31,746	19.6	45.7	25.7	281.0	13,377	34,914	69,417	83,355	34.6	6.2	9.1	5.8	9.3
Winston-Salem, NC	NA	NA	158,231	17.0	41.5	26.8	967.1	9,654	29,693	52,607	66,563	47.6	4.3	15.3	11.0	17.9
Worcester, MA-CT	8,555	981.2	234,150	20.8	37.3	35.4	2,309.4	16,252	38,399	75,705	96,860	33.9	9.8	9.9	6.6	10.2
Yakima, WA	6,835	2,725.4	68,089	9.1	52.9	17.6	759.3	13,744	24,305	54,917	62,783	45.0	3.6	16.5	12.8	19.7
York-Hanover, PA	NA	NA	98,846	19.2	48.9	25.2	1,007.3	15,009	33,587	68,940	82,154	34.6	4.8	8.7	5.7	9.4
Youngstown-Warren-Boardman, OH-PA	NA	NA	112,747	14.7	50.4	22.2	1,026.5	14,447	27,993	48,020	63,220	51.7	2.7	16.8	12.9	23.4
Yuba City, CA	4,266	2,439.7	48,171	8.8	42.5	19.1	500.7	13,063	27,836	61,655	69,812	41.1	5.0	14.0	10.9	15.9
Yuma, AZ	3,235	1,492.0	54,040	5.2	52.1	15.4	295.8	7,792	23,507	48,790	54,897	50.9	2.2	18.2	15.5	21.5

1. Data for serious crimes have not been adjusted for underreporting; this may affect comparability between geographic areas and over time. 2. Per 100,000 population estimated by the FBI. 3. All persons 3 years old and over enrolled in nursery school through college. 4. Persons 25 years old and over. 5. Elementary and secondary education expenditures. 6. Based on population estimated by the American Community Survey, 2015.

Area name	Personal income, 2019										Earnings, 2019		
			Per capita[1]			Supplements to wages and salaries, employer contributions (mil dol)						Contributrions for government social insurance (mil dol)	
	Total (mil dol)	Percent change, 2018–2019	Dollars	Rank	Wages and Salaries (mil dol)	Pension and insurance	Government social insurance	Proprietors' income	Dividends, interest, and rent (mil dol)	Personal transfer receipts (mil dol)	Total (mil dol)	From employee and self-employed	From employer
	62	63	64	65	66	67	68	69	70	71	72	73	74
Texarkana, TX-AR	6,179	6.7	41,516	359	2,669	478	197	374	987	2,004	3,718	243	197
The Villages, FL	7,581	6.1	54,533	128	1,630	280	118	671	2,457	3,003	2,699	304	118
Toledo, OH	32,981	6.4	51,408	173	16,250	2,820	1,201	2,593	4,786	8,860	22,864	1,363	1,201
Topeka, KS	11,654	6.4	50,479	191	5,710	898	442	863	1,887	2,996	7,913	528	442
Trenton-Princeton, NJ	27,256	4.8	74,218	15	19,072	2,782	1,343	2,042	5,128	4,898	25,238	1,484	1,343
Tucson, AZ	51,332	9.6	48,373	235	21,306	3,664	1,555	3,264	10,065	14,927	29,789	2,049	1,555
Tulsa, OK	58,443	3.2	58,071	84	24,127	3,619	1,794	9,726	11,632	11,516	39,266	2,280	1,794
Tuscaloosa, AL	10,656	6.7	42,084	349	5,196	916	382	549	1,843	2,972	7,044	471	382
Twin Falls, ID	4,940	9.5	43,725	330	2,069	336	185	864	750	1,169	3,454	203	185
Tyler, TX	13,459	3.2	57,076	93	5,334	815	374	3,087	2,233	2,935	9,610	506	374
Urban Honolulu, HI	60,522	4.8	62,793	43	28,500	6,299	2,314	4,644	10,929	12,702	41,757	2,499	2,314
Utica-Rome, NY	14,294	7.6	49,581	212	5,688	1,440	463	959	1,893	4,617	8,550	511	463
Valdosta, GA	5,941	8.6	40,046	373	2,686	573	196	306	972	1,718	3,761	217	196
Vallejo, CA	26,230	13.0	58,688	76	10,042	1,970	712	1,217	3,454	6,337	13,941	838	712
Victoria, TX	5,331	2.4	53,547	136	1,887	319	129	603	1,082	1,341	2,939	169	129
Vineland-Bridgeton, NJ	6,689	8.6	45,498	293	3,157	632	255	525	809	2,312	4,570	289	255
Virginia Beach-Norfolk-Newport News, VA-NC	94,883	7.4	53,310	137	46,907	9,070	3,575	3,480	17,691	21,586	63,032	3,847	3,575
Visalia, CA	21,723	16.5	46,348	280	7,677	1,806	596	2,796	2,339	6,790	12,875	651	596
Waco, TX	12,577	8.4	45,403	294	6,245	1,009	434	944	1,878	3,293	8,633	503	434
Walla Walla, WA	3,173	11.4	51,767	167	1,395	276	129	391	593	819	2,191	119	129
Warner Robins, GA	8,630	8.1	45,888	286	4,036	995	304	306	1,462	2,210	5,641	323	304
Washington-Arlington-Alexandria, DC-VA-MD-WV	485,551	5.5	76,771	13	286,149	44,333	19,918	33,833	89,481	63,367	384,232	22,102	19,918
Frederick-Gaithersburg-Rockville, MD Div 23,224	111,868	4.6	84,943	X	48,204	7,304	3,373	11,169	23,244	13,346	70,051	4,070	3,373
Washington-Arlington-Alexandria, DC-VA-MD-WV Div 47,894	373,682	5.8	74,622	X	237,945	37,029	16,545	22,664	66,238	50,021	314,182	18,032	16,545
Waterloo-Cedar Falls, IA	8,437	6.6	50,126	198	4,398	759	354	449	1,540	2,114	5,960	403	354
Watertown-Fort Drum, NY	5,833	8.3	53,964	134	2,802	835	255	258	902	1,581	4,150	204	255
Wausau-Weston, WI	8,860	5.7	54,305	130	4,320	806	320	780	1,331	1,867	6,226	397	320
Weirton-Steubenville, WV-OH	5,299	7.7	46,007	285	1,697	339	132	260	707	1,911	2,429	181	132
Wenatchee, WA	6,668	10.4	55,047	120	2,520	458	242	755	1,339	1,682	3,974	229	242
Wheeling, WV-OH	6,716	1.9	48,947	223	2,920	500	223	448	1,205	2,125	4,090	288	223
Wichita, KS	35,407	4.8	55,000	121	15,612	2,453	1,208	3,989	7,686	7,216	23,261	1,460	1,208
Wichita Falls, TX	7,160	5.6	46,954	266	2,858	581	210	527	1,424	1,999	4,176	239	210
Williamsport, PA	5,516	8.7	48,721	228	2,446	522	190	312	792	1,768	3,470	227	190
Wilmington, NC	14,686	5.9	48,744	227	7,109	1,065	500	1,039	3,397	3,582	9,712	643	500
Winchester, VA-WV	7,438	6.7	52,377	154	3,491	557	256	477	1,202	1,568	4,781	313	256
Winston-Salem, NC	32,729	6.1	48,151	239	14,658	2,077	1,056	2,099	5,348	8,368	19,891	1,365	1,056
Worcester, MA-CT	58,392	8.6	61,741	52	23,356	4,307	1,675	3,985	7,183	13,883	33,322	1,823	1,675
Yakima, WA	12,367	12.0	49,099	218	4,988	889	508	1,500	1,759	3,602	7,885	404	508
York-Hanover, PA	25,117	7.5	55,761	109	9,594	1,739	746	1,528	3,643	6,311	13,608	868	746
Youngstown-Warren-Boardman, OH-PA	24,783	7.6	46,635	272	9,152	1,696	699	1,790	3,831	8,522	13,337	909	699
Yuba City, CA	8,607	13.0	48,752	226	2,992	714	230	731	1,030	2,744	4,667	267	230
Yuma, AZ	8,887	18.3	40,800	366	3,355	667	290	1,092	1,117	2,912	5,404	316	290

1. Based on the resident population estimated as of July 1 of the year shown.

Area name	Earnings, 2019 (cont.) — Percent by selected industries: Farm	Mining, quarrying, and extracting	Construc-tion	Manufac-turing	Informa-tion; pro-fessional, scientific, and technical serviecs	Retail trade	Finance, insur-ance, real estate, rental and leasing	Health care and social assistance	Govern-ment	Social Security beneficiaries, December 2019: Number	Rate[1]	Supple-mental Security Income Recipi-ents, December 2019	Housing units, 2020: Total	Percent change, 2010–2020
	75	76	77	78	79	80	81	82	83	84	85	86	87	88
Texarkana, TX-AR	0.8	D	5.6	12.1	4.2	7.9	5.4	D	23.5	33,565	228	6,351	65,546	0.2
The Villages, FL	1.0	0.3	24.3	4.9	5.0	7.4	7.4	D	15.7	77,025	568	1,693	79,678	4.8
Toledo, OH	0.5	D	6.4	18.2	D	5.9	7.7	D	15.3	133,455	207	19,197	304,638	0.4
Topeka, KS	1.0	0.4	5.9	7.4	D	4.9	D	15.8	22.0	53,515	230	5,488	104,842	0.4
Trenton-Princeton, NJ	0.0	D	2.8	7.1	19.8	3.2	13.2	9.0	16.3	66,295	172	9,374	150,657	0.1
Tucson, AZ	0.2	0.8	5.5	11.4	9.6	6.5	7.2	14.5	23.4	240,875	229	21,066	474,807	0.8
Tulsa, OK	0.0	8.9	6.4	12.4	8.4	5.6	D	11.4	9.2	200,385	196	22,418	442,622	1.0
Tuscaloosa, AL	0.7	2.5	6.2	20.3	D	6.1	D	D	27.2	53,380	199	8,390	123,469	1.1
Twin Falls, ID	16.3	D	5.1	13.4	D	7.7	D	13.2	10.3	22,130	189	2,216	44,511	2.4
Tyler, TX	0.1	19.7	5.9	5.0	6.9	8.8	6.3	17.6	10.6	48,220	203	5,441	98,655	1.0
Urban Honolulu, HI	0.2	0.1	8.5	1.8	8.2	4.9	7.6	11.5	32.6	184,365	184	14,635	372,626	0.4
Utica-Rome, NY	0.9	0.3	4.5	9.1	6.2	6.8	7.5	16.4	29.5	72,510	250	9,252	137,668	0.3
Valdosta, GA	1.6	D	D	D	5.7	D	5.0	D	34.1	27,495	184	5,439	63,227	2.1
Vallejo, CA	0.8	0.3	10.7	13.2	4.0	6.3	4.3	16.9	24.5	82,590	183	11,137	163,356	0.5
Victoria, TX	0.2	14.5	7.2	7.4	D	8.3	5.9	D	14.8	20,495	209	2,498	42,692	0.4
Vineland-Bridgeton, NJ	2.7	0.3	7.2	14.4	D	7.8	2.8	16.2	24.8	30,980	202	5,834	57,210	0.1
Virginia Beach-Norfolk-Newport News, VA-NC	0.1	D	D	8.1	9.8	5.2	D	10.8	33.3	333,620	185	35,979	766,797	0.7
Visalia, CA	16.1	0.0	5.2	7.7	2.7	5.9	3.7	7.6	22.8	68,015	143	18,525	152,700	1.1
Waco, TX	0.2	D	8.4	15.5	7.1	6.8	D	D	15.8	51,415	183	7,707	114,673	1.0
Walla Walla, WA	14.6	D	4.5	14.7	D	4.5	4.8	D	22.5	13,900	222	1,397	25,165	0.6
Warner Robins, GA	0.7	D	D	D	9.0	5.8	D	5.8	51.0	34,010	174	4,804	80,162	1.6
Washington-Arlington-Alexandria, DC-VA-MD-WV	0.0	D	D	D	D	3.4	D	D	27.3	822,832	129	87,708	2,525,522	0.8
Frederick-Gaithersburg-Rockville, MD Div 23,224	0.1	D	D	D	20.2	4.2	D	D	22.7	191,855	144	16,268	512,161	0.6
Washington-Arlington-Alexandria, DC-VA-MD-WV Div 47,894	0.0	0.0	D	1.2	28.0	3.2	5.7	6.4	28.3	630,977	126	71,440	2,013,361	0.9
Waterloo-Cedar Falls, IA	1.3	D	5.6	24.5	4.6	6.7	D	12.9	15.5	36,755	219	3,534	74,854	0.3
Watertown-Fort Drum, NY	2.2	0.2	4.1	3.2	2.6	6.1	2.4	10.7	57.4	23,060	198	2,733	61,726	0.2
Wausau-Weston, WI	2.6	0.0	5.7	24.6	5.1	5.3	10.9	14.0	11.4	38,560	232	2,373	76,434	0.6
Weirton-Steubenville, WV-OH	-0.1	D	5.5	17.1	3.6	7.1	4.3	D	15.0	32,845	284	3,828	55,992	-0.1
Wenatchee, WA	9.6	D	10.5	4.0	D	7.6	5.0	15.2	20.6	26,980	219	1,923	55,816	1.8
Wheeling, WV-OH	-0.2	D	D	6.7	10.0	7.4	6.0	D	14.3	36,375	264	3,931	67,423	-0.1
Wichita, KS	0.5	2.2	6.4	20.1	D	5.9	7.3	D	13.0	124,460	192	12,683	277,661	0.6
Wichita Falls, TX	0.9	3.8	4.5	9.0	D	7.0	6.0	D	29.9	31,265	210	4,232	64,718	0.3
Williamsport, PA	0.7	2.6	5.5	16.3	5.4	6.8	5.4	18.5	18.6	29,390	259	3,186	52,662	0.1
Wilmington, NC	0.7	D	9.5	5.2	D	7.9	8.4	10.5	19.5	64,010	219	5,083	147,777	2.5
Winchester, VA-WV	0.1	D	D	13.2	4.7	7.7	8.8	D	17.8	30,620	211	2,239	61,527	1.2
Winston-Salem, NC	0.2	0.1	6.2	12.2	6.6	7.4	9.7	17.8	10.4	153,160	225	14,214	306,152	1.3
Worcester, MA-CT	0.1	0.1	7.2	12.2	10.3	6.1	7.0	16.5	16.3	183,255	187	24,210	403,626	0.5
Yakima, WA	17.8	0.0	4.5	7.5	2.8	6.9	3.5	13.6	17.9	45,830	179	7,089	91,356	0.7
York-Hanover, PA	0.3	D	9.1	18.9	6.2	5.8	5.1	14.6	13.3	100,160	218	8,385	188,598	0.6
Youngstown-Warren-Boardman, OH-PA	0.3	0.4	7.5	13.9	4.5	8.5	5.5	18.1	15.3	144,380	268	18,913	253,238	0.0
Yuba City, CA	6.2	D	6.5	3.8	3.2	6.8	3.8	D	33.3	32,105	176	7,512	64,617	0.8
Yuma, AZ	13.4	0.0	4.7	4.1	5.3	7.9	4.1	10.7	26.6	42,110	203	4,767	93,796	1.5

1. Per 1,000 resident population estimated as of July 1 of the year shown.

Area name	Occupied housing units, 2016-2020: Occupied units: Total	Owner-occupied: Percent	Owner-occupied: Median value[1]	Median owner cost as a percent of income: With a mortgage	Median owner cost as a percent of income: Without a mortgage[2]	Renter-occupied: Median rent[3]	Renter-occupied: Median rent as a percent of income	Renter-occupied: Substandard units[4] (percent)	Civilian labor force, 2021: Total	Civilian labor force, 2021: Percent change 2020-2021	Unemployment: Total	Unemployment: Rate[5]	Civilian employment[6], 2016-2020: Total	Percent: Management, business, science, and arts	Percent: Construction, production, and maintenance occupations
	89	90	91	92	93	94	95	96	97	98	99	100	101	102	103
Texarkana, TX-AR	55,812	65.8	114,100	18.3	10.7	753	28.0	3.6	63,284	0.3	3,425	5.4	60,059	31.8	28.2
The Villages, FL	59,076	88.6	267,100	23.6	10.0	935	38.7	0.9	34,621	6.0	1,831	5.3	26,114	31.5	21.4
Toledo, OH	266,939	63.5	134,900	19.0	11.4	767	27.3	1.4	316,440	-1.0	18,005	5.7	308,706	34.9	26.6
Topeka, KS	95,356	69.4	137,900	19.2	11.6	808	27.1	2.2	120,516	0.3	3,660	3.0	111,589	37.8	24.9
Trenton-Princeton, NJ	131,440	63.5	290,100	23.2	14.6	1,311	30.6	2.7	212,752	0.6	10,997	5.2	179,189	46.6	17.5
Tucson, AZ	410,942	64.0	199,400	20.9	10.4	931	30.6	4.0	480,903	0.3	23,808	5.0	451,995	38.4	17.8
Tulsa, OK	384,369	65.3	155,000	19.1	10.5	863	27.0	3.2	481,573	0.5	19,296	4.0	468,969	36.7	24.0
Tuscaloosa, AL	91,112	65.0	165,800	19.7	10.0	833	30.7	1.8	117,390	-2.8	4,503	3.8	111,965	35.4	27.6
Twin Falls, ID	39,762	69.3	181,500	21.3	10.5	810	27.6	2.9	54,451	1.4	1,915	3.5	51,808	31.9	34.3
Tyler, TX	77,809	67.2	164,200	20.4	10.8	955	27.6	3.3	110,095	2.4	5,656	5.1	104,190	33.9	25.2
Urban Honolulu, HI	316,928	57.5	702,300	25.5	10.0	1,779	33.4	9.3	451,661	0.5	23,881	5.3	464,037	37.5	17.8
Utica-Rome, NY	115,768	69.9	127,000	18.6	11.6	760	26.9	2.2	127,691	-2.1	6,661	5.2	131,741	37.8	20.7
Valdosta, GA	54,469	55.8	137,300	19.9	10.2	790	30.7	2.9	64,287	0.6	2,557	4.0	60,235	29.6	25.2
Vallejo, CA	151,191	62.1	437,900	23.7	10.3	1,684	31.6	5.9	199,365	-1.1	14,860	7.5	209,436	33.7	24.2
Victoria, TX	35,360	68.3	151,700	19.9	10.0	955	29.2	3.5	43,938	0.5	2,817	6.4	45,264	30.7	28.6
Vineland-Bridgeton, NJ	50,947	66.3	166,400	24.1	14.6	1,082	37.4	3.5	68,943	0.6	5,288	7.7	60,369	27.4	32.9
Virginia Beach-Norfolk-Newport News, VA-NC	672,053	62.3	253,800	22.6	10.6	1,187	30.3	2.0	846,917	-2.9	38,255	4.5	818,682	39.9	20.9
Visalia, CA	139,044	57.1	223,600	24.4	10.0	974	31.3	10.4	200,896	-0.6	21,435	10.7	183,876	27.0	35.0
Waco, TX	96,974	60.2	148,100	20.0	12.2	880	32.1	3.3	128,768	3.2	6,295	4.9	121,599	32.5	26.9
Walla Walla, WA	22,773	64.0	244,400	20.5	10.7	946	31.8	2.7	31,593	1.8	1,456	4.6	26,563	36.2	22.2
Warner Robins, GA	68,257	66.0	155,200	18.5	10.0	907	28.7	2.6	83,770	1.8	3,130	3.7	82,810	35.4	23.8
Washington-Arlington-Alexandria, DC-VA-MD-WV	2,244,311	63.9	436,600	21.3	10.0	1,718	28.7	3.3	3,362,843	-1.9	163,989	4.9	3,339,285	53.9	13.2
Frederick-Gaithersburg-Rockville, MD Div 23,224	467,124	67.7	451,900	21.0	10.0	1,739	30.0	3.0	682,191	-1.7	36,499	5.4	694,592	55.4	12.5
Washington-Arlington-Alexandria, DC-VA-MD-WV Div 47,894	1,777,187	62.9	431,800	21.3	10.0	1,713	28.4	3.4	2,680,652	-1.9	127,490	4.8	2,644,693	53.5	13.4
Waterloo-Cedar Falls, IA	68,165	69.3	152,300	18.8	10.6	806	27.4	1.8	87,412	-0.6	3,761	4.3	87,374	34.3	27.2
Watertown-Fort Drum, NY	43,046	55.7	150,100	19.4	11.3	1,018	28.9	2.4	43,765	-0.7	2,201	5.0	42,808	33.3	23.4
Wausau-Weston, WI	68,652	72.3	158,200	18.3	10.8	767	25.0	2.3	89,265	1.3	2,754	3.1	84,856	34.8	29.8
Weirton-Steubenville, WV-OH	50,009	71.0	95,400	17.0	10.0	650	25.4	1.3	50,278	0.2	3,190	6.3	50,799	30.1	29.0
Wenatchee, WA	44,818	65.1	299,500	22.1	10.0	942	25.3	4.6	66,817	0.8	3,576	5.4	55,863	31.7	30.4
Wheeling, WV-OH	55,376	74.5	115,200	16.8	10.0	657	28.7	1.1	61,592	-0.9	3,581	5.8	60,507	30.7	27.0
Wichita, KS	247,011	64.3	144,200	19.0	11.4	829	27.7	2.6	315,195	-0.7	13,775	4.4	308,166	36.7	25.6
Wichita Falls, TX	56,210	63.9	106,500	19.6	11.8	818	28.9	2.6	64,131	0.6	3,330	5.2	65,849	32.3	26.4
Williamsport, PA	46,160	68.6	161,900	20.1	12.0	797	28.9	1.7	55,322	-2.5	3,715	6.7	52,692	32.3	26.8
Wilmington, NC	120,810	62.6	243,700	21.6	12.0	1,046	31.7	1.4	151,775	3.9	6,422	4.2	141,945	40.9	18.3
Winchester, VA-WV	51,928	71.4	242,500	19.7	10.0	1,071	27.2	1.9	74,501	-0.4	2,301	3.1	66,781	36.4	26.3
Winston-Salem, NC	267,603	67.9	157,700	19.0	10.0	790	28.9	2.4	320,815	1.9	15,055	4.7	309,335	36.3	26.3
Worcester, MA-CT	359,670	66.0	283,600	21.5	13.6	1,061	29.2	1.9	505,517	0.1	29,925	5.9	482,773	42.1	20.1
Yakima, WA	83,765	62.3	191,400	22.0	10.2	868	27.8	8.5	131,217	-1.6	9,146	7.0	106,673	27.1	38.2
York-Hanover, PA	174,425	74.8	183,300	21.0	12.9	972	28.8	1.6	234,914	-0.6	12,733	5.4	226,081	34.8	27.8
Youngstown-Warren-Boardman, OH-PA	231,607	70.3	110,300	18.7	11.4	683	29.0	1.5	229,831	-1.6	15,024	6.5	237,740	31.5	26.6
Yuba City, CA	59,020	59.9	288,900	23.7	10.5	1,062	29.9	6.0	75,966	-0.2	6,673	8.8	69,976	28.6	29.8
Yuma, AZ	74,624	68.6	139,200	22.0	10.0	851	27.2	8.9	93,693	-1.1	12,102	12.9	78,723	25.4	31.3

1. Specified owner-occupied units. 2. A value of 10.0 represents 10 percent or less; a value of 50.0 represents 50 percent or more. 3. Specified renter-occupied units. 4. Overcrowded or lacking complete plumbing facilities. 5. Percent of civilian labor force. 6. Civilian employed persons 16 years old and over.

Area name	Private nonfarm establishments, employment and payroll, 2019									Agriculture, 2017			
		Employment						Annual payroll		Farms			Farm producers whose primary occupation is farming (percent)
											Percent with:		
	Number of establish-ments	Total	Health care and social assistance	Manufactur-ing	Retail trade	Finance and insurance	Professional, scientific, and technical services	Total (mil dol)	Average per employee (dollars)	Number	Fewer than 50 acres	1000 acres or more	
	104	105	106	107	108	109	110	111	112	113	114	115	116
Texarkana, TX-AR	3,052	48,088	8,682	6,425	7,644	1,562	2,644	1,880	39,091	2,433	40.1	4.3	36.1
The Villages, FL	1,706	27,829	5,360	1,091	4,421	786	665	1,062	38,179	1,307	75.7	1.9	37.0
Toledo, OH	13,950	272,237	48,930	49,012	31,676	7,130	12,002	13,328	48,959	2,791	48.8	5.7	38.1
Topeka, KS	4,971	82,944	19,947	8,367	10,553	6,027	3,586	3,892	46,927	4,511	29.0	9.4	34.9
Trenton-Princeton, NJ	9,669	202,228	29,320	6,572	26,035	16,730	25,194	15,031	74,326	323	72.1	0.6	35.1
Tucson, AZ	20,408	330,431	65,722	21,689	48,551	13,025	19,064	14,979	45,332	661	79.7	7.9	42.9
Tulsa, OK	24,627	411,327	61,926	52,512	47,808	16,417	25,619	20,077	48,811	9,398	44.7	4.8	33.5
Tuscaloosa, AL	4,607	88,000	13,778	20,227	10,738	1,984	2,163	3,876	44,040	1,652	33.4	8.2	37.5
Twin Falls, ID	3,349	39,224	6,970	5,603	6,244	967	1,294	1,471	37,510	1,697	51.1	6.4	51.2
Tyler, TX	5,931	95,866	22,649	8,517	13,097	3,317	4,618	4,232	44,144	2,928	58.8	1.1	31.7
Urban Honolulu, HI	21,237	364,092	55,287	9,617	45,977	18,724	19,009	16,854	46,290	927	91.3	1.7	55.4
Utica-Rome, NY	5,853	100,021	22,682	12,065	13,409	6,721	4,207	4,145	41,442	1,563	30.4	2.0	46.2
Valdosta, GA	3,130	45,054	8,712	3,726	7,026	1,327	1,364	1,669	37,035	909	42.2	9.2	37.5
Vallejo, CA	7,267	118,253	22,974	10,379	18,797	3,441	3,798	6,349	53,690	849	65.3	8.1	44.6
Victoria, TX	2,399	33,519	6,983	2,047	6,012	787	1,150	1,410	42,051	2,541	42.0	5.9	32.3
Vineland-Bridgeton, NJ	2,746	46,305	10,357	7,541	6,820	906	986	1,994	43,067	560	63.6	2.0	48.0
Virginia Beach-Norfolk-Newport News, VA-NC	38,996	643,616	102,753	60,104	89,654	26,800	52,531	29,713	46,166	1,840	54.3	10.2	41.6
Visalia, CA	6,632	100,314	17,702	13,589	16,400	3,061	2,368	4,334	43,209	4,187	57.6	5.4	52.3
Waco, TX	5,646	109,477	16,990	15,959	13,454	5,166	4,494	4,482	40,941	4,469	54.3	4.4	32.7
Walla Walla, WA	1,405	20,686	4,585	3,687	2,456	723	558	975	47,143	903	54.2	18.4	41.7
Warner Robins, GA	3,099	48,985	7,590	7,350	8,755	1,254	4,311	1,808	36,909	505	53.5	3.2	30.7
Washington-Arlington-Alexandria, DC-VA-MD-WV	157,315	2,816,183	355,042	50,208	280,076	106,288	595,874	199,349	70,787	9,392	58.4	2.5	38.7
Frederick-Gaithersburg-Rockville, MD Div 23,224	33,740	543,584	92,349	13,373	60,068	26,043	91,034	35,839	65,931	1,931	58.2	2.5	40.3
Washington-Arlington-Alexandria, DC-VA-MD-WV Div 47,894	123,575	2,272,599	262,693	36,835	220,008	80,245	504,840	163,510	71,949	7,461	58.5	2.5	38.2
Waterloo-Cedar Falls, IA	4,013	75,157	13,691	13,153	10,943	3,470	3,302	3,460	46,035	2,691	38.2	8.2	42.6
Watertown-Fort Drum, NY	2,370	28,834	6,746	2,214	5,989	766	825	1,150	39,899	792	26.5	5.6	51.5
Wausau-Weston, WI	4,072	74,245	11,504	20,923	8,836	5,110	1,512	3,456	46,542	2,663	33.2	2.7	48.7
Weirton-Steubenville, WV-OH	2,101	33,404	7,306	5,342	4,355	759	615	1,274	38,132	781	32.5	0.1	36.3
Wenatchee, WA	3,425	39,957	7,599	2,111	6,362	940	1,375	1,809	45,270	1,564	57.9	12.1	48.4
Wheeling, WV-OH	3,165	53,588	11,116	2,257	8,021	2,142	2,570	2,182	40,714	1,596	29.6	0.8	38.0
Wichita, KS	14,797	264,442	41,458	50,974	32,848	8,050	12,683	12,313	46,562	4,536	35.5	15.0	36.7
Wichita Falls, TX	3,339	46,405	11,538	4,735	7,229	1,840	1,025	1,759	37,901	1,997	28.8	18.1	36.5
Williamsport, PA	2,711	45,220	9,874	7,447	6,863	1,547	1,581	1,844	40,768	1,043	32.2	1.3	38.6
Wilmington, NC	9,132	114,424	20,745	6,416	18,405	4,066	6,275	5,363	46,865	395	58.2	3.3	47.5
Winchester, VA-WV	3,238	56,630	10,223	7,397	10,109	3,346	1,772	2,508	44,291	1,645	53.2	2.2	34.8
Winston-Salem, NC	13,656	252,351	52,283	31,968	31,060	12,271	9,211	11,959	47,390	3,825	52.9	1.2	40.0
Worcester, MA-CT	20,434	346,152	75,102	40,298	44,072	15,427	21,536	18,059	52,172	2,214	66.4	0.3	38.5
Yakima, WA	4,760	71,520	14,373	9,134	10,330	1,520	2,323	3,115	43,550	2,952	74.1	3.8	44.3
York-Hanover, PA	8,574	167,260	25,906	30,588	22,055	4,769	6,579	7,649	45,733	2,067	62.0	2.0	39.3
Youngstown-Warren-Boardman, OH-PA	11,799	184,285	38,548	26,081	29,536	5,120	4,755	7,088	38,461	2,978	48.3	1.4	37.7
Yuba City, CA	2,766	35,212	6,796	1,937	5,850	1,049	1,134	1,644	46,694	1,921	53.5	5.2	53.1
Yuma, AZ	3,116	46,323	8,741	3,480	8,334	1,299	1,272	1,760	37,990	456	60.7	13.2	50.4

Area name	Agriculture, 2017 (cont.) — Land in farms: Acreage (1,000)	Land in farms: Percent change, 2012–2017	Land in farms — Acres: Average size of farm	Acres: Total irrigated (1,000)	Acres: Total cropland (1,000)	Value of land and buildings (dollars): Average per farm	Value of land and buildings (dollars): Average per acre	Value of machinery and equipmnet, average per farm (dollars)	Value of products sold: Total (mil dol)	Value of products sold: Average per farm (acres)	Value of products sold — Percent from: Crops	Percent from: Livestock and poultry products	Organic farms (number)	Farms with internet access (percent)	Government payments: Total ($1,000)	Government payments: Percent of farms
	117	118	119	120	121	122	123	124	125	126	127	128	129	130	131	132
Texarkana, TX-AR	580	-4.6	239.0	24.8	191.5	655,739	2,749	84,649	180.5	74,199	24.9	75.1	0	73.4	6,849	17.8
The Villages, FL	177	-3.4	135.0	2.0	21.3	816,314	6,025	50,217	54.5	41,666	36.7	63.3	8	74.7	1,099	16.7
Toledo, OH	652	2.1	234.0	5.6	613.0	1,562,388	6,687	175,895	442.3	158,461	79.5	20.5	17	77.9	20,571	63.8
Topeka, KS	1,610	0.3	357.0	29.6	815.2	852,691	2,389	103,730	351.5	77,915	61.6	38.4	7	77.1	10,303	43.2
Trenton-Princeton, NJ	25	27.8	78.0	1.0	15.8	1,414,873	18,114	83,437	25.0	77,344	80.1	19.9	12	73.4	149	8.0
Tucson, AZ	2,618	NA	3,960.0	30.0	40.7	2,088,809	527	79,142	75.5	114,174	84.3	15.7	3	72.0	1,234	5.4
Tulsa, OK	2,653	-3.7	282.0	16.9	518.9	615,238	2,179	60,741	314.7	33,485	25.0	75.0	3	74.1	9,321	10.3
Tuscaloosa, AL	511	8.8	309.0	3.9	91.8	750,702	2,427	86,005	216.8	131,242	9.3	90.7	4	70.8	5,338	41.8
Twin Falls, ID	640	-4.7	377.0	376.3	391.9	1,837,189	4,868	280,963	1,319.8	777,738	22.0	78.0	42	87.0	6,506	30.8
Tyler, TX	272	-10.1	93.0	1.9	64.3	487,136	5,248	52,759	53.6	18,308	68.6	31.4	0	71.8	94	1.2
Urban Honolulu, HI	72	3.8	77.0	11.7	23.1	1,920,260	24,794	92,037	151.4	163,305	90.4	9.6	25	71.1	350	10.8
Utica-Rome, NY	311	-10.1	199.0	0.9	188.7	500,447	2,519	115,581	158.4	101,364	27.4	72.6	43	73.4	1,533	19.1
Valdosta, GA	310	15.6	341.0	39.8	150.6	1,283,208	3,764	154,355	195.2	214,726	73.2	26.8	3	73.3	5,651	41.6
Vallejo, CA	343	-15.8	404.0	110.4	152.1	3,691,320	9,148	178,302	296.6	349,337	83.8	16.2	63	85.2	2,554	13.9
Victoria, TX	806	-13.6	317.0	8.2	119.4	887,059	2,796	65,326	76.0	29,923	51.0	49.0	0	70.1	3,621	8.9
Vineland-Bridgeton, NJ	66	2.7	118.0	20.0	49.6	1,159,638	9,801	150,220	212.6	379,730	97.5	2.5	8	77.5	665	9.6
Virginia Beach-Norfolk-Newport News, VA-NC	564	2.3	307.0	7.3	415.8	1,278,266	4,170	163,276	387.9	210,824	73.4	26.6	9	82.6	19,010	38.2
Visalia, CA	1,250	0.9	299.0	568.2	721.4	3,501,053	11,726	218,462	4,474.8	1,068,739	49.7	50.3	104	78.2	13,824	10.4
Waco, TX	965	3.1	216.0	6.2	466.3	683,249	3,164	81,994	337.6	75,544	30.2	69.8	4	72.7	9,061	14.2
Walla Walla, WA	703	8.9	778.0	101.7	565.8	1,968,909	2,531	208,241	D	D	D	D	13	85.3	16,092	40.1
Warner Robins, GA	97	17.5	193.0	24.0	52.1	975,172	5,064	133,780	83.5	165,396	80.9	19.1	0	82.2	699	17.4
Washington-Arlington-Alexandria, DC-VA-MD-WV	1,254	-3.5	134.0	7.2	645.0	1,047,921	7,849	82,594	476.9	50,780	58.4	41.6	78	82.9	9,865	11.6
Frederick-Gaithersburg-Rockville, MD Div 23,224	254	3.7	132.0	2.3	189.4	1,208,668	9,185	116,267	174.2	90,193	58.2	41.8	35	83.1	5,159	23.0
Washington-Arlington-Alexandria, DC-VA-MD-WV Div 47,894	1,000	-5.2	134.0	4.8	455.6	1,006,318	7,509	73,879	302.8	40,580	58.5	41.5	43	82.9	4,706	8.6
Waterloo-Cedar Falls, IA	862	-2.7	320.0	0.9	812.7	2,765,372	8,630	252,938	757.9	281,635	64.3	35.7	15	82.2	22,822	76.4
Watertown-Fort Drum, NY	247	-14.9	312.0	0.4	168.8	836,501	2,677	170,553	165.1	208,404	21.6	78.4	31	74.7	1,986	22.3
Wausau-Weston, WI	551	-0.8	207.0	7.3	365.9	939,424	4,537	152,474	450.6	169,203	26.1	73.9	63	73.3	1,432	27.0
Weirton-Steubenville, WV-OH	100	8.4	128.0	0.1	40.7	639,277	5,011	79,855	11.0	14,059	47.4	52.6	0	77.8	192	6.9
Wenatchee, WA	883	-0.8	564.0	40.1	573.5	1,209,012	2,143	104,421	444.4	284,169	97.9	2.1	77	80.9	16,065	24.6
Wheeling, WV-OH	229	-0.2	143.0	0.1	75.0	486,981	3,396	79,205	31.9	19,969	28.2	71.8	5	71.1	169	3.9
Wichita, KS	2,397	3.6	528.0	109.2	1,660.7	1,325,671	2,509	155,663	680.7	150,073	57.4	42.6	16	79.5	26,736	50.6
Wichita Falls, TX	1,578	2.4	790.0	10.7	378.0	1,314,140	1,663	86,950	161.9	81,049	16.3	83.7	0	77.4	8,463	28.4
Williamsport, PA	186	17.5	178.0	0.2	79.0	913,566	5,119	69,673	63.7	61,086	48.1	51.9	8	67.0	2,683	40.6
Wilmington, NC	65	11.4	165.0	1.9	41.4	948,987	5,735	100,043	201.1	509,147	19.1	80.9	9	79.2	583	17.7
Winchester, VA-WV	242	-0.4	147.0	0.2	82.1	723,372	4,922	61,643	72.5	44,068	40.9	59.1	6	73.3	322	8.3
Winston-Salem, NC	385	1.3	101.0	2.1	181.5	551,408	5,485	63,812	267.0	69,798	29.0	71.0	15	73.6	1,509	10.4
Worcester, MA-CT	147	-8.0	67.0	1.9	56.8	751,336	11,293	57,343	110.3	49,813	57.0	43.0	32	81.4	1,147	7.3
Yakima, WA	1,781	0.1	603.0	260.0	344.0	1,662,431	2,755	174,332	1,988.0	673,451	71.3	28.7	84	79.0	5,221	6.5
York-Hanover, PA	253	-3.6	122.0	0.7	199.2	1,002,707	8,201	105,569	260.9	126,235	51.7	48.3	25	74.5	4,781	17.8
Youngstown-Warren-Boardman, OH-PA	355	0.7	119.0	1.0	236.8	555,675	4,667	104,689	190.4	63,938	50.5	49.5	39	74.0	4,148	22.0
Yuba City, CA	560	-0.4	292.0	271.2	336.7	2,657,292	9,107	207,693	591.3	307,805	96.0	4.0	63	80.4	10,515	10.3
Yuma, AZ	247	15.2	542.0	181.4	234.3	5,006,515	9,235	462,680	D	D	D	D	34	84.4	3,789	14.9

Area name	Water use, 2015		Wholesale Trade[1], 2017				Retail Trade[2], 2017				Real estate and rental and leasing,[2] 2017			
	Public supply water withdrawn (mil gal/ day)	Public supply gallons withdrawn per person per day	Number of establish- ments	Number of employees	Sales (mil dol)	Average payroll (mil dol)	Number of establish- ments	Number of employees	Sales (mil dol)	Average payroll (mil dol)	Number of establish- ments	Number of employees	Sales (mil dol)	Average payroll (mil dol)
	133	134	135	136	137	138	139	140	141	142	143	144	145	146
Texarkana, TX-AR	19.8	132.4	121	1,323	651.1	61.1	563	7,969	2,287.6	204.8	110	519	95.7	19.5
The Villages, FL	24.1	203.0	49	450	267.0	22.4	241	3,726	1,089.7	88.2	137	652	90.5	18.3
Toledo, OH	93.8	145.0	671	11,704	7,969.7	671.8	2,016	34,717	9,289.3	850.5	595	3,721	4,522.0	227.9
Topeka, KS	18.7	79.8	180	2,231	2,067.4	127.1	757	10,726	2,656.9	249.9	236	999	181.3	33.4
Trenton-Princeton, NJ	37.6	101.3	352	D	10,156.9	D	1,249	25,101	7,573.9	702.8	355	2,142	721.0	109.9
Tucson, AZ	175.4	173.7	666	6,524	3,723.2	321.7	2,721	46,749	12,230.9	1,271.8	1,347	6,396	1,271.3	243.8
Tulsa, OK	133.4	135.9	1,168	17,421	12,726.9	1,037.9	3,020	48,857	14,386.1	1,280.6	1,189	7,509	1,359.6	302.8
Tuscaloosa, AL	38.9	156.7	152	1,532	926.0	83.9	836	10,974	2,963.9	267.2	215	1,870	251.1	62.4
Twin Falls, ID	19.4	184.5	163	1,628	1,333.3	81.5	443	6,070	1,830.9	165.2	157	370	75.2	11.0
Tyler, TX	42.9	192.4	226	2,841	1,180.6	145.3	839	13,251	4,074.6	364.5	333	1,177	262.1	51.6
Urban Honolulu, HI	168.8	169.0	1,036	13,217	9,376.4	689.4	2,856	48,609	14,266.1	1,437.5	1,288	8,864	3,150.9	483.1
Utica-Rome, NY	61.7	208.6	211	3,044	1,488.1	142.4	958	13,710	3,721.6	348.9	197	749	147.0	25.5
Valdosta, GA	14.5	101.3	120	1,216	1,012.0	56.4	586	7,496	2,230.2	177.8	143	701	124.2	23.0
Vallejo, CA	52.2	119.7	253	4,043	3,119.4	261.9	1,061	20,104	6,244.8	601.4	393	1,603	503.6	68.8
Victoria, TX	12.4	124.1	D	D	D	83.7	385	5,866	1,796.0	162.6	127	1,141	527.0	61.0
Vineland-Bridgeton, NJ	15.7	100.9	153	4,405	2,833.3	200.5	492	7,027	2,011.0	182.1	102	486	108.7	18.9
Virginia Beach-Norfolk-Newport News, VA-NC	169.8	96.4	1,190	16,618	14,933.4	1,050.5	5,874	90,028	22,507.3	2,224.1	2,225	14,425	3,195.9	650.5
Visalia, CA	70.3	152.9	338	4,898	8,105.4	270.5	1,098	16,622	4,599.0	429.3	330	1,500	256.8	49.1
Waco, TX	43.7	166.3	246	2,789	1,828.0	142.6	885	13,322	3,879.3	352.7	262	1,708	379.5	78.3
Walla Walla, WA	12.7	210.8	D	D	D	15.1	171	2,225	560.8	62.1	70	234	36.5	8.4
Warner Robins, GA	26.1	147.4	43	320	175.8	13.7	587	8,555	2,432.6	209.0	148	514	127.2	18.2
Washington-Arlington-Alexandria, DC-VA-MD-WV	568.5	93.0	3,488	51,603	63,173.9	4,094.5	16,174	279,083	82,640.2	8,372.9	7,968	57,264	21,101.4	3,809.5
Frederick-Gaithersburg-Rockville, MD Div 23,224	368.7	286.9	879	11,155	9,027.7	930.3	3,299	59,294	18,565.8	1,866.4	1,743	13,221	6,231.6	927.0
Washington-Arlington-Alexandria, DC-VA-MD-WV Div 47,894	199.8	41.4	2,609	40,448	54,146.2	3,164.3	12,875	219,789	64,074.5	6,506.5	6,225	44,043	14,869.8	2,882.5
Waterloo-Cedar Falls, IA	18.3	107.4	187	3,034	2,533.2	161.0	629	10,706	2,597.8	264.8	152	786	143.2	26.8
Watertown-Fort Drum, NY	9.3	79.0	56	678	285.3	33.0	484	6,485	1,911.8	171.6	128	624	102.3	24.3
Wausau-Weston, WI	12.4	75.4	192	3,024	1,454.3	152.7	560	11,941	3,500.3	290.2	108	543	99.5	19.0
Weirton-Steubenville, WV-OH	15.4	128.1	10	141	74.6	5.7	354	4,884	1,310.0	115.2	66	179	43.2	5.5
Wenatchee, WA	16.7	144.1	136	3,828	1,752.9	160.7	480	6,014	1,664.5	174.6	183	678	129.8	25.5
Wheeling, WV-OH	20.0	138.6	117	1,727	4,194.9	78.2	561	8,470	2,357.8	199.9	123	693	129.8	24.8
Wichita, KS	73.1	114.7	678	9,590	8,643.7	573.4	2,064	34,237	9,245.6	876.1	729	3,463	802.0	130.5
Wichita Falls, TX	11.7	77.6	165	1,322	505.0	60.7	515	7,255	2,002.9	180.6	162	783	132.2	26.3
Williamsport, PA	8.8	75.7	114	1,788	1,083.6	75.3	451	7,031	1,896.4	167.4	109	731	142.6	30.4
Wilmington, NC	9.0	32.4	339	3,331	1,801.0	183.1	1,239	17,899	5,344.2	489.6	563	2,153	531.0	93.2
Winchester, VA-WV	5.8	43.3	36	459	463.9	102.2	545	8,511	2,437.0	227.2	139	306	159.9	11.5
Winston-Salem, NC	68.6	104.0	516	7,702	6,868.0	413.0	2,173	31,179	8,631.3	809.9	560	2,296	813.8	104.9
Worcester, MA-CT	259.4	277.2	801	13,268	8,527.3	796.7	2,861	44,753	14,689.5	1,262.5	735	3,479	841.4	171.0
Yakima, WA	30.0	120.6	220	4,707	3,634.3	241.2	730	10,415	3,136.8	301.2	263	1,013	180.5	33.1
York-Hanover, PA	34.8	78.6	340	7,055	6,755.3	384.1	1,212	21,792	6,119.8	538.5	291	1,983	410.2	81.0
Youngstown-Warren-Boardman, OH-PA	51.9	94.4	492	6,968	4,350.1	361.6	2,001	31,490	7,922.6	757.7	417	2,711	504.2	97.0
Yuba City, CA	22.6	132.0	93	2,073	1,368.5	118.3	408	5,904	1,795.0	167.5	124	460	92.1	15.1
Yuma, AZ	36.3	177.7	128	1,856	1,438.4	102.1	472	8,292	2,219.1	210.0	177	761	148.3	23.3

1. Merchant wholesalers, except manufacturers' sales branches and offices. 2. Employer establishments.

Area name	Professional, scientific, and technical services, 2017				Manufacturing, 2017				Accommodation and food services, 2017			
	Number of establish-ments	Number of employees	Sales (mil dol)	Average payroll (mil dol)	Number of establish-ments	Number of employees	Receipts (mil dol)	Annual payroll (mil dol)	Number of establish-ments	Number of employees	Receipts (mil dol)	Annual payroll (mil dol)
	147	148	149	150	151	152	153	154	155	156	157	158
Texarkana, TX-AR	48	222	23.5	7.9	105	5,572	2,438.6	323.0	197	5,006	227.7	65.5
The Villages, FL	160	753	103.6	40.1	39	943	474.7	49.1	143	3,614	177.1	56.6
Toledo, OH	899	10,321	1,609.1	652.7	765	43,621	32,045.4	2,599.0	1,626	29,502	1,477.7	420.4
Topeka, KS	34	131	11.5	3.9	119	D	3,436.3	D	43	1,117	151.3	28.1
Trenton-Princeton, NJ	1,614	24,223	5,681.5	2,299.6	231	6,743	2,217.8	423.3	867	14,034	912.8	260.6
Tucson, AZ	2,554	17,645	2,636.6	1,069.3	617	23,392	9,958.9	1,965.6	1,852	44,608	2,877.5	808.1
Tulsa, OK	2,826	22,722	4,022.0	1,557.3	1,196	47,793	21,280.0	2,790.4	2,138	44,035	2,597.0	708.5
Tuscaloosa, AL	25	124	10.6	3.2	175	16,030	21,097.0	977.2	21	194	9.8	2.3
Twin Falls, ID	259	1,171	153.5	51.3	116	5,158	2,623.2	235.0	236	4,079	203.9	55.7
Tyler, TX	624	4,570	917.0	301.9	184	6,614	4,305.0	340.6	490	10,739	596.4	182.9
Urban Honolulu, HI	2,473	18,527	3,231.9	1,238.8	501	9,240	5,325.4	439.0	2,569	67,611	6,805.4	1,767.8
Utica-Rome, NY	477	4,081	676.7	231.5	289	11,866	3,714.7	625.3	773	13,624	1,092.3	282.4
Valdosta, GA	18	66	4.8	1.5	D	D	D	D	290	6,087	315.3	83.5
Vallejo, CA	590	3,726	627.2	233.5	245	9,085	7,191.2	610.6	775	13,222	848.6	237.8
Victoria, TX	13	25	2.5	0.7	D	D	D	D	D	D	D	D
Vineland-Bridgeton, NJ	D	D	D	D	158	8,509	2,612.5	408.6	243	3,541	184.5	49.1
Virginia Beach-Norfolk-Newport News, VA-NC	2,420	30,613	5,486.4	2,214.5	857	D	17,037.4	D	4,078	79,461	4,617.9	1,281.0
Visalia, CA	D	D	D	D	231	13,534	8,119.7	719.1	640	9,898	641.4	173.1
Waco, TX	400	2,772	525.7	165.9	258	13,907	7,639.8	836.8	536	D	629.7	D
Walla Walla, WA	D	D	D	D	D	D	D	D	127	2,030	120.1	36.8
Warner Robins, GA	28	134	15.5	5.8	D	D	D	D	329	7,252	347.1	103.8
Washington-Arlington-Alexandria, DC-VA-MD-WV	26,766	486,249	122,883.5	48,710.3	2,127	50,350	16,724.2	3,298.7	13,545	290,254	23,267.5	6,515.6
Frederick-Gaithersburg-Rockville, MD Div 23,224	6,618	88,743	16,077.2	7,187.8	523	14,072	5,274.6	988.7	2,425	44,590	3,130.8	891.9
Washington-Arlington-Alexandria, DC-VA-MD-WV Div 47,894	20,148	397,506	106,806.4	41,522.4	1,604	36,278	11,449.6	2,310.0	11,120	245,664	20,136.8	5,623.7
Waterloo-Cedar Falls, IA	41	258	28.0	8.1	191	15,029	6,653.4	750.2	390	7,436	394.8	105.4
Watertown-Fort Drum, NY	D	D	D	D	68	2,334	906.1	113.5	333	4,376	249.2	81.6
Wausau-Weston, WI	36	111	12.8	4.5	285	19,353	6,419.8	968.6	410	6,129	280.7	82.8
Weirton-Steubenville, WV-OH	49	341	80.4	14.0	72	5,592	2,952.0	324.1	235	3,965	300.7	65.4
Wenatchee, WA	242	1,188	145.0	57.8	126	1,879	421.2	85.7	385	5,280	346.8	114.2
Wheeling, WV-OH	87	560	58.2	22.3	105	2,255	987.0	106.5	327	6,727	424.8	105.1
Wichita, KS	1,264	11,911	1,954.9	728.2	632	46,542	22,259.5	3,216.9	1,393	27,549	1,306.2	385.8
Wichita Falls, TX	22	43	7.5	1.9	133	4,397	1,273.5	239.6	6	60	1.8	0.6
Williamsport, PA	D	D	D	D	156	7,422	3,192.1	376.5	273	4,720	253.7	76.5
Wilmington, NC	D	D	D	D	225	6,515	2,315.1	485.4	881	16,694	934.8	266.5
Winchester, VA-WV	D	D	D	53.1	119	7,290	4,672.7	414.7	144	3,320	160.2	48.4
Winston-Salem, NC	1,222	7,732	1,178.7	437.2	660	30,149	30,921.3	1,536.0	1,225	24,340	1,266.0	355.7
Worcester, MA-CT	1,833	18,742	4,100.8	1,706.7	1,087	40,300	14,068.7	2,587.4	2,047	29,986	1,835.8	533.3
Yakima, WA	D	D	D	D	245	9,487	3,536.6	453.2	445	6,498	418.3	118.8
York-Hanover, PA	697	6,496	884.4	397.1	517	29,074	11,501.2	1,589.0	785	14,306	706.4	195.4
Youngstown-Warren-Boardman, OH-PA	266	1,937	193.7	70.8	690	26,356	11,314.5	1,467.0	1,190	21,655	959.5	275.9
Yuba City, CA	210	1,113	166.5	62.4	92	1,971	686.0	102.3	233	3,409	225.9	59.7
Yuma, AZ	D	D	D	D	75	3,095	967.4	132.4	345	6,823	371.6	101.7

Area name	Health care and social assistance, 2017				Other services, 2017				Nonemployer businesses, 2018		Value of residential construction authorized by building permits, 2020	
	Number of establish-ments	Number of employees	Receipts (mil dol)	Annual payroll (mil dol)	Number of establish-ments	Number of employees	Receipts (mil dol)	Annual payroll (mil dol)	Number	Receipts (mil dol)	New construc-tion ($1,000)	Number of housing units
	159	160	161	162	163	164	165	166	167	168	169	170
Texarkana, TX-AR	401	8,720	1,075.3	390.8	156	1,108	108.2	37.0	9,078	413.9	42,720	259
The Villages, FL	202	4,682	635.1	217.7	82	436	34.6	11.4	8,147	364.3	1,203,827	4,611
Toledo, OH	1,856	49,629	5,525.2	2,190.7	1,053	6,872	727.5	201.9	39,572	1,780.8	292,444	1,210
Topeka, KS	584	18,286	2,078.8	874.9	389	2,534	341.6	98.0	13,168	593.1	145,599	717
Trenton-Princeton, NJ	1,192	30,342	3,364.8	1,424.9	854	6,011	1,423.0	276.7	28,098	1,542.4	53,329	544
Tucson, AZ	2,862	61,632	7,137.9	2,861.4	1,485	10,873	1,229.4	305.4	72,626	3,003.4	1,753,992	6,284
Tulsa, OK	2,658	62,823	7,948.4	2,887.0	1,503	9,701	1,834.3	351.9	78,418	3,776.6	1,087,487	4,920
Tuscaloosa, AL	503	14,657	1,562.5	655.4	241	1,463	168.3	47.9	15,968	743.6	297,333	1,496
Twin Falls, ID	432	6,980	723.5	263.4	194	1,106	110.2	32.3	7,406	355.1	220,837	1,068
Tyler, TX	685	22,449	2,985.8	1,095.4	374	2,239	239.2	67.8	20,568	1,099.2	201,056	912
Urban Honolulu, HI	2,578	54,227	7,522.5	2,994.2	2,064	15,687	1,965.5	500.9	71,327	3,675.4	468,351	1,438
Utica-Rome, NY	719	23,182	2,122.9	974.0	523	5,660	349.6	119.4	15,625	657.1	90,042	456
Valdosta, GA	479	8,429	941.7	347.0	147	670	70.0	17.4	9,735	462.9	273,096	1,535
Vallejo, CA	931	22,704	3,667.2	1,608.3	576	3,920	630.6	159.5	26,856	1,173.8	387,484	1,378
Victoria, TX	306	6,952	761.9	320.2	154	1,148	170.9	46.9	7,792	340.4	59,296	391
Vineland-Bridgeton, NJ	405	11,257	1,121.9	531.6	240	1,246	120.9	31.9	6,406	317.4	20,529	185
Virginia Beach-Norfolk-Newport News, VA-NC	4,069	99,251	13,154.4	4,927.8	2,882	18,665	2,503.6	596.4	115,164	4,620.6	1,449,487	7,377
Visalia, CA	884	16,822	1,970.5	745.0	405	2,313	267.4	75.4	21,732	1,097.8	347,316	1,510
Waco, TX	611	18,206	1,830.9	773.5	D	D	D	80.0	18,973	920.4	131,486	1,107
Walla Walla, WA	155	4,730	566.2	245.5	D	D	D	D	3,456	164.5	51,701	261
Warner Robins, GA	382	7,960	796.9	286.7	191	1,103	104.1	29.4	13,147	444.5	300,094	1,534
Washington-Arlington-Alexandria, DC-VA-MD-WV	16,579	335,348	44,708.1	17,766.5	13,529	167,501	42,933.8	10,506.4	598,268	28,684.1	5,337,620	27,414
Frederick-Gaithersburg-Rockville, MD Div 23,224	4,406	84,304	10,678.2	4,591.1	2,395	23,025	4,919.7	1,377.1	141,864	7,434.2	960,458	4,660
Washington-Arlington-Alexandria, DC-VA-MD-WV Div 47,894	12,173	251,044	34,029.9	13,175.4	11,134	144,476	38,014.1	9,129.4	456,404	21,249.9	4,377,162	22,754
Waterloo-Cedar Falls, IA	462	13,506	1,354.2	565.2	281	1,762	181.1	49.1	10,158	485.4	76,492	205
Watertown-Fort Drum, NY	273	6,535	660.4	304.3	183	866	102.3	22.8	5,278	210.0	32,572	161
Wausau-Weston, WI	390	10,447	1,418.3	529.0	270	1,507	184.8	47.6	9,503	482.6	140,934	680
Weirton-Steubenville, WV-OH	297	7,311	745.1	283.7	181	1,017	94.9	27.6	5,263	198.3	8,379	34
Wenatchee, WA	300	7,442	1,008.9	444.0	225	821	95.4	25.0	7,150	338.6	234,043	1,000
Wheeling, WV-OH	504	11,607	1,248.2	476.2	278	1,852	187.6	55.2	6,667	288.6	15,012	96
Wichita, KS	1,812	43,963	4,786.3	1,922.0	960	5,960	807.6	187.6	42,069	1,967.8	683,433	2,384
Wichita Falls, TX	432	11,260	1,162.4	432.5	255	1,204	162.2	36.7	9,843	476.1	45,583	191
Williamsport, PA	302	8,805	1,146.5	415.6	225	1,591	143.2	36.9	6,323	294.6	15,123	56
Wilmington, NC	936	20,349	2,432.9	951.6	586	3,449	346.9	103.4	27,550	1,421.9	987,203	4,418
Winchester, VA-WV	269	7,080	1,125.3	407.1	92	536	45.5	14.0	9,600	466.0	244,248	1,022
Winston-Salem, NC	1,180	44,180	5,013.7	1,776.7	946	4,851	768.9	151.8	48,502	2,044.6	1,085,525	4,206
Worcester, MA-CT	2,409	75,856	9,076.9	3,576.6	1,628	9,090	983.4	280.5	65,536	3,180.7	438,444	2,053
Yakima, WA	576	14,031	1,779.2	692.5	283	1,580	168.1	44.4	9,633	490.4	223,483	1,103
York-Hanover, PA	988	26,954	3,178.4	1,260.7	795	5,081	513.5	146.4	26,978	1,354.1	250,114	1,316
Youngstown-Warren-Boardman, OH-PA	1,740	43,420	4,298.0	1,741.2	908	5,462	459.2	130.8	35,862	1,609.2	82,861	400
Yuba City, CA	323	6,566	938.1	354.1	180	808	88.2	25.2	10,147	614.0	212,300	981
Yuma, AZ	411	8,367	1,074.7	365.5	214	1,124	102.6	30.6	10,540	419.6	205,136	1,291

Area name	Government employment and payroll, 2017									Local government finances, 2017				
			March payroll (percent of total)							General revenue				
												Taxes		
	Full-time equivalent employees	March payroll (dollars)	Adminis-tration, judicial, and legal	Police and corrections	Fire protection	Highways and transpor-tation	Health and welfare	Natural resources and utilities	Education and libraries	Total (mil dol)	Inter-govern-mental (mil dol)	Total (mil dol)	Per capita[1] (dollars) Total	Per capita[1] (dollars) Property
	171	172	173	174	175	176	177	178	179	180	181	182	183	184
Texarkana, TX-AR	6,643	21,508,073	5.4	9.3	3.1	3.7	4.9	3.0	68.5	526.9	242.1	196.5	1,314	971
The Villages, FL	1,805	6,376,591	5.2	22.2	6.8	3.6	0.3	3.5	57.8	324.6	40.6	147.5	1,180	970
Toledo, OH	24,493	107,114,923	8.8	12.1	6.3	4.4	8.7	5.6	52.6	3,019.3	1,079.9	1,364.7	2,118	1,291
Topeka, KS	11,945	42,626,815	5.2	10.2	3.8	3.0	2.4	5.2	69.1	998.3	428.4	389.1	1,670	1,193
Trenton-Princeton, NJ	14,557	89,476,151	6.3	11.2	3.5	2.2	5.1	4.7	64.1	2,186.7	669.9	1,243.6	3,378	3,332
Tucson, AZ	31,752	127,346,777	11.2	14.7	7.2	3.8	2.7	7.1	50.9	3,446.6	1,195.6	1,540.0	1,500	1,074
Tulsa, OK	33,401	114,906,377	6.2	10.6	6.4	4.2	3.1	5.6	61.7	3,225.9	963.8	1,545.5	1,559	847
Tuscaloosa, AL	11,664	43,638,673	3.8	7.8	3.4	3.7	41.3	4.9	33.7	1,237.6	312.4	235.4	938	418
Twin Falls, ID	4,105	14,151,701	9.2	10.2	2.8	3.4	2.9	5.0	65.3	406.5	194.9	124.4	1,140	1,068
Tyler, TX	9,437	33,803,613	7.5	10.5	4.0	2.3	8.3	2.9	63.7	757.5	230.3	392.1	1,726	1,338
Urban Honolulu, HI	10,620	59,188,205	13.8	33.1	16.0	4.1	4.2	22.8	0.0	2,959.6	435.8	1,639.6	1,662	1,115
Utica-Rome, NY	13,452	58,809,562	5.8	7.7	2.6	5.3	5.3	4.4	67.7	1,786.8	886.4	698.0	2,389	1,565
Valdosta, GA	7,071	26,126,999	3.8	6.9	2.0	1.5	39.9	2.8	42.7	762.4	191.0	181.0	1,245	813
Vallejo, CA	14,181	85,279,873	8.8	16.3	3.9	2.8	11.4	6.1	48.9	2,297.4	1,058.2	776.7	1,751	1,193
Victoria, TX	6,080	21,925,876	4.5	8.6	3.6	1.8	31.4	2.9	46.5	550.7	111.0	212.5	2,134	1,688
Vineland-Bridgeton, NJ	7,181	38,072,311	3.2	10.2	0.7	1.1	5.7	5.9	71.6	897.5	508.3	274.3	1,812	1,776
Virginia Beach-Norfolk-Newport News, VA-NC	75,966	315,130,045	6.3	10.6	5.0	3.1	9.0	8.1	55.3	8,674.7	3,342.3	3,461.8	1,966	1,368
Visalia, CA	23,861	111,821,006	5.1	7.4	1.9	1.1	31.0	4.0	48.3	3,798.6	1,982.9	537.8	1,163	700
Waco, TX	11,821	45,018,230	5.7	11.5	3.0	1.9	5.9	7.1	63.9	1,169.9	425.7	490.2	1,822	1,460
Walla Walla, WA	2,255	10,369,781	7.3	9.6	5.1	6.8	5.0	3.7	60.2	278.3	123.5	98.1	1,622	997
Warner Robins, GA	6,934	24,839,122	5.3	9.1	3.4	1.7	1.6	4.1	71.8	607.2	234.4	247.8	1,376	805
Washington-Arlington-Alexandria, DC-VA-MD-WV	258,342	1,509,069,206	6.9	10.2	4.2	8.5	7.5	6.0	52.1	43,753.3	12,391.1	24,630.6	3,965	2,276
Frederick-Gaithersburg-Rockville, MD Div 23,224	48,208	318,667,676	3.8	7.8	4.6	3.1	6.6	3.5	66.2	8,252.9	1,639.9	5,030.5	3,877	1,996
Washington-Arlington-Alexandria, DC-VA-MD-WV Div 47,894	210,134	1,190,401,530	7.7	10.9	4.0	9.9	7.8	6.7	48.3	35,500.4	10,751.2	19,600.1	3,989	2,349
Waterloo-Cedar Falls, IA	7,541	32,145,689	3.9	7.9	3.1	4.0	6.0	7.6	66.3	893.8	364.1	294.5	1,739	1,465
Watertown-Fort Drum, NY	5,641	24,270,939	5.8	5.5	1.8	7.2	5.7	3.2	67.8	739.1	370.0	279.4	2,469	1,419
Wausau-Weston, WI	6,471	28,685,366	5.1	7.6	1.7	5.0	14.3	2.6	62.4	983.4	576.8	263.2	1,613	1,489
Weirton-Steubenville, WV-OH	4,386	14,172,355	7.0	10.7	1.9	4.2	8.4	6.2	59.6	409.0	169.6	155.1	1,314	930
Wenatchee, WA	5,674	30,515,741	4.2	5.5	1.9	5.6	8.1	28.8	44.1	700.3	303.3	217.8	1,840	1,109
Wheeling, WV-OH	5,775	19,162,949	8.4	8.1	3.0	4.5	7.0	11.4	55.5	533.8	145.6	266.2	1,885	1,396
Wichita, KS	26,450	98,085,385	6.4	10.8	4.3	3.2	4.7	5.0	63.6	2,643.6	1,204.6	868.1	1,362	1,003
Wichita Falls, TX	6,575	24,216,273	5.5	12.2	8.9	2.7	9.6	5.4	54.0	516.7	194.9	221.4	1,467	1,204
Williamsport, PA	3,735	16,093,813	7.9	7.7	1.8	4.2	1.8	6.8	69.3	504.9	219.4	183.1	1,606	1,169
Wilmington, NC	15,220	62,968,999	3.0	6.9	2.4	1.0	45.3	2.9	34.3	2,227.0	380.5	481.4	1,663	1,146
Winchester, VA-WV	5,700	19,768,233	6.5	14.6	4.0	1.8	1.5	4.5	65.2	489.1	173.5	238.9	1,731	1,250
Winston-Salem, NC	23,586	79,865,777	4.7	9.2	4.1	1.3	8.1	4.4	65.8	1,988.4	946.2	794.0	1,191	897
Worcester, MA-CT	28,812	140,488,525	4.6	9.2	5.9	3.5	2.6	3.8	68.6	3,855.5	1,573.8	1,843.1	1,956	1,906
Yakima, WA	9,179	43,173,358	6.3	9.8	3.4	2.4	1.2	5.9	69.1	1,163.9	708.0	278.4	1,114	636
York-Hanover, PA	11,962	52,520,313	6.6	13.8	1.8	2.1	5.9	3.5	63.6	1,957.2	680.8	911.8	2,047	1,668
Youngstown-Warren-Boardman, OH-PA	21,031	78,440,663	6.9	9.9	3.3	3.3	8.0	5.3	62.1	2,015.0	897.1	796.5	1,471	991
Yuba City, CA	6,944	37,149,999	6.6	8.3	2.0	1.9	11.3	3.0	64.0	1,032.8	685.7	203.7	1,179	919
Yuma, AZ	7,776	27,599,788	11.8	12.2	3.2	2.3	2.4	7.4	59.2	761.8	338.4	336.9	1,608	1,179

1. Based on the resident population estimated as of July 1 of the year shown

Area name	Local government finances, 2017 (cont.)										Government employment, 2019			Individual income tax returns, 2018		
	Direct general expenditure							Debt outstanding								
			Percent of total for:													
	Total (mil dol)	Per capita[1] (dollars)	Educa-tion	Health and hospitals	Police protection	Public welfare	Highways	Total (mil dol)	Per capita[1] (dollars)	Federal civilian	Federal military	State and local	Number of returns	Mean adjusted gross income	Mean income tax
	185	186	187	188	189	190	191	192	193	194	195	196	197	198	199
Texarkana, TX-AR	514.4	3,439	55.9	2.9	5.8	1.3	4.6	447.7	2,994	3,494	391	8,927	64,440	52,764	4,996
The Villages, FL	307.7	2,461	27.6	1.1	7.3	0.5	7.7	579.9	4,640	1,748	232	3,126	65,400	86,555	11,166
Toledo, OH	3,180.8	4,936	41.9	5.9	8.0	4.8	3.6	2,963.6	4,599	2,536	1,722	42,201	315,790	60,278	6,421
Topeka, KS	1,071.6	4,599	53.5	1.6	6.2	0.1	7.4	1,320.2	5,666	3,583	943	22,695	112,100	58,289	5,562
Trenton-Princeton, NJ	2,256.8	6,130	55.2	1.0	5.6	3.2	1.4	1,839.7	4,997	2,348	708	36,844	180,880	97,512	14,623
Tucson, AZ	3,167.0	3,086	39.3	2.2	12.8	1.8	6.9	5,952.8	5,800	13,387	8,654	66,885	483,760	63,458	6,795
Tulsa, OK	3,004.1	3,030	47.3	5.0	6.9	0.7	6.7	4,200.9	4,238	5,056	3,639	47,532	446,850	68,746	7,910
Tuscaloosa, AL	1,269.6	5,060	32.1	41.0	4.8	0.0	5.0	1,146.1	4,567	2,156	1,016	25,513	102,750	57,768	5,826
Twin Falls, ID	418.0	3,829	55.1	2.2	4.5	1.0	5.8	408.5	3,742	458	340	5,612	49,190	52,038	4,617
Tyler, TX	736.2	3,240	58.0	4.9	5.9	0.1	3.6	1,714.9	7,548	751	472	13,279	106,810	65,827	7,741
Urban Honolulu, HI	1,981.5	2,009	0.0	2.2	14.5	1.1	9.1	6,208.2	6,294	32,296	47,560	60,496	496,000	71,953	8,050
Utica-Rome, NY	1,774.6	6,074	54.6	2.2	2.9	10.4	5.4	1,252.8	4,288	2,500	499	26,218	135,280	57,101	5,597
Valdosta, GA	850.3	5,850	33.0	44.0	4.0	0.0	2.8	547.4	3,766	1,203	5,067	11,463	58,830	49,696	4,638
Vallejo, CA	2,261.9	5,100	38.2	8.0	9.9	6.9	4.7	2,036.9	4,593	3,731	7,697	20,732	218,670	72,136	7,757
Victoria, TX	550.0	5,522	37.5	32.8	5.6	0.0	3.4	534.8	5,369	227	196	6,543	46,170	62,949	7,103
Vineland-Bridgeton, NJ	984.1	6,499	63.7	2.4	3.2	1.9	4.6	340.3	2,247	667	291	11,348	67,830	51,455	4,672
Virginia Beach-Norfolk-Newport News, VA-NC	8,517.6	4,837	42.8	6.4	5.1	3.2	3.5	8,791.4	4,992	60,463	64,369	102,963	852,190	65,400	6,984
Visalia, CA	3,763.9	8,141	41.8	26.6	3.2	6.7	3.0	1,853.2	4,009	1,078	683	30,684	191,210	47,860	4,068
Waco, TX	1,017.8	3,784	52.9	6.2	6.8	0.8	2.1	1,287.1	4,785	3,359	622	15,828	121,080	57,386	5,914
Walla Walla, WA	265.3	4,384	46.0	3.5	5.4	0.1	9.6	233.0	3,850	1,983	147	4,149	27,360	64,917	6,608
Warner Robins, GA	569.0	3,158	58.9	3.6	6.7	0.0	3.4	157.1	872	15,929	4,006	11,477	85,010	56,610	5,131
Washington-Arlington-Alexandria, DC-VA-MD-WV	43,681.9	7,033	40.5	3.3	5.2	10.7	3.0	56,275.1	9,060	386,559	67,221	328,266	3,167,250	100,896	14,860
Frederick-Gaithersburg-Rockville, MD Div 23,224	8,887.0	6,850	42.7	1.8	3.9	0.9	3.1	13,431.9	10,353	52,665	10,407	54,201	668,390	110,074	17,059
Washington-Arlington-Alexandria, DC-VA-MD-WV Div 47,894	34,794.8	7,081	40.0	3.7	5.5	13.2	3.0	42,843.2	8,719	333,894	56,814	274,065	2,498,860	98,442	14,271
Waterloo-Cedar Falls, IA	867.4	5,122	53.7	6.5	4.7	1.0	5.9	655.4	3,870	652	613	12,833	77,020	64,207	6,455
Watertown-Fort Drum, NY	718.8	6,352	52.7	3.0	2.3	8.1	6.8	408.3	3,608	3,345	15,659	7,719	50,300	52,786	4,558
Wausau-Weston, WI	1,065.5	6,529	37.8	8.6	3.6	26.0	8.2	547.1	3,352	466	419	9,014	83,600	65,691	7,175
Weirton-Steubenville, WV-OH	710.0	6,014	69.1	3.6	3.3	1.8	2.8	298.3	2,527	283	393	6,036	55,340	52,155	4,675
Wenatchee, WA	619.1	5,232	46.3	12.2	4.6	0.2	6.5	1,381.8	11,678	907	297	8,180	61,470	65,834	7,126
Wheeling, WV-OH	517.7	3,665	46.5	0.8	5.6	2.8	5.3	494.0	3,497	632	484	8,193	65,350	60,715	6,561
Wichita, KS	2,608.4	4,092	51.4	3.3	5.7	0.1	6.5	5,720.1	8,973	5,422	5,248	37,265	303,990	65,541	7,082
Wichita Falls, TX	568.1	3,763	51.7	9.2	6.3	0.8	3.6	695.8	4,610	1,964	6,050	10,169	65,630	58,437	5,900
Williamsport, PA	510.6	4,479	56.7	0.0	2.8	2.6	4.3	983.6	8,627	402	277	8,168	54,910	55,739	5,352
Wilmington, NC	2,146.0	7,414	23.7	51.7	4.3	2.5	0.6	1,816.5	6,276	1,225	822	22,927	138,940	72,824	9,053
Winchester, VA-WV	494.1	3,580	56.3	0.6	5.2	3.1	1.1	509.0	3,688	2,510	493	7,828	68,530	65,756	6,851
Winston-Salem, NC	2,150.2	3,225	50.0	3.2	8.3	4.7	2.3	1,936.0	2,904	2,104	1,501	28,159	310,960	61,939	6,615
Worcester, MA-CT	4,150.9	4,406	62.3	0.6	4.1	0.3	4.0	2,690.1	2,855	3,406	2,121	56,332	470,790	76,748	9,359
Yakima, WA	1,133.6	4,536	60.9	0.9	4.8	0.2	4.6	803.9	3,217	1,289	711	16,132	116,870	53,353	5,008
York-Hanover, PA	1,967.7	4,417	49.6	3.5	3.5	10.0	2.9	2,310.6	5,187	4,354	1,410	14,968	230,650	65,754	6,869
Youngstown-Warren-Boardman, OH-PA	2,147.6	3,966	54.3	3.7	6.6	4.1	3.3	1,548.0	2,858	2,005	1,325	25,885	265,510	51,823	4,904
Yuba City, CA	1,093.9	6,331	47.0	6.3	5.3	8.8	2.0	998.8	5,781	1,612	4,281	10,698	75,120	54,599	4,677
Yuma, AZ	662.2	3,161	48.5	1.4	7.5	2.1	4.6	438.5	2,093	3,761	4,376	10,355	94,520	45,331	3,514

1. Based on the resident population estimated as of July 1 of the year shown.

PART D.

Cities of 25,000 or More

(For explanation of symbols, see page viii)

City Highlights and Rankings

Figure D-1. Ten Fastest Growing Cities Among the 75 Largest, 2020–2021

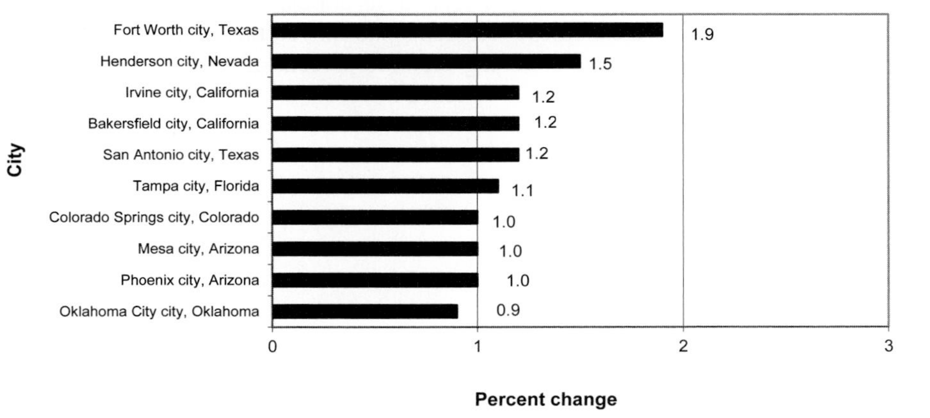

In 2021, 9 cities had more than 1 million residents, led by New York City with nearly 8.5 million people, Los Angeles with over 3.8 million people, and Chicago with nearly 2.7 million people. California had 15 cities among the nation's 75 most populous, as well as 3 among the top 15 (Los Angeles, San Diego, and San Jose). Texas had 9 cities in the top 75 and 5 among the top 15 (Houston, San Antonio, Dallas, Austin, and Fort Worth).

Among the largest cities, 53 had growth rates equaling 5 percent or higher from 2010 to 2020 and 35 had growth rates at 10 percent or higher. Many of these cities were in the South. Irvine, CA, had the highest growth rate at 43.9 percent. Texas had two cities in the top 10 (Austin and Fort Worth), as did Colorado (Denver and Aurora) and North Carolina (Charlotte and Durham). Forty-seven of the largest cities equaled or exceeded the U.S. growth rate of 7.4 percent.

Among the 75 largest cities, 9 lost population between 2010 and 2020. Detroit lost 10.4 percent of its population, while Cleveland dropped by 6.0 percent.

New Orleans, with an 11.7 percent increase, was among the top 30 cities for population growth. Though New Orleans lost more than half of its population after Hurricane Katrina in 2005, it has grown by more than two-thirds between 2006 and 2020. It was the 28th fastest growing city from 2010 to 2020, but its 2021 population is still about 18 percent below its pre-Katrina total.

Among all cities of 25,000 or more, 65 cities had unemployment rates of 10 percent or more, significantly lower than in 2020 when 345 cities had unemployment rates of 10 percent or more. Fourteen of the 25 cities with the highest unemployment rates were located in California; 3 were in New Jersey; 2 each were in Texas, Pennsylvania, and Michigan; while Arizona and Illinois each had one. Among the largest cities, Detroit, MI, had the highest unemployment rate at 13.5 percent followed by Newark, NJ, at 10.6 percent. Two cities in Nebraska had the lowest unemployment rates among the large cities: Lincoln at 2.5 percent and Omaha at 3.1 percent.

Among all cities, 439 had unemployment rates of 4.0 percent or lower compared with only 26 from last year. Zionsville, IN, had the lowest unemployment rate at 1.8 percent followed by Kearney City, NE; Trussville, AL; and Logan City, UT, at 2.0 percent. No unemployment data are available for Hawaiian cities, but Honolulu County had an unemployment rate of 5.3 percent.

While the 2020 census provides updated counts of the population and basic demographic characteristics, updated information on social and economic characteristics is now obtained through the ongoing American Community Survey (ACS). For states, counties, and metropolitan areas, the official intercensal estimates are provided by age, sex, race, and Hispanic origin through the Population Estimates Program. Estimates of these demographic characteristics are not included for cities through the Population Estimates Program but are available through the ACS. This book includes ACS 5-year estimates for 2016 through 2020; including data on education, income, housing characteristics, and more.

Among the largest cities, San Francisco, San Jose, and Irvine were the top 3 for both median income and median housing value from 2016 to 2020. Seattle, San Diego, and Washington, DC, also ranked in the top 10 for both median income and housing value. Plano, TX, ranked 5th for median household income, but its median housing value ranked only 22nd among large cities. Los Angeles and New York ranked 7th and 8th for median housing value, but their median household incomes ranked 30th and 24th among large cities. San Francisco topped the ranking with an estimated median housing value of $1,152,300. Detroit and Cleveland had the lowest median housing values among large cities, from 2016 to 2020, at $52,700 and $73,400, respectively. They also had the lowest median incomes among the largest cities.

Among the 75 largest cities from 2016 to 2020, there were 6 cities where 10 percent or more of residents had moved from another state or county within the 5-year period. This may result from population growth: Irvine, CA, had one of the highest growth rates in recent years as well as one of the highest proportions of people who had moved there in the past year. Irvine has a strong technological economy as well as a large university. Other cities have large shifts because of student or military population groups: East Lansing, MI—site of Michigan State University—lost 3.0 percent of its population from 2010 to 2020 but 26.4 percent of its residents had moved there during the 2016–2020 period, reflecting the 60.0 percent of residents who were between the ages of 18 and 24.

75 Largest Cities by 2021 Population
Selected rankings

Population, 2021			Land area, 2021				Population density, 2021			
Population rank	City	Population [col 2]	Population rank	Land area rank	City	Land area (square miles) [col 1]	Population rank	Density rank	City	Density (per square kilometer) [col 4]
1	New York city, New York	8,467,513	73	1	Anchorage municipality, Alaska	1,706.9	1	1	New York city, New York	28,178
2	Los Angeles city, California	3,849,297	12	2	Jacksonville city, Florida	747.3	75	2	Jersey City city, New Jersey	19,315
3	Chicago city, Illinois	2,696,555	4	3	Houston city, Texas	640.4	17	3	San Francisco city, California	17,382
4	Houston city, Texas	2,288,250	20	4	Oklahoma City city, Oklahoma	606.5	24	4	Boston city, Massachusetts	13,556
5	Phoenix city, Arizona	1,624,569	5	5	Phoenix city, Arizona	518.3	66	5	Newark city, New Jersey	12,748
6	Philadelphia city, Pennsylvania	1,576,251	7	6	San Antonio city, Texas	498.4	44	6	Miami city, Florida	12,219
7	San Antonio city, Texas	1,451,853	21	7	Nashville-Davidson metro, Tennessee	475.8	3	7	Chicago city, Illinois	11,843
8	San Diego city, California	1,381,611	2	8	Los Angeles city, California	469.5	6	8	Philadelphia city, Pennsylvania	11,728
9	Dallas city, Texas	1,288,457	15	9	Indianapolis city, Indiana	361.6	62	9	Santa Ana city, California	11,294
10	San Jose city, California	983,489	13	10	Fort Worth city, Texas	348.6	23	10	Washington city, District of Columbia	10,966
11	Austin city, Texas	964,177	9	11	Dallas city, Texas	339.6	43	11	Long Beach city, California	8,995
12	Jacksonville city, Florida	954,614	8	12	San Diego city, California	325.9	18	12	Seattle city, Washington	8,748
13	Fort Worth city, Texas	935,508	11	13	Austin city, Texas	319.9	2	13	Los Angeles city, California	8,199
14	Columbus city, Ohio	906,528	37	14	Kansas City city, Missouri	314.7	46	14	Minneapolis city, Minnesota	7,877
15	Indianapolis city, Indiana	882,039	16	15	Charlotte city, North Carolina	309.2	45	15	Oakland city, California	7,761
16	Charlotte city, North Carolina	879,709	1	16	New York city, New York	300.5	30	16	Baltimore city, Maryland	7,126
17	San Francisco city, California	815,201	29	17	Memphis city, Tennessee	294.9	55	17	Anaheim city, California	6,878
18	Seattle city, Washington	733,919	59	18	Lexington-Fayette urban county, Kentucky	283.6	31	18	Milwaukee city, Wisconsin	5,918
19	Denver city, Colorado	711,463	28	19	Louisville/Jefferson County metro, Kentucky	263.2	67	19	St. Paul city, Minnesota	5,908
20	Oklahoma City city, Oklahoma	687,725	22	20	El Paso city, Texas	258.4	56	20	Urban Honolulu CDP, Hawaii	5,711
21	Nashville-Davidson metro, Tennessee	678,851	42	21	Virginia Beach city, Virginia	244.7	10	21	San Jose city, California	5,516
22	El Paso city, Texas	678,415	34	22	Tucson city, Arizona	241.0	68	22	Pittsburgh city, Pennsylvania	5,423
23	Washington city, District of Columbia	670,050	3	23	Chicago city, Illinois	227.7	35	23	Sacramento city, California	5,325
24	Boston city, Massachusetts	654,776	14	24	Columbus city, Ohio	220.1	58	24	Stockton city, California	5,162
25	Las Vegas city, Nevada	646,790	47	25	Tulsa city, Oklahoma	197.8	26	25	Portland city, Oregon	4,803
26	Portland city, Oregon	641,162	40	26	Colorado Springs city, Colorado	195.8	70	26	St. Louis city, Missouri	4,754
27	Detroit city, Michigan	632,464	32	27	Albuquerque city, New Mexico	187.3	54	27	Cleveland city, Ohio	4,736
28	Louisville/Jefferson County metro, Kentucky	628,594	10	28	San Jose city, California	178.3	64	28	Irvine city, California	4,711
29	Memphis city, Tennessee	628,127	53	29	New Orleans city, Louisiana	169.5	33	29	Fresno city, California	4,710
30	Baltimore city, Maryland	576,498	60	30	Corpus Christi city, Texas	162.2	19	30	Denver city, Colorado	4,647
31	Milwaukee city, Wisconsin	569,330	49	31	Wichita city, Kansas	162.0	25	31	Las Vegas city, Nevada	4,561
32	Albuquerque city, New Mexico	562,599	51	32	Aurora city, Colorado	160.0	27	32	Detroit city, Michigan	4,560
33	Fresno city, California	544,510	19	33	Denver city, Colorado	153.1	8	33	San Diego city, California	4,239
34	Tucson city, Arizona	543,242	48	34	Bakersfield city, California	149.8	14	34	Columbus city, Ohio	4,119
35	Sacramento city, California	525,041	41	35	Raleigh city, North Carolina	147.1	50	35	Arlington city, Texas	4,100
36	Mesa city, Arizona	509,475	39	36	Omaha city, Nebraska	142.5	72	36	Plano city, Texas	4,020
37	Kansas City city, Missouri	508,394	25	37	Las Vegas city, Nevada	141.8	65	37	Cincinnati city, Ohio	3,966
38	Atlanta city, Georgia	496,461	36	38	Mesa city, Arizona	138.8	61	38	Riverside city, California	3,907
39	Omaha city, Nebraska	487,300	27	39	Detroit city, Michigan	138.7	9	39	Dallas city, Texas	3,794
40	Colorado Springs city, Colorado	483,956	38	40	Atlanta city, Georgia	135.3	36	40	Mesa city, Arizona	3,671
41	Raleigh city, North Carolina	469,124	6	41	Philadelphia city, Pennsylvania	134.4	38	41	Atlanta city, Georgia	3,669
42	Virginia Beach city, Virginia	457,672	26	42	Portland city, Oregon	133.5	4	42	Houston city, Texas	3,573
43	Long Beach city, California	456,062	69	43	Greensboro city, North Carolina	130.3	39	43	Omaha city, Nebraska	3,420
44	Miami city, Florida	439,890	33	44	Fresno city, California	115.6	52	44	Tampa city, Florida	3,395
45	Oakland city, California	433,823	52	45	Tampa city, Florida	114.0	41	45	Raleigh city, North Carolina	3,189
46	Minneapolis city, Minnesota	425,336	74	46	Durham city, North Carolina	113.5	5	46	Phoenix city, Arizona	3,134
47	Tulsa city, Oklahoma	411,401	63	47	Orlando city, Florida	110.9	57	47	Henderson city, Nevada	3,028
48	Bakersfield city, California	407,615	57	48	Henderson city, Nevada	106.4	11	48	Austin city, Texas	3,014
49	Wichita city, Kansas	395,699	35	49	Sacramento city, California	98.6	32	49	Albuquerque city, New Mexico	3,004
50	Arlington city, Texas	392,786	71	50	Lincoln city, Nebraska	97.7	71	50	Lincoln city, Nebraska	2,996
51	Aurora city, Colorado	389,347	31	51	Milwaukee city, Wisconsin	96.2	7	51	San Antonio city, Texas	2,913
52	Tampa city, Florida	387,050	50	52	Arlington city, Texas	95.8	16	52	Charlotte city, North Carolina	2,845
53	New Orleans city, Louisiana	376,971	18	53	Seattle city, Washington	83.9	63	53	Orlando city, Florida	2,788
54	Cleveland city, Ohio	367,991	61	54	Riverside city, California	81.2	48	54	Bakersfield city, California	2,721
55	Anaheim city, California	345,940	30	55	Baltimore city, Maryland	80.9	13	55	Fort Worth city, Texas	2,684
56	Urban Honolulu CDP, Hawaii	345,510	65	56	Cincinnati city, Ohio	77.9	22	56	El Paso city, Texas	2,625
57	Henderson city, Nevada	322,178	54	57	Cleveland city, Ohio	77.7	74	57	Durham city, North Carolina	2,516
58	Stockton city, California	322,120	72	58	Plano city, Texas	71.7	40	58	Colorado Springs city, Colorado	2,472
59	Lexington-Fayette urban county, Kentucky	321,793	64	59	Irvine city, California	65.6	49	59	Wichita city, Kansas	2,443
60	Corpus Christi city, Texas	317,773	58	60	Stockton city, California	62.4	15	60	Indianapolis city, Indiana	2,439
61	Riverside city, California	317,261	70	61	St. Louis city, Missouri	61.7	51	61	Aurora city, Colorado	2,433
62	Santa Ana city, California	309,441	23	62	Washington city, District of Columbia	61.1	28	62	Louisville/Jefferson County metro, Kentucky	2,388
63	Orlando city, Florida	309,154	56	63	Urban Honolulu CDP, Hawaii	60.5	69	63	Greensboro city, North Carolina	2,289
64	Irvine city, California	309,031	45	64	Oakland city, California	55.9	34	64	Tucson city, Arizona	2,254
65	Cincinnati city, Ohio	308,935	68	65	Pittsburgh city, Pennsylvania	55.4	53	65	New Orleans city, Louisiana	2,224
66	Newark city, New Jersey	307,220	46	66	Minneapolis city, Minnesota	54.0	29	66	Memphis city, Tennessee	2,130
67	St. Paul city, Minnesota	307,193	67	67	St. Paul city, Minnesota	52.0	47	67	Tulsa city, Oklahoma	2,080
68	Pittsburgh city, Pennsylvania	300,431	43	68	Long Beach city, California	50.7	60	68	Corpus Christi city, Texas	1,959
69	Greensboro city, North Carolina	298,263	55	69	Anaheim city, California	50.3	42	69	Virginia Beach city, Virginia	1,870
70	St. Louis city, Missouri	293,310	24	70	Boston city, Massachusetts	48.3	37	70	Kansas City city, Missouri	1,616
71	Lincoln city, Nebraska	292,657	17	71	San Francisco city, California	46.9	21	71	Nashville-Davidson metro, Tennessee	1,427
72	Plano city, Texas	288,253	44	72	Miami city, Florida	36.0	12	72	Jacksonville city, Florida	1,277
73	Anchorage municipality, Alaska	288,121	62	73	Santa Ana city, California	27.4	59	73	Lexington-Fayette urban county, Kentucky	1,135
74	Durham city, North Carolina	285,527	66	74	Newark city, New Jersey	24.1	20	74	Oklahoma City city, Oklahoma	1,134
75	Jersey City city, New Jersey	283,927	75	75	Jersey City city, New Jersey	14.7	73	75	Anchorage municipality, Alaska	169

75 Largest Cities by 2021 Population
Selected rankings

Percent population change, 2010–2020

Population rank	Percent change rank	City	Percent change [col 26]
64	1	Irvine city, California	43.9
63	2	Orlando city, Florida	28.9
57	3	Henderson city, Nevada	23.6
13	4	Fort Worth city, Texas	23.3
74	5	Durham city, North Carolina	22.9
18	6	Seattle city, Washington	20.8
11	7	Austin city, Texas	19.7
19	8	Denver city, Colorado	19.4
16	9	Charlotte city, North Carolina	18.9
51	9	Aurora city, Colorado	18.9
75	11	Jersey City city, New Jersey	18.1
20	12	Oklahoma City city, Oklahoma	17.4
38	13	Atlanta city, Georgia	16.8
48	14	Bakersfield city, California	15.9
41	15	Raleigh city, North Carolina	15.7
12	16	Jacksonville city, Florida	15.6
14	17	Columbus city, Ohio	14.8
40	17	Colorado Springs city, Colorado	14.8
36	19	Mesa city, Arizona	14.7
23	20	Washington city, District of Columbia	14.6
21	21	Nashville-Davidson metro, Tennessee	14.3
52	22	Tampa city, Florida	13.8
71	23	Lincoln city, Nebraska	12.5
45	24	Oakland city, California	12.4
66	25	Newark city, New Jersey	12.3
35	26	Sacramento city, California	12.1
46	27	Minneapolis city, Minnesota	12.0
26	28	Portland city, Oregon	11.7
53	28	New Orleans city, Louisiana	11.7
5	30	Phoenix city, Arizona	11.1
69	31	Greensboro city, North Carolina	10.8
44	32	Miami city, Florida	10.7
37	33	Kansas City city, Missouri	10.5
4	34	Houston city, Texas	10.0
72	34	Plano city, Texas	10.0
25	36	Las Vegas city, Nevada	9.8
58	37	Stockton city, California	9.7
24	38	Boston city, Massachusetts	9.5
67	39	St. Paul city, Minnesota	9.2
33	40	Fresno city, California	9.1
59	41	Lexington-Fayette urban county, Kentucky	9.0
9	42	Dallas city, Texas	8.9
17	43	San Francisco city, California	8.5
15	44	Indianapolis city, Indiana	8.2
7	45	San Antonio city, Texas	8.1
50	46	Arlington city, Texas	8.0
1	47	New York city, New York	7.7
39	48	Omaha city, Nebraska	6.9
8	49	San Diego city, California	6.5
10	49	San Jose city, California	6.5
28	51	Louisville/Jefferson County metro, Kentucky	6.2
47	52	Tulsa city, Oklahoma	5.3
6	53	Philadelphia city, Pennsylvania	5.1
42	54	Virginia Beach city, Virginia	4.9
22	55	El Paso city, Texas	4.7
65	56	Cincinnati city, Ohio	4.4
60	57	Corpus Christi city, Texas	4.2
56	58	Urban Honolulu CDP, Hawaii	3.9
49	59	Wichita city, Kansas	3.8
32	60	Albuquerque city, New Mexico	3.4
61	60	Riverside city, California	3.4
55	62	Anaheim city, California	3.2
34	63	Tucson city, Arizona	2.8
2	64	Los Angeles city, California	2.7
3	65	Chicago city, Illinois	1.9
43	66	Long Beach city, California	0.9
73	67	Anchorage municipality, Alaska	-0.3
68	68	Pittsburgh city, Pennsylvania	-0.7
31	69	Milwaukee city, Wisconsin	-2.9
29	70	Memphis city, Tennessee	-3.0
62	71	Santa Ana city, California	-4.4
30	72	Baltimore city, Maryland	-5.6
70	72	St. Louis city, Missouri	-5.6
54	74	Cleveland city, Ohio	-6.0
27	75	Detroit city, Michigan	-10.4

Percent White alone, 2020

Population rank	White rank	City	Percent White [col 5]
71	1	Lincoln city, Nebraska	78.7
40	2	Colorado Springs city, Colorado	70.3
26	3	Portland city, Oregon	68.8
59	4	Lexington-Fayette urban county, Kentucky	68.3
36	5	Mesa city, Arizona	65.7
39	6	Omaha city, Nebraska	65.5
28	7	Louisville/Jefferson County metro, Kentucky	63.8
49	8	Wichita city, Kansas	63.4
57	9	Henderson city, Nevada	63.2
68	10	Pittsburgh city, Pennsylvania	62.7
18	11	Seattle city, Washington	61.3
42	12	Virginia Beach city, Virginia	60.7
19	13	Denver city, Colorado	60.6
46	14	Minneapolis city, Minnesota	59.5
73	15	Anchorage municipality, Alaska	56.5
21	16	Nashville-Davidson metro, Tennessee	56.0
37	17	Kansas City city, Missouri	55.3
11	18	Austin city, Texas	54.7
34	19	Tucson city, Arizona	54.5
20	20	Oklahoma City city, Oklahoma	53.6
60	20	Corpus Christi city, Texas	53.6
41	22	Raleigh city, North Carolina	53.3
14	23	Columbus city, Ohio	53.2
15	24	Indianapolis city, Indiana	52.2
32	24	Albuquerque city, New Mexico	52.2
47	26	Tulsa city, Oklahoma	51.8
67	27	St. Paul city, Minnesota	50.5
12	28	Jacksonville city, Florida	50.1
5	29	Phoenix city, Arizona	49.7
52	29	Tampa city, Florida	49.7
72	31	Plano city, Texas	49.5
65	32	Cincinnati city, Ohio	47.7
24	33	Boston city, Massachusetts	47.1
51	33	Aurora city, Colorado	47.1
8	35	San Diego city, California	46.4
25	36	Las Vegas city, Nevada	46.0
13	37	Fort Worth city, Texas	44.9
7	38	San Antonio city, Texas	44.3
70	39	St. Louis city, Missouri	43.9
16	40	Charlotte city, North Carolina	41.7
17	41	San Francisco city, California	41.3
50	42	Arlington city, Texas	40.5
74	43	Durham city, North Carolina	40.2
63	44	Orlando city, Florida	40.0
69	44	Greensboro city, North Carolina	40.0
38	46	Atlanta city, Georgia	39.8
23	47	Washington city, District of Columbia	39.6
48	48	Bakersfield city, California	38.9
64	49	Irvine city, California	37.7
22	50	El Paso city, Texas	36.8
61	51	Riverside city, California	36.5
6	52	Philadelphia city, Pennsylvania	36.3
9	53	Dallas city, Texas	36.1
31	53	Milwaukee city, Wisconsin	36.1
3	55	Chicago city, Illinois	35.9
2	56	Los Angeles city, California	34.9
35	57	Sacramento city, California	34.8
54	58	Cleveland city, Ohio	34.5
1	59	New York city, New York	34.1
33	60	Fresno city, California	33.2
53	61	New Orleans city, Louisiana	32.9
4	62	Houston city, Texas	32.1
43	63	Long Beach city, California	32.0
55	64	Anaheim city, California	31.1
44	65	Miami city, Florida	30.2
45	66	Oakland city, California	30.0
30	67	Baltimore city, Maryland	27.8
10	68	San Jose city, California	27.3
75	68	Jersey City city, New Jersey	27.3
29	70	Memphis city, Tennessee	25.0
58	71	Stockton city, California	23.5
62	72	Santa Ana city, California	18.5
56	73	Urban Honolulu CDP, Hawaii	16.4
66	74	Newark city, New Jersey	12.1
27	75	Detroit city, Michigan	10.7

Percent Black alone, 2020

Population rank	Black rank	City	Percent Black [col 6]
27	1	Detroit city, Michigan	77.7
29	2	Memphis city, Tennessee	61.6
30	3	Baltimore city, Maryland	57.8
53	4	New Orleans city, Louisiana	54.2
66	5	Newark city, New Jersey	49.4
54	6	Cleveland city, Ohio	48.4
38	7	Atlanta city, Georgia	47.2
70	8	St. Louis city, Missouri	43.0
69	9	Greensboro city, North Carolina	42.0
23	10	Washington city, District of Columbia	41.4
65	11	Cincinnati city, Ohio	40.6
6	12	Philadelphia city, Pennsylvania	39.3
31	13	Milwaukee city, Wisconsin	38.6
74	14	Durham city, North Carolina	36.2
16	15	Charlotte city, North Carolina	33.1
12	16	Jacksonville city, Florida	30.6
3	17	Chicago city, Illinois	29.2
14	18	Columbus city, Ohio	28.6
15	19	Indianapolis city, Indiana	27.8
41	20	Raleigh city, North Carolina	26.3
37	21	Kansas City city, Missouri	26.1
21	22	Nashville-Davidson metro, Tennessee	24.2
63	23	Orlando city, Florida	23.8
9	24	Dallas city, Texas	23.3
50	25	Arlington city, Texas	22.9
68	26	Pittsburgh city, Pennsylvania	22.8
4	27	Houston city, Texas	22.6
1	28	New York city, New York	22.1
52	29	Tampa city, Florida	21.9
28	30	Louisville/Jefferson County metro, Kentucky	21.6
45	31	Oakland city, California	21.3
24	32	Boston city, Massachusetts	20.6
75	33	Jersey City city, New Jersey	19.9
13	34	Fort Worth city, Texas	19.6
46	35	Minneapolis city, Minnesota	19.1
42	36	Virginia Beach city, Virginia	18.6
67	37	St. Paul city, Minnesota	16.8
51	38	Aurora city, Colorado	15.9
47	39	Tulsa city, Oklahoma	14.9
59	39	Lexington-Fayette urban county, Kentucky	14.9
20	41	Oklahoma City city, Oklahoma	14.0
35	42	Sacramento city, California	13.2
25	43	Las Vegas city, Nevada	12.9
44	43	Miami city, Florida	12.9
58	45	Stockton city, California	12.6
43	46	Long Beach city, California	12.5
39	47	Omaha city, Nebraska	12.4
49	48	Wichita city, Kansas	11.0
19	49	Denver city, Colorado	8.9
72	49	Plano city, Texas	8.9
2	51	Los Angeles city, California	8.6
5	52	Phoenix city, Arizona	7.8
33	53	Fresno city, California	7.6
11	54	Austin city, Texas	7.3
7	55	San Antonio city, Texas	7.2
18	56	Seattle city, Washington	7.0
48	56	Bakersfield city, California	7.0
57	58	Henderson city, Nevada	6.7
61	59	Riverside city, California	6.4
8	60	San Diego city, California	5.9
26	60	Portland city, Oregon	5.9
40	60	Colorado Springs city, Colorado	5.9
34	63	Tucson city, Arizona	5.6
17	64	San Francisco city, California	5.3
73	65	Anchorage municipality, Alaska	5.0
71	66	Lincoln city, Nebraska	4.7
60	67	Corpus Christi city, Texas	4.4
36	68	Mesa city, Arizona	4.2
22	69	El Paso city, Texas	3.7
32	70	Albuquerque city, New Mexico	3.5
10	71	San Jose city, California	2.9
55	72	Anaheim city, California	2.7
64	73	Irvine city, California	2.3
56	74	Urban Honolulu CDP, Hawaii	1.7
62	75	Santa Ana city, California	1.1

75 Largest Cities by 2021 Population
Selected rankings

Percent American Indian, Alaska Native alone, 2020

Population rank	American Indian, Alaska Native rank	City	Percent American Indian, Alaska Native [col 7]
73	1	Anchorage municipality, Alaska	8.1
32	2	Albuquerque city, New Mexico	5.6
47	3	Tulsa city, Oklahoma	5.2
62	4	Santa Ana city, California	3.7
20	5	Oklahoma City city, Oklahoma	3.4
34	6	Tucson city, Arizona	2.9
36	7	Mesa city, Arizona	2.7
5	8	Phoenix city, Arizona	2.6
33	9	Fresno city, California	2.4
61	10	Riverside city, California	2.0
45	11	Oakland city, California	1.9
48	12	Bakersfield city, California	1.8
55	12	Anaheim city, California	1.8
2	14	Los Angeles city, California	1.7
46	14	Minneapolis city, Minnesota	1.7
58	14	Stockton city, California	1.7
19	17	Denver city, Colorado	1.5
43	17	Long Beach city, California	1.5
10	19	San Jose city, California	1.4
35	19	Sacramento city, California	1.4
51	19	Aurora city, Colorado	1.4
3	22	Chicago city, Illinois	1.3
49	22	Wichita city, Kansas	1.3
4	24	Houston city, Texas	1.2
7	24	San Antonio city, Texas	1.2
9	24	Dallas city, Texas	1.2
22	27	El Paso city, Texas	1.1
25	27	Las Vegas city, Nevada	1.1
26	27	Portland city, Oregon	1.1
39	27	Omaha city, Nebraska	1.1
40	27	Colorado Springs city, Colorado	1.1
50	27	Arlington city, Texas	1.1
1	33	New York city, New York	1.0
11	33	Austin city, Texas	1.0
67	33	St. Paul city, Minnesota	1.0
8	36	San Diego city, California	0.9
13	36	Fort Worth city, Texas	0.9
31	36	Milwaukee city, Wisconsin	0.9
60	36	Corpus Christi city, Texas	0.9
71	36	Lincoln city, Nebraska	0.9
17	41	San Francisco city, California	0.7
18	41	Seattle city, Washington	0.7
57	41	Henderson city, Nevada	0.7
66	41	Newark city, New Jersey	0.7
72	41	Plano city, Texas	0.7
74	41	Durham city, North Carolina	0.7
75	41	Jersey City city, New Jersey	0.7
16	48	Charlotte city, North Carolina	0.6
21	48	Nashville-Davidson metro, Tennessee	0.6
37	48	Kansas City city, Missouri	0.6
41	48	Raleigh city, North Carolina	0.6
69	48	Greensboro city, North Carolina	0.6
15	53	Indianapolis city, Indiana	0.5
23	53	Washington city, District of Columbia	0.5
27	53	Detroit city, Michigan	0.5
6	56	Philadelphia city, Pennsylvania	0.4
12	56	Jacksonville city, Florida	0.4
14	56	Columbus city, Ohio	0.4
24	56	Boston city, Massachusetts	0.4
29	56	Memphis city, Tennessee	0.4
30	56	Baltimore city, Maryland	0.4
42	56	Virginia Beach city, Virginia	0.4
44	56	Miami city, Florida	0.4
52	56	Tampa city, Florida	0.4
54	56	Cleveland city, Ohio	0.4
63	56	Orlando city, Florida	0.4
28	67	Louisville/Jefferson County metro, Kentucky	0.3
38	67	Atlanta city, Georgia	0.3
53	67	New Orleans city, Louisiana	0.3
59	67	Lexington-Fayette urban county, Kentucky	0.3
64	67	Irvine city, California	0.3
65	67	Cincinnati city, Ohio	0.3
70	67	St. Louis city, Missouri	0.3
56	74	Urban Honolulu CDP, Hawaii	0.2
68	74	Pittsburgh city, Pennsylvania	0.2

Percent Asian and Pacific Islander alone, 2020

Population rank	Asian and Pacific Islander rank	City	Percent Asian and Pacific Islander [col 8]
56	1	Urban Honolulu CDP, Hawaii	52.9
64	2	Irvine city, California	45.6
10	3	San Jose city, California	38.5
17	4	San Francisco city, California	33.9
75	5	Jersey City city, New Jersey	28.0
72	6	Plano city, Texas	24.2
58	7	Stockton city, California	22.0
35	8	Sacramento city, California	19.9
67	9	St. Paul city, Minnesota	19.2
8	10	San Diego city, California	17.9
55	11	Anaheim city, California	17.7
18	12	Seattle city, Washington	17.1
45	13	Oakland city, California	16.1
1	14	New York city, New York	15.7
33	15	Fresno city, California	14.7
43	16	Long Beach city, California	13.0
62	17	Santa Ana city, California	12.3
2	18	Los Angeles city, California	11.9
24	19	Boston city, Massachusetts	11.3
73	20	Anchorage municipality, Alaska	9.5
57	21	Henderson city, Nevada	9.3
11	22	Austin city, Texas	9.0
6	23	Philadelphia city, Pennsylvania	8.3
26	24	Portland city, Oregon	8.1
48	25	Bakersfield city, California	7.8
50	26	Arlington city, Texas	7.7
42	27	Virginia Beach city, Virginia	7.5
61	28	Riverside city, California	7.4
4	29	Houston city, Texas	7.3
25	30	Las Vegas city, Nevada	7.2
16	31	Charlotte city, North Carolina	7.1
3	32	Chicago city, Illinois	7.0
68	33	Pittsburgh city, Pennsylvania	6.5
51	34	Aurora city, Colorado	6.4
14	35	Columbus city, Ohio	6.2
46	36	Minneapolis city, Minnesota	5.8
74	37	Durham city, North Carolina	5.6
52	38	Tampa city, Florida	5.4
13	39	Fort Worth city, Texas	5.2
31	39	Milwaukee city, Wisconsin	5.2
12	41	Jacksonville city, Florida	5.1
49	41	Wichita city, Kansas	5.1
69	41	Greensboro city, North Carolina	5.1
41	44	Raleigh city, North Carolina	5.0
23	45	Washington city, District of Columbia	4.9
71	46	Lincoln city, Nebraska	4.8
20	47	Oklahoma City city, Oklahoma	4.6
39	47	Omaha city, Nebraska	4.6
38	49	Atlanta city, Georgia	4.5
63	50	Orlando city, Florida	4.3
15	51	Indianapolis city, Indiana	4.2
59	51	Lexington-Fayette urban county, Kentucky	4.2
5	53	Phoenix city, Arizona	4.1
70	53	St. Louis city, Missouri	4.1
19	55	Denver city, Colorado	3.9
21	55	Nashville-Davidson metro, Tennessee	3.9
9	57	Dallas city, Texas	3.7
30	58	Baltimore city, Maryland	3.6
28	59	Louisville/Jefferson County metro, Kentucky	3.5
47	59	Tulsa city, Oklahoma	3.5
32	61	Albuquerque city, New Mexico	3.4
40	61	Colorado Springs city, Colorado	3.4
7	63	San Antonio city, Texas	3.3
34	64	Tucson city, Arizona	3.2
37	65	Kansas City city, Missouri	3.1
53	66	New Orleans city, Louisiana	2.8
54	66	Cleveland city, Ohio	2.8
36	68	Mesa city, Arizona	2.6
60	69	Corpus Christi city, Texas	2.5
65	69	Cincinnati city, Ohio	2.5
29	71	Memphis city, Tennessee	1.8
27	72	Detroit city, Michigan	1.6
66	72	Newark city, New Jersey	1.6
22	74	El Paso city, Texas	1.5
44	75	Miami city, Florida	1.4

Percent Hispanic or Latino,[1] 2020

Population rank	Hispanic or Latino rank	City	Percent Hispanic or Latino [col 12]
22	1	El Paso city, Texas	81.2
62	2	Santa Ana city, California	76.7
44	3	Miami city, Florida	70.2
7	4	San Antonio city, Texas	63.9
60	5	Corpus Christi city, Texas	60.7
61	6	Riverside city, California	54.7
55	7	Anaheim city, California	53.8
48	8	Bakersfield city, California	52.7
33	9	Fresno city, California	50.5
32	10	Albuquerque city, New Mexico	47.7
2	11	Los Angeles city, California	46.9
58	12	Stockton city, California	44.1
4	13	Houston city, Texas	44.0
43	14	Long Beach city, California	43.3
9	15	Dallas city, Texas	42.3
34	16	Tucson city, Arizona	42.2
5	17	Phoenix city, Arizona	41.1
66	18	Newark city, New Jersey	36.4
13	19	Fort Worth city, Texas	34.8
25	20	Las Vegas city, Nevada	33.3
63	21	Orlando city, Florida	32.9
11	22	Austin city, Texas	32.5
10	23	San Jose city, California	31.2
50	24	Arlington city, Texas	30.7
51	25	Aurora city, Colorado	30.3
3	26	Chicago city, Illinois	29.8
8	27	San Diego city, California	29.7
35	28	Sacramento city, California	28.8
45	28	Oakland city, California	28.8
1	30	New York city, New York	28.3
19	31	Denver city, Colorado	27.9
36	32	Mesa city, Arizona	27.3
52	33	Tampa city, Florida	25.6
75	34	Jersey City city, New Jersey	24.9
20	35	Oklahoma City city, Oklahoma	21.3
31	36	Milwaukee city, Wisconsin	20.1
47	37	Tulsa city, Oklahoma	19.1
24	38	Boston city, Massachusetts	18.7
40	39	Colorado Springs city, Colorado	18.4
49	40	Wichita city, Kansas	18.3
57	41	Henderson city, Nevada	17.9
16	42	Charlotte city, North Carolina	16.3
72	43	Plano city, Texas	16.0
17	44	San Francisco city, California	15.6
39	45	Omaha city, Nebraska	15.5
74	46	Durham city, North Carolina	15.3
6	47	Philadelphia city, Pennsylvania	14.9
21	48	Nashville-Davidson metro, Tennessee	13.7
54	49	Cleveland city, Ohio	13.1
15	50	Indianapolis city, Indiana	13.0
41	51	Raleigh city, North Carolina	12.9
37	52	Kansas City city, Missouri	12.0
64	53	Irvine city, California	11.7
12	54	Jacksonville city, Florida	11.6
23	55	Washington city, District of Columbia	11.3
26	56	Portland city, Oregon	11.1
46	57	Minneapolis city, Minnesota	10.4
69	58	Greensboro city, North Carolina	10.2
29	59	Memphis city, Tennessee	9.8
67	60	St. Paul city, Minnesota	9.7
59	61	Lexington-Fayette urban county, Kentucky	9.2
73	62	Anchorage municipality, Alaska	9.1
42	63	Virginia Beach city, Virginia	8.8
71	64	Lincoln city, Nebraska	8.6
18	65	Seattle city, Washington	8.2
53	66	New Orleans city, Louisiana	8.1
27	67	Detroit city, Michigan	8.0
30	68	Baltimore city, Maryland	7.8
14	69	Columbus city, Ohio	7.7
28	70	Louisville/Jefferson County metro, Kentucky	7.5
56	71	Urban Honolulu CDP, Hawaii	6.3
38	72	Atlanta city, Georgia	6.0
65	73	Cincinnati city, Ohio	5.1
70	73	St. Louis city, Missouri	5.1
68	75	Pittsburgh city, Pennsylvania	3.8

75 Largest Cities by 2021 Population
Selected rankings

Percent under 18 years old, 2016-2020				Percent 65 years old and over, 2016-2020				Percent high school graduate or less, 2016-2020			
Population rank	Under 18 years old rank	City	Percent under 18 years old [col 14]	Population rank	65 years old and over rank	City	Percent 65 years old and over [col 20]	Population rank	Percent high school graduate or less rank	City	Percent high school graduate or less [col 40]
48	1	Bakersfield city, California	29.9	56	1	Urban Honolulu CDP, Hawaii	20.4	62	1	Santa Ana city, California	61.2
33	2	Fresno city, California	28.2	57	2	Henderson city, Nevada	20.3	66	2	Newark city, New Jersey	59.9
58	3	Stockton city, California	27.8	36	3	Mesa city, Arizona	16.6	58	3	Stockton city, California	51.6
13	4	Fort Worth city, Texas	27.2	44	3	Miami city, Florida	16.6	54	4	Cleveland city, Ohio	50.9
22	5	El Paso city, Texas	26.6	28	5	Louisville/Jefferson County metro, Kentucky	16.1	27	5	Detroit city, Michigan	50.3
31	6	Milwaukee city, Wisconsin	26.1	17	6	San Francisco city, California	15.8	44	6	Miami city, Florida	48.7
50	7	Arlington city, Texas	25.8	32	7	Albuquerque city, New Mexico	15.7	31	7	Milwaukee city, Wisconsin	46.7
5	8	Phoenix city, Arizona	25.7	68	8	Pittsburgh city, Pennsylvania	15.0	6	8	Philadelphia city, Pennsylvania	46.1
20	9	Oklahoma City city, Oklahoma	25.5	1	9	New York city, New York	14.9	55	9	Anaheim city, California	45.1
62	10	Santa Ana city, California	25.2	25	9	Las Vegas city, Nevada	14.9	61	10	Riverside city, California	45.0
49	11	Wichita city, Kansas	25.0	34	11	Tucson city, Arizona	14.8	60	11	Corpus Christi city, Texas	44.7
51	12	Aurora city, Colorado	24.9	53	11	New Orleans city, Louisiana	14.8	48	12	Bakersfield city, California	44.0
7	13	San Antonio city, Texas	24.8	49	13	Wichita city, Kansas	14.5	29	13	Memphis city, Tennessee	43.9
9	13	Dallas city, Texas	24.8	47	14	Tulsa city, Oklahoma	14.4	33	14	Fresno city, California	43.6
27	13	Detroit city, Michigan	24.8	54	15	Cleveland city, Ohio	14.3	7	15	San Antonio city, Texas	43.3
29	13	Memphis city, Tennessee	24.8	42	16	Virginia Beach city, Virginia	14.2	30	16	Baltimore city, Maryland	43.0
39	13	Omaha city, Nebraska	24.8	30	17	Baltimore city, Maryland	14.0	9	17	Dallas city, Texas	42.7
67	13	St. Paul city, Minnesota	24.8	60	17	Corpus Christi city, Texas	14.0	4	18	Houston city, Texas	42.4
4	19	Houston city, Texas	24.7	27	19	Detroit city, Michigan	13.9	25	19	Las Vegas city, Nevada	42.3
15	20	Indianapolis city, Indiana	24.6	12	20	Jacksonville city, Florida	13.8	22	20	El Paso city, Texas	41.9
60	20	Corpus Christi city, Texas	24.6	6	21	Philadelphia city, Pennsylvania	13.7	13	21	Fort Worth city, Texas	41.7
47	22	Tulsa city, Oklahoma	24.5	70	21	St. Louis city, Missouri	13.7	15	22	Indianapolis city, Indiana	40.9
66	23	Newark city, New Jersey	24.4	40	23	Colorado Springs city, Colorado	13.6	1	23	New York city, New York	40.8
73	24	Anchorage municipality, Alaska	24.3	69	24	Greensboro city, North Carolina	13.5	2	24	Los Angeles city, California	40.6
61	25	Riverside city, California	24.0	29	25	Memphis city, Tennessee	13.4	5	25	Phoenix city, Arizona	40.5
36	26	Mesa city, Arizona	23.9	45	25	Oakland city, California	13.4	51	26	Aurora city, Colorado	39.2
25	27	Las Vegas city, Nevada	23.7	59	25	Lexington-Fayette urban county, Kentucky	13.4	12	27	Jacksonville city, Florida	39.0
55	28	Anaheim city, California	23.5	71	25	Lincoln city, Nebraska	13.4	50	28	Arlington city, Texas	38.4
16	29	Charlotte city, North Carolina	23.4	8	29	San Diego city, California	13.3	49	29	Wichita city, Kansas	38.0
40	30	Colorado Springs city, Colorado	22.9	35	29	Sacramento city, California	13.3	20	30	Oklahoma City city, Oklahoma	37.9
12	31	Jacksonville city, Florida	22.8	37	29	Kansas City city, Missouri	13.3	47	31	Tulsa city, Oklahoma	37.8
37	31	Kansas City city, Missouri	22.8	39	29	Omaha city, Nebraska	13.3	43	32	Long Beach city, California	37.3
35	33	Sacramento city, California	22.7	26	33	Portland city, Oregon	13.2	34	33	Tucson city, Arizona	37.0
64	34	Irvine city, California	22.5	72	33	Plano city, Texas	13.2	52	34	Tampa city, Florida	36.6
14	35	Columbus city, Ohio	22.3	10	35	San Jose city, California	13.0	3	35	Chicago city, Illinois	36.1
71	35	Lincoln city, Nebraska	22.3	2	36	Los Angeles city, California	12.9	14	36	Columbus city, Ohio	35.5
72	35	Plano city, Texas	22.3	22	36	El Paso city, Texas	12.9	70	37	St. Louis city, Missouri	35.4
42	38	Virginia Beach city, Virginia	22.2	3	38	Chicago city, Illinois	12.7	28	38	Louisville/Jefferson County metro, Kentucky	35.3
28	39	Louisville/Jefferson County metro, Kentucky	22.1	52	38	Tampa city, Florida	12.7	65	39	Cincinnati city, Ohio	35.2
10	40	San Jose city, California	22.0	20	40	Oklahoma City city, Oklahoma	12.6	53	40	New Orleans city, Louisiana	35.1
69	40	Greensboro city, North Carolina	22.0	15	41	Indianapolis city, Indiana	12.5	36	41	Mesa city, Arizona	34.7
32	42	Albuquerque city, New Mexico	21.9	18	41	Seattle city, Washington	12.5	35	42	Sacramento city, California	34.6
6	43	Philadelphia city, Pennsylvania	21.7	65	41	Cincinnati city, Ohio	12.5	37	43	Kansas City city, Missouri	34.5
43	43	Long Beach city, California	21.7	58	44	Stockton city, California	12.4	56	44	Urban Honolulu CDP, Hawaii	33.5
54	43	Cleveland city, Ohio	21.7	7	45	San Antonio city, Texas	12.3	67	44	St. Paul city, Minnesota	33.5
65	46	Cincinnati city, Ohio	21.6	21	45	Nashville-Davidson metro, Tennessee	12.3	75	46	Jersey City city, New Jersey	33.4
52	47	Tampa city, Florida	21.4	23	47	Washington city, District of Columbia	12.2	39	47	Omaha city, Nebraska	32.2
63	47	Orlando city, Florida	21.4	51	48	Aurora city, Colorado	11.9	45	48	Oakland city, California	31.8
74	49	Durham city, North Carolina	21.3	74	48	Durham city, North Carolina	11.9	63	48	Orlando city, Florida	31.8
57	50	Henderson city, Nevada	21.1	19	50	Denver city, Colorado	11.8	21	50	Nashville-Davidson metro, Tennessee	31.7
59	51	Lexington-Fayette urban county, Kentucky	20.9	24	50	Boston city, Massachusetts	11.8	68	50	Pittsburgh city, Pennsylvania	31.7
21	52	Nashville-Davidson metro, Tennessee	20.8	55	50	Anaheim city, California	11.8	10	52	San Jose city, California	31.5
1	53	New York city, New York	20.7	43	53	Long Beach city, California	11.7	32	53	Albuquerque city, New Mexico	31.4
75	53	Jersey City city, New Jersey	20.7	33	54	Fresno city, California	11.6	57	53	Henderson city, Nevada	31.4
34	55	Tucson city, Arizona	20.6	38	54	Atlanta city, Georgia	11.6	69	53	Greensboro city, North Carolina	31.4
3	56	Chicago city, Illinois	20.5	61	56	Riverside city, California	11.1	24	56	Boston city, Massachusetts	31.0
30	56	Baltimore city, Maryland	20.5	73	56	Anchorage municipality, Alaska	11.1	73	57	Anchorage municipality, Alaska	29.7
2	58	Los Angeles city, California	20.4	75	56	Jersey City city, New Jersey	11.1	19	58	Denver city, Colorado	28.0
41	58	Raleigh city, North Carolina	20.4	4	59	Houston city, Texas	11.0	71	59	Lincoln city, Nebraska	27.9
53	60	New Orleans city, Louisiana	20.0	5	59	Phoenix city, Arizona	11.0	16	60	Charlotte city, North Carolina	27.4
11	61	Austin city, Texas	19.9	67	59	St. Paul city, Minnesota	11.0	59	61	Lexington-Fayette urban county, Kentucky	27.1
46	62	Minneapolis city, Minnesota	19.8	41	62	Raleigh city, North Carolina	10.8	38	62	Atlanta city, Georgia	26.9
8	63	San Diego city, California	19.6	9	63	Dallas city, Texas	10.6	42	63	Virginia Beach city, Virginia	26.7
19	64	Denver city, Colorado	19.4	66	63	Newark city, New Jersey	10.6	74	64	Durham city, North Carolina	26.6
45	64	Oakland city, California	19.4	31	65	Milwaukee city, Wisconsin	10.5	8	65	San Diego city, California	26.3
70	66	St. Louis city, Missouri	19.1	50	65	Arlington city, Texas	10.5	40	66	Colorado Springs city, Colorado	25.4
23	67	Washington city, District of Columbia	18.0	14	67	Columbus city, Ohio	10.4	23	67	Washington city, District of Columbia	24.7
38	68	Atlanta city, Georgia	17.6	16	67	Charlotte city, North Carolina	10.4	11	68	Austin city, Texas	24.4
26	69	Portland city, Oregon	17.4	63	69	Orlando city, Florida	10.1	46	69	Minneapolis city, Minnesota	24.1
56	70	Urban Honolulu CDP, Hawaii	17.3	48	70	Bakersfield city, California	10.0	41	70	Raleigh city, North Carolina	23.5
44	71	Miami city, Florida	17.2	13	71	Fort Worth city, Texas	9.9	17	71	San Francisco city, California	23.0
24	72	Boston city, Massachusetts	15.8	46	71	Minneapolis city, Minnesota	9.9	26	72	Portland city, Oregon	22.6
68	73	Pittsburgh city, Pennsylvania	14.6	64	71	Irvine city, California	9.9	72	73	Plano city, Texas	19.0
18	74	Seattle city, Washington	14.5	62	74	Santa Ana city, California	9.8	18	74	Seattle city, Washington	14.3
17	75	San Francisco city, California	13.4	11	75	Austin city, Texas	9.4	64	75	Irvine city, California	11.5

75 Largest Cities by 2021 Population
Selected rankings

Percent college graduates (bachelor's degree or more), 2016–2020

Population rank	Percent college graduate rank	City	Percent college graduates [col 41]
64	1	Irvine city, California	69.5
18	2	Seattle city, Washington	65.0
23	3	Washington city, District of Columbia	59.8
17	4	San Francisco city, California	58.8
72	5	Plano city, Texas	57.6
11	6	Austin city, Texas	53.4
38	6	Atlanta city, Georgia	53.4
46	8	Minneapolis city, Minnesota	51.8
41	9	Raleigh city, North Carolina	51.4
24	10	Boston city, Massachusetts	51.3
74	11	Durham city, North Carolina	51.2
26	12	Portland city, Oregon	51.0
19	13	Denver city, Colorado	50.3
75	14	Jersey City city, New Jersey	49.8
8	15	San Diego city, California	46.7
45	16	Oakland city, California	46.1
68	17	Pittsburgh city, Pennsylvania	45.4
59	18	Lexington-Fayette urban county, Kentucky	45.0
10	19	San Jose city, California	44.8
16	19	Charlotte city, North Carolina	44.8
21	21	Nashville-Davidson metro, Tennessee	43.3
67	22	St. Paul city, Minnesota	41.3
3	23	Chicago city, Illinois	41.1
52	24	Tampa city, Florida	39.9
63	24	Orlando city, Florida	39.9
71	24	Lincoln city, Nebraska	39.9
40	27	Colorado Springs city, Colorado	39.6
69	28	Greensboro city, North Carolina	39.4
1	29	New York city, New York	39.1
65	30	Cincinnati city, Ohio	38.7
39	31	Omaha city, Nebraska	38.3
53	32	New Orleans city, Louisiana	38.0
56	33	Urban Honolulu CDP, Hawaii	37.8
42	34	Virginia Beach city, Virginia	37.3
70	35	St. Louis city, Missouri	37.2
14	36	Columbus city, Ohio	36.8
73	37	Anchorage municipality, Alaska	36.6
32	38	Albuquerque city, New Mexico	36.5
37	39	Kansas City city, Missouri	35.7
2	40	Los Angeles city, California	35.6
9	41	Dallas city, Texas	34.7
4	42	Houston city, Texas	34.3
35	42	Sacramento city, California	34.3
57	44	Henderson city, Nevada	34.0
28	45	Louisville/Jefferson County metro, Kentucky	33.9
30	46	Baltimore city, Maryland	32.9
15	47	Indianapolis city, Indiana	32.2
43	48	Long Beach city, California	31.8
20	49	Oklahoma City city, Oklahoma	31.5
44	49	Miami city, Florida	31.5
47	51	Tulsa city, Oklahoma	31.3
6	52	Philadelphia city, Pennsylvania	31.2
50	53	Arlington city, Texas	30.9
49	54	Wichita city, Kansas	30.7
13	55	Fort Worth city, Texas	30.1
51	56	Aurora city, Colorado	30.0
5	57	Phoenix city, Arizona	29.4
12	58	Jacksonville city, Florida	29.3
34	59	Tucson city, Arizona	28.2
36	60	Mesa city, Arizona	28.1
29	61	Memphis city, Tennessee	26.6
55	61	Anaheim city, California	26.6
7	63	San Antonio city, Texas	26.4
22	64	El Paso city, Texas	25.9
25	65	Las Vegas city, Nevada	25.2
31	66	Milwaukee city, Wisconsin	24.6
61	67	Riverside city, California	24.1
33	68	Fresno city, California	22.9
48	69	Bakersfield city, California	22.6
60	70	Corpus Christi city, Texas	22.0
54	71	Cleveland city, Ohio	18.6
58	71	Stockton city, California	18.6
62	73	Santa Ana city, California	16.8
27	74	Detroit city, Michigan	16.4
66	75	Newark city, New Jersey	15.5

Percent married couple family households, 2016–2020

Population rank	Married-couple households rank	City	Percent married couple households [col 30]
72	1	Plano city, Texas	57.5
10	2	San Jose city, California	55.3
62	3	Santa Ana city, California	54.9
64	4	Irvine city, California	52.5
61	5	Riverside city, California	51.6
42	6	Virginia Beach city, Virginia	51.1
55	7	Anaheim city, California	50.6
48	8	Bakersfield city, California	50.2
57	9	Henderson city, Nevada	49.5
73	10	Anchorage municipality, Alaska	49.2
40	11	Colorado Springs city, Colorado	48.3
36	12	Mesa city, Arizona	47.8
50	13	Arlington city, Texas	47.4
13	14	Fort Worth city, Texas	46.2
51	15	Aurora city, Colorado	46.0
22	16	El Paso city, Texas	45.5
58	17	Stockton city, California	45.2
8	18	San Diego city, California	45.0
60	19	Corpus Christi city, Texas	44.9
71	20	Lincoln city, Nebraska	43.8
39	21	Omaha city, Nebraska	43.0
20	22	Oklahoma City city, Oklahoma	42.7
49	23	Wichita city, Kansas	42.6
25	24	Las Vegas city, Nevada	42.2
5	25	Phoenix city, Arizona	42.0
59	26	Lexington-Fayette urban county, Kentucky	41.1
56	27	Urban Honolulu CDP, Hawaii	41.0
33	28	Fresno city, California	40.7
7	29	San Antonio city, Texas	40.6
12	30	Jacksonville city, Florida	40.4
28	31	Louisville/Jefferson County metro, Kentucky	40.2
16	32	Charlotte city, North Carolina	40.0
75	33	Jersey City city, New Jersey	39.4
35	34	Sacramento city, California	38.9
2	35	Los Angeles city, California	38.7
41	36	Raleigh city, North Carolina	38.6
11	37	Austin city, Texas	38.2
26	38	Portland city, Oregon	38.1
4	39	Houston city, Texas	38.0
43	40	Long Beach city, California	37.9
47	41	Tulsa city, Oklahoma	37.8
21	42	Nashville-Davidson metro, Tennessee	37.2
74	43	Durham city, North Carolina	37.1
1	44	New York city, New York	36.9
32	45	Albuquerque city, New Mexico	36.4
9	46	Dallas city, Texas	36.2
17	47	San Francisco city, California	35.7
15	48	Indianapolis city, Indiana	35.6
67	48	St. Paul city, Minnesota	35.6
37	50	Kansas City city, Missouri	35.5
45	51	Oakland city, California	35.4
18	52	Seattle city, Washington	35.2
19	53	Denver city, Colorado	35.1
52	53	Tampa city, Florida	35.1
69	55	Greensboro city, North Carolina	35.0
63	56	Orlando city, Florida	34.3
34	57	Tucson city, Arizona	33.6
3	58	Chicago city, Illinois	32.5
14	59	Columbus city, Ohio	32.3
44	60	Miami city, Florida	32.1
46	61	Minneapolis city, Minnesota	30.7
24	62	Boston city, Massachusetts	28.6
29	63	Memphis city, Tennessee	28.5
6	64	Philadelphia city, Pennsylvania	28.2
66	65	Newark city, New Jersey	27.4
31	66	Milwaukee city, Wisconsin	26.9
68	67	Pittsburgh city, Pennsylvania	26.7
23	68	Washington city, District of Columbia	26.1
53	69	New Orleans city, Louisiana	25.9
70	70	St. Louis city, Missouri	25.4
38	71	Atlanta city, Georgia	24.7
65	72	Cincinnati city, Ohio	24.2
30	73	Baltimore city, Maryland	23.9
54	74	Cleveland city, Ohio	19.8
27	75	Detroit city, Michigan	19.5

Percent of households composed of one person, 2016–2020

Population rank	One-person household rank	City	Percent one-person households [col 33]
53	1	New Orleans city, Louisiana	46.5
38	2	Atlanta city, Georgia	46.0
70	3	St. Louis city, Missouri	45.4
23	4	Washington city, District of Columbia	45.1
54	5	Cleveland city, Ohio	45.0
65	6	Cincinnati city, Ohio	44.6
68	7	Pittsburgh city, Pennsylvania	44.2
27	8	Detroit city, Michigan	41.6
30	9	Baltimore city, Maryland	40.8
46	10	Minneapolis city, Minnesota	40.3
18	11	Seattle city, Washington	39.9
19	12	Denver city, Colorado	38.4
29	13	Memphis city, Tennessee	37.9
3	14	Chicago city, Illinois	37.5
31	15	Milwaukee city, Wisconsin	37.4
6	16	Philadelphia city, Pennsylvania	37.2
15	16	Indianapolis city, Indiana	37.2
37	18	Kansas City city, Missouri	37.1
44	19	Miami city, Florida	36.5
17	20	San Francisco city, California	36.3
14	21	Columbus city, Ohio	36.0
24	21	Boston city, Massachusetts	36.0
47	21	Tulsa city, Oklahoma	36.0
67	21	St. Paul city, Minnesota	36.0
32	25	Albuquerque city, New Mexico	35.9
52	26	Tampa city, Florida	35.8
66	27	Newark city, New Jersey	35.6
9	28	Dallas city, Texas	35.5
34	29	Tucson city, Arizona	35.1
69	29	Greensboro city, North Carolina	35.1
21	31	Nashville-Davidson metro, Tennessee	35.0
74	32	Durham city, North Carolina	34.9
56	33	Urban Honolulu CDP, Hawaii	34.7
26	34	Portland city, Oregon	34.1
41	34	Raleigh city, North Carolina	34.1
28	36	Louisville/Jefferson County metro, Kentucky	34.0
11	37	Austin city, Texas	33.9
16	38	Charlotte city, North Carolina	33.5
45	39	Oakland city, California	33.4
39	40	Omaha city, Nebraska	33.2
49	40	Wichita city, Kansas	33.2
63	40	Orlando city, Florida	33.2
4	43	Houston city, Texas	32.7
59	44	Lexington-Fayette urban county, Kentucky	32.4
1	45	New York city, New York	32.1
20	46	Oklahoma City city, Oklahoma	31.8
12	47	Jacksonville city, Florida	31.7
71	48	Lincoln city, Nebraska	31.0
7	49	San Antonio city, Texas	30.8
35	50	Sacramento city, California	30.7
43	51	Long Beach city, California	30.6
2	52	Los Angeles city, California	30.5
75	53	Jersey City city, New Jersey	30.3
25	54	Las Vegas city, Nevada	30.0
5	55	Phoenix city, Arizona	28.2
40	56	Colorado Springs city, Colorado	28.0
8	57	San Diego city, California	27.6
57	57	Henderson city, Nevada	27.6
60	59	Corpus Christi city, Texas	26.7
13	60	Fort Worth city, Texas	26.3
51	60	Aurora city, Colorado	26.3
36	62	Mesa city, Arizona	26.0
73	63	Anchorage municipality, Alaska	25.9
22	64	El Paso city, Texas	25.5
33	65	Fresno city, California	25.3
50	66	Arlington city, Texas	25.2
42	67	Virginia Beach city, Virginia	24.0
72	68	Plano city, Texas	23.4
64	69	Irvine city, California	22.8
58	70	Stockton city, California	22.2
48	71	Bakersfield city, California	19.7
55	72	Anaheim city, California	19.6
10	73	San Jose city, California	19.5
61	74	Riverside city, California	18.9
62	75	Santa Ana city, California	13.3

75 Largest Cities by 2021 Population

Selected rankings

Median household income, 2016–2020

Population rank	Median income rank	City	Median income (dollars) [col 42]
17	1	San Francisco city, California	119,136
10	2	San Jose city, California	117,324
64	3	Irvine city, California	108,318
18	4	Seattle city, Washington	97,185
72	5	Plano city, Texas	96,348
23	6	Washington city, District of Columbia	90,842
73	7	Anchorage municipality, Alaska	84,813
8	8	San Diego city, California	83,454
45	9	Oakland city, California	80,143
42	10	Virginia Beach city, Virginia	78,136
55	11	Anaheim city, California	76,723
75	12	Jersey City city, New Jersey	76,444
24	13	Boston city, Massachusetts	76,298
11	14	Austin city, Texas	75,752
57	15	Henderson city, Nevada	75,430
26	16	Portland city, Oregon	73,159
61	17	Riverside city, California	72,738
19	18	Denver city, Colorado	72,661
56	19	Urban Honolulu CDP, Hawaii	72,454
62	20	Santa Ana city, California	72,406
41	21	Raleigh city, North Carolina	69,720
51	22	Aurora city, Colorado	67,723
40	23	Colorado Springs city, Colorado	67,719
1	24	New York city, New York	67,046
43	25	Long Beach city, California	66,410
46	26	Minneapolis city, Minnesota	66,068
35	27	Sacramento city, California	65,847
48	28	Bakersfield city, California	65,687
16	29	Charlotte city, North Carolina	65,359
2	30	Los Angeles city, California	65,290
13	31	Fort Worth city, Texas	64,567
38	32	Atlanta city, Georgia	64,179
50	33	Arlington city, Texas	63,351
21	34	Nashville-Davidson metro, Tennessee	62,515
39	35	Omaha city, Nebraska	62,213
3	36	Chicago city, Illinois	62,097
74	37	Durham city, North Carolina	61,962
36	38	Mesa city, Arizona	61,640
5	39	Phoenix city, Arizona	60,914
71	40	Lincoln city, Nebraska	60,063
67	41	St. Paul city, Minnesota	59,717
59	42	Lexington-Fayette urban county, Kentucky	58,954
58	43	Stockton city, California	58,393
25	44	Las Vegas city, Nevada	58,377
28	45	Louisville/Jefferson County metro, Kentucky	58,196
60	46	Corpus Christi city, Texas	57,387
20	47	Oklahoma City city, Oklahoma	56,456
37	48	Kansas City city, Missouri	56,179
52	49	Tampa city, Florida	55,634
12	50	Jacksonville city, Florida	55,531
63	51	Orlando city, Florida	55,183
14	52	Columbus city, Ohio	54,902
9	53	Dallas city, Texas	54,747
32	54	Albuquerque city, New Mexico	53,936
4	55	Houston city, Texas	53,600
49	56	Wichita city, Kansas	53,466
7	57	San Antonio city, Texas	53,420
33	58	Fresno city, California	53,368
30	59	Baltimore city, Maryland	52,164
15	60	Indianapolis city, Indiana	50,939
68	61	Pittsburgh city, Pennsylvania	50,536
69	62	Greensboro city, North Carolina	49,492
47	63	Tulsa city, Oklahoma	49,474
6	64	Philadelphia city, Pennsylvania	49,127
22	65	El Paso city, Texas	48,866
70	66	St. Louis city, Missouri	45,782
34	67	Tucson city, Arizona	45,227
44	68	Miami city, Florida	44,268
53	69	New Orleans city, Louisiana	43,258
31	70	Milwaukee city, Wisconsin	43,125
65	71	Cincinnati city, Ohio	42,663
29	72	Memphis city, Tennessee	41,864
66	73	Newark city, New Jersey	37,476
27	74	Detroit city, Michigan	32,498
54	75	Cleveland city, Ohio	31,838

Median value of owner-occupied housing units, 2016–2020

Population rank	Median value rank	City	Median value (dollars) [col 53]
17	1	San Francisco city, California	1,152,300
10	2	San Jose city, California	925,800
64	3	Irvine city, California	861,700
45	4	Oakland city, California	730,000
18	5	Seattle city, Washington	713,600
56	6	Urban Honolulu CDP, Hawaii	707,400
2	7	Los Angeles city, California	670,700
1	8	New York city, New York	635,200
8	9	San Diego city, California	629,500
23	10	Washington city, District of Columbia	618,100
55	11	Anaheim city, California	602,400
43	12	Long Beach city, California	584,200
24	13	Boston city, Massachusetts	581,200
62	14	Santa Ana city, California	525,900
26	15	Portland city, Oregon	438,500
19	16	Denver city, Colorado	427,600
75	17	Jersey City city, New Jersey	406,200
61	18	Riverside city, California	389,500
35	19	Sacramento city, California	361,300
11	20	Austin city, Texas	358,600
44	21	Miami city, Florida	344,300
72	22	Plano city, Texas	341,800
57	23	Henderson city, Nevada	341,100
51	24	Aurora city, Colorado	322,200
73	25	Anchorage municipality, Alaska	320,100
38	26	Atlanta city, Georgia	314,400
58	27	Stockton city, California	298,200
40	28	Colorado Springs city, Colorado	294,500
42	29	Virginia Beach city, Virginia	287,400
25	30	Las Vegas city, Nevada	279,700
46	31	Minneapolis city, Minnesota	268,100
3	32	Chicago city, Illinois	267,600
21	33	Nashville-Davidson metro, Tennessee	267,400
41	34	Raleigh city, North Carolina	266,900
63	35	Orlando city, Florida	262,500
48	36	Bakersfield city, California	258,700
33	37	Fresno city, California	256,000
66	38	Newark city, New Jersey	254,900
52	39	Tampa city, Florida	254,600
5	40	Phoenix city, Arizona	250,800
53	41	New Orleans city, Louisiana	250,000
36	42	Mesa city, Arizona	245,500
74	43	Durham city, North Carolina	243,000
16	44	Charlotte city, North Carolina	235,000
67	45	St. Paul city, Minnesota	217,100
9	46	Dallas city, Texas	208,700
32	47	Albuquerque city, New Mexico	204,100
59	48	Lexington-Fayette urban county, Kentucky	200,900
13	49	Fort Worth city, Texas	190,400
50	50	Arlington city, Texas	188,100
12	51	Jacksonville city, Florida	187,700
4	52	Houston city, Texas	186,800
71	53	Lincoln city, Nebraska	180,400
28	54	Louisville/Jefferson County metro, Kentucky	178,100
6	55	Philadelphia city, Pennsylvania	171,600
39	56	Omaha city, Nebraska	167,800
30	57	Baltimore city, Maryland	167,300
34	58	Tucson city, Arizona	165,900
37	59	Kansas City city, Missouri	163,300
69	60	Greensboro city, North Carolina	163,000
20	61	Oklahoma City city, Oklahoma	161,800
14	62	Columbus city, Ohio	160,000
7	63	San Antonio city, Texas	156,700
60	64	Corpus Christi city, Texas	150,100
65	65	Cincinnati city, Ohio	148,700
15	66	Indianapolis city, Indiana	145,300
70	67	St. Louis city, Missouri	143,700
47	68	Tulsa city, Oklahoma	143,400
49	69	Wichita city, Kansas	138,100
68	70	Pittsburgh city, Pennsylvania	134,800
22	71	El Paso city, Texas	132,800
31	72	Milwaukee city, Wisconsin	128,300
29	73	Memphis city, Tennessee	107,100
54	74	Cleveland city, Ohio	73,400
27	75	Detroit city, Michigan	52,700

Mean travel time to work, 2016–2020

Population rank	Mean travel time to work rank	City	Mean travel time to work (minutes) [col 56]
1	1	New York city, New York	41.4
75	2	Jersey City city, New Jersey	37.2
3	3	Chicago city, Illinois	34.7
66	4	Newark city, New Jersey	34.5
6	5	Philadelphia city, Pennsylvania	33.4
17	6	San Francisco city, California	33.3
45	7	Oakland city, California	32.9
61	8	Riverside city, California	32.0
2	9	Los Angeles city, California	31.9
58	9	Stockton city, California	31.9
30	11	Baltimore city, Maryland	31.1
43	12	Long Beach city, California	31.0
23	13	Washington city, District of Columbia	30.9
10	14	San Jose city, California	30.8
24	15	Boston city, Massachusetts	30.7
51	16	Aurora city, Colorado	29.8
55	17	Anaheim city, California	29.1
44	18	Miami city, Florida	28.6
18	19	Seattle city, Washington	27.7
4	20	Houston city, Texas	27.6
13	21	Fort Worth city, Texas	27.5
38	21	Atlanta city, Georgia	27.5
50	23	Arlington city, Texas	27.2
9	24	Dallas city, Texas	26.9
72	25	Plano city, Texas	26.8
63	25	Orlando city, Florida	26.8
5	27	Phoenix city, Arizona	26.2
26	27	Portland city, Oregon	26.2
35	29	Sacramento city, California	26.0
27	30	Detroit city, Michigan	25.8
25	31	Las Vegas city, Nevada	25.7
19	31	Denver city, Colorado	25.7
62	31	Santa Ana city, California	25.7
16	34	Charlotte city, North Carolina	25.6
64	35	Irvine city, California	25.5
36	36	Mesa city, Arizona	25.4
21	37	Nashville-Davidson metropolitan Tennessee	25.3
12	38	Jacksonville city, Florida	24.9
52	38	Tampa city, Florida	24.9
11	40	Austin city, Texas	24.6
7	40	San Antonio city, Texas	24.6
8	42	San Diego city, California	24.5
41	43	Raleigh city, North Carolina	24.4
67	44	St. Paul city, Minnesota	24.2
68	44	Pittsburgh city, Pennsylvania	24.2
57	46	Henderson city, Nevada	23.9
70	46	St. Louis city, Missouri	23.9
15	46	Indianapolis city	23.9
54	49	Cleveland city, Ohio	23.8
53	50	New Orleans city, Louisiana	23.7
42	51	Virginia Beach city, Virginia	23.6
65	52	Cincinnati city, Ohio	23.5
22	53	El Paso city, Texas	23.4
48	53	Bakersfield city, California	23.4
40	55	Colorado Springs city, Colorado	23.3
56	56	Urban Honolulu CDP, Hawaii	23.2
46	56	Minneapolis city, Minnesota	23.2
74	58	Durham city, North Carolina	22.8
28	59	Louisville/Jefferson County metro Kentucky	22.6
31	60	Milwaukee city, Wisconsin	22.4
34	60	Tucson city, Arizona	22.4
33	62	Fresno city, California	22.3
14	63	Columbus city, Ohio	22.0
32	63	Albuquerque city, New Mexico	22.0
37	63	Kansas City city, Missouri	22.0
29	66	Memphis city, Tennessee	21.7
20	67	Oklahoma City city, Oklahoma	21.4
69	67	Greensboro city, North Carolina	21.4
59	69	Lexington-Fayette urban county, Kentucky	20.8
60	70	Corpus Christi city, Texas	19.4
39	71	Omaha city, Nebraska	19.3
71	72	Lincoln city, Nebraska	18.9
49	73	Wichita city, Kansas	18.8
73	74	Anchorage municipality, Alaska	18.6
47	74	Tulsa city, Oklahoma	18.6

75 Largest Cities by 2021 Population
Selected rankings

Median Non-Family Household Income, 2016–2020

Population rank	Non-family income rank	City	Median non-family income [col 46]
17	1	San Francisco city, California	96,421
23	2	Washington city, District of Columbia	75,477
10	3	San Jose city, California	72,962
64	4	Irvine city, California	70,151
18	5	Seattle city, Washington	69,092
45	6	Oakland city, California	64,498
24	7	Boston city, Massachusetts	61,649
8	8	San Diego city, California	61,539
75	9	Jersey City city, New Jersey	61,273
72	10	Plano city, Texas	58,573
73	11	Anchorage municipality, Alaska	57,311
11	12	Austin city, Texas	56,825
19	13	Denver city, Colorado	56,719
55	14	Anaheim city, California	54,593
43	15	Long Beach city, California	52,951
26	16	Portland city, Oregon	52,247
38	17	Atlanta city, Georgia	51,840
41	18	Raleigh city, North Carolina	51,512
62	19	Santa Ana city, California	51,064
42	20	Virginia Beach city, Virginia	50,798
35	21	Sacramento city, California	50,534
46	22	Minneapolis city, Minnesota	50,484
1	23	New York city, New York	50,460
57	24	Henderson city, Nevada	48,995
2	25	Los Angeles city, California	48,887
3	26	Chicago city, Illinois	48,764
56	27	Urban Honolulu CDP, Hawaii	48,636
16	28	Charlotte city, North Carolina	48,539
21	29	Nashville-Davidson metro, Tennessee	47,954
51	30	Aurora city, Colorado	47,636
63	31	Orlando city, Florida	46,973
9	32	Dallas city, Texas	45,658
67	33	St. Paul city, Minnesota	43,971
74	34	Durham city, North Carolina	43,386
40	35	Colorado Springs city, Colorado	43,001
14	36	Columbus city, Ohio	42,789
13	37	Fort Worth city, Texas	42,438
5	38	Phoenix city, Arizona	42,310
50	39	Arlington city, Texas	42,281
61	40	Riverside city, California	41,976
4	41	Houston city, Texas	41,950
36	42	Mesa city, Arizona	41,160
39	43	Omaha city, Nebraska	39,536
48	44	Bakersfield city, California	39,210
30	45	Baltimore city, Maryland	39,140
52	46	Tampa city, Florida	38,591
12	47	Jacksonville city, Florida	38,558
37	48	Kansas City city, Missouri	38,204
20	49	Oklahoma City city, Oklahoma	38,161
28	50	Louisville/Jefferson County metro, Kentucky	37,784
25	51	Las Vegas city, Nevada	37,389
71	52	Lincoln city, Nebraska	37,297
59	53	Lexington-Fayette urban county, Kentucky	37,282
68	54	Pittsburgh city, Pennsylvania	36,418
15	55	Indianapolis city, Indiana	36,023
6	56	Philadelphia city, Pennsylvania	35,827
7	57	San Antonio city, Texas	35,786
60	58	Corpus Christi city, Texas	35,770
69	59	Greensboro city, North Carolina	35,553
32	60	Albuquerque city, New Mexico	35,418
70	61	St. Louis city, Missouri	34,523
58	62	Stockton city, California	34,401
47	63	Tulsa city, Oklahoma	34,236
65	64	Cincinnati city, Ohio	33,510
33	65	Fresno city, California	33,323
49	66	Wichita city, Kansas	32,677
44	67	Miami city, Florida	32,001
34	68	Tucson city, Arizona	31,876
31	69	Milwaukee city, Wisconsin	31,698
29	70	Memphis city, Tennessee	30,493
53	71	New Orleans city, Louisiana	28,770
22	72	El Paso city, Texas	27,694
66	73	Newark city, New Jersey	25,456
27	74	Detroit city, Michigan	23,484
54	75	Cleveland city, Ohio	23,197

Unemployment rate, 2021

Population rank	Unemployment rate rank	City	Unemployment rate [col 64]
27	1	Detroit city, Michigan	13.5
66	2	Newark city, New Jersey	10.6
58	3	Stockton city, California	10.0
1	4	New York city, New York	9.9
43	5	Long Beach city, California	9.6
6	6	Philadelphia city, Pennsylvania	9.2
2	7	Los Angeles city, California	8.9
54	8	Cleveland city, Ohio	8.5
25	9	Las Vegas city, Nevada	8.4
53	10	New Orleans city, Louisiana	8.3
29	11	Memphis city, Tennessee	8.2
33	11	Fresno city, California	8.2
48	13	Bakersfield city, California	8.0
3	14	Chicago city, Illinois	7.6
30	14	Baltimore city, Maryland	7.6
35	16	Sacramento city, California	7.4
45	17	Oakland city, California	7.3
75	18	Jersey City city, New Jersey	7.0
55	19	Anaheim city, California	6.9
57	19	Henderson city, Nevada	6.9
60	19	Corpus Christi city, Texas	6.9
61	22	Riverside city, California	6.7
23	23	Washington city, District of Columbia	6.6
51	23	Aurora city, Colorado	6.6
31	25	Milwaukee city, Wisconsin	6.5
4	26	Houston city, Texas	6.4
70	26	St. Louis city, Missouri	6.4
32	28	Albuquerque city, New Mexico	6.3
8	29	San Diego city, California	6.2
62	29	Santa Ana city, California	6.2
68	29	Pittsburgh city, Pennsylvania	6.2
19	32	Denver city, Colorado	5.9
22	32	El Paso city, Texas	5.9
69	32	Greensboro city, North Carolina	5.9
24	35	Boston city, Massachusetts	5.8
73	35	Anchorage municipality, Alaska	5.8
9	37	Dallas city, Texas	5.7
13	38	Fort Worth city, Texas	5.6
40	38	Colorado Springs city, Colorado	5.6
63	38	Orlando city, Florida	5.6
65	38	Cincinnati city, Ohio	5.6
34	42	Tucson city, Arizona	5.5
26	43	Portland city, Oregon	5.4
37	43	Kansas City city, Missouri	5.4
50	43	Arlington city, Texas	5.4
10	46	San Jose city, California	5.3
64	46	Irvine city, California	5.3
7	48	San Antonio city, Texas	5.2
14	48	Columbus city, Ohio	5.2
44	48	Miami city, Florida	5.2
16	51	Charlotte city, North Carolina	5.1
38	51	Atlanta city, Georgia	5.1
17	53	San Francisco city, California	5.0
5	54	Phoenix city, Arizona	4.9
49	54	Wichita city, Kansas	4.9
28	56	Louisville/Jefferson County metro, Kentucky	4.8
12	57	Jacksonville city, Florida	4.6
52	57	Tampa city, Florida	4.6
15	59	Indianapolis city, Indiana	4.5
41	59	Raleigh city, North Carolina	4.5
47	59	Tulsa city, Oklahoma	4.5
36	62	Mesa city, Arizona	4.4
72	62	Plano city, Texas	4.4
21	64	Nashville-Davidson metro, Tennessee	4.2
67	64	St. Paul city, Minnesota	4.2
74	64	Durham city, North Carolina	4.2
20	67	Oklahoma City city, Oklahoma	4.0
11	68	Austin city, Texas	3.9
59	68	Lexington-Fayette urban county, Kentucky	3.9
46	70	Minneapolis city, Minnesota	3.8
18	71	Seattle city, Washington	3.7
42	71	Virginia Beach city, Virginia	3.7
39	73	Omaha city, Nebraska	3.1
71	74	Lincoln city, Nebraska	2.5
56		Urban Honolulu CDP, Hawaii	NA

Percent change in civilian labor force, 2020–2021

Population rank	Percent change rank	City	Percent change [col 62]
11	1	Austin city, Texas	5.4
72	2	Plano city, Texas	4.0
9	3	Dallas city, Texas	3.7
41	4	Raleigh city, North Carolina	3.4
74	5	Durham city, North Carolina	3.2
13	6	Fort Worth city, Texas	2.9
12	7	Jacksonville city, Florida	2.5
36	7	Mesa city, Arizona	2.5
44	7	Miami city, Florida	2.5
40	10	Colorado Springs city, Colorado	2.4
50	10	Arlington city, Texas	2.4
5	12	Phoenix city, Arizona	2.2
73	13	Anchorage municipality, Alaska	2.1
7	14	San Antonio city, Texas	2.0
16	14	Charlotte city, North Carolina	2.0
51	16	Aurora city, Colorado	1.9
19	17	Denver city, Colorado	1.8
38	17	Atlanta city, Georgia	1.8
20	19	Oklahoma City city, Oklahoma	1.6
32	19	Albuquerque city, New Mexico	1.6
21	21	Nashville-Davidson metro, Tennessee	1.4
61	21	Riverside city, California	1.4
52	23	Tampa city, Florida	1.3
57	23	Henderson city, Nevada	1.3
22	25	El Paso city, Texas	1.2
28	25	Louisville/Jefferson County metro, Kentucky	1.2
26	27	Portland city, Oregon	1.1
14	28	Columbus city, Ohio	1.0
4	29	Houston city, Texas	0.9
15	29	Indianapolis city, Indiana	0.9
59	31	Lexington-Fayette urban county, Kentucky	0.8
37	32	Kansas City city, Missouri	0.7
69	32	Greensboro city, North Carolina	0.7
35	34	Sacramento city, California	0.6
43	34	Long Beach city, California	0.6
64	34	Irvine city, California	0.6
2	37	Los Angeles city, California	0.4
25	37	Las Vegas city, Nevada	0.4
39	39	Omaha city, Nebraska	0.3
47	39	Tulsa city, Oklahoma	0.3
60	39	Corpus Christi city, Texas	0.3
70	39	St. Louis city, Missouri	0.3
8	43	San Diego city, California	0.1
31	43	Milwaukee city, Wisconsin	0.1
34	43	Tucson city, Arizona	0.1
71	43	Lincoln city, Nebraska	0.1
18	47	Seattle city, Washington	0.0
65	47	Cincinnati city, Ohio	0.0
75	49	Jersey City city, New Jersey	-0.1
24	50	Boston city, Massachusetts	-0.3
29	50	Memphis city, Tennessee	-0.3
58	52	Stockton city, California	-0.4
63	52	Orlando city, Florida	-0.4
62	54	Santa Ana city, California	-0.6
33	55	Fresno city, California	-0.8
66	55	Newark city, New Jersey	-0.8
48	57	Bakersfield city, California	-1.1
53	57	New Orleans city, Louisiana	-1.1
49	59	Wichita city, Kansas	-1.2
55	60	Anaheim city, California	-1.3
3	61	Chicago city, Illinois	-1.4
10	61	San Jose city, California	-1.4
1	63	New York city, New York	-1.5
45	64	Oakland city, California	-1.6
30	65	Baltimore city, Maryland	-1.7
54	66	Cleveland city, Ohio	-1.8
6	67	Philadelphia city, Pennsylvania	-2.0
23	67	Washington city, District of Columbia	-2.0
17	69	San Francisco city, California	-2.2
68	70	Pittsburgh city, Pennsylvania	-2.6
42	71	Virginia Beach city, Virginia	-2.9
67	72	St. Paul city, Minnesota	-3.4
46	73	Minneapolis city, Minnesota	-3.5
27	74	Detroit city, Michigan	-4.4
56		Urban Honolulu CDP, Hawaii	NA

75 Largest Cities by 2021 Population
Selected rankings

Per capita local government taxes, 2017

Population rank	Local taxes rank	City	Local per capita taxes (dollars) [col 121]
23	1	Washington city, District of Columbia	10,729
1	2	New York city, New York	6,555
17	3	San Francisco city, California	4,255
24	4	Boston city, Massachusetts	3,439
30	5	Baltimore city, Maryland	2,438
6	6	Philadelphia city, Pennsylvania	2,346
21	7	Nashville-Davidson metro, Tennessee	2,329
42	8	Virginia Beach city, Virginia	2,107
73	9	Anchorage municipality, Alaska	2,070
18	10	Seattle city, Washington	1,966
45	11	Oakland city, California	1,915
19	12	Denver city, Colorado	1,893
70	13	St. Louis city, Missouri	1,875
65	14	Cincinnati city, Ohio	1,810
37	15	Kansas City city, Missouri	1,513
53	16	New Orleans city, Louisiana	1,416
68	17	Pittsburgh city, Pennsylvania	1,385
26	18	Portland city, Oregon	1,371
3	19	Chicago city, Illinois	1,314
38	20	Atlanta city, Georgia	1,300
59	21	Lexington-Fayette urban county, Kentucky	1,277
66	22	Newark city, New Jersey	1,234
54	23	Cleveland city, Ohio	1,225
10	24	San Jose city, California	1,200
44	25	Miami city, Florida	1,196
2	26	Los Angeles city, California	1,184
46	27	Minneapolis city, Minnesota	1,120
12	28	Jacksonville city, Florida	1,114
27	29	Detroit city, Michigan	1,108
4	30	Houston city, Texas	1,080
14	31	Columbus city, Ohio	1,074
75	32	Jersey City city, New Jersey	1,055
55	33	Anaheim city, California	1,052
72	34	Plano city, Texas	1,050
8	35	San Diego city, California	1,001
16	36	Charlotte city, North Carolina	999
20	36	Oklahoma City city, Oklahoma	999
9	38	Dallas city, Texas	990
47	39	Tulsa city, Oklahoma	967
63	40	Orlando city, Florida	954
43	41	Long Beach city, California	939
11	42	Austin city, Texas	937
35	43	Sacramento city, California	913
39	44	Omaha city, Nebraska	898
13	45	Fort Worth city, Texas	875
51	46	Aurora city, Colorado	857
28	47	Louisville/Jefferson County metro, Kentucky	838
52	48	Tampa city, Florida	791
74	49	Durham city, North Carolina	783
64	50	Irvine city, California	777
5	51	Phoenix city, Arizona	767
41	52	Raleigh city, North Carolina	765
58	53	Stockton city, California	732
60	54	Corpus Christi city, Texas	722
50	55	Arlington city, Texas	714
69	56	Greensboro city, North Carolina	709
40	57	Colorado Springs city, Colorado	707
29	58	Memphis city, Tennessee	696
32	59	Albuquerque city, New Mexico	690
61	60	Riverside city, California	686
22	61	El Paso city, Texas	673
62	62	Santa Ana city, California	634
7	63	San Antonio city, Texas	626
33	64	Fresno city, California	613
71	65	Lincoln city, Nebraska	600
34	66	Tucson city, Arizona	578
67	67	St. Paul city, Minnesota	574
15	68	Indianapolis city, Indiana	492
57	68	Henderson city, Nevada	492
31	70	Milwaukee city, Wisconsin	482
49	71	Wichita city, Kansas	471
48	72	Bakersfield city, California	462
36	73	Mesa city, Arizona	439
25	74	Las Vegas city, Nevada	354
56		Urban Honolulu CDP, Hawaii	NA

Per capita city government debt outstanding, 2017

Population rank	Debt rank	City	Debt per capita (dollars) [col 138]
21	1	Nashville-Davidson metro, Tennessee	21,246
23	2	Washington city, District of Columbia	20,747
17	3	San Francisco city, California	19,138
1	4	New York city, New York	16,666
38	5	Atlanta city, Georgia	14,652
12	6	Jacksonville city, Florida	9,830
19	7	Denver city, Colorado	8,885
3	8	Chicago city, Illinois	8,683
9	9	Dallas city, Texas	8,129
67	10	St. Paul city, Minnesota	7,809
7	11	San Antonio city, Texas	7,751
37	12	Kansas City city, Missouri	7,339
2	13	Los Angeles city, California	6,949
18	14	Seattle city, Washington	6,929
46	15	Minneapolis city, Minnesota	6,898
49	16	Wichita city, Kansas	6,380
54	17	Cleveland city, Ohio	6,253
70	18	St. Louis city, Missouri	6,173
53	19	New Orleans city, Louisiana	6,166
4	20	Houston city, Texas	6,083
11	21	Austin city, Texas	5,669
61	22	Riverside city, California	5,477
40	23	Colorado Springs city, Colorado	5,335
73	24	Anchorage municipality, Alaska	5,331
45	25	Oakland city, California	5,255
55	26	Anaheim city, California	5,203
60	27	Corpus Christi city, Texas	5,145
43	28	Long Beach city, California	5,073
14	29	Columbus city, Ohio	4,871
26	30	Portland city, Oregon	4,863
71	31	Lincoln city, Nebraska	4,811
16	32	Charlotte city, North Carolina	4,736
5	33	Phoenix city, Arizona	4,729
27	34	Detroit city, Michigan	4,726
10	35	San Jose city, California	4,618
35	36	Sacramento city, California	4,559
63	37	Orlando city, Florida	4,406
52	38	Tampa city, Florida	4,284
15	39	Indianapolis city, Indiana	4,137
64	40	Irvine city, California	3,866
41	41	Raleigh city, North Carolina	3,608
47	42	Tulsa city, Oklahoma	3,512
22	43	El Paso city, Texas	3,339
42	44	Virginia Beach city, Virginia	3,299
6	45	Philadelphia city, Pennsylvania	3,162
29	46	Memphis city, Tennessee	3,082
36	47	Mesa city, Arizona	3,073
39	48	Omaha city, Nebraska	2,912
20	49	Oklahoma City city, Oklahoma	2,857
59	50	Lexington-Fayette urban county, Kentucky	2,856
65	51	Cincinnati city, Ohio	2,846
24	52	Boston city, Massachusetts	2,806
32	53	Albuquerque city, New Mexico	2,800
28	54	Louisville/Jefferson County metro, Kentucky	2,783
50	55	Arlington city, Texas	2,643
31	56	Milwaukee city, Wisconsin	2,538
75	57	Jersey City city, New Jersey	2,512
33	58	Fresno city, California	2,296
51	59	Aurora city, Colorado	2,203
8	60	San Diego city, California	1,968
58	61	Stockton city, California	1,899
34	62	Tucson city, Arizona	1,858
48	63	Bakersfield city, California	1,751
69	64	Greensboro city, North Carolina	1,704
13	65	Fort Worth city, Texas	1,694
68	66	Pittsburgh city, Pennsylvania	1,570
66	67	Newark city, New Jersey	1,543
44	68	Miami city, Florida	1,429
30	69	Baltimore city, Maryland	1,341
25	70	Las Vegas city, Nevada	1,255
74	71	Durham city, North Carolina	1,232
57	72	Henderson city, Nevada	772
62	73	Santa Ana city, California	671
72	74	Plano city, Texas	471
56		Urban Honolulu CDP, Hawaii	NA

Violent crime rate, 2020 (violent crimes known to police)

Population rank	Violent crime rate rank	City	Violent crimes (per 100,000) population) [col 36]
29	1	Memphis city, Tennessee	2,352.0
27	2	Detroit city, Michigan	2,178.5
70	3	St. Louis city, Missouri	2,016.3
54	4	Cleveland city, Ohio	1,656.7
31	5	Milwaukee city, Wisconsin	1,596.8
37	6	Kansas City city, Missouri	1,585.9
32	7	Albuquerque city, New Mexico	1,343.6
53	8	New Orleans city, Louisiana	1,324.3
45	9	Oakland city, California	1,290.9
58	10	Stockton city, California	1,277.2
4	11	Houston city, Texas	1,256.3
73	12	Anchorage municipality, Alaska	1,212.3
46	13	Minneapolis city, Minnesota	1,154.9
47	14	Tulsa city, Oklahoma	1,132.6
3	15	Chicago city, Illinois	986.9
23	16	Washington city, District of Columbia	957.9
69	17	Greensboro city, North Carolina	901.7
51	18	Aurora city, Colorado	900.4
65	19	Cincinnati city, Ohio	892.9
63	20	Orlando city, Florida	860.4
74	21	Durham city, North Carolina	858.8
19	22	Denver city, Colorado	857.9
9	23	Dallas city, Texas	844.7
60	24	Corpus Christi city, Texas	842.4
16	25	Charlotte city, North Carolina	836.3
5	26	Phoenix city, Arizona	798.5
67	27	St. Paul city, Minnesota	748.7
7	28	San Antonio city, Texas	735.4
20	29	Oklahoma City city, Oklahoma	726.0
2	30	Los Angeles city, California	721.9
34	31	Tucson city, Arizona	698.2
12	32	Jacksonville city, Florida	697.9
35	33	Sacramento city, California	683.4
33	34	Fresno city, California	664.8
39	35	Omaha city, Nebraska	631.3
18	36	Seattle city, Washington	626.3
24	37	Boston city, Massachusetts	624.4
40	38	Colorado Springs city, Colorado	597.0
1	39	New York city, New York	577.8
14	40	Columbus city, Ohio	555.6
44	40	Miami city, Florida	555.6
17	42	San Francisco city, California	544.1
13	43	Fort Worth city, Texas	541.0
50	44	Arlington city, Texas	531.9
66	45	Newark city, New Jersey	528.6
25	46	Las Vegas city, Nevada	527.7
26	47	Portland city, Oregon	522.7
52	48	Tampa city, Florida	520.2
48	49	Bakersfield city, California	516.9
43	50	Long Beach city, California	506.4
11	51	Austin city, Texas	467.0
61	52	Riverside city, California	445.9
75	53	Jersey City city, New Jersey	443.3
62	54	Santa Ana city, California	429.0
10	55	San Jose city, California	424.9
41	56	Raleigh city, North Carolina	392.1
36	57	Mesa city, Arizona	371.7
8	58	San Diego city, California	368.9
55	59	Anaheim city, California	352.6
59	60	Lexington-Fayette urban county, Kentucky	320.1
22	61	El Paso city, Texas	316.2
57	62	Henderson city, Nevada	207.9
72	63	Plano city, Texas	155.4
42	64	Virginia Beach city, Virginia	98.7
64	65	Irvine city, California	51.2
6		Philadelphia city, Pennsylvania	NA
15		Indianapolis city, Indiana	NA
21		Nashville-Davidson metro, Tennessee	NA
28		Louisville/Jefferson County metro, Kentucky	NA
30		Baltimore city, Maryland	NA
38		Atlanta city, Georgia	NA
49		Wichita city, Kansas	NA
56		Urban Honolulu CDP, Hawaii	NA
68		Pittsburgh city, Pennsylvania	NA
71		Lincoln city, Nebraska	NA

75 Largest Cities by 2021 Population

Selected rankings

Property crime rate, 2020 (property crimes known to police)

Population rank	Property crime rank	City	Property crimes (per 100,000) population) [col 38]
70	1	St. Louis city, Missouri	5,830.3
29	2	Memphis city, Tennessee	5,560.8
45	3	Oakland city, California	5,165.7
47	4	Tulsa city, Oklahoma	5,111.6
32	5	Albuquerque city, New Mexico	5,012.1
18	6	Seattle city, Washington	4,872.6
26	7	Portland city, Oregon	4,738.9
19	8	Denver city, Colorado	4,648.7
46	9	Minneapolis city, Minnesota	4,558.1
53	10	New Orleans city, Louisiana	4,539.6
17	11	San Francisco city, California	4,394.4
4	12	Houston city, Texas	4,178.9
37	13	Kansas City city, Missouri	4,119.5
54	14	Cleveland city, Ohio	4,070.7
48	15	Bakersfield city, California	4,022.8
20	16	Oklahoma City city, Oklahoma	3,895.5
63	17	Orlando city, Florida	3,803.5
67	18	St. Paul city, Minnesota	3,802.7
74	19	Durham city, North Carolina	3,737.8
65	20	Cincinnati city, Ohio	3,683.3
11	21	Austin city, Texas	3,631.2
7	22	San Antonio city, Texas	3,626.8
34	23	Tucson city, Arizona	3,620.9
69	24	Greensboro city, North Carolina.	3,611.4
73	25	Anchorage municipality, Alaska .	3,447.1
9	26	Dallas city, Texas	3,446.3
23	27	Washington city, District of Columbia	3,431.3
51	28	Aurora city, Colorado	3,390.8
40	29	Colorado Springs city, Colorado	3,379.6
60	30	Corpus Christi city, Texas	3,266.1
16	31	Charlotte city, North Carolina	3,240.2
27	32	Detroit city, Michigan	3,210.7
39	33	Omaha city, Nebraska	3,174.5
14	34	Columbus city, Ohio	3,130.4
33	35	Fresno city, California	3,076.7
5	36	Phoenix city, Arizona	2,989.5
61	37	Riverside city, California	2,984.7
58	38	Stockton city, California	2,981.4
59	39	Lexington-Fayette urban county, Kentucky	2,871.6
12	40	Jacksonville city, Florida	2,871.5
44	41	Miami city, Florida	2,749.8
43	42	Long Beach city, California	2,746.5
35	43	Sacramento city, California	2,745.0
13	44	Fort Worth city, Texas	2,733.2
31	45	Milwaukee city, Wisconsin	2,728.5
50	46	Arlington city, Texas	2,550.5
55	47	Anaheim city, California	2,519.1
10	48	San Jose city, California	2,316.3
25	49	Las Vegas city, Nevada	2,210.6
2	50	Los Angeles city, California	2,148.0
62	51	Santa Ana city, California	2,079.2
41	52	Raleigh city, North Carolina	2,020.7
24	53	Boston city, Massachusetts	1,866.4
36	54	Mesa city, Arizona	1,846.4
8	55	San Diego city, California	1,691.8
72	56	Plano city, Texas	1,645.2
66	57	Newark city, New Jersey	1,618.1
1	58	New York city, New York	1,558.5
42	59	Virginia Beach city, Virginia	1,511.8
64	60	Irvine city, California	1,498.6
75	61	Jersey City city, New Jersey	1,496.5
57	62	Henderson city, Nevada	1,426.3
52	63	Tampa city, Florida	1,365.2
22	64	El Paso city, Texas	1,241.4
3		Chicago city, Illinois	NA
6		Philadelphia city, Pennsylvania	NA
15		Indianapolis city, Indiana	NA
21		Nashville-Davidson metro, Tennessee	NA
28		Louisville/Jefferson County metro, Kentucky	NA
30		Baltimore city, Maryland	NA
38		Atlanta city, Georgia	NA
49		Wichita city, Kansas	NA
56		Urban Honolulu CDP, Hawaii	NA
68		Pittsburgh city, Pennsylvania	NA
71		Lincoln city, Nebraska	NA

Full-time equivalent local government employees, 2017

Population rank	Government employees rank	City	Government employees [col 108]
1	1	New York city, New York	434,443
2	2	Los Angeles city, California	52,287
23	3	Washington city, District of Columbia	40,352
17	4	San Francisco city, California	33,660
3	5	Chicago city, Illinois	31,798
6	6	Philadelphia city, Pennsylvania	30,557
30	7	Baltimore city, Maryland	25,611
4	8	Houston city, Texas	21,657
21	9	Nashville-Davidson metro, Tennessee	21,283
24	10	Boston city, Massachusetts	19,672
42	11	Virginia Beach city, Virginia	17,638
7	12	San Antonio city, Texas	15,585
9	13	Dallas city, Texas	14,767
19	14	Denver city, Colorado	14,162
11	15	Austin city, Texas	13,610
15	16	Indianapolis city, Indiana	13,456
5	17	Phoenix city, Arizona	12,939
18	18	Seattle city, Washington	11,912
8	19	San Diego city, California	10,832
29	20	Memphis city, Tennessee	10,740
73	21	Anchorage municipality, Alaska	9,255
12	22	Jacksonville city, Florida	9,087
27	23	Detroit city, Michigan	8,795
14	24	Columbus city, Ohio	8,528
38	25	Atlanta city, Georgia	8,317
16	26	Charlotte city, North Carolina	8,026
54	27	Cleveland city, Ohio	7,046
53	28	New Orleans city, Louisiana	6,939
32	29	Albuquerque city, New Mexico	6,938
13	30	Fort Worth city, Texas	6,703
70	31	St. Louis city, Missouri	6,658
22	32	El Paso city, Texas	6,522
31	33	Milwaukee city, Wisconsin	6,507
37	34	Kansas City city, Missouri	6,334
26	35	Portland city, Oregon	6,225
65	36	Cincinnati city, Ohio	5,538
43	37	Long Beach city, California	5,477
34	38	Tucson city, Arizona	4,956
46	39	Minneapolis city, Minnesota	4,811
41	40	Raleigh city, North Carolina	4,767
20	41	Oklahoma City city, Oklahoma	4,494
52	42	Tampa city, Florida	4,198
35	43	Sacramento city, California	4,106
45	44	Oakland city, California	4,077
40	45	Colorado Springs city, Colorado	4,068
44	46	Miami city, Florida	3,951
47	47	Tulsa city, Oklahoma	3,773
59	48	Lexington-Fayette urban county, Kentucky	3,756
66	49	Newark city, New Jersey	3,735
36	50	Mesa city, Arizona	3,715
33	51	Fresno city, California	3,451
10	52	San Jose city, California	3,403
68	53	Pittsburgh city, Pennsylvania	3,293
69	54	Greensboro city, North Carolina	3,249
67	55	St. Paul city, Minnesota	3,186
63	56	Orlando city, Florida	3,145
60	57	Corpus Christi city, Texas	2,997
75	58	Jersey City city, New Jersey	2,982
49	59	Wichita city, Kansas	2,961
39	60	Omaha city, Nebraska	2,910
51	61	Aurora city, Colorado	2,891
25	62	Las Vegas city, Nevada	2,867
74	63	Durham city, North Carolina	2,861
71	64	Lincoln city, Nebraska	2,642
50	65	Arlington city, Texas	2,558
55	66	Anaheim city, California	2,310
57	66	Henderson city, Nevada	2,310
72	68	Plano city, Texas	2,302
61	69	Riverside city, California	2,170
58	70	Stockton city, California	1,598
48	71	Bakersfield city, California	1,490
62	72	Santa Ana city, California	1,094
64	73	Irvine city, California	1,045
28		Louisville/Jefferson County metro, Kentucky	NA
56		Urban Honolulu CDP, Hawaii	NA

Local government employee payroll for March 2017

Population rank	Government employee payroll rank	City	Government payroll (thousands of dollars) [col 109]
1	1	New York city, New York	2,716,087,055
2	2	Los Angeles city, California	452,879,430
23	3	Washington city, District of Columbia	276,215,832
17	4	San Francisco city, California	260,920,281
3	5	Chicago city, Illinois	220,385,761
6	6	Philadelphia city, Pennsylvania	177,705,357
30	7	Baltimore city, Maryland	138,264,675
24	8	Boston city, Massachusetts	132,820,934
4	9	Houston city, Texas	108,741,222
21	10	Nashville-Davidson metro, Tennessee	101,098,567
5	11	Phoenix city, Arizona	98,028,340
18	12	Seattle city, Washington	94,722,910
7	13	San Antonio city, Texas	91,157,442
19	14	Denver city, Colorado	86,682,654
9	15	Dallas city, Texas	85,321,347
11	16	Austin city, Texas	84,706,545
8	17	San Diego city, California	75,006,131
42	18	Virginia Beach city, Virginia	70,561,307
15	19	Indianapolis city, Indiana	61,603,859
73	20	Anchorage municipality, Alaska	52,804,925
14	21	Columbus city, Ohio	52,605,234
29	22	Memphis city, Tennessee	51,032,329
26	23	Portland city, Oregon	42,536,596
12	24	Jacksonville city, Florida	42,343,407
16	25	Charlotte city, North Carolina	40,618,050
38	26	Atlanta city, Georgia	39,867,373
43	27	Long Beach city, California	39,697,152
13	28	Fort Worth city, Texas	38,281,122
32	29	Albuquerque city, New Mexico	37,997,192
70	30	St. Louis city, Missouri	37,801,592
31	31	Milwaukee city, Wisconsin	37,635,419
45	32	Oakland city, California	36,522,164
28	33	Louisville/Jefferson County metro, Kentucky	36,302,120
54	34	Cleveland city, Ohio	35,836,530
53	35	New Orleans city, Louisiana	33,679,953
27	36	Detroit city, Michigan	32,957,680
35	37	Sacramento city, California	31,089,039
65	38	Cincinnati city, Ohio	30,765,986
46	39	Minneapolis city, Minnesota	29,451,317
37	40	Kansas City city, Missouri	28,199,434
40	41	Colorado Springs city, Colorado	27,500,431
20	42	Oklahoma City city, Oklahoma	27,224,626
34	43	Tucson city, Arizona	25,663,881
22	44	El Paso city, Texas	25,566,174
52	45	Tampa city, Florida	25,536,216
36	46	Mesa city, Arizona	22,765,005
10	47	San Jose city, California	22,735,265
44	48	Miami city, Florida	21,993,811
75	49	Jersey City city, New Jersey	20,957,923
33	50	Fresno city, California	20,907,203
41	51	Raleigh city, North Carolina	20,560,599
25	52	Las Vegas city, Nevada	20,161,448
61	53	Riverside city, California	19,847,957
55	54	Anaheim city, California	19,689,571
47	55	Tulsa city, Oklahoma	19,022,256
59	56	Lexington-Fayette urban county, Kentucky	18,866,699
67	57	St. Paul city, Minnesota	18,549,813
39	58	Omaha city, Nebraska	18,004,814
63	59	Orlando city, Florida	17,935,004
51	60	Aurora city, Colorado	17,630,608
68	61	Pittsburgh city, Pennsylvania	17,441,555
57	62	Henderson city, Nevada	16,130,348
66	63	Newark city, New Jersey	15,962,973
71	64	Lincoln city, Nebraska	14,836,126
49	65	Wichita city, Kansas	14,226,610
50	66	Arlington city, Texas	13,968,727
60	67	Corpus Christi city, Texas	13,665,749
69	68	Greensboro city, North Carolina	13,016,203
72	69	Plano city, Texas	12,930,116
74	70	Durham city, North Carolina	12,296,323
58	71	Stockton city, California	11,211,014
64	72	Irvine city, California	10,354,501
48	73	Bakersfield city, California	9,653,365
62	74	Santa Ana city, California	9,302,161
56		Urban Honolulu CDP, Hawaii	NA

Table D. Cities — **Land Area and Population**

STATE Place code	City	Land area[1] (sq. mi)	Population, 2021			Race 2020						
						Race alone[2] (percent)						Two or more races (percent)
			Total persons 2021	Rank	Per square mile	White	Black or African American	American Indian, Alaskan Native	Asian	Hawaiian Pacific Islander	Some other race	
		1	2	3	4	5	6	7	8	9	10	11

1. Dry land or land partially or temporarily covered by water. 2. Hispanic or Latino persons may be of any race.

Table D. Cities — **Population**

City	Percent Hispanic or Latino[1], 2020	Percent foreign born, 2016–2020	Age of population (percent), 2016–2020							Median age, 2016–2020	Percent female, 2016–2020	Population			
												Census counts		Percent change	
			Under 18 years	18 to 24 years	25 to 34 years	35 to 44 years	45 to 54 years	55 to 64 years	65 years and over			2010	2020	2010-2020	2020-2021
	12	13	14	15	16	17	18	19	20	21	22	23	24	25	26

1. May be of any race.

Table D. Cities — **Households, Group Quarters, Crime, and Education**

City	Households, 2016-2020							Persons in group quarters, 2016–2020	Serious crimes known to police[1], 2020				Educational attainment, 2016–2020		
			Percent						Violent		Property			Attainment[3] (percent)	
	Number	Persons per household	Family	Married couple family	Female family	Non-family	One person		Number	Rate[2]	Number	Rate[2]	Population age 25 and over	High school graduate or less	Bachelor's degree or more
	27	28	29	30	31	32	33	34	35	36	37	38	39	40	41

1. Data for serious crimes have not been adjusted for underreporting. This may affect comparability between geographic areas and over time. 2. Per 100,000 population estimated by the FBI. 3. Persons 25 years old and over.

Table D. Cities — **Income, Poverty, and Housing**

City	Money income, 2016-2020					Median earnings of Full year, Full-time workers, 2016–2020			Housing units, 2016-2020				
	Households												
	Median household income	Percent with income less than $25,000	Percent with income of $200,000 or more	Median family income	Median non-family household income	All persons	Men	Women	Total	Occupied	Percent owner occupied	Median value[1] (dollars)	Median gross rent (dollars)
	42	43	44	45	46	47	48	49	50	51	52	53	54

1. Specified owner-occupied units

Table D. Cities — Commuting, Computer Access, Migration, Labor Force, and Employment

City	Commuting, 2016–2020[1]		Computer access[2], 2016–2020		Migration, 2016–2020		Civilian labor force, 2021				Civilian Employment, 2016–2020[4]			
	Percent		Percent		Percent who lived in the same house one year ago	Percent who lived in another state or county one year ago	Total	Percent change 2020–2021	Unemployment[3]		Population age 16 and older		Population age 16 to 64	
	Drove alone	Mean travel time to work	With a computer in the house	With Internet access					Total	Rate	Number	Percent in labor force	Number	Percent who worked full-year full-time
	55	56	57	58	59	60	61	62	63	64	65	66	67	68

1. Employed persons. 2. Households. 3. Percent of civilian labor force. 4. Persons 16 years old and over.

Table D. Cities — Construction, Wholesale Trade, and Retail Trade

City	Value of residential construction authorized by building permits, 2021			Wholesale trade[1], 2017				Retail trade[2], 2017			
	New construction ($1,000)	Number of housing units	Percent single family	Number of establishments	Number of employees	Sales (mil dol)	Annual payroll (mil dol)	Number of establish-ments	Number of employees	Sales (mil dol)	Annual payroll (mil dol)
	69	70	71	72	73	74	75	76	77	78	79

1. Merchant wholesalers except manufacturers' sales branches and offices. 2. Establishments with payroll.

Table D. Cities — Real Estate, Professional Services, and Manufacturing

City	Real estate and rental and leasing, 2017				Professional, scientific, and technical services[1], 2017				Manufacturing, 2017			
	Number of establish-ments	Number of employees	Receipts (mil dol)	Annual payroll (mil dol)	Number of establish-ments	Number of employees	Receipts (mil dol)	Annual payroll (mil dol)	Number of establish-ments	Number of employees	Receipts (mil dol)	Annual payroll (mil dol)
	80	81	82	83	84	85	86	87	88	89	90	91

1. Establishments subject to federal tax.

Table D. Cities — Accommodation and Food Services, Arts, Entertainment, and Recreation, and Health Care and Social Assistance

City	Accommodation and food services, 2017				Arts, entertainment, and recreation[1], 2017				Health care and social assistance[1], 2017			
	Number of establish-ments	Number of employees	Receipts (mil dol)	Annual payroll (mil dol)	Number of establish-ments	Number of employees	Receipts (mil dol)	Annual payroll (mil dol)	Number of establish-ments	Number of employees	Receipts (mil dol)	Annual payroll (mil dol)
	92	93	94	95	96	97	98	99	100	101	102	103

1. Establishments subject to federal tax.

Table D. Cities — Other Services and Government Employment and Payroll

City	Other services[1]				Government employment and payroll, 2017								
						March payroll							
							Perent of total for:						
	Number of establish- ments	Number of employees	Receipts (mil dol)	Annual payroll (mil dol)	Full-time equivalent employees	Total (dollars)	Admin- istrative, judicial, and legal	Police and corrections	Fire protection	Highways and trans- portation	Health and welfare	Natural resources and utilities	Education and libraries
	104	105	106	107	108	109	110	111	112	113	114	115	116

1. Establishments subject to federal tax.

Table D. Cities — City Government Finances

City	City government finances, 2017									
	General revenue							General expenditure		
		Intergovernmental		Taxes						
					Per capita[1] (dollars)				Per capita[1] (dollars)	
	Total (mil dol)	Total (mil dol)	Percent from state government	Total (mil dol)	Total	Property	Sales and gross receipts	Total (mil dol)	Total	Capital outlays
	117	118	119	120	121	122	123	124	125	126

1. Based on population estimated as of July 1 of the year shown.

Table D. Cities — City Government Finances

City	City government finances, 2017 (cont.)												
	General expenditure (cont.)										Debt outstanding		
	Percent of total for:												
	Public welfare	Highways	Parking facilities	Education	Health and hospitals	Police protection	Sewerage and sanitation	Parks and recreation	Housing and community development	Interest on debt	Total (mil dol)	Per capita[1] (dollars)	Debt issued during year
	127	128	129	130	131	132	133	134	135	136	137	138	139

1. Based on the population estimated as of July 1 of the year shown.

Table D. Cities — **Land Area and Population**

STATE	Place code	City	Land area[1] (sq. mi)	Population, 2021: Total persons 2021	Population, 2021: Rank	Population, 2021: Per square mile	Race 2020, Race alone[2] (percent): White	Black or African American	American Indian, Alaskan Native	Asian	Hawaiian Pacific Islander	Some other race	Two or more races (percent)
			1	2	3	4	5	6	7	8	9	10	11
00	00000	UNITED STATES	3,533,043.7	331,893,745	X	93.9	61.6	12.4	1.1	6.0	0.2	8.4	10.2
01	00000	ALABAMA	50,646.6	5,039,877	X	99.5	64.1	25.8	0.7	1.5	0.1	2.7	5.1
01	00820	Alabaster	25.4	33,676	1,178	1,325.8	67.1	16.1	0.7	1.2	0.1	7.3	7.6
01	02956	Athens	40.6	27,027	1,438	665.7	69.3	17.0	0.8	0.9	0.1	5.5	6.4
01	03076	Auburn	61.0	78,564	463	1,287.9	64.2	18.4	0.3	9.7	0.0	2.1	5.2
01	05980	Bessemer	40.4	25,615	1,511	634.0	19.8	69.9	0.4	0.3	0.0	5.2	4.5
01	07000	Birmingham	147.0	197,575	124	1,344.0	23.5	68.4	0.4	1.6	0.1	2.7	3.3
01	19648	Daphne	19.0	28,777	1,358	1,514.6	79.2	10.8	0.5	1.5	0.1	1.4	6.6
01	20104	Decatur	54.4	57,804	685	1,062.6	57.3	23.2	0.7	0.9	0.1	10.3	7.4
01	21184	Dothan	89.8	71,175	522	792.6	57.0	33.6	0.4	1.6	0.1	2.0	5.3
01	24184	Enterprise	31.0	29,395	1,328	948.2	61.9	20.5	1.0	2.8	0.2	4.2	9.5
01	26896	Florence	26.5	39,933	992	1,506.9	70.7	18.9	0.4	1.3	0.1	2.7	5.9
01	28696	Gadsden	37.4	33,769	1,175	902.9	51.7	35.7	1.2	0.8	0.1	4.9	5.6
01	35800	Homewood	8.3	26,054	1,489	3,139.0	69.9	19.9	0.2	2.7	0.0	2.0	5.3
01	35896	Hoover	48.1	92,589	365	1,924.9	68.7	16.9	0.3	6.4	0.0	2.1	5.6
01	37000	Huntsville	219.3	216,963	106	989.3	56.6	29.3	0.7	2.5	0.1	3.4	7.3
01	45784	Madison	30.4	58,357	674	1,919.6	66.6	14.9	0.5	7.8	0.1	1.9	8.2
01	50000	Mobile	139.5	184,952	138	1,325.8	40.8	51.3	0.3	1.8	0.1	1.4	4.3
01	51000	Montgomery	159.9	198,665	123	1,242.4	29.2	60.3	0.4	3.6	0.1	2.9	3.6
01	55200	Northport	17.5	31,009	1,271	1,771.9	64.8	25.0	1.0	1.2	0.1	3.6	4.3
01	57048	Opelika	61.2	31,538	1,256	515.3	48.8	38.8	0.6	2.2	0.0	5.1	4.4
01	59472	Phenix City	28.1	38,428	1,036	1,367.5	41.6	49.1	0.4	1.0	0.2	2.2	5.6
01	62328	Prattville	35.4	38,286	1,039	1,081.5	68.8	21.1	0.4	2.3	0.1	1.7	5.7
01	76944	Trussville	34.7	26,388	1,472	760.5	81.6	11.0	0.2	2.1	0.0	0.7	4.4
01	77256	Tuscaloosa	61.9	100,618	327	1,625.5	48.7	41.2	0.3	2.4	0.1	2.1	5.3
01	78552	Vestavia Hills	20.0	38,801	1,026	1,940.1	83.9	4.7	0.2	5.6	0.0	1.1	4.5
02	00000	ALASKA	571,016.9	732,673	X	1.3	59.4	3.0	15.2	6.0	1.7	2.5	12.2
02	03000	Anchorage	1,706.9	288,121	73	168.8	56.5	5.0	8.1	9.5	3.4	3.5	14.0
02	24230	Fairbanks	31.7	32,702	1,211	1,031.6	57.8	8.1	10.7	4.8	1.2	3.3	14.0
02	36400	Juneau	2,704.0	31,973	1,235	11.8	62.4	1.1	11.2	6.5	1.5	2.0	15.3
04	00000	ARIZONA	113,653.1	7,276,316	X	64.0	60.4	4.7	4.5	3.6	0.2	12.6	13.9
04	02830	Apache Junction	35.1	39,981	988	1,139.1	80.8	1.2	1.2	1.0	0.1	6.9	8.7
04	04720	Avondale	47.6	90,564	377	1,902.6	37.7	10.0	2.1	4.1	0.4	25.7	20.0
04	07940	Buckeye	393.0	101,315	317	257.8	56.6	7.2	1.8	1.7	0.3	16.2	16.1
04	08220	Bullhead City	59.4	42,232	945	711.0	73.6	1.4	1.4	1.5	0.2	10.0	11.8
04	10530	Casa Grande	112.0	57,699	686	515.2	56.4	4.9	4.2	2.0	0.3	15.4	16.8
04	12000	Chandler	65.5	279,458	76	4,266.5	58.4	6.0	1.9	12.0	0.2	8.2	13.3
04	22220	El Mirage	9.9	36,016	1,099	3,638.0	47.4	7.4	2.0	2.0	0.4	22.0	18.9
04	23620	Flagstaff	66.0	76,989	473	1,166.5	66.2	2.1	11.2	2.6	0.3	7.1	10.6
04	23760	Florence town	62.6	26,205	1,478	418.6	60.0	7.6	4.6	0.9	0.2	18.7	8.0
04	27400	Gilbert town	68.6	273,136	80	3,981.6	71.5	3.8	1.0	6.7	0.2	4.5	12.1
04	27820	Glendale	64.7	249,630	91	3,858.3	51.1	7.7	2.0	4.7	0.2	18.6	15.7
04	28380	Goodyear	191.3	101,733	316	531.8	59.2	7.7	1.4	4.1	0.3	12.3	15.0
04	37620	Kingman	37.5	33,822	1,174	901.9	80.2	1.3	1.9	2.1	0.3	4.5	9.7
04	39370	Lake Havasu City	46.3	58,284	675	1,258.8	83.6	0.6	1.0	1.1	0.1	4.5	9.0
04	44270	Marana town	121.1	54,895	725	453.3	70.5	2.8	1.2	4.1	0.2	6.8	14.4
04	44410	Maricopa	42.5	62,720	613	1,475.8	56.0	12.4	2.4	2.9	0.5	10.5	15.3
04	46000	Mesa	138.8	509,475	36	3,670.6	65.7	4.2	2.7	2.6	0.4	12.0	12.3
04	51600	Oro Valley	34.9	47,879	831	1,371.9	79.6	1.6	0.5	4.3	0.1	3.1	10.8
04	54050	Peoria	176.1	194,917	131	1,106.9	71.4	4.0	1.1	4.6	0.2	6.8	11.9
04	55000	Phoenix	518.3	1,624,569	5	3,134.4	49.7	7.8	2.6	4.1	0.2	20.1	15.5
04	57380	Prescott	45.0	46,833	852	1,040.7	86.2	0.7	1.0	1.8	0.1	2.5	7.7
04	57450	Prescott Valley town	40.5	48,188	825	1,189.8	78.7	0.9	1.3	1.6	0.2	6.9	10.4
04	58150	Queen Creek	40.8	66,346	576	1,626.1	77.2	3.3	0.9	2.5	0.2	4.2	11.7
04	62140	Sahuarita	31.7	35,337	1,128	1,114.7	63.2	2.9	1.3	1.9	0.3	10.2	20.3
04	63470	San Luis	34.0	37,333	1,064	1,098.0	23.2	2.7	1.2	0.1	0.0	39.6	33.1
04	65000	Scottsdale	184.0	242,753	92	1,319.3	81.0	2.0	0.8	5.0	0.1	3.3	7.8
04	66820	Sierra Vista	152.3	45,479	870	298.6	63.9	8.2	1.0	4.4	0.8	6.9	14.9
04	71510	Surprise	110.3	149,191	179	1,352.6	71.7	5.5	0.9	2.8	0.2	6.3	12.6
04	73000	Tempe	39.9	184,118	140	4,614.5	59.8	6.7	3.1	9.7	0.4	8.0	12.4
04	77000	Tucson	241.0	543,242	34	2,254.1	54.5	5.6	2.9	3.2	0.3	15.2	18.3
04	85540	Yuma	120.8	97,093	340	803.8	46.4	2.6	1.8	2.1	0.2	23.1	23.9
05	00000	ARKANSAS	52,037.5	3,025,891	X	58.1	70.2	15.1	0.9	1.7	0.5	4.5	7.1
05	04840	Bella Vista	45.3	30,808	1,280	680.1	88.6	0.7	1.0	0.7	0.1	1.3	7.5
05	05290	Benton	22.9	35,675	1,114	1,557.9	78.8	9.8	0.6	1.4	0.0	2.8	6.4
05	05320	Bentonville	34.1	56,734	697	1,663.8	66.3	3.1	1.2	15.6	0.4	4.0	9.3
05	10300	Cabot	20.7	26,655	1,457	1,287.7	84.4	2.9	0.6	1.7	0.1	1.9	8.4

1. Dry land or land partially or temporarily covered by water. 2. Hispanic or Latino persons may be of any race.

City	Percent Hispanic or Latino[1], 2020	Percent foreign born, 2016–2020	Age of population (percent), 2016–2020							Median age, 2016–2020	Percent female, 2016–2020	Population			
			Under 18 years	18 to 24 years	25 to 34 years	35 to 44 years	45 to 54 years	55 to 64 years	65 years and over			Census counts		Percent change	
												2010	2020	2010–2020	2020–2021
	12	13	14	15	16	17	18	19	20	21	22	23	24	25	26
UNITED STATES	18.7	13.5	22.4	9.3	13.9	12.7	12.7	12.9	16.0	38.2	50.8	308,758,105	331,449,281	7.3	0.1
ALABAMA	5.3	3.4	22.3	9.3	13.1	12.2	12.8	13.4	16.9	39.2	51.7	4,780,118	5,024,279	5.1	0.3
Alabaster	12.7	5.6	26.5	8.3	11.2	16.9	14.5	11.2	11.3	37.0	52.4	31,095	33,360	7.3	0.9
Athens	9.5	5.0	19.7	7.2	15.3	11.5	12.5	15.4	18.3	41.3	50.2	21,877	25,420	16.2	6.3
Auburn	4.8	10.3	18.2	31.2	14.2	10.8	10.3	6.9	8.4	25.2	50.6	53,426	76,000	42.3	3.4
Bessemer	8.9	2.8	20.0	9.7	11.3	11.5	12.7	14.6	20.3	42.4	54.1	27,439	26,044	-5.1	-1.6
Birmingham	4.6	4.0	19.3	11.0	18.2	11.3	11.0	13.5	15.6	36.2	53.3	212,013	200,763	-5.3	-1.6
Daphne	4.5	3.5	23.4	7.7	12.6	12.3	11.4	13.9	18.7	39.5	51.5	21,638	27,525	27.2	4.5
Decatur	15.7	6.7	23.2	8.1	11.9	12.0	13.8	12.5	18.5	40.4	51.1	55,779	57,851	3.7	-0.1
Dothan	4.4	3.1	22.8	7.7	13.5	12.2	12.5	13.2	18.1	40.0	52.2	66,002	71,182	7.8	0.0
Enterprise	11.9	4.5	25.8	7.4	15.1	13.6	11.0	11.2	16.0	36.2	51.9	26,519	28,752	8.4	2.2
Florence	5.2	3.1	19.3	16.4	15.1	10.7	8.8	11.7	17.9	34.5	53.5	39,601	39,783	0.5	0.4
Gadsden	8.1	4.2	21.6	9.8	11.2	13.6	12.1	13.6	18.1	40.3	52.3	36,930	34,070	-7.7	-0.9
Homewood	5.4	6.3	24.4	15.8	15.5	13.3	11.6	8.4	11.1	30.6	54.7	25,157	26,388	4.9	-1.3
Hoover	5.1	8.6	25.5	6.4	13.5	15.0	13.7	10.6	15.4	37.9	52.8	80,477	92,651	15.1	-0.1
Huntsville	7.8	6.4	19.9	12.1	15.5	11.7	11.7	12.8	16.4	36.8	51.4	180,370	214,372	18.9	1.2
Madison	5.8	7.6	26.2	6.0	11.8	13.9	16.0	13.2	12.7	39.6	50.9	43,193	57,124	32.3	2.2
Mobile	3.2	3.4	21.3	10.6	15.2	11.9	11.5	12.9	16.6	37.3	53.0	194,665	186,833	-4.0	-1.0
Montgomery	4.8	5.1	23.8	10.3	14.8	12.6	11.8	12.2	14.6	36.0	53.1	205,488	200,567	-2.4	-0.9
Northport	6.6	3.0	26.4	7.6	18.2	13.6	9.9	11.2	13.1	33.3	54.0	23,765	31,119	30.9	-0.4
Opelika	7.8	3.4	22.1	7.9	15.2	10.9	14.6	12.8	16.4	40.7	52.1	26,441	31,039	17.4	1.6
Phenix City	6.0	4.0	24.9	9.2	14.6	14.2	12.3	12.4	12.4	35.6	51.8	32,810	38,819	18.3	-1.0
Prattville	4.0	3.6	24.2	8.9	13.7	13.4	13.9	11.5	14.5	37.3	51.2	34,280	37,813	10.3	1.3
Trussville	2.2	1.7	25.5	5.7	7.6	14.4	15.9	16.6	14.4	42.9	50.5	19,959	26,160	31.1	0.9
Tuscaloosa	5.5	4.1	17.8	24.0	14.9	10.5	9.7	10.0	13.0	29.5	51.7	90,228	99,706	10.5	0.9
Vestavia Hills	3.2	5.7	25.1	6.3	9.8	13.8	13.4	14.3	17.3	39.9	52.3	33,826	39,166	15.8	-0.9
ALASKA	6.8	7.8	24.9	9.5	16.1	12.8	12.1	12.7	11.9	34.6	47.8	710,246	733,391	3.3	-0.1
Anchorage	9.1	10.8	24.3	9.9	17.4	13.1	12.2	12.0	11.1	33.9	49.0	292,252	291,247	-0.3	-1.1
Fairbanks	11.4	6.4	25.0	17.5	20.9	9.5	9.2	7.6	10.3	27.9	46.9	31,551	32,744	3.8	-0.1
Juneau	6.4	8.4	21.4	8.2	15.4	13.7	13.5	14.3	13.6	38.5	48.7	31,276	32,255	3.1	-0.9
ARIZONA	30.7	13.2	22.9	9.6	13.8	12.3	11.9	12.0	17.6	37.9	50.3	6,392,292	7,151,502	11.9	1.7
Apache Junction	17.3	8.3	15.1	5.9	10.3	8.3	10.6	14.9	34.9	54.7	51.6	35,709	38,675	8.3	3.4
Avondale	55.6	18.4	28.1	10.3	16.8	13.4	12.3	10.3	8.8	31.6	51.0	76,068	89,490	17.6	1.2
Buckeye	38.9	10.5	29.4	7.6	15.1	16.2	11.2	8.5	12.1	33.7	45.3	50,829	91,154	79.3	11.1
Bullhead City	23.8	9.0	17.6	6.1	11.6	8.4	9.5	15.9	31.0	51.6	50.6	39,545	41,403	4.7	2.0
Casa Grande	40.2	11.1	25.6	10.2	13.1	11.0	10.5	9.9	19.7	36.1	50.0	48,571	53,891	11.0	7.1
Chandler	22.6	15.2	24.4	7.5	15.1	15.4	14.3	11.4	12.0	36.7	51.1	236,158	276,330	17.0	1.1
El Mirage	49.3	13.7	29.6	9.6	16.4	13.5	11.5	8.7	10.7	32.0	52.3	31,797	35,858	12.8	0.4
Flagstaff	19.7	5.3	18.4	31.8	14.6	10.4	7.7	8.3	8.8	24.9	50.1	66,018	76,781	16.3	0.3
Florence town	29.5	12.8	7.2	7.0	23.4	20.5	10.9	14.0	17.0	40.3	22.8	25,424	25,428	0.0	3.1
Gilbert town	16.8	9.1	29.7	8.7	12.4	15.1	14.6	9.9	9.7	34.5	51.2	208,439	268,302	28.7	1.8
Glendale	39.3	16.5	25.7	10.8	14.9	11.9	13.3	11.6	11.9	33.8	50.7	226,134	248,345	9.8	0.5
Goodyear	30.7	11.0	24.5	7.0	12.1	14.7	13.5	11.1	17.1	39.6	52.5	65,249	95,003	45.6	7.1
Kingman	14.4	3.9	20.2	6.7	14.5	10.7	8.8	15.1	24.0	42.8	48.1	28,071	32,680	16.4	3.5
Lake Havasu City	13.8	7.6	15.1	6.0	10.0	8.5	12.5	14.9	32.9	53.5	50.2	52,533	57,204	8.9	1.9
Marana town	25.1	8.7	22.8	7.7	10.7	14.8	11.5	11.1	21.3	41.3	50.8	34,541	52,020	50.6	5.5
Maricopa	27.8	9.5	28.5	7.2	12.8	16.0	12.5	9.9	13.1	35.9	52.3	43,493	58,442	34.4	7.3
Mesa	27.3	11.9	23.9	9.2	15.3	12.2	11.6	11.2	16.6	36.2	50.6	439,941	504,500	14.7	1.0
Oro Valley	13.7	9.7	18.1	6.0	7.6	8.8	10.4	14.4	34.7	54.0	51.6	41,027	47,185	15.0	1.5
Peoria	20.3	9.9	23.3	7.7	11.9	12.9	12.6	13.9	17.5	40.3	52.0	154,069	191,052	24.0	2.0
Phoenix	41.1	19.3	25.7	9.8	16.2	13.9	12.6	10.9	11.0	33.9	50.1	1,446,682	1,607,739	11.1	1.0
Prescott	9.2	5.7	11.9	8.3	7.6	6.1	9.7	17.6	38.8	59.1	51.1	39,662	45,683	15.2	2.5
Prescott Valley town	18.8	7.7	20.2	6.3	11.4	9.1	11.0	13.4	28.5	47.4	52.4	38,858	46,811	20.5	2.9
Queen Creek	16.2	5.6	31.3	6.5	9.7	15.3	13.6	10.3	13.3	36.6	51.9	26,732	59,590	122.9	11.3
Sahuarita	36.8	9.5	28.2	7.3	9.9	14.9	9.2	9.3	21.2	37.1	52.7	26,001	34,222	31.6	3.3
San Luis	90.1	46.7	29.1	11.8	16.1	12.7	12.5	9.6	8.3	30.7	45.6	27,922	35,905	28.6	4.0
Scottsdale	9.8	12.3	15.1	6.8	13.5	11.2	13.4	15.5	24.4	47.7	51.1	217,486	241,488	11.0	0.5
Sierra Vista	23.6	9.5	22.5	10.6	14.1	12.5	10.3	10.8	19.2	36.7	49.9	45,258	45,321	0.1	0.3
Surprise	19.8	8.3	24.9	6.6	9.7	12.9	12.9	9.8	23.1	41.9	52.6	117,436	143,261	22.0	4.1
Tempe	22.0	15.4	14.4	22.2	22.8	11.3	8.8	9.7	10.8	29.8	47.6	161,772	179,765	11.1	2.4
Tucson	42.2	14.6	20.6	15.3	15.5	12.0	10.8	11.0	14.8	34.0	50.5	526,510	541,349	2.8	0.3
Yuma	60.9	20.9	25.8	12.5	15.7	11.5	9.5	9.3	15.6	31.8	48.4	90,672	95,814	5.7	1.3
ARKANSAS	8.5	4.9	23.3	9.4	13.1	12.3	12.2	12.7	16.9	38.3	50.9	2,916,029	3,011,524	3.3	0.5
Bella Vista	4.5	2.0	18.3	4.6	9.0	13.4	8.2	14.7	31.8	50.6	50.5	26,510	30,202	13.9	2.0
Benton	5.8	3.6	24.8	8.0	13.3	15.3	12.7	10.6	15.3	37.5	51.4	30,765	35,011	13.8	1.9
Bentonville	10.0	17.0	27.9	8.2	19.6	17.1	11.3	8.1	7.8	32.0	48.2	35,344	54,120	53.1	4.8
Cabot	5.9	3.5	28.1	7.4	14.4	15.0	12.4	11.1	11.7	35.1	51.5	24,116	26,573	10.2	0.3

1. May be of any race.

City	Households, 2016–2020							Persons in group quarters, 2016–2020	Serious crimes known to police[1], 2020				Educational attainment, 2016–2020		
			Percent						Violent		Property			Attainment[3] (percent)	
	Number	Persons per household	Family	Married couple family	Female family	Non-family	One person		Number	Rate[2]	Number	Rate[2]	Population age 25 and over	High school graduate or less	Bachelor's degree or more
	27	28	29	30	31	32	33	34	35	36	37	38	39	40	41
UNITED STATES	122,354,219	2.60	65.3	48.1	12.3	34.7	28.0	8,073,334	1,313,105	398.5	6,452,038	1,958.2	222,836,834	38.1	32.9
ALABAMA	1,888,504	2.53	65.4	47.3	13.9	34.6	30.0	117,179	22,322	453.6	105,161	2,136.8	3,344,006	43.5	26.2
Alabaster	11,751	2.82	74.1	61.3	10.0	25.9	22.8	284	NA	NA	NA	NA	21,747	29.6	38.0
Athens	9,709	2.69	67.4	52.6	11.8	32.6	28.7	592	NA	NA	NA	NA	19,501	39.9	28.3
Auburn	24,386	2.47	51.9	40.1	10.0	48.1	32.7	5,324	NA	NA	NA	NA	33,156	17.0	59.1
Bessemer	11,084	2.28	53.1	25.7	22.9	46.9	41.8	821	NA	NA	NA	NA	18,341	54.7	14.6
Birmingham	91,598	2.20	49.6	24.7	20.2	50.4	42.9	9,203	NA	NA	NA	NA	146,978	40.5	28.9
Daphne	10,608	2.48	62.6	52.5	7.2	37.4	30.0	220	NA	NA	NA	NA	18,314	24.9	39.4
Decatur	22,345	2.39	60.0	43.1	13.1	40.0	34.7	836	NA	NA	NA	NA	37,320	45.8	23.0
Dothan	26,681	2.53	63.0	42.8	16.2	37.0	33.2	986	NA	NA	NA	NA	47,659	40.5	26.5
Enterprise	10,908	2.56	67.3	46.9	16.4	32.7	28.2	270	128	448.0	715	2,502.7	18,843	33.4	27.2
Florence	17,493	2.22	53.5	35.2	14.8	46.5	36.8	1,893	NA	NA	NA	NA	26,114	42.6	27.8
Gadsden	13,740	2.49	57.1	30.9	21.9	42.9	37.5	961	NA	NA	NA	NA	24,188	52.9	16.0
Homewood	9,551	2.42	57.5	45.5	9.8	42.5	34.6	2,073	NA	NA	NA	NA	15,059	13.3	69.4
Hoover	32,551	2.61	72.4	58.8	9.9	27.6	23.8	431	NA	NA	NA	NA	58,178	16.3	58.7
Huntsville	86,961	2.20	57.1	39.1	13.7	42.9	36.5	8,253	NA	NA	NA	NA	135,821	27.3	44.0
Madison	20,111	2.51	67.7	56.2	9.5	32.3	26.8	227	NA	NA	NA	NA	34,354	14.2	62.2
Mobile	78,089	2.36	55.7	34.2	17.8	44.3	38.8	5,875	NA	NA	NA	NA	129,306	40.1	31.0
Montgomery	79,331	2.43	58.6	33.2	20.3	41.4	36.4	6,516	NA	NA	NA	NA	131,256	37.2	33.4
Northport	9,813	2.58	69.8	49.0	17.7	30.2	24.2	649	NA	NA	NA	NA	17,154	31.6	34.7
Opelika	12,240	2.45	61.6	42.7	17.0	38.4	33.8	610	NA	NA	NA	NA	21,417	39.1	31.7
Phenix City	15,329	2.34	59.0	35.1	18.6	41.0	37.0	566	NA	NA	NA	NA	24,029	40.7	22.2
Prattville	14,271	2.53	70.7	52.2	13.9	29.3	25.4	504	NA	NA	NA	NA	24,515	36.5	34.7
Trussville	8,093	2.78	81.7	69.6	10.9	18.3	16.3	113	NA	NA	NA	NA	15,558	20.6	46.9
Tuscaloosa	36,749	2.49	53.9	35.1	15.0	46.1	36.3	9,162	NA	NA	NA	NA	58,511	35.6	38.3
Vestavia Hills	13,029	2.63	73.2	63.5	7.9	26.8	24.4	158	NA	NA	NA	NA	23,676	14.3	66.7
ALASKA	255,173	2.78	65.8	49.9	10.3	34.2	26.3	27,095	6,126	837.8	16,528	2,260.5	483,436	35.3	30.0
Anchorage	106,970	2.66	65.0	49.2	10.7	35.0	25.9	7,259	3,472	1,212.3	9,872	3,447.1	192,345	29.7	36.6
Fairbanks	11,175	2.56	66.2	50.6	10.4	33.8	23.8	2,828	260	843.3	1,276	4,138.6	18,073	34.3	26.8
Juneau	12,878	2.45	58.1	45.3	8.3	41.9	32.0	539	296	927.2	946	2,963.2	22,607	25.3	38.8
ARIZONA	2,643,430	2.65	65.1	47.5	12.1	34.9	27.5	157,934	35,980	484.8	165,323	2,227.7	4,846,056	35.9	30.3
Apache Junction	18,277	2.28	56.4	45.4	8.3	43.6	34.7	166	93	214.4	770	1,774.8	33,091	45.8	17.3
Avondale	26,427	3.25	75.0	48.2	17.9	25.0	18.0	169	310	347.0	3,025	3,386.0	53,042	44.6	19.8
Buckeye	20,443	3.33	82.8	67.3	10.7	17.2	12.6	6,403	145	173.4	1,184	1,416.1	46,946	39.5	20.7
Bullhead City	18,014	2.26	60.6	41.5	12.8	39.4	33.5	157	108	263.2	1,110	2,705.0	31,163	53.4	11.1
Casa Grande	19,016	3.00	69.8	49.5	14.1	30.2	23.7	237	338	565.0	1,200	2,006.0	36,761	47.4	18.7
Chandler	93,887	2.73	68.6	52.0	11.6	31.4	23.2	884	543	205.6	4,898	1,854.8	174,999	23.9	44.6
El Mirage	10,873	3.28	78.2	49.2	21.3	21.8	15.5	11	106	292.6	803	2,216.9	21,714	52.3	14.9
Flagstaff	24,466	2.45	50.7	36.5	9.5	49.3	28.4	13,301	NA	NA	NA	NA	36,513	19.7	50.7
Florence town	4,601	2.46	66.5	53.8	8.2	33.5	26.9	15,468	25	90.7	73	264.8	22,949	57.8	11.4
Gilbert town	79,714	3.11	77.0	61.9	10.2	23.0	17.5	488	284	109.4	2,798	1,077.7	152,938	20.1	45.3
Glendale	83,083	2.96	66.7	42.9	16.0	33.3	26.1	4,076	1,123	439.6	6,956	2,722.8	158,928	45.1	21.9
Goodyear	27,016	2.94	78.0	66.6	8.1	22.0	16.5	4,173	199	222.1	1,922	2,144.9	57,204	28.7	31.9
Kingman	12,582	2.29	63.4	43.6	11.5	36.6	29.3	1,563	124	395.5	1,106	3,527.8	22,240	40.1	18.9
Lake Havasu City	25,131	2.20	61.3	50.5	6.7	38.7	31.6	248	105	186.7	790	1,404.6	43,721	42.9	16.1
Marana town	17,277	2.69	76.9	65.4	8.7	23.1	18.7	666	39	76.6	1,165	2,286.9	32,766	21.3	46.5
Maricopa	15,309	3.29	78.5	62.8	10.4	21.5	15.9	0	67	126.0	615	1,156.8	32,383	37.6	23.9
Mesa	186,503	2.71	66.0	47.8	12.9	34.0	26.0	3,966	1,960	371.7	9,737	1,846.4	340,732	34.7	28.1
Oro Valley	20,039	2.26	67.2	58.4	6.4	32.8	26.4	61	27	57.9	559	1,198.7	34,378	16.0	55.4
Peoria	62,180	2.75	71.3	55.1	11.5	28.7	24.3	1,328	471	263.9	2,683	1,503.2	118,593	30.6	34.1
Phoenix	580,835	2.82	63.8	42.0	14.9	36.2	28.2	19,102	13,646	798.5	51,089	2,989.5	1,070,083	40.5	29.4
Prescott	19,797	2.07	58.9	49.9	6.4	41.1	33.9	2,481	168	374.7	657	1,465.4	34,712	22.6	37.7
Prescott Valley town	18,977	2.39	65.1	49.3	10.9	34.9	28.0	221	80	168.6	374	788.0	33,487	40.0	22.0
Queen Creek	15,988	3.26	83.6	74.0	6.6	16.4	13.4	49	NA	NA	NA	NA	32,457	25.4	38.1
Sahuarita	10,557	2.90	78.8	67.0	8.0	21.2	18.4	111	36	112.3	273	851.7	19,798	21.6	42.4
San Luis	8,356	3.74	87.9	60.4	21.9	12.1	8.6	2,599	25	70.3	323	908.0	20,001	67.5	8.4
Scottsdale	117,974	2.15	55.8	46.1	6.9	44.2	35.4	1,719	470	178.7	4,945	1,880.2	199,062	14.8	59.4
Sierra Vista	17,817	2.31	62.3	46.9	10.4	37.7	32.8	2,616	82	191.6	888	2,074.8	29,275	26.3	31.7
Surprise	50,199	2.76	76.4	63.0	10.3	23.6	18.8	366	209	144.5	2,006	1,387.1	95,206	33.7	29.2
Tempe	76,218	2.37	47.1	30.9	9.7	52.9	33.7	10,682	1,100	550.2	7,124	3,563.2	121,374	21.8	46.5
Tucson	215,943	2.40	54.6	33.6	14.8	45.4	35.1	26,763	3,843	698.2	19,931	3,620.9	349,743	37.0	28.2
Yuma	35,344	2.67	71.2	50.5	14.9	28.8	22.2	3,135	498	502.5	1,927	1,944.6	60,075	43.8	19.9
ARKANSAS	1,170,544	2.50	65.8	48.2	13.1	34.2	28.7	83,757	20,363	671.9	79,200	2,613.4	2,026,722	46.7	23.8
Bella Vista	11,796	2.43	72.1	64.8	5.8	27.9	23.6	147	55	188.8	170	583.4	22,236	31.0	34.4
Benton	13,993	2.57	66.1	47.1	15.5	33.9	27.9	440	215	572.7	1,241	3,305.6	24,440	39.0	26.9
Bentonville	19,178	2.67	67.8	55.0	8.8	32.2	24.6	844	183	317.8	857	1,488.5	33,274	25.6	51.8
Cabot	10,066	2.60	70.8	51.1	13.2	29.2	24.1	179	102	383.6	372	1,398.9	17,004	38.3	25.1

1. Data for serious crimes have not been adjusted for underreporting. This may affect comparability between geographic areas and over time. 2. Per 100,000 population estimated by the FBI. 3. Persons 25 years old and over.

City	Money income, 2016–2020					Median earnings of full year, full-time workers, 2016–2020			Housing units, 2016–2020				
	Households												
	Median household income	Percent with income less than $25,000	Percent with income of $200,000 or more	Median family income	Median non-family household income	All persons	Men	Women	Total	Occupied	Percent owner occupied	Median value[1] (dollars)	Median gross rent (dollars)
	42	43	44	45	46	47	48	49	50	51	52	53	54
UNITED STATES	64,994	18.4	8.3	80,069	39,027	50,459	54,601	44,344	138,432,751	122,354,219	64.4	229,800	1,096
ALABAMA	52,035	24.6	4.4	66,772	28,529	43,900	50,891	37,549	2,270,398	1,888,504	69.2	149,600	811
Alabaster	80,871	8.6	5.2	92,895	46,536	53,085	59,616	46,524	12,350	11,751	84.0	178,300	1,140
Athens	53,144	26.0	6.0	76,875	23,859	42,791	49,651	37,823	10,566	9,709	65.9	171,900	657
Auburn	49,028	32.4	7.6	94,720	20,560	50,689	60,933	44,326	29,344	24,386	48.2	270,400	887
Bessemer	30,284	40.6	1.0	45,399	22,281	39,897	48,198	36,454	13,371	11,084	52.9	100,100	764
Birmingham	38,832	33.5	2.7	49,417	27,157	38,508	42,305	34,076	114,135	91,598	45.9	97,500	870
Daphne	71,105	13.0	6.2	86,222	48,793	51,480	62,560	42,246	11,623	10,608	70.4	218,900	1,126
Decatur	49,296	24.6	4.4	63,673	31,044	41,028	47,636	33,072	24,811	22,345	64.4	141,000	692
Dothan	48,377	26.0	4.8	66,447	27,942	42,402	50,107	36,597	31,811	26,681	59.6	152,700	767
Enterprise	62,182	21.1	3.0	70,850	41,528	47,540	52,849	39,159	12,307	10,908	58.1	174,500	855
Florence	39,735	32.4	2.7	56,010	24,611	36,556	40,345	31,802	20,371	17,493	50.5	142,000	655
Gadsden	34,062	38.1	0.9	47,550	22,119	30,965	39,951	26,028	17,474	13,740	58.2	80,400	645
Homewood	84,418	12.7	14.4	122,234	48,357	66,790	85,011	54,247	11,303	9,551	62.6	379,800	1,206
Hoover	92,984	10.0	16.0	113,375	50,170	63,226	78,720	52,661	35,487	32,551	70.4	298,400	1,155
Huntsville	56,758	22.8	7.3	78,039	36,846	50,824	60,831	40,406	94,882	86,961	56.7	184,500	868
Madison	94,214	8.8	11.9	121,960	53,306	73,758	95,530	51,599	20,958	20,111	72.6	263,800	986
Mobile	43,456	30.4	3.8	56,873	28,041	41,477	48,788	35,508	92,398	78,089	51.8	134,100	873
Montgomery	49,608	26.4	4.0	60,275	34,118	40,732	45,461	36,986	93,258	79,331	54.1	121,100	905
Northport	64,814	21.5	1.6	80,330	38,963	50,559	56,167	42,153	10,983	9,813	63.9	187,500	838
Opelika	50,488	25.8	2.6	69,173	27,410	41,934	46,881	35,974	13,392	12,240	67.9	153,400	754
Phenix City	41,842	33.1	3.6	53,923	25,900	40,100	47,268	31,745	17,783	15,329	50.8	130,100	822
Prattville	64,613	16.7	4.5	76,123	44,434	46,667	56,231	39,365	15,002	14,271	65.4	170,600	1,084
Trussville	104,976	6.0	18.1	118,802	57,679	71,140	82,148	57,179	8,520	8,093	92.5	273,100	1,180
Tuscaloosa	44,507	30.6	5.4	66,990	27,261	40,170	42,879	37,603	48,572	36,749	48.2	190,100	858
Vestavia Hills	110,478	8.4	26.0	143,998	43,650	72,852	98,459	57,396	14,531	13,029	77.5	380,600	1,313
ALASKA	77,790	13.0	8.8	92,648	51,651	57,634	64,449	51,541	318,370	255,173	64.8	275,600	1,240
Anchorage	84,813	10.2	10.8	100,775	57,311	59,401	65,625	52,883	118,293	106,970	62.2	320,100	1,310
Fairbanks	64,397	12.4	4.8	70,265	49,020	49,578	54,833	43,935	13,233	11,175	37.8	217,700	1,327
Juneau	88,077	11.0	10.0	106,066	63,801	58,548	63,469	56,397	13,792	12,878	64.6	355,100	1,262
ARIZONA	61,529	18.3	6.4	73,456	39,829	46,403	50,573	42,179	3,040,595	2,643,430	65.3	242,000	1,097
Apache Junction	46,708	24.9	2.1	61,419	28,313	43,269	48,731	36,987	23,343	18,277	78.0	122,000	811
Avondale	67,886	13.0	3.7	72,214	44,036	43,783	46,089	40,342	27,985	26,427	60.7	232,500	1,271
Buckeye	79,156	9.7	4.9	82,389	50,255	47,730	51,791	39,627	23,328	20,443	80.4	246,400	1,320
Bullhead City	43,442	26.6	3.1	51,019	28,423	36,918	40,426	34,301	24,146	18,014	61.7	152,100	825
Casa Grande	55,236	19.8	3.5	61,656	34,012	39,980	42,800	36,657	22,795	19,016	64.4	162,000	1,022
Chandler	85,796	9.4	11.8	101,922	58,073	59,654	65,492	52,752	100,267	93,887	64.9	324,500	1,381
El Mirage	59,975	14.5	1.4	60,618	46,589	39,017	42,151	36,243	11,750	10,873	64.2	177,200	1,308
Flagstaff	58,685	21.9	5.5	81,259	38,270	43,849	46,346	41,254	28,401	24,466	46.8	362,700	1,286
Florence town	58,363	17.4	5.0	61,494	33,825	36,561	43,714	34,082	6,468	4,601	81.4	188,000	827
Gilbert town	99,154	6.8	12.8	109,808	58,368	62,819	74,059	52,693	84,437	79,714	73.5	348,000	1,580
Glendale	56,991	20.4	4.1	65,763	36,549	42,413	45,928	38,957	89,156	83,083	55.8	231,200	1,051
Goodyear	85,217	8.0	8.7	94,167	58,003	53,431	58,187	47,809	30,520	27,016	79.1	310,500	1,435
Kingman	51,081	22.0	2.4	57,811	28,815	42,604	50,644	35,375	13,823	12,582	64.9	162,200	883
Lake Havasu City	55,887	19.6	3.3	67,147	39,212	42,965	43,600	42,702	32,777	25,131	72.1	267,500	943
Marana town	89,689	7.2	7.3	96,075	54,579	59,848	70,491	50,795	18,988	17,277	83.1	271,200	1,295
Maricopa	75,229	9.7	4.0	79,814	50,242	49,760	54,524	44,707	18,091	15,309	81.1	217,400	1,425
Mesa	61,640	16.7	5.3	72,907	41,160	44,019	47,257	41,146	214,831	186,503	62.4	245,500	1,105
Oro Valley	86,863	10.1	12.4	103,465	54,925	66,667	76,605	56,881	22,629	20,039	76.0	330,400	1,326
Peoria	76,423	12.9	8.1	90,352	43,219	52,318	57,186	47,188	68,149	62,180	74.2	282,200	1,340
Phoenix	60,914	17.5	7.0	70,803	42,310	43,534	45,676	41,405	626,977	580,835	55.6	250,800	1,100
Prescott	58,562	19.6	6.8	77,827	38,170	45,810	50,282	41,879	22,826	19,797	70.1	362,300	904
Prescott Valley town	54,315	19.7	2.6	63,239	33,727	42,894	43,868	40,744	20,609	18,977	71.6	260,400	1,061
Queen Creek	104,161	7.6	14.3	111,208	57,901	67,060	80,501	48,538	17,445	15,988	88.4	363,800	1,640
Sahuarita	85,247	10.1	5.8	89,790	53,042	53,440	65,635	43,284	11,855	10,557	79.3	237,300	1,350
San Luis	41,648	28.4	2.1	41,801	30,291	31,522	33,697	26,795	8,680	8,356	66.4	128,500	649
Scottsdale	91,042	11.7	18.2	122,110	62,020	71,096	82,303	58,363	139,189	117,974	66.5	493,200	1,452
Sierra Vista	59,585	18.7	3.5	76,287	38,934	52,944	59,686	39,271	20,118	17,817	59.0	174,100	977
Surprise	71,192	10.5	4.0	79,142	45,534	50,471	55,081	44,009	56,632	50,199	75.5	258,700	1,443
Tempe	61,290	20.0	5.6	79,609	46,985	46,769	50,032	44,349	83,039	76,218	40.3	287,600	1,230
Tucson	45,227	27.7	2.3	56,969	31,876	38,270	40,101	36,437	240,782	215,943	51.7	165,900	861
Yuma	52,183	23.5	2.7	59,364	31,358	40,601	46,347	34,399	41,714	35,344	64.4	152,300	917
ARKANSAS	49,475	25.0	4.0	62,067	27,792	41,104	45,355	36,583	1,379,778	1,170,544	65.8	133,600	760
Bella Vista	71,258	11.5	7.3	83,855	38,267	51,946	59,502	46,465	13,116	11,796	87.6	173,300	959
Benton	59,994	18.7	4.2	74,525	38,049	46,294	56,328	38,061	15,263	13,993	67.5	148,700	841
Bentonville	84,340	11.3	14.5	106,607	54,989	63,936	75,606	46,263	20,764	19,178	51.1	258,300	978
Cabot	59,167	18.8	2.2	71,889	35,082	44,430	50,272	39,364	10,811	10,066	64.7	162,200	858

1. Specified owner-occupied units.

Table D. Cities — Commuting, Computer Access, Migration, Labor Force, and Employment

City	Commuting, 2016–2020[1]: Percent: Drove alone	Commuting, 2016–2020[1]: Mean travel time to work	Computer access[2], 2016–2020: Percent: With a computer in the house	Computer access[2], 2016–2020: Percent: With Internet access	Migration, 2016–2020: Percent who lived in the same house one year ago	Migration, 2016–2020: Percent who lived in another state or county one year ago	Civilian labor force, 2021: Total	Civilian labor force, 2021: Percent change 2020-2021	Civilian labor force, 2021: Unemployment[3]: Total	Civilian labor force, 2021: Unemployment[3]: Rate	Civilian Employment, 2016–2020[4]: Population age 16 and older: Number	Civilian Employment, 2016–2020[4]: Population age 16 and older: Percent in labor force	Civilian Employment, 2016–2020[4]: Population age 16 to 64: Number	Civilian Employment, 2016–2020[4]: Population age 16 to 64: Percent who worked full-year full-time
	55	56	57	58	59	60	61	62	63	64	65	66	67	68
UNITED STATES	74.9	26.9	91.9	84.8	86.2	6.1	162,930,448	1.1	8,751,466	5.4	261,649,873	63.0	209,287,056	51.3
ALABAMA	84.9	25.2	87.9	79.4	86.8	5.6	2,246,993	-0.9	77,272	3.4	3,926,842	57.2	3,099,408	49.0
Alabaster	83.1	31.6	97.0	91.7	86.9	6.7	18,474	0.4	391	2.1	25,507	68.6	21,744	57.8
Athens	89.6	23.2	88.3	81.1	87.2	6.4	13,154	1.6	299	2.3	22,073	58.4	17,183	51.0
Auburn	79.8	20.2	97.3	88.2	74.7	15.5	31,490	0.4	840	2.7	54,914	58.0	49,385	37.4
Bessemer	76.8	23.7	84.1	71.7	85.1	3.4	9,878	-2.9	602	6.1	21,407	53.0	16,115	39.0
Birmingham	77.9	21.7	85.6	75.5	79.1	6.4	92,652	-2.4	4,605	5.0	174,370	59.1	141,457	45.4
Daphne	88.5	24.9	95.9	92.3	85.4	6.0	12,877	0.8	386	3.0	20,969	62.2	16,005	57.4
Decatur	88.1	19.5	86.4	76.2	87.7	4.8	27,666	-1.2	827	3.0	43,399	58.0	33,338	51.6
Dothan	86.3	19.5	88.1	80.1	87.2	5.5	30,540	-1.1	1,106	3.6	54,688	56.6	42,286	49.1
Enterprise	86.4	20.1	93.0	87.9	80.1	11.5	11,451	-1.1	344	3.0	21,664	56.5	17,167	49.9
Florence	86.1	18.1	87.5	76.5	71.1	13.6	18,535	-1.9	600	3.2	33,630	55.3	26,353	42.9
Gadsden	86.1	20.3	83.8	73.4	84.0	5.4	12,197	-6.5	684	5.6	28,455	53.8	22,089	42.8
Homewood	81.2	17.0	94.9	91.4	82.3	8.6	14,114	0.9	298	2.1	19,616	70.0	16,823	52.7
Hoover	81.6	24.5	97.4	94.3	84.5	6.8	46,121	0.3	1,058	2.3	66,109	68.1	52,963	58.3
Huntsville	84.1	19.3	92.9	86.3	79.2	7.7	102,244	0.8	2,993	2.9	163,956	63.4	131,211	51.8
Madison	87.6	20.1	98.1	94.6	85.4	6.3	27,679	2.2	623	2.3	39,479	65.4	33,027	58.0
Mobile	84.3	22.3	86.9	75.0	85.7	3.6	87,206	-2.4	4,691	5.4	154,011	57.4	122,523	47.4
Montgomery	82.5	20.0	89.6	82.1	78.3	8.3	92,636	-1.8	4,765	5.1	156,860	59.3	127,787	47.8
Northport	90.3	22.3	92.1	86.3	86.5	3.3	13,384	-1.6	411	3.1	19,606	66.7	16,194	58.9
Opelika	84.3	19.3	87.5	80.6	85.5	5.7	14,500	-1.3	506	3.5	24,368	61.9	19,337	52.9
Phenix City	86.5	22.0	88.9	74.4	86.1	8.8	14,780	-1.7	436	2.9	28,503	58.8	23,987	49.5
Prattville	86.4	21.6	93.5	87.8	83.4	10.8	17,573	-0.3	474	2.7	29,052	58.4	23,743	54.2
Trussville	88.0	27.1	93.9	91.4	92.0	4.2	11,840	0.7	239	2.0	17,542	65.5	14,300	56.8
Tuscaloosa	81.5	19.1	88.7	78.9	76.1	12.7	46,849	-3.2	1,945	4.2	84,700	58.0	71,632	42.0
Vestavia Hills	83.9	21.4	94.9	90.4	88.4	4.2	18,064	1.2	420	2.3	26,885	64.0	20,922	56.5
ALASKA	68.1	18.9	95.0	87.2	82.7	7.6	354,936	2.3	22,670	6.4	572,684	64.2	485,055	48.2
Anchorage	75.0	18.6	96.7	91.6	81.2	6.9	150,276	2.1	8,737	5.8	228,657	67.3	196,280	53.2
Fairbanks	69.0	14.1	94.9	83.6	71.5	17.2	12,305	1.4	794	6.5	24,139	53.2	20,892	55.0
Juneau	66.5	15.3	95.2	90.9	83.4	6.9	16,734	2.6	794	4.7	25,962	66.0	21,586	52.4
ARIZONA	74.5	25.8	93.3	86.2	83.0	6.2	3,518,425	1.8	172,106	4.9	5,720,956	59.7	4,458,752	49.8
Apache Junction	76.6	27.7	91.7	81.9	80.0	14.5	15,835	1.0	884	5.6	36,448	45.3	21,842	43.1
Avondale	76.7	29.1	95.1	87.7	83.5	4.9	46,429	3.3	2,531	5.5	64,300	68.7	56,745	56.5
Buckeye	76.9	31.9	97.4	94.2	85.5	6.1	34,970	3.2	2,076	5.9	54,504	55.6	45,524	48.0
Bullhead City	74.5	22.8	89.3	82.7	83.9	8.2	17,314	1.2	1,078	6.2	34,294	47.5	21,639	42.6
Casa Grande	79.4	22.6	92.2	86.4	80.0	8.1	26,573	2.6	1,322	5.0	43,985	56.6	32,669	48.9
Chandler	76.0	24.9	97.2	92.7	82.4	6.0	152,461	2.6	5,830	3.8	201,078	71.8	170,354	58.9
El Mirage	76.8	30.4	93.4	87.4	87.3	2.4	17,104	2.8	931	5.4	26,195	67.8	22,372	53.8
Flagstaff	67.4	15.4	96.4	86.1	65.4	21.1	40,905	1.0	1,720	4.2	61,561	65.0	55,134	36.1
Florence town	74.5	33.8	93.4	88.0	78.7	15.8	4,305	2.3	241	5.6	25,030	15.5	20,491	14.0
Gilbert town	75.6	27.1	98.7	96.1	82.8	5.6	142,725	2.8	4,797	3.4	183,980	71.4	160,001	56.5
Glendale	75.0	28.6	93.5	81.1	83.1	4.6	126,539	2.4	6,276	5.0	192,886	64.1	163,217	50.8
Goodyear	75.2	31.3	98.1	94.2	84.9	6.0	43,488	3.0	1,964	4.5	65,781	58.0	51,481	52.0
Kingman	82.0	18.5	92.7	87.7	75.4	9.5	14,194	2.5	776	5.5	24,821	49.7	17,520	47.5
Lake Havasu City	77.9	19.3	92.4	84.7	80.2	10.3	25,175	1.0	1,173	4.7	48,313	46.7	30,056	46.6
Marana town	77.6	29.8	98.0	94.7	86.2	6.4	25,127	0.8	832	3.3	37,210	59.4	27,150	55.4
Maricopa	74.5	38.1	97.3	94.4	85.7	8.8	27,518	2.5	1,405	5.1	37,361	64.9	30,766	53.9
Mesa	73.3	25.4	93.9	88.5	81.1	5.6	261,960	2.5	11,472	4.4	400,797	64.5	316,091	53.6
Oro Valley	77.3	27.5	97.1	92.9	82.0	8.3	19,616	0.5	762	3.9	38,386	47.3	22,684	49.0
Peoria	76.1	29.4	96.0	91.5	84.5	4.2	93,608	2.5	3,908	4.2	136,030	62.2	105,842	54.7
Phoenix	72.9	26.2	93.8	85.5	83.9	3.9	863,731	2.2	41,990	4.9	1,280,078	67.9	1,098,076	53.7
Prescott	73.3	16.8	93.1	88.4	82.2	10.2	18,234	2.0	817	4.5	38,973	40.9	22,121	37.6
Prescott Valley town	79.3	21.4	92.9	86.5	84.9	9.0	22,581	2.3	871	3.9	37,344	52.1	24,347	46.3
Queen Creek	72.4	32.7	99.3	97.2	81.7	10.3	28,722	3.0	969	3.4	38,280	65.5	31,367	53.5
Sahuarita	81.7	28.0	96.6	93.5	83.9	6.9	13,295	1.1	568	4.3	22,840	52.7	16,333	49.8
San Luis	75.5	31.8	83.8	76.8	88.7	3.8	16,846	0.4	4,890	29.0	25,205	56.2	22,397	35.4
Scottsdale	72.0	21.8	96.7	93.2	83.8	6.6	148,944	2.2	5,161	3.5	221,614	61.8	159,328	56.8
Sierra Vista	75.2	17.9	94.6	88.2	77.9	15.1	18,060	-2.5	692	3.8	34,695	47.8	26,275	54.6
Surprise	79.1	30.7	96.7	93.0	86.7	4.2	62,146	2.7	2,948	4.7	108,964	54.5	76,798	52.2
Tempe	68.1	21.3	97.1	90.2	73.0	8.8	120,296	2.2	4,811	4.0	166,970	69.2	146,198	47.8
Tucson	73.1	22.4	92.9	86.2	77.0	7.3	257,721	0.1	14,262	5.5	444,852	60.7	364,024	44.3
Yuma	78.2	16.7	91.3	83.5	79.8	8.1	43,858	-1.8	3,730	8.5	74,898	56.8	59,706	50.6
ARKANSAS	82.3	21.8	88.2	76.5	85.4	6.3	1,332,620	-1.8	53,636	4.0	2,388,169	57.8	1,878,052	50.0
Bella Vista	83.8	25.9	96.7	87.5	84.6	8.2	12,277	0.0	450	3.7	24,293	53.6	15,115	59.0
Benton	86.0	24.0	93.8	85.4	86.7	6.0	17,237	-1.8	535	3.1	28,247	66.3	22,692	62.0
Bentonville	83.9	16.6	95.8	78.8	81.2	9.2	29,655	0.5	731	2.5	38,815	70.7	34,765	62.8
Cabot	85.8	28.5	92.6	87.1	82.7	9.7	11,697	-1.7	397	3.4	20,038	63.0	16,958	55.0

1. Employed persons. 2. Households. 3. Percent of civilian labor force. 4. Persons 16 years old and over.

City	Value of residential construction authorized by building permits, 2021			Wholesale trade[1], 2017				Retail trade[2], 2017			
	New construction ($1,000)	Number of housing units	Percent single family	Number of establishments	Number of employees	Sales (mil dol)	Annual payroll (mil dol)	Number of establish-ments	Number of employees	Sales (mil dol)	Annual payroll (mil dol)
	69	70	71	72	73	74	75	76	77	78	79
UNITED STATES	380,036,187	1,736,982	64.2	352,065	5,156,359	5,700,966.9	337,908.8	1,064,087	15,938,821	4,949,601.5	441,795.6
ALABAMA	4,816,174	22,100	80.9	4,410	63,468	66,906.3	3,461.1	17,958	230,069	63,740.4	5,819.1
Alabaster	27,696	80	100.0	42	981	528.5	46.0	96	2,013	450.5	48.7
Athens	139,180	624	74.7	19	306	239.2	12.8	148	1,980	554.2	51.2
Auburn	219,279	820	89.1	37	477	123.2	18.5	211	3,609	890.8	84.2
Bessemer	3,026	24	100.0	59	1,163	559.7	63.6	172	2,610	756.9	70.1
Birmingham	66,273	637	14.1	472	8,998	8,242.3	524.6	906	11,179	3,084.1	295.6
Daphne	118,228	443	100.0	41	303	157.0	20.4	102	2,548	960.7	75.4
Decatur	32,062	109	100.0	78	1,316	1,091.5	71.3	D	D	D	D
Dothan	77,984	249	100.0	D	D	D	D	461	7,378	2,097.5	193.5
Enterprise	42,334	166	100.0	9	197	39.0	9.2	164	2,150	689.2	58.2
Florence	13,672	114	75.4	46	945	432.2	43.2	283	4,404	1,066.5	106.9
Gadsden	0	0	0.0	30	283	197.6	14.1	214	3,079	819.3	72.2
Homewood	18,686	24	100.0	67	910	583.5	58.5	208	3,108	723.7	84.3
Hoover	185,357	385	100.0	80	706	1,970.1	90.2	398	7,989	2,568.6	227.9
Huntsville	272,200	2,811	52.8	210	3,744	4,340.2	233.0	952	15,387	4,332.5	421.5
Madison	187,677	801	43.1	48	776	463.4	56.8	137	2,050	499.8	54.0
Mobile	22,654	99	100.0	355	4,062	2,318.3	215.9	987	15,065	4,116.9	400.4
Montgomery	45,624	282	92.6	250	4,664	3,772.5	242.8	869	12,352	3,349.2	318.0
Northport	55,652	175	100.0	23	386	199.6	21.0	141	2,115	500.1	51.3
Opelika	131,715	632	67.9	36	500	333.2	29.0	199	3,063	848.4	70.0
Phenix City	11,615	118	88.1	9	59	83.7	2.6	115	1,691	405.6	38.2
Prattville	91,286	277	100.0	D	D	D	6.3	156	2,930	687.9	66.3
Trussville	75,991	204	100.0	31	208	144.5	11.8	127	1,810	415.6	39.7
Tuscaloosa	211,722	1,126	35.6	84	873	439.0	47.6	470	7,117	1,962.2	175.0
Vestavia Hills	20,237	34	100.0	34	178	163.3	12.6	145	2,084	514.6	59.7
ALASKA	413,299	1,552	74.6	643	7,529	5,557.3	457.5	2,480	34,498	10,384.8	1,095.1
Anchorage	312,471	1,133	74.1	338	5,162	3,807.4	314.0	849	15,445	4,903.2	507.6
Fairbanks	0	0	0.0	44	492	368.8	28.0	195	3,783	1,190.8	123.5
Juneau	12,930	62	79.0	33	278	203.1	16.0	148	1,790	464.8	53.3
ARIZONA	15,322,691	65,334	71.3	5,508	79,541	71,206.1	4,826.6	17,918	324,912	104,365.6	9,505.5
Apache Junction	63,152	254	93.7	13	116	48.4	6.7	102	1,835	461.7	46.9
Avondale	214,310	743	99.7	12	208	70.3	11.0	120	4,077	1,843.6	146.0
Buckeye	727,776	2,618	100.0	17	150	87.4	7.6	65	1,422	476.8	38.3
Bullhead City	88,157	400	99.5	11	75	35.9	3.4	109	2,192	630.1	59.6
Casa Grande	391,309	1,539	100.0	25	451	233.4	22.6	182	3,417	973.1	87.1
Chandler	465,478	2,083	32.2	273	4,128	4,528.6	310.6	760	15,938	4,480.8	439.5
El Mirage	22,419	155	7.1	4	40	20.9	1.7	31	548	141.4	15.5
Flagstaff	136,765	657	31.4	74	682	325.8	31.5	328	5,763	1,632.6	148.4
Florence town	117,560	386	100.0	NA	NA	NA	NA	12	172	46.9	4.1
Gilbert town	337,799	1,919	76.6	160	1,175	780.7	70.1	526	11,863	3,953.4	371.9
Glendale	163,788	713	100.0	122	1,462	1,080.7	68.1	673	14,394	5,251.1	405.7
Goodyear	762,950	3,233	61.1	30	559	1,022.3	28.6	149	4,398	1,444.5	120.6
Kingman	53,487	374	93.0	17	318	137.1	15.5	137	2,654	964.4	71.9
Lake Havasu City	84,103	464	85.3	45	546	132.4	24.2	236	3,146	1,010.9	86.8
Marana town	440,659	1,461	85.7	29	244	84.8	8.7	179	3,671	1,067.8	98.2
Maricopa	546,143	1,846	100.0	6	15	3.4	0.7	34	926	283.8	23.6
Mesa	1,099,600	4,635	44.1	334	4,852	2,656.5	314.0	1,283	23,696	6,961.2	671.2
Oro Valley	123,023	340	100.0	24	93	50.5	4.7	87	2,182	557.9	54.5
Peoria	250,762	1,903	82.1	63	413	217.9	18.3	400	10,761	3,795.6	349.1
Phoenix	2,034,641	11,492	42.8	1,823	36,641	36,110.3	2,317.8	3,753	73,994	27,061.7	2,313.4
Prescott	150,335	461	83.1	54	685	444.5	41.2	271	4,206	1,214.3	123.0
Prescott Valley town	193,254	832	64.2	27	462	388.9	19.5	106	1,920	503.5	50.0
Queen Creek	863,191	2,639	83.2	14	18	6.2	0.9	81	1,257	277.2	25.7
Sahuarita	152,730	533	100.0	9	40	14.2	2.0	31	918	246.0	22.9
San Luis	40,029	255	100.0	D	D	D	D	33	653	161.5	15.2
Scottsdale	388,504	1,700	32.5	481	4,119	2,902.8	251.2	1,358	21,051	7,973.4	726.5
Sierra Vista	9,372	55	100.0	9	67	13.5	2.5	148	2,714	741.7	70.3
Surprise	912,791	2,699	99.5	20	504	256.9	19.1	200	5,435	1,803.4	153.8
Tempe	310,391	1,758	7.0	379	6,993	7,053.0	454.6	771	16,650	5,905.2	553.4
Tucson	431,615	2,093	54.2	410	4,469	2,698.8	218.2	1,812	32,262	8,459.9	887.3
Yuma	132,583	823	76.3	74	1,287	1,028.9	68.9	313	6,228	1,686.4	159.7
ARKANSAS	2,857,616	14,198	74.4	2,812	36,528	29,242.1	1,882.8	10,925	142,857	40,174.1	3,665.3
Bella Vista	175,737	584	100.0	12	49	16.2	3.2	26	386	73.2	8.5
Benton	89,921	326	100.0	26	187	170.9	7.1	145	2,224	808.2	62.8
Bentonville	183,807	603	75.8	97	1,137	995.6	85.8	141	3,347	1,385.9	112.2
Cabot	36,454	121	80.2	13	82	38.4	3.8	85	1,239	320.6	30.4

1. Merchant wholesalers except manufacturers' sales branches and offices. 2. Establishments with payroll.

City	Real estate and rental and leasing, 2017				Professional, scientific, and technical services[1], 2017				Manufacturing, 2017			
	Number of establish-ments	Number of employees	Receipts (mil dol)	Annual payroll (mil dol)	Number of establish-ments	Number of employees	Receipts (mil dol)	Annual payroll (mil dol)	Number of establish-ments	Number of employees	Receipts (mil dol)	Annual payroll (mil dol)
	80	81	82	83	84	85	86	87	88	89	90	91
UNITED STATES	410,820	2,194,885	674,147.0	113,409.6	913,624	9,015,366	1,844,781.0	729,370.9	291,586	11,522,039	5,548,796.8	670,678.4
ALABAMA	4,362	22,778	5,785.1	968.2	9,496	100,857	20,681.0	7,188.4	4,133	245,725	137,441.2	12,916.0
Alabaster	20	79	30.0	3.5	62	455	58.1	16.2	NA	NA	NA	NA
Athens	39	100	17.6	3.2	72	514	92.6	38.9	NA	NA	NA	NA
Auburn	86	344	85.4	13.6	158	820	107.6	39.0	NA	NA	NA	NA
Bessemer	25	134	29.7	6.0	53	577	105.9	28.0	NA	NA	NA	NA
Birmingham	303	3,308	646.8	172.9	909	11,420	2,374.7	911.5	NA	NA	NA	NA
Daphne	50	115	31.8	4.0	90	443	60.9	26.1	NA	NA	NA	NA
Decatur	69	297	72.3	12.3	133	1,716	438.7	110.1	NA	NA	NA	NA
Dothan	D	D	D	D	197	1,044	150.7	54.0	NA	NA	NA	NA
Enterprise	31	144	20.0	4.7	52	728	135.2	54.2	NA	NA	NA	NA
Florence	D	D	D	D	126	645	65.1	24.7	NA	NA	NA	NA
Gadsden	40	141	48.6	5.2	91	454	54.6	19.7	NA	NA	NA	NA
Homewood	71	473	114.4	24.6	176	1,551	362.2	120.2	NA	NA	NA	NA
Hoover	119	559	400.7	38.3	326	2,571	404.4	155.1	NA	NA	NA	NA
Huntsville	321	1,509	464.7	60.9	1,146	33,606	9,011.1	3,053.7	NA	NA	NA	NA
Madison	57	247	85.7	10.3	130	1,793	668.6	137.9	NA	NA	NA	NA
Mobile	319	1,869	423.5	72.2	707	8,917	1,348.6	537.0	NA	NA	NA	NA
Montgomery	248	1,556	333.7	67.0	580	5,887	1,079.0	395.1	NA	NA	NA	NA
Northport	28	271	31.4	8.0	60	423	35.8	13.2	NA	NA	NA	NA
Opelika	44	216	32.9	7.7	80	421	50.9	16.4	NA	NA	NA	NA
Phenix City	D	D	D	D	45	174	20.4	6.5	NA	NA	NA	NA
Prattville	46	124	28.4	4.4	46	257	27.1	9.6	NA	NA	NA	NA
Trussville	29	80	31.8	4.4	65	292	36.5	15.6	NA	NA	NA	NA
Tuscaloosa	143	1,386	192.9	47.5	D	D	D	D	NA	NA	NA	NA
Vestavia Hills	88	466	803.5	46.9	D	D	D	D	NA	NA	NA	NA
ALASKA	965	4,622	1,188.3	222.8	1,959	17,869	3,235.5	1,268.6	535	12,515	8,616.9	585.3
Anchorage	437	2,519	681.0	124.4	1,188	14,219	2,583.0	1,044.9	NA	NA	NA	NA
Fairbanks	92	537	124.4	31.5	116	984	251.9	67.1	NA	NA	NA	NA
Juneau	64	195	60.0	8.0	91	471	74.6	29.7	NA	NA	NA	NA
ARIZONA	9,937	48,305	12,992.2	2,267.2	18,100	146,970	24,118.9	10,563.0	4,343	142,809	56,635.9	9,148.7
Apache Junction	38	130	31.5	2.8	20	54	6.0	1.6	NA	NA	NA	NA
Avondale	50	149	33.9	5.5	68	357	25.6	10.0	NA	NA	NA	NA
Buckeye	41	100	16.2	2.8	63	165	20.3	6.3	NA	NA	NA	NA
Bullhead City	62	268	35.7	5.6	39	198	28.3	11.0	NA	NA	NA	NA
Casa Grande	53	246	46.5	7.8	52	249	25.4	8.2	NA	NA	NA	NA
Chandler	459	1,494	506.3	80.6	801	13,130	1,022.3	1,570.0	NA	NA	NA	NA
El Mirage	16	55	10.6	1.7	10	47	6.1	1.5	NA	NA	NA	NA
Flagstaff	160	657	148.2	22.0	273	1,419	188.3	69.2	NA	NA	NA	NA
Florence town	7	35	4.4	0.8	15	29	4.7	1.8	NA	NA	NA	NA
Gilbert town	491	1,220	398.3	59.7	739	4,785	976.8	330.2	NA	NA	NA	NA
Glendale	239	1,017	268.6	38.0	339	2,031	240.8	135.1	NA	NA	NA	NA
Goodyear	98	1,004	190.1	23.6	134	504	69.3	25.0	NA	NA	NA	NA
Kingman	34	94	22.1	2.8	51	269	23.7	10.1	NA	NA	NA	NA
Lake Havasu City	113	318	83.0	10.4	96	308	44.8	12.3	NA	NA	NA	NA
Marana town	45	154	43.9	6.1	78	221	30.1	9.2	NA	NA	NA	NA
Maricopa	19	34	12.3	1.2	48	207	12.3	7.3	NA	NA	NA	NA
Mesa	669	2,481	609.1	96.3	1,168	6,599	948.8	361.5	NA	NA	NA	NA
Oro Valley	77	131	35.1	6.3	144	397	60.0	22.4	NA	NA	NA	NA
Peoria	212	688	177.3	30.4	306	871	127.7	41.2	NA	NA	NA	NA
Phoenix	2,336	16,218	4,524.0	876.1	5,288	53,825	9,296.5	3,733.8	NA	NA	NA	NA
Prescott	159	349	82.8	13.8	229	845	104.1	42.0	NA	NA	NA	NA
Prescott Valley town	43	111	33.6	4.9	62	350	39.2	14.8	NA	NA	NA	NA
Queen Creek	55	101	15.6	3.2	98	225	33.6	10.9	NA	NA	NA	NA
Sahuarita	18	23	5.9	0.9	11	31	3.7	1.8	NA	NA	NA	NA
San Luis	D	D	D	D	10	36	2.3	0.7	NA	NA	NA	NA
Scottsdale	1,223	6,842	2,478.1	387.9	2,332	17,664	3,929.3	1,445.3	NA	NA	NA	NA
Sierra Vista	56	283	40.2	8.1	97	1,507	239.7	105.6	NA	NA	NA	NA
Surprise	89	221	61.0	8.3	D	D	D	D	NA	NA	NA	NA
Tempe	469	2,844	921.7	152.2	D	D	D	D	NA	NA	NA	NA
Tucson	739	3,980	762.3	148.4	1,574	12,594	1,976.5	796.9	NA	NA	NA	NA
Yuma	145	612	106.9	17.8	170	786	97.1	37.3	NA	NA	NA	NA
ARKANSAS	3,115	12,776	2,588.2	473.3	5,914	38,088	5,564.9	2,070.7	2,571	152,696	58,363.7	7,024.8
Bella Vista	22	94	9.7	2.4	38	97	21.5	4.1	NA	NA	NA	NA
Benton	35	117	30.1	4.7	69	385	60.7	18.4	NA	NA	NA	NA
Bentonville	88	358	100.9	15.9	264	4,158	747.7	313.1	NA	NA	NA	NA
Cabot	28	95	17.2	4.4	49	270	27.8	11.3	NA	NA	NA	NA

1. Establishments subject to federal tax.

Table D. Cities — Accommodation and Food Services, Arts, Entertainment, and Recreation, and Health Care and Social Assistance

City	Accommodation and food services, 2017				Arts, entertainment, and recreation[1], 2017				Health care and social assistance[1], 2017			
	Number of establish-ments	Number of employees	Receipts (mil dol)	Annual payroll (mil dol)	Number of establish-ments	Number of employees	Receipts (mil dol)	Annual payroll (mil dol)	Number of establish-ments	Number of employees	Receipts (mil dol)	Annual payroll (mil dol)
	92	93	94	95	96	97	98	99	100	101	102	103
UNITED STATES	726,081	14,002,624	938,237.1	264,603.6	142,938.0	2,390,279	265,620.0	82,256.0	892,245	20,506,502	2,527,903.3	990,056.2
ALABAMA	9,085	183,590	10,527.7	2,761.5	1,168.0	17,939	1,158.3	333.3	10,636	258,399	31,238.9	11,948.8
Alabaster	54	1,373	74.2	20.8	11.0	261	18.4	8.4	82	2,649	321.5	119.5
Athens	77	1,784	84.0	21.8	D	D	D	D	98	1,980	186.6	77.1
Auburn	226	4,598	227.6	58.7	15.0	256	12.9	4.4	132	1,631	141.7	48.2
Bessemer	91	1,807	90.2	23.7	8.0	103	6.4	2.4	87	2,594	258.4	97.6
Birmingham	608	13,704	774.8	232.3	83.0	1,873	136.5	39.1	730	40,064	7,422.7	2,527.5
Daphne	77	1,650	90.6	22.9	D	D	D	D	92	1,580	151.7	69.8
Decatur	149	3,322	160.1	48.5	21.0	264	12.4	3.9	285	4,439	440.7	184.3
Dothan	239	5,102	273.9	72.0	D	D	D	5.4	312	9,741	1,175.5	491.6
Enterprise	91	1,560	78.5	20.8	D	D	D	D	87	1,547	150.6	59.4
Florence	136	3,898	174.1	53.6	16.0	250	7.4	2.3	208	4,768	556.1	192.6
Gadsden	115	2,641	136.3	37.6	8.0	168	7.3	2.5	211	5,388	631.8	237.2
Homewood	139	2,629	159.1	44.4	13.0	160	6.9	1.7	208	6,546	955.2	367.3
Hoover	220	5,140	354.5	95.5	33.0	683	39.8	12.6	258	3,618	366.7	170.7
Huntsville	580	13,530	716.2	207.2	88.0	1,943	78.8	31.8	773	21,639	3,099.9	1,103.1
Madison	120	2,157	109.4	29.3	14.0	242	8.6	3.1	147	2,469	262.4	99.9
Mobile	510	11,756	626.1	176.1	73.0	1,465	58.7	19.0	627	18,940	2,505.9	928.2
Montgomery	492	11,361	842.2	182.1	53.0	1,283	66.1	24.8	649	18,128	2,103.9	880.7
Northport	75	1,468	74.8	23.9	D	D	D	D	99	3,141	274.0	118.4
Opelika	112	2,796	134.2	39.0	D	D	D	D	102	5,116	535.5	221.2
Phenix City	78	1,429	76.4	18.9	6.0	36	2.3	0.5	62	1,407	155.6	52.4
Prattville	D	D	D	D	D	D	D	D	86	1,447	124.0	49.7
Trussville	63	1,645	81.6	23.1	10.0	239	7.0	2.2	62	841	71.8	29.2
Tuscaloosa	332	8,245	443.0	122.8	35.0	388	22.5	5.5	303	9,957	1,176.4	488.5
Vestavia Hills	83	1,836	85.5	24.2	21.0	758	65.1	17.6	156	2,826	403.0	157.9
ALASKA	2,214	28,853	2,536.5	741.7	575.0	5,433	449.2	103.9	2,679	52,125	7,856.2	3,048.1
Anchorage	798	15,618	1,224.8	386.2	158.0	2,795	199.0	49.5	1,291	27,333	4,482.7	1,673.1
Fairbanks	155	2,470	174.7	50.5	47.0	508	47.6	6.8	216	5,826	778.2	335.3
Juneau	124	1,390	112.9	31.2	38.0	593	24.3	7.1	133	2,288	310.2	134.4
ARIZONA	13,079	299,628	19,848.7	5,636.1	2,041.0	47,060	4,812.4	1,581.7	18,816	379,015	48,130.1	18,409.1
Apache Junction	48	869	37.2	11.4	9.0	140	14.5	3.0	76	990	80.6	34.9
Avondale	113	2,255	134.3	36.1	10.0	D	59.2	D	124	1,519	167.4	58.2
Buckeye	49	1,101	59.5	15.7	9.0	154	5.4	2.0	38	385	63.3	25.4
Bullhead City	89	1,286	74.9	20.4	7.0	49	3.4	1.4	120	1,774	225.9	79.2
Casa Grande	102	2,531	123.2	36.6	10.0	113	6.9	1.7	188	3,444	355.9	158.5
Chandler	556	14,304	1,059.6	286.0	89.0	1,974	292.5	42.2	839	14,927	1,832.9	622.0
El Mirage	12	183	9.8	2.8	NA	NA	NA	NA	10	88	6.4	2.5
Flagstaff	329	7,249	459.8	129.4	56.0	874	48.4	18.1	346	6,592	903.5	314.3
Florence town	18	311	13.5	3.7	D	D	D	D	24	601	80.9	35.3
Gilbert town	420	9,804	507.4	150.2	69.0	1,767	80.6	27.4	827	11,909	1,573.9	555.0
Glendale	420	9,413	584.7	151.5	52.0	2,386	760.3	344.5	713	14,020	1,911.7	658.1
Goodyear	138	4,035	224.3	66.3	16.0	553	27.1	8.4	176	5,066	638.1	216.3
Kingman	105	1,927	117.9	32.0	7.0	42	2.5	0.7	126	3,496	442.0	172.2
Lake Havasu City	139	2,824	166.3	48.9	15.0	210	13.0	4.4	191	2,571	342.4	115.0
Marana town	116	2,646	190.3	48.7	19.0	370	20.9	7.6	69	1,220	110.1	58.2
Maricopa	41	726	38.8	10.6	5.0	D	5.2	D	45	475	46.2	18.5
Mesa	841	17,855	978.9	289.7	113.0	2,023	139.6	47.2	1,432	31,274	3,630.5	1,366.2
Oro Valley	74	1,916	136.3	36.5	20.0	415	26.0	9.6	149	2,038	261.1	96.6
Peoria	293	7,172	410.8	124.1	39.0	702	53.3	14.8	501	7,793	830.4	346.7
Phoenix	2,958	69,330	4,789.3	1,382.1	416.0	10,741	1,300.2	485.0	4,267	107,483	15,036.4	5,882.0
Prescott	176	2,921	162.5	50.7	26.0	472	22.9	8.4	365	7,049	844.7	325.9
Prescott Valley town	76	1,329	75.4	22.5	9.0	203	5.9	2.3	139	2,746	331.2	102.3
Queen Creek	48	1,114	58.8	19.3	D	D	D	D	89	587	58.2	21.2
Sahuarita	28	527	26.3	7.4	NA	NA	NA	NA	23	111	11.8	4.6
San Luis	15	178	10.0	2.9	NA	NA	NA	NA	27	388	51.2	20.6
Scottsdale	886	26,231	1,872.7	564.3	220.0	5,835	478.9	150.3	1,726	25,334	3,725.9	1,362.9
Sierra Vista	97	1,783	95.8	30.3	D	D	D	D	167	2,918	280.1	110.6
Surprise	178	4,625	281.8	75.4	14.0	452	19.6	6.7	256	3,111	317.1	122.4
Tempe	633	14,895	875.9	255.7	82.0	1,551	102.3	31.5	633	11,539	1,177.8	477.5
Tucson	1,271	27,909	1,587.8	472.0	165.0	2,921	153.1	47.2	1,822	44,082	5,236.0	2,119.3
Yuma	244	5,753	307.2	86.2	D	D	D	D	328	7,066	938.6	313.8
ARKANSAS	5,977	106,280	5,484.8	1,572.8	787.0	9,919	1,056.6	217.6	7,878	182,126	19,845.4	7,960.7
Bella Vista	22	282	17.0	5.0	6.0	73	2.7	0.9	29	435	39.2	15.3
Benton	73	1,281	74.5	21.2	D	D	D	D	114	2,776	272.8	102.1
Bentonville	159	3,352	209.6	56.7	20.0	579	89.4	16.8	156	2,936	250.0	113.7
Cabot	57	1,085	55.5	15.7	D	D	D	D	68	830	65.6	26.1

1. Establishments subject to federal tax.

City	Other services[1]				Government employment and payroll, 2017								
						March payroll							
							Perent of total for:						
	Number of establish-ments	Number of employees	Receipts (mil dol)	Annual payroll (mil dol)	Full-time equivalent employees	Total (dollars)	Admin-istrative, judicial, and legal	Police and corrections	Fire protection	Highways and trans-portation	Health and welfare	Natural resources and utilities	Education and libraries
	104	105	106	107	108	109	110	111	112	113	114	115	116
UNITED STATES	560,845	3,696,831	544,127.7	133,751.1	X	X	X	X	X	X	X	X	X
ALABAMA	6,149	38,476	5,844.4	1,302.6	X	X	X	X	X	X	X	X	X
Alabaster	D	D	D	D	217	1,013,772	0.0	41.6	31.3	0.8	0.0	22.9	3.4
Athens	48	271	22.6	6.8	401	1,548,473	15.5	16.3	10.2	8.7	0.0	49.3	0.0
Auburn	95	501	47.6	13.1	559	2,135,112	15.3	25.8	16.5	9.6	0.9	24.3	4.1
Bessemer	50	547	98.9	25.7	585	2,499,951	9.9	30.6	19.8	1.9	0.8	34.1	1.3
Birmingham	407	4,323	1,642.0	191.7	4,994	23,334,276	10.4	26.6	16.6	3.9	0.8	30.1	4.0
Daphne	58	325	33.6	10.1	261	981,697	12.7	31.3	20.1	12.6	1.2	11.1	3.9
Decatur	D	D	D	D	671	2,952,604	7.3	21.2	16.9	3.8	1.4	45.3	0.0
Dothan	174	888	101.8	24.7	1,008	4,064,982	12.2	22.8	19.5	2.7	0.7	34.1	0.0
Enterprise	D	D	D	D	578	1,587,934	5.2	17.1	8.9	3.7	44.1	14.3	0.7
Florence	D	D	D	12.0	818	3,265,818	5.8	17.1	11.8	6.4	0.9	52.0	0.0
Gadsden	D	D	D	D	693	2,605,616	8.9	20.9	22.0	8.5	0.8	28.5	3.1
Homewood	84	1,625	239.4	65.1	372	1,292,236	8.0	27.9	20.4	1.1	0.0	19.4	6.2
Hoover	115	640	66.8	20.7	698	3,829,422	11.1	31.1	26.2	5.3	0.5	8.5	8.4
Huntsville	336	3,146	412.7	116.6	2,677	13,501,024	8.7	20.9	15.5	7.7	1.6	26.7	0.0
Madison	57	511	66.7	17.3	388	1,635,565	14.8	30.4	20.9	6.1	0.2	15.3	0.0
Mobile	381	3,075	321.9	85.9	2,711	10,723,431	10.9	28.1	19.2	4.4	0.8	27.7	3.5
Montgomery	412	2,611	401.8	107.1	2,677	10,755,405	8.1	24.1	18.4	6.6	0.2	28.9	1.9
Northport	D	D	D	D	299	1,174,861	10.9	30.8	24.1	5.9	0.0	27.3	0.0
Opelika	D	D	D	D	388	1,689,321	9.6	27.2	17.1	3.0	0.5	39.3	2.2
Phenix City	50	248	25.6	7.6	433	1,405,644	9.7	27.0	19.5	7.3	0.4	31.1	1.2
Prattville	D	D	D	D	330	1,254,033	11.7	32.8	30.7	2.7	0.0	21.2	0.0
Trussville	52	281	48.1	12.9	205	926,849	7.8	33.0	29.0	5.7	0.0	12.0	6.0
Tuscaloosa	144	1,117	121.8	35.5	1,303	5,456,667	12.2	28.7	21.6	13.3	0.3	16.9	0.0
Vestavia Hills	66	381	46.8	13.5	276	1,301,919	7.8	27.1	43.8	1.9	0.0	7.0	5.3
ALASKA	1,357	7,271	1,351.3	269.7	X	X	X	X	X	X	X	X	X
Anchorage	571	3,928	886.5	150.5	9,255	52,804,925	4.8	9.0	7.0	4.8	1.7	10.0	60.7
Fairbanks	110	568	84.1	20.8	204	1,433,298	8.8	26.3	28.8	33.1	0.0	0.0	0.0
Juneau	76	393	62.4	16.6	1,761	11,406,328	5.4	5.8	2.9	7.2	30.8	7.3	40.6
ARIZONA	9,271	68,350	8,727.5	2,305.9	X	X	X	X	X	X	X	X	X
Apache Junction	43	217	20.6	6.4	243	1,192,738	27.1	39.3	0.0	8.9	3.0	12.5	8.1
Avondale	72	453	51.7	13.8	505	3,064,120	15.5	33.9	18.1	3.2	2.8	13.1	1.9
Buckeye	21	84	8.4	1.8	437	2,212,861	26.8	19.3	29.1	3.5	1.7	9.8	2.0
Bullhead City	50	270	23.1	6.6	300	1,339,366	21.2	44.1	0.0	14.0	1.8	13.0	0.0
Casa Grande	71	436	34.5	11.3	401	2,083,036	21.3	30.1	18.8	5.8	0.4	16.6	3.3
Chandler	356	2,389	285.3	77.2	1,718	10,949,371	15.7	33.7	16.5	7.1	4.8	15.3	2.8
El Mirage	D	D	D	D	160	934,594	15.7	36.3	17.4	4.5	0.0	8.3	0.0
Flagstaff	166	932	89.4	27.8	786	3,843,359	18.9	21.9	13.2	4.0	3.2	21.7	5.2
Florence town	D	D	D	D	176	806,986	19.4	24.2	22.3	8.2	0.0	20.2	2.5
Gilbert town	332	1,816	185.3	53.9	1,200	7,163,116	17.5	33.5	18.7	2.9	0.1	18.8	0.0
Glendale	285	1,476	161.0	43.3	1,656	9,914,002	11.9	34.4	20.1	4.8	2.1	20.0	2.2
Goodyear	66	384	34.2	11.1	483	3,126,807	20.7	27.4	25.5	7.2	0.0	14.5	0.0
Kingman	51	331	29.4	8.9	328	1,497,786	17.9	22.6	22.4	10.9	0.0	24.1	0.0
Lake Havasu City	147	598	61.2	15.5	503	2,453,216	17.0	26.8	20.7	7.9	0.0	23.6	0.0
Marana town	D	D	D	D	357	1,812,592	27.3	34.1	0.0	17.1	1.7	14.3	0.0
Maricopa	D	D	D	D	313	1,580,935	9.7	31.5	29.8	3.3	0.7	17.7	1.7
Mesa	631	4,133	436.3	129.7	3,715	22,765,005	16.0	35.4	16.4	3.8	3.0	19.0	1.3
Oro Valley	58	526	44.3	12.7	385	1,998,940	22.1	41.7	0.0	11.6	0.0	17.9	0.0
Peoria	232	1,393	137.0	40.9	1,301	7,486,848	23.2	25.0	19.2	6.4	0.0	21.0	2.0
Phoenix	2,204	20,997	2,767.6	777.9	12,939	98,028,340	11.5	34.9	19.2	9.7	4.4	17.4	1.5
Prescott	130	620	69.1	18.9	499	2,456,719	13.2	24.4	17.9	14.1	2.8	20.5	3.8
Prescott Valley town	82	350	32.5	9.7	237	1,085,810	17.3	43.8	0.0	9.2	4.8	10.0	7.3
Queen Creek	41	180	24.2	5.9	245	1,271,018	22.7	0.0	16.1	7.9	22.5	25.3	0.0
Sahuarita	20	139	8.8	3.8	139	750,836	39.8	41.0	0.0	9.5	0.0	9.7	0.0
San Luis	D	D	D	D	350	1,191,616	38.6	20.9	12.5	4.5	0.0	20.3	0.0
Scottsdale	743	6,676	690.2	214.2	2,358	13,918,114	21.5	30.6	15.2	5.1	1.8	17.6	3.3
Sierra Vista	67	338	33.8	7.7	363	1,670,914	13.4	29.1	18.3	8.9	2.7	14.3	2.4
Surprise	101	964	83.6	25.0	871	5,256,566	16.8	25.0	21.5	5.7	6.9	18.8	0.0
Tempe	378	3,909	1,414.7	244.8	1,813	10,766,295	16.8	31.8	14.1	5.5	9.6	17.4	1.4
Tucson	935	6,299	837.9	197.3	4,956	25,663,881	13.1	31.8	18.1	9.1	3.0	19.6	0.0
Yuma	152	819	75.6	22.5	970	4,031,433	16.1	29.4	15.9	6.7	4.4	24.7	0.0
ARKANSAS	3,910	21,132	2,873.8	655.4	X	X	X	X	X	X	X	X	X
Bella Vista	22	206	25.5	7.5	138	573,617	6.8	29.1	40.2	12.3	6.7	0.0	2.8
Benton	D	D	D	D	231	838,938	11.8	38.5	33.7	5.0	0.0	7.5	0.0
Bentonville	D	D	D	21.1	515	2,182,740	12.4	23.9	18.5	3.0	0.0	33.9	2.9
Cabot	31	153	13.1	3.7	196	715,133	13.1	28.2	20.7	8.2	0.0	27.0	0.0

1. Establishments subject to federal tax.

Table D. Cities — City Government Finances

City	City government finances, 2017 — General revenue: Total (mil dol)	General revenue: Intergovernmental: Total (mil dol)	General revenue: Intergovernmental: Percent from state government	General revenue: Taxes: Total (mil dol)	General revenue: Taxes: Per capita[1] (dollars): Total	General revenue: Taxes: Per capita[1] (dollars): Property	General revenue: Taxes: Per capita[1] (dollars): Sales and gross receipts	General expenditure: Total (mil dol)	General expenditure: Per capita[1] (dollars): Total	General expenditure: Per capita[1] (dollars): Capital outlays
	117	118	119	120	121	122	123	124	125	126
UNITED STATES	X	X	X	X	X	X	X	X	X	X
ALABAMA	X	X	X	X	X	X	X	X	X	X
Alabaster	39.5	0.8	51.1	29.4	883	108	775	27.7	833	48
Athens	24.7	2.7	48.3	21.8	849	50	800	20.5	798	68
Auburn	122.1	1.2	41.6	91.7	1,435	372	1,062	88.5	1,384	296
Bessemer	64.1	4.8	86.0	48.3	1,813	297	1,274	74.3	2,791	379
Birmingham	517.2	49.6	71.5	413.2	1,954	280	1,249	531.4	2,512	433
Daphne	35.6	3.4	100.0	28.4	1,093	200	892	30.2	1,161	189
Decatur	125.1	15.5	63.0	68.0	1,250	235	967	93.8	1,723	414
Dothan	112.3	5.2	29.5	78.1	1,144	56	1,088	126.9	1,858	387
Enterprise	37.0	0.8	98.1	29.5	1,050	94	956	25.7	913	49
Florence	72.6	3.6	91.0	51.0	1,273	307	962	63.6	1,588	154
Gadsden	66.4	2.8	25.7	50.5	1,419	73	869	58.0	1,631	64
Homewood	56.0	0.9	100.0	51.9	2,037	718	1,319	45.3	1,778	418
Hoover	126.2	8.8	62.7	103.6	1,216	131	1,050	129.2	1,516	351
Huntsville	440.2	35.8	93.6	307.8	1,575	296	1,279	413.8	2,117	620
Madison	53.5	1.3	100.0	41.5	843	276	567	53.2	1,081	269
Mobile	401.3	18.8	47.7	285.1	1,499	104	1,395	358.2	1,883	362
Montgomery	270.3	30.4	77.7	196.9	984	148	836	225.3	1,126	69
Northport	30.1	4.4	22.1	19.2	740	122	601	35.3	1,360	339
Opelika	74.7	1.5	51.6	57.3	1,892	321	1,236	53.6	1,769	228
Phenix City	47.6	1.5	100.0	33.8	938	164	774	50.3	1,395	233
Prattville	45.9	1.3	38.6	35.3	994	79	915	37.9	1,069	190
Trussville	41.8	1.2	57.5	37.3	1,717	212	1,505	34.7	1,598	323
Tuscaloosa	191.2	52.2	36.2	89.3	896	138	758	157.0	1,576	355
Vestavia Hills	36.2	0.0	0.0	35.4	1,029	448	577	18.6	542	0
ALASKA	X	X	X	X	X	X	X	X	X	X
Anchorage	1,432.3	620.4	93.7	609.3	2,070	1,797	273	1,395.3	4,741	734
Fairbanks	60.0	20.9	99.4	24.3	767	472	296	49.4	1,558	484
Juneau	341.6	89.2	91.3	102.9	3,206	1,520	1,686	327.3	10,198	1,922
ARIZONA	X	X	X	X	X	X	X	X	X	X
Apache Junction	24.7	10.1	100.0	13.1	323	0	323	37.5	923	0
Avondale	112.5	33.6	96.8	53.4	630	80	550	103.1	1,216	200
Buckeye	80.9	19.3	96.6	45.1	659	88	571	68.0	993	33
Bullhead City	54.2	17.2	100.0	14.4	358	0	358	53.4	1,327	205
Casa Grande	83.0	23.6	90.5	35.3	633	134	500	79.4	1,426	154
Chandler	375.8	99.9	91.8	175.2	691	117	574	449.0	1,771	404
El Mirage	37.5	11.3	100.0	12.0	339	110	229	41.4	1,168	105
Flagstaff	146.3	37.1	86.3	66.6	924	167	757	133.5	1,854	273
Florence town	28.0	12.0	90.8	7.6	294	82	200	22.7	878	57
Gilbert town	317.7	88.6	94.1	164.7	679	98	577	260.6	1,074	161
Glendale	390.7	98.4	88.8	200.2	808	105	703	401.4	1,620	269
Goodyear	152.2	31.4	100.0	85.3	1,066	257	809	136.3	1,705	357
Kingman	49.9	13.2	91.4	19.3	656	0	656	41.2	1,402	179
Lake Havasu City	105.1	27.6	80.7	32.6	599	219	380	88.8	1,633	130
Marana town	98.7	44.7	34.4	47.8	1,062	11	1,046	87.0	1,936	787
Maricopa	56.0	22.4	87.0	27.5	573	295	278	65.7	1,368	411
Mesa	651.7	206.3	77.4	219.6	439	69	370	699.2	1,398	157
Oro Valley	47.3	19.0	100.0	21.3	479	0	479	48.2	1,081	117
Peoria	266.7	67.5	100.0	114.9	683	129	554	253.6	1,508	168
Phoenix	3,254.8	900.6	75.3	1,253.3	767	201	563	2,422.3	1,483	157
Prescott	85.6	21.9	75.6	37.4	877	40	817	91.6	2,146	485
Prescott Valley town	57.3	18.3	88.6	25.1	564	35	529	49.4	1,111	172
Queen Creek	88.5	11.2	100.0	44.5	1,029	140	889	57.7	1,335	137
Sahuarita	26.2	12.3	98.6	9.3	312	16	296	26.3	883	123
San Luis	27.7	10.5	99.4	8.8	270	0	270	31.3	955	74
Scottsdale	495.2	97.2	90.8	280.4	1,115	256	860	496.6	1,975	371
Sierra Vista	58.2	17.4	99.8	22.4	521	10	511	59.6	1,388	187
Surprise	158.0	43.3	100.0	71.4	530	78	452	196.0	1,454	345
Tempe	392.5	81.3	75.2	206.6	1,112	247	865	351.6	1,892	261
Tucson	745.4	264.8	75.1	313.1	578	94	485	721.2	1,332	185
Yuma	223.8	34.0	93.8	155.5	1,613	1,118	495	133.1	1,380	141
ARKANSAS	X	X	X	X	X	X	X	X	X	X
Bella Vista	14.4	10.4	33.0	0.1	5	0	5	15.7	549	42
Benton	32.2	3.2	89.3	20.6	574	60	513	36.4	1,013	354
Bentonville	84.0	14.9	51.0	38.9	788	157	631	83.7	1,694	699
Cabot	23.7	5.0	44.8	12.2	462	57	406	22.2	841	78

1. Based on population estimated as of July 1 of the year shown.

City	City government finances, 2017 (cont.)												
	General expenditure (cont.)												
	Percent of total for:									Debt outstanding			
	Public welfare	Highways	Parking facilities	Education	Health and hospitals	Police protection	Sewerage and sanitation	Parks and recreation	Housing and community development	Interest on debt	Total (mil dol)	Per capita[1] (dollars)	Debt issued during year
	127	128	129	130	131	132	133	134	135	136	137	138	139
UNITED STATES	X	X	X	X	X	X	X	X	X	X	X	X	X
ALABAMA	X	X	X	X	X	X	X	X	X	X	X	X	X
Alabaster	0.0	7.5	0.0	0.0	0.0	20.3	20.0	8.7	0.0	9.8	113.1	3,400	6.6
Athens	0.1	0.0	0.0	0.0	0.0	24.7	0.0	0.0	0.0	0.0	171.4	6,663	62.3
Auburn	0.2	5.5	0.5	0.0	2.6	15.0	12.7	6.2	0.5	10.2	305.1	4,773	23.0
Bessemer	0.0	6.1	0.0	0.0	0.5	16.5	5.8	2.7	1.5	3.5	152.1	5,708	0.0
Birmingham	0.0	14.6	1.0	0.0	0.0	18.5	0.0	5.4	2.1	3.2	1,451.7	6,863	539.5
Daphne	0.0	10.1	0.0	0.0	0.6	15.9	5.5	10.3	0.0	4.2	33.3	1,279	8.6
Decatur	0.2	5.2	0.0	0.0	0.9	13.9	34.8	8.7	3.0	7.1	200.5	3,683	21.6
Dothan	0.2	6.5	0.0	0.0	0.7	13.5	24.7	17.5	0.3	0.0	122.5	1,794	49.6
Enterprise	0.8	5.0	0.0	0.0	0.0	18.4	15.5	8.1	0.0	0.0	87.7	3,120	2.0
Florence	0.0	8.1	0.1	0.0	1.1	15.7	16.9	11.6	0.0	2.7	99.0	2,470	0.0
Gadsden	0.0	5.6	0.0	0.0	0.0	17.1	14.9	9.4	0.7	3.3	93.1	2,618	0.0
Homewood	0.0	8.7	0.0	0.0	0.0	23.7	4.7	8.4	0.0	5.5	65.6	2,574	2.7
Hoover	0.0	9.5	0.0	0.0	0.1	18.6	7.1	16.6	0.0	2.5	141.6	1,661	68.6
Huntsville	0.0	8.9	0.4	0.0	0.8	11.3	5.4	9.4	1.3	7.8	983.4	5,032	137.4
Madison	0.0	15.5	0.0	0.0	0.0	12.2	19.2	6.8	0.0	14.7	276.7	5,622	72.8
Mobile	0.0	4.0	1.9	0.0	2.0	12.5	20.1	8.0	1.4	5.1	483.5	2,542	81.6
Montgomery	0.0	8.1	0.3	0.0	0.0	20.3	8.2	12.4	0.7	5.5	356.0	1,780	31.2
Northport	0.0	32.5	0.0	0.0	0.0	20.3	10.4	0.0	0.0	2.6	51.2	1,976	10.7
Opelika	0.0	8.9	0.0	0.0	0.7	17.6	10.2	10.6	0.6	9.1	204.8	6,756	16.4
Phenix City	0.0	4.1	0.0	0.0	0.3	14.2	16.2	11.9	0.0	5.3	121.9	3,383	15.2
Prattville	0.0	5.9	0.0	0.0	0.0	18.2	21.4	4.8	0.0	0.0	60.5	1,707	7.4
Trussville	0.0	13.3	0.0	0.0	0.0	18.5	3.9	9.5	0.0	17.1	134.9	6,212	3.7
Tuscaloosa	0.0	16.1	0.0	0.0	0.2	19.4	10.3	6.2	1.6	2.2	191.8	1,925	33.4
Vestavia Hills	0.0	0.0	0.0	0.0	0.0	32.1	4.1	4.1	0.0	12.2	46.5	1,352	0.0
ALASKA	X	X	X	X	X	X	X	X	X	X	X	X	X
Anchorage	0.1	8.5	0.0	49.8	1.5	9.5	5.2	2.5	0.9	2.1	1,569.1	5,331	55.9
Fairbanks	0.0	19.7	0.0	0.0	0.0	13.5	0.0	0.0	0.0	0.4	4.8	152	0.4
Juneau	0.0	4.0	0.1	22.6	31.8	4.3	4.0	4.5	0.9	2.3	149.8	4,667	20.3
ARIZONA	X	X	X	X	X	X	X	X	X	X	X	X	X
Apache Junction	0.0	23.7	0.0	0.0	0.0	33.4	0.0	11.3	4.9	0.9	6.1	149	0.0
Avondale	3.4	4.8	0.0	0.0	3.4	33.2	18.0	4.4	1.5	3.2	60.1	709	0.0
Buckeye	0.0	5.5	0.0	0.0	0.0	24.0	25.7	3.0	0.0	4.8	89.2	1,302	0.0
Bullhead City	0.0	7.5	0.0	0.0	4.3	24.9	23.3	5.7	0.3	3.7	42.5	1,057	0.0
Casa Grande	0.0	12.1	0.0	0.0	0.6	21.0	13.6	12.9	0.0	2.5	90.7	1,629	0.0
Chandler	0.0	6.6	0.0	0.0	0.0	25.6	34.8	5.8	1.9	2.9	318.9	1,257	39.1
El Mirage	0.0	8.4	0.0	0.0	1.5	32.0	26.6	3.9	0.3	1.4	25.6	724	0.0
Flagstaff	0.0	13.2	0.0	0.0	0.0	15.5	18.2	6.1	6.8	1.8	79.8	1,108	0.0
Florence town	0.0	12.6	0.0	0.0	0.0	12.8	13.1	8.2	0.0	12.3	70.6	2,728	5.5
Gilbert town	0.0	13.0	0.0	0.0	0.0	21.0	15.2	8.8	0.5	4.4	407.8	1,680	121.7
Glendale	0.0	10.6	0.0	0.0	0.0	23.2	13.2	6.2	5.4	6.8	804.4	3,246	0.0
Goodyear	0.0	16.2	0.0	0.0	0.0	15.8	10.4	4.8	1.2	9.4	269.2	3,367	0.0
Kingman	0.0	12.6	0.0	0.0	0.0	26.7	15.7	10.6	0.0	3.7	36.0	1,224	0.0
Lake Havasu City	0.0	6.8	0.0	0.0	0.0	16.8	19.9	4.2	0.5	9.2	259.3	4,768	0.0
Marana town	0.0	41.8	0.0	0.0	0.0	17.7	1.3	6.7	0.7	4.5	104.3	2,320	61.8
Maricopa	0.0	13.3	0.0	0.0	0.0	17.7	0.1	8.7	0.0	3.1	41.4	863	0.0
Mesa	0.0	6.8	0.0	0.0	0.0	25.6	11.8	8.4	3.9	9.3	1,536.5	3,073	293.9
Oro Valley	0.0	28.3	0.0	0.0	0.0	43.1	2.2	18.8	0.0	4.0	47.5	1,066	0.0
Peoria	0.0	17.1	0.0	0.0	0.0	18.9	13.7	11.3	0.0	5.1	274.9	1,634	0.0
Phoenix	0.0	3.8	0.1	1.3	0.0	18.7	12.1	6.7	5.6	11.9	7,724.4	4,729	1,130.0
Prescott	0.0	23.0	0.1	0.0	0.0	16.3	23.3	9.0	0.1	3.0	98.9	2,318	1.0
Prescott Valley town	0.0	16.1	0.0	0.0	0.0	20.5	12.2	7.7	0.0	5.9	68.4	1,538	0.0
Queen Creek	0.0	10.1	0.0	0.0	0.0	0.0	18.3	7.1	0.8	6.7	154.7	3,580	0.0
Sahuarita	0.0	17.7	0.0	0.0	0.0	27.0	12.9	6.7	0.0	6.6	46.0	1,545	9.9
San Luis	0.7	11.9	0.0	0.0	0.0	15.8	11.1	7.1	0.6	17.5	197.1	6,021	0.0
Scottsdale	0.0	5.6	0.0	0.0	0.0	19.7	12.4	8.5	1.3	8.5	1,218.6	4,847	247.0
Sierra Vista	0.0	24.3	0.0	0.0	0.0	21.1	16.1	6.1	2.3	1.2	19.9	464	0.0
Surprise	0.0	12.9	0.0	0.0	0.0	14.1	13.9	11.3	6.3	1.7	73.8	547	0.0
Tempe	0.0	4.7	0.0	0.0	0.0	27.4	13.2	7.5	5.4	3.5	446.0	2,401	0.0
Tucson	0.0	13.6	0.7	0.0	0.0	28.6	7.2	5.4	9.2	1.5	1,005.8	1,858	133.1
Yuma	0.0	9.7	0.0	0.0	0.6	22.2	13.2	14.6	1.3	3.6	24.2	251	0.0
ARKANSAS	X	X	X	X	X	X	X	X	X	X	X	X	X
Bella Vista	0.0	26.5	0.0	0.0	0.0	20.9	0.0	9.6	0.0	0.0	0.0	0	0.0
Benton	0.0	26.8	0.0	0.0	1.3	16.6	12.5	9.0	0.0	9.3	98.6	2,741	2.0
Bentonville	0.0	20.0	0.0	0.0	0.0	10.9	16.0	10.4	0.2	2.4	59.1	1,196	0.0
Cabot	0.2	8.4	0.0	0.0	0.1	18.3	19.2	12.2	0.0	8.2	12.3	469	0.0

1. Based on population estimated as of July 1 of the year shown.

STATE Place code	City	Land area[1] (sq. mi)	Population, 2021: Total persons 2021	Population, 2021: Rank	Population, 2021: Per square mile	Race 2020: Race alone[2] (percent): White	Race 2020: Race alone[2] (percent): Black or African American	Race 2020: Race alone[2] (percent): American Indian, Alaskan Native	Race 2020: Race alone[2] (percent): Asian	Race 2020: Race alone[2] (percent): Hawaiian Pacific Islander	Race 2020: Race alone[2] (percent): Some other race	Race 2020: Two or more races (percent)
		1	2	3	4	5	6	7	8	9	10	11
	ARKANSAS—Cont'd											
05 15190	Conway	46.3	65,121	586	1,406.5	67.3	18.4	0.5	1.9	0.1	3.5	8.4
05 23290	Fayetteville	54.4	95,230	349	1,750.6	75.9	6.5	1.1	3.2	0.5	3.4	9.3
05 24550	Fort Smith	64.0	89,576	382	1,399.6	60.8	8.7	2.2	5.8	0.1	10.9	11.4
05 33400	Hot Springs	37.5	38,114	1,044	1,016.4	66.9	16.5	0.9	1.4	0.1	5.0	9.1
05 34750	Jacksonville	28.6	29,305	1,336	1,024.7	44.9	40.3	0.6	1.9	0.2	3.3	8.8
05 35710	Jonesboro	80.2	79,324	455	989.1	64.5	22.8	0.3	2.1	0.1	3.8	6.4
05 41000	Little Rock	120.0	201,998	118	1,683.3	43.5	40.6	0.6	3.5	0.0	6.0	5.7
05 50450	North Little Rock	53.0	64,162	595	1,210.6	45.4	42.8	0.5	1.2	0.0	4.0	6.1
05 53390	Paragould	31.9	29,906	1,313	937.5	87.6	3.0	0.4	0.5	1.0	2.0	5.6
05 55310	Pine Bluff	44.2	40,244	985	910.5	17.8	77.2	0.3	0.8	0.1	1.2	2.5
05 60410	Rogers	38.9	71,112	524	1,828.1	61.0	1.5	1.6	2.8	1.5	18.5	13.1
05 61670	Russellville	28.3	29,338	1,331	1,036.7	72.2	6.3	1.0	1.7	0.1	9.4	9.3
05 63800	Sherwood	20.7	33,020	1,192	1,595.2	62.4	25.3	0.5	2.0	0.0	2.6	7.2
05 66080	Springdale	49.2	87,609	393	1,780.7	46.7	2.2	1.6	2.2	10.4	24.2	12.6
05 68810	Texarkana	42.0	29,314	1,333	698.0	55.9	35.4	0.6	0.6	0.0	2.1	5.4
06 00000	CALIFORNIA	155,854.0	39,237,836	X	251.8	41.2	5.7	1.6	15.4	0.4	21.2	14.6
06 00296	Adelanto	52.9	38,118	1,043	720.6	22.2	19.4	2.2	2.8	0.7	38.6	14.0
06 00562	Alameda	10.4	76,362	477	7,342.5	43.6	5.9	0.6	32.5	0.5	4.1	12.9
06 00884	Alhambra	7.6	81,211	434	10,685.7	14.4	1.9	1.3	51.9	0.1	17.6	13.0
06 00947	Aliso Viejo	6.9	51,824	768	7,510.7	60.0	1.9	0.4	16.6	0.3	6.6	14.1
06 02000	Anaheim	50.3	345,940	55	6,877.5	31.1	2.7	1.8	17.7	0.4	29.3	17.0
06 02252	Antioch	29.2	114,794	256	3,931.3	28.4	20.9	1.5	13.0	1.3	20.8	14.1
06 02364	Apple Valley	77.0	76,224	480	989.9	54.7	8.3	1.8	3.4	0.4	16.4	15.0
06 02462	Arcadia	10.9	55,345	717	5,077.5	20.1	1.7	0.4	64.9	0.1	5.6	7.3
06 03064	Atascadero	26.1	29,708	1,318	1,138.2	73.7	1.6	1.2	3.1	0.1	6.4	14.0
06 03162	Atwater	6.6	31,978	1,233	4,845.2	40.6	3.4	3.0	5.6	0.3	27.9	19.2
06 03386	Azusa	9.7	48,676	818	5,018.1	27.6	3.5	2.6	14.8	0.1	31.2	20.1
06 03526	Bakersfield	149.8	407,615	48	2,721.1	38.9	7.0	1.8	7.8	0.2	27.6	16.6
06 03666	Baldwin Park	6.6	70,629	533	10,701.4	15.7	1.0	2.0	20.5	0.1	41.9	18.7
06 03820	Banning	23.2	30,273	1,301	1,304.9	46.3	7.7	2.4	6.0	0.1	23.8	13.6
06 04030	Barstow	41.3	25,442	1,519	616.0	37.2	19.5	2.7	2.9	1.4	19.5	16.7
06 04758	Beaumont	30.3	55,280	721	1,824.4	45.4	8.3	1.8	8.7	0.2	19.5	16.2
06 04870	Bell	2.5	32,831	1,204	13,132.4	18.5	0.6	2.7	0.8	0.1	55.0	22.4
06 04982	Bellflower	6.1	77,408	467	12,689.8	21.5	13.3	1.7	12.8	0.7	33.3	16.6
06 04996	Bell Gardens	2.5	38,552	1,032	15,420.8	14.0	0.7	3.2	0.7	0.1	61.9	19.4
06 05108	Belmont	4.6	27,225	1,429	5,918.5	50.3	1.3	0.4	29.6	0.5	5.4	12.5
06 05290	Benicia	12.8	26,819	1,446	2,095.2	63.1	5.1	0.6	12.0	0.4	3.9	14.9
06 06000	Berkeley	10.4	117,145	244	11,263.9	53.3	7.9	0.5	20.0	0.2	6.3	11.7
06 06308	Beverly Hills	5.7	31,896	1,239	5,595.8	77.9	2.1	0.1	8.8	0.0	2.3	8.7
06 08058	Brawley	8.1	26,539	1,464	3,276.4	31.5	1.6	1.4	1.6	0.1	37.1	26.7
06 08100	Brea	12.2	47,589	838	3,900.7	45.1	1.8	0.8	28.0	0.2	10.3	14.0
06 08142	Brentwood	14.9	64,870	590	4,353.7	51.4	6.9	1.0	13.4	0.5	10.8	15.9
06 08786	Buena Park	10.5	83,011	422	7,905.8	25.9	3.2	1.3	33.2	0.5	22.4	13.5
06 08954	Burbank	17.3	105,401	302	6,092.5	60.9	2.9	0.8	11.7	0.1	10.1	13.6
06 09066	Burlingame	4.4	30,106	1,304	6,842.3	53.0	0.9	0.4	27.6	0.4	6.1	11.7
06 09710	Calexico	8.6	38,534	1,033	4,480.7	19.7	0.2	1.3	1.1	0.0	45.4	32.2
06 10046	Camarillo	19.7	70,858	527	3,596.9	59.6	2.3	0.9	11.3	0.3	10.0	15.6
06 10345	Campbell	6.1	42,754	934	7,008.9	51.0	2.5	0.8	24.2	0.3	8.4	12.8
06 11194	Carlsbad	37.8	115,302	255	3,050.3	72.6	1.2	0.6	8.0	0.2	4.8	12.7
06 11530	Carson	18.7	93,535	361	5,001.9	11.9	22.8	1.1	26.7	1.8	23.6	12.2
06 12048	Cathedral City	22.5	52,220	762	2,320.9	36.9	2.4	1.9	6.0	0.1	35.0	17.6
06 12524	Ceres	9.5	49,282	809	5,187.6	33.0	2.1	2.1	8.6	0.8	35.6	18.0
06 12552	Cerritos	8.7	48,394	822	5,562.5	15.0	6.6	0.4	62.6	0.4	5.7	9.2
06 13014	Chico	34.5	102,338	313	2,966.3	70.4	2.0	1.6	4.4	0.4	9.1	12.1
06 13210	Chino	29.6	92,975	364	3,141.0	29.9	6.1	1.5	19.3	0.2	25.5	17.7
06 13214	Chino Hills	44.7	78,665	462	1,759.8	29.0	4.2	0.8	40.5	0.2	11.3	14.0
06 13392	Chula Vista	49.6	277,220	77	5,589.1	26.2	5.1	1.3	15.5	0.5	25.3	26.1
06 13588	Citrus Heights	14.2	87,402	395	6,155.1	68.9	3.9	1.2	4.2	0.5	8.3	13.0
06 13756	Claremont	13.3	35,703	1,113	2,684.4	52.8	5.1	0.8	15.8	0.1	8.8	16.5
06 14218	Clovis	25.8	122,989	231	4,767.0	55.7	2.8	1.4	13.0	0.3	11.8	15.1
06 14260	Coachella	30.1	42,554	938	1,413.8	17.3	0.5	2.1	0.6	0.0	55.7	23.7
06 14890	Colton	15.6	54,285	735	3,479.8	24.7	8.8	2.4	4.8	0.3	42.2	16.9
06 15044	Compton	10.0	93,597	360	9,359.7	8.1	26.0	2.1	0.5	0.6	50.1	12.7
06 16000	Concord	30.6	124,074	228	4,054.7	47.7	3.8	1.1	15.0	0.6	17.0	14.9
06 16350	Corona	39.9	159,743	162	4,003.6	40.1	5.5	1.5	12.0	0.4	23.0	17.3
06 16532	Costa Mesa	15.8	110,750	278	7,009.5	54.1	1.3	1.3	8.7	0.4	19.1	15.1
06 16742	Covina	7.0	50,411	792	7,201.6	31.0	3.8	1.9	15.3	0.2	25.5	22.3
06 17568	Culver City	5.1	39,970	989	7,837.3	49.2	7.9	0.6	17.0	0.2	9.2	15.8

1. Dry land or land partially or temporarily covered by water. 2. Hispanic or Latino persons may be of any race.

City	Percent Hispanic or Latino[1], 2020	Percent foreign born, 2016–2020	Age of population (percent), 2016–2020: Under 18 years	18 to 24 years	25 to 34 years	35 to 44 years	45 to 54 years	55 to 64 years	65 years and over	Median age, 2016–2020	Percent female, 2016–2020	Population: Census counts: 2010	2020	Percent change: 2010–2020	2020–2021
	12	13	14	15	16	17	18	19	20	21	22	23	24	25	26
ARKANSAS—Cont'd															
Conway	6.7	4.5	20.8	21.4	15.9	12.7	9.5	8.9	10.8	29.5	53.1	58,872	63,656	8.1	2.3
Fayetteville	8.6	5.8	17.9	26.5	17.8	11.5	8.8	8.8	8.7	27.7	50.7	73,584	93,582	27.2	1.8
Fort Smith	19.6	11.7	23.8	10.3	13.8	12.7	12.0	12.5	14.9	36.7	50.7	86,266	89,177	3.4	0.4
Hot Springs	9.6	7.9	18.9	9.8	12.0	10.7	11.4	15.2	22.0	43.6	54.3	37,937	38,053	0.3	0.2
Jacksonville	7.4	4.2	24.0	11.3	18.3	11.2	10.0	12.5	12.6	33.2	52.6	28,368	29,469	3.9	-0.6
Jonesboro	7.3	5.1	24.3	13.3	13.7	13.6	11.2	10.7	13.2	34.0	51.7	67,291	78,524	16.7	1.0
Little Rock	10.1	7.3	23.5	9.1	15.5	13.3	11.9	12.4	14.3	36.5	52.5	193,534	202,514	4.6	-0.3
North Little Rock	7.1	3.2	24.8	8.9	16.4	11.8	10.6	11.8	15.7	35.0	52.4	62,333	64,633	3.7	-0.7
Paragould	4.4	0.9	24.5	9.2	15.3	13.4	11.5	11.9	14.2	35.6	51.6	26,315	29,439	11.9	1.6
Pine Bluff	1.8	1.7	22.8	11.9	13.7	12.2	11.2	13.0	15.2	36.4	52.8	49,060	41,246	-15.9	-2.4
Rogers	33.4	20.4	27.7	9.4	16.0	13.7	14.5	9.3	9.4	33.0	51.9	56,104	69,753	24.3	1.9
Russellville	16.9	9.8	23.7	21.0	15.0	10.1	8.7	9.8	11.8	27.6	50.9	28,106	29,150	3.7	0.6
Sherwood	5.6	2.5	23.4	8.4	12.1	13.8	12.0	13.6	16.7	38.8	52.5	29,609	32,780	10.7	0.7
Springdale	39.6	23.4	30.7	9.5	14.7	14.1	11.7	9.7	9.7	31.8	48.7	70,808	87,441	23.5	0.2
Texarkana	4.2	2.2	22.6	8.5	14.3	11.7	12.8	13.3	16.9	40.2	52.3	29,888	29,314	-1.9	0.0
CALIFORNIA	39.4	26.6	22.8	9.5	15.3	13.3	12.8	12.0	14.3	36.7	50.3	37,254,522	39,538,223	6.1	-0.8
Adelanto	63.5	17.4	34.0	12.0	15.5	14.4	9.9	7.9	6.2	27.6	46.6	31,760	37,817	19.1	0.8
Alameda	12.1	25.3	21.4	5.4	15.2	15.6	13.7	12.2	16.6	40.2	51.3	73,812	78,611	6.5	-2.9
Alhambra	36.1	48.1	17.4	7.7	15.7	13.5	14.1	13.0	18.6	41.4	51.5	83,073	83,001	-0.1	-2.2
Aliso Viejo	18.9	22.9	25.5	7.4	13.3	15.6	16.6	13.0	8.5	37.4	53.1	47,668	52,174	9.5	-0.7
Anaheim	53.8	35.0	23.5	10.4	16.5	13.0	13.1	11.7	11.8	34.8	51.2	336,332	347,015	3.2	-0.3
Antioch	36.4	21.4	24.2	9.5	14.6	12.9	12.5	13.7	12.7	36.4	52.3	102,745	115,360	12.3	-0.5
Apple Valley	38.2	10.3	28.2	8.1	12.2	11.7	10.7	12.6	16.4	36.4	52.0	69,146	75,913	9.8	0.4
Arcadia	13.1	47.4	22.0	6.6	10.9	12.6	14.6	14.1	19.2	43.3	51.6	56,242	56,737	0.9	-2.5
Atascadero	19.6	6.7	20.8	9.5	13.7	11.3	11.9	16.8	16.0	38.6	50.4	28,306	29,794	5.3	-0.3
Atwater	59.6	22.6	28.4	9.3	14.1	13.9	12.3	10.0	12.0	33.6	51.1	28,552	31,819	11.4	0.5
Azusa	64.0	28.8	21.4	19.2	15.0	12.7	10.7	10.0	11.0	30.4	51.5	46,574	49,757	6.8	-2.2
Bakersfield	52.7	19.2	29.9	10.1	16.2	12.6	11.4	9.8	10.0	31.0	50.6	347,783	402,907	15.9	1.2
Baldwin Park	74.4	45.6	22.9	10.1	16.3	13.7	13.1	11.2	12.7	35.5	49.8	75,397	72,323	-4.1	-2.3
Banning	45.5	19.5	22.6	8.3	9.3	11.3	9.8	9.4	29.3	43.6	52.0	28,684	29,528	2.9	2.5
Barstow	44.4	10.9	31.0	10.4	14.4	11.2	10.3	11.1	11.5	30.3	53.3	22,747	25,433	11.8	0.0
Beaumont	42.5	17.6	31.1	6.5	13.6	15.5	10.0	9.8	13.6	34.4	51.9	36,932	53,101	43.8	4.1
Bell	93.5	42.6	26.4	11.4	16.6	13.0	13.8	9.6	9.2	31.8	48.3	35,469	33,656	-5.1	-2.5
Bellflower	57.1	31.6	24.5	9.7	16.3	14.0	13.8	10.7	11.1	34.7	51.0	76,625	79,298	3.5	-2.4
Bell Gardens	96.2	41.0	29.8	12.0	15.9	13.4	12.7	8.8	7.5	29.6	49.0	42,058	39,556	-5.9	-2.5
Belmont	12.4	30.3	23.5	5.1	13.1	16.5	15.3	11.7	14.8	39.3	50.1	25,900	28,313	9.3	-3.8
Benicia	14.8	13.2	20.4	5.5	9.4	13.2	13.3	17.0	21.1	46.1	50.8	27,035	27,092	0.2	-1.0
Berkeley	13.7	21.2	12.3	24.0	17.8	10.9	9.1	10.4	15.5	32.1	51.1	112,443	119,693	6.4	-2.1
Beverly Hills	6.8	34.6	19.9	5.9	10.5	11.3	15.9	13.6	22.8	46.9	52.7	33,923	32,782	-3.4	-2.7
Brawley	86.1	26.6	33.3	9.8	16.4	8.9	11.0	9.0	11.6	29.1	52.3	24,977	26,443	5.9	0.4
Brea	27.4	22.1	22.0	9.0	13.1	13.2	15.2	12.5	15.0	39.6	53.7	39,195	47,415	21.0	0.4
Brentwood	26.6	14.2	26.0	9.2	8.9	12.6	15.9	12.4	15.0	40.9	52.1	51,627	64,355	24.7	0.8
Buena Park	40.9	36.3	22.3	9.3	15.8	13.4	11.9	13.0	14.3	36.7	50.4	80,456	84,173	4.6	-1.4
Burbank	24.2	30.2	18.4	7.9	17.4	13.6	14.2	12.9	15.6	39.6	51.5	103,360	107,563	4.1	-2.0
Burlingame	13.6	29.2	23.0	3.7	13.0	17.6	15.9	11.8	15.1	41.0	49.4	28,815	31,374	8.9	-4.0
Calexico	97.2	44.9	28.0	9.3	13.1	11.6	12.1	10.4	15.5	34.6	53.2	38,573	38,649	0.2	-0.3
Camarillo	27.4	14.5	21.1	9.8	13.3	11.2	12.4	12.5	19.7	40.5	51.7	65,175	70,797	8.6	0.1
Campbell	19.2	28.8	21.4	5.9	15.7	15.6	13.8	13.4	14.3	38.9	50.5	40,578	44,080	8.6	-3.0
Carlsbad	15.1	15.5	23.2	6.7	10.3	14.1	14.9	14.3	16.5	41.8	50.7	105,349	114,972	9.1	0.3
Carson	39.4	34.1	20.6	9.2	13.8	12.5	13.5	13.3	17.1	40.1	51.1	91,711	95,367	4.0	-1.9
Cathedral City	60.0	30.6	21.9	8.4	12.6	12.7	12.5	14.2	17.6	40.6	49.4	51,233	51,535	0.6	1.3
Ceres	64.1	24.4	29.4	11.3	15.6	13.5	11.4	8.3	10.5	30.8	48.2	45,878	49,276	7.4	0.0
Cerritos	14.3	42.7	19.3	7.2	10.9	12.6	12.1	13.4	24.5	45.0	50.1	49,043	49,683	1.3	-2.6
Chico	20.3	7.7	19.1	22.0	15.7	11.5	9.5	9.7	12.5	29.8	51.4	89,013	102,849	15.5	-0.5
Chino	51.2	23.4	21.4	7.7	16.5	16.9	13.4	12.4	11.6	37.3	45.1	78,074	90,989	16.5	2.2
Chino Hills	28.2	29.9	22.8	9.3	13.9	11.6	14.6	15.8	12.1	38.6	50.6	74,792	78,573	5.1	0.1
Chula Vista	59.8	30.1	24.7	9.3	14.7	14.4	13.4	11.5	12.1	36.0	50.5	243,912	276,025	13.2	0.4
Citrus Heights	19.6	13.7	20.5	8.7	16.8	12.5	12.2	12.6	16.8	37.6	51.4	83,118	88,018	5.9	-0.7
Claremont	25.3	17.9	16.8	16.7	10.8	10.5	12.8	12.7	19.7	40.4	51.8	34,867	36,462	4.6	-2.1
Clovis	30.5	12.9	28.8	8.0	13.6	13.5	12.0	11.1	13.0	34.8	50.7	95,987	120,254	25.3	2.3
Coachella	96.4	39.5	20.9	8.2	18.3	16.3	15.7	11.1	9.5	36.4	52.3	40,712	41,987	3.1	1.4
Colton	73.8	22.1	26.8	10.1	18.2	12.5	11.7	10.3	10.5	31.8	51.5	52,118	53,945	3.5	0.6
Compton	70.8	30.1	29.0	10.7	14.3	13.0	12.7	10.7	9.6	31.8	51.6	96,373	95,959	-0.4	-2.5
Concord	31.1	24.4	21.7	7.5	15.8	14.3	12.5	13.4	14.8	38.1	50.3	122,162	125,389	2.6	-1.0
Corona	46.5	24.0	25.3	10.1	14.9	14.1	13.9	11.6	10.1	34.8	50.0	152,283	157,265	3.3	1.6
Costa Mesa	36.5	24.7	19.8	9.0	19.9	15.0	13.6	10.8	11.9	35.6	49.6	110,082	111,915	1.7	-1.0
Covina	58.7	24.6	21.6	10.0	14.3	15.2	13.4	12.0	13.5	37.5	50.4	47,797	51,373	7.5	-1.9
Culver City	21.4	25.7	19.0	4.9	15.1	14.8	14.1	14.0	18.2	42.6	53.7	38,833	40,795	5.1	-2.0

1. May be of any race.

City	Households, 2016–2020							Persons in group quarters, 2016–2020	Serious crimes known to police[2], 2020				Educational attainment, 2016–2020		
			Percent						Violent		Property			Attainment[4] (percent)	
	Number	Persons per household	Family	Married couple family	Female family	Non-family	One person		Number	Rate	Number	Rate	Population age 25 and over	High school graduate or less	Bachelor's degree or more
	27	28	29	30	31	32	33	34	35	36	37	38	39	40	41
ARKANSAS—Cont'd															
Conway	24,789	2.49	57.7	41.9	12.6	42.3	31.0	4,944	359	523.3	1,915	2,791.6	38,642	31.7	41.1
Fayetteville	35,716	2.23	46.9	33.1	8.3	53.1	34.4	6,885	517	579.3	4,611	5,166.3	48,214	24.8	50.3
Fort Smith	36,347	2.38	61.8	40.7	15.3	38.2	32.0	1,455	1,031	1,170.6	4,871	5,530.8	57,900	45.2	24.3
Hot Springs	16,614	2.22	54.5	34.2	16.1	45.5	40.4	1,778	287	737.9	2,276	5,852.0	27,607	45.1	21.1
Jacksonville	10,642	2.59	66.4	46.5	16.2	33.6	29.4	862	327	1,158.9	1,263	4,476.0	18,392	41.0	21.8
Jonesboro	30,123	2.45	63.0	42.0	16.8	37.0	28.1	3,584	642	805.5	2,825	3,544.5	48,275	40.4	29.7
Little Rock	83,525	2.33	55.6	34.7	17.3	44.4	37.7	3,612	3,657	1,849.9	9,602	4,857.1	133,634	30.6	42.6
North Little Rock	28,350	2.30	53.8	31.7	17.8	46.2	38.4	795	665	1,003.0	2,433	3,669.5	43,845	39.0	29.2
Paragould	11,032	2.55	70.0	46.8	17.4	30.0	24.3	655	378	1,290.6	1,329	4,537.7	19,103	52.2	19.2
Pine Bluff	16,808	2.28	58.8	29.5	24.0	41.2	35.4	4,038	746	1,832.1	1,990	4,887.3	27,637	50.0	19.6
Rogers	24,508	2.75	71.7	53.0	13.7	28.3	23.5	492	274	390.3	1,822	2,595.7	42,653	46.9	30.6
Russellville	9,824	2.64	59.6	43.5	14.2	40.4	31.8	3,310	139	475.0	1,133	3,871.4	16,171	43.1	29.0
Sherwood	12,547	2.48	65.3	45.5	14.7	34.7	30.2	100	202	638.5	847	2,677.3	21,284	30.9	32.5
Springdale	27,093	2.93	73.1	49.1	16.0	26.9	22.5	938	NA	NA	NA	NA	48,090	53.2	21.3
Texarkana	11,370	2.51	64.2	39.5	20.8	35.8	30.3	1,354	273	921.6	922	3,112.6	20,589	47.9	18.8
CALIFORNIA	13,103,114	2.94	68.6	49.7	12.9	31.4	23.8	824,735	174,026	442.0	842,054	2,138.9	26,665,143	36.4	34.7
Adelanto	7,753	4.06	82.4	48.5	25.4	17.6	14.0	2,769	274	798.1	304	885.5	18,505	60.6	6.2
Alameda	30,514	2.58	62.3	48.2	10.6	37.7	28.5	1,134	193	247.3	2,485	3,184.0	58,431	19.6	56.7
Alhambra	30,297	2.76	68.8	46.3	16.0	31.2	23.1	786	175	208.8	1,551	1,850.5	63,252	38.9	36.4
Aliso Viejo	18,428	2.71	68.3	53.8	9.9	31.7	25.2	417	28	54.6	387	755.2	33,789	14.3	56.3
Anaheim	103,704	3.36	72.7	50.6	15.7	27.3	19.6	4,939	1,241	352.6	8,865	2,519.1	233,455	45.1	26.6
Antioch	33,803	3.28	74.6	48.8	19.1	25.4	18.9	567	591	525.4	2,719	2,417.3	73,897	40.4	21.1
Apple Valley	23,936	3.04	74.9	54.0	15.7	25.1	19.9	524	427	577.6	861	1,164.6	46,661	43.6	17.8
Arcadia	19,207	2.94	79.5	56.7	17.1	20.5	16.2	669	87	149.7	1,034	1,779.0	40,765	22.1	56.9
Atascadero	11,681	2.57	68.6	54.7	8.8	31.4	24.2	369	84	277.5	393	1,298.5	21,233	29.2	29.8
Atwater	10,090	2.99	75.8	50.3	18.6	24.2	19.6	141	152	511.7	889	2,992.9	18,895	50.0	14.0
Azusa	13,279	3.34	73.9	49.3	17.4	26.1	18.1	5,231	155	307.7	975	1,935.6	29,472	44.8	27.3
Bakersfield	118,568	3.17	74.6	50.2	17.2	25.4	19.7	4,409	2,007	516.9	15,619	4,022.8	227,859	44.0	22.6
Baldwin Park	17,708	4.25	86.0	56.0	19.8	14.0	10.6	481	161	214.0	862	1,145.8	50,652	63.2	13.3
Banning	11,163	2.69	65.7	43.4	15.5	34.3	30.0	298	125	398.2	543	1,729.7	20,911	48.7	16.4
Barstow	8,166	2.85	67.7	27.5	33.4	32.3	26.2	299	275	1,143.9	928	3,860.1	13,793	46.0	10.5
Beaumont	14,299	3.36	79.9	58.3	13.9	20.1	16.1	176	116	219.3	874	1,652.7	30,103	36.7	25.9
Bell	8,930	3.85	83.2	48.6	25.0	16.8	14.3	878	182	512.3	502	1,413.0	21,945	72.8	8.3
Bellflower	22,998	3.29	74.6	46.2	18.7	25.4	19.3	689	348	455.4	1,799	2,354.2	50,291	48.8	17.7
Bell Gardens	9,657	4.28	86.2	46.8	26.4	13.8	9.7	406	150	357.1	618	1,471.1	24,311	76.7	6.1
Belmont	10,379	2.54	69.7	61.4	5.6	30.3	24.0	636	52	192.1	422	1,559.3	19,256	11.9	67.5
Benicia	11,455	2.46	67.5	53.2	8.7	32.5	27.9	24	25	88.1	400	1,409.7	20,864	22.2	42.7
Berkeley	45,884	2.40	46.9	36.7	7.3	53.1	33.9	13,101	537	438.9	5,535	4,524.1	78,378	10.8	73.1
Beverly Hills	14,685	2.29	56.6	44.9	7.2	43.4	37.4	25	111	328.6	1,244	3,683.1	25,006	15.7	63.9
Brawley	6,957	3.71	75.9	46.2	21.3	24.1	19.7	116	120	455.2	616	2,336.6	14,759	49.9	15.0
Brea	15,518	2.84	72.9	56.2	13.6	27.1	21.9	115	63	144.1	1,178	2,695.3	30,500	23.0	46.8
Brentwood	20,410	3.08	79.6	65.2	10.5	20.4	16.8	212	169	255.8	1,292	1,955.8	40,818	26.3	35.5
Buena Park	23,276	3.50	82.6	59.3	16.3	17.4	13.1	856	181	221.0	2,147	2,621.5	56,254	37.5	30.5
Burbank	41,473	2.48	59.6	43.5	11.3	40.4	30.9	524	174	169.9	2,474	2,415.6	76,188	23.8	44.4
Burlingame	12,047	2.46	63.0	53.3	7.4	37.0	29.5	490	67	215.3	1,151	3,697.9	22,035	12.8	66.6
Calexico	9,333	4.26	77.4	52.6	20.4	22.6	20.6	83	71	177.7	805	2,014.7	24,956	54.1	18.9
Camarillo	24,429	2.76	69.7	57.1	9.9	30.3	23.5	1,099	53	75.3	817	1,160.1	47,356	21.7	41.3
Campbell	16,121	2.64	64.5	50.2	9.8	35.5	25.6	319	110	262.4	1,365	3,256.1	31,177	21.9	53.5
Carlsbad	43,107	2.64	71.6	57.8	10.4	28.4	22.1	525	224	192.2	1,841	1,580.0	80,241	14.8	59.1
Carson	24,882	3.64	82.6	54.8	19.4	17.4	14.8	824	392	429.0	2,044	2,237.0	64,094	40.0	28.8
Cathedral City	19,716	2.76	60.9	43.8	11.8	39.1	31.7	374	130	234.6	651	1,174.7	38,168	48.1	23.8
Ceres	13,302	3.58	80.4	52.1	19.0	19.6	16.6	709	190	387.5	898	1,831.6	28,642	58.0	11.3
Cerritos	15,406	3.20	84.8	67.2	12.1	15.2	13.3	155	100	200.2	1,362	2,726.6	36,275	20.0	53.6
Chico	37,628	2.53	53.2	35.1	11.8	46.8	29.3	3,667	540	512.6	2,113	2,005.6	58,058	24.4	38.5
Chino	23,062	3.33	79.1	59.0	14.1	20.9	15.5	12,417	335	347.8	2,075	2,154.5	63,214	42.4	23.4
Chino Hills	25,874	3.20	83.2	67.1	10.8	16.8	13.3	125	112	131.9	833	981.1	56,255	22.4	48.1
Chula Vista	79,486	3.36	80.2	59.9	14.8	19.8	15.5	2,003	916	329.5	3,257	1,171.5	177,566	37.3	29.2
Citrus Heights	33,835	2.57	63.0	43.5	13.3	37.0	27.6	678	286	323.8	2,121	2,401.7	62,104	34.1	21.6
Claremont	11,981	2.62	70.8	57.0	10.7	29.2	23.7	4,258	51	140.0	696	1,910.9	23,678	16.2	56.3
Clovis	37,726	2.97	74.8	54.0	14.7	25.2	20.2	512	240	205.5	2,334	1,998.1	71,227	28.3	34.5
Coachella	17,508	2.61	51.9	36.8	11.1	48.1	45.1	0	139	300.2	715	1,544.1	32,358	84.3	3.3
Colton	16,467	3.27	76.3	45.8	20.8	23.7	18.4	323	191	346.5	1,429	2,592.7	34,220	53.2	18.5
Compton	23,915	3.98	82.4	46.3	25.4	17.6	14.0	615	1,125	1,177.9	2,249	2,354.7	57,727	66.0	9.3
Concord	46,402	2.76	67.5	50.8	11.8	32.5	24.5	1,238	423	325.2	3,783	2,908.3	91,384	29.8	37.4
Corona	47,953	3.49	81.0	62.0	13.1	19.0	14.8	720	240	139.7	3,610	2,100.7	108,544	38.3	27.9
Costa Mesa	40,660	2.73	60.3	44.6	9.8	39.7	25.1	1,922	488	430.7	3,581	3,160.2	80,481	31.2	41.1
Covina	15,296	3.10	72.7	48.5	15.7	27.3	21.4	436	152	320.6	1,110	2,341.1	32,667	37.9	25.9
Culver City	17,378	2.22	54.0	42.7	8.6	46.0	38.7	335	196	499.8	1,600	4,079.8	29,627	16.2	60.4

2. Data for serious crimes have not been adjusted for underreporting. This may affect comparability between geographic areas and over time.

4. Persons 25 years old and over.

City	Money income, 2016–2020					Median earnings Full year, Full-time workers, 2016–2020			Housing units, 2016–2020				
	Households												
	Median household income	Percent with income less than $25,000	Percent with income of $200,000 or more	Median family income	Median non-family household income	All persons	Men	Women	Total	Occupied	Percent owner occupied	Median value[1] (dollars)	Median gross rent (dollars)
	42	43	44	45	46	47	48	49	50	51	52	53	54
ARKANSAS—Cont'd													
Conway	47,999	24.7	4.2	70,763	30,890	40,617	43,189	37,741	27,485	24,789	47.1	179,400	820
Fayetteville	47,350	28.9	6.0	75,530	31,030	47,046	49,990	43,968	38,270	35,716	37.9	232,100	837
Fort Smith	45,233	24.8	3.6	55,596	28,942	37,957	41,604	35,098	39,868	36,347	50.6	132,800	703
Hot Springs	40,125	31.1	2.7	55,964	23,496	32,421	35,657	31,370	20,897	16,614	53.6	127,500	749
Jacksonville	48,587	26.4	2.0	64,752	29,000	37,280	41,314	34,236	12,602	10,642	48.4	126,900	838
Jonesboro	47,062	26.0	4.8	61,537	28,949	40,018	45,511	36,418	32,901	30,123	52.3	161,500	786
Little Rock	53,620	22.9	7.6	72,970	36,718	45,533	49,596	41,868	96,399	83,525	54.6	172,500	889
North Little Rock	43,831	27.7	3.3	53,819	33,980	41,089	44,133	37,358	32,476	28,350	47.6	144,100	867
Paragould	48,276	25.4	2.2	53,010	26,399	40,559	43,463	34,798	11,801	11,032	58.7	137,400	736
Pine Bluff	34,410	37.5	1.9	43,163	22,711	34,617	35,367	34,209	21,203	16,808	51.4	74,900	734
Rogers	65,511	15.9	10.1	74,855	42,565	40,862	44,647	35,405	25,883	24,508	56.8	185,200	937
Russellville	37,436	30.0	2.5	52,308	21,362	33,798	41,274	25,672	11,345	9,824	58.4	133,100	695
Sherwood	63,877	16.2	5.1	79,009	45,382	48,640	51,360	44,427	13,974	12,547	69.4	155,800	859
Springdale	51,868	16.3	4.8	57,186	34,192	35,839	39,111	31,451	28,402	27,093	50.0	161,000	782
Texarkana	41,873	31.8	2.6	55,979	23,481	39,240	49,225	32,857	13,564	11,370	56.7	127,500	747
CALIFORNIA	78,672	15.5	13.3	89,798	50,894	54,399	58,750	50,827	14,210,945	13,103,114	55.3	538,500	1,586
Adelanto	49,493	23.4	2.7	53,021	31,412	38,448	41,353	33,192	8,586	7,753	57.2	213,800	1,186
Alameda	106,737	11.2	22.6	130,234	70,452	81,436	85,184	77,565	32,494	30,514	48.2	920,200	1,973
Alhambra	66,593	19.0	7.1	72,982	49,169	48,372	49,825	46,537	32,137	30,297	40.0	630,200	1,495
Aliso Viejo	118,540	9.5	19.3	136,651	82,933	85,059	96,545	75,826	19,548	18,428	58.0	656,600	2,335
Anaheim	76,723	14.4	9.2	81,408	54,593	45,302	48,609	41,341	108,561	103,704	45.6	602,400	1,743
Antioch	80,234	13.2	8.6	89,430	54,295	52,111	54,960	48,461	34,996	33,803	61.4	428,800	1,911
Apple Valley	54,929	18.4	5.3	61,623	32,947	50,612	56,482	40,615	25,529	23,936	64.7	270,400	1,084
Arcadia	95,736	10.7	17.8	104,587	57,381	64,201	75,368	55,402	21,057	19,207	60.4	1,136,700	1,700
Atascadero	79,620	9.6	8.6	91,996	53,237	53,412	61,270	45,430	12,049	11,681	63.5	529,600	1,439
Atwater	57,052	19.6	2.5	60,040	35,798	41,695	44,139	37,242	10,448	10,090	52.4	251,100	1,044
Azusa	65,912	13.1	6.0	72,326	56,788	41,024	41,542	40,000	14,120	13,279	55.2	438,700	1,524
Bakersfield	65,687	17.9	5.9	71,655	39,210	48,829	52,668	42,323	125,143	118,568	59.4	258,700	1,124
Baldwin Park	68,741	15.4	4.3	69,299	31,526	36,258	39,286	32,456	18,223	17,708	57.6	436,800	1,523
Banning	43,442	25.5	3.4	49,884	27,028	36,224	37,161	34,685	11,968	11,163	68.6	242,000	1,097
Barstow	42,912	29.3	2.1	47,166	28,217	41,277	41,940	39,574	9,135	8,166	41.0	130,100	812
Beaumont	88,932	10.5	7.4	94,363	46,163	60,989	66,318	51,943	14,863	14,299	79.6	338,700	1,318
Bell	47,740	24.5	3.1	50,309	20,601	31,619	33,306	28,709	9,173	8,930	32.0	436,400	1,216
Bellflower	63,848	17.5	3.7	69,936	39,542	42,429	45,147	40,296	24,341	22,998	38.2	483,100	1,432
Bell Gardens	45,289	22.8	1.5	44,775	23,236	28,918	30,824	26,228	9,874	9,657	21.6	402,600	1,296
Belmont	160,046	10.2	41.1	212,155	81,435	121,152	139,180	104,705	11,084	10,379	57.5	1,604,700	2,546
Benicia	106,989	10.6	16.7	124,846	60,881	77,376	90,426	66,978	11,984	11,455	71.2	597,500	1,995
Berkeley	91,259	18.1	20.9	145,151	54,545	79,236	85,579	71,368	50,046	45,884	42.9	1,059,500	1,767
Beverly Hills	101,241	15.4	25.8	150,986	66,864	84,683	108,783	72,578	17,269	14,685	43.3	2,000,000	2,259
Brawley	46,177	32.0	3.5	44,223	50,747	47,978	57,500	36,320	8,331	6,957	52.9	214,900	840
Brea	100,969	8.7	16.2	118,139	62,169	65,382	70,695	60,831	16,231	15,518	62.9	687,700	1,958
Brentwood	113,298	9.4	17.1	120,775	51,107	77,432	88,258	68,204	21,180	20,410	78.6	610,000	2,215
Buena Park	84,680	10.6	8.4	86,363	51,495	50,234	52,141	46,681	24,244	23,276	56.6	608,800	1,723
Burbank	79,212	17.8	13.0	101,550	51,201	63,972	71,026	56,984	43,986	41,473	42.8	790,300	1,763
Burlingame	138,344	5.8	33.7	190,272	80,579	105,524	109,760	101,712	12,655	12,047	51.3	2,000,000	2,305
Calexico	42,732	32.1	2.1	54,353	15,201	37,354	44,236	30,028	11,458	9,333	52.9	219,600	934
Camarillo	98,039	10.5	14.2	115,572	61,577	66,089	76,190	57,326	25,717	24,429	63.8	619,100	2,161
Campbell	122,644	10.6	26.8	142,212	85,055	89,393	101,881	81,149	17,442	16,121	49.2	1,156,000	2,323
Carlsbad	112,933	9.3	25.0	133,412	67,729	91,679	103,241	76,417	46,918	43,107	62.5	857,300	2,054
Carson	86,040	11.5	10.9	91,073	44,326	50,754	51,830	50,022	25,923	24,882	73.7	494,800	1,569
Cathedral City	50,350	25.6	5.0	61,986	29,050	39,828	39,696	39,946	23,897	19,716	61.6	302,500	1,241
Ceres	59,247	17.6	3.3	62,491	31,270	42,469	46,280	35,726	13,651	13,302	60.0	284,300	1,289
Cerritos	109,229	8.2	19.6	116,996	62,122	70,506	77,155	67,405	15,934	15,406	76.2	716,000	2,455
Chico	57,357	25.6	6.5	77,030	34,632	46,418	51,159	42,885	41,337	37,628	45.4	349,300	1,145
Chino	85,659	10.1	7.1	89,762	53,599	50,724	54,994	42,971	24,670	23,062	61.9	476,800	1,697
Chino Hills	104,661	8.1	17.3	113,664	61,016	65,336	67,389	60,968	27,187	25,874	73.0	642,500	2,226
Chula Vista	86,132	12.6	10.1	95,950	43,015	52,716	57,280	47,322	85,860	79,486	60.1	526,500	1,729
Citrus Heights	65,867	14.1	3.4	76,311	47,513	50,721	53,267	47,449	35,119	33,835	58.5	326,700	1,364
Claremont	101,080	9.3	20.9	132,894	51,722	80,049	84,461	70,092	12,685	11,981	66.0	688,600	1,604
Clovis	84,119	11.8	10.8	95,580	44,309	60,768	64,478	54,762	39,375	37,726	65.1	341,800	1,247
Coachella	33,999	36.4	1.3	51,716	21,527	32,087	32,930	31,055	17,772	17,508	71.5	238,500	830
Colton	56,762	19.5	2.0	61,928	33,615	40,439	43,865	35,466	18,275	16,467	52.4	292,300	1,213
Compton	58,703	21.0	2.8	62,045	30,025	35,710	35,699	35,728	24,823	23,915	55.9	383,500	1,236
Concord	92,706	11.3	12.7	105,056	60,995	64,909	69,917	60,178	47,771	46,402	60.1	581,900	1,800
Corona	88,434	11.4	11.3	97,058	48,677	53,012	56,947	48,153	49,804	47,953	63.6	491,000	1,705
Costa Mesa	90,370	10.8	14.4	97,842	78,248	59,063	59,955	58,168	42,391	40,660	40.5	807,000	1,927
Covina	77,913	14.0	7.4	85,231	50,081	50,280	51,226	49,007	15,920	15,296	57.4	549,500	1,587
Culver City	97,540	12.5	17.3	134,617	72,406	84,484	91,170	77,047	18,171	17,378	53.8	920,900	2,071

1. Specified owner-occupied units

City	Commuting, 2016–2020[1]		Computer access[2], 2016–2020		Migration, 2016–2020		Civilian labor force, 2021				Civilian Employment, 2016–2020[4]			
	Percent		Percent						Unemployment[3]		Population age 16 and older		Population age 16 to 64	
	Drove alone	Mean travel time to work	With a computer in the house	With Internet access	Percent who lived in the same house one year ago	Percent who lived in another state or county one year ago	Total	Percent change 2020–2021	Total	Rate	Number	Percent in labor force	Number	Percent who worked full-year full-time
	55	56	57	58	59	60	61	62	63	64	65	66	67	68
ARKANSAS—Cont'd														
Conway	83.6	21.1	93.3	86.6	86.7	7.0	33,617	-1.7	1,184	3.5	54,280	63.3	47,068	50.9
Fayetteville	72.0	18.1	96.0	86.1	72.7	12.5	48,756	-0.2	1,574	3.2	72,250	63.8	64,686	43.4
Fort Smith	79.9	16.6	89.6	78.2	81.6	7.2	37,707	-3.3	1,419	3.8	69,438	62.2	56,316	51.3
Hot Springs	77.8	17.0	88.4	76.2	83.3	7.5	15,169	-2.5	922	6.1	32,262	51.6	23,734	45.4
Jacksonville	82.8	20.1	92.8	80.8	84.6	9.6	11,457	-2.5	683	6.0	22,335	56.6	18,759	51.6
Jonesboro	83.9	17.9	89.9	81.4	75.3	10.1	39,368	-1.2	1,331	3.4	60,709	63.5	50,466	49.1
Little Rock	80.8	18.2	90.9	82.8	85.6	5.8	95,325	-2.1	4,901	5.1	156,376	65.2	127,958	55.9
North Little Rock	82.5	19.5	89.2	76.4	84.2	6.0	29,386	-3.0	1,580	5.4	50,994	63.4	40,635	51.4
Paragould	83.3	19.5	91.8	83.6	75.1	8.6	12,321	-2.0	465	3.8	22,648	59.8	18,562	47.2
Pine Bluff	88.4	17.7	86.5	66.1	83.6	7.2	15,574	-4.5	1,199	7.7	33,608	52.3	27,189	39.3
Rogers	83.0	16.0	93.0	74.8	88.7	4.8	36,445	0.2	961	2.6	51,053	69.7	44,691	61.5
Russellville	77.7	15.7	93.5	82.8	79.3	10.2	12,591	-2.0	463	3.7	23,009	58.7	19,552	38.1
Sherwood	83.1	23.8	92.7	85.4	86.7	4.8	15,772	-2.1	597	3.8	24,722	61.9	19,499	57.2
Springdale	77.6	18.9	90.6	75.5	84.5	7.3	38,782	0.4	1,103	2.8	58,120	69.1	50,342	56.4
Texarkana	83.0	17.0	87.3	78.8	84.5	7.7	13,071	-2.1	706	5.4	24,063	54.9	19,028	46.8
CALIFORNIA	72.1	29.8	94.3	88.5	87.6	4.8	18,923,194	0.0	1,381,250	7.3	31,403,964	63.3	25,759,467	48.5
Adelanto	79.1	41.7	94.6	87.7	84.9	7.9	10,384	2.5	1,537	14.8	23,823	50.5	21,687	33.1
Alameda	54.4	35.0	95.9	92.1	85.7	6.9	39,932	-0.9	2,216	5.5	64,177	67.3	50,949	58.5
Alhambra	76.3	30.9	93.6	88.7	91.6	2.1	45,228	-0.8	3,577	7.9	71,744	62.6	56,026	53.0
Aliso Viejo	76.1	26.7	98.5	96.2	86.4	3.4	28,466	0.0	1,454	5.1	38,746	75.8	34,460	56.5
Anaheim	77.8	29.1	94.8	89.9	88.5	3.8	167,683	-1.3	11,563	6.9	279,776	67.0	238,086	51.0
Antioch	65.8	46.4	95.5	91.2	88.3	4.5	50,078	-1.1	4,602	9.2	88,027	64.6	73,922	44.2
Apple Valley	80.5	36.3	96.2	90.2	88.9	3.2	29,959	2.8	2,524	8.4	55,118	52.3	43,083	39.3
Arcadia	74.7	31.6	96.2	93.2	89.5	3.4	28,149	0.8	1,849	6.6	46,325	59.0	35,378	48.3
Atascadero	77.3	22.7	94.9	88.0	90.4	3.3	14,852	1.1	723	4.9	24,745	65.3	19,872	52.1
Atwater	82.3	28.8	94.6	90.2	85.0	3.1	12,052	-0.3	1,195	9.9	22,622	63.3	18,971	46.9
Azusa	71.8	29.8	95.0	79.3	87.7	3.8	24,695	1.3	2,101	8.5	40,038	64.6	34,571	42.9
Bakersfield	82.0	23.4	95.1	89.3	85.6	3.8	176,495	-1.1	14,121	8.0	278,768	63.2	240,772	44.2
Baldwin Park	75.2	32.7	94.7	87.9	95.2	1.0	33,924	0.1	3,199	9.4	60,312	63.9	50,729	47.8
Banning	80.4	26.8	88.6	77.2	89.5	5.2	11,181	0.4	1,059	9.5	24,285	46.7	15,425	38.7
Barstow	77.2	26.1	89.3	72.3	79.6	4.9	10,201	3.1	940	9.2	17,010	51.3	14,292	40.0
Beaumont	80.3	36.0	98.0	91.6	88.3	7.1	24,179	1.5	1,525	6.3	34,561	62.0	28,017	51.6
Bell	75.8	33.2	90.7	76.7	94.5	0.6	14,740	0.9	1,429	9.7	27,030	62.0	23,782	46.8
Bellflower	80.7	30.8	93.4	82.9	91.8	1.4	35,963	0.8	3,937	10.9	59,782	66.6	51,320	50.1
Bell Gardens	77.2	31.3	89.8	80.5	95.6	0.3	17,581	0.9	1,727	9.8	30,884	61.7	27,763	44.8
Belmont	68.5	30.2	96.5	93.6	84.7	7.6	15,596	-0.6	613	3.9	21,393	71.1	17,394	57.1
Benicia	72.7	36.0	96.4	93.7	89.9	6.3	13,819	-1.0	723	5.2	23,090	65.0	17,138	53.9
Berkeley	30.9	31.3	96.7	92.5	73.1	16.2	60,226	0.2	2,886	4.8	110,138	61.2	91,087	37.9
Beverly Hills	66.6	25.3	94.0	90.4	89.9	3.5	17,368	1.1	1,223	7.0	28,380	59.6	20,699	44.7
Brawley	77.0	22.7	88.9	81.1	86.6	3.5	10,058	-0.8	1,571	15.6	18,369	53.2	15,371	33.6
Brea	80.6	33.3	96.7	94.1	87.5	4.9	22,782	-0.4	1,294	5.7	35,577	67.8	28,938	54.1
Brentwood	75.1	45.1	96.4	94.3	87.7	5.0	28,917	-0.6	1,835	6.3	48,969	63.1	39,518	48.1
Buena Park	81.5	30.3	95.9	91.8	89.3	4.7	38,690	-1.6	2,742	7.1	65,676	67.4	53,940	51.3
Burbank	74.0	29.2	92.2	86.5	89.4	3.7	58,031	0.0	5,697	9.8	86,581	66.6	70,481	51.0
Burlingame	63.1	33.3	95.8	93.7	85.2	8.9	16,998	-1.2	673	4.0	23,994	72.0	19,460	59.7
Calexico	76.0	24.7	87.0	79.7	91.0	1.3	16,810	-8.0	4,447	26.5	30,155	52.9	23,994	31.8
Camarillo	80.6	24.2	94.2	92.5	88.2	5.2	33,204	-1.0	1,698	5.1	56,081	62.0	42,568	50.8
Campbell	77.5	26.9	96.2	91.7	84.1	6.4	26,101	-0.5	1,110	4.3	34,744	68.7	28,608	59.4
Carlsbad	72.6	28.0	97.5	94.4	85.9	5.5	53,354	0.1	2,865	5.4	90,962	64.8	72,046	51.0
Carson	81.4	28.2	93.8	89.4	93.5	1.4	45,177	0.7	4,476	9.9	75,165	62.7	59,583	50.0
Cathedral City	81.2	20.4	89.0	84.3	89.5	3.9	26,898	-1.1	1,851	6.9	44,211	57.1	34,547	42.9
Ceres	85.0	32.7	90.6	86.4	87.4	4.3	21,220	-0.4	2,052	9.7	35,638	60.8	30,576	40.5
Cerritos	79.7	34.0	96.0	93.6	90.8	3.1	24,130	0.7	1,772	7.3	41,035	58.3	28,929	53.1
Chico	73.8	17.2	95.8	90.2	77.7	9.0	51,662	-1.2	2,747	5.3	82,069	65.8	69,772	39.2
Chino	79.3	34.6	96.9	91.9	82.8	12.7	44,207	1.0	2,766	6.3	72,327	56.3	61,945	43.9
Chino Hills	78.6	38.8	98.3	95.8	87.9	8.7	46,238	1.5	2,237	4.8	66,340	65.1	56,300	49.6
Chula Vista	77.4	29.8	94.8	90.2	90.6	2.5	121,969	-0.1	9,183	7.5	210,502	64.7	178,111	46.7
Citrus Heights	75.9	28.2	94.7	89.0	85.1	6.1	43,083	0.5	2,838	6.6	71,775	64.8	57,062	49.2
Claremont	62.9	28.1	95.2	92.4	85.1	9.4	16,198	2.2	1,109	6.8	30,353	59.5	23,353	40.8
Clovis	82.9	23.2	95.1	91.4	85.8	4.0	55,917	-0.4	3,006	5.4	83,433	65.7	68,802	50.5
Coachella	85.0	23.1	89.5	80.5	97.7	0.5	20,665	1.2	2,788	13.5	37,435	70.7	33,094	46.5
Colton	77.0	27.7	92.2	85.6	92.2	3.6	25,089	1.6	1,967	7.8	41,474	61.0	35,785	47.7
Compton	78.4	31.5	91.0	74.0	95.2	0.6	38,937	0.7	5,000	12.8	71,245	61.8	62,072	45.0
Concord	67.3	35.2	95.7	90.8	86.2	6.0	62,895	-0.9	3,716	5.9	103,783	67.4	84,709	51.7
Corona	79.8	37.2	95.6	89.7	88.2	5.9	85,921	1.3	4,944	5.8	130,471	65.9	113,491	51.4
Costa Mesa	73.2	22.7	95.9	92.1	85.4	4.0	62,824	-0.3	3,417	5.4	92,866	72.6	79,393	53.0
Covina	74.7	34.5	94.8	86.5	90.2	2.4	23,642	0.7	2,252	9.5	38,808	67.4	32,349	50.8
Culver City	74.2	27.8	94.4	85.6	89.5	3.3	22,161	0.8	1,628	7.3	32,123	69.7	25,026	57.8

1. Employed persons. 2. Households. 3. Percent of civilian labor force. 4. Persons 16 years old and over.

Table D. Cities — Construction, Wholesale Trade, and Retail Trade

City	Value of residential construction authorized by building permits, 2021			Wholesale trade[1], 2017				Retail trade[2], 2017			
	New construction ($1,000)	Number of housing units	Percent single family	Number of establishments	Number of employees	Sales (mil dol)	Annual payroll (mil dol)	Number of establish-ments	Number of employees	Sales (mil dol)	Annual payroll (mil dol)
	69	70	71	72	73	74	75	76	77	78	79
ARKANSAS—Cont'd											
Conway	111,747	829	68.5	52	595	505.8	29.3	296	5,085	1,531.7	132.4
Fayetteville	261,645	1,339	49.7	64	761	732.3	35.0	428	7,523	1,993.3	187.1
Fort Smith	47,578	325	58.8	165	2,568	1,523.5	133.4	515	7,673	2,045.0	186.8
Hot Springs	37,597	330	23.6	42	317	116.3	12.6	354	4,926	1,310.9	123.9
Jacksonville	7,613	42	100.0	14	136	42.8	5.9	93	1,375	406.9	37.3
Jonesboro	102,611	868	61.4	91	1,129	728.4	53.9	408	6,221	1,704.7	155.2
Little Rock	217,083	1,126	59.1	376	7,115	4,385.1	397.7	1,065	15,813	4,575.2	433.9
North Little Rock	62,070	523	34.0	162	3,705	3,897.8	220.8	396	6,015	1,607.8	147.4
Paragould	27,373	184	84.8	20	176	79.6	7.1	126	1,785	451.3	45.6
Pine Bluff	1,978	10	100.0	39	319	171.1	14.5	233	2,714	646.0	65.6
Rogers	145,790	851	67.7	50	702	807.3	42.1	341	6,215	1,400.7	147.2
Russellville	5,652	67	67.2	43	507	358.5	23.4	215	2,860	798.6	71.1
Sherwood	37,902	138	100.0	30	275	155.2	13.7	99	1,817	806.4	66.2
Springdale	76,771	226	100.0	133	1,486	1,331.9	83.4	268	4,261	1,386.0	132.3
Texarkana	6,153	28	100.0	D	D	D	D	120	1,253	366.0	31.0
CALIFORNIA	28,724,878	119,436	55.2	52,861	735,916	806,282.5	55,597.1	108,233	1,723,278	594,861.4	54,229.4
Adelanto	39,134	208	100.0	5	102	41.3	5.1	18	222	68.1	6.8
Alameda	129,544	618	32.0	60	1,746	2,266.7	183.0	180	2,415	655.0	80.5
Alhambra	61,294	218	36.7	255	977	924.2	35.7	251	4,511	1,938.0	145.4
Aliso Viejo	0	0	0.0	74	687	556.6	64.8	72	1,546	388.5	44.8
Anaheim	173,660	919	9.2	792	10,365	7,471.9	604.8	841	12,856	4,282.0	404.2
Antioch	174,867	675	85.6	27	491	288.1	25.4	222	4,012	1,120.2	127.6
Apple Valley	25,573	147	89.1	18	108	26.7	2.8	118	2,452	685.1	62.3
Arcadia	76,560	197	50.8	309	1,348	644.7	62.7	298	5,034	978.5	117.1
Atascadero	20,035	127	52.8	23	128	39.1	5.9	117	1,224	350.2	34.7
Atwater	26,156	77	100.0	6	76	58.9	3.0	70	1,253	281.3	28.2
Azusa	22,984	146	14.4	90	1,064	904.9	63.6	101	1,378	492.2	43.8
Bakersfield	290,929	1,162	96.5	283	3,708	2,799.6	218.6	989	20,027	6,145.7	575.6
Baldwin Park	8,436	41	58.5	147	829	421.1	38.6	133	2,330	967.1	67.9
Banning	33,874	212	100.0	10	247	64.0	8.0	61	757	235.7	21.8
Barstow	252	1	100.0	8	51	14.1	1.8	127	2,257	691.4	51.7
Beaumont	124,346	442	100.0	8	30	7.2	1.1	78	1,574	494.7	43.3
Bell	11,376	82	13.4	82	1,874	1,504.6	124.2	59	566	157.7	13.9
Bellflower	7,959	120	24.2	35	240	112.3	9.5	183	1,962	569.6	61.7
Bell Gardens	2,127	14	35.7	41	617	233.0	26.3	74	1,153	277.2	29.7
Belmont	3,144	4	100.0	17	61	31.2	3.5	50	782	342.4	37.3
Benicia	1,037	4	50.0	61	1,149	695.1	71.6	64	1,129	275.4	32.9
Berkeley	56,590	316	27.8	108	1,225	1,092.6	89.1	483	6,425	1,586.0	215.2
Beverly Hills	124,935	25	100.0	133	929	695.8	60.8	485	6,976	3,840.1	354.7
Brawley	29,729	227	69.6	19	203	282.9	12.9	51	784	175.5	19.7
Brea	9,095	29	13.8	327	5,016	4,197.4	325.9	315	5,969	1,175.2	140.4
Brentwood	69,558	742	38.8	13	62	83.6	4.2	155	2,722	760.6	73.1
Buena Park	53,776	182	100.0	190	4,392	3,967.7	275.3	228	4,460	1,862.6	151.1
Burbank	34,552	234	73.5	199	3,680	1,937.6	279.4	418	7,965	2,730.3	235.1
Burlingame	109,348	446	6.1	137	1,350	1,227.6	85.1	165	2,368	946.5	112.8
Calexico	3,970	65	92.3	53	309	417.2	9.2	159	2,461	465.6	48.2
Camarillo	42,559	154	85.7	137	2,467	2,328.5	211.2	330	5,612	1,367.9	136.2
Campbell	40,634	82	100.0	77	754	714.9	83.3	D	D	D	87.9
Carlsbad	29,951	107	100.0	281	5,854	3,783.6	497.0	487	8,305	3,111.0	270.7
Carson	11,234	56	12.5	346	6,630	5,045.4	360.1	221	4,827	2,085.0	196.4
Cathedral City	36,319	220	68.2	21	89	34.9	3.8	134	2,455	1,072.6	92.5
Ceres	5,171	17	100.0	23	482	334.9	29.9	102	1,795	446.6	41.6
Cerritos	76	1	100.0	237	5,003	3,916.5	328.0	251	7,796	4,022.1	280.9
Chico	109,431	769	31.2	81	1,187	585.2	60.3	393	7,340	2,240.4	214.6
Chino	141,994	575	69.4	526	7,891	6,620.7	423.5	298	4,951	1,424.3	131.5
Chino Hills	8,230	30	100.0	126	428	267.3	20.3	165	2,535	697.7	65.6
Chula Vista	266,810	1,756	16.6	289	2,134	2,323.1	107.5	624	12,160	3,155.8	337.1
Citrus Heights	56,599	215	100.0	15	67	37.6	3.6	246	4,525	1,136.6	113.3
Claremont	3,993	8	100.0	25	351	141.5	17.8	86	1,268	440.4	40.7
Clovis	274,606	1,037	79.5	45	216	134.1	9.8	306	6,679	2,026.5	184.0
Coachella	26,724	119	100.0	18	272	124.7	19.4	60	1,000	312.6	25.5
Colton	7,462	44	100.0	41	758	757.8	39.7	112	2,051	662.1	65.5
Compton	4,376	53	96.2	122	2,107	1,457.1	112.2	160	2,414	574.3	53.9
Concord	4,491	62	96.8	151	1,391	737.8	88.3	420	8,211	3,164.2	288.3
Corona	48,739	177	100.0	305	7,018	13,069.1	482.5	441	8,810	3,106.4	269.0
Costa Mesa	9,772	23	100.0	262	3,735	6,242.6	280.7	766	15,676	4,557.6	485.9
Covina	1,408	5	100.0	70	535	284.4	24.0	173	3,350	912.2	102.1
Culver City	19,317	110	96.4	109	1,363	946.9	88.1	301	5,726	1,905.3	182.2

1. Merchant wholesalers except manufacturers' sales branches and offices. 2. Establishments with payroll.

City	Real estate and rental and leasing, 2017				Professional, scientific, and technical services[1], 2017				Manufacturing, 2017			
	Number of establish-ments	Number of employees	Receipts (mil dol)	Annual payroll (mil dol)	Number of establish-ments	Number of employees	Receipts (mil dol)	Annual payroll (mil dol)	Number of establish-ments	Number of employees	Receipts (mil dol)	Annual payroll (mil dol)
	80	81	82	83	84	85	86	87	88	89	90	91
ARKANSAS—Cont'd												
Conway	115	486	93.0	15.8	184	717	93.3	32.0	NA	NA	NA	NA
Fayetteville	180	667	157.9	24.9	413	2,501	340.3	142.0	NA	NA	NA	NA
Fort Smith	143	1,137	185.6	44.5	D	D	D	D	NA	NA	NA	NA
Hot Springs	72	375	57.7	13.2	148	798	81.0	34.2	NA	NA	NA	NA
Jacksonville	43	194	32.0	6.3	41	335	46.8	18.5	NA	NA	NA	NA
Jonesboro	117	483	117.8	18.8	183	1,321	166.1	55.1	NA	NA	NA	NA
Little Rock	432	2,196	535.8	109.2	1,245	9,394	1,631.2	576.7	NA	NA	NA	NA
North Little Rock	109	495	110.8	17.8	D	D	D	D	NA	NA	NA	NA
Paragould	31	70	11.7	1.6	48	336	31.5	12.6	NA	NA	NA	NA
Pine Bluff	49	173	27.7	5.1	D	D	17.2	D	NA	NA	NA	NA
Rogers	98	410	114.5	20.2	238	2,763	372.9	150.4	NA	NA	NA	NA
Russellville	67	175	32.3	4.8	121	701	78.1	41.9	NA	NA	NA	NA
Sherwood	43	126	30.6	4.0	39	163	16.9	6.4	NA	NA	NA	NA
Springdale	71	290	60.9	10.8	149	988	121.4	49.3	NA	NA	NA	NA
Texarkana	38	147	35.2	6.1	D	D	D	D	NA	NA	NA	NA
CALIFORNIA	57,434	314,273	110,821.5	18,275.0	127,023	1,241,452	300,626.2	118,663.9	37,887	1,160,890	510,858.5	76,483.1
Adelanto	9	15	3.4	0.5	4	79	10.4	4.6	NA	NA	NA	NA
Alameda	90	349	97.6	14.0	248	2,483	796.9	263.0	NA	NA	NA	NA
Alhambra	140	469	105.5	23.3	281	1,058	166.3	48.0	NA	NA	NA	NA
Aliso Viejo	86	1,883	415.0	135.0	307	4,789	986.8	482.1	NA	NA	NA	NA
Anaheim	446	3,853	970.0	168.8	D	D	D	D	NA	NA	NA	NA
Antioch	65	395	280.3	24.3	90	529	76.2	29.3	NA	NA	NA	NA
Apple Valley	44	137	24.8	4.4	77	301	29.2	11.0	NA	NA	NA	NA
Arcadia	275	890	197.2	33.0	314	1,023	158.7	54.8	NA	NA	NA	NA
Atascadero	D	D	D	D	75	285	37.2	12.9	NA	NA	NA	NA
Atwater	12	37	9.4	0.8	11	64	9.0	3.0	NA	NA	NA	NA
Azusa	30	65	12.7	2.7	42	422	80.1	33.5	NA	NA	NA	NA
Bakersfield	377	2,017	388.2	79.8	790	5,270	779.0	300.7	NA	NA	NA	NA
Baldwin Park	23	75	16.8	3.7	40	196	19.2	7.3	NA	NA	NA	NA
Banning	25	89	14.9	3.0	14	122	8.5	2.9	NA	NA	NA	NA
Barstow	32	204	20.5	3.0	21	644	106.6	40.1	NA	NA	NA	NA
Beaumont	28	93	16.7	2.8	33	77	9.3	3.0	NA	NA	NA	NA
Bell	D	D	D	D	26	244	39.6	12.5	NA	NA	NA	NA
Bellflower	71	286	67.3	15.9	63	218	20.6	5.7	NA	NA	NA	NA
Bell Gardens	D	D	D	D	9	128	14.7	6.2	NA	NA	NA	NA
Belmont	39	D	77.9	D	102	429	67.3	46.5	NA	NA	NA	NA
Benicia	44	180	82.7	10.5	111	964	202.3	72.4	NA	NA	NA	NA
Berkeley	216	904	273.4	53.4	663	4,639	995.4	432.1	NA	NA	NA	NA
Beverly Hills	604	3,494	1,251.4	201.8	1,053	6,182	1,863.3	595.4	NA	NA	NA	NA
Brawley	31	109	27.1	4.1	D	D	D	D	NA	NA	NA	NA
Brea	131	633	174.9	33.2	312	2,532	440.0	168.7	NA	NA	NA	NA
Brentwood	58	154	60.1	6.8	100	399	67.0	22.6	NA	NA	NA	NA
Buena Park	78	309	80.0	13.7	141	758	130.6	37.8	NA	NA	NA	NA
Burbank	297	3,111	2,178.9	221.7	665	8,516	1,622.5	643.2	NA	NA	NA	NA
Burlingame	165	830	425.7	57.6	307	2,963	773.3	284.4	NA	NA	NA	NA
Calexico	34	118	16.0	3.1	41	115	9.9	3.2	NA	NA	NA	NA
Camarillo	115	598	158.4	33.4	339	2,751	589.9	216.1	NA	NA	NA	NA
Campbell	99	376	103.6	20.8	327	3,576	899.1	382.6	NA	NA	NA	NA
Carlsbad	394	1,345	425.8	81.7	1,089	8,040	1,596.7	624.4	NA	NA	NA	NA
Carson	80	1,227	576.8	93.1	115	855	161.5	54.7	NA	NA	NA	NA
Cathedral City	38	160	46.9	5.8	43	95	12.9	3.6	NA	NA	NA	NA
Ceres	33	133	51.1	5.9	30	433	52.6	23.8	NA	NA	NA	NA
Cerritos	101	410	185.0	29.7	206	1,389	336.8	121.1	NA	NA	NA	NA
Chico	165	705	126.6	22.9	303	1,949	423.3	105.5	NA	NA	NA	NA
Chino	82	417	140.3	18.8	164	940	154.4	48.9	NA	NA	NA	NA
Chino Hills	97	223	70.0	9.6	194	644	127.0	35.9	NA	NA	NA	NA
Chula Vista	310	931	285.8	36.7	455	2,438	348.8	112.6	NA	NA	NA	NA
Citrus Heights	83	320	129.1	10.4	104	649	85.1	32.4	NA	NA	NA	NA
Claremont	D	D	D	D	152	575	129.0	41.3	NA	NA	NA	NA
Clovis	98	344	101.8	13.5	186	1,595	174.2	68.6	NA	NA	NA	NA
Coachella	21	65	14.0	2.2	7	39	6.5	1.5	NA	NA	NA	NA
Colton	40	240	57.6	9.1	45	1,800	118.6	50.2	NA	NA	NA	NA
Compton	21	198	44.2	11.1	18	325	26.2	9.0	NA	NA	NA	NA
Concord	182	1,414	454.9	71.7	298	4,687	1,044.6	400.3	NA	NA	NA	NA
Corona	203	765	321.4	45.5	384	3,434	406.9	178.8	NA	NA	NA	NA
Costa Mesa	347	3,889	994.4	184.4	812	8,989	2,232.0	771.9	NA	NA	NA	NA
Covina	99	589	93.7	28.8	183	934	123.3	48.4	NA	NA	NA	NA
Culver City	128	1,475	260.7	74.2	459	5,140	917.4	364.0	NA	NA	NA	NA

1. Establishments subject to federal tax.

City	Accommodation and food services, 2017				Arts, entertainment, and recreation[1], 2017				Health care and social assistance[1], 2017			
	Number of establish-ments	Number of employees	Receipts (mil dol)	Annual payroll (mil dol)	Number of establish-ments	Number of employees	Receipts (mil dol)	Annual payroll (mil dol)	Number of establish-ments	Number of employees	Receipts (mil dol)	Annual payroll (mil dol)
	92	93	94	95	96	97	98	99	100	101	102	103
ARKANSAS—Cont'd												
Conway	180	3,851	193.4	59.4	16.0	224	11.2	3.9	253	5,012	487.9	198.1
Fayetteville	367	7,796	392.5	115.8	48.0	700	53.6	13.8	375	9,954	1,212.4	565.7
Fort Smith	273	5,742	291.6	86.6	28.0	288	22.1	6.5	374	10,671	1,376.9	530.3
Hot Springs	218	4,441	233.4	69.4	37.0	1,445	182.7	30.9	256	7,527	982.1	344.4
Jacksonville	58	835	41.2	11.4	4.0	35	2.0	0.8	61	1,765	124.9	53.4
Jonesboro	D	D	D	D	20.0	354	12.7	5.0	325	9,650	1,152.9	462.4
Little Rock	660	13,362	754.9	222.3	92.0	1,681	155.3	37.1	1,049	37,064	5,684.2	2,240.6
North Little Rock	237	4,761	234.0	70.0	D	D	D	8.7	245	5,693	654.6	240.0
Paragould	D	D	D	D	D	D	D	D	94	1,840	182.5	66.6
Pine Bluff	99	1,584	81.1	19.9	D	D	D	D	167	3,541	372.8	154.8
Rogers	194	5,028	274.8	84.7	17.0	362	19.2	7.0	229	4,669	704.3	229.5
Russellville	127	2,624	126.6	37.2	12.0	D	1.3	D	160	3,425	311.7	114.6
Sherwood	42	833	45.0	12.2	D	D	D	0.4	62	1,095	133.5	52.1
Springdale	144	2,633	147.0	40.1	D	D	D	D	165	4,952	542.9	223.2
Texarkana	67	1,347	56.7	16.3	D	D	D	D	D	D	D	D
CALIFORNIA	89,596	1,739,010	133,716.9	37,677.2	26,390.0	349,752	53,107.2	17,209.0	113,390	2,043,117	311,312.2	119,500.6
Adelanto	17	228	12.8	3.3	NA	NA	NA	NA	16	199	19.7	10.1
Alameda	237	3,611	241.4	70.1	42.0	1,149	375.5	244.3	228	4,027	429.7	169.2
Alhambra	256	4,275	254.6	78.9	24.0	250	17.8	4.5	302	3,588	504.2	154.6
Aliso Viejo	90	1,689	121.4	37.3	25.0	491	40.1	10.9	140	2,692	461.6	168.0
Anaheim	799	27,327	2,536.2	694.4	94.0	34,259	4,594.7	1,387.6	970	20,597	2,891.9	1,118.3
Antioch	139	2,028	132.2	37.4	28.0	375	22.3	6.2	261	5,922	1,059.8	428.9
Apple Valley	95	1,565	86.6	24.0	8.0	117	8.8	2.4	208	3,512	617.9	197.9
Arcadia	224	4,170	265.7	78.3	71.0	2,277	248.8	56.4	441	5,310	706.8	255.3
Atascadero	78	1,087	72.4	18.7	12.0	180	6.1	2.3	119	3,123	354.3	190.8
Atwater	39	536	36.1	8.7	D	D	D	D	29	621	36.6	17.5
Azusa	95	1,319	78.3	23.3	6.0	84	3.4	1.4	60	698	48.2	21.3
Bakersfield	799	15,215	961.7	267.0	79.0	1,580	93.9	27.5	1,210	23,324	3,792.1	1,273.2
Baldwin Park	103	1,504	111.2	27.3	NA	NA	NA	NA	86	5,226	957.8	367.5
Banning	57	730	48.7	13.1	NA	NA	NA	NA	59	1,619	164.1	72.7
Barstow	93	1,625	110.7	27.7	NA	NA	NA	NA	58	763	106.4	40.0
Beaumont	58	966	60.7	17.9	5.0	62	3.3	1.2	50	686	55.5	22.3
Bell	63	863	67.0	16.7	NA	NA	NA	NA	38	531	44.7	20.3
Bellflower	136	1,855	123.7	32.1	17.0	181	13.4	2.7	176	2,584	367.7	113.4
Bell Gardens	66	2,578	208.2	69.9	NA	NA	NA	NA	39	1,012	79.1	37.7
Belmont	68	824	79.4	20.8	5.0	57	4.9	1.1	71	650	72.0	26.9
Benicia	68	1,055	65.9	18.6	16.0	137	7.3	2.8	64	320	41.8	14.3
Berkeley	538	8,416	617.1	201.1	115.0	1,619	252.3	62.3	491	8,402	1,340.5	552.1
Beverly Hills	238	9,436	952.5	319.6	1,036.0	5,821	3,620.8	1,061.4	1,209	6,751	1,492.8	433.3
Brawley	46	570	35.9	9.2	D	D	D	D	54	1,540	198.1	79.3
Brea	180	4,673	303.8	94.0	D	D	D	2.5	187	2,463	264.4	117.3
Brentwood	128	2,151	143.1	40.6	11.0	270	14.8	4.0	150	1,392	139.0	50.9
Buena Park	231	4,492	296.7	78.5	D	D	D	D	220	2,215	183.7	75.0
Burbank	353	8,431	746.5	181.6	447.0	1,793	503.1	156.1	629	9,383	1,426.4	478.5
Burlingame	161	5,155	586.8	175.5	24.0	433	21.1	6.5	211	4,729	936.7	350.4
Calexico	62	896	51.1	13.3	NA	NA	NA	NA	25	360	43.0	16.4
Camarillo	177	3,362	218.3	62.4	33.0	474	22.2	9.1	274	4,745	403.9	171.5
Campbell	153	3,485	245.7	78.9	20.0	195	26.7	4.4	221	3,215	420.1	155.9
Carlsbad	314	9,150	733.5	225.8	86.0	3,603	367.4	78.7	450	7,009	652.4	266.1
Carson	186	3,440	239.3	64.1	19.0	561	104.4	37.3	197	2,260	210.2	84.1
Cathedral City	109	1,777	110.6	30.5	12.0	261	15.7	5.2	70	765	87.2	41.8
Ceres	75	1,067	67.8	17.0	6.0	67	4.2	1.1	56	677	73.5	28.9
Cerritos	208	4,794	320.2	92.1	12.0	169	14.5	3.7	245	3,003	361.9	135.9
Chico	292	5,709	315.4	93.8	26.0	540	24.4	8.6	443	9,129	1,188.1	457.4
Chino	190	3,425	179.7	53.8	28.0	815	44.9	11.8	231	2,926	326.2	115.3
Chino Hills	178	3,343	189.5	55.3	23.0	389	26.8	7.7	166	1,722	201.7	74.2
Chula Vista	431	7,956	523.8	149.5	60.0	1,968	113.3	32.8	613	10,464	1,533.3	579.9
Citrus Heights	D	D	D	D	15.0	590	33.8	11.8	166	2,475	205.6	85.3
Claremont	121	1,918	127.9	36.6	18.0	469	26.6	11.7	182	2,377	244.0	93.3
Clovis	247	4,677	271.5	76.1	29.0	580	49.2	9.4	272	5,829	678.8	240.9
Coachella	54	751	44.1	11.0	D	D	D	D	22	204	19.7	8.7
Colton	93	1,304	86.8	21.3	NA	NA	NA	NA	120	5,057	943.2	289.0
Compton	D	D	D	D	D	D	D	0.7	91	1,038	76.2	31.9
Concord	299	5,364	378.7	103.6	49.0	1,046	67.3	17.5	432	8,766	1,422.3	484.5
Corona	346	6,667	411.6	116.8	43.0	487	39.8	9.5	424	5,741	630.2	229.6
Costa Mesa	471	10,378	770.9	226.1	73.0	1,894	514.8	262.1	454	5,715	569.9	208.9
Covina	143	2,147	138.7	36.5	13.0	128	7.8	1.6	242	4,622	418.7	178.0
Culver City	247	4,719	366.8	101.4	184.0	572	266.5	105.0	236	4,667	691.2	198.2

1. Establishments subject to federal tax.

City	Other services[1]				Government employment and payroll, 2017								
						March payroll							
							Perent of total for:						
	Number of establish-ments	Number of employees	Receipts (mil dol)	Annual payroll (mil dol)	Full-time equivalent employees	Total (dollars)	Admin-istrative, judicial, and legal	Police and corrections	Fire protection	Highways and trans-portation	Health and welfare	Natural resources and utilities	Education and libraries
	104	105	106	107	108	109	110	111	112	113	114	115	116
ARKANSAS—Cont'd													
Conway	106	566	51.8	14.9	517	1,734,322	12.3	31.7	27.5	7.8	0.0	17.9	0.0
Fayetteville	164	874	364.3	27.7	703	2,692,445	14.4	26.1	17.5	11.7	2.7	20.8	0.0
Fort Smith	D	D	83.3	D	927	3,748,677	9.6	22.4	20.8	11.9	1.7	32.7	0.0
Hot Springs	115	520	42.3	13.6	635	2,314,170	11.8	25.0	16.9	9.6	3.4	25.8	5.2
Jacksonville	31	125	14.2	3.9	356	1,336,592	12.7	28.5	22.3	3.9	0.0	25.8	0.0
Jonesboro	113	724	72.9	18.9	703	2,662,047	8.1	23.5	12.7	9.5	1.2	45.0	0.0
Little Rock	501	3,692	746.3	152.1	3,175	14,264,399	7.6	26.2	17.4	11.3	12.9	18.7	0.0
North Little Rock	147	908	95.8	28.2	990	3,992,647	7.7	24.2	20.1	6.6	1.3	34.0	2.6
Paragould	32	146	13.6	3.6	285	1,104,826	4.7	15.3	11.2	7.6	0.0	34.1	0.0
Pine Bluff	57	340	33.3	8.8	359	1,141,415	11.2	44.7	24.8	13.3	2.4	3.5	0.0
Rogers	87	574	63.3	20.3	520	2,122,890	10.2	28.2	27.6	5.1	1.2	20.4	4.1
Russellville	74	416	33.3	12.3	262	988,177	6.5	23.9	24.5	7.1	0.0	27.4	0.0
Sherwood	54	247	31.2	7.2	235	824,999	18.5	44.3	0.0	6.5	0.0	25.7	0.0
Springdale	119	939	105.5	31.7	629	2,484,976	9.5	31.9	23.1	6.1	0.3	19.8	3.5
Texarkana	33	163	21.1	4.6	216	992,096	9.2	49.5	27.6	3.3	0.0	1.7	0.0
CALIFORNIA	62,302	437,372	64,253.9	15,637.9	X	X	X	X	X	X	X	X	X
Adelanto	D	D	8.9	D	130	635,090	18.0	62.9	0.0	6.8	0.0	11.6	0.0
Alameda	155	1,493	206.5	61.8	569	4,984,205	8.7	25.4	26.0	10.9	5.0	20.7	3.3
Alhambra	125	503	64.5	17.4	417	3,094,298	8.1	35.3	29.1	3.4	3.7	16.1	4.1
Aliso Viejo	63	472	78.0	27.3	23	150,158	88.7	0.0	0.0	4.0	0.0	7.2	0.0
Anaheim	430	3,672	407.2	130.7	2,310	19,689,571	11.0	34.3	16.7	2.4	1.2	28.3	2.0
Antioch	98	554	58.0	17.0	307	2,742,360	9.7	58.4	0.0	7.2	5.7	16.1	0.0
Apple Valley	48	310	20.4	8.2	91	500,285	44.5	0.6	0.0	8.9	4.7	31.2	0.0
Arcadia	119	555	57.0	16.5	327	2,702,545	12.3	35.0	26.1	6.3	0.0	10.5	5.5
Atascadero	47	193	19.8	6.1	133	836,599	14.1	33.9	21.9	3.5	6.0	12.6	0.0
Atwater	21	117	10.6	2.4	77	468,259	21.2	53.5	0.0	8.3	0.0	16.2	0.0
Azusa	78	402	39.3	10.7	291	2,124,946	13.2	41.8	0.0	3.8	2.9	34.4	2.7
Bakersfield	454	3,674	362.5	113.6	1,490	9,653,365	6.6	42.2	18.5	7.2	0.6	16.9	0.0
Baldwin Park	50	137	16.6	3.5	234	1,398,737	11.8	58.8	0.0	10.2	3.0	10.9	0.0
Banning	33	203	17.6	4.9	174	1,229,485	21.3	29.0	0.0	11.9	0.0	34.9	0.0
Barstow	31	329	20.0	7.8	163	1,216,100	13.4	37.1	16.0	10.2	1.2	12.0	0.0
Beaumont	D	D	D	D	128	830,132	3.7	57.6	0.0	13.2	4.5	12.1	0.0
Bell	33	154	14.9	4.9	112	614,180	15.4	57.0	0.0	0.0	13.8	13.8	0.0
Bellflower	125	539	61.2	17.6	146	689,645	32.6	10.7	0.0	28.8	9.0	19.0	0.0
Bell Gardens	D	D	D	D	191	1,176,849	11.3	58.6	0.0	13.1	3.7	11.8	0.0
Belmont	57	317	39.1	11.5	169	1,475,781	12.6	30.9	20.2	9.8	5.6	21.0	0.0
Benicia	79	749	119.5	40.7	310	2,026,006	13.0	23.5	18.0	3.4	0.0	29.9	7.0
Berkeley	326	2,358	336.9	117.8	1,668	15,534,530	10.4	41.0	11.9	4.6	13.5	10.3	4.7
Beverly Hills	404	2,441	611.1	87.5	568	5,900,462	0.0	44.0	27.2	2.1	2.8	17.9	6.0
Brawley	27	136	12.3	4.0	150	830,182	13.1	30.3	13.1	7.3	4.2	22.4	5.4
Brea	103	768	66.7	21.3	466	3,431,286	14.7	42.8	17.4	2.4	1.3	14.0	0.0
Brentwood	96	528	57.0	15.3	290	2,391,198	16.9	35.1	0.0	11.2	5.8	27.1	0.0
Buena Park	96	615	130.2	29.2	296	2,162,651	10.3	57.0	0.0	10.5	1.8	12.2	0.0
Burbank	281	2,509	325.4	94.8	1,299	11,787,918	11.7	21.9	14.1	5.4	3.5	34.6	2.8
Burlingame	141	866	132.3	39.2	225	1,879,269	7.4	34.5	16.3	5.8	0.0	25.6	10.6
Calexico	D	D	D	D	123	666,071	6.0	26.1	26.7	4.9	7.5	22.8	3.9
Camarillo	134	1,027	95.6	29.4	140	1,011,277	33.6	1.4	0.0	31.3	0.7	25.3	1.3
Campbell	183	1,409	147.3	50.0	211	1,800,103	21.1	40.8	0.0	4.7	1.3	11.7	0.0
Carlsbad	230	1,896	296.5	67.1	801	4,595,548	14.4	15.2	22.6	6.9	6.8	13.1	8.9
Carson	127	1,854	238.3	72.8	533	2,931,854	28.7	6.7	0.0	15.1	7.8	25.7	0.0
Cathedral City	101	725	69.9	22.2	173	1,659,811	17.2	47.0	24.8	6.1	0.0	0.5	0.0
Ceres	48	472	138.0	29.1	176	1,162,295	11.2	37.0	25.2	8.1	0.0	9.9	0.0
Cerritos	71	1,113	65.6	36.1	340	1,728,051	29.0	5.6	0.0	1.7	2.6	16.5	11.0
Chico	178	2,840	158.7	52.1	354	2,577,844	9.9	44.5	22.6	7.6	0.4	7.3	0.0
Chino	163	1,715	122.3	43.7	473	3,264,265	13.5	49.5	0.0	3.6	3.9	16.2	0.0
Chino Hills	72	433	24.5	8.2	190	1,055,324	42.7	0.0	0.0	5.5	1.9	39.5	0.0
Chula Vista	275	1,852	139.2	44.0	1,035	7,321,658	10.7	37.4	18.4	18.0	3.8	6.5	2.8
Citrus Heights	90	562	94.4	21.4	207	1,592,325	17.1	67.1	0.0	5.1	2.9	1.8	0.0
Claremont	50	214	24.7	7.2	202	1,271,964	23.8	43.5	0.0	4.6	0.0	28.2	0.0
Clovis	145	1,047	94.0	27.3	560	3,609,832	9.9	34.4	16.0	6.0	9.6	15.0	0.0
Coachella	16	59	5.8	1.5	84	642,472	15.2	4.5	0.0	6.5	11.2	45.1	0.0
Colton	57	500	69.2	15.1	316	2,313,222	14.2	30.5	18.4	3.1	0.4	30.3	0.8
Compton	D	D	D	D	329	2,108,515	20.1	6.2	37.0	8.5	4.0	13.5	0.0
Concord	251	1,589	199.6	62.6	475	3,242,924	14.9	60.4	0.0	9.1	1.3	10.8	0.0
Corona	240	1,634	154.3	43.5	670	5,204,685	11.4	38.4	24.9	6.0	0.2	15.5	1.9
Costa Mesa	386	2,850	324.1	88.8	530	4,404,296	15.6	41.6	24.5	3.9	0.0	7.6	0.0
Covina	141	681	75.2	21.0	177	1,447,454	16.4	61.5	0.0	2.4	0.7	12.6	2.8
Culver City	167	1,521	212.6	57.2	686	5,240,715	10.1	24.2	21.8	25.1	6.8	10.6	0.0

1. Establishments subject to federal tax.

City	City government finances, 2017									
	General revenue							General expenditure		
		Intergovernmental		Taxes						
					Per capita[1] (dollars)				Per capita[1] (dollars)	
	Total (mil dol)	Total (mil dol)	Percent from state government	Total (mil dol)	Total	Property	Sales and gross receipts	Total (mil dol)	Total	Capital outlays
	117	118	119	120	121	122	123	124	125	126
ARKANSAS—Cont'd										
Conway	113.6	9.1	67.7	37.8	574	81	493	120.1	1,822	548
Fayetteville	139.3	27.3	43.7	68.5	801	115	685	129.7	1,516	452
Fort Smith	173.9	40.9	49.7	65.8	749	155	594	154.1	1,754	639
Hot Springs	73.3	6.4	56.4	32.3	838	0	838	83.2	2,162	544
Jacksonville	32.6	10.9	44.6	10.7	377	29	348	34.3	1,205	148
Jonesboro	79.1	22.7	27.0	28.1	370	65	305	75.6	995	130
Little Rock	461.4	90.4	24.4	186.2	939	276	663	513.3	2,589	710
North Little Rock	104.1	20.4	26.0	52.2	793	287	506	109.4	1,661	285
Paragould	33.8	6.0	39.4	7.2	251	34	218	33.4	1,169	142
Pine Bluff	47.5	14.3	39.1	20.6	478	93	386	48.7	1,129	102
Rogers	93.3	23.7	40.6	46.3	694	79	615	87.2	1,309	540
Russellville	35.1	7.4	33.9	17.6	605	33	573	39.5	1,354	529
Sherwood	25.6	9.3	26.2	8.8	284	21	263	25.1	809	94
Springdale	92.0	27.1	36.9	39.1	490	88	402	81.1	1,016	253
Texarkana	32.0	6.6	59.3	15.3	510	127	384	29.0	964	24
CALIFORNIA	X	X	X	X	X	X	X	X	X	X
Adelanto	19.0	0.3	84.0	11.8	347	191	147	19.6	577	70
Alameda	173.1	14.1	38.1	96.2	1,217	633	405	128.2	1,622	63
Alhambra	98.6	3.5	86.4	56.5	665	295	364	102.9	1,212	144
Aliso Viejo	24.2	2.6	58.7	17.5	344	140	197	33.5	657	95
Anaheim	796.8	150.7	10.4	368.6	1,052	279	768	705.4	2,013	241
Antioch	81.7	6.2	56.5	52.0	466	202	260	74.9	672	95
Apple Valley	65.8	11.5	85.7	27.8	381	155	185	73.3	1,005	111
Arcadia	82.7	4.7	38.9	51.7	886	379	495	76.4	1,309	143
Atascadero	30.9	2.4	40.5	20.0	660	294	328	32.3	1,065	306
Atwater	35.4	2.6	68.1	11.5	393	142	150	46.1	1,574	573
Azusa	57.5	2.5	81.1	31.6	634	193	374	51.7	1,038	37
Bakersfield	444.4	118.4	11.1	174.7	462	215	244	467.9	1,238	485
Baldwin Park	47.8	10.4	77.3	27.6	364	154	207	49.6	653	52
Banning	30.6	6.8	72.7	10.7	345	152	188	29.7	954	248
Barstow	29.6	2.8	91.0	17.7	738	164	572	37.0	1,545	236
Beaumont	82.2	5.5	7.7	18.3	390	166	218	95.8	2,046	957
Bell	33.2	4.4	37.1	20.2	569	364	202	36.5	1,024	248
Bellflower	39.3	4.0	54.2	28.9	373	138	232	38.1	493	78
Bell Gardens	43.7	2.1	58.8	26.6	627	130	496	38.8	912	86
Belmont	66.3	2.5	54.7	30.2	1,114	656	399	50.4	1,863	64
Benicia	51.9	2.1	75.2	36.4	1,287	597	481	63.0	2,231	715
Berkeley	381.9	35.9	58.7	186.7	1,528	738	539	364.8	2,986	172
Beverly Hills	340.2	3.5	32.8	214.1	6,251	1,804	4,270	308.6	9,012	1,169
Brawley	22.8	2.3	82.3	10.6	403	150	195	32.7	1,249	334
Brea	75.4	5.8	21.8	44.8	1,053	420	613	91.7	2,153	615
Brentwood	141.4	5.2	48.2	46.8	752	311	253	106.1	1,704	231
Buena Park	88.2	4.1	85.8	63.1	764	322	424	107.4	1,300	279
Burbank	249.2	21.0	38.4	141.7	1,360	596	756	318.8	3,060	0
Burlingame	112.1	1.3	99.3	66.5	2,173	561	1,378	82.4	2,693	481
Calexico	34.3	5.5	30.7	14.8	369	131	237	30.2	754	106
Camarillo	85.5	9.2	34.0	43.9	652	247	397	106.9	1,586	278
Campbell	56.2	3.6	34.8	41.3	969	333	614	68.9	1,619	167
Carlsbad	226.5	19.6	44.8	141.1	1,233	593	627	213.3	1,863	385
Carson	166.8	42.6	6.6	97.5	1,058	462	592	242.2	2,627	429
Cathedral City	60.3	11.5	14.7	33.6	617	139	461	61.6	1,132	141
Ceres	56.3	6.5	45.0	16.9	350	123	225	55.9	1,157	94
Cerritos	65.1	1.7	97.2	52.3	1,032	218	795	79.6	1,570	181
Chico	111.0	16.6	33.2	68.5	736	270	461	102.8	1,105	310
Chino	169.7	15.9	97.5	64.5	719	325	358	129.7	1,448	148
Chino Hills	118.1	3.8	49.9	47.2	589	157	426	104.1	1,299	209
Chula Vista	494.5	23.3	41.6	136.6	508	208	259	298.0	1,108	224
Citrus Heights	53.7	5.7	55.1	36.1	411	143	264	59.7	681	143
Claremont	42.5	2.4	48.7	24.9	696	265	425	48.2	1,346	128
Clovis	162.5	15.3	30.7	59.0	540	224	310	140.0	1,281	213
Coachella	41.1	9.3	95.3	19.3	426	128	256	54.5	1,203	535
Colton	70.4	5.9	44.7	26.1	478	219	257	81.5	1,490	134
Compton	83.0	15.1	17.1	44.7	461	184	275	122.5	1,262	118
Concord	193.1	37.8	21.5	100.4	775	259	401	160.4	1,238	106
Corona	238.9	18.6	60.0	114.1	682	313	344	300.5	1,796	709
Costa Mesa	139.3	7.5	94.0	117.8	1,036	331	698	130.7	1,150	145
Covina	52.1	2.1	87.3	31.4	651	238	407	47.3	981	145
Culver City	192.9	53.9	10.5	88.9	2,279	322	1,627	166.5	4,268	531

1. Based on population estimated as of July 1 of the year shown.

City	City government finances, 2017 (cont.)												
	General expenditure (cont.)												
	Percent of total for:										Debt outstanding		
	Public welfare	Highways	Parking facilities	Education	Health and hospitals	Police protection	Sewerage and sanitation	Parks and recreation	Housing and community development	Interest on debt	Total (mil dol)	Per capita[1] (dollars)	Debt issued during year
	127	128	129	130	131	132	133	134	135	136	137	138	139
ARKANSAS—Cont'd													
Conway	0.0	14.5	0.0	0.0	0.3	10.2	16.0	5.2	0.6	10.3	438.3	6,646	31.0
Fayetteville	0.0	14.9	1.0	0.0	0.6	11.0	23.3	8.9	0.5	3.1	107.0	1,250	17.3
Fort Smith	0.0	22.8	0.1	0.0	0.1	9.4	21.0	2.4	1.4	11.6	745.0	8,482	178.0
Hot Springs	0.0	4.2	0.1	0.0	0.8	13.7	38.9	2.2	0.3	4.2	100.4	2,609	9.9
Jacksonville	0.0	5.1	0.0	0.0	7.9	21.1	15.9	11.5	0.7	3.2	43.5	1,526	16.1
Jonesboro	0.0	12.3	0.0	0.0	1.3	15.8	14.6	6.8	0.8	14.4	272.8	3,592	0.4
Little Rock	0.0	8.2	0.3	0.0	7.4	13.9	12.9	8.4	1.4	4.2	592.8	2,989	52.7
North Little Rock	0.1	8.1	0.0	0.0	1.0	18.4	22.3	6.8	0.6	3.9	146.2	2,220	21.3
Paragould	0.3	10.2	0.0	0.0	0.5	11.4	20.1	9.3	0.0	0.8	14.3	501	5.6
Pine Bluff	0.7	8.3	0.0	0.0	0.1	30.4	17.3	5.6	4.7	1.9	23.4	543	0.0
Rogers	0.0	29.7	0.0	0.0	0.5	11.6	8.8	13.2	0.0	4.3	117.6	1,766	26.6
Russellville	0.0	12.4	0.0	0.0	0.9	11.4	34.0	15.4	0.0	1.9	47.5	1,628	0.0
Sherwood	0.0	13.7	0.0	0.0	1.3	27.2	14.8	17.6	0.0	0.7	12.2	392	0.0
Springdale	0.0	14.6	0.0	0.0	0.9	19.7	16.2	11.5	0.9	6.2	198.8	2,491	75.5
Texarkana	0.0	5.5	0.0	0.0	1.3	24.4	22.5	1.2	0.9	2.9	32.4	1,078	0.0
CALIFORNIA	X	X	X	X	X	X	X	X	X	X	X	X	X
Adelanto	0.0	9.4	0.0	0.0	0.0	31.7	0.0	3.1	9.6	10.7	27.8	819	1.0
Alameda	0.0	4.2	0.0	0.0	3.1	24.1	3.3	5.5	19.5	3.1	142.2	1,799	12.9
Alhambra	0.0	6.1	2.0	0.0	0.0	26.2	11.2	7.3	6.0	2.1	56.1	661	8.4
Aliso Viejo	0.0	11.6	0.0	0.0	1.6	46.3	0.0	9.3	0.4	3.8	31.2	612	0.0
Anaheim	0.0	3.6	0.0	0.0	0.4	21.0	7.7	19.9	16.0	11.5	1,823.7	5,203	321.8
Antioch	0.0	17.3	0.0	0.0	2.5	47.4	6.7	7.7	5.4	0.5	30.1	270	0.2
Apple Valley	0.0	5.8	0.0	0.0	2.6	36.1	20.2	6.0	8.4	1.3	16.8	230	0.0
Arcadia	0.0	9.3	0.0	0.0	4.6	27.3	2.3	4.3	0.4	0.6	11.8	202	0.0
Atascadero	0.0	7.0	0.0	0.0	0.7	21.4	6.1	11.3	19.3	3.8	40.7	1,343	0.0
Atwater	0.0	4.4	0.0	0.0	0.0	14.1	51.4	1.0	1.4	8.9	77.1	2,635	0.0
Azusa	0.0	3.7	0.0	0.0	1.1	35.5	10.1	6.9	1.5	5.3	171.8	3,449	0.0
Bakersfield	0.0	7.0	0.0	0.0	0.4	17.8	13.6	7.6	3.6	1.6	661.7	1,751	23.2
Baldwin Park	0.0	15.5	0.0	0.0	0.7	37.1	0.6	8.4	14.7	1.3	13.9	183	1.6
Banning	0.0	12.7	0.0	0.0	0.5	25.3	20.2	3.8	13.3	1.2	63.2	2,028	0.2
Barstow	0.0	14.0	0.0	0.0	0.7	25.6	15.4	7.0	5.7	1.1	9.1	378	0.0
Beaumont	0.0	1.3	0.0	0.0	0.6	9.8	8.1	2.5	0.0	11.9	216.6	4,624	0.1
Bell	0.0	11.9	0.0	0.0	0.0	25.9	4.5	5.9	20.2	9.6	69.0	1,938	0.9
Bellflower	0.0	32.1	0.0	0.0	0.0	31.8	0.0	6.1	5.9	3.5	36.5	472	0.0
Bell Gardens	0.0	13.6	0.0	0.0	0.0	40.5	7.2	14.5	2.2	2.5	20.6	485	0.0
Belmont	0.0	5.0	0.0	0.0	0.0	22.9	20.2	9.4	0.5	4.5	66.6	2,462	0.0
Benicia	0.0	6.3	0.0	0.0	0.0	15.1	10.1	8.7	0.1	2.0	59.7	2,114	11.0
Berkeley	0.0	10.3	2.8	0.0	10.7	18.0	13.8	5.3	3.4	1.9	201.8	1,652	49.0
Beverly Hills	0.0	5.8	16.7	0.0	6.2	23.1	8.0	11.0	5.0	1.5	214.1	6,252	0.0
Brawley	0.0	6.1	0.0	0.0	0.5	18.6	22.8	4.8	4.9	0.9	19.2	732	8.4
Brea	0.0	18.2	0.0	0.0	5.8	24.6	6.5	11.6	9.2	1.4	75.2	1,766	0.0
Brentwood	0.0	12.6	0.0	0.0	0.3	20.7	21.1	13.3	6.8	6.1	177.3	2,848	0.3
Buena Park	0.0	14.4	0.0	0.0	0.7	22.4	3.3	6.0	15.4	4.1	96.2	1,165	9.8
Burbank	0.0	5.6	0.2	0.1	4.2	16.5	7.5	3.2	3.5	1.6	281.5	2,702	0.5
Burlingame	0.0	9.6	0.9	0.0	0.0	18.5	18.4	11.1	0.0	5.1	88.6	2,897	17.6
Calexico	0.0	8.2	0.0	0.0	0.5	24.4	22.5	1.9	8.3	4.8	63.6	1,586	0.0
Camarillo	0.0	21.5	0.0	0.0	0.7	30.2	13.3	1.1	4.4	3.1	82.4	1,222	41.6
Campbell	0.0	14.0	0.0	0.0	0.0	24.3	0.1	10.9	2.2	1.0	10.4	243	8.2
Carlsbad	0.0	12.5	0.0	0.0	8.3	16.1	8.2	13.1	5.6	0.3	37.0	324	0.2
Carson	0.0	7.1	0.0	0.0	0.1	17.2	0.0	8.4	18.7	4.9	204.7	2,220	33.8
Cathedral City	0.0	12.3	0.0	0.0	5.5	24.4	1.1	2.0	8.0	11.1	195.3	3,589	0.0
Ceres	0.0	8.6	0.0	0.0	0.9	22.2	13.0	3.7	8.0	1.6	22.5	466	0.0
Cerritos	0.0	10.8	0.0	0.0	0.0	33.0	6.4	12.8	5.1	0.1	11.0	217	0.0
Chico	0.0	21.2	0.6	0.0	1.2	23.0	5.7	2.4	11.7	5.3	128.4	1,379	0.5
Chino	0.0	7.6	0.0	0.0	0.0	26.4	24.2	5.1	12.2	2.2	69.6	777	0.0
Chino Hills	0.0	14.0	0.0	0.0	0.4	25.5	12.3	7.2	0.4	3.9	115.1	1,436	0.0
Chula Vista	0.0	9.3	0.2	0.0	1.0	20.9	9.3	19.9	1.8	2.2	669.1	2,487	0.0
Citrus Heights	0.0	22.5	0.0	0.0	1.2	34.7	1.3	1.3	11.0	2.0	26.6	303	0.0
Claremont	0.0	16.2	0.0	0.0	1.6	24.2	14.6	7.8	4.8	1.2	13.7	383	0.0
Clovis	0.0	9.4	0.0	0.0	1.3	22.3	25.8	4.9	9.4	6.7	177.8	1,627	3.7
Coachella	0.0	33.4	0.0	0.0	0.5	15.0	14.2	15.2	0.3	2.1	93.3	2,060	25.5
Colton	0.0	8.0	0.0	0.0	1.0	32.5	24.8	4.0	7.2	3.3	94.4	1,726	0.3
Compton	0.0	3.4	0.0	0.0	0.2	19.5	9.3	0.8	13.3	1.9	103.5	1,067	28.7
Concord	0.0	19.3	0.0	0.0	0.0	33.3	15.8	7.5	2.3	1.6	76.2	588	0.0
Corona	0.0	14.5	0.0	0.0	0.0	15.7	19.2	1.7	4.3	1.4	218.3	1,305	26.7
Costa Mesa	0.0	8.3	0.0	0.0	0.2	34.1	0.0	7.3	1.4	0.8	25.0	220	0.0
Covina	0.0	9.3	0.3	0.0	0.3	33.5	4.0	6.7	8.4	4.0	64.5	1,338	0.0
Culver City	0.0	5.5	1.2	0.0	4.4	22.4	13.6	5.0	10.2	0.5	15.0	384	0.0

1. Based on population estimated as of July 1 of the year shown.

STATE Place code	City	Land area[1] (sq. mi)	Population, 2021: Total persons 2021	Population, 2021: Rank	Population, 2021: Per square mile	Race 2020, Race alone[2] (percent): White	Black or African American	American Indian, Alaskan Native	Asian	Hawaiian Pacific Islander	Some other race	Two or more races (percent)
		1	2	3	4	5	6	7	8	9	10	11
	CALIFORNIA—Cont'd											
06 17610	Cupertino	11.3	58,622	670	5,187.8	22.3	0.6	0.2	70.2	0.0	1.5	5.2
06 17750	Cypress	6.6	49,926	800	7,564.5	37.4	3.2	0.7	37.7	0.6	8.6	11.8
06 17918	Daly City	7.6	101,243	318	13,321.4	14.3	2.4	0.9	57.5	0.7	15.2	9.0
06 17946	Dana Point	6.5	32,821	1,206	5,049.4	74.7	0.9	0.6	4.1	0.1	6.4	13.4
06 17988	Danville town	18.1	43,240	926	2,389.0	70.8	0.9	0.2	15.2	0.1	1.7	11.0
06 18100	Davis	10.0	66,799	568	6,679.9	54.7	2.5	0.7	22.1	0.2	7.3	12.6
06 18394	Delano	14.7	52,173	764	3,549.2	14.0	5.4	2.0	14.5	0.1	50.0	14.0
06 18996	Desert Hot Springs	30.3	32,716	1,210	1,079.7	34.2	8.1	2.4	2.4	0.2	35.7	17.0
06 19192	Diamond Bar	14.9	53,857	741	3,614.6	18.5	3.3	0.6	59.7	0.2	7.6	10.2
06 19766	Downey	12.4	111,645	273	9,003.6	23.4	3.7	2.1	6.7	0.3	40.0	23.9
06 20018	Dublin	15.2	71,674	514	4,715.4	29.1	4.0	0.7	53.8	0.3	3.6	8.5
06 20956	East Palo Alto	2.5	28,847	1,351	11,538.8	11.9	10.9	2.3	5.3	6.9	48.0	14.6
06 21230	Eastvale	12.7	71,375	518	5,620.1	26.5	9.1	0.9	30.1	0.3	15.9	17.2
06 21712	El Cajon	14.5	105,432	301	7,271.2	58.1	6.7	1.1	4.9	0.5	14.5	14.1
06 21782	El Centro	12.0	44,158	902	3,679.8	26.3	2.0	1.9	1.8	0.1	38.3	29.5
06 21796	El Cerrito	3.7	25,845	1,500	6,985.1	46.2	5.5	0.5	29.8	0.2	5.5	12.4
06 22020	Elk Grove	42.0	178,997	145	4,261.8	32.6	10.1	0.8	33.5	1.5	7.7	13.8
06 22230	El Monte	9.6	106,907	293	11,136.1	12.8	0.8	2.2	30.3	0.1	38.5	15.3
06 22300	El Paso de Robles (Paso Robles)	19.6	31,759	1,246	1,620.4	61.0	1.7	1.6	2.4	0.3	17.3	15.8
06 22678	Encinitas	19.1	61,762	625	3,233.6	77.3	0.5	0.6	4.4	0.1	5.4	11.7
06 22804	Escondido	37.3	150,665	175	4,039.3	41.9	2.4	1.8	7.9	0.3	29.0	16.7
06 23042	Eureka	9.5	26,489	1,467	2,788.3	68.1	2.0	4.3	5.6	0.9	6.7	12.4
06 23182	Fairfield	41.6	119,705	239	2,877.5	32.5	14.9	1.3	18.7	1.1	16.3	15.2
06 24638	Folsom	27.9	81,224	433	2,911.3	58.7	4.2	0.5	19.7	0.3	5.4	11.1
06 24680	Fontana	43.1	210,761	109	4,890.0	23.9	9.0	2.2	8.5	0.3	38.1	18.1
06 25338	Foster City	3.8	32,517	1,215	8,557.1	33.0	1.5	0.2	53.5	0.6	2.9	8.3
06 25380	Fountain Valley	9.1	56,495	698	6,208.2	41.9	1.0	0.5	39.8	0.2	6.4	10.1
06 26000	Fremont	78.1	227,514	97	2,913.1	18.4	2.3	0.6	64.0	0.5	6.6	7.6
06 27000	Fresno	115.6	544,510	33	4,710.3	33.2	7.6	2.4	14.7	0.2	26.8	15.2
06 28000	Fullerton	22.4	141,874	194	6,333.7	36.3	2.3	1.3	26.7	0.2	18.2	14.9
06 28112	Galt	7.1	25,495	1,516	3,590.8	50.7	1.9	1.7	4.1	0.4	22.8	18.4
06 28168	Gardena	5.8	59,702	648	10,293.4	11.9	21.8	1.2	26.5	0.7	25.9	11.9
06 29000	Garden Grove	18.0	170,488	154	9,471.6	21.9	1.0	1.2	42.4	0.5	20.9	12.1
06 29504	Gilroy	16.5	58,101	680	3,521.3	35.0	2.3	2.6	10.6	0.4	29.6	19.5
06 30000	Glendale	30.5	192,366	133	6,307.1	65.3	1.8	0.6	15.2	0.1	8.1	9.0
06 30014	Glendora	19.5	51,569	773	2,644.6	52.9	2.2	1.1	13.0	0.1	13.2	17.5
06 30378	Goleta	7.9	32,855	1,203	4,158.9	52.0	1.6	1.5	12.1	0.1	15.8	17.0
06 31960	Hanford	17.5	58,496	672	3,342.6	45.5	4.7	2.0	4.3	0.2	25.2	18.1
06 32548	Hawthorne	6.1	86,091	406	14,113.3	16.1	24.2	2.0	7.7	0.8	33.8	15.5
06 33000	Hayward	45.8	159,827	161	3,489.7	17.2	9.0	1.6	29.6	3.1	26.6	12.9
06 33182	Hemet	29.3	90,436	379	3,086.6	46.0	9.8	2.0	3.5	0.5	23.1	15.2
06 33308	Hercules	6.4	26,091	1,485	4,076.7	16.2	16.1	0.6	46.9	0.5	8.6	11.1
06 33434	Hesperia	72.7	100,971	322	1,388.9	40.3	5.6	1.9	2.4	0.2	33.9	15.6
06 33588	Highland	18.6	57,159	692	3,073.1	34.1	9.3	1.8	8.3	0.3	30.2	16.0
06 34120	Hollister	8.0	43,346	922	5,418.3	36.1	1.0	2.8	4.1	0.3	37.5	18.2
06 36000	Huntington Beach	27.0	196,652	129	7,283.4	63.7	1.2	0.7	13.3	0.3	7.9	13.0
06 36056	Huntington Park	3.0	53,644	743	17,881.3	14.5	0.8	2.8	0.7	0.1	61.1	20.0
06 36294	Imperial Beach	4.3	26,059	1,488	6,060.2	43.4	3.7	1.2	6.2	0.6	23.9	21.0
06 36448	Indio	33.2	90,416	380	2,723.4	35.0	2.3	1.6	2.6	0.1	37.7	20.8
06 36546	Inglewood	9.1	105,181	303	11,558.4	9.5	38.7	2.0	2.1	0.3	33.9	13.4
06 36770	Irvine	65.6	309,031	64	4,710.8	37.7	2.3	0.3	45.6	0.1	4.3	9.7
06 37692	Jurupa Valley	42.9	106,941	292	2,492.8	28.7	3.6	2.1	5.3	0.3	41.9	18.1
06 39122	Lafayette	15.0	25,208	1,534	1,680.5	72.8	0.7	0.2	12.6	0.1	1.8	11.7
06 39220	Laguna Hills	6.5	30,965	1,273	4,763.8	57.9	1.4	0.7	15.2	0.2	10.7	13.8
06 39248	Laguna Niguel	14.7	64,239	594	4,370.0	69.7	1.3	0.5	9.9	0.1	6.0	12.6
06 39290	La Habra	7.6	62,609	614	8,238.0	35.0	1.9	1.7	12.7	0.2	27.9	20.6
06 39486	Lake Elsinore	38.2	71,563	516	1,873.4	39.5	6.8	1.5	7.4	0.5	25.3	18.9
06 39496	Lake Forest	16.7	85,742	408	5,134.3	52.0	1.7	1.0	19.6	0.2	10.9	14.5
06 39892	Lakewood	9.4	80,611	439	8,575.6	37.6	8.3	1.1	18.9	0.9	16.0	17.3
06 40004	La Mesa	9.1	60,721	636	6,672.6	59.5	6.9	1.0	6.7	0.6	9.5	15.8
06 40032	La Mirada	7.8	46,658	853	5,981.8	36.8	2.3	1.3	22.9	0.2	17.1	19.3
06 40130	Lancaster	94.3	170,150	155	1,804.3	32.6	21.3	1.7	4.7	0.2	23.8	15.7
06 40340	La Puente	3.5	37,303	1,066	10,658.0	16.7	1.2	2.1	13.0	0.2	47.4	19.4
06 40354	La Quinta	35.3	38,181	1,041	1,081.6	62.7	1.9	0.9	4.1	0.2	16.7	13.5
06 40704	Lathrop	19.8	30,659	1,291	1,548.4	24.2	7.6	1.2	30.3	1.3	21.3	14.1
06 40830	La Verne	8.4	30,680	1,287	3,652.4	55.3	3.1	1.1	11.2	0.2	11.9	17.3
06 40886	Lawndale	2.0	31,121	1,267	15,560.5	21.2	8.5	2.5	10.4	0.6	39.3	17.5
06 41124	Lemon Grove	3.9	27,413	1,419	7,029.0	35.3	12.1	1.4	9.0	1.0	22.9	18.4

1. Dry land or land partially or temporarily covered by water. 2. Hispanic or Latino persons may be of any race.

City	Percent Hispanic or Latino[1], 2020	Percent foreign born, 2016–2020	Age of population (percent), 2016–2020: Under 18 years	18 to 24 years	25 to 34 years	35 to 44 years	45 to 54 years	55 to 64 years	65 years and over	Median age, 2016–2020	Percent female, 2016–2020	Population: Census counts: 2010	2020	Percent change: 2010–2020	2020–2021
	12	13	14	15	16	17	18	19	20	21	22	23	24	25	26
CALIFORNIA—Cont'd															
Cupertino	3.9	52.4	26.1	6.5	8.3	16.3	18.0	10.3	14.5	41.2	49.1	58,547	60,575	3.5	-3.2
Cypress	21.3	29.8	23.7	7.2	10.2	13.9	15.4	13.9	15.7	41.8	51.7	47,858	50,269	5.0	-0.7
Daly City	24.1	51.3	15.6	9.1	16.9	13.7	12.2	14.1	18.3	40.4	51.1	101,322	104,940	3.6	-3.5
Dana Point	19.0	13.4	17.4	5.5	10.2	10.2	18.3	17.9	20.4	48.9	50.7	33,291	33,165	-0.4	-1.0
Danville town	9.1	16.5	24.1	7.1	4.4	11.6	18.2	15.8	18.8	46.6	51.7	41,871	43,602	4.1	-0.8
Davis	17.0	20.8	14.7	33.1	13.3	8.3	9.2	8.8	12.6	26.2	53.5	65,675	66,796	1.7	0.0
Delano	74.8	36.5	25.6	12.0	18.5	15.0	11.9	8.5	8.6	31.1	41.3	53,048	51,845	-2.3	0.6
Desert Hot Springs	61.2	22.8	25.7	9.1	13.3	13.5	11.9	12.9	13.5	36.4	51.5	27,063	32,529	20.2	0.6
Diamond Bar	19.6	45.4	20.3	7.0	13.3	11.9	14.8	15.7	17.0	42.9	51.4	55,566	55,226	-0.6	-2.5
Downey	75.1	31.3	24.0	9.1	16.1	13.2	14.0	11.0	12.5	35.5	51.2	111,775	114,558	2.5	-2.5
Dublin	11.5	38.8	26.5	5.0	15.3	20.0	14.5	9.5	9.2	36.3	50.7	46,036	72,142	56.7	-0.6
East Palo Alto	66.5	43.1	24.6	9.4	20.1	14.8	12.7	10.3	8.2	32.4	50.8	28,185	30,050	6.6	-4.0
Eastvale	37.5	27.0	30.9	9.0	12.8	17.1	13.7	8.8	7.8	33.0	50.6	53,712	69,849	30.0	2.2
El Cajon	29.4	28.8	25.5	8.8	15.7	13.3	11.2	12.8	12.7	35.0	50.9	99,589	106,286	6.7	-0.8
El Centro	87.0	27.9	30.9	9.8	13.6	11.9	9.9	10.6	13.3	31.9	50.7	42,686	44,347	3.9	-0.4
El Cerrito	11.8	31.6	17.6	6.2	14.1	16.6	13.0	13.3	19.2	41.8	52.8	23,598	25,977	10.1	-0.5
Elk Grove	19.0	24.2	26.4	8.4	11.4	14.8	14.4	12.3	12.3	37.7	51.9	152,988	177,145	15.8	1.0
El Monte	64.7	49.7	23.0	10.6	15.5	13.0	13.2	11.5	13.3	35.6	49.5	113,580	109,554	-3.5	-2.4
El Paso de Robles (Paso Robles)	38.0	16.2	22.1	8.9	13.3	12.8	12.7	12.2	18.1	39.0	51.9	29,744	31,513	5.9	0.8
Encinitas	15.1	12.7	21.2	5.6	11.6	14.0	14.4	14.7	18.6	43.0	50.3	59,500	62,082	4.3	-0.5
Escondido	51.8	27.1	24.0	9.6	16.2	12.5	12.4	12.2	13.1	35.1	49.8	143,990	151,271	5.1	-0.4
Eureka	15.1	7.6	18.5	10.2	15.4	13.7	13.0	13.1	16.1	38.6	50.8	27,196	26,547	-2.4	-0.2
Fairfield	30.6	22.0	25.0	9.0	16.0	13.0	12.7	11.2	13.1	35.0	50.7	105,453	119,793	13.6	-0.1
Folsom	13.1	16.6	24.8	6.2	11.8	15.4	17.2	11.9	12.7	40.2	49.1	72,147	79,036	9.5	2.8
Fontana	67.8	26.0	28.9	11.8	14.6	14.7	13.1	8.7	8.2	31.2	50.1	196,457	208,766	6.3	1.0
Foster City	7.2	47.9	23.2	4.3	16.2	16.9	12.2	10.5	16.7	38.9	50.1	30,563	33,818	10.7	-3.8
Fountain Valley	15.5	31.9	19.5	8.1	11.3	11.8	14.3	14.8	20.3	44.5	51.9	55,360	57,175	3.3	-1.2
Fremont	12.6	49.0	23.5	5.9	15.5	16.9	14.2	11.3	12.7	38.2	50.4	214,065	232,084	8.4	-2.0
Fresno	50.5	19.6	28.2	10.7	16.6	12.6	10.6	9.7	11.6	31.4	50.6	497,059	542,161	9.1	0.4
Fullerton	37.8	28.7	23.1	11.1	15.4	12.1	12.7	12.3	13.2	35.2	50.4	135,183	143,367	6.1	-1.0
Galt	45.7	18.7	25.1	7.4	13.6	13.5	13.1	14.8	12.4	37.5	50.6	23,717	25,525	7.6	-0.1
Gardena	40.2	37.4	19.9	7.6	14.8	13.6	13.4	13.8	16.9	40.5	51.6	58,829	61,069	3.8	-2.2
Garden Grove	37.3	43.7	21.4	9.4	14.6	12.0	14.8	13.7	14.1	39.0	49.7	170,960	172,144	0.7	-1.0
Gilroy	56.5	24.2	28.6	9.7	11.7	14.4	13.2	10.6	11.8	34.9	51.5	48,969	59,669	21.9	-2.6
Glendale	17.1	52.4	17.7	7.4	16.2	12.9	14.2	13.8	17.9	41.6	53.1	191,682	196,841	2.7	-2.3
Glendora	36.2	19.0	22.9	6.7	13.1	13.5	13.3	14.4	16.1	40.4	52.6	50,247	52,610	4.7	-2.0
Goleta	35.3	22.6	20.5	14.4	14.6	13.1	11.1	11.8	14.7	35.6	49.5	30,096	32,753	8.8	0.3
Hanford	53.0	17.7	28.3	9.3	14.6	14.0	11.8	9.8	12.3	33.4	49.5	54,457	57,932	6.4	1.0
Hawthorne	53.7	33.3	26.5	9.2	18.2	13.8	13.6	10.2	8.5	32.6	51.1	84,171	88,255	4.9	-2.5
Hayward	41.2	38.9	20.9	9.7	17.7	13.9	12.7	12.5	12.5	36.0	50.2	144,319	163,635	13.4	-2.3
Hemet	45.4	17.1	26.0	8.5	12.1	10.2	10.4	11.0	21.8	38.5	51.8	78,695	89,855	14.2	0.6
Hercules	16.6	33.4	19.4	8.2	13.1	13.3	13.5	16.3	16.3	41.7	51.5	24,089	26,045	8.1	0.2
Hesperia	58.8	17.9	29.4	10.2	13.2	13.3	12.0	10.8	11.0	32.8	49.8	90,096	100,038	11.0	0.9
Highland	55.5	22.4	30.5	10.0	13.9	12.4	12.8	10.6	9.8	31.2	50.4	53,110	57,083	7.5	0.1
Hollister	68.9	20.4	28.4	9.6	14.8	14.2	13.5	10.0	9.6	33.4	50.6	35,221	41,702	18.4	3.9
Huntington Beach	19.9	16.0	18.5	7.6	14.0	12.4	14.9	14.4	18.2	43.2	49.7	190,987	199,140	4.3	-1.2
Huntington Park	96.5	45.7	27.2	12.4	15.0	14.2	13.0	8.7	9.4	31.7	49.1	58,127	55,005	-5.4	-2.5
Imperial Beach	51.1	18.3	23.7	12.2	18.4	13.9	11.3	10.4	10.1	32.6	48.3	26,329	26,190	-0.5	-0.5
Indio	69.1	22.9	22.2	8.4	13.3	12.6	12.5	11.4	19.6	39.8	51.2	79,225	89,127	12.5	1.4
Inglewood	51.7	28.8	22.1	9.6	15.4	14.0	13.9	12.3	12.7	37.1	51.1	109,605	107,961	-1.5	-2.6
Irvine	11.7	39.5	22.5	13.0	16.6	14.8	13.9	9.3	9.9	33.8	50.8	212,125	305,313	43.9	1.2
Jurupa Valley	70.5	27.1	27.2	11.1	15.2	13.6	12.2	10.3	10.4	32.9	49.8	94,983	105,107	10.7	1.7
Lafayette	8.2	15.4	25.4	4.6	7.4	11.8	18.0	13.8	19.0	45.5	51.3	23,789	25,426	6.9	-0.9
Laguna Hills	23.9	24.5	19.5	7.8	13.0	13.3	15.5	12.9	17.9	41.8	52.3	30,679	31,402	2.4	-1.4
Laguna Niguel	16.3	22.4	18.6	8.1	11.1	10.7	14.5	18.5	18.4	46.4	51.7	62,993	64,519	2.4	-0.4
La Habra	59.3	26.6	22.5	9.2	15.8	12.5	12.9	13.4	13.7	37.3	50.3	61,447	63,200	2.9	-0.9
Lake Elsinore	51.0	22.2	29.9	9.1	17.9	13.0	12.4	8.9	8.9	31.4	51.7	53,301	70,366	32.0	1.7
Lake Forest	25.6	24.7	21.8	7.6	14.4	14.4	15.6	12.6	13.5	39.2	51.3	77,445	86,070	11.1	-0.4
Lakewood	35.7	21.9	21.3	8.9	14.1	14.5	13.4	13.8	13.9	38.5	51.8	80,086	82,727	3.3	-2.6
La Mesa	25.7	15.0	20.7	8.7	19.3	13.5	11.4	11.9	14.6	35.8	53.1	57,014	61,191	7.3	-0.8
La Mirada	43.0	25.4	18.2	14.0	10.6	11.2	12.7	14.1	19.2	41.8	51.0	48,527	47,831	-1.4	-2.5
Lancaster	45.1	11.1	28.4	9.2	14.5	13.4	12.3	11.8	10.5	33.3	49.8	156,653	173,305	10.6	-1.8
La Puente	81.7	40.2	22.4	11.0	16.5	11.0	15.0	11.5	12.5	35.0	49.2	39,832	38,166	-4.2	-2.3
La Quinta	34.2	14.7	20.1	7.3	10.0	8.3	12.9	14.3	27.1	48.6	50.6	37,462	37,600	0.4	1.5
Lathrop	39.7	32.4	28.4	10.0	15.3	13.5	11.9	10.5	10.4	32.7	51.3	17,588	28,789	63.7	6.5
La Verne	35.7	16.3	19.6	9.5	9.7	10.6	13.4	16.5	20.7	45.8	52.4	30,917	31,408	1.6	-2.3
Lawndale	62.9	39.9	23.0	9.2	18.2	13.9	14.3	11.5	9.8	34.8	48.3	32,769	31,895	-2.7	-2.4
Lemon Grove	46.5	17.9	23.8	8.5	16.3	13.0	10.1	14.3	14.0	35.9	51.0	25,318	27,656	9.2	-0.9

1. May be of any race.

City	Households, 2016–2020							Persons in group quarters, 2016–2020	Serious crimes known to police[2], 2020				Educational attainment, 2016–2020		
	Number	Persons per household	Percent						Violent		Property		Population age 25 and over	Attainment[4] (percent)	
			Family	Married couple family	Female family	Non-family	One person		Number	Rate	Number	Rate		High school graduate or less	Bachelor's degree or more
	27	28	29	30	31	32	33	34	35	36	37	38	39	40	41
CALIFORNIA—Cont'd															
Cupertino	20,506	2.90	76.9	68.4	5.8	23.1	19.1	420	69	116.3	830	1,398.6	40,327	8.2	79.6
Cypress	15,833	3.09	80.6	62.0	15.3	19.4	14.1	141	60	122.1	727	1,479.9	33,955	23.6	47.3
Daly City	32,242	3.30	72.7	50.5	14.9	27.3	18.6	826	192	179.7	1,460	1,366.3	80,696	33.1	39.3
Dana Point	14,392	2.34	62.8	52.8	5.7	37.2	29.0	136	32	95.2	450	1,339.1	26,029	17.2	53.9
Danville town	16,499	2.72	78.1	66.7	8.8	21.9	17.9	124	21	46.9	239	533.5	30,901	9.0	68.6
Davis	24,973	2.68	51.1	41.4	7.3	48.9	23.7	1,789	98	140.3	2,452	3,510.2	35,850	9.4	74.6
Delano	11,444	3.87	86.5	63.7	15.8	13.5	10.2	8,558	185	345.0	856	1,596.3	32,946	70.4	7.4
Desert Hot Springs	10,776	2.70	56.6	30.8	18.6	43.4	36.2	157	218	749.8	480	1,651.0	19,090	53.9	15.7
Diamond Bar	17,642	3.16	81.8	65.7	11.1	18.2	14.7	200	62	111.2	793	1,422.8	40,640	20.9	54.0
Downey	33,433	3.31	80.0	51.4	19.5	20.0	15.8	688	301	271.0	2,153	1,938.7	74,348	43.7	24.6
Dublin	20,883	2.99	78.7	65.9	8.0	21.3	15.3	1,369	110	163.3	892	1,324.1	43,764	14.6	67.5
East Palo Alto	7,900	3.71	75.0	52.4	17.2	25.0	14.5	177	146	495.9	669	2,272.5	19,434	51.1	23.8
Eastvale	15,649	4.20	88.8	74.2	10.5	11.2	8.7	18	83	126.9	816	1,247.9	39,543	28.0	39.8
El Cajon	33,496	3.01	71.6	48.6	16.4	28.4	22.3	2,399	512	496.9	1,846	1,791.6	67,853	43.4	22.1
El Centro	11,750	3.70	79.3	49.4	21.6	20.7	17.0	445	158	357.2	1,003	2,267.3	26,012	51.9	16.7
El Cerrito	10,258	2.45	64.7	52.3	9.8	35.3	25.9	129	114	443.1	931	3,619.0	19,280	16.1	64.2
Elk Grove	53,627	3.22	80.2	61.0	14.3	19.8	16.8	852	398	224.4	2,380	1,342.1	113,101	26.0	36.7
El Monte	29,077	3.87	81.5	48.9	20.0	18.5	14.1	1,327	348	300.8	1,775	1,534.3	75,709	66.0	13.4
El Paso de Robles (Paso Robles)	12,107	2.59	68.9	50.9	12.7	31.1	24.6	117	53	163.4	363	1,119.4	21,715	34.8	24.8
Encinitas	23,893	2.62	66.5	56.4	6.6	33.5	22.7	347	133	210.9	676	1,072.1	46,110	14.5	61.7
Escondido	48,724	3.04	68.6	48.5	13.1	31.4	24.1	2,355	569	373.2	2,697	1,769.2	99,829	43.7	24.6
Eureka	11,216	2.29	47.8	30.2	11.5	52.2	37.8	1,234	182	682.8	1,041	3,905.3	19,216	34.7	29.0
Fairfield	36,843	3.12	76.2	54.7	14.2	23.8	18.1	1,746	542	457.4	2,990	2,523.4	76,892	34.7	27.9
Folsom	27,717	2.69	72.2	60.1	8.2	27.8	22.4	5,029	83	100.7	1,198	1,453.4	54,953	19.5	50.2
Fontana	55,369	3.83	85.6	59.6	19.1	14.4	10.9	556	666	307.5	2,504	1,156.3	126,188	51.3	19.0
Foster City	12,243	2.69	71.9	60.9	8.1	28.1	20.4	177	41	119.6	482	1,405.6	23,961	10.6	71.4
Fountain Valley	18,369	3.03	73.9	58.4	10.1	26.1	19.9	509	67	121.1	1,338	2,417.6	40,673	27.3	42.3
Fremont	74,479	3.13	81.1	68.9	8.4	18.9	14.9	1,478	407	166.6	5,722	2,342.6	165,845	23.0	58.7
Fresno	170,137	3.04	67.8	40.7	18.9	32.2	25.3	9,589	3,560	664.8	16,475	3,076.7	321,425	43.6	22.9
Fullerton	45,092	3.05	71.0	54.4	11.2	29.0	20.8	3,443	422	303.6	3,337	2,400.5	92,780	28.1	42.9
Galt	8,458	3.08	80.2	61.4	14.5	19.8	14.2	170	63	234.5	445	1,656.3	17,695	44.7	19.4
Gardena	20,391	2.88	67.3	46.1	15.3	32.7	26.2	744	269	453.0	1,324	2,229.5	43,053	41.5	26.6
Garden Grove	47,837	3.57	78.8	54.5	15.9	21.2	15.6	2,005	512	298.2	3,938	2,293.6	119,567	48.9	22.8
Gilroy	15,677	3.50	80.0	57.1	17.2	20.0	14.6	412	260	431.4	1,507	2,500.5	34,032	39.5	28.6
Glendale	74,766	2.64	66.0	48.0	12.1	34.0	27.9	1,803	206	102.9	3,197	1,597.2	149,420	33.4	41.6
Glendora	16,523	3.03	77.0	59.5	12.1	23.0	17.2	989	101	195.4	1,200	2,322.2	35,956	27.5	38.7
Goleta	11,652	2.74	62.2	47.4	11.5	37.8	24.9	235	60	193.6	583	1,880.8	20,945	24.1	47.8
Hanford	18,960	3.00	76.6	51.1	17.9	23.4	17.6	471	321	552.7	1,119	1,926.8	35,801	43.8	18.9
Hawthorne	28,056	3.02	66.7	36.8	20.5	33.3	26.9	666	675	782.4	1,631	1,890.6	54,917	46.5	23.5
Hayward	47,467	3.27	73.9	50.5	16.5	26.1	18.7	3,514	528	328.2	5,350	3,325.2	110,157	42.7	29.8
Hemet	28,533	2.94	66.3	46.5	13.5	33.7	27.5	783	347	403.2	2,063	2,397.2	55,488	49.8	13.7
Hercules	8,980	2.90	74.5	54.7	15.2	25.5	21.9	65	30	113.1	238	897.3	18,888	24.1	43.9
Hesperia	27,207	3.49	80.3	54.2	15.9	19.7	15.8	153	549	569.6	1,173	1,217.1	57,389	57.7	10.2
Highland	15,870	3.48	80.7	51.3	19.2	19.3	15.5	155	379	680.8	739	1,327.5	32,887	47.7	22.4
Hollister	11,438	3.50	81.6	57.6	16.5	18.4	14.7	118	131	316.1	393	948.4	24,845	48.8	16.1
Huntington Beach	77,589	2.56	64.4	48.4	10.8	35.6	26.4	998	493	246.3	3,928	1,962.7	147,714	23.3	43.6
Huntington Park	14,621	3.94	83.5	45.2	26.1	16.5	12.6	146	421	732.9	1,720	2,994.3	34,890	73.2	7.8
Imperial Beach	9,361	2.81	67.7	37.5	17.3	32.3	24.5	1,022	95	344.7	283	1,026.9	17,530	42.2	24.0
Indio	33,806	2.63	61.2	46.6	9.7	38.8	35.2	926	534	572.8	1,376	1,476.1	62,411	55.1	18.0
Inglewood	36,104	2.97	67.7	35.6	24.4	32.3	27.2	2,055	679	628.8	2,495	2,310.5	74,633	45.0	22.2
Irvine	96,707	2.74	65.3	52.5	8.5	34.7	22.8	7,615	152	51.2	4,452	1,498.6	175,764	11.5	69.5
Jurupa Valley	24,829	4.26	83.0	59.1	15.2	17.0	12.3	853	286	257.2	2,347	2,110.6	65,777	58.1	14.4
Lafayette	9,470	2.73	77.8	69.1	5.2	22.2	17.0	120	15	55.6	261	967.9	18,156	6.1	73.1
Laguna Hills	11,260	2.77	69.3	55.6	9.9	30.7	22.3	470	57	182.3	419	1,340.2	22,968	21.8	50.4
Laguna Niguel	24,838	2.60	73.1	59.4	10.2	26.9	20.9	357	41	61.4	579	867.3	47,670	17.6	54.6
La Habra	19,515	3.19	75.7	55.0	12.8	24.3	18.0	456	156	257.1	1,107	1,824.6	42,891	38.4	28.3
Lake Elsinore	17,435	3.68	81.6	59.2	15.0	18.4	14.7	19	199	279.2	1,648	2,311.8	39,156	42.8	21.8
Lake Forest	29,342	2.87	73.3	59.2	9.8	26.7	20.8	555	95	109.9	850	983.0	59,791	20.9	49.2
Lakewood	25,560	3.11	76.9	54.3	15.7	23.1	18.3	126	236	297.9	1,707	2,154.7	55,553	31.2	31.1
La Mesa	23,523	2.53	58.2	40.2	14.1	41.8	33.3	775	181	304.3	1,036	1,741.5	42,534	24.4	37.1
La Mirada	14,777	3.07	79.0	60.6	13.3	21.0	18.3	2,919	92	191.1	698	1,449.8	32,746	32.1	36.0
Lancaster	47,883	3.15	73.6	47.4	19.2	26.4	22.3	6,914	1,198	759.7	2,690	1,705.9	98,478	47.7	19.1
La Puente	9,706	4.09	86.8	52.8	20.7	13.2	9.9	89	124	313.2	387	977.5	26,472	64.9	11.5
La Quinta	16,292	2.55	67.4	54.8	8.1	32.6	27.7	72	46	108.9	852	2,017.6	30,245	30.0	34.4
Lathrop	5,819	4.10	86.8	65.6	12.0	13.2	10.2	22	NA	NA	NA	NA	14,691	47.7	18.8
La Verne	11,775	2.68	71.7	53.2	13.4	28.3	23.7	736	44	137.2	642	2,001.7	22,923	25.4	39.1
Lawndale	9,726	3.33	73.7	47.7	14.4	26.3	19.0	144	154	476.1	484	1,496.3	22,059	52.3	20.5
Lemon Grove	8,617	3.08	70.3	46.3	18.2	29.7	22.9	202	147	544.9	420	1,557.0	18,105	42.4	17.6

2. Data for serious crimes have not been adjusted for underreporting. This may affect comparability between geographic areas and over time. 4. Persons 25 years old and over.

City	Money income, 2016–2020					Median earnings Full year, Full-time workers, 2016–2020			Housing units, 2016–2020				
	Households												
	Median household income	Percent with income less than $25,000	Percent with income of $200,000 or more	Median family income	Median non-family household income	All persons	Men	Women	Total	Occupied	Percent owner occupied	Median value[1] (dollars)	Median gross rent (dollars)
	42	43	44	45	46	47	48	49	50	51	52	53	54
CALIFORNIA—Cont'd													
Cupertino	182,857	8.9	45.5	213,446	66,929	152,690	163,696	122,630	21,753	20,506	60.8	1,866,200	3,299
Cypress	102,005	10.2	15.5	111,440	53,500	64,956	71,583	61,314	16,481	15,833	69.1	665,100	1,965
Daly City	99,910	10.7	15.7	109,627	62,768	53,818	54,027	53,449	33,540	32,242	60.0	851,800	2,240
Dana Point	105,250	9.0	23.0	127,350	66,641	82,097	96,100	70,858	17,080	14,392	62.7	923,100	2,219
Danville town	167,827	8.1	42.4	197,965	73,484	129,937	162,153	101,120	16,966	16,499	84.7	1,152,300	2,414
Davis	75,394	22.5	15.6	139,966	39,016	72,398	81,955	62,195	26,373	24,973	44.7	675,900	1,659
Delano	47,042	25.6	1.6	50,442	17,837	36,282	40,144	30,628	12,047	11,444	59.4	202,900	916
Desert Hot Springs	37,818	35.2	1.0	47,111	23,722	33,225	32,251	34,247	12,853	10,776	47.5	218,000	1,046
Diamond Bar	100,723	11.7	15.7	110,926	50,538	62,741	67,300	54,157	18,269	17,642	76.4	690,500	2,101
Downey	75,974	10.4	8.3	79,836	40,281	46,562	51,694	41,525	34,653	33,433	49.0	582,500	1,569
Dublin	152,745	5.4	35.7	169,526	93,906	108,233	130,777	83,603	21,507	20,883	63.7	934,500	2,775
East Palo Alto	83,511	12.1	14.2	79,792	67,813	45,335	46,492	43,292	8,387	7,900	48.8	941,300	1,765
Eastvale	127,881	6.0	22.1	134,229	58,836	66,518	73,861	57,639	16,341	15,649	78.8	596,200	2,584
El Cajon	56,367	22.1	5.2	65,434	35,284	45,873	47,374	43,226	34,716	33,496	41.9	470,800	1,398
El Centro	47,366	29.7	3.4	49,001	24,254	41,647	42,323	39,710	13,890	11,750	49.8	210,100	821
El Cerrito	108,294	11.5	21.3	133,492	66,528	80,207	86,055	73,074	10,880	10,258	57.8	858,000	2,031
Elk Grove	101,776	9.4	11.9	109,123	61,119	65,091	70,816	59,081	54,920	53,627	73.9	437,100	1,734
El Monte	53,874	21.6	3.1	57,083	24,568	32,260	33,910	30,982	30,214	29,077	42.3	480,100	1,351
El Paso de Robles (Paso Robles)	69,297	12.3	5.7	81,940	45,790	47,196	52,087	40,991	12,633	12,107	59.4	481,700	1,391
Encinitas	120,488	8.3	26.8	151,169	67,134	84,135	97,940	74,372	26,129	23,893	63.8	992,100	2,124
Escondido	65,326	18.8	7.2	74,983	38,413	42,904	47,631	39,260	50,509	48,724	51.3	473,700	1,550
Eureka	43,199	27.9	3.2	59,914	29,582	38,977	39,002	38,916	12,450	11,216	44.1	295,500	951
Fairfield	86,204	10.9	10.6	93,907	56,033	54,580	59,410	50,228	38,539	36,843	59.0	433,300	1,734
Folsom	118,006	9.0	21.3	141,437	58,416	87,757	104,758	72,520	28,583	27,717	68.4	558,900	1,818
Fontana	75,681	12.5	7.3	78,459	48,860	44,809	48,194	41,060	57,105	55,369	66.3	393,200	1,368
Foster City	163,322	5.8	38.2	186,773	104,324	123,191	136,026	106,927	12,962	12,243	53.3	1,399,600	3,303
Fountain Valley	89,924	13.7	14.2	105,945	45,631	60,621	66,586	53,902	18,748	18,369	67.7	777,200	2,100
Fremont	142,374	7.5	31.6	157,457	69,717	95,779	106,136	78,377	78,038	74,479	61.4	999,500	2,453
Fresno	53,368	25.6	4.6	59,533	33,323	42,194	44,003	40,288	180,020	170,137	46.8	256,000	1,041
Fullerton	85,471	12.9	13.2	102,290	53,562	56,872	61,680	51,835	47,722	45,092	53.7	667,300	1,718
Galt	73,969	12.9	5.4	89,358	38,205	51,913	54,900	50,577	8,827	8,458	73.5	356,700	1,198
Gardena	64,015	18.6	5.0	76,171	37,173	44,808	47,158	42,010	21,373	20,391	49.1	519,000	1,377
Garden Grove	73,611	15.4	7.4	79,247	45,287	44,757	48,544	40,675	49,144	47,837	53.7	580,300	1,631
Gilroy	107,729	9.2	18.0	118,979	54,507	64,958	71,863	57,650	16,282	15,677	63.6	717,800	1,929
Glendale	70,596	22.2	11.5	80,056	47,529	58,932	61,357	55,128	79,743	74,766	34.0	821,500	1,711
Glendora	99,153	10.3	15.1	107,549	53,061	63,929	72,429	54,593	17,258	16,523	70.4	637,500	1,772
Goleta	98,035	10.7	14.3	110,842	74,721	56,250	57,681	53,919	12,359	11,652	51.9	813,000	1,955
Hanford	65,974	15.8	4.2	70,651	43,836	47,731	50,962	42,476	19,784	18,960	59.9	231,600	1,026
Hawthorne	57,849	18.8	4.5	63,598	42,135	41,679	43,526	40,102	29,282	28,056	27.5	602,100	1,335
Hayward	91,490	11.1	13.6	98,779	59,789	54,498	57,393	51,196	49,895	47,467	55.1	622,700	1,914
Hemet	43,152	28.6	2.4	51,578	25,375	42,327	47,087	36,580	31,971	28,533	59.8	213,000	1,157
Hercules	110,669	9.7	18.4	125,933	56,304	69,601	67,196	72,287	9,223	8,980	80.6	564,600	2,592
Hesperia	54,149	22.3	2.9	60,583	26,246	41,436	47,334	33,498	28,435	27,207	62.2	255,500	1,217
Highland	62,956	18.0	8.1	67,632	29,236	43,752	45,126	42,203	16,447	15,870	67.4	338,500	1,143
Hollister	80,670	10.4	6.4	85,643	46,100	50,277	55,718	42,088	11,775	11,438	62.5	526,900	1,505
Huntington Beach	97,469	10.4	16.9	113,315	70,152	71,689	77,516	63,320	81,846	77,589	56.6	803,400	1,965
Huntington Park	46,738	24.4	1.5	48,677	18,564	31,056	31,499	30,181	14,977	14,621	27.4	426,700	1,143
Imperial Beach	59,795	15.4	5.1	64,818	40,133	40,834	41,095	40,345	10,551	9,361	32.3	593,400	1,487
Indio	53,434	24.4	4.0	66,922	30,943	43,503	51,852	36,586	38,875	33,806	72.2	290,200	1,113
Inglewood	58,536	19.7	5.1	64,124	38,166	42,470	41,552	43,636	38,318	36,104	36.1	555,000	1,414
Irvine	108,318	13.9	21.2	130,522	70,151	86,899	101,042	71,563	104,553	96,707	45.2	861,700	2,425
Jurupa Valley	77,787	12.8	8.8	81,730	39,320	41,389	42,252	38,481	26,042	24,829	68.9	393,200	1,398
Lafayette	188,140	5.8	47.0	228,042	84,018	133,750	152,799	108,917	10,014	9,470	71.4	1,557,200	2,273
Laguna Hills	102,358	11.0	21.3	120,513	66,808	74,385	80,965	70,493	11,709	11,260	70.2	744,800	2,163
Laguna Niguel	119,608	8.8	25.0	139,270	75,105	81,475	95,069	65,996	26,583	24,838	68.6	863,600	2,331
La Habra	83,532	12.2	8.3	85,503	57,802	48,831	51,010	46,883	20,142	19,515	57.7	577,900	1,639
Lake Elsinore	74,490	13.3	6.4	79,357	37,398	52,259	58,570	41,023	18,642	17,435	68.8	366,200	1,501
Lake Forest	112,988	7.7	19.5	130,000	64,591	73,317	84,022	62,880	30,740	29,342	70.4	682,700	2,121
Lakewood	96,487	10.6	11.0	105,253	50,215	62,030	66,989	56,197	26,339	25,560	73.6	595,200	1,905
La Mesa	71,287	17.0	7.2	84,567	49,570	56,725	61,561	52,084	25,117	23,523	42.9	564,900	1,607
La Mirada	92,493	12.5	11.5	103,676	42,703	60,364	62,207	58,016	14,996	14,777	77.4	606,200	1,555
Lancaster	58,413	22.7	4.7	64,621	35,582	46,960	50,562	43,763	51,796	47,883	53.8	280,300	1,274
La Puente	66,132	14.4	3.3	69,074	39,737	36,454	38,694	33,701	10,023	9,706	59.1	446,800	1,429
La Quinta	75,724	14.0	15.1	99,172	45,671	55,966	59,174	51,600	25,875	16,292	72.4	405,200	1,408
Lathrop	90,179	11.6	7.0	92,054	52,548	50,896	55,057	43,053	6,290	5,819	79.7	385,900	1,751
La Verne	93,473	15.4	13.6	116,530	35,827	67,091	73,358	62,184	12,165	11,775	72.5	602,000	1,637
Lawndale	65,923	13.6	2.8	67,079	45,960	42,411	45,206	40,443	10,268	9,726	37.2	551,800	1,564
Lemon Grove	66,953	18.0	2.5	73,584	38,344	47,870	51,054	45,386	8,993	8,617	52.5	456,400	1,389

1. Specified owner-occupied units

City	Commuting, 2016–2020[1] Percent: Drove alone	Commuting, 2016–2020[1] Percent: Mean travel time to work	Computer access[2], 2016–2020 Percent: With a computer in the house	Computer access[2], 2016–2020 Percent: With Internet access	Migration, 2016–2020: Percent who lived in the same house one year ago	Migration, 2016–2020: Percent who lived in another state or county one year ago	Civilian labor force, 2021: Total	Civilian labor force, 2021: Percent change 2020–2021	Civilian labor force, 2021: Unemployment[3] Total	Civilian labor force, 2021: Unemployment[3] Rate	Civilian Employment, 2016–2020[4]: Population age 16 and older Number	Civilian Employment, 2016–2020[4]: Population age 16 and older Percent in labor force	Civilian Employment, 2016–2020[4]: Population age 16 to 64 Number	Civilian Employment, 2016–2020[4]: Population age 16 to 64 Percent who worked full-year full-time
	55	56	57	58	59	60	61	62	63	64	65	66	67	68
CALIFORNIA—Cont'd														
Cupertino	74.7	29.1	96.4	93.4	85.5	7.2	28,075	0.4	1,028	3.7	46,235	60.8	37,587	54.7
Cypress	78.9	31.5	96.6	92.9	91.7	4.9	24,255	-0.9	1,497	6.2	39,054	63.2	31,342	49.2
Daly City	58.1	31.7	94.7	89.6	90.9	5.9	62,642	-3.1	3,695	5.9	92,723	67.5	73,106	56.5
Dana Point	70.8	28.0	97.8	94.6	85.2	5.7	17,882	-0.1	950	5.3	29,000	62.9	22,093	47.9
Danville town	68.3	33.3	96.4	95.0	89.3	5.1	19,794	0.2	866	4.4	35,727	64.0	27,272	51.5
Davis	54.4	22.9	98.5	94.3	69.5	15.6	34,545	1.8	1,305	3.8	59,962	57.2	51,332	33.4
Delano	78.5	18.3	75.7	69.0	87.7	9.1	21,448	0.9	5,174	24.1	40,797	49.2	36,278	28.4
Desert Hot Springs	81.2	27.4	88.3	79.0	87.7	3.2	12,263	-1.9	1,281	10.4	22,751	58.2	18,800	44.2
Diamond Bar	77.8	36.7	97.0	94.0	90.2	4.6	29,141	0.8	2,051	7.0	45,892	62.9	36,390	51.0
Downey	78.3	32.4	95.0	88.6	92.6	1.2	55,663	0.7	4,962	8.9	87,896	66.3	73,934	51.5
Dublin	62.3	41.0	98.3	96.7	80.6	10.5	32,643	0.2	1,490	4.6	48,313	69.7	42,422	57.5
East Palo Alto	69.5	24.8	96.2	85.9	92.4	3.5	14,392	-1.8	928	6.4	23,313	71.8	20,902	53.1
Eastvale	75.6	39.5	99.5	98.3	90.3	7.1	34,065	1.0	1,916	5.6	47,717	68.8	42,580	54.3
El Cajon	76.5	26.5	95.1	90.1	82.3	5.0	44,569	-0.4	4,009	9.0	79,704	62.1	66,567	43.7
El Centro	79.8	20.3	89.3	83.9	88.4	4.4	18,117	-2.6	2,574	14.2	31,524	56.8	25,700	38.3
El Cerrito	48.7	33.8	96.2	93.2	85.3	10.4	13,223	-0.6	701	5.3	21,236	65.2	16,375	52.0
Elk Grove	76.8	32.9	97.4	93.7	89.2	4.1	83,920	0.8	4,899	5.8	134,079	64.6	112,837	50.0
El Monte	73.7	29.7	91.6	81.1	93.2	1.1	50,154	-0.6	4,542	9.1	90,926	62.0	75,781	45.6
El Paso de Robles (Paso Robles)	77.9	24.7	95.5	89.5	89.6	4.7	15,515	0.8	857	5.5	25,134	63.6	19,450	50.6
Encinitas	70.8	24.4	96.1	92.9	87.2	4.2	31,865	0.5	1,433	4.5	51,188	64.4	39,501	49.6
Escondido	77.7	27.9	94.5	89.8	87.2	2.8	66,739	0.3	4,240	6.4	118,292	64.5	98,629	50.7
Eureka	73.9	15.3	94.5	86.4	79.0	9.4	11,879	-2.0	724	6.1	22,369	61.5	18,020	41.5
Fairfield	76.8	32.5	95.8	91.9	84.5	7.2	51,303	-1.0	3,720	7.3	90,620	64.3	75,339	50.6
Folsom	72.4	26.1	97.5	94.6	83.7	8.4	38,328	1.5	1,677	4.4	62,067	62.0	51,936	51.6
Fontana	77.1	34.5	96.1	88.9	89.8	4.4	102,095	1.8	7,298	7.1	158,624	66.0	141,132	49.7
Foster City	66.6	33.4	98.1	96.3	77.8	10.9	18,347	-0.7	656	3.6	26,215	67.0	20,688	60.0
Fountain Valley	80.1	27.3	95.2	90.2	88.6	3.2	27,164	-0.9	1,657	6.1	46,755	59.6	35,391	46.4
Fremont	65.3	35.5	97.3	94.1	89.3	5.7	113,596	0.1	5,575	4.9	185,060	67.3	155,211	58.5
Fresno	77.7	22.3	91.4	82.7	84.9	3.8	230,590	-0.8	18,863	8.2	393,157	61.5	332,248	42.3
Fullerton	77.0	30.7	96.1	92.0	86.5	4.8	68,278	-0.9	4,372	6.4	111,519	65.4	92,884	47.6
Galt	76.6	32.3	94.8	89.4	88.5	5.5	11,549	1.4	919	8.0	20,212	64.1	16,948	48.8
Gardena	76.9	29.1	91.1	83.1	92.0	2.6	29,840	0.0	2,979	10.0	48,603	62.1	38,566	51.8
Garden Grove	77.7	29.6	94.1	87.9	92.0	2.4	79,339	-2.1	5,953	7.5	140,214	64.0	115,785	48.2
Gilroy	73.7	37.1	97.6	93.6	89.5	2.0	28,146	-1.4	1,754	6.2	41,035	69.0	34,545	49.6
Glendale	74.8	28.5	89.3	84.4	89.4	2.9	101,632	0.2	9,167	9.0	167,821	62.1	132,091	49.5
Glendora	75.5	34.1	95.3	88.1	88.8	2.5	24,980	1.4	1,883	7.5	40,944	63.4	32,705	49.9
Goleta	70.2	18.3	96.0	93.0	85.4	5.2	18,144	0.2	704	3.9	26,341	70.2	21,621	52.6
Hanford	79.7	23.7	93.2	85.0	85.4	6.1	24,669	-1.9	2,074	8.4	42,885	60.0	35,849	47.2
Hawthorne	73.8	30.7	94.4	87.1	88.0	2.4	43,606	-0.6	4,539	10.4	65,183	69.1	57,885	49.1
Hayward	68.0	35.6	95.3	90.5	90.5	4.7	74,995	-1.4	5,470	7.3	129,463	67.4	109,536	54.3
Hemet	78.8	35.9	90.2	81.6	85.2	4.0	30,483	0.9	3,224	10.6	65,338	49.1	46,917	39.5
Hercules	67.4	41.7	98.1	95.6	89.6	4.3	13,792	-0.2	872	6.3	21,465	68.1	17,216	56.8
Hesperia	81.4	41.7	94.8	91.2	92.1	2.3	37,592	2.6	3,691	9.8	70,370	55.2	59,898	40.1
Highland	82.8	29.3	92.8	82.8	90.9	2.8	25,345	1.6	1,998	7.9	40,224	61.9	34,823	46.6
Hollister	78.1	36.7	96.3	93.0	86.3	7.6	20,715	-1.7	1,678	8.1	30,058	69.0	26,226	45.2
Huntington Beach	77.7	30.5	96.5	91.1	87.5	5.0	103,723	-0.5	6,000	5.8	167,488	66.4	131,061	51.5
Huntington Park	65.3	31.6	90.5	80.9	92.9	0.8	25,733	1.4	2,286	8.9	43,791	66.5	38,354	48.4
Imperial Beach	76.9	28.2	95.1	88.3	83.7	5.3	11,872	-0.6	1,065	9.0	21,607	65.2	18,843	48.0
Indio	82.6	22.4	91.6	85.0	92.0	2.6	41,696	-0.2	3,433	8.2	72,124	58.0	54,523	46.1
Inglewood	72.1	31.2	93.8	85.7	90.8	1.6	52,181	-1.0	5,825	11.2	87,709	67.0	73,873	48.3
Irvine	71.1	25.5	98.3	94.6	77.7	10.4	142,618	0.6	7,551	5.3	217,846	64.5	190,758	47.5
Jurupa Valley	76.7	33.7	95.2	89.2	91.1	3.9	50,093	1.9	3,522	7.0	80,689	63.6	69,607	46.7
Lafayette	56.1	32.0	97.8	95.9	87.5	6.3	11,748	0.5	471	4.0	20,109	63.8	15,170	51.0
Laguna Hills	74.3	24.5	97.4	94.6	89.8	2.9	16,454	0.1	844	5.1	26,066	66.8	20,403	51.7
Laguna Niguel	75.7	28.8	98.2	95.1	87.0	4.4	33,368	0.1	1,823	5.5	54,541	65.5	42,553	51.3
La Habra	78.4	30.5	95.9	90.6	89.4	5.4	30,076	-0.4	1,938	6.4	50,322	68.3	41,731	51.3
Lake Elsinore	79.4	42.9	97.3	91.2	88.6	5.9	30,136	0.7	2,297	7.6	46,924	64.5	41,220	46.5
Lake Forest	78.2	25.6	96.5	94.2	88.0	3.2	47,085	0.6	2,430	5.2	68,328	70.0	56,857	55.1
Lakewood	81.7	30.3	95.2	91.0	91.8	1.9	41,504	0.4	3,449	8.3	64,442	66.5	53,390	52.1
La Mesa	77.3	26.3	94.1	91.0	82.0	4.1	29,874	0.0	1,948	6.5	48,673	66.4	39,891	52.9
La Mirada	78.2	32.5	95.9	90.0	91.5	4.2	23,323	0.4	1,857	8.0	40,802	60.9	31,521	47.4
Lancaster	79.9	31.0	90.0	83.2	91.1	2.6	64,508	1.9	7,986	12.4	118,397	52.8	101,843	43.1
La Puente	73.7	31.3	94.2	86.4	94.0	1.2	18,684	0.7	1,740	9.3	31,919	62.5	26,927	48.1
La Quinta	75.6	24.2	94.6	91.6	88.4	5.0	19,498	-0.1	1,277	6.5	34,383	52.6	23,083	44.4
Lathrop	75.9	44.5	96.4	91.9	87.4	8.3	10,179	0.3	936	9.2	17,746	61.4	15,272	45.7
La Verne	72.2	31.5	95.0	91.2	91.1	3.1	15,768	1.6	1,192	7.6	26,787	61.2	20,099	46.0
Lawndale	74.3	26.2	95.5	89.0	91.6	1.1	16,231	-1.2	1,505	9.3	25,856	72.1	22,659	50.3
Lemon Grove	73.7	29.5	91.8	86.7	86.9	3.3	12,125	-0.8	1,010	8.3	20,960	62.3	17,226	47.2

1. Employed persons. 2. Households. 3. Percent of civilian labor force. 4. Persons 16 years old and over.

Table D. Cities — Construction, Wholesale Trade, and Retail Trade

City	Value of residential construction authorized by building permits, 2021			Wholesale trade[1], 2017				Retail trade[2], 2017			
	New construction ($1,000)	Number of housing units	Percent single family	Number of establishments	Number of employees	Sales (mil dol)	Annual payroll (mil dol)	Number of establish-ments	Number of employees	Sales (mil dol)	Annual payroll (mil dol)
	69	70	71	72	73	74	75	76	77	78	79
CALIFORNIA—Cont'd											
Cupertino	24,226	67	67.2	61	791	722.0	81.2	D	D	D	116.6
Cypress	2,531	11	72.7	112	3,556	4,376.3	276.5	90	1,569	643.2	49.2
Daly City	92,307	183	19.7	28	148	55.0	6.1	190	4,048	1,151.0	117.4
Dana Point	38,361	49	100.0	58	159	166.9	9.3	97	1,027	379.9	32.4
Danville town	9,748	38	100.0	34	152	234.7	10.8	121	1,633	596.6	51.9
Davis	49,715	324	8.3	20	213	153.0	14.4	122	2,136	595.3	56.8
Delano	5,397	28	100.0	12	133	179.4	8.7	92	1,683	415.5	40.3
Desert Hot Springs	35,920	186	96.8	4	9	1.4	0.3	44	588	160.5	15.9
Diamond Bar	7,360	20	100.0	289	1,205	2,133.2	56.2	144	1,000	424.7	31.8
Downey	27,009	121	100.0	86	921	428.8	59.0	294	5,829	1,712.4	165.7
Dublin	230,329	770	13.1	63	477	202.3	26.6	189	4,330	1,758.0	166.5
East Palo Alto	3,283	17	100.0	8	38	7.4	2.6	22	858	306.2	27.6
Eastvale	960	2	100.0	77	675	991.3	28.2	78	1,362	366.8	31.1
El Cajon	5,647	41	90.2	124	1,324	661.4	69.3	456	7,318	2,313.7	209.2
El Centro	11,815	74	24.3	57	424	327.7	19.8	194	4,454	1,004.9	107.6
El Cerrito	9,162	45	55.6	12	51	34.6	1.7	62	1,551	441.1	45.3
Elk Grove	128,281	563	100.0	D	D	D	23.9	279	7,241	2,561.7	231.7
El Monte	16,638	77	46.8	312	2,338	1,050.6	98.7	308	3,677	1,567.2	146.9
El Paso de Robles (Paso Robles)	10,671	51	76.5	42	352	147.9	15.3	143	2,245	670.3	63.7
Encinitas	26,092	132	100.0	87	432	410.5	31.9	284	4,402	1,262.7	127.7
Escondido	125,280	432	78.2	132	998	524.5	56.2	511	10,528	3,318.7	316.6
Eureka	2,534	26	84.6	47	448	227.5	23.0	222	3,418	1,008.0	101.9
Fairfield	122,453	365	100.0	77	1,377	1,081.5	90.9	313	5,691	1,837.5	167.5
Folsom	302,621	949	100.0	32	240	1,485.1	36.6	288	6,285	2,036.4	189.8
Fontana	215,290	1,052	62.0	184	3,468	5,602.1	175.7	337	7,334	2,995.0	232.7
Foster City	30,717	43	65.1	35	586	563.0	56.1	31	788	315.7	28.2
Fountain Valley	18,946	80	37.5	102	1,474	9,572.9	127.7	213	3,139	1,296.5	97.1
Fremont	217,174	719	19.6	454	9,727	15,444.9	962.7	447	8,938	4,108.6	356.0
Fresno	549,704	2,178	87.7	510	8,150	6,495.3	453.2	1,537	25,256	7,265.6	698.2
Fullerton	10,112	40	17.5	291	2,839	2,214.7	157.7	428	5,476	1,767.2	152.5
Galt	19,567	119	100.0	8	328	229.0	23.1	39	629	636.3	18.3
Gardena	9,706	64	100.0	172	1,688	956.2	85.5	172	2,534	954.2	80.0
Garden Grove	32,557	274	100.0	227	2,364	1,248.8	111.4	444	5,988	2,236.9	179.4
Gilroy	49,079	248	39.9	47	593	473.3	42.9	302	5,409	1,789.1	150.9
Glendale	22,654	167	80.2	241	1,913	1,307.9	147.8	726	12,197	3,899.9	384.3
Glendora	9,342	53	100.0	48	405	218.6	27.3	132	2,743	866.7	83.3
Goleta	2,294	28	3.6	58	1,147	1,597.3	89.7	123	2,414	727.3	72.9
Hanford	88,852	290	91.7	27	386	249.1	23.8	160	2,778	847.8	77.2
Hawthorne	25,225	36	86.1	72	1,354	555.2	61.4	154	3,841	1,667.9	122.8
Hayward	70,205	334	62.6	442	6,836	5,408.2	406.7	412	6,899	2,267.2	216.2
Hemet	54,348	219	100.0	18	82	81.9	3.0	212	4,534	1,202.9	125.3
Hercules	NA	NA	NA	D	D	D	D	18	383	107.1	10.2
Hesperia	38,623	253	96.8	42	194	168.7	7.2	179	2,602	690.9	66.5
Highland	7,646	31	100.0	11	81	19.9	2.6	57	764	231.9	22.4
Hollister	100,421	396	100.0	20	167	72.3	7.3	79	1,267	393.9	40.7
Huntington Beach	39,595	162	61.7	372	4,541	3,571.7	295.4	624	10,253	3,560.3	316.4
Huntington Park	120	3	100.0	60	775	340.3	30.8	184	2,301	642.5	60.1
Imperial Beach	5,740	38	52.6	6	12	4.5	0.4	35	251	52.1	6.1
Indio	116,461	738	70.7	44	514	287.4	25.0	169	3,206	1,167.3	107.4
Inglewood	33,773	158	96.8	77	615	317.3	27.5	239	4,197	1,296.4	123.8
Irvine	605,647	2,362	47.8	1,095	19,409	35,190.8	1,684.3	700	11,702	4,999.7	437.3
Jurupa Valley	51,314	315	100.0	102	2,654	3,717.7	160.8	142	1,995	680.2	52.8
Lafayette	NA	NA	NA	22	111	257.7	9.4	81	1,267	298.7	39.2
Laguna Hills	209	1	100.0	105	568	311.8	37.9	171	1,819	485.7	51.2
Laguna Niguel	37,000	192	0.0	77	486	259.5	28.2	157	2,890	1,217.2	100.8
La Habra	11,296	63	100.0	60	332	191.1	16.1	183	3,876	1,079.6	105.1
Lake Elsinore	62,550	221	100.0	35	207	84.7	9.8	193	3,314	958.6	89.9
Lake Forest	124,559	409	100.0	216	3,427	4,292.9	283.9	214	3,951	1,218.6	140.3
Lakewood	1,335	14	100.0	26	118	63.5	5.6	215	5,494	1,305.2	132.0
La Mesa	11,965	142	47.9	21	220	53.7	8.8	224	4,099	1,296.5	124.5
La Mirada	18,392	94	100.0	130	3,395	2,139.1	235.7	91	1,547	418.7	46.0
Lancaster	96,271	677	38.8	63	642	643.8	34.4	310	5,519	1,814.6	167.1
La Puente	1,587	21	100.0	22	101	24.1	2.7	102	1,258	307.5	31.4
La Quinta	65,825	256	100.0	24	44	30.2	2.1	90	2,405	670.0	66.0
Lathrop	319,628	937	90.6	15	724	1,699.2	44.1	26	482	179.3	14.2
La Verne	3,355	14	100.0	58	545	484.7	33.0	80	1,224	302.7	29.6
Lawndale	3,304	15	100.0	16	113	50.8	6.8	83	751	227.9	22.1
Lemon Grove	9,630	38	100.0	12	59	34.1	1.9	78	1,629	619.0	50.7

1. Merchant wholesalers except manufacturers' sales branches and offices. 2. Establishments with payroll.

City	Real estate and rental and leasing, 2017				Professional, scientific, and technical services[1], 2017				Manufacturing, 2017			
	Number of establish-ments	Number of employees	Receipts (mil dol)	Annual payroll (mil dol)	Number of establish-ments	Number of employees	Receipts (mil dol)	Annual payroll (mil dol)	Number of establish-ments	Number of employees	Receipts (mil dol)	Annual payroll (mil dol)
	80	81	82	83	84	85	86	87	88	89	90	91
CALIFORNIA—Cont'd												
Cupertino	122	696	188.2	33.7	413	2,420	527.9	251.4	NA	NA	NA	NA
Cypress	83	236	74.2	12.9	146	1,553	375.9	106.5	NA	NA	NA	NA
Daly City	57	367	238.6	17.3	81	437	44.5	16.4	NA	NA	NA	NA
Dana Point	90	191	80.5	14.1	204	606	138.5	46.3	NA	NA	NA	NA
Danville town	128	439	170.1	29.7	212	827	222.9	73.0	NA	NA	NA	NA
Davis	130	586	75.6	21.8	238	1,627	297.8	126.3	NA	NA	NA	NA
Delano	17	46	13.0	1.7	D	D	7.8	D	NA	NA	NA	NA
Desert Hot Springs	18	43	12.9	1.8	11	282	6.6	4.5	NA	NA	NA	NA
Diamond Bar	145	D	73.2	D	273	1,194	245.1	67.8	NA	NA	NA	NA
Downey	165	990	202.9	41.1	162	665	83.5	24.8	NA	NA	NA	NA
Dublin	60	251	111.4	14.3	276	1,972	496.3	187.8	NA	NA	NA	NA
East Palo Alto	18	76	94.4	12.3	24	469	183.8	62.2	NA	NA	NA	NA
Eastvale	D	D	D	D	D	D	D	D	NA	NA	NA	NA
El Cajon	144	920	238.1	40.4	208	1,187	171.7	57.9	NA	NA	NA	NA
El Centro	50	229	56.9	7.1	91	494	59.2	24.2	NA	NA	NA	NA
El Cerrito	24	37	27.5	2.1	70	187	26.6	8.5	NA	NA	NA	NA
Elk Grove	136	413	102.3	14.1	241	1,053	185.5	55.0	NA	NA	NA	NA
El Monte	75	361	78.9	18.7	129	588	101.5	34.2	NA	NA	NA	NA
El Paso de Robles (Paso Robles)	63	284	61.8	9.5	82	368	49.1	18.9	NA	NA	NA	NA
Encinitas	243	647	164.4	39.0	621	2,235	500.3	169.7	NA	NA	NA	NA
Escondido	205	825	196.4	35.0	339	1,776	276.7	99.9	NA	NA	NA	NA
Eureka	49	257	70.1	9.7	91	789	111.3	45.6	NA	NA	NA	NA
Fairfield	109	499	163.1	20.5	163	909	138.7	48.9	NA	NA	NA	NA
Folsom	123	782	185.4	48.0	411	10,954	1,129.9	1,591.9	NA	NA	NA	NA
Fontana	112	570	221.7	30.5	131	474	68.7	22.3	NA	NA	NA	NA
Foster City	64	651	323.4	54.8	139	1,523	390.6	175.0	NA	NA	NA	NA
Fountain Valley	126	407	110.9	18.1	233	2,226	509.1	163.1	NA	NA	NA	NA
Fremont	284	1,174	525.9	67.8	1,251	13,598	3,166.0	1,414.2	NA	NA	NA	NA
Fresno	558	3,657	784.4	157.6	1,150	8,428	1,269.8	498.7	NA	NA	NA	NA
Fullerton	247	917	207.9	31.6	448	2,968	443.0	200.3	NA	NA	NA	NA
Galt	7	11	1.9	0.2	21	60	5.8	1.7	NA	NA	NA	NA
Gardena	55	284	49.0	10.4	79	283	33.2	12.2	NA	NA	NA	NA
Garden Grove	167	818	242.9	34.2	275	1,724	189.7	73.5	NA	NA	NA	NA
Gilroy	46	171	62.4	7.9	73	470	88.3	29.5	NA	NA	NA	NA
Glendale	401	2,913	1,695.7	233.7	1,086	6,902	1,732.8	556.1	NA	NA	NA	NA
Glendora	87	295	70.1	11.6	141	934	118.5	44.0	NA	NA	NA	NA
Goleta	47	288	56.8	11.3	D	D	D	D	NA	NA	NA	NA
Hanford	63	250	54.4	8.9	61	368	38.7	16.0	NA	NA	NA	NA
Hawthorne	79	342	45.5	11.9	73	606	112.2	27.3	NA	NA	NA	NA
Hayward	188	1,450	411.4	76.5	319	5,858	2,297.4	932.9	NA	NA	NA	NA
Hemet	84	416	95.2	19.2	58	379	31.2	13.4	NA	NA	NA	NA
Hercules	9	16	3.6	1.1	28	215	35.1	14.7	NA	NA	NA	NA
Hesperia	52	227	58.8	8.9	57	238	25.2	7.8	NA	NA	NA	NA
Highland	14	31	8.9	0.8	34	155	25.2	6.1	NA	NA	NA	NA
Hollister	37	96	24.9	3.5	48	179	24.3	8.4	NA	NA	NA	NA
Huntington Beach	403	1,436	477.2	70.5	837	4,436	1,052.7	307.4	NA	NA	NA	NA
Huntington Park	28	146	26.4	4.9	33	194	17.8	6.2	NA	NA	NA	NA
Imperial Beach	19	64	13.3	2.4	35	115	13.8	5.7	NA	NA	NA	NA
Indio	65	353	69.5	12.8	79	403	54.3	18.4	NA	NA	NA	NA
Inglewood	76	736	326.6	33.1	86	604	79.4	22.2	NA	NA	NA	NA
Irvine	945	12,200	4,969.4	1,209.1	3,259	47,066	9,985.8	4,614.0	NA	NA	NA	NA
Jurupa Valley	45	455	123.0	23.6	48	253	32.4	8.5	NA	NA	NA	NA
Lafayette	54	144	57.7	8.0	216	1,010	210.1	75.9	NA	NA	NA	NA
Laguna Hills	96	594	73.5	27.2	367	1,995	405.4	142.0	NA	NA	NA	NA
Laguna Niguel	159	481	269.1	35.4	354	922	175.9	51.6	NA	NA	NA	NA
La Habra	70	255	59.3	9.2	94	461	54.5	18.7	NA	NA	NA	NA
Lake Elsinore	40	232	80.8	9.6	67	397	36.9	12.4	NA	NA	NA	NA
Lake Forest	129	970	201.9	51.7	465	3,203	629.3	228.9	NA	NA	NA	NA
Lakewood	54	300	47.1	9.3	97	531	40.4	15.4	NA	NA	NA	NA
La Mesa	151	824	147.8	29.7	252	1,091	165.2	62.3	NA	NA	NA	NA
La Mirada	56	585	110.1	38.7	74	292	55.5	20.5	NA	NA	NA	NA
Lancaster	125	533	153.7	20.3	145	1,179	145.6	54.9	NA	NA	NA	NA
La Puente	23	72	15.2	2.7	19	436	14.3	5.9	NA	NA	NA	NA
La Quinta	99	270	72.8	13.1	98	337	80.1	26.2	NA	NA	NA	NA
Lathrop	16	55	17.9	1.9	7	99	15.6	5.9	NA	NA	NA	NA
La Verne	43	154	37.4	6.9	73	402	60.9	20.8	NA	NA	NA	NA
Lawndale	23	285	70.8	12.1	38	110	51.4	9.2	NA	NA	NA	NA
Lemon Grove	27	75	23.1	2.3	24	156	11.7	3.9	NA	NA	NA	NA

1. Establishments subject to federal tax.

City	Accommodation and food services, 2017				Arts, entertainment, and recreation[1], 2017				Health care and social assistance[1], 2017			
	Number of establish-ments	Number of employees	Receipts (mil dol)	Annual payroll (mil dol)	Number of establish-ments	Number of employees	Receipts (mil dol)	Annual payroll (mil dol)	Number of establish-ments	Number of employees	Receipts (mil dol)	Annual payroll (mil dol)
	92	93	94	95	96	97	98	99	100	101	102	103
CALIFORNIA—Cont'd												
Cupertino	192	3,440	259.3	83.1	28.0	538	30.1	9.5	233	2,482	287.8	117.3
Cypress	129	2,082	145.0	40.0	D	D	D	D	132	1,424	255.6	57.7
Daly City	198	3,416	271.2	75.7	14.0	553	42.4	13.1	263	4,620	721.6	255.7
Dana Point	112	3,795	448.0	127.4	D	D	D	7.2	129	1,248	124.5	48.3
Danville town	114	2,217	134.2	41.0	33.0	497	38.6	14.1	168	1,796	204.5	80.8
Davis	188	3,392	187.3	57.5	25.0	289	14.4	4.8	172	2,626	368.1	130.5
Delano	64	922	52.4	14.8	D	D	D	D	74	1,507	170.1	66.6
Desert Hot Springs	47	470	31.5	7.5	D	D	D	D	37	497	28.7	13.8
Diamond Bar	141	1,950	120.9	35.0	11.0	185	14.0	3.7	208	1,587	155.1	62.7
Downey	292	5,840	398.4	111.5	20.0	262	29.0	5.8	355	12,312	1,941.9	800.6
Dublin	183	3,288	264.6	73.8	D	D	D	D	184	1,850	257.5	100.2
East Palo Alto	23	565	75.7	27.2	D	D	D	D	35	483	48.9	26.0
Eastvale	53	1,096	62.8	17.2	D	D	D	D	59	262	29.1	9.4
El Cajon	229	3,532	200.7	52.3	15.0	333	16.5	4.8	287	6,238	521.3	231.4
El Centro	123	2,311	138.8	40.5	11.0	104	3.9	1.1	153	2,915	304.5	117.0
El Cerrito	58	694	56.2	14.3	9.0	38	3.0	0.9	83	597	72.1	24.3
Elk Grove	276	5,122	309.6	86.1	27.0	546	31.6	8.3	384	4,044	593.3	190.4
El Monte	204	2,109	153.1	34.8	9.0	D	6.9	D	216	3,203	265.0	107.4
El Paso de Robles (Paso Robles)	133	2,514	174.3	50.1	14.0	325	15.8	4.9	88	1,154	71.8	31.0
Encinitas	230	4,455	284.8	89.8	70.0	853	65.5	21.4	438	5,156	758.3	267.4
Escondido	276	4,875	316.6	91.2	34.0	708	36.9	12.6	426	8,246	1,248.5	441.4
Eureka	147	2,034	123.7	35.7	17.0	150	7.6	2.3	153	3,477	527.9	193.5
Fairfield	210	3,507	221.3	63.8	22.0	580	22.0	7.9	283	7,141	1,195.3	414.0
Folsom	231	4,867	279.4	84.0	36.0	605	32.4	10.3	292	4,017	827.2	264.2
Fontana	270	4,779	309.8	80.2	18.0	370	27.4	6.2	207	8,480	1,981.1	689.1
Foster City	72	1,394	115.2	32.6	5.0	232	8.8	3.8	101	1,249	170.1	68.8
Fountain Valley	193	3,109	194.6	55.2	D	D	D	9.0	430	7,277	1,113.4	380.1
Fremont	464	7,787	620.2	165.3	52.0	966	60.2	19.6	732	12,827	2,152.1	874.2
Fresno	1,018	20,209	1,208.6	342.6	123.0	3,647	171.4	58.8	1,734	35,901	5,347.5	2,130.6
Fullerton	365	7,803	416.1	142.1	40.0	762	46.3	16.3	449	8,509	1,320.4	582.1
Galt	D	D	D	D	5.0	39	2.9	0.8	30	249	23.3	9.0
Gardena	235	3,065	223.2	57.7	13.0	1,260	90.9	38.7	144	2,797	314.4	117.5
Garden Grove	484	8,175	673.6	158.9	D	D	D	D	509	6,152	746.0	242.4
Gilroy	155	2,711	189.1	52.1	D	D	D	D	D	D	D	D
Glendale	489	8,105	640.4	171.2	236.0	1,382	189.8	59.8	1,167	16,964	2,012.7	748.6
Glendora	118	1,711	105.1	30.2	D	D	D	D	223	3,712	422.2	162.4
Goleta	107	2,812	316.7	72.8	14.0	372	16.7	5.6	132	1,728	273.9	87.1
Hanford	D	D	D	28.9	D	D	D	D	165	4,184	575.8	198.5
Hawthorne	129	1,955	147.5	34.6	D	D	D	D	172	2,666	305.4	135.1
Hayward	326	4,417	317.2	85.4	25.0	D	36.8	D	331	7,052	753.5	292.2
Hemet	149	2,374	144.8	41.1	D	D	D	D	222	4,585	547.5	195.0
Hercules	33	358	24.6	6.3	NA	NA	NA	NA	45	274	41.1	13.9
Hesperia	121	2,192	124.1	31.5	12.0	77	4.0	1.1	104	1,050	91.3	36.5
Highland	60	1,038	65.0	17.9	D	D	D	D	58	1,684	108.0	36.5
Hollister	63	946	58.1	16.5	11.0	141	6.8	1.7	77	1,168	168.1	73.2
Huntington Beach	546	12,331	814.5	237.1	113.0	1,459	119.0	28.9	751	6,662	832.1	309.9
Huntington Park	128	1,772	117.4	30.6	3.0	69	6.8	1.7	124	1,823	235.3	69.9
Imperial Beach	45	431	29.4	7.8	4.0	9	0.5	0.1	25	436	37.2	16.0
Indio	140	3,549	319.5	86.8	14.0	532	206.6	16.0	131	2,200	245.2	93.1
Inglewood	186	2,872	219.7	55.6	27.0	1,699	209.1	38.2	264	5,128	684.8	221.7
Irvine	736	16,000	1,176.5	334.4	154.0	2,714	259.4	72.6	1,294	15,404	2,105.6	771.9
Jurupa Valley	91	1,379	86.4	22.3	D	D	D	D	78	1,253	89.3	37.2
Lafayette	67	1,643	115.4	39.2	27.0	336	40.0	9.1	139	1,546	230.2	120.8
Laguna Hills	90	1,956	130.0	37.6	D	D	D	D	374	5,753	825.4	286.3
Laguna Niguel	122	1,796	121.3	33.9	D	D	D	D	241	1,891	195.3	75.5
La Habra	145	2,128	138.9	38.3	D	D	D	D	130	1,265	118.8	49.2
Lake Elsinore	108	1,654	103.3	28.9	16.0	509	30.0	10.0	80	519	57.4	22.0
Lake Forest	230	3,814	263.7	68.4	43.0	452	27.3	7.0	252	2,526	260.7	91.9
Lakewood	D	D	D	D	14.0	283	24.9	5.4	203	2,719	398.7	142.1
La Mesa	176	3,565	202.7	67.1	21.0	546	22.3	9.5	351	8,597	1,447.4	537.8
La Mirada	107	1,407	112.9	24.6	14.0	224	17.0	4.9	108	1,430	134.3	53.9
Lancaster	239	3,950	250.1	64.4	19.0	274	26.2	6.5	423	10,408	1,469.7	537.1
La Puente	90	1,106	74.5	18.7	4.0	15	1.6	0.2	63	472	39.9	14.4
La Quinta	D	D	D	D	23.0	1,049	86.8	32.8	104	841	76.7	33.1
Lathrop	34	469	32.3	7.8	NA	NA	NA	NA	21	99	8.9	2.9
La Verne	74	1,443	86.6	25.1	D	D	D	D	79	927	82.3	32.6
Lawndale	52	700	51.0	13.5	7.0	14	7.1	1.0	79	459	47.4	16.2
Lemon Grove	55	907	57.4	15.0	3.0	18	1.2	0.4	50	969	76.6	30.7

1. Establishments subject to federal tax.

City	Other services[1]				Government employment and payroll, 2017								
						March payroll							
							Perent of total for:						
	Number of establish-ments	Number of employees	Receipts (mil dol)	Annual payroll (mil dol)	Full-time equivalent employees	Total (dollars)	Admin-istrative, judicial, and legal	Police and corrections	Fire protection	Highways and trans-portation	Health and welfare	Natural resources and utilities	Education and libraries
	104	105	106	107	108	109	110	111	112	113	114	115	116
CALIFORNIA—Cont'd													
Cupertino	79	470	79.0	14.7	164	1,353,372	34.4	0.0	0.0	21.5	0.0	26.3	0.0
Cypress	86	733	96.1	38.4	165	1,155,562	23.2	47.9	0.0	2.6	1.0	12.6	0.0
Daly City	98	442	44.6	12.3	539	4,366,533	8.6	29.3	24.4	3.1	2.8	20.4	2.4
Dana Point	76	378	42.3	10.6	72	562,904	20.2	0.0	0.0	25.2	33.7	14.3	0.0
Danville town	77	374	38.8	10.3	117	658,459	35.3	4.1	0.0	26.7	0.0	26.5	0.0
Davis	97	532	57.8	16.2	303	2,032,567	11.2	34.4	18.5	6.2	0.0	29.8	0.0
Delano	20	69	6.9	1.5	282	1,386,031	7.7	60.6	0.0	4.4	2.3	21.2	0.0
Desert Hot Springs	13	52	4.7	1.4	70	371,024	28.6	58.7	0.0	0.0	12.7	0.0	0.0
Diamond Bar	81	369	76.0	17.5	77	445,656	41.9	0.0	0.0	14.0	13.8	30.3	0.0
Downey	162	895	89.2	24.4	545	3,855,947	8.6	41.9	25.6	4.8	1.5	12.6	2.5
Dublin	107	671	92.7	26.7	114	848,938	28.9	3.1	0.6	8.7	16.8	40.9	0.0
East Palo Alto	17	98	12.9	4.3	100	889,558	28.0	52.0	0.0	6.1	3.3	5.2	0.0
Eastvale	D	D	D	D	16	69,663	100.0	0.0	0.0	0.0	0.0	0.0	0.0
El Cajon	213	1,678	200.2	57.0	404	2,768,459	10.9	47.1	17.9	5.9	2.1	12.1	0.0
El Centro	72	324	37.9	9.8	1,192	5,563,406	3.0	7.7	4.3	1.4	75.7	5.3	0.6
El Cerrito	36	248	24.1	6.9	181	1,559,103	8.8	30.6	33.0	6.2	5.9	15.5	0.0
Elk Grove	180	1,265	166.0	41.0	326	2,978,726	22.2	73.7	0.0	2.6	0.0	1.0	0.0
El Monte	129	497	61.4	13.3	348	2,600,084	8.9	60.6	0.0	18.7	5.2	6.6	0.0
El Paso de Robles (Paso Robles)	62	300	32.4	9.2	184	1,253,520	11.0	27.5	15.4	4.3	3.4	23.8	3.7
Encinitas	183	1,141	117.6	39.4	196	1,339,981	35.6	0.0	3.7	7.1	21.5	25.4	0.0
Escondido	279	1,541	179.8	50.9	875	5,261,351	15.1	30.9	15.9	6.8	0.7	24.6	2.7
Eureka	90	552	60.6	18.1	311	1,656,604	9.1	31.6	18.9	8.5	4.5	19.6	0.0
Fairfield	150	1,131	282.7	52.5	599	3,818,932	10.2	37.1	15.8	12.4	2.9	11.2	0.0
Folsom	129	974	74.9	24.5	456	3,094,854	10.4	26.3	21.1	6.2	5.5	26.9	1.6
Fontana	212	1,257	151.3	34.3	772	5,316,586	10.6	51.7	0.0	7.4	6.0	21.1	0.0
Foster City	31	148	14.7	5.4	207	1,825,425	19.7	32.2	19.4	5.7	0.0	22.9	0.0
Fountain Valley	102	739	65.2	23.7	227	1,874,378	11.0	39.3	27.2	8.0	0.0	11.7	0.0
Fremont	350	2,386	406.3	87.0	957	9,501,136	16.3	31.8	22.4	8.3	8.5	8.5	0.0
Fresno	661	6,346	745.7	208.6	3,451	20,907,203	6.8	36.3	15.6	19.6	0.0	16.7	0.0
Fullerton	238	2,771	268.7	79.1	694	4,622,092	7.9	39.7	19.5	7.1	4.2	10.1	3.5
Galt	D	D	D	D	186	1,023,415	19.5	33.6	0.0	4.0	0.0	31.3	0.0
Gardena	117	625	74.8	20.1	454	2,464,867	7.9	42.6	0.0	28.2	6.3	8.7	0.0
Garden Grove	271	1,572	124.4	37.6	691	5,437,306	10.6	42.6	15.3	7.1	4.6	17.8	0.0
Gilroy	111	890	109.1	30.1	300	2,453,398	12.5	37.2	18.1	7.2	2.7	17.5	0.0
Glendale	410	1,865	231.7	60.3	1,735	12,571,242	12.4	21.4	18.8	6.5	3.9	26.6	2.9
Glendora	92	554	140.9	30.7	348	1,891,522	10.6	43.7	0.0	11.9	6.9	19.8	7.2
Goleta	D	D	D	64.9	62	536,263	73.6	0.0	0.0	14.1	0.0	12.3	0.0
Hanford	69	311	33.2	8.1	281	1,593,527	8.0	32.3	15.1	8.8	0.7	23.6	0.0
Hawthorne	119	683	67.8	18.2	299	2,186,109	15.5	56.8	0.0	7.3	6.5	8.6	0.0
Hayward	259	2,031	296.4	73.7	818	8,184,527	10.0	41.9	21.2	2.7	1.4	10.8	2.8
Hemet	95	461	42.8	11.5	427	3,039,134	11.5	33.8	20.3	7.4	2.2	11.7	3.6
Hercules	D	D	D	D	142	795,040	19.6	36.4	0.0	9.2	0.8	24.9	0.0
Hesperia	101	601	73.0	20.1	120	670,338	31.5	0.0	0.0	15.9	14.5	0.0	0.0
Highland	35	155	16.0	3.9	41	318,191	66.6	0.0	0.0	21.6	0.6	1.5	0.0
Hollister	D	D	D	8.1	168	1,323,462	9.0	22.7	31.6	10.8	0.7	10.9	0.0
Huntington Beach	411	2,525	251.5	75.3	1,039	8,450,607	10.6	36.4	21.4	3.7	1.8	15.1	2.7
Huntington Park	D	D	D	D	164	1,072,674	15.5	61.0	0.0	5.9	7.4	4.5	0.0
Imperial Beach	32	138	10.5	2.8	96	610,849	21.7	0.0	23.5	5.7	24.4	16.3	0.0
Indio	85	664	62.0	18.5	242	1,977,846	5.8	55.4	0.0	8.3	5.9	19.1	0.0
Inglewood	142	1,308	153.3	41.7	533	2,366,678	24.9	19.9	0.0	3.7	11.2	17.9	4.5
Irvine	410	3,869	609.8	145.6	1,045	10,354,501	15.2	43.5	0.0	10.4	5.8	18.3	0.0
Jurupa Valley	D	D	61.7	D	12	81,726	90.6	0.0	0.0	9.4	0.0	0.0	0.0
Lafayette	76	467	46.0	13.5	55	336,040	14.8	10.7	0.0	21.6	22.8	17.6	3.4
Laguna Hills	86	458	61.0	14.8	43	291,744	40.0	0.0	0.0	14.4	18.8	26.2	0.0
Laguna Niguel	109	482	48.6	14.3	88	587,478	23.1	2.6	0.0	13.7	17.8	40.1	0.0
La Habra	112	559	55.8	16.3	333	1,951,632	11.4	46.4	0.0	0.0	0.0	0.0	0.0
Lake Elsinore	72	330	40.2	11.7	87	501,292	31.3	0.0	0.0	27.7	4.7	19.5	0.0
Lake Forest	140	881	91.0	27.4	84	557,618	58.8	1.2	0.0	5.1	13.9	20.9	0.0
Lakewood	82	607	78.7	18.4	266	1,877,960	24.0	6.4	0.0	14.6	2.1	42.8	0.0
La Mesa	130	814	75.9	23.4	254	1,896,004	11.5	43.4	25.0	3.7	1.0	9.9	0.0
La Mirada	48	166	13.3	3.5	153	780,641	15.8	8.6	0.0	21.2	0.0	50.2	0.0
Lancaster	170	840	92.0	26.4	392	2,055,333	23.1	3.9	0.0	25.0	8.5	35.4	0.0
La Puente	44	188	14.5	4.1	42	185,307	35.3	0.0	0.0	2.3	21.6	32.2	0.0
La Quinta	50	299	44.6	8.0	91	505,915	26.4	0.0	0.0	19.0	0.0	11.6	0.0
Lathrop	D	D	D	D	72	497,755	33.2	4.0	0.0	7.4	9.2	22.2	0.0
La Verne	D	D	D	D	182	1,379,456	14.7	37.1	26.8	3.4	0.0	13.2	0.0
Lawndale	D	D	D	D	70	429,954	31.3	0.0	0.0	28.0	5.8	17.5	0.0
Lemon Grove	55	174	15.2	4.3	52	391,345	15.0	0.0	50.2	14.0	7.5	5.9	0.0

1. Establishments subject to federal tax.

City	City government finances, 2017									
	General revenue							General expenditure		
		Intergovernmental		Taxes						
					Per capita[1] (dollars)				Per capita[1] (dollars)	
	Total (mil dol)	Total (mil dol)	Percent from state government	Total (mil dol)	Total	Property	Sales and gross receipts	Total (mil dol)	Total	Capital outlays
	117	118	119	120	121	122	123	124	125	126
CALIFORNIA—Cont'd										
Cupertino	107.6	2.6	70.2	65.5	1,080	344	705	87.7	1,448	86
Cypress	45.6	3.9	42.7	32.2	659	280	362	47.0	962	245
Daly City	115.4	7.9	55.4	66.5	623	315	305	116.1	1,088	126
Dana Point	40.3	1.8	97.3	35.2	1,044	341	655	55.3	1,636	132
Danville town	37.0	2.0	100.0	25.2	564	298	251	40.1	897	248
Davis	118.3	15.5	24.7	57.2	832	318	297	102.4	1,488	159
Delano	62.7	7.4	53.0	23.6	446	184	259	42.6	805	70
Desert Hot Springs	27.6	1.9	99.5	17.3	603	277	307	29.4	1,026	233
Diamond Bar	30.6	3.0	64.6	21.5	381	190	182	44.7	794	349
Downey	111.2	19.1	37.6	63.9	568	235	331	107.6	957	62
Dublin	120.9	3.3	82.5	99.2	1,632	608	695	86.1	1,416	109
East Palo Alto	39.8	5.0	39.0	23.9	805	387	378	29.1	981	159
Eastvale	26.7	2.0	77.1	22.3	358	130	221	31.5	505	4
El Cajon	105.2	6.5	47.2	68.4	661	215	443	110.7	1,070	173
El Centro	191.6	8.4	11.5	26.3	596	236	351	215.7	4,890	918
El Cerrito	52.3	11.5	15.3	21.3	836	436	393	49.4	1,938	343
Elk Grove	226.4	24.4	53.8	69.4	405	146	254	112.2	654	122
El Monte	98.8	9.8	38.9	76.4	662	301	346	101.6	880	144
El Paso de Robles (Paso Robles)	65.9	3.1	51.7	39.3	1,238	450	781	53.3	1,677	326
Encinitas	88.6	5.2	31.5	61.8	982	695	279	126.4	2,010	420
Escondido	175.6	12.6	60.9	89.9	595	263	320	180.6	1,195	122
Eureka	75.2	30.1	12.4	26.2	965	158	803	58.5	2,158	302
Fairfield	170.2	42.3	10.2	105.8	913	367	541	135.2	1,167	236
Folsom	133.3	13.5	49.9	71.0	913	413	406	117.5	1,510	228
Fontana	297.6	16.5	39.6	168.6	799	514	268	224.3	1,063	269
Foster City	83.7	1.2	100.0	41.1	1,198	794	363	46.9	1,366	53
Fountain Valley	60.2	5.5	35.7	40.1	715	330	371	69.1	1,233	219
Fremont	311.6	20.1	58.8	244.3	1,042	381	652	283.4	1,208	128
Fresno	767.4	154.7	39.0	322.1	613	244	366	440.5	838	4
Fullerton	171.6	30.6	86.1	88.9	636	367	241	170.1	1,217	287
Galt	34.2	1.5	70.7	13.3	509	216	235	30.6	1,170	97
Gardena	106.7	46.4	11.0	47.9	800	213	433	81.6	1,363	161
Garden Grove	219.2	9.9	56.9	120.8	697	362	313	248.1	1,431	418
Gilroy	82.8	3.1	67.7	41.8	727	250	468	90.6	1,575	375
Glendale	379.8	20.7	57.5	182.9	906	378	523	322.1	1,596	90
Glendora	42.2	4.8	51.6	29.4	566	211	286	35.6	684	66
Goleta	44.5	2.4	47.4	25.3	812	196	611	41.2	1,326	419
Hanford	52.2	3.7	56.8	28.6	507	177	237	58.1	1,031	125
Hawthorne	99.1	7.4	54.1	65.9	755	232	519	106.4	1,219	103
Hayward	250.4	23.7	56.5	165.7	1,034	356	606	226.4	1,412	262
Hemet	55.4	4.7	66.2	37.3	440	168	268	64.6	762	134
Hercules	51.3	14.5	53.3	23.2	911	608	298	30.5	1,197	269
Hesperia	66.9	5.5	46.8	48.4	512	278	232	97.6	1,033	326
Highland	28.0	3.8	51.8	21.1	383	210	94	47.5	861	214
Hollister	56.8	7.1	19.6	20.7	539	112	326	38.8	1,010	13
Huntington Beach	276.3	14.8	68.9	178.5	888	418	464	265.2	1,320	135
Huntington Park	62.4	8.7	52.6	37.0	633	311	310	54.1	925	74
Imperial Beach	26.3	2.6	93.2	11.7	428	204	204	26.8	982	88
Indio	96.2	10.1	49.7	59.5	666	255	406	105.8	1,183	132
Inglewood	191.4	30.2	9.2	120.3	1,095	441	571	240.1	2,184	279
Irvine	307.9	12.6	60.1	214.3	777	225	343	305.3	1,106	84
Jurupa Valley	39.5	2.6	94.6	26.4	250	58	157	35.2	333	0
Lafayette	25.6	3.1	23.2	15.4	585	308	243	29.4	1,113	225
Laguna Hills	24.2	1.8	61.8	20.1	634	309	314	30.9	978	258
Laguna Niguel	46.6	2.5	69.8	38.3	581	314	258	58.8	890	195
La Habra	70.0	12.2	59.7	37.1	610	261	345	89.7	1,472	318
Lake Elsinore	71.6	6.0	94.4	30.1	455	116	278	72.6	1,099	172
Lake Forest	90.9	4.9	40.8	45.4	541	204	328	95.5	1,139	355
Lakewood	60.0	7.4	86.5	39.8	495	185	305	57.4	712	89
La Mesa	64.2	4.4	76.6	42.1	705	240	461	72.1	1,207	186
La Mirada	54.3	6.4	17.5	36.2	742	225	512	57.1	1,169	438
Lancaster	116.7	9.7	57.7	85.9	539	237	240	149.5	937	185
La Puente	18.8	1.7	78.1	12.8	319	149	168	18.2	455	83
La Quinta	79.8	6.9	22.5	54.9	1,332	790	528	64.0	1,555	228
Lathrop	64.8	1.7	37.1	24.1	1,085	246	280	35.4	1,594	191
La Verne	41.5	1.9	86.0	22.6	700	315	381	41.8	1,295	58
Lawndale	18.7	3.5	23.9	13.6	413	139	252	29.3	892	217
Lemon Grove	24.9	3.4	96.0	13.4	498	177	317	34.3	1,272	196

1. Based on population estimated as of July 1 of the year shown.

City	City government finances, 2017 (cont.)												
	General expenditure (cont.)												
	Percent of total for:									Debt outstanding			
	Public welfare	Highways	Parking facilities	Education	Health and hospitals	Police protection	Sewerage and sanitation	Parks and recreation	Housing and community development	Interest on debt	Total (mil dol)	Per capita[1] (dollars)	Debt issued during year
	127	128	129	130	131	132	133	134	135	136	137	138	139
CALIFORNIA—Cont'd													
Cupertino	0.0	8.7	0.0	0.0	0.0	26.3	3.4	17.0	8.9	1.2	33.7	556	0.0
Cypress	0.0	22.2	0.0	0.0	1.2	33.2	3.1	14.1	8.2	0.1	1.8	37	0.0
Daly City	0.0	9.3	0.0	0.0	0.0	28.3	15.2	7.9	5.8	0.5	29.2	273	0.0
Dana Point	0.0	16.2	0.0	0.0	0.6	44.0	0.0	13.7	0.0	1.4	18.8	558	0.0
Danville town	0.0	18.2	0.0	0.0	1.8	19.2	0.0	21.5	0.0	1.5	10.4	232	0.0
Davis	0.0	8.1	0.0	0.0	0.0	18.8	21.6	18.7	1.8	0.9	154.1	2,239	32.1
Delano	0.0	7.5	0.0	0.0	0.0	24.8	11.0	5.0	2.3	4.1	65.2	1,233	1.3
Desert Hot Springs	0.0	18.2	0.0	0.0	1.3	21.9	0.0	3.3	10.6	15.3	75.9	2,650	35.4
Diamond Bar	0.0	14.6	0.0	0.0	0.5	14.2	1.3	13.8	1.1	1.0	9.6	171	0.0
Downey	0.0	4.2	0.0	0.0	4.8	33.4	2.9	13.2	5.2	1.1	28.4	253	0.7
Dublin	0.0	8.8	0.0	0.0	0.7	20.1	4.5	14.7	2.4	0.2	10.4	171	5.5
East Palo Alto	0.0	15.9	0.0	0.0	0.0	34.0	8.6	4.3	7.2	0.0	27.1	914	0.1
Eastvale	0.0	3.7	0.0	0.0	1.2	50.4	0.0	0.0	0.0	0.0	0.0	0	0.0
El Cajon	0.0	7.0	0.0	0.0	2.8	31.1	16.8	4.8	10.0	2.9	61.5	594	0.0
El Centro	0.0	3.2	0.0	0.0	75.2	5.1	3.9	2.4	1.3	2.3	157.7	3,576	0.0
El Cerrito	0.0	11.2	0.0	0.0	0.0	21.8	5.7	10.5	6.8	3.8	36.9	1,450	0.0
Elk Grove	0.0	17.2	0.0	0.0	0.0	31.8	14.5	0.6	5.0	0.7	14.4	84	4.9
El Monte	0.0	6.9	0.1	0.0	0.4	25.0	1.7	7.4	11.4	3.4	72.6	629	32.0
El Paso de Robles (Paso Robles)	0.0	13.9	0.0	0.0	0.0	19.8	11.1	9.4	0.7	6.0	87.9	2,767	0.0
Encinitas	0.0	7.4	0.0	0.0	1.4	20.7	8.2	8.7	1.6	2.7	60.8	967	0.0
Escondido	0.0	6.3	0.1	0.0	0.8	23.1	23.6	5.0	0.9	3.5	242.8	1,606	3.2
Eureka	0.0	6.4	0.2	0.0	0.1	21.4	18.5	5.5	11.8	5.4	60.6	2,234	0.0
Fairfield	0.0	25.5	0.0	0.0	0.2	27.4	0.1	10.7	11.6	1.6	162.8	1,406	40.3
Folsom	0.0	7.1	0.0	0.0	0.9	19.2	10.4	11.4	5.8	4.2	219.5	2,821	0.0
Fontana	0.0	13.0	0.0	0.0	0.0	26.6	7.9	6.8	13.0	7.3	390.2	1,848	0.0
Foster City	0.0	3.9	0.0	0.0	0.0	24.3	15.9	17.2	1.2	0.0	0.0	0	0.0
Fountain Valley	0.0	17.8	0.0	0.0	5.3	23.9	7.7	6.2	8.3	1.5	44.7	797	2.8
Fremont	0.1	14.7	0.0	0.0	6.2	25.6	12.5	5.4	1.7	2.1	204.3	871	85.2
Fresno	0.0	9.2	0.9	0.0	1.5	31.3	14.3	5.5	1.8	10.7	1,206.3	2,296	272.4
Fullerton	0.0	28.7	0.0	0.0	0.8	26.7	7.8	5.4	1.0	4.9	106.7	763	2.5
Galt	0.0	7.5	0.0	0.0	0.0	25.2	26.3	9.5	0.0	4.1	41.7	1,594	6.2
Gardena	0.0	11.0	0.0	0.0	1.0	39.1	2.3	10.4	3.0	1.6	21.9	365	1.6
Garden Grove	0.0	5.9	0.0	0.0	2.2	22.2	2.5	2.3	43.4	3.3	127.7	736	16.0
Gilroy	0.0	3.9	0.0	0.0	0.1	23.4	10.7	1.8	25.0	4.4	84.8	1,474	0.0
Glendale	0.0	3.5	2.3	0.0	1.8	23.9	14.6	5.2	10.9	1.9	382.6	1,896	0.0
Glendora	0.0	9.6	0.0	0.0	0.4	44.6	0.0	10.3	9.3	1.5	34.3	660	0.0
Goleta	0.0	32.2	0.0	0.0	0.9	18.7	0.0	7.5	9.8	2.8	14.9	479	0.0
Hanford	0.0	11.0	0.0	0.0	1.5	20.3	26.9	6.5	1.7	1.4	41.6	737	0.0
Hawthorne	0.0	12.8	0.0	0.0	0.0	33.4	0.8	3.4	12.7	3.4	70.2	804	0.0
Hayward	0.0	19.0	0.0	0.1	0.9	30.5	10.1	0.5	0.7	2.6	211.4	1,318	0.9
Hemet	0.0	15.4	0.0	0.0	0.5	33.1	5.7	2.4	10.2	0.7	10.1	119	0.0
Hercules	0.0	11.4	0.0	0.0	0.0	19.7	10.4	6.2	10.6	13.0	153.0	6,000	6.8
Hesperia	0.0	21.6	0.0	0.0	1.5	15.9	0.0	0.0	21.9	10.4	185.2	1,961	0.0
Highland	0.0	26.0	0.0	0.0	6.8	36.4	0.0	2.3	7.1	0.0	11.2	204	0.0
Hollister	0.0	6.0	0.0	0.0	1.4	17.1	17.9	2.6	0.0	8.6	69.0	1,797	1.5
Huntington Beach	0.0	11.0	0.8	0.0	2.3	31.7	7.5	7.0	3.2	2.2	142.1	707	5.8
Huntington Park	0.0	7.2	1.5	0.0	1.3	32.4	0.5	3.4	4.5	33.0	259.7	4,441	13.7
Imperial Beach	0.0	8.0	0.0	0.0	1.1	32.3	15.4	2.1	5.4	5.7	37.8	1,385	0.0
Indio	0.0	9.0	0.0	0.0	4.0	23.1	0.0	4.8	12.8	5.3	181.1	2,025	16.3
Inglewood	0.0	6.2	2.6	0.0	0.6	25.7	7.7	6.9	16.9	4.4	236.9	2,155	0.0
Irvine	0.0	16.5	0.0	0.2	1.9	23.9	0.0	20.8	2.7	12.5	1,066.9	3,866	166.0
Jurupa Valley	0.0	9.1	0.0	0.0	2.4	49.2	0.0	0.1	1.1	0.3	7.9	75	8.2
Lafayette	0.0	25.1	1.1	0.0	0.5	33.2	0.0	10.9	2.6	0.7	4.8	183	2.1
Laguna Hills	0.0	20.6	0.0	0.0	0.8	25.2	0.0	25.9	0.2	1.5	8.7	276	0.0
Laguna Niguel	0.0	20.3	0.0	0.0	1.2	40.5	0.0	15.2	0.1	0.0	0.3	4	0.0
La Habra	0.0	21.3	0.0	0.0	1.9	20.6	7.7	10.6	6.1	1.7	112.3	1,845	1.2
Lake Elsinore	0.0	1.5	0.0	0.0	1.1	16.1	0.0	22.1	11.9	15.6	246.2	3,727	0.0
Lake Forest	0.0	31.5	0.0	0.0	1.2	16.7	0.0	15.6	1.0	0.6	14.4	171	0.0
Lakewood	0.0	17.7	0.0	0.0	0.7	21.4	8.8	23.0	4.5	0.2	2.0	25	0.0
La Mesa	0.0	17.1	0.3	0.0	0.8	25.0	21.1	5.5	0.7	1.7	43.6	730	1.9
La Mirada	0.0	43.0	0.0	0.0	0.0	14.8	0.0	22.7	3.7	5.2	70.8	1,450	1.0
Lancaster	0.0	23.2	0.0	0.0	0.4	19.9	0.0	8.1	10.0	5.9	233.7	1,466	80.5
La Puente	0.0	15.6	0.0	0.0	0.0	33.5	2.9	17.7	2.9	4.0	33.7	842	11.7
La Quinta	0.0	12.4	0.0	0.0	2.3	23.1	0.0	10.8	8.9	14.6	211.7	5,140	37.8
Lathrop	0.0	29.9	0.0	0.0	0.7	13.0	16.3	3.5	1.7	5.3	60.5	2,722	22.9
La Verne	0.0	6.2	0.0	0.0	8.0	31.9	8.4	9.0	3.5	2.0	10.6	327	0.0
Lawndale	0.0	9.8	0.0	0.0	0.2	37.4	0.0	9.2	20.0	3.6	19.6	597	0.0
Lemon Grove	0.0	7.0	0.0	0.0	0.6	31.7	13.1	0.0	9.4	3.3	27.7	1,028	0.0

1. Based on population estimated as of July 1 of the year shown.

STATE Place code	City	Land area[1] (sq. mi)	Population, 2021: Total persons 2021	Population, 2021: Rank	Population, 2021: Per square mile	Race 2020: Race alone[2] (percent): White	Race 2020: Race alone[2] (percent): Black or African American	Race 2020: Race alone[2] (percent): American Indian, Alaskan Native	Race 2020: Race alone[2] (percent): Asian	Race 2020: Race alone[2] (percent): Hawaiian Pacific Islander	Race 2020: Race alone[2] (percent): Some other race	Race 2020: Two or more races (percent)
		1	2	3	4	5	6	7	8	9	10	11
	CALIFORNIA—Cont'd											
06 41,152	Lemoore	8.8	27,259	1,427	3,097.6	41.5	6.2	2.1	8.7	0.4	24.0	17.2
06 41,474	Lincoln	24.2	50,649	787	2,092.9	70.3	1.8	0.8	6.3	0.3	7.6	12.9
06 41,992	Livermore	26.4	86,803	399	3,288.0	59.7	2.0	0.8	14.6	0.3	8.6	14.1
06 42,202	Lodi	13.6	67,021	562	4,928.0	51.8	1.3	1.2	9.6	0.2	22.1	13.7
06 42,524	Lompoc	11.6	43,834	908	3,778.8	42.4	4.5	2.6	4.0	0.3	25.4	20.9
06 43,000	Long Beach	50.7	456,062	43	8,995.3	32.0	12.5	1.5	13.0	0.9	25.6	14.4
06 43,280	Los Altos	6.5	30,700	1,285	4,723.1	53.6	0.6	0.1	35.3	0.1	1.4	8.7
06 44,000	Los Angeles	469.5	3,849,297	2	8,198.7	34.9	8.6	1.7	11.9	0.2	29.5	13.3
06 44,028	Los Banos	10.0	46,398	859	4,639.8	31.2	2.5	2.8	3.3	0.7	40.1	19.4
06 44,112	Los Gatos	11.6	32,538	1,213	2,805.0	67.3	0.9	0.3	18.4	0.1	2.6	10.4
06 44,574	Lynwood	4.8	65,505	581	13,646.9	13.3	8.2	3.0	0.7	0.3	56.4	18.0
06 45,022	Madera	16.5	67,944	556	4,117.8	25.8	2.6	6.9	2.8	0.1	43.3	18.6
06 45,400	Manhattan Beach	3.9	34,668	1,147	8,889.2	73.6	0.9	0.2	11.4	0.1	2.0	11.8
06 45,484	Manteca	21.4	85,792	407	4,009.0	42.4	4.5	1.8	14.4	0.8	20.5	15.6
06 46,114	Martinez	12.6	36,819	1,077	2,922.1	64.9	3.7	0.7	10.3	0.3	5.5	14.6
06 46,492	Maywood	1.2	24,562	1,552	20,468.3	13.1	0.6	2.8	0.4	0.0	61.3	21.8
06 46,842	Menifee	46.5	106,401	296	2,288.2	52.2	6.8	1.3	6.5	0.5	16.5	16.4
06 46,870	Menlo Park	10.0	32,475	1,216	3,247.5	57.3	3.1	0.7	17.2	1.1	9.4	11.2
06 46,898	Merced	23.3	89,308	384	3,833.0	35.8	5.4	2.5	11.1	0.3	27.1	17.8
06 47,766	Milpitas	13.5	79,066	457	5,856.7	11.3	2.1	0.6	71.7	0.4	7.5	6.3
06 48,256	Mission Viejo	17.7	92,449	367	5,223.1	65.7	1.3	0.5	11.8	0.2	6.6	13.8
06 48,354	Modesto	43.0	218,771	104	5,087.7	46.6	4.1	1.9	8.1	1.1	23.1	15.1
06 48,648	Monrovia	13.6	37,500	1,059	2,757.4	41.3	5.6	1.2	16.7	0.1	18.5	16.5
06 48,788	Montclair	5.5	38,061	1,047	6,920.2	20.4	4.4	2.5	11.5	0.2	42.6	18.4
06 48,816	Montebello	8.3	61,204	629	7,374.0	21.3	1.0	2.2	12.8	0.1	41.9	20.6
06 48,872	Monterey	8.6	29,874	1,315	3,473.7	67.4	3.2	1.0	7.9	0.7	7.3	12.4
06 48,914	Monterey Park	7.7	59,667	650	7,749.0	8.4	0.7	0.9	66.7	0.1	13.5	9.8
06 49,138	Moorpark	12.3	35,975	1,100	2,924.8	57.8	1.7	1.0	8.9	0.1	14.4	16.0
06 49,270	Moreno Valley	51.3	211,600	108	4,124.8	22.5	15.9	1.9	6.0	0.6	35.8	17.4
06 49,278	Morgan Hill	12.9	45,342	875	3,514.9	49.7	2.2	1.4	14.8	0.4	16.0	15.5
06 49,670	Mountain View	12.0	81,516	431	6,793.0	42.4	1.5	0.8	35.1	0.3	8.6	11.4
06 50,076	Murrieta	33.6	112,991	265	3,362.8	53.3	6.0	1.1	10.4	0.5	11.4	17.3
06 50,258	Napa	18.0	78,818	460	4,378.8	58.3	0.8	1.6	2.6	0.2	20.4	16.1
06 50,398	National City	7.3	55,912	700	7,659.2	19.8	4.0	1.7	19.7	0.6	32.2	22.0
06 50,916	Newark	13.9	47,434	843	3,412.5	22.6	3.3	1.2	41.7	1.5	17.5	12.2
06 51,182	Newport Beach	23.8	84,792	415	3,562.7	78.2	0.8	0.3	8.8	0.1	2.7	9.1
06 51,560	Norco	13.9	26,077	1,487	1,876.0	55.9	6.1	1.2	3.4	0.2	20.1	13.1
06 52,526	Norwalk	9.7	100,373	328	10,347.7	20.1	4.1	2.4	13.7	0.4	38.3	21.1
06 52,582	Novato	27.5	52,708	757	1,916.7	61.1	2.7	1.8	7.5	0.2	13.3	13.4
06 53,000	Oakland	55.9	433,823	45	7,760.7	30.0	21.3	1.9	16.1	0.7	18.3	11.8
06 53,070	Oakley	15.9	43,771	910	2,752.9	45.9	8.4	1.0	9.5	0.7	16.9	17.6
06 53,322	Oceanside	41.3	172,982	152	4,188.4	51.5	4.1	1.4	7.6	1.2	18.0	16.2
06 53,896	Ontario	50.0	177,963	146	3,559.3	24.2	6.3	2.4	9.3	0.3	38.0	19.5
06 53,980	Orange	25.7	137,264	202	5,341.0	46.5	1.7	1.3	13.1	0.3	20.7	16.3
06 54,652	Oxnard	26.5	201,879	119	7,618.1	24.8	2.4	3.3	7.7	0.3	39.6	22.0
06 54,806	Pacifica	12.6	37,099	1,072	2,944.4	53.0	1.9	0.8	21.7	0.7	6.3	15.6
06 55,156	Palmdale	106.1	165,761	159	1,562.3	26.6	13.6	2.1	4.4	0.2	35.8	17.3
06 55,184	Palm Desert	26.8	51,541	774	1,923.2	68.7	2.0	0.8	4.8	0.1	12.0	11.5
06 55,254	Palm Springs	94.5	45,019	880	476.4	66.7	4.4	1.2	4.7	0.2	12.9	10.1
06 55,282	Palo Alto	24.1	66,680	569	2,766.8	49.9	1.8	0.2	35.5	0.2	3.0	9.5
06 55,618	Paramount	4.7	52,506	758	11,171.5	14.8	9.6	2.6	3.4	0.5	48.5	20.5
06 56,000	Pasadena	23.0	135,732	206	5,901.4	41.7	8.1	1.4	17.7	0.1	15.9	15.1
06 56,700	Perris	31.5	79,835	448	2,534.4	18.8	10.5	2.2	3.7	0.3	45.8	18.6
06 56,784	Petaluma	14.4	59,403	657	4,125.2	68.1	1.4	1.2	4.8	0.3	10.9	13.3
06 56,924	Pico Rivera	8.3	60,764	635	7,321.0	21.3	0.8	2.7	3.6	0.1	44.6	26.9
06 57,456	Pittsburg	17.7	76,544	476	4,324.5	20.8	16.8	1.4	19.7	1.2	25.7	14.3
06 57,526	Placentia	6.6	51,274	778	7,768.8	43.4	2.0	1.1	19.5	0.2	17.5	16.4
06 57,764	Pleasant Hill	7.1	34,304	1,161	4,831.5	63.1	2.7	0.6	15.4	0.3	4.6	13.4
06 57,792	Pleasanton	24.1	78,252	465	3,247.0	45.1	1.7	0.4	39.6	0.2	3.5	9.4
06 58,072	Pomona	23.0	148,338	182	6,449.5	21.0	5.8	2.3	10.7	0.2	41.3	18.7
06 58,240	Porterville	18.6	62,742	612	3,373.2	37.4	0.9	2.5	4.4	0.2	36.8	17.8
06 58,520	Poway	39.1	48,421	821	1,238.4	62.6	1.5	0.6	13.8	0.2	7.2	14.0
06 59,444	Rancho Cordova	34.6	80,413	441	2,324.1	48.8	9.3	1.2	15.6	1.1	10.5	13.5
06 59,451	Rancho Cucamonga	46.5	175,142	150	3,766.5	42.6	9.2	1.1	14.8	0.3	15.1	16.9
06 59,514	Rancho Palos Verdes	13.5	41,295	955	3,058.9	50.8	2.7	0.3	32.0	0.1	2.8	11.3
06 59,587	Rancho Santa Margarita	12.9	47,442	842	3,677.7	62.9	1.7	0.6	12.2	0.2	7.1	15.3
06 59,920	Redding	59.6	93,462	362	1,568.2	77.0	1.5	2.4	4.4	0.2	3.5	11.0
06 59,962	Redlands	36.0	73,288	503	2,035.8	53.3	5.1	1.2	9.7	0.3	14.4	16.2
06 60,018	Redondo Beach	6.2	69,781	538	11,255.0	62.0	3.1	0.6	14.3	0.3	5.1	14.5
06 60,102	Redwood City	19.3	81,643	429	4,230.2	44.5	1.8	1.6	16.2	0.8	21.0	14.0

1. Dry land or land partially or temporarily covered by water. 2. Hispanic or Latino persons may be of any race.

City	Percent Hispanic or Latino[1], 2020	Percent foreign born, 2016–2020	Age of population (percent), 2016–2020: Under 18 years	18 to 24 years	25 to 34 years	35 to 44 years	45 to 54 years	55 to 64 years	65 years and over	Median age, 2016–2020	Percent female, 2016–2020	Population: Census counts 2010	Census counts 2020	Percent change 2010–2020	Percent change 2020–2021
	12	13	14	15	16	17	18	19	20	21	22	23	24	25	26
CALIFORNIA—Cont'd															
Lemoore	48.0	14.4	25.3	11.9	19.3	11.8	12.0	8.7	11.0	31.3	46.8	24,534	26,989	10.0	1.0
Lincoln	20.2	12.3	22.6	5.6	10.3	12.8	11.3	9.8	27.6	43.7	52.4	42,922	49,808	16.0	1.7
Livermore	21.6	17.0	22.6	6.7	13.2	13.8	15.6	14.9	13.2	40.4	50.9	81,497	88,614	8.7	-2.0
Lodi	39.1	18.4	27.3	8.2	14.9	13.0	10.8	12.0	13.7	34.7	50.8	62,121	66,409	6.9	0.9
Lompoc	57.3	21.9	27.4	10.1	15.2	13.4	11.6	11.1	11.2	33.4	44.8	42,436	44,398	4.6	-1.3
Long Beach	43.3	25.1	21.7	10.2	17.5	13.8	13.1	11.9	11.7	35.3	50.7	462,189	466,302	0.9	-2.2
Los Altos	4.9	31.0	25.5	5.3	6.8	11.5	18.1	13.9	18.8	45.7	50.7	29,075	31,706	9.0	-3.2
Los Angeles	46.9	36.3	20.4	10.0	18.2	14.4	13.0	11.2	12.9	35.9	50.5	3,793,206	3,893,986	2.7	-1.1
Los Banos	73.8	28.0	35.0	9.0	12.8	12.1	10.9	9.8	10.3	29.4	49.3	35,967	45,287	25.9	2.5
Los Gatos	9.0	24.0	21.7	4.5	8.1	11.7	18.8	14.4	20.9	47.1	50.6	29,717	33,587	13.0	-3.1
Lynwood	88.3	38.3	27.0	11.7	17.8	14.7	10.8	10.5	7.6	31.1	51.2	69,758	67,139	-3.8	-2.4
Madera	80.7	28.1	33.1	10.7	15.1	13.1	10.9	8.2	8.9	28.7	51.0	61,909	66,316	7.1	2.5
Manhattan Beach	8.7	13.0	27.2	3.3	8.6	14.1	16.7	14.4	15.7	42.9	51.6	35,130	35,610	1.4	-2.6
Manteca	40.6	17.5	25.9	9.0	13.4	12.9	13.7	11.6	13.5	36.4	49.4	67,338	83,678	24.3	2.5
Martinez	17.9	11.8	20.4	7.3	12.2	14.8	13.4	15.4	16.4	42.2	51.2	36,037	37,206	3.2	-1.0
Maywood	97.1	50.0	27.9	10.4	17.1	12.9	13.2	8.3	10.2	31.6	49.3	27,380	25,191	-8.0	-2.5
Menifee	37.8	14.9	24.7	7.4	14.5	11.7	10.8	13.1	17.7	38.0	50.9	77,384	102,654	32.7	3.7
Menlo Park	17.7	26.9	24.6	8.6	12.7	14.3	12.4	12.7	14.6	37.6	51.1	32,014	33,785	5.5	-3.9
Merced	56.3	24.0	29.2	13.1	16.0	11.9	10.3	9.2	10.3	29.8	50.0	78,959	86,141	9.1	3.7
Milpitas	13.2	52.1	22.1	6.7	20.5	14.8	12.5	11.9	11.5	35.4	47.5	66,824	80,275	20.1	-1.5
Mission Viejo	19.2	21.7	20.1	6.8	10.6	12.1	14.2	14.7	21.3	45.3	50.5	93,101	93,759	0.7	-1.4
Modesto	42.9	18.0	26.3	8.7	15.5	12.1	11.8	11.9	13.8	34.7	50.9	203,057	218,471	7.6	0.1
Monrovia	39.5	25.3	21.6	7.8	13.3	15.4	15.0	13.2	13.7	39.6	51.7	36,600	38,022	3.9	-1.4
Montclair	71.9	32.9	25.6	13.4	15.8	12.1	11.8	10.1	11.1	32.1	52.5	36,649	37,936	3.5	0.3
Montebello	78.2	36.7	21.9	9.0	16.7	12.6	12.5	11.7	15.6	36.9	51.4	62,483	62,771	0.5	-2.5
Monterey	18.6	13.7	15.6	12.1	19.8	11.4	10.2	12.0	19.0	36.9	51.3	27,774	30,102	8.4	-0.8
Monterey Park	27.4	53.0	18.0	6.8	14.1	12.7	13.0	13.7	21.7	43.7	51.9	60,271	61,259	1.6	-2.6
Moorpark	33.2	16.4	23.1	8.6	12.8	11.6	14.6	15.2	14.1	39.7	50.3	34,594	36,344	5.1	-1.0
Moreno Valley	61.4	25.1	28.1	11.7	15.9	13.4	12.1	9.8	9.0	31.3	51.1	193,330	208,865	8.0	1.3
Morgan Hill	33.1	19.2	26.6	7.2	12.2	13.3	14.0	13.1	13.6	37.8	51.4	37,973	45,558	20.0	-0.5
Mountain View	17.2	42.1	20.2	6.9	22.6	16.9	12.1	10.2	11.2	35.2	48.6	73,565	82,592	12.3	-1.3
Murrieta	30.6	14.4	28.2	9.0	13.1	13.6	13.4	10.8	11.8	34.7	50.9	103,726	111,050	7.1	1.7
Napa	39.8	19.8	22.2	8.0	13.7	13.3	13.1	12.3	17.3	39.4	51.1	77,094	79,276	2.8	-0.6
National City	66.0	36.9	20.2	14.1	17.5	12.2	11.0	11.0	13.9	33.9	49.2	58,557	56,235	-4.0	-0.6
Newark	30.2	38.2	20.6	7.7	18.6	13.7	13.4	13.5	12.5	36.6	49.7	42,573	47,947	12.6	-1.1
Newport Beach	9.6	14.5	16.7	5.4	13.4	11.5	13.9	15.1	24.0	47.5	51.7	85,211	85,411	0.2	-0.7
Norco	36.1	10.4	17.9	8.4	13.0	13.8	17.1	14.9	15.0	41.8	45.6	27,216	25,960	-4.6	0.5
Norwalk	71.6	32.2	23.6	9.6	16.4	13.6	12.1	11.4	13.3	35.3	49.8	105,549	102,910	-2.5	-2.5
Novato	25.6	20.6	18.6	7.5	8.6	10.8	14.9	16.4	23.3	48.6	49.9	51,873	53,130	2.4	-0.8
Oakland	28.8	26.5	19.4	7.4	20.3	15.9	12.4	11.2	13.4	36.6	51.6	390,781	439,349	12.4	-1.3
Oakley	36.7	15.3	28.1	9.4	11.8	15.6	12.1	13.6	9.4	35.4	50.7	35,421	43,390	22.5	0.9
Oceanside	36.4	20.2	21.6	9.5	15.9	12.8	11.5	13.2	15.5	37.1	50.8	167,560	174,352	4.1	-0.8
Ontario	68.4	26.8	26.3	10.6	17.5	13.6	12.2	10.3	9.5	32.3	51.0	163,931	175,518	7.1	1.4
Orange	41.2	22.3	20.6	11.3	16.2	12.9	13.1	12.0	13.8	36.2	49.6	136,778	138,992	1.6	-1.2
Oxnard	74.7	33.9	26.7	10.6	15.7	13.6	12.6	10.8	10.0	32.8	49.5	198,066	202,185	2.1	-0.2
Pacifica	19.1	20.9	19.2	6.4	14.3	12.8	14.4	14.5	18.5	42.9	49.6	37,341	38,655	3.5	-4.0
Palmdale	61.8	24.8	29.9	10.3	13.1	12.5	13.2	11.0	10.0	32.3	50.8	152,731	169,913	11.2	-2.4
Palm Desert	26.0	17.2	14.1	7.0	10.4	9.0	9.4	14.4	35.8	55.1	53.0	48,449	51,163	5.6	0.7
Palm Springs	24.8	18.9	10.6	5.8	8.1	8.1	15.1	20.0	32.4	56.1	40.4	44,554	44,561	0.0	1.0
Palo Alto	7.4	34.0	22.8	5.8	12.0	12.7	14.6	12.8	19.3	42.6	51.4	64,347	68,724	6.8	-3.0
Paramount	81.2	35.4	27.4	12.3	15.5	13.1	14.0	9.1	8.6	31.5	49.5	54,107	53,828	-0.5	-2.5
Pasadena	33.0	30.3	17.8	7.5	18.6	14.9	13.3	11.5	16.3	38.8	51.8	137,085	138,679	1.2	-2.1
Perris	75.7	30.6	31.2	12.0	16.1	13.1	12.0	9.0	6.6	28.8	49.8	68,562	78,786	14.9	1.3
Petaluma	22.8	15.2	19.9	7.1	12.8	13.0	13.6	15.2	18.4	42.8	49.8	57,977	59,713	3.0	-0.5
Pico Rivera	90.6	31.1	21.2	10.1	14.2	12.8	13.8	12.2	15.8	38.6	52.0	62,964	62,215	-1.2	-2.3
Pittsburg	42.3	32.3	23.4	10.0	16.9	13.6	11.9	12.3	12.0	34.8	50.9	63,266	76,439	20.8	0.1
Placentia	38.0	24.3	24.5	9.5	13.5	12.9	13.4	12.3	13.9	36.8	50.7	50,902	51,911	2.0	-1.2
Pleasant Hill	14.3	19.5	20.1	8.1	13.3	13.3	14.2	14.5	16.5	42.2	51.5	33,075	34,595	4.6	-0.8
Pleasanton	9.9	32.8	24.4	5.8	10.1	14.9	16.1	13.6	15.1	41.6	50.6	70,274	80,421	14.4	-2.7
Pomona	71.2	34.1	24.6	13.0	14.5	13.1	12.4	10.9	11.5	33.3	51.1	149,235	151,554	1.6	-2.1
Porterville	69.5	24.1	30.3	10.8	13.7	13.3	10.6	9.0	12.4	30.9	49.4	58,095	62,607	7.8	0.2
Poway	18.5	19.0	23.2	6.8	11.3	12.5	13.3	14.5	18.4	41.4	50.0	47,805	48,918	2.3	-1.0
Rancho Cordova	21.6	24.5	25.3	7.9	18.2	13.7	11.7	11.7	11.5	34.3	51.0	64,805	79,666	22.9	0.9
Rancho Cucamonga	37.4	20.2	22.9	9.1	15.9	12.1	14.6	12.9	12.5	36.8	51.1	165,373	174,628	5.6	0.3
Rancho Palos Verdes	10.7	27.7	21.8	6.3	5.0	10.0	15.8	15.5	25.6	49.8	51.5	41,688	42,365	1.6	-2.5
Rancho Santa Margarita	21.5	18.1	24.1	7.6	11.9	15.1	16.2	15.6	9.5	39.2	51.3	47,855	48,119	0.6	-1.4
Redding	11.2	7.0	22.3	8.5	14.8	11.5	10.7	12.8	19.3	38.2	51.7	89,877	93,559	4.1	-0.1
Redlands	35.2	13.7	23.2	10.3	15.6	13.2	10.6	12.5	14.6	35.7	52.7	68,699	73,004	6.3	0.4
Redondo Beach	17.5	19.6	22.6	4.4	14.6	16.4	15.4	13.6	13.1	39.9	50.2	66,870	71,520	7.0	-2.4
Redwood City	35.7	32.9	21.6	7.2	17.9	15.3	14.2	10.9	12.9	36.8	50.1	76,935	84,234	9.5	-3.1

1. May be of any race.

City	Households, 2016–2020							Persons in group quarters, 2016–2020	Serious crimes known to police[2], 2020				Educational attainment, 2016–2020		
			Percent						Violent		Property			Attainment[4] (percent)	
	Number	Persons per household	Family	Married couple family	Female family	Non-family	One person		Number	Rate	Number	Rate	Population age 25 and over	High school graduate or less	Bachelor's degree or more
	27	28	29	30	31	32	33	34	35	36	37	38	39	40	41
CALIFORNIA—Cont'd															
Lemoore	8,803	2.94	74.9	49.9	14.6	25.1	20.4	15	104	385.5	363	1,345.4	16,232	39.4	22.0
Lincoln	18,417	2.61	71.5	61.4	7.7	28.5	24.1	152	38	77.7	556	1,137.3	34,547	25.3	35.3
Livermore	32,196	2.84	74.0	62.4	8.4	26.0	21.1	424	164	179.8	1,526	1,673.2	64,857	22.4	45.1
Lodi	23,017	2.86	70.8	50.7	12.9	29.2	23.4	701	225	329.9	1,262	1,850.2	42,914	45.0	21.4
Lompoc	13,216	3.00	70.2	46.0	15.2	29.8	23.4	3,117	239	556.9	972	2,264.9	26,724	50.7	12.3
Long Beach	166,236	2.72	59.8	37.9	15.5	40.2	30.6	9,265	2,343	506.4	12,707	2,746.5	314,509	37.3	31.8
Los Altos	10,557	2.90	82.3	74.3	6.9	17.7	15.8	285	23	76.2	323	1,069.4	21,344	5.0	84.6
Los Angeles	1,402,522	2.77	59.2	38.7	14.0	40.8	30.5	90,266	28,882	721.9	85,932	2,148.0	2,767,578	40.6	35.6
Los Banos	10,799	3.64	80.4	57.7	15.0	19.6	16.6	139	220	528.5	933	2,241.1	22,075	61.0	9.9
Los Gatos	12,573	2.51	70.0	60.0	6.9	30.0	25.5	395	20	66.1	406	1,341.2	23,602	11.0	71.5
Lynwood	15,313	4.35	87.5	56.3	20.7	12.5	10.1	3,008	441	630.7	1,511	2,161.0	42,715	70.9	7.8
Madera	17,598	3.68	81.1	54.6	19.0	18.9	14.2	866	310	467.2	1,141	1,719.6	36,879	61.9	10.0
Manhattan Beach	13,313	2.63	69.2	58.1	6.2	30.8	23.5	26	46	130.7	784	2,227.9	24,367	7.4	76.8
Manteca	25,670	3.13	75.7	55.3	13.4	24.3	17.8	622	217	255.5	1,429	1,682.6	52,767	46.1	17.0
Martinez	14,853	2.55	66.9	51.3	10.1	33.1	25.4	581	76	197.2	559	1,450.3	27,755	21.2	42.5
Maywood	6,753	4.00	84.8	53.8	19.8	15.2	10.9	127	117	434.5	459	1,704.5	16,728	78.1	7.5
Menifee	29,325	3.16	75.8	60.7	10.9	24.2	20.2	171	139	143.5	1,659	1,713.2	63,098	39.0	20.4
Menlo Park	12,174	2.80	67.1	55.6	9.1	32.9	23.3	1,105	52	148.6	781	2,231.3	23,494	14.1	70.5
Merced	26,626	3.12	69.9	40.8	19.4	30.1	22.9	1,089	672	798.1	1,949	2,314.8	48,579	50.3	16.5
Milpitas	22,132	3.29	79.5	64.4	10.7	20.5	13.0	2,434	111	128.4	2,103	2,433.6	53,563	26.4	53.2
Mission Viejo	33,000	2.85	77.7	66.2	8.1	22.3	17.2	1,602	71	75.1	853	902.5	69,883	19.9	49.6
Modesto	71,113	2.98	71.8	48.9	16.0	28.2	22.7	2,710	1,603	740.2	5,340	2,465.8	139,468	46.2	19.3
Monrovia	13,322	2.81	68.2	44.7	15.5	31.8	24.3	213	69	190.1	914	2,517.8	26,560	30.1	40.5
Montclair	10,564	3.76	80.7	49.4	22.7	19.3	15.0	317	252	622.6	1,447	3,575.2	24,419	50.5	17.7
Montebello	18,842	3.30	78.0	44.7	22.8	22.0	16.6	465	NA	NA	NA	NA	43,307	52.1	19.3
Monterey	12,373	2.10	46.9	38.1	5.9	53.1	41.0	2,554	96	340.3	903	3,201.1	20,670	15.6	55.7
Monterey Park	20,221	2.98	75.6	52.3	16.7	24.4	18.6	255	113	189.6	1,230	2,063.4	45,550	44.4	33.0
Moorpark	11,557	3.15	81.9	70.2	6.1	18.1	14.9	0	17	46.5	225	615.2	24,898	22.9	45.8
Moreno Valley	51,545	4.04	84.4	55.6	20.6	15.6	11.0	761	833	387.0	5,126	2,381.3	125,521	51.0	17.1
Morgan Hill	14,320	3.10	80.1	64.0	12.0	19.9	15.3	435	59	125.7	766	1,632.4	29,649	26.5	42.7
Mountain View	33,029	2.42	56.3	46.4	6.5	43.7	31.1	290	144	172.0	2,177	2,599.6	58,370	14.8	71.0
Murrieta	33,095	3.43	80.7	64.3	12.3	19.3	15.3	586	95	80.8	1,205	1,024.3	71,598	30.9	29.8
Napa	28,232	2.74	66.4	51.2	10.3	33.6	26.7	989	267	341.3	1,320	1,687.2	54,616	34.0	35.4
National City	17,169	3.21	70.9	42.4	21.8	29.1	23.7	6,242	351	568.8	1,160	1,879.8	40,264	52.1	15.8
Newark	14,356	3.34	82.1	61.7	13.8	17.9	12.8	141	119	238.3	1,443	2,889.8	34,518	35.9	37.8
Newport Beach	38,596	2.23	57.7	49.2	5.8	42.3	32.6	477	141	167.0	1,785	2,113.7	67,581	9.5	67.2
Norco	7,354	3.26	78.6	62.3	11.4	21.4	17.5	3,076	39	147.0	605	2,279.9	19,911	45.0	19.2
Norwalk	26,748	3.81	83.3	55.6	18.5	16.7	12.2	2,622	437	421.1	1,771	1,706.6	69,804	51.5	20.3
Novato	21,555	2.46	66.0	53.9	8.4	34.0	27.7	658	238	425.6	851	1,521.7	39,759	23.7	46.3
Oakland	160,095	2.60	54.3	35.4	13.2	45.7	33.4	6,638	5,653	1,290.9	22,622	5,165.7	309,242	31.8	46.1
Oakley	12,133	3.42	82.9	65.9	11.6	17.1	14.7	102	42	96.8	478	1,101.8	26,013	40.7	20.1
Oceanside	61,111	2.86	68.1	52.1	10.8	31.9	24.3	755	717	406.0	3,180	1,800.5	120,965	32.6	31.6
Ontario	50,599	3.51	78.3	50.3	19.1	21.7	16.5	761	686	365.9	3,994	2,130.5	112,476	51.2	18.0
Orange	43,327	3.04	71.5	54.9	11.6	28.5	20.0	7,502	180	129.6	2,396	1,725.7	94,844	31.2	38.9
Oxnard	51,020	4.04	81.1	54.0	18.1	18.9	13.3	1,515	743	353.7	4,323	2,057.9	130,296	54.9	18.5
Pacifica	13,819	2.78	70.7	54.4	10.2	29.3	20.6	187	82	212.0	715	1,848.6	28,800	20.9	46.7
Palmdale	42,687	3.58	79.8	52.9	19.0	20.2	15.2	231	744	479.0	2,134	1,373.9	91,601	52.8	15.7
Palm Desert	24,335	2.17	56.9	44.6	8.5	43.1	34.4	290	125	232.3	1,564	2,906.5	41,862	26.2	38.0
Palm Springs	24,767	1.93	42.2	31.9	6.4	57.8	45.0	502	257	525.0	1,690	3,452.4	40,454	25.8	42.1
Palo Alto	26,150	2.58	66.9	56.3	7.8	33.1	25.5	543	81	123.7	1,931	2,949.9	48,553	6.7	82.7
Paramount	14,156	3.79	81.8	48.6	22.0	18.2	14.6	311	263	487.6	1,309	2,426.8	32,546	62.7	12.2
Pasadena	56,718	2.44	55.1	40.4	9.9	44.9	34.7	3,871	414	292.6	3,021	2,135.4	106,063	25.0	53.0
Perris	17,470	4.43	88.4	60.3	18.1	11.6	8.0	297	306	380.0	1,890	2,347.1	44,117	64.2	10.2
Petaluma	22,766	2.64	68.2	54.7	8.7	31.8	24.7	672	255	419.4	756	1,243.3	44,407	26.0	40.5
Pico Rivera	17,060	3.64	79.6	54.0	18.3	20.4	16.8	452	173	279.4	1,166	1,882.9	42,990	59.3	13.6
Pittsburg	21,349	3.34	77.2	51.7	16.8	22.8	16.7	369	477	647.5	1,580	2,144.6	47,801	45.4	21.4
Placentia	16,378	3.15	77.4	57.9	12.9	22.6	17.0	524	232	452.6	1,066	2,079.6	34,336	29.0	40.7
Pleasant Hill	13,762	2.51	64.3	47.8	12.0	35.7	28.2	403	95	271.2	1,354	3,865.0	25,063	15.3	54.9
Pleasanton	27,815	2.86	78.5	68.9	6.8	21.5	17.4	302	94	113.0	1,188	1,428.5	55,832	14.0	65.5
Pomona	40,367	3.64	75.6	48.3	17.9	24.4	17.8	4,305	780	513.2	4,759	3,131.3	94,396	53.3	17.5
Porterville	17,649	3.27	76.8	47.5	20.9	23.2	18.9	1,358	236	394.9	1,016	1,700.2	34,821	55.2	12.3
Poway	16,015	3.07	79.3	64.8	9.4	20.7	15.6	627	53	107.1	366	739.7	34,847	20.2	50.4
Rancho Cordova	25,364	2.91	68.9	48.3	14.6	31.1	21.9	532	322	422.1	1,555	2,038.2	49,683	35.5	27.4
Rancho Cucamonga	57,485	3.04	76.6	55.8	14.7	23.4	18.9	3,082	551	308.0	3,265	1,824.9	121,108	27.6	35.8
Rancho Palos Verdes	15,181	2.71	78.2	69.1	7.3	21.8	19.3	492	43	103.6	335	807.0	29,942	10.5	69.1
Rancho Santa Margarita	16,960	2.85	75.9	63.3	9.4	24.1	20.4	0	19	39.7	282	588.8	33,007	19.8	48.8
Redding	36,365	2.46	62.9	44.5	12.7	37.1	28.8	2,471	513	552.2	2,323	2,500.7	63,629	31.7	25.2
Redlands	24,582	2.80	68.4	48.8	15.2	31.6	23.9	2,782	238	331.4	1,865	2,596.8	47,634	29.2	42.3
Redondo Beach	27,414	2.43	59.1	47.5	7.6	40.9	30.0	165	167	250.3	1,422	2,131.0	48,682	13.3	62.4
Redwood City	30,175	2.75	66.0	51.9	10.0	34.0	24.7	1,536	187	215.0	1,489	1,711.8	60,153	27.7	52.3

2. Data for serious crimes have not been adjusted for underreporting. This may affect comparability between geographic areas and over time.   4. Persons 25 years old and over.

City	Money income, 2016–2020					Median earnings Full year, Full-time workers, 2016–2020			Housing units, 2016–2020				
	Households												
	Median household income	Percent with income less than $25,000	Percent with income of $200,000 or more	Median family income	Median non-family household income	All persons	Men	Women	Total	Occupied	Percent owner occupied	Median value[1] (dollars)	Median gross rent (dollars)
	42	43	44	45	46	47	48	49	50	51	52	53	54
CALIFORNIA—Cont'd													
Lemoore	68,658	14.0	5.6	69,931	49,196	46,714	51,292	41,829	9,262	8,803	52.5	242,700	1,097
Lincoln	88,991	12.1	11.4	102,458	50,978	66,020	75,664	54,334	18,999	18,417	81.0	468,400	1,837
Livermore	131,664	6.2	27.4	149,855	69,672	88,394	97,381	75,759	33,330	32,196	72.6	806,100	2,164
Lodi	64,153	17.5	5.9	72,562	38,699	46,497	50,939	42,195	24,190	23,017	52.8	345,400	1,260
Lompoc	57,071	20.9	3.0	64,333	38,188	40,617	40,984	39,738	13,726	13,216	45.3	337,100	1,224
Long Beach	66,410	17.8	8.4	75,310	52,951	49,455	50,869	46,887	175,725	166,236	40.2	584,200	1,391
Los Altos	240,094	4.6	59.0	250	100,662	182,988	207,824	135,068	11,054	10,557	79.8	2,000,000	3,375
Los Angeles	65,290	20.6	10.9	74,471	48,887	46,960	47,609	46,195	1,513,791	1,402,522	37.0	670,700	1,523
Los Banos	64,567	14.7	3.1	71,724	37,306	42,115	46,187	34,594	11,358	10,799	57.3	315,500	1,253
Los Gatos	156,270	7.8	40.0	198,064	93,500	131,932	157,879	105,441	13,480	12,573	65.9	1,775,500	2,482
Lynwood	57,063	17.1	3.0	57,080	27,214	32,861	36,373	30,477	15,676	15,313	47.7	422,200	1,261
Madera	49,335	21.0	1.8	50,309	29,182	37,152	40,607	32,931	18,713	17,598	50.6	237,500	1,079
Manhattan Beach	153,926	5.3	39.8	195,510	92,562	125,498	146,071	96,711	14,952	13,313	67.7	2,000,000	2,582
Manteca	76,846	13.2	7.8	85,197	46,547	54,029	59,704	48,056	26,774	25,670	65.2	407,600	1,588
Martinez	109,994	9.2	19.3	130,649	65,731	81,165	97,636	65,516	15,340	14,853	69.6	622,800	1,854
Maywood	50,996	22.4	1.8	52,397	27,474	30,039	30,903	28,689	6,908	6,753	27.7	427,300	1,153
Menifee	76,824	13.8	6.3	87,466	33,382	56,943	62,287	47,781	31,677	29,325	78.6	353,000	1,657
Menlo Park	167,567	8.9	42.7	203,861	88,629	111,123	147,924	84,646	13,280	12,174	58.2	2,000,000	2,531
Merced	49,973	26.2	3.8	54,699	31,952	41,189	41,993	39,004	28,120	26,626	42.6	251,500	1,032
Milpitas	137,000	8.8	30.4	139,973	94,216	86,547	100,753	72,794	22,966	22,132	63.7	927,200	2,626
Mission Viejo	121,299	7.4	21.4	133,922	66,678	78,020	88,034	66,605	34,385	33,000	77.2	732,100	2,326
Modesto	62,182	16.7	5.2	69,425	40,507	50,115	52,828	45,522	73,906	71,113	55.7	300,700	1,254
Monrovia	81,990	13.0	11.9	89,329	53,257	56,129	60,156	53,478	14,230	13,322	47.3	694,700	1,696
Montclair	63,245	18.7	2.7	67,338	34,904	39,625	39,768	39,217	10,774	10,564	53.5	388,100	1,477
Montebello	62,781	17.0	5.5	66,367	31,855	39,481	39,694	39,195	19,900	18,842	44.3	519,000	1,443
Monterey	80,908	11.0	13.0	110,018	63,618	64,817	73,750	57,261	13,615	12,373	34.3	813,600	1,855
Monterey Park	63,389	19.5	9.2	68,116	42,959	46,542	50,838	41,624	21,424	20,221	50.7	641,700	1,505
Moorpark	119,597	6.2	23.9	132,750	63,250	72,572	78,400	64,176	11,981	11,557	77.9	662,400	2,080
Moreno Valley	70,385	13.4	4.2	70,957	44,570	41,900	44,566	38,326	54,089	51,545	62.2	335,700	1,587
Morgan Hill	128,373	5.5	29.4	140,563	73,167	81,094	89,538	70,896	14,715	14,320	72.6	886,300	1,836
Mountain View	144,116	9.0	35.3	180,236	107,646	123,434	133,330	101,966	35,842	33,029	41.4	1,560,600	2,490
Murrieta	91,654	8.2	13.0	99,755	55,998	64,277	70,662	51,743	35,207	33,095	66.1	435,700	1,859
Napa	85,953	11.4	12.9	101,698	53,235	56,394	56,379	56,406	30,522	28,232	58.6	644,100	1,779
National City	49,176	24.1	3.3	53,820	31,433	34,144	36,072	32,716	18,179	17,169	32.9	428,800	1,266
Newark	127,619	6.5	24.5	132,526	90,676	64,934	70,000	59,466	14,942	14,356	68.5	816,100	2,366
Newport Beach	133,849	10.5	34.2	176,264	89,165	100,174	117,281	76,968	45,527	38,596	54.3	1,976,400	2,409
Norco	106,370	10.7	14.4	119,735	52,188	64,287	71,959	52,470	7,678	7,354	82.3	559,100	1,831
Norwalk	77,425	12.3	4.7	80,070	38,938	43,122	46,045	40,064	27,701	26,748	66.1	461,000	1,678
Novato	101,629	10.2	20.9	130,357	60,787	75,000	84,788	64,333	22,290	21,555	69.9	804,900	1,975
Oakland	80,143	18.1	15.7	92,046	64,498	63,250	63,935	62,711	171,749	160,095	40.9	730,000	1,539
Oakley	103,552	12.5	12.7	107,969	27,482	63,943	78,309	52,160	12,378	12,133	75.8	469,100	1,779
Oceanside	75,411	13.3	8.2	88,477	48,160	50,202	53,486	43,623	65,829	61,111	57.1	538,200	1,803
Ontario	67,357	14.9	3.9	70,337	51,804	41,945	43,727	40,209	52,575	50,599	54.6	408,000	1,557
Orange	96,605	10.2	15.9	110,116	62,557	59,090	62,523	53,725	45,157	43,327	59.2	680,300	1,857
Oxnard	77,050	11.0	6.3	76,754	50,841	40,033	40,246	39,448	54,992	51,020	54.5	471,400	1,659
Pacifica	130,466	6.9	25.0	144,953	78,011	76,734	80,682	72,179	14,246	13,819	69.2	943,500	2,535
Palmdale	65,444	16.8	5.1	68,634	37,054	44,170	49,063	38,122	45,334	42,687	63.9	302,800	1,333
Palm Desert	64,295	19.7	10.2	79,526	42,196	49,115	52,713	42,391	39,058	24,335	64.6	361,200	1,353
Palm Springs	57,916	23.7	10.4	78,995	43,845	57,236	62,123	50,343	37,762	24,767	63.7	398,100	1,199
Palo Alto	174,003	10.0	45.6	221,650	95,868	145,160	169,645	110,818	28,309	26,150	56.3	2,000,000	2,679
Paramount	57,313	16.4	2.4	58,299	38,994	35,434	37,242	32,616	14,660	14,156	42.1	388,300	1,462
Pasadena	85,129	17.8	15.5	106,979	62,063	65,577	70,140	62,183	62,659	56,718	42.0	822,100	1,787
Perris	66,926	13.2	2.7	66,773	34,560	38,211	41,298	32,297	18,243	17,470	65.1	309,500	1,453
Petaluma	92,762	10.7	14.9	114,680	53,781	70,478	79,470	62,377	23,503	22,766	64.1	664,200	2,027
Pico Rivera	70,620	18.5	7.7	76,449	27,014	41,155	45,179	36,391	17,461	17,060	70.2	464,700	1,393
Pittsburg	83,163	13.3	8.5	87,124	51,583	51,441	54,079	47,947	22,299	21,349	59.4	425,300	1,827
Placentia	100,707	10.0	16.3	113,698	50,448	59,726	66,864	54,003	16,829	16,378	63.9	653,400	1,856
Pleasant Hill	125,573	9.7	21.4	144,258	80,240	87,186	99,205	79,612	14,286	13,762	64.2	777,700	2,102
Pleasanton	160,689	8.0	37.8	184,053	75,740	112,487	131,738	94,812	29,069	27,815	67.9	1,056,100	2,570
Pomona	62,407	18.4	4.0	64,519	40,018	38,026	40,283	35,917	42,008	40,367	53.3	420,600	1,406
Porterville	44,095	30.1	2.4	45,993	25,008	34,776	40,518	31,779	18,654	17,649	50.4	182,100	943
Poway	115,332	7.1	23.6	129,286	65,873	73,452	85,899	59,415	16,713	16,015	78.9	716,300	1,630
Rancho Cordova	69,963	13.8	6.1	75,713	52,511	50,050	52,066	47,173	26,338	25,364	56.3	325,300	1,327
Rancho Cucamonga	92,290	10.3	13.8	103,094	56,761	60,750	66,464	52,869	59,916	57,485	62.5	515,600	1,855
Rancho Palos Verdes	146,163	7.3	35.1	164,320	66,889	104,856	128,623	83,926	16,405	15,181	77.6	1,209,200	2,839
Rancho Santa Margarita	125,329	6.9	26.1	152,500	64,085	81,378	100,788	67,335	17,226	16,960	72.7	679,500	2,133
Redding	56,098	20.7	4.7	68,340	36,162	48,648	53,077	42,984	39,244	36,365	55.4	274,800	1,112
Redlands	81,265	14.4	12.6	92,108	48,070	59,732	65,206	50,535	26,273	24,582	58.5	424,900	1,464
Redondo Beach	116,832	6.7	24.6	149,190	82,004	91,907	99,192	84,143	29,904	27,414	53.3	974,200	2,165
Redwood City	123,294	8.8	29.5	137,470	95,547	83,931	88,769	79,091	31,583	30,175	47.5	1,424,200	2,427

1. Specified owner-occupied units

City	Commuting, 2016–2020[1]: Percent: Drove alone	Commuting, 2016–2020[1]: Percent: Mean travel time to work	Computer access[2], 2016–2020: Percent: With a computer in the house	Computer access[2], 2016–2020: Percent: With Internet access	Migration, 2016–2020: Percent who lived in the same house one year ago	Migration, 2016–2020: Percent who lived in another state or county one year ago	Civilian labor force, 2021: Total	Civilian labor force, 2021: Percent change 2020–2021	Civilian labor force, 2021: Unemployment[3]: Total	Civilian labor force, 2021: Unemployment[3]: Rate	Civilian Employment, 2016–2020[4]: Population age 16 and older: Number	Civilian Employment, 2016–2020[4]: Population age 16 and older: Percent in labor force	Civilian Employment, 2016–2020[4]: Population age 16 to 64: Number	Civilian Employment, 2016–2020[4]: Population age 16 to 64: Percent who worked full-year full-time
	55	56	57	58	59	60	61	62	63	64	65	66	67	68
CALIFORNIA—Cont'd														
Lemoore	80.4	21.0	92.9	88.6	81.5	6.2	11,630	-1.8	891	7.7	20,014	59.8	17,162	50.1
Lincoln	81.1	29.6	96.9	90.2	90.0	5.7	19,227	0.9	1,051	5.5	38,327	53.9	25,051	54.1
Livermore	73.8	32.4	96.6	94.1	88.0	4.7	46,819	-0.5	2,147	4.6	73,292	70.6	61,209	56.6
Lodi	78.1	26.3	92.6	87.1	83.5	5.1	30,372	0.5	2,414	7.9	50,594	63.9	41,445	47.4
Lompoc	68.8	27.3	90.4	83.6	82.8	3.2	17,382	-0.7	1,413	8.1	31,979	59.1	27,208	43.8
Long Beach	73.1	31.0	94.8	87.3	88.5	3.7	232,540	0.6	22,208	9.6	371,987	66.5	317,826	49.7
Los Altos	71.6	23.9	98.0	96.4	89.9	5.2	14,207	0.9	483	3.4	24,163	58.9	18,358	51.2
Los Angeles	67.7	31.9	93.3	85.8	88.9	3.0	2,050,398	0.4	181,615	8.9	3,254,012	66.5	2,743,225	48.5
Los Banos	79.5	44.5	94.4	83.6	89.4	5.3	16,995	-1.0	2,220	13.1	26,937	61.8	22,866	45.1
Los Gatos	75.9	29.7	94.0	91.9	87.4	4.1	15,515	-0.2	644	4.2	25,880	61.6	19,195	53.5
Lynwood	74.8	30.9	94.6	73.3	94.7	0.6	28,003	0.8	3,099	11.1	52,669	60.4	47,408	43.9
Madera	71.8	28.0	90.2	83.1	88.0	3.7	28,048	0.3	2,544	9.1	46,289	62.1	40,477	40.5
Manhattan Beach	72.5	32.1	98.0	94.9	89.4	3.7	18,485	2.4	970	5.2	26,918	63.0	21,403	53.0
Manteca	78.7	39.8	93.8	89.0	87.7	5.4	39,082	0.2	2,863	7.3	62,145	60.4	51,208	46.3
Martinez	70.9	33.8	95.7	93.1	86.7	4.0	19,576	-0.3	1,070	5.5	31,341	68.3	25,035	53.5
Maywood	70.6	30.7	86.7	74.5	95.6	0.8	11,979	1.5	1,024	8.5	20,316	65.6	17,562	51.0
Menifee	80.0	42.9	94.5	89.9	86.8	4.6	42,191	1.3	3,173	7.5	72,597	56.1	56,135	45.8
Menlo Park	59.7	26.5	98.3	93.9	81.0	14.3	19,102	0.1	625	3.3	27,319	66.0	22,184	52.9
Merced	77.8	27.6	92.0	88.6	84.7	5.3	35,515	-0.5	3,275	9.2	62,158	59.1	53,460	37.2
Milpitas	72.4	28.1	98.1	96.0	83.3	5.1	40,004	-1.3	2,127	5.3	60,282	67.1	51,616	57.0
Mission Viejo	77.5	28.0	97.5	94.9	89.3	3.0	47,297	-0.1	2,599	5.5	78,951	64.3	58,534	53.8
Modesto	80.9	28.7	93.5	87.7	86.4	4.9	94,068	-1.3	7,580	8.1	164,029	60.8	134,363	44.5
Monrovia	76.6	32.5	94.7	88.3	91.2	2.3	21,157	1.2	1,509	7.1	30,351	66.0	25,179	53.4
Montclair	75.6	31.1	94.3	85.9	92.4	5.0	20,033	1.1	1,277	6.4	31,086	63.0	26,628	44.6
Montebello	73.4	34.1	89.5	79.0	92.8	1.8	28,453	0.4	2,772	9.7	50,529	65.1	40,745	48.9
Monterey	62.6	19.2	94.9	90.8	71.8	21.5	14,954	-1.8	706	4.7	24,695	57.0	19,267	55.5
Monterey Park	76.8	30.6	91.3	86.2	91.5	1.6	28,733	-2.3	2,426	8.4	50,988	57.2	37,834	50.8
Moorpark	79.4	28.8	96.0	94.1	93.5	2.4	18,627	-1.2	925	5.0	29,084	66.5	23,929	52.4
Moreno Valley	79.8	36.6	96.6	91.8	89.3	4.5	98,504	1.5	8,219	8.3	156,788	63.6	138,087	46.1
Morgan Hill	75.0	36.4	98.0	93.0	89.3	2.7	23,983	-1.0	1,140	4.8	33,991	68.0	27,889	54.1
Mountain View	64.0	24.3	96.7	92.6	80.3	10.7	49,160	0.7	1,497	3.0	65,276	73.3	56,308	60.5
Murrieta	80.3	36.5	97.4	93.8	83.5	6.7	56,838	0.7	3,307	5.8	85,862	62.5	72,361	45.4
Napa	76.7	22.9	94.5	89.4	88.4	5.3	39,072	-0.8	2,504	6.4	63,251	67.9	49,715	52.4
National City	66.0	27.4	88.0	78.7	89.1	4.4	24,497	-0.8	2,281	9.3	50,388	55.3	41,865	52.8
Newark	67.5	32.6	97.9	94.9	90.7	3.4	24,960	-0.6	1,377	5.5	39,477	69.4	33,472	61.5
Newport Beach	75.0	26.2	97.0	94.0	83.2	5.2	43,822	0.6	2,056	4.7	74,138	62.6	53,338	55.0
Norco	80.0	36.0	95.1	90.8	87.2	8.6	12,223	1.6	696	5.7	22,881	55.5	18,830	43.9
Norwalk	81.1	30.7	94.5	87.7	93.9	1.9	49,381	0.6	4,804	9.7	82,651	61.9	68,739	49.8
Novato	69.7	32.6	94.0	91.3	88.7	4.8	26,523	-1.5	1,250	4.7	45,208	62.3	32,700	50.8
Oakland	49.9	32.9	92.6	85.9	86.6	6.2	206,661	-1.6	15,184	7.3	348,494	68.8	291,910	52.2
Oakley	76.7	43.2	97.7	92.4	91.4	3.6	19,590	-0.6	1,449	7.4	31,083	69.3	27,160	48.0
Oceanside	76.1	30.0	95.6	91.8	84.5	5.1	79,781	-0.4	5,424	6.8	141,502	65.0	114,219	52.0
Ontario	80.6	32.1	95.9	88.4	90.1	5.1	90,952	1.6	6,200	6.8	136,660	67.0	119,735	49.3
Orange	76.7	26.9	96.0	92.9	87.7	3.9	68,908	-0.2	3,852	5.6	114,192	65.7	95,003	49.7
Oxnard	78.3	26.0	94.0	84.9	92.4	2.4	97,041	-0.6	7,260	7.5	157,842	68.0	137,066	48.8
Pacifica	68.8	31.1	97.5	94.5	90.4	5.4	22,930	-1.5	1,166	5.1	32,111	69.0	24,967	60.5
Palmdale	76.6	42.0	93.9	88.2	90.6	1.7	62,877	1.4	7,776	12.4	112,948	59.3	97,652	44.9
Palm Desert	69.2	20.3	93.2	87.9	85.4	7.0	25,058	-0.6	1,677	6.7	46,328	49.0	27,348	46.2
Palm Springs	66.7	21.8	92.1	87.3	83.3	8.1	23,399	-0.4	1,564	6.7	43,958	50.5	28,285	41.5
Palo Alto	57.7	24.6	97.4	94.0	84.5	8.8	34,751	0.7	1,021	2.9	54,584	62.9	41,451	54.9
Paramount	79.0	28.7	94.0	82.6	92.7	1.2	24,208	0.6	2,522	10.4	41,072	65.4	36,424	47.0
Pasadena	65.9	28.7	92.7	87.1	86.0	4.3	77,603	1.5	5,688	7.3	119,112	66.1	95,958	52.5
Perris	79.3	37.0	96.1	88.2	91.0	3.9	31,774	1.8	2,991	9.4	56,046	63.8	50,953	48.2
Petaluma	73.0	31.1	94.2	89.8	88.6	5.5	31,729	-1.1	1,503	4.7	50,500	64.4	39,306	48.1
Pico Rivera	82.5	31.1	90.0	82.7	95.1	0.8	29,590	0.8	2,861	9.7	51,035	62.2	41,152	53.0
Pittsburg	68.2	42.0	93.8	90.0	88.8	4.2	33,718	-1.4	2,785	8.3	56,757	65.4	48,151	48.0
Placentia	79.5	28.7	96.9	93.0	89.6	2.7	24,824	-0.6	1,437	5.8	40,707	68.0	33,492	54.2
Pleasant Hill	65.0	34.2	95.7	93.1	87.7	5.8	17,266	-0.2	903	5.2	28,897	65.4	23,147	53.5
Pleasanton	66.6	35.6	97.5	95.4	87.9	6.6	38,110	0.2	1,700	4.5	62,919	65.9	50,834	55.2
Pomona	73.0	31.7	94.6	87.2	89.4	4.2	66,867	1.1	6,701	10.0	118,402	63.5	101,045	44.6
Porterville	78.7	22.4	88.6	82.5	86.6	2.7	24,809	-0.7	3,296	13.3	43,233	61.6	35,938	42.5
Poway	76.7	25.3	97.9	93.7	88.0	2.5	24,458	1.2	1,143	4.7	39,412	63.0	30,257	53.1
Rancho Cordova	74.4	26.9	95.3	90.9	84.7	5.1	35,778	0.8	2,505	7.0	57,085	66.3	48,553	49.7
Rancho Cucamonga	80.5	32.1	96.9	93.0	86.4	5.4	97,461	1.6	5,300	5.4	141,712	66.2	119,441	48.6
Rancho Palos Verdes	76.6	35.2	96.5	93.8	90.3	4.1	18,627	2.0	1,124	6.0	34,058	56.3	23,398	48.0
Rancho Santa Margarita	77.6	29.2	97.5	95.7	88.0	2.7	26,156	0.1	1,284	4.9	38,096	73.2	33,524	55.9
Redding	80.8	17.5	93.0	85.9	81.9	6.9	39,405	-0.7	2,509	6.4	73,622	57.2	55,876	42.3
Redlands	78.4	23.4	92.7	86.2	87.0	4.9	36,140	1.9	1,971	5.5	57,069	61.8	46,621	47.2
Redondo Beach	77.3	30.3	97.0	93.4	87.0	4.6	39,330	1.2	2,563	6.5	52,992	73.0	44,257	59.9
Redwood City	67.5	26.6	96.8	91.1	85.8	7.6	47,772	-0.8	1,853	3.9	68,078	71.4	57,147	55.4

1. Employed persons. 2. Households. 3. Percent of civilian labor force. 4. Persons 16 years old and over.

City	Value of residential construction authorized by building permits, 2021			Wholesale trade[1], 2017				Retail trade[2], 2017			
	New construction ($1,000)	Number of housing units	Percent single family	Number of establishments	Number of employees	Sales (mil dol)	Annual payroll (mil dol)	Number of establish-ments	Number of employees	Sales (mil dol)	Annual payroll (mil dol)
	69	70	71	72	73	74	75	76	77	78	79
CALIFORNIA—Cont'd											
Lemoore	22,571	99	100.0	5	27	59.1	1.6	52	559	129.8	14.3
Lincoln	305,894	1,016	100.0	18	140	75.0	7.8	68	1,220	340.1	33.0
Livermore	10,389	36	100.0	164	2,753	2,261.5	189.3	366	6,829	2,295.0	249.3
Lodi	97,890	357	100.0	40	280	843.7	16.6	214	3,991	1,271.4	112.0
Lompoc	6,192	41	90.2	9	53	17.2	2.0	108	1,553	408.8	40.3
Long Beach	163,642	908	33.5	309	4,118	9,446.9	311.2	921	13,603	4,095.0	382.7
Los Altos	69,655	134	57.5	15	87	68.4	7.0	D	D	D	34.6
Los Angeles	2,754,493	14,088	17.6	8,196	79,204	58,687.6	4,521.8	11,728	151,931	50,763.6	4,828.2
Los Banos	56,826	114	100.0	8	110	100.0	3.7	80	1,473	356.5	36.8
Los Gatos	53,214	139	85.6	21	D	597.4	D	D	D	D	73.9
Lynwood	11,583	98	91.8	39	487	328.8	31.1	102	1,250	368.5	30.6
Madera	52,206	251	100.0	27	363	298.2	23.1	156	2,282	644.2	59.7
Manhattan Beach	19,058	71	94.4	40	364	1,335.9	63.9	175	2,822	777.4	85.1
Manteca	229,277	711	98.6	29	462	515.7	26.7	193	3,614	1,082.2	106.2
Martinez	14,215	63	100.0	23	212	61.3	10.4	69	1,060	327.9	34.8
Maywood	1,840	11	81.8	16	652	426.2	31.4	45	508	124.8	12.3
Menifee	546,280	1,264	100.0	15	58	25.5	1.8	109	2,109	546.0	52.8
Menlo Park	89,120	173	19.1	32	745	1,787.4	69.5	113	1,798	486.0	92.3
Merced	198,248	723	100.0	37	643	1,090.6	37.3	225	4,134	1,156.9	108.7
Milpitas	43,754	201	36.3	160	8,560	9,497.6	1,380.9	295	5,471	1,352.1	143.8
Mission Viejo	65,611	210	15.2	102	530	374.9	38.5	336	6,221	1,874.0	189.0
Modesto	43,580	311	61.4	100	2,035	2,779.0	133.2	691	11,082	2,557.7	275.4
Monrovia	4,902	45	82.2	86	855	490.7	56.7	105	2,918	1,120.7	100.3
Montclair	620	6	100.0	90	695	323.5	31.6	217	4,086	1,241.5	124.6
Montebello	21,128	185	17.3	109	1,709	1,097.7	96.6	209	3,885	1,053.0	98.1
Monterey	8,000	18	22.2	35	335	1,005.9	24.0	200	2,232	495.9	64.6
Monterey Park	5,258	15	100.0	185	1,227	977.0	46.8	194	1,787	619.1	51.6
Moorpark	1,226	17	100.0	55	1,072	602.4	68.6	60	900	245.6	22.2
Moreno Valley	100,940	383	98.4	D	D	D	D	326	9,094	2,941.6	269.3
Morgan Hill	32,568	94	91.5	56	2,108	1,221.7	144.6	D	D	D	67.1
Mountain View	88,195	298	57.7	92	1,867	8,098.8	192.2	210	4,054	1,305.0	141.9
Murrieta	77,981	440	5.7	106	968	855.4	62.2	228	4,930	1,666.5	150.8
Napa	185,815	977	12.3	75	505	371.0	32.2	295	4,518	1,317.9	139.5
National City	13,838	83	15.7	93	1,571	985.3	73.8	295	6,265	1,758.9	181.2
Newark	125,679	398	66.8	55	1,167	868.0	68.6	161	4,149	883.0	114.3
Newport Beach	142,853	209	70.3	224	1,915	1,571.1	135.6	472	7,370	3,007.4	281.0
Norco	874	7	100.0	28	534	361.5	34.5	108	1,527	557.9	44.0
Norwalk	734	3	100.0	96	1,431	1,304.2	69.6	172	3,479	1,391.2	110.0
Novato	22,220	82	57.3	67	627	525.5	51.0	162	2,656	883.2	93.5
Oakland	274,603	1,351	8.4	341	4,811	4,228.9	299.6	995	11,810	3,804.3	425.4
Oakley	130,333	488	100.0	7	D	23.5	D	37	403	143.0	12.7
Oceanside	110,162	491	14.7	144	1,563	1,038.8	93.0	398	6,639	1,757.8	173.5
Ontario	152,011	882	83.7	775	13,440	11,718.8	704.9	590	14,963	7,007.9	503.5
Orange	19,011	131	60.3	334	4,361	6,801.5	267.4	538	8,816	2,639.1	273.5
Oxnard	78,052	347	15.0	211	3,685	7,400.6	244.6	437	8,471	3,150.9	274.8
Pacifica	11,715	42	81.0	10	29	27.6	1.7	58	681	172.0	18.6
Palmdale	51,216	288	64.9	30	147	67.1	5.1	308	7,566	1,833.8	190.6
Palm Desert	81,625	157	90.4	77	569	271.2	28.4	453	6,849	2,286.5	190.8
Palm Springs	91,571	288	100.0	32	182	76.4	7.0	208	3,280	973.1	94.2
Palo Alto	56,676	129	98.4	87	4,217	26,497.2	1,840.2	323	5,426	1,940.0	236.6
Paramount	4,551	22	100.0	219	2,167	1,177.5	94.3	123	1,632	419.2	46.0
Pasadena	34,934	330	13.9	167	1,143	1,084.0	78.8	559	9,940	3,730.3	334.5
Perris	31,086	201	77.6	29	348	363.9	20.4	103	3,071	1,319.5	106.8
Petaluma	28,316	111	100.0	103	2,461	1,854.9	231.5	273	3,900	1,259.4	134.5
Pico Rivera	4,144	50	96.0	86	2,223	1,683.9	130.2	117	2,477	573.4	63.5
Pittsburg	111,477	676	30.9	33	771	331.4	41.5	106	2,234	665.2	67.1
Placentia	90,955	480	12.9	106	1,078	624.8	70.6	99	1,337	506.2	45.5
Pleasant Hill	4,117	11	100.0	25	139	97.8	9.3	135	3,149	733.0	77.9
Pleasanton	54,930	153	50.3	129	3,227	2,019.8	171.0	314	6,397	1,864.7	207.0
Pomona	14,073	120	98.3	316	3,279	2,922.1	174.0	330	4,329	1,304.9	119.0
Porterville	63,917	227	64.8	24	207	566.7	13.7	151	2,652	619.9	65.9
Poway	21,430	78	42.3	95	1,987	1,180.8	148.7	140	3,001	1,121.5	99.5
Rancho Cordova	171,195	552	100.0	165	2,261	1,573.3	165.6	282	3,851	1,104.5	124.6
Rancho Cucamonga	129,630	973	11.0	377	4,598	4,372.4	247.2	476	8,566	2,281.1	232.3
Rancho Palos Verdes	5,890	5	100.0	35	95	57.6	4.8	50	482	161.5	14.1
Rancho Santa Margarita	0	0	0.0	65	488	259.9	31.3	73	1,967	643.9	64.2
Redding	60,011	201	76.1	110	1,223	760.7	66.5	442	7,306	2,251.6	218.7
Redlands	56,825	392	16.3	53	622	403.4	29.1	213	4,753	1,711.2	140.1
Redondo Beach	39,827	117	65.0	73	425	391.4	29.3	261	4,055	963.0	105.1
Redwood City	51,754	193	29.0	69	2,137	1,358.7	268.9	222	4,818	2,088.8	196.0

1. Merchant wholesalers except manufacturers' sales branches and offices. 2. Establishments with payroll.

City	Real estate and rental and leasing, 2017				Professional, scientific, and technical services[1], 2017				Manufacturing, 2017			
	Number of establish-ments	Number of employees	Receipts (mil dol)	Annual payroll (mil dol)	Number of establish-ments	Number of employees	Receipts (mil dol)	Annual payroll (mil dol)	Number of establish-ments	Number of employees	Receipts (mil dol)	Annual payroll (mil dol)
	80	81	82	83	84	85	86	87	88	89	90	91
CALIFORNIA—Cont'd												
Lemoore	24	57	13.5	1.9	20	66	6.7	2.5	NA	NA	NA	NA
Lincoln	42	101	21.4	3.9	58	478	40.8	19.4	NA	NA	NA	NA
Livermore	110	716	261.2	51.7	250	12,580	3,354.8	1,138.0	NA	NA	NA	NA
Lodi	65	441	43.4	15.6	99	418	52.8	17.8	NA	NA	NA	NA
Lompoc	38	217	28.7	5.9	41	272	37.7	14.0	NA	NA	NA	NA
Long Beach	571	3,040	1,215.7	151.1	1,123	8,457	1,589.0	573.7	NA	NA	NA	NA
Los Altos	110	446	217.3	32.0	277	4,124	1,079.3	614.1	NA	NA	NA	NA
Los Angeles	7,059	44,587	19,766.6	2,717.1	16,741	155,056	38,074.8	13,648.8	NA	NA	NA	NA
Los Banos	25	58	14.4	1.8	22	114	14.8	5.1	NA	NA	NA	NA
Los Gatos	140	571	211.8	35.7	270	1,786	337.7	146.6	NA	NA	NA	NA
Lynwood	13	129	11.6	4.2	26	92	10.6	3.5	NA	NA	NA	NA
Madera	47	177	31.4	5.8	38	152	15.1	4.8	NA	NA	NA	NA
Manhattan Beach	171	546	183.3	31.4	407	3,584	732.2	338.5	NA	NA	NA	NA
Manteca	63	269	57.2	12.8	61	274	31.1	10.6	NA	NA	NA	NA
Martinez	46	204	51.7	8.8	91	402	64.3	23.9	NA	NA	NA	NA
Maywood	5	11	1.0	0.2	4	10	0.4	0.2	NA	NA	NA	NA
Menifee	55	204	43.9	6.4	65	175	20.5	6.2	NA	NA	NA	NA
Menlo Park	80	320	160.7	27.1	346	6,125	1,996.2	865.7	NA	NA	NA	NA
Merced	69	359	72.5	13.0	90	462	45.9	17.1	NA	NA	NA	NA
Milpitas	93	762	197.9	40.6	343	7,472	2,425.6	975.0	NA	NA	NA	NA
Mission Viejo	170	750	283.3	50.1	496	2,675	625.8	251.5	NA	NA	NA	NA
Modesto	213	952	237.2	37.6	377	3,116	402.6	176.9	NA	NA	NA	NA
Monrovia	70	298	55.3	14.9	173	1,927	417.3	159.7	NA	NA	NA	NA
Montclair	32	226	62.5	10.0	36	224	31.8	9.1	NA	NA	NA	NA
Montebello	63	412	101.4	18.0	71	325	34.9	11.2	NA	NA	NA	NA
Monterey	95	411	133.7	16.9	240	4,470	493.0	203.4	NA	NA	NA	NA
Monterey Park	112	279	77.3	12.1	190	1,597	212.2	96.4	NA	NA	NA	NA
Moorpark	40	185	27.3	7.2	114	388	74.2	24.2	NA	NA	NA	NA
Moreno Valley	88	336	99.9	12.9	87	538	55.6	19.3	NA	NA	NA	NA
Morgan Hill	74	255	73.0	11.3	130	858	131.6	53.3	NA	NA	NA	NA
Mountain View	145	812	208.5	42.3	537	13,889	4,426.6	1,850.8	NA	NA	NA	NA
Murrieta	167	603	141.6	24.2	282	1,317	215.9	74.4	NA	NA	NA	NA
Napa	120	569	166.9	27.9	D	D	D	D	NA	NA	NA	NA
National City	55	306	85.7	13.5	54	585	74.5	29.0	NA	NA	NA	NA
Newark	51	247	105.8	13.4	157	2,442	956.1	287.7	NA	NA	NA	NA
Newport Beach	841	4,996	2,407.4	415.6	1,348	9,092	2,133.2	804.6	NA	NA	NA	NA
Norco	37	89	25.2	3.2	79	1,338	127.6	60.6	NA	NA	NA	NA
Norwalk	55	204	50.1	9.2	68	1,383	374.4	159.9	NA	NA	NA	NA
Novato	81	391	95.8	19.7	247	2,294	448.4	188.7	NA	NA	NA	NA
Oakland	544	3,196	934.2	159.2	1,628	14,453	3,276.0	1,340.8	NA	NA	NA	NA
Oakley	21	61	17.9	4.0	23	121	16.4	4.8	NA	NA	NA	NA
Oceanside	187	678	208.4	29.4	350	1,814	254.5	95.2	NA	NA	NA	NA
Ontario	218	1,786	665.6	97.1	D	D	D	D	NA	NA	NA	NA
Orange	300	2,196	656.8	110.4	744	9,814	1,165.7	476.9	NA	NA	NA	NA
Oxnard	168	627	189.0	25.8	257	2,222	394.9	138.4	NA	NA	NA	NA
Pacifica	30	52	17.9	2.9	83	236	43.9	11.1	NA	NA	NA	NA
Palmdale	112	373	89.9	12.8	157	3,894	749.9	322.7	NA	NA	NA	NA
Palm Desert	165	1,056	209.1	55.5	296	1,079	184.8	58.1	NA	NA	NA	NA
Palm Springs	151	676	174.8	31.0	190	639	131.0	40.1	NA	NA	NA	NA
Palo Alto	209	1,820	1,059.3	138.6	904	17,354	6,631.6	2,693.8	NA	NA	NA	NA
Paramount	28	190	48.9	8.7	37	370	27.2	13.4	NA	NA	NA	NA
Pasadena	434	2,153	569.1	108.7	1,352	17,626	5,094.7	1,866.5	NA	NA	NA	NA
Perris	29	130	32.4	10.0	39	121	17.0	4.8	NA	NA	NA	NA
Petaluma	72	360	105.7	15.9	D	D	D	D	NA	NA	NA	NA
Pico Rivera	43	215	95.2	12.8	33	197	33.4	9.6	NA	NA	NA	NA
Pittsburg	34	219	56.6	11.5	49	283	48.8	14.7	NA	NA	NA	NA
Placentia	70	388	88.0	16.1	121	465	63.4	22.5	NA	NA	NA	NA
Pleasant Hill	55	340	94.3	24.4	160	840	147.9	60.8	NA	NA	NA	NA
Pleasanton	218	1,075	400.5	73.6	634	8,558	2,014.1	1,049.7	NA	NA	NA	NA
Pomona	102	652	156.9	28.6	132	1,085	156.3	52.2	NA	NA	NA	NA
Porterville	25	90	14.2	2.7	44	184	20.0	5.5	NA	NA	NA	NA
Poway	92	343	103.5	14.0	265	1,479	263.7	103.4	NA	NA	NA	NA
Rancho Cordova	90	447	119.1	30.4	243	5,602	1,173.6	491.5	NA	NA	NA	NA
Rancho Cucamonga	256	1,003	356.3	47.5	491	3,294	506.0	174.5	NA	NA	NA	NA
Rancho Palos Verdes	76	172	68.5	8.7	157	642	105.9	43.3	NA	NA	NA	NA
Rancho Santa Margarita	75	249	169.0	35.3	221	1,731	221.0	66.5	NA	NA	NA	NA
Redding	165	672	144.9	25.4	288	1,748	231.3	101.7	NA	NA	NA	NA
Redlands	98	477	117.1	15.9	245	1,199	190.0	66.0	NA	NA	NA	NA
Redondo Beach	168	888	205.9	51.1	476	7,910	1,427.0	846.4	NA	NA	NA	NA
Redwood City	163	858	326.7	48.4	477	10,934	3,716.2	1,589.5	NA	NA	NA	NA

1. Establishments subject to federal tax.

Table D. Cities — Accommodation and Food Services, Arts, Entertainment, and Recreation, and Health Care and Social Assistance

City	Accommodation and food services, 2017				Arts, entertainment, and recreation[1], 2017				Health care and social assistance[1], 2017			
	Number of establish-ments	Number of employees	Receipts (mil dol)	Annual payroll (mil dol)	Number of establish-ments	Number of employees	Receipts (mil dol)	Annual payroll (mil dol)	Number of establish-ments	Number of employees	Receipts (mil dol)	Annual payroll (mil dol)
	92	93	94	95	96	97	98	99	100	101	102	103
CALIFORNIA—Cont'd												
Lemoore	D	D	D	D	3.0	D	1.2	D	26	178	19.0	7.2
Lincoln	63	942	57.5	15.9	11.0	190	12.5	4.6	87	949	165.0	46.7
Livermore	219	3,592	263.8	78.1	38.0	1,079	102.6	24.1	214	2,551	363.2	136.7
Lodi	144	2,288	143.8	41.0	14.0	352	17.7	5.8	195	3,498	499.1	177.2
Lompoc	90	1,224	83.6	22.6	5.0	46	2.6	0.6	84	1,582	192.6	70.6
Long Beach	993	20,426	1,508.7	408.3	145.0	2,242	187.7	60.3	1,263	29,063	4,152.6	1,682.3
Los Altos	88	1,323	124.0	34.7	20.0	D	10.2	D	172	1,962	287.5	118.2
Los Angeles	9,300	179,751	14,223.6	3,971.4	10,363.0	49,334	14,957.1	5,540.6	12,429	226,723	34,620.9	12,523.4
Los Banos	73	1,044	60.1	15.5	D	D	D	D	54	774	115.9	40.4
Los Gatos	127	2,550	169.6	58.6	24.0	762	56.6	18.0	339	3,386	525.4	193.2
Lynwood	87	1,400	104.7	24.4	NA	NA	NA	NA	135	3,667	749.5	212.1
Madera	98	1,339	87.0	21.5	8.0	78	4.0	1.0	135	2,349	241.6	82.4
Manhattan Beach	151	4,437	319.3	102.5	96.0	428	52.9	19.9	237	1,416	221.7	87.3
Manteca	144	2,779	162.7	46.2	D	D	D	D	167	4,019	575.6	202.5
Martinez	90	999	70.0	18.4	7.0	35	2.0	0.5	97	5,436	866.9	362.6
Maywood	41	462	33.0	8.9	NA	NA	NA	NA	26	336	35.2	11.1
Menifee	95	2,379	139.2	41.3	12.0	174	10.4	2.9	119	2,141	181.4	70.6
Menlo Park	97	1,690	127.9	40.0	20.0	243	23.4	9.3	163	2,418	269.8	128.2
Merced	138	2,513	148.4	37.7	20.0	221	12.2	3.6	288	5,102	688.9	262.6
Milpitas	314	5,598	500.7	121.8	26.0	584	43.9	12.1	285	3,405	495.8	174.7
Mission Viejo	214	3,880	230.2	66.9	39.0	661	50.6	14.2	508	7,651	1,219.1	491.5
Modesto	430	8,484	483.4	140.1	47.0	858	59.2	16.8	683	16,649	2,967.9	1,109.8
Monrovia	119	2,024	128.5	37.6	23.0	182	18.6	3.9	104	1,651	173.4	68.1
Montclair	93	1,627	93.1	27.8	D	D	D	D	126	2,517	213.9	75.7
Montebello	142	2,355	135.9	39.2	7.0	182	15.7	4.6	194	3,248	476.4	163.7
Monterey	234	6,544	567.1	163.5	39.0	994	163.3	52.1	307	6,055	1,131.4	425.9
Monterey Park	242	3,327	208.9	62.8	12.0	132	13.0	2.9	282	4,342	703.8	227.3
Moorpark	54	817	50.3	14.6	15.0	45	5.0	1.6	67	692	66.8	26.5
Moreno Valley	257	4,746	294.4	78.6	22.0	310	22.4	5.0	248	6,376	1,035.4	400.7
Morgan Hill	128	1,904	141.6	39.0	15.0	368	16.4	7.0	D	D	D	53.5
Mountain View	366	6,514	486.3	185.3	24.0	838	91.6	21.8	324	7,574	2,048.2	774.0
Murrieta	195	3,737	212.9	62.5	37.0	548	31.1	9.2	340	5,494	735.3	281.8
Napa	229	5,716	553.0	148.2	30.0	451	57.8	8.9	306	5,637	914.4	334.9
National City	177	2,997	215.1	54.5	12.0	139	7.4	1.9	177	3,842	441.7	137.1
Newark	176	2,471	201.2	50.5	4.0	52	4.1	1.3	104	773	79.9	27.7
Newport Beach	411	13,281	1,227.6	344.9	131.0	1,708	217.6	67.6	1,036	13,306	2,612.4	872.7
Norco	D	D	D	D	9.0	117	12.8	3.1	47	557	53.4	20.2
Norwalk	148	2,106	141.3	37.4	11.0	209	14.8	3.9	160	4,090	460.3	281.1
Novato	127	2,081	138.6	41.8	27.0	438	32.7	10.5	194	2,670	431.3	174.7
Oakland	1,108	17,173	1,293.0	372.9	164.0	3,257	815.2	352.8	1,279	30,875	5,002.0	2,205.9
Oakley	D	D	D	D	3.0	D	7.0	D	39	248	20.6	8.2
Oceanside	359	7,350	586.5	144.1	47.0	1,100	70.1	25.3	363	5,870	761.1	297.1
Ontario	364	7,906	529.3	147.0	30.0	872	73.8	19.0	268	6,152	1,061.2	343.7
Orange	450	8,572	591.4	173.3	53.0	731	59.5	15.0	687	20,941	3,789.6	1,363.0
Oxnard	312	6,273	416.3	114.4	36.0	398	32.4	8.0	455	7,068	847.1	347.5
Pacifica	72	1,008	67.5	19.0	D	D	D	2.3	45	563	52.0	23.7
Palmdale	235	4,743	299.5	84.5	17.0	520	23.6	8.5	261	2,704	332.8	108.5
Palm Desert	195	6,563	497.5	153.5	48.0	2,602	216.3	72.6	286	3,891	352.6	137.5
Palm Springs	276	6,406	503.2	145.8	49.0	1,363	264.4	47.1	283	5,879	1,027.4	364.3
Palo Alto	321	7,457	709.9	216.1	57.0	1,219	100.4	37.1	412	27,393	7,345.7	2,683.1
Paramount	69	830	60.2	15.6	4.0	42	2.6	1.0	70	1,603	153.0	68.8
Pasadena	557	11,645	883.9	253.2	249.0	2,311	390.4	100.8	1,104	19,293	2,798.4	1,131.5
Perris	77	1,310	92.7	23.1	D	D	D	3.7	57	829	80.6	33.3
Petaluma	180	2,830	176.1	54.7	41.0	631	55.4	12.1	193	3,342	405.3	176.4
Pico Rivera	115	2,022	141.2	35.9	5.0	98	6.7	1.6	83	1,570	143.6	55.0
Pittsburg	94	1,514	104.4	29.1	5.0	80	4.0	1.1	85	1,059	98.3	41.1
Placentia	106	1,479	94.5	26.2	D	D	D	4.2	137	1,375	182.5	60.5
Pleasant Hill	114	2,104	183.4	44.5	18.0	446	23.3	11.1	157	2,631	441.6	116.9
Pleasanton	252	4,537	381.8	101.7	44.0	1,109	96.2	27.3	338	7,384	1,570.6	548.0
Pomona	237	4,464	259.0	79.3	18.0	394	82.5	16.2	322	9,677	1,540.6	540.4
Porterville	92	1,422	83.6	22.3	D	D	D	D	154	3,293	339.8	140.3
Poway	112	1,542	90.0	25.3	31.0	452	37.3	12.7	191	2,727	418.0	143.5
Rancho Cordova	165	3,165	217.6	57.4	24.0	491	31.5	8.7	133	5,321	851.2	325.0
Rancho Cucamonga	402	8,913	542.5	160.7	51.0	658	55.9	15.0	535	6,858	718.9	278.1
Rancho Palos Verdes	40	1,532	161.6	49.0	20.0	328	29.6	10.8	132	914	118.0	38.8
Rancho Santa Margarita	78	1,861	107.0	32.4	26.0	365	36.0	10.0	97	900	95.4	35.3
Redding	260	4,767	283.9	82.4	35.0	494	28.1	9.3	565	10,007	1,419.3	525.5
Redlands	185	3,318	190.6	55.8	27.0	602	26.0	7.6	379	7,221	952.8	366.1
Redondo Beach	231	4,891	322.1	104.5	D	D	D	D	260	1,792	222.3	86.8
Redwood City	244	3,724	292.5	86.5	38.0	931	76.1	20.0	346	6,563	1,107.4	564.9

1. Establishments subject to federal tax.

City	Other services[1]				Government employment and payroll, 2017								
						March payroll							
							Perent of total for:						
	Number of establish-ments	Number of employees	Receipts (mil dol)	Annual payroll (mil dol)	Full-time equivalent employees	Total (dollars)	Admin-istrative, judicial, and legal	Police and corrections	Fire protection	Highways and trans-portation	Health and welfare	Natural resources and utilities	Education and libraries
	104	105	106	107	108	109	110	111	112	113	114	115	116
CALIFORNIA—Cont'd													
Lemoore	D	D	D	D	107	511,098	13.0	52.1	0.0	1.2	2.3	29.9	0.0
Lincoln	D	D	D	6.0	214	1,281,023	18.7	28.4	11.2	10.5	9.3	10.6	1.8
Livermore	148	828	107.0	29.9	429	3,798,311	15.9	36.7	0.0	16.7	5.5	16.2	6.3
Lodi	123	606	72.3	21.4	495	3,158,229	10.3	27.2	16.3	7.0	1.8	29.1	2.7
Lompoc	51	351	25.1	8.3	380	2,298,679	13.3	22.5	12.5	4.9	0.0	32.5	2.5
Long Beach	699	5,912	627.9	179.9	5,477	39,697,152	7.1	26.3	14.1	21.8	5.4	12.7	1.5
Los Altos	78	726	1,802.6	58.7	139	1,212,302	9.9	34.6	0.0	13.3	6.0	32.0	0.0
Los Angeles	7,114	53,813	8,661.8	1,932.4	52,287	452,879,430	10.9	25.7	10.2	11.1	2.7	30.9	1.2
Los Banos	29	175	13.2	4.3	159	915,005	11.4	40.1	15.6	5.1	2.1	19.2	0.0
Los Gatos	112	715	78.4	20.7	161	1,481,593	16.6	44.7	0.0	10.6	7.3	6.5	7.7
Lynwood	D	D	D	D	250	1,095,158	42.8	2.5	0.0	20.8	5.6	28.3	0.0
Madera	55	239	25.3	6.5	294	1,462,912	16.2	35.5	0.0	9.9	12.4	22.5	0.0
Manhattan Beach	90	705	131.3	25.7	351	2,662,902	14.7	46.2	8.1	8.8	8.8	11.7	0.0
Manteca	90	440	50.6	11.8	366	2,635,747	13.0	35.1	16.5	6.2	1.2	25.5	0.0
Martinez	62	248	38.7	11.0	59	491,580	13.6	76.6	0.0	2.7	3.6	3.1	0.0
Maywood	D	D	D	D	23	76,222	44.2	0.0	0.0	0.0	6.9	36.6	0.0
Menifee	54	314	39.4	9.7	83	474,674	40.9	0.0	0.0	24.1	0.0	20.8	0.0
Menlo Park	93	584	91.5	22.2	293	2,219,306	10.4	33.8	0.0	5.7	1.0	8.5	5.5
Merced	77	433	43.1	11.6	448	2,854,185	10.0	35.2	18.2	2.5	1.4	22.1	0.0
Milpitas	133	1,011	156.9	47.7	375	3,499,150	15.0	37.9	22.9	7.2	1.2	9.3	0.0
Mission Viejo	215	1,253	134.6	42.1	196	1,146,333	30.3	0.0	0.0	15.1	7.1	23.9	17.8
Modesto	309	1,761	183.2	51.3	1,148	8,001,264	13.2	29.7	18.7	9.0	0.8	25.7	0.0
Monrovia	85	575	102.8	20.1	280	1,931,644	18.1	34.8	23.5	1.6	3.3	14.1	3.7
Montclair	D	D	39.7	D	278	1,588,376	24.9	33.6	17.3	1.8	13.6	5.5	0.0
Montebello	106	571	58.6	17.0	392	2,384,162	7.9	36.5	21.6	29.5	0.0	2.7	0.0
Monterey	99	897	171.8	26.9	505	3,608,460	10.0	15.7	24.8	5.7	0.6	13.7	3.4
Monterey Park	87	378	39.6	9.3	333	2,214,654	9.7	35.3	26.2	4.9	2.6	16.0	5.3
Moorpark	33	148	18.1	4.6	74	567,743	35.0	0.0	0.0	14.4	20.1	30.5	0.0
Moreno Valley	132	572	51.0	14.4	412	2,054,931	30.4	4.2	2.5	17.0	20.1	17.5	3.7
Morgan Hill	93	388	41.7	12.4	224	1,286,104	12.5	25.6	0.0	4.5	0.4	11.8	0.0
Mountain View	152	901	318.1	87.6	671	5,866,700	11.3	25.8	15.6	12.6	6.2	15.5	4.4
Murrieta	186	1,259	123.1	36.4	316	2,365,710	12.9	42.9	23.5	5.3	0.3	5.1	3.5
Napa	173	1,100	143.7	37.7	449	4,001,327	10.5	30.6	19.6	10.0	3.1	21.2	0.0
National City	124	687	63.4	20.1	405	2,542,406	8.6	41.8	20.2	3.0	4.4	9.9	7.7
Newark	92	587	61.2	19.0	176	878,820	14.6	51.4	0.0	5.5	1.7	15.2	0.0
Newport Beach	322	2,215	340.1	70.5	784	8,009,294	13.2	35.6	19.4	8.3	1.1	10.9	4.5
Norco	72	412	39.2	12.3	89	348,976	36.5	0.0	0.0	0.0	1.6	35.4	0.0
Norwalk	89	419	53.6	13.1	339	1,819,034	18.9	5.9	0.0	43.1	10.1	12.8	0.0
Novato	113	881	247.9	44.1	208	1,580,041	7.8	47.8	0.0	4.1	8.2	13.5	0.0
Oakland	945	7,498	1,499.8	345.3	4,077	36,522,164	10.8	32.3	18.6	18.4	6.4	5.6	3.0
Oakley	D	D	D	D	75	669,513	13.2	61.2	0.0	10.3	4.3	6.0	0.0
Oceanside	231	1,596	155.8	48.6	1,010	7,245,519	14.3	40.5	19.0	3.1	2.9	16.1	2.4
Ontario	231	2,627	346.2	114.2	1,177	10,470,584	9.1	39.3	21.9	0.0	1.2	16.1	2.3
Orange	353	2,549	282.5	85.7	650	5,729,395	7.6	37.2	26.7	7.7	3.1	11.4	3.7
Oxnard	227	1,132	130.8	35.5	1,254	8,375,994	8.4	32.1	18.0	4.2	7.7	22.5	1.9
Pacifica	52	157	16.9	4.4	189	1,420,456	8.7	25.9	18.2	10.1	0.0	28.7	0.0
Palmdale	121	664	47.6	14.8	259	1,371,327	21.8	4.9	0.0	23.4	8.3	26.4	0.0
Palm Desert	189	1,388	114.9	35.5	115	977,448	44.6	0.0	0.0	25.9	3.5	4.6	0.0
Palm Springs	114	868	77.8	21.3	452	3,754,400	16.6	29.9	19.3	18.5	1.5	3.9	2.1
Palo Alto	185	1,962	970.0	136.9	1,032	9,194,693	18.4	13.2	14.3	3.1	0.8	34.4	3.7
Paramount	66	480	67.5	19.9	165	844,493	21.3	19.0	0.0	23.3	10.7	24.9	0.0
Pasadena	448	2,941	338.0	88.0	1,903	14,743,235	14.4	23.4	13.4	4.8	4.4	30.0	3.2
Perris	39	166	29.8	5.4	259	1,448,110	17.9	0.0	0.0	6.2	9.0	33.0	0.0
Petaluma	139	899	89.6	28.1	319	2,597,477	11.3	31.4	22.1	13.6	0.9	19.4	0.0
Pico Rivera	67	518	70.1	18.6	266	1,253,039	21.6	0.0	0.0	31.8	12.8	33.8	0.0
Pittsburg	80	681	63.2	21.5	292	2,210,692	11.4	47.3	0.0	8.1	2.4	20.8	0.0
Placentia	D	D	D	13.3	135	872,042	14.9	63.3	0.0	14.1	0.3	7.3	0.0
Pleasant Hill	75	513	49.3	16.4	129	1,083,557	21.9	52.8	0.0	22.8	2.3	0.0	0.0
Pleasanton	169	1,401	202.5	63.3	532	4,798,853	11.6	23.7	32.0	5.5	1.2	18.0	4.1
Pomona	163	968	111.3	34.0	654	3,272,255	8.4	51.9	0.0	5.9	6.4	15.2	2.9
Porterville	43	281	26.4	8.5	564	2,144,104	8.1	22.4	11.8	4.1	3.0	45.3	2.2
Poway	108	540	51.1	15.1	247	1,657,178	20.5	0.0	32.3	3.2	0.0	23.0	0.0
Rancho Cordova	118	761	102.2	31.8	79	502,805	38.0	0.0	0.0	24.4	3.0	0.0	0.0
Rancho Cucamonga	282	1,496	162.3	47.6	625	3,766,895	15.6	0.0	36.6	11.6	0.0	26.4	4.9
Rancho Palos Verdes	40	100	12.9	2.8	92	602,068	100.0	0.0	0.0	0.0	0.0	0.0	0.0
Rancho Santa Margarita	71	346	36.3	10.3	33	223,919	44.4	2.7	0.0	21.3	18.6	13.0	0.0
Redding	206	1,272	168.3	38.8	789	5,878,787	9.6	20.4	13.4	6.2	1.1	39.5	0.0
Redlands	143	970	97.4	30.7	493	3,384,099	9.8	30.4	20.7	4.5	0.4	24.3	3.4
Redondo Beach	158	762	75.9	21.6	505	3,899,259	11.8	37.3	21.3	8.1	5.9	9.4	3.4
Redwood City	163	1,846	1,298.3	195.8	585	5,213,786	13.5	23.5	18.2	7.9	8.8	16.4	7.2

1. Establishments subject to federal tax.

City	City government finances, 2017									
	General revenue							General expenditure		
		Intergovernmental		Taxes						
					Per capita[1] (dollars)				Per capita[1] (dollars)	
	Total (mil dol)	Total (mil dol)	Percent from state government	Total (mil dol)	Total	Property	Sales and gross receipts	Total (mil dol)	Total	Capital outlays
	117	118	119	120	121	122	123	124	125	126
CALIFORNIA—Cont'd										
Lemoore	20.2	2.1	67.1	7.4	283	166	114	22.5	856	207
Lincoln	90.3	4.5	56.1	20.4	429	215	205	56.7	1,192	150
Livermore	172.3	7.9	46.6	94.0	1,043	456	546	203.7	2,260	338
Lodi	102.0	17.6	62.1	42.1	640	222	409	117.6	1,789	210
Lompoc	74.0	8.9	33.8	20.2	468	173	292	67.0	1,549	185
Long Beach	1,548.9	258.1	27.0	438.3	939	415	516	1,647.7	3,531	933
Los Altos	48.7	2.3	54.4	34.1	1,112	645	461	47.1	1,535	191
Los Angeles	10,825.2	1,131.0	26.5	4,708.7	1,184	490	639	9,618.2	2,419	399
Los Banos	42.4	2.4	87.9	18.6	479	146	155	34.2	878	150
Los Gatos	41.5	1.8	97.4	33.2	1,073	456	596	51.1	1,653	437
Lynwood	49.1	6.3	92.4	27.8	393	176	216	47.5	671	126
Madera	58.4	10.0	35.2	23.8	366	145	219	61.5	947	233
Manhattan Beach	88.6	4.2	40.2	53.7	1,503	790	691	86.2	2,415	205
Manteca	112.8	7.4	56.0	44.4	561	165	249	113.5	1,435	392
Martinez	29.9	1.6	99.2	25.1	654	346	290	27.3	711	54
Maywood	11.1	1.2	50.2	8.7	318	113	161	12.4	454	27
Menifee	49.7	4.5	76.4	31.6	350	136	208	88.6	983	190
Menlo Park	74.1	3.2	58.0	56.4	1,650	790	842	71.0	2,076	363
Merced	93.5	7.8	72.2	38.6	467	169	291	107.0	1,296	274
Milpitas	177.5	4.8	40.4	99.9	1,282	606	667	133.4	1,713	410
Mission Viejo	83.9	4.0	59.8	59.8	626	359	260	101.3	1,060	131
Modesto	285.6	70.5	69.9	107.5	505	158	347	214.1	1,005	131
Monrovia	66.4	8.2	16.0	42.1	1,142	706	418	73.2	1,986	229
Montclair	63.7	3.6	40.7	43.7	1,117	579	518	61.8	1,579	455
Montebello	132.5	36.4	14.0	71.6	1,140	451	652	82.4	1,312	178
Monterey	143.5	7.0	74.5	68.4	2,407	471	1,778	136.1	4,790	363
Monterey Park	70.1	7.6	76.0	42.6	701	421	266	65.7	1,083	51
Moorpark	34.9	2.8	27.0	15.6	426	246	172	38.5	1,053	85
Moreno Valley	149.0	14.7	73.5	100.5	486	201	250	212.2	1,026	177
Morgan Hill	71.1	1.4	96.9	34.6	769	232	369	75.3	1,674	425
Mountain View	300.9	4.1	65.6	148.3	1,827	1,064	661	272.8	3,360	740
Murrieta	70.0	5.8	59.5	48.4	428	182	241	95.9	849	299
Napa	139.8	17.2	22.1	75.2	951	389	546	138.2	1,747	158
National City	92.6	18.8	28.8	54.2	888	297	588	100.6	1,646	378
Newark	72.2	3.5	46.7	50.2	1,059	347	661	55.8	1,177	85
Newport Beach	259.8	10.8	20.0	174.0	2,029	1,095	900	296.0	3,452	1,350
Norco	32.4	1.4	72.7	15.0	559	151	349	55.6	2,070	522
Norwalk	101.3	33.2	24.6	56.4	535	217	304	73.6	698	64
Novato	54.3	3.2	58.5	38.1	685	346	319	58.8	1,055	220
Oakland	1,639.3	137.8	49.4	812.7	1,915	893	747	1,319.3	3,109	273
Oakley	34.6	1.2	100.0	18.0	432	134	133	31.7	762	250
Oceanside	270.0	23.3	44.3	108.3	616	344	259	277.8	1,579	262
Ontario	416.0	25.1	35.3	233.8	1,333	384	944	458.7	2,616	619
Orange	147.1	9.9	56.4	105.8	754	324	424	170.6	1,217	330
Oxnard	374.7	21.2	48.0	132.9	636	395	237	301.2	1,442	24
Pacifica	52.4	3.6	45.5	27.0	692	377	266	50.3	1,289	119
Palmdale	171.9	15.6	66.9	131.3	839	545	278	101.3	647	100
Palm Desert	125.3	2.9	50.5	55.5	1,052	192	829	128.0	2,424	451
Palm Springs	207.4	13.3	24.7	108.5	2,258	704	1,266	184.2	3,834	753
Palo Alto	274.2	6.8	36.9	127.2	1,899	654	1,133	338.4	5,054	1,472
Paramount	33.7	5.9	70.5	24.7	452	142	308	35.8	656	100
Pasadena	403.5	42.8	27.6	217.6	1,535	669	763	323.3	2,281	0
Perris	60.3	4.6	79.9	29.4	379	153	222	87.6	1,129	150
Petaluma	103.1	16.4	31.3	42.1	694	241	416	90.5	1,491	229
Pico Rivera	59.3	12.6	42.1	37.1	588	165	281	76.7	1,214	345
Pittsburg	141.1	50.7	8.2	40.8	567	253	290	109.5	1,520	198
Placentia	41.0	3.1	50.8	28.4	546	264	276	56.1	1,081	129
Pleasant Hill	29.5	3.0	58.6	23.6	677	174	495	42.2	1,208	220
Pleasanton	171.1	6.6	67.3	113.8	1,374	734	512	130.7	1,578	0
Pomona	180.3	22.1	26.2	100.2	657	316	328	171.9	1,127	154
Porterville	67.1	14.5	44.9	25.5	427	109	256	55.9	936	180
Poway	116.0	1.9	91.9	89.0	1,786	1,379	370	141.5	2,840	930
Rancho Cordova	91.1	11.0	34.5	66.5	907	197	509	107.3	1,462	309
Rancho Cucamonga	210.2	17.9	47.5	156.2	883	583	276	193.8	1,095	233
Rancho Palos Verdes	36.1	1.7	79.9	29.9	711	305	371	32.6	773	72
Rancho Santa Margarita	20.4	1.6	73.4	16.6	342	138	196	19.6	404	63
Redding	156.2	21.3	32.8	56.4	616	254	339	146.5	1,600	127
Redlands	115.4	6.2	73.8	55.0	771	369	389	110.8	1,553	311
Redondo Beach	123.4	6.9	79.8	64.0	948	471	440	122.5	1,815	106
Redwood City	210.3	12.6	40.6	110.9	1,284	678	591	221.0	2,559	262

1. Based on population estimated as of July 1 of the year shown.

City	City government finances, 2017 (cont.)												
	General expenditure (cont.)												
	Percent of total for:										Debt outstanding		
	Public welfare	Highways	Parking facilities	Education	Health and hospitals	Police protection	Sewerage and sanitation	Parks and recreation	Housing and community development	Interest on debt	Total (mil dol)	Per capita[1] (dollars)	Debt issued during year
	127	128	129	130	131	132	133	134	135	136	137	138	139
CALIFORNIA—Cont'd													
Lemoore	0.0	13.8	0.0	0.0	0.0	23.2	19.7	13.5	8.9	0.1	5.8	222	0.0
Lincoln	0.0	13.6	0.0	0.0	0.0	9.5	23.9	14.9	4.0	2.6	27.9	588	27.6
Livermore	0.0	12.0	0.0	0.9	0.4	15.8	10.9	1.6	4.6	1.9	124.3	1,379	25.1
Lodi	0.0	7.4	0.0	0.0	0.4	16.9	11.8	5.0	1.3	2.5	152.6	2,321	0.0
Lompoc	0.0	9.1	0.0	0.0	0.7	16.4	22.6	6.8	7.7	5.5	41.1	950	0.0
Long Beach	0.0	6.8	0.0	0.0	4.4	14.4	5.2	6.3	4.8	2.8	2,367.5	5,073	171.7
Los Altos	0.0	14.1	0.0	0.0	0.0	23.1	14.6	6.0	0.7	0.1	1.4	47	0.0
Los Angeles	0.0	5.7	0.4	0.0	3.9	22.8	12.1	4.8	2.5	5.6	27,626.9	6,949	3,433.3
Los Banos	0.0	9.6	0.0	0.0	0.0	24.1	30.3	15.8	1.9	0.4	2.0	52	0.0
Los Gatos	0.0	13.5	0.0	0.0	0.4	26.0	0.0	6.4	1.2	2.0	24.6	794	0.0
Lynwood	0.0	20.1	0.0	0.0	5.7	23.8	0.0	9.2	11.3	2.0	40.3	571	7.7
Madera	0.0	25.7	0.1	0.0	1.2	19.2	19.5	8.8	3.7	4.8	94.5	1,455	0.0
Manhattan Beach	0.0	7.9	4.5	0.0	2.8	31.7	7.5	15.0	0.0	0.9	25.0	700	5.9
Manteca	0.0	17.2	0.0	0.0	0.3	17.7	29.0	7.3	8.0	1.6	69.7	882	0.0
Martinez	0.0	9.8	0.8	0.0	0.0	39.8	0.2	13.3	0.0	4.4	33.7	877	0.0
Maywood	0.0	18.8	0.0	0.0	0.6	30.0	0.0	3.3	4.3	1.6	2.8	104	0.0
Menifee	0.0	28.4	0.0	0.0	0.8	26.9	0.0	0.8	3.2	1.0	18.3	203	0.0
Menlo Park	0.0	21.2	1.1	0.0	0.0	21.9	0.0	21.5	3.9	4.9	78.5	2,297	0.0
Merced	0.0	14.8	0.1	0.0	1.2	19.3	25.2	4.8	7.4	1.1	49.6	600	0.0
Milpitas	0.0	10.8	0.0	0.0	11.9	20.3	6.2	3.7	19.2	5.3	125.6	1,613	0.0
Mission Viejo	0.0	13.8	0.0	0.6	3.2	19.9	0.0	14.2	5.5	1.6	38.0	398	0.0
Modesto	0.0	4.4	0.6	0.0	0.5	25.4	31.1	6.2	3.4	3.6	516.5	2,425	140.3
Monrovia	0.0	4.0	0.0	0.0	0.5	33.1	1.9	3.4	11.1	10.8	149.8	4,066	27.7
Montclair	0.0	6.1	0.0	0.0	5.7	15.9	10.6	5.9	34.0	6.5	86.9	2,221	0.0
Montebello	0.0	5.7	0.0	0.0	0.0	26.0	3.9	8.0	13.9	6.0	130.2	2,073	55.4
Monterey	0.0	14.2	4.6	0.0	0.0	11.5	1.8	9.7	5.8	5.2	97.5	3,432	3.8
Monterey Park	0.0	7.6	0.0	0.0	15.8	28.3	12.6	6.3	2.6	8.4	90.6	1,494	3.8
Moorpark	0.0	21.2	0.0	0.0	0.7	19.3	0.7	16.7	12.7	3.1	29.0	793	0.0
Moreno Valley	0.0	12.6	0.0	0.0	1.2	38.0	0.0	4.4	4.0	2.4	144.4	698	24.7
Morgan Hill	0.0	9.8	0.0	0.0	0.0	20.7	9.0	11.8	25.4	3.9	90.4	2,010	0.0
Mountain View	0.0	3.4	0.2	1.8	0.0	11.6	12.0	16.6	1.2	0.6	44.0	541	0.0
Murrieta	0.0	28.5	0.0	0.0	0.5	27.8	0.0	10.9	9.1	2.8	52.1	461	0.0
Napa	0.0	11.7	0.1	0.0	4.7	18.8	16.7	7.2	13.3	0.1	56.9	719	12.5
National City	0.0	2.7	0.0	0.0	1.2	24.6	7.3	1.6	36.4	2.5	60.4	988	1.3
Newark	0.0	16.2	0.0	0.0	0.4	31.7	0.1	10.2	0.8	1.4	18.3	385	0.0
Newport Beach	0.0	10.8	0.0	0.0	2.8	17.5	3.1	8.2	2.3	2.5	226.9	2,646	0.0
Norco	0.0	7.5	0.0	0.0	3.0	19.6	13.5	4.2	10.9	5.6	149.1	5,552	0.0
Norwalk	0.0	14.6	0.5	0.0	8.7	18.9	1.3	12.1	14.9	4.3	119.3	1,131	1.0
Novato	0.0	11.6	0.0	0.0	2.1	24.9	0.3	20.3	5.9	6.1	66.4	1,193	0.0
Oakland	0.0	3.4	0.6	0.0	6.1	21.0	4.4	3.0	5.2	9.5	2,230.3	5,255	51.8
Oakley	0.0	31.4	0.0	0.0	0.7	25.7	0.0	7.7	10.6	5.1	61.8	1,484	20.1
Oceanside	0.0	10.5	0.3	0.0	0.2	21.3	15.8	10.4	12.8	2.1	171.6	975	0.0
Ontario	0.0	22.0	0.0	0.0	0.3	20.5	9.4	11.1	4.1	4.6	250.9	1,431	2.1
Orange	0.0	13.0	0.0	0.0	7.6	24.8	3.7	14.2	8.0	1.4	107.7	768	0.0
Oxnard	0.0	4.7	0.0	0.0	0.0	22.1	21.5	6.7	3.4	8.0	442.7	2,120	0.0
Pacifica	0.0	8.9	1.0	0.2	1.1	19.9	20.6	10.9	0.2	6.5	72.2	1,852	36.8
Palmdale	0.0	15.1	0.0	0.0	0.7	23.6	3.3	14.7	13.5	5.3	184.4	1,178	18.1
Palm Desert	0.0	12.7	0.0	0.0	0.8	15.7	0.0	16.1	20.1	9.0	416.8	7,895	245.7
Palm Springs	0.0	12.7	1.5	0.0	1.4	13.7	2.9	14.8	3.6	4.9	211.4	4,400	11.5
Palo Alto	0.0	2.9	0.8	0.0	0.0	12.5	28.6	8.8	0.5	1.4	132.9	1,984	3.2
Paramount	0.0	17.9	0.0	0.0	0.0	29.7	0.0	14.5	11.3	0.0	5.0	92	0.3
Pasadena	0.0	5.7	3.4	0.0	4.6	22.5	5.5	8.6	7.3	6.2	946.5	6,677	197.8
Perris	0.0	10.1	0.0	0.0	0.9	33.8	3.5	3.6	11.9	8.0	311.0	4,010	5.4
Petaluma	0.0	13.6	0.0	0.0	0.5	20.2	16.1	6.0	9.3	8.1	136.4	2,247	23.4
Pico Rivera	0.0	33.9	0.0	0.0	0.0	16.0	0.0	12.0	8.8	0.9	69.4	1,099	0.0
Pittsburg	0.0	12.2	0.0	0.0	0.5	23.3	2.1	5.2	25.3	14.7	367.7	5,107	36.4
Placentia	0.0	14.0	0.7	0.0	1.0	22.1	5.6	3.9	3.2	1.3	14.3	275	0.0
Pleasant Hill	0.0	37.9	0.0	0.0	0.9	26.3	0.3	0.0	6.0	0.1	11.9	342	0.0
Pleasanton	0.0	7.3	0.0	0.0	0.0	21.0	10.4	18.9	7.2	0.0	65.9	795	11.6
Pomona	0.0	15.7	0.0	0.0	0.4	30.7	7.5	1.9	11.5	10.0	275.6	1,808	71.9
Porterville	0.0	7.6	0.0	0.0	0.2	21.5	23.9	10.4	0.6	6.2	78.6	1,315	0.0
Poway	0.0	7.7	0.0	0.0	0.3	15.9	8.0	5.7	32.2	4.1	159.2	3,197	0.2
Rancho Cordova	0.0	24.3	0.0	0.0	0.5	35.5	2.9	0.0	7.1	0.5	17.8	243	0.0
Rancho Cucamonga	0.0	13.3	0.0	0.0	1.9	18.7	1.0	7.8	12.1	7.0	298.0	1,684	56.9
Rancho Palos Verdes	0.0	16.0	0.0	0.0	0.3	17.8	0.7	13.3	1.6	3.2	25.9	615	0.0
Rancho Santa Margarita	0.0	21.3	0.0	0.0	4.4	45.1	0.0	6.4	0.0	1.7	9.6	198	0.0
Redding	0.0	4.3	0.0	0.0	0.5	19.5	32.8	4.4	6.9	3.7	231.1	2,525	4.2
Redlands	0.0	11.1	0.0	0.0	4.6	22.8	19.3	6.2	3.4	2.1	61.2	858	0.0
Redondo Beach	0.0	6.2	0.0	0.0	4.4	29.2	6.6	7.5	5.5	0.7	32.0	475	0.0
Redwood City	0.0	10.8	1.2	0.0	0.7	17.7	12.3	7.4	3.0	2.2	96.0	1,111	6.3

1. Based on population estimated as of July 1 of the year shown.

Table D. Cities — **Land Area and Population**

STATE	Place code	City	Land area[1] (sq. mi)	Population, 2021: Total persons 2021	Population, 2021: Rank	Population, 2021: Per square mile	Race 2020: Race alone[2] (percent): White	Race 2020: Race alone[2] (percent): Black or African American	Race 2020: Race alone[2] (percent): American Indian, Alaskan Native	Race 2020: Race alone[2] (percent): Asian	Race 2020: Race alone[2] (percent): Hawaiian Pacific Islander	Race 2020: Race alone[2] (percent): Some other race	Race 2020: Two or more races (percent)
			1	2	3	4	5	6	7	8	9	10	11
		CALIFORNIA—Cont'd											
06	60242	Reedley	5.6	25,232	1,531	4,505.7	29.4	0.5	1.6	3.0	0.0	43.7	21.9
06	60466	Rialto	24.1	104,394	306	4,331.7	21.0	11.9	2.6	2.6	0.4	43.1	18.4
06	60620	Richmond	30.1	115,639	251	3,841.8	20.1	19.1	2.1	14.4	0.6	30.7	13.1
06	60704	Ridgecrest	20.9	28,105	1,386	1,344.7	65.9	4.8	1.2	5.5	0.6	8.5	13.5
06	62000	Riverside	81.2	317,261	61	3,907.2	36.5	6.4	2.0	7.4	0.4	30.3	17.2
06	62364	Rocklin	19.8	72,975	505	3,685.6	68.7	1.8	0.7	11.9	0.3	3.8	12.8
06	62546	Rohnert Park	7.3	44,411	897	6,083.7	59.2	2.2	1.6	6.4	0.4	15.6	14.6
06	62896	Rosemead	5.2	50,245	796	9,662.5	7.7	0.6	1.1	64.4	0.0	17.3	8.9
06	62938	Roseville	44.1	151,901	173	3,444.5	65.6	2.5	0.8	12.7	0.4	5.3	12.7
06	64000	Sacramento	98.6	525,041	35	5,325.0	34.8	13.2	1.4	19.9	1.6	15.3	13.8
06	64224	Salinas	23.5	162,791	160	6,927.3	23.0	1.4	3.3	5.9	0.3	45.6	20.4
06	65000	San Bernardino	62.1	222,203	100	3,578.1	24.2	12.6	2.3	4.2	0.4	39.6	16.8
06	65028	San Bruno	5.5	42,275	944	7,686.4	33.8	1.8	1.0	32.2	2.6	14.8	13.8
06	65042	San Buenaventura (Ventura)	21.9	109,925	279	5,019.4	61.5	1.8	1.5	4.0	0.2	14.2	16.8
06	65070	San Carlos	5.4	30,034	1,306	5,561.9	63.4	0.9	0.3	19.1	0.3	3.5	12.5
06	65084	San Clemente	18.4	63,896	600	3,472.6	75.6	0.7	0.7	4.0	0.2	5.9	13.0
06	66000	San Diego	325.9	1,381,611	8	4,239.4	46.4	5.9	0.9	17.9	0.4	14.1	14.4
06	66070	San Dimas	15.0	34,064	1,165	2,270.9	49.5	3.8	1.1	14.4	0.1	12.5	18.6
06	67000	San Francisco	46.9	815,201	17	17,381.7	41.3	5.3	0.7	33.9	0.4	8.4	9.9
06	67042	San Gabriel	4.1	38,670	1,030	9,431.7	12.6	1.0	0.9	63.7	0.1	12.4	9.2
06	67056	Sanger	5.8	26,716	1,453	4,606.2	31.3	1.0	1.6	3.3	0.1	42.2	20.5
06	67112	San Jacinto	26.0	55,290	720	2,126.5	33.5	8.8	2.9	3.4	0.5	33.1	17.8
06	68000	San Jose	178.3	983,489	10	5,515.9	27.3	2.9	1.4	38.5	0.4	18.2	11.2
06	68028	San Juan Capistrano	14.4	34,955	1,139	2,427.4	58.6	0.5	1.6	3.5	0.1	20.6	15.1
06	68084	San Leandro	13.3	88,868	387	6,681.8	23.1	11.1	1.2	35.9	0.9	16.3	11.5
06	68154	San Luis Obispo	13.3	47,545	840	3,574.8	72.6	1.1	0.7	6.2	0.1	6.7	12.5
06	68196	San Marcos	24.6	94,926	351	3,858.8	50.8	2.2	1.2	11.0	0.3	18.4	16.0
06	68252	San Mateo	12.1	102,200	314	8,446.3	41.5	1.7	0.8	26.5	1.6	15.2	12.6
06	68294	San Pablo	2.6	31,773	1,245	12,220.4	13.0	12.5	2.2	15.6	0.5	43.0	13.2
06	68364	San Rafael	16.6	60,769	634	3,660.8	54.6	1.7	3.7	6.6	0.3	20.8	12.4
06	68378	San Ramon	20.1	86,947	396	4,325.7	34.0	2.6	0.3	51.1	0.2	2.6	9.1
06	69000	Santa Ana	27.4	309,441	62	11,293.5	18.5	1.1	3.7	12.3	0.3	45.1	19.1
06	69070	Santa Barbara	19.5	88,255	391	4,525.9	58.5	1.4	1.5	3.6	0.1	17.6	17.3
06	69084	Santa Clara	18.3	127,151	217	6,948.1	30.9	2.2	0.8	47.0	0.4	8.9	9.8
06	69088	Santa Clarita	70.8	224,593	99	3,172.2	50.8	4.2	1.1	12.0	0.1	16.1	15.6
06	69112	Santa Cruz	12.7	61,950	622	4,878.0	63.2	2.6	1.1	8.5	0.2	11.3	13.2
06	69196	Santa Maria	22.8	109,711	281	4,811.9	28.3	1.2	3.8	5.0	0.2	40.8	20.8
06	70000	Santa Monica	8.4	91,105	375	10,845.8	68.1	4.1	0.6	9.2	0.1	5.7	12.1
06	70042	Santa Paula	5.5	30,759	1,282	5,592.5	32.1	0.4	2.7	0.8	0.1	42.4	21.5
06	70098	Santa Rosa	42.5	176,938	149	4,163.2	55.7	2.3	2.3	6.1	0.6	19.1	13.9
06	70224	Santee	16.5	59,703	647	3,618.4	68.7	2.3	0.8	5.9	0.5	7.4	14.3
06	70280	Saratoga	12.8	30,163	1,303	2,356.5	37.9	0.3	0.1	54.3	0.2	1.1	6.1
06	70686	Seal Beach	11.3	24,937	1,547	2,206.8	70.1	1.6	0.4	14.5	0.2	3.0	10.1
06	70742	Seaside	8.9	32,085	1,228	3,605.1	34.7	5.8	2.1	9.7	1.5	28.9	17.3
06	72016	Simi Valley	41.5	125,975	221	3,035.5	60.0	1.6	0.9	10.7	0.2	12.4	14.2
06	73080	South Gate	7.2	91,154	373	12,660.3	15.2	1.1	3.5	0.8	0.1	57.2	22.1
06	73220	South Pasadena	3.4	26,314	1,473	7,739.4	39.6	2.5	0.7	34.4	0.1	7.1	15.7
06	73262	South San Francisco	9.2	64,251	593	6,983.8	22.1	2.0	1.1	41.4	1.6	18.5	13.4
06	73962	Stanton	3.1	37,970	1,049	12,248.4	22.5	1.9	1.7	29.9	0.6	30.4	13.0
06	75000	Stockton	62.4	322,120	58	5,162.2	23.5	12.6	1.7	22.0	0.8	25.5	13.8
06	75630	Suisun City	4.0	29,165	1,341	7,291.3	28.5	19.0	1.7	19.8	1.3	13.4	16.4
06	77000	Sunnyvale	22.1	152,258	171	6,889.5	29.9	1.4	0.7	50.0	0.3	9.1	8.6
06	78120	Temecula	37.3	110,846	276	2,971.7	55.6	4.7	1.5	11.3	0.4	10.2	16.3
06	78148	Temple City	4.0	35,763	1,110	8,940.8	17.1	0.9	0.7	63.9	0.1	8.9	8.5
06	78582	Thousand Oaks	55.3	125,754	225	2,274.0	66.9	1.4	0.7	10.0	0.1	7.8	13.0
06	80000	Torrance	20.5	143,600	190	7,004.9	39.0	3.4	0.5	35.7	0.4	7.7	13.2
06	80238	Tracy	26.2	95,387	346	3,640.7	33.8	6.4	1.3	21.2	1.1	19.4	16.7
06	80644	Tulare	20.6	70,733	531	3,433.6	41.0	3.0	1.9	2.5	0.1	31.8	19.7
06	80812	Turlock	16.8	72,682	508	4,326.3	52.8	2.1	2.0	7.5	0.4	20.9	14.2
06	80854	Tustin	11.1	79,430	454	7,155.9	34.4	2.2	1.3	24.0	0.3	22.7	15.1
06	80994	Twentynine Palms	58.7	27,435	1,418	467.4	59.1	11.8	1.4	5.8	1.3	8.1	12.4
06	81204	Union City	19.4	68,681	549	3,540.3	13.7	4.5	1.0	57.9	1.2	11.5	10.2
06	81344	Upland	15.6	79,274	456	5,081.7	44.3	6.4	1.4	10.2	0.2	20.0	17.5
06	81554	Vacaville	29.9	103,078	309	3,447.4	51.8	9.6	1.1	9.0	0.8	11.9	16.0
06	81666	Vallejo	30.4	124,886	227	4,108.1	24.2	19.9	1.1	23.6	1.1	17.5	12.6
06	82590	Victorville	73.7	135,950	205	1,844.6	29.5	17.9	2.1	4.2	0.6	29.5	16.3
06	82954	Visalia	38.0	142,978	192	3,762.6	46.2	2.1	2.0	5.8	0.2	26.9	16.9
06	82996	Vista	18.7	98,655	335	5,275.7	43.9	2.7	2.4	5.3	0.7	26.5	18.5
06	83332	Walnut	9.0	27,830	1,397	3,092.2	12.1	2.5	0.4	67.5	0.1	7.9	9.5
06	83346	Walnut Creek	19.8	69,695	539	3,519.9	66.3	2.2	0.3	16.7	0.2	3.5	10.9

1. Dry land or land partially or temporarily covered by water. 2. Hispanic or Latino persons may be of any race.

City	Percent Hispanic or Latino[1], 2020	Percent foreign born, 2016–2020	Age of population (percent), 2016–2020							Median age, 2016–2020	Percent female, 2016–2020	Population			
												Census counts		Percent change	
			Under 18 years	18 to 24 years	25 to 34 years	35 to 44 years	45 to 54 years	55 to 64 years	65 years and over			2010	2020	2010–2020	2020–2021
	12	13	14	15	16	17	18	19	20	21	22	23	24	25	26
CALIFORNIA—Cont'd															
Reedley	79.1	29.8	31.7	10.2	15.6	10.9	10.4	11.0	10.2	30.7	49.9	24,306	25,221	3.8	0.0
Rialto	74.4	26.0	27.4	12.3	16.4	13.3	11.5	9.6	9.5	30.7	50.6	99,301	104,216	4.9	0.2
Richmond	44.6	34.5	21.5	9.9	15.9	13.5	14.4	11.1	13.7	37.2	50.9	103,337	116,287	12.5	-0.6
Ridgecrest	21.9	7.2	24.6	7.3	14.0	15.0	12.8	12.0	14.3	37.2	50.6	27,616	27,918	1.1	0.7
Riverside	54.7	22.7	24.0	14.2	16.3	12.8	11.7	10.0	11.1	31.8	50.2	303,905	314,347	3.4	0.9
Rocklin	13.9	12.3	25.9	9.8	11.2	14.3	14.1	11.1	13.5	36.9	51.1	57,135	71,571	25.3	2.0
Rohnert Park	29.6	14.5	19.2	12.6	18.2	12.2	11.9	13.2	12.6	35.0	51.8	41,163	44,330	7.7	0.2
Rosemead	31.1	58.0	19.7	8.7	13.6	12.2	14.2	13.9	17.7	41.3	49.9	53,753	51,268	-4.6	-2.0
Roseville	16.3	13.7	23.5	7.5	12.6	14.4	13.5	11.9	16.7	39.4	51.4	119,277	147,817	23.9	2.8
Sacramento	28.8	21.3	22.7	8.9	18.7	13.7	11.5	11.2	13.3	34.9	50.9	466,369	522,754	12.1	0.4
Salinas	79.6	36.5	30.7	10.1	15.8	14.3	10.8	9.2	9.2	31.0	49.2	150,560	163,687	8.7	-0.5
San Bernardino	68.0	22.0	28.7	11.5	15.7	13.2	11.3	9.9	9.6	30.9	50.6	210,309	221,898	5.5	0.1
San Bruno	28.0	39.0	18.3	8.3	16.8	15.9	13.7	11.8	15.2	38.8	49.4	41,143	43,906	6.7	-3.7
San Buenaventura (Ventura)	35.1	14.4	20.9	7.9	13.8	13.3	11.7	14.8	17.7	40.4	50.1	107,212	110,600	3.2	-0.6
San Carlos	11.1	21.7	23.9	5.1	10.8	15.7	15.2	14.4	15.0	40.7	52.1	28,268	30,743	8.8	-2.3
San Clemente	18.2	11.7	22.6	6.1	10.4	12.0	15.0	15.1	18.8	44.2	50.3	63,500	64,409	1.4	-0.8
San Diego	29.7	25.6	19.6	10.9	19.2	14.1	12.2	10.8	13.3	35.2	49.5	1,301,927	1,385,922	6.5	-0.3
San Dimas	37.1	20.8	20.4	7.6	13.5	10.8	13.7	14.7	19.2	42.5	53.5	33,373	34,939	4.7	-2.5
San Francisco	15.6	34.2	13.4	7.0	23.4	15.8	13.1	11.6	15.8	38.3	49.0	805,184	873,965	8.5	-6.7
San Gabriel	25.0	55.9	17.4	7.4	14.3	12.5	15.2	15.6	17.6	43.4	51.8	39,644	39,611	-0.1	-2.4
Sanger	82.6	19.7	31.7	8.8	14.8	14.7	12.9	7.3	9.7	31.6	48.1	24,265	26,635	9.8	0.3
San Jacinto	61.3	18.6	27.2	11.5	15.0	12.8	12.9	9.5	11.1	31.9	50.7	44,200	53,946	22.0	2.5
San Jose	31.2	40.5	22.0	8.7	16.1	14.6	13.7	12.0	13.0	37.1	49.4	952,354	1,014,545	6.5	-3.1
San Juan Capistrano	38.9	20.4	24.4	7.7	10.9	9.8	14.9	14.2	18.0	42.3	54.0	34,411	35,253	2.4	-0.8
San Leandro	28.5	35.9	18.4	7.7	15.0	13.5	14.3	14.8	16.4	41.1	51.2	84,963	91,675	7.9	-3.1
San Luis Obispo	18.5	8.7	11.6	35.3	13.6	8.3	8.3	9.4	13.5	26.7	48.6	45,141	47,085	4.3	1.0
San Marcos	36.8	24.6	26.5	10.3	13.2	14.9	12.4	10.1	12.7	35.0	49.9	83,638	94,914	13.5	0.0
San Mateo	25.7	35.0	20.6	6.9	17.3	15.6	12.9	10.9	15.8	37.8	50.0	97,130	105,674	8.8	-3.3
San Pablo	61.0	43.1	26.4	10.5	15.3	16.0	12.6	9.3	10.0	33.1	49.1	29,505	32,109	8.8	-1.0
San Rafael	34.3	27.5	20.1	8.2	10.8	13.5	13.8	12.9	20.7	42.6	50.7	57,693	61,287	6.2	-0.8
San Ramon	8.4	36.2	27.8	6.3	8.7	15.7	19.0	11.3	11.2	40.8	50.0	71,404	86,426	21.0	0.6
Santa Ana	76.7	42.7	25.2	11.1	17.2	14.0	12.8	10.0	9.8	32.6	48.5	324,778	310,538	-4.4	-0.4
Santa Barbara	38.7	21.6	16.8	12.0	16.3	11.4	11.3	12.6	19.6	38.9	50.2	88,383	88,730	0.4	-0.5
Santa Clara	17.7	44.4	19.4	10.8	21.9	15.7	11.7	9.4	11.1	34.0	47.8	116,328	127,452	9.6	-0.2
Santa Clarita	34.4	20.1	26.4	8.5	12.8	13.5	14.7	12.6	11.6	36.6	49.9	208,778	229,213	9.8	-2.0
Santa Cruz	24.0	13.7	12.7	32.1	12.7	10.1	10.2	9.7	12.5	28.1	50.6	59,948	62,341	4.0	-0.6
Santa Maria	76.5	33.9	31.1	12.6	14.2	12.7	10.8	8.3	10.3	29.0	50.6	99,596	109,903	10.3	-0.2
Santa Monica	14.6	22.6	15.1	5.5	20.4	14.7	13.5	12.9	17.9	40.5	50.6	89,742	93,028	3.7	-2.1
Santa Paula	81.7	28.0	28.8	9.5	14.8	13.3	11.4	8.9	13.3	32.4	50.6	29,648	30,713	3.6	0.1
Santa Rosa	34.3	20.9	21.4	8.2	14.0	13.5	12.5	12.6	17.6	39.6	52.0	175,015	178,155	1.8	-0.7
Santee	20.9	10.1	22.5	7.6	14.5	14.0	12.4	13.6	15.3	38.9	52.1	53,413	60,075	12.5	-0.6
Saratoga	3.6	41.6	20.1	4.1	6.5	11.0	17.6	16.8	23.9	50.5	50.4	30,034	31,164	3.8	-3.2
Seal Beach	12.5	15.1	13.0	3.5	8.6	8.2	10.7	14.3	41.7	59.4	54.7	24,165	25,272	4.6	-1.3
Seaside	47.9	27.1	23.3	11.8	16.6	11.7	12.7	11.6	12.4	33.8	50.0	33,024	32,385	-1.9	-0.9
Simi Valley	28.4	18.0	21.0	8.3	13.2	12.8	14.8	14.3	15.7	41.0	51.2	124,247	126,487	1.8	-0.4
South Gate	94.9	42.1	26.2	11.6	15.4	13.7	12.9	9.8	10.4	32.3	50.7	94,396	92,971	-1.5	-2.0
South Pasadena	20.7	24.1	23.3	4.7	13.3	18.1	15.7	12.0	12.8	39.5	50.2	25,605	27,001	5.5	-2.5
South San Francisco	32.8	38.7	17.8	7.6	15.6	13.9	14.3	14.4	16.3	40.9	50.2	63,613	66,119	3.9	-2.8
Stanton	49.5	41.2	23.9	8.7	16.2	14.6	12.8	11.3	12.5	35.7	51.4	37,829	37,953	0.3	0.0
Stockton	44.1	25.6	27.8	10.5	14.5	13.2	11.4	10.2	12.4	33.0	51.8	292,348	320,759	9.7	0.4
Suisun City	29.1	20.7	23.3	10.3	16.9	13.0	12.1	12.6	11.9	34.7	50.7	28,116	29,471	4.8	-1.0
Sunnyvale	16.3	49.4	20.9	6.1	22.9	16.1	12.0	10.2	11.9	35.1	48.6	140,492	156,291	11.2	-2.6
Temecula	27.6	15.7	29.1	7.7	12.6	14.6	13.7	11.8	10.5	35.3	51.0	99,970	110,130	10.2	0.7
Temple City	19.5	48.5	21.4	7.7	11.2	12.4	16.6	13.0	17.8	42.7	52.7	35,557	36,545	2.8	-2.1
Thousand Oaks	19.9	17.3	21.0	8.3	10.0	11.4	14.7	15.0	19.6	44.4	51.2	126,490	126,926	0.3	-0.9
Torrance	19.1	30.6	21.4	6.3	13.2	13.3	14.7	14.3	16.8	41.8	51.7	145,309	147,323	1.4	-2.5
Tracy	38.7	26.0	27.9	9.6	13.7	13.5	15.3	10.8	9.2	33.9	49.6	83,426	93,356	11.9	2.2
Tulare	63.3	17.8	34.2	11.5	15.3	11.1	11.2	8.5	8.2	28.0	50.4	59,328	68,880	16.1	2.7
Turlock	41.2	22.6	26.0	10.1	15.0	12.2	12.8	10.2	13.8	34.5	51.9	68,632	72,645	5.8	0.1
Tustin	40.7	31.4	24.7	8.4	15.8	14.5	13.7	10.5	12.3	35.5	50.0	75,299	80,142	6.4	-0.9
Twentynine Palms	24.4	6.6	28.5	25.1	20.2	9.6	4.8	5.9	5.9	24.0	44.3	25,048	27,420	9.5	0.1
Union City	21.5	46.4	18.5	8.1	15.9	14.5	13.2	13.3	16.5	39.8	48.4	69,547	70,650	1.6	-2.8
Upland	44.5	17.6	21.8	9.9	15.9	11.2	14.0	12.3	14.9	37.6	51.9	73,719	79,110	7.3	0.2
Vacaville	26.8	12.3	22.3	8.3	15.5	13.1	13.3	12.8	14.7	37.8	47.8	92,422	102,675	11.1	0.4
Vallejo	28.4	26.2	21.0	9.3	14.2	13.2	12.2	14.6	15.7	39.1	51.5	115,908	126,035	8.7	-0.9
Victorville	55.4	18.9	31.3	9.3	14.8	13.8	11.2	9.4	10.3	31.9	50.3	115,895	134,550	16.1	1.0
Visalia	52.7	12.7	29.0	9.3	15.6	12.6	10.4	10.0	13.2	32.5	51.5	124,526	141,561	13.7	1.0
Vista	50.6	25.3	25.1	10.4	16.2	13.4	13.7	10.5	10.7	33.9	49.4	93,157	98,484	5.7	0.2
Walnut	18.7	50.5	18.4	7.5	11.9	10.9	13.1	17.2	21.1	46.1	51.4	29,166	28,522	-2.2	-2.4
Walnut Creek	10.4	23.8	15.6	4.7	14.6	11.8	10.5	12.5	30.4	48.3	52.8	64,145	70,078	9.2	-0.5

1. May be of any race.

City	Households, 2016–2020: Number	Households, 2016–2020: Persons per household	Households, 2016–2020: Percent: Family	Households, 2016–2020: Percent: Married couple family	Households, 2016–2020: Percent: Female family	Households, 2016–2020: Percent: Non-family	Households, 2016–2020: Percent: One person	Persons in group quarters, 2016–2020	Serious crimes known to police[2], 2020: Violent: Number	Serious crimes known to police[2], 2020: Violent: Rate	Serious crimes known to police[2], 2020: Property: Number	Serious crimes known to police[2], 2020: Property: Rate	Educational attainment, 2016–2020: Population age 25 and over	Educational attainment, 2016–2020: Attainment[4] (percent): High school graduate or less	Educational attainment, 2016–2020: Attainment[4] (percent): Bachelor's degree or more
	27	28	29	30	31	32	33	34	35	36	37	38	39	40	41
CALIFORNIA—Cont'd															
Reedley	7,030	3.61	84.6	57.6	16.2	15.4	12.4	334	127	492.2	232	899.2	14,928	58.9	13.2
Rialto	26,134	3.94	82.6	52.8	20.2	17.4	13.7	554	500	480.8	2,525	2,427.8	62,438	59.6	11.8
Richmond	37,450	2.90	67.0	44.2	15.0	33.0	25.2	1,360	1,074	964.4	3,679	3,303.5	75,498	42.4	30.0
Ridgecrest	11,667	2.46	60.2	45.6	10.3	39.8	32.3	199	158	542.6	320	1,098.9	19,679	29.3	32.0
Riverside	90,663	3.44	73.6	51.6	15.4	26.4	18.9	15,900	1,491	445.9	9,980	2,984.7	202,593	45.0	24.1
Rocklin	22,912	2.88	72.3	60.3	9.2	27.7	21.9	972	70	99.7	1,135	1,616.4	43,141	18.1	46.9
Rohnert Park	16,315	2.60	59.0	41.4	11.9	41.0	25.6	63	280	642.6	709	1,627.2	28,996	31.5	29.9
Rosemead	14,413	3.70	82.8	58.9	15.1	17.2	13.0	571	189	349.4	895	1,654.7	38,563	59.2	21.1
Roseville	51,799	2.66	70.1	55.2	9.8	29.9	24.6	997	277	192.2	2,843	1,972.6	95,817	19.9	43.5
Sacramento	187,683	2.63	59.4	38.9	14.0	40.6	30.7	9,144	3,547	683.4	14,248	2,745.0	344,699	34.6	34.3
Salinas	41,296	3.74	79.3	53.6	17.6	20.7	16.0	1,543	866	555.2	3,481	2,231.6	92,486	59.8	16.0
San Bernardino	59,770	3.45	75.1	41.3	23.7	24.9	19.5	10,788	3,033	1,401.8	6,059	2,800.4	129,614	59.8	11.8
San Bruno	15,229	2.90	69.0	54.7	9.2	31.0	22.3	469	100	232.6	938	2,181.5	32,788	28.1	43.5
San Buenaventura (Ventura)	40,841	2.61	64.2	47.1	11.4	35.8	28.2	1,964	328	300.1	3,086	2,823.6	77,247	27.1	37.5
San Carlos	10,955	2.69	72.1	61.5	7.6	27.9	20.2	127	NA	NA	NA	NA	21,044	10.0	68.3
San Clemente	24,388	2.65	70.6	59.9	8.0	29.4	23.0	333	92	142.3	866	1,339.2	46,330	18.0	50.3
San Diego	511,662	2.69	60.2	45.0	10.8	39.8	27.6	37,680	5,303	368.9	24,321	1,691.8	982,945	26.3	46.7
San Dimas	11,396	2.90	73.1	56.5	10.9	26.9	22.8	799	83	246.7	761	2,261.6	24,336	25.1	38.1
San Francisco	362,141	2.36	47.1	35.7	7.9	52.9	36.3	20,169	4,796	544.1	38,737	4,394.4	696,575	23.0	58.8
San Gabriel	12,278	3.21	76.6	50.8	16.6	23.4	17.2	686	75	187.8	525	1,314.9	30,139	46.9	33.1
Sanger	7,419	3.58	82.5	46.2	22.2	17.5	16.5	168	111	436.0	371	1,457.4	15,908	53.9	11.5
San Jacinto	13,049	3.72	77.8	51.7	18.2	22.2	16.0	199	98	196.9	1,462	2,937.0	29,895	51.6	13.6
San Jose	324,340	3.13	72.7	55.3	11.4	27.3	19.5	13,967	4,375	424.9	23,847	2,316.3	713,674	31.5	44.8
San Juan Capistrano	12,238	2.93	72.5	60.8	8.3	27.5	23.5	146	63	174.6	303	839.9	24,418	31.1	39.0
San Leandro	31,274	2.88	66.1	48.3	12.4	33.9	26.5	482	462	517.7	3,416	3,827.9	66,908	40.1	31.6
San Luis Obispo	19,114	2.40	40.3	30.1	6.6	59.7	31.9	1,437	207	433.8	1,620	3,394.7	25,193	19.3	50.0
San Marcos	29,749	3.20	75.0	57.5	12.0	25.0	19.0	960	194	197.6	971	988.8	60,846	32.2	38.5
San Mateo	39,072	2.61	63.3	50.0	9.2	36.7	28.8	1,534	274	260.3	2,306	2,191.1	75,064	21.7	56.4
San Pablo	9,154	3.33	76.5	42.9	21.4	23.5	20.1	444	168	539.1	854	2,740.3	19,542	55.8	14.7
San Rafael	23,703	2.41	58.8	45.5	9.3	41.2	32.5	2,096	229	391.4	1,912	3,267.7	42,444	24.4	51.8
San Ramon	27,524	2.95	79.1	68.5	8.0	20.9	17.4	107	54	70.6	796	1,040.5	53,672	10.9	70.9
Santa Ana	79,142	4.15	80.6	54.9	17.0	19.4	13.3	4,550	1,429	429.0	6,926	2,079.2	211,957	61.2	16.8
Santa Barbara	37,806	2.37	53.9	40.0	8.7	46.1	32.1	1,384	389	424.2	2,188	2,386.2	64,737	24.2	50.1
Santa Clara	44,198	2.75	67.3	54.9	7.9	32.7	21.8	5,224	206	156.1	3,301	2,501.2	88,544	19.0	62.1
Santa Clarita	68,406	3.08	76.0	59.7	10.7	24.0	18.7	1,970	291	131.1	2,013	907.0	138,326	26.9	37.4
Santa Cruz	22,644	2.41	47.2	35.4	7.4	52.8	31.2	10,354	309	474.9	2,237	3,437.7	35,900	16.4	54.3
Santa Maria	28,013	3.73	80.3	51.7	18.9	19.7	15.4	1,092	834	771.2	2,472	2,285.9	59,375	59.4	13.4
Santa Monica	45,706	1.97	41.8	31.8	6.5	58.2	46.9	1,626	541	598.0	3,852	4,257.6	72,746	14.0	68.0
Santa Paula	8,994	3.35	73.9	51.9	15.9	26.1	21.6	136	102	341.6	437	1,463.4	18,690	58.5	13.9
Santa Rosa	66,580	2.63	62.3	46.3	10.0	37.7	28.4	3,258	913	516.0	2,838	1,604.0	125,575	32.2	33.8
Santee	19,450	2.85	72.7	53.3	13.4	27.3	20.3	1,961	167	285.0	452	771.4	40,108	32.4	28.2
Saratoga	11,064	2.79	83.6	76.1	5.6	16.4	13.8	215	18	59.7	216	716.1	23,557	8.6	77.9
Seal Beach	12,555	1.91	47.1	38.2	5.6	52.9	46.8	239	26	108.9	561	2,349.9	20,277	19.7	49.1
Seaside	10,709	3.06	67.5	46.7	12.7	32.5	24.7	1,286	72	212.9	498	1,472.4	22,116	42.8	24.1
Simi Valley	42,902	2.91	72.0	54.6	12.0	28.0	21.7	768	167	132.8	1,318	1,048.2	88,961	29.2	33.9
South Gate	23,989	3.95	84.1	51.3	20.4	15.9	12.1	68	637	682.5	2,946	3,156.3	58,966	66.8	10.2
South Pasadena	9,671	2.62	65.8	50.3	10.9	34.2	27.0	116	26	102.8	631	2,494.2	18,333	9.0	70.6
South San Francisco	21,388	3.09	74.9	55.0	13.7	25.1	17.3	777	155	227.1	1,560	2,285.4	49,887	33.1	37.6
Stanton	11,723	3.25	69.4	46.5	15.2	30.6	26.6	227	128	335.4	804	2,106.6	25,815	53.1	20.9
Stockton	95,236	3.20	72.5	45.2	19.0	27.5	22.2	6,566	4,023	1,277.2	9,391	2,981.4	191,861	51.6	18.6
Suisun City	9,293	3.16	76.0	53.6	15.5	24.0	19.7	128	134	449.0	585	1,960.3	19,580	39.5	19.9
Sunnyvale	55,807	2.72	66.2	55.4	6.7	33.8	21.9	975	229	148.6	3,178	2,061.9	111,506	16.5	65.9
Temecula	34,299	3.30	81.6	66.7	11.2	18.4	13.8	65	148	127.1	2,262	1,942.6	71,509	25.5	35.0
Temple City	11,183	3.15	79.5	58.4	12.8	20.5	16.3	476	49	136.7	322	898.4	25,338	34.2	41.4
Thousand Oaks	46,341	2.71	68.4	57.0	8.2	31.6	25.8	1,970	76	59.9	1,315	1,036.9	90,181	18.2	50.0
Torrance	53,995	2.65	68.1	53.5	10.6	31.9	26.6	1,439	274	191.0	2,935	2,046.4	104,419	21.4	51.7
Tracy	27,007	3.38	79.3	58.7	13.5	20.7	16.1	259	174	181.1	1,629	1,695.7	57,131	41.3	22.0
Tulare	18,381	3.49	81.3	53.0	19.4	18.7	13.4	348	300	453.1	1,486	2,244.5	35,049	57.0	10.2
Turlock	25,444	2.83	70.0	47.3	14.5	30.0	22.7	612	408	550.0	2,062	2,779.6	46,529	43.0	24.8
Tustin	26,501	3.01	71.3	52.6	13.1	28.7	21.1	967	148	185.5	2,131	2,670.6	54,030	28.5	44.8
Twentynine Palms	8,416	2.78	66.3	50.7	9.8	33.7	27.0	3,360	141	538.5	236	901.3	12,420	33.9	22.9
Union City	21,723	3.42	82.4	65.8	11.2	17.6	13.2	729	222	297.5	1,897	2,542.0	55,139	34.3	41.4
Upland	26,654	2.88	71.5	51.3	13.3	28.5	20.0	676	363	468.3	1,759	2,269.4	52,829	31.2	32.7
Vacaville	33,026	2.81	72.8	55.2	12.1	27.2	21.2	7,111	247	243.1	1,760	1,732.0	69,400	33.7	24.9
Vallejo	41,863	2.86	69.6	45.2	16.7	30.4	23.6	1,501	1,212	990.8	4,078	3,333.7	84,627	37.2	26.7
Victorville	33,742	3.52	77.8	49.4	20.9	22.2	17.9	4,200	1,084	880.7	1,958	1,590.8	73,061	51.4	10.9
Visalia	43,867	2.99	73.4	51.0	16.0	26.6	22.2	1,988	555	408.9	3,077	2,267.0	82,168	39.6	22.5
Vista	30,917	3.19	73.0	50.8	15.6	27.0	19.9	2,008	345	336.3	1,203	1,172.5	64,933	44.0	25.1
Walnut	9,106	3.26	87.4	69.8	12.3	12.6	10.2	53	38	127.8	326	1,096.2	22,058	20.7	54.9
Walnut Creek	32,163	2.14	56.7	47.9	5.9	43.3	35.6	1,028	91	128.4	2,063	2,911.8	55,698	10.6	68.4

2. Data for serious crimes have not been adjusted for underreporting. This may affect comparability between geographic areas and over time.

4. Persons 25 years old and over.

City	Money income, 2016–2020					Median earnings Full year, Full-time workers, 2016–2020			Housing units, 2016–2020				
	Households												
	Median household income	Percent with income less than $25,000	Percent with income of $200,000 or more	Median family income	Median non-family household income	All persons	Men	Women	Total	Occupied	Percent owner occupied	Median value[1] (dollars)	Median gross rent (dollars)
	42	43	44	45	46	47	48	49	50	51	52	53	54
CALIFORNIA—Cont'd													
Reedley	45,850	22.2	2.6	50,727	23,715	37,907	40,111	33,765	7,401	7,030	58.1	218,200	973
Rialto	65,538	16.3	3.7	72,030	29,812	39,004	41,347	34,652	27,422	26,134	63.8	330,000	1,302
Richmond	72,463	15.1	7.4	77,971	55,363	50,008	50,349	49,279	39,765	37,450	53.0	505,800	1,574
Ridgecrest	71,774	18.2	4.3	84,641	42,172	62,969	76,903	45,641	12,673	11,667	61.0	184,600	928
Riverside	72,738	15.3	7.4	80,586	41,976	44,861	48,577	41,329	95,553	90,663	54.9	389,500	1,466
Rocklin	100,664	9.6	15.6	119,096	49,676	76,287	84,945	63,565	23,892	22,912	67.0	513,600	1,740
Rohnert Park	77,831	11.2	9.0	92,788	53,566	54,964	60,577	50,414	16,872	16,315	50.7	508,000	1,823
Rosemead	60,006	19.6	4.2	64,607	31,504	38,838	38,936	38,623	15,210	14,413	49.8	576,000	1,398
Roseville	95,519	11.7	14.6	116,884	51,340	74,787	81,658	66,950	54,116	51,799	67.5	473,300	1,678
Sacramento	65,847	18.7	7.6	76,108	50,534	51,525	52,356	50,670	197,948	187,683	49.8	361,300	1,328
Salinas	67,914	14.1	6.5	69,147	45,656	40,726	41,790	38,928	42,675	41,296	47.9	451,000	1,492
San Bernardino	49,287	24.6	2.9	52,590	29,842	36,780	39,689	33,050	64,173	59,770	48.6	272,600	1,109
San Bruno	113,103	8.9	21.1	129,774	74,413	66,956	70,278	61,859	15,922	15,229	60.5	958,300	2,459
San Buenaventura (Ventura)	79,986	13.4	10.4	93,503	50,324	58,430	63,699	52,860	43,402	40,841	55.5	593,700	1,675
San Carlos	189,739	5.5	47.4	230,735	102,295	140,119	156,219	124,042	11,549	10,955	69.5	1,756,800	2,423
San Clemente	108,183	10.5	24.8	141,456	55,293	85,501	95,891	68,003	27,299	24,388	65.7	931,400	1,915
San Diego	83,454	13.7	13.6	99,450	61,539	59,870	64,703	53,514	548,931	511,662	47.5	629,500	1,770
San Dimas	90,234	16.0	14.1	110,968	40,720	66,109	73,750	61,498	11,947	11,396	69.3	604,600	1,829
San Francisco	119,136	14.8	29.0	138,207	96,421	89,931	100,178	81,267	398,613	362,141	38.0	1,152,300	2,010
San Gabriel	70,892	17.0	9.0	73,651	47,148	44,732	46,363	42,841	13,311	12,278	46.7	712,400	1,545
Sanger	52,349	21.0	3.2	55,203	21,271	37,941	36,847	39,703	7,795	7,419	58.7	257,900	950
San Jacinto	56,933	19.7	3.9	62,347	36,718	41,949	43,375	39,151	14,483	13,049	66.3	266,500	1,250
San Jose	117,324	10.2	25.1	129,879	72,962	71,138	80,801	61,339	338,109	324,340	56.6	925,800	2,232
San Juan Capistrano	103,922	12.6	21.4	120,528	51,156	66,315	76,073	60,423	13,230	12,238	74.7	760,400	2,136
San Leandro	86,604	13.6	12.0	97,031	49,792	58,798	60,393	56,756	32,778	31,274	56.2	624,900	1,759
San Luis Obispo	58,546	25.6	10.9	100,991	36,270	56,075	67,750	47,934	20,926	19,114	41.1	662,300	1,611
San Marcos	86,408	13.4	12.8	101,983	44,390	55,287	62,086	51,112	31,239	29,749	62.6	584,600	1,802
San Mateo	126,102	9.7	29.5	148,368	85,185	95,413	102,855	86,302	41,784	39,072	52.7	1,186,400	2,658
San Pablo	60,819	17.0	1.6	64,647	32,929	42,814	44,149	40,384	9,666	9,154	38.7	380,700	1,550
San Rafael	97,009	12.6	22.1	128,299	62,796	73,472	80,270	70,868	24,443	23,703	49.4	975,500	2,037
San Ramon	167,345	6.6	41.5	193,547	86,168	120,061	143,345	92,416	28,370	27,524	71.8	1,001,600	2,395
Santa Ana	72,406	12.5	6.2	70,974	51,064	36,342	37,439	33,733	81,362	79,142	46.2	525,900	1,626
Santa Barbara	81,618	13.7	16.9	105,513	61,596	58,232	60,622	56,263	40,238	37,806	41.3	1,082,300	1,874
Santa Clara	136,870	7.6	29.5	152,359	93,368	98,577	109,943	79,326	47,174	44,198	43.5	1,120,400	2,523
Santa Clarita	100,932	9.9	15.3	113,304	55,869	67,709	76,127	58,645	70,976	68,406	69.6	564,500	2,003
Santa Cruz	86,618	20.3	16.5	135,117	43,899	71,451	81,348	62,544	24,450	22,644	46.3	895,800	2,038
Santa Maria	67,634	13.2	4.4	64,930	39,339	35,748	36,822	32,178	29,231	28,013	50.4	359,700	1,475
Santa Monica	98,300	17.4	21.5	130,933	78,176	88,698	99,024	81,414	51,445	45,706	27.9	1,452,100	1,900
Santa Paula	62,241	18.0	3.4	62,403	46,471	36,622	40,277	33,932	9,520	8,994	54.1	421,900	1,383
Santa Rosa	80,472	13.1	9.0	95,178	51,678	53,305	54,715	51,880	69,515	66,580	55.2	571,600	1,728
Santee	85,826	11.5	7.7	95,105	55,580	60,527	65,963	52,473	20,193	19,450	71.4	478,000	1,757
Saratoga	201,046	5.7	51.2	229,630	80,500	154,379	176,114	119,052	11,486	11,064	86.1	2,000,000	3,339
Seal Beach	72,596	15.6	14.8	117,674	45,229	88,973	100,709	73,269	13,866	12,555	76.4	417,700	2,031
Seaside	68,399	15.4	7.9	76,000	40,031	41,006	41,990	39,198	11,594	10,709	39.3	539,200	1,877
Simi Valley	99,245	9.5	15.0	114,601	56,257	66,666	76,525	58,135	44,357	42,902	71.5	612,700	2,137
South Gate	55,084	17.8	3.0	55,681	32,362	35,930	38,197	32,594	24,472	23,989	44.2	438,100	1,211
South Pasadena	109,927	8.9	26.2	143,519	79,382	86,875	98,933	74,157	10,485	9,671	49.0	1,113,100	1,830
South San Francisco	106,005	9.7	22.1	113,687	75,348	62,570	64,267	60,127	22,284	21,388	61.6	911,000	2,279
Stanton	66,017	18.3	5.1	73,152	41,083	45,379	47,815	42,038	11,992	11,723	48.2	432,600	1,641
Stockton	58,393	20.5	5.1	64,711	34,401	42,659	44,424	40,426	101,954	95,236	49.9	298,200	1,183
Suisun City	82,325	11.1	6.5	91,346	52,757	53,867	55,248	51,960	9,553	9,293	60.6	381,000	1,737
Sunnyvale	150,464	7.3	35.5	162,789	117,883	107,852	124,854	90,801	58,618	55,807	44.9	1,397,200	2,699
Temecula	98,631	8.6	13.2	105,061	63,671	64,921	74,725	53,500	35,980	34,299	65.9	464,900	1,935
Temple City	84,442	14.2	11.6	91,836	44,894	59,030	62,840	53,111	11,816	11,183	59.5	732,200	1,701
Thousand Oaks	108,377	11.3	22.7	136,187	57,575	80,269	93,408	65,785	48,224	46,341	69.4	751,900	2,207
Torrance	94,781	11.3	16.0	114,227	57,856	70,803	77,772	65,170	58,394	53,995	54.6	796,800	1,803
Tracy	95,741	8.6	10.8	101,501	64,857	60,893	67,008	51,234	27,787	27,007	61.8	470,400	1,862
Tulare	56,024	19.3	3.0	60,193	33,139	41,507	42,686	40,152	19,526	18,381	57.2	226,500	1,103
Turlock	60,799	20.5	5.6	67,118	33,718	49,323	53,937	42,260	26,238	25,444	53.7	329,900	1,159
Tustin	88,386	11.1	15.9	102,282	65,620	60,614	64,397	55,745	27,806	26,501	49.7	693,000	1,885
Twentynine Palms	42,959	24.5	1.0	43,583	36,781	41,543	44,260	34,498	9,768	8,416	31.0	139,400	975
Union City	120,772	7.9	23.3	127,014	66,250	64,719	71,562	58,516	22,540	21,723	65.0	812,000	2,322
Upland	76,259	13.4	9.8	86,758	50,033	54,288	60,133	47,384	27,344	26,654	54.6	547,100	1,571
Vacaville	93,291	8.7	12.6	105,620	59,855	62,193	73,461	51,737	34,579	33,026	65.2	448,700	1,757
Vallejo	73,869	14.4	7.3	83,268	48,548	52,492	56,579	49,545	44,280	41,863	57.1	404,600	1,624
Victorville	55,155	21.5	3.4	61,299	30,716	41,990	45,497	34,609	35,960	33,742	55.7	235,700	1,298
Visalia	66,668	15.7	5.3	73,018	44,691	47,514	50,118	45,318	46,139	43,867	59.2	254,600	1,085
Vista	73,163	13.5	7.4	81,022	47,083	42,222	44,263	40,179	32,219	30,917	49.6	503,500	1,731
Walnut	108,264	9.2	17.6	117,244	54,239	59,766	63,734	53,296	9,555	9,106	83.3	806,900	2,518
Walnut Creek	108,689	10.0	24.2	145,141	72,316	100,207	119,617	82,879	33,689	32,163	63.9	814,900	2,247

1. Specified owner-occupied units

City	Commuting, 2016–2020[1]		Computer access[2], 2016–2020		Migration, 2016–2020		Civilian labor force, 2021				Civilian Employment, 2016–2020[4]			
	Percent		Percent						Unemployment[3]		Population age 16 and older		Population age 16 to 64	
	Drove alone	Mean travel time to work	With a computer in the house	With Internet access	Percent who lived in the same house one year ago	Percent who lived in another state or county one year ago	Total	Percent change 2020–2021	Total	Rate	Number	Percent in labor force	Number	Percent who worked full-year full-time
	55	56	57	58	59	60	61	62	63	64	65	66	67	68
CALIFORNIA—Cont'd														
Reedley	74.4	23.4	90.3	71.4	92.9	1.8	12,399	0.1	1,993	16.1	18,166	62.5	15,550	38.3
Rialto	79.3	33.2	95.4	82.4	90.2	3.1	46,100	1.7	3,983	8.6	78,637	65.5	68,797	46.1
Richmond	63.2	35.4	94.5	89.7	90.3	5.2	51,709	-1.4	4,155	8.0	89,303	66.1	74,180	48.5
Ridgecrest	72.1	15.6	90.6	85.1	85.3	5.2	13,419	1.6	550	4.1	22,525	61.8	18,406	50.6
Riverside	76.1	32.0	95.1	89.4	87.4	5.7	156,286	1.4	10,466	6.7	258,626	62.6	222,355	45.2
Rocklin	77.0	26.5	96.3	93.2	83.5	9.5	34,066	0.8	1,602	4.7	51,807	64.2	42,732	49.6
Rohnert Park	75.2	27.9	96.4	91.8	79.2	7.1	22,503	-1.7	1,273	5.7	35,042	70.6	29,664	51.1
Rosemead	78.0	30.0	92.3	83.8	93.6	1.5	24,713	-3.0	2,303	9.3	44,614	59.2	35,103	47.9
Roseville	75.0	27.2	96.4	92.2	85.1	8.6	70,442	0.6	3,418	4.9	110,708	63.6	87,511	52.3
Sacramento	71.9	26.0	94.7	89.1	83.6	6.2	237,783	0.6	17,499	7.4	401,161	64.3	334,032	49.7
Salinas	71.4	24.5	92.4	86.8	91.3	2.8	77,305	-0.9	7,990	10.3	113,191	64.1	98,761	45.0
San Bernardino	77.1	29.0	91.9	76.8	86.9	4.2	87,759	1.3	8,601	9.8	161,547	58.9	140,635	40.7
San Bruno	63.9	28.0	95.4	91.6	88.4	6.5	26,605	-2.1	1,359	5.1	37,309	72.2	30,520	59.8
San Buenaventura (Ventura)	77.3	25.7	92.9	89.1	87.7	4.0	52,524	-1.5	3,055	5.8	88,795	63.0	69,638	47.8
San Carlos	68.8	29.0	97.3	95.1	88.5	6.0	16,500	-0.6	595	3.6	23,214	72.8	18,780	60.7
San Clemente	74.9	30.2	97.8	93.7	86.3	6.0	30,491	-0.1	1,656	5.4	52,366	63.3	40,154	49.7
San Diego	72.0	24.5	96.2	92.0	83.1	6.3	699,411	0.1	43,450	6.2	1,166,581	64.9	978,669	51.9
San Dimas	74.9	33.3	92.6	85.7	89.2	3.6	17,196	1.2	1,267	7.4	27,770	60.4	21,272	48.6
San Francisco	30.5	33.3	94.3	89.1	85.4	7.3	545,953	-2.2	27,519	5.0	768,889	71.2	630,732	58.2
San Gabriel	75.8	30.6	93.5	87.4	94.4	2.0	20,800	-1.6	1,565	7.5	34,088	62.3	27,047	52.5
Sanger	83.1	25.8	87.1	79.1	93.3	1.1	11,934	0.2	1,167	9.8	19,525	61.2	16,927	44.1
San Jacinto	77.8	39.6	93.7	86.0	88.2	3.5	20,353	1.5	1,964	9.6	37,513	58.9	32,122	41.9
San Jose	72.6	30.8	96.0	92.3	87.3	4.4	536,588	-1.4	28,174	5.3	828,880	68.4	695,468	54.5
San Juan Capistrano	76.6	25.2	95.1	90.5	88.7	1.8	16,430	-0.2	818	5.0	28,514	61.2	22,028	48.7
San Leandro	66.4	33.8	94.0	89.2	92.3	2.8	44,867	-2.0	3,157	7.0	75,640	65.6	60,780	54.3
San Luis Obispo	69.4	15.3	95.4	90.5	66.3	12.6	24,688	0.8	1,225	5.0	42,547	64.0	36,129	35.3
San Marcos	76.9	26.5	97.0	93.4	85.6	3.0	41,459	0.1	2,289	5.5	72,751	66.1	60,524	51.2
San Mateo	66.3	29.1	96.2	93.1	85.5	8.0	60,566	-1.3	2,484	4.1	84,338	70.5	67,958	57.5
San Pablo	63.5	36.2	94.5	91.1	91.6	2.9	13,449	-1.7	1,084	8.1	23,795	64.6	20,710	45.7
San Rafael	61.5	28.1	95.6	91.4	85.7	7.1	30,120	-1.3	1,320	4.4	48,630	65.9	36,359	48.7
San Ramon	67.6	38.4	98.6	96.4	87.2	7.7	41,178	0.3	1,803	4.4	61,603	69.1	52,488	55.7
Santa Ana	72.8	25.7	94.4	85.7	90.1	2.4	152,088	-0.6	9,429	6.2	258,730	67.7	226,085	49.9
Santa Barbara	67.2	17.2	95.0	90.4	81.9	6.6	50,068	-0.5	2,146	4.3	77,289	66.6	59,457	50.8
Santa Clara	68.5	24.3	97.4	94.7	78.5	10.8	70,697	-0.3	2,820	4.0	104,579	70.1	90,451	54.9
Santa Clarita	77.4	36.8	96.6	93.8	88.2	2.4	111,506	0.5	8,787	7.9	162,776	67.0	138,144	50.8
Santa Cruz	58.1	23.0	95.6	91.9	71.0	16.2	31,340	-1.0	1,542	4.9	57,944	63.0	49,827	35.1
Santa Maria	69.1	22.0	91.4	87.5	88.0	2.8	49,470	0.4	4,242	8.6	75,980	66.5	65,105	53.2
Santa Monica	63.3	26.1	94.4	89.7	85.5	4.9	54,255	0.9	3,795	7.0	79,202	68.7	62,791	54.7
Santa Paula	78.9	26.8	81.7	77.4	94.8	0.8	13,670	0.2	1,475	10.8	22,389	61.0	18,353	43.8
Santa Rosa	77.2	23.3	94.8	90.5	84.7	4.6	85,167	-1.1	4,987	5.9	144,760	66.4	113,280	49.9
Santee	81.9	28.1	95.4	91.8	84.6	2.8	28,204	0.3	1,553	5.5	45,988	62.1	37,209	50.7
Saratoga	72.0	29.3	98.0	95.4	92.6	2.8	14,366	0.6	544	3.8	25,933	55.5	18,504	51.7
Seal Beach	78.4	33.0	90.7	85.9	88.9	5.8	9,522	0.2	570	6.0	21,483	44.2	11,358	50.1
Seaside	74.6	22.0	93.4	89.1	82.4	10.8	17,003	-2.8	871	5.1	27,059	62.4	22,840	45.6
Simi Valley	78.6	30.3	94.7	92.2	91.3	3.3	64,755	-1.7	3,402	5.3	102,692	66.4	82,890	52.9
South Gate	71.4	32.5	91.9	84.8	93.6	1.1	42,188	0.7	4,173	9.9	73,107	64.8	63,261	46.3
South Pasadena	72.3	32.8	97.5	94.8	90.1	2.8	14,239	1.2	952	6.7	20,147	71.7	16,878	61.5
South San Francisco	61.0	29.0	93.6	90.3	91.2	4.2	37,700	-2.6	2,136	5.7	56,432	68.6	45,510	57.3
Stanton	77.0	29.4	93.5	88.9	90.5	2.8	17,863	-1.5	1,261	7.1	30,133	66.6	25,333	50.2
Stockton	79.4	31.9	91.8	82.7	88.4	4.0	132,126	-0.4	13,253	10.0	234,639	59.8	196,034	44.3
Suisun City	80.7	35.5	95.9	89.6	89.9	5.2	13,591	-1.1	1,061	7.8	23,260	66.6	19,767	51.3
Sunnyvale	67.6	24.7	97.6	93.8	80.0	8.8	84,621	0.1	3,039	3.6	123,472	71.7	105,269	61.4
Temecula	77.7	36.1	98.5	95.6	84.2	7.9	55,032	0.5	3,104	5.6	84,272	64.2	72,355	48.0
Temple City	74.4	33.3	94.9	89.9	92.8	2.1	17,699	-0.8	1,391	7.9	29,078	61.0	22,734	50.2
Thousand Oaks	76.7	25.9	93.9	91.2	90.6	4.6	61,594	-1.5	3,022	4.9	104,286	62.3	79,251	49.1
Torrance	78.3	29.2	95.5	91.4	87.5	3.0	74,836	0.8	5,107	6.8	116,671	63.9	92,421	53.3
Tracy	75.5	44.5	96.9	92.0	87.0	6.0	45,287	-0.5	2,953	6.5	68,895	68.7	60,457	51.8
Tulare	82.9	20.9	91.1	83.2	87.9	3.7	28,639	-0.2	2,308	8.1	44,945	62.8	39,658	45.1
Turlock	82.5	26.0	91.7	84.8	87.5	4.7	33,050	-0.6	2,278	6.9	56,513	60.2	46,466	43.1
Tustin	76.2	24.4	97.3	93.2	84.7	4.5	41,275	0.0	2,441	5.9	63,210	69.5	53,263	54.6
Twentynine Palms	67.2	15.6	94.0	87.8	65.5	23.7	7,329	2.7	575	7.8	19,523	38.3	17,943	58.2
Union City	67.7	34.7	97.2	92.6	90.6	4.1	35,545	-0.7	2,142	6.0	62,354	66.2	49,951	58.9
Upland	76.1	31.1	94.7	89.9	86.5	6.6	40,470	1.6	2,581	6.4	62,352	66.3	50,821	49.6
Vacaville	81.1	29.0	95.6	93.4	85.3	7.0	44,067	-0.8	2,778	6.3	79,940	57.6	65,296	47.8
Vallejo	70.3	36.7	95.2	90.1	87.1	7.3	54,046	-1.7	4,748	8.8	98,993	64.1	79,976	47.2
Victorville	75.8	39.3	94.7	88.6	86.3	4.7	48,742	2.4	5,323	10.9	88,825	55.7	76,204	38.6
Visalia	80.7	20.9	94.9	88.0	88.9	3.2	61,314	-0.9	4,209	6.9	98,645	62.0	81,133	46.6
Vista	81.9	27.1	96.1	90.5	87.5	3.3	43,684	-0.3	2,965	6.8	78,624	66.5	67,902	53.1
Walnut	75.9	36.9	97.3	94.8	91.8	3.2	15,389	0.9	1,041	6.8	24,997	58.5	18,720	49.7
Walnut Creek	55.6	37.4	96.1	92.3	84.3	9.8	32,849	0.3	1,561	4.8	60,334	57.4	39,106	53.0

1. Employed persons. 2. Households. 3. Percent of civilian labor force. 4. Persons 16 years old and over.

City	Value of residential construction authorized by building permits, 2021			Wholesale trade[1], 2017				Retail trade[2], 2017			
	New construction ($1,000)	Number of housing units	Percent single family	Number of establishments	Number of employees	Sales (mil dol)	Annual payroll (mil dol)	Number of establish-ments	Number of employees	Sales (mil dol)	Annual payroll (mil dol)
	69	70	71	72	73	74	75	76	77	78	79
CALIFORNIA—Cont'd											
Reedley	34,964	146	100.0	14	124	66.5	6.2	54	562	145.4	15.6
Rialto	12,300	47	100.0	54	1,109	1,194.7	56.7	150	3,299	1,219.2	90.9
Richmond	12,539	94	81.9	100	1,730	1,933.7	114.7	228	4,845	1,815.4	175.4
Ridgecrest	12,495	152	52.6	5	29	19.8	1.2	78	1,333	301.3	32.2
Riverside	150,148	883	33.2	324	5,890	5,221.6	347.2	867	15,315	4,981.2	463.0
Rocklin	206,009	657	70.5	70	1,816	1,079.5	106.1	171	2,627	972.7	97.5
Rohnert Park	53,489	272	83.1	34	698	347.6	50.8	110	2,176	715.6	65.4
Rosemead	22,304	144	78.5	129	593	294.6	20.0	177	1,807	473.3	47.9
Roseville	474,599	1,883	100.0	98	1,165	1,403.1	81.5	613	14,350	4,869.1	462.5
Sacramento	576,846	3,083	32.6	454	8,275	9,019.9	476.9	1,198	19,969	5,281.6	550.2
Salinas	22,513	198	32.3	134	2,729	2,879.4	178.2	443	7,831	2,663.9	227.1
San Bernardino	47,935	207	69.1	135	3,386	3,479.5	158.6	515	13,661	5,216.1	417.9
San Bruno	5,722	11	100.0	31	366	477.1	30.7	138	1,990	7,807.2	62.7
San Buenaventura (Ventura)	64,918	477	3.1	162	1,753	1,029.4	102.2	497	7,449	2,103.8	217.0
San Carlos	11,861	46	82.6	94	943	612.1	64.8	137	3,217	615.4	75.0
San Clemente	38,988	189	18.5	163	1,672	1,989.0	155.9	239	3,320	806.8	87.3
San Diego	925,452	4,788	11.3	1,866	22,288	22,459.1	1,652.3	4,240	66,413	20,732.3	2,025.1
San Dimas	5,370	18	100.0	100	571	314.3	29.6	128	1,816	586.7	51.3
San Francisco	819,407	2,519	1.3	963	14,014	24,706.6	1,245.9	3,396	49,883	19,362.3	2,119.1
San Gabriel	7,568	55	100.0	126	513	305.2	17.5	218	1,627	481.4	41.4
Sanger	4,782	43	16.3	11	97	91.9	3.7	50	715	194.9	19.7
San Jacinto	21,595	123	100.0	15	71	31.7	2.8	68	1,092	319.0	31.0
San Jose	144,003	658	45.4	1,055	35,492	71,189.3	5,865.6	2,204	43,442	15,756.1	1,896.5
San Juan Capistrano	5,150	16	100.0	62	323	300.2	20.6	126	1,975	789.0	78.2
San Leandro	7,534	54	88.9	234	3,337	2,575.9	206.9	301	7,348	5,522.2	239.2
San Luis Obispo	102,353	602	47.7	74	933	530.8	55.0	342	5,770	1,882.5	187.0
San Marcos	87,589	335	43.0	134	1,139	565.7	61.9	268	4,415	1,414.2	144.0
San Mateo	91,112	264	25.8	83	2,791	4,211.1	403.0	349	6,371	2,035.2	210.9
San Pablo	2,140	6	100.0	10	61	28.0	2.7	78	1,024	248.4	27.6
San Rafael	14,791	80	31.3	112	936	896.0	68.8	318	5,235	1,764.6	201.4
San Ramon	26,670	89	24.7	97	1,608	2,703.6	128.5	109	1,975	666.6	68.0
Santa Ana	144,492	851	27.1	540	6,092	7,320.9	352.6	841	12,828	3,828.2	386.0
Santa Barbara	11,044	229	68.1	112	2,017	1,715.8	242.8	544	6,220	1,658.1	181.2
Santa Clara	134,019	409	88.0	344	9,949	9,994.0	1,558.2	335	4,802	2,059.9	200.2
Santa Clarita	91,554	366	99.5	219	3,121	9,702.3	186.4	555	10,464	3,538.6	326.5
Santa Cruz	56,272	267	19.9	62	851	758.2	86.2	268	4,052	984.7	112.7
Santa Maria	61,878	592	22.3	105	1,347	803.2	73.4	357	6,048	1,761.8	174.1
Santa Monica	76,899	185	41.6	156	2,220	1,317.6	147.9	672	10,704	4,606.9	476.7
Santa Paula	73,268	210	100.0	15	283	160.7	8.6	51	693	202.2	18.9
Santa Rosa	321,649	1,451	28.9	156	1,909	1,641.0	128.5	679	11,842	3,621.5	387.0
Santee	18,450	141	48.9	41	368	490.2	20.9	146	3,306	892.9	89.4
Saratoga	53,880	90	100.0	14	33	22.2	2.7	D	D	D	7.8
Seal Beach	10,352	18	100.0	24	803	727.8	99.2	80	1,598	386.6	38.0
Seaside	0	0	0.0	12	35	13.3	1.4	91	1,585	710.7	62.3
Simi Valley	13,405	52	86.5	149	1,332	748.6	78.1	410	6,234	2,026.3	193.0
South Gate	51,149	442	31.2	54	795	748.1	39.6	161	3,177	892.9	81.7
South Pasadena	2,513	17	100.0	35	203	195.5	13.2	56	831	244.3	25.2
South San Francisco	33,129	147	17.7	289	4,212	4,456.9	429.6	213	3,774	1,200.0	135.3
Stanton	63,864	437	31.4	31	298	87.3	13.9	96	1,347	514.0	41.2
Stockton	197,670	855	64.1	228	5,449	5,720.2	299.3	702	11,974	3,947.4	339.8
Suisun City	5,168	25	40.0	D	D	D	D	32	604	153.7	15.7
Sunnyvale	221,815	1,400	13.6	163	8,817	7,504.0	1,698.5	256	4,782	1,870.9	173.7
Temecula	92,246	503	86.9	163	2,442	2,600.0	138.9	460	9,426	3,164.0	284.6
Temple City	10,304	66	100.0	74	247	138.1	8.7	103	1,188	308.0	28.9
Thousand Oaks	15,719	16	100.0	191	3,365	11,379.3	442.0	531	9,044	3,434.4	318.5
Torrance	14,540	72	55.6	620	5,573	7,454.0	380.1	709	13,168	4,685.5	413.2
Tracy	306,775	958	72.2	71	2,418	3,128.8	199.9	230	4,578	1,454.3	138.0
Tulare	24,948	158	79.7	54	726	1,565.5	44.1	187	3,241	896.7	81.9
Turlock	30,746	113	98.2	64	891	472.2	48.0	239	4,311	1,109.7	114.4
Tustin	10,199	34	8.8	185	2,558	1,571.2	197.1	297	6,742	2,749.1	223.5
Twentynine Palms	243	4	100.0	4	18	8.7	0.9	32	286	85.6	7.6
Union City	3,152	23	100.0	143	4,672	4,430.6	367.4	112	2,177	791.6	73.0
Upland	28,993	112	44.6	119	754	282.7	33.9	253	4,112	1,141.5	112.5
Vacaville	152,321	594	63.0	40	333	319.1	18.0	328	6,309	1,798.7	175.1
Vallejo	6,740	30	100.0	30	592	395.1	46.9	237	4,529	1,381.4	146.8
Victorville	200,337	642	100.0	44	281	165.4	11.4	314	6,756	2,034.1	193.4
Visalia	192,793	840	89.0	138	1,934	3,799.2	112.0	423	7,865	2,199.2	204.0
Vista	12,100	95	100.0	193	3,641	2,108.0	229.5	258	4,526	1,469.2	140.6
Walnut	8,830	27	100.0	240	884	562.2	35.2	125	1,172	355.0	28.3
Walnut Creek	27,821	83	7.2	69	700	2,060.6	70.6	301	6,960	2,503.9	281.8

1. Merchant wholesalers except manufacturers' sales branches and offices. 2. Establishments with payroll.

Table D. Cities — **Real Estate, Professional Services, and Manufacturing**

City	Real estate and rental and leasing, 2017				Professional, scientific, and technical services[1], 2017				Manufacturing, 2017			
	Number of establish-ments	Number of employees	Receipts (mil dol)	Annual payroll (mil dol)	Number of establish-ments	Number of employees	Receipts (mil dol)	Annual payroll (mil dol)	Number of establish-ments	Number of employees	Receipts (mil dol)	Annual payroll (mil dol)
	80	81	82	83	84	85	86	87	88	89	90	91
CALIFORNIA—Cont'd												
Reedley	D	D	D	D	23	70	9.3	2.8	NA	NA	NA	NA
Rialto	49	211	49.1	6.9	39	266	22.9	8.1	NA	NA	NA	NA
Richmond	78	395	127.9	20.1	172	2,147	224.9	201.2	NA	NA	NA	NA
Ridgecrest	26	104	23.0	3.3	56	848	144.6	56.3	NA	NA	NA	NA
Riverside	370	1,809	430.8	75.9	674	5,250	791.7	295.5	NA	NA	NA	NA
Rocklin	127	352	92.0	16.2	211	1,853	292.9	108.3	NA	NA	NA	NA
Rohnert Park	55	232	74.3	9.9	75	459	69.3	29.6	NA	NA	NA	NA
Rosemead	55	156	41.2	8.7	100	358	40.1	12.1	NA	NA	NA	NA
Roseville	337	2,177	608.3	126.2	560	5,821	960.6	400.0	NA	NA	NA	NA
Sacramento	634	3,406	923.5	176.0	1,847	17,260	4,126.9	1,488.6	NA	NA	NA	NA
Salinas	116	542	176.3	26.6	D	D	D	D	NA	NA	NA	NA
San Bernardino	118	523	117.3	20.4	220	1,925	238.7	115.5	NA	NA	NA	NA
San Bruno	44	164	104.4	10.2	77	707	148.1	82.0	NA	NA	NA	NA
San Buenaventura (Ventura)	217	996	248.4	45.9	497	3,948	722.9	331.1	NA	NA	NA	NA
San Carlos	61	341	111.7	24.9	243	2,208	578.9	241.9	NA	NA	NA	NA
San Clemente	154	887	244.7	34.8	448	1,530	339.4	96.8	NA	NA	NA	NA
San Diego	3,293	18,066	7,824.7	1,125.2	8,428	115,825	32,669.9	12,606.7	NA	NA	NA	NA
San Dimas	61	518	76.8	18.2	148	2,068	352.6	130.2	NA	NA	NA	NA
San Francisco	2,132	19,351	9,399.2	1,564.4	7,193	117,838	41,004.8	14,435.8	NA	NA	NA	NA
San Gabriel	92	194	41.2	6.2	160	905	94.8	27.6	NA	NA	NA	NA
Sanger	D	D	D	D	13	40	3.4	0.9	NA	NA	NA	NA
San Jacinto	D	D	D	D	23	113	13.6	4.5	NA	NA	NA	NA
San Jose	1,139	6,062	2,776.9	409.6	3,276	45,002	10,651.4	5,087.4	NA	NA	NA	NA
San Juan Capistrano	104	323	78.5	22.9	234	1,209	216.1	93.0	NA	NA	NA	NA
San Leandro	137	834	187.6	41.2	131	686	157.0	53.0	NA	NA	NA	NA
San Luis Obispo	142	876	174.3	39.5	358	2,507	464.2	173.3	NA	NA	NA	NA
San Marcos	148	494	129.5	25.4	263	1,510	246.7	86.6	NA	NA	NA	NA
San Mateo	199	1,107	513.6	79.4	577	6,189	1,418.6	591.2	NA	NA	NA	NA
San Pablo	17	51	14.6	1.9	13	110	11.7	4.3	NA	NA	NA	NA
San Rafael	170	948	965.7	54.8	518	2,619	565.1	212.0	NA	NA	NA	NA
San Ramon	128	878	451.6	65.6	566	5,263	1,312.7	509.7	NA	NA	NA	NA
Santa Ana	315	2,503	853.6	183.2	1,067	10,446	1,926.0	726.4	NA	NA	NA	NA
Santa Barbara	353	1,362	339.6	65.6	670	4,249	1,064.6	340.0	NA	NA	NA	NA
Santa Clara	204	2,162	670.1	144.0	1,000	21,327	7,151.3	2,850.5	NA	NA	NA	NA
Santa Clarita	285	1,204	314.6	61.5	630	3,375	593.8	205.6	NA	NA	NA	NA
Santa Cruz	83	267	100.2	11.5	308	1,607	256.2	147.7	NA	NA	NA	NA
Santa Maria	88	403	95.8	16.0	154	983	136.5	53.4	NA	NA	NA	NA
Santa Monica	523	3,086	969.4	231.2	1,259	10,777	2,915.2	1,104.5	NA	NA	NA	NA
Santa Paula	23	135	42.2	9.5	D	D	18.4	D	NA	NA	NA	NA
Santa Rosa	246	1,106	307.4	54.3	617	3,918	603.9	258.9	NA	NA	NA	NA
Santee	56	189	52.8	7.8	93	411	51.7	17.5	NA	NA	NA	NA
Saratoga	D	D	D	D	178	554	115.6	42.3	NA	NA	NA	NA
Seal Beach	D	D	D	D	137	613	164.2	51.8	NA	NA	NA	NA
Seaside	14	99	15.9	3.5	D	D	D	D	NA	NA	NA	NA
Simi Valley	142	508	161.1	24.2	377	2,085	358.0	134.4	NA	NA	NA	NA
South Gate	54	160	52.7	8.2	35	664	63.4	19.4	NA	NA	NA	NA
South Pasadena	D	D	D	D	D	D	D	D	NA	NA	NA	NA
South San Francisco	97	917	203.7	42.4	239	9,444	4,595.5	2,331.4	NA	NA	NA	NA
Stanton	25	93	39.1	4.1	44	274	35.3	12.3	NA	NA	NA	NA
Stockton	215	1,352	283.4	53.4	359	2,836	346.5	154.3	NA	NA	NA	NA
Suisun City	9	30	6.9	1.6	19	74	7.2	3.1	NA	NA	NA	NA
Sunnyvale	198	1,109	429.0	72.8	835	26,102	8,381.8	3,283.7	NA	NA	NA	NA
Temecula	224	710	203.8	30.3	430	2,149	361.1	131.8	NA	NA	NA	NA
Temple City	68	153	45.3	8.1	77	258	27.6	9.1	NA	NA	NA	NA
Thousand Oaks	311	1,224	353.0	69.2	D	D	D	D	NA	NA	NA	NA
Torrance	401	1,907	466.3	82.9	D	D	D	D	NA	NA	NA	NA
Tracy	93	216	79.6	9.9	140	580	83.3	31.0	NA	NA	NA	NA
Tulare	52	219	34.4	6.0	41	285	43.1	18.8	NA	NA	NA	NA
Turlock	64	230	54.6	8.0	101	749	81.7	32.1	NA	NA	NA	NA
Tustin	196	1,123	258.3	60.8	626	3,688	658.0	247.5	NA	NA	NA	NA
Twentynine Palms	15	166	35.1	3.4	12	90	9.8	5.4	NA	NA	NA	NA
Union City	48	175	64.0	9.6	117	523	95.2	39.1	NA	NA	NA	NA
Upland	120	1,096	370.7	71.0	230	1,530	217.9	77.4	NA	NA	NA	NA
Vacaville	107	485	139.3	18.8	133	1,077	183.4	73.3	NA	NA	NA	NA
Vallejo	77	272	70.4	11.3	105	526	67.2	26.1	NA	NA	NA	NA
Victorville	101	451	111.3	13.2	90	699	66.0	21.4	NA	NA	NA	NA
Visalia	154	923	171.9	34.1	256	1,457	226.1	77.5	NA	NA	NA	NA
Vista	155	724	251.0	32.9	267	1,561	266.4	100.2	NA	NA	NA	NA
Walnut	75	164	54.0	7.5	153	444	74.5	23.3	NA	NA	NA	NA
Walnut Creek	238	1,482	424.4	106.8	724	6,893	1,425.3	620.0	NA	NA	NA	NA

1. Establishments subject to federal tax.

City	Accommodation and food services, 2017				Arts, entertainment, and recreation[1], 2017				Health care and social assistance[1], 2017			
	Number of establish-ments	Number of employees	Receipts (mil dol)	Annual payroll (mil dol)	Number of establish-ments	Number of employees	Receipts (mil dol)	Annual payroll (mil dol)	Number of establish-ments	Number of employees	Receipts (mil dol)	Annual payroll (mil dol)
	92	93	94	95	96	97	98	99	100	101	102	103
CALIFORNIA—Cont'd												
Reedley	D	D	D	D	3.0	39	1.6	0.3	54	1,631	163.6	64.6
Rialto	113	1,999	125.2	32.5	8.0	123	17.9	2.4	96	936	92.0	33.1
Richmond	138	1,408	109.9	30.6	35.0	1,417	94.3	27.0	150	4,940	676.9	284.3
Ridgecrest	68	1,012	69.0	17.9	D	D	D	1.2	67	1,315	159.1	58.2
Riverside	628	12,935	771.0	225.0	69.0	1,186	89.3	26.8	969	21,881	3,070.2	1,114.9
Rocklin	132	1,950	115.5	32.2	18.0	409	22.5	6.8	192	1,663	160.6	59.1
Rohnert Park	102	4,092	767.5	119.7	13.0	255	20.3	5.1	93	1,001	139.4	50.6
Rosemead	177	2,780	182.6	49.6	D	D	D	3.2	147	2,155	203.2	79.0
Roseville	405	8,923	557.4	168.4	58.0	1,894	116.1	34.8	583	15,615	3,209.7	1,327.6
Sacramento	1,210	24,804	1,613.8	466.3	148.0	3,862	485.3	207.8	1,351	46,565	9,153.8	3,549.5
Salinas	300	4,775	318.4	87.5	26.0	451	34.8	9.1	345	7,217	1,303.6	492.8
San Bernardino	362	6,183	393.2	107.1	22.0	467	38.0	10.5	452	12,967	1,868.1	631.0
San Bruno	117	1,655	133.8	36.7	D	D	D	D	107	1,131	207.1	59.3
San Buenaventura (Ventura)	353	6,364	430.0	126.2	72.0	718	60.3	15.4	583	11,196	1,544.0	576.1
San Carlos	105	1,698	128.1	42.4	21.0	145	13.3	3.8	113	1,787	249.1	111.4
San Clemente	174	2,918	194.2	53.1	48.0	444	49.0	17.3	249	2,870	339.3	131.7
San Diego	4,076	98,278	7,986.3	2,290.6	629.0	18,611	1,675.6	529.3	4,712	97,758	16,500.6	6,428.0
San Dimas	89	1,800	107.4	31.8	18.0	244	33.5	7.9	141	2,450	241.9	87.4
San Francisco	4,559	89,123	9,426.2	2,717.4	616.0	15,360	2,541.2	852.2	3,330	69,425	13,052.4	5,235.7
San Gabriel	184	2,381	146.6	43.0	10.0	127	12.0	4.7	231	3,617	397.0	162.6
Sanger	38	766	34.6	8.4	3.0	14	0.6	0.2	39	367	36.3	14.3
San Jacinto	48	629	41.2	10.1	NA	NA	NA	NA	36	283	31.2	11.8
San Jose	2,215	39,154	2,850.9	824.8	251.0	8,417	751.4	312.9	2,617	38,211	5,677.6	2,322.5
San Juan Capistrano	76	1,463	98.7	28.9	D	D	D	D	151	1,867	213.7	76.1
San Leandro	233	3,441	257.9	70.1	20.0	D	24.7	D	279	8,061	1,509.7	600.4
San Luis Obispo	237	5,150	310.2	92.6	25.0	311	14.7	5.0	389	6,129	871.5	333.3
San Marcos	211	3,820	226.0	66.9	23.0	237	17.6	4.3	201	3,183	327.7	150.1
San Mateo	371	5,655	482.9	141.1	40.0	818	67.6	20.6	553	7,558	1,190.9	442.1
San Pablo	71	878	64.4	15.8	NA	NA	NA	NA	57	1,357	129.5	54.7
San Rafael	228	3,418	252.5	77.5	80.0	602	100.1	24.8	365	6,843	777.0	427.9
San Ramon	158	2,702	208.3	54.6	33.0	502	34.2	11.0	360	4,323	721.5	270.9
Santa Ana	602	9,481	656.6	177.2	58.0	1,140	141.4	31.7	876	14,624	1,920.3	660.1
Santa Barbara	487	9,711	726.5	225.2	117.0	1,434	133.8	37.8	590	9,902	1,779.8	562.8
Santa Clara	455	7,951	773.3	217.1	46.0	2,126	605.1	243.2	304	9,674	1,906.0	916.7
Santa Clarita	384	7,810	504.8	149.5	177.0	1,201	108.5	35.3	619	8,461	1,123.0	419.7
Santa Cruz	279	5,496	384.6	113.5	41.0	2,033	95.1	37.8	263	3,569	408.8	160.4
Santa Maria	197	3,198	224.3	61.3	23.0	340	18.6	6.3	335	6,512	1,087.2	348.8
Santa Monica	503	13,766	1,260.8	386.3	772.0	3,131	792.1	329.2	949	10,936	1,966.1	690.8
Santa Paula	43	723	40.3	11.9	D	D	D	D	43	390	59.3	18.8
Santa Rosa	422	6,895	455.0	127.3	81.0	1,419	125.6	38.4	766	14,989	2,265.7	1,021.5
Santee	133	2,420	148.0	43.5	D	D	D	D	120	956	143.9	35.1
Saratoga	57	628	58.8	15.9	16.0	258	35.0	7.5	116	1,411	150.6	66.6
Seal Beach	97	2,199	147.4	44.1	D	D	D	D	93	828	87.9	31.0
Seaside	80	1,451	97.1	26.7	NA	NA	NA	NA	21	290	22.4	8.2
Simi Valley	247	4,200	274.7	74.9	73.0	634	42.1	15.2	375	4,312	525.8	201.8
South Gate	127	2,090	138.3	37.8	9.0	204	21.3	5.2	83	895	95.6	33.5
South Pasadena	66	1,057	61.9	18.5	68.0	296	49.5	19.9	128	731	80.4	30.4
South San Francisco	262	5,006	539.1	138.1	22.0	295	27.7	8.7	203	3,351	457.5	277.3
Stanton	84	1,072	73.9	17.8	D	D	D	D	41	801	44.2	19.7
Stockton	492	7,809	504.4	136.2	50.0	989	63.2	23.3	761	19,134	2,218.3	896.8
Suisun City	39	609	38.8	10.8	D	D	D	D	23	144	10.8	4.4
Sunnyvale	431	6,502	599.9	170.7	48.0	958	69.2	20.0	475	5,651	756.5	286.4
Temecula	332	7,648	455.5	141.4	51.0	741	52.5	14.5	422	4,413	531.4	198.1
Temple City	74	1,338	78.5	23.2	4.0	6	1.0	0.1	111	1,140	94.8	38.4
Thousand Oaks	335	7,485	478.4	144.6	123.0	1,455	113.3	37.3	723	8,242	1,322.2	437.4
Torrance	480	10,197	695.6	197.5	88.0	1,430	112.3	33.5	1,112	17,983	2,765.7	1,089.4
Tracy	185	3,065	196.4	54.2	21.0	418	20.9	7.5	197	2,677	414.0	132.2
Tulare	89	1,527	98.8	26.7	D	D	D	D	115	1,602	144.9	61.6
Turlock	173	3,395	204.6	57.8	17.0	325	19.2	5.4	213	4,512	578.5	211.3
Tustin	293	5,630	363.4	102.7	40.0	541	34.9	9.6	472	4,110	565.3	207.2
Twentynine Palms	48	773	61.2	14.0	4.0	46	2.3	0.8	15	236	36.3	14.8
Union City	128	2,158	148.1	41.9	D	D	D	D	165	2,453	371.5	153.2
Upland	185	3,288	188.0	55.1	32.0	484	33.2	8.9	387	6,621	887.9	294.6
Vacaville	198	3,994	251.0	72.4	24.0	436	35.6	5.6	215	5,747	1,105.3	465.9
Vallejo	190	2,998	204.4	54.9	28.0	1,760	105.6	30.5	291	8,968	1,283.3	697.7
Victorville	190	3,915	216.8	62.7	15.0	343	16.9	4.8	257	6,432	764.3	247.7
Visalia	271	4,990	317.4	88.1	29.0	589	33.2	9.2	467	10,168	1,326.5	479.8
Vista	200	2,926	191.1	53.0	28.0	360	33.4	9.5	257	4,034	387.4	166.1
Walnut	62	747	52.8	13.8	17.0	41	8.1	2.6	98	632	60.1	24.8
Walnut Creek	235	4,912	372.3	111.9	60.0	655	253.5	20.0	533	13,584	3,012.3	1,265.2

1. Establishments subject to federal tax.

City	Other services[1]				Government employment and payroll, 2017								
						March payroll							
							Perent of total for:						
	Number of establish-ments	Number of employees	Receipts (mil dol)	Annual payroll (mil dol)	Full-time equivalent employees	Total (dollars)	Admin-istrative, judicial, and legal	Police and corrections	Fire protection	Highways and trans-portation	Health and welfare	Natural resources and utilities	Education and libraries
	104	105	106	107	108	109	110	111	112	113	114	115	116
CALIFORNIA—Cont'd													
Reedley	D	D	D	D	133	633,561	13.4	36.5	2.6	12.2	0.0	29.2	0.0
Rialto	81	388	45.4	12.1	375	3,064,779	11.6	40.5	27.8	7.5	1.9	4.9	0.0
Richmond	133	719	101.6	30.1	737	6,812,090	9.5	42.1	17.8	1.6	1.0	9.0	3.2
Ridgecrest	34	149	15.5	4.3	107	593,787	13.3	50.8	0.0	14.7	4.7	14.5	0.0
Riverside	456	2,928	362.8	91.5	2,170	19,847,957	12.0	34.9	11.5	5.4	1.1	23.8	1.3
Rocklin	90	483	54.7	15.7	253	1,929,938	16.9	36.8	18.9	5.5	1.5	4.7	0.0
Rohnert Park	71	418	47.4	14.2	192	1,356,881	17.9	57.4	0.0	0.0	1.6	23.1	0.0
Rosemead	100	300	27.1	7.0	85	486,146	31.5	13.4	0.0	10.6	6.6	37.9	0.0
Roseville	250	2,574	330.9	98.7	1,320	9,827,383	15.4	18.1	15.2	2.8	0.7	40.5	2.0
Sacramento	1,017	8,213	1,321.9	395.9	4,106	31,089,039	8.1	36.2	19.8	10.7	3.7	19.8	0.0
Salinas	214	1,236	166.0	42.8	543	3,681,676	11.2	41.1	19.5	14.4	2.8	4.0	4.9
San Bernardino	226	1,537	130.0	37.5	1,186	7,552,176	7.2	42.0	17.0	0.3	0.0	26.4	1.1
San Bruno	95	670	95.8	24.7	252	2,135,604	10.4	36.3	20.5	2.1	2.2	15.9	3.3
San Buenaventura (Ventura)	262	1,266	148.1	38.4	693	4,722,938	13.8	29.9	21.1	8.7	1.1	23.0	0.0
San Carlos	97	963	98.8	34.1	80	649,694	35.3	0.0	1.8	10.4	6.6	29.9	0.0
San Clemente	129	745	81.5	25.1	216	921,067	22.0	0.0	0.0	24.0	5.9	44.8	0.0
San Diego	2,801	23,453	2,828.0	779.6	10,832	75,006,131	16.1	26.5	14.4	3.1	0.0	24.7	2.9
San Dimas	60	924	71.8	13.5	137	641,242	26.1	0.0	0.0	17.1	0.0	39.6	0.0
San Francisco	2,470	25,451	5,265.1	1,112.6	33,660	260,920,281	11.9	17.2	8.2	23.9	23.9	11.9	1.7
San Gabriel	141	477	50.4	14.0	191	1,632,525	19.5	37.5	23.1	10.7	0.0	4.2	0.0
Sanger	18	228	16.3	4.3	103	668,749	12.1	35.4	28.0	3.3	1.7	15.8	0.0
San Jacinto	38	131	12.9	3.1	43	215,583	42.8	0.0	0.0	5.1	0.0	34.1	0.0
San Jose	1,569	10,237	1,296.8	374.0	3,403	22,735,265	8.9	30.6	16.9	9.7	9.5	14.9	5.1
San Juan Capistrano	73	336	41.7	11.4	94	671,052	28.9	0.0	0.0	18.8	17.0	35.3	0.0
San Leandro	201	1,346	176.3	52.3	421	3,019,956	12.5	39.1	0.0	9.3	6.0	17.4	5.4
San Luis Obispo	139	837	87.0	25.2	480	3,327,790	11.0	24.3	16.6	4.2	6.6	21.9	0.0
San Marcos	178	1,179	97.8	32.1	298	2,077,947	15.8	0.0	40.1	13.9	5.5	17.3	0.0
San Mateo	245	1,601	149.2	51.2	501	4,613,844	9.4	37.3	24.2	0.0	2.7	20.7	5.9
San Pablo	D	D	D	D	79	471,449	49.3	1.6	0.0	13.4	12.2	22.1	0.0
San Rafael	258	1,899	251.6	79.1	486	3,267,504	7.4	29.5	27.2	2.5	3.9	8.1	5.0
San Ramon	148	980	126.7	38.6	294	2,297,560	12.7	38.3	0.0	33.0	0.0	12.5	0.0
Santa Ana	469	3,298	405.2	107.3	1,094	9,302,161	14.8	60.9	0.0	8.8	7.8	5.2	2.4
Santa Barbara	306	2,304	312.0	75.9	1,161	7,949,171	14.5	23.5	15.4	13.5	1.6	20.9	2.9
Santa Clara	292	2,126	262.7	78.6	1,095	11,426,450	10.1	24.7	20.0	6.2	0.5	28.7	3.6
Santa Clarita	333	2,013	227.2	61.4	509	2,841,241	22.0	0.0	0.0	10.5	0.5	34.8	0.2
Santa Cruz	138	1,169	140.0	54.3	1,069	6,006,317	13.1	18.8	13.5	4.5	1.8	33.3	9.0
Santa Maria	165	1,181	138.8	37.6	614	4,153,499	8.6	38.2	16.7	5.8	1.8	24.2	2.8
Santa Monica	482	3,854	573.4	150.9	2,218	17,156,068	15.4	22.9	10.8	21.6	2.9	13.1	3.4
Santa Paula	45	261	16.3	5.4	114	769,663	12.5	41.5	18.2	4.2	4.4	14.0	0.0
Santa Rosa	348	2,603	311.2	96.7	1,260	9,471,990	10.7	25.7	17.1	10.1	3.6	21.9	0.0
Santee	109	602	69.6	18.7	155	1,209,222	28.3	0.6	51.2	9.9	1.2	8.9	0.0
Saratoga	44	108	18.5	4.1	63	533,502	27.2	0.0	0.0	25.1	17.6	20.4	0.0
Seal Beach	42	470	35.4	12.7	104	918,526	12.9	53.1	0.0	25.4	4.8	2.6	0.0
Seaside	54	251	30.6	8.8	159	1,184,921	8.9	38.8	23.1	14.9	2.1	9.4	0.0
Simi Valley	190	1,043	145.3	27.0	564	3,481,556	15.4	32.5	0.0	21.3	13.6	17.2	0.0
South Gate	74	269	37.1	7.3	335	2,078,258	10.7	47.2	0.0	15.4	7.1	19.8	0.0
South Pasadena	41	168	23.3	5.8	183	1,136,265	11.5	35.7	20.8	5.1	8.3	7.4	9.4
South San Francisco	129	1,495	203.5	64.8	544	4,433,064	10.8	26.5	24.1	2.6	0.4	24.4	5.5
Stanton	D	D	D	D	46	243,289	36.7	0.0	0.0	19.1	21.5	22.6	0.0
Stockton	364	2,813	254.1	79.9	1,598	11,211,014	9.4	45.5	17.6	4.4	3.4	13.9	3.0
Suisun City	D	D	D	D	98	561,250	17.9	44.2	4.2	11.9	5.5	16.3	0.0
Sunnyvale	197	1,086	129.2	40.1	849	8,013,441	9.5	44.6	7.9	9.3	8.7	16.5	3.5
Temecula	255	1,450	134.2	41.0	213	1,366,140	29.5	0.0	0.9	26.1	17.0	26.3	0.0
Temple City	63	191	22.6	5.7	65	335,559	28.2	0.0	0.0	0.0	21.0	38.3	0.0
Thousand Oaks	259	1,238	152.6	40.6	418	2,687,417	30.3	1.3	0.0	26.3	0.6	22.9	9.9
Torrance	307	2,220	247.1	70.8	1,383	11,106,855	10.5	31.9	18.8	15.6	4.4	10.4	3.1
Tracy	124	598	62.1	17.5	484	4,115,746	12.7	30.5	22.4	11.2	0.0	13.9	0.0
Tulare	53	302	45.6	12.3	366	2,119,156	10.1	34.1	16.1	2.4	2.1	24.7	1.8
Turlock	116	1,104	139.5	55.0	388	2,061,200	13.3	36.8	14.9	9.8	1.1	24.1	0.0
Tustin	166	1,415	142.3	43.4	309	3,042,614	10.1	58.6	0.0	13.9	6.2	11.1	0.0
Twentynine Palms	18	95	8.7	2.5	29	180,695	29.6	0.0	0.0	16.9	6.4	29.2	0.0
Union City	94	880	138.9	34.8	265	2,232,787	13.7	48.9	0.0	17.3	8.0	12.1	0.0
Upland	189	1,091	103.0	32.5	364	2,707,926	7.5	39.1	22.6	6.7	5.1	11.5	3.2
Vacaville	143	883	85.6	24.1	588	4,471,583	12.8	33.2	21.7	10.8	3.5	18.1	0.0
Vallejo	132	711	77.1	24.3	686	6,718,823	9.5	48.0	15.1	6.7	0.9	19.7	0.0
Victorville	122	585	57.2	15.1	381	2,014,212	29.2	0.0	0.0	26.2	2.1	32.7	2.0
Visalia	182	1,184	127.8	37.2	659	3,951,120	12.2	35.5	16.8	5.7	4.2	19.4	0.0
Vista	141	834	92.9	28.6	300	2,120,925	26.4	0.0	39.2	4.1	2.1	13.5	0.0
Walnut	63	328	36.7	11.1	54	314,058	52.2	0.0	0.0	3.0	0.0	44.8	0.0
Walnut Creek	222	3,127	333.3	153.2	414	3,171,980	17.0	38.0	0.0	4.8	0.6	21.8	0.0

1. Establishments subject to federal tax.

City	City government finances, 2017									
	General revenue							General expenditure		
		Intergovernmental		Taxes						
					Per capita[1] (dollars)				Per capita[1] (dollars)	
	Total (mil dol)	Total (mil dol)	Percent from state government	Total (mil dol)	Total	Property	Sales and gross receipts	Total (mil dol)	Total	Capital outlays
	117	118	119	120	121	122	123	124	125	126
CALIFORNIA—Cont'd										
Reedley	38.3	18.0	4.0	8.1	318	124	148	21.3	830	90
Rialto	191.8	13.8	91.1	68.3	662	316	342	126.7	1,227	1
Richmond	293.7	44.7	30.8	153.3	1,395	587	692	295.9	2,693	389
Ridgecrest	27.3	4.2	45.0	12.5	434	69	271	21.2	740	141
Riverside	451.5	47.0	68.3	224.3	686	263	409	404.3	1,237	92
Rocklin	73.2	4.2	62.4	41.4	641	236	395	65.9	1,020	66
Rohnert Park	80.3	3.5	67.8	28.8	674	177	492	66.5	1,557	291
Rosemead	27.5	2.5	75.1	20.9	385	160	223	50.2	927	295
Roseville	382.4	49.9	36.9	108.1	800	335	457	251.2	1,859	129
Sacramento	1,022.4	59.0	46.8	457.1	913	358	530	776.0	1,550	8
Salinas	172.1	18.9	50.3	127.9	817	203	613	160.6	1,026	131
San Bernardino	204.8	9.3	64.2	128.3	592	146	442	195.1	900	97
San Bruno	79.9	1.5	85.8	32.7	757	299	410	70.9	1,641	133
San Buenaventura (Ventura)	160.9	7.0	77.9	91.3	830	331	474	172.0	1,562	156
San Carlos	67.6	1.3	72.8	37.8	1,244	457	704	55.9	1,841	159
San Clemente	86.1	3.8	68.1	50.7	780	468	289	96.0	1,478	316
San Diego	3,177.9	331.0	12.6	1,414.4	1,001	419	576	2,575.2	1,823	217
San Dimas	28.8	1.5	84.5	20.9	612	238	368	40.2	1,179	110
San Francisco	9,978.8	2,985.9	47.3	3,736.2	4,255	2,354	1,434	10,297.3	11,728	921
San Gabriel	42.8	2.6	78.2	30.3	754	400	349	49.2	1,223	193
Sanger	31.5	4.6	54.5	11.3	451	68	359	24.7	986	114
San Jacinto	28.5	2.6	76.5	16.9	351	207	140	28.5	593	42
San Jose	2,270.4	98.5	51.3	1,238.6	1,200	578	522	1,558.9	1,510	112
San Juan Capistrano	48.2	3.9	64.4	31.3	871	483	368	40.9	1,140	183
San Leandro	157.1	14.0	29.2	99.5	1,100	317	723	151.4	1,674	144
San Luis Obispo	103.5	6.4	29.3	60.5	1,279	319	953	105.3	2,225	372
San Marcos	130.3	5.0	63.0	77.1	806	479	321	154.1	1,612	288
San Mateo	207.2	7.8	62.0	124.9	1,197	526	554	177.3	1,698	256
San Pablo	52.2	2.4	100.0	39.5	1,271	102	1,166	50.7	1,631	394
San Rafael	103.5	6.4	43.4	68.8	1,170	327	756	102.4	1,741	51
San Ramon	90.1	19.4	20.1	45.4	599	294	255	85.2	1,125	164
Santa Ana	403.8	93.2	23.6	210.9	634	246	380	470.9	1,416	212
Santa Barbara	270.3	18.5	35.9	108.1	1,181	578	594	236.5	2,584	222
Santa Clara	494.1	28.3	15.1	146.7	1,158	402	710	407.6	3,217	304
Santa Clarita	191.7	46.0	48.5	103.3	483	194	265	187.6	878	180
Santa Cruz	154.6	5.8	49.8	76.9	1,187	380	754	157.4	2,429	335
Santa Maria	144.0	21.0	26.1	63.6	598	165	341	140.1	1,318	239
Santa Monica	690.5	116.4	22.6	338.1	3,685	813	2,718	501.6	5,468	194
Santa Paula	30.7	2.5	63.2	10.5	350	209	139	32.2	1,068	160
Santa Rosa	302.6	56.3	79.2	116.7	643	238	384	318.4	1,753	301
Santee	53.5	4.7	38.6	35.8	619	283	330	74.9	1,295	192
Saratoga	24.9	2.1	45.3	19.1	620	399	180	33.0	1,070	192
Seal Beach	34.7	2.0	52.7	22.9	947	429	505	51.7	2,136	470
Seaside	32.8	2.7	81.0	25.7	760	198	560	32.0	945	207
Simi Valley	113.4	15.7	38.8	68.4	543	279	258	107.1	849	135
South Gate	90.0	12.9	43.5	47.0	495	195	299	75.7	798	135
South Pasadena	34.7	2.7	43.7	23.0	894	512	351	29.1	1,134	0
South San Francisco	146.8	4.5	80.0	88.6	1,319	462	801	144.8	2,156	262
Stanton	26.8	3.0	81.9	18.4	479	150	327	37.1	967	228
Stockton	401.2	37.4	30.9	227.1	732	211	519	320.3	1,033	16
Suisun City	20.0	4.3	20.6	8.7	296	150	127	21.7	735	122
Sunnyvale	373.0	27.0	70.5	141.5	923	462	450	290.0	1,893	92
Temecula	118.3	9.4	30.8	78.1	685	193	486	180.1	1,580	527
Temple City	19.2	3.2	75.3	11.6	321	199	116	18.2	502	15
Thousand Oaks	151.8	12.3	30.0	88.0	687	269	392	178.4	1,391	218
Torrance	287.9	51.9	8.4	181.7	1,247	346	878	239.5	1,643	2
Tracy	182.9	29.4	12.1	70.7	780	276	500	151.2	1,667	399
Tulare	101.5	10.5	36.7	34.8	549	161	385	103.4	1,628	464
Turlock	85.6	7.1	56.0	37.4	510	154	293	101.8	1,389	436
Tustin	140.3	4.2	80.5	51.4	642	229	404	112.9	1,409	334
Twentynine Palms	11.9	1.2	100.0	9.1	344	180	163	13.0	491	101
Union City	109.2	21.9	54.3	64.3	854	393	358	124.9	1,660	319
Upland	81.3	3.1	88.4	41.9	546	260	259	78.7	1,025	64
Vacaville	199.7	29.9	16.0	87.9	883	391	486	192.1	1,929	553
Vallejo	191.9	33.5	23.0	90.3	743	248	473	172.0	1,415	128
Victorville	151.4	33.7	18.0	60.1	492	220	270	212.0	1,738	191
Visalia	227.5	55.7	38.4	81.8	618	167	448	156.9	1,185	239
Vista	138.9	8.9	71.4	71.6	711	329	376	176.0	1,747	208
Walnut	18.7	3.0	29.6	10.6	354	196	151	23.1	769	29
Walnut Creek	107.6	2.6	76.0	63.3	908	317	527	110.7	1,589	128

1. Based on population estimated as of July 1 of the year shown.

City	City government finances, 2017 (cont.)												
	General expenditure (cont.)												
	Percent of total for:									Debt outstanding			
	Public welfare	Highways	Parking facilities	Education	Health and hospitals	Police protection	Sewerage and sanitation	Parks and recreation	Housing and community development	Interest on debt	Total (mil dol)	Per capita[1] (dollars)	Debt issued during year
	127	128	129	130	131	132	133	134	135	136	137	138	139
CALIFORNIA—Cont'd													
Reedley	0.0	8.4	0.0	0.0	0.0	28.4	31.2	8.2	0.0	5.6	36.1	1,408	0.0
Rialto	0.0	4.4	0.0	0.0	3.2	25.3	10.1	4.7	0.3	15.2	312.1	3,023	0.0
Richmond	0.0	10.4	0.0	0.0	0.2	22.6	4.5	1.7	16.8	5.9	627.7	5,714	13.1
Ridgecrest	0.0	9.0	0.0	0.0	1.7	32.6	5.6	8.9	15.6	7.8	32.3	1,126	0.0
Riverside	0.0	3.9	0.9	0.0	1.2	23.6	19.6	6.8	1.3	11.8	1,790.3	5,477	7.4
Rocklin	0.0	10.5	0.0	0.0	0.3	20.6	0.0	12.2	0.8	3.6	70.5	1,090	17.9
Rohnert Park	0.0	6.6	0.0	0.0	0.8	25.7	19.2	6.3	15.4	3.0	61.4	1,438	0.4
Rosemead	0.0	3.1	0.0	0.0	0.5	31.9	0.0	8.9	10.3	3.7	45.3	836	0.0
Roseville	2.2	5.0	0.0	0.0	0.5	13.8	23.6	7.9	5.2	6.3	996.9	7,380	165.0
Sacramento	0.7	3.4	2.3	0.0	2.5	20.6	13.9	7.9	3.4	11.6	2,283.1	4,559	57.5
Salinas	0.0	9.6	0.9	0.0	1.2	30.1	3.4	3.9	8.4	2.4	57.8	370	4.9
San Bernardino	0.0	10.7	0.0	0.0	1.0	32.4	12.1	4.1	8.4	3.8	220.1	1,015	104.5
San Bruno	0.0	4.1	0.0	0.0	1.7	20.1	16.5	10.1	0.0	1.6	29.8	691	1.9
San Buenaventura (Ventura)	0.0	9.0	0.5	0.0	0.3	21.4	10.6	9.4	2.4	2.5	151.2	1,373	0.0
San Carlos	0.0	15.4	0.1	0.0	0.0	16.5	20.6	8.0	4.7	0.3	3.9	130	0.0
San Clemente	0.0	7.5	0.2	0.0	1.2	14.5	14.4	24.3	2.2	1.0	82.5	1,269	65.3
San Diego	0.0	7.2	0.1	0.0	1.9	12.4	20.0	11.3	14.7	6.4	2,779.5	1,968	40.6
San Dimas	0.0	15.7	0.0	0.0	0.4	31.3	0.1	8.9	4.8	1.7	15.2	446	0.1
San Francisco	13.9	1.1	1.7	2.1	31.7	5.1	4.1	2.5	4.0	5.2	16,803.8	19,138	3,535.7
San Gabriel	0.0	9.1	0.0	0.0	0.0	28.5	2.5	12.9	2.7	0.9	10.8	267	0.0
Sanger	0.0	6.5	0.0	0.0	5.6	26.7	27.3	4.4	0.0	4.0	25.7	1,026	0.0
San Jacinto	0.0	22.1	0.0	0.0	0.0	36.4	3.0	1.1	2.5	1.5	26.2	545	0.0
San Jose	0.0	4.1	0.7	0.0	0.2	16.5	22.2	10.1	2.8	14.8	4,767.7	4,618	645.5
San Juan Capistrano	0.0	7.1	0.0	0.0	1.7	22.2	9.0	10.9	9.7	6.9	89.7	2,500	32.1
San Leandro	0.0	5.6	0.2	0.0	0.1	21.8	7.3	5.9	7.1	3.7	100.9	1,115	19.5
San Luis Obispo	0.0	13.1	3.1	0.0	0.0	16.3	10.2	9.9	2.2	1.9	66.7	1,408	0.0
San Marcos	0.0	13.8	0.0	0.0	2.0	22.7	0.0	8.9	12.4	9.3	291.6	3,049	0.0
San Mateo	0.0	3.0	1.2	0.0	0.3	21.6	27.9	8.8	0.2	4.5	223.2	2,138	0.7
San Pablo	0.0	21.4	0.0	0.0	0.3	33.0	0.0	7.5	5.6	3.3	46.4	1,492	0.3
San Rafael	0.0	10.6	3.5	0.0	7.3	23.6	0.0	11.2	1.2	0.5	28.2	479	0.0
San Ramon	0.0	13.0	0.0	0.0	0.0	23.4	0.4	22.7	6.6	4.5	89.4	1,179	0.0
Santa Ana	0.0	8.2	1.3	0.0	1.2	28.1	6.4	7.6	12.8	2.5	223.3	671	2.1
Santa Barbara	0.0	4.9	3.2	0.0	0.3	16.4	22.3	10.4	1.6	3.8	211.0	2,306	52.1
Santa Clara	0.0	6.8	0.4	0.0	0.3	15.3	14.6	23.9	0.5	5.8	704.2	5,558	4.0
Santa Clarita	0.0	37.9	0.0	0.0	0.0	12.4	0.0	12.3	7.1	1.6	57.5	269	0.0
Santa Cruz	0.0	5.8	4.6	0.0	0.0	17.9	21.9	11.5	8.3	2.5	124.5	1,921	23.6
Santa Maria	0.0	6.0	0.0	0.0	0.0	21.0	31.1	9.6	0.4	0.9	53.7	505	0.0
Santa Monica	0.0	2.7	2.9	0.0	4.7	17.1	8.2	10.7	8.9	3.1	345.2	3,762	0.0
Santa Paula	0.0	8.1	0.0	0.0	0.5	20.2	16.6	14.0	0.0	12.2	124.9	4,144	0.0
Santa Rosa	0.0	10.5	1.5	0.0	1.0	16.6	19.8	6.1	5.4	3.4	404.9	2,230	112.5
Santee	0.0	8.1	0.0	0.2	4.8	36.2	0.0	6.1	10.9	3.3	58.1	1,004	44.6
Saratoga	0.0	19.0	0.0	0.0	3.3	31.4	0.0	15.1	0.6	1.1	9.6	311	0.0
Seal Beach	0.0	15.0	0.0	0.0	0.2	23.8	10.8	4.6	2.3	0.9	17.1	708	0.0
Seaside	0.0	10.3	0.0	0.0	0.7	35.3	0.0	10.4	5.9	1.8	13.2	391	0.0
Simi Valley	0.0	9.8	0.0	0.0	0.8	30.4	18.7	0.6	6.5	1.7	180.0	1,427	19.9
South Gate	0.0	24.7	0.0	0.0	0.0	32.1	5.0	9.2	10.6	5.2	84.8	894	0.3
South Pasadena	0.0	5.3	0.1	0.0	2.7	28.5	3.1	13.5	0.0	0.2	55.4	2,155	0.0
South San Francisco	0.0	15.1	0.7	0.0	7.5	18.2	15.0	10.3	3.8	0.8	48.4	720	0.0
Stanton	0.0	4.9	0.0	0.0	0.9	27.7	1.5	5.8	25.9	8.8	80.6	2,101	0.0
Stockton	0.0	3.3	1.5	0.0	0.9	38.5	14.4	7.2	1.0	5.7	589.0	1,899	35.1
Suisun City	0.0	12.1	0.0	0.0	1.2	28.0	0.0	9.5	26.4	0.4	4.4	149	2.0
Sunnyvale	0.0	4.5	0.1	0.0	0.4	19.4	35.2	7.6	1.1	0.9	72.2	471	3.9
Temecula	0.0	14.1	0.0	0.0	0.3	14.7	4.3	3.8	1.6	3.1	151.3	1,328	66.3
Temple City	0.0	8.5	0.8	0.0	1.9	25.2	0.0	13.0	2.4	1.5	6.4	177	0.0
Thousand Oaks	0.0	21.0	0.0	0.0	0.2	31.6	9.9	5.1	2.3	0.6	74.2	578	0.3
Torrance	0.0	8.2	0.0	0.0	5.3	32.3	6.1	8.9	2.8	2.0	82.3	564	5.6
Tracy	0.0	7.8	0.0	0.0	0.6	15.7	21.9	11.8	1.7	2.7	91.6	1,010	0.0
Tulare	0.0	19.8	0.0	0.0	1.7	15.0	25.3	4.4	0.7	11.8	262.9	4,141	58.3
Turlock	0.0	8.8	0.0	0.0	0.5	28.3	12.8	3.8	11.5	6.7	104.2	1,423	0.0
Tustin	0.0	25.6	0.0	0.0	0.0	20.9	0.0	3.5	5.7	3.4	164.0	2,047	16.9
Twentynine Palms	0.0	15.0	0.0	0.0	4.7	28.1	0.0	19.0	4.4	3.6	11.5	435	0.0
Union City	0.0	7.4	0.0	0.0	0.4	21.3	0.5	12.1	11.8	6.3	163.3	2,170	4.7
Upland	0.0	9.1	0.0	0.0	0.1	24.1	22.1	2.9	10.4	0.0	8.4	110	0.0
Vacaville	0.0	10.4	0.0	0.0	6.1	18.0	23.3	6.0	15.5	1.1	52.6	528	0.0
Vallejo	0.0	11.0	0.5	0.0	1.9	24.0	13.4	2.7	15.6	1.9	126.1	1,038	0.4
Victorville	0.0	4.0	0.0	0.0	0.3	10.8	20.0	4.2	9.1	9.8	412.3	3,380	1.0
Visalia	0.0	4.6	0.0	1.8	0.0	21.2	42.6	8.6	2.1	1.0	27.1	205	0.0
Vista	0.0	3.6	0.0	0.0	2.4	36.7	26.7	5.0	1.8	5.5	222.8	2,212	5.3
Walnut	0.0	19.9	0.0	0.0	1.0	30.8	0.1	15.2	3.1	5.3	28.7	956	0.0
Walnut Creek	0.0	10.5	6.2	0.0	0.7	23.2	0.0	24.3	5.2	0.0	0.9	14	0.2

1. Based on population estimated as of July 1 of the year shown.

STATE Place code	City	Land area[1] (sq. mi)	Population, 2021: Total persons 2021	Population, 2021: Rank	Population, 2021: Per square mile	Race 2020, Race alone[2] (percent): White	Black or African American	American Indian, Alaskan Native	Asian	Hawaiian Pacific Islander	Some other race	Race 2020: Two or more races (percent)
		1	2	3	4	5	6	7	8	9	10	11
	CALIFORNIA—Cont'd											
06 83542	Wasco	9.4	28,173	1,382	2,997.1	20.2	5.6	2.1	0.6	0.1	54.9	16.6
06 83668	Watsonville	6.8	52,067	765	7,656.9	22.3	0.6	2.7	3.1	0.1	51.7	19.6
06 84200	West Covina	16.0	107,017	289	6,688.6	20.1	3.7	1.6	30.7	0.2	25.3	18.4
06 84410	West Hollywood	1.9	34,938	1,140	18,388.4	73.8	3.8	0.3	6.5	0.1	4.8	10.6
06 84550	Westminster	10.0	90,195	381	9,019.5	23.1	1.0	0.8	51.4	0.5	14.3	8.8
06 84816	West Sacramento	21.5	53,637	744	2,494.7	47.3	5.0	1.8	13.6	1.2	14.6	16.6
06 85292	Whittier	14.6	85,311	413	5,843.2	35.2	1.4	2.2	5.0	0.2	31.4	24.7
06 85446	Wildomar	23.7	37,189	1,068	1,569.2	51.6	3.8	1.6	5.6	0.6	19.7	17.1
06 85922	Windsor town	7.4	26,039	1,492	3,518.8	61.8	0.9	2.4	3.0	0.2	17.8	13.8
06 86328	Woodland	15.3	61,398	628	4,012.9	44.6	1.9	2.0	8.7	0.4	23.6	18.8
06 86832	Yorba Linda	20.0	67,989	555	3,399.5	57.1	1.2	0.5	23.0	0.1	5.0	13.1
06 86972	Yuba City	15.0	69,536	542	4,635.7	43.2	2.4	2.0	22.3	0.3	17.3	12.5
06 87042	Yucaipa	28.3	54,739	730	1,934.2	64.1	1.5	1.5	2.9	0.2	15.3	14.4
08 00000	COLORADO	103,637.5	5,812,069	X	56.1	70.7	4.1	1.3	3.5	0.2	8.0	12.3
08 03455	Arvada	38.9	123,436	230	3,173.2	80.7	1.1	1.0	2.6	0.1	3.7	10.8
08 04000	Aurora	160.0	389,347	51	2,433.4	47.1	15.9	1.4	6.4	0.4	13.5	15.1
08 07850	Boulder	26.3	104,175	307	3,961.0	78.8	1.3	0.6	6.4	0.1	4.7	8.1
08 08675	Brighton	21.3	40,693	971	1,910.5	60.6	1.6	2.0	1.9	0.2	15.6	18.1
08 09280	Broomfield	33.0	75,325	490	2,282.6	76.0	1.3	0.6	6.9	0.1	4.1	10.9
08 12415	Castle Rock town	34.3	76,353	479	2,226.0	82.3	1.5	0.6	2.2	0.1	2.8	10.5
08 12815	Centennial	29.7	106,966	291	3,601.5	77.6	3.4	0.4	6.4	0.1	2.6	9.6
08 16000	Colorado Springs	195.8	483,956	40	2,471.7	70.3	5.9	1.1	3.4	0.3	6.2	12.8
08 16495	Commerce City	36.4	64,287	592	1,766.1	51.3	4.2	1.7	3.2	0.2	20.0	19.3
08 20000	Denver	153.1	711,463	19	4,647.0	60.6	8.9	1.5	3.9	0.2	11.3	13.5
08 24785	Englewood	6.6	33,516	1,181	5,078.2	74.6	2.7	1.4	2.5	0.1	7.0	11.6
08 24950	Erie town	20.5	31,686	1,250	1,545.7	80.7	0.9	0.4	5.5	0.1	2.2	10.3
08 27425	Fort Collins	57.2	168,538	158	2,946.5	80.8	1.5	0.8	3.6	0.1	3.6	9.6
08 27865	Fountain	22.3	29,677	1,319	1,330.8	61.4	9.6	1.2	2.5	1.2	6.9	17.2
08 31660	Grand Junction	40.4	66,964	564	1,657.5	81.2	1.0	1.1	1.6	0.2	5.1	9.8
08 32155	Greeley	48.9	109,323	283	2,235.6	62.0	2.7	1.8	2.0	0.1	14.8	16.6
08 41835	Lafayette	9.2	31,002	1,272	3,369.8	74.9	1.1	0.9	4.2	0.1	6.7	12.0
08 43000	Lakewood	43.5	156,605	166	3,600.1	72.1	1.9	1.6	3.8	0.1	7.7	12.7
08 45255	Littleton	12.6	45,191	877	3,586.6	81.0	1.4	0.9	2.3	0.1	4.4	10.0
08 45970	Longmont	28.8	100,758	326	3,498.5	71.1	1.0	1.3	3.6	0.1	10.3	12.7
08 46465	Loveland	34.5	77,194	469	2,237.5	84.0	0.9	0.9	1.2	0.1	4.0	9.0
08 54330	Northglenn	7.4	37,333	1,064	5,045.0	62.0	2.3	2.2	4.0	0.2	12.0	17.4
08 57630	Parker town	22.3	60,313	642	2,704.6	78.8	2.0	0.5	5.9	0.1	2.3	10.4
08 62000	Pueblo	56.2	112,368	271	1,999.4	59.3	2.7	2.7	1.1	0.1	14.7	19.3
08 77290	Thornton	35.9	142,610	193	3,972.4	60.1	2.1	1.5	6.0	0.1	13.1	17.2
08 83835	Westminster	31.6	114,561	257	3,625.3	70.3	1.7	1.3	5.6	0.1	7.7	13.3
08 84440	Wheat Ridge	9.3	32,722	1,209	3,518.5	74.5	1.4	1.6	2.1	0.1	7.4	12.8
08 85485	Windsor town	25.6	35,788	1,109	1,398.0	86.7	0.6	0.6	1.5	0.1	2.4	8.2
09 00000	CONNECTICUT	4,842.7	3,605,597	X	744.5	66.4	10.8	0.4	4.8	0.0	8.3	9.2
09 08000	Bridgeport	16.1	148,333	183	9,213.2	22.7	35.1	0.9	2.8	0.1	24.6	13.9
09 08420	Bristol	26.4	60,661	638	2,297.8	75.2	5.9	0.3	2.6	0.0	6.4	9.6
09 18430	Danbury	42.0	86,759	401	2,065.7	48.1	7.2	0.6	6.2	0.0	21.6	16.1
09 37000	Hartford	17.4	120,576	237	6,929.7	19.4	38.2	0.8	3.5	0.1	25.5	12.5
09 46450	Meriden	23.7	60,517	639	2,553.5	55.6	10.6	0.7	2.2	0.1	16.6	14.3
09 47290	Middletown	41.0	47,108	847	1,149.0	66.2	14.1	0.4	5.5	0.0	4.3	9.5
09 47500	Milford	21.9	50,541	791	2,307.8	81.6	3.2	0.2	5.5	0.0	2.4	7.1
09 49880	Naugatuck	16.4	31,433	1,260	1,916.6	71.4	7.8	0.2	2.4	0.1	7.4	10.8
09 50370	New Britain	13.4	73,841	499	5,510.5	46.0	14.8	0.5	2.6	0.1	21.0	14.9
09 52000	New Haven	18.7	135,081	208	7,223.6	32.7	32.2	1.0	6.8	0.1	15.3	12.0
09 52280	New London	5.6	27,635	1,407	4,934.8	48.1	17.3	1.1	2.5	0.1	16.6	14.3
09 55990	Norwalk	22.9	91,194	372	3,982.3	52.9	12.8	0.7	5.3	0.0	15.7	12.5
09 56200	Norwich	28.1	40,014	987	1,424.0	57.8	12.6	0.9	7.2	0.2	8.6	12.8
09 68100	Shelton	30.6	41,474	953	1,355.4	80.1	4.8	0.1	4.5	0.0	3.3	7.2
09 73000	Stamford	37.6	136,309	204	3,625.2	51.4	12.6	0.7	8.5	0.0	15.1	11.7
09 76500	Torrington	39.8	35,357	1,125	888.4	76.7	3.5	0.5	2.5	0.0	7.6	9.1
09 80000	Waterbury	28.5	113,811	262	3,993.4	40.8	21.9	0.7	2.1	0.1	20.0	14.3
09 82800	West Haven	10.8	55,294	718	5,119.8	50.9	21.9	0.7	4.9	0.0	11.4	10.3
10 00000	DELAWARE	1,948.5	1,003,384	X	515.0	60.4	22.1	0.5	4.3	0.0	4.9	7.7
10 21200	Dover	23.7	38,992	1,018	1,645.2	39.6	43.6	0.6	3.3	0.1	3.6	9.2
10 50670	Newark	9.4	31,155	1,266	3,314.4	67.0	15.1	0.1	9.1	0.0	2.1	6.7
10 77580	Wilmington	10.9	70,750	530	6,490.8	28.7	56.2	0.4	1.3	0.0	6.2	7.2

1. Dry land or land partially or temporarily covered by water. 2. Hispanic or Latino persons may be of any race.

City	Percent Hispanic or Latino[1], 2020	Percent foreign born, 2016–2020	Age of population (percent), 2016–2020: Under 18 years	18 to 24 years	25 to 34 years	35 to 44 years	45 to 54 years	55 to 64 years	65 years and over	Median age, 2016–2020	Percent female, 2016–2020	Population: Census counts: 2010	2020	Percent change: 2010–2020	2020–2021
	12	13	14	15	16	17	18	19	20	21	22	23	24	25	26
CALIFORNIA—Cont'd															
Wasco	84.7	29.8	25.1	11.1	24.6	13.2	9.7	10.7	5.6	30.4	39.6	25,549	27,275	6.8	3.3
Watsonville	82.3	36.1	30.6	10.4	14.3	12.6	11.8	9.5	10.8	30.9	50.2	51,186	52,739	3.0	-1.3
West Covina	53.1	35.7	20.7	9.2	15.4	12.2	12.9	13.7	15.9	38.5	51.4	106,109	109,772	3.5	-2.5
West Hollywood	12.6	24.6	3.9	4.7	32.7	18.0	11.9	13.1	15.8	38.7	45.1	34,335	35,848	4.4	-2.5
Westminster	24.6	44.9	21.4	8.0	13.8	11.7	15.2	13.5	16.5	40.7	50.8	89,511	91,089	1.8	-1.0
West Sacramento	32.0	24.8	26.5	9.7	15.0	15.3	10.7	11.7	11.1	34.4	51.2	48,744	53,666	10.1	-0.1
Whittier	70.8	16.6	23.0	9.6	13.5	14.1	12.7	11.9	15.1	37.8	51.7	85,313	87,383	2.4	-2.4
Wildomar	40.9	16.2	25.2	9.5	15.1	12.9	10.8	13.2	13.2	35.1	50.8	32,211	36,914	14.6	0.7
Windsor town	33.8	15.5	23.9	8.3	10.2	13.0	14.4	14.8	15.4	41.8	50.6	26,792	26,307	-1.8	-1.0
Woodland	48.5	23.1	23.9	10.3	14.2	14.0	12.8	11.4	13.4	36.1	49.7	55,557	60,852	9.5	0.9
Yorba Linda	18.0	19.0	23.3	7.0	9.5	11.6	15.4	15.2	18.0	43.9	51.0	64,176	68,460	6.7	-0.7
Yuba City	30.9	23.2	25.4	9.5	14.5	12.2	11.6	11.4	15.3	35.4	50.5	65,634	70,101	6.8	-0.8
Yucaipa	34.4	11.4	24.5	9.3	14.0	10.4	12.8	14.5	14.6	36.8	51.1	51,279	54,620	6.5	0.2
COLORADO	21.9	9.5	22.1	9.2	15.7	13.8	12.5	12.4	14.2	36.9	49.7	5,029,319	5,773,714	14.8	0.7
Arvada	15.0	5.1	21.0	6.6	14.9	14.3	13.8	12.5	17.0	40.0	50.9	106,759	124,539	16.7	-0.9
Aurora	30.3	20.6	24.9	8.8	16.6	14.4	12.5	10.9	11.9	34.8	50.3	324,976	386,241	18.9	0.8
Boulder	10.6	10.5	12.3	29.3	17.1	10.2	10.1	9.4	11.6	28.8	48.4	97,613	105,414	8.0	-1.2
Brighton	42.5	7.4	27.3	7.6	16.3	15.4	12.3	10.5	10.6	34.0	48.2	33,840	39,990	18.2	1.8
Broomfield	13.4	10.0	22.7	7.5	15.4	14.6	14.1	11.8	13.8	38.4	50.0	55,848	74,112	32.7	1.6
Castle Rock town	11.7	5.5	28.8	7.7	12.8	16.1	14.0	10.3	10.4	35.5	50.3	48,238	73,012	51.4	4.6
Centennial	9.6	8.8	23.2	6.4	11.7	14.4	13.9	14.6	15.9	41.3	49.6	100,391	108,353	7.9	-1.3
Colorado Springs	18.4	7.5	22.9	10.6	16.9	12.7	11.7	11.5	13.6	34.7	50.0	417,450	479,260	14.8	1.0
Commerce City	48.9	14.4	31.9	7.1	14.9	16.4	12.8	8.3	8.5	32.6	50.2	45,849	62,477	36.3	2.9
Denver	27.9	14.0	19.4	8.0	23.4	16.1	11.6	9.9	11.8	34.6	49.9	599,454	715,522	19.4	-0.6
Englewood	19.1	5.9	16.4	9.1	21.7	14.9	10.4	13.3	14.2	36.4	51.1	30,260	33,609	11.1	-0.3
Erie town	10.2	8.1	30.8	4.2	11.0	18.9	15.2	9.6	10.3	37.1	51.5	18,177	30,230	66.3	4.8
Fort Collins	12.4	6.9	17.9	21.9	17.9	11.9	9.7	9.7	10.9	29.9	49.9	144,861	168,972	16.6	-0.3
Fountain	23.7	8.5	29.5	9.1	18.4	16.3	12.9	8.1	5.8	30.3	50.8	25,899	29,848	15.2	-0.6
Grand Junction	15.8	5.0	18.8	11.8	14.2	12.2	11.0	12.7	19.3	39.2	51.1	59,034	65,733	11.3	1.9
Greeley	40.2	11.2	24.6	14.2	16.0	11.9	11.0	10.3	12.2	31.6	49.7	92,953	108,935	17.2	0.4
Lafayette	18.5	8.6	23.0	4.9	14.4	14.5	14.7	13.6	14.8	39.7	49.8	24,482	30,792	25.8	0.7
Lakewood	22.7	8.6	17.7	9.0	18.0	13.4	11.7	13.3	16.9	38.5	50.7	142,592	155,944	9.4	0.4
Littleton	13.6	6.7	18.0	7.2	17.9	12.9	11.1	15.1	17.7	40.2	51.5	41,624	45,644	9.7	-1.0
Longmont	24.7	11.3	22.7	8.7	12.8	14.0	12.9	13.1	15.7	39.1	51.2	86,330	100,119	16.0	0.6
Loveland	13.0	3.3	21.5	8.3	13.4	13.8	11.4	12.6	18.9	39.6	51.0	67,005	76,677	14.4	0.7
Northglenn	36.8	10.9	24.0	10.8	18.7	13.5	11.0	10.6	11.5	32.8	49.3	35,690	38,143	6.9	-2.1
Parker town	10.8	7.5	29.4	8.0	12.1	17.7	14.0	9.9	8.9	35.3	50.1	45,352	58,477	28.9	3.1
Pueblo	49.3	3.2	22.2	9.3	14.1	12.1	11.5	12.6	18.2	38.2	50.3	106,539	111,925	5.1	0.4
Thornton	36.2	13.3	27.8	8.5	16.1	14.9	13.4	10.0	9.3	33.5	50.0	118,859	141,935	19.4	0.5
Westminster	23.4	9.0	21.2	8.5	16.8	14.1	12.7	13.5	13.3	37.2	49.8	106,142	116,375	9.6	-1.6
Wheat Ridge	22.3	3.5	17.0	6.2	16.2	14.1	12.2	14.0	20.3	41.9	52.8	30,179	32,380	7.3	1.1
Windsor town	10.0	3.3	26.6	5.4	10.2	14.1	14.0	13.5	16.1	40.7	49.9	18,650	32,758	75.6	9.2
CONNECTICUT	17.3	14.6	20.6	9.7	12.4	11.9	13.8	14.3	17.2	41.1	51.2	3,574,151	3,605,944	0.9	0.0
Bridgeport	42.3	29.8	23.3	12.0	15.4	13.6	12.6	11.4	11.8	34.6	52.1	144,247	148,692	3.1	-0.2
Bristol	16.3	8.6	20.9	7.7	13.3	13.0	13.9	14.2	17.1	40.5	51.8	60,491	60,783	0.5	-0.2
Danbury	33.2	31.1	20.3	10.6	13.4	14.1	12.8	13.7	15.1	38.9	50.3	80,834	86,550	7.1	0.2
Hartford	44.0	21.1	23.2	13.7	16.2	12.7	11.9	10.6	11.7	32.9	52.5	124,756	121,219	-2.8	-0.5
Meriden	36.6	10.8	19.8	8.5	14.2	13.8	12.8	15.1	15.9	40.8	53.7	60,825	60,859	0.1	-0.6
Middletown	11.8	12.0	15.7	14.5	15.4	11.6	12.5	14.1	16.2	38.7	51.3	47,650	47,057	-1.2	0.1
Milford	7.9	11.8	17.4	6.9	14.1	11.7	13.8	16.5	19.6	44.8	50.5	51,251	50,587	-1.4	-0.1
Naugatuck	15.5	14.0	19.9	8.9	13.7	12.7	14.9	15.2	14.5	39.8	48.9	31,871	31,593	-0.9	-0.5
New Britain	44.0	18.5	23.7	13.4	16.2	11.4	11.1	11.0	13.2	32.9	51.8	73,203	74,217	1.4	-0.5
New Haven	30.6	17.4	22.6	15.3	18.9	12.7	10.9	8.7	10.9	30.7	53.4	129,864	133,924	3.1	0.9
New London	34.1	18.8	18.5	20.3	13.7	12.3	10.2	12.4	12.6	31.8	51.9	27,620	27,641	0.1	0.0
Norwalk	30.3	28.5	19.4	8.2	15.2	13.5	14.5	13.8	15.3	40.1	50.9	85,609	91,143	6.5	0.1
Norwich	19.3	14.4	20.4	8.7	16.0	11.5	12.2	14.2	17.0	38.8	52.0	40,503	40,018	-1.2	0.0
Shelton	10.0	11.8	16.9	8.6	10.4	10.6	15.6	16.4	21.5	48.1	52.4	39,563	40,872	3.3	1.5
Stamford	28.0	33.0	19.3	8.8	17.4	14.2	12.4	12.4	15.4	37.9	51.2	122,633	135,445	10.4	0.6
Torrington	15.3	8.9	18.6	7.7	12.6	10.8	15.2	15.8	19.2	45.2	49.3	36,395	35,484	-2.5	-0.4
Waterbury	39.6	16.8	24.0	9.5	14.9	11.1	13.7	12.7	14.1	36.4	51.8	110,305	114,446	3.8	-0.6
West Haven	23.7	19.6	20.9	13.5	15.6	11.6	12.6	13.0	12.8	35.0	50.4	55,564	55,560	0.0	-0.5
DELAWARE	10.5	9.4	21.1	8.6	13.3	11.6	12.6	14.0	18.8	41.0	51.7	897,947	989,948	10.2	1.4
Dover	8.3	8.9	19.1	17.7	14.8	10.4	11.5	9.8	16.7	33.8	53.5	35,795	39,614	10.7	-1.6
Newark	7.0	13.7	11.8	38.9	14.1	6.3	7.1	8.6	13.3	24.7	52.9	31,776	31,314	-1.5	-0.5
Wilmington	13.3	7.7	22.3	8.6	18.1	12.4	11.9	13.4	13.4	35.9	53.4	70,941	70,941	0.0	-0.3

1. May be of any race.

City	Households, 2016–2020							Persons in group quarters, 2016–2020	Serious crimes known to police[2], 2020				Educational attainment, 2016–2020		
			Percent						Violent		Property			Attainment[4] (percent)	
	Number	Persons per household	Family	Married couple family	Female family	Non-family	One person		Number	Rate	Number	Rate	Population age 25 and over	High school graduate or less	Bachelor's degree or more
	27	28	29	30	31	32	33	34	35	36	37	38	39	40	41
CALIFORNIA—Cont'd															
Wasco	6,464	3.40	84.0	57.9	18.0	16.0	15.4	5,588	NA	NA	NA	NA	17,578	72.1	4.4
Watsonville	14,317	3.63	77.7	51.3	17.6	22.3	16.5	419	299	552.2	1,132	2,090.5	30,926	61.0	13.3
West Covina	30,855	3.40	78.2	52.8	17.5	21.8	16.2	914	206	196.2	2,212	2,106.9	74,177	40.6	30.3
West Hollywood	22,845	1.55	21.1	16.4	3.3	78.9	59.3	179	205	558.3	1,205	3,281.7	32,465	15.2	60.1
Westminster	27,144	3.34	77.6	56.1	14.6	22.4	18.0	303	259	285.4	2,549	2,809.1	64,193	45.1	27.0
West Sacramento	18,356	2.89	70.3	49.8	14.6	29.7	21.5	458	211	390.2	1,505	2,783.5	34,208	34.9	30.7
Whittier	27,093	3.07	70.9	49.2	15.4	29.1	23.2	1,704	237	278.6	1,634	1,920.7	57,147	40.2	26.7
Wildomar	10,318	3.49	81.6	61.6	11.9	18.4	14.2	88	58	153.4	416	1,100.3	23,537	46.6	16.1
Windsor town	9,378	2.94	77.0	62.1	8.2	23.0	17.8	65	38	139.9	234	861.4	18,728	29.2	34.5
Woodland	20,530	2.86	73.4	53.3	14.1	26.6	20.9	1,138	227	371.4	1,376	2,251.2	39,317	42.0	27.9
Yorba Linda	22,528	3.01	82.4	70.6	7.0	17.6	14.8	312	32	47.0	573	842.4	47,423	17.6	53.8
Yuba City	22,958	2.87	70.8	49.9	12.8	29.2	23.3	824	242	360.3	1,850	2,754.4	43,380	43.3	20.4
Yucaipa	18,438	2.92	71.9	55.3	10.8	28.1	24.3	485	153	282.3	601	1,108.9	35,973	40.5	24.2
COLORADO	2,137,402	2.60	63.6	50.0	9.1	36.4	27.7	119,595	24,570	423.1	164,582	2,833.8	3,900,754	29.1	41.6
Arvada	46,983	2.55	66.7	54.3	8.6	33.3	26.1	528	280	227.7	3,891	3,163.9	87,084	28.1	43.1
Aurora	133,062	2.83	65.6	46.0	13.4	34.4	26.3	2,205	3,473	900.4	13,079	3,390.8	251,550	39.2	30.0
Boulder	43,378	2.26	40.7	33.5	4.7	59.3	36.2	10,931	343	321.8	4,019	3,770.2	63,441	8.5	76.7
Brighton	11,861	3.09	71.8	55.1	12.8	28.2	22.8	1,732	192	451.4	1,308	3,075.0	24,966	44.6	20.9
Broomfield	27,199	2.54	64.0	54.0	6.6	36.0	27.5	317	76	105.9	2,145	2,987.7	48,449	17.1	56.1
Castle Rock town	21,536	2.99	77.0	65.5	7.2	23.0	17.9	689	45	63.2	1,183	1,662.7	41,416	18.4	50.0
Centennial	40,697	2.69	74.1	61.8	8.2	25.9	21.2	2,049	144	128.5	1,979	1,765.3	78,443	16.4	58.9
Colorado Springs	184,788	2.51	63.4	48.3	10.2	36.6	28.0	7,508	2,896	597.0	16,394	3,379.6	313,413	25.4	39.6
Commerce City	17,282	3.21	75.9	57.3	12.5	24.1	19.5	372	298	479.4	2,051	3,299.3	34,088	45.4	24.9
Denver	287,756	2.44	48.1	35.1	8.9	51.9	38.4	14,290	6,329	857.9	34,294	4,648.7	519,573	28.0	50.3
Englewood	15,756	2.18	46.1	33.6	8.2	53.9	42.1	445	90	253.8	2,010	5,667.7	25,963	30.1	43.2
Erie town	8,912	3.04	81.3	70.2	7.5	18.7	14.1	58	28	99.3	326	1,156.1	17,647	12.3	64.1
Fort Collins	61,526	2.56	54.6	43.3	7.2	45.4	25.1	8,297	NA	NA	NA	NA	99,868	18.2	55.6
Fountain	9,870	3.06	76.3	63.6	7.6	23.7	17.2	0	129	412.2	617	1,971.4	18,579	28.5	27.8
Grand Junction	25,760	2.32	52.5	39.9	8.6	47.5	37.6	2,572	348	542.5	2,966	4,623.6	43,179	35.2	33.5
Greeley	34,721	2.91	66.7	49.5	12.6	33.3	26.3	6,265	470	425.3	2,722	2,463.2	65,815	43.6	25.1
Lafayette	11,696	2.39	61.9	47.4	7.9	38.1	28.3	11	61	193.9	647	2,056.8	20,141	16.3	61.0
Lakewood	64,844	2.37	56.7	41.3	10.1	43.3	33.2	2,280	903	565.4	8,050	5,040.1	114,151	30.3	42.0
Littleton	20,300	2.25	55.9	43.7	7.8	44.1	34.6	543	72	147.5	1,176	2,409.6	34,581	20.5	53.6
Longmont	36,773	2.59	65.3	50.2	10.8	34.7	27.7	651	394	399.8	2,715	2,755.1	65,808	27.8	44.2
Loveland	32,716	2.48	64.7	50.6	8.8	35.3	27.6	482	NA	NA	NA	NA	57,380	29.3	36.7
Northglenn	13,496	2.89	66.8	45.8	13.9	33.2	24.9	138	190	485.2	1,447	3,695.0	25,566	45.0	20.0
Parker town	18,944	2.93	75.3	63.9	7.1	24.7	18.9	37	73	123.2	875	1,476.9	34,698	17.3	52.4
Pueblo	44,817	2.41	56.3	36.0	14.7	43.7	37.4	3,910	1,181	1,045.1	5,233	4,630.9	76,527	42.2	20.4
Thornton	46,868	3.07	71.8	55.0	11.3	28.2	20.8	455	415	287.9	4,538	3,148.0	91,846	39.5	28.3
Westminster	44,887	2.55	62.9	47.4	9.9	37.1	28.2	332	326	286.1	4,033	3,539.6	80,685	29.5	39.3
Wheat Ridge	14,264	2.19	51.5	38.0	9.0	48.5	36.8	613	173	550.1	1,674	5,322.6	24,490	30.8	39.6
Windsor town	8,419	2.80	79.0	65.5	9.9	21.0	16.8	98	NA	NA	NA	NA	16,104	20.7	45.4
CONNECTICUT	1,385,437	2.50	65.2	48.0	12.5	34.8	28.5	112,075	6,459	181.6	55,670	1,565.1	2,489,205	35.4	40.0
Bridgeport	51,638	2.72	62.5	32.2	22.5	37.5	30.9	4,593	829	574.3	2,514	1,741.6	93,854	55.9	19.7
Bristol	24,408	2.43	62.4	43.4	13.7	37.6	30.0	781	69	115.2	766	1,279.1	42,875	42.2	26.5
Danbury	31,074	2.61	64.4	46.4	13.5	35.6	28.3	3,396	98	115.2	806	947.3	58,479	42.5	33.5
Hartford	47,722	2.41	54.0	20.4	26.4	46.0	39.3	7,752	1,208	992.2	3,787	3,110.5	77,258	59.2	17.0
Meriden	25,222	2.32	57.8	34.8	17.0	42.2	37.4	1,039	151	254.9	1,254	2,116.9	42,710	50.5	21.8
Middletown	19,876	2.12	52.4	36.6	12.9	47.6	38.9	4,294	38	82.4	597	1,294.8	32,364	33.7	39.8
Milford	22,360	2.42	63.3	51.3	8.7	36.7	31.1	429	NA	NA	NA	NA	41,245	28.6	45.5
Naugatuck	11,843	2.61	68.2	50.5	13.1	31.8	23.4	295	36	116.0	445	1,434.4	22,190	37.7	30.1
New Britain	27,683	2.52	59.4	31.7	21.4	40.6	33.0	2,703	297	410.2	1,805	2,492.7	45,640	55.2	18.5
New Haven	49,051	2.47	51.2	24.7	21.5	48.8	37.3	9,349	922	707.6	4,575	3,511.2	80,999	45.8	35.2
New London	10,991	2.11	53.4	27.9	20.2	46.6	38.4	3,838	67	250.2	500	1,867.3	16,515	43.5	27.2
Norwalk	34,427	2.56	65.4	48.5	11.6	34.6	28.5	617	143	160.4	1,222	1,370.9	64,192	33.6	43.6
Norwich	16,382	2.36	61.7	39.5	16.2	38.3	31.4	440	134	347.4	542	1,405.0	27,753	48.8	21.4
Shelton	16,516	2.46	67.3	55.1	8.5	32.7	27.1	513	17	41.2	371	898.3	30,655	31.5	43.0
Stamford	50,952	2.53	62.3	46.6	11.8	37.7	28.9	1,128	284	217.7	NA	NA	93,469	29.8	52.2
Torrington	14,377	2.33	61.3	42.2	13.6	38.7	31.4	811	32	94.7	388	1,148.1	25,266	47.2	22.6
Waterbury	42,135	2.51	59.9	33.0	20.5	40.1	34.5	1,979	400	372.9	2,843	2,650.5	71,644	56.6	17.1
West Haven	19,729	2.61	63.7	39.9	16.7	36.3	29.1	3,247	87	159.6	1,218	2,234.2	35,848	49.3	25.1
DELAWARE	370,953	2.54	65.5	48.0	12.7	34.5	28.1	24,952	4,262	431.9	19,355	1,961.4	679,870	40.4	32.7
Dover	14,740	2.28	53.5	28.6	19.6	46.5	37.8	4,285	329	856.1	1,549	4,030.9	23,924	42.0	25.5
Newark	10,736	2.49	48.3	41.4	4.7	51.7	32.3	7,141	80	237.0	636	1,884.3	16,696	21.0	54.8
Wilmington	29,708	2.26	46.2	21.2	20.4	53.8	47.1	3,431	1,115	1,590.6	2,598	3,706.1	48,827	49.7	28.8

2. Data for serious crimes have not been adjusted for underreporting. This may affect comparability between geographic areas and over time.
4. Persons 25 years old and over.

City	Money income, 2016–2020					Median earnings Full year, Full-time workers, 2016–2020			Housing units, 2016–2020				
	Households												
	Median household income	Percent with income less than $25,000	Percent with income of $200,000 or more	Median family income	Median non-family household income	All persons	Men	Women	Total	Occupied	Percent owner occupied	Median value[1] (dollars)	Median gross rent (dollars)
	42	43	44	45	46	47	48	49	50	51	52	53	54
CALIFORNIA—Cont'd													
Wasco	39,291	27.4	1.6	42,652	14,565	34,792	36,159	29,869	6,859	6,464	59.4	179,500	785
Watsonville	61,496	20.4	5.6	66,430	34,394	38,673	42,654	35,164	14,881	14,317	45.0	500,300	1,502
West Covina	85,626	13.6	9.6	93,654	41,220	50,109	51,491	45,996	32,102	30,855	62.7	578,800	1,745
West Hollywood	71,692	20.1	13.7	110,886	63,098	71,859	78,974	65,277	25,501	22,845	19.8	743,700	1,744
Westminster	67,142	20.7	9.6	73,841	39,740	48,266	50,233	45,204	28,144	27,144	53.4	624,000	1,686
West Sacramento	73,979	19.7	10.2	84,393	46,269	61,544	66,254	57,166	19,375	18,356	56.6	372,700	1,120
Whittier	76,026	16.0	7.5	87,313	37,571	50,752	54,954	47,515	28,136	27,093	57.7	598,000	1,407
Wildomar	76,791	12.9	8.9	81,472	44,068	51,292	61,023	39,148	10,833	10,318	73.4	378,100	1,655
Windsor town	117,533	8.2	15.3	130,867	55,873	71,010	76,634	61,094	9,705	9,378	78.0	620,600	2,003
Woodland	71,477	14.1	6.2	78,846	43,799	48,613	53,336	41,988	21,023	20,530	52.5	381,800	1,197
Yorba Linda	133,088	7.2	27.7	150,176	55,045	90,025	104,481	75,369	23,502	22,528	82.4	862,900	2,323
Yuba City	60,910	17.1	5.9	68,657	37,271	43,552	47,017	40,171	23,922	22,958	54.6	304,600	1,111
Yucaipa	73,196	15.8	6.6	94,865	32,218	56,387	61,201	49,543	19,682	18,438	71.6	345,100	1,217
COLORADO	75,231	14.2	9.6	92,752	47,627	53,517	58,990	48,348	2,361,372	2,137,402	66.2	369,900	1,335
Arvada	92,669	8.8	10.7	113,548	54,644	62,303	70,912	54,347	48,408	46,983	75.9	424,100	1,444
Aurora	67,723	12.7	5.6	80,249	47,636	45,786	47,205	44,067	139,091	133,062	61.6	322,200	1,401
Boulder	72,279	21.0	16.2	130,729	46,377	65,765	69,369	61,273	46,333	43,378	49.6	736,000	1,588
Brighton	74,813	12.4	5.2	85,283	44,685	49,626	55,832	44,450	12,183	11,861	64.8	337,100	1,363
Broomfield	101,206	8.0	16.3	129,207	64,300	70,114	80,322	60,014	28,037	27,199	66.3	450,600	1,711
Castle Rock town	113,585	5.8	16.4	128,917	59,682	71,580	84,745	55,030	22,225	21,536	79.9	444,800	1,630
Centennial	109,767	5.3	18.6	129,346	63,166	72,276	81,546	64,671	41,744	40,697	81.9	458,300	1,728
Colorado Springs	67,719	16.2	6.9	81,479	43,001	48,281	52,047	43,940	194,008	184,788	60.2	294,500	1,196
Commerce City	82,939	13.2	5.8	92,338	55,265	52,769	56,844	46,386	17,739	17,282	75.2	340,100	1,400
Denver	72,661	15.6	11.4	93,236	56,719	55,589	59,283	52,376	306,269	287,756	50.4	427,600	1,397
Englewood	66,399	18.5	5.8	90,571	48,230	52,153	55,210	46,264	16,755	15,756	48.1	379,300	1,224
Erie town	124,480	4.9	19.5	138,348	80,747	83,489	103,858	65,080	9,073	8,912	85.4	514,000	2,128
Fort Collins	70,528	17.4	7.7	97,296	44,005	51,507	56,806	44,668	64,262	61,526	55.3	398,800	1,373
Fountain	68,194	13.4	3.4	71,906	42,428	43,903	50,679	40,063	10,343	9,870	69.6	259,000	1,505
Grand Junction	54,570	21.9	4.1	73,943	35,524	46,403	49,837	41,673	27,219	25,760	60.6	251,400	895
Greeley	57,537	20.2	3.3	72,204	32,782	43,598	49,479	38,346	36,449	34,721	60.7	274,800	1,063
Lafayette	85,909	8.3	14.3	109,969	56,417	66,530	72,932	59,881	12,089	11,696	70.5	458,300	1,685
Lakewood	71,233	14.2	7.0	91,546	50,078	52,656	55,241	47,722	67,597	64,844	59.0	398,200	1,430
Littleton	76,375	15.3	11.0	104,242	46,840	58,714	62,500	54,011	21,189	20,300	58.9	446,500	1,359
Longmont	79,140	13.5	8.2	96,609	44,392	54,226	60,427	47,112	38,399	36,773	64.1	396,000	1,437
Loveland	72,515	15.3	4.7	84,065	41,193	50,605	55,133	44,196	33,936	32,716	62.8	339,500	1,330
Northglenn	71,104	11.3	3.5	80,301	49,445	45,346	49,631	39,655	13,937	13,496	56.6	331,200	1,372
Parker town	114,802	6.4	16.9	132,634	57,636	74,328	85,184	62,956	19,750	18,944	76.0	446,100	1,676
Pueblo	42,902	30.4	2.2	54,651	28,161	41,579	43,292	39,862	48,823	44,817	57.1	149,600	826
Thornton	80,732	10.4	6.9	91,789	54,840	52,599	57,711	45,584	48,549	46,868	72.6	349,000	1,485
Westminster	76,378	10.8	8.4	95,837	49,956	54,037	59,068	48,375	46,402	44,887	65.1	363,500	1,472
Wheat Ridge	63,333	21.6	7.2	90,365	38,060	52,272	56,299	46,696	14,959	14,264	52.9	426,500	1,164
Windsor town	103,933	6.9	12.5	116,925	55,399	64,800	75,457	53,962	8,586	8,419	82.7	425,300	1,397
CONNECTICUT	79,855	15.2	13.2	102,061	45,539	62,627	69,364	55,737	1,521,199	1,385,437	66.1	279,700	1,201
Bridgeport	47,484	28.3	3.2	55,622	30,876	42,328	42,984	41,518	58,114	51,638	42.3	186,000	1,171
Bristol	68,485	16.5	5.3	85,562	43,562	53,039	54,532	51,343	26,275	24,408	63.4	198,600	1,093
Danbury	73,204	15.8	9.2	85,556	51,815	53,691	55,601	50,008	33,592	31,074	57.0	311,200	1,475
Hartford	36,154	36.8	2.0	43,794	25,105	39,417	41,726	36,335	55,205	47,722	24.9	170,200	1,004
Meriden	58,472	17.5	4.3	77,465	44,516	51,295	57,492	46,673	27,870	25,222	57.8	171,700	1,041
Middletown	62,022	19.1	6.6	85,807	42,506	57,072	63,373	51,123	21,549	19,876	52.3	234,300	1,138
Milford	95,627	10.3	14.5	118,510	56,931	74,202	78,819	68,673	24,424	22,360	74.5	321,800	1,608
Naugatuck	77,967	11.8	6.1	91,089	42,254	57,951	63,057	52,612	12,606	11,843	67.6	187,900	1,099
New Britain	47,393	27.2	2.3	56,361	34,679	43,397	47,564	38,880	31,011	27,683	40.6	161,900	1,030
New Haven	44,507	30.9	4.9	51,434	35,128	47,219	49,653	44,048	55,956	49,051	28.0	205,100	1,219
New London	47,424	27.9	3.3	53,902	38,531	41,735	52,234	37,974	12,233	10,991	39.8	186,900	1,034
Norwalk	89,486	11.2	17.6	102,314	64,294	64,117	69,501	61,396	36,946	34,427	57.3	438,900	1,691
Norwich	57,565	20.4	4.8	67,982	37,537	45,641	52,391	38,668	19,120	16,382	53.0	170,800	1,058
Shelton	98,873	12.7	13.7	119,036	48,807	72,995	80,983	67,938	17,276	16,516	79.6	345,200	1,375
Stamford	96,885	12.8	19.6	111,519	67,599	72,422	76,914	68,065	55,039	50,952	50.3	541,600	1,877
Torrington	60,662	17.3	4.3	79,474	38,367	49,519	53,081	46,043	16,599	14,377	68.9	153,800	951
Waterbury	46,329	28.9	2.6	56,237	30,656	45,025	48,799	40,790	48,390	42,135	45.0	132,700	986
West Haven	64,255	18.0	5.3	75,394	41,988	50,727	52,229	42,485	21,750	19,729	51.4	196,800	1,164
DELAWARE	69,110	15.5	7.6	84,825	41,157	51,913	56,426	47,490	438,438	370,953	71.4	258,300	1,150
Dover	48,500	24.8	2.4	58,578	34,734	40,658	41,342	37,132	16,062	14,740	47.9	182,100	1,066
Newark	60,767	24.6	6.3	94,541	32,286	54,012	52,855	57,766	11,817	10,736	53.4	277,700	1,282
Wilmington	45,139	29.8	5.1	56,682	34,730	47,260	51,209	44,593	33,849	29,708	43.8	173,500	1,030

1. Specified owner-occupied units

City	Commuting, 2016–2020[1] Percent Drove alone	Commuting, 2016–2020[1] Mean travel time to work	Computer access[2], 2016–2020 Percent With a computer in the house	Computer access[2], 2016–2020 Percent With Internet access	Migration, 2016–2020 Percent who lived in the same house one year ago	Migration, 2016–2020 Percent who lived in another state or county one year ago	Civilian labor force, 2021 Total	Civilian labor force, 2021 Percent change 2020–2021	Civilian labor force, 2021 Unemployment[3] Total	Civilian labor force, 2021 Unemployment[3] Rate	Civilian Employment, 2016–2020[4] Population age 16 and older Number	Civilian Employment, 2016–2020[4] Population age 16 and older Percent in labor force	Civilian Employment, 2016–2020[4] Population age 16 to 64 Number	Civilian Employment, 2016–2020[4] Population age 16 to 64 Percent who worked full-year full-time
	55	56	57	58	59	60	61	62	63	64	65	66	67	68
CALIFORNIA—Cont'd														
Wasco	84.9	24.2	68.6	61.2	82.8	13.2	8,905	0.3	1,241	13.9	21,132	46.3	19,592	30.6
Watsonville	70.6	26.9	86.8	78.8	93.3	2.0	24,313	-0.2	3,303	13.6	38,340	65.3	32,705	45.5
West Covina	79.8	33.9	94.8	88.2	89.9	2.3	51,384	0.5	4,722	9.2	86,094	64.5	69,223	51.6
West Hollywood	69.1	29.4	94.3	90.1	84.9	6.2	25,851	-0.2	2,458	9.5	34,142	79.3	28,537	60.7
Westminster	76.3	28.7	93.7	89.0	91.3	2.4	40,613	-1.8	3,225	7.9	73,770	60.7	58,781	44.8
West Sacramento	72.2	25.0	94.8	90.2	88.8	6.6	25,241	0.4	1,530	6.1	40,798	65.1	34,866	47.3
Whittier	80.7	34.0	91.2	83.7	92.0	1.7	42,089	1.0	3,671	8.7	67,730	61.5	54,901	52.1
Wildomar	80.3	38.4	96.1	89.5	85.0	6.7	17,480	0.9	1,162	6.6	28,361	60.6	23,598	44.4
Windsor town	77.9	22.4	94.4	92.1	90.8	2.2	13,419	-0.7	717	5.3	21,968	70.0	17,719	50.8
Woodland	78.5	23.2	90.0	84.8	87.1	4.6	30,120	1.5	2,206	7.3	46,978	63.8	38,995	49.5
Yorba Linda	78.3	32.2	97.8	95.6	89.6	3.3	33,590	0.2	1,635	4.9	54,237	63.7	41,988	50.0
Yuba City	77.9	29.0	90.7	85.0	83.8	7.9	31,270	-0.7	2,880	9.2	51,578	58.9	41,349	44.0
Yucaipa	82.8	30.5	94.4	87.3	90.8	3.6	25,838	1.8	1,476	5.7	42,361	62.9	34,434	50.4
COLORADO	72.9	25.8	94.9	89.4	82.4	9.6	3,156,110	2.2	169,399	5.4	4,568,027	67.4	3,759,690	53.7
Arvada	78.0	27.6	95.2	91.9	85.2	8.1	69,106	2.0	3,451	5.0	98,013	70.3	77,519	59.6
Aurora	74.1	29.8	95.5	89.9	82.0	9.9	206,815	1.9	13,709	6.6	295,295	70.7	250,313	56.9
Boulder	48.5	19.8	97.9	93.4	66.1	17.0	65,211	2.3	2,488	3.8	97,119	65.3	84,533	37.5
Brighton	78.6	32.0	92.5	86.2	85.8	7.4	20,392	2.6	1,321	6.5	28,951	67.6	24,903	57.4
Broomfield	72.7	26.8	97.8	94.2	80.8	14.9	41,167	1.9	1,848	4.5	55,755	72.8	46,168	59.6
Castle Rock town	76.4	30.0	96.9	95.3	82.1	9.7	37,968	2.4	1,567	4.1	49,035	71.8	42,285	56.1
Centennial	75.4	26.6	98.1	94.9	85.6	8.6	62,757	2.2	2,629	4.2	88,498	70.1	70,825	57.8
Colorado Springs	76.2	23.3	95.4	91.3	77.9	9.4	243,486	2.4	13,728	5.6	374,692	64.7	310,407	52.5
Commerce City	74.1	30.4	92.6	86.4	85.6	7.7	30,331	2.3	1,899	6.3	40,193	73.6	35,420	57.4
Denver	66.1	25.7	94.9	89.1	80.2	11.6	427,421	1.8	25,298	5.9	590,529	72.3	506,326	57.4
Englewood	73.3	25.2	92.8	86.0	77.7	15.0	21,417	1.9	1,248	5.8	29,647	71.8	24,694	58.5
Erie town	66.6	28.5	97.7	96.7	83.0	12.7	17,854	1.9	597	3.3	19,529	73.5	16,728	57.2
Fort Collins	69.7	20.7	97.3	90.9	73.5	12.6	99,936	2.3	4,479	4.5	139,834	70.3	121,693	45.7
Fountain	80.0	26.6	95.7	93.4	78.5	12.0	13,327	2.5	796	6.0	22,395	60.1	20,654	49.0
Grand Junction	74.9	15.9	91.3	86.3	75.5	8.9	31,156	3.2	1,812	5.8	51,632	61.9	39,626	46.2
Greeley	78.1	24.7	93.7	84.1	79.8	9.9	51,355	0.5	3,534	6.9	83,668	63.5	70,612	46.6
Lafayette	69.4	25.1	95.4	92.3	81.7	8.2	17,568	2.6	820	4.7	22,055	74.2	17,908	57.2
Lakewood	75.3	27.2	94.6	89.9	82.2	10.9	87,805	1.8	5,194	5.9	131,440	68.4	105,172	57.3
Littleton	72.8	26.5	96.1	91.5	81.0	12.1	25,034	1.8	1,206	4.8	38,758	69.4	30,565	56.9
Longmont	74.3	24.9	94.2	88.9	81.7	10.1	55,767	2.9	2,911	5.2	76,800	69.0	61,721	53.6
Loveland	79.0	25.7	95.6	89.0	84.2	6.5	45,839	2.7	2,298	5.0	65,591	65.3	50,101	56.2
Northglenn	79.5	28.2	95.8	86.5	83.0	6.0	21,407	2.0	1,457	6.8	30,591	71.9	26,083	60.4
Parker town	77.9	26.7	99.1	96.6	81.5	12.3	33,746	2.0	1,452	4.3	40,987	75.9	36,038	59.1
Pueblo	80.9	19.4	87.3	76.7	82.1	6.0	49,801	2.0	4,510	9.1	89,423	54.9	69,122	43.3
Thornton	77.3	30.5	97.7	92.3	84.3	6.9	81,850	2.2	4,427	5.4	108,452	72.9	95,056	56.5
Westminster	77.8	27.1	94.3	89.7	82.7	11.4	66,419	1.7	3,657	5.5	93,264	73.0	77,987	59.8
Wheat Ridge	69.6	25.8	91.1	85.4	83.6	9.4	17,404	1.7	1,171	6.7	26,811	66.6	20,341	57.5
Windsor town	80.5	25.7	97.6	94.9	83.8	11.2	15,125	0.6	684	4.5	17,981	68.9	14,160	57.2
CONNECTICUT	76.3	26.7	92.0	86.8	88.3	5.0	1,855,923	-2.2	116,108	6.3	2,927,839	65.7	2,312,373	51.3
Bridgeport	68.1	29.6	88.2	80.3	85.2	4.8	67,830	-1.8	6,741	9.9	114,781	66.5	97,684	42.4
Bristol	81.1	24.6	90.5	85.0	87.8	5.1	32,486	-2.8	2,321	7.1	48,892	68.5	38,638	56.3
Danbury	74.2	28.6	92.1	86.8	87.1	5.3	45,677	-1.8	2,462	5.4	69,025	70.0	56,229	49.6
Hartford	61.5	22.3	86.5	74.9	82.6	5.3	52,686	-3.8	5,804	11.0	97,426	60.1	83,092	39.8
Meriden	78.2	23.7	86.8	78.0	88.4	3.1	32,240	-1.8	2,441	7.6	48,880	64.9	39,426	52.2
Middletown	76.4	21.4	88.4	81.1	83.7	11.1	25,531	-2.5	1,580	6.2	40,083	64.4	32,572	50.3
Milford	82.1	26.6	93.1	88.8	89.8	4.9	29,844	-1.3	1,771	5.9	46,596	67.9	35,908	57.7
Naugatuck	80.0	30.5	92.0	87.3	89.6	3.0	16,738	-2.4	1,138	6.8	25,977	70.9	21,438	53.8
New Britain	77.4	20.5	85.9	74.7	87.3	4.0	36,651	-2.5	3,543	9.7	57,059	63.1	47,514	46.6
New Haven	59.1	22.4	88.6	82.6	80.4	7.8	65,844	-1.5	5,098	7.7	104,010	65.1	89,857	40.9
New London	66.9	19.3	89.4	83.4	80.7	11.2	11,667	-3.6	1,180	10.1	22,367	59.2	18,972	44.6
Norwalk	72.2	27.6	94.7	90.4	90.2	4.0	49,320	-2.1	2,882	5.8	73,244	71.2	59,625	53.8
Norwich	78.3	22.3	86.0	81.2	85.8	4.3	19,272	-5.6	1,723	8.9	31,947	65.5	25,286	47.7
Shelton	82.6	27.6	90.2	86.8	88.3	5.0	21,392	-1.4	1,334	6.2	35,151	64.7	26,283	55.0
Stamford	64.9	28.4	93.4	89.1	84.1	6.1	69,294	-2.1	3,952	5.7	107,654	72.4	87,579	53.9
Torrington	85.4	26.2	89.9	85.1	88.2	3.8	18,677	-2.5	1,306	7.0	28,667	65.5	22,073	51.2
Waterbury	77.6	25.8	84.1	73.7	87.4	4.4	49,767	-2.3	5,050	10.1	84,582	61.7	69,425	43.7
West Haven	75.2	23.5	92.6	89.0	85.8	6.3	30,243	-2.5	2,031	6.7	44,649	67.3	37,653	47.7
DELAWARE	78.8	26.2	93.1	86.9	88.0	5.3	496,430	2.2	26,555	5.3	787,102	61.6	605,078	52.2
Dover	79.6	20.8	89.3	84.2	78.5	12.0	16,137	1.3	1,406	8.7	31,193	58.4	24,870	44.9
Newark	64.4	21.4	95.0	88.6	72.1	13.9	16,523	2.3	677	4.1	30,448	52.9	25,955	30.3
Wilmington	62.9	23.3	90.6	77.4	81.3	5.7	34,519	0.5	2,911	8.4	56,415	63.1	46,961	47.5

1. Employed persons. 2. Households. 3. Percent of civilian labor force. 4. Persons 16 years old and over.

Table D. Cities — **Construction, Wholesale Trade, and Retail Trade**

City	Value of residential construction authorized by building permits, 2021			Wholesale trade[1], 2017				Retail trade[2], 2017			
	New construction ($1,000)	Number of housing units	Percent single family	Number of establishments	Number of employees	Sales (mil dol)	Annual payroll (mil dol)	Number of establish-ments	Number of employees	Sales (mil dol)	Annual payroll (mil dol)
	69	70	71	72	73	74	75	76	77	78	79
CALIFORNIA—Cont'd											
Wasco	9,038	66	100.0	4	20	7.1	0.8	36	450	111.8	11.1
Watsonville	12,982	144	45.8	63	1,053	1,207.9	64.0	150	2,378	2,046.0	69.2
West Covina	6,030	22	100.0	91	234	118.7	8.2	284	5,745	1,800.8	155.2
West Hollywood	42,225	193	10.9	100	620	503.8	36.8	306	3,710	1,424.4	136.4
Westminster	15,510	127	93.7	113	535	452.2	24.8	397	5,144	1,708.0	149.7
West Sacramento	109,474	628	30.3	144	4,360	7,097.8	247.5	157	2,413	740.7	72.1
Whittier	56,170	253	74.7	63	399	169.5	17.7	215	3,587	897.3	93.5
Wildomar	12,908	52	100.0	7	51	30.2	2.0	34	424	150.5	13.1
Windsor town	17,284	68	23.5	23	525	481.4	35.4	61	1,179	341.8	37.8
Woodland	43,451	155	100.0	71	1,253	1,041.7	68.4	152	2,362	804.9	71.2
Yorba Linda	3,348	14	100.0	131	1,361	904.3	104.6	133	1,732	643.3	58.3
Yuba City	19,015	56	92.9	38	378	236.4	21.8	243	4,174	1,180.1	114.2
Yucaipa	22,790	60	100.0	20	106	27.2	3.3	99	1,081	297.6	28.8
COLORADO	13,743,890	56,524	53.5	5,953	80,365	83,316.2	5,376.3	19,056	279,982	84,930.6	8,419.7
Arvada	102,573	373	100.0	93	1,033	549.0	56.7	258	3,970	1,350.6	121.3
Aurora	790,889	4,176	50.2	229	6,441	10,715.8	388.5	973	17,442	4,945.2	471.9
Boulder	126,238	294	13.9	210	3,228	1,784.7	282.4	593	9,518	2,646.5	293.8
Brighton	114,624	374	99.2	25	712	512.7	44.8	106	2,210	841.6	72.6
Broomfield	176,997	501	53.5	70	845	430.1	55.9	286	5,338	1,280.6	139.7
Castle Rock town	383,775	1,697	68.0	D	D	D	10.0	206	3,790	1,011.5	97.9
Centennial	9,274	9	100.0	185	3,450	14,662.0	362.0	293	5,719	2,403.0	212.6
Colorado Springs	NA	NA	NA	347	3,869	2,521.2	260.7	1,698	26,651	8,162.1	777.7
Commerce City	356,503	1,702	58.7	142	3,380	2,446.0	205.9	131	1,949	646.6	57.6
Denver	1,514,650	10,000	15.5	1,191	20,941	20,105.5	1,388.8	2,471	32,753	9,218.5	1,047.9
Englewood	40,757	247	20.2	105	1,508	1,577.0	115.1	206	3,574	1,149.9	152.5
Erie town	222,654	1,082	60.3	10	82	31.1	4.3	29	453	151.5	13.1
Fort Collins	153,728	839	45.4	129	2,126	1,815.4	178.5	606	10,749	3,052.3	304.9
Fountain	NA	NA	NA	NA	NA	NA	NA	58	1,731	563.7	45.9
Grand Junction	NA	NA	NA	147	1,390	776.7	71.9	433	6,851	1,990.0	196.0
Greeley	196,606	915	34.4	88	833	621.9	45.8	311	5,520	1,814.6	161.1
Lafayette	23,490	76	77.6	38	384	149.5	27.9	79	1,114	275.8	30.0
Lakewood	62,578	364	25.5	140	920	646.8	63.4	677	11,479	3,123.0	314.9
Littleton	13,640	35	100.0	63	1,245	1,120.5	89.8	228	4,331	2,122.5	173.6
Longmont	125,289	621	21.4	75	654	448.1	43.6	292	5,383	1,648.5	163.8
Loveland	240,972	1,023	51.8	77	1,489	1,339.0	110.5	336	6,144	1,879.7	165.6
Northglenn	83,967	460	16.3	18	123	60.1	6.0	120	2,346	775.9	81.9
Parker town	311,462	1,015	63.0	35	199	119.6	11.0	193	3,741	1,278.2	107.4
Pueblo	NA	NA	NA	59	647	293.2	34.7	383	6,341	1,744.0	168.2
Thornton	313,678	1,148	61.0	34	182	83.2	14.2	220	5,547	1,622.7	168.9
Westminster	106,079	459	32.0	66	905	715.8	62.4	325	6,752	1,822.0	179.8
Wheat Ridge	86,021	439	35.8	69	711	298.5	48.0	177	2,271	791.1	81.3
Windsor town	278,038	1,121	71.9	22	271	122.9	17.6	65	669	236.3	21.2
CONNECTICUT	1,224,866	4,651	63.2	3,504	62,298	102,896.5	5,173.7	12,391	186,297	55,404.5	5,560.8
Bridgeport	5,644	62	45.2	D	D	D	D	284	3,179	939.5	112.2
Bristol	19,755	94	100.0	39	434	359.9	22.4	161	2,904	877.6	84.1
Danbury	16,415	71	97.2	90	1,302	998.1	93.0	444	8,143	2,510.1	251.1
Hartford	1,480	11	100.0	94	1,962	1,354.0	104.0	371	3,334	1,374.1	115.7
Meriden	1,000	10	100.0	39	337	179.3	18.5	227	3,049	752.4	74.9
Middletown	3,609	22	100.0	45	1,190	642.0	71.2	124	1,633	572.9	55.2
Milford	NA	NA	NA	95	1,239	815.2	76.7	312	6,036	1,781.2	168.9
Naugatuck	4,484	25	64.0	18	469	188.2	30.3	60	1,139	413.6	35.9
New Britain	1,199	9	100.0	41	378	227.8	25.6	162	1,797	734.8	57.4
New Haven	26,059	299	4.3	69	2,269	1,990.8	660.7	344	3,671	1,272.5	117.8
New London	7,501	45	95.6	16	726	527.5	52.6	105	1,538	513.1	48.5
Norwalk	54,859	149	16.8	131	2,254	2,364.9	172.0	345	6,332	2,094.3	236.6
Norwich	785	4	50.0	18	419	247.8	27.4	128	1,912	533.1	54.7
Shelton	13,866	92	63.0	60	1,926	2,109.7	197.6	91	1,817	603.8	59.9
Stamford	19,163	55	43.6	236	5,349	41,814.6	654.0	460	6,250	2,042.7	221.2
Torrington	1,013	7	100.0	24	190	63.2	10.5	151	2,666	829.8	82.2
Waterbury	1,877	23	56.5	68	770	531.0	48.2	432	5,994	1,692.3	163.4
West Haven	1,060	9	100.0	55	1,291	727.9	77.5	111	1,295	317.7	36.9
DELAWARE	1,175,682	8,500	85.4	962	9,315	7,224.6	522.6	3,648	58,201	17,667.9	1,558.0
Dover	17,113	81	100.0	46	232	173.5	16.0	258	4,087	1,070.8	91.4
Newark	404	2	100.0	42	346	125.8	17.3	147	2,924	986.7	91.6
Wilmington	66,805	525	1.7	129	1,078	1,286.6	69.3	287	3,360	1,129.4	101.3

1. Merchant wholesalers except manufacturers' sales branches and offices. 2. Establishments with payroll.

City	Real estate and rental and leasing, 2017				Professional, scientific, and technical services[1], 2017				Manufacturing, 2017			
	Number of establish-ments	Number of employees	Receipts (mil dol)	Annual payroll (mil dol)	Number of establish-ments	Number of employees	Receipts (mil dol)	Annual payroll (mil dol)	Number of establish-ments	Number of employees	Receipts (mil dol)	Annual payroll (mil dol)
	80	81	82	83	84	85	86	87	88	89	90	91
CALIFORNIA—Cont'd												
Wasco	15	46	7.1	1.3	5	21	3.9	0.7	NA	NA	NA	NA
Watsonville	57	255	50.9	8.6	78	470	63.4	30.0	NA	NA	NA	NA
West Covina	107	453	81.4	17.7	155	710	109.9	35.6	NA	NA	NA	NA
West Hollywood	185	1,104	372.8	60.4	446	3,140	844.5	295.8	NA	NA	NA	NA
Westminster	124	406	106.9	14.6	162	755	186.4	36.7	NA	NA	NA	NA
West Sacramento	94	765	160.9	35.2	93	1,262	360.6	108.7	NA	NA	NA	NA
Whittier	D	D	D	D	176	1,057	110.8	40.1	NA	NA	NA	NA
Wildomar	20	154	27.4	5.1	40	94	12.0	3.2	NA	NA	NA	NA
Windsor town	25	494	52.8	15.1	55	244	46.7	12.0	NA	NA	NA	NA
Woodland	53	241	75.2	10.5	85	446	64.4	23.0	NA	NA	NA	NA
Yorba Linda	135	387	124.5	18.2	278	906	177.7	55.1	NA	NA	NA	NA
Yuba City	66	306	61.4	10.2	97	456	53.3	18.8	NA	NA	NA	NA
Yucaipa	53	164	32.2	5.2	68	198	23.3	7.7	NA	NA	NA	NA
COLORADO	12,087	47,642	12,757.1	2,387.8	26,404	192,964	39,654.7	15,801.4	5,111	121,372	50,809.1	7,356.9
Arvada	158	347	71.3	14.7	413	1,662	256.0	94.6	NA	NA	NA	NA
Aurora	403	1,857	429.6	85.4	733	7,726	1,383.7	671.7	NA	NA	NA	NA
Boulder	393	1,608	383.3	72.9	1,524	16,400	3,244.9	1,490.0	NA	NA	NA	NA
Brighton	50	143	23.9	6.1	64	415	65.0	22.5	NA	NA	NA	NA
Broomfield	150	425	170.4	22.9	404	4,147	944.9	366.4	NA	NA	NA	NA
Castle Rock town	122	324	79.2	12.6	258	828	163.1	54.1	NA	NA	NA	NA
Centennial	356	1,100	425.5	73.1	744	4,758	1,073.9	377.1	NA	NA	NA	NA
Colorado Springs	1,092	3,867	843.4	161.2	2,097	20,579	4,151.6	1,668.0	NA	NA	NA	NA
Commerce City	60	672	151.5	33.8	D	D	D	D	NA	NA	NA	NA
Denver	2,033	11,307	3,866.6	710.4	5,133	50,003	12,642.8	4,747.1	NA	NA	NA	NA
Englewood	96	430	111.9	24.3	D	D	D	D	NA	NA	NA	NA
Erie town	D	D	D	D	119	215	38.1	13.1	NA	NA	NA	NA
Fort Collins	420	1,369	368.1	56.6	943	5,898	1,129.8	486.5	NA	NA	NA	NA
Fountain	12	41	8.3	1.2	23	93	6.6	2.1	NA	NA	NA	NA
Grand Junction	222	727	180.2	30.5	359	3,120	490.9	198.3	NA	NA	NA	NA
Greeley	142	754	122.2	31.5	213	1,068	154.1	53.0	NA	NA	NA	NA
Lafayette	D	D	D	D	202	2,330	361.0	135.9	NA	NA	NA	NA
Lakewood	295	1,151	328.5	51.6	871	7,165	1,285.5	520.5	NA	NA	NA	NA
Littleton	116	376	69.9	14.0	379	2,009	372.0	143.8	NA	NA	NA	NA
Longmont	136	393	92.5	15.9	402	5,245	1,024.6	524.3	NA	NA	NA	NA
Loveland	146	433	121.9	23.3	301	2,032	329.5	115.2	NA	NA	NA	NA
Northglenn	35	71	23.4	3.1	64	307	30.5	13.7	NA	NA	NA	NA
Parker town	121	223	50.9	9.9	247	802	144.9	46.1	NA	NA	NA	NA
Pueblo	110	567	101.5	16.6	D	D	D	D	NA	NA	NA	NA
Thornton	121	434	113.7	18.8	182	1,160	237.1	84.6	NA	NA	NA	NA
Westminster	198	645	134.6	27.8	D	D	D	D	NA	NA	NA	NA
Wheat Ridge	69	188	39.5	7.6	201	1,360	188.6	84.4	NA	NA	NA	NA
Windsor town	59	302	43.9	11.5	102	418	75.1	22.2	NA	NA	NA	NA
CONNECTICUT	3,459	20,224	6,691.3	1,114.8	9,184	108,479	21,600.1	9,709.8	3,986	156,822	57,882.0	11,021.6
Bridgeport	92	518	119.0	24.7	197	1,285	270.0	113.5	NA	NA	NA	NA
Bristol	33	101	27.7	4.1	71	322	66.9	18.7	NA	NA	NA	NA
Danbury	90	1,951	477.0	143.0	222	2,269	377.8	163.1	NA	NA	NA	NA
Hartford	169	1,270	307.9	65.2	410	8,800	2,163.7	824.9	NA	NA	NA	NA
Meriden	45	491	60.6	21.7	64	841	153.6	69.4	NA	NA	NA	NA
Middletown	45	301	56.4	15.0	101	1,022	228.4	82.7	NA	NA	NA	NA
Milford	58	264	1,109.2	15.8	181	1,189	232.3	96.6	NA	NA	NA	NA
Naugatuck	D	D	D	D	35	210	32.7	11.3	NA	NA	NA	NA
New Britain	38	174	40.6	7.2	74	601	84.5	42.8	NA	NA	NA	NA
New Haven	132	809	200.2	34.2	356	3,485	781.2	336.0	NA	NA	NA	NA
New London	26	139	27.8	6.2	86	642	129.9	56.2	NA	NA	NA	NA
Norwalk	110	393	114.3	21.3	325	5,218	1,429.6	518.7	NA	NA	NA	NA
Norwich	35	126	25.1	4.3	56	878	122.4	57.4	NA	NA	NA	NA
Shelton	47	331	161.0	26.3	154	2,421	732.9	203.6	NA	NA	NA	NA
Stamford	246	1,605	680.3	145.9	743	16,984	4,348.0	1,735.9	NA	NA	NA	NA
Torrington	22	87	14.2	3.4	56	377	51.3	19.7	NA	NA	NA	NA
Waterbury	87	344	93.0	14.8	121	742	100.0	39.0	NA	NA	NA	NA
West Haven	39	110	38.9	4.8	60	315	40.4	14.0	NA	NA	NA	NA
DELAWARE	1,286	6,096	5,163.7	287.7	2,991	29,716	7,003.0	2,942.2	558	27,536	16,689.2	1,543.9
Dover	80	334	147.9	13.2	189	1,347	237.4	106.1	NA	NA	NA	NA
Newark	52	219	543.8	9.0	140	1,560	268.1	103.8	NA	NA	NA	NA
Wilmington	202	833	833.1	51.5	686	9,685	3,225.0	1,471.1	NA	NA	NA	NA

1. Establishments subject to federal tax.

Table D. Cities — Accommodation and Food Services, Arts, Entertainment, and Recreation, and Health Care and Social Assistance

City	Accommodation and food services, 2017				Arts, entertainment, and recreation[1], 2017				Health care and social assistance[1], 2017			
	Number of establish-ments	Number of employees	Receipts (mil dol)	Annual payroll (mil dol)	Number of establish-ments	Number of employees	Receipts (mil dol)	Annual payroll (mil dol)	Number of establish-ments	Number of employees	Receipts (mil dol)	Annual payroll (mil dol)
	92	93	94	95	96	97	98	99	100	101	102	103
CALIFORNIA—Cont'd												
Wasco	D	D	D	D	NA	NA	NA	NA	18	427	45.4	16.1
Watsonville	105	1,508	105.3	27.6	10.0	D	7.9	D	190	2,927	394.5	146.4
West Covina	231	3,955	247.7	67.0	18.0	437	33.1	8.9	345	7,319	1,040.8	353.5
West Hollywood	258	10,190	968.3	287.8	D	D	D	D	302	14,861	3,599.4	1,373.7
Westminster	277	3,077	202.2	48.4	D	D	D	D	301	2,899	384.0	120.1
West Sacramento	D	D	D	D	11.0	737	27.2	7.1	92	1,445	155.4	62.0
Whittier	215	3,604	225.4	66.7	13.0	486	22.8	8.3	319	10,435	1,332.3	471.5
Wildomar	47	581	36.8	10.6	13.0	161	10.8	3.0	66	1,695	203.4	84.5
Windsor town	48	994	59.1	17.3	D	D	D	D	45	603	52.9	23.2
Woodland	D	D	D	D	20.0	288	11.7	3.5	130	2,586	360.0	135.9
Yorba Linda	113	1,908	119.0	32.5	D	D	D	D	211	1,644	156.9	66.6
Yuba City	129	2,191	145.8	38.2	17.0	283	14.0	4.2	216	3,527	463.1	174.8
Yucaipa	75	1,374	71.4	21.6	18.0	145	7.9	2.2	98	1,310	114.7	41.4
COLORADO	14,121	290,915	19,455.8	5,804.1	3,028.0	58,229	5,681.1	1,935.3	16,659	320,813	40,055.8	15,719.7
Arvada	208	4,129	223.9	69.4	44.0	672	36.6	13.5	281	4,503	370.6	168.2
Aurora	680	13,457	813.3	241.1	69.0	D	71.3	D	791	26,587	3,301.0	1,370.6
Boulder	433	10,606	680.7	210.0	148.0	1,525	108.2	33.3	671	8,626	1,072.3	444.9
Brighton	85	1,534	94.1	26.3	4.0	D	1.4	D	88	1,851	273.4	97.6
Broomfield	178	3,689	261.1	77.9	35.0	398	21.8	6.5	197	2,472	287.5	117.3
Castle Rock town	116	2,307	138.0	41.9	D	D	D	D	180	2,166	258.3	90.0
Centennial	245	6,353	363.9	140.6	48.0	897	52.5	15.1	450	6,621	667.5	270.6
Colorado Springs	1,111	26,615	1,681.5	479.3	219.0	3,178	202.1	58.1	1,850	35,415	4,064.0	1,616.4
Commerce City	78	1,207	76.9	20.9	D	D	D	D	44	630	59.6	23.3
Denver	2,354	55,545	4,477.0	1,297.4	473.0	11,883	1,655.6	660.8	2,302	56,165	8,008.4	3,078.4
Englewood	117	1,934	109.0	34.0	D	D	D	D	232	8,097	1,140.1	359.7
Erie town	25	408	18.4	5.5	6.0	53	4.6	1.5	45	259	23.0	9.2
Fort Collins	483	10,162	561.3	175.2	105.0	1,269	76.8	21.5	713	11,970	1,293.1	564.1
Fountain	54	1,187	64.9	17.9	D	D	D	D	D	D	D	D
Grand Junction	247	5,101	281.7	90.5	39.0	524	27.1	8.8	367	10,487	1,348.1	498.4
Greeley	220	4,284	215.3	64.4	32.0	275	17.4	3.5	334	6,318	901.6	348.4
Lafayette	74	D	61.5	D	10.0	518	7.4	2.9	152	4,464	600.3	213.8
Lakewood	413	8,801	554.9	166.6	67.0	815	47.5	15.4	665	13,975	1,653.5	634.5
Littleton	152	2,885	160.6	49.4	39.0	666	42.6	13.4	275	4,712	736.6	252.6
Longmont	239	4,154	221.6	71.0	45.0	248	17.6	4.5	312	4,766	489.5	197.3
Loveland	224	4,916	277.3	81.9	41.0	246	14.9	3.8	275	5,868	839.8	299.2
Northglenn	57	1,668	96.6	31.5	11.0	D	15.7	D	79	868	68.0	27.9
Parker town	137	2,732	161.3	47.1	22.0	755	36.0	11.0	216	3,788	596.5	195.5
Pueblo	273	4,962	250.8	74.0	34.0	674	92.0	18.6	369	12,940	1,373.5	588.9
Thornton	189	4,025	249.1	71.7	31.0	D	14.8	D	209	3,899	496.9	197.7
Westminster	258	6,014	384.3	122.8	47.0	880	48.6	16.2	304	6,846	827.8	313.7
Wheat Ridge	91	1,515	89.2	26.8	19.0	119	9.3	2.6	206	5,239	655.6	276.5
Windsor town	50	693	34.8	11.1	15.0	118	10.7	2.9	85	983	80.0	33.1
CONNECTICUT	8,762	146,456	10,791.5	3,069.7	1,744.0	30,320	2,406.1	785.3	11,065	295,083	35,302.4	14,069.0
Bridgeport	239	2,581	175.4	47.8	35.0	838	47.6	14.0	350	15,223	1,772.7	766.0
Bristol	104	1,421	92.5	24.3	16.0	403	37.9	11.1	172	4,618	404.2	178.0
Danbury	232	3,958	272.7	81.6	29.0	467	25.7	7.7	286	9,809	1,368.3	636.8
Hartford	340	5,544	390.0	110.7	35.0	1,477	107.9	32.0	471	24,473	3,630.6	1,575.8
Meriden	119	1,316	80.5	19.7	7.0	483	14.9	7.0	148	5,315	547.7	222.0
Middletown	126	1,535	105.7	32.5	20.0	334	14.9	5.5	183	9,759	1,171.4	592.5
Milford	194	3,121	194.6	54.1	33.0	522	32.8	11.1	189	3,429	372.0	173.8
Naugatuck	49	546	31.2	7.8	3.0	120	3.9	1.4	51	1,326	93.6	44.2
New Britain	103	1,280	85.9	23.1	15.0	397	19.2	8.9	169	8,866	807.3	362.2
New Haven	366	4,686	352.6	102.3	44.0	639	49.0	16.0	422	21,715	3,572.0	1,228.6
New London	99	1,383	85.6	26.5	17.0	146	9.9	3.2	132	4,300	566.5	237.6
Norwalk	297	3,778	303.6	85.3	73.0	1,559	167.0	63.8	298	6,606	889.2	344.8
Norwich	82	1,487	87.5	27.0	11.0	113	7.9	2.0	192	5,301	619.1	260.6
Shelton	117	1,752	119.5	33.0	19.0	246	17.5	5.1	133	3,368	446.3	220.6
Stamford	410	6,333	520.2	155.5	79.0	1,789	231.5	58.4	475	10,082	3,737.3	607.8
Torrington	92	1,010	62.7	17.9	17.0	229	11.4	3.4	156	4,105	403.0	174.3
Waterbury	237	3,084	180.2	49.8	15.0	347	24.9	6.7	346	11,499	1,276.8	529.9
West Haven	114	1,463	92.2	25.9	NA	NA	NA	NA	82	3,470	638.1	252.8
DELAWARE	2,141	39,950	2,554.4	714.1	440.0	8,466	853.9	223.7	2,648	68,348	8,855.3	3,720.5
Dover	135	4,329	333.9	76.5	D	D	D	D	240	7,734	993.3	389.4
Newark	140	3,456	195.2	60.0	21.0	271	14.9	4.7	162	10,649	1,831.1	808.6
Wilmington	222	3,407	235.0	67.8	55.0	741	53.0	17.9	373	9,984	1,173.3	468.9

1. Establishments subject to federal tax.

City	Other services[1]				Government employment and payroll, 2017								
						March payroll							
							Perent of total for:						
	Number of establish-ments	Number of employees	Receipts (mil dol)	Annual payroll (mil dol)	Full-time equivalent employees	Total (dollars)	Admin-istrative, judicial, and legal	Police and corrections	Fire protection	Highways and trans-portation	Health and welfare	Natural resources and utilities	Education and libraries
	104	105	106	107	108	109	110	111	112	113	114	115	116
CALIFORNIA—Cont'd													
Wasco	11	37	4.4	1.0	61	297,732	32.8	0.0	0.0	23.1	9.1	29.1	0.0
Watsonville	83	391	42.5	12.2	440	3,980,296	8.4	25.4	14.9	6.0	3.9	29.8	10.4
West Covina	109	518	50.4	12.8	399	2,822,262	11.7	43.5	31.8	5.3	3.0	4.6	0.0
West Hollywood	241	1,936	609.8	90.8	240	2,150,704	28.3	1.7	0.6	4.7	13.0	9.8	0.0
Westminster	147	852	114.9	26.1	244	1,811,637	10.3	61.2	0.0	7.1	2.8	11.3	0.0
West Sacramento	115	985	137.2	44.7	424	3,883,022	14.1	25.4	25.1	1.9	6.5	14.5	0.0
Whittier	131	820	70.0	20.2	496	3,040,149	10.2	45.5	0.0	4.8	5.7	20.6	6.0
Wildomar	39	243	18.6	6.5	16	94,814	32.9	0.0	0.0	7.0	0.0	0.0	0.0
Windsor town	48	174	19.1	5.7	101	704,741	24.5	0.0	0.0	8.4	4.4	43.8	0.0
Woodland	96	490	48.0	14.1	317	2,079,464	9.5	30.7	19.4	5.7	3.0	24.0	2.8
Yorba Linda	96	582	53.5	17.6	123	752,679	20.8	0.0	0.0	20.3	7.3	25.2	19.6
Yuba City	109	557	60.4	18.3	300	1,946,414	9.0	33.8	24.7	2.6	0.0	19.1	0.0
Yucaipa	58	301	28.3	8.0	58	349,100	32.6	1.0	0.0	27.3	7.7	23.9	0.0
COLORADO	11,667	74,317	10,973.6	2,785.1	X	X	X	X	X	X	X	X	X
Arvada	202	1,187	137.3	35.7	406	2,487,923	10.4	56.5	0.0	9.1	2.7	21.3	0.0
Aurora	526	3,512	441.6	135.0	2,891	17,630,608	14.5	37.8	14.5	7.0	2.4	21.1	1.4
Boulder	387	2,873	422.1	123.2	1,112	7,993,053	16.7	23.2	11.2	5.4	2.1	25.5	4.7
Brighton	59	290	33.7	9.8	308	1,473,623	20.4	31.6	0.0	6.9	7.8	26.1	0.0
Broomfield	145	732	158.2	36.2	765	4,448,301	17.0	35.1	0.0	2.2	18.5	18.7	3.6
Castle Rock town	133	636	64.1	20.7	543	3,305,326	16.7	18.9	20.8	6.4	0.0	27.4	0.0
Centennial	259	1,657	252.8	70.8	73	420,544	100.0	0.0	0.0	0.0	0.0	0.0	0.0
Colorado Springs	995	8,956	2,133.3	391.6	4,068	27,500,431	5.4	23.6	13.1	5.4	0.0	50.4	0.0
Commerce City	106	722	89.9	26.2	475	2,708,700	22.4	41.2	0.0	11.4	8.1	16.3	0.0
Denver	1,874	15,112	2,404.0	600.2	14,162	86,682,654	14.4	30.4	10.0	11.2	10.9	18.3	2.6
Englewood	137	862	100.9	35.8	441	2,466,812	14.6	27.1	0.0	5.3	2.3	38.5	1.3
Erie town	26	152	12.6	4.8	167	809,525	21.2	23.7	0.0	2.8	0.0	35.6	0.0
Fort Collins	358	2,052	394.2	65.6	1,708	9,440,627	28.8	23.4	0.0	10.5	0.4	32.6	0.0
Fountain	24	148	15.1	4.5	221	1,182,395	15.6	23.1	12.8	4.1	3.0	32.4	0.0
Grand Junction	251	1,478	170.2	50.8	654	3,742,842	11.3	34.8	20.3	5.9	2.2	21.7	0.0
Greeley	170	1,085	125.9	32.5	966	4,912,944	13.1	27.7	16.1	10.6	0.7	27.1	0.0
Lafayette	64	305	43.5	13.5	250	1,287,475	10.8	25.6	15.5	6.1	4.9	29.7	5.9
Lakewood	352	2,080	226.2	68.4	1,077	6,308,895	17.4	49.7	0.0	3.9	1.6	16.9	0.0
Littleton	146	965	123.5	35.2	462	3,320,019	11.3	21.6	46.6	4.9	4.3	5.3	3.9
Longmont	202	1,224	108.9	34.8	940	5,985,157	12.9	27.6	12.3	3.8	3.9	29.2	5.3
Loveland	154	1,173	126.9	42.1	706	3,643,996	23.8	24.4	13.4	6.1	0.0	25.5	3.1
Northglenn	66	411	49.9	13.0	264	1,420,139	20.9	39.4	0.0	7.1	0.0	29.4	0.0
Parker town	158	992	94.0	30.1	418	2,100,948	21.8	33.8	0.0	10.9	0.0	27.2	0.0
Pueblo	179	1,056	97.9	28.4	893	5,127,375	9.0	34.5	18.8	8.4	0.5	26.6	0.0
Thornton	138	1,196	244.6	44.8	882	5,877,074	20.3	28.2	10.4	10.5	4.4	23.8	0.0
Westminster	191	1,227	109.7	38.5	1,038	6,205,205	18.9	27.9	15.4	4.0	3.6	25.8	2.5
Wheat Ridge	123	585	77.7	22.7	353	1,288,582	18.3	41.7	0.0	10.6	0.0	29.4	0.0
Windsor town	53	287	34.8	10.1	154	694,687	23.0	24.4	0.0	11.9	0.4	30.1	0.0
CONNECTICUT	7,507	46,490	6,055.5	1,645.5	X	X	X	X	X	X	X	X	X
Bridgeport	211	1,092	122.2	34.0	4,257	22,084,090	4.1	24.4	10.9	1.7	1.1	3.8	53.0
Bristol	98	458	53.1	14.3	1,484	8,479,799	3.6	13.0	7.6	2.4	1.5	6.1	62.8
Danbury	198	1,205	177.1	39.8	1,853	11,285,779	3.3	10.4	8.2	4.2	1.1	3.0	68.3
Hartford	293	2,187	415.4	88.9	5,025	26,287,752	2.7	8.4	5.0	0.3	4.3	1.5	77.7
Meriden	101	477	44.0	14.3	1,672	9,671,134	4.0	12.7	7.8	2.3	1.5	4.8	66.5
Middletown	106	513	72.8	18.5	1,538	8,328,920	3.1	12.3	8.7	2.3	5.9	5.5	59.0
Milford	157	1,010	87.3	29.2	1,561	7,897,551	5.0	10.0	9.4	2.5	3.1	4.2	62.7
Naugatuck	43	163	21.3	5.1	871	4,716,756	3.4	12.2	5.5	1.8	0.1	1.5	74.3
New Britain	97	434	58.0	13.5	2,015	12,472,801	2.9	10.7	9.6	3.0	1.5	5.1	64.5
New Haven	256	1,708	266.4	70.2	5,852	26,236,826	3.6	13.4	8.2	2.1	3.1	2.3	65.6
New London	69	439	61.9	14.0	777	3,886,300	4.7	16.1	10.9	1.2	1.5	4.6	57.8
Norwalk	231	1,432	190.4	51.2	3,068	15,640,214	3.7	13.1	8.8	3.2	1.1	1.8	66.9
Norwich	76	518	49.0	11.6	1,217	6,728,759	2.7	10.6	6.3	0.3	2.2	4.4	52.8
Shelton	73	514	36.0	13.0	923	5,479,085	4.1	9.8	0.7	3.0	1.9	2.7	75.5
Stamford	340	1,882	264.1	66.3	3,071	21,670,742	4.7	9.0	9.2	0.0	0.0	0.0	77.1
Torrington	83	414	52.7	12.9	1,032	5,822,835	5.0	13.4	7.1	2.7	2.0	2.5	65.9
Waterbury	159	1,251	117.4	32.3	4,072	21,297,073	3.5	10.6	6.3	1.4	2.3	4.7	71.2
West Haven	88	427	54.2	14.1	1,336	8,036,488	4.6	16.4	4.3	4.4	2.4	0.5	67.3
DELAWARE	1,608	10,252	1,220.8	339.1	X	X	X	X	X	X	X	X	X
Dover	91	627	62.2	17.6	360	1,823,318	20.1	46.0	1.1	5.2	0.4	23.3	3.9
Newark	65	503	65.8	21.9	293	1,596,221	12.5	38.5	0.4	6.2	1.0	27.7	0.0
Wilmington	226	1,638	307.6	64.1	1,168	6,098,980	18.3	40.8	17.3	2.0	4.4	11.5	0.0

1. Establishments subject to federal tax.

City	City government finances, 2017									
	General revenue							General expenditure		
		Intergovernmental		Taxes						
					Per capita[1] (dollars)				Per capita[1] (dollars)	
	Total (mil dol)	Total (mil dol)	Percent from state government	Total (mil dol)	Total	Property	Sales and gross receipts	Total (mil dol)	Total	Capital outlays
	117	118	119	120	121	122	123	124	125	126
CALIFORNIA—Cont'd										
Wasco	20.1	4.1	16.6	7.0	260	116	136	17.6	657	79
Watsonville	84.7	4.7	41.1	35.4	656	407	246	91.2	1,691	117
West Covina	108.8	7.5	52.1	67.2	628	340	283	120.4	1,126	314
West Hollywood	141.9	3.4	63.9	78.3	2,129	696	1,407	157.3	4,274	682
Westminster	78.1	6.6	38.4	61.0	669	309	346	130.0	1,426	529
West Sacramento	123.0	7.0	62.1	60.7	1,138	546	419	152.7	2,864	838
Whittier	85.8	4.6	63.1	49.1	569	249	311	85.0	984	119
Wildomar	15.6	4.0	83.6	9.2	252	108	137	18.3	498	38
Windsor town	30.7	1.7	43.6	16.0	583	254	324	36.0	1,312	280
Woodland	119.7	3.5	62.5	53.4	891	260	622	107.5	1,794	417
Yorba Linda	63.3	4.8	31.7	37.8	557	341	186	67.7	997	284
Yuba City	68.5	7.7	28.7	31.7	476	174	299	65.2	979	162
Yucaipa	28.8	2.4	95.0	18.7	350	271	61	39.5	738	131
COLORADO	X	X	X	X	X	X	X	X	X	X
Arvada	5.5	0.0	0.0	5.5	46	46	0	0.0	0	0
Aurora	505.2	45.7	47.5	315.2	857	99	758	493.8	1,343	228
Boulder	359.7	29.1	75.3	205.8	1,934	365	1,568	346.4	3,254	629
Brighton	62.8	7.1	100.0	40.5	1,005	191	814	56.3	1,396	256
Broomfield	248.1	15.6	98.1	133.9	1,962	670	1,156	145.7	2,134	227
Castle Rock town	111.2	4.7	100.0	56.6	908	103	805	89.6	1,438	176
Centennial	89.5	11.6	0.0	63.4	574	133	434	74.6	676	164
Colorado Springs	591.9	59.6	43.2	328.7	707	75	631	480.5	1,033	192
Commerce City	77.5	2.5	73.9	63.6	1,138	50	1,088	65.0	1,162	0
Denver	3,390.9	279.3	90.4	1,334.7	1,893	580	1,313	3,002.8	4,260	770
Englewood	69.6	4.1	48.3	39.3	1,140	139	1,001	61.2	1,775	4
Erie town	50.7	1.8	86.0	16.6	689	219	470	30.3	1,255	423
Fort Collins	333.0	50.6	39.7	176.4	1,065	149	906	271.2	1,638	177
Fountain	20.3	1.5	8.0	17.1	575	68	507	28.6	962	104
Grand Junction	118.1	16.4	40.4	58.3	940	163	778	128.1	2,066	240
Greeley	159.2	15.9	53.7	100.0	936	167	769	147.4	1,380	343
Lafayette	54.0	1.6	100.0	25.1	882	270	612	40.4	1,419	155
Lakewood	221.3	27.3	33.1	138.8	896	142	695	212.5	1,371	173
Littleton	101.2	17.9	100.0	44.7	935	141	793	87.6	1,833	105
Longmont	173.3	25.8	25.7	91.7	969	185	784	194.3	2,054	524
Loveland	146.6	8.5	95.8	85.0	1,105	326	780	137.1	1,783	287
Northglenn	41.8	3.8	100.0	27.4	703	80	623	35.1	900	202
Parker town	79.5	9.0	30.8	51.2	943	35	909	82.1	1,514	474
Pueblo	158.4	18.4	74.1	91.1	820	178	643	144.0	1,297	103
Thornton	208.1	28.6	84.5	125.0	914	102	812	178.3	1,303	288
Westminster	243.5	29.5	16.8	131.9	1,168	141	1,027	245.1	2,170	712
Wheat Ridge	34.1	1.8	63.8	28.8	919	26	893	45.1	1,440	262
Windsor town	29.0	1.5	69.0	14.8	558	212	346	27.0	1,016	349
CONNECTICUT	X	X	X	X	X	X	X	X	X	X
Bridgeport	786.6	412.0	97.2	318.0	2,188	2,150	38	813.6	5,597	834
Bristol	236.3	76.2	98.8	144.8	2,408	2,352	39	223.4	3,716	424
Danbury	313.9	77.3	98.3	207.3	2,449	2,405	44	284.1	3,357	249
Hartford	843.8	535.8	87.8	267.1	2,173	2,108	55	801.4	6,521	381
Meriden	264.9	120.4	98.7	122.5	2,054	2,054	0	265.4	4,449	547
Middletown	211.6	45.0	95.5	111.0	2,389	2,374	15	230.4	4,958	313
Milford	230.1	27.6	97.1	182.3	3,452	3,433	2	228.5	4,327	259
Naugatuck	125.3	40.5	89.5	77.1	2,460	2,436	24	133.6	4,261	14
New Britain	242.9	120.2	99.1	121.9	1,679	1,679	0	176.8	2,434	20
New Haven	846.0	506.3	91.8	267.9	2,051	1,932	104	872.2	6,675	998
New London	130.0	63.2	92.6	49.6	1,839	1,824	15	132.6	4,918	110
Norwalk	402.6	51.9	98.5	311.3	3,524	3,411	64	383.0	4,335	353
Norwich	224.3	127.5	94.6	79.9	2,034	2,019	0	171.1	4,355	209
Shelton	132.3	19.1	94.1	103.5	2,520	2,469	19	114.9	2,798	75
Stamford	621.5	69.0	99.3	524.4	4,037	3,802	173	542.9	4,180	36
Torrington	146.8	40.0	97.1	90.9	2,643	2,625	11	130.7	3,798	82
Waterbury	531.0	249.6	98.6	242.3	2,238	2,207	19	576.6	5,325	358
West Haven	199.3	76.8	99.3	99.4	1,813	1,780	33	197.6	3,602	135
DELAWARE	X	X	X	X	X	X	X	X	X	X
Dover	38.6	5.3	41.6	16.8	449	335	70	47.6	1,272	137
Newark	25.0	1.5	86.4	9.8	292	186	63	38.2	1,135	133
Wilmington	217.8	54.1	36.6	118.8	1,681	575	97	184.0	2,604	186

1. Based on population estimated as of July 1 of the year shown.

City	City government finances, 2017 (cont.)												
	General expenditure (cont.)												
	Percent of total for:									Debt outstanding			
	Public welfare	Highways	Parking facilities	Education	Health and hospitals	Police protection	Sewerage and sanitation	Parks and recreation	Housing and community development	Interest on debt	Total (mil dol)	Per capita[1] (dollars)	Debt issued during year
	127	128	129	130	131	132	133	134	135	136	137	138	139
CALIFORNIA—Cont'd													
Wasco	0.0	14.5	0.0	0.0	0.9	19.7	23.3	0.0	5.8	0.4	1.5	56	0.0
Watsonville	0.0	9.3	0.2	0.0	1.2	20.9	21.2	4.9	2.5	0.4	4.9	91	0.0
West Covina	0.0	11.3	0.3	0.0	1.8	28.7	0.0	5.1	20.1	3.1	81.7	764	15.4
West Hollywood	0.0	10.9	1.6	0.0	4.0	25.4	1.7	4.6	5.9	7.4	155.2	4,217	0.0
Westminster	0.0	7.0	0.0	0.0	1.4	20.6	0.0	3.0	33.2	5.0	126.7	1,390	77.5
West Sacramento	0.0	17.1	0.0	0.0	0.7	12.6	19.4	6.2	8.9	5.5	334.7	6,279	0.4
Whittier	0.0	10.3	0.4	0.0	0.0	38.4	10.6	14.2	2.3	2.3	61.6	714	0.0
Wildomar	0.0	18.3	0.0	0.0	2.7	29.0	0.0	0.0	8.1	0.0	0.0	0	0.0
Windsor town	0.0	12.2	0.0	0.0	0.7	19.5	21.6	7.4	7.5	1.0	15.2	554	0.0
Woodland	0.2	10.6	0.0	0.0	0.6	18.1	11.1	4.9	1.6	5.4	381.6	6,368	60.2
Yorba Linda	0.0	33.4	0.0	0.0	0.0	15.8	0.0	19.1	1.0	1.2	20.0	294	0.1
Yuba City	0.0	11.2	0.0	0.0	1.1	22.0	20.6	6.8	3.7	1.6	100.6	1,512	15.8
Yucaipa	0.0	23.5	0.0	0.0	0.0	19.5	0.3	14.0	9.1	0.0	38.1	712	0.0
COLORADO	X	X	X	X	X	X	X	X	X	X	X	X	X
Arvada	0.0	0.0	0.0	0.0	0.0	0.0	0.0	0.0	0.0	0.0	71.8	604	0.0
Aurora	0.0	12.1	0.0	0.0	0.0	21.4	15.1	11.6	3.6	1.7	809.7	2,203	471.7
Boulder	0.0	18.1	2.6	0.0	0.0	11.5	7.9	16.8	4.7	2.1	125.5	1,179	0.0
Brighton	0.0	15.7	0.0	0.0	0.5	17.4	7.8	13.5	0.0	4.6	61.4	1,522	0.0
Broomfield	9.9	7.0	0.0	0.0	1.7	12.3	14.4	15.5	0.7	8.1	261.2	3,826	0.0
Castle Rock town	0.0	17.0	0.0	0.0	0.0	12.1	16.7	16.9	0.0	2.8	93.4	1,499	0.0
Centennial	0.0	35.8	0.0	0.0	0.0	28.9	0.0	3.0	0.0	0.2	2.9	26	0.0
Colorado Springs	0.0	17.0	0.6	0.0	0.3	19.2	9.5	6.0	2.2	4.3	2,481.6	5,335	127.9
Commerce City	0.0	11.8	0.0	0.0	0.0	24.1	0.0	16.8	5.0	15.8	312.5	5,588	66.8
Denver	4.5	4.9	0.6	0.0	2.1	7.9	4.2	8.0	4.0	8.2	6,263.5	8,885	1,361.6
Englewood	0.0	6.2	0.0	0.0	0.0	20.6	22.3	13.3	3.5	4.7	55.5	1,610	0.6
Erie town	0.2	13.9	0.0	0.0	0.0	11.2	9.4	26.4	1.0	0.0	87.8	3,636	16.7
Fort Collins	1.6	25.5	0.9	0.0	0.7	16.0	5.2	14.9	2.3	2.4	143.2	865	0.0
Fountain	0.0	8.8	0.0	0.0	0.0	22.5	0.0	3.9	10.4	0.0	49.4	1,662	7.2
Grand Junction	0.0	12.6	0.3	0.0	0.0	22.9	12.5	12.1	1.3	0.0	92.6	1,494	1.6
Greeley	0.0	19.1	0.1	0.0	0.0	15.2	9.2	13.7	5.7	1.4	158.8	1,487	58.2
Lafayette	0.0	10.6	0.0	0.0	3.9	17.1	12.6	21.4	3.6	4.0	30.3	1,067	0.0
Lakewood	0.0	10.8	0.0	0.0	0.9	27.9	2.2	12.2	1.2	1.2	37.1	239	0.0
Littleton	0.5	7.0	0.0	0.0	0.0	13.9	10.4	4.8	0.3	2.1	42.8	895	0.0
Longmont	0.6	12.6	0.1	0.0	0.0	9.6	15.6	13.7	4.0	2.3	191.2	2,020	0.0
Loveland	0.0	13.9	0.0	0.0	0.0	17.3	12.0	14.0	6.5	0.2	2.5	32	0.0
Northglenn	0.0	15.2	0.0	0.0	0.0	25.0	20.5	10.7	6.5	0.0	0.2	6	0.0
Parker town	0.0	27.2	0.0	0.0	0.0	18.6	1.4	32.7	2.2	4.1	65.0	1,198	0.0
Pueblo	0.0	8.2	0.9	0.0	0.0	23.4	12.7	5.6	9.3	1.9	120.5	1,085	0.0
Thornton	0.0	10.3	0.0	0.0	0.3	19.2	12.5	15.7	0.1	2.8	112.8	825	0.0
Westminster	0.0	3.8	0.0	0.0	0.0	9.4	5.3	9.6	28.6	1.2	397.6	3,519	78.8
Wheat Ridge	0.0	9.8	0.0	0.0	0.0	22.4	0.0	27.6	3.1	0.1	0.1	3	0.0
Windsor town	0.0	27.0	0.0	0.0	0.4	12.2	11.8	25.3	0.0	1.0	11.0	413	0.0
CONNECTICUT	X	X	X	X	X	X	X	X	X	X	X	X	X
Bridgeport	0.2	4.1	0.0	44.6	0.3	13.6	5.2	0.9	0.5	4.7	686.8	4,725	62.8
Bristol	0.0	6.5	0.0	55.6	3.4	7.0	3.4	1.3	0.7	1.0	89.1	1,482	25.3
Danbury	0.2	3.5	0.4	53.8	1.9	6.0	3.6	2.1	0.4	2.1	232.3	2,745	29.6
Hartford	1.7	2.2	0.1	56.0	1.8	6.9	0.8	0.7	8.9	2.5	619.6	5,042	0.0
Meriden	0.0	2.9	0.1	58.7	2.1	5.2	5.4	1.2	0.0	2.0	157.0	2,633	0.0
Middletown	0.2	3.0	0.5	40.8	0.5	6.6	16.7	1.2	0.2	2.3	107.0	2,302	0.0
Milford	0.6	2.4	0.0	53.6	1.3	7.3	5.1	0.6	0.3	1.9	102.6	1,942	0.0
Naugatuck	0.1	3.2	0.0	54.1	0.0	5.2	3.4	0.1	0.2	3.1	30.8	982	0.0
New Britain	0.0	0.0	0.0	94.6	0.0	0.0	0.0	0.0	0.0	5.4	189.1	2,604	0.0
New Haven	0.0	2.4	2.7	49.9	0.4	4.7	0.8	0.7	1.3	2.7	605.0	4,630	125.2
New London	0.0	7.6	0.4	54.1	0.2	7.4	4.2	3.1	1.1	0.4	44.8	1,663	0.0
Norwalk	0.1	4.4	1.6	54.8	1.2	5.6	3.3	1.2	0.3	2.5	261.1	2,955	38.2
Norwich	1.9	9.6	0.0	55.4	0.0	13.4	5.8	1.0	0.5	0.0	67.6	1,721	13.8
Shelton	0.3	5.1	0.0	67.2	1.8	5.5	2.0	1.6	0.8	1.2	48.1	1,171	4.0
Stamford	0.3	2.5	0.7	57.5	1.5	11.4	4.9	0.7	2.2	3.7	559.7	4,309	47.7
Torrington	0.0	6.6	0.0	60.3	5.7	7.5	3.9	1.4	0.1	0.9	16.2	472	0.0
Waterbury	0.7	4.1	0.0	54.8	0.7	5.8	2.0	0.4	0.5	4.7	448.9	4,145	0.0
West Haven	0.2	3.6	0.0	53.3	0.9	8.3	6.3	1.1	0.4	1.7	30.7	560	0.0
DELAWARE	X	X	X	X	X	X	X	X	X	X	X	X	X
Dover	0.2	6.5	0.0	0.0	0.0	41.5	22.4	1.5	0.7	0.3	36.9	987	0.0
Newark	0.0	5.5	4.3	0.0	0.0	31.7	19.8	7.2	0.5	0.1	9.9	296	0.0
Wilmington	0.0	4.1	3.8	0.0	0.0	35.0	11.2	5.2	2.8	2.7	367.9	5,207	59.7

1. Based on population estimated as of July 1 of the year shown.

STATE Place code	City	Land area[1] (sq. mi)	Population, 2021: Total persons 2021	Population, 2021: Rank	Population, 2021: Per square mile	Race 2020: Race alone[2] (percent): White	Race 2020: Race alone[2] (percent): Black or African American	Race 2020: Race alone[2] (percent): American Indian, Alaskan Native	Race 2020: Race alone[2] (percent): Asian	Race 2020: Race alone[2] (percent): Hawaiian Pacific Islander	Race 2020: Race alone[2] (percent): Some other race	Race 2020: Two or more races (percent)
		1	2	3	4	5	6	7	8	9	10	11
11 00000	DISTRICT OF COLUMBIA....	61.1	670,050	X	10,966.4	39.6	41.4	0.5	4.9	0.1	5.4	8.1
11 50000	Washington	61.1	670,050	23	10,966.4	39.6	41.4	0.5	4.9	0.1	5.4	8.1
12 00000	FLORIDA	53,647.9	21,781,128	X	406.0	57.7	15.1	0.4	3.0	0.1	7.3	16.5
12 00950	Altamonte Springs	9.1	45,517	868	5,001.9	51.7	16.5	0.5	3.6	0.1	9.4	18.2
12 01700	Apopka	34.6	55,496	714	1,603.9	43.7	25.8	0.5	3.1	0.1	11.1	15.7
12 02681	Aventura	2.6	39,237	1,012	15,091.2	60.8	2.9	0.2	2.1	0.0	6.5	27.5
12 07300	Boca Raton	29.2	95,787	344	3,280.4	74.7	5.5	0.3	3.3	0.0	3.7	12.4
12 07525	Bonita Springs	38.4	54,904	724	1,429.8	77.9	0.9	0.6	1.4	0.1	9.3	9.7
12 07875	Boynton Beach	16.2	80,089	443	4,943.8	50.9	31.2	0.3	2.4	0.0	4.9	10.2
12 07950	Bradenton	14.3	55,905	701	3,909.4	64.7	14.5	0.4	1.4	0.1	8.3	10.6
12 10275	Cape Coral	106.0	204,510	116	1,929.3	72.3	4.3	0.3	1.7	0.1	5.8	15.6
12 11050	Casselberry	7.0	29,093	1,345	4,156.1	59.9	10.2	0.4	3.3	0.1	9.3	16.8
12 12875	Clearwater	26.1	116,674	246	4,470.3	68.0	10.5	0.7	2.9	0.1	7.1	10.7
12 12925	Clermont	18.1	44,530	895	2,460.2	60.1	12.8	0.3	4.5	0.1	8.3	13.9
12 13275	Coconut Creek	11.2	57,117	693	5,099.7	49.9	16.6	0.2	3.8	0.1	8.4	21.0
12 14125	Cooper City	8.0	33,972	1,170	4,246.5	59.3	5.9	0.3	7.6	0.0	5.5	21.3
12 14250	Coral Gables	12.9	48,375	823	3,750.0	43.0	5.0	0.1	2.6	0.1	8.3	40.9
12 14400	Coral Springs	22.9	132,822	213	5,800.1	43.0	23.2	0.3	5.6	0.0	9.0	18.8
12 15475	Crestview	17.0	27,820	1,399	1,636.5	61.8	18.8	0.6	2.9	0.3	3.4	12.2
12 15968	Cutler Bay town	9.9	44,291	898	4,473.8	36.9	9.9	0.3	2.2	0.0	9.7	41.0
12 16335	Dania Beach	7.8	31,454	1,258	4,032.6	49.1	21.0	0.6	2.2	0.1	9.7	17.4
12 16475	Davie town	34.9	104,882	305	3,005.2	50.9	8.8	0.4	6.1	0.1	9.4	24.3
12 16525	Daytona Beach	65.6	74,437	495	1,134.7	54.0	32.3	0.3	2.7	0.1	3.5	7.2
12 16725	Deerfield Beach	14.9	86,339	404	5,794.6	46.0	24.9	0.3	1.9	0.0	9.7	17.1
12 16875	DeLand	19.3	38,764	1,027	2,008.5	65.4	14.0	0.3	2.5	0.1	6.3	11.4
12 17100	Delray Beach	15.9	66,573	572	4,187.0	60.1	25.5	0.3	1.9	0.0	3.7	8.5
12 17200	Deltona	37.3	95,782	345	2,567.9	54.7	11.6	0.5	1.5	0.1	12.5	19.1
12 17935	Doral	13.8	75,966	484	5,504.8	26.1	1.4	0.2	3.1	0.0	15.4	53.8
12 18575	Dunedin	10.4	35,949	1,102	3,456.6	86.3	2.7	0.3	1.7	0.1	2.0	7.0
12 21150	Estero	24.4	37,522	1,058	1,537.8	88.1	1.4	0.1	2.1	0.1	2.2	6.1
12 24000	Fort Lauderdale	34.6	181,668	143	5,250.5	51.8	27.6	0.3	2.0	0.0	5.9	12.3
12 24125	Fort Myers	39.8	92,245	370	2,317.7	52.2	22.5	0.9	2.5	0.0	9.9	12.0
12 24300	Fort Pierce	23.8	47,927	830	2,013.7	38.1	38.5	0.6	1.0	0.0	10.3	11.4
12 25175	Gainesville	63.4	140,398	195	2,214.5	57.5	20.6	0.3	7.8	0.0	3.7	10.0
12 27322	Greenacres	6.0	43,813	909	7,302.2	35.6	22.2	1.0	3.8	0.0	16.3	21.1
12 28400	Haines City	18.8	29,070	1,346	1,546.3	36.4	22.2	0.8	1.5	0.1	19.4	19.7
12 28452	Hallandale Beach	4.2	41,005	962	9,763.1	48.7	16.4	0.4	1.9	0.1	11.0	21.6
12 30000	Hialeah	21.6	220,490	102	10,207.9	27.4	1.2	0.2	0.4	0.0	12.5	58.3
12 32000	Hollywood	27.3	152,131	172	5,572.6	46.4	17.3	0.7	2.7	0.0	10.7	22.1
12 32275	Homestead	15.1	80,528	440	5,333.0	29.5	18.6	1.5	1.2	0.1	16.9	32.3
12 35000	Jacksonville	747.3	954,614	12	1,277.4	50.1	30.6	0.4	5.1	0.1	4.6	9.1
12 35875	Jupiter	21.6	60,802	633	2,814.9	79.3	1.5	0.6	3.2	0.1	4.5	10.8
12 36550	Key West	5.6	26,527	1,465	4,737.0	67.5	10.3	0.5	2.4	0.1	5.6	13.7
12 36950	Kissimmee	21.5	79,436	453	3,694.7	29.7	10.6	0.7	3.6	0.1	26.7	28.6
12 38250	Lakeland	66.3	115,425	254	1,741.0	59.2	19.3	0.5	2.2	0.1	7.3	11.4
12 39081	Lake Worth Beach	5.9	42,496	940	7,202.7	39.0	19.1	5.8	1.0	0.1	19.1	16.0
12 39425	Largo	18.6	82,341	426	4,426.9	75.5	6.5	0.4	3.2	0.1	4.5	9.7
12 39525	Lauderdale Lakes	3.7	35,609	1,115	9,624.1	6.9	84.2	0.2	1.2	0.0	2.5	5.0
12 39550	Lauderhill	8.5	73,458	502	8,642.1	10.8	76.6	0.2	1.8	0.0	3.5	7.1
12 39875	Leesburg	38.4	27,810	1,400	724.2	55.9	26.0	0.4	2.0	0.3	5.4	10.0
12 43125	Margate	8.8	58,001	681	6,591.0	36.6	32.2	0.4	4.4	0.0	9.4	17.0
12 43975	Melbourne	44.2	85,064	414	1,924.5	71.3	9.9	0.4	3.7	0.1	4.2	10.5
12 45000	Miami	36.0	439,890	44	12,219.2	30.2	12.9	0.4	1.4	0.0	14.3	40.7
12 45025	Miami Beach	7.7	80,671	437	10,476.8	51.2	3.1	0.4	2.0	0.0	10.6	32.6
12 45060	Miami Gardens	18.2	110,867	275	6,091.6	9.3	63.5	0.2	0.7	0.0	7.7	18.6
12 45100	Miami Lakes	5.7	30,388	1,296	5,331.2	30.8	2.5	0.2	1.7	0.0	11.3	53.6
12 45975	Miramar	28.9	135,077	209	4,673.9	16.5	42.4	0.3	5.9	0.0	9.9	25.1
12 48625	New Smyrna Beach	37.8	31,120	1,268	823.3	87.4	4.0	0.3	1.2	0.0	1.2	5.8
12 49425	North Lauderdale	4.6	44,239	899	9,617.2	14.2	58.4	0.5	2.9	0.0	10.9	13.0
12 49450	North Miami	8.5	59,229	660	6,968.1	17.8	51.7	0.4	1.6	0.0	9.3	19.2
12 49475	North Miami Beach	4.8	42,507	939	8,855.6	26.2	34.1	0.5	3.5	0.0	11.0	24.6
12 49675	North Port	99.4	80,021	444	805.0	80.7	5.3	0.3	1.7	0.1	3.2	8.7
12 50575	Oakland Park	7.5	43,650	911	5,820.0	43.2	25.8	0.4	2.3	0.1	11.2	17.0
12 50750	Ocala	47.3	64,096	597	1,355.1	60.0	19.3	0.3	3.9	0.0	5.3	11.2
12 51075	Ocoee	15.6	47,452	841	3,041.8	43.2	23.6	0.5	6.5	0.1	11.5	14.6
12 53000	Orlando	110.9	309,154	63	2,787.7	40.0	23.8	0.4	4.3	0.1	12.3	19.0
12 53150	Ormond Beach	34.8	43,517	918	1,250.5	84.1	4.0	0.3	3.1	0.0	1.7	6.8
12 53575	Oviedo	15.5	39,559	1,002	2,552.2	65.7	7.7	0.3	6.0	0.0	5.0	15.4

1. Dry land or land partially or temporarily covered by water. 2. Hispanic or Latino persons may be of any race.

Table D. Cities — **Population**

City	Percent Hispanic or Latino[1], 2020	Percent foreign born, 2016–2020	Age of population (percent), 2016–2020: Under 18 years	18 to 24 years	25 to 34 years	35 to 44 years	45 to 54 years	55 to 64 years	65 years and over	Median age, 2016–2020	Percent female, 2016–2020	Population: Census counts: 2010	2020	Percent change: 2010–2020	2020–2021
	12	13	14	15	16	17	18	19	20	21	22	23	24	25	26
DISTRICT OF COLUMBIA	11.3	13.4	18.0	10.5	23.3	15.1	10.8	10.0	12.2	34.1	52.5	601,767	689,545	14.6	-2.8
Washington	11.3	13.4	18.0	10.5	23.3	15.1	10.8	10.0	12.2	34.1	52.5	601,767	689,545	14.6	-2.8
FLORIDA	26.5	20.8	19.9	8.2	13.0	12.1	12.9	13.4	20.5	42.2	51.1	18,804,589	21,538,187	14.5	1.1
Altamonte Springs	30.6	19.1	18.6	7.6	20.5	16.5	11.0	11.1	14.6	36.7	54.1	41,573	46,335	11.5	-1.8
Apopka	29.1	17.9	24.9	7.5	13.2	12.8	15.2	11.6	14.8	38.0	50.3	42,235	54,897	30.0	1.1
Aventura	40.3	49.6	16.5	4.9	9.3	12.3	14.7	13.7	28.6	50.3	54.3	35,762	40,225	12.5	-2.5
Boca Raton	15.2	19.0	17.4	8.9	9.6	10.2	12.3	14.3	27.3	48.2	52.8	84,409	96,358	14.2	-0.6
Bonita Springs	21.2	22.4	12.6	4.7	9.0	9.2	9.6	14.4	40.6	58.3	49.7	43,936	53,820	22.5	2.0
Boynton Beach	15.4	25.7	16.5	7.9	15.8	14.4	12.0	12.7	20.7	41.3	51.2	68,297	80,401	17.7	-0.4
Bradenton	20.2	13.5	19.9	6.6	13.7	9.4	11.1	14.4	24.9	45.3	52.4	49,221	55,423	12.6	0.9
Cape Coral	23.8	16.6	17.6	6.7	10.6	11.2	13.8	16.3	24.0	47.8	50.5	154,307	194,979	26.4	4.9
Casselberry	29.9	16.2	19.4	8.4	17.8	12.3	12.3	14.5	15.3	37.4	51.0	26,030	28,791	10.6	1.0
Clearwater	17.4	17.2	18.9	5.9	12.8	12.1	13.2	14.3	22.8	45.2	52.2	109,091	117,227	7.5	-0.5
Clermont	21.7	18.3	22.0	7.5	10.0	11.3	12.8	12.9	23.5	44.2	52.9	28,811	43,040	49.4	3.5
Coconut Creek	25.1	29.6	21.2	7.4	12.8	14.3	14.2	12.2	17.9	40.8	52.4	53,046	57,818	9.0	-1.2
Cooper City	31.8	25.9	25.3	9.1	9.2	14.4	15.1	13.2	13.6	39.7	52.5	28,534	34,394	20.5	-1.2
Coral Gables	58.8	39.8	19.9	15.6	10.2	10.5	13.5	11.5	18.8	39.7	54.5	46,744	49,495	5.9	-2.3
Coral Springs	29.4	29.4	26.2	8.6	12.1	14.0	14.2	13.2	11.6	37.0	52.3	122,591	134,366	9.6	-1.1
Crestview	11.0	4.1	23.6	12.3	20.7	12.5	8.5	11.5	10.9	32.2	50.9	21,050	27,480	30.5	1.2
Cutler Bay town	64.5	42.1	24.6	7.2	13.5	12.7	16.4	11.8	13.9	38.4	52.1	40,289	45,407	12.7	-2.5
Dania Beach	31.1	29.6	20.6	5.6	16.3	13.6	13.4	13.6	17.0	40.5	52.6	29,689	31,772	7.0	-1.0
Davie town	39.5	30.7	21.8	10.4	16.1	12.7	15.3	11.5	12.2	36.2	51.2	91,950	105,719	15.0	-0.8
Daytona Beach	9.3	9.0	17.0	12.9	15.4	10.5	11.0	13.0	20.1	39.3	51.0	61,587	71,681	16.4	3.8
Deerfield Beach	20.2	37.6	18.1	7.3	14.1	12.3	12.1	13.3	22.7	43.2	54.6	75,096	86,873	15.7	-0.6
DeLand	18.8	8.3	20.1	13.3	10.5	12.4	11.4	11.4	21.0	40.6	54.7	26,872	37,404	39.2	3.6
Delray Beach	11.6	23.9	14.3	7.5	13.3	10.9	12.7	15.9	25.4	48.3	51.7	60,611	66,911	10.4	-0.5
Deltona	37.6	9.1	23.5	8.2	14.1	12.6	12.9	12.6	16.1	38.1	52.0	85,133	94,158	10.6	1.7
Doral	83.0	68.5	26.2	8.4	14.4	16.8	16.8	9.9	7.6	35.8	50.7	45,704	75,803	65.9	0.2
Dunedin	7.1	9.7	12.4	4.3	9.4	9.1	12.4	19.0	33.4	56.8	54.7	35,353	36,074	2.0	-0.3
Estero	7.8	10.7	11.1	2.8	6.1	6.0	7.0	14.9	52.0	65.9	51.6	27,991	37,127	32.6	1.1
Fort Lauderdale	19.2	24.5	17.9	7.1	15.9	13.0	13.5	14.7	17.9	42.0	48.3	165,998	182,817	10.1	-0.6
Fort Myers	23.6	18.5	20.7	7.8	13.1	13.3	11.2	11.8	22.2	40.9	51.7	62,308	85,525	37.3	7.9
Fort Pierce	24.5	15.3	22.8	8.3	14.5	9.7	13.4	12.5	18.7	39.5	51.6	41,933	47,279	12.7	1.4
Gainesville	13.8	11.9	13.3	33.4	17.8	9.0	7.4	7.8	11.3	26.4	52.1	124,492	139,835	12.3	0.4
Greenacres	44.7	40.7	21.6	10.1	15.0	12.4	13.3	11.7	15.8	37.2	52.1	37,560	44,152	17.6	-0.8
Haines City	48.9	19.0	25.3	8.4	13.5	14.9	9.9	12.4	15.6	37.0	52.9	20,379	26,750	31.3	8.7
Hallandale Beach	38.0	48.7	16.2	7.2	13.9	11.5	11.8	15.5	24.0	45.9	52.5	37,113	41,211	11.0	-0.5
Hialeah	94.0	75.2	16.6	8.2	12.4	12.3	16.3	13.5	20.7	45.3	51.9	224,697	223,017	-0.7	-1.1
Hollywood	39.9	37.4	19.2	8.1	14.7	13.8	14.7	13.6	15.9	40.6	49.9	140,694	153,061	8.8	-0.6
Homestead	68.2	37.4	33.2	8.3	16.6	16.7	10.3	7.4	7.5	30.8	50.1	60,753	80,697	32.8	-0.2
Jacksonville	11.6	11.7	22.8	9.0	16.6	12.8	12.4	12.5	13.8	35.9	51.6	821,758	949,577	15.6	0.5
Jupiter	16.0	13.7	19.1	7.0	10.7	11.3	14.4	14.4	23.1	46.5	51.7	55,222	61,100	10.6	-0.5
Key West	22.4	22.1	14.4	6.6	16.4	15.4	14.3	15.0	17.9	42.1	46.5	24,635	26,983	9.5	-1.7
Kissimmee	67.1	26.1	23.0	9.0	17.3	14.7	12.4	11.1	12.4	35.3	49.2	59,546	79,242	33.1	0.2
Lakeland	20.2	11.1	19.5	10.1	13.1	12.0	11.1	11.9	22.2	40.8	51.8	97,287	111,881	15.0	3.2
Lake Worth Beach	45.8	38.9	22.8	8.2	16.0	14.8	12.1	11.0	15.2	36.6	46.5	34,890	42,175	20.9	0.8
Largo	12.8	12.8	16.0	7.0	12.1	10.9	12.6	15.2	26.3	48.7	52.2	79,338	82,632	4.2	-0.4
Lauderdale Lakes	6.5	50.2	25.0	8.3	12.9	11.5	12.6	10.9	18.7	37.4	52.4	32,773	35,955	9.7	-1.0
Lauderhill	9.4	37.3	26.4	8.7	13.6	13.0	13.1	12.2	13.0	35.9	54.1	66,936	74,495	11.3	-1.4
Leesburg	15.7	10.9	21.4	7.6	14.0	11.7	10.3	9.6	25.5	42.3	52.6	20,332	26,942	32.5	3.2
Margate	27.1	36.4	16.2	5.8	13.3	12.4	12.0	15.9	24.4	47.1	53.8	53,116	58,697	10.5	-1.2
Melbourne	12.6	10.7	17.8	10.0	15.1	10.1	11.8	14.3	20.9	41.4	51.1	76,221	84,313	10.6	0.9
Miami	70.2	58.1	17.2	7.6	17.3	14.7	14.4	12.2	16.6	40.1	50.1	399,500	442,265	10.7	-0.5
Miami Beach	50.6	55.4	15.5	6.1	17.2	16.2	16.0	12.2	16.7	41.6	48.3	87,380	82,826	-5.2	-2.6
Miami Gardens	32.9	33.3	23.6	9.5	14.7	12.3	12.7	12.2	14.9	36.8	52.5	107,173	111,579	4.1	-0.6
Miami Lakes	84.1	50.9	20.7	8.5	12.3	13.7	16.6	12.5	15.7	41.6	53.0	29,373	30,435	3.6	-0.2
Miramar	41.1	37.9	23.1	8.4	13.7	17.0	14.6	11.7	11.6	38.1	51.8	121,958	134,676	10.4	0.3
New Smyrna Beach	4.9	6.8	10.9	4.5	8.6	7.6	10.0	20.2	38.1	59.3	51.1	23,430	30,233	29.0	2.9
North Lauderdale	26.1	45.1	25.1	10.4	16.0	14.8	14.9	9.6	9.2	33.9	52.1	41,089	44,781	9.0	-1.2
North Miami	33.8	55.5	22.7	8.7	15.0	15.3	11.9	13.0	13.3	37.5	49.8	60,169	60,250	0.1	-1.7
North Miami Beach	42.4	54.1	23.0	9.4	15.8	12.0	14.0	11.8	13.9	36.5	51.7	40,855	43,645	6.8	-2.6
North Port	10.5	9.4	18.6	8.0	9.3	8.8	12.6	16.1	26.7	48.8	52.5	57,320	75,175	31.1	6.4
Oakland Park	30.5	34.7	18.6	7.9	14.7	14.8	16.7	14.8	12.5	40.7	46.2	41,299	44,214	7.1	-1.3
Ocala	17.1	9.9	22.1	8.6	13.5	13.7	11.5	11.9	18.7	38.6	50.2	56,559	63,455	12.2	1.0
Ocoee	25.3	22.6	26.0	7.6	16.5	15.8	14.1	10.5	9.5	34.9	50.4	35,730	47,331	32.5	0.3
Orlando	32.9	23.0	21.4	8.1	22.7	15.8	11.6	10.3	10.1	33.9	52.0	238,723	307,674	28.9	0.5
Ormond Beach	6.6	7.6	17.9	5.9	9.7	7.9	12.4	14.3	32.0	52.5	52.3	39,429	43,159	9.5	0.8
Oviedo	20.9	13.9	25.8	8.6	13.9	13.4	15.6	13.3	9.4	36.3	50.8	33,475	40,183	20.0	-1.6

1. May be of any race.

Table D. Cities — **Households, Group Quarters, Crime, and Education**

City	Households, 2016–2020							Persons in group quarters, 2016–2020	Serious crimes known to police[2], 2020				Educational attainment, 2016–2020		
			Percent						Violent		Property			Attainment[4] (percent)	
	Number	Persons per household	Family	Married couple family	Female family	Non-family	One person		Number	Rate	Number	Rate	Population age 25 and over	High school graduate or less	Bachelor's degree or more
	27	28	29	30	31	32	33	34	35	36	37	38	39	40	41
DISTRICT OF COLUMBIA	288,307	2.30	42.8	26.1	13.3	57.2	45.1	38,992	7,127	999.8	24,899	3,493.0	501,986	24.7	59.8
Washington	288,307	2.30	42.8	26.1	13.3	57.2	45.1	38,992	6,828	957.9	24,459	3,431.3	501,986	24.7	59.8
FLORIDA	7,931,313	2.62	64.5	46.9	12.7	35.5	28.6	431,523	83,368	383.6	384,556	1,769.4	15,255,326	39.7	30.5
Altamonte Springs	19,732	2.21	51.5	32.5	14.3	48.5	38.4	286	140	315.0	999	2,248.0	32,430	24.3	39.0
Apopka	17,312	3.04	74.1	55.3	13.5	25.9	20.5	215	247	450.4	1,395	2,543.7	35,701	36.6	30.4
Aventura	17,770	2.08	52.6	41.8	7.2	47.4	42.8	105	68	183.2	1,232	3,319.5	29,215	17.3	53.0
Boca Raton	42,235	2.25	54.6	45.0	6.5	45.4	37.6	3,712	206	202.8	1,996	1,964.9	72,800	18.6	57.2
Bonita Springs	24,377	2.37	66.7	59.5	4.8	33.3	27.9	34	NA	NA	NA	NA	47,758	34.7	37.5
Boynton Beach	30,370	2.55	56.9	38.4	13.6	43.1	34.3	703	523	654.5	1,794	2,244.9	59,022	39.6	28.4
Bradenton	22,350	2.51	58.3	41.3	12.2	41.7	36.0	1,337	306	504.2	1,322	2,178.4	42,131	46.3	24.9
Cape Coral	69,912	2.70	69.2	56.1	8.8	30.8	25.8	682	255	127.8	2,130	1,067.7	143,612	45.5	23.1
Casselberry	12,092	2.35	55.6	38.5	11.7	44.4	32.9	95	103	354.2	778	2,675.4	20,593	32.9	31.2
Clearwater	48,211	2.36	56.5	40.7	12.0	43.5	35.7	2,312	460	390.3	2,232	1,893.8	87,211	39.3	30.2
Clermont	13,032	2.81	70.4	58.3	8.6	29.6	26.2	198	93	232.9	612	1,532.6	25,930	32.3	34.0
Coconut Creek	24,137	2.51	58.4	39.6	13.2	41.6	33.5	272	88	141.4	662	1,064.0	43,517	34.6	34.4
Cooper City	11,319	3.15	84.4	65.9	13.6	15.6	13.1	24	35	95.3	324	882.5	23,424	25.9	45.1
Coral Gables	18,457	2.45	60.1	49.3	8.8	39.9	33.9	4,702	51	102.0	1,167	2,333.2	32,187	14.0	68.8
Coral Springs	42,504	3.13	76.5	54.5	16.0	23.5	19.1	276	164	121.5	1,664	1,232.3	86,897	29.5	39.1
Crestview	8,984	2.62	66.5	49.3	14.2	33.5	28.8	1,182	93	360.6	602	2,334.5	15,807	38.6	25.4
Cutler Bay town	13,000	3.35	79.3	54.9	17.9	20.7	15.4	388	114	258.5	814	1,845.9	29,979	38.8	31.0
Dania Beach	12,234	2.61	61.8	41.5	15.2	38.2	32.4	183	203	623.5	1,023	3,142.2	23,702	37.6	29.5
Davie town	35,644	2.92	69.0	45.6	17.0	31.0	22.0	1,529	263	243.5	2,445	2,264.1	71,624	32.3	38.1
Daytona Beach	28,763	2.27	50.8	29.7	14.8	49.2	38.8	3,409	725	1,034.5	2,145	3,060.6	48,111	44.6	22.6
Deerfield Beach	32,297	2.46	53.4	35.8	12.9	46.6	39.6	1,470	285	348.6	1,603	1,960.9	60,277	45.3	25.9
DeLand	12,675	2.44	61.2	45.5	12.7	38.8	32.4	2,651	188	524.1	870	2,425.2	22,407	34.7	30.6
Delray Beach	28,914	2.34	52.8	38.1	11.2	47.2	38.0	1,182	401	568.9	2,412	3,421.9	53,933	34.7	39.3
Deltona	30,585	3.00	75.1	54.2	12.2	24.9	18.6	179	NA	NA	NA	NA	62,711	46.1	16.5
Doral	18,791	3.32	81.5	61.6	12.2	18.5	14.0	0	63	92.1	1,238	1,809.3	40,817	24.0	52.9
Dunedin	17,794	2.01	52.7	42.4	7.8	47.3	40.6	629	53	144.5	376	1,025.2	30,395	33.6	33.8
Estero	15,763	2.12	67.9	62.8	2.5	32.1	24.8	0	NA	NA	NA	NA	28,789	22.3	48.3
Fort Lauderdale	74,968	2.38	50.4	33.8	12.1	49.6	39.1	3,101	1,158	628.2	7,662	4,156.3	136,387	35.6	37.5
Fort Myers	31,598	2.53	58.0	40.3	13.2	42.0	34.0	3,429	467	516.7	1,699	1,879.8	59,715	44.6	29.3
Fort Pierce	16,687	2.71	60.0	33.7	19.6	40.0	32.9	699	251	538.9	938	2,014.0	31,585	56.2	15.6
Gainesville	51,180	2.33	37.1	24.0	9.9	62.9	42.8	14,314	1,042	771.4	4,297	3,181.2	71,243	25.5	47.9
Greenacres	14,215	2.89	67.5	40.9	21.1	32.5	26.7	161	119	286.6	711	1,712.5	28,156	48.4	22.0
Haines City	7,640	3.27	73.2	50.1	15.5	26.8	22.4	222	45	168.4	403	1,508.3	16,700	54.4	13.7
Hallandale Beach	18,001	2.21	50.7	32.0	14.0	49.3	41.1	65	200	498.1	1,047	2,607.5	30,467	39.9	34.1
Hialeah	76,459	3.03	73.3	44.5	20.5	26.7	22.0	2,067	447	190.8	3,851	1,644.1	175,902	62.1	17.6
Hollywood	57,095	2.66	62.1	40.3	14.5	37.9	32.1	1,677	542	346.5	3,316	2,119.7	111,783	40.9	28.5
Homestead	19,392	3.53	80.5	43.7	24.7	19.5	16.1	543	610	864.8	1,704	2,415.7	40,335	48.6	23.5
Jacksonville	348,809	2.53	61.1	40.4	15.4	38.9	31.7	21,453	6,424	697.9	26,432	2,871.5	615,004	39.0	29.3
Jupiter	26,597	2.43	62.0	49.2	9.8	38.0	31.7	437	83	123.8	701	1,045.4	48,172	22.9	49.3
Key West	10,788	2.15	52.8	42.7	7.4	47.2	32.3	1,284	106	440.6	450	1,870.3	19,361	33.7	37.8
Kissimmee	22,836	3.14	68.9	44.2	18.8	31.1	23.1	686	318	427.8	1,707	2,296.3	49,240	46.4	19.2
Lakeland	41,750	2.52	58.5	41.0	11.7	41.5	33.7	5,089	404	354.8	2,813	2,470.2	77,619	42.9	25.8
Lake Worth Beach	12,947	2.90	54.4	28.6	14.9	45.6	32.7	696	410	1,052.8	1,251	3,212.2	26,412	53.8	20.1
Largo	36,926	2.27	50.7	35.8	11.0	49.3	38.7	866	332	387.9	1,810	2,114.6	65,207	41.2	24.0
Lauderdale Lakes	12,736	2.80	61.1	29.1	23.6	38.9	35.9	379	276	754.4	781	2,134.6	24,047	55.9	17.2
Lauderhill	24,036	2.96	65.6	32.9	26.8	34.4	29.5	577	632	872.7	1,909	2,636.0	46,633	51.0	19.3
Leesburg	9,142	2.48	63.2	42.6	17.2	36.8	30.9	435	159	660.8	949	3,943.8	16,433	52.8	14.7
Margate	24,577	2.37	59.3	42.1	13.1	40.7	34.9	233	105	176.6	675	1,135.4	45,594	48.1	21.6
Melbourne	32,874	2.42	55.5	38.9	11.6	44.5	36.6	2,566	757	903.3	2,531	3,020.1	59,386	36.1	30.9
Miami	180,676	2.50	55.7	32.1	16.6	44.3	36.5	9,878	2,645	555.6	13,092	2,749.8	346,471	48.7	31.5
Miami Beach	43,237	2.05	45.1	33.3	6.7	54.9	44.9	886	668	750.4	5,109	5,739.4	70,100	29.8	47.7
Miami Gardens	30,946	3.53	74.8	36.6	30.3	25.2	21.5	1,444	782	709.1	2,775	2,516.2	74,078	57.7	15.4
Miami Lakes	10,393	2.98	75.2	53.9	16.4	24.8	19.2	42	31	98.2	425	1,345.6	21,952	32.7	37.2
Miramar	42,256	3.32	77.0	50.3	19.6	23.0	16.7	161	349	243.3	1,500	1,045.5	96,297	39.3	28.6
New Smyrna Beach	13,223	2.04	57.9	47.0	6.5	42.1	37.4	232	75	264.3	458	1,613.8	23,001	31.9	35.3
North Lauderdale	14,049	3.14	67.0	35.4	24.1	33.0	29.4	57	192	430.3	646	1,447.8	28,509	56.1	17.4
North Miami	19,529	3.13	65.7	36.6	18.4	34.3	29.4	1,354	481	762.2	2,008	3,181.8	42,841	54.4	19.1
North Miami Beach	13,617	3.13	70.1	42.0	20.3	29.9	26.1	242	318	734.9	1,172	2,708.4	28,935	44.2	24.8
North Port	25,592	2.68	77.0	61.4	12.2	23.0	16.4	126	117	161.6	743	1,026.4	50,465	41.3	24.8
Oakland Park	16,971	2.64	52.8	32.2	14.0	47.2	35.4	208	258	565.2	1,613	3,533.7	33,038	42.6	28.3
Ocala	23,893	2.39	55.4	34.8	15.5	44.6	38.4	2,933	413	674.0	1,936	3,159.5	41,629	42.4	27.3
Ocoee	14,428	3.27	79.5	59.6	12.7	20.5	15.4	209	132	264.7	1,131	2,267.6	31,477	37.4	32.9
Orlando	113,238	2.50	54.5	34.3	15.1	45.5	33.2	2,120	2,524	860.4	11,158	3,803.5	200,804	31.8	39.9
Ormond Beach	18,554	2.30	59.9	46.6	8.2	40.1	33.8	547	161	363.7	1,035	2,337.9	32,956	35.1	32.9
Oviedo	13,054	3.14	82.7	67.4	10.7	17.3	12.6	103	52	121.2	247	575.7	26,937	17.1	53.2

2. Data for serious crimes have not been adjusted for underreporting. This may affect comparability between geographic areas and over time.

4. Persons 25 years old and over.

City	Money income, 2016–2020					Median earnings Full year, Full-time workers, 2016–2020			Housing units, 2016–2020				
	Households												
	Median household income	Percent with income less than $25,000	Percent with income of $200,000 or more	Median family income	Median non-family household income	All persons	Men	Women	Total	Occupied	Percent owner occupied	Median value[1] (dollars)	Median gross rent (dollars)
	42	43	44	45	46	47	48	49	50	51	52	53	54
DISTRICT OF COLUMBIA....	90,842	17.7	19.8	120,337	75,477	78,545	84,331	73,784	319,192	288,307	42.5	618,100	1,607
Washington	90,842	17.7	19.8	120,337	75,477	78,545	84,331	73,784	319,192	288,307	42.5	618,100	1,607
FLORIDA	57,703	19.7	6.4	69,670	36,698	42,467	46,040	39,606	9,562,324	7,931,313	66.2	232,000	1,218
Altamonte Springs	55,312	16.2	3.4	63,027	47,127	41,414	43,617	39,670	22,205	19,732	39.6	188,000	1,260
Apopka	69,343	11.2	6.6	80,733	40,093	43,782	45,127	42,065	18,642	17,312	74.5	251,800	1,394
Aventura	65,893	23.0	13.8	94,953	40,064	58,028	77,845	44,112	28,058	17,770	64.6	354,100	1,911
Boca Raton	84,445	15.3	18.4	115,849	51,209	69,215	82,119	53,057	51,693	42,235	68.1	480,800	1,837
Bonita Springs	72,475	12.4	10.7	87,799	45,256	41,435	42,027	39,898	37,689	24,377	80.5	314,600	1,333
Boynton Beach	56,850	19.7	4.7	65,984	42,841	40,505	42,629	38,120	37,498	30,370	60.7	229,100	1,551
Bradenton	48,369	23.0	2.9	60,926	34,254	36,666	39,062	34,120	28,310	22,350	58.2	192,800	1,158
Cape Coral	61,780	15.4	4.6	71,743	40,403	43,474	45,986	41,291	86,898	69,912	76.4	237,400	1,367
Casselberry	49,377	23.4	0.7	60,484	37,079	41,395	44,289	36,772	12,970	12,092	60.7	182,700	1,174
Clearwater	50,335	24.0	5.2	66,327	33,978	43,693	49,002	40,096	58,981	48,211	58.5	225,600	1,167
Clermont	71,726	13.9	4.6	86,190	43,798	44,196	51,915	41,658	14,937	13,032	71.0	261,800	1,460
Coconut Creek	65,578	17.3	4.7	79,630	40,768	46,785	53,889	41,723	27,365	24,137	64.9	192,900	1,700
Cooper City	108,763	8.3	15.6	120,669	54,955	63,842	70,255	57,159	11,730	11,319	84.0	411,700	2,089
Coral Gables	103,999	14.4	26.9	163,166	60,718	80,985	102,753	64,467	21,336	18,457	64.3	856,600	1,794
Coral Springs	77,488	11.8	10.3	87,827	47,821	51,151	59,246	45,976	45,344	42,504	62.2	370,600	1,567
Crestview	50,188	20.2	3.6	69,100	27,953	41,495	55,181	35,974	9,896	8,984	58.7	171,200	1,036
Cutler Bay town	75,699	13.4	6.2	77,625	42,461	43,686	47,075	40,768	13,836	13,000	66.1	304,100	1,586
Dania Beach	45,187	26.1	4.1	59,394	33,790	42,240	44,846	41,030	15,294	12,234	48.8	201,600	1,323
Davie town	74,523	15.5	10.6	83,117	49,431	47,550	54,070	42,007	38,951	35,644	66.8	322,300	1,558
Daytona Beach	38,686	33.3	1.7	50,332	27,755	33,444	34,064	32,686	35,503	28,763	43.5	164,400	979
Deerfield Beach	47,183	26.0	3.3	57,211	32,268	39,283	40,430	38,478	41,638	32,297	59.9	182,100	1,394
DeLand	54,397	24.8	6.1	69,544	26,370	43,272	50,391	35,336	13,986	12,675	59.0	222,500	1,005
Delray Beach	66,245	17.4	10.8	75,481	48,024	45,490	49,386	42,796	35,923	28,914	62.7	298,600	1,600
Deltona	56,760	17.2	1.9	61,909	33,733	40,030	43,302	34,882	33,123	30,585	77.5	170,000	1,189
Doral	75,138	15.3	8.6	74,331	63,861	43,033	49,043	36,640	23,086	18,791	46.9	412,500	2,082
Dunedin	51,730	26.6	4.6	69,333	32,911	50,498	54,552	47,321	21,058	17,794	68.2	219,300	1,127
Estero	88,803	9.7	13.0	100,080	59,619	63,951	80,060	53,972	23,949	15,763	85.5	345,500	1,576
Fort Lauderdale	64,313	17.9	11.2	76,796	54,057	48,723	52,629	43,747	95,057	74,968	53.9	350,900	1,353
Fort Myers	48,848	24.3	7.0	60,184	33,458	39,018	40,472	37,099	41,329	31,598	48.2	248,400	1,096
Fort Pierce	37,624	31.9	1.1	45,520	25,369	30,865	31,195	30,592	21,398	16,687	47.4	124,700	961
Gainesville	38,028	36.0	3.3	62,158	26,460	37,854	41,189	35,860	60,885	51,180	38.7	179,500	965
Greenacres	47,840	21.7	4.6	54,235	36,250	35,007	33,877	35,904	16,887	14,215	62.7	173,100	1,397
Haines City	43,259	28.5	3.8	47,686	30,166	31,794	35,908	25,471	10,019	7,640	64.4	160,500	1,023
Hallandale Beach	40,237	31.1	3.9	48,779	32,241	36,564	39,051	35,004	27,314	18,001	52.8	229,300	1,289
Hialeah	38,471	34.3	1.4	44,419	16,522	30,954	33,085	27,197	78,718	76,459	47.0	256,900	1,210
Hollywood	54,317	19.4	6.4	65,886	36,113	40,878	42,144	38,479	69,538	57,095	56.9	281,300	1,262
Homestead	50,723	25.2	1.9	50,485	35,938	34,702	36,708	32,473	21,053	19,392	41.4	235,800	1,303
Jacksonville	55,531	20.2	4.7	67,443	38,558	43,366	46,595	40,641	389,130	348,809	56.4	187,700	1,089
Jupiter	87,163	11.9	15.8	107,470	57,288	58,179	66,665	52,570	33,277	26,597	76.8	384,800	1,684
Key West	73,029	13.5	9.8	84,935	54,223	43,956	47,730	40,497	13,748	10,788	41.8	686,700	1,877
Kissimmee	41,399	27.6	1.9	43,975	30,007	31,932	33,225	31,239	28,868	22,836	44.5	201,300	1,177
Lakeland	50,136	22.7	4.3	61,846	33,103	41,021	44,056	36,788	50,078	41,750	54.8	160,400	1,056
Lake Worth Beach	41,997	24.1	2.5	48,750	35,107	32,278	30,987	36,301	15,365	12,947	43.7	223,300	1,139
Largo	46,733	22.1	2.0	59,800	34,037	40,177	40,656	39,365	46,962	36,926	59.2	134,800	1,131
Lauderdale Lakes	36,103	37.0	0.4	47,699	16,541	29,695	30,917	26,864	15,669	12,736	50.0	122,300	1,123
Lauderhill	43,658	26.0	1.3	52,510	31,413	34,059	34,302	33,942	28,361	24,036	51.3	178,500	1,265
Leesburg	38,026	31.5	1.7	52,689	25,794	31,707	33,417	30,261	10,515	9,142	50.3	160,000	926
Margate	46,460	24.6	2.3	60,605	31,526	41,596	43,878	39,040	27,810	24,577	73.4	215,300	1,330
Melbourne	51,934	24.3	4.0	65,032	34,545	41,886	48,808	36,917	38,304	32,874	57.8	186,000	1,087
Miami	44,268	31.5	6.7	48,003	32,001	36,605	38,501	33,678	209,161	180,676	30.4	344,300	1,242
Miami Beach	57,211	23.8	11.7	74,893	41,711	46,990	52,258	39,396	66,947	43,237	36.9	441,300	1,432
Miami Gardens	46,760	22.8	1.6	51,660	27,363	32,562	31,890	34,047	33,242	30,946	66.6	216,500	1,320
Miami Lakes	77,535	9.9	11.0	88,060	52,184	54,229	57,279	51,302	10,896	10,393	64.7	410,300	1,608
Miramar	70,477	11.5	7.4	77,215	46,871	45,157	46,144	43,571	44,929	42,256	68.9	314,200	1,485
New Smyrna Beach	61,885	19.0	6.6	80,577	39,708	48,271	53,092	46,228	19,063	13,223	78.1	272,100	1,260
North Lauderdale	46,594	22.7	1.4	53,532	31,768	35,365	35,864	34,357	15,068	14,049	55.5	185,000	1,506
North Miami	43,562	27.3	3.6	46,939	29,548	30,777	31,396	29,442	21,865	19,529	44.1	232,600	1,205
North Miami Beach	46,761	22.9	2.6	50,544	28,450	32,133	33,180	30,828	15,985	13,617	52.1	212,300	1,220
North Port	64,543	10.7	5.4	73,394	38,125	41,845	48,415	36,517	30,765	25,592	81.0	216,400	1,248
Oakland Park	53,744	20.0	4.2	59,896	45,725	40,675	42,804	37,276	19,004	16,971	57.4	243,200	1,277
Ocala	42,361	29.0	4.9	53,446	29,594	39,474	42,431	36,766	27,029	23,893	45.9	149,800	973
Ocoee	79,273	11.2	5.4	85,008	51,667	46,956	51,517	39,928	15,467	14,428	71.8	266,100	1,415
Orlando	55,183	21.8	6.6	62,143	46,973	42,494	46,956	39,387	136,180	113,238	37.3	262,500	1,253
Ormond Beach	55,189	19.1	6.7	73,016	32,387	44,675	52,114	41,656	21,026	18,554	75.5	219,400	1,145
Oviedo	98,922	8.0	13.5	105,817	46,957	58,850	70,464	51,526	13,765	13,054	77.8	315,200	1,674

1. Specified owner-occupied units

Table D. Cities — **Commuting, Computer Access, Migration, Labor Force, and Employment**

City	Commuting, 2016–2020[1]		Computer access[2], 2016–2020		Migration, 2016–2020		Civilian labor force, 2021				Civilian Employment, 2016–2020[4]			
	Percent		Percent						Unemployment[3]		Population age 16 and older		Population age 16 to 64	
	Drove alone	Mean travel time to work	With a computer in the house	With Internet access	Percent who lived in the same house one year ago	Percent who lived in another state or county one year ago	Total	Percent change 2020–2021	Total	Rate	Number	Percent in labor force	Number	Percent who worked full-year full-time
	55	56	57	58	59	60	61	62	63	64	65	66	67	68
DISTRICT OF COLUMBIA	32.1	30.9	93.0	85.0	80.7	9.6	381,673	-2.0	25,095	6.6	586,181	70.2	500,269	57.3
Washington	32.1	30.9	93.0	85.0	80.7	9.6	381,673	-2.0	25,095	6.6	586,181	70.2	500,269	57.3
FLORIDA	77.7	27.9	93.1	85.0	84.9	7.0	10,312,768	2.2	469,711	4.6	17,486,583	58.6	13,138,671	51.0
Altamonte Springs	81.1	27.1	95.7	90.6	80.3	11.2	24,495	1.5	1,128	4.6	36,565	70.8	30,144	60.2
Apopka	78.6	31.6	93.8	86.8	92.6	3.6	27,386	3.0	1,207	4.4	41,277	67.5	33,444	57.7
Aventura	73.0	31.6	92.8	79.0	87.1	7.4	15,885	3.3	712	4.5	31,783	55.4	21,159	54.2
Boca Raton	74.8	21.5	95.3	90.9	82.9	9.7	52,543	3.3	1,779	3.4	83,563	56.2	56,595	46.6
Bonita Springs	71.1	23.0	95.8	88.9	87.0	8.8	26,308	4.2	882	3.4	51,631	46.0	28,186	51.1
Boynton Beach	80.1	25.9	94.1	85.3	82.7	6.7	39,944	1.2	2,030	5.1	66,399	65.2	50,221	56.8
Bradenton	77.7	25.9	92.5	84.7	83.9	8.3	26,747	3.4	1,150	4.3	47,109	55.2	32,823	50.0
Cape Coral	80.9	28.5	94.5	88.1	87.7	5.8	95,237	3.4	4,014	4.2	160,230	58.0	114,805	52.6
Casselberry	72.2	25.8	96.0	87.4	84.8	9.1	15,364	2.1	694	4.5	23,484	62.9	19,120	52.0
Clearwater	71.9	23.3	90.0	82.0	81.6	6.0	57,865	2.1	2,415	4.2	96,312	58.9	69,875	52.5
Clermont	77.6	35.6	96.9	92.7	81.0	13.6	17,608	1.0	723	4.1	29,457	57.4	20,816	54.6
Coconut Creek	79.4	28.4	93.4	88.1	84.5	5.4	32,473	1.5	1,268	3.9	49,699	67.3	38,813	58.9
Cooper City	80.4	29.9	98.1	95.8	89.7	3.6	19,838	2.7	633	3.2	27,993	68.4	23,123	51.9
Coral Gables	71.9	25.2	97.5	92.8	81.1	10.4	24,423	4.4	786	3.2	41,068	58.8	31,658	49.2
Coral Springs	79.6	29.3	97.8	93.8	86.0	5.5	73,023	1.5	3,153	4.3	103,241	71.2	87,744	53.0
Crestview	83.4	29.2	89.9	84.8	74.2	14.1	11,293	4.5	432	3.8	19,482	58.9	16,801	49.2
Cutler Bay town	75.8	43.3	95.9	87.4	89.3	1.7	21,841	3.6	996	4.6	34,714	68.0	28,629	57.9
Dania Beach	72.0	29.1	93.3	83.3	86.2	6.5	16,616	-1.9	945	5.7	26,060	65.0	20,608	47.2
Davie town	79.0	28.7	97.3	92.9	84.5	5.7	58,647	1.9	2,239	3.8	85,229	68.5	72,322	52.0
Daytona Beach	76.6	19.3	89.5	73.6	78.6	11.3	31,668	1.0	2,126	6.7	58,070	54.6	44,288	45.3
Deerfield Beach	77.3	26.0	90.6	82.9	79.5	7.7	40,558	0.8	1,988	4.9	67,195	61.7	48,840	51.0
DeLand	79.6	25.7	90.8	81.2	80.7	10.0	15,114	2.7	760	5.0	27,687	51.3	20,633	47.6
Delray Beach	75.4	22.6	92.9	86.8	83.6	7.7	36,075	1.2	1,612	4.5	60,340	61.6	42,859	51.5
Deltona	82.9	34.7	95.5	85.3	90.5	5.5	44,563	2.3	2,232	5.0	72,757	58.8	57,949	51.7
Doral	76.2	27.6	98.4	94.5	78.8	8.3	33,631	3.5	1,410	4.2	47,842	67.3	43,078	54.8
Dunedin	77.2	24.8	91.4	81.9	82.9	7.8	17,826	2.2	630	3.5	32,547	52.4	20,345	49.3
Estero	78.3	27.0	97.8	93.5	88.1	7.5	12,752	2.9	516	4.0	30,085	39.3	12,683	50.7
Fort Lauderdale	75.2	26.8	93.6	84.6	82.7	6.3	98,249	-0.2	5,456	5.6	153,271	64.4	120,765	52.7
Fort Myers	74.5	24.0	90.3	82.8	77.4	8.0	38,712	2.6	1,867	4.8	67,604	54.9	49,063	49.9
Fort Pierce	76.0	25.6	87.7	78.3	88.0	4.6	18,880	1.3	1,304	6.9	36,594	55.3	28,017	45.2
Gainesville	66.3	18.7	95.3	84.1	69.5	15.3	68,626	2.7	2,801	4.1	117,774	57.2	102,652	35.7
Greenacres	79.7	29.2	93.1	85.6	85.3	4.5	21,714	2.7	904	4.2	33,417	66.0	26,901	51.2
Haines City	86.9	32.5	89.0	63.9	86.3	6.8	11,821	-1.8	802	6.8	19,258	56.0	15,318	44.1
Hallandale Beach	73.2	31.6	90.7	80.9	82.2	10.2	18,312	-0.9	1,128	6.2	33,850	61.7	24,297	49.5
Hialeah	76.0	29.3	87.1	73.8	91.7	2.3	107,233	3.0	6,093	5.7	199,673	59.5	151,311	53.9
Hollywood	77.1	29.5	94.9	87.5	86.0	6.6	80,753	0.1	4,147	5.1	127,587	67.6	103,179	53.3
Homestead	67.0	40.1	94.9	86.1	87.1	2.7	30,600	3.5	1,803	5.9	48,179	67.2	43,017	49.6
Jacksonville	78.7	24.9	92.8	85.2	81.8	6.0	465,672	2.5	21,194	4.6	717,384	63.8	592,783	54.5
Jupiter	78.1	22.4	96.8	90.7	86.7	6.4	34,197	3.8	957	2.8	54,255	62.6	39,218	53.5
Key West	57.8	13.1	93.4	84.5	77.4	11.6	15,607	1.2	430	2.8	21,467	65.9	17,080	63.2
Kissimmee	75.2	31.6	89.8	77.6	84.3	9.4	37,167	-3.7	2,567	6.9	57,521	63.7	48,510	45.3
Lakeland	80.3	23.0	88.3	74.4	79.2	11.1	50,302	4.0	2,681	5.3	90,888	55.1	66,339	49.2
Lake Worth Beach	63.8	28.6	93.1	75.6	85.7	4.5	19,583	2.3	910	4.6	30,334	63.9	24,517	50.7
Largo	78.8	23.6	88.9	80.7	82.4	6.3	41,012	2.1	1,727	4.2	72,587	58.6	50,301	54.4
Lauderdale Lakes	76.4	29.6	87.9	67.5	85.4	3.1	18,066	-0.3	1,298	7.2	27,666	63.1	20,912	49.8
Lauderhill	78.4	29.8	90.9	74.1	86.5	3.1	36,049	-0.7	2,702	7.5	54,508	65.2	45,159	48.2
Leesburg	74.5	23.3	87.8	82.9	78.5	8.8	9,526	2.7	614	6.4	18,865	50.4	12,965	45.0
Margate	79.2	28.1	93.4	82.9	89.1	4.4	30,424	0.8	1,581	5.2	50,270	62.4	36,028	55.0
Melbourne	77.6	22.1	90.5	85.4	81.7	8.3	40,609	2.8	1,782	4.4	69,493	57.4	52,311	48.8
Miami	67.9	28.6	88.7	69.1	85.7	4.2	225,503	2.5	11,734	5.2	389,114	63.1	312,516	55.6
Miami Beach	52.1	27.1	94.1	78.9	77.7	8.7	51,641	2.0	1,958	3.8	76,735	69.6	61,827	59.6
Miami Gardens	83.5	33.3	90.6	73.8	90.7	2.4	50,314	3.0	4,224	8.4	88,040	60.0	71,506	48.9
Miami Lakes	81.8	32.2	97.1	92.1	90.7	2.5	15,722	3.9	595	3.8	25,559	68.6	20,674	55.9
Miramar	86.2	29.7	97.9	86.3	93.7	3.7	76,655	1.2	3,850	5.0	111,042	70.3	94,781	58.8
New Smyrna Beach	72.0	27.0	94.4	85.1	84.9	10.2	12,212	2.5	498	4.1	24,497	43.1	14,141	52.7
North Lauderdale	77.4	30.6	95.0	87.6	85.7	4.3	23,732	1.1	1,491	6.3	34,569	73.1	30,490	51.5
North Miami	74.3	31.8	92.5	73.4	85.8	4.9	30,054	0.9	2,084	6.9	49,879	64.8	41,572	50.1
North Miami Beach	73.7	33.1	93.8	76.5	90.6	3.3	21,287	1.6	1,301	6.1	34,054	66.8	28,111	52.3
North Port	82.7	31.6	95.4	89.2	86.4	6.9	31,318	4.2	1,307	4.2	57,459	52.2	39,095	51.8
Oakland Park	73.8	27.5	96.1	88.2	86.2	5.0	26,064	0.1	1,311	5.0	37,617	73.1	31,990	54.7
Ocala	80.1	19.8	87.3	80.2	79.7	8.9	26,069	1.9	1,341	5.1	48,162	57.7	36,945	49.2
Ocoee	71.9	32.9	96.8	92.5	84.1	7.7	26,684	1.2	1,132	4.2	36,305	71.8	31,820	56.3
Orlando	77.0	26.8	95.2	87.9	78.6	10.3	164,578	-0.4	9,179	5.6	229,914	72.0	201,037	55.2
Ormond Beach	80.6	21.3	89.1	83.3	88.0	5.2	19,641	2.9	762	3.9	36,279	51.1	22,458	50.1
Oviedo	77.7	28.6	97.7	95.6	86.4	8.2	21,507	3.7	728	3.4	32,026	70.4	28,163	50.7

1. Employed persons. 2. Households. 3. Percent of civilian labor force. 4. Persons 16 years old and over.

City	Value of residential construction authorized by building permits, 2021			Wholesale trade[1], 2017				Retail trade[2], 2017			
	New construction ($1,000)	Number of housing units	Percent single family	Number of establishments	Number of employees	Sales (mil dol)	Annual payroll (mil dol)	Number of establish-ments	Number of employees	Sales (mil dol)	Annual payroll (mil dol)
	69	70	71	72	73	74	75	76	77	78	79
DISTRICT OF COLUMBIA	625,841	4,740	7.9	321	3,851	3,387.1	292.5	1,743	23,133	5,533.9	672.6
Washington	625,841	4,740	7.9	321	3,851	3,387.1	292.5	1,743	23,133	5,533.9	672.6
FLORIDA	49,325,935	213,494	69.7	27,230	283,295	288,642.2	16,241.2	74,496	1,086,052	333,134.6	29,686.2
Altamonte Springs	0	0	0.0	67	568	348.5	33.9	317	6,186	1,895.6	161.1
Apopka	207,247	604	100.0	55	985	372.3	44.3	155	2,489	831.4	68.2
Aventura	0	0	0.0	137	586	1,797.2	39.7	399	8,877	2,092.9	240.7
Boca Raton	213,558	179	82.1	436	5,801	8,008.4	457.6	742	10,317	2,874.0	354.5
Bonita Springs	231,218	796	93.2	48	357	191.9	18.2	195	2,501	700.3	67.1
Boynton Beach	112,950	363	10.2	113	928	592.7	48.5	332	5,615	1,378.2	131.9
Bradenton	49,934	412	65.8	31	317	168.8	17.8	244	3,834	1,064.2	95.3
Cape Coral	991,634	5,412	79.1	118	494	317.3	23.8	455	6,550	1,793.8	165.1
Casselberry	35,660	353	8.5	29	296	102.6	15.5	149	2,571	505.6	56.1
Clearwater	34,263	125	100.0	160	1,850	855.3	108.7	682	10,337	3,133.6	300.8
Clermont	124,283	662	100.0	22	85	62.8	3.4	160	3,289	1,103.3	85.6
Coconut Creek	0	0	0.0	53	304	257.9	15.5	169	3,510	1,568.2	134.3
Cooper City	2,487	6	100.0	49	159	119.7	8.4	96	1,753	442.2	51.9
Coral Gables	38,536	28	100.0	199	1,657	7,635.4	180.5	326	4,954	1,901.8	185.2
Coral Springs	5,741	25	100.0	238	2,010	1,252.2	118.0	470	8,318	2,490.0	229.1
Crestview	45,110	176	84.1	5	12	3.0	0.4	109	1,672	482.5	40.3
Cutler Bay town	1,669	7	100.0	27	113	35.4	3.1	157	2,524	796.0	64.4
Dania Beach	12,676	45	100.0	129	1,005	629.6	49.0	155	1,846	536.5	57.0
Davie town	22,149	165	39.4	268	1,753	988.0	83.8	443	7,614	2,973.0	232.8
Daytona Beach	340,540	1,320	92.8	74	679	374.4	30.5	519	7,165	2,113.8	192.7
Deerfield Beach	17,461	98	100.0	213	3,650	13,808.6	206.7	315	3,668	1,150.2	108.6
DeLand	216,382	763	100.0	48	401	269.8	29.0	164	2,872	863.6	80.4
Delray Beach	87,640	273	35.5	129	1,019	776.7	59.0	401	5,475	2,172.0	183.9
Deltona	135,586	479	89.1	13	27	10.8	1.3	114	1,930	474.1	45.1
Doral	108,973	586	35.2	1,480	14,646	30,046.8	926.3	546	7,535	2,565.1	244.5
Dunedin	21,480	69	97.1	26	256	111.0	9.3	134	1,462	455.9	40.8
Estero	6,901	29	100.0	18	66	54.2	3.7	246	4,718	1,006.9	104.6
Fort Lauderdale	184,628	646	31.3	576	5,970	5,648.1	350.2	1,120	13,335	5,091.7	434.4
Fort Myers	209,196	1,137	36.6	168	2,615	1,367.2	126.7	717	11,773	3,651.6	323.2
Fort Pierce	85,961	373	68.4	40	463	284.8	21.7	246	3,345	1,351.7	104.0
Gainesville	59,944	1,258	13.6	109	1,224	1,218.7	62.6	549	9,697	2,663.3	237.7
Greenacres	2,565	14	100.0	18	39	23.7	1.4	105	1,684	616.1	55.0
Haines City	489,165	1,521	99.6	13	135	36.9	6.8	67	1,191	355.3	29.2
Hallandale Beach	12,467	54	22.2	87	436	296.2	21.2	154	1,816	456.9	45.4
Hialeah	100,654	620	0.3	534	4,518	1,676.4	165.5	1,000	11,423	2,891.4	263.8
Hollywood	28,055	106	71.7	293	2,731	1,914.4	155.3	605	7,898	2,329.2	225.4
Homestead	80,248	559	100.0	43	307	183.0	12.2	182	2,610	727.9	63.9
Jacksonville	1,382,446	9,969	62.1	1,099	22,090	20,467.2	1,375.5	3,145	50,554	16,703.8	1,410.1
Jupiter	46,976	50	100.0	120	679	422.1	44.8	318	3,528	841.6	96.4
Key West	2,610	12	100.0	D	D	D	2.8	296	2,785	660.6	71.1
Kissimmee	130,619	614	40.4	58	305	104.1	11.3	370	5,535	1,275.6	130.3
Lakeland	239,379	1,249	68.7	156	3,245	10,452.0	171.7	581	10,502	3,221.4	287.5
Lake Worth Beach	30,033	272	7.0	NA	NA	NA	NA	NA	NA	NA	NA
Largo	22,116	75	100.0	99	1,300	2,337.6	64.2	350	5,260	1,510.9	142.6
Lauderdale Lakes	13,104	46	100.0	20	145	44.3	5.4	83	1,183	293.7	28.4
Lauderhill	0	0	0.0	39	154	36.2	3.7	175	1,564	414.2	40.6
Leesburg	86,414	513	97.3	52	421	143.6	15.4	216	2,891	869.0	86.5
Margate	1,655	12	100.0	52	268	149.2	12.7	189	2,820	949.4	89.9
Melbourne	48,008	149	100.0	113	1,504	717.3	91.0	449	6,935	2,085.2	195.6
Miami	1,526,128	6,255	1.6	1,436	9,090	13,043.8	512.2	2,624	32,942	10,232.7	876.6
Miami Beach	51,798	50	100.0	155	519	322.3	28.2	551	6,909	1,823.1	191.0
Miami Gardens	3,402	24	62.5	182	3,849	2,085.0	206.9	307	5,021	2,133.4	162.1
Miami Lakes	61,099	279	100.0	101	1,402	901.5	84.7	85	1,357	567.2	46.3
Miramar	75,887	545	39.3	199	3,278	3,316.9	200.7	201	3,383	1,005.5	87.4
New Smyrna Beach	135,151	588	90.8	17	57	23.8	2.2	155	2,029	696.6	53.1
North Lauderdale	5,785	46	100.0	6	18	3.2	0.5	65	1,234	306.7	32.2
North Miami	24,890	206	4.9	71	411	260.9	22.3	198	2,544	807.9	69.9
North Miami Beach	60,705	369	0.5	73	236	79.5	9.0	190	2,670	1,084.1	77.9
North Port	683,711	2,388	84.3	24	194	60.8	8.8	99	1,951	467.4	46.7
Oakland Park	3,700	29	65.5	108	931	426.0	70.4	242	2,121	722.5	64.4
Ocala	86,533	776	24.2	158	2,741	1,837.0	145.5	629	10,971	3,461.8	312.9
Ocoee	84,436	299	100.0	25	660	815.6	46.0	139	2,224	515.3	50.8
Orlando	683,089	3,724	26.6	661	10,635	7,905.2	631.2	1,639	30,854	9,404.0	802.8
Ormond Beach	56,125	153	100.0	48	355	127.2	17.1	219	3,105	778.6	76.4
Oviedo	1,843	10	100.0	30	201	99.4	10.4	146	2,127	438.7	48.4

1. Merchant wholesalers except manufacturers' sales branches and offices. 2. Establishments with payroll.

City	Real estate and rental and leasing, 2017				Professional, scientific, and technical services[1], 2017				Manufacturing, 2017			
	Number of establish-ments	Number of employees	Receipts (mil dol)	Annual payroll (mil dol)	Number of establish-ments	Number of employees	Receipts (mil dol)	Annual payroll (mil dol)	Number of establish-ments	Number of employees	Receipts (mil dol)	Annual payroll (mil dol)
	80	81	82	83	84	85	86	87	88	89	90	91
DISTRICT OF COLUMBIA	1,350	11,000	4,524.7	883.3	5,812	108,016	37,245.0	13,126.0	113	1,092	277.4	49.8
Washington	1,350	11,000	4,524.7	883.3	5,812	108,016	37,245.0	13,126.0	NA	NA	NA	NA
FLORIDA	37,660	176,886	49,175.2	8,183.6	79,224	513,798	89,601.2	34,672.5	13,471	296,389	106,341.9	16,575.6
Altamonte Springs	116	982	185.6	40.1	275	2,978	211.0	211.3	NA	NA	NA	NA
Apopka	52	139	23.9	4.5	115	400	58.8	19.0	NA	NA	NA	NA
Aventura	285	907	235.3	44.6	440	1,156	299.7	85.8	NA	NA	NA	NA
Boca Raton	578	4,591	957.6	237.6	1,769	13,203	2,821.2	945.2	NA	NA	NA	NA
Bonita Springs	147	539	128.9	26.3	219	1,097	187.5	68.9	NA	NA	NA	NA
Boynton Beach	114	455	97.7	17.0	328	1,364	183.5	54.2	NA	NA	NA	NA
Bradenton	97	269	74.2	10.2	228	1,315	179.6	77.8	NA	NA	NA	NA
Cape Coral	413	667	142.9	24.6	456	1,409	186.1	61.2	NA	NA	NA	NA
Casselberry	51	218	50.6	9.0	85	350	42.3	14.6	NA	NA	NA	NA
Clearwater	330	1,187	262.0	50.3	726	5,378	785.2	332.8	NA	NA	NA	NA
Clermont	99	247	58.8	8.7	107	342	41.7	15.3	NA	NA	NA	NA
Coconut Creek	67	294	154.8	14.9	198	1,234	183.5	62.2	NA	NA	NA	NA
Cooper City	D	D	D	D	208	671	94.4	36.2	NA	NA	NA	NA
Coral Gables	450	1,736	532.9	102.5	1,708	10,129	2,184.5	786.7	NA	NA	NA	NA
Coral Springs	267	1,222	301.1	44.7	D	D	D	D	NA	NA	NA	NA
Crestview	30	68	13.5	2.0	49	248	35.1	13.1	NA	NA	NA	NA
Cutler Bay town	34	59	11.5	2.2	85	196	18.1	5.2	NA	NA	NA	NA
Dania Beach	72	578	117.9	31.6	145	600	112.9	36.6	NA	NA	NA	NA
Davie town	223	1,049	276.6	48.3	597	2,084	348.3	103.9	NA	NA	NA	NA
Daytona Beach	166	825	234.7	32.9	309	2,256	271.1	110.5	NA	NA	NA	NA
Deerfield Beach	139	944	249.8	48.7	403	2,764	432.2	177.2	NA	NA	NA	NA
DeLand	62	240	45.8	8.3	127	664	88.4	28.8	NA	NA	NA	NA
Delray Beach	216	539	129.3	24.4	488	2,350	474.1	144.3	NA	NA	NA	NA
Deltona	25	31	6.8	1.2	57	178	22.9	7.0	NA	NA	NA	NA
Doral	360	2,441	431.0	103.1	691	4,103	766.2	226.6	NA	NA	NA	NA
Dunedin	D	D	D	D	177	544	88.7	30.3	NA	NA	NA	NA
Estero	113	1,022	191.5	157.8	120	534	92.4	31.6	NA	NA	NA	NA
Fort Lauderdale	823	3,876	1,796.5	227.3	2,491	16,701	3,568.6	1,301.1	NA	NA	NA	NA
Fort Myers	248	1,123	418.3	48.4	563	5,444	1,166.1	589.6	NA	NA	NA	NA
Fort Pierce	60	493	80.2	19.2	149	944	145.4	48.5	NA	NA	NA	NA
Gainesville	228	1,375	230.3	49.2	477	3,104	396.9	160.9	NA	NA	NA	NA
Greenacres	31	283	40.5	11.6	110	367	54.8	17.2	NA	NA	NA	NA
Haines City	32	142	25.9	4.8	15	44	4.2	1.6	NA	NA	NA	NA
Hallandale Beach	123	519	114.4	27.0	186	973	196.3	52.5	NA	NA	NA	NA
Hialeah	240	702	153.0	23.4	383	1,282	151.1	42.6	NA	NA	NA	NA
Hollywood	346	2,367	270.3	93.6	D	D	D	D	NA	NA	NA	NA
Homestead	48	144	24.8	4.7	86	526	35.0	13.3	NA	NA	NA	NA
Jacksonville	1,333	8,415	3,040.7	471.7	3,058	35,882	6,386.5	2,533.6	NA	NA	NA	NA
Jupiter	205	1,015	148.2	48.0	538	3,335	581.5	212.5	NA	NA	NA	NA
Key West	131	546	152.1	20.5	154	404	63.7	20.3	NA	NA	NA	NA
Kissimmee	190	1,028	191.4	36.5	196	889	90.2	31.9	NA	NA	NA	NA
Lakeland	207	1,135	283.3	50.1	374	2,330	317.8	121.3	NA	NA	NA	NA
Lake Worth Beach	NA	NA	NA	NA	NA	NA	NA	NA	NA	NA	NA	NA
Largo	126	511	133.4	21.4	244	2,878	481.5	160.1	NA	NA	NA	NA
Lauderdale Lakes	28	432	388.9	16.3	27	48	6.3	2.1	NA	NA	NA	NA
Lauderhill	50	285	60.1	10.3	96	264	38.7	12.0	NA	NA	NA	NA
Leesburg	50	222	50.0	7.5	72	308	37.7	14.6	NA	NA	NA	NA
Margate	56	201	43.7	4.7	147	729	89.6	27.1	NA	NA	NA	NA
Melbourne	197	682	163.2	25.4	468	8,212	1,901.0	703.6	NA	NA	NA	NA
Miami	1,541	6,240	2,578.4	380.0	4,279	28,985	7,076.9	2,694.8	NA	NA	NA	NA
Miami Beach	564	1,981	588.0	91.4	767	2,353	504.5	143.6	NA	NA	NA	NA
Miami Gardens	75	453	94.4	18.2	95	315	34.8	14.6	NA	NA	NA	NA
Miami Lakes	116	492	145.1	28.7	309	1,628	323.1	100.2	NA	NA	NA	NA
Miramar	135	560	171.0	26.1	339	1,882	364.0	130.3	NA	NA	NA	NA
New Smyrna Beach	68	198	35.8	6.1	111	294	43.5	17.4	NA	NA	NA	NA
North Lauderdale	18	57	19.9	1.9	37	585	30.0	15.7	NA	NA	NA	NA
North Miami	120	402	73.9	16.6	192	597	97.5	32.6	NA	NA	NA	NA
North Miami Beach	91	190	38.0	6.9	223	833	132.1	45.4	NA	NA	NA	NA
North Port	D	D	D	D	56	151	16.5	5.6	NA	NA	NA	NA
Oakland Park	110	450	95.8	24.9	225	1,069	216.6	81.6	NA	NA	NA	NA
Ocala	194	954	218.3	30.1	400	1,912	240.0	86.2	NA	NA	NA	NA
Ocoee	41	327	53.3	13.9	102	612	126.4	35.3	NA	NA	NA	NA
Orlando	987	8,964	3,542.0	536.0	2,332	22,012	4,146.5	1,677.5	NA	NA	NA	NA
Ormond Beach	95	D	70.8	D	191	1,069	181.1	54.8	NA	NA	NA	NA
Oviedo	D	D	D	6.2	149	745	93.1	39.6	NA	NA	NA	NA

1. Establishments subject to federal tax.

City	Accommodation and food services, 2017				Arts, entertainment, and recreation[1], 2017				Health care and social assistance[1], 2017			
	Number of establish-ments	Number of employees	Receipts (mil dol)	Annual payroll (mil dol)	Number of establish-ments	Number of employees	Receipts (mil dol)	Annual payroll (mil dol)	Number of establish-ments	Number of employees	Receipts (mil dol)	Annual payroll (mil dol)
	92	93	94	95	96	97	98	99	100	101	102	103
DISTRICT OF COLUMBIA	2,733	72,890	6,739.8	2,060.2	380.0	9,817	1,736.5	830.1	2,203	74,134	11,400.2	4,376.0
Washington	2,733	72,890	6,739.8	2,060.2	380.0	9,817	1,736.5	830.1	2,203	74,134	11,400.2	4,376.0
FLORIDA	42,071	955,006	67,950.4	18,462.3	8,883.0	208,733	23,434.9	6,639.1	61,554	1,127,155	155,283.6	55,472.2
Altamonte Springs	156	3,722	233.4	69.8	23.0	229	21.8	4.1	243	5,741	885.1	289.2
Apopka	76	1,484	81.8	23.1	15.0	60	9.4	1.7	112	1,499	172.7	80.3
Aventura	111	3,330	286.5	83.0	32.0	262	24.8	5.9	295	3,544	708.0	226.8
Boca Raton	439	12,240	950.4	273.8	120.0	2,287	267.8	73.0	849	11,616	1,850.3	686.9
Bonita Springs	135	3,366	213.4	66.6	48.0	1,813	226.5	49.8	164	1,572	192.1	59.4
Boynton Beach	207	4,508	253.5	78.4	38.0	765	53.1	20.0	363	6,057	864.0	306.4
Bradenton	124	2,490	141.0	41.4	29.0	309	20.1	6.7	315	9,649	1,162.7	423.8
Cape Coral	238	4,856	265.3	80.3	56.0	420	26.1	7.2	321	5,242	677.7	253.5
Casselberry	80	1,261	68.2	19.2	18.0	179	11.1	2.2	66	558	64.0	20.0
Clearwater	397	9,686	746.3	194.5	86.0	1,711	133.9	34.7	578	11,955	1,652.5	587.2
Clermont	107	3,032	167.0	50.5	27.0	402	24.8	7.8	194	3,912	476.4	169.5
Coconut Creek	91	1,585	89.2	24.7	25.0	1,914	368.8	66.4	117	1,598	1,090.1	66.0
Cooper City	61	810	43.1	12.5	15.0	72	3.4	1.4	151	892	81.4	29.7
Coral Gables	267	5,925	443.3	138.2	79.0	954	95.6	33.4	522	6,673	1,494.2	472.6
Coral Springs	318	5,280	317.3	91.3	D	D	D	D	505	3,192	405.8	139.9
Crestview	70	1,432	73.7	19.7	D	D	D	D	93	1,732	211.3	78.8
Cutler Bay town	71	1,297	84.2	21.8	9.0	64	4.4	1.0	94	1,220	174.3	42.1
Dania Beach	84	1,750	155.4	34.2	23.0	521	50.6	16.0	57	519	50.4	17.2
Davie town	257	7,377	940.7	190.1	69.0	696	55.6	16.3	317	3,315	289.4	106.7
Daytona Beach	301	6,918	449.4	118.7	47.0	2,501	439.4	69.3	305	11,086	1,517.9	503.4
Deerfield Beach	179	3,367	223.0	60.2	43.0	436	38.3	10.4	198	4,009	340.0	125.0
DeLand	123	2,147	105.0	30.0	21.0	284	12.2	4.0	141	3,703	395.2	144.1
Delray Beach	259	6,536	551.9	139.4	56.0	772	66.9	21.9	460	7,196	1,128.3	347.9
Deltona	47	688	37.9	9.8	12.0	240	6.3	2.2	90	724	72.0	24.9
Doral	316	6,946	507.2	143.6	80.0	496	57.4	12.5	231	3,692	416.0	147.2
Dunedin	D	D	D	D	22.0	209	14.1	3.7	132	2,413	257.3	103.6
Estero	78	1,826	106.0	32.8	20.0	742	47.0	15.5	75	764	73.7	35.4
Fort Lauderdale	736	18,456	1,534.8	419.3	187.0	1,572	201.6	49.4	945	15,261	1,950.6	756.5
Fort Myers	353	8,181	471.7	145.6	51.0	1,870	124.4	36.4	456	17,839	2,375.1	1,100.1
Fort Pierce	135	2,597	133.9	39.4	D	D	D	D	202	3,879	584.0	191.3
Gainesville	421	9,768	516.0	150.8	58.0	721	35.4	11.8	447	18,947	3,259.8	1,183.1
Greenacres	68	1,086	65.5	17.8	12.0	127	6.0	1.6	110	807	106.4	34.6
Haines City	50	916	58.7	12.3	4.0	58	4.1	1.4	57	1,477	256.6	74.9
Hallandale Beach	87	2,464	160.3	52.5	40.0	1,176	302.2	43.4	153	1,006	107.9	38.1
Hialeah	377	6,741	431.5	106.3	44.0	D	81.0	D	796	10,440	1,382.9	437.8
Hollywood	381	6,057	519.6	138.3	95.0	811	75.1	16.9	550	12,593	1,653.1	697.2
Homestead	101	2,025	138.9	35.3	D	D	D	D	182	3,867	401.5	122.1
Jacksonville	1,998	41,498	2,489.3	687.4	294.0	6,482	776.2	370.6	2,601	68,647	10,016.0	3,670.9
Jupiter	181	4,756	290.3	86.1	65.0	1,505	127.1	38.9	376	4,974	696.0	262.0
Key West	278	6,071	757.0	173.7	55.0	476	70.2	14.2	105	1,050	185.8	56.0
Kissimmee	236	5,337	409.3	98.7	23.0	1,201	120.8	33.9	310	6,050	987.5	325.7
Lakeland	300	7,573	416.5	119.6	37.0	703	37.1	12.4	427	13,942	1,897.2	678.0
Lake Worth Beach	NA	NA	NA	NA	NA	NA	NA	NA	NA	NA	NA	NA
Largo	181	2,931	167.0	46.4	31.0	277	17.6	3.9	316	10,599	1,190.9	504.5
Lauderdale Lakes	35	596	32.4	9.2	D	D	D	D	96	2,515	308.6	106.0
Lauderhill	83	1,073	71.3	16.4	18.0	112	13.4	1.9	154	1,894	144.8	59.2
Leesburg	90	1,804	103.9	29.9	12.0	D	4.6	D	225	5,512	612.3	234.2
Margate	93	1,221	80.0	20.8	18.0	323	19.7	5.3	168	2,519	445.1	129.6
Melbourne	265	5,501	340.0	97.7	36.0	508	30.6	10.5	450	12,706	1,740.9	587.8
Miami	1,460	35,124	2,753.6	743.2	318.0	7,230	1,317.8	490.4	1,858	41,128	6,459.9	2,228.5
Miami Beach	691	28,900	3,170.4	848.2	144.0	1,182	170.2	41.2	426	7,303	1,066.5	429.6
Miami Gardens	104	1,440	103.0	24.8	D	D	D	D	193	2,883	365.0	175.3
Miami Lakes	75	1,902	132.9	38.9	23.0	144	30.0	6.2	235	3,060	348.2	117.4
Miramar	124	2,084	140.8	36.2	39.0	252	18.5	5.1	290	3,714	567.3	216.8
New Smyrna Beach	115	1,987	99.5	33.2	31.0	252	32.4	7.2	109	1,581	188.2	63.5
North Lauderdale	27	497	29.3	7.4	D	D	D	0.3	34	311	21.8	7.4
North Miami	111	1,874	110.5	28.0	20.0	208	28.3	5.0	167	4,020	283.5	139.0
North Miami Beach	112	1,775	125.6	32.4	17.0	85	8.3	1.6	222	4,407	581.1	209.1
North Port	53	1,031	55.6	16.4	5.0	37	1.3	0.5	80	717	83.2	26.8
Oakland Park	114	2,283	133.8	41.5	26.0	231	13.8	3.4	197	1,963	229.0	87.5
Ocala	301	6,783	385.4	106.3	29.0	383	22.3	6.0	583	12,284	1,658.1	582.7
Ocoee	80	1,191	68.5	18.4	22.0	113	11.1	2.6	127	3,085	574.9	142.2
Orlando	1,129	33,869	2,950.3	703.4	242.0	28,497	3,500.8	818.8	1,144	38,074	6,331.1	2,136.2
Ormond Beach	147	2,991	174.6	49.8	31.0	396	22.7	9.7	234	3,595	454.2	200.1
Oviedo	D	D	D	D	20.0	189	12.3	2.9	128	1,279	152.8	50.8

1. Establishments subject to federal tax.

Table D. Cities — Other Services and Government Employment and Payroll

City	Other services[1]				Government employment and payroll, 2017								
						March payroll							
							Perent of total for:						
	Number of establish- ments	Number of employees	Receipts (mil dol)	Annual payroll (mil dol)	Full-time equivalent employees	Total (dollars)	Admin- istrative, judicial, and legal	Police and corrections	Fire protection	Highways and trans- portation	Health and welfare	Natural resources and utilities	Education and libraries
	104	105	106	107	108	109	110	111	112	113	114	115	116
DISTRICT OF COLUMBIA....	3,502	73,756	24,225.6	5,459.1	X	X	X	X	X	X	X	X	X
Washington	3,502	73,756	24,225.6	5,459.1	40,352	276,215,832	14.5	18.1	5.3	2.1	17.4	9.3	22.4
FLORIDA	38,932	222,512	29,616.9	6,946.2	X	X	X	X	X	X	X	X	X
Altamonte Springs	125	592	47.9	15.6	461	2,055,913	21.8	29.0	0.0	2.0	0.0	38.0	1.0
Apopka	69	335	29.0	7.8	405	2,056,784	13.9	34.9	25.1	3.2	0.0	15.0	0.0
Aventura	112	1,287	153.6	39.3	346	1,474,105	18.1	28.6	27.1	8.9	0.5	15.7	0.0
Boca Raton	492	2,666	396.9	92.6	1,616	8,328,920	12.4	23.5	25.3	3.1	0.1	27.9	2.4
Bonita Springs	137	632	78.9	20.1	60	279,533	45.7	0.0	0.0	15.4	13.0	22.2	0.0
Boynton Beach	201	1,520	125.4	40.5	747	4,245,982	11.5	28.4	26.7	0.2	0.3	24.1	2.5
Bradenton	101	400	57.8	13.3	507	2,184,357	11.9	33.9	19.1	3.1	0.5	24.0	0.0
Cape Coral	280	1,099	93.4	28.4	1,377	7,666,811	18.1	24.1	18.5	3.6	5.3	27.0	0.0
Casselberry	71	212	18.2	4.9	167	747,193	11.6	38.1	0.0	4.6	1.4	32.5	0.0
Clearwater	284	1,164	143.5	36.4	1,649	7,771,554	13.0	26.2	16.5	4.0	0.6	29.1	3.1
Clermont	81	434	39.8	12.4	277	1,070,366	12.9	27.5	23.7	9.3	0.0	23.5	0.0
Coconut Creek	106	705	63.2	21.4	370	2,242,383	21.0	42.8	1.5	3.4	0.0	20.8	0.0
Cooper City	66	495	66.0	14.5	136	578,526	17.3	0.0	0.0	0.0	0.0	48.9	0.0
Coral Gables	229	1,124	157.6	36.7	829	4,496,506	21.0	28.6	24.5	4.0	0.0	13.5	0.0
Coral Springs	294	1,159	119.4	29.7	919	5,422,682	13.9	39.6	26.9	1.9	0.0	11.2	0.0
Crestview	33	133	13.8	4.0	222	748,433	10.8	25.9	26.6	16.0	0.8	15.8	4.1
Cutler Bay town	D	D	D	D	53	224,074	39.6	1.1	0.0	9.7	0.0	35.7	0.0
Dania Beach	112	586	76.6	20.0	128	624,214	23.2	0.0	0.0	4.1	8.4	24.5	39.8
Davie town	315	1,530	220.4	48.0	667	4,500,059	10.5	42.7	25.9	4.5	0.9	10.1	0.0
Daytona Beach	173	1,297	390.5	69.7	964	4,588,181	12.0	39.1	11.5	5.1	1.4	26.4	0.0
Deerfield Beach	231	892	106.6	25.7	330	1,569,268	23.0	0.0	0.0	6.8	1.7	60.9	0.0
DeLand	94	422	36.5	10.4	370	1,617,265	12.3	22.7	13.3	4.8	7.2	32.6	0.0
Delray Beach	272	1,035	128.4	28.0	819	4,654,723	13.3	31.2	29.7	2.8	0.5	18.2	0.0
Deltona	D	D	D	D	308	1,299,004	19.7	0.0	34.0	4.6	0.0	32.3	0.0
Doral	202	1,917	348.6	75.4	368	1,893,403	13.6	55.1	0.0	6.7	0.0	8.2	0.0
Dunedin	78	323	28.8	7.6	361	1,657,266	8.3	0.0	21.7	5.8	3.6	40.4	5.7
Estero	71	509	50.9	14.7	14	56,874	81.5	0.0	0.0	7.3	11.2	0.0	0.0
Fort Lauderdale	793	5,081	662.0	188.9	2,525	15,897,679	11.4	31.2	21.8	1.5	6.9	19.5	0.0
Fort Myers	302	1,850	253.3	59.0	819	3,768,648	14.5	35.0	19.2	1.8	1.2	24.7	0.0
Fort Pierce	94	405	30.9	10.8	594	2,513,558	8.1	25.4	0.0	1.8	0.4	43.1	0.0
Gainesville	274	2,770	448.7	89.6	2,166	10,629,345	18.4	17.1	9.0	12.5	1.5	35.1	0.0
Greenacres	66	291	29.1	8.0	186	1,059,161	15.1	34.8	33.0	2.2	0.0	2.2	0.0
Haines City	26	79	6.2	1.9	262	928,258	13.9	34.0	13.4	3.8	0.0	28.1	2.6
Hallandale Beach	147	683	76.9	19.0	514	3,159,677	15.0	34.5	21.0	4.5	3.7	19.1	0.0
Hialeah	442	1,790	187.9	44.4	1,278	6,831,692	5.6	31.9	32.4	3.6	4.8	19.3	0.9
Hollywood	351	1,913	245.6	67.8	1,367	7,734,587	10.9	35.3	22.5	3.5	2.3	17.9	0.0
Homestead	71	318	28.2	7.0	402	2,558,562	11.3	39.9	0.0	3.3	1.3	34.7	0.0
Jacksonville	1,614	11,019	1,530.6	387.6	9,087	42,343,407	12.8	31.9	15.2	6.4	1.9	17.7	2.2
Jupiter	219	1,339	173.5	44.2	375	2,229,268	12.5	45.1	0.0	3.8	0.0	20.2	0.0
Key West	73	276	36.6	9.8	488	2,501,175	20.4	32.6	22.8	10.9	0.0	6.2	0.0
Kissimmee	144	758	86.5	21.7	897	4,628,057	6.0	20.8	13.6	3.6	0.2	51.6	0.0
Lakeland	196	1,294	145.4	37.1	2,180	11,663,514	11.3	17.1	10.6	4.3	2.7	47.2	1.4
Lake Worth Beach	NA	NA	NA	NA	NA	NA	NA	NA	NA	NA	NA	NA	NA
Largo	186	1,040	112.8	33.3	846	4,172,007	10.7	28.2	21.0	5.0	6.0	25.3	3.0
Lauderdale Lakes	47	187	23.6	5.6	81	311,550	38.5	0.0	0.0	5.3	19.3	16.6	0.0
Lauderhill	106	387	39.1	9.7	483	3,060,756	11.9	35.9	22.8	4.3	0.0	21.3	0.0
Leesburg	71	482	55.3	12.6	445	1,950,959	14.9	21.1	13.7	2.4	1.0	37.6	3.1
Margate	128	411	47.7	14.0	478	3,000,546	7.0	33.3	30.5	0.3	1.5	7.3	0.0
Melbourne	205	1,002	80.9	27.4	876	3,893,511	12.8	26.3	21.8	12.8	0.7	22.8	0.0
Miami	1,195	7,218	1,343.8	223.0	3,951	21,993,811	8.7	37.7	30.2	1.1	0.9	10.1	0.0
Miami Beach	305	2,250	209.0	50.4	1,868	11,648,570	17.6	25.1	20.0	2.2	3.5	14.7	0.0
Miami Gardens	73	226	26.4	6.2	482	3,036,273	10.1	66.9	0.0	4.2	0.7	5.9	0.0
Miami Lakes	60	613	64.4	18.4	46	234,782	44.8	0.0	0.0	0.0	0.0	28.4	0.0
Miramar	129	986	105.5	30.6	868	5,621,208	15.4	36.4	23.5	2.2	2.7	15.9	0.0
New Smyrna Beach	95	427	38.6	9.9	226	1,017,053	20.4	22.4	23.6	8.5	0.0	12.8	0.0
North Lauderdale	33	160	25.0	5.2	160	737,670	14.1	0.0	34.5	6.4	9.5	25.3	0.0
North Miami	118	550	49.1	14.0	398	1,769,654	18.8	49.8	0.0	2.7	1.4	25.8	1.4
North Miami Beach	96	482	41.8	10.1	464	2,379,780	13.4	37.8	0.0	7.0	0.3	17.7	1.3
North Port	57	225	31.6	9.1	535	2,621,666	13.9	24.6	20.6	9.8	0.5	18.4	0.0
Oakland Park	194	668	97.8	20.9	246	1,355,506	20.1	0.0	34.6	4.3	1.0	27.3	2.0
Ocala	243	1,427	143.1	42.5	958	4,546,983	11.3	25.4	15.8	6.5	0.6	35.7	0.0
Ocoee	D	D	D	D	342	1,635,673	11.3	31.2	19.8	7.4	8.7	21.6	0.0
Orlando	729	6,858	719.9	204.9	3,145	17,935,004	15.1	34.3	25.7	1.6	1.1	14.2	0.0
Ormond Beach	108	536	44.9	12.7	357	1,444,897	17.0	25.9	17.2	6.6	0.0	25.5	0.0
Oviedo	D	D	D	D	287	1,289,540	12.1	28.9	25.3	2.1	0.0	27.0	0.0

1. Establishments subject to federal tax.

City	City government finances, 2017									
	General revenue							General expenditure		
		Intergovernmental		Taxes						
					Per capita[1] (dollars)				Per capita[1] (dollars)	
	Total (mil dol)	Total (mil dol)	Percent from state government	Total (mil dol)	Total	Property	Sales and gross receipts	Total (mil dol)	Total	Capital outlays
	117	118	119	120	121	122	123	124	125	126
DISTRICT OF COLUMBIA	X	X	X	X	X	X	X	X	X	X
Washington	13,057.2	4,055.8	5.5	7,455.9	10,729	3,500	2,877	13,938.0	20,057	2,232
FLORIDA	X	X	X	X	X	X	X	X	X	X
Altamonte Springs	56.5	5.7	97.3	26.0	588	231	358	65.9	1,490	618
Apopka	57.7	10.4	93.8	20.9	399	151	249	56.8	1,087	68
Aventura	54.7	13.1	89.1	31.8	845	399	444	48.8	1,296	148
Boca Raton	253.8	34.3	33.5	133.4	1,358	796	561	238.8	2,431	185
Bonita Springs	28.0	6.0	92.4	14.7	261	117	144	27.6	491	219
Boynton Beach	139.5	11.3	86.3	69.1	889	628	261	134.4	1,729	194
Bradenton	78.5	9.4	71.4	30.7	541	319	219	64.5	1,138	56
Cape Coral	295.7	50.1	91.6	112.6	613	416	197	286.5	1,560	106
Casselberry	36.9	3.8	91.7	12.7	449	122	327	42.3	1,494	434
Clearwater	247.2	31.1	48.2	88.7	768	380	389	229.3	1,986	143
Clermont	47.9	4.9	67.0	21.0	596	250	346	49.8	1,416	373
Coconut Creek	76.0	7.2	90.4	34.1	558	322	236	69.4	1,136	151
Cooper City	42.0	4.5	73.2	23.5	659	415	244	41.8	1,171	48
Coral Gables	172.9	6.4	89.0	105.2	2,077	1,411	666	185.2	3,659	687
Coral Springs	155.2	15.5	85.5	87.8	657	312	327	155.9	1,168	151
Crestview	24.6	4.1	76.9	12.4	519	270	249	20.2	842	100
Cutler Bay town	23.1	8.5	55.8	12.0	271	104	166	22.4	504	7
Dania Beach	58.6	3.7	84.9	29.5	919	555	364	60.0	1,867	698
Davie town	123.5	15.1	80.3	76.2	725	425	300	129.3	1,230	98
Daytona Beach	147.0	15.6	54.6	50.3	739	378	361	130.4	1,916	201
Deerfield Beach	134.4	17.0	63.1	60.8	755	467	285	139.6	1,733	74
DeLand	49.6	6.4	83.5	20.1	623	289	323	43.2	1,336	89
Delray Beach	183.4	31.3	25.7	95.6	1,391	1,053	336	141.7	2,062	155
Deltona	59.1	10.4	90.8	28.5	315	152	163	55.8	615	100
Doral	72.5	8.3	84.1	52.7	875	298	577	74.0	1,228	466
Dunedin	49.5	5.0	81.6	20.9	574	226	347	61.5	1,686	97
Estero	20.6	3.5	97.7	12.6	382	101	281	21.8	662	46
Fort Lauderdale	444.4	48.0	44.3	205.9	1,145	663	482	400.8	2,228	92
Fort Myers	180.2	13.7	71.5	79.6	994	526	468	183.9	2,298	177
Fort Pierce	74.1	8.0	55.9	26.0	571	387	184	78.2	1,718	49
Gainesville	209.3	36.9	50.5	62.1	470	221	250	226.8	1,717	263
Greenacres	26.6	5.2	89.5	16.6	408	203	204	29.5	725	122
Haines City	34.7	2.4	91.2	14.4	600	324	276	27.2	1,133	72
Hallandale Beach	90.6	10.6	35.9	35.3	888	598	290	111.4	2,798	525
Hialeah	254.1	63.3	73.3	101.2	428	199	229	241.2	1,021	37
Hollywood	316.5	29.1	64.7	146.5	955	680	275	282.9	1,844	165
Homestead	84.6	16.7	62.7	24.5	355	173	182	112.8	1,632	354
Jacksonville	2,264.4	558.5	39.1	993.4	1,114	625	488	1,680.4	1,884	121
Jupiter	68.3	9.7	73.5	42.2	651	379	272	56.6	872	73
Key West	117.3	20.7	48.5	30.0	1,198	570	627	121.8	4,865	1,125
Kissimmee	104.6	42.0	43.7	30.8	430	165	266	100.5	1,407	248
Lakeland	230.0	26.2	67.3	57.0	529	289	239	230.6	2,141	340
Lake Worth Beach	NA	NA	NA	NA	NA	NA	NA	NA	NA	NA
Largo	121.7	13.3	83.9	46.2	545	228	315	168.2	1,986	657
Lauderdale Lakes	35.3	7.4	63.7	15.9	438	221	217	28.6	790	28
Lauderhill	84.8	11.1	79.7	34.6	481	252	229	78.6	1,093	28
Leesburg	48.2	4.2	62.8	16.3	721	220	500	52.0	2,299	274
Margate	78.0	7.5	82.4	35.1	602	364	238	75.0	1,289	123
Melbourne	172.2	57.3	84.5	54.4	665	352	313	138.1	1,688	62
Miami	929.9	173.7	37.2	546.2	1,196	739	457	894.4	1,959	193
Miami Beach	565.7	66.3	17.5	347.5	3,834	1,627	2,207	646.2	7,129	1,755
Miami Gardens	92.6	16.5	78.9	52.3	466	244	221	83.7	746	42
Miami Lakes	24.6	6.1	78.3	15.0	489	195	294	23.2	756	144
Miramar	169.4	19.1	71.6	84.5	602	369	233	195.4	1,394	225
New Smyrna Beach	60.6	5.0	43.9	22.6	856	428	428	51.6	1,952	474
North Lauderdale	43.1	5.5	91.8	16.4	371	184	187	40.0	906	25
North Miami	92.9	10.1	76.4	32.2	520	302	218	89.1	1,438	26
North Miami Beach	72.7	6.7	80.4	29.1	679	328	351	90.2	2,107	174
North Port	104.1	10.3	72.6	31.9	481	152	328	96.6	1,457	288
Oakland Park	68.5	8.8	49.2	27.6	614	336	278	63.3	1,410	99
Ocala	136.2	15.3	69.7	44.3	750	433	318	130.0	2,199	252
Ocoee	58.7	12.4	98.0	18.6	399	237	161	51.7	1,109	123
Orlando	873.9	254.3	23.9	268.8	954	523	431	851.2	3,020	169
Ormond Beach	58.4	10.5	44.0	25.7	603	295	305	57.2	1,340	215
Oviedo	48.1	10.2	41.0	22.1	542	274	268	50.1	1,228	133

1. Based on population estimated as of July 1 of the year shown.

City	City government finances, 2017 (cont.) — General expenditure (cont.) — Percent of total for: Public welfare	Highways	Parking facilities	Education	Health and hospitals	Police protection	Sewerage and sanitation	Parks and recreation	Housing and community development	Interest on debt	Debt outstanding: Total (mil dol)	Debt outstanding: Per capita[1] (dollars)	Debt issued during year
	127	128	129	130	131	132	133	134	135	136	137	138	139
DISTRICT OF COLUMBIA	X	X	X	X	X	X	X	X	X	X	X	X	X
Washington	28.2	3.3	0.2	20.9	4.7	4.5	4.9	1.9	5.5	4.2	14,417.4	20,747	2,739.2
FLORIDA	X	X	X	X	X	X	X	X	X	X	X	X	X
Altamonte Springs	0.0	27.8	0.0	0.0	0.0	16.2	15.4	8.4	0.0	0.0	0.0	0	0.0
Apopka	0.0	5.9	0.0	0.0	9.8	28.5	18.3	6.4	0.0	0.5	24.8	475	1.8
Aventura	0.0	10.9	0.0	17.1	0.0	38.7	0.0	7.7	0.0	1.5	20.2	536	0.0
Boca Raton	0.0	4.6	0.0	0.0	0.0	18.6	13.9	16.0	0.3	2.1	68.8	700	0.0
Bonita Springs	0.0	15.9	0.0	0.0	0.4	6.1	0.0	10.9	0.0	2.5	23.0	409	0.0
Boynton Beach	0.0	1.0	0.0	0.0	0.0	23.0	22.7	6.7	0.2	0.8	108.1	1,391	0.0
Bradenton	0.0	5.4	0.6	0.0	0.0	22.5	24.9	4.6	8.1	2.0	43.3	764	14.3
Cape Coral	0.0	8.7	0.0	8.0	0.0	12.2	8.7	7.1	0.6	3.4	820.4	4,466	1.0
Casselberry	0.0	12.7	0.0	0.0	0.0	13.8	24.0	13.2	0.0	0.8	21.6	762	0.0
Clearwater	0.0	5.2	1.8	0.0	3.1	17.4	26.1	14.0	0.2	0.7	205.6	1,780	0.0
Clermont	0.0	3.1	0.0	0.0	0.0	32.6	20.9	10.1	0.0	1.4	22.8	648	10.6
Coconut Creek	0.0	2.9	0.0	0.0	0.0	24.7	1.3	10.0	0.6	0.6	6.3	103	0.0
Cooper City	0.0	3.7	0.3	0.0	0.0	29.0	18.4	8.3	0.0	0.1	0.7	18	0.0
Coral Gables	0.0	3.2	3.9	0.0	0.0	22.8	10.6	13.8	0.0	1.2	100.2	1,979	23.8
Coral Springs	0.0	3.9	0.0	0.0	5.9	31.6	8.8	11.4	0.0	1.2	121.0	906	42.1
Crestview	0.0	8.1	0.0	0.0	0.0	22.5	20.6	5.4	0.0	1.0	27.7	1,154	15.3
Cutler Bay town	0.0	0.0	0.0	0.0	0.0	40.1	0.0	9.6	0.0	2.4	15.7	353	0.0
Dania Beach	0.0	4.5	1.0	0.0	0.0	21.6	11.6	7.7	0.0	0.6	29.6	922	0.0
Davie town	0.0	5.8	0.0	0.0	17.1	32.8	0.0	4.5	0.8	1.1	186.7	1,776	0.4
Daytona Beach	0.3	4.9	0.2	0.0	0.0	23.8	16.6	11.3	1.1	1.9	138.9	2,040	0.8
Deerfield Beach	1.6	3.3	0.4	0.0	0.0	16.8	26.2	4.8	1.4	1.5	64.4	800	0.0
DeLand	0.0	6.9	0.0	0.0	0.0	18.0	24.6	8.0	0.0	0.7	9.3	288	0.0
Delray Beach	0.0	3.2	0.8	0.0	0.0	25.4	3.6	12.7	0.2	1.7	68.6	998	0.0
Deltona	0.0	11.8	0.0	0.0	0.0	18.2	18.6	6.9	1.7	1.5	166.8	1,841	39.2
Doral	0.0	22.3	0.0	0.0	0.0	27.2	0.0	24.2	0.0	1.3	21.5	356	0.0
Dunedin	0.0	4.7	0.0	0.0	0.0	6.7	22.6	14.8	0.0	1.0	35.2	964	0.0
Estero	0.0	10.7	0.0	0.0	0.0	32.1	3.2	23.7	0.0	0.0	0.0	0	0.0
Fort Lauderdale	0.0	4.2	4.1	0.0	0.0	24.8	4.7	8.0	2.4	3.3	719.8	4,001	158.9
Fort Myers	0.0	5.5	0.6	0.0	0.0	20.4	25.0	7.9	0.4	2.3	342.2	4,277	52.1
Fort Pierce	0.0	3.5	0.0	0.0	0.0	17.0	21.1	17.2	4.2	6.3	151.0	3,315	0.0
Gainesville	0.5	10.9	0.2	0.0	0.2	17.6	21.3	7.3	9.7	3.2	1,090.1	8,256	18.6
Greenacres	0.0	5.7	0.0	0.0	20.1	31.0	4.0	17.4	0.0	0.4	2.4	60	0.0
Haines City	0.0	3.2	0.0	0.0	0.0	22.8	19.0	10.2	0.0	6.9	54.3	2,257	24.1
Hallandale Beach	0.0	2.1	0.0	0.0	0.0	22.7	21.7	16.8	0.0	2.0	110.6	2,780	102.8
Hialeah	0.0	3.9	0.0	2.2	0.0	21.7	28.2	5.7	0.8	2.0	155.7	659	46.1
Hollywood	0.0	3.3	2.5	0.0	0.0	24.4	19.5	4.9	0.7	3.3	329.1	2,145	103.3
Homestead	0.7	5.8	0.0	0.0	0.0	30.9	21.1	5.6	1.4	1.2	27.4	397	4.6
Jacksonville	0.7	2.8	0.2	0.0	4.9	21.0	9.8	6.7	1.1	6.7	8,768.9	9,830	476.4
Jupiter	0.0	12.1	0.0	0.0	0.0	34.8	0.0	4.9	0.0	1.6	40.7	627	0.0
Key West	0.0	6.6	0.0	0.0	1.6	12.1	20.1	8.2	9.8	0.7	21.3	852	0.0
Kissimmee	0.0	17.0	0.0	3.9	0.0	23.8	7.7	9.8	0.1	1.8	305.3	4,273	216.5
Lakeland	0.0	7.2	0.5	0.0	0.0	16.7	14.3	23.6	1.0	0.3	988.0	9,173	149.3
Lake Worth Beach	NA	NA	NA	NA	NA	NA	NA	NA	NA	NA	NA	NA	NA
Largo	0.0	1.3	0.0	0.0	0.0	12.9	45.7	7.0	1.0	0.2	36.2	428	21.9
Lauderdale Lakes	0.0	1.8	0.0	0.0	0.0	22.4	3.9	4.6	0.0	3.2	20.5	566	0.0
Lauderhill	0.0	1.2	0.0	0.0	5.7	23.3	6.9	8.9	1.6	3.8	99.6	1,385	12.7
Leesburg	0.0	2.8	0.0	0.0	0.0	14.5	21.3	3.1	0.6	5.0	117.9	5,217	0.0
Margate	0.0	2.0	0.0	0.0	0.0	23.3	13.2	5.4	0.8	2.0	26.3	451	0.0
Melbourne	0.0	9.1	0.0	0.0	0.4	13.9	19.1	6.9	0.9	0.3	97.8	1,195	38.6
Miami	0.3	1.6	3.9	0.0	0.0	26.4	4.2	10.3	3.3	4.2	652.3	1,429	67.9
Miami Beach	0.2	1.8	7.2	0.0	3.0	15.9	11.2	29.8	0.7	4.9	982.5	10,839	575.8
Miami Gardens	0.0	5.4	0.0	0.0	0.0	41.0	0.0	8.1	1.7	8.9	160.8	1,433	12.4
Miami Lakes	0.0	14.9	0.0	0.0	0.0	29.8	0.0	18.0	0.0	2.9	8.6	281	0.2
Miramar	0.0	1.5	0.0	0.0	4.7	28.6	6.4	10.4	1.0	3.3	213.8	1,525	2.2
New Smyrna Beach	0.0	8.3	0.2	0.0	0.0	11.3	24.2	17.6	0.0	1.4	23.3	879	2.0
North Lauderdale	0.0	4.0	0.0	0.0	0.0	23.2	19.3	12.8	0.8	0.3	1.7	38	0.0
North Miami	0.0	6.6	0.0	0.0	0.0	26.8	21.1	11.5	0.6	1.4	18.7	302	0.0
North Miami Beach	0.0	2.5	0.0	0.0	0.0	26.2	20.3	3.6	0.0	1.0	99.0	2,310	6.2
North Port	0.3	22.8	0.0	0.0	4.2	15.6	20.8	2.8	0.0	0.7	70.2	1,059	0.4
Oakland Park	0.0	7.0	0.0	0.0	0.0	23.0	17.8	8.3	0.0	1.4	56.6	1,261	0.7
Ocala	0.0	7.8	2.7	0.0	0.0	20.0	22.4	7.4	1.3	0.5	173.3	2,932	0.0
Ocoee	0.0	3.2	0.0	0.0	0.0	20.0	18.1	3.8	0.0	1.5	38.8	833	0.0
Orlando	0.0	2.2	1.6	0.0	0.0	17.5	12.6	12.6	1.1	5.9	1,241.5	4,406	131.3
Ormond Beach	0.0	7.8	0.0	0.0	0.0	13.0	25.8	12.5	0.0	0.5	45.0	1,053	0.0
Oviedo	0.0	21.1	0.0	0.0	8.6	16.8	12.3	9.1	0.0	1.3	74.1	1,817	2.2

1. Based on population estimated as of July 1 of the year shown.

STATE Place code	City	Land area[1] (sq. mi)	Population, 2021: Total persons 2021	Population, 2021: Rank	Population, 2021: Per square mile	Race 2020, Race alone[2] (percent): White	Black or African American	American Indian, Alaskan Native	Asian	Hawaiian Pacific Islander	Some other race	Two or more races (percent)
		1	2	3	4	5	6	7	8	9	10	11
	FLORIDA—Cont'd											
12 54000	Palm Bay	86.4	122,942	232	1,422.9	60.9	17.9	0.4	2.0	0.1	5.9	12.9
12 54075	Palm Beach Gardens	58.7	59,449	655	1,012.8	79.6	3.9	0.2	4.5	0.0	2.6	9.2
12 54200	Palm Coast	95.4	93,833	358	983.6	72.9	10.8	0.3	2.5	0.1	3.5	9.9
12 54450	Palm Springs	4.2	26,780	1,450	6,376.2	34.7	14.2	1.6	1.8	0.1	18.8	28.9
12 54700	Panama City	35.1	34,045	1,166	969.9	63.5	19.2	0.6	2.2	0.1	4.9	9.6
12 55125	Parkland	12.5	35,265	1,131	2,821.2	64.5	6.1	0.1	8.9	0.0	3.6	16.8
12 55775	Pembroke Pines	32.7	169,391	157	5,180.2	32.1	20.3	0.3	5.7	0.1	11.0	30.5
12 55925	Pensacola	22.8	53,678	742	2,354.3	66.2	22.4	0.4	2.5	0.1	1.4	7.0
12 56975	Pinellas Park	16.1	53,202	752	3,304.5	67.3	6.9	0.4	9.8	0.1	5.1	10.4
12 57425	Plantation	21.8	92,986	363	4,265.4	47.9	21.3	0.3	4.6	0.0	6.9	19.0
12 57550	Plant City	28.2	39,653	999	1,406.1	54.8	13.9	0.6	1.6	0.1	12.8	16.2
12 58050	Pompano Beach	24.0	111,348	274	4,639.5	45.4	28.6	0.6	1.6	0.0	9.1	14.7
12 58575	Port Orange	26.8	63,486	604	2,368.9	83.0	4.0	0.3	3.2	0.1	2.1	7.3
12 58715	Port St. Lucie	119.2	217,523	105	1,824.9	58.0	18.5	0.4	2.2	0.1	6.8	14.1
12 60975	Riviera Beach	8.3	38,074	1,046	4,587.2	24.5	61.7	0.3	3.0	0.0	3.4	7.0
12 61500	Rockledge	13.2	28,316	1,374	2,145.2	70.6	13.6	0.4	2.3	0.1	2.7	10.2
12 62100	Royal Palm Beach	11.3	39,043	1,016	3,455.1	47.8	22.7	0.3	5.0	0.0	7.2	16.9
12 62625	St. Cloud	25.5	62,043	621	2,433.1	51.4	7.0	0.5	2.0	0.1	15.2	23.9
12 63000	St. Petersburg	61.9	258,201	86	4,171.3	64.2	21.0	0.3	3.5	0.1	2.5	8.4
12 63650	Sanford	23.6	60,681	637	2,571.2	43.0	26.6	0.5	5.1	0.1	9.9	14.8
12 64175	Sarasota	14.7	54,764	728	3,725.4	66.2	12.4	0.5	3.1	0.1	7.4	10.4
12 64825	Sebastian	14.0	25,703	1,507	1,835.9	83.5	4.7	0.2	1.4	0.0	2.3	7.9
12 69700	Sunrise	16.2	96,021	343	5,927.2	32.7	32.0	0.2	4.2	0.1	9.4	21.4
12 70600	Tallahassee	101.9	197,102	128	1,934.3	50.5	35.0	0.3	4.5	0.1	2.2	7.5
12 70675	Tamarac	11.6	71,541	517	6,167.3	36.5	32.8	0.3	3.2	0.0	9.0	18.1
12 71000	Tampa	114.0	387,050	52	3,395.2	49.7	21.9	0.4	5.4	0.1	7.6	14.8
12 71150	Tarpon Springs	9.3	25,560	1,515	2,748.4	80.9	6.3	0.3	1.4	0.1	3.0	7.9
12 71400	Temple Terrace	7.5	27,013	1,440	3,601.7	53.1	23.2	0.3	5.8	0.1	5.0	12.4
12 71900	Titusville	29.2	48,874	816	1,673.8	72.5	13.6	0.4	1.9	0.1	2.5	9.0
12 73900	Venice	16.1	26,047	1,491	1,617.8	93.1	0.7	0.2	1.0	0.0	1.0	3.9
12 75812	Wellington	45.0	61,448	627	1,365.5	61.5	10.9	0.2	5.3	0.0	5.4	16.8
12 76500	West Melbourne	10.7	27,830	1,397	2,600.9	72.1	5.5	0.4	7.5	0.1	3.2	11.3
12 76582	Weston	24.6	67,312	559	2,736.3	41.3	3.7	0.3	7.0	0.0	8.4	39.3
12 76600	West Palm Beach	53.8	117,286	243	2,180.0	43.3	31.6	0.8	2.5	0.0	8.6	13.1
12 78250	Winter Garden	16.3	46,502	856	2,852.9	56.6	12.8	0.3	5.9	0.1	8.3	16.1
12 78275	Winter Haven	32.8	52,710	756	1,607.0	51.8	25.3	0.4	2.5	0.0	8.7	11.2
12 78300	Winter Park	8.8	29,131	1,343	3,310.3	76.7	7.2	0.2	3.6	0.0	2.7	9.6
12 78325	Winter Springs	14.9	38,317	1,038	2,571.6	70.0	6.7	0.3	3.6	0.1	5.6	13.7
13 00000	GEORGIA	57,716.3	10,799,566	X	187.1	51.9	31.0	0.5	4.5	0.1	5.2	6.9
13 01052	Albany	55.1	69,048	546	1,253.1	20.1	74.9	0.2	0.8	0.0	1.2	2.8
13 01696	Alpharetta	26.9	66,127	578	2,458.3	57.2	10.3	0.3	20.1	0.0	3.6	8.5
13 03436	Athens-Clarke County	116.3	127,358	216	1,095.1	58.2	24.6	0.5	3.9	0.1	6.1	6.7
13 04000	Atlanta	135.3	496,461	38	3,669.3	39.8	47.2	0.3	4.5	0.0	2.4	5.8
13 04200	Augusta-Richmond County	302.3	201,196	121	665.6	34.4	55.3	0.3	1.9	0.2	2.3	5.6
13 10944	Brookhaven	11.7	55,366	716	4,732.1	57.9	11.6	1.1	7.3	0.0	12.3	9.9
13 12988	Canton	18.3	34,576	1,154	1,889.4	65.3	9.8	1.4	1.1	0.0	11.5	11.0
13 13492	Carrollton	22.5	27,493	1,414	1,221.9	50.7	32.0	0.6	1.7	0.0	8.1	6.9
13 15172	Chamblee	7.7	29,781	1,316	3,867.7	35.0	13.8	2.3	8.7	0.0	28.3	11.9
13 19000	Columbus	216.5	205,617	115	949.7	39.9	46.5	0.4	2.7	0.3	3.2	7.1
13 21380	Dalton	21.1	34,285	1,162	1,624.9	46.1	6.5	3.3	2.5	0.1	25.8	15.8
13 23900	Douglasville	22.9	35,561	1,119	1,552.9	21.5	65.2	0.4	1.9	0.1	4.6	6.4
13 24600	Duluth	10.2	31,864	1,242	3,123.9	34.2	22.0	0.4	24.9	0.1	8.2	10.2
13 24768	Dunwoody	13.0	50,901	784	3,915.5	55.5	11.9	0.5	17.1	0.0	6.4	8.4
13 25720	East Point	14.7	38,141	1,042	2,594.6	10.3	76.8	0.5	0.7	0.0	6.2	5.4
13 31908	Gainesville	33.4	43,417	920	1,299.9	48.1	14.6	1.1	3.5	0.1	20.2	12.5
13 38964	Hinesville	18.3	35,420	1,122	1,935.5	31.1	49.9	0.4	2.6	1.0	4.5	10.5
13 42425	Johns Creek	30.8	82,065	427	2,664.4	49.0	10.6	0.2	29.9	0.0	2.6	7.8
13 43192	Kennesaw	9.7	33,049	1,189	3,407.1	54.4	24.3	0.4	5.0	0.1	5.4	10.4
13 44340	LaGrange	42.1	31,551	1,255	749.4	36.6	51.0	0.3	3.8	0.0	4.1	4.0
13 45488	Lawrenceville	13.7	30,516	1,293	2,227.4	29.7	35.1	1.1	7.6	0.0	14.9	11.5
13 48624	McDonough	12.9	30,356	1,298	2,353.2	18.0	70.2	0.3	2.1	0.1	3.1	6.1
13 49008	Macon-Bibb County	249.4	156,762	165	628.6	36.7	54.6	0.2	2.1	0.0	2.4	4.0
13 49756	Marietta	23.5	61,497	626	2,616.9	45.1	29.3	1.2	2.9	0.1	11.3	10.1
13 51670	Milton	38.5	41,259	956	1,071.7	63.9	9.6	0.3	15.6	0.0	2.1	8.5
13 55020	Newnan	19.5	43,298	924	2,220.4	51.7	31.1	0.3	4.5	0.1	4.9	7.4
13 59724	Peachtree City	25.1	38,818	1,024	1,546.5	71.4	8.5	0.2	9.0	0.0	2.6	8.2
13 59735	Peachtree Corners	16.1	42,108	948	2,615.4	47.4	23.2	0.6	9.4	0.1	9.1	10.3
13 62104	Pooler	27.7	26,930	1,443	972.2	54.3	26.9	0.5	6.0	0.2	4.1	8.0
13 66668	Rome	31.7	37,746	1,053	1,190.7	50.3	26.9	1.2	2.0	0.0	9.9	9.7

1. Dry land or land partially or temporarily covered by water. 2. Hispanic or Latino persons may be of any race.

City	Percent Hispanic or Latino[1], 2020	Percent foreign born, 2016–2020	Age of population (percent), 2016–2020: Under 18 years	18 to 24 years	25 to 34 years	35 to 44 years	45 to 54 years	55 to 64 years	65 years and over	Median age, 2016–2020	Percent female, 2016–2020	Population: Census counts: 2010	2020	Percent change: 2010–2020	2020–2021
	12	13	14	15	16	17	18	19	20	21	22	23	24	25	26
FLORIDA—Cont'd															
Palm Bay	17.9	13.4	22.2	7.8	12.8	12.0	10.6	15.8	18.8	40.6	50.8	104,006	119,874	15.3	2.6
Palm Beach Gardens	11.4	15.0	16.9	4.4	10.4	11.7	11.8	14.9	29.9	51.0	54.4	49,906	59,218	18.7	0.4
Palm Coast	12.3	14.2	17.7	6.8	9.7	10.3	12.0	14.4	29.0	49.3	52.5	75,203	89,310	18.8	5.1
Palm Springs	60.2	48.1	23.5	9.5	15.2	14.4	16.6	10.0	10.9	36.2	49.8	23,166	26,972	16.4	-0.7
Panama City	10.7	6.9	21.5	8.8	14.6	11.0	13.4	12.4	18.3	39.8	54.4	34,632	32,967	-4.8	3.3
Parkland	18.5	23.4	33.5	5.3	6.3	14.9	17.1	11.5	11.5	38.3	48.4	22,523	34,664	53.9	1.7
Pembroke Pines	49.7	37.3	20.1	8.5	12.4	13.1	14.1	13.3	18.4	42.2	52.6	154,898	171,163	10.5	-1.0
Pensacola	5.2	3.7	23.2	7.3	17.0	10.3	10.3	13.6	18.3	36.8	52.2	52,015	54,394	4.6	-1.3
Pinellas Park	13.8	16.1	18.7	5.7	13.7	13.2	12.2	14.6	22.0	43.6	52.9	49,568	53,116	7.2	0.2
Plantation	28.0	31.5	21.1	7.0	14.5	13.2	14.7	13.2	16.3	40.3	51.7	84,883	91,736	8.1	1.4
Plant City	33.9	13.4	25.2	8.2	15.8	14.6	12.6	11.4	12.4	35.7	53.1	34,712	39,794	14.6	-0.4
Pompano Beach	23.8	29.6	19.1	6.8	15.6	11.7	12.7	14.7	19.3	42.1	47.2	99,752	112,117	12.4	-0.7
Port Orange	7.3	8.4	17.7	8.5	11.4	11.1	12.6	14.1	24.6	45.7	50.9	56,621	62,872	11.0	1.0
Port St. Lucie	21.8	18.1	21.7	7.6	12.0	11.9	13.5	12.8	20.5	42.7	51.0	164,200	204,913	24.8	6.2
Riviera Beach	10.7	20.5	23.3	7.9	15.3	10.5	10.8	14.9	17.4	37.4	51.6	32,540	37,606	15.6	1.2
Rockledge	10.2	5.6	18.0	6.8	9.9	12.8	14.3	16.7	21.5	47.2	50.3	24,916	27,688	11.1	2.3
Royal Palm Beach	27.0	27.7	23.3	7.7	12.9	12.8	13.3	14.8	15.3	39.9	53.1	34,196	39,048	14.2	0.0
St. Cloud	47.6	10.0	28.5	8.3	11.7	15.3	12.8	10.7	12.6	36.0	52.7	37,793	58,973	56.0	5.2
St. Petersburg	9.0	10.0	16.6	8.1	15.4	12.3	13.3	15.1	19.3	43.1	51.5	245,173	258,277	5.3	0.0
Sanford	27.6	15.7	24.1	7.6	18.8	14.9	11.1	10.7	12.8	34.7	49.6	53,925	60,795	12.7	-0.2
Sarasota	17.9	16.7	14.6	7.3	13.5	10.0	11.8	14.7	28.0	48.9	52.5	52,106	54,108	3.8	1.2
Sebastian	8.9	6.7	14.4	4.2	8.5	6.9	13.0	17.5	35.5	57.0	51.6	21,941	25,084	14.3	2.5
Sunrise	35.0	41.2	20.4	7.9	13.6	13.5	11.5	13.8	19.3	40.9	53.2	84,297	97,313	15.4	-1.3
Tallahassee	8.5	7.4	16.8	28.3	16.8	10.0	9.0	8.7	10.4	27.2	52.9	181,049	196,068	8.3	0.5
Tamarac	30.4	35.1	17.1	6.3	11.1	11.8	12.9	13.5	27.2	47.8	54.2	60,781	71,891	18.3	-0.5
Tampa	25.6	17.8	21.4	10.2	17.2	13.5	13.2	11.8	12.7	35.9	50.7	336,249	382,769	13.8	1.1
Tarpon Springs	9.1	13.6	15.7	5.8	8.4	8.9	13.8	17.2	30.2	53.3	52.4	23,507	25,138	6.9	1.7
Temple Terrace	17.8	15.7	19.3	14.4	17.8	12.0	9.7	11.8	15.0	34.1	48.8	24,585	26,684	8.5	1.2
Titusville	9.6	4.9	18.7	7.6	13.7	9.0	12.0	15.4	23.5	45.6	54.1	43,687	48,791	11.7	0.2
Venice	3.7	9.5	6.4	3.6	3.2	3.6	7.4	13.9	61.9	68.7	54.6	20,800	25,290	21.6	3.0
Wellington	24.2	23.6	25.0	7.6	10.1	12.0	15.5	12.7	17.1	41.2	52.3	56,697	61,854	9.1	-0.7
West Melbourne	12.4	11.2	23.2	7.7	10.3	11.2	14.2	11.7	21.8	41.9	49.6	18,289	25,877	41.5	7.5
Weston	54.1	46.3	28.6	8.2	6.5	13.4	19.6	12.9	10.7	41.2	52.3	65,427	68,094	4.1	-1.1
West Palm Beach	24.6	26.6	17.6	10.3	16.6	12.1	12.0	12.1	19.2	39.1	51.8	100,670	117,151	16.4	0.1
Winter Garden	22.4	25.4	24.4	7.7	11.1	14.9	17.2	10.7	14.1	40.4	53.0	34,764	46,998	35.2	-1.1
Winter Haven	23.4	8.3	20.7	6.9	12.9	10.1	12.6	11.5	25.5	44.6	52.7	34,643	50,247	45.0	4.9
Winter Park	11.8	11.0	17.3	10.4	11.8	10.0	13.4	14.8	22.3	45.3	53.9	27,724	29,784	7.4	-2.2
Winter Springs	20.5	10.2	17.9	7.3	14.0	13.2	13.2	15.2	19.3	43.3	50.1	33,306	38,484	15.5	-0.4
GEORGIA	10.5	10.2	23.8	9.6	13.9	13.2	13.4	12.2	13.9	36.9	51.4	9,688,737	10,711,908	10.6	0.8
Albany	2.4	1.8	24.0	12.7	14.4	11.6	10.6	11.5	15.2	34.4	54.1	77,430	69,832	-9.8	-1.1
Alpharetta	9.3	29.1	25.7	6.5	10.5	14.8	18.3	14.1	10.1	39.9	50.0	57,383	65,852	14.8	0.4
Athens-Clarke County	11.1	9.5	17.3	26.0	16.5	11.3	9.0	9.0	10.9	28.3	52.4	115,370	127,320	10.4	0.0
Atlanta	6.0	8.0	17.6	13.9	21.8	13.8	11.6	9.7	11.6	33.2	51.3	427,042	498,602	16.8	-0.4
Augusta-Richmond County	5.5	3.5	22.9	11.4	16.4	11.6	11.1	12.6	13.9	34.4	51.6	195,862	202,123	3.2	-0.5
Brookhaven	22.1	19.9	22.3	6.8	22.0	16.8	11.8	10.2	10.1	34.4	51.0	49,895	55,143	10.5	0.4
Canton	24.5	15.9	25.4	10.1	15.5	15.3	11.5	8.9	13.2	34.4	49.7	23,522	32,951	40.1	4.9
Carrollton	14.3	6.3	20.6	24.0	15.4	10.1	10.8	7.1	11.9	27.5	54.0	24,379	27,118	11.2	1.4
Chamblee	43.5	31.8	23.9	7.1	22.6	16.9	12.5	8.0	9.0	33.3	47.4	26,993	30,133	11.6	-1.2
Columbus	8.0	5.2	24.7	9.9	16.2	12.7	11.4	11.7	13.3	34.4	51.3	190,570	206,922	8.6	-0.6
Dalton	50.8	26.7	25.7	12.2	13.9	12.3	12.0	11.8	12.0	33.6	51.4	33,104	34,348	3.8	-0.2
Douglasville	9.1	8.9	24.5	9.7	13.7	15.4	13.8	11.5	11.6	36.7	55.2	29,892	34,698	16.1	2.5
Duluth	16.9	34.2	23.3	6.8	13.1	15.2	15.5	14.7	11.3	40.2	53.9	26,672	31,908	19.6	-0.1
Dunwoody	12.8	21.4	25.9	5.8	14.9	16.8	13.0	9.1	14.5	36.7	52.1	46,428	51,629	11.2	-1.4
East Point	10.5	5.6	23.5	9.2	17.6	14.3	12.6	11.9	10.8	34.8	54.4	33,452	38,384	14.7	-0.6
Gainesville	37.0	23.4	26.6	11.5	14.7	12.4	9.7	9.6	15.5	32.6	54.1	34,045	42,339	24.4	2.5
Hinesville	13.1	7.6	29.0	11.2	21.4	12.5	9.6	8.8	7.5	29.0	51.7	33,309	35,265	5.9	0.4
Johns Creek	7.0	31.0	26.6	6.6	7.8	15.2	18.5	14.7	10.5	41.6	50.9	76,639	82,499	7.6	-0.5
Kennesaw	12.9	16.2	23.3	12.4	15.9	13.7	13.2	11.2	10.3	34.1	52.2	30,618	33,001	7.8	0.1
LaGrange	6.1	5.5	25.5	10.9	14.8	11.8	12.2	11.6	13.2	34.1	54.4	29,365	30,917	5.3	2.1
Lawrenceville	27.9	24.0	25.5	9.9	18.7	13.1	11.3	9.4	12.0	32.9	51.6	27,215	30,436	11.8	0.3
McDonough	6.7	9.2	27.8	13.1	15.4	13.8	12.0	8.9	8.9	29.9	53.6	21,800	29,182	33.9	4.0
Macon-Bibb County	4.3	3.2	24.3	10.3	13.9	11.5	11.8	12.7	15.6	36.3	53.0	155,844	157,346	1.0	-0.4
Marietta	20.5	16.6	21.8	11.7	16.1	15.1	11.4	10.6	13.2	35.2	49.9	56,369	60,969	8.2	0.9
Milton	7.3	18.9	28.7	4.8	10.5	14.7	19.7	13.7	8.0	39.3	49.3	32,828	41,318	25.9	-0.1
Newnan	10.6	10.6	25.3	8.4	15.0	15.1	13.0	11.0	12.3	35.8	54.0	32,874	42,383	28.9	2.2
Peachtree City	7.8	12.8	24.8	6.3	7.6	12.6	15.1	14.6	19.1	44.2	52.7	34,409	38,248	11.2	1.5
Peachtree Corners	18.1	18.0	22.1	10.7	16.7	13.6	11.9	12.8	12.2	35.3	50.7	38,006	42,309	11.3	-0.5
Pooler	9.3	11.6	23.4	8.8	13.7	16.6	13.9	12.2	11.4	36.6	52.0	18,491	25,560	38.2	5.4
Rome	19.7	13.1	24.8	9.0	12.7	13.8	12.5	11.6	15.6	37.8	54.1	36,417	37,719	3.6	0.1

1. May be of any race.

City	Households, 2016–2020							Persons in group quarters, 2016–2020	Serious crimes known to police[2], 2020				Educational attainment, 2016–2020		
			Percent						Violent		Property			Attainment[4] (percent)	
	Number	Persons per household	Family	Married couple family	Female family	Non-family	One person		Number	Rate	Number	Rate	Population age 25 and over	High school graduate or less	Bachelor's degree or more
	27	28	29	30	31	32	33	34	35	36	37	38	39	40	41
FLORIDA—Cont'd															
Palm Bay	39,109	2.90	68.7	50.0	13.3	31.3	25.6	519	328	280.6	1,770	1,514.2	79,643	43.4	19.6
Palm Beach Gardens	24,359	2.32	63.7	53.4	7.7	36.3	30.1	458	65	110.9	999	1,703.9	44,836	18.4	54.8
Palm Coast	33,264	2.65	73.6	57.7	11.6	26.4	20.7	189	NA	NA	NA	NA	66,568	42.3	23.2
Palm Springs	8,066	3.11	70.2	38.9	22.9	29.8	22.6	123	288	1,131.6	784	3,080.4	16,872	57.4	16.5
Panama City	15,733	2.25	56.3	33.9	17.4	43.7	36.4	623	303	873.9	1,453	4,190.7	25,079	38.7	25.3
Parkland	9,819	3.35	86.8	77.1	7.9	13.2	10.8	10	8	22.4	201	561.9	20,137	16.6	63.0
Pembroke Pines	60,210	2.84	68.4	49.9	14.0	31.6	26.1	717	209	118.9	2,495	1,419.6	122,727	36.2	33.6
Pensacola	22,926	2.29	53.4	35.7	14.3	46.6	36.7	503	327	616.0	1,543	2,906.8	36,783	28.6	40.0
Pinellas Park	20,746	2.54	59.5	42.6	10.2	40.5	32.6	886	187	345.6	1,788	3,304.1	40,478	46.7	23.0
Plantation	34,532	2.72	65.8	47.5	12.9	34.2	26.5	359	199	208.0	1,942	2,029.9	67,810	25.8	45.4
Plant City	14,223	2.76	66.4	46.6	14.3	33.6	27.0	176	199	493.4	906	2,246.5	26,296	49.1	22.7
Pompano Beach	42,757	2.50	55.8	35.9	13.9	44.2	35.9	4,240	837	737.2	3,142	2,767.2	82,336	45.7	26.5
Port Orange	26,547	2.40	61.2	47.6	8.7	38.8	30.0	174	50	76.0	953	1,447.7	47,119	35.4	28.1
Port St. Lucie	68,241	2.86	75.0	56.8	13.3	25.0	19.7	693	264	127.9	1,666	807.0	138,440	42.8	23.4
Riviera Beach	12,045	2.88	61.6	32.8	21.8	38.4	31.1	322	428	1,195.6	1,174	3,279.5	24,106	47.1	25.5
Rockledge	10,768	2.55	69.5	54.1	10.8	30.5	25.8	263	60	209.7	343	1,198.7	20,856	33.5	31.0
Royal Palm Beach	12,398	3.19	78.3	59.7	14.9	21.7	17.2	114	85	206.6	637	1,548.3	27,363	34.2	33.7
St. Cloud	15,986	3.29	71.9	49.4	16.6	28.1	22.7	557	99	174.2	599	1,054.1	33,565	40.2	22.1
St. Petersburg	111,957	2.30	53.1	37.6	11.2	46.9	37.4	6,226	1,772	662.0	6,841	2,555.6	198,834	31.7	37.1
Sanford	22,236	2.66	63.3	40.4	17.2	36.7	28.8	1,185	511	819.7	1,396	2,239.3	41,219	41.0	25.4
Sarasota	25,209	2.15	49.5	35.0	11.7	50.5	41.7	3,539	349	591.5	1,622	2,749.1	45,151	36.8	37.2
Sebastian	10,684	2.39	62.6	55.5	4.7	37.4	32.2	49	21	78.9	155	582.1	20,843	42.5	27.1
Sunrise	34,356	2.73	63.6	44.2	14.2	36.4	31.4	727	195	202.2	1,324	1,373.0	67,871	38.0	29.1
Tallahassee	78,283	2.28	44.2	27.7	12.9	55.8	36.5	14,357	1,516	773.4	5,786	2,951.9	105,902	24.2	48.4
Tamarac	27,330	2.42	56.5	34.9	15.5	43.5	38.2	291	146	216.6	1,009	1,497.1	50,836	41.3	26.8
Tampa	156,705	2.45	54.4	35.1	14.0	45.6	35.8	11,742	2,119	520.2	5,561	1,365.2	270,708	36.6	39.9
Tarpon Springs	10,971	2.27	56.4	44.9	9.7	43.6	38.1	482	109	422.2	348	1,347.9	19,919	37.7	31.3
Temple Terrace	10,490	2.51	53.9	37.9	11.0	46.1	33.3	557	72	267.8	483	1,796.2	17,844	28.1	42.7
Titusville	18,930	2.42	58.2	43.4	10.7	41.8	34.4	521	295	628.7	1,081	2,304.0	34,124	40.8	23.0
Venice	12,521	1.84	54.4	49.4	3.7	45.6	38.8	477	16	65.7	346	1,420.0	21,220	31.0	42.4
Wellington	21,495	3.02	77.5	62.8	9.0	22.5	17.5	5	67	100.9	489	736.1	43,766	26.0	44.6
West Melbourne	8,941	2.59	59.6	48.7	8.3	40.4	34.3	306	48	191.8	385	1,538.8	16,210	28.1	38.7
Weston	21,297	3.33	88.5	75.4	9.5	11.5	9.5	0	36	50.1	307	427.5	44,850	14.2	64.3
West Palm Beach	43,849	2.46	51.9	33.1	13.0	48.1	38.4	3,239	863	761.9	3,862	3,409.6	80,028	36.6	35.6
Winter Garden	15,089	2.94	77.2	58.8	13.0	22.8	18.9	488	153	322.2	810	1,705.8	30,496	34.1	41.5
Winter Haven	15,423	2.74	66.5	43.4	17.4	33.5	28.1	676	171	369.5	920	1,988.1	31,104	48.4	19.4
Winter Park	13,072	2.22	54.0	41.0	8.2	46.0	37.3	1,701	87	279.0	685	2,196.7	22,229	16.1	62.1
Winter Springs	14,949	2.46	68.8	53.5	10.1	31.2	26.9	41	66	174.7	285	754.2	27,581	17.5	49.6
GEORGIA	3,830,264	2.68	67.0	47.4	14.9	33.0	27.3	262,691	42,850	400.1	214,988	2,007.4	6,996,425	39.6	32.2
Albany	28,184	2.42	56.8	25.8	26.1	43.2	38.1	4,414	1,234	1,724.3	3,148	4,398.7	46,028	46.2	20.8
Alpharetta	23,958	2.76	74.3	63.2	8.1	25.7	20.4	323	151	221.0	689	1,008.4	45,100	12.4	69.9
Athens-Clarke County	50,284	2.30	48.3	30.8	13.4	51.7	34.3	11,411	NA	NA	NA	NA	72,056	30.4	45.4
Atlanta	215,179	2.14	42.5	24.7	14.3	57.5	46.0	37,476	NA	NA	NA	NA	340,883	26.9	53.4
Augusta-Richmond County	72,526	2.65	59.1	33.0	21.6	40.9	35.0	9,973	NA	NA	NA	NA	132,953	46.3	22.5
Brookhaven	23,203	2.32	52.4	42.4	7.3	47.6	36.4	815	222	394.7	1,412	2,510.3	38,788	19.8	69.6
Canton	10,340	2.83	68.8	50.7	12.4	31.2	22.6	233	NA	NA	NA	NA	18,985	40.3	27.8
Carrollton	9,293	2.55	63.0	36.1	20.9	37.0	27.1	3,138	NA	NA	NA	NA	14,890	41.5	32.5
Chamblee	11,710	2.54	50.5	34.6	10.4	49.5	36.1	136	NA	NA	NA	NA	20,611	38.0	45.5
Columbus	73,648	2.56	60.9	37.7	18.9	39.1	34.2	6,996	NA	NA	NA	NA	127,636	38.3	27.5
Dalton	11,777	2.72	66.8	39.5	17.9	33.2	28.2	1,449	NA	NA	NA	NA	20,806	58.0	20.2
Douglasville	12,672	2.52	63.8	36.9	24.3	36.2	29.5	1,088	195	566.7	1,792	5,207.9	21,734	32.1	36.6
Duluth	11,195	2.63	66.9	50.5	12.0	33.1	27.7	74	50	167.0	414	1,382.5	20,640	23.3	50.8
Dunwoody	20,628	2.40	59.6	50.0	7.2	40.4	35.6	29	83	167.0	1,386	2,789.5	33,766	12.3	71.9
East Point	14,782	2.33	48.6	20.7	23.4	51.4	43.5	518	NA	NA	NA	NA	23,575	37.2	35.1
Gainesville	14,156	2.85	63.3	41.4	17.9	36.7	29.1	1,106	184	414.4	1,116	2,513.6	25,668	49.2	25.3
Hinesville	13,302	2.48	69.9	44.3	20.9	30.1	26.2	305	NA	NA	NA	NA	19,924	31.8	20.7
Johns Creek	28,748	2.93	80.2	68.7	8.8	19.8	17.2	242	33	38.6	384	449.6	56,485	13.2	68.6
Kennesaw	13,030	2.62	68.0	50.1	16.3	32.0	24.2	91	NA	NA	NA	NA	22,017	27.6	44.8
LaGrange	11,309	2.63	60.8	32.3	24.1	39.2	34.7	802	176	578.8	1,729	5,686.4	19,394	49.6	22.2
Lawrenceville	10,672	2.79	65.8	38.9	21.7	34.2	29.6	326	NA	NA	NA	NA	19,439	41.1	25.6
McDonough	8,036	3.06	68.5	42.2	22.6	31.5	26.7	955	88	321.9	714	2,611.7	15,114	35.5	29.2
Macon-Bibb County	58,154	2.53	59.6	35.4	19.9	40.4	35.3	6,075	NA	NA	NA	NA	100,107	44.6	25.3
Marietta	24,148	2.39	56.1	37.5	14.5	43.9	35.3	3,040	301	490.6	1,802	2,937.3	40,355	30.4	44.0
Milton	14,248	2.75	76.6	67.4	7.0	23.4	20.8	5	15	37.2	207	512.8	26,119	12.0	72.3
Newnan	15,234	2.61	64.0	45.0	17.3	36.0	30.2	472	532	1,247.1	837	1,962.1	26,645	33.2	36.1
Peachtree City	13,705	2.60	72.9	61.7	8.9	27.1	23.8	166	16	43.9	388	1,065.3	24,717	16.0	58.9
Peachtree Corners	17,093	2.55	62.9	48.3	10.7	37.1	32.3	2	NA	NA	NA	NA	29,223	24.3	51.4
Pooler	9,452	2.59	62.7	49.4	9.3	37.3	29.6	70	36	135.2	537	2,016.2	16,654	26.5	35.2
Rome	14,227	2.46	62.0	39.6	18.1	38.0	34.0	1,526	NA	NA	NA	NA	24,166	47.6	25.7

2. Data for serious crimes have not been adjusted for underreporting. This may affect comparability between geographic areas and over time.

4. Persons 25 years old and over.

City	Money income, 2016–2020					Median earnings Full year, Full-time workers, 2016–2020			Housing units, 2016–2020				
	Households												
	Median household income	Percent with income less than $25,000	Percent with income of $200,000 or more	Median family income	Median non-family household income	All persons	Men	Women	Total	Occupied	Percent owner occupied	Median value[1] (dollars)	Median gross rent (dollars)
	42	43	44	45	46	47	48	49	50	51	52	53	54
FLORIDA—Cont'd													
Palm Bay	52,435	19.5	3.0	59,498	31,391	36,101	40,865	32,482	43,771	39,109	76.9	172,200	1,101
Palm Beach Gardens	89,736	12.4	20.4	119,002	53,847	60,501	73,332	53,264	29,775	24,359	74.7	395,300	1,808
Palm Coast	57,872	16.6	3.7	64,172	38,493	40,284	42,152	37,112	37,747	33,264	74.6	226,100	1,374
Palm Springs	47,808	20.4	1.5	50,658	37,697	35,039	35,508	33,571	9,291	8,066	43.9	160,400	1,228
Panama City	48,185	25.4	3.5	61,239	32,297	40,362	42,590	36,763	17,788	15,733	52.5	169,100	964
Parkland	159,692	5.2	39.1	166,717	74,145	100,129	104,059	79,736	10,364	9,819	83.3	631,000	2,670
Pembroke Pines	68,683	18.5	6.3	85,697	39,583	47,656	51,999	43,479	65,001	60,210	70.6	302,900	1,564
Pensacola	56,199	21.1	6.0	75,548	39,564	47,658	53,357	42,336	25,912	22,926	61.6	199,300	998
Pinellas Park	50,546	24.3	2.6	62,813	31,500	41,034	44,818	38,530	24,130	20,746	68.0	169,000	1,126
Plantation	75,780	13.4	9.4	86,673	51,831	50,429	54,248	46,831	38,006	34,532	64.4	343,000	1,735
Plant City	54,933	18.4	2.6	65,772	34,080	40,470	42,889	36,143	15,337	14,223	60.0	179,100	1,056
Pompano Beach	52,565	23.0	4.8	59,483	40,028	40,649	41,794	38,468	55,421	42,757	52.9	227,600	1,314
Port Orange	56,242	20.5	2.9	74,539	31,814	43,813	50,977	37,215	30,123	26,547	72.5	202,800	1,214
Port St. Lucie	62,380	14.7	4.3	66,834	40,736	41,440	45,905	36,384	75,749	68,241	78.8	224,400	1,485
Riviera Beach	48,228	26.4	4.9	61,374	33,310	37,599	40,758	35,029	16,380	12,045	54.7	218,300	1,209
Rockledge	70,028	13.9	4.6	79,275	46,366	47,487	44,004	48,945	12,471	10,768	80.9	226,800	1,333
Royal Palm Beach	83,636	7.9	7.0	92,129	52,070	51,890	55,453	44,940	13,745	12,398	81.3	284,600	1,708
St. Cloud	58,623	16.1	2.6	65,022	36,354	40,976	41,742	39,741	19,678	15,986	70.3	218,800	1,193
St. Petersburg	60,798	18.0	7.1	81,434	41,073	46,131	48,845	43,663	138,225	111,957	62.4	222,900	1,168
Sanford	52,664	22.5	2.7	60,621	35,765	40,676	42,323	37,620	24,340	22,236	51.2	176,600	1,171
Sarasota	56,093	21.4	8.4	72,828	40,003	39,701	42,984	36,291	31,885	25,209	58.0	291,500	1,177
Sebastian	54,986	16.7	2.4	67,856	36,288	40,863	41,585	40,199	12,285	10,684	82.5	200,700	1,156
Sunrise	54,701	21.4	3.2	67,637	32,375	42,010	44,224	40,517	38,440	34,356	68.6	220,600	1,617
Tallahassee	46,461	27.5	4.9	69,864	31,844	41,277	44,601	38,794	89,418	78,283	39.7	212,800	1,022
Tamarac	51,799	22.1	2.6	59,199	36,698	41,215	44,547	38,803	30,979	27,330	73.5	186,600	1,449
Tampa	55,634	23.3	9.9	72,497	38,591	46,647	50,366	43,005	174,041	156,705	49.3	254,600	1,178
Tarpon Springs	53,713	24.1	8.4	71,209	30,050	45,583	46,861	42,302	12,917	10,971	75.5	231,900	908
Temple Terrace	56,209	12.6	6.4	72,984	43,750	43,004	46,094	41,250	11,190	10,490	49.7	229,800	1,146
Titusville	48,757	21.7	2.3	61,473	33,801	42,359	50,346	36,274	23,812	18,930	70.9	160,700	967
Venice	61,953	18.7	7.0	81,125	40,044	45,366	55,094	40,234	18,174	12,521	78.3	282,700	1,275
Wellington	90,924	9.1	16.6	103,511	52,301	60,395	75,404	49,778	24,555	21,495	74.2	411,200	1,955
West Melbourne	75,552	11.5	2.9	90,065	45,713	56,810	68,511	47,272	9,856	8,941	79.9	240,800	1,353
Weston	113,032	7.3	24.4	120,124	60,113	68,892	85,786	52,739	24,156	21,297	73.9	505,400	2,229
West Palm Beach	54,603	21.7	5.6	65,519	43,794	41,802	43,460	40,058	54,463	43,849	48.2	263,400	1,381
Winter Garden	85,065	11.4	11.8	97,156	39,174	51,368	66,284	47,648	16,217	15,089	68.7	323,800	1,268
Winter Haven	48,560	23.6	3.8	54,282	32,198	36,625	38,697	33,521	18,624	15,423	60.6	162,400	946
Winter Park	80,500	17.1	19.4	130,120	51,160	69,375	83,738	58,321	14,511	13,072	64.7	470,800	1,372
Winter Springs	76,550	14.0	10.5	96,008	50,478	55,776	66,543	47,541	15,713	14,949	79.5	260,800	1,337
GEORGIA	61,224	19.7	7.1	74,127	37,306	46,648	51,346	41,609	4,329,675	3,830,264	64.0	190,200	1,042
Albany	38,826	36.4	1.6	43,104	27,464	36,397	40,879	33,151	33,621	28,184	40.3	100,300	766
Alpharetta	119,568	8.3	28.9	153,102	70,521	90,177	102,690	70,704	25,457	23,958	67.7	447,400	1,464
Athens-Clarke County	40,363	33.8	3.8	61,621	25,685	39,344	42,372	36,909	53,452	50,284	40.5	186,800	872
Atlanta	64,179	23.8	13.4	84,851	51,840	61,365	70,260	53,300	250,533	215,179	44.8	314,400	1,227
Augusta-Richmond County	43,882	29.7	2.6	53,033	30,851	36,709	41,205	33,323	89,055	72,526	51.6	115,300	908
Brookhaven	101,607	12.3	23.8	149,271	71,677	76,768	80,926	73,286	25,455	23,203	51.6	524,800	1,444
Canton	61,459	19.7	4.1	76,296	37,500	45,563	47,444	40,636	10,986	10,340	50.5	237,800	1,259
Carrollton	44,736	27.8	5.0	63,548	31,477	41,188	45,956	36,315	10,123	9,293	40.0	180,500	837
Chamblee	66,607	16.8	8.4	72,867	61,778	50,622	44,612	53,750	12,690	11,710	38.0	301,500	1,372
Columbus	47,418	27.2	3.9	63,709	29,351	40,909	45,912	35,921	85,012	73,648	49.1	142,900	925
Dalton	46,894	25.4	4.1	56,213	29,409	34,590	34,522	34,826	13,250	11,777	46.9	154,200	714
Douglasville	63,858	18.8	5.7	73,547	41,355	47,545	48,540	45,663	13,655	12,672	47.9	196,400	1,141
Duluth	74,377	13.8	6.8	86,605	55,854	54,954	65,364	49,032	11,713	11,195	56.2	254,200	1,423
Dunwoody	96,470	10.0	19.9	137,492	61,226	82,848	90,926	73,583	22,628	20,628	54.1	446,800	1,457
East Point	45,411	24.5	2.5	55,823	38,005	41,171	41,495	40,986	17,539	14,782	42.8	159,900	1,069
Gainesville	53,662	22.0	5.4	61,032	33,502	31,896	35,092	30,162	16,525	14,156	41.8	230,700	958
Hinesville	48,580	19.1	0.5	51,808	41,244	39,796	41,609	34,918	15,559	13,302	42.8	130,100	1,024
Johns Creek	125,862	6.6	25.5	137,237	64,491	85,940	103,503	59,930	30,211	28,748	75.3	423,600	1,702
Kennesaw	72,972	15.2	6.2	84,314	43,929	51,089	54,248	47,625	13,707	13,030	67.5	215,800	1,347
LaGrange	36,690	34.8	3.0	48,736	22,230	36,742	41,943	31,265	12,927	11,309	40.3	131,700	854
Lawrenceville	52,312	21.7	3.3	65,783	35,942	39,600	41,490	37,744	11,154	10,672	46.5	183,300	1,094
McDonough	69,916	14.9	4.5	73,457	43,242	46,564	52,193	44,380	8,720	8,036	50.0	173,200	1,197
Macon-Bibb County	41,317	31.9	4.0	56,802	26,538	40,326	44,969	36,726	70,138	58,154	51.7	125,300	834
Marietta	59,594	17.2	9.5	76,936	40,502	47,736	50,545	45,021	26,401	24,148	44.0	310,100	1,145
Milton	127,487	8.0	33.7	156,478	71,146	91,268	108,537	71,655	14,645	14,248	75.7	544,600	1,395
Newnan	66,384	16.4	4.6	86,325	41,321	48,061	55,049	39,226	15,879	15,234	55.9	214,600	1,122
Peachtree City	100,768	9.5	19.6	127,601	54,366	80,540	103,595	58,723	14,465	13,705	73.8	353,400	1,509
Peachtree Corners	65,328	13.8	14.1	95,156	40,516	50,278	51,365	49,016	17,805	17,093	52.0	360,100	1,201
Pooler	79,004	6.3	5.9	89,639	62,287	55,013	67,008	50,311	9,978	9,452	56.5	223,500	1,295
Rome	38,987	29.6	4.3	56,335	29,669	36,063	38,663	34,699	15,947	14,227	48.8	158,000	752

City	Commuting, 2016–2020[1]		Computer access[2], 2016–2020		Migration, 2016–2020		Civilian labor force, 2021				Civilian Employment, 2016–2020[4]			
	Percent		Percent						Unemployment[3]		Population age 16 and older		Population age 16 to 64	
	Drove alone	Mean travel time to work	With a computer in the house	With Internet access	Percent who lived in the same house one year ago	Percent who lived in another state or county one year ago	Total	Percent change 2020–2021	Total	Rate	Number	Percent in labor force	Number	Percent who worked full-year full-time
	55	56	57	58	59	60	61	62	63	64	65	66	67	68
FLORIDA—Cont'd														
Palm Bay	84.2	27.5	92.5	88.1	88.9	4.5	56,559	2.8	2,574	4.6	91,926	57.6	70,582	48.5
Palm Beach Gardens	78.5	23.7	96.1	92.8	87.8	5.2	29,824	3.2	948	3.2	48,675	56.6	31,632	54.2
Palm Coast	80.9	26.7	92.2	76.4	88.1	8.8	38,059	2.5	1,766	4.6	74,434	51.2	48,856	48.6
Palm Springs	78.3	27.5	94.4	84.6	84.9	3.9	12,919	2.7	578	4.5	19,921	69.2	17,189	54.2
Panama City	78.3	20.4	91.4	83.0	77.0	7.1	15,900	4.0	742	4.7	29,003	60.3	22,417	49.0
Parkland	74.5	30.4	96.0	95.0	82.3	8.6	18,396	3.6	517	2.8	23,350	62.3	19,569	54.1
Pembroke Pines	84.8	31.7	94.6	85.6	89.1	4.6	91,926	1.2	3,847	4.2	141,250	62.7	109,521	57.7
Pensacola	75.4	20.4	92.6	84.7	80.8	8.3	27,366	1.6	1,045	3.8	41,749	61.7	32,072	51.9
Pinellas Park	82.7	22.4	91.3	83.0	85.2	5.6	27,010	2.0	1,110	4.1	44,504	59.6	32,757	54.9
Plantation	78.7	27.0	96.6	90.5	83.3	6.1	54,614	1.5	2,109	3.9	76,910	68.1	61,496	55.4
Plant City	83.5	26.8	93.5	86.3	83.6	5.7	19,835	2.7	788	4.0	30,703	67.0	25,828	53.9
Pompano Beach	71.3	25.9	90.4	83.3	81.5	6.1	53,182	0.5	3,143	5.9	91,857	60.5	70,406	48.2
Port Orange	81.2	22.8	94.1	85.8	86.5	5.5	31,599	2.8	1,162	3.7	53,972	57.6	38,262	50.0
Port St. Lucie	81.4	28.6	96.1	91.7	88.0	7.0	99,931	2.5	4,450	4.5	158,176	60.0	118,104	53.7
Riviera Beach	74.1	22.6	89.0	80.8	85.1	6.2	16,767	0.5	1,087	6.5	27,660	61.1	21,579	45.4
Rockledge	86.2	25.7	95.4	91.4	89.3	4.0	14,833	2.8	523	3.5	23,449	60.3	17,497	53.7
Royal Palm Beach	82.1	28.0	97.1	92.8	91.1	4.0	21,835	2.6	822	3.8	31,461	69.9	25,400	53.8
St. Cloud	81.0	37.3	95.8	90.7	86.9	7.1	26,633	0.4	1,519	5.7	39,637	61.0	32,928	48.6
St. Petersburg	75.8	23.5	93.2	86.5	84.6	6.5	141,300	1.5	6,092	4.3	225,117	63.6	174,291	56.5
Sanford	80.7	25.9	92.6	84.6	77.9	12.9	28,036	1.4	1,768	6.3	47,081	64.4	39,342	52.8
Sarasota	75.5	22.2	92.5	84.1	81.1	8.0	28,273	3.7	1,130	4.0	50,268	53.6	34,072	50.2
Sebastian	81.4	30.8	91.0	84.3	87.2	6.9	10,678	1.4	485	4.5	22,386	45.6	13,286	46.7
Sunrise	79.7	27.7	95.1	80.3	86.6	3.7	51,897	0.7	2,498	4.8	77,541	64.9	59,247	53.8
Tallahassee	77.3	18.6	95.8	88.6	70.0	13.1	102,030	2.1	4,766	4.7	163,753	65.5	143,643	42.1
Tamarac	79.6	30.4	91.4	83.9	84.2	5.9	34,698	0.5	1,744	5.0	56,213	60.1	38,151	55.2
Tampa	74.0	24.9	93.8	87.4	78.5	8.8	208,326	1.3	9,525	4.6	320,112	65.3	269,774	52.7
Tarpon Springs	75.2	29.3	90.3	80.6	87.2	6.8	11,848	2.2	504	4.3	21,859	51.2	14,193	47.4
Temple Terrace	79.7	26.0	96.3	92.0	79.3	8.6	14,909	1.3	709	4.8	22,452	65.9	18,429	53.9
Titusville	81.6	23.7	93.5	89.1	85.7	6.5	21,596	2.2	989	4.6	38,656	53.6	27,753	47.3
Venice	79.7	23.1	90.9	80.9	84.6	9.8	7,086	4.0	354	5.0	22,418	31.2	7,826	44.6
Wellington	77.9	30.8	96.7	94.2	87.1	5.1	34,146	3.6	1,126	3.3	50,781	64.4	39,677	50.7
West Melbourne	81.9	21.8	92.3	87.0	87.6	6.3	13,362	3.7	480	3.6	18,658	59.0	13,546	54.8
Weston	74.7	33.0	98.9	96.6	86.6	6.7	35,799	2.5	1,128	3.2	53,606	65.3	46,008	50.1
West Palm Beach	76.1	23.7	93.1	82.7	81.2	8.0	59,674	2.0	2,773	4.6	93,748	64.0	72,396	54.0
Winter Garden	79.5	29.4	96.2	90.8	86.2	3.9	23,379	-1.5	1,100	4.7	35,344	67.8	29,033	53.4
Winter Haven	83.0	27.5	88.0	71.8	81.4	9.4	19,940	2.5	1,283	6.4	35,306	51.2	24,373	49.4
Winter Park	73.4	24.4	93.7	88.1	81.0	9.5	14,167	3.7	565	4.0	26,178	57.0	19,313	51.4
Winter Springs	80.7	32.3	96.3	91.7	88.9	7.5	19,371	3.1	726	3.7	31,104	65.0	23,996	55.2
GEORGIA	77.7	28.7	92.0	83.8	85.5	8.0	5,186,969	2.1	203,237	3.9	8,296,817	62.7	6,837,456	51.9
Albany	78.1	18.4	86.2	73.8	76.6	8.4	30,422	0.0	2,026	6.7	56,969	57.1	45,898	42.1
Alpharetta	72.4	29.1	97.0	94.8	83.1	9.5	36,965	3.1	974	2.6	51,322	72.0	44,572	58.3
Athens-Clarke County	72.8	20.0	93.6	86.1	71.4	17.0	59,167	2.0	2,245	3.8	106,931	60.6	93,048	38.7
Atlanta	63.0	27.5	92.1	84.8	78.7	11.0	268,954	1.8	13,601	5.1	417,995	65.9	360,387	51.4
Augusta-Richmond County	78.0	20.9	89.3	79.0	82.1	8.7	0	0.4	4,515	5.3	160,601	57.0	132,408	44.9
Brookhaven	67.4	25.1	93.2	90.4	84.8	9.7	35,043	3.7	786	2.2	43,219	78.7	37,712	67.0
Canton	66.6	31.1	95.2	91.5	82.8	9.4	16,809	3.6	390	2.3	22,860	67.7	18,969	56.4
Carrollton	72.9	18.0	90.9	82.7	66.2	13.5	11,682	2.3	512	4.4	22,238	56.4	19,035	37.0
Chamblee	60.8	27.4	89.6	82.1	84.9	8.1	20,887	3.6	490	2.3	23,682	76.2	21,007	65.4
Columbus	79.7	20.3	89.6	81.0	78.9	10.7	76,629	-0.8	4,076	5.3	151,808	56.8	125,867	47.6
Dalton	80.3	18.4	88.5	81.7	88.3	5.4	13,614	0.1	537	3.9	26,190	62.6	22,153	53.2
Douglasville	82.5	34.2	95.3	82.4	80.4	11.7	17,167	1.8	832	4.8	25,617	69.7	21,801	55.0
Duluth	80.7	32.3	96.5	90.1	81.0	9.1	15,968	2.3	511	3.2	23,350	69.9	20,003	59.2
Dunwoody	69.7	25.5	96.9	94.3	84.2	11.8	27,061	3.5	773	2.9	38,155	67.8	31,007	60.7
East Point	63.2	33.4	93.1	84.8	82.1	8.4	17,068	-0.6	1,337	7.8	27,356	69.7	23,565	56.2
Gainesville	73.9	23.4	92.2	84.6	83.1	9.8	21,132	2.2	617	2.9	31,737	62.7	25,324	56.0
Hinesville	86.1	22.1	97.4	90.6	69.8	18.1	15,549	2.6	583	3.7	24,622	58.3	22,114	52.4
Johns Creek	69.8	32.6	98.9	97.4	86.5	8.2	44,736	3.0	1,240	2.8	65,928	67.8	57,015	56.0
Kennesaw	77.3	34.2	97.9	95.8	83.4	7.4	20,088	2.7	598	3.0	27,318	71.4	23,799	51.4
LaGrange	77.3	21.2	84.2	73.1	82.3	5.5	15,658	-0.3	851	5.4	23,276	61.6	19,266	48.0
Lawrenceville	77.7	34.2	93.1	83.1	83.3	8.9	14,848	2.7	667	4.5	22,889	69.1	19,279	51.7
McDonough	80.0	31.0	94.1	91.4	82.0	9.0	12,717	0.4	787	6.2	19,605	66.3	17,325	52.2
Macon-Bibb County	81.7	20.7	88.0	78.6	84.0	7.6	67,875	1.0	3,404	5.0	120,074	56.7	96,188	43.6
Marietta	73.1	28.5	95.1	86.3	77.9	10.6	35,180	2.8	1,211	3.4	48,579	67.2	40,562	56.0
Milton	76.3	28.8	98.9	97.0	87.6	8.3	20,232	3.3	522	2.6	29,589	71.2	26,440	56.0
Newnan	79.2	28.1	93.4	86.9	80.9	9.0	19,720	1.8	825	4.2	31,122	66.7	26,187	57.3
Peachtree City	74.0	29.8	95.6	90.4	87.0	8.7	18,672	3.7	397	2.1	28,149	60.3	21,308	53.1
Peachtree Corners	73.3	27.8	97.2	90.2	89.4	8.0	25,157	3.0	840	3.3	35,013	70.1	29,697	60.4
Pooler	86.0	21.7	97.9	93.6	80.0	11.4	14,249	3.7	456	3.2	19,586	70.9	16,775	57.0
Rome	74.4	24.3	86.6	80.0	82.0	6.6	15,352	1.1	665	4.3	28,374	55.7	22,668	44.8

1. Employed persons. 2. Households. 3. Percent of civilian labor force. 4. Persons 16 years old and over.

City	Value of residential construction authorized by building permits, 2021			Wholesale trade[1], 2017				Retail trade[2], 2017			
	New construction ($1,000)	Number of housing units	Percent single family	Number of establishments	Number of employees	Sales (mil dol)	Annual payroll (mil dol)	Number of establish-ments	Number of employees	Sales (mil dol)	Annual payroll (mil dol)
	69	70	71	72	73	74	75	76	77	78	79
FLORIDA—Cont'd											
Palm Bay	674,077	2,486	100.0	33	230	120.7	14.1	192	3,537	949.9	88.7
Palm Beach Gardens	141,485	367	77.7	72	550	455.3	40.3	374	6,904	1,703.3	183.2
Palm Coast	535,150	2,280	85.0	35	187	83.2	10.1	169	3,177	871.3	79.5
Palm Springs	10,272	59	15.3	14	228	164.7	13.7	131	2,080	857.1	58.0
Panama City	63,223	181	80.1	62	854	328.4	35.6	305	4,724	1,422.8	133.6
Parkland	187,383	498	100.0	56	87	96.3	4.6	32	316	96.8	7.8
Pembroke Pines	945	4	100.0	186	506	305.6	25.8	577	12,099	3,743.5	327.7
Pensacola	36,543	215	16.7	72	638	276.6	34.2	381	6,068	1,400.3	141.2
Pinellas Park	18,392	217	21.2	195	2,598	1,286.8	131.0	312	4,188	1,449.6	126.3
Plantation	124,921	1,190	1.2	118	586	386.7	45.5	333	5,054	1,262.9	123.3
Plant City	57,587	214	100.0	71	2,397	3,680.6	139.3	183	3,768	1,836.5	110.9
Pompano Beach	45,426	404	24.0	456	7,001	5,731.1	386.5	635	8,230	3,492.6	291.8
Port Orange	123,293	551	47.7	34	284	186.0	13.7	186	3,186	777.7	73.6
Port St. Lucie	1,212,544	6,512	79.2	104	614	217.8	27.4	371	6,893	1,890.8	179.0
Riviera Beach	27,041	121	70.2	97	2,769	2,008.0	176.0	126	1,376	482.9	46.6
Rockledge	13,297	43	48.8	38	295	256.2	19.9	99	1,215	296.8	29.7
Royal Palm Beach	40,429	103	90.3	24	166	121.0	8.7	161	3,605	1,089.8	95.6
St. Cloud	442,265	1,209	100.0	11	90	22.7	3.6	132	2,369	612.1	58.8
St. Petersburg	400,665	1,635	27.8	184	2,380	1,303.8	159.0	911	15,594	5,651.5	450.1
Sanford	138,200	883	41.0	97	1,476	639.5	75.6	364	6,148	2,136.8	184.5
Sarasota	229,216	805	20.5	80	678	375.2	41.3	451	4,662	1,306.9	140.3
Sebastian	71,072	288	100.0	D	D	D	3.5	47	887	220.5	21.6
Sunrise	0	0	0.0	257	2,861	2,753.3	175.0	557	11,840	2,874.9	273.1
Tallahassee	262,554	1,853	29.1	153	2,117	1,745.3	148.1	877	13,577	3,391.5	331.8
Tamarac	15,418	70	100.0	71	1,522	1,112.5	91.4	126	2,934	731.6	110.0
Tampa	604,905	2,405	54.6	642	10,930	9,610.2	639.4	1,867	25,775	7,846.7	757.7
Tarpon Springs	34,051	174	63.8	34	219	86.6	9.8	138	1,634	452.4	45.1
Temple Terrace	2,761	16	100.0	26	390	168.1	18.2	88	1,339	294.8	28.4
Titusville	24,519	149	100.0	20	105	33.0	4.3	176	2,893	751.3	73.5
Venice	225,852	823	85.2	34	184	139.2	9.0	140	1,663	388.5	40.4
Wellington	27,226	45	100.0	85	311	236.6	18.3	260	3,485	710.6	85.2
West Melbourne	52,335	399	18.8	35	231	137.4	12.8	159	2,720	695.7	61.6
Weston	6,220	26	100.0	234	1,705	3,365.3	118.3	138	1,834	816.2	53.6
West Palm Beach	370,597	1,676	6.1	144	1,668	2,115.5	83.6	595	9,297	3,433.9	290.1
Winter Garden	104,062	250	100.0	57	637	1,304.8	30.9	202	3,678	994.9	89.0
Winter Haven	241,226	1,007	100.0	37	481	281.5	19.1	219	3,493	1,082.9	96.1
Winter Park	60,935	103	97.1	47	443	254.0	20.2	250	2,871	978.8	94.1
Winter Springs	29,843	191	53.4	27	128	54.3	8.1	49	424	116.8	11.5
GEORGIA	14,437,233	67,223	79.5	10,832	165,088	188,899.2	10,594.4	34,100	485,505	148,624.6	12,560.5
Albany	8,413	25	100.0	103	1,804	989.8	84.6	407	5,724	1,502.7	129.7
Alpharetta	162,501	449	90.0	173	3,956	7,862.4	391.5	406	7,575	2,103.0	201.2
Athens-Clarke County	145,120	1,166	15.4	94	2,042	2,980.2	95.9	513	8,212	1,982.0	195.5
Atlanta	418,900	2,413	35.4	671	11,052	16,286.0	798.0	1,991	28,468	7,416.3	781.8
Augusta-Richmond County	108,868	671	97.2	D	D	D	D	752	10,886	2,799.6	261.7
Brookhaven	161,099	559	38.8	35	269	500.1	23.5	111	1,796	407.2	42.0
Canton	105,460	495	69.3	30	125	50.5	7.0	145	2,859	816.0	76.3
Carrollton	45,075	152	100.0	38	376	175.8	16.9	189	2,723	702.5	62.5
Chamblee	24,872	75	100.0	86	676	494.4	35.9	218	3,776	2,410.9	177.6
Columbus	118,533	675	43.9	152	1,978	1,683.1	109.0	794	11,547	2,979.2	268.9
Dalton	NA	NA	NA	124	2,737	814.0	115.3	230	2,748	779.6	66.0
Douglasville	256,556	1,275	19.7	26	879	1,692.9	76.2	243	4,655	1,231.6	104.4
Duluth	37,028	117	47.0	172	3,427	3,026.2	289.6	191	3,017	1,130.6	98.1
Dunwoody	111,146	631	5.2	53	1,559	7,628.2	140.0	242	5,137	991.4	124.1
East Point	12,228	126	100.0	27	768	896.6	49.3	108	1,686	400.2	35.5
Gainesville	130,861	863	26.5	97	1,874	5,939.6	104.0	306	5,089	1,586.6	152.9
Hinesville	40,621	179	100.0	6	28	15.2	1.2	123	1,765	472.5	44.1
Johns Creek	48,915	122	100.0	73	395	804.2	37.5	160	2,089	477.7	46.4
Kennesaw	41,343	157	92.4	93	1,646	1,691.3	113.6	250	4,989	1,186.8	115.9
LaGrange	29,322	138	31.9	33	387	260.7	17.5	172	2,453	650.6	64.0
Lawrenceville	11,644	83	100.0	105	3,086	1,981.7	282.9	292	4,128	1,163.2	112.5
McDonough	46,238	239	100.0	37	1,198	822.1	74.8	140	3,089	1,202.4	88.6
Macon-Bibb County	31,112	177	100.0	178	2,913	1,943.5	149.2	D	D	D	D
Marietta	116,570	484	99.2	237	3,882	2,644.2	237.7	428	5,858	2,099.7	192.5
Milton	52,113	206	100.0	31	150	180.0	13.6	70	892	198.7	20.2
Newnan	126,924	580	35.9	37	513	668.3	29.5	220	4,095	1,127.7	95.2
Peachtree City	124,143	369	93.2	79	1,377	1,203.8	103.7	170	3,335	825.4	74.7
Peachtree Corners	21,906	76	100.0	149	3,019	2,594.4	255.1	91	789	187.2	20.5
Pooler	138,783	710	52.4	41	756	876.5	50.8	167	2,677	665.2	57.4
Rome	NA	NA	NA	48	899	616.7	45.5	295	3,723	1,055.8	94.7

1. Merchant wholesalers except manufacturers' sales branches and offices. 2. Establishments with payroll.

City	Real estate and rental and leasing, 2017				Professional, scientific, and technical services[1], 2017				Manufacturing, 2017			
	Number of establish-ments	Number of employees	Receipts (mil dol)	Annual payroll (mil dol)	Number of establish-ments	Number of employees	Receipts (mil dol)	Annual payroll (mil dol)	Number of establish-ments	Number of employees	Receipts (mil dol)	Annual payroll (mil dol)
	80	81	82	83	84	85	86	87	88	89	90	91
FLORIDA—Cont'd												
Palm Bay	67	237	44.8	9.4	128	607	92.6	32.4	NA	NA	NA	NA
Palm Beach Gardens	170	765	627.7	50.6	543	3,060	611.9	230.5	NA	NA	NA	NA
Palm Coast	D	D	D	D	137	342	45.4	15.4	NA	NA	NA	NA
Palm Springs	28	95	23.4	3.3	55	249	43.1	13.3	NA	NA	NA	NA
Panama City	98	497	113.7	16.7	222	1,556	261.2	99.1	NA	NA	NA	NA
Parkland	D	D	D	D	189	237	59.9	14.9	NA	NA	NA	NA
Pembroke Pines	233	863	237.8	43.0	640	1,857	318.5	93.9	NA	NA	NA	NA
Pensacola	149	768	169.0	25.4	484	5,270	797.5	326.6	NA	NA	NA	NA
Pinellas Park	73	454	103.8	19.2	161	1,096	131.6	64.8	NA	NA	NA	NA
Plantation	254	2,278	632.4	104.7	743	6,356	778.1	566.4	NA	NA	NA	NA
Plant City	46	202	41.9	8.3	103	419	52.0	19.5	NA	NA	NA	NA
Pompano Beach	279	1,140	351.3	52.9	523	2,179	421.5	122.6	NA	NA	NA	NA
Port Orange	111	396	68.5	12.6	132	850	88.7	42.9	NA	NA	NA	NA
Port St. Lucie	185	385	97.7	12.6	294	1,097	134.6	46.6	NA	NA	NA	NA
Riviera Beach	50	271	53.6	17.0	80	319	69.3	18.7	NA	NA	NA	NA
Rockledge	34	151	26.3	5.6	80	525	64.0	22.3	NA	NA	NA	NA
Royal Palm Beach	37	62	31.6	2.1	119	467	51.5	17.7	NA	NA	NA	NA
St. Cloud	52	124	25.4	4.1	64	192	21.4	6.8	NA	NA	NA	NA
St. Petersburg	467	2,667	476.2	106.6	1,312	12,571	1,947.8	764.6	NA	NA	NA	NA
Sanford	92	443	176.0	18.9	145	1,222	152.1	58.1	NA	NA	NA	NA
Sarasota	262	708	170.7	30.9	656	4,895	1,011.2	390.1	NA	NA	NA	NA
Sebastian	34	72	20.1	2.1	57	178	22.2	8.2	NA	NA	NA	NA
Sunrise	137	763	233.0	32.2	396	2,528	420.2	165.0	NA	NA	NA	NA
Tallahassee	376	2,652	413.2	90.2	1,194	9,135	1,673.3	686.6	NA	NA	NA	NA
Tamarac	74	217	57.8	8.0	203	683	85.6	33.1	NA	NA	NA	NA
Tampa	1,110	5,982	2,105.8	321.7	2,971	41,022	8,562.9	3,659.3	NA	NA	NA	NA
Tarpon Springs	54	312	43.2	7.8	96	334	68.2	14.9	NA	NA	NA	NA
Temple Terrace	45	109	38.8	5.1	126	1,254	212.7	92.3	NA	NA	NA	NA
Titusville	39	141	25.1	4.1	102	521	83.0	26.0	NA	NA	NA	NA
Venice	93	293	77.2	11.0	129	421	56.5	20.3	NA	NA	NA	NA
Wellington	168	1,070	239.5	60.4	383	915	165.6	50.7	NA	NA	NA	NA
West Melbourne	27	108	19.4	3.7	65	453	82.1	27.3	NA	NA	NA	NA
Weston	252	472	141.6	22.5	D	D	D	D	NA	NA	NA	NA
West Palm Beach	333	1,462	397.5	81.6	1,190	7,989	1,761.7	733.5	NA	NA	NA	NA
Winter Garden	103	334	72.4	14.2	165	598	92.9	36.6	NA	NA	NA	NA
Winter Haven	60	346	90.1	13.0	124	670	77.1	32.4	NA	NA	NA	NA
Winter Park	171	604	164.3	29.9	525	3,559	637.2	238.4	NA	NA	NA	NA
Winter Springs	55	98	17.0	3.7	116	659	100.2	36.9	NA	NA	NA	NA
GEORGIA	12,426	63,935	23,009.0	3,795.4	29,737	266,523	55,149.4	20,188.6	7,510	368,836	169,058.5	19,071.6
Albany	109	451	103.0	16.2	191	1,391	186.0	71.2	NA	NA	NA	NA
Alpharetta	226	1,549	966.7	113.8	907	15,625	4,113.1	1,455.6	NA	NA	NA	NA
Athens-Clarke County	202	1,392	242.9	54.2	321	1,530	194.1	72.0	NA	NA	NA	NA
Atlanta	1,461	13,207	6,524.6	1,012.1	3,987	68,768	18,727.5	6,780.7	NA	NA	NA	NA
Augusta-Richmond County	D	D	D	D	465	4,947	877.6	282.8	NA	NA	NA	NA
Brookhaven	172	1,286	277.1	68.8	377	3,665	669.5	281.8	NA	NA	NA	NA
Canton	37	80	23.2	3.3	104	629	129.0	34.7	NA	NA	NA	NA
Carrollton	45	224	43.9	5.9	75	356	56.4	20.4	NA	NA	NA	NA
Chamblee	67	312	58.1	12.9	237	2,252	421.6	176.4	NA	NA	NA	NA
Columbus	242	1,314	342.8	54.5	330	2,613	311.8	122.1	NA	NA	NA	NA
Dalton	32	115	27.0	4.1	136	1,108	134.0	66.2	NA	NA	NA	NA
Douglasville	53	171	62.8	6.6	107	552	67.3	25.9	NA	NA	NA	NA
Duluth	111	487	222.7	28.0	305	4,196	815.8	305.9	NA	NA	NA	NA
Dunwoody	167	699	269.5	53.2	523	7,645	1,287.1	588.9	NA	NA	NA	NA
East Point	38	322	63.4	11.2	55	466	37.7	15.6	NA	NA	NA	NA
Gainesville	88	261	75.7	11.2	177	846	132.6	43.4	NA	NA	NA	NA
Hinesville	41	136	25.9	4.2	33	220	22.5	7.6	NA	NA	NA	NA
Johns Creek	129	291	767.7	29.7	638	2,987	740.0	201.8	NA	NA	NA	NA
Kennesaw	65	471	132.7	17.5	138	975	153.9	49.6	NA	NA	NA	NA
LaGrange	52	152	45.4	6.0	69	307	42.1	16.6	NA	NA	NA	NA
Lawrenceville	68	399	127.4	21.2	219	1,194	162.8	62.6	NA	NA	NA	NA
McDonough	35	99	63.2	4.6	87	589	99.7	32.0	NA	NA	NA	NA
Macon-Bibb County	203	1,050	208.6	40.3	356	2,611	414.5	141.3	NA	NA	NA	NA
Marietta	190	958	326.8	56.7	537	5,093	1,259.1	319.0	NA	NA	NA	NA
Milton	56	132	41.3	7.9	244	1,356	313.8	96.9	NA	NA	NA	NA
Newnan	81	212	61.1	8.8	103	781	113.6	44.1	NA	NA	NA	NA
Peachtree City	101	225	63.8	11.5	D	D	D	D	NA	NA	NA	NA
Peachtree Corners	117	1,034	235.4	60.0	345	7,505	1,750.2	555.2	NA	NA	NA	NA
Pooler	30	223	57.6	8.6	40	264	68.6	13.8	NA	NA	NA	NA
Rome	58	207	44.3	7.6	139	706	108.8	27.3	NA	NA	NA	NA

1. Establishments subject to federal tax.

City	Accommodation and food services, 2017				Arts, entertainment, and recreation[1], 2017				Health care and social assistance[1], 2017			
	Number of establish-ments	Number of employees	Receipts (mil dol)	Annual payroll (mil dol)	Number of establish-ments	Number of employees	Receipts (mil dol)	Annual payroll (mil dol)	Number of establish-ments	Number of employees	Receipts (mil dol)	Annual payroll (mil dol)
	92	93	94	95	96	97	98	99	100	101	102	103
FLORIDA—Cont'd												
Palm Bay	118	1,954	110.5	29.4	16.0	92	4.8	1.4	151	2,335	223.3	82.0
Palm Beach Gardens	165	4,965	292.3	103.9	62.0	1,313	310.3	58.6	409	4,790	788.7	237.6
Palm Coast	110	2,182	119.2	33.0	D	D	D	7.2	194	3,467	473.0	156.2
Palm Springs	47	636	45.3	11.7	NA	NA	NA	NA	156	1,932	248.3	83.6
Panama City	166	3,534	191.5	58.6	14.0	152	7.3	2.5	354	8,121	1,058.5	403.1
Parkland	22	356	11.3	3.8	10.0	39	2.4	1.0	87	274	46.1	13.0
Pembroke Pines	324	7,639	462.4	132.4	76.0	536	52.9	8.6	638	9,390	1,296.8	496.8
Pensacola	195	5,482	286.0	92.4	34.0	736	29.5	9.8	456	14,133	1,961.8	776.1
Pinellas Park	133	2,501	182.4	44.5	22.0	232	12.9	3.1	183	3,189	295.8	115.3
Plantation	212	3,869	295.3	75.8	42.0	555	38.4	13.2	611	7,486	1,094.6	369.2
Plant City	84	1,927	100.4	28.6	10.0	714	13.9	3.1	134	2,237	370.5	104.2
Pompano Beach	279	4,425	379.4	92.3	73.0	1,567	140.9	24.9	335	5,819	589.5	205.9
Port Orange	126	2,714	141.9	44.8	20.0	393	11.4	4.6	182	1,915	194.5	75.3
Port St. Lucie	239	4,613	252.5	69.4	48.0	379	28.2	7.0	488	7,881	1,058.2	343.1
Riviera Beach	37	886	61.5	18.0	5.0	361	24.2	4.3	72	3,543	517.8	197.4
Rockledge	64	1,200	58.9	17.3	11.0	205	9.1	2.7	131	3,319	404.6	146.5
Royal Palm Beach	105	2,109	125.3	35.5	11.0	98	7.6	2.2	154	1,544	191.1	75.6
St. Cloud	82	1,475	84.7	24.5	D	D	D	2.7	98	1,643	197.9	65.1
St. Petersburg	568	10,140	658.0	179.1	116.0	2,201	307.4	164.1	1,021	20,818	3,081.4	1,081.0
Sanford	150	3,039	169.1	49.2	15.0	262	8.2	3.4	144	2,690	377.6	142.0
Sarasota	272	6,120	447.2	121.4	70.0	1,573	127.6	37.5	470	11,452	1,674.8	560.0
Sebastian	D	D	D	D	9.0	35	3.1	0.8	D	D	D	D
Sunrise	203	4,158	256.9	73.2	38.0	D	145.8	D	289	7,051	1,006.2	527.9
Tallahassee	647	14,587	774.0	211.9	84.0	1,268	96.3	24.6	680	17,885	2,343.0	917.4
Tamarac	67	1,053	69.7	16.6	21.0	269	17.4	4.7	230	3,849	548.2	158.1
Tampa	1,130	28,032	2,072.4	557.1	213.0	10,239	1,388.0	512.3	1,526	38,844	6,863.8	2,268.7
Tarpon Springs	75	1,375	84.9	23.1	20.0	200	17.2	4.8	81	1,757	221.9	83.1
Temple Terrace	73	1,378	80.0	21.5	11.0	61	6.8	1.7	104	1,501	191.2	73.4
Titusville	102	2,018	105.9	29.4	12.0	177	10.8	2.5	147	2,868	332.1	120.6
Venice	100	2,004	112.8	38.2	17.0	159	10.4	3.1	142	3,601	534.9	168.3
Wellington	120	2,830	140.6	42.5	81.0	956	132.5	24.5	264	2,789	389.7	140.3
West Melbourne	59	1,492	86.3	24.4	6.0	63	5.5	1.7	68	1,310	117.3	43.1
Weston	118	2,530	182.8	48.5	32.0	685	50.0	14.2	291	3,950	735.1	294.2
West Palm Beach	389	8,290	567.9	163.1	81.0	1,945	286.8	68.4	621	13,961	1,840.3	639.8
Winter Garden	102	2,328	130.5	40.3	35.0	271	26.5	4.7	106	1,272	118.6	45.5
Winter Haven	117	2,369	131.0	35.2	18.0	1,971	171.2	35.6	191	5,761	644.4	288.3
Winter Park	163	4,692	258.4	86.2	50.0	937	84.9	24.9	357	5,942	771.2	277.8
Winter Springs	29	263	14.5	3.9	19.0	145	10.4	3.5	62	323	21.1	8.7
GEORGIA	21,201	426,884	26,010.1	6,999.7	3,452.0	50,796	5,245.3	1,752.1	25,260	521,146	68,759.7	25,771.5
Albany	D	D	D	D	23.0	258	14.7	4.5	295	8,386	1,149.2	453.7
Alpharetta	350	7,192	467.5	129.0	53.0	1,536	158.7	28.5	478	5,378	741.3	287.3
Athens-Clarke County	360	7,878	396.0	110.0	66.0	959	50.8	15.2	456	10,263	1,666.8	621.3
Atlanta	1,896	54,165	4,270.9	1,201.8	469.0	9,271	1,414.3	406.8	1,798	43,378	8,249.2	2,530.6
Augusta-Richmond County	461	10,227	558.3	148.0	53.0	1,298	179.5	40.3	605	24,637	3,881.6	1,370.2
Brookhaven	139	2,468	170.8	49.6	30.0	416	41.5	8.8	175	3,685	474.9	185.6
Canton	108	2,290	129.4	40.2	15.0	195	9.3	2.7	127	3,136	510.6	155.5
Carrollton	114	2,371	117.6	32.2	D	D	D	D	132	3,606	548.5	229.8
Chamblee	128	1,559	119.8	31.7	14.0	117	8.8	2.2	123	1,920	197.7	93.9
Columbus	474	10,818	574.5	162.6	50.0	1,047	56.4	18.0	666	15,924	1,829.0	701.9
Dalton	134	2,741	170.3	44.8	15.0	275	12.9	4.7	164	D	638.8	D
Douglasville	152	3,226	173.1	46.7	16.0	D	17.1	D	146	2,754	421.3	145.1
Duluth	186	2,349	136.7	33.9	27.0	310	28.3	11.7	D	D	D	D
Dunwoody	149	3,804	234.7	74.3	25.0	527	32.8	13.7	230	3,485	335.6	122.3
East Point	98	2,035	153.3	39.7	13.0	12	30.0	1.7	90	1,815	233.1	79.7
Gainesville	157	3,290	181.4	51.3	24.0	D	19.6	D	309	11,054	1,540.2	596.8
Hinesville	91	1,757	87.9	21.4	3.0	15	1.3	0.2	69	1,137	106.2	45.2
Johns Creek	162	2,402	133.0	38.0	43.0	1,131	81.7	31.7	216	2,864	419.3	150.3
Kennesaw	168	3,962	188.7	58.4	24.0	467	21.4	5.4	111	1,687	142.2	64.6
LaGrange	90	1,742	94.3	25.0	D	D	D	D	D	D	D	D
Lawrenceville	130	2,173	122.9	32.7	24.0	492	31.3	7.4	281	8,469	1,281.5	482.6
McDonough	94	1,988	121.7	30.5	5.0	38	2.4	0.6	100	1,426	152.7	60.2
Macon-Bibb County	D	D	D	D	39.0	630	30.8	8.6	619	16,894	2,123.3	756.1
Marietta	269	4,571	282.9	79.7	49.0	929	112.0	27.6	434	12,131	2,324.9	852.2
Milton	58	925	51.4	13.7	18.0	225	16.8	5.2	45	412	49.7	19.6
Newnan	118	3,262	167.0	49.2	20.0	251	13.7	3.2	124	2,881	695.7	150.2
Peachtree City	120	2,937	167.8	51.1	35.0	488	71.5	13.4	146	1,473	161.1	57.4
Peachtree Corners	86	1,467	105.7	27.3	25.0	725	99.9	20.9	93	1,452	156.5	71.0
Pooler	126	3,144	169.1	47.9	14.0	191	14.2	4.3	48	470	51.9	19.1
Rome	156	3,639	195.4	54.9	20.0	177	9.9	3.2	268	7,906	1,104.3	379.0

1. Establishments subject to federal tax.

City	Other services[1]				Government employment and payroll, 2017								
						March payroll							
							Perent of total for:						
	Number of establish-ments	Number of employees	Receipts (mil dol)	Annual payroll (mil dol)	Full-time equivalent employees	Total (dollars)	Admin-istrative, judicial, and legal	Police and corrections	Fire protection	Highways and trans-portation	Health and welfare	Natural resources and utilities	Education and libraries
	104	105	106	107	108	109	110	111	112	113	114	115	116
FLORIDA—Cont'd													
Palm Bay	101	441	44.3	13.8	770	3,203,187	10.8	28.6	22.0	10.0	3.1	22.5	0.0
Palm Beach Gardens	184	1,754	201.5	77.1	559	3,461,550	10.2	36.5	29.6	7.0	2.1	11.6	0.0
Palm Coast	89	407	33.1	8.9	399	1,699,178	26.6	0.0	18.5	15.6	0.0	37.3	0.0
Palm Springs	73	287	24.5	6.4	168	751,015	10.9	43.3	0.0	6.3	0.0	35.0	4.5
Panama City	106	677	53.8	16.1	550	1,043,351	11.7	24.2	13.2	27.6	3.7	18.9	0.0
Parkland	29	91	11.8	2.2	111	485,381	28.5	0.0	0.0	39.7	0.0	7.4	5.2
Pembroke Pines	255	1,522	146.9	42.8	656	3,958,045	11.6	46.1	35.1	0.0	0.4	4.4	0.0
Pensacola	149	1,205	104.0	32.2	715	2,886,335	11.8	26.2	16.1	12.5	3.9	23.3	0.0
Pinellas Park	182	1,202	130.6	43.3	493	2,244,205	13.6	31.7	19.5	4.0	5.6	17.8	3.9
Plantation	195	875	124.4	28.3	808	4,245,516	9.8	41.1	3.4	5.2	10.2	17.7	1.0
Plant City	67	314	34.4	10.7	361	1,349,864	10.5	31.6	14.7	10.8	0.4	23.7	3.0
Pompano Beach	396	2,075	303.0	70.5	776	4,045,084	17.8	0.0	32.1	14.3	1.5	22.6	0.0
Port Orange	104	386	33.5	8.2	406	1,668,896	15.4	26.7	15.6	3.8	4.4	27.5	0.0
Port St. Lucie	234	828	79.6	22.5	1,002	4,813,985	17.2	37.8	0.0	6.1	3.3	22.2	0.0
Riviera Beach	90	648	75.6	21.7	492	2,387,288	16.7	31.0	21.2	5.6	2.0	15.3	1.1
Rockledge	49	109	17.6	4.7	237	843,910	7.5	34.1	20.9	10.8	0.8	19.4	0.0
Royal Palm Beach	90	488	47.1	13.5	124	571,750	27.0	0.0	0.0	29.0	10.1	29.6	0.0
St. Cloud	D	D	D	D	423	1,704,067	14.6	30.3	15.2	7.6	2.5	24.2	0.0
St. Petersburg	531	3,176	402.0	108.6	3,230	17,086,876	13.0	29.4	13.2	0.8	1.5	31.2	1.6
Sanford	125	655	57.0	18.3	565	2,407,854	7.2	25.6	17.2	16.4	0.0	24.5	0.0
Sarasota	258	1,373	246.9	41.4	704	3,740,313	13.4	37.7	0.0	3.5	1.2	27.0	0.0
Sebastian	36	166	13.7	3.8	131	539,565	15.8	47.1	0.0	10.5	0.0	17.6	0.0
Sunrise	148	760	146.2	31.3	1,004	6,575,439	9.0	31.4	20.5	1.2	9.1	28.1	0.0
Tallahassee	524	4,124	693.0	185.1	3,177	16,131,062	17.5	17.2	11.0	8.8	1.6	36.8	0.0
Tamarac	93	274	30.3	9.0	363	1,876,467	25.5	0.0	24.3	8.4	1.2	29.3	0.0
Tampa	1,043	9,738	1,446.1	278.3	4,198	25,536,216	11.1	34.9	18.1	2.0	4.0	24.4	0.0
Tarpon Springs	62	221	27.4	6.8	262	1,196,345	12.0	28.9	20.0	2.2	0.0	30.6	4.0
Temple Terrace	32	140	15.3	3.5	339	1,405,996	12.2	26.3	19.4	1.2	2.7	32.5	2.4
Titusville	80	406	34.1	11.3	462	1,914,251	19.1	30.0	15.9	4.2	0.8	24.8	0.0
Venice	82	467	89.1	14.1	287	1,412,424	21.2	23.6	17.7	5.7	0.0	31.8	0.0
Wellington	129	582	119.0	19.1	334	1,637,284	28.0	0.0	0.0	2.6	2.1	33.3	0.0
West Melbourne	67	283	31.9	7.8	110	487,088	18.9	43.0	0.0	9.0	0.0	16.8	0.0
Weston	123	483	41.6	13.0	11	69,116	100.0	0.0	0.0	0.0	0.0	0.0	0.0
West Palm Beach	383	2,254	377.2	79.7	1,432	7,321,395	15.2	31.5	18.1	1.4	1.0	21.8	2.1
Winter Garden	90	581	53.0	16.8	290	1,318,942	12.7	36.5	18.3	0.0	4.8	19.1	0.0
Winter Haven	81	317	32.5	9.6	458	1,781,107	14.2	26.9	18.4	5.2	0.0	28.0	2.4
Winter Park	159	878	97.5	27.2	524	2,722,952	10.4	22.3	21.4	4.0	0.6	34.6	0.0
Winter Springs	39	99	11.1	3.0	171	748,571	18.0	44.8	0.0	10.4	2.7	24.1	0.0
GEORGIA	14,976	97,721	14,342.5	3,347.6	X	X	X	X	X	X	X	X	X
Albany	123	851	76.6	23.8	1,093	4,003,560	13.8	19.3	17.5	7.0	1.1	33.3	0.0
Alpharetta	179	1,439	1,864.2	58.1	429	2,208,992	16.6	30.6	22.6	10.4	2.7	7.5	0.0
Athens-Clarke County	196	1,403	275.9	48.3	1,814	7,225,052	17.1	30.3	11.4	6.0	0.5	21.1	2.5
Atlanta	1,345	15,249	3,022.3	622.8	8,317	39,867,373	17.0	31.7	11.9	11.0	1.8	25.6	0.0
Augusta-Richmond County	287	1,789	218.9	58.9	2,658	9,166,187	21.2	32.9	13.3	7.7	2.3	17.6	2.5
Brookhaven	84	737	158.6	35.3	131	660,056	21.6	61.6	0.7	0.0	6.1	6.3	0.0
Canton	60	340	28.6	9.3	116	467,903	20.5	45.4	0.0	8.3	0.0	5.9	0.0
Carrollton	D	D	D	D	346	1,228,502	9.6	25.4	19.9	1.8	0.0	43.0	0.0
Chamblee	122	634	76.1	24.4	121	493,397	14.4	63.8	0.0	1.4	0.0	17.8	0.0
Columbus	D	D	D	62.2	3,208	11,274,331	11.9	33.3	13.6	6.3	3.3	19.7	2.6
Dalton	76	624	90.1	23.7	606	2,675,375	3.3	15.1	13.5	10.4	0.4	28.8	0.0
Douglasville	D	D	D	D	245	935,953	16.1	54.4	0.0	7.1	0.0	15.9	0.0
Duluth	162	852	89.7	25.3	156	752,142	21.0	55.6	0.0	0.0	5.4	18.0	0.0
Dunwoody	108	557	70.1	23.3	87	436,150	14.3	85.7	0.0	0.0	0.0	0.0	0.0
East Point	D	D	D	12.0	477	1,946,198	19.1	37.4	16.3	2.8	0.0	24.4	0.0
Gainesville	125	613	72.5	17.3	662	2,501,132	10.0	16.9	17.1	7.8	1.7	42.3	0.0
Hinesville	47	355	25.9	7.3	198	737,647	9.3	50.7	24.2	0.0	3.7	2.3	0.0
Johns Creek	D	D	D	26.5	9	49,581	86.8	13.2	0.0	0.0	0.0	0.0	0.0
Kennesaw	121	1,099	146.2	54.3	204	787,343	15.1	36.8	0.0	6.2	0.0	25.0	0.0
LaGrange	62	286	36.3	8.6	402	1,914,641	4.8	28.3	13.5	4.2	0.5	28.0	0.0
Lawrenceville	153	1,135	158.5	52.4	296	1,211,161	17.4	38.5	0.0	6.0	0.0	24.9	0.0
McDonough	D	D	D	D	160	617,022	25.6	32.2	18.2	6.4	0.0	16.7	0.0
Macon-Bibb County	D	D	D	D	1,723	6,541,305	22.3	35.2	21.2	3.4	0.6	5.7	2.3
Marietta	248	1,352	164.5	49.7	691	3,014,616	14.4	24.7	22.2	4.6	1.0	23.3	0.0
Milton	55	362	23.0	7.8	124	630,689	0.0	29.3	47.9	8.2	0.0	2.1	0.0
Newnan	D	D	D	10.8	357	1,574,402	7.1	24.9	14.7	5.0	0.5	21.7	0.8
Peachtree City	107	968	69.7	24.8	276	1,143,737	9.7	26.0	28.3	11.0	0.0	4.5	3.9
Peachtree Corners	62	330	55.1	13.0	10	39,282	0.0	0.0	0.0	0.0	0.0	0.0	0.0
Pooler	41	337	35.5	9.9	193	775,425	7.3	27.8	30.6	3.8	0.0	21.8	0.0
Rome	D	D	D	D	600	2,163,223	8.1	18.6	28.7	12.7	1.2	26.4	0.0

1. Establishments subject to federal tax.

City	City government finances, 2017									
	General revenue							General expenditure		
		Intergovernmental		Taxes						
					Per capita[1] (dollars)				Per capita[1] (dollars)	
	Total (mil dol)	Total (mil dol)	Percent from state government	Total (mil dol)	Total	Property	Sales and gross receipts	Total (mil dol)	Total	Capital outlays
	117	118	119	120	121	122	123	124	125	126
FLORIDA—Cont'd										
Palm Bay	92.1	15.6	88.0	47.0	419	220	199	87.5	780	104
Palm Beach Gardens	89.6	7.3	87.4	66.7	1,183	922	261	93.2	1,655	215
Palm Coast	64.3	10.2	51.6	25.4	295	197	98	88.6	1,028	205
Palm Springs	24.0	2.9	96.5	9.1	364	143	222	21.4	860	67
Panama City	70.8	10.1	89.8	33.0	888	305	583	60.7	1,634	156
Parkland	43.9	3.0	82.9	22.9	723	463	260	33.5	1,060	255
Pembroke Pines	281.9	67.5	90.0	106.7	625	359	266	368.2	2,157	318
Pensacola	133.3	44.9	20.4	44.2	841	261	580	133.4	2,539	460
Pinellas Park	76.0	10.6	77.2	34.8	658	297	361	82.7	1,563	164
Plantation	133.9	11.4	83.9	78.3	835	493	341	117.8	1,256	100
Plant City	58.3	9.5	70.5	24.4	623	220	325	56.4	1,437	304
Pompano Beach	186.5	21.7	67.8	101.5	919	569	351	209.6	1,899	300
Port Orange	68.6	7.5	90.5	25.6	406	193	213	69.2	1,097	61
Port St. Lucie	265.6	31.7	71.6	95.4	504	348	157	253.7	1,341	219
Riviera Beach	99.2	9.6	43.5	56.7	1,633	1,286	347	124.3	3,583	557
Rockledge	28.3	2.9	99.8	14.2	519	282	237	26.3	962	85
Royal Palm Beach	56.2	4.7	94.8	15.1	392	111	281	27.7	717	120
St. Cloud	82.9	7.0	65.0	18.1	351	141	210	67.7	1,310	106
St. Petersburg	428.7	81.9	37.9	161.8	616	367	249	438.3	1,669	153
Sanford	139.1	36.8	23.1	38.3	643	321	322	101.2	1,700	265
Sarasota	158.5	23.4	57.3	63.7	1,114	498	616	151.6	2,650	420
Sebastian	19.7	3.4	99.4	12.5	497	157	341	15.9	631	71
Sunrise	218.9	14.3	73.2	76.1	807	404	402	196.2	2,081	261
Tallahassee	381.8	68.3	56.9	103.4	540	204	336	350.7	1,830	159
Tamarac	105.1	13.6	50.8	40.3	609	312	297	101.6	1,537	128
Tampa	700.5	94.9	65.7	309.4	791	369	422	732.5	1,873	273
Tarpon Springs	41.7	5.2	57.6	17.0	673	310	363	45.2	1,792	325
Temple Terrace	36.8	4.0	81.7	17.3	648	316	331	43.2	1,617	160
Titusville	63.8	9.9	51.9	24.7	535	271	254	51.1	1,108	39
Venice	61.1	14.1	38.8	24.1	1,044	444	599	69.5	3,009	944
Wellington	69.4	8.9	72.0	34.4	530	255	275	75.1	1,159	266
West Melbourne	20.2	3.6	73.5	9.8	447	122	317	19.3	882	324
Weston	85.2	6.2	100.0	35.3	498	242	256	107.2	1,512	53
West Palm Beach	266.9	46.7	31.3	130.3	1,181	762	419	272.2	2,467	138
Winter Garden	55.1	10.7	76.4	24.1	552	229	323	58.2	1,332	312
Winter Haven	67.9	6.7	85.5	23.4	572	250	322	68.4	1,675	231
Winter Park	67.6	9.4	66.3	31.8	1,031	620	411	78.9	2,555	327
Winter Springs	34.6	4.4	79.0	15.7	429	123	306	28.8	787	171
GEORGIA	X	X	X	X	X	X	X	X	X	X
Albany	112.3	27.8	20.8	28.0	382	211	172	118.2	1,614	5
Alpharetta	116.0	31.6	21.4	52.0	790	411	373	115.0	1,749	695
Athens-Clarke County	227.6	61.2	4.7	80.3	634	424	207	216.1	1,704	241
Atlanta	1,874.4	322.1	4.6	639.3	1,300	728	572	1,608.0	3,270	839
Augusta-Richmond County	393.7	123.9	3.7	123.4	627	358	268	325.8	1,654	217
Brookhaven	85.2	19.9	3.4	23.1	431	230	201	96.4	1,797	224
Canton	34.1	7.2	4.4	11.9	421	183	233	21.6	762	132
Carrollton	37.1	8.4	3.1	11.9	444	181	251	35.8	1,339	208
Chamblee	24.1	2.1	37.8	15.5	529	241	285	19.6	667	72
Columbus	331.5	90.7	8.2	141.2	728	426	298	329.2	1,698	185
Dalton	88.1	17.4	1.8	14.6	434	263	168	75.6	2,252	290
Douglasville	34.3	7.6	11.4	18.4	557	253	268	27.3	828	27
Duluth	27.1	7.8	5.3	14.9	505	277	226	21.8	741	90
Dunwoody	38.0	8.7	6.0	21.5	434	137	290	52.0	1,048	363
East Point	56.9	14.2	1.4	22.4	640	372	268	41.1	1,174	0
Gainesville	116.3	17.4	4.9	28.8	714	396	315	82.0	2,032	241
Hinesville	30.2	4.3	10.0	13.0	395	240	153	29.9	906	26
Johns Creek	57.3	22.1	9.5	31.0	368	195	171	79.1	939	427
Kennesaw	33.5	7.6	3.1	17.1	499	308	189	39.4	1,151	479
LaGrange	49.5	11.9	3.3	6.2	202	13	184	52.2	1,714	110
Lawrenceville	21.7	6.1	9.8	5.7	191	90	93	43.1	1,455	393
McDonough	22.6	4.8	3.8	9.0	363	150	209	23.0	932	211
Macon-Bibb County	136.5	57.0	3.3	39.8	261	162	99	138.4	906	70
Marietta	104.6	19.1	0.6	38.9	642	285	349	104.2	1,717	485
Milton	31.8	11.3	3.4	17.3	445	287	157	33.0	850	302
Newnan	42.7	15.2	2.3	15.1	389	148	227	38.3	985	156
Peachtree City	57.1	7.7	5.1	22.9	650	401	246	39.6	1,122	82
Peachtree Corners	38.6	7.6	5.1	13.1	304	217	87	39.6	916	18
Pooler	34.7	9.9	5.4	11.1	468	213	250	46.0	1,945	987
Rome	73.4	20.2	3.4	23.1	635	296	284	92.4	2,541	342

1. Based on population estimated as of July 1 of the year shown.

City	City government finances, 2017 (cont.)												
	General expenditure (cont.)												
	Percent of total for:									Debt outstanding			
	Public welfare	Highways	Parking facilities	Education	Health and hospitals	Police protection	Sewerage and sanitation	Parks and recreation	Housing and community development	Interest on debt	Total (mil dol)	Per capita[1] (dollars)	Debt issued during year
	127	128	129	130	131	132	133	134	135	136	137	138	139
FLORIDA—Cont'd													
Palm Bay	0.0	19.1	0.0	0.0	0.0	20.8	21.1	4.4	1.6	5.1	134.5	1,199	28.6
Palm Beach Gardens	0.0	4.0	0.0	0.0	0.0	24.7	0.0	9.7	0.0	0.6	12.7	226	0.0
Palm Coast	0.0	15.4	0.0	0.0	0.0	3.1	39.9	8.0	0.0	1.0	166.2	1,930	45.9
Palm Springs	0.0	7.7	0.0	0.0	0.0	0.0	33.2	5.6	0.0	0.6	17.0	683	0.0
Panama City	0.0	6.3	0.0	0.0	0.4	17.5	12.1	10.5	0.6	0.5	53.6	1,443	0.0
Parkland	0.0	4.2	0.0	0.0	0.0	20.1	0.0	29.1	0.0	1.6	10.7	340	0.0
Pembroke Pines	0.4	1.5	0.0	0.0	0.0	15.3	13.3	12.1	2.4	3.9	327.5	1,918	7.6
Pensacola	0.0	5.4	0.3	0.0	0.0	18.9	5.5	7.4	12.4	6.2	203.0	3,865	26.8
Pinellas Park	0.0	6.6	0.0	0.0	3.9	17.5	24.4	6.8	0.0	0.2	19.2	362	0.0
Plantation	0.0	2.3	0.0	0.0	6.9	30.9	17.0	13.5	0.9	0.6	43.9	467	0.0
Plant City	0.0	4.9	0.0	0.0	0.0	16.5	37.6	8.3	1.9	0.5	36.9	940	0.0
Pompano Beach	0.0	2.2	0.6	0.0	6.8	19.8	14.2	6.1	1.4	0.8	104.8	950	0.0
Port Orange	0.0	9.7	0.0	0.0	0.0	17.3	34.6	7.4	0.4	3.0	101.9	1,616	0.0
Port St. Lucie	0.0	34.0	0.0	0.0	0.5	16.0	17.3	6.4	0.1	9.3	806.9	4,266	372.1
Riviera Beach	3.1	2.6	0.0	0.0	0.0	14.1	11.5	9.2	0.0	3.3	176.6	5,089	43.2
Rockledge	0.0	12.1	0.0	0.0	8.5	21.7	24.0	0.0	0.0	0.8	3.0	109	0.2
Royal Palm Beach	0.0	9.6	0.0	0.0	0.0	27.6	4.2	18.8	0.0	1.3	0.0	0	0.0
St. Cloud	0.0	5.3	0.0	0.0	3.8	16.3	28.3	5.5	0.0	4.7	96.6	1,868	0.0
St. Petersburg	0.0	5.0	1.3	0.0	2.8	23.5	19.5	14.9	1.3	0.5	653.5	2,489	139.7
Sanford	0.7	6.8	0.0	0.0	7.3	15.1	25.4	6.9	0.5	0.6	72.0	1,209	8.4
Sarasota	0.0	9.8	1.2	0.0	0.0	23.0	24.8	13.3	2.7	3.0	109.2	1,910	2.9
Sebastian	0.0	19.8	0.0	0.0	0.0	32.5	0.0	17.0	0.0	0.8	3.2	126	0.0
Sunrise	0.0	1.6	8.3	0.0	0.0	22.3	22.3	7.1	0.4	1.1	258.1	2,737	0.0
Tallahassee	0.0	15.8	0.0	0.0	0.0	17.2	18.0	7.0	1.0	2.0	1,413.0	7,373	257.0
Tamarac	0.0	6.6	0.0	0.0	0.0	15.0	16.6	7.2	0.6	1.2	52.3	791	0.0
Tampa	0.0	4.6	2.1	0.0	0.0	20.9	25.8	9.6	2.3	2.0	1,675.3	4,284	315.8
Tarpon Springs	0.0	3.7	0.0	0.0	0.0	19.0	25.6	10.5	0.0	0.0	33.7	1,337	0.0
Temple Terrace	0.0	2.4	0.0	0.0	0.0	23.6	24.7	6.4	0.0	1.6	39.5	1,478	24.4
Titusville	0.0	10.3	0.0	0.0	0.0	21.5	15.5	2.0	1.6	0.4	37.7	817	0.4
Venice	0.0	0.7	0.0	0.0	0.0	12.7	26.9	12.7	0.0	0.2	43.1	1,867	0.0
Wellington	0.0	12.4	0.0	0.0	0.0	11.2	9.2	20.1	0.0	0.1	5.5	84	3.2
West Melbourne	0.0	15.0	0.0	0.0	0.0	26.9	11.6	8.8	0.0	0.0	13.6	619	0.0
Weston	0.0	0.4	0.0	0.0	8.6	10.7	33.8	9.3	0.0	2.7	68.3	963	6.2
West Palm Beach	0.0	6.1	2.1	0.0	0.6	21.4	24.5	7.3	2.5	2.8	452.1	4,098	120.2
Winter Garden	2.1	9.0	0.0	0.0	0.0	18.8	24.9	4.1	0.2	0.8	36.2	828	19.8
Winter Haven	0.2	2.6	0.0	0.0	0.0	17.3	25.8	14.0	0.0	1.2	73.8	1,807	0.0
Winter Park	0.0	1.9	0.0	0.0	0.0	16.7	12.9	11.2	0.0	0.8	145.9	4,726	0.0
Winter Springs	0.0	17.0	0.0	0.0	0.0	25.3	25.2	7.4	0.0	0.7	22.1	602	0.0
GEORGIA	X	X	X	X	X	X	X	X	X	X	X	X	X
Albany	0.0	5.9	0.0	0.0	0.0	14.0	42.5	4.1	0.8	1.5	29.9	408	0.0
Alpharetta	0.0	19.5	0.0	0.0	0.0	17.4	2.8	11.2	0.0	3.7	222.0	3,377	123.4
Athens-Clarke County	0.3	5.9	0.0	0.0	0.9	14.5	10.4	5.5	0.0	7.6	264.0	2,082	0.0
Atlanta	1.2	6.3	0.0	0.0	0.1	11.9	3.4	3.4	0.5	10.9	7,204.2	14,652	548.9
Augusta-Richmond County	0.6	12.3	0.0	0.0	1.4	13.2	24.6	6.1	0.5	0.9	604.8	3,070	66.1
Brookhaven	0.0	6.6	0.0	0.0	0.0	18.0	24.0	6.8	1.6	0.0	21.5	400	0.0
Canton	0.0	18.9	0.0	0.0	0.0	21.3	17.3	5.0	0.0	5.2	38.1	1,345	3.7
Carrollton	0.0	10.6	0.0	0.0	0.0	18.9	22.0	15.8	0.0	1.1	13.3	499	0.0
Chamblee	0.0	10.7	0.0	0.0	0.4	40.4	6.6	9.0	0.0	0.1	0.0	0	0.0
Columbus	0.2	10.9	0.0	0.0	9.7	15.4	8.9	5.2	1.3	1.9	452.8	2,336	0.0
Dalton	0.0	10.6	0.0	0.0	0.0	11.8	29.6	9.2	0.0	0.8	70.8	2,107	0.1
Douglasville	0.0	5.5	0.0	0.0	0.0	35.7	7.4	13.9	0.0	4.7	46.5	1,410	13.6
Duluth	0.0	13.9	0.0	0.0	0.0	36.4	0.0	12.0	0.0	0.9	16.5	561	0.0
Dunwoody	0.0	19.7	0.0	0.0	0.0	15.2	4.2	7.8	0.0	0.2	1.5	29	0.0
East Point	0.0	3.4	0.0	0.0	0.0	23.3	11.1	2.8	0.0	12.0	116.1	3,317	50.9
Gainesville	0.1	6.6	0.0	0.0	0.0	11.0	26.1	11.3	0.0	8.7	779.5	19,311	0.0
Hinesville	0.9	5.5	0.0	0.0	0.0	22.2	28.9	1.5	2.4	2.6	31.0	940	12.7
Johns Creek	0.0	26.8	0.0	0.0	0.0	11.9	0.0	30.7	0.0	0.2	3.9	46	0.2
Kennesaw	0.0	11.8	0.0	0.0	0.0	17.1	4.2	7.0	15.8	3.3	32.1	940	0.0
LaGrange	0.0	8.4	0.0	0.0	0.7	20.0	30.3	3.8	0.0	1.5	37.9	1,243	2.4
Lawrenceville	0.0	6.7	0.0	0.0	0.0	24.0	11.6	0.8	1.9	0.0	0.0	0	0.0
McDonough	0.0	8.2	0.0	0.0	0.0	31.2	17.1	6.2	0.0	0.6	9.8	399	4.2
Macon-Bibb County	0.0	3.0	0.1	0.0	0.0	19.4	7.5	1.4	7.8	1.1	35.9	235	0.0
Marietta	0.3	23.3	0.0	0.0	0.0	18.9	13.4	2.1	8.6	4.6	115.1	1,898	0.0
Milton	0.0	21.9	0.0	0.0	0.0	14.8	0.0	7.2	0.0	1.1	9.6	247	0.7
Newnan	0.0	15.1	0.0	0.0	0.0	20.4	14.2	4.4	0.1	0.0	32.3	829	0.0
Peachtree City	0.0	13.2	0.0	0.0	0.8	16.5	0.0	6.3	0.0	1.6	13.0	370	3.2
Peachtree Corners	0.0	8.3	0.0	0.0	0.0	22.9	22.8	1.9	3.8	2.0	0.0	0	0.0
Pooler	0.0	7.6	0.0	0.0	0.0	10.6	13.2	8.1	0.0	2.0	18.0	762	1.3
Rome	0.1	5.9	0.1	0.0	0.2	8.3	36.3	11.0	0.9	3.2	43.9	1,207	0.0

1. Based on population estimated as of July 1 of the year shown.

Table D. Cities — **Land Area and Population**

STATE	Place code	City	Land area[1] (sq. mi)	Population, 2021: Total persons 2021	Population, 2021: Rank	Population, 2021: Per square mile	Race 2020: Race alone[2] (percent): White	Race 2020: Race alone[2] (percent): Black or African American	Race 2020: Race alone[2] (percent): American Indian, Alaskan Native	Race 2020: Race alone[2] (percent): Asian	Race 2020: Race alone[2] (percent): Hawaiian Pacific Islander	Race 2020: Race alone[2] (percent): Some other race	Race 2020: Two or more races (percent)
			1	2	3	4	5	6	7	8	9	10	11
		GEORGIA—Cont'd											
13	67284	Roswell	40.7	92,530	366	2,273.5	65.4	11.8	0.4	5.0	0.0	6.8	10.6
13	68516	Sandy Springs	37.7	107,180	288	2,843.0	55.6	18.7	0.4	9.4	0.1	6.7	9.1
13	69000	Savannah	108.5	147,088	187	1,355.6	37.9	49.1	0.3	3.8	0.2	3.1	5.5
13	71492	Smyrna	15.6	55,685	708	3,569.6	45.6	31.3	0.5	6.7	0.0	6.2	9.7
13	72122	South Fulton	85.2	108,575	284	1,274.4	3.5	90.5	0.2	0.4	0.0	1.9	3.4
13	73256	Statesboro	15.0	33,399	1,184	2,226.6	50.2	40.4	0.3	1.9	0.1	2.3	4.8
13	73704	Stockbridge	13.7	29,163	1,342	2,128.7	13.8	66.1	0.5	8.7	0.1	4.7	6.2
13	73784	Stonecrest	37.4	59,863	646	1,600.6	2.6	92.3	0.2	0.4	0.0	1.3	3.2
13	74180	Sugar Hill	11.1	25,259	1,528	2,275.6	52.2	12.7	0.7	15.3	0.1	8.3	10.9
13	77652	Tucker	20.2	36,855	1,076	1,824.5	40.2	36.2	0.5	8.3	0.0	7.4	7.3
13	78324	Union City	19.7	27,359	1,423	1,388.8	5.5	85.4	0.3	0.5	0.0	4.3	3.9
13	78800	Valdosta	36.0	55,567	711	1,543.5	35.4	54.8	0.3	1.6	0.1	2.8	5.0
13	80508	Warner Robins	37.8	81,446	432	2,154.7	43.2	41.5	0.4	3.7	0.1	3.6	7.6
13	84176	Woodstock	12.6	36,198	1,095	2,872.9	69.9	11.3	0.2	4.4	0.1	4.1	10.1
15	00000	HAWAII	6,422.4	1,441,553	X	224.5	22.9	1.6	0.3	37.2	10.8	1.8	25.3
15	06290	East Honolulu CDP	23.0	NA	NA	NA	24.1	0.6	0.1	47.6	2.9	0.9	23.8
15	07470	Ewa Gentry CDP	2.1	NA	NA	NA	12.9	2.8	0.3	46.3	6.9	1.7	29.1
15	14650	Hilo CDP	53.6	NA	NA	NA	16.4	0.6	0.3	31.1	15.6	1.1	34.9
15	22700	Kahului CDP	14.4	NA	NA	NA	10.5	0.5	0.4	51.5	14.2	1.8	21.2
15	23150	Kailua CDP (Honolulu County)	7.8	NA	NA	NA	43.3	0.7	0.2	17.9	6.0	1.7	30.1
15	28250	Kaneohe CDP	6.5	NA	NA	NA	19.3	0.7	0.2	34.4	9.7	1.2	34.4
15	51050	Mililani Town CDP	4.0	NA	NA	NA	13.6	1.6	0.2	44.5	5.3	1.3	33.6
15	62600	Pearl City CDP	9.1	NA	NA	NA	9.3	1.7	0.2	55.6	7.2	1.4	24.7
15	71550	Urban Honolulu CDP	60.5	345,510	56	5,710.9	16.4	1.7	0.2	52.9	9.2	1.3	18.2
15	79700	Waipahu CDP	2.7	NA	NA	NA	2.4	0.6	0.1	72.2	12.4	0.5	11.8
16	00000	IDAHO	82,645.1	1,900,923	X	23.0	82.1	0.9	1.4	1.5	0.2	5.6	8.3
16	08830	Boise City	84.1	237,446	94	2,823.4	81.2	2.3	0.7	3.6	0.3	3.5	8.5
16	12250	Caldwell	23.0	63,629	603	2,766.5	64.7	0.9	1.5	0.9	0.2	16.6	15.2
16	16750	Coeur d'Alene	16.1	55,904	702	3,472.3	88.5	0.4	1.0	1.1	0.2	1.5	7.3
16	23410	Eagle	31.0	32,100	1,227	1,035.5	88.0	0.4	0.4	1.7	0.1	1.7	7.7
16	39700	Idaho Falls	25.6	66,898	566	2,613.2	81.6	0.7	1.3	1.3	0.1	7.2	7.8
16	46540	Lewiston	17.3	34,447	1,156	1,991.2	89.3	0.5	1.8	0.9	0.1	1.0	6.3
16	52120	Meridian	35.6	125,963	222	3,538.3	84.1	1.0	0.5	2.6	0.2	2.8	8.8
16	54550	Moscow	6.9	25,850	1,498	3,746.4	84.3	1.2	0.8	3.5	0.2	2.0	8.0
16	56260	Nampa	34.3	106,186	297	3,095.8	73.3	0.9	1.2	1.1	0.5	11.2	11.9
16	64090	Pocatello	33.4	57,092	694	1,709.3	83.6	1.2	2.2	1.7	0.4	3.7	7.3
16	64810	Post Falls	16.2	42,610	937	2,630.2	88.3	0.4	1.0	0.8	0.2	1.5	7.9
16	67420	Rexburg	10.1	35,300	1,130	3,495.0	84.0	1.8	0.5	2.2	0.5	5.3	5.7
16	82810	Twin Falls	19.5	53,213	751	2,728.9	78.1	1.8	1.1	2.5	0.4	6.9	9.3
17	00000	ILLINOIS	55,513.7	12,671,469	X	228.3	61.4	14.1	0.8	5.9	0.0	8.9	8.9
17	00243	Addison	9.8	35,353	1,126	3,607.4	47.7	3.5	1.7	8.1	0.0	23.0	16.0
17	00685	Algonquin	12.1	29,944	1,311	2,474.7	77.3	2.4	0.4	7.3	0.0	4.1	8.4
17	01114	Alton	15.7	25,422	1,522	1,619.2	63.8	26.8	0.5	0.7	0.0	1.1	7.1
17	02154	Arlington Heights	16.6	76,000	483	4,578.3	79.0	1.6	0.2	10.8	0.0	2.6	5.8
17	03012	Aurora	45.0	179,266	144	3,983.7	40.6	10.9	1.6	11.0	0.0	20.7	15.1
17	04013	Bartlett	15.7	40,539	975	2,582.1	66.2	2.5	0.4	17.9	0.0	4.5	8.3
17	04078	Batavia	10.7	26,092	1,484	2,438.5	84.2	2.5	0.2	2.3	0.0	3.3	7.5
17	04845	Belleville	23.2	41,751	950	1,799.6	58.0	32.2	0.3	1.0	0.1	1.4	7.0
17	05092	Belvidere	12.1	25,134	1,541	2,077.2	61.8	3.0	1.5	1.1	0.1	18.1	14.5
17	05573	Berwyn	3.9	55,772	703	14,300.5	33.3	8.5	2.8	2.5	0.0	31.6	21.2
17	06613	Bloomington	27.1	78,283	464	2,888.7	71.2	10.9	0.4	7.2	0.0	3.3	6.9
17	07133	Bolingbrook	24.9	73,597	500	2,955.7	40.1	19.5	0.9	13.9	0.0	12.7	12.9
17	09447	Buffalo Grove	9.6	42,794	930	4,457.7	63.1	1.2	0.3	27.5	0.0	2.3	5.6
17	09642	Burbank	4.2	28,789	1,356	6,854.5	60.3	1.9	1.6	3.1	0.0	17.4	15.6
17	10487	Calumet City	7.2	35,159	1,133	4,883.2	9.7	72.6	0.6	0.2	0.0	10.4	6.3
17	11332	Carol Stream	9.1	39,333	1,010	4,322.3	57.1	6.9	0.6	18.7	0.0	7.9	8.7
17	11358	Carpentersville	7.9	37,598	1,056	4,759.2	37.5	5.9	2.4	5.3	0.0	32.0	16.8
17	12385	Champaign	23.0	89,114	386	3,874.5	53.5	18.0	0.4	16.7	0.0	4.0	7.5
17	14000	Chicago	227.7	2,696,555	3	11,842.6	35.9	29.2	1.3	7.0	0.0	15.8	10.8
17	14026	Chicago Heights	10.3	26,905	1,444	2,612.1	21.0	42.5	1.3	0.3	0.1	23.3	11.4
17	14351	Cicero town	5.9	83,161	421	14,095.1	19.2	3.7	4.3	0.6	0.0	46.9	25.3
17	17887	Crystal Lake	18.9	40,411	979	2,138.1	79.8	1.5	0.4	2.8	0.0	6.1	9.3
17	18563	Danville	17.9	28,787	1,357	1,608.2	54.4	33.4	0.3	1.5	0.0	3.9	6.4
17	18823	Decatur	42.9	69,646	540	1,623.4	63.7	26.6	0.2	1.3	0.0	1.5	6.7
17	19161	DeKalb	17.0	40,486	976	2,381.5	58.7	18.5	0.8	3.9	0.0	8.0	10.1

1. Dry land or land partially or temporarily covered by water. 2. Hispanic or Latino persons may be of any race.

Table D. Cities — **Population**

City	Percent Hispanic or Latino[1], 2020	Percent foreign born, 2016–2020	Age of population (percent), 2016–2020: Under 18 years	18 to 24 years	25 to 34 years	35 to 44 years	45 to 54 years	55 to 64 years	65 years and over	Median age, 2016–2020	Percent female, 2016–2020	Population: Census counts: 2010	2020	Percent change: 2010–2020	2020–2021
	12	13	14	15	16	17	18	19	20	21	22	23	24	25	26
GEORGIA—Cont'd															
Roswell	15.2	19.3	25.1	7.2	11.2	14.0	15.5	12.8	14.3	39.5	50.8	88,333	92,892	5.2	-0.4
Sandy Springs	13.6	18.9	19.1	7.6	19.5	15.9	12.8	11.5	13.6	36.7	51.8	93,828	108,134	15.2	-0.9
Savannah	6.6	6.0	20.8	13.7	18.9	11.9	9.9	11.2	13.6	32.9	52.1	136,919	148,095	8.2	-0.7
Smyrna	13.8	16.5	23.2	6.2	20.5	16.9	14.1	9.8	9.3	35.0	53.0	50,864	55,689	9.5	0.0
South Fulton	3.3	5.2	24.8	8.9	13.2	14.8	16.7	9.7	11.9	37.3	53.3	85,589	107,524	25.6	1.0
Statesboro	5.8	4.4	14.1	45.4	13.8	6.2	5.7	6.2	8.6	22.4	51.9	28,370	33,159	16.9	0.7
Stockbridge	8.7	14.1	26.7	9.2	13.0	15.8	15.9	9.3	10.0	35.7	57.8	26,369	28,944	9.8	0.8
Stonecrest	2.8	8.8	25.7	10.0	16.6	13.5	14.4	11.1	8.7	33.6	54.6	50,195	59,148	17.8	1.2
Sugar Hill	18.9	20.6	27.9	8.2	12.5	18.0	15.3	10.0	8.1	35.8	52.5	18,688	25,093	34.3	0.7
Tucker	12.5	16.4	18.1	6.8	13.4	12.1	15.6	14.0	20.0	44.7	50.7	33,379	36,989	10.8	-0.4
Union City	7.4	5.8	28.9	8.4	15.4	13.4	8.9	11.7	13.3	32.8	54.5	19,335	26,839	38.8	1.9
Valdosta	6.1	3.2	22.6	20.5	16.0	10.9	8.5	8.8	12.7	28.4	53.0	54,753	55,485	1.3	0.1
Warner Robins	8.1	7.6	26.1	9.0	17.5	13.2	11.1	11.1	12.0	33.3	53.1	69,859	80,324	15.0	1.4
Woodstock	11.1	9.8	24.2	6.7	17.8	14.3	12.8	10.3	13.9	36.1	53.2	23,788	34,985	47.1	3.5
HAWAII	9.5	18.3	21.3	8.5	14.3	12.7	12.1	12.7	18.4	39.4	49.8	1,360,304	1,455,271	7.0	-0.9
East Honolulu CDP	5.4	15.8	19.1	6.1	8.2	10.9	14.6	14.3	26.8	48.7	50.4	NA	NA	NA	NA
Ewa Gentry CDP	11.6	16.8	27.2	6.5	19.1	16.5	12.6	10.0	8.0	33.0	50.2	NA	NA	NA	NA
Hilo CDP	11.5	9.0	21.1	9.4	13.1	11.6	10.5	13.2	21.1	40.4	51.1	NA	NA	NA	NA
Kahului CDP	8.5	32.6	23.6	7.9	12.7	13.0	13.5	11.5	17.7	39.4	49.2	NA	NA	NA	NA
Kailua CDP (Honolulu County)	8.7	9.0	21.6	6.8	12.8	13.7	11.7	14.2	19.3	41.4	51.3	NA	NA	NA	NA
Kaneohe CDP	9.9	8.3	19.0	6.8	14.6	11.5	11.4	15.1	21.6	43.1	50.8	NA	NA	NA	NA
Mililani Town CDP	10.6	11.0	20.2	6.2	13.4	12.9	11.3	12.8	23.2	42.6	48.8	NA	NA	NA	NA
Pearl City CDP	8.1	13.1	18.0	9.4	12.7	12.3	11.0	11.3	25.3	42.3	49.7	NA	NA	NA	NA
Urban Honolulu CDP	6.3	27.5	17.3	8.3	15.4	13.2	12.7	12.8	20.4	41.7	49.8	337,721	350,943	3.9	-1.5
Waipahu CDP	4.7	41.1	21.4	8.4	15.6	11.6	12.2	10.3	20.4	39.5	51.8	NA	NA	NA	NA
IDAHO	13.0	5.9	25.3	9.4	13.1	12.6	11.5	12.2	15.8	36.6	49.9	1,567,658	1,839,106	17.3	3.4
Boise City	9.0	6.6	19.9	10.7	15.7	13.9	12.8	12.4	14.6	37.5	49.8	209,382	235,670	12.6	0.8
Caldwell	36.7	10.7	33.5	9.4	15.2	12.9	10.4	8.8	9.8	29.5	50.9	46,353	59,985	29.4	6.1
Coeur d'Alene	5.5	3.0	21.6	9.6	16.0	13.5	10.6	11.3	17.4	37.3	50.3	44,161	54,515	23.4	2.5
Eagle	6.7	5.4	25.4	4.1	8.2	11.2	13.6	16.7	20.9	46.1	51.8	19,984	30,471	52.5	5.3
Idaho Falls	15.5	5.5	28.8	8.4	15.1	13.0	10.4	11.3	13.1	33.4	50.1	57,833	65,413	13.1	2.3
Lewiston	4.1	2.2	21.0	9.3	13.6	11.8	11.6	13.2	19.4	39.8	51.1	31,893	34,193	7.2	0.7
Meridian	9.5	4.5	28.2	8.1	12.6	14.9	13.5	10.3	12.4	35.9	50.3	76,983	118,099	53.4	6.7
Moscow	6.4	6.6	14.9	34.6	15.3	10.4	6.9	7.7	10.2	25.2	48.4	23,807	25,414	6.8	1.7
Nampa	25.3	7.8	25.8	11.5	15.1	13.4	9.9	9.7	14.6	33.3	49.8	81,892	100,252	22.4	5.9
Pocatello	10.3	3.7	24.2	12.0	16.6	13.2	9.7	10.8	13.5	32.9	49.3	54,235	56,238	3.7	1.5
Post Falls	6.1	1.6	30.3	7.0	15.7	15.0	9.6	10.3	12.1	32.9	52.0	27,785	38,538	38.7	10.6
Rexburg	10.8	5.4	23.7	38.6	16.9	6.0	5.4	4.2	5.2	23.1	49.3	25,497	34,931	37.0	1.1
Twin Falls	17.3	10.5	26.1	9.6	16.3	12.7	10.4	10.0	14.8	33.6	50.8	44,313	51,593	16.4	3.1
ILLINOIS	18.2	13.9	22.5	9.2	13.9	12.9	12.9	13.0	15.7	38.3	50.9	12,831,572	12,812,508	-0.1	-1.1
Addison	45.6	33.5	22.7	9.3	14.1	12.4	13.9	11.9	15.6	37.8	50.7	37,084	35,742	-3.6	-1.1
Algonquin	11.3	12.3	22.3	8.2	10.9	11.9	16.7	17.0	13.1	42.5	51.3	30,065	29,719	-1.2	0.8
Alton	2.6	1.5	24.3	7.0	14.6	12.8	11.8	12.9	16.6	38.1	52.1	27,936	25,701	-8.0	-1.1
Arlington Heights	6.9	19.7	22.9	4.7	10.4	14.0	13.5	14.9	19.6	43.4	51.2	75,185	77,595	3.2	-2.1
Aurora	41.5	25.6	28.2	9.6	12.9	16.1	13.9	9.4	9.8	34.4	50.3	197,964	180,688	-8.7	-0.8
Bartlett	12.0	20.0	23.7	7.7	10.9	12.9	15.8	14.3	14.6	40.6	49.4	41,235	41,164	-0.2	-1.5
Batavia	9.2	5.3	26.3	5.9	12.2	13.3	14.4	13.0	15.0	38.8	50.9	26,236	26,093	-0.5	0.0
Belleville	3.8	2.4	22.4	9.1	14.4	14.0	13.5	12.7	13.9	38.1	51.8	44,239	42,333	-4.3	-1.4
Belvidere	35.9	13.8	24.2	10.2	13.2	12.0	13.3	12.3	14.8	36.4	51.3	25,641	25,327	-1.2	-0.8
Berwyn	64.2	27.1	26.1	8.7	14.5	14.3	12.3	11.7	12.5	35.6	49.6	56,650	57,120	0.8	-2.4
Bloomington	7.5	10.1	22.5	12.1	14.7	13.3	12.2	12.1	13.0	35.5	50.8	76,683	78,273	2.1	0.0
Bolingbrook	26.8	21.7	25.6	10.3	12.3	14.5	15.1	11.5	10.8	36.6	50.8	73,362	73,956	0.8	-0.5
Buffalo Grove	6.6	34.9	22.8	7.2	10.8	14.9	15.5	14.7	14.0	41.5	52.7	41,509	43,225	4.1	-1.0
Burbank	39.6	27.5	25.8	8.8	12.6	13.6	11.5	13.5	14.2	37.8	48.1	28,906	29,408	1.7	-2.1
Calumet City	18.0	8.6	23.5	11.0	14.0	12.1	12.3	13.7	13.5	36.9	55.0	37,159	35,968	-3.2	-2.2
Carol Stream	17.2	26.8	21.0	9.2	13.4	12.5	13.5	15.4	15.1	40.1	50.8	39,497	39,849	0.9	-1.3
Carpentersville	56.3	29.7	30.2	10.9	11.8	14.1	14.2	9.6	9.2	32.1	50.5	37,679	37,946	0.7	-0.9
Champaign	8.7	15.8	17.0	29.0	15.2	10.6	8.8	9.0	10.5	27.3	47.6	81,245	88,421	8.8	0.8
Chicago	29.8	20.3	20.5	9.8	20.1	14.0	11.9	11.1	12.7	34.8	51.4	2,695,674	2,747,231	1.9	-1.8
Chicago Heights	39.0	14.8	26.9	10.7	11.9	12.3	13.0	10.3	14.9	35.4	51.4	30,393	27,519	-9.5	-2.2
Cicero town	89.0	38.7	28.0	12.3	14.5	13.6	12.9	10.3	8.5	31.7	50.8	84,241	85,180	1.1	-2.4
Crystal Lake	14.8	9.4	24.4	8.6	9.7	14.3	14.9	12.7	15.4	39.9	49.7	40,749	40,243	-1.2	0.4
Danville	7.5	3.1	24.9	9.1	13.1	11.8	10.8	13.4	16.9	37.6	50.4	33,027	29,214	-11.5	-1.5
Decatur	3.1	2.5	21.0	9.9	13.7	10.6	10.7	13.8	20.3	39.8	53.4	76,122	70,765	-7.0	-1.6
DeKalb	17.8	9.2	17.9	31.8	14.7	9.4	8.6	8.6	9.1	25.1	50.6	44,124	40,506	-8.2	0.0

1. May be of any race.

Table D. Cities — **Households, Group Quarters, Crime, and Education**

City	Households, 2016–2020							Persons in group quarters, 2016–2020	Serious crimes known to police[2], 2020				Educational attainment, 2016–2020		
			Percent						Violent		Property			Attainment[4] (percent)	
	Number	Persons per household	Family	Married couple family	Female family	Non-family	One person		Number	Rate	Number	Rate	Population age 25 and over	High school graduate or less	Bachelor's degree or more
	27	28	29	30	31	32	33	34	35	36	37	38	39	40	41
GEORGIA—Cont'd															
Roswell	34,885	2.71	69.7	56.4	9.4	30.3	24.2	474	357	374.2	1,079	1,131.1	64,257	19.4	60.8
Sandy Springs	49,537	2.18	51.4	39.5	8.7	48.6	38.9	436	164	147.5	1,539	1,383.8	79,308	15.5	66.5
Savannah	52,918	2.55	56.1	31.0	20.3	43.9	33.2	10,533	NA	NA	NA	NA	95,269	38.4	29.1
Smyrna	24,760	2.27	55.5	39.1	12.1	44.5	36.1	186	214	373.4	1,176	2,051.7	39,764	19.7	55.7
South Fulton	35,149	2.80	63.4	35.5	20.8	36.6	31.8	289	1,034	1,027.2	2,694	2,676.4	65,347	32.0	37.5
Statesboro	10,441	2.33	43.4	23.1	17.2	56.6	33.2	7,789	NA	NA	NA	NA	13,005	45.1	24.9
Stockbridge	11,136	2.64	67.8	37.0	25.8	32.2	27.8	5	NA	NA	NA	NA	18,849	33.3	30.2
Stonecrest	19,897	2.74	58.0	24.4	26.5	42.0	35.4	243	NA	NA	NA	NA	35,157	37.3	28.3
Sugar Hill	7,746	3.10	80.2	65.1	8.8	19.8	16.3	7	NA	NA	NA	NA	15,327	36.8	40.5
Tucker	14,538	2.46	60.8	43.1	13.4	39.2	31.8	451	NA	NA	NA	NA	27,262	24.7	49.9
Union City	9,722	2.25	53.3	20.0	27.0	46.7	44.6	53	NA	NA	NA	NA	13,782	36.7	24.5
Valdosta	21,961	2.46	51.9	28.9	18.2	48.1	36.4	2,264	220	388.5	1,848	3,263.4	32,038	46.4	27.0
Warner Robins	30,192	2.54	64.4	42.4	17.2	35.6	28.8	297	495	630.5	3,154	4,017.4	49,945	36.2	29.8
Woodstock	13,226	2.43	64.7	52.1	8.3	35.3	30.6	139	61	178.1	333	972.2	22,322	21.7	48.6
HAWAII	467,932	2.94	69.3	51.2	12.4	30.7	24.3	43,130	3,576	254.2	33,928	2,411.4	996,423	34.8	33.6
East Honolulu CDP	16,436	2.85	79.0	64.1	10.2	21.0	17.0	250	NA	NA	NA	NA	35,274	16.9	59.7
Ewa Gentry CDP	7,379	3.57	80.9	61.2	12.8	19.1	9.9	0	NA	NA	NA	NA	17,462	34.7	27.1
Hilo CDP	16,225	2.71	65.4	43.3	16.1	34.6	26.7	1,288	NA	NA	NA	NA	31,436	33.9	33.9
Kahului CDP	8,369	3.40	82.0	55.7	17.7	18.0	14.4	1,573	NA	NA	NA	NA	20,533	48.0	19.7
Kailua CDP (Honolulu County)	12,387	3.04	74.4	59.2	10.6	25.6	18.5	239	NA	NA	NA	NA	27,170	23.1	49.4
Kaneohe CDP	10,378	3.15	75.3	56.5	13.8	24.7	20.0	858	NA	NA	NA	NA	24,886	34.2	37.9
Mililani Town CDP	8,934	3.07	80.2	62.5	13.0	19.8	15.5	0	NA	NA	NA	NA	20,220	26.2	38.1
Pearl City CDP	14,172	3.06	75.1	56.1	13.9	24.9	20.6	1,730	NA	NA	NA	NA	32,769	31.2	35.8
Urban Honolulu CDP	131,081	2.55	57.8	41.0	11.5	42.2	34.7	12,738	NA	NA	NA	NA	258,456	33.5	37.8
Waipahu CDP	8,342	4.42	80.7	52.4	19.4	19.3	15.8	1,432	NA	NA	NA	NA	26,869	51.1	17.1
IDAHO	649,299	2.66	68.0	54.9	8.7	32.0	25.7	30,437	4,432	242.6	20,313	1,111.9	1,145,344	35.4	28.7
Boise City	94,449	2.38	56.7	44.5	8.5	43.3	33.4	3,263	677	292.8	3,793	1,640.4	158,258	25.3	42.7
Caldwell	17,494	3.17	69.6	49.9	14.0	30.4	23.0	1,317	NA	NA	NA	NA	32,391	51.1	15.5
Coeur d'Alene	22,095	2.27	58.3	44.4	9.4	41.7	31.4	1,252	209	391.3	835	1,563.5	35,415	31.3	27.7
Eagle	10,610	2.65	78.2	68.9	5.9	21.8	19.6	9	NA	NA	NA	NA	19,865	18.5	47.4
Idaho Falls	23,575	2.60	64.6	48.1	11.7	35.4	29.2	1,067	291	458.6	1,152	1,815.4	39,229	34.4	30.0
Lewiston	13,686	2.33	62.8	48.1	8.9	37.2	31.2	959	61	185.5	767	2,332.3	22,891	38.0	24.7
Meridian	38,049	2.82	74.1	59.6	9.3	25.9	21.9	303	190	159.4	1,006	843.9	68,610	22.5	41.1
Moscow	10,127	2.21	44.1	38.9	3.5	55.9	35.8	3,245	10	38.6	391	1,508.6	12,954	16.2	53.7
Nampa	34,164	2.78	67.6	50.7	10.8	32.4	24.8	1,948	319	314.6	1,666	1,642.8	60,642	45.0	19.9
Pocatello	20,766	2.49	58.6	44.1	10.0	41.4	32.8	4,297	206	362.0	1,223	2,149.4	35,736	35.1	28.2
Post Falls	12,481	2.78	73.4	54.2	11.9	26.6	21.8	270	NA	NA	NA	NA	21,929	34.9	21.7
Rexburg	9,170	3.13	79.9	74.9	3.7	20.1	12.1	358	9	30.1	101	338.2	10,964	14.8	43.4
Twin Falls	19,094	2.56	65.0	50.7	9.0	35.0	27.3	925	259	509.1	892	1,753.4	32,006	38.6	23.4
ILLINOIS	4,884,061	2.54	63.8	47.1	12.1	36.2	29.8	296,806	53,612	425.9	196,287	1,559.4	8,686,700	35.9	35.5
Addison	12,799	2.86	71.6	54.5	12.7	28.4	23.2	153	65	178.5	NA	NA	24,944	51.4	24.6
Algonquin	11,176	2.76	77.1	64.3	8.5	22.9	17.7	0	27	87.1	NA	NA	21,445	24.3	44.0
Alton	11,325	2.29	55.2	31.3	19.7	44.8	35.6	568	216	829.9	NA	NA	18,211	40.8	19.8
Arlington Heights	30,672	2.42	65.2	56.7	6.0	34.8	30.0	772	43	57.6	NA	NA	54,400	19.6	58.1
Aurora	65,128	3.03	73.1	52.3	14.6	26.9	21.4	1,760	659	333.3	NA	NA	124,012	42.0	33.1
Bartlett	13,515	3.02	80.4	68.7	8.1	19.6	16.8	93	9	22.2	NA	NA	28,038	27.4	45.6
Batavia	9,728	2.71	71.4	63.7	6.3	28.6	24.0	96	18	68.1	NA	NA	17,956	18.4	53.8
Belleville	17,824	2.25	52.8	35.8	12.2	47.2	40.4	1,184	236	582.2	NA	NA	28,252	32.4	26.8
Belvidere	8,940	2.76	65.9	42.4	16.4	34.1	28.4	272	NA	NA	NA	NA	16,348	55.6	15.0
Berwyn	18,277	2.99	67.6	45.0	16.1	32.4	25.9	186	NA	NA	NA	NA	35,764	49.0	22.2
Bloomington	32,125	2.35	58.0	45.2	9.6	42.0	34.2	2,184	314	405.8	NA	NA	50,827	27.0	46.5
Bolingbrook	23,165	3.19	79.2	60.2	14.5	20.8	16.4	353	130	174.1	NA	NA	47,645	32.7	38.5
Buffalo Grove	15,276	2.66	74.8	64.8	7.4	25.2	22.8	139	5	12.4	NA	NA	28,548	13.2	66.3
Burbank	9,108	3.10	74.9	55.0	12.2	25.1	23.2	231	83	294.1	NA	NA	18,607	55.5	16.2
Calumet City	14,166	2.56	60.8	26.6	26.4	39.2	36.8	19	158	441.6	NA	NA	23,754	41.3	18.6
Carol Stream	14,209	2.75	72.8	57.8	13.0	27.2	21.3	347	42	107.2	NA	NA	27,541	28.9	41.1
Carpentersville	11,004	3.42	75.8	55.9	13.1	24.2	18.0	7	27	72.6	NA	NA	22,145	52.8	20.4
Champaign	34,851	2.30	44.8	32.6	8.8	55.2	40.0	7,973	827	921.1	NA	NA	47,675	23.5	51.3
Chicago	1,081,143	2.44	52.3	32.5	14.8	47.7	37.5	59,104	26,583	986.9	NA	NA	1,883,017	36.1	41.1
Chicago Heights	9,736	2.96	68.9	37.5	20.7	31.1	28.3	766	205	701.9	NA	NA	18,480	51.9	17.1
Cicero town	22,698	3.55	77.1	47.8	19.6	22.9	19.0	817	325	404.1	NA	NA	48,693	68.2	9.8
Crystal Lake	14,393	2.73	76.2	62.5	8.8	23.8	20.4	346	37	93.1	NA	NA	26,565	28.3	40.2
Danville	12,181	2.35	56.7	31.5	19.6	43.3	38.7	2,303	505	1,671.7	NA	NA	20,425	49.8	17.3
Decatur	31,073	2.20	53.9	35.9	14.3	46.1	40.0	3,489	489	696.8	NA	NA	49,666	46.0	21.5
DeKalb	15,839	2.45	49.3	32.0	13.1	50.7	34.5	4,102	252	590.0	NA	NA	21,616	30.9	38.0

2. Data for serious crimes have not been adjusted for underreporting. This may affect comparability between geographic areas and over time. 4. Persons 25 years old and over.

City	Money income, 2016–2020					Median earnings Full year, Full-time workers, 2016–2020			Housing units, 2016–2020				
	Households												
	Median household income	Percent with income less than $25,000	Percent with income of $200,000 or more	Median family income	Median non-family household income	All persons	Men	Women	Total	Occupied	Percent owner occupied	Median value[1] (dollars)	Median gross rent (dollars)
	42	43	44	45	46	47	48	49	50	51	52	53	54
GEORGIA—Cont'd													
Roswell	105,913	7.9	20.9	125,641	64,144	71,153	82,545	61,117	36,760	34,885	70.1	385,800	1,361
Sandy Springs	80,998	10.6	18.9	123,432	61,929	63,316	72,642	56,701	53,360	49,537	49.7	474,000	1,383
Savannah	46,149	28.2	3.7	55,743	33,236	36,996	41,286	34,613	61,991	52,918	44.0	162,300	1,049
Smyrna	77,713	10.7	11.0	102,342	59,176	62,260	71,002	57,205	26,924	24,760	55.5	309,000	1,326
South Fulton	65,104	14.5	4.7	77,536	45,012	46,866	48,154	45,100	38,299	35,149	69.3	176,800	1,193
Statesboro	32,790	41.0	1.1	45,235	23,373	31,406	31,592	31,143	12,130	10,441	24.6	115,100	776
Stockbridge	58,401	10.5	3.9	71,521	47,779	47,330	50,743	46,771	11,691	11,136	45.2	187,900	1,175
Stonecrest	51,439	21.6	2.1	64,984	37,945	41,404	42,373	40,619	21,766	19,897	45.6	136,400	1,146
Sugar Hill	90,205	10.0	10.5	95,951	58,617	53,938	58,981	47,746	8,009	7,746	83.1	249,300	1,195
Tucker	74,069	13.4	8.2	94,574	47,351	53,931	56,510	51,723	15,942	14,538	62.6	272,500	1,132
Union City	39,768	24.7	0.5	53,103	32,115	34,950	38,098	34,142	10,734	9,722	37.1	150,600	994
Valdosta	33,583	39.9	3.2	46,117	22,374	33,174	37,541	31,239	25,146	21,961	39.0	129,800	788
Warner Robins	55,163	19.8	3.0	64,743	37,273	42,664	49,276	38,175	33,066	30,192	52.7	129,000	944
Woodstock	81,268	9.4	7.9	99,072	50,677	59,388	73,059	48,731	13,805	13,226	67.3	265,300	1,386
HAWAII	83,173	13.0	11.3	97,813	49,031	50,760	55,191	45,467	546,571	467,932	60.3	636,400	1,651
East Honolulu CDP	139,487	5.2	26.9	151,349	73,212	74,626	83,038	65,170	18,537	16,436	84.3	968,200	2,690
Ewa Gentry CDP	112,385	1.8	13.1	118,595	91,000	52,203	64,223	46,914	7,560	7,379	71.9	594,500	1,965
Hilo CDP	65,727	21.7	4.9	78,764	33,457	45,731	49,861	43,479	18,524	16,225	62.0	341,500	1,098
Kahului CDP	83,238	12.0	8.4	88,394	30,321	40,982	44,667	37,374	8,903	8,369	57.8	617,500	1,333
Kailua CDP (Honolulu County)	122,706	6.8	24.6	139,423	64,462	65,675	75,685	57,176	13,303	12,387	74.6	992,100	2,510
Kaneohe CDP	116,118	6.0	16.8	126,611	59,028	56,627	65,553	51,121	10,949	10,378	72.8	805,700	2,001
Mililani Town CDP	104,409	5.2	14.3	117,377	60,112	58,125	62,617	53,486	9,149	8,934	79.7	683,700	1,922
Pearl City CDP	101,517	7.7	15.1	116,042	52,793	54,294	61,313	50,059	14,652	14,172	70.6	691,900	2,044
Urban Honolulu CDP	72,454	16.0	10.0	92,019	48,636	50,876	54,492	46,076	152,576	131,081	46.3	707,400	1,520
Waipahu CDP	78,351	15.1	10.0	83,609	37,250	37,241	40,913	34,753	8,721	8,342	56.3	648,200	1,338
IDAHO	58,915	18.2	4.7	70,885	34,270	43,599	49,848	37,189	737,411	649,299	70.8	235,600	887
Boise City	63,778	16.8	7.2	83,074	40,080	48,844	51,683	43,289	99,452	94,449	61.7	282,900	1,009
Caldwell	55,069	20.3	2.0	61,264	30,833	37,132	40,352	32,515	18,159	17,494	67.0	188,300	910
Coeur d'Alene	54,763	21.3	3.1	66,751	35,940	39,517	42,382	33,180	23,567	22,095	54.1	276,600	1,037
Eagle	91,414	11.9	17.9	107,607	41,708	70,200	90,532	56,690	11,092	10,610	85.5	455,800	1,275
Idaho Falls	56,590	20.0	4.5	67,198	33,875	38,934	47,566	30,629	25,043	23,575	61.5	179,600	787
Lewiston	54,912	23.5	3.5	76,185	31,708	48,127	53,968	38,827	14,531	13,686	72.2	204,600	724
Meridian	76,403	10.4	9.0	88,961	43,555	49,794	58,534	42,497	39,143	38,049	76.8	304,500	1,200
Moscow	42,262	30.4	3.8	74,183	26,086	42,932	46,711	39,526	10,688	10,127	39.3	240,500	722
Nampa	53,205	18.2	1.2	62,530	33,716	37,098	41,878	32,558	35,261	34,164	66.3	191,800	972
Pocatello	46,882	25.2	2.4	63,909	30,115	41,378	46,191	37,991	22,865	20,766	63.0	154,000	661
Post Falls	62,033	15.2	1.4	72,283	32,774	43,701	48,628	38,673	13,044	12,481	70.9	246,400	1,049
Rexburg	33,278	39.9	3.5	40,921	21,055	34,116	39,168	26,184	11,832	9,170	29.9	221,700	765
Twin Falls	50,839	20.2	2.0	58,965	35,550	41,698	45,556	35,190	19,960	19,094	64.4	175,900	841
ILLINOIS	68,428	17.9	8.8	86,251	40,774	53,252	59,651	47,170	5,373,385	4,884,061	66.3	202,100	1,038
Addison	68,534	17.9	5.7	79,011	39,018	45,577	50,004	39,304	13,187	12,799	64.8	259,000	1,089
Algonquin	109,819	7.9	15.4	127,660	53,357	74,264	85,664	60,444	11,604	11,176	85.0	268,100	1,659
Alton	43,291	29.3	1.5	55,228	29,585	40,887	47,395	35,291	13,287	11,325	60.0	80,400	796
Arlington Heights	100,221	11.6	16.3	126,753	56,784	75,659	85,973	65,480	32,467	30,672	74.0	352,000	1,441
Aurora	74,659	12.7	8.7	83,464	45,638	47,112	51,804	41,530	68,523	65,128	65.1	194,100	1,274
Bartlett	109,980	7.2	14.4	123,249	53,452	66,186	71,982	57,817	13,905	13,515	85.0	286,200	1,702
Batavia	97,995	12.4	17.2	123,247	38,305	70,930	86,557	55,466	10,056	9,728	77.2	310,300	1,168
Belleville	52,843	22.4	2.7	71,835	32,329	41,759	46,885	38,292	20,761	17,824	62.0	97,500	817
Belvidere	52,609	21.5	0.7	67,518	30,397	38,435	41,133	33,343	9,515	8,940	73.2	114,600	854
Berwyn	61,915	15.8	4.3	72,241	37,436	41,260	43,038	38,753	20,059	18,277	59.1	227,100	995
Bloomington	66,861	21.1	7.3	91,227	37,283	55,440	63,970	48,340	35,110	32,125	60.6	165,300	844
Bolingbrook	92,184	10.2	11.7	102,174	53,452	53,399	60,855	48,174	23,958	23,165	80.4	231,100	1,385
Buffalo Grove	117,921	10.0	22.0	140,920	54,528	81,304	89,663	68,081	15,775	15,276	79.3	338,400	1,700
Burbank	70,052	12.1	5.3	79,422	40,717	49,105	52,367	41,772	9,600	9,108	79.0	201,300	1,120
Calumet City	50,640	27.8	0.6	55,612	31,358	41,966	43,550	41,020	16,451	14,166	57.2	111,500	959
Carol Stream	89,820	8.5	8.8	103,332	52,759	58,449	62,971	52,877	14,669	14,209	69.3	257,800	1,291
Carpentersville	73,105	11.8	6.7	79,102	51,970	43,903	48,475	38,697	11,369	11,004	73.3	176,800	1,270
Champaign	49,467	29.5	6.6	78,118	30,508	45,741	49,594	42,241	39,586	34,851	44.0	167,000	922
Chicago	62,097	22.9	9.6	74,580	48,764	54,448	56,978	52,259	1,217,686	1,081,143	45.3	267,600	1,154
Chicago Heights	49,880	28.5	1.7	59,536	25,033	40,847	42,903	36,263	11,293	9,736	63.5	107,700	918
Cicero town	53,726	17.9	2.2	56,632	30,487	34,455	37,389	31,326	24,736	22,698	51.8	174,400	951
Crystal Lake	91,456	8.9	9.6	104,910	46,033	61,420	72,044	51,353	15,195	14,393	75.9	233,400	1,224
Danville	37,328	33.6	2.1	46,418	26,804	39,972	44,524	36,910	14,730	12,181	58.5	67,200	680
Decatur	45,404	27.2	2.8	62,699	32,863	42,500	49,200	36,289	36,458	31,073	61.8	85,500	688
DeKalb	44,223	28.9	3.9	67,155	30,048	40,948	48,721	35,131	17,161	15,839	41.2	165,500	889

1. Specified owner-occupied units

City	Commuting, 2016–2020[1]		Computer access[2], 2016–2020		Migration, 2016–2020		Civilian labor force, 2021				Civilian Employment, 2016–2020[4]			
	Percent		Percent						Unemployment[3]		Population age 16 and older		Population age 16 to 64	
	Drove alone	Mean travel time to work	With a computer in the house	With Internet access	Percent who lived in the same house one year ago	Percent who lived in another state or county one year ago	Total	Percent change 2020–2021	Total	Rate	Number	Percent in labor force	Number	Percent who worked full-year full-time
	55	56	57	58	59	60	61	62	63	64	65	66	67	68
GEORGIA—Cont'd														
Roswell	70.5	30.0	97.5	93.8	86.2	7.3	53,341	3.1	1,371	2.6	73,513	69.7	59,992	58.8
Sandy Springs	68.8	26.1	97.3	92.2	81.3	11.0	65,495	3.2	1,944	3.0	90,303	73.2	75,605	64.9
Savannah	71.3	20.7	91.5	83.6	75.8	10.6	68,685	2.4	3,640	5.3	117,733	63.3	97,954	47.9
Smyrna	78.8	29.0	97.9	95.7	81.1	9.6	34,677	2.7	1,187	3.4	44,138	77.8	38,895	64.6
South Fulton	77.5	33.7	95.6	91.0	89.0	7.5	NA	NA	NA	NA	77,356	69.3	65,646	55.5
Statesboro	73.7	18.4	90.7	73.6	57.1	23.2	14,358	1.4	774	5.4	27,981	56.1	25,210	26.6
Stockbridge	81.4	30.9	96.4	86.6	78.8	14.6	14,636	1.0	768	5.2	22,479	72.3	19,533	58.9
Stonecrest	72.6	37.3	94.1	81.2	79.9	11.0	NA	NA	NA	NA	42,333	70.0	37,568	51.4
Sugar Hill	78.7	32.9	94.1	83.6	89.2	6.6	13,246	2.7	392	3.0	17,943	70.3	15,999	58.2
Tucker	72.7	31.4	94.5	90.4	84.9	7.8	19,986	2.3	698	3.5	30,331	65.0	23,073	57.7
Union City	82.7	26.8	90.8	81.8	83.8	10.6	10,478	0.8	829	7.9	16,260	67.5	13,348	63.5
Valdosta	79.6	17.7	83.1	60.2	81.2	9.7	25,146	0.1	1,244	4.9	44,799	56.1	37,642	43.1
Warner Robins	85.0	21.4	92.1	84.7	84.3	7.5	34,296	1.6	1,371	4.0	58,738	64.8	49,534	53.9
Woodstock	81.1	37.2	98.3	95.3	84.8	10.8	17,831	3.4	474	2.7	25,129	74.2	20,627	58.5
HAWAII	67.6	27.1	92.7	86.7	86.8	5.4	668,413	0.9	38,226	5.7	1,148,836	61.5	887,629	55.7
East Honolulu CDP	66.1	32.3	95.8	93.0	91.1	2.7	NA	NA	NA	NA	39,119	60.5	26,474	59.2
Ewa Gentry CDP	73.8	37.8	99.0	93.7	88.4	2.3	NA	NA	NA	NA	20,099	69.7	17,989	61.5
Hilo CDP	72.9	18.3	87.9	78.5	90.8	4.0	NA	NA	NA	NA	36,818	57.8	27,274	45.6
Kahului CDP	73.6	20.4	87.8	82.0	87.2	5.9	NA	NA	NA	NA	23,499	65.4	18,180	59.9
Kailua CDP (Honolulu County)	74.2	29.5	95.5	92.3	86.0	6.7	NA	NA	NA	NA	30,549	61.1	23,236	56.2
Kaneohe CDP	70.4	28.2	93.1	89.7	91.6	2.5	NA	NA	NA	NA	27,865	62.1	20,605	58.0
Mililani Town CDP	81.8	30.8	96.8	92.9	90.5	2.6	NA	NA	NA	NA	22,453	63.0	16,090	58.8
Pearl City CDP	72.9	28.4	91.7	88.6	87.9	4.3	NA	NA	NA	NA	37,887	56.7	26,483	63.8
Urban Honolulu CDP	57.9	23.2	91.2	85.0	85.5	5.5	NA	NA	NA	NA	293,946	62.9	223,106	55.2
Waipahu CDP	59.3	36.5	89.3	76.6	87.9	2.7	NA	NA	NA	NA	31,017	60.1	23,215	55.3
IDAHO	77.8	21.2	93.2	86.0	83.2	7.9	917,056	2.2	32,728	3.6	1,360,062	62.8	1,082,318	49.4
Boise City	76.5	18.8	94.0	86.2	82.5	7.4	132,804	2.6	4,373	3.3	188,557	68.9	155,343	53.0
Caldwell	77.5	25.8	94.3	87.3	79.1	8.6	28,621	2.8	1,163	4.1	39,314	64.2	33,743	48.6
Coeur d'Alene	82.6	18.7	92.7	86.1	80.8	8.6	26,589	0.6	1,176	4.4	41,230	64.6	32,267	51.4
Eagle	76.5	22.5	93.6	91.2	86.5	8.5	15,301	3.4	477	3.1	22,100	57.2	16,215	50.2
Idaho Falls	79.6	16.8	94.3	88.4	80.2	8.1	32,368	3.2	992	3.1	46,187	64.8	38,026	52.5
Lewiston	81.8	15.8	90.3	83.0	85.1	6.9	17,620	0.0	550	3.1	26,619	61.6	20,247	51.4
Meridian	79.5	22.5	96.0	91.4	84.6	7.2	62,005	3.1	1,947	3.1	80,559	70.8	67,147	55.3
Moscow	60.3	15.6	96.3	88.1	67.3	16.5	12,833	0.3	404	3.1	22,371	65.8	19,751	36.2
Nampa	79.6	23.4	92.9	86.9	78.4	9.1	47,167	2.6	1,834	3.9	74,667	63.5	60,572	50.0
Pocatello	78.6	16.2	93.9	85.7	79.2	9.4	28,683	1.0	1,039	3.6	43,806	57.8	36,250	40.3
Post Falls	80.4	20.0	93.0	87.0	84.9	5.0	20,088	1.0	769	3.8	25,252	65.7	21,009	49.9
Rexburg	62.8	12.1	98.6	70.5	59.5	24.5	17,018	4.2	370	2.2	22,978	69.0	21,457	25.5
Twin Falls	81.4	17.5	93.4	85.1	80.1	9.8	24,708	1.1	932	3.8	37,866	65.6	30,498	52.2
ILLINOIS	71.5	29.0	91.5	84.9	87.5	4.7	6,318,915	-0.8	382,941	6.1	10,193,604	65.1	8,203,178	52.4
Addison	79.8	25.7	89.5	82.7	91.2	4.7	18,853	-1.1	1,034	5.5	29,448	68.5	23,726	56.8
Algonquin	80.8	33.7	95.6	92.6	90.5	6.2	16,863	-1.3	786	4.7	25,114	74.8	21,087	56.4
Alton	80.0	24.4	88.9	80.7	83.8	5.1	11,212	-0.5	846	7.5	20,728	61.7	16,319	45.4
Arlington Heights	75.5	29.6	94.3	90.5	89.3	3.6	39,665	-0.6	1,635	4.1	59,813	66.7	45,077	59.0
Aurora	74.3	29.2	94.4	87.2	85.3	6.9	97,607	-0.5	5,576	5.7	150,384	72.1	130,763	55.0
Bartlett	76.8	33.9	94.5	91.5	92.5	4.2	22,516	-1.0	1,048	4.7	32,574	68.3	26,598	58.5
Batavia	73.5	29.2	93.7	89.4	89.5	5.7	13,265	-0.2	603	4.5	20,359	70.9	16,383	56.3
Belleville	83.6	26.7	90.1	80.8	84.5	6.1	21,606	-0.7	1,430	6.6	32,977	65.8	27,252	55.9
Belvidere	80.5	24.8	92.0	84.8	90.8	5.4	11,271	-1.4	1,235	11.0	19,618	67.8	15,916	47.5
Berwyn	70.2	31.1	93.7	87.2	91.4	1.2	26,615	-1.7	2,023	7.6	42,127	67.2	35,278	54.4
Bloomington	79.0	16.3	93.3	85.6	85.2	6.0	38,799	0.8	1,981	5.1	62,161	64.9	52,054	51.6
Bolingbrook	82.1	32.0	96.5	92.6	90.1	6.3	39,800	-1.5	2,203	5.5	57,419	72.1	49,406	57.9
Buffalo Grove	72.8	30.3	95.1	92.4	88.3	7.1	23,612	-0.3	901	3.8	32,781	71.2	27,050	59.7
Burbank	76.7	35.8	89.7	84.5	91.2	1.3	13,773	-0.9	988	7.2	21,918	64.4	17,869	49.6
Calumet City	67.6	36.6	87.8	81.0	86.8	2.1	16,337	0.6	2,066	12.6	28,570	65.1	23,691	47.5
Carol Stream	79.6	29.5	95.9	92.4	86.5	6.0	22,840	-1.2	1,013	4.4	32,209	70.3	26,271	57.4
Carpentersville	82.0	31.3	95.1	90.2	90.3	5.5	18,009	-0.9	1,430	7.9	27,455	73.8	23,982	53.1
Champaign	65.2	15.2	95.6	85.2	74.1	13.4	46,455	1.4	2,260	4.9	74,593	60.9	65,313	41.0
Chicago	48.1	34.7	90.4	81.9	85.0	3.7	1,350,133	-1.4	103,073	7.6	2,204,754	67.2	1,862,580	52.1
Chicago Heights	77.9	27.7	85.2	77.6	91.3	1.2	12,760	1.0	1,437	11.3	22,816	61.1	18,408	45.4
Cicero town	70.4	30.4	89.5	80.0	93.4	1.0	35,174	-1.3	2,536	7.2	61,689	64.5	54,752	51.0
Crystal Lake	77.2	30.2	95.7	93.9	90.7	3.7	21,844	-1.3	921	4.2	31,404	69.7	25,304	54.8
Danville	78.7	15.1	80.9	74.4	88.9	3.3	11,716	-2.3	911	7.8	24,032	49.9	18,804	40.8
Decatur	82.9	17.1	86.4	78.1	81.5	5.5	30,535	-1.3	2,768	9.1	58,327	57.4	43,771	47.5
DeKalb	75.4	21.5	93.2	86.6	75.6	12.6	21,497	0.5	1,408	6.5	36,069	67.7	32,181	37.5

1. Employed persons. 2. Households. 3. Percent of civilian labor force. 4. Persons 16 years old and over.

City	Value of residential construction authorized by building permits, 2021			Wholesale trade[1], 2017				Retail trade[2], 2017			
	New construction ($1,000)	Number of housing units	Percent single family	Number of establishments	Number of employees	Sales (mil dol)	Annual payroll (mil dol)	Number of establish-ments	Number of employees	Sales (mil dol)	Annual payroll (mil dol)
	69	70	71	72	73	74	75	76	77	78	79
GEORGIA—Cont'd											
Roswell	93,109	199	100.0	169	2,445	2,483.0	207.6	340	5,875	2,680.2	204.1
Sandy Springs	86,213	305	85.2	153	3,193	4,650.5	364.9	271	4,407	1,527.4	146.2
Savannah	115,808	492	99.0	173	2,139	2,079.8	121.2	853	12,466	3,130.3	309.0
Smyrna	55,465	235	100.0	75	2,883	3,780.0	314.2	206	3,557	1,605.3	114.1
South Fulton	189,445	802	100.0	NA	NA	NA	NA	NA	NA	NA	NA
Statesboro	17,822	184	100.0	20	130	159.8	7.1	180	2,793	724.6	64.6
Stockbridge	27,962	118	100.0	7	58	32.3	5.0	97	1,738	442.4	42.4
Stonecrest	139,434	588	100.0	39	491	261.7	27.9	180	3,293	772.7	76.5
Sugar Hill	14,139	73	100.0	19	79	27.2	4.7	41	583	146.9	13.4
Tucker	12,351	54	90.7	177	2,850	1,789.9	171.6	171	2,674	762.8	79.9
Union City	46,535	247	100.0	8	149	56.3	10.2	63	2,164	1,180.1	87.7
Valdosta	127,316	603	100.0	71	820	741.6	40.1	387	5,792	1,613.0	135.3
Warner Robins	81,730	453	100.0	20	210	88.2	8.6	314	4,805	1,235.7	116.4
Woodstock	142,698	485	100.0	58	576	279.4	35.1	229	3,902	1,031.8	93.1
HAWAII	1,396,040	3,459	70.7	1,423	16,829	11,342.6	858.8	4,644	72,908	21,658.9	2,184.7
East Honolulu CDP	NA	NA	NA	29	61	20.4	2.8	48	894	358.2	29.8
Ewa Gentry CDP	NA	NA	NA	NA	NA	NA	NA	8	122	29.1	2.4
Hilo CDP	NA	NA	NA	61	800	386.4	35.1	213	4,395	1,293.5	126.3
Kahului CDP	NA	NA	NA	57	836	631.1	42.5	191	4,485	1,527.1	148.2
Kailua CDP (Honolulu County)	NA	NA	NA	19	57	22.5	3.4	96	1,571	407.0	46.0
Kaneohe CDP	NA	NA	NA	15	78	17.2	2.7	104	1,743	562.9	55.1
Mililani Town CDP	NA	NA	NA	5	10	1.6	0.3	32	1,062	254.8	27.2
Pearl City CDP	NA	NA	NA	24	372	290.0	21.0	67	2,136	720.5	58.3
Urban Honolulu CDP	NA	NA	NA	674	8,497	6,625.0	455.2	1,763	26,810	8,039.6	826.4
Waipahu CDP	NA	NA	NA	42	624	277.6	33.0	98	1,585	504.6	52.2
IDAHO	4,949,319	21,732	74.3	1,870	23,878	23,736.5	1,259.7	6,133	82,312	24,936.1	2,312.2
Boise City	456,175	2,021	42.4	383	5,346	6,486.4	338.8	920	15,803	5,042.7	498.2
Caldwell	144,117	1,105	74.9	34	388	188.1	18.7	110	1,626	552.4	52.5
Coeur d'Alene	114,645	582	53.3	45	485	462.4	22.8	289	4,457	1,428.4	128.2
Eagle	202,231	463	100.0	28	271	372.6	22.9	80	1,147	344.1	31.7
Idaho Falls	97,882	555	100.0	114	1,243	2,099.0	60.7	353	5,664	1,650.8	145.3
Lewiston	20,877	79	82.3	43	489	432.6	21.3	194	2,478	702.9	68.7
Meridian	616,656	2,735	67.5	104	2,882	2,544.4	168.0	310	5,788	1,534.8	159.5
Moscow	19,309	97	44.3	9	181	86.4	8.3	103	1,660	308.4	37.7
Nampa	315,159	2,392	60.1	89	1,098	1,043.9	54.6	310	5,758	2,073.7	167.8
Pocatello	29,498	223	65.0	67	704	541.8	30.4	226	3,127	944.4	82.1
Post Falls	141,335	835	54.4	24	365	257.1	24.2	109	2,133	815.5	68.8
Rexburg	40,694	201	62.2	25	456	252.2	18.0	167	1,590	448.0	41.0
Twin Falls	107,027	558	74.9	84	904	540.0	41.9	307	4,694	1,424.1	127.0
ILLINOIS	4,272,625	19,658	55.6	15,409	272,391	311,140.6	19,071.8	38,189	629,878	173,473.9	16,246.9
Addison	7,709	35	100.0	193	4,874	2,720.5	346.1	108	1,738	847.2	70.5
Algonquin	27,586	105	100.0	17	108	279.7	6.8	151	3,470	716.6	70.1
Alton	0	0	0.0	21	192	122.9	9.9	141	2,175	421.4	46.6
Arlington Heights	26,405	105	27.6	155	2,334	2,837.7	205.1	219	4,147	1,107.4	112.2
Aurora	18,825	71	77.5	164	4,319	21,447.6	298.8	568	9,559	2,173.0	213.3
Bartlett	8,354	24	100.0	62	1,409	1,245.2	87.7	45	383	102.5	9.3
Batavia	13,323	64	14.1	70	1,431	1,567.5	83.3	91	1,890	430.6	44.0
Belleville	6,070	28	100.0	41	517	258.3	27.0	178	2,788	695.4	72.2
Belvidere	9,356	61	100.0	11	89	41.2	3.4	72	1,083	337.4	27.9
Berwyn	1,944	11	100.0	10	67	42.9	2.7	102	1,273	258.5	29.0
Bloomington	24,729	157	60.5	72	1,180	6,395.6	100.5	323	5,767	1,311.3	125.5
Bolingbrook	47,616	383	16.4	117	5,995	5,967.2	422.4	216	5,336	1,315.4	133.5
Buffalo Grove	27,432	72	100.0	125	2,881	3,499.3	221.5	101	1,282	479.9	46.6
Burbank	2,165	11	100.0	9	25	8.8	1.0	90	1,504	346.7	30.9
Calumet City	0	0	0.0	D	D	D	D	136	2,172	429.4	49.3
Carol Stream	0	0	0.0	105	3,112	5,024.5	209.6	101	2,073	542.5	53.5
Carpentersville	230	1	100.0	11	42	36.8	2.5	49	1,151	348.1	29.9
Champaign	44,440	284	19.4	67	1,404	656.0	64.5	389	6,358	1,516.8	142.8
Chicago	694,065	5,341	7.8	2,245	39,863	40,410.4	2,840.6	6,945	97,034	23,313.0	2,568.5
Chicago Heights	175	1	100.0	36	746	759.4	41.6	63	639	161.6	14.4
Cicero town	273	1	100.0	34	947	647.5	50.6	133	2,454	741.3	62.3
Crystal Lake	62,835	225	45.8	D	D	D	D	208	3,792	1,054.2	101.1
Danville	0	0	0.0	35	1,528	3,298.6	78.0	151	2,587	595.3	58.8
Decatur	1,846	8	75.0	69	1,085	1,041.0	61.4	285	4,159	1,198.3	114.0
DeKalb	12,328	103	8.7	21	263	96.3	11.7	113	2,387	498.1	50.5

1. Merchant wholesalers except manufacturers' sales branches and offices. 2. Establishments with payroll.

City	Real estate and rental and leasing, 2017: Number of establish-ments	Number of employees	Receipts (mil dol)	Annual payroll (mil dol)	Professional, scientific, and technical services[1], 2017: Number of establish-ments	Number of employees	Receipts (mil dol)	Annual payroll (mil dol)	Manufacturing, 2017: Number of establish-ments	Number of employees	Receipts (mil dol)	Annual payroll (mil dol)
	80	81	82	83	84	85	86	87	88	89	90	91
GEORGIA—Cont'd												
Roswell	227	1,071	260.1	55.0	764	5,455	1,197.8	454.7	NA	NA	NA	NA
Sandy Springs	393	2,815	845.2	152.5	1,016	15,440	3,777.2	1,409.6	NA	NA	NA	NA
Savannah	273	1,551	344.3	56.2	523	4,117	561.7	216.7	NA	NA	NA	NA
Smyrna	126	665	138.9	30.6	292	3,710	741.0	313.2	NA	NA	NA	NA
South Fulton	NA	NA	NA	NA	NA	NA	NA	NA	NA	NA	NA	NA
Statesboro	55	253	43.0	7.9	91	468	53.4	19.8	NA	NA	NA	NA
Stockbridge	34	141	33.3	5.5	61	324	85.7	17.2	NA	NA	NA	NA
Stonecrest	24	172	52.6	9.1	38	205	10.2	13.7	NA	NA	NA	NA
Sugar Hill	28	75	16.6	2.6	64	142	20.8	6.3	NA	NA	NA	NA
Tucker	78	201	65.9	12.0	217	1,928	308.1	100.3	NA	NA	NA	NA
Union City	24	134	29.3	4.6	13	77	7.1	1.9	NA	NA	NA	NA
Valdosta	109	552	108.0	18.5	176	903	145.7	49.4	NA	NA	NA	NA
Warner Robins	75	318	85.8	10.9	195	2,855	454.7	179.4	NA	NA	NA	NA
Woodstock	66	265	98.3	14.2	197	1,070	200.7	64.1	NA	NA	NA	NA
HAWAII	2,069	13,101	4,409.0	675.2	3,380	22,668	3,799.4	1,465.6	783	11,850	6,055.9	558.5
East Honolulu CDP	56	122	28.1	6.1	101	300	43.7	16.6	NA	NA	NA	NA
Ewa Gentry CDP	4	17	1.0	0.5	3	3	0.4	0.1	NA	NA	NA	NA
Hilo CDP	87	337	71.6	11.6	98	602	85.7	33.9	NA	NA	NA	NA
Kahului CDP	47	379	93.0	16.0	47	259	30.1	10.7	NA	NA	NA	NA
Kailua CDP (Honolulu County)	55	173	45.7	10.6	101	313	47.8	17.8	NA	NA	NA	NA
Kaneohe CDP	31	145	26.7	5.3	51	190	33.2	11.8	NA	NA	NA	NA
Mililani Town CDP	10	36	11.5	2.1	24	70	5.3	1.8	NA	NA	NA	NA
Pearl City CDP	21	95	14.0	3.8	45	313	75.8	18.6	NA	NA	NA	NA
Urban Honolulu CDP	858	6,154	1,902.5	338.0	1,725	13,894	2,557.5	979.6	NA	NA	NA	NA
Waipahu CDP	29	152	28.8	5.7	17	549	36.1	17.9	NA	NA	NA	NA
IDAHO	2,644	7,521	1,635.4	276.7	4,686	33,246	5,045.5	1,921.0	1,877	58,746	20,263.4	3,486.1
Boise City	555	2,156	476.1	84.8	1,298	9,518	1,498.3	576.9	NA	NA	NA	NA
Caldwell	41	215	32.3	6.2	43	212	25.6	7.9	NA	NA	NA	NA
Coeur d'Alene	153	456	127.6	18.1	265	1,505	182.1	83.2	NA	NA	NA	NA
Eagle	D	D	D	D	146	611	82.4	31.1	NA	NA	NA	NA
Idaho Falls	105	366	107.6	15.3	305	7,969	1,447.2	578.0	NA	NA	NA	NA
Lewiston	D	D	D	D	71	518	50.7	21.2	NA	NA	NA	NA
Meridian	177	527	164.6	24.8	268	3,002	522.4	181.5	NA	NA	NA	NA
Moscow	40	144	18.4	3.5	58	444	49.2	17.6	NA	NA	NA	NA
Nampa	87	230	47.1	8.5	152	885	106.0	41.2	NA	NA	NA	NA
Pocatello	78	D	45.4	D	D	D	D	D	NA	NA	NA	NA
Post Falls	54	129	22.7	4.7	65	549	136.3	30.3	NA	NA	NA	NA
Rexburg	45	230	28.4	4.3	D	D	D	D	NA	NA	NA	NA
Twin Falls	104	278	58.5	8.7	D	D	D	D	NA	NA	NA	NA
ILLINOIS	13,589	82,763	32,355.2	4,824.5	38,805	404,450	87,118.6	33,951.1	13,162	527,862	241,484.3	30,116.3
Addison	48	167	37.0	7.2	90	480	102.1	27.7	NA	NA	NA	NA
Algonquin	30	55	13.5	3.1	97	258	35.3	11.9	NA	NA	NA	NA
Alton	32	126	25.8	4.6	57	303	40.2	17.8	NA	NA	NA	NA
Arlington Heights	118	3,547	321.8	93.4	480	3,446	419.6	303.3	NA	NA	NA	NA
Aurora	140	544	160.4	20.6	494	2,379	439.7	147.2	NA	NA	NA	NA
Bartlett	26	161	42.7	11.1	144	444	110.5	28.4	NA	NA	NA	NA
Batavia	26	77	20.1	3.8	139	555	115.6	36.0	NA	NA	NA	NA
Belleville	50	233	36.7	7.9	150	1,025	150.7	68.2	NA	NA	NA	NA
Belvidere	14	45	8.1	1.3	28	240	49.8	24.7	NA	NA	NA	NA
Berwyn	30	60	15.3	1.5	80	278	49.3	13.9	NA	NA	NA	NA
Bloomington	106	455	98.6	15.9	232	1,584	246.7	101.7	NA	NA	NA	NA
Bolingbrook	48	229	65.0	8.6	190	1,455	169.2	66.0	NA	NA	NA	NA
Buffalo Grove	57	269	88.0	18.0	308	2,571	469.4	214.7	NA	NA	NA	NA
Burbank	12	30	7.2	1.0	32	96	9.9	3.9	NA	NA	NA	NA
Calumet City	18	126	23.4	3.3	22	66	5.8	2.4	NA	NA	NA	NA
Carol Stream	36	278	75.0	11.0	96	503	76.6	29.0	NA	NA	NA	NA
Carpentersville	21	94	19.0	4.4	28	67	8.3	2.8	NA	NA	NA	NA
Champaign	136	1,541	304.5	68.2	257	1,783	264.1	109.5	NA	NA	NA	NA
Chicago	3,684	28,995	13,429.1	2,102.7	10,735	174,661	48,101.5	17,622.3	NA	NA	NA	NA
Chicago Heights	14	96	29.0	4.5	27	203	37.0	8.3	NA	NA	NA	NA
Cicero town	28	98	23.9	3.6	41	299	23.5	8.8	NA	NA	NA	NA
Crystal Lake	54	228	38.7	8.7	191	947	259.5	51.6	NA	NA	NA	NA
Danville	33	93	17.7	2.5	54	323	51.6	15.2	NA	NA	NA	NA
Decatur	72	433	63.3	12.5	114	919	105.0	44.6	NA	NA	NA	NA
DeKalb	47	326	69.5	10.5	42	146	14.8	4.6	NA	NA	NA	NA

1. Establishments subject to federal tax.

City	Accommodation and food services, 2017				Arts, entertainment, and recreation[1], 2017				Health care and social assistance[1], 2017			
	Number of establish-ments	Number of employees	Receipts (mil dol)	Annual payroll (mil dol)	Number of establish-ments	Number of employees	Receipts (mil dol)	Annual payroll (mil dol)	Number of establish-ments	Number of employees	Receipts (mil dol)	Annual payroll (mil dol)
	92	93	94	95	96	97	98	99	100	101	102	103
GEORGIA—Cont'd												
Roswell	276	5,642	320.0	95.0	70.0	634	45.2	15.0	432	6,894	757.3	299.0
Sandy Springs	297	5,436	382.0	105.4	60.0	1,153	101.1	29.2	689	22,581	3,657.6	1,410.6
Savannah	638	14,866	1,077.9	272.3	75.0	872	57.0	16.8	580	19,038	2,347.5	899.2
Smyrna	188	3,573	228.5	63.0	D	D	D	D	233	2,981	302.6	120.2
South Fulton	NA	NA	NA	NA	NA	NA	NA	NA	NA	NA	NA	NA
Statesboro	137	3,679	162.9	44.1	D	D	D	D	167	3,121	329.0	118.8
Stockbridge	71	1,258	72.5	19.9	10.0	D	11.4	D	151	2,390	286.4	103.9
Stonecrest	104	2,109	128.3	32.0	8.0	71	4.7	0.9	133	2,046	213.4	82.9
Sugar Hill	20	325	13.7	4.3	7.0	9	1.8	0.4	33	325	35.0	11.7
Tucker	134	2,415	137.1	34.0	23.0	223	16.2	4.8	167	3,936	504.3	173.5
Union City	40	798	45.5	10.7	NA	NA	NA	NA	43	777	56.7	22.4
Valdosta	204	4,588	241.4	64.1	17.0	213	8.1	2.4	362	7,379	855.6	309.9
Warner Robins	201	4,703	221.1	60.5	D	D	D	D	227	5,750	624.2	221.8
Woodstock	120	2,998	159.8	47.4	D	D	D	7.2	152	1,764	239.6	81.7
HAWAII	3,865	112,743	12,101.8	3,296.8	510.0	11,912	1,025.8	314.3	3,677	73,551	9,785.7	3,998.4
East Honolulu CDP	66	1,189	74.1	21.7	23.0	526	44.9	14.5	82	990	105.5	38.8
Ewa Gentry CDP	5	77	4.4	1.3	NA	NA	NA	NA	4	14	2.4	1.0
Hilo CDP	153	2,711	191.0	49.9	12.0	132	8.4	2.6	233	4,621	473.3	247.8
Kahului CDP	D	D	D	D	D	D	D	D	97	1,757	187.0	83.4
Kailua CDP (Honolulu County)	106	1,784	112.2	31.9	15.0	205	16.4	5.4	147	2,022	316.4	127.2
Kaneohe CDP	87	1,483	97.1	25.2	D	D	D	D	109	2,232	204.3	96.8
Mililani Town CDP	45	1,002	66.0	16.5	5.0	238	14.9	3.9	30	306	31.7	15.9
Pearl City CDP	79	1,608	101.4	27.7	D	D	D	D	71	909	93.9	38.8
Urban Honolulu CDP	1,575	45,827	5,301.5	1,318.1	124.0	2,727	241.0	73.2	1,529	34,983	5,292.8	2,084.4
Waipahu CDP	63	1,183	82.1	21.8	NA	NA	NA	NA	92	1,074	119.6	45.7
IDAHO	3,856	65,463	3,598.1	1,006.2	804.0	9,644	601.6	174.1	5,310	98,100	10,469.0	4,292.3
Boise City	663	13,262	723.5	216.8	115.0	2,511	114.8	35.5	979	26,996	3,415.2	1,483.9
Caldwell	68	1,358	66.7	17.0	12.0	220	7.5	2.8	126	1,977	232.5	80.7
Coeur d'Alene	210	4,714	260.5	81.8	45.0	286	26.7	7.4	293	7,752	826.3	389.1
Eagle	59	1,082	54.5	15.7	18.0	196	15.3	4.3	99	885	92.2	37.1
Idaho Falls	184	3,892	188.0	58.4	25.0	571	14.7	4.8	455	7,585	997.7	328.4
Lewiston	D	D	D	D	D	D	D	D	139	3,288	309.4	124.4
Meridian	220	5,201	265.9	77.3	42.0	610	32.9	9.8	355	6,486	637.6	248.4
Moscow	102	1,806	79.1	23.6	D	D	D	D	78	1,507	133.1	54.7
Nampa	180	3,676	185.8	51.6	21.0	555	11.8	4.4	219	4,737	371.2	176.4
Pocatello	146	2,608	133.7	35.3	21.0	296	8.9	2.7	314	5,003	585.7	198.5
Post Falls	D	D	D	D	12.0	94	5.7	1.8	123	1,982	184.0	76.9
Rexburg	60	1,141	47.5	12.1	8.0	84	3.1	0.6	D	D	D	D
Twin Falls	165	3,406	167.0	46.7	32.0	234	12.3	3.4	321	5,857	635.8	225.1
ILLINOIS	29,025	536,245	35,314.4	10,188.5	5,218.0	91,647	10,067.4	2,830.2	34,235	817,733	97,626.1	38,088.6
Addison	87	1,503	91.0	26.2	10.0	429	32.4	11.6	80	1,252	105.1	57.1
Algonquin	93	1,984	104.3	34.1	17.0	407	19.9	5.6	102	799	75.4	33.0
Alton	96	1,734	87.4	26.4	D	D	D	D	125	4,265	420.4	172.8
Arlington Heights	176	3,295	211.3	59.1	42.0	594	44.1	15.0	414	10,686	1,347.7	561.8
Aurora	287	4,738	281.8	75.5	57.0	1,398	172.3	36.0	390	9,379	1,366.2	525.9
Bartlett	42	807	40.9	12.0	7.0	44	4.3	1.6	63	787	80.8	34.1
Batavia	62	1,197	66.1	19.1	10.0	145	6.4	1.7	69	928	84.6	32.0
Belleville	D	D	D	29.3	14.0	412	10.8	3.7	190	5,448	669.9	280.7
Belvidere	40	578	31.8	8.2	D	D	D	0.4	46	800	73.4	28.1
Berwyn	111	1,977	113.9	34.3	11.0	74	2.7	0.9	146	4,445	452.0	208.7
Bloomington	248	4,975	238.6	73.5	38.0	1,163	47.3	14.0	243	5,071	636.7	257.0
Bolingbrook	150	3,362	195.0	55.6	17.0	363	24.7	10.2	175	2,527	265.7	103.4
Buffalo Grove	D	D	D	D	25.0	459	26.4	6.7	172	1,810	210.8	92.4
Burbank	63	871	54.0	14.6	4.0	D	6.1	D	50	683	71.9	24.0
Calumet City	74	1,113	68.8	16.8	6.0	58	4.6	1.4	58	2,316	76.7	38.4
Carol Stream	69	1,320	77.0	22.4	14.0	113	9.9	1.7	62	998	103.8	40.2
Carpentersville	43	677	36.5	10.2	5.0	15	1.3	0.2	28	246	24.6	8.3
Champaign	357	7,960	411.2	122.3	42.0	367	22.2	8.1	204	3,952	450.8	188.7
Chicago	6,770	142,220	12,308.5	3,607.4	1,101.0	25,651	3,865.1	1,179.9	6,778	186,215	22,877.1	8,947.8
Chicago Heights	42	491	31.7	8.2	4.0	83	2.2	1.1	72	2,582	184.8	85.6
Cicero town	104	1,255	85.2	22.0	10.0	40	4.5	0.8	91	1,575	120.2	53.1
Crystal Lake	116	2,992	177.1	50.9	26.0	711	47.4	10.5	220	2,851	302.2	133.8
Danville	95	1,663	73.6	20.9	13.0	152	5.4	1.8	114	4,311	490.4	238.7
Decatur	199	3,342	158.4	48.7	35.0	622	24.3	8.0	240	7,644	941.3	328.4
DeKalb	103	1,843	90.1	25.5	14.0	88	6.7	2.0	65	2,360	290.8	95.2

1. Establishments subject to federal tax.

City	Other services[1]				Government employment and payroll, 2017								
						March payroll							
							Perent of total for:						
	Number of establish-ments	Number of employees	Receipts (mil dol)	Annual payroll (mil dol)	Full-time equivalent employees	Total (dollars)	Admin-istrative, judicial, and legal	Police and corrections	Fire protection	Highways and trans-portation	Health and welfare	Natural resources and utilities	Education and libraries
	104	105	106	107	108	109	110	111	112	113	114	115	116
GEORGIA—Cont'd													
Roswell	D	D	D	55.9	765	3,218,687	15.4	31.3	13.3	8.0	0.0	29.5	0.0
Sandy Springs	251	1,914	274.6	79.8	296	1,627,788	9.1	55.2	32.9	0.0	0.0	2.8	0.0
Savannah	287	1,976	227.8	66.7	2,671	10,853,045	7.1	32.7	14.8	9.4	3.1	24.2	0.1
Smyrna	131	598	78.1	21.9	412	1,616,640	9.7	36.1	22.3	5.4	2.9	14.9	2.8
South Fulton	NA	NA	NA	NA	NA	NA	NA	NA	NA	NA	NA	NA	NA
Statesboro	D	D	D	D	274	940,840	12.4	28.4	12.4	12.1	0.0	32.0	0.0
Stockbridge	56	251	32.6	9.0	75	274,091	32.7	0.0	0.0	21.7	0.0	33.2	0.0
Stonecrest	D	D	D	D	NA	NA	NA	NA	NA	NA	NA	NA	NA
Sugar Hill	34	136	16.4	4.8	79	306,812	39.9	0.0	0.0	13.3	0.0	37.6	0.0
Tucker	126	842	197.9	37.0	0	2,944	100.0	0.0	0.0	0.0	0.0	0.0	0.0
Union City	D	D	D	6.3	171	624,319	13.7	36.8	30.7	4.0	1.5	7.9	0.0
Valdosta	99	458	42.4	11.4	564	2,010,839	9.1	33.7	18.6	5.9	4.1	26.6	0.0
Warner Robins	112	658	64.5	17.8	576	1,911,076	8.8	29.3	21.8	7.2	1.2	24.8	0.0
Woodstock	84	444	49.1	14.9	149	584,179	9.4	34.7	36.7	3.1	6.0	10.0	0.0
HAWAII	2,912	20,219	2,561.2	652.4	X	X	X	X	X	X	X	X	X
East Honolulu CDP	60	290	40.3	9.1	NA	NA	NA	NA	NA	NA	NA	NA	NA
Ewa Gentry CDP	10	42	5.2	0.9	NA	NA	NA	NA	NA	NA	NA	NA	NA
Hilo CDP	89	392	76.9	14.7	NA	NA	NA	NA	NA	NA	NA	NA	NA
Kahului CDP	56	659	63.6	20.6	NA	NA	NA	NA	NA	NA	NA	NA	NA
Kailua CDP (Honolulu County)	74	518	42.0	10.6	NA	NA	NA	NA	NA	NA	NA	NA	NA
Kaneohe CDP	73	325	38.1	10.7	NA	NA	NA	NA	NA	NA	NA	NA	NA
Mililani Town CDP	32	486	24.9	8.4	NA	NA	NA	NA	NA	NA	NA	NA	NA
Pearl City CDP	69	329	46.5	10.2	NA	NA	NA	NA	NA	NA	NA	NA	NA
Urban Honolulu CDP	1,333	11,192	1,492.8	375.2	NA	NA	NA	NA	NA	NA	NA	NA	NA
Waipahu CDP	72	459	42.0	10.6	NA	NA	NA	NA	NA	NA	NA	NA	NA
IDAHO	2,749	14,016	1,574.0	434.6	X	X	X	X	X	X	X	X	X
Boise City	531	3,282	426.9	116.3	1,769	9,161,227	20.4	25.7	23.8	5.2	0.7	16.1	3.6
Caldwell	52	315	29.0	9.9	249	1,042,008	10.2	31.6	22.9	12.0	0.0	15.7	3.4
Coeur d'Alene	110	653	65.6	19.4	354	1,949,936	16.9	30.0	21.8	7.8	0.2	19.1	3.3
Eagle	53	327	26.5	8.7	41	171,701	45.6	0.0	0.0	0.0	0.0	20.8	24.7
Idaho Falls	122	556	63.7	16.2	754	3,562,474	11.0	18.6	21.6	8.2	0.0	34.2	2.7
Lewiston	D	D	D	D	314	1,471,501	14.1	22.5	25.9	7.3	0.0	16.0	3.2
Meridian	134	709	72.0	24.9	411	2,074,414	17.0	34.0	23.0	8.2	0.0	17.5	0.0
Moscow	49	363	31.2	9.4	157	772,655	17.1	27.5	4.5	11.7	5.3	31.0	0.0
Nampa	124	748	69.5	21.3	593	2,877,951	5.7	38.0	19.0	3.3	1.5	14.5	2.5
Pocatello	D	D	59.3	D	578	2,751,585	7.3	28.4	18.9	12.9	1.5	21.7	2.5
Post Falls	59	334	31.7	9.9	189	811,810	16.7	41.2	0.0	10.0	1.2	23.4	0.0
Rexburg	27	144	10.4	3.0	141	586,398	21.7	31.4	3.2	11.0	4.4	16.7	0.0
Twin Falls	115	802	70.7	23.1	297	1,445,319	12.5	33.2	15.8	13.0	3.3	12.8	4.2
ILLINOIS	24,296	171,261	29,599.4	7,164.3	X	X	X	X	X	X	X	X	X
Addison	133	892	122.3	33.4	288	1,938,386	9.8	48.7	0.0	3.4	8.0	18.2	6.8
Algonquin	70	324	30.8	10.0	147	845,145	11.3	26.1	0.0	11.5	0.3	33.9	0.0
Alton	55	279	24.3	6.6	212	1,055,343	10.1	42.8	26.7	4.4	2.6	12.1	0.0
Arlington Heights	201	1,262	193.8	50.5	570	4,103,045	12.1	28.1	24.2	9.9	2.6	7.2	15.3
Aurora	236	1,387	164.2	39.3	1,439	9,828,813	9.4	32.8	18.5	7.5	8.1	14.4	5.4
Bartlett	D	D	D	D	169	1,154,138	11.7	47.0	0.0	11.2	4.4	18.2	0.0
Batavia	77	642	76.8	23.8	174	666,982	8.5	27.3	17.7	8.7	6.8	30.9	0.0
Belleville	100	629	55.6	17.8	327	1,705,639	5.8	36.5	25.1	6.5	0.0	16.1	4.0
Belvidere	44	210	21.7	6.2	136	768,644	12.9	38.7	22.9	7.6	0.0	10.9	4.1
Berwyn	71	425	32.8	9.0	410	2,424,924	7.2	43.9	29.7	5.6	1.1	2.4	4.9
Bloomington	176	1,706	184.5	61.4	789	4,402,455	5.9	27.1	19.2	17.7	0.1	20.9	4.8
Bolingbrook	99	530	52.1	16.0	327	2,409,853	8.3	43.5	29.9	8.9	0.0	9.4	0.0
Buffalo Grove	83	504	62.1	17.3	221	1,816,394	10.0	37.7	29.5	2.8	0.4	10.4	0.0
Burbank	D	D	D	D	119	865,103	7.4	46.2	32.6	10.9	0.0	0.0	0.0
Calumet City	46	155	17.0	4.7	335	1,941,229	3.7	46.0	24.2	5.8	4.4	5.3	10.6
Carol Stream	80	425	47.1	12.7	193	1,270,083	12.0	49.5	0.0	12.4	5.1	5.3	11.7
Carpentersville	D	D	10.7	D	185	1,271,922	7.5	39.2	25.5	10.6	5.7	10.3	0.0
Champaign	168	1,360	104.4	32.7	553	3,543,612	19.7	30.0	23.2	3.7	1.6	2.7	8.3
Chicago	5,308	48,556	13,066.3	2,554.7	31,798	220,385,761	6.4	42.8	16.1	10.9	3.0	7.7	2.2
Chicago Heights	38	175	21.4	6.4	270	1,550,273	6.9	46.8	27.8	6.2	0.8	5.6	2.8
Cicero town	82	310	34.6	8.7	718	3,280,911	10.2	40.5	16.5	2.6	4.5	16.1	1.9
Crystal Lake	134	797	73.0	24.0	288	2,009,773	12.4	27.0	27.6	5.9	2.3	10.0	9.4
Danville	57	281	24.6	7.0	276	1,339,199	8.0	31.9	22.2	13.0	0.3	12.7	5.8
Decatur	121	843	277.4	30.5	507	3,126,016	9.1	41.0	25.8	9.0	1.6	6.8	3.9
DeKalb	58	323	28.1	7.6	213	1,617,137	9.4	43.9	28.1	9.0	2.7	4.3	0.0

1. Establishments subject to federal tax.

City	City government finances, 2017									
	General revenue							General expenditure		
		Intergovernmental		Taxes						
					Per capita[1] (dollars)				Per capita[1] (dollars)	
	Total (mil dol)	Total (mil dol)	Percent from state government	Total (mil dol)	Total	Property	Sales and gross receipts	Total (mil dol)	Total	Capital outlays
	117	118	119	120	121	122	123	124	125	126
GEORGIA—Cont'd										
Roswell	102.6	28.0	4.6	44.4	469	283	184	131.2	1,385	191
Sandy Springs	117.1	31.0	4.3	70.4	660	307	353	208.1	1,951	1,186
Savannah	375.3	86.7	1.1	122.2	838	451	379	378.2	2,594	304
Smyrna	72.5	12.1	4.2	34.1	606	391	213	50.0	889	2
South Fulton	NA	NA	NA	NA	NA	NA	NA	NA	NA	NA
Statesboro	35.0	6.1	6.2	10.7	341	145	192	29.7	948	53
Stockbridge	16.2	6.7	7.2	4.9	167	4	160	10.9	375	24
Stonecrest	NA	NA	NA	NA	NA	NA	NA	NA	NA	NA
Sugar Hill	22.0	3.2	6.4	6.2	271	134	137	17.2	748	434
Tucker	61.7	16.9	8.2	26.3	730	427	299	61.3	1,701	185
Union City	28.6	5.7	10.5	13.9	652	405	245	21.8	1,025	35
Valdosta	75.0	24.2	6.6	25.8	461	221	236	67.2	1,199	106
Warner Robins	68.2	8.0	12.1	31.9	423	233	188	70.3	932	87
Woodstock	32.7	4.3	12.0	17.2	543	293	243	22.7	717	0
HAWAII	X	X	X	X	X	X	X	X	X	X
East Honolulu CDP	NA	NA	NA	NA	NA	NA	NA	NA	NA	NA
Ewa Gentry CDP	NA	NA	NA	NA	NA	NA	NA	NA	NA	NA
Hilo CDP	NA	NA	NA	NA	NA	NA	NA	NA	NA	NA
Kahului CDP	NA	NA	NA	NA	NA	NA	NA	NA	NA	NA
Kailua CDP (Honolulu County)	NA	NA	NA	NA	NA	NA	NA	NA	NA	NA
Kaneohe CDP	NA	NA	NA	NA	NA	NA	NA	NA	NA	NA
Mililani Town CDP	NA	NA	NA	NA	NA	NA	NA	NA	NA	NA
Pearl City CDP	NA	NA	NA	NA	NA	NA	NA	NA	NA	NA
Urban Honolulu CDP	NA	NA	NA	NA	NA	NA	NA	NA	NA	NA
Waipahu CDP	NA	NA	NA	NA	NA	NA	NA	NA	NA	NA
IDAHO	X	X	X	X	X	X	X	X	X	X
Boise City	349.8	37.5	63.7	145.7	640	564	76	321.0	1,410	270
Caldwell	48.2	7.2	57.6	17.6	322	282	39	45.9	838	154
Coeur d'Alene	59.1	10.6	56.7	26.8	529	410	119	58.8	1,162	208
Eagle	7.0	2.1	100.0	4.5	172	58	114	6.0	229	0
Idaho Falls	87.3	18.6	87.5	33.3	538	509	30	79.1	1,280	271
Lewiston	55.4	11.6	100.0	21.2	649	596	53	51.2	1,565	84
Meridian	63.0	7.8	99.7	34.5	343	274	69	66.9	665	177
Moscow	27.9	6.3	49.1	7.3	287	215	72	25.9	1,019	161
Nampa	104.6	12.6	95.8	47.6	508	461	47	89.0	950	93
Pocatello	72.2	16.3	60.3	31.9	577	538	39	60.0	1,085	85
Post Falls	29.7	6.2	100.0	11.0	332	332	0	20.5	617	37
Rexburg	22.7	4.8	99.7	4.1	144	126	18	23.7	830	103
Twin Falls	60.0	12.5	47.2	31.1	631	551	81	45.4	922	176
ILLINOIS	X	X	X	X	X	X	X	X	X	X
Addison	45.9	15.4	92.6	17.2	465	379	86	64.9	1,756	476
Algonquin	27.7	12.9	94.2	12.9	418	203	215	36.0	1,165	353
Alton	54.8	21.1	68.7	16.9	632	371	261	70.2	2,627	1,106
Arlington Heights	183.9	38.4	97.1	131.1	1,737	1,229	507	170.3	2,257	174
Aurora	231.6	70.3	91.8	140.7	702	422	280	236.7	1,181	81
Bartlett	38.1	8.1	93.7	20.0	486	354	132	59.3	1,441	374
Batavia	35.0	10.7	94.0	16.6	626	284	343	34.5	1,302	226
Belleville	59.5	21.2	100.0	24.8	595	473	122	77.8	1,865	675
Belvidere	21.4	7.3	100.0	9.0	358	228	130	23.8	946	104
Berwyn	72.7	16.4	86.9	45.7	825	601	224	76.1	1,373	57
Bloomington	136.1	29.6	98.3	70.9	907	307	600	131.3	1,681	115
Bolingbrook	105.9	26.6	90.5	54.0	720	271	450	104.4	1,392	106
Buffalo Grove	53.0	11.7	100.0	25.7	624	377	247	54.5	1,323	138
Burbank	22.8	7.3	100.0	13.6	475	209	266	23.7	823	87
Calumet City	53.3	13.3	80.0	34.4	940	693	247	55.7	1,524	144
Carol Stream	33.4	14.2	98.0	15.0	377	112	265	28.8	723	3
Carpentersville	41.7	11.9	82.1	21.4	565	369	195	41.3	1,088	116
Champaign	109.6	36.0	85.2	61.2	696	300	396	104.6	1,191	206
Chicago	8,260.8	1,710.7	63.4	3,561.4	1,314	477	734	7,769.2	2,866	464
Chicago Heights	43.6	9.9	86.9	26.9	901	651	251	45.9	1,538	99
Cicero town	107.6	24.4	88.4	67.8	823	581	242	129.2	1,568	206
Crystal Lake	55.5	17.9	99.4	24.8	618	421	197	53.7	1,341	118
Danville	49.7	31.1	87.9	10.0	319	204	115	48.1	1,535	60
Decatur	91.9	32.5	94.6	39.1	544	217	327	86.9	1,210	6
DeKalb	55.5	17.6	93.5	29.9	699	344	355	57.4	1,341	262

1. Based on population estimated as of July 1 of the year shown.

City	City government finances, 2017 (cont.)												
	General expenditure (cont.)												
	Percent of total for:									Debt outstanding			
	Public welfare	Highways	Parking facilities	Education	Health and hospitals	Police protection	Sewerage and sanitation	Parks and recreation	Housing and community development	Interest on debt	Total (mil dol)	Per capita[1] (dollars)	Debt issued during year
	127	128	129	130	131	132	133	134	135	136	137	138	139
GEORGIA—Cont'd													
Roswell	0.0	8.9	0.0	0.0	0.0	14.4	18.6	15.4	1.8	0.4	23.9	253	0.0
Sandy Springs	0.0	12.2	0.0	0.0	0.0	9.4	0.0	52.3	0.0	3.5	178.3	1,672	2.8
Savannah	3.7	11.1	1.9	0.0	0.0	18.0	18.4	7.6	0.0	1.3	158.9	1,090	64.3
Smyrna	0.0	5.1	0.0	0.5	0.0	13.2	20.7	6.0	0.0	7.9	86.0	1,528	29.1
South Fulton	NA	NA	NA	NA	NA	NA	NA	NA	NA	NA	NA	NA	NA
Statesboro	0.0	10.1	0.0	0.0	0.2	21.8	36.8	2.0	0.0	3.3	15.0	480	0.0
Stockbridge	0.0	17.3	0.0	0.0	0.0	1.2	26.5	2.6	0.0	6.3	14.5	499	0.0
Stonecrest	NA	NA	NA	NA	NA	NA	NA	NA	NA	NA	NA	NA	NA
Sugar Hill	0.0	7.8	0.0	0.0	0.0	0.7	0.2	27.7	34.0	0.0	0.0	0	0.0
Tucker	0.2	10.9	0.0	0.0	9.7	15.4	8.9	5.2	1.3	1.9	66.5	1,845	0.0
Union City	0.0	10.7	0.0	0.0	0.0	22.6	16.1	2.4	0.0	2.4	19.2	906	0.0
Valdosta	0.0	12.4	0.0	0.0	0.0	24.4	22.9	0.1	0.1	5.0	89.7	1,601	3.9
Warner Robins	0.0	9.0	0.0	0.0	0.6	20.4	25.5	5.1	0.7	2.7	34.5	458	0.0
Woodstock	0.0	4.2	0.0	0.0	0.0	20.8	19.3	4.4	0.0	0.3	3.3	104	2.5
HAWAII	X	X	X	X	X	X	X	X	X	X	X	X	X
East Honolulu CDP	NA	NA	NA	NA	NA	NA	NA	NA	NA	NA	NA	NA	NA
Ewa Gentry CDP	NA	NA	NA	NA	NA	NA	NA	NA	NA	NA	NA	NA	NA
Hilo CDP	NA	NA	NA	NA	NA	NA	NA	NA	NA	NA	NA	NA	NA
Kahului CDP	NA	NA	NA	NA	NA	NA	NA	NA	NA	NA	NA	NA	NA
Kailua CDP (Honolulu County)	NA	NA	NA	NA	NA	NA	NA	NA	NA	NA	NA	NA	NA
Kaneohe CDP	NA	NA	NA	NA	NA	NA	NA	NA	NA	NA	NA	NA	NA
Mililani Town CDP	NA	NA	NA	NA	NA	NA	NA	NA	NA	NA	NA	NA	NA
Pearl City CDP	NA	NA	NA	NA	NA	NA	NA	NA	NA	NA	NA	NA	NA
Urban Honolulu CDP	NA	NA	NA	NA	NA	NA	NA	NA	NA	NA	NA	NA	NA
Waipahu CDP	NA	NA	NA	NA	NA	NA	NA	NA	NA	NA	NA	NA	NA
IDAHO	X	X	X	X	X	X	X	X	X	X	X	X	X
Boise City	0.0	0.6	0.0	0.0	0.3	16.9	29.0	10.0	1.0	0.8	109.3	480	0.0
Caldwell	0.0	10.8	0.0	0.0	0.0	18.5	25.1	7.0	0.4	1.9	25.4	464	2.5
Coeur d'Alene	0.0	9.4	0.1	0.0	0.0	22.6	24.7	5.5	0.9	1.3	35.7	706	0.0
Eagle	0.0	2.1	0.0	0.0	1.0	32.5	0.0	6.5	0.0	0.0	3.4	131	0.0
Idaho Falls	0.0	7.0	0.0	0.0	5.2	17.5	11.2	13.6	5.1	1.3	29.3	475	0.9
Lewiston	0.0	13.7	0.0	0.0	7.2	15.3	20.5	7.6	0.0	0.5	4.2	129	0.0
Meridian	0.0	0.0	0.0	0.0	0.0	21.6	22.7	13.0	5.1	0.0	0.6	6	0.0
Moscow	0.0	13.1	0.0	0.0	0.0	19.2	31.4	10.8	0.3	1.5	10.3	403	1.3
Nampa	0.0	7.9	0.0	0.0	0.0	21.5	16.6	17.4	1.3	0.4	0.0	0	0.0
Pocatello	0.0	12.1	0.0	0.0	1.7	21.0	17.9	7.6	3.0	2.2	40.0	723	0.0
Post Falls	0.0	16.4	0.0	0.0	0.0	30.3	9.7	9.4	0.0	1.5	5.9	178	0.0
Rexburg	0.0	13.4	0.0	0.0	0.0	9.9	18.0	7.4	0.0	1.5	6.9	243	0.0
Twin Falls	0.0	11.0	0.0	0.0	0.9	17.8	14.7	6.2	1.8	6.9	109.0	2,211	13.7
ILLINOIS	X	X	X	X	X	X	X	X	X	X	X	X	X
Addison	0.0	11.1	0.0	0.0	0.0	38.0	11.9	0.0	0.0	2.4	59.2	1,603	17.3
Algonquin	0.0	43.9	0.0	0.0	0.0	25.8	7.1	1.7	0.0	3.7	29.9	968	1.8
Alton	0.0	6.4	0.0	0.0	0.2	17.1	8.9	5.6	0.0	0.5	12.1	453	0.2
Arlington Heights	0.5	12.9	0.0	0.0	1.8	24.6	1.2	0.7	5.8	2.3	66.3	878	34.5
Aurora	4.8	11.8	1.7	0.0	0.0	32.5	0.0	3.4	0.2	3.5	1,034.8	5,164	205.8
Bartlett	0.0	6.0	0.3	0.0	0.0	20.3	7.2	4.2	0.0	4.0	77.8	1,890	26.0
Batavia	0.0	14.3	0.0	0.0	0.0	25.7	13.0	0.0	0.0	3.5	35.9	1,356	0.0
Belleville	0.0	3.5	0.0	0.0	1.2	19.3	25.9	2.2	0.0	7.3	74.5	1,788	0.0
Belvidere	4.6	20.2	0.0	0.0	0.1	26.0	10.1	0.0	0.0	5.6	32.4	1,288	0.7
Berwyn	0.0	9.6	0.1	0.0	0.0	34.6	6.3	2.4	0.3	11.3	264.9	4,779	30.4
Bloomington	0.0	7.0	0.1	0.0	0.0	21.0	9.8	12.3	0.6	8.0	257.7	3,298	19.5
Bolingbrook	0.0	9.0	0.0	0.0	0.0	23.5	10.1	12.0	0.0	5.8	236.7	3,156	5.1
Buffalo Grove	0.0	16.7	0.0	0.0	0.0	26.3	10.0	0.0	0.0	5.9	68.8	1,671	13.2
Burbank	0.0	17.5	0.0	0.0	0.0	34.2	0.0	0.0	0.0	14.0	83.9	2,920	14.1
Calumet City	2.7	9.5	0.0	0.0	0.0	27.8	0.0	0.0	0.2	3.8	44.4	1,215	6.0
Carol Stream	0.0	13.1	0.0	0.0	0.0	47.7	0.0	0.0	0.0	1.0	7.0	175	0.0
Carpentersville	0.0	14.8	0.0	0.0	0.0	27.3	1.9	0.4	0.0	9.8	99.4	2,617	8.7
Champaign	4.7	16.6	3.1	0.0	0.0	22.8	2.4	0.0	0.0	4.0	136.1	1,550	9.0
Chicago	3.9	8.6	0.1	0.0	1.7	18.7	5.7	0.4	3.1	12.0	23,539.6	8,683	2,428.3
Chicago Heights	0.0	4.0	0.0	0.0	0.0	27.9	0.0	1.0	0.0	6.3	182.5	6,109	15.7
Cicero town	4.0	14.1	0.0	0.0	1.4	21.7	0.0	2.0	0.0	9.2	299.4	3,633	24.5
Crystal Lake	0.0	15.4	0.0	0.0	0.2	23.9	6.2	3.1	0.0	2.0	45.3	1,131	10.2
Danville	0.0	11.6	0.0	0.0	0.0	0.0	12.3	4.4	0.0	0.6	5.3	170	0.0
Decatur	0.0	14.6	0.0	0.0	0.0	30.3	2.9	1.4	0.0	7.0	133.5	1,859	24.3
DeKalb	0.0	7.5	0.0	0.0	0.0	21.5	3.9	0.0	0.4	2.2	33.7	788	0.0

1. Based on population estimated as of July 1 of the year shown.

STATE	Place code	City	Land area[1] (sq. mi)	Population, 2021: Total persons 2021	Population, 2021: Rank	Population, 2021: Per square mile	Race 2020: Race alone[2] (percent): White	Race 2020: Race alone[2] (percent): Black or African American	Race 2020: Race alone[2] (percent): American Indian, Alaskan Native	Race 2020: Race alone[2] (percent): Asian	Race 2020: Race alone[2] (percent): Hawaiian Pacific Islander	Race 2020: Race alone[2] (percent): Some other race	Race 2020: Two or more races (percent)
			1	2	3	4	5	6	7	8	9	10	11
		ILLINOIS—Cont'd											
17	19642	Des Plaines	14.2	59,459	654	4,187.3	62.4	2.4	1.0	15.2	0.0	9.2	9.7
17	20591	Downers Grove	14.6	49,654	806	3,401.0	81.9	3.7	0.2	5.9	0.0	1.6	6.7
17	22697	Edwardsville	19.8	25,218	1,533	1,273.6	79.4	10.2	0.2	3.1	0.1	1.1	5.8
17	23074	Elgin	38.0	113,911	261	2,997.7	43.4	6.6	2.4	6.5	0.1	24.3	16.7
17	23256	Elk Grove Village	11.6	32,066	1,229	2,764.3	73.3	1.9	0.5	12.0	0.0	4.9	7.3
17	23620	Elmhurst	10.2	45,326	876	4,443.7	80.5	2.1	0.3	6.5	0.0	2.9	7.7
17	24582	Evanston	7.8	77,517	466	9,938.1	59.1	16.1	0.7	9.9	0.1	4.5	9.8
17	28326	Galesburg	17.8	29,712	1,317	1,669.2	72.9	14.4	0.3	1.0	0.0	3.4	8.0
17	29730	Glendale Heights	5.4	32,796	1,207	6,073.3	36.6	7.3	1.3	25.3	0.1	16.9	12.6
17	29756	Glen Ellyn	6.9	28,533	1,367	4,135.2	78.8	3.3	0.2	8.2	0.0	2.8	6.7
17	29938	Glenview	14.0	47,856	832	3,418.3	72.3	1.1	0.3	16.6	0.0	3.0	6.6
17	30926	Granite City	19.0	27,484	1,415	1,446.5	77.0	11.3	0.4	0.7	0.0	3.3	7.4
17	32018	Gurnee	13.5	30,521	1,292	2,260.8	59.9	9.0	0.6	12.3	0.1	7.8	10.3
17	32746	Hanover Park	6.4	36,774	1,079	5,745.9	37.1	7.1	1.6	17.0	0.1	21.4	15.7
17	34722	Highland Park	12.2	30,177	1,302	2,473.5	83.7	1.6	0.6	3.7	0.0	3.2	7.3
17	35411	Hoffman Estates	21.1	51,350	776	2,433.6	52.1	4.9	0.6	26.3	0.0	7.5	8.7
17	36750	Huntley	14.3	28,008	1,391	1,958.6	82.4	1.7	0.2	5.5	0.0	3.0	7.2
17	38570	Joliet	65.1	150,372	176	2,309.9	51.3	16.3	1.0	2.0	0.0	15.2	14.3
17	41183	Lake in the Hills	10.2	28,945	1,349	2,837.7	75.1	2.4	0.6	5.7	0.0	6.5	9.7
17	42028	Lansing	7.5	28,379	1,370	3,783.9	32.2	46.6	0.7	0.9	0.0	10.7	8.9
17	44225	Lockport	11.5	26,118	1,482	2,271.1	86.4	1.6	0.3	1.8	0.0	2.5	7.5
17	44407	Lombard	10.2	43,891	905	4,303.0	70.8	4.6	0.4	13.1	0.0	3.8	7.2
17	45694	McHenry	14.5	27,372	1,422	1,887.7	80.7	1.1	0.5	1.9	0.0	6.5	9.3
17	49867	Moline	16.8	42,418	943	2,524.9	70.1	8.8	0.8	3.0	0.0	7.1	10.0
17	50647	Morton Grove	5.1	24,712	1,550	4,845.5	54.2	1.9	0.4	34.0	0.0	3.1	6.4
17	51089	Mount Prospect	10.7	55,541	712	5,190.7	66.4	2.7	0.7	14.5	0.0	8.0	7.7
17	51349	Mundelein	9.6	31,560	1,254	3,287.5	56.6	2.0	1.2	11.1	0.0	16.6	12.4
17	51622	Naperville	39.1	149,104	180	3,813.4	63.4	5.0	0.2	22.3	0.0	2.2	6.9
17	52584	New Lenox	15.7	27,477	1,416	1,750.1	89.9	1.2	0.1	1.1	0.0	1.4	6.3
17	53000	Niles	5.8	30,345	1,299	5,231.9	67.2	1.7	0.4	19.6	0.0	5.0	6.0
17	53234	Normal town	17.9	53,594	745	2,994.1	74.9	11.6	0.2	4.4	0.0	2.3	6.6
17	53481	Northbrook	13.2	34,587	1,152	2,620.2	77.5	0.8	0.1	16.4	0.0	0.8	4.5
17	53559	North Chicago	8.0	30,029	1,307	3,753.6	34.4	27.7	1.3	5.6	0.4	20.2	10.5
17	54638	Oak Forest	6.0	26,793	1,447	4,465.5	71.6	7.5	0.6	4.8	0.0	6.6	8.8
17	54820	Oak Lawn	8.6	57,013	695	6,629.4	68.3	7.7	0.9	2.8	0.0	9.4	10.9
17	54885	Oak Park	4.7	53,224	749	11,324.3	62.0	19.1	0.3	5.5	0.0	2.7	10.4
17	55249	O'Fallon	15.6	32,292	1,220	2,070.0	70.6	16.4	0.2	2.7	0.1	1.4	8.5
17	56640	Orland Park	22.0	57,850	684	2,629.5	82.5	3.4	0.2	5.4	0.0	2.5	6.0
17	56887	Oswego	14.9	35,316	1,129	2,370.2	71.2	7.7	0.4	4.7	0.0	5.0	11.0
17	57225	Palatine	14.1	66,321	577	4,703.6	63.9	3.1	0.9	12.9	0.0	9.8	9.4
17	57875	Park Ridge	7.1	38,810	1,025	5,466.2	86.1	0.5	0.2	4.9	0.0	1.8	6.5
17	58447	Pekin	15.7	31,448	1,259	2,003.1	91.3	2.3	0.4	0.7	0.0	0.7	4.6
17	59000	Peoria	48.0	111,666	272	2,326.4	54.6	27.9	0.4	6.4	0.0	3.8	7.0
17	60287	Plainfield	24.7	45,398	873	1,838.0	70.6	7.0	0.4	9.7	0.0	3.2	9.1
17	62367	Quincy	15.8	39,131	1,014	2,476.6	86.3	5.9	0.2	1.0	0.1	0.9	5.6
17	65000	Rockford	64.9	147,711	185	2,276.0	52.2	23.0	0.8	3.5	0.0	9.9	10.5
17	65078	Rock Island	16.9	36,636	1,082	2,167.8	61.9	19.6	0.4	4.3	0.1	4.3	9.3
17	65442	Romeoville	19.1	40,469	977	2,118.8	47.6	13.8	1.0	6.9	0.0	15.6	15.0
17	66040	Round Lake Beach	5.0	27,081	1,436	5,416.2	41.6	4.8	2.1	3.1	0.1	28.4	19.9
17	66703	St. Charles	14.4	33,009	1,194	2,292.3	81.2	1.7	0.4	4.4	0.0	4.6	7.7
17	68003	Schaumburg	19.3	77,082	471	3,993.9	57.5	4.3	0.4	26.5	0.0	4.3	7.0
17	70122	Skokie	10.1	66,422	575	6,576.4	51.4	7.9	0.5	27.8	0.0	4.6	7.8
17	72000	Springfield	61.2	113,394	263	1,852.8	68.9	20.4	0.3	2.9	0.0	1.1	6.4
17	73157	Streamwood	7.8	38,651	1,031	4,955.3	46.6	5.9	1.7	16.0	0.0	16.3	13.4
17	75484	Tinley Park	16.1	54,864	726	3,407.7	80.6	6.4	0.1	4.2	0.0	2.3	6.4
17	77005	Urbana	11.8	38,681	1,029	3,278.1	51.6	18.9	0.3	18.3	0.0	3.6	7.4
17	77694	Vernon Hills	7.7	26,786	1,449	3,478.7	57.9	2.5	0.7	25.9	0.1	5.1	7.9
17	79293	Waukegan	24.2	88,614	389	3,661.7	23.1	17.0	2.7	5.2	0.1	35.0	16.9
17	80060	West Chicago	15.4	25,370	1,525	1,647.4	41.0	2.9	2.2	8.0	0.0	28.9	17.0
17	81048	Wheaton	11.3	53,126	753	4,701.4	79.0	4.3	0.2	7.5	0.0	2.2	6.8
17	81087	Wheeling	8.7	38,499	1,034	4,425.2	50.3	2.4	1.4	16.7	0.0	17.3	11.8
17	82075	Wilmette	5.4	27,587	1,409	5,108.7	78.8	0.9	0.2	11.8	0.0	1.0	7.3
17	83245	Woodridge	9.6	33,826	1,173	3,523.5	60.8	10.0	0.5	13.3	0.1	6.6	8.7
17	83349	Woodstock	13.2	25,646	1,510	1,942.9	69.2	3.0	0.9	2.1	0.0	12.9	12.0
18	00000	INDIANA	35,826.4	6,805,985	X	190.0	77.2	9.6	0.4	2.5	0.0	3.9	6.4
18	01468	Anderson	41.6	54,817	727	1,317.7	73.4	14.6	0.5	0.6	0.0	4.1	6.9
18	05860	Bloomington	23.3	79,968	447	3,432.1	76.5	5.2	0.3	9.0	0.0	2.0	7.0

1. Dry land or land partially or temporarily covered by water. 2. Hispanic or Latino persons may be of any race.

City	Percent Hispanic or Latino[1], 2020	Percent foreign born, 2016–2020	Age of population (percent), 2016–2020: Under 18 years	18 to 24 years	25 to 34 years	35 to 44 years	45 to 54 years	55 to 64 years	65 years and over	Median age, 2016–2020	Percent female, 2016–2020	Population: Census counts 2010	Census counts 2020	Percent change 2010–2020	Percent change 2020–2021
	12	13	14	15	16	17	18	19	20	21	22	23	24	25	26
ILLINOIS—Cont'd															
Des Plaines	20.5	30.5	20.4	6.5	12.9	12.8	13.3	15.4	18.8	42.8	51.3	58,252	60,681	4.2	-2.0
Downers Grove	6.8	10.3	21.5	7.4	11.5	11.7	13.1	15.6	19.1	43.1	51.3	48,880	50,230	2.8	-1.1
Edwardsville	3.7	3.5	20.5	24.3	11.1	11.3	11.9	10.1	10.8	29.9	52.2	24,409	25,354	3.9	-0.5
Elgin	47.4	26.0	26.6	9.2	14.4	12.7	12.9	11.9	12.2	34.9	49.4	108,218	114,809	6.1	-0.8
Elk Grove Village	12.2	22.5	20.2	6.6	10.6	14.2	14.3	14.4	19.7	43.6	52.4	33,166	32,769	-1.2	-2.1
Elmhurst	9.3	9.6	25.1	8.6	8.8	12.5	14.2	14.3	16.5	40.7	50.8	44,120	45,713	3.6	-0.8
Evanston	11.2	18.0	19.9	16.0	12.7	12.3	11.5	11.5	16.0	36.2	52.2	74,483	79,035	6.1	-1.9
Galesburg	8.5	4.6	17.5	12.8	11.9	11.4	11.4	13.6	21.3	41.2	48.2	32,192	30,139	-6.4	-1.4
Glendale Heights	32.8	35.7	23.0	9.9	18.0	14.3	11.1	11.2	12.5	34.3	50.1	34,326	33,241	-3.2	-1.3
Glen Ellyn	7.5	10.9	26.6	6.5	8.1	14.1	14.1	12.8	17.8	41.0	50.9	27,656	28,872	4.4	-1.2
Glenview	7.4	20.9	24.5	5.3	6.8	11.7	14.7	14.0	23.1	46.2	51.3	44,726	48,769	9.0	-1.9
Granite City	7.3	2.8	22.6	6.4	14.0	13.3	10.8	16.2	16.6	39.2	49.7	29,753	27,764	-6.7	-1.0
Gurnee	17.7	15.4	22.9	11.7	10.6	13.4	15.8	13.6	12.0	39.2	52.5	31,231	30,746	-1.6	-0.7
Hanover Park	41.5	32.0	27.9	9.1	14.0	14.5	12.1	12.1	10.4	34.2	52.4	38,215	37,444	-2.0	-1.8
Highland Park	8.9	11.0	24.8	4.3	5.1	12.6	13.1	15.5	24.6	47.2	51.9	29,745	30,217	1.6	-0.1
Hoffman Estates	16.1	31.6	23.1	7.3	15.1	12.6	15.3	13.1	13.5	38.2	50.6	51,891	52,460	1.1	-2.1
Huntley	9.3	8.8	20.9	4.0	6.5	12.5	12.1	10.0	34.0	48.8	50.2	24,312	27,782	14.3	0.8
Joliet	33.6	13.8	27.1	10.7	13.8	14.2	14.2	9.8	10.2	33.8	50.5	147,307	150,352	2.1	0.0
Lake in the Hills	16.2	11.2	27.2	10.8	11.7	14.6	16.5	11.6	7.6	35.2	51.6	28,946	29,000	0.2	-0.2
Lansing	20.6	10.2	24.2	7.2	11.9	12.9	14.1	12.4	17.2	40.2	56.3	28,353	29,038	2.4	-2.3
Lockport	9.8	7.9	27.6	7.5	12.9	14.4	15.7	11.4	10.5	36.8	51.3	24,873	26,101	4.9	0.1
Lombard	10.2	16.6	20.4	9.0	16.3	12.7	12.2	13.7	15.7	37.7	51.8	43,462	44,441	2.3	-1.2
McHenry	15.5	9.2	20.8	8.7	11.6	14.4	15.0	13.2	16.3	41.3	51.5	27,025	27,123	0.4	0.9
Moline	18.7	9.6	22.9	7.2	13.4	12.7	11.1	12.6	20.0	39.6	51.2	43,439	42,954	-1.1	-1.2
Morton Grove	8.1	38.3	19.4	5.2	7.5	14.3	14.3	13.1	26.2	47.2	50.7	23,241	25,269	8.7	-2.2
Mount Prospect	16.2	30.0	22.9	5.3	13.8	13.4	14.7	11.8	18.1	40.8	50.3	55,037	56,749	3.1	-2.1
Mundelein	32.0	30.0	22.6	8.6	14.6	12.4	14.5	12.8	14.5	38.0	49.4	30,987	31,603	2.0	-0.1
Naperville	6.9	21.0	25.3	7.9	11.1	14.0	15.1	13.5	13.0	39.1	50.8	142,175	149,427	5.1	-0.2
New Lenox	7.1	2.2	29.4	7.1	11.1	15.6	13.5	12.9	10.4	36.0	49.8	24,296	27,218	12.0	1.0
Niles	11.2	40.4	16.4	7.0	12.4	11.5	13.1	14.6	25.1	47.6	51.7	29,847	31,014	3.9	-2.2
Normal town	6.5	5.7	16.9	32.9	11.8	10.1	9.1	8.5	10.9	25.2	53.1	52,555	53,585	2.0	0.0
Northbrook	3.4	20.1	20.8	5.5	7.2	10.4	14.6	16.0	25.6	49.7	52.6	33,200	35,237	6.1	-1.8
North Chicago	36.2	16.3	17.0	36.2	19.5	7.6	5.9	7.1	6.7	24.1	40.0	32,594	30,173	-7.4	-0.5
Oak Forest	16.5	11.0	21.3	8.7	11.6	11.7	15.5	14.8	16.4	42.0	49.8	28,001	27,403	-2.1	-2.2
Oak Lawn	22.6	18.6	21.7	7.0	12.9	12.3	12.4	15.2	18.5	41.0	50.9	56,690	58,271	2.8	-2.2
Oak Park	9.3	8.9	23.8	6.1	11.7	15.1	14.8	12.7	15.7	40.6	53.3	51,878	54,486	5.0	-2.3
O'Fallon	5.0	4.6	26.2	5.9	13.3	14.5	14.3	10.3	15.5	37.7	52.2	28,767	32,360	12.5	-0.2
Orland Park	7.9	15.7	20.9	6.3	10.6	10.6	12.7	16.0	23.0	46.1	50.3	56,602	58,648	3.6	-1.4
Oswego	15.7	13.1	30.0	8.2	9.6	15.9	15.3	10.3	10.6	37.0	51.2	30,452	34,607	13.6	2.0
Palatine	19.6	24.6	24.0	6.3	16.0	12.9	12.9	13.9	13.9	37.8	52.3	68,551	67,771	-1.1	-2.1
Park Ridge	7.2	14.1	23.5	5.7	7.5	13.1	14.6	15.3	20.3	45.2	51.2	37,460	39,645	5.8	-2.1
Pekin	2.4	0.8	21.6	7.1	14.8	11.1	12.7	14.1	18.6	40.8	50.6	34,042	31,727	-6.8	-0.9
Peoria	7.0	8.1	24.0	10.5	14.9	12.2	11.0	11.6	15.7	35.4	51.9	115,141	113,173	-1.7	-1.3
Plainfield	11.4	11.7	30.5	8.2	9.3	15.2	18.2	9.3	9.3	37.1	51.5	39,881	44,733	12.2	1.5
Quincy	2.3	1.4	21.4	8.7	13.7	11.3	11.3	13.0	20.7	40.3	52.0	40,717	39,560	-2.8	-1.1
Rockford	19.9	12.6	24.4	8.7	13.4	11.5	12.0	12.6	17.4	37.8	51.6	153,311	149,009	-2.8	-0.9
Rock Island	11.6	9.9	21.7	15.1	12.2	10.9	10.3	13.3	16.5	35.8	51.1	38,979	37,159	-4.7	-1.4
Romeoville	34.6	21.1	24.5	13.7	12.5	14.0	15.0	9.7	10.7	34.6	50.6	39,645	39,873	0.6	1.5
Round Lake Beach	55.6	23.6	28.1	9.9	14.7	14.7	12.8	11.6	8.3	33.5	47.3	28,090	27,294	-2.8	-0.8
St. Charles	11.3	9.5	21.5	10.1	12.2	10.3	15.9	13.7	16.3	41.3	50.9	32,289	33,091	2.5	-0.2
Schaumburg	10.5	31.0	22.7	5.3	15.9	15.8	12.3	12.5	15.5	38.5	51.4	74,233	78,691	6.0	-2.0
Skokie	10.6	38.1	23.3	6.7	9.5	12.7	13.1	14.6	20.0	42.9	52.9	64,826	67,775	4.5	-2.0
Springfield	3.1	4.2	21.9	8.8	13.6	11.4	12.2	14.1	17.9	39.9	52.5	116,995	114,461	-2.2	-0.9
Streamwood	33.8	28.5	22.8	8.0	14.1	15.4	14.0	12.1	13.6	38.2	50.4	39,842	39,519	-0.8	-2.2
Tinley Park	8.4	9.3	21.4	7.4	13.6	12.3	12.1	15.5	17.5	40.5	50.2	56,827	55,922	-1.6	-1.9
Urbana	8.5	18.3	11.7	38.2	18.0	8.1	5.7	7.8	10.5	25.0	50.6	42,137	38,530	-8.6	0.4
Vernon Hills	12.2	32.2	26.1	6.6	9.6	15.2	14.4	12.5	15.8	40.2	51.4	25,005	26,894	7.6	-0.4
Waukegan	59.5	29.3	26.7	11.5	14.5	14.4	12.2	10.4	10.3	33.1	50.1	89,119	89,361	0.3	-0.8
West Chicago	51.9	32.2	28.0	11.0	12.4	13.0	15.1	11.2	9.2	34.0	50.5	27,239	25,632	-5.9	-1.0
Wheaton	6.5	11.7	22.8	11.4	13.6	11.0	11.6	13.4	16.2	36.7	50.4	53,170	53,718	1.0	-1.1
Wheeling	33.3	42.4	19.9	6.4	17.5	15.7	11.6	12.9	16.0	38.4	51.4	37,644	39,158	4.0	-1.7
Wilmette	4.9	15.5	28.6	3.8	4.3	10.8	17.1	15.0	20.3	46.5	51.2	27,060	28,119	3.9	-1.9
Woodridge	14.8	21.1	22.7	8.2	15.5	15.2	12.3	15.1	11.0	37.5	49.5	32,989	34,182	3.6	-1.0
Woodstock	27.0	11.7	22.6	10.5	14.1	12.2	13.5	12.1	15.0	36.7	51.2	24,789	25,551	3.1	0.4
INDIANA	8.2	5.3	23.5	9.9	13.1	12.3	12.5	13.0	15.7	37.8	50.7	6,484,050	6,785,528	4.6	0.3
Anderson	7.6	2.7	20.5	10.3	14.1	11.1	12.1	12.7	19.2	39.4	51.4	56,083	54,745	-2.4	0.1
Bloomington	5.8	11.4	11.4	41.0	15.3	8.5	6.7	7.1	10.0	24.0	49.7	80,299	79,912	-0.5	0.1

1. May be of any race.

City	Households, 2016–2020: Number	Households, 2016–2020: Persons per household	Households, 2016–2020: Percent: Family	Households, 2016–2020: Percent: Married couple family	Households, 2016–2020: Percent: Female family	Households, 2016–2020: Percent: Non-family	Households, 2016–2020: Percent: One person	Persons in group quarters, 2016–2020	Serious crimes known to police[2], 2020: Violent: Number	Serious crimes known to police[2], 2020: Violent: Rate	Serious crimes known to police[2], 2020: Property: Number	Serious crimes known to police[2], 2020: Property: Rate	Educational attainment, 2016–2020: Population age 25 and over	Educational attainment, 2016–2020: Attainment[4] (percent): High school graduate or less	Educational attainment, 2016–2020: Attainment[4] (percent): Bachelor's degree or more
	27	28	29	30	31	32	33	34	35	36	37	38	39	40	41
ILLINOIS—Cont'd															
Des Plaines	21,849	2.62	67.7	52.6	10.3	32.3	27.4	1,109	43	72.9	NA	NA	42,652	33.6	38.3
Downers Grove	20,115	2.42	63.8	53.5	6.0	36.2	31.5	622	47	95.8	NA	NA	34,984	17.7	58.6
Edwardsville	8,814	2.52	60.0	51.3	6.3	40.0	25.3	3,130	8	31.6	NA	NA	13,984	19.9	55.5
Elgin	36,825	2.99	71.4	52.3	13.6	28.6	24.1	1,802	260	234.0	NA	NA	71,906	44.4	25.1
Elk Grove Village	12,835	2.51	69.1	55.8	9.5	30.9	27.7	256	25	77.4	NA	NA	23,754	28.7	37.4
Elmhurst	16,808	2.70	72.0	63.4	6.5	28.0	24.4	1,271	39	82.9	NA	NA	30,897	16.4	61.3
Evanston	27,918	2.40	54.4	42.4	8.7	45.6	34.8	7,079	NA	NA	NA	NA	47,450	17.3	67.1
Galesburg	12,495	2.10	48.5	33.9	10.0	51.5	44.9	4,116	144	480.2	NA	NA	21,179	49.4	18.6
Glendale Heights	11,654	2.90	71.2	51.8	14.5	28.8	21.5	33	50	149.1	NA	NA	22,715	42.8	28.3
Glen Ellyn	10,747	2.58	70.1	61.6	6.6	29.9	26.8	43	20	72.2	NA	NA	18,577	14.4	68.9
Glenview	18,058	2.57	71.2	61.1	7.5	28.8	26.9	770	47	98.7	NA	NA	33,166	15.1	66.6
Granite City	12,125	2.33	60.5	40.4	14.5	39.5	34.2	281	218	779.1	NA	NA	20,277	47.1	12.5
Gurnee	11,403	2.67	70.9	57.7	10.2	29.1	24.3	45	43	142.0	NA	NA	19,946	18.7	55.4
Hanover Park	11,064	3.42	82.9	59.0	17.0	17.1	12.4	4	48	128.5	NA	NA	23,845	43.6	27.3
Highland Park	11,700	2.50	73.8	67.2	3.9	26.2	23.6	295	NA	NA	NA	NA	20,979	11.1	75.6
Hoffman Estates	18,110	2.77	77.6	61.7	12.0	22.4	18.1	211	NA	NA	NA	NA	35,118	26.0	48.3
Huntley	12,113	2.26	64.6	54.5	7.7	35.4	33.1	0	11	39.9	NA	NA	20,585	30.8	36.8
Joliet	48,516	2.98	71.6	51.1	14.6	28.4	24.0	2,921	NA	NA	NA	NA	91,701	44.5	23.2
Lake in the Hills	9,783	2.93	77.8	61.4	10.1	22.2	17.6	0	23	80.4	NA	NA	17,751	25.5	38.8
Lansing	10,741	2.56	63.5	35.2	22.0	36.5	31.8	98	116	425.0	NA	NA	18,934	41.1	26.2
Lockport	8,975	2.82	73.1	57.3	12.7	26.9	22.0	195	26	101.2	NA	NA	16,557	31.2	37.2
Lombard	17,030	2.54	64.1	51.2	9.8	35.9	29.5	571	34	76.6	NA	NA	30,918	24.6	48.4
McHenry	10,504	2.54	67.1	54.3	8.4	32.9	27.0	227	34	125.6	NA	NA	18,954	36.7	29.7
Moline	17,937	2.28	61.9	47.1	10.7	38.1	33.7	294	204	496.0	NA	NA	28,786	36.4	28.9
Morton Grove	8,786	2.59	72.1	60.9	7.6	27.9	25.9	181	33	145.1	NA	NA	17,276	29.7	47.9
Mount Prospect	20,855	2.59	72.1	60.1	8.1	27.9	23.6	108	26	48.5	NA	NA	38,908	31.7	44.0
Mundelein	11,085	2.82	74.1	62.3	8.2	25.9	20.9	315	18	58.0	NA	NA	21,742	31.4	42.3
Naperville	52,648	2.76	74.9	64.6	7.4	25.1	20.4	2,580	99	66.4	NA	NA	98,590	12.6	69.9
New Lenox	8,720	3.06	81.6	72.6	7.1	18.4	16.0	105	24	88.1	NA	NA	16,996	23.2	44.4
Niles	11,065	2.52	64.9	51.6	9.6	35.1	29.8	1,289	15	52.0	NA	NA	22,367	39.0	36.7
Normal town	19,520	2.50	52.3	39.4	9.8	47.7	29.4	5,965	105	192.0	NA	NA	27,493	20.6	51.2
Northbrook	12,749	2.55	73.3	66.6	5.8	26.7	25.0	707	10	30.4	NA	NA	24,502	14.7	70.6
North Chicago	7,694	2.55	57.4	36.8	14.8	42.6	32.5	10,343	NA	NA	NA	NA	14,020	45.8	22.5
Oak Forest	10,102	2.71	71.5	56.7	8.3	28.5	23.4	56	48	177.2	NA	NA	19,162	36.1	30.3
Oak Lawn	21,154	2.60	64.0	46.9	11.6	36.0	32.2	520	93	169.6	NA	NA	39,526	36.2	33.4
Oak Park	21,701	2.38	58.9	45.6	9.9	41.1	35.3	520	194	370.0	NA	NA	36,527	11.8	70.8
O'Fallon	11,493	2.57	74.8	59.1	11.4	25.2	23.4	0	72	242.7	NA	NA	20,019	18.7	49.7
Orland Park	22,487	2.57	70.9	59.3	8.0	29.1	26.6	553	22	37.9	NA	NA	42,515	29.4	42.5
Oswego	11,566	3.06	80.4	67.0	8.4	19.6	17.4	85	27	73.1	NA	NA	21,915	26.0	44.3
Palatine	26,804	2.52	63.9	47.0	11.6	36.1	28.3	222	33	49.0	NA	NA	47,290	24.4	50.4
Park Ridge	14,384	2.56	71.8	59.6	9.9	28.2	25.3	565	19	51.5	NA	NA	26,496	17.6	61.3
Pekin	13,777	2.26	54.9	37.7	12.1	45.1	37.5	1,670	NA	NA	NA	NA	23,386	47.2	17.6
Peoria	46,430	2.34	54.8	35.6	15.6	45.2	39.5	4,066	1,084	986.1	NA	NA	73,788	34.7	35.0
Plainfield	13,365	3.35	85.3	73.1	8.6	14.7	11.9	131	NA	NA	NA	NA	27,503	21.2	55.3
Quincy	17,226	2.26	57.7	42.5	11.3	42.3	36.1	1,203	197	494.2	NA	NA	28,060	42.2	24.1
Rockford	62,011	2.32	59.0	35.5	18.1	41.0	35.3	3,880	2,101	1,451.0	4,104	2,834.4	98,553	45.4	22.3
Rock Island	15,538	2.24	55.2	35.6	14.8	44.8	36.4	2,861	213	576.0	NA	NA	23,807	41.5	22.2
Romeoville	11,675	3.29	74.8	59.1	10.9	25.2	19.4	1,230	NA	NA	NA	NA	24,501	44.1	21.0
Round Lake Beach	8,502	3.20	76.7	56.2	13.1	23.3	20.6	133	NA	NA	NA	NA	16,948	53.2	16.5
St. Charles	12,342	2.60	71.0	57.8	10.5	29.0	23.5	497	NA	NA	NA	NA	22,319	22.9	47.7
Schaumburg	30,249	2.41	61.8	50.4	8.3	38.2	33.0	442	78	107.2	NA	NA	52,864	24.1	49.8
Skokie	22,503	2.78	72.0	55.7	11.2	28.0	25.5	775	125	200.1	NA	NA	44,267	27.1	49.8
Springfield	51,064	2.18	54.7	35.0	15.4	45.3	38.5	3,686	1,078	946.3	NA	NA	79,739	34.7	34.8
Streamwood	13,170	3.01	74.7	58.7	10.4	25.3	21.5	242	59	150.7	NA	NA	27,614	43.1	27.2
Tinley Park	21,871	2.56	67.5	54.7	10.0	32.5	29.0	55	38	68.3	NA	NA	39,911	29.5	37.5
Urbana	17,295	2.06	38.6	25.6	9.0	61.4	44.6	6,885	NA	NA	NA	NA	21,268	20.5	58.8
Vernon Hills	10,006	2.63	72.1	58.0	11.1	27.9	23.8	46	21	78.7	NA	NA	17,785	19.4	60.8
Waukegan	29,822	2.85	67.9	44.1	17.4	32.1	26.3	2,282	316	368.6	NA	NA	53,832	53.1	19.8
West Chicago	7,838	3.40	77.0	58.7	12.7	23.0	19.3	360	36	134.5	NA	NA	16,465	47.9	29.0
Wheaton	19,218	2.61	68.3	58.7	6.3	31.7	26.5	2,951	46	87.3	NA	NA	34,962	15.0	63.8
Wheeling	15,148	2.52	63.9	48.4	9.8	36.1	29.7	529	28	72.3	NA	NA	28,525	34.0	41.3
Wilmette	10,210	2.64	73.3	65.4	5.2	26.7	25.0	133	NA	NA	NA	NA	18,310	5.7	84.5
Woodridge	13,023	2.56	67.3	53.0	11.1	32.7	26.7	97	33	98.6	NA	NA	23,133	20.6	49.5
Woodstock	9,706	2.52	70.6	46.4	18.7	29.4	23.8	897	17	67.2	NA	NA	16,977	38.9	30.3
INDIANA	2,602,770	2.50	64.5	48.1	11.5	35.5	29.0	189,435	24,161	357.7	120,453	1,783.2	4,466,180	43.9	27.2
Anderson	23,312	2.24	56.0	33.5	17.3	44.0	37.5	2,352	NA	NA	NA	NA	37,683	55.3	15.1
Bloomington	31,979	2.18	38.6	27.1	8.9	61.4	41.0	15,073	480	555.9	2,079	2,407.7	40,259	23.5	55.7

2. Data for serious crimes have not been adjusted for underreporting. This may affect comparability between geographic areas and over time. 4. Persons 25 years old and over.

City	Money income, 2016–2020					Median earnings Full year, Full-time workers, 2016–2020			Housing units, 2016–2020				
	Households												
	Median household income	Percent with income less than $25,000	Percent with income of $200,000 or more	Median family income	Median non-family household income	All persons	Men	Women	Total	Occupied	Percent owner occupied	Median value[1] (dollars)	Median gross rent (dollars)
	42	43	44	45	46	47	48	49	50	51	52	53	54
ILLINOIS—Cont'd													
Des Plaines	73,639	13.1	8.3	93,205	42,609	57,795	63,570	49,114	23,212	21,849	78.3	267,200	1,167
Downers Grove	97,197	13.8	17.7	131,733	45,193	76,148	88,676	62,784	21,116	20,115	75.1	360,100	1,364
Edwardsville	75,271	15.0	12.4	118,914	36,593	66,394	83,379	55,851	9,547	8,814	66.5	238,000	921
Elgin	72,999	12.9	5.4	82,334	44,317	45,418	49,446	40,729	38,623	36,825	70.1	196,100	1,087
Elk Grove Village	85,240	7.0	9.6	105,398	53,537	62,189	69,776	51,999	13,507	12,835	73.7	286,300	1,307
Elmhurst	123,869	6.6	24.9	148,663	54,565	86,683	100,857	69,252	17,551	16,808	81.0	442,400	1,490
Evanston	82,335	16.0	18.7	130,494	49,164	73,759	80,980	68,658	31,129	27,918	56.7	409,900	1,433
Galesburg	37,322	34.3	1.2	63,118	22,773	40,576	42,118	36,368	14,632	12,495	57.8	76,400	622
Glendale Heights	70,034	10.5	3.2	71,226	53,050	43,462	47,425	38,874	12,266	11,654	62.8	203,200	1,316
Glen Ellyn	118,208	11.1	29.5	169,358	45,353	95,278	118,194	73,791	11,133	10,747	76.9	465,200	1,109
Glenview	118,019	11.4	25.7	148,277	51,546	94,651	104,757	80,805	19,245	18,058	79.0	498,000	1,810
Granite City	53,545	27.4	1.9	67,927	28,785	45,995	53,327	40,936	13,865	12,125	64.8	83,100	716
Gurnee	100,892	10.7	17.0	129,858	53,084	67,392	84,830	55,563	11,969	11,403	71.6	269,000	1,252
Hanover Park	77,367	12.6	4.9	80,815	49,515	46,053	50,862	40,694	11,306	11,064	73.0	206,400	1,320
Highland Park	147,067	8.8	37.0	185,101	50,490	109,386	129,826	90,904	12,292	11,700	83.9	535,000	1,666
Hoffman Estates	92,423	8.4	10.5	103,641	53,197	62,081	67,282	55,966	18,818	18,110	72.3	286,600	1,417
Huntley	77,420	17.5	7.3	94,495	31,273	70,218	76,746	56,833	12,562	12,113	87.5	256,100	1,278
Joliet	72,871	15.0	4.6	86,198	41,122	50,491	57,038	41,270	51,837	48,516	70.0	193,100	1,077
Lake in the Hills	96,470	4.9	12.4	107,708	59,327	62,174	68,948	51,010	9,997	9,783	82.5	236,000	1,487
Lansing	57,659	19.4	3.8	70,775	43,528	47,483	53,739	43,115	11,668	10,741	66.5	132,000	1,036
Lockport	87,817	10.7	7.9	100,928	49,744	63,314	71,349	57,107	9,351	8,975	80.9	244,900	1,305
Lombard	86,167	9.8	8.8	100,420	53,894	62,977	72,198	52,623	18,203	17,030	69.8	264,300	1,482
McHenry	77,004	13.0	8.4	101,855	35,076	61,568	65,396	55,128	10,796	10,504	73.0	194,800	1,328
Moline	57,475	20.4	3.5	75,696	33,129	45,623	48,768	41,960	19,673	17,937	66.1	125,000	779
Morton Grove	87,063	11.9	9.5	110,549	42,108	69,964	76,200	64,155	9,414	8,786	87.5	326,100	2,022
Mount Prospect	84,353	13.7	10.7	103,946	40,330	61,416	66,053	55,883	22,019	20,855	69.2	332,100	1,172
Mundelein	91,535	6.5	11.4	102,531	65,153	53,053	59,867	46,888	11,502	11,085	73.7	236,400	1,396
Naperville	127,648	6.8	26.2	150,075	65,069	90,372	107,203	69,319	55,224	52,648	74.3	424,800	1,546
New Lenox	115,327	5.0	15.1	128,767	55,225	75,007	87,470	60,063	9,118	8,720	91.4	308,500	1,163
Niles	63,490	17.4	7.5	85,270	33,577	53,263	58,702	49,267	11,660	11,065	75.9	289,800	1,133
Normal town	58,381	26.6	6.2	97,427	27,976	53,449	61,069	46,836	21,465	19,520	56.8	169,300	852
Northbrook	128,883	6.6	32.9	173,545	55,156	106,536	115,850	81,385	14,106	12,749	86.8	563,200	1,949
North Chicago	47,213	26.5	1.4	57,061	30,847	32,287	33,315	30,620	8,605	7,694	34.8	107,900	1,250
Oak Forest	78,865	10.2	4.5	94,225	51,924	52,500	66,055	46,858	10,354	10,102	81.9	202,400	1,095
Oak Lawn	69,352	16.2	7.4	90,690	45,304	57,466	63,282	51,817	22,745	21,154	80.2	211,500	1,115
Oak Park	96,945	14.4	20.8	142,785	53,321	83,839	93,786	72,476	23,155	21,701	60.2	403,200	1,213
O'Fallon	90,432	7.6	11.6	108,467	51,406	63,026	73,862	52,940	12,286	11,493	71.8	214,600	1,134
Orland Park	84,676	10.9	11.2	104,343	43,702	66,488	74,397	55,239	23,473	22,487	86.5	289,000	1,203
Oswego	97,330	5.2	11.5	114,437	47,688	59,620	64,588	55,427	11,655	11,566	88.4	254,200	1,513
Palatine	83,495	10.6	11.9	108,166	54,916	62,028	68,602	55,481	28,395	26,804	67.7	286,600	1,236
Park Ridge	113,809	10.1	24.5	145,995	55,463	85,946	97,019	71,996	15,466	14,384	82.8	451,200	1,360
Pekin	50,552	22.9	2.2	69,156	37,744	44,539	51,097	36,625	15,159	13,777	68.6	104,000	671
Peoria	51,736	27.4	5.4	69,414	30,691	49,740	54,945	43,092	53,681	46,430	56.3	127,900	817
Plainfield	131,241	4.6	23.3	141,664	58,602	75,982	91,617	61,726	13,675	13,365	89.5	322,500	1,737
Quincy	46,935	24.3	3.7	64,891	31,228	40,216	43,757	32,644	19,093	17,226	63.5	118,800	688
Rockford	44,771	28.3	3.1	55,199	28,741	40,732	44,376	35,848	68,369	62,011	53.5	95,200	784
Rock Island	48,120	25.8	2.5	61,081	35,217	43,047	45,345	38,802	17,402	15,538	61.4	106,300	714
Romeoville	85,888	8.7	4.8	93,563	48,284	50,551	53,778	42,892	12,366	11,675	83.9	198,800	1,631
Round Lake Beach	77,207	10.2	3.2	90,392	46,635	44,176	47,174	38,838	8,961	8,502	76.4	149,000	1,255
St. Charles	102,414	8.0	18.1	124,032	53,472	68,643	81,282	54,043	12,999	12,342	70.6	303,000	1,382
Schaumburg	82,387	10.9	8.1	98,640	59,080	64,816	71,943	56,803	31,972	30,249	63.2	261,900	1,458
Skokie	74,725	14.4	10.6	93,491	42,788	56,049	61,402	51,798	24,153	22,503	72.2	324,200	1,269
Springfield	54,164	23.4	4.8	75,045	37,380	48,844	51,776	45,390	56,578	51,064	62.9	131,300	820
Streamwood	88,917	10.2	6.3	97,537	54,426	48,297	51,517	43,758	13,628	13,170	85.8	205,900	1,705
Tinley Park	82,163	10.6	8.9	103,902	49,889	62,878	74,433	52,349	22,802	21,871	85.8	238,200	1,227
Urbana	35,984	38.1	4.1	66,955	24,168	41,186	43,662	39,000	19,699	17,295	33.5	151,700	833
Vernon Hills	100,725	10.5	19.8	123,919	60,862	78,637	90,990	63,134	10,726	10,006	65.0	341,500	1,672
Waukegan	53,778	20.6	4.5	63,401	34,692	36,749	40,129	33,448	31,789	29,822	48.1	140,300	976
West Chicago	77,098	13.4	11.0	88,509	45,402	42,144	46,584	36,171	8,218	7,838	70.4	247,100	1,130
Wheaton	105,764	9.5	19.7	129,579	56,973	76,588	90,630	58,021	20,368	19,218	72.9	371,700	1,464
Wheeling	71,966	12.8	6.9	83,406	59,075	49,256	51,887	45,333	15,705	15,148	61.2	202,000	1,270
Wilmette	161,765	7.1	42.0	206,483	71,619	121,964	157,781	98,286	10,827	10,210	88.4	685,600	1,498
Woodridge	88,803	8.6	10.9	104,957	57,373	61,744	66,230	54,784	13,557	13,023	64.7	282,200	1,367
Woodstock	69,470	15.0	6.2	83,231	39,099	47,723	52,072	42,753	10,133	9,706	62.8	174,600	1,056
INDIANA	58,235	19.5	4.5	73,265	33,840	46,287	52,537	39,890	2,903,720	2,602,770	69.5	148,900	844
Anderson	37,110	33.0	0.9	46,960	26,763	36,546	40,715	32,115	28,255	23,312	56.1	78,600	781
Bloomington	41,354	35.9	4.1	72,350	26,022	43,849	51,012	39,422	35,252	31,979	35.3	219,200	946

1. Specified owner-occupied units

City	Commuting, 2016–2020[1]		Computer access[2], 2016–2020		Migration, 2016–2020		Civilian labor force, 2021				Civilian Employment, 2016–2020[4]			
	Percent		Percent						Unemployment[3]		Population age 16 and older		Population age 16 to 64	
	Drove alone	Mean travel time to work	With a computer in the house	With Internet access	Percent who lived in the same house one year ago	Percent who lived in another state or county one year ago	Total	Percent change 2020–2021	Total	Rate	Number	Percent in labor force	Number	Percent who worked full-year full-time
	55	56	57	58	59	60	61	62	63	64	65	66	67	68
ILLINOIS—Cont'd														
Des Plaines	75.0	30.5	92.8	87.0	91.8	2.2	32,314	-1.3	1,805	5.6	48,039	66.4	37,089	55.7
Downers Grove	68.9	30.3	93.2	90.8	88.8	4.7	26,579	-0.3	1,087	4.1	39,704	66.0	30,277	56.7
Edwardsville	83.7	25.3	97.4	89.3	74.7	13.9	13,259	0.5	459	3.5	20,814	63.6	18,081	41.0
Elgin	78.0	28.3	94.5	88.8	88.9	5.9	55,255	-0.8	4,043	7.3	85,666	68.6	71,954	54.1
Elk Grove Village	76.8	27.6	93.9	89.1	89.8	2.2	18,285	-1.5	887	4.9	26,648	66.8	20,254	62.6
Elmhurst	68.3	29.3	94.2	91.5	90.5	5.1	23,286	-0.4	924	4.0	36,391	67.7	28,694	54.5
Evanston	46.4	30.6	96.1	91.0	81.1	7.8	37,803	-0.4	1,847	4.9	61,047	62.3	49,177	45.5
Galesburg	80.4	14.8	80.7	71.2	89.7	5.8	11,452	-3.2	819	7.2	25,695	49.3	19,228	36.1
Glendale Heights	79.4	25.5	96.3	92.7	85.4	5.7	18,650	-1.0	1,035	5.5	26,746	73.1	22,509	59.2
Glen Ellyn	63.2	31.6	92.7	90.2	87.6	6.4	13,700	-0.5	562	4.1	21,314	64.9	16,363	53.0
Glenview	68.7	30.7	93.1	89.4	90.3	2.6	22,543	-1.1	915	4.1	37,510	60.7	26,624	52.6
Granite City	83.4	23.1	88.2	80.3	89.9	3.3	12,706	-0.4	783	6.2	22,898	60.2	18,153	46.4
Gurnee	79.5	28.7	95.4	91.8	86.2	5.9	16,871	0.3	788	4.7	24,576	71.9	20,919	58.4
Hanover Park	71.8	29.6	97.1	91.1	87.2	6.8	20,029	-1.3	1,198	6.0	28,822	69.9	24,880	55.4
Highland Park	67.1	30.5	94.8	91.9	88.8	7.2	14,967	0.5	555	3.7	23,244	64.2	15,974	55.0
Hoffman Estates	78.3	31.6	97.4	94.1	89.5	3.5	28,974	-1.2	1,335	4.6	40,726	69.1	33,934	56.1
Huntley	83.7	32.9	94.9	90.8	88.8	7.9	11,721	-1.2	549	4.7	22,484	53.4	13,162	56.1
Joliet	83.3	30.4	93.5	87.6	88.8	4.7	73,697	-1.4	5,343	7.2	111,385	70.3	96,348	53.4
Lake in the Hills	82.3	35.1	98.0	96.5	91.1	5.0	15,640	-1.7	753	4.8	21,840	77.2	19,657	58.1
Lansing	80.1	31.8	92.7	86.4	86.8	1.9	14,092	0.0	1,325	9.4	22,284	63.3	17,539	47.8
Lockport	84.9	36.5	95.7	90.6	88.8	5.1	14,037	-0.8	676	4.8	19,505	73.0	16,823	57.2
Lombard	74.5	29.4	92.8	89.1	86.8	5.6	25,004	-1.0	1,135	4.5	35,543	69.9	28,665	56.2
McHenry	81.9	32.4	93.4	91.4	87.4	5.5	14,099	-0.9	656	4.7	21,898	68.8	17,510	56.9
Moline	82.5	18.5	92.5	86.8	86.2	3.6	20,621	-1.5	1,130	5.5	32,816	64.2	24,563	52.8
Morton Grove	73.2	31.8	90.0	87.9	95.0	1.4	11,175	-2.0	583	5.2	19,058	61.0	13,045	55.9
Mount Prospect	75.3	29.8	93.0	88.0	88.2	2.2	28,536	-1.0	1,220	4.3	43,037	66.3	33,207	57.5
Mundelein	81.3	28.0	95.3	92.7	89.3	4.9	17,961	0.2	908	5.1	25,169	71.1	20,579	58.7
Naperville	68.7	33.8	97.2	95.3	87.3	7.6	77,478	-0.3	3,021	3.9	115,315	69.1	96,078	55.8
New Lenox	83.3	34.6	97.2	94.8	92.9	2.5	14,728	-0.9	614	4.2	19,735	72.5	16,948	58.5
Niles	77.4	29.2	84.1	79.0	92.5	1.6	13,280	-2.1	738	5.6	24,927	58.9	17,599	50.1
Normal town	77.3	16.7	95.6	80.2	76.7	12.5	27,553	1.2	1,165	4.2	46,477	62.1	40,532	38.2
Northbrook	66.0	29.5	95.2	92.0	91.5	2.8	15,701	-1.0	695	4.4	27,305	58.4	18,804	54.3
North Chicago	44.1	18.2	91.2	82.7	63.9	28.4	9,052	1.2	716	7.9	25,311	44.3	23,315	50.5
Oak Forest	76.7	32.2	93.4	89.9	94.3	1.5	14,517	-1.3	870	6.0	22,192	70.5	17,697	57.0
Oak Lawn	78.3	35.1	89.3	81.6	93.6	1.0	27,543	-1.2	1,761	6.4	44,234	61.1	33,993	51.9
Oak Park	52.7	35.1	95.8	89.3	87.9	4.1	29,196	-0.5	1,410	4.8	41,380	70.5	33,174	57.7
O'Fallon	86.3	24.9	96.8	92.0	85.8	8.2	13,971	-0.4	660	4.7	22,490	65.2	17,913	60.6
Orland Park	79.5	34.4	93.2	88.5	90.2	3.0	29,367	-0.9	1,426	4.9	48,094	60.5	34,682	53.0
Oswego	77.0	31.7	97.9	95.8	88.9	10.0	19,739	-0.9	817	4.1	25,950	70.1	22,187	56.9
Palatine	73.1	29.2	95.8	91.9	85.5	5.8	37,751	-0.7	1,738	4.6	53,283	73.5	43,836	58.2
Park Ridge	67.4	30.1	94.2	91.1	91.5	2.0	18,751	-1.0	808	4.3	29,678	64.1	22,088	56.5
Pekin	84.8	22.2	87.4	81.8	84.3	8.1	14,198	-0.9	840	5.9	26,409	58.5	20,306	48.8
Peoria	81.1	17.3	88.9	80.1	85.5	5.0	50,078	-0.8	4,006	8.0	88,088	60.9	70,399	46.3
Plainfield	79.1	35.8	97.2	94.0	90.7	5.3	22,851	-1.2	967	4.2	32,926	73.9	28,752	59.0
Quincy	82.7	13.5	85.2	78.5	86.3	4.2	18,416	-1.2	765	4.2	32,523	63.4	24,202	56.9
Rockford	78.3	21.8	88.5	80.0	83.7	4.9	63,709	-1.7	6,540	10.3	115,323	60.6	89,684	44.4
Rock Island	78.2	18.2	89.4	83.8	81.4	5.8	17,108	-1.1	1,021	6.0	30,329	62.3	24,102	44.2
Romeoville	79.3	32.8	96.1	92.6	91.9	3.8	19,831	-1.7	1,278	6.4	31,266	71.2	27,033	51.6
Round Lake Beach	79.0	31.7	95.5	91.8	91.7	3.1	14,684	0.5	1,186	8.1	20,790	73.2	18,523	56.6
St. Charles	76.6	30.4	95.3	92.4	83.2	6.3	17,738	-0.6	782	4.4	26,748	69.2	21,441	55.7
Schaumburg	79.5	30.2	96.2	92.8	86.4	6.1	42,281	-1.0	1,954	4.6	58,467	70.4	47,067	60.6
Skokie	68.1	28.4	93.1	88.8	91.0	2.4	31,709	-2.2	1,745	5.5	50,056	61.4	37,369	48.8
Springfield	80.3	17.9	89.3	79.6	83.1	4.8	55,736	1.1	3,454	6.2	93,010	60.5	72,390	49.7
Streamwood	83.3	29.4	97.3	94.7	91.9	2.4	22,611	-1.1	1,352	6.0	31,736	69.4	26,297	57.7
Tinley Park	79.2	33.5	93.8	90.8	91.8	2.7	30,869	-1.2	1,527	4.9	45,457	68.4	35,635	54.2
Urbana	53.6	15.3	92.7	77.6	68.0	19.8	21,508	1.3	1,016	4.7	38,008	57.0	33,539	31.8
Vernon Hills	72.7	28.7	95.5	93.6	87.9	5.1	15,077	0.0	580	3.8	20,536	68.0	16,378	56.8
Waukegan	72.2	27.1	92.6	85.3	81.9	5.8	43,973	1.2	3,359	7.6	66,684	68.1	57,717	51.7
West Chicago	72.9	26.3	95.6	89.7	90.6	4.7	13,716	-0.2	669	4.9	20,495	73.0	18,011	52.4
Wheaton	70.5	27.5	96.5	93.4	85.6	7.0	27,911	-0.4	1,024	3.7	42,461	65.6	33,874	51.8
Wheeling	74.6	25.2	96.2	89.0	89.4	4.2	22,820	-0.6	1,085	4.8	31,837	71.5	25,639	62.1
Wilmette	52.7	36.3	94.9	92.1	91.2	3.0	12,437	0.0	472	3.8	20,555	60.6	15,042	52.1
Woodridge	72.4	32.4	95.8	92.6	88.2	6.3	19,964	-0.7	932	4.7	26,517	77.2	22,823	59.4
Woodstock	87.5	28.1	95.2	92.0	81.9	7.0	12,731	-0.7	635	5.0	20,448	67.4	16,643	54.6
INDIANA	81.3	23.9	90.3	82.7	85.7	6.3	3,321,548	0.0	118,382	3.6	5,306,367	63.7	4,255,541	51.8
Anderson	77.3	24.8	85.7	76.8	83.3	4.9	23,219	-0.6	1,230	5.3	44,473	56.2	34,020	43.0
Bloomington	61.0	16.7	94.4	84.9	60.6	20.4	37,825	1.7	1,177	3.1	76,306	57.6	67,858	28.0

1. Employed persons. 2. Households. 3. Percent of civilian labor force. 4. Persons 16 years old and over.

Table D. Cities — **Construction, Wholesale Trade, and Retail Trade**

City	Value of residential construction authorized by building permits, 2021			Wholesale trade[1], 2017				Retail trade[2], 2017			
	New construction ($1,000)	Number of housing units	Percent single family	Number of establishments	Number of employees	Sales (mil dol)	Annual payroll (mil dol)	Number of establish-ments	Number of employees	Sales (mil dol)	Annual payroll (mil dol)
	69	70	71	72	73	74	75	76	77	78	79
ILLINOIS—Cont'd											
Des Plaines	5,734	10	100.0	125	3,192	2,652.4	261.8	178	3,134	886.1	88.4
Downers Grove	24,568	43	100.0	116	2,557	6,219.5	272.0	228	5,096	1,598.5	140.2
Edwardsville	14,627	46	93.5	18	924	1,181.7	50.1	105	1,800	386.0	40.2
Elgin	36,114	167	100.0	176	4,035	5,637.2	284.3	208	3,703	1,186.2	107.1
Elk Grove Village	1,410	6	100.0	426	8,055	13,689.1	551.7	131	2,463	1,209.7	86.1
Elmhurst	53,931	97	100.0	126	4,038	3,055.2	458.5	154	2,963	1,215.1	89.5
Evanston	14,881	25	44.0	41	298	447.4	19.8	205	4,000	1,011.7	99.9
Galesburg	207	1	100.0	21	450	331.8	20.9	142	3,326	793.8	90.7
Glendale Heights	927	1	100.0	73	1,386	1,199.3	96.8	85	2,212	661.8	61.8
Glen Ellyn	13,070	18	100.0	33	210	278.2	18.1	92	1,226	324.0	30.0
Glenview	36,971	66	93.9	92	1,690	1,901.0	133.0	159	4,446	1,775.8	196.6
Granite City	633	4	100.0	26	391	440.7	22.0	81	1,293	360.5	36.5
Gurnee	675	1	100.0	61	634	503.7	36.5	241	5,817	1,183.3	117.4
Hanover Park	0	0	0.0	28	1,390	1,142.1	74.1	66	962	255.0	24.1
Highland Park	30,461	95	29.5	46	160	648.6	16.8	159	2,623	1,229.4	96.0
Hoffman Estates	415	1	100.0	68	1,016	845.5	101.7	118	2,755	838.9	77.0
Huntley	26,484	143	100.0	36	421	157.3	26.8	52	1,168	275.1	27.2
Joliet	63,635	331	66.8	91	2,124	3,044.7	108.7	392	8,204	2,099.7	192.9
Lake in the Hills	450	1	100.0	19	197	90.9	15.1	55	817	263.6	25.1
Lansing	0	0	0.0	25	210	107.2	9.2	96	1,894	484.2	47.5
Lockport	27,561	89	86.5	18	78	86.3	6.0	60	921	236.9	22.0
Lombard	21,712	128	7.8	122	1,888	1,115.0	109.4	236	4,109	1,049.8	106.0
McHenry	18,840	392	26.5	42	1,859	775.2	114.4	122	2,138	526.0	54.5
Moline	3,631	45	37.8	38	711	1,001.1	54.6	213	4,452	1,156.9	110.8
Morton Grove	635	1	100.0	59	729	562.5	56.9	97	1,352	483.6	41.9
Mount Prospect	4,218	14	50.0	79	1,334	1,474.0	99.1	151	2,723	2,642.2	66.5
Mundelein	17,789	112	100.0	55	612	348.7	37.2	95	1,044	269.6	26.8
Naperville	216,644	735	37.6	243	2,458	2,900.8	175.2	460	10,909	3,927.8	317.7
New Lenox	44,582	134	100.0	19	259	156.3	18.0	76	1,922	431.5	42.0
Niles	1,652	3	100.0	93	2,154	1,236.7	195.9	248	6,140	2,080.4	178.6
Normal town	17,414	84	81.0	D	D	D	D	129	3,210	802.8	71.7
Northbrook	27,880	49	100.0	169	3,492	5,559.8	411.2	219	4,044	1,298.8	139.5
North Chicago	480	4	100.0	8	273	201.9	19.0	33	125	71.6	2.8
Oak Forest	200	1	100.0	23	96	47.9	5.2	55	637	179.1	14.1
Oak Lawn	3,862	13	100.0	28	80	30.7	2.7	172	3,707	1,249.8	105.1
Oak Park	12,900	43	2.3	D	D	D	23.6	146	1,736	357.8	35.8
O'Fallon	36,523	128	90.6	11	47	21.8	2.8	92	2,537	921.6	85.7
Orland Park	36,456	174	100.0	52	292	134.2	17.7	342	8,662	2,169.1	224.3
Oswego	24,848	160	73.8	D	D	D	D	96	2,497	519.3	49.7
Palatine	2,295	6	100.0	61	401	372.8	19.7	179	3,328	842.4	87.2
Park Ridge	16,410	24	100.0	43	192	456.6	16.5	72	1,245	433.2	37.4
Pekin	2,380	14	42.9	18	300	181.6	16.0	110	1,992	556.6	54.1
Peoria	15,560	51	100.0	129	2,216	992.4	107.0	509	8,716	1,988.5	205.9
Plainfield	81,137	356	100.0	25	236	276.0	17.3	111	2,443	611.0	56.2
Quincy	14,580	68	100.0	67	1,366	648.5	58.0	250	4,591	1,019.6	105.8
Rockford	6,705	30	46.7	167	2,509	1,845.1	128.7	517	8,093	2,239.1	206.3
Rock Island	6,487	47	100.0	48	1,021	719.9	55.6	75	887	168.9	22.3
Romeoville	2,699	9	100.0	68	2,516	9,742.6	169.1	68	1,695	414.1	35.6
Round Lake Beach	0	0	0.0	6	25	6.8	1.3	57	1,703	376.1	36.9
St. Charles	12,636	25	100.0	113	1,307	1,410.9	84.8	146	3,705	1,181.8	109.5
Schaumburg	19,138	110	10.9	263	4,993	8,377.2	430.3	465	12,304	3,075.3	323.2
Skokie	3,709	12	100.0	112	971	616.7	58.9	334	6,593	1,453.6	170.6
Springfield	34,537	224	61.2	116	1,917	2,522.9	102.8	570	10,751	2,645.6	257.5
Streamwood	0	0	0.0	18	118	86.9	7.1	78	1,673	480.3	41.6
Tinley Park	6,947	41	24.4	52	779	282.1	46.6	161	3,816	1,397.1	109.1
Urbana	14,307	58	100.0	22	797	820.8	36.5	76	1,430	389.9	37.3
Vernon Hills	46,048	73	100.0	66	3,002	2,004.7	255.5	193	4,474	730.9	91.1
Waukegan	381	3	100.0	74	2,909	2,927.6	210.8	222	3,120	746.3	73.1
West Chicago	787	2	100.0	74	1,591	1,063.0	116.0	70	1,191	337.7	34.4
Wheaton	6,835	24	100.0	42	145	350.9	10.8	157	3,182	542.2	58.3
Wheeling	730	3	100.0	D	D	D	D	89	1,293	358.6	42.5
Wilmette	15,860	21	100.0	27	93	95.1	6.0	87	1,202	267.6	31.9
Woodridge	11,371	25	100.0	68	2,848	2,346.0	198.9	103	2,534	760.4	62.8
Woodstock	8,447	65	100.0	27	503	216.8	37.5	80	1,639	560.5	50.2
INDIANA	7,583,248	29,860	74.4	6,271	96,880	87,596.7	5,505.8	21,327	336,615	102,106.0	8,660.1
Anderson	8,543	67	100.0	39	576	591.0	30.8	206	3,634	1,131.3	90.9
Bloomington	NA	NA	NA	37	401	170.4	27.5	361	5,762	1,659.4	140.7

1. Merchant wholesalers except manufacturers' sales branches and offices. 2. Establishments with payroll.

City	Real estate and rental and leasing, 2017				Professional, scientific, and technical services[1], 2017				Manufacturing, 2017			
	Number of establish-ments	Number of employees	Receipts (mil dol)	Annual payroll (mil dol)	Number of establish-ments	Number of employees	Receipts (mil dol)	Annual payroll (mil dol)	Number of establish-ments	Number of employees	Receipts (mil dol)	Annual payroll (mil dol)
	80	81	82	83	84	85	86	87	88	89	90	91
ILLINOIS—Cont'd												
Des Plaines	82	1,248	1,382.0	82.4	254	2,276	420.2	151.6	NA	NA	NA	NA
Downers Grove	119	816	433.3	52.6	347	4,485	1,015.6	396.4	NA	NA	NA	NA
Edwardsville	49	141	53.0	7.5	140	1,198	267.0	89.2	NA	NA	NA	NA
Elgin	90	474	135.6	22.7	276	1,678	283.6	100.6	NA	NA	NA	NA
Elk Grove Village	57	630	179.0	39.5	164	2,308	489.7	170.4	NA	NA	NA	NA
Elmhurst	85	364	86.3	19.2	259	1,457	244.3	77.7	NA	NA	NA	NA
Evanston	120	408	119.8	23.7	410	3,350	646.9	252.0	NA	NA	NA	NA
Galesburg	29	102	13.5	2.7	49	246	29.4	10.8	NA	NA	NA	NA
Glendale Heights	22	103	126.3	5.1	46	295	59.0	18.8	NA	NA	NA	NA
Glen Ellyn	55	214	244.7	16.2	163	632	148.8	38.3	NA	NA	NA	NA
Glenview	106	244	75.9	13.6	288	1,900	258.1	140.9	NA	NA	NA	NA
Granite City	25	145	30.9	5.7	39	261	23.7	11.6	NA	NA	NA	NA
Gurnee	34	202	80.1	11.3	139	592	74.7	33.3	NA	NA	NA	NA
Hanover Park	16	51	9.7	1.9	36	113	11.0	3.6	NA	NA	NA	NA
Highland Park	78	385	110.7	24.7	221	1,146	194.9	81.3	NA	NA	NA	NA
Hoffman Estates	51	139	40.3	7.7	208	1,576	271.7	104.6	NA	NA	NA	NA
Huntley	19	205	48.1	9.4	54	293	41.1	17.6	NA	NA	NA	NA
Joliet	99	464	100.0	21.5	223	1,370	227.3	87.7	NA	NA	NA	NA
Lake in the Hills	9	23	3.9	0.9	62	219	34.8	13.2	NA	NA	NA	NA
Lansing	24	86	12.1	3.7	37	161	17.7	6.8	NA	NA	NA	NA
Lockport	16	23	6.0	0.9	42	172	21.3	7.7	NA	NA	NA	NA
Lombard	82	433	91.7	22.8	250	2,556	489.0	202.4	NA	NA	NA	NA
McHenry	26	102	25.3	3.6	73	461	74.3	27.2	NA	NA	NA	NA
Moline	62	291	69.3	11.4	101	1,114	157.4	49.7	NA	NA	NA	NA
Morton Grove	D	D	D	D	82	421	67.0	25.4	NA	NA	NA	NA
Mount Prospect	44	168	59.2	9.6	175	652	115.6	41.9	NA	NA	NA	NA
Mundelein	23	50	16.1	2.2	105	3,090	638.5	248.5	NA	NA	NA	NA
Naperville	235	931	348.0	51.7	1,149	9,144	1,417.0	841.6	NA	NA	NA	NA
New Lenox	27	48	16.9	1.5	54	296	36.7	17.0	NA	NA	NA	NA
Niles	44	280	50.9	12.0	80	286	42.3	14.5	NA	NA	NA	NA
Normal town	D	D	D	8.1	59	515	86.6	30.6	NA	NA	NA	NA
Northbrook	174	643	211.4	52.7	586	5,959	1,553.2	669.4	NA	NA	NA	NA
North Chicago	6	27	5.6	1.1	15	156	19.9	9.2	NA	NA	NA	NA
Oak Forest	20	81	23.0	4.8	43	177	26.4	7.8	NA	NA	NA	NA
Oak Lawn	40	146	24.5	4.1	90	324	34.4	15.2	NA	NA	NA	NA
Oak Park	86	378	79.9	17.0	306	1,168	171.5	68.7	NA	NA	NA	NA
O'Fallon	46	160	33.2	6.3	91	1,064	186.5	77.1	NA	NA	NA	NA
Orland Park	108	337	138.8	13.0	258	1,358	174.8	68.3	NA	NA	NA	NA
Oswego	33	92	17.3	3.4	88	285	45.6	12.7	NA	NA	NA	NA
Palatine	83	271	61.7	11.7	328	1,360	206.3	78.9	NA	NA	NA	NA
Park Ridge	87	387	64.3	18.7	243	792	134.1	46.2	NA	NA	NA	NA
Pekin	22	52	8.5	1.5	40	238	21.8	10.0	NA	NA	NA	NA
Peoria	146	859	151.3	32.1	341	4,342	671.5	276.5	NA	NA	NA	NA
Plainfield	37	88	28.7	4.0	143	924	137.9	87.6	NA	NA	NA	NA
Quincy	51	184	30.7	5.5	105	685	65.7	27.7	NA	NA	NA	NA
Rockford	151	1,051	207.0	46.9	384	4,093	637.5	231.9	NA	NA	NA	NA
Rock Island	30	129	17.9	3.0	103	1,232	211.5	82.6	NA	NA	NA	NA
Romeoville	25	252	81.3	18.9	44	259	34.1	12.3	NA	NA	NA	NA
Round Lake Beach	10	19	6.2	0.6	17	52	4.8	1.8	NA	NA	NA	NA
St. Charles	75	579	760.8	34.7	D	D	D	D	NA	NA	NA	NA
Schaumburg	151	1,460	560.1	93.4	683	12,555	2,542.1	1,155.4	NA	NA	NA	NA
Skokie	111	506	109.2	29.1	366	10,099	1,182.4	429.8	NA	NA	NA	NA
Springfield	186	762	212.2	26.8	391	4,850	712.1	304.9	NA	NA	NA	NA
Streamwood	19	212	62.1	14.7	75	241	42.3	9.0	NA	NA	NA	NA
Tinley Park	39	146	27.4	6.5	140	866	99.2	38.9	NA	NA	NA	NA
Urbana	30	197	30.4	5.5	71	560	67.1	28.0	NA	NA	NA	NA
Vernon Hills	33	138	66.7	8.5	153	1,971	437.1	163.5	NA	NA	NA	NA
Waukegan	59	268	62.0	8.8	161	861	200.8	63.1	NA	NA	NA	NA
West Chicago	19	101	35.0	6.5	80	869	308.5	70.1	NA	NA	NA	NA
Wheaton	82	272	64.5	14.0	372	1,716	310.1	124.3	NA	NA	NA	NA
Wheeling	34	115	39.0	4.9	127	882	108.4	38.5	NA	NA	NA	NA
Wilmette	52	333	47.9	12.6	168	359	68.3	23.4	NA	NA	NA	NA
Woodridge	37	397	84.7	17.9	D	D	D	D	NA	NA	NA	NA
Woodstock	28	92	19.2	2.6	75	303	40.3	14.5	NA	NA	NA	NA
INDIANA	6,686	34,736	8,392.2	1,519.7	13,061	121,821	22,390.7	8,537.8	8,064	496,083	246,671.7	28,131.2
Anderson	65	303	70.3	8.7	87	395	37.0	13.0	NA	NA	NA	NA
Bloomington	158	848	166.9	30.9	213	1,555	208.0	81.4	NA	NA	NA	NA

1. Establishments subject to federal tax.

Table D. Cities — Accommodation and Food Services, Arts, Entertainment, and Recreation, and Health Care and Social Assistance

City	Accommodation and food services, 2017				Arts, entertainment, and recreation[1], 2017				Health care and social assistance[1], 2017			
	Number of establish-ments	Number of employees	Receipts (mil dol)	Annual payroll (mil dol)	Number of establish-ments	Number of employees	Receipts (mil dol)	Annual payroll (mil dol)	Number of establish-ments	Number of employees	Receipts (mil dol)	Annual payroll (mil dol)
	92	93	94	95	96	97	98	99	100	101	102	103
ILLINOIS—Cont'd												
Des Plaines	180	3,881	318.7	85.2	D	D	D	D	265	8,581	841.8	274.6
Downers Grove	168	3,000	199.2	56.3	26.0	463	20.3	6.7	265	5,695	945.3	332.5
Edwardsville	87	2,365	112.6	36.3	17.0	560	18.0	6.8	77	890	73.4	30.0
Elgin	180	3,329	173.1	49.2	26.0	1,037	175.3	37.6	294	7,370	935.3	387.0
Elk Grove Village	123	2,556	158.7	50.3	16.0	92	21.7	4.9	147	5,466	695.3	283.8
Elmhurst	128	2,135	128.3	37.2	30.0	505	27.1	7.4	218	7,388	1,033.4	340.8
Evanston	249	4,741	318.5	102.7	53.0	728	46.8	17.1	365	10,751	1,678.0	803.9
Galesburg	97	1,498	73.0	19.9	14.0	146	6.1	1.8	122	3,375	344.0	112.2
Glendale Heights	60	1,015	61.8	17.2	10.0	184	21.5	4.3	45	871	122.2	45.8
Glen Ellyn	D	D	D	D	10.0	367	11.9	4.8	109	1,338	209.8	97.4
Glenview	170	3,400	210.3	74.1	41.0	688	56.7	24.0	288	5,687	753.3	267.5
Granite City	74	1,132	57.0	15.6	5.0	67	1.5	0.7	81	2,083	235.9	92.0
Gurnee	123	3,378	167.2	51.4	15.0	1,622	149.5	20.3	173	2,452	205.6	82.3
Hanover Park	52	481	34.1	7.8	3.0	D	3.7	D	41	618	41.3	17.3
Highland Park	87	1,525	89.5	27.6	43.0	721	108.7	33.8	163	3,022	483.3	153.1
Hoffman Estates	105	2,032	138.4	42.5	17.0	173	13.6	3.4	237	5,751	747.6	283.2
Huntley	29	526	28.1	8.5	7.0	227	10.3	3.7	58	645	56.1	26.3
Joliet	268	6,012	557.8	131.1	31.0	832	66.5	17.4	366	8,710	964.3	427.3
Lake in the Hills	29	548	27.2	7.8	9.0	91	6.4	2.5	47	402	48.8	17.6
Lansing	58	1,127	62.5	16.1	9.0	91	5.3	1.9	59	635	39.9	15.7
Lockport	49	594	32.4	8.3	D	D	D	D	D	D	D	D
Lombard	147	3,286	236.7	71.2	D	D	D	D	172	2,853	305.1	109.4
McHenry	D	D	D	D	8.0	72	5.5	1.7	112	3,918	645.0	213.5
Moline	149	3,051	146.0	44.0	16.0	507	15.4	5.9	201	3,886	478.6	166.0
Morton Grove	63	826	55.4	17.3	12.0	188	10.4	3.2	80	771	106.4	30.2
Mount Prospect	110	1,621	103.2	28.5	13.0	276	9.8	3.1	134	1,161	104.6	44.8
Mundelein	83	1,110	65.3	18.7	9.0	106	8.7	3.0	61	306	28.3	10.1
Naperville	372	9,203	575.5	181.9	86.0	2,147	286.6	41.2	691	12,766	1,625.9	672.8
New Lenox	49	1,256	67.6	18.4	8.0	100	7.4	1.6	91	5,513	622.4	232.0
Niles	120	1,551	112.3	28.3	13.0	243	13.0	3.7	148	3,735	377.3	116.8
Normal town	119	3,146	154.6	44.8	D	D	D	D	106	3,133	388.1	130.9
Northbrook	99	2,121	147.2	49.7	40.0	700	53.4	21.5	273	5,498	406.8	188.1
North Chicago	31	372	19.9	5.3	3.0	22	0.8	0.3	D	D	D	D
Oak Forest	D	D	D	D	7.0	48	2.7	0.8	53	1,068	54.7	25.3
Oak Lawn	120	2,905	238.8	55.9	12.0	142	8.1	2.2	240	9,338	1,688.8	545.0
Oak Park	108	1,834	109.9	33.0	38.0	412	28.0	8.7	312	5,360	568.5	236.8
O'Fallon	70	1,491	81.8	23.7	10.0	421	11.8	4.6	85	1,828	254.6	94.8
Orland Park	D	D	D	D	45.0	1,176	62.1	19.6	339	3,934	398.0	167.2
Oswego	78	1,851	95.4	27.1	10.0	117	5.3	1.5	82	911	81.9	29.5
Palatine	116	1,571	102.1	27.0	28.0	583	27.6	8.9	161	1,761	137.4	56.6
Park Ridge	70	1,121	69.2	20.0	21.0	206	19.7	6.5	243	11,564	1,981.9	758.8
Pekin	71	1,275	57.8	16.7	14.0	107	3.9	1.4	101	1,882	170.3	70.1
Peoria	315	6,046	322.0	94.7	51.0	1,391	58.8	21.3	439	23,741	3,175.1	1,336.5
Plainfield	D	D	D	D	21.0	496	16.8	5.2	161	1,449	124.3	48.9
Quincy	128	2,568	115.2	33.8	29.0	366	13.2	5.4	129	5,782	988.7	305.7
Rockford	342	7,811	409.8	123.1	58.0	926	46.0	13.2	480	17,434	2,370.2	901.3
Rock Island	75	1,686	125.2	30.8	D	D	D	2.6	114	3,488	326.0	152.1
Romeoville	60	1,324	71.1	21.7	16.0	625	30.9	9.8	40	892	68.7	32.0
Round Lake Beach	43	798	49.4	12.8	5.0	90	5.5	1.2	39	414	33.3	13.9
St. Charles	133	3,305	258.0	67.7	30.0	374	21.3	5.8	184	2,229	242.2	90.1
Schaumburg	305	8,473	627.7	181.4	43.0	1,320	82.8	21.8	330	4,671	518.6	189.5
Skokie	176	4,284	309.7	88.4	33.0	697	64.3	17.9	435	8,878	827.1	346.5
Springfield	420	8,603	425.8	130.3	67.0	1,124	183.3	23.9	401	21,292	2,965.3	1,018.1
Streamwood	74	1,063	68.8	17.2	D	D	D	D	56	979	105.4	32.9
Tinley Park	122	2,781	171.7	48.0	19.0	385	87.1	13.8	169	2,923	269.1	101.8
Urbana	108	1,969	105.5	30.7	15.0	141	4.1	1.2	75	7,531	1,404.6	565.0
Vernon Hills	97	2,048	127.9	37.6	21.0	619	36.3	11.2	139	1,320	172.7	61.7
Waukegan	169	2,522	163.7	43.1	25.0	401	26.9	6.9	154	3,066	399.0	153.7
West Chicago	58	679	37.2	10.7	10.0	93	8.0	2.2	39	529	49.4	17.5
Wheaton	D	D	D	D	37.0	464	27.8	8.9	215	4,709	427.3	194.9
Wheeling	76	2,017	163.5	44.9	12.0	45	3.7	0.7	77	2,002	144.5	61.0
Wilmette	54	848	57.5	19.0	22.0	151	20.4	6.0	115	829	90.0	31.9
Woodridge	56	1,439	70.7	21.5	15.0	254	22.4	5.7	D	D	D	D
Woodstock	57	805	45.1	12.3	8.0	45	2.7	0.8	85	2,065	304.3	97.5
INDIANA	13,647	280,340	15,250.0	4,288.5	2,320.0	37,937	3,998.5	1,119.5	16,668	436,616	51,837.3	19,641.2
Anderson	138	3,244	145.4	43.8	D	D	D	D	191	5,536	638.1	233.1
Bloomington	363	7,661	394.3	111.8	36.0	688	21.4	7.8	356	9,307	920.2	392.3

1. Establishments subject to federal tax.

City	Other services[1]				Government employment and payroll, 2017								
						March payroll							
							Perent of total for:						
	Number of establish-ments	Number of employees	Receipts (mil dol)	Annual payroll (mil dol)	Full-time equivalent employees	Total (dollars)	Admin-istrative, judicial, and legal	Police and corrections	Fire protection	Highways and trans-portation	Health and welfare	Natural resources and utilities	Education and libraries
	104	105	106	107	108	109	110	111	112	113	114	115	116
ILLINOIS—Cont'd													
Des Plaines	175	1,145	173.7	47.6	417	2,951,169	7.2	33.7	28.6	7.9	0.5	9.4	0.0
Downers Grove	129	1,512	243.7	87.1	402	2,513,313	16.2	30.8	26.2	1.6	2.8	10.9	8.4
Edwardsville	53	377	37.8	11.6	221	1,085,833	9.0	34.2	22.3	10.6	0.0	13.3	5.2
Elgin	187	1,566	212.1	70.0	744	5,184,943	10.3	39.1	24.6	3.4	0.0	18.7	0.0
Elk Grove Village	125	1,240	169.7	58.5	314	2,010,165	11.6	35.1	30.0	3.3	6.8	6.5	0.0
Elmhurst	116	730	79.8	23.6	608	3,539,277	10.6	25.1	12.8	8.0	0.0	13.7	22.0
Evanston	202	1,705	315.1	92.8	966	6,323,487	13.1	28.4	15.3	4.8	5.4	22.9	4.8
Galesburg	51	369	119.8	11.4	259	1,317,865	13.4	30.0	20.6	8.0	2.2	15.7	4.8
Glendale Heights	33	253	36.6	10.0	234	1,355,867	13.8	38.4	0.0	9.3	4.9	32.0	0.0
Glen Ellyn	64	423	29.5	11.5	194	1,112,684	8.7	33.3	0.2	5.1	0.4	24.2	17.6
Glenview	169	969	118.4	35.6	360	2,839,149	3.9	24.6	27.1	5.0	1.8	7.4	12.1
Granite City	51	345	39.6	12.3	221	1,244,240	7.8	32.9	29.0	10.7	0.3	14.3	0.0
Gurnee	67	421	45.0	14.4	205	1,419,542	9.8	37.0	31.1	12.8	0.0	4.4	0.0
Hanover Park	D	D	D	D	216	1,390,130	8.8	44.4	23.2	4.2	0.0	8.2	0.0
Highland Park	122	590	64.5	20.2	228	1,596,297	8.6	30.8	26.4	9.8	1.3	11.6	0.0
Hoffman Estates	72	349	30.4	9.7	354	2,698,643	12.5	31.9	31.4	5.3	1.4	10.0	0.0
Huntley	46	205	22.0	6.7	90	599,687	20.2	47.8	0.0	13.4	0.0	9.6	0.0
Joliet	187	1,167	130.3	37.1	892	6,910,248	6.0	39.1	27.6	5.2	2.5	9.2	3.4
Lake in the Hills	D	D	D	D	131	814,212	11.4	47.5	0.0	11.5	3.7	13.6	0.0
Lansing	46	514	42.3	15.3	201	1,089,482	7.3	48.7	20.2	7.5	0.0	6.4	6.6
Lockport	57	249	22.7	7.1	99	625,754	12.4	49.7	0.0	15.8	2.4	16.6	0.0
Lombard	124	1,253	187.7	51.0	245	1,816,412	10.2	35.6	31.2	6.3	0.7	8.4	0.0
McHenry	76	390	36.9	10.9	163	1,093,776	7.1	48.9	0.0	13.6	2.6	24.1	0.0
Moline	91	642	55.9	18.3	377	2,369,164	10.8	27.4	18.3	9.7	0.8	18.3	6.5
Morton Grove	55	297	29.7	9.5	198	1,397,175	7.9	32.8	28.0	6.2	1.3	9.0	9.8
Mount Prospect	107	735	122.3	32.9	418	2,902,387	7.1	30.0	23.5	3.6	4.3	8.5	15.7
Mundelein	69	322	30.6	10.1	191	1,191,472	8.4	42.9	18.0	7.9	2.1	7.1	0.0
Naperville	297	2,529	211.5	83.6	1,105	7,205,462	9.0	28.8	17.5	14.5	0.0	20.5	9.6
New Lenox	69	341	36.4	9.9	109	763,892	13.7	41.2	0.0	14.9	2.6	17.3	0.0
Niles	88	515	61.8	17.6	294	2,022,452	10.0	27.9	24.3	16.5	5.7	10.1	0.0
Normal town	59	515	41.5	14.8	462	2,875,904	10.5	27.4	19.9	6.0	0.0	24.5	5.8
Northbrook	131	684	114.5	26.1	356	2,326,042	7.7	35.3	24.0	6.6	0.0	7.5	11.6
North Chicago	21	86	10.7	2.6	168	1,037,212	6.0	51.1	20.0	8.7	1.4	7.3	2.7
Oak Forest	D	D	D	D	164	947,676	3.1	49.0	26.3	7.2	2.6	11.7	0.0
Oak Lawn	108	682	67.3	17.9	383	2,606,591	4.2	39.0	29.5	5.7	0.8	7.1	8.8
Oak Park	130	646	63.4	17.2	336	2,470,159	9.5	42.0	23.8	5.3	1.2	4.4	0.0
O'Fallon	56	340	29.3	9.8	247	1,130,264	16.4	30.9	2.1	7.2	10.0	25.1	4.0
Orland Park	133	1,063	109.3	36.4	443	2,445,732	9.3	42.6	0.0	6.9	0.0	19.7	9.3
Oswego	68	353	38.7	11.7	109	699,543	20.4	64.0	0.0	0.0	0.0	15.5	0.0
Palatine	155	765	77.4	23.9	340	2,512,137	9.4	39.7	32.7	3.3	1.1	4.4	0.0
Park Ridge	97	677	128.8	30.2	263	1,488,872	5.8	37.5	22.9	2.2	0.0	6.4	12.6
Pekin	60	287	22.2	6.5	260	1,406,663	4.4	32.4	24.7	8.6	2.1	6.3	19.0
Peoria	198	3,953	413.4	191.9	791	5,667,304	7.3	41.8	27.6	6.1	4.0	0.4	5.1
Plainfield	78	531	53.7	16.8	138	1,144,565	12.2	62.6	0.0	10.6	0.0	10.1	0.0
Quincy	109	525	58.6	14.9	352	1,613,922	7.4	26.6	22.9	15.4	1.2	14.9	5.7
Rockford	282	2,023	243.9	62.0	1,103	7,086,162	5.6	33.2	36.5	5.3	7.4	4.8	4.2
Rock Island	59	388	38.8	11.9	368	1,968,792	6.9	32.3	18.7	14.5	4.8	16.7	4.2
Romeoville	64	450	60.6	16.1	281	1,619,462	9.5	41.7	17.8	4.2	0.9	22.7	0.0
Round Lake Beach	28	130	9.2	3.3	66	418,314	12.0	67.5	0.0	14.4	4.9	1.2	0.0
St. Charles	113	738	66.5	22.6	265	2,077,030	19.1	27.9	20.1	11.8	0.0	16.2	0.0
Schaumburg	245	2,381	442.5	133.2	514	3,870,281	10.7	31.8	28.6	5.7	6.8	8.8	0.0
Skokie	189	1,522	174.0	54.1	600	3,841,807	7.9	30.1	23.6	2.7	5.7	10.7	13.4
Springfield	355	2,754	349.7	115.0	1,431	9,424,523	4.4	19.7	17.0	8.4	1.4	47.3	1.8
Streamwood	73	320	30.2	9.5	192	1,343,293	8.6	36.1	29.5	5.2	0.6	11.9	0.0
Tinley Park	74	397	43.3	10.8	361	2,034,117	10.1	44.4	14.2	7.5	0.5	9.3	9.8
Urbana	53	570	613.9	45.0	260	1,906,717	11.3	40.6	24.1	11.2	3.7	2.4	0.0
Vernon Hills	65	543	56.5	17.5	107	859,465	9.6	66.5	0.0	18.1	5.8	0.0	0.0
Waukegan	114	478	57.9	13.8	514	3,531,059	9.2	37.9	27.1	2.8	0.5	7.5	5.3
West Chicago	46	251	47.4	13.3	115	873,891	18.2	48.2	0.0	10.8	0.7	19.0	0.0
Wheaton	118	762	79.1	20.4	461	2,894,226	8.6	34.0	12.6	8.3	0.0	11.5	18.4
Wheeling	83	404	67.1	13.7	244	1,910,542	10.0	43.3	24.9	2.4	7.2	8.2	0.0
Wilmette	77	550	58.6	17.7	205	1,652,110	14.0	33.5	24.5	12.1	0.9	12.5	0.0
Woodridge	55	368	23.5	12.0	164	1,100,802	17.3	45.2	0.0	6.2	0.0	12.3	13.6
Woodstock	63	245	23.5	6.9	164	891,099	8.4	40.3	0.0	5.3	0.0	19.9	8.6
INDIANA	10,777	75,446	11,120.7	2,561.7	X	X	X	X	X	X	X	X	X
Anderson	86	599	53.0	14.0	814	3,297,848	7.5	21.4	15.7	10.1	3.5	36.0	0.0
Bloomington	150	1,205	393.3	45.0	775	3,297,022	15.0	21.4	16.5	13.3	4.4	24.2	0.0

1. Establishments subject to federal tax.

City	City government finances, 2017									
	General revenue							General expenditure		
		Intergovernmental		Taxes						
					Per capita[1] (dollars)				Per capita[1] (dollars)	
	Total (mil dol)	Total (mil dol)	Percent from state government	Total (mil dol)	Total	Property	Sales and gross receipts	Total (mil dol)	Total	Capital outlays
	117	118	119	120	121	122	123	124	125	126
ILLINOIS—Cont'd										
Des Plaines	122.0	50.6	96.2	59.0	1,016	608	408	109.0	1,876	332
Downers Grove	71.0	28.6	94.7	30.3	612	443	169	65.1	1,313	78
Edwardsville	35.5	13.2	100.0	12.6	502	420	82	41.5	1,654	573
Elgin	157.5	43.0	96.2	76.4	681	452	230	147.7	1,318	182
Elk Grove Village	94.2	16.8	97.9	51.8	1,570	785	785	73.0	2,213	136
Elmhurst	79.1	21.2	99.0	39.7	851	460	391	96.7	2,075	548
Evanston	147.8	26.7	81.6	79.3	1,063	698	365	171.5	2,298	245
Galesburg	41.3	13.6	97.6	21.3	692	340	352	40.3	1,312	154
Glendale Heights	39.5	13.6	91.2	19.4	569	268	302	40.7	1,190	164
Glen Ellyn	44.4	8.2	88.7	19.2	683	437	246	44.6	1,590	322
Glenview	117.6	27.8	98.4	69.3	1,458	1,112	346	102.0	2,146	192
Granite City	47.2	12.9	92.6	21.8	762	612	149	45.9	1,603	105
Gurnee	45.8	28.0	87.5	12.2	396	0	396	41.0	1,335	109
Hanover Park	45.9	11.1	97.7	25.6	674	417	258	43.4	1,140	111
Highland Park	58.8	13.4	98.5	32.7	1,101	574	527	58.7	1,976	301
Hoffman Estates	99.5	17.6	82.4	53.6	1,042	725	317	79.1	1,537	126
Huntley	21.7	6.1	95.9	10.1	374	258	116	24.3	897	72
Joliet	228.2	72.2	97.7	88.9	601	284	318	191.7	1,297	312
Lake in the Hills	20.1	7.4	95.4	8.5	296	213	83	20.9	726	85
Lansing	38.1	9.8	88.6	20.6	740	514	225	35.4	1,267	102
Lockport	23.7	9.0	92.4	9.2	364	256	109	22.1	875	113
Lombard	99.3	29.3	90.0	19.6	447	205	243	109.0	2,485	141
McHenry	30.1	12.8	98.8	6.6	247	204	43	53.2	1,983	1,081
Moline	66.5	25.5	97.3	34.3	818	466	352	97.8	2,333	669
Morton Grove	36.7	7.9	96.6	22.9	991	564	427	31.9	1,383	32
Mount Prospect	78.3	11.8	72.8	55.8	1,020	596	425	81.9	1,498	60
Mundelein	40.6	16.9	99.5	14.5	463	410	53	39.4	1,257	109
Naperville	266.4	106.0	94.7	137.4	930	659	236	255.7	1,732	133
New Lenox	36.1	9.1	98.1	11.7	442	127	315	32.8	1,240	199
Niles	60.3	25.7	99.5	28.2	957	290	667	64.4	2,187	459
Normal town	81.4	18.9	99.2	43.1	791	259	532	92.6	1,700	396
Northbrook	65.3	17.7	99.2	35.8	1,074	659	416	74.0	2,219	195
North Chicago	28.9	7.2	89.4	16.4	548	353	195	36.5	1,218	143
Oak Forest	26.4	5.9	90.1	16.2	587	399	188	31.2	1,129	234
Oak Lawn	77.6	20.0	96.2	39.5	705	393	312	67.1	1,199	2
Oak Park	90.3	17.8	72.6	57.3	1,099	755	344	95.1	1,825	361
O'Fallon	42.6	17.4	96.6	13.1	447	239	208	37.9	1,294	187
Orland Park	88.8	30.5	98.6	29.6	506	258	248	93.4	1,594	526
Oswego	24.1	14.9	98.7	4.6	131	38	93	23.6	676	121
Palatine	83.0	21.8	84.1	45.1	659	454	205	84.1	1,228	151
Park Ridge	53.3	8.8	99.5	39.2	1,049	667	382	46.7	1,249	84
Pekin	46.0	12.8	96.9	13.7	420	206	214	50.5	1,552	347
Peoria	185.9	55.2	92.1	84.6	752	323	429	197.8	1,756	250
Plainfield	42.6	10.9	93.7	18.1	412	154	258	38.4	876	131
Quincy	47.4	25.0	85.7	14.8	368	67	300	33.8	838	4
Rockford	252.5	107.4	66.7	90.8	618	401	217	240.9	1,639	286
Rock Island	63.7	18.4	90.0	24.2	640	430	210	73.5	1,945	290
Romeoville	61.5	14.1	85.7	27.2	685	415	271	71.2	1,797	440
Round Lake Beach	15.3	7.9	97.2	6.2	225	91	133	17.3	627	182
St. Charles	57.2	16.9	99.2	28.5	875	429	446	59.3	1,822	384
Schaumburg	168.9	48.1	91.1	67.7	915	274	641	196.8	2,658	351
Skokie	115.0	29.8	98.1	64.7	1,013	491	522	100.9	1,580	187
Springfield	160.6	54.6	86.9	83.7	723	243	480	204.1	1,763	454
Streamwood	33.3	10.0	98.8	19.9	500	291	209	29.4	736	58
Tinley Park	68.2	21.5	98.0	38.5	681	446	235	57.6	1,018	165
Urbana	46.8	15.9	76.4	23.7	553	228	325	43.7	1,022	111
Vernon Hills	31.5	17.5	100.0	10.4	399	0	399	28.8	1,098	35
Waukegan	90.9	29.2	92.3	52.4	598	395	202	118.0	1,347	267
West Chicago	30.0	8.6	99.8	9.0	329	164	165	30.0	1,101	36
Wheaton	59.3	14.1	100.0	35.4	663	473	190	52.9	990	57
Wheeling	57.4	14.4	85.4	34.3	891	611	280	63.5	1,650	281
Wilmette	48.1	7.4	99.4	29.6	1,083	603	479	48.4	1,769	192
Woodridge	33.5	11.5	91.6	16.5	490	221	269	28.3	843	58
Woodstock	27.6	9.7	88.2	11.2	446	398	47	24.8	984	117
INDIANA	X	X	X	X	X	X	X	X	X	X
Anderson	65.9	9.6	48.7	29.9	544	525	19	172.4	3,140	78
Bloomington	188.3	58.2	35.3	79.0	932	909	23	263.9	3,110	107

1. Based on population estimated as of July 1 of the year shown.

City	City government finances, 2017 (cont.)												
	General expenditure (cont.)												
	Percent of total for:									Debt outstanding			
	Public welfare	Highways	Parking facilities	Education	Health and hospitals	Police protection	Sewerage and sanitation	Parks and recreation	Housing and community development	Interest on debt	Total (mil dol)	Per capita[1] (dollars)	Debt issued during year
	127	128	129	130	131	132	133	134	135	136	137	138	139
ILLINOIS—Cont'd													
Des Plaines	0.0	18.6	0.0	0.0	0.0	21.3	0.2	0.1	1.4	0.7	200.2	3,447	8.0
Downers Grove	1.2	12.3	2.1	0.0	0.0	25.2	1.1	0.0	0.0	4.2	75.7	1,528	8.7
Edwardsville	0.0	15.1	0.0	0.0	0.0	27.8	11.1	11.7	0.0	2.4	30.5	1,216	8.5
Elgin	0.7	16.8	0.0	0.0	0.0	30.0	3.9	12.2	0.0	2.3	87.5	781	25.0
Elk Grove Village	0.0	11.2	0.0	0.0	0.0	26.9	2.6	0.0	0.0	5.0	75.6	2,294	0.0
Elmhurst	0.2	16.2	2.1	0.0	0.4	17.0	25.5	1.4	0.0	3.2	90.0	1,930	25.0
Evanston	0.0	7.9	5.0	0.0	1.8	22.0	5.1	6.9	0.0	8.5	393.9	5,279	57.4
Galesburg	0.0	14.3	0.5	0.0	0.0	16.6	0.0	8.3	0.0	8.2	105.2	3,423	31.7
Glendale Heights	0.0	16.2	0.0	0.0	0.0	19.2	0.6	9.6	0.0	5.8	34.4	1,008	0.0
Glen Ellyn	0.0	6.5	0.6	0.0	0.0	18.9	13.9	10.2	0.0	3.1	23.2	825	0.0
Glenview	0.0	15.7	0.0	0.0	0.0	13.1	2.4	0.0	0.0	2.4	62.2	1,309	3.9
Granite City	0.0	11.1	0.0	0.0	0.0	20.1	4.9	1.2	0.0	8.6	100.4	3,500	5.9
Gurnee	0.0	11.5	0.0	0.0	0.0	31.9	0.0	0.0	0.0	5.6	52.4	1,707	0.3
Hanover Park	0.0	11.4	0.7	0.0	0.0	30.7	4.5	0.0	0.0	6.0	66.9	1,759	3.2
Highland Park	0.0	3.3	2.2	0.0	0.0	28.0	7.9	0.0	0.0	2.7	53.2	1,789	11.4
Hoffman Estates	0.0	15.8	0.0	0.0	2.3	24.2	2.6	14.2	0.0	5.9	205.4	3,991	17.8
Huntley	0.0	12.2	0.0	0.0	0.0	24.0	14.4	0.0	0.0	4.6	24.6	910	3.1
Joliet	0.0	11.7	0.6	0.0	0.0	22.2	20.0	3.7	5.8	0.6	84.2	569	12.8
Lake in the Hills	0.0	12.5	0.0	0.0	0.0	38.7	0.0	8.1	1.8	3.4	16.3	568	0.3
Lansing	0.0	10.1	0.0	0.0	0.0	34.8	0.0	0.0	0.0	12.2	106.4	3,812	16.8
Lockport	0.0	26.3	0.0	0.0	0.0	35.4	22.2	0.0	0.0	5.9	16.7	661	0.0
Lombard	0.0	3.8	0.1	0.0	0.0	13.3	0.1	0.0	0.0	8.0	210.5	4,798	0.0
McHenry	0.0	14.8	0.0	0.0	0.0	21.2	48.2	6.2	0.0	0.9	38.3	1,428	19.2
Moline	0.0	7.7	0.4	0.0	0.0	16.2	17.1	4.1	2.5	7.7	182.0	4,343	37.8
Morton Grove	0.0	12.1	0.0	0.0	0.1	30.9	5.6	0.0	0.0	3.3	20.5	889	0.0
Mount Prospect	1.9	10.0	0.0	0.0	0.2	20.8	5.4	0.6	0.6	15.2	157.4	2,878	32.4
Mundelein	0.0	30.8	0.0	0.0	0.0	29.2	6.7	0.0	0.0	1.5	12.6	404	0.0
Naperville	0.0	21.6	0.0	0.0	0.0	25.2	2.9	4.3	0.0	4.7	154.5	1,047	140.5
New Lenox	0.0	31.4	0.6	0.0	0.0	23.1	11.3	0.0	6.0	5.0	53.9	2,036	4.6
Niles	0.0	13.4	0.0	0.0	3.0	22.0	15.4	2.5	0.0	0.4	8.9	301	0.9
Normal town	0.0	10.8	0.0	0.0	0.0	14.1	8.4	11.5	0.0	4.2	92.3	1,695	22.4
Northbrook	0.0	14.8	0.2	0.0	0.0	19.8	3.2	0.0	0.9	4.8	100.5	3,015	0.0
North Chicago	0.0	5.0	0.0	0.0	0.0	27.0	0.0	0.0	0.0	14.2	121.3	4,048	12.9
Oak Forest	0.0	11.8	0.8	0.0	0.0	31.7	0.0	0.0	0.0	8.3	63.8	2,310	11.3
Oak Lawn	0.2	9.6	0.0	0.0	0.0	28.4	7.4	0.6	0.0	5.0	71.7	1,281	14.5
Oak Park	0.0	17.2	3.9	0.0	1.1	21.1	3.3	0.0	10.8	10.6	288.3	5,529	64.9
O'Fallon	0.0	21.0	0.0	0.0	0.0	20.2	13.7	12.8	0.0	6.4	54.9	1,872	9.5
Orland Park	0.0	16.6	16.7	0.0	0.0	21.4	8.0	11.1	0.0	2.6	109.6	1,871	8.5
Oswego	0.0	10.0	0.0	0.0	0.0	47.9	10.0	0.0	0.0	6.6	49.9	1,432	27.6
Palatine	0.0	12.2	0.9	0.0	0.0	26.2	8.9	0.0	4.8	9.8	197.8	2,887	11.0
Park Ridge	0.0	15.9	0.7	0.0	0.0	18.4	8.8	1.0	0.0	2.6	35.8	955	12.4
Pekin	0.0	25.5	0.0	0.0	0.0	20.4	8.1	0.0	0.2	2.5	11.4	351	0.0
Peoria	0.0	14.1	0.0	0.0	0.0	20.0	5.2	0.0	0.1	4.2	191.9	1,704	34.9
Plainfield	0.0	24.7	0.0	0.0	0.0	30.2	15.0	0.0	0.0	8.2	60.4	1,377	1.1
Quincy	0.0	8.2	0.0	0.0	0.6	26.6	11.6	2.7	0.2	1.3	15.4	381	4.1
Rockford	6.9	20.8	0.8	0.0	0.0	21.2	5.4	5.7	5.4	2.7	104.8	713	31.6
Rock Island	0.0	19.4	0.0	0.0	0.0	19.5	9.7	8.8	0.1	5.5	66.4	1,757	5.6
Romeoville	0.0	12.0	0.8	0.0	0.0	19.2	12.6	6.8	0.0	3.6	169.3	4,273	10.2
Round Lake Beach	0.0	38.1	0.1	0.0	0.0	37.0	0.8	1.3	8.3	3.7	20.0	727	0.0
St. Charles	0.0	13.4	0.0	0.0	0.0	19.5	12.4	0.0	0.0	6.8	105.9	3,254	26.4
Schaumburg	0.6	18.5	0.1	0.0	0.3	14.5	2.2	19.7	0.1	5.4	519.0	7,010	91.1
Skokie	0.0	21.3	0.0	0.0	2.1	22.8	4.7	2.2	0.0	3.1	57.5	900	14.2
Springfield	0.0	24.9	0.5	0.0	0.0	22.3	4.6	1.2	3.5	2.6	1,436.9	12,412	75.1
Streamwood	0.0	9.3	0.0	0.0	0.0	38.9	0.0	1.2	0.0	0.7	4.5	114	0.0
Tinley Park	0.0	14.7	0.0	0.0	0.0	30.6	10.3	0.0	0.0	5.0	67.8	1,199	3.1
Urbana	0.0	26.4	2.1	0.0	0.0	20.5	0.2	0.0	11.8	0.3	11.5	270	0.0
Vernon Hills	0.0	16.5	0.0	0.0	0.0	33.7	0.0	2.9	0.0	7.8	50.8	1,939	0.1
Waukegan	0.0	15.1	0.0	0.0	0.0	30.3	4.1	0.8	3.9	3.0	339.5	3,875	11.8
West Chicago	0.0	0.0	0.2	0.0	0.0	32.9	19.8	0.0	0.0	0.5	49.4	1,814	3.2
Wheaton	0.3	18.4	1.3	0.0	0.0	26.5	7.2	1.1	0.0	1.5	23.9	448	0.0
Wheeling	0.0	18.6	0.1	0.0	0.0	23.8	2.1	0.0	0.0	4.8	66.3	1,721	18.0
Wilmette	0.0	5.9	0.8	0.0	0.5	22.1	9.2	0.0	0.0	6.1	135.7	4,960	0.3
Woodridge	0.0	10.6	0.0	0.0	0.0	35.6	4.5	0.0	0.0	7.1	54.5	1,622	5.9
Woodstock	0.0	5.1	0.0	0.0	7.0	29.5	11.0	11.8	0.0	2.2	34.0	1,347	0.1
INDIANA	X	X	X	X	X	X	X	X	X	X	X	X	X
Anderson	0.0	1.7	0.0	0.0	0.0	6.8	27.9	0.9	0.0	1.3	189.0	3,442	63.2
Bloomington	0.0	3.0	0.7	0.0	0.0	5.6	14.2	3.4	51.1	6.9	350.1	4,127	44.6

1. Based on population estimated as of July 1 of the year shown.

STATE	Place code	City	Land area[1] (sq. mi)	Population, 2021: Total persons 2021	Population, 2021: Rank	Population, 2021: Per square mile	Race 2020: Race alone[2] (percent): White	Race 2020: Race alone[2] (percent): Black or African American	Race 2020: Race alone[2] (percent): American Indian, Alaskan Native	Race 2020: Race alone[2] (percent): Asian	Race 2020: Race alone[2] (percent): Hawaiian Pacific Islander	Race 2020: Race alone[2] (percent): Some other race	Race 2020: Two or more races (percent)
			1	2	3	4	5	6	7	8	9	10	11
		INDIANA—Cont'd											
18	08416	Brownsburg town	16.3	30,068	1,305	1,844.7	82.1	6.6	0.2	2.6	0.1	1.8	6.7
18	10342	Carmel	49.1	100,777	325	2,052.5	76.5	3.3	0.1	12.0	0.0	1.4	6.5
18	14734	Columbus	28.4	50,569	789	1,780.6	74.4	3.1	0.4	10.4	0.1	4.8	6.9
18	16138	Crown Point	17.9	34,621	1,150	1,934.1	78.2	7.4	0.4	2.9	0.0	2.9	8.2
18	19486	East Chicago	14.1	26,099	1,483	1,851.0	16.5	41.1	1.1	0.3	0.1	26.2	14.7
18	20728	Elkhart	27.5	53,949	740	1,961.8	53.0	14.0	1.0	1.1	0.1	19.0	11.8
18	22000	Evansville	47.4	116,486	248	2,457.5	75.3	13.6	0.3	1.2	0.5	2.0	7.0
18	23278	Fishers	35.7	101,171	319	2,833.9	76.5	6.7	0.2	8.0	0.0	1.7	6.7
18	25000	Fort Wayne	110.8	265,974	84	2,400.5	65.0	15.3	0.5	5.8	0.0	5.6	7.8
18	25450	Franklin	14.7	25,437	1,521	1,730.4	89.6	1.7	0.4	1.1	0.0	1.8	5.3
18	27000	Gary	49.9	68,325	552	1,369.2	10.6	80.2	0.4	0.2	0.0	3.3	5.2
18	28386	Goshen	17.6	34,756	1,145	1,974.8	63.8	3.3	1.1	1.4	0.0	18.4	12.0
18	29898	Greenwood	27.9	64,918	589	2,326.8	77.7	4.3	0.3	9.0	0.1	2.2	6.5
18	31000	Hammond	22.7	76,984	474	3,391.4	39.2	26.0	1.2	0.8	0.0	18.5	14.2
18	34114	Hobart	26.2	29,521	1,324	1,126.8	72.0	9.6	0.5	1.2	0.1	5.3	11.3
18	36000	Indianapolis	361.6	882,039	15	2,439.3	52.2	27.8	0.5	4.2	0.0	7.6	7.5
18	38358	Jeffersonville	34.1	50,315	795	1,475.5	72.9	14.1	0.4	1.5	0.2	2.8	8.1
18	40392	Kokomo	36.7	59,691	649	1,626.5	79.1	10.6	0.3	1.5	0.0	1.6	6.9
18	40788	Lafayette	29.4	70,835	528	2,409.4	71.1	10.5	0.5	1.8	0.0	6.9	9.1
18	42426	Lawrence	20.1	49,357	808	2,455.6	47.7	29.0	0.8	1.5	0.1	11.4	9.4
18	46908	Marion	15.7	28,177	1,381	1,794.7	72.0	14.7	0.4	1.0	0.1	2.8	9.0
18	48528	Merrillville town	33.2	36,524	1,087	1,100.1	32.7	51.1	0.6	1.3	0.0	5.5	8.6
18	48798	Michigan City	20.4	32,033	1,230	1,570.2	59.2	27.8	0.4	0.9	0.0	3.4	8.2
18	49932	Mishawaka	17.9	51,074	780	2,853.3	77.2	9.5	0.4	2.8	0.0	2.1	7.9
18	51876	Muncie	27.4	65,292	585	2,382.9	78.0	11.6	0.3	1.5	0.1	2.1	6.5
18	52326	New Albany	15.4	37,411	1,060	2,429.3	79.4	9.2	0.5	0.9	0.0	2.4	7.7
18	54180	Noblesville	34.4	70,926	526	2,061.8	83.4	4.6	0.2	2.6	0.1	2.3	6.8
18	60246	Plainfield town	26.0	35,592	1,116	1,368.9	78.2	9.1	0.2	4.3	0.0	2.1	6.0
18	61092	Portage	25.6	38,192	1,040	1,491.9	69.2	11.7	0.5	1.0	0.1	5.5	11.9
18	64260	Richmond	24.0	35,817	1,108	1,492.4	79.4	8.0	0.4	1.7	0.0	3.3	7.2
18	68220	Schererville town	15.1	29,589	1,321	1,959.5	75.0	8.2	0.3	3.5	0.0	3.6	9.3
18	71000	South Bend	42.0	103,353	308	2,460.8	53.5	25.7	0.7	1.5	0.1	8.4	10.1
18	75428	Terre Haute	34.8	58,525	671	1,681.8	79.0	10.8	0.4	1.8	0.0	1.9	6.1
18	78326	Valparaiso	16.4	34,428	1,157	2,099.3	82.3	4.1	0.3	2.3	0.0	3.4	7.6
18	82700	Westfield	31.9	50,630	788	1,587.1	84.0	3.3	0.2	3.3	0.1	2.8	6.3
18	82862	West Lafayette	13.6	44,672	889	3,284.7	61.8	3.9	0.2	19.2	0.0	3.3	11.6
18	86372	Zionsville town	67.2	31,702	1,249	471.8	86.5	1.9	0.2	4.3	0.0	1.0	6.0
19	00000	IOWA	55,853.7	3,193,079	X	57.2	84.5	4.1	0.5	2.4	0.2	2.8	5.6
19	01855	Ames	27.6	66,424	574	2,406.7	77.5	4.2	0.3	7.9	0.0	3.1	6.9
19	02305	Ankeny	30.5	70,287	535	2,304.5	87.9	2.5	0.2	2.4	0.1	1.5	5.5
19	06355	Bettendorf	21.3	39,327	1,011	1,846.3	82.4	3.7	0.2	6.2	0.0	1.3	6.2
19	11755	Cedar Falls	29.4	40,388	981	1,373.7	87.5	3.1	0.2	3.2	0.3	1.0	4.7
19	12000	Cedar Rapids	72.1	136,467	203	1,892.7	77.8	10.4	0.3	2.7	0.4	1.7	6.8
19	16860	Council Bluffs	43.0	62,415	617	1,451.5	83.7	2.7	0.9	1.0	0.1	4.7	6.9
19	19000	Davenport	63.8	101,009	321	1,583.2	74.1	12.0	0.4	2.2	0.0	2.6	8.7
19	21000	Des Moines	88.2	212,031	107	2,404.0	64.5	11.7	0.7	6.8	0.1	6.6	9.6
19	22395	Dubuque	30.9	59,119	661	1,913.2	85.1	6.3	0.4	1.2	1.3	1.3	4.4
19	38595	Iowa City	25.6	74,596	494	2,913.9	72.5	10.2	0.2	7.3	0.0	3.0	6.7
19	49485	Marion	17.8	41,703	952	2,342.9	88.2	3.1	0.2	2.2	0.0	0.9	5.4
19	49755	Marshalltown	19.2	27,388	1,420	1,426.5	64.8	2.7	1.1	5.3	0.1	14.4	11.6
19	50160	Mason City	27.9	27,138	1,432	972.7	87.0	2.9	0.5	1.5	0.5	1.9	5.7
19	60465	Ottumwa	16.1	25,350	1,526	1,574.5	74.3	5.4	0.8	2.3	2.0	8.6	6.7
19	73335	Sioux City	58.5	85,617	410	1,463.5	68.0	5.9	2.8	3.3	0.7	9.2	10.2
19	79950	Urbandale	22.5	45,923	864	2,041.0	83.1	4.0	0.2	5.5	0.0	1.6	5.6
19	82425	Waterloo	61.6	66,941	565	1,086.7	67.5	18.0	0.5	3.0	1.1	3.3	6.5
19	83910	West Des Moines	47.2	69,792	537	1,478.6	78.1	5.4	0.3	7.0	0.1	2.3	6.7
20	00000	KANSAS	81,758.5	2,934,582	X	35.9	75.6	5.7	1.1	2.9	0.1	4.9	9.5
20	17800	Derby	10.3	25,847	1,499	2,509.4	83.4	2.4	0.9	1.9	0.1	1.6	9.7
20	18250	Dodge City	14.7	27,690	1,404	1,883.7	44.6	3.4	2.4	1.4	0.0	27.7	20.5
20	25325	Garden City	10.9	27,856	1,396	2,555.6	47.4	5.2	0.9	5.3	0.1	17.4	23.8
20	33625	Hutchinson	24.6	39,712	998	1,614.3	81.7	4.3	1.0	0.7	0.1	3.8	8.5
20	36000	Kansas City	124.7	154,545	170	1,239.3	41.0	21.5	1.1	4.8	0.2	16.1	15.2
20	38900	Lawrence	34.2	95,256	348	2,785.3	75.3	5.3	2.8	4.8	0.1	2.4	9.3
20	39000	Leavenworth	24.3	37,176	1,069	1,529.9	71.0	13.8	1.1	1.8	0.3	2.0	10.0
20	39075	Leawood	15.1	33,743	1,176	2,234.6	86.5	1.5	0.2	5.1	0.0	0.7	6.1
20	39350	Lenexa	34.1	58,388	673	1,712.3	78.0	6.4	0.4	4.1	0.1	2.9	8.1
20	44250	Manhattan	19.9	54,763	729	2,751.9	76.0	5.9	0.5	5.3	0.3	3.5	8.4

1. Dry land or land partially or temporarily covered by water. 2. Hispanic or Latino persons may be of any race.

City	Percent Hispanic or Latino[1], 2020	Percent foreign born, 2016–2020	Age of population (percent), 2016–2020: Under 18 years	18 to 24 years	25 to 34 years	35 to 44 years	45 to 54 years	55 to 64 years	65 years and over	Median age, 2016–2020	Percent female, 2016–2020	Population: Census counts 2010	Census counts 2020	Percent change 2010–2020	Percent change 2020–2021
	12	13	14	15	16	17	18	19	20	21	22	23	24	25	26
INDIANA—Cont'd															
Brownsburg town	4.8	6.3	28.0	6.5	13.6	17.0	11.9	9.8	13.1	35.9	48.2	21,954	28,952	31.9	3.9
Carmel	4.5	12.8	25.9	7.1	10.0	14.9	15.5	12.9	13.8	40.0	51.7	83,885	99,777	18.9	1.0
Columbus	9.6	15.6	23.7	9.1	16.5	12.9	11.3	11.4	15.1	35.5	50.3	44,088	50,423	14.4	0.3
Crown Point	11.5	6.2	24.0	6.0	14.7	13.5	12.1	12.3	17.4	39.1	49.8	27,866	34,439	23.6	0.5
East Chicago	52.6	15.5	26.9	8.7	13.9	13.0	11.6	11.7	14.3	35.4	51.1	29,698	26,314	-11.4	-0.8
Elkhart	30.7	13.3	27.7	9.2	14.7	12.0	12.9	10.2	13.2	33.4	52.6	51,911	54,044	4.1	-0.2
Evansville	4.3	3.2	21.2	9.6	15.6	12.0	12.0	13.4	16.1	37.7	51.9	120,069	117,298	-2.3	-0.7
Fishers	5.1	10.1	28.2	7.3	12.7	15.9	15.3	11.2	9.6	36.5	51.6	77,287	99,053	28.2	2.1
Fort Wayne	10.6	8.1	24.7	10.0	14.9	12.3	11.8	12.2	14.2	35.3	51.6	253,703	263,852	4.0	0.8
Franklin	4.2	1.3	24.0	11.5	13.3	12.6	11.1	12.6	14.9	35.7	52.6	23,710	25,124	6.0	1.2
Gary	7.6	1.7	25.7	8.4	12.1	11.2	10.5	12.6	19.3	37.5	53.8	80,256	68,982	-14.0	-1.0
Goshen	33.7	13.5	25.2	10.1	12.2	11.7	11.5	10.7	18.7	37.6	51.7	32,572	34,849	7.0	-0.3
Greenwood	5.4	7.5	26.5	7.9	14.6	14.5	11.8	9.9	14.9	35.7	51.5	51,110	63,903	25.0	1.6
Hammond	40.2	11.3	25.4	10.6	13.0	14.0	11.3	13.8	11.9	35.7	51.6	80,828	77,754	-3.8	-1.0
Hobart	18.9	4.5	22.6	8.7	11.9	14.4	12.6	13.7	16.0	39.5	53.1	29,336	29,713	1.3	-0.6
Indianapolis	13.0	9.6	24.6	9.5	17.0	12.8	11.6	12.0	12.5	34.3	51.8	820,443	887,752	8.2	-0.6
Jeffersonville	6.1	3.8	22.3	8.0	15.4	12.4	12.0	13.9	15.9	38.2	52.6	45,007	49,413	9.8	1.8
Kokomo	4.2	2.5	22.4	8.3	13.0	11.2	12.4	13.7	19.0	40.0	52.9	58,189	59,609	2.4	0.1
Lafayette	14.8	8.2	23.0	11.6	18.5	12.5	10.4	10.8	13.3	33.0	50.5	68,864	70,906	3.0	-0.1
Lawrence	19.8	9.7	26.6	8.3	15.6	13.7	12.2	12.3	11.4	34.8	50.9	45,916	49,322	7.4	0.1
Marion	8.0	1.7	19.0	18.0	11.5	8.4	10.9	13.8	18.4	36.4	54.2	29,892	28,337	-5.2	-0.6
Merrillville town	14.7	7.4	22.9	8.3	12.3	13.7	12.9	12.6	17.4	40.1	53.0	34,966	36,603	4.7	-0.2
Michigan City	7.7	3.1	23.0	9.3	16.4	11.6	11.7	12.6	15.4	36.1	48.2	31,553	32,081	1.7	-0.1
Mishawaka	6.1	5.6	21.6	10.6	18.2	12.0	10.3	12.0	15.3	34.7	50.0	48,292	51,201	6.0	-0.2
Muncie	4.2	2.6	16.2	28.3	11.9	9.3	9.6	10.6	14.0	28.8	52.3	70,206	65,382	-6.9	-0.1
New Albany	5.1	2.3	21.1	8.9	15.7	13.8	11.4	12.8	16.3	38.4	52.0	36,375	37,688	3.6	-0.7
Noblesville	6.1	3.6	27.5	9.0	15.0	14.6	13.2	9.3	11.4	34.1	50.4	52,378	69,517	32.7	2.0
Plainfield town	4.9	6.4	22.9	9.0	13.5	14.3	12.5	12.5	15.4	38.6	49.2	27,700	34,771	25.5	2.4
Portage	19.0	3.3	22.5	8.4	15.4	11.8	13.2	14.1	14.6	37.6	52.6	36,826	37,934	3.0	0.7
Richmond	5.6	3.6	20.7	11.6	13.2	11.0	11.7	13.0	18.7	38.6	51.9	36,779	35,915	-2.3	-0.3
Schererville town	13.7	10.2	19.5	8.7	11.1	12.7	15.2	14.3	18.4	44.0	51.3	29,217	29,570	1.2	0.1
South Bend	16.7	8.6	26.9	9.8	15.0	12.5	11.8	10.5	13.6	33.7	52.6	101,239	103,675	2.4	-0.3
Terre Haute	3.9	3.7	18.9	19.7	14.2	10.4	11.2	10.3	15.3	32.6	48.7	60,791	58,621	-3.6	-0.2
Valparaiso	9.5	5.5	19.4	14.3	13.8	12.0	10.2	12.5	17.8	36.5	50.9	31,740	34,154	7.6	0.8
Westfield	6.5	8.2	29.1	7.2	11.9	15.7	13.6	9.6	12.8	36.3	51.8	30,138	46,427	54.0	9.1
West Lafayette	6.3	22.6	9.8	58.7	9.1	5.8	4.5	4.9	7.2	21.6	44.8	41,997	44,332	5.6	0.8
Zionsville town	3.7	5.4	28.0	5.7	8.3	14.2	17.5	13.3	12.9	41.0	49.5	24,394	30,605	25.5	3.6
IOWA	6.8	5.4	23.1	10.1	12.6	12.1	11.8	13.2	17.1	38.3	50.3	3,046,877	3,190,369	4.7	0.1
Ames	5.9	13.2	12.0	42.6	13.7	8.4	6.3	6.9	10.2	23.5	46.4	59,035	65,955	11.7	0.7
Ankeny	4.2	3.6	27.3	9.9	17.1	15.6	12.0	7.8	10.2	32.5	49.5	45,602	67,892	48.9	3.5
Bettendorf	5.3	5.9	26.1	5.9	11.3	14.0	12.8	12.6	17.3	39.7	52.1	33,207	39,106	17.8	0.6
Cedar Falls	2.9	5.5	18.1	27.7	12.0	9.9	7.9	9.4	15.1	27.3	52.5	39,284	40,536	3.2	-0.4
Cedar Rapids	4.7	6.2	22.3	10.3	15.1	13.0	11.5	11.7	16.1	36.5	50.6	126,609	137,664	8.7	-0.9
Council Bluffs	10.4	5.0	22.3	9.6	13.2	12.5	12.1	13.3	16.9	38.7	51.3	62,213	62,701	0.8	-0.5
Davenport	8.8	4.9	22.2	9.9	15.2	12.4	11.9	13.1	15.3	37.0	50.7	99,697	101,728	2.0	-0.7
Des Moines	15.6	12.9	24.0	10.7	16.9	12.7	11.8	11.9	12.0	34.0	50.9	204,216	214,137	4.9	-1.0
Dubuque	3.7	3.1	20.1	12.3	14.4	10.3	10.8	13.1	19.0	37.5	51.5	57,605	59,639	3.5	-0.9
Iowa City	7.3	13.7	14.4	32.7	15.7	9.8	8.2	8.0	11.2	26.3	50.1	67,963	74,373	9.4	0.3
Marion	3.1	2.2	24.8	6.5	14.0	14.2	12.9	11.6	16.0	38.0	52.6	35,225	41,572	18.0	0.3
Marshalltown	31.3	16.7	26.3	9.7	12.4	11.9	10.5	11.3	17.9	35.7	49.9	27,558	27,610	0.2	-0.8
Mason City	6.7	2.4	20.6	8.8	13.4	10.3	11.8	14.1	21.0	41.9	51.5	28,072	27,353	-2.6	-0.8
Ottumwa	15.7	10.7	22.3	10.3	14.0	10.5	13.6	13.8	15.6	38.1	50.2	25,028	25,528	2.0	-0.7
Sioux City	20.9	10.4	26.9	10.7	13.7	12.4	11.5	11.3	13.5	34.1	50.5	82,685	85,731	3.7	-0.1
Urbandale	4.9	7.5	26.4	5.1	13.5	13.5	13.6	13.3	14.6	38.9	50.8	39,472	45,582	15.5	0.7
Waterloo	7.1	9.6	23.3	9.7	14.7	11.8	11.4	13.1	16.1	36.7	50.4	68,490	67,453	-1.5	-0.8
West Des Moines	6.6	11.1	23.2	7.4	18.6	13.8	12.1	11.3	13.6	35.7	50.5	56,707	68,717	21.2	1.6
KANSAS	13.0	7.0	24.2	10.1	13.1	12.3	11.6	12.8	15.8	36.9	50.2	2,853,120	2,937,880	3.0	-0.1
Derby	7.7	3.3	27.7	7.5	13.6	14.5	9.8	11.8	15.0	35.6	51.7	22,294	25,761	15.6	0.3
Dodge City	63.9	27.8	31.9	10.5	14.7	12.5	11.3	10.3	8.7	29.6	49.0	27,324	27,803	1.8	-0.4
Garden City	54.1	23.8	28.5	10.9	14.5	11.5	11.0	11.4	12.2	31.9	47.8	26,736	28,138	5.2	-1.0
Hutchinson	12.9	3.2	22.3	9.5	11.6	13.1	11.7	12.5	19.3	39.5	50.3	42,180	40,068	-5.0	-0.9
Kansas City	34.6	17.5	27.8	9.0	15.2	13.1	11.2	11.6	12.1	33.5	49.9	145,781	156,602	7.4	-1.3
Lawrence	7.7	8.4	17.1	26.6	16.0	11.7	9.1	8.1	11.4	28.2	50.2	87,944	94,909	7.9	0.4
Leavenworth	8.8	2.8	23.5	9.6	14.3	16.0	10.8	12.6	13.3	36.4	45.6	35,245	37,416	6.2	-0.6
Leawood	3.2	6.3	22.4	4.8	7.2	11.4	12.7	19.2	22.3	48.5	51.5	31,888	33,933	6.4	-0.6
Lenexa	8.3	7.9	21.7	7.8	15.5	14.6	11.6	13.7	15.2	38.2	50.6	48,214	57,425	19.1	1.7
Manhattan	9.2	7.9	15.4	35.6	15.9	9.0	7.4	7.7	8.8	24.6	48.9	52,161	54,507	4.5	0.5

1. May be of any race.

City	Households, 2016–2020							Persons in group quarters, 2016–2020	Serious crimes known to police[2], 2020				Educational attainment, 2016–2020		
			Percent						Violent		Property			Attainment[4] (percent)	
	Number	Persons per household	Family	Married couple family	Female family	Non-family	One person		Number	Rate	Number	Rate	Population age 25 and over	High school graduate or less	Bachelor's degree or more
	27	28	29	30	31	32	33	34	35	36	37	38	39	40	41
INDIANA—Cont'd															
Brownsburg town	9,122	2.88	76.1	62.5	8.4	23.9	18.8	284	23	83.3	266	963.0	17,378	27.0	44.3
Carmel	37,369	2.64	74.4	64.8	7.2	25.6	21.4	469	51	49.5	605	586.8	66,507	10.7	71.9
Columbus	19,466	2.46	60.9	46.2	10.6	39.1	32.7	912	NA	NA	NA	NA	32,811	33.9	41.8
Crown Point	10,938	2.65	72.0	58.7	8.9	28.0	22.7	1,425	NA	NA	NA	NA	21,257	36.9	32.1
East Chicago	10,645	2.62	60.0	30.1	21.5	40.0	34.2	116	NA	NA	NA	NA	18,076	64.3	10.1
Elkhart	20,777	2.49	58.5	32.7	21.2	41.5	35.7	907	NA	NA	NA	NA	33,242	58.0	15.0
Evansville	51,706	2.21	54.5	33.2	15.8	45.5	36.9	4,159	1,185	1,006.4	4,252	3,611.1	81,900	46.1	21.5
Fishers	33,853	2.76	75.3	64.3	6.6	24.7	20.1	45	64	65.7	630	646.3	60,343	12.8	65.4
Fort Wayne	108,207	2.44	59.6	40.5	13.8	40.4	32.8	4,840	1,124	412.8	6,117	2,246.7	175,125	39.8	28.2
Franklin	9,160	2.63	66.8	49.0	12.6	33.2	26.9	1,226	34	131.7	479	1,854.8	16,287	47.4	21.2
Gary	31,207	2.39	57.7	22.1	28.8	42.3	37.5	777	NA	NA	NA	NA	49,706	54.4	13.5
Goshen	12,701	2.61	62.7	46.9	11.4	37.3	32.2	1,379	NA	NA	NA	NA	22,368	51.7	24.7
Greenwood	22,981	2.53	65.9	47.7	11.4	34.1	27.7	551	62	102.5	1,226	2,027.8	38,589	40.5	30.9
Hammond	28,836	2.60	61.9	36.2	19.9	38.1	31.7	1,029	NA	NA	NA	NA	48,724	56.5	14.7
Hobart	11,182	2.49	62.0	46.3	11.4	38.0	30.7	249	48	172.7	790	2,842.6	19,308	41.6	25.2
Indianapolis	346,940	2.49	54.5	35.6	14.2	45.5	37.2	15,888	NA	NA	NA	NA	579,504	40.9	32.2
Jeffersonville	18,775	2.51	65.5	45.8	15.1	34.5	28.8	897	NA	NA	NA	NA	33,377	42.7	21.6
Kokomo	25,536	2.23	57.4	37.3	16.6	42.6	37.8	1,108	437	753.4	1,152	1,986.2	40,216	50.7	17.5
Lafayette	31,189	2.28	55.6	35.8	13.7	44.4	36.2	1,384	428	594.1	2,198	3,051.1	47,439	44.3	27.7
Lawrence	18,981	2.57	61.7	45.3	12.5	38.3	30.9	155	167	334.9	972	1,949.3	31,930	37.2	35.0
Marion	11,251	2.09	56.4	31.6	16.9	43.6	37.2	4,234	NA	NA	NA	NA	17,486	54.7	16.2
Merrillville town	14,533	2.37	59.5	38.3	13.6	40.5	35.3	420	48	138.0	472	1,357.3	23,981	45.8	24.6
Michigan City	12,057	2.34	56.6	31.1	19.2	43.4	36.8	2,937	NA	NA	NA	NA	21,138	50.4	16.5
Mishawaka	21,875	2.22	51.0	33.0	12.6	49.0	42.8	1,052	80	158.1	1,207	2,384.9	33,709	45.1	25.1
Muncie	27,439	2.21	49.3	29.6	14.2	50.7	35.9	7,197	NA	NA	NA	NA	37,592	45.9	25.6
New Albany	14,759	2.41	55.2	35.5	14.7	44.8	37.9	1,145	144	390.3	1,258	3,410.0	25,707	47.4	22.2
Noblesville	23,868	2.67	69.9	58.5	7.5	30.1	23.3	788	60	90.7	551	833.2	40,861	22.5	48.9
Plainfield town	12,651	2.56	68.1	50.6	12.0	31.9	27.3	1,845	42	115.9	480	1,324.5	23,316	39.1	32.0
Portage	14,386	2.52	65.9	44.8	15.9	34.1	29.1	261	NA	NA	NA	NA	25,237	50.8	15.7
Richmond	14,860	2.22	58.4	37.7	17.1	41.6	32.4	2,426	NA	NA	NA	NA	23,986	48.5	20.4
Schererville town	11,519	2.46	68.4	53.6	8.7	31.6	27.6	173	NA	NA	NA	NA	20,500	32.0	35.9
South Bend	39,709	2.50	56.1	33.7	18.0	43.9	36.8	3,227	1,765	1,728.4	3,741	3,663.4	65,055	43.0	28.2
Terre Haute	23,665	2.25	53.2	34.3	13.6	46.8	37.1	7,552	837	1,381.1	2,886	4,762.1	37,217	45.6	23.0
Valparaiso	13,965	2.17	52.0	39.3	8.1	48.0	37.8	3,375	NA	NA	NA	NA	22,364	33.5	37.8
Westfield	15,572	2.66	78.8	61.2	14.0	21.2	17.5	176	23	50.6	340	747.8	26,547	21.3	54.4
West Lafayette	14,498	2.37	37.4	31.3	4.7	62.6	37.0	15,251	NA	NA	NA	NA	15,674	12.7	71.0
Zionsville town	10,061	2.78	84.3	77.6	4.6	15.7	13.7	82	14	48.6	86	298.4	18,584	10.7	71.9
IOWA	1,273,941	2.40	62.9	49.6	9.1	37.1	29.8	97,553	9,601	303.5	53,725	1,698.2	2,104,864	38.3	29.3
Ames	25,174	2.21	40.6	34.2	4.2	59.4	33.4	10,651	122	181.8	1,189	1,771.7	30,167	15.7	61.6
Ankeny	24,532	2.61	64.5	54.5	6.8	35.5	26.0	738	116	165.0	806	1,146.5	40,637	18.2	52.2
Bettendorf	14,267	2.53	67.2	53.6	10.7	32.8	29.2	172	37	100.2	571	1,546.3	24,645	21.1	51.2
Cedar Falls	15,157	2.45	53.9	45.8	4.9	46.1	30.1	3,653	NA	NA	NA	NA	22,125	22.0	48.5
Cedar Rapids	55,784	2.33	57.7	42.4	10.1	42.3	33.1	3,381	432	321.6	4,254	3,166.8	89,770	32.6	32.9
Council Bluffs	25,039	2.41	60.1	41.1	14.0	39.9	32.6	2,084	574	923.7	2,976	4,788.9	42,459	46.5	19.5
Davenport	40,261	2.46	58.2	41.4	12.5	41.8	33.7	3,191	750	736.7	3,996	3,925.1	69,333	40.0	26.6
Des Moines	85,667	2.46	55.3	35.9	14.3	44.7	34.8	5,000	1,517	704.6	8,400	3,901.7	140,676	42.6	27.9
Dubuque	24,151	2.24	57.6	43.6	10.2	42.4	34.8	3,884	231	398.9	1,165	2,012.0	39,200	39.9	31.7
Iowa City	31,483	2.20	42.1	34.3	5.7	57.9	35.4	6,458	151	198.8	1,335	1,757.4	40,131	17.8	59.6
Marion	15,656	2.53	65.2	52.7	8.5	34.8	27.1	299	60	146.5	NA	NA	27,412	29.0	36.0
Marshalltown	9,980	2.58	63.8	49.7	10.5	36.2	28.7	1,164	128	481.9	470	1,769.3	17,257	51.8	20.8
Mason City	12,611	2.08	57.1	42.4	10.4	42.9	36.5	806	114	425.2	854	3,185.3	19,104	43.3	20.5
Ottumwa	10,152	2.34	62.1	42.3	12.9	37.9	32.0	780	230	946.8	949	3,906.5	16,532	47.4	20.1
Sioux City	31,430	2.54	63.5	42.3	15.2	36.5	29.0	2,723	477	577.3	2,682	3,245.9	51,532	46.1	22.4
Urbandale	16,614	2.62	71.9	58.9	8.3	28.1	21.6	323	47	104.5	458	1,018.7	30,050	21.0	49.1
Waterloo	28,710	2.32	58.4	39.4	13.6	41.6	35.0	932	419	623.5	1,718	2,556.5	45,364	44.7	22.6
West Des Moines	29,440	2.25	56.1	43.4	9.1	43.9	34.5	366	93	134.3	1,140	1,646.2	46,301	19.5	54.0
KANSAS	1,141,985	2.48	64.6	50.5	9.8	35.4	29.1	79,708	12,385	425.0	64,077	2,199.1	1,911,990	34.5	33.9
Derby	9,090	2.68	73.2	57.5	11.8	26.8	23.5	57	29	114.9	472	1,870.9	15,831	25.8	38.4
Dodge City	8,615	3.08	69.3	49.5	14.1	30.7	23.3	610	124	458.1	681	2,516.1	15,641	55.1	15.7
Garden City	9,416	2.74	66.2	47.8	11.2	33.8	28.3	614	139	527.3	904	3,429.4	16,005	54.6	16.7
Hutchinson	16,282	2.35	59.6	44.8	11.6	40.4	33.1	2,481	NA	NA	NA	NA	27,742	39.3	20.0
Kansas City	55,644	2.73	63.7	39.7	16.8	36.3	30.9	1,218	NA	NA	NA	NA	96,633	52.9	17.9
Lawrence	39,422	2.28	50.1	39.6	7.1	49.9	31.1	7,390	NA	NA	NA	NA	54,819	20.7	54.9
Leavenworth	12,836	2.54	64.8	49.0	9.8	35.2	29.7	3,480	294	816.1	NA	NA	24,182	35.7	33.0
Leawood	13,404	2.58	78.5	73.5	3.4	21.5	18.6	76	15	42.8	571	1,628.9	25,277	6.1	76.0
Lenexa	22,864	2.38	65.8	54.3	8.5	34.2	27.8	383	103	182.3	903	1,598.0	38,671	16.9	55.2
Manhattan	20,629	2.36	46.4	34.2	6.8	53.6	34.3	6,309	NA	NA	NA	NA	26,922	17.9	52.9

2. Data for serious crimes have not been adjusted for underreporting. This may affect comparability between geographic areas and over time.

4. Persons 25 years old and over.

City	Money income, 2016–2020					Median earnings Full year, Full-time workers, 2016–2020			Housing units, 2016–2020				
	Households												
	Median household income	Percent with income less than $25,000	Percent with income of $200,000 or more	Median family income	Median non-family household income	All persons	Men	Women	Total	Occupied	Percent owner occupied	Median value[1] (dollars)	Median gross rent (dollars)
	42	43	44	45	46	47	48	49	50	51	52	53	54
INDIANA—Cont'd													
Brownsburg town	89,089	9.7	7.2	98,797	44,051	51,898	57,339	44,392	9,626	9,122	75.5	211,900	1,140
Carmel	115,109	5.9	24.1	143,130	61,308	86,455	102,130	68,152	39,652	37,369	75.7	352,400	1,247
Columbus	67,387	17.5	5.6	82,205	42,088	54,065	66,164	41,344	20,922	19,466	61.3	174,300	956
Crown Point	82,222	12.2	5.4	91,519	48,404	59,477	71,712	42,864	11,223	10,938	85.9	206,400	1,119
East Chicago	35,396	35.8	1.0	41,363	23,680	35,576	37,582	31,608	13,771	10,645	43.8	73,100	658
Elkhart	40,101	32.3	1.1	46,796	27,708	37,065	40,990	32,998	23,522	20,777	50.5	96,500	787
Evansville	42,623	27.8	1.8	53,968	30,574	39,061	44,524	34,375	58,695	51,706	54.8	98,600	797
Fishers	108,361	5.3	16.5	124,839	54,472	72,750	84,390	60,707	34,999	33,853	76.9	280,300	1,240
Fort Wayne	51,454	22.4	3.1	64,127	32,594	41,719	47,577	36,744	118,465	108,207	62.6	121,600	777
Franklin	60,500	17.5	1.9	74,014	34,395	45,894	50,606	40,303	9,829	9,160	63.3	145,200	904
Gary	31,315	39.6	0.9	36,885	22,601	34,110	38,363	31,523	42,124	31,207	50.3	68,400	792
Goshen	50,224	22.7	2.4	63,127	30,279	41,657	46,542	33,926	13,993	12,701	63.1	131,400	815
Greenwood	66,103	13.4	3.4	76,188	40,281	48,460	53,492	41,810	24,784	22,981	60.2	167,600	1,041
Hammond	46,974	26.2	1.8	56,401	31,801	40,019	46,179	33,948	32,054	28,836	61.4	98,700	883
Hobart	63,356	16.5	2.4	78,004	39,080	51,396	62,255	41,348	12,226	11,182	73.5	155,900	979
Indianapolis	50,939	23.2	4.7	64,448	36,023	43,640	48,354	40,649	391,500	346,940	54.1	145,300	910
Jeffersonville	56,667	15.5	1.6	63,253	41,218	42,279	45,784	39,036	21,447	18,775	69.1	145,500	872
Kokomo	48,830	24.1	2.0	61,181	33,788	45,838	52,196	37,311	29,561	25,536	65.4	93,300	741
Lafayette	46,925	24.5	1.3	59,503	32,039	39,221	44,804	33,880	33,570	31,189	49.3	119,400	853
Lawrence	62,257	19.4	4.1	85,533	36,370	49,263	54,761	43,198	20,187	18,981	63.9	159,500	945
Marion	35,252	34.9	1.8	43,162	27,184	37,607	39,952	32,122	13,311	11,251	55.8	69,800	685
Merrillville town	63,381	17.9	3.2	76,217	38,240	52,234	55,663	44,567	15,737	14,533	65.8	140,600	1,075
Michigan City	44,930	27.3	1.7	58,769	31,790	39,774	44,094	34,781	14,402	12,057	53.7	95,100	764
Mishawaka	44,792	26.8	2.8	59,621	30,108	39,145	44,440	33,935	24,922	21,875	49.5	105,800	823
Muncie	34,602	37.3	1.5	52,581	23,163	37,793	41,088	34,115	32,047	27,439	50.0	76,500	714
New Albany	49,415	25.3	2.1	64,634	33,601	41,921	46,308	38,240	17,319	14,759	57.5	128,700	791
Noblesville	85,314	9.5	8.0	105,031	43,266	58,138	66,324	47,249	25,598	23,868	72.9	230,100	1,041
Plainfield town	65,306	12.7	5.6	78,712	40,987	49,975	53,720	42,300	13,089	12,651	64.7	185,800	1,053
Portage	59,731	20.2	2.8	71,822	34,183	45,539	55,971	33,348	15,235	14,386	68.6	156,600	936
Richmond	40,871	30.8	1.9	54,688	25,076	35,245	39,096	32,468	17,676	14,860	53.8	86,300	704
Schererville town	75,327	10.0	8.7	94,199	46,908	54,994	66,216	44,027	12,149	11,519	80.4	237,500	985
South Bend	42,657	28.5	2.6	54,229	30,734	40,151	43,062	37,081	46,489	39,709	57.6	88,600	814
Terre Haute	37,299	32.9	2.1	50,100	24,509	37,076	41,806	33,899	26,757	23,665	54.1	83,800	754
Valparaiso	56,027	21.3	5.5	83,825	36,719	48,873	62,420	37,087	14,874	13,965	53.3	188,400	937
Westfield	99,855	6.7	15.8	108,306	56,405	66,405	80,269	53,330	16,227	15,572	79.0	281,400	1,200
West Lafayette	31,460	45.0	7.1	93,377	18,801	54,077	57,589	46,760	16,054	14,498	34.6	235,300	915
Zionsville town	137,265	6.6	29.1	158,631	54,176	91,852	103,512	75,357	10,673	10,061	84.6	406,800	1,408
IOWA	61,836	17.7	5.0	79,186	36,253	48,030	52,902	41,420	1,407,819	1,273,941	71.2	153,900	806
Ames	50,783	26.7	4.6	91,099	30,209	51,312	55,139	43,707	27,125	25,174	41.2	213,500	944
Ankeny	89,484	6.7	8.6	104,864	54,612	60,763	67,154	51,999	25,913	24,532	73.7	239,300	1,108
Bettendorf	85,404	10.2	11.7	103,636	44,257	63,514	75,161	50,379	15,438	14,267	76.3	232,600	933
Cedar Falls	64,809	16.6	7.7	97,563	39,616	52,518	60,387	44,709	16,118	15,157	64.4	204,300	944
Cedar Rapids	60,787	16.2	4.9	78,899	41,462	47,928	54,654	41,571	60,341	55,784	70.1	144,500	791
Council Bluffs	53,449	20.8	2.7	64,365	31,867	41,520	45,153	37,375	27,171	25,039	62.7	122,400	860
Davenport	53,140	22.1	3.5	69,285	34,967	45,320	49,782	40,773	45,085	40,261	63.2	135,200	786
Des Moines	54,843	20.3	3.8	66,420	40,322	44,010	47,295	40,299	93,052	85,667	59.6	141,300	881
Dubuque	54,938	20.6	3.5	74,164	33,520	44,288	50,131	37,863	26,214	24,151	64.5	147,900	807
Iowa City	48,148	29.7	5.5	86,192	29,968	50,116	53,448	43,194	34,062	31,483	46.7	223,900	976
Marion	72,500	13.2	7.5	95,217	39,521	54,607	65,544	44,576	16,438	15,656	77.1	177,200	724
Marshalltown	54,778	21.5	1.7	67,204	33,692	41,609	47,556	35,321	10,912	9,980	66.2	93,300	719
Mason City	53,406	19.6	3.5	67,787	33,360	45,531	52,682	39,056	13,665	12,611	64.9	112,500	733
Ottumwa	42,418	27.9	1.6	55,083	29,302	39,419	42,383	35,383	11,371	10,152	61.4	75,800	765
Sioux City	57,750	21.2	3.8	68,962	33,299	42,365	46,555	38,068	33,702	31,430	63.6	123,100	797
Urbandale	95,961	8.7	13.6	114,975	51,215	60,311	69,811	52,780	17,302	16,614	78.0	242,500	944
Waterloo	46,942	25.1	3.2	59,437	30,902	39,914	42,569	36,506	31,823	28,710	59.9	117,000	776
West Des Moines	74,159	10.9	9.2	99,914	53,977	58,063	64,054	53,154	31,756	29,440	59.5	228,300	1,058
KANSAS	61,091	18.0	5.7	77,620	34,826	46,824	52,422	40,845	1,280,376	1,141,985	66.2	157,600	863
Derby	74,447	11.8	6.0	87,805	42,750	53,185	60,292	45,514	9,569	9,090	71.7	173,800	978
Dodge City	52,654	16.8	3.4	61,993	32,364	38,515	41,203	32,479	9,199	8,615	59.2	106,200	785
Garden City	56,274	17.7	1.7	71,853	38,360	39,780	44,263	31,589	10,183	9,416	59.2	156,900	838
Hutchinson	48,889	21.3	3.4	62,975	31,145	39,171	46,515	31,741	18,695	16,282	64.5	101,300	765
Kansas City	46,424	26.3	1.9	54,955	28,018	38,607	41,381	34,750	63,156	55,644	57.5	101,300	882
Lawrence	55,598	22.5	5.9	88,286	34,792	46,536	51,223	41,761	42,033	39,422	44.6	204,800	953
Leavenworth	60,870	19.7	3.2	81,133	33,629	41,491	44,539	38,227	14,331	12,836	49.1	136,800	967
Leawood	156,538	5.3	41.2	194,974	76,116	116,568	143,329	86,583	14,022	13,404	89.8	472,500	1,629
Lenexa	90,487	8.4	12.1	110,925	53,462	61,267	70,998	53,205	24,260	22,864	58.7	278,100	1,183
Manhattan	50,957	24.5	4.2	79,601	35,005	41,340	42,717	40,461	23,992	20,629	39.7	213,200	911

1. Specified owner-occupied units

City	Commuting, 2016–2020[1]		Computer access[2], 2016–2020		Migration, 2016–2020		Civilian labor force, 2021				Civilian Employment, 2016–2020[4]			
	Percent		Percent						Unemployment[3]		Population age 16 and older		Population age 16 to 64	
	Drove alone	Mean travel time to work	With a computer in the house	With Internet access	Percent who lived in the same house one year ago	Percent who lived in another state or county one year ago	Total	Percent change 2020–2021	Total	Rate	Number	Percent in labor force	Number	Percent who worked full-year full-time
	55	56	57	58	59	60	61	62	63	64	65	66	67	68
INDIANA—Cont'd														
Brownsburg town	80.6	25.3	96.2	92.8	85.6	9.4	15,794	2.0	375	2.4	19,973	71.4	16,504	60.2
Carmel	77.5	24.4	97.9	96.1	86.3	8.7	54,689	2.0	1,136	2.1	76,514	70.9	62,809	59.0
Columbus	81.2	17.6	91.9	86.5	80.4	9.4	24,491	-2.0	709	2.9	38,494	65.2	31,123	52.8
Crown Point	89.2	27.6	92.4	89.8	88.2	3.2	15,126	-2.0	556	3.7	23,737	60.9	18,448	54.6
East Chicago	73.6	24.1	78.0	63.6	85.4	8.1	9,739	-1.2	1,028	10.6	21,373	54.1	17,367	41.5
Elkhart	75.3	18.6	87.5	79.5	82.1	5.0	26,933	3.3	939	3.5	39,614	64.1	32,676	48.7
Evansville	82.9	18.8	89.6	81.9	79.7	6.7	57,488	-1.5	2,471	4.3	95,663	63.0	76,559	51.0
Fishers	79.5	25.9	98.0	96.3	86.8	8.3	53,677	2.3	1,138	2.1	69,782	74.4	60,853	62.2
Fort Wayne	82.0	21.3	91.9	85.7	83.6	4.9	128,158	-1.1	5,210	4.1	209,568	66.2	171,536	52.1
Franklin	82.2	25.2	89.2	84.0	82.2	6.0	12,488	0.6	385	3.1	20,029	65.4	16,264	53.9
Gary	76.2	28.6	82.5	68.0	82.3	6.9	26,636	-1.4	3,279	12.3	58,271	49.8	43,668	37.5
Goshen	72.4	18.2	89.0	81.3	82.1	6.9	18,398	4.4	443	2.4	26,583	64.6	20,117	50.7
Greenwood	83.7	25.1	94.3	88.9	79.7	12.4	31,368	0.9	895	2.9	44,899	68.1	36,152	60.9
Hammond	80.1	25.2	86.8	76.6	86.2	6.5	32,993	-1.0	2,354	7.1	59,037	61.4	50,009	44.9
Hobart	85.6	27.5	93.0	90.0	88.7	3.4	14,084	-2.9	799	5.7	22,428	63.6	17,931	48.7
Indianapolis	79.9	23.9	89.5	82.4	84.9	5.3	455,555	0.9	20,466	4.5	685,354	66.6	575,552	52.2
Jeffersonville	81.8	21.0	92.5	80.7	90.4	4.2	25,504	-0.1	883	3.5	38,348	63.8	30,709	54.9
Kokomo	82.8	17.6	89.6	80.4	82.5	5.8	24,032	-7.0	1,646	6.8	46,706	58.0	35,669	48.4
Lafayette	79.6	17.5	92.2	83.4	78.8	7.0	36,123	0.3	1,585	4.4	57,164	68.5	47,542	56.6
Lawrence	81.9	24.4	86.8	80.4	90.0	4.7	26,986	1.5	972	3.6	37,138	72.4	31,542	52.4
Marion	70.3	14.7	85.2	70.3	81.6	7.5	12,249	-1.9	563	4.6	23,022	53.8	17,914	33.3
Merrillville town	84.9	30.1	90.4	85.9	87.2	3.8	16,557	-1.8	1,216	7.3	28,120	64.8	22,065	52.5
Michigan City	79.1	21.5	89.1	76.6	78.3	10.8	12,471	-3.6	876	7.0	24,705	56.7	19,905	40.7
Mishawaka	83.2	21.0	88.2	79.7	84.7	5.0	25,599	-2.3	964	3.8	39,884	67.9	32,283	53.3
Muncie	73.2	18.0	91.0	79.9	71.0	13.1	29,895	-1.5	1,297	4.3	58,231	57.6	48,759	33.3
New Albany	85.8	20.2	87.4	74.9	86.2	7.1	18,538	-1.0	696	3.8	29,905	61.7	23,922	51.9
Noblesville	82.7	26.3	96.5	94.3	83.2	9.2	36,620	1.7	873	2.4	48,673	72.7	41,325	58.0
Plainfield town	77.7	23.5	95.6	89.0	81.0	11.6	17,569	1.7	476	2.7	27,381	64.4	22,110	55.5
Portage	88.3	28.5	91.8	82.7	86.8	6.3	17,396	-2.3	901	5.2	29,411	62.7	24,074	50.7
Richmond	77.6	16.9	87.2	76.6	79.3	7.5	14,413	-3.0	624	4.3	28,850	57.5	22,209	45.1
Schererville town	87.7	31.4	92.5	89.6	91.9	3.5	15,304	-1.2	553	3.6	23,843	66.6	18,591	57.8
South Bend	75.0	20.1	85.6	74.9	85.4	5.6	46,620	-2.6	2,695	5.8	78,171	63.5	64,198	47.9
Terre Haute	75.6	17.1	89.5	80.6	76.0	11.1	23,897	-2.1	1,144	4.8	50,393	55.1	41,107	38.3
Valparaiso	77.2	23.7	92.5	83.0	78.9	10.3	16,043	-1.2	564	3.5	27,987	59.3	21,988	46.4
Westfield	79.8	23.8	98.7	95.1	87.0	6.0	25,329	2.3	522	2.1	30,779	73.2	25,434	60.1
West Lafayette	56.1	15.6	96.9	86.6	57.5	27.2	22,207	3.7	463	2.1	45,513	49.0	41,943	18.0
Zionsville town	75.6	28.1	96.7	94.0	86.2	8.9	15,253	2.5	272	1.8	21,124	68.0	17,499	59.2
IOWA	80.2	19.5	90.4	82.9	85.6	6.4	1,676,075	-0.4	70,869	4.2	2,504,540	67.0	1,967,139	56.1
Ames	65.9	16.8	95.7	69.5	61.6	18.5	39,651	0.4	1,127	2.8	59,285	63.9	52,520	32.2
Ankeny	85.1	21.6	96.8	90.7	82.8	6.3	39,431	1.1	1,301	3.3	48,688	77.9	42,072	67.0
Bettendorf	87.6	18.5	92.2	88.1	87.0	5.7	18,337	0.1	815	4.4	28,090	66.0	21,837	57.8
Cedar Falls	79.8	15.5	94.3	87.8	70.9	12.2	21,584	-0.4	687	3.2	34,051	71.6	27,902	42.1
Cedar Rapids	82.6	18.0	93.0	86.6	84.2	6.3	70,721	-1.6	3,964	5.6	107,119	68.7	85,732	56.3
Council Bluffs	83.0	19.3	88.6	77.9	85.9	5.6	30,829	-1.1	1,442	4.7	50,147	64.5	39,636	54.7
Davenport	85.2	17.9	86.9	80.4	87.4	4.4	50,213	-0.7	3,128	6.2	81,889	63.5	66,272	51.2
Des Moines	78.6	19.1	91.6	82.5	82.2	6.2	110,123	0.1	6,160	5.6	169,569	69.8	143,721	54.5
Dubuque	78.2	14.6	90.1	82.6	84.2	6.1	32,189	-1.4	1,513	4.7	47,685	65.4	36,672	52.6
Iowa City	58.6	17.3	95.6	88.5	68.9	14.0	41,553	-1.3	1,564	3.8	66,125	66.9	57,623	37.8
Marion	82.5	19.5	94.3	88.6	84.9	6.0	20,779	-1.0	898	4.3	31,002	71.8	24,632	60.9
Marshalltown	76.3	16.6	87.8	78.5	86.3	5.2	11,320	-1.7	875	7.7	20,596	62.8	15,761	52.7
Mason City	81.6	15.7	87.7	81.5	86.6	5.8	14,225	-3.5	641	4.5	22,221	66.8	16,544	56.4
Ottumwa	82.7	16.1	87.8	78.1	83.3	6.5	11,617	-2.9	651	5.6	19,647	62.8	15,819	50.6
Sioux City	83.7	17.3	90.2	79.8	90.0	4.5	43,768	-0.3	1,968	4.5	62,547	69.8	51,408	56.2
Urbandale	82.0	19.1	96.8	91.2	86.5	6.7	25,161	0.8	804	3.2	33,565	72.9	27,159	63.2
Waterloo	78.2	16.4	88.6	79.5	81.6	4.9	33,231	-1.3	1,870	5.6	53,663	65.5	42,788	52.8
West Des Moines	80.8	17.3	96.9	90.7	80.6	11.1	40,436	0.8	1,452	3.6	52,833	73.4	43,762	64.5
KANSAS	80.7	19.6	91.7	84.0	84.1	7.0	1,495,665	0.1	48,342	3.2	2,285,921	65.9	1,825,004	55.4
Derby	88.3	22.2	96.8	93.0	83.8	5.2	12,930	-0.1	474	3.7	18,234	65.8	14,559	58.6
Dodge City	80.2	12.3	87.3	80.3	82.3	9.9	14,070	2.4	309	2.2	19,498	71.8	17,140	56.0
Garden City	82.1	13.4	88.9	78.6	82.0	4.9	14,756	-1.3	316	2.1	19,597	71.2	16,377	58.1
Hutchinson	83.5	15.5	89.9	82.9	82.9	8.0	18,869	-0.2	653	3.5	32,615	59.8	24,773	52.7
Kansas City	79.3	21.6	90.0	78.8	85.9	6.6	70,862	-0.2	3,349	4.7	114,867	65.8	96,359	52.6
Lawrence	74.9	19.6	96.7	88.7	70.6	12.6	52,210	0.9	1,644	3.1	82,092	71.6	71,021	47.0
Leavenworth	80.6	17.3	93.7	84.5	68.8	22.0	13,822	0.0	501	3.6	28,367	49.7	23,567	50.4
Leawood	79.9	21.9	98.1	96.5	88.8	5.4	17,482	1.4	414	2.4	27,791	63.0	20,045	53.3
Lenexa	81.0	20.0	96.3	93.5	82.0	8.2	32,813	0.5	900	2.7	44,228	72.7	35,908	63.8
Manhattan	70.4	15.0	96.6	88.9	65.9	17.2	28,161	0.6	717	2.5	47,465	67.1	42,595	39.7

1. Employed persons. 2. Households. 3. Percent of civilian labor force. 4. Persons 16 years old and over.

Table D. Cities — Construction, Wholesale Trade, and Retail Trade

City	Value of residential construction authorized by building permits, 2021: New construction ($1,000)	Value of residential construction authorized by building permits, 2021: Number of housing units	Value of residential construction authorized by building permits, 2021: Percent single family	Wholesale trade[1], 2017: Number of establishments	Wholesale trade[1], 2017: Number of employees	Wholesale trade[1], 2017: Sales (mil dol)	Wholesale trade[1], 2017: Annual payroll (mil dol)	Retail trade[2], 2017: Number of establishments	Retail trade[2], 2017: Number of employees	Retail trade[2], 2017: Sales (mil dol)	Retail trade[2], 2017: Annual payroll (mil dol)
	69	70	71	72	73	74	75	76	77	78	79
INDIANA—Cont'd											
Brownsburg town	128,571	443	100.0	25	142	202.8	8.6	87	2,007	594.6	52.8
Carmel	286,115	943	59.2	130	1,337	1,188.5	111.1	291	6,092	2,128.1	180.1
Columbus	NA	NA	NA	46	734	563.1	37.4	193	3,525	966.7	85.1
Crown Point	92,250	274	100.0	34	200	147.1	10.7	86	1,091	277.0	26.3
East Chicago	0	0	0.0	29	400	504.3	23.9	53	397	94.4	8.5
Elkhart	13,910	123	43.9	168	3,845	3,111.3	200.8	286	4,227	1,171.1	112.6
Evansville	92,446	356	89.3	211	3,167	2,197.0	168.7	698	11,649	3,187.2	294.4
Fishers	240,902	723	88.2	96	1,758	1,025.7	109.7	206	4,188	1,468.5	122.9
Fort Wayne	NA	NA	NA	372	6,095	5,211.5	320.4	1,081	20,457	6,048.8	544.8
Franklin	44,360	175	100.0	30	547	176.3	19.6	69	1,546	507.2	47.0
Gary	1,879	10	100.0	34	624	578.9	30.3	173	1,393	441.4	28.0
Goshen	14,158	57	100.0	27	623	733.5	32.1	158	3,272	959.4	88.4
Greenwood	118,614	590	44.1	31	1,547	1,246.7	107.7	321	7,324	2,334.7	180.5
Hammond	2,410	18	55.6	73	1,109	793.4	72.1	210	3,522	1,101.0	87.5
Hobart	13,643	43	100.0	27	299	1,025.8	16.4	206	4,367	1,224.4	108.4
Indianapolis	481,659	2,189	55.8	D	D	D	D	2,711	46,121	14,347.3	1,256.6
Jeffersonville	106,137	747	39.2	50	917	1,501.3	51.8	131	5,105	1,852.8	148.9
Kokomo	40,142	169	98.8	45	439	284.4	25.1	308	4,935	1,316.4	112.8
Lafayette	58,490	519	1.0	76	1,217	1,034.4	64.8	425	7,654	2,231.4	194.2
Lawrence	9,646	49	100.0	41	797	750.6	47.2	118	1,767	462.7	43.5
Marion	875	4	100.0	24	243	113.3	10.7	153	2,291	630.6	53.1
Merrillville town	7,875	38	100.0	32	242	153.8	13.9	207	3,834	1,296.8	117.2
Michigan City	10,808	36	100.0	30	638	420.1	27.1	230	3,803	776.0	74.9
Mishawaka	8,518	40	92.5	52	569	543.2	28.7	366	7,700	2,775.5	199.2
Muncie	4,139	18	100.0	55	580	372.1	26.7	348	5,310	1,373.6	125.2
New Albany	10,865	57	100.0	36	465	261.1	21.2	135	2,381	606.7	61.1
Noblesville	226,683	1,063	57.9	81	766	439.3	51.1	230	4,502	1,220.1	105.8
Plainfield town	88,580	276	100.0	39	2,742	3,943.2	146.9	136	5,233	2,516.5	171.1
Portage	20,988	143	100.0	27	727	586.2	43.9	93	2,016	567.1	49.1
Richmond	3,112	24	100.0	32	542	280.6	25.6	198	3,313	839.7	76.1
Schererville town	29,076	77	94.8	25	101	41.8	5.1	122	2,717	713.0	67.0
South Bend	NA	NA	NA	148	2,801	2,729.0	160.4	322	5,303	1,763.9	145.0
Terre Haute	5,567	33	57.6	76	1,081	434.8	46.0	311	4,366	986.5	94.9
Valparaiso	55,214	158	89.9	44	621	302.4	35.2	193	3,755	996.3	91.2
Westfield	582,050	1,853	76.5	46	1,071	910.5	85.4	99	2,256	662.6	56.9
West Lafayette	28,066	149	20.8	D	D	D	1.1	86	1,845	413.7	36.8
Zionsville town	231,560	292	100.0	20	140	154.5	9.3	D	D	D	16.5
IOWA	3,182,377	13,686	66.9	4,426	62,658	64,162.6	3,389.3	11,479	181,416	50,063.1	4,518.5
Ames	42,490	201	45.3	33	855	502.9	22.9	208	4,362	1,015.0	103.4
Ankeny	283,929	1,175	77.5	46	1,458	2,346.5	92.4	157	4,450	1,535.9	125.2
Bettendorf	57,679	219	48.4	48	619	549.0	31.8	95	1,514	362.7	36.7
Cedar Falls	28,920	92	100.0	42	920	857.9	55.3	168	3,444	883.7	85.2
Cedar Rapids	68,838	438	36.1	204	3,953	2,737.6	265.2	479	11,763	5,379.0	275.7
Council Bluffs	19,908	92	60.9	57	926	952.5	52.8	200	5,265	1,397.9	126.7
Davenport	20,430	84	100.0	162	2,646	1,330.3	142.2	472	9,446	2,487.8	248.2
Des Moines	145,605	628	39.5	272	5,365	4,952.1	289.0	597	9,699	2,299.8	247.9
Dubuque	59,757	200	20.0	81	991	1,195.5	51.1	326	6,228	1,509.9	153.2
Iowa City	82,605	294	46.6	35	508	554.6	26.2	216	4,292	1,167.2	117.6
Marion	26,223	233	87.1	36	582	222.0	32.0	108	1,896	462.8	46.2
Marshalltown	3,937	17	100.0	22	291	194.6	16.6	115	1,879	409.9	43.7
Mason City	1,932	6	100.0	50	630	482.7	32.2	165	3,105	744.2	73.6
Ottumwa	737	5	100.0	21	136	200.2	7.9	114	2,123	527.6	52.4
Sioux City	27,869	106	100.0	140	2,129	1,808.3	112.7	363	7,005	1,912.0	168.5
Urbandale	147,502	497	67.2	107	1,588	933.7	102.8	148	3,533	1,564.3	127.1
Waterloo	9,800	13	84.6	77	1,226	889.4	59.5	281	4,867	1,155.4	123.9
West Des Moines	189,783	789	53.2	56	623	2,252.1	46.2	385	8,858	1,732.4	192.4
KANSAS	2,592,906	9,538	68.9	3,755	52,611	61,889.4	3,159.9	10,095	149,845	39,337.5	3,784.9
Derby	39,825	148	77.0	D	D	D	D	79	1,677	393.0	37.1
Dodge City	12,488	66	66.7	44	547	232.0	26.8	102	1,651	436.6	39.4
Garden City	9,100	57	86.0	26	128	143.1	7.4	149	2,653	638.2	60.0
Hutchinson	7,199	34	29.4	54	805	1,022.0	33.8	182	2,715	676.5	63.3
Kansas City	33,469	167	85.0	194	5,554	7,273.3	391.8	399	7,034	1,958.3	193.9
Lawrence	78,078	441	42.4	57	375	165.5	19.5	333	6,119	1,451.8	141.3
Leavenworth	7,403	35	77.1	D	D	D	0.9	97	1,615	478.7	42.5
Leawood	46,918	64	100.0	35	281	430.8	18.7	148	2,427	431.9	60.0
Lenexa	102,366	229	100.0	312	5,800	3,662.6	390.1	202	4,112	1,168.2	124.6
Manhattan	20,890	68	97.1	35	610	192.6	24.8	238	4,998	1,044.2	119.2

1. Merchant wholesalers except manufacturers' sales branches and offices. 2. Establishments with payroll.

Table D. Cities — **Real Estate, Professional Services, and Manufacturing**

City	Real estate and rental and leasing, 2017: Number of establish-ments	Number of employees	Receipts (mil dol)	Annual payroll (mil dol)	Professional, scientific, and technical services[1], 2017: Number of establish-ments	Number of employees	Receipts (mil dol)	Annual payroll (mil dol)	Manufacturing, 2017: Number of establish-ments	Number of employees	Receipts (mil dol)	Annual payroll (mil dol)
	80	81	82	83	84	85	86	87	88	89	90	91
INDIANA—Cont'd												
Brownsburg town	35	94	18.4	3.2	71	273	35.2	13.0	NA	NA	NA	NA
Carmel	247	1,808	846.7	157.4	645	7,416	1,456.8	584.2	NA	NA	NA	NA
Columbus	58	216	44.7	7.9	128	2,145	205.7	143.4	NA	NA	NA	NA
Crown Point	39	191	49.7	9.9	104	661	84.8	33.4	NA	NA	NA	NA
East Chicago	13	95	21.0	5.6	15	187	26.6	11.8	NA	NA	NA	NA
Elkhart	67	428	93.7	16.9	131	885	119.0	42.1	NA	NA	NA	NA
Evansville	186	1,083	242.3	40.2	366	3,391	483.3	193.4	NA	NA	NA	NA
Fishers	127	468	116.6	22.9	396	2,434	419.2	137.0	NA	NA	NA	NA
Fort Wayne	352	2,004	503.1	81.8	660	4,865	774.6	269.0	NA	NA	NA	NA
Franklin	20	61	14.3	2.1	55	434	41.8	17.1	NA	NA	NA	NA
Gary	35	193	31.0	6.0	33	157	32.5	6.6	NA	NA	NA	NA
Goshen	46	161	28.0	5.4	71	434	45.8	17.0	NA	NA	NA	NA
Greenwood	96	339	101.1	12.2	117	807	109.0	37.7	NA	NA	NA	NA
Hammond	45	201	34.3	7.4	87	926	143.3	63.7	NA	NA	NA	NA
Hobart	28	124	35.0	4.6	48	345	40.0	16.0	NA	NA	NA	NA
Indianapolis	D	D	D	D	D	D	D	D	NA	NA	NA	NA
Jeffersonville	61	271	68.3	11.5	101	765	117.0	36.6	NA	NA	NA	NA
Kokomo	68	288	61.1	9.6	100	626	85.4	26.9	NA	NA	NA	NA
Lafayette	138	821	148.5	32.6	190	1,584	218.0	82.6	NA	NA	NA	NA
Lawrence	47	277	49.6	11.4	112	2,460	259.4	127.9	NA	NA	NA	NA
Marion	37	139	18.8	3.6	44	229	27.1	9.3	NA	NA	NA	NA
Merrillville town	66	406	76.8	17.2	179	1,382	181.7	71.5	NA	NA	NA	NA
Michigan City	36	180	37.0	8.5	48	265	33.5	12.0	NA	NA	NA	NA
Mishawaka	71	488	93.5	17.1	100	1,765	1,082.2	128.1	NA	NA	NA	NA
Muncie	74	272	56.9	8.7	108	1,105	170.4	31.6	NA	NA	NA	NA
New Albany	45	187	22.3	4.9	121	1,035	165.6	53.9	NA	NA	NA	NA
Noblesville	77	250	79.6	8.1	220	799	132.0	46.1	NA	NA	NA	NA
Plainfield town	36	144	39.3	5.5	53	671	61.1	20.7	NA	NA	NA	NA
Portage	32	165	39.1	7.0	42	252	35.1	15.3	NA	NA	NA	NA
Richmond	41	180	37.1	7.2	53	303	29.2	11.3	NA	NA	NA	NA
Schererville town	41	204	56.8	7.4	108	551	84.5	30.8	NA	NA	NA	NA
South Bend	93	956	157.3	38.1	259	2,208	392.4	135.4	NA	NA	NA	NA
Terre Haute	65	428	79.3	13.5	147	969	105.3	44.9	NA	NA	NA	NA
Valparaiso	67	360	71.2	12.2	166	810	144.3	42.9	NA	NA	NA	NA
Westfield	41	100	34.4	3.6	119	1,864	336.0	126.5	NA	NA	NA	NA
West Lafayette	40	321	41.1	9.5	89	814	154.8	65.1	NA	NA	NA	NA
Zionsville town	50	118	34.5	5.2	125	466	104.6	30.6	NA	NA	NA	NA
IOWA	3,130	13,999	2,890.1	575.6	6,460	52,607	7,936.8	3,172.3	3,489	210,722	109,727.8	11,373.9
Ames	84	358	59.5	13.7	145	912	115.2	55.1	NA	NA	NA	NA
Ankeny	84	236	67.7	10.3	115	574	76.0	33.6	NA	NA	NA	NA
Bettendorf	50	222	34.9	8.7	102	493	54.8	18.7	NA	NA	NA	NA
Cedar Falls	52	248	52.0	10.5	95	2,158	139.0	148.6	NA	NA	NA	NA
Cedar Rapids	185	925	222.9	40.1	385	5,043	762.9	375.2	NA	NA	NA	NA
Council Bluffs	64	279	50.3	9.9	100	634	90.6	30.9	NA	NA	NA	NA
Davenport	125	552	136.8	20.7	253	2,116	341.1	123.3	NA	NA	NA	NA
Des Moines	239	1,505	311.3	66.4	638	6,647	1,234.6	479.3	NA	NA	NA	NA
Dubuque	83	329	80.6	12.1	144	1,941	306.0	107.7	NA	NA	NA	NA
Iowa City	79	379	77.8	17.4	147	961	159.6	57.0	NA	NA	NA	NA
Marion	D	D	D	D	55	385	45.3	22.2	NA	NA	NA	NA
Marshalltown	24	473	98.1	16.9	35	311	54.9	13.8	NA	NA	NA	NA
Mason City	49	132	22.8	3.3	71	421	54.0	24.2	NA	NA	NA	NA
Ottumwa	23	119	24.5	3.8	30	161	21.6	6.6	NA	NA	NA	NA
Sioux City	87	479	76.1	14.7	181	994	145.7	50.1	NA	NA	NA	NA
Urbandale	84	624	155.6	28.9	203	3,499	747.2	233.7	NA	NA	NA	NA
Waterloo	90	524	89.7	16.0	96	807	98.0	41.8	NA	NA	NA	NA
West Des Moines	164	1,550	271.8	86.4	424	4,496	835.0	340.2	NA	NA	NA	NA
KANSAS	3,415	14,532	3,942.5	586.4	7,201	65,648	10,971.8	4,174.3	2,760	155,968	83,418.1	9,032.0
Derby	21	66	12.3	1.5	26	94	10.2	3.5	NA	NA	NA	NA
Dodge City	D	D	D	D	D	D	D	D	NA	NA	NA	NA
Garden City	31	115	21.8	3.4	45	249	31.3	10.7	NA	NA	NA	NA
Hutchinson	55	193	32.6	6.5	77	551	69.1	29.4	NA	NA	NA	NA
Kansas City	123	652	131.4	26.5	178	1,464	336.6	91.0	NA	NA	NA	NA
Lawrence	140	691	109.0	23.5	259	4,867	311.8	124.6	NA	NA	NA	NA
Leavenworth	37	172	51.3	4.9	D	D	128.4	D	NA	NA	NA	NA
Leawood	104	566	251.7	26.4	256	1,435	411.8	151.0	NA	NA	NA	NA
Lenexa	133	881	236.9	45.3	337	6,854	1,485.6	561.3	NA	NA	NA	NA
Manhattan	122	483	78.2	15.1	D	D	D	D	NA	NA	NA	NA

1. Establishments subject to federal tax.

City	Accommodation and food services, 2017				Arts, entertainment, and recreation[1], 2017				Health care and social assistance[1], 2017			
	Number of establish-ments	Number of employees	Receipts (mil dol)	Annual payroll (mil dol)	Number of establish-ments	Number of employees	Receipts (mil dol)	Annual payroll (mil dol)	Number of establish-ments	Number of employees	Receipts (mil dol)	Annual payroll (mil dol)
	92	93	94	95	96	97	98	99	100	101	102	103
INDIANA—Cont'd												
Brownsburg town	69	1,645	76.2	20.9	27.0	337	78.1	20.0	67	1,361	119.4	49.1
Carmel	240	6,795	408.4	131.4	74.0	1,025	80.1	25.5	509	11,468	1,576.5	577.5
Columbus	140	3,536	172.6	49.9	23.0	171	7.5	2.5	203	5,011	597.5	225.1
Crown Point	79	1,494	72.2	20.0	17.0	238	8.0	2.3	116	3,782	513.2	155.4
East Chicago	46	1,748	222.9	49.3	NA	NA	NA	NA	39	1,597	296.1	77.9
Elkhart	185	3,470	178.0	49.1	19.0	210	12.1	3.7	166	5,527	772.7	252.6
Evansville	411	9,952	581.3	156.7	66.0	1,379	81.2	22.8	542	18,755	2,354.2	831.6
Fishers	207	4,614	240.1	69.7	52.0	831	58.5	18.5	280	4,402	459.4	203.4
Fort Wayne	649	15,505	746.5	226.1	103.0	2,232	121.5	40.2	876	28,627	3,167.8	1,345.5
Franklin	72	1,394	68.4	18.8	D	D	D	D	76	2,372	194.1	95.8
Gary	72	959	90.9	17.4	D	D	D	D	121	3,033	258.9	122.3
Goshen	100	2,019	97.0	25.4	10.0	99	4.8	1.7	110	4,120	508.7	186.4
Greenwood	163	4,298	226.2	65.2	17.0	183	11.0	3.7	187	4,900	484.3	198.9
Hammond	145	2,194	120.6	31.3	D	D	D	D	99	4,089	558.4	201.7
Hobart	67	1,461	73.5	19.8	D	D	D	D	63	2,130	351.7	100.1
Indianapolis	2,138	50,367	3,119.5	887.2	336.0	8,487	1,440.0	535.2	2,700	88,524	12,566.1	4,846.7
Jeffersonville	108	2,090	102.3	30.8	D	D	D	D	157	4,457	554.8	214.7
Kokomo	183	3,933	181.4	52.9	D	D	D	D	222	5,155	579.8	217.2
Lafayette	244	5,346	278.9	78.6	44.0	436	16.9	5.7	377	10,181	1,408.5	514.6
Lawrence	D	D	D	D	D	D	D	D	75	1,167	77.4	34.8
Marion	83	1,629	74.0	21.2	D	D	D	D	139	4,305	396.8	154.8
Merrillville town	135	3,233	181.9	52.3	13.0	192	9.9	2.8	266	4,964	649.8	234.9
Michigan City	99	3,042	279.2	63.7	13.0	126	7.1	2.3	97	2,617	344.6	125.4
Mishawaka	204	4,544	242.7	67.5	D	D	D	D	193	5,793	734.2	260.6
Muncie	177	4,511	196.8	58.4	32.0	449	14.5	5.3	327	9,324	991.1	385.1
New Albany	99	1,995	100.3	28.5	13.0	231	8.2	2.3	182	5,619	597.4	231.9
Noblesville	138	3,573	174.9	54.5	32.0	347	58.2	8.6	179	3,425	379.6	141.3
Plainfield town	109	2,540	129.6	37.1	11.0	109	9.1	1.4	78	1,144	108.6	43.6
Portage	86	1,955	97.5	27.9	10.0	222	5.1	1.7	68	1,121	123.1	42.5
Richmond	108	2,400	118.6	37.1	14.0	70	3.9	1.0	136	4,518	629.5	205.0
Schererville town	102	2,466	122.0	37.0	12.0	416	17.5	5.4	104	2,013	134.3	55.0
South Bend	245	4,627	238.6	67.3	35.0	664	32.7	11.1	312	10,192	1,377.5	449.6
Terre Haute	235	4,807	237.4	67.7	26.0	174	7.8	2.6	266	7,482	1,127.6	380.8
Valparaiso	128	2,707	137.4	40.7	13.0	412	16.2	5.7	192	4,102	410.9	161.4
Westfield	76	1,747	85.5	26.4	25.0	324	22.7	5.6	77	892	68.0	28.7
West Lafayette	165	3,249	171.3	43.9	11.0	72	3.0	0.8	70	2,193	195.8	87.2
Zionsville town	47	757	35.8	10.7	24.0	98	13.7	3.6	66	754	59.3	26.4
IOWA	7,283	123,866	7,110.7	1,897.4	1,451.0	18,336	1,158.2	315.5	8,610	216,965	22,419.8	9,241.6
Ames	205	4,628	225.1	64.4	27.0	376	17.7	6.7	165	4,962	608.3	243.6
Ankeny	137	3,252	160.2	48.6	22.0	441	12.0	4.3	134	2,049	175.0	74.0
Bettendorf	75	2,058	151.6	32.3	14.0	211	6.4	1.8	143	3,423	358.3	147.2
Cedar Falls	125	2,838	120.9	38.1	19.0	132	6.8	2.0	115	2,687	225.3	79.4
Cedar Rapids	417	8,001	400.8	125.2	60.0	1,504	75.2	25.6	467	13,259	1,611.7	610.3
Council Bluffs	157	5,186	575.4	109.8	D	D	D	D	209	4,863	534.4	203.0
Davenport	301	6,766	382.6	105.3	47.0	863	47.2	17.6	331	8,939	895.0	372.6
Des Moines	562	9,920	566.8	169.3	78.0	1,608	100.0	31.7	528	22,243	2,987.2	1,266.9
Dubuque	194	4,323	243.7	71.1	42.0	1,279	115.9	23.6	229	7,792	882.2	381.5
Iowa City	240	4,078	185.4	56.8	23.0	295	11.4	3.0	271	16,070	2,421.8	885.5
Marion	56	898	40.3	11.8	8.0	127	3.7	1.0	91	1,037	74.2	32.4
Marshalltown	70	993	48.5	14.0	D	D	D	D	D	D	D	D
Mason City	86	1,472	70.2	20.6	D	D	D	D	110	2,935	311.9	140.1
Ottumwa	D	D	D	14.4	D	D	D	D	89	2,851	254.1	98.7
Sioux City	D	D	D	D	41.0	553	20.9	6.1	301	9,030	1,024.5	399.5
Urbandale	93	1,833	107.8	31.1	23.0	644	38.1	11.2	110	2,848	242.5	103.6
Waterloo	174	3,672	233.4	56.9	35.0	578	24.0	8.6	238	8,396	943.0	400.7
West Des Moines	246	5,390	331.9	99.0	38.0	660	41.2	15.2	322	6,055	809.6	351.1
KANSAS	6,253	118,905	5,907.5	1,723.7	1,092.0	17,313	1,230.8	323.3	8,104	195,941	21,439.7	8,522.4
Derby	56	1,362	51.2	17.1	D	D	D	D	50	615	55.8	23.9
Dodge City	88	1,503	99.2	26.8	D	D	D	D	D	D	D	D
Garden City	82	1,519	81.5	22.2	7.0	D	4.8	D	D	D	D	D
Hutchinson	106	2,245	98.0	29.8	11.0	339	12.6	4.5	144	3,807	447.1	171.0
Kansas City	243	5,600	318.5	90.5	30.0	D	184.5	D	280	15,926	1,901.4	837.3
Lawrence	296	6,936	313.0	92.5	44.0	652	64.5	9.6	283	6,166	628.3	250.8
Leavenworth	61	1,044	55.1	16.5	D	D	D	D	75	2,375	283.2	114.1
Leawood	68	2,908	142.8	56.5	17.0	279	21.1	7.9	192	2,377	334.6	122.9
Lenexa	122	3,094	172.5	50.6	32.0	727	40.9	13.9	162	5,278	821.6	260.2
Manhattan	D	D	D	D	18.0	233	12.3	3.7	212	3,714	391.1	138.2

1. Establishments subject to federal tax.

City	Other services[1]				Government employment and payroll, 2017								
						March payroll							
							Perent of total for:						
	Number of establish-ments	Number of employees	Receipts (mil dol)	Annual payroll (mil dol)	Full-time equivalent employees	Total (dollars)	Admin-istrative, judicial, and legal	Police and corrections	Fire protection	Highways and trans-portation	Health and welfare	Natural resources and utilities	Education and libraries
	104	105	106	107	108	109	110	111	112	113	114	115	116
INDIANA—Cont'd													
Brownsburg town	59	304	31.5	9.6	242	1,094,913	12.6	26.1	41.1	3.2	0.0	13.7	0.0
Carmel	195	1,598	181.3	58.1	541	3,323,712	11.6	24.8	35.4	6.7	0.0	18.1	0.0
Columbus	92	659	80.0	19.5	449	1,866,119	6.7	23.7	24.0	7.9	3.0	33.8	0.0
Crown Point	76	506	69.7	18.7	206	901,061	10.4	28.3	20.4	8.1	0.0	25.4	0.0
East Chicago	37	169	20.5	4.0	753	3,206,403	8.4	26.2	16.2	7.5	4.5	37.1	0.0
Elkhart	130	1,151	180.0	44.0	571	2,684,118	5.8	28.3	25.7	9.1	0.7	14.9	0.0
Evansville	303	2,498	274.0	76.1	1,284	5,829,082	2.6	29.5	23.4	14.2	1.7	23.2	0.0
Fishers	136	1,146	77.6	24.4	419	2,279,967	9.1	28.9	37.3	5.7	2.0	9.7	0.0
Fort Wayne	538	4,331	471.7	147.5	2,015	9,797,922	5.7	33.5	19.2	13.2	4.7	20.5	0.0
Franklin	39	242	22.1	6.7	224	806,113	7.4	28.7	27.2	6.4	1.3	22.6	0.0
Gary	73	375	49.7	12.1	1,141	3,176,242	11.7	16.3	20.2	6.4	10.1	27.0	0.0
Goshen	67	463	44.2	15.3	252	1,147,950	9.3	31.3	23.9	6.9	1.3	16.0	0.0
Greenwood	123	848	91.5	29.7	297	1,295,362	18.8	27.9	28.4	9.1	0.0	12.2	0.0
Hammond	116	896	98.8	29.3	805	4,079,099	5.1	37.3	26.7	4.3	3.5	19.0	0.0
Hobart	65	425	42.5	13.2	232	1,033,616	6.4	34.5	25.9	5.8	3.9	19.1	0.0
Indianapolis	1,518	16,940	4,074.8	743.8	13,456	61,603,859	8.7	15.6	10.9	6.1	41.6	15.3	0.0
Jeffersonville	76	731	97.6	23.0	344	1,489,946	7.7	29.2	30.8	7.7	0.9	22.2	0.0
Kokomo	D	D	D	D	431	1,773,018	8.0	31.6	24.1	11.7	3.4	16.8	0.0
Lafayette	D	D	D	D	752	3,450,984	5.5	27.2	22.7	18.1	0.8	20.5	0.0
Lawrence	73	443	59.0	15.0	282	1,291,474	6.7	31.9	43.0	2.1	0.9	13.3	0.0
Marion	63	316	28.8	8.9	239	862,860	8.3	40.0	31.7	20.1	0.0	0.0	0.0
Merrillville town	81	685	72.5	22.4	146	491,875	20.8	35.9	14.7	24.0	0.0	4.2	0.0
Michigan City	70	369	37.9	9.8	407	1,649,855	6.5	27.1	22.3	9.1	0.8	32.6	0.0
Mishawaka	112	709	69.0	21.9	503	2,309,841	6.7	25.0	27.1	4.6	1.9	32.5	0.0
Muncie	124	874	104.3	24.5	566	2,111,689	7.0	23.9	22.9	16.3	1.8	23.4	0.0
New Albany	76	415	46.1	11.7	261	1,199,198	6.4	29.6	38.6	4.7	2.2	17.6	0.0
Noblesville	102	755	55.1	17.5	355	1,910,485	9.9	24.2	42.0	9.6	0.7	12.7	0.0
Plainfield town	59	742	66.6	29.3	248	1,039,451	10.1	25.1	34.3	4.5	0.0	23.0	0.0
Portage	62	465	51.1	18.6	243	1,025,489	8.0	34.2	28.8	15.7	1.2	12.1	0.0
Richmond	64	392	35.5	9.5	489	1,912,770	4.8	18.8	15.3	6.8	4.7	48.6	0.0
Schererville town	78	676	72.9	21.5	200	817,686	14.8	38.0	17.9	15.1	0.0	13.8	0.0
South Bend	192	1,595	217.5	57.2	1,244	5,813,124	6.4	27.3	24.2	14.0	2.6	20.8	0.0
Terre Haute	121	761	91.2	21.6	578	2,421,306	5.9	26.7	33.9	15.6	0.0	15.9	0.0
Valparaiso	108	745	79.8	18.8	284	1,314,343	5.9	21.1	26.3	6.8	0.0	39.9	0.0
Westfield	55	340	34.3	11.3	176	992,602	19.6	28.0	32.8	8.5	1.6	9.5	0.0
West Lafayette	40	626	340.0	31.2	236	1,028,818	5.8	33.3	21.8	4.2	5.4	24.8	0.0
Zionsville town	44	308	25.2	7.8	147	698,161	20.4	22.3	39.7	4.6	0.0	8.8	0.0
IOWA	5,975	31,306	4,186.5	1,021.5	X	X	X	X	X	X	X	X	X
Ames	110	1,006	262.4	33.1	635	3,374,874	8.8	11.7	9.7	22.4	1.9	31.1	5.3
Ankeny	98	911	99.1	24.1	282	1,457,235	18.7	25.1	18.9	13.1	0.0	19.5	4.8
Bettendorf	69	395	35.3	10.9	283	1,575,986	10.7	22.8	12.6	12.8	3.3	22.8	9.5
Cedar Falls	59	449	45.0	13.8	430	2,364,435	8.8	11.4	7.2	7.5	0.4	57.7	3.0
Cedar Rapids	248	2,058	228.8	68.4	1,293	7,127,614	10.4	23.5	12.1	17.6	1.8	23.8	3.4
Council Bluffs	107	544	92.6	17.0	451	2,613,092	8.2	32.9	24.9	9.2	3.9	14.0	4.5
Davenport	189	1,495	142.1	44.5	855	4,516,209	10.1	25.5	18.9	13.0	2.7	16.5	5.2
Des Moines	447	3,030	431.1	116.0	1,933	12,154,999	7.4	25.8	16.5	12.1	5.5	26.5	3.2
Dubuque	144	873	96.3	22.8	648	3,329,064	12.8	20.3	16.1	22.9	5.6	13.5	4.5
Iowa City	118	883	254.7	37.5	836	3,543,459	10.2	17.4	10.4	18.2	6.6	18.5	8.6
Marion	56	389	36.9	13.0	187	1,102,380	6.1	30.3	21.4	10.1	6.2	19.2	6.6
Marshalltown	D	D	D	D	202	961,826	5.7	31.5	15.6	13.4	0.0	22.8	5.4
Mason City	72	352	34.0	9.5	264	1,250,056	6.8	23.1	16.1	12.2	7.7	23.4	4.4
Ottumwa	37	180	14.9	4.4	233	968,202	9.3	23.7	15.9	11.4	2.7	30.4	3.5
Sioux City	D	D	D	D	787	4,258,995	9.0	24.9	17.8	17.5	2.5	19.1	5.1
Urbandale	112	776	114.9	35.1	237	1,286,100	9.6	29.1	16.1	13.3	4.8	13.9	8.0
Waterloo	117	929	85.6	23.3	634	3,494,655	4.9	30.4	23.1	11.5	2.2	19.3	3.7
West Des Moines	161	1,498	293.8	80.1	458	2,735,559	9.7	18.5	15.1	12.7	11.2	17.1	4.7
KANSAS	5,069	27,987	3,986.2	927.7	X	X	X	X	X	X	X	X	X
Derby	D	D	D	D	206	838,515	22.6	29.1	15.1	8.2	2.9	12.2	7.2
Dodge City	44	243	33.8	7.2	237	841,843	14.1	29.4	13.0	11.1	0.7	20.1	7.2
Garden City	53	243	33.0	8.0	322	1,330,163	19.8	27.5	12.1	6.5	0.7	32.0	0.0
Hutchinson	78	405	43.9	9.8	388	1,692,937	9.1	29.1	25.0	8.2	2.0	22.6	0.0
Kansas City	190	1,349	355.5	47.6	2,690	15,933,139	8.2	25.9	22.3	5.8	3.8	25.6	0.1
Lawrence	178	1,198	216.5	41.1	2,243	13,193,908	3.7	9.6	8.5	2.5	59.8	13.5	0.0
Leavenworth	59	313	23.9	7.7	240	958,374	11.8	31.3	23.8	7.3	4.6	17.3	0.0
Leawood	77	1,039	178.6	59.6	260	1,468,797	17.9	29.1	24.0	12.4	1.6	11.8	0.0
Lenexa	84	722	102.7	30.9	428	2,250,458	15.8	31.7	22.7	11.5	2.6	10.9	0.0
Manhattan	107	1,081	290.4	47.6	407	1,733,009	13.8	0.0	29.3	14.3	3.7	37.6	0.0

1. Establishments subject to federal tax.

City	City government finances, 2017									
	General revenue							General expenditure		
		Intergovernmental		Taxes						
					Per capita[1] (dollars)				Per capita[1] (dollars)	
	Total (mil dol)	Total (mil dol)	Percent from state government	Total (mil dol)	Total	Property	Sales and gross receipts	Total (mil dol)	Total	Capital outlays
	117	118	119	120	121	122	123	124	125	126
INDIANA—Cont'd										
Brownsburg town	30.4	3.5	93.1	13.2	511	461	51	36.6	1,414	292
Carmel	102.8	23.2	88.3	46.4	477	431	46	123.4	1,267	54
Columbus	46.4	14.7	29.1	25.3	536	501	35	46.8	992	175
Crown Point	36.5	4.4	84.2	12.6	428	378	50	24.8	839	99
East Chicago	83.4	31.3	97.0	37.4	1,329	1,302	27	73.6	2,614	393
Elkhart	84.0	13.2	96.2	34.5	658	645	13	62.0	1,184	55
Evansville	196.3	45.3	74.1	65.4	553	511	30	197.1	1,665	283
Fishers	86.7	6.6	88.0	60.1	656	366	60	66.7	728	57
Fort Wayne	240.6	46.2	100.0	183.9	694	467	17	183.4	692	51
Franklin	21.8	3.0	88.6	12.8	514	477	37	35.3	1,414	144
Gary	125.1	22.3	84.0	39.1	516	498	18	133.1	1,757	240
Goshen	38.2	4.0	92.1	17.3	517	490	27	33.9	1,012	144
Greenwood	62.6	7.3	92.8	22.4	391	378	13	36.7	639	41
Hammond	168.6	61.9	98.7	52.0	680	641	33	170.7	2,231	365
Hobart	43.0	4.9	93.2	16.8	598	559	39	37.1	1,318	311
Indianapolis	3,008.5	919.2	61.9	424.6	492	325	0	2,462.1	2,851	95
Jeffersonville	91.7	2.1	100.0	46.7	988	709	0	58.9	1,246	332
Kokomo	82.7	29.4	45.6	37.9	655	651	4	60.4	1,044	59
Lafayette	122.9	19.0	86.6	46.8	649	623	15	91.6	1,271	380
Lawrence	36.2	4.4	86.5	14.7	302	289	13	30.7	631	17
Marion	40.6	8.6	97.2	19.5	692	688	4	30.1	1,067	72
Merrillville town	15.5	0.6	100.0	14.9	427	345	27	11.5	332	58
Michigan City	74.6	22.2	98.5	20.9	673	643	30	65.1	2,099	353
Mishawaka	95.6	3.7	0.0	70.8	1,446	1,245	14	98.6	2,014	760
Muncie	143.2	20.0	81.2	23.5	342	321	10	96.7	1,405	349
New Albany	71.7	6.7	92.1	23.2	637	602	21	56.1	1,538	228
Noblesville	88.8	18.0	88.6	43.7	706	609	98	64.9	1,050	167
Plainfield town	54.8	5.2	94.5	29.2	886	826	60	55.2	1,677	635
Portage	46.0	1.2	100.0	26.8	730	579	42	31.1	846	78
Richmond	52.0	15.0	80.1	15.9	449	432	16	55.1	1,554	99
Schererville town	34.0	2.7	87.8	9.0	316	265	51	18.9	661	42
South Bend	222.5	56.4	85.4	82.2	806	780	17	191.1	1,873	278
Terre Haute	102.6	20.5	62.6	33.5	551	539	10	89.2	1,467	429
Valparaiso	55.7	4.7	93.1	26.5	792	770	23	45.6	1,364	214
Westfield	28.2	4.8	76.6	18.7	474	404	69	48.8	1,236	369
West Lafayette	74.3	4.6	92.8	17.3	365	359	7	56.2	1,184	581
Zionsville town	31.5	14.2	99.7	12.5	455	397	58	23.7	862	49
IOWA	X	X	X	X	X	X	X	X	X	X
Ames	279.3	24.1	60.4	39.5	595	409	186	247.2	3,729	504
Ankeny	81.8	8.7	94.3	45.1	723	631	92	68.9	1,104	228
Bettendorf	69.7	11.7	60.9	35.2	984	757	227	68.3	1,908	569
Cedar Falls	83.0	14.2	55.4	34.2	834	627	208	73.4	1,788	694
Cedar Rapids	381.2	99.4	38.3	137.5	1,037	739	298	387.8	2,925	1,067
Council Bluffs	131.3	37.5	66.4	66.9	1,073	732	341	114.8	1,840	507
Davenport	188.2	41.4	54.1	98.4	961	715	247	167.1	1,633	381
Des Moines	463.7	96.0	39.3	183.3	846	663	183	411.3	1,898	251
Dubuque	147.4	46.1	38.9	53.5	918	597	321	125.0	2,144	533
Iowa City	146.2	39.2	60.6	64.0	845	761	85	128.1	1,693	507
Marion	51.0	6.9	76.0	29.8	754	590	165	55.2	1,399	438
Marshalltown	38.7	9.3	50.5	18.2	670	425	245	35.6	1,314	305
Mason City	40.6	7.3	69.5	21.7	793	561	232	42.0	1,538	324
Ottumwa	44.8	5.8	59.1	19.1	781	576	205	40.3	1,648	284
Sioux City	155.2	34.8	62.7	75.8	922	626	295	157.5	1,915	438
Urbandale	55.8	9.1	71.1	36.7	842	758	84	55.9	1,282	536
Waterloo	144.8	46.8	41.1	65.3	964	688	276	129.8	1,916	485
West Des Moines	121.3	24.1	64.0	71.4	1,088	981	108	127.0	1,937	640
KANSAS	X	X	X	X	X	X	X	X	X	X
Derby	30.3	5.6	27.0	15.0	636	427	209	27.2	1,150	243
Dodge City	48.6	8.1	47.4	20.7	752	400	352	49.4	1,793	438
Garden City	63.0	16.3	5.6	15.2	571	246	325	55.5	2,086	588
Hutchinson	55.4	8.0	48.2	34.4	841	305	536	83.1	2,032	932
Kansas City	398.0	65.7	90.9	233.0	1,525	694	824	397.1	2,600	393
Lawrence	389.1	24.2	49.3	74.5	771	369	402	374.2	3,873	598
Leavenworth	39.6	6.6	26.9	21.9	605	200	405	37.9	1,047	202
Leawood	52.6	5.4	57.2	40.3	1,163	549	614	54.6	1,576	225
Lenexa	110.3	17.8	47.3	68.0	1,269	638	632	134.2	2,507	1,242
Manhattan	100.8	9.0	35.2	66.0	1,197	538	659	76.7	1,391	228

1. Based on population estimated as of July 1 of the year shown.

City	City government finances, 2017 (cont.)												
	General expenditure (cont.)												
	Percent of total for:										Debt outstanding		
	Public welfare	Highways	Parking facilities	Education	Health and hospitals	Police protection	Sewerage and sanitation	Parks and recreation	Housing and community development	Interest on debt	Total (mil dol)	Per capita[1] (dollars)	Debt issued during year
	127	128	129	130	131	132	133	134	135	136	137	138	139
INDIANA—Cont'd													
Brownsburg town	0.0	2.8	0.0	0.0	0.0	15.2	16.5	6.5	0.0	3.9	35.5	1,373	0.0
Carmel	0.0	11.8	0.0	0.0	1.1	15.1	6.0	10.0	0.0	16.4	753.7	7,738	0.0
Columbus	0.0	11.2	0.0	0.0	1.1	20.2	12.4	13.6	0.6	0.0	14.9	316	0.0
Crown Point	0.0	15.2	0.0	0.0	0.3	36.3	1.3	13.2	0.1	2.4	27.2	921	0.0
East Chicago	0.0	10.9	0.0	0.0	0.7	16.0	8.5	2.9	2.5	4.8	98.2	3,488	0.0
Elkhart	0.0	16.5	0.0	0.0	0.2	17.1	1.8	3.5	1.3	2.4	47.7	910	0.0
Evansville	0.0	4.1	0.2	0.0	2.9	17.7	15.3	5.5	1.9	12.9	745.6	6,301	0.0
Fishers	0.0	6.3	0.0	0.0	0.0	22.1	0.1	1.9	1.6	0.0	325.6	3,554	66.3
Fort Wayne	0.0	22.0	0.3	0.0	1.4	34.1	5.0	7.3	5.5	0.0	497.7	1,877	24.6
Franklin	0.0	21.2	0.0	0.0	0.0	12.0	6.0	8.1	0.0	2.5	21.7	868	0.0
Gary	0.0	1.6	0.0	0.0	2.2	13.0	19.5	4.1	2.9	3.3	84.3	1,113	0.0
Goshen	0.0	8.1	2.5	0.0	0.0	16.8	11.1	6.6	0.7	3.8	85.8	2,562	0.0
Greenwood	0.0	16.5	0.0	0.0	0.0	14.6	28.3	7.2	0.0	5.7	58.3	1,017	0.0
Hammond	0.0	6.3	0.0	0.0	0.1	14.2	21.4	6.3	2.0	4.9	260.5	3,406	0.0
Hobart	0.0	22.8	0.0	0.0	0.0	15.6	24.2	2.3	0.0	3.0	26.8	954	0.0
Indianapolis	0.0	0.0	0.0	0.0	53.8	9.0	1.8	3.4	0.0	8.3	3,572.6	4,137	238.3
Jeffersonville	0.0	7.1	0.0	0.0	1.0	14.4	15.5	10.0	0.0	0.0	115.6	2,447	3.6
Kokomo	0.0	0.0	0.0	0.0	0.0	20.5	19.8	5.6	0.0	1.7	31.1	538	11.8
Lafayette	0.0	25.7	0.3	0.0	0.3	17.0	2.4	5.1	1.2	6.0	148.0	2,052	0.0
Lawrence	0.0	8.9	0.0	0.0	5.7	19.7	23.7	3.5	0.0	3.4	26.3	541	0.0
Marion	0.0	15.2	0.0	0.0	0.3	21.5	4.9	3.5	0.0	4.5	22.7	806	0.0
Merrillville town	0.0	31.2	0.0	0.0	0.3	30.2	1.3	1.2	0.0	0.0	31.2	896	3.2
Michigan City	0.0	4.9	0.0	0.0	0.5	22.3	24.0	5.8	1.1	1.0	80.9	2,608	0.0
Mishawaka	0.0	18.9	0.0	0.0	0.0	13.5	0.0	4.4	22.6	0.4	76.1	1,554	0.0
Muncie	0.0	3.9	0.3	0.0	0.6	11.8	37.9	2.0	0.4	7.3	176.4	2,562	0.0
New Albany	0.0	8.3	0.1	0.0	0.9	14.0	28.0	3.8	0.1	5.3	74.7	2,049	0.0
Noblesville	0.0	13.6	0.1	0.0	0.0	14.2	7.3	5.6	0.0	14.4	233.6	3,775	0.0
Plainfield town	0.0	2.1	0.0	0.0	0.0	10.3	9.6	7.9	0.0	9.4	168.9	5,128	0.0
Portage	0.0	10.2	0.0	0.0	0.0	19.1	28.4	3.0	0.0	8.8	68.2	1,856	0.0
Richmond	0.0	3.4	0.1	0.0	0.0	13.1	27.7	4.4	0.0	4.9	70.1	1,979	0.0
Schererville town	0.0	7.9	0.0	0.0	4.6	29.1	28.0	6.4	0.0	5.4	46.2	1,617	0.0
South Bend	0.0	5.1	0.4	0.0	3.9	16.7	12.6	6.3	0.0	3.9	219.6	2,152	0.3
Terre Haute	0.0	4.0	0.0	0.0	1.6	13.7	12.7	3.1	4.8	6.7	223.0	3,666	0.0
Valparaiso	0.0	20.7	0.1	0.0	0.0	8.7	7.0	6.4	0.0	7.2	81.6	2,442	0.0
Westfield	0.0	12.0	0.0	0.0	0.3	13.0	4.8	15.1	0.0	4.5	100.3	2,540	0.0
West Lafayette	0.2	2.9	0.0	0.0	0.0	11.8	12.5	3.6	0.3	10.7	150.3	3,165	0.0
Zionsville town	0.0	0.5	0.0	0.0	0.0	13.2	9.7	18.3	0.0	2.7	22.1	804	0.0
IOWA	X	X	X	X	X	X	X	X	X	X	X	X	X
Ames	0.5	1.7	0.4	0.0	71.4	3.6	5.2	1.6	0.2	2.2	221.7	3,344	0.0
Ankeny	0.0	19.9	0.0	0.0	5.0	12.4	23.1	12.6	0.0	7.6	148.9	2,387	0.0
Bettendorf	0.0	4.2	0.0	0.0	0.0	10.8	12.8	2.9	0.0	7.3	133.4	3,728	0.0
Cedar Falls	0.0	12.3	0.2	0.0	0.4	6.8	9.3	6.4	2.0	1.2	67.3	1,640	0.0
Cedar Rapids	0.0	5.0	0.3	0.0	0.3	11.7	15.8	2.9	2.0	3.7	489.6	3,694	0.0
Council Bluffs	0.2	5.8	0.1	0.0	2.7	15.1	12.5	7.4	0.5	0.0	90.8	1,455	0.0
Davenport	0.0	10.4	0.6	0.0	0.0	15.0	12.4	4.4	4.4	5.4	317.3	3,101	0.0
Des Moines	2.2	7.1	2.1	0.0	0.2	15.6	14.0	2.5	4.9	5.5	561.4	2,591	0.0
Dubuque	0.4	5.4	1.3	0.0	2.2	11.7	8.3	6.6	7.2	6.9	271.2	4,652	0.0
Iowa City	0.2	5.1	2.9	0.0	0.6	9.8	13.3	5.6	8.8	2.0	128.7	1,701	0.0
Marion	0.0	7.2	0.0	0.0	0.1	13.1	19.2	4.6	1.5	2.7	59.9	1,518	0.0
Marshalltown	0.1	21.5	0.1	0.0	3.7	16.6	11.7	4.5	3.7	2.9	58.8	2,169	7.1
Mason City	0.7	6.9	0.3	0.0	0.7	14.6	8.0	4.8	0.0	2.4	36.6	1,339	0.0
Ottumwa	0.2	9.3	1.4	0.0	1.2	11.4	34.4	3.2	0.0	1.8	46.3	1,897	0.0
Sioux City	0.0	6.1	0.8	0.0	0.4	12.5	16.2	8.5	5.6	4.2	255.9	3,112	0.0
Urbandale	0.0	9.0	0.0	0.0	0.1	14.3	4.3	9.1	1.2	2.8	77.7	1,783	0.0
Waterloo	0.2	12.8	0.5	0.0	1.7	14.3	9.8	6.1	9.8	2.2	112.0	1,653	0.0
West Des Moines	0.9	7.3	0.0	0.0	4.0	7.9	15.5	4.1	0.5	3.2	128.9	1,966	0.1
KANSAS	X	X	X	X	X	X	X	X	X	X	X	X	X
Derby	0.0	16.1	0.0	0.0	0.3	13.1	8.9	1.9	0.0	7.1	64.6	2,733	5.8
Dodge City	0.0	5.9	0.0	0.0	0.9	10.4	14.8	34.1	0.4	14.3	233.4	8,462	43.1
Garden City	0.0	6.0	0.0	0.0	0.0	15.3	8.5	6.9	0.0	1.6	41.0	1,539	2.0
Hutchinson	0.0	13.1	0.0	0.0	0.7	11.6	9.4	35.8	1.8	1.4	78.3	1,916	31.1
Kansas City	0.0	3.1	0.1	0.0	5.4	13.0	8.8	1.8	0.8	11.0	1,749.6	11,455	297.3
Lawrence	0.0	2.5	0.3	0.0	58.3	5.1	12.2	2.8	0.3	2.4	388.7	4,022	73.7
Leavenworth	0.0	16.8	0.0	0.0	0.7	17.5	14.5	7.4	8.9	2.2	29.1	803	6.6
Leawood	0.0	34.8	0.0	0.0	0.0	19.5	0.0	14.7	0.0	4.3	48.9	1,411	10.2
Lenexa	0.0	55.9	0.0	0.0	0.0	11.2	1.8	4.5	0.0	9.9	397.5	7,423	85.3
Manhattan	0.0	6.6	0.0	0.0	0.7	20.6	11.0	10.1	0.8	16.1	373.6	6,777	22.6

1. Based on population estimated as of July 1 of the year shown.

Table D. Cities — Land Area and Population

STATE	Place code	City	Land area[1] (sq. mi)	Population, 2021: Total persons 2021	Population, 2021: Rank	Population, 2021: Per square mile	Race 2020, Race alone[2] (percent): White	Black or African American	American Indian, Alaskan Native	Asian	Hawaiian Pacific Islander	Some other race	Two or more races (percent)
			1	2	3	4	5	6	7	8	9	10	11
		KANSAS—Cont'd											
20	52575	Olathe	62.0	143,014	191	2,306.7	73.9	6.0	0.5	4.5	0.1	4.8	10.3
20	53775	Overland Park	75.2	197,106	127	2,621.1	75.0	4.6	0.4	9.3	0.1	2.6	8.1
20	62700	Salina	25.8	46,481	857	1,801.6	78.1	3.8	0.7	2.3	0.1	4.5	10.4
20	64500	Shawnee	42.0	67,511	557	1,607.4	78.2	5.7	0.5	3.2	0.0	3.1	9.3
20	71000	Topeka	61.6	125,963	222	2,044.9	68.4	10.4	1.4	1.6	0.1	6.1	11.9
20	79000	Wichita	162.0	395,699	49	2,442.6	63.4	11.0	1.3	5.1	0.1	7.4	11.7
21	00000	KENTUCKY	39,491.4	4,509,394	X	114.2	82.4	8.0	0.3	1.7	0.1	2.1	5.4
21	08902	Bowling Green	40.4	73,529	501	1,820.0	64.3	13.8	0.4	8.0	0.8	5.5	7.1
21	17848	Covington	13.2	40,837	967	3,093.7	75.7	11.6	0.5	0.6	0.1	3.7	7.8
21	24274	Elizabethtown	27.5	31,931	1,237	1,161.1	74.9	11.5	0.4	2.8	0.2	1.9	8.2
21	27982	Florence	10.7	32,132	1,225	3,003.0	76.9	8.3	0.5	2.8	0.3	4.1	7.2
21	28900	Frankfort	14.8	28,595	1,366	1,932.1	74.6	12.9	0.4	2.2	0.0	2.6	7.2
21	30700	Georgetown	17.0	37,730	1,054	2,219.4	82.6	7.0	0.3	1.3	0.0	2.0	6.7
21	35866	Henderson	16.1	27,716	1,403	1,721.5	78.1	12.3	0.3	0.7	0.1	2.3	6.2
21	37918	Hopkinsville	31.8	30,683	1,286	964.9	58.5	31.2	0.5	1.3	0.1	2.1	6.3
21	39142	Independence	17.6	28,920	1,350	1,643.2	89.5	2.2	0.1	1.0	0.1	1.2	5.9
21	40222	Jeffersontown	10.6	28,671	1,361	2,704.8	72.4	11.8	0.3	4.4	0.1	3.5	7.5
21	46027	Lexington-Fayette	283.6	321,793	59	1,134.7	68.3	14.9	0.3	4.2	0.0	5.2	7.1
21	48003	Louisville/Jefferson County	263.2	628,594	28	2,388.3	63.8	21.6	0.3	3.5	0.1	3.4	7.3
21	56136	Nicholasville	14.8	31,490	1,257	2,127.7	84.2	6.1	0.2	0.8	0.1	2.0	6.6
21	58620	Owensboro	20.7	60,011	644	2,899.1	80.7	7.1	0.3	3.5	0.1	2.3	6.0
21	58836	Paducah	20.3	26,278	1,475	1,294.5	67.7	22.2	0.4	1.0	0.0	1.9	6.8
21	65226	Richmond	20.3	35,756	1,112	1,761.4	80.8	7.5	0.3	1.4	0.1	1.8	8.0
22	00000	LOUISIANA	43,204.5	4,624,047	X	107.0	57.1	31.4	0.7	1.9	0.0	3.1	5.9
22	00975	Alexandria	28.5	44,787	886	1,571.5	37.1	54.9	0.4	2.2	0.0	1.1	4.2
22	05000	Baton Rouge	86.3	222,185	101	2,574.6	35.2	53.8	0.3	3.2	0.0	3.0	4.4
22	08920	Bossier City	43.9	62,865	611	1,432.0	52.7	30.7	0.6	2.4	0.1	5.6	7.9
22	13960	Central	62.3	29,958	1,309	480.9	79.9	11.7	0.3	0.8	0.0	1.9	5.5
22	36255	Houma	14.5	33,018	1,193	2,277.1	59.3	24.3	4.5	1.4	0.0	4.0	6.4
22	39475	Kenner	14.9	65,364	584	4,386.8	44.8	21.9	0.6	4.8	0.0	14.8	13.1
22	40735	Lafayette	55.9	121,771	234	2,178.4	58.1	30.7	0.4	2.6	0.0	2.3	5.8
22	41155	Lake Charles	45.7	81,097	436	1,774.6	42.5	46.2	0.4	2.6	0.1	2.6	5.6
22	51410	Monroe	29.7	47,284	844	1,592.1	30.6	63.5	0.2	1.8	0.0	0.9	3.0
22	54035	New Iberia	11.1	27,989	1,393	2,521.5	45.3	44.4	0.3	2.8	0.0	2.0	5.1
22	55000	New Orleans	169.5	376,971	53	2,224.0	32.9	54.2	0.3	2.8	0.0	3.2	6.4
22	70000	Shreveport	108.1	184,021	141	1,702.3	36.0	56.0	0.4	1.6	0.1	1.6	4.3
22	70805	Slidell	15.0	28,658	1,362	1,910.5	62.1	23.9	0.7	1.8	0.0	2.8	8.5
23	00000	MAINE	30,844.8	1,372,247	X	44.5	90.8	1.9	0.6	1.2	0.0	0.7	4.7
23	02795	Bangor	34.3	31,921	1,238	930.6	88.0	2.3	1.0	2.2	0.0	0.9	5.6
23	38740	Lewiston	34.1	36,617	1,084	1,073.8	77.9	13.9	0.4	1.2	0.1	1.0	5.5
23	60545	Portland	21.5	68,313	553	3,177.3	79.0	10.2	0.3	3.2	0.0	1.6	5.6
23	71990	South Portland	12.1	26,993	1,442	2,230.8	83.9	5.9	0.4	3.4	0.1	1.4	5.0
24	00000	MARYLAND	9,711.1	6,165,129	X	634.9	48.7	29.5	0.5	6.8	0.1	6.7	7.8
24	01600	Annapolis	7.2	40,687	972	5,651.0	52.4	21.7	0.7	2.5	0.0	14.5	8.1
24	04000	Baltimore	80.9	576,498	30	7,126.1	27.8	57.8	0.4	3.6	0.0	4.8	5.5
24	08775	Bowie	20.4	57,644	688	2,825.7	29.0	53.5	0.4	4.6	0.0	4.7	7.9
24	18750	College Park	5.6	35,110	1,137	6,269.6	50.2	14.9	0.5	17.2	0.0	8.9	8.3
24	30325	Frederick	23.9	79,588	452	3,330.0	52.1	19.1	0.7	5.7	0.1	10.9	11.4
24	31175	Gaithersburg	10.3	69,101	545	6,708.8	34.8	16.6	0.9	19.1	0.1	17.1	11.4
24	36075	Hagerstown	12.6	43,487	919	3,451.3	62.4	19.9	0.4	2.1	0.1	4.5	10.7
24	45900	Laurel	4.8	29,490	1,326	6,143.8	18.4	50.3	1.0	8.2	0.0	12.5	9.6
24	67675	Rockville	13.6	67,139	560	4,936.7	47.4	10.9	0.6	21.6	0.1	7.9	11.5
24	69925	Salisbury	13.8	32,930	1,197	2,386.2	41.2	42.0	0.5	3.7	0.1	5.0	7.4
25	00000	MASSACHUSETTS	7,801.0	6,984,723	X	895.4	69.6	7.0	0.3	7.2	0.0	7.1	8.7
25	00840	Agawam Town	23.3	28,494	1,368	1,222.9	87.3	2.1	0.2	2.6	0.0	2.0	5.8
25	01370	Amherst Town	27.6	39,378	1,007	1,426.7	63.1	6.1	0.4	17.8	0.0	3.4	9.3
25	02690	Attleboro	26.8	46,580	855	1,738.1	77.1	5.8	0.3	4.7	0.0	4.5	7.4
25	03690	Barnstable Town	59.9	49,583	807	827.8	77.2	4.6	0.5	1.8	0.1	4.7	11.1
25	05595	Beverly	15.1	42,446	942	2,811.0	86.0	2.3	0.1	2.2	0.0	2.8	6.5
25	07000	Boston	48.3	654,776	24	13,556.4	47.1	20.6	0.4	11.3	0.1	10.1	10.5
25	07740	Braintree Town	13.8	38,822	1,023	2,813.2	70.8	3.4	0.2	17.2	0.0	2.4	6.0
25	08130	Bridgewater Town	27.2	28,805	1,355	1,059.0	82.5	7.2	0.2	1.9	0.0	1.8	6.4
25	09000	Brockton	21.3	105,446	300	4,950.5	29.4	35.0	0.5	2.2	0.0	12.3	20.7
25	11000	Cambridge	6.4	117,090	245	18,295.3	57.3	10.6	0.2	19.2	0.0	3.4	9.2

1. Dry land or land partially or temporarily covered by water. 2. Hispanic or Latino persons may be of any race.

City	Percent Hispanic or Latino[1], 2020	Percent foreign born, 2016–2020	Age of population (percent), 2016–2020: Under 18 years	18 to 24 years	25 to 34 years	35 to 44 years	45 to 54 years	55 to 64 years	65 years and over	Median age, 2016–2020	Percent female, 2016–2020	Population: Census counts: 2010	2020	Percent change: 2010–2020	2020–2021
	12	13	14	15	16	17	18	19	20	21	22	23	24	25	26
KANSAS—Cont'd															
Olathe	12.4	10.9	28.3	7.6	13.8	15.4	13.4	9.9	11.6	35.2	50.8	125,900	141,238	12.2	1.3
Overland Park	7.8	11.5	22.9	8.3	14.1	13.3	13.4	12.6	15.4	38.5	50.6	173,329	197,295	13.8	-0.1
Salina	13.4	5.4	23.3	9.2	13.5	11.8	12.0	13.4	16.8	38.0	50.3	47,777	46,868	-1.9	-0.8
Shawnee	9.2	6.8	24.4	9.4	11.9	14.2	14.5	12.0	13.5	38.2	51.7	62,205	67,340	8.3	0.3
Topeka	16.4	4.9	22.9	9.4	13.4	12.0	11.3	12.8	18.1	38.1	52.3	127,630	126,515	-0.9	-0.4
Wichita	18.3	9.9	25.0	9.7	14.9	12.2	11.4	12.2	14.5	35.3	50.6	382,424	397,070	3.8	-0.3
KENTUCKY	4.6	4.0	22.6	9.4	13.0	12.4	12.9	13.3	16.4	39.0	50.8	4,339,330	4,505,836	3.8	0.1
Bowling Green	9.7	13.3	21.4	23.5	15.4	11.6	8.1	8.4	11.5	27.6	51.5	59,405	72,524	22.1	1.4
Covington	7.0	4.6	21.9	6.1	18.9	14.2	12.3	13.6	13.0	36.7	49.1	40,482	41,058	1.4	-0.5
Elizabethtown	5.5	5.5	23.6	8.5	15.3	15.0	11.1	11.5	15.0	36.7	51.9	28,053	31,447	12.1	1.5
Florence	8.7	8.7	24.4	8.1	15.1	12.4	12.0	11.1	16.9	37.6	50.0	29,531	31,830	7.8	0.9
Frankfort	5.2	5.5	22.2	10.5	17.2	11.5	11.6	12.2	14.8	35.1	52.3	27,272	28,641	5.0	-0.2
Georgetown	5.3	3.3	25.7	11.6	16.4	14.8	11.5	10.0	10.0	33.0	52.1	29,137	37,048	27.2	1.8
Henderson	4.1	1.7	23.2	7.9	14.1	11.9	12.0	13.8	17.1	39.6	52.5	28,928	28,013	-3.2	-1.1
Hopkinsville	5.0	2.5	25.1	9.5	13.1	11.2	11.7	12.2	17.2	37.3	51.4	31,975	30,839	-3.6	-0.5
Independence	3.2	2.9	27.0	7.8	16.5	14.0	14.9	10.1	9.6	34.2	50.4	24,759	28,557	15.3	1.3
Jeffersontown	7.7	10.0	23.2	5.7	14.7	12.8	12.3	14.3	17.0	39.8	52.0	27,813	28,904	3.9	-0.8
Lexington-Fayette	9.2	10.0	20.9	13.9	15.4	13.1	11.7	11.5	13.4	34.8	51.0	295,875	322,570	9.0	-0.2
Louisville/Jefferson County	7.5	8.1	22.1	8.6	14.8	12.5	12.4	13.4	16.1	38.4	51.7	595,730	632,689	6.2	-0.6
Nicholasville	5.1	4.3	25.6	8.1	12.5	14.6	13.7	11.8	13.8	37.7	52.9	28,018	31,112	11.0	1.2
Owensboro	4.8	4.0	23.8	9.5	13.4	11.1	11.1	12.6	18.5	38.4	52.3	57,477	60,205	4.7	-0.3
Paducah	3.9	2.0	19.0	8.2	11.4	13.2	13.5	15.3	19.4	43.8	53.6	25,008	26,538	6.1	-1.0
Richmond	4.3	3.3	18.3	28.8	14.6	12.3	7.1	8.3	10.5	26.2	53.5	31,320	34,716	10.8	3.0
LOUISIANA	6.9	4.1	23.5	9.2	14.3	12.6	12.1	12.9	15.4	37.2	51.2	4,533,500	4,657,757	2.7	-0.7
Alexandria	2.8	3.3	23.0	9.3	14.5	11.8	11.9	12.6	16.9	37.2	52.0	47,901	45,407	-5.2	-1.4
Baton Rouge	5.9	5.5	21.3	17.3	15.2	10.1	10.0	11.4	14.7	32.0	52.9	229,279	225,128	-1.8	-1.3
Bossier City	10.7	4.8	23.6	10.2	16.6	13.1	10.4	11.5	14.8	34.8	51.1	61,596	62,722	1.8	0.2
Central	4.6	2.0	26.0	8.0	10.0	15.0	11.9	13.3	15.9	38.4	49.6	27,215	29,962	10.1	0.0
Houma	7.3	2.6	24.8	7.7	15.4	11.2	12.9	12.5	15.5	36.3	50.2	33,694	33,368	-1.0	-1.0
Kenner	30.0	20.0	24.6	7.4	15.4	11.9	11.7	13.1	15.9	36.5	52.0	66,663	66,474	-0.3	-1.7
Lafayette	6.2	4.6	20.8	11.2	15.7	11.9	11.1	13.8	15.6	36.4	51.9	121,724	122,018	0.2	-0.2
Lake Charles	5.6	3.6	22.8	9.9	16.6	11.8	11.6	11.4	15.9	35.5	52.0	72,375	85,434	18.0	-5.1
Monroe	2.1	2.0	27.0	12.5	13.3	11.7	9.5	11.7	14.3	33.0	52.1	48,927	47,780	-2.3	-1.0
New Iberia	5.1	2.7	27.0	7.8	13.7	12.1	11.9	11.7	15.8	36.4	52.0	30,607	28,518	-6.8	-1.9
New Orleans	8.1	5.4	20.0	8.6	17.8	13.7	11.9	13.2	14.8	37.2	52.7	343,828	383,997	11.7	-1.8
Shreveport	3.5	2.7	24.0	8.7	15.6	12.1	10.6	12.5	16.5	36.1	52.9	200,941	187,993	-6.4	-2.1
Slidell	8.3	3.7	24.0	7.1	12.3	13.7	11.3	11.5	20.0	39.5	53.1	27,290	28,699	5.2	-0.1
MAINE	2.0	3.6	18.7	8.0	12.0	11.5	13.4	15.7	20.6	44.8	51.0	1,328,354	1,362,359	2.6	0.7
Bangor	2.4	4.3	17.8	11.3	18.6	9.4	12.7	12.7	17.5	37.9	52.6	33,031	31,821	-3.7	0.3
Lewiston	2.5	6.9	20.2	11.2	13.6	10.0	11.9	14.4	18.8	39.5	50.9	36,594	36,806	0.6	-0.5
Portland	3.9	11.0	15.4	10.0	21.8	14.1	11.3	12.0	15.4	36.5	51.2	66,190	68,402	3.3	-0.1
South Portland	3.4	9.6	16.6	11.9	14.2	10.2	12.9	15.4	18.7	42.2	51.8	25,021	26,492	5.9	1.9
MARYLAND	11.8	15.2	22.2	8.8	13.7	12.9	13.5	13.4	15.4	38.8	51.5	5,773,787	6,177,224	7.0	-0.2
Annapolis	22.9	13.2	22.2	8.6	14.3	12.8	11.2	13.7	17.2	38.3	50.7	38,334	40,788	6.4	-0.2
Baltimore	7.8	8.1	20.5	9.6	19.0	12.6	11.6	12.7	14.0	35.5	53.1	620,777	585,708	-5.6	-1.6
Bowie	9.0	13.9	21.5	7.0	11.9	12.1	16.1	16.5	14.9	42.7	52.8	54,822	58,310	6.4	-1.1
College Park	15.3	22.8	10.0	50.7	12.8	7.9	6.1	6.2	6.3	21.7	47.6	30,410	35,423	16.5	-0.9
Frederick	20.9	19.2	21.7	9.7	16.6	13.7	13.2	11.7	13.5	36.4	51.5	65,339	78,062	19.5	2.0
Gaithersburg	28.5	39.1	22.0	9.1	14.1	16.2	13.6	12.3	12.7	37.6	51.5	59,891	69,657	16.3	-0.8
Hagerstown	9.8	7.0	25.6	7.6	15.4	12.5	13.7	10.7	14.6	35.9	52.1	39,652	43,489	9.7	0.0
Laurel	21.0	28.9	24.7	6.8	17.6	14.7	13.9	11.6	10.7	36.0	52.8	24,909	30,036	20.6	-1.8
Rockville	16.9	33.5	21.2	7.1	14.1	15.6	12.5	11.8	17.7	39.5	53.0	61,298	67,101	9.5	0.1
Salisbury	9.2	12.2	21.6	21.0	15.9	10.0	8.0	11.2	12.3	29.2	53.4	30,268	32,849	8.5	0.2
MASSACHUSETTS	12.6	16.9	19.8	10.1	14.3	12.2	13.3	13.6	16.5	39.6	51.5	6,547,788	7,029,917	7.4	-0.6
Agawam Town	6.4	6.9	18.1	6.8	12.6	10.3	15.1	16.2	20.9	47.1	52.0	28,438	28,699	0.9	-0.7
Amherst Town	9.7	17.2	9.2	58.4	7.0	5.6	5.3	6.3	8.2	21.4	50.1	37,819	39,470	4.4	-0.2
Attleboro	8.9	10.0	21.7	7.0	14.4	13.6	13.4	14.1	15.8	40.1	51.1	43,570	46,429	6.6	0.3
Barnstable Town	5.4	15.3	18.1	7.1	10.8	11.4	13.0	16.3	23.3	47.5	51.2	45,195	48,923	8.2	1.3
Beverly	6.3	8.9	19.0	12.5	12.4	10.8	13.5	14.2	17.7	40.6	53.1	39,504	42,714	8.1	-0.6
Boston	18.7	28.2	15.8	14.8	24.4	12.5	10.6	10.1	11.8	32.4	52.0	617,779	676,216	9.5	-3.2
Braintree Town	4.8	19.1	21.8	7.4	12.1	13.9	14.0	14.1	16.7	41.1	51.9	35,726	39,168	9.6	-0.9
Bridgewater Town	4.4	5.9	16.2	20.1	12.4	11.4	12.8	11.2	15.9	35.9	47.6	26,569	28,432	7.0	1.3
Brockton	12.1	32.5	25.9	9.3	13.9	12.6	12.9	12.3	13.0	35.6	52.6	93,767	105,652	12.7	-0.2
Cambridge	9.1	29.2	12.4	19.4	28.3	12.9	8.1	7.2	11.6	30.6	49.8	105,155	117,779	12.0	-0.6

1. May be of any race.

City	Households, 2016–2020							Persons in group quarters, 2016–2020	Serious crimes known to police[2], 2020				Educational attainment, 2016–2020		
			Percent						Violent		Property			Attainment[4] (percent)	
	Number	Persons per household	Family	Married couple family	Female family	Non-family	One person		Number	Rate	Number	Rate	Population age 25 and over	High school graduate or less	Bachelor's degree or more
	27	28	29	30	31	32	33	34	35	36	37	38	39	40	41
KANSAS—Cont'd															
Olathe	48,919	2.81	74.5	60.1	9.6	25.5	19.7	1,519	355	249.6	1,940	1,364.0	89,279	22.2	50.1
Overland Park	79,894	2.41	63.5	51.7	8.6	36.5	30.0	1,200	411	207.5	3,906	1,972.4	133,179	15.0	61.3
Salina	19,245	2.35	58.0	43.7	10.2	42.0	36.9	1,401	NA	NA	NA	NA	31,555	38.1	27.1
Shawnee	24,309	2.69	71.9	61.3	8.1	28.1	22.0	357	191	288.5	1,130	1,706.7	43,561	20.2	49.7
Topeka	54,092	2.24	56.1	38.4	13.5	43.9	37.3	4,646	NA	NA	NA	NA	85,220	42.2	28.5
Wichita	154,683	2.49	60.1	42.6	12.6	39.9	33.2	5,090	NA	NA	NA	NA	254,991	38.0	30.7
KENTUCKY	1,748,053	2.48	65.2	48.0	12.2	34.8	28.7	131,825	11,600	259.1	79,673	1,779.5	3,034,491	45.5	25.0
Bowling Green	27,504	2.34	54.0	33.4	14.7	46.0	33.6	7,151	247	343.7	3,195	4,446.1	39,451	38.8	31.6
Covington	17,397	2.26	49.5	28.2	15.0	50.5	39.1	1,094	154	381.9	1,049	2,601.4	29,128	45.0	28.3
Elizabethtown	13,039	2.23	56.5	38.2	13.0	43.5	35.0	1,155	44	144.2	286	937.6	20,507	31.1	27.7
Florence	13,238	2.45	60.8	39.8	15.5	39.2	33.0	318	55	164.7	1,561	4,674.1	22,092	40.7	25.1
Frankfort	11,913	2.21	55.6	30.9	17.1	44.4	37.9	1,394	69	248.2	855	3,075.2	18,641	39.4	30.1
Georgetown	13,297	2.49	70.5	50.9	14.0	29.5	22.8	1,270	63	176.5	798	2,235.2	21,546	36.2	29.6
Henderson	12,060	2.24	60.5	38.8	15.6	39.5	34.9	1,435	82	291.5	737	2,620.4	19,615	50.4	17.6
Hopkinsville	13,225	2.21	58.1	32.2	19.1	41.9	34.0	1,860	89	291.5	930	3,046.0	20,291	46.6	19.5
Independence	9,507	2.96	74.9	58.1	10.5	25.1	18.0	5	21	72.5	130	448.9	18,322	35.6	30.7
Jeffersontown	11,572	2.40	64.5	50.1	10.1	35.5	30.9	197	29	104.7	706	2,548.7	19,845	30.2	36.6
Lexington-Fayette	130,926	2.36	56.9	41.1	11.3	43.1	32.4	12,680	1,043	320.1	9,357	2,871.6	210,053	27.1	45.0
Louisville/Jefferson County	316,411	2.38	59.0	40.2	13.9	41.0	34.0	16,228	NA	NA	NA	NA	532,550	35.3	33.9
Nicholasville	11,244	2.69	67.3	44.4	18.7	32.7	24.6	266	67	214.8	852	2,731.6	20,257	51.0	20.5
Owensboro	25,414	2.27	59.5	39.7	14.1	40.5	33.2	2,165	161	266.4	2,326	3,849.1	39,877	43.5	24.6
Paducah	11,592	2.05	49.7	31.2	14.8	50.3	42.1	1,176	85	342.1	993	3,996.0	18,147	41.3	26.5
Richmond	13,351	2.33	47.0	30.2	13.0	53.0	38.4	4,631	67	182.6	950	2,589.2	18,902	36.7	32.1
LOUISIANA	1,751,956	2.59	63.7	43.4	15.5	36.3	30.7	129,391	29,704	639.4	133,989	2,884.4	3,139,520	47.4	24.9
Alexandria	17,738	2.50	59.9	31.3	23.5	40.1	35.7	2,160	850	1,848.4	3,317	7,213.1	31,533	50.7	24.1
Baton Rouge	85,091	2.51	52.3	30.2	17.4	47.7	38.8	8,344	2,087	951.9	10,580	4,825.7	136,316	39.7	34.9
Bossier City	27,277	2.41	61.2	40.2	16.1	38.8	32.0	2,627	609	884.3	3,201	4,648.0	45,259	40.7	23.3
Central	9,891	2.95	78.7	62.4	13.2	21.3	17.2	45	NA	NA	NA	NA	19,305	41.4	26.8
Houma	12,909	2.54	63.3	39.6	15.4	36.7	29.8	235	NA	NA	NA	NA	22,326	51.8	18.6
Kenner	24,249	2.73	63.8	43.0	16.8	36.2	31.1	473	178	268.4	1,781	2,686.0	45,391	46.4	26.2
Lafayette	50,252	2.43	58.8	41.2	13.7	41.2	32.0	4,586	712	562.1	5,725	4,519.3	86,174	35.1	39.3
Lake Charles	33,093	2.27	56.5	34.4	18.5	43.5	34.6	2,781	409	517.2	2,511	3,175.4	52,368	42.0	26.3
Monroe	17,162	2.59	53.1	26.8	21.8	46.9	41.6	3,430	1,399	2,969.1	2,883	6,118.6	29,004	48.1	25.8
New Iberia	11,285	2.53	65.4	37.6	18.2	34.6	29.3	398	NA	NA	NA	NA	18,888	58.4	19.9
New Orleans	154,826	2.43	46.2	25.9	16.9	53.8	46.5	14,514	5,215	1,324.3	17,876	4,539.6	279,378	35.1	38.0
Shreveport	75,680	2.44	57.1	33.3	19.6	42.9	37.5	4,972	1,713	923.0	8,907	4,799.3	127,689	43.8	26.1
Slidell	10,805	2.53	61.5	38.6	16.8	38.5	29.9	414	77	278.3	878	3,173.2	19,142	40.0	23.4
MAINE	569,551	2.29	61.4	48.3	8.9	38.6	29.8	36,347	1,466	108.6	15,610	1,156.2	982,385	38.1	32.5
Bangor	13,968	2.12	52.1	36.1	13.5	47.9	36.2	2,414	51	158.5	1,207	3,750.9	22,699	34.9	36.7
Lewiston	15,844	2.14	53.1	36.5	10.8	46.9	37.5	2,291	97	268.1	639	1,765.9	24,818	51.2	20.2
Portland	30,796	2.10	42.5	32.7	7.1	57.5	39.2	2,097	129	194.8	1,143	1,725.8	49,795	21.6	53.7
South Portland	11,242	2.22	54.9	39.2	9.3	45.1	34.8	682	32	125.0	402	1,570.7	18,358	26.7	45.5
MARYLAND	2,230,527	2.64	66.3	47.6	14.0	33.7	27.5	140,207	24,215	399.9	97,487	1,609.8	4,164,698	33.6	40.9
Annapolis	16,291	2.38	56.7	41.2	12.4	43.3	36.4	604	NA	NA	NA	NA	27,236	27.5	50.0
Baltimore	242,499	2.39	49.2	23.9	20.9	50.8	40.8	23,909	NA	NA	NA	NA	421,442	43.0	32.9
Bowie	20,822	2.77	71.8	53.2	15.0	28.2	23.7	392	61	103.4	548	928.7	41,604	24.8	48.7
College Park	7,620	2.83	43.3	33.7	6.1	56.7	33.3	10,676	NA	NA	NA	NA	12,674	29.9	49.9
Frederick	28,754	2.43	61.2	42.5	14.2	38.8	31.0	1,869	NA	NA	NA	NA	49,300	32.6	40.6
Gaithersburg	24,713	2.73	67.0	50.2	13.7	33.0	25.7	382	NA	NA	NA	NA	46,774	27.1	53.5
Hagerstown	16,669	2.34	54.4	31.2	17.9	45.6	38.9	1,001	NA	NA	NA	NA	26,758	51.2	17.8
Laurel	9,647	2.65	57.6	36.1	16.8	42.4	33.9	171	NA	NA	NA	NA	17,626	30.4	43.8
Rockville	26,439	2.55	64.6	48.6	11.3	35.4	28.6	795	NA	NA	NA	NA	48,838	17.8	64.2
Salisbury	12,705	2.48	52.1	25.3	20.1	47.9	33.3	1,405	NA	NA	NA	NA	18,877	44.4	28.0
MASSACHUSETTS	2,646,980	2.50	63.2	46.9	12.0	36.8	28.4	248,305	21,288	308.8	72,602	1,053.2	4,815,331	32.5	44.5
Agawam Town	11,668	2.41	63.1	49.0	11.2	36.9	30.9	529	66	231.3	299	1,047.9	21,494	36.0	35.3
Amherst Town	9,488	2.44	49.0	37.0	9.9	51.0	30.4	16,839	62	154.8	104	259.6	12,968	15.4	71.0
Attleboro	17,491	2.54	65.4	47.9	13.1	34.6	28.0	567	137	303.2	528	1,168.6	32,094	40.3	31.7
Barnstable Town	19,060	2.31	64.7	50.7	10.1	35.3	27.9	504	188	425.6	350	792.4	33,271	30.6	40.9
Beverly	16,568	2.33	58.8	47.1	9.3	41.2	33.8	3,507	60	142.1	163	386.0	28,827	27.6	49.4
Boston	273,188	2.35	47.6	28.6	14.9	52.4	36.0	47,189	4,354	624.4	13,015	1,866.4	478,864	31.0	51.3
Braintree Town	13,751	2.67	68.2	53.2	11.5	31.8	25.2	532	85	228.0	323	866.5	26,314	30.7	44.4
Bridgewater Town	8,367	2.71	70.0	54.6	8.6	30.0	22.3	4,757	NA	NA	NA	NA	17,488	35.6	38.6
Brockton	31,459	2.99	71.4	39.8	23.9	28.6	24.9	1,654	752	758.3	1,659	1,672.9	61,996	55.2	18.4
Cambridge	47,449	2.13	42.5	32.9	6.7	57.5	35.5	16,812	341	284.3	2,200	1,834.3	80,317	11.2	79.1

2. Data for serious crimes have not been adjusted for underreporting. This may affect comparability between geographic areas and over time. 4. Persons 25 years old and over.

City	Money income, 2016–2020					Median earnings Full year, Full-time workers, 2016–2020			Housing units, 2016–2020				
	Households												
	Median household income	Percent with income less than $25,000	Percent with income of $200,000 or more	Median family income	Median non-family household income	All persons	Men	Women	Total	Occupied	Percent owner occupied	Median value[1] (dollars)	Median gross rent (dollars)
	42	43	44	45	46	47	48	49	50	51	52	53	54
KANSAS—Cont'd													
Olathe	96,548	8.2	9.3	105,927	54,195	58,962	69,956	51,013	50,738	48,919	73.0	252,900	1,070
Overland Park	87,629	8.2	14.2	114,957	53,844	65,857	75,691	54,795	83,650	79,894	63.0	295,800	1,200
Salina	49,870	22.7	2.8	68,074	29,154	40,304	45,673	33,799	21,024	19,245	61.8	133,500	769
Shawnee	88,941	9.4	13.8	106,647	49,983	56,414	68,508	48,187	25,163	24,309	74.6	247,100	1,022
Topeka	49,647	21.7	2.7	64,454	34,137	42,521	44,471	39,494	60,489	54,092	58.6	105,700	815
Wichita	53,466	21.6	4.2	69,930	32,677	42,958	48,660	38,383	172,801	154,683	58.0	138,100	821
KENTUCKY	52,238	24.0	4.2	65,893	30,352	44,129	49,784	38,919	1,994,554	1,748,053	67.6	147,100	783
Bowling Green	42,044	30.9	3.2	50,853	32,290	37,980	42,658	33,720	30,080	27,504	39.1	168,000	815
Covington	46,035	29.0	3.7	59,221	33,851	43,765	45,382	42,431	19,866	17,397	49.6	120,100	722
Elizabethtown	47,270	22.8	3.1	68,940	29,561	45,256	49,795	41,599	14,338	13,039	45.6	175,400	765
Florence	60,018	15.9	4.8	72,389	40,225	47,279	51,047	41,518	14,171	13,238	54.9	154,900	979
Frankfort	50,602	20.1	1.6	62,557	36,974	41,910	46,040	38,888	13,072	11,913	46.7	132,500	779
Georgetown	66,972	14.8	4.1	76,676	43,963	47,178	54,173	37,864	13,925	13,297	63.0	176,300	940
Henderson	40,360	33.6	1.7	60,677	23,651	38,646	43,476	33,678	13,357	12,060	51.6	119,800	687
Hopkinsville	39,743	30.0	3.6	48,833	28,003	39,007	43,488	36,105	15,178	13,225	46.7	117,500	729
Independence	79,929	8.0	3.4	86,118	63,471	48,583	53,933	44,467	9,806	9,507	79.7	179,700	949
Jeffersontown	70,951	7.7	3.1	81,378	53,174	53,010	59,051	50,068	12,211	11,572	67.6	186,600	1,015
Lexington-Fayette	58,954	19.9	6.9	80,115	37,282	47,333	51,336	42,724	142,813	130,926	54.6	200,900	920
Louisville/Jefferson County	58,196	19.6	5.7	75,482	37,784	47,714	52,083	42,795	347,172	316,411	61.5	178,100	901
Nicholasville	54,575	21.2	2.4	63,965	36,774	42,999	50,161	36,196	11,994	11,244	59.8	149,500	801
Owensboro	46,193	26.5	2.4	57,067	32,286	42,440	48,722	35,510	27,609	25,414	55.6	125,600	812
Paducah	39,061	34.8	3.9	56,442	24,961	40,729	43,890	36,546	13,713	11,592	51.0	118,100	695
Richmond	39,329	33.2	1.9	57,520	26,689	39,202	40,975	35,272	14,700	13,351	38.5	148,900	713
LOUISIANA	50,800	26.6	4.7	65,427	28,909	45,264	53,302	37,832	2,074,664	1,751,956	66.6	168,100	876
Alexandria	41,845	34.4	5.0	50,807	24,575	41,035	44,235	37,011	21,361	17,738	50.3	151,100	833
Baton Rouge	44,177	32.0	5.3	62,906	29,070	42,315	51,968	36,020	102,556	85,091	49.9	185,000	886
Bossier City	48,385	25.5	2.3	59,752	36,155	42,385	46,461	38,466	31,404	27,277	51.9	165,600	956
Central	90,183	7.6	10.8	101,825	50,579	58,200	71,227	44,992	11,277	9,891	88.7	240,200	996
Houma	44,956	32.4	3.9	63,333	24,527	46,012	57,500	32,225	14,280	12,909	65.9	163,700	750
Kenner	54,493	22.8	5.4	68,296	32,943	41,854	49,079	37,657	27,169	24,249	58.7	190,800	987
Lafayette	54,139	24.4	6.9	76,212	34,519	44,390	52,983	37,374	57,329	50,252	58.4	197,900	899
Lake Charles	44,785	31.4	5.1	59,921	30,643	41,929	50,698	31,120	38,180	33,093	54.6	155,700	830
Monroe	31,926	42.1	4.5	41,929	19,881	35,839	45,493	29,717	20,804	17,162	42.6	150,000	711
New Iberia	43,938	31.1	2.1	45,929	33,087	39,560	50,216	32,260	13,376	11,285	53.1	116,200	794
New Orleans	43,258	33.2	6.2	64,873	28,770	45,702	51,665	40,869	192,012	154,826	49.8	250,000	1,025
Shreveport	40,809	32.9	4.5	54,023	26,628	40,163	48,626	34,276	89,523	75,680	54.2	151,700	827
Slidell	55,874	22.6	5.1	68,902	31,305	46,074	55,690	39,158	11,687	10,805	67.0	167,900	1,227
MAINE	59,489	19.9	4.9	76,192	34,126	47,317	51,674	42,224	746,793	569,551	72.9	198,000	873
Bangor	47,538	26.5	4.4	67,217	31,169	41,913	44,061	39,183	15,635	13,968	47.9	155,200	834
Lewiston	42,969	30.3	1.6	62,215	24,522	40,582	42,066	38,389	16,836	15,844	48.0	150,100	748
Portland	61,695	20.3	6.6	87,088	44,944	50,847	52,464	47,259	34,187	30,796	45.2	302,700	1,204
South Portland	67,198	14.8	5.6	88,397	48,678	49,736	53,320	47,588	11,869	11,242	64.3	276,100	1,346
MARYLAND	87,063	12.8	13.4	105,790	52,712	62,007	66,509	56,863	2,459,650	2,230,527	67.1	325,400	1,415
Annapolis	87,897	12.4	14.8	110,545	56,764	60,128	63,420	55,455	17,727	16,291	55.3	414,000	1,491
Baltimore	52,164	26.5	6.2	64,814	39,140	51,299	53,546	49,100	293,936	242,499	47.7	167,300	1,094
Bowie	116,796	5.0	19.8	132,600	90,117	78,302	80,233	77,453	21,458	20,822	85.0	350,000	1,937
College Park	68,825	27.1	9.6	112,093	33,555	53,632	52,779	56,250	8,374	7,620	42.8	345,800	1,583
Frederick	78,400	12.1	8.4	96,314	56,295	58,645	65,496	51,025	30,648	28,754	57.2	277,300	1,378
Gaithersburg	91,845	12.1	15.1	104,817	69,036	60,075	63,243	55,939	26,069	24,713	50.6	413,500	1,754
Hagerstown	41,905	32.1	1.7	52,374	25,434	42,080	47,070	37,684	18,665	16,669	41.8	160,000	864
Laurel	80,255	11.4	8.9	92,546	66,420	56,409	56,441	56,377	10,256	9,647	43.7	281,500	1,611
Rockville	111,797	9.4	20.5	130,367	81,112	76,954	86,126	68,119	27,757	26,439	54.9	540,100	1,914
Salisbury	44,474	27.0	2.1	55,764	32,179	41,625	46,271	36,886	14,317	12,705	27.5	167,800	1,061
MASSACHUSETTS	84,385	15.9	14.3	106,526	48,876	64,762	71,335	57,913	2,913,009	2,646,980	62.5	398,800	1,336
Agawam Town	72,396	15.5	7.1	95,694	40,117	59,168	62,456	53,500	12,079	11,668	75.7	233,400	1,126
Amherst Town	56,906	27.9	13.5	113,913	29,191	56,231	66,250	54,534	10,550	9,488	47.9	369,600	1,275
Attleboro	77,107	16.4	10.2	97,495	36,431	59,344	64,877	52,849	19,040	17,491	68.0	313,400	1,125
Barnstable Town	77,227	12.6	10.3	100,075	53,660	58,001	64,718	50,977	26,666	19,060	73.8	399,700	1,446
Beverly	84,354	20.0	16.4	119,000	46,457	70,975	77,436	61,014	17,159	16,568	60.4	463,000	1,308
Boston	76,298	23.0	14.1	89,270	61,649	63,750	66,487	61,221	298,708	273,188	35.3	581,200	1,685
Braintree Town	101,544	11.5	17.9	130,308	61,171	75,718	79,692	67,958	14,481	13,751	74.2	489,600	1,501
Bridgewater Town	100,747	9.0	14.1	121,523	50,326	66,558	75,461	58,890	8,755	8,367	73.4	380,700	1,658
Brockton	62,249	21.3	5.5	74,630	29,410	48,076	51,387	44,458	33,588	31,459	56.0	279,600	1,193
Cambridge	107,490	14.0	22.7	142,889	83,935	79,717	86,742	72,312	51,828	47,449	34.9	843,100	2,293

1. Specified owner-occupied units

City	Commuting, 2016–2020[1]		Computer access[2], 2016–2020		Migration, 2016–2020		Civilian labor force, 2021				Civilian Employment, 2016–2020[4]			
	Percent		Percent						Unemployment[3]		Population age 16 and older		Population age 16 to 64	
	Drove alone	Mean travel time to work	With a computer in the house	With Internet access	Percent who lived in the same house one year ago	Percent who lived in another state or county one year ago	Total	Percent change 2020–2021	Total	Rate	Number	Percent in labor force	Number	Percent who worked full-year full-time
	55	56	57	58	59	60	61	62	63	64	65	66	67	68
KANSAS—Cont'd														
Olathe	80.2	21.9	96.3	93.3	86.9	4.4	80,671	0.7	2,030	2.5	104,455	74.9	88,341	60.9
Overland Park	80.3	20.0	96.4	93.9	83.1	7.8	112,496	0.7	3,008	2.7	154,784	71.8	124,904	59.7
Salina	80.5	13.9	90.0	83.8	81.5	8.5	24,944	-0.5	772	3.1	37,030	66.3	29,186	54.2
Shawnee	79.8	21.5	96.7	93.0	87.8	5.5	36,803	0.6	1,074	2.9	51,617	74.4	42,710	61.2
Topeka	80.2	17.0	87.3	73.4	85.8	5.7	63,037	-0.2	2,125	3.4	100,203	62.1	77,382	54.3
Wichita	82.5	18.8	91.8	84.6	81.4	5.2	191,672	-1.2	9,323	4.9	303,433	66.6	246,694	53.9
KENTUCKY	81.2	23.7	88.5	81.0	85.5	6.4	2,036,942	1.0	95,205	4.7	3,567,512	59.1	2,837,584	48.8
Bowling Green	77.2	19.8	92.0	86.6	70.1	15.3	33,099	1.4	1,444	4.4	57,747	67.3	49,474	39.4
Covington	74.1	22.4	87.2	79.7	78.9	10.7	18,685	0.7	920	4.9	32,454	66.2	27,196	52.8
Elizabethtown	83.0	20.2	87.0	75.1	80.4	8.2	13,371	-2.0	581	4.3	23,930	61.2	19,399	52.8
Florence	80.0	22.2	92.8	87.8	81.1	11.7	16,921	1.0	689	4.1	25,850	66.8	20,331	59.7
Frankfort	79.2	17.1	91.3	79.5	77.4	9.4	14,179	1.5	658	4.6	22,124	63.1	18,031	50.4
Georgetown	81.0	20.1	93.0	88.0	79.3	9.5	18,382	-0.8	687	3.7	26,309	70.1	22,858	58.2
Henderson	85.2	21.0	83.6	75.4	84.0	5.3	12,523	0.4	597	4.8	22,834	55.4	17,975	48.4
Hopkinsville	87.9	17.6	87.1	76.6	79.8	8.1	12,034	0.4	786	6.5	24,098	52.2	18,765	43.5
Independence	84.0	28.4	97.9	93.6	87.0	6.9	15,338	1.5	603	3.9	21,282	74.8	18,569	59.1
Jeffersontown	77.2	22.2	93.1	90.1	86.9	4.2	15,877	1.7	614	3.9	22,204	69.3	17,455	60.8
Lexington-Fayette	77.9	20.8	94.7	88.6	77.1	8.5	173,189	0.8	6,796	3.9	261,526	67.9	218,349	51.0
Louisville/Jefferson County	78.5	22.6	91.3	85.9	84.6	4.6	394,151	1.2	18,941	4.8	617,396	65.9	493,408	53.3
Nicholasville	81.5	23.7	89.1	82.2	82.3	8.5	15,083	0.4	632	4.2	23,555	62.4	19,352	51.8
Owensboro	83.9	17.5	87.4	82.0	82.1	5.6	26,282	0.6	1,213	4.6	46,873	58.7	35,818	49.4
Paducah	82.3	17.7	87.3	79.8	88.1	3.5	10,479	1.9	568	5.4	20,741	57.6	15,905	48.7
Richmond	78.9	20.1	92.2	81.9	68.3	15.1	18,418	1.5	795	4.3	29,870	65.1	26,120	37.8
LOUISIANA	81.9	25.8	88.1	78.2	87.4	5.2	2,062,492	0.0	113,089	5.5	3,688,107	58.7	2,968,563	48.0
Alexandria	79.7	19.7	85.4	76.3	83.0	5.6	18,707	0.8	897	4.8	37,489	55.8	29,617	45.1
Baton Rouge	79.1	21.3	89.1	81.2	81.3	6.2	110,081	0.0	6,714	6.1	180,842	62.4	148,139	44.1
Bossier City	84.5	18.0	91.9	67.5	84.8	8.5	29,934	0.4	1,277	4.3	53,931	52.7	43,811	53.2
Central	87.3	30.4	94.5	91.1	91.5	4.4	15,554	1.7	533	3.4	22,283	64.6	17,643	59.1
Houma	83.4	22.4	85.1	78.7	83.3	4.8	13,520	-1.8	847	6.3	25,931	56.2	20,804	48.3
Kenner	80.2	26.0	86.6	78.3	88.6	4.3	32,204	-0.6	1,907	5.9	51,777	66.5	41,136	57.1
Lafayette	83.1	20.7	91.8	86.6	82.9	6.7	59,770	0.8	2,920	4.9	103,272	63.4	83,536	50.6
Lake Charles	83.3	17.8	87.3	76.5	85.2	5.6	37,495	-2.4	2,448	6.5	61,802	61.0	49,415	50.3
Monroe	76.9	16.3	79.5	71.0	86.0	3.7	19,544	-0.3	1,261	6.5	36,706	54.3	29,832	38.8
New Iberia	84.1	22.9	80.5	73.7	82.7	4.5	10,526	0.8	925	8.8	21,748	57.2	17,159	42.4
New Orleans	66.5	23.7	88.8	77.2	86.1	5.9	177,776	-1.1	14,796	8.3	321,207	60.9	263,340	44.8
Shreveport	84.1	19.1	87.4	72.0	86.3	4.4	79,771	-0.1	5,292	6.6	149,727	56.9	118,452	46.3
Slidell	80.0	28.6	87.1	82.8	82.7	10.1	11,915	-0.6	617	5.2	21,711	59.5	16,142	51.2
MAINE	77.2	24.3	91.1	84.3	87.1	5.8	681,884	1.0	31,550	4.6	1,120,778	62.8	844,211	51.7
Bangor	71.3	16.9	92.2	84.8	79.1	8.7	16,404	0.5	758	4.6	27,202	60.4	21,600	48.3
Lewiston	72.0	20.2	86.7	78.7	81.3	7.1	16,794	0.2	955	5.7	29,722	60.4	22,910	49.2
Portland	62.3	19.7	92.2	86.8	79.1	10.4	37,795	0.8	1,734	4.6	57,525	70.5	47,264	54.9
South Portland	76.4	18.0	94.2	90.3	86.1	5.4	14,537	0.9	602	4.1	22,168	70.7	17,360	55.7
MARYLAND	72.1	33.0	93.6	88.1	86.8	6.4	3,175,550	-1.6	183,322	5.8	4,846,076	66.9	3,915,201	55.9
Annapolis	70.7	29.7	92.9	87.3	81.6	7.0	22,335	-1.8	1,102	4.9	31,397	71.1	24,638	60.3
Baltimore	59.2	31.1	87.9	77.2	84.3	6.8	277,525	-1.7	21,223	7.6	491,582	62.0	407,023	49.1
Bowie	69.8	36.9	97.4	95.3	90.6	4.5	33,770	-2.4	2,045	6.1	47,491	72.2	38,845	60.5
College Park	51.1	28.7	96.9	85.7	65.8	25.1	14,641	-0.9	1,049	7.2	29,361	52.6	27,329	28.1
Frederick	75.5	32.1	94.0	89.5	81.3	8.8	37,857	-2.3	2,000	5.3	57,916	70.0	48,223	57.4
Gaithersburg	64.3	32.8	97.1	91.2	80.5	7.0	35,650	-2.0	2,069	5.8	54,226	73.7	45,631	57.3
Hagerstown	72.8	27.7	88.1	77.6	81.1	5.4	18,321	-1.5	1,271	6.9	30,656	60.7	24,812	45.6
Laurel	70.3	35.9	97.1	92.6	78.9	11.2	15,601	-2.9	1,286	8.2	19,821	76.6	17,065	62.2
Rockville	57.1	32.2	96.7	93.1	82.6	9.1	37,438	-1.7	1,750	4.7	55,195	68.9	43,127	59.6
Salisbury	78.5	21.8	90.2	79.2	72.8	10.5	14,993	0.3	1,108	7.4	26,427	66.4	22,391	40.2
MASSACHUSETTS	68.0	30.0	92.6	87.7	87.4	6.0	3,750,870	0.2	215,392	5.7	5,678,025	67.1	4,541,459	52.1
Agawam Town	87.1	21.7	90.3	85.5	93.6	1.7	16,136	0.8	904	5.6	24,010	65.0	18,039	56.4
Amherst Town	42.6	18.5	98.0	93.4	50.2	26.5	19,392	2.3	797	4.1	36,739	56.4	33,457	17.2
Attleboro	81.9	31.3	91.4	85.8	90.7	4.8	25,465	-0.1	1,385	5.4	36,233	68.7	29,099	56.0
Barnstable Town	75.8	23.7	96.1	92.0	91.5	3.6	24,087	1.5	1,559	6.5	37,426	66.2	27,067	52.7
Beverly	67.3	29.2	90.0	86.0	86.5	5.9	23,271	0.3	1,124	4.8	34,759	67.5	27,335	52.4
Boston	37.5	30.7	92.5	86.2	80.0	10.8	392,960	-0.3	22,875	5.8	591,878	69.7	510,594	51.0
Braintree Town	67.0	34.3	94.5	90.4	91.8	4.4	20,785	-0.7	1,128	5.4	30,120	69.6	23,909	57.4
Bridgewater Town	77.2	30.7	96.1	92.7	87.4	7.5	14,974	-0.2	762	5.1	23,672	64.5	19,304	44.3
Brockton	74.5	31.4	90.0	82.0	85.6	6.2	48,960	-1.6	4,358	8.9	74,084	68.5	61,635	48.4
Cambridge	24.3	26.5	95.5	89.7	72.8	17.7	71,468	2.2	2,506	3.5	104,804	69.4	91,079	49.7

1. Employed persons. 2. Households. 3. Percent of civilian labor force. 4. Persons 16 years old and over.

City	Value of residential construction authorized by building permits, 2021			Wholesale trade[1], 2017				Retail trade[2], 2017			
	New construction ($1,000)	Number of housing units	Percent single family	Number of establishments	Number of employees	Sales (mil dol)	Annual payroll (mil dol)	Number of establish-ments	Number of employees	Sales (mil dol)	Annual payroll (mil dol)
	69	70	71	72	73	74	75	76	77	78	79
KANSAS—Cont'd											
Olathe	394,107	1,206	53.1	145	3,415	3,652.1	210.4	331	7,589	2,551.2	207.1
Overland Park	237,052	705	90.1	228	4,117	15,131.2	394.9	712	13,744	3,194.5	367.3
Salina	13,347	61	100.0	73	1,047	529.8	56.0	229	3,997	1,090.2	93.0
Shawnee	158,340	816	26.8	63	939	995.4	62.0	193	3,527	855.1	88.1
Topeka	62,869	384	28.6	124	1,441	1,078.7	81.4	525	8,881	2,180.3	210.2
Wichita	309,752	1,128	67.4	510	7,717	7,207.0	477.1	1,467	26,178	7,133.4	679.0
KENTUCKY	2,912,471	14,841	68.0	3,646	55,784	80,128.5	3,171.6	15,021	225,127	64,294.3	5,630.0
Bowling Green	154,912	1,362	22.6	125	1,516	2,180.8	80.8	460	7,420	1,862.9	180.8
Covington	44,199	230	17.8	30	1,023	313.1	38.5	121	1,526	402.8	38.1
Elizabethtown	25,584	105	75.2	40	489	343.8	23.2	255	4,735	1,234.5	117.0
Florence	NA	NA	NA	D	D	D	10.2	301	6,867	1,901.3	171.4
Frankfort	4,684	23	100.0	43	440	497.6	25.5	143	1,960	469.4	44.3
Georgetown	NA	NA	NA	14	93	32.2	3.6	97	1,653	476.1	39.7
Henderson	6,367	32	87.5	31	418	230.3	23.3	134	1,866	631.0	48.0
Hopkinsville	6,809	52	88.5	44	620	656.7	31.3	168	2,320	667.2	61.3
Independence	31,294	128	100.0	D	D	D	20.1	39	1,006	203.0	16.0
Jeffersontown	16,528	69	100.0	152	3,127	2,996.6	212.7	157	2,869	1,117.1	94.6
Lexington-Fayette	260,249	1,655	47.9	328	4,645	3,402.9	258.8	1,211	23,102	6,341.8	597.9
Louisville/Jefferson County	346,275	1,848	74.8	682	10,313	6,561.4	619.1	1,987	32,443	9,077.9	851.0
Nicholasville	31,080	241	98.3	31	878	1,443.8	41.6	111	2,003	737.6	58.1
Owensboro	36,118	388	100.0	60	853	475.2	42.7	329	4,867	1,295.1	115.5
Paducah	11,188	53	28.3	72	1,161	4,238.8	52.9	307	5,255	1,489.8	136.7
Richmond	67,717	389	69.2	23	180	142.3	6.3	196	3,220	918.6	78.6
LOUISIANA	4,054,061	19,147	88.5	4,673	63,503	59,523.7	3,493.7	16,564	233,385	65,000.8	5,988.4
Alexandria	24,765	94	100.0	76	971	1,027.7	48.3	340	5,180	1,478.7	136.5
Baton Rouge	90,337	266	100.0	305	3,987	2,625.0	232.5	1,211	18,219	4,601.5	474.1
Bossier City	58,210	332	100.0	74	1,354	862.5	67.5	368	6,775	1,860.0	164.1
Central	50,493	218	99.1	9	37	257.5	5.0	44	910	217.6	21.8
Houma	NA	NA	NA	63	552	254.5	26.9	157	2,072	428.5	50.7
Kenner	20,631	55	100.0	94	974	355.0	53.0	274	4,419	1,358.5	119.6
Lafayette	NA	NA	NA	263	3,325	1,659.8	176.0	822	13,685	3,594.5	355.6
Lake Charles	52,271	365	92.3	79	978	628.5	45.7	469	7,026	2,120.0	178.3
Monroe	35,493	221	45.7	74	1,270	1,257.9	58.6	361	5,912	1,485.2	143.5
New Iberia	1,814	8	100.0	49	795	562.3	43.4	193	2,601	744.7	67.6
New Orleans	298,269	1,576	45.4	255	3,124	2,506.4	187.2	1,327	14,795	3,499.1	387.0
Shreveport	59,357	218	100.0	283	3,848	2,686.2	202.8	799	12,031	3,386.1	319.5
Slidell	3,611	20	100.0	D	D	D	7.4	277	4,972	1,273.3	118.9
MAINE	1,593,799	6,530	80.2	1,309	15,527	13,951.8	803.4	6,250	81,733	23,878.7	2,249.6
Bangor	9,661	42	42.9	66	888	459.1	49.4	283	5,699	1,801.0	141.4
Lewiston	11,663	65	46.2	39	702	299.3	34.1	150	1,731	567.6	46.2
Portland	49,298	283	10.2	173	2,580	1,804.5	166.6	388	5,340	2,248.3	175.7
South Portland	13,303	85	25.9	45	714	2,158.4	42.6	253	4,674	1,171.8	122.8
MARYLAND	4,011,527	18,496	67.7	4,598	73,388	62,762.8	4,872.3	17,911	291,814	84,966.2	8,240.9
Annapolis	10,717	24	50.0	75	621	985.1	43.5	423	6,433	1,515.6	168.3
Baltimore	314,765	1,557	12.3	508	7,678	9,253.2	509.0	1,912	21,064	7,175.3	600.3
Bowie	NA	NA	NA	18	100	43.3	7.1	157	4,235	1,199.4	119.6
College Park	NA	NA	NA	7	90	22.8	5.9	64	1,374	414.3	39.6
Frederick	166,801	1,023	49.0	89	1,048	669.7	58.9	337	6,207	1,942.3	185.1
Gaithersburg	12,726	111	33.3	62	722	537.1	55.9	301	6,469	2,211.4	202.7
Hagerstown	10,497	94	100.0	52	503	243.3	27.1	211	4,439	1,247.2	108.7
Laurel	35,763	125	8.8	19	610	189.5	32.8	144	2,544	644.1	67.5
Rockville	15,220	86	100.0	83	2,003	2,010.1	281.9	279	4,451	1,726.6	155.1
Salisbury	3,986	27	100.0	51	642	446.6	31.1	218	4,500	1,277.1	113.1
MASSACHUSETTS	4,941,794	19,853	36.4	6,324	120,957	137,010.9	10,129.9	23,928	364,204	110,194.5	10,911.5
Agawam Town	4,573	20	100.0	43	658	451.0	44.9	87	967	318.9	30.2
Amherst Town	9,358	63	9.5	NA	NA	NA	NA	NA	NA	NA	NA
Attleboro	14,122	58	89.7	32	560	504.9	34.6	151	3,018	870.3	75.4
Barnstable Town	45,404	58	96.6	46	602	315.9	35.1	355	4,187	1,338.3	129.2
Beverly	7,748	25	68.0	44	364	194.2	24.4	141	2,006	582.6	58.8
Boston	836,293	3,512	1.5	512	11,960	10,100.5	1,475.5	2,191	32,451	12,080.2	1,103.5
Braintree Town	4,675	12	100.0	48	518	370.2	40.3	284	5,936	1,724.2	180.5
Bridgewater Town	27,647	99	51.5	NA	NA	NA	NA	NA	NA	NA	NA
Brockton	16,512	143	19.6	69	1,455	931.5	100.3	327	5,070	1,349.9	148.4
Cambridge	124,661	661	6.5	82	2,489	932.3	197.5	387	5,773	1,286.8	151.6

1. Merchant wholesalers except manufacturers' sales branches and offices. 2. Establishments with payroll.

City	Real estate and rental and leasing, 2017				Professional, scientific, and technical services[1], 2017				Manufacturing, 2017			
	Number of establish-ments	Number of employees	Receipts (mil dol)	Annual payroll (mil dol)	Number of establish-ments	Number of employees	Receipts (mil dol)	Annual payroll (mil dol)	Number of establish-ments	Number of employees	Receipts (mil dol)	Annual payroll (mil dol)
	80	81	82	83	84	85	86	87	88	89	90	91
KANSAS—Cont'd												
Olathe	156	517	141.6	25.1	355	2,571	257.0	98.4	NA	NA	NA	NA
Overland Park	439	2,325	1,053.0	123.4	D	D	D	D	NA	NA	NA	NA
Salina	59	181	40.6	5.3	105	1,064	93.3	39.9	NA	NA	NA	NA
Shawnee	81	323	87.8	12.9	158	752	116.5	43.5	NA	NA	NA	NA
Topeka	189	882	160.2	30.2	343	3,527	553.2	221.1	NA	NA	NA	NA
Wichita	527	2,896	720.0	113.8	1,050	10,366	1,782.7	642.7	NA	NA	NA	NA
KENTUCKY	3,902	18,070	5,125.3	731.1	8,125	67,615	10,271.7	3,636.2	3,699	234,010	133,415.5	12,768.7
Bowling Green	116	484	104.0	15.8	175	1,610	178.1	59.8	NA	NA	NA	NA
Covington	34	246	60.4	12.0	119	1,104	211.6	86.3	NA	NA	NA	NA
Elizabethtown	62	403	67.4	11.4	87	430	50.0	20.6	NA	NA	NA	NA
Florence	51	198	51.8	7.9	105	955	137.5	55.7	NA	NA	NA	NA
Frankfort	29	142	14.6	3.8	100	957	110.1	41.9	NA	NA	NA	NA
Georgetown	41	115	24.8	3.1	62	324	39.5	16.0	NA	NA	NA	NA
Henderson	45	182	21.7	4.9	64	382	32.8	11.1	NA	NA	NA	NA
Hopkinsville	50	147	25.5	3.8	50	305	32.8	10.6	NA	NA	NA	NA
Independence	5	9	1.8	0.3	D	D	2.1	D	NA	NA	NA	NA
Jeffersontown	97	574	170.0	29.6	170	3,063	447.7	153.2	NA	NA	NA	NA
Lexington-Fayette	486	2,223	580.8	86.3	1,163	11,126	2,006.1	701.2	NA	NA	NA	NA
Louisville/Jefferson County	766	4,023	1,019.4	177.0	1,697	17,890	3,088.5	1,146.6	NA	NA	NA	NA
Nicholasville	25	106	16.2	3.3	55	515	106.0	31.2	NA	NA	NA	NA
Owensboro	76	453	60.6	11.9	128	734	96.2	37.1	NA	NA	NA	NA
Paducah	49	341	72.6	10.0	126	959	119.7	45.2	NA	NA	NA	NA
Richmond	54	197	42.6	5.9	82	507	88.7	23.7	NA	NA	NA	NA
LOUISIANA	5,121	29,345	7,300.6	1,386.0	12,072	95,652	16,082.1	6,185.4	3,190	117,910	187,439.9	8,257.3
Alexandria	108	423	83.5	16.3	196	1,345	168.1	64.6	NA	NA	NA	NA
Baton Rouge	384	2,005	498.2	97.7	1,137	14,263	2,593.3	1,012.7	NA	NA	NA	NA
Bossier City	104	546	131.0	20.7	126	1,093	98.9	37.6	NA	NA	NA	NA
Central	15	30	6.2	0.9	27	90	9.4	3.9	NA	NA	NA	NA
Houma	61	382	121.9	20.4	134	1,429	155.4	83.9	NA	NA	NA	NA
Kenner	99	868	259.5	36.6	150	803	144.5	49.4	NA	NA	NA	NA
Lafayette	341	1,792	505.4	95.4	1,018	6,933	1,267.9	451.6	NA	NA	NA	NA
Lake Charles	141	642	161.2	24.9	303	1,789	293.8	96.5	NA	NA	NA	NA
Monroe	137	747	184.2	27.8	289	1,854	279.9	91.8	NA	NA	NA	NA
New Iberia	55	339	69.3	17.0	89	426	60.6	19.0	NA	NA	NA	NA
New Orleans	470	2,327	573.6	99.7	1,622	15,845	3,414.6	1,318.6	NA	NA	NA	NA
Shreveport	321	1,780	367.5	69.1	598	4,408	736.4	248.8	NA	NA	NA	NA
Slidell	41	235	61.9	10.3	131	584	70.4	22.2	NA	NA	NA	NA
MAINE	1,821	7,138	1,484.2	287.4	3,543	23,381	3,873.6	1,488.1	1,691	48,620	15,089.2	2,598.7
Bangor	105	622	225.1	19.8	141	993	117.6	53.4	NA	NA	NA	NA
Lewiston	54	226	36.2	8.1	78	1,014	259.6	60.7	NA	NA	NA	NA
Portland	303	1,577	374.9	76.6	677	6,052	1,132.5	484.8	NA	NA	NA	NA
South Portland	55	346	78.1	17.1	96	1,283	206.7	84.2	NA	NA	NA	NA
MARYLAND	6,811	49,157	18,087.4	2,851.5	20,974	283,999	55,404.7	23,645.2	2,967	97,992	41,776.9	6,343.2
Annapolis	101	557	138.4	35.6	368	2,338	480.1	211.8	NA	NA	NA	NA
Baltimore	748	5,107	1,607.3	314.5	1,698	25,853	5,762.5	2,378.0	NA	NA	NA	NA
Bowie	38	110	36.5	4.4	198	2,443	518.2	196.4	NA	NA	NA	NA
College Park	26	307	59.9	10.4	90	547	77.9	39.0	NA	NA	NA	NA
Frederick	121	473	134.0	23.6	390	6,056	878.6	431.2	NA	NA	NA	NA
Gaithersburg	96	357	228.4	22.8	471	8,464	1,457.0	890.3	NA	NA	NA	NA
Hagerstown	62	458	105.5	16.1	112	941	108.8	46.0	NA	NA	NA	NA
Laurel	50	853	140.2	35.9	90	1,037	159.4	79.3	NA	NA	NA	NA
Rockville	148	1,862	1,116.8	143.2	891	24,125	3,585.6	1,573.8	NA	NA	NA	NA
Salisbury	76	491	84.6	19.1	146	1,058	146.3	54.1	NA	NA	NA	NA
MASSACHUSETTS	7,584	52,315	17,912.1	3,369.5	21,985	310,313	78,597.9	32,256.2	6,437	231,593	82,308.5	15,749.4
Agawam Town	24	98	28.3	5.6	60	762	112.0	45.3	NA	NA	NA	NA
Amherst Town	NA	NA	NA	NA	NA	NA	NA	NA	NA	NA	NA	NA
Attleboro	25	125	25.5	5.4	72	298	45.1	16.1	NA	NA	NA	NA
Barnstable Town	95	303	96.2	14.1	215	999	200.8	92.8	NA	NA	NA	NA
Beverly	50	314	123.2	19.4	174	1,961	364.1	155.9	NA	NA	NA	NA
Boston	1,263	13,923	5,397.4	1,124.2	3,485	86,292	25,456.4	9,928.6	NA	NA	NA	NA
Braintree Town	83	1,659	355.1	110.2	201	1,919	362.0	166.0	NA	NA	NA	NA
Bridgewater Town	NA	NA	NA	NA	NA	NA	NA	NA	NA	NA	NA	NA
Brockton	62	226	53.2	9.5	129	672	98.5	37.7	NA	NA	NA	NA
Cambridge	210	1,392	724.6	94.7	983	33,024	11,262.9	4,389.3	NA	NA	NA	NA

1. Establishments subject to federal tax.

City	Accommodation and food services, 2017				Arts, entertainment, and recreation[1], 2017				Health care and social assistance[1], 2017			
	Number of establish-ments	Number of employees	Receipts (mil dol)	Annual payroll (mil dol)	Number of establish-ments	Number of employees	Receipts (mil dol)	Annual payroll (mil dol)	Number of establish-ments	Number of employees	Receipts (mil dol)	Annual payroll (mil dol)
	92	93	94	95	96	97	98	99	100	101	102	103
KANSAS—Cont'd												
Olathe	236	5,655	318.2	92.2	42.0	939	29.8	10.5	294	6,486	880.2	286.7
Overland Park	486	11,539	675.1	212.3	103.0	2,758	144.7	48.0	804	17,310	2,709.0	958.5
Salina	135	2,800	129.2	37.0	D	D	D	D	D	D	D	D
Shawnee	120	2,614	125.0	36.9	22.0	353	23.1	5.4	143	1,480	135.1	56.3
Topeka	326	6,472	324.6	92.4	51.0	976	45.6	16.4	454	15,708	1,919.6	800.2
Wichita	1,011	21,150	1,035.0	306.1	133.0	2,702	142.4	40.9	1,336	34,913	4,016.7	1,599.2
KENTUCKY	8,228	174,910	9,191.2	2,621.2	1,406.0	19,605	1,965.0	440.6	11,597	268,711	32,369.5	12,412.1
Bowling Green	259	6,307	323.8	99.7	33.0	633	41.1	11.4	351	8,704	1,166.7	423.6
Covington	126	2,329	156.1	42.1	13.0	106	10.2	2.2	95	2,049	157.3	71.9
Elizabethtown	122	3,322	170.5	46.9	12.0	100	6.9	1.9	225	6,032	632.7	275.2
Florence	168	4,045	236.9	68.6	23.0	577	39.0	9.7	179	3,864	411.1	171.2
Frankfort	87	1,870	97.9	27.8	10.0	96	2.8	0.9	131	1,920	300.8	92.8
Georgetown	100	2,138	122.0	34.2	11.0	81	5.0	1.8	98	1,312	137.8	54.7
Henderson	72	1,350	69.3	18.0	D	D	D	D	140	2,463	217.9	89.5
Hopkinsville	76	1,614	79.5	23.1	D	D	D	D	136	3,051	352.6	127.0
Independence	19	370	19.1	6.9	3.0	D	0.3	D	21	192	13.0	5.2
Jeffersontown	124	3,215	180.8	52.3	25.0	451	41.5	9.9	138	2,322	207.6	79.9
Lexington-Fayette	849	20,035	1,112.4	325.4	173.0	3,186	349.4	91.4	1,154	32,976	4,708.5	1,706.1
Louisville/Jefferson County	1,397	32,702	1,910.5	540.9	261.0	5,035	789.1	133.2	1,703	50,488	7,015.0	2,601.7
Nicholasville	64	1,424	62.8	19.5	D	D	D	D	81	912	75.7	34.2
Owensboro	160	3,623	185.8	54.8	24.0	460	25.9	7.3	286	9,004	1,011.9	441.7
Paducah	175	3,931	187.4	55.9	19.0	309	10.7	3.6	213	6,571	876.2	299.0
Richmond	111	2,903	136.4	42.3	12.0	158	5.2	1.6	157	2,773	284.7	107.5
LOUISIANA	9,877	215,048	14,553.0	3,808.8	1,526.0	25,649	2,788.6	845.4	12,685	302,408	34,618.0	12,912.7
Alexandria	179	3,685	195.0	52.7	D	D	D	D	381	8,649	1,175.1	413.7
Baton Rouge	755	18,801	1,180.7	318.0	97.0	2,389	144.7	41.5	857	25,744	3,331.5	1,077.8
Bossier City	222	8,315	747.4	159.9	28.0	778	76.2	14.5	189	4,194	433.4	169.5
Central	D	D	D	D	D	D	D	D	40	585	39.7	17.6
Houma	99	1,395	81.9	22.8	8.0	34	2.5	0.6	154	4,240	428.6	182.2
Kenner	182	3,541	253.4	64.9	23.0	972	130.5	28.2	173	3,184	415.5	140.0
Lafayette	606	13,551	898.6	229.2	66.0	1,296	67.6	20.9	978	22,460	2,794.4	990.6
Lake Charles	263	9,425	955.2	222.0	36.0	335	22.2	5.1	391	11,114	1,211.8	467.8
Monroe	168	3,769	193.1	51.9	26.0	483	23.1	5.5	420	9,475	1,027.1	373.9
New Iberia	92	1,605	75.9	21.3	D	D	D	D	171	3,524	304.5	109.9
New Orleans	1,510	42,732	3,768.7	1,026.2	234.0	6,789	656.9	153.8	994	26,020	3,804.3	1,273.3
Shreveport	474	11,625	753.5	193.0	74.0	1,014	62.9	18.3	843	28,006	4,126.8	1,487.0
Slidell	194	3,884	191.2	54.5	9.0	106	6.9	2.0	187	5,057	585.2	237.1
MAINE	4,257	55,746	4,017.7	1,167.1	887.0	8,027	676.8	188.4	4,771	112,594	11,777.3	5,000.0
Bangor	146	3,659	242.8	66.2	22.0	211	42.3	5.5	286	11,651	1,415.4	630.0
Lewiston	90	1,258	75.0	23.7	14.0	168	6.2	2.5	185	7,223	879.7	383.6
Portland	413	7,068	499.7	159.0	75.0	1,058	90.1	25.5	462	15,910	2,285.5	850.4
South Portland	134	2,782	172.6	52.0	D	D	D	D	136	3,289	399.9	209.3
MARYLAND	12,139	237,730	16,930.7	4,624.5	2,172.0	43,573	4,970.1	1,588.3	16,800	384,096	48,675.7	19,294.2
Annapolis	196	5,866	383.1	114.9	54.0	838	72.1	22.5	204	2,005	246.7	95.8
Baltimore	1,542	25,190	1,980.5	550.7	203.0	7,484	936.0	389.1	1,494	77,508	12,756.8	4,397.6
Bowie	96	2,601	150.1	46.9	D	D	D	D	265	2,585	248.3	97.3
College Park	120	2,022	128.1	33.5	10.0	172	9.8	4.4	34	297	24.8	12.0
Frederick	265	5,127	307.2	90.5	D	D	D	14.4	440	8,565	1,056.9	410.4
Gaithersburg	220	4,686	358.7	98.2	37.0	918	59.9	18.9	227	4,744	588.6	212.1
Hagerstown	139	2,672	142.3	40.8	17.0	362	18.5	4.7	210	3,935	390.7	166.6
Laurel	98	2,213	134.7	38.3	D	D	D	D	131	1,517	171.0	66.6
Rockville	268	4,157	318.7	86.7	38.0	1,139	69.4	27.8	374	8,387	1,447.4	803.6
Salisbury	142	3,017	157.1	41.0	12.0	111	5.6	1.6	206	6,774	797.1	345.9
MASSACHUSETTS	17,773	311,058	22,892.8	6,857.1	3,477.0	66,160	7,037.2	2,360.4	19,349	635,012	74,024.0	32,038.2
Agawam Town	65	769	38.9	11.3	12.0	1,715	91.7	22.2	62	1,369	103.3	46.2
Amherst Town	NA	NA	NA	NA	NA	NA	NA	NA	NA	NA	NA	NA
Attleboro	85	1,813	101.2	33.9	15.0	249	8.3	3.6	128	4,657	473.6	217.1
Barnstable Town	189	3,118	238.1	77.4	55.0	635	77.9	25.1	253	8,175	1,109.8	458.0
Beverly	119	1,823	111.6	36.7	28.0	750	42.6	14.6	180	4,732	652.3	281.6
Boston	2,456	61,705	6,072.9	1,769.1	361.0	13,163	2,180.8	877.9	1,747	133,669	21,411.9	9,308.2
Braintree Town	123	2,746	196.3	56.8	21.0	328	46.5	7.7	126	3,818	377.2	143.9
Bridgewater Town	NA	NA	NA	NA	NA	NA	NA	NA	NA	NA	NA	NA
Brockton	168	2,447	165.1	48.8	15.0	337	17.5	6.2	294	12,717	1,444.9	636.8
Cambridge	476	12,601	1,004.6	326.5	82.0	1,284	247.2	34.9	361	9,551	1,323.0	613.4

1. Establishments subject to federal tax.

City	Other services[1]: Number of establish-ments	Other services[1]: Number of employees	Other services[1]: Receipts (mil dol)	Other services[1]: Annual payroll (mil dol)	Government employment and payroll, 2017: Full-time equivalent employees	March payroll: Total (dollars)	Perent of total for: Admin-istrative, judicial, and legal	Police and corrections	Fire protection	Highways and trans-portation	Health and welfare	Natural resources and utilities	Education and libraries
	104	105	106	107	108	109	110	111	112	113	114	115	116
KANSAS—Cont'd													
Olathe	197	1,292	131.7	39.0	697	4,432,327	16.2	28.8	19.2	8.3	0.6	27.0	0.0
Overland Park	401	2,392	261.8	77.8	1,086	3,243,332	17.6	35.9	19.4	13.1	1.0	8.8	0.0
Salina	95	535	99.0	15.5	478	2,114,081	9.9	21.9	23.4	10.8	4.0	26.8	0.0
Shawnee	93	605	47.4	16.2	296	1,917,070	13.7	38.3	20.0	14.6	0.0	8.0	0.0
Topeka	312	2,171	295.9	85.7	1,196	5,881,517	14.4	30.7	24.7	9.1	3.1	14.8	0.0
Wichita	659	4,761	676.1	149.8	2,961	14,226,610	10.6	32.3	18.4	12.0	3.7	14.4	2.7
KENTUCKY	5,900	38,040	4,755.2	1,198.2	X	X	X	X	X	X	X	X	X
Bowling Green	179	1,128	104.7	28.3	681	3,194,750	7.2	22.3	20.4	5.2	1.6	26.6	0.0
Covington	71	527	44.2	13.5	376	1,896,750	10.8	32.1	32.5	2.6	12.6	5.9	0.0
Elizabethtown	74	458	49.4	12.8	317	1,236,052	12.4	23.5	20.6	9.5	0.0	25.9	0.0
Florence	74	514	39.7	13.3	198	1,566,875	5.7	36.0	33.0	3.7	0.0	11.0	0.0
Frankfort	76	436	62.2	16.1	575	2,644,113	4.0	11.4	17.3	5.4	2.3	28.9	0.0
Georgetown	D	D	D	6.6	191	758,457	10.3	39.3	33.4	6.9	0.0	6.2	0.0
Henderson	D	D	D	D	467	1,970,799	10.6	18.3	15.0	6.0	5.7	40.9	0.0
Hopkinsville	54	258	23.5	5.6	443	1,859,036	5.8	19.4	20.4	1.6	5.4	33.0	0.0
Independence	13	65	6.8	2.5	42	207,642	9.8	71.7	0.0	13.2	2.9	2.4	0.0
Jeffersontown	100	787	118.6	39.5	128	667,386	10.4	69.3	0.0	11.8	2.6	2.0	0.0
Lexington-Fayette	595	4,860	961.7	165.0	3,756	18,866,699	10.5	30.8	20.8	5.8	7.3	14.2	3.0
Louisville/Jefferson County	969	8,330	1,156.7	272.1	0	36,302,120	9.1	28.8	6.5	12.3	17.3	18.8	2.3
Nicholasville	59	234	20.1	5.7	225	925,322	16.2	30.8	22.3	3.4	0.0	15.4	0.0
Owensboro	D	D	D	D	776	3,786,398	6.5	16.5	12.2	5.6	2.5	41.7	0.0
Paducah	D	D	D	D	531	2,391,618	5.3	17.2	15.0	8.5	6.2	37.4	0.2
Richmond	50	247	25.1	7.1	259	421,250	9.3	26.8	23.5	5.7	16.0	10.0	0.0
LOUISIANA	6,531	43,472	5,702.0	1,571.6	X	X	X	X	X	X	X	X	X
Alexandria	92	571	76.2	19.3	888	3,077,029	19.1	24.1	16.5	8.4	1.3	26.5	0.0
Baton Rouge	570	4,281	680.4	165.3	6,100	25,370,879	15.8	29.2	14.6	12.1	19.0	3.3	5.8
Bossier City	105	897	78.3	24.8	690	2,672,349	12.1	33.0	34.0	2.8	1.1	13.0	0.0
Central	D	D	D	D	12	21,138	55.9	44.1	0.0	0.0	0.0	0.0	0.0
Houma	57	593	79.3	33.7	2,640	10,714,118	9.5	14.0	2.1	2.1	60.4	8.5	3.4
Kenner	121	793	109.7	30.7	628	2,559,064	14.9	44.2	18.6	5.8	2.7	8.1	0.0
Lafayette	316	2,479	283.5	79.0	3,190	10,047,868	16.8	32.5	12.1	8.6	3.1	20.9	3.4
Lake Charles	139	970	107.5	30.4	927	2,945,183	13.5	25.6	23.5	4.3	0.0	27.3	0.0
Monroe	104	708	58.3	17.0	1,055	3,346,633	13.6	22.2	21.2	8.7	6.9	25.7	0.0
New Iberia	64	282	35.0	10.0	167	549,275	13.6	0.0	41.3	11.6	8.3	25.2	0.0
New Orleans	722	5,256	751.2	181.7	6,939	33,679,953	12.6	41.0	9.3	3.1	7.9	17.4	2.1
Shreveport	330	2,326	249.3	67.4	2,693	9,834,778	8.5	29.4	28.3	4.3	1.3	15.1	6.0
Slidell	105	416	33.4	9.8	326	1,145,559	17.2	40.7	0.0	12.9	0.0	24.0	0.0
MAINE	2,921	14,477	1,809.2	474.8	X	X	X	X	X	X	X	X	X
Bangor	93	687	83.2	22.0	1,151	5,026,690	4.0	9.1	8.6	16.7	3.1	4.8	51.5
Lewiston	78	429	42.7	13.6	1,348	5,468,002	3.8	8.7	7.2	4.0	0.6	3.6	69.4
Portland	286	1,905	275.2	72.3	2,684	12,071,737	6.5	9.9	9.3	5.6	11.3	3.7	46.7
South Portland	84	612	49.8	15.5	886	3,012,021	7.2	10.5	11.2	5.0	1.1	9.1	51.8
MARYLAND	10,355	81,469	12,118.3	3,518.8	X	X	X	X	X	X	X	X	X
Annapolis	202	1,802	232.6	76.0	671	3,640,943	12.5	28.3	24.5	16.4	0.0	13.9	0.0
Baltimore	996	9,183	1,395.2	359.6	25,611	138,264,675	6.7	17.7	8.7	3.1	3.8	8.7	49.4
Bowie	64	401	32.7	11.8	368	1,787,807	17.1	24.4	0.0	6.4	4.1	29.9	0.0
College Park	51	282	66.3	13.2	113	647,321	27.1	11.9	0.0	6.8	9.6	19.4	0.0
Frederick	205	1,639	233.4	63.2	600	2,869,188	10.7	38.9	0.0	7.5	6.3	22.0	0.0
Gaithersburg	151	1,236	132.0	41.8	347	2,140,618	25.2	25.7	0.0	10.7	8.4	23.5	0.0
Hagerstown	106	696	69.4	19.7	411	1,913,537	8.7	17.2	19.2	8.0	2.4	32.8	0.0
Laurel	65	487	41.3	15.6	207	1,129,796	17.3	48.9	0.0	5.3	0.0	14.7	0.0
Rockville	249	3,193	685.4	273.2	596	3,495,551	18.6	17.9	0.0	8.5	9.3	45.2	0.0
Salisbury	108	920	100.5	29.1	393	1,584,284	9.7	34.4	19.1	8.4	3.2	21.1	0.0
MASSACHUSETTS	14,810	100,088	13,093.7	3,605.7	X	X	X	X	X	X	X	X	X
Agawam Town	57	385	161.7	15.3	1,031	4,421,652	3.8	8.1	8.9	3.8	1.9	2.8	65.4
Amherst Town	NA	NA	NA	NA	NA	NA	NA	NA	NA	NA	NA	NA	NA
Attleboro	82	320	35.9	9.2	1,224	6,646,168	3.6	9.7	10.1	1.4	1.5	7.5	65.7
Barnstable Town	175	1,169	121.7	42.1	1,354	7,736,084	7.5	15.0	0.0	6.0	1.8	6.2	59.3
Beverly	100	591	70.6	19.5	857	5,000,348	4.2	11.7	9.4	4.7	1.9	2.7	64.5
Boston	1,852	19,411	3,450.7	820.3	19,672	132,820,934	3.5	21.3	11.1	1.9	6.9	5.2	48.7
Braintree Town	117	808	94.7	28.2	1,353	8,370,821	2.4	9.0	10.9	2.5	1.8	13.7	59.5
Bridgewater Town	NA	NA	NA	NA	NA	NA	NA	NA	NA	NA	NA	NA	NA
Brockton	184	1,369	127.1	41.8	3,379	18,208,042	2.5	10.9	5.1	1.3	0.7	2.6	76.1
Cambridge	284	2,154	353.0	104.3	7,136	36,213,738	5.0	8.2	5.6	2.0	46.6	3.5	26.1

1. Establishments subject to federal tax.

City	City government finances, 2017									
	General revenue							General expenditure		
		Intergovernmental		Taxes						
					Per capita[1] (dollars)				Per capita[1] (dollars)	
	Total (mil dol)	Total (mil dol)	Percent from state government	Total (mil dol)	Total	Property	Sales and gross receipts	Total (mil dol)	Total	Capital outlays
	117	118	119	120	121	122	123	124	125	126
KANSAS—Cont'd										
Olathe	208.3	13.0	62.7	117.9	858	300	558	224.7	1,634	444
Overland Park	303.5	66.1	20.9	125.5	656	210	445	229.9	1,202	268
Salina	68.3	4.8	55.8	40.1	857	312	545	63.7	1,361	104
Shawnee	77.4	19.9	55.8	46.2	704	329	375	70.6	1,078	230
Topeka	196.4	25.9	75.3	123.5	976	392	584	193.8	1,532	380
Wichita	638.0	175.1	49.8	184.0	471	318	154	575.7	1,475	346
KENTUCKY	X	X	X	X	X	X	X	X	X	X
Bowling Green	118.3	11.8	29.8	73.4	1,082	191	103	83.0	1,223	173
Covington	73.7	16.1	15.1	45.9	1,134	179	254	70.5	1,739	553
Elizabethtown	51.5	6.0	45.2	32.7	1,107	124	348	36.8	1,247	138
Florence	47.0	3.4	91.6	33.5	1,034	244	162	27.4	847	236
Frankfort	77.8	3.5	49.5	28.2	1,021	134	135	63.9	2,309	412
Georgetown	36.5	3.8	40.2	23.1	684	71	160	25.5	756	35
Henderson	43.6	12.8	10.6	20.3	709	313	197	39.8	1,388	269
Hopkinsville	40.1	6.0	8.4	28.6	932	173	164	33.1	1,078	57
Independence	9.1	0.7	94.2	8.1	292	160	38	6.7	242	73
Jeffersontown	50.0	21.0	15.8	21.2	755	140	132	40.0	1,422	119
Lexington-Fayette	690.2	86.8	23.5	411.2	1,277	324	229	589.9	1,832	481
Louisville/Jefferson County	1,127.6	192.7	37.9	645.2	838	204	126	1,215.3	1,579	151
Nicholasville	25.4	2.4	64.4	18.4	604	140	203	16.5	543	57
Owensboro	112.1	20.8	17.6	42.1	707	185	141	91.5	1,537	220
Paducah	68.5	14.3	52.9	36.4	1,459	253	197	52.6	2,106	561
Richmond	49.2	9.2	16.7	25.7	728	98	164	27.6	780	104
LOUISIANA	X	X	X	X	X	X	X	X	X	X
Alexandria	85.5	19.2	4.6	50.0	1,064	224	840	103.6	2,204	375
Baton Rouge	991.7	113.8	42.8	550.0	2,451	919	1,532	1,138.2	5,072	742
Bossier City	134.8	4.4	42.7	78.9	1,152	204	948	95.4	1,393	230
Central	16.5	5.1	5.8	9.6	330	0	330	8.4	287	251
Houma	482.7	85.3	11.7	103.7	3,121	1,587	1,534	524.9	15,790	2,430
Kenner	102.1	51.4	4.8	31.3	467	128	339	107.2	1,601	333
Lafayette	378.0	37.9	19.2	233.7	1,847	998	848	399.6	3,158	621
Lake Charles	140.1	24.1	52.8	89.4	1,152	121	1,031	122.0	1,573	270
Monroe	134.6	22.5	14.2	84.6	1,752	237	1,515	106.1	2,199	145
New Iberia	35.1	6.4	6.8	21.3	724	152	572	31.5	1,066	169
New Orleans	1,508.9	379.6	17.7	554.4	1,416	658	747	1,359.1	3,472	920
Shreveport	393.6	43.1	35.0	239.8	1,249	474	775	378.3	1,970	218
Slidell	38.8	0.0	0.0	31.2	1,117	255	862	13.7	491	0
MAINE	X	X	X	X	X	X	X	X	X	X
Bangor	147.3	41.4	94.0	62.0	1,935	1,915	20	143.1	4,465	506
Lewiston	149.3	67.9	95.1	60.4	1,680	1,665	15	143.4	3,987	476
Portland	296.3	49.7	91.9	167.4	2,512	2,441	71	330.9	4,964	237
South Portland	100.0	18.4	90.3	68.8	2,701	2,696	5	100.6	3,950	570
MARYLAND	X	X	X	X	X	X	X	X	X	X
Annapolis	97.1	10.0	44.7	58.7	1,495	1,150	175	89.8	2,289	20
Baltimore	3,446.7	1,447.1	96.3	1,488.2	2,438	1,405	323	3,478.8	5,698	601
Bowie	52.8	3.1	86.1	42.5	726	482	51	49.8	850	0
College Park	20.5	1.8	80.6	14.7	456	286	100	16.0	496	2
Frederick	122.6	18.9	65.5	67.1	945	763	55	92.6	1,305	25
Gaithersburg	66.7	4.5	54.7	46.5	683	400	117	57.3	842	19
Hagerstown	64.4	4.0	44.0	33.9	843	648	130	62.5	1,554	5
Laurel	36.1	2.3	65.0	26.2	1,018	791	94	34.5	1,339	0
Rockville	111.6	8.8	51.2	60.8	896	594	101	104.8	1,545	28
Salisbury	58.8	12.6	76.7	26.4	808	690	58	51.9	1,591	54
MASSACHUSETTS	X	X	X	X	X	X	X	X	X	X
Agawam Town	101.2	30.5	96.6	61.6	2,147	2,117	30	115.5	4,027	196
Amherst Town	NA	NA	NA	NA	NA	NA	NA	NA	NA	NA
Attleboro	149.9	54.0	98.0	74.9	1,672	1,619	52	133.3	2,976	164
Barnstable Town	185.8	28.1	84.0	126.3	2,848	2,753	95	183.8	4,143	394
Beverly	171.4	44.1	92.5	101.7	2,426	2,367	59	162.2	3,869	1,021
Boston	3,800.8	945.0	91.1	2,365.0	3,439	3,077	362	3,728.9	5,422	605
Braintree Town	140.0	35.0	95.9	96.0	2,578	2,438	140	133.2	3,574	177
Bridgewater Town	NA	NA	NA	NA	NA	NA	NA	NA	NA	NA
Brockton	415.3	229.7	98.4	145.2	1,518	1,460	58	375.7	3,927	65
Cambridge	1,207.0	357.5	73.2	431.5	3,692	3,255	437	1,102.8	9,436	808

1. Based on population estimated as of July 1 of the year shown.

City	City government finances, 2017 (cont.)												
	General expenditure (cont.)												
	Percent of total for:										Debt outstanding		
	Public welfare	Highways	Parking facilities	Education	Health and hospitals	Police protection	Sewerage and sanitation	Parks and recreation	Housing and community development	Interest on debt	Total (mil dol)	Per capita[1] (dollars)	Debt issued during year
	127	128	129	130	131	132	133	134	135	136	137	138	139
KANSAS—Cont'd													
Olathe	0.0	23.1	0.0	0.0	0.0	11.0	6.9	12.9	0.0	15.8	964.4	7,012	31.1
Overland Park	0.0	20.2	0.0	0.0	0.0	14.7	4.3	5.5	0.1	21.1	480.0	2,509	31.6
Salina	0.0	10.7	0.0	0.0	1.6	16.7	11.7	10.7	3.7	2.5	135.1	2,884	0.0
Shawnee	0.0	22.8	0.0	0.0	0.0	22.3	2.4	8.7	0.4	6.9	128.3	1,957	25.2
Topeka	0.3	15.9	1.3	0.0	0.0	19.3	19.7	1.5	2.1	3.2	392.1	3,099	74.7
Wichita	0.0	14.8	0.2	0.0	0.4	14.4	11.4	5.9	0.1	18.3	2,489.8	6,380	153.3
KENTUCKY	X	X	X	X	X	X	X	X	X	X	X	X	X
Bowling Green	0.0	14.6	0.0	0.0	0.0	13.1	14.0	12.0	6.3	4.4	165.8	2,443	0.8
Covington	0.0	16.7	1.2	0.0	0.0	13.4	2.0	9.8	21.0	2.6	106.0	2,615	21.2
Elizabethtown	0.0	14.6	0.0	0.0	0.0	8.7	13.4	11.4	0.0	0.0	54.1	1,832	4.9
Florence	0.0	36.3	0.0	0.0	0.0	20.0	7.7	6.5	0.0	1.9	18.3	566	0.0
Frankfort	0.0	4.9	0.0	0.0	0.0	10.1	19.3	5.2	0.0	0.0	60.1	2,172	5.1
Georgetown	0.0	5.1	0.0	0.5	0.0	15.0	29.4	3.5	1.4	1.6	443.9	13,183	0.0
Henderson	0.0	6.2	0.0	0.0	0.0	11.3	6.8	3.6	17.7	3.4	116.1	4,051	10.2
Hopkinsville	0.0	4.7	0.0	0.0	0.0	15.6	0.0	2.6	23.2	1.7	165.1	5,381	5.3
Independence	0.0	36.5	0.0	0.0	0.0	36.1	0.0	2.4	0.0	4.2	5.9	215	0.0
Jeffersontown	0.0	9.4	0.0	0.0	54.0	16.6	2.8	5.2	4.4	0.0	102.5	3,642	0.0
Lexington-Fayette	1.9	2.8	0.0	0.0	2.7	10.2	20.6	10.0	1.4	4.0	919.4	2,856	199.2
Louisville/Jefferson County	1.2	6.8	2.2	4.4	8.0	15.2	2.2	4.9	4.4	10.0	2,142.7	2,783	329.7
Nicholasville	0.0	12.2	0.0	0.0	0.0	26.5	19.4	0.0	2.3	2.8	35.8	1,175	0.0
Owensboro	0.0	7.4	0.2	0.0	0.0	9.1	24.4	6.5	9.0	6.0	450.1	7,562	32.9
Paducah	0.0	21.8	0.0	0.0	0.0	12.4	5.6	5.6	16.1	1.9	180.3	7,222	7.1
Richmond	0.0	4.9	0.0	0.0	0.0	13.1	23.0	8.1	8.3	4.0	74.4	2,106	6.6
LOUISIANA	X	X	X	X	X	X	X	X	X	X	X	X	X
Alexandria	0.0	8.4	0.0	0.0	0.0	16.4	12.4	6.2	4.2	8.1	201.5	4,285	12.0
Baton Rouge	0.5	3.9	0.1	1.0	12.8	13.7	19.6	1.2	5.9	6.9	1,319.4	5,879	0.0
Bossier City	0.7	10.6	0.0	0.0	0.6	20.5	11.3	5.0	4.6	9.2	528.8	7,723	38.2
Central	0.0	3.0	0.0	0.0	0.0	3.5	84.0	0.0	0.0	0.0	0.0	0	0.0
Houma	0.5	6.5	0.0	0.0	53.2	7.6	3.5	1.0	4.7	1.3	113.8	3,422	2.0
Kenner	1.2	7.3	0.0	0.0	0.4	15.9	19.8	9.6	11.3	0.0	91.1	1,361	8.7
Lafayette	0.3	12.0	0.2	0.0	0.4	23.8	8.9	7.5	4.3	3.9	484.1	3,826	20.4
Lake Charles	0.0	23.6	0.0	0.0	0.4	15.7	7.7	7.7	17.3	4.0	56.8	732	0.0
Monroe	0.0	7.1	0.0	0.0	0.0	16.1	12.7	8.5	11.1	0.0	206.8	4,285	6.1
New Iberia	0.5	7.1	0.0	0.0	0.0	20.0	40.1	3.5	3.6	0.2	1.2	41	0.0
New Orleans	0.0	4.2	0.0	0.0	3.4	6.3	10.2	6.1	18.9	6.1	2,414.1	6,166	137.3
Shreveport	0.0	5.4	0.2	0.0	0.0	16.1	15.0	9.0	6.0	5.4	206.4	1,075	0.0
Slidell	0.0	0.0	0.0	0.0	0.0	0.0	39.4	11.0	0.0	0.0	0.0	0	0.0
MAINE	X	X	X	X	X	X	X	X	X	X	X	X	X
Bangor	0.0	0.0	0.5	33.2	2.2	6.2	7.3	4.9	0.8	3.3	134.0	4,181	4.3
Lewiston	0.8	3.0	0.0	50.2	0.0	4.5	8.0	0.6	1.8	2.5	125.1	3,479	11.7
Portland	11.1	5.0	0.7	33.1	1.9	5.2	7.8	2.8	1.1	5.5	392.1	5,883	0.0
South Portland	0.5	6.1	0.0	46.4	0.0	5.1	7.0	3.6	0.0	1.7	56.6	2,221	12.7
MARYLAND	X	X	X	X	X	X	X	X	X	X	X	X	X
Annapolis	0.0	9.0	6.1	0.0	0.0	21.2	11.6	11.7	0.6	1.5	161.8	4,122	17.0
Baltimore	0.0	2.8	0.7	39.7	3.4	14.3	14.6	1.1	1.5	0.9	818.8	1,341	139.9
Bowie	0.0	13.4	0.0	0.0	0.5	22.6	19.8	16.0	0.7	1.1	13.2	225	0.1
College Park	0.0	15.6	1.0	0.0	0.7	7.3	20.8	7.8	1.2	3.8	12.3	382	0.5
Frederick	0.0	11.8	4.0	0.0	0.0	32.5	12.6	8.6	0.4	5.4	210.7	2,970	11.2
Gaithersburg	0.0	5.7	0.0	0.0	0.8	17.4	5.1	14.3	4.6	8.5	102.7	1,511	0.0
Hagerstown	0.0	5.7	1.1	0.0	0.0	22.5	23.9	7.1	1.4	7.1	109.4	2,723	10.6
Laurel	0.0	21.7	0.0	0.0	0.0	32.3	3.7	5.3	0.2	0.9	7.1	274	0.0
Rockville	0.0	15.1	0.5	0.0	0.4	10.7	15.6	22.9	1.7	5.1	130.8	1,929	17.5
Salisbury	0.0	11.1	1.2	0.0	0.3	23.1	20.3	5.6	0.5	6.7	102.0	3,127	39.6
MASSACHUSETTS	X	X	X	X	X	X	X	X	X	X	X	X	X
Agawam Town	0.1	3.8	0.0	56.3	1.8	4.5	4.6	0.7	0.3	0.6	25.8	899	0.0
Amherst Town	NA	NA	NA	NA	NA	NA	NA	NA	NA	NA	NA	NA	NA
Attleboro	0.7	3.2	0.0	61.6	2.2	5.9	5.6	1.4	0.4	1.2	60.0	1,340	0.0
Barnstable Town	0.2	2.9	0.0	47.6	0.7	7.3	3.8	3.6	0.4	1.7	105.5	2,378	12.4
Beverly	0.4	4.7	0.0	60.7	0.3	4.9	5.4	1.1	0.1	1.8	87.5	2,086	31.9
Boston	0.1	3.2	0.1	37.5	7.6	10.1	6.9	2.5	2.7	1.9	1,929.8	2,806	378.7
Braintree Town	0.2	5.3	0.0	63.9	0.2	7.6	1.1	2.1	0.0	0.7	121.4	3,259	8.6
Bridgewater Town	NA	NA	NA	NA	NA	NA	NA	NA	NA	NA	NA	NA	NA
Brockton	0.3	2.4	0.1	68.3	0.3	6.1	4.8	0.5	0.0	1.9	199.6	2,086	5.0
Cambridge	0.1	1.5	0.1	20.3	53.9	3.5	3.9	1.7	0.1	1.2	422.1	3,612	77.4

1. Based on population estimated as of July 1 of the year shown.

STATE Place code	City	Land area[1] (sq. mi)	Population, 2021: Total persons 2021	Population, 2021: Rank	Population, 2021: Per square mile	Race 2020, Race alone[2] (percent): White	Black or African American	American Indian, Alaskan Native	Asian	Hawaiian Pacific Islander	Some other race	Race 2020: Two or more races (percent)
		1	2	3	4	5	6	7	8	9	10	11
	MASSACHUSETTS—Cont'd											
25 13205	Chelsea	2.2	38,889	1,020	17,676.8	27.4	7.3	1.4	3.3	0.0	44.6	15.9
25 13660	Chicopee	22.9	55,190	722	2,410.0	71.9	4.8	0.4	1.7	0.1	10.3	10.9
25 21990	Everett	3.4	48,557	819	14,281.5	37.4	14.6	0.7	7.6	0.0	22.5	17.2
25 23000	Fall River	33.1	93,884	357	2,836.4	73.4	5.6	0.4	2.7	0.0	6.8	11.1
25 23875	Fitchburg	27.8	41,732	951	1,501.2	60.3	7.2	0.6	3.6	0.0	14.0	14.1
25 24960	Framingham	25.0	71,265	520	2,850.6	56.2	6.2	0.5	7.3	0.0	16.0	13.7
25 25172	Franklin Town	26.6	33,036	1,190	1,242.0	86.0	2.0	0.1	5.5	0.1	1.4	5.0
25 26150	Gloucester	26.2	29,952	1,310	1,143.2	89.1	1.1	0.3	1.1	0.1	2.8	5.5
25 29405	Haverhill	33.0	67,361	558	2,041.2	70.3	4.6	0.4	2.0	0.0	12.9	9.8
25 30840	Holyoke	21.2	37,929	1,051	1,789.1	52.3	4.3	0.7	1.1	0.1	25.9	15.7
25 34550	Lawrence	6.9	88,508	390	12,827.2	20.0	5.5	1.4	1.9	0.1	51.0	20.1
25 35075	Leominster	28.8	43,613	913	1,514.3	67.7	7.0	0.3	3.2	0.0	9.3	12.4
25 37000	Lowell	13.6	113,994	260	8,381.9	45.5	9.0	0.4	22.3	0.1	12.1	10.7
25 37490	Lynn	10.7	100,843	324	9,424.6	38.2	12.1	1.4	6.9	0.0	27.8	13.6
25 37875	Malden	5.0	65,074	587	13,014.8	41.4	14.7	0.3	25.9	0.0	7.3	10.4
25 38715	Marlborough	20.9	41,110	957	1,967.0	61.3	3.4	0.5	5.9	0.0	14.4	14.5
25 39835	Medford	8.1	62,098	620	7,666.4	67.8	8.3	0.1	11.5	0.0	3.9	8.3
25 40115	Melrose	4.7	29,312	1,334	6,236.6	80.5	3.2	0.1	7.4	0.0	1.7	6.9
25 40710	Methuen Town	22.2	52,798	755	2,378.3	62.9	5.1	0.4	4.0	0.0	17.4	10.1
25 45000	New Bedford	20.0	100,941	323	5,047.1	60.8	5.8	1.4	1.0	0.1	14.9	16.1
25 45560	Newton	17.8	87,453	394	4,913.1	71.1	3.0	0.2	16.6	0.0	2.2	6.9
25 46330	Northampton	34.2	29,311	1,335	857.0	80.0	3.1	0.3	4.4	0.0	3.7	8.4
25 46598	North Attleborough Town	18.9	30,854	1,279	1,632.5	83.8	3.1	0.1	5.9	0.0	1.7	5.4
25 52490	Peabody	16.2	54,119	738	3,340.7	79.2	3.6	0.2	2.5	0.0	6.3	8.3
25 53960	Pittsfield	40.5	43,641	912	1,077.6	79.5	6.8	0.2	1.4	0.0	4.0	8.0
25 55745	Quincy	16.6	101,119	320	6,091.5	55.1	5.7	0.2	30.8	0.0	2.7	5.5
25 56000	Randolph Town	9.8	34,715	1,146	3,542.3	27.5	43.2	0.4	12.9	0.0	7.1	8.8
25 56585	Revere	5.7	59,075	662	10,364.0	49.1	5.2	0.7	5.6	0.0	23.9	15.5
25 59105	Salem	8.3	44,819	885	5,399.9	71.5	5.1	0.3	2.9	0.1	9.7	10.5
25 62535	Somerville	4.1	79,815	450	19,467.1	67.1	5.5	0.2	10.6	0.0	6.3	10.2
25 67000	Springfield	31.9	154,789	168	4,852.3	36.7	20.8	0.9	2.9	0.1	24.1	14.4
25 69170	Taunton	46.7	59,600	651	1,276.2	74.7	8.7	0.3	1.2	0.1	5.0	10.1
25 72600	Waltham	12.7	64,015	598	5,040.6	62.4	7.0	0.5	12.2	0.0	10.6	7.3
25 73440	Watertown Town	4.0	35,149	1,135	8,787.3	74.6	3.6	0.2	9.6	0.0	4.1	7.9
25 76030	Westfield	46.3	40,575	974	876.3	84.5	2.0	0.3	2.3	0.0	3.9	6.9
25 77890	West Springfield Town	16.7	28,629	1,364	1,714.3	74.8	4.1	0.2	6.4	0.0	5.8	8.6
25 78972	Weymouth Town	16.8	57,670	687	3,432.7	78.3	4.9	0.2	7.0	0.0	3.0	6.7
25 81035	Woburn	12.7	41,056	958	3,232.8	74.0	5.5	0.2	8.5	0.0	4.1	7.7
25 82000	Worcester	37.4	205,918	114	5,505.8	53.3	14.8	0.5	7.1	0.0	12.9	11.3
26 00000	MICHIGAN	56,605.9	10,050,811	X	177.6	73.9	13.7	0.6	3.3	0.0	2.2	6.3
26 01380	Allen Park	7.0	28,237	1,378	4,033.9	81.3	4.0	0.5	1.3	0.0	3.7	9.2
26 03000	Ann Arbor	28.2	121,536	235	4,309.8	67.6	6.8	0.2	15.7	0.1	1.8	7.9
26 05920	Battle Creek	42.6	52,335	759	1,228.5	63.8	17.9	0.8	5.1	0.0	3.6	8.9
26 06020	Bay City	10.2	32,404	1,218	3,176.9	84.1	3.3	0.6	0.5	0.0	2.3	9.2
26 12060	Burton	23.4	29,500	1,325	1,260.7	80.4	9.8	0.6	0.6	0.0	1.3	7.2
26 21000	Dearborn	24.2	108,420	285	4,480.2	86.4	4.0	0.2	2.5	0.0	1.3	5.6
26 21020	Dearborn Heights	11.7	62,451	616	5,337.7	80.4	9.8	0.3	1.7	0.0	1.7	6.1
26 22000	Detroit	138.7	632,464	27	4,559.9	10.7	77.7	0.5	1.6	0.0	4.6	4.9
26 24120	East Lansing	13.4	46,854	851	3,496.6	71.4	12.1	0.4	8.8	0.1	2.0	5.2
26 24290	Eastpointe	5.2	34,037	1,167	6,545.6	39.4	52.7	0.3	1.1	0.0	1.0	5.5
26 27440	Farmington Hills	33.3	83,292	419	2,501.3	59.7	18.3	0.2	15.3	0.0	1.1	5.4
26 29000	Flint	33.4	80,628	438	2,414.0	33.9	56.3	0.5	0.5	0.0	2.0	6.9
26 31420	Garden City	5.9	26,994	1,441	4,575.3	84.0	6.1	0.4	1.1	0.0	1.1	7.3
26 34000	Grand Rapids	44.8	197,416	125	4,406.6	60.3	18.9	0.9	2.3	0.0	9.0	8.7
26 36280	Hamtramck	2.1	28,000	1,392	13,333.3	55.9	10.0	0.1	26.9	0.0	1.0	6.0
26 38640	Holland	16.7	34,024	1,168	2,037.4	71.2	4.2	0.8	2.8	0.1	9.4	11.5
26 40680	Inkster	6.3	25,725	1,506	4,083.3	18.0	73.3	0.4	0.8	0.0	1.4	6.0
26 41420	Jackson	10.8	31,347	1,262	2,902.5	66.8	19.3	0.5	1.1	0.0	2.5	9.8
26 42160	Kalamazoo	24.7	73,257	504	2,965.9	60.3	23.2	0.7	2.2	0.0	4.6	9.0
26 42820	Kentwood	20.9	54,141	737	2,590.5	55.9	19.4	0.7	11.3	0.0	5.1	7.6
26 46000	Lansing	39.1	112,684	268	2,881.9	55.0	23.4	0.8	4.2	0.0	5.0	11.6
26 47800	Lincoln Park	5.8	39,643	1,000	6,835.0	64.0	9.6	0.9	0.6	0.1	12.6	12.3
26 49000	Livonia	35.7	94,422	353	2,644.9	85.1	4.8	0.3	3.2	0.0	0.9	5.8
26 50560	Madison Heights	7.1	28,238	1,377	3,977.2	77.1	7.8	0.3	7.0	0.0	1.3	6.4
26 53780	Midland	34.4	42,472	941	1,234.7	86.5	2.0	0.4	3.4	0.2	1.1	6.5
26 56320	Muskegon	14.1	37,552	1,057	2,663.3	52.7	34.2	1.0	0.4	0.0	4.1	7.5
26 59140	Norton Shores	23.2	25,185	1,536	1,085.6	86.6	3.6	0.5	1.4	0.0	1.3	6.6
26 59440	Novi	30.2	66,560	573	2,204.0	58.1	7.6	0.2	26.9	0.0	1.4	5.8

1. Dry land or land partially or temporarily covered by water. 2. Hispanic or Latino persons may be of any race.

City	Percent Hispanic or Latino[1], 2020	Percent foreign born, 2016–2020	Age of population (percent), 2016–2020: Under 18 years	18 to 24 years	25 to 34 years	35 to 44 years	45 to 54 years	55 to 64 years	65 years and over	Median age, 2016–2020	Percent female, 2016–2020	Population: Census counts 2010	2020	Percent change 2010–2020	2020–2021
	12	13	14	15	16	17	18	19	20	21	22	23	24	25	26
MASSACHUSETTS—Cont'd															
Chelsea	65.8	47.1	24.5	8.7	18.9	16.7	11.8	9.7	9.7	33.8	49.2	35,181	40,615	15.4	-4.2
Chicopee	23.4	8.9	19.5	9.2	13.5	11.8	12.1	14.7	19.1	41.3	51.8	55,307	55,576	0.5	-0.7
Everett	28.5	43.0	22.0	7.6	20.3	14.6	14.0	10.2	11.3	35.1	49.0	41,553	49,165	18.3	-1.2
Fall River	13.4	21.3	21.0	7.9	15.1	12.9	13.4	13.1	16.6	39.4	51.5	88,865	93,938	5.7	-0.1
Fitchburg	30.1	10.2	21.7	12.8	14.6	11.6	13.3	13.0	13.1	35.6	51.3	40,325	41,945	4.0	-0.5
Framingham	16.8	28.4	20.1	9.0	15.5	13.0	13.5	12.7	16.2	38.9	50.5	68,325	72,342	5.9	-1.5
Franklin Town	3.7	8.5	22.3	11.3	9.6	11.8	18.8	12.9	13.3	40.9	52.0	31,633	33,243	5.1	-0.6
Gloucester	4.7	8.4	16.3	5.8	11.3	10.2	13.5	18.8	24.1	50.6	50.4	28,789	29,726	3.3	0.8
Haverhill	23.6	11.6	21.9	8.8	14.5	12.5	13.3	14.6	14.5	38.4	51.6	60,878	67,764	11.3	-0.6
Holyoke	51.3	5.8	22.8	9.8	16.2	12.2	12.1	11.8	15.1	35.8	50.6	39,881	38,247	-4.1	-0.8
Lawrence	81.8	40.8	26.8	10.9	17.1	13.3	10.9	10.7	10.2	32.2	50.0	76,343	89,152	16.8	-0.7
Leominster	18.9	16.1	20.7	7.9	13.8	11.8	13.8	14.7	17.2	41.5	51.3	40,762	43,782	7.4	-0.4
Lowell	21.7	26.7	21.0	13.9	17.0	13.0	11.8	12.0	11.5	33.8	50.6	106,529	115,441	8.4	-1.3
Lynn	44.0	36.7	24.0	10.0	15.6	13.5	13.6	11.0	12.3	35.3	49.7	90,319	101,238	12.1	-0.4
Malden	10.4	42.3	18.4	9.4	22.0	12.7	12.3	12.0	13.1	35.1	50.5	59,533	66,353	11.5	-1.9
Marlborough	15.9	24.0	20.0	7.4	16.5	13.3	13.6	14.1	15.2	39.4	52.2	38,501	41,838	8.7	-1.7
Medford	6.2	22.1	13.1	14.7	21.6	12.3	10.5	13.4	14.4	35.4	52.0	56,280	59,662	6.0	4.1
Melrose	4.5	12.1	19.7	6.7	11.9	16.4	14.7	11.8	18.9	41.7	52.0	26,971	29,860	10.7	-1.8
Methuen Town	29.3	23.1	20.8	9.7	12.2	15.1	13.2	13.0	16.0	39.6	52.3	47,332	53,026	12.0	-0.4
New Bedford	24.3	19.0	23.4	9.8	15.1	12.7	12.5	11.3	15.1	36.4	51.1	95,063	101,044	6.3	-0.1
Newton	5.1	21.3	21.3	12.7	9.1	11.9	14.1	12.6	18.3	41.1	53.0	85,074	88,787	4.4	-1.5
Northampton	9.1	7.6	15.7	16.4	12.0	12.3	12.1	12.5	19.1	40.0	58.7	28,559	29,549	3.5	-0.8
North Attleborough Town	4.1	9.0	22.6	7.0	14.1	13.3	13.6	14.6	14.8	40.2	50.4	28,699	30,795	7.3	0.2
Peabody	9.9	15.6	18.3	8.5	11.7	10.0	13.6	15.3	22.6	46.6	53.1	51,270	54,486	6.3	-0.7
Pittsfield	8.1	5.7	17.8	7.5	14.0	12.3	12.5	15.8	20.2	43.9	51.8	44,743	43,917	-1.8	-0.6
Quincy	5.1	32.9	14.6	7.9	21.6	14.3	11.7	13.0	16.8	38.5	50.8	92,260	101,685	10.2	-0.6
Randolph Town	10.9	35.8	19.1	9.6	14.4	12.2	12.5	15.3	16.7	40.8	52.2	32,099	34,995	9.0	-0.8
Revere	37.3	40.1	20.6	7.6	15.3	15.7	14.7	12.3	13.7	39.2	49.3	51,715	61,878	19.7	-4.5
Salem	19.8	14.5	15.6	12.5	17.7	12.1	13.0	12.6	16.4	38.2	56.0	41,311	44,501	7.7	0.7
Somerville	11.3	23.9	11.0	14.5	32.9	15.0	9.2	8.7	8.8	31.5	50.2	75,693	81,054	7.1	-1.5
Springfield	46.7	10.0	24.5	12.8	14.4	12.2	11.6	11.7	12.8	33.6	52.7	153,132	155,913	1.8	-0.7
Taunton	7.9	12.0	22.4	7.7	14.3	12.0	13.4	15.4	14.7	39.0	52.6	55,834	59,359	6.3	0.4
Waltham	16.4	26.6	13.7	20.0	17.7	12.9	9.9	11.3	14.5	34.3	51.7	60,660	64,994	7.1	-1.5
Watertown Town	7.7	23.2	14.4	5.9	21.5	16.0	11.2	14.1	16.9	39.5	53.6	31,963	35,374	10.7	-0.6
Westfield	9.7	8.4	18.9	15.1	11.7	11.2	12.4	13.2	17.5	39.3	51.7	41,093	40,795	-0.7	-0.5
West Springfield Town	13.9	16.9	21.1	8.2	17.7	12.5	14.7	11.0	14.8	37.1	50.5	28,391	28,843	1.6	-0.7
Weymouth Town	4.5	12.7	17.6	8.1	14.0	11.7	13.8	16.0	18.9	43.8	52.0	53,762	57,513	7.0	0.3
Woburn	6.4	19.2	19.3	8.1	16.1	12.9	13.2	14.4	16.1	39.7	50.8	38,908	40,934	5.2	0.3
Worcester	24.6	21.0	19.0	15.5	16.1	12.0	11.8	12.1	13.6	34.6	50.8	180,892	206,601	14.2	-0.3
MICHIGAN	5.6	6.9	21.7	9.6	12.9	11.7	12.9	14.0	17.2	39.8	50.8	9,884,112	10,077,331	2.0	-0.3
Allen Park	12.2	4.0	21.1	6.1	12.1	13.3	16.0	13.9	17.6	43.4	51.0	28,212	28,629	1.5	-1.4
Ann Arbor	5.5	19.7	12.4	32.3	17.3	9.9	8.0	8.1	11.9	27.5	50.6	114,008	122,830	7.7	-1.1
Battle Creek	7.7	6.6	25.8	8.0	14.0	13.5	11.8	11.8	15.2	36.5	51.5	52,388	52,631	0.5	-0.6
Bay City	10.0	1.3	21.7	9.7	13.7	13.0	12.4	14.7	14.8	38.5	52.3	34,929	32,655	-6.5	-0.8
Burton	5.0	1.7	21.4	8.8	10.9	12.8	13.9	14.7	17.6	42.5	54.2	30,003	29,680	-1.1	-0.6
Dearborn	3.6	29.5	28.9	10.7	14.4	11.7	11.4	10.1	12.9	32.1	50.3	98,146	109,910	12.0	-1.4
Dearborn Heights	5.0	21.5	25.1	8.0	14.9	11.2	11.5	13.7	15.6	36.1	51.0	57,774	63,257	9.5	-1.3
Detroit	8.0	6.1	24.8	10.1	15.5	11.8	11.8	12.1	13.9	34.6	52.7	713,956	639,614	-10.4	-1.1
East Lansing	5.2	13.1	8.3	60.0	9.4	5.1	4.4	4.2	8.5	21.4	50.9	48,573	47,127	-3.0	-0.6
Eastpointe	2.4	3.1	22.8	9.0	14.5	13.7	13.9	13.2	13.0	38.1	52.6	32,403	34,342	6.0	-0.9
Farmington Hills	3.1	21.1	18.0	8.0	14.3	11.7	14.2	13.5	20.4	42.8	51.4	79,725	83,991	5.4	-0.8
Flint	4.9	1.9	24.5	10.4	13.6	11.4	13.0	13.5	13.6	36.3	51.5	102,258	81,381	-20.4	-0.9
Garden City	4.4	5.3	19.6	8.4	12.5	11.6	17.9	14.4	15.5	43.0	51.4	27,636	27,360	-1.0	-1.3
Grand Rapids	16.5	11.1	22.3	13.8	20.1	11.3	9.9	10.1	12.4	31.2	51.0	187,999	198,487	5.6	-0.5
Hamtramck	1.1	40.3	33.2	12.7	15.0	13.1	10.1	8.4	7.4	27.5	48.6	22,443	28,413	26.6	-1.5
Holland	23.4	6.9	20.8	18.0	13.7	11.1	10.4	10.0	16.1	32.9	51.4	33,099	34,242	3.5	-0.6
Inkster	3.1	5.1	31.4	7.5	15.1	11.4	12.1	11.3	11.2	31.6	52.8	25,366	26,066	2.8	-1.3
Jackson	6.8	2.4	25.1	9.5	15.3	12.1	13.6	13.5	11.0	35.1	51.6	33,474	31,505	-5.9	-0.5
Kalamazoo	9.1	6.1	18.9	28.2	15.3	10.1	8.2	8.7	10.6	26.4	50.8	74,263	73,808	-0.6	-0.7
Kentwood	10.9	18.2	25.2	8.0	18.1	12.3	11.3	11.0	14.1	34.1	52.1	48,698	54,375	11.7	-0.4
Lansing	13.7	10.0	23.2	11.9	18.5	12.3	11.0	10.9	12.2	32.7	51.2	114,269	112,954	-1.2	-0.2
Lincoln Park	25.8	8.8	24.7	8.6	15.1	13.2	12.8	12.2	13.5	36.1	51.0	38,085	40,201	5.6	-1.4
Livonia	3.6	8.3	18.5	7.6	13.0	10.6	13.1	16.6	20.6	45.3	51.3	96,857	95,531	-1.4	-1.2
Madison Heights	3.6	14.9	16.9	8.1	17.0	14.7	15.5	13.1	14.8	40.5	50.6	29,694	28,473	-4.1	-0.8
Midland	3.9	5.9	21.7	10.3	14.6	12.0	11.1	12.6	17.6	37.9	52.1	41,872	42,543	1.6	-0.2
Muskegon	9.2	3.3	23.4	11.2	15.4	13.6	11.0	12.2	13.1	34.9	49.4	38,397	37,519	-2.3	0.1
Norton Shores	5.2	2.8	23.3	7.7	14.1	10.5	9.5	13.8	21.0	39.1	52.0	24,002	25,166	4.8	0.1
Novi	4.1	26.8	23.9	6.7	13.1	13.8	15.3	13.1	14.1	39.2	51.2	55,232	66,252	20.0	0.5

1. May be of any race.

Table D. Cities — Households, Group Quarters, Crime, and Education

City	Households, 2016–2020: Number	Households, 2016–2020: Persons per household	Households, 2016–2020: Percent: Family	Households, 2016–2020: Percent: Married couple family	Households, 2016–2020: Percent: Female family	Households, 2016–2020: Percent: Non-family	Households, 2016–2020: Percent: One person	Persons in group quarters, 2016–2020	Serious crimes known to police[2], 2020: Violent: Number	Serious crimes known to police[2], 2020: Violent: Rate	Serious crimes known to police[2], 2020: Property: Number	Serious crimes known to police[2], 2020: Property: Rate	Educational attainment, 2016–2020: Population age 25 and over	Educational attainment, 2016–2020: Attainment[4] (percent): High school graduate or less	Educational attainment, 2016–2020: Attainment[4] (percent): Bachelor's degree or more
	27	28	29	30	31	32	33	34	35	36	37	38	39	40	41
MASSACHUSETTS—Cont'd															
Chelsea	13,174	2.97	57.6	31.1	19.4	42.4	32.9	765	249	622.6	570	1,425.2	26,615	60.9	19.9
Chicopee	23,447	2.31	59.9	37.0	17.6	40.1	33.5	1,133	294	535.3	1,148	2,090.4	39,299	49.4	20.8
Everett	16,107	2.86	68.2	41.6	18.6	31.8	25.1	178	181	387.0	674	1,441.2	32,584	51.8	23.7
Fall River	38,709	2.28	59.3	34.3	17.8	40.7	35.0	1,371	779	873.9	994	1,115.1	63,765	58.3	15.9
Fitchburg	15,555	2.50	60.1	36.8	16.7	39.9	30.2	1,761	221	546.4	584	1,444.0	26,587	46.5	21.4
Framingham	28,401	2.45	65.1	49.5	11.7	34.9	27.9	3,158	264	353.5	862	1,154.3	51,656	31.6	49.8
Franklin Town	12,414	2.62	71.5	60.8	9.2	28.5	21.7	1,125	6	17.5	32	93.3	22,322	20.3	55.3
Gloucester	13,410	2.23	61.4	48.0	9.3	38.6	30.9	355	72	236.5	96	315.3	23,621	32.2	39.2
Haverhill	24,612	2.55	63.0	40.0	17.2	37.0	27.5	964	304	474.9	638	996.6	44,205	40.7	29.4
Holyoke	15,464	2.52	60.1	28.3	25.5	39.9	32.0	1,212	362	905.0	1,246	3,114.8	27,068	53.1	22.0
Lawrence	26,551	2.97	68.5	32.0	27.5	31.5	26.4	1,171	358	447.5	647	808.8	49,817	63.0	12.5
Leominster	16,983	2.43	61.3	43.7	12.6	38.7	31.2	375	199	478.4	697	1,675.6	29,672	39.5	29.8
Lowell	40,260	2.65	60.6	34.7	18.8	39.4	28.6	4,749	348	313.9	1,629	1,469.2	72,534	49.0	27.3
Lynn	33,261	2.81	64.9	37.8	18.7	35.1	29.2	757	418	443.6	910	965.8	62,169	55.3	19.5
Malden	23,367	2.59	64.5	46.4	12.0	35.5	25.5	281	162	269.0	751	1,246.9	43,787	38.0	40.6
Marlborough	16,044	2.44	62.1	47.2	11.0	37.9	29.0	550	149	377.2	353	893.7	28,799	35.5	40.4
Medford	23,807	2.35	54.6	40.5	10.6	45.4	29.7	2,351	72	126.0	537	939.8	42,099	27.1	54.7
Melrose	11,238	2.47	65.3	55.6	4.9	34.7	26.7	322	26	92.9	132	471.8	20,657	20.6	61.1
Methuen Town	17,611	2.84	73.4	49.6	17.2	26.6	22.0	471	62	122.0	441	867.9	35,088	39.8	29.6
New Bedford	39,059	2.39	58.5	32.2	19.8	41.5	34.3	1,930	596	628.1	1,684	1,774.8	63,676	57.4	16.9
Newton	30,756	2.62	72.3	61.5	8.3	27.7	21.4	7,645	48	54.4	486	550.5	58,261	10.4	78.7
Northampton	11,352	2.18	54.4	40.9	10.9	45.6	33.9	3,825	92	323.6	469	1,649.8	19,395	21.3	60.8
North Attleborough Town	11,317	2.57	64.3	51.0	9.5	35.7	30.0	192	32	109.3	312	1,065.6	20,621	32.0	41.7
Peabody	22,049	2.38	61.4	45.7	11.4	38.6	33.3	545	114	215.2	423	798.5	38,836	39.0	34.6
Pittsfield	19,072	2.17	54.9	36.9	14.4	45.1	35.9	1,035	341	814.5	664	1,586.1	31,771	37.9	31.2
Quincy	41,322	2.26	52.1	39.4	8.5	47.9	36.0	1,188	303	320.6	1,146	1,212.5	73,200	33.0	45.6
Randolph Town	11,727	2.89	73.2	47.9	19.8	26.8	22.5	346	86	268.3	298	929.7	24,368	43.9	27.6
Revere	18,555	2.86	62.3	41.3	13.6	37.7	30.1	255	196	370.3	657	1,241.3	38,344	55.4	24.1
Salem	19,094	2.18	51.4	34.1	14.3	48.6	36.9	1,746	108	250.3	650	1,506.2	31,174	31.7	45.1
Somerville	34,046	2.29	39.8	29.9	7.1	60.2	31.6	3,059	153	187.6	966	1,184.5	60,517	22.4	65.7
Springfield	56,804	2.61	62.1	29.6	25.7	37.9	32.2	5,649	1,480	966.8	3,730	2,436.6	96,334	53.0	19.0
Taunton	22,077	2.57	64.8	40.6	17.8	35.2	28.7	676	237	413.3	275	479.6	40,061	48.7	22.7
Waltham	23,891	2.29	51.9	39.7	9.0	48.1	31.8	7,818	85	136.4	385	617.6	41,499	28.2	52.5
Watertown Town	16,142	2.20	55.0	41.8	9.4	45.0	33.1	300	31	85.6	253	698.9	28,470	19.3	66.0
Westfield	15,099	2.51	67.9	51.5	10.5	32.1	26.9	3,348	84	204.5	324	788.9	27,244	38.8	32.2
West Springfield Town	12,402	2.29	54.8	40.1	9.8	45.2	39.1	139	134	471.2	879	3,091.0	20,187	37.8	32.4
Weymouth Town	24,392	2.33	62.0	45.4	11.3	38.0	30.5	477	130	223.8	441	759.2	42,513	32.0	40.0
Woburn	15,901	2.52	65.4	48.6	11.5	34.6	25.3	304	54	134.5	394	981.5	29,274	30.9	47.1
Worcester	72,289	2.36	53.4	32.4	15.8	46.6	36.8	14,736	1,169	632.4	3,695	1,998.9	121,348	43.3	31.2
MICHIGAN	3,980,408	2.45	63.5	46.9	11.8	36.5	29.9	225,743	47,641	478.0	135,633	1,360.9	6,853,674	37.2	30.0
Allen Park	11,368	2.37	64.5	48.8	10.4	35.5	31.0	179	98	365.5	381	1,421.2	19,719	34.1	28.5
Ann Arbor	48,109	2.25	44.3	36.3	5.5	55.7	34.2	12,910	294	243.7	1,592	1,319.6	66,901	9.4	77.3
Battle Creek	20,690	2.40	57.2	34.3	18.0	42.8	36.9	1,352	540	892.9	1,569	2,594.3	33,856	45.1	21.1
Bay City	14,327	2.27	54.3	32.3	16.4	45.7	38.4	426	276	849.6	500	1,539.2	22,563	47.6	16.2
Burton	12,240	2.33	60.3	39.2	16.7	39.7	31.6	109	192	675.4	648	2,279.5	19,973	46.4	16.1
Dearborn	31,797	2.96	65.4	50.4	10.0	34.6	29.4	360	277	296.2	1,662	1,777.4	57,010	39.4	32.8
Dearborn Heights	20,214	2.73	66.8	46.1	14.4	33.2	29.2	483	291	528.1	769	1,395.5	37,223	44.9	23.6
Detroit	270,446	2.44	52.0	19.5	25.7	48.0	41.6	13,159	14,370	2,178.5	21,178	3,210.7	437,572	50.3	16.4
East Lansing	13,430	2.43	36.9	28.8	5.6	63.1	34.9	15,739	74	153.9	817	1,698.6	15,337	12.7	69.4
Eastpointe	12,856	2.49	62.0	32.3	23.6	38.0	32.4	163	241	752.0	668	2,084.5	21,995	45.8	16.6
Farmington Hills	34,803	2.30	59.6	47.3	9.4	40.4	34.5	722	84	104.1	558	691.4	59,911	19.2	55.2
Flint	40,807	2.29	56.9	23.3	26.4	43.1	36.3	2,705	996	1,050.2	1,614	1,701.8	62,504	50.9	12.3
Garden City	11,007	2.41	63.9	44.0	14.1	36.1	30.5	64	54	205.5	204	776.2	19,118	48.2	13.7
Grand Rapids	76,360	2.51	55.5	36.8	12.7	44.5	33.0	7,913	1,443	712.5	3,956	1,953.5	127,357	34.7	37.7
Hamtramck	5,880	3.57	70.9	54.1	11.7	29.1	24.0	713	180	836.7	320	1,487.4	11,730	63.9	13.7
Holland	12,283	2.42	59.6	44.4	10.1	40.4	34.0	3,618	132	397.3	527	1,586.0	20,400	37.3	32.5
Inkster	8,953	2.69	62.0	22.7	31.7	38.0	31.8	336	318	1,315.5	543	2,246.3	14,912	53.7	10.5
Jackson	13,467	2.34	54.8	28.1	19.8	45.2	37.6	781	350	1,082.5	1,001	3,096.0	21,094	47.9	16.0
Kalamazoo	29,208	2.36	46.0	28.5	13.0	54.0	36.2	7,142	1,094	1,431.7	3,670	4,803.0	40,278	30.8	35.9
Kentwood	20,223	2.54	61.3	42.3	13.9	38.7	31.0	446	229	438.2	1,207	2,309.5	34,637	35.3	33.6
Lansing	49,539	2.35	49.5	29.6	14.6	50.5	39.7	1,019	1,699	1,431.9	3,565	3,004.6	76,257	36.1	26.3
Lincoln Park	14,734	2.47	56.5	36.3	13.5	43.5	36.5	81	NA	NA	NA	NA	24,343	57.7	11.5
Livonia	37,650	2.45	68.5	56.7	7.8	31.5	26.6	1,556	209	223.9	1,196	1,281.3	69,435	27.3	37.4
Madison Heights	13,824	2.16	50.1	33.8	12.1	49.9	41.5	138	70	234.1	458	1,531.5	22,502	39.9	28.0
Midland	17,626	2.31	61.2	48.1	10.6	38.8	31.8	1,163	62	148.7	329	789.3	28,502	27.5	44.6
Muskegon	13,530	2.36	53.9	26.7	21.8	46.1	38.4	5,354	254	698.0	1,004	2,758.9	24,391	50.5	13.4
Norton Shores	9,586	2.54	70.4	53.3	11.5	29.6	25.5	164	45	181.9	537	2,170.4	16,944	30.2	30.1
Novi	24,130	2.49	65.4	54.3	7.7	34.6	29.7	338	60	97.5	429	696.9	41,959	16.6	59.0

2. Data for serious crimes have not been adjusted for underreporting. This may affect comparability between geographic areas and over time.
4. Persons 25 years old and over.

City	Money income, 2016–2020: Households: Median household income	Money income, 2016–2020: Households: Percent with income less than $25,000	Money income, 2016–2020: Households: Percent with income of $200,000 or more	Money income, 2016–2020: Median family income	Money income, 2016–2020: Median non-family household income	Median earnings Full year, Full-time workers, 2016–2020: All persons	Median earnings Full year, Full-time workers, 2016–2020: Men	Median earnings Full year, Full-time workers, 2016–2020: Women	Housing units, 2016–2020: Total	Housing units, 2016–2020: Occupied	Housing units, 2016–2020: Percent owner occupied	Housing units, 2016–2020: Median value[1] (dollars)	Housing units, 2016–2020: Median gross rent (dollars)
	42	43	44	45	46	47	48	49	50	51	52	53	54
MASSACHUSETTS—Cont'd													
Chelsea	60,370	22.4	4.4	62,985	33,903	43,631	43,206	44,077	13,791	13,174	26.9	369,900	1,474
Chicopee	52,702	24.5	2.5	64,481	31,657	48,182	52,864	41,874	25,044	23,447	58.9	188,400	941
Everett	70,627	19.3	5.7	75,847	41,519	49,147	49,093	49,200	17,026	16,107	39.4	434,300	1,587
Fall River	46,007	30.1	2.6	53,809	27,264	46,436	52,238	40,817	42,513	38,709	36.8	256,200	834
Fitchburg	54,683	19.6	3.5	62,929	43,024	48,750	51,835	43,385	16,972	15,555	53.2	216,500	964
Framingham	86,322	13.2	14.2	106,770	50,625	64,545	67,426	59,484	29,423	28,401	56.1	439,400	1,421
Franklin Town	118,193	9.6	24.8	148,002	54,250	81,146	90,979	64,886	12,711	12,414	80.5	432,800	1,468
Gloucester	76,260	17.5	10.0	96,083	43,051	59,958	64,165	50,287	15,004	13,410	62.7	435,200	1,233
Haverhill	69,237	16.7	7.3	84,693	46,210	55,315	62,393	45,934	25,627	24,612	58.2	319,400	1,222
Holyoke	42,537	33.6	3.6	51,704	31,047	46,767	47,419	45,898	17,097	15,464	40.0	197,700	847
Lawrence	45,045	28.8	2.2	50,038	21,273	37,334	42,378	34,252	27,922	26,551	29.7	280,800	1,188
Leominster	63,119	17.4	6.6	86,480	42,457	51,351	57,722	47,353	17,645	16,983	60.4	261,300	1,006
Lowell	62,196	24.3	5.1	74,808	38,382	50,292	53,778	43,513	42,025	40,260	43.4	285,200	1,229
Lynn	61,329	24.7	4.1	70,286	30,958	45,095	49,443	40,228	34,524	33,261	46.4	354,400	1,241
Malden	73,399	18.8	8.3	86,006	46,740	60,009	61,787	54,639	24,759	23,367	42.0	447,000	1,650
Marlborough	83,469	12.8	10.8	101,700	48,368	60,461	61,663	57,862	17,099	16,044	57.9	365,200	1,498
Medford	101,168	12.4	16.4	125,332	75,562	69,943	74,964	64,505	25,018	23,807	55.5	551,900	2,003
Melrose	114,604	12.2	20.8	148,070	55,469	84,950	87,173	80,788	11,632	11,238	66.9	599,600	1,638
Methuen Town	83,527	14.9	9.7	97,293	40,783	55,664	61,504	48,639	18,334	17,611	73.5	350,200	1,276
New Bedford	48,999	27.9	2.2	61,449	29,044	46,638	52,178	40,791	42,222	39,059	39.8	239,000	869
Newton	154,398	8.8	37.2	189,656	70,441	105,467	121,653	86,817	32,504	30,756	71.5	952,100	1,897
Northampton	71,866	17.5	10.2	99,154	39,955	60,697	68,750	56,193	12,137	11,352	58.4	337,100	1,189
North Attleborough Town	91,994	11.5	13.1	117,703	45,757	67,627	74,235	61,009	11,635	11,317	68.2	355,600	1,087
Peabody	80,681	14.5	9.6	102,908	43,197	57,101	65,849	51,895	22,766	22,049	65.2	419,500	1,503
Pittsfield	56,620	22.3	4.5	75,452	32,566	49,972	53,197	42,733	21,483	19,072	62.8	176,800	907
Quincy	80,462	16.7	8.6	96,639	62,920	62,443	65,080	60,045	43,581	41,322	44.4	453,100	1,659
Randolph Town	87,803	13.4	9.6	95,259	54,597	54,714	61,850	47,572	12,190	11,727	68.9	351,700	1,626
Revere	68,331	22.3	5.9	80,563	36,620	50,803	53,949	45,190	20,170	18,555	49.5	388,900	1,462
Salem	66,428	22.4	7.7	84,944	47,676	57,393	60,634	55,565	20,069	19,094	49.8	379,400	1,325
Somerville	102,311	13.4	16.4	108,532	95,851	66,345	75,230	59,503	36,161	34,046	33.5	709,800	2,026
Springfield	41,571	32.2	2.1	51,364	25,671	43,520	46,052	41,792	61,668	56,804	47.4	162,900	908
Taunton	63,433	19.8	5.0	79,547	40,148	52,035	56,298	45,227	23,553	22,077	62.5	291,100	1,024
Waltham	95,851	12.1	14.6	118,376	72,048	65,982	71,840	57,496	25,293	23,891	50.0	574,000	1,774
Watertown Town	100,434	12.4	17.0	116,917	77,748	76,134	77,939	75,178	16,960	16,142	51.1	599,100	1,876
Westfield	74,456	13.2	6.9	92,163	42,743	57,475	65,164	47,479	15,998	15,099	68.0	247,300	964
West Springfield Town	54,516	19.1	6.8	74,077	37,002	52,222	54,810	48,763	12,691	12,402	56.7	235,200	912
Weymouth Town	85,536	13.2	9.9	108,958	55,085	66,985	67,972	65,976	25,260	24,392	68.2	384,700	1,552
Woburn	92,084	10.7	14.6	108,489	63,350	69,137	75,293	59,756	16,718	15,901	58.3	486,600	1,763
Worcester	51,647	27.1	4.5	66,924	35,513	49,425	52,765	45,226	78,258	72,289	42.0	241,800	1,115
MICHIGAN	59,234	19.7	5.7	75,470	35,002	50,100	54,975	42,586	4,611,913	3,980,408	71.7	162,600	892
Allen Park	69,331	13.4	4.4	86,644	41,843	55,964	60,048	52,670	11,932	11,368	84.6	133,600	1,016
Ann Arbor	69,456	21.7	12.0	115,479	45,152	65,275	73,878	59,604	51,010	48,109	45.4	346,800	1,299
Battle Creek	42,285	28.4	3.2	58,466	27,252	41,275	43,999	38,031	23,474	20,690	60.6	91,700	770
Bay City	38,014	30.7	1.4	49,319	28,272	37,580	42,752	32,323	15,973	14,327	67.6	68,000	635
Burton	48,174	24.3	1.6	62,223	31,676	40,893	43,149	35,358	13,153	12,240	74.5	96,300	810
Dearborn	56,302	23.3	5.3	64,601	41,734	52,673	53,057	52,100	34,758	31,797	66.7	154,100	1,019
Dearborn Heights	50,987	22.5	3.5	57,430	34,804	47,012	52,217	40,551	21,702	20,214	70.8	122,200	1,049
Detroit	32,498	39.9	1.4	40,138	23,484	36,336	37,016	35,600	358,145	270,446	47.6	52,700	850
East Lansing	40,800	35.9	7.6	106,951	24,847	55,381	62,361	47,314	15,335	13,430	39.5	194,100	969
Eastpointe	49,800	20.0	0.9	57,295	39,586	42,253	46,725	36,945	13,871	12,856	67.5	83,800	1,086
Farmington Hills	85,152	13.8	11.3	111,021	52,108	69,058	81,357	55,638	36,694	34,803	62.0	270,000	1,211
Flint	30,383	41.8	0.8	35,173	22,944	33,420	36,874	31,347	52,792	40,807	56.9	31,700	730
Garden City	57,011	15.9	1.2	68,815	36,385	44,483	51,927	35,495	11,437	11,007	79.5	119,900	967
Grand Rapids	51,333	24.8	2.8	64,166	38,108	42,146	45,605	39,243	81,640	76,360	55.0	156,500	947
Hamtramck	29,230	40.7	0.6	30,362	23,349	31,088	32,963	28,926	7,134	5,880	55.9	72,600	743
Holland	58,796	16.4	4.4	76,395	35,552	42,290	48,762	36,163	13,177	12,283	64.6	165,400	908
Inkster	32,109	40.1	1.2	41,344	23,076	36,297	35,411	36,705	10,739	8,953	41.1	51,500	915
Jackson	37,192	32.8	1.2	49,143	25,761	35,404	39,164	32,251	15,574	13,467	55.2	71,400	729
Kalamazoo	43,222	28.9	3.0	53,417	31,827	39,100	41,615	35,070	32,438	29,208	44.0	113,700	825
Kentwood	55,046	17.0	4.9	70,743	36,621	42,960	50,037	37,756	20,692	20,223	57.9	169,700	967
Lansing	44,233	26.9	0.9	53,143	36,481	40,372	41,998	37,050	55,312	49,539	51.5	87,700	847
Lincoln Park	47,094	24.7	1.2	57,220	32,278	40,740	44,215	34,258	15,864	14,734	70.8	81,000	850
Livonia	82,158	9.7	7.0	98,634	48,102	61,290	69,796	52,515	39,022	37,650	86.9	204,300	1,095
Madison Heights	54,668	20.2	1.6	64,563	43,434	49,476	51,865	44,294	14,523	13,824	61.1	137,700	992
Midland	63,867	19.5	8.2	83,153	34,892	54,091	63,373	45,825	18,804	17,626	65.5	154,800	818
Muskegon	35,323	37.0	0.6	44,639	21,931	35,184	36,096	33,581	15,744	13,530	49.9	77,200	741
Norton Shores	65,727	13.4	5.3	76,789	39,786	47,484	54,287	41,534	10,479	9,586	83.2	151,000	978
Novi	93,943	7.8	16.6	118,886	57,689	75,973	91,657	61,489	25,275	24,130	66.5	325,500	1,352

1. Specified owner-occupied units

City	Commuting, 2016–2020[1]		Computer access[2], 2016–2020		Migration, 2016–2020		Civilian labor force, 2021				Civilian Employment, 2016–2020[4]			
	Percent		Percent						Unemployment[3]		Population age 16 and older		Population age 16 to 64	
	Drove alone	Mean travel time to work	With a computer in the house	With Internet access	Percent who lived in the same house one year ago	Percent who lived in another state or county one year ago	Total	Percent change 2020–2021	Total	Rate	Number	Percent in labor force	Number	Percent who worked full-year full-time
	55	56	57	58	59	60	61	62	63	64	65	66	67	68
MASSACHUSETTS—Cont'd														
Chelsea	46.0	33.9	90.0	82.2	85.4	7.1	20,496	-2.4	1,436	7.0	31,145	69.3	27,268	49.4
Chicopee	85.2	19.1	87.9	83.0	89.5	3.5	27,885	0.3	2,073	7.4	45,784	60.4	35,260	46.8
Everett	51.4	36.2	90.8	85.9	86.8	5.5	26,685	-2.0	1,592	6.0	37,035	73.2	31,806	53.1
Fall River	78.7	25.1	83.4	72.3	86.6	3.6	41,210	-0.2	3,741	9.1	72,648	59.5	57,778	45.6
Fitchburg	73.8	26.3	91.7	84.7	88.3	4.3	19,923	-0.9	1,657	8.3	32,510	66.4	27,211	44.5
Framingham	72.4	30.6	94.6	91.5	87.1	6.0	40,659	-0.7	1,766	4.3	59,733	72.2	47,957	54.4
Franklin Town	76.8	36.2	96.4	94.2	90.1	5.1	19,068	0.7	916	4.8	27,424	71.7	22,958	56.2
Gloucester	77.3	26.7	92.5	88.6	90.6	1.7	16,366	0.6	1,125	6.9	25,952	64.3	18,639	50.2
Haverhill	80.2	27.5	93.2	85.0	90.1	2.8	35,672	0.0	2,346	6.6	51,371	69.4	42,140	52.1
Holyoke	75.3	20.5	86.6	76.6	88.4	4.2	16,649	-0.3	1,516	9.1	32,155	54.8	26,101	38.4
Lawrence	70.3	23.3	87.0	73.2	88.3	3.7	37,371	-2.4	4,634	12.4	60,945	67.5	52,769	44.5
Leominster	82.7	28.3	92.5	86.7	91.0	3.8	22,577	-0.5	1,441	6.4	33,877	68.2	26,706	55.4
Lowell	75.6	26.4	86.2	78.1	84.6	5.6	57,530	0.1	4,053	7.0	90,093	67.2	77,346	49.0
Lynn	65.9	32.4	88.7	81.2	89.2	4.4	48,215	-1.8	3,885	8.1	74,024	67.2	62,422	50.4
Malden	51.1	36.8	93.1	87.4	82.8	8.1	34,040	-2.2	2,152	6.3	50,367	68.9	42,430	51.9
Marlborough	75.8	30.2	94.3	91.7	86.2	4.8	22,904	-0.8	1,166	5.1	32,555	72.8	26,508	57.9
Medford	54.2	31.8	94.7	92.0	84.9	7.5	36,314	0.5	1,694	4.7	51,616	73.4	43,225	57.1
Melrose	56.9	37.0	93.8	91.5	92.8	4.7	16,335	0.5	705	4.3	23,271	69.5	17,974	61.8
Methuen Town	81.6	27.3	92.9	88.4	90.5	3.4	27,856	0.5	2,001	7.2	41,666	69.8	33,577	53.0
New Bedford	74.0	26.0	84.9	78.3	86.7	3.6	47,461	-1.2	4,164	8.8	75,699	62.7	61,302	46.3
Newton	58.5	28.4	95.7	93.9	87.1	7.8	47,185	1.6	1,868	4.0	72,190	65.2	56,016	49.5
Northampton	66.3	21.8	93.1	87.5	82.7	9.3	16,326	0.7	675	4.1	24,745	61.6	19,304	42.9
North Attleborough Town	79.4	31.5	95.4	91.9	88.8	6.2	16,654	0.1	832	5.0	23,662	72.0	19,333	54.2
Peabody	84.2	27.4	88.6	84.3	88.4	4.3	29,144	-0.8	1,691	5.8	44,612	64.9	32,653	56.8
Pittsfield	81.0	17.3	89.3	83.6	88.8	2.9	20,590	0.0	1,584	7.7	35,709	63.2	27,136	47.2
Quincy	54.7	36.1	92.1	88.4	84.2	10.1	55,271	-2.2	3,341	6.0	82,129	69.7	66,247	57.3
Randolph Town	72.8	38.0	95.3	91.7	92.0	5.8	18,607	-1.9	1,370	7.4	28,613	67.4	22,891	51.9
Revere	57.7	33.5	90.1	83.8	87.7	5.0	28,916	-4.2	2,090	7.2	43,450	68.5	36,110	51.5
Salem	63.7	31.1	90.5	86.3	86.8	5.3	24,240	-0.8	1,536	6.3	37,349	68.7	30,224	52.8
Somerville	34.1	32.3	93.7	90.3	76.4	12.5	52,414	1.0	2,146	4.1	73,124	80.0	66,018	61.1
Springfield	75.6	21.1	83.9	74.9	87.9	3.5	65,318	-0.4	6,831	10.5	120,038	57.6	100,371	39.0
Taunton	82.2	29.5	89.1	81.8	88.2	7.0	30,384	-1.3	2,111	6.9	46,072	66.3	37,621	50.3
Waltham	66.3	25.4	94.5	89.4	81.9	10.1	37,563	1.2	1,820	4.8	54,987	69.2	45,904	51.9
Watertown Town	60.8	28.0	94.4	92.2	85.2	8.8	23,127	0.7	934	4.0	30,974	73.9	24,948	61.2
Westfield	84.4	24.3	92.3	86.5	85.8	5.4	21,318	1.3	1,275	6.0	34,710	61.9	27,500	47.1
West Springfield Town	83.4	19.2	89.1	85.8	84.9	5.3	14,883	0.0	953	6.4	23,088	67.9	18,868	52.4
Weymouth Town	73.5	33.9	94.7	88.2	87.5	6.0	32,596	-0.3	1,957	6.0	48,650	70.2	37,865	55.3
Woburn	75.9	26.9	93.2	89.9	87.3	4.3	23,634	-0.2	1,189	5.0	33,542	71.2	27,068	58.3
Worcester	69.0	24.6	89.2	82.7	84.7	6.7	93,502	-0.3	6,594	7.1	154,033	61.1	128,876	44.7
MICHIGAN	80.7	24.6	91.1	83.8	86.6	5.6	4,776,110	-1.4	280,459	5.9	8,070,619	61.4	6,357,778	48.2
Allen Park	86.4	23.4	91.7	87.5	92.7	1.9	14,045	1.7	732	5.2	21,965	63.6	17,199	56.7
Ann Arbor	51.5	19.7	97.0	91.1	66.3	17.6	62,342	-1.4	2,210	3.5	107,728	60.8	93,373	36.3
Battle Creek	78.0	18.3	89.0	82.1	86.0	5.7	21,569	-4.5	1,663	7.7	39,662	61.1	31,917	47.8
Bay City	80.5	20.2	87.8	83.5	86.5	5.0	14,864	-3.9	1,165	7.8	26,705	60.8	21,824	42.2
Burton	81.9	23.8	89.5	81.0	84.5	2.3	12,824	-2.8	980	7.6	23,346	59.1	18,325	44.5
Dearborn	82.8	21.3	91.9	85.7	86.3	5.4	38,607	1.6	2,020	5.2	70,566	56.0	58,428	39.5
Dearborn Heights	83.8	24.2	90.6	84.0	87.3	2.1	25,067	1.1	1,474	5.9	43,087	56.3	34,436	42.7
Detroit	68.8	25.8	85.7	70.4	85.9	3.7	254,132	-4.4	34,217	13.5	523,622	54.7	429,906	36.4
East Lansing	53.0	16.4	96.2	85.7	52.3	26.4	21,852	-2.5	863	3.9	45,118	54.8	40,989	18.5
Eastpointe	79.9	25.5	90.5	82.7	87.4	4.9	15,084	-3.3	1,300	8.6	25,870	61.9	21,694	45.3
Farmington Hills	82.6	25.5	93.0	89.0	86.5	7.0	43,343	2.8	1,299	3.0	68,175	66.1	51,667	55.3
Flint	75.7	22.4	80.7	65.8	84.4	3.7	32,737	-5.9	4,387	13.4	74,963	53.1	61,941	30.5
Garden City	84.3	25.5	91.2	85.9	92.3	1.4	14,671	1.5	796	5.4	21,927	65.0	17,799	49.7
Grand Rapids	73.1	19.4	90.2	83.1	78.3	7.9	101,663	-2.9	6,336	6.2	159,770	67.6	135,063	48.3
Hamtramck	69.7	24.4	87.3	73.7	90.8	2.3	7,799	-1.5	730	9.4	15,413	43.1	13,805	28.4
Holland	75.1	17.1	91.0	85.5	78.5	11.1	16,450	-2.1	770	4.7	27,392	66.5	22,023	46.4
Inkster	78.0	26.7	88.1	76.3	81.5	5.5	9,052	-3.2	1,055	11.7	17,322	58.8	14,601	39.6
Jackson	76.7	18.5	89.8	82.0	85.2	4.3	13,703	-5.5	1,294	9.4	25,081	62.5	21,526	40.2
Kalamazoo	75.4	17.7	93.0	84.4	67.7	13.7	35,744	-3.0	2,228	6.2	63,495	65.2	55,461	36.7
Kentwood	82.7	18.8	93.0	87.6	83.5	4.9	29,055	-1.7	1,291	4.4	39,680	70.9	32,380	58.0
Lansing	74.7	19.7	91.6	80.6	78.4	8.7	56,473	-4.1	4,457	7.9	93,099	67.3	78,769	46.1
Lincoln Park	84.4	26.0	88.4	72.7	90.1	2.4	17,206	1.0	1,053	6.1	28,224	60.1	23,304	45.3
Livonia	85.0	24.1	93.2	90.3	90.4	4.2	51,887	3.0	1,848	3.6	78,688	63.7	59,350	54.8
Madison Heights	81.9	24.3	93.0	86.4	87.4	4.7	15,327	-0.9	1,017	6.6	25,362	69.6	20,927	58.9
Midland	83.6	19.6	91.3	87.8	82.9	8.0	19,474	-1.8	771	4.0	33,685	60.1	26,313	50.3
Muskegon	79.9	20.4	84.6	74.7	76.0	9.3	13,254	-5.7	1,641	12.4	29,506	51.9	24,631	35.7
Norton Shores	84.4	20.6	92.4	85.2	86.9	5.8	11,790	-1.6	662	5.6	19,435	63.8	14,270	55.6
Novi	85.0	26.9	96.9	92.8	86.9	7.4	33,344	2.6	1,046	3.1	47,848	68.8	39,300	57.3

1. Employed persons. 2. Households. 3. Percent of civilian labor force. 4. Persons 16 years old and over.

City	Value of residential construction authorized by building permits, 2021			Wholesale trade[1], 2017				Retail trade[2], 2017			
	New construction ($1,000)	Number of housing units	Percent single family	Number of establishments	Number of employees	Sales (mil dol)	Annual payroll (mil dol)	Number of establishments	Number of employees	Sales (mil dol)	Annual payroll (mil dol)
	69	70	71	72	73	74	75	76	77	78	79
MASSACHUSETTS—Cont'd											
Chelsea	12,889	77	0.0	84	1,512	2,289.8	106.1	109	1,882	492.3	51.2
Chicopee	4,131	24	100.0	42	1,458	1,399.9	72.2	166	2,576	840.9	74.6
Everett	77,143	415	0.0	49	1,229	1,146.6	80.1	125	2,009	510.4	56.9
Fall River	8,117	72	95.8	69	1,486	783.0	79.9	276	3,329	932.6	97.1
Fitchburg	6,234	26	100.0	34	349	223.8	25.4	122	1,643	371.9	40.6
Framingham	8,469	33	100.0	NA	NA	NA	NA	NA	NA	NA	NA
Franklin Town	48,991	300	32.7	47	1,179	1,689.5	81.2	107	1,771	524.8	54.9
Gloucester	27,824	46	50.0	37	368	496.0	21.0	126	1,550	387.9	43.4
Haverhill	10,795	38	92.1	49	460	294.5	35.1	137	2,525	807.5	76.6
Holyoke	0	0	0.0	19	365	97.5	19.8	207	3,651	694.4	88.6
Lawrence	2,131	19	47.4	53	1,319	699.1	141.5	227	1,729	553.0	57.0
Leominster	10,371	80	15.0	39	439	279.9	25.8	213	4,390	1,055.4	103.1
Lowell	6,616	37	78.4	48	622	411.3	52.9	229	2,591	847.0	77.5
Lynn	77,342	209	4.8	40	396	191.5	23.0	218	2,266	770.4	83.1
Malden	500	1	100.0	36	623	294.9	35.8	129	1,184	397.7	34.9
Marlborough	4,086	29	100.0	82	2,126	2,537.3	175.1	213	3,293	1,029.6	86.6
Medford	66,534	1,667	0.4	41	578	272.8	38.5	143	1,810	662.5	61.6
Melrose	3,578	14	7.1	9	45	22.8	2.6	59	777	242.8	26.5
Methuen Town	68,645	274	27.7	40	647	2,882.2	41.8	126	2,260	600.3	57.6
New Bedford	4,864	30	93.3	91	2,012	1,205.2	101.6	291	2,945	827.1	77.9
Newton	29,639	62	100.0	92	1,205	1,375.4	142.8	320	4,964	1,182.2	157.6
Northampton	8,360	34	70.6	D	D	D	8.7	159	2,149	559.9	61.7
North Attleborough Town	14,545	58	100.0	NA	NA	NA	NA	NA	NA	NA	NA
Peabody	9,023	31	87.1	54	1,250	3,285.7	85.7	290	5,289	1,357.7	162.2
Pittsfield	7,504	25	20.0	46	688	269.8	34.9	192	3,125	936.8	92.3
Quincy	47,517	621	1.0	64	1,095	1,580.1	65.6	243	4,402	1,308.9	130.3
Randolph Town	2,081	12	66.7	NA	NA	NA	NA	NA	NA	NA	NA
Revere	8,666	54	22.2	21	191	1,137.2	11.9	122	2,085	546.9	48.4
Salem	20,810	77	9.1	33	191	97.1	10.5	177	2,205	508.6	57.9
Somerville	28,142	140	20.7	48	637	360.7	51.2	206	3,555	942.3	95.3
Springfield	828	3	100.0	95	1,405	1,187.8	93.8	460	5,693	1,382.8	155.0
Taunton	19,945	135	74.8	63	3,567	2,970.0	274.6	195	2,861	668.6	77.5
Waltham	22,256	57	45.6	93	3,195	4,481.3	310.8	237	3,454	1,076.2	109.3
Watertown Town	5,629	20	90.0	33	509	177.7	33.5	133	2,985	857.6	96.9
Westfield	10,239	52	100.0	33	1,000	1,871.7	52.1	134	2,127	577.5	55.4
West Springfield Town	1,956	8	100.0	57	730	260.8	46.8	181	3,417	1,228.3	112.3
Weymouth Town	16,376	67	37.3	49	473	397.4	29.0	192	2,735	827.4	91.5
Woburn	42,977	203	11.8	208	3,983	2,743.6	313.7	182	3,582	1,649.0	121.9
Worcester	27,629	178	37.1	161	2,114	938.7	107.9	552	7,378	2,036.3	207.2
MICHIGAN	5,684,341	21,732	77.1	9,173	147,939	138,545.8	9,136.3	34,201	469,987	143,437.1	12,481.8
Allen Park	0	0	0.0	12	174	127.2	8.5	109	2,073	424.9	41.7
Ann Arbor	56,477	227	77.1	69	453	346.1	31.0	540	8,265	1,978.1	213.2
Battle Creek	3,397	11	100.0	33	431	302.5	23.2	230	3,109	821.8	73.8
Bay City	0	0	0.0	29	511	213.0	21.5	133	1,125	272.8	31.5
Burton	15,902	81	100.0	D	D	D	37.1	126	1,964	485.8	48.2
Dearborn	7,614	23	100.0	138	1,765	2,290.6	102.1	556	6,600	2,110.5	165.9
Dearborn Heights	4,389	14	100.0	41	123	40.0	5.0	214	1,846	496.5	41.1
Detroit	411,409	1,023	1.0	377	7,476	7,244.5	481.5	1,945	13,065	3,564.7	310.9
East Lansing	6,642	26	15.4	10	30	11.8	1.7	85	1,588	319.6	38.3
Eastpointe	4,468	14	100.0	10	39	8.8	1.5	111	934	289.6	26.6
Farmington Hills	4,409	13	100.0	168	3,414	4,609.0	285.7	270	3,983	1,539.6	124.3
Flint	0	0	0.0	61	948	503.5	38.9	331	3,025	3,230.9	74.0
Garden City	925	4	100.0	17	123	28.4	4.8	106	744	296.1	22.2
Grand Rapids	41,364	286	15.0	209	4,832	3,439.6	269.4	575	7,642	2,287.5	219.5
Hamtramck	0	0	0.0	5	24	8.8	0.8	116	470	126.4	10.1
Holland	3,014	11	100.0	40	618	461.3	39.7	156	2,218	770.8	67.4
Inkster	0	0	0.0	7	89	57.4	7.0	51	291	79.3	5.7
Jackson	500	2	100.0	52	743	576.4	42.0	152	1,606	384.1	40.9
Kalamazoo	4,242	17	100.0	84	1,564	712.3	76.8	264	2,768	778.0	78.8
Kentwood	24,046	110	100.0	133	3,588	2,041.6	217.8	285	4,828	1,338.8	135.0
Lansing	48,096	362	8.3	115	1,800	3,531.6	100.0	450	6,257	1,733.0	167.8
Lincoln Park	0	0	0.0	D	D	D	D	125	1,319	344.5	31.4
Livonia	8,828	30	100.0	242	4,365	5,037.7	260.9	434	7,510	2,316.1	200.7
Madison Heights	8,201	141	5.7	118	2,526	1,475.0	165.7	168	3,126	1,310.7	97.5
Midland	10,475	79	77.2	35	612	2,621.3	66.8	200	3,468	988.7	86.8
Muskegon	6,097	34	52.9	34	473	215.1	23.7	117	1,699	512.0	44.2
Norton Shores	7,565	23	100.0	25	331	139.3	20.0	105	1,852	473.6	40.6
Novi	16,126	114	100.0	171	3,161	6,133.3	253.6	343	7,145	2,059.1	191.3

1. Merchant wholesalers except manufacturers' sales branches and offices. 2. Establishments with payroll.

City	Real estate and rental and leasing, 2017				Professional, scientific, and technical services[1], 2017				Manufacturing, 2017			
	Number of establish-ments	Number of employees	Receipts (mil dol)	Annual payroll (mil dol)	Number of establish-ments	Number of employees	Receipts (mil dol)	Annual payroll (mil dol)	Number of establish-ments	Number of employees	Receipts (mil dol)	Annual payroll (mil dol)
	80	81	82	83	84	85	86	87	88	89	90	91
MASSACHUSETTS—Cont'd												
Chelsea	35	178	28.4	5.9	36	219	47.4	22.1	NA	NA	NA	NA
Chicopee	41	188	44.4	6.8	43	618	47.7	19.8	NA	NA	NA	NA
Everett	24	76	24.0	4.3	D	D	D	D	NA	NA	NA	NA
Fall River	75	719	73.7	17.2	159	1,058	136.8	47.7	NA	NA	NA	NA
Fitchburg	31	155	28.6	6.3	45	303	38.6	14.6	NA	NA	NA	NA
Framingham	NA	NA	NA	NA	NA	NA	NA	NA	NA	NA	NA	NA
Franklin Town	35	153	72.9	9.8	96	804	159.9	62.3	NA	NA	NA	NA
Gloucester	27	71	13.7	3.3	85	292	73.0	18.9	NA	NA	NA	NA
Haverhill	48	325	67.6	15.4	84	612	88.8	32.7	NA	NA	NA	NA
Holyoke	42	348	53.7	14.9	64	386	65.9	23.6	NA	NA	NA	NA
Lawrence	45	318	51.8	13.4	65	390	61.5	25.3	NA	NA	NA	NA
Leominster	44	476	101.0	22.4	95	577	71.2	33.4	NA	NA	NA	NA
Lowell	78	553	91.7	20.2	135	1,631	297.0	116.2	NA	NA	NA	NA
Lynn	46	180	51.9	8.7	80	343	41.0	15.9	NA	NA	NA	NA
Malden	53	374	80.6	18.6	58	204	26.7	9.8	NA	NA	NA	NA
Marlborough	53	210	99.3	11.8	198	4,420	2,039.1	475.3	NA	NA	NA	NA
Medford	46	193	71.0	11.6	144	2,803	782.3	277.8	NA	NA	NA	NA
Melrose	23	95	38.6	5.9	77	276	36.7	17.4	NA	NA	NA	NA
Methuen Town	39	D	27.2	D	78	359	70.2	19.4	NA	NA	NA	NA
New Bedford	80	452	86.9	15.8	177	1,065	134.9	49.1	NA	NA	NA	NA
Newton	155	3,059	2,648.6	302.4	606	4,535	957.1	487.0	NA	NA	NA	NA
Northampton	33	92	25.9	3.5	122	682	112.9	41.2	NA	NA	NA	NA
North Attleborough Town	NA	NA	NA	NA	NA	NA	NA	NA	NA	NA	NA	NA
Peabody	45	285	75.3	14.4	115	856	176.4	65.7	NA	NA	NA	NA
Pittsfield	43	265	36.6	9.2	134	2,709	569.6	261.5	NA	NA	NA	NA
Quincy	107	651	160.5	39.5	283	2,860	506.8	230.8	NA	NA	NA	NA
Randolph Town	NA	NA	NA	NA	NA	NA	NA	NA	NA	NA	NA	NA
Revere	28	233	45.2	8.3	47	153	16.4	5.6	NA	NA	NA	NA
Salem	42	232	58.2	10.0	159	682	106.9	43.1	NA	NA	NA	NA
Somerville	79	445	116.7	22.6	208	1,315	284.1	107.1	NA	NA	NA	NA
Springfield	118	780	135.3	35.1	270	2,349	380.1	151.0	NA	NA	NA	NA
Taunton	38	126	39.3	6.3	93	567	92.6	41.3	NA	NA	NA	NA
Waltham	122	849	308.9	58.4	420	17,227	3,652.8	2,020.3	NA	NA	NA	NA
Watertown Town	41	167	35.2	7.9	133	2,782	594.7	297.4	NA	NA	NA	NA
Westfield	35	150	39.8	6.1	64	602	85.4	40.9	NA	NA	NA	NA
West Springfield Town	40	158	38.8	6.8	73	665	123.0	50.8	NA	NA	NA	NA
Weymouth Town	44	127	37.3	5.4	99	544	113.7	40.5	NA	NA	NA	NA
Woburn	91	1,979	298.6	109.9	329	6,002	1,420.9	581.6	NA	NA	NA	NA
Worcester	175	762	170.6	31.9	419	3,958	665.3	350.5	NA	NA	NA	NA
MICHIGAN	8,467	54,808	17,782.6	2,374.4	21,832	282,246	39,436.5	19,669.9	12,418	582,365	262,495.4	33,349.3
Allen Park	D	D	D	3.6	54	556	160.4	34.4	NA	NA	NA	NA
Ann Arbor	167	1,864	396.7	105.5	646	7,279	1,434.3	589.5	NA	NA	NA	NA
Battle Creek	44	271	40.3	8.6	100	2,176	95.3	189.2	NA	NA	NA	NA
Bay City	21	93	9.7	2.0	81	588	57.4	28.7	NA	NA	NA	NA
Burton	20	79	14.1	2.3	36	329	25.4	9.0	NA	NA	NA	NA
Dearborn	D	D	D	D	271	15,810	713.9	917.7	NA	NA	NA	NA
Dearborn Heights	D	D	D	D	89	291	29.4	12.2	NA	NA	NA	NA
Detroit	268	1,832	389.7	95.9	764	16,904	3,975.1	1,397.8	NA	NA	NA	NA
East Lansing	44	398	45.8	13.6	125	1,551	280.5	103.7	NA	NA	NA	NA
Eastpointe	14	56	17.3	2.3	33	182	18.9	7.6	NA	NA	NA	NA
Farmington Hills	193	1,998	405.4	116.7	724	14,791	1,924.7	1,089.2	NA	NA	NA	NA
Flint	66	519	83.0	20.1	123	631	74.6	35.2	NA	NA	NA	NA
Garden City	D	D	D	1.6	24	72	7.7	1.9	NA	NA	NA	NA
Grand Rapids	197	1,401	227.4	69.8	635	8,130	1,530.3	544.6	NA	NA	NA	NA
Hamtramck	5	19	1.6	0.3	9	61	7.0	2.9	NA	NA	NA	NA
Holland	57	274	65.0	12.1	90	2,365	434.0	236.1	NA	NA	NA	NA
Inkster	D	D	D	3.1	10	42	4.6	1.1	NA	NA	NA	NA
Jackson	36	163	40.3	6.3	70	1,108	111.6	57.5	NA	NA	NA	NA
Kalamazoo	87	639	95.5	19.3	195	1,686	287.9	102.6	NA	NA	NA	NA
Kentwood	51	188	65.2	8.9	115	1,431	226.8	88.6	NA	NA	NA	NA
Lansing	98	690	127.7	39.4	250	2,760	521.0	189.5	NA	NA	NA	NA
Lincoln Park	D	D	D	5.2	34	317	36.7	11.3	NA	NA	NA	NA
Livonia	96	808	199.8	38.9	368	7,825	1,471.7	599.4	NA	NA	NA	NA
Madison Heights	40	491	128.3	29.5	119	1,663	195.8	119.7	NA	NA	NA	NA
Midland	51	316	66.2	16.9	125	2,298	131.9	340.2	NA	NA	NA	NA
Muskegon	19	126	22.2	3.3	83	768	98.6	40.7	NA	NA	NA	NA
Norton Shores	18	270	28.2	10.5	41	282	38.6	15.6	NA	NA	NA	NA
Novi	79	321	147.5	14.0	350	5,183	896.6	405.4	NA	NA	NA	NA

1. Establishments subject to federal tax.

City	Accommodation and food services, 2017				Arts, entertainment, and recreation[1], 2017				Health care and social assistance[1], 2017			
	Number of establish-ments	Number of employees	Receipts (mil dol)	Annual payroll (mil dol)	Number of establish-ments	Number of employees	Receipts (mil dol)	Annual payroll (mil dol)	Number of establish-ments	Number of employees	Receipts (mil dol)	Annual payroll (mil dol)
	92	93	94	95	96	97	98	99	100	101	102	103
MASSACHUSETTS—Cont'd												
Chelsea	84	941	71.6	19.4	D	D	D	D	82	2,574	160.5	83.3
Chicopee	101	1,665	97.9	29.0	9.0	115	7.2	1.9	95	1,903	120.3	58.2
Everett	90	1,153	88.4	24.4	7.0	123	5.9	2.1	53	1,122	178.1	70.4
Fall River	189	2,538	149.3	44.4	19.0	310	16.4	5.6	306	11,860	1,265.2	548.1
Fitchburg	81	1,032	60.3	16.1	7.0	63	7.0	2.9	124	3,604	227.8	104.4
Framingham	NA	NA	NA	NA	NA	NA	NA	NA	NA	NA	NA	NA
Franklin Town	67	1,420	74.9	23.3	D	D	D	D	73	1,100	98.3	44.7
Gloucester	106	1,313	104.9	34.7	27.0	336	28.0	10.5	87	1,783	244.6	83.2
Haverhill	134	1,903	120.8	34.8	32.0	743	38.3	14.1	143	3,560	301.8	131.7
Holyoke	98	1,603	99.6	27.8	15.0	197	9.1	3.3	143	5,845	536.9	255.9
Lawrence	125	1,239	84.5	22.3	D	D	D	0.8	190	10,384	869.6	420.4
Leominster	114	2,172	124.2	36.6	16.0	127	6.9	1.8	129	3,902	466.8	187.8
Lowell	207	2,972	185.9	53.4	22.0	291	15.8	5.0	227	10,190	1,148.1	443.4
Lynn	159	1,625	111.6	29.8	16.0	207	9.4	3.2	204	7,025	520.1	248.8
Malden	120	1,345	85.9	24.3	11.0	111	12.7	3.7	118	2,984	325.2	115.3
Marlborough	153	2,429	182.8	52.5	21.0	367	25.7	7.4	145	7,591	981.6	379.6
Medford	128	2,288	160.1	45.0	D	D	D	D	128	3,305	422.1	181.7
Melrose	43	605	37.6	11.8	12.0	276	10.6	4.8	81	2,114	257.8	118.5
Methuen Town	98	1,889	125.6	32.8	11.0	340	15.8	5.4	116	3,894	403.6	181.2
New Bedford	210	2,719	158.2	45.8	24.0	361	23.1	6.6	226	8,588	837.1	355.2
Newton	235	4,069	323.6	99.4	79.0	1,401	177.2	73.3	490	11,068	1,291.0	629.1
Northampton	105	1,806	97.6	34.9	28.0	402	22.1	7.2	175	5,830	674.2	320.9
North Attleborough Town	NA	NA	NA	NA	NA	NA	NA	NA	NA	NA	NA	NA
Peabody	145	2,698	190.4	57.2	13.0	334	18.9	6.6	170	5,803	650.7	274.6
Pittsfield	146	1,822	105.8	32.7	30.0	400	47.3	11.7	227	7,371	874.8	382.0
Quincy	246	3,397	244.3	69.0	35.0	892	50.7	18.0	287	8,035	809.2	337.1
Randolph Town	NA	NA	NA	NA	NA	NA	NA	NA	NA	NA	NA	NA
Revere	105	1,463	96.0	25.5	D	D	D	D	81	1,179	96.9	45.9
Salem	155	2,353	162.5	49.9	32.0	688	66.1	24.0	134	5,978	823.3	360.4
Somerville	243	4,058	280.8	94.3	32.0	470	83.5	15.2	159	4,179	561.3	201.2
Springfield	252	4,603	267.4	81.0	20.0	349	30.5	7.6	445	24,004	3,136.4	1,283.6
Taunton	118	2,103	107.2	32.7	13.0	283	12.5	4.0	133	3,589	439.4	165.0
Waltham	328	4,343	345.0	102.3	32.0	581	50.2	13.0	219	5,244	612.5	278.5
Watertown Town	98	1,354	94.8	28.3	25.0	310	28.4	6.6	119	1,585	188.0	73.5
Westfield	75	1,217	62.4	19.7	13.0	324	9.2	4.2	96	2,421	231.4	106.2
West Springfield Town	101	2,114	125.1	37.6	17.0	399	37.0	9.2	116	3,126	221.3	98.3
Weymouth Town	105	1,443	91.1	25.8	17.0	363	19.6	9.1	165	8,909	1,018.3	476.5
Woburn	120	2,209	187.8	46.9	30.0	615	36.5	10.1	178	4,761	442.9	186.7
Worcester	487	7,323	460.0	131.8	44.0	1,661	83.3	27.7	648	33,563	4,889.0	1,812.7
MICHIGAN	20,696	399,032	23,056.4	6,562.7	3,469.0	49,733	4,998.3	1,749.8	26,977	627,808	74,194.5	29,309.9
Allen Park	72	1,394	78.2	22.5	6.0	120	7.2	2.1	84	1,210	128.5	54.8
Ann Arbor	434	10,233	624.8	189.6	71.0	849	46.2	15.5	372	24,404	3,919.2	1,641.2
Battle Creek	D	D	D	D	19.0	298	13.7	5.2	171	6,712	823.5	327.0
Bay City	96	1,648	78.4	22.1	17.0	248	10.0	3.2	150	3,562	436.7	161.4
Burton	57	985	44.7	12.1	7.0	57	6.0	0.8	90	1,564	68.2	30.0
Dearborn	293	4,836	280.9	76.5	28.0	D	492.8	D	464	9,746	1,326.5	499.7
Dearborn Heights	117	1,739	97.9	26.3	8.0	73	3.8	1.4	133	1,287	114.4	46.0
Detroit	963	25,115	2,729.6	647.9	92.0	4,307	730.0	405.6	982	50,181	7,484.8	2,858.2
East Lansing	136	2,704	127.7	37.7	10.0	149	10.6	2.8	130	2,818	313.0	133.6
Eastpointe	54	848	40.6	11.1	4.0	19	0.7	0.3	94	432	39.2	15.7
Farmington Hills	182	3,003	175.9	49.3	40.0	675	39.6	15.3	421	15,018	1,340.5	602.9
Flint	171	2,787	142.1	43.6	15.0	547	44.2	12.7	201	9,385	1,278.8	463.2
Garden City	45	623	32.2	8.0	D	D	D	D	81	1,990	247.3	85.5
Grand Rapids	477	11,352	591.7	196.8	75.0	1,717	132.8	39.0	559	30,484	4,131.9	1,397.9
Hamtramck	45	381	23.8	6.0	NA	NA	NA	NA	35	444	47.5	16.0
Holland	79	2,118	102.0	36.1	9.0	238	9.5	2.9	135	4,238	400.0	193.2
Inkster	17	140	10.2	2.0	NA	NA	NA	NA	38	691	51.7	20.3
Jackson	86	1,392	77.7	20.2	19.0	118	8.8	2.5	178	7,385	868.5	392.0
Kalamazoo	228	5,225	238.2	81.0	41.0	912	44.3	15.6	232	13,832	2,177.0	841.8
Kentwood	103	2,415	129.3	38.9	19.0	549	25.1	6.8	147	4,146	471.4	240.9
Lansing	226	4,437	211.2	67.5	30.0	786	107.9	18.3	271	14,168	1,859.0	723.2
Lincoln Park	67	1,066	57.9	14.5	3.0	27	1.2	0.5	60	1,048	104.8	41.1
Livonia	282	6,259	343.7	101.5	40.0	635	38.5	10.6	492	11,622	1,341.3	586.8
Madison Heights	114	1,890	114.6	31.8	10.0	74	4.3	1.3	115	2,645	325.0	129.8
Midland	126	2,973	154.8	46.5	24.0	394	35.9	10.6	249	6,583	865.9	285.4
Muskegon	85	1,442	73.2	20.7	14.0	260	17.2	6.6	118	7,161	1,115.0	410.9
Norton Shores	48	1,115	37.0	11.6	10.0	100	6.9	1.7	91	1,352	132.8	51.8
Novi	187	4,586	265.0	78.9	32.0	847	180.4	21.8	296	7,623	911.6	378.1

1. Establishments subject to federal tax.

City	Other services[1]				Government employment and payroll, 2017								
						March payroll							
							Perent of total for:						
	Number of establish-ments	Number of employees	Receipts (mil dol)	Annual payroll (mil dol)	Full-time equivalent employees	Total (dollars)	Admin-istrative, judicial, and legal	Police and corrections	Fire protection	Highways and trans-portation	Health and welfare	Natural resources and utilities	Education and libraries
	104	105	106	107	108	109	110	111	112	113	114	115	116
MASSACHUSETTS—Cont'd													
Chelsea	52	674	51.4	16.7	1,366	6,341,623	2.8	12.7	12.0	0.5	1.4	0.7	68.5
Chicopee	96	536	46.3	14.2	2,238	11,063,107	2.6	7.9	7.8	0.8	0.9	8.5	69.6
Everett	76	404	43.9	14.7	1,308	7,801,522	3.6	12.8	9.3	1.1	0.9	1.3	64.8
Fall River	158	873	84.0	25.3	2,318	11,491,808	2.3	16.8	9.0	2.1	1.1	2.1	65.4
Fitchburg	61	316	35.5	9.9	1,190	5,658,922	3.8	10.3	8.1	2.9	1.5	5.6	67.2
Framingham	NA	NA	NA	NA	NA	NA	NA	NA	NA	NA	NA	NA	NA
Franklin Town	D	D	D	21.5	983	5,249,148	3.5	5.6	5.1	1.4	0.5	3.1	79.9
Gloucester	80	400	35.9	11.8	973	4,543,657	5.4	10.2	10.4	1.1	3.3	1.2	63.2
Haverhill	100	500	47.5	15.6	1,778	9,771,010	3.6	7.9	7.8	2.3	3.5	5.6	67.9
Holyoke	56	397	21.9	7.5	2,086	9,796,872	2.5	12.7	7.6	1.8	1.4	14.9	58.7
Lawrence	131	812	78.7	22.7	497	3,463,746	14.0	35.2	24.6	16.7	5.0	3.0	1.7
Leominster	71	329	29.4	8.2	1,050	5,639,777	2.0	7.4	7.8	1.3	0.6	1.9	79.0
Lowell	183	906	96.1	27.4	3,063	17,623,297	2.6	11.7	7.9	1.7	2.4	2.9	70.2
Lynn	142	590	56.6	18.5	3,251	15,409,664	1.5	7.2	7.1	0.5	1.9	1.6	78.3
Malden	119	738	66.7	18.4	1,320	7,778,185	2.4	8.1	5.9	0.9	0.5	1.3	78.4
Marlborough	100	984	131.8	57.6	1,235	6,146,989	2.4	10.2	7.4	2.1	2.6	3.0	69.8
Medford	115	1,034	307.4	59.0	1,533	6,856,790	3.8	14.8	13.1	4.6	0.5	2.3	60.8
Melrose	56	343	33.9	10.1	705	4,004,590	4.7	11.5	9.7	0.5	3.4	3.4	59.5
Methuen Town	67	364	30.1	10.3	1,188	8,629,719	2.0	11.8	7.5	1.9	1.0	3.8	71.3
New Bedford	161	1,036	109.2	31.2	2,810	13,820,091	3.1	13.6	9.2	2.0	2.1	3.7	61.4
Newton	241	1,967	337.8	78.9	3,271	19,625,415	3.7	7.6	6.7	3.4	1.9	3.9	71.3
Northampton	86	554	59.5	19.3	1,368	7,743,025	7.0	16.4	15.1	3.4	4.9	8.4	44.6
North Attleborough Town	NA	NA	NA	NA	NA	NA	NA	NA	NA	NA	NA	NA	NA
Peabody	142	679	67.1	20.1	1,434	7,145,303	4.0	8.9	8.3	1.9	3.6	10.2	62.2
Pittsfield	95	712	56.0	17.9	1,363	6,147,139	1.6	7.8	5.6	0.1	1.2	1.6	80.6
Quincy	214	1,482	297.5	67.0	2,574	15,779,182	3.1	12.8	13.6	3.0	1.4	3.6	59.4
Randolph Town	NA	NA	NA	NA	NA	NA	NA	NA	NA	NA	NA	NA	NA
Revere	84	364	43.1	10.3	1,206	7,117,092	4.2	9.9	8.8	1.8	2.3	0.7	71.5
Salem	124	709	67.2	21.0	1,295	6,526,007	3.6	9.7	7.2	2.1	1.1	1.9	72.5
Somerville	132	1,436	125.4	41.2	1,839	11,122,600	5.3	8.5	11.4	3.3	5.9	1.9	55.6
Springfield	227	2,584	265.2	82.6	5,718	28,054,091	3.0	12.3	5.8	1.7	1.7	2.4	72.1
Taunton	103	462	40.8	12.4	1,684	8,439,690	2.6	11.6	9.2	1.1	6.2	4.2	63.5
Waltham	176	1,075	140.1	51.8	1,717	9,886,003	4.5	13.4	12.2	5.0	1.6	2.7	57.2
Watertown Town	101	1,116	311.3	81.3	644	3,642,899	6.4	19.9	15.6	1.2	1.7	3.9	51.1
Westfield	64	452	36.6	12.0	1,487	7,427,763	3.8	9.6	7.8	1.7	1.4	12.9	62.0
West Springfield Town	61	467	50.9	15.3	991	5,114,134	2.9	11.0	8.8	5.2	0.7	0.4	69.0
Weymouth Town	131	1,086	76.7	26.4	1,301	6,282,223	0.0	0.0	0.0	0.0	0.0	0.0	100.0
Woburn	143	1,188	278.0	48.2	901	5,716,920	3.6	10.0	8.0	4.0	1.7	2.3	69.6
Worcester	358	2,286	232.1	69.5	1,745	10,914,232	11.0	35.4	26.7	5.4	6.3	10.3	3.4
MICHIGAN	16,545	104,291	13,205.0	3,415.1	X	X	X	X	X	X	X	X	X
Allen Park	57	239	24.5	5.2	138	630,053	8.1	35.8	20.6	5.1	5.1	19.4	4.8
Ann Arbor	235	1,855	297.0	78.4	949	5,739,709	12.5	35.7	10.7	11.2	2.3	11.7	0.0
Battle Creek	96	845	478.4	45.0	505	2,561,641	12.1	28.3	18.5	10.7	1.5	16.6	0.0
Bay City	73	458	44.8	12.6	268	1,253,021	17.2	24.6	10.6	5.6	1.2	36.7	0.0
Burton	D	D	D	D	94	426,834	23.9	46.3	2.8	10.1	2.4	10.1	0.0
Dearborn	227	1,444	137.4	34.9	919	3,774,428	12.9	29.4	13.0	3.9	5.8	11.8	4.5
Dearborn Heights	110	365	34.2	8.3	301	1,416,010	13.7	40.6	19.1	3.5	0.6	11.8	3.5
Detroit	785	5,867	1,028.8	216.3	8,795	32,957,680	15.3	46.9	11.2	6.3	2.8	6.9	2.0
East Lansing	57	682	139.2	34.7	380	1,883,723	16.9	28.6	14.7	3.7	3.3	19.2	4.0
Eastpointe	57	215	25.3	6.0	178	824,608	14.8	39.6	19.5	6.0	0.0	11.0	3.5
Farmington Hills	168	2,344	162.0	74.1	461	2,518,181	14.5	38.0	21.3	10.6	0.5	13.1	0.0
Flint	116	1,227	359.3	45.0	3,499	17,528,973	1.8	3.9	4.4	1.0	84.8	3.1	0.0
Garden City	D	D	D	D	87	459,448	16.9	45.3	27.3	0.0	0.0	5.7	3.8
Grand Rapids	382	2,679	344.0	83.9	1,515	8,401,875	15.7	28.8	15.5	4.6	4.4	15.1	4.6
Hamtramck	28	51	4.7	0.9	95	487,995	23.5	36.3	31.1	1.9	1.8	1.5	3.6
Holland	72	575	65.8	18.4	211	1,062,551	15.8	37.5	13.5	7.0	2.6	10.6	0.0
Inkster	19	65	3.4	1.1	115	478,647	13.6	33.1	24.0	0.0	18.9	10.5	0.0
Jackson	74	484	73.4	14.8	217	1,090,462	14.9	29.2	12.6	4.0	2.6	31.8	0.0
Kalamazoo	162	1,809	247.1	53.0	542	2,984,444	11.0	48.8	7.8	2.5	3.2	23.1	0.0
Kentwood	83	1,052	114.9	38.4	1	6,650	0.0	100.0	0.0	0.0	0.0	0.0	0.0
Lansing	266	2,122	339.1	87.7	1,717	10,111,886	7.4	14.2	9.5	3.6	2.0	37.7	0.0
Lincoln Park	75	323	48.9	10.8	134	591,702	11.0	45.0	24.3	3.6	4.3	7.6	0.1
Livonia	245	1,811	274.1	67.2	677	3,317,307	15.1	30.3	17.5	7.3	2.2	11.8	4.9
Madison Heights	88	543	69.8	20.7	158	872,404	13.8	41.4	19.0	4.9	5.5	8.8	3.0
Midland	104	845	146.2	26.7	384	1,874,862	12.5	15.8	14.4	16.3	3.5	24.7	7.3
Muskegon	58	428	48.3	11.2	270	1,123,408	10.3	39.2	16.9	6.3	6.9	13.7	0.0
Norton Shores	38	280	21.7	8.3	103	528,221	11.3	36.1	23.2	15.3	1.0	11.3	0.0
Novi	119	1,192	160.1	49.0	328	1,626,861	15.0	34.0	15.0	7.2	1.6	10.4	7.2

1. Establishments subject to federal tax.

City	City government finances, 2017									
	General revenue							General expenditure		
		Intergovernmental		Taxes						
					Per capita[1] (dollars)				Per capita[1] (dollars)	
	Total (mil dol)	Total (mil dol)	Percent from state government	Total (mil dol)	Total	Property	Sales and gross receipts	Total (mil dol)	Total	Capital outlays
	117	118	119	120	121	122	123	124	125	126
MASSACHUSETTS—Cont'd										
Chelsea	207.0	112.4	98.5	69.4	1,722	1,626	95	196.4	4,875	717
Chicopee	221.8	88.8	98.6	86.2	1,558	1,509	49	207.4	3,748	80
Everett	202.2	89.5	97.3	102.0	2,213	2,164	48	189.0	4,099	291
Fall River	329.3	178.6	93.9	105.0	1,176	1,114	62	287.9	3,224	161
Fitchburg	156.4	80.9	94.7	56.0	1,374	1,299	75	137.9	3,384	257
Framingham	NA	NA	NA	NA	NA	NA	NA	NA	NA	NA
Franklin Town	129.9	36.9	99.8	77.5	2,336	2,270	66	139.5	4,208	376
Gloucester	129.8	21.6	95.7	85.6	2,838	2,719	120	129.9	4,307	530
Haverhill	250.3	102.9	98.3	108.3	1,702	1,624	78	230.2	3,616	480
Holyoke	185.1	109.1	95.9	56.9	1,415	1,355	60	176.0	4,375	34
Lawrence	335.3	249.5	84.5	74.9	937	880	56	326.4	4,080	130
Leominster	149.3	63.5	95.5	72.1	1,732	1,697	35	134.7	3,238	234
Lowell	405.0	222.8	93.0	138.2	1,236	1,190	46	399.9	3,579	212
Lynn	366.0	218.6	97.5	131.5	1,401	1,364	36	387.6	4,127	66
Malden	195.3	85.7	99.6	92.7	1,518	1,440	78	167.7	2,746	134
Marlborough	161.2	40.1	99.6	102.9	2,587	2,496	91	157.5	3,959	89
Medford	176.5	37.5	94.6	116.7	2,020	1,936	84	176.8	3,060	81
Melrose	100.8	20.1	96.7	63.0	2,234	2,220	13	107.4	3,808	173
Methuen Town	175.5	67.6	99.1	91.7	1,823	1,763	60	155.7	3,094	200
New Bedford	418.3	235.2	96.1	129.2	1,359	1,281	78	425.1	4,471	1,168
Newton	456.5	57.7	89.2	344.9	3,882	3,730	152	459.3	5,170	747
Northampton	107.4	22.5	88.9	60.9	2,131	2,038	94	98.5	3,447	136
North Attleborough Town	NA	NA	NA	NA	NA	NA	NA	NA	NA	NA
Peabody	182.5	47.1	88.6	115.7	2,185	2,063	122	196.7	3,714	469
Pittsfield	194.8	95.9	97.7	87.8	2,054	1,993	61	216.1	5,054	1,134
Quincy	381.7	81.4	91.5	228.2	2,419	2,361	59	445.3	4,721	383
Randolph Town	NA	NA	NA	NA	NA	NA	NA	NA	NA	NA
Revere	185.6	87.1	99.2	89.3	1,652	1,558	94	196.3	3,631	382
Salem	191.3	54.4	91.2	92.3	2,133	2,082	51	172.8	3,992	7
Somerville	266.5	70.4	93.4	155.7	1,917	1,742	175	274.1	3,376	167
Springfield	729.9	475.9	94.2	210.9	1,368	1,283	85	727.3	4,716	336
Taunton	220.1	89.0	96.9	104.1	1,827	1,748	79	221.4	3,885	193
Waltham	260.4	33.3	96.5	194.1	3,090	2,886	204	224.3	3,571	209
Watertown Town	138.2	18.9	97.1	100.7	2,817	2,784	33	127.2	3,560	237
Westfield	151.2	56.9	93.5	75.3	1,820	1,784	35	141.0	3,405	513
West Springfield Town	113.9	38.9	94.4	67.1	2,349	2,251	98	101.8	3,564	238
Weymouth Town	183.3	49.4	97.6	110.1	1,941	1,848	93	176.6	3,115	190
Woburn	156.6	26.9	99.2	111.4	2,758	2,599	159	160.1	3,966	428
Worcester	757.5	367.1	95.0	307.5	1,659	1,601	58	808.0	4,360	644
MICHIGAN	X	X	X	X	X	X	X	X	X	X
Allen Park	60.4	8.4	61.7	22.6	830	783	47	58.5	2,148	308
Ann Arbor	258.5	61.0	37.2	102.6	844	781	63	255.8	2,105	318
Battle Creek	107.9	26.0	63.0	48.7	950	606	20	101.7	1,984	308
Bay City	55.3	16.0	51.5	14.6	440	423	17	46.0	1,388	287
Burton	24.2	6.9	84.1	7.7	269	248	21	34.3	1,198	229
Dearborn	207.9	41.5	86.3	100.3	1,059	1,017	42	229.5	2,423	287
Dearborn Heights	69.1	15.6	91.2	32.7	586	532	54	66.8	1,195	62
Detroit	1,894.3	608.6	59.6	747.8	1,108	290	372	2,108.5	3,125	876
East Lansing	67.1	14.0	84.6	25.0	509	464	45	74.2	1,512	312
Eastpointe	30.5	6.9	97.7	13.0	400	356	44	39.6	1,219	79
Farmington Hills	100.0	17.0	89.4	48.6	597	574	23	115.9	1,423	182
Flint	614.5	175.2	89.6	35.9	372	176	34	577.5	5,987	164
Garden City	31.1	7.2	74.1	12.2	456	432	24	39.0	1,459	51
Grand Rapids	361.4	81.9	48.0	154.6	776	279	26	371.7	1,866	207
Hamtramck	38.0	9.5	62.1	10.9	500	331	61	31.2	1,427	159
Holland	53.4	11.8	78.8	18.1	542	518	24	77.0	2,304	1,046
Inkster	48.7	25.5	61.8	9.8	401	353	48	33.3	1,358	63
Jackson	60.4	21.9	36.7	20.5	627	339	12	61.2	1,872	366
Kalamazoo	129.0	32.1	65.7	41.4	546	515	32	98.8	1,303	131
Kentwood	42.2	11.1	87.1	20.9	404	366	38	47.2	912	96
Lansing	238.2	55.9	49.7	82.1	697	381	13	218.3	1,854	80
Lincoln Park	37.7	9.7	84.6	13.3	362	334	29	36.7	1,000	85
Livonia	121.6	18.8	92.8	58.3	619	590	29	111.0	1,178	30
Madison Heights	40.1	7.7	94.0	18.9	627	601	25	44.0	1,455	211
Midland	81.6	21.3	85.8	36.4	869	851	18	70.1	1,674	104
Muskegon	56.0	12.1	74.2	18.6	490	213	50	56.4	1,484	66
Norton Shores	29.4	4.8	98.4	11.9	485	443	43	26.0	1,063	129
Novi	70.4	10.4	97.0	35.5	593	552	41	71.4	1,191	312

1. Based on population estimated as of July 1 of the year shown.

City	City government finances, 2017 (cont.)												
	General expenditure (cont.)												
	Percent of total for:									Debt outstanding			
	Public welfare	Highways	Parking facilities	Education	Health and hospitals	Police protection	Sewerage and sanitation	Parks and recreation	Housing and community development	Interest on debt	Total (mil dol)	Per capita[1] (dollars)	Debt issued during year
	127	128	129	130	131	132	133	134	135	136	137	138	139
MASSACHUSETTS—Cont'd													
Chelsea	0.3	2.2	0.0	62.1	0.0	5.3	5.5	0.1	3.1	0.5	38.0	944	9.4
Chicopee	0.4	1.4	0.0	55.2	0.3	5.5	9.9	1.7	0.5	1.8	179.9	3,251	50.7
Everett	0.2	4.4	0.0	62.2	1.2	7.0	1.9	0.4	0.6	1.3	85.9	1,862	14.4
Fall River	0.9	3.3	0.2	58.8	0.1	7.1	7.3	0.5	2.3	1.9	262.7	2,942	9.4
Fitchburg	0.5	5.4	0.2	60.5	0.5	5.6	7.7	0.5	0.8	1.1	72.0	1,766	1.2
Framingham	NA	NA	NA	NA	NA	NA	NA	NA	NA	NA	NA	NA	NA
Franklin Town	0.2	4.8	0.0	57.5	0.2	3.8	5.0	0.5	0.0	2.1	98.8	2,978	0.0
Gloucester	0.4	3.5	0.0	46.5	0.3	4.9	8.0	0.2	0.8	2.5	159.0	5,272	22.1
Haverhill	0.5	3.1	0.2	58.9	0.3	4.7	6.7	1.1	0.5	1.1	109.5	1,720	1.1
Holyoke	0.3	2.8	0.1	61.8	0.4	7.3	4.7	0.5	1.7	1.0	86.8	2,157	5.0
Lawrence	0.3	2.5	0.1	70.3	0.0	3.9	1.2	0.0	0.3	1.2	142.6	1,783	46.3
Leominster	0.4	4.7	0.0	66.4	0.3	5.7	6.2	0.6	0.3	0.8	50.9	1,224	0.0
Lowell	0.2	2.7	0.5	58.5	0.6	6.6	5.4	0.7	1.6	1.8	252.2	2,257	20.4
Lynn	0.3	2.1	0.2	59.7	0.0	5.3	1.4	0.1	1.1	1.4	63.2	673	0.0
Malden	0.2	3.1	0.0	63.0	0.6	6.8	1.7	0.5	0.0	1.8	86.1	1,409	4.0
Marlborough	0.2	6.2	0.0	58.5	0.3	4.9	10.7	0.2	0.0	2.9	147.3	3,701	12.0
Medford	0.2	2.7	0.0	46.6	0.3	7.0	11.4	0.5	0.9	1.3	56.5	978	0.0
Melrose	0.4	5.7	0.0	46.2	0.8	4.2	8.1	1.6	0.1	1.8	60.7	2,153	0.0
Methuen Town	0.3	5.9	0.0	64.3	0.5	8.2	3.9	0.1	0.3	1.0	66.5	1,321	11.9
New Bedford	0.7	0.7	0.1	66.8	1.0	5.8	4.3	0.7	0.9	1.7	244.0	2,566	18.4
Newton	0.1	3.0	0.0	59.5	0.7	4.2	8.4	1.4	1.0	1.9	316.4	3,562	109.3
Northampton	0.9	5.6	0.6	44.4	0.3	5.9	3.3	0.3	0.3	1.7	55.5	1,942	3.4
North Attleborough Town	NA	NA	NA	NA	NA	NA	NA	NA	NA	NA	NA	NA	NA
Peabody	0.2	2.8	0.0	54.5	0.7	5.5	6.2	1.7	1.3	1.2	88.6	1,673	10.0
Pittsfield	0.5	3.2	0.1	60.7	0.3	4.4	5.5	0.4	0.6	1.3	133.3	3,116	36.1
Quincy	0.3	2.5	0.0	44.7	0.9	6.0	8.4	0.7	1.4	1.4	257.5	2,730	43.6
Randolph Town	NA	NA	NA	NA	NA	NA	NA	NA	NA	NA	NA	NA	NA
Revere	0.4	2.6	0.0	56.1	0.3	4.9	9.7	0.2	0.3	1.4	135.9	2,513	53.5
Salem	0.4	3.4	0.5	48.5	0.3	5.9	4.7	0.8	0.5	1.2	79.2	1,829	17.2
Somerville	0.2	3.4	0.0	39.3	0.9	6.1	10.4	0.8	1.3	1.4	154.7	1,905	32.2
Springfield	0.3	1.6	0.0	62.3	0.2	6.1	1.4	1.2	1.1	1.2	200.5	1,300	71.4
Taunton	3.4	2.8	0.0	52.0	0.4	6.9	4.8	0.6	0.8	1.2	144.8	2,541	4.2
Waltham	0.1	5.6	0.2	51.3	0.3	7.4	9.4	0.8	0.6	1.2	93.7	1,491	25.7
Watertown Town	0.2	3.0	0.0	46.7	0.5	6.9	8.4	0.5	0.0	1.1	34.1	955	0.8
Westfield	0.5	5.8	0.0	55.5	3.6	5.3	6.2	0.2	0.5	2.3	98.1	2,370	0.0
West Springfield Town	0.6	4.2	0.0	58.5	0.3	6.9	4.4	0.5	1.0	2.2	71.4	2,498	0.0
Weymouth Town	0.4	2.4	0.0	54.9	0.3	6.4	10.8	0.3	0.5	0.7	77.9	1,374	6.4
Woburn	0.4	3.5	0.0	52.5	0.6	5.3	8.4	0.5	0.0	0.9	74.3	1,839	9.5
Worcester	0.3	3.9	0.2	53.8	0.4	5.9	6.0	0.8	1.0	3.3	722.7	3,899	102.0
MICHIGAN	X	X	X	X	X	X	X	X	X	X	X	X	X
Allen Park	0.0	17.2	0.0	0.0	0.0	10.3	18.9	2.5	0.6	5.3	74.2	2,724	1.5
Ann Arbor	0.0	13.0	8.6	0.0	0.0	10.7	19.5	5.9	8.6	2.6	313.7	2,582	38.6
Battle Creek	0.0	13.6	1.4	0.0	0.0	19.2	18.9	5.8	1.1	1.7	105.2	2,053	57.0
Bay City	0.0	16.2	0.0	0.0	0.0	14.2	25.0	2.2	8.3	5.2	81.2	2,450	10.4
Burton	0.0	8.9	0.0	0.0	1.0	15.9	41.6	0.5	0.0	0.9	30.2	1,055	8.6
Dearborn	0.0	7.8	0.1	0.0	0.0	16.3	33.2	7.9	1.3	1.7	226.7	2,394	21.6
Dearborn Heights	0.0	15.2	0.0	0.0	0.0	20.9	25.2	1.2	1.7	1.9	48.2	863	18.8
Detroit	0.0	4.2	0.2	0.1	1.4	12.9	17.2	26.4	5.5	7.1	3,188.4	4,726	982.5
East Lansing	0.0	7.0	10.4	0.0	0.2	14.8	19.8	8.4	0.7	2.3	62.1	1,265	17.3
Eastpointe	0.0	12.0	0.0	0.0	0.0	21.3	21.1	1.5	0.0	1.1	16.6	512	4.7
Farmington Hills	0.0	25.0	0.0	0.0	0.0	16.9	14.2	8.0	0.0	0.3	51.9	637	25.1
Flint	0.0	1.9	0.0	0.0	78.9	4.5	5.6	0.1	1.4	1.1	145.4	1,507	0.0
Garden City	0.0	13.6	0.0	0.0	3.2	16.8	37.4	3.1	0.0	0.5	34.3	1,284	2.1
Grand Rapids	0.0	6.2	4.1	0.0	0.2	13.9	13.6	3.2	9.9	5.5	676.1	3,395	84.7
Hamtramck	0.0	5.4	0.0	0.0	0.0	14.7	31.1	0.1	11.4	0.2	10.3	473	6.0
Holland	0.0	13.9	0.2	0.0	0.2	10.0	31.7	15.2	0.4	1.2	243.1	7,279	21.7
Inkster	0.0	6.8	0.0	0.0	0.7	12.8	14.5	1.0	28.7	4.0	38.2	1,556	0.3
Jackson	0.0	24.9	0.5	0.0	0.0	14.4	11.0	5.8	10.7	3.8	45.6	1,395	18.2
Kalamazoo	0.0	12.2	0.0	0.0	0.7	0.0	26.0	4.0	1.8	5.6	512.6	6,763	8.0
Kentwood	0.0	27.1	0.0	0.0	0.0	21.9	14.2	7.4	0.0	0.7	16.4	317	0.0
Lansing	0.0	11.5	1.7	0.0	0.0	17.8	10.2	7.9	9.4	4.0	565.6	4,804	37.6
Lincoln Park	0.0	12.1	0.0	0.0	0.0	26.4	19.5	1.3	1.9	0.0	11.9	324	2.3
Livonia	0.0	13.8	0.0	0.0	0.0	18.1	26.7	8.1	1.7	1.2	47.6	505	10.5
Madison Heights	0.0	12.4	0.0	0.0	0.0	22.8	31.3	2.4	0.0	0.7	23.2	767	15.3
Midland	0.0	15.9	0.2	0.0	0.0	11.2	16.7	17.5	5.0	0.8	22.6	540	0.0
Muskegon	0.0	8.8	0.0	0.0	0.0	16.4	37.4	6.3	4.7	0.6	20.1	529	0.2
Norton Shores	0.0	19.6	0.0	0.0	0.0	16.0	27.4	2.2	0.0	0.1	2.7	110	0.0
Novi	0.0	26.8	0.0	0.0	0.0	15.7	13.8	11.2	0.1	1.0	23.4	390	0.0

1. Based on population estimated as of July 1 of the year shown.

STATE	Place code	City	Land area[1] (sq. mi)	Population, 2021: Total persons 2021	Population, 2021: Rank	Population, 2021: Per square mile	Race 2020: Race alone[2] (percent): White	Black or African American	American Indian, Alaskan Native	Asian	Hawaiian Pacific Islander	Some other race	Two or more races (percent)
			1	2	3	4	5	6	7	8	9	10	11
		MICHIGAN—Cont'd											
26	59920	Oak Park	5.1	29,322	1,332	5,749.4	36.8	55.6	0.2	1.5	0.0	1.0	4.9
26	65440	Pontiac	19.9	60,984	632	3,064.5	27.5	48.2	0.7	2.3	0.0	11.1	10.1
26	65560	Portage	32.3	48,844	817	1,512.2	81.4	5.2	0.4	4.6	0.0	1.6	6.8
26	65820	Port Huron	8.1	28,826	1,354	3,558.8	80.0	8.3	0.8	0.7	0.0	1.5	8.8
26	69035	Rochester Hills	32.8	76,028	482	2,317.9	72.8	3.7	0.3	15.2	0.0	1.6	6.4
26	69420	Romulus	35.6	25,097	1,543	705.0	42.1	46.8	0.4	1.3	0.1	2.0	7.4
26	69800	Roseville	9.8	47,154	846	4,811.6	68.5	20.9	0.4	1.9	0.0	0.9	7.3
26	70040	Royal Oak	11.8	57,953	682	4,911.3	85.8	3.7	0.2	3.3	0.0	1.0	6.1
26	70520	Saginaw	17.1	43,854	907	2,564.6	39.0	44.9	0.6	0.5	0.0	5.6	9.4
26	70760	St. Clair Shores	11.7	58,200	676	4,974.4	86.0	6.4	0.2	1.1	0.0	0.7	5.5
26	74900	Southfield	26.3	75,898	485	2,885.9	21.4	70.5	0.2	2.4	0.0	1.3	4.2
26	74960	Southgate	6.9	29,896	1,314	4,332.8	77.9	7.8	0.7	2.5	0.0	2.5	8.6
26	76460	Sterling Heights	36.4	133,269	211	3,661.2	79.7	6.6	0.2	8.2	0.0	0.7	4.7
26	79000	Taylor	23.6	62,573	615	2,651.4	66.1	20.1	0.5	2.1	0.0	2.7	8.4
26	80700	Troy	33.4	86,836	398	2,599.9	62.2	4.0	0.2	27.3	0.0	1.2	5.1
26	82960	Walker	24.6	25,153	1,539	1,022.5	84.4	3.7	0.5	2.8	0.0	2.5	6.1
26	84000	Warren	34.4	138,130	198	4,015.4	62.4	20.4	0.3	10.3	0.0	1.0	5.7
26	86000	Westland	20.4	84,515	417	4,142.9	64.8	21.8	0.5	4.3	0.0	1.6	6.9
26	88900	Wyandotte	5.3	24,684	1,551	4,657.4	87.9	2.0	0.5	0.5	0.0	1.7	7.4
26	88940	Wyoming	24.7	76,749	475	3,107.2	62.2	9.0	1.0	3.2	0.0	13.3	11.2
27	00000	MINNESOTA	79,625.9	5,707,390	X	71.7	77.5	7.0	1.2	5.2	0.1	3.0	6.1
27	01486	Andover	33.9	32,926	1,198	971.3	87.2	3.0	0.3	3.1	0.0	0.9	5.5
27	01900	Apple Valley	16.9	55,638	709	3,292.2	72.0	8.9	0.5	6.7	0.0	4.2	7.7
27	02908	Austin	13.3	26,225	1,476	1,971.8	68.0	6.0	0.6	7.6	1.0	9.0	7.8
27	06382	Blaine	32.9	70,935	525	2,156.1	74.0	7.1	0.6	9.0	0.0	2.6	6.7
27	06616	Bloomington	34.7	89,298	385	2,573.4	69.3	9.9	0.8	6.6	0.1	6.2	7.1
27	07948	Brooklyn Center	8.0	32,880	1,200	4,110.0	34.4	28.0	1.4	19.0	0.0	8.2	9.0
27	07966	Brooklyn Park	26.1	84,526	416	3,238.5	39.7	29.5	0.6	18.9	0.0	4.6	6.8
27	08794	Burnsville	24.9	63,943	599	2,568.0	62.9	15.5	0.6	5.7	0.1	7.0	8.2
27	10918	Chanhassen	20.4	26,037	1,493	1,276.3	85.2	1.4	0.2	6.2	0.0	1.4	5.7
27	10972	Chaska	17.0	28,047	1,389	1,649.8	78.9	4.6	0.5	4.0	0.0	5.4	6.6
27	13114	Coon Rapids	22.6	63,385	606	2,804.6	73.7	10.4	0.7	6.1	0.0	2.2	6.9
27	13456	Cottage Grove	33.6	39,926	993	1,188.3	76.3	6.1	0.5	7.1	0.0	2.5	7.5
27	17000	Duluth	71.7	86,372	402	1,204.6	85.0	3.6	2.6	1.6	0.0	0.8	6.5
27	17288	Eagan	31.2	68,642	550	2,200.1	71.2	9.3	0.4	9.5	0.0	2.7	6.8
27	18116	Eden Prairie	32.5	63,161	608	1,943.4	70.4	7.2	0.3	13.9	0.0	1.9	6.2
27	18188	Edina	15.5	53,318	747	3,439.9	79.6	3.6	0.2	9.0	0.0	1.6	6.0
27	18674	Elk River	42.3	26,192	1,480	619.2	85.9	4.1	0.6	1.8	0.0	1.5	6.1
27	22814	Fridley	10.2	30,313	1,300	2,971.9	58.8	18.2	1.0	7.0	0.0	6.3	8.6
27	31076	Inver Grove Heights	27.9	35,541	1,120	1,273.9	74.6	6.1	0.7	4.4	0.1	6.2	8.0
27	35180	Lakeville	36.6	72,812	507	1,989.4	79.9	4.3	0.4	5.8	0.0	2.9	6.6
27	39878	Mankato	19.4	44,693	888	2,303.8	79.0	8.4	0.5	3.8	0.1	2.3	5.8
27	40166	Maple Grove	32.6	70,726	532	2,169.5	78.0	6.4	0.4	7.7	0.0	1.5	6.1
27	40382	Maplewood	17.0	40,940	965	2,408.2	57.6	11.2	0.6	19.1	0.1	4.5	6.9
27	43000	Minneapolis	54.0	425,336	46	7,876.6	59.5	19.1	1.7	5.8	0.0	5.9	8.0
27	43252	Minnetonka	26.9	53,266	748	1,980.1	83.4	4.6	0.2	4.6	0.0	1.3	5.9
27	43864	Moorhead	22.3	44,668	890	2,003.0	81.6	6.7	2.1	1.6	0.0	1.6	6.4
27	47680	Oakdale	11.0	27,974	1,394	2,543.1	67.6	10.3	0.5	12.3	0.0	2.8	6.5
27	49300	Owatonna	15.1	26,398	1,471	1,748.2	83.5	5.0	0.3	1.1	0.1	4.2	5.8
27	51730	Plymouth	32.7	79,828	449	2,441.2	74.5	6.3	0.3	11.4	0.0	1.6	5.9
27	52594	Prior Lake	16.3	28,086	1,387	1,723.1	83.4	2.8	2.1	4.7	0.1	1.1	5.9
27	53026	Ramsey	28.9	28,202	1,380	975.8	82.7	6.5	0.4	3.2	0.0	1.5	5.7
27	54214	Richfield	6.8	36,527	1,086	5,371.6	61.0	9.8	1.4	6.6	0.1	12.0	9.1
27	54880	Rochester	55.6	121,465	236	2,184.6	73.2	8.9	0.4	7.9	0.1	2.9	6.6
27	55726	Rosemount	33.3	26,642	1,458	800.1	80.1	4.8	0.3	5.9	0.0	2.3	6.5
27	55852	Roseville	13.0	35,874	1,104	2,759.5	72.2	8.9	0.6	9.5	0.1	2.4	6.3
27	56896	St. Cloud	40.0	68,818	548	1,720.5	68.8	19.2	0.6	3.5	0.1	1.9	5.8
27	57220	St. Louis Park	10.6	49,158	812	4,637.5	78.1	8.0	0.7	4.2	0.1	2.5	6.4
27	58000	St. Paul	52.0	307,193	67	5,907.6	50.5	16.8	1.0	19.2	0.0	4.8	7.6
27	58738	Savage	15.6	32,983	1,195	2,114.3	73.5	8.7	0.5	9.0	0.1	2.2	6.0
27	59350	Shakopee	28.5	44,547	894	1,563.1	64.9	9.4	1.5	11.8	0.0	5.0	7.4
27	59998	Shoreview	10.8	26,670	1,454	2,469.4	78.6	3.7	0.4	10.3	0.0	1.2	5.8
27	71032	Winona	19.0	25,964	1,496	1,366.5	89.3	2.8	0.3	2.2	0.0	1.3	4.2
27	71428	Woodbury	34.9	76,990	472	2,206.0	72.3	7.4	0.3	11.4	0.0	1.4	7.0
28	00000	MISSISSIPPI	46,925.5	2,949,965	X	62.9	56.0	36.6	0.6	1.1	0.0	1.9	3.7
28	06220	Biloxi	42.9	49,241	810	1,147.8	60.2	22.2	0.5	4.4	0.2	4.4	8.2
28	08300	Brandon	25.7	25,373	1,523	987.3	74.2	20.1	0.3	0.9	0.0	0.9	3.6

1. Dry land or land partially or temporarily covered by water. 2. Hispanic or Latino persons may be of any race.

City	Percent Hispanic or Latino[1], 2020	Percent foreign born, 2016–2020	Age of population (percent), 2016–2020: Under 18 years	18 to 24 years	25 to 34 years	35 to 44 years	45 to 54 years	55 to 64 years	65 years and over	Median age, 2016–2020	Percent female, 2016–2020	Population: Census counts 2010	2020	Percent change 2010–2020	2020–2021
	12	13	14	15	16	17	18	19	20	21	22	23	24	25	26
MICHIGAN—Cont'd															
Oak Park	2.2	9.5	19.6	10.1	17.1	12.8	11.6	12.3	16.6	37.1	53.5	29,408	29,580	0.6	-0.9
Pontiac	21.8	9.2	25.0	10.6	16.2	10.9	13.6	11.5	12.2	33.6	52.1	59,695	61,572	3.1	-1.0
Portage	4.5	6.4	22.9	10.6	13.9	12.1	12.1	12.2	16.3	37.1	51.2	46,304	48,846	5.5	0.0
Port Huron	5.8	2.8	22.0	10.0	14.2	11.7	11.8	14.0	16.2	38.3	50.5	30,206	29,038	-3.9	-0.7
Rochester Hills	4.7	19.8	22.7	7.2	10.7	14.3	13.9	13.6	17.6	41.4	51.6	70,987	76,293	7.5	-0.3
Romulus	4.4	3.1	25.6	8.6	14.5	12.0	13.3	12.0	14.0	36.5	50.4	23,989	25,157	4.9	-0.2
Roseville	2.8	4.0	20.3	8.4	15.2	11.2	13.9	14.6	16.4	40.9	51.5	47,322	47,714	0.8	-1.2
Royal Oak	3.7	7.3	15.5	8.5	25.3	12.5	11.0	13.2	13.9	35.3	49.5	57,232	58,217	1.7	-0.5
Saginaw	15.8	1.3	26.7	8.8	14.0	12.5	11.9	12.5	13.6	35.4	50.5	51,493	44,166	-14.2	-0.7
St. Clair Shores	2.8	3.9	17.4	6.6	15.0	12.5	11.7	16.2	20.4	43.5	50.8	59,765	58,893	-1.5	-1.2
Southfield	2.2	7.9	18.7	8.8	14.2	11.5	13.0	14.0	19.9	42.2	53.8	71,715	76,579	6.8	-0.9
Southgate	9.1	6.3	18.7	7.2	16.8	11.1	12.4	15.5	18.4	42.2	52.2	30,047	30,000	-0.2	-0.3
Sterling Heights	2.4	27.3	19.8	9.0	14.7	11.1	13.7	14.4	17.3	40.7	51.2	129,675	134,348	3.6	-0.8
Taylor	7.9	4.8	20.3	10.1	15.7	10.2	14.2	14.2	15.3	39.0	50.6	63,131	63,384	0.4	-1.3
Troy	3.4	28.9	21.1	9.2	10.8	12.6	14.6	14.4	17.3	42.1	49.0	80,970	87,316	7.8	-0.5
Walker	6.2	5.2	21.8	8.4	16.7	12.1	10.7	13.2	17.0	37.2	53.9	23,545	25,159	6.9	0.0
Warren	2.6	13.8	21.9	8.6	15.2	12.2	13.0	13.5	15.6	38.4	51.3	134,072	139,407	4.0	-0.9
Westland	4.5	8.8	22.0	8.0	15.3	12.0	12.8	13.3	16.6	38.8	53.4	84,150	85,433	1.5	-1.1
Wyandotte	7.1	3.0	20.9	5.8	16.8	11.6	12.5	16.2	16.2	39.9	53.5	25,883	25,016	-3.3	-1.3
Wyoming	25.4	11.4	24.4	9.9	17.8	13.4	11.9	12.1	10.5	33.6	50.8	72,117	76,574	6.2	0.2
MINNESOTA	6.1	8.4	23.2	8.9	13.6	12.7	12.4	13.4	15.8	38.1	50.2	5,303,933	5,706,494	7.6	0.0
Andover	2.7	4.2	26.2	7.7	10.5	14.2	15.7	13.2	12.5	39.4	50.2	30,588	32,624	6.7	0.9
Apple Valley	8.1	13.2	24.0	8.5	13.2	13.2	13.4	13.3	14.3	37.8	50.9	49,092	56,246	14.6	-1.1
Austin	17.7	15.5	25.1	8.8	12.6	12.9	10.3	12.3	18.0	37.9	49.9	24,923	26,152	4.9	0.3
Blaine	5.6	11.9	26.4	7.4	12.4	14.9	12.9	13.7	12.2	37.4	50.4	57,179	70,293	22.9	0.9
Bloomington	9.9	14.2	20.1	6.7	13.6	12.5	12.9	14.4	19.8	42.6	51.5	82,893	90,012	8.6	-0.8
Brooklyn Center	13.8	23.6	28.3	7.6	19.5	12.9	10.1	10.2	11.5	31.9	51.3	30,180	33,824	12.1	-2.8
Brooklyn Park	7.6	24.2	28.2	8.5	14.6	14.4	12.5	11.2	10.8	34.4	50.9	75,776	86,688	14.4	-2.5
Burnsville	11.9	14.1	23.3	8.7	14.2	12.3	11.3	14.0	16.3	37.1	52.4	60,286	64,352	6.7	-0.6
Chanhassen	3.7	7.5	26.4	7.3	10.2	13.4	15.4	15.2	12.2	39.6	51.0	22,938	25,967	13.2	0.3
Chaska	9.7	6.3	26.6	8.6	12.1	14.4	14.9	12.5	10.9	36.9	51.4	23,865	27,828	16.6	0.8
Coon Rapids	4.7	9.0	21.6	8.0	14.3	12.9	13.7	13.3	16.2	39.2	51.1	61,485	63,660	3.5	-0.4
Cottage Grove	6.8	5.7	27.8	7.3	11.5	17.3	13.0	10.8	12.2	36.5	49.8	34,601	38,882	12.4	2.7
Duluth	2.4	3.5	17.9	19.6	14.1	11.0	10.1	11.7	15.6	33.7	51.3	86,266	86,645	0.4	-0.3
Eagan	6.1	14.9	22.5	7.9	13.6	14.5	13.0	15.0	13.6	38.9	51.1	64,150	68,905	7.4	-0.4
Eden Prairie	4.6	18.2	24.5	5.0	12.0	14.9	14.0	14.8	14.7	40.2	51.2	60,797	64,375	5.9	-1.9
Edina	3.7	10.4	23.0	4.9	10.7	12.4	14.2	13.4	21.4	44.3	52.6	47,988	53,563	11.6	-0.5
Elk River	3.8	5.6	26.6	6.9	15.5	14.4	12.8	11.6	12.3	35.5	50.0	22,960	25,798	12.4	1.5
Fridley	11.1	19.2	22.7	8.7	18.3	12.8	11.6	11.0	14.8	35.1	49.4	27,222	29,568	8.6	2.5
Inver Grove Heights	12.0	10.4	21.9	7.2	13.6	13.7	13.2	14.1	16.3	40.1	49.4	33,986	35,783	5.3	-0.7
Lakeville	5.7	8.2	28.2	7.8	12.3	13.5	15.3	13.7	9.3	36.0	49.9	55,998	69,654	24.4	4.5
Mankato	5.8	7.8	17.3	30.0	15.0	9.7	7.3	8.7	12.0	26.4	50.2	39,862	44,417	11.4	0.6
Maple Grove	3.5	9.2	25.5	5.0	12.1	14.3	14.9	15.3	12.9	40.5	52.7	61,548	70,509	14.6	0.3
Maplewood	8.9	13.7	22.1	7.4	16.5	12.7	10.3	13.7	17.2	38.4	49.2	38,016	42,100	10.7	-2.8
Minneapolis	10.4	15.2	19.8	13.5	22.2	14.0	10.5	10.1	9.9	32.3	49.3	382,603	428,403	12.0	-0.7
Minnetonka	3.6	10.1	20.4	4.2	14.7	12.6	11.6	15.2	21.3	43.3	50.7	49,750	53,962	8.5	-1.3
Moorhead	5.3	6.3	23.1	19.2	14.8	12.0	9.4	9.9	11.7	30.7	51.1	39,437	44,443	12.7	0.5
Oakdale	6.2	9.5	20.4	10.2	14.4	9.1	12.8	16.7	16.4	41.0	53.2	27,364	28,322	3.5	-1.2
Owatonna	9.6	5.3	25.1	8.2	11.7	12.2	13.1	12.2	17.5	38.6	50.4	25,622	26,438	3.2	-0.2
Plymouth	3.9	14.1	23.6	5.0	13.5	14.5	12.9	14.8	15.7	40.4	50.4	70,589	81,181	15.0	-1.7
Prior Lake	3.3	6.0	26.4	7.5	10.5	15.2	15.0	12.3	13.1	39.1	51.3	23,022	27,624	20.0	1.7
Ramsey	3.5	6.2	26.8	7.8	13.7	12.5	15.8	11.6	11.7	36.1	50.0	23,683	27,682	16.9	1.9
Richfield	18.4	16.6	19.3	7.1	20.3	14.4	11.0	11.8	16.0	36.8	49.4	35,228	37,074	5.2	-1.5
Rochester	6.6	13.5	24.1	8.2	16.2	13.3	11.1	12.0	15.1	35.9	51.1	106,825	121,244	13.5	0.2
Rosemount	5.2	6.6	27.7	7.8	11.9	14.6	15.1	11.8	11.1	36.6	50.2	21,881	25,679	17.4	3.8
Roseville	5.4	10.9	19.1	11.3	13.5	11.4	10.0	13.4	21.3	39.8	51.6	33,631	36,251	7.8	-1.0
St. Cloud	4.1	11.8	20.2	20.3	15.2	11.0	9.8	10.5	13.0	30.5	49.0	66,082	68,774	4.1	0.1
St. Louis Park	5.3	10.0	16.9	6.4	24.8	13.6	9.9	11.4	17.0	36.1	52.3	45,197	50,016	10.7	-1.7
St. Paul	9.7	19.7	24.8	11.0	18.5	13.2	10.9	10.6	11.0	32.5	51.1	285,103	311,448	9.2	-1.4
Savage	4.7	11.2	26.8	7.4	13.1	14.7	15.8	12.7	9.5	36.6	49.6	26,911	32,495	20.7	1.5
Shakopee	9.2	17.1	27.7	8.8	13.4	17.4	14.7	8.8	9.2	35.1	51.3	36,993	43,641	18.0	2.1
Shoreview	3.4	9.8	21.7	5.2	10.3	10.8	14.5	16.5	20.9	46.3	51.6	25,043	26,952	7.6	-1.0
Winona	3.2	3.4	12.0	30.5	11.9	8.3	8.5	11.8	16.9	30.3	51.7	27,583	26,030	-5.6	-0.3
Woodbury	4.8	12.1	27.9	7.6	10.3	15.2	14.8	12.4	11.7	37.9	50.7	61,963	75,163	21.3	2.4
MISSISSIPPI	3.6	2.3	23.7	9.8	12.9	12.5	12.3	12.9	15.9	37.7	51.6	2,968,129	2,961,279	-0.2	-0.4
Biloxi	9.5	6.4	22.0	12.5	15.2	11.2	11.2	13.4	14.4	35.2	49.7	44,250	49,523	11.9	-0.6
Brandon	2.1	3.5	23.1	8.1	12.0	13.7	14.8	10.9	17.4	40.9	52.0	22,054	25,100	13.8	1.1

1. May be of any race.

City	Households, 2016–2020: Number	Households, 2016–2020: Persons per household	Households, 2016–2020: Percent: Family	Households, 2016–2020: Percent: Married couple family	Households, 2016–2020: Percent: Female family	Households, 2016–2020: Percent: Non-family	Households, 2016–2020: Percent: One person	Persons in group quarters, 2016–2020	Serious crimes known to police[2], 2020: Violent: Number	Serious crimes known to police[2], 2020: Violent: Rate	Serious crimes known to police[2], 2020: Property: Number	Serious crimes known to police[2], 2020: Property: Rate	Educational attainment, 2016–2020: Population age 25 and over	Educational attainment, 2016–2020: Attainment[4] (percent): High school graduate or less	Educational attainment, 2016–2020: Attainment[4] (percent): Bachelor's degree or more
	27	28	29	30	31	32	33	34	35	36	37	38	39	40	41
MICHIGAN—Cont'd															
Oak Park	11,804	2.49	56.3	32.1	19.8	43.7	34.7	57	94	319.4	388	1,318.3	20,722	28.7	33.4
Pontiac	23,529	2.45	51.6	21.2	23.2	48.4	41.9	1,961	840	1,413.9	1,096	1,844.8	38,439	54.9	13.5
Portage	20,098	2.44	62.5	49.6	10.1	37.5	30.0	150	111	222.9	1,340	2,690.9	32,748	24.2	46.5
Port Huron	12,331	2.31	57.3	33.3	18.1	42.7	33.1	449	225	786.7	631	2,206.1	19,666	46.9	16.9
Rochester Hills	28,766	2.54	71.0	60.7	7.3	29.0	25.8	1,245	51	68.1	331	441.8	52,109	18.2	58.9
Romulus	8,769	2.66	65.8	43.2	15.7	34.2	28.3	199	246	1,045.3	474	2,014.2	15,481	46.1	19.1
Roseville	20,599	2.28	57.9	33.6	17.5	42.1	35.7	284	217	461.9	1,138	2,422.2	33,642	47.7	14.1
Royal Oak	28,933	2.04	45.2	36.6	5.4	54.8	41.6	278	42	70.6	398	668.8	45,015	17.7	59.5
Saginaw	19,605	2.40	54.3	24.7	22.8	45.7	38.9	1,393	1,029	2,154.2	720	1,507.3	31,204	52.2	12.9
St. Clair Shores	27,039	2.17	57.3	42.4	10.3	42.7	37.6	377	103	174.9	436	740.3	44,951	34.5	26.5
Southfield	31,965	2.24	53.2	33.1	17.3	46.8	41.4	1,424	288	395.6	1,309	1,798.2	52,921	26.3	38.9
Southgate	12,454	2.33	59.4	41.4	13.1	40.6	32.7	116	85	294.6	505	1,750.6	21,581	43.1	20.1
Sterling Heights	50,516	2.60	68.2	52.9	10.2	31.8	27.8	938	233	175.5	1,140	858.8	94,278	40.4	30.0
Taylor	25,005	2.42	63.8	38.8	17.5	36.2	28.4	714	371	611.2	1,108	1,825.4	42,551	51.8	13.7
Troy	31,660	2.64	71.5	62.8	5.7	28.5	24.2	339	86	101.8	732	866.9	58,595	16.7	62.6
Walker	10,169	2.42	63.4	51.9	8.3	36.6	30.8	278	48	191.8	513	2,050.4	17,399	32.8	32.2
Warren	52,428	2.53	63.6	41.7	15.8	36.4	30.7	1,352	672	501.8	1,938	1,447.0	93,293	47.5	19.0
Westland	34,953	2.31	57.0	37.9	14.1	43.0	38.0	845	330	406.2	883	1,086.8	57,208	40.5	22.7
Wyandotte	10,799	2.30	57.8	40.5	12.9	42.2	34.8	65	NA	NA	NA	NA	18,288	40.7	18.7
Wyoming	27,803	2.72	66.5	47.1	13.1	33.5	25.1	458	411	540.3	1,143	1,502.5	49,926	43.7	22.4
MINNESOTA	2,207,988	2.48	63.6	50.3	9.0	36.4	28.8	130,618	15,698	277.5	120,212	2,124.9	3,802,438	30.9	36.8
Andover	10,821	3.05	83.1	71.3	8.3	16.9	12.7	43	NA	NA	NA	NA	21,829	23.8	36.4
Apple Valley	20,601	2.59	71.0	56.8	9.1	29.0	23.1	305	60	107.4	907	1,624.1	36,286	23.9	44.4
Austin	10,097	2.43	62.6	45.0	11.9	37.4	32.3	624	70	277.0	402	1,591.0	16,652	46.8	22.8
Blaine	23,151	2.80	72.0	57.5	10.1	28.0	21.8	131	83	124.6	1,457	2,188.1	43,020	32.4	34.0
Bloomington	35,064	2.40	61.0	47.1	9.3	39.0	31.7	1,031	266	312.4	2,889	3,392.5	62,380	26.9	42.8
Brooklyn Center	10,570	2.89	67.7	39.0	18.6	32.3	25.3	200	148	481.4	1,109	3,607.2	19,724	41.2	21.7
Brooklyn Park	27,837	2.87	72.4	46.8	19.2	27.6	22.9	247	350	432.6	2,756	3,406.8	50,820	34.0	30.5
Burnsville	23,898	2.56	66.1	49.8	13.0	33.9	27.3	402	150	244.1	1,560	2,538.9	41,875	28.7	39.7
Chanhassen	9,396	2.76	76.3	66.6	7.5	23.7	19.4	5	NA	NA	NA	NA	17,223	10.2	63.4
Chaska	10,262	2.59	64.3	51.6	8.6	35.7	27.2	133	11	40.2	258	943.2	17,337	24.2	45.6
Coon Rapids	24,121	2.58	65.2	46.7	13.4	34.8	26.8	418	121	191.6	1,379	2,183.3	44,151	37.9	25.4
Cottage Grove	12,266	3.02	79.7	66.4	8.8	20.3	16.0	74	21	55.4	570	1,502.4	24,087	26.6	37.8
Duluth	36,526	2.18	49.1	36.1	9.5	50.9	36.6	6,289	257	300.4	3,224	3,768.3	53,674	27.3	39.0
Eagan	26,805	2.46	65.1	52.2	9.2	34.9	27.6	327	NA	NA	NA	NA	46,191	18.2	51.9
Eden Prairie	24,606	2.61	70.7	61.0	6.4	29.3	24.2	175	43	65.8	921	1,409.3	45,401	14.6	64.4
Edina	22,269	2.33	63.8	55.7	5.8	36.2	32.2	312	43	80.5	932	1,744.6	37,650	9.4	71.6
Elk River	8,529	2.83	70.2	52.3	11.6	29.8	22.5	774	24	94.2	444	1,743.4	16,578	34.4	23.7
Fridley	10,767	2.57	62.4	42.2	12.5	37.6	29.9	132	95	340.6	1,280	4,589.1	19,053	39.0	29.6
Inver Grove Heights	14,481	2.44	65.6	50.2	11.2	34.4	26.5	189	87	242.6	766	2,136.0	25,166	29.3	40.1
Lakeville	22,820	2.87	78.8	66.3	9.6	21.2	16.9	187	NA	NA	NA	NA	42,050	18.6	49.2
Mankato	16,828	2.33	49.8	34.5	9.0	50.2	27.7	3,542	108	249.6	1,033	2,387.0	22,483	30.2	38.3
Maple Grove	27,845	2.57	72.3	62.7	6.8	27.7	21.8	59	56	75.7	1,206	1,631.1	49,753	16.6	54.4
Maplewood	14,790	2.68	62.3	44.2	11.2	37.7	28.8	1,004	133	323.6	1,901	4,625.8	28,665	34.7	35.0
Minneapolis	178,886	2.28	43.9	30.7	9.5	56.1	40.3	17,346	5,025	1,154.9	19,833	4,558.1	283,237	24.1	51.8
Minnetonka	23,293	2.29	61.4	51.2	7.0	38.6	31.2	406	22	40.3	717	1,314.1	40,570	15.0	61.3
Moorhead	16,798	2.38	57.3	44.9	8.9	42.7	33.0	3,430	189	428.3	1,303	2,952.5	25,034	25.5	36.6
Oakdale	11,229	2.47	64.7	46.3	13.1	35.3	29.1	209	32	114.3	936	3,344.1	19,377	36.3	31.3
Owatonna	10,616	2.38	63.7	55.2	6.5	36.3	31.3	490	47	182.7	398	1,547.4	17,166	36.5	29.4
Plymouth	31,470	2.48	68.0	58.7	6.4	32.0	25.2	934	53	65.6	1,157	1,431.2	56,299	13.5	62.0
Prior Lake	9,802	2.73	72.0	61.8	6.1	28.0	23.2	40	47	169.4	596	2,147.9	17,702	17.1	48.3
Ramsey	9,630	2.82	75.1	60.2	9.0	24.9	17.4	5	21	74.5	219	776.5	17,804	30.7	30.8
Richfield	15,322	2.35	58.2	44.0	9.4	41.8	32.5	321	NA	NA	NA	NA	26,668	30.0	43.0
Rochester	48,468	2.37	60.2	47.7	8.9	39.8	30.6	2,340	300	249.3	2,314	1,922.9	79,196	24.2	48.0
Rosemount	8,698	2.85	78.3	64.6	9.3	21.7	17.2	33	7	27.3	175	683.7	15,994	19.4	48.5
Roseville	15,166	2.29	57.9	47.8	7.6	42.1	36.7	1,457	116	316.3	2,370	6,462.2	25,147	23.6	52.1
St. Cloud	26,878	2.37	52.5	35.8	12.5	47.5	34.4	4,798	NA	NA	NA	NA	40,714	35.5	30.8
St. Louis Park	23,774	2.03	44.5	35.4	6.0	55.5	42.0	690	63	128.4	1,475	3,006.6	37,479	15.7	59.9
St. Paul	114,742	2.59	53.7	35.6	13.1	46.3	36.0	8,571	2,320	748.7	11,783	3,802.7	196,431	33.5	41.3
Savage	10,802	2.94	79.8	65.1	10.5	20.2	13.7	9	33	99.9	406	1,229.6	20,887	18.8	50.6
Shakopee	14,125	2.86	71.4	51.9	11.9	28.6	20.8	971	NA	NA	NA	NA	26,316	32.2	37.1
Shoreview	11,377	2.35	65.2	55.3	7.0	34.8	30.9	230	NA	NA	NA	NA	19,659	15.7	57.6
Winona	10,521	2.21	45.5	36.1	6.0	54.5	40.1	3,508	45	169.9	683	2,578.6	15,376	32.3	33.8
Woodbury	25,969	2.73	73.5	62.0	7.8	26.5	21.2	291	71	95.8	1,522	2,053.7	45,938	13.7	61.0
MISSISSIPPI	1,116,649	2.59	66.3	44.7	17.0	33.7	29.2	94,430	8,638	291.2	62,351	2,101.6	1,983,112	44.8	22.8
Biloxi	18,096	2.38	60.8	43.8	12.8	39.2	32.4	3,039	NA	NA	NA	NA	30,175	37.2	26.6
Brandon	8,564	2.71	78.3	61.7	12.7	21.7	18.6	902	24	97.8	179	729.3	16,575	22.9	41.9

2. Data for serious crimes have not been adjusted for underreporting. This may affect comparability between geographic areas and over time.

4. Persons 25 years old and over.

City	Money income, 2016–2020: Households: Median household income	Money income, 2016–2020: Households: Percent with income less than $25,000	Money income, 2016–2020: Households: Percent with income of $200,000 or more	Money income, 2016–2020: Median family income	Money income, 2016–2020: Median non-family household income	Median earnings Full year, Full-time workers, 2016–2020: All persons	Median earnings Full year, Full-time workers, 2016–2020: Men	Median earnings Full year, Full-time workers, 2016–2020: Women	Housing units, 2016–2020: Total	Housing units, 2016–2020: Occupied	Housing units, 2016–2020: Percent owner occupied	Housing units, 2016–2020: Median value[1] (dollars)	Housing units, 2016–2020: Median gross rent (dollars)
	42	43	44	45	46	47	48	49	50	51	52	53	54
MICHIGAN—Cont'd													
Oak Park	54,202	20.5	4.3	66,639	39,113	44,573	50,313	41,840	12,468	11,804	56.0	129,800	1,123
Pontiac	34,673	34.7	0.7	46,719	25,950	33,516	36,314	32,353	27,089	23,529	43.4	73,800	811
Portage	66,571	14.4	6.1	88,878	41,222	53,238	60,015	46,785	21,323	20,098	67.6	174,600	889
Port Huron	41,165	30.0	1.8	50,411	27,161	37,181	41,166	32,948	13,651	12,331	56.3	96,900	805
Rochester Hills	99,666	9.1	15.7	118,880	48,329	82,373	93,272	65,613	30,303	28,766	77.4	303,800	1,311
Romulus	61,314	21.0	1.7	71,109	32,664	46,193	52,901	39,561	9,582	8,769	69.2	109,900	913
Roseville	49,426	22.9	1.1	60,832	32,350	41,198	47,389	37,160	21,604	20,599	62.8	97,600	1,027
Royal Oak	83,194	11.6	9.3	114,414	65,124	68,349	77,905	58,619	31,115	28,933	65.2	236,600	1,129
Saginaw	30,845	40.2	1.3	38,105	21,217	32,975	36,637	29,164	23,378	19,605	55.6	41,500	747
St. Clair Shores	62,935	15.7	3.6	81,355	40,250	52,458	59,425	45,930	28,324	27,039	82.4	144,500	945
Southfield	58,076	19.8	4.2	75,055	41,386	51,816	53,666	50,607	34,685	31,965	48.6	164,800	1,126
Southgate	59,975	19.1	3.3	74,133	37,572	51,488	56,089	43,653	13,203	12,454	66.7	125,800	905
Sterling Heights	66,346	15.0	4.1	78,458	42,081	51,898	57,661	43,172	52,085	50,516	74.4	198,300	1,051
Taylor	52,872	22.2	1.7	61,398	36,651	41,821	44,823	38,915	26,787	25,005	64.4	109,400	877
Troy	104,132	10.1	17.8	126,117	53,921	81,333	91,444	62,113	33,255	31,660	74.5	318,600	1,239
Walker	63,878	14.2	3.6	82,948	34,701	47,121	50,950	42,441	10,558	10,169	61.4	201,300	867
Warren	51,796	21.8	2.4	62,567	34,681	43,715	47,063	40,226	56,820	52,428	70.3	132,900	962
Westland	51,956	22.2	2.2	68,125	34,811	44,119	50,222	39,241	37,350	34,953	60.8	131,600	923
Wyandotte	54,419	21.4	2.3	72,054	34,328	51,129	56,647	44,140	11,762	10,799	70.3	118,900	776
Wyoming	57,088	17.1	2.1	66,796	37,278	40,660	44,864	36,694	29,320	27,803	67.4	135,500	910
MINNESOTA	73,382	14.6	8.5	92,692	42,913	54,146	59,993	49,047	2,458,030	2,207,988	71.9	235,700	1,010
Andover	112,967	4.2	13.0	121,187	70,011	65,769	72,745	56,069	11,014	10,821	92.9	305,900	1,684
Apple Valley	90,162	8.6	10.4	108,093	51,791	61,624	66,660	55,134	21,151	20,601	77.7	270,600	1,396
Austin	48,730	24.2	2.7	63,423	27,857	41,001	42,051	38,548	10,949	10,097	65.4	114,100	815
Blaine	86,796	9.8	8.1	101,605	49,099	58,256	63,828	51,482	24,091	23,151	87.0	240,700	1,475
Bloomington	78,224	12.1	9.5	98,276	48,907	56,513	61,645	51,974	36,521	35,064	67.8	265,700	1,220
Brooklyn Center	64,023	16.7	2.5	67,681	44,803	41,107	43,445	38,253	10,889	10,570	59.6	187,400	1,120
Brooklyn Park	73,207	11.6	6.5	82,669	43,712	49,370	51,565	45,664	28,953	27,837	68.1	233,700	1,150
Burnsville	76,017	11.3	6.3	92,366	47,988	54,399	60,112	50,563	24,841	23,898	68.2	263,700	1,297
Chanhassen	124,184	6.5	27.3	144,961	67,857	82,310	102,326	65,658	9,828	9,396	87.9	400,300	1,469
Chaska	90,161	9.9	13.4	121,250	48,386	62,418	71,840	52,520	10,485	10,262	69.7	290,300	1,160
Coon Rapids	76,169	9.3	4.3	88,089	47,706	51,261	54,004	46,998	24,601	24,121	74.8	216,000	1,208
Cottage Grove	102,600	3.9	11.1	110,860	55,641	62,121	67,906	56,991	12,661	12,266	88.9	261,500	1,470
Duluth	54,084	23.1	5.0	77,341	33,584	47,643	51,120	43,130	38,812	36,526	60.2	167,300	854
Eagan	93,332	9.3	14.0	119,657	52,602	69,037	77,574	58,606	27,481	26,805	70.3	298,700	1,262
Eden Prairie	115,227	6.4	21.5	134,413	63,908	82,648	91,516	69,896	25,446	24,606	75.4	374,700	1,450
Edina	108,576	11.8	26.4	151,352	49,851	91,662	107,587	70,760	23,621	22,269	69.7	501,400	1,442
Elk River	87,755	7.2	5.5	95,303	48,082	58,881	63,315	51,706	8,889	8,529	78.0	243,500	1,040
Fridley	65,669	12.1	3.9	73,690	44,798	48,496	51,129	45,442	11,175	10,767	62.0	211,900	1,036
Inver Grove Heights	83,155	10.3	9.7	101,337	49,339	61,736	66,548	54,589	15,059	14,481	69.1	273,000	1,214
Lakeville	112,020	5.7	16.2	126,885	51,913	69,673	81,963	55,684	23,168	22,820	87.2	325,400	1,464
Mankato	52,411	23.0	2.9	75,309	35,029	43,733	47,845	37,411	18,306	16,828	49.9	188,900	927
Maple Grove	113,793	6.3	17.3	131,515	66,414	78,138	86,548	70,290	28,671	27,845	85.2	299,700	1,609
Maplewood	72,959	12.5	6.4	94,597	44,221	50,254	50,824	48,890	15,295	14,790	72.0	230,100	1,160
Minneapolis	66,068	20.3	9.4	91,899	50,484	55,812	58,938	53,465	190,105	178,886	47.4	268,100	1,078
Minnetonka	100,363	8.6	19.4	129,493	60,902	75,237	82,066	66,159	24,432	23,293	71.3	362,100	1,467
Moorhead	61,220	21.4	3.0	86,463	32,112	50,699	56,457	44,218	18,245	16,798	58.6	200,300	880
Oakdale	74,303	14.0	5.8	95,137	45,216	56,160	61,597	52,188	11,530	11,229	77.1	232,900	1,097
Owatonna	66,037	16.0	5.4	90,804	36,029	51,500	54,089	45,022	11,083	10,616	72.6	171,400	811
Plymouth	112,631	7.6	23.0	142,881	59,455	82,673	91,389	74,347	32,897	31,470	72.7	368,600	1,418
Prior Lake	108,481	8.4	21.8	125,957	55,000	70,024	81,595	59,145	10,165	9,802	84.5	328,400	1,220
Ramsey	97,779	6.1	8.6	105,878	69,621	60,862	65,929	54,732	9,866	9,630	85.1	264,900	1,510
Richfield	70,091	11.5	5.4	86,023	47,426	52,916	54,818	50,905	15,802	15,322	62.5	241,100	1,150
Rochester	76,034	14.0	8.4	96,417	47,937	57,825	62,801	53,307	50,944	48,468	67.1	219,400	1,044
Rosemount	110,573	6.6	16.5	123,469	53,050	65,140	67,230	61,165	8,920	8,698	85.4	295,800	1,372
Roseville	74,571	12.8	8.8	98,456	48,450	57,687	63,542	51,579	16,031	15,166	67.4	266,100	1,092
St. Cloud	50,335	24.1	2.8	68,109	32,627	43,020	44,147	41,670	28,559	26,878	49.5	158,500	821
St. Louis Park	84,694	12.1	10.9	118,408	63,498	64,856	71,235	59,297	24,749	23,774	57.7	290,500	1,267
St. Paul	59,717	19.7	6.5	74,852	43,971	48,043	50,279	45,668	121,887	114,742	51.0	217,100	1,013
Savage	116,895	4.2	18.4	127,328	67,382	67,096	77,150	55,336	10,960	10,802	85.0	326,800	1,370
Shakopee	90,642	7.2	11.6	105,677	54,602	58,070	65,727	48,605	14,556	14,125	74.2	280,500	1,213
Shoreview	97,633	7.5	12.3	127,906	55,758	77,874	81,498	71,671	11,695	11,377	85.1	285,500	1,246
Winona	48,653	24.5	2.1	78,487	32,657	41,654	44,909	39,185	11,502	10,521	64.1	153,500	648
Woodbury	108,055	6.2	17.8	128,107	61,586	77,638	83,402	70,184	26,576	25,969	81.3	336,600	1,503
MISSISSIPPI	46,511	28.4	3.4	58,923	25,314	40,306	45,780	34,357	1,330,867	1,116,649	68.8	125,500	789
Biloxi	48,999	25.9	3.3	64,474	30,741	42,327	47,016	35,732	21,907	18,096	44.4	166,500	865
Brandon	80,924	6.1	6.1	84,233	58,428	50,029	56,711	45,395	9,044	8,564	82.5	202,500	981

1. Specified owner-occupied units

City	Commuting, 2016–2020[1]: Percent: Drove alone	Commuting, 2016–2020[1]: Mean travel time to work	Computer access[2], 2016–2020: Percent: With a computer in the house	Computer access[2], 2016–2020: Percent: With Internet access	Migration, 2016–2020: Percent who lived in the same house one year ago	Migration, 2016–2020: Percent who lived in another state or county one year ago	Civilian labor force, 2021: Total	Civilian labor force, 2021: Percent change 2020–2021	Civilian labor force, 2021: Unemployment[3]: Total	Civilian labor force, 2021: Unemployment[3]: Rate	Civilian Employment, 2016–2020[4]: Population age 16 and older: Number	Civilian Employment, 2016–2020[4]: Population age 16 and older: Percent in labor force	Civilian Employment, 2016–2020[4]: Population age 16 to 64: Number	Civilian Employment, 2016–2020[4]: Population age 16 to 64: Percent who worked full-year full-time
	55	56	57	58	59	60	61	62	63	64	65	66	67	68
MICHIGAN—Cont'd														
Oak Park	76.9	22.1	92.6	85.7	86.4	6.1	14,219	-1.9	1,104	7.8	24,271	65.7	19,392	50.4
Pontiac	73.4	21.9	84.0	75.0	81.6	6.0	25,030	-4.8	2,712	10.8	46,247	60.3	38,946	42.6
Portage	85.4	19.6	93.7	91.0	84.6	5.6	24,656	-2.1	1,131	4.6	39,258	69.1	31,258	55.3
Port Huron	74.2	21.2	89.0	82.8	79.2	6.0	12,504	-2.7	1,003	8.0	23,231	59.8	18,538	41.7
Rochester Hills	84.3	26.2	95.5	92.1	88.7	5.2	39,259	1.9	1,518	3.9	59,477	63.4	46,356	54.2
Romulus	86.3	24.6	91.6	80.9	89.2	2.5	11,628	0.1	836	7.2	18,039	65.1	14,754	53.1
Roseville	84.0	26.2	89.1	83.7	86.5	4.5	22,861	-2.2	1,736	7.6	38,566	63.6	30,816	50.9
Royal Oak	83.7	25.1	95.1	91.1	82.1	8.6	37,923	2.9	1,088	2.9	50,900	74.7	42,635	63.6
Saginaw	77.8	18.1	83.7	72.6	84.7	3.8	17,866	-6.1	2,184	12.2	36,778	55.4	30,177	36.3
St. Clair Shores	85.1	26.5	91.0	86.5	89.7	4.7	30,595	-0.3	1,751	5.7	49,924	64.7	37,870	55.5
Southfield	82.6	24.5	91.4	85.9	87.4	5.2	34,467	-0.9	2,298	6.7	61,215	61.0	46,707	49.9
Southgate	84.7	25.6	88.4	82.2	86.4	3.6	15,816	2.0	750	4.7	24,154	63.6	18,804	54.5
Sterling Heights	83.1	26.4	93.8	89.5	90.1	3.7	66,685	-0.2	3,763	5.6	109,681	62.7	86,734	48.1
Taylor	84.9	22.5	91.2	79.3	88.0	2.4	29,052	-0.4	2,301	7.9	50,236	61.1	40,888	50.0
Troy	82.3	25.8	96.9	94.4	89.8	5.3	43,131	1.9	1,657	3.8	68,665	64.2	54,118	54.1
Walker	82.8	19.1	94.1	86.7	87.6	3.3	14,693	-1.3	568	3.9	19,991	69.9	15,751	61.1
Warren	83.8	25.2	89.3	83.5	87.8	5.0	62,763	-1.8	4,468	7.1	108,235	62.4	87,262	48.1
Westland	83.6	25.8	91.3	85.5	87.8	2.7	43,802	1.4	2,458	5.6	65,374	64.4	51,788	51.7
Wyandotte	83.9	23.9	90.0	81.4	91.8	2.3	13,363	1.5	732	5.5	20,364	62.2	16,325	52.0
Wyoming	78.0	20.7	92.1	86.8	83.5	5.4	43,303	-2.1	2,225	5.1	59,358	71.0	51,361	51.9
MINNESOTA	76.0	23.8	92.7	86.8	86.3	6.8	3,021,360	-3.3	102,967	3.4	4,444,556	69.2	3,556,980	55.5
Andover	81.7	29.1	97.0	94.5	91.4	3.2	18,528	-2.7	479	2.6	25,591	73.5	21,477	60.7
Apple Valley	76.3	26.1	95.4	92.0	86.9	6.5	30,709	-3.1	914	3.0	42,148	72.9	34,457	61.0
Austin	77.0	15.8	89.8	81.7	80.3	7.3	12,371	-3.7	412	3.3	19,504	62.2	14,978	51.7
Blaine	78.1	25.2	95.0	92.9	89.0	6.0	36,913	-2.8	1,170	3.2	49,921	71.6	41,991	57.0
Bloomington	74.5	22.4	94.4	89.0	86.7	5.4	44,711	-3.8	1,652	3.7	70,156	69.1	53,248	59.0
Brooklyn Center	73.6	24.8	91.7	82.5	85.3	7.7	14,862	-4.0	826	5.6	22,648	74.5	19,119	55.3
Brooklyn Park	74.6	25.0	96.3	89.7	91.3	4.2	41,434	-3.2	1,948	4.7	60,506	73.5	51,851	58.4
Burnsville	75.3	24.4	95.9	91.1	85.1	8.5	35,194	-3.5	1,269	3.6	48,780	71.9	38,754	58.6
Chanhassen	78.2	24.6	98.6	95.4	89.8	8.0	14,228	-2.9	341	2.4	19,981	73.6	16,826	58.6
Chaska	80.5	25.6	95.8	93.4	88.6	6.9	15,269	-3.0	454	3.0	20,587	74.3	17,681	62.0
Coon Rapids	81.0	24.9	94.4	90.0	87.4	7.4	34,700	-3.2	1,239	3.6	51,127	71.5	40,946	57.9
Cottage Grove	82.3	25.1	95.7	93.3	89.9	6.0	20,642	-2.7	620	3.0	27,974	72.6	23,429	59.2
Duluth	75.9	16.7	91.4	84.2	76.1	10.4	44,129	-3.9	1,457	3.3	71,945	66.2	58,533	44.0
Eagan	76.9	24.2	96.8	92.2	87.3	7.4	38,408	-3.1	1,118	2.9	53,178	74.9	44,177	60.4
Eden Prairie	76.1	23.9	97.1	94.0	85.4	6.3	35,784	-2.4	940	2.6	50,578	69.6	41,110	59.6
Edina	75.6	21.3	94.2	89.7	85.7	6.0	25,376	-2.4	635	2.5	41,669	65.0	30,509	58.9
Elk River	81.0	29.7	93.2	88.1	86.3	8.6	13,517	-2.9	411	3.0	19,002	72.1	15,932	59.0
Fridley	74.9	24.3	93.9	90.1	84.7	11.8	14,589	-3.5	667	4.6	21,852	71.7	17,749	57.8
Inver Grove Heights	77.0	24.5	95.4	88.9	87.7	7.7	19,490	-2.7	627	3.2	28,544	69.7	22,767	57.0
Lakeville	77.8	26.8	97.5	94.6	88.7	5.2	38,118	-2.5	1,016	2.7	49,339	77.1	43,244	58.7
Mankato	77.4	16.4	94.2	85.4	70.4	15.6	25,576	-4.1	811	3.2	36,122	70.6	30,995	40.8
Maple Grove	76.0	25.7	98.2	95.9	88.9	3.9	41,196	-2.4	1,062	2.6	55,831	73.1	46,604	62.6
Maplewood	78.1	25.1	91.9	87.5	87.5	5.8	20,281	-3.5	847	4.2	32,644	67.0	25,654	56.3
Minneapolis	59.0	23.2	93.9	85.7	76.7	9.5	241,696	-3.5	9,148	3.8	347,944	74.1	305,714	51.5
Minnetonka	74.1	22.2	94.5	92.4	84.3	5.9	30,699	-2.3	848	2.8	43,955	69.3	32,511	60.5
Moorhead	77.3	17.6	91.9	83.3	78.5	13.3	24,746	-1.2	630	2.5	34,369	70.9	29,302	48.6
Oakdale	79.0	23.2	92.2	87.6	90.7	7.4	15,527	-3.0	561	3.6	22,814	68.5	18,229	53.1
Owatonna	84.3	15.8	91.7	87.4	85.9	6.2	13,921	-3.6	455	3.3	19,989	67.6	15,477	59.2
Plymouth	77.2	23.9	97.1	94.1	84.6	6.6	43,763	-2.3	1,173	2.7	62,199	71.4	49,806	62.7
Prior Lake	76.1	26.1	95.8	91.6	91.3	5.5	14,862	-3.0	425	2.9	20,426	73.7	16,906	60.5
Ramsey	83.2	29.4	97.1	94.3	90.1	5.1	16,117	-2.9	469	2.9	20,870	75.9	17,676	61.4
Richfield	72.0	23.4	92.6	86.6	84.8	6.0	19,697	-3.6	696	3.5	30,136	72.5	24,334	58.1
Rochester	68.7	17.0	93.9	88.2	82.8	8.5	66,898	-2.5	1,935	2.9	91,791	71.5	74,120	56.4
Rosemount	78.3	28.7	97.9	95.4	90.0	4.5	13,903	-2.6	364	2.6	18,614	77.9	15,862	67.8
Roseville	75.2	21.4	92.6	88.4	84.2	7.9	18,894	-2.8	593	3.1	29,795	65.4	22,110	56.8
St. Cloud	78.3	19.1	92.7	85.4	72.7	16.1	36,065	-4.5	1,781	4.9	55,874	68.5	46,982	43.4
St. Louis Park	73.0	21.7	94.5	90.4	80.7	7.1	29,744	-2.7	840	2.8	41,328	75.2	33,009	65.4
St. Paul	64.9	24.2	93.5	87.3	81.5	9.4	154,964	-3.4	6,469	4.2	238,008	69.8	204,478	50.1
Savage	82.3	26.6	98.6	94.7	91.4	6.6	18,776	-2.9	538	2.9	24,351	78.5	21,345	60.9
Shakopee	79.9	22.7	95.5	92.0	89.1	8.0	23,787	-3.0	789	3.3	31,252	75.0	27,450	57.5
Shoreview	81.2	25.2	96.0	92.2	88.9	5.7	14,673	-2.6	371	2.5	21,913	66.8	16,279	58.1
Winona	71.9	14.3	91.8	86.5	72.1	12.9	14,510	-4.2	430	3.0	23,822	68.7	19,291	39.4
Woodbury	77.9	24.5	97.6	95.7	85.8	7.5	40,521	-2.5	986	2.4	53,677	73.6	45,303	57.7
MISSISSIPPI	84.6	25.2	86.5	75.1	87.5	5.9	1,254,239	0.9	69,838	5.6	2,357,026	56.8	1,882,756	47.5
Biloxi	73.0	20.7	89.5	79.5	72.3	16.6	19,476	0.1	997	5.1	36,961	57.1	30,313	51.1
Brandon	89.6	25.0	96.8	92.8	83.1	8.3	12,266	1.6	428	3.5	19,250	66.1	15,058	61.9

1. Employed persons. 2. Households. 3. Percent of civilian labor force. 4. Persons 16 years old and over.

City	Value of residential construction authorized by building permits, 2021			Wholesale trade[1], 2017				Retail trade[2], 2017			
	New construction ($1,000)	Number of housing units	Percent single family	Number of establishments	Number of employees	Sales (mil dol)	Annual payroll (mil dol)	Number of establish-ments	Number of employees	Sales (mil dol)	Annual payroll (mil dol)
	69	70	71	72	73	74	75	76	77	78	79
MICHIGAN—Cont'd											
Oak Park	0	0	0.0	48	588	332.1	38.2	114	1,166	310.6	28.1
Pontiac	716	5	100.0	41	774	838.8	38.7	197	1,966	586.6	60.5
Portage	27,289	127	91.3	50	1,213	639.7	82.4	296	5,658	1,211.2	120.1
Port Huron	345	4	100.0	22	247	184.6	11.9	100	1,168	346.4	32.7
Rochester Hills	74,381	191	100.0	86	861	624.8	62.7	252	5,660	1,727.8	147.8
Romulus	4,503	55	89.1	71	1,806	1,693.0	90.6	79	814	271.3	26.8
Roseville	150	1	100.0	44	780	763.5	40.1	233	4,877	1,364.3	117.3
Royal Oak	49,003	169	100.0	50	312	726.5	26.5	210	2,419	665.6	65.9
Saginaw	1,144	6	100.0	30	548	318.8	29.1	133	738	165.4	16.9
St. Clair Shores	2,551	13	100.0	33	183	81.2	8.4	171	1,880	581.4	54.0
Southfield	7,878	43	39.5	124	2,349	3,121.6	227.2	362	5,298	2,018.3	173.5
Southgate	4,292	11	100.0	9	29	9.2	1.4	123	2,586	931.9	73.9
Sterling Heights	45,324	144	100.0	153	1,877	883.6	106.7	458	6,921	2,223.5	196.6
Taylor	24,938	69	100.0	61	962	1,342.2	56.2	290	4,978	1,556.5	126.7
Troy	32,882	125	96.0	320	7,383	7,017.5	507.3	582	12,256	3,595.0	401.3
Walker	9,743	30	93.3	79	2,531	1,422.7	143.2	120	2,445	632.1	54.7
Warren	2,078	8	100.0	180	4,105	2,934.1	255.5	463	5,697	1,784.4	154.8
Westland	9,553	74	100.0	52	507	170.0	23.0	277	4,331	1,189.6	102.7
Wyandotte	5,730	18	100.0	7	36	8.1	1.2	76	510	153.5	12.7
Wyoming	23,544	185	80.5	176	4,245	3,808.5	258.6	251	4,629	1,341.7	135.0
MINNESOTA	7,726,133	33,652	49.6	6,397	108,895	106,476.5	7,091.2	18,827	302,886	91,993.6	8,117.5
Andover	43,949	140	100.0	17	62	24.8	3.1	47	949	208.7	20.2
Apple Valley	35,337	235	26.8	23	121	42.1	5.0	118	3,478	976.0	94.6
Austin	3,008	14	100.0	7	38	30.7	1.9	87	1,517	313.1	35.0
Blaine	161,879	610	63.0	69	1,107	559.2	56.2	227	4,730	1,054.5	109.6
Bloomington	12,820	74	8.1	193	5,285	6,246.6	435.3	529	11,577	3,030.3	309.3
Brooklyn Center	438	2	100.0	23	597	420.6	31.6	64	2,053	830.8	66.2
Brooklyn Park	47,525	220	33.6	89	1,645	1,588.8	126.3	153	4,081	1,292.6	116.5
Burnsville	44,420	464	6.7	151	2,570	1,256.6	174.7	325	6,637	2,540.0	205.7
Chanhassen	65,470	208	47.1	51	1,773	1,561.2	179.4	69	1,462	383.4	39.1
Chaska	74,928	227	100.0	25	315	119.7	19.2	45	814	229.6	21.3
Coon Rapids	15,338	61	100.0	33	405	218.8	23.7	192	4,948	1,504.5	131.9
Cottage Grove	162,767	590	100.0	11	339	423.2	24.9	49	1,136	299.6	33.5
Duluth	18,778	141	47.5	94	1,041	494.5	53.5	405	6,344	1,323.6	144.8
Eagan	11,379	33	100.0	146	2,657	1,915.8	197.7	265	5,074	1,114.3	110.1
Eden Prairie	76,049	283	13.1	170	4,053	13,176.3	305.0	224	6,654	3,525.8	275.4
Edina	71,421	102	73.5	108	934	691.3	77.7	277	5,064	1,061.8	133.2
Elk River	41,310	199	69.8	23	140	110.4	7.2	93	1,778	460.5	46.0
Fridley	20,672	136	0.0	67	1,923	1,509.3	133.6	81	2,035	653.8	59.9
Inver Grove Heights	70,895	311	43.4	18	152	225.8	9.6	74	1,979	849.4	65.3
Lakeville	261,140	1,119	65.1	59	856	622.5	58.3	108	2,799	824.6	73.2
Mankato	53,240	264	46.6	53	915	1,595.0	56.3	267	5,849	1,390.2	136.5
Maple Grove	111,307	590	49.2	97	2,632	2,243.1	217.7	229	5,183	1,189.7	123.8
Maplewood	1,910	4	100.0	37	379	258.9	24.7	215	4,384	1,455.1	126.4
Minneapolis	585,614	3,182	2.0	466	7,907	7,532.9	548.8	1,135	13,609	5,706.8	363.4
Minnetonka	71,255	226	15.9	115	1,814	2,068.3	134.0	288	6,346	1,965.6	186.4
Moorhead	49,860	284	38.0	27	569	327.3	30.0	107	2,123	535.4	54.2
Oakdale	16,311	50	60.0	38	728	444.6	50.8	60	1,891	452.5	43.7
Owatonna	19,074	121	34.7	16	305	190.1	16.1	106	2,014	475.9	49.3
Plymouth	66,411	217	79.3	186	5,545	5,445.6	396.8	186	3,574	1,340.1	116.7
Prior Lake	52,843	132	100.0	14	55	26.3	2.9	48	431	113.6	10.6
Ramsey	44,767	183	94.5	30	504	266.6	22.9	64	563	210.4	17.8
Richfield	56,069	466	0.2	12	77	21.3	2.8	110	3,253	6,501.7	140.1
Rochester	137,505	625	40.2	72	790	412.7	43.7	493	10,464	2,639.3	274.0
Rosemount	89,469	340	66.5	17	150	83.6	9.1	39	397	90.1	9.1
Roseville	57,552	315	4.4	78	1,157	1,190.2	72.1	281	6,334	1,426.2	153.0
St. Cloud	29,316	128	98.4	84	2,399	1,442.5	123.4	326	6,467	1,739.8	166.2
St. Louis Park	77,027	332	2.1	89	1,412	840.5	100.8	183	4,203	1,503.0	134.8
St. Paul	260,093	2,120	3.6	246	6,243	4,223.5	398.6	725	9,284	1,851.8	224.7
Savage	29,460	93	74.2	49	894	1,077.9	61.1	70	991	286.6	34.3
Shakopee	132,895	593	26.0	56	1,566	1,549.5	111.2	109	2,354	776.0	72.9
Shoreview	55,844	278	7.2	16	567	157.2	62.4	32	620	140.8	13.8
Winona	10,156	49	12.2	27	301	346.8	14.3	104	2,126	523.1	51.2
Woodbury	240,470	927	58.1	33	303	172.7	18.9	255	5,566	1,180.1	121.1
MISSISSIPPI	1,541,523	7,988	92.4	2,347	32,051	31,126.7	1,616.8	11,525	141,410	36,920.6	3,384.5
Biloxi	22,030	90	100.0	32	226	116.6	9.0	205	2,578	553.6	58.7
Brandon	17,846	67	100.0	18	384	556.2	24.0	96	1,580	801.9	53.8

1. Merchant wholesalers except manufacturers' sales branches and offices. 2. Establishments with payroll.

City	Real estate and rental and leasing, 2017: Number of establish-ments	Number of employees	Receipts (mil dol)	Annual payroll (mil dol)	Professional, scientific, and technical services[1], 2017: Number of establish-ments	Number of employees	Receipts (mil dol)	Annual payroll (mil dol)	Manufacturing, 2017: Number of establish-ments	Number of employees	Receipts (mil dol)	Annual payroll (mil dol)
	80	81	82	83	84	85	86	87	88	89	90	91
MICHIGAN—Cont'd												
Oak Park	23	461	30.1	12.2	26	250	36.1	19.3	NA	NA	NA	NA
Pontiac	37	198	50.7	9.3	48	3,042	427.3	234.5	NA	NA	NA	NA
Portage	56	1,375	124.2	53.0	136	1,453	226.4	85.1	NA	NA	NA	NA
Port Huron	19	708	23.8	14.5	68	400	66.4	30.4	NA	NA	NA	NA
Rochester Hills	54	318	64.0	11.8	236	3,533	427.3	218.7	NA	NA	NA	NA
Romulus	41	898	284.5	34.8	16	173	37.9	7.8	NA	NA	NA	NA
Roseville	35	231	51.1	8.5	44	212	23.1	11.6	NA	NA	NA	NA
Royal Oak	81	412	81.0	17.6	292	2,200	371.4	154.8	NA	NA	NA	NA
Saginaw	20	97	17.2	3.3	75	693	79.7	41.9	NA	NA	NA	NA
St. Clair Shores	44	137	30.3	3.9	168	766	87.9	35.4	NA	NA	NA	NA
Southfield	233	2,549	570.5	153.4	720	14,277	2,819.1	1,301.7	NA	NA	NA	NA
Southgate	D	D	D	2.4	27	235	20.7	9.6	NA	NA	NA	NA
Sterling Heights	105	693	214.3	29.4	255	7,854	1,046.9	566.5	NA	NA	NA	NA
Taylor	52	359	106.2	13.4	81	791	126.7	42.8	NA	NA	NA	NA
Troy	181	1,354	453.4	61.7	902	16,472	3,026.0	1,259.7	NA	NA	NA	NA
Walker	31	126	41.2	7.1	54	433	68.4	22.3	NA	NA	NA	NA
Warren	95	982	263.9	42.8	172	21,392	263.2	1,262.1	NA	NA	NA	NA
Westland	D	D	D	14.3	64	285	35.1	9.6	NA	NA	NA	NA
Wyandotte	D	D	D	1.1	40	149	18.6	7.3	NA	NA	NA	NA
Wyoming	60	540	205.2	26.2	117	822	121.6	41.4	NA	NA	NA	NA
MINNESOTA	7,218	38,077	10,432.9	1,915.0	16,689	186,597	34,697.3	14,711.9	7,198	309,097	122,013.5	17,925.8
Andover	60	184	25.5	5.2	66	157	23.1	7.4	NA	NA	NA	NA
Apple Valley	67	176	42.5	7.2	160	469	80.5	30.5	NA	NA	NA	NA
Austin	17	215	11.1	4.4	D	D	24.7	D	NA	NA	NA	NA
Blaine	80	198	96.8	9.3	D	D	D	D	NA	NA	NA	NA
Bloomington	199	4,618	1,235.7	276.4	542	9,590	1,880.7	829.4	NA	NA	NA	NA
Brooklyn Center	34	148	39.5	5.1	60	490	89.2	45.5	NA	NA	NA	NA
Brooklyn Park	70	395	87.8	18.6	135	738	129.4	45.2	NA	NA	NA	NA
Burnsville	124	675	160.2	29.5	268	1,786	329.3	122.5	NA	NA	NA	NA
Chanhassen	43	358	64.8	16.8	136	3,125	563.4	202.5	NA	NA	NA	NA
Chaska	D	D	D	D	83	678	193.8	63.9	NA	NA	NA	NA
Coon Rapids	70	241	58.7	7.6	118	866	128.3	50.2	NA	NA	NA	NA
Cottage Grove	D	D	D	D	47	103	16.2	4.7	NA	NA	NA	NA
Duluth	137	638	118.0	21.4	D	D	D	D	NA	NA	NA	NA
Eagan	141	770	291.7	41.3	346	3,219	622.3	247.9	NA	NA	NA	NA
Eden Prairie	131	820	225.1	40.8	436	4,273	885.7	351.0	NA	NA	NA	NA
Edina	225	1,665	631.9	128.9	D	D	D	D	NA	NA	NA	NA
Elk River	43	110	30.8	4.7	79	436	39.7	18.5	NA	NA	NA	NA
Fridley	32	415	50.1	13.0	65	282	64.1	15.8	NA	NA	NA	NA
Inver Grove Heights	34	134	28.4	4.9	81	445	63.6	29.0	NA	NA	NA	NA
Lakeville	91	308	74.6	13.4	196	556	92.1	31.6	NA	NA	NA	NA
Mankato	72	561	88.0	16.8	D	D	D	D	NA	NA	NA	NA
Maple Grove	117	265	87.8	14.1	314	1,435	261.3	108.6	NA	NA	NA	NA
Maplewood	D	D	D	D	85	351	41.1	17.3	NA	NA	NA	NA
Minneapolis	794	5,194	1,612.6	320.7	2,555	36,745	8,637.0	3,444.9	NA	NA	NA	NA
Minnetonka	160	1,085	377.0	81.5	436	4,098	982.1	305.0	NA	NA	NA	NA
Moorhead	33	149	21.8	4.3	D	D	D	D	NA	NA	NA	NA
Oakdale	32	71	17.6	3.9	89	1,107	161.7	81.5	NA	NA	NA	NA
Owatonna	20	253	16.9	4.6	37	158	32.0	5.6	NA	NA	NA	NA
Plymouth	167	976	318.2	64.1	489	7,686	1,212.2	461.8	NA	NA	NA	NA
Prior Lake	30	77	17.1	2.8	97	261	36.3	14.4	NA	NA	NA	NA
Ramsey	29	37	10.0	1.9	42	178	26.7	11.4	NA	NA	NA	NA
Richfield	32	162	29.3	5.9	96	601	71.0	29.3	NA	NA	NA	NA
Rochester	155	716	148.7	26.0	D	D	5,483.6	D	NA	NA	NA	NA
Rosemount	17	36	14.8	2.1	71	986	81.1	69.5	NA	NA	NA	NA
Roseville	65	391	119.0	22.4	187	1,787	379.4	136.6	NA	NA	NA	NA
St. Cloud	117	606	150.0	25.3	D	D	D	D	NA	NA	NA	NA
St. Louis Park	148	1,005	175.3	43.5	352	3,666	591.3	302.1	NA	NA	NA	NA
St. Paul	393	2,413	533.6	112.6	939	7,440	1,668.8	577.8	NA	NA	NA	NA
Savage	45	155	45.6	7.4	111	268	46.9	16.8	NA	NA	NA	NA
Shakopee	52	151	31.5	4.9	96	1,003	45.4	122.9	NA	NA	NA	NA
Shoreview	D	D	D	D	100	425	80.6	26.2	NA	NA	NA	NA
Winona	28	89	16.0	2.2	52	232	22.1	8.5	NA	NA	NA	NA
Woodbury	98	585	172.4	39.3	279	1,119	200.8	77.0	NA	NA	NA	NA
MISSISSIPPI	2,403	9,683	1,996.9	345.4	4,746	30,477	4,597.6	1,617.7	2,142	138,460	60,906.5	6,653.7
Biloxi	56	231	59.7	7.8	138	984	104.5	35.2	NA	NA	NA	NA
Brandon	33	69	14.9	2.0	75	273	37.5	12.4	NA	NA	NA	NA

1. Establishments subject to federal tax.

City	Accommodation and food services, 2017				Arts, entertainment, and recreation[1], 2017				Health care and social assistance[1], 2017			
	Number of establish-ments	Number of employees	Receipts (mil dol)	Annual payroll (mil dol)	Number of establish-ments	Number of employees	Receipts (mil dol)	Annual payroll (mil dol)	Number of establish-ments	Number of employees	Receipts (mil dol)	Annual payroll (mil dol)
	92	93	94	95	96	97	98	99	100	101	102	103
MICHIGAN—Cont'd												
Oak Park	45	551	32.7	8.1	4.0	26	3.0	0.6	98	827	155.7	29.0
Pontiac	98	1,458	92.9	25.2	14.0	66	11.2	1.7	140	6,071	774.3	280.5
Portage	152	3,547	166.0	52.8	15.0	288	14.0	4.5	198	2,769	252.8	117.8
Port Huron	53	967	42.8	13.3	D	D	D	D	158	4,564	551.7	217.0
Rochester Hills	154	3,301	166.0	49.0	28.0	239	22.7	6.5	327	3,839	424.6	184.9
Romulus	82	3,020	249.0	69.3	NA	NA	NA	NA	53	850	53.2	23.7
Roseville	105	2,898	142.4	40.8	6.0	98	5.9	1.4	143	1,479	151.7	68.8
Royal Oak	177	3,633	207.4	64.9	27.0	204	22.7	4.8	221	11,738	2,025.1	703.9
Saginaw	75	1,356	61.3	18.9	10.0	204	12.3	3.3	173	10,734	1,423.2	555.7
St. Clair Shores	D	D	D	D	23.0	179	17.0	4.1	261	3,285	363.4	171.7
Southfield	244	4,307	272.5	75.0	24.0	337	28.9	9.5	719	13,913	1,672.8	680.2
Southgate	86	2,135	105.7	32.8	8.0	159	7.7	2.0	99	1,513	140.1	59.1
Sterling Heights	262	5,168	263.3	74.6	28.0	295	21.2	5.1	453	6,039	581.1	236.2
Taylor	151	2,919	151.7	39.7	17.0	218	20.5	3.2	141	3,198	343.5	134.2
Troy	319	7,054	467.5	123.9	38.0	626	42.5	14.3	499	12,559	1,619.1	617.7
Walker	76	2,247	108.5	31.5	D	D	D	D	70	1,198	111.0	49.0
Warren	295	5,414	309.8	86.2	24.0	301	34.5	4.9	447	7,385	859.8	354.3
Westland	153	2,911	135.7	40.1	15.0	236	14.3	3.4	190	2,733	248.4	100.3
Wyandotte	67	846	42.5	11.6	6.0	31	3.4	0.6	58	2,832	385.8	146.2
Wyoming	143	2,763	139.3	39.7	19.0	665	37.4	9.4	149	5,085	625.4	245.1
MINNESOTA	12,022	239,194	14,234.3	4,271.9	3,012.0	48,380	4,161.5	1,560.7	17,066	473,338	50,491.0	21,206.5
Andover	34	582	27.9	8.0	12.0	362	12.9	3.9	59	717	61.9	26.4
Apple Valley	81	2,022	103.7	33.1	20.0	D	12.4	D	147	2,011	194.3	77.5
Austin	54	870	43.9	13.3	8.0	176	5.7	2.5	82	2,369	239.9	93.7
Blaine	D	D	D	D	25.0	480	46.5	12.5	135	2,826	216.1	85.7
Bloomington	286	8,771	622.1	183.2	52.0	1,329	77.7	24.6	296	7,142	641.5	315.6
Brooklyn Center	59	1,067	70.5	17.9	6.0	115	4.7	1.3	141	2,781	204.0	89.0
Brooklyn Park	101	1,675	95.3	28.2	18.0	159	14.5	2.8	176	4,282	265.8	138.2
Burnsville	134	2,830	166.8	47.2	46.0	1,166	39.4	12.2	269	6,896	746.6	313.4
Chanhassen	56	1,132	70.9	20.9	17.0	847	56.0	18.2	76	1,324	154.7	62.1
Chaska	41	700	40.7	12.2	6.0	167	11.2	4.0	76	1,330	110.7	50.4
Coon Rapids	115	2,968	163.5	51.2	22.0	454	18.7	5.9	200	7,113	1,163.1	409.5
Cottage Grove	42	667	36.6	10.8	4.0	17	1.3	0.2	63	729	66.3	30.0
Duluth	254	6,157	318.0	101.6	63.0	950	44.3	13.6	470	17,433	2,210.1	935.8
Eagan	176	3,519	228.1	65.8	28.0	D	461.2	D	206	5,045	390.1	170.9
Eden Prairie	154	3,507	209.9	68.2	50.0	1,066	84.7	24.8	186	3,152	304.5	144.7
Edina	127	3,340	201.6	67.8	34.0	1,153	62.4	22.2	424	9,300	1,551.8	603.1
Elk River	D	D	D	D	D	D	D	D	83	2,006	126.7	56.5
Fridley	D	D	D	D	8.0	513	66.7	15.0	95	3,034	393.6	185.9
Inver Grove Heights	47	959	51.4	15.3	D	D	D	D	75	1,454	102.6	49.7
Lakeville	73	2,040	101.9	33.7	17.0	585	27.5	8.8	120	1,685	118.8	51.3
Mankato	151	4,014	172.3	52.6	33.0	564	19.0	7.0	228	7,128	730.4	339.7
Maple Grove	122	3,673	212.7	67.9	25.0	476	32.3	10.1	212	4,452	679.7	223.2
Maplewood	98	2,028	118.2	36.7	20.0	241	17.3	4.0	212	5,254	778.5	260.0
Minneapolis	1,298	30,932	1,998.7	652.2	313.0	6,730	910.1	446.2	1,392	60,986	8,089.3	3,256.7
Minnetonka	101	2,445	166.0	52.2	31.0	788	31.1	12.7	233	4,100	357.6	170.6
Moorhead	71	1,425	73.5	22.7	D	D	D	D	151	4,001	254.2	108.8
Oakdale	44	1,459	80.2	26.5	15.0	487	24.0	5.8	81	1,102	95.0	31.3
Owatonna	72	1,448	62.2	19.7	12.0	132	7.7	2.4	120	2,457	240.0	105.5
Plymouth	127	2,954	179.6	53.6	34.0	729	38.0	10.4	286	5,263	680.7	303.5
Prior Lake	D	D	D	D	D	D	D	D	45	590	52.0	19.2
Ramsey	21	362	15.5	4.2	8.0	73	4.2	1.4	D	D	D	D
Richfield	69	1,357	78.4	23.8	10.0	111	6.4	1.8	124	2,753	170.3	75.9
Rochester	308	7,631	476.8	146.6	54.0	979	42.1	15.0	431	20,978	2,733.2	928.8
Rosemount	28	600	25.0	7.2	10.0	49	4.6	0.6	D	D	D	D
Roseville	121	3,509	201.4	66.6	19.0	289	28.8	7.0	202	3,857	378.7	134.7
St. Cloud	180	4,324	207.2	58.6	41.0	529	38.8	9.7	284	13,312	1,787.4	746.3
St. Louis Park	96	2,412	157.4	49.4	34.0	668	44.6	16.4	234	9,950	1,448.7	634.3
St. Paul	674	13,422	728.0	235.7	152.0	4,543	552.1	199.1	1,112	45,769	4,992.4	2,230.6
Savage	D	D	D	D	11.0	226	11.8	3.9	67	836	65.0	29.1
Shakopee	D	D	D	D	25.0	949	105.4	44.8	89	2,666	319.8	119.0
Shoreview	29	571	33.9	10.4	13.0	317	13.7	3.8	98	1,325	93.9	46.2
Winona	96	2,017	78.3	22.8	25.0	363	12.0	5.1	103	2,794	218.4	99.3
Woodbury	130	3,497	187.1	57.7	33.0	741	32.7	9.8	235	3,797	593.4	265.3
MISSISSIPPI	5,651	129,836	8,181.3	2,134.3	694.0	8,203	582.8	156.3	6,391	169,010	18,752.3	7,533.3
Biloxi	156	12,235	1,271.7	326.1	23.0	771	70.9	18.5	150	5,455	888.4	390.0
Brandon	73	1,251	64.9	17.4	7.0	126	3.9	1.3	D	D	D	D

1. Establishments subject to federal tax.

City	Other services[1]: Number of establishments	Other services[1]: Number of employees	Other services[1]: Receipts (mil dol)	Other services[1]: Annual payroll (mil dol)	Government employment and payroll, 2017: Full-time equivalent employees	March payroll: Total (dollars)	Perent of total for: Administrative, judicial, and legal	Police and corrections	Fire protection	Highways and transportation	Health and welfare	Natural resources and utilities	Education and libraries
	104	105	106	107	108	109	110	111	112	113	114	115	116
MICHIGAN—Cont'd													
Oak Park	D	D	D	D	166	785,044	29.1	51.5	0.0	11.1	1.5	3.5	3.3
Pontiac	68	577	67.8	19.3	81	335,718	66.2	4.7	0.0	4.4	7.5	2.5	10.9
Portage	101	795	68.5	23.0	217	1,041,792	13.2	39.3	19.8	13.5	4.5	5.0	0.0
Port Huron	38	197	22.8	5.9	261	1,240,671	10.8	29.7	17.5	6.5	0.4	24.2	0.0
Rochester Hills	111	774	77.7	27.3	230	1,363,246	24.3	0.4	27.8	7.3	0.0	24.8	0.0
Romulus	51	633	78.5	19.5	183	845,806	19.5	35.1	10.2	3.7	0.0	11.0	2.0
Roseville	83	411	36.9	11.8	262	1,316,999	19.5	36.4	18.4	4.5	4.7	5.3	4.4
Royal Oak	138	774	73.8	23.1	372	1,893,874	21.0	31.8	17.9	5.8	1.3	7.0	3.8
Saginaw	60	436	44.9	11.6	364	1,601,557	12.6	21.9	16.7	7.3	0.9	34.1	0.0
St. Clair Shores	117	716	49.6	14.8	282	1,529,888	15.0	42.8	21.6	1.7	0.7	11.6	5.1
Southfield	177	1,164	216.4	50.3	591	3,132,241	17.7	31.5	20.2	6.2	1.1	9.2	5.0
Southgate	D	D	D	D	146	681,169	15.3	37.6	21.8	7.8	0.6	9.3	2.6
Sterling Heights	215	1,092	102.3	32.5	520	3,085,789	14.4	39.5	21.3	5.3	3.0	10.2	3.8
Taylor	109	1,028	133.0	45.5	358	1,747,951	13.5	40.2	18.9	6.4	4.6	14.1	0.3
Troy	243	2,000	645.7	83.4	430	2,226,427	16.6	44.1	3.6	9.7	0.0	14.3	6.2
Walker	67	761	80.5	27.4	116	580,999	17.4	39.1	11.2	10.9	0.0	7.8	0.0
Warren	260	1,305	190.6	50.7	868	4,546,706	14.8	32.4	17.1	5.7	1.9	18.8	2.7
Westland	129	851	116.5	30.7	332	1,685,200	18.2	35.8	25.8	3.2	4.4	9.7	0.0
Wyandotte	50	238	20.2	7.4	318	1,538,335	5.8	16.0	10.7	7.7	0.0	25.4	0.0
Wyoming	119	1,167	104.8	32.1	403	2,036,612	15.8	32.1	9.9	11.4	3.1	21.2	0.0
MINNESOTA	11,339	77,400	10,077.4	2,553.6	X	X	X	X	X	X	X	X	X
Andover	D	D	D	D	79	409,816	15.8	0.0	14.9	21.5	0.0	30.4	0.0
Apple Valley	66	629	61.9	18.7	234	1,365,809	19.0	33.2	5.4	7.5	0.0	23.9	0.0
Austin	57	329	53.0	6.7	147	728,388	9.7	29.7	8.5	15.0	0.0	26.2	6.7
Blaine	136	1,068	133.8	38.1	199	1,535,440	13.4	43.7	5.0	10.1	2.9	15.0	0.0
Bloomington	200	2,179	352.9	90.8	605	4,022,432	18.0	30.1	1.7	11.3	12.4	17.3	0.0
Brooklyn Center	27	344	21.2	7.9	200	1,270,549	11.0	39.2	3.3	9.7	1.6	21.9	0.0
Brooklyn Park	93	638	57.7	19.3	462	2,049,529	8.1	36.7	10.5	11.0	10.1	15.7	0.0
Burnsville	133	821	76.5	31.1	269	1,904,343	11.2	34.9	18.8	8.2	1.4	15.0	0.0
Chanhassen	65	482	53.9	15.8	75	434,679	17.9	0.5	3.9	10.4	7.6	34.3	0.0
Chaska	34	222	17.2	5.4	166	971,733	13.8	21.6	1.9	7.1	0.0	48.4	0.0
Coon Rapids	104	896	94.6	28.3	255	1,606,439	14.7	33.7	14.5	7.5	2.6	15.1	0.0
Cottage Grove	43	265	16.8	5.9	169	951,197	9.2	35.4	12.7	9.6	8.7	19.2	0.0
Duluth	185	1,372	137.3	34.9	1,059	5,770,250	10.4	20.8	15.6	19.1	1.3	21.2	3.8
Eagan	155	1,725	205.6	66.7	281	1,785,151	11.9	37.7	3.8	10.0	4.4	27.5	0.0
Eden Prairie	148	1,152	220.0	52.6	377	2,135,836	12.9	32.9	6.2	9.6	2.3	24.9	0.0
Edina	141	1,451	203.2	59.5	368	2,156,450	6.1	26.4	12.0	10.9	1.0	23.7	0.0
Elk River	50	316	41.5	10.3	0	919,663	20.2	23.0	6.1	7.0	0.0	26.8	0.0
Fridley	59	486	57.3	14.3	160	931,644	14.7	37.8	7.6	12.3	5.1	17.9	0.0
Inver Grove Heights	54	405	48.4	15.5	195	1,026,882	11.1	32.7	12.0	13.1	7.2	24.0	0.0
Lakeville	89	599	75.6	19.0	226	1,415,893	9.5	34.3	3.7	8.8	3.2	18.1	0.0
Mankato	85	806	77.6	22.5	279	1,560,674	17.7	27.6	8.5	14.4	4.3	18.7	0.0
Maple Grove	147	1,617	115.4	50.6	328	1,813,759	14.7	34.2	6.4	6.7	2.2	22.6	0.0
Maplewood	74	450	58.7	16.9	178	1,136,916	18.5	38.7	17.6	10.6	0.4	6.5	0.0
Minneapolis	1,033	10,041	1,928.2	425.9	4,811	29,451,317	16.8	26.3	10.8	8.7	5.4	22.5	0.0
Minnetonka	123	837	123.1	25.4	294	1,683,951	17.0	28.2	7.2	12.2	1.4	22.3	0.0
Moorhead	78	386	42.9	11.9	341	1,807,198	8.0	22.9	12.5	9.7	1.8	40.2	0.0
Oakdale	38	138	15.7	4.6	111	690,728	9.6	37.3	11.0	5.1	4.1	22.6	0.0
Owatonna	63	422	57.9	12.4	214	1,258,086	10.3	21.6	4.1	9.9	0.5	44.1	4.6
Plymouth	131	1,101	101.4	38.8	315	1,920,231	12.4	35.6	5.8	4.2	2.9	28.3	0.0
Prior Lake	D	D	18.7	D	100	570,637	15.6	32.8	4.8	20.0	4.8	12.7	0.0
Ramsey	29	180	25.6	4.1	79	475,833	13.6	42.3	29.3	3.3	0.0	4.5	0.0
Richfield	66	742	124.6	31.2	157	885,604	14.7	33.5	0.0	13.8	5.8	23.9	0.0
Rochester	216	1,850	169.2	52.5	915	6,209,034	14.5	22.7	12.7	6.8	0.0	32.3	5.6
Rosemount	37	225	21.4	6.0	84	548,277	15.7	32.3	0.0	26.0	6.6	13.7	0.0
Roseville	112	1,143	300.3	43.8	218	1,300,355	16.4	31.0	9.9	8.6	3.6	20.6	0.0
St. Cloud	142	1,217	128.4	36.4	514	2,603,968	10.3	32.2	15.4	10.8	5.3	18.8	0.0
St. Louis Park	143	1,088	91.5	31.7	276	1,991,961	10.1	28.0	11.8	8.0	13.9	19.8	0.0
St. Paul	634	5,191	859.4	214.3	3,186	18,549,813	11.3	28.4	19.3	6.9	3.5	22.3	4.2
Savage	57	604	37.9	13.3	132	726,106	15.8	36.8	2.3	13.5	0.0	19.2	0.0
Shakopee	67	383	39.9	11.6	219	1,326,235	15.2	28.9	4.5	3.9	0.0	36.4	0.0
Shoreview	27	152	13.3	4.0	123	722,231	15.2	0.0	36.9	15.9	11.6	15.9	0.0
Winona	43	204	27.4	5.2	180	907,619	9.3	26.6	14.9	10.1	3.7	23.8	5.0
Woodbury	122	998	71.1	26.0	211	1,311,828	7.1	20.7	13.8	10.0	0.0	38.6	5.6
MISSISSIPPI	3,417	18,345	2,278.6	603.2	X	X	X	X	X	X	X	X	X
Biloxi	66	326	30.4	8.2	637	2,469,007	10.2	27.3	33.8	9.0	2.0	12.4	0.0
Brandon	37	137	16.5	4.2	157	539,308	15.4	33.3	34.3	2.9	0.0	12.8	0.0

1. Establishments subject to federal tax.

City	City government finances, 2017									
	General revenue							General expenditure		
		Intergovernmental		Taxes						
					Per capita[1] (dollars)				Per capita[1] (dollars)	
	Total (mil dol)	Total (mil dol)	Percent from state government	Total (mil dol)	Total	Property	Sales and gross receipts	Total (mil dol)	Total	Capital outlays
	117	118	119	120	121	122	123	124	125	126
MICHIGAN—Cont'd										
Oak Park	41.6	6.1	91.1	18.0	604	586	17	46.4	1,558	27
Pontiac	52.2	16.9	93.5	27.8	463	204	40	48.1	800	73
Portage	57.0	11.9	96.2	24.0	493	458	34	51.9	1,063	181
Port Huron	62.9	20.0	45.2	19.0	653	398	26	54.1	1,865	144
Rochester Hills	80.4	15.2	77.0	34.2	459	420	39	78.4	1,053	57
Romulus	46.1	8.9	75.5	16.8	714	628	87	42.3	1,801	191
Roseville	55.0	12.7	90.4	22.3	470	444	26	52.2	1,099	83
Royal Oak	107.6	13.0	81.4	51.6	869	780	89	108.0	1,819	331
Saginaw	83.1	31.9	44.3	21.2	435	133	30	92.3	1,896	114
St. Clair Shores	79.2	13.6	80.9	34.0	569	524	45	80.7	1,353	243
Southfield	104.3	23.0	61.3	64.4	878	809	69	113.2	1,542	265
Southgate	34.4	6.4	87.3	16.4	563	540	23	34.0	1,168	3
Sterling Heights	152.6	36.8	75.4	64.5	486	467	19	172.6	1,301	207
Taylor	104.3	25.8	54.6	43.4	707	657	49	100.5	1,637	20
Troy	103.7	17.4	88.7	52.7	625	593	33	102.4	1,217	230
Walker	24.1	4.8	88.3	15.4	622	94	32	23.8	958	137
Warren	191.1	49.0	89.8	97.5	721	687	34	167.7	1,241	94
Westland	103.2	26.6	62.0	33.8	412	396	17	105.4	1,286	27
Wyandotte	45.2	6.3	91.7	16.3	651	623	28	97.8	3,905	135
Wyoming	74.2	23.3	56.0	28.1	370	330	40	69.7	916	46
MINNESOTA	X	X	X	X	X	X	X	X	X	X
Andover	22.2	1.6	87.0	12.5	382	363	19	17.8	542	121
Apple Valley	55.9	2.7	74.9	27.5	525	459	66	43.1	823	188
Austin	34.6	14.2	84.4	7.9	314	216	98	40.2	1,602	440
Blaine	48.3	3.4	78.6	25.9	403	348	56	50.4	784	185
Bloomington	152.9	20.6	44.3	78.0	912	635	277	163.4	1,909	388
Brooklyn Center	48.4	4.0	67.7	22.3	721	632	89	47.5	1,534	276
Brooklyn Park	82.7	7.8	71.6	49.0	610	512	98	73.2	911	183
Burnsville	66.5	5.2	55.4	35.7	580	523	58	63.9	1,040	278
Chanhassen	19.2	1.0	57.8	12.0	469	416	52	19.3	755	117
Chaska	34.7	2.9	77.1	12.8	483	285	198	40.1	1,511	289
Coon Rapids	59.4	5.6	83.0	31.4	502	407	95	68.6	1,099	321
Cottage Grove	31.0	4.2	64.3	16.2	441	405	36	0.0	0	0
Duluth	223.9	79.1	70.4	63.8	742	338	404	227.7	2,649	727
Eagan	63.3	4.9	87.1	34.6	520	474	46	67.4	1,013	278
Eden Prairie	64.0	2.4	59.2	40.6	632	533	99	74.1	1,154	259
Edina	70.6	6.1	97.2	39.4	761	605	155	73.5	1,419	407
Elk River	31.6	2.2	97.6	13.4	547	520	27	32.9	1,342	736
Fridley	34.3	7.6	97.9	13.7	493	441	52	32.6	1,175	323
Inver Grove Heights	34.9	2.8	37.2	21.4	606	574	0	35.7	1,008	266
Lakeville	69.5	9.3	69.3	29.8	469	410	58	71.3	1,119	591
Mankato	95.3	20.1	67.0	27.3	646	416	230	102.9	2,438	789
Maple Grove	78.0	7.7	93.7	37.4	528	484	43	68.1	962	282
Maplewood	49.4	5.6	98.8	24.3	597	517	80	36.5	896	95
Minneapolis	1,215.6	223.1	41.2	471.3	1,120	744	376	1,582.3	3,759	1,427
Minnetonka	65.4	6.1	89.3	39.4	744	643	101	63.0	1,190	272
Moorhead	72.2	27.1	87.4	9.5	219	216	4	74.0	1,712	743
Oakdale	23.9	1.1	88.1	11.6	416	365	51	24.2	863	146
Owatonna	27.7	7.0	84.4	12.0	466	436	30	24.6	956	146
Plymouth	92.1	18.8	75.5	37.3	478	418	60	103.0	1,319	406
Prior Lake	23.3	1.7	52.2	13.0	493	464	28	24.1	913	296
Ramsey	18.2	1.5	91.1	11.3	427	401	26	16.0	606	124
Richfield	46.3	10.3	37.8	22.2	617	523	94	54.0	1,499	496
Rochester	289.2	56.0	76.0	88.5	766	491	274	326.3	2,823	1,037
Rosemount	21.1	0.7	85.8	12.0	492	444	43	21.6	888	222
Roseville	32.5	3.4	68.0	20.4	566	554	12	37.4	1,036	273
St. Cloud	118.2	24.7	92.7	40.8	599	360	239	125.8	1,847	821
St. Louis Park	60.9	4.5	85.1	35.1	719	568	151	71.5	1,464	437
St. Paul	658.5	197.0	57.5	174.9	574	373	200	811.0	2,660	316
Savage	35.8	5.7	99.2	17.9	573	531	41	35.7	1,142	438
Shakopee	34.2	3.3	97.6	21.7	532	444	77	65.1	1,598	880
Shoreview	27.5	1.4	99.9	13.4	504	430	74	25.7	965	116
Winona	32.3	13.1	93.8	8.9	333	273	60	32.0	1,192	390
Woodbury	80.3	6.2	87.4	36.3	522	454	68	71.1	1,022	329
MISSISSIPPI	X	X	X	X	X	X	X	X	X	X
Biloxi	111.4	64.0	55.6	23.0	499	383	116	107.8	2,343	605
Brandon	19.9	7.0	88.5	6.4	265	227	38	18.4	768	55

1. Based on population estimated as of July 1 of the year shown.

City	City government finances, 2017 (cont.)												
	General expenditure (cont.)												
	Percent of total for:									Debt outstanding			
	Public welfare	Highways	Parking facilities	Education	Health and hospitals	Police protection	Sewerage and sanitation	Parks and recreation	Housing and community development	Interest on debt	Total (mil dol)	Per capita[1] (dollars)	Debt issued during year
	127	128	129	130	131	132	133	134	135	136	137	138	139
MICHIGAN—Cont'd													
Oak Park	0.0	11.3	0.0	0.0	0.0	0.0	38.6	1.4	0.0	2.2	40.2	1,349	0.0
Pontiac	0.0	21.3	0.0	0.0	0.0	25.5	7.2	1.6	3.2	2.3	22.5	373	0.0
Portage	0.3	18.0	0.0	0.0	2.8	19.0	23.9	5.9	0.4	1.5	67.5	1,383	3.6
Port Huron	0.0	12.6	0.0	0.0	0.0	16.1	18.9	8.1	13.2	3.7	89.3	3,076	1.9
Rochester Hills	0.0	13.1	0.0	0.0	0.0	22.6	22.3	14.1	0.0	0.5	28.1	377	0.1
Romulus	0.0	15.4	0.0	0.0	0.0	21.9	16.6	5.7	2.1	2.1	38.9	1,654	1.6
Roseville	0.0	8.8	0.0	0.0	0.0	20.6	27.5	0.5	1.3	0.6	12.0	253	1.1
Royal Oak	0.0	18.8	0.9	0.0	0.6	17.4	22.5	4.0	1.3	1.0	221.1	3,724	140.1
Saginaw	0.0	14.4	0.0	0.0	0.0	14.6	35.1	0.4	7.3	0.6	62.8	1,291	26.5
St. Clair Shores	0.0	7.9	0.0	0.0	0.0	24.4	28.8	10.1	2.6	1.7	24.1	404	8.6
Southfield	0.0	22.2	0.0	0.0	2.6	22.9	2.3	7.5	0.7	2.1	76.0	1,035	0.0
Southgate	0.0	0.0	0.0	0.0	0.0	21.3	19.2	4.5	0.0	1.1	14.8	508	1.0
Sterling Heights	0.0	20.7	0.0	0.0	0.0	17.8	28.5	2.6	0.6	1.7	147.8	1,114	97.1
Taylor	0.0	7.7	0.0	0.1	0.0	10.7	14.7	5.7	8.0	2.5	67.1	1,092	4.2
Troy	0.0	18.9	0.0	0.0	0.0	22.6	21.9	9.7	0.0	1.4	34.5	410	0.0
Walker	0.0	27.8	0.0	0.0	0.0	20.1	0.0	9.0	0.0	0.6	4.5	183	2.7
Warren	0.0	14.3	0.0	0.0	0.3	25.5	14.1	4.2	2.4	1.1	189.7	1,404	53.8
Westland	1.2	6.4	0.0	0.0	0.8	17.5	19.6	6.1	7.4	1.2	34.5	421	8.8
Wyandotte	0.0	3.3	0.0	0.0	0.0	6.1	10.5	1.5	0.0	0.5	83.9	3,351	0.5
Wyoming	0.0	12.8	0.0	0.0	0.0	17.8	20.0	7.9	12.5	1.8	69.6	915	0.0
MINNESOTA	X	X	X	X	X	X	X	X	X	X	X	X	X
Andover	0.0	13.2	0.0	0.0	0.0	16.5	12.7	18.4	2.7	0.0	27.6	841	4.5
Apple Valley	0.0	30.1	0.0	0.0	0.0	20.9	0.0	21.0	0.0	2.5	42.3	807	0.0
Austin	0.0	13.9	0.0	0.0	0.0	11.4	14.9	9.9	2.2	0.0	50.1	1,998	1.0
Blaine	0.0	30.8	0.0	0.0	0.0	20.3	18.7	4.0	0.0	1.8	45.2	703	11.2
Bloomington	0.0	19.3	0.0	0.0	3.8	15.1	7.3	9.0	8.3	1.2	72.4	846	13.5
Brooklyn Center	0.3	13.3	0.0	0.0	0.0	16.9	13.0	16.3	14.3	0.0	99.2	3,204	38.3
Brooklyn Park	0.0	24.6	0.0	0.0	0.0	28.7	0.0	16.6	0.9	2.4	70.8	881	7.9
Burnsville	0.0	18.1	0.2	0.0	0.0	21.0	19.7	14.1	0.8	0.0	66.2	1,078	9.3
Chanhassen	0.0	27.0	0.0	0.0	0.0	8.9	14.7	18.7	0.0	2.5	29.0	1,135	10.0
Chaska	0.0	20.1	0.0	0.0	0.0	10.2	9.0	29.3	0.8	8.0	108.3	4,078	0.0
Coon Rapids	0.0	25.1	0.0	0.0	0.9	15.2	12.9	23.1	2.8	2.0	95.9	1,535	9.5
Cottage Grove	0.0	0.0	0.0	0.0	0.0	0.0	0.0	0.0	0.0	0.0	46.2	1,260	0.0
Duluth	0.0	13.2	0.8	0.0	0.0	10.1	10.8	15.0	1.7	3.3	263.8	3,068	56.1
Eagan	0.0	26.7	0.0	0.0	0.0	19.8	9.7	15.1	0.0	1.1	64.0	961	8.1
Eden Prairie	0.0	18.2	0.0	0.0	0.0	18.7	8.1	23.1	1.2	1.7	83.0	1,293	4.2
Edina	0.0	30.3	0.0	0.0	0.0	15.5	2.2	21.4	0.1	3.5	135.3	2,612	16.4
Elk River	0.0	0.0	0.0	0.0	0.0	7.9	60.3	10.3	2.9	0.0	69.9	2,854	12.4
Fridley	0.0	13.5	0.0	0.0	0.0	19.5	21.5	20.5	0.0	0.0	13.8	495	6.0
Inver Grove Heights	0.0	22.4	0.0	0.0	0.0	19.8	18.1	0.0	2.7	5.3	51.7	1,462	8.5
Lakeville	0.0	46.2	0.0	0.0	0.0	14.5	8.9	9.2	2.1	0.0	126.5	1,987	31.1
Mankato	0.0	18.4	1.2	0.0	0.0	8.6	9.9	4.1	7.5	0.0	120.9	2,866	18.5
Maple Grove	0.0	29.2	0.0	0.0	0.0	16.3	9.1	16.0	1.1	6.4	197.9	2,794	8.1
Maplewood	0.0	15.8	0.0	0.0	0.1	23.6	14.8	12.1	2.1	0.0	117.7	2,893	9.5
Minneapolis	0.0	11.8	2.8	0.0	1.6	10.1	7.8	6.8	11.9	6.6	2,903.4	6,898	163.0
Minnetonka	0.0	23.7	0.0	0.0	0.6	20.8	12.9	17.4	2.9	0.3	136.2	2,574	29.9
Moorhead	0.0	47.2	0.0	0.0	0.0	12.6	12.0	7.4	0.9	0.0	381.7	8,824	128.5
Oakdale	0.0	26.1	0.0	0.0	3.7	21.8	14.8	5.9	0.0	3.0	23.7	846	7.8
Owatonna	0.0	25.5	0.0	0.0	0.0	19.2	8.1	13.1	4.2	0.0	45.8	1,780	5.7
Plymouth	0.0	26.4	0.0	0.0	0.0	12.6	8.3	22.0	5.8	0.0	75.0	960	0.0
Prior Lake	0.0	33.6	0.0	0.0	0.0	15.0	10.9	10.9	2.1	7.7	45.9	1,738	3.6
Ramsey	0.0	24.7	0.6	0.0	0.0	20.3	11.1	8.6	6.1	0.0	40.5	1,527	1.7
Richfield	0.0	34.8	0.0	0.0	0.1	15.3	0.0	9.4	12.9	3.1	116.0	3,218	14.2
Rochester	0.0	13.4	1.4	0.0	0.1	8.7	4.3	22.2	0.4	27.4	2,610.2	22,582	45.1
Rosemount	0.0	27.6	0.0	0.0	0.0	17.5	7.9	15.0	0.0	2.3	25.8	1,061	0.0
Roseville	0.0	7.4	0.0	0.0	0.0	19.5	15.1	16.1	12.3	3.4	31.8	882	0.0
St. Cloud	0.0	13.6	1.5	0.0	0.9	13.8	12.2	29.3	2.1	0.0	398.0	5,845	55.9
St. Louis Park	0.0	19.3	0.0	0.0	0.0	12.8	14.5	26.5	0.9	2.2	187.1	3,830	39.4
St. Paul	0.0	10.7	0.8	0.0	1.1	12.7	9.1	9.1	17.1	5.0	2,381.0	7,809	126.2
Savage	0.0	44.6	0.0	0.0	0.0	15.3	12.6	7.1	0.0	5.1	62.5	1,999	3.3
Shakopee	0.0	11.7	0.0	0.0	0.0	11.9	13.6	43.5	4.1	0.0	93.5	2,295	29.5
Shoreview	0.0	12.0	0.0	0.0	0.0	8.2	15.8	20.4	2.2	1.4	52.8	1,983	7.6
Winona	0.0	18.4	0.0	0.0	0.0	15.2	18.1	18.5	0.0	0.5	3.1	114	0.0
Woodbury	0.0	40.2	0.0	0.0	3.3	15.0	9.5	13.1	0.8	2.2	95.4	1,372	3.6
MISSISSIPPI	X	X	X	X	X	X	X	X	X	X	X	X	X
Biloxi	0.8	9.7	0.0	0.0	0.2	13.8	23.9	4.5	1.2	2.7	113.5	2,467	25.2
Brandon	0.0	12.4	0.0	0.0	0.7	20.9	21.4	7.1	0.0	4.1	15.2	631	0.0

1. Based on population estimated as of July 1 of the year shown.

STATE Place code	City	Land area[1] (sq. mi)	Population, 2021: Total persons 2021	Population, 2021: Rank	Population, 2021: Per square mile	Race 2020, Race alone[2] (percent): White	Black or African American	American Indian, Alaskan Native	Asian	Hawaiian Pacific Islander	Some other race	Two or more races (percent)
		1	2	3	4	5	6	7	8	9	10	11
	MISSISSIPPI—Cont'd											
28 14420	Clinton	41.9	27,451	1,417	655.2	51.7	38.3	0.2	4.6	0.0	1.6	3.7
28 29180	Greenville	26.9	28,777	1,358	1,069.8	16.4	80.5	0.1	0.9	0.0	0.5	1.6
28 29700	Gulfport	55.6	72,105	510	1,296.9	48.5	39.1	0.5	1.6	0.2	3.2	6.9
28 31020	Hattiesburg	53.4	47,068	848	881.4	40.0	51.2	0.2	1.7	0.1	3.2	3.5
28 33700	Horn Lake	16.0	26,737	1,452	1,671.1	38.7	49.5	0.3	0.8	0.1	5.5	5.2
28 36000	Jackson	111.7	149,761	177	1,340.7	16.8	78.9	0.2	0.5	0.0	1.3	2.4
28 44520	Madison	25.3	27,719	1,402	1,095.6	79.0	11.7	0.1	4.8	0.0	0.9	3.4
28 46640	Meridian	53.7	34,424	1,158	641.0	28.7	65.8	0.2	1.0	0.1	1.4	2.8
28 54040	Olive Branch	37.2	40,276	984	1,082.7	55.3	35.0	0.3	1.8	0.1	2.6	5.1
28 54840	Oxford	26.6	26,430	1,469	993.6	66.2	22.4	0.1	5.0	0.0	1.7	4.6
28 55760	Pearl	25.5	27,258	1,428	1,068.9	62.8	26.8	0.2	1.2	0.3	3.7	4.9
28 69280	Southaven	41.3	55,429	715	1,342.1	54.4	34.0	0.3	2.4	0.1	3.5	5.3
28 74840	Tupelo	64.4	37,667	1,055	584.9	53.7	37.3	0.3	1.8	0.0	3.1	3.8
29 00000	MISSOURI	68,745.5	6,168,187	X	89.7	77.0	11.4	0.5	2.2	0.2	2.1	6.7
29 03160	Ballwin	9.0	30,870	1,277	3,430.0	81.1	3.0	0.2	8.8	0.0	1.0	5.8
29 06652	Blue Springs	22.4	59,430	656	2,653.1	78.5	7.8	0.5	1.5	0.2	2.0	9.5
29 11242	Cape Girardeau	29.1	39,820	995	1,368.4	74.6	14.5	0.3	2.6	0.0	1.6	6.3
29 13600	Chesterfield	31.9	49,703	803	1,558.1	75.8	3.2	0.2	14.4	0.0	1.1	5.4
29 15670	Columbia	66.6	126,853	218	1,904.7	72.5	11.9	0.3	5.6	0.1	2.2	7.4
29 24778	Florissant	12.6	52,003	766	4,127.2	46.3	44.8	0.2	1.0	0.0	1.5	6.1
29 27190	Gladstone	8.1	27,017	1,439	3,335.4	75.5	8.2	0.6	2.1	1.1	2.6	9.9
29 28324	Grandview	14.7	25,844	1,501	1,758.1	42.0	38.2	0.8	1.6	0.2	6.5	10.8
29 31276	Hazelwood	16.0	25,241	1,530	1,577.6	45.2	43.8	0.3	1.5	0.0	2.6	6.5
29 35000	Independence	78.0	122,088	233	1,565.2	72.6	8.7	0.8	1.2	0.7	5.5	10.6
29 37000	Jefferson City	36.1	42,772	932	1,184.8	74.3	15.8	0.3	1.8	0.1	1.3	6.3
29 37592	Joplin	38.1	51,846	767	1,360.8	79.8	3.2	2.1	1.9	0.6	2.5	9.9
29 38000	Kansas City	314.7	508,394	37	1,615.5	55.3	26.1	0.6	3.1	0.3	5.5	9.0
29 39044	Kirkwood	9.2	29,371	1,329	3,192.5	86.1	5.7	0.2	1.6	0.0	0.8	5.7
29 41348	Lee's Summit	63.9	102,781	311	1,608.5	78.6	8.9	0.3	2.4	0.1	1.7	7.9
29 42032	Liberty	28.8	30,377	1,297	1,054.8	84.2	4.6	0.5	1.0	0.2	1.6	8.1
29 46586	Maryland Heights	21.9	28,024	1,390	1,279.6	58.5	15.4	0.4	16.4	0.1	2.8	6.5
29 54074	O'Fallon	30.0	93,644	359	3,121.5	82.3	5.1	0.2	4.1	0.1	1.5	6.8
29 60788	Raytown	9.9	29,580	1,322	2,987.9	53.3	32.7	0.5	1.1	0.2	3.0	9.2
29 64082	St. Charles	24.8	70,820	529	2,855.6	79.2	7.7	0.2	3.3	0.1	2.7	6.7
29 64550	St. Joseph	44.0	71,602	515	1,627.3	80.8	6.0	0.6	1.4	0.6	2.6	8.0
29 65000	St. Louis	61.7	293,310	70	4,753.8	43.9	43.0	0.3	4.1	0.0	2.6	6.1
29 65126	St. Peters	22.5	58,129	679	2,583.5	83.4	5.6	0.2	2.6	0.1	1.5	6.7
29 70000	Springfield	82.5	169,724	156	2,057.3	81.1	4.8	0.8	2.3	0.2	2.2	8.7
29 75220	University City	5.9	34,629	1,149	5,869.3	48.9	36.6	0.2	6.5	0.1	2.0	5.8
29 78442	Wentzville	20.7	45,452	871	2,195.7	84.9	5.9	0.2	1.5	0.0	1.0	6.5
29 79820	Wildwood	66.6	35,255	1,132	529.4	85.6	1.6	0.1	6.0	0.0	0.7	5.9
30 00000	MONTANA	145,547.7	1,104,271	X	7.6	84.5	0.5	6.2	0.8	0.1	1.3	6.6
30 06550	Billings	44.8	117,445	242	2,621.5	83.5	1.0	4.9	0.9	0.2	1.9	7.5
30 08950	Bozeman	20.8	54,539	731	2,622.1	88.2	0.6	1.2	1.8	0.1	1.7	6.4
30 11390	Butte-Silver Bow	715.8	34,768	1,144	48.6	90.5	0.4	1.6	0.6	0.1	1.0	5.9
30 32800	Great Falls	23.1	60,403	641	2,614.8	82.2	1.2	5.7	1.2	0.1	1.3	8.3
30 35600	Helena	16.8	33,120	1,187	1,971.4	88.1	0.6	2.1	1.1	0.1	1.1	7.0
30 50200	Missoula	34.6	74,822	493	2,162.5	84.4	0.9	2.9	1.4	0.1	3.1	7.2
31 00000	NEBRASKA	76,816.5	1,963,692	X	25.6	78.4	4.9	1.2	2.7	0.1	5.4	7.3
31 03950	Bellevue	21.5	63,737	601	2,964.5	71.8	5.9	0.8	2.4	0.2	6.7	12.3
31 17670	Fremont	10.8	27,373	1,421	2,534.5	79.2	0.8	1.1	0.6	0.1	9.9	8.3
31 19595	Grand Island	30.1	52,335	759	1,738.7	65.8	3.5	1.6	1.3	0.1	17.3	10.3
31 21415	Hastings	14.9	25,037	1,545	1,680.3	83.2	1.0	0.7	1.6	0.0	5.9	7.6
31 25055	Kearney	14.8	33,959	1,171	2,294.5	85.0	1.6	0.6	1.9	0.1	4.6	6.2
31 28000	Lincoln	97.7	292,657	71	2,995.5	78.7	4.7	0.9	4.8	0.1	3.5	7.5
31 37000	Omaha	142.5	487,300	39	3,419.6	65.5	12.4	1.1	4.6	0.1	7.2	9.1
32 00000	NEVADA	109,860.4	3,143,991	X	28.6	51.2	9.8	1.4	8.8	0.8	14.0	14.0
32 09700	Carson City	144.5	58,993	663	408.3	68.0	1.9	2.5	2.4	0.2	12.1	12.9
32 31900	Henderson	106.4	322,178	57	3,028.0	63.2	6.7	0.7	9.3	0.8	6.1	13.2
32 40000	Las Vegas	141.8	646,790	25	4,561.3	46.0	12.9	1.1	7.2	0.7	17.0	15.0
32 51800	North Las Vegas	102.3	274,133	79	2,679.7	31.0	22.1	1.2	6.7	1.0	21.9	16.1
32 60600	Reno	108.9	268,851	82	2,468.8	62.7	3.1	1.4	7.1	0.8	12.0	13.0
32 68400	Sparks	36.5	109,796	280	3,008.1	58.8	3.0	1.6	6.7	1.0	14.7	14.1
33 00000	NEW HAMPSHIRE	8,953.4	1,388,992	X	155.1	88.3	1.5	0.2	2.6	0.0	1.7	5.6
33 14200	Concord	64.0	44,006	904	687.6	85.4	3.8	0.3	4.1	0.0	1.2	5.2
33 18820	Dover	26.7	33,171	1,186	1,242.4	85.7	1.7	0.2	5.5	0.0	1.2	5.6

1. Dry land or land partially or temporarily covered by water. 2. Hispanic or Latino persons may be of any race.

City	Percent Hispanic or Latino[1], 2020	Percent foreign born, 2016–2020	Age of population (percent), 2016–2020							Median age, 2016–2020	Percent female, 2016–2020	Population			
			Under 18 years	18 to 24 years	25 to 34 years	35 to 44 years	45 to 54 years	55 to 64 years	65 years and over			Census counts		Percent change	
												2010	2020	2010–2020	2020–2021
	12	13	14	15	16	17	18	19	20	21	22	23	24	25	26
MISSISSIPPI—Cont'd															
Clinton	2.8	5.8	26.6	9.4	14.6	12.5	9.9	10.5	16.6	34.6	55.0	25,230	28,047	11.2	-2.1
Greenville	0.9	1.0	26.3	7.4	13.4	10.6	11.8	14.2	16.3	37.3	54.7	34,396	29,658	-13.8	-3.0
Gulfport	6.9	3.8	24.0	9.8	16.0	12.1	12.2	11.9	14.0	35.2	51.9	67,785	72,961	7.6	-1.2
Hattiesburg	4.6	3.2	20.9	19.2	18.5	11.0	8.8	8.8	12.8	29.4	54.0	45,732	47,289	3.4	-0.5
Horn Lake	7.8	4.8	26.5	11.3	14.1	14.9	13.3	9.4	10.5	34.0	52.7	26,068	26,772	2.7	-0.1
Jackson	2.1	1.1	24.5	11.9	15.6	12.0	10.9	12.1	13.0	33.5	54.0	173,556	153,643	-11.5	-2.5
Madison	2.0	6.7	27.9	6.4	7.4	14.2	14.7	15.2	14.2	40.8	52.1	24,073	27,767	15.3	-0.2
Meridian	2.3	2.2	24.1	9.3	14.3	10.8	12.0	13.5	16.2	36.8	52.3	41,126	35,001	-14.9	-1.6
Olive Branch	4.7	5.0	24.5	7.7	13.6	14.2	14.5	11.6	13.9	37.9	52.4	33,487	39,784	18.8	1.2
Oxford	4.1	4.9	17.5	26.6	16.2	11.7	8.0	7.7	12.4	27.7	50.4	22,145	25,821	16.6	2.4
Pearl	5.7	2.0	23.5	7.9	17.1	13.9	10.4	11.6	15.6	35.7	54.1	25,675	27,027	5.3	0.9
Southaven	6.1	4.0	25.8	9.1	12.3	13.8	13.7	11.9	13.4	37.0	52.9	48,982	54,640	11.6	1.4
Tupelo	4.9	2.7	25.4	8.9	14.3	12.5	12.6	11.7	14.6	36.1	53.8	37,622	37,843	0.6	-0.5
MISSOURI	4.9	4.2	22.5	9.3	13.4	12.2	12.3	13.5	16.9	38.7	50.9	5,988,941	6,154,913	2.8	0.2
Ballwin	3.1	7.3	22.5	6.6	11.7	10.7	14.0	14.1	20.3	43.5	51.2	30,417	31,151	2.4	-0.9
Blue Springs	6.7	2.7	28.3	6.8	13.8	11.9	13.8	12.5	13.0	35.8	51.9	52,587	58,648	11.5	1.3
Cape Girardeau	3.7	4.6	18.1	20.6	12.0	10.0	9.9	11.0	18.4	34.4	52.0	37,966	39,345	3.6	1.2
Chesterfield	3.5	16.1	22.1	6.1	8.1	11.0	14.3	15.2	23.2	46.8	51.7	47,483	50,014	5.3	-0.6
Columbia	4.9	8.6	18.7	24.5	15.6	11.5	9.2	9.4	11.0	28.8	51.7	109,041	125,691	15.3	0.9
Florissant	3.0	4.2	23.7	8.6	15.3	12.7	12.2	13.6	13.9	36.9	52.4	52,260	52,548	0.6	-1.0
Gladstone	8.5	5.6	20.0	7.4	14.4	12.2	12.7	14.3	19.0	41.6	49.2	25,436	27,064	6.4	-0.2
Grandview	13.2	5.4	23.2	9.9	17.5	11.2	12.0	12.6	13.5	34.7	52.2	24,455	26,211	7.2	-1.4
Hazelwood	4.2	8.6	21.5	13.2	12.3	12.3	11.4	13.5	15.9	38.4	52.5	25,723	25,505	-0.8	-1.0
Independence	12.2	4.6	22.5	8.0	13.6	12.5	11.6	13.6	18.2	39.5	52.3	116,823	123,028	5.3	-0.8
Jefferson City	3.6	3.9	20.3	10.1	15.1	13.6	12.5	12.8	15.5	38.0	48.5	43,124	42,969	-0.4	-0.5
Joplin	6.3	4.3	22.2	10.8	14.8	12.0	10.3	11.9	17.9	36.6	50.9	50,780	51,719	1.8	0.2
Kansas City	12.0	8.0	22.8	9.0	17.6	13.1	11.8	12.3	13.3	35.4	51.5	459,883	507,969	10.5	0.1
Kirkwood	2.8	3.7	25.7	5.5	10.6	12.2	12.6	12.8	20.7	42.0	53.5	27,561	29,487	7.0	-0.4
Lee's Summit	5.3	4.6	26.3	6.4	11.6	14.6	12.8	12.9	15.3	38.4	52.4	91,369	101,160	10.7	1.6
Liberty	5.6	3.0	26.3	8.7	13.6	14.2	10.9	13.6	12.7	35.8	50.1	29,242	30,244	3.4	0.4
Maryland Heights	4.8	20.9	18.4	9.8	19.7	15.0	11.3	12.3	13.6	36.4	51.7	27,469	28,307	3.1	-1.0
O'Fallon	4.0	4.5	26.3	7.0	13.1	14.3	14.8	12.4	12.0	37.5	50.7	79,599	91,390	14.8	2.5
Raytown	7.8	5.8	20.4	8.5	13.6	11.7	14.3	14.2	17.2	41.1	52.8	29,611	30,010	1.3	-1.4
St. Charles	5.6	5.8	17.3	13.6	15.9	11.7	10.1	14.4	17.1	37.6	52.1	66,207	70,384	6.3	0.6
St. Joseph	7.3	4.2	22.3	10.2	14.3	12.7	11.7	13.0	15.9	37.6	49.7	76,782	72,456	-5.6	-1.2
St. Louis	5.1	6.9	19.1	9.2	20.1	13.3	11.6	13.1	13.7	36.0	51.5	319,308	301,578	-5.6	-2.7
St. Peters	3.8	3.4	22.5	7.4	12.9	14.0	12.6	14.5	16.3	39.9	52.4	52,595	57,725	9.8	0.7
Springfield	5.9	3.2	17.5	19.3	15.4	10.8	10.2	11.0	15.8	33.2	51.8	159,333	169,767	6.5	0.0
University City	3.9	8.4	17.4	14.2	15.7	11.3	8.0	14.0	19.4	37.8	55.4	35,286	35,009	-0.8	-1.1
Wentzville	3.3	2.4	32.5	6.3	13.5	17.1	11.8	7.7	11.0	33.5	50.3	29,134	44,559	52.9	2.0
Wildwood	3.3	8.7	25.6	6.2	6.7	11.1	16.9	16.3	17.1	45.2	51.3	35,301	35,467	0.5	-0.6
MONTANA	4.2	2.2	21.5	9.3	12.9	12.0	11.4	14.3	18.7	40.1	49.7	989,400	1,084,225	9.6	1.8
Billings	6.8	2.3	23.1	8.8	15.3	13.0	10.5	12.1	17.3	37.3	50.6	104,294	117,077	12.3	0.3
Bozeman	5.0	4.5	13.2	30.0	20.2	10.5	8.4	7.5	10.2	27.8	47.4	37,271	52,855	41.8	3.2
Butte-Silver Bow	4.7	2.0	20.4	11.2	12.1	11.4	11.5	14.4	18.9	40.1	48.9	33,507	34,495	2.9	0.8
Great Falls	4.5	2.0	21.8	9.1	14.7	11.4	11.1	12.8	19.0	38.3	50.6	59,113	60,506	2.4	-0.2
Helena	4.0	1.4	19.0	10.5	12.4	12.9	11.1	13.5	20.6	41.0	52.6	28,811	32,257	12.0	2.7
Missoula	6.2	3.2	17.4	17.6	17.8	13.6	10.0	10.5	13.0	33.1	50.2	67,386	73,746	9.4	1.5
NEBRASKA	12.0	7.4	24.7	9.8	13.3	12.5	11.5	12.6	15.7	36.6	50.1	1,826,311	1,961,504	7.4	0.1
Bellevue	16.9	8.8	24.5	10.7	14.9	12.9	11.2	12.2	13.6	34.9	49.5	51,525	64,208	24.6	-0.7
Fremont	19.2	8.1	24.2	10.3	12.0	11.6	11.2	12.6	18.1	37.7	50.8	26,415	27,182	2.9	0.7
Grand Island	34.3	16.8	28.2	8.2	13.7	12.6	11.6	11.2	14.5	35.0	49.2	48,678	53,083	9.0	-1.4
Hastings	13.8	7.2	23.6	13.2	12.5	10.4	11.2	11.8	17.3	36.0	51.0	25,234	25,175	-0.2	-0.5
Kearney	10.8	5.0	20.9	19.4	13.2	12.4	9.1	10.2	14.7	32.1	50.7	30,949	33,695	8.9	0.8
Lincoln	8.6	9.0	22.3	16.0	14.7	12.5	10.4	10.7	13.4	32.9	49.8	258,791	291,114	12.5	0.5
Omaha	15.5	10.7	24.8	9.7	15.6	13.0	11.7	11.9	13.3	34.9	50.7	458,992	490,627	6.9	-0.7
NEVADA	28.7	19.4	22.7	8.2	14.6	13.3	13.0	12.4	15.8	38.2	49.8	2,700,683	3,104,614	15.0	1.3
Carson City	25.4	12.8	20.4	7.5	13.0	11.7	12.4	14.7	20.3	42.2	48.5	55,269	58,639	6.1	0.6
Henderson	17.9	13.7	21.1	6.4	12.5	12.8	13.7	13.2	20.3	43.0	50.5	256,995	317,521	23.6	1.5
Las Vegas	33.3	20.6	23.7	8.2	14.4	13.6	13.1	12.1	14.9	37.7	50.1	584,500	641,825	9.8	0.8
North Las Vegas	40.7	21.0	28.3	9.5	14.9	13.8	12.9	9.7	10.9	33.1	50.9	216,670	262,678	21.2	4.4
Reno	25.4	16.4	20.9	10.3	17.1	12.8	11.7	12.2	15.1	36.1	49.6	225,325	263,436	16.9	2.1
Sparks	30.1	15.7	23.2	9.0	14.0	13.4	13.6	11.4	15.5	37.8	50.4	91,112	108,772	19.4	0.9
NEW HAMPSHIRE	4.3	6.1	19.0	9.3	12.5	11.5	14.0	15.6	18.1	43.0	50.4	1,316,457	1,377,529	4.6	0.8
Concord	3.1	8.9	18.7	8.5	15.9	11.7	13.8	13.7	17.6	40.2	49.3	42,686	43,694	2.4	0.7
Dover	3.2	5.9	17.8	10.7	20.0	12.3	11.2	11.6	16.3	35.7	50.6	29,999	32,758	9.2	1.3

1. May be of any race.

City	Households, 2016–2020							Persons in group quarters, 2016–2020	Serious crimes known to police[2], 2020				Educational attainment, 2016–2020		
			Percent						Violent		Property			Attainment[4] (percent)	
	Number	Persons per household	Family	Married couple family	Female family	Non-family	One person		Number	Rate	Number	Rate	Population age 25 and over	High school graduate or less	Bachelor's degree or more
	27	28	29	30	31	32	33	34	35	36	37	38	39	40	41
MISSISSIPPI—Cont'd															
Clinton	8,800	2.76	68.4	45.9	19.2	31.6	27.4	475	16	65.7	463	1,901.5	15,871	23.2	46.2
Greenville	11,945	2.46	62.5	30.1	27.6	37.5	34.7	443	NA	NA	NA	NA	19,795	50.9	19.8
Gulfport	28,193	2.48	63.1	36.4	21.3	36.9	30.7	1,700	317	439.4	3,078	4,266.6	47,475	41.4	23.3
Hattiesburg	17,828	2.39	53.3	26.6	22.0	46.7	36.4	3,431	171	372.8	2,418	5,271.4	27,559	33.6	31.3
Horn Lake	9,270	2.93	72.1	42.0	22.6	27.9	21.9	58	47	171.5	605	2,207.7	16,947	48.7	18.5
Jackson	62,861	2.49	57.4	27.9	24.8	42.6	36.8	7,077	NA	NA	NA	NA	104,107	38.3	28.4
Madison	8,720	2.89	79.3	73.7	4.3	20.7	18.7	456	NA	NA	NA	NA	16,868	11.1	68.7
Meridian	15,665	2.29	57.7	31.8	22.2	42.3	37.2	1,416	NA	NA	NA	NA	24,818	44.9	21.4
Olive Branch	13,931	2.75	70.8	54.4	12.8	29.2	24.8	0	89	224.9	862	2,178.6	25,940	35.5	27.5
Oxford	10,844	2.49	46.2	35.1	10.6	53.8	36.6	714	45	155.9	609	2,109.7	15,479	19.7	61.3
Pearl	10,565	2.50	62.4	41.6	17.0	37.6	31.6	74	NA	NA	NA	NA	18,153	44.0	20.9
Southaven	20,226	2.71	70.9	48.0	14.2	29.1	23.4	250	NA	NA	NA	NA	35,825	37.5	23.1
Tupelo	15,004	2.50	62.4	40.5	17.0	37.6	34.4	716	NA	NA	NA	NA	25,116	34.4	33.8
MISSOURI	2,440,212	2.44	63.6	47.8	11.4	36.4	29.8	172,576	33,385	542.7	155,698	2,531.0	4,176,792	40.0	29.9
Ballwin	11,934	2.53	70.1	61.1	7.1	29.9	26.3	5	19	63.2	255	848.8	21,400	15.4	59.4
Blue Springs	20,344	2.71	75.3	57.2	13.9	24.7	20.3	225	119	211.8	1,311	2,333.0	36,012	31.4	33.5
Cape Girardeau	15,855	2.34	51.8	38.4	10.2	48.2	34.5	2,928	362	886.3	1,204	2,947.7	24,612	35.7	34.1
Chesterfield	19,378	2.41	69.4	61.9	6.0	30.6	27.2	875	43	90.4	834	1,754.2	34,161	11.9	69.4
Columbia	49,371	2.31	50.9	38.7	8.7	49.1	34.7	8,689	552	442.2	3,326	2,664.4	69,599	21.8	53.3
Florissant	19,702	2.56	62.6	39.3	17.6	37.4	30.7	836	196	385.7	1,167	2,296.7	34,679	40.9	23.3
Gladstone	11,598	2.36	61.8	43.8	11.5	38.2	33.7	24	130	469.0	666	2,402.7	19,868	36.7	30.0
Grandview	10,255	2.42	55.8	34.8	16.2	44.2	36.5	178	199	799.3	1,038	4,169.0	16,729	44.3	20.8
Hazelwood	11,205	2.24	56.4	34.9	16.7	43.6	38.7	170	164	654.7	789	3,149.6	16,481	36.1	30.9
Independence	48,836	2.37	59.3	40.1	15.0	40.7	33.5	1,260	791	678.1	5,338	4,576.2	81,371	46.8	20.0
Jefferson City	16,882	2.24	55.2	40.2	10.8	44.8	39.6	4,786	109	255.6	821	1,924.8	29,679	38.2	33.1
Joplin	21,012	2.32	57.0	40.7	10.8	43.0	33.7	1,829	338	663.6	3,276	6,431.7	33,878	42.9	24.7
Kansas City	206,295	2.34	53.7	35.5	13.7	46.3	37.1	9,035	7,919	1,585.9	20,570	4,119.5	334,831	34.5	35.7
Kirkwood	11,423	2.41	64.2	53.6	8.3	35.8	30.9	258	42	150.9	493	1,771.2	19,125	13.3	63.8
Lee's Summit	37,664	2.61	72.5	58.6	9.7	27.5	22.9	668	NA	NA	NA	NA	66,601	21.9	47.9
Liberty	10,816	2.82	70.3	53.4	13.7	29.7	23.6	1,249	129	128.7	2,050	2,044.5	20,633	33.3	36.9
Maryland Heights	11,980	2.20	57.1	43.2	10.5	42.9	34.3	587	NA	NA	NA	NA	19,376	22.5	50.8
O'Fallon	31,681	2.77	75.0	60.5	10.3	25.0	19.9	415	109	121.5	1,020	1,137.1	58,717	27.4	42.8
Raytown	12,720	2.26	55.2	34.8	16.3	44.8	37.3	491	197	681.1	1,172	4,052.3	20,739	40.7	21.5
St. Charles	29,051	2.21	57.8	46.4	8.5	42.2	33.5	6,538	192	268.3	1,368	1,911.6	48,854	29.3	40.1
St. Joseph	29,008	2.46	58.1	40.1	12.9	41.9	34.8	4,103	414	554.4	3,843	5,146.0	50,936	49.0	21.4
St. Louis	143,566	2.05	45.2	25.4	15.9	54.8	45.4	10,045	6,017	2,016.3	17,399	5,830.3	218,594	35.4	37.2
St. Peters	22,766	2.52	66.8	54.8	9.2	33.2	28.7	243	153	260.0	1,085	1,843.7	40,363	26.9	39.1
Springfield	78,027	2.01	47.8	33.1	10.1	52.2	39.4	10,932	2,545	1,507.2	11,738	6,951.5	105,938	37.8	28.7
University City	15,904	2.14	50.7	37.2	10.7	49.3	38.5	293	146	428.8	855	2,511.4	23,495	19.6	60.8
Wentzville	13,458	2.99	77.3	64.3	9.6	22.7	18.4	149	NA	NA	NA	NA	24,730	26.3	39.0
Wildwood	12,655	2.80	84.8	75.3	6.5	15.2	12.8	93	NA	NA	NA	NA	24,192	11.1	65.0
MONTANA	436,048	2.37	61.3	49.3	7.7	38.7	30.8	28,885	5,077	469.8	22,917	2,120.8	734,688	34.1	33.1
Billings	47,484	2.25	57.8	43.9	8.7	42.2	34.1	3,094	939	852.4	5,249	4,765.0	74,758	32.5	35.6
Bozeman	20,457	2.17	45.4	35.4	5.9	54.6	30.6	3,995	157	305.1	697	1,354.5	27,465	12.9	63.1
Butte-Silver Bow	15,026	2.23	54.9	42.1	8.9	45.1	39.4	1,371	NA	NA	NA	NA	23,865	41.1	27.5
Great Falls	25,742	2.21	56.8	39.4	11.5	43.2	36.5	1,774	266	455.9	2,999	5,140.1	40,582	38.4	27.7
Helena	14,668	2.11	50.2	38.1	8.2	49.8	40.4	1,633	216	642.3	1,227	3,648.6	23,036	23.2	49.0
Missoula	32,555	2.21	47.5	35.4	8.5	52.5	35.7	3,073	376	491.7	2,745	3,589.7	48,747	20.5	51.0
NEBRASKA	766,663	2.44	63.8	50.0	9.3	36.2	29.4	51,208	6,473	334.1	36,991	1,909.2	1,259,540	34.2	32.5
Bellevue	24,335	2.62	67.7	49.2	11.3	32.3	25.1	226	NA	NA	NA	NA	41,430	31.1	33.7
Fremont	10,948	2.33	62.5	48.2	10.4	37.5	29.7	861	NA	NA	NA	NA	17,273	48.5	19.1
Grand Island	19,601	2.57	66.2	46.5	14.1	33.8	27.5	941	216	419.0	1,258	2,440.5	32,622	45.5	20.3
Hastings	10,137	2.30	60.6	44.1	11.5	39.4	33.6	1,553	NA	NA	NA	NA	15,738	37.0	26.1
Kearney	13,361	2.38	58.2	44.2	10.8	41.8	32.3	1,983	122	356.7	678	1,982.4	20,139	31.0	36.8
Lincoln	115,930	2.36	58.0	43.8	10.0	42.0	31.0	13,176	NA	NA	NA	NA	176,852	27.9	39.9
Omaha	189,922	2.46	59.6	43.0	11.5	40.4	33.2	11,931	3,032	631.3	15,247	3,174.5	313,871	32.2	38.3
NEVADA	1,130,011	2.65	63.7	44.4	13.0	36.3	28.2	37,525	14,445	460.3	60,462	1,926.6	2,093,820	41.0	25.5
Carson City	22,858	2.32	62.7	43.0	12.9	37.3	31.5	2,265	NA	NA	NA	NA	39,827	38.5	22.9
Henderson	120,735	2.55	65.1	49.5	10.7	34.9	27.6	1,557	682	207.9	4,679	1,426.3	224,917	31.4	34.0
Las Vegas	237,308	2.68	62.6	42.2	14.1	37.4	30.0	7,914	8,934	527.7	37,426	2,210.6	438,997	42.3	25.2
North Las Vegas	76,223	3.22	74.1	47.6	18.5	25.9	20.2	2,164	1,337	521.8	4,160	1,623.6	153,832	49.8	17.2
Reno	105,321	2.33	55.0	38.8	10.4	45.0	32.5	5,417	1,460	563.3	5,564	2,146.9	172,810	32.6	34.8
Sparks	39,500	2.60	67.3	48.3	12.9	32.7	25.1	289	446	418.1	2,087	1,956.6	69,829	40.8	23.4
NEW HAMPSHIRE	539,116	2.44	65.2	52.2	8.6	34.8	26.7	41,423	2,000	146.4	15,014	1,098.9	971,162	34.0	37.6
Concord	17,761	2.28	60.1	44.9	9.8	39.9	31.6	3,094	84	192.1	727	1,662.2	31,647	34.6	38.5
Dover	13,860	2.23	56.7	45.4	7.5	43.3	30.1	948	24	73.9	315	969.8	22,806	26.4	46.5

2. Data for serious crimes have not been adjusted for underreporting. This may affect comparability between geographic areas and over time.

4. Persons 25 years old and over.

City	Money income, 2016–2020					Median earnings Full year, Full-time workers, 2016–2020			Housing units, 2016–2020				
	Households												
	Median household income	Percent with income less than $25,000	Percent with income of $200,000 or more	Median family income	Median non-family household income	All persons	Men	Women	Total	Occupied	Percent owner occupied	Median value[1] (dollars)	Median gross rent (dollars)
	42	43	44	45	46	47	48	49	50	51	52	53	54
MISSISSIPPI—Cont'd													
Clinton	64,403	14.4	6.2	77,939	34,690	44,493	53,429	41,355	9,797	8,800	69.4	177,500	1,004
Greenville	29,013	43.4	2.2	40,896	18,557	34,084	40,804	29,150	14,464	11,945	49.6	79,900	720
Gulfport	40,554	31.1	2.0	50,214	27,167	34,579	39,142	30,251	33,642	28,193	50.8	132,700	887
Hattiesburg	36,111	38.3	2.3	46,712	24,324	33,730	37,780	30,081	21,228	17,828	38.1	110,500	808
Horn Lake	52,181	17.4	1.0	55,061	40,722	36,195	40,484	32,113	10,023	9,270	57.3	114,300	1,067
Jackson	40,064	31.8	2.5	49,366	27,468	34,630	38,383	32,413	74,759	62,861	49.0	91,400	856
Madison	119,855	4.9	23.1	139,665	54,809	73,495	90,269	60,742	9,086	8,720	94.3	271,100	1,566
Meridian	30,088	41.9	3.0	41,269	21,072	35,004	41,327	30,852	18,888	15,665	47.3	84,300	709
Olive Branch	78,939	11.3	4.1	87,381	51,832	48,772	55,489	40,694	14,576	13,931	77.2	188,800	1,182
Oxford	48,566	31.1	5.3	76,563	31,363	46,826	55,625	40,055	15,972	10,844	43.5	270,000	973
Pearl	50,614	16.8	0.9	63,163	37,848	38,721	42,490	33,931	11,390	10,565	60.0	131,600	953
Southaven	63,321	16.1	3.3	70,720	40,411	45,408	50,000	41,544	21,484	20,226	71.1	160,500	1,055
Tupelo	54,691	24.0	4.9	67,251	31,011	41,769	49,430	35,059	17,091	15,004	59.6	148,900	795
MISSOURI	57,290	20.1	5.2	72,834	33,731	45,502	51,118	40,276	2,804,664	2,440,212	67.1	163,600	843
Ballwin	97,174	9.2	13.2	119,913	46,684	69,943	81,983	55,652	12,461	11,934	85.4	277,100	1,157
Blue Springs	72,846	8.9	4.1	83,058	46,345	51,444	56,745	44,861	21,195	20,344	69.8	174,800	1,013
Cape Girardeau	45,713	27.7	3.2	66,886	26,762	40,338	44,646	37,545	18,390	15,855	53.7	153,400	762
Chesterfield	120,394	7.7	25.4	150,240	55,067	99,781	109,530	73,548	20,263	19,378	80.6	374,100	1,212
Columbia	53,447	24.6	7.4	81,392	32,382	45,381	50,465	40,293	53,746	49,371	47.4	208,300	890
Florissant	58,769	14.7	0.9	73,794	36,798	44,209	45,231	43,391	21,769	19,702	65.4	99,900	1,054
Gladstone	63,225	13.7	3.7	75,905	41,855	44,519	47,308	40,953	12,483	11,598	65.0	153,800	939
Grandview	47,670	25.2	2.2	57,476	33,182	39,736	42,316	37,629	11,228	10,255	49.6	117,700	843
Hazelwood	52,201	14.6	3.0	65,118	34,369	40,742	46,219	36,929	12,028	11,205	59.7	119,700	869
Independence	50,797	21.7	2.3	64,271	33,769	41,467	45,662	36,189	54,120	48,836	59.4	121,200	871
Jefferson City	54,003	21.4	2.5	75,490	34,392	41,797	48,285	37,874	18,942	16,882	57.1	161,400	653
Joplin	45,091	28.4	2.7	57,169	27,920	38,128	42,942	32,763	23,851	21,012	57.9	125,400	774
Kansas City	56,179	21.3	5.1	73,786	38,204	46,833	51,493	42,319	233,432	206,295	53.8	163,300	979
Kirkwood	94,067	9.7	14.8	124,621	51,477	75,694	93,036	60,114	12,486	11,423	73.6	337,100	1,116
Lee's Summit	93,295	10.5	11.9	108,397	46,094	65,037	73,350	56,319	39,495	37,664	76.5	234,700	1,069
Liberty	78,184	10.1	5.2	90,839	38,349	51,689	58,330	46,260	11,505	10,816	74.6	194,900	905
Maryland Heights	69,973	12.2	3.4	89,805	52,753	56,572	64,776	49,734	12,412	11,980	55.2	162,800	1,025
O'Fallon	92,498	8.6	9.2	106,419	50,057	60,310	70,777	51,340	32,740	31,681	82.7	235,200	1,153
Raytown	55,940	17.6	1.2	71,461	36,723	43,856	47,126	41,339	13,640	12,720	60.2	113,100	966
St. Charles	71,232	12.6	7.9	90,211	47,714	53,318	59,495	48,738	30,986	29,051	66.1	212,000	989
St. Joseph	48,716	25.9	2.9	60,272	28,206	41,421	43,502	39,224	33,760	29,008	58.9	117,800	785
St. Louis	45,782	28.6	4.1	60,978	34,523	45,867	49,444	42,216	176,955	143,566	44.1	143,700	840
St. Peters	80,119	10.8	5.6	97,777	44,408	54,697	63,976	48,584	23,715	22,766	82.5	191,900	1,058
Springfield	37,491	32.9	1.9	52,296	25,499	35,179	37,720	32,374	83,116	78,027	42.4	122,200	760
University City	66,466	19.7	15.0	97,022	46,040	62,602	68,466	57,671	17,208	15,904	52.7	260,600	1,088
Wentzville	93,602	6.6	7.7	99,855	54,637	61,870	66,325	51,917	14,004	13,458	84.0	234,800	1,042
Wildwood	135,177	4.3	27.1	146,996	60,417	90,304	107,155	70,495	13,043	12,655	92.4	384,200	1,284
MONTANA	56,539	20.2	4.7	72,773	33,606	44,061	50,208	38,405	514,956	436,048	68.5	244,900	836
Billings	60,032	18.0	6.2	78,284	38,735	47,163	53,253	40,554	50,959	47,484	63.2	233,700	923
Bozeman	59,695	19.7	7.6	89,664	41,957	45,456	51,253	40,954	22,057	20,457	42.6	412,500	1,145
Butte-Silver Bow	49,359	27.2	2.7	62,138	27,823	47,158	52,247	38,285	17,318	15,026	69.6	155,300	680
Great Falls	49,809	24.5	2.9	67,780	31,421	40,336	43,373	36,434	28,152	25,742	64.4	181,500	748
Helena	60,074	20.2	4.9	84,068	41,643	48,401	51,772	45,074	15,716	14,668	57.3	263,300	845
Missoula	50,947	22.5	4.3	75,000	33,613	40,539	42,231	38,281	34,887	32,555	47.4	301,700	900
NEBRASKA	63,015	17.0	5.2	80,125	36,396	47,206	52,311	40,947	844,248	766,663	66.2	164,000	857
Bellevue	70,647	13.7	3.8	83,314	42,878	47,072	53,180	41,624	25,586	24,335	63.4	165,900	1,010
Fremont	54,291	20.7	1.9	72,318	30,168	42,508	48,430	36,353	11,685	10,948	55.8	140,400	771
Grand Island	56,513	20.4	3.8	66,755	31,980	40,873	45,038	36,645	20,758	19,601	58.8	148,200	780
Hastings	52,747	24.6	3.7	72,458	30,032	41,261	46,497	34,450	11,103	10,137	63.0	127,300	730
Kearney	60,755	21.9	2.9	85,444	31,332	47,097	53,566	40,362	14,370	13,361	61.2	188,800	793
Lincoln	60,063	17.4	5.0	79,395	37,297	45,699	50,574	39,840	122,048	115,930	56.2	180,400	871
Omaha	62,213	18.0	6.4	80,956	39,536	49,305	52,973	43,835	203,215	189,922	59.0	167,800	948
NEVADA	62,043	17.8	5.9	74,077	40,355	44,567	48,599	41,182	1,268,533	1,130,011	57.1	290,200	1,159
Carson City	58,305	18.7	4.9	69,727	36,023	43,033	45,905	39,178	24,132	22,858	58.2	299,900	982
Henderson	75,430	13.0	9.7	89,151	48,995	54,579	63,867	47,884	131,804	120,735	64.3	341,100	1,360
Las Vegas	58,377	20.3	5.7	71,684	37,389	43,379	46,099	41,265	259,521	237,308	53.4	279,700	1,153
North Las Vegas	60,972	15.3	2.5	66,864	40,759	40,904	42,143	39,248	81,881	76,223	59.8	260,100	1,253
Reno	61,860	18.2	6.1	78,843	43,134	45,693	49,536	41,478	112,516	105,321	47.7	361,100	1,107
Sparks	67,187	14.1	4.8	80,012	42,756	46,451	51,272	41,221	41,743	39,500	57.5	324,000	1,244
NEW HAMPSHIRE	77,923	13.3	9.7	97,001	43,777	55,224	61,725	49,228	638,611	539,116	71.2	272,300	1,145
Concord	70,004	17.5	7.2	88,661	40,178	52,223	56,727	47,058	18,810	17,761	54.6	239,300	1,104
Dover	74,833	13.2	7.8	97,359	49,209	53,232	59,548	46,343	14,514	13,860	53.2	274,100	1,184

1. Specified owner-occupied units

City	Commuting, 2016–2020[1] Percent Drove alone	Commuting, 2016–2020[1] Percent Mean travel time to work	Computer access[2], 2016–2020 Percent With a computer in the house	Computer access[2], 2016–2020 Percent With Internet access	Migration, 2016–2020 Percent who lived in the same house one year ago	Migration, 2016–2020 Percent who lived in another state or county one year ago	Civilian labor force, 2021 Total	Civilian labor force, 2021 Percent change 2020–2021	Civilian labor force, 2021 Unemployment[3] Total	Civilian labor force, 2021 Unemployment[3] Rate	Civilian Employment, 2016–2020[4] Population age 16 and older Number	Civilian Employment, 2016–2020[4] Population age 16 and older Percent in labor force	Civilian Employment, 2016–2020[4] Population age 16 to 64 Number	Civilian Employment, 2016–2020[4] Population age 16 to 64 Percent who worked full-year full-time
	55	56	57	58	59	60	61	62	63	64	65	66	67	68
MISSISSIPPI—Cont'd														
Clinton	78.6	24.4	91.4	88.5	87.8	6.1	12,112	1.5	485	4.0	18,747	63.6	14,635	56.2
Greenville	84.3	16.1	80.7	64.0	87.5	3.4	10,638	-2.0	862	8.1	22,893	54.0	18,024	41.0
Gulfport	85.1	21.2	87.9	79.3	77.5	9.8	28,678	0.1	1,728	6.0	56,017	59.6	45,978	48.9
Hattiesburg	79.9	16.9	87.8	77.9	75.4	13.7	21,461	2.1	1,182	5.5	37,259	62.3	31,390	40.9
Horn Lake	87.9	27.1	95.3	90.6	83.6	7.6	12,789	0.3	595	4.7	21,029	68.3	18,165	55.4
Jackson	81.7	21.0	88.7	82.3	81.6	6.0	68,563	-0.8	4,548	6.6	127,660	62.9	106,400	45.9
Madison	87.4	22.3	98.4	95.4	92.3	5.5	12,874	1.6	415	3.2	19,367	66.0	15,733	56.9
Meridian	84.3	17.7	86.0	73.9	84.0	7.2	13,748	-0.7	814	5.9	28,926	53.5	22,905	45.8
Olive Branch	88.0	24.6	94.6	88.1	86.5	6.9	20,624	2.4	707	3.4	30,136	67.3	24,827	58.3
Oxford	83.3	21.5	96.3	88.4	73.1	12.8	15,054	4.9	565	3.8	23,155	62.8	19,736	39.7
Pearl	84.9	22.6	93.0	85.4	84.3	7.9	12,500	1.2	496	4.0	20,968	68.0	16,851	62.2
Southaven	83.8	25.2	95.0	88.1	84.4	6.2	28,508	2.0	1,079	3.8	42,618	66.6	35,247	57.6
Tupelo	89.5	18.1	86.7	77.0	87.0	5.9	17,757	0.1	871	4.9	29,547	63.2	23,963	54.2
MISSOURI	80.8	23.9	90.7	82.7	85.5	6.8	3,062,449	0.8	134,081	4.4	4,903,578	62.6	3,870,194	53.0
Ballwin	83.3	25.0	94.9	93.2	90.5	3.9	16,683	0.7	486	2.9	24,185	66.8	18,049	59.8
Blue Springs	86.7	27.4	97.1	90.8	87.2	3.9	30,849	1.1	1,386	4.5	41,537	70.8	34,327	60.1
Cape Girardeau	78.0	17.1	89.4	83.9	76.6	10.6	20,744	0.0	805	3.9	33,606	59.6	26,218	42.6
Chesterfield	81.2	22.6	96.3	94.3	85.9	5.8	24,668	1.4	781	3.2	39,027	62.2	27,978	56.1
Columbia	75.8	16.5	94.7	85.0	72.8	11.7	67,551	3.2	2,028	3.0	102,321	65.5	88,794	45.3
Florissant	84.9	25.8	93.4	87.8	84.0	4.7	27,859	0.9	1,648	5.9	40,548	69.2	33,414	52.8
Gladstone	81.5	22.0	93.9	88.1	83.5	8.9	14,696	0.9	773	5.3	22,400	66.1	17,191	57.2
Grandview	77.5	23.3	94.5	88.9	83.6	6.3	12,766	1.1	746	5.8	19,799	67.2	16,420	52.6
Hazelwood	80.7	22.4	94.1	88.7	84.0	4.1	13,696	0.8	811	5.9	20,352	68.9	16,336	59.7
Independence	86.3	24.2	90.3	82.5	91.2	3.2	56,776	0.9	3,629	6.4	93,697	63.1	72,359	54.0
Jefferson City	83.7	15.8	90.2	72.4	82.8	8.4	20,224	-0.6	689	3.4	34,755	60.6	28,122	54.5
Joplin	79.8	17.6	90.0	80.9	83.1	9.2	24,651	1.9	990	4.0	40,411	62.7	31,335	49.4
Kansas City	79.9	22.0	91.9	82.8	82.2	7.9	259,161	0.7	14,042	5.4	390,383	69.3	324,847	56.9
Kirkwood	82.6	23.1	94.6	91.2	88.7	4.8	15,830	1.3	479	3.0	21,609	63.2	15,860	57.6
Lee's Summit	81.9	26.9	95.8	91.0	86.8	5.2	55,613	1.3	1,816	3.3	76,115	70.6	60,941	60.4
Liberty	83.0	22.2	95.2	93.8	78.1	10.4	16,721	1.9	864	5.2	24,433	68.2	20,408	55.9
Maryland Heights	79.2	21.0	96.8	93.0	80.1	10.7	15,933	1.0	610	3.8	22,696	70.9	19,028	62.3
O'Fallon	83.9	27.0	96.5	92.6	91.5	3.8	50,111	0.8	1,681	3.4	67,471	72.8	56,909	60.7
Raytown	87.6	23.2	93.5	85.6	89.4	4.4	14,805	0.8	984	6.6	23,846	69.0	18,829	57.0
St. Charles	82.1	21.4	94.8	88.8	85.4	7.6	39,494	0.8	1,433	3.6	59,753	67.2	47,655	54.1
St. Joseph	81.9	15.9	86.8	77.7	81.6	7.6	36,376	-0.7	1,422	3.9	60,570	59.7	48,609	49.3
St. Louis	71.0	23.9	87.0	78.1	82.8	8.7	150,531	0.3	9,583	6.4	252,148	66.3	210,536	53.4
St. Peters	85.1	24.7	94.5	91.7	90.9	4.3	34,301	0.8	1,128	3.3	45,974	70.8	36,623	60.9
Springfield	80.1	18.1	89.0	74.8	76.8	9.4	86,837	1.4	3,238	3.7	141,432	59.7	114,869	46.2
University City	74.8	19.7	92.2	87.0	81.1	8.6	18,347	0.8	814	4.4	28,996	61.2	22,327	52.5
Wentzville	86.2	27.7	97.5	93.5	86.6	5.0	23,275	1.2	919	3.9	28,747	72.3	24,289	61.3
Wildwood	80.6	30.2	98.8	97.1	88.9	4.2	18,727	1.3	527	2.8	27,692	66.1	21,611	53.8
MONTANA	75.2	18.4	90.5	83.2	84.5	7.5	549,743	1.3	18,541	3.4	859,185	63.2	661,066	50.2
Billings	82.3	17.3	92.0	85.9	82.5	5.9	56,867	0.5	1,818	3.2	87,146	66.6	68,126	55.7
Bozeman	69.3	14.8	97.0	90.2	68.9	16.3	33,402	4.0	786	2.4	42,897	71.8	37,966	41.1
Butte-Silver Bow	80.5	15.0	86.8	78.3	85.2	7.3	17,489	0.7	635	3.6	28,540	60.0	21,947	45.7
Great Falls	81.8	14.8	86.8	79.7	79.8	8.2	27,812	-0.5	912	3.3	47,293	61.5	36,122	53.1
Helena	72.5	13.0	90.6	83.5	77.0	10.2	18,618	1.4	508	2.7	27,072	65.8	20,358	57.5
Missoula	71.5	15.8	95.0	90.2	74.0	13.0	42,194	0.6	1,405	3.3	63,454	73.3	53,676	45.0
NEBRASKA	80.7	18.9	91.5	85.4	84.7	6.7	1,049,033	0.4	26,371	2.5	1,500,813	69.0	1,198,782	57.9
Bellevue	84.6	20.7	95.2	90.6	83.6	8.9	26,903	0.5	755	2.8	49,897	66.2	41,187	58.4
Fremont	83.0	18.7	90.1	83.6	81.7	6.3	14,686	0.5	356	2.4	20,480	67.2	15,704	58.4
Grand Island	82.8	16.8	90.6	84.0	80.1	6.0	27,021	0.8	809	3.0	38,343	69.9	30,919	59.5
Hastings	83.8	15.2	88.8	82.7	83.4	6.2	13,349	-0.7	327	2.4	19,804	66.9	15,499	54.0
Kearney	83.7	14.0	92.7	86.5	73.5	10.4	19,703	1.0	385	2.0	27,422	71.9	22,446	54.3
Lincoln	79.7	18.9	94.6	89.0	77.9	8.5	161,196	0.1	3,971	2.5	229,432	70.8	190,925	54.2
Omaha	79.2	19.3	91.7	85.9	84.1	5.6	249,169	0.3	7,771	3.1	372,998	69.9	309,278	55.9
NEVADA	76.8	24.6	93.6	85.1	83.0	5.7	1,504,761	0.1	108,822	7.2	2,419,552	63.0	1,941,532	51.0
Carson City	79.4	20.0	92.0	85.7	83.1	9.7	25,665	0.4	1,231	4.8	45,189	60.3	33,968	54.3
Henderson	80.2	23.9	95.1	90.7	84.5	5.5	160,278	1.3	11,004	6.9	252,866	60.2	190,059	52.2
Las Vegas	76.7	25.7	92.9	82.2	82.3	5.4	303,377	0.4	25,518	8.4	509,426	62.4	413,662	49.7
North Las Vegas	80.4	27.6	95.0	86.6	84.1	4.5	115,025	0.9	10,839	9.4	185,300	63.3	158,248	50.4
Reno	73.0	20.6	93.6	84.7	79.6	7.6	137,492	1.7	5,978	4.3	204,125	67.9	166,276	52.9
Sparks	78.1	22.9	94.9	88.4	82.6	5.0	56,747	1.9	2,421	4.3	81,732	67.7	65,746	55.0
NEW HAMPSHIRE	79.5	27.4	93.7	88.5	86.4	6.8	755,422	-0.6	26,482	3.5	1,130,008	67.1	884,866	55.2
Concord	79.1	22.8	91.1	85.0	85.6	7.5	22,168	-2.6	720	3.2	36,242	62.7	28,570	54.0
Dover	80.1	23.1	95.1	90.6	79.5	11.0	18,495	-0.8	608	3.3	26,753	71.4	21,554	61.1

1. Employed persons. 2. Households. 3. Percent of civilian labor force. 4. Persons 16 years old and over.

City	Value of residential construction authorized by building permits, 2021			Wholesale trade[1], 2017				Retail trade[2], 2017			
	New construction ($1,000)	Number of housing units	Percent single family	Number of establishments	Number of employees	Sales (mil dol)	Annual payroll (mil dol)	Number of establish-ments	Number of employees	Sales (mil dol)	Annual payroll (mil dol)
	69	70	71	72	73	74	75	76	77	78	79
MISSISSIPPI—Cont'd											
Clinton	17,750	70	100.0	14	49	16.0	2.0	89	1,236	372.4	35.6
Greenville	995	7	42.9	30	336	552.4	16.2	166	2,238	485.3	47.3
Gulfport	74,401	216	99.1	78	868	465.5	44.2	382	5,972	1,589.2	144.9
Hattiesburg	13,514	47	100.0	73	822	564.4	38.6	454	6,900	1,749.2	163.5
Horn Lake	1,252	21	100.0	D	D	D	5.8	84	1,341	386.8	35.4
Jackson	2,724	11	100.0	216	2,962	2,908.9	175.7	624	8,303	2,630.8	234.5
Madison	40,313	81	100.0	20	102	86.1	10.2	97	2,097	596.2	48.4
Meridian	2,814	11	100.0	50	1,315	1,778.7	56.8	314	4,497	1,091.7	108.1
Olive Branch	32,101	237	100.0	55	1,592	1,641.7	84.3	148	2,660	861.6	69.7
Oxford	41,300	170	78.8	14	222	174.8	7.7	195	2,866	584.3	57.5
Pearl	25,867	151	100.0	52	680	421.5	37.1	172	2,756	560.9	58.1
Southaven	81,561	569	100.0	33	1,381	3,059.2	71.8	274	4,680	1,318.7	121.0
Tupelo	25,939	101	98.0	113	1,633	943.4	76.8	380	6,235	1,377.0	142.4
MISSOURI	4,747,590	21,372	65.2	6,293	95,156	102,651.6	5,631.7	20,694	312,616	100,394.0	8,147.5
Ballwin	2,746	6	100.0	12	49	45.1	2.5	83	1,667	690.3	54.4
Blue Springs	32,946	272	65.1	39	355	319.4	24.3	157	3,621	1,051.4	90.5
Cape Girardeau	35,382	112	91.1	67	793	549.8	39.4	286	4,769	1,217.1	116.4
Chesterfield	NA	NA	NA	137	1,932	1,285.5	159.9	380	5,835	1,219.3	128.1
Columbia	172,459	676	72.0	112	1,441	745.3	79.1	494	10,223	2,762.9	249.0
Florissant	75	1	100.0	10	33	12.1	0.9	157	3,510	807.9	83.1
Gladstone	969	4	100.0	13	49	30.9	2.6	74	1,853	561.6	52.7
Grandview	1,625	11	100.0	34	424	217.0	23.2	80	1,017	257.3	26.7
Hazelwood	4,600	38	2.6	58	1,472	1,114.6	83.7	97	1,873	789.2	67.5
Independence	25,071	143	69.2	73	483	207.1	22.8	400	8,576	2,357.9	212.0
Jefferson City	16,273	62	93.5	60	926	1,273.2	43.6	243	5,176	1,307.2	127.7
Joplin	52,905	457	42.2	85	1,715	752.7	73.0	360	6,311	1,846.8	156.2
Kansas City	415,311	2,338	38.1	590	11,714	20,250.1	750.5	1,456	25,405	9,130.3	694.1
Kirkwood	37,271	96	87.5	31	172	102.3	10.6	110	2,386	810.7	73.4
Lee's Summit	234,876	712	89.6	104	1,522	834.9	87.9	288	5,910	1,681.4	158.5
Liberty	40,367	257	25.7	20	206	171.6	13.6	96	1,881	431.6	48.4
Maryland Heights	617	2	100.0	204	5,207	6,856.6	458.0	115	1,536	527.1	56.4
O'Fallon	79,935	357	97.2	78	1,183	4,092.0	61.2	227	3,670	1,162.4	105.3
Raytown	8,669	11	45.5	18	153	58.6	8.6	86	1,449	360.2	36.8
St. Charles	112,117	413	100.0	78	1,584	3,034.0	98.3	267	4,163	1,087.1	99.7
St. Joseph	10,989	47	91.5	90	1,162	1,601.5	61.8	287	5,638	1,387.1	131.8
St. Louis	118,427	955	15.3	401	6,973	6,103.3	425.4	878	9,928	2,857.2	276.4
St. Peters	43,133	405	17.0	73	846	431.2	44.8	337	6,893	2,033.5	189.0
Springfield	65,218	877	6.6	320	7,221	5,038.3	361.4	940	16,834	4,676.9	450.4
University City	2,130	5	100.0	20	236	170.2	17.1	82	770	162.9	19.7
Wentzville	173,937	775	49.4	35	280	196.1	17.7	118	2,967	930.9	83.3
Wildwood	NA	NA	NA	33	53	28.4	3.0	39	475	104.5	13.0
MONTANA	1,411,199	7,272	43.6	1,366	13,078	11,214.5	677.3	4,754	59,032	16,935.8	1,622.6
Billings	194,572	910	58.2	247	3,468	2,559.4	201.1	606	9,384	2,944.8	276.9
Bozeman	189,016	1,215	25.6	65	830	440.2	40.7	363	5,443	1,458.0	149.0
Butte-Silver Bow	9,057	72	87.5	D	D	D	D	162	2,175	573.3	54.5
Great Falls	12,068	97	50.5	88	970	641.4	46.9	325	5,075	1,364.3	133.5
Helena	42,848	211	25.1	44	401	321.6	17.7	223	3,525	1,007.0	99.1
Missoula	225,310	1,556	13.7	108	1,298	777.1	70.7	459	6,865	1,857.1	185.7
NEBRASKA	2,016,001	10,723	59.0	2,782	35,143	39,908.6	1,964.7	7,154	109,729	31,214.7	2,853.4
Bellevue	89,356	415	46.0	18	90	148.9	7.0	98	2,325	792.2	69.2
Fremont	25,668	117	39.3	31	592	673.9	33.6	115	2,209	686.9	60.8
Grand Island	45,645	232	42.2	73	1,084	615.1	61.8	279	4,879	1,217.2	125.7
Hastings	6,532	26	100.0	36	444	242.3	20.4	126	1,853	474.9	48.4
Kearney	44,589	158	72.8	49	763	712.1	38.3	191	3,604	845.8	88.2
Lincoln	499,373	2,320	47.1	251	3,847	4,163.0	210.6	951	18,008	4,681.2	466.0
Omaha	329,717	3,167	51.2	677	10,090	11,536.0	660.1	1,597	33,315	9,418.6	897.1
NEVADA	5,293,432	23,406	69.6	2,665	32,879	25,395.7	1,915.2	8,745	145,773	45,110.7	4,220.2
Carson City	64,422	307	66.1	81	620	335.2	29.4	220	3,141	1,170.8	102.3
Henderson	1,008,122	4,743	70.8	240	1,925	1,111.1	113.8	768	14,462	5,280.3	436.8
Las Vegas	881,857	3,748	72.0	409	2,708	1,937.9	150.7	1,923	35,708	10,767.9	1,000.4
North Las Vegas	886,447	3,746	75.7	191	4,000	3,174.4	245.7	344	7,295	2,093.9	185.0
Reno	721,235	3,953	35.8	306	5,519	4,685.3	306.0	1,015	17,305	5,933.3	548.6
Sparks	158,924	676	88.0	226	3,757	2,271.8	200.0	322	5,258	1,439.3	150.3
NEW HAMPSHIRE	1,260,568	4,892	70.0	1,509	22,314	20,328.4	1,577.3	6,032	96,591	30,039.4	2,804.6
Concord	13,201	102	33.3	55	1,075	1,831.3	60.2	278	5,108	1,572.1	156.7
Dover	24,246	98	55.1	32	500	167.4	30.3	91	1,369	412.4	46.8

1. Merchant wholesalers except manufacturers' sales branches and offices. 2. Establishments with payroll.

City	Real estate and rental and leasing, 2017				Professional, scientific, and technical services[1], 2017				Manufacturing, 2017			
	Number of establish-ments	Number of employees	Receipts (mil dol)	Annual payroll (mil dol)	Number of establish-ments	Number of employees	Receipts (mil dol)	Annual payroll (mil dol)	Number of establish-ments	Number of employees	Receipts (mil dol)	Annual payroll (mil dol)
	80	81	82	83	84	85	86	87	88	89	90	91
MISSISSIPPI—Cont'd												
Clinton	37	117	22.9	2.8	56	256	37.5	12.3	NA	NA	NA	NA
Greenville	31	113	18.4	4.1	59	250	29.5	10.2	NA	NA	NA	NA
Gulfport	111	575	129.8	18.5	183	1,154	182.6	59.6	NA	NA	NA	NA
Hattiesburg	104	507	115.5	19.0	163	1,519	188.4	65.8	NA	NA	NA	NA
Horn Lake	23	83	22.6	2.9	14	65	6.9	2.6	NA	NA	NA	NA
Jackson	222	1,037	254.1	47.9	576	4,964	836.3	316.4	NA	NA	NA	NA
Madison	D	D	D	D	138	592	118.0	35.0	NA	NA	NA	NA
Meridian	66	321	67.5	12.5	112	870	93.6	36.3	NA	NA	NA	NA
Olive Branch	27	81	27.3	3.6	39	151	13.3	4.2	NA	NA	NA	NA
Oxford	55	219	55.5	7.8	115	896	226.0	68.5	NA	NA	NA	NA
Pearl	37	216	35.5	8.7	25	147	29.4	6.6	NA	NA	NA	NA
Southaven	50	208	84.6	10.0	79	497	80.9	23.3	NA	NA	NA	NA
Tupelo	78	340	74.9	11.7	160	983	124.7	51.7	NA	NA	NA	NA
MISSOURI	6,644	37,144	8,975.9	1,625.7	14,171	161,595	30,111.6	11,584.3	5,797	259,462	118,633.7	14,216.5
Ballwin	29	82	19.4	3.1	69	111	17.0	5.8	NA	NA	NA	NA
Blue Springs	70	656	88.2	22.9	119	464	61.5	20.7	NA	NA	NA	NA
Cape Girardeau	89	264	61.9	9.3	120	864	88.2	35.1	NA	NA	NA	NA
Chesterfield	129	852	219.5	39.2	403	14,366	2,770.4	979.1	NA	NA	NA	NA
Columbia	228	1,163	213.1	37.7	367	4,365	501.5	226.3	NA	NA	NA	NA
Florissant	31	112	22.9	3.7	57	260	20.5	8.2	NA	NA	NA	NA
Gladstone	47	162	60.3	7.7	D	D	D	D	NA	NA	NA	NA
Grandview	31	285	44.2	9.9	D	D	13.0	D	NA	NA	NA	NA
Hazelwood	34	136	54.7	5.6	49	620	111.9	41.5	NA	NA	NA	NA
Independence	94	426	119.6	14.4	224	894	110.2	49.2	NA	NA	NA	NA
Jefferson City	64	221	56.5	8.3	212	1,425	210.3	88.6	NA	NA	NA	NA
Joplin	85	449	85.3	13.9	137	940	122.6	44.6	NA	NA	NA	NA
Kansas City	631	4,863	1,778.8	291.4	1,957	32,540	7,384.6	2,765.6	NA	NA	NA	NA
Kirkwood	49	152	48.7	4.7	133	576	111.2	38.3	NA	NA	NA	NA
Lee's Summit	143	382	126.4	19.5	349	1,816	262.8	100.5	NA	NA	NA	NA
Liberty	37	161	36.0	5.1	D	D	D	D	NA	NA	NA	NA
Maryland Heights	66	391	115.4	21.3	146	2,268	338.2	142.6	NA	NA	NA	NA
O'Fallon	88	488	105.2	19.0	146	591	113.1	38.5	NA	NA	NA	NA
Raytown	17	73	9.5	2.4	D	D	D	D	NA	NA	NA	NA
St. Charles	96	546	283.6	31.1	265	3,046	268.8	99.2	NA	NA	NA	NA
St. Joseph	100	393	64.6	11.2	132	1,246	233.3	87.7	NA	NA	NA	NA
St. Louis	412	2,388	632.7	108.5	1,114	18,010	3,685.1	1,388.8	NA	NA	NA	NA
St. Peters	84	273	77.9	10.9	D	D	D	D	NA	NA	NA	NA
Springfield	380	2,844	453.5	96.7	681	6,162	872.7	356.9	NA	NA	NA	NA
University City	46	762	117.4	26.6	90	257	33.9	12.4	NA	NA	NA	NA
Wentzville	D	D	D	D	48	1,695	198.3	75.6	NA	NA	NA	NA
Wildwood	D	D	D	D	115	421	54.3	22.1	NA	NA	NA	NA
MONTANA	2,036	5,951	1,144.6	205.6	3,836	17,711	2,517.4	938.6	1,328	17,944	10,943.6	935.7
Billings	277	1,033	231.9	44.0	520	3,536	619.3	217.8	NA	NA	NA	NA
Bozeman	219	526	129.8	20.0	490	2,309	386.5	140.0	NA	NA	NA	NA
Butte-Silver Bow	57	156	20.4	3.9	107	546	66.4	28.7	NA	NA	NA	NA
Great Falls	103	353	65.0	11.6	170	1,088	161.9	57.6	NA	NA	NA	NA
Helena	91	226	57.6	8.1	215	1,569	221.5	90.1	NA	NA	NA	NA
Missoula	196	718	143.5	25.9	481	2,940	353.7	149.1	NA	NA	NA	NA
NEBRASKA	2,354	11,293	2,291.9	486.8	4,699	39,566	6,278.4	2,385.3	1,760	93,510	53,129.3	4,728.4
Bellevue	51	189	34.7	5.5	90	1,172	196.8	71.9	NA	NA	NA	NA
Fremont	38	168	30.6	5.5	34	168	18.3	6.4	NA	NA	NA	NA
Grand Island	66	249	43.3	7.8	91	640	75.5	32.7	NA	NA	NA	NA
Hastings	45	110	23.6	3.1	56	266	29.1	11.0	NA	NA	NA	NA
Kearney	57	144	47.3	5.4	85	967	98.6	43.8	NA	NA	NA	NA
Lincoln	391	1,957	362.1	80.7	835	8,293	1,431.9	486.8	NA	NA	NA	NA
Omaha	803	5,999	1,241.9	286.0	1,672	19,019	3,188.8	1,290.8	NA	NA	NA	NA
NEVADA	4,684	30,562	7,359.0	1,312.2	9,018	60,168	10,815.7	3,951.1	1,828	44,182	16,408.1	2,516.7
Carson City	118	361	94.1	13.0	246	1,126	189.0	74.4	NA	NA	NA	NA
Henderson	513	1,719	472.4	79.5	1,020	4,993	852.1	308.3	NA	NA	NA	NA
Las Vegas	1,081	5,775	1,309.4	283.5	2,610	17,301	3,413.1	1,206.3	NA	NA	NA	NA
North Las Vegas	131	839	228.2	37.1	153	2,526	409.9	189.9	NA	NA	NA	NA
Reno	540	2,960	722.2	116.7	1,270	8,428	1,401.1	532.4	NA	NA	NA	NA
Sparks	132	817	165.7	32.1	136	920	111.9	41.3	NA	NA	NA	NA
NEW HAMPSHIRE	1,523	7,920	2,000.3	381.4	3,674	32,387	5,583.3	2,382.8	1,790	65,211	20,304.1	3,875.2
Concord	D	D	D	D	207	2,034	327.3	161.2	NA	NA	NA	NA
Dover	32	122	25.2	4.8	86	469	80.1	34.6	NA	NA	NA	NA

1. Establishments subject to federal tax.

City	Accommodation and food services, 2017				Arts, entertainment, and recreation[1], 2017				Health care and social assistance[1], 2017			
	Number of establish-ments	Number of employees	Receipts (mil dol)	Annual payroll (mil dol)	Number of establish-ments	Number of employees	Receipts (mil dol)	Annual payroll (mil dol)	Number of establish-ments	Number of employees	Receipts (mil dol)	Annual payroll (mil dol)
	92	93	94	95	96	97	98	99	100	101	102	103
MISSISSIPPI—Cont'd												
Clinton	65	1,295	62.5	15.4	13.0	144	11.5	1.7	53	1,285	70.7	28.0
Greenville	78	2,140	140.2	35.9	11.0	90	4.5	1.9	126	2,934	278.5	112.2
Gulfport	205	5,964	451.1	99.8	20.0	274	41.9	4.9	252	7,631	915.0	391.2
Hattiesburg	254	6,028	308.2	87.0	21.0	355	14.2	4.7	229	9,360	1,232.3	526.5
Horn Lake	59	1,561	83.9	22.9	5.0	D	20.1	D	D	D	D	D
Jackson	374	8,801	433.6	122.1	46.0	813	68.3	22.8	624	30,160	3,812.3	1,733.1
Madison	D	D	D	D	25.0	413	18.2	5.9	93	5,051	187.4	90.0
Meridian	162	3,874	185.5	50.3	D	D	D	D	200	6,596	889.9	318.9
Olive Branch	95	2,241	109.8	28.7	D	D	D	D	74	1,183	98.9	41.7
Oxford	167	3,644	190.8	61.1	D	D	D	D	134	2,720	455.9	122.2
Pearl	80	1,715	110.7	26.8	8.0	23	3.0	0.7	D	D	D	D
Southaven	154	3,728	192.9	51.4	D	D	D	D	159	3,613	575.1	189.9
Tupelo	182	3,932	193.8	54.1	25.0	173	9.4	2.4	245	8,839	1,179.8	434.2
MISSOURI	12,896	263,644	15,082.4	4,274.7	2,274.0	40,484	3,953.3	1,554.3	19,097	423,057	48,192.5	18,682.2
Ballwin	52	1,128	54.0	16.6	14.0	516	22.1	9.0	44	553	34.4	16.4
Blue Springs	123	2,659	137.4	38.2	22.0	231	9.5	3.1	144	1,868	169.9	67.7
Cape Girardeau	141	3,417	163.4	49.4	D	D	D	D	272	9,492	1,269.9	462.4
Chesterfield	199	4,217	244.3	73.8	47.0	639	29.7	10.3	281	7,862	1,043.4	454.5
Columbia	417	9,877	463.7	135.7	60.0	923	37.5	12.4	584	18,346	2,544.2	870.5
Florissant	D	D	D	D	D	D	D	D	211	2,589	225.8	93.4
Gladstone	44	946	43.5	13.7	4.0	D	1.7	D	76	776	65.9	26.8
Grandview	45	1,026	46.5	15.4	3.0	13	1.3	0.3	64	531	36.4	16.9
Hazelwood	55	949	47.5	14.2	4.0	6	0.6	0.1	111	984	94.8	34.7
Independence	229	5,721	290.0	85.9	26.0	333	22.9	6.3	342	6,465	837.7	313.0
Jefferson City	151	3,194	154.2	44.8	20.0	426	31.8	8.3	254	6,697	788.3	308.5
Joplin	193	4,606	208.8	64.9	23.0	354	11.4	4.6	276	10,140	1,130.7	455.9
Kansas City	1,186	30,485	2,100.0	594.3	221.0	6,819	1,187.0	604.8	1,770	45,482	6,381.5	2,403.9
Kirkwood	71	1,877	94.9	32.8	21.0	515	29.6	9.8	120	1,915	151.4	62.5
Lee's Summit	198	4,846	229.9	71.0	40.0	423	17.1	5.0	330	6,882	944.5	340.8
Liberty	76	1,747	87.9	26.4	13.0	64	3.5	0.9	134	3,209	334.9	143.8
Maryland Heights	96	3,063	366.5	74.0	20.0	544	52.9	9.6	96	3,886	359.2	157.7
O'Fallon	169	3,947	186.0	57.5	25.0	673	25.7	9.8	226	3,365	300.7	122.0
Raytown	51	1,169	49.5	13.8	4.0	41	2.0	0.5	88	966	67.9	28.0
St. Charles	228	7,324	562.2	138.3	33.0	343	17.6	5.2	261	5,464	554.8	209.3
St. Joseph	192	3,990	195.1	57.1	20.0	566	43.5	9.9	D	D	D	D
St. Louis	1,002	22,623	1,685.1	451.0	148.0	4,609	616.8	221.1	1,554	39,629	4,647.7	1,753.1
St. Peters	171	3,748	190.6	58.2	35.0	712	31.9	8.9	299	4,540	439.0	170.7
Springfield	702	14,999	760.5	221.1	75.0	1,334	87.7	22.9	768	28,280	3,729.7	1,389.8
University City	85	1,439	76.7	23.2	12.0	D	23.5	D	169	1,682	127.9	39.4
Wentzville	84	1,954	97.9	27.4	9.0	113	6.3	1.6	88	1,292	98.4	47.3
Wildwood	26	664	35.4	10.2	9.0	330	7.8	2.3	58	581	51.7	22.9
MONTANA	3,568	52,415	3,126.0	898.6	1,234.0	10,492	876.7	179.5	3,716	73,254	8,447.9	3,303.9
Billings	347	8,420	489.0	140.5	148.0	1,550	149.6	25.9	534	13,921	2,029.2	786.9
Bozeman	241	4,553	273.2	79.7	83.0	462	48.9	9.6	305	4,646	534.7	194.6
Butte-Silver Bow	137	2,184	114.3	35.8	46.0	328	24.0	4.6	169	3,114	295.5	113.6
Great Falls	208	3,739	207.7	60.0	72.0	689	58.8	11.9	269	6,664	792.4	317.6
Helena	157	3,072	164.3	49.3	55.0	756	53.6	8.9	D	D	D	D
Missoula	293	6,180	341.4	97.0	84.0	1,299	75.7	19.5	453	9,689	1,151.0	401.3
NEBRASKA	4,621	76,386	3,957.8	1,135.9	913.0	14,879	891.3	249.2	5,817	135,691	16,060.4	6,116.9
Bellevue	119	2,415	117.7	36.1	D	D	D	D	131	2,384	247.4	92.8
Fremont	69	1,132	54.5	15.3	12.0	414	8.7	3.7	106	2,629	252.4	102.1
Grand Island	151	2,565	139.5	40.9	25.0	464	43.0	8.0	182	4,408	506.3	193.8
Hastings	80	1,400	65.9	17.1	D	D	D	D	103	2,826	319.0	134.3
Kearney	129	2,613	123.4	37.4	22.0	490	17.2	5.4	183	3,892	662.3	167.6
Lincoln	746	14,706	745.7	211.9	129.0	2,878	119.9	36.2	1,012	24,568	2,869.8	1,093.9
Omaha	1,340	27,002	1,509.1	442.7	244.0	6,172	433.1	119.8	1,828	51,418	6,936.8	2,683.5
NEVADA	6,810	319,584	33,979.9	9,578.4	1,635.0	31,918	5,143.2	1,068.0	7,372	132,093	18,111.8	6,620.4
Carson City	170	3,036	193.0	54.1	51.0	1,019	118.5	41.7	215	3,865	623.8	214.4
Henderson	535	16,075	1,341.9	366.7	197.0	3,474	343.7	89.6	879	12,658	1,848.3	646.0
Las Vegas	1,403	45,459	3,979.4	1,177.9	332.0	6,476	1,598.5	307.0	2,077	39,266	5,199.3	1,914.2
North Las Vegas	270	7,756	628.8	169.1	D	D	D	D	274	6,983	1,140.6	439.3
Reno	821	23,651	1,802.0	518.4	151.0	3,008	340.8	74.5	1,019	22,180	3,181.6	1,225.2
Sparks	210	5,393	386.1	108.8	46.0	1,317	94.6	23.2	182	3,102	367.0	127.6
NEW HAMPSHIRE	3,784	59,531	3,722.0	1,132.7	815.0	12,442	978.1	290.7	3,737	94,594	11,931.6	4,741.7
Concord	131	2,877	176.4	59.1	25.0	401	20.9	7.3	237	9,984	1,132.2	516.0
Dover	110	1,905	108.6	33.3	17.0	179	10.5	3.5	139	4,200	572.7	203.7

1. Establishments subject to federal tax.

City	Other services[1]: Number of establish-ments	Other services[1]: Number of employees	Other services[1]: Receipts (mil dol)	Other services[1]: Annual payroll (mil dol)	Government employment and payroll, 2017: Full-time equivalent employees	March payroll: Total (dollars)	Perent of total for: Admin-istrative, judicial, and legal	Police and corrections	Fire protection	Highways and trans-portation	Health and welfare	Natural resources and utilities	Education and libraries
	104	105	106	107	108	109	110	111	112	113	114	115	116
MISSISSIPPI—Cont'd													
Clinton	41	246	31.0	9.4	208	675,547	9.7	34.6	25.8	5.2	0.0	19.5	0.0
Greenville	D	D	D	D	308	932,163	9.8	40.2	26.7	16.1	0.0	3.9	0.0
Gulfport	114	767	80.6	23.5	3,674	19,047,459	1.4	4.1	3.2	0.8	88.3	1.0	0.0
Hattiesburg	106	746	73.6	18.8	671	2,076,495	12.8	27.9	23.0	11.6	3.7	18.3	0.0
Horn Lake	20	121	15.0	4.2	188	670,233	8.3	43.2	29.3	4.5	0.0	14.0	0.0
Jackson	312	2,097	286.8	86.1	2,154	6,153,172	13.1	31.3	19.3	5.2	5.2	17.5	0.0
Madison	36	217	33.8	9.3	218	779,511	10.1	42.5	19.2	9.3	0.0	11.4	0.0
Meridian	D	D	D	D	532	1,624,537	10.4	23.6	27.2	11.8	3.7	19.2	0.0
Olive Branch	D	D	D	D	404	1,656,189	13.0	24.3	31.2	3.9	0.7	21.3	0.0
Oxford	48	318	79.4	11.2	326	1,071,974	7.5	33.2	19.9	5.5	1.1	26.3	0.0
Pearl	46	299	37.5	11.1	216	903,023	8.6	31.3	29.5	10.4	2.5	17.7	0.0
Southaven	59	389	31.8	9.1	383	1,549,716	10.7	38.5	33.1	2.9	0.4	14.3	0.0
Tupelo	D	D	D	D	514	1,914,110	12.7	24.8	21.0	9.8	0.0	29.2	0.0
MISSOURI	10,513	68,206	8,693.9	2,297.4	X	X	X	X	X	X	X	X	X
Ballwin	47	287	21.8	7.6	157	685,445	12.2	43.3	0.0	16.6	0.0	22.4	0.0
Blue Springs	110	540	53.7	16.4	291	1,550,352	12.7	51.1	0.0	8.7	6.1	19.7	0.0
Cape Girardeau	99	594	57.5	16.8	437	1,558,764	8.5	25.5	18.1	9.3	0.0	26.1	0.0
Chesterfield	151	1,213	172.3	42.2	238	1,140,711	13.9	49.2	0.0	15.7	0.0	16.3	0.0
Columbia	289	1,947	196.6	60.8	1,480	5,541,903	22.8	14.8	13.4	7.9	7.4	29.8	0.0
Florissant	93	516	48.7	15.8	381	1,461,910	12.2	33.9	0.4	11.0	11.9	30.2	0.0
Gladstone	54	279	27.0	7.7	209	831,442	13.9	32.9	20.6	5.2	1.7	22.0	0.0
Grandview	34	191	20.4	5.7	216	732,142	14.6	31.0	24.9	7.4	3.9	17.1	0.0
Hazelwood	46	279	28.2	10.1	126	751,106	8.0	58.1	33.9	0.0	0.0	0.0	0.0
Independence	179	1,005	102.3	31.1	1,031	6,155,008	6.7	24.6	16.4	3.2	3.5	44.3	0.0
Jefferson City	192	1,151	191.0	50.0	370	1,669,553	10.6	27.1	18.2	11.2	0.6	21.0	0.0
Joplin	111	890	72.1	24.4	548	1,905,882	10.0	29.4	19.6	11.0	8.6	13.7	4.2
Kansas City	860	7,708	1,753.3	295.8	6,334	28,199,434	11.8	19.0	28.8	11.7	7.4	20.5	0.0
Kirkwood	61	459	46.9	11.1	298	1,535,998	6.7	27.5	22.4	3.4	1.8	32.8	0.0
Lee's Summit	171	1,052	99.7	32.5	703	3,810,408	15.9	25.3	24.9	9.9	7.9	16.1	0.0
Liberty	55	336	30.2	9.5	191	864,609	20.2	33.8	25.2	7.2	1.2	7.0	0.0
Maryland Heights	64	632	73.0	26.9	195	1,125,065	18.7	52.2	0.0	7.5	0.0	12.9	0.0
O'Fallon	142	1,225	114.1	37.1	458	2,119,939	12.3	37.5	0.0	9.1	0.2	28.6	0.0
Raytown	48	396	44.3	11.8	141	692,893	12.7	54.6	0.0	11.8	12.3	5.8	2.8
St. Charles	162	1,035	112.7	32.8	501	2,735,489	7.7	34.1	22.1	15.6	0.0	6.7	0.0
St. Joseph	148	1,175	178.9	48.1	693	2,714,225	9.4	27.2	21.4	11.5	6.6	20.9	0.0
St. Louis	625	5,377	827.8	199.1	6,658	37,801,592	16.1	37.5	15.7	12.1	2.0	12.5	0.0
St. Peters	166	1,255	115.2	34.2	541	2,548,634	15.4	27.5	0.0	11.9	9.0	36.2	0.0
Springfield	476	4,094	448.9	134.1	2,825	14,818,819	5.5	15.9	8.3	10.0	2.8	33.9	0.0
University City	57	513	59.3	21.2	286	1,206,503	5.9	47.1	16.2	8.1	0.0	13.6	7.0
Wentzville	56	379	37.8	10.2	248	1,084,085	15.8	40.5	0.0	9.5	1.6	22.4	0.0
Wildwood	24	111	6.2	2.0	21	145,661	74.2	0.0	0.0	11.7	0.0	0.0	0.0
MONTANA	2,409	12,077	1,608.6	403.0	X	X	X	X	X	X	X	X	X
Billings	302	1,927	230.4	63.9	907	5,144,967	10.7	22.3	17.6	14.0	1.0	18.4	2.7
Bozeman	183	1,103	193.2	43.4	366	1,782,896	18.3	22.4	16.2	4.9	0.0	21.9	4.9
Butte-Silver Bow	65	277	38.2	8.1	450	2,205,916	15.6	24.3	18.9	14.3	2.0	21.5	0.0
Great Falls	D	D	D	D	494	2,452,526	16.7	30.1	17.3	11.4	3.8	17.6	2.9
Helena	170	1,022	146.7	46.0	313	1,491,616	18.9	27.1	14.4	7.5	0.3	21.5	0.0
Missoula	252	2,039	336.9	73.8	561	2,768,191	12.6	29.8	24.1	9.6	1.7	17.8	0.0
NEBRASKA	4,107	21,757	3,608.2	701.0	X	X	X	X	X	X	X	X	X
Bellevue	85	474	41.9	12.5	330	1,482,766	6.4	48.5	24.0	8.2	1.6	5.8	3.6
Fremont	62	258	26.1	6.7	289	1,563,109	14.4	16.4	9.1	6.0	0.5	49.7	2.9
Grand Island	136	920	85.9	22.4	618	3,076,295	9.6	16.4	15.9	8.2	0.3	43.8	3.8
Hastings	D	D	D	D	395	2,129,773	2.7	11.3	6.8	5.2	0.0	52.1	2.5
Kearney	98	554	75.2	13.3	311	1,416,471	11.1	26.4	7.2	8.3	0.0	34.7	4.8
Lincoln	678	4,126	757.0	150.3	2,642	14,836,126	7.7	18.2	13.0	10.8	9.1	36.5	2.7
Omaha	1,043	7,314	1,650.8	249.5	2,910	18,004,814	5.5	37.8	29.6	8.1	1.6	10.8	3.3
NEVADA	4,032	28,825	3,281.5	914.2	X	X	X	X	X	X	X	X	X
Carson City	132	618	100.6	22.3	650	3,550,570	21.0	28.3	16.0	8.6	5.8	14.8	2.1
Henderson	423	3,209	325.5	91.9	2,310	16,130,348	16.1	32.6	16.9	1.1	1.7	21.9	0.0
Las Vegas	921	6,955	777.1	215.5	2,867	20,161,448	18.7	14.2	33.0	5.9	2.9	16.3	0.0
North Las Vegas	182	2,045	202.1	66.9	1,081	8,065,862	13.5	40.2	21.3	3.6	4.3	14.1	1.2
Reno	523	3,845	453.3	129.3	1,251	8,747,437	13.9	33.3	27.4	3.9	0.0	11.5	0.0
Sparks	172	1,071	132.9	37.6	499	3,235,999	20.7	26.9	24.1	4.5	0.0	23.9	0.0
NEW HAMPSHIRE	3,011	17,864	2,096.2	619.2	X	X	X	X	X	X	X	X	X
Concord	222	1,356	233.0	56.0	463	2,884,048	13.0	23.4	17.7	8.5	9.1	13.8	3.4
Dover	74	467	37.5	11.0	847	3,683,989	5.2	10.3	8.4	1.8	1.1	5.8	64.8

1. Establishments subject to federal tax.

City	City government finances, 2017									
	General revenue							General expenditure		
		Intergovernmental		Taxes						
					Per capita[1] (dollars)				Per capita[1] (dollars)	
	Total (mil dol)	Total (mil dol)	Percent from state government	Total (mil dol)	Total	Property	Sales and gross receipts	Total (mil dol)	Total	Capital outlays
	117	118	119	120	121	122	123	124	125	126
MISSISSIPPI—Cont'd										
Clinton	22.8	7.3	94.7	9.4	369	333	36	21.3	839	121
Greenville	34.6	11.5	68.2	14.1	461	383	78	31.4	1,026	158
Gulfport	597.0	45.1	93.7	32.3	449	332	117	586.8	8,156	509
Hattiesburg	80.5	32.7	79.9	28.5	620	422	198	86.7	1,883	400
Horn Lake	21.3	6.0	100.0	7.9	290	262	28	21.9	806	102
Jackson	219.6	57.8	68.0	80.6	483	420	64	201.3	1,206	166
Madison	31.5	12.1	70.3	12.9	503	429	75	29.7	1,160	270
Meridian	44.5	15.4	99.1	18.5	488	413	75	38.4	1,012	68
Olive Branch	42.7	9.9	100.0	18.9	502	452	50	39.0	1,039	114
Oxford	43.0	15.0	81.4	15.1	559	332	228	36.1	1,333	149
Pearl	33.2	13.7	91.9	8.8	332	288	44	32.6	1,232	83
Southaven	61.0	21.2	75.6	27.9	514	453	62	54.8	1,011	207
Tupelo	63.2	32.0	85.0	16.1	421	395	25	74.4	1,949	748
MISSOURI	X	X	X	X	X	X	X	X	X	X
Ballwin	21.3	2.8	74.0	14.2	471	0	471	19.2	637	115
Blue Springs	50.1	3.9	100.0	31.3	571	112	452	46.4	845	85
Cape Girardeau	72.6	6.5	100.0	47.6	1,214	63	1,074	69.5	1,775	755
Chesterfield	35.2	3.3	100.0	31.9	671	0	671	35.3	743	210
Columbia	182.1	38.8	12.9	73.5	605	99	506	156.7	1,289	337
Florissant	36.3	15.5	5.5	13.6	265	13	179	32.2	627	60
Gladstone	32.3	4.0	59.0	17.1	632	124	508	29.2	1,079	204
Grandview	30.2	3.7	100.0	17.0	675	183	492	29.2	1,160	266
Hazelwood	34.1	1.9	49.9	29.9	1,181	319	862	36.7	1,451	99
Independence	140.0	11.0	92.8	81.4	694	80	614	162.7	1,388	233
Jefferson City	63.2	6.7	100.0	36.4	848	123	725	63.1	1,471	315
Joplin	135.2	59.2	7.9	49.9	988	59	930	120.1	2,380	1,063
Kansas City	1,617.5	101.0	39.7	739.0	1,513	254	698	1,710.9	3,504	476
Kirkwood	27.9	1.9	100.0	21.6	780	166	614	27.5	993	124
Lee's Summit	160.3	22.0	13.8	84.5	870	318	552	143.0	1,472	356
Liberty	43.7	1.0	1.0	27.3	865	206	659	57.1	1,812	572
Maryland Heights	39.3	11.9	21.0	22.0	815	168	647	61.4	2,275	1,209
O'Fallon	73.2	8.9	59.3	45.8	524	121	402	70.6	807	280
Raytown	28.9	1.7	100.0	16.9	578	74	499	24.9	849	92
St. Charles	98.3	10.3	27.9	64.5	917	256	661	105.1	1,493	396
St. Joseph	119.4	10.2	81.3	66.4	872	184	689	115.6	1,520	374
St. Louis	919.8	110.5	55.9	578.0	1,875	303	907	1,030.2	3,342	243
St. Peters	89.6	7.8	28.3	46.1	806	178	628	103.0	1,801	372
Springfield	348.8	57.1	68.6	173.3	1,037	137	900	306.3	1,833	334
University City	36.5	2.2	100.0	26.3	765	139	626	35.6	1,034	67
Wentzville	49.6	5.6	38.8	30.5	778	168	611	41.3	1,056	246
Wildwood	16.1	9.2	15.4	5.8	164	0	164	14.7	415	176
MONTANA	X	X	X	X	X	X	X	X	X	X
Billings	163.2	26.0	60.8	46.5	424	339	79	152.7	1,391	332
Bozeman	64.9	9.1	100.0	24.7	526	482	43	62.0	1,323	234
Butte-Silver Bow	70.0	14.8	94.8	33.0	947	917	30	89.0	2,558	739
Great Falls	64.9	11.6	77.8	22.2	377	334	43	60.1	1,021	120
Helena	46.1	10.1	53.2	13.1	410	351	58	39.2	1,223	127
Missoula	89.1	23.0	96.4	40.4	546	491	55	90.8	1,226	110
NEBRASKA	X	X	X	X	X	X	X	X	X	X
Bellevue	53.8	6.9	95.9	31.1	582	298	285	54.1	1,013	147
Fremont	42.9	5.5	72.3	17.0	640	193	447	51.2	1,931	366
Grand Island	76.4	5.7	100.0	34.7	679	226	453	86.1	1,685	581
Hastings	34.9	9.0	57.5	12.9	516	212	290	35.3	1,408	413
Kearney	47.4	7.3	100.0	18.8	560	97	463	56.5	1,683	597
Lincoln	350.3	70.6	35.0	170.9	600	250	350	373.6	1,313	297
Omaha	717.8	70.6	65.3	427.8	898	326	572	540.2	1,134	81
NEVADA	X	X	X	X	X	X	X	X	X	X
Carson City	144.0	47.5	62.8	47.6	873	505	368	129.7	2,379	315
Henderson	393.0	141.9	79.6	147.4	492	253	239	368.1	1,230	97
Las Vegas	851.6	399.8	74.1	224.7	354	180	173	796.5	1,254	161
North Las Vegas	290.7	116.1	95.7	93.9	390	226	164	259.9	1,081	128
Reno	392.3	90.5	88.5	146.5	594	264	330	348.5	1,413	235
Sparks	129.3	41.6	94.3	44.8	448	262	187	117.5	1,175	158
NEW HAMPSHIRE	X	X	X	X	X	X	X	X	X	X
Concord	13.7	0.0	0.0	0.0	0	0	0	21.2	489	0
Dover	126.3	28.7	86.1	83.3	2,637	2,596	40	128.6	4,070	976

1. Based on population estimated as of July 1 of the year shown.

City	City government finances, 2017 (cont.)												
	General expenditure (cont.)												
	Percent of total for:										Debt outstanding		
	Public welfare	Highways	Parking facilities	Education	Health and hospitals	Police protection	Sewerage and sanitation	Parks and recreation	Housing and community development	Interest on debt	Total (mil dol)	Per capita[1] (dollars)	Debt issued during year
	127	128	129	130	131	132	133	134	135	136	137	138	139
MISSISSIPPI—Cont'd													
Clinton	0.0	11.5	0.0	0.0	0.0	23.0	26.1	8.1	0.0	2.7	34.2	1,351	10.4
Greenville	0.0	11.2	0.0	0.0	1.3	24.2	14.3	3.2	0.0	0.7	17.0	556	1.9
Gulfport	0.0	2.1	0.0	0.0	81.8	3.2	4.1	1.8	0.3	1.7	177.0	2,460	60.2
Hattiesburg	0.0	10.0	0.3	0.0	1.1	14.4	22.7	7.9	0.9	2.1	126.5	2,747	47.7
Horn Lake	0.0	3.8	0.0	0.0	0.0	25.1	12.9	6.6	0.0	6.1	24.6	906	0.0
Jackson	1.0	8.9	0.0	0.0	0.5	17.7	18.9	8.1	0.8	4.7	443.6	2,659	54.1
Madison	0.0	25.9	0.0	0.0	0.0	22.1	14.4	6.7	0.0	4.5	57.5	2,244	13.9
Meridian	0.0	12.6	0.2	0.0	0.0	20.9	14.9	7.4	4.0	3.6	51.6	1,360	9.5
Olive Branch	0.0	14.4	0.0	0.0	2.5	24.6	16.3	6.8	0.0	2.4	47.5	1,266	0.6
Oxford	0.0	10.1	2.3	0.0	0.4	17.9	15.1	14.8	0.0	2.0	44.2	1,635	7.4
Pearl	0.0	13.1	0.0	0.0	1.4	20.5	22.1	4.5	0.0	4.0	81.1	3,063	16.5
Southaven	0.0	12.5	0.0	0.0	0.8	20.2	9.8	9.2	0.0	2.7	81.9	1,513	13.9
Tupelo	0.0	17.4	0.0	0.0	0.0	22.2	14.7	21.2	0.1	3.0	97.9	2,565	31.8
MISSOURI	X	X	X	X	X	X	X	X	X	X	X	X	X
Ballwin	0.0	25.9	0.0	0.0	0.0	26.0	1.6	27.0	0.0	0.0	16.6	548	0.0
Blue Springs	0.0	7.7	0.0	0.0	0.0	32.6	13.3	11.2	1.7	10.1	123.5	2,252	0.0
Cape Girardeau	0.0	10.7	0.0	0.0	0.6	11.8	31.8	9.5	3.4	1.4	40.1	1,023	0.0
Chesterfield	0.0	0.0	0.0	0.0	0.0	26.6	0.0	17.8	0.0	0.0	43.8	920	0.0
Columbia	0.6	13.3	1.7	0.0	3.4	11.3	25.5	12.3	0.9	3.2	365.2	3,005	24.7
Florissant	0.0	12.8	0.0	0.0	2.3	36.1	0.7	15.9	3.1	0.7	16.4	320	0.0
Gladstone	0.0	16.9	0.0	0.0	0.6	17.8	16.7	17.5	5.2	0.0	41.9	1,545	1.2
Grandview	0.0	12.0	0.0	0.0	0.0	19.2	9.9	9.2	0.9	3.0	20.6	818	0.0
Hazelwood	0.0	0.1	0.0	0.0	0.0	21.8	0.4	8.8	0.0	3.7	32.2	1,273	0.9
Independence	0.0	5.2	0.0	0.0	1.8	21.6	18.5	7.4	3.0	10.2	464.8	3,966	0.0
Jefferson City	0.0	8.6	0.0	0.0	0.0	15.9	19.7	18.7	0.0	3.0	88.2	2,055	15.6
Joplin	0.0	21.5	0.0	0.0	2.9	8.0	19.5	4.0	5.2	1.1	37.6	744	3.3
Kansas City	0.7	4.3	0.2	0.0	3.2	13.1	13.0	4.2	3.3	4.6	3,583.8	7,339	363.8
Kirkwood	0.0	12.5	0.0	0.0	0.0	26.6	10.1	17.3	0.0	0.0	15.6	562	1.5
Lee's Summit	0.0	11.7	0.0	0.0	0.0	13.9	11.2	5.7	2.7	2.2	62.7	645	0.0
Liberty	0.0	10.2	0.0	0.0	0.4	12.3	43.0	7.8	8.1	0.9	0.2	5	0.0
Maryland Heights	0.0	13.7	0.0	0.0	0.0	17.6	4.6	49.2	0.5	1.7	23.5	871	0.0
O'Fallon	0.0	19.4	0.0	0.0	0.0	31.5	14.3	12.7	0.4	0.0	207.8	2,374	47.1
Raytown	0.0	6.3	0.0	0.0	0.0	30.6	19.3	6.3	3.0	9.2	51.5	1,757	0.0
St. Charles	0.7	14.6	0.3	0.0	1.1	18.0	13.9	4.9	0.0	8.7	209.1	2,970	3.2
St. Joseph	0.0	12.8	3.4	0.0	3.1	15.5	23.8	7.2	0.2	5.8	726.2	9,545	15.6
St. Louis	0.0	2.4	0.9	0.0	5.5	18.5	1.8	2.5	2.1	8.5	1,902.6	6,173	426.3
St. Peters	0.0	13.3	0.0	0.0	0.7	12.6	26.8	15.8	0.2	0.0	126.3	2,208	24.2
Springfield	0.5	14.1	0.1	0.0	3.0	24.9	11.3	11.0	1.1	3.3	896.0	5,361	0.0
University City	0.0	18.3	0.3	0.0	0.0	25.1	11.3	5.6	5.9	0.2	3.4	98	0.0
Wentzville	0.0	17.3	0.0	0.0	0.1	18.3	21.3	10.5	0.0	6.5	62.0	1,584	0.0
Wildwood	0.0	42.0	0.0	0.0	0.0	21.4	0.0	16.8	0.0	1.1	1.3	38	0.0
MONTANA	X	X	X	X	X	X	X	X	X	X	X	X	X
Billings	0.0	22.7	1.2	0.0	0.5	14.5	22.0	4.3	3.7	1.8	198.4	1,807	64.0
Bozeman	12.5	9.6	1.2	0.0	0.0	20.5	15.3	0.8	0.4	2.3	36.7	782	0.0
Butte-Silver Bow	0.4	7.4	0.3	0.0	5.4	9.9	30.0	3.7	3.3	1.6	41.6	1,194	0.0
Great Falls	0.0	9.3	0.9	0.0	0.0	21.3	25.8	6.9	2.6	1.6	57.9	984	14.7
Helena	0.0	11.3	2.2	0.0	0.6	19.3	21.6	12.6	0.1	0.8	23.5	733	14.2
Missoula	0.2	9.3	2.1	0.0	2.1	19.4	7.6	8.5	3.6	2.2	66.5	898	0.0
NEBRASKA	X	X	X	X	X	X	X	X	X	X	X	X	X
Bellevue	0.3	10.0	0.0	0.0	0.3	26.8	22.5	4.8	1.0	3.6	52.5	984	11.4
Fremont	0.0	29.4	0.0	0.0	0.0	11.4	24.6	11.0	0.0	5.5	71.0	2,679	0.2
Grand Island	0.0	1.7	0.0	0.0	0.0	17.1	26.9	5.5	3.9	3.8	86.2	1,687	2.6
Hastings	0.0	16.6	0.0	0.0	0.0	13.7	17.2	10.8	2.4	1.2	33.7	1,343	0.8
Kearney	0.5	23.4	0.0	0.0	0.4	10.7	19.6	20.7	1.6	1.1	55.8	1,661	14.0
Lincoln	2.2	16.8	1.7	0.0	7.8	11.0	10.9	4.6	1.3	13.4	1,368.8	4,811	174.3
Omaha	0.5	14.7	0.4	0.0	0.6	25.2	10.5	5.1	0.1	9.8	1,386.7	2,912	175.4
NEVADA	X	X	X	X	X	X	X	X	X	X	X	X	X
Carson City	5.0	11.1	0.0	0.0	7.2	14.7	5.9	7.8	1.6	3.3	277.0	5,079	31.3
Henderson	0.0	3.2	0.0	0.0	0.0	22.8	8.7	12.7	4.3	2.5	230.9	772	12.7
Las Vegas	0.0	12.1	1.0	0.0	0.5	18.8	7.7	7.9	2.2	4.3	797.5	1,255	22.9
North Las Vegas	0.0	6.4	0.0	0.0	0.0	32.5	6.9	5.5	1.7	8.5	415.5	1,728	0.0
Reno	0.0	5.0	0.2	0.0	0.0	18.2	17.5	3.3	3.2	4.6	621.2	2,519	48.5
Sparks	0.0	7.9	0.0	0.0	0.0	22.3	17.3	7.2	1.1	9.9	198.9	1,988	56.3
NEW HAMPSHIRE	X	X	X	X	X	X	X	X	X	X	X	X	X
Concord	0.0	0.0	5.0	0.0	0.0	0.0	0.0	19.2	0.0	12.0	46.1	1,066	0.0
Dover	0.6	5.5	0.6	65.0	0.0	6.4	0.7	1.6	0.0	8.3	165.5	5,238	10.1

1. Based on population estimated as of July 1 of the year shown.

Table D. Cities — **Land Area and Population**

STATE	Place code	City	Land area[1] (sq. mi)	Population, 2021: Total persons 2021	Population, 2021: Rank	Population, 2021: Per square mile	Race 2020: Race alone[2] (percent): White	Black or African American	American Indian, Alaskan Native	Asian	Hawaiian Pacific Islander	Some other race	Two or more races (percent)
			1	2	3	4	5	6	7	8	9	10	11
		NEW HAMPSHIRE—Cont'd											
33	45140	Manchester	33.1	115,462	253	3,488.3	76.7	5.5	0.3	4.2	0.0	5.2	7.9
33	50260	Nashua	30.8	91,124	374	2,958.6	73.1	3.0	0.3	7.8	0.0	6.8	9.0
33	65140	Rochester	45.0	32,869	1,201	730.4	90.3	1.1	0.2	1.6	0.0	0.8	6.0
34	00000	NEW JERSEY	7,354.8	9,267,130	X	1,260.0	55.0	13.1	0.6	10.2	0.0	11.3	9.7
34	02080	Atlantic City	10.8	38,466	1,035	3,561.7	19.2	35.6	0.7	16.2	0.6	17.1	10.6
34	03580	Bayonne	5.8	69,211	544	11,932.9	50.7	11.2	0.6	9.9	0.0	15.5	12.1
34	05170	Bergenfield	2.9	28,206	1,379	9,726.2	36.4	7.5	0.5	25.8	0.0	18.5	11.3
34	07600	Bridgeton	6.2	26,610	1,460	4,291.9	16.6	26.4	3.5	0.4	0.0	42.5	10.5
34	10000	Camden	8.9	71,773	513	8,064.4	10.4	42.0	1.1	1.8	0.1	32.5	12.1
34	10750	Carteret	4.4	25,152	1,540	5,716.4	27.6	16.2	0.7	22.9	0.0	19.9	12.7
34	13570	Cliffside Park	1.0	25,594	1,512	25,594.0	48.7	3.1	1.2	14.9	0.0	18.2	13.9
34	13690	Clifton	11.3	89,367	383	7,908.6	48.8	5.2	0.9	9.5	0.0	22.1	13.4
34	19390	East Orange	3.9	68,903	547	17,667.4	3.0	80.3	0.5	0.7	0.0	7.6	7.9
34	21000	Elizabeth	12.3	135,407	207	11,008.7	20.1	17.7	1.1	2.1	0.0	37.4	21.6
34	21480	Englewood	4.9	29,113	1,344	5,941.4	33.6	26.1	0.7	9.8	0.1	17.0	12.7
34	22470	Fair Lawn	5.1	35,159	1,133	6,893.9	69.3	2.6	0.2	12.9	0.0	5.7	9.4
34	24420	Fort Lee	2.5	39,871	994	15,948.4	40.8	3.4	0.1	42.3	0.0	5.9	7.5
34	25770	Garfield	2.1	32,469	1,217	15,461.4	55.8	6.2	0.8	3.2	0.0	21.3	12.6
34	28680	Hackensack	4.2	45,646	867	10,868.1	29.3	22.1	1.2	10.4	0.0	24.1	12.8
34	32250	Hoboken	1.3	58,690	668	45,146.2	70.7	4.1	0.2	10.9	0.1	5.3	8.7
34	36000	Jersey City	14.7	283,927	75	19,314.8	27.3	19.9	0.7	28.0	0.1	14.4	9.7
34	36510	Kearny	8.8	40,370	983	4,587.5	42.0	3.5	0.8	5.0	0.1	29.2	19.3
34	40350	Linden	10.7	43,594	914	4,074.2	37.0	28.0	0.5	3.5	0.0	17.7	13.3
34	41100	Lodi	2.3	25,966	1,495	11,289.6	45.2	8.8	0.5	8.4	0.0	21.6	15.5
34	41310	Long Branch	5.1	32,383	1,219	6,349.6	45.8	10.7	1.4	1.9	0.0	23.3	16.8
34	46680	Millville	42.0	27,638	1,406	658.0	56.9	22.6	0.7	1.2	0.0	6.6	12.0
34	51000	Newark	24.1	307,220	66	12,747.7	12.1	49.4	0.7	1.6	0.1	23.9	12.1
34	51210	New Brunswick	5.2	55,708	707	10,713.1	24.2	12.4	1.7	10.5	0.1	39.1	12.0
34	55950	Paramus	10.4	26,416	1,470	2,540.0	60.3	1.9	0.1	26.2	0.0	3.8	7.7
34	56550	Passaic	3.1	69,633	541	22,462.3	21.5	7.5	3.2	3.9	0.1	48.6	15.2
34	57000	Paterson	8.4	157,794	163	18,785.0	14.1	24.9	1.5	5.1	0.1	40.2	14.1
34	58200	Perth Amboy	4.7	55,291	719	11,764.0	17.4	8.3	1.3	1.2	0.1	51.0	20.8
34	59190	Plainfield	6.0	54,936	723	9,156.0	10.0	35.9	1.9	1.0	0.1	38.6	12.5
34	60900	Princeton	17.9	30,872	1,276	1,724.7	59.2	6.0	0.3	22.0	0.0	3.9	8.5
34	61530	Rahway	3.9	29,911	1,312	7,669.5	34.4	31.6	0.8	5.6	0.0	14.3	13.4
34	63000	Ridgewood	5.7	26,202	1,479	4,596.8	70.2	1.4	0.1	17.6	0.0	1.8	8.7
34	65790	Sayreville	15.8	45,086	879	2,853.5	52.8	13.3	0.3	16.9	0.0	7.0	9.7
34	74000	Trenton	7.6	90,457	378	11,902.2	13.2	43.7	1.5	0.7	0.1	30.0	10.9
34	74630	Union City	1.3	65,638	580	50,490.8	20.7	3.4	2.4	3.7	0.0	46.6	23.2
34	76070	Vineland	68.4	61,156	630	894.1	47.0	14.0	1.1	2.2	0.0	20.5	15.3
34	79040	Westfield	6.7	30,754	1,284	4,590.1	78.2	2.6	0.1	8.9	0.0	1.8	8.4
34	79610	West New York	1.0	52,242	761	52,242.0	22.3	3.4	2.5	7.2	0.0	42.6	22.0
35	00000	NEW MEXICO	121,312.2	2,115,877	X	17.4	51.0	2.2	10.0	1.8	0.1	15.0	19.9
35	01780	Alamogordo	21.4	31,652	1,251	1,479.1	62.9	6.2	1.7	2.4	0.4	9.4	17.0
35	02000	Albuquerque	187.3	562,599	32	3,003.7	52.2	3.5	5.6	3.4	0.1	14.2	21.0
35	12150	Carlsbad	31.5	31,888	1,241	1,012.3	57.0	2.3	1.5	1.4	0.1	19.8	17.9
35	16420	Clovis	23.6	37,988	1,048	1,609.7	55.6	6.9	1.3	1.9	0.1	17.7	16.5
35	25800	Farmington	34.5	46,422	858	1,345.6	48.8	1.0	30.7	1.1	0.1	7.8	10.6
35	32520	Hobbs	26.4	39,756	997	1,505.9	42.3	5.6	1.4	1.2	0.0	26.5	22.8
35	39380	Las Cruces	76.9	112,914	267	1,468.3	51.9	2.7	2.3	1.9	0.1	16.6	24.5
35	63460	Rio Rancho	103.4	105,834	299	1,023.5	60.2	2.9	4.2	2.1	0.2	10.5	19.8
35	64930	Roswell	29.7	48,081	827	1,618.9	54.8	2.2	1.5	1.2	0.1	20.9	19.2
35	70500	Santa Fe	52.2	88,193	392	1,689.5	55.7	1.1	2.4	1.9	0.1	16.0	22.8
36	00000	NEW YORK	47,123.8	19,835,913	X	420.9	55.2	14.8	0.7	9.6	0.1	10.9	8.7
36	01000	Albany	21.4	98,617	336	4,608.3	46.8	31.3	0.4	8.1	0.1	5.5	8.0
36	03078	Auburn	8.3	26,664	1,455	3,212.5	81.9	7.9	0.4	0.7	0.0	1.3	7.8
36	06607	Binghamton	10.5	47,566	839	4,530.1	66.8	14.7	0.5	6.0	0.0	2.8	9.2
36	11000	Buffalo	40.4	276,807	78	6,851.7	41.9	36.9	0.7	7.6	0.1	5.3	7.5
36	24229	Elmira	7.3	26,299	1,474	3,602.6	72.3	14.9	0.4	0.8	0.0	2.0	9.6
36	27485	Freeport	4.6	44,199	900	9,608.5	21.8	30.4	1.2	1.9	0.1	30.4	14.2
36	29113	Glen Cove	6.7	28,131	1,385	4,198.7	57.1	6.2	0.8	5.2	0.0	17.3	13.4
36	32402	Harrison	16.8	28,774	1,360	1,712.7	70.2	3.2	0.3	11.5	0.1	6.4	8.3
36	33139	Hempstead	3.7	58,734	667	15,874.1	9.3	40.2	1.2	2.1	0.1	35.3	11.8
36	38077	Ithaca	5.4	31,710	1,248	5,872.2	63.8	6.4	0.3	16.6	0.0	4.4	8.3
36	38264	Jamestown	8.9	28,393	1,369	3,190.2	78.7	4.6	0.6	0.6	0.1	4.9	10.6
36	39853	Kiryas Joel	1.5	36,229	1,094	24,152.7	70.7	0.2	0.1	0.1	0.0	26.7	2.2

1. Dry land or land partially or temporarily covered by water. 2. Hispanic or Latino persons may be of any race.

City	Percent Hispanic or Latino[1], 2020	Percent foreign born, 2016–2020	Age of population (percent), 2016–2020: Under 18 years	18 to 24 years	25 to 34 years	35 to 44 years	45 to 54 years	55 to 64 years	65 years and over	Median age, 2016–2020	Percent female, 2016–2020	Population: Census counts: 2010	Census counts: 2020	Percent change: 2010–2020	Percent change: 2020–2021
	12	13	14	15	16	17	18	19	20	21	22	23	24	25	26
NEW HAMPSHIRE—Cont'd															
Manchester	11.8	14.6	18.4	10.3	18.8	13.0	12.9	13.0	13.7	36.7	49.2	109,542	115,555	5.5	-0.1
Nashua	13.9	16.0	19.7	8.3	16.1	11.9	13.4	14.0	16.5	39.5	49.9	86,475	91,405	5.7	-0.3
Rochester	3.1	3.3	20.6	8.0	11.5	12.8	13.6	14.8	18.7	43.3	49.5	29,789	32,518	9.2	1.1
NEW JERSEY	21.6	22.7	22.0	8.6	12.9	12.8	13.9	13.6	16.2	40.0	51.1	8,791,959	9,288,994	5.7	-0.2
Atlantic City	29.9	30.8	25.1	9.2	12.7	11.6	12.8	13.5	15.1	37.1	50.0	39,552	38,504	-2.6	-0.1
Bayonne	30.8	30.3	22.6	7.4	14.7	14.1	12.7	13.6	14.8	38.3	51.1	63,015	71,555	13.6	-3.3
Bergenfield	32.2	36.1	22.1	9.4	13.2	12.4	11.8	15.7	15.5	38.8	51.8	26,839	28,345	5.6	-0.5
Bridgeton	60.0	21.9	30.6	9.3	18.1	17.1	9.5	8.0	7.5	30.2	45.6	25,377	26,759	5.4	-0.6
Camden	52.8	15.1	28.8	10.5	14.1	13.6	11.4	11.1	10.4	32.2	52.6	76,874	72,001	-6.3	-0.3
Carteret	36.9	36.0	22.9	7.7	16.8	10.9	13.0	15.5	13.3	38.0	51.0	22,846	25,308	10.8	-0.6
Cliffside Park	34.8	47.0	18.7	6.6	16.3	12.4	12.4	13.3	20.3	42.1	52.6	23,551	25,700	9.1	-0.4
Clifton	40.0	37.6	20.1	9.0	14.4	13.5	12.0	13.9	17.2	39.5	52.3	84,175	90,222	7.2	-0.9
East Orange	13.0	27.3	23.2	9.3	17.3	13.2	11.6	11.7	13.7	35.2	53.8	64,346	69,725	8.4	-1.2
Elizabeth	65.7	47.5	26.1	9.8	14.2	14.6	13.3	11.2	10.7	34.9	50.6	124,974	137,316	9.9	-1.4
Englewood	32.9	36.2	21.6	7.4	11.5	12.9	15.8	13.6	17.2	43.1	54.1	27,116	29,313	8.1	-0.7
Fair Lawn	15.4	31.2	23.2	7.2	8.7	14.6	13.9	13.5	18.7	41.5	52.4	32,379	34,940	7.9	0.6
Fort Lee	13.4	49.3	16.6	5.0	12.2	14.4	13.0	13.8	25.0	46.5	51.6	35,426	40,206	13.5	-0.8
Garfield	39.1	45.3	19.9	10.1	15.6	13.0	14.1	13.3	13.9	37.9	51.3	30,497	32,662	7.1	-0.6
Hackensack	41.8	38.6	16.7	7.4	18.7	15.2	12.8	13.1	16.0	39.2	52.9	43,024	45,977	6.9	-0.7
Hoboken	14.1	19.4	13.5	10.7	35.1	18.0	9.1	6.6	6.9	32.0	50.2	50,020	60,675	21.3	-3.3
Jersey City	24.9	42.5	20.7	7.7	23.4	16.4	10.8	9.9	11.1	34.2	50.0	247,608	292,412	18.1	-2.9
Kearny	48.7	46.8	21.2	8.1	16.8	14.3	13.6	12.4	13.7	37.6	47.8	40,711	42,165	3.6	-4.3
Linden	34.4	34.0	21.0	7.7	14.1	13.7	15.2	13.7	14.6	40.5	51.9	40,533	43,717	7.9	-0.3
Lodi	41.4	38.6	20.0	9.6	15.3	13.1	13.7	12.8	15.6	39.4	54.0	24,091	26,207	8.8	-0.9
Long Branch	32.6	29.4	22.1	10.9	13.3	14.2	11.3	12.0	16.1	37.2	50.9	30,717	31,661	3.1	2.3
Millville	19.0	6.0	20.8	7.6	11.7	11.0	16.4	14.4	18.1	44.1	52.1	28,422	27,789	-2.2	-0.5
Newark	36.4	32.5	24.4	10.3	16.1	14.0	13.4	11.2	10.6	34.5	51.1	276,941	310,876	12.3	-1.2
New Brunswick	56.8	31.3	21.9	30.8	13.9	12.1	8.6	6.3	6.3	23.5	49.5	54,500	55,443	1.7	0.5
Paramus	10.5	30.2	18.6	7.2	9.1	11.3	12.2	16.1	25.6	48.5	49.8	26,342	26,661	1.2	-0.9
Passaic	73.1	40.6	32.8	11.0	14.0	13.8	11.1	8.6	8.7	29.6	50.6	69,751	70,466	1.0	-1.2
Paterson	61.9	42.5	27.0	10.1	15.1	12.8	12.6	10.7	11.7	33.4	51.2	146,184	159,674	9.2	-1.2
Perth Amboy	83.2	43.9	24.7	10.9	14.8	13.0	13.9	10.9	11.8	34.8	50.5	50,827	55,414	9.0	-0.2
Plainfield	54.6	36.2	27.2	8.5	15.7	14.4	12.5	10.1	11.7	34.2	48.5	49,549	54,609	10.2	0.6
Princeton	9.8	29.7	19.2	22.5	10.6	8.7	12.9	10.3	15.7	31.8	50.3	28,584	31,026	8.5	-0.5
Rahway	30.0	23.0	20.0	8.5	17.0	13.8	12.8	12.9	14.9	38.2	49.4	27,320	29,538	8.1	1.3
Ridgewood	8.0	20.1	29.3	6.5	6.4	12.1	19.3	12.2	14.2	42.1	51.0	24,950	25,985	4.1	0.8
Sayreville	17.4	30.7	20.8	6.4	16.9	13.8	13.8	14.7	13.6	39.0	50.7	42,775	45,315	5.9	-0.5
Trenton	45.0	22.6	26.4	8.7	15.0	14.0	12.6	12.1	11.3	35.0	51.3	84,962	90,857	6.9	-0.4
Union City	82.4	54.9	21.9	9.6	15.5	15.7	15.1	10.3	11.9	36.9	51.9	66,467	68,512	3.1	-4.2
Vineland	43.3	10.2	24.6	9.7	12.5	11.9	12.0	12.5	16.7	37.8	52.2	60,717	61,305	1.0	-0.2
Westfield	7.2	11.5	28.4	6.7	7.3	12.7	16.3	14.0	14.6	40.8	52.0	30,296	31,004	2.3	-0.8
West New York	75.8	59.4	22.1	6.6	20.1	16.1	13.7	9.2	12.3	35.8	49.2	49,686	52,798	6.3	-1.1
NEW MEXICO	47.7	9.2	23.1	9.5	13.5	12.1	11.5	13.0	17.4	38.1	50.5	2,059,199	2,117,522	2.8	-0.1
Alamogordo	33.2	6.5	22.7	8.7	14.8	12.2	10.9	12.0	18.6	38.2	50.4	30,402	31,358	3.1	0.9
Albuquerque	47.7	9.8	21.9	9.1	15.8	13.1	11.9	12.5	15.7	37.1	51.3	546,121	564,563	3.4	-0.3
Carlsbad	50.6	5.3	22.9	10.1	15.3	13.1	10.3	13.3	15.1	36.7	48.1	26,245	32,241	22.8	-1.1
Clovis	47.1	10.5	26.9	11.3	18.2	12.3	9.5	10.2	11.6	31.5	48.8	37,808	38,324	1.4	-0.9
Farmington	22.4	3.0	28.7	9.1	12.7	15.1	11.4	9.8	13.1	34.6	49.7	45,947	46,684	1.6	-0.6
Hobbs	61.9	17.8	30.0	10.5	15.7	12.0	11.4	10.6	9.9	30.8	47.5	34,051	40,508	19.0	-1.9
Las Cruces	60.3	11.5	23.0	15.8	14.4	11.1	9.9	9.7	16.1	32.5	50.6	97,700	111,507	14.1	1.3
Rio Rancho	41.6	5.1	24.6	8.0	12.9	13.3	12.4	12.8	15.9	38.4	51.2	87,389	103,977	19.0	1.8
Roswell	58.8	13.3	26.5	10.6	13.0	11.2	11.7	11.7	15.3	34.9	51.2	48,421	48,539	0.2	-0.9
Santa Fe	51.0	14.2	18.1	8.6	11.9	12.1	12.5	13.2	23.7	44.4	52.5	80,879	87,497	8.2	0.8
NEW YORK	19.5	22.4	20.9	9.2	14.7	12.4	13.1	13.2	16.5	39.0	51.5	19,378,117	20,201,249	4.2	-1.8
Albany	11.6	15.5	17.1	21.9	16.8	10.8	10.1	10.1	13.2	30.7	53.4	97,836	99,345	1.5	-0.7
Auburn	4.1	2.7	18.4	7.2	16.7	13.6	10.8	14.3	19.0	40.4	49.2	27,690	26,868	-3.0	-0.8
Binghamton	8.7	10.3	17.9	17.9	13.3	10.5	11.0	13.6	15.8	35.6	50.9	47,403	48,007	1.3	-0.9
Buffalo	12.8	10.4	22.4	12.0	18.1	11.6	10.9	12.1	13.0	33.4	52.4	261,346	278,302	6.5	-0.5
Elmira	6.0	2.2	23.2	10.8	15.0	13.2	12.4	11.4	13.9	35.5	50.5	29,245	26,379	-9.8	-0.3
Freeport	47.9	32.1	21.0	9.4	14.0	13.2	13.7	12.2	16.6	39.2	51.9	42,856	44,479	3.8	-0.6
Glen Cove	34.4	31.8	20.0	10.0	12.1	11.6	14.8	12.0	19.5	41.8	53.8	26,952	28,313	5.0	-0.6
Harrison	15.6	22.2	23.8	17.9	8.1	14.2	14.0	9.6	12.4	35.2	52.6	27,469	28,652	4.3	0.4
Hempstead	50.1	39.3	25.9	9.5	14.2	15.6	12.1	10.2	12.4	35.2	53.0	54,018	59,113	9.4	-0.6
Ithaca	10.0	17.5	8.3	53.4	12.4	8.5	5.2	6.0	6.3	22.1	49.3	30,013	31,853	6.1	-0.4
Jamestown	13.4	2.1	23.9	8.3	15.3	10.9	12.0	13.1	16.6	37.2	51.9	31,160	28,643	-8.1	-0.9
Kiryas Joel	1.4	6.7	59.5	13.4	11.2	8.7	3.3	1.4	2.4	14.1	47.7	20,365	32,996	62.0	9.8

1. May be of any race.

City	Households, 2016–2020: Number	Households, 2016–2020: Persons per household	Households, 2016–2020: Percent: Family	Households, 2016–2020: Percent: Married couple family	Households, 2016–2020: Percent: Female family	Households, 2016–2020: Percent: Non-family	Households, 2016–2020: Percent: One person	Persons in group quarters, 2016–2020	Serious crimes known to police[2], 2020: Violent: Number	Serious crimes known to police[2], 2020: Violent: Rate	Serious crimes known to police[2], 2020: Property: Number	Serious crimes known to police[2], 2020: Property: Rate	Educational attainment, 2016–2020: Population age 25 and over	Educational attainment, 2016–2020: Attainment[4] (percent): High school graduate or less	Educational attainment, 2016–2020: Attainment[4] (percent): Bachelor's degree or more
	27	28	29	30	31	32	33	34	35	36	37	38	39	40	41
NEW HAMPSHIRE—Cont'd															
Manchester	47,239	2.33	53.9	36.7	11.0	46.1	33.8	2,502	670	592.8	2,560	2,265.1	80,221	41.2	30.8
Nashua	36,446	2.40	59.0	43.6	11.3	41.0	31.8	1,584	107	119.3	818	912.2	64,089	34.7	37.1
Rochester	13,151	2.37	62.8	47.7	8.8	37.2	28.7	171	72	226.7	NA	NA	22,351	45.6	20.9
NEW JERSEY	3,272,054	2.66	68.7	51.0	12.8	31.3	26.0	182,577	17,353	195.4	102,875	1,158.2	6,169,501	36.5	40.7
Atlantic City	15,775	2.36	53.2	24.7	21.5	46.8	40.4	638	309	822.9	1,013	2,697.7	24,834	59.4	18.2
Bayonne	24,784	2.62	65.5	44.3	15.5	34.5	30.6	270	118	181.5	647	995.2	45,582	41.3	37.8
Bergenfield	9,037	3.02	73.8	55.7	13.0	26.2	21.3	62	13	47.5	84	307.2	18,749	32.1	46.2
Bridgeton	6,270	3.25	64.8	25.4	30.7	35.2	27.8	3,891	234	973.7	737	3,066.7	14,592	74.8	6.9
Camden	25,411	2.80	65.6	17.9	37.7	34.4	29.8	2,547	1,172	1,602.7	1,579	2,159.3	44,734	67.0	10.0
Carteret	8,036	2.92	70.8	50.8	14.3	29.2	24.9	10	39	166.4	263	1,121.8	16,311	49.3	28.2
Cliffside Park	10,592	2.40	64.9	50.0	9.8	35.1	30.4	5	15	56.8	87	329.5	18,979	33.3	46.6
Clifton	29,863	2.83	71.1	50.0	14.6	28.9	24.0	626	82	96.4	1,334	1,568.3	60,409	43.5	33.8
East Orange	24,210	2.63	56.9	23.4	25.4	43.1	36.8	1,045	294	457.1	810	1,259.3	43,650	50.0	20.0
Elizabeth	41,729	3.03	71.1	39.8	21.4	28.9	24.2	1,915	774	597.6	2,897	2,236.8	82,375	62.7	14.4
Englewood	11,064	2.55	69.7	46.5	18.1	30.3	26.7	205	51	178.9	327	1,146.8	20,162	33.7	45.5
Fair Lawn	11,488	2.85	78.0	65.2	9.8	22.0	19.1	191	12	36.5	244	741.4	22,954	21.7	58.5
Fort Lee	17,396	2.17	57.2	45.8	8.5	42.8	36.9	12	39	100.2	374	960.9	29,699	22.3	60.2
Garfield	11,629	2.72	72.1	45.2	17.9	27.9	23.3	42	35	109.7	357	1,118.8	22,183	55.1	22.3
Hackensack	19,537	2.21	50.5	29.8	15.7	49.5	41.0	1,149	54	122.0	573	1,294.5	33,582	38.3	39.4
Hoboken	24,983	2.07	44.8	35.1	7.4	55.2	32.4	1,465	66	124.8	774	1,463.1	40,387	12.8	79.6
Jersey City	103,880	2.50	59.0	39.4	14.4	41.0	30.3	2,581	1,167	443.3	3,940	1,496.5	187,996	33.4	49.8
Kearny	13,710	2.85	75.8	51.5	15.8	24.2	20.1	2,067	45	109.7	473	1,152.6	29,122	52.8	26.7
Linden	14,728	2.85	73.0	49.0	16.9	27.0	23.8	302	142	334.0	1,106	2,601.4	30,169	47.5	23.2
Lodi	8,825	2.75	66.7	43.2	18.2	33.3	26.1	131	22	90.4	183	751.8	17,171	47.4	25.6
Long Branch	12,098	2.50	61.9	39.4	16.8	38.1	29.9	171	92	304.9	560	1,855.8	20,366	48.9	28.3
Millville	11,500	2.37	64.2	42.4	15.6	35.8	29.5	246	173	634.4	928	3,402.8	19,665	54.0	17.9
Newark	102,195	2.63	59.8	27.4	25.4	40.2	35.6	13,496	1,492	528.6	4,567	1,618.1	184,100	59.9	15.5
New Brunswick	15,546	3.03	57.7	28.9	20.3	42.3	26.2	8,812	285	511.7	964	1,730.7	26,476	60.9	23.0
Paramus	8,334	2.96	79.9	66.0	10.8	20.1	18.4	1,719	23	87.7	455	1,735.2	19,587	28.8	48.3
Passaic	19,817	3.51	76.0	35.9	31.8	24.0	20.7	328	279	400.8	1,028	1,476.8	39,198	68.9	15.6
Paterson	45,627	3.14	73.8	35.6	29.9	26.2	21.5	2,112	1,433	988.6	2,160	1,490.2	91,525	67.6	11.5
Perth Amboy	16,527	3.09	75.0	38.5	24.8	25.0	20.5	590	137	266.6	508	988.6	33,207	64.7	15.3
Plainfield	15,626	3.13	71.1	38.7	22.0	28.9	24.2	1,340	228	453.0	733	1,456.3	32,319	58.4	20.8
Princeton	9,806	2.59	67.6	58.5	5.9	32.4	24.7	5,747	11	35.0	196	623.1	18,152	8.1	84.5
Rahway	11,621	2.54	64.8	40.0	16.8	35.2	31.0	136	43	142.6	201	666.5	21,232	45.1	30.3
Ridgewood	8,417	2.96	79.5	68.3	8.9	20.5	17.4	221	8	32.0	133	531.2	16,119	12.9	75.9
Sayreville	16,780	2.64	67.4	49.6	11.7	32.6	28.5	15	55	124.2	260	587.1	32,185	37.6	35.8
Trenton	28,581	2.79	58.1	27.4	24.5	41.9	36.3	3,570	969	1,168.8	1,733	2,090.2	54,129	62.3	14.2
Union City	25,528	2.65	66.0	36.0	19.8	34.0	26.8	488	203	298.3	1,185	1,741.2	46,640	58.7	23.1
Vineland	21,199	2.70	68.5	44.4	16.2	31.5	26.2	2,128	227	382.9	1,239	2,089.8	39,015	52.6	21.2
Westfield	10,188	2.88	76.8	69.4	6.0	23.2	21.2	323	8	27.2	172	585.3	19,249	13.2	74.7
West New York	18,951	2.78	67.1	39.8	17.7	32.9	23.5	111	106	200.1	587	1,108.0	37,665	51.9	32.7
NEW MEXICO	792,755	2.59	62.7	43.0	13.7	37.3	31.0	42,919	16,393	778.3	59,859	2,841.9	1,415,298	39.7	28.1
Alamogordo	12,830	2.42	55.7	42.1	9.8	44.3	38.1	582	NA	NA	NA	NA	21,696	37.1	21.8
Albuquerque	229,701	2.42	56.6	36.4	14.2	43.4	35.9	5,633	7,552	1,343.6	28,171	5,012.1	386,527	31.4	36.5
Carlsbad	11,088	2.59	66.6	45.7	11.2	33.4	29.5	562	195	645.0	1,039	3,436.6	19,621	46.7	19.4
Clovis	14,758	2.59	63.3	40.7	16.1	36.7	31.4	517	NA	NA	NA	NA	23,931	45.7	20.2
Farmington	15,910	2.74	69.7	48.9	13.2	30.3	25.4	1,425	529	1,197.1	1,447	3,274.4	27,947	36.2	20.7
Hobbs	12,627	2.89	70.0	46.9	15.4	30.0	25.5	1,973	NA	NA	NA	NA	22,908	54.6	16.3
Las Cruces	41,467	2.45	57.8	36.7	14.9	42.2	31.5	1,472	NA	NA	NA	NA	63,021	31.2	36.8
Rio Rancho	35,476	2.75	73.6	55.8	13.0	26.4	19.6	523	NA	NA	NA	NA	66,018	30.2	31.6
Roswell	17,576	2.61	65.6	41.5	17.3	34.4	31.3	1,866	NA	NA	NA	NA	30,028	47.1	18.6
Santa Fe	36,096	2.30	53.8	36.8	12.2	46.2	38.3	1,412	NA	NA	NA	NA	61,897	33.3	42.0
NEW YORK	7,417,224	2.55	63.0	44.0	14.0	37.0	29.8	569,176	70,339	363.8	272,788	1,410.7	13,649,157	38.2	37.5
Albany	41,614	2.08	42.6	23.5	15.7	57.4	41.8	10,266	869	902.2	2,650	2,751.3	59,128	32.6	42.5
Auburn	11,411	2.10	49.9	27.9	16.3	50.1	38.8	2,407	NA	NA	NA	NA	19,624	44.3	19.5
Binghamton	20,052	2.15	46.0	26.9	16.1	54.0	39.5	1,655	372	843.9	1,775	4,026.5	28,767	43.8	27.9
Buffalo	110,896	2.23	49.9	24.4	20.0	50.1	40.5	8,925	2,592	1,018.0	7,844	3,080.6	167,836	41.8	28.6
Elmira	9,999	2.38	57.9	32.4	19.1	42.1	36.9	3,400	59	220.0	812	3,027.6	17,978	55.2	15.4
Freeport	14,345	2.96	70.0	42.2	20.1	30.0	24.3	482	NA	NA	NA	NA	29,962	48.2	25.7
Glen Cove	10,201	2.59	66.1	43.0	15.3	33.9	28.7	712	3	11.0	107	393.6	19,012	42.8	39.9
Harrison	8,262	3.00	76.5	65.3	6.5	23.5	17.2	3,598	6	20.6	126	432.8	16,520	23.8	58.0
Hempstead	16,290	3.33	73.7	33.4	33.0	26.3	22.3	842	357	646.4	568	1,028.4	35,630	57.9	18.4
Ithaca	11,732	1.99	28.6	21.7	5.6	71.4	38.1	7,399	98	316.9	1,157	3,741.1	11,762	16.0	69.0
Jamestown	12,979	2.20	52.7	30.4	16.1	47.3	39.1	683	NA	NA	NA	NA	19,863	46.2	19.3
Kiryas Joel	4,588	5.60	98.3	96.5	1.7	1.7	1.6	231	NA	NA	NA	NA	7,010	72.6	7.2

2. Data for serious crimes have not been adjusted for underreporting. This may affect comparability between geographic areas and over time. 4. Persons 25 years old and over.

City	Money income, 2016–2020					Median earnings Full year, Full-time workers, 2016–2020			Housing units, 2016–2020				
	Households												
	Median household income	Percent with income less than $25,000	Percent with income of $200,000 or more	Median family income	Median non-family household income	All persons	Men	Women	Total	Occupied	Percent owner occupied	Median value[1] (dollars)	Median gross rent (dollars)
	42	43	44	45	46	47	48	49	50	51	52	53	54
NEW HAMPSHIRE—Cont'd													
Manchester	62,087	17.3	4.0	74,559	44,544	46,516	50,127	42,535	50,177	47,239	45.0	241,600	1,160
Nashua	73,785	13.9	8.0	92,400	45,496	54,725	61,554	48,406	37,767	36,446	54.7	279,800	1,309
Rochester	66,831	16.9	3.1	75,258	34,222	48,457	51,234	45,685	13,791	13,151	67.1	186,600	1,071
NEW JERSEY	85,245	14.5	14.8	104,804	47,603	62,597	70,131	55,118	3,628,732	3,272,054	64.0	343,500	1,368
Atlantic City	29,526	44.2	2.5	36,066	20,927	32,670	32,655	32,695	20,664	15,775	28.2	150,000	927
Bayonne	69,511	18.2	8.5	80,661	44,489	53,144	57,093	47,123	27,237	24,784	40.6	346,000	1,325
Bergenfield	102,724	12.3	12.4	115,333	54,974	60,162	64,944	51,770	9,376	9,037	68.5	369,500	1,420
Bridgeton	38,319	34.5	1.8	38,604	24,639	32,083	32,019	32,164	7,090	6,270	35.6	107,500	1,127
Camden	28,623	44.0	1.7	32,426	17,415	34,683	35,598	33,088	29,242	25,411	40.3	82,500	938
Carteret	76,276	16.5	7.1	80,000	52,109	49,397	49,386	49,413	8,456	8,036	57.8	281,000	1,521
Cliffside Park	83,989	16.4	13.9	91,464	58,973	66,078	74,048	59,601	11,444	10,592	50.3	454,400	1,552
Clifton	83,086	14.5	10.7	96,087	43,921	52,702	55,829	46,935	31,373	29,863	56.2	354,700	1,428
East Orange	50,990	27.1	2.6	60,334	37,293	43,914	44,292	43,392	28,019	24,210	24.0	226,000	1,156
Elizabeth	50,647	20.8	2.9	53,541	31,625	36,774	39,546	32,375	45,133	41,729	25.9	291,300	1,201
Englewood	86,485	13.7	22.6	96,467	67,892	63,110	70,153	57,538	11,894	11,064	53.1	403,800	1,511
Fair Lawn	129,965	7.7	25.8	154,100	71,474	83,637	95,518	73,620	11,824	11,488	80.4	439,100	1,826
Fort Lee	88,457	15.0	13.1	112,464	61,150	76,027	85,479	69,071	18,768	17,396	58.1	348,300	1,909
Garfield	64,242	18.6	8.1	70,917	41,880	48,305	53,773	41,330	12,336	11,629	44.6	357,000	1,355
Hackensack	71,079	17.8	7.9	76,563	57,736	55,835	56,352	55,145	20,836	19,537	33.7	306,700	1,493
Hoboken	153,438	9.5	36.9	200,132	122,266	101,348	114,887	89,198	27,740	24,983	34.6	759,800	2,360
Jersey City	76,444	18.6	14.7	83,554	61,273	65,737	69,822	61,569	113,854	103,880	29.6	406,200	1,485
Kearny	73,554	13.2	5.2	77,046	47,332	48,082	51,679	43,250	14,420	13,710	46.6	354,700	1,338
Linden	75,084	12.4	4.2	85,093	41,122	50,376	54,108	46,732	15,720	14,728	59.9	293,700	1,362
Lodi	64,249	20.4	10.4	75,606	48,958	49,323	57,882	41,779	9,267	8,825	39.9	389,400	1,373
Long Branch	62,027	22.2	6.3	65,662	43,952	44,330	48,500	41,416	14,757	12,098	40.4	367,000	1,370
Millville	63,182	24.5	7.3	71,250	33,757	47,005	53,323	39,231	12,656	11,500	67.7	165,900	1,003
Newark	37,476	35.2	2.0	45,507	25,456	37,844	41,081	34,248	114,410	102,195	23.5	254,900	1,116
New Brunswick	43,930	34.4	5.0	48,452	33,163	38,984	42,391	34,539	16,605	15,546	19.5	267,200	1,524
Paramus	130,273	10.1	24.0	141,619	48,868	80,720	84,987	71,936	8,776	8,334	82.6	614,900	2,503
Passaic	44,779	27.9	3.4	43,926	24,411	32,344	34,374	30,524	20,642	19,817	21.5	348,000	1,189
Paterson	45,141	30.1	2.4	49,352	24,255	36,361	38,364	32,829	49,034	45,627	26.0	257,700	1,213
Perth Amboy	54,188	24.0	3.6	52,279	34,590	38,118	41,642	32,772	17,388	16,527	30.5	270,500	1,387
Plainfield	58,400	20.1	6.4	64,140	33,206	38,239	40,208	35,585	16,848	15,626	43.4	268,000	1,260
Princeton	146,127	11.8	39.7	225,065	61,761	101,892	131,646	91,320	10,931	9,806	56.4	872,400	1,704
Rahway	77,393	15.9	8.1	94,247	47,336	61,841	72,188	51,459	12,249	11,621	57.5	276,500	1,271
Ridgewood	178,958	4.2	47.2	222,147	102,941	140,266	153,621	91,351	8,740	8,417	81.1	744,200	2,062
Sayreville	82,693	11.0	9.3	98,618	47,574	59,198	66,275	53,153	17,252	16,780	62.4	312,500	1,351
Trenton	37,002	37.9	2.4	51,073	20,502	37,083	39,307	35,664	34,514	28,581	38.4	97,000	1,085
Union City	49,457	27.6	4.4	53,090	34,095	36,149	37,670	33,251	27,462	25,528	19.8	360,000	1,247
Vineland	55,740	21.4	4.6	68,528	32,903	45,616	48,262	40,651	22,636	21,199	67.4	170,300	1,064
Westfield	158,323	7.9	41.7	202,331	58,672	113,069	131,824	91,296	10,670	10,188	80.8	773,200	1,713
West New York	64,378	20.7	6.8	61,506	58,602	43,220	45,222	40,126	20,690	18,951	22.4	340,800	1,366
NEW MEXICO	51,243	25.3	4.1	62,611	31,640	42,385	46,641	38,017	943,568	792,755	68.0	175,700	857
Alamogordo	45,786	24.6	2.2	61,396	33,472	36,873	43,981	31,533	14,964	12,830	60.0	125,400	787
Albuquerque	53,936	23.2	4.6	68,567	35,418	44,559	48,070	41,652	247,926	229,701	60.3	204,100	889
Carlsbad	69,786	19.3	3.5	84,063	37,897	51,308	61,572	36,714	13,023	11,088	70.7	150,300	1,050
Clovis	47,794	25.9	1.6	53,426	33,707	35,454	40,470	29,862	16,725	14,758	54.8	132,300	867
Farmington	56,576	20.6	3.1	65,490	37,461	48,179	52,216	42,718	17,943	15,910	63.0	188,500	892
Hobbs	57,646	20.2	5.2	65,840	31,837	50,401	60,542	35,892	14,569	12,627	60.1	144,000	923
Las Cruces	45,140	32.0	2.1	55,377	26,475	38,148	41,941	34,227	45,889	41,467	55.3	161,100	805
Rio Rancho	66,733	13.1	4.9	75,504	42,885	47,812	52,007	41,609	37,411	35,476	79.4	200,800	1,157
Roswell	45,493	29.8	2.3	54,177	24,635	36,741	41,108	31,209	20,134	17,576	64.3	110,000	819
Santa Fe	57,274	18.2	6.2	68,559	43,648	44,185	44,340	44,048	42,142	36,096	63.2	290,800	1,125
NEW YORK	71,117	19.1	11.5	87,270	43,646	56,743	61,136	52,786	8,362,971	7,417,224	54.1	325,000	1,315
Albany	48,512	27.2	4.3	66,070	38,611	47,216	49,408	45,273	48,665	41,614	36.7	186,800	992
Auburn	43,555	28.8	1.7	61,164	30,077	45,828	51,575	39,910	12,996	11,411	47.1	107,500	743
Binghamton	35,730	37.1	2.9	47,493	25,831	40,532	44,945	36,838	23,391	20,052	41.2	92,800	753
Buffalo	39,677	34.8	2.8	50,038	29,691	42,441	45,677	40,624	131,044	110,896	41.5	101,000	801
Elmira	36,543	34.3	1.4	46,152	23,183	38,149	42,760	34,787	12,324	9,999	50.8	76,200	727
Freeport	85,540	14.0	13.2	100,872	47,500	52,728	53,379	51,398	14,885	14,345	66.9	361,000	1,663
Glen Cove	79,131	19.4	14.0	98,673	38,125	55,795	64,851	48,324	10,743	10,201	54.2	509,500	1,828
Harrison	128,393	7.1	33.3	155,625	61,723	81,379	101,619	67,964	8,920	8,262	64.6	871,800	2,286
Hempstead	68,946	19.3	7.6	72,721	45,430	42,553	43,565	41,627	17,580	16,290	43.8	339,500	1,483
Ithaca	38,019	40.0	5.4	98,542	22,884	51,190	55,464	47,875	12,885	11,732	25.1	261,900	1,171
Jamestown	34,767	38.5	1.0	46,529	22,388	36,290	40,519	32,618	14,938	12,979	48.4	66,400	611
Kiryas Joel	35,437	34.7	1.5	35,542	23,571	45,279	49,315	30,625	4,942	4,588	29.0	530,700	1,245

1. Specified owner-occupied units

City	Commuting, 2016–2020[1]		Computer access[2], 2016–2020		Migration, 2016–2020		Civilian labor force, 2021				Civilian Employment, 2016–2020[4]			
	Percent		Percent						Unemployment[3]		Population age 16 and older		Population age 16 to 64	
	Drove alone	Mean travel time to work	With a computer in the house	With Internet access	Percent who lived in the same house one year ago	Percent who lived in another state or county one year ago	Total	Percent change 2020–2021	Total	Rate	Number	Percent in labor force	Number	Percent who worked full-year full-time
	55	56	57	58	59	60	61	62	63	64	65	66	67	68
NEW HAMPSHIRE—Cont'd														
Manchester	79.2	24.0	92.2	86.9	78.4	9.8	63,436	-2.1	2,528	4.0	94,053	70.7	78,673	56.7
Nashua	79.2	26.1	93.2	89.5	83.3	8.5	50,140	-1.2	2,097	4.2	73,472	69.9	58,778	56.9
Rochester	79.9	27.8	90.9	85.3	89.1	4.3	17,582	-1.0	618	3.5	25,701	65.5	19,834	58.8
NEW JERSEY	69.6	32.0	92.9	87.4	89.7	5.0	4,661,087	0.4	295,690	6.3	7,161,184	65.6	5,718,246	53.0
Atlantic City	45.7	21.8	82.2	68.2	80.6	3.8	15,294	-6.3	2,008	13.1	29,679	59.2	23,969	36.8
Bayonne	53.5	35.4	90.8	84.4	90.0	3.9	34,049	-1.2	2,792	8.2	51,762	64.4	42,097	52.9
Bergenfield	71.8	35.0	93.6	89.8	94.3	3.4	15,097	-0.2	825	5.5	21,820	70.3	17,588	54.7
Bridgeton	60.3	27.7	85.1	72.1	86.4	5.9	8,421	1.5	673	8.0	17,354	48.9	15,542	40.3
Camden	57.1	27.4	83.1	68.3	86.3	5.9	27,474	0.3	3,444	12.5	54,624	55.4	46,927	34.5
Carteret	74.7	30.6	88.2	75.9	89.3	6.1	12,115	0.2	922	7.6	18,567	63.6	15,453	51.2
Cliffside Park	53.8	37.2	92.3	88.1	88.4	7.0	13,663	0.0	755	5.5	21,527	62.1	16,376	54.3
Clifton	74.2	28.2	90.5	85.6	90.3	4.8	46,035	-0.8	3,289	7.1	69,767	67.9	55,138	56.2
East Orange	55.3	33.0	90.8	82.9	86.7	5.5	30,894	-0.9	3,125	10.1	51,349	66.0	42,465	49.8
Elizabeth	60.5	25.9	85.8	77.6	89.4	5.1	64,765	-0.8	5,243	8.1	98,220	68.1	84,458	52.5
Englewood	60.4	31.4	96.0	88.9	90.9	4.8	15,404	-0.3	985	6.4	23,074	67.2	18,181	55.3
Fair Lawn	64.9	34.4	95.2	91.7	92.4	5.2	18,479	0.2	1,081	5.8	26,023	68.9	19,843	58.7
Fort Lee	50.7	38.0	94.3	89.6	91.4	4.4	20,373	0.1	995	4.9	32,287	62.3	22,808	58.1
Garfield	71.7	27.1	89.9	83.2	93.0	3.2	16,722	-1.2	1,708	10.2	26,055	63.3	21,655	54.4
Hackensack	61.9	31.4	93.4	89.8	86.0	6.7	24,723	-0.9	1,815	7.3	37,522	69.0	30,441	60.4
Hoboken	21.7	39.0	95.8	94.0	80.1	10.5	36,673	1.9	1,205	3.3	46,372	79.4	42,689	67.8
Jersey City	30.2	37.2	93.2	87.4	85.9	7.1	143,989	-0.1	10,143	7.0	212,899	69.4	183,849	57.4
Kearny	68.4	31.9	93.3	88.0	90.0	5.1	20,692	-1.7	1,649	8.0	33,351	65.4	27,697	51.4
Linden	70.8	31.0	91.8	86.4	90.3	4.6	22,545	-0.3	1,710	7.6	34,574	68.5	28,380	52.6
Lodi	69.4	28.1	92.3	88.3	89.2	3.9	12,989	-1.7	1,173	9.0	20,217	65.1	16,418	55.3
Long Branch	61.7	31.1	91.8	83.0	88.0	5.5	16,683	1.5	968	5.8	24,511	65.7	19,598	45.3
Millville	85.9	25.5	90.5	82.9	91.0	1.2	13,775	-0.2	1,068	7.8	22,262	63.8	17,283	50.6
Newark	53.9	34.5	87.7	70.1	89.3	4.1	122,573	-0.8	13,033	10.6	219,996	61.1	190,082	42.9
New Brunswick	48.0	27.8	89.3	75.7	80.1	11.4	28,017	2.1	1,589	5.7	45,311	54.2	41,759	33.9
Paramus	68.6	31.1	91.6	89.7	91.4	3.8	12,799	-0.4	758	5.9	22,150	58.8	15,395	50.7
Passaic	48.6	26.8	89.0	83.4	91.7	2.8	29,866	-1.5	2,662	8.9	49,216	64.4	43,132	43.3
Paterson	66.0	24.3	87.0	75.3	91.4	2.0	63,836	-3.0	8,125	12.7	110,329	61.9	93,306	49.9
Perth Amboy	66.8	26.5	89.5	65.9	91.9	1.9	26,055	-1.5	2,676	10.3	40,393	63.0	34,303	47.1
Plainfield	65.9	32.9	86.5	74.2	89.7	5.2	27,275	0.5	2,197	8.1	37,889	68.5	32,010	53.1
Princeton	42.1	26.4	97.5	88.9	75.2	18.3	17,574	1.9	527	3.0	25,855	60.7	20,953	41.7
Rahway	68.2	33.2	91.2	86.1	84.3	7.8	15,494	0.2	1,147	7.4	24,203	68.3	19,772	57.0
Ridgewood	55.8	38.5	97.6	96.2	88.8	3.5	11,907	1.7	550	4.6	18,706	64.9	15,130	53.7
Sayreville	72.4	35.0	94.5	89.4	89.9	5.1	24,772	1.6	1,557	6.3	36,011	70.9	30,002	56.0
Trenton	59.8	25.6	84.2	66.7	84.9	5.0	41,613	0.1	3,372	8.1	63,544	57.1	54,158	40.3
Union City	33.3	34.3	91.3	81.7	92.4	3.0	35,218	-2.3	3,019	8.6	54,862	68.0	46,728	52.6
Vineland	81.0	22.3	89.8	82.5	89.1	4.0	29,549	0.2	2,221	7.5	46,287	60.2	36,353	45.9
Westfield	58.0	38.5	94.7	91.7	92.9	3.7	13,958	1.7	581	4.2	22,089	65.4	17,750	56.3
West New York	30.5	37.2	92.0	82.5	90.2	4.6	29,203	-1.1	1,994	6.8	41,953	71.4	35,460	57.2
NEW MEXICO	79.1	22.7	88.1	77.5	87.0	5.7	943,356	0.8	64,027	6.8	1,672,029	56.9	1,307,129	46.6
Alamogordo	82.9	17.1	91.3	85.4	77.6	11.8	13,060	0.5	812	6.2	25,243	53.0	19,346	51.5
Albuquerque	78.5	22.0	92.4	83.5	84.5	5.0	281,575	1.6	17,605	6.3	452,264	63.6	364,247	51.0
Carlsbad	82.6	20.7	89.2	81.5	87.0	4.3	15,905	-4.3	1,128	7.1	23,538	61.6	19,106	52.1
Clovis	83.8	16.1	89.0	82.4	76.1	9.9	17,430	0.6	900	5.2	29,496	57.9	24,997	51.5
Farmington	83.2	19.0	92.6	80.5	84.8	5.5	19,187	-1.5	1,434	7.5	33,535	58.3	27,632	46.1
Hobbs	84.3	22.4	89.1	79.8	88.2	5.9	15,040	-3.8	1,549	10.3	28,424	61.6	24,611	46.1
Las Cruces	77.1	18.5	92.1	80.7	83.3	7.1	47,907	1.0	3,010	6.3	82,179	58.0	65,653	41.2
Rio Rancho	79.3	27.9	95.7	90.5	87.8	6.9	47,142	1.9	3,053	6.5	76,708	62.5	61,106	51.1
Roswell	84.1	17.0	83.5	71.5	82.4	6.3	20,557	0.5	1,516	7.4	36,619	58.2	29,315	48.4
Santa Fe	77.2	19.7	91.2	82.4	87.9	5.8	41,766	1.7	2,667	6.4	71,186	60.2	51,184	50.1
NEW YORK	52.3	33.5	91.1	84.5	89.6	4.6	9,441,458	-1.4	655,178	6.9	15,908,940	62.9	12,687,238	50.6
Albany	57.8	18.5	89.9	81.9	77.1	10.8	46,175	-2.5	2,633	5.7	82,266	64.4	69,471	44.4
Auburn	81.2	19.6	87.9	78.3	80.7	7.8	11,249	-3.3	650	5.8	21,937	54.0	16,928	41.9
Binghamton	69.7	17.3	85.9	79.0	75.1	10.2	17,406	-3.1	1,089	6.3	37,840	57.8	30,770	34.7
Buffalo	67.9	20.0	88.3	79.3	82.7	4.7	107,599	-3.5	8,286	7.7	204,931	59.3	171,667	41.9
Elmira	71.4	18.1	88.5	79.3	85.2	4.4	9,543	-4.7	677	7.1	21,520	54.2	17,722	35.2
Freeport	69.6	32.1	92.6	89.1	94.7	1.4	22,963	-1.3	1,406	6.1	35,186	65.4	28,059	51.9
Glen Cove	71.4	30.5	91.2	86.2	91.5	4.3	14,123	0.0	626	4.4	22,456	60.2	17,150	52.9
Harrison	54.3	31.6	95.4	93.0	88.8	7.6	13,674	0.0	573	4.2	22,717	61.7	19,208	42.2
Hempstead	59.0	32.7	92.0	81.3	91.2	3.8	27,898	-1.2	1,807	6.5	41,980	66.2	35,135	52.8
Ithaca	28.6	17.4	96.9	79.7	55.8	24.8	13,257	-1.2	512	3.9	28,664	53.8	26,742	21.0
Jamestown	76.0	14.7	85.4	76.2	85.2	5.0	11,191	-3.3	659	5.9	22,936	58.3	18,084	44.5
Kiryas Joel	34.5	22.4	30.6	20.4	95.2	1.0	5,678	-0.8	238	4.2	11,751	45.4	11,135	26.1

1. Employed persons. 2. Households. 3. Percent of civilian labor force. 4. Persons 16 years old and over.

City	Value of residential construction authorized by building permits, 2021			Wholesale trade[1], 2017				Retail trade[2], 2017			
	New construction ($1,000)	Number of housing units	Percent single family	Number of establishments	Number of employees	Sales (mil dol)	Annual payroll (mil dol)	Number of establish-ments	Number of employees	Sales (mil dol)	Annual payroll (mil dol)
	69	70	71	72	73	74	75	76	77	78	79
NEW HAMPSHIRE—Cont'd											
Manchester	22,725	134	94.0	195	3,163	2,757.7	244.2	419	7,274	2,476.3	237.5
Nashua	15,224	55	96.4	119	1,527	1,299.5	106.3	464	9,984	3,300.7	292.0
Rochester	23,438	150	41.3	11	167	71.3	14.2	131	2,897	800.4	89.2
NEW JERSEY	5,234,056	37,094	37.5	12,289	230,006	312,405.1	18,970.9	31,200	469,615	149,171.3	13,453.1
Atlantic City	21,158	168	4.8	5	D	106.9	D	275	2,970	647.7	63.4
Bayonne	39,129	371	1.6	55	905	754.8	48.3	178	2,011	504.7	49.8
Bergenfield	2,840	7	100.0	33	234	144.6	12.8	84	818	213.4	22.1
Bridgeton	0	0	0.0	23	366	130.1	11.4	90	594	258.1	16.3
Camden	1,496	14	85.7	50	1,214	985.2	66.9	190	940	280.2	22.3
Carteret	2,121	19	26.3	35	1,147	1,060.2	93.0	43	3,101	1,155.9	97.2
Cliffside Park	12,557	58	24.1	25	43	18.1	1.9	53	167	54.5	4.2
Clifton	3,792	40	30.0	178	1,802	908.6	100.2	300	4,875	1,535.1	142.1
East Orange	40,405	246	11.0	18	140	480.9	6.7	151	1,275	346.0	30.4
Elizabeth	9,082	92	4.3	106	3,450	4,803.1	241.0	532	7,489	1,694.7	154.9
Englewood	17,554	60	15.0	93	1,303	812.9	80.5	156	2,084	1,572.3	101.4
Fair Lawn	11,010	222	73.0	56	589	239.6	24.1	88	872	339.7	31.7
Fort Lee	29,477	178	9.6	153	1,109	1,919.5	97.8	135	1,340	392.3	29.8
Garfield	2,484	89	1.1	41	477	225.0	23.8	71	912	269.5	24.5
Hackensack	28,651	66	0.0	181	1,562	1,674.5	97.7	260	3,615	989.9	102.7
Hoboken	67,105	93	9.7	34	229	155.0	14.6	167	1,480	420.0	37.6
Jersey City	397,033	3,232	7.6	189	5,929	5,916.0	460.1	818	12,319	3,302.1	294.5
Kearny	0	0	0.0	49	904	1,213.3	54.9	98	1,838	517.4	51.0
Linden	9,206	69	68.1	113	1,948	1,818.7	114.8	196	2,696	1,087.2	102.6
Lodi	0	0	0.0	48	530	223.2	35.1	92	1,107	337.6	27.3
Long Branch	48,290	671	20.6	28	125	73.0	5.8	86	1,112	408.2	36.8
Millville	5,739	49	100.0	25	545	322.1	35.5	86	1,703	442.6	42.4
Newark	151,362	1,328	0.1	333	6,003	6,820.3	440.3	903	7,325	3,104.3	288.4
New Brunswick	29,787	169	1.8	62	840	513.5	44.5	123	679	203.2	17.0
Paramus	54,486	50	90.0	93	1,476	2,095.5	128.9	586	14,840	4,146.7	410.8
Passaic	13,773	119	18.5	86	1,104	473.6	46.9	252	2,189	566.6	54.4
Paterson	42,654	665	2.3	185	2,284	1,196.6	119.5	555	3,641	1,061.8	91.3
Perth Amboy	14,366	100	5.0	39	1,152	1,425.1	81.7	208	1,353	467.1	39.6
Plainfield	14,946	279	1.4	21	D	38.7	D	124	615	201.5	19.8
Princeton	0	0	0.0	D	D	D	D	137	3,170	776.1	85.9
Rahway	14,019	203	7.4	64	791	1,413.1	54.7	72	578	232.4	16.8
Ridgewood	9,794	30	40.0	29	111	67.3	7.2	97	1,031	225.8	27.4
Sayreville	7,508	111	19.8	59	652	711.1	40.7	107	1,316	471.1	37.0
Trenton	5,195	73	1.4	42	610	655.5	36.3	233	1,343	363.2	35.2
Union City	10,726	110	0.0	39	182	103.1	8.2	271	1,269	322.9	31.7
Vineland	10,019	90	30.0	71	1,999	1,720.8	97.7	261	3,815	1,060.0	99.3
Westfield	12,442	29	100.0	15	D	22.3	D	109	1,352	274.4	31.2
West New York	65,691	639	23.0	24	166	40.3	4.8	215	1,287	332.8	32.4
NEW MEXICO	1,622,288	7,753	70.5	1,507	16,914	11,936.9	834.9	6,335	92,557	26,404.3	2,511.3
Alamogordo	NA	NA	NA	8	42	11.9	1.1	123	2,084	533.7	51.9
Albuquerque	278,860	1,667	46.4	633	8,376	5,131.6	431.1	1,806	32,482	9,618.9	933.5
Carlsbad	18,769	86	96.5	D	D	D	D	111	1,805	563.9	55.3
Clovis	26,869	156	50.0	25	277	102.1	9.4	163	2,240	603.8	57.5
Farmington	11,401	49	100.0	91	764	395.6	44.8	298	4,754	1,362.3	134.2
Hobbs	53,033	211	100.0	66	965	473.1	48.8	151	2,682	894.1	78.9
Las Cruces	199,041	862	88.5	71	665	355.0	31.7	394	7,221	1,887.5	174.3
Rio Rancho	268,752	1,538	68.9	24	154	91.9	8.6	112	2,859	801.4	77.5
Roswell	10,524	67	100.0	33	335	172.8	13.7	179	2,985	829.2	75.4
Santa Fe	133,831	840	27.1	72	695	841.9	37.0	710	8,126	2,326.8	244.2
NEW YORK	7,652,184	40,135	27.7	26,900	330,990	367,972.4	22,510.3	78,260	945,360	291,724.9	27,814.8
Albany	93,252	428	1.9	98	1,373	3,169.1	85.1	468	6,947	1,905.1	198.1
Auburn	100	1	100.0	D	D	D	9.8	114	1,893	468.6	44.9
Binghamton	12,179	65	0.0	54	621	254.6	23.8	169	1,745	483.1	46.4
Buffalo	62,892	292	12.0	233	4,611	2,814.3	266.0	877	8,134	1,689.5	183.2
Elmira	13,000	116	0.0	36	442	191.0	19.7	80	1,115	312.5	30.7
Freeport	3,547	10	100.0	74	589	297.3	30.3	186	1,904	777.7	60.7
Glen Cove	2,587	6	66.7	49	594	197.8	12.4	101	1,146	658.5	42.8
Harrison	14,248	35	100.0	56	1,030	4,255.8	108.5	53	352	120.0	11.6
Hempstead	2,600	22	45.5	34	245	115.3	13.6	208	2,482	1,268.4	86.9
Ithaca	79,423	464	2.6	14	111	31.0	4.1	173	3,000	748.7	77.9
Jamestown	0	0	0.0	33	236	109.7	9.1	106	1,411	433.3	41.5
Kiryas Joel	83,286	650	0.5	59	229	115.7	7.0	152	926	474.9	27.0

1. Merchant wholesalers except manufacturers' sales branches and offices. 2. Establishments with payroll.

City	Real estate and rental and leasing, 2017				Professional, scientific, and technical services[1], 2017				Manufacturing, 2017			
	Number of establish-ments	Number of employees	Receipts (mil dol)	Annual payroll (mil dol)	Number of establish-ments	Number of employees	Receipts (mil dol)	Annual payroll (mil dol)	Number of establish-ments	Number of employees	Receipts (mil dol)	Annual payroll (mil dol)
	80	81	82	83	84	85	86	87	88	89	90	91
NEW HAMPSHIRE—Cont'd												
Manchester	156	1,589	297.1	71.7	457	4,859	902.9	426.0	NA	NA	NA	NA
Nashua	124	505	120.5	23.9	306	3,316	763.2	375.9	NA	NA	NA	NA
Rochester	25	76	17.1	2.6	36	295	28.5	12.1	NA	NA	NA	NA
NEW JERSEY	9,622	61,052	21,184.3	3,435.2	28,962	325,516	67,232.3	28,735.5	7,332	219,835	95,483.0	13,908.6
Atlantic City	45	452	143.6	18.1	D	D	D	67.5	NA	NA	NA	NA
Bayonne	37	182	37.0	8.4	71	492	63.5	37.3	NA	NA	NA	NA
Bergenfield	D	D	D	D	42	228	31.8	12.9	NA	NA	NA	NA
Bridgeton	14	123	25.3	4.1	29	112	10.1	3.4	NA	NA	NA	NA
Camden	41	198	45.7	8.2	58	1,013	584.8	96.9	NA	NA	NA	NA
Carteret	12	51	27.1	3.0	28	432	123.0	34.1	NA	NA	NA	NA
Cliffside Park	D	D	D	D	50	206	34.3	10.5	NA	NA	NA	NA
Clifton	107	596	120.0	25.8	242	1,413	231.7	82.3	NA	NA	NA	NA
East Orange	49	248	55.7	7.9	47	147	18.5	5.4	NA	NA	NA	NA
Elizabeth	100	434	229.9	21.9	D	D	84.2	D	NA	NA	NA	NA
Englewood	63	236	93.7	13.9	130	649	99.2	37.0	NA	NA	NA	NA
Fair Lawn	D	D	D	D	209	1,168	216.9	84.2	NA	NA	NA	NA
Fort Lee	135	610	204.8	28.3	248	1,554	321.5	134.3	NA	NA	NA	NA
Garfield	16	68	14.6	2.6	31	209	21.3	6.7	NA	NA	NA	NA
Hackensack	138	615	260.3	33.9	411	2,870	610.9	236.7	NA	NA	NA	NA
Hoboken	112	529	245.9	25.8	225	1,286	317.0	108.2	NA	NA	NA	NA
Jersey City	263	1,583	499.1	84.9	655	8,057	2,184.2	793.0	NA	NA	NA	NA
Kearny	33	238	68.1	16.8	54	264	57.2	13.5	NA	NA	NA	NA
Linden	39	209	80.6	11.7	55	934	49.7	39.3	NA	NA	NA	NA
Lodi	27	126	31.2	5.6	25	90	15.3	3.8	NA	NA	NA	NA
Long Branch	D	D	D	D	53	155	26.9	6.8	NA	NA	NA	NA
Millville	16	78	14.9	2.2	37	240	33.4	9.2	NA	NA	NA	NA
Newark	227	2,413	683.3	95.8	473	8,271	1,794.0	842.7	NA	NA	NA	NA
New Brunswick	58	395	100.4	19.2	125	1,084	241.7	87.3	NA	NA	NA	NA
Paramus	70	470	350.6	28.1	206	2,412	507.4	168.7	NA	NA	NA	NA
Passaic	51	157	32.3	5.2	68	350	51.8	12.7	NA	NA	NA	NA
Paterson	84	402	67.0	14.2	89	368	59.1	20.0	NA	NA	NA	NA
Perth Amboy	32	158	49.6	6.7	58	211	23.9	8.8	NA	NA	NA	NA
Plainfield	26	84	21.2	3.2	D	D	28.2	D	NA	NA	NA	NA
Princeton	48	323	186.8	21.0	238	1,592	393.2	155.7	NA	NA	NA	NA
Rahway	23	197	42.2	11.4	D	D	24.8	D	NA	NA	NA	NA
Ridgewood	50	229	87.3	10.4	130	389	77.2	25.0	NA	NA	NA	NA
Sayreville	32	130	36.3	4.7	88	1,149	173.9	85.3	NA	NA	NA	NA
Trenton	58	310	85.5	10.6	125	840	189.9	78.2	NA	NA	NA	NA
Union City	54	138	28.4	4.4	108	357	59.5	16.0	NA	NA	NA	NA
Vineland	57	252	62.9	11.5	104	580	63.8	23.5	NA	NA	NA	NA
Westfield	30	107	43.6	4.0	142	822	168.9	62.1	NA	NA	NA	NA
West New York	51	234	75.2	13.0	79	219	36.1	12.2	NA	NA	NA	NA
NEW MEXICO	2,408	9,229	2,185.6	375.8	4,728	56,695	10,081.7	4,190.4	1,332	23,235	13,723.6	1,286.8
Alamogordo	35	138	20.3	3.5	D	D	D	D	NA	NA	NA	NA
Albuquerque	897	3,942	967.2	158.4	D	D	2,773.4	D	NA	NA	NA	NA
Carlsbad	30	147	42.8	7.3	52	386	100.7	23.4	NA	NA	NA	NA
Clovis	57	190	31.7	4.9	66	302	31.3	10.8	NA	NA	NA	NA
Farmington	79	433	124.3	25.1	157	897	93.9	40.4	NA	NA	NA	NA
Hobbs	62	408	110.2	26.5	55	348	43.0	16.6	NA	NA	NA	NA
Las Cruces	D	D	D	16.6	251	2,801	331.1	134.3	NA	NA	NA	NA
Rio Rancho	63	214	44.0	9.1	106	457	58.1	24.1	NA	NA	NA	NA
Roswell	64	164	32.3	5.0	88	691	124.3	47.4	NA	NA	NA	NA
Santa Fe	224	703	181.7	37.1	516	2,060	347.0	129.8	NA	NA	NA	NA
NEW YORK	34,076	193,442	70,693.0	11,356.8	61,744	668,196	172,936.2	60,227.2	15,499	411,100	155,571.9	23,751.3
Albany	143	882	222.0	39.3	451	10,628	2,021.4	757.5	NA	NA	NA	NA
Auburn	35	84	21.6	2.7	46	258	27.6	11.9	NA	NA	NA	NA
Binghamton	53	217	30.0	6.9	115	1,485	183.7	67.1	NA	NA	NA	NA
Buffalo	275	2,354	483.4	90.1	717	14,519	2,220.6	894.4	NA	NA	NA	NA
Elmira	28	102	19.6	3.8	46	239	31.6	10.0	NA	NA	NA	NA
Freeport	47	233	62.1	8.9	123	377	61.9	22.4	NA	NA	NA	NA
Glen Cove	25	99	22.4	4.5	85	310	56.8	19.8	NA	NA	NA	NA
Harrison	82	933	308.8	70.7	166	2,225	971.7	207.4	NA	NA	NA	NA
Hempstead	53	278	72.8	9.7	D	D	D	D	NA	NA	NA	NA
Ithaca	55	412	71.5	14.2	133	991	131.8	53.4	NA	NA	NA	NA
Jamestown	28	110	19.7	3.4	57	280	34.8	13.5	NA	NA	NA	NA
Kiryas Joel	47	114	18.0	3.6	101	383	43.5	12.5	NA	NA	NA	NA

1. Establishments subject to federal tax.

City	Accommodation and food services, 2017				Arts, entertainment, and recreation[1], 2017				Health care and social assistance[1], 2017			
	Number of establishments	Number of employees	Receipts (mil dol)	Annual payroll (mil dol)	Number of establishments	Number of employees	Receipts (mil dol)	Annual payroll (mil dol)	Number of establishments	Number of employees	Receipts (mil dol)	Annual payroll (mil dol)
	92	93	94	95	96	97	98	99	100	101	102	103
NEW HAMPSHIRE—Cont'd												
Manchester	307	6,151	372.5	109.4	49.0	1,035	84.1	42.3	350	14,010	1,804.7	767.4
Nashua	228	4,686	271.5	81.3	45.0	592	37.7	13.3	370	9,314	1,276.6	470.1
Rochester	73	1,164	65.8	18.1	8.0	133	4.8	2.2	74	1,883	259.2	100.8
NEW JERSEY	21,495	318,734	23,785.1	6,431.5	3,842.0	65,529	5,967.2	1,934.1	28,005	613,406	74,723.4	30,134.1
Atlantic City	199	26,558	3,006.3	852.9	D	D	D	D	68	3,300	461.5	175.6
Bayonne	D	D	D	D	17.0	300	25.1	5.5	170	2,708	308.4	108.8
Bergenfield	41	370	25.7	6.4	D	D	D	D	77	643	53.5	19.5
Bridgeton	30	216	13.6	3.3	D	D	D	D	40	1,397	98.9	42.4
Camden	90	482	42.8	8.8	10.0	357	73.8	11.2	161	13,231	1,958.9	876.9
Carteret	22	268	18.6	3.9	NA	NA	NA	NA	D	D	D	D
Cliffside Park	56	372	22.8	5.4	4.0	108	4.1	1.0	61	359	41.1	12.7
Clifton	D	D	D	D	26.0	314	36.0	10.0	442	5,344	578.0	217.1
East Orange	55	681	36.8	9.8	D	D	D	D	150	6,677	771.9	354.8
Elizabeth	260	3,291	304.4	73.5	10.0	101	6.3	1.7	219	6,377	630.0	277.4
Englewood	59	776	68.5	18.2	24.0	359	28.8	9.1	242	5,205	1,165.4	338.4
Fair Lawn	76	891	64.7	16.5	15.0	143	8.3	2.0	202	3,115	281.7	116.5
Fort Lee	136	1,364	118.9	25.6	16.0	95	7.0	1.8	214	1,504	199.7	53.5
Garfield	49	575	46.0	11.7	NA	NA	NA	NA	34	501	21.4	11.0
Hackensack	137	2,313	157.4	47.4	15.0	448	18.8	6.6	373	18,335	2,906.0	1,139.1
Hoboken	260	4,079	288.8	85.7	D	D	D	D	153	2,674	432.4	127.8
Jersey City	564	7,109	612.5	163.6	81.0	1,057	134.6	29.9	532	11,874	1,306.9	536.7
Kearny	68	743	50.8	13.8	D	D	D	D	67	1,016	89.8	39.6
Linden	D	D	D	D	D	D	D	D	72	1,801	191.8	66.3
Lodi	57	501	33.7	6.5	7.0	20	2.3	0.3	33	207	16.3	5.8
Long Branch	102	1,456	99.0	28.3	12.0	92	10.6	2.6	94	5,100	1,021.6	422.3
Millville	58	803	45.4	12.9	10.0	D	17.7	D	93	1,688	132.5	60.8
Newark	582	9,177	861.5	216.5	36.0	2,295	287.8	137.2	471	18,615	2,716.5	1,051.5
New Brunswick	182	2,307	178.4	43.4	13.0	448	28.7	9.4	123	9,944	1,771.7	705.8
Paramus	154	3,653	249.4	69.9	26.0	785	67.4	19.2	273	6,281	754.1	324.5
Passaic	D	D	D	D	8.0	D	2.5	D	131	2,776	322.0	110.7
Paterson	D	D	D	D	14.0	186	9.4	1.8	238	8,526	1,049.3	485.7
Perth Amboy	111	670	50.7	10.7	6.0	15	1.5	0.5	80	1,375	106.9	45.3
Plainfield	D	D	D	D	D	D	D	D	106	1,964	144.5	73.6
Princeton	102	2,101	149.2	48.9	37.0	850	54.8	19.9	140	2,371	408.6	135.1
Rahway	59	603	42.1	11.1	6.0	106	3.1	1.3	52	1,479	181.9	72.7
Ridgewood	89	1,117	70.8	23.6	14.0	199	13.1	4.2	216	5,958	1,062.4	424.1
Sayreville	D	D	D	D	12.0	196	17.4	5.2	65	524	42.4	16.4
Trenton	142	916	67.4	16.6	13.0	177	12.4	4.7	160	8,046	790.1	400.8
Union City	154	1,144	76.7	18.1	D	D	D	D	193	2,147	152.7	65.2
Vineland	118	2,099	105.5	27.4	13.0	90	8.0	2.5	219	7,064	807.8	387.8
Westfield	D	D	D	D	21.0	436	16.8	8.2	146	2,125	214.6	96.8
West New York	95	756	49.0	13.2	13.0	53	7.0	2.6	117	3,153	133.5	73.1
NEW MEXICO	4,392	91,601	5,526.0	1,583.2	700.0	12,062	1,119.7	271.6	5,134	127,808	13,602.4	5,405.5
Alamogordo	D	D	D	D	D	D	D	D	98	2,501	297.2	104.1
Albuquerque	1,399	31,062	1,778.9	525.7	215.0	3,659	254.2	68.2	1,818	50,897	6,106.6	2,390.6
Carlsbad	77	1,565	114.2	27.4	D	D	D	D	73	1,920	189.0	76.9
Clovis	D	D	D	D	12.0	50	2.9	0.8	D	D	D	D
Farmington	169	3,710	183.7	53.2	15.0	179	7.8	3.5	237	6,045	658.5	266.2
Hobbs	104	2,236	194.0	39.0	D	D	D	D	D	D	D	D
Las Cruces	283	6,408	328.6	95.6	24.0	237	10.1	3.5	453	11,917	1,126.2	467.6
Rio Rancho	108	2,640	128.4	37.5	D	D	D	D	174	3,483	492.6	150.7
Roswell	119	2,359	122.7	34.7	16.0	132	7.5	1.9	163	3,997	406.7	179.2
Santa Fe	370	8,091	569.3	184.7	115.0	1,524	141.3	42.2	426	7,348	1,050.5	381.7
NEW YORK	54,797	824,806	66,963.5	19,792.9	13,019.0	185,076	29,269.9	8,695.5	58,902	1,654,593	193,507.6	80,687.9
Albany	446	6,343	405.5	127.4	53.0	1,159	56.4	19.2	356	23,957	3,316.5	1,266.6
Auburn	83	1,189	67.9	18.3	18.0	478	14.5	5.6	157	3,631	335.1	167.7
Binghamton	176	3,255	159.7	48.0	22.0	355	20.0	7.4	154	7,381	744.6	332.0
Buffalo	697	13,799	706.1	228.9	104.0	2,974	423.1	162.1	687	38,916	5,125.9	2,155.4
Elmira	D	D	D	D	14.0	238	8.8	3.4	127	4,622	490.9	241.4
Freeport	108	848	65.3	19.7	18.0	54	15.2	2.2	159	1,902	170.7	70.7
Glen Cove	D	D	D	D	19.0	396	27.5	9.4	112	2,819	315.1	151.6
Harrison	D	D	D	D	27.0	985	117.3	46.3	127	3,331	504.5	200.2
Hempstead	134	2,710	266.6	62.7	8.0	151	10.3	4.1	203	4,169	298.3	133.6
Ithaca	204	3,447	182.6	59.7	25.0	191	18.5	5.2	104	1,510	124.1	54.7
Jamestown	79	895	47.3	13.5	18.0	275	18.7	4.0	91	2,870	249.8	110.2
Kiryas Joel	17	61	10.4	1.4	9.0	22	2.7	0.6	23	1,213	98.1	46.9

1. Establishments subject to federal tax.

City	Other services[1]				Government employment and payroll, 2017								
						March payroll							
							Perent of total for:						
	Number of establish-ments	Number of employees	Receipts (mil dol)	Annual payroll (mil dol)	Full-time equivalent employees	Total (dollars)	Admin-istrative, judicial, and legal	Police and corrections	Fire protection	Highways and trans-portation	Health and welfare	Natural resources and utilities	Education and libraries
	104	105	106	107	108	109	110	111	112	113	114	115	116
NEW HAMPSHIRE—Cont'd													
Manchester	284	2,389	354.7	98.6	3,155	16,041,295	3.6	12.7	9.5	10.2	2.5	7.4	51.8
Nashua	191	1,645	165.8	55.4	2,699	13,478,642	3.8	13.3	8.9	3.9	1.1	8.7	58.6
Rochester	63	349	37.3	9.9	973	4,205,963	5.0	9.8	5.2	3.1	0.5	2.8	71.9
NEW JERSEY	19,162	113,846	14,025.6	3,679.3	X	X	X	X	X	X	X	X	X
Atlantic City	64	844	65.2	18.3	1,546	9,801,157	8.1	41.5	24.4	1.3	7.0	9.0	1.9
Bayonne	131	491	35.0	9.4	2,463	14,984,419	2.7	17.0	11.6	3.4	3.0	0.9	60.5
Bergenfield	63	149	18.2	3.6	175	1,201,986	7.5	54.7	4.8	0.0	2.5	22.9	5.5
Bridgeton	17	86	9.6	2.6	18	68,880	0.0	0.0	0.0	0.0	100.0	0.0	0.0
Camden	54	393	42.2	10.5	662	3,756,554	15.9	9.6	39.9	2.6	11.2	9.8	0.0
Carteret	23	89	17.0	4.5	192	1,316,091	15.9	49.3	13.9	3.8	9.8	5.2	2.1
Cliffside Park	55	161	23.2	4.2	255	1,278,180	10.5	44.7	1.3	0.0	12.9	13.8	5.3
Clifton	209	1,103	108.5	37.5	564	3,939,877	6.3	35.4	29.0	0.9	2.6	4.4	3.7
East Orange	69	309	34.4	9.3	2,811	18,542,586	3.9	14.2	7.7	1.3	3.4	2.7	66.7
Elizabeth	208	1,671	122.0	67.1	1,415	9,391,483	9.0	36.6	26.7	7.6	8.9	2.7	1.6
Englewood	112	652	62.8	20.5	731	5,467,310	3.0	22.8	11.8	2.1	2.7	4.5	50.4
Fair Lawn	90	463	36.7	11.6	227	1,783,449	9.9	43.8	1.2	4.8	2.6	20.6	5.9
Fort Lee	153	663	119.9	22.2	306	2,105,983	8.9	50.5	3.4	9.7	7.3	3.7	4.5
Garfield	D	D	D	D	189	1,367,252	7.9	65.3	1.3	7.9	10.3	4.1	2.4
Hackensack	151	916	119.2	33.0	415	3,031,478	6.8	42.5	34.2	0.6	3.6	5.8	4.5
Hoboken	150	980	79.3	27.4	635	3,716,486	3.2	33.9	30.3	1.0	8.6	9.4	4.2
Jersey City	419	1,860	213.6	50.4	2,982	20,957,923	8.1	44.0	27.5	3.2	7.0	6.4	2.0
Kearny	D	D	D	D	325	2,322,529	4.7	46.4	33.1	8.1	1.8	1.7	1.4
Linden	105	951	115.6	37.7	527	2,710,901	5.9	24.0	26.3	7.6	10.6	22.3	0.0
Lodi	D	D	54.4	D	110	745,951	8.2	64.2	0.0	10.2	11.5	1.3	4.7
Long Branch	63	255	33.3	6.7	374	2,326,716	10.2	41.5	11.0	5.3	11.1	8.6	3.1
Millville	52	229	19.1	5.8	218	1,119,395	14.2	45.0	6.2	9.5	8.4	16.6	0.0
Newark	563	3,527	505.2	123.6	3,735	15,962,973	11.5	35.4	18.0	0.6	15.6	9.9	2.9
New Brunswick	92	975	259.0	45.1	2,218	13,176,046	2.4	13.9	6.4	0.7	1.0	3.6	69.5
Paramus	79	669	108.1	30.2	348	2,063,276	9.3	52.9	1.6	0.8	6.7	19.5	6.9
Passaic	91	426	45.7	10.0	607	3,264,367	6.8	43.4	27.5	4.2	13.1	1.6	2.1
Paterson	232	1,348	122.9	32.6	1,538	9,711,177	7.0	44.9	28.3	1.1	7.5	6.4	1.5
Perth Amboy	D	D	D	17.5	451	2,622,482	10.6	41.9	17.2	3.2	10.1	8.5	1.7
Plainfield	87	325	29.3	8.7	596	3,705,643	11.8	31.9	21.7	0.6	6.8	7.2	5.4
Princeton	103	973	731.4	63.6	247	1,607,979	14.1	41.8	0.0	14.5	14.0	6.6	0.0
Rahway	D	D	26.6	D	286	1,963,091	7.4	40.5	21.7	9.0	8.2	6.9	4.4
Ridgewood	85	590	36.0	12.9	257	2,000,250	10.5	26.9	19.9	5.7	1.6	35.4	0.0
Sayreville	D	D	D	9.7	279	1,964,301	15.0	52.5	0.8	3.0	0.6	15.9	4.1
Trenton	139	805	112.2	37.3	2,465	17,459,250	3.1	11.0	9.2	0.9	3.3	5.4	66.0
Union City	117	308	39.1	7.3	2,489	12,749,167	2.2	14.6	0.2	0.0	2.9	3.8	75.1
Vineland	121	731	68.3	17.8	683	4,105,814	10.9	28.8	5.0	1.5	11.3	38.5	2.2
Westfield	100	561	54.6	17.3	225	1,462,240	9.5	33.3	21.2	15.5	9.7	5.1	5.1
West New York	86	262	25.8	5.1	1,604	9,705,140	3.1	15.4	0.8	0.2	2.5	2.6	74.4
NEW MEXICO	2,963	17,547	2,085.4	558.2	X	X	X	X	X	X	X	X	X
Alamogordo	54	288	21.3	6.0	295	867,629	16.4	29.5	8.3	3.3	8.9	20.4	4.0
Albuquerque	1,004	6,871	800.4	225.7	6,938	37,997,192	9.8	30.8	14.7	16.1	9.2	14.1	1.6
Carlsbad	47	462	65.1	14.5	494	2,632,596	10.6	23.9	17.4	12.8	0.0	25.7	1.7
Clovis	71	404	46.0	9.9	379	1,260,854	7.8	24.0	27.7	9.2	4.8	17.3	2.4
Farmington	145	959	158.1	31.8	954	4,000,911	9.5	22.8	11.6	5.0	2.4	39.0	3.8
Hobbs	57	500	97.8	22.5	479	2,228,763	9.1	31.1	16.8	7.7	3.6	23.9	2.2
Las Cruces	176	908	73.8	23.2	1,470	5,706,100	9.2	24.4	13.4	5.3	4.6	21.3	1.8
Rio Rancho	89	500	45.2	14.0	659	2,861,344	12.1	35.1	23.2	7.1	0.0	10.6	3.9
Roswell	64	443	32.0	8.8	543	2,039,709	8.2	29.5	20.0	10.0	1.5	24.5	3.3
Santa Fe	306	1,752	267.4	72.3	1,444	6,129,397	10.7	17.5	12.2	10.8	5.9	32.3	2.4
NEW YORK	48,436	299,209	51,749.9	11,845.9	X	X	X	X	X	X	X	X	X
Albany	289	1,909	365.6	97.8	1,247	8,694,425	6.8	44.9	17.0	4.1	8.7	17.4	0.0
Auburn	59	254	25.6	6.5	302	1,533,311	12.9	28.7	25.7	7.6	4.2	20.2	0.0
Binghamton	108	652	65.7	17.1	554	2,898,702	5.9	31.4	28.3	6.0	6.3	15.3	0.0
Buffalo	431	3,135	311.2	79.9	9,147	51,448,265	3.0	13.1	8.5	0.6	1.9	6.0	64.6
Elmira	39	216	25.7	5.9	303	1,797,692	5.8	37.9	27.4	6.1	4.8	16.5	0.0
Freeport	130	773	70.7	21.8	378	2,751,992	11.1	46.7	0.7	1.8	1.1	34.7	0.0
Glen Cove	79	292	30.7	8.7	229	1,410,099	9.8	44.1	1.8	7.3	7.3	17.9	0.0
Harrison	66	1,415	336.9	55.5	282	1,765,849	14.2	43.2	8.0	7.9	2.8	13.9	7.8
Hempstead	125	752	69.5	20.0	398	3,062,661	9.0	50.1	2.5	8.5	2.1	19.5	3.9
Ithaca	86	575	126.6	18.9	436	2,235,422	10.2	23.5	20.2	8.2	0.6	27.6	0.0
Jamestown	64	360	43.1	9.5	614	3,020,128	3.6	13.4	11.8	9.4	1.4	3.1	57.2
Kiryas Joel	17	71	10.4	1.8	40	212,704	16.5	0.0	1.0	39.0	17.1	26.4	0.0

1. Establishments subject to federal tax.

City	City government finances, 2017									
	General revenue							General expenditure		
		Intergovernmental		Taxes						
					Per capita[1] (dollars)				Per capita[1] (dollars)	
	Total (mil dol)	Total (mil dol)	Percent from state government	Total (mil dol)	Total	Property	Sales and gross receipts	Total (mil dol)	Total	Capital outlays
	117	118	119	120	121	122	123	124	125	126
NEW HAMPSHIRE—Cont'd										
Manchester	431.5	144.0	88.3	198.5	1,769	1,720	49	376.7	3,356	80
Nashua	331.6	71.6	99.0	215.4	2,421	2,403	17	291.4	3,274	188
Rochester	114.2	36.3	94.0	52.6	1,695	1,512	183	75.4	2,429	232
NEW JERSEY	X	X	X	X	X	X	X	X	X	X
Atlantic City	263.3	125.2	79.9	118.3	3,131	3,008	123	213.7	5,653	178
Bayonne	234.7	90.2	87.3	88.4	1,352	1,310	42	278.2	4,257	70
Bergenfield	35.9	2.6	90.5	32.3	1,177	1,136	41	33.7	1,226	133
Bridgeton	35.6	8.1	61.2	14.5	591	549	42	33.9	1,386	33
Camden	262.1	21.3	3.7	48.4	656	632	24	180.7	2,451	0
Carteret	50.9	13.6	0.0	27.3	1,154	1,109	45	40.7	1,722	0
Cliffside Park	42.7	7.6	25.1	30.6	1,242	1,207	35	39.0	1,582	122
Clifton	122.3	14.3	80.2	89.7	1,052	1,005	48	112.4	1,318	185
East Orange	388.8	267.5	93.5	101.3	1,575	1,535	40	403.7	6,278	121
Elizabeth	307.8	58.5	62.1	189.2	1,476	1,323	153	276.9	2,160	245
Englewood	90.4	27.5	70.3	54.6	1,907	1,838	69	146.8	5,129	455
Fair Lawn	49.7	4.2	97.2	43.3	1,308	1,247	61	43.0	1,300	129
Fort Lee	83.6	9.3	24.7	68.8	1,844	1,739	105	81.1	2,174	186
Garfield	79.0	1.8	1.1	55.4	1,739	1,729	10	31.3	984	73
Hackensack	103.5	7.1	73.1	86.4	1,940	1,856	84	110.2	2,476	369
Hoboken	136.9	25.0	55.1	69.1	1,288	1,181	106	178.6	3,328	1,145
Jersey City	796.7	175.1	49.5	277.6	1,055	946	109	622.6	2,365	136
Kearny	78.4	24.3	100.0	46.4	1,116	1,083	33	73.0	1,754	100
Linden	107.0	25.5	81.8	71.6	1,689	1,519	169	101.9	2,404	286
Lodi	33.1	8.2	29.1	19.5	796	758	37	31.2	1,274	75
Long Branch	77.8	18.7	27.0	43.9	1,438	1,370	68	80.5	2,633	366
Millville	35.4	5.3	100.0	22.1	799	745	54	36.0	1,302	0
Newark	845.4	353.0	39.2	347.1	1,234	910	192	891.1	3,168	187
New Brunswick	300.6	192.9	92.9	37.2	664	603	60	347.2	6,186	237
Paramus	60.0	5.1	89.5	48.2	1,812	1,649	162	65.0	2,443	292
Passaic	124.4	37.1	40.7	67.5	963	942	21	124.7	1,778	57
Paterson	340.1	108.9	54.7	175.5	1,202	1,175	27	333.3	2,283	141
Perth Amboy	111.5	24.1	44.3	60.7	1,171	1,124	47	98.4	1,899	110
Plainfield	124.7	23.1	1.0	95.8	1,902	1,886	16	129.5	2,571	32
Princeton	60.0	3.8	90.3	38.0	1,211	1,179	31	59.8	1,908	436
Rahway	57.5	5.0	88.8	43.0	1,450	1,334	116	50.9	1,719	88
Ridgewood	44.6	2.3	92.3	37.9	1,502	1,415	87	49.3	1,950	263
Sayreville	56.1	12.1	80.9	36.2	814	759	55	57.0	1,280	187
Trenton	467.1	382.8	92.0	54.3	651	608	42	512.0	6,131	103
Union City	356.8	265.5	97.4	70.5	1,029	993	36	386.4	5,642	312
Vineland	96.1	18.4	22.9	36.1	604	577	26	86.8	1,450	428
Westfield	47.1	4.1	79.0	37.2	1,244	1,160	84	41.1	1,374	117
West New York	212.3	137.3	94.9	41.5	787	739	48	241.7	4,584	336
NEW MEXICO	X	X	X	X	X	X	X	X	X	X
Alamogordo	48.3	14.7	76.8	19.0	605	127	478	39.5	1,260	311
Albuquerque	979.8	270.0	87.5	386.0	690	261	429	814.4	1,455	218
Carlsbad	79.2	5.3	93.6	55.1	1,908	93	1,815	71.8	2,489	862
Clovis	56.3	10.0	60.5	30.4	780	52	729	55.9	1,435	463
Farmington	87.9	33.5	11.4	29.9	659	42	617	93.5	2,060	126
Hobbs	127.2	50.8	98.1	54.0	1,428	66	1,362	98.4	2,601	451
Las Cruces	180.7	17.6	55.4	123.3	1,210	148	1,062	101.7	998	174
Rio Rancho	113.0	15.7	46.9	61.1	634	203	432	89.6	931	133
Roswell	66.7	42.3	94.4	7.8	163	129	34	64.8	1,351	264
Santa Fe	185.8	70.3	80.8	48.4	577	134	442	231.5	2,758	332
NEW YORK	X	X	X	X	X	X	X	X	X	X
Albany	189.8	62.4	36.0	64.4	659	578	81	188.6	1,930	240
Auburn	49.3	19.6	50.5	13.0	487	442	45	45.3	1,702	184
Binghamton	111.1	50.1	34.4	38.3	850	814	35	125.6	2,788	1,159
Buffalo	1,439.0	1,218.1	89.2	106.4	415	335	80	1,482.7	5,785	348
Elmira	33.7	15.0	40.8	13.4	492	458	34	39.2	1,437	184
Freeport	66.8	1.8	82.2	45.7	1,059	985	74	76.9	1,782	73
Glen Cove	59.7	19.7	43.5	33.4	1,226	1,101	125	54.0	1,982	213
Harrison	14.0	1.3	54.4	11.8	422	378	44	18.3	656	252
Hempstead	80.6	2.0	65.7	67.4	1,218	1,168	50	75.8	1,369	58
Ithaca	66.0	10.2	63.2	38.2	1,246	715	531	67.2	2,191	286
Jamestown	76.2	35.4	57.8	16.6	562	534	28	82.7	2,803	72
Kiryas Joel	11.3	5.5	22.8	3.5	144	95	22	10.1	415	35

1. Based on population estimated as of July 1 of the year shown.

City	City government finances, 2017 (cont.)												
	General expenditure (cont.)												
	Percent of total for:									Debt outstanding			
	Public welfare	Highways	Parking facilities	Education	Health and hospitals	Police protection	Sewerage and sanitation	Parks and recreation	Housing and community development	Interest on debt	Total (mil dol)	Per capita[1] (dollars)	Debt issued during year
	127	128	129	130	131	132	133	134	135	136	137	138	139
NEW HAMPSHIRE—Cont'd													
Manchester	0.2	4.3	0.6	46.8	0.7	6.1	3.4	1.7	0.0	4.9	437.7	3,899	21.0
Nashua	0.3	5.4	0.0	54.5	0.4	9.9	6.0	2.1	0.9	5.6	189.4	2,128	13.3
Rochester	0.2	6.2	0.0	86.1	0.0	0.0	0.0	1.0	0.0	4.0	39.3	1,265	0.0
NEW JERSEY	X	X	X	X	X	X	X	X	X	X	X	X	X
Atlantic City	0.5	0.9	0.0	0.0	0.6	17.3	1.0	1.7	10.4	6.1	188.2	4,979	0.0
Bayonne	0.0	0.8	0.4	51.9	0.3	8.3	2.0	1.9	6.2	3.1	238.9	3,657	1.7
Bergenfield	0.0	4.7	0.0	0.0	1.5	22.1	16.9	2.2	0.2	0.3	8.9	325	0.0
Bridgeton	0.0	4.4	0.0	0.0	0.6	16.3	23.8	2.2	13.0	0.5	14.3	584	0.0
Camden	0.0	5.1	0.0	0.0	0.0	37.9	7.0	1.7	0.0	0.1	3.2	44	0.0
Carteret	0.0	3.2	0.7	0.0	0.0	19.1	11.1	2.3	22.6	1.9	54.1	2,293	0.8
Cliffside Park	0.0	3.8	0.0	0.0	2.4	16.3	10.7	3.8	15.6	3.3	42.0	1,703	0.0
Clifton	0.0	2.6	0.0	0.0	1.1	18.5	11.1	1.4	2.9	2.2	84.9	995	15.8
East Orange	0.0	1.1	0.1	62.7	1.8	6.2	2.8	1.0	5.4	0.4	78.6	1,223	0.0
Elizabeth	0.1	4.9	1.5	0.0	1.6	16.7	12.2	3.4	9.6	1.6	183.8	1,434	49.1
Englewood	0.0	0.8	0.0	51.8	0.5	9.0	4.4	1.0	5.8	1.0	71.7	2,504	1.5
Fair Lawn	0.1	7.0	0.0	0.0	0.6	20.9	12.4	5.4	0.0	2.5	34.7	1,049	18.9
Fort Lee	0.4	3.0	2.7	0.0	2.7	18.1	3.5	1.9	8.4	2.2	57.6	1,543	11.6
Garfield	0.0	5.0	0.0	0.0	0.9	27.2	11.5	3.5	11.9	0.0	43.8	1,375	7.7
Hackensack	0.0	2.1	0.6	0.0	0.8	15.0	11.0	9.2	4.4	1.0	57.0	1,281	0.0
Hoboken	0.0	12.5	7.7	0.0	0.4	9.3	2.8	0.9	9.4	1.5	132.1	2,461	0.0
Jersey City	0.0	1.4	0.4	0.0	1.5	16.6	7.8	1.8	15.0	4.1	661.4	2,512	0.0
Kearny	0.0	4.0	0.0	0.0	0.7	21.0	17.8	1.2	0.0	2.3	69.8	1,678	34.0
Linden	0.0	5.9	0.0	0.0	0.9	15.4	4.7	2.1	5.2	1.3	52.9	1,249	1.0
Lodi	0.0	5.2	0.0	0.0	0.4	21.6	5.1	1.3	23.6	1.1	22.7	927	0.0
Long Branch	0.0	1.9	0.2	0.0	0.8	14.7	12.3	2.4	21.7	2.7	82.5	2,699	0.0
Millville	0.0	7.0	0.0	0.0	0.6	19.1	20.9	1.7	0.5	3.0	31.1	1,122	0.1
Newark	0.3	1.8	0.5	0.0	3.4	16.1	9.6	1.8	21.3	2.0	433.8	1,543	0.0
New Brunswick	0.0	0.7	4.5	58.2	0.3	5.8	4.4	0.5	4.4	5.5	575.5	10,256	190.1
Paramus	0.1	3.1	0.0	0.0	2.4	20.3	8.5	8.0	0.0	0.9	37.7	1,416	0.0
Passaic	0.0	2.9	0.6	0.0	2.2	17.4	9.3	1.3	21.7	0.5	5.6	80	0.0
Paterson	0.0	2.9	1.9	0.0	3.7	15.7	7.3	1.9	16.4	1.3	82.4	564	0.0
Perth Amboy	0.2	1.4	0.6	0.0	0.6	13.1	8.7	1.5	20.4	9.1	175.2	3,381	4.3
Plainfield	0.0	3.5	0.0	0.0	0.7	13.1	1.0	0.7	11.7	0.0	36.3	720	0.0
Princeton	0.3	11.2	2.8	0.0	2.1	12.3	12.6	1.6	1.2	4.3	95.1	3,031	12.3
Rahway	0.0	9.5	0.0	0.0	1.5	17.9	14.3	1.7	0.0	3.5	79.0	2,667	20.6
Ridgewood	0.1	4.9	3.6	0.0	0.6	14.0	10.1	3.0	0.0	2.0	57.7	2,286	27.2
Sayreville	0.0	8.1	0.0	0.0	0.2	21.8	14.8	2.3	4.3	1.2	51.1	1,148	7.0
Trenton	0.0	0.8	0.1	57.7	0.9	7.3	3.5	0.5	3.5	1.5	321.1	3,846	24.4
Union City	0.1	0.6	0.6	71.1	0.5	6.5	2.6	0.6	0.4	0.7	108.9	1,590	10.3
Vineland	0.0	29.2	0.0	0.0	4.3	16.9	13.7	0.8	11.1	0.1	59.6	995	29.8
Westfield	0.0	0.7	0.6	0.0	2.0	15.8	8.4	2.1	0.0	0.3	25.7	859	0.0
West New York	0.0	1.0	0.8	64.6	0.6	5.8	1.7	1.1	4.5	0.6	46.5	882	11.6
NEW MEXICO	X	X	X	X	X	X	X	X	X	X	X	X	X
Alamogordo	5.3	8.8	0.0	0.0	0.0	17.3	10.2	19.5	2.9	0.0	63.6	2,027	17.5
Albuquerque	3.5	3.4	0.5	0.0	3.9	20.8	20.1	12.8	0.2	2.0	1,567.1	2,800	129.9
Carlsbad	0.0	14.5	0.0	0.0	0.5	17.3	18.5	14.6	0.0	1.1	52.0	1,801	0.0
Clovis	0.0	18.0	0.0	0.0	0.1	12.9	12.9	7.1	6.0	1.6	22.0	564	1.2
Farmington	0.0	11.1	0.0	0.0	1.9	18.0	10.7	14.5	0.4	0.0	1,684.2	37,082	30.6
Hobbs	0.0	7.6	0.0	0.0	1.1	17.1	18.7	21.2	0.0	0.4	39.9	1,055	0.0
Las Cruces	0.0	1.6	0.0	0.0	0.3	24.4	29.1	6.7	1.5	0.0	202.4	1,985	40.3
Rio Rancho	1.1	16.0	0.0	0.0	0.0	20.9	15.1	7.1	0.5	0.0	228.9	2,377	61.3
Roswell	0.0	11.4	0.0	0.0	0.0	21.1	10.8	12.5	0.0	0.6	8.8	184	0.0
Santa Fe	3.4	6.5	2.4	0.0	0.0	11.2	17.1	9.4	13.3	0.1	259.0	3,085	46.8
NEW YORK	X	X	X	X	X	X	X	X	X	X	X	X	X
Albany	0.0	6.8	0.0	0.0	0.3	31.9	3.9	2.1	0.0	7.7	288.2	2,949	23.7
Auburn	0.0	7.9	0.3	0.0	0.1	14.8	19.1	3.0	1.9	5.8	67.1	2,518	4.9
Binghamton	0.0	6.6	0.5	0.0	0.1	9.6	40.1	2.7	2.8	5.2	172.1	3,820	39.5
Buffalo	0.0	3.8	0.2	61.6	0.1	6.3	2.8	1.2	0.0	2.5	1,263.9	4,931	157.9
Elmira	0.0	9.6	0.6	0.0	0.7	19.4	2.5	4.3	2.8	3.2	26.8	983	0.0
Freeport	0.0	6.3	0.1	0.0	0.0	24.3	4.3	4.3	0.0	10.6	109.3	2,534	17.1
Glen Cove	7.9	10.8	0.0	0.0	1.5	27.9	5.3	10.5	0.7	7.2	57.5	2,109	5.0
Harrison	0.0	17.3	0.0	0.0	0.0	1.6	22.9	0.0	0.0	20.8	62.1	2,223	0.0
Hempstead	0.0	3.3	0.4	0.0	0.0	30.3	4.1	4.4	0.4	4.4	49.2	888	6.5
Ithaca	0.0	9.3	3.2	0.0	0.1	12.4	6.6	10.5	0.0	8.9	127.5	4,154	36.9
Jamestown	0.0	6.2	0.1	39.5	0.1	6.8	8.3	2.1	0.0	3.0	32.4	1,098	0.0
Kiryas Joel	0.0	8.9	0.1	0.0	0.0	5.6	27.5	0.5	0.0	8.6	44.0	1,814	36.1

1. Based on population estimated as of July 1 of the year shown.

STATE Place code	City	Land area[1] (sq. mi)	Population, 2021 Total persons 2021	Rank	Per square mile	Race 2020 Race alone[2] (percent) White	Black or African American	American Indian, Alaskan Native	Asian	Hawaiian Pacific Islander	Some other race	Two or more races (percent)
		1	2	3	4	5	6	7	8	9	10	11
	NEW YORK—Cont'd											
36 42554	Lindenhurst	3.7	27,138	1,432	7,334.6	78.9	2.5	0.3	2.7	0.0	7.2	8.4
36 43335	Long Beach	2.2	34,778	1,143	15,808.2	76.0	5.6	0.3	3.2	0.1	7.3	7.6
36 47042	Middletown	5.3	30,452	1,294	5,745.7	32.9	23.5	1.4	3.8	0.0	24.0	14.4
36 49121	Mount Vernon	4.4	72,581	509	16,495.7	14.0	62.4	0.6	2.0	0.0	11.3	9.6
36 50034	Newburgh	3.8	28,834	1,353	7,587.9	22.7	28.3	2.3	0.9	0.1	33.7	12.0
36 50617	New Rochelle	10.3	81,587	430	7,921.1	44.4	18.9	1.2	4.9	0.1	18.9	11.6
36 51000	New York	300.5	8,467,513	1	28,178.1	34.1	22.1	1.0	15.7	0.1	17.0	10.1
36 51055	Niagara Falls	14.1	48,360	824	3,429.8	61.1	24.6	1.8	2.1	0.0	2.2	8.4
36 53682	North Tonawanda	10.1	30,409	1,295	3,010.8	91.8	1.5	0.5	0.7	0.0	0.8	4.7
36 55530	Ossining	3.2	27,298	1,426	8,530.6	37.7	14.7	1.1	4.4	0.0	27.5	14.6
36 56979	Peekskill	4.3	25,740	1,504	5,986.0	35.9	20.1	0.9	2.9	0.0	27.7	12.5
36 59223	Port Chester	2.3	31,190	1,265	13,560.9	32.1	4.7	1.9	2.3	0.0	41.0	17.9
36 59641	Poughkeepsie	5.1	31,850	1,243	6,245.1	37.4	37.2	0.8	1.7	0.0	12.4	10.5
36 63000	Rochester	35.8	210,606	111	5,882.8	36.4	40.1	0.4	4.0	0.1	9.6	9.4
36 63264	Rockville Centre	3.3	25,814	1,503	7,822.4	80.5	5.3	0.1	2.4	0.0	4.2	7.4
36 63418	Rome	74.9	31,974	1,234	426.9	81.8	6.9	0.5	1.4	0.1	2.2	7.2
36 65255	Saratoga Springs	28.1	28,301	1,376	1,007.2	86.6	2.7	0.2	3.0	0.0	1.5	6.0
36 65508	Schenectady	10.8	66,990	563	6,202.8	45.9	22.0	1.4	6.6	0.2	10.7	13.3
36 70420	Spring Valley	2.0	33,033	1,191	16,516.5	33.9	29.8	1.0	3.6	0.0	23.9	7.9
36 73000	Syracuse	25.1	146,103	188	5,820.8	47.9	30.7	0.9	7.0	0.0	4.4	9.0
36 75484	Troy	10.4	50,394	793	4,845.6	61.2	19.7	0.4	5.0	0.0	3.8	9.9
36 76540	Utica	16.7	64,501	591	3,862.3	55.3	17.3	0.3	12.7	0.1	6.2	8.1
36 76705	Valley Stream	3.5	40,414	978	11,546.9	31.6	24.2	0.8	16.1	0.1	15.5	11.6
36 81677	White Plains	9.7	59,526	652	6,136.7	48.0	12.0	1.2	8.1	0.1	18.4	12.2
36 84000	Yonkers	18.0	209,530	112	11,640.6	37.3	18.0	1.2	6.2	0.0	24.6	12.6
37 00000	NORTH CAROLINA	48,620.3	10,551,162	X	217.0	62.2	20.5	1.2	3.3	0.1	5.9	6.8
37 01520	Apex	22.0	62,911	610	2,859.6	68.8	6.7	0.3	12.4	0.0	3.0	8.7
37 02080	Asheboro	18.9	27,124	1,434	1,435.1	57.4	12.3	1.3	1.4	0.0	16.9	10.8
37 02140	Asheville	45.5	94,067	355	2,067.4	75.8	10.5	0.4	1.6	0.3	4.1	7.3
37 09060	Burlington	30.2	58,818	664	1,947.6	47.4	28.5	1.0	2.4	0.1	13.5	7.1
37 10740	Cary	59.3	176,987	148	2,984.6	58.2	7.9	0.3	22.4	0.1	3.5	7.6
37 11800	Chapel Hill	21.6	61,128	631	2,830.0	64.2	9.6	0.4	15.0	0.0	3.0	7.7
37 12000	Charlotte	309.2	879,709	16	2,845.1	41.7	33.1	0.6	7.1	0.1	9.6	7.9
37 12860	Clayton	15.3	28,306	1,375	1,850.1	57.8	23.6	0.5	1.6	0.0	6.2	10.2
37 14100	Concord	63.7	107,697	286	1,690.7	54.4	22.4	0.5	6.7	0.1	7.7	8.2
37 14700	Cornelius	12.7	31,650	1,252	2,492.1	81.4	6.3	0.2	2.4	0.0	2.9	6.7
37 19000	Durham	113.5	285,527	74	2,515.7	40.2	36.2	0.7	5.6	0.0	9.8	7.4
37 22920	Fayetteville	148.3	208,778	113	1,407.8	37.3	43.0	1.2	3.2	0.5	4.9	9.8
37 25300	Fuquay-Varina	17.6	36,736	1,081	2,087.3	70.9	14.0	0.6	2.4	0.1	3.7	8.3
37 25480	Garner	16.6	31,935	1,236	1,923.8	52.6	29.9	0.8	2.2	0.1	7.0	7.4
37 25580	Gastonia	51.7	81,161	435	1,569.8	52.6	30.7	0.5	1.7	0.0	7.1	7.4
37 26880	Goldsboro	28.6	32,749	1,208	1,145.1	34.2	53.8	0.5	2.4	0.1	3.0	6.1
37 28000	Greensboro	130.3	298,263	69	2,289.0	40.0	42.0	0.6	5.1	0.0	5.6	6.6
37 28080	Greenville	37.1	88,728	388	2,391.6	46.8	41.4	0.4	2.8	0.1	3.1	5.5
37 31060	Hickory	30.8	43,532	915	1,413.4	66.5	13.8	0.7	3.9	0.1	7.1	8.0
37 31400	High Point	56.5	114,086	258	2,019.2	45.5	32.1	0.6	8.8	0.1	6.4	6.5
37 32260	Holly Springs	17.3	43,524	917	2,515.8	75.1	8.7	0.3	5.5	0.0	2.3	8.1
37 33120	Huntersville	41.3	61,839	624	1,497.3	71.4	12.0	0.3	4.2	0.0	4.2	7.8
37 33560	Indian Trail	22.4	40,953	964	1,828.3	68.3	11.6	0.5	2.8	0.1	7.3	9.4
37 34200	Jacksonville	48.8	72,876	506	1,493.4	58.0	18.2	0.7	3.4	0.6	7.5	11.6
37 35200	Kannapolis	33.5	54,446	733	1,625.3	56.8	22.3	0.6	2.5	0.0	9.2	8.5
37 35600	Kernersville	18.0	26,793	1,447	1,488.5	68.5	15.6	0.7	2.0	0.0	5.2	7.9
37 41960	Matthews	17.1	29,623	1,320	1,732.3	72.5	10.5	0.4	4.8	0.0	4.0	7.8
37 43480	Mint Hill	24.4	26,633	1,459	1,091.5	66.0	15.8	0.5	3.9	0.0	5.9	7.7
37 43920	Monroe	30.9	34,888	1,142	1,129.1	44.1	23.0	1.1	1.2	0.1	21.4	9.2
37 44220	Mooresville	25.3	51,594	772	2,039.3	71.6	11.1	0.4	5.2	0.1	3.9	7.7
37 44520	Morrisville	8.8	31,278	1,264	3,554.3	35.2	9.9	0.3	46.3	0.0	2.5	5.7
37 46340	New Bern	28.4	31,346	1,263	1,103.7	56.7	26.9	0.3	6.5	0.1	3.2	6.3
37 55000	Raleigh	147.1	469,124	41	3,189.2	53.3	26.3	0.6	5.0	0.1	7.5	7.4
37 57500	Rocky Mount	45.0	53,957	739	1,199.0	27.3	63.8	0.6	1.4	0.1	3.0	3.8
37 58860	Salisbury	21.9	35,760	1,111	1,632.9	46.4	36.1	0.7	1.4	0.1	8.8	6.6
37 59280	Sanford	29.6	30,678	1,288	1,036.4	47.3	24.0	0.9	1.5	0.1	16.4	9.8
37 64740	Statesville	25.1	28,844	1,352	1,149.2	51.7	32.4	0.3	1.9	0.0	6.1	7.6
37 67420	Thomasville	16.8	27,203	1,430	1,619.2	59.4	20.5	0.8	1.5	0.0	9.9	7.9
37 70540	Wake Forest	18.0	49,657	805	2,758.7	69.1	16.1	0.3	3.7	0.1	2.7	8.1
37 74440	Wilmington	51.4	117,643	240	2,288.8	70.9	16.5	0.4	1.6	0.1	3.9	6.6
37 74540	Wilson	31.2	47,731	836	1,529.8	37.8	48.3	0.5	1.7	0.0	6.6	5.0
37 75000	Winston-Salem	133.1	250,320	90	1,880.7	45.8	32.5	0.7	2.5	0.1	10.7	7.6

1. Dry land or land partially or temporarily covered by water. 2. Hispanic or Latino persons may be of any race.

City	Percent Hispanic or Latino[1], 2020	Percent foreign born, 2016–2020	Age of population (percent), 2016–2020: Under 18 years	18 to 24 years	25 to 34 years	35 to 44 years	45 to 54 years	55 to 64 years	65 years and over	Median age, 2016–2020	Percent female, 2016–2020	Population: Census counts: 2010	2020	Percent change: 2010–2020	2020–2021
	12	13	14	15	16	17	18	19	20	21	22	23	24	25	26
NEW YORK—Cont'd															
Lindenhurst	16.4	14.3	19.6	9.4	13.6	11.2	16.7	15.1	14.4	41.4	50.2	27,269	27,150	-0.4	0.0
Long Beach	15.3	15.0	14.0	7.4	16.4	11.7	13.2	18.6	18.6	45.2	50.2	33,333	34,968	4.9	-0.5
Middletown	43.6	16.1	26.6	9.8	12.0	12.2	13.1	11.9	14.3	36.4	50.5	28,126	30,421	8.2	0.1
Mount Vernon	19.0	30.4	19.3	7.3	14.9	13.2	13.9	13.3	17.9	41.4	56.2	67,324	73,693	9.5	-1.5
Newburgh	52.3	24.6	26.0	11.6	16.1	12.6	11.6	10.2	11.8	31.8	51.5	28,906	28,931	0.1	-0.3
New Rochelle	32.9	29.7	20.3	12.1	11.4	11.8	13.5	13.4	17.4	40.0	51.7	77,060	79,996	3.8	2.0
New York	28.3	36.4	20.7	8.5	17.8	13.6	12.5	11.9	14.9	36.9	52.3	8,174,930	8,804,190	7.7	-3.8
Niagara Falls	5.4	5.1	21.0	8.3	13.2	11.6	12.2	16.2	17.6	40.8	52.8	50,031	48,709	-2.6	-0.7
North Tonawanda	3.1	2.9	16.4	7.1	16.8	8.7	15.0	16.8	19.2	46.0	51.1	31,574	30,528	-3.3	-0.4
Ossining	47.4	34.3	18.8	6.1	14.1	15.4	16.9	12.8	15.9	42.1	47.2	25,058	27,693	10.5	-1.4
Peekskill	43.9	26.6	22.5	7.5	11.8	16.4	12.7	14.0	15.2	39.6	52.3	23,575	25,377	7.6	1.4
Port Chester	65.2	44.5	21.8	9.0	15.1	16.7	12.0	11.4	13.9	38.1	48.0	28,922	31,673	9.5	-1.5
Poughkeepsie	22.5	19.4	19.1	9.6	16.3	13.7	14.3	10.7	16.3	38.7	52.7	30,812	31,490	2.2	1.1
Rochester	19.8	9.4	22.5	12.3	19.5	11.7	10.9	11.4	11.6	32.4	51.6	210,645	211,233	0.3	-0.3
Rockville Centre	11.6	9.9	22.8	6.0	10.1	11.8	14.3	14.7	20.2	44.4	53.9	24,039	25,977	8.1	-0.6
Rome	7.2	3.4	21.3	7.2	15.5	10.9	11.6	14.8	18.7	40.1	50.0	33,715	32,138	-4.7	-0.5
Saratoga Springs	4.9	7.5	14.1	14.2	14.2	11.0	12.6	13.5	20.3	41.4	52.3	26,567	28,143	5.9	0.6
Schenectady	13.1	15.8	19.3	12.1	15.9	12.3	12.6	13.7	14.0	37.3	50.8	66,157	67,000	1.3	0.0
Spring Valley	32.3	40.2	34.1	10.4	13.7	14.5	10.1	7.9	9.2	28.5	50.3	31,328	33,062	5.5	-0.1
Syracuse	10.5	13.4	21.1	17.4	16.1	10.5	10.8	11.1	12.9	31.7	52.3	145,047	147,363	1.6	-0.9
Troy	10.6	7.7	19.3	18.2	18.6	11.1	10.2	11.0	11.7	31.2	51.1	50,162	50,760	1.2	-0.7
Utica	13.8	21.6	24.7	12.5	13.7	10.8	12.2	11.0	15.1	34.2	50.8	62,245	65,263	4.8	-1.2
Valley Stream	26.3	36.7	20.0	8.7	12.3	13.2	15.2	15.3	15.4	42.4	53.8	37,385	40,685	8.8	-0.7
White Plains	32.6	31.9	17.7	9.2	14.9	12.5	12.6	14.3	18.9	41.5	51.8	56,824	59,555	4.8	0.0
Yonkers	42.1	30.7	21.6	9.3	14.2	12.9	12.8	12.6	16.7	38.7	51.7	196,129	211,237	7.7	-0.8
NORTH CAROLINA	10.7	8.0	22.2	9.5	13.4	12.6	13.2	12.9	16.3	38.9	51.4	9,535,762	10,439,388	9.5	1.1
Apex	8.3	10.7	29.5	6.3	12.2	17.8	16.6	9.7	7.9	36.1	51.6	37,802	58,797	55.5	7.0
Asheboro	29.4	13.7	25.3	9.9	14.0	13.7	10.1	9.1	18.0	35.6	52.3	25,391	26,954	6.2	0.6
Asheville	8.1	7.3	17.5	8.2	17.4	14.7	12.5	10.8	18.9	39.6	52.0	83,359	94,539	13.4	-0.5
Burlington	20.1	11.8	22.3	8.4	14.1	11.7	13.2	12.5	17.8	39.3	52.7	51,062	57,346	12.3	2.6
Cary	8.2	22.4	25.6	6.1	11.5	16.0	15.9	12.5	12.5	39.6	51.0	135,869	174,754	28.6	1.3
Chapel Hill	7.6	15.7	17.1	32.5	11.8	9.6	10.1	7.9	11.0	25.2	52.5	57,221	61,326	7.2	-0.3
Charlotte	16.3	17.2	23.4	9.4	18.3	14.8	12.9	10.8	10.4	34.4	52.0	735,580	874,541	18.9	0.6
Clayton	14.3	10.0	24.0	8.2	18.7	12.7	13.4	10.4	12.6	34.6	49.2	16,210	26,323	62.4	7.5
Concord	13.9	11.5	25.7	7.8	13.1	15.1	14.2	12.0	12.1	37.7	50.9	79,342	105,186	32.6	2.4
Cornelius	7.3	8.2	22.8	6.3	8.7	15.2	17.3	13.0	16.8	43.0	51.3	24,906	31,432	26.2	0.7
Durham	15.3	14.7	21.3	11.0	19.4	13.7	11.8	10.8	11.9	34.1	53.1	230,740	283,547	22.9	0.7
Fayetteville	12.6	7.5	23.5	15.4	18.9	11.1	9.2	10.0	12.0	30.1	49.6	200,565	208,871	4.1	0.0
Fuquay-Varina	9.4	7.7	28.7	8.6	12.6	16.7	13.9	7.4	12.0	35.0	52.7	18,053	34,152	89.2	7.6
Garner	12.2	6.5	23.3	7.9	18.7	11.2	13.4	11.3	14.2	35.1	52.4	25,786	31,163	20.9	2.5
Gastonia	12.6	6.5	24.9	7.9	13.5	13.2	13.3	11.4	15.7	37.8	53.0	71,729	80,367	12.0	1.0
Goldsboro	7.1	5.2	21.2	11.6	15.2	10.7	11.0	12.2	18.0	36.9	51.8	35,413	33,107	-6.5	-1.1
Greensboro	10.2	12.0	22.0	13.1	15.8	12.1	12.4	11.1	13.5	34.4	53.7	268,936	297,899	10.8	0.1
Greenville	5.8	4.2	19.9	26.4	15.5	11.2	9.5	7.8	9.7	26.8	54.9	84,630	87,882	3.8	1.0
Hickory	12.8	9.9	22.6	10.8	13.1	11.8	13.6	11.9	16.2	37.8	52.0	40,186	43,279	7.7	0.6
High Point	11.2	12.8	23.1	10.4	13.1	12.9	12.6	12.2	15.7	37.7	51.9	104,517	113,887	9.0	0.2
Holly Springs	7.0	7.8	35.1	4.7	9.2	18.5	17.7	7.3	7.5	35.8	52.6	24,737	41,251	66.8	5.5
Huntersville	9.7	9.1	26.6	6.1	11.6	15.8	16.1	11.5	12.3	38.5	50.5	46,924	61,403	30.9	0.7
Indian Trail	14.4	10.2	28.9	10.1	11.1	14.7	15.5	10.1	9.6	35.0	52.3	33,618	40,079	19.2	2.2
Jacksonville	18.6	5.2	21.4	36.9	16.9	8.0	4.7	5.4	6.7	23.2	38.8	70,285	73,339	4.3	-0.6
Kannapolis	15.9	7.3	26.2	8.1	15.0	13.1	13.2	9.7	14.8	35.5	51.5	42,618	53,145	24.7	2.4
Kernersville	10.7	7.3	20.3	9.8	13.6	12.3	14.6	12.3	17.1	40.1	52.4	23,100	26,481	14.6	1.2
Matthews	9.2	10.6	21.1	8.2	15.2	11.0	14.5	13.0	17.0	39.7	50.5	27,189	29,429	8.2	0.7
Mint Hill	11.1	7.8	19.5	7.2	12.1	11.3	16.6	14.4	19.0	45.0	53.7	22,731	26,468	16.4	0.6
Monroe	31.7	14.9	26.4	11.6	11.7	13.8	13.5	9.6	13.4	35.2	50.8	32,909	34,551	5.0	1.0
Mooresville	8.8	11.0	25.8	8.8	14.7	14.2	14.5	10.1	11.8	35.4	52.4	34,377	50,205	46.0	2.8
Morrisville	5.8	34.9	25.5	7.6	19.6	18.6	12.5	10.0	6.3	34.0	49.8	18,585	29,633	59.4	5.6
New Bern	6.7	8.0	21.3	7.5	14.7	11.5	11.2	11.1	22.7	40.7	52.5	29,317	31,116	6.1	0.7
Raleigh	12.9	12.8	20.4	12.4	18.9	14.3	12.8	10.4	10.8	34.0	51.7	404,118	467,592	15.7	0.3
Rocky Mount	4.9	4.0	21.7	9.4	11.7	11.9	12.8	13.8	18.7	41.1	54.2	57,701	54,351	-5.8	-0.7
Salisbury	14.2	5.7	23.4	12.2	13.0	10.5	12.1	12.0	16.9	36.4	49.4	33,514	35,567	6.1	0.5
Sanford	28.2	12.5	28.4	8.3	14.3	13.2	12.6	10.5	12.6	34.2	52.6	28,217	30,227	7.1	1.5
Statesville	11.6	8.6	23.7	8.3	13.7	14.4	12.9	11.6	15.5	38.6	50.6	24,520	28,120	14.7	2.6
Thomasville	16.7	10.1	24.9	7.2	12.6	12.3	13.0	12.9	17.2	39.3	53.9	26,802	27,147	1.3	0.2
Wake Forest	7.9	6.0	28.2	6.4	11.5	16.0	17.5	9.3	11.1	37.7	52.4	30,135	47,625	58.0	4.3
Wilmington	8.3	4.7	17.1	16.4	14.4	11.6	10.7	12.6	17.2	37.1	53.6	106,465	115,955	8.9	1.5
Wilson	10.1	6.2	23.3	9.6	12.5	10.7	12.4	13.9	17.5	38.7	54.0	49,149	47,941	-2.5	-0.4
Winston-Salem	17.2	9.9	23.5	10.9	14.4	12.1	12.2	12.3	14.5	35.9	53.2	229,624	249,443	8.6	0.4

1. May be of any race.

City	Households, 2016–2020							Persons in group quarters, 2016–2020	Serious crimes known to police[2], 2020				Educational attainment, 2016–2020		
			Percent						Violent		Property			Attainment[4] (percent)	
	Number	Persons per household	Family	Married couple family	Female family	Non-family	One person		Number	Rate	Number	Rate	Population age 25 and over	High school graduate or less	Bachelor's degree or more
	27	28	29	30	31	32	33	34	35	36	37	38	39	40	41
NEW YORK—Cont'd															
Lindenhurst	8,727	3.08	75.2	58.4	12.7	24.8	19.8	35	NA	NA	NA	NA	19,079	43.3	26.0
Long Beach	14,010	2.31	56.9	41.8	10.7	43.1	33.2	1,065	13	38.9	46	137.5	26,305	26.1	49.7
Middletown	9,838	2.80	64.1	43.5	17.1	35.9	30.5	434	90	319.2	383	1,358.4	17,834	48.1	19.4
Mount Vernon	27,180	2.45	57.2	29.2	22.1	42.8	37.8	926	382	567.3	879	1,305.3	49,612	41.1	30.9
Newburgh	10,268	2.65	57.7	30.2	19.2	42.3	34.1	916	285	1,014.4	720	2,562.7	17,545	57.1	18.6
New Rochelle	29,004	2.63	65.7	48.1	13.2	34.3	30.0	3,065	NA	NA	NA	NA	53,595	36.7	44.4
New York	3,191,691	2.57	59.6	36.9	17.2	40.4	32.1	183,020	47,959	577.8	129,361	1,558.5	5,933,426	40.8	39.1
Niagara Falls	22,330	2.13	52.3	30.6	16.2	47.7	40.4	366	NA	NA	NA	NA	33,924	46.7	19.8
North Tonawanda	13,870	2.18	57.7	42.9	11.3	42.3	34.2	150	37	122.9	330	1,096.2	23,221	40.3	26.5
Ossining	9,141	2.53	66.8	48.7	12.8	33.2	27.8	1,869	17	68.6	196	790.8	18,749	40.3	34.2
Peekskill	9,679	2.47	60.7	36.0	16.7	39.3	33.1	156	33	135.4	176	722.2	16,865	46.2	31.2
Port Chester	9,236	3.14	73.2	54.7	12.9	26.8	21.8	243	22	75.4	209	716.2	20,199	49.7	29.7
Poughkeepsie	12,839	2.29	50.1	26.6	19.8	49.9	40.4	934	243	797.2	529	1,735.6	21,653	43.6	27.0
Rochester	88,006	2.24	47.6	20.5	22.2	52.4	41.7	9,435	1,680	818.7	6,887	3,356.3	134,522	43.7	27.1
Rockville Centre	9,792	2.48	67.0	56.2	8.4	33.0	31.0	249	14	56.9	106	430.8	17,474	19.7	60.4
Rome	13,092	2.28	57.3	37.0	15.6	42.7	37.0	2,367	65	203.3	570	1,782.5	23,039	45.8	21.5
Saratoga Springs	12,550	2.03	53.7	43.4	7.8	46.3	33.7	2,612	53	186.6	449	1,581.2	20,108	20.7	58.7
Schenectady	24,617	2.51	50.4	29.8	15.4	49.6	41.9	3,612	468	718.1	1,622	2,488.6	44,801	47.3	21.5
Spring Valley	9,818	3.28	70.8	42.8	19.3	29.2	25.9	80	96	296.7	343	1,060.1	17,931	54.7	17.6
Syracuse	56,384	2.25	49.4	24.7	19.2	50.6	38.9	15,436	1,192	839.4	4,009	2,823.0	87,543	43.3	29.0
Troy	20,228	2.20	48.4	23.7	19.9	51.6	39.8	4,721	330	672.8	1,411	2,876.5	30,818	38.2	30.6
Utica	22,443	2.55	59.9	34.5	19.1	40.1	33.2	2,733	298	501.0	2,017	3,390.9	37,637	50.5	20.1
Valley Stream	11,857	3.16	81.1	60.2	15.8	18.9	16.9	39	NA	NA	NA	NA	26,739	33.6	40.2
White Plains	23,222	2.45	61.8	46.8	10.1	38.2	31.7	1,219	NA	NA	NA	NA	42,520	30.5	51.2
Yonkers	75,864	2.60	64.0	41.2	16.7	36.0	30.9	3,090	653	325.2	1,990	991.0	138,335	42.4	34.5
NORTH CAROLINA	4,031,592	2.51	65.1	47.9	12.8	34.9	28.7	279,287	44,451	419.3	236,026	2,226.5	7,096,773	36.9	32.0
Apex	19,228	2.86	76.2	63.7	9.2	23.8	18.7	189	30	48.1	697	1,118.4	35,431	13.2	62.3
Asheboro	10,741	2.33	57.9	37.1	15.8	42.1	38.6	826	NA	NA	NA	NA	16,779	49.8	18.0
Asheville	39,895	2.23	46.3	35.0	8.6	53.7	40.8	3,442	761	809.7	5,395	5,740.6	68,570	24.6	49.9
Burlington	22,739	2.36	57.4	34.3	17.4	42.6	35.3	914	527	958.1	2,391	4,347.0	37,808	41.6	26.2
Cary	63,519	2.66	72.4	60.7	7.4	27.6	22.4	327	116	66.5	1,651	946.5	115,678	12.4	68.6
Chapel Hill	19,856	2.54	54.6	44.0	7.8	45.4	29.9	11,503	93	143.4	1,140	1,757.8	31,171	10.7	76.9
Charlotte	338,985	2.54	58.1	40.0	13.7	41.9	33.5	12,892	8,015	836.3	31,053	3,240.2	586,883	27.4	44.8
Clayton	8,337	2.77	70.0	52.4	10.3	30.0	25.6	104	38	145.7	597	2,288.5	15,699	30.3	30.7
Concord	33,059	2.81	70.2	53.0	12.9	29.8	24.8	1,315	118	119.9	1,375	1,397.2	62,617	33.2	38.3
Cornelius	12,363	2.41	66.0	54.1	8.1	34.0	28.0	7	NA	NA	NA	NA	21,164	16.0	54.4
Durham	114,420	2.31	55.6	37.1	14.0	44.4	34.9	11,666	2,447	858.8	10,650	3,737.8	187,292	26.6	51.2
Fayetteville	82,242	2.39	58.9	37.1	17.3	41.1	35.7	14,853	2,074	978.1	7,210	3,400.4	129,197	32.9	27.3
Fuquay-Varina	9,940	2.91	74.3	60.7	10.2	25.7	20.7	162	23	71.7	303	944.2	18,244	24.4	46.4
Garner	11,784	2.56	64.9	48.9	12.5	35.1	23.9	196	84	261.7	979	3,050.5	20,853	24.8	44.1
Gastonia	29,306	2.57	61.7	41.6	14.2	38.3	31.0	1,421	720	924.0	3,172	4,070.9	51,457	41.3	25.6
Goldsboro	14,632	2.22	55.6	31.8	21.5	44.4	39.9	2,069	397	1,165.9	1,709	5,018.9	23,231	45.3	20.5
Greensboro	118,126	2.36	56.6	35.0	17.1	43.4	35.1	15,912	2,704	901.7	10,830	3,611.4	190,993	31.4	39.4
Greenville	36,859	2.34	50.6	29.0	17.9	49.4	32.4	6,550	415	439.7	2,481	2,629.0	49,900	30.2	37.8
Hickory	16,704	2.37	59.5	42.1	11.9	40.5	34.2	1,531	223	540.0	1,718	4,159.8	27,353	35.8	35.0
High Point	42,840	2.52	64.2	41.8	17.2	35.8	30.1	4,443	773	679.7	3,417	3,004.6	74,771	39.7	32.2
Holly Springs	11,573	3.16	84.3	70.4	8.0	15.7	12.3	15	31	78.3	370	934.3	22,009	14.4	59.6
Huntersville	20,666	2.76	74.3	60.7	8.4	25.7	20.7	290	99	166.5	881	1,481.4	38,561	17.9	53.9
Indian Trail	12,693	3.12	81.5	68.8	8.0	18.5	15.5	0	NA	NA	NA	NA	24,197	30.2	38.6
Jacksonville	21,126	2.62	70.9	54.2	13.4	29.1	23.6	18,914	245	341.0	1,481	2,061.5	31,010	35.6	25.0
Kannapolis	17,569	2.82	71.7	49.7	17.4	28.3	22.6	270	122	235.4	1,460	2,816.5	32,697	41.3	24.9
Kernersville	10,731	2.30	57.9	42.8	11.5	42.1	37.6	190	81	326.2	1,036	4,171.5	17,395	34.3	32.0
Matthews	12,125	2.67	72.8	61.1	7.8	27.2	23.2	297	61	180.2	1,082	3,195.5	23,101	20.7	53.7
Mint Hill	10,474	2.60	76.0	61.1	11.3	24.0	21.3	39	59	209.2	361	1,279.7	19,994	25.8	40.3
Monroe	11,509	3.02	70.1	46.4	17.7	29.9	23.2	626	364	1,015.7	1,736	4,844.3	21,916	48.9	17.8
Mooresville	14,729	2.60	70.4	52.0	13.1	29.6	23.8	269	80	201.6	972	2,448.9	25,142	25.5	41.7
Morrisville	10,426	2.65	65.8	56.0	8.6	34.2	27.9	0	24	79.3	639	2,111.4	18,471	12.1	70.0
New Bern	13,666	2.17	57.3	40.2	11.8	42.7	36.9	396	190	632.3	930	3,095.2	21,357	36.5	27.7
Raleigh	187,517	2.40	54.9	38.6	12.5	45.1	34.1	20,203	1,891	392.1	9,745	2,020.7	315,693	23.5	51.4
Rocky Mount	22,475	2.37	63.8	34.9	22.9	36.2	31.9	1,153	615	1,149.1	1,564	2,922.3	37,428	49.7	21.1
Salisbury	12,401	2.44	61.3	35.6	19.9	38.7	32.3	3,655	251	737.3	1,218	3,577.6	21,882	41.3	25.0
Sanford	10,202	2.84	67.3	43.0	17.5	32.7	27.5	760	NA	NA	NA	NA	18,815	45.6	21.3
Statesville	10,963	2.40	64.2	35.5	23.0	35.8	30.7	782	NA	NA	NA	NA	18,433	40.3	27.1
Thomasville	10,850	2.43	65.3	42.7	16.0	34.7	31.1	435	118	443.1	735	2,759.9	18,239	54.4	13.8
Wake Forest	15,734	2.78	74.6	59.8	12.5	25.4	19.2	364	66	138.3	519	1,087.2	28,844	18.4	55.5
Wilmington	53,830	2.17	47.6	34.3	10.3	52.4	39.1	5,615	791	628.8	3,204	2,547.0	81,333	26.7	43.9
Wilson	19,463	2.46	60.5	37.3	18.6	39.5	33.9	1,435	270	545.6	1,439	2,907.9	33,060	48.4	22.8
Winston-Salem	96,611	2.44	58.2	38.1	15.7	41.8	35.5	10,506	NA	NA	NA	NA	161,205	36.7	34.3

2. Data for serious crimes have not been adjusted for underreporting. This may affect comparability between geographic areas and over time.

4. Persons 25 years old and over.

City	Money income, 2016–2020					Median earnings Full year, Full-time workers, 2016–2020			Housing units, 2016–2020				
	Households												
	Median household income	Percent with income less than $25,000	Percent with income of $200,000 or more	Median family income	Median non-family household income	All persons	Men	Women	Total	Occupied	Percent owner occupied	Median value[1] (dollars)	Median gross rent (dollars)
	42	43	44	45	46	47	48	49	50	51	52	53	54
NEW YORK—Cont'd													
Lindenhurst	101,867	9.0	12.3	113,270	48,921	63,285	74,859	50,734	9,258	8,727	84.1	384,400	1,750
Long Beach	106,709	9.9	20.3	124,890	75,976	75,458	79,449	70,402	15,855	14,010	60.2	555,900	2,026
Middletown	58,235	22.1	5.8	73,526	31,560	46,750	48,322	45,128	11,197	9,838	54.8	186,200	1,284
Mount Vernon	59,291	23.3	8.1	81,875	34,122	51,124	51,712	50,474	28,632	27,180	38.1	367,200	1,327
Newburgh	43,435	28.8	2.3	60,010	30,972	40,322	42,344	36,935	11,937	10,268	32.1	159,500	1,139
New Rochelle	81,735	17.4	19.3	110,077	44,286	71,243	72,030	69,506	30,407	29,004	53.3	562,300	1,537
New York	67,046	22.4	12.1	75,865	50,460	57,312	59,710	55,094	3,519,595	3,191,691	32.8	635,200	1,489
Niagara Falls	41,137	33.4	2.4	55,015	26,764	41,122	46,230	36,247	26,696	22,330	58.6	78,500	649
North Tonawanda	60,673	18.9	2.3	78,300	35,953	48,472	53,467	42,328	14,980	13,870	69.9	129,200	735
Ossining	83,060	13.0	13.1	95,788	57,614	60,944	62,452	58,549	9,816	9,141	52.5	363,200	1,770
Peekskill	66,067	20.4	7.8	81,495	35,689	51,360	53,701	42,283	10,561	9,679	49.6	288,300	1,524
Port Chester	81,586	15.8	12.8	86,651	42,260	45,970	44,125	49,340	9,768	9,236	41.3	458,000	1,778
Poughkeepsie	47,008	26.7	5.4	64,228	36,919	44,026	45,212	42,865	14,262	12,839	35.9	204,000	1,127
Rochester	37,395	35.5	2.7	43,873	30,398	41,370	44,231	39,103	100,276	88,006	36.2	88,100	875
Rockville Centre	118,254	12.2	30.9	172,476	51,166	97,665	124,648	85,545	10,198	9,792	73.3	653,300	1,645
Rome	51,752	25.5	2.5	66,714	31,602	43,847	50,892	38,264	15,202	13,092	57.2	101,200	779
Saratoga Springs	85,946	11.5	13.5	117,299	56,230	71,084	80,981	59,169	14,357	12,550	55.8	360,000	1,328
Schenectady	47,773	27.5	1.8	56,642	34,238	42,147	43,210	40,498	31,819	24,617	45.1	113,200	919
Spring Valley	45,646	27.3	3.4	51,034	26,954	36,106	37,584	35,627	10,485	9,818	25.6	312,100	1,377
Syracuse	38,893	34.4	2.2	48,072	29,662	43,243	45,170	41,628	67,961	56,384	39.2	95,800	830
Troy	48,834	27.7	2.4	61,167	36,564	48,771	50,917	46,295	23,794	20,228	33.8	149,900	964
Utica	42,624	31.6	2.6	50,770	28,274	38,632	40,940	36,280	27,334	22,443	51.7	102,400	750
Valley Stream	116,746	7.3	17.3	129,079	44,021	64,766	64,106	65,328	12,594	11,857	82.1	450,100	1,634
White Plains	96,715	14.6	19.9	118,785	61,730	70,135	73,032	66,700	25,038	23,222	52.0	558,100	1,781
Yonkers	69,825	19.6	10.3	83,571	41,835	57,053	60,468	54,731	81,020	75,864	47.3	414,200	1,461
NORTH CAROLINA	56,642	20.7	6.0	70,978	34,473	44,831	49,745	40,904	4,687,122	4,031,592	65.7	182,100	932
Apex	112,549	7.3	15.6	130,392	65,177	78,195	89,867	61,617	20,483	19,228	74.9	348,500	1,415
Asheboro	37,171	31.6	1.1	45,589	25,252	33,857	36,300	32,296	11,735	10,741	48.6	119,700	685
Asheville	53,621	22.9	6.5	74,348	36,472	40,937	42,681	38,759	47,165	39,895	49.1	291,800	1,084
Burlington	45,587	28.3	2.8	56,343	30,604	38,204	41,332	35,370	25,221	22,739	53.5	137,000	823
Cary	107,463	7.1	20.1	132,620	57,209	80,019	96,069	63,463	67,287	63,519	67.4	376,600	1,312
Chapel Hill	75,249	20.6	20.7	140,189	39,011	67,418	81,190	57,140	22,152	19,856	51.8	435,500	1,221
Charlotte	65,359	15.4	9.7	80,247	48,539	50,043	54,740	44,475	367,252	338,985	52.8	235,000	1,185
Clayton	61,954	16.9	5.9	71,912	34,487	46,478	49,284	45,295	9,020	8,337	64.1	200,700	1,060
Concord	70,973	14.9	9.0	85,746	41,591	49,159	53,773	44,042	37,098	33,059	69.6	220,300	1,011
Cornelius	90,377	11.3	19.2	127,500	50,217	70,838	83,233	58,721	13,485	12,363	71.5	352,600	1,236
Durham	61,962	17.1	7.4	83,610	43,386	50,703	52,645	48,389	122,422	114,420	51.6	243,000	1,098
Fayetteville	46,321	25.6	2.5	54,563	33,168	37,934	40,767	35,315	95,045	82,242	44.4	134,800	960
Fuquay-Varina	81,914	14.2	7.0	98,513	41,250	54,063	59,488	50,243	10,420	9,940	69.7	278,100	1,279
Garner	67,571	11.4	6.7	84,766	49,690	50,996	56,375	47,593	12,436	11,784	63.7	214,400	1,218
Gastonia	50,266	24.9	3.1	67,220	29,754	41,924	46,745	37,359	32,689	29,306	55.0	162,900	902
Goldsboro	37,556	36.0	2.4	48,005	24,852	33,430	37,853	31,411	16,894	14,632	39.7	134,200	799
Greensboro	49,492	24.3	5.0	64,570	35,553	41,372	44,684	39,252	131,171	118,126	49.4	163,000	893
Greenville	42,612	28.8	4.0	58,968	33,148	40,588	44,799	36,309	42,996	36,859	33.6	159,400	823
Hickory	48,653	26.3	4.8	68,045	27,930	39,718	44,733	34,201	18,640	16,704	55.9	189,100	771
High Point	49,649	22.2	4.2	65,270	32,477	42,745	47,171	37,972	48,013	42,840	57.9	162,000	880
Holly Springs	110,758	5.2	17.6	120,369	53,842	79,310	89,694	65,192	12,059	11,573	81.7	354,500	1,489
Huntersville	100,789	7.4	16.1	116,102	63,642	74,222	82,218	60,288	21,562	20,666	73.6	318,000	1,363
Indian Trail	86,512	8.2	9.6	94,606	44,768	53,736	60,918	45,756	13,144	12,693	86.6	238,800	1,488
Jacksonville	45,754	18.0	2.5	48,426	36,163	33,441	35,911	31,333	23,504	21,126	33.0	157,000	1,032
Kannapolis	55,923	22.0	4.1	66,499	30,567	40,659	42,672	38,474	20,119	17,569	61.3	160,200	875
Kernersville	56,991	21.8	4.8	79,222	35,436	48,488	51,486	44,846	11,559	10,731	51.8	196,400	851
Matthews	89,881	9.7	9.7	109,419	43,170	57,370	67,210	50,425	12,727	12,125	68.7	283,100	1,350
Mint Hill	80,093	12.5	7.6	93,400	39,463	52,417	62,055	49,021	11,071	10,474	78.5	281,200	1,025
Monroe	53,064	18.4	3.7	62,828	38,218	38,793	40,463	35,906	12,627	11,509	58.6	174,100	997
Mooresville	70,625	14.0	6.4	79,240	43,679	54,826	62,549	43,914	15,426	14,729	57.2	245,900	1,176
Morrisville	100,495	6.3	13.9	123,101	81,331	77,753	92,645	63,059	11,132	10,426	52.1	333,500	1,459
New Bern	43,406	25.0	3.9	61,390	29,543	37,894	39,588	35,373	15,889	13,666	56.9	160,500	863
Raleigh	69,720	13.9	9.2	88,922	51,512	52,006	55,160	48,901	206,328	187,517	51.5	266,900	1,175
Rocky Mount	42,691	29.1	3.1	50,651	23,821	37,948	44,832	33,603	26,839	22,475	50.9	109,700	782
Salisbury	43,364	29.5	4.3	52,136	27,235	42,044	44,687	36,621	14,451	12,401	49.5	140,000	818
Sanford	47,017	25.5	2.5	57,627	27,724	35,666	38,389	32,555	11,309	10,202	52.3	144,900	780
Statesville	42,004	26.2	2.5	57,609	28,522	37,048	43,504	33,233	12,190	10,963	52.1	161,200	762
Thomasville	42,257	27.1	0.7	51,561	28,088	37,054	38,484	35,019	11,832	10,850	59.4	118,000	707
Wake Forest	100,162	6.9	9.3	107,491	54,022	63,779	74,349	53,388	16,488	15,734	70.1	314,200	1,190
Wilmington	51,137	26.5	6.9	76,329	34,916	43,967	49,190	40,394	60,289	53,830	46.0	264,600	1,008
Wilson	43,126	31.4	3.5	57,351	25,169	38,046	42,273	34,058	22,140	19,463	51.1	146,000	747
Winston-Salem	47,269	25.6	4.8	62,568	31,286	40,467	41,620	38,549	109,657	96,611	54.6	152,000	827

1. Specified owner-occupied units

Table D. Cities — Commuting, Computer Access, Migration, Labor Force, and Employment

City	Commuting, 2016–2020[1]: Percent: Drove alone	Commuting, 2016–2020[1]: Mean travel time to work	Computer access[2], 2016–2020: Percent: With a computer in the house	Computer access[2], 2016–2020: Percent: With Internet access	Migration, 2016–2020: Percent who lived in the same house one year ago	Migration, 2016–2020: Percent who lived in another state or county one year ago	Civilian labor force, 2021: Total	Civilian labor force, 2021: Percent change 2020–2021	Civilian labor force, 2021: Unemployment[3]: Total	Civilian labor force, 2021: Unemployment[3]: Rate	Civilian Employment, 2016–2020[4]: Population age 16 and older: Number	Civilian Employment, 2016–2020[4]: Population age 16 and older: Percent in labor force	Civilian Employment, 2016–2020[4]: Population age 16 to 64: Number	Civilian Employment, 2016–2020[4]: Population age 16 to 64: Percent who worked full-year full-time
	55	56	57	58	59	60	61	62	63	64	65	66	67	68
NEW YORK—Cont'd														
Lindenhurst	77.4	32.8	95.4	91.3	91.9	3.0	15,250	-0.8	691	4.5	22,357	69.0	18,491	52.8
Long Beach	61.7	42.3	94.7	91.2	89.4	1.8	19,809	0.2	831	4.2	29,309	67.9	23,077	57.8
Middletown	72.6	30.6	92.5	76.9	86.8	5.2	13,912	-2.2	800	5.8	21,725	62.2	17,714	48.6
Mount Vernon	49.8	37.3	89.4	70.2	90.4	4.6	33,095	-2.4	2,479	7.5	55,953	64.9	43,818	55.6
Newburgh	62.5	25.4	81.2	74.0	90.8	3.6	12,205	-2.6	813	6.7	21,751	62.5	18,421	45.6
New Rochelle	55.2	33.0	91.0	84.4	89.8	4.6	39,920	-1.2	2,079	5.2	65,773	64.3	51,992	45.8
New York	22.3	41.4	90.8	83.4	90.1	4.4	4,043,671	-1.5	398,364	9.9	6,821,791	63.4	5,569,278	50.6
Niagara Falls	76.1	19.6	84.0	75.6	90.3	3.2	20,339	-4.5	1,562	7.7	38,875	57.8	30,441	45.3
North Tonawanda	85.5	20.8	88.6	82.6	92.0	3.5	14,936	-2.9	731	4.9	26,108	64.4	20,277	53.5
Ossining	60.4	34.6	93.4	87.3	86.4	6.2	12,963	-0.7	585	4.5	20,920	64.6	16,954	51.3
Peekskill	61.5	38.8	88.3	82.2	90.2	4.4	13,089	-1.2	605	4.6	19,182	69.1	15,523	55.5
Port Chester	54.5	26.0	91.5	87.3	89.4	3.3	16,313	-0.9	591	3.6	23,420	68.8	19,360	50.8
Poughkeepsie	65.3	25.7	88.3	80.7	83.7	6.9	13,502	-2.8	884	6.5	25,174	63.0	20,216	47.1
Rochester	68.1	19.8	87.7	78.9	79.1	6.3	89,949	-2.9	7,151	8.0	164,716	61.9	140,769	41.8
Rockville Centre	54.9	39.4	90.9	88.1	92.6	2.9	12,387	0.6	504	4.1	19,636	66.6	14,665	56.9
Rome	79.2	18.1	86.8	81.7	87.1	3.9	13,336	-2.5	729	5.5	25,962	52.5	19,932	48.4
Saratoga Springs	71.7	25.3	94.8	91.2	80.3	11.5	14,134	-2.5	552	3.9	24,671	63.3	18,964	51.6
Schenectady	72.0	21.5	91.4	81.1	86.4	6.6	30,403	-2.8	2,010	6.6	53,962	61.1	44,803	45.2
Spring Valley	54.6	25.0	82.3	72.2	88.1	4.6	14,834	-1.1	660	4.4	22,511	67.2	19,527	38.9
Syracuse	63.4	17.6	84.2	72.2	76.6	9.6	58,122	-3.1	4,018	6.9	115,719	56.4	97,291	36.6
Troy	65.8	22.3	91.4	83.7	75.3	14.3	22,847	-2.5	1,342	5.9	40,994	60.9	35,236	41.2
Utica	72.2	16.9	87.8	80.3	81.8	7.7	23,182	-3.1	1,586	6.8	46,658	56.8	37,598	41.0
Valley Stream	62.4	41.9	96.6	93.7	93.0	4.7	19,719	-1.3	1,006	5.1	30,916	69.2	25,141	56.0
White Plains	53.7	28.3	94.8	91.9	88.1	5.7	32,055	-1.0	1,272	4.0	49,059	66.3	38,080	54.3
Yonkers	52.0	34.6	90.7	82.6	90.5	4.4	96,270	-2.8	6,078	6.3	162,646	63.9	129,142	50.7
NORTH CAROLINA	79.3	24.9	90.7	82.9	85.4	7.3	4,959,672	2.3	238,474	4.8	8,352,255	61.2	6,663,901	51.3
Apex	77.3	24.4	97.6	94.6	85.2	7.5	33,594	4.6	974	2.9	40,769	74.5	36,384	61.2
Asheboro	80.8	19.7	89.7	81.0	83.1	4.4	10,558	0.6	596	5.6	20,019	58.1	15,374	48.0
Asheville	74.1	17.7	88.8	83.6	82.3	9.0	49,583	0.8	2,235	4.5	77,828	63.9	60,392	50.8
Burlington	87.2	22.3	89.5	78.9	85.3	7.5	25,969	2.2	1,417	5.5	43,435	62.7	33,708	52.7
Cary	74.0	22.9	98.3	95.6	82.4	9.2	93,305	4.4	3,072	3.3	131,064	70.6	109,876	59.2
Chapel Hill	53.7	20.3	97.6	89.3	67.0	22.6	31,773	4.2	1,183	3.7	52,634	59.0	45,853	34.2
Charlotte	72.6	25.6	94.9	89.0	82.4	7.2	493,015	2.0	24,943	5.1	690,712	71.7	599,953	57.2
Clayton	78.2	30.5	96.6	83.5	77.4	12.7	13,487	4.6	494	3.7	18,221	68.7	15,308	56.0
Concord	78.9	28.6	94.5	88.6	85.0	7.0	49,255	2.1	2,292	4.7	72,658	69.6	61,282	55.4
Cornelius	72.0	28.1	98.0	94.0	86.3	6.1	17,821	2.6	660	3.7	24,029	64.5	19,016	56.1
Durham	74.8	22.8	94.2	87.8	80.0	10.0	154,522	3.2	6,413	4.2	223,304	68.9	190,389	54.6
Fayetteville	76.4	19.3	91.4	84.9	76.0	12.7	75,372	1.2	5,688	7.5	166,195	51.3	140,881	54.1
Fuquay-Varina	76.2	32.5	94.2	91.1	87.0	7.0	15,546	4.3	620	4.0	21,423	68.7	17,932	55.0
Garner	78.2	28.0	95.4	92.2	78.1	13.6	17,615	3.8	757	4.3	23,896	70.0	19,596	60.0
Gastonia	84.6	25.6	89.6	81.3	84.7	7.1	36,329	1.6	2,191	6.0	59,996	64.2	47,936	52.3
Goldsboro	77.6	18.4	83.4	78.7	77.8	10.0	11,370	0.7	842	7.4	28,087	49.0	21,872	41.5
Greensboro	79.5	21.4	89.6	79.0	82.5	7.6	141,807	0.7	8,400	5.9	236,505	65.1	196,831	48.4
Greenville	78.7	18.0	92.4	84.3	67.4	18.4	46,883	1.7	2,559	5.5	76,149	63.2	67,139	40.3
Hickory	77.3	19.6	90.7	83.5	82.7	10.3	19,923	1.3	977	4.9	33,095	61.6	26,444	47.7
High Point	80.6	20.7	91.8	84.6	82.7	8.1	52,493	0.9	3,273	6.2	89,731	62.3	72,080	48.6
Holly Springs	77.4	28.7	97.6	95.9	86.8	6.3	19,582	4.0	637	3.3	25,223	72.0	22,473	58.6
Huntersville	77.5	29.2	97.1	93.7	87.1	7.3	33,709	2.4	1,200	3.6	43,538	70.9	36,493	57.6
Indian Trail	79.9	32.2	97.5	94.3	84.7	9.2	21,075	2.7	774	3.7	29,444	74.8	25,621	57.3
Jacksonville	60.8	15.0	96.1	89.8	63.5	26.4	19,931	3.6	1,196	6.0	59,590	34.7	54,583	65.7
Kannapolis	79.9	25.0	91.6	84.6	86.5	8.2	24,001	2.0	1,260	5.2	38,071	65.3	30,727	55.5
Kernersville	81.1	23.1	92.9	86.8	83.8	10.2	13,278	1.9	553	4.2	20,523	65.8	16,257	56.3
Matthews	78.4	28.2	96.0	91.8	87.8	6.8	18,022	2.9	672	3.7	26,481	66.8	20,931	56.7
Mint Hill	79.3	29.2	96.0	93.5	88.3	6.4	14,562	2.6	574	3.9	22,717	65.2	17,547	56.5
Monroe	76.9	28.1	92.0	85.6	85.3	6.2	17,001	2.8	901	5.3	27,504	64.7	22,783	50.5
Mooresville	77.6	24.7	95.9	91.2	78.8	11.9	20,836	1.4	1,000	4.8	29,750	67.6	25,188	53.9
Morrisville	72.8	21.8	96.7	94.3	74.3	11.5	16,903	4.7	490	2.9	21,226	73.5	19,486	61.7
New Bern	82.5	19.2	89.6	77.7	84.8	7.9	12,498	1.7	627	5.0	24,283	56.8	17,485	53.2
Raleigh	75.3	24.4	96.8	92.1	79.8	8.2	252,626	3.4	11,337	4.5	384,617	70.2	333,820	54.8
Rocky Mount	84.7	22.2	85.0	72.3	85.0	10.2	22,269	1.0	2,086	9.4	44,097	57.0	33,929	44.0
Salisbury	76.0	22.0	87.9	79.8	82.8	10.0	13,496	1.6	944	7.0	26,957	57.5	21,214	42.0
Sanford	82.7	24.6	87.6	69.0	86.2	6.1	11,993	0.7	725	6.0	22,114	63.9	18,361	52.6
Statesville	79.1	21.3	88.6	80.9	84.1	5.4	11,928	1.5	799	6.7	21,373	66.5	17,175	51.7
Thomasville	83.2	24.2	87.6	80.9	86.0	8.2	11,837	0.9	704	5.9	21,066	59.2	16,460	46.2
Wake Forest	79.4	30.9	97.2	95.7	76.9	9.5	23,734	4.0	883	3.7	33,185	71.5	28,291	57.7
Wilmington	77.8	18.4	92.8	83.2	79.7	10.8	64,352	3.6	2,901	4.5	103,702	61.8	82,631	47.1
Wilson	80.8	20.0	82.2	73.5	84.6	5.2	19,591	-0.7	1,534	7.8	39,050	59.2	30,410	47.1
Winston-Salem	79.3	21.1	92.0	81.5	85.3	6.7	115,889	1.7	6,356	5.5	194,924	60.7	159,278	47.6

1. Employed persons. 2. Households. 3. Percent of civilian labor force. 4. Persons 16 years old and over.

City	Value of residential construction authorized by building permits, 2021			Wholesale trade[1], 2017				Retail trade[2], 2017			
	New construction ($1,000)	Number of housing units	Percent single family	Number of establishments	Number of employees	Sales (mil dol)	Annual payroll (mil dol)	Number of establish-ments	Number of employees	Sales (mil dol)	Annual payroll (mil dol)
	69	70	71	72	73	74	75	76	77	78	79
NEW YORK—Cont'd											
Lindenhurst	3,470	34	11.8	41	290	117.1	14.8	91	516	175.1	20.9
Long Beach	4,200	21	100.0	28	98	34.7	6.0	84	906	325.2	35.8
Middletown	18,348	76	100.0	27	210	115.0	11.2	115	1,509	465.4	39.0
Mount Vernon	200	2	100.0	86	962	665.3	56.0	226	2,264	559.3	59.6
Newburgh	9,356	28	100.0	34	271	162.6	13.2	84	756	250.8	22.9
New Rochelle	177,865	863	0.2	70	382	338.0	24.2	237	3,025	1,338.9	106.3
New York	615,409	5,348	0.0	13,813	150,295	190,586.3	10,284.5	35,488	353,094	116,309.8	11,294.6
Niagara Falls	1,200	7	14.3	D	D	D	D	287	4,335	856.0	81.2
North Tonawanda	3,465	16	43.8	D	D	D	19.2	75	1,166	256.2	28.5
Ossining	680	4	0.0	12	D	86.3	D	75	609	169.2	18.7
Peekskill	3,800	37	5.4	27	318	119.6	13.5	95	916	242.2	25.0
Port Chester	0	0	0.0	39	484	313.8	31.4	155	2,397	703.4	69.5
Poughkeepsie	4,546	33	6.1	23	219	183.4	11.2	125	1,649	296.7	36.6
Rochester	6,508	45	100.0	242	3,356	1,616.0	178.7	743	7,184	1,437.2	178.2
Rockville Centre	1,897	4	100.0	35	259	131.2	21.0	120	1,163	391.4	37.1
Rome	15,850	98	5.1	19	215	111.9	9.4	117	2,083	536.1	54.3
Saratoga Springs	47,267	71	91.5	24	554	283.9	30.2	146	1,947	640.9	58.3
Schenectady	15,478	121	0.0	38	362	350.3	23.9	197	1,520	414.5	39.3
Spring Valley	4,075	22	45.5	45	371	496.0	14.2	164	1,380	553.2	45.4
Syracuse	2,622	19	89.5	120	1,855	1,947.4	101.4	593	7,219	1,770.9	184.3
Troy	6,603	45	11.1	26	347	878.6	21.6	142	1,338	352.5	36.2
Utica	0	0	0.0	54	846	475.9	39.8	186	2,619	619.4	63.4
Valley Stream	3,949	33	36.4	59	432	357.5	31.6	178	2,151	728.2	65.9
White Plains	86,250	296	1.4	105	1,757	4,032.0	242.2	396	7,271	2,111.7	227.9
Yonkers	56,183	579	2.1	149	1,270	844.4	70.0	715	10,095	2,895.5	290.1
NORTH CAROLINA	20,485,854	94,874	22.3	9,831	154,877	132,342.1	10,273.4	34,926	496,081	141,134.3	12,673.3
Apex	301,489	1,444	84.1	46	451	359.1	28.4	148	3,034	960.6	85.1
Asheboro	9,045	89	97.8	33	323	179.4	11.7	187	2,619	729.0	65.2
Asheville	117,220	549	82.5	160	1,660	1,185.9	101.4	872	14,168	3,501.8	358.6
Burlington	80,984	623	46.7	74	1,213	487.2	72.2	354	5,770	1,446.4	135.4
Cary	496,385	2,305	41.8	158	3,619	6,133.0	362.3	544	9,914	3,169.6	279.7
Chapel Hill	68,023	450	9.3	25	141	197.2	9.6	168	2,741	826.4	80.3
Charlotte	NA	NA	NA	1,606	27,225	22,741.5	1,831.8	2,758	46,761	13,772.2	1,307.5
Clayton	88,119	513	100.0	14	208	188.6	9.7	84	1,412	419.4	34.7
Concord	NA	NA	NA	109	1,785	1,935.2	123.4	507	10,139	2,490.6	240.2
Cornelius	NA	NA	NA	46	515	196.6	29.9	112	1,603	547.2	49.2
Durham	742,485	3,321	59.0	216	5,244	4,486.4	539.2	867	14,593	3,700.2	368.3
Fayetteville	70,697	397	84.9	95	1,710	668.2	60.8	861	14,319	3,941.0	360.1
Fuquay-Varina	375,686	1,807	100.0	16	208	127.2	10.0	118	2,158	706.8	54.5
Garner	136,095	992	71.0	66	1,411	957.4	72.5	156	3,136	784.4	67.2
Gastonia	230,377	924	66.9	84	882	353.3	35.6	365	5,816	1,419.2	137.6
Goldsboro	15,344	68	100.0	61	1,302	1,092.6	47.5	296	4,265	1,138.7	97.2
Greensboro	336,968	1,892	28.0	538	9,612	10,399.4	850.7	1,246	20,654	5,768.7	538.6
Greenville	137,865	843	44.2	54	503	370.3	29.0	414	6,765	1,782.8	169.9
Hickory	NA	NA	NA	118	4,143	3,412.8	233.6	410	7,136	2,240.3	191.9
High Point	91,000	524	100.0	307	4,428	4,430.5	256.8	388	5,018	1,523.8	134.1
Holly Springs	193,675	1,056	67.4	15	63	49.9	3.9	67	1,289	337.7	31.5
Huntersville	NA	NA	NA	53	924	1,346.6	73.7	173	3,872	1,141.2	97.9
Indian Trail	NA	NA	NA	88	927	500.9	58.7	107	2,226	741.2	64.0
Jacksonville	3,964	17	100.0	27	139	70.3	6.2	329	6,247	1,701.0	153.4
Kannapolis	NA	NA	NA	21	297	225.7	14.9	155	1,807	527.9	44.0
Kernersville	72,267	557	51.9	65	839	727.2	51.1	157	3,315	1,105.5	112.2
Matthews	NA	NA	NA	54	944	325.0	58.6	164	3,091	996.3	84.7
Mint Hill	NA	NA	NA	26	124	85.2	8.9	66	949	235.3	22.3
Monroe	76,803	556	89.2	63	1,077	565.9	58.9	226	3,026	778.0	70.4
Mooresville	NA	NA	NA	105	998	579.3	66.0	258	4,663	1,415.5	118.1
Morrisville	42,489	242	74.4	88	4,185	12,734.1	521.8	106	1,782	492.9	44.1
New Bern	4,306	18	100.0	28	307	796.2	16.7	205	3,162	856.3	77.9
Raleigh	1,213,136	6,487	20.9	596	10,466	8,105.1	673.8	1,798	29,789	9,238.1	845.8
Rocky Mount	26,961	219	100.0	83	1,534	933.5	69.2	300	4,016	1,041.0	91.7
Salisbury	NA	NA	NA	53	844	593.4	44.9	200	3,193	939.9	82.0
Sanford	24,370	116	100.0	33	550	569.6	25.4	210	2,741	771.3	66.6
Statesville	NA	NA	NA	59	835	527.0	43.9	204	3,062	896.1	79.1
Thomasville	15,845	97	97.9	31	711	226.6	27.2	131	1,350	339.7	30.1
Wake Forest	154,348	753	100.0	31	296	236.4	20.0	D	D	D	D
Wilmington	NA	NA	NA	138	1,385	743.7	85.0	801	11,925	3,747.0	329.9
Wilson	29,939	201	45.3	80	811	532.1	43.4	272	3,456	909.7	83.9
Winston-Salem	195,194	1,087	100.0	236	3,954	3,454.2	218.7	1,009	16,801	4,562.7	424.0

1. Merchant wholesalers except manufacturers' sales branches and offices. 2. Establishments with payroll.

City	Real estate and rental and leasing, 2017				Professional, scientific, and technical services[1], 2017				Manufacturing, 2017			
	Number of establish-ments	Number of employees	Receipts (mil dol)	Annual payroll (mil dol)	Number of establish-ments	Number of employees	Receipts (mil dol)	Annual payroll (mil dol)	Number of establish-ments	Number of employees	Receipts (mil dol)	Annual payroll (mil dol)
	80	81	82	83	84	85	86	87	88	89	90	91
NEW YORK—Cont'd												
Lindenhurst	16	33	10.1	1.1	58	161	26.4	7.9	NA	NA	NA	NA
Long Beach	49	129	43.9	5.8	105	195	35.3	9.3	NA	NA	NA	NA
Middletown	26	95	22.3	2.7	45	165	20.9	8.2	NA	NA	NA	NA
Mount Vernon	127	549	95.4	22.6	101	377	59.7	21.0	NA	NA	NA	NA
Newburgh	18	81	14.3	2.6	56	416	51.0	20.9	NA	NA	NA	NA
New Rochelle	200	692	226.8	34.2	215	719	130.4	47.7	NA	NA	NA	NA
New York	20,435	127,520	53,248.7	8,226.3	28,631	406,156	126,759.0	42,531.8	NA	NA	NA	NA
Niagara Falls	46	306	54.0	8.0	79	391	54.9	15.1	NA	NA	NA	NA
North Tonawanda	8	20	2.5	0.9	31	151	10.8	4.8	NA	NA	NA	NA
Ossining	29	101	35.4	3.3	52	166	32.6	10.2	NA	NA	NA	NA
Peekskill	31	176	36.7	12.4	53	207	38.4	13.5	NA	NA	NA	NA
Port Chester	31	107	32.1	5.8	72	229	41.5	10.7	NA	NA	NA	NA
Poughkeepsie	47	198	32.4	7.2	121	921	130.9	54.1	NA	NA	NA	NA
Rochester	286	2,481	416.1	108.5	637	9,109	1,513.0	610.9	NA	NA	NA	NA
Rockville Centre	89	180	56.1	9.5	206	710	142.9	46.8	NA	NA	NA	NA
Rome	33	97	16.8	2.8	85	1,444	327.1	106.5	NA	NA	NA	NA
Saratoga Springs	83	380	89.7	16.3	184	1,294	267.0	96.0	NA	NA	NA	NA
Schenectady	59	264	61.9	10.2	125	1,234	154.0	71.7	NA	NA	NA	NA
Spring Valley	104	567	93.5	21.1	89	245	36.4	12.7	NA	NA	NA	NA
Syracuse	209	1,615	320.6	77.6	462	7,318	1,197.2	442.4	NA	NA	NA	NA
Troy	40	235	41.6	8.4	98	754	102.1	49.2	NA	NA	NA	NA
Utica	52	177	31.0	5.4	137	1,238	180.9	68.0	NA	NA	NA	NA
Valley Stream	52	227	48.9	9.4	146	1,574	229.8	92.7	NA	NA	NA	NA
White Plains	203	771	263.0	45.7	690	5,859	1,448.4	521.3	NA	NA	NA	NA
Yonkers	345	1,475	359.5	65.8	264	1,596	321.2	140.0	NA	NA	NA	NA
NORTH CAROLINA	12,450	56,360	14,647.0	2,638.6	24,766	221,438	40,877.5	16,047.7	8,834	422,891	200,380.8	21,480.2
Apex	D	D	D	4.6	196	617	99.0	31.9	NA	NA	NA	NA
Asheboro	35	174	29.4	6.8	62	334	35.8	13.0	NA	NA	NA	NA
Asheville	354	1,204	272.7	48.9	693	3,657	503.8	213.4	NA	NA	NA	NA
Burlington	78	289	79.0	9.5	94	774	87.7	37.6	NA	NA	NA	NA
Cary	292	1,138	354.2	54.4	1,049	11,172	2,078.5	943.6	NA	NA	NA	NA
Chapel Hill	D	D	D	D	D	D	D	D	NA	NA	NA	NA
Charlotte	1,936	11,022	4,012.6	693.7	3,655	47,392	10,078.0	3,863.8	NA	NA	NA	NA
Clayton	25	67	25.3	3.1	60	259	30.5	11.4	NA	NA	NA	NA
Concord	151	629	153.3	22.5	254	993	140.7	49.4	NA	NA	NA	NA
Cornelius	114	470	134.7	16.9	188	720	118.4	43.3	NA	NA	NA	NA
Durham	337	2,013	443.3	102.0	D	D	D	D	NA	NA	NA	NA
Fayetteville	249	1,457	350.7	52.5	434	5,417	652.6	276.2	NA	NA	NA	NA
Fuquay-Varina	26	55	15.2	3.0	68	266	43.6	16.0	NA	NA	NA	NA
Garner	35	145	50.4	7.3	87	1,302	85.5	37.9	NA	NA	NA	NA
Gastonia	106	470	152.8	17.6	154	1,040	93.2	40.3	NA	NA	NA	NA
Goldsboro	48	287	45.3	9.2	87	523	59.6	23.4	NA	NA	NA	NA
Greensboro	508	3,933	744.9	203.2	965	7,972	1,276.8	491.0	NA	NA	NA	NA
Greenville	130	559	116.9	19.4	238	1,182	148.7	56.4	NA	NA	NA	NA
Hickory	110	472	106.0	18.8	197	1,712	706.0	100.2	NA	NA	NA	NA
High Point	125	708	104.6	26.1	289	2,867	470.1	181.4	NA	NA	NA	NA
Holly Springs	D	D	D	D	106	470	84.0	30.1	NA	NA	NA	NA
Huntersville	109	306	97.3	16.8	217	1,715	269.9	105.7	NA	NA	NA	NA
Indian Trail	45	111	30.1	5.2	72	341	43.9	14.0	NA	NA	NA	NA
Jacksonville	118	450	91.7	15.7	139	943	101.9	38.1	NA	NA	NA	NA
Kannapolis	45	153	31.5	6.0	53	463	43.2	16.4	NA	NA	NA	NA
Kernersville	44	102	33.0	4.6	91	465	66.7	20.9	NA	NA	NA	NA
Matthews	63	385	76.9	14.8	141	771	105.6	40.5	NA	NA	NA	NA
Mint Hill	35	59	16.6	2.4	61	627	52.8	20.0	NA	NA	NA	NA
Monroe	39	147	25.8	5.3	107	745	94.2	32.9	NA	NA	NA	NA
Mooresville	96	263	86.1	10.7	179	1,812	243.1	98.4	NA	NA	NA	NA
Morrisville	59	624	221.0	29.6	200	7,841	2,051.1	826.0	NA	NA	NA	NA
New Bern	59	193	36.0	6.4	101	615	95.5	42.9	NA	NA	NA	NA
Raleigh	962	6,090	1,652.3	365.0	2,494	33,853	7,201.2	2,813.7	NA	NA	NA	NA
Rocky Mount	68	440	75.0	16.0	110	730	107.9	32.4	NA	NA	NA	NA
Salisbury	44	134	23.1	4.4	90	548	83.5	25.7	NA	NA	NA	NA
Sanford	31	91	22.9	4.0	71	322	34.8	14.2	NA	NA	NA	NA
Statesville	46	184	24.5	6.0	83	533	106.2	27.9	NA	NA	NA	NA
Thomasville	D	D	D	3.0	35	165	21.2	4.2	NA	NA	NA	NA
Wake Forest	52	158	59.2	7.4	154	1,530	426.8	116.3	NA	NA	NA	NA
Wilmington	305	1,117	286.1	48.2	674	4,243	676.7	247.9	NA	NA	NA	NA
Wilson	71	258	44.1	7.4	90	542	65.0	25.9	NA	NA	NA	NA
Winston-Salem	351	1,687	661.1	77.2	694	5,556	912.5	348.5	NA	NA	NA	NA

1. Establishments subject to federal tax.

City	Accommodation and food services, 2017				Arts, entertainment, and recreation[1], 2017				Health care and social assistance[1], 2017			
	Number of establish-ments	Number of employees	Receipts (mil dol)	Annual payroll (mil dol)	Number of establish-ments	Number of employees	Receipts (mil dol)	Annual payroll (mil dol)	Number of establish-ments	Number of employees	Receipts (mil dol)	Annual payroll (mil dol)
	92	93	94	95	96	97	98	99	100	101	102	103
NEW YORK—Cont'd												
Lindenhurst	68	848	49.8	14.0	D	D	D	D	49	386	32.2	11.8
Long Beach	96	927	70.1	18.7	19.0	170	10.9	2.8	88	1,205	150.1	55.2
Middletown	72	659	39.5	13.0	D	D	D	D	92	2,064	145.2	67.7
Mount Vernon	100	1,009	66.7	17.3	14.0	170	13.6	5.1	150	3,251	279.7	123.6
Newburgh	79	904	58.2	18.5	7.0	45	2.5	0.9	112	3,323	410.3	143.3
New Rochelle	213	2,172	158.8	41.8	41.0	641	55.7	15.8	272	5,879	641.5	267.3
New York	24,871	396,907	38,941.9	11,578.9	6,771.0	96,960	20,763.6	6,078.4	NA	NA	NA	NA
Niagara Falls	202	5,417	620.5	123.8	17.0	175	10.7	3.1	103	2,607	235.1	101.5
North Tonawanda	55	751	38.2	12.7	18.0	78	6.8	1.4	61	1,165	68.3	51.9
Ossining	50	321	25.0	6.6	7.0	28	3.7	1.6	44	900	79.1	43.4
Peekskill	70	753	45.4	13.5	11.0	55	3.7	0.9	61	866	71.1	31.0
Port Chester	109	1,073	98.1	28.0	12.0	375	25.4	5.4	49	1,233	133.4	52.4
Poughkeepsie	102	1,540	78.3	27.6	13.0	227	14.2	4.0	145	5,520	981.3	290.1
Rochester	590	7,749	402.9	133.6	100.0	2,162	150.4	47.7	484	37,839	4,114.8	1,709.6
Rockville Centre	127	1,943	136.7	41.1	24.0	187	14.5	2.8	209	2,823	414.6	134.3
Rome	87	1,273	59.4	18.7	14.0	63	4.3	1.3	108	2,528	201.2	94.1
Saratoga Springs	169	3,889	321.4	100.6	51.0	1,085	200.1	34.0	165	4,024	500.4	205.3
Schenectady	170	2,208	121.3	36.6	25.0	1,859	236.0	57.5	212	8,001	808.2	370.2
Spring Valley	D	D	D	D	D	D	D	D	71	4,054	185.0	103.0
Syracuse	425	7,156	398.8	132.5	47.0	1,243	59.6	21.4	446	26,170	3,421.5	1,442.9
Troy	166	2,298	133.4	40.9	12.0	239	12.8	4.4	187	5,567	618.1	250.2
Utica	D	D	D	D	20.0	D	21.5	D	221	10,854	1,024.3	468.6
Valley Stream	91	1,444	81.2	24.3	19.0	343	20.7	7.2	171	5,562	313.7	151.7
White Plains	231	3,544	288.4	83.8	44.0	778	56.6	17.7	391	13,062	1,958.1	877.0
Yonkers	387	4,822	368.3	101.9	56.0	1,491	281.0	55.4	493	10,893	1,265.3	555.2
NORTH CAROLINA	21,437	429,125	24,913.0	6,865.6	3,868.0	69,027	6,354.3	2,056.8	24,080	602,444	72,732.3	27,627.2
Apex	96	2,156	111.4	33.3	19.0	202	15.8	3.1	128	1,143	129.7	46.6
Asheboro	108	2,391	118.1	32.0	11.0	188	5.5	2.0	143	3,276	288.6	126.7
Asheville	646	15,437	963.8	288.7	126.0	2,342	168.4	53.5	739	24,227	3,350.7	1,328.8
Burlington	196	4,568	230.1	63.8	24.0	492	15.7	6.5	247	10,615	1,590.3	599.4
Cary	432	9,309	541.1	162.5	81.0	2,675	107.4	35.8	D	D	D	D
Chapel Hill	221	4,537	268.2	86.2	39.0	471	31.4	11.8	274	15,270	1,943.2	838.6
Charlotte	2,214	50,810	3,396.2	925.1	413.0	12,043	1,343.5	614.1	2,288	60,916	9,331.0	3,379.3
Clayton	65	1,376	62.9	17.8	D	D	D	D	90	1,326	150.1	65.5
Concord	265	7,952	436.7	118.3	56.0	2,328	495.6	130.5	271	7,600	955.0	418.4
Cornelius	86	1,401	80.2	20.8	38.0	704	49.3	12.8	D	D	D	D
Durham	709	15,662	1,000.3	290.9	106.0	2,162	98.2	35.9	823	27,001	4,717.5	1,479.9
Fayetteville	534	12,325	631.8	174.8	56.0	661	32.6	8.9	612	18,776	2,231.4	887.4
Fuquay-Varina	82	1,737	76.6	20.4	10.0	167	5.8	1.9	63	1,313	84.1	37.4
Garner	86	2,259	124.8	31.7	8.0	130	7.4	2.0	100	1,375	149.7	59.0
Gastonia	209	4,659	256.3	70.7	23.0	447	15.2	5.5	311	9,322	1,100.0	439.8
Goldsboro	161	3,371	165.7	45.8	12.0	214	7.2	1.8	186	6,299	695.8	272.0
Greensboro	884	20,121	1,076.6	310.4	122.0	2,541	138.5	44.2	890	24,398	3,050.0	1,153.4
Greenville	298	7,275	363.9	97.1	27.0	396	22.0	6.8	386	14,873	2,069.6	733.4
Hickory	193	4,176	219.2	65.0	27.0	551	23.4	9.0	286	9,735	1,227.6	464.3
High Point	236	5,662	280.7	80.0	31.0	526	55.6	7.3	274	8,440	811.7	369.7
Holly Springs	63	1,336	66.6	20.6	21.0	285	17.9	7.1	94	732	62.7	25.6
Huntersville	121	3,005	168.3	48.7	D	D	D	D	181	3,106	595.4	170.8
Indian Trail	83	1,371	64.5	16.8	D	D	D	D	D	D	D	D
Jacksonville	246	5,373	297.3	80.7	15.0	263	18.7	4.5	198	4,155	527.5	172.8
Kannapolis	82	1,591	81.5	21.8	D	D	D	D	63	907	89.5	35.6
Kernersville	93	1,914	94.7	25.1	21.0	239	11.4	3.1	81	1,011	93.1	30.5
Matthews	112	2,578	134.6	38.6	31.0	684	24.6	7.7	144	3,779	578.7	175.7
Mint Hill	40	648	30.8	8.2	11.0	67	5.0	1.4	44	567	87.2	21.8
Monroe	115	2,384	142.6	37.6	11.0	135	7.9	3.0	158	4,048	459.1	185.4
Mooresville	190	3,895	215.6	60.4	57.0	1,341	294.7	77.7	206	3,055	373.7	137.1
Morrisville	124	2,441	173.5	46.0	11.0	142	8.7	3.0	64	848	111.6	40.5
New Bern	124	2,588	142.1	38.6	D	D	D	D	187	5,467	598.5	244.4
Raleigh	1,259	29,257	1,829.4	510.3	244.0	7,406	512.5	184.4	1,635	43,361	5,535.4	2,256.4
Rocky Mount	149	3,372	170.8	45.7	24.0	397	15.9	5.1	219	6,098	513.4	226.8
Salisbury	143	3,027	167.9	46.6	19.0	300	14.3	4.4	187	7,950	993.5	481.0
Sanford	105	1,915	96.5	26.3	11.0	121	5.6	1.4	145	2,519	255.7	97.6
Statesville	123	2,452	124.4	32.6	11.0	129	19.9	5.0	181	4,835	446.9	200.7
Thomasville	72	1,137	62.2	16.1	4.0	122	3.3	1.5	49	1,568	166.5	56.5
Wake Forest	100	2,045	108.7	29.7	26.0	278	16.5	4.2	D	D	D	D
Wilmington	525	11,091	601.3	173.5	88.0	1,467	81.4	25.4	673	16,330	2,078.0	815.8
Wilson	144	3,010	157.9	42.8	D	D	D	D	206	4,782	407.5	162.2
Winston-Salem	578	13,249	715.1	206.6	91.0	2,611	509.1	81.7	631	32,573	4,106.2	1,412.9

1. Establishments subject to federal tax.

City	Other services[1]				Government employment and payroll, 2017								
						March payroll							
							Perent of total for:						
	Number of establish-ments	Number of employees	Receipts (mil dol)	Annual payroll (mil dol)	Full-time equivalent employees	Total (dollars)	Admin-istrative, judicial, and legal	Police and corrections	Fire protection	Highways and trans-portation	Health and welfare	Natural resources and utilities	Education and libraries
	104	105	106	107	108	109	110	111	112	113	114	115	116
NEW YORK—Cont'd													
Lindenhurst	103	345	41.2	11.2	64	218,306	22.1	0.0	6.6	25.3	0.0	19.0	0.0
Long Beach	104	318	38.8	6.9	460	2,820,272	8.6	31.5	11.6	18.0	4.8	21.8	0.0
Middletown	55	301	28.0	8.5	244	1,425,159	14.6	45.0	10.0	5.9	1.7	22.8	0.0
Mount Vernon	151	677	106.3	26.1	561	3,698,608	8.2	43.3	29.4	3.1	1.4	14.6	0.0
Newburgh	59	540	58.6	17.1	301	1,577,058	7.4	34.2	35.6	2.1	2.3	13.7	0.0
New Rochelle	214	1,034	128.3	27.6	563	3,923,869	9.2	29.5	34.6	4.8	5.9	16.0	0.0
New York	23,119	159,346	35,687.9	7,493.0	434,443	2,716,087,055	3.5	16.6	4.9	15.4	17.7	4.9	34.4
Niagara Falls	73	425	38.4	10.4	565	2,503,768	9.9	35.5	30.5	7.3	8.2	6.5	0.0
North Tonawanda	59	186	14.9	3.7	287	1,463,894	6.8	28.1	17.2	18.6	0.6	25.4	0.0
Ossining	60	207	25.8	7.6	196	1,432,560	12.7	41.6	0.4	13.2	0.9	25.0	0.0
Peekskill	80	938	73.5	32.1	215	1,650,670	10.8	34.5	15.2	13.5	4.1	21.8	0.0
Port Chester	97	398	73.6	17.5	178	1,284,288	14.9	52.6	1.0	8.2	1.6	13.6	0.0
Poughkeepsie	90	519	59.0	17.7	317	1,831,845	7.5	41.6	20.7	7.3	6.0	15.5	0.0
Rochester	376	2,559	398.7	96.5	9,569	52,522,336	2.9	12.1	7.5	0.7	3.0	4.9	64.9
Rockville Centre	117	635	71.1	20.3	293	2,074,606	14.2	40.8	0.0	5.6	0.7	34.4	0.0
Rome	68	412	41.0	9.5	335	1,649,030	9.3	27.6	32.0	13.4	2.2	12.1	0.0
Saratoga Springs	94	496	82.3	15.1	356	1,861,287	9.5	32.3	19.3	23.6	4.3	7.5	0.0
Schenectady	105	776	159.8	34.0	500	2,823,338	0.0	44.8	24.5	7.3	10.9	10.2	0.0
Spring Valley	62	207	22.0	5.5	113	907,428	10.8	68.5	0.7	18.2	1.8	0.0	0.0
Syracuse	258	1,642	175.0	50.2	5,554	31,911,402	1.7	12.2	7.1	4.7	3.0	4.0	67.3
Troy	81	497	39.9	14.6	461	2,294,977	9.2	28.7	25.0	1.6	14.8	14.3	0.0
Utica	106	3,141	140.7	55.3	538	2,824,997	6.7	40.3	25.9	3.4	11.4	8.8	0.0
Valley Stream	D	D	D	D	211	1,315,477	13.1	0.0	0.5	17.7	0.0	36.8	6.5
White Plains	243	1,590	245.7	67.4	1,000	6,983,033	8.3	27.0	18.6	8.9	8.3	10.3	3.3
Yonkers	442	1,635	227.3	50.8	6,946	47,004,207	4.3	17.5	11.1	1.3	2.3	7.1	55.1
NORTH CAROLINA	15,118	93,642	13,022.2	3,152.9	X	X	X	X	X	X	X	X	X
Apex	D	D	D	D	429	2,099,202	17.2	21.4	16.7	4.0	4.8	27.2	0.0
Asheboro	45	325	35.8	8.7	323	1,215,465	8.0	27.6	17.9	9.0	0.0	27.8	0.0
Asheville	334	2,077	233.2	67.3	1,209	5,026,530	11.5	19.7	22.7	5.0	2.9	15.5	0.0
Burlington	105	696	56.6	17.8	763	2,690,756	10.6	28.9	15.3	6.7	2.8	26.4	0.0
Cary	305	2,251	290.1	104.1	1,388	6,713,498	13.5	19.4	17.6	12.2	0.0	25.2	0.0
Chapel Hill	102	1,334	291.4	59.5	886	3,497,343	12.7	26.9	15.5	18.7	2.7	8.0	3.6
Charlotte	1,608	14,437	2,394.5	510.2	8,026	40,618,050	9.9	29.8	16.7	16.6	2.7	18.7	0.0
Clayton	D	D	D	D	212	898,827	17.7	24.4	15.2	0.0	4.6	25.8	3.2
Concord	178	1,070	124.8	31.5	986	3,991,786	9.6	20.2	19.6	8.6	3.0	24.0	0.0
Cornelius	75	467	33.0	11.7	121	496,775	18.5	12.1	52.5	4.5	0.0	12.3	0.0
Durham	445	5,545	1,598.6	316.4	2,861	12,296,323	9.4	29.9	17.6	5.2	2.6	22.2	0.0
Fayetteville	304	1,788	175.1	51.2	2,364	9,863,073	7.3	26.2	14.5	7.1	0.9	27.2	0.0
Fuquay-Varina	51	319	30.1	8.1	181	781,273	15.0	22.6	21.9	6.8	0.0	22.7	0.0
Garner	D	D	D	D	186	891,895	12.2	46.9	0.0	5.3	1.2	9.3	0.0
Gastonia	150	931	89.4	24.7	901	3,649,318	15.7	23.2	15.5	9.8	1.3	28.5	0.0
Goldsboro	90	596	48.7	14.7	437	1,702,043	11.2	24.2	18.9	7.0	0.6	29.8	0.0
Greensboro	564	3,979	953.6	139.1	3,249	13,016,203	8.6	26.8	20.0	7.1	1.7	20.5	2.4
Greenville	138	859	77.7	23.4	1,200	5,562,532	7.2	18.7	9.5	7.6	4.7	35.3	2.0
Hickory	123	754	71.4	22.1	682	2,418,912	10.9	23.6	22.8	6.8	0.2	25.1	6.1
High Point	196	1,743	251.7	53.8	1,550	6,874,503	10.3	32.5	13.2	5.0	2.2	31.8	3.1
Holly Springs	46	189	17.3	5.4	284	1,287,759	20.3	24.7	13.5	11.6	0.0	29.9	0.0
Huntersville	95	525	46.2	13.3	161	770,414	21.0	57.5	0.0	8.9	0.0	11.0	0.0
Indian Trail	D	D	D	D	50	166,386	56.9	0.0	0.0	9.1	0.0	9.1	0.0
Jacksonville	106	702	58.0	18.6	564	2,057,785	15.4	29.8	16.0	4.0	0.4	25.1	0.0
Kannapolis	D	D	D	D	327	1,248,082	12.2	26.9	33.3	5.3	0.0	17.8	0.0
Kernersville	75	491	59.6	14.6	252	961,038	10.1	38.2	29.7	5.3	0.0	13.6	0.0
Matthews	85	465	57.0	14.6	161	662,976	14.6	47.6	12.7	19.2	0.0	6.0	0.0
Mint Hill	D	D	D	D	13	70,791	100.0	0.0	0.0	0.0	0.0	0.0	0.0
Monroe	90	496	54.3	18.4	529	2,183,062	15.7	21.3	17.2	5.6	0.0	34.5	0.0
Mooresville	118	653	75.0	20.2	461	1,929,534	12.5	25.3	20.5	3.7	0.0	23.6	4.8
Morrisville	47	289	44.9	12.4	196	812,811	15.8	22.7	29.5	3.3	0.0	12.6	0.0
New Bern	74	287	32.7	8.1	444	1,841,764	14.7	24.1	15.9	4.3	0.8	34.8	0.0
Raleigh	1,106	8,160	1,090.2	313.7	4,767	20,560,599	11.1	20.7	14.3	9.8	2.2	34.5	0.0
Rocky Mount	76	458	157.2	13.0	947	3,736,932	14.0	24.0	17.1	5.0	0.6	34.4	0.0
Salisbury	62	330	33.5	9.4	421	1,754,807	15.6	18.4	19.4	9.3	0.8	24.7	0.0
Sanford	71	366	27.3	8.9	354	1,485,156	13.2	32.0	15.6	6.2	0.0	20.7	0.0
Statesville	70	446	40.3	11.9	419	1,597,177	13.6	25.4	17.6	3.7	0.0	33.8	0.0
Thomasville	D	D	D	D	288	1,047,940	9.0	28.4	22.2	5.1	0.0	25.6	0.0
Wake Forest	80	473	47.3	15.4	228	1,161,132	10.6	37.5	0.0	5.5	0.9	17.8	0.0
Wilmington	317	2,137	210.8	60.8	1,005	4,472,124	15.5	34.8	21.4	8.6	1.7	16.0	0.0
Wilson	91	565	52.4	15.1	774	3,369,718	16.1	18.6	12.8	3.4	0.6	39.9	0.0
Winston-Salem	418	2,661	523.9	86.4	2,230	8,672,025	13.0	33.4	17.5	7.9	5.0	22.2	0.0

1. Establishments subject to federal tax.

City	City government finances, 2017									
	General revenue							General expenditure		
		Intergovernmental		Taxes						
					Per capita[1] (dollars)				Per capita[1] (dollars)	
	Total (mil dol)	Total (mil dol)	Percent from state government	Total (mil dol)	Total	Property	Sales and gross receipts	Total (mil dol)	Total	Capital outlays
	117	118	119	120	121	122	123	124	125	126
NEW YORK—Cont'd										
Lindenhurst	14.4	2.2	83.2	8.8	328	268	60	13.3	493	78
Long Beach	82.5	11.3	63.3	43.0	1,280	1,070	209	89.9	2,679	253
Middletown	44.1	14.2	24.4	20.4	731	674	57	47.8	1,711	208
Mount Vernon	115.4	14.9	64.6	85.0	1,251	874	352	114.0	1,677	63
Newburgh	55.5	19.3	46.5	23.1	820	737	82	59.6	2,114	54
New Rochelle	148.7	22.9	40.5	95.7	1,210	733	477	143.1	1,809	129
New York	106,595.1	37,653.5	81.2	55,310.4	6,555	2,933	1,159	102,551.2	12,154	1,303
Niagara Falls	113.7	62.5	73.5	42.0	870	586	284	125.2	2,594	346
North Tonawanda	43.1	17.0	33.9	18.7	615	534	55	44.6	1,465	139
Ossining	40.0	10.9	5.5	23.2	923	863	60	45.3	1,803	176
Peekskill	46.7	15.4	27.2	18.7	779	695	84	51.8	2,159	281
Port Chester	40.0	5.6	17.6	25.4	863	782	82	43.2	1,468	181
Poughkeepsie	60.4	23.5	28.2	23.7	778	682	97	61.4	2,018	141
Rochester	1,347.3	1,042.1	79.9	121.0	586	523	63	1,473.5	7,139	748
Rockville Centre	44.2	4.3	28.1	31.7	1,285	1,166	117	54.7	2,220	379
Rome	50.6	14.9	86.9	26.2	813	479	334	51.3	1,592	101
Saratoga Springs	54.0	3.9	50.3	34.7	1,239	666	573	58.8	2,101	224
Schenectady	102.2	38.5	55.0	35.7	546	465	82	109.7	1,680	257
Spring Valley	37.0	11.4	8.0	24.5	757	707	50	43.8	1,356	12
Syracuse	712.0	591.5	83.3	66.0	464	412	53	765.2	5,378	223
Troy	73.4	33.1	44.6	24.8	502	451	51	74.3	1,503	122
Utica	90.4	35.8	72.5	43.4	719	464	253	83.2	1,378	157
Valley Stream	39.5	2.3	48.3	31.9	849	773	74	41.3	1,098	140
White Plains	175.5	7.3	96.7	117.4	2,010	967	1,043	184.9	3,167	198
Yonkers	1,011.1	527.2	98.9	401.7	2,010	1,104	589	1,167.9	5,843	306
NORTH CAROLINA	X	X	X	X	X	X	X	X	X	X
Apex	62.9	8.4	68.1	36.5	722	455	267	57.1	1,130	217
Asheboro	37.2	6.2	96.4	20.6	799	613	185	31.9	1,236	31
Asheville	142.3	24.4	51.5	88.1	960	639	322	132.6	1,445	226
Burlington	55.8	9.0	67.6	40.7	766	523	243	50.9	957	113
Cary	248.7	23.3	71.8	130.5	786	542	244	178.3	1,075	232
Chapel Hill	0.0	0.0	0.0	0.0	0	0	0	2.2	37	0
Charlotte	2,085.7	502.2	46.8	858.8	999	530	468	1,536.3	1,786	485
Clayton	34.9	8.2	100.0	11.2	521	471	50	26.5	1,237	179
Concord	133.7	30.0	59.0	67.6	734	555	178	110.5	1,199	159
Cornelius	25.5	6.3	84.8	17.7	603	468	135	23.2	790	212
Durham	376.8	58.6	61.8	211.3	783	584	199	308.6	1,144	164
Fayetteville	200.8	64.8	42.7	108.3	518	344	174	192.2	919	110
Fuquay-Varina	34.4	5.0	50.1	18.8	676	461	215	30.6	1,101	153
Garner	30.0	3.2	95.0	24.0	836	620	216	33.9	1,178	283
Gastonia	88.1	15.5	79.5	45.6	597	396	201	91.4	1,198	155
Goldsboro	39.1	7.8	95.3	25.6	747	458	289	37.5	1,095	95
Greensboro	385.0	52.6	74.1	206.8	709	494	216	415.0	1,423	219
Greenville	151.2	24.4	86.8	49.2	535	363	172	138.2	1,502	236
Hickory	67.5	10.8	73.8	37.7	925	659	267	58.4	1,431	198
High Point	175.5	32.5	64.3	85.2	762	550	212	156.2	1,398	79
Holly Springs	42.1	13.9	100.0	19.9	565	517	48	30.3	861	88
Huntersville	42.7	6.2	80.5	29.4	521	347	175	39.7	704	148
Indian Trail	14.3	2.2	37.6	9.9	254	181	73	17.4	448	171
Jacksonville	70.8	9.7	74.7	35.7	490	296	194	59.6	819	99
Kannapolis	48.9	7.0	65.5	34.8	713	510	204	49.2	1,009	130
Kernersville	29.8	1.8	100.0	23.0	945	631	314	30.5	1,254	200
Matthews	25.5	4.0	71.3	17.1	532	362	170	20.1	625	106
Mint Hill	13.8	2.0	100.0	8.5	318	318	0	13.7	512	20
Monroe	51.7	10.3	61.3	26.7	759	576	183	61.5	1,747	755
Mooresville	83.0	8.9	75.3	45.4	1,201	946	255	76.8	2,030	462
Morrisville	31.9	3.8	97.0	25.5	966	699	268	30.5	1,155	272
New Bern	0.0	0.0	0.0	0.0	0	0	0	2.5	85	0
Raleigh	724.2	109.0	54.2	356.1	765	523	242	552.4	1,186	194
Rocky Mount	82.8	17.9	58.2	35.9	658	449	208	78.4	1,436	146
Salisbury	59.4	6.1	91.3	25.2	749	523	226	61.1	1,812	87
Sanford	41.0	5.6	73.0	21.5	730	520	210	39.6	1,347	51
Statesville	44.3	10.5	99.8	14.4	539	521	18	36.0	1,350	173
Thomasville	23.8	4.9	94.7	16.8	631	443	188	25.4	955	135
Wake Forest	46.4	7.5	47.6	35.5	842	582	260	45.0	1,067	291
Wilmington	150.3	20.4	74.4	95.8	793	472	321	150.5	1,245	156
Wilson	81.9	10.8	91.9	30.4	619	452	167	70.3	1,430	133
Winston-Salem	324.1	51.4	57.9	171.5	701	500	202	412.9	1,689	523

1. Based on population estimated as of July 1 of the year shown.

City	City government finances, 2017 (cont.)												
	General expenditure (cont.)												
	Percent of total for:									Debt outstanding			
	Public welfare	Highways	Parking facilities	Education	Health and hospitals	Police protection	Sewerage and sanitation	Parks and recreation	Housing and community development	Interest on debt	Total (mil dol)	Per capita[1] (dollars)	Debt issued during year
	127	128	129	130	131	132	133	134	135	136	137	138	139
NEW YORK—Cont'd													
Lindenhurst	0.0	28.8	0.1	0.0	0.0	0.8	4.9	7.3	0.7	2.2	9.0	333	0.0
Long Beach	0.0	4.3	0.0	0.2	0.1	15.5	12.1	8.6	0.5	6.7	142.6	4,248	6.9
Middletown	0.0	5.2	0.0	0.0	0.0	17.9	9.4	4.5	1.8	6.5	56.3	2,016	3.5
Mount Vernon	0.8	2.3	0.0	0.0	0.5	21.2	5.7	5.9	3.7	2.3	29.5	435	0.0
Newburgh	0.0	3.2	0.0	0.0	0.1	27.0	14.2	2.1	2.4	9.7	91.0	3,226	0.0
New Rochelle	6.9	8.2	1.4	0.0	0.3	23.3	4.9	2.5	1.2	3.9	125.9	1,592	0.0
New York	13.8	1.9	0.0	31.0	9.9	5.5	3.6	1.3	5.7	6.1	140,617.8	16,666	16,835.6
Niagara Falls	2.3	13.2	0.0	0.0	0.2	17.0	3.2	2.4	2.8	5.4	55.1	1,142	37.5
North Tonawanda	0.0	12.3	0.0	0.0	0.0	13.6	12.5	4.8	0.4	2.0	13.6	448	9.1
Ossining	6.9	8.3	0.1	0.0	0.3	19.2	8.3	5.8	7.7	4.1	33.7	1,343	6.4
Peekskill	11.9	10.6	0.3	0.0	0.5	16.6	4.4	6.7	2.6	8.8	78.0	3,252	0.0
Port Chester	0.0	9.6	0.9	0.0	0.6	21.7	8.9	3.5	0.0	6.0	43.2	1,470	12.5
Poughkeepsie	8.3	7.8	0.4	0.0	0.2	20.5	7.4	0.8	1.0	7.7	71.0	2,334	0.0
Rochester	0.0	2.8	1.1	58.0	0.1	6.2	3.2	1.2	0.8	1.3	804.2	3,896	37.5
Rockville Centre	4.9	13.6	0.3	0.0	0.1	20.2	5.8	7.5	0.2	4.9	60.7	2,466	9.4
Rome	0.0	9.8	0.4	0.0	0.2	12.9	10.0	2.0	2.8	7.0	73.5	2,277	18.9
Saratoga Springs	0.2	8.3	0.2	0.0	0.2	21.0	8.9	9.3	0.6	6.4	52.5	1,877	3.0
Schenectady	0.0	8.4	0.6	0.0	0.1	18.5	14.4	2.0	2.7	2.8	113.6	1,739	21.5
Spring Valley	19.5	4.0	0.1	0.0	0.0	19.1	0.1	0.6	19.5	2.3	11.1	343	0.0
Syracuse	0.0	3.8	0.0	60.4	0.0	6.2	2.7	1.1	0.9	2.6	441.8	3,105	52.8
Troy	0.0	6.3	0.0	0.0	0.2	25.5	7.5	3.0	2.4	7.1	70.2	1,420	0.0
Utica	7.5	5.7	0.4	0.0	1.1	18.4	3.5	3.4	1.9	4.0	68.6	1,137	2.9
Valley Stream	0.0	14.9	0.9	0.0	0.3	0.5	13.7	10.2	0.0	4.3	30.3	805	4.7
White Plains	0.0	8.9	0.1	0.0	0.0	20.3	5.4	5.0	0.1	5.2	160.2	2,743	38.5
Yonkers	0.0	0.4	0.0	51.9	0.1	8.5	1.9	0.9	0.0	3.1	732.1	3,663	65.8
NORTH CAROLINA	X	X	X	X	X	X	X	X	X	X	X	X	X
Apex	0.0	7.9	0.0	0.0	3.2	17.9	18.0	8.3	3.2	4.1	81.0	1,604	0.0
Asheboro	0.0	7.7	0.0	0.0	0.1	24.1	23.4	10.0	2.9	0.2	5.8	225	0.0
Asheville	0.0	12.7	2.4	0.0	0.2	20.4	8.8	11.9	7.2	1.2	118.4	1,291	0.0
Burlington	0.0	5.0	0.0	0.0	0.0	34.7	5.6	16.3	1.4	0.2	38.2	720	0.0
Cary	0.0	14.2	0.0	0.0	0.0	13.9	5.0	14.9	2.4	4.7	407.8	2,458	32.0
Chapel Hill	0.0	0.0	0.0	0.0	0.0	0.0	0.0	0.0	0.0	100.0	59.5	1,010	10.5
Charlotte	0.0	8.0	0.0	0.0	0.0	17.6	17.1	7.6	4.6	7.9	4,073.0	4,736	779.3
Clayton	11.8	4.7	0.0	0.0	0.0	16.8	19.5	7.8	0.0	0.4	26.9	1,254	6.5
Concord	0.0	6.3	0.0	0.0	0.0	20.0	18.7	7.8	11.1	2.1	106.6	1,156	0.0
Cornelius	0.0	11.8	0.0	0.0	0.0	30.4	8.4	26.0	6.6	1.8	11.2	381	0.0
Durham	0.0	7.3	0.9	0.0	0.0	28.5	17.3	6.1	9.1	3.9	332.3	1,232	83.4
Fayetteville	0.2	8.6	0.2	0.0	0.0	27.9	8.2	7.5	2.8	6.9	312.5	1,495	1.9
Fuquay-Varina	0.0	10.6	0.0	0.0	0.0	12.8	17.5	10.5	4.4	6.5	58.2	2,093	0.0
Garner	0.0	13.2	0.0	0.0	0.0	23.0	5.6	24.3	3.9	3.8	36.5	1,268	6.2
Gastonia	0.0	15.9	1.2	0.0	0.9	19.1	23.3	6.7	6.4	2.7	78.9	1,034	5.0
Goldsboro	0.0	8.1	0.0	0.0	0.0	27.1	7.6	11.9	10.3	4.8	57.6	1,683	26.8
Greensboro	0.0	11.8	1.1	0.0	0.1	18.6	23.3	14.9	3.7	2.2	496.9	1,704	133.2
Greenville	0.0	9.0	0.0	0.0	0.0	18.2	28.8	6.5	9.1	2.1	303.6	3,299	22.1
Hickory	0.0	6.0	0.0	0.0	0.0	20.6	26.1	6.8	7.4	0.7	31.2	764	0.0
High Point	0.0	8.0	0.2	0.0	0.1	17.9	15.7	13.3	7.1	5.4	225.3	2,017	70.9
Holly Springs	0.0	4.9	0.0	0.0	0.0	19.3	10.6	18.9	10.1	4.5	81.4	2,317	0.0
Huntersville	0.0	19.4	0.0	0.0	0.7	27.6	1.5	25.6	3.6	3.9	41.1	728	11.4
Indian Trail	0.0	18.6	0.0	0.0	0.2	13.0	13.9	4.9	8.1	2.2	15.5	399	0.0
Jacksonville	0.0	7.9	0.0	0.0	0.0	23.6	30.4	11.0	2.3	4.3	92.1	1,265	0.0
Kannapolis	0.0	9.1	0.0	0.0	0.0	17.3	18.0	7.7	6.6	7.3	96.6	1,980	0.0
Kernersville	0.0	6.9	0.0	0.0	0.0	32.3	8.7	7.1	1.2	0.7	15.8	652	8.3
Matthews	0.0	16.6	0.0	0.0	3.2	30.2	7.9	10.2	2.4	1.1	6.4	198	0.0
Mint Hill	0.0	15.2	0.0	0.0	0.0	24.7	21.8	5.0	0.0	0.4	1.1	41	0.0
Monroe	0.0	5.2	0.0	0.0	0.1	16.6	4.0	7.4	2.6	1.2	74.5	2,115	20.7
Mooresville	0.0	6.9	0.0	0.0	0.1	13.3	14.5	15.8	9.7	8.4	192.3	5,083	0.0
Morrisville	0.0	33.1	0.0	0.0	0.0	12.1	4.5	9.4	6.2	1.8	19.3	729	14.3
New Bern	0.0	0.0	0.0	0.0	0.0	0.0	0.0	0.0	0.0	100.0	56.7	1,897	0.8
Raleigh	0.3	9.4	1.7	0.0	0.0	18.8	16.9	16.7	3.8	5.8	1,680.4	3,608	262.9
Rocky Mount	0.6	5.0	0.0	0.0	0.0	21.2	26.3	19.7	3.9	1.3	57.0	1,044	36.8
Salisbury	0.0	8.4	0.0	0.1	0.0	11.9	18.9	3.0	4.8	7.0	55.6	1,650	29.7
Sanford	0.0	8.0	0.0	0.0	0.1	24.1	17.6	1.9	15.3	7.4	59.4	2,019	0.0
Statesville	0.0	6.9	0.0	0.0	0.1	21.8	23.3	9.5	0.6	4.0	33.1	1,239	0.0
Thomasville	0.0	8.9	0.0	0.0	0.1	25.9	10.8	6.2	3.0	3.4	32.4	1,216	0.0
Wake Forest	0.0	5.4	0.0	0.0	0.0	20.9	7.4	28.9	6.0	1.4	22.5	535	0.0
Wilmington	0.0	7.3	2.7	0.0	0.0	21.5	9.8	7.1	6.1	5.4	185.7	1,537	11.8
Wilson	0.9	5.7	0.1	0.0	0.0	18.1	12.8	9.3	7.5	1.4	74.2	1,508	0.0
Winston-Salem	0.0	8.4	0.4	0.0	0.0	19.2	23.8	11.5	7.6	9.9	778.9	3,186	88.3

1. Based on population estimated as of July 1 of the year shown.

STATE Place code	City	Land area[1] (sq. mi)	Population, 2021: Total persons 2021	Population, 2021: Rank	Population, 2021: Per square mile	Race 2020: Race alone[2] (percent): White	Race 2020: Race alone[2] (percent): Black or African American	Race 2020: Race alone[2] (percent): American Indian, Alaskan Native	Race 2020: Race alone[2] (percent): Asian	Race 2020: Race alone[2] (percent): Hawaiian Pacific Islander	Race 2020: Race alone[2] (percent): Some other race	Race 2020: Two or more races (percent)
		1	2	3	4	5	6	7	8	9	10	11
38 00000	NORTH DAKOTA	68,994.8	774,948	X	11.2	82.9	3.4	5.0	1.7	0.1	1.5	5.4
38 07200	Bismarck	34.7	74,138	497	2,136.5	84.7	2.9	4.8	1.3	0.4	1.3	4.5
38 19620	Dickinson	14.1	25,167	1,537	1,784.9	83.6	4.0	1.6	1.2	0.2	3.3	6.1
38 25700	Fargo	50.2	126,748	219	2,524.9	78.9	8.8	1.6	4.1	0.1	1.2	5.3
38 32060	Grand Forks	27.9	58,781	665	2,106.8	80.6	4.8	2.8	4.0	0.1	1.4	6.3
38 53380	Minot	27.7	47,789	833	1,725.2	79.7	5.2	2.9	1.9	0.2	2.0	8.1
38 84780	West Fargo	16.2	39,487	1,005	2,437.5	85.6	4.7	1.2	2.2	0.0	1.0	5.3
38 86220	Williston	23.2	27,332	1,425	1,178.1	75.1	6.7	2.6	1.9	0.3	4.3	9.0
39 00000	OHIO	40,858.8	11,780,017	X	288.3	77.0	12.5	0.3	2.5	0.0	1.9	5.8
39 01000	Akron	61.9	189,347	136	3,058.9	54.7	31.4	0.3	5.3	0.0	1.6	6.6
39 03464	Avon Lake	11.1	25,588	1,513	2,305.2	90.6	1.1	0.2	2.0	0.1	0.9	5.2
39 03828	Barberton	9.0	24,983	1,546	2,775.9	84.1	8.0	0.3	0.5	0.1	0.8	6.2
39 04720	Beavercreek	26.6	46,636	854	1,753.2	83.1	3.2	0.2	6.0	0.0	1.0	6.5
39 07972	Bowling Green	12.9	30,677	1,289	2,378.1	83.1	5.5	0.3	2.4	0.0	2.0	6.7
39 09680	Brunswick	13.0	35,340	1,127	2,718.5	90.5	1.6	0.1	1.5	0.0	1.0	5.3
39 12000	Canton	26.3	70,426	534	2,677.8	62.1	24.8	0.7	0.4	0.1	2.4	9.5
39 15000	Cincinnati	77.9	308,935	65	3,965.8	47.7	40.6	0.3	2.5	0.1	3.0	5.8
39 16000	Cleveland	77.7	367,991	54	4,736.0	34.5	48.4	0.4	2.8	0.0	6.3	7.6
39 16014	Cleveland Heights	8.1	44,652	891	5,512.6	46.3	41.3	0.2	5.0	0.0	1.4	5.7
39 18000	Columbus	220.1	906,528	14	4,118.7	53.2	28.6	0.4	6.2	0.0	4.3	7.2
39 19778	Cuyahoga Falls	25.8	50,810	786	1,969.4	83.9	4.7	0.2	5.0	0.0	0.8	5.3
39 21000	Dayton	55.8	137,571	200	2,465.4	47.6	40.7	0.4	1.4	0.1	3.3	6.6
39 21434	Delaware	20.0	42,814	929	2,140.7	83.2	4.3	0.2	3.9	0.1	1.7	6.7
39 22694	Dublin	24.7	49,085	813	1,987.2	71.3	2.0	0.1	20.4	0.0	0.8	5.4
39 25256	Elyria	20.5	52,816	754	2,576.4	72.2	14.7	0.3	0.8	0.0	2.4	9.6
39 25704	Euclid	10.7	48,928	814	4,572.7	29.8	64.0	0.2	0.6	0.0	1.1	4.2
39 25914	Fairborn	14.6	34,620	1,151	2,371.2	77.9	8.8	0.3	3.4	0.1	1.4	8.1
39 25970	Fairfield	20.8	44,562	893	2,142.4	64.8	17.5	0.4	5.9	0.1	4.5	6.7
39 27048	Findlay	19.6	39,942	991	2,037.9	86.1	2.6	0.3	2.7	0.0	2.1	6.2
39 29106	Gahanna	12.4	35,440	1,121	2,858.1	74.0	14.5	0.3	3.1	0.1	1.5	6.5
39 29428	Garfield Heights	7.2	29,369	1,330	4,079.0	36.0	56.5	0.1	0.9	0.0	1.6	4.9
39 31860	Green	32.0	27,337	1,424	854.3	89.5	2.6	0.1	2.0	0.0	0.5	5.2
39 32592	Grove City	17.6	41,787	949	2,374.3	86.3	3.7	0.2	1.9	0.0	1.7	6.3
39 33012	Hamilton	21.5	62,947	609	2,927.8	74.6	9.9	0.6	0.9	0.4	6.1	7.5
39 35476	Hilliard	14.3	36,892	1,075	2,579.9	80.3	4.3	0.2	6.8	0.0	1.8	6.6
39 36610	Huber Heights	22.2	43,272	925	1,949.2	71.5	15.5	0.3	3.1	0.1	1.7	7.8
39 39872	Kent	9.2	27,751	1,401	3,016.4	76.9	10.1	0.3	4.6	0.0	1.1	7.0
39 40040	Kettering	18.7	57,377	690	3,068.3	84.5	5.3	0.2	1.9	0.1	1.2	6.8
39 41664	Lakewood	5.5	50,104	798	9,109.8	84.3	5.5	0.2	2.4	0.0	1.3	6.3
39 41720	Lancaster	19.0	40,763	969	2,145.4	91.2	2.0	0.3	0.6	0.0	0.8	5.1
39 43554	Lima	13.6	35,868	1,105	2,637.4	60.6	27.8	0.4	0.6	0.1	1.9	8.7
39 44856	Lorain	23.6	65,430	582	2,772.5	57.7	17.1	0.6	0.5	0.0	9.7	14.3
39 47138	Mansfield	30.8	47,669	837	1,547.7	70.4	21.0	0.3	0.7	0.1	1.1	6.4
39 47754	Marion	13.0	35,868	1,105	2,759.1	81.9	10.5	0.4	0.4	0.0	1.6	5.2
39 48160	Marysville	16.1	26,223	1,477	1,628.8	85.5	3.8	0.2	3.9	0.0	1.2	5.5
39 48188	Mason	19.3	35,089	1,138	1,818.1	68.6	4.2	0.2	18.4	0.2	1.7	6.6
39 48244	Massillon	19.0	32,231	1,223	1,696.4	82.9	7.9	0.4	0.4	0.0	1.5	6.9
39 48790	Medina	11.6	25,934	1,497	2,235.7	88.3	3.5	0.2	0.9	0.0	1.3	5.8
39 49056	Mentor	27.8	47,221	845	1,698.6	91.7	1.5	0.1	1.7	0.0	0.6	4.4
39 49840	Middletown	26.1	50,998	783	1,953.9	73.7	12.7	0.3	0.9	0.1	4.2	8.0
39 54040	Newark	20.9	50,383	794	2,410.7	88.5	3.4	0.3	0.7	0.0	0.8	6.3
39 56882	North Olmsted	11.7	31,991	1,232	2,734.3	86.4	3.1	0.2	2.8	0.0	1.6	6.0
39 56966	North Ridgeville	23.4	36,240	1,092	1,548.7	89.3	1.9	0.2	1.6	0.0	1.2	5.9
39 57008	North Royalton	21.4	30,965	1,273	1,447.0	88.8	1.8	0.1	4.3	0.0	0.8	4.2
39 61000	Parma	20.0	79,982	445	3,999.1	84.2	4.3	0.2	2.5	0.0	2.5	6.4
39 62148	Perrysburg	11.9	25,114	1,542	2,110.4	86.1	2.0	0.2	4.4	0.0	1.2	6.2
39 66390	Reynoldsburg	11.3	41,050	959	3,632.7	50.6	29.1	0.3	9.8	0.0	3.1	7.0
39 70380	Sandusky	9.6	24,758	1,549	2,579.0	63.8	23.4	0.4	0.4	0.0	1.8	10.2
39 71682	Shaker Heights	6.3	28,970	1,348	4,598.4	53.8	34.0	0.1	4.4	0.0	1.2	6.5
39 74118	Springfield	26.0	58,763	666	2,260.1	69.5	18.8	0.3	0.8	0.1	2.6	7.9
39 74944	Stow	17.1	34,342	1,160	2,008.3	87.5	3.6	0.1	3.1	0.0	0.6	5.2
39 75098	Strongsville	24.6	46,042	862	1,871.6	84.9	2.6	0.1	6.3	0.0	1.0	4.9
39 77000	Toledo	80.5	268,508	83	3,335.5	58.3	28.8	0.4	1.2	0.0	3.0	8.3
39 77588	Troy	12.1	26,432	1,468	2,184.5	85.4	4.1	0.1	3.0	0.0	1.2	6.1
39 79002	Upper Arlington	9.8	36,295	1,089	3,703.6	86.1	1.0	0.1	6.6	0.0	0.6	5.6
39 80892	Warren	16.0	39,020	1,017	2,438.8	62.7	27.9	0.2	0.4	0.0	1.1	7.6
39 83342	Westerville	12.6	38,862	1,022	3,084.3	82.2	7.7	0.2	2.9	0.0	1.1	5.9
39 83622	Westlake	15.9	33,986	1,169	2,137.5	85.8	2.3	0.1	5.7	0.0	1.2	4.9
39 86548	Wooster	17.1	26,751	1,451	1,564.4	86.9	3.6	0.2	2.0	0.0	1.2	6.1

1. Dry land or land partially or temporarily covered by water. 2. Hispanic or Latino persons may be of any race.

City	Percent Hispanic or Latino[1], 2020	Percent foreign born, 2016–2020	Age of population (percent), 2016–2020							Median age, 2016–2020	Percent female, 2016–2020	Population			
			Under 18 years	18 to 24 years	25 to 34 years	35 to 44 years	45 to 54 years	55 to 64 years	65 years and over			Census counts		Percent change	
												2010	2020	2010–2020	2020–2021
	12	13	14	15	16	17	18	19	20	21	22	23	24	25	26
NORTH DAKOTA	4.3	4.3	23.4	11.2	15.2	11.9	10.6	12.4	15.3	35.2	48.8	672,575	779,094	15.8	-0.5
Bismarck	3.5	3.1	22.2	9.2	15.0	12.8	10.8	12.6	17.3	37.4	50.8	61,324	73,651	20.1	0.7
Dickinson	8.0	3.7	26.2	10.2	18.5	11.3	11.5	10.8	11.6	32.6	48.8	17,876	25,656	43.5	-1.9
Fargo	3.7	9.9	19.9	17.0	18.3	12.4	9.4	10.0	12.8	31.4	49.6	105,612	125,830	19.1	0.7
Grand Forks	5.0	6.3	19.8	21.5	17.8	10.1	8.3	9.9	12.6	29.4	47.8	52,921	59,022	11.5	-0.4
Minot	6.8	5.4	21.4	13.5	20.2	12.1	9.3	10.0	13.5	32.1	48.3	41,095	48,353	17.7	-1.2
West Fargo	3.1	4.2	27.3	9.4	17.6	15.4	11.1	10.4	8.7	33.1	49.8	25,854	38,733	49.8	1.9
Williston	10.8	9.2	27.4	8.7	21.7	15.0	9.9	9.3	8.1	30.9	46.3	15,939	29,158	82.9	-6.3
OHIO	4.4	4.6	22.2	9.1	13.2	12.0	12.7	13.8	17.0	39.5	51.0	11,536,763	11,799,448	2.3	-0.2
Akron	3.3	6.8	21.2	11.5	15.5	11.2	12.1	13.4	15.1	36.5	52.4	199,077	190,534	-4.3	-0.6
Avon Lake	3.6	4.5	24.5	3.9	9.1	12.7	17.1	12.8	20.0	44.7	52.1	22,581	25,269	11.9	1.3
Barberton	1.9	1.4	22.2	5.5	15.2	9.5	10.1	17.4	20.0	41.6	53.1	26,538	25,185	-5.1	-0.8
Beavercreek	3.6	7.1	21.8	6.6	13.9	12.5	12.9	14.2	18.1	40.7	49.9	45,191	46,507	2.9	0.3
Bowling Green	7.1	3.4	13.9	44.3	12.4	6.4	6.6	7.3	9.1	22.5	52.2	30,113	30,630	1.7	0.2
Brunswick	3.3	4.1	22.9	8.4	11.9	13.4	13.8	13.5	16.1	39.8	51.6	34,283	35,440	3.4	-0.3
Canton	5.0	2.5	24.7	9.7	15.6	11.2	11.9	12.9	14.0	34.9	51.5	73,430	70,947	-3.4	-0.7
Cincinnati	5.1	6.1	21.6	13.6	18.7	11.5	10.5	11.6	12.5	32.4	51.6	297,098	310,242	4.4	-0.4
Cleveland	13.1	6.1	21.7	10.1	16.4	11.6	12.1	13.8	14.3	36.3	52.0	396,831	373,091	-6.0	-1.4
Cleveland Heights	3.4	9.0	20.4	11.7	16.0	11.3	9.9	11.4	19.4	36.5	55.6	46,139	45,306	-1.8	-1.4
Columbus	7.7	12.8	22.3	11.3	21.1	13.1	11.2	10.6	10.4	32.4	51.2	789,007	905,672	14.8	0.1
Cuyahoga Falls	2.2	6.3	19.9	7.7	17.1	13.6	12.2	13.1	16.6	38.5	52.5	49,588	51,109	3.1	-0.6
Dayton	5.7	4.9	20.9	15.4	15.9	10.4	11.4	13.0	13.0	33.5	50.5	141,930	138,310	-2.6	-0.5
Delaware	4.4	3.8	24.0	10.7	12.7	17.1	12.2	10.3	13.0	36.5	50.6	34,800	41,252	18.5	3.8
Dublin	2.9	20.2	29.4	5.1	9.3	16.0	15.9	12.7	11.7	39.3	49.1	41,396	49,359	19.2	-0.6
Elyria	8.4	2.5	21.5	10.0	12.8	11.9	12.4	14.3	17.1	40.5	52.9	54,562	52,738	-3.3	0.1
Euclid	2.1	3.1	20.9	9.2	12.9	11.1	12.2	16.6	17.1	41.4	54.4	48,901	49,628	1.5	-1.4
Fairborn	3.8	5.4	18.9	13.3	18.8	13.1	10.0	11.4	14.5	34.4	52.2	32,955	34,488	4.7	0.4
Fairfield	8.0	11.9	21.7	8.9	13.4	12.8	11.2	14.6	17.4	40.0	52.4	42,501	44,936	5.7	-0.8
Findlay	6.7	5.1	20.0	11.3	16.1	11.1	11.4	12.4	17.7	37.3	52.1	41,189	40,078	-2.7	-0.3
Gahanna	3.7	5.8	23.8	5.9	13.6	14.1	13.6	13.3	15.7	39.6	53.3	33,230	35,749	7.6	-0.9
Garfield Heights	3.9	3.5	23.6	8.9	12.0	12.3	11.0	15.8	16.4	39.5	55.0	28,884	29,786	3.1	-1.4
Green	1.8	3.0	24.4	6.9	10.4	13.1	13.0	14.1	18.0	42.0	49.1	25,742	27,477	6.7	-0.5
Grove City	3.6	3.1	24.5	6.4	14.0	13.6	13.5	11.5	16.4	37.9	51.2	35,633	41,276	15.8	1.2
Hamilton	10.0	3.6	23.1	11.7	14.3	11.9	10.9	13.2	14.9	35.7	51.5	62,253	63,386	1.8	-0.7
Hilliard	4.4	7.0	26.4	7.4	13.7	15.2	13.7	13.0	10.5	36.7	51.1	28,235	37,132	31.5	-0.6
Huber Heights	3.9	5.8	24.9	8.4	12.9	12.5	13.2	12.6	15.6	37.5	52.1	38,110	43,341	13.7	-0.2
Kent	3.4	7.1	14.3	38.2	11.7	10.0	7.5	7.5	11.0	24.1	52.0	28,904	27,813	-3.8	-0.2
Kettering	3.4	5.3	21.5	7.4	15.7	11.8	11.0	13.8	18.7	39.1	52.2	56,128	57,743	2.9	-0.6
Lakewood	4.9	8.0	16.7	8.7	26.3	12.7	10.2	12.1	13.4	34.0	51.3	52,166	50,848	-2.5	-1.5
Lancaster	1.9	1.2	22.3	8.2	14.8	11.2	13.4	12.5	17.4	39.2	50.5	38,764	40,522	4.5	0.6
Lima	4.2	1.4	24.9	11.6	15.4	11.5	12.6	10.4	13.6	33.5	48.1	38,620	36,175	-6.3	-0.8
Lorain	29.2	2.6	24.9	9.3	12.8	12.0	11.7	13.3	16.0	38.0	51.9	64,027	65,340	2.1	0.1
Mansfield	2.8	2.2	19.5	10.8	15.5	13.0	12.2	12.2	16.8	38.3	47.0	47,811	47,540	-0.6	0.3
Marion	3.7	1.8	20.3	9.3	17.7	12.5	12.9	13.4	13.9	37.2	43.6	36,831	35,971	-2.3	-0.3
Marysville	3.3	3.6	21.4	8.2	17.5	16.9	13.6	11.7	10.7	36.9	55.1	22,145	25,324	14.4	3.5
Mason	4.5	13.1	27.0	5.9	7.2	15.6	16.5	14.7	13.1	42.9	48.9	30,860	34,787	12.7	0.9
Massillon	3.6	0.9	21.3	7.3	12.8	13.8	10.5	14.0	20.3	41.2	50.6	32,297	32,148	-0.5	0.3
Medina	3.3	2.6	23.9	7.9	13.5	13.3	13.2	13.1	15.1	38.9	49.1	26,639	25,969	-2.5	-0.1
Mentor	2.1	4.8	19.2	6.7	10.2	11.1	13.1	16.7	23.1	47.3	51.3	47,161	47,435	0.6	-0.5
Middletown	8.1	2.4	22.5	10.1	13.7	10.3	12.2	14.0	17.2	38.4	52.3	48,691	51,033	4.8	-0.1
Newark	2.0	2.7	22.6	10.9	13.2	12.3	12.4	12.9	15.8	37.3	51.1	47,551	49,913	5.0	0.9
North Olmsted	5.0	10.5	20.8	7.8	11.4	10.5	13.8	16.1	19.6	44.6	50.1	32,753	32,409	-1.1	-1.3
North Ridgeville	4.6	5.3	24.3	5.6	13.6	12.6	12.2	12.8	18.9	40.1	51.2	29,476	35,370	20.0	2.5
North Royalton	2.7	10.7	18.4	8.6	14.7	10.6	14.2	14.3	19.1	42.7	52.2	30,470	31,292	2.7	-1.0
Parma	6.9	10.5	17.7	8.8	14.9	11.3	13.1	14.4	19.9	43.0	51.2	81,618	81,047	-0.7	-1.3
Perrysburg	5.1	6.6	26.8	7.3	11.0	15.3	14.2	10.9	14.4	37.2	49.9	20,751	25,068	20.8	0.2
Reynoldsburg	5.6	10.0	25.8	8.1	14.0	12.8	13.1	12.4	13.8	36.2	51.3	35,929	41,091	14.4	-0.1
Sandusky	5.8	1.7	22.3	9.7	14.4	10.3	12.6	14.1	16.6	37.9	52.3	25,909	25,065	-3.3	-1.2
Shaker Heights	3.2	7.4	25.4	5.9	11.1	13.5	12.9	12.4	19.0	40.4	54.0	28,395	29,400	3.5	-1.5
Springfield	4.9	2.3	24.5	11.5	13.4	10.2	11.0	12.3	17.1	35.4	53.1	60,564	58,940	-2.7	-0.3
Stow	2.2	3.8	20.4	9.0	13.3	12.8	12.9	12.7	18.8	40.1	52.0	34,832	34,491	-1.0	-0.4
Strongsville	3.5	10.5	20.1	6.0	10.8	10.7	14.6	15.5	22.3	46.6	50.6	44,750	46,449	3.8	-0.9
Toledo	8.9	3.4	23.4	10.3	15.7	11.6	12.0	12.6	14.4	35.4	51.5	287,357	270,726	-5.8	-0.8
Troy	2.5	3.7	25.0	8.5	13.1	14.3	13.8	9.7	15.6	36.9	51.2	25,232	26,308	4.3	0.5
Upper Arlington	2.4	8.5	28.1	3.9	10.5	14.9	13.9	11.7	17.0	39.4	49.6	33,675	36,810	9.3	-1.4
Warren	2.8	1.3	20.5	9.9	12.8	12.1	11.8	14.9	18.1	40.5	51.1	41,584	39,217	-5.7	-0.5
Westerville	2.9	5.8	22.1	8.2	12.2	12.9	11.6	12.8	20.3	40.8	53.2	36,268	39,160	8.0	-0.8
Westlake	3.4	10.9	20.4	6.5	11.7	9.2	13.5	16.1	22.5	47.0	52.3	32,726	34,283	4.8	-0.9
Wooster	3.1	4.5	17.6	16.4	11.9	10.7	11.2	12.1	20.2	38.5	53.0	26,177	26,780	2.3	-0.1

1. May be of any race.

City	Households, 2016–2020: Number	Households, 2016–2020: Persons per household	Households, 2016–2020: Percent: Family	Households, 2016–2020: Percent: Married couple family	Households, 2016–2020: Percent: Female family	Households, 2016–2020: Percent: Non-family	Households, 2016–2020: Percent: One person	Persons in group quarters, 2016–2020	Serious crimes known to police[2], 2020: Violent: Number	Serious crimes known to police[2], 2020: Violent: Rate	Serious crimes known to police[2], 2020: Property: Number	Serious crimes known to police[2], 2020: Property: Rate	Educational attainment, 2016–2020: Population age 25 and over	Educational attainment, 2016–2020: Attainment[4] (percent): High school graduate or less	Educational attainment, 2016–2020: Attainment[4] (percent): Bachelor's degree or more
	27	28	29	30	31	32	33	34	35	36	37	38	39	40	41
NORTH DAKOTA	320,873	2.29	59.0	47.6	7.5	41.0	32.5	25,410	2,518	329.0	16,256	2,124.1	497,525	33.0	30.7
Bismarck	32,393	2.20	58.5	44.9	9.9	41.5	33.5	2,107	260	346.7	2,471	3,294.8	50,347	28.6	36.9
Dickinson	9,459	2.34	56.6	45.2	7.2	43.4	34.6	702	39	163.9	456	1,915.9	14,540	39.6	25.2
Fargo	55,478	2.14	49.8	38.8	7.5	50.2	37.1	4,848	584	460.1	4,403	3,468.9	77,856	24.7	40.9
Grand Forks	25,780	2.06	46.3	33.8	9.0	53.7	39.8	3,575	164	292.0	1,315	2,341.4	33,222	26.0	37.8
Minot	21,156	2.20	52.8	41.7	6.4	47.2	37.6	1,222	155	322.2	800	1,662.9	31,156	37.2	29.6
West Fargo	14,059	2.58	68.4	58.4	7.4	31.6	22.5	78	55	142.6	730	1,893.1	23,011	20.8	43.0
Williston	11,674	2.34	57.6	41.4	6.9	42.4	32.3	478	116	373.6	725	2,335.2	17,781	39.6	27.5
OHIO	4,717,226	2.41	62.6	45.5	12.3	37.4	30.9	314,246	36,104	308.8	216,363	1,850.3	8,014,966	42.0	28.9
Akron	85,170	2.25	53.2	29.4	18.3	46.8	38.1	5,392	1,797	910.2	6,971	3,530.8	132,779	46.1	21.5
Avon Lake	9,912	2.44	66.8	59.3	5.3	33.2	28.9	122	4	16.2	53	214.4	17,407	19.6	51.6
Barberton	11,221	2.29	56.3	37.3	15.8	43.7	35.6	359	65	251.1	651	2,514.5	18,824	60.1	15.8
Beavercreek	19,125	2.45	70.6	58.3	7.6	29.4	24.8	398	24	50.0	989	2,059.2	33,937	18.9	51.8
Bowling Green	11,178	2.32	40.7	25.2	11.6	59.3	35.8	5,753	14	44.3	436	1,378.8	13,246	32.0	42.7
Brunswick	13,844	2.50	65.3	52.1	8.4	34.7	29.4	285	NA	NA	NA	NA	23,991	38.8	27.5
Canton	30,260	2.26	53.7	26.3	21.7	46.3	39.5	2,568	1,002	1,428.9	3,411	4,864.2	46,420	51.7	13.7
Cincinnati	138,696	2.09	45.1	24.2	16.5	54.9	44.6	13,120	2,721	892.9	11,224	3,683.3	196,143	35.2	38.7
Cleveland	174,920	2.12	47.0	19.8	20.7	53.0	45.0	12,867	6,281	1,656.7	15,433	4,070.7	261,397	50.9	18.6
Cleveland Heights	18,976	2.28	53.3	35.4	14.7	46.7	35.8	896	115	263.0	527	1,205.3	30,004	18.9	57.9
Columbus	362,626	2.39	52.8	32.3	15.2	47.2	36.0	23,756	5,064	555.6	28,530	3,130.4	589,763	35.5	36.8
Cuyahoga Falls	21,954	2.22	56.2	43.4	9.0	43.8	36.0	496	37	75.4	961	1,958.8	35,642	35.0	34.1
Dayton	58,748	2.16	49.8	24.1	20.8	50.2	42.2	13,762	1,523	1,086.4	5,391	3,845.4	89,465	44.9	18.4
Delaware	15,471	2.57	66.9	51.8	10.5	33.1	27.6	2,121	57	135.5	367	872.5	27,321	30.6	42.5
Dublin	16,819	2.83	79.1	71.9	4.1	20.9	19.0	186	22	44.0	372	744.7	31,360	11.1	73.8
Elyria	23,136	2.30	57.4	34.2	16.2	42.6	36.7	739	136	253.4	785	1,462.5	36,901	46.8	15.2
Euclid	22,374	2.07	49.8	23.9	22.4	50.2	44.1	640	240	518.7	1,327	2,867.8	32,728	40.9	20.9
Fairborn	14,931	2.20	53.8	36.1	13.3	46.2	34.2	673	100	294.5	529	1,558.1	22,710	34.6	29.8
Fairfield	17,447	2.41	64.4	48.4	11.0	35.6	30.2	542	NA	NA	NA	NA	29,593	42.2	30.6
Findlay	18,288	2.15	51.8	36.3	11.4	48.2	39.4	1,757	65	157.6	777	1,884.2	28,237	42.8	27.9
Gahanna	13,775	2.56	70.0	55.3	10.9	30.0	24.7	178	60	167.9	615	1,720.9	24,918	24.8	48.6
Garfield Heights	11,863	2.30	57.3	29.7	23.3	42.7	35.7	402	NA	NA	NA	NA	18,680	50.5	14.6
Green	10,055	2.54	70.4	57.0	9.3	29.6	25.3	184	NA	NA	NA	NA	17,678	30.1	39.8
Grove City	16,251	2.53	72.4	57.1	10.7	27.6	23.1	292	80	188.0	1,054	2,477.0	28,618	36.5	33.4
Hamilton	24,116	2.50	61.8	37.3	18.3	38.2	31.9	1,838	NA	NA	NA	NA	40,531	54.2	17.4
Hilliard	13,896	2.65	74.6	60.1	10.5	25.4	22.0	166	24	63.9	265	705.1	24,479	20.8	55.0
Huber Heights	15,901	2.53	68.6	49.4	13.1	31.4	25.8	191	67	175.6	682	1,787.3	27,003	35.4	24.3
Kent	10,792	2.24	46.5	31.4	10.4	53.5	41.0	5,529	27	90.8	452	1,520.2	14,128	30.2	44.5
Kettering	25,018	2.19	57.9	44.2	10.4	42.1	35.2	498	NA	NA	NA	NA	39,291	26.5	38.6
Lakewood	25,421	1.95	40.5	29.7	7.3	59.5	46.3	316	64	129.6	744	1,506.4	37,299	24.3	47.8
Lancaster	16,451	2.39	60.5	41.9	12.9	39.5	31.3	1,081	101	248.2	1,212	2,977.9	28,089	50.1	19.1
Lima	14,426	2.36	56.1	27.1	22.9	43.9	36.8	2,834	NA	NA	NA	NA	23,444	55.6	10.6
Lorain	26,110	2.42	58.2	32.0	20.3	41.8	35.8	680	323	506.0	1,510	2,365.6	41,981	51.8	13.1
Mansfield	18,580	2.15	50.2	28.3	17.0	49.8	40.0	6,421	NA	NA	NA	NA	32,354	54.5	15.4
Marion	12,694	2.40	57.8	38.0	14.8	42.2	36.4	5,548	NA	NA	NA	NA	25,352	59.2	10.7
Marysville	8,786	2.44	63.8	49.1	8.2	36.2	29.2	3,134	NA	NA	NA	NA	17,292	38.3	31.9
Mason	12,470	2.66	76.4	64.8	8.4	23.6	19.6	361	NA	NA	NA	NA	22,537	19.7	60.0
Massillon	14,075	2.25	60.2	40.5	14.0	39.8	31.9	835	56	171.7	759	2,327.0	23,197	51.9	17.5
Medina	10,302	2.48	68.3	49.9	13.3	31.7	28.2	482	21	81.1	196	757.3	17,738	34.7	35.1
Mentor	19,416	2.41	67.5	54.8	8.6	32.5	28.2	377	63	133.3	616	1,303.0	34,916	36.5	32.6
Middletown	20,057	2.39	60.0	36.8	16.4	40.0	32.4	744	147	301.1	1,170	2,396.9	32,867	56.1	15.6
Newark	19,336	2.52	59.9	39.1	16.1	40.1	32.4	1,253	139	274.6	1,748	3,452.8	33,213	47.3	21.4
North Olmsted	12,941	2.41	65.6	52.8	8.4	34.4	29.1	417	13	41.7	371	1,190.0	22,541	36.5	31.4
North Ridgeville	12,688	2.66	70.7	55.9	9.2	29.3	25.4	258	NA	NA	NA	NA	23,799	34.5	30.9
North Royalton	13,196	2.26	63.7	50.0	9.8	36.3	30.2	333	13	43.3	155	516.5	22,015	30.7	39.0
Parma	33,702	2.30	61.2	42.1	13.8	38.8	31.6	1,045	135	173.8	688	885.6	57,832	44.2	22.8
Perrysburg	8,695	2.45	62.8	50.4	8.5	37.2	31.8	228	13	59.8	181	833.2	14,211	16.6	55.7
Reynoldsburg	14,678	2.59	63.3	45.0	14.1	36.7	30.9	35	NA	NA	NA	NA	25,121	32.7	32.2
Sandusky	11,171	2.17	55.2	31.1	19.2	44.8	37.4	458	NA	NA	NA	NA	16,778	52.6	17.4
Shaker Heights	11,505	2.34	61.8	45.8	12.6	38.2	32.8	177	NA	NA	NA	NA	18,668	11.8	69.9
Springfield	23,868	2.35	56.9	31.0	19.5	43.1	35.3	2,799	338	575.8	3,014	5,134.9	37,709	55.1	15.2
Stow	14,331	2.40	64.0	52.3	7.5	36.0	28.3	399	18	51.8	485	1,394.4	24,548	26.2	48.0
Strongsville	18,491	2.40	67.5	58.0	6.7	32.5	28.0	352	19	42.6	608	1,362.5	33,018	25.2	48.5
Toledo	119,215	2.25	53.6	28.6	18.5	46.4	37.9	7,306	2,729	1,006.1	7,849	2,893.8	182,438	45.8	18.8
Troy	10,025	2.58	62.1	46.4	10.8	37.9	29.8	324	NA	NA	NA	NA	17,418	42.8	25.7
Upper Arlington	13,627	2.58	69.9	61.3	6.7	30.1	26.1	145	11	30.9	336	945.0	24,033	7.8	78.7
Warren	17,448	2.08	50.1	23.3	21.0	49.9	43.1	2,617	173	449.8	1,073	2,789.8	27,130	59.5	15.1
Westerville	15,053	2.55	72.2	60.0	8.8	27.8	23.7	2,011	39	93.6	685	1,644.6	28,211	19.5	55.5
Westlake	13,779	2.28	59.3	50.2	6.5	40.7	35.1	805	NA	NA	NA	NA	23,495	21.2	55.1
Wooster	11,127	2.11	56.0	42.1	9.5	44.0	38.7	3,109	70	264.9	661	2,501.5	17,531	42.8	28.2

2. Data for serious crimes have not been adjusted for underreporting. This may affect comparability between geographic areas and over time. 4. Persons 25 years old and over.

City	Money income, 2016–2020					Median earnings Full year, Full-time workers, 2016–2020			Housing units, 2016–2020				
	Households												
	Median household income	Percent with income less than $25,000	Percent with income of $200,000 or more	Median family income	Median non-family household income	All persons	Men	Women	Total	Occupied	Percent owner occupied	Median value[1] (dollars)	Median gross rent (dollars)
	42	43	44	45	46	47	48	49	50	51	52	53	54
NORTH DAKOTA	65,315	17.6	6.0	86,798	39,781	50,234	54,826	42,455	376,597	320,873	62.5	199,900	828
Bismarck	67,629	16.1	6.2	89,656	41,241	52,796	59,104	48,781	35,119	32,393	65.0	249,200	874
Dickinson	66,306	19.3	7.0	100,113	41,557	51,930	62,352	41,104	10,884	9,459	55.9	237,900	904
Fargo	57,520	20.5	5.4	81,873	39,861	44,808	46,453	42,608	60,929	55,478	44.4	225,500	821
Grand Forks	50,194	24.6	3.6	81,317	34,773	47,440	51,831	41,252	27,628	25,780	43.9	209,800	817
Minot	64,401	17.3	4.7	85,731	39,985	49,719	53,400	42,670	24,395	21,156	55.5	211,000	882
West Fargo	87,674	9.4	12.1	101,988	48,813	53,602	57,221	47,249	14,746	14,059	66.3	241,800	957
Williston	76,873	12.7	9.0	92,743	51,229	55,692	68,595	41,527	15,372	11,674	46.3	244,400	1,009
OHIO	58,116	20.5	5.2	74,391	34,626	48,501	53,408	41,952	5,217,090	4,717,226	66.3	151,400	825
Akron	40,281	31.3	1.9	50,102	28,539	38,684	41,945	35,878	95,900	85,170	50.4	83,500	795
Avon Lake	82,994	12.4	13.0	110,228	37,866	77,774	90,162	60,414	10,472	9,912	81.0	260,000	1,170
Barberton	41,119	28.7	1.6	52,167	27,979	38,718	48,164	31,442	12,163	11,221	58.5	88,400	756
Beavercreek	94,632	9.3	10.7	108,866	54,357	66,066	75,728	58,275	20,215	19,125	73.5	201,100	1,229
Bowling Green	39,210	32.7	3.2	63,590	26,459	36,828	40,914	34,525	11,922	11,178	36.6	171,800	737
Brunswick	70,384	13.0	3.4	86,867	43,044	51,767	59,017	41,717	14,388	13,844	74.0	178,000	926
Canton	32,735	38.5	1.0	42,849	24,173	33,739	37,672	30,437	34,727	30,260	47.7	73,300	705
Cincinnati	42,663	31.4	5.3	58,437	33,510	46,791	50,440	42,943	161,166	138,696	38.9	148,700	760
Cleveland	31,838	41.1	1.9	39,721	23,197	38,893	41,505	36,472	211,212	174,920	41.9	73,400	735
Cleveland Heights	59,086	22.1	7.6	77,877	41,840	54,303	57,076	52,929	21,538	18,976	56.4	133,700	1,005
Columbus	54,902	20.9	3.4	66,161	42,789	45,935	48,898	42,950	395,162	362,626	44.9	160,000	989
Cuyahoga Falls	60,280	16.8	2.9	76,675	39,539	48,387	50,904	44,330	23,555	21,954	61.8	134,800	865
Dayton	34,457	38.9	1.5	43,485	24,837	38,245	42,121	34,714	73,554	58,748	47.1	69,400	724
Delaware	74,130	15.3	6.1	90,934	37,773	57,541	64,966	48,060	16,248	15,471	62.7	197,600	963
Dublin	138,372	6.7	29.5	159,495	67,934	94,593	109,823	73,896	17,577	16,819	75.8	394,500	1,362
Elyria	43,816	27.3	1.2	55,149	31,855	39,927	43,791	35,256	25,468	23,136	59.6	107,600	740
Euclid	40,342	33.4	1.3	50,586	27,724	42,609	44,423	41,038	25,474	22,374	45.3	84,500	810
Fairborn	48,825	23.6	1.5	62,995	36,295	42,289	48,089	36,291	16,200	14,931	46.7	123,700	846
Fairfield	63,655	16.0	5.1	77,111	38,329	46,702	49,383	42,271	18,679	17,447	62.5	166,000	961
Findlay	48,547	22.4	4.2	65,600	31,363	42,553	50,067	37,634	19,605	18,288	56.1	140,600	759
Gahanna	89,945	9.3	9.6	105,959	49,995	62,032	65,608	59,752	14,083	13,775	72.5	228,800	1,153
Garfield Heights	43,901	29.5	0.7	55,278	29,486	40,909	44,763	37,390	13,134	11,863	58.0	75,400	937
Green	81,899	13.0	9.8	95,981	43,877	60,944	72,613	51,256	10,743	10,055	74.6	206,300	919
Grove City	77,865	9.9	6.5	97,491	42,803	53,142	60,577	44,869	16,974	16,251	71.8	199,700	1,089
Hamilton	47,937	25.2	1.9	57,446	31,653	39,504	44,965	34,740	26,875	24,116	54.7	108,000	829
Hilliard	102,283	9.6	13.5	119,603	44,471	68,441	76,045	61,787	14,306	13,896	71.5	265,600	1,218
Huber Heights	66,134	13.8	3.6	75,794	42,283	46,255	52,971	39,432	16,821	15,901	74.0	121,300	966
Kent	36,809	37.7	4.2	77,532	22,060	40,639	40,059	42,139	13,131	10,792	41.2	154,400	789
Kettering	61,974	17.1	5.0	79,063	37,745	48,069	51,274	44,507	26,479	25,018	63.4	142,700	835
Lakewood	54,487	21.1	4.9	81,955	42,400	51,238	54,229	46,692	27,652	25,421	42.6	171,600	813
Lancaster	44,794	26.0	1.5	59,930	27,287	42,025	49,527	38,265	18,250	16,451	57.8	131,700	835
Lima	34,586	34.6	0.8	39,331	26,007	34,490	37,830	32,236	16,644	14,426	46.4	68,900	687
Lorain	40,486	33.1	1.0	51,493	25,792	39,256	43,541	34,234	29,557	26,110	55.5	90,700	719
Mansfield	36,318	35.7	1.1	46,106	27,425	34,988	40,023	31,184	21,547	18,580	48.6	80,300	640
Marion	40,223	29.8	0.9	51,152	26,630	38,342	40,398	33,279	14,844	12,694	55.0	77,800	737
Marysville	79,016	11.3	7.9	100,750	52,045	61,193	68,814	49,582	9,173	8,786	69.4	206,700	1,015
Mason	104,462	7.6	22.6	124,609	54,920	77,097	89,141	60,769	12,692	12,470	79.0	313,400	1,381
Massillon	48,268	24.5	1.2	56,916	30,750	41,309	43,487	38,344	15,511	14,075	63.4	107,400	711
Medina	66,691	16.8	5.0	85,885	35,876	54,042	61,146	48,657	10,709	10,302	67.9	176,100	851
Mentor	73,208	11.5	6.7	91,009	42,588	56,988	65,377	50,387	20,610	19,416	84.0	183,600	958
Middletown	42,290	27.4	1.7	54,835	29,948	38,069	41,355	34,738	22,990	20,057	53.2	105,100	817
Newark	48,609	25.3	2.6	60,218	28,032	41,567	45,404	38,218	22,170	19,336	54.7	129,500	795
North Olmsted	72,666	13.8	4.8	85,208	45,026	53,649	54,574	51,696	13,465	12,941	76.0	161,300	965
North Ridgeville	77,560	8.3	4.8	84,337	52,141	54,411	57,666	50,577	13,267	12,688	87.5	188,400	1,049
North Royalton	69,788	10.5	7.3	95,041	44,933	54,301	64,792	45,182	14,001	13,196	67.9	215,900	891
Parma	58,011	16.4	1.8	70,495	39,038	46,884	50,981	42,378	36,002	33,702	70.9	118,600	882
Perrysburg	89,223	11.0	16.4	114,746	57,561	71,947	85,779	56,992	9,325	8,695	60.8	228,800	1,068
Reynoldsburg	65,623	12.8	3.8	86,822	37,814	49,553	51,805	45,341	15,483	14,678	61.8	171,900	1,030
Sandusky	41,082	30.3	1.6	52,125	27,835	37,490	44,043	31,671	13,771	11,171	51.9	85,300	742
Shaker Heights	88,635	13.1	21.6	123,906	48,567	72,008	85,967	59,299	12,736	11,505	60.3	241,900	1,012
Springfield	39,344	29.3	1.1	46,891	27,225	35,781	41,159	31,639	28,088	23,868	50.3	80,600	733
Stow	76,883	11.4	6.8	92,083	48,371	57,331	65,263	50,640	15,324	14,331	69.4	190,800	1,009
Strongsville	90,377	8.8	10.3	111,663	51,694	66,116	75,204	59,297	19,231	18,491	81.5	215,900	1,057
Toledo	39,155	33.2	0.9	50,428	27,397	40,234	42,596	36,955	137,738	119,215	50.7	83,600	737
Troy	61,216	19.3	4.0	77,458	31,946	44,584	51,176	39,195	10,902	10,025	63.5	144,100	782
Upper Arlington	124,688	5.2	26.2	154,326	64,278	87,670	97,164	71,677	14,326	13,627	78.9	429,100	1,248
Warren	27,108	46.1	0.8	37,552	21,257	34,038	41,491	28,364	20,282	17,448	52.0	66,100	658
Westerville	92,287	7.9	9.6	109,168	55,895	66,462	72,755	61,608	15,879	15,053	77.7	244,500	1,113
Westlake	92,917	10.0	17.8	123,194	54,507	72,994	79,777	66,839	14,931	13,779	71.8	263,500	1,223
Wooster	52,366	23.3	3.3	65,625	30,922	42,302	47,516	35,217	11,974	11,127	60.3	147,200	766

1. Specified owner-occupied units

City	Commuting, 2016–2020[1]		Computer access[2], 2016–2020		Migration, 2016–2020		Civilian labor force, 2021				Civilian Employment, 2016–2020[4]			
	Percent		Percent						Unemployment[3]		Population age 16 and older		Population age 16 to 64	
	Drove alone	Mean travel time to work	With a computer in the house	With Internet access	Percent who lived in the same house one year ago	Percent who lived in another state or county one year ago	Total	Percent change 2020–2021	Total	Rate	Number	Percent in labor force	Number	Percent who worked full-year full-time
	55	56	57	58	59	60	61	62	63	64	65	66	67	68
NORTH DAKOTA	80.8	17.6	91.3	82.5	82.5	8.6	406,187	-1.3	14,932	3.7	599,849	69.1	483,443	57.7
Bismarck	84.9	16.5	91.5	84.0	84.2	6.5	39,580	0.6	1,213	3.1	58,881	67.6	46,143	60.3
Dickinson	81.3	16.4	89.7	82.3	80.7	9.8	13,026	-5.5	618	4.7	17,560	69.5	14,913	55.6
Fargo	81.3	15.2	93.5	84.9	74.2	11.2	72,689	0.6	2,058	2.8	101,230	74.6	85,387	56.1
Grand Forks	81.6	13.7	91.5	80.9	76.0	12.5	30,912	-0.6	943	3.1	46,611	71.6	39,477	50.1
Minot	81.1	18.8	93.4	86.3	77.5	10.1	23,152	-1.3	969	4.2	38,830	69.7	32,378	58.4
West Fargo	83.7	17.9	95.8	93.2	79.8	7.8	23,103	1.2	625	2.7	27,124	82.1	23,948	66.6
Williston	85.3	15.0	93.6	79.7	79.7	12.3	15,986	-11.1	1,019	6.4	20,717	75.8	18,469	58.5
OHIO	81.5	23.7	90.7	84.0	86.0	5.4	5,736,882	0.0	295,003	5.1	9,385,593	63.0	7,394,972	51.4
Akron	78.3	21.9	88.0	81.0	84.3	4.9	88,753	-1.9	5,933	6.7	160,188	63.4	130,353	45.2
Avon Lake	83.5	27.9	95.6	88.5	91.9	4.2	12,519	1.3	540	4.3	19,271	65.4	14,412	56.1
Barberton	83.8	22.7	82.4	75.7	90.7	1.9	12,160	-1.8	714	5.9	20,831	58.1	15,614	48.3
Beavercreek	86.8	19.4	95.4	92.5	86.6	9.3	23,580	0.5	909	3.9	38,427	61.4	29,860	57.8
Bowling Green	72.7	16.8	95.7	86.2	55.3	22.5	16,251	0.3	605	3.7	27,854	71.6	24,961	29.4
Brunswick	86.6	27.0	95.9	88.4	92.1	3.3	19,720	0.1	830	4.2	27,955	69.9	22,341	60.5
Canton	79.4	20.7	87.5	74.8	81.4	4.2	30,737	-1.3	2,030	6.6	55,019	60.4	45,119	42.4
Cincinnati	70.6	23.5	89.5	82.5	76.4	8.0	148,149	0.0	8,258	5.6	243,879	66.5	206,141	47.2
Cleveland	68.8	23.8	85.5	71.5	82.1	4.3	155,813	-1.8	13,206	8.5	309,886	59.5	254,905	41.5
Cleveland Heights	72.0	22.8	93.6	86.4	83.3	6.3	22,106	0.4	1,320	6.0	36,228	63.0	27,666	48.4
Columbus	77.7	22.0	93.8	87.7	78.7	7.1	485,107	1.0	25,102	5.2	708,694	70.2	616,384	53.1
Cuyahoga Falls	87.3	22.8	90.4	85.8	87.6	5.4	25,809	-0.9	1,286	5.0	40,622	68.8	32,464	57.5
Dayton	71.1	20.8	85.6	77.5	74.4	7.3	58,036	-2.1	4,134	7.1	113,916	58.4	95,630	37.0
Delaware	80.2	26.9	94.9	90.6	84.2	8.6	22,933	1.6	886	3.9	32,854	69.7	27,431	53.7
Dublin	79.4	24.5	98.5	97.3	87.5	6.6	26,915	2.8	1,060	3.9	35,545	71.2	29,946	57.3
Elyria	85.0	22.7	88.6	76.2	85.1	4.1	26,647	-1.1	1,638	6.1	43,589	61.8	34,369	48.9
Euclid	74.0	25.9	85.0	74.7	85.2	3.0	22,130	-1.4	1,839	8.3	38,327	61.2	30,330	51.4
Fairborn	81.7	21.1	93.5	87.8	78.4	13.0	16,936	-0.7	816	4.8	27,770	62.6	22,910	47.7
Fairfield	88.2	24.2	92.7	87.9	89.0	5.3	24,250	0.2	1,045	4.3	34,518	68.1	27,120	58.9
Findlay	82.1	15.7	92.9	86.1	80.6	9.0	21,456	-1.5	997	4.6	33,690	64.2	26,433	53.2
Gahanna	81.3	20.8	96.3	94.5	89.4	3.6	20,466	1.7	848	4.1	28,315	68.8	22,739	61.3
Garfield Heights	84.9	23.8	88.5	79.2	86.3	2.1	13,376	-1.6	1,090	8.1	22,180	64.2	17,633	49.8
Green	84.4	23.1	94.8	91.3	90.7	3.6	13,471	-0.5	630	4.7	20,306	64.0	15,665	54.4
Grove City	85.5	25.0	96.0	92.5	83.1	4.0	22,949	2.1	980	4.3	32,302	70.7	25,499	63.3
Hamilton	80.6	26.4	90.1	83.9	84.7	4.8	28,095	0.3	1,530	5.4	49,073	61.2	39,813	50.0
Hilliard	85.4	24.7	97.5	93.8	85.5	5.9	20,046	2.3	736	3.7	28,703	74.6	24,809	60.1
Huber Heights	86.1	23.7	93.5	90.5	87.0	6.7	18,028	-1.3	982	5.4	31,461	64.4	25,145	53.1
Kent	73.5	21.9	92.6	79.4	71.6	18.4	15,941	0.0	673	4.2	25,839	65.3	22,585	31.2
Kettering	84.6	20.2	93.5	89.5	85.6	4.5	28,375	-0.8	1,298	4.6	44,648	65.9	34,298	58.4
Lakewood	77.0	24.0	93.5	87.1	80.2	5.4	28,953	-0.6	1,462	5.0	42,428	74.9	35,744	60.5
Lancaster	81.1	28.0	88.4	80.7	81.2	9.2	18,467	0.9	925	5.0	32,403	58.7	25,352	48.2
Lima	81.0	17.7	87.0	77.7	81.8	4.5	14,413	-1.8	1,047	7.3	28,663	60.3	23,634	42.1
Lorain	79.5	24.5	88.6	71.4	86.4	3.5	27,144	-1.8	2,214	8.2	49,881	56.4	39,691	42.6
Mansfield	83.4	19.7	85.7	75.0	77.6	10.6	17,110	-1.2	1,182	6.9	38,525	47.9	30,721	33.8
Marion	78.9	20.4	88.3	80.8	82.6	7.3	13,555	-1.6	749	5.5	29,315	49.6	24,320	37.4
Marysville	78.3	23.8	95.4	92.0	78.0	14.1	11,387	1.1	436	3.8	19,791	63.6	17,153	53.2
Mason	81.4	24.7	97.3	95.0	86.9	8.9	17,575	1.3	651	3.7	25,989	67.2	21,589	57.6
Massillon	83.5	21.9	90.2	84.8	86.9	2.9	15,297	-0.7	870	5.7	26,492	60.9	19,896	51.4
Medina	83.1	26.8	94.9	88.6	87.8	6.5	12,853	-0.2	609	4.7	20,475	69.7	16,545	56.1
Mentor	85.5	23.4	93.3	89.9	92.0	2.3	26,006	0.8	1,182	4.5	39,074	62.5	28,204	58.6
Middletown	85.2	23.1	87.8	79.3	81.1	7.5	21,231	-0.4	1,393	6.6	38,819	59.2	30,417	48.1
Newark	81.0	24.2	91.1	84.2	85.9	4.0	24,533	0.8	1,104	4.5	39,758	59.8	31,880	49.8
North Olmsted	82.7	25.2	92.9	88.7	89.3	4.5	16,836	0.2	885	5.3	25,814	65.9	19,643	56.1
North Ridgeville	83.8	26.3	95.9	90.9	89.7	5.6	18,340	0.5	820	4.5	26,578	63.9	20,154	60.3
North Royalton	86.7	27.9	94.6	91.8	86.6	4.6	17,018	1.2	849	5.0	25,108	68.2	19,346	60.2
Parma	84.3	24.8	90.3	85.1	86.5	2.9	40,680	-0.6	2,407	5.9	66,523	65.8	50,907	55.4
Perrysburg	82.8	20.3	94.5	90.4	81.9	10.5	12,047	0.6	473	3.9	16,478	70.5	13,378	56.9
Reynoldsburg	81.8	25.3	95.5	88.9	85.5	8.6	21,411	1.1	1,086	5.1	29,292	70.1	24,043	57.9
Sandusky	80.9	17.8	88.3	73.6	87.3	4.2	11,760	0.5	946	8.0	19,742	64.0	15,654	48.8
Shaker Heights	75.6	24.1	94.9	89.4	83.9	5.7	13,619	1.5	707	5.2	21,181	68.3	16,027	56.5
Springfield	77.2	20.0	88.2	81.8	77.6	6.4	24,950	-0.9	1,524	6.1	46,050	58.1	35,990	42.1
Stow	85.4	24.9	93.0	90.9	85.9	5.5	18,190	-0.4	830	4.6	28,520	66.9	21,981	55.9
Strongsville	81.1	28.0	92.2	89.4	88.0	4.3	23,886	1.2	1,133	4.7	36,691	66.4	26,743	60.5
Toledo	81.3	20.0	89.8	81.6	82.5	5.0	124,298	-2.4	8,886	7.1	217,948	61.7	178,346	44.8
Troy	83.9	20.8	92.2	88.4	89.0	5.1	13,760	-1.1	575	4.2	20,404	67.0	16,330	57.5
Upper Arlington	81.4	20.0	98.1	96.1	87.8	3.9	18,550	3.0	715	3.9	26,433	68.5	20,436	61.5
Warren	85.0	24.3	82.5	72.7	87.7	4.7	13,232	-2.7	1,051	7.9	31,929	45.3	24,890	34.8
Westerville	79.0	21.8	96.1	94.5	89.5	5.0	23,275	2.1	944	4.1	32,365	66.1	24,143	58.4
Westlake	80.0	24.7	93.9	90.0	87.8	4.5	16,619	1.3	820	4.9	26,629	63.7	19,395	57.8
Wooster	75.7	16.3	89.0	84.4	75.5	9.6	13,545	-0.7	528	3.9	22,330	60.4	16,967	46.5

1. Employed persons. 2. Households. 3. Percent of civilian labor force. 4. Persons 16 years old and over.

City	Value of residential construction authorized by building permits, 2021			Wholesale trade[1], 2017				Retail trade[2], 2017			
	New construction ($1,000)	Number of housing units	Percent single family	Number of establishments	Number of employees	Sales (mil dol)	Annual payroll (mil dol)	Number of establish-ments	Number of employees	Sales (mil dol)	Annual payroll (mil dol)
	69	70	71	72	73	74	75	76	77	78	79
NORTH DAKOTA	865,569	3,600	62.9	1,563	20,075	23,276.8	1,203.6	3,277	49,579	19,251.1	1,453.9
Bismarck	124,943	542	44.8	132	2,460	1,859.0	155.4	388	7,549	2,074.0	213.9
Dickinson	28,049	68	100.0	54	623	433.8	40.1	139	2,054	701.2	69.0
Fargo	218,142	1,146	35.8	253	5,174	4,102.0	310.2	539	11,419	7,915.5	363.0
Grand Forks	38,776	146	100.0	57	953	630.5	53.3	282	5,846	1,551.3	149.6
Minot	27,782	145	57.2	79	1,305	1,706.2	79.6	268	5,160	1,384.7	143.9
West Fargo	101,877	289	86.9	52	546	398.6	29.3	101	1,531	508.6	41.9
Williston	11,738	32	100.0	76	1,034	912.1	70.3	112	1,857	730.2	68.2
OHIO	7,339,454	30,418	67.4	11,430	193,412	172,949.1	11,316.0	35,500	588,060	174,299.7	14,861.4
Akron	NA	NA	NA	229	3,602	1,875.3	189.2	549	7,127	1,804.0	178.7
Avon Lake	31,597	67	73.1	16	66	45.2	4.3	39	440	118.5	9.8
Barberton	1,215	9	100.0	22	228	236.8	10.6	61	718	175.7	16.4
Beavercreek	NA	NA	NA	25	265	226.2	15.9	270	6,178	1,184.1	117.7
Bowling Green	NA	NA	NA	12	78	21.7	3.1	92	1,780	413.9	38.8
Brunswick	3,825	11	100.0	45	401	312.1	21.8	83	1,487	881.1	46.6
Canton	3,617	31	100.0	79	1,257	1,966.4	67.3	281	3,843	941.7	91.7
Cincinnati	149,714	1,138	18.1	309	5,562	5,482.8	363.0	866	15,048	3,907.5	370.6
Cleveland	16,274	131	79.4	511	9,019	5,965.9	514.5	1,136	9,648	2,487.4	223.9
Cleveland Heights	0	0	0.0	13	65	13.7	2.5	91	1,201	283.7	31.5
Columbus	665,698	4,468	20.4	788	18,425	19,175.9	1,168.1	2,600	48,299	15,623.8	1,326.4
Cuyahoga Falls	NA	NA	NA	44	643	264.6	31.8	168	3,559	1,137.9	99.1
Dayton	4,203	14	100.0	141	2,405	5,432.2	174.7	346	3,707	858.1	84.7
Delaware	158,466	493	92.7	20	191	85.7	10.3	112	1,940	745.6	53.3
Dublin	99,947	143	100.0	90	1,815	4,740.7	157.3	107	2,358	1,224.8	82.9
Elyria	33,050	146	72.6	53	296	163.9	13.4	198	3,164	803.5	74.8
Euclid	0	0	0.0	37	453	210.9	25.8	83	1,034	292.7	27.2
Fairborn	37,937	216	44.9	D	D	D	D	69	878	307.6	18.6
Fairfield	4,449	11	100.0	75	2,299	1,815.9	128.4	167	4,069	1,233.8	114.3
Findlay	3,865	26	34.6	43	772	894.8	44.7	201	3,900	1,048.9	94.2
Gahanna	3,629	6	100.0	48	904	976.7	42.4	91	1,468	547.5	40.6
Garfield Heights	0	0	0.0	31	413	131.6	27.8	66	876	202.0	17.4
Green	NA	NA	NA	39	645	511.4	43.4	62	1,869	912.7	65.5
Grove City	108,901	409	100.0	29	936	902.0	57.8	121	3,115	1,116.1	74.5
Hamilton	12,162	79	100.0	40	769	728.6	50.2	190	3,518	776.7	73.5
Hilliard	54,806	334	35.3	44	724	533.2	42.3	87	1,613	478.4	47.1
Huber Heights	NA	NA	NA	23	516	358.8	32.3	111	2,553	570.4	55.9
Kent	2,201	12	33.3	10	91	100.6	7.4	74	940	342.1	26.0
Kettering	0	0	0.0	28	196	188.2	13.6	150	4,391	2,074.1	94.4
Lakewood	1,820	3	100.0	20	366	631.3	40.8	114	1,067	291.6	26.0
Lancaster	18,127	263	20.9	28	231	55.0	9.7	188	2,858	729.1	68.5
Lima	6,884	60	0.0	42	528	402.3	29.2	109	1,374	344.5	33.8
Lorain	18,496	119	100.0	25	397	262.7	22.4	124	1,894	414.0	40.9
Mansfield	4,057	14	85.7	52	677	315.9	35.4	172	2,288	497.1	58.9
Marion	2,203	9	100.0	16	202	143.7	9.3	71	684	248.7	18.8
Marysville	NA	NA	NA	20	189	326.3	10.6	79	1,923	677.3	53.6
Mason	72,361	149	96.6	55	3,326	1,473.3	250.3	125	2,143	507.2	49.4
Massillon	13,848	159	35.8	22	391	221.8	21.3	111	2,561	744.1	65.7
Medina	5,407	35	100.0	45	463	340.5	23.3	108	1,677	398.5	38.7
Mentor	16,138	74	100.0	88	717	328.8	37.5	276	5,755	1,554.5	139.5
Middletown	32,146	175	100.0	D	D	D	D	124	3,340	1,686.6	94.2
Newark	NA	NA	NA	25	296	138.0	14.5	136	1,828	557.4	45.7
North Olmsted	862	2	100.0	18	163	250.5	17.9	241	5,236	1,538.4	133.8
North Ridgeville	67,664	321	94.4	29	180	130.2	10.9	50	592	176.8	14.4
North Royalton	9,081	35	100.0	33	537	202.1	38.5	69	606	179.6	16.6
Parma	10,265	44	100.0	58	1,095	588.9	53.6	219	3,650	999.7	88.8
Perrysburg	NA	NA	NA	46	725	498.9	41.1	89	1,735	519.9	42.1
Reynoldsburg	20,167	117	24.8	10	36	16.4	1.6	118	2,455	1,136.8	62.8
Sandusky	4,756	14	100.0	21	819	400.0	56.3	93	1,184	342.5	29.6
Shaker Heights	2,040	6	100.0	12	25	9.7	1.2	44	522	96.9	11.3
Springfield	22,105	86	88.4	46	1,044	1,418.1	51.3	224	4,171	1,043.7	90.2
Stow	16,762	41	80.5	49	400	411.3	24.5	98	2,294	587.0	54.5
Strongsville	11,136	30	100.0	71	1,897	874.1	97.5	240	5,320	1,190.8	116.8
Toledo	3,766	23	100.0	242	3,619	2,463.3	167.6	880	13,410	2,854.4	290.3
Troy	NA	NA	NA	20	573	522.8	34.1	87	2,451	662.8	56.0
Upper Arlington	23,884	30	80.0	15	34	11.3	1.7	83	1,065	222.4	22.9
Warren	0	0	0.0	25	448	350.2	23.3	142	3,681	643.7	98.4
Westerville	4,453	20	40.0	50	475	270.0	29.7	121	2,156	664.2	62.8
Westlake	46,308	132	100.0	81	1,018	940.8	62.0	182	2,658	798.9	78.6
Wooster	4,962	21	38.1	32	439	360.9	19.4	169	2,864	758.3	68.7

1. Merchant wholesalers except manufacturers' sales branches and offices. 2. Establishments with payroll.

City	Real estate and rental and leasing, 2017				Professional, scientific, and technical services[1], 2017				Manufacturing, 2017			
	Number of establish-ments	Number of employees	Receipts (mil dol)	Annual payroll (mil dol)	Number of establish-ments	Number of employees	Receipts (mil dol)	Annual payroll (mil dol)	Number of establish-ments	Number of employees	Receipts (mil dol)	Annual payroll (mil dol)
	80	81	82	83	84	85	86	87	88	89	90	91
NORTH DAKOTA	1,100	5,440	1,279.6	242.3	1,821	14,880	2,424.9	947.2	701	24,214	13,604.9	1,266.4
Bismarck	140	446	104.1	16.1	261	2,335	474.8	165.9	NA	NA	NA	NA
Dickinson	43	180	62.2	10.6	74	443	73.0	25.6	NA	NA	NA	NA
Fargo	277	1,716	292.8	66.5	449	5,007	726.6	315.1	NA	NA	NA	NA
Grand Forks	80	569	90.1	20.5	119	1,301	172.8	77.0	NA	NA	NA	NA
Minot	D	D	D	D	121	737	115.3	45.1	NA	NA	NA	NA
West Fargo	D	D	D	D	48	821	187.8	62.5	NA	NA	NA	NA
Williston	96	421	157.1	34.1	98	403	77.9	28.2	NA	NA	NA	NA
OHIO	10,782	62,902	20,524.3	2,986.2	23,854	250,438	43,625.0	17,058.7	13,922	652,462	306,222.2	36,256.8
Akron	165	977	191.9	38.4	440	4,411	854.1	305.1	NA	NA	NA	NA
Avon Lake	18	63	12.2	2.0	50	115	16.2	5.3	NA	NA	NA	NA
Barberton	12	37	6.3	0.8	D	D	D	D	NA	NA	NA	NA
Beavercreek	47	171	75.0	6.1	229	5,170	1,037.5	434.0	NA	NA	NA	NA
Bowling Green	40	168	24.9	5.5	49	273	35.5	15.1	NA	NA	NA	NA
Brunswick	29	85	26.5	3.2	62	298	33.6	13.5	NA	NA	NA	NA
Canton	66	307	47.1	13.9	127	677	96.1	31.4	NA	NA	NA	NA
Cincinnati	435	2,689	758.7	155.5	1,115	20,598	4,137.9	1,629.3	NA	NA	NA	NA
Cleveland	395	2,997	615.4	135.2	1,091	20,238	4,542.7	1,782.7	NA	NA	NA	NA
Cleveland Heights	52	226	32.1	6.8	95	259	35.3	12.2	NA	NA	NA	NA
Columbus	1,040	8,225	2,665.3	442.2	2,259	30,953	6,164.9	2,285.1	NA	NA	NA	NA
Cuyahoga Falls	45	209	24.8	6.7	96	578	60.7	24.0	NA	NA	NA	NA
Dayton	113	501	136.1	20.0	290	3,387	593.5	222.1	NA	NA	NA	NA
Delaware	34	210	41.3	9.7	79	429	85.1	26.6	NA	NA	NA	NA
Dublin	113	698	147.5	39.7	443	7,332	1,131.1	593.6	NA	NA	NA	NA
Elyria	56	258	50.7	9.7	77	440	55.2	26.7	NA	NA	NA	NA
Euclid	45	287	44.4	8.2	48	326	49.3	18.3	NA	NA	NA	NA
Fairborn	31	105	19.4	2.9	73	2,138	594.9	191.1	NA	NA	NA	NA
Fairfield	57	340	83.8	13.2	81	912	102.2	35.0	NA	NA	NA	NA
Findlay	49	419	59.4	15.3	86	1,241	156.1	64.1	NA	NA	NA	NA
Gahanna	46	401	238.9	16.8	141	1,278	162.2	67.1	NA	NA	NA	NA
Garfield Heights	22	87	18.8	4.1	31	328	50.9	23.6	NA	NA	NA	NA
Green	27	195	52.7	7.5	73	802	168.1	54.4	NA	NA	NA	NA
Grove City	43	152	74.5	6.7	51	366	43.4	13.7	NA	NA	NA	NA
Hamilton	39	194	38.4	6.7	86	353	35.6	13.3	NA	NA	NA	NA
Hilliard	51	217	44.3	11.8	112	796	104.0	56.0	NA	NA	NA	NA
Huber Heights	26	136	23.4	5.7	30	377	30.5	12.8	NA	NA	NA	NA
Kent	30	153	32.1	4.7	37	234	26.5	11.3	NA	NA	NA	NA
Kettering	60	324	51.4	10.6	108	2,721	468.9	173.1	NA	NA	NA	NA
Lakewood	46	160	36.9	6.4	125	470	70.9	27.6	NA	NA	NA	NA
Lancaster	49	143	28.3	5.0	70	416	43.3	16.2	NA	NA	NA	NA
Lima	23	114	14.8	3.0	71	529	49.4	20.6	NA	NA	NA	NA
Lorain	39	143	21.6	4.5	52	185	24.4	7.7	NA	NA	NA	NA
Mansfield	55	314	44.9	9.7	117	576	65.5	25.3	NA	NA	NA	NA
Marion	17	50	10.6	1.4	33	116	11.0	4.2	NA	NA	NA	NA
Marysville	28	127	23.4	3.8	36	1,089	112.2	62.4	NA	NA	NA	NA
Mason	45	214	71.2	11.9	126	784	121.3	49.3	NA	NA	NA	NA
Massillon	22	177	45.3	9.4	51	242	19.0	7.5	NA	NA	NA	NA
Medina	41	155	36.0	5.9	101	639	73.2	30.9	NA	NA	NA	NA
Mentor	52	201	59.4	7.2	147	1,330	152.4	65.5	NA	NA	NA	NA
Middletown	43	153	34.2	5.0	70	413	46.6	19.6	NA	NA	NA	NA
Newark	50	203	33.7	5.7	D	D	D	D	NA	NA	NA	NA
North Olmsted	50	185	49.7	8.2	66	284	34.2	15.4	NA	NA	NA	NA
North Ridgeville	12	57	11.6	2.0	40	212	29.6	12.3	NA	NA	NA	NA
North Royalton	27	177	35.6	8.8	79	288	47.7	14.7	NA	NA	NA	NA
Parma	55	316	82.4	12.9	102	632	83.6	25.9	NA	NA	NA	NA
Perrysburg	25	126	32.7	6.0	78	1,094	210.1	75.3	NA	NA	NA	NA
Reynoldsburg	36	D	58.2	D	79	498	49.5	21.6	NA	NA	NA	NA
Sandusky	D	D	D	3.3	51	270	33.6	13.8	NA	NA	NA	NA
Shaker Heights	31	75	12.0	2.9	102	461	80.5	36.7	NA	NA	NA	NA
Springfield	55	222	42.1	6.6	85	508	61.4	21.7	NA	NA	NA	NA
Stow	D	D	D	D	79	801	95.3	45.1	NA	NA	NA	NA
Strongsville	54	295	105.0	11.6	130	718	114.2	41.2	NA	NA	NA	NA
Toledo	247	2,232	4,129.9	163.8	412	4,285	761.7	266.2	NA	NA	NA	NA
Troy	19	104	23.0	4.0	51	350	53.3	21.9	NA	NA	NA	NA
Upper Arlington	62	385	117.4	15.7	153	647	124.1	45.1	NA	NA	NA	NA
Warren	26	104	16.4	2.6	76	322	32.5	13.3	NA	NA	NA	NA
Westerville	69	673	114.5	35.7	224	2,691	405.0	174.0	NA	NA	NA	NA
Westlake	80	289	88.3	16.1	244	2,136	536.0	180.4	NA	NA	NA	NA
Wooster	28	114	20.0	3.6	68	555	68.4	28.0	NA	NA	NA	NA

1. Establishments subject to federal tax.

City	Accommodation and food services, 2017				Arts, entertainment, and recreation[1], 2017				Health care and social assistance[1], 2017			
	Number of establish-ments	Number of employees	Receipts (mil dol)	Annual payroll (mil dol)	Number of establish-ments	Number of employees	Receipts (mil dol)	Annual payroll (mil dol)	Number of establish-ments	Number of employees	Receipts (mil dol)	Annual payroll (mil dol)
	92	93	94	95	96	97	98	99	100	101	102	103
NORTH DAKOTA	2,080	36,648	2,118.0	619.9	470.0	5,418	272.8	84.5	2,057	62,455	7,297.8	2,913.3
Bismarck	197	5,353	287.6	94.2	42.0	914	38.7	14.3	292	10,316	1,254.7	483.8
Dickinson	72	1,288	77.1	24.6	D	D	D	D	90	1,809	201.3	74.0
Fargo	371	8,857	432.6	138.0	79.0	1,717	78.2	26.7	426	19,053	2,867.3	977.7
Grand Forks	182	4,165	188.0	61.0	45.0	938	30.3	8.7	147	7,143	804.8	370.3
Minot	164	3,558	173.7	56.3	36.0	440	25.3	6.6	144	4,809	593.6	278.0
West Fargo	46	969	45.2	13.9	15.0	62	2.7	0.8	66	942	60.3	27.5
Williston	D	D	D	35.9	13.0	49	5.0	1.4	66	1,194	184.5	60.0
OHIO	24,346	474,616	24,560.6	7,078.1	3,999.0	76,914	8,595.6	2,832.1	29,595	856,794	97,117.4	39,468.5
Akron	414	6,196	312.4	89.2	48.0	1,348	104.1	38.3	492	31,388	3,589.0	1,640.0
Avon Lake	45	536	26.0	7.6	11.0	114	5.2	2.0	45	525	36.9	17.4
Barberton	42	682	28.5	8.4	NA	NA	NA	NA	78	2,110	213.0	81.7
Beavercreek	136	4,131	200.0	61.7	13.0	221	13.0	3.2	154	3,520	363.1	171.8
Bowling Green	106	2,628	99.9	28.5	10.0	106	5.8	1.5	105	2,853	226.0	88.8
Brunswick	69	1,309	54.2	14.5	13.0	82	6.5	1.6	59	1,095	98.4	46.3
Canton	155	2,735	133.7	36.3	23.0	470	49.3	10.6	205	10,591	1,307.8	504.3
Cincinnati	813	17,343	1,027.6	314.7	146.0	6,496	1,327.9	538.1	896	55,181	7,650.0	3,301.8
Cleveland	1,014	17,408	1,172.4	335.3	127.0	8,202	1,361.4	666.7	758	79,004	11,017.7	5,036.5
Cleveland Heights	79	1,137	65.9	18.3	16.0	58	5.9	1.8	99	1,182	70.1	33.7
Columbus	2,072	46,502	2,800.7	795.5	238.0	6,805	748.1	244.4	NA	NA	NA	NA
Cuyahoga Falls	138	3,002	147.5	42.3	15.0	123	32.7	2.7	143	4,101	322.8	145.9
Dayton	266	5,041	256.8	78.1	33.0	1,165	175.2	30.9	NA	NA	NA	NA
Delaware	91	1,709	85.7	24.0	12.0	299	19.6	4.3	140	3,088	284.3	117.7
Dublin	136	3,437	194.3	57.7	32.0	745	81.3	20.1	NA	NA	NA	NA
Elyria	112	2,125	100.6	27.6	D	D	D	D	144	4,257	451.4	187.8
Euclid	61	665	41.1	10.7	7.0	125	8.1	2.1	98	3,581	261.8	124.0
Fairborn	72	1,326	73.3	20.0	4.0	103	1.9	0.9	53	919	71.2	30.0
Fairfield	103	2,241	121.8	32.3	10.0	94	5.3	1.2	NA	NA	NA	NA
Findlay	152	3,994	182.1	54.6	19.0	309	15.0	4.7	159	4,521	504.5	195.3
Gahanna	97	2,017	109.8	32.5	17.0	299	9.2	2.8	170	3,722	326.0	163.0
Garfield Heights	39	654	34.5	9.2	NA	NA	NA	NA	73	2,580	292.5	130.7
Green	55	1,124	51.7	14.0	D	D	D	D	89	2,108	197.7	82.1
Grove City	123	3,348	167.3	48.2	17.0	403	14.4	5.4	127	1,910	271.4	78.9
Hamilton	141	2,958	151.1	42.3	16.0	167	12.5	3.1	173	3,561	391.4	157.0
Hilliard	78	1,651	82.9	25.3	20.0	375	25.3	8.1	138	1,738	189.7	73.4
Huber Heights	82	1,754	86.2	26.7	9.0	215	4.2	1.8	NA	NA	NA	NA
Kent	91	1,921	81.5	26.4	D	D	D	D	57	1,044	85.5	30.9
Kettering	D	D	D	D	20.0	628	22.2	9.1	NA	NA	NA	NA
Lakewood	138	2,031	109.8	32.5	19.0	340	13.6	4.9	110	1,415	111.5	51.9
Lancaster	105	2,235	105.7	31.9	18.0	266	11.5	3.3	182	5,043	603.6	226.6
Lima	73	1,304	68.7	17.9	14.0	205	8.9	2.1	162	8,181	1,132.7	437.7
Lorain	D	D	D	D	D	D	D	D	145	4,186	464.4	208.7
Mansfield	104	1,960	92.7	27.5	12.0	256	9.5	3.2	248	6,291	634.1	250.5
Marion	48	926	45.5	12.3	9.0	51	4.0	0.9	141	3,495	404.2	165.4
Marysville	59	1,440	75.2	21.2	D	D	D	D	68	1,716	206.0	76.0
Mason	105	2,460	144.7	38.4	20.0	303	40.0	8.5	131	2,596	205.4	88.3
Massillon	80	1,352	65.6	18.3	9.0	82	3.0	1.0	87	2,931	287.7	112.9
Medina	61	1,182	52.5	15.7	7.0	29	3.4	0.7	87	2,210	259.6	105.3
Mentor	163	3,824	186.0	52.5	15.0	132	10.0	2.9	178	3,056	271.5	119.4
Middletown	94	2,103	106.7	30.9	15.0	131	6.1	1.6	NA	NA	NA	NA
Newark	97	1,474	81.8	22.5	19.0	220	16.9	4.9	159	5,008	576.9	230.8
North Olmsted	120	2,547	129.1	38.2	9.0	66	5.1	1.4	85	1,468	133.1	45.9
North Ridgeville	42	765	44.9	11.9	9.0	74	4.7	1.3	39	555	41.5	17.1
North Royalton	D	D	D	D	10.0	163	6.1	1.8	68	1,174	89.5	39.3
Parma	169	2,827	139.5	39.8	17.0	216	8.5	2.3	202	5,401	417.0	199.7
Perrysburg	79	2,188	103.6	30.4	15.0	D	5.9	D	113	1,910	141.2	66.5
Reynoldsburg	77	1,854	91.3	27.2	4.0	22	1.1	0.3	NA	NA	NA	NA
Sandusky	83	1,106	99.3	18.9	D	D	D	D	93	3,513	367.5	153.2
Shaker Heights	32	400	23.4	5.8	8.0	194	14.2	5.7	70	2,223	146.3	60.9
Springfield	162	3,487	161.6	47.3	16.0	286	8.8	3.0	229	5,888	641.2	241.2
Stow	97	1,951	85.6	24.5	18.0	156	12.3	2.4	84	1,603	122.5	49.4
Strongsville	124	2,812	146.3	43.2	22.0	306	27.8	6.8	113	1,939	213.3	80.3
Toledo	649	11,380	582.7	168.0	90.0	4,552	389.1	84.8	739	24,505	3,066.2	1,188.5
Troy	75	1,897	88.6	25.4	8.0	102	4.2	1.6	97	1,542	111.1	48.2
Upper Arlington	69	1,524	77.2	23.6	13.0	269	19.7	7.3	97	2,137	173.5	79.1
Warren	69	1,061	47.3	13.4	14.0	134	4.3	1.5	164	5,512	717.4	242.8
Westerville	117	2,767	133.9	37.4	19.0	163	9.7	2.8	NA	NA	NA	NA
Westlake	105	2,656	160.9	47.9	23.0	445	32.4	9.7	236	4,520	458.3	189.1
Wooster	92	2,023	99.9	29.4	11.0	187	8.5	2.7	139	3,869	372.3	162.1

1. Establishments subject to federal tax.

City	Other services[1]				Government employment and payroll, 2017								
						March payroll							
							Perent of total for:						
	Number of establish-ments	Number of employees	Receipts (mil dol)	Annual payroll (mil dol)	Full-time equivalent employees	Total (dollars)	Admin-istrative, judicial, and legal	Police and corrections	Fire protection	Highways and trans-portation	Health and welfare	Natural resources and utilities	Education and libraries
	104	105	106	107	108	109	110	111	112	113	114	115	116
NORTH DAKOTA	1,763	9,706	1,246.0	318.3	X	X	X	X	X	X	X	X	X
Bismarck	248	1,656	241.2	68.4	721	3,561,718	9.6	26.1	12.6	8.3	6.5	21.2	3.4
Dickinson	D	D	D	D	158	719,090	11.7	36.5	6.4	9.0	0.0	28.9	5.2
Fargo	307	2,393	288.5	70.9	982	4,940,787	10.6	21.8	13.8	19.8	13.0	13.9	3.8
Grand Forks	109	656	83.4	21.3	547	2,676,157	12.6	21.0	16.2	14.3	8.2	19.6	3.7
Minot	121	710	86.9	23.3	459	2,044,359	10.1	25.5	17.0	15.3	0.0	19.3	3.1
West Fargo	66	506	56.4	15.1	178	824,064	32.5	39.9	0.0	4.5	0.0	18.2	4.9
Williston	72	431	89.7	18.7	269	1,553,384	5.6	22.7	19.1	19.9	0.0	20.8	1.8
OHIO	18,425	126,378	15,268.0	4,043.9	X	X	X	X	X	X	X	X	X
Akron	337	2,022	225.4	58.1	2,074	9,349,114	18.6	29.1	22.6	3.7	1.6	18.7	0.0
Avon Lake	35	224	17.0	5.0	171	1,019,117	8.5	23.5	20.7	15.5	0.0	29.0	0.0
Barberton	D	D	D	D	258	1,204,287	17.1	23.7	20.5	6.9	9.8	22.1	0.0
Beavercreek	69	460	34.9	11.9	154	824,107	6.7	51.2	0.0	23.2	4.2	14.6	0.0
Bowling Green	46	237	16.7	5.2	318	1,651,866	14.3	19.1	19.6	9.5	0.6	31.7	0.0
Brunswick	62	359	40.6	12.6	153	819,758	12.2	40.0	24.1	9.9	1.9	6.3	0.0
Canton	125	909	154.6	34.7	936	4,445,774	14.7	23.0	20.0	7.9	7.6	22.3	0.0
Cincinnati	542	4,633	642.4	163.5	5,538	30,765,986	7.2	25.0	18.8	5.1	8.7	27.8	0.0
Cleveland	705	5,805	757.4	202.3	7,046	35,836,530	13.7	31.1	12.4	9.6	8.0	23.2	0.0
Cleveland Heights	54	308	30.2	10.7	424	2,142,030	9.1	30.1	26.9	4.6	2.1	17.5	0.0
Columbus	1,251	11,396	1,776.5	426.8	8,528	52,605,234	13.2	32.1	23.7	4.3	7.2	15.7	0.0
Cuyahoga Falls	107	706	48.4	15.2	472	2,354,361	12.7	20.1	19.6	8.9	2.6	29.6	0.0
Dayton	197	1,667	247.0	61.7	1,981	10,478,912	13.9	23.0	17.3	12.2	2.9	23.9	0.0
Delaware	56	273	29.0	7.8	302	1,895,429	23.2	22.5	30.3	7.2	0.0	14.8	0.0
Dublin	65	1,445	247.7	102.3	461	2,663,324	24.2	27.9	0.0	10.6	0.0	26.1	0.0
Elyria	76	382	46.9	9.5	481	2,392,714	14.7	27.7	15.8	6.3	3.3	26.1	0.0
Euclid	52	266	26.9	7.6	370	1,840,187	12.9	32.1	25.9	3.4	3.1	16.0	0.0
Fairborn	39	263	27.4	8.2	259	1,399,619	23.2	27.0	26.0	5.6	3.1	10.6	0.0
Fairfield	86	669	84.6	21.2	336	1,864,962	19.6	30.1	17.5	8.7	0.0	22.0	0.0
Findlay	113	837	116.4	27.8	314	1,518,041	15.3	27.3	23.0	11.4	0.0	22.3	0.0
Gahanna	67	594	70.1	20.5	185	1,054,288	18.7	49.7	0.0	2.7	0.0	25.6	0.0
Garfield Heights	D	D	D	D	204	1,043,312	14.7	40.3	27.0	1.0	4.2	1.7	0.0
Green	D	D	D	42.7	135	745,011	17.8	0.0	50.1	29.1	0.0	3.0	0.0
Grove City	65	809	83.2	24.4	196	1,110,362	16.8	55.0	0.0	4.9	0.0	18.2	0.0
Hamilton	85	637	64.5	18.6	641	3,621,843	14.5	21.0	17.4	6.5	2.4	29.5	0.0
Hilliard	58	381	45.0	15.4	140	748,456	19.1	53.6	0.0	3.8	0.0	18.4	0.0
Huber Heights	61	313	30.3	7.9	179	1,076,657	14.1	36.4	32.1	11.3	0.0	0.1	0.0
Kent	46	311	29.4	9.3	211	1,399,013	8.2	36.2	19.1	14.6	6.8	13.7	0.0
Kettering	87	688	47.1	15.6	523	2,665,641	21.1	26.8	15.4	13.8	0.8	15.2	0.0
Lakewood	71	443	39.1	11.5	446	2,594,885	14.0	30.6	25.2	3.6	6.1	18.6	0.0
Lancaster	78	537	58.7	15.7	414	2,070,670	11.8	26.0	23.6	5.5	0.8	32.0	0.0
Lima	64	435	36.3	9.9	436	1,962,792	20.4	24.3	19.8	9.9	3.7	21.8	0.0
Lorain	74	494	52.7	10.8	480	2,336,209	16.9	29.7	18.4	4.8	1.3	24.5	0.0
Mansfield	107	629	65.1	16.3	443	1,978,647	18.0	27.5	22.9	3.0	2.3	18.7	0.0
Marion	46	374	23.8	7.1	274	1,190,214	13.5	29.1	23.9	12.5	2.1	17.0	0.0
Marysville	D	D	D	D	201	1,039,002	17.1	25.4	27.1	3.8	0.0	20.8	0.0
Mason	70	642	54.5	18.3	272	1,438,726	19.1	23.2	24.1	7.9	0.0	20.0	0.0
Massillon	64	484	50.4	14.6	245	1,236,148	23.3	19.2	23.2	6.6	4.2	22.1	0.0
Medina	64	406	39.7	13.4	222	1,012,513	22.9	28.6	5.2	5.7	3.9	25.0	0.0
Mentor	125	830	65.4	22.3	423	2,061,016	15.1	31.4	26.9	13.8	1.8	11.1	0.0
Middletown	81	551	63.0	15.7	370	1,804,982	15.7	31.1	22.6	8.3	3.4	15.5	0.0
Newark	77	493	56.8	13.5	390	1,895,696	15.2	30.1	24.2	8.0	3.0	18.9	0.0
North Olmsted	94	682	72.0	20.2	263	1,477,873	11.0	37.0	18.8	8.1	4.1	17.8	0.0
North Ridgeville	44	240	23.3	6.2	208	1,174,498	12.6	26.7	20.2	11.5	1.9	22.1	0.0
North Royalton	65	289	28.3	9.0	164	1,004,069	8.3	32.8	26.6	14.2	5.6	12.6	0.0
Parma	125	822	87.9	27.2	594	2,839,358	17.2	31.9	23.1	15.6	1.8	3.7	0.0
Perrysburg	57	413	25.3	10.0	171	952,133	24.1	28.2	19.8	9.0	0.0	18.9	0.0
Reynoldsburg	45	238	28.2	9.6	144	800,384	20.4	60.7	0.0	3.6	1.3	9.5	0.0
Sandusky	43	175	20.9	4.4	238	1,128,593	18.9	23.6	21.7	4.9	5.4	24.5	0.0
Shaker Heights	39	122	24.4	3.7	393	2,183,740	15.6	30.6	18.3	3.1	3.1	14.1	0.0
Springfield	113	860	136.2	31.9	566	2,572,119	18.6	27.5	25.5	5.9	2.6	16.4	0.0
Stow	69	385	30.5	10.4	256	1,403,473	24.1	28.5	25.3	9.0	0.5	11.1	0.0
Strongsville	96	870	70.6	23.8	374	2,259,326	6.6	41.4	20.4	16.2	4.6	9.5	0.0
Toledo	387	2,543	317.7	72.9	2,644	14,297,353	12.4	29.7	29.2	8.2	1.1	15.7	0.0
Troy	60	307	36.5	7.8	190	1,073,928	12.4	26.5	23.2	10.8	2.0	24.0	0.0
Upper Arlington	40	293	40.0	10.5	223	1,554,960	16.3	28.4	31.5	3.7	2.6	15.8	0.0
Warren	69	323	31.5	9.0	349	1,255,656	20.8	16.0	18.3	9.6	3.0	32.2	0.0
Westerville	84	1,100	363.4	70.6	493	2,982,891	16.1	24.1	22.7	4.1	0.2	27.6	0.0
Westlake	80	714	53.6	18.8	291	1,529,306	10.5	35.2	23.7	2.4	2.7	17.9	0.0
Wooster	52	335	41.2	8.6	1,020	4,971,173	2.5	5.3	5.6	1.7	82.8	2.1	0.0

1. Establishments subject to federal tax.

City	City government finances, 2017									
	General revenue							General expenditure		
		Intergovernmental		Taxes						
					Per capita[1] (dollars)				Per capita[1] (dollars)	
	Total (mil dol)	Total (mil dol)	Percent from state government	Total (mil dol)	Total	Property	Sales and gross receipts	Total (mil dol)	Total	Capital outlays
	117	118	119	120	121	122	123	124	125	126
NORTH DAKOTA	X	X	X	X	X	X	X	X	X	X
Bismarck	128.8	25.4	55.2	44.5	608	276	331	161.7	2,211	740
Dickinson	54.9	25.3	100.0	14.7	660	235	425	41.3	1,856	667
Fargo	278.9	77.2	92.7	91.8	750	220	516	373.1	3,048	1,949
Grand Forks	116.8	24.1	58.9	42.2	743	325	419	63.8	1,124	139
Minot	138.2	63.8	29.5	40.3	839	354	485	119.5	2,487	990
West Fargo	52.2	2.9	100.0	22.6	635	292	343	65.3	1,832	1,119
Williston	109.7	23.7	59.5	68.7	2,648	1,726	920	53.5	2,061	246
OHIO	X	X	X	X	X	X	X	X	X	X
Akron	445.0	37.7	36.9	214.3	1,082	153	5	416.1	2,100	70
Avon Lake	36.2	5.0	100.0	19.5	808	259	15	34.5	1,430	310
Barberton	35.9	6.0	87.2	15.2	582	45	25	35.0	1,342	119
Beavercreek	36.7	10.2	100.0	21.4	456	438	19	33.5	714	211
Bowling Green	40.4	3.3	100.0	27.8	872	86	12	36.6	1,150	122
Brunswick	34.1	4.3	63.7	22.3	640	53	58	25.4	730	68
Canton	122.5	20.0	100.0	66.5	934	72	26	164.0	2,305	712
Cincinnati	1,158.1	403.9	11.7	545.9	1,810	261	101	928.7	3,079	635
Cleveland	985.2	205.9	83.4	471.8	1,225	128	177	1,056.0	2,741	374
Cleveland Heights	55.1	5.9	54.6	38.7	869	232	67	54.6	1,225	153
Columbus	1,640.6	186.4	27.9	947.2	1,074	49	74	1,749.5	1,984	416
Cuyahoga Falls	71.2	1.1	55.9	44.7	908	229	23	63.9	1,299	209
Dayton	314.5	46.9	63.0	144.1	1,026	116	12	276.9	1,973	164
Delaware	65.8	7.8	30.9	27.8	706	43	27	60.3	1,532	319
Dublin	129.7	3.7	100.0	100.0	2,094	76	133	239.4	5,013	3,117
Elyria	66.2	5.4	80.9	38.9	723	68	77	62.4	1,161	107
Euclid	101.9	43.2	97.9	30.6	649	91	25	132.4	2,806	829
Fairborn	42.7	4.9	64.7	22.4	666	190	37	33.5	995	150
Fairfield	64.5	6.0	100.0	38.9	913	191	101	53.8	1,262	158
Findlay	53.8	5.3	100.0	29.8	718	68	8	49.0	1,181	260
Gahanna	42.6	3.4	91.9	22.6	640	57	48	38.8	1,097	194
Garfield Heights	33.7	6.0	100.0	20.0	721	257	29	32.0	1,149	196
Green	32.3	5.5	36.5	25.1	974	59	21	36.9	1,430	167
Grove City	46.1	10.6	99.9	29.6	719	64	66	56.7	1,378	606
Hamilton	88.8	9.6	78.7	39.4	634	169	20	97.5	1,570	288
Hilliard	46.0	3.2	56.0	30.0	833	35	43	25.3	701	70
Huber Heights	36.0	5.7	40.7	21.6	567	71	36	37.5	985	246
Kent	37.7	7.3	43.1	19.9	663	107	26	34.6	1,155	350
Kettering	86.6	7.2	89.2	60.5	1,097	169	12	83.0	1,506	205
Lakewood	68.6	8.5	70.6	40.0	796	274	46	64.4	1,282	229
Lancaster	76.4	9.7	92.0	28.7	712	145	1	63.8	1,585	233
Lima	71.1	29.4	68.5	19.4	523	30	29	77.0	2,075	739
Lorain	47.1	13.1	24.5	27.8	436	49	14	51.4	806	115
Mansfield	64.2	9.8	50.6	38.1	826	46	42	59.9	1,299	61
Marion	39.4	5.3	100.0	19.4	537	36	13	36.0	997	92
Marysville	35.1	1.3	74.8	19.6	818	55	33	35.7	1,496	121
Mason	79.8	5.1	100.0	45.2	1,361	349	79	79.7	2,398	742
Massillon	44.8	4.8	100.0	21.2	655	63	17	41.3	1,275	53
Medina	63.3	2.9	43.0	53.3	2,036	1,291	24	43.4	1,659	281
Mentor	74.0	6.7	98.6	54.5	1,156	106	57	74.5	1,580	0
Middletown	63.3	13.1	43.5	28.7	587	113	17	57.9	1,184	289
Newark	62.7	16.0	97.4	28.9	583	84	2	65.9	1,332	303
North Olmsted	47.6	14.1	9.0	24.7	780	289	13	44.4	1,401	123
North Ridgeville	35.6	3.1	100.0	18.2	546	154	63	42.0	1,258	318
North Royalton	32.3	2.0	97.8	21.0	694	171	8	31.3	1,033	138
Parma	85.9	12.9	100.0	59.4	751	133	42	85.5	1,081	20
Perrysburg	38.6	1.8	98.3	24.2	1,128	163	90	30.8	1,436	284
Reynoldsburg	35.7	4.4	26.9	16.1	423	12	10	24.5	647	28
Sandusky	40.6	6.0	72.8	22.3	897	96	408	28.7	1,156	26
Shaker Heights	66.1	8.6	30.5	42.2	1,542	276	44	70.8	2,584	315
Springfield	66.0	14.9	78.9	35.6	602	33	34	86.8	1,467	267
Stow	42.8	7.7	98.7	26.1	749	204	51	38.4	1,104	197
Strongsville	75.1	5.7	42.2	46.0	1,029	208	37	68.3	1,527	260
Toledo	499.8	101.1	92.9	214.9	777	42	11	480.1	1,735	249
Troy	43.5	1.6	63.6	23.5	910	86	30	36.2	1,399	177
Upper Arlington	56.5	8.9	100.0	35.9	1,015	272	21	47.4	1,338	391
Warren	56.2	7.5	59.2	18.9	479	32	21	52.2	1,324	124
Westerville	99.2	11.1	54.2	67.5	1,694	423	57	135.1	3,392	1,197
Westlake	77.7	8.4	88.4	44.1	1,367	407	92	75.2	2,329	967
Wooster	170.2	5.0	93.2	22.6	850	86	48	181.4	6,808	293

1. Based on population estimated as of July 1 of the year shown.

City	City government finances, 2017 (cont.)												
	General expenditure (cont.)												
	Percent of total for:										Debt outstanding		
	Public welfare	Highways	Parking facilities	Education	Health and hospitals	Police protection	Sewerage and sanitation	Parks and recreation	Housing and community development	Interest on debt	Total (mil dol)	Per capita[1] (dollars)	Debt issued during year
	127	128	129	130	131	132	133	134	135	136	137	138	139
NORTH DAKOTA	X	X	X	X	X	X	X	X	X	X	X	X	X
Bismarck	0.0	24.3	0.8	0.0	1.7	10.0	20.6	7.2	0.2	5.5	222.9	3,048	20.3
Dickinson	0.0	26.2	0.0	0.0	0.0	12.3	32.9	2.0	0.0	6.3	85.7	3,848	6.9
Fargo	0.1	29.7	0.5	0.0	2.9	5.0	5.1	4.2	0.4	6.3	795.4	6,497	169.8
Grand Forks	0.0	11.9	0.7	0.0	3.1	16.0	23.3	3.6	3.0	0.0	352.1	6,204	21.4
Minot	0.0	49.7	0.1	0.0	2.6	8.3	8.1	2.2	0.0	0.0	108.4	2,255	18.2
West Fargo	0.0	52.9	0.0	0.0	0.0	9.4	20.4	0.0	0.0	0.0	250.1	7,015	27.1
Williston	0.0	13.0	0.0	0.0	1.4	8.9	9.0	13.0	0.0	13.3	249.5	9,621	39.4
OHIO	X	X	X	X	X	X	X	X	X	X	X	X	X
Akron	0.2	5.9	1.2	0.1	1.1	14.3	21.2	2.3	6.0	5.2	674.3	3,404	0.0
Avon Lake	0.0	17.4	0.0	0.0	0.6	14.4	30.2	2.6	0.0	1.6	17.1	706	0.0
Barberton	0.0	6.5	0.0	0.0	0.0	14.7	25.7	3.9	2.3	0.6	4.5	172	0.0
Beavercreek	0.0	50.2	0.0	0.0	0.0	28.1	0.0	11.3	1.8	1.8	6.3	134	0.0
Bowling Green	0.0	6.6	0.0	0.0	0.6	16.7	18.0	7.1	2.7	4.3	13.3	417	0.0
Brunswick	0.4	13.4	0.0	0.0	0.0	29.5	13.3	7.6	2.6	1.2	7.4	213	0.0
Canton	0.0	26.1	0.4	0.0	4.2	11.6	18.8	2.0	6.3	0.1	2.4	33	0.0
Cincinnati	0.0	12.4	1.4	0.6	2.3	17.0	15.4	6.0	2.6	2.8	858.4	2,846	0.0
Cleveland	0.0	3.2	0.7	0.0	3.9	22.8	4.8	3.2	8.0	6.1	2,408.9	6,253	270.6
Cleveland Heights	0.0	13.7	2.5	0.0	1.8	13.8	5.9	6.0	3.6	1.3	23.5	527	3.1
Columbus	0.0	10.3	0.2	0.3	3.0	17.8	16.1	8.8	1.0	6.3	4,294.7	4,871	1,008.1
Cuyahoga Falls	0.0	6.6	0.0	0.0	0.0	16.3	18.9	12.9	3.1	0.4	0.6	13	0.0
Dayton	0.0	7.2	0.0	0.0	0.0	20.3	14.2	3.5	5.0	2.1	53.5	381	0.0
Delaware	0.0	7.3	0.1	0.0	0.0	12.7	12.4	4.7	0.1	0.0	110.0	2,794	0.0
Dublin	0.0	57.2	0.0	0.0	0.2	5.9	2.7	11.2	0.0	1.6	158.6	3,322	32.6
Elyria	0.0	2.5	0.0	0.0	2.8	20.2	26.5	3.3	1.8	2.2	48.4	900	0.0
Euclid	0.0	1.4	0.0	0.0	0.3	8.9	71.8	2.8	0.8	0.8	31.1	660	1.5
Fairborn	0.0	16.9	0.0	0.0	0.2	16.2	22.1	1.0	2.2	1.7	12.2	361	0.0
Fairfield	0.0	10.7	0.0	0.0	0.0	20.2	15.6	9.9	0.0	1.8	16.3	382	0.0
Findlay	0.0	19.2	0.2	0.0	3.2	13.7	19.6	3.3	0.0	2.1	10.9	263	0.0
Gahanna	0.0	15.4	0.2	0.0	0.7	24.9	16.8	11.0	1.2	2.5	23.1	652	0.0
Garfield Heights	0.0	12.8	0.0	0.0	1.7	0.0	17.8	7.9	1.4	2.5	19.5	700	1.4
Green	0.0	29.6	0.0	0.0	0.8	0.0	0.0	16.4	0.0	8.0	75.5	2,929	12.5
Grove City	0.0	17.4	0.0	0.0	0.0	19.4	2.3	8.5	0.0	0.0	54.5	1,324	21.4
Hamilton	0.0	14.7	0.3	0.0	4.6	15.1	20.7	3.8	2.9	4.7	227.6	3,664	0.0
Hilliard	0.0	10.6	0.0	0.0	0.0	28.8	7.0	13.1	0.0	0.0	63.9	1,774	10.4
Huber Heights	0.0	14.3	0.0	0.0	0.0	17.8	8.7	2.5	4.7	8.5	83.3	2,188	24.7
Kent	0.6	0.0	0.1	0.0	2.0	19.0	13.5	6.4	4.1	0.0	30.0	1,002	0.0
Kettering	0.0	12.1	0.0	0.0	2.1	20.1	0.0	18.3	2.6	0.7	14.7	267	0.0
Lakewood	2.0	12.2	0.6	0.0	0.6	17.0	22.7	6.5	3.7	0.0	79.7	1,587	41.2
Lancaster	0.0	15.8	0.0	0.0	0.8	13.6	17.9	3.6	1.9	1.5	0.0	0	0.0
Lima	0.0	8.9	0.1	0.0	0.0	11.1	46.5	3.2	3.3	0.0	115.5	3,113	13.9
Lorain	0.0	15.1	0.0	0.0	1.7	26.8	0.0	0.9	5.8	8.9	125.1	1,961	4.7
Mansfield	0.8	16.2	0.0	0.4	0.0	16.4	7.9	0.7	2.8	0.4	6.9	150	0.0
Marion	0.0	9.0	0.0	0.0	1.3	18.7	29.4	3.6	0.0	3.3	24.0	666	0.0
Marysville	0.0	6.6	0.0	0.0	0.0	14.3	41.8	1.7	0.0	0.0	188.0	7,870	93.1
Mason	0.0	19.4	0.0	0.0	0.0	12.7	8.3	14.4	4.9	5.0	70.0	2,108	0.0
Massillon	0.0	8.0	0.0	0.0	1.7	18.2	22.2	9.4	0.1	2.8	0.0	0	0.0
Medina	0.0	19.5	0.0	0.0	3.2	11.6	8.4	14.0	0.4	3.4	12.6	482	0.0
Mentor	0.0	26.0	0.0	0.0	0.0	19.1	0.0	13.2	0.0	1.6	18.1	384	0.0
Middletown	0.6	17.0	0.0	0.0	0.8	17.8	23.6	1.3	0.8	0.0	204.9	4,195	0.0
Newark	0.0	6.7	0.0	0.0	0.1	16.2	30.9	1.2	0.0	1.6	20.2	409	0.0
North Olmsted	0.0	16.4	0.0	0.0	0.0	14.8	11.1	9.6	0.0	7.6	76.8	2,422	0.0
North Ridgeville	0.0	10.7	0.0	0.0	3.7	14.1	37.9	1.4	0.0	1.9	18.1	542	0.0
North Royalton	0.8	14.9	0.0	0.0	0.0	17.9	28.9	2.1	0.0	3.2	23.6	781	0.0
Parma	0.0	6.9	0.0	0.0	0.4	40.1	0.5	5.2	9.0	2.0	24.3	307	0.0
Perrysburg	0.0	18.3	0.0	0.0	0.1	15.1	14.4	7.6	0.0	0.0	37.8	1,760	0.0
Reynoldsburg	0.0	4.7	0.0	0.0	1.1	38.0	30.5	6.0	0.0	0.0	17.8	470	1.1
Sandusky	0.0	7.0	0.0	0.0	0.0	17.9	25.0	2.1	1.5	2.0	14.4	580	0.0
Shaker Heights	0.0	9.8	0.0	0.0	0.7	17.7	7.9	6.2	4.5	1.1	15.2	556	0.0
Springfield	0.0	10.5	0.0	0.0	0.1	28.6	19.0	0.8	6.0	3.1	43.3	732	4.2
Stow	0.0	10.9	0.0	0.0	2.5	14.1	5.6	6.8	0.3	1.5	6.8	195	0.0
Strongsville	0.0	25.9	0.0	0.0	0.5	17.7	12.1	9.1	0.0	2.8	49.2	1,100	18.4
Toledo	0.0	9.4	0.0	0.0	0.8	18.0	20.5	2.3	3.7	4.4	422.8	1,528	0.0
Troy	0.0	6.9	0.1	0.0	0.9	12.3	17.3	10.7	3.0	1.0	9.8	378	0.0
Upper Arlington	0.0	26.4	0.0	0.0	0.6	16.8	6.1	11.1	0.0	0.0	68.7	1,939	15.2
Warren	0.0	10.9	0.2	0.0	1.9	12.2	20.5	1.3	4.3	0.0	30.6	776	0.0
Westerville	0.0	18.0	1.3	0.0	0.0	10.2	9.9	10.0	0.0	1.6	65.2	1,637	0.0
Westlake	0.0	20.1	20.4	0.0	0.0	10.7	6.0	9.3	0.0	0.0	90.4	2,803	0.0
Wooster	0.0	2.4	0.0	0.0	74.0	4.1	6.1	1.0	0.8	0.4	17.2	644	0.0

1. Based on population estimated as of July 1 of the year shown.

Table D. Cities — **Land Area and Population**

STATE Place code	City	Land area[1] (sq. mi)	Population, 2021: Total persons 2021	Population, 2021: Rank	Population, 2021: Per square mile	Race 2020: Race alone[2] (percent): White	Race alone: Black or African American	Race alone: American Indian, Alaskan Native	Race alone: Asian	Race alone: Hawaiian Pacific Islander	Race alone: Some other race	Race 2020: Two or more races (percent)
		1	2	3	4	5	6	7	8	9	10	11
	OHIO—Cont'd											
39 86772	Xenia	13.0	25,463	1,518	1,958.7	79.2	11.1	0.4	0.7	0.1	1.0	7.6
39 88000	Youngstown	33.9	60,270	643	1,777.9	43.0	43.4	0.4	0.4	0.0	5.0	7.7
40 00000	OKLAHOMA	68,595.9	3,986,639	X	58.1	63.5	7.3	8.4	2.3	0.2	5.4	12.8
40 04450	Bartlesville	22.5	37,384	1,062	1,661.5	68.4	3.3	9.0	2.4	0.0	2.7	14.2
40 06400	Bixby	24.9	29,242	1,339	1,174.4	71.8	2.1	6.1	3.7	0.0	3.0	13.3
40 09050	Broken Arrow	63.0	116,330	250	1,846.5	66.2	5.1	5.6	4.6	0.1	3.9	14.6
40 23200	Edmond	84.4	95,341	347	1,129.6	74.0	6.6	2.4	3.6	0.1	2.3	11.1
40 23950	Enid	73.9	50,566	790	684.2	68.7	3.3	2.7	1.3	5.7	7.6	10.8
40 37800	Jenks	17.1	26,661	1,456	1,559.1	66.4	3.2	5.5	9.7	0.0	2.2	13.1
40 41850	Lawton	81.4	91,055	376	1,118.6	52.5	20.4	5.1	3.1	0.8	4.9	13.2
40 48350	Midwest City	24.4	58,145	678	2,383.0	55.3	22.8	4.0	1.7	0.2	2.6	13.4
40 49200	Moore	22.1	63,462	605	2,871.6	68.1	6.0	4.3	2.8	0.1	4.0	14.7
40 50050	Muskogee	42.9	36,790	1,078	857.6	49.3	14.3	15.8	1.0	0.1	4.7	14.8
40 52500	Norman	178.6	128,097	215	717.2	69.7	5.0	4.4	4.0	0.1	4.2	12.6
40 55000	Oklahoma City	606.5	687,725	20	1,133.9	53.6	14.0	3.4	4.6	0.2	11.1	13.1
40 56650	Owasso	17.0	38,732	1,028	2,278.4	67.9	4.0	7.3	2.8	0.1	3.1	14.8
40 66800	Shawnee	43.6	31,576	1,253	724.2	65.9	4.6	13.7	1.0	0.1	2.8	11.9
40 70300	Stillwater	29.8	48,134	826	1,615.2	71.8	4.6	3.8	5.2	0.1	2.5	12.0
40 75000	Tulsa	197.8	411,401	47	2,079.9	51.8	14.9	5.2	3.5	0.2	9.8	14.6
41 00000	OREGON	95,988.0	4,246,155	X	44.2	74.8	2.0	1.5	4.6	0.5	6.3	10.5
41 01000	Albany	17.7	56,828	696	3,210.6	79.5	0.8	1.4	1.8	0.3	5.3	10.9
41 05350	Beaverton	19.6	98,216	337	5,011.0	62.3	2.9	1.0	12.2	0.5	8.7	12.5
41 05800	Bend	33.6	102,059	315	3,037.5	84.5	0.5	0.7	1.6	0.1	3.6	9.0
41 15800	Corvallis	14.3	59,864	645	4,186.3	74.3	1.3	0.9	9.7	0.4	3.9	9.6
41 23850	Eugene	44.2	175,096	151	3,961.4	77.8	1.8	1.2	4.1	0.3	4.1	10.7
41 26200	Forest Grove	5.8	26,089	1,486	4,498.1	68.2	1.0	1.3	2.7	0.3	13.6	12.9
41 30550	Grants Pass	11.5	39,364	1,008	3,423.0	83.6	0.6	1.3	1.3	0.2	3.2	9.8
41 31250	Gresham	23.5	113,103	264	4,812.9	62.9	5.2	1.6	6.0	1.1	11.5	11.7
41 34100	Hillsboro	25.8	106,633	295	4,133.1	57.8	2.9	1.3	12.6	0.5	12.5	12.3
41 38500	Keizer	7.2	39,157	1,013	5,438.5	72.4	1.0	1.6	2.1	1.0	9.5	12.3
41 40550	Lake Oswego	10.8	40,411	979	3,741.8	80.2	0.8	0.3	8.3	0.1	1.4	8.9
41 45000	McMinnville	10.6	34,666	1,148	3,270.4	72.9	0.6	1.5	1.4	0.3	11.7	11.7
41 47000	Medford	25.9	86,367	403	3,334.6	76.0	1.0	1.4	2.1	0.6	6.3	12.6
41 52100	Newberg	5.9	25,477	1,517	4,318.1	78.2	0.9	1.1	2.0	0.2	7.0	10.7
41 55200	Oregon City	10.0	37,411	1,060	3,741.1	82.4	1.0	0.8	2.2	0.3	3.6	9.7
41 59000	Portland	133.5	641,162	26	4,802.7	68.8	5.9	1.1	8.1	0.6	4.8	10.7
41 61200	Redmond	18.3	35,582	1,117	1,944.4	81.2	0.6	1.2	1.2	0.1	5.7	10.0
41 64900	Salem	48.8	177,723	147	3,641.9	69.1	1.7	1.7	3.2	1.4	10.9	12.1
41 69600	Springfield	15.9	62,256	619	3,915.5	78.1	1.2	1.4	1.5	0.4	6.4	11.0
41 73650	Tigard	12.7	55,767	704	4,391.1	69.9	2.1	0.9	8.9	1.0	6.8	10.4
41 74950	Tualatin	8.4	27,537	1,411	3,278.2	71.2	1.3	0.9	4.3	1.2	8.6	12.7
41 80150	West Linn	7.4	27,103	1,435	3,662.6	82.8	0.8	0.3	5.0	0.1	1.5	9.5
41 82800	Wilsonville	7.6	26,519	1,466	3,489.3	76.2	1.6	1.1	5.0	0.4	6.0	9.7
41 83750	Woodburn	5.9	26,054	1,489	4,415.9	42.1	0.5	5.0	1.1	0.3	32.4	18.6
42 00000	PENNSYLVANIA	44,741.7	12,964,056	X	289.8	75.0	10.9	0.2	3.9	0.0	3.9	6.0
42 02000	Allentown	17.6	125,944	224	7,155.9	38.3	13.2	0.8	2.1	0.1	30.1	15.5
42 02184	Altoona	9.8	43,525	916	4,441.3	88.8	4.3	0.2	0.6	0.0	0.8	5.3
42 06064	Bethel Park	11.7	33,110	1,188	2,829.9	91.1	1.5	0.1	2.8	0.0	0.6	4.0
42 06088	Bethlehem	19.1	75,624	487	3,959.4	62.3	8.7	0.5	3.5	0.1	13.0	12.0
42 13208	Chester	4.8	32,535	1,214	6,778.1	15.2	70.6	0.5	0.7	0.0	6.9	6.1
42 21648	Easton	4.3	28,057	1,388	6,524.9	55.6	17.5	0.6	2.4	0.1	11.9	11.8
42 24000	Erie	19.1	93,999	356	4,921.4	66.2	18.0	0.2	3.7	0.0	3.5	8.2
42 32800	Harrisburg	8.1	50,135	797	6,189.5	26.5	44.8	0.5	3.6	0.0	14.1	10.6
42 33408	Hazleton	6.0	29,970	1,308	4,995.0	38.8	4.1	0.7	0.8	0.1	38.1	17.6
42 41216	Lancaster	7.2	57,503	689	7,986.5	45.6	15.0	0.6	3.9	0.0	20.3	14.4
42 42168	Lebanon	4.2	26,581	1,461	6,328.8	55.2	5.3	0.5	0.9	0.1	22.9	15.0
42 50528	Monroeville	19.7	28,334	1,372	1,438.3	70.1	15.3	0.1	7.5	0.0	1.5	5.4
42 54656	Norristown	3.5	35,829	1,107	10,236.9	29.0	32.3	1.4	2.3	0.0	21.7	13.1
42 60000	Philadelphia	134.4	1,576,251	6	11,728.1	36.3	39.3	0.4	8.3	0.1	8.7	6.9
42 61000	Pittsburgh	55.4	300,431	68	5,422.9	62.7	22.8	0.2	6.5	0.0	1.8	5.9
42 61536	Plum	28.6	26,877	1,445	939.8	89.5	4.4	0.1	1.2	0.0	0.7	4.2
42 63624	Reading	9.8	94,844	352	9,678.0	30.0	11.4	1.5	0.8	0.1	37.6	18.6
42 69000	Scranton	25.3	75,874	486	2,999.0	69.5	8.1	0.5	5.6	0.0	7.9	8.3
42 73808	State College	4.6	39,525	1,003	8,592.4	78.8	2.9	0.1	9.7	0.1	1.6	6.8
42 85152	Wilkes-Barre	6.8	44,453	896	6,537.2	58.9	15.4	0.6	1.8	0.0	13.0	10.2
42 85312	Williamsport	8.8	27,603	1,408	3,136.7	72.6	16.2	0.2	1.1	0.0	1.7	8.1
42 87048	York	5.3	44,834	884	8,459.2	37.7	25.9	0.7	1.0	0.1	21.3	13.4

1. Dry land or land partially or temporarily covered by water. 2. Hispanic or Latino persons may be of any race.

City	Percent Hispanic or Latino[1], 2020	Percent foreign born, 2016–2020	Age of population (percent), 2016–2020: Under 18 years	18 to 24 years	25 to 34 years	35 to 44 years	45 to 54 years	55 to 64 years	65 years and over	Median age, 2016–2020	Percent female, 2016–2020	Population: Census counts, 2010	Census counts, 2020	Percent change, 2010–2020	Percent change, 2020–2021
	12	13	14	15	16	17	18	19	20	21	22	23	24	25	26
OHIO—Cont'd															
Xenia	2.3	1.1	22.3	6.9	15.6	12.0	11.3	12.4	19.5	39.7	51.6	25,643	25,408	-0.9	0.2
Youngstown	11.5	2.5	21.1	10.9	12.6	10.9	11.8	14.7	17.9	39.8	50.3	66,946	60,774	-9.2	-0.8
OKLAHOMA	11.9	6.0	24.2	9.7	13.8	12.5	11.7	12.5	15.7	36.7	50.5	3,751,582	3,959,353	5.5	0.7
Bartlesville	7.5	5.5	23.9	8.6	14.1	11.1	11.3	12.2	19.0	38.0	52.2	35,726	37,197	4.1	0.5
Bixby	7.9	5.1	28.3	6.3	12.4	14.8	12.7	11.6	13.8	37.0	52.0	20,907	28,700	37.3	1.9
Broken Arrow	10.3	7.1	25.4	7.5	13.9	13.1	12.8	11.4	15.8	37.2	51.0	98,674	113,730	15.3	2.3
Edmond	7.0	6.2	25.5	9.8	12.5	11.7	12.1	13.5	15.1	36.8	52.0	81,130	94,498	16.5	0.9
Enid	16.3	9.5	25.5	9.5	14.7	12.9	10.2	11.8	15.4	35.1	50.4	49,386	51,327	3.9	-1.5
Jenks	6.9	9.2	30.9	7.2	12.6	15.5	13.4	10.1	10.4	34.5	52.1	16,915	26,017	53.8	2.5
Lawton	15.3	6.5	23.6	13.9	17.9	12.6	9.8	10.7	11.4	31.5	48.0	96,862	90,537	-6.5	0.6
Midwest City	8.4	2.9	24.0	8.9	15.2	12.0	10.9	11.9	17.0	36.0	52.4	54,372	58,459	7.5	-0.5
Moore	12.1	5.2	25.0	9.2	17.3	12.9	11.5	11.2	12.9	34.1	52.5	55,082	63,308	14.9	0.2
Muskogee	9.4	3.5	25.5	9.9	13.7	11.4	11.4	12.8	15.2	36.2	51.5	39,184	36,989	-5.6	-0.5
Norman	9.2	7.1	19.1	21.4	15.1	12.3	9.7	10.2	12.3	30.9	50.4	110,876	127,224	14.7	0.7
Oklahoma City	21.3	11.7	25.5	9.1	16.2	13.6	11.4	11.6	12.6	34.4	50.7	580,494	681,387	17.4	0.9
Owasso	9.1	3.8	29.4	8.4	15.8	13.6	11.3	10.6	11.1	32.9	50.0	29,813	38,415	28.9	0.8
Shawnee	7.4	2.2	22.5	12.6	13.5	11.3	10.8	12.5	16.8	35.7	52.8	29,796	31,300	5.0	0.9
Stillwater	7.5	10.0	14.5	38.9	13.6	9.4	6.4	7.2	10.1	24.0	49.4	45,717	47,901	4.8	0.5
Tulsa	19.1	11.2	24.5	9.6	15.6	12.5	11.3	12.1	14.4	35.2	51.5	391,873	412,458	5.3	-0.3
OREGON	13.9	9.8	20.8	8.7	14.2	13.4	12.3	13.0	17.6	39.5	50.4	3,831,083	4,237,256	10.6	0.2
Albany	14.1	5.9	25.2	8.6	14.4	13.7	11.6	10.8	15.7	36.2	51.2	50,147	56,412	12.5	0.7
Beaverton	18.1	20.3	19.4	8.3	18.8	14.3	12.3	12.6	14.3	36.8	49.8	89,768	97,521	8.6	0.7
Bend	9.2	5.0	21.6	6.7	15.8	14.3	12.9	11.9	16.8	39.5	51.5	76,655	99,126	29.3	3.0
Corvallis	10.1	12.7	13.4	32.1	15.5	9.7	7.4	9.0	12.9	27.1	48.9	54,498	59,696	9.5	0.3
Eugene	10.6	7.4	16.8	18.2	14.9	12.4	10.0	11.0	16.6	35.0	51.1	156,406	174,753	11.7	0.2
Forest Grove	27.3	9.8	23.2	13.2	14.4	12.0	11.4	11.2	14.5	34.6	51.3	21,291	26,172	22.9	-0.3
Grants Pass	10.0	3.1	23.0	8.9	13.4	12.7	9.7	12.3	20.0	39.7	51.6	35,884	39,205	9.3	0.4
Gresham	21.0	16.5	23.9	9.5	14.5	13.2	12.2	12.6	14.1	36.5	50.4	105,607	114,507	8.4	-1.2
Hillsboro	24.1	20.5	23.5	8.8	19.8	16.0	12.0	9.4	10.6	33.9	50.0	92,002	106,448	15.7	0.2
Keizer	22.0	9.0	24.1	10.0	12.9	14.1	10.9	12.6	15.4	37.0	52.9	36,468	39,408	8.1	-0.6
Lake Oswego	5.3	12.5	22.5	4.9	8.6	11.7	16.5	14.6	21.4	46.4	50.2	36,727	40,786	11.1	-0.9
McMinnville	23.9	11.3	21.9	12.1	12.6	11.7	11.0	11.4	19.3	38.0	51.1	32,210	34,319	6.5	1.0
Medford	17.1	6.8	23.9	7.8	15.0	12.4	11.3	11.4	18.3	37.4	51.7	75,010	85,828	14.4	0.6
Newberg	14.9	8.5	23.4	14.3	15.5	13.5	10.4	9.2	13.7	33.9	50.8	22,143	25,447	14.9	0.1
Oregon City	9.2	4.9	23.0	8.5	14.8	14.4	13.2	12.1	14.1	36.9	50.6	32,630	37,466	14.8	-0.1
Portland	11.1	13.4	17.4	7.7	19.9	17.3	13.3	11.1	13.2	37.5	50.4	583,810	652,089	11.7	-1.7
Redmond	14.0	4.7	23.1	9.6	14.3	16.1	9.8	12.1	15.0	36.2	52.8	26,212	33,315	27.1	6.8
Salem	23.5	10.9	23.9	9.8	15.1	13.9	11.7	10.8	14.7	35.9	49.4	154,905	175,432	13.3	1.3
Springfield	14.5	4.9	21.3	10.6	15.3	12.5	12.3	13.0	15.0	36.9	50.9	59,407	62,360	5.0	-0.2
Tigard	13.6	14.0	21.8	6.9	15.1	16.5	12.5	11.6	15.6	38.0	50.4	47,979	54,832	14.3	1.7
Tualatin	18.5	10.2	23.7	9.2	13.8	16.9	13.3	11.6	11.4	37.0	51.2	26,112	27,958	7.1	-1.5
West Linn	5.7	9.5	25.4	6.8	7.6	12.1	16.5	15.4	16.3	43.5	51.0	25,137	27,376	8.9	-1.0
Wilsonville	13.5	8.2	20.4	8.7	18.5	14.1	12.0	11.8	14.6	36.5	54.1	19,542	26,594	36.1	-0.3
Woodburn	61.6	26.4	28.5	7.0	12.4	11.6	10.6	11.8	18.1	38.1	54.0	24,131	26,030	7.9	0.1
PENNSYLVANIA	8.1	7.0	20.7	9.0	13.2	11.7	12.9	14.1	18.3	40.9	51.0	12,702,891	13,002,700	2.4	-0.3
Allentown	54.2	18.8	26.4	12.4	16.6	11.6	10.7	10.4	11.8	31.2	51.6	118,018	126,092	6.8	-0.1
Altoona	1.8	0.8	22.1	8.8	14.5	11.8	12.6	13.7	16.5	39.1	51.4	45,967	43,997	-4.3	-1.1
Bethel Park	1.8	4.9	18.2	5.4	12.1	11.1	13.3	16.5	23.3	47.6	51.5	32,385	33,573	3.7	-1.4
Bethlehem	29.2	9.8	18.4	15.6	15.0	12.0	10.7	11.2	17.2	36.1	52.1	74,964	75,710	1.0	-0.1
Chester	12.4	3.8	23.6	15.5	15.5	10.8	10.5	11.2	12.9	31.6	51.0	33,889	32,718	-3.5	-0.6
Easton	25.8	12.0	19.2	17.9	12.9	12.7	11.8	11.9	13.6	35.0	50.2	26,814	28,027	4.5	0.1
Erie	8.5	7.1	22.4	11.7	16.5	10.3	11.7	12.5	14.9	34.5	51.2	101,735	94,823	-6.8	-0.9
Harrisburg	25.8	9.0	27.6	9.7	18.0	10.8	11.2	11.7	11.1	31.5	51.8	49,528	50,090	1.1	0.1
Hazleton	63.1	33.2	24.3	9.7	13.3	12.8	13.2	11.4	15.3	37.1	50.9	25,416	29,896	17.6	0.2
Lancaster	40.2	12.5	22.2	13.8	18.4	13.5	10.9	11.3	9.9	32.7	52.0	59,262	57,842	-2.4	-0.6
Lebanon	46.2	7.2	24.5	9.5	13.9	12.8	12.3	12.1	14.9	36.8	50.9	25,492	26,764	5.0	-0.7
Monroeville	2.8	8.5	18.0	6.9	13.1	11.7	13.0	15.0	22.4	45.4	54.0	28,348	28,640	1.0	-1.1
Norristown	35.2	19.6	25.5	9.7	18.4	14.0	11.6	10.2	10.6	32.9	50.8	34,341	35,783	4.2	0.1
Philadelphia	14.9	14.3	21.7	9.8	19.1	12.6	11.4	11.6	13.7	34.6	52.7	1,525,999	1,603,797	5.1	-1.7
Pittsburgh	3.8	9.0	14.6	16.5	21.6	11.0	9.7	11.6	15.0	33.4	51.0	305,306	303,160	-0.7	-0.9
Plum	1.7	1.4	21.5	5.8	10.3	13.0	12.9	16.3	20.2	44.6	51.0	27,110	27,153	0.2	-1.0
Reading	69.0	18.6	29.1	12.4	14.8	11.4	11.9	10.0	10.5	30.6	51.4	87,996	95,097	8.1	-0.3
Scranton	16.0	10.0	21.0	13.1	13.1	11.2	11.8	12.5	17.3	37.3	50.0	76,077	76,110	0.0	-0.3
State College	5.5	14.4	6.9	61.4	11.7	5.1	4.3	4.7	6.0	21.5	47.3	41,980	39,848	-5.1	-0.8
Wilkes-Barre	25.0	12.9	22.9	13.4	14.9	12.6	10.2	10.8	15.2	34.1	50.7	41,510	44,498	7.2	-0.1
Williamsport	4.2	3.0	20.9	19.4	17.1	9.0	10.5	10.7	12.4	29.8	48.9	29,374	27,764	-5.5	-0.6
York	38.1	9.8	25.7	12.6	15.6	12.0	12.4	11.3	10.3	32.2	50.3	43,807	44,810	2.3	0.1

1. May be of any race.

City	Households, 2016–2020							Persons in group quarters, 2016–2020	Serious crimes known to police[2], 2020				Educational attainment, 2016–2020		
			Percent						Violent		Property			Attainment[4] (percent)	
	Number	Persons per household	Family	Married couple family	Female family	Non-family	One person		Number	Rate	Number	Rate	Population age 25 and over	High school graduate or less	Bachelor's degree or more
	27	28	29	30	31	32	33	34	35	36	37	38	39	40	41
OHIO—Cont'd															
Xenia	11,188	2.30	59.8	42.3	14.2	40.2	33.2	1,051	75	276.8	588	2,170.1	18,933	47.5	19.1
Youngstown	28,303	2.11	51.1	21.4	23.8	48.9	42.5	4,483	NA	NA	NA	NA	43,577	56.3	14.6
OKLAHOMA	1,493,569	2.57	65.3	48.1	12.2	34.7	29.0	109,738	18,255	458.6	107,705	2,705.6	2,611,680	42.6	26.1
Bartlesville	14,425	2.48	63.4	48.1	11.5	36.6	32.3	655	88	243.2	1,144	3,161.7	24,649	40.0	32.5
Bixby	9,752	2.80	72.6	61.0	7.8	27.4	23.6	40	20	69.3	373	1,293.3	17,843	25.1	45.4
Broken Arrow	40,189	2.70	73.7	58.7	9.8	26.3	22.0	516	192	172.2	2,158	1,935.6	73,037	29.3	34.5
Edmond	34,750	2.64	71.4	58.4	10.0	28.6	21.7	1,437	139	145.4	1,484	1,552.8	60,282	17.8	54.8
Enid	19,356	2.50	62.3	46.7	11.5	37.7	32.0	1,634	233	468.7	1,420	2,856.7	32,616	49.4	23.3
Jenks	7,860	2.91	80.0	63.5	10.9	20.0	16.8	45	26	105.5	262	1,063.4	14,203	25.7	43.7
Lawton	33,052	2.55	61.6	37.8	17.3	38.4	33.0	9,214	727	785.9	2,071	2,238.7	58,455	42.7	22.1
Midwest City	23,366	2.44	60.0	38.0	17.3	40.0	34.7	335	183	317.0	1,632	2,827.0	38,463	38.2	23.4
Moore	23,195	2.64	71.3	50.9	14.2	28.7	22.9	389	131	208.5	1,452	2,310.6	40,542	37.2	27.0
Muskogee	14,945	2.40	62.5	37.9	18.6	37.5	33.4	1,396	446	1,209.2	1,291	3,500.2	24,109	48.9	20.2
Norman	48,977	2.37	57.0	41.3	10.3	43.0	30.1	7,822	366	289.4	3,261	2,578.3	73,938	25.3	44.1
Oklahoma City	246,904	2.58	61.0	42.7	13.2	39.0	31.8	13,263	4,818	726.0	25,853	3,895.5	424,700	37.9	31.5
Owasso	13,477	2.68	66.8	51.9	9.4	33.2	27.3	249	78	206.3	703	1,859.1	22,662	32.0	33.8
Shawnee	11,906	2.50	61.1	39.5	15.3	38.9	33.7	1,621	155	490.4	1,340	4,239.7	20,341	45.0	23.8
Stillwater	19,741	2.18	42.1	31.3	7.9	57.9	39.6	7,061	146	287.2	1,248	2,455.2	23,404	24.5	49.2
Tulsa	163,368	2.42	56.5	37.8	14.0	43.5	36.0	6,940	4,555	1,132.6	20,557	5,111.6	265,210	37.8	31.3
OREGON	1,642,579	2.49	63.0	48.3	10.1	37.0	27.4	88,758	12,380	291.9	112,782	2,659.0	2,944,830	31.5	34.4
Albany	20,278	2.64	65.5	48.7	11.4	34.5	25.7	903	83	148.4	1,545	2,762.6	36,055	31.1	27.7
Beaverton	41,026	2.38	59.5	43.9	10.1	40.5	29.3	957	235	234.8	2,197	2,195.1	71,273	23.7	47.2
Bend	39,842	2.42	62.3	48.8	8.5	37.7	26.9	578	174	168.1	1,959	1,893.0	69,554	22.1	44.9
Corvallis	23,243	2.27	48.1	35.7	8.7	51.9	30.1	5,792	NA	NA	NA	NA	31,942	13.3	58.5
Eugene	71,738	2.29	50.3	36.8	9.8	49.7	33.3	6,423	681	390.2	6,980	3,999.7	110,696	22.4	43.0
Forest Grove	8,601	2.76	63.0	50.4	9.2	37.0	27.8	1,074	56	214.8	526	2,018.0	15,798	34.8	31.0
Grants Pass	16,050	2.30	63.5	43.9	13.6	36.5	29.2	992	133	346.2	1,160	3,019.3	25,851	40.0	16.6
Gresham	39,932	2.72	66.0	45.7	15.1	34.0	25.8	1,742	510	464.6	3,078	2,804.1	73,611	39.4	22.7
Hillsboro	38,903	2.74	68.6	52.3	11.4	31.4	21.2	1,381	257	231.2	2,147	1,931.7	73,173	28.6	41.4
Keizer	14,432	2.71	67.5	46.3	14.7	32.5	23.8	358	70	174.6	758	1,890.9	25,948	35.6	26.1
Lake Oswego	16,153	2.43	69.1	59.3	6.9	30.9	26.1	164	27	67.2	659	1,640.5	28,670	8.3	73.0
McMinnville	12,897	2.54	62.7	44.2	14.0	37.3	29.9	1,763	95	271.1	782	2,231.7	22,748	35.3	25.8
Medford	33,131	2.42	61.9	45.1	12.8	38.1	29.5	1,763	388	461.8	3,615	4,302.8	56,131	36.8	26.2
Newberg	8,305	2.64	68.3	52.5	12.3	31.7	25.3	1,734	NA	NA	NA	NA	14,737	31.2	35.7
Oregon City	13,404	2.70	68.0	54.0	10.2	32.0	22.5	894	114	300.9	593	1,565.0	25,395	31.9	29.3
Portland	277,142	2.29	50.7	38.1	8.8	49.3	34.1	16,443	3,465	522.7	31,416	4,738.9	486,812	22.6	51.0
Redmond	11,850	2.63	66.1	50.7	11.0	33.9	25.6	226	88	265.1	1,055	3,177.9	21,104	38.7	21.5
Salem	62,988	2.60	62.6	44.1	13.7	37.4	29.6	8,180	698	395.2	6,698	3,792.1	113,919	34.9	29.6
Springfield	25,210	2.46	61.9	42.1	13.3	38.1	28.7	683	194	304.7	1,760	2,764.4	42,742	39.7	18.9
Tigard	21,257	2.53	65.6	51.9	9.7	34.4	24.1	407	107	189.8	1,472	2,611.0	38,617	22.0	44.3
Tualatin	10,584	2.59	68.1	54.8	10.6	31.9	23.5	154	64	228.3	726	2,590.1	18,506	20.0	45.8
West Linn	9,887	2.69	74.7	64.0	8.5	25.3	20.6	181	12	44.6	314	1,166.6	18,147	12.6	62.2
Wilsonville	9,685	2.37	60.3	48.5	7.0	39.7	29.7	1,500	NA	NA	NA	NA	17,325	23.3	44.7
Woodburn	8,660	2.98	69.6	49.0	13.2	30.4	25.7	180	87	328.0	872	3,288.0	16,783	57.6	17.0
PENNSYLVANIA	5,106,601	2.42	63.7	47.4	11.7	36.3	29.8	419,905	49,793	389.5	210,167	1,644.1	8,989,998	43.2	32.3
Allentown	42,801	2.70	62.6	32.2	22.9	37.4	28.6	5,445	NA	NA	NA	NA	74,133	57.7	16.6
Altoona	18,545	2.30	60.5	38.2	16.3	39.5	32.9	1,010	NA	NA	NA	NA	30,179	56.4	18.1
Bethel Park	14,457	2.21	64.2	54.4	7.5	35.8	32.4	293	NA	NA	NA	NA	24,676	25.9	48.1
Bethlehem	29,359	2.37	57.0	36.6	14.2	43.0	34.1	6,080	NA	NA	NA	NA	49,938	43.0	31.3
Chester	12,030	2.52	55.5	16.5	32.3	44.5	38.0	3,598	NA	NA	NA	NA	20,614	62.3	13.5
Easton	9,577	2.48	63.0	38.6	20.4	37.0	28.8	3,527	NA	NA	NA	NA	17,162	54.3	25.3
Erie	40,180	2.27	52.9	30.0	17.1	47.1	37.1	5,470	NA	NA	NA	NA	63,668	52.0	22.0
Harrisburg	20,986	2.29	50.2	20.7	23.8	49.8	41.2	1,115	422	857.0	876	1,778.9	30,872	50.2	22.6
Hazleton	9,672	2.54	61.0	35.4	18.4	39.0	33.0	282	NA	NA	NA	NA	16,376	64.6	12.4
Lancaster	22,055	2.53	58.4	34.2	18.5	41.6	31.1	3,494	NA	NA	NA	NA	37,962	53.2	23.5
Lebanon	10,119	2.51	57.9	30.6	19.2	42.1	31.9	340	NA	NA	NA	NA	17,014	67.7	10.3
Monroeville	12,137	2.23	64.7	49.4	10.6	35.3	30.3	556	NA	NA	NA	NA	20,714	27.6	42.8
Norristown	12,848	2.61	63.8	33.3	23.1	36.2	30.3	908	NA	NA	NA	NA	22,291	52.4	22.2
Philadelphia	613,125	2.50	54.0	28.2	20.0	46.0	37.2	47,468	NA	NA	NA	NA	1,082,283	46.1	31.2
Pittsburgh	140,496	1.98	41.6	26.7	11.6	58.4	44.2	22,525	NA	NA	NA	NA	207,544	31.7	45.4
Plum	11,058	2.45	71.6	60.7	6.3	28.4	24.8	91	NA	NA	NA	NA	19,713	30.5	37.6
Reading	30,053	2.85	64.1	28.4	28.3	35.9	29.2	2,781	NA	NA	NA	NA	51,736	66.2	10.1
Scranton	31,363	2.28	55.7	34.7	14.4	44.3	37.8	5,378	NA	NA	NA	NA	50,759	52.5	22.7
State College	12,369	2.42	28.5	23.7	3.1	71.5	42.5	12,216	NA	NA	NA	NA	13,352	12.3	72.1
Wilkes-Barre	15,467	2.43	59.7	34.3	18.6	40.3	34.6	3,259	NA	NA	NA	NA	26,001	55.4	18.4
Williamsport	11,505	2.17	52.9	29.8	17.9	47.1	35.9	3,416	NA	NA	NA	NA	16,976	47.1	24.9
York	17,012	2.51	56.1	26.1	23.9	43.9	34.6	1,281	NA	NA	NA	NA	27,138	62.1	14.8

2. Data for serious crimes have not been adjusted for underreporting. This may affect comparability between geographic areas and over time.

4. Persons 25 years old and over.

City	Money income, 2016–2020					Median earnings Full year, Full-time workers, 2016–2020			Housing units, 2016–2020				
	Households												
	Median household income	Percent with income less than $25,000	Percent with income of $200,000 or more	Median family income	Median non-family household income	All persons	Men	Women	Total	Occupied	Percent owner occupied	Median value[1] (dollars)	Median gross rent (dollars)
	42	43	44	45	46	47	48	49	50	51	52	53	54
OHIO—Cont'd													
Xenia	46,202	27.6	1.6	59,077	27,420	42,787	47,850	40,517	12,239	11,188	56.1	108,800	744
Youngstown	30,129	43.2	0.9	36,621	22,869	32,660	35,620	30,910	33,824	28,303	56.2	46,900	638
OKLAHOMA	53,840	22.1	4.5	67,511	31,846	42,518	49,448	36,900	1,740,972	1,493,569	66.1	142,400	818
Bartlesville	53,098	22.0	6.1	68,385	32,012	41,441	47,868	35,840	16,721	14,425	66.9	128,600	730
Bixby	83,955	14.1	12.4	103,131	35,417	59,260	70,942	47,111	10,310	9,752	77.3	242,500	1,062
Broken Arrow	74,070	9.9	6.5	84,984	46,183	50,395	56,431	43,251	42,608	40,189	73.0	168,500	1,065
Edmond	84,223	12.6	14.6	109,071	43,275	59,438	75,431	46,375	37,232	34,750	70.6	253,500	1,092
Enid	51,784	23.1	2.3	61,409	36,133	39,231	47,730	31,609	21,931	19,356	61.0	112,800	809
Jenks	87,306	8.4	10.4	102,002	46,210	62,576	77,314	52,321	8,406	7,860	76.6	224,700	1,272
Lawton	47,690	24.1	1.9	55,892	34,640	35,652	40,711	32,241	39,916	33,052	44.4	111,000	810
Midwest City	49,368	23.6	1.4	59,533	33,743	39,484	43,812	34,332	25,349	23,366	57.5	117,700	840
Moore	67,851	13.1	2.3	76,983	44,889	42,783	49,428	36,962	24,316	23,195	68.8	148,500	1,064
Muskogee	38,218	32.3	1.5	48,130	23,860	35,963	38,806	33,398	17,723	14,945	53.6	98,800	683
Norman	58,111	20.5	5.2	79,435	34,653	44,533	50,548	39,085	53,310	48,977	53.4	184,300	882
Oklahoma City	56,456	20.3	5.5	71,130	38,161	43,317	48,554	39,433	276,084	246,904	59.3	161,800	884
Owasso	66,897	13.7	4.7	85,632	42,029	50,660	59,647	40,710	14,084	13,477	65.9	180,100	1,049
Shawnee	41,123	30.8	2.4	57,049	26,365	38,721	42,177	34,631	13,645	11,906	57.1	113,300	707
Stillwater	34,906	36.4	2.9	71,536	20,920	41,792	46,005	38,461	22,769	19,741	39.2	185,300	826
Tulsa	49,474	24.6	6.2	64,316	34,236	41,852	46,523	37,349	187,543	163,368	51.5	143,400	839
OREGON	65,667	17.3	7.2	80,630	40,246	50,818	54,962	44,911	1,788,855	1,642,579	62.8	336,700	1,173
Albany	62,172	16.1	3.5	72,850	39,226	48,379	52,509	41,822	21,408	20,278	61.2	244,000	1,047
Beaverton	77,745	13.0	7.9	94,637	48,753	56,427	62,122	50,870	42,481	41,026	50.1	400,500	1,416
Bend	67,973	14.2	8.2	85,853	42,277	50,141	55,313	42,925	43,357	39,842	59.6	415,100	1,374
Corvallis	55,390	26.1	6.1	83,054	33,558	50,933	56,340	45,317	25,025	23,243	42.6	361,800	1,164
Eugene	52,689	24.3	5.5	80,285	32,791	45,315	48,377	42,343	75,138	71,738	47.7	304,500	1,075
Forest Grove	69,513	19.0	4.7	87,367	36,925	48,726	55,613	41,631	8,955	8,601	61.2	346,400	1,152
Grants Pass	46,580	27.4	1.7	55,538	29,108	39,765	41,869	36,418	16,837	16,050	52.5	260,400	945
Gresham	58,250	18.7	3.5	68,342	39,017	44,086	47,854	41,502	41,866	39,932	55.0	318,300	1,233
Hillsboro	85,586	9.1	9.3	91,455	65,567	58,003	67,009	50,712	40,532	38,903	52.6	363,600	1,551
Keizer	64,671	15.8	3.0	77,473	42,181	46,027	48,702	41,627	15,064	14,432	59.9	279,900	1,096
Lake Oswego	114,444	7.3	26.1	146,938	57,074	91,529	104,798	71,812	17,287	16,153	72.1	659,400	1,725
McMinnville	53,628	22.6	5.0	68,150	36,199	43,138	42,813	43,599	13,459	12,897	62.7	282,000	1,010
Medford	52,243	21.3	3.5	65,933	34,310	43,343	47,118	36,247	35,103	33,131	52.8	278,100	1,052
Newberg	75,225	12.2	4.3	88,292	43,139	50,941	55,414	48,369	8,700	8,305	63.7	341,400	1,281
Oregon City	81,039	9.9	5.6	92,888	47,152	54,404	59,240	47,659	14,022	13,404	65.8	382,100	1,314
Portland	73,159	16.9	10.9	96,975	52,247	56,760	60,639	52,953	293,208	277,142	53.1	438,500	1,325
Redmond	64,852	13.8	1.6	70,291	36,922	39,606	43,731	36,283	12,131	11,850	62.4	279,700	1,153
Salem	58,726	18.6	3.8	70,693	36,970	45,164	48,783	40,907	66,767	62,988	54.9	266,200	1,034
Springfield	49,938	22.2	1.9	59,335	30,604	40,688	43,289	36,407	25,754	25,210	53.8	226,300	969
Tigard	86,757	12.8	10.8	107,321	50,723	59,953	65,068	53,066	22,091	21,257	63.0	431,700	1,363
Tualatin	92,454	10.8	12.0	105,632	51,582	58,109	67,637	51,576	11,172	10,584	54.3	443,400	1,408
West Linn	119,415	10.1	23.3	140,376	49,566	89,679	107,995	64,739	10,166	9,887	82.0	528,600	1,597
Wilsonville	72,541	13.8	11.5	96,903	52,989	60,080	68,170	51,311	10,058	9,685	48.7	441,800	1,415
Woodburn	52,251	20.1	1.9	57,388	28,210	35,563	35,610	35,421	8,946	8,660	63.1	230,500	1,066
PENNSYLVANIA	63,627	18.7	7.1	80,996	36,247	51,469	56,481	44,898	5,713,345	5,106,601	69.0	187,500	958
Allentown	43,816	27.7	2.1	47,271	32,124	36,288	40,734	32,412	46,143	42,801	41.5	135,800	1,035
Altoona	42,244	29.9	1.9	57,224	22,921	38,803	42,069	35,853	20,724	18,545	63.2	92,900	701
Bethel Park	84,304	12.8	8.3	108,696	37,137	66,803	75,672	54,730	15,111	14,457	79.8	204,400	990
Bethlehem	56,034	21.3	5.2	70,034	36,277	44,484	50,387	40,827	31,287	29,359	50.6	175,600	1,076
Chester	32,867	38.3	1.4	38,468	23,142	36,650	37,820	35,184	14,193	12,030	37.1	70,300	878
Easton	55,201	22.4	3.5	62,264	37,072	41,920	45,821	38,170	10,852	9,577	47.8	129,700	1,023
Erie	38,655	32.9	1.3	51,035	25,879	36,467	39,685	33,659	44,856	40,180	52.0	90,500	725
Harrisburg	41,831	30.3	2.1	45,902	36,297	38,116	40,321	35,858	25,044	20,986	35.1	85,500	846
Hazleton	38,010	28.4	0.8	41,840	30,609	32,474	37,555	29,054	11,162	9,672	46.9	98,300	825
Lancaster	49,628	24.5	2.2	56,843	35,870	38,777	43,441	34,291	23,432	22,055	46.1	127,500	920
Lebanon	40,380	30.3	0.7	41,714	31,445	34,721	38,052	30,803	11,139	10,119	42.5	99,100	821
Monroeville	70,634	15.0	3.7	89,207	41,528	54,180	60,171	50,880	13,414	12,137	70.0	155,400	1,049
Norristown	54,409	20.5	3.1	60,652	34,012	40,126	42,189	38,605	14,432	12,848	40.6	158,900	1,106
Philadelphia	49,127	28.5	5.3	58,090	35,827	47,871	51,058	44,849	689,121	613,125	52.8	171,600	1,084
Pittsburgh	50,536	27.7	5.6	71,453	36,418	50,156	53,592	45,627	159,339	140,496	46.7	134,800	984
Plum	82,704	10.9	6.4	100,599	42,492	59,146	65,410	51,406	11,664	11,058	81.8	159,800	951
Reading	35,745	36.2	1.3	43,114	21,489	32,391	36,063	30,525	34,077	30,053	39.4	79,500	817
Scranton	41,687	30.2	2.3	56,042	27,438	39,927	41,550	37,327	36,669	31,363	48.2	106,700	795
State College	38,076	35.7	6.7	105,219	26,983	47,222	47,925	44,587	13,872	12,369	26.9	332,100	1,083
Wilkes-Barre	40,505	31.7	1.4	51,455	25,004	38,084	40,843	34,661	19,321	15,467	48.5	78,000	757
Williamsport	41,190	32.9	2.7	52,016	27,308	36,584	42,958	32,814	13,377	11,505	40.7	113,200	765
York	36,320	32.1	1.1	39,587	28,550	36,746	39,915	35,012	19,043	17,012	41.7	77,100	848

1. Specified owner-occupied units

City	Commuting, 2016–2020[1]		Computer access[2], 2016–2020		Migration, 2016–2020		Civilian labor force, 2021				Civilian Employment, 2016–2020[4]			
	Percent		Percent		Percent who lived in the same house one year ago	Percent who lived in another state or county one year ago	Total	Percent change 2020–2021	Unemployment[3]		Population age 16 and older		Population age 16 to 64	
	Drove alone	Mean travel time to work	With a computer in the house	With Internet access					Total	Rate	Number	Percent in labor force	Number	Percent who worked full-year full-time
	55	56	57	58	59	60	61	62	63	64	65	66	67	68
OHIO—Cont'd														
Xenia	84.9	24.1	87.8	82.3	86.1	5.3	11,527	-1.1	660	5.7	21,672	57.2	16,444	48.3
Youngstown	72.8	19.9	82.4	73.4	82.5	7.8	21,680	-2.6	1,820	8.4	52,279	52.3	40,776	33.9
OKLAHOMA	81.6	22.0	90.6	81.2	83.8	7.1	1,854,234	1.0	71,154	3.8	3,097,358	60.5	2,478,163	51.0
Bartlesville	79.1	17.9	89.3	82.8	84.2	8.1	15,913	1.3	604	3.8	28,635	58.5	21,716	49.9
Bixby	85.9	23.2	97.2	93.4	84.9	5.0	13,498	0.8	413	3.1	20,415	67.9	16,637	59.1
Broken Arrow	84.5	21.5	96.8	92.7	86.7	5.7	58,171	0.3	1,967	3.4	84,220	68.8	67,025	58.6
Edmond	80.3	22.8	96.2	93.3	82.5	6.3	49,299	2.2	1,407	2.9	72,382	65.0	58,370	53.2
Enid	79.7	16.9	90.3	79.2	83.1	8.5	21,282	-0.2	785	3.7	38,727	59.7	30,987	52.1
Jenks	83.7	21.7	98.0	95.6	83.0	6.3	12,589	1.3	400	3.2	16,657	69.1	14,279	56.9
Lawton	71.6	15.9	92.5	85.2	71.4	15.7	35,611	-0.2	1,591	4.5	73,746	52.8	63,047	48.3
Midwest City	84.0	21.7	90.4	83.5	82.4	5.2	26,785	1.3	1,222	4.6	44,985	62.1	35,218	55.3
Moore	84.1	23.6	96.3	92.0	83.2	7.5	31,965	1.5	1,107	3.5	47,773	69.1	39,832	59.0
Muskogee	83.3	17.9	86.6	70.0	81.7	7.1	16,081	-0.2	752	4.7	28,805	55.8	23,113	46.3
Norman	78.2	22.3	94.8	87.4	74.3	12.5	63,692	1.7	1,998	3.1	102,787	64.9	87,527	46.1
Oklahoma City	81.4	21.4	92.6	85.4	82.0	7.1	327,626	1.6	13,254	4.0	501,602	66.3	419,963	54.2
Owasso	83.0	21.3	93.3	90.1	80.6	9.9	19,265	0.7	640	3.3	26,692	70.4	22,656	56.5
Shawnee	84.5	20.3	87.8	79.7	80.6	9.4	14,501	1.4	613	4.2	25,074	55.5	19,820	41.5
Stillwater	75.9	16.5	95.2	83.0	63.7	20.9	24,152	1.5	669	2.8	43,585	57.4	38,522	31.2
Tulsa	79.7	18.6	91.8	83.7	80.2	6.3	195,780	0.3	8,736	4.5	313,901	65.3	255,992	51.4
OREGON	70.5	23.9	94.1	87.9	83.4	7.5	2,148,333	2.1	112,195	5.2	3,408,422	62.5	2,673,490	48.7
Albany	81.4	20.7	95.1	88.8	84.0	7.4	26,416	1.9	1,440	5.5	42,249	62.9	33,696	49.2
Beaverton	67.9	25.2	96.4	91.2	81.1	8.7	55,928	1.8	2,445	4.4	81,134	71.1	66,996	56.1
Bend	70.7	16.6	95.2	90.4	80.2	10.1	56,374	4.3	2,620	4.6	78,218	67.8	61,875	49.9
Corvallis	59.4	16.8	96.6	91.7	67.3	19.6	30,315	2.0	1,187	3.9	51,810	60.6	44,260	32.7
Eugene	64.8	18.5	96.0	88.9	72.3	11.2	84,988	1.5	4,365	5.1	145,282	63.1	116,971	39.7
Forest Grove	73.5	29.9	93.8	87.0	84.2	5.8	12,265	2.9	633	5.2	19,795	67.2	16,186	49.1
Grants Pass	76.3	15.3	89.6	82.7	81.1	7.7	16,735	2.4	1,098	6.6	30,451	56.0	22,852	42.2
Gresham	71.9	28.5	93.6	87.0	85.3	5.0	55,619	2.3	3,577	6.4	86,879	64.7	71,307	47.8
Hillsboro	71.1	24.0	97.5	93.1	81.1	7.9	60,064	2.7	2,519	4.2	85,189	71.5	73,760	55.6
Keizer	80.5	22.8	96.7	91.0	87.7	5.3	20,044	2.9	959	4.8	30,978	64.7	24,924	53.3
Lake Oswego	73.3	24.6	97.1	94.5	85.6	10.6	21,189	2.4	791	3.7	31,791	62.3	23,356	52.2
McMinnville	73.5	21.6	90.8	83.0	83.6	5.7	17,314	2.2	923	5.3	27,719	57.4	21,069	47.1
Medford	78.7	16.9	93.6	86.9	80.8	5.4	41,613	2.5	2,343	5.6	64,492	61.3	49,441	48.7
Newberg	71.4	26.3	97.1	88.3	81.5	10.4	13,611	2.0	581	4.3	18,780	66.2	15,547	52.1
Oregon City	77.9	29.8	94.5	90.1	84.0	6.7	19,731	1.7	974	4.9	29,359	68.7	24,139	58.5
Portland	55.7	26.2	95.3	90.2	81.7	8.4	381,655	1.1	20,725	5.4	549,154	70.8	463,352	52.5
Redmond	75.1	20.4	94.0	88.6	79.0	5.9	14,706	4.7	954	6.5	24,618	68.7	19,921	53.4
Salem	73.4	22.7	94.3	88.1	82.9	8.4	84,535	3.0	4,362	5.2	135,651	61.3	110,317	47.9
Springfield	74.2	21.2	93.5	86.6	81.8	4.9	31,049	1.6	1,867	6.0	51,007	65.5	41,622	45.2
Tigard	71.1	24.2	96.5	93.1	86.2	6.3	32,195	1.9	1,393	4.3	43,614	69.4	35,151	56.6
Tualatin	76.3	22.4	96.0	93.7	84.8	9.8	15,163	1.9	636	4.2	21,919	73.0	18,779	57.0
West Linn	69.9	27.3	96.3	92.4	89.8	7.0	14,627	2.5	545	3.7	20,842	61.5	16,492	47.5
Wilsonville	77.4	28.3	96.4	88.7	78.9	14.9	12,679	2.4	619	4.9	19,924	62.9	16,369	50.4
Woodburn	73.0	25.9	87.5	78.8	94.7	3.8	11,963	3.0	557	4.7	19,376	61.1	14,681	54.5
PENNSYLVANIA	74.4	27.1	89.6	83.6	87.8	5.2	6,406,185	-1.2	406,743	6.3	10,456,049	62.7	8,120,945	52.3
Allentown	68.5	23.2	89.1	80.6	82.2	6.9	57,475	0.1	6,156	10.7	92,677	63.4	78,333	45.0
Altoona	81.6	18.7	84.9	78.1	86.7	5.1	19,797	-2.4	1,362	6.9	35,118	57.0	27,916	45.8
Bethel Park	72.7	30.5	93.4	90.5	91.9	3.2	16,990	-1.7	856	5.0	26,923	65.5	19,393	61.0
Bethlehem	75.8	23.3	89.1	82.3	80.7	10.4	38,091	0.0	2,708	7.1	63,380	59.0	50,357	47.8
Chester	60.5	22.3	86.2	78.6	82.9	8.6	13,512	-1.3	1,676	12.4	26,539	56.0	22,166	38.1
Easton	69.7	27.6	88.9	79.3	78.5	11.0	12,364	-0.2	1,003	8.1	22,920	59.9	19,202	45.7
Erie	71.4	18.0	87.0	79.1	81.1	5.7	42,744	-2.6	3,674	8.6	77,290	59.8	62,914	43.8
Harrisburg	60.4	19.2	87.8	76.8	74.1	11.5	22,250	-2.1	2,460	11.1	36,635	67.2	31,153	49.8
Hazleton	67.6	21.1	84.9	75.7	82.2	8.5	11,930	-1.9	1,722	14.4	19,607	63.6	15,803	51.8
Lancaster	65.1	22.8	89.5	78.7	81.1	7.2	27,416	-1.9	2,344	8.5	47,714	67.5	41,854	46.7
Lebanon	74.9	19.5	84.9	76.8	76.0	10.8	11,967	-1.4	1,157	9.7	20,110	61.4	16,264	46.3
Monroeville	71.4	28.9	93.6	87.8	90.1	3.7	14,120	-1.7	839	5.9	23,420	63.3	17,255	58.1
Norristown	65.9	26.7	88.7	77.9	83.1	5.4	18,374	-0.7	1,340	7.3	26,106	71.9	22,464	53.1
Philadelphia	49.5	33.4	88.5	79.6	85.8	5.1	721,225	-2.0	66,071	9.2	1,272,154	61.5	1,054,751	46.7
Pittsburgh	53.6	24.2	89.8	83.6	78.2	9.4	152,756	-2.6	9,444	6.2	261,870	64.1	216,691	48.7
Plum	79.8	29.0	93.0	89.4	92.5	2.0	14,529	-1.5	806	5.5	22,080	67.7	16,607	59.8
Reading	59.8	24.3	85.4	75.8	79.3	7.9	34,674	-3.3	4,205	12.1	65,420	61.0	56,119	40.9
Scranton	73.2	20.0	87.1	79.2	83.5	7.3	35,924	-2.2	2,664	7.4	62,990	56.7	49,681	44.9
State College	43.0	16.3	96.9	86.8	51.5	29.5	15,490	-1.5	728	4.7	39,589	46.4	37,067	19.4
Wilkes-Barre	71.3	19.1	85.5	78.3	78.1	11.0	18,492	-2.8	1,841	10.0	32,765	57.5	26,564	42.1
Williamsport	69.3	15.6	89.7	81.4	77.7	7.2	12,890	-3.4	1,009	7.8	23,243	59.5	19,719	44.1
York	68.3	22.5	87.5	78.8	79.8	7.5	18,300	-3.4	2,346	12.8	33,879	64.2	29,335	42.4

1. Employed persons. 2. Households. 3. Percent of civilian labor force. 4. Persons 16 years old and over.

City	Value of residential construction authorized by building permits, 2021			Wholesale trade[1], 2017				Retail trade[2], 2017			
	New construction ($1,000)	Number of housing units	Percent single family	Number of establishments	Number of employees	Sales (mil dol)	Annual payroll (mil dol)	Number of establish-ments	Number of employees	Sales (mil dol)	Annual payroll (mil dol)
	69	70	71	72	73	74	75	76	77	78	79
OHIO—Cont'd											
Xenia	NA	NA	NA	11	83	30.8	4.6	75	1,837	441.3	44.1
Youngstown	NA	NA	NA	83	1,223	660.1	56.9	162	1,441	336.2	33.3
OKLAHOMA	3,454,208	14,733	90.4	3,859	50,233	42,221.4	2,757.0	12,963	180,451	53,382.1	4,682.9
Bartlesville	23,458	85	100.0	18	72	33.5	2.9	148	2,237	657.2	56.8
Bixby	68,983	290	100.0	27	168	75.6	8.7	67	873	243.2	21.6
Broken Arrow	166,813	785	92.6	141	1,577	910.1	89.6	264	5,160	1,858.4	142.5
Edmond	305,598	725	99.7	113	1,196	726.2	57.6	355	5,653	1,551.0	151.3
Enid	10,609	33	100.0	55	679	1,044.5	35.4	244	3,628	911.1	94.1
Jenks	74,580	238	100.0	D	D	D	D	41	501	120.3	10.8
Lawton	15,879	66	100.0	D	D	D	D	336	4,833	1,250.3	119.5
Midwest City	26,420	159	96.2	11	81	25.6	3.1	170	4,077	1,267.0	111.7
Moore	75,309	275	91.3	D	D	D	D	167	2,913	721.1	68.6
Muskogee	8,212	43	100.0	46	594	311.8	26.5	204	3,027	780.3	72.9
Norman	196,444	742	76.1	64	943	579.0	53.5	434	7,673	2,234.1	194.0
Oklahoma City	990,341	4,267	96.7	1,026	16,717	18,804.1	987.4	2,234	33,933	10,999.8	965.6
Owasso	62,817	324	79.6	19	99	155.1	5.1	121	3,206	814.3	69.5
Shawnee	15,735	76	65.8	20	151	70.0	7.0	184	2,590	682.3	60.4
Stillwater	48,365	210	82.9	26	178	85.1	6.8	198	3,294	770.3	74.4
Tulsa	187,437	817	79.8	694	11,740	8,296.9	727.8	1,664	28,067	8,171.4	762.0
OREGON	5,128,318	21,916	60.2	4,452	67,900	58,205.2	4,306.2	14,318	211,222	61,699.3	6,066.6
Albany	27,859	110	100.0	50	493	437.2	25.3	191	3,094	844.6	84.8
Beaverton	32,226	110	100.0	163	3,933	3,365.8	272.4	409	9,745	4,788.3	311.1
Bend	311,203	1,457	51.3	141	1,204	891.2	64.9	597	8,285	2,596.6	250.4
Corvallis	40,407	155	92.9	25	213	100.9	12.8	217	3,632	848.0	90.4
Eugene	273,975	1,398	21.8	251	3,325	1,805.6	198.9	747	11,990	3,210.8	362.5
Forest Grove	62,734	386	34.5	9	104	46.4	6.7	40	483	124.0	13.1
Grants Pass	31,182	162	58.0	36	244	175.4	11.8	237	3,701	1,047.2	109.5
Gresham	76,105	399	55.4	53	1,756	1,098.5	98.9	279	4,385	1,511.0	128.1
Hillsboro	218,407	909	70.5	109	2,182	1,449.8	220.6	328	6,986	2,119.5	200.7
Keizer	11,404	62	40.3	17	45	41.4	2.8	88	1,425	295.3	30.3
Lake Oswego	29,055	47	100.0	90	1,643	1,265.9	200.4	108	1,168	269.4	31.7
McMinnville	38,486	143	100.0	17	143	116.8	8.4	146	2,296	665.6	65.0
Medford	105,315	437	72.8	115	1,223	853.8	60.8	473	8,072	2,737.4	239.3
Newberg	76,283	269	42.8	D	D	D	1.9	69	1,116	357.8	33.4
Oregon City	19,212	62	82.3	16	239	99.5	13.1	123	1,919	587.7	53.1
Portland	622,218	3,028	15.7	1,103	22,237	24,079.4	1,517.7	2,703	37,084	9,800.8	1,112.8
Redmond	139,326	650	70.5	42	253	118.3	11.5	126	2,090	681.8	59.6
Salem	168,341	846	52.8	155	1,722	1,274.8	89.0	621	10,944	3,408.8	319.3
Springfield	65,345	247	94.3	49	1,024	519.7	51.7	211	3,698	969.9	96.6
Tigard	93,113	357	59.7	170	2,629	2,150.5	201.8	321	7,553	2,166.1	238.1
Tualatin	37,595	268	1.5	114	1,860	1,095.6	122.4	105	2,130	634.7	67.7
West Linn	18,119	37	100.0	20	73	75.5	4.5	40	568	142.9	16.1
Wilsonville	43,330	117	100.0	79	2,237	4,157.6	153.6	79	1,824	851.9	69.7
Woodburn	105,561	561	46.5	16	231	189.9	9.7	179	2,867	513.8	55.4
PENNSYLVANIA	9,311,131	47,894	39.2	12,071	204,256	199,203.8	12,958.8	42,514	662,560	234,836.3	17,354.0
Allentown	0	0	0.0	124	2,582	2,071.4	244.2	374	5,997	2,473.3	179.2
Altoona	567	2	100.0	46	791	520.2	41.5	228	4,940	1,252.3	113.0
Bethel Park	6,038	23	100.0	37	272	126.4	15.9	101	2,627	730.0	72.5
Bethlehem	9,462	99	3.0	73	3,434	10,488.3	176.4	219	3,576	1,641.5	90.7
Chester	1,350	10	60.0	20	201	188.1	13.6	63	341	93.5	8.4
Easton	9,903	154	0.0	27	401	659.4	29.2	136	1,859	441.4	45.4
Erie	230	12	8.3	102	1,741	755.8	85.7	339	4,889	906.2	104.6
Harrisburg	6,330	53	0.0	60	1,502	2,726.5	85.7	181	2,266	636.3	53.2
Hazleton	0	0	0.0	32	482	162.5	25.0	110	1,055	248.8	22.8
Lancaster	644	4	100.0	53	869	514.8	40.1	345	5,430	1,222.1	135.3
Lebanon	0	0	0.0	17	116	43.0	5.5	99	1,396	320.3	34.4
Monroeville	12,850	124	30.6	38	317	128.0	16.6	268	5,533	1,798.1	137.4
Norristown	0	0	0.0	35	399	382.6	33.7	90	627	239.2	21.8
Philadelphia	4,144,779	25,257	6.1	1,006	17,207	16,323.4	1,169.1	4,540	53,157	14,973.0	1,305.4
Pittsburgh	119,478	815	24.3	380	7,665	7,477.5	531.4	1,121	17,273	5,116.2	479.8
Plum	12,798	41	100.0	29	217	108.6	11.0	50	572	143.8	15.5
Reading	0	0	0.0	51	1,282	1,249.3	78.2	226	3,225	827.7	77.2
Scranton	749	3	100.0	76	1,235	1,910.8	62.9	303	3,802	1,075.3	102.0
State College	0	0	0.0	8	51	39.4	3.1	115	1,654	254.0	29.9
Wilkes-Barre	519	2	100.0	41	313	145.2	15.4	242	4,820	1,328.0	113.2
Williamsport	25	1	100.0	35	938	657.7	34.3	98	1,410	313.8	35.6
York	11,325	56	100.0	54	901	627.9	54.3	128	1,482	541.4	41.3

1. Merchant wholesalers except manufacturers' sales branches and offices. 2. Establishments with payroll.

City	Real estate and rental and leasing, 2017				Professional, scientific, and technical services[1], 2017				Manufacturing, 2017			
	Number of establish-ments	Number of employees	Receipts (mil dol)	Annual payroll (mil dol)	Number of establish-ments	Number of employees	Receipts (mil dol)	Annual payroll (mil dol)	Number of establish-ments	Number of employees	Receipts (mil dol)	Annual payroll (mil dol)
	80	81	82	83	84	85	86	87	88	89	90	91
OHIO—Cont'd												
Xenia	18	54	13.5	1.6	21	96	18.6	5.7	NA	NA	NA	NA
Youngstown	D	D	D	D	85	724	100.2	42.2	NA	NA	NA	NA
OKLAHOMA	4,461	22,135	4,696.2	941.8	9,736	70,920	11,246.9	4,455.8	3,376	123,138	61,143.3	6,740.0
Bartlesville	D	D	D	D	82	1,557	137.5	136.8	NA	NA	NA	NA
Bixby	D	D	D	D	55	139	23.6	6.0	NA	NA	NA	NA
Broken Arrow	97	324	69.1	11.1	257	1,640	219.5	93.3	NA	NA	NA	NA
Edmond	233	561	204.9	25.9	510	2,554	330.4	119.6	NA	NA	NA	NA
Enid	83	337	62.3	11.2	108	560	71.2	27.9	NA	NA	NA	NA
Jenks	D	D	D	D	67	310	39.1	19.0	NA	NA	NA	NA
Lawton	122	431	72.3	12.4	124	1,288	153.6	57.7	NA	NA	NA	NA
Midwest City	65	257	58.3	8.2	88	615	67.3	32.0	NA	NA	NA	NA
Moore	56	248	67.9	11.8	76	374	38.3	13.1	NA	NA	NA	NA
Muskogee	43	164	25.7	4.8	64	499	41.1	17.4	NA	NA	NA	NA
Norman	224	1,006	179.2	38.4	464	2,302	310.7	115.7	NA	NA	NA	NA
Oklahoma City	1,058	6,008	1,618.3	323.5	2,577	25,695	4,406.1	1,799.4	NA	NA	NA	NA
Owasso	55	190	51.4	7.1	74	200	31.0	9.1	NA	NA	NA	NA
Shawnee	38	167	21.8	4.8	72	577	76.0	26.1	NA	NA	NA	NA
Stillwater	68	344	58.6	9.7	108	973	131.4	47.4	NA	NA	NA	NA
Tulsa	773	6,322	1,104.5	262.4	1,854	17,646	3,178.4	1,247.9	NA	NA	NA	NA
OREGON	6,771	29,773	6,773.7	1,263.2	12,620	92,358	14,719.7	6,902.0	5,557	172,210	62,411.2	10,667.7
Albany	67	226	38.2	8.2	114	701	90.8	31.3	NA	NA	NA	NA
Beaverton	281	1,150	301.7	45.9	D	D	D	D	NA	NA	NA	NA
Bend	323	808	212.1	34.4	638	2,520	383.8	151.9	NA	NA	NA	NA
Corvallis	D	D	D	D	195	1,555	361.1	117.0	NA	NA	NA	NA
Eugene	355	1,469	337.1	54.9	720	4,231	543.0	220.0	NA	NA	NA	NA
Forest Grove	28	82	12.6	2.0	35	166	16.0	6.8	NA	NA	NA	NA
Grants Pass	79	365	54.3	15.0	93	739	67.2	23.7	NA	NA	NA	NA
Gresham	118	442	88.1	14.4	123	458	59.8	21.5	NA	NA	NA	NA
Hillsboro	152	603	170.6	29.5	255	9,104	771.6	1,273.5	NA	NA	NA	NA
Keizer	32	151	30.6	4.3	54	259	33.6	10.4	NA	NA	NA	NA
Lake Oswego	167	909	303.3	56.3	D	D	D	D	NA	NA	NA	NA
McMinnville	35	107	20.8	3.6	83	338	44.8	15.6	NA	NA	NA	NA
Medford	191	745	159.8	26.5	257	1,493	180.7	66.4	NA	NA	NA	NA
Newberg	D	D	D	D	48	186	22.7	9.7	NA	NA	NA	NA
Oregon City	D	D	D	D	106	515	68.9	23.8	NA	NA	NA	NA
Portland	1,527	10,487	2,229.6	507.9	3,934	35,617	6,945.5	2,805.5	NA	NA	NA	NA
Redmond	54	126	33.8	3.9	54	308	39.3	24.0	NA	NA	NA	NA
Salem	311	1,335	300.0	57.5	500	2,972	402.1	159.5	NA	NA	NA	NA
Springfield	71	272	56.5	11.1	95	671	61.0	26.8	NA	NA	NA	NA
Tigard	132	614	293.6	45.1	347	3,296	493.3	214.5	NA	NA	NA	NA
Tualatin	78	326	161.3	16.2	107	1,264	183.6	61.0	NA	NA	NA	NA
West Linn	D	D	D	D	131	415	67.9	25.7	NA	NA	NA	NA
Wilsonville	62	282	60.5	11.8	91	2,260	638.8	332.6	NA	NA	NA	NA
Woodburn	16	76	27.1	2.0	31	134	12.6	4.6	NA	NA	NA	NA
PENNSYLVANIA	10,662	66,715	18,860.6	3,472.2	29,991	340,361	64,179.4	26,673.7	13,537	536,967	227,812.0	30,392.5
Allentown	102	509	150.1	23.4	215	1,282	204.5	89.7	NA	NA	NA	NA
Altoona	48	213	38.8	7.3	84	659	78.4	34.9	NA	NA	NA	NA
Bethel Park	27	97	32.6	4.4	95	504	78.8	34.7	NA	NA	NA	NA
Bethlehem	70	520	109.6	22.6	187	1,481	312.4	107.0	NA	NA	NA	NA
Chester	15	44	9.6	2.0	16	262	72.9	23.2	NA	NA	NA	NA
Easton	24	70	15.3	2.5	76	531	57.3	33.3	NA	NA	NA	NA
Erie	54	284	47.5	9.7	181	1,735	292.9	101.4	NA	NA	NA	NA
Harrisburg	57	263	76.6	12.7	250	3,168	592.1	256.2	NA	NA	NA	NA
Hazleton	15	38	9.8	1.4	42	139	16.9	5.4	NA	NA	NA	NA
Lancaster	49	328	53.6	13.3	225	2,087	308.3	128.3	NA	NA	NA	NA
Lebanon	29	170	25.5	5.9	47	325	48.7	15.2	NA	NA	NA	NA
Monroeville	60	409	86.0	18.5	89	1,291	168.9	100.5	NA	NA	NA	NA
Norristown	25	139	24.4	4.9	77	491	78.6	34.1	NA	NA	NA	NA
Philadelphia	1,293	10,704	3,027.6	617.0	3,123	58,180	13,016.2	5,289.6	NA	NA	NA	NA
Pittsburgh	453	4,909	1,258.7	233.7	1,569	30,512	6,465.2	2,643.1	NA	NA	NA	NA
Plum	18	48	8.9	2.5	35	502	176.4	49.5	NA	NA	NA	NA
Reading	137	D	120.8	D	125	1,973	252.6	141.8	NA	NA	NA	NA
Scranton	60	334	59.9	11.0	206	1,237	175.6	74.9	NA	NA	NA	NA
State College	D	D	D	D	85	551	94.0	35.3	NA	NA	NA	NA
Wilkes-Barre	48	312	90.7	15.8	109	1,356	195.6	77.0	NA	NA	NA	NA
Williamsport	34	260	43.6	10.2	74	661	82.0	34.8	NA	NA	NA	NA
York	33	296	57.0	14.2	136	1,913	272.5	105.1	NA	NA	NA	NA

1. Establishments subject to federal tax.

Table D. Cities — Accommodation and Food Services, Arts, Entertainment, and Recreation, and Health Care and Social Assistance

City	Accommodation and food services, 2017				Arts, entertainment, and recreation[1], 2017				Health care and social assistance[1], 2017			
	Number of establish-ments	Number of employees	Receipts (mil dol)	Annual payroll (mil dol)	Number of establish-ments	Number of employees	Receipts (mil dol)	Annual payroll (mil dol)	Number of establish-ments	Number of employees	Receipts (mil dol)	Annual payroll (mil dol)
	92	93	94	95	96	97	98	99	100	101	102	103
OHIO—Cont'd												
Xenia	45	1,053	48.4	14.4	7.0	106	8.6	2.1	87	1,586	147.1	60.0
Youngstown	D	D	D	D	D	D	D	D	NA	NA	NA	NA
OKLAHOMA	8,397	159,826	9,250.8	2,469.9	1,152.0	26,523	3,470.1	798.8	11,035	226,462	27,031.0	9,952.8
Bartlesville	98	1,749	85.4	24.5	D	D	D	D	153	2,874	282.6	116.7
Bixby	36	686	32.2	9.9	10.0	115	4.9	2.0	45	311	28.5	10.3
Broken Arrow	221	4,732	234.8	68.8	36.0	554	29.5	10.5	244	4,451	352.8	142.5
Edmond	262	5,149	262.8	75.1	54.0	1,095	54.6	18.2	510	5,338	637.2	224.3
Enid	124	2,396	127.0	32.4	21.0	244	11.5	4.2	D	D	D	D
Jenks	30	617	30.8	10.2	7.0	190	6.4	3.5	61	578	71.9	26.0
Lawton	217	4,576	265.6	69.1	D	D	D	D	232	5,609	628.8	261.1
Midwest City	133	2,792	137.3	39.5	11.0	228	6.3	2.5	196	2,732	397.6	128.0
Moore	139	3,063	149.6	40.7	14.0	112	6.6	1.7	104	924	80.9	30.4
Muskogee	112	2,125	95.8	26.7	D	D	D	D	191	5,417	726.3	295.2
Norman	363	7,908	419.3	119.9	D	D	D	D	486	8,811	924.8	403.5
Oklahoma City	1,597	33,987	1,959.2	541.5	195.0	5,273	931.8	256.0	2,436	54,538	8,613.2	2,865.2
Owasso	101	2,601	124.5	35.5	9.0	214	5.3	1.4	105	1,984	211.5	74.5
Shawnee	117	2,546	129.8	35.7	12.0	196	11.0	3.8	139	2,639	229.3	101.0
Stillwater	188	3,600	166.7	44.8	15.0	151	4.5	1.5	126	3,016	271.5	127.2
Tulsa	1,205	25,731	1,502.8	419.7	172.0	3,351	177.9	66.3	1,588	45,593	6,447.2	2,298.3
OREGON	11,708	182,613	11,803.9	3,504.5	1,992.0	29,222	2,255.9	775.5	13,948	263,278	33,083.8	13,106.2
Albany	133	2,191	118.0	34.9	16.0	135	8.8	2.2	138	3,041	344.3	138.2
Beaverton	341	5,608	356.4	107.9	76.0	1,544	77.2	24.7	473	6,216	692.3	277.8
Bend	382	6,525	434.8	139.4	87.0	1,770	86.4	24.5	533	9,929	1,387.6	551.5
Corvallis	193	3,535	195.0	55.8	23.0	329	10.2	4.3	251	5,425	686.0	299.6
Eugene	576	9,516	569.0	166.4	96.0	1,793	93.1	23.9	829	12,879	1,217.8	502.0
Forest Grove	49	795	47.2	13.9	7.0	34	2.0	0.5	D	D	D	D
Grants Pass	162	2,499	139.6	40.9	19.0	348	12.2	4.6	253	4,939	506.0	212.9
Gresham	237	4,217	245.4	72.7	37.0	510	29.9	8.9	413	5,934	633.8	237.7
Hillsboro	293	5,784	403.0	116.2	48.0	952	48.3	15.4	350	7,724	1,088.1	406.7
Keizer	74	1,187	63.7	17.8	16.0	178	12.9	3.7	111	1,536	121.8	53.3
Lake Oswego	114	2,189	140.1	42.8	42.0	429	24.2	9.6	240	2,419	252.4	98.3
McMinnville	94	1,534	88.3	26.9	D	D	D	D	155	2,634	272.1	108.7
Medford	278	4,872	281.8	84.8	41.0	539	38.0	11.5	435	12,307	1,649.9	639.5
Newberg	66	1,333	73.4	23.5	7.0	54	1.8	0.5	106	2,031	239.4	92.3
Oregon City	D	D	D	D	16.0	145	7.9	2.7	157	2,617	327.5	125.2
Portland	2,882	47,324	3,281.5	998.7	494.0	7,257	935.4	351.5	2,906	67,025	9,249.7	3,544.8
Redmond	104	1,452	99.4	26.9	9.0	30	2.6	0.7	126	1,884	224.8	90.6
Salem	457	7,454	431.7	131.0	74.0	984	58.8	18.0	724	15,658	1,962.5	821.1
Springfield	178	3,149	176.8	52.4	20.0	248	8.7	2.6	216	8,193	1,515.9	540.2
Tigard	181	3,223	207.5	62.2	32.0	359	26.0	8.5	277	3,308	368.2	139.4
Tualatin	87	1,691	102.7	31.2	D	D	D	D	D	D	D	D
West Linn	53	767	44.1	13.9	8.0	39	2.6	0.8	114	870	78.5	32.0
Wilsonville	87	1,607	114.9	31.3	D	D	D	D	76	2,999	249.1	131.8
Woodburn	72	1,144	64.4	18.4	7.0	75	6.6	2.1	D	D	D	D
PENNSYLVANIA	28,843	481,682	28,849.4	7,931.4	4,862.0	101,095	10,655.4	3,265.1	37,699	1,035,971	116,621.8	47,885.2
Allentown	278	4,016	212.4	60.1	38.0	696	60.4	16.1	340	9,317	1,240.4	472.9
Altoona	136	2,437	123.5	34.4	19.0	188	8.6	3.1	231	7,152	761.1	336.6
Bethel Park	74	1,865	97.9	29.5	D	D	D	D	142	1,850	174.3	80.1
Bethlehem	232	5,777	822.9	159.2	26.0	444	31.5	8.5	NA	NA	NA	NA
Chester	31	452	26.5	8.2	4.0	1,605	315.3	64.9	75	2,020	304.0	162.2
Easton	114	1,558	90.7	25.1	11.0	399	26.4	9.1	75	1,993	217.2	77.1
Erie	211	4,197	177.2	51.1	43.0	962	45.4	16.0	458	16,369	1,860.0	806.3
Harrisburg	180	2,571	163.8	45.8	31.0	334	29.5	9.5	207	8,012	992.2	408.7
Hazleton	63	722	40.3	9.0	7.0	16	1.0	0.2	103	2,938	279.4	110.2
Lancaster	193	4,075	247.0	73.6	27.0	572	32.0	10.0	201	10,120	1,535.0	574.2
Lebanon	D	D	D	D	D	D	D	D	90	2,944	355.0	138.7
Monroeville	118	2,580	141.9	39.1	20.0	296	12.6	4.5	236	6,094	704.1	290.0
Norristown	68	416	32.8	6.7	12.0	128	11.4	4.0	106	2,563	226.7	123.4
Philadelphia	3,953	61,893	4,480.2	1,278.3	451.0	15,371	2,496.1	979.7	3,992	161,976	21,515.8	8,284.7
Pittsburgh	1,311	26,134	1,724.2	511.2	209.0	9,309	1,740.5	668.2	1,383	60,636	8,315.3	3,525.8
Plum	35	588	24.8	7.7	7.0	9	1.2	0.4	35	727	45.5	16.1
Reading	146	1,910	122.5	26.5	22.0	769	36.0	11.0	159	4,881	342.7	160.7
Scranton	209	2,681	160.6	44.1	D	D	D	D	337	11,865	1,273.7	537.6
State College	143	3,014	145.3	40.0	18.0	343	16.2	5.6	120	3,795	568.5	213.6
Wilkes-Barre	140	2,407	125.8	35.5	13.0	511	22.6	7.5	146	7,076	1,091.7	384.0
Williamsport	88	1,792	102.1	34.7	13.0	139	18.7	2.7	113	5,462	846.9	294.6
York	95	1,533	79.5	21.4	17.0	363	21.6	6.6	129	7,828	1,265.8	427.7

1. Establishments subject to federal tax.

City	Other services[1]: Number of establish-ments	Other services[1]: Number of employees	Other services[1]: Receipts (mil dol)	Other services[1]: Annual payroll (mil dol)	Government employment and payroll, 2017: Full-time equivalent employees	March payroll: Total (dollars)	Perent of total for: Admin-istrative, judicial, and legal	Police and corrections	Fire protection	Highways and trans-portation	Health and welfare	Natural resources and utilities	Education and libraries
	104	105	106	107	108	109	110	111	112	113	114	115	116
OHIO—Cont'd													
Xenia	39	270	26.6	6.5	226	1,273,227	21.5	25.0	35.1	3.1	0.4	14.9	0.0
Youngstown	99	1,165	97.5	28.2	803	3,326,951	12.0	27.5	20.0	5.8	3.5	27.9	0.0
OKLAHOMA	5,565	31,947	4,933.6	1,083.6	X	X	X	X	X	X	X	X	X
Bartlesville	68	428	40.7	12.1	340	1,394,623	12.3	24.7	24.0	3.6	4.2	21.9	5.3
Bixby	D	D	D	D	117	491,696	16.3	33.6	25.8	4.3	0.0	13.0	0.0
Broken Arrow	167	1,188	146.8	42.8	727	3,786,247	11.8	30.9	30.0	6.7	0.0	16.9	0.0
Edmond	206	996	99.3	28.1	749	4,157,091	15.5	24.6	24.9	6.6	1.5	21.4	0.0
Enid	101	530	59.7	14.5	463	1,922,891	13.9	26.7	24.5	7.7	0.3	14.5	2.6
Jenks	21	81	6.3	2.4	87	360,597	6.8	26.9	28.5	2.2	0.9	11.2	0.0
Lawton	D	D	D	D	872	3,517,667	14.1	30.3	18.8	7.2	2.2	20.5	1.9
Midwest City	58	338	29.3	9.0	468	2,438,934	15.0	26.6	24.2	3.5	3.3	19.5	0.0
Moore	74	331	33.3	9.3	328	2,094,680	12.1	38.6	30.4	2.3	2.5	8.6	0.0
Muskogee	D	D	D	13.2	452	1,676,180	14.9	28.8	25.0	5.3	0.0	21.3	0.0
Norman	170	984	236.6	30.6	3,444	18,975,140	2.4	7.4	5.5	2.4	75.8	4.7	0.0
Oklahoma City	1,140	8,064	1,120.2	298.2	4,494	27,224,626	9.9	34.3	27.2	8.5	4.4	15.6	0.0
Owasso	D	D	D	D	267	1,294,440	13.7	28.3	27.8	6.2	0.8	16.5	0.0
Shawnee	53	275	28.7	7.8	310	1,418,292	11.2	26.5	23.3	8.7	0.4	23.6	0.0
Stillwater	81	753	237.1	26.7	1,610	8,774,509	3.4	7.3	5.3	2.0	70.8	8.7	0.8
Tulsa	900	6,379	1,438.9	241.4	3,773	19,022,256	13.6	28.1	21.7	14.1	0.3	15.1	0.0
OREGON	7,414	43,543	6,288.8	1,555.0	X	X	X	X	X	X	X	X	X
Albany	82	612	40.0	14.5	384	2,174,784	11.3	25.4	25.1	12.6	0.0	19.7	3.7
Beaverton	203	1,350	154.4	46.2	588	2,785,440	34.7	25.0	0.0	4.9	0.0	8.8	11.5
Bend	260	1,326	163.5	44.8	583	4,017,372	18.8	22.1	24.0	9.8	6.4	12.1	0.0
Corvallis	118	899	215.4	37.1	439	2,570,510	11.3	24.1	19.5	7.7	6.8	19.3	8.2
Eugene	381	2,529	428.1	85.2	1,880	12,757,120	7.9	18.3	14.0	8.0	2.6	24.7	3.3
Forest Grove	31	117	18.3	3.8	167	1,210,756	14.2	23.7	15.7	5.9	0.0	29.8	5.4
Grants Pass	80	377	33.7	9.8	219	1,202,000	17.5	44.2	16.7	2.1	0.0	13.7	0.0
Gresham	145	753	69.6	22.7	495	3,476,105	12.8	35.9	23.6	5.2	6.4	12.3	0.0
Hillsboro	165	2,021	545.5	132.3	874	5,270,127	17.5	22.8	17.1	4.6	0.0	25.0	6.6
Keizer	43	176	18.3	4.8	91	565,772	21.9	52.4	0.0	4.6	4.2	15.4	0.0
Lake Oswego	102	526	60.4	18.9	344	2,197,219	16.0	24.2	20.9	3.3	0.3	16.8	6.2
McMinnville	54	289	21.6	7.2	259	1,535,550	14.1	21.9	18.5	5.3	1.7	32.2	4.0
Medford	163	1,169	132.0	35.5	485	2,896,083	13.3	33.7	22.0	15.4	0.0	10.2	0.0
Newberg	37	148	13.6	3.7	134	773,657	21.7	38.4	0.0	2.3	0.0	17.5	6.5
Oregon City	75	404	40.3	11.9	187	1,094,799	19.9	35.4	0.0	13.3	0.4	17.6	5.3
Portland	1,926	13,837	2,463.4	556.9	6,225	42,536,596	20.1	23.8	14.9	10.8	1.8	26.6	0.0
Redmond	55	431	52.5	14.1	152	837,919	12.7	34.6	0.0	20.5	5.9	18.5	0.0
Salem	322	1,811	175.6	55.7	1,212	7,311,691	13.3	28.9	16.6	3.3	5.3	16.4	2.9
Springfield	96	538	56.1	15.0	547	3,697,459	13.5	23.1	22.1	8.5	5.0	15.3	2.1
Tigard	155	1,116	226.8	43.5	284	1,707,823	26.8	34.9	0.0	8.0	1.1	11.4	11.2
Tualatin	97	561	61.9	19.5	150	925,011	22.7	37.3	0.0	2.3	4.8	12.4	11.1
West Linn	46	185	14.0	4.7	121	640,406	23.9	20.3	0.0	12.5	0.0	21.4	12.7
Wilsonville	52	312	41.9	15.1	147	808,750	29.5	0.0	0.0	33.6	0.0	13.5	9.8
Woodburn	25	121	11.9	3.5	134	715,033	22.4	38.1	0.0	7.2	1.1	20.3	4.5
PENNSYLVANIA	26,075	161,337	22,982.2	5,136.6	X	X	X	X	X	X	X	X	X
Allentown	247	1,606	171.0	52.4	848	5,261,837	8.4	33.2	19.8	5.0	8.9	19.7	0.0
Altoona	118	613	49.0	14.5	237	1,025,045	9.3	37.4	29.4	17.3	4.7	2.1	0.0
Bethel Park	85	561	38.8	14.6	128	661,011	12.1	56.2	0.0	16.2	0.0	15.0	0.0
Bethlehem	157	1,163	110.7	37.7	692	3,608,415	7.3	31.6	18.2	3.3	7.0	18.2	0.0
Chester	D	D	D	D	341	1,905,322	7.9	48.0	28.7	4.3	0.2	5.0	0.0
Easton	71	391	39.4	11.8	230	1,255,442	10.8	32.9	26.6	2.9	2.4	13.1	0.0
Erie	215	1,446	153.5	35.8	637	3,968,930	7.4	35.9	25.5	11.9	2.3	17.1	0.0
Harrisburg	185	1,394	249.5	77.4	441	2,045,074	7.3	35.1	22.6	7.3	1.7	16.8	0.0
Hazleton	48	194	14.4	4.2	91	483,561	10.3	46.5	20.9	13.6	6.5	0.4	0.0
Lancaster	148	1,295	108.5	30.1	546	3,002,028	5.8	40.3	18.3	5.0	2.8	23.9	0.0
Lebanon	63	255	29.3	7.1	146	754,384	5.1	39.4	16.9	5.7	2.1	30.9	0.0
Monroeville	91	599	36.7	13.6	143	920,606	14.4	52.5	0.0	6.2	4.2	15.3	6.2
Norristown	D	D	D	5.9	164	1,032,999	11.9	61.7	14.9	5.6	0.0	1.7	0.0
Philadelphia	2,687	20,004	2,958.1	785.8	30,557	177,705,357	16.8	37.8	10.4	3.8	12.0	15.6	1.8
Pittsburgh	912	7,796	1,614.1	277.4	3,293	17,441,555	10.9	40.2	19.8	11.5	11.5	5.1	0.0
Plum	44	232	23.3	6.9	67	393,790	66.5	0.0	0.0	0.0	0.0	0.0	0.0
Reading	107	738	91.0	21.7	595	3,156,585	7.9	37.4	22.1	0.8	5.7	24.4	1.3
Scranton	148	771	90.7	22.2	487	2,362,715	5.0	37.1	34.4	4.4	1.2	8.8	6.9
State College	53	285	19.9	8.2	174	970,917	23.1	48.0	0.0	13.8	2.1	3.8	0.0
Wilkes-Barre	91	540	55.3	15.6	282	1,551,214	9.7	36.6	28.4	2.1	5.0	9.8	0.0
Williamsport	73	728	54.5	14.1	205	1,066,708	6.4	32.8	21.5	33.0	1.9	4.1	0.0
York	77	681	117.1	23.6	341	1,850,502	12.1	40.3	22.6	2.5	4.1	13.6	0.0

1. Establishments subject to federal tax.

City	City government finances, 2017									
	General revenue							General expenditure		
		Intergovernmental		Taxes						
					Per capita[1] (dollars)				Per capita[1] (dollars)	
	Total (mil dol)	Total (mil dol)	Percent from state government	Total (mil dol)	Total	Property	Sales and gross receipts	Total (mil dol)	Total	Capital outlays
	117	118	119	120	121	122	123	124	125	126
OHIO—Cont'd										
Xenia	32.8	5.1	97.5	16.2	609	26	38	22.7	855	412
Youngstown	128.6	18.3	33.3	74.6	1,155	52	163	102.3	1,584	38
OKLAHOMA	X	X	X	X	X	X	X	X	X	X
Bartlesville	44.2	2.0	69.8	25.4	698	132	555	45.2	1,242	286
Bixby	23.4	0.7	92.5	16.0	599	109	455	17.2	645	120
Broken Arrow	116.7	12.0	92.4	68.2	629	136	466	110.7	1,021	211
Edmond	124.9	8.7	89.1	72.3	789	0	788	106.8	1,165	169
Enid	71.4	2.5	51.3	39.3	784	11	756	65.2	1,300	182
Jenks	24.1	0.4	51.9	12.3	548	180	368	23.0	1,023	250
Lawton	109.7	12.3	64.3	58.0	617	40	577	127.3	1,354	402
Midwest City	57.8	4.7	14.7	14.5	253	48	205	63.2	1,106	114
Moore	75.6	12.8	4.1	43.2	708	99	609	87.8	1,441	190
Muskogee	53.5	6.5	37.9	30.6	809	7	803	55.7	1,475	370
Norman	560.6	9.8	33.7	103.1	836	119	716	544.1	4,410	588
Oklahoma City	1,268.2	197.6	44.4	642.5	999	161	839	1,026.0	1,596	398
Owasso	48.9	2.3	40.1	33.4	919	3	917	42.9	1,180	384
Shawnee	37.0	4.2	76.2	22.4	716	2	704	39.0	1,246	219
Stillwater	55.4	2.2	63.3	32.8	656	21	636	43.3	866	132
Tulsa	821.1	74.2	10.1	388.8	967	184	784	720.9	1,793	554
OREGON	X	X	X	X	X	X	X	X	X	X
Albany	76.2	9.9	51.9	38.3	715	561	154	84.7	1,582	447
Beaverton	108.9	19.8	56.1	55.9	572	417	155	90.6	926	69
Bend	126.6	13.2	59.6	69.3	732	358	374	125.8	1,330	367
Corvallis	83.7	13.3	50.5	39.9	681	484	198	78.3	1,337	137
Eugene	313.9	42.6	46.5	143.6	848	683	164	284.7	1,681	228
Forest Grove	26.1	1.9	100.0	10.5	435	332	103	29.1	1,203	18
Grants Pass	41.1	5.0	73.1	25.4	674	492	182	46.1	1,223	315
Gresham	132.1	36.2	30.6	59.4	534	281	253	129.8	1,167	140
Hillsboro	189.9	12.9	87.3	101.0	940	635	305	165.3	1,538	110
Keizer	20.8	3.6	89.6	8.5	216	128	88	19.4	494	28
Lake Oswego	98.4	19.2	18.5	47.5	1,210	1,011	200	88.0	2,239	446
McMinnville	41.8	5.1	66.4	19.0	556	442	114	49.2	1,441	365
Medford	131.9	15.9	49.9	72.4	892	517	375	134.0	1,651	339
Newberg	31.2	4.0	76.9	15.2	651	329	279	28.5	1,216	185
Oregon City	57.0	7.9	100.0	23.0	631	417	214	39.1	1,074	75
Portland	1,734.3	204.2	41.5	888.0	1,371	823	548	1,449.1	2,236	419
Redmond	59.0	12.1	51.4	19.3	644	366	278	67.1	2,236	894
Salem	313.6	73.5	61.1	127.4	751	546	205	285.2	1,682	224
Springfield	149.8	9.5	99.0	44.6	715	546	169	101.0	1,619	129
Tigard	63.9	10.3	61.9	31.2	585	349	237	52.0	974	107
Tualatin	33.3	4.9	48.9	13.7	497	358	139	32.3	1,168	71
West Linn	27.1	5.2	59.9	12.9	481	324	157	28.2	1,054	281
Wilsonville	57.6	5.5	60.2	28.3	1,171	675	266	27.8	1,151	278
Woodburn	29.0	2.8	95.8	15.2	590	395	195	19.6	760	21
PENNSYLVANIA	X	X	X	X	X	X	X	X	X	X
Allentown	149.9	31.8	50.9	70.6	584	254	117	182.3	1,506	101
Altoona	34.7	6.4	52.1	23.7	539	227	82	34.4	783	69
Bethel Park	32.3	3.2	57.4	17.9	555	185	68	36.7	1,136	170
Bethlehem	96.8	23.1	92.4	42.8	566	341	100	97.3	1,288	0
Chester	56.7	9.9	87.5	22.2	653	273	96	55.4	1,633	14
Easton	54.0	9.3	57.4	19.1	705	333	71	52.9	1,951	80
Erie	120.0	23.3	35.3	53.8	554	362	58	108.3	1,114	65
Harrisburg	89.4	19.2	54.3	44.7	909	353	314	139.6	2,838	1,046
Hazleton	22.2	7.4	92.0	13.0	522	187	65	13.3	535	11
Lancaster	94.4	10.8	67.2	38.0	638	456	68	133.5	2,244	382
Lebanon	17.0	2.7	67.3	10.6	410	153	39	14.1	548	15
Monroeville	31.3	2.7	91.5	27.3	986	323	355	27.1	981	37
Norristown	32.6	4.1	58.3	23.1	671	320	78	27.8	807	41
Philadelphia	7,149.5	2,318.6	66.7	3,708.3	2,346	362	419	6,861.4	4,341	276
Pittsburgh	628.6	115.8	64.2	417.5	1,385	470	516	757.1	2,511	54
Plum	15.5	1.7	85.0	10.8	398	209	42	17.1	629	70
Reading	129.9	14.0	94.7	58.8	668	277	91	125.2	1,421	26
Scranton	115.7	9.2	76.7	73.5	952	419	133	107.4	1,391	6
State College	44.0	4.9	58.0	16.4	386	174	49	41.4	975	129
Wilkes-Barre	54.7	14.0	55.1	28.6	699	267	82	50.9	1,244	133
Williamsport	37.4	15.5	69.5	19.9	698	472	144	26.6	933	107
York	76.8	7.8	61.0	30.2	685	450	128	66.9	1,519	48

1. Based on population estimated as of July 1 of the year shown.

City	City government finances, 2017 (cont.)												
	General expenditure (cont.)												
	Percent of total for:									Debt outstanding			
	Public welfare	Highways	Parking facilities	Education	Health and hospitals	Police protection	Sewerage and sanitation	Parks and recreation	Housing and community development	Interest on debt	Total (mil dol)	Per capita[1] (dollars)	Debt issued during year
	127	128	129	130	131	132	133	134	135	136	137	138	139
OHIO—Cont'd													
Xenia	0.0	7.7	0.2	0.0	0.0	4.9	31.4	0.9	1.2	0.2	1.2	44	0.0
Youngstown	0.0	6.5	0.1	0.0	1.5	22.5	27.0	2.7	6.9	0.4	8.6	134	0.0
OKLAHOMA	X	X	X	X	X	X	X	X	X	X	X	X	X
Bartlesville	0.0	5.9	0.0	0.0	0.0	15.6	22.9	11.2	0.8	3.3	86.5	2,378	0.0
Bixby	0.0	12.6	0.0	0.0	0.0	25.7	3.0	7.5	0.0	4.8	20.7	778	0.0
Broken Arrow	0.0	14.9	0.0	0.0	0.0	21.4	9.8	7.2	1.2	5.1	226.6	2,091	45.7
Edmond	0.7	11.6	0.0	0.0	0.7	25.2	13.5	13.0	0.0	3.3	129.0	1,407	41.8
Enid	0.3	4.0	0.0	1.8	8.3	15.6	13.8	3.0	14.0	2.3	65.6	1,308	15.2
Jenks	0.0	19.3	0.0	0.0	0.3	15.6	9.2	23.3	0.0	8.0	46.5	2,064	0.0
Lawton	0.0	15.5	0.0	2.0	0.0	16.7	19.2	5.0	0.6	0.0	124.2	1,322	34.4
Midwest City	0.0	10.7	0.0	0.0	0.7	25.6	9.9	5.3	7.0	0.0	76.5	1,338	0.0
Moore	0.2	10.3	0.0	0.0	0.0	13.6	9.2	7.5	8.7	1.7	95.1	1,559	1.8
Muskogee	0.0	9.2	0.0	0.0	0.7	16.7	7.9	11.4	0.0	0.1	66.9	1,771	0.0
Norman	0.0	5.8	0.0	0.0	65.8	5.4	8.2	3.5	1.0	2.9	407.2	3,300	218.8
Oklahoma City	0.0	7.5	0.4	0.0	0.5	17.9	7.3	22.5	4.9	3.5	1,836.8	2,857	321.1
Owasso	0.0	11.2	0.0	0.0	4.8	20.4	12.4	7.6	6.3	2.0	42.3	1,163	21.3
Shawnee	0.0	15.8	0.0	0.0	0.0	22.0	8.8	10.0	5.5	0.3	23.3	746	4.2
Stillwater	0.0	17.5	0.0	0.0	0.1	27.3	17.5	6.3	0.0	0.9	94.3	1,885	12.9
Tulsa	2.5	16.9	0.5	0.0	10.6	14.5	17.3	5.7	1.0	4.7	1,412.1	3,512	296.0
OREGON	X	X	X	X	X	X	X	X	X	X	X	X	X
Albany	0.0	4.8	0.0	0.0	0.2	27.4	14.9	7.0	3.4	3.8	90.4	1,689	0.0
Beaverton	0.0	8.7	0.0	0.0	0.0	34.3	11.8	0.3	1.2	0.6	8.4	86	0.0
Bend	0.0	14.6	0.4	0.0	0.0	15.9	22.8	0.0	2.5	3.3	152.2	1,609	0.0
Corvallis	0.0	6.4	0.2	0.0	0.0	19.0	13.0	10.2	7.4	0.0	41.0	701	0.0
Eugene	0.0	3.4	1.8	0.0	0.0	18.8	13.1	10.1	3.2	0.5	307.6	1,816	163.6
Forest Grove	0.0	5.5	0.0	0.0	0.0	19.1	17.3	4.5	1.6	16.0	123.8	5,117	31.1
Grants Pass	0.0	15.5	0.0	0.0	0.0	33.5	17.1	4.8	0.3	0.5	7.9	209	0.0
Gresham	0.0	8.8	0.0	0.0	0.0	22.9	20.2	2.6	1.1	2.1	80.5	724	6.5
Hillsboro	0.0	9.8	0.0	0.0	0.0	18.6	23.5	14.2	1.6	1.4	92.7	863	35.2
Keizer	0.0	5.0	0.0	0.0	0.0	33.3	28.1	1.9	0.0	0.0	15.5	396	0.0
Lake Oswego	0.0	7.6	0.0	0.0	0.0	14.7	10.3	11.5	0.0	0.0	183.1	4,661	0.0
McMinnville	0.0	20.4	0.0	0.0	9.5	15.2	12.4	8.3	0.4	2.3	33.9	991	6.1
Medford	0.0	8.3	0.3	0.0	0.0	28.3	9.2	5.4	0.7	17.0	535.1	6,591	0.0
Newberg	0.0	12.4	0.0	0.0	0.0	20.9	21.9	0.0	0.0	0.0	42.1	1,796	0.3
Oregon City	0.0	9.5	1.1	0.0	0.0	22.4	20.2	9.8	1.2	3.9	23.9	658	0.0
Portland	0.0	12.4	0.6	0.0	0.0	14.2	16.2	9.4	9.8	7.9	3,150.5	4,863	631.1
Redmond	0.0	9.6	0.0	0.0	0.0	11.6	17.7	6.2	12.0	4.4	80.6	2,686	3.9
Salem	0.0	13.2	0.9	0.0	0.8	14.4	14.7	2.7	12.9	7.4	416.0	2,452	0.0
Springfield	0.0	6.6	0.0	0.0	6.3	18.9	31.1	0.0	0.8	5.8	122.3	1,961	0.0
Tigard	0.4	7.3	0.0	0.0	0.0	31.5	10.0	7.4	1.1	2.2	119.4	2,237	0.0
Tualatin	0.0	7.5	0.0	0.0	0.0	22.6	27.0	9.1	0.3	0.7	10.0	360	0.0
West Linn	0.0	9.9	0.0	0.0	0.0	20.6	16.1	22.7	0.0	1.4	16.5	616	0.0
Wilsonville	0.2	12.9	0.0	0.0	0.0	14.9	16.3	8.1	0.0	0.0	70.7	2,928	0.0
Woodburn	0.0	8.9	0.0	0.0	0.0	35.9	22.2	9.4	0.3	5.5	36.9	1,430	0.0
PENNSYLVANIA	X	X	X	X	X	X	X	X	X	X	X	X	X
Allentown	0.0	17.2	0.0	0.0	4.0	18.2	16.0	5.4	4.2	1.8	97.4	805	3.2
Altoona	0.0	21.4	0.0	0.0	0.0	26.0	0.0	1.0	11.6	2.7	25.3	575	1.3
Bethel Park	0.0	14.7	0.0	0.0	0.0	19.6	30.0	6.5	0.3	2.1	20.2	625	0.0
Bethlehem	0.0	7.4	0.0	0.0	3.9	14.8	20.8	3.9	2.9	8.7	195.1	2,582	3.6
Chester	0.0	5.0	0.0	0.0	1.1	31.2	2.7	5.1	1.8	0.9	6.7	197	0.0
Easton	0.0	6.0	0.3	0.0	0.2	19.7	20.5	3.6	3.4	4.0	47.7	1,759	1.2
Erie	0.0	13.2	0.0	0.0	0.0	16.1	16.9	2.1	5.1	3.6	178.4	1,835	14.6
Harrisburg	0.0	8.3	0.0	0.0	0.0	13.8	6.8	0.7	48.4	5.3	98.9	2,009	13.0
Hazleton	0.0	15.3	0.0	0.0	0.6	31.5	0.0	0.8	15.7	2.2	8.4	337	0.0
Lancaster	0.0	7.1	0.0	0.0	0.0	14.6	34.5	3.7	2.9	6.0	258.7	4,348	133.0
Lebanon	0.0	8.4	0.3	0.0	1.7	29.6	5.0	3.5	1.6	0.1	0.2	6	0.1
Monroeville	0.0	15.3	0.0	0.0	0.3	39.1	5.2	7.7	1.7	2.3	19.3	699	0.3
Norristown	0.0	7.5	0.0	0.0	2.7	30.9	10.7	1.7	3.3	3.1	14.4	418	0.8
Philadelphia	2.9	3.0	0.0	2.0	24.6	9.8	7.0	1.5	5.8	3.4	4,997.9	3,162	99.9
Pittsburgh	0.0	14.1	0.0	0.0	2.5	12.5	2.3	1.3	1.7	3.2	473.2	1,570	27.8
Plum	0.0	31.5	0.0	0.0	0.0	26.9	10.1	7.0	0.0	3.4	17.0	627	24.0
Reading	0.0	5.6	0.0	0.0	3.6	27.8	21.0	1.2	6.1	10.0	257.4	2,921	25.5
Scranton	0.0	6.1	0.0	0.0	0.0	23.2	18.4	0.7	0.0	6.6	152.8	1,979	33.4
State College	0.0	14.3	9.0	0.0	1.0	20.9	22.3	3.7	4.1	2.0	36.3	856	6.1
Wilkes-Barre	0.0	13.3	1.7	0.0	5.9	20.0	10.1	2.8	12.8	4.5	67.4	1,646	8.8
Williamsport	0.0	14.2	0.0	0.0	0.0	30.5	0.0	7.7	5.7	3.2	22.5	791	4.3
York	0.0	7.0	2.6	0.0	2.3	15.9	23.9	1.7	3.1	9.2	94.3	2,140	0.0

1. Based on population estimated as of July 1 of the year shown.

Table D. Cities — **Land Area and Population**

STATE	Place code	City	Land area[1] (sq. mi)	Population, 2021: Total persons 2021	Population, 2021: Rank	Population, 2021: Per square mile	Race 2020, Race alone[2] (percent): White	Race 2020, Race alone[2] (percent): Black or African American	Race 2020, Race alone[2] (percent): American Indian, Alaskan Native	Race 2020, Race alone[2] (percent): Asian	Race 2020, Race alone[2] (percent): Hawaiian Pacific Islander	Race 2020, Race alone[2] (percent): Some other race	Race 2020: Two or more races (percent)
			1	2	3	4	5	6	7	8	9	10	11
44	00000	RHODE ISLAND	1,033.9	1,095,610	X	1,059.7	71.3	5.7	0.7	3.6	0.0	9.4	9.3
44	19180	Cranston	28.3	82,566	424	2,917.5	68.1	5.6	0.6	7.0	0.1	10.0	8.6
44	22960	East Providence	13.3	46,929	849	3,528.5	77.4	5.4	0.4	2.1	0.0	4.8	9.8
44	49960	Newport	7.7	25,156	1,538	3,267.0	75.9	5.9	0.9	1.8	0.1	6.1	9.4
44	54640	Pawtucket	8.7	75,387	489	8,665.2	49.6	13.0	0.6	1.5	0.1	16.4	18.7
44	59000	Providence	18.4	189,692	135	10,309.3	37.7	13.5	1.5	6.1	0.1	26.9	14.2
44	74300	Warwick	35.0	83,011	422	2,371.7	85.7	2.1	0.3	3.1	0.0	2.6	6.2
44	80780	Woonsocket	7.7	43,118	927	5,599.7	64.4	7.9	0.6	5.8	0.1	9.6	11.6
45	00000	SOUTH CAROLINA	30,063.7	5,190,705	X	172.7	63.4	25.0	0.5	1.8	0.1	3.5	5.8
45	00550	Aiken	21.2	31,895	1,240	1,504.5	62.5	28.5	0.2	2.0	0.1	1.5	5.2
45	01360	Anderson	14.7	29,284	1,337	1,992.1	59.5	29.7	0.2	1.5	0.0	2.5	6.6
45	07210	Bluffton	52.0	32,191	1,224	619.1	73.0	8.4	0.4	2.1	0.0	6.6	9.5
45	13330	Charleston	114.8	151,612	174	1,320.7	73.5	17.0	0.3	2.2	0.1	1.6	5.3
45	16000	Columbia	137.2	137,541	201	1,002.5	50.7	38.5	0.3	3.1	0.1	2.3	5.1
45	25810	Florence	23.4	39,958	990	1,707.6	45.5	46.9	0.2	2.3	0.0	1.1	3.9
45	29815	Goose Creek	42.3	46,229	861	1,092.9	60.3	21.8	0.6	3.5	0.1	4.9	8.7
45	30850	Greenville	29.8	72,095	511	2,419.3	65.8	22.9	0.2	2.2	0.1	3.3	5.6
45	30985	Greer	23.5	38,865	1,021	1,653.8	60.9	16.0	0.5	5.3	0.0	8.2	9.0
45	34045	Hilton Head Island	41.4	38,076	1,045	919.7	79.2	5.8	0.4	0.8	0.0	7.1	6.7
45	48535	Mount Pleasant	49.5	92,398	368	1,866.6	88.6	3.3	0.2	2.2	0.0	0.9	4.8
45	49075	Myrtle Beach	23.5	37,100	1,071	1,578.7	68.7	13.2	0.5	2.3	0.1	7.0	8.0
45	50875	North Charleston	77.6	117,472	241	1,513.8	39.8	40.6	0.7	2.9	0.1	8.8	7.1
45	61405	Rock Hill	39.8	74,102	498	1,861.9	48.7	38.8	0.6	2.0	0.1	3.9	5.9
45	68290	Spartanburg	20.3	38,401	1,037	1,891.7	45.3	44.1	0.3	2.1	0.2	2.9	5.1
45	70270	Summerville	21.6	51,216	779	2,371.1	66.8	20.8	0.5	1.6	0.1	2.5	7.8
45	70405	Sumter	32.8	42,976	928	1,310.2	41.3	48.7	0.3	2.1	0.1	2.0	5.6
46	00000	SOUTH DAKOTA	75,809.7	895,376	X	11.8	80.7	2.0	8.8	1.5	0.1	1.7	5.3
46	00100	Aberdeen	16.5	28,324	1,373	1,716.6	83.6	1.9	3.7	3.1	0.2	2.2	5.3
46	52980	Rapid City	54.7	76,184	481	1,392.8	74.6	1.5	13.2	1.6	0.1	1.2	7.8
46	59020	Sioux Falls	79.4	196,528	130	2,475.2	79.0	6.3	2.7	2.8	0.0	2.9	6.1
47	00000	TENNESSEE	41,238.0	6,975,218	X	169.1	72.2	15.8	0.4	2.0	0.1	3.6	6.0
47	03440	Bartlett	32.3	57,318	691	1,774.6	68.6	20.1	0.3	3.3	0.1	1.8	5.8
47	08280	Brentwood	41.1	45,491	869	1,106.8	82.1	3.2	0.1	8.1	0.0	0.8	5.7
47	08540	Bristol	32.7	27,530	1,412	841.9	89.9	3.0	0.2	0.9	0.0	1.1	4.9
47	14000	Chattanooga	142.4	182,113	142	1,278.9	56.1	29.1	0.7	2.8	0.0	4.4	6.9
47	15160	Clarksville	99.5	170,957	153	1,718.2	57.0	24.4	0.5	2.5	0.5	4.2	10.9
47	15400	Cleveland	27.1	47,955	829	1,769.6	74.4	8.2	0.5	1.8	0.2	5.9	9.1
47	16420	Collierville	36.4	51,343	777	1,410.5	68.0	11.8	0.2	12.8	0.0	1.6	5.6
47	16540	Columbia	33.2	43,340	923	1,305.4	66.5	18.5	0.5	1.0	0.1	5.5	7.8
47	16920	Cookeville	35.8	35,138	1,136	981.5	80.2	4.8	1.2	2.3	0.1	5.3	6.2
47	27740	Franklin	43.1	85,469	411	1,983.0	76.4	5.2	0.3	7.7	0.1	3.6	6.8
47	28540	Gallatin	33.0	46,902	850	1,421.3	70.6	14.8	0.5	1.7	0.1	4.5	7.9
47	28960	Germantown	20.0	41,034	960	2,051.7	83.0	4.1	0.2	6.9	0.0	0.8	5.0
47	33280	Hendersonville	31.6	62,257	618	1,970.2	78.8	8.7	0.3	2.1	0.1	2.5	7.4
47	37640	Jackson	58.4	68,114	554	1,166.3	46.7	44.0	0.3	1.6	0.0	2.8	4.6
47	38320	Johnson City	43.4	71,278	519	1,642.4	80.1	6.9	0.4	2.4	0.1	2.9	7.2
47	39560	Kingsport	52.6	55,582	710	1,056.7	87.9	3.7	0.3	1.4	0.0	1.4	5.4
47	40000	Knoxville	98.7	192,648	132	1,951.9	69.6	16.0	0.7	2.3	0.1	4.1	7.3
47	41200	La Vergne	24.7	39,091	1,015	1,582.6	45.9	25.4	0.9	3.7	0.1	13.9	10.2
47	41520	Lebanon	39.7	40,888	966	1,029.9	75.4	11.4	0.6	1.5	0.0	4.3	6.9
47	46380	Maryville	17.3	32,263	1,221	1,864.9	86.2	3.0	0.4	2.0	0.0	2.3	6.1
47	48000	Memphis	294.9	628,127	29	2,130.0	25.0	61.6	0.4	1.8	0.0	6.5	4.7
47	50280	Morristown	27.6	30,777	1,281	1,115.1	68.1	5.6	1.2	1.5	0.9	13.4	9.3
47	50780	Mount Juliet	25.5	40,766	968	1,598.7	77.1	8.2	0.3	5.1	0.0	2.5	6.7
47	51560	Murfreesboro	63.4	157,519	164	2,484.5	64.0	19.5	0.5	3.8	0.1	4.3	7.8
47	52004	Nashville-Davidson	475.8	678,851	21	1,426.8	56.0	24.2	0.6	3.9	0.0	7.9	7.5
47	55120	Oak Ridge	85.3	31,824	1,244	373.1	78.6	7.5	0.4	2.6	0.1	2.7	8.0
47	69420	Smyrna	33.2	55,518	713	1,672.2	58.9	16.3	0.6	5.9	0.1	9.2	9.0
47	70580	Spring Hill	27.0	53,339	746	1,975.5	81.4	6.0	0.3	2.2	0.1	2.6	7.5
48	00000	TEXAS	261,263.1	29,527,941	X	113.0	50.1	12.2	1.0	5.4	0.1	13.6	17.6
48	01000	Abilene	106.7	125,070	226	1,172.2	64.9	10.4	0.9	2.2	0.1	9.3	12.2
48	01924	Allen	26.4	106,874	294	4,048.3	53.7	9.8	0.5	21.4	0.1	3.8	10.6
48	02272	Alvin	24.3	27,576	1,410	1,134.8	64.1	4.3	0.8	1.4	0.0	13.5	15.9
48	03000	Amarillo	102.8	201,234	120	1,957.5	61.2	7.3	1.1	4.2	0.0	10.5	15.6
48	04000	Arlington	95.8	392,786	50	4,100.1	40.5	22.9	1.1	7.7	0.1	13.6	14.1

1. Dry land or land partially or temporarily covered by water. 2. Hispanic or Latino persons may be of any race.

City	Percent Hispanic or Latino[1], 2020	Percent foreign born, 2016–2020	Age of population (percent), 2016–2020: Under 18 years	18 to 24 years	25 to 34 years	35 to 44 years	45 to 54 years	55 to 64 years	65 years and over	Median age, 2016–2020	Percent female, 2016–2020	Population: Census counts 2010	Census counts 2020	Percent change 2010–2020	Percent change 2020–2021
	12	13	14	15	16	17	18	19	20	21	22	23	24	25	26
RHODE ISLAND	16.6	14.0	19.4	10.5	13.9	11.7	13.2	14.1	17.3	40.0	51.4	1,052,970	1,097,379	4.2	-0.2
Cranston	18.2	15.0	20.6	8.0	14.5	13.7	12.3	14.5	16.4	39.8	49.8	80,666	82,935	2.8	-0.4
East Providence	7.1	15.4	17.2	7.1	15.9	12.7	12.3	15.6	19.3	41.6	51.2	47,071	47,228	0.3	-0.6
Newport	11.8	6.6	14.7	16.1	18.5	10.1	10.7	11.2	18.7	35.6	51.4	24,924	25,330	1.6	-0.7
Pawtucket	24.8	25.8	20.9	8.4	17.6	13.7	13.6	13.1	12.8	37.2	49.7	71,160	75,842	6.6	-0.6
Providence	43.9	30.2	21.3	16.9	17.4	12.0	11.0	9.8	11.6	31.2	52.1	177,732	190,284	7.1	-0.3
Warwick	6.1	6.7	17.9	6.8	13.4	11.9	13.4	15.7	20.9	45.1	52.9	82,687	82,976	0.3	0.0
Woonsocket	21.0	13.4	22.0	8.0	18.1	11.6	13.1	13.5	13.6	35.9	51.4	41,202	43,322	5.1	-0.5
SOUTH CAROLINA	6.9	5.2	21.8	9.2	13.2	12.1	12.7	13.3	17.7	39.7	51.5	4,625,358	5,118,425	10.7	1.4
Aiken	3.8	2.9	18.5	9.7	12.6	8.2	11.8	13.1	26.1	46.1	53.5	29,609	31,800	7.4	0.3
Anderson	6.2	3.0	22.8	12.8	14.8	9.8	11.3	11.0	17.5	34.7	54.0	26,410	29,170	10.5	0.4
Bluffton	14.6	8.2	25.1	5.4	11.0	16.5	12.7	10.3	19.0	41.2	51.5	13,001	28,121	116.3	14.5
Charleston	4.5	5.1	16.5	12.2	20.9	12.2	10.4	12.4	15.4	35.3	53.1	120,415	150,522	25.0	0.7
Columbia	5.9	5.0	16.4	27.4	17.2	9.9	10.3	8.5	10.2	28.2	49.3	130,550	137,300	5.2	0.2
Florence	2.8	5.1	24.4	6.8	14.1	11.9	12.2	12.2	18.4	39.1	54.7	37,886	39,970	5.5	0.0
Goose Creek	9.5	6.7	23.0	15.1	14.8	12.3	12.7	11.5	10.6	32.4	49.3	36,428	45,533	25.0	1.5
Greenville	7.0	6.9	17.5	11.7	20.7	12.8	11.6	11.3	14.4	35.0	52.5	59,325	70,633	19.1	2.1
Greer	15.9	17.0	27.0	7.1	16.1	15.2	12.8	9.2	12.7	34.9	50.2	25,882	35,367	36.6	9.9
Hilton Head Island	13.4	10.9	12.8	3.7	9.8	7.7	11.0	18.2	36.8	57.9	50.6	37,097	38,191	2.9	-0.3
Mount Pleasant	3.6	5.2	22.9	4.6	14.2	14.5	14.2	12.8	16.7	40.8	50.7	68,400	90,668	32.6	1.9
Myrtle Beach	11.9	12.9	20.2	5.8	13.4	11.4	13.2	15.2	20.9	44.4	51.8	26,950	35,868	33.1	3.4
North Charleston	14.0	10.8	23.8	9.9	19.8	13.2	11.2	11.0	11.1	33.2	50.2	97,591	115,113	18.0	2.0
Rock Hill	7.7	6.1	23.3	12.5	15.7	11.9	11.3	11.1	14.3	34.1	53.9	66,867	73,905	10.5	0.3
Spartanburg	5.9	4.9	22.7	11.3	15.9	11.1	10.4	12.1	16.6	35.1	54.5	36,717	38,567	5.0	-0.4
Summerville	6.3	5.4	24.2	8.9	13.8	13.5	11.4	14.5	13.8	36.7	52.0	42,966	50,933	18.5	0.6
Sumter	4.8	4.7	27.0	11.3	14.9	10.3	10.3	10.8	15.3	31.8	52.4	40,530	43,420	7.1	-1.0
SOUTH DAKOTA	4.4	4.0	24.5	9.5	13.1	11.9	11.0	13.3	16.7	37.2	49.6	814,198	886,667	8.9	1.0
Aberdeen	5.1	6.2	22.0	12.2	14.3	10.8	10.3	12.8	17.6	35.8	51.1	26,112	28,510	9.2	-0.7
Rapid City	5.3	2.6	23.3	8.9	14.6	12.2	10.4	12.3	18.3	37.2	50.0	68,975	74,194	7.6	2.7
Sioux Falls	6.4	9.2	25.0	9.8	16.5	13.3	11.1	11.4	12.9	34.2	50.1	153,976	192,683	25.1	2.0
TENNESSEE	6.9	5.1	22.3	9.1	13.8	12.5	13.0	13.1	16.4	38.8	51.2	6,346,281	6,910,840	8.9	0.9
Bartlett	4.3	6.4	23.3	6.7	10.5	13.5	13.4	14.7	17.8	42.1	51.5	56,938	57,791	1.5	-0.8
Brentwood	3.6	9.0	29.2	7.5	5.0	12.2	18.1	14.4	13.5	42.6	50.5	37,067	45,377	22.4	0.3
Bristol	2.5	2.1	21.2	8.6	14.0	11.0	12.7	14.2	18.3	40.8	52.5	26,765	27,178	1.5	1.3
Chattanooga	9.2	6.7	19.8	10.7	17.0	12.3	10.8	12.9	16.6	36.7	53.0	170,319	181,234	6.4	0.5
Clarksville	11.8	5.8	26.9	11.9	20.8	13.4	9.8	8.7	8.4	30.0	49.8	132,881	166,634	25.4	2.6
Cleveland	11.8	8.6	21.0	15.3	14.5	11.6	11.4	9.6	16.7	34.1	52.9	41,251	47,263	14.6	1.5
Collierville	4.3	11.5	26.8	5.8	10.5	13.0	15.8	13.6	14.5	40.6	51.6	45,599	51,198	12.3	0.3
Columbia	10.7	4.6	25.5	8.4	15.6	12.9	11.3	11.6	14.7	35.5	52.9	34,648	41,556	19.9	4.3
Cookeville	9.9	5.9	18.7	23.4	13.9	11.0	11.0	8.3	13.7	29.9	51.8	31,120	34,438	10.7	2.0
Franklin	8.0	12.2	25.5	6.8	13.1	15.2	14.5	12.2	12.7	37.5	52.1	62,572	83,347	33.2	2.5
Gallatin	9.9	6.2	23.1	7.4	14.6	12.7	12.8	12.8	16.6	38.4	49.9	30,347	44,352	46.1	5.7
Germantown	3.0	8.3	25.5	4.4	7.5	14.1	13.3	13.4	21.7	44.2	51.4	38,835	41,256	6.2	-0.5
Hendersonville	6.4	5.0	22.7	7.3	12.8	13.8	14.3	13.5	15.7	40.1	52.9	51,333	61,756	20.3	0.8
Jackson	5.1	3.4	24.4	11.9	13.0	11.7	10.8	13.0	15.2	35.5	53.8	66,844	68,211	2.0	-0.1
Johnson City	6.3	6.4	18.7	16.2	14.2	12.1	12.0	12.3	14.5	35.6	52.2	63,376	70,588	11.4	1.0
Kingsport	3.1	2.1	19.8	7.0	11.7	11.7	12.3	12.6	25.0	44.9	53.8	53,006	55,444	4.6	0.2
Knoxville	7.9	6.1	18.9	17.6	16.1	11.5	11.3	10.7	13.9	32.9	52.0	178,137	190,011	6.7	1.4
La Vergne	24.3	13.1	29.6	9.0	15.3	13.7	14.5	10.5	7.4	32.0	50.2	32,597	38,783	19.0	0.8
Lebanon	8.6	6.7	23.2	11.1	15.5	13.6	10.3	9.9	16.4	35.1	52.5	26,193	38,204	45.9	7.0
Maryville	5.1	3.7	23.2	10.9	11.0	11.6	14.0	11.1	18.2	40.3	52.9	27,436	31,765	15.8	1.6
Memphis	9.8	6.0	24.8	10.2	16.1	12.1	11.5	12.0	13.4	34.2	52.7	651,874	632,207	-3.0	-0.6
Morristown	25.6	8.9	24.6	8.6	13.2	13.9	11.9	11.3	16.4	37.4	51.9	28,947	30,585	5.7	0.6
Mount Juliet	6.1	9.2	26.4	6.8	11.8	16.0	13.4	11.9	13.6	38.5	50.6	24,783	39,354	58.8	3.6
Murfreesboro	9.1	6.5	23.3	16.8	16.6	14.1	10.9	9.1	9.2	30.6	51.4	109,100	152,437	39.7	3.3
Nashville-Davidson	13.7	12.9	20.8	9.8	20.3	13.7	11.6	11.4	12.3	34.4	51.8	603,465	689,504	14.3	-1.5
Oak Ridge	6.2	7.7	24.5	6.4	13.9	11.4	12.5	13.5	17.7	39.3	51.2	29,328	31,389	7.0	1.4
Smyrna	16.9	10.4	25.9	9.6	16.1	14.1	12.9	10.2	11.0	33.8	50.5	40,420	53,138	31.5	4.5
Spring Hill	7.9	4.5	30.4	7.1	13.3	17.3	13.0	8.2	10.7	34.4	51.5	29,107	50,021	71.9	6.6
TEXAS	39.3	16.8	25.8	9.8	14.7	13.6	12.4	11.2	12.5	34.8	50.3	25,146,072	29,145,505	15.9	1.3
Abilene	26.9	7.1	23.2	15.1	16.3	12.5	9.3	10.5	13.2	32.0	48.6	117,509	124,797	6.2	0.2
Allen	12.6	20.2	27.3	8.6	11.5	15.2	16.6	11.7	9.0	37.0	49.0	84,273	104,786	24.3	2.0
Alvin	37.7	9.2	27.9	10.0	16.0	13.0	11.9	7.9	13.2	32.2	51.2	24,172	27,110	12.2	1.7
Amarillo	32.6	11.9	26.8	8.9	15.5	13.0	10.8	11.1	13.8	34.1	50.7	190,675	200,904	5.4	0.2
Arlington	30.7	20.8	25.8	11.5	15.8	13.0	12.7	10.8	10.5	32.9	51.4	365,125	394,218	8.0	-0.4

1. May be of any race.

City	Households, 2016–2020: Number	Households, 2016–2020: Persons per household	Households, 2016–2020: Percent: Family	Households, 2016–2020: Percent: Married couple family	Households, 2016–2020: Percent: Female family	Households, 2016–2020: Percent: Non-family	Households, 2016–2020: Percent: One person	Persons in group quarters, 2016–2020	Serious crimes known to police[2], 2020: Violent: Number	Serious crimes known to police[2], 2020: Violent: Rate	Serious crimes known to police[2], 2020: Property: Number	Serious crimes known to police[2], 2020: Property: Rate	Educational attainment, 2016–2020: Population age 25 and over	Educational attainment, 2016–2020: Attainment[4] (percent): High school graduate or less	Educational attainment, 2016–2020: Attainment[4] (percent): Bachelor's degree or more
	27	28	29	30	31	32	33	34	35	36	37	38	39	40	41
RHODE ISLAND	414,730	2.45	62.2	44.5	13.0	37.8	30.6	41,441	2,440	230.8	13,166	1,245.5	741,370	38.8	35.0
Cranston	31,362	2.47	62.2	46.3	12.2	37.8	32.2	3,705	111	136.5	858	1,055.2	57,997	38.1	33.9
East Providence	19,988	2.34	57.6	40.6	12.0	42.4	36.9	716	112	235.6	349	734.1	35,911	43.3	31.1
Newport	10,065	2.12	49.5	33.7	11.9	50.5	39.3	3,342	74	305.8	370	1,528.8	17,091	24.0	53.4
Pawtucket	27,903	2.56	61.6	35.2	18.6	38.4	30.9	501	288	399.9	1,496	2,077.3	50,785	51.0	23.1
Providence	64,190	2.57	55.8	31.1	19.2	44.2	33.6	14,551	873	486.1	4,337	2,414.8	110,910	48.5	32.3
Warwick	35,465	2.27	59.6	45.6	9.7	40.4	33.4	550	66	81.9	993	1,231.9	61,055	35.9	32.5
Woonsocket	16,515	2.48	57.5	32.1	19.5	42.5	35.3	736	209	501.3	756	1,813.3	29,125	52.4	17.8
SOUTH CAROLINA	1,961,481	2.53	65.3	47.1	13.9	34.7	29.1	135,224	27,691	530.7	141,987	2,721.1	3,512,626	40.5	29.0
Aiken	13,094	2.29	63.7	46.7	13.8	36.3	32.3	1,496	250	806.3	1,493	4,815.0	22,563	31.2	42.4
Anderson	11,494	2.22	52.6	30.3	17.1	47.4	43.3	1,818	NA	NA	NA	NA	17,643	43.8	23.1
Bluffton	8,504	2.71	72.5	61.3	10.3	27.5	20.4	117	25	90.7	199	722.3	16,107	20.5	46.3
Charleston	57,226	2.29	51.6	40.5	9.0	48.4	35.8	5,743	650	465.7	3,218	2,305.5	97,671	21.8	54.4
Columbia	47,306	2.22	47.7	29.5	14.5	52.3	39.2	29,051	991	752.0	5,898	4,475.7	75,264	29.9	43.4
Florence	15,874	2.39	61.8	40.5	18.9	38.2	34.9	645	562	1,456.1	2,390	6,192.2	26,503	38.6	31.1
Goose Creek	14,460	2.81	74.8	54.8	14.9	25.2	19.9	2,267	NA	NA	NA	NA	26,576	34.6	27.3
Greenville	31,859	2.05	48.3	34.5	10.8	51.7	42.0	4,313	502	697.1	2,929	4,067.3	49,276	26.7	50.8
Greer	11,849	2.70	68.3	50.3	13.4	31.7	26.4	195	97	282.6	1,051	3,062.4	21,239	35.2	35.4
Hilton Head Island	17,910	2.22	62.9	54.3	6.3	37.1	29.8	184	NA	NA	NA	NA	33,397	23.8	53.9
Mount Pleasant	36,407	2.45	65.5	56.4	6.3	34.5	27.6	372	94	99.3	1,257	1,327.3	64,845	12.1	64.2
Myrtle Beach	14,205	2.36	56.2	41.0	10.7	43.8	37.9	140	492	1,379.8	3,108	8,716.1	24,884	38.6	30.4
North Charleston	43,372	2.50	52.8	32.4	16.8	47.2	39.6	5,309	1,345	1,144.7	5,998	5,104.6	75,531	43.7	25.1
Rock Hill	29,353	2.44	58.4	36.5	17.7	41.6	33.1	2,924	NA	NA	NA	NA	47,801	34.4	30.6
Spartanburg	15,319	2.30	55.7	30.9	20.2	44.3	39.0	2,256	536	1,430.5	2,286	6,101.0	24,700	41.4	33.1
Summerville	19,888	2.68	66.3	48.7	13.8	33.7	27.7	302	183	340.7	1,497	2,787.1	35,914	33.0	29.6
Sumter	15,354	2.49	62.9	38.6	19.2	37.1	34.0	1,581	491	1,241.7	1,459	3,689.7	24,515	39.4	25.6
SOUTH DAKOTA	347,878	2.43	62.9	49.4	9.0	37.1	30.6	34,019	4,476	501.4	17,468	1,956.7	580,244	38.0	29.3
Aberdeen	12,187	2.23	54.9	41.8	8.4	45.1	37.6	1,190	159	558.0	666	2,337.3	18,616	36.7	32.9
Rapid City	30,316	2.40	56.4	41.1	11.8	43.6	36.0	3,678	673	857.4	3,137	3,996.6	51,877	33.3	33.5
Sioux Falls	73,818	2.37	59.2	44.0	10.7	40.8	32.7	6,102	1,120	597.7	5,867	3,131.2	117,957	32.7	35.1
TENNESSEE	2,639,455	2.51	65.4	48.2	12.7	34.6	28.6	158,180	46,328	672.7	171,675	2,492.8	4,649,847	43.6	28.2
Bartlett	20,615	2.83	79.5	66.5	9.5	20.5	17.9	859	153	256.2	1,156	1,935.9	41,439	32.3	35.9
Brentwood	14,027	3.04	84.1	76.1	6.5	15.9	14.2	86	19	43.7	332	764.0	27,033	9.0	76.0
Bristol	11,652	2.26	59.7	42.1	14.3	40.3	34.6	619	155	573.8	774	2,865.3	18,924	45.2	27.0
Chattanooga	77,179	2.24	51.7	33.8	14.0	48.3	40.7	8,846	2,504	1,359.3	11,709	6,356.3	126,115	38.9	31.4
Clarksville	57,803	2.64	69.3	49.3	14.6	30.7	24.2	3,450	983	609.9	3,615	2,243.0	95,448	33.6	28.3
Cleveland	16,989	2.47	59.6	41.3	13.9	40.4	32.4	3,219	454	987.1	2,312	5,026.7	28,743	42.1	27.9
Collierville	17,598	2.87	81.5	72.1	6.8	18.5	16.0	104	91	176.1	637	1,232.7	34,054	17.6	57.6
Columbia	15,144	2.54	66.5	43.0	17.7	33.5	28.2	1,057	303	738.8	1,289	3,142.9	26,140	44.6	21.6
Cookeville	13,912	2.23	54.4	37.2	13.0	45.6	33.6	2,839	NA	NA	NA	NA	19,661	42.8	35.1
Franklin	30,847	2.60	71.4	60.3	9.0	28.6	22.5	350	195	227.5	792	923.9	54,562	16.8	62.6
Gallatin	15,459	2.53	68.5	50.2	13.5	31.5	26.9	1,091	137	307.3	439	984.7	27,996	40.0	28.8
Germantown	14,944	2.62	76.3	70.5	4.2	23.7	22.2	101	42	107.0	531	1,352.4	27,463	11.0	66.0
Hendersonville	21,681	2.66	69.6	55.0	10.1	30.4	26.5	186	95	161.3	585	993.2	40,544	29.0	38.4
Jackson	26,027	2.43	60.0	35.6	19.8	40.0	35.0	3,774	703	1,045.6	2,414	3,590.4	42,718	45.2	27.1
Johnson City	29,141	2.16	53.8	37.7	12.7	46.2	36.5	3,957	296	439.9	2,717	4,037.6	43,593	33.3	39.0
Kingsport	23,987	2.20	59.2	40.9	14.4	40.8	34.4	946	372	685.6	2,426	4,471.1	39,298	44.1	28.4
Knoxville	82,088	2.18	48.0	30.5	13.7	52.0	39.9	8,518	1,528	809.9	7,977	4,228.0	119,112	37.6	33.5
La Vergne	11,968	2.97	78.5	53.6	13.7	21.5	17.1	13	187	518.5	619	1,716.3	21,806	41.5	25.0
Lebanon	12,618	2.63	69.1	47.1	15.4	30.9	24.8	1,605	216	570.9	1,059	2,799.2	22,837	42.8	28.8
Maryville	10,937	2.52	66.2	52.1	11.1	33.8	29.9	1,805	64	213.3	324	1,079.8	19,344	34.1	35.7
Memphis	255,756	2.49	55.8	28.5	22.2	44.2	37.9	15,260	15,310	2,352.0	36,197	5,560.8	422,698	43.9	26.6
Morristown	11,757	2.46	56.8	37.3	13.6	43.2	36.2	926	258	850.6	1,290	4,253.2	19,950	58.9	15.1
Mount Juliet	12,998	2.75	75.5	64.8	6.9	24.5	20.6	95	71	183.5	636	1,644.0	23,933	24.7	46.4
Murfreesboro	52,252	2.63	63.0	45.1	13.2	37.0	24.2	4,209	740	487.6	3,772	2,485.4	84,977	28.6	39.3
Nashville-Davidson	289,191	2.31	54.1	37.2	12.7	45.9	35.0	21,402	NA	NA	NA	NA	478,719	31.7	43.3
Oak Ridge	12,073	2.39	63.7	45.4	14.1	36.3	32.0	325	168	576.5	621	2,131.2	20,103	32.2	36.1
Smyrna	18,274	2.76	68.3	46.8	15.6	31.7	25.0	332	204	385.0	1,242	2,344.1	32,734	40.9	26.2
Spring Hill	14,011	2.98	81.1	67.1	10.0	18.9	15.9	58	75	163.9	389	850.0	26,103	21.0	47.4
TEXAS	9,906,070	2.83	69.0	50.2	13.7	31.0	25.3	595,587	131,084	446.5	659,160	2,245.0	18,449,851	40.3	30.7
Abilene	43,607	2.55	64.5	46.1	13.6	35.5	27.6	13,525	514	414.3	2,649	2,135.2	76,957	44.3	24.9
Allen	33,649	3.09	79.9	67.1	9.5	20.1	15.6	208	105	97.0	996	920.4	66,658	17.6	55.3
Alvin	9,710	2.73	71.0	45.2	20.0	29.0	23.0	77	83	307.2	731	2,705.9	16,509	43.3	18.5
Amarillo	76,778	2.57	65.1	46.1	13.4	34.9	30.4	1,867	1,676	836.8	7,369	3,679.1	128,036	43.1	23.3
Arlington	135,240	2.90	68.9	47.4	15.6	31.1	25.2	4,415	2,142	531.9	10,271	2,550.5	249,339	38.4	30.9

2. Data for serious crimes have not been adjusted for underreporting. This may affect comparability between geographic areas and over time. 4. Persons 25 years old and over.

City	Money income, 2016–2020					Median earnings Full year, Full-time workers, 2016–2020			Housing units, 2016–2020				
	Households												
	Median household income	Percent with income less than $25,000	Percent with income of $200,000 or more	Median family income	Median non-family household income	All persons	Men	Women	Total	Occupied	Percent owner occupied	Median value[1] (dollars)	Median gross rent (dollars)
	42	43	44	45	46	47	48	49	50	51	52	53	54
RHODE ISLAND	70,305	18.5	7.7	89,330	39,713	53,847	59,214	48,005	469,289	414,730	61.6	276,600	1,031
Cranston	74,425	16.5	6.7	89,180	39,792	56,582	60,818	50,980	33,284	31,362	67.7	257,400	1,107
East Providence	63,158	23.1	5.0	88,973	28,162	54,160	57,750	51,086	21,243	19,988	61.0	233,100	988
Newport	68,201	18.9	8.3	96,161	48,525	55,864	59,579	51,446	13,029	10,065	43.9	495,000	1,326
Pawtucket	52,902	23.4	2.8	66,544	35,063	42,366	47,469	38,076	30,793	27,903	47.5	213,700	933
Providence	49,065	29.0	5.6	58,607	35,300	42,704	46,542	40,957	74,769	64,190	37.8	225,200	1,015
Warwick	73,285	16.7	6.5	90,027	41,378	56,159	60,412	51,029	37,502	35,465	70.2	238,300	1,168
Woonsocket	44,310	28.2	2.5	55,818	27,722	42,918	47,787	38,775	18,680	16,515	37.2	191,500	921
SOUTH CAROLINA	54,864	22.1	5.1	68,813	32,023	43,174	49,041	38,066	2,319,112	1,961,481	70.1	170,100	918
Aiken	56,202	20.5	6.0	80,874	32,140	47,157	64,278	37,159	14,725	13,094	66.1	199,100	971
Anderson	33,569	35.9	2.5	46,976	23,225	38,019	41,961	34,312	12,847	11,494	47.2	138,000	743
Bluffton	85,844	6.5	9.7	93,695	66,713	52,789	56,212	47,816	9,345	8,504	82.2	299,700	1,761
Charleston	72,071	17.6	10.8	100,187	49,043	52,423	57,140	48,917	65,278	57,226	55.4	349,000	1,318
Columbia	47,416	29.0	6.7	70,539	33,414	43,241	47,431	39,779	55,015	47,306	47.0	186,000	956
Florence	51,073	27.1	4.4	66,039	28,545	42,021	50,474	36,288	18,348	15,874	56.6	155,000	776
Goose Creek	74,730	10.5	5.7	86,094	52,194	48,964	59,395	41,983	15,399	14,460	71.2	199,600	1,353
Greenville	58,259	21.5	10.9	93,087	40,074	50,952	56,831	44,595	35,255	31,859	43.1	332,700	1,013
Greer	65,516	15.7	5.8	78,218	40,659	46,328	52,126	40,388	12,893	11,849	66.7	184,200	945
Hilton Head Island	86,171	13.0	17.5	110,022	56,300	50,166	52,946	44,643	34,665	17,910	80.2	488,000	1,330
Mount Pleasant	104,772	9.3	21.3	134,720	62,401	68,610	81,875	58,401	39,442	36,407	71.8	472,900	1,702
Myrtle Beach	43,378	29.4	4.9	55,714	28,414	34,517	34,762	33,736	25,410	14,205	56.8	237,200	924
North Charleston	47,201	24.9	3.2	60,492	34,757	38,416	43,353	33,855	48,285	43,372	46.9	184,600	1,084
Rock Hill	51,874	21.2	3.7	66,078	34,763	39,592	41,538	37,668	31,259	29,353	51.8	167,600	1,017
Spartanburg	42,841	30.0	3.1	52,304	31,631	40,850	46,192	35,927	17,601	15,319	50.2	133,200	839
Summerville	60,271	16.6	5.0	80,226	37,560	50,324	52,379	44,850	21,671	19,888	64.5	215,800	1,157
Sumter	40,760	31.7	3.2	50,975	22,940	38,319	44,626	33,121	17,891	15,354	50.0	131,800	858
SOUTH DAKOTA	59,896	18.1	4.4	77,042	35,803	44,100	49,603	38,663	396,817	347,878	68.0	174,600	761
Aberdeen	56,455	20.3	3.5	82,123	35,178	44,050	49,741	39,931	13,435	12,187	57.6	169,400	669
Rapid City	53,760	22.1	5.0	72,263	33,536	40,885	45,071	37,491	33,123	30,316	61.0	194,100	855
Sioux Falls	61,738	16.3	4.9	81,770	38,618	45,635	51,003	40,790	78,437	73,818	59.5	205,100	838
TENNESSEE	54,833	21.6	5.1	68,793	32,825	43,502	48,705	39,201	2,996,127	2,639,455	66.5	177,600	897
Bartlett	81,568	8.1	6.5	90,031	52,206	56,586	61,710	51,618	21,452	20,615	85.4	195,900	1,379
Brentwood	160,174	6.4	38.5	184,528	59,873	108,205	139,071	67,145	14,497	14,027	90.3	682,100	2,033
Bristol	42,067	29.0	2.5	57,527	27,345	39,009	42,336	33,065	13,002	11,652	65.6	135,800	709
Chattanooga	47,165	25.1	5.1	65,462	33,688	41,904	46,374	39,331	86,684	77,179	52.8	174,900	891
Clarksville	55,819	17.7	2.6	65,387	35,584	39,980	43,331	36,323	63,968	57,803	54.3	164,800	963
Cleveland	44,542	27.1	3.1	57,657	29,712	36,041	40,013	32,297	18,495	16,989	47.3	175,100	786
Collierville	117,327	6.2	20.4	124,937	63,728	75,881	93,235	60,873	18,284	17,598	78.5	332,900	1,354
Columbia	50,378	22.1	3.4	61,812	33,253	39,768	43,503	36,128	16,964	15,144	61.7	169,200	908
Cookeville	40,836	33.4	2.9	63,542	22,465	39,206	41,713	36,250	15,332	13,912	41.8	170,300	740
Franklin	100,169	9.6	15.9	115,544	57,077	67,724	79,091	56,477	32,382	30,847	65.4	438,800	1,553
Gallatin	60,930	20.7	5.3	72,495	32,151	45,870	49,195	41,304	16,744	15,459	60.4	243,600	1,026
Germantown	123,387	6.2	24.6	141,043	52,307	85,407	101,178	68,029	15,521	14,944	86.4	337,600	1,358
Hendersonville	75,146	9.2	8.8	91,466	48,395	51,945	60,380	45,579	22,794	21,681	71.0	282,000	1,169
Jackson	42,549	32.1	3.6	53,469	29,223	39,683	44,409	34,605	29,843	26,027	52.2	138,900	878
Johnson City	42,174	31.3	5.1	65,512	26,518	39,913	40,641	39,334	32,499	29,141	49.5	170,700	775
Kingsport	42,066	28.8	4.2	59,047	29,455	41,167	50,203	33,055	27,007	23,987	62.1	149,100	666
Knoxville	41,598	30.3	3.0	55,835	30,756	38,192	41,796	35,337	92,394	82,088	46.9	142,700	883
La Vergne	66,360	13.8	3.8	72,656	42,707	44,110	47,632	41,144	12,630	11,968	73.1	184,600	1,299
Lebanon	58,859	19.1	4.9	71,351	30,883	42,242	44,771	38,701	13,540	12,618	57.3	261,400	971
Maryville	66,038	17.8	5.0	85,359	36,167	49,299	55,808	41,623	12,099	10,937	68.2	212,700	882
Memphis	41,864	30.9	4.2	51,954	30,493	38,611	41,370	35,959	299,599	255,756	46.2	107,100	915
Morristown	33,511	37.6	1.4	43,054	21,623	31,318	31,261	31,420	13,161	11,757	48.7	119,500	714
Mount Juliet	93,096	10.6	8.7	107,870	50,244	56,341	62,013	48,957	13,971	12,998	75.2	288,500	1,562
Murfreesboro	60,683	14.8	4.8	79,246	40,495	43,585	49,853	40,455	55,940	52,252	51.9	257,500	1,095
Nashville-Davidson	62,515	17.0	7.2	77,046	47,954	47,051	49,953	44,650	319,739	289,191	54.4	267,400	1,172
Oak Ridge	55,869	18.0	5.4	67,282	35,906	46,200	51,462	41,113	14,152	12,073	60.7	157,700	868
Smyrna	66,003	12.2	2.6	74,647	43,146	45,258	48,825	42,595	19,199	18,274	57.2	211,700	1,104
Spring Hill	90,322	8.6	5.2	100,366	50,705	62,158	70,505	52,165	14,463	14,011	75.0	299,900	1,429
TEXAS	63,826	18.3	7.8	76,073	39,925	47,635	52,184	41,798	11,112,975	9,906,070	62.3	187,200	1,082
Abilene	52,518	21.7	3.0	67,079	30,537	38,233	42,059	33,798	50,003	43,607	54.0	131,300	918
Allen	113,719	5.8	20.6	124,926	68,538	74,860	90,450	59,553	35,339	33,649	73.4	323,500	1,497
Alvin	57,114	18.9	4.1	62,657	40,514	41,862	47,312	37,201	10,775	9,710	56.9	157,700	1,053
Amarillo	52,941	22.3	4.4	64,632	31,663	41,279	46,393	35,567	85,902	76,778	59.1	138,900	876
Arlington	63,351	16.0	5.6	74,135	42,281	44,265	47,024	41,759	146,438	135,240	55.7	188,100	1,089

1. Specified owner-occupied units

City	Commuting, 2016–2020[1]		Computer access[2], 2016–2020		Migration, 2016–2020		Civilian labor force, 2021				Civilian Employment, 2016–2020[4]			
	Percent		Percent						Unemployment[3]		Population age 16 and older		Population age 16 to 64	
	Drove alone	Mean travel time to work	With a computer in the house	With Internet access	Percent who lived in the same house one year ago	Percent who lived in another state or county one year ago	Total	Percent change 2020–2021	Total	Rate	Number	Percent in labor force	Number	Percent who worked full-year full-time
	55	56	57	58	59	60	61	62	63	64	65	66	67	68
RHODE ISLAND	79.7	25.3	90.7	85.8	88.1	5.7	571,034	0.7	32,065	5.6	878,121	64.5	695,635	51.1
Cranston	81.7	23.2	90.1	86.1	90.2	3.5	42,743	0.5	2,451	5.7	66,153	64.7	52,821	52.6
East Providence	81.2	24.2	88.0	81.2	87.2	5.0	24,988	0.6	1,473	5.9	39,849	65.0	30,695	55.8
Newport	60.2	18.4	92.3	86.7	74.2	19.6	13,990	0.9	670	4.8	21,441	57.7	16,833	50.1
Pawtucket	80.0	25.9	89.8	82.9	89.5	3.3	37,615	-0.6	2,447	6.5	58,533	70.5	49,357	54.6
Providence	65.1	24.1	88.0	81.6	82.8	7.4	89,176	-0.4	5,946	6.7	146,037	61.7	125,297	42.6
Warwick	86.2	24.9	90.6	86.5	89.3	6.1	47,137	1.0	2,321	4.9	68,130	65.6	51,162	56.4
Woonsocket	78.7	25.9	90.9	82.9	83.3	6.6	19,674	-0.4	1,416	7.2	33,318	64.7	27,649	47.6
SOUTH CAROLINA	81.5	25.1	90.2	80.7	86.2	7.1	2,364,366	1.4	94,553	4.0	4,111,745	59.5	3,211,049	50.9
Aiken	83.4	23.9	93.4	88.2	82.4	8.5	13,061	0.4	540	4.1	26,156	53.8	17,950	45.5
Anderson	80.5	19.7	87.5	77.1	81.2	7.2	11,393	1.2	502	4.4	21,822	59.1	17,018	46.7
Bluffton	80.8	24.9	99.0	92.8	82.6	9.7	12,928	1.7	387	3.0	18,182	65.6	13,777	57.5
Charleston	76.3	22.9	94.5	83.2	82.3	9.4	74,260	1.9	2,524	3.4	116,546	66.0	95,509	56.9
Columbia	63.4	16.2	93.7	82.8	63.4	25.5	56,789	1.0	2,482	4.4	114,749	56.7	101,052	40.7
Florence	80.8	19.5	87.5	73.8	87.8	3.8	19,398	0.6	783	4.0	30,407	61.5	23,332	55.9
Goose Creek	77.1	25.1	97.3	93.3	78.5	16.5	20,248	3.0	682	3.4	34,167	60.7	29,601	59.6
Greenville	78.4	19.9	90.6	84.6	74.1	11.6	36,610	1.7	1,267	3.5	58,691	68.1	48,662	55.1
Greer	82.4	24.3	93.1	87.5	83.3	10.5	18,041	1.7	530	2.9	24,465	70.2	20,366	59.2
Hilton Head Island	73.9	19.6	96.3	90.3	86.0	6.1	17,045	1.3	510	3.0	35,556	50.9	20,818	53.1
Mount Pleasant	78.4	24.0	96.4	83.1	83.2	5.9	49,369	3.1	1,199	2.4	71,856	67.3	56,939	59.9
Myrtle Beach	80.2	17.6	93.3	81.1	85.4	6.7	15,564	1.1	904	5.8	27,346	59.2	20,309	49.2
North Charleston	80.6	23.8	92.1	73.3	82.2	9.6	56,068	1.9	2,571	4.6	88,923	63.9	76,252	56.7
Rock Hill	80.7	24.4	92.9	86.9	81.3	10.2	39,690	1.3	1,911	4.8	59,085	66.4	48,455	53.5
Spartanburg	81.0	20.5	84.0	75.0	81.4	6.8	16,873	-0.6	955	5.7	29,730	59.3	23,532	45.4
Summerville	86.1	30.2	96.2	87.3	84.0	10.6	24,984	2.9	909	3.6	42,149	65.7	34,759	53.8
Sumter	83.5	19.5	86.3	77.9	80.8	9.3	15,252	-0.7	757	5.0	30,071	53.9	23,970	49.4
SOUTH DAKOTA	80.0	17.3	90.2	82.9	84.9	8.1	468,015	1.4	14,504	3.1	686,885	67.5	540,054	56.8
Aberdeen	82.1	10.9	90.4	81.5	82.4	6.5	14,897	0.1	470	3.2	22,807	68.9	17,835	58.3
Rapid City	81.9	17.4	91.9	84.4	81.6	8.3	38,495	2.3	1,198	3.1	60,443	64.2	46,412	53.8
Sioux Falls	83.5	16.7	94.4	89.0	80.2	9.9	109,138	1.4	3,169	2.9	140,490	73.9	117,169	60.5
TENNESSEE	81.9	25.4	89.1	80.9	85.8	6.4	3,327,966	0.9	142,703	4.3	5,437,242	61.1	4,329,678	51.2
Bartlett	88.1	25.2	95.0	90.9	89.6	3.4	30,904	0.8	1,025	3.3	46,959	61.3	36,399	55.5
Brentwood	79.4	25.8	96.9	95.0	91.0	5.5	22,133	3.6	543	2.5	32,709	64.5	26,926	49.9
Bristol	87.2	21.9	87.6	80.3	86.8	5.7	11,518	-0.5	478	4.2	22,127	57.9	17,200	46.1
Chattanooga	78.6	19.0	87.6	79.7	82.6	7.0	87,879	0.0	4,322	4.9	149,161	62.6	119,085	51.3
Clarksville	85.8	25.3	94.8	88.5	77.8	12.6	63,966	0.5	3,217	5.0	117,858	58.3	104,727	52.1
Cleveland	77.7	19.6	88.2	81.1	79.9	7.6	20,894	-3.7	953	4.6	36,441	61.5	28,904	45.9
Collierville	84.5	26.1	97.0	94.8	87.4	6.5	26,095	1.3	723	2.8	38,795	65.8	31,474	54.3
Columbia	83.8	27.6	92.0	83.0	86.8	8.9	20,327	1.2	1,238	6.1	30,525	63.9	24,713	53.7
Cookeville	84.5	19.8	88.9	79.0	73.6	13.0	14,565	0.8	597	4.1	28,486	59.9	23,832	42.5
Franklin	76.0	25.2	97.0	94.1	82.4	12.3	49,198	3.2	1,170	2.4	62,309	70.0	52,079	58.2
Gallatin	80.1	27.4	90.0	82.5	84.1	9.4	23,462	2.0	947	4.0	31,627	61.9	24,948	54.7
Germantown	83.4	21.6	94.3	91.7	88.9	4.4	19,671	1.4	545	2.8	30,494	62.5	21,998	58.5
Hendersonville	81.8	27.6	95.5	91.1	84.9	8.8	33,699	2.3	1,079	3.2	46,363	69.6	37,283	57.9
Jackson	76.7	17.0	87.3	80.3	86.9	6.8	32,605	-0.4	1,647	5.1	52,364	57.4	42,178	44.0
Johnson City	83.2	18.1	91.1	82.3	77.2	12.3	31,875	1.3	1,137	3.6	55,781	61.7	46,076	46.0
Kingsport	81.9	19.2	87.7	78.8	82.3	8.3	22,583	-1.1	1,057	4.7	44,244	52.5	30,823	47.2
Knoxville	78.1	20.6	90.2	78.8	77.8	9.3	98,002	1.1	3,711	3.8	155,487	63.8	129,482	47.4
La Vergne	82.2	31.5	96.1	86.0	89.8	6.8	19,523	0.7	809	4.1	26,180	74.0	23,546	55.9
Lebanon	77.6	24.7	92.5	83.6	81.2	8.6	18,273	2.0	733	4.0	27,516	62.3	21,832	54.0
Maryville	90.2	21.5	91.7	84.7	88.8	4.3	14,197	1.6	448	3.2	23,946	57.9	18,602	48.4
Memphis	81.6	21.7	84.0	73.3	84.2	3.7	299,438	-0.3	24,477	8.2	506,045	63.0	419,058	48.6
Morristown	85.8	18.8	83.3	75.6	87.9	5.3	11,749	-0.4	528	4.5	23,158	55.4	18,260	43.7
Mount Juliet	79.3	31.1	98.0	92.4	85.2	9.0	21,118	2.0	684	3.2	27,339	70.7	22,466	62.1
Murfreesboro	79.0	27.2	94.9	88.5	78.2	9.9	86,169	2.0	3,105	3.6	112,097	71.4	99,001	53.2
Nashville-Davidson	75.5	25.3	94.0	87.8	81.2	8.1	404,747	1.4	16,991	4.2	560,745	71.8	475,997	56.9
Oak Ridge	82.1	22.5	92.0	86.5	81.2	11.8	14,207	1.4	520	3.7	22,744	58.2	17,592	48.5
Smyrna	83.5	29.2	95.4	89.3	84.4	8.5	29,704	1.2	1,033	3.5	39,043	72.6	33,443	58.3
Spring Hill	81.1	30.3	98.6	96.3	84.1	11.7	25,675	2.7	862	3.4	29,946	73.2	25,463	59.9
TEXAS	78.7	26.6	92.7	84.5	84.8	6.5	14,220,446	2.5	807,410	5.7	22,078,090	64.4	18,484,721	52.4
Abilene	78.3	15.7	91.3	81.7	76.6	11.5	57,264	2.4	2,534	4.4	98,715	58.1	82,287	50.1
Allen	79.3	28.6	99.1	96.9	83.3	7.6	60,874	4.1	2,555	4.2	78,984	72.0	69,573	57.8
Alvin	83.5	31.7	91.8	85.7	84.8	7.4	12,517	1.7	938	7.5	19,799	63.2	16,284	56.5
Amarillo	82.8	18.6	92.3	82.1	82.4	7.9	101,798	2.7	3,914	3.8	151,504	65.5	123,933	56.6
Arlington	80.9	27.2	95.8	87.4	85.8	5.8	213,982	2.4	11,519	5.4	307,858	69.4	266,237	54.2

1. Employed persons. 2. Households. 3. Percent of civilian labor force. 4. Persons 16 years old and over.

City	Value of residential construction authorized by building permits, 2021			Wholesale trade[1], 2017				Retail trade[2], 2017			
	New construction ($1,000)	Number of housing units	Percent single family	Number of establishments	Number of employees	Sales (mil dol)	Annual payroll (mil dol)	Number of establish-ments	Number of employees	Sales (mil dol)	Annual payroll (mil dol)
	69	70	71	72	73	74	75	76	77	78	79
RHODE ISLAND	328,495	1,392	74.2	1,107	16,847	13,636.5	1,042.1	3,769	48,753	13,843.5	1,444.4
Cranston	9,950	50	92.0	122	2,081	1,401.9	138.3	300	5,101	1,283.7	156.8
East Providence	1,576	7	100.0	68	1,363	934.2	92.8	132	1,884	775.6	63.9
Newport	6,992	11	100.0	22	70	123.2	5.1	207	1,482	331.6	39.4
Pawtucket	3,807	31	25.8	64	2,278	1,082.4	93.7	195	1,783	501.9	51.9
Providence	3,915	54	1.9	179	1,926	2,554.8	159.3	649	6,659	1,479.9	171.8
Warwick	9,108	80	50.0	133	1,845	1,056.6	125.5	417	8,259	2,412.3	239.3
Woonsocket	6,015	35	100.0	39	658	296.1	38.7	131	1,372	422.3	47.7
SOUTH CAROLINA	11,652,262	50,690	85.4	4,360	61,421	57,337.4	3,537.8	17,700	253,384	69,980.1	6,205.6
Aiken	48,549	195	100.0	20	94	124.9	5.1	209	3,610	865.9	81.0
Anderson	20,941	169	100.0	25	202	73.1	8.2	243	3,951	812.9	86.8
Bluffton	509,550	1,245	65.9	24	132	77.1	7.1	94	1,292	460.8	41.6
Charleston	192,222	1,469	74.3	138	2,180	2,513.5	158.5	784	11,100	3,703.9	329.5
Columbia	303,808	1,700	47.3	140	3,118	2,507.0	191.3	670	11,864	3,260.1	287.1
Florence	35,905	240	99.2	55	1,006	795.1	54.8	365	6,543	1,671.2	151.2
Goose Creek	75,446	372	100.0	D	D	D	D	83	1,944	501.4	46.6
Greenville	100,642	363	89.0	233	3,016	6,272.3	207.0	684	11,380	3,245.3	306.8
Greer	228,587	1,490	65.6	45	418	223.2	23.4	148	3,210	995.2	90.9
Hilton Head Island	85,708	554	45.7	55	299	142.6	13.4	262	2,722	670.6	72.3
Mount Pleasant	308,083	1,014	68.8	84	428	205.6	25.0	390	6,224	1,573.6	157.6
Myrtle Beach	227,197	691	100.0	82	795	394.3	46.0	668	10,778	2,578.8	250.8
North Charleston	89,212	748	35.3	211	3,594	2,150.9	205.3	570	9,439	2,545.4	239.2
Rock Hill	122,677	680	45.0	80	1,453	1,176.8	88.3	322	5,741	1,424.9	133.7
Spartanburg	9,931	42	100.0	58	432	313.4	25.4	344	6,234	1,424.1	141.6
Summerville	53,518	236	75.0	35	409	504.2	20.4	223	4,891	1,221.5	112.5
Sumter	NA	NA	NA	29	269	109.0	12.6	250	3,754	907.0	85.0
SOUTH DAKOTA	1,565,480	7,917	54.6	1,392	16,630	17,314.3	887.0	3,884	53,134	14,673.7	1,372.0
Aberdeen	8,535	74	75.7	41	714	1,180.7	36.7	160	2,746	736.5	73.5
Rapid City	171,412	1,099	25.5	127	1,514	905.9	77.6	478	8,423	2,566.7	232.6
Sioux Falls	524,969	3,132	41.9	326	5,479	4,037.9	321.9	783	16,116	4,349.4	435.1
TENNESSEE	11,477,551	57,484	64.3	5,864	100,044	111,030.0	5,824.7	22,593	322,218	101,978.3	8,574.3
Bartlett	19,815	58	75.9	61	857	466.3	55.5	127	1,869	667.0	60.4
Brentwood	166,899	147	100.0	67	644	638.0	52.2	169	3,386	1,259.8	111.3
Bristol	4,324	27	100.0	41	303	93.1	12.9	152	2,932	786.9	72.6
Chattanooga	190,683	1,232	46.7	375	5,996	3,883.2	364.4	1,084	20,026	6,223.9	564.4
Clarksville	352,811	3,265	44.5	70	915	400.0	41.9	491	8,241	2,097.8	210.0
Cleveland	75,559	278	91.0	46	556	769.2	41.9	280	4,265	1,149.8	112.5
Collierville	70,716	271	100.0	43	894	804.1	48.8	207	3,877	1,142.6	94.9
Columbia	128,024	1,212	65.7	47	540	256.3	28.3	214	2,597	933.6	77.7
Cookeville	54,356	248	60.5	54	551	311.7	27.1	282	4,187	1,210.8	112.9
Franklin	285,704	1,180	24.8	153	2,437	6,863.7	197.8	481	8,792	2,878.2	269.3
Gallatin	234,284	778	98.1	35	530	691.5	24.8	145	2,411	743.1	67.6
Germantown	NA	NA	NA	33	937	1,143.1	85.9	147	2,120	430.2	49.2
Hendersonville	160,727	454	100.0	53	487	229.0	32.8	203	3,222	839.6	76.4
Jackson	46,751	191	100.0	122	2,199	1,218.7	94.7	439	6,871	1,986.7	174.9
Johnson City	53,005	247	97.6	83	1,527	1,062.8	88.9	436	7,718	2,123.7	187.7
Kingsport	45,501	182	95.1	71	989	492.6	44.1	317	5,487	1,463.5	132.2
Knoxville	166,741	960	27.2	395	6,266	3,640.6	356.8	1,264	21,652	6,318.7	605.9
La Vergne	18,249	103	100.0	62	2,827	12,427.3	191.4	65	898	290.7	34.4
Lebanon	235,812	1,258	100.0	57	1,265	2,091.1	75.3	222	2,979	983.7	82.8
Maryville	33,800	143	100.0	33	334	824.6	19.4	173	2,686	619.9	63.5
Memphis	NA	NA	NA	906	22,618	25,130.2	1,282.4	2,306	35,216	18,895.6	973.1
Morristown	57,902	510	85.9	40	788	753.7	38.0	249	4,054	1,153.4	105.7
Mount Juliet	231,350	609	100.0	21	280	147.9	16.7	152	2,666	641.2	59.3
Murfreesboro	552,888	2,376	86.9	101	974	740.4	55.2	575	11,809	3,738.5	328.0
Nashville-Davidson	1,936,711	16,137	24.4	907	18,710	17,092.0	1,243.1	2,426	36,463	10,889.1	1,056.4
Oak Ridge	34,904	303	37.0	27	203	923.4	11.4	107	1,535	420.2	38.1
Smyrna	88,414	453	64.0	29	860	1,464.3	51.5	157	2,569	609.8	58.7
Spring Hill	98,070	926	68.6	D	D	D	8.3	89	1,613	378.0	39.3
TEXAS	52,319,224	265,955	67.5	28,861	435,728	779,742.5	27,818.6	80,874	1,304,540	417,231.9	36,627.8
Abilene	147,725	869	56.6	D	D	D	D	503	7,962	2,321.7	208.2
Allen	269,339	1,711	33.0	D	D	D	59.6	325	6,374	1,380.4	130.2
Alvin	70,038	345	100.0	D	D	D	18.6	107	1,969	816.0	64.6
Amarillo	133,003	574	94.4	211	3,039	3,151.0	172.5	777	13,450	3,663.7	346.0
Arlington	311,581	2,226	43.8	332	5,236	3,938.7	326.0	1,196	21,315	6,710.0	596.0

1. Merchant wholesalers except manufacturers' sales branches and offices. 2. Establishments with payroll.

City	Real estate and rental and leasing, 2017				Professional, scientific, and technical services[1], 2017				Manufacturing, 2017			
	Number of establish-ments	Number of employees	Receipts (mil dol)	Annual payroll (mil dol)	Number of establish-ments	Number of employees	Receipts (mil dol)	Annual payroll (mil dol)	Number of establish-ments	Number of employees	Receipts (mil dol)	Annual payroll (mil dol)
	80	81	82	83	84	85	86	87	88	89	90	91
RHODE ISLAND	1,110	5,287	1,351.1	247.7	3,026	23,910	4,043.5	1,565.7	1,340	40,221	12,416.3	2,390.2
Cranston	83	333	85.2	15.8	227	1,775	337.2	102.7	NA	NA	NA	NA
East Providence	47	231	46.3	11.1	130	1,099	191.6	68.1	NA	NA	NA	NA
Newport	51	275	50.0	12.2	125	677	124.1	44.8	NA	NA	NA	NA
Pawtucket	64	225	51.6	11.3	111	819	117.3	46.7	NA	NA	NA	NA
Providence	213	1,354	353.6	67.5	792	6,865	1,354.8	552.0	NA	NA	NA	NA
Warwick	118	939	252.2	42.1	353	3,072	333.7	131.2	NA	NA	NA	NA
Woonsocket	35	135	25.9	5.7	39	302	71.4	25.1	NA	NA	NA	NA
SOUTH CAROLINA	5,890	26,764	6,509.7	1,128.5	10,859	100,377	17,037.8	6,497.6	3,827	225,237	138,586.5	12,777.4
Aiken	45	162	31.9	5.5	112	1,291	206.4	91.0	NA	NA	NA	NA
Anderson	55	162	36.5	5.2	124	711	76.0	28.6	NA	NA	NA	NA
Bluffton	44	118	26.4	5.1	100	491	89.4	31.4	NA	NA	NA	NA
Charleston	434	1,617	397.8	100.0	855	6,668	1,193.8	490.2	NA	NA	NA	NA
Columbia	254	1,548	753.1	93.0	825	8,579	1,684.3	586.6	NA	NA	NA	NA
Florence	64	304	67.2	13.3	140	1,111	180.4	55.6	NA	NA	NA	NA
Goose Creek	27	105	41.2	4.1	65	838	143.8	60.3	NA	NA	NA	NA
Greenville	333	1,878	372.5	81.9	954	15,341	3,704.0	1,296.4	NA	NA	NA	NA
Greer	42	162	35.7	5.1	87	638	98.4	36.7	NA	NA	NA	NA
Hilton Head Island	252	1,119	276.3	52.7	249	982	170.6	62.5	NA	NA	NA	NA
Mount Pleasant	323	818	240.2	36.4	530	3,244	704.5	274.9	NA	NA	NA	NA
Myrtle Beach	242	1,712	317.7	64.9	258	1,452	211.1	77.0	NA	NA	NA	NA
North Charleston	191	1,412	450.5	60.9	376	7,183	1,375.2	534.3	NA	NA	NA	NA
Rock Hill	106	433	112.6	19.6	173	1,204	155.8	62.8	NA	NA	NA	NA
Spartanburg	91	403	193.0	14.6	187	1,269	197.5	78.0	NA	NA	NA	NA
Summerville	84	305	83.4	10.8	142	1,498	153.8	54.1	NA	NA	NA	NA
Sumter	52	271	39.8	7.7	100	581	60.1	19.2	NA	NA	NA	NA
SOUTH DAKOTA	1,143	4,330	829.0	155.0	1,967	13,063	1,763.4	654.9	1,051	42,935	16,779.5	2,057.4
Aberdeen	54	280	48.7	10.7	54	340	43.6	15.9	NA	NA	NA	NA
Rapid City	193	598	155.6	20.1	273	1,863	255.9	91.4	NA	NA	NA	NA
Sioux Falls	297	1,649	357.0	75.1	577	5,461	764.4	303.2	NA	NA	NA	NA
TENNESSEE	6,048	36,212	10,679.1	1,759.7	11,411	116,205	18,739.1	7,661.2	5,811	321,195	155,422.4	17,021.9
Bartlett	36	189	175.4	7.4	115	2,305	163.6	74.0	NA	NA	NA	NA
Brentwood	125	674	240.7	49.4	333	4,095	796.0	329.0	NA	NA	NA	NA
Bristol	36	99	21.0	3.5	65	624	71.6	34.4	NA	NA	NA	NA
Chattanooga	316	1,802	581.4	111.1	650	7,162	1,210.8	455.5	NA	NA	NA	NA
Clarksville	162	728	154.8	23.4	174	1,777	207.2	78.4	NA	NA	NA	NA
Cleveland	59	212	50.8	8.2	114	652	76.8	26.3	NA	NA	NA	NA
Collierville	48	170	62.2	7.9	107	482	59.6	21.9	NA	NA	NA	NA
Columbia	50	199	45.2	5.8	59	471	58.5	25.5	NA	NA	NA	NA
Cookeville	53	207	48.2	7.0	102	594	71.0	23.6	NA	NA	NA	NA
Franklin	163	804	1,097.8	56.4	480	5,922	978.2	438.5	NA	NA	NA	NA
Gallatin	47	618	172.9	44.9	63	444	41.2	16.6	NA	NA	NA	NA
Germantown	45	325	275.0	28.5	110	602	86.8	35.0	NA	NA	NA	NA
Hendersonville	85	312	97.1	13.5	126	2,199	246.4	114.8	NA	NA	NA	NA
Jackson	105	513	103.2	19.1	146	1,117	133.8	55.0	NA	NA	NA	NA
Johnson City	117	737	128.0	24.5	155	1,070	134.4	51.2	NA	NA	NA	NA
Kingsport	60	311	64.3	8.5	123	834	105.7	35.1	NA	NA	NA	NA
Knoxville	389	2,840	648.4	126.2	732	6,824	936.5	403.3	NA	NA	NA	NA
La Vergne	17	108	45.4	7.0	22	858	26.1	45.6	NA	NA	NA	NA
Lebanon	58	259	83.8	13.3	91	478	63.6	19.9	NA	NA	NA	NA
Maryville	37	120	31.0	3.4	D	D	D	D	NA	NA	NA	NA
Memphis	753	7,045	1,629.8	366.6	1,243	14,880	2,337.0	964.3	NA	NA	NA	NA
Morristown	D	D	D	D	58	233	28.7	12.4	NA	NA	NA	NA
Mount Juliet	42	D	53.9	D	61	632	115.1	33.5	NA	NA	NA	NA
Murfreesboro	169	1,164	326.3	51.5	D	D	D	D	NA	NA	NA	NA
Nashville-Davidson	1,032	8,141	2,738.3	458.6	2,094	29,524	5,523.6	2,329.4	NA	NA	NA	NA
Oak Ridge	40	134	31.8	5.6	153	8,104	2,163.8	771.8	NA	NA	NA	NA
Smyrna	43	179	81.1	10.3	48	730	125.7	51.5	NA	NA	NA	NA
Spring Hill	26	115	46.8	5.1	46	156	19.3	7.1	NA	NA	NA	NA
TEXAS	32,290	198,712	56,443.4	10,559.8	70,033	735,744	150,903.3	59,488.2	19,844	758,722	575,217.8	48,003.6
Abilene	167	776	187.1	31.1	256	1,600	211.9	83.7	NA	NA	NA	NA
Allen	106	347	132.7	16.7	372	1,706	303.5	119.9	NA	NA	NA	NA
Alvin	41	297	42.8	16.3	31	188	34.1	8.7	NA	NA	NA	NA
Amarillo	289	1,246	270.5	51.3	478	2,665	391.9	160.3	NA	NA	NA	NA
Arlington	370	2,014	540.9	96.6	784	6,083	1,073.3	371.6	NA	NA	NA	NA

1. Establishments subject to federal tax.

City	Accommodation and food services, 2017				Arts, entertainment, and recreation[1], 2017				Health care and social assistance[1], 2017			
	Number of establish-ments	Number of employees	Receipts (mil dol)	Annual payroll (mil dol)	Number of establish-ments	Number of employees	Receipts (mil dol)	Annual payroll (mil dol)	Number of establish-ments	Number of employees	Receipts (mil dol)	Annual payroll (mil dol)
	92	93	94	95	96	97	98	99	100	101	102	103
RHODE ISLAND	3,167	50,642	3,617.9	1,016.4	575.0	8,673	739.5	219.4	3,177	87,546	9,574.0	4,092.1
Cranston	209	3,249	196.0	55.5	D	D	D	D	293	5,980	472.6	229.7
East Providence	D	D	D	D	26.0	546	29.7	11.5	160	4,521	407.3	209.6
Newport	192	3,595	377.7	113.1	46.0	619	100.5	24.3	62	1,726	184.8	76.5
Pawtucket	D	D	D	D	21.0	448	31.2	11.7	160	4,131	358.0	149.8
Providence	642	11,268	770.9	227.2	60.0	2,110	164.4	48.4	577	29,944	4,426.6	1,785.4
Warwick	258	5,497	334.8	94.3	41.0	746	45.9	14.8	357	8,635	983.5	449.1
Woonsocket	85	1,200	62.6	17.5	7.0	107	7.4	2.2	139	4,136	376.2	166.3
SOUTH CAROLINA	10,847	223,081	13,385.0	3,666.5	1,687.0	28,317	1,880.7	541.6	10,588	244,198	29,454.9	11,050.5
Aiken	158	3,200	164.1	47.8	27.0	350	30.2	8.1	205	4,442	462.8	169.4
Anderson	155	2,959	151.7	42.5	13.0	327	8.6	2.7	189	5,932	763.8	254.7
Bluffton	64	1,817	107.7	36.7	D	D	D	D	89	1,305	105.7	46.1
Charleston	641	16,356	1,263.9	349.8	122.0	2,001	185.4	49.6	540	17,068	3,281.1	1,071.1
Columbia	573	13,902	729.8	205.7	60.0	766	56.6	14.6	563	24,289	3,736.4	1,365.9
Florence	211	4,806	249.3	73.9	16.0	330	11.5	5.9	267	12,687	1,817.8	669.4
Goose Creek	74	1,570	75.1	20.7	6.0	103	4.6	1.3	52	562	49.0	18.5
Greenville	471	12,028	737.2	212.1	69.0	1,338	99.8	28.5	478	16,083	1,672.0	735.6
Greer	99	1,843	95.8	25.2	11.0	73	4.2	1.2	82	1,403	141.9	57.0
Hilton Head Island	259	6,802	586.9	171.5	61.0	1,358	98.1	29.7	186	2,655	354.1	110.7
Mount Pleasant	254	5,290	330.1	94.0	81.0	913	63.3	17.4	D	D	D	D
Myrtle Beach	585	15,481	1,195.2	288.8	100.0	2,325	215.0	48.4	260	3,600	782.7	211.0
North Charleston	363	8,051	521.6	135.2	24.0	852	28.8	9.5	363	8,192	1,215.7	402.5
Rock Hill	199	5,221	267.4	75.5	28.0	369	23.5	5.8	298	7,059	860.1	283.4
Spartanburg	216	4,658	257.9	73.6	23.0	301	10.5	3.5	208	9,385	1,049.0	577.7
Summerville	167	3,571	191.3	54.3	D	D	D	D	190	3,165	315.6	119.4
Sumter	140	2,999	148.2	40.6	10.0	223	7.1	2.7	162	4,648	578.3	185.8
SOUTH DAKOTA	2,495	40,704	2,315.5	659.2	697.0	6,799	540.7	129.5	2,420	71,821	8,714.4	3,458.2
Aberdeen	88	1,873	96.1	28.8	27.0	270	11.1	3.4	102	3,072	357.0	145.2
Rapid City	263	6,179	348.3	106.5	86.0	659	51.2	13.0	365	10,448	1,443.2	540.3
Sioux Falls	466	11,856	660.6	192.3	159.0	2,761	174.0	43.5	560	29,192	3,927.9	1,597.1
TENNESSEE	13,518	287,534	17,181.8	4,839.4	2,824.0	37,967	5,036.9	1,719.9	15,891	414,598	52,088.8	20,219.5
Bartlett	98	1,613	89.9	23.3	16.0	163	10.7	5.0	134	4,208	393.7	144.9
Brentwood	115	2,905	192.5	49.9	64.0	931	85.3	29.7	261	7,021	968.5	439.6
Bristol	101	2,124	95.7	26.8	17.0	254	68.4	10.0	134	3,617	540.6	202.7
Chattanooga	730	17,030	1,023.3	287.6	110.0	2,533	149.9	46.9	915	27,089	3,481.5	1,389.5
Clarksville	350	7,637	373.7	107.1	38.0	407	17.1	5.1	335	8,076	813.8	348.6
Cleveland	182	3,941	202.0	56.7	D	D	D	D	211	4,578	584.6	200.7
Collierville	124	2,595	142.7	39.7	D	D	D	D	119	1,715	190.6	74.6
Columbia	101	2,042	101.5	30.7	12.0	106	8.2	2.0	181	4,691	521.6	210.8
Cookeville	154	3,745	189.7	55.8	17.0	203	7.4	2.0	217	5,820	552.7	234.4
Franklin	321	8,352	540.3	153.6	176.0	1,379	175.5	44.6	387	8,667	1,093.3	436.3
Gallatin	84	1,658	89.6	25.4	16.0	181	15.6	5.0	120	2,937	345.8	119.8
Germantown	89	2,112	118.5	35.9	D	D	D	D	213	7,539	1,347.4	496.7
Hendersonville	123	2,797	158.9	47.1	D	D	D	D	188	2,791	382.3	133.1
Jackson	216	5,218	270.5	76.6	26.0	330	16.8	5.2	320	13,468	1,474.8	603.7
Johnson City	269	6,674	322.5	96.7	32.0	261	15.7	4.8	334	13,174	1,722.0	764.3
Kingsport	210	4,926	246.5	71.4	22.0	383	11.1	4.3	277	7,487	1,030.0	395.1
Knoxville	777	19,947	1,110.2	339.0	108.0	1,985	128.7	35.3	969	32,083	4,216.3	1,582.8
La Vergne	35	531	31.5	8.1	D	D	D	0.1	21	174	19.5	4.5
Lebanon	123	2,597	145.4	40.6	16.0	124	9.3	2.8	170	2,573	306.3	109.4
Maryville	87	1,866	97.3	28.5	12.0	85	4.0	1.1	162	4,624	494.5	202.1
Memphis	1,399	31,459	1,857.8	529.7	148.0	4,111	447.3	225.0	1,667	55,489	7,615.4	2,872.2
Morristown	D	D	D	D	D	D	D	D	169	4,246	416.4	159.1
Mount Juliet	102	2,340	129.6	41.6	15.0	177	10.5	2.7	103	1,060	104.9	40.8
Murfreesboro	397	9,538	495.8	150.5	46.0	624	28.5	8.7	446	11,923	1,492.2	579.3
Nashville-Davidson	1,982	50,360	3,954.7	1,071.8	827.0	9,720	2,700.0	951.0	1,912	75,503	12,112.0	4,645.1
Oak Ridge	75	1,567	82.9	23.9	11.0	130	5.9	2.1	152	3,707	451.5	164.9
Smyrna	123	2,887	168.3	45.3	14.0	270	12.9	3.5	148	2,214	316.8	97.9
Spring Hill	78	1,814	80.8	26.9	11.0	76	3.1	1.2	65	677	61.6	23.0
TEXAS	57,098	1,201,419	74,369.4	20,610.6	7,620.0	153,566	14,841.6	4,513.5	69,952	1,581,577	186,108.7	69,899.0
Abilene	295	6,704	345.9	102.4	D	D	D	D	382	11,855	1,311.6	505.9
Allen	214	4,572	272.7	77.8	35.0	672	33.2	10.3	363	3,832	441.7	155.8
Alvin	77	1,360	76.5	21.8	7.0	122	5.2	1.5	59	1,054	59.9	28.3
Amarillo	530	11,165	632.4	169.3	68.0	957	51.3	16.5	679	17,186	2,233.3	795.6
Arlington	774	19,755	1,232.9	327.2	85.0	5,408	796.5	272.6	1,011	22,351	2,502.4	981.7

1. Establishments subject to federal tax.

City	Other services[1]				Government employment and payroll, 2017								
						March payroll							
							Perent of total for:						
	Number of establish-ments	Number of employees	Receipts (mil dol)	Annual payroll (mil dol)	Full-time equivalent employees	Total (dollars)	Admin-istrative, judicial, and legal	Police and corrections	Fire protection	Highways and trans-portation	Health and welfare	Natural resources and utilities	Education and libraries
	104	105	106	107	108	109	110	111	112	113	114	115	116
RHODE ISLAND	2,318	13,882	1,772.9	471.0	X	X	X	X	X	X	X	X	X
Cranston	181	1,300	136.6	47.5	2,260	12,721,944	2.0	7.1	9.3	1.7	1.1	0.8	76.5
East Providence	103	576	59.9	18.2	1,176	5,613,335	3.9	9.4	8.4	3.5	0.6	5.0	68.8
Newport	80	552	39.5	15.4	733	4,389,852	5.1	16.8	14.3	2.2	0.8	9.4	51.2
Pawtucket	140	787	75.0	22.0	1,646	9,798,066	3.3	7.3	10.2	0.7	0.2	3.7	73.7
Providence	421	3,336	529.5	130.7	4,460	27,543,641	4.4	13.6	13.1	1.6	1.2	7.2	58.1
Warwick	229	1,598	212.1	54.4	2,411	13,058,247	3.0	10.9	13.1	2.2	0.7	3.6	64.0
Woonsocket	62	242	23.7	6.7	1,220	6,074,841	2.3	9.6	10.0	2.5	0.7	2.3	71.6
SOUTH CAROLINA	7,068	46,847	5,653.1	1,528.9	X	X	X	X	X	X	X	X	X
Aiken	70	366	39.8	9.6	380	1,309,295	17.3	36.2	4.4	23.2	0.0	18.6	0.0
Anderson	72	444	35.9	12.0	458	1,433,486	12.4	30.6	14.0	4.1	1.1	30.3	0.0
Bluffton	D	D	D	D	120	595,675	32.9	45.8	0.0	2.9	0.6	4.8	0.0
Charleston	320	2,118	347.2	74.1	2,017	8,885,603	9.7	29.2	19.7	2.8	0.5	36.0	0.0
Columbia	358	3,793	406.7	123.1	2,387	8,437,005	13.1	19.3	24.7	7.8	3.1	27.1	0.0
Florence	90	694	74.0	18.9	483	1,631,926	11.0	26.8	16.8	7.1	2.7	33.3	0.0
Goose Creek	48	282	35.1	8.3	261	1,051,887	14.5	35.9	21.6	3.7	0.0	20.1	0.0
Greenville	262	1,810	390.2	61.4	1,090	4,394,459	9.2	17.3	14.9	5.4	1.5	42.0	0.0
Greer	61	341	47.5	11.9	201	750,291	19.0	37.1	19.5	5.3	0.0	11.8	0.0
Hilton Head Island	133	1,144	142.8	42.6	241	1,412,148	20.9	0.0	54.8	2.2	13.1	1.7	0.0
Mount Pleasant	190	1,122	97.2	34.0	576	2,297,312	20.1	29.1	22.7	2.1	0.0	23.1	0.0
Myrtle Beach	186	1,284	161.4	36.3	941	3,847,183	11.3	31.4	19.4	7.4	0.3	23.5	2.2
North Charleston	235	2,101	281.0	87.9	1,139	4,423,364	11.2	38.6	22.7	5.8	0.2	14.7	0.0
Rock Hill	118	865	105.5	31.0	889	3,624,179	24.2	21.2	13.9	2.5	8.3	29.0	0.0
Spartanburg	129	1,077	140.1	32.6	598	2,385,343	8.6	23.3	11.2	2.7	1.9	43.7	0.0
Summerville	117	669	56.2	20.9	419	1,532,008	8.7	31.0	21.9	7.4	0.0	21.5	0.0
Sumter	81	541	49.9	13.6	570	1,922,091	13.7	24.8	18.4	2.3	1.8	25.3	0.0
SOUTH DAKOTA	1,860	8,713	1,224.4	277.6	X	X	X	X	X	X	X	X	X
Aberdeen	65	296	28.3	7.8	292	1,227,627	9.9	21.1	17.4	15.0	0.0	30.7	4.5
Rapid City	257	1,486	174.5	47.9	972	3,985,284	6.4	19.8	19.1	15.6	0.3	30.0	3.4
Sioux Falls	368	2,769	401.9	96.7	1,310	6,656,200	14.3	23.7	16.3	10.0	8.2	19.3	4.7
TENNESSEE	8,570	61,744	8,650.0	2,149.1	X	X	X	X	X	X	X	X	X
Bartlett	D	D	D	18.4	565	2,426,976	15.2	29.5	20.5	6.6	1.2	19.6	0.0
Brentwood	110	904	137.7	37.2	273	1,548,644	19.2	27.9	30.0	6.4	0.0	11.3	5.2
Bristol	52	276	32.2	9.1	906	3,310,594	4.7	11.0	6.2	3.8	0.2	7.9	63.5
Chattanooga	464	3,310	497.9	119.2	3,216	13,851,575	7.3	16.4	12.1	11.9	4.6	41.4	1.8
Clarksville	D	D	D	D	1,062	3,844,522	7.4	32.3	23.3	14.7	0.6	18.7	0.0
Cleveland	D	D	D	D	1,072	4,229,059	2.1	9.9	17.4	4.8	1.2	2.7	60.1
Collierville	70	509	36.4	12.3	501	2,125,507	17.9	29.8	19.9	6.9	0.8	19.1	0.0
Columbia	D	D	D	D	501	2,162,900	7.1	18.0	18.8	5.3	0.0	44.4	0.0
Cookeville	D	D	D	12.7	2,932	11,250,845	1.3	1.8	1.9	1.2	87.0	5.9	0.0
Franklin	197	1,716	152.9	55.8	720	3,140,176	14.1	20.1	26.1	5.7	0.0	19.6	0.0
Gallatin	75	390	53.1	14.2	465	1,858,965	10.3	20.0	18.0	3.7	0.0	40.0	0.0
Germantown	72	575	46.3	15.6	428	2,182,982	10.9	33.0	23.7	9.3	6.0	15.6	0.0
Hendersonville	102	540	57.5	17.2	338	1,603,915	10.1	35.4	37.5	3.5	0.4	5.0	0.0
Jackson	D	D	D	23.2	808	3,216,351	9.7	35.4	25.6	9.8	0.3	16.5	0.0
Johnson City	161	920	74.1	22.1	2,115	8,311,535	4.7	8.0	6.6	7.3	0.4	23.9	47.6
Kingsport	110	960	107.2	37.7	1,935	7,226,954	6.5	8.5	6.8	2.7	0.4	13.3	61.0
Knoxville	493	3,430	483.1	111.1	2,530	12,561,702	6.6	19.5	11.9	3.9	0.8	53.5	0.0
La Vergne	27	868	114.3	45.4	212	793,706	12.9	37.3	19.0	3.4	0.0	16.5	3.2
Lebanon	78	1,065	133.6	44.5	510	1,431,893	14.2	22.4	14.7	6.5	3.9	38.2	0.0
Maryville	72	375	41.0	11.3	937	4,626,698	5.0	7.6	4.0	3.9	0.0	13.9	64.8
Memphis	904	8,775	2,537.5	395.4	10,740	51,032,329	4.9	26.4	16.9	5.0	1.3	41.4	1.6
Morristown	73	449	34.3	11.3	464	2,152,548	6.8	17.2	15.1	7.8	0.0	43.9	0.0
Mount Juliet	63	436	42.5	15.6	166	686,313	14.0	41.0	12.2	7.6	0.0	14.3	0.0
Murfreesboro	231	1,510	149.0	47.3	2,460	9,533,413	4.0	14.7	9.0	3.2	0.1	19.1	49.4
Nashville-Davidson	1,293	13,383	1,681.5	479.3	21,283	101,098,567	6.3	14.3	6.5	1.1	6.4	14.5	48.8
Oak Ridge	58	268	21.6	6.8	1,068	4,685,105	7.1	6.8	7.0	0.9	0.0	10.5	66.6
Smyrna	D	D	D	D	398	1,846,459	18.2	26.3	24.5	1.9	0.0	25.6	0.0
Spring Hill	42	233	23.6	6.3	224	834,881	8.4	29.3	27.1	7.0	0.0	19.4	4.4
TEXAS	37,506	285,777	39,008.3	10,468.1	X	X	X	X	X	X	X	X	X
Abilene	D	D	D	D	1,201	5,368,188	10.4	31.9	22.2	4.8	5.8	18.2	1.8
Allen	118	912	84.1	29.2	770	3,819,781	10.4	27.7	21.8	2.6	4.9	25.2	3.8
Alvin	43	274	42.9	10.2	227	895,337	15.6	39.7	2.5	10.3	10.5	13.8	0.0
Amarillo	376	2,926	358.7	95.5	1,992	8,436,582	7.0	32.1	22.7	7.2	5.7	17.8	2.2
Arlington	476	3,291	659.1	102.9	2,558	13,968,727	12.5	39.5	21.2	5.3	4.9	14.5	1.2

1. Establishments subject to federal tax.

City	City government finances, 2017									
	General revenue							General expenditure		
		Intergovernmental		Taxes						
					Per capita[1] (dollars)				Per capita[1] (dollars)	
	Total (mil dol)	Total (mil dol)	Percent from state government	Total (mil dol)	Total	Property	Sales and gross receipts	Total (mil dol)	Total	Capital outlays
	117	118	119	120	121	122	123	124	125	126
RHODE ISLAND	X	X	X	X	X	X	X	X	X	X
Cranston	332.8	96.2	87.6	190.1	2,346	2,309	37	306.0	3,777	209
East Providence	121.8	53.9	96.7	45.7	966	943	22	174.6	3,686	132
Newport	140.5	26.4	92.9	78.9	3,199	2,958	241	146.8	5,955	1,028
Pawtucket	236.7	122.6	95.0	104.2	1,456	1,442	13	239.4	3,343	193
Providence	898.0	401.5	93.5	371.9	2,075	1,986	88	790.6	4,411	148
Warwick	337.8	55.9	96.2	240.3	2,974	2,888	86	334.7	4,141	181
Woonsocket	176.1	86.4	95.2	65.1	1,567	1,511	56	162.0	3,903	229
SOUTH CAROLINA	X	X	X	X	X	X	X	X	X	X
Aiken	49.4	1.9	50.1	28.8	936	352	391	44.4	1,445	145
Anderson	44.7	2.7	20.5	22.0	808	475	333	39.5	1,448	92
Bluffton	25.1	2.4	67.4	18.9	919	348	572	23.4	1,139	305
Charleston	262.8	12.4	45.3	176.6	1,302	563	739	176.9	1,304	117
Columbia	262.9	66.2	40.5	98.9	738	299	440	309.0	2,306	614
Florence	54.7	3.4	49.5	28.6	742	94	647	66.3	1,719	684
Goose Creek	24.8	1.2	3.3	18.7	448	80	367	23.5	563	71
Greenville	181.3	8.3	100.0	92.9	1,357	682	675	120.2	1,755	201
Greer	37.6	3.1	26.0	22.8	735	373	362	31.1	1,002	76
Hilton Head Island	73.0	1.8	57.9	59.3	1,476	596	881	63.2	1,572	349
Mount Pleasant	146.0	7.3	57.7	88.5	1,014	447	564	145.8	1,670	714
Myrtle Beach	211.7	18.1	76.5	111.3	3,409	1,004	2,405	133.5	4,089	352
North Charleston	148.4	9.4	31.1	122.0	1,101	549	497	134.6	1,214	193
Rock Hill	105.3	11.1	22.6	45.2	616	379	238	102.3	1,394	317
Spartanburg	68.0	23.8	10.1	36.1	963	487	476	42.6	1,138	63
Summerville	39.8	3.9	77.4	27.7	537	246	291	35.3	684	81
Sumter	61.5	6.9	23.6	28.4	715	244	471	48.0	1,209	168
SOUTH DAKOTA	X	X	X	X	X	X	X	X	X	X
Aberdeen	45.9	8.4	13.9	28.3	992	296	696	32.6	1,144	0
Rapid City	146.3	13.5	53.6	85.5	1,137	212	925	96.2	1,278	104
Sioux Falls	292.5	18.1	50.7	204.6	1,152	324	828	270.6	1,523	550
TENNESSEE	X	X	X	X	X	X	X	X	X	X
Bartlett	65.4	23.9	40.6	23.8	403	320	84	66.0	1,116	224
Brentwood	58.7	25.6	37.8	19.9	468	273	194	51.3	1,204	285
Bristol	114.3	57.2	43.5	37.0	1,379	1,252	127	75.3	2,804	156
Chattanooga	533.7	132.3	32.3	168.7	940	760	180	391.0	2,178	187
Clarksville	158.6	54.0	69.4	42.1	275	221	54	123.3	806	100
Cleveland	138.1	89.8	50.5	28.2	633	543	90	136.6	3,069	837
Collierville	68.5	5.8	100.0	46.5	925	510	414	45.6	908	64
Columbia	61.0	16.8	9.1	16.4	426	290	136	52.2	1,361	87
Cookeville	306.3	19.4	36.1	14.3	429	299	130	316.2	9,463	494
Franklin	128.0	55.8	41.4	30.3	387	230	157	91.3	1,167	86
Gallatin	59.2	31.7	58.4	16.6	443	326	117	39.7	1,061	103
Germantown	68.7	17.3	45.7	32.6	834	740	94	59.4	1,518	122
Hendersonville	44.9	15.1	48.4	22.4	389	290	99	43.8	760	115
Jackson	75.7	16.4	12.6	37.5	562	469	93	82.5	1,236	168
Johnson City	251.9	136.2	41.3	59.0	892	745	147	200.8	3,035	199
Kingsport	197.0	110.3	42.0	52.8	988	731	257	179.2	3,350	605
Knoxville	402.4	43.6	51.1	223.9	1,198	663	535	290.1	1,552	498
La Vergne	36.6	17.7	73.2	10.3	288	212	76	22.7	637	68
Lebanon	34.6	17.8	33.3	13.1	402	208	194	41.6	1,279	288
Maryville	115.4	59.0	48.8	42.8	1,471	1,335	136	85.3	2,936	212
Memphis	1,242.1	318.8	34.2	453.0	696	588	108	1,048.8	1,611	143
Morristown	63.3	19.7	28.0	15.0	506	371	135	61.7	2,074	335
Mount Juliet	41.9	12.4	99.2	16.6	480	49	431	34.8	1,005	426
Murfreesboro	224.3	109.0	62.9	100.5	738	288	450	260.0	1,909	614
Nashville-Davidson	2,657.7	644.9	94.4	1,600.6	2,329	1,414	914	2,894.0	4,212	698
Oak Ridge	149.5	89.2	33.4	43.3	1,493	919	574	113.2	3,900	218
Smyrna	66.5	22.7	25.1	15.7	314	201	113	53.3	1,067	190
Spring Hill	31.8	5.2	92.1	14.2	358	135	223	30.0	759	227
TEXAS	X	X	X	X	X	X	X	X	X	X
Abilene	150.3	11.5	24.2	99.6	815	312	504	185.5	1,518	545
Allen	150.6	1.4	39.5	103.7	1,024	535	490	97.5	963	145
Alvin	29.2	0.3	13.3	19.1	725	352	373	22.9	870	109
Amarillo	285.4	34.4	43.6	151.2	757	213	543	289.4	1,449	217
Arlington	514.4	28.7	23.4	283.7	714	323	391	463.3	1,166	129

1. Based on population estimated as of July 1 of the year shown.

City	City government finances, 2017 (cont.)												
	General expenditure (cont.)												
	Percent of total for:										Debt outstanding		
	Public welfare	Highways	Parking facilities	Education	Health and hospitals	Police protection	Sewerage and sanitation	Parks and recreation	Housing and community development	Interest on debt	Total (mil dol)	Per capita[1] (dollars)	Debt issued during year
	127	128	129	130	131	132	133	134	135	136	137	138	139
RHODE ISLAND	X	X	X	X	X	X	X	X	X	X	X	X	X
Cranston	0.0	6.2	0.0	59.9	1.0	8.1	7.0	1.0	0.4	1.1	93.9	1,159	2.2
East Providence	0.0	4.6	0.0	54.0	0.2	8.9	6.7	0.5	0.6	1.0	86.1	1,818	0.0
Newport	0.3	0.2	1.1	30.4	7.2	12.0	18.0	0.2	0.2	2.2	171.6	6,963	16.7
Pawtucket	0.0	1.1	0.0	61.6	0.0	11.3	1.7	0.7	0.6	0.9	188.3	2,630	30.5
Providence	0.0	1.2	0.0	55.7	0.0	12.0	1.5	1.4	2.0	4.2	711.1	3,967	18.6
Warwick	0.2	2.8	0.0	54.9	0.1	6.8	4.7	0.7	0.4	1.2	145.6	1,801	8.5
Woonsocket	0.2	2.7	0.0	57.8	0.0	5.7	9.7	0.4	0.6	5.3	152.8	3,679	62.7
SOUTH CAROLINA	X	X	X	X	X	X	X	X	X	X	X	X	X
Aiken	0.0	4.8	0.0	0.0	0.0	18.7	25.4	10.5	0.4	0.0	0.0	0	0.0
Anderson	0.0	0.0	0.0	0.0	0.0	22.1	37.9	5.0	2.1	0.0	179.0	6,566	0.0
Bluffton	0.0	7.9	0.0	0.0	0.0	28.2	7.9	1.5	3.1	2.7	15.1	732	0.9
Charleston	0.3	4.6	6.7	0.0	0.0	27.8	5.4	9.8	2.3	0.6	26.3	194	0.0
Columbia	0.0	3.3	1.2	0.0	0.6	14.2	40.0	4.5	2.7	0.0	595.0	4,440	211.5
Florence	0.0	12.2	1.2	0.0	0.0	13.1	22.0	30.8	0.3	0.0	191.7	4,975	51.5
Goose Creek	0.0	0.0	1.6	0.0	0.0	29.2	6.1	26.2	0.0	0.0	26.7	638	13.3
Greenville	0.0	8.2	2.6	0.0	0.5	23.5	21.0	7.0	5.4	1.7	108.8	1,589	0.0
Greer	0.0	4.9	0.0	0.0	0.0	20.3	23.7	10.7	0.0	8.1	78.1	2,513	0.0
Hilton Head Island	0.0	3.4	0.0	0.0	0.0	5.9	4.4	18.2	13.3	5.7	90.1	2,243	0.0
Mount Pleasant	0.0	9.5	0.0	0.0	5.9	8.4	10.3	5.2	1.9	0.0	226.4	2,594	119.9
Myrtle Beach	0.0	6.6	3.8	0.0	0.0	20.8	15.3	12.1	1.4	0.0	208.4	6,382	55.5
North Charleston	0.0	5.0	0.6	0.0	0.0	27.0	6.4	5.4	0.3	0.0	199.6	1,801	80.0
Rock Hill	0.0	7.9	0.0	0.0	0.0	16.0	16.6	20.2	2.1	0.0	287.3	3,914	105.4
Spartanburg	0.0	5.7	3.0	0.0	0.5	25.5	10.7	3.7	1.4	0.0	192.7	5,149	65.6
Summerville	0.0	7.9	0.0	0.0	0.0	26.5	9.8	8.5	1.3	1.2	7.1	137	0.0
Sumter	0.0	2.5	0.0	0.0	0.0	25.6	20.0	7.9	6.9	0.4	34.8	878	0.0
SOUTH DAKOTA	X	X	X	X	X	X	X	X	X	X	X	X	X
Aberdeen	0.0	8.5	0.0	0.0	0.4	13.7	9.7	16.3	0.0	4.2	62.0	2,175	10.6
Rapid City	0.1	9.1	0.4	0.0	4.6	16.9	13.0	18.4	0.4	2.7	148.0	1,967	0.0
Sioux Falls	0.0	25.1	0.8	0.0	4.0	11.0	15.7	14.9	2.1	2.4	380.9	2,144	38.9
TENNESSEE	X	X	X	X	X	X	X	X	X	X	X	X	X
Bartlett	0.0	18.3	0.0	0.0	0.0	21.7	14.8	10.9	0.1	0.0	46.1	780	7.9
Brentwood	0.0	12.2	0.0	0.0	0.1	17.9	10.7	4.0	0.8	2.5	44.9	1,054	3.9
Bristol	0.0	5.4	0.0	57.9	0.0	9.9	7.1	5.0	0.7	0.3	2.2	82	0.0
Chattanooga	1.2	5.9	0.6	2.9	0.7	18.1	21.1	6.1	2.5	3.9	706.5	3,935	38.4
Clarksville	0.0	10.4	0.2	0.0	0.0	22.4	21.3	6.0	1.5	0.0	795.3	5,201	0.0
Cleveland	0.0	5.3	0.0	39.4	0.5	7.6	8.8	4.4	1.0	2.0	121.3	2,724	0.0
Collierville	0.0	8.2	0.0	0.0	0.0	27.2	12.4	13.2	0.0	10.9	123.5	2,458	0.0
Columbia	0.1	9.8	0.0	0.0	0.4	15.0	20.8	3.7	0.4	2.0	57.4	1,496	9.0
Cookeville	0.0	1.0	0.0	0.0	88.1	2.6	1.6	1.0	0.0	0.9	91.8	2,746	0.0
Franklin	0.0	10.8	0.0	0.0	0.2	17.0	25.9	4.7	0.3	0.0	195.9	2,503	40.2
Gallatin	0.8	3.7	0.0	0.0	0.0	20.9	20.6	10.8	0.0	1.4	68.0	1,816	0.0
Germantown	0.0	6.5	0.0	0.0	3.4	19.1	15.0	13.1	0.0	1.5	32.0	817	0.0
Hendersonville	0.0	13.7	0.0	0.0	0.0	26.9	12.2	7.0	0.0	0.9	4.8	84	0.0
Jackson	0.0	15.7	0.0	0.0	0.0	32.6	17.4	5.5	0.0	0.0	124.2	1,861	7.3
Johnson City	0.0	6.3	0.0	39.3	0.0	6.8	14.8	4.3	0.4	5.8	382.6	5,783	83.4
Kingsport	0.0	3.5	0.0	44.4	0.0	6.9	5.6	4.7	0.2	0.0	241.2	4,509	30.3
Knoxville	0.0	8.4	0.5	0.0	0.0	11.4	35.5	10.0	0.5	5.7	542.4	2,902	0.0
La Vergne	0.5	5.2	0.0	0.0	0.0	26.7	20.6	4.0	0.0	0.0	35.7	1,003	4.3
Lebanon	0.0	13.3	0.0	0.0	0.3	24.7	12.8	5.8	0.4	0.0	69.5	2,137	13.1
Maryville	0.0	3.7	0.0	68.1	0.3	6.2	5.5	1.8	0.0	2.7	104.2	3,587	0.0
Memphis	0.0	2.1	0.2	0.0	0.0	24.1	11.6	4.6	2.6	7.8	2,006.0	3,082	220.9
Morristown	0.4	10.3	0.0	0.0	0.6	13.3	24.5	3.2	0.4	3.9	231.6	7,786	15.8
Mount Juliet	0.3	34.1	0.0	0.0	0.0	13.9	20.2	3.6	0.0	0.0	13.7	395	0.0
Murfreesboro	0.0	6.7	0.0	32.7	0.0	26.2	2.4	13.8	0.4	0.0	368.8	2,708	51.9
Nashville-Davidson	1.7	4.7	0.1	38.6	5.6	7.4	7.1	4.5	0.0	5.2	14,599.2	21,246	901.2
Oak Ridge	0.0	2.5	0.0	52.3	0.3	5.8	10.9	4.2	1.4	3.1	125.2	4,313	0.0
Smyrna	0.4	9.3	0.0	0.0	0.0	18.6	12.1	15.6	0.0	0.0	61.2	1,226	1.9
Spring Hill	0.0	18.4	0.0	0.0	0.0	19.3	26.8	1.6	0.0	0.0	32.0	807	0.0
TEXAS	X	X	X	X	X	X	X	X	X	X	X	X	X
Abilene	0.0	3.7	0.0	0.0	3.0	14.2	42.6	4.7	0.7	1.2	256.2	2,096	0.0
Allen	0.0	3.5	0.0	0.0	0.4	19.5	8.7	25.1	0.9	0.0	149.6	1,478	47.0
Alvin	0.0	17.9	0.0	0.0	8.7	28.0	23.4	7.0	0.0	0.0	30.3	1,152	0.0
Amarillo	0.0	8.1	0.0	0.0	6.6	16.1	16.6	12.0	5.1	2.4	366.7	1,836	0.0
Arlington	0.0	10.7	0.0	0.0	1.2	21.4	15.8	7.3	1.0	13.8	1,049.6	2,643	0.0

1. Based on population estimated as of July 1 of the year shown.

STATE Place code	City	Land area[1] (sq. mi)	Population, 2021: Total persons 2021	Population, 2021: Rank	Population, 2021: Per square mile	Race 2020: Race alone[2] (percent): White	Race 2020: Race alone[2] (percent): Black or African American	Race 2020: Race alone[2] (percent): American Indian, Alaskan Native	Race 2020: Race alone[2] (percent): Asian	Race 2020: Race alone[2] (percent): Hawaiian Pacific Islander	Race 2020: Race alone[2] (percent): Some other race	Race 2020: Two or more races (percent)
		1	2	3	4	5	6	7	8	9	10	11
	TEXAS —Cont'd											
48 05000	Austin	319.9	964,177	11	3,014.0	54.7	7.3	1.0	9.0	0.1	11.9	16.1
48 05372	Balch Springs	9.0	27,160	1,431	3,017.8	27.1	22.7	2.1	1.0	0.1	26.4	20.5
48 06128	Baytown	37.0	82,480	425	2,229.2	41.9	16.9	1.2	1.8	0.1	18.8	19.3
48 07000	Beaumont	82.5	112,556	269	1,364.3	31.1	47.3	0.6	3.8	0.0	9.6	7.5
48 07132	Bedford	10.0	49,187	811	4,918.7	64.2	11.7	0.6	5.3	0.8	5.0	12.3
48 08236	Big Spring	18.9	25,735	1,505	1,361.6	64.6	6.1	1.2	1.3	0.1	11.9	14.9
48 10768	Brownsville	131.7	187,831	137	1,426.2	34.9	0.3	0.7	0.6	0.0	20.5	42.9
48 10912	Bryan	54.2	86,866	397	1,602.7	50.4	15.8	0.9	2.5	0.1	14.5	15.8
48 11428	Burleson	28.3	51,618	771	1,824.0	77.2	4.6	0.8	1.6	0.1	4.7	11.1
48 13024	Carrollton	36.7	133,251	212	3,630.8	43.3	10.1	1.1	16.9	0.1	12.3	16.3
48 13492	Cedar Hill	35.8	48,557	819	1,356.3	22.0	53.2	0.9	2.1	0.1	10.0	11.7
48 13552	Cedar Park	25.6	78,693	461	3,073.9	62.1	4.4	0.6	14.2	0.1	5.1	13.5
48 14920	Cibolo	21.0	33,475	1,182	1,594.0	51.8	16.4	0.7	3.4	0.4	7.5	19.8
48 15364	Cleburne	32.3	31,999	1,231	990.7	68.7	4.1	1.1	0.6	1.2	12.3	12.0
48 15976	College Station	51.2	120,019	238	2,344.1	63.5	8.1	0.5	10.2	0.1	7.4	10.2
48 15988	Colleyville	13.1	25,986	1,494	1,983.7	77.1	2.5	0.4	10.0	0.1	1.4	8.6
48 16432	Conroe	72.0	94,400	354	1,311.1	57.2	10.3	1.2	2.7	0.1	14.8	13.6
48 16468	Converse	9.4	28,643	1,363	3,047.1	39.7	22.1	1.0	2.9	0.6	11.9	21.8
48 16612	Coppell	14.4	42,221	946	2,932.0	51.8	5.4	0.4	27.1	0.1	4.0	11.3
48 16624	Copperas Cove	18.0	37,041	1,074	2,057.8	54.4	18.5	0.8	3.0	2.2	6.1	14.9
48 17000	Corpus Christi	162.2	317,773	60	1,959.1	53.6	4.4	0.9	2.5	0.1	12.7	25.9
48 19000	Dallas	339.6	1,288,457	9	3,794.0	36.1	23.3	1.2	3.7	0.1	19.5	16.2
48 19624	Deer Park	10.5	33,676	1,178	3,207.2	67.0	2.4	0.9	1.4	0.1	10.9	17.4
48 19792	Del Rio	20.4	34,584	1,153	1,695.3	44.0	1.4	0.7	0.8	0.1	17.2	35.8
48 19972	Denton	96.8	148,146	184	1,530.4	61.2	11.4	1.0	4.4	0.1	8.9	13.1
48 20092	DeSoto	21.6	55,729	705	2,580.0	12.7	70.1	0.6	0.9	0.0	7.4	8.3
48 21628	Duncanville	11.2	39,797	996	3,553.3	29.7	30.1	2.0	1.4	0.1	19.3	17.5
48 21892	Eagle Pass	9.4	28,596	1,365	3,042.1	30.5	0.5	0.7	0.6	0.0	24.3	43.4
48 22660	Edinburg	44.7	102,483	312	2,292.7	35.6	1.6	0.7	2.6	0.0	19.6	39.8
48 24000	El Paso	258.4	678,415	22	2,625.4	36.8	3.7	1.1	1.5	0.2	20.6	36.0
48 24768	Euless	16.1	60,500	640	3,757.8	46.4	16.2	0.7	14.7	2.0	7.4	12.5
48 25452	Farmers Branch	11.9	36,442	1,088	3,062.4	45.3	8.4	1.2	8.8	0.0	17.8	18.5
48 26232	Flower Mound	42.0	77,243	468	1,839.1	68.7	3.5	0.6	14.2	0.0	2.7	10.4
48 27000	Fort Worth	348.6	935,508	13	2,683.6	44.9	19.6	0.9	5.2	0.1	14.2	15.1
48 27648	Friendswood	20.8	41,004	963	1,971.3	73.9	3.6	0.4	6.4	0.1	3.6	12.0
48 27684	Frisco	68.6	210,719	110	3,071.7	50.5	9.0	0.5	26.3	0.1	3.5	10.1
48 28068	Galveston	41.1	53,219	750	1,294.9	54.6	16.8	1.0	3.2	0.1	11.0	13.3
48 29000	Garland	57.1	242,035	93	4,238.8	35.1	15.1	1.3	12.0	0.1	19.2	17.2
48 29336	Georgetown	57.3	75,420	488	1,316.2	73.9	4.7	0.7	2.1	0.1	6.1	12.4
48 30464	Grand Prairie	72.5	197,347	126	2,722.0	29.3	24.1	1.2	7.6	0.1	19.4	18.1
48 30644	Grapevine	32.1	50,872	785	1,584.8	68.3	4.6	0.9	6.3	0.1	7.1	12.8
48 30920	Greenville	32.3	29,578	1,323	915.7	58.4	14.2	1.2	1.3	0.2	11.5	13.2
48 31928	Haltom City	12.3	45,746	865	3,719.2	45.7	7.6	1.4	7.9	0.2	20.9	16.3
48 32312	Harker Heights	15.6	33,560	1,180	2,151.3	46.8	23.0	0.8	4.8	1.3	7.4	15.9
48 32372	Harlingen	40.1	71,925	512	1,793.6	45.8	1.0	0.7	1.3	0.1	15.4	35.7
48 35000	Houston	640.4	2,288,250	4	3,573.2	32.1	22.6	1.2	7.3	0.1	20.7	16.1
48 35528	Huntsville	42.6	46,288	860	1,086.6	50.0	25.3	0.6	2.2	0.1	15.0	6.8
48 35576	Hurst	10.0	40,055	986	4,005.5	62.4	10.2	0.9	3.0	0.6	9.1	13.9
48 35624	Hutto	12.6	30,855	1,278	2,448.8	52.5	13.3	1.0	2.2	0.2	10.8	20.0
48 37000	Irving	67.0	254,198	88	3,794.0	27.7	12.7	1.4	22.4	0.1	19.2	16.5
48 38632	Keller	18.4	45,397	874	2,467.2	77.4	3.1	0.5	7.0	0.1	2.3	9.7
48 39148	Killeen	54.8	156,261	167	2,851.5	30.0	37.3	0.9	4.0	1.8	10.0	15.9
48 39352	Kingsville	13.9	25,069	1,544	1,803.5	53.8	4.3	0.8	3.1	0.0	12.3	25.7
48 39952	Kyle	31.1	51,789	769	1,665.2	53.4	5.4	1.0	1.8	0.1	14.9	23.4
48 40588	Lake Jackson	19.7	27,879	1,395	1,415.2	66.7	5.7	0.8	3.3	0.0	9.5	14.0
48 41212	Lancaster	33.1	40,728	970	1,230.5	12.0	66.3	0.7	0.4	0.0	11.3	9.3
48 41440	La Porte	18.6	35,964	1,101	1,933.5	62.5	6.0	0.9	1.1	0.1	11.9	17.5
48 41464	Laredo	106.8	256,153	87	2,398.4	38.1	0.4	0.6	0.5	0.0	19.6	40.6
48 41980	League City	51.3	115,595	252	2,253.3	66.2	7.5	0.5	6.3	0.1	5.6	13.8
48 42016	Leander	37.7	67,124	561	1,780.5	62.9	5.1	0.8	10.0	0.1	6.4	14.6
48 42508	Lewisville	37.0	112,944	266	3,052.5	41.9	15.8	1.2	11.3	0.1	14.1	15.6
48 43012	Little Elm	18.1	51,042	782	2,820.0	47.1	18.4	0.9	9.8	0.1	8.3	15.4
48 43888	Longview	55.8	81,762	428	1,465.3	54.2	23.8	0.6	1.6	0.0	10.2	9.6
48 45000	Lubbock	134.7	260,993	85	1,937.6	59.5	10.1	1.1	3.7	0.1	11.7	13.9
48 45072	Lufkin	34.2	34,074	1,164	996.3	47.0	26.8	0.7	2.0	0.1	12.5	10.9
48 45384	McAllen	62.3	143,920	189	2,310.1	34.4	0.8	0.8	2.6	0.0	18.2	43.1
48 45744	McKinney	67.0	202,690	117	3,025.2	56.2	13.0	0.7	12.3	0.1	5.6	12.1
48 46452	Mansfield	36.7	74,368	496	2,026.4	53.3	21.8	0.7	5.6	0.1	6.5	12.1

1. Dry land or land partially or temporarily covered by water. 2. Hispanic or Latino persons may be of any race.

City	Percent Hispanic or Latino[1], 2020	Percent foreign born, 2016–2020	Age of population (percent), 2016–2020: Under 18 years	18 to 24 years	25 to 34 years	35 to 44 years	45 to 54 years	55 to 64 years	65 years and over	Median age, 2016–2020	Percent female, 2016–2020	Population: Census counts: 2010	2020	Percent change: 2010–2020	2020–2021
	12	13	14	15	16	17	18	19	20	21	22	23	24	25	26
TEXAS —Cont'd															
Austin	32.5	18.0	19.9	10.2	22.5	16.4	11.8	9.8	9.4	33.7	49.2	801,862	959,549	19.7	0.5
Balch Springs	59.5	24.3	31.4	10.3	14.7	12.1	12.0	10.8	8.7	30.4	49.3	23,831	27,717	16.3	-2.0
Baytown	49.5	18.6	28.5	9.8	14.5	13.4	12.5	9.7	11.6	33.2	50.2	72,075	83,698	16.1	-1.5
Beaumont	17.9	11.6	24.4	11.2	14.2	12.2	10.9	12.0	15.1	35.1	51.2	117,243	114,586	-2.3	-1.8
Bedford	16.9	11.2	22.6	6.6	15.1	14.6	11.1	13.4	16.4	38.5	52.2	46,990	49,965	6.3	-1.6
Big Spring	53.0	13.3	21.5	10.8	15.5	15.3	14.2	11.0	11.7	36.3	43.3	27,250	26,274	-3.6	-2.1
Brownsville	93.9	28.0	29.6	12.7	12.0	12.8	11.0	9.5	12.4	30.9	52.0	174,448	186,611	7.0	0.7
Bryan	39.1	15.4	24.3	13.4	18.5	12.0	10.2	10.1	11.3	31.2	49.5	76,233	85,461	12.1	1.6
Burleson	16.3	2.6	29.3	7.8	13.0	16.2	12.3	9.8	11.5	34.9	51.5	36,876	47,807	29.6	8.0
Carrollton	31.7	27.9	21.2	8.5	15.7	14.9	14.7	13.4	11.6	37.8	51.4	119,213	133,348	11.9	-0.1
Cedar Hill	24.2	10.5	29.0	8.7	14.1	13.5	13.4	12.0	9.2	34.0	52.9	44,935	49,175	9.4	-1.3
Cedar Park	18.5	14.6	27.8	6.1	15.5	17.7	14.1	9.4	9.5	35.4	50.7	55,113	77,646	40.9	1.3
Cibolo	30.7	7.0	30.0	8.8	13.0	15.9	14.7	8.2	9.5	34.2	49.2	20,180	32,279	60.0	3.7
Cleburne	29.9	4.9	26.5	9.4	13.9	12.2	10.2	11.3	16.6	35.2	49.1	29,634	31,136	5.1	2.8
College Station	19.4	12.2	17.1	38.2	14.7	10.3	6.8	6.2	6.7	23.1	49.3	94,250	118,180	25.4	1.6
Colleyville	7.1	9.1	23.7	6.3	6.5	9.5	16.3	19.5	18.2	47.1	47.8	22,809	26,084	14.4	-0.4
Conroe	32.8	16.6	24.2	10.8	17.0	12.7	11.3	10.4	13.7	33.7	50.3	65,368	89,148	36.4	5.9
Converse	42.9	8.4	29.7	9.4	13.2	15.2	12.6	9.8	10.1	33.2	49.2	21,535	27,677	28.5	3.5
Coppell	13.9	27.0	27.8	5.5	9.5	16.0	18.1	14.2	8.9	39.8	52.4	38,666	43,002	11.2	-1.8
Copperas Cove	19.9	7.9	26.2	9.8	19.3	15.0	11.2	8.5	10.1	32.4	52.0	32,253	36,224	12.3	2.3
Corpus Christi	60.7	9.1	24.6	10.2	14.8	13.1	11.7	11.7	14.0	35.3	50.4	305,202	317,929	4.2	0.0
Dallas	42.3	23.9	24.8	9.8	18.9	13.8	11.8	10.4	10.6	32.9	50.4	1,197,672	1,304,442	8.9	-1.2
Deer Park	36.9	10.2	25.3	10.9	11.6	11.9	13.0	12.0	15.3	36.3	48.8	31,999	34,503	7.8	-2.4
Del Rio	83.9	24.7	28.8	9.8	14.1	13.5	10.2	9.1	14.5	33.5	49.8	35,921	34,688	-3.4	-0.3
Denton	24.6	13.1	19.8	21.0	17.6	11.6	9.6	9.1	11.3	29.5	51.4	116,329	141,123	21.3	5.0
DeSoto	16.6	6.6	25.0	7.5	12.3	12.2	15.8	13.1	14.2	39.3	55.7	49,056	56,155	14.5	-0.8
Duncanville	44.6	13.3	25.8	9.6	11.2	13.3	10.9	13.4	15.7	36.8	51.4	38,559	40,721	5.6	-2.3
Eagle Pass	94.8	30.2	27.7	13.3	15.2	10.0	12.2	9.3	12.2	30.2	51.9	26,606	28,392	6.7	0.7
Edinburg	88.4	19.2	28.9	13.4	15.7	15.3	9.9	8.1	8.7	29.2	48.2	82,058	99,678	21.5	2.8
El Paso	81.2	23.0	26.6	11.1	15.1	12.3	11.4	10.6	12.9	33.0	51.0	648,079	678,587	4.7	0.0
Euless	20.1	21.1	22.8	8.5	17.6	15.2	13.4	12.0	10.6	35.9	49.8	51,263	61,089	19.2	-1.0
Farmers Branch	43.5	27.2	23.7	8.7	18.6	14.6	12.4	10.2	11.8	34.5	51.2	29,139	36,019	23.6	1.2
Flower Mound	11.1	13.7	28.7	6.0	8.4	14.1	18.0	14.4	10.3	40.6	49.5	64,658	75,859	17.3	1.8
Fort Worth	34.8	16.3	27.2	9.7	16.7	14.2	12.1	10.2	9.9	33.0	51.0	744,800	918,377	23.3	1.9
Friendswood	16.4	9.3	26.7	8.7	10.0	11.5	15.9	12.9	14.3	38.9	51.7	35,911	41,218	14.8	-0.5
Frisco	11.5	23.2	29.8	7.1	9.4	18.8	17.2	8.5	9.1	37.4	51.2	117,159	200,675	71.3	5.0
Galveston	29.4	13.7	16.0	12.2	15.6	11.5	12.3	14.8	17.5	39.9	49.9	47,742	53,585	12.2	-0.7
Garland	42.7	30.3	26.9	10.2	14.0	12.3	12.4	12.5	11.8	34.2	50.4	226,857	246,132	8.5	-1.7
Georgetown	21.5	7.6	19.2	8.6	9.7	11.9	10.3	11.9	28.4	45.5	52.8	47,491	66,964	41.0	12.6
Grand Prairie	45.3	22.7	28.5	9.6	13.7	14.1	13.6	10.4	10.1	33.6	51.3	175,435	196,272	11.9	0.5
Grapevine	20.0	18.0	21.4	8.2	14.3	12.8	15.5	15.6	12.1	39.7	49.9	46,336	50,651	9.3	0.4
Greenville	28.0	10.0	25.2	7.9	15.3	13.5	10.8	10.8	16.5	36.0	49.9	25,528	28,187	10.4	4.9
Haltom City	46.3	25.6	29.3	8.9	14.6	15.1	12.0	9.4	10.7	32.8	51.4	42,566	46,120	8.3	-0.8
Harker Heights	22.2	9.8	27.5	8.6	14.2	16.4	12.9	10.9	9.5	34.5	50.0	26,730	32,997	23.4	1.7
Harlingen	81.7	14.5	31.6	8.3	15.5	10.6	10.4	8.6	15.0	31.3	51.5	64,924	71,802	10.6	0.2
Houston	44.0	28.9	24.7	9.7	18.5	14.0	11.7	10.5	11.0	33.3	50.2	2,092,919	2,302,792	10.0	-0.6
Huntsville	23.8	10.4	11.3	29.6	15.2	11.9	11.0	10.3	10.8	30.6	40.9	38,524	45,769	18.8	1.1
Hurst	24.2	12.8	25.0	7.3	13.0	13.3	12.4	12.1	16.9	37.9	50.5	37,344	40,442	8.3	-1.0
Hutto	35.6	9.1	25.7	7.9	15.4	22.4	15.5	7.7	5.3	35.5	51.8	16,462	27,605	67.7	11.8
Irving	41.1	39.1	27.0	9.1	19.1	16.0	12.0	8.7	8.0	32.0	50.0	216,285	256,793	18.7	-1.0
Keller	10.3	9.7	27.0	6.4	8.3	11.9	17.8	14.5	14.1	42.4	50.4	39,627	45,792	15.6	-0.9
Killeen	27.1	9.1	29.2	11.3	19.6	13.6	10.6	8.5	7.2	29.4	50.6	127,733	152,570	19.4	2.4
Kingsville	71.9	7.7	23.7	22.5	14.7	10.6	8.5	8.1	11.9	27.3	48.1	26,453	25,408	-4.0	-1.3
Kyle	48.9	8.1	29.8	9.3	17.9	15.8	10.5	9.5	7.3	31.7	49.4	28,227	45,752	62.1	13.2
Lake Jackson	28.5	9.3	25.8	9.4	16.8	12.3	10.2	12.7	12.8	33.6	50.2	26,830	28,212	5.2	-1.2
Lancaster	23.7	4.8	31.0	7.6	13.6	13.2	11.7	12.9	9.9	32.6	55.5	36,651	41,290	12.7	-1.4
La Porte	37.1	8.8	24.8	8.1	14.9	12.2	13.2	14.5	12.3	36.5	51.8	33,808	35,137	3.9	2.4
Laredo	95.1	25.6	32.9	11.4	13.7	12.8	11.4	8.4	9.3	28.9	51.0	235,781	255,181	8.2	0.4
League City	20.9	10.6	27.7	7.1	14.8	15.3	14.2	10.6	10.3	35.2	50.2	83,589	114,426	36.9	1.0
Leander	22.1	12.6	29.6	7.5	13.5	17.0	13.4	10.4	8.5	34.7	51.3	27,279	59,345	117.5	13.1
Lewisville	32.1	21.6	24.1	8.4	20.7	15.0	12.8	10.7	8.3	33.2	51.0	95,474	111,676	17.0	1.1
Little Elm	24.1	17.5	29.2	7.5	13.3	23.2	12.9	7.1	6.8	35.0	49.1	25,877	46,361	79.2	10.1
Longview	20.7	9.9	25.6	9.7	14.8	12.0	10.6	11.7	15.4	34.9	51.2	80,419	81,760	1.7	0.0
Lubbock	35.6	7.0	22.8	18.8	15.4	11.4	9.6	9.7	12.3	29.9	50.8	229,944	257,180	11.8	1.5
Lufkin	27.6	12.9	26.1	9.9	16.1	11.9	11.0	10.2	14.8	32.8	52.6	35,136	34,148	-2.8	-0.2
McAllen	86.7	26.5	29.2	10.1	14.0	12.9	11.6	9.5	12.7	32.6	50.5	131,565	142,242	8.1	1.2
McKinney	17.1	16.3	28.8	7.6	11.4	17.6	14.3	9.8	10.6	36.5	51.0	131,154	195,057	48.7	3.9
Mansfield	18.5	10.3	29.2	8.6	10.7	14.8	14.5	11.4	10.6	36.3	52.4	56,654	72,654	28.2	2.4

1. May be of any race.

City	Households, 2016–2020							Persons in group quarters, 2016–2020	Serious crimes known to police[2], 2020				Educational attainment, 2016–2020		
			Percent						Violent		Property			Attainment[4] (percent)	
	Number	Persons per household	Family	Married couple family	Female family	Non-family	One person		Number	Rate	Number	Rate	Population age 25 and over	High school graduate or less	Bachelor's degree or more
	27	28	29	30	31	32	33	34	35	36	37	38	39	40	41
TEXAS —Cont'd															
Austin	395,280	2.39	51.9	38.2	9.7	48.1	33.9	22,041	4,671	467.0	36,322	3,631.2	675,347	24.4	53.4
Balch Springs	6,916	3.62	79.8	48.6	20.9	20.2	15.8	109	180	714.6	822	3,263.3	14,633	63.9	7.6
Baytown	26,592	2.84	68.3	43.5	16.7	31.7	25.8	612	338	434.3	2,917	3,748.2	46,962	50.0	14.4
Beaumont	46,935	2.43	61.6	39.9	17.0	38.4	33.4	3,311	1,431	1,225.5	3,863	3,308.3	75,499	45.1	24.5
Bedford	20,089	2.43	61.9	45.2	12.5	38.1	32.6	361	122	247.6	1,096	2,224.3	34,753	25.0	37.9
Big Spring	8,458	2.74	60.6	40.6	12.4	39.4	34.4	4,711	141	498.3	805	2,845.1	18,873	57.1	11.7
Brownsville	53,506	3.38	78.9	50.2	21.6	21.1	18.7	1,313	738	401.9	3,394	1,848.3	105,150	57.5	19.7
Bryan	30,647	2.65	60.9	37.5	17.7	39.1	31.9	4,278	463	529.5	1,718	1,964.9	53,311	46.0	26.6
Burleson	15,979	2.95	77.2	57.0	16.2	22.8	19.3	78	108	217.5	671	1,351.2	29,645	35.5	27.2
Carrollton	49,675	2.75	68.7	53.7	10.7	31.3	25.4	671	NA	NA	NA	NA	96,537	33.1	40.2
Cedar Hill	15,537	3.08	71.5	50.6	16.0	28.5	25.1	500	69	142.7	920	1,902.7	30,109	32.0	30.6
Cedar Park	25,061	3.07	74.2	62.0	9.2	25.8	19.9	245	83	100.4	1,059	1,281.3	50,992	20.1	49.2
Cibolo	9,106	3.33	86.3	66.3	15.4	13.7	11.7	0	37	112.9	271	826.8	18,575	26.8	39.1
Cleburne	10,982	2.73	67.8	48.6	13.3	32.2	27.2	847	104	330.3	522	1,657.9	19,748	55.8	16.1
College Station	41,682	2.50	49.2	35.4	10.3	50.8	30.5	11,665	217	179.6	2,299	1,902.7	51,803	17.8	57.8
Colleyville	9,249	2.89	87.4	79.2	4.4	12.6	11.1	0	8	29.0	154	557.9	18,735	8.7	63.7
Conroe	32,547	2.67	65.7	48.1	12.0	34.3	26.9	1,557	175	185.3	2,336	2,473.2	57,464	43.1	27.9
Converse	8,435	3.25	73.2	52.3	16.0	26.8	23.0	143	NA	NA	NA	NA	16,777	32.5	27.3
Coppell	15,231	2.72	80.0	68.2	9.1	20.0	18.5	13	29	69.4	632	1,511.7	27,670	10.7	69.5
Copperas Cove	12,632	2.58	70.5	50.0	15.5	29.5	25.3	325	144	432.0	712	2,136.0	21,091	32.5	20.8
Corpus Christi	117,789	2.70	67.1	44.9	15.9	32.9	26.7	8,368	2,772	842.4	10,747	3,266.1	212,737	44.7	22.0
Dallas	524,498	2.52	56.2	36.2	14.7	43.8	35.5	16,654	11,514	844.7	46,974	3,446.3	876,582	42.7	34.7
Deer Park	11,637	2.88	75.7	59.1	12.7	24.3	21.9	122	45	133.8	573	1,703.8	21,423	40.0	20.9
Del Rio	12,300	2.82	72.3	49.0	17.3	27.7	24.5	1,199	58	162.3	563	1,575.6	21,983	54.9	19.6
Denton	47,777	2.72	59.5	44.4	11.5	40.5	27.6	9,854	NA	NA	NA	NA	82,721	28.0	39.5
DeSoto	19,041	2.76	68.8	44.1	21.0	31.2	28.1	572	189	353.2	1,177	2,199.4	35,886	32.9	26.7
Duncanville	13,573	2.86	73.7	47.0	19.8	26.3	24.1	230	140	360.4	866	2,229.3	25,242	44.3	24.0
Eagle Pass	8,850	3.29	79.7	52.1	19.5	20.3	16.6	193	43	143.2	553	1,841.6	17,270	52.6	23.1
Edinburg	29,899	3.07	72.4	44.0	20.1	27.6	21.0	5,935	325	314.0	2,310	2,232.1	56,366	44.6	27.0
El Paso	230,905	2.92	70.4	45.5	18.7	29.6	25.5	6,066	2,167	316.2	8,507	1,241.4	423,060	41.9	25.9
Euless	21,967	2.56	60.3	40.3	14.0	39.7	31.8	133	NA	NA	NA	NA	38,698	32.1	34.2
Farmers Branch	16,015	2.66	63.2	44.8	15.0	36.8	28.3	124	77	150.7	1,011	1,979.3	28,866	35.6	41.7
Flower Mound	26,233	3.00	83.7	74.2	6.5	16.3	14.5	203	45	55.6	552	682.3	51,433	14.8	62.1
Fort Worth	307,248	2.85	67.2	46.2	15.3	32.8	26.3	15,898	5,029	541.0	25,405	2,733.2	562,928	41.7	30.1
Friendswood	13,540	2.93	77.0	64.9	8.8	23.0	20.0	237	36	88.2	234	573.6	25,754	22.2	48.1
Frisco	64,151	2.93	75.6	65.8	7.3	24.4	21.4	348	183	86.1	2,066	971.7	118,960	13.3	64.4
Galveston	21,683	2.15	52.4	35.1	13.4	47.6	38.9	3,723	327	644.3	1,694	3,337.9	36,113	38.7	30.3
Garland	75,886	3.14	74.9	52.5	14.7	25.1	19.6	701	695	287.4	6,104	2,523.9	150,223	46.8	23.1
Georgetown	28,075	2.62	68.3	56.6	8.5	31.7	27.6	1,947	123	146.1	1,077	1,278.9	54,494	27.0	43.6
Grand Prairie	62,679	3.09	74.0	52.4	15.5	26.0	21.9	426	483	245.2	3,791	1,924.5	119,974	47.1	23.9
Grapevine	21,838	2.47	63.6	51.9	7.7	36.4	27.5	236	99	175.7	1,183	2,099.6	38,095	22.9	50.6
Greenville	10,454	2.61	63.2	40.6	15.6	36.8	31.4	793	62	212.3	493	1,687.8	18,791	52.9	17.8
Haltom City	14,601	3.03	72.0	46.7	19.4	28.0	22.3	104	138	313.4	1,354	3,074.7	27,390	63.0	11.5
Harker Heights	11,067	2.84	73.0	50.8	18.3	27.0	22.8	192	58	175.3	429	1,296.4	20,220	30.6	35.2
Harlingen	21,752	2.92	71.5	44.7	21.6	28.5	24.4	1,519	269	413.8	2,437	3,748.4	39,140	52.6	18.5
Houston	874,827	2.61	60.2	38.0	15.8	39.8	32.7	33,826	29,474	1,256.3	98,043	4,178.9	1,517,559	42.4	34.3
Huntsville	13,187	2.22	44.7	28.6	13.8	55.3	36.7	12,450	157	368.1	674	1,580.4	24,641	53.5	18.8
Hurst	14,340	2.69	66.6	50.5	12.9	33.4	27.3	254	97	250.0	1,018	2,624.0	26,265	34.1	32.5
Hutto	8,106	3.30	76.7	59.2	10.4	23.3	16.7	0	25	84.5	199	672.5	17,771	36.0	30.7
Irving	86,023	2.78	66.6	47.3	13.0	33.4	27.2	1,310	780	321.0	6,223	2,561.2	153,704	39.3	38.6
Keller	16,383	2.85	80.3	71.0	6.3	19.7	18.2	270	39	81.1	333	692.1	31,232	16.4	57.6
Killeen	54,840	2.71	67.0	44.3	18.1	33.0	27.6	151	1,033	669.0	NA	NA	88,336	33.7	20.5
Kingsville	9,399	2.52	61.8	38.7	15.2	38.2	28.7	1,727	118	468.3	581	2,306.0	13,648	49.3	24.6
Kyle	14,701	3.09	70.5	52.6	12.8	29.5	21.2	447	81	157.9	544	1,060.3	27,945	35.3	30.7
Lake Jackson	10,074	2.70	69.8	56.4	8.8	30.2	22.4	68	46	168.7	600	2,200.6	17,691	31.7	33.8
Lancaster	13,646	2.85	70.8	39.5	25.9	29.2	25.5	421	204	515.3	948	2,394.7	24,097	38.1	22.8
La Porte	12,342	2.86	74.1	52.9	15.6	25.9	21.6	86	81	230.8	441	1,256.3	23,724	44.8	16.2
Laredo	72,328	3.56	80.6	52.0	21.7	19.4	17.1	3,099	859	323.5	3,836	1,444.7	145,110	55.5	19.3
League City	37,662	2.79	73.1	60.8	8.6	26.9	22.0	448	127	114.9	1,493	1,350.9	68,736	21.1	48.3
Leander	18,505	3.28	81.7	66.7	9.9	18.3	15.1	8	62	90.4	600	875.0	38,130	25.0	41.0
Lewisville	39,664	2.70	61.9	44.1	13.0	38.1	30.1	455	324	292.4	1,949	1,759.0	72,701	35.6	32.9
Little Elm	15,942	3.12	78.1	59.2	12.4	21.9	18.5	0	85	147.9	219	381.0	31,505	29.0	38.8
Longview	31,450	2.49	63.5	42.4	16.8	36.5	29.9	3,734	276	337.6	2,362	2,889.3	53,121	43.5	20.4
Lubbock	98,849	2.49	57.4	39.5	13.2	42.6	30.6	11,266	2,852	1,087.9	10,770	4,108.4	149,916	36.8	33.7
Lufkin	12,755	2.67	64.9	42.7	17.9	35.1	29.8	1,245	284	811.3	NA	NA	22,602	45.7	22.0
McAllen	45,429	3.12	75.1	48.4	21.5	24.9	20.6	999	123	85.1	2,791	1,930.6	86,600	42.5	31.3
McKinney	65,065	2.92	77.4	62.4	10.7	22.6	19.2	1,378	280	134.4	1,950	936.0	121,601	22.5	49.3
Mansfield	22,760	3.12	79.4	65.2	10.8	20.6	17.8	399	68	91.4	863	1,160.6	44,367	23.7	39.9

2. Data for serious crimes have not been adjusted for underreporting. This may affect comparability between geographic areas and over time.

4. Persons 25 years old and over.

Table D. Cities — Income, Poverty, and Housing

City	Money income, 2016–2020					Median earnings Full year, Full-time workers, 2016–2020			Housing units, 2016–2020				
	Households												
	Median household income	Percent with income less than $25,000	Percent with income of $200,000 or more	Median family income	Median non-family household income	All persons	Men	Women	Total	Occupied	Percent owner occupied	Median value[1] (dollars)	Median gross rent (dollars)
	42	43	44	45	46	47	48	49	50	51	52	53	54
TEXAS —Cont'd													
Austin	75,752	14.4	11.3	98,014	56,825	54,397	59,036	51,323	426,899	395,280	45.5	358,600	1,346
Balch Springs	52,696	18.3	1.7	53,367	33,919	37,313	38,094	35,699	7,826	6,916	66.9	120,000	1,024
Baytown	54,454	21.9	2.7	65,204	34,648	45,178	54,463	32,940	29,259	26,592	55.9	126,500	969
Beaumont	48,168	26.5	5.2	57,413	31,961	41,578	46,609	37,280	53,693	46,935	54.5	123,700	868
Bedford	71,644	10.2	5.3	91,115	44,373	53,244	58,120	50,493	21,135	20,089	53.1	234,700	1,166
Big Spring	55,637	22.7	3.1	61,058	37,226	40,802	54,866	30,797	9,828	8,458	60.8	94,700	881
Brownsville	40,924	33.2	1.8	45,998	17,690	31,306	33,934	28,324	58,467	53,506	60.4	92,400	754
Bryan	46,813	26.8	3.8	56,596	33,596	38,403	40,230	35,115	34,162	30,647	49.9	158,000	925
Burleson	77,329	9.5	5.7	83,531	44,805	52,176	56,467	47,684	16,557	15,979	70.1	198,200	1,326
Carrollton	82,345	9.3	9.7	95,235	58,811	53,933	56,856	51,723	52,039	49,675	59.7	267,100	1,299
Cedar Hill	75,715	11.8	6.0	84,645	47,361	51,584	53,748	49,249	16,166	15,537	71.4	189,700	1,475
Cedar Park	108,194	8.0	13.8	122,575	61,974	68,049	81,111	54,671	25,982	25,061	71.5	327,400	1,475
Cibolo	102,109	5.9	8.9	106,595	60,668	58,056	64,849	52,193	9,705	9,106	85.9	237,300	1,711
Cleburne	51,475	19.5	2.5	60,666	31,117	37,130	43,509	29,319	11,716	10,982	62.6	130,200	994
College Station	47,456	31.3	6.7	80,795	26,452	50,582	58,852	41,768	47,796	41,682	36.8	256,600	1,001
Colleyville	171,485	4.1	40.7	181,856	86,563	113,750	153,785	85,240	9,436	9,249	95.9	567,600	2,261
Conroe	61,997	17.6	7.4	75,687	41,264	45,125	50,290	38,275	35,412	32,547	54.5	208,100	1,106
Converse	69,048	16.9	2.2	85,547	39,126	45,567	50,072	41,403	8,748	8,435	75.1	170,400	1,281
Coppell	128,476	4.8	28.4	148,511	61,454	91,151	108,857	70,649	15,768	15,231	71.9	414,000	1,538
Copperas Cove	53,640	17.8	1.5	60,801	32,054	37,180	41,128	33,171	14,192	12,632	56.3	116,900	851
Corpus Christi	57,387	21.3	4.7	68,907	35,770	42,158	49,408	35,972	132,965	117,789	57.0	150,100	1,055
Dallas	54,747	21.0	8.6	60,895	45,658	43,881	45,210	42,193	581,987	524,498	41.3	208,700	1,111
Deer Park	75,838	9.9	6.6	91,935	40,950	58,854	64,108	50,983	12,457	11,637	73.8	183,000	1,165
Del Rio	45,561	30.6	1.2	56,196	19,097	36,113	43,222	31,755	13,617	12,300	61.4	102,900	733
Denton	62,542	18.6	5.9	84,190	34,346	44,535	51,235	38,391	52,220	47,777	50.0	237,700	1,121
DeSoto	71,124	12.4	4.0	82,061	51,748	50,455	50,979	50,024	20,140	19,041	64.6	195,900	1,208
Duncanville	57,614	17.1	3.7	67,542	38,569	42,143	44,796	40,396	14,422	13,573	64.8	164,800	1,240
Eagle Pass	46,005	32.1	1.1	53,236	21,518	34,579	41,808	25,191	9,841	8,850	57.5	129,900	669
Edinburg	51,220	27.5	2.9	57,689	33,797	41,534	48,309	35,475	32,749	29,899	56.2	132,400	810
El Paso	48,866	26.5	3.1	55,638	27,694	37,891	40,991	34,054	252,526	230,905	59.6	132,800	857
Euless	67,181	11.5	5.0	74,472	51,675	47,646	50,561	45,194	23,504	21,967	41.6	213,700	1,220
Farmers Branch	73,695	9.2	7.7	83,605	62,146	51,411	52,909	47,892	17,577	16,015	51.1	210,600	1,423
Flower Mound	139,703	4.7	27.6	156,995	56,985	88,026	105,233	64,356	26,883	26,233	85.7	376,500	1,787
Fort Worth	64,567	17.0	5.8	75,537	42,438	47,042	50,326	42,463	336,468	307,248	57.0	190,400	1,115
Friendswood	108,135	8.0	22.0	133,400	46,954	72,532	86,464	61,491	14,402	13,540	76.6	300,100	1,394
Frisco	128,761	7.0	25.5	152,433	60,559	92,142	108,313	66,329	68,274	64,151	70.1	420,700	1,508
Galveston	51,280	27.5	5.1	69,046	33,539	45,150	50,963	40,554	32,421	21,683	45.0	196,400	1,024
Garland	63,192	12.7	4.3	69,586	45,174	39,740	41,676	36,226	79,749	75,886	63.2	172,600	1,182
Georgetown	77,188	12.8	8.1	94,563	45,274	51,385	56,232	44,825	29,438	28,075	73.5	287,100	1,278
Grand Prairie	69,171	13.3	3.9	77,943	45,993	45,329	48,027	41,994	66,678	62,679	61.3	174,300	1,142
Grapevine	94,363	8.5	15.0	119,357	62,177	60,406	76,110	52,770	22,924	21,838	53.8	338,700	1,444
Greenville	48,979	25.9	3.0	55,015	30,680	38,135	41,542	33,549	11,175	10,454	51.1	113,800	967
Haltom City	51,067	18.4	1.6	56,053	36,096	36,472	41,338	31,919	15,595	14,601	51.5	131,800	1,050
Harker Heights	73,685	15.7	5.1	81,547	46,301	46,130	54,325	37,893	12,291	11,067	55.7	200,700	912
Harlingen	43,003	31.1	2.4	47,652	28,280	34,173	39,404	30,257	25,623	21,752	56.7	92,000	748
Houston	53,600	22.6	8.4	61,128	41,950	44,055	45,899	41,717	982,694	874,827	42.9	186,800	1,086
Huntsville	31,020	37.5	0.8	47,704	23,161	33,392	36,258	31,280	14,795	13,187	30.4	168,800	887
Hurst	64,441	12.0	5.5	74,677	41,467	47,123	51,592	45,350	15,520	14,340	59.8	209,000	1,120
Hutto	87,333	7.7	4.6	90,842	67,027	46,566	50,336	43,853	8,325	8,106	78.0	213,800	1,779
Irving	66,567	12.8	6.5	74,116	52,122	45,205	49,937	40,625	92,873	86,023	37.7	196,500	1,192
Keller	149,342	5.8	34.9	166,167	72,679	102,452	121,683	70,229	16,667	16,383	82.4	412,800	1,544
Killeen	50,335	20.4	2.0	55,969	36,714	36,884	40,139	34,474	62,287	54,840	44.5	132,000	948
Kingsville	46,053	32.2	1.3	55,642	23,315	45,417	49,815	33,680	11,097	9,399	46.6	96,200	898
Kyle	75,413	8.2	5.5	83,119	52,058	49,574	51,418	44,828	15,265	14,701	66.4	209,300	1,484
Lake Jackson	81,207	8.9	10.3	93,850	50,119	60,313	70,182	46,088	10,834	10,074	62.7	200,800	1,217
Lancaster	57,832	18.6	1.4	65,758	50,416	45,255	45,444	45,208	14,463	13,646	63.4	154,900	1,193
La Porte	75,810	15.9	6.3	87,440	44,387	53,185	63,896	46,097	13,067	12,342	71.6	158,500	1,124
Laredo	51,120	26.6	3.6	54,885	25,687	35,512	40,482	29,393	78,996	72,328	62.4	140,100	858
League City	108,979	8.6	16.7	125,643	55,066	74,360	86,222	61,332	39,204	37,662	75.2	258,800	1,387
Leander	106,108	5.7	15.1	114,421	54,256	62,005	67,952	52,277	19,248	18,505	76.2	292,000	1,516
Lewisville	67,026	11.4	3.9	77,754	50,773	47,441	50,069	44,047	42,845	39,664	42.5	232,800	1,228
Little Elm	94,446	7.6	9.5	102,818	56,089	60,374	64,820	56,993	16,506	15,942	68.8	270,600	1,660
Longview	50,019	24.1	4.2	58,524	31,057	41,575	46,900	36,439	35,528	31,450	53.6	143,300	855
Lubbock	51,623	24.6	4.3	68,905	32,071	42,039	47,656	37,062	109,243	98,849	51.8	147,900	958
Lufkin	48,369	27.0	3.4	54,358	26,143	34,594	39,409	29,028	14,533	12,755	51.0	118,500	841
McAllen	49,259	29.0	4.4	54,649	33,108	39,245	42,648	35,010	51,237	45,429	59.5	131,500	829
McKinney	100,775	9.9	14.3	113,500	53,907	66,129	81,967	54,716	68,543	65,065	65.6	327,800	1,442
Mansfield	102,388	7.3	12.9	113,445	54,866	62,455	73,929	55,344	23,675	22,760	74.9	279,200	1,447

1. Specified owner-occupied units

City	Commuting, 2016–2020[1]		Computer access[2], 2016–2020		Migration, 2016–2020		Civilian labor force, 2021				Civilian Employment, 2016–2020[4]			
	Percent		Percent						Unemployment[3]		Population age 16 and older		Population age 16 to 64	
	Drove alone	Mean travel time to work	With a computer in the house	With Internet access	Percent who lived in the same house one year ago	Percent who lived in another state or county one year ago	Total	Percent change 2020–2021	Total	Rate	Number	Percent in labor force	Number	Percent who worked full-year full-time
	55	56	57	58	59	60	61	62	63	64	65	66	67	68
TEXAS —Cont'd														
Austin	70.1	24.6	96.2	89.4	79.0	8.9	610,454	5.4	23,630	3.9	792,215	74.3	701,182	58.3
Balch Springs	67.8	35.5	93.7	83.0	88.4	3.3	10,619	4.4	730	6.9	18,075	70.1	15,892	47.5
Baytown	85.9	25.3	91.9	82.4	83.5	6.8	34,074	-0.9	4,231	12.4	56,799	63.3	47,983	49.8
Beaumont	87.9	18.7	91.2	76.5	86.6	5.3	48,521	-2.3	4,381	9.0	91,344	59.5	73,655	49.4
Bedford	79.9	25.7	96.0	91.3	77.6	6.9	28,767	2.3	1,505	5.2	39,372	69.0	31,296	61.0
Big Spring	78.1	18.0	90.4	78.9	83.1	10.8	9,575	-0.8	676	7.1	22,345	49.9	19,090	38.4
Brownsville	81.8	20.1	83.9	57.9	90.1	2.2	78,866	3.0	6,595	8.4	135,191	56.7	112,561	43.3
Bryan	81.4	16.7	91.4	78.0	76.8	9.8	45,082	4.0	2,019	4.5	67,024	62.9	57,319	50.7
Burleson	89.1	30.2	96.6	91.1	86.8	7.2	26,200	3.1	1,206	4.6	34,803	71.7	29,379	64.1
Carrollton	78.4	25.6	97.8	90.5	87.1	7.3	83,975	3.8	3,696	4.4	112,147	73.6	96,261	59.6
Cedar Hill	82.5	30.9	98.2	93.6	87.6	3.4	26,865	4.0	1,826	6.8	36,027	71.1	31,568	57.8
Cedar Park	72.9	27.8	98.0	95.6	83.1	10.1	44,901	5.8	1,717	3.8	58,276	71.2	50,950	57.7
Cibolo	82.3	30.7	96.7	93.5	84.2	11.4	15,908	2.9	714	4.5	22,345	60.2	19,469	53.0
Cleburne	88.8	27.8	90.7	84.4	89.3	4.3	14,216	3.0	723	5.1	23,675	59.1	18,565	52.8
College Station	76.3	16.8	98.2	85.3	64.6	17.5	62,380	4.2	2,400	3.8	98,251	59.9	90,550	35.1
Colleyville	72.7	26.5	99.7	99.0	90.8	3.2	14,817	4.0	539	3.6	21,034	63.8	16,162	49.4
Conroe	82.0	27.5	94.0	88.3	81.5	7.1	44,856	1.5	2,629	5.9	68,838	65.7	56,752	55.6
Converse	83.0	28.1	97.3	90.8	84.2	9.2	14,546	2.3	889	6.1	20,106	65.4	17,333	52.6
Coppell	79.2	24.8	99.7	96.3	87.4	5.7	23,604	4.2	1,036	4.4	31,588	73.8	27,877	60.8
Copperas Cove	81.8	25.5	94.5	89.9	78.3	14.4	12,794	2.3	742	5.8	25,059	57.2	21,726	51.2
Corpus Christi	82.4	19.4	91.3	84.8	83.3	5.6	148,791	0.3	10,214	6.9	255,131	62.2	209,600	52.1
Dallas	74.3	26.9	89.8	80.9	83.5	6.2	696,594	3.7	39,624	5.7	1,040,423	68.7	898,324	56.2
Deer Park	86.2	25.0	95.1	92.2	88.0	4.7	16,071	1.4	1,150	7.2	26,268	65.0	21,129	51.9
Del Rio	81.2	18.6	83.6	64.9	85.8	6.8	16,229	3.4	1,030	6.3	26,775	58.2	21,592	48.4
Denton	74.5	23.9	96.0	89.3	73.9	12.4	81,078	3.7	3,738	4.6	116,400	67.2	100,664	46.7
DeSoto	79.5	31.0	96.1	88.6	88.7	3.3	28,855	4.0	2,108	7.3	41,691	69.0	34,162	57.0
Duncanville	80.8	27.9	93.0	86.8	94.3	1.9	19,936	3.5	1,245	6.2	30,269	61.5	24,136	49.1
Eagle Pass	84.4	21.6	82.1	69.5	85.1	6.7	12,797	-1.8	1,810	14.1	22,321	58.2	18,731	45.6
Edinburg	78.7	19.0	88.7	76.5	85.9	4.8	48,358	2.7	3,072	6.4	71,855	62.3	63,395	45.8
El Paso	80.2	23.4	89.3	81.7	84.9	4.8	302,594	1.2	17,933	5.9	518,769	60.3	430,965	48.0
Euless	83.9	24.5	97.5	92.9	80.8	7.2	32,968	1.6	1,813	5.5	44,574	74.4	38,626	62.2
Farmers Branch	80.3	23.1	97.2	89.8	84.7	7.3	27,803	4.6	1,288	4.6	33,957	73.5	28,939	63.0
Flower Mound	76.7	27.9	98.9	97.0	85.4	7.0	45,517	4.3	1,646	3.6	59,371	71.8	51,256	58.1
Fort Worth	79.1	27.5	94.4	87.5	83.8	6.2	455,572	2.9	25,601	5.6	675,618	68.1	587,332	54.5
Friendswood	80.5	31.2	97.7	96.1	87.0	7.8	19,369	2.1	993	5.1	30,484	68.7	24,775	56.8
Frisco	72.7	29.5	99.0	96.0	83.3	10.8	116,296	4.2	4,326	3.7	138,602	71.1	121,392	58.4
Galveston	72.1	20.8	91.0	84.3	77.0	11.3	23,148	-0.3	1,523	6.6	43,238	57.9	34,410	43.7
Garland	77.7	29.7	96.1	90.3	88.9	3.4	125,213	3.6	6,371	5.1	182,153	69.5	154,038	54.9
Georgetown	77.6	27.4	96.4	92.6	82.3	8.2	36,447	6.3	1,765	4.8	62,247	51.3	40,841	49.1
Grand Prairie	80.1	29.2	94.3	86.2	89.0	6.2	102,076	3.2	5,739	5.6	145,479	69.4	125,986	56.0
Grapevine	79.2	24.0	97.0	95.0	81.2	10.1	33,589	2.9	1,368	4.1	43,912	76.9	37,374	61.7
Greenville	81.9	24.7	90.9	82.2	76.5	9.2	12,347	4.5	713	5.8	21,808	62.8	17,176	52.6
Haltom City	78.5	26.1	92.6	87.1	84.9	4.8	22,215	3.1	1,177	5.3	32,672	67.8	27,923	56.6
Harker Heights	82.4	23.3	95.7	90.9	79.0	10.4	13,119	2.6	723	5.5	24,245	58.8	21,227	51.9
Harlingen	83.1	17.1	86.0	71.9	91.1	3.2	25,589	3.3	1,875	7.3	47,270	58.9	37,491	46.0
Houston	75.9	27.6	91.5	83.1	82.0	5.2	1,127,860	0.9	71,904	6.4	1,799,877	66.7	1,545,749	52.2
Huntsville	77.9	23.6	92.2	85.2	75.6	15.3	11,866	-0.1	834	7.0	37,499	41.4	33,020	26.7
Hurst	80.1	24.9	95.9	87.5	86.9	3.0	20,050	2.6	1,063	5.3	30,079	66.6	23,530	57.4
Hutto	79.4	30.0	98.1	94.6	83.7	7.3	16,891	6.0	705	4.2	20,537	77.0	19,119	59.6
Irving	77.6	24.4	96.4	87.9	79.9	8.8	133,494	3.4	6,864	5.1	182,062	73.3	162,769	59.0
Keller	75.6	30.0	97.5	95.8	86.2	5.2	24,129	3.4	936	3.9	36,205	67.9	29,591	55.4
Killeen	81.1	22.7	94.4	87.1	72.7	13.0	58,202	2.4	4,076	7.0	109,665	60.2	99,023	49.2
Kingsville	79.0	19.5	89.1	78.9	83.2	10.0	10,781	0.3	777	7.2	20,198	58.1	17,171	38.6
Kyle	82.7	38.1	94.7	90.9	86.7	7.9	27,975	5.7	1,176	4.2	33,333	73.4	29,999	62.1
Lake Jackson	85.3	20.6	96.2	91.6	79.6	9.2	13,325	1.3	1,045	7.8	20,875	68.5	17,383	56.3
Lancaster	83.3	30.9	93.1	83.7	82.4	3.9	19,349	3.8	1,637	8.5	28,299	71.1	24,398	55.7
La Porte	83.4	26.9	94.2	89.0	85.9	3.6	18,313	1.2	1,322	7.2	27,520	65.7	23,185	53.9
Laredo	80.7	21.1	86.1	72.3	89.7	2.5	111,574	1.0	6,975	6.3	184,020	61.3	159,812	47.9
League City	84.1	29.8	97.7	93.9	86.8	6.7	57,353	1.9	2,979	5.2	79,927	70.3	69,105	59.6
Leander	74.9	30.4	98.7	94.9	79.3	9.7	37,621	6.4	1,433	3.8	44,235	73.2	39,081	59.8
Lewisville	78.2	25.3	98.1	93.4	78.1	10.6	69,391	3.3	3,256	4.7	84,474	76.3	75,491	60.3
Little Elm	78.0	37.6	98.2	95.6	84.4	12.1	29,602	4.0	1,315	4.4	36,905	74.3	33,543	58.1
Longview	84.5	19.7	90.0	82.9	79.7	8.3	36,722	0.4	2,497	6.8	63,519	60.4	50,849	52.3
Lubbock	79.8	16.0	93.3	81.7	74.1	11.3	135,384	2.8	6,200	4.6	204,516	64.8	173,020	48.8
Lufkin	79.2	16.1	91.2	86.3	80.6	7.6	14,665	1.5	942	6.4	27,074	60.4	21,850	49.8
McAllen	76.1	20.1	91.2	84.8	88.2	3.4	68,224	2.3	4,439	6.5	106,298	61.6	88,179	46.9
McKinney	78.2	29.2	97.7	92.1	84.0	7.8	111,026	3.9	4,908	4.4	141,267	71.0	120,937	60.8
Mansfield	83.0	30.0	97.1	94.2	85.0	7.3	39,107	3.3	1,848	4.7	53,250	70.2	45,648	57.3

1. Employed persons. 2. Households. 3. Percent of civilian labor force. 4. Persons 16 years old and over.

City	Value of residential construction authorized by building permits, 2021			Wholesale trade[1], 2017				Retail trade[2], 2017			
	New construction ($1,000)	Number of housing units	Percent single family	Number of establishments	Number of employees	Sales (mil dol)	Annual payroll (mil dol)	Number of establish-ments	Number of employees	Sales (mil dol)	Annual payroll (mil dol)
	69	70	71	72	73	74	75	76	77	78	79
TEXAS —Cont'd											
Austin	3,117,892	18,722	22.3	1,028	21,202	79,057.2	1,738.1	3,359	57,095	18,284.1	1,789.7
Balch Springs	2,147	9	100.0	12	291	256.8	16.8	82	1,307	394.5	30.5
Baytown	73,504	309	100.0	54	612	287.7	30.3	287	5,915	1,982.3	150.0
Beaumont	62,749	308	90.9	178	2,276	1,896.8	134.6	599	9,023	2,833.2	260.4
Bedford	775	2	100.0	31	140	96.3	10.9	128	1,982	650.7	57.2
Big Spring	587	2	100.0	24	151	163.4	9.2	103	1,392	484.2	40.2
Brownsville	114,759	1,129	78.2	184	1,317	761.4	48.1	513	9,075	2,244.0	214.5
Bryan	207,857	1,220	82.5	82	1,574	1,098.5	88.5	301	4,049	1,399.6	114.6
Burleson	79,138	615	35.8	28	228	213.5	11.9	181	3,925	1,369.5	108.1
Carrollton	94,285	467	70.0	404	6,804	5,736.1	426.9	442	6,032	2,248.2	226.5
Cedar Hill	33,906	74	100.0	15	242	140.8	15.4	147	3,360	625.0	67.6
Cedar Park	18,696	103	100.0	50	469	233.7	24.6	278	4,438	1,293.4	120.7
Cibolo	120,255	493	100.0	D	D	D	D	24	440	108.8	12.6
Cleburne	84,224	584	45.2	36	417	227.0	19.0	139	2,469	836.9	78.6
College Station	169,655	992	67.9	38	277	152.2	14.0	311	6,258	1,544.6	134.8
Colleyville	33,714	52	100.0	34	103	112.2	9.3	86	1,051	240.9	27.8
Conroe	679,698	3,081	83.5	123	1,557	5,416.1	94.3	385	7,488	2,739.2	236.2
Converse	65,169	377	100.0	13	299	521.5	22.4	34	706	178.1	20.2
Coppell	6,706	20	100.0	94	2,704	2,902.8	191.2	89	3,727	1,821.6	202.2
Copperas Cove	24,327	211	32.7	D	D	D	0.0	76	1,169	309.4	29.2
Corpus Christi	350,967	1,470	100.0	355	5,276	2,845.6	279.7	978	17,527	5,160.2	471.3
Dallas	1,426,686	10,014	22.4	1,969	32,922	27,651.6	1,951.3	4,129	65,708	20,463.0	2,023.3
Deer Park	3,521	15	100.0	45	794	397.9	55.3	68	1,379	396.8	35.9
Del Rio	21,750	100	100.0	D	D	D	4.8	140	2,078	638.6	50.4
Denton	428,698	1,665	72.3	93	1,158	1,214.5	69.3	445	7,546	2,280.5	182.5
DeSoto	67,484	283	99.3	31	338	238.4	16.5	87	2,484	1,079.9	77.4
Duncanville	1,232	6	100.0	20	276	106.5	17.7	112	1,606	617.8	49.0
Eagle Pass	35,862	135	93.3	33	165	175.2	9.1	148	2,641	637.0	57.1
Edinburg	141,174	930	50.9	79	1,692	731.7	66.4	220	4,634	1,420.7	112.7
El Paso	495,339	2,233	87.8	852	9,401	7,535.4	415.2	1,984	34,562	9,051.9	814.6
Euless	33,733	141	100.0	40	734	373.6	54.6	171	2,506	735.0	64.8
Farmers Branch	73,382	309	100.0	214	6,108	4,636.7	409.0	192	3,002	1,118.0	110.0
Flower Mound	105,189	445	99.1	87	1,922	1,651.9	108.8	155	3,358	941.7	78.7
Fort Worth	1,944,022	11,574	62.5	699	17,277	17,429.4	1,216.1	2,246	39,925	13,691.4	1,123.3
Friendswood	37,695	81	100.0	20	127	164.1	9.1	90	1,292	399.4	31.7
Frisco	627,320	3,390	55.4	131	2,676	21,828.4	197.5	540	11,660	4,102.1	353.4
Galveston	51,908	251	100.0	34	298	196.3	10.1	217	2,707	726.8	71.7
Garland	138,842	427	100.0	182	3,339	2,039.5	177.5	612	9,410	2,938.4	247.4
Georgetown	859,759	5,941	39.3	48	408	282.8	24.4	205	3,806	1,510.1	122.7
Grand Prairie	427,027	2,293	53.8	295	6,961	6,160.8	428.2	371	5,732	2,134.6	170.4
Grapevine	61,642	380	14.7	101	2,152	3,344.0	161.0	312	5,614	2,845.4	199.7
Greenville	62,871	505	98.0	D	D	D	7.5	139	2,540	856.2	75.1
Haltom City	28,934	101	100.0	111	1,524	1,188.0	79.1	147	1,545	548.8	51.7
Harker Heights	58,198	222	72.1	3	D	2.1	D	57	1,246	322.2	31.4
Harlingen	11,050	84	0.0	73	716	1,063.1	28.8	289	5,440	1,486.2	139.7
Houston	2,474,713	15,249	46.9	4,721	81,680	364,405.6	5,882.7	9,493	159,513	53,089.2	4,696.5
Huntsville	91,047	652	37.9	22	224	177.9	10.3	144	2,490	843.1	61.6
Hurst	1,196	5	100.0	27	173	139.2	9.7	274	5,553	1,350.0	126.0
Hutto	729,773	2,080	100.0	7	55	18.6	3.1	29	574	270.7	19.0
Irving	193,515	1,094	33.5	351	12,141	13,991.2	1,035.2	668	12,263	5,172.6	379.8
Keller	60,448	101	100.0	25	74	30.6	3.5	103	1,689	881.4	40.5
Killeen	190,038	1,204	49.2	D	D	D	4.1	402	6,892	2,005.1	174.4
Kingsville	5,259	44	61.4	D	D	D	D	88	1,310	411.8	35.5
Kyle	382,544	2,133	66.4	12	118	71.8	6.7	68	1,872	522.3	45.5
Lake Jackson	6,475	21	100.0	7	20	3.0	0.6	104	2,664	772.4	70.7
Lancaster	7,866	37	100.0	23	900	1,135.0	38.1	64	1,075	278.6	26.1
La Porte	74,218	320	100.0	46	1,422	700.2	87.1	72	576	195.3	16.9
Laredo	251,974	1,684	86.8	D	D	D	109.8	795	13,447	3,357.2	314.3
League City	92,827	388	100.0	61	590	320.2	32.4	213	4,426	1,560.8	124.6
Leander	599,116	3,233	74.2	13	57	22.8	2.5	58	835	244.6	22.4
Lewisville	340,402	1,885	28.4	126	3,335	9,848.5	229.0	438	7,375	2,595.3	210.1
Little Elm	400,656	1,555	81.5	17	114	65.4	6.7	52	985	293.0	23.9
Longview	64,242	325	69.2	165	2,129	1,040.1	107.9	490	7,419	2,094.0	201.2
Lubbock	649,071	3,131	78.4	312	4,860	5,343.4	271.2	889	17,441	5,351.4	481.6
Lufkin	15,660	72	100.0	45	589	272.3	30.6	254	4,462	1,294.0	117.2
McAllen	195,762	1,012	79.7	360	3,343	2,380.4	134.8	847	14,186	3,520.4	333.8
McKinney	504,460	1,727	100.0	130	1,730	1,923.4	121.6	395	8,136	3,100.3	266.9
Mansfield	348,569	1,050	100.0	58	2,147	1,224.9	111.9	160	3,527	994.7	82.5

1. Merchant wholesalers except manufacturers' sales branches and offices. 2. Establishments with payroll.

City	Real estate and rental and leasing, 2017				Professional, scientific, and technical services[1], 2017				Manufacturing, 2017			
	Number of establish-ments	Number of employees	Receipts (mil dol)	Annual payroll (mil dol)	Number of establish-ments	Number of employees	Receipts (mil dol)	Annual payroll (mil dol)	Number of establish-ments	Number of employees	Receipts (mil dol)	Annual payroll (mil dol)
	80	81	82	83	84	85	86	87	88	89	90	91
TEXAS —Cont'd												
Austin	2,089	14,255	4,160.0	887.0	6,026	84,531	19,150.5	8,355.5	NA	NA	NA	NA
Balch Springs	13	41	10.1	1.2	7	43	2.4	0.9	NA	NA	NA	NA
Baytown	87	607	173.4	32.8	107	1,685	168.5	116.4	NA	NA	NA	NA
Beaumont	202	1,513	387.9	69.8	349	4,657	847.9	354.9	NA	NA	NA	NA
Bedford	70	353	82.8	25.8	155	731	138.8	48.6	NA	NA	NA	NA
Big Spring	32	109	31.5	3.9	34	155	18.0	6.1	NA	NA	NA	NA
Brownsville	138	621	97.0	17.7	271	1,956	198.1	66.9	NA	NA	NA	NA
Bryan	111	632	105.5	22.4	196	1,050	144.2	62.5	NA	NA	NA	NA
Burleson	50	224	62.0	15.5	65	255	32.9	9.8	NA	NA	NA	NA
Carrollton	179	1,544	393.9	86.8	430	3,556	591.5	203.6	NA	NA	NA	NA
Cedar Hill	27	92	31.0	4.9	58	177	19.0	5.7	NA	NA	NA	NA
Cedar Park	97	356	113.3	12.9	241	1,310	197.7	79.8	NA	NA	NA	NA
Cibolo	10	26	3.3	0.5	16	38	6.1	1.8	NA	NA	NA	NA
Cleburne	43	260	29.1	5.8	73	298	43.0	15.3	NA	NA	NA	NA
College Station	149	726	147.5	22.0	205	2,008	288.6	120.1	NA	NA	NA	NA
Colleyville	68	149	34.3	6.3	183	686	181.5	44.8	NA	NA	NA	NA
Conroe	111	515	121.7	21.9	227	1,007	145.4	54.3	NA	NA	NA	NA
Converse	15	50	13.3	2.2	16	56	7.8	2.2	NA	NA	NA	NA
Coppell	85	829	217.8	58.6	278	5,864	948.7	563.7	NA	NA	NA	NA
Copperas Cove	32	119	14.4	3.9	26	117	12.0	3.5	NA	NA	NA	NA
Corpus Christi	413	2,647	670.5	135.0	786	7,070	1,153.2	439.5	NA	NA	NA	NA
Dallas	2,555	24,594	8,069.8	1,686.4	5,875	83,897	19,110.6	7,385.4	NA	NA	NA	NA
Deer Park	39	476	156.1	34.1	73	2,057	307.8	147.2	NA	NA	NA	NA
Del Rio	35	105	24.1	3.7	35	213	23.8	6.4	NA	NA	NA	NA
Denton	187	990	197.5	37.5	292	1,417	159.7	77.5	NA	NA	NA	NA
DeSoto	44	225	50.4	9.0	42	240	26.8	13.2	NA	NA	NA	NA
Duncanville	40	D	30.2	D	55	286	23.7	10.4	NA	NA	NA	NA
Eagle Pass	D	D	D	D	34	196	20.8	7.6	NA	NA	NA	NA
Edinburg	69	204	27.9	5.3	154	1,195	135.2	40.9	NA	NA	NA	NA
El Paso	793	3,791	832.8	139.5	1,211	9,756	1,508.2	458.7	NA	NA	NA	NA
Euless	D	D	D	D	92	839	180.9	64.3	NA	NA	NA	NA
Farmers Branch	101	1,235	464.2	83.1	395	6,430	1,367.4	580.9	NA	NA	NA	NA
Flower Mound	D	D	D	D	334	1,949	333.7	118.1	NA	NA	NA	NA
Fort Worth	910	5,596	1,653.2	273.3	1,891	20,570	3,489.9	1,424.4	NA	NA	NA	NA
Friendswood	48	122	26.6	4.4	142	551	81.1	30.1	NA	NA	NA	NA
Frisco	251	946	307.1	44.9	954	5,484	1,154.9	461.8	NA	NA	NA	NA
Galveston	75	334	66.8	12.9	111	606	129.3	36.4	NA	NA	NA	NA
Garland	175	1,385	316.7	53.3	298	2,261	277.2	125.4	NA	NA	NA	NA
Georgetown	87	319	112.8	17.9	203	807	115.0	43.8	NA	NA	NA	NA
Grand Prairie	144	1,367	331.3	63.1	187	1,289	242.1	77.2	NA	NA	NA	NA
Grapevine	115	1,177	432.3	68.0	253	1,725	356.8	132.7	NA	NA	NA	NA
Greenville	39	167	38.1	9.0	45	501	61.0	23.1	NA	NA	NA	NA
Haltom City	31	197	59.9	10.1	53	276	38.7	12.7	NA	NA	NA	NA
Harker Heights	27	89	22.0	3.9	27	139	12.4	5.0	NA	NA	NA	NA
Harlingen	113	552	90.9	14.6	151	941	110.7	34.1	NA	NA	NA	NA
Houston	4,321	35,135	10,879.3	1,938.1	10,488	153,689	36,911.7	14,228.3	NA	NA	NA	NA
Huntsville	52	161	37.5	5.1	65	412	31.6	10.3	NA	NA	NA	NA
Hurst	41	222	59.2	11.1	143	747	92.2	42.1	NA	NA	NA	NA
Hutto	9	18	4.7	1.0	16	59	5.2	1.7	NA	NA	NA	NA
Irving	381	4,869	2,280.8	296.9	1,235	25,765	5,415.4	2,290.2	NA	NA	NA	NA
Keller	62	172	63.6	8.2	177	604	113.2	39.6	NA	NA	NA	NA
Killeen	152	630	123.3	21.3	110	984	110.2	47.0	NA	NA	NA	NA
Kingsville	29	116	29.0	4.5	D	D	D	D	NA	NA	NA	NA
Kyle	D	D	D	D	26	89	11.4	4.1	NA	NA	NA	NA
Lake Jackson	31	136	21.1	3.6	39	204	28.5	8.9	NA	NA	NA	NA
Lancaster	19	78	22.0	2.9	18	62	13.9	3.0	NA	NA	NA	NA
La Porte	33	370	161.7	24.5	68	2,355	374.8	189.1	NA	NA	NA	NA
Laredo	247	890	214.1	28.8	D	D	D	D	NA	NA	NA	NA
League City	86	295	75.2	13.2	189	1,921	268.8	110.3	NA	NA	NA	NA
Leander	35	63	14.2	2.7	87	281	46.9	17.4	NA	NA	NA	NA
Lewisville	141	746	242.4	36.8	248	2,665	477.5	177.9	NA	NA	NA	NA
Little Elm	19	51	16.3	1.8	65	141	18.6	7.0	NA	NA	NA	NA
Longview	146	683	164.2	29.4	306	2,240	406.7	132.1	NA	NA	NA	NA
Lubbock	412	1,912	398.0	72.0	606	4,324	585.5	223.4	NA	NA	NA	NA
Lufkin	64	314	94.3	11.2	116	659	87.7	32.5	NA	NA	NA	NA
McAllen	242	858	195.9	29.0	502	3,860	392.0	136.0	NA	NA	NA	NA
McKinney	214	755	211.8	36.3	514	2,206	361.5	155.1	NA	NA	NA	NA
Mansfield	58	207	66.1	10.8	129	505	76.6	29.4	NA	NA	NA	NA

1. Establishments subject to federal tax.

Table D. Cities — Accommodation and Food Services, Arts, Entertainment, and Recreation, and Health Care and Social Assistance

City	Accommodation and food services, 2017				Arts, entertainment, and recreation[1], 2017				Health care and social assistance[1], 2017			
	Number of establish-ments	Number of employees	Receipts (mil dol)	Annual payroll (mil dol)	Number of establish-ments	Number of employees	Receipts (mil dol)	Annual payroll (mil dol)	Number of establish-ments	Number of employees	Receipts (mil dol)	Annual payroll (mil dol)
	92	93	94	95	96	97	98	99	100	101	102	103
TEXAS —Cont'd												
Austin	2,981	73,697	5,336.9	1,510.1	545.0	9,671	1,121.4	264.7	3,150	71,118	8,839.3	3,392.5
Balch Springs	41	721	52.8	11.8	D	D	D	D	11	122	9.9	3.8
Baytown	206	4,458	264.7	71.6	14.0	194	12.1	3.3	226	4,800	621.8	217.9
Beaumont	299	6,662	382.1	102.3	43.0	561	26.9	8.3	618	13,552	1,408.1	513.8
Bedford	116	2,380	141.2	38.7	10.0	95	7.4	2.3	232	6,185	904.1	316.0
Big Spring	81	1,295	72.0	19.4	D	D	D	D	D	D	D	D
Brownsville	342	6,555	313.1	81.1	30.0	441	19.3	7.0	479	17,053	965.5	431.9
Bryan	175	3,446	167.3	48.1	24.0	645	26.7	12.4	242	4,796	667.2	240.3
Burleson	109	2,547	135.5	36.6	13.0	D	2.9	D	108	1,308	120.8	42.8
Carrollton	351	4,655	291.3	81.5	40.0	984	74.1	18.0	427	6,935	837.1	309.9
Cedar Hill	91	2,145	115.3	31.2	D	D	D	D	100	1,309	98.2	39.5
Cedar Park	185	3,925	223.4	66.8	36.0	785	48.2	11.1	261	3,764	461.6	187.1
Cibolo	16	147	9.4	2.2	4.0	52	3.9	1.5	D	D	D	3.3
Cleburne	88	1,594	78.8	21.6	D	D	D	D	119	1,774	222.1	77.4
College Station	339	9,157	496.9	125.2	37.0	698	29.1	9.0	180	5,705	759.5	256.9
Colleyville	65	1,119	61.2	18.4	18.0	398	39.9	8.1	D	D	D	D
Conroe	196	4,483	335.3	86.4	27.0	542	36.4	8.2	278	4,808	654.8	241.2
Converse	28	673	31.9	9.3	D	D	D	D	29	552	29.3	14.8
Coppell	78	1,927	114.5	35.7	12.0	293	10.3	3.7	173	1,685	176.6	72.7
Copperas Cove	57	1,002	46.4	11.9	D	D	D	D	34	461	29.2	12.7
Corpus Christi	827	18,028	986.9	272.0	86.0	1,963	105.0	35.7	1,071	27,875	2,870.3	1,119.4
Dallas	3,172	73,679	5,436.1	1,525.4	433.0	12,428	1,468.9	493.3	4,386	121,052	18,432.0	6,827.8
Deer Park	66	1,786	90.0	26.4	7.0	10	2.1	0.2	52	787	64.9	26.2
Del Rio	82	1,767	96.8	24.4	D	D	D	0.4	D	D	D	D
Denton	325	7,433	385.5	111.9	D	D	D	D	480	8,327	1,156.4	406.8
DeSoto	76	1,638	81.3	22.8	7.0	85	6.5	2.2	175	4,565	317.1	139.6
Duncanville	67	1,788	98.8	25.1	D	D	D	D	131	1,970	130.3	51.0
Eagle Pass	72	1,407	72.9	19.6	D	D	D	D	101	3,998	237.1	96.3
Edinburg	142	2,768	146.6	39.0	D	D	D	D	332	10,504	578.8	251.9
El Paso	1,448	32,400	1,566.2	435.8	148.0	2,663	142.4	48.8	1,635	45,067	4,614.4	1,704.1
Euless	96	1,756	106.5	26.2	15.0	417	23.9	6.4	85	1,191	87.1	34.6
Farmers Branch	106	2,964	196.2	57.0	18.0	474	32.1	11.5	191	5,030	666.8	282.5
Flower Mound	D	D	D	D	29.0	494	25.1	7.9	274	3,895	497.3	176.0
Fort Worth	1,644	37,634	2,349.7	654.7	205.0	6,153	613.7	147.5	2,113	59,067	8,752.7	2,973.0
Friendswood	66	1,136	58.8	16.6	13.0	113	7.8	2.5	139	1,243	112.9	42.7
Frisco	434	9,494	624.5	175.1	98.0	2,919	1,130.6	362.3	647	7,966	1,132.1	390.2
Galveston	240	7,318	524.9	149.2	36.0	546	46.7	11.0	128	8,418	824.2	365.1
Garland	364	6,701	389.6	106.8	34.0	678	37.7	9.0	492	10,093	700.5	286.5
Georgetown	127	2,822	160.1	48.2	23.0	344	25.5	7.7	197	4,577	428.9	204.5
Grand Prairie	249	4,808	309.6	77.5	25.0	628	107.3	16.1	282	4,994	327.2	114.0
Grapevine	217	9,464	824.1	210.4	27.0	736	59.1	13.3	254	3,640	676.2	204.3
Greenville	80	1,770	97.8	27.6	9.0	84	6.2	1.3	130	2,922	319.5	132.5
Haltom City	72	905	52.3	13.0	D	D	D	D	43	489	37.7	17.0
Harker Heights	62	912	33.7	9.0	8.0	35	1.8	0.4	D	D	D	D
Harlingen	173	4,065	216.6	62.3	20.0	D	10.7	D	375	15,455	1,149.4	463.7
Houston	7,240	159,256	11,039.1	3,058.4	783.0	25,027	3,042.3	1,088.9	8,402	220,087	32,073.4	11,737.5
Huntsville	D	D	D	32.3	D	D	D	D	96	2,188	243.5	87.5
Hurst	136	4,142	167.6	45.6	17.0	208	10.3	2.8	152	1,581	168.5	70.2
Hutto	25	468	28.5	7.9	D	D	D	D	D	D	D	8.9
Irving	656	13,735	1,080.8	288.2	62.0	773	84.0	21.6	676	12,494	1,927.2	719.0
Keller	78	1,384	71.8	21.1	19.0	199	20.7	4.1	153	1,670	175.8	59.1
Killeen	274	6,252	322.7	84.7	D	D	D	D	211	2,898	308.8	120.8
Kingsville	68	1,238	65.8	18.3	3.0	D	1.3	D	72	1,305	103.5	41.0
Kyle	59	1,337	72.6	21.4	8.0	145	16.6	3.3	82	1,950	274.1	103.7
Lake Jackson	83	1,943	114.3	31.8	D	D	D	D	145	2,214	222.2	95.9
Lancaster	46	862	44.6	12.0	3.0	19	0.9	0.3	47	1,304	103.2	38.8
La Porte	68	1,391	88.5	24.6	NA	NA	NA	NA	44	448	36.5	15.2
Laredo	D	D	D	D	D	D	D	D	D	D	D	D
League City	169	3,453	183.5	55.1	D	D	D	D	200	2,907	259.7	99.2
Leander	D	D	D	D	D	D	D	D	57	407	38.2	15.8
Lewisville	275	5,161	323.9	85.6	44.0	1,023	66.8	19.4	284	5,698	846.3	345.8
Little Elm	56	949	48.9	14.4	15.0	83	6.3	1.7	36	294	40.6	14.2
Longview	274	5,630	286.5	86.2	30.0	328	17.8	5.6	393	10,308	1,186.9	453.4
Lubbock	668	15,930	904.2	255.1	84.0	1,923	86.9	28.4	819	23,907	2,964.2	1,013.4
Lufkin	124	2,849	158.2	43.7	15.0	184	9.0	3.3	263	7,245	605.9	250.8
McAllen	439	10,773	542.4	152.2	46.0	574	52.4	12.5	821	18,470	1,717.3	607.3
McKinney	288	6,578	373.6	110.0	55.0	1,078	64.3	23.4	516	7,979	994.5	363.4
Mansfield	139	3,622	199.6	55.1	25.0	693	42.4	12.0	D	D	D	D

1. Establishments subject to federal tax.

City	Other services[1]				Government employment and payroll, 2017								
						March payroll							
							Perent of total for:						
	Number of establish-ments	Number of employees	Receipts (mil dol)	Annual payroll (mil dol)	Full-time equivalent employees	Total (dollars)	Admin-istrative, judicial, and legal	Police and corrections	Fire protection	Highways and trans-portation	Health and welfare	Natural resources and utilities	Education and libraries
	104	105	106	107	108	109	110	111	112	113	114	115	116
TEXAS —Cont'd													
Austin	2,203	19,625	2,930.9	834.6	13,610	84,706,545	10.3	25.1	12.4	6.3	7.8	32.4	1.9
Balch Springs	36	216	26.7	7.5	169	1,117,916	11.0	34.2	30.4	5.9	1.4	11.1	1.2
Baytown	116	1,119	133.0	47.8	871	4,767,592	12.1	29.2	25.9	2.7	3.1	19.6	2.2
Beaumont	225	2,630	238.3	125.1	1,065	5,508,111	7.0	32.3	26.9	5.2	6.6	16.1	1.5
Bedford	63	508	56.1	13.8	365	1,912,040	12.3	26.5	26.1	6.2	0.0	13.2	3.9
Big Spring	37	286	25.5	6.5	244	1,004,920	14.6	24.2	30.1	6.4	2.3	20.7	0.0
Brownsville	139	625	50.4	12.5	1,466	6,013,698	8.8	29.9	19.9	11.0	3.3	23.5	2.6
Bryan	150	962	149.2	31.8	722	3,508,034	16.8	29.1	23.3	6.0	0.9	18.3	3.7
Burleson	D	D	D	D	366	1,929,487	11.7	23.3	16.5	8.0	5.1	22.9	2.2
Carrollton	234	1,673	176.3	54.1	880	3,924,840	15.9	22.5	26.7	8.8	4.6	11.3	3.3
Cedar Hill	D	D	D	D	344	1,659,912	11.5	28.9	23.5	4.3	5.2	20.0	2.6
Cedar Park	161	1,034	107.0	36.2	441	2,303,041	13.9	30.9	21.7	5.9	0.6	13.7	2.3
Cibolo	D	D	D	D	104	424,190	11.6	42.1	15.3	11.1	0.0	18.5	0.0
Cleburne	71	442	43.8	14.4	342	1,450,782	7.2	26.9	22.2	3.2	5.3	23.6	1.7
College Station	111	1,071	459.1	40.6	902	4,439,747	21.2	23.7	20.1	5.8	0.0	24.1	0.0
Colleyville	81	657	69.6	20.6	197	1,044,356	15.0	27.6	24.1	3.0	0.4	13.4	4.6
Conroe	152	1,014	105.0	30.9	584	2,887,973	11.2	30.4	23.3	8.9	0.4	16.8	0.0
Converse	D	D	D	D	161	598,967	10.3	36.2	24.3	5.9	0.0	9.8	1.6
Coppell	80	1,046	137.2	47.9	376	1,874,509	21.0	8.1	33.0	8.0	0.0	27.0	2.8
Copperas Cove	52	296	27.5	7.6	264	1,107,609	17.2	31.6	11.6	1.3	8.3	18.8	2.2
Corpus Christi	487	3,837	575.6	130.5	2,997	13,665,749	12.9	27.4	20.1	7.2	2.6	25.0	0.9
Dallas	1,883	18,163	3,603.5	793.1	14,767	85,321,347	8.2	29.6	18.5	18.5	4.0	15.6	1.4
Deer Park	D	D	D	D	372	1,670,930	18.5	32.4	5.3	2.7	0.0	32.5	2.9
Del Rio	D	D	D	D	522	1,616,515	13.5	25.6	21.8	5.8	8.5	17.9	0.0
Denton	205	1,328	177.4	50.9	1,496	8,533,833	14.1	16.8	16.4	5.2	1.6	40.8	2.3
DeSoto	52	214	18.3	5.4	358	1,779,783	8.0	33.4	23.2	1.4	0.4	13.5	2.8
Duncanville	68	445	44.4	19.5	278	1,360,082	13.8	29.8	21.9	5.3	0.4	16.7	3.3
Eagle Pass	33	149	10.4	3.3	393	1,137,666	7.7	31.4	17.9	16.1	3.9	20.4	1.6
Edinburg	80	339	26.1	7.4	873	3,090,023	9.4	34.0	9.3	3.6	1.5	27.4	2.9
El Paso	D	D	D	D	6,522	25,566,174	8.6	25.6	20.7	13.2	6.2	13.5	1.7
Euless	67	522	88.5	24.7	423	2,376,427	13.0	35.4	23.0	3.6	1.8	16.8	4.0
Farmers Branch	85	1,144	154.4	37.8	385	2,278,646	11.1	24.5	24.6	3.4	0.7	19.4	0.0
Flower Mound	110	959	107.2	31.7	554	3,000,454	9.0	24.5	28.6	2.9	3.5	16.7	2.5
Fort Worth	1,001	9,263	1,154.8	287.3	6,703	38,281,122	9.2	37.3	19.2	4.6	5.5	19.7	1.9
Friendswood	59	297	26.2	9.3	220	1,012,376	22.9	46.4	0.5	5.2	7.5	9.5	6.1
Frisco	237	1,660	195.0	58.2	636	3,316,154	9.9	30.4	23.9	5.3	1.2	19.8	3.8
Galveston	116	650	248.5	20.7	905	4,048,763	14.8	27.8	16.8	24.0	4.1	12.2	0.0
Garland	265	1,418	141.4	42.1	2,118	11,691,722	10.3	24.2	16.5	3.5	2.9	28.9	2.3
Georgetown	118	654	74.3	22.4	665	3,544,984	15.9	18.2	21.2	3.2	2.1	27.1	3.0
Grand Prairie	202	1,382	153.2	43.6	1,359	7,454,175	10.2	33.3	24.0	3.8	6.2	12.9	1.5
Grapevine	101	1,418	275.9	44.3	649	3,495,468	12.7	24.0	20.6	7.7	0.7	14.6	2.9
Greenville	41	206	19.2	5.2	388	1,877,528	0.0	22.0	16.8	1.6	0.2	56.7	1.4
Haltom City	81	540	78.4	20.5	240	1,343,974	12.6	34.3	37.7	3.6	0.0	7.5	4.3
Harker Heights	34	198	14.0	3.8	219	967,994	17.1	30.7	21.9	3.2	0.5	17.4	3.2
Harlingen	113	698	59.5	18.1	765	2,944,522	7.3	29.0	19.4	8.3	1.4	21.9	1.9
Houston	4,429	40,422	5,805.8	1,502.3	21,657	108,741,222	7.1	36.9	21.1	7.4	5.3	8.6	1.6
Huntsville	48	316	26.9	7.3	346	1,383,500	24.2	27.0	5.3	6.5	0.0	23.7	2.5
Hurst	85	537	45.7	14.5	396	2,083,352	10.9	34.9	19.8	2.4	3.0	15.5	4.2
Hutto	17	69	7.9	2.6	60	309,656	21.4	60.5	0.0	3.6	0.0	11.0	3.5
Irving	324	6,050	1,256.9	278.1	1,975	10,564,254	10.5	26.4	23.0	6.1	2.7	20.3	4.1
Keller	72	434	41.1	14.5	321	1,555,104	14.1	30.2	22.2	2.4	5.0	21.8	3.8
Killeen	182	1,068	105.5	27.8	1,201	4,971,267	12.2	33.8	25.0	4.9	1.1	16.6	1.4
Kingsville	36	155	16.7	3.1	283	966,742	14.4	26.1	16.5	4.7	2.8	22.8	2.8
Kyle	35	221	18.0	5.1	184	801,895	11.6	38.9	0.0	6.8	0.8	18.8	3.6
Lake Jackson	33	229	13.1	4.9	230	1,227,377	12.7	28.9	0.9	5.6	0.0	33.5	0.0
Lancaster	26	170	23.2	6.8	227	1,083,542	7.2	31.0	33.3	3.6	0.8	18.4	2.3
La Porte	D	D	439.4	D	381	1,918,813	14.2	39.2	4.9	4.6	8.0	19.5	0.0
Laredo	D	D	D	D	2,590	12,767,862	6.2	34.8	23.4	10.1	8.4	14.7	1.3
League City	117	802	67.8	19.6	550	2,481,831	14.5	36.3	2.2	9.6	9.0	16.5	3.8
Leander	43	172	22.0	6.8	243	1,175,001	11.2	25.8	24.8	8.8	0.0	15.5	0.0
Lewisville	178	1,131	142.5	40.9	813	3,202,868	11.3	32.7	23.1	4.7	6.3	14.4	2.1
Little Elm	29	154	13.5	4.1	224	1,387,532	9.0	25.4	29.4	6.9	2.1	16.6	2.0
Longview	183	1,531	158.1	51.0	857	3,771,794	8.9	27.7	26.8	2.0	4.5	20.6	1.6
Lubbock	405	3,610	366.7	103.9	2,204	10,549,253	8.5	28.8	24.8	3.9	2.1	29.2	1.2
Lufkin	96	628	88.6	19.7	436	1,707,473	10.8	29.9	21.4	5.6	0.0	22.8	1.8
McAllen	195	1,286	106.3	30.4	1,845	6,873,623	11.7	27.9	14.5	11.7	3.0	26.1	3.0
McKinney	193	1,398	153.4	45.7	1,059	6,033,670	14.3	28.5	22.3	9.4	0.1	13.4	2.5
Mansfield	93	771	77.9	22.9	502	2,465,516	12.0	32.8	24.1	6.2	1.4	17.2	1.4

1. Establishments subject to federal tax.

City	City government finances, 2017: General revenue: Total (mil dol)	General revenue: Intergovernmental: Total (mil dol)	General revenue: Intergovernmental: Percent from state government	General revenue: Taxes: Total (mil dol)	General revenue: Taxes: Per capita[1] (dollars): Total	General revenue: Taxes: Per capita[1] (dollars): Property	General revenue: Taxes: Per capita[1] (dollars): Sales and gross receipts	General expenditure: Total (mil dol)	General expenditure: Per capita[1] (dollars): Total	General expenditure: Per capita[1] (dollars): Capital outlays
	117	118	119	120	121	122	123	124	125	126
TEXAS —Cont'd										
Austin	1,949.7	96.4	22.6	891.1	937	523	413	2,010.4	2,113	417
Balch Springs	17.4	1.3	43.0	14.4	567	235	332	22.7	899	328
Baytown	135.9	8.8	74.7	60.0	782	324	458	130.7	1,704	322
Beaumont	206.3	46.5	77.5	100.5	845	407	438	192.2	1,616	248
Bedford	47.4	0.7	100.0	32.5	655	338	317	50.8	1,024	118
Big Spring	24.9	1.2	60.4	13.2	479	236	243	18.3	662	31
Brownsville	191.7	21.5	18.3	80.9	443	241	202	175.0	960	98
Bryan	88.2	2.4	6.5	53.3	633	353	280	144.1	1,711	173
Burleson	62.5	0.5	78.3	41.9	911	452	459	60.4	1,312	376
Carrollton	156.7	2.9	82.0	117.2	862	498	363	151.3	1,112	262
Cedar Hill	61.9	0.8	9.7	42.7	876	463	412	56.6	1,160	104
Cedar Park	97.2	6.9	100.0	58.2	770	348	422	79.8	1,057	259
Cibolo	21.7	0.3	9.1	13.0	448	270	178	15.4	531	44
Cleburne	51.7	2.6	36.2	29.5	979	515	464	53.4	1,768	611
College Station	111.1	3.0	36.1	69.6	608	283	325	104.6	914	184
Colleyville	39.6	0.6	100.0	30.7	1,153	780	373	33.2	1,245	99
Conroe	108.1	10.9	10.2	78.5	926	310	616	118.9	1,402	494
Converse	17.6	0.6	2.2	9.9	368	202	165	14.2	526	35
Coppell	91.7	3.4	2.3	75.8	1,805	864	941	106.3	2,531	963
Copperas Cove	28.8	0.2	18.8	18.9	581	446	135	19.3	593	0
Corpus Christi	448.0	30.4	41.2	234.9	722	340	381	436.0	1,339	248
Dallas	3,128.3	142.0	62.3	1,329.3	990	617	373	3,235.6	2,410	631
Deer Park	47.0	0.2	32.7	23.2	682	431	251	43.5	1,281	75
Del Rio	43.6	4.9	53.7	19.1	532	240	292	41.6	1,158	177
Denton	211.0	10.9	57.7	116.4	858	415	443	216.0	1,593	330
DeSoto	58.2	2.6	100.0	37.0	690	453	237	52.6	982	124
Duncanville	42.1	0.6	35.1	24.4	618	345	274	37.4	945	15
Eagle Pass	33.1	3.4	100.0	12.2	417	249	167	256.8	8,761	209
Edinburg	82.3	6.1	80.7	48.8	512	266	246	83.1	871	162
El Paso	868.3	87.0	35.9	458.5	673	352	320	744.6	1,093	214
Euless	82.2	0.7	46.8	56.7	1,025	267	758	92.3	1,671	322
Farmers Branch	61.0	0.6	24.4	48.9	1,302	710	592	61.6	1,639	287
Flower Mound	93.1	2.7	21.1	73.3	956	493	463	78.7	1,026	110
Fort Worth	1,311.3	102.9	69.5	765.5	875	503	372	1,299.6	1,486	214
Friendswood	33.0	0.7	77.3	24.3	609	411	199	36.5	915	238
Frisco	413.0	46.0	1.7	160.5	903	547	355	374.1	2,105	1,072
Galveston	203.8	59.1	87.4	77.9	1,540	570	969	166.1	3,284	1,001
Garland	237.9	17.5	6.5	122.7	515	330	185	219.5	921	62
Georgetown	89.0	4.0	99.9	52.2	738	304	434	100.4	1,421	460
Grand Prairie	281.1	34.0	13.0	152.1	784	395	389	243.5	1,255	143
Grapevine	149.9	3.1	76.6	115.1	2,132	586	1,545	146.8	2,720	716
Greenville	49.2	1.8	4.5	21.5	787	390	398	18.6	679	446
Haltom City	44.7	0.2	28.2	30.5	687	268	419	40.2	904	130
Harker Heights	28.2	0.6	98.9	19.1	618	352	265	29.4	951	247
Harlingen	87.8	7.4	39.0	45.9	704	278	427	83.6	1,283	136
Houston	4,568.5	320.9	35.7	2,501.5	1,080	623	457	4,066.6	1,755	271
Huntsville	37.8	2.9	97.3	17.2	413	140	273	36.6	876	185
Hurst	57.7	1.1	44.0	40.2	1,025	359	667	57.1	1,458	184
Hutto	14.6	0.1	100.0	9.2	364	191	173	16.2	638	104
Irving	325.6	15.8	80.6	241.2	1,002	517	485	349.4	1,452	254
Keller	64.1	5.9	62.8	41.7	886	545	340	53.8	1,142	160
Killeen	131.7	6.4	21.1	68.8	474	264	210	157.8	1,087	152
Kingsville	19.9	0.1	100.0	12.8	504	255	249	13.0	511	53
Kyle	21.0	1.6	24.4	12.8	297	172	125	24.9	576	143
Lake Jackson	33.2	0.0	100.0	18.1	661	214	447	31.9	1,166	117
Lancaster	44.1	0.3	15.0	28.7	728	398	330	41.6	1,056	33
La Porte	65.7	1.0	9.5	36.9	1,042	681	361	48.7	1,378	137
Laredo	426.9	40.9	42.8	151.4	584	297	287	370.2	1,427	193
League City	103.7	3.4	75.8	66.4	635	368	267	88.1	844	154
Leander	44.5	5.6	1.6	29.4	589	395	195	46.0	923	350
Lewisville	126.6	1.5	54.3	90.7	852	330	522	130.2	1,223	341
Little Elm	44.1	0.8	59.4	30.7	667	353	315	30.7	667	13
Longview	128.3	11.1	30.8	80.4	993	405	588	111.7	1,379	135
Lubbock	322.9	37.2	12.6	168.4	662	316	346	366.4	1,440	487
Lufkin	47.9	1.5	73.5	27.8	780	299	481	49.7	1,397	110
McAllen	218.2	11.1	13.2	114.7	806	284	522	205.1	1,442	299
McKinney	269.3	8.6	10.8	161.9	889	498	391	220.2	1,209	260
Mansfield	106.2	1.0	99.1	72.3	1,050	607	443	122.4	1,778	523

1. Based on population estimated as of July 1 of the year shown.

City	City government finances, 2017 (cont.)												
	General expenditure (cont.)												
	Percent of total for:										Debt outstanding		
	Public welfare	Highways	Parking facilities	Education	Health and hospitals	Police protection	Sewerage and sanitation	Parks and recreation	Housing and community development	Interest on debt	Total (mil dol)	Per capita[1] (dollars)	Debt issued during year
	127	128	129	130	131	132	133	134	135	136	137	138	139
TEXAS —Cont'd													
Austin	0.0	8.5	0.0	0.0	7.5	17.3	13.6	8.6	3.4	4.5	5,394.5	5,669	0.0
Balch Springs	0.0	10.7	0.0	0.0	0.0	15.6	0.0	1.1	3.6	1.9	9.8	388	0.0
Baytown	0.0	10.5	0.0	0.0	2.2	25.0	8.1	9.6	0.4	3.4	204.4	2,666	53.2
Beaumont	0.0	15.8	0.0	0.0	13.5	19.8	9.8	4.8	2.7	5.1	372.6	3,132	79.9
Bedford	0.0	5.0	0.0	0.0	0.9	25.5	13.1	6.5	0.0	4.3	49.7	1,003	0.0
Big Spring	0.0	13.4	0.0	0.0	0.0	27.6	0.0	10.0	0.0	0.0	27.4	990	8.0
Brownsville	0.7	7.6	0.3	0.0	1.1	20.6	12.2	5.3	2.3	3.3	311.4	1,707	0.0
Bryan	0.0	6.6	0.0	0.0	0.6	12.5	12.0	4.2	0.9	0.0	440.9	5,238	118.9
Burleson	0.0	18.9	0.0	0.0	0.7	18.6	12.8	11.0	0.0	5.3	158.2	3,439	46.7
Carrollton	0.0	16.3	0.0	0.0	1.8	19.4	12.8	9.4	0.9	4.4	192.5	1,415	33.8
Cedar Hill	0.0	11.7	0.0	0.0	0.0	18.0	13.5	5.0	0.0	10.8	138.5	2,840	0.0
Cedar Park	0.0	17.1	0.0	0.0	0.4	12.8	16.6	4.4	0.0	8.7	52.2	691	0.0
Cibolo	0.2	8.8	0.0	0.0	2.8	20.7	31.5	5.5	0.0	0.0	52.2	1,797	3.6
Cleburne	0.0	4.9	0.0	0.0	0.7	14.2	13.6	34.4	0.0	0.0	172.8	5,723	35.5
College Station	0.0	17.4	0.5	0.0	0.0	14.8	18.4	8.9	1.3	3.6	278.9	2,437	75.8
Colleyville	0.0	10.3	0.0	0.0	0.0	15.5	9.6	10.8	0.8	3.5	13.6	512	0.0
Conroe	0.0	15.1	0.0	0.0	0.0	26.1	14.3	7.1	0.8	3.9	265.3	3,128	25.1
Converse	0.0	11.3	0.0	0.0	0.0	23.4	20.8	4.3	0.0	0.0	19.6	727	11.5
Coppell	0.0	22.7	0.0	0.0	0.8	10.4	5.8	26.1	0.0	0.0	106.6	2,538	15.1
Copperas Cove	0.0	0.0	0.0	0.0	2.0	25.6	23.9	8.7	0.0	0.0	70.3	2,164	15.9
Corpus Christi	0.0	12.2	0.1	0.0	1.6	19.6	19.6	8.4	2.5	5.4	1,675.1	5,145	225.0
Dallas	0.3	6.8	0.0	0.0	0.9	12.7	12.1	6.0	1.2	10.7	10,912.7	8,129	1,019.4
Deer Park	0.0	3.8	0.0	0.0	0.6	17.9	14.9	15.5	0.0	3.8	41.5	1,222	0.0
Del Rio	3.4	15.0	0.0	0.0	1.5	18.0	15.9	4.3	0.0	3.6	38.3	1,067	0.0
Denton	0.0	10.4	0.0	0.0	0.0	13.9	27.2	6.7	0.2	3.5	569.3	4,198	0.0
DeSoto	0.0	7.5	0.0	0.0	0.0	17.0	22.9	8.1	0.0	6.3	106.1	1,982	0.0
Duncanville	0.0	7.8	0.0	0.0	1.0	21.6	20.1	9.7	0.0	0.6	6.5	165	0.0
Eagle Pass	0.0	3.2	0.0	0.0	0.0	2.7	1.6	1.3	0.0	1.1	63.4	2,161	4.9
Edinburg	0.0	4.7	0.0	0.0	2.1	18.5	25.7	14.7	1.6	2.8	93.0	974	0.0
El Paso	0.1	4.3	0.0	0.0	2.7	16.1	19.2	8.0	2.2	11.8	2,275.1	3,339	586.9
Euless	0.0	11.9	0.0	0.0	2.5	16.8	5.0	11.5	0.0	0.0	62.5	1,132	20.8
Farmers Branch	0.0	13.9	0.0	0.0	0.7	25.9	3.4	18.7	0.0	6.0	103.3	2,748	30.2
Flower Mound	0.0	10.4	0.0	0.0	1.7	20.1	13.8	9.3	0.3	4.4	145.9	1,902	37.1
Fort Worth	0.0	10.6	0.3	0.0	1.0	21.9	20.2	7.0	1.6	5.2	1,482.3	1,694	0.0
Friendswood	0.0	9.4	0.0	0.0	1.1	25.3	8.4	14.4	1.2	0.0	67.7	1,701	36.1
Frisco	0.0	12.4	0.0	4.0	0.6	8.2	11.7	6.8	0.0	0.0	809.1	4,552	181.3
Galveston	0.0	8.2	0.0	0.0	0.4	9.7	23.7	15.5	2.1	3.5	209.7	4,147	20.6
Garland	0.2	7.1	0.0	0.0	1.8	21.9	15.4	6.4	5.9	6.0	963.3	4,042	121.8
Georgetown	0.0	3.3	0.0	0.0	0.8	13.3	7.5	8.7	1.2	3.7	127.0	1,797	0.0
Grand Prairie	0.0	5.8	0.0	0.0	1.0	21.2	16.3	8.7	13.6	3.8	268.0	1,382	0.0
Grapevine	0.0	4.8	0.0	0.0	0.0	10.1	3.4	10.8	0.0	4.3	164.5	3,048	9.4
Greenville	0.0	26.4	0.0	0.0	0.0	0.2	4.6	0.8	0.0	8.3	98.3	3,593	1.9
Haltom City	0.0	13.5	0.0	0.0	0.0	24.0	14.1	4.2	0.0	3.1	50.7	1,141	0.0
Harker Heights	0.0	13.5	0.0	0.0	1.8	19.5	22.4	8.0	0.0	0.0	45.8	1,482	6.5
Harlingen	0.0	5.2	0.0	0.0	0.8	15.6	21.9	6.7	1.8	3.6	99.8	1,532	23.9
Houston	0.0	4.5	0.3	0.0	3.0	17.9	15.1	2.6	1.6	17.3	14,092.4	6,083	362.0
Huntsville	0.0	8.7	0.0	0.0	0.0	19.5	39.0	3.7	0.0	1.1	29.8	714	0.0
Hurst	0.0	14.8	0.0	0.0	2.2	25.6	11.9	15.1	0.0	4.0	67.0	1,711	4.7
Hutto	0.0	11.6	0.0	0.0	0.0	20.7	18.0	14.5	0.0	2.1	46.6	1,837	0.0
Irving	0.0	7.5	0.0	0.0	0.5	16.5	18.5	15.6	1.0	6.2	668.0	2,776	304.7
Keller	0.0	15.0	0.0	0.0	0.0	18.3	7.5	12.7	0.0	8.1	84.0	1,783	0.0
Killeen	0.0	17.4	0.0	0.0	0.7	18.9	17.2	5.5	1.1	7.1	284.6	1,961	53.0
Kingsville	0.0	14.2	0.0	0.0	2.5	37.0	18.4	1.0	0.0	8.9	27.0	1,064	0.0
Kyle	0.0	2.7	0.0	0.0	0.8	18.1	24.5	10.5	0.0	10.3	63.8	1,479	0.0
Lake Jackson	0.0	17.3	0.0	0.0	0.0	16.7	18.1	10.7	0.0	3.1	53.1	1,938	7.8
Lancaster	0.4	1.0	0.0	0.0	0.5	16.7	21.3	9.8	0.0	8.3	135.2	3,431	0.0
La Porte	0.0	7.6	0.0	0.0	0.0	25.7	10.8	11.9	1.7	0.0	35.5	1,003	3.2
Laredo	0.1	1.7	0.5	0.0	4.7	18.1	14.3	4.1	3.6	9.1	524.2	2,021	0.0
League City	0.0	8.9	0.0	0.0	4.7	21.1	21.7	7.7	0.2	4.4	210.4	2,015	0.0
Leander	0.0	35.9	0.0	0.0	0.2	13.7	15.5	7.5	0.0	0.0	127.2	2,555	0.0
Lewisville	0.0	13.4	0.0	0.0	0.0	19.2	12.9	7.1	5.4	8.0	164.0	1,541	0.0
Little Elm	0.0	3.7	0.0	0.0	0.5	17.9	12.0	9.5	0.0	6.1	92.5	2,012	27.8
Longview	0.0	8.7	0.0	0.0	1.4	17.9	13.5	11.2	6.7	2.1	69.9	863	0.0
Lubbock	0.0	7.3	0.0	0.0	1.3	14.6	25.0	4.2	0.7	7.9	1,242.5	4,883	135.5
Lufkin	0.0	11.7	0.0	0.0	1.4	19.2	26.3	6.6	0.5	4.2	158.4	4,451	9.1
McAllen	0.8	11.1	0.5	0.0	1.3	16.6	27.7	8.8	1.0	2.0	253.6	1,783	52.7
McKinney	0.0	7.1	0.0	0.0	0.8	12.4	12.7	7.2	0.5	0.0	383.2	2,104	100.2
Mansfield	0.0	22.3	0.0	0.0	1.8	14.6	5.8	13.6	0.0	5.7	199.3	2,894	79.2

1. Based on population estimated as of July 1 of the year shown.

STATE	Place code	City	Land area[1] (sq. mi)	Population, 2021: Total persons 2021	Population, 2021: Rank	Population, 2021: Per square mile	Race 2020: Race alone[2] (percent): White	Black or African American	American Indian, Alaskan Native	Asian	Hawaiian Pacific Islander	Some other race	Two or more races (percent)
			1	2	3	4	5	6	7	8	9	10	11
		TEXAS —Cont'd											
48	47892	Mesquite	49.1	147,691	186	3,008.0	33.5	25.1	1.4	2.9	0.1	19.9	17.2
48	48072	Midland	75.5	131,325	214	1,739.4	57.6	7.9	0.9	2.6	0.1	12.5	18.4
48	48096	Midlothian	63.6	37,053	1,073	582.6	73.5	9.2	0.7	1.1	0.1	5.3	10.2
48	48768	Mission	36.3	86,223	405	2,375.3	34.0	0.6	0.6	1.5	0.0	19.4	43.8
48	48804	Missouri City	29.0	74,850	492	2,581.0	22.2	41.1	0.5	18.3	0.0	7.9	9.8
48	50256	Nacogdoches	27.6	32,118	1,226	1,163.7	53.5	26.4	0.7	1.7	0.0	9.5	8.3
48	50820	New Braunfels	45.0	98,857	334	2,196.8	67.9	2.9	0.7	1.5	0.2	8.5	18.4
48	52356	North Richland Hills	18.2	70,209	536	3,857.6	69.3	7.0	0.8	4.2	0.3	5.8	12.6
48	53388	Odessa	51.5	112,483	270	2,184.1	49.6	6.6	1.0	2.2	0.2	18.6	21.8
48	56000	Pasadena	43.7	148,626	181	3,401.1	43.5	3.6	1.2	2.3	0.0	24.6	24.8
48	56348	Pearland	48.7	125,990	220	2,587.1	42.5	19.9	0.5	15.0	0.1	7.3	14.7
48	57176	Pflugerville	25.6	66,884	567	2,612.7	47.0	15.4	0.9	8.5	0.2	9.7	18.3
48	57200	Pharr	23.6	79,697	451	3,377.0	32.4	0.3	0.6	0.4	0.0	26.5	39.7
48	58016	Plano	71.7	288,253	72	4,020.3	49.5	8.9	0.7	24.2	0.1	6.0	10.6
48	58820	Port Arthur	75.9	55,724	706	734.2	24.1	38.0	1.0	5.9	0.0	18.9	12.0
48	59696	Prosper	25.2	34,136	1,163	1,354.6	70.9	8.4	0.6	7.2	0.1	2.8	10.2
48	61796	Richardson	28.6	116,382	249	4,069.3	54.2	10.7	0.6	17.2	0.1	6.3	11.0
48	62828	Rockwall	29.5	49,669	804	1,683.7	69.2	8.1	0.8	3.7	0.1	6.0	12.2
48	63284	Rosenberg	37.3	39,468	1,006	1,058.1	33.9	17.0	0.9	4.4	0.0	22.9	20.8
48	63500	Round Rock	37.6	123,876	229	3,294.6	53.8	10.2	0.8	8.2	0.2	9.6	17.1
48	63572	Rowlett	20.7	63,671	602	3,075.9	53.1	17.7	0.8	8.0	0.1	6.7	13.6
48	64064	Sachse	9.8	29,042	1,347	2,963.5	53.8	11.3	0.7	17.7	0.1	5.0	11.2
48	64472	San Angelo	60.0	99,667	330	1,661.1	62.8	4.4	0.9	1.7	0.2	11.2	18.9
48	65000	San Antonio	498.4	1,451,853	7	2,913.0	44.3	7.2	1.2	3.3	0.1	16.7	27.1
48	65516	San Juan	11.7	35,577	1,118	3,040.8	30.1	0.3	0.6	0.2	0.0	23.8	45.0
48	65600	San Marcos	36.3	68,580	551	1,889.3	54.9	7.2	0.9	3.0	0.1	12.7	21.2
48	66128	Schertz	32.1	42,622	936	1,327.8	57.1	12.3	0.8	3.0	0.3	7.0	19.4
48	66644	Seguin	38.8	30,902	1,275	796.4	53.5	6.5	0.8	1.1	0.1	17.2	20.8
48	67496	Sherman	46.2	44,873	883	971.3	60.3	10.5	1.7	3.2	0.1	12.3	11.8
48	68636	Socorro	21.9	36,236	1,093	1,654.6	29.4	0.4	3.1	0.2	0.0	29.6	37.3
48	69032	Southlake	21.8	31,105	1,269	1,426.8	70.5	2.4	0.3	15.5	0.0	1.4	9.9
48	70808	Sugar Land	40.5	109,373	282	2,700.6	40.7	7.3	0.3	38.6	0.0	3.1	9.9
48	72176	Temple	71.5	85,416	412	1,194.6	58.9	15.4	0.9	2.6	0.2	9.2	12.7
48	72368	Texarkana	31.4	36,017	1,098	1,147.0	47.9	37.8	0.7	2.1	0.1	4.9	6.5
48	72392	Texas City	66.3	54,247	736	818.2	45.1	28.0	0.9	1.4	0.1	10.8	13.7
48	72530	The Colony	14.0	45,000	881	3,214.3	57.8	10.0	0.9	8.8	0.1	8.1	14.2
48	74144	Tyler	57.5	107,192	287	1,864.2	52.4	23.1	0.7	2.9	0.1	11.2	9.6
48	74492	University Park	3.7	24,849	1,548	6,715.9	82.2	1.4	0.3	7.7	0.0	1.5	6.9
48	75428	Victoria	37.4	65,377	583	1,748.0	53.5	7.8	0.8	2.1	0.1	14.1	21.7
48	76000	Waco	88.7	139,594	196	1,573.8	49.9	20.1	1.0	2.6	0.1	13.4	12.8
48	76816	Waxahachie	49.5	43,368	921	876.1	60.7	14.6	0.8	0.9	0.1	8.5	14.4
48	76864	Weatherford	27.3	33,710	1,177	1,234.8	81.0	2.1	0.9	1.1	0.1	5.0	10.0
48	77272	Weslaco	16.4	41,024	961	2,501.5	41.4	0.6	0.9	1.0	0.0	19.5	36.6
48	79000	Wichita Falls	72.0	102,988	310	1,430.4	62.4	13.0	1.1	2.5	0.2	9.4	11.4
48	80356	Wylie	22.1	59,394	658	2,687.5	55.4	13.8	0.8	10.0	0.1	8.1	11.8
49	00000	UTAH	82,376.9	3,337,975	X	40.5	78.7	1.2	1.3	2.5	1.1	6.7	8.5
49	01310	American Fork	11.2	34,422	1,159	3,073.4	85.4	0.6	0.6	1.5	0.9	4.0	7.0
49	07690	Bountiful	13.2	45,438	872	3,442.3	86.4	0.8	0.5	1.6	1.2	2.8	6.7
49	11320	Cedar City	36.0	37,206	1,067	1,033.5	83.7	1.1	2.3	1.5	0.6	4.1	6.6
49	13850	Clearfield	7.7	32,238	1,222	4,186.8	73.7	2.8	1.2	2.5	1.2	7.7	10.9
49	16270	Cottonwood Heights	9.2	32,864	1,202	3,572.2	85.2	0.7	0.5	3.4	0.3	2.2	7.7
49	20120	Draper	29.9	51,749	770	1,730.7	81.5	1.3	0.7	4.5	0.5	3.5	7.9
49	20810	Eagle Mountain	50.4	49,738	801	986.9	83.9	0.7	0.5	0.8	1.0	3.9	9.2
49	34970	Herriman	21.6	58,198	677	2,694.4	81.2	1.0	0.7	2.4	1.2	4.7	8.8
49	36070	Holladay	8.5	31,390	1,261	3,692.9	87.5	0.9	0.3	3.1	0.4	1.6	6.3
49	40360	Kaysville	10.5	32,976	1,196	3,140.6	90.7	0.6	0.4	1.0	0.4	1.6	5.3
49	40470	Kearns	4.6	36,747	1,080	7,988.5	53.3	1.4	2.0	2.1	3.0	23.7	14.5
49	43660	Layton	22.5	83,291	420	3,701.8	80.0	1.5	0.9	2.3	0.7	5.7	9.0
49	44320	Lehi	28.5	79,978	446	2,806.2	84.9	0.5	0.5	2.5	0.9	2.8	7.8
49	45860	Logan	17.9	54,436	734	3,041.1	79.3	1.6	1.3	2.8	0.9	6.7	7.5
49	47290	Magna	15.1	29,268	1,338	1,938.3	61.8	1.5	1.3	1.2	2.8	20.6	10.8
49	49710	Midvale	5.9	35,938	1,103	6,091.2	67.0	3.0	1.4	4.2	1.5	11.0	11.7
49	50150	Millcreek	12.9	64,110	596	4,969.8	77.9	2.9	0.9	4.6	0.7	4.4	8.5
49	53230	Murray	12.3	49,729	802	4,043.0	78.7	2.3	1.0	3.4	0.8	4.6	9.3
49	55980	Ogden	27.5	86,798	400	3,156.3	67.2	2.3	1.7	1.5	0.4	14.9	12.0
49	57300	Orem	18.6	97,861	338	5,261.3	74.0	0.9	1.0	2.1	1.5	9.5	11.1
49	60930	Pleasant Grove	9.2	37,949	1,050	4,124.9	83.7	0.6	0.5	1.3	0.8	4.5	8.7
49	62470	Provo	41.7	114,084	259	2,735.8	74.6	0.9	1.0	2.5	1.5	8.2	11.3

1. Dry land or land partially or temporarily covered by water. 2. Hispanic or Latino persons may be of any race.

City	Percent Hispanic or Latino[1], 2020	Percent foreign born, 2016–2020	Age of population (percent), 2016–2020							Median age, 2016–2020	Percent female, 2016–2020	Population			
			Under 18 years	18 to 24 years	25 to 34 years	35 to 44 years	45 to 54 years	55 to 64 years	65 years and over			Census counts		Percent change	
												2010	2020	2010–2020	2020–2021
	12	13	14	15	16	17	18	19	20	21	22	23	24	25	26
TEXAS —Cont'd															
Mesquite	44.1	19.9	29.0	10.1	13.4	12.3	13.3	10.9	11.0	33.0	52.2	139,768	150,308	7.5	-1.7
Midland	41.6	14.9	27.8	9.3	18.7	13.7	10.2	10.0	10.3	31.4	49.1	111,192	132,448	19.1	-0.8
Midlothian	16.1	4.0	29.7	8.2	11.6	14.9	14.5	10.3	10.8	35.7	51.4	22,975	35,183	53.1	5.3
Mission	88.5	29.1	31.3	8.8	12.6	12.3	12.5	9.7	12.9	33.0	50.8	77,704	85,868	10.5	0.4
Missouri City	18.9	22.3	22.5	8.3	12.0	12.9	14.0	15.7	14.6	40.3	53.7	66,653	74,244	11.4	0.8
Nacogdoches	20.2	6.6	19.7	31.8	12.5	8.9	7.2	8.1	11.8	24.4	52.9	32,804	32,213	-1.8	-0.3
New Braunfels	34.6	7.1	25.7	8.5	14.7	13.9	12.3	11.1	13.9	36.0	51.2	57,674	90,136	56.3	9.7
North Richland Hills	18.8	10.2	22.3	8.2	13.7	12.0	13.0	14.2	16.5	39.7	52.6	63,147	69,968	10.8	0.3
Odessa	56.1	12.0	29.8	10.4	17.4	12.4	10.2	9.8	9.9	30.4	50.3	99,878	114,368	14.5	-1.6
Pasadena	67.8	26.4	30.0	10.6	14.5	12.5	12.4	10.4	9.6	31.2	50.3	149,389	151,955	1.7	-2.2
Pearland	24.7	17.2	28.4	7.1	14.0	16.2	13.4	10.3	10.6	35.3	51.0	93,159	125,944	35.2	0.0
Pflugerville	31.2	14.9	24.1	6.7	15.9	15.2	17.5	11.1	9.4	37.1	51.8	48,370	65,678	35.8	1.8
Pharr	94.3	30.7	33.5	9.4	14.5	12.7	10.5	7.1	12.2	30.0	52.8	70,537	79,779	13.1	-0.1
Plano	16.0	27.4	22.3	8.2	13.7	15.1	14.1	13.2	13.2	38.9	50.7	259,860	285,900	10.0	0.8
Port Arthur	37.8	20.0	28.1	8.4	15.1	11.6	11.3	12.7	12.8	34.0	51.2	54,376	55,610	2.3	0.2
Prosper	10.2	9.6	35.0	5.9	8.6	17.6	17.8	7.6	7.5	35.5	49.5	9,547	30,225	216.6	12.9
Richardson	17.2	23.2	22.4	11.1	16.3	12.4	12.2	11.6	14.0	35.1	51.1	99,251	117,973	18.9	-1.3
Rockwall	18.3	9.2	24.7	8.8	10.3	15.4	15.6	11.3	13.8	39.0	51.3	37,562	47,283	25.9	5.0
Rosenberg	55.1	21.6	28.5	10.9	16.0	13.5	10.0	10.0	11.1	30.9	51.7	31,225	38,279	22.6	3.1
Round Rock	29.9	14.3	25.9	9.1	14.4	16.6	14.4	10.5	9.1	35.4	50.7	100,019	119,519	19.5	3.6
Rowlett	21.2	15.6	24.4	6.5	14.2	13.4	15.8	14.9	10.7	38.9	50.5	56,223	62,543	11.2	1.8
Sachse	15.7	22.8	22.3	10.0	9.8	14.5	18.7	12.0	12.7	39.8	53.3	20,291	27,142	33.8	7.0
San Angelo	42.4	6.0	23.2	13.0	15.2	11.9	10.1	11.0	15.7	34.0	50.1	93,219	100,006	7.3	-0.3
San Antonio	63.9	14.0	24.8	10.5	16.4	13.4	11.9	10.7	12.3	33.8	50.6	1,326,819	1,434,270	8.1	1.2
San Juan	96.4	23.6	32.6	11.3	12.6	12.9	12.5	6.7	11.3	29.3	51.9	33,972	35,329	4.0	0.7
San Marcos	40.6	9.0	13.1	36.5	17.3	9.4	7.6	6.7	9.4	25.1	53.0	45,129	67,290	49.1	1.9
Schertz	31.3	6.1	23.8	9.3	12.1	14.3	14.2	12.9	13.4	37.9	51.2	31,826	41,997	32.0	1.5
Seguin	53.7	7.1	23.3	11.9	13.6	12.9	10.3	11.3	16.6	35.9	53.1	25,606	29,419	14.9	5.0
Sherman	24.2	10.5	25.0	11.7	13.7	11.4	11.5	11.4	15.1	34.6	52.1	38,853	43,625	12.3	2.9
Socorro	96.5	33.4	27.0	11.4	13.0	13.4	12.5	10.6	12.0	34.1	54.1	32,039	34,276	7.0	5.7
Southlake	7.6	15.2	33.1	4.1	4.5	13.4	19.9	14.0	10.9	42.0	51.6	26,573	31,289	17.7	-0.6
Sugar Land	12.1	35.1	22.4	7.6	11.7	12.9	14.8	14.7	15.8	41.5	51.0	107,700	111,046	3.1	-1.5
Temple	26.2	7.6	27.7	8.9	15.8	12.8	9.8	10.2	14.8	33.6	53.2	66,076	81,938	24.0	4.2
Texarkana	8.5	4.6	24.9	9.2	12.9	12.9	11.5	12.2	16.5	37.3	52.7	36,306	36,234	-0.2	-0.6
Texas City	31.1	7.1	25.9	9.2	14.6	11.5	11.1	12.6	15.0	35.2	53.0	45,105	51,898	15.1	4.5
The Colony	22.5	11.7	22.2	5.9	21.4	15.2	15.0	12.0	8.3	35.2	50.3	36,341	44,437	22.3	1.3
Tyler	22.7	11.3	23.1	12.2	15.6	10.6	11.5	10.8	16.2	34.3	52.6	96,761	105,735	9.3	1.4
University Park	5.6	7.0	27.2	17.7	4.3	12.2	17.4	12.4	8.7	35.4	52.5	23,067	25,078	8.7	-0.9
Victoria	51.8	8.1	25.6	10.0	15.1	11.9	10.4	12.3	14.8	34.5	51.8	62,619	65,643	4.8	-0.4
Waco	31.7	10.8	23.8	19.8	14.1	10.9	9.2	9.6	12.5	28.9	51.6	124,787	137,948	10.5	1.2
Waxahachie	25.9	6.3	25.4	11.0	17.2	11.9	11.4	9.9	13.1	32.3	51.2	29,536	40,925	38.6	6.0
Weatherford	14.6	7.0	24.1	7.8	15.6	12.5	10.1	12.3	17.6	36.9	49.5	25,744	30,630	19.0	10.1
Weslaco	89.1	17.0	32.3	10.0	13.9	10.9	11.6	9.0	12.3	30.1	51.4	36,835	40,165	9.0	2.1
Wichita Falls	22.7	7.2	22.8	15.1	15.9	11.6	10.4	11.1	13.2	32.4	47.4	104,682	102,498	-2.1	0.5
Wylie	19.6	18.2	28.5	9.2	14.7	16.0	16.3	8.6	6.7	34.0	51.7	41,706	57,602	38.1	3.1
UTAH	15.1	8.4	29.4	11.3	14.8	13.7	10.3	9.5	11.1	31.1	49.6	2,763,891	3,271,616	18.4	2.0
American Fork	9.6	5.3	32.8	11.3	15.1	13.4	9.4	8.6	9.4	28.1	49.3	26,553	33,422	25.9	3.0
Bountiful	7.6	4.8	29.4	7.7	17.5	12.6	8.5	9.8	14.5	32.4	50.2	42,577	45,811	7.6	-0.8
Cedar City	10.8	4.7	29.0	18.9	15.3	11.1	7.2	7.8	10.7	26.1	49.5	28,867	35,078	21.5	6.1
Clearfield	18.3	7.7	30.5	12.5	17.9	14.2	9.8	8.0	7.1	29.0	48.7	29,890	31,908	6.8	1.0
Cottonwood Heights	6.9	6.7	21.8	8.4	13.4	14.1	12.9	12.7	16.7	39.0	51.8	33,586	33,681	0.3	-2.4
Draper	9.3	9.3	31.7	7.4	13.7	16.0	14.3	8.7	8.1	32.9	48.4	42,272	50,510	19.5	2.5
Eagle Mountain	11.5	4.1	48.0	7.8	16.9	15.7	6.8	2.7	2.0	19.0	48.4	21,936	43,760	99.5	13.7
Herriman	13.0	4.6	39.2	6.8	15.6	16.5	10.8	6.7	4.5	28.3	51.7	21,768	55,312	154.1	5.2
Holladay	5.6	6.6	25.1	7.5	11.6	13.4	12.0	13.5	17.0	39.1	50.9	30,127	32,024	6.3	-2.0
Kaysville	5.9	2.1	36.5	7.6	10.2	14.6	11.5	9.9	9.6	30.9	49.0	27,573	32,902	19.3	0.2
Kearns	42.3	17.5	32.1	10.7	14.1	14.3	12.6	9.4	6.9	29.6	50.7	35,769	36,825	3.0	-0.2
Layton	13.9	6.2	30.7	9.6	14.8	15.1	10.7	9.7	9.4	31.4	49.9	67,531	81,759	21.1	1.9
Lehi	8.7	6.1	39.6	9.3	13.7	17.1	8.8	5.9	5.6	26.0	49.8	47,757	76,107	59.4	5.1
Logan	15.1	9.4	23.8	30.9	18.8	8.3	5.8	5.5	7.0	23.8	49.1	48,205	52,673	9.3	3.3
Magna	34.4	14.1	29.1	9.3	14.7	17.0	11.9	10.3	7.8	32.8	50.4	26,513	29,327	10.6	-0.2
Midvale	23.3	15.5	25.6	8.0	24.3	16.6	8.1	9.3	8.1	31.5	49.6	28,000	36,057	28.8	-0.3
Millcreek	10.8	10.8	22.4	8.3	17.1	14.6	11.6	11.1	15.0	36.5	50.8	58,750	63,899	8.8	0.3
Murray	13.1	8.9	20.7	8.5	17.8	12.7	10.8	11.8	17.7	37.2	52.3	46,680	50,743	8.7	-2.0
Ogden	30.8	11.9	25.4	10.7	17.3	13.6	10.3	11.4	11.1	33.0	48.6	82,893	86,830	4.7	0.0
Orem	20.2	12.1	28.3	18.5	15.9	11.2	8.1	7.7	10.3	26.5	49.8	88,344	98,070	11.0	-0.2
Pleasant Grove	11.8	6.0	32.0	12.8	14.4	12.5	10.5	8.1	9.8	28.3	47.6	33,547	37,817	12.7	0.3
Provo	18.6	11.2	20.6	37.7	16.5	8.3	5.6	5.0	6.2	23.7	50.6	112,485	114,189	1.5	-0.1

1. May be of any race.

City	Households, 2016–2020							Persons in group quarters, 2016–2020	Serious crimes known to police[2], 2020				Educational attainment, 2016–2020		
			Percent						Violent		Property			Attainment[4] (percent)	
	Number	Persons per household	Family	Married couple family	Female family	Non-family	One person		Number	Rate	Number	Rate	Population age 25 and over	High school graduate or less	Bachelor's degree or more
	27	28	29	30	31	32	33	34	35	36	37	38	39	40	41
TEXAS —Cont'd															
Mesquite	46,586	3.04	74.4	46.9	20.2	25.6	22.1	608	619	438.0	4,997	3,535.8	86,619	49.6	17.7
Midland	47,682	2.93	68.4	51.0	11.7	31.6	26.8	1,661	549	364.7	3,119	2,072.0	88,845	41.5	29.2
Midlothian	10,462	3.01	84.3	67.0	13.8	15.7	13.1	8	32	91.5	308	881.0	19,598	31.1	32.0
Mission	25,172	3.32	80.0	56.1	18.6	20.0	17.4	188	132	155.2	1,304	1,533.2	50,173	48.0	27.0
Missouri City	24,827	3.02	81.0	59.5	16.2	19.0	16.5	456	130	170.0	689	900.9	52,132	29.1	43.1
Nacogdoches	11,895	2.32	52.0	32.6	13.6	48.0	33.0	5,262	120	365.0	943	2,868.6	15,961	39.5	28.9
New Braunfels	30,855	2.71	67.9	53.2	9.9	32.1	25.7	960	219	231.1	1,230	1,298.1	55,730	35.7	35.5
North Richland Hills	27,200	2.58	69.6	53.1	12.4	30.4	25.9	323	NA	NA	NA	NA	49,037	31.0	35.4
Odessa	41,942	2.89	67.3	43.7	17.6	32.7	27.9	1,549	1,020	807.7	3,163	2,504.6	73,386	49.5	18.6
Pasadena	48,174	3.15	75.1	51.2	16.6	24.9	20.0	977	866	571.9	3,533	2,333.2	90,645	59.3	15.0
Pearland	42,098	2.98	76.4	65.0	8.3	23.6	19.6	562	125	99.1	1,799	1,426.5	81,120	20.3	49.7
Pflugerville	22,210	2.85	74.8	58.9	11.4	25.2	19.9	232	81	119.9	926	1,370.7	43,976	30.5	37.0
Pharr	22,668	3.47	81.3	50.0	24.9	18.7	16.2	96	364	454.4	1,255	1,566.8	44,901	59.6	16.8
Plano	107,320	2.68	71.0	57.5	9.8	29.0	23.4	794	452	155.4	4,784	1,645.2	200,684	19.0	57.6
Port Arthur	20,599	2.62	62.8	36.0	21.1	37.2	32.7	635	422	777.8	1,253	2,309.4	34,779	59.7	11.2
Prosper	7,512	3.45	91.5	84.0	4.6	8.5	6.6	0	33	121.1	231	847.7	15,302	12.8	62.3
Richardson	44,136	2.64	66.0	50.0	11.8	34.0	25.8	2,198	158	127.2	2,424	1,951.8	78,827	20.0	53.4
Rockwall	16,151	2.78	79.1	67.4	8.1	20.9	17.7	318	59	125.9	805	1,717.6	30,013	22.0	45.8
Rosenberg	12,636	2.98	68.2	47.0	16.2	31.8	28.2	176	161	411.1	629	1,606.1	22,920	49.3	20.4
Round Rock	41,896	3.06	71.5	54.4	12.3	28.5	22.6	597	185	134.5	2,282	1,658.5	83,675	27.0	41.3
Rowlett	21,628	3.01	84.1	68.9	11.7	15.9	12.5	313	100	145.3	1,057	1,536.1	45,197	28.9	35.7
Sachse	8,736	2.96	77.9	64.3	11.2	22.1	20.0	0	16	59.7	167	623.2	17,530	29.8	37.0
San Angelo	36,843	2.56	62.5	44.9	12.2	37.5	31.0	6,112	357	350.5	3,039	2,983.5	64,128	42.1	25.1
San Antonio	509,550	2.96	62.7	40.6	16.9	37.3	30.8	21,466	11,569	735.4	57,057	3,626.8	988,008	43.3	26.4
San Juan	9,875	3.71	86.7	56.3	25.1	13.3	11.9	135	139	372.3	738	1,976.6	20,617	64.6	13.8
San Marcos	23,769	2.44	44.7	28.3	11.5	55.3	31.6	6,012	283	419.7	1,419	2,104.3	32,288	36.2	34.6
Schertz	14,853	2.84	77.9	62.7	10.9	22.1	18.9	257	61	140.8	460	1,062.0	28,396	29.4	37.2
Seguin	10,252	2.73	63.8	40.9	17.1	36.2	28.2	1,480	69	226.1	672	2,202.3	19,071	60.7	16.3
Sherman	15,687	2.65	64.4	43.7	16.3	35.6	29.8	1,616	197	441.6	1,095	2,454.6	27,371	39.3	21.2
Socorro	9,964	3.44	84.7	53.9	22.8	15.3	13.5	14	48	138.6	217	626.7	21,151	64.9	7.8
Southlake	9,323	3.40	90.1	82.8	5.6	9.9	8.0	26	14	42.3	236	713.4	19,900	11.5	68.9
Sugar Land	38,852	3.04	80.6	70.5	8.0	19.4	15.8	282	68	56.8	1,277	1,067.1	83,012	18.7	59.6
Temple	28,276	2.65	63.8	43.5	15.5	36.2	30.8	1,558	297	371.8	2,098	2,626.5	48,570	35.8	28.8
Texarkana	14,148	2.48	62.0	36.6	21.9	38.0	33.9	1,625	NA	NA	NA	NA	24,232	40.2	24.9
Texas City	17,499	2.75	67.4	40.5	21.5	32.6	26.9	1,338	178	351.4	1,396	2,755.6	32,081	49.0	16.1
The Colony	17,401	2.52	63.0	50.0	9.3	37.0	30.6	0	NA	NA	NA	NA	31,472	26.3	42.0
Tyler	37,114	2.72	62.2	44.8	13.6	37.8	31.5	4,912	472	436.5	3,296	3,047.9	68,492	34.2	29.5
University Park	7,593	2.95	83.7	74.3	6.5	16.3	11.7	2,606	4	15.8	239	946.4	13,788	4.5	88.8
Victoria	23,724	2.78	65.6	44.3	15.2	34.4	27.5	1,119	311	461.4	1,823	2,704.5	43,180	47.2	19.6
Waco	50,108	2.58	57.9	36.4	17.1	42.1	32.2	8,528	905	642.4	4,854	3,445.7	77,656	44.4	25.4
Waxahachie	12,522	2.83	72.5	52.1	15.9	27.5	24.6	1,293	71	181.9	701	1,795.6	23,358	39.5	24.3
Weatherford	11,528	2.67	66.3	54.5	6.6	33.7	29.1	1,310	85	246.2	561	1,625.1	21,879	41.7	21.5
Weslaco	12,671	3.21	78.9	49.4	24.0	21.1	19.4	444	136	322.4	1,350	3,200.3	23,719	45.8	24.3
Wichita Falls	37,297	2.44	61.9	41.7	13.7	38.1	31.1	13,797	405	386.9	3,222	3,078.2	65,016	44.0	23.9
Wylie	15,730	3.25	81.8	62.6	15.2	18.2	11.7	115	41	75.3	374	686.7	31,954	29.0	36.8
UTAH	1,003,345	3.09	74.4	60.9	9.0	25.6	19.5	47,887	8,471	260.7	80,091	2,464.4	1,868,472	29.8	34.7
American Fork	9,254	3.37	83.5	70.6	10.1	16.5	13.9	464	NA	NA	NA	NA	17,691	22.6	38.9
Bountiful	14,178	3.07	75.8	64.1	7.9	24.2	20.3	417	35	79.3	363	822.6	27,643	19.4	47.6
Cedar City	10,914	3.01	70.9	55.7	9.9	29.1	19.9	550	63	177.5	533	1,502.0	17,404	28.6	33.7
Clearfield	10,210	3.06	71.7	53.1	11.8	28.3	22.0	369	69	213.2	525	1,622.5	18,016	38.2	22.1
Cottonwood Heights	12,549	2.70	69.7	58.6	8.4	30.3	24.0	40	48	141.7	924	2,728.0	23,644	18.0	51.6
Draper	14,390	3.21	81.3	68.8	8.0	18.7	14.4	2,397	71	143.9	1,138	2,307.1	29,579	19.4	47.6
Eagle Mountain	8,002	4.43	95.5	83.6	7.5	4.5	2.8	0	NA	NA	NA	NA	15,643	21.2	35.4
Herriman	12,211	3.70	85.4	72.5	11.6	14.6	12.0	0	37	65.7	492	873.7	24,430	21.4	38.5
Holladay	11,170	2.71	73.1	56.5	10.6	26.9	22.0	187	NA	NA	NA	NA	20,541	13.6	56.5
Kaysville	8,832	3.62	86.9	79.3	6.3	13.1	9.8	0	NA	NA	NA	NA	17,847	14.3	49.8
Kearns	10,126	3.60	84.6	63.1	15.6	15.4	11.3	18	NA	NA	NA	NA	20,849	51.2	13.4
Layton	24,722	3.12	77.7	63.5	9.3	22.3	18.1	112	142	179.2	1,409	1,778.1	46,112	29.5	34.6
Lehi	17,781	3.76	85.7	79.3	4.3	14.3	10.3	73	NA	NA	NA	NA	34,242	18.3	45.3
Logan	17,256	2.81	66.1	53.1	9.7	33.9	18.8	2,703	100	192.7	592	1,140.7	23,250	27.9	37.0
Magna	8,214	3.28	77.1	53.8	15.5	22.9	17.3	65	NA	NA	NA	NA	16,670	57.5	11.8
Midvale	13,348	2.52	58.5	39.9	12.7	41.5	32.1	117	NA	NA	NA	NA	22,400	32.5	30.4
Millcreek	23,959	2.50	59.6	47.0	8.3	40.4	31.5	909	NA	NA	NA	NA	42,186	20.2	51.9
Murray	19,084	2.55	61.5	47.0	9.7	38.5	29.9	261	237	482.0	3,271	6,652.6	34,666	27.4	36.0
Ogden	31,199	2.71	63.1	44.3	12.3	36.9	28.9	2,558	446	505.0	2,915	3,300.9	55,627	43.5	22.4
Orem	29,912	3.22	77.3	64.1	9.1	22.7	14.8	1,575	106	107.2	2,033	2,055.6	52,078	22.7	40.8
Pleasant Grove	11,733	3.27	78.0	66.2	7.0	22.0	16.9	60	31	79.9	336	865.9	21,260	19.9	40.9
Provo	33,447	3.14	69.5	57.1	8.3	30.5	14.5	11,839	NA	NA	NA	NA	48,746	22.0	42.9

2. Data for serious crimes have not been adjusted for underreporting. This may affect comparability between geographic areas and over time.
4. Persons 25 years old and over.

Table D. Cities — Income, Poverty, and Housing

City	Money income, 2016–2020: Households: Median household income	Households: Percent with income less than $25,000	Households: Percent with income of $200,000 or more	Median family income	Median non-family household income	Median earnings Full year, Full-time workers, 2016–2020: All persons	Men	Women	Housing units, 2016–2020: Total	Occupied	Percent owner occupied	Median value[1] (dollars)	Median gross rent (dollars)
	42	43	44	45	46	47	48	49	50	51	52	53	54
TEXAS —Cont'd													
Mesquite	60,715	15.4	2.0	65,942	39,097	41,617	43,931	38,874	49,648	46,586	59.2	160,000	1,157
Midland	83,616	13.5	12.5	98,123	50,744	54,200	66,801	43,199	51,190	47,682	64.4	238,000	1,256
Midlothian	95,603	9.8	11.2	104,188	47,708	63,458	69,284	55,727	10,843	10,462	80.1	254,100	1,266
Mission	49,358	25.2	4.6	55,651	26,454	40,270	44,669	33,529	29,549	25,172	70.0	125,600	847
Missouri City	83,491	7.5	10.7	90,143	51,747	53,426	58,003	50,540	25,820	24,827	81.9	213,000	1,662
Nacogdoches	35,050	39.7	3.0	53,839	22,341	35,724	40,087	28,985	14,032	11,895	37.2	151,800	768
New Braunfels	71,274	13.3	6.6	85,101	45,229	49,626	51,061	46,300	33,523	30,855	61.7	237,900	1,217
North Richland Hills	75,563	11.0	8.2	91,164	43,726	52,082	57,418	48,223	28,535	27,200	64.9	232,200	1,209
Odessa	63,829	17.1	5.0	75,424	40,106	49,435	55,058	38,979	46,214	41,942	60.9	159,700	1,104
Pasadena	57,781	19.2	3.8	64,703	35,380	42,009	48,185	31,821	53,220	48,174	52.5	132,300	993
Pearland	102,764	7.5	15.0	116,220	57,879	66,722	75,072	60,680	44,891	42,098	77.2	260,300	1,431
Pflugerville	95,471	5.5	8.1	104,947	59,356	56,306	65,497	50,578	23,046	22,210	75.1	252,300	1,401
Pharr	40,513	34.2	2.1	44,109	26,146	35,712	37,555	27,179	25,770	22,668	59.1	81,600	774
Plano	96,348	8.9	15.9	113,796	58,573	65,912	80,313	56,040	113,254	107,320	58.9	341,800	1,447
Port Arthur	37,794	35.1	1.9	45,668	24,538	40,107	44,109	34,474	25,468	20,599	56.6	68,700	826
Prosper	153,777	2.5	32.3	157,974	85,750	99,615	111,792	67,308	8,217	7,512	89.3	482,700	1,634
Richardson	85,350	11.9	11.5	101,488	51,076	58,028	65,345	54,512	47,070	44,136	56.3	295,500	1,452
Rockwall	100,894	6.9	15.1	112,973	48,902	67,471	72,620	63,835	16,834	16,151	77.4	276,400	1,338
Rosenberg	58,633	18.6	3.4	64,788	43,410	43,060	49,397	40,250	13,769	12,636	51.4	172,900	1,125
Round Rock	86,121	8.0	11.1	101,009	56,024	52,989	60,130	47,006	44,896	41,896	58.6	259,400	1,345
Rowlett	103,627	7.2	11.6	107,497	67,196	58,220	65,084	53,146	22,280	21,628	83.4	237,300	1,602
Sachse	109,098	5.3	14.6	112,940	84,795	65,350	80,091	55,661	8,945	8,736	88.9	259,100	1,444
San Angelo	55,682	20.4	3.4	70,137	32,768	37,413	45,311	32,927	41,616	36,843	62.3	143,300	902
San Antonio	53,420	22.7	4.3	64,030	35,786	40,406	42,277	37,547	555,138	509,550	53.8	156,700	1,025
San Juan	45,263	28.5	1.1	47,512	19,356	32,884	34,260	31,836	10,763	9,875	78.0	91,900	752
San Marcos	42,030	29.6	1.8	54,261	28,252	32,954	35,142	30,010	25,940	23,769	29.1	185,300	1,099
Schertz	84,527	6.3	8.1	97,076	54,082	52,810	58,613	47,942	15,435	14,853	77.2	223,400	1,374
Seguin	49,976	23.6	2.5	61,289	27,863	35,382	37,717	33,130	11,310	10,252	63.3	143,800	916
Sherman	50,627	21.4	3.0	59,184	32,585	36,900	38,699	35,106	17,683	15,687	54.9	131,300	902
Socorro	40,065	31.6	0.5	42,098	17,340	30,382	34,009	24,733	10,475	9,964	78.2	99,100	725
Southlake	223,621	3.9	56.5	235,227	0	146,750	185,893	89,688	9,663	9,323	94.5	697,000	1,337
Sugar Land	123,261	6.8	25.0	138,436	65,430	76,105	92,119	62,793	40,527	38,852	81.2	337,600	1,768
Temple	53,723	24.5	3.2	67,883	31,900	45,144	50,319	40,059	31,282	28,276	53.9	145,900	911
Texarkana	46,408	31.3	4.7	65,965	25,239	42,051	54,087	34,383	16,591	14,148	52.3	143,300	797
Texas City	49,229	21.7	5.5	63,462	32,361	41,209	50,526	35,836	19,887	17,499	54.1	131,400	1,006
The Colony	87,748	7.9	10.3	107,089	59,349	57,276	60,377	55,900	18,307	17,401	59.7	244,400	1,481
Tyler	54,883	23.0	6.4	69,799	32,194	40,403	44,734	35,222	42,915	37,114	53.3	164,900	945
University Park	247,716	6.7	57.3	250	70,417	200,997	237,073	103,750	8,232	7,593	83.0	1,351,400	2,095
Victoria	56,332	21.6	4.3	67,754	37,626	42,001	49,868	33,537	27,185	23,724	60.8	146,400	963
Waco	40,349	32.7	3.5	54,645	24,003	36,360	39,715	33,339	56,748	50,108	47.0	133,500	879
Waxahachie	68,496	13.8	4.3	76,817	47,480	45,224	49,611	39,906	13,502	12,522	57.5	201,200	1,129
Weatherford	68,184	17.7	6.0	85,370	33,474	46,199	54,684	34,175	12,502	11,528	64.2	202,800	1,093
Weslaco	47,094	29.6	2.5	54,103	25,332	38,192	44,223	32,662	16,593	12,671	60.3	91,500	742
Wichita Falls	47,335	26.9	3.2	62,463	28,461	38,752	44,276	33,967	43,223	37,297	56.5	104,800	828
Wylie	98,484	5.7	9.8	105,562	65,509	55,266	60,524	50,934	16,320	15,730	74.3	253,100	1,585
UTAH	74,197	12.4	7.0	84,590	41,986	49,819	56,548	40,381	1,110,369	1,003,345	70.5	305,400	1,090
American Fork	78,690	8.9	6.0	85,475	38,683	51,951	60,807	40,166	9,562	9,254	73.8	322,500	1,256
Bountiful	83,660	7.8	10.2	93,040	52,051	53,540	62,480	42,295	14,961	14,178	75.5	343,900	1,148
Cedar City	52,524	23.5	1.8	64,007	27,685	39,378	42,424	32,976	12,109	10,914	54.0	227,500	809
Clearfield	62,374	16.2	2.4	70,788	41,676	43,410	49,183	36,426	10,752	10,210	59.1	222,300	1,117
Cottonwood Heights	95,427	8.9	14.4	116,816	55,866	63,419	76,236	53,548	13,474	12,549	71.8	402,100	1,288
Draper	112,541	6.6	23.0	123,806	64,620	71,510	95,017	51,472	14,995	14,390	77.8	517,100	1,436
Eagle Mountain	87,094	3.5	4.5	87,098	71,800	56,553	62,339	43,385	8,256	8,002	91.6	317,500	1,634
Herriman	102,096	3.3	9.4	107,875	65,888	59,180	74,850	47,469	12,440	12,211	85.0	414,600	1,368
Holladay	92,635	8.5	18.8	108,983	43,736	65,470	75,904	53,606	11,933	11,170	77.8	481,100	1,305
Kaysville	103,730	8.2	12.2	111,903	53,294	69,091	81,270	44,915	8,920	8,832	86.8	368,700	1,077
Kearns	68,870	8.7	2.0	70,454	42,121	39,945	42,412	34,941	10,252	10,126	82.4	220,400	1,417
Layton	81,067	10.0	5.9	90,404	47,958	52,218	59,273	41,842	25,506	24,722	72.0	285,100	1,084
Lehi	101,429	6.1	8.5	107,299	55,798	62,698	79,003	43,226	18,371	17,781	78.9	378,300	1,510
Logan	43,056	24.0	1.7	49,390	32,078	34,470	39,374	29,434	18,592	17,256	38.6	216,200	783
Magna	68,765	10.7	0.7	73,402	39,606	41,585	46,370	35,704	8,442	8,214	78.5	229,200	1,109
Midvale	62,354	17.4	2.2	70,246	46,327	45,810	47,304	44,026	14,484	13,348	44.7	285,200	1,160
Millcreek	74,325	14.7	10.1	95,349	47,682	55,009	59,952	47,252	25,417	23,959	61.8	392,700	1,149
Murray	65,397	12.9	4.9	84,726	42,567	49,340	52,294	43,193	20,213	19,084	65.5	313,800	1,162
Ogden	55,974	19.3	3.6	65,540	36,621	40,131	43,417	35,211	34,154	31,199	60.1	195,600	872
Orem	65,622	14.3	5.8	71,076	40,917	42,599	51,254	35,297	31,597	29,912	59.3	296,900	1,057
Pleasant Grove	76,672	8.8	7.9	84,261	43,932	51,183	60,035	39,131	12,063	11,733	67.5	324,100	1,227
Provo	50,072	23.3	4.2	56,894	35,072	37,309	40,925	32,700	35,488	33,447	40.5	298,000	901

1. Specified owner-occupied units

City	Commuting, 2016–2020[1]		Computer access[2], 2016–2020		Migration, 2016–2020		Civilian labor force, 2021				Civilian Employment, 2016–2020[4]			
	Percent		Percent						Unemployment[3]		Population age 16 and older		Population age 16 to 64	
	Drove alone	Mean travel time to work	With a computer in the house	With Internet access	Percent who lived in the same house one year ago	Percent who lived in another state or county one year ago	Total	Percent change 2020–2021	Total	Rate	Number	Percent in labor force	Number	Percent who worked full-year full-time
	55	56	57	58	59	60	61	62	63	64	65	66	67	68
TEXAS —Cont'd														
Mesquite	78.6	32.4	94.0	88.3	84.3	3.1	74,581	3.9	4,356	5.8	105,566	68.3	89,966	53.8
Midland	83.4	19.0	93.6	86.2	81.0	9.1	81,887	1.7	4,573	5.6	105,266	70.6	90,777	57.6
Midlothian	81.8	30.7	97.8	95.2	87.3	6.9	18,185	4.6	754	4.1	23,214	71.8	19,810	58.2
Mission	80.0	21.3	91.6	82.2	89.2	3.2	35,833	2.2	3,207	8.9	60,328	57.8	49,551	44.0
Missouri City	79.0	31.2	97.4	93.4	89.7	7.0	39,506	1.1	2,599	6.6	60,707	66.2	49,691	52.9
Nacogdoches	77.9	17.2	92.6	84.1	64.8	15.2	14,152	2.5	837	5.9	26,937	60.8	23,069	34.8
New Braunfels	81.9	24.3	94.4	90.2	81.6	13.0	47,423	2.6	2,065	4.4	65,008	65.4	53,265	57.1
North Richland Hills	80.1	27.1	96.9	93.7	83.0	5.6	40,514	2.9	1,883	4.6	56,677	68.4	45,027	57.7
Odessa	82.4	22.0	92.4	85.3	81.2	7.9	61,649	-1.4	4,608	7.5	90,027	69.6	77,826	55.6
Pasadena	78.9	25.8	93.2	88.6	81.9	3.0	64,468	0.4	5,175	8.0	111,671	66.7	97,012	48.9
Pearland	84.0	34.9	98.0	95.3	89.0	7.1	64,452	1.9	3,118	4.8	94,062	70.2	80,682	60.7
Pflugerville	78.8	28.8	99.0	95.4	84.3	7.3	39,044	5.6	2,019	5.2	50,332	74.6	44,372	60.5
Pharr	79.9	20.7	86.7	59.0	93.7	1.3	32,316	1.8	3,154	9.8	55,068	58.5	45,431	45.0
Plano	76.9	26.8	98.4	94.9	87.2	7.5	165,412	4.0	7,225	4.4	232,271	69.6	194,064	59.2
Port Arthur	88.2	24.2	87.1	68.5	89.1	3.6	21,142	-2.5	2,889	13.7	40,880	53.0	33,878	42.3
Prosper	75.2	34.0	99.0	97.0	83.0	10.8	12,583	4.2	687	5.5	17,690	69.5	15,749	57.9
Richardson	75.2	24.7	98.3	93.1	81.5	9.1	66,919	4.2	3,024	4.5	95,122	68.2	78,542	55.5
Rockwall	78.3	30.6	96.4	93.4	84.6	10.4	24,658	4.3	1,118	4.5	35,611	68.6	29,358	58.1
Rosenberg	81.4	29.2	88.6	79.1	83.5	5.3	18,288	1.5	1,184	6.5	28,321	66.4	24,134	51.0
Round Rock	75.7	25.3	98.1	95.3	79.8	12.0	76,521	6.2	2,853	3.7	99,810	74.4	88,086	57.5
Rowlett	81.3	33.1	98.7	96.3	85.3	5.4	38,655	4.3	1,812	4.7	51,396	71.9	44,391	61.1
Sachse	76.2	32.1	98.4	92.8	91.2	4.7	15,270	4.0	608	4.0	21,107	71.0	17,809	61.0
San Angelo	78.2	17.4	90.7	79.4	82.0	8.9	45,213	1.3	2,276	5.0	79,709	62.7	63,935	55.2
San Antonio	76.3	24.6	91.9	81.6	83.7	5.1	730,583	2.0	38,288	5.2	1,192,216	64.0	1,004,058	50.1
San Juan	85.2	24.6	86.6	56.2	92.4	0.5	15,939	1.8	1,735	10.9	26,201	58.7	22,045	45.4
San Marcos	74.7	22.5	94.7	76.2	66.8	16.4	35,171	4.6	1,651	4.7	56,608	65.7	50,558	39.8
Schertz	84.9	29.5	97.4	93.7	84.7	9.9	19,665	2.7	927	4.7	33,441	63.9	27,735	56.8
Seguin	82.7	20.0	88.9	79.2	84.9	4.9	13,443	2.0	651	4.8	23,083	58.7	18,185	51.4
Sherman	78.3	21.3	93.0	77.5	79.0	6.8	21,084	3.3	994	4.7	33,469	62.9	26,925	52.8
Socorro	78.2	26.2	90.4	77.2	90.9	2.0	15,206	1.2	1,039	6.8	26,393	59.0	22,271	45.7
Southlake	68.4	28.9	99.2	98.5	87.6	7.8	15,125	4.0	599	4.0	22,772	62.5	19,316	51.1
Sugar Land	78.1	31.1	98.6	96.4	88.8	6.3	58,923	2.1	3,152	5.3	95,399	65.1	76,613	52.7
Temple	82.0	19.2	91.7	84.8	80.5	7.8	36,796	2.7	1,769	4.8	57,121	59.6	45,815	50.0
Texarkana	86.7	15.9	79.8	70.0	91.0	4.4	14,976	1.1	932	6.2	28,555	55.1	22,510	46.2
Texas City	83.2	22.5	89.0	83.5	78.8	7.5	22,448	0.4	1,934	8.6	37,809	60.8	30,390	48.8
The Colony	80.5	28.2	98.5	93.7	84.4	10.2	29,364	3.1	1,347	4.6	34,881	78.9	31,247	68.3
Tyler	84.3	20.5	93.1	83.3	84.9	7.3	52,058	2.4	2,678	5.1	83,936	62.4	66,739	53.4
University Park	73.4	18.9	98.8	98.2	84.4	6.4	11,249	5.9	463	4.1	19,180	60.0	17,004	41.0
Victoria	78.8	18.9	90.2	73.4	83.1	5.9	29,431	0.3	1,920	6.5	51,598	64.0	41,672	50.6
Waco	80.1	17.3	88.9	78.7	77.3	9.2	62,973	3.0	3,323	5.3	107,788	59.9	90,542	44.3
Waxahachie	84.6	26.2	95.2	90.1	80.6	7.8	20,423	4.1	970	4.7	28,478	66.1	23,653	56.7
Weatherford	80.9	27.4	95.0	85.5	81.3	8.8	15,566	3.1	675	4.3	25,330	60.2	19,693	55.6
Weslaco	77.3	29.4	92.4	84.5	84.4	4.2	17,463	3.5	1,677	9.6	29,386	58.3	24,347	44.7
Wichita Falls	73.0	14.3	89.8	80.3	77.3	11.8	42,757	0.4	2,338	5.5	83,196	55.7	69,428	47.0
Wylie	78.2	33.9	98.5	94.3	84.5	9.7	30,090	3.9	1,257	4.2	38,489	76.4	35,034	60.1
UTAH	74.4	22.0	96.1	89.2	83.8	6.9	1,681,494	2.5	45,344	2.7	2,325,169	68.6	1,976,159	50.5
American Fork	77.0	21.1	96.6	90.1	86.5	4.5	16,427	4.4	433	2.6	22,349	66.3	19,365	46.3
Bountiful	76.1	22.9	96.5	92.2	84.5	8.9	21,121	1.4	580	2.7	32,331	66.3	25,951	52.4
Cedar City	78.2	13.6	96.6	85.4	81.4	11.7	17,134	3.8	506	3.0	24,884	63.5	21,310	41.5
Clearfield	78.3	22.4	95.4	85.7	81.9	8.8	15,155	1.1	488	3.2	22,571	68.6	20,315	54.5
Cottonwood Heights	70.9	22.3	96.6	90.9	86.9	5.0	19,793	1.3	517	2.6	27,269	70.8	21,606	55.0
Draper	72.3	23.8	99.4	92.6	84.2	7.3	23,892	2.1	654	2.7	35,083	67.6	31,162	51.3
Eagle Mountain	72.5	33.2	99.9	94.4	85.8	5.7	19,096	4.8	463	2.4	19,572	74.8	18,847	50.4
Herriman	73.1	28.3	100.0	96.5	83.9	6.3	25,603	2.3	712	2.8	29,316	75.3	27,293	56.2
Holladay	75.8	19.5	97.3	93.7	85.8	5.3	15,804	1.1	449	2.8	23,693	66.6	18,520	53.3
Kaysville	78.3	23.9	98.1	94.8	90.0	4.8	15,317	2.1	338	2.2	21,507	66.8	18,425	47.1
Kearns	77.8	24.5	96.3	92.6	90.1	1.3	19,878	1.7	572	2.9	26,169	74.3	23,659	56.4
Layton	78.4	23.2	96.7	89.8	85.7	6.5	40,700	1.5	1,019	2.5	56,279	71.0	49,043	54.7
Lehi	72.3	23.3	98.8	95.8	85.1	7.2	33,301	4.7	798	2.4	43,272	72.7	39,525	50.8
Logan	68.9	14.3	96.4	84.5	68.9	13.2	29,406	4.2	586	2.0	40,156	71.4	36,582	36.9
Magna	80.3	24.3	94.7	91.5	86.7	3.5	14,148	1.8	513	3.6	20,269	74.0	18,174	55.1
Midvale	73.0	21.0	96.6	89.7	77.9	8.0	21,504	1.1	641	3.0	25,967	75.0	23,234	56.7
Millcreek	73.8	20.2	95.1	88.7	83.6	6.6	35,178	1.4	935	2.7	48,791	68.5	39,647	54.1
Murray	74.5	19.7	94.1	87.2	85.2	5.1	29,437	1.3	841	2.9	39,877	69.7	31,215	56.8
Ogden	77.4	20.8	92.7	86.2	81.1	6.8	42,250	0.7	1,469	3.5	67,115	66.6	57,405	53.4
Orem	74.2	19.5	98.1	90.8	77.9	7.0	53,558	4.6	1,331	2.5	72,950	70.1	62,895	46.3
Pleasant Grove	78.0	21.8	98.6	91.5	84.8	5.2	19,611	4.7	483	2.5	27,412	69.9	23,640	50.3
Provo	59.8	19.0	97.5	70.6	62.6	16.1	68,695	5.1	1,450	2.1	95,443	71.3	88,157	31.0

1. Employed persons. 2. Households. 3. Percent of civilian labor force. 4. Persons 16 years old and over.

City	Value of residential construction authorized by building permits, 2021			Wholesale trade[1], 2017				Retail trade[2], 2017			
	New construction ($1,000)	Number of housing units	Percent single family	Number of establishments	Number of employees	Sales (mil dol)	Annual payroll (mil dol)	Number of establish-ments	Number of employees	Sales (mil dol)	Annual payroll (mil dol)
	69	70	71	72	73	74	75	76	77	78	79
TEXAS —Cont'd											
Mesquite	133,016	560	100.0	71	642	621.8	37.2	435	7,849	2,217.2	220.8
Midland	174,724	858	100.0	168	2,646	4,981.8	184.2	463	8,368	3,036.9	269.3
Midlothian	164,924	695	99.7	D	D	D	D	60	848	285.5	23.6
Mission	89,305	564	95.0	85	613	344.8	21.1	208	3,852	1,219.1	96.7
Missouri City	164,836	693	100.0	71	851	747.0	51.3	176	3,402	814.2	79.5
Nacogdoches	4,554	28	100.0	29	286	148.0	13.9	193	2,640	800.0	72.4
New Braunfels	498,573	2,388	74.8	D	D	D	119.1	321	5,707	2,185.0	178.6
North Richland Hills	89,529	489	51.9	37	371	183.6	18.0	171	3,994	1,945.1	130.3
Odessa	330,810	1,406	97.7	188	2,973	2,083.6	195.5	407	7,700	2,864.7	256.0
Pasadena	19,776	119	100.0	159	2,859	1,643.0	185.1	419	6,655	1,721.3	158.5
Pearland	170,032	715	100.0	66	546	283.1	32.3	300	6,635	1,756.4	163.8
Pflugerville	110,548	503	86.1	48	672	346.5	38.7	120	1,970	579.9	50.5
Pharr	77,380	451	50.8	130	1,514	864.7	64.1	174	2,543	768.9	66.5
Plano	109,762	668	48.1	402	6,240	8,208.8	563.9	1,085	23,966	9,763.5	790.0
Port Arthur	39,879	261	99.2	31	577	549.8	32.6	181	3,235	1,014.7	85.2
Prosper	289,633	1,220	100.0	D	D	D	7.3	36	600	210.6	20.8
Richardson	116,037	751	5.3	231	5,702	12,071.6	569.7	351	5,337	2,801.4	201.2
Rockwall	172,494	989	43.2	42	316	373.7	23.9	223	4,656	1,531.0	142.4
Rosenberg	122,510	513	99.6	25	420	360.9	25.8	184	3,544	1,143.8	102.9
Round Rock	401,394	1,931	42.3	98	912	1,385.0	68.8	426	10,564	4,354.7	422.9
Rowlett	117,424	738	44.9	33	144	74.9	8.3	98	1,903	514.6	45.4
Sachse	159,130	596	67.6	6	7	2.1	0.4	25	619	189.5	15.5
San Angelo	71,863	333	100.0	97	1,194	700.9	63.6	406	6,498	1,919.7	187.2
San Antonio	2,315,591	11,158	58.9	1,280	25,669	16,371.7	1,461.3	4,419	81,646	24,317.9	2,200.2
San Juan	27,242	213	100.0	14	182	118.5	6.7	55	990	430.9	34.3
San Marcos	134,559	721	100.0	26	183	279.3	14.8	397	10,611	3,612.4	254.0
Schertz	55,372	234	100.0	52	1,602	1,250.3	103.7	55	1,464	426.7	37.4
Seguin	252,693	1,124	87.7	23	322	111.8	15.5	124	1,959	599.4	51.1
Sherman	0	0	0.0	40	372	448.9	19.3	217	4,035	1,281.7	109.4
Socorro	133,227	597	89.6	15	103	67.5	4.9	61	716	197.0	15.4
Southlake	126,137	96	100.0	66	731	459.4	47.6	216	4,760	1,439.3	138.4
Sugar Land	50,748	151	100.0	203	2,947	6,729.9	171.1	546	8,629	2,637.0	219.4
Temple	283,446	1,922	55.6	62	2,208	4,015.4	118.5	269	4,836	1,490.5	128.9
Texarkana	12,312	54	100.0	52	579	264.2	26.9	292	5,078	1,327.8	129.9
Texas City	196,542	867	95.6	36	504	269.9	32.0	189	2,747	730.5	69.6
The Colony	37,187	156	100.0	19	339	311.9	23.9	76	2,811	910.4	100.6
Tyler	115,934	533	81.2	121	1,503	635.5	85.2	634	10,870	3,293.9	298.3
University Park	39,442	72	88.9	16	45	10.0	1.6	99	1,116	240.2	31.5
Victoria	58,282	349	51.9	81	1,133	861.7	63.8	342	5,539	1,694.7	155.0
Waco	63,036	737	89.7	148	1,864	1,023.0	96.7	564	8,748	2,401.0	229.0
Waxahachie	190,484	871	95.8	D	D	D	21.3	156	2,946	830.2	79.0
Weatherford	93,746	446	100.0	D	D	D	19.1	196	3,561	1,445.8	112.6
Weslaco	158,526	685	95.9	29	444	248.4	15.5	158	3,378	970.7	84.2
Wichita Falls	25,736	93	100.0	125	1,116	418.6	52.4	417	6,438	1,797.1	159.3
Wylie	121,380	516	97.3	19	166	104.2	10.1	83	1,893	465.0	40.5
UTAH	9,188,026	39,058	62.5	3,109	46,631	41,834.1	2,880.8	9,995	153,633	50,008.3	4,445.9
American Fork	245,243	1,297	22.1	32	821	617.9	44.0	159	3,079	1,208.3	96.3
Bountiful	27,733	72	58.3	D	D	D	9.6	144	2,207	980.0	76.0
Cedar City	121,276	602	43.7	23	165	124.2	7.9	161	2,091	614.5	51.3
Clearfield	135,442	960	12.0	18	245	391.8	9.8	66	571	148.0	12.4
Cottonwood Heights	63,881	144	50.0	41	709	659.1	82.6	74	1,778	931.0	55.2
Draper	116,524	267	100.0	68	1,995	2,304.4	155.2	212	4,439	2,045.6	157.6
Eagle Mountain	416,627	1,538	96.4	6	27	2.5	0.3	19	182	49.7	3.2
Herriman	179,601	749	83.0	8	8	4.1	0.4	34	385	129.9	10.4
Holladay	20,976	71	31.0	21	83	27.5	1.8	68	609	167.1	14.7
Kaysville	62,796	159	100.0	24	250	91.9	13.4	84	1,019	262.8	27.8
Kearns	NA	NA	NA	4	23	6.4	1.3	34	441	109.7	11.3
Layton	132,003	450	95.6	46	338	156.8	15.6	294	5,222	1,406.8	138.0
Lehi	480,292	2,030	76.9	36	1,233	873.4	76.5	178	2,707	846.8	73.2
Logan	45,870	175	100.0	71	691	508.3	34.6	275	4,271	1,309.0	105.1
Magna	NA	NA	NA	5	36	9.3	2.2	26	439	126.6	11.1
Midvale	45,766	245	10.6	52	577	293.9	29.9	157	3,646	2,408.4	163.2
Millcreek	45,529	145	65.5	69	634	238.3	36.7	174	2,573	684.6	74.3
Murray	102,041	415	24.3	93	868	399.3	45.5	340	6,394	2,170.6	201.6
Ogden	70,539	505	26.1	96	1,835	1,628.9	100.5	349	4,272	1,226.0	121.0
Orem	59,908	269	46.5	103	1,203	592.7	60.1	478	7,756	2,197.7	212.9
Pleasant Grove	81,669	282	41.5	30	135	93.3	10.7	97	1,144	285.0	32.7
Provo	98,802	715	13.7	60	1,983	816.6	144.6	396	4,673	1,149.9	118.4

1. Merchant wholesalers except manufacturers' sales branches and offices. 2. Establishments with payroll.

City	Real estate and rental and leasing, 2017				Professional, scientific, and technical services[1], 2017				Manufacturing, 2017			
	Number of establish-ments	Number of employees	Receipts (mil dol)	Annual payroll (mil dol)	Number of establish-ments	Number of employees	Receipts (mil dol)	Annual payroll (mil dol)	Number of establish-ments	Number of employees	Receipts (mil dol)	Annual payroll (mil dol)
	80	81	82	83	84	85	86	87	88	89	90	91
TEXAS —Cont'd												
Mesquite	98	452	120.6	20.1	112	736	62.7	20.9	NA	NA	NA	NA
Midland	293	1,719	559.0	90.1	443	2,948	675.4	212.4	NA	NA	NA	NA
Midlothian	29	111	31.8	4.4	42	177	21.9	7.4	NA	NA	NA	NA
Mission	73	208	33.1	6.0	86	366	42.1	13.9	NA	NA	NA	NA
Missouri City	62	221	60.5	8.8	183	781	151.6	53.4	NA	NA	NA	NA
Nacogdoches	47	184	27.0	5.6	73	367	49.1	14.6	NA	NA	NA	NA
New Braunfels	149	540	128.7	23.1	199	1,126	144.1	50.2	NA	NA	NA	NA
North Richland Hills	64	501	59.3	17.6	151	460	83.2	25.5	NA	NA	NA	NA
Odessa	154	1,446	589.3	82.8	213	1,549	257.4	89.8	NA	NA	NA	NA
Pasadena	134	892	234.5	42.1	185	4,077	570.6	291.7	NA	NA	NA	NA
Pearland	108	380	108.9	18.7	236	1,286	256.3	84.1	NA	NA	NA	NA
Pflugerville	39	114	32.6	5.4	93	540	83.6	39.8	NA	NA	NA	NA
Pharr	46	251	54.7	7.8	69	831	50.4	20.4	NA	NA	NA	NA
Plano	570	5,611	1,423.5	355.3	1,750	31,565	8,237.1	3,202.8	NA	NA	NA	NA
Port Arthur	33	343	57.9	15.2	41	365	46.6	22.4	NA	NA	NA	NA
Prosper	29	85	26.3	3.2	62	156	29.0	7.5	NA	NA	NA	NA
Richardson	201	1,275	458.6	60.8	D	D	D	D	NA	NA	NA	NA
Rockwall	73	235	70.7	9.4	198	923	143.2	56.8	NA	NA	NA	NA
Rosenberg	34	459	37.5	16.3	52	194	33.4	11.3	NA	NA	NA	NA
Round Rock	165	555	198.9	27.8	444	13,529	3,171.9	1,286.9	NA	NA	NA	NA
Rowlett	22	44	11.6	1.9	92	480	76.7	25.6	NA	NA	NA	NA
Sachse	11	28	5.6	0.8	35	119	12.6	5.2	NA	NA	NA	NA
San Angelo	136	557	112.8	19.3	189	1,231	162.4	53.8	NA	NA	NA	NA
San Antonio	1,783	12,132	2,899.6	632.0	3,644	46,677	7,090.7	2,899.3	NA	NA	NA	NA
San Juan	9	40	4.6	1.5	10	24	2.1	0.4	NA	NA	NA	NA
San Marcos	92	612	136.6	19.9	94	799	103.7	25.1	NA	NA	NA	NA
Schertz	38	211	41.7	8.3	51	466	91.2	24.8	NA	NA	NA	NA
Seguin	34	134	25.8	5.2	45	255	24.8	11.4	NA	NA	NA	NA
Sherman	46	171	49.9	6.8	105	400	61.1	21.4	NA	NA	NA	NA
Socorro	16	31	4.1	0.7	18	121	31.5	4.4	NA	NA	NA	NA
Southlake	105	800	104.5	33.4	243	1,572	278.4	97.6	NA	NA	NA	NA
Sugar Land	212	516	157.7	23.9	643	9,908	3,584.3	1,037.9	NA	NA	NA	NA
Temple	85	450	63.8	15.6	103	652	90.1	32.9	NA	NA	NA	NA
Texarkana	81	395	72.5	15.8	123	2,248	206.4	84.5	NA	NA	NA	NA
Texas City	41	910	209.3	58.1	54	671	76.1	31.5	NA	NA	NA	NA
The Colony	32	104	48.6	4.8	80	480	60.9	17.2	NA	NA	NA	NA
Tyler	226	911	199.6	39.4	450	3,518	733.5	238.0	NA	NA	NA	NA
University Park	64	117	39.8	9.3	113	282	70.8	17.7	NA	NA	NA	NA
Victoria	107	792	415.9	38.7	140	1,016	136.0	43.4	NA	NA	NA	NA
Waco	182	1,462	333.5	68.3	278	2,307	464.1	145.6	NA	NA	NA	NA
Waxahachie	48	179	46.2	5.8	81	402	48.3	20.9	NA	NA	NA	NA
Weatherford	52	230	64.1	12.2	106	551	81.0	26.2	NA	NA	NA	NA
Weslaco	41	194	34.6	5.8	52	404	41.4	13.3	NA	NA	NA	NA
Wichita Falls	150	756	127.2	25.4	193	1,279	131.7	52.4	NA	NA	NA	NA
Wylie	40	123	25.4	4.9	64	213	37.2	11.8	NA	NA	NA	NA
UTAH	5,577	19,457	5,296.5	876.9	10,873	92,444	15,304.7	5,610.4	3,377	121,527	55,788.0	7,171.0
American Fork	67	216	40.4	6.2	143	1,229	120.8	47.2	NA	NA	NA	NA
Bountiful	93	170	30.6	6.7	223	1,003	127.3	46.7	NA	NA	NA	NA
Cedar City	83	151	34.4	5.3	116	429	51.6	17.5	NA	NA	NA	NA
Clearfield	27	82	37.6	3.9	67	1,198	150.2	81.2	NA	NA	NA	NA
Cottonwood Heights	172	600	234.5	30.9	228	1,497	367.2	119.5	NA	NA	NA	NA
Draper	142	499	127.7	21.2	307	2,099	341.8	110.5	NA	NA	NA	NA
Eagle Mountain	28	35	5.0	1.0	48	100	17.1	6.3	NA	NA	NA	NA
Herriman	51	66	9.1	2.5	66	132	14.5	4.6	NA	NA	NA	NA
Holladay	D	D	D	D	199	1,638	365.1	196.0	NA	NA	NA	NA
Kaysville	43	75	21.4	2.6	130	872	106.6	50.6	NA	NA	NA	NA
Kearns	11	35	7.7	1.2	7	11	0.6	0.2	NA	NA	NA	NA
Layton	127	512	118.9	17.2	213	1,552	201.4	79.2	NA	NA	NA	NA
Lehi	D	D	D	D	325	3,937	848.3	355.2	NA	NA	NA	NA
Logan	124	361	67.4	10.6	189	1,868	246.1	76.9	NA	NA	NA	NA
Magna	12	19	2.4	0.7	D	D	D	D	NA	NA	NA	NA
Midvale	83	534	145.3	31.6	127	3,481	251.7	153.1	NA	NA	NA	NA
Millcreek	143	590	109.8	28.2	295	1,843	327.0	106.7	NA	NA	NA	NA
Murray	169	1,143	233.2	55.1	D	D	D	D	NA	NA	NA	NA
Ogden	114	381	56.3	11.3	275	2,689	348.1	131.5	NA	NA	NA	NA
Orem	210	724	180.7	28.2	D	D	D	D	NA	NA	NA	NA
Pleasant Grove	D	D	D	D	140	985	177.7	68.4	NA	NA	NA	NA
Provo	136	556	99.0	18.2	415	2,798	427.1	163.6	NA	NA	NA	NA

1. Establishments subject to federal tax.

Table D. Cities — **Accommodation and Food Services, Arts, Entertainment, and Recreation, and Health Care and Social Assistance**

City	Accommodation and food services, 2017				Arts, entertainment, and recreation[1], 2017				Health care and social assistance[1], 2017			
	Number of establish-ments	Number of employees	Receipts (mil dol)	Annual payroll (mil dol)	Number of establish-ments	Number of employees	Receipts (mil dol)	Annual payroll (mil dol)	Number of establish-ments	Number of employees	Receipts (mil dol)	Annual payroll (mil dol)
	92	93	94	95	96	97	98	99	100	101	102	103
TEXAS —Cont'd												
Mesquite	236	5,700	347.6	94.2	D	D	D	D	355	8,370	615.1	235.8
Midland	333	7,990	608.9	154.4	48.0	D	95.0	D	393	7,444	882.0	348.9
Midlothian	52	936	51.7	15.9	5.0	31	1.7	0.5	56	773	45.5	20.1
Mission	142	2,593	137.4	34.9	13.0	266	18.4	6.2	306	10,015	419.6	212.2
Missouri City	125	1,889	109.0	27.7	18.0	261	11.0	3.7	230	2,249	181.8	65.4
Nacogdoches	108	2,168	114.9	34.9	13.0	92	6.4	0.9	179	3,196	363.7	130.1
New Braunfels	260	6,136	344.5	101.1	47.0	1,173	82.4	26.8	285	5,296	613.7	231.6
North Richland Hills	145	3,074	155.4	43.4	21.0	296	13.7	3.6	175	2,577	356.9	128.5
Odessa	264	6,434	449.2	115.2	33.0	483	38.7	10.7	290	8,055	1,010.6	380.6
Pasadena	238	5,473	303.9	85.3	17.0	330	20.5	4.4	352	7,459	846.0	324.7
Pearland	236	5,726	338.1	93.4	25.0	499	23.3	7.1	372	4,937	651.0	200.3
Pflugerville	93	2,267	119.9	36.8	D	D	D	3.3	94	1,025	91.9	37.5
Pharr	109	2,209	131.6	31.1	8.0	63	4.3	1.4	162	5,088	264.2	99.8
Plano	922	19,346	1,259.2	367.9	117.0	2,399	180.6	45.8	1,632	29,943	4,556.9	1,516.6
Port Arthur	117	2,263	118.9	32.2	D	D	D	D	D	D	D	113.8
Prosper	D	D	D	D	11.0	42	3.6	0.5	51	231	32.1	11.4
Richardson	459	7,531	512.3	139.4	68.0	716	45.4	12.9	599	8,892	959.9	342.3
Rockwall	153	3,973	215.0	62.1	21.0	369	24.5	6.7	224	2,933	444.7	139.2
Rosenberg	120	2,461	149.0	43.7	8.0	37	5.2	0.7	76	850	64.5	24.3
Round Rock	333	7,804	482.1	135.4	42.0	1,317	81.2	20.0	364	8,980	1,325.5	506.8
Rowlett	85	1,455	86.1	23.5	13.0	153	11.1	2.3	120	2,283	358.5	96.2
Sachse	26	401	19.1	6.2	D	D	D	D	D	D	D	4.4
San Angelo	248	4,816	257.9	72.5	32.0	597	25.5	8.6	263	7,868	815.0	351.4
San Antonio	3,546	93,890	5,969.7	1,652.2	D	D	D	D	4,263	113,466	13,591.5	4,917.8
San Juan	23	428	27.2	6.7	D	D	D	D	55	1,382	57.9	31.5
San Marcos	256	5,899	288.2	82.8	22.0	156	8.8	3.2	169	3,732	413.2	166.5
Schertz	59	1,596	80.5	23.3	4.0	162	4.9	1.6	69	1,042	110.4	42.4
Seguin	88	1,569	85.3	23.7	D	D	D	D	101	1,914	220.4	86.3
Sherman	112	2,739	158.6	45.7	D	D	D	D	213	3,898	415.2	161.9
Socorro	29	499	20.8	4.8	NA	NA	NA	NA	15	293	9.5	4.8
Southlake	128	3,408	203.1	62.8	29.0	588	38.1	11.4	269	2,900	458.5	148.4
Sugar Land	377	8,118	525.6	145.4	45.0	D	133.8	D	740	12,100	1,644.1	581.8
Temple	187	4,019	209.3	59.7	25.0	353	19.8	6.4	199	21,426	3,170.3	1,522.6
Texarkana	148	3,886	180.4	52.3	D	D	D	D	247	6,804	943.5	339.4
Texas City	88	1,518	80.6	21.1	6.0	50	3.2	1.1	103	2,264	217.0	93.4
The Colony	83	1,919	119.1	33.8	12.0	485	31.0	8.5	61	632	51.0	21.3
Tyler	358	8,501	457.2	140.2	44.0	768	47.1	16.5	569	20,676	2,852.0	1,033.3
University Park	61	1,619	112.8	41.7	D	D	D	D	72	419	68.0	23.0
Victoria	185	3,663	191.3	55.8	D	D	D	D	277	6,721	742.3	312.6
Waco	367	8,862	505.4	130.0	53.0	1,382	74.0	22.3	454	16,024	1,651.2	697.6
Waxahachie	100	2,669	140.5	41.0	10.0	138	4.6	1.6	116	2,078	287.2	94.6
Weatherford	121	2,541	139.7	38.8	D	D	D	0.9	150	2,414	296.8	103.4
Weslaco	91	2,073	110.9	27.4	8.0	64	2.5	1.1	195	7,892	400.7	186.5
Wichita Falls	260	5,438	265.4	76.6	33.0	440	14.3	4.9	365	10,507	1,108.2	408.4
Wylie	49	985	59.4	15.7	D	D	D	D	69	1,074	74.4	33.7
UTAH	5,931	118,734	7,098.2	2,003.5	1,180.0	28,240	1,760.2	552.6	8,254	146,365	18,708.2	6,703.4
American Fork	89	1,968	102.5	27.3	15.0	122	9.8	2.1	152	2,603	356.4	111.5
Bountiful	74	1,562	73.5	21.9	15.0	98	8.0	1.7	223	3,291	348.1	133.1
Cedar City	D	D	D	D	16.0	86	4.8	1.2	144	2,182	182.2	68.4
Clearfield	D	D	D	D	NA	NA	NA	NA	61	1,672	119.1	45.4
Cottonwood Heights	D	D	D	D	13.0	165	17.6	3.9	147	1,559	153.8	57.7
Draper	117	2,066	110.2	32.2	D	D	D	D	174	1,671	210.2	73.0
Eagle Mountain	8	112	3.7	1.1	NA	NA	NA	NA	16	68	7.0	2.3
Herriman	19	431	18.8	4.9	6.0	11	0.9	0.2	38	338	18.7	8.0
Holladay	55	803	50.1	13.1	D	D	D	D	126	934	88.2	35.3
Kaysville	24	508	20.3	5.7	11.0	190	10.4	2.3	77	668	55.8	24.2
Kearns	18	232	11.0	2.9	NA	NA	NA	NA	9	130	8.4	4.0
Layton	166	3,673	210.3	56.8	19.0	296	10.0	3.2	214	3,915	473.2	167.0
Lehi	98	2,154	129.1	37.2	25.0	674	71.1	12.4	114	1,058	141.6	51.4
Logan	128	3,069	141.9	40.9	28.0	248	14.2	4.4	220	3,667	452.7	141.4
Magna	23	343	18.3	4.7	NA	NA	NA	NA	23	391	26.8	13.4
Midvale	109	1,961	113.1	32.0	13.0	451	21.0	6.6	81	781	61.3	26.1
Millcreek	D	D	D	D	33.0	290	15.6	5.7	371	5,110	728.5	241.3
Murray	125	2,927	166.4	50.6	19.0	384	21.8	5.9	370	10,971	1,963.1	653.8
Ogden	216	3,798	188.5	55.0	D	D	D	D	309	7,156	1,050.0	346.0
Orem	186	3,680	204.0	56.0	57.0	522	30.7	8.1	314	5,771	537.7	193.1
Pleasant Grove	34	654	48.2	13.1	14.0	49	14.5	1.7	82	660	57.0	19.6
Provo	202	4,386	240.0	70.7	47.0	305	20.7	5.6	323	10,535	1,322.3	494.7

1. Establishments subject to federal tax.

City	Other services[1]				Government employment and payroll, 2017								
						March payroll							
							Perent of total for:						
	Number of establish-ments	Number of employees	Receipts (mil dol)	Annual payroll (mil dol)	Full-time equivalent employees	Total (dollars)	Admin-istrative, judicial, and legal	Police and corrections	Fire protection	Highways and trans-portation	Health and welfare	Natural resources and utilities	Education and libraries
	104	105	106	107	108	109	110	111	112	113	114	115	116
TEXAS —Cont'd													
Mesquite	115	823	100.9	28.7	1,114	6,060,197	11.2	33.9	27.2	3.7	3.8	14.6	1.7
Midland	252	2,152	396.2	87.9	968	4,871,703	11.3	25.9	23.9	14.0	2.7	16.7	0.0
Midlothian	30	242	22.5	6.6	218	1,076,225	12.9	32.1	29.2	4.7	0.5	14.0	0.0
Mission	78	391	37.6	10.2	643	2,364,235	11.4	38.2	17.4	2.8	1.6	23.9	2.8
Missouri City	D	D	D	D	315	1,632,986	9.5	42.4	22.9	9.3	0.0	4.5	0.0
Nacogdoches	D	D	D	D	312	1,270,092	11.7	30.5	23.0	6.5	1.2	17.7	1.7
New Braunfels	147	1,096	101.1	33.0	827	3,664,065	7.8	24.5	26.2	5.9	1.3	26.6	2.5
North Richland Hills	93	487	60.5	15.9	626	2,982,868	13.0	32.5	21.9	7.4	4.8	15.6	3.3
Odessa	193	1,687	210.5	59.3	943	4,456,802	14.2	28.4	22.6	8.6	2.0	16.1	0.0
Pasadena	167	2,056	604.7	109.3	1,024	5,195,001	10.3	46.0	2.5	8.3	5.2	17.2	2.9
Pearland	165	1,227	109.5	35.3	689	3,375,508	10.7	37.0	16.5	6.6	6.6	15.5	0.0
Pflugerville	64	449	57.9	18.9	340	1,586,208	16.4	48.0	0.0	4.9	0.0	12.2	3.5
Pharr	64	487	52.8	13.0	641	2,300,354	11.6	36.5	14.0	8.4	1.0	18.4	2.2
Plano	524	4,256	824.3	154.5	2,302	12,930,116	10.1	29.9	23.6	2.7	0.0	13.4	4.4
Port Arthur	52	248	35.5	10.2	664	3,432,181	8.3	26.8	21.8	5.6	9.0	25.1	1.7
Prosper	20	114	11.8	3.6	152	828,179	12.9	19.2	27.0	1.7	0.0	21.6	0.9
Richardson	201	1,718	236.8	76.3	1,053	6,535,292	15.4	24.9	18.9	4.9	1.8	18.8	3.4
Rockwall	92	639	59.6	19.0	283	1,555,754	17.3	39.5	14.2	3.1	0.0	15.8	0.0
Rosenberg	61	269	36.4	9.9	220	935,709	12.4	48.5	20.9	5.4	1.4	5.0	0.0
Round Rock	211	1,942	197.1	63.9	853	4,179,488	7.4	31.9	20.1	4.9	0.0	18.8	2.9
Rowlett	77	399	45.7	14.3	353	1,833,057	9.9	33.6	27.4	3.5	6.0	10.8	0.5
Sachse	D	D	D	D	127	478,491	4.0	39.9	26.7	7.9	8.1	10.5	2.9
San Angelo	191	1,052	147.8	34.6	911	3,997,824	15.6	26.1	24.2	5.3	3.8	19.3	0.0
San Antonio	2,132	16,568	1,683.3	497.3	15,585	91,157,442	7.9	22.6	14.9	3.9	5.3	41.7	1.5
San Juan	12	99	10.7	2.1	209	675,652	0.0	34.8	11.6	1.6	4.4	30.4	3.6
San Marcos	92	529	62.0	17.7	604	3,071,174	14.5	27.8	14.5	5.5	4.9	23.9	2.6
Schertz	D	D	47.6	D	327	1,451,552	16.4	24.9	14.8	4.2	18.6	9.0	3.0
Seguin	51	351	37.7	10.9	933	4,361,087	6.2	9.2	6.8	2.3	63.3	10.6	1.3
Sherman	59	387	44.4	12.0	422	1,937,884	11.7	24.1	24.6	5.8	2.9	25.8	1.5
Socorro	18	101	7.6	2.2	100	322,769	27.7	45.1	0.0	16.3	0.0	5.2	0.0
Southlake	91	733	58.3	21.3	338	1,703,855	25.8	22.7	21.3	7.0	2.9	18.1	2.2
Sugar Land	190	1,559	129.4	39.6	730	4,005,280	19.7	30.4	17.3	7.8	12.3	10.7	0.0
Temple	132	876	77.8	31.5	809	3,363,934	13.3	28.5	21.7	6.4	2.2	23.7	2.6
Texarkana	108	788	75.4	25.8	529	2,087,616	14.8	23.8	17.2	9.5	3.2	18.4	1.8
Texas City	48	281	37.5	9.9	493	2,285,519	7.5	27.9	21.2	9.3	1.4	27.1	2.0
The Colony	53	242	20.8	6.1	331	1,585,838	5.5	28.7	28.8	3.9	0.0	14.9	3.3
Tyler	244	1,569	173.4	48.3	840	4,220,921	7.2	33.3	30.5	9.7	1.2	15.4	1.6
University Park	28	222	24.8	6.9	240	1,527,224	7.9	25.7	19.4	4.8	0.0	24.1	1.0
Victoria	128	889	115.1	32.5	589	2,437,506	10.7	27.7	27.2	5.4	0.0	22.2	3.3
Waco	253	1,621	205.5	53.0	1,545	6,661,214	9.5	30.2	17.6	4.5	6.7	25.0	2.2
Waxahachie	61	352	38.0	10.6	290	1,418,072	12.4	28.0	25.4	3.4	3.0	21.1	0.0
Weatherford	64	444	38.7	14.1	380	1,292,771	16.2	21.4	16.6	5.4	0.4	24.3	3.0
Weslaco	61	517	43.6	16.4	302	1,190,869	14.3	38.2	27.2	7.7	0.0	5.7	2.6
Wichita Falls	189	970	135.6	29.9	1,165	5,879,646	6.8	23.8	36.5	7.4	5.0	15.9	0.9
Wylie	D	D	D	D	320	1,388,780	13.6	15.1	31.5	6.4	1.7	21.2	6.9
UTAH	4,763	29,903	3,526.9	957.5	X	X	X	X	X	X	X	X	X
American Fork	69	413	42.2	11.3	217	914,048	15.9	22.7	17.7	2.6	5.0	23.4	4.8
Bountiful	79	565	50.7	14.6	205	1,038,767	13.9	29.3	0.0	14.2	0.0	42.2	0.0
Cedar City	63	222	25.0	6.0	208	699,101	9.9	26.3	7.2	12.9	2.1	29.8	3.2
Clearfield	D	D	D	D	180	685,812	19.1	29.5	17.6	2.9	0.9	22.2	0.0
Cottonwood Heights	34	190	14.6	4.9	74	361,371	9.4	71.8	0.0	14.8	0.0	0.0	3.8
Draper	95	693	56.6	19.0	186	849,667	18.8	29.5	3.8	14.1	0.6	18.3	0.0
Eagle Mountain	10	20	2.7	0.7	147	584,820	16.8	0.0	0.0	4.9	52.2	12.9	2.6
Herriman	18	124	9.4	5.6	97	435,304	30.8	0.0	0.0	20.1	0.0	33.9	0.0
Holladay	55	260	18.0	5.9	21	101,357	82.9	0.0	0.0	0.0	0.0	17.1	0.0
Kaysville	36	210	21.7	5.7	145	558,493	10.8	23.0	8.8	7.7	0.0	39.0	0.0
Kearns	16	63	8.3	2.5	NA	NA	NA	NA	NA	NA	NA	NA	NA
Layton	123	825	74.9	20.2	352	1,629,092	18.5	35.0	21.5	9.4	0.1	14.0	0.0
Lehi	60	527	83.9	17.8	387	1,583,383	14.0	19.3	14.8	5.3	0.6	36.3	4.3
Logan	115	586	66.4	17.5	483	2,025,945	8.9	17.1	14.8	10.0	3.6	37.3	3.2
Magna	D	D	D	D	NA	NA	NA	NA	NA	NA	NA	NA	NA
Midvale	77	447	53.6	14.4	78	365,027	59.3	0.0	0.0	11.8	4.3	21.6	0.0
Millcreek	115	742	73.3	22.3	52	190,207	100.0	0.0	0.0	0.0	0.0	0.0	0.0
Murray	165	1,220	136.0	43.0	452	2,231,784	15.7	22.8	15.9	4.1	1.5	30.0	3.0
Ogden	141	1,120	125.1	34.5	636	2,957,540	17.5	29.6	16.0	5.3	12.6	16.6	0.0
Orem	172	1,007	93.4	27.5	522	2,253,204	20.2	27.0	15.7	5.2	2.4	19.7	7.2
Pleasant Grove	50	214	25.1	7.2	188	671,019	18.2	26.3	13.0	6.9	0.5	26.2	4.6
Provo	141	727	92.6	20.8	814	3,480,203	17.3	23.0	13.0	5.3	1.4	31.9	3.9

1. Establishments subject to federal tax.

City	City government finances, 2017									
	General revenue							General expenditure		
		Intergovernmental		Taxes						
					Per capita[1] (dollars)				Per capita[1] (dollars)	
	Total (mil dol)	Total (mil dol)	Percent from state government	Total (mil dol)	Total	Property	Sales and gross receipts	Total (mil dol)	Total	Capital outlays
	117	118	119	120	121	122	123	124	125	126
TEXAS —Cont'd										
Mesquite	171.2	13.7	7.2	98.8	685	287	397	166.9	1,157	118
Midland	201.0	10.0	29.8	132.1	970	312	658	154.6	1,135	141
Midlothian	43.1	8.5	2.8	26.3	893	649	244	47.2	1,600	427
Mission	79.0	8.1	45.4	40.1	480	239	242	69.6	833	73
Missouri City	66.8	5.4	33.9	46.3	621	421	201	70.2	941	185
Nacogdoches	35.1	1.2	69.7	18.2	547	261	287	35.2	1,059	126
New Braunfels	103.4	0.7	54.9	62.0	786	275	511	102.6	1,300	268
North Richland Hills	91.2	19.9	64.5	41.1	582	213	370	85.6	1,213	338
Odessa	141.4	3.3	59.9	92.3	792	228	565	122.2	1,049	93
Pasadena	174.4	19.0	46.1	98.4	640	274	366	159.7	1,038	275
Pearland	153.6	1.9	64.2	107.5	901	543	357	130.9	1,098	188
Pflugerville	59.3	2.9	4.1	33.7	533	331	202	65.9	1,041	451
Pharr	50.0	4.0	48.7	18.6	236	193	41	0.0	0	0
Plano	457.1	8.4	67.3	302.0	1,050	574	476	369.7	1,285	111
Port Arthur	117.2	13.6	86.7	47.5	857	363	493	105.1	1,896	171
Prosper	44.2	0.1	56.3	21.4	1,052	600	452	23.1	1,139	2
Richardson	203.1	5.0	77.6	138.9	1,195	678	517	195.5	1,682	188
Rockwall	55.5	0.3	100.0	47.7	1,080	486	594	39.6	897	0
Rosenberg	45.0	5.4	29.3	27.4	736	255	480	32.7	878	159
Round Rock	171.4	1.2	49.6	135.8	1,098	340	758	150.9	1,220	285
Rowlett	64.3	2.4	7.1	40.1	637	436	201	63.0	1,000	196
Sachse	38.7	0.4	9.3	35.2	1,355	397	958	35.5	1,368	709
San Angelo	114.5	5.2	11.1	70.9	712	352	359	120.3	1,207	234
San Antonio	2,328.5	464.5	36.9	946.1	626	295	322	2,273.7	1,505	273
San Juan	20.5	1.1	30.8	11.6	316	194	123	21.7	592	93
San Marcos	103.9	19.8	100.0	50.1	789	282	507	87.5	1,377	240
Schertz	54.8	3.2	8.9	31.3	780	406	374	45.9	1,144	255
Seguin	142.7	16.4	93.8	16.9	581	273	308	172.4	5,928	1,084
Sherman	48.9	1.3	61.2	28.9	681	220	461	53.2	1,257	114
Socorro	10.3	0.2	30.2	8.8	263	201	62	8.3	247	0
Southlake	89.5	0.7	65.5	73.2	2,303	1,197	1,106	84.3	2,655	496
Sugar Land	167.8	6.0	38.5	102.0	857	326	532	226.1	1,900	931
Temple	108.4	4.6	95.0	58.3	784	373	411	101.4	1,363	242
Texarkana	49.3	1.5	25.8	36.4	987	439	548	43.3	1,175	139
Texas City	61.0	1.7	83.3	43.5	899	467	432	70.1	1,448	199
The Colony	51.5	5.0	92.3	37.6	877	494	383	37.9	883	49
Tyler	139.8	18.1	7.0	79.6	760	174	586	126.2	1,205	228
University Park	57.4	0.2	100.0	25.1	994	695	299	59.4	2,353	222
Victoria	86.5	3.5	30.2	55.9	833	355	479	88.3	1,318	298
Waco	320.4	51.1	25.6	122.7	896	470	427	194.5	1,420	146
Waxahachie	51.1	0.2	100.0	36.6	1,037	533	504	41.8	1,185	71
Weatherford	37.5	1.7	48.3	24.0	780	324	456	43.1	1,403	192
Weslaco	35.3	1.8	91.3	21.6	538	265	273	32.5	808	80
Wichita Falls	114.8	16.7	37.5	65.7	630	331	299	124.1	1,189	131
Wylie	57.6	4.6	64.4	39.0	788	548	240	50.0	1,010	109
UTAH	X	X	X	X	X	X	X	X	X	X
American Fork	49.1	7.5	17.8	17.6	596	249	346	42.8	1,451	229
Bountiful	32.9	3.0	58.4	15.6	354	84	269	43.0	978	204
Cedar City	28.5	2.3	69.2	16.4	519	183	335	23.3	737	97
Clearfield	34.8	1.3	73.8	14.8	474	213	260	29.9	956	103
Cottonwood Heights	23.2	1.4	97.1	16.5	484	212	273	27.4	806	336
Draper	117.0	8.7	40.0	60.8	1,274	570	703	67.5	1,415	555
Eagle Mountain	19.1	1.1	100.0	6.2	193	43	150	20.9	651	150
Herriman	38.6	7.8	48.1	15.4	393	47	346	45.8	1,169	887
Holladay	2.1	0.0	0.0	1.7	56	2	54	2.9	94	1
Kaysville	23.3	1.2	100.0	11.2	352	102	250	19.3	610	53
Kearns	NA	NA	NA	NA	NA	NA	NA	NA	NA	NA
Layton	49.3	6.8	23.0	19.7	258	100	158	52.7	689	143
Lehi	74.4	3.2	28.2	26.9	423	144	279	77.5	1,217	413
Logan	70.4	9.9	62.4	26.1	511	114	391	52.8	1,034	118
Magna	NA	NA	NA	NA	NA	NA	NA	NA	NA	NA
Midvale	29.7	2.2	56.1	14.1	421	108	313	26.8	798	289
Millcreek	3.7	1.3	0.0	2.4	39	0	39	3.9	64	0
Murray	57.2	4.6	45.2	36.8	745	225	520	91.5	1,855	279
Ogden	101.2	9.9	71.6	49.5	568	274	294	100.6	1,155	201
Orem	86.3	6.0	88.2	45.8	469	103	366	71.5	732	151
Pleasant Grove	29.6	1.3	99.8	11.4	293	104	189	23.3	600	25
Provo	81.0	6.1	51.3	37.8	321	119	202	91.3	776	23

1. Based on population estimated as of July 1 of the year shown.

City	City government finances, 2017 (cont.) — General expenditure (cont.) — Percent of total for: Public welfare	Highways	Parking facilities	Education	Health and hospitals	Police protection	Sewerage and sanitation	Parks and recreation	Housing and community development	Interest on debt	Debt outstanding: Total (mil dol)	Debt outstanding: Per capita[1] (dollars)	Debt issued during year
	127	128	129	130	131	132	133	134	135	136	137	138	139
TEXAS —Cont'd													
Mesquite	0.3	5.0	0.0	0.0	0.8	24.1	11.4	8.4	9.9	3.9	145.4	1,008	0.0
Midland	0.0	4.9	0.0	0.0	3.4	17.7	15.2	12.9	1.0	1.6	78.3	575	0.0
Midlothian	0.3	8.0	0.0	0.0	1.4	12.9	8.7	22.0	0.0	8.0	90.3	3,063	8.8
Mission	0.0	5.9	0.0	0.0	0.6	20.7	14.0	5.0	1.6	17.7	361.0	4,320	0.0
Missouri City	0.0	11.5	0.0	0.0	0.4	19.9	10.7	11.3	0.5	6.6	160.9	2,156	0.0
Nacogdoches	0.0	6.4	0.0	0.0	1.4	23.2	22.6	4.7	0.0	0.8	46.6	1,402	1.7
New Braunfels	0.0	18.2	0.0	0.0	1.6	14.8	15.9	7.8	0.0	4.9	112.8	1,430	0.0
North Richland Hills	0.0	12.3	0.0	0.0	0.0	19.9	3.2	11.5	0.0	6.7	136.7	1,939	8.5
Odessa	0.0	10.1	0.0	0.0	0.8	19.3	19.0	5.5	0.4	2.7	52.9	454	0.0
Pasadena	0.0	10.7	0.0	0.0	2.3	30.4	14.2	7.9	9.5	1.7	215.9	1,403	158.1
Pearland	0.0	9.3	0.0	0.0	3.6	16.6	18.5	8.2	0.0	10.6	231.7	1,942	0.0
Pflugerville	0.0	20.8	0.0	0.0	0.9	22.0	18.1	13.9	0.1	0.0	222.8	3,521	69.0
Pharr	0.0	0.0	0.0	0.0	0.0	0.0	0.0	0.0	0.0	0.0	109.7	1,395	0.0
Plano	0.0	4.7	0.0	0.0	1.0	17.6	17.0	12.3	0.7	3.6	135.4	471	0.0
Port Arthur	2.1	10.1	0.0	0.0	1.7	21.6	14.2	4.6	2.3	2.5	57.3	1,033	0.0
Prosper	0.0	0.8	0.0	0.0	0.0	9.8	30.4	8.5	0.0	12.7	83.0	4,082	17.6
Richardson	0.0	12.3	0.0	0.0	0.9	13.6	21.5	14.9	0.0	5.9	238.9	2,056	35.4
Rockwall	0.0	6.7	0.0	0.0	0.0	26.5	11.9	10.5	0.0	12.4	125.1	2,834	0.0
Rosenberg	0.0	16.8	0.0	0.0	0.9	25.3	18.0	3.5	0.0	4.8	17.0	456	0.0
Round Rock	0.0	17.8	0.0	0.0	0.4	16.5	7.1	11.2	1.2	7.5	247.2	1,999	0.0
Rowlett	0.0	7.5	0.0	0.0	1.5	18.2	24.0	8.3	0.3	4.4	98.5	1,564	7.0
Sachse	0.0	5.2	0.0	0.0	0.4	9.3	7.5	3.3	0.0	5.3	40.4	1,555	0.0
San Angelo	0.1	5.3	0.0	0.0	2.8	16.8	9.8	14.0	2.3	3.7	207.7	2,084	0.0
San Antonio	5.6	6.2	0.6	2.8	1.3	17.1	15.5	10.3	2.2	6.1	11,712.5	7,751	1,820.6
San Juan	0.0	7.8	0.0	0.0	0.0	18.9	24.1	7.7	0.0	3.6	19.6	535	0.0
San Marcos	0.0	10.9	0.0	0.0	3.8	19.5	17.4	4.6	0.4	7.3	70.8	1,115	0.0
Schertz	0.1	4.4	0.0	0.0	12.2	11.4	17.1	18.8	0.0	4.2	70.3	1,752	13.9
Seguin	0.0	4.9	0.0	0.0	60.4	4.2	7.0	2.5	0.0	4.7	228.6	7,861	148.9
Sherman	0.1	10.3	0.0	0.0	1.3	17.9	16.1	5.9	0.7	0.0	175.0	4,131	75.3
Socorro	0.0	15.4	0.0	0.0	4.7	33.3	0.0	9.6	0.0	10.4	23.4	697	3.6
Southlake	0.0	5.1	0.0	0.0	0.0	10.9	6.2	27.9	0.0	0.0	171.2	5,389	26.8
Sugar Land	0.0	12.9	0.0	0.0	0.5	9.7	7.6	34.4	0.0	6.6	469.7	3,948	88.4
Temple	0.0	5.2	0.0	0.0	1.0	17.8	20.7	10.4	0.0	4.0	49.6	667	0.0
Texarkana	0.0	12.6	0.0	0.0	2.2	20.7	19.0	5.2	2.7	4.3	55.6	1,508	0.0
Texas City	0.0	15.9	0.0	0.0	0.5	17.9	17.0	12.8	0.4	3.4	69.9	1,444	0.0
The Colony	0.0	10.2	0.0	0.0	0.0	22.4	9.3	7.8	0.0	3.9	121.3	2,827	17.7
Tyler	0.0	10.1	0.0	0.0	0.5	21.9	21.9	3.3	8.1	0.1	55.5	530	0.0
University Park	0.0	10.4	0.0	0.0	0.0	12.1	11.9	5.7	0.0	34.2	640.9	25,404	143.8
Victoria	0.1	12.8	0.0	0.0	0.0	15.6	19.5	7.8	0.7	4.4	163.7	2,442	2.4
Waco	0.0	4.6	0.0	0.0	4.7	21.4	16.2	13.0	1.9	5.6	269.6	1,968	0.0
Waxahachie	0.0	7.5	0.0	0.0	2.3	19.1	14.2	8.4	0.0	8.0	159.0	4,511	0.0
Weatherford	0.0	13.7	0.0	0.0	2.9	18.7	16.3	5.5	0.0	5.6	107.3	3,493	6.1
Weslaco	0.0	6.7	0.0	0.0	0.0	20.5	23.0	5.2	0.0	0.0	80.5	2,003	0.0
Wichita Falls	0.0	7.6	0.0	0.0	4.2	19.0	14.3	6.1	4.3	1.4	186.9	1,792	101.4
Wylie	0.0	15.2	0.0	0.0	1.0	17.3	14.5	10.4	0.0	6.3	89.5	1,807	35.9
UTAH	X	X	X	X	X	X	X	X	X	X	X	X	X
American Fork	1.2	5.7	0.0	0.8	11.8	15.4	6.6	13.4	2.8	0.3	0.0	0	0.0
Bountiful	0.0	13.7	0.0	0.0	0.0	28.7	6.9	13.3	0.8	0.0	0.0	0	0.0
Cedar City	0.0	12.2	0.1	0.0	0.9	19.1	9.7	18.0	7.2	0.2	1.6	51	1.6
Clearfield	0.0	1.6	0.0	0.0	0.0	14.9	0.0	0.0	17.7	2.1	2.4	77	2.4
Cottonwood Heights	0.0	1.6	0.0	0.0	0.5	19.4	0.0	0.0	3.9	0.2	4.1	120	4.1
Draper	0.0	10.9	0.0	0.0	0.0	0.0	3.9	9.8	10.1	0.7	13.5	283	3.8
Eagle Mountain	0.0	18.7	0.0	0.0	0.1	9.7	13.8	20.0	1.1	0.2	24.1	751	0.0
Herriman	0.0	33.0	0.0	0.0	0.0	0.5	0.0	5.4	0.5	0.1	21.8	556	21.8
Holladay	0.0	0.0	9.3	0.0	1.6	0.0	0.5	0.9	4.9	0.0	0.0	0	0.0
Kaysville	0.0	10.1	0.0	0.0	3.7	17.9	22.5	9.6	0.0	0.1	0.0	0	0.0
Kearns	NA	NA	NA	NA	NA	NA	NA	NA	NA	NA	NA	NA	NA
Layton	0.0	7.8	0.0	0.0	7.9	16.8	22.6	6.4	2.5	0.0	0.0	0	0.0
Lehi	0.2	8.3	0.0	0.3	0.2	10.0	14.6	20.9	0.7	5.7	120.3	1,890	4.2
Logan	1.1	7.7	0.0	0.0	4.7	14.0	17.5	14.7	4.6	0.2	0.0	0	0.0
Magna	NA	NA	NA	NA	NA	NA	NA	NA	NA	NA	NA	NA	NA
Midvale	0.0	1.8	0.0	0.0	0.5	24.1	10.8	1.5	27.0	0.6	18.5	552	18.3
Millcreek	0.0	88.3	0.0	0.0	0.0	10.2	0.0	0.0	0.0	0.0	0.0	0	0.0
Murray	1.2	4.8	0.0	0.0	0.6	22.5	7.6	14.2	9.0	0.6	10.3	209	10.0
Ogden	0.0	8.9	0.0	0.0	4.9	19.4	3.2	1.3	6.8	1.7	117.4	1,348	17.0
Orem	0.2	7.3	0.0	0.0	0.4	16.8	11.7	10.6	2.2	0.2	3.7	38	2.9
Pleasant Grove	5.5	12.8	0.0	0.0	0.5	14.9	19.3	9.0	3.3	0.6	15.7	404	15.7
Provo	0.0	5.6	0.0	0.0	0.5	16.5	12.7	10.4	6.4	0.3	4.6	39	2.1

1. Based on population estimated as of July 1 of the year shown.

STATE	Place code	City	Land area[1] (sq. mi)	Population, 2021: Total persons 2021	Population, 2021: Rank	Population, 2021: Per square mile	Race 2020, Race alone[2] (percent): White	Black or African American	American Indian, Alaskan Native	Asian	Hawaiian Pacific Islander	Some other race	Two or more races (percent)
			1	2	3	4	5	6	7	8	9	10	11
		UTAH —Cont'd											
49	64340	Riverton	12.6	45,148	878	3,583.2	86.5	0.7	0.4	2.4	0.8	2.7	6.4
49	65110	Roy	8.1	39,358	1,009	4,859.0	78.2	1.2	1.0	2.0	0.6	7.6	9.4
49	65330	St. George	78.5	99,958	329	1,273.4	81.1	0.7	1.4	1.2	1.2	6.4	7.9
49	67000	Salt Lake City	110.3	200,478	122	1,817.6	68.4	2.9	1.4	5.5	2.1	9.7	9.9
49	67440	Sandy	24.2	95,050	350	3,927.7	81.0	1.0	0.6	4.2	0.7	4.1	8.3
49	67825	Saratoga Springs	23.1	44,164	901	1,911.9	85.0	0.8	0.5	1.2	1.0	3.0	8.5
49	70850	South Jordan	22.2	80,139	442	3,609.9	81.6	1.0	0.4	5.3	1.1	2.9	7.7
49	71070	South Salt Lake	6.9	26,166	1,481	3,792.2	58.8	6.3	2.2	8.5	1.6	11.5	11.0
49	71290	Spanish Fork	16.3	43,870	906	2,691.4	83.2	0.5	0.7	0.6	0.8	5.7	8.5
49	72280	Springville	14.4	36,135	1,097	2,509.4	80.5	0.6	0.9	0.8	0.9	6.9	9.3
49	74810	Syracuse	10.2	33,331	1,185	3,267.7	86.3	1.1	0.4	2.0	0.5	2.8	6.9
49	75360	Taylorsville	10.8	59,242	659	5,485.4	66.5	2.4	1.4	4.6	2.5	11.4	11.2
49	76680	Tooele	24.1	37,104	1,070	1,539.6	81.6	0.7	1.2	0.9	1.0	5.8	8.8
49	81960	Washington	34.8	31,035	1,270	891.8	85.9	0.5	0.9	1.1	0.9	3.8	6.9
49	82950	West Jordan	32.3	116,541	247	3,608.1	71.1	1.3	1.0	3.3	2.1	10.0	11.2
49	83470	West Valley City	35.8	139,110	197	3,885.8	49.5	2.8	1.9	5.7	4.6	22.5	13.1
50	00000	VERMONT	9,217.9	645,570	X	70.0	89.8	1.4	0.4	1.8	0.0	0.8	5.8
50	10675	Burlington	10.3	44,781	887	4,347.7	82.2	4.8	0.2	5.4	0.0	1.1	6.2
51	00000	VIRGINIA	39,482.1	8,642,274	X	218.9	60.3	18.6	0.5	7.1	0.1	5.2	8.2
51	01000	Alexandria	14.9	154,706	169	10,383.0	51.5	20.0	0.6	7.1	0.1	9.9	10.8
51	07784	Blacksburg	19.7	44,949	882	2,281.7	70.9	4.5	0.1	16.3	0.1	1.6	6.5
51	14968	Charlottesville	10.2	45,672	866	4,477.6	65.2	15.3	0.4	8.8	0.0	2.7	7.7
51	16000	Chesapeake	338.5	251,269	89	742.3	56.0	29.0	0.5	3.6	0.2	2.7	8.1
51	21344	Danville	42.8	42,215	947	986.3	40.5	51.4	0.4	1.2	0.0	2.6	3.8
51	29744	Fredericksburg	10.5	28,367	1,371	2,701.6	56.7	21.9	0.6	4.8	0.1	6.3	9.6
51	35000	Hampton	51.5	137,746	199	2,674.7	37.3	49.5	0.5	2.6	0.2	2.3	7.6
51	35624	Harrisonburg	17.3	51,430	775	2,972.8	65.2	8.1	0.6	4.1	0.1	11.6	10.3
51	44984	Leesburg	12.6	48,908	815	3,881.6	58.0	8.4	0.5	8.8	0.1	13.0	11.2
51	47672	Lynchburg	49.0	79,009	458	1,612.4	61.4	27.2	0.3	2.2	0.1	3.0	5.8
51	48952	Manassas	9.8	42,708	935	4,358.0	39.1	12.0	1.3	6.4	0.1	28.0	13.2
51	56000	Newport News	69.0	184,587	139	2,675.2	40.1	42.2	0.5	3.4	0.2	4.8	8.7
51	57000	Norfolk	53.3	235,089	95	4,410.7	43.2	40.2	0.6	3.8	0.2	4.0	8.1
51	61832	Petersburg	22.7	33,429	1,183	1,472.6	16.2	74.2	0.4	1.0	0.1	3.4	4.7
51	64000	Portsmouth	33.3	97,840	339	2,938.1	36.7	53.3	0.4	1.3	0.1	1.8	6.4
51	67000	Richmond	59.9	226,604	98	3,783.0	43.3	40.4	0.4	2.8	0.1	6.8	6.2
51	68000	Roanoke	42.5	98,865	333	2,326.2	57.3	27.5	0.4	2.5	0.1	4.8	7.5
51	70000	Salem	14.5	25,373	1,523	1,749.9	82.5	7.7	0.2	2.1	0.0	2.0	5.4
51	75216	Staunton	19.9	25,661	1,509	1,289.5	78.5	11.4	0.3	1.3	0.0	1.8	6.7
51	76432	Suffolk	399.2	96,194	342	241.0	47.4	42.1	0.4	1.8	0.1	1.7	6.5
51	82000	Virginia Beach	244.7	457,672	42	1,870.3	60.7	18.6	0.4	7.5	0.2	3.0	9.6
51	86720	Winchester	9.2	28,136	1,384	3,058.3	65.2	10.2	0.9	2.5	0.1	12.6	8.5
53	00000	WASHINGTON	66,455.1	7,738,692	X	116.4	66.6	4.0	1.6	9.5	0.8	6.7	10.9
53	03180	Auburn	29.6	85,699	409	2,895.2	51.6	7.8	2.3	13.1	3.2	10.3	11.7
53	05210	Bellevue	33.5	149,440	178	4,460.9	44.7	2.6	0.4	40.6	0.2	3.4	8.1
53	05280	Bellingham	28.1	92,289	369	3,284.3	77.3	1.4	1.2	6.0	0.3	3.7	10.1
53	07380	Bothell	13.6	47,784	834	3,513.5	65.0	1.9	0.6	17.7	0.2	4.0	10.6
53	07695	Bremerton	28.4	44,122	903	1,553.6	66.7	7.0	1.6	6.3	1.5	4.6	12.3
53	08850	Burien	10.0	51,073	781	5,107.3	47.6	7.7	1.6	14.1	1.8	14.8	12.5
53	09480	Camas	14.1	27,054	1,437	1,918.7	76.3	1.0	0.4	9.9	0.2	1.9	10.1
53	17635	Des Moines	6.4	32,689	1,212	5,107.7	49.4	12.2	1.1	12.7	2.6	10.3	11.5
53	20750	Edmonds	8.9	42,758	933	4,804.3	74.9	3.2	0.6	8.0	0.4	2.9	10.1
53	22640	Everett	33.2	110,812	277	3,337.7	61.7	5.4	1.3	9.6	1.3	8.9	11.9
53	23515	Federal Way	22.3	99,037	332	4,441.1	41.0	14.4	1.2	15.5	4.1	11.5	12.4
53	33805	Issaquah	12.1	39,505	1,004	3,264.9	59.8	2.0	0.3	25.9	0.2	2.5	9.3
53	35275	Kennewick	27.9	84,488	418	3,028.2	65.3	1.9	1.1	2.8	0.5	15.3	13.0
53	35415	Kent	33.8	134,835	210	3,989.2	39.7	12.8	1.0	23.6	2.6	9.7	10.7
53	35940	Kirkland	17.8	92,107	371	5,174.6	65.5	2.1	0.5	17.9	0.2	3.6	10.3
53	36745	Lacey	17.3	54,461	732	3,148.0	63.7	5.9	1.2	9.1	2.5	4.5	13.1
53	37900	Lake Stevens	9.2	36,288	1,090	3,944.3	74.3	2.4	0.7	5.8	0.5	4.1	12.3
53	38038	Lakewood	17.1	63,331	607	3,703.6	49.2	13.1	1.3	9.1	3.9	9.0	14.3
53	40245	Longview	14.8	37,824	1,052	2,555.7	79.0	1.2	1.7	2.5	0.6	5.1	9.7
53	40840	Lynnwood	7.9	40,592	973	5,138.2	52.4	7.4	1.1	19.2	0.7	8.1	11.2
53	43150	Maple Valley	6.0	28,153	1,383	4,692.2	72.7	2.7	0.6	8.9	0.3	2.6	12.3
53	43955	Marysville	20.8	71,144	523	3,420.4	68.1	2.6	2.1	7.5	0.8	6.6	12.4
53	45005	Mercer Island	6.4	25,442	1,519	3,975.3	64.6	1.1	0.2	23.0	0.1	1.3	9.6

1. Dry land or land partially or temporarily covered by water. 2. Hispanic or Latino persons may be of any race.

City	Percent Hispanic or Latino[1], 2020	Percent foreign born, 2016–2020	Age of population (percent), 2016–2020: Under 18 years	18 to 24 years	25 to 34 years	35 to 44 years	45 to 54 years	55 to 64 years	65 years and over	Median age, 2016–2020	Percent female, 2016–2020	Population: Census counts 2010	Census counts 2020	Percent change 2010–2020	Percent change 2020–2021
	12	13	14	15	16	17	18	19	20	21	22	23	24	25	26
UTAH —Cont'd															
Riverton	7.9	4.7	34.5	7.4	11.9	16.7	11.1	10.1	8.3	32.6	50.0	38,832	45,402	16.9	-0.6
Roy	17.4	5.2	28.9	9.3	16.8	13.4	9.8	10.9	10.9	31.4	48.5	37,450	39,420	5.3	-0.2
St. George	13.7	7.0	24.7	10.2	11.9	10.5	9.1	9.9	23.8	38.1	51.3	72,759	95,284	31.0	4.9
Salt Lake City	20.8	16.3	19.5	13.5	21.5	14.1	9.8	10.0	11.6	32.5	48.5	186,430	198,746	6.6	0.9
Sandy	10.8	10.3	25.5	8.4	14.6	12.9	12.1	12.2	14.3	36.0	49.1	90,176	97,430	8.0	-2.4
Saratoga Springs	9.6	4.6	45.7	7.2	15.1	16.9	6.8	4.6	3.7	22.0	47.2	17,842	37,783	111.8	16.9
South Jordan	9.0	5.8	32.5	6.5	13.4	15.0	12.1	9.2	11.3	33.1	51.7	50,473	77,661	53.9	3.2
South Salt Lake	24.7	24.9	22.8	12.5	20.2	18.1	10.5	9.2	6.8	31.9	49.9	23,576	26,382	11.9	-0.8
Spanish Fork	13.9	5.1	37.1	10.9	14.1	13.9	9.9	6.2	7.9	26.4	50.0	34,764	42,663	22.7	2.8
Springville	16.2	7.8	37.0	11.2	15.7	12.3	8.1	6.9	8.8	26.0	51.3	29,563	35,335	19.5	2.3
Syracuse	8.6	2.0	38.9	8.6	11.0	16.0	9.9	8.3	7.2	27.6	50.6	24,377	32,110	31.7	3.8
Taylorsville	23.7	18.3	27.0	8.6	16.9	13.4	11.1	10.6	12.5	33.3	50.3	58,691	60,552	3.2	-2.2
Tooele	15.3	3.9	30.4	10.6	13.7	15.3	11.6	8.3	10.0	31.8	51.7	31,603	35,670	12.9	4.0
Washington	9.6	4.0	29.2	7.4	13.8	14.6	9.8	7.7	17.4	34.7	52.2	18,766	28,087	49.7	10.5
West Jordan	22.3	10.8	29.8	9.4	15.4	15.5	12.1	9.7	8.1	32.1	49.1	103,605	117,190	13.1	-0.6
West Valley City	39.4	21.4	31.3	10.1	16.3	13.5	11.1	9.0	8.6	30.2	49.0	129,487	140,571	8.6	-1.0
VERMONT	2.4	4.6	18.5	10.7	11.9	11.3	12.9	15.3	19.4	42.8	50.6	625,727	643,077	2.8	0.4
Burlington	3.7	10.7	12.0	34.7	16.8	8.4	8.1	8.5	11.5	27.1	51.4	42,413	44,890	5.8	-0.2
VIRGINIA	10.5	12.6	22.0	9.5	13.9	13.0	13.2	13.0	15.4	38.4	50.8	8,001,046	8,631,393	7.9	0.1
Alexandria	18.4	26.1	18.4	5.9	21.3	18.4	13.4	11.0	11.6	36.8	51.8	139,998	159,467	13.9	-3.0
Blacksburg	5.8	14.2	10.4	53.7	11.9	7.0	5.4	5.0	6.5	21.8	46.1	42,521	44,268	4.1	1.5
Charlottesville	6.9	11.3	15.5	20.2	19.6	12.5	10.2	10.2	11.8	32.3	52.0	43,425	46,553	7.2	-1.9
Chesapeake	7.1	6.0	24.3	8.5	14.2	13.8	13.0	13.1	13.2	37.0	51.1	222,268	249,422	12.2	0.7
Danville	4.9	3.4	21.9	8.5	12.7	10.4	11.7	14.2	20.7	40.9	54.0	43,071	42,590	-1.1	-0.9
Fredericksburg	12.4	10.2	20.8	18.7	17.6	10.9	10.3	10.7	10.9	30.7	54.1	24,178	27,982	15.7	1.4
Hampton	6.1	4.7	21.1	11.8	15.7	11.3	11.2	13.6	15.3	36.3	51.9	137,463	137,148	-0.2	0.4
Harrisonburg	23.2	16.3	16.4	32.5	14.0	10.5	9.3	8.1	9.1	25.8	51.4	48,902	51,814	6.0	-0.7
Leesburg	22.1	20.9	28.2	7.9	13.8	16.2	15.1	10.7	8.2	35.1	49.5	42,614	48,307	13.4	1.2
Lynchburg	4.9	5.0	19.0	25.0	14.3	8.9	8.8	9.8	14.3	28.5	53.2	75,535	79,009	4.6	0.0
Manassas	42.9	26.5	26.7	8.6	15.1	15.4	12.3	11.6	10.4	34.7	49.6	37,799	42,772	13.2	-0.1
Newport News	10.4	7.5	23.2	11.8	17.0	12.1	11.0	11.8	12.9	33.8	51.6	180,956	186,247	2.9	-0.9
Norfolk	9.7	7.3	19.6	17.6	19.5	11.5	9.8	10.8	11.2	30.8	47.8	242,840	238,005	-2.0	-1.2
Petersburg	5.9	3.3	21.0	9.3	16.3	10.8	12.2	13.6	16.8	37.2	54.4	32,441	33,458	3.1	-0.1
Portsmouth	4.5	3.4	23.3	9.5	16.5	12.0	11.3	12.6	14.7	35.5	51.7	95,531	97,915	2.5	-0.1
Richmond	10.5	7.3	17.4	12.2	21.9	12.1	10.9	12.4	13.1	34.1	52.6	204,440	226,610	10.8	0.0
Roanoke	8.5	6.6	22.2	7.4	15.5	12.7	12.6	13.1	16.5	38.2	52.6	96,910	100,011	3.2	-1.1
Salem	4.3	4.3	18.6	13.0	11.8	10.7	12.8	13.9	19.3	41.2	52.6	24,834	25,346	2.1	0.1
Staunton	4.2	4.2	19.0	9.2	13.2	12.4	11.6	13.4	21.2	41.5	54.2	23,745	25,750	8.4	-0.3
Suffolk	4.5	3.8	24.1	8.0	13.5	12.9	13.7	13.4	14.5	38.1	51.6	84,606	94,324	11.5	2.0
Virginia Beach	8.8	9.7	22.2	9.3	16.5	13.2	12.4	12.3	14.2	36.4	50.9	437,885	459,470	4.9	-0.4
Winchester	19.5	13.8	22.8	10.4	13.5	12.5	12.8	11.4	16.7	37.3	51.1	26,223	28,120	7.2	0.1
WASHINGTON	13.7	14.5	22.0	8.8	15.3	13.4	12.4	12.7	15.4	37.8	50.0	6,724,540	7,705,281	14.6	0.4
Auburn	18.6	21.4	26.3	8.0	15.0	14.5	12.7	12.0	11.4	35.4	50.4	70,299	87,351	24.3	-1.9
Bellevue	7.3	39.3	20.9	6.1	18.8	14.7	13.5	11.8	14.3	37.6	48.9	127,885	152,045	18.9	-1.7
Bellingham	9.3	9.4	13.9	23.8	15.0	11.4	9.2	11.1	15.7	32.9	51.6	81,610	91,231	11.8	1.2
Bothell	9.2	21.4	23.1	7.1	15.2	15.9	13.8	11.8	13.0	37.7	48.8	39,830	48,184	21.0	-0.8
Bremerton	13.0	7.1	17.2	16.1	21.5	12.4	8.9	11.2	12.6	32.4	47.5	37,839	43,886	16.0	0.5
Burien	24.5	25.1	22.3	7.2	14.5	15.4	13.4	12.8	14.4	38.1	48.2	48,079	52,121	8.4	-2.0
Camas	7.2	12.3	27.3	6.4	8.0	14.2	19.2	12.5	12.3	41.9	50.2	19,818	26,095	31.7	3.7
Des Moines	17.7	21.2	21.0	7.2	15.4	15.6	11.3	11.6	17.9	39.0	51.7	29,685	32,891	10.8	-0.6
Edmonds	7.6	14.8	18.5	6.9	12.8	11.7	14.4	14.2	21.4	45.0	52.9	39,686	42,852	8.0	-0.2
Everett	17.2	20.3	20.5	9.6	18.5	12.9	12.1	13.2	13.1	35.9	48.4	102,864	110,723	7.6	0.1
Federal Way	20.1	26.7	23.6	9.7	15.2	12.5	11.9	13.6	13.5	36.2	49.8	89,259	101,131	13.3	-2.1
Issaquah	7.1	27.8	22.1	5.2	18.1	18.6	14.6	9.7	11.7	37.2	52.2	30,436	40,103	31.8	-1.5
Kennewick	30.2	13.3	26.6	8.5	14.8	12.8	10.3	12.1	15.0	35.1	50.2	73,994	83,943	13.4	0.6
Kent	16.4	32.1	24.7	9.2	16.9	13.9	12.3	12.2	10.8	34.6	49.2	118,620	136,750	15.3	-1.4
Kirkland	7.9	24.0	20.2	7.3	17.9	16.1	12.9	12.1	13.5	37.4	50.5	80,585	92,247	14.5	-0.2
Lacey	12.6	12.1	21.1	10.0	16.8	13.3	9.7	10.6	18.5	36.8	52.7	42,559	53,442	25.6	1.9
Lake Stevens	11.0	7.0	28.7	6.7	16.6	16.4	12.0	10.0	9.5	33.9	49.9	28,270	35,601	25.9	1.9
Lakewood	18.1	15.6	20.1	10.5	18.3	11.7	10.5	12.9	15.9	35.6	50.6	57,532	63,666	10.7	-0.5
Longview	11.8	4.6	21.8	9.1	13.0	11.7	11.2	12.0	21.1	39.4	52.1	36,833	37,861	2.8	-0.1
Lynnwood	15.7	30.3	20.2	8.0	14.2	14.2	13.6	13.1	16.6	40.2	51.1	35,853	38,583	7.6	5.2
Maple Valley	8.0	8.4	31.7	5.8	11.8	18.0	13.8	10.8	8.0	35.4	50.6	22,724	28,078	23.6	0.3
Marysville	14.4	10.4	22.9	9.2	14.1	14.2	13.6	13.0	13.1	37.6	50.9	60,022	70,683	17.8	0.7
Mercer Island	4.6	22.3	23.6	5.2	8.2	11.5	16.9	14.1	20.6	45.9	52.5	22,699	25,792	13.6	-1.4

1. May be of any race.

City	Households, 2016–2020							Persons in group quarters, 2016–2020	Serious crimes known to police[2], 2020				Educational attainment, 2016–2020		
			Percent						Violent		Property			Attainment[4] (percent)	
	Number	Persons per household	Family	Married couple family	Female family	Non-family	One person		Number	Rate	Number	Rate	Population age 25 and over	High school graduate or less	Bachelor's degree or more
	27	28	29	30	31	32	33	34	35	36	37	38	39	40	41
UTAH —Cont'd															
Riverton	12,597	3.47	86.8	73.7	9.0	13.2	11.7	78	31	68.7	580	1,286.2	25,435	25.3	38.0
Roy	12,767	3.06	76.0	58.1	9.6	24.0	19.4	141	52	130.5	505	1,267.3	24,250	43.2	18.6
St. George	31,447	2.74	72.2	58.6	10.1	27.8	22.6	921	148	161.4	1,025	1,118.1	56,809	27.5	29.4
Salt Lake City	81,688	2.37	49.1	37.5	7.6	50.9	37.3	6,606	1,865	922.4	14,865	7,352.1	134,078	26.6	48.7
Sandy	31,446	3.04	77.2	64.6	8.2	22.8	17.6	432	175	180.2	2,979	3,068.3	63,484	23.2	43.0
Saratoga Springs	7,521	4.16	90.7	84.3	4.6	9.3	6.6	20	39	109.5	272	763.6	14,733	14.3	45.8
South Jordan	22,184	3.32	79.5	70.6	6.7	20.5	16.8	7	105	131.1	1,441	1,799.2	44,952	19.3	42.9
South Salt Lake	9,210	2.59	57.7	36.9	13.5	42.3	33.1	1,309	249	964.5	2,376	9,203.6	16,256	44.3	27.1
Spanish Fork	10,500	3.73	87.2	76.8	7.0	12.8	11.4	908	31	74.5	469	1,127.3	20,856	28.3	34.8
Springville	9,287	3.57	80.7	68.7	8.8	19.3	15.9	124	26	77.1	440	1,304.6	17,237	25.8	36.7
Syracuse	7,946	3.81	89.8	73.1	10.2	10.2	8.2	88	24	74.2	232	717.3	15,944	23.5	35.6
Taylorsville	19,821	3.02	72.8	53.0	13.8	27.2	21.2	140	NA	NA	NA	NA	38,585	41.5	22.7
Tooele	11,277	3.11	77.5	58.5	12.1	22.5	18.5	246	107	292.9	815	2,231.2	20,811	45.3	15.8
Washington	9,300	3.03	79.1	71.1	5.1	20.9	16.7	28	32	104.5	434	1,417.3	17,876	25.8	33.0
West Jordan	34,549	3.32	79.9	64.6	10.0	20.1	15.0	557	291	246.7	2,979	2,525.5	69,990	35.9	26.4
West Valley City	37,078	3.65	79.9	56.4	15.2	20.1	14.0	337	718	528.4	4,525	3,330.0	79,431	51.4	15.4
VERMONT	262,852	2.28	59.8	47.2	8.6	40.2	30.7	25,476	1,081	173.4	7,586	1,217.0	442,089	34.8	39.7
Burlington	16,189	2.19	37.9	27.3	7.9	62.1	35.7	7,226	151	352.3	1,032	2,407.7	22,712	25.7	54.0
VIRGINIA	3,184,121	2.60	66.0	50.2	11.5	34.0	27.5	244,432	17,925	208.7	125,114	1,456.4	5,831,949	33.5	39.5
Alexandria	71,289	2.20	47.5	36.5	7.8	52.5	42.3	1,469	295	182.6	2,793	1,729.1	119,957	17.3	65.1
Blacksburg	12,935	2.72	36.9	31.1	4.6	63.1	29.9	9,155	29	65.3	310	697.9	15,952	13.9	70.2
Charlottesville	18,814	2.36	47.6	32.5	11.0	52.4	33.7	2,764	189	396.5	916	1,921.5	30,341	25.6	55.7
Chesapeake	86,524	2.75	74.3	56.2	13.9	25.7	21.5	5,114	1,020	412.8	4,413	1,785.8	163,257	30.5	34.6
Danville	18,266	2.14	54.7	30.5	20.1	45.3	39.0	1,584	109	274.5	1,129	2,843.5	28,313	50.0	18.4
Fredericksburg	11,059	2.40	51.1	37.8	8.8	48.9	37.9	2,541	117	395.4	809	2,733.8	17,572	31.2	42.4
Hampton	54,847	2.38	59.2	36.8	16.6	40.8	33.7	4,601	357	266.3	3,338	2,489.5	90,627	37.8	26.7
Harrisonburg	16,751	2.76	55.9	37.0	12.4	44.1	28.7	7,284	117	218.9	811	1,517.5	27,384	42.6	35.2
Leesburg	18,093	2.96	73.0	60.4	7.9	27.0	18.5	254	122	221.5	535	971.5	34,358	25.2	54.3
Lynchburg	28,223	2.50	59.3	39.7	16.1	40.7	29.5	10,362	367	442.9	1,350	1,629.0	45,393	35.7	36.0
Manassas	13,066	3.13	74.4	53.6	14.3	25.6	20.9	86	128	309.3	662	1,599.6	26,581	41.1	31.3
Newport News	70,376	2.43	60.5	37.6	17.8	39.5	32.9	8,862	1,119	625.5	3,648	2,039.2	116,686	36.6	28.0
Norfolk	89,398	2.43	57.1	35.0	17.7	42.9	33.3	26,935	1,543	636.2	6,591	2,717.8	153,359	36.7	30.0
Petersburg	13,231	2.28	47.2	20.1	21.0	52.8	46.6	638	197	631.5	807	2,587.0	21,459	51.6	20.3
Portsmouth	36,650	2.49	59.8	34.8	20.2	40.2	32.7	3,877	867	920.3	4,277	4,540.1	63,775	41.3	20.8
Richmond	91,005	2.40	44.2	25.3	14.5	55.8	43.1	10,528	814	348.8	6,816	2,920.9	161,426	34.4	41.2
Roanoke	41,694	2.33	52.5	31.4	15.9	47.5	38.6	1,797	448	451.0	3,809	3,834.5	69,800	47.6	24.8
Salem	9,876	2.30	62.7	45.0	12.5	37.3	29.6	2,599	13	51.3	480	1,895.3	17,300	36.8	30.3
Staunton	10,638	2.19	58.2	39.8	15.2	41.8	36.6	1,351	45	179.7	549	2,191.8	17,697	39.7	31.1
Suffolk	34,603	2.63	71.6	53.4	14.3	28.4	24.3	438	366	394.1	1,715	1,846.4	62,050	35.7	29.6
Virginia Beach	172,452	2.56	68.8	51.1	12.9	31.2	24.0	9,520	445	98.7	6,816	1,511.8	309,067	26.7	37.3
Winchester	10,669	2.52	57.4	37.3	14.5	42.6	35.6	1,054	72	254.6	586	2,072.2	18,643	38.6	34.3
WASHINGTON	2,905,822	2.53	64.5	50.1	9.7	35.5	26.7	146,985	22,596	293.7	210,223	2,732.4	5,199,771	30.1	36.7
Auburn	29,220	2.75	67.6	49.0	12.7	32.4	24.7	578	362	437.3	3,394	4,100.1	53,140	39.1	26.8
Bellevue	58,293	2.48	65.9	56.9	6.1	34.1	26.3	1,384	175	116.2	4,526	3,006.4	106,647	13.2	69.1
Bellingham	38,680	2.23	45.2	34.8	8.2	54.8	34.4	4,516	240	256.3	4,306	4,599.0	56,569	22.7	45.4
Bothell	17,746	2.57	68.0	59.3	5.5	32.0	23.9	720	39	80.7	1,187	2,456.4	32,350	20.3	53.2
Bremerton	16,750	2.23	50.9	35.4	10.8	49.1	35.4	3,843	143	342.0	1,342	3,209.2	27,486	29.7	25.6
Burien	19,235	2.66	61.4	41.3	12.3	38.6	29.6	399	231	445.3	2,183	4,207.9	36,371	40.5	27.9
Camas	8,263	2.90	80.4	71.6	6.6	19.6	16.1	60	8	32.0	283	1,133.0	15,920	20.8	51.4
Des Moines	12,284	2.56	64.7	45.1	12.2	35.3	28.4	581	109	333.8	1,152	3,528.1	22,966	37.9	28.9
Edmonds	17,845	2.35	64.6	53.7	7.5	35.4	28.3	352	90	209.6	1,201	2,797.3	31,568	19.5	48.9
Everett	43,293	2.46	57.2	38.2	11.9	42.8	32.3	4,312	379	337.1	3,654	3,249.8	77,425	39.7	23.7
Federal Way	34,956	2.74	66.5	47.1	12.9	33.5	26.2	870	344	354.4	2,542	2,618.7	64,562	36.8	29.4
Issaquah	16,129	2.38	63.7	51.6	8.6	36.3	26.1	265	22	54.1	1,159	2,850.5	28,158	12.8	66.7
Kennewick	30,232	2.69	67.9	49.4	13.0	32.1	26.2	1,273	215	251.4	2,836	3,316.0	53,623	38.2	26.6
Kent	44,487	2.87	69.8	48.3	14.9	30.2	22.9	2,231	470	351.1	5,393	4,028.1	85,967	39.5	27.1
Kirkland	37,142	2.42	62.9	52.2	7.2	37.1	26.9	1,340	109	115.4	2,010	2,127.7	66,119	14.5	62.3
Lacey	20,214	2.47	64.0	49.0	11.2	36.0	28.4	948	83	154.2	1,386	2,575.0	35,002	28.7	32.2
Lake Stevens	11,536	2.90	76.8	58.8	12.3	23.2	17.1	42	56	161.8	328	948.0	21,621	33.0	27.8
Lakewood	24,821	2.39	59.8	40.6	14.5	40.2	32.1	1,255	381	620.2	2,620	4,264.9	42,021	39.7	22.2
Longview	15,912	2.32	56.6	36.0	14.3	43.4	36.9	965	99	256.3	1,196	3,096.1	26,204	42.5	15.1
Lynnwood	14,559	2.59	61.2	43.8	12.7	38.8	27.3	814	92	232.8	1,637	4,142.5	27,677	32.1	29.2
Maple Valley	8,855	3.02	82.9	67.9	11.4	17.1	13.4	0	15	54.1	358	1,290.7	16,696	23.1	43.3
Marysville	25,428	2.72	71.1	54.9	12.3	28.9	22.0	440	96	134.2	1,006	1,406.6	47,321	38.4	20.2
Mercer Island	10,128	2.54	70.4	62.5	5.5	29.6	22.6	145	4	15.2	400	1,522.8	18,397	8.2	76.2

2. Data for serious crimes have not been adjusted for underreporting. This may affect comparability between geographic areas and over time. 4. Persons 25 years old and over.

City	Money income, 2016–2020					Median earnings Full year, Full-time workers, 2016–2020			Housing units, 2016–2020				
	Households												
	Median household income	Percent with income less than $25,000	Percent with income of $200,000 or more	Median family income	Median non-family household income	All persons	Men	Women	Total	Occupied	Percent owner occupied	Median value[1] (dollars)	Median gross rent (dollars)
	42	43	44	45	46	47	48	49	50	51	52	53	54
UTAH —Cont'd													
Riverton	101,810	4.9	9.6	106,021	44,781	63,278	74,626	42,280	12,889	12,597	87.1	375,900	1,447
Roy	72,739	8.6	2.3	77,451	46,813	45,712	53,879	35,756	13,185	12,767	84.1	222,900	1,094
St. George	59,989	16.4	5.2	69,883	32,912	42,077	47,112	34,984	37,720	31,447	65.2	302,300	1,088
Salt Lake City	63,156	19.7	8.5	84,561	43,801	48,237	50,645	45,264	88,155	81,688	48.3	346,100	1,050
Sandy	95,715	8.5	12.6	107,681	54,092	60,247	69,536	49,624	32,966	31,446	78.5	375,800	1,399
Saratoga Springs	101,592	4.4	7.6	103,109	55,614	68,958	78,433	43,125	7,791	7,521	83.4	365,400	1,603
South Jordan	106,824	6.5	14.7	119,787	54,882	67,230	80,381	51,130	22,960	22,184	83.2	430,300	1,504
South Salt Lake	49,616	19.5	3.7	54,568	43,271	40,124	41,965	36,932	10,006	9,210	40.6	248,400	968
Spanish Fork	79,846	7.5	5.4	83,798	37,648	48,125	54,975	35,549	10,761	10,500	75.3	300,600	1,144
Springville	72,356	12.0	3.9	80,696	39,450	48,686	54,012	36,133	9,695	9,287	70.4	290,900	1,151
Syracuse	103,522	3.7	11.2	106,832	50,278	62,176	79,340	41,629	8,175	7,946	91.5	340,900	1,766
Taylorsville	67,249	11.8	3.9	76,300	45,274	42,865	47,333	38,205	20,679	19,821	69.9	263,800	1,119
Tooele	65,740	10.7	1.8	69,995	33,333	44,587	52,421	36,213	11,793	11,277	79.3	212,400	1,042
Washington	75,389	13.9	7.1	87,505	29,011	49,002	64,514	40,108	11,011	9,300	70.5	330,700	1,168
West Jordan	84,722	6.1	4.4	90,312	51,354	48,908	55,512	40,705	35,516	34,549	76.8	316,600	1,269
West Valley City	70,427	10.8	3.4	74,696	42,521	40,255	44,352	35,056	38,476	37,078	69.6	242,500	1,170
VERMONT	63,477	18.1	6.0	83,023	37,947	49,689	52,538	45,734	337,214	262,852	71.3	230,900	999
Burlington	55,461	27.1	6.7	89,765	38,190	51,427	55,968	43,295	16,853	16,189	37.6	312,200	1,279
VIRGINIA	76,398	15.0	11.6	93,284	46,317	54,896	61,977	49,098	3,537,788	3,184,121	66.7	282,800	1,257
Alexandria	102,227	9.2	19.8	137,135	84,547	78,134	82,039	74,468	76,361	71,289	43.4	572,700	1,774
Blacksburg	41,711	38.8	8.2	103,519	22,336	57,236	64,932	50,683	15,521	12,935	33.7	309,800	1,141
Charlottesville	59,598	23.8	9.0	90,051	43,579	51,179	56,758	47,286	20,736	18,814	40.1	329,100	1,188
Chesapeake	81,261	11.4	8.5	94,474	47,908	53,507	63,990	45,935	91,707	86,524	72.3	286,000	1,300
Danville	37,147	35.5	1.7	47,603	24,634	36,830	41,963	32,148	22,017	18,266	50.3	95,500	688
Fredericksburg	69,528	18.2	7.9	94,833	50,168	52,211	62,714	42,424	11,887	11,059	39.8	376,700	1,287
Hampton	57,041	19.8	3.4	70,165	40,306	45,333	52,652	39,914	60,145	54,847	56.9	188,600	1,115
Harrisonburg	49,117	25.8	3.3	65,160	30,732	41,441	45,089	36,234	18,317	16,751	40.5	220,100	911
Leesburg	113,933	6.8	20.9	129,989	71,268	71,662	84,874	59,063	18,610	18,093	69.2	459,100	1,649
Lynchburg	49,201	22.2	2.6	62,038	33,283	37,145	41,567	32,747	32,533	28,223	49.8	162,900	859
Manassas	86,227	10.4	10.6	96,157	54,096	52,215	55,625	48,438	13,823	13,066	69.3	338,100	1,549
Newport News	54,511	21.1	3.0	67,050	37,427	43,823	50,216	38,149	77,851	70,376	48.3	194,700	1,075
Norfolk	53,026	22.8	4.1	64,390	39,122	41,940	46,243	37,773	98,142	89,398	43.5	215,800	1,077
Petersburg	43,029	30.7	1.2	51,659	34,533	36,898	41,628	34,463	16,346	13,231	36.1	111,800	958
Portsmouth	53,213	23.4	2.6	61,738	38,076	42,306	47,867	37,440	40,879	36,650	55.3	174,200	1,083
Richmond	51,421	25.8	6.7	68,988	38,512	45,178	47,458	42,964	100,930	91,005	43.7	244,200	1,070
Roanoke	45,664	29.1	4.0	55,345	30,519	38,911	40,864	37,614	46,991	41,694	52.3	134,900	804
Salem	63,411	17.0	5.7	78,898	40,148	50,437	52,976	44,823	10,846	9,876	64.4	200,000	926
Staunton	52,292	22.3	3.5	71,661	32,120	43,440	50,656	39,075	11,847	10,638	59.0	171,600	864
Suffolk	79,899	15.3	7.8	94,393	42,857	52,708	61,098	43,327	37,394	34,603	70.3	265,600	1,231
Virginia Beach	78,136	10.5	8.3	91,553	50,798	51,101	56,565	45,910	185,735	172,452	64.7	287,400	1,380
Winchester	61,102	16.6	7.3	73,708	37,753	45,536	48,186	42,740	11,980	10,669	44.7	247,800	1,096
WASHINGTON	77,006	14.0	10.5	92,422	48,399	59,178	65,578	51,132	3,150,194	2,905,822	63.3	366,800	1,337
Auburn	76,410	13.2	8.4	89,245	46,587	54,676	60,535	50,076	30,828	29,220	59.6	356,200	1,314
Bellevue	129,497	8.3	29.1	157,851	88,031	103,265	119,684	85,033	62,486	58,293	53.3	887,700	2,104
Bellingham	56,198	23.7	4.5	84,769	37,087	44,887	49,122	41,502	40,656	38,680	46.4	405,700	1,133
Bothell	107,651	7.9	16.5	127,008	67,062	74,985	91,376	58,874	18,732	17,746	64.9	587,900	1,797
Bremerton	57,963	21.4	3.6	66,199	40,782	51,361	57,821	41,535	18,203	16,750	45.9	270,100	1,135
Burien	71,233	14.7	9.1	83,214	45,222	52,038	55,525	48,065	20,301	19,235	55.0	419,500	1,365
Camas	115,993	7.0	19.8	130,402	43,598	76,281	90,417	62,478	8,626	8,263	78.0	458,000	1,214
Des Moines	70,268	8.4	5.8	80,649	50,445	53,443	58,571	47,256	12,950	12,284	58.6	379,300	1,390
Edmonds	91,499	6.4	17.1	118,208	54,485	74,137	85,139	61,917	18,847	17,845	71.6	587,200	1,508
Everett	66,023	17.0	4.5	77,941	48,405	50,105	53,357	43,475	45,853	43,293	47.5	359,900	1,316
Federal Way	68,672	14.9	6.9	80,692	46,530	50,974	55,214	45,981	36,726	34,956	54.3	359,000	1,411
Issaquah	122,053	8.6	24.6	147,703	84,893	95,603	115,139	84,494	16,797	16,129	59.9	677,500	2,095
Kennewick	62,283	17.2	5.6	75,419	35,513	51,325	58,452	43,173	32,123	30,232	65.0	239,200	955
Kent	73,891	13.2	7.1	80,876	54,509	51,875	55,339	48,228	46,779	44,487	55.2	378,800	1,495
Kirkland	116,595	9.2	23.3	143,767	73,989	88,125	103,371	74,559	39,594	37,142	62.2	724,700	1,894
Lacey	69,752	13.7	3.2	87,590	50,468	49,156	55,813	42,911	20,933	20,214	56.8	286,200	1,421
Lake Stevens	93,087	7.4	6.4	100,201	61,368	60,457	68,542	51,984	11,822	11,536	75.8	384,400	1,663
Lakewood	55,723	19.6	3.6	67,113	39,817	42,871	47,142	40,239	26,830	24,821	43.2	309,600	1,095
Longview	48,028	25.6	2.4	64,573	28,247	45,281	52,275	40,675	16,783	15,912	52.2	212,300	883
Lynnwood	62,926	20.8	7.4	81,518	36,605	51,700	54,723	49,084	15,309	14,559	53.0	443,100	1,350
Maple Valley	117,706	8.1	15.0	123,438	58,150	80,448	93,514	61,513	9,068	8,855	85.0	451,900	1,984
Marysville	83,239	10.1	6.2	93,754	51,123	54,609	62,212	45,321	26,144	25,428	70.2	353,100	1,445
Mercer Island	150,506	7.9	41.4	213,675	60,233	123,228	143,681	103,179	10,886	10,128	66.9	1,386,300	2,166

1. Specified owner-occupied units

City	Commuting, 2016–2020[1]		Computer access[2], 2016–2020		Migration, 2016–2020		Civilian labor force, 2021				Civilian Employment, 2016–2020[4]			
	Percent		Percent						Unemployment[3]		Population age 16 and older		Population age 16 to 64	
	Drove alone	Mean travel time to work	With a computer in the house	With Internet access	Percent who lived in the same house one year ago	Percent who lived in another state or county one year ago	Total	Percent change 2020–2021	Total	Rate	Number	Percent in labor force	Number	Percent who worked full-year full-time
	55	56	57	58	59	60	61	62	63	64	65	66	67	68
UTAH —Cont'd														
Riverton	74.3	27.4	97.4	93.5	88.8	4.6	24,891	2.5	547	2.2	30,134	72.0	26,503	55.5
Roy	78.8	22.2	97.0	92.4	87.0	7.6	19,812	1.4	586	3.0	28,890	71.4	24,602	58.6
St. George	77.0	15.3	92.4	85.6	81.9	9.0	41,990	4.2	1,225	2.9	68,027	55.9	47,285	46.3
Salt Lake City	66.0	19.8	94.7	86.4	79.3	8.9	120,252	1.1	3,295	2.7	164,689	72.3	141,412	53.9
Sandy	73.7	23.2	96.9	90.8	85.9	5.2	54,351	1.8	1,436	2.6	74,284	69.2	60,575	54.9
Saratoga Springs	75.2	31.4	99.6	96.8	83.0	9.0	15,559	4.8	392	2.5	18,156	69.6	16,997	49.6
South Jordan	73.8	24.6	98.2	91.4	84.4	6.4	40,966	2.2	1,014	2.5	52,565	70.1	44,255	53.3
South Salt Lake	74.5	21.0	93.8	79.6	78.5	5.8	13,451	-0.1	520	3.9	20,057	71.1	18,350	50.7
Spanish Fork	77.8	21.3	97.5	93.7	84.3	5.6	19,418	4.8	465	2.4	26,776	69.0	23,601	50.5
Springville	75.3	21.3	96.8	90.8	81.4	7.5	17,362	4.9	441	2.5	22,059	66.8	19,136	47.4
Syracuse	76.9	29.4	99.7	96.2	90.0	5.7	16,022	2.3	349	2.2	20,170	74.1	17,986	52.1
Taylorsville	74.4	21.9	95.0	89.5	84.4	4.4	34,304	1.6	972	2.8	45,131	71.4	37,650	57.9
Tooele	72.6	29.7	94.5	90.5	86.4	6.8	18,364	2.0	591	3.2	25,598	68.8	22,062	53.4
Washington	80.3	14.5	96.1	88.4	89.6	4.4	15,161	5.1	400	2.6	20,875	58.1	15,959	46.6
West Jordan	76.7	25.1	98.3	95.6	86.5	3.6	65,553	2.1	1,731	2.6	84,930	75.9	75,616	57.2
West Valley City	76.7	22.5	95.8	90.0	85.1	4.7	71,502	1.5	2,279	3.2	98,457	72.1	86,735	55.6
VERMONT	74.4	23.3	91.3	82.9	86.7	6.4	328,216	-3.8	11,275	3.4	523,065	65.3	402,193	51.8
Burlington	50.2	18.8	93.7	84.7	64.3	16.7	23,398	-3.8	758	3.2	38,270	64.3	33,347	37.3
VIRGINIA	74.9	28.6	92.3	85.7	85.2	8.8	4,267,656	-2.3	166,853	3.9	6,849,454	64.0	5,535,109	55.0
Alexandria	56.6	32.0	96.4	92.2	80.1	13.8	97,365	-2.0	3,673	3.8	131,691	76.0	113,267	67.3
Blacksburg	58.8	13.8	97.1	93.8	65.6	18.1	19,871	1.2	618	3.1	40,434	48.4	37,544	20.0
Charlottesville	58.9	17.3	93.8	84.8	71.6	17.5	24,609	-2.6	903	3.7	40,513	63.5	34,959	46.1
Chesapeake	82.2	26.3	96.0	92.0	85.2	9.8	119,733	-2.7	4,608	3.8	190,497	62.2	158,402	54.9
Danville	79.0	18.6	83.4	71.3	86.5	5.6	18,394	-4.4	1,204	6.5	32,638	53.3	24,230	42.6
Fredericksburg	69.9	30.4	94.3	87.4	73.4	19.5	13,853	-2.3	646	4.7	23,554	69.2	20,384	50.8
Hampton	80.8	22.7	92.8	84.2	83.1	9.9	62,844	-3.3	3,566	5.7	109,189	60.2	88,530	52.3
Harrisonburg	70.8	16.5	91.8	79.2	70.7	20.6	23,996	-1.6	969	4.0	45,748	59.6	40,856	35.7
Leesburg	72.7	31.3	96.0	92.8	87.0	6.1	28,683	-2.0	804	2.8	40,371	76.5	35,961	59.0
Lynchburg	73.6	17.7	91.7	85.0	78.5	13.5	34,699	-3.2	1,760	5.1	67,343	59.1	55,787	40.4
Manassas	73.8	35.8	94.3	92.1	82.1	12.0	20,983	-2.4	821	3.9	31,490	73.0	27,238	57.0
Newport News	76.8	23.5	92.4	78.8	83.6	10.3	86,364	-3.6	4,837	5.6	141,773	61.2	118,537	57.2
Norfolk	71.8	21.4	92.1	83.9	75.5	14.7	107,879	-3.5	6,185	5.7	200,825	56.4	173,476	55.5
Petersburg	74.5	24.4	83.8	72.3	76.9	15.8	12,529	-4.1	1,319	10.5	24,904	60.0	19,737	47.3
Portsmouth	77.6	23.2	90.9	83.2	84.1	9.3	43,482	-3.3	2,908	6.7	75,059	58.4	61,062	54.0
Richmond	70.2	21.8	89.9	77.7	77.7	12.2	116,270	-3.5	6,378	5.5	192,898	66.2	162,758	49.4
Roanoke	79.0	22.2	86.8	77.1	83.1	8.5	47,664	-3.4	2,309	4.8	78,847	64.5	62,494	55.4
Salem	80.7	18.8	91.5	80.9	85.9	10.7	12,390	-2.8	440	3.6	21,168	61.3	16,289	52.6
Staunton	82.4	22.4	87.9	77.3	81.4	12.7	11,849	-3.3	452	3.8	20,378	61.1	15,154	54.3
Suffolk	85.7	29.4	92.7	84.1	85.5	9.5	44,227	-2.5	1,944	4.4	71,731	64.8	58,522	56.6
Virginia Beach	80.3	23.6	95.7	91.1	83.0	8.8	224,179	-2.9	8,300	3.7	362,268	64.4	298,277	57.9
Winchester	68.3	23.8	88.2	78.4	85.8	10.1	14,437	-1.7	505	3.5	22,314	66.0	17,645	51.0
WASHINGTON	69.7	28.0	94.8	89.9	83.0	7.2	3,913,513	-0.4	204,775	5.2	6,038,812	63.7	4,878,208	51.3
Auburn	74.9	32.7	94.4	90.3	82.2	6.6	41,613	-0.8	2,367	5.7	61,585	68.9	52,350	52.9
Bellevue	57.6	24.3	97.8	95.2	79.7	7.9	80,779	1.0	2,873	3.6	118,944	66.5	98,099	55.7
Bellingham	68.1	19.0	94.9	88.9	72.4	10.8	48,178	-3.0	2,697	5.6	79,264	64.5	65,031	42.4
Bothell	63.7	31.6	96.0	93.4	82.0	10.2	26,270	0.2	1,074	4.1	36,751	70.3	30,733	55.0
Bremerton	57.7	26.7	93.4	88.5	74.2	12.5	18,325	-0.3	1,162	6.3	34,646	51.6	29,445	54.5
Burien	66.7	28.4	93.2	89.6	85.1	4.3	27,016	-1.6	1,498	5.5	41,497	67.8	34,085	50.2
Camas	73.7	27.1	97.0	94.8	88.2	6.3	12,529	1.0	583	4.7	18,653	66.8	15,692	52.3
Des Moines	75.7	30.2	95.6	92.2	84.2	5.3	16,982	-1.3	1,002	5.9	25,867	64.1	20,136	52.0
Edmonds	68.8	31.6	97.0	93.8	87.4	7.2	22,875	0.1	951	4.2	35,557	64.0	26,502	54.7
Everett	70.3	28.3	93.6	86.8	82.5	6.1	57,347	-1.0	3,431	6.0	90,560	64.8	75,987	52.5
Federal Way	70.5	35.5	96.0	89.5	80.5	7.3	49,598	-1.2	2,901	5.8	76,950	66.4	63,846	50.6
Issaquah	56.6	30.5	98.2	95.3	79.2	7.6	21,840	1.1	773	3.5	30,856	73.5	26,332	60.5
Kennewick	80.6	21.4	93.7	86.1	85.5	6.3	42,943	-1.1	2,398	5.6	62,747	60.5	50,355	47.5
Kent	69.6	31.9	95.8	92.8	83.2	5.3	66,447	-1.1	4,027	6.1	101,324	68.8	87,225	51.3
Kirkland	67.1	27.4	97.6	94.2	82.8	7.2	55,699	0.8	2,008	3.6	74,723	70.9	62,393	56.6
Lacey	78.5	26.2	93.8	90.1	80.3	8.9	23,745	-1.3	1,355	5.7	41,203	56.8	31,822	52.9
Lake Stevens	78.9	35.2	97.4	92.7	84.8	5.1	18,110	-0.5	959	5.3	24,746	72.1	21,567	58.7
Lakewood	73.1	29.3	93.7	88.6	81.5	7.4	26,935	-0.9	1,827	6.8	49,622	58.2	40,019	50.4
Longview	82.0	22.8	90.4	82.7	80.6	7.5	15,971	-1.0	1,076	6.7	30,531	54.6	22,529	41.9
Lynnwood	66.7	31.4	92.6	86.8	85.0	6.6	20,560	-1.2	1,117	5.4	31,507	63.1	25,103	47.4
Maple Valley	76.3	41.1	97.2	95.0	84.9	4.0	14,378	0.5	614	4.3	19,047	72.9	16,909	56.0
Marysville	78.7	32.2	96.0	91.8	86.1	4.5	36,310	-1.3	2,079	5.7	55,789	66.4	46,675	54.6
Mercer Island	60.8	25.9	94.7	92.6	84.4	6.6	12,289	1.1	432	3.5	20,583	62.6	15,266	52.3

1. Employed persons. 2. Households. 3. Percent of civilian labor force. 4. Persons 16 years old and over.

City	Value of residential construction authorized by building permits, 2021			Wholesale trade[1], 2017				Retail trade[2], 2017			
	New construction ($1,000)	Number of housing units	Percent single family	Number of establishments	Number of employees	Sales (mil dol)	Annual payroll (mil dol)	Number of establish-ments	Number of employees	Sales (mil dol)	Annual payroll (mil dol)
	69	70	71	72	73	74	75	76	77	78	79
UTAH —Cont'd											
Riverton	73,832	283	56.2	16	43	23.1	2.0	64	1,283	331.3	31.4
Roy	13,500	57	87.7	D	D	D	D	71	1,056	252.9	23.8
St. George	244,421	1,500	98.0	108	743	353.9	33.3	436	6,553	2,022.1	188.7
Salt Lake City	510,972	3,691	4.7	601	13,791	14,430.6	960.6	919	15,363	5,192.0	483.3
Sandy	22,216	77	66.2	120	1,177	826.6	62.2	405	7,001	2,504.1	215.2
Saratoga Springs	388,807	1,763	87.0	5	5	2.1	0.1	39	293	117.5	9.6
South Jordan	358,614	1,793	62.1	41	122	55.7	4.5	174	4,012	1,658.9	145.7
South Salt Lake	69,344	250	4.0	226	4,226	3,808.4	248.3	223	3,239	1,331.3	142.1
Spanish Fork	105,070	481	95.0	23	210	176.8	9.1	112	1,783	546.3	46.2
Springville	70,060	263	69.2	23	320	134.2	16.7	96	1,213	371.2	35.5
Syracuse	147,187	866	51.8	7	49	44.9	1.4	21	587	183.1	18.2
Taylorsville	2,845	10	100.0	21	99	53.8	3.3	79	1,388	346.8	34.0
Tooele	106,683	448	100.0	9	60	31.0	3.7	70	1,365	399.5	34.5
Washington	240,265	934	94.9	18	80	24.0	3.4	70	1,174	328.4	30.4
West Jordan	219,939	946	48.9	73	1,496	1,705.6	97.0	210	4,371	1,053.4	106.2
West Valley City	72,941	267	65.9	145	2,504	2,304.7	155.0	291	5,682	2,153.9	173.6
VERMONT	499,725	2,319	58.7	671	9,395	6,032.4	502.6	3,219	38,390	10,811.3	1,102.5
Burlington	20,573	133	6.0	43	477	378.7	35.9	213	2,856	591.7	77.1
VIRGINIA	7,750,202	39,388	63.8	5,937	86,698	98,904.6	5,734.1	27,134	429,072	120,162.1	11,476.0
Alexandria	41,568	200	6.0	72	872	651.9	60.4	475	7,862	2,548.9	258.9
Blacksburg	22,157	97	75.3	9	310	340.2	13.5	96	1,468	270.3	23.7
Charlottesville	39,434	191	42.4	44	451	330.2	24.3	281	3,282	714.9	77.4
Chesapeake	303,610	1,383	68.1	241	3,552	2,790.8	205.7	785	14,925	4,182.0	387.9
Danville	21,249	244	6.6	45	560	255.9	29.6	302	4,558	1,144.0	104.0
Fredericksburg	39,453	142	100.0	24	254	123.6	10.8	261	4,326	1,015.0	109.9
Hampton	15,095	242	100.0	60	921	425.1	47.0	423	6,748	1,569.0	168.8
Harrisonburg	6,672	36	25.0	58	864	438.7	43.9	325	5,341	1,378.8	136.1
Leesburg	24,139	109	100.0	17	277	157.8	17.7	279	5,980	1,765.5	153.1
Lynchburg	28,160	143	72.0	74	898	479.1	43.2	355	6,890	2,162.9	165.3
Manassas	22,829	97	100.0	47	458	227.6	23.4	176	2,153	961.8	77.1
Newport News	16,903	106	100.0	112	1,887	1,539.2	129.7	648	10,091	2,596.7	242.7
Norfolk	174,524	1,473	20.6	187	2,714	2,296.8	146.3	830	11,729	2,696.3	293.1
Petersburg	11,694	116	23.3	D	D	D	15.2	141	2,454	940.7	67.1
Portsmouth	23,737	196	100.0	43	659	226.8	33.6	261	3,060	627.3	69.4
Richmond	149,313	1,067	47.0	253	3,815	3,581.9	212.4	790	9,088	2,260.4	241.1
Roanoke	55,083	393	14.5	155	2,211	1,381.3	116.4	533	8,966	2,603.5	215.5
Salem	0	0	0.0	68	1,552	1,120.6	100.8	151	1,995	524.5	49.7
Staunton	9,128	63	68.3	21	227	80.2	8.7	133	1,834	449.7	46.3
Suffolk	228,588	1,363	60.7	36	1,117	1,443.4	78.9	238	3,997	1,160.6	99.6
Virginia Beach	137,486	463	72.4	351	4,770	5,596.5	359.4	1,506	24,023	6,155.3	607.2
Winchester	32,136	209	9.6	36	459	463.9	22.2	284	4,317	1,017.2	109.6
WASHINGTON	12,501,328	56,941	44.0	7,755	120,320	112,352.6	7,649.3	21,751	347,728	160,284.8	11,412.9
Auburn	31,904	79	100.0	180	4,529	6,417.0	304.1	291	5,174	1,746.6	165.0
Bellevue	534,666	2,367	8.4	281	4,021	7,101.4	446.1	653	14,690	5,123.3	555.7
Bellingham	151,406	1,115	20.1	146	1,497	751.8	74.0	515	8,719	2,489.3	250.8
Bothell	102,127	268	79.9	54	1,754	2,375.4	287.8	110	1,725	468.9	52.7
Bremerton	115,020	532	58.3	22	190	95.5	10.1	151	2,050	832.1	81.8
Burien	27,388	163	26.4	23	128	44.8	5.6	151	2,055	735.9	72.3
Camas	99,094	286	100.0	20	324	820.4	35.9	52	417	104.8	10.3
Des Moines	13,007	33	36.4	12	237	188.9	16.7	40	303	94.6	10.7
Edmonds	21,978	79	41.8	43	176	153.5	11.7	132	1,902	638.0	68.2
Everett	102,460	630	4.9	132	2,680	2,085.2	142.5	439	7,422	2,380.1	245.4
Federal Way	11,411	29	100.0	57	433	441.7	24.3	260	4,913	1,384.7	142.5
Issaquah	33,136	155	49.7	50	532	462.8	38.3	160	3,736	4,809.3	142.9
Kennewick	89,231	280	99.3	78	749	654.3	38.8	378	6,713	1,909.6	181.6
Kent	131,040	424	80.9	407	10,147	11,483.4	655.4	343	7,603	3,673.0	252.7
Kirkland	151,769	596	54.9	130	1,405	970.9	92.5	250	4,905	2,020.3	194.3
Lacey	111,672	917	11.7	30	538	625.9	30.7	158	3,697	1,029.0	106.4
Lake Stevens	78,609	215	99.1	13	48	23.1	1.8	46	893	247.4	24.9
Lakewood	27,444	83	73.5	68	1,157	1,296.6	66.2	242	3,016	798.6	82.3
Longview	7,260	68	14.7	42	568	342.7	30.8	174	3,223	992.0	95.2
Lynnwood	190,463	1,299	1.1	84	822	411.9	57.9	411	8,806	2,784.3	279.5
Maple Valley	63,138	164	97.6	10	59	22.5	4.3	49	923	272.4	27.6
Marysville	113,272	616	48.4	38	355	185.8	19.5	179	3,699	1,182.8	118.1
Mercer Island	26,724	31	100.0	30	115	187.9	9.2	36	488	133.4	16.2

1. Merchant wholesalers except manufacturers' sales branches and offices. 2. Establishments with payroll.

City	Real estate and rental and leasing, 2017: Number of establish-ments	Real estate and rental and leasing, 2017: Number of employees	Real estate and rental and leasing, 2017: Receipts (mil dol)	Real estate and rental and leasing, 2017: Annual payroll (mil dol)	Professional, scientific, and technical services[1], 2017: Number of establish-ments	Professional, scientific, and technical services[1], 2017: Number of employees	Professional, scientific, and technical services[1], 2017: Receipts (mil dol)	Professional, scientific, and technical services[1], 2017: Annual payroll (mil dol)	Manufacturing, 2017: Number of establish-ments	Manufacturing, 2017: Number of employees	Manufacturing, 2017: Receipts (mil dol)	Manufacturing, 2017: Annual payroll (mil dol)
	80	81	82	83	84	85	86	87	88	89	90	91
UTAH —Cont'd												
Riverton	D	D	D	D	111	241	25.2	7.6	NA	NA	NA	NA
Roy	24	45	9.5	1.1	29	176	19.6	8.2	NA	NA	NA	NA
St. George	262	607	147.7	19.4	447	2,103	280.1	83.3	NA	NA	NA	NA
Salt Lake City	608	3,524	1,376.8	200.3	1,616	20,088	3,814.2	1,472.0	NA	NA	NA	NA
Sandy	276	1,350	389.1	69.7	D	D	D	D	NA	NA	NA	NA
Saratoga Springs	24	25	5.5	0.9	61	114	18.4	6.5	NA	NA	NA	NA
South Jordan	173	454	92.4	16.4	323	1,951	321.4	136.4	NA	NA	NA	NA
South Salt Lake	70	421	122.3	27.1	134	1,694	348.3	98.1	NA	NA	NA	NA
Spanish Fork	48	81	19.9	2.8	108	358	68.5	16.9	NA	NA	NA	NA
Springville	30	D	15.5	D	82	342	52.4	19.9	NA	NA	NA	NA
Syracuse	33	32	4.4	0.9	63	118	23.0	8.0	NA	NA	NA	NA
Taylorsville	D	D	D	D	115	7,775	1,432.5	436.6	NA	NA	NA	NA
Tooele	30	74	14.5	2.1	43	190	18.4	6.3	NA	NA	NA	NA
Washington	65	142	19.9	4.4	62	133	19.6	5.9	NA	NA	NA	NA
West Jordan	93	211	44.7	7.5	160	601	82.3	26.4	NA	NA	NA	NA
West Valley City	94	462	242.4	22.5	149	2,326	299.1	120.0	NA	NA	NA	NA
VERMONT	784	2,938	651.8	119.3	2,096	12,563	2,079.2	841.5	1,033	28,629	8,652.4	1,610.0
Burlington	66	334	81.3	15.9	308	3,009	525.5	226.6	NA	NA	NA	NA
VIRGINIA	10,051	55,778	17,207.8	2,949.2	31,431	470,265	101,433.2	41,552.8	5,038	232,695	99,343.9	12,987.4
Alexandria	282	1,580	555.7	84.0	1,211	19,170	4,414.4	1,910.1	NA	NA	NA	NA
Blacksburg	42	346	69.9	13.1	146	1,499	247.8	116.1	NA	NA	NA	NA
Charlottesville	84	555	110.8	26.2	334	2,763	446.3	191.7	NA	NA	NA	NA
Chesapeake	307	1,421	382.9	66.8	519	9,596	1,369.0	565.6	NA	NA	NA	NA
Danville	53	237	31.6	6.9	64	393	43.3	18.4	NA	NA	NA	NA
Fredericksburg	75	314	76.9	14.8	181	1,401	175.6	80.7	NA	NA	NA	NA
Hampton	123	784	154.5	26.7	290	4,585	828.6	363.1	NA	NA	NA	NA
Harrisonburg	71	373	99.1	14.0	140	1,091	127.4	52.9	NA	NA	NA	NA
Leesburg	60	252	88.8	12.4	371	3,208	550.6	268.3	NA	NA	NA	NA
Lynchburg	119	458	87.4	16.6	192	2,919	622.3	217.2	NA	NA	NA	NA
Manassas	45	226	61.4	10.7	216	1,693	295.6	122.7	NA	NA	NA	NA
Newport News	280	1,419	348.7	59.2	363	5,003	815.3	312.7	NA	NA	NA	NA
Norfolk	317	3,133	608.6	145.4	707	10,576	2,009.4	727.5	NA	NA	NA	NA
Petersburg	37	163	30.9	4.9	36	239	27.6	10.1	NA	NA	NA	NA
Portsmouth	77	388	80.4	14.0	144	1,450	160.3	69.9	NA	NA	NA	NA
Richmond	329	2,197	939.5	106.3	910	11,464	2,524.0	1,058.2	NA	NA	NA	NA
Roanoke	174	938	193.3	36.6	308	2,688	421.0	171.2	NA	NA	NA	NA
Salem	43	199	60.0	9.8	78	450	68.3	20.3	NA	NA	NA	NA
Staunton	38	142	17.0	5.1	64	298	40.6	15.4	NA	NA	NA	NA
Suffolk	74	279	53.5	12.5	145	923	132.8	53.8	NA	NA	NA	NA
Virginia Beach	761	5,451	1,198.7	261.4	1,494	21,755	4,109.6	1,619.2	NA	NA	NA	NA
Winchester	66	306	97.6	11.5	142	995	103.4	48.5	NA	NA	NA	NA
WASHINGTON	11,826	53,706	15,626.7	2,756.8	22,144	214,628	42,429.3	17,333.1	7,017	263,132	140,381.5	17,943.8
Auburn	95	380	98.1	16.2	151	707	110.2	38.5	NA	NA	NA	NA
Bellevue	613	3,693	1,354.6	270.2	1,361	22,379	4,638.1	2,102.0	NA	NA	NA	NA
Bellingham	234	993	348.9	43.4	446	2,086	333.0	119.1	NA	NA	NA	NA
Bothell	99	249	109.4	14.8	273	4,074	840.9	327.9	NA	NA	NA	NA
Bremerton	67	242	38.3	7.5	75	798	127.0	52.1	NA	NA	NA	NA
Burien	75	232	73.0	9.2	95	484	41.4	16.8	NA	NA	NA	NA
Camas	26	107	27.3	4.9	79	939	194.6	77.7	NA	NA	NA	NA
Des Moines	30	71	17.8	2.8	31	123	15.3	4.9	NA	NA	NA	NA
Edmonds	D	D	D	D	213	1,061	158.8	66.9	NA	NA	NA	NA
Everett	173	1,115	226.6	43.3	323	3,467	493.7	236.9	NA	NA	NA	NA
Federal Way	130	597	209.1	26.4	188	1,621	194.8	90.1	NA	NA	NA	NA
Issaquah	96	392	160.8	27.2	207	1,232	182.6	115.5	NA	NA	NA	NA
Kennewick	173	729	177.3	26.8	190	1,342	211.7	76.1	NA	NA	NA	NA
Kent	196	985	373.4	52.5	246	2,534	461.7	133.9	NA	NA	NA	NA
Kirkland	272	1,159	882.1	76.9	594	6,422	1,503.9	658.8	NA	NA	NA	NA
Lacey	62	241	55.4	8.3	82	1,729	217.3	103.7	NA	NA	NA	NA
Lake Stevens	38	167	47.0	7.5	29	85	12.1	4.5	NA	NA	NA	NA
Lakewood	117	686	156.4	27.2	106	710	94.3	35.7	NA	NA	NA	NA
Longview	70	263	53.4	8.6	71	448	47.1	20.0	NA	NA	NA	NA
Lynnwood	103	398	164.2	17.9	191	2,320	463.3	169.5	NA	NA	NA	NA
Maple Valley	22	32	10.3	2.1	47	174	23.0	10.0	NA	NA	NA	NA
Marysville	72	240	63.5	9.8	67	281	27.5	9.6	NA	NA	NA	NA
Mercer Island	D	D	D	D	150	510	90.4	34.4	NA	NA	NA	NA

1. Establishments subject to federal tax.

Table D. Cities — **Accommodation and Food Services, Arts, Entertainment, and Recreation, and Health Care and Social Assistance**

City	Accommodation and food services, 2017				Arts, entertainment, and recreation[1], 2017				Health care and social assistance[1], 2017			
	Number of establish-ments	Number of employees	Receipts (mil dol)	Annual payroll (mil dol)	Number of establish-ments	Number of employees	Receipts (mil dol)	Annual payroll (mil dol)	Number of establish-ments	Number of employees	Receipts (mil dol)	Annual payroll (mil dol)
	92	93	94	95	96	97	98	99	100	101	102	103
UTAH —Cont'd												
Riverton	53	1,111	54.8	16.5	11.0	167	6.1	1.5	100	1,672	205.8	69.9
Roy	41	674	38.2	9.5	4.0	D	1.1	D	56	595	60.6	26.7
St. George	241	5,083	283.4	77.3	50.0	594	34.7	9.2	479	7,927	1,101.3	347.0
Salt Lake City	835	19,340	1,387.6	378.6	143.0	3,336	288.9	75.9	741	25,849	3,998.9	1,621.3
Sandy	213	3,892	228.2	64.7	47.0	1,217	107.1	30.0	315	3,567	383.7	156.4
Saratoga Springs	16	310	14.9	3.8	9.0	42	4.0	1.1	30	297	36.0	10.6
South Jordan	111	2,570	133.8	38.8	24.0	434	26.0	7.6	174	2,436	248.4	113.2
South Salt Lake	93	1,079	60.5	16.7	14.0	160	16.9	2.7	65	1,542	231.8	53.8
Spanish Fork	54	1,179	53.9	13.6	4.0	71	2.6	0.8	D	D	D	D
Springville	41	837	39.0	12.2	D	D	D	D	83	773	66.7	23.0
Syracuse	19	269	11.5	2.8	D	D	D	D	D	D	D	D
Taylorsville	D	D	D	D	11.0	165	8.2	2.1	110	1,444	115.8	46.1
Tooele	51	905	45.9	12.2	9.0	72	3.8	1.3	D	D	D	D
Washington	D	D	D	D	D	D	D	D	36	159	14.1	5.2
West Jordan	133	2,622	146.9	39.8	13.0	171	8.4	2.1	209	4,575	516.3	142.2
West Valley City	226	4,126	249.0	66.8	D	D	D	D	140	4,106	550.3	187.1
VERMONT	1,979	32,891	2,019.8	620.5	457.0	7,739	517.0	150.9	2,102	48,285	5,451.6	2,229.4
Burlington	172	3,588	234.0	72.4	37.0	794	50.2	18.0	176	8,863	1,485.8	456.2
VIRGINIA	18,199	358,010	22,074.7	6,226.9	3,071.0	61,703	4,446.8	1,283.0	20,522	454,501	58,792.5	22,721.6
Alexandria	402	8,518	691.8	193.3	75.0	1,283	252.7	43.6	426	7,386	1,056.3	379.4
Blacksburg	112	2,249	114.7	31.3	22.0	202	6.1	2.1	D	D	D	D
Charlottesville	292	5,491	329.6	98.3	53.0	750	111.0	36.4	158	9,293	1,742.6	877.9
Chesapeake	486	10,068	530.7	148.8	54.0	1,280	59.2	18.7	514	10,002	1,239.6	503.6
Danville	143	2,925	148.8	41.4	15.0	189	8.1	2.7	180	5,096	489.0	210.3
Fredericksburg	186	4,460	227.5	72.2	19.0	447	22.7	6.1	225	5,189	883.6	329.9
Hampton	256	5,902	304.4	89.2	D	D	D	D	281	7,833	1,299.2	454.5
Harrisonburg	208	5,138	259.0	81.3	24.0	234	12.2	4.8	185	3,080	281.4	124.0
Leesburg	142	2,924	239.9	60.5	25.0	364	15.8	5.1	182	3,129	308.2	128.9
Lynchburg	270	6,023	292.1	83.4	35.0	567	23.9	8.2	289	10,123	1,393.7	516.1
Manassas	126	1,947	117.3	32.6	17.0	184	9.8	2.9	177	3,231	376.1	158.6
Newport News	411	7,516	390.0	111.5	52.0	1,025	40.7	16.4	452	15,710	1,843.3	782.2
Norfolk	612	11,326	659.3	181.7	75.0	1,558	110.0	35.7	582	20,755	3,181.5	1,090.6
Petersburg	94	930	50.5	13.8	10.0	72	2.3	0.8	126	4,361	479.6	190.8
Portsmouth	163	2,414	119.9	34.2	D	D	D	D	227	7,627	1,142.0	385.7
Richmond	677	14,306	793.6	258.9	114.0	2,455	178.9	53.9	607	27,376	4,123.1	1,644.4
Roanoke	302	7,205	371.9	112.9	49.0	545	39.8	11.0	316	13,827	2,050.3	743.0
Salem	97	1,885	95.9	28.0	13.0	195	9.8	3.5	143	5,424	990.3	365.2
Staunton	84	1,333	66.2	21.8	12.0	241	8.6	3.6	95	2,486	190.0	89.8
Suffolk	150	3,029	163.2	45.4	16.0	348	12.7	4.7	240	4,979	593.0	226.0
Virginia Beach	1,292	25,108	1,494.1	419.4	202.0	3,598	249.3	66.8	1,162	21,729	2,767.4	1,052.8
Winchester	144	3,320	160.2	48.4	18.0	258	15.5	5.2	269	7,080	1,125.3	407.1
WASHINGTON	17,828	289,371	21,068.6	6,395.3	3,097.0	65,091	6,483.5	2,078.4	21,264	438,835	56,442.2	22,849.3
Auburn	159	2,514	146.0	46.1	D	D	D	D	215	3,917	474.7	214.2
Bellevue	512	10,576	918.7	271.9	89.0	2,418	192.1	66.8	1,053	15,245	2,298.3	841.8
Bellingham	359	6,023	348.4	118.1	76.0	1,058	40.9	14.5	519	9,046	1,208.4	415.7
Bothell	143	2,270	141.4	43.5	17.0	414	20.4	8.1	174	2,487	231.7	106.4
Bremerton	114	2,053	129.7	36.5	15.0	370	13.2	4.3	138	4,816	749.9	250.3
Burien	D	D	D	D	18.0	278	18.4	6.9	194	2,908	473.0	168.6
Camas	39	456	23.7	7.5	D	D	D	D	53	370	29.9	12.5
Des Moines	55	831	57.1	17.6	6.0	59	3.3	2.1	80	1,389	115.1	48.0
Edmonds	133	2,032	143.5	44.2	18.0	251	12.4	4.3	219	4,195	495.9	207.9
Everett	377	5,036	329.7	99.8	39.0	645	41.9	13.0	444	14,553	1,787.7	737.2
Federal Way	242	3,796	264.1	76.7	37.0	693	46.4	14.7	367	6,243	733.6	289.4
Issaquah	130	2,324	159.8	48.1	25.0	828	39.1	18.3	234	4,383	484.2	179.9
Kennewick	214	3,894	241.9	71.8	28.0	584	32.4	11.4	302	5,911	594.6	266.2
Kent	290	3,799	257.5	72.6	28.0	411	41.2	12.3	336	4,085	368.7	156.9
Kirkland	240	4,007	334.0	99.3	59.0	1,002	57.1	22.7	427	9,426	1,262.3	607.4
Lacey	139	2,366	140.7	42.9	D	D	D	D	148	2,832	224.3	100.0
Lake Stevens	40	724	43.8	13.4	D	D	D	D	44	407	39.7	17.7
Lakewood	180	2,568	166.9	50.0	24.0	875	35.6	19.8	218	5,847	607.3	304.9
Longview	110	1,694	90.6	27.5	D	D	D	D	159	4,602	526.2	216.5
Lynnwood	220	3,626	271.9	76.8	15.0	204	13.6	3.5	242	2,899	281.2	120.5
Maple Valley	53	861	47.9	15.0	14.0	201	6.9	2.4	55	493	43.4	18.0
Marysville	123	1,795	115.1	33.9	14.0	201	12.8	3.1	134	1,625	187.2	82.1
Mercer Island	36	581	36.6	11.0	20.0	390	16.4	7.4	93	959	102.3	36.3

1. Establishments subject to federal tax.

City	Other services[1]				Government employment and payroll, 2017								
						March payroll							
							Perent of total for:						
	Number of establish- ments	Number of employees	Receipts (mil dol)	Annual payroll (mil dol)	Full-time equivalent employees	Total (dollars)	Admin- istrative, judicial, and legal	Police and corrections	Fire protection	Highways and trans- portation	Health and welfare	Natural resources and utilities	Education and libraries
	104	105	106	107	108	109	110	111	112	113	114	115	116
UTAH —Cont'd													
Riverton	D	D	D	D	89	466,875	26.0	0.0	0.0	12.9	0.2	32.1	0.0
Roy	D	D	D	D	183	833,799	15.4	26.1	33.7	3.8	0.0	15.6	0.0
St. George	182	1,092	107.5	28.2	798	3,348,441	12.7	23.8	5.5	7.5	0.0	44.5	0.0
Salt Lake City	699	5,916	775.2	219.3	3,055	15,732,443	15.4	21.7	14.3	21.9	0.4	15.4	4.3
Sandy	169	1,079	108.0	32.0	514	2,541,559	23.0	27.1	17.0	9.4	0.9	18.6	0.0
Saratoga Springs	D	D	D	D	136	573,104	28.9	33.3	15.4	8.0	0.0	1.7	1.5
South Jordan	81	505	41.0	13.5	373	1,630,405	22.5	19.1	20.9	3.2	2.5	16.6	0.0
South Salt Lake	143	924	116.0	32.7	271	1,139,494	14.4	29.1	26.9	5.6	4.6	14.9	0.0
Spanish Fork	D	D	D	D	344	1,474,006	26.9	14.8	2.0	4.1	4.4	17.7	2.3
Springville	D	D	D	D	247	1,106,787	13.2	23.7	5.3	8.2	0.4	40.9	4.2
Syracuse	15	71	6.7	1.9	99	413,284	25.3	29.7	17.4	5.2	0.0	19.0	0.0
Taylorsville	41	272	27.1	8.6	42	171,501	76.3	0.0	0.0	0.0	1.2	0.0	0.0
Tooele	D	D	D	D	155	572,952	22.0	34.1	1.4	5.1	0.0	19.0	5.5
Washington	31	127	12.4	3.9	220	768,746	17.9	16.6	6.8	3.5	0.0	38.7	0.0
West Jordan	125	815	124.4	38.9	513	2,455,676	17.7	31.8	22.0	4.8	3.1	9.9	0.0
West Valley City	130	741	91.5	24.4	728	3,395,984	16.7	37.1	17.6	7.5	6.7	10.1	0.0
VERMONT	1,603	7,339	922.1	244.0	X	X	X	X	X	X	X	X	X
Burlington	128	814	116.6	27.6	740	4,083,314	21.2	18.4	11.7	14.6	2.6	25.3	2.7
VIRGINIA	15,700	118,537	20,344.4	5,188.4	X	X	X	X	X	X	X	X	X
Alexandria	611	9,983	3,295.4	767.9	5,558	29,910,334	9.3	14.2	7.3	1.9	12.9	8.3	42.1
Blacksburg	54	382	248.2	14.0	356	1,357,428	31.4	22.5	0.6	26.7	4.0	11.9	0.0
Charlottesville	158	1,729	580.2	105.1	2,026	8,850,434	10.6	8.3	5.6	9.5	7.6	8.1	45.4
Chesapeake	438	3,057	349.2	110.8	9,189	35,172,070	5.6	11.9	5.5	2.0	5.6	4.8	61.2
Danville	89	424	59.0	11.3	2,182	7,837,955	10.7	13.4	6.7	4.0	5.6	10.5	44.5
Fredericksburg	113	762	68.7	23.4	1,157	4,653,781	12.7	8.2	5.1	5.8	4.6	6.6	50.3
Hampton	169	953	111.9	28.0	5,164	20,964,935	7.4	11.7	7.5	0.9	6.1	7.1	56.6
Harrisonburg	131	715	84.9	25.7	1,563	6,085,265	3.9	7.3	6.4	5.5	0.3	14.2	55.8
Leesburg	114	658	81.0	25.9	384	2,292,277	20.8	25.7	0.0	7.3	0.7	34.2	1.2
Lynchburg	171	1,013	107.3	31.5	2,987	9,939,533	10.6	8.8	5.9	5.0	6.0	6.7	55.9
Manassas	137	902	142.6	35.8	1,566	8,259,510	5.8	8.8	4.1	2.6	2.7	7.8	66.3
Newport News	283	1,731	186.4	49.2	7,911	33,653,408	6.2	12.5	6.1	1.7	5.3	11.1	56.0
Norfolk	396	3,023	459.0	106.2	10,850	48,264,655	7.3	13.9	4.9	3.9	8.8	7.0	51.3
Petersburg	75	576	67.5	15.8	1,237	4,738,339	12.0	11.3	11.6	3.7	5.3	1.4	54.7
Portsmouth	143	1,143	140.7	42.2	3,846	15,956,245	6.4	12.4	6.7	1.7	8.2	4.8	58.0
Richmond	520	4,950	609.4	174.3	8,650	35,398,423	8.7	16.8	6.2	1.8	8.0	10.1	44.9
Roanoke	252	1,629	154.5	48.3	3,798	15,653,992	8.7	13.0	8.1	2.0	7.5	2.4	56.3
Salem	88	474	41.1	12.5	1,107	4,279,865	10.4	10.3	7.5	3.9	1.3	10.9	51.7
Staunton	86	456	43.9	14.0	775	3,017,755	14.3	11.1	3.5	4.6	0.0	7.3	55.8
Suffolk	137	715	65.1	19.2	3,372	14,209,808	10.1	8.4	10.9	3.5	3.3	7.4	55.5
Virginia Beach	943	5,762	918.6	174.6	17,638	70,561,307	6.4	10.4	4.2	1.5	6.9	8.9	59.0
Winchester	92	536	45.5	14.0	1,576	6,043,273	8.0	23.5	5.5	2.1	3.5	6.9	47.2
WASHINGTON	13,444	78,480	14,513.7	3,004.6	X	X	X	X	X	X	X	X	X
Auburn	162	1,180	157.4	51.2	454	3,059,866	23.3	34.7	0.0	16.4	4.4	18.2	0.0
Bellevue	443	3,020	336.1	109.2	1,360	10,639,183	16.4	17.5	21.4	10.1	2.5	22.5	0.0
Bellingham	276	1,771	220.6	66.2	825	5,436,962	14.6	24.5	27.3	6.7	0.5	13.6	3.3
Bothell	82	500	40.4	16.5	323	2,501,428	16.0	29.3	26.4	6.8	4.2	7.3	0.0
Bremerton	90	440	48.8	14.2	314	2,214,919	17.1	24.0	23.9	10.9	3.1	16.8	0.0
Burien	107	598	63.2	17.3	77	479,562	40.5	0.0	0.0	16.2	0.0	33.6	0.0
Camas	30	96	8.4	2.6	167	1,195,112	14.0	17.7	30.2	4.9	9.0	16.8	5.9
Des Moines	35	150	18.5	5.4	134	897,466	25.3	38.4	0.0	12.9	0.0	17.4	0.0
Edmonds	115	531	52.0	17.7	176	1,267,743	14.9	41.2	0.0	12.6	1.5	28.6	0.0
Everett	253	1,966	240.7	78.1	1,191	8,542,797	9.5	21.4	21.8	14.5	2.7	22.5	3.1
Federal Way	154	694	62.9	22.8	365	2,495,462	19.6	53.5	0.0	6.7	0.0	16.4	0.0
Issaquah	106	828	118.8	30.8	247	1,614,855	48.4	23.8	0.0	5.7	0.0	22.0	0.0
Kennewick	169	963	90.1	29.3	400	2,756,636	19.0	32.2	24.4	6.7	1.8	16.0	0.0
Kent	242	1,449	158.0	50.0	702	4,511,920	26.0	35.1	0.0	12.2	1.1	21.8	0.0
Kirkland	237	1,286	156.2	59.8	605	4,373,154	28.2	22.1	23.3	2.8	0.0	11.2	0.0
Lacey	100	685	91.0	24.7	276	1,821,023	16.6	31.1	0.0	5.4	3.4	25.6	0.0
Lake Stevens	D	D	13.0	D	75	564,484	26.3	52.4	0.0	19.6	0.0	1.7	0.0
Lakewood	131	801	92.0	30.7	222	1,614,522	14.8	62.1	0.0	9.7	5.5	4.9	0.0
Longview	82	547	60.1	19.1	329	2,272,290	14.1	25.8	21.5	13.6	0.0	19.2	5.7
Lynnwood	153	1,066	113.9	36.7	397	3,100,998	18.4	30.5	20.5	2.5	0.0	16.4	0.0
Maple Valley	50	213	19.1	6.5	54	298,951	50.9	1.8	0.0	12.0	0.0	31.3	0.0
Marysville	113	505	53.3	16.2	275	1,964,954	26.6	35.3	0.0	7.9	0.0	22.7	0.0
Mercer Island	48	170	21.2	5.8	204	1,736,301	11.9	17.9	24.3	2.7	3.5	11.9	0.0

1. Establishments subject to federal tax.

City	City government finances, 2017									
	General revenue							General expenditure		
		Intergovernmental		Taxes						
					Per capita[1] (dollars)				Per capita[1] (dollars)	
	Total (mil dol)	Total (mil dol)	Percent from state government	Total (mil dol)	Total	Property	Sales and gross receipts	Total (mil dol)	Total	Capital outlays
	117	118	119	120	121	122	123	124	125	126
UTAH —Cont'd										
Riverton	21.2	1.6	82.1	9.1	209	7	202	16.7	385	54
Roy	25.8	1.6	91.2	13.0	332	102	231	20.9	532	68
St. George	108.1	6.0	58.0	51.0	604	143	461	86.4	1,022	251
Salt Lake City	639.8	16.5	11.4	264.4	1,316	846	470	776.5	3,865	1,588
Sandy	90.3	5.1	81.7	50.5	524	160	364	107.7	1,117	581
Saratoga Springs	26.7	1.3	84.8	10.8	365	97	268	17.5	593	115
South Jordan	61.4	3.1	89.1	45.5	642	327	315	37.1	523	418
South Salt Lake	34.2	4.3	13.2	24.0	963	234	728	33.3	1,334	118
Spanish Fork	34.7	1.5	76.0	11.0	279	64	215	26.5	672	164
Springville	33.2	1.8	93.0	19.0	573	208	365	40.8	1,229	322
Syracuse	24.6	2.6	64.9	9.1	310	73	208	15.5	528	64
Taylorsville	23.4	0.6	100.0	18.6	309	133	177	20.9	348	20
Tooele	24.8	1.6	84.9	15.1	437	152	285	18.8	543	21
Washington	27.2	1.2	94.5	12.0	453	167	286	28.8	1,090	65
West Jordan	83.0	4.8	87.4	46.8	411	155	256	74.3	652	138
West Valley City	125.9	13.4	40.4	78.2	574	284	290	125.1	918	18
VERMONT	X	X	X	X	X	X	X	X	X	X
Burlington	136.5	22.6	44.8	45.1	1,065	732	332	120.2	2,835	661
VIRGINIA	X	X	X	X	X	X	X	X	X	X
Alexandria	931.2	216.1	74.5	611.7	3,842	2,970	872	953.5	5,989	792
Blacksburg	46.5	15.2	48.5	19.9	449	153	297	37.4	841	161
Charlottesville	284.7	117.4	65.7	115.9	2,442	1,469	928	279.0	5,879	627
Chesapeake	1,034.6	456.8	82.5	465.8	1,939	1,356	564	974.9	4,060	455
Danville	227.3	124.1	77.6	56.2	1,369	721	616	228.3	5,562	202
Fredericksburg	219.2	87.6	50.6	81.0	2,842	1,463	1,362	170.1	5,970	511
Hampton	602.6	274.9	77.6	244.4	1,814	1,233	581	585.8	4,348	378
Harrisonburg	203.2	81.0	85.6	79.3	1,479	722	735	220.5	4,111	1,090
Leesburg	74.1	22.4	90.3	32.4	599	274	325	69.9	1,292	277
Lynchburg	379.8	190.6	73.1	136.8	1,699	1,007	675	330.5	4,104	978
Manassas	219.2	85.2	84.8	99.7	2,423	1,844	553	209.5	5,092	470
Newport News	904.3	403.4	73.8	368.0	2,051	1,455	581	911.6	5,080	625
Norfolk	1,219.1	544.7	73.0	443.6	1,814	1,104	690	1,240.6	5,073	704
Petersburg	147.0	79.1	86.4	55.2	1,772	1,308	450	145.4	4,669	116
Portsmouth	418.6	204.0	83.7	166.4	1,755	1,255	500	491.0	5,177	314
Richmond	1,288.8	545.0	79.3	525.3	2,312	1,451	819	1,217.7	5,359	668
Roanoke	488.0	259.4	83.9	184.9	1,868	1,142	726	450.1	4,547	298
Salem	118.2	39.8	89.6	60.4	2,380	1,562	792	124.0	4,888	743
Staunton	98.1	45.6	88.9	36.9	1,518	1,018	492	89.9	3,697	152
Suffolk	393.1	171.0	88.9	168.9	1,874	1,377	481	396.4	4,399	928
Virginia Beach	1,932.4	740.4	80.9	948.1	2,107	1,432	651	1,859.0	4,132	485
Winchester	221.6	109.2	45.2	75.6	2,683	1,545	1,138	157.8	5,600	561
WASHINGTON	X	X	X	X	X	X	X	X	X	X
Auburn	145.3	13.7	74.7	61.1	751	222	477	122.3	1,504	244
Bellevue	414.6	47.4	27.0	221.7	1,526	284	1,086	402.8	2,773	690
Bellingham	169.4	13.8	60.9	98.1	1,101	250	809	139.2	1,564	165
Bothell	89.7	10.8	90.1	44.2	968	277	623	77.7	1,701	385
Bremerton	71.9	4.6	83.1	36.5	898	238	628	60.0	1,476	129
Burien	41.5	4.0	68.6	27.3	525	144	342	30.5	586	58
Camas	49.7	5.0	97.1	20.7	889	563	246	43.1	1,849	395
Des Moines	42.2	9.1	94.7	19.4	618	152	421	35.8	1,140	332
Edmonds	67.4	8.8	78.0	36.3	859	347	437	60.4	1,432	180
Everett	228.6	15.2	75.1	139.7	1,268	382	829	198.5	1,802	219
Federal Way	90.4	22.8	74.2	48.3	497	108	334	92.2	948	295
Issaquah	78.4	8.7	80.9	43.2	1,146	253	805	68.3	1,812	354
Kennewick	88.9	8.2	87.6	53.9	661	154	473	86.9	1,065	208
Kent	197.9	23.2	69.2	101.7	772	171	553	169.4	1,286	257
Kirkland	166.4	8.7	65.8	99.7	1,120	321	683	151.3	1,700	270
Lacey	78.1	6.5	61.3	34.0	685	141	492	56.2	1,132	96
Lake Stevens	19.8	2.2	99.9	14.3	435	131	235	18.3	558	151
Lakewood	61.1	15.6	70.9	35.6	591	123	432	56.9	943	281
Longview	69.2	9.6	49.4	29.3	780	248	520	61.8	1,644	158
Lynnwood	84.4	6.9	71.5	49.1	1,283	310	916	77.0	2,012	209
Maple Valley	19.5	2.7	96.9	13.0	500	141	297	18.2	703	136
Marysville	82.6	4.4	83.4	45.0	653	232	385	75.7	1,099	177
Mercer Island	49.2	1.4	78.5	30.2	1,176	483	549	46.6	1,814	151

1. Based on population estimated as of July 1 of the year shown.

City	City government finances, 2017 (cont.)												
	General expenditure (cont.)												
	Percent of total for:									Debt outstanding			
	Public welfare	Highways	Parking facilities	Education	Health and hospitals	Police protection	Sewerage and sanitation	Parks and recreation	Housing and community development	Interest on debt	Total (mil dol)	Per capita[1] (dollars)	Debt issued during year
	127	128	129	130	131	132	133	134	135	136	137	138	139
UTAH —Cont'd													
Riverton	0.9	11.5	0.0	0.0	1.4	0.0	7.5	18.1	2.8	1.7	427.2	9,851	0.0
Roy	0.0	13.8	0.0	0.0	0.0	23.2	7.7	14.3	1.7	0.0	1.8	45	0.0
St. George	0.2	4.1	0.0	0.0	0.0	15.3	15.8	19.1	3.7	0.6	109.0	1,289	0.0
Salt Lake City	0.0	2.3	0.0	0.1	0.7	12.6	2.5	5.0	2.9	1.7	1,677.2	8,347	1,236.3
Sandy	0.0	2.0	0.0	0.0	0.5	12.4	3.5	12.6	1.2	0.2	0.0	0	0.0
Saratoga Springs	0.0	5.5	0.0	0.0	0.0	0.0	16.9	12.8	0.0	0.0	15.1	511	15.1
South Jordan	0.0	0.0	0.0	0.0	0.0	0.0	0.0	0.0	0.0	1.2	23.7	335	23.7
South Salt Lake	0.0	6.5	0.0	3.8	4.0	22.3	5.5	2.7	8.8	3.3	13.5	541	0.1
Spanish Fork	0.8	9.0	0.0	0.0	3.2	14.6	13.9	21.4	4.9	0.2	0.0	0	0.0
Springville	0.0	3.6	0.0	17.0	0.0	12.8	11.2	8.0	3.4	0.1	35.8	1,078	1.2
Syracuse	0.0	11.8	0.0	0.0	0.0	16.8	13.7	12.6	0.0	3.1	10.4	353	0.0
Taylorsville	0.5	0.0	0.0	0.0	0.0	42.5	0.0	0.3	4.8	0.0	0.5	9	0.0
Tooele	0.0	7.0	0.0	0.0	1.3	23.5	13.6	14.0	5.0	4.6	11.4	328	11.4
Washington	0.0	11.0	0.0	0.0	0.0	20.2	13.8	26.5	4.9	3.6	18.3	693	8.7
West Jordan	0.0	10.1	0.0	0.0	0.0	24.2	7.6	6.9	0.4	0.3	55.3	486	49.9
West Valley City	4.7	12.6	0.0	0.0	2.7	19.3	3.8	8.3	17.1	1.2	76.2	559	119.1
VERMONT	X	X	X	X	X	X	X	X	X	X	X	X	X
Burlington	0.0	9.6	4.6	0.0	0.1	12.9	5.9	9.7	3.9	3.9	185.1	4,365	37.2
VIRGINIA	X	X	X	X	X	X	X	X	X	X	X	X	X
Alexandria	5.1	6.3	0.0	29.3	5.1	9.9	8.8	4.0	3.4	0.4	802.7	5,042	130.9
Blacksburg	0.0	21.0	0.0	0.0	1.6	21.3	17.3	6.5	6.3	0.1	0.0	0	0.0
Charlottesville	10.5	7.0	0.1	28.5	7.9	6.5	5.0	4.4	6.3	0.0	140.6	2,963	15.2
Chesapeake	2.1	5.8	0.0	50.7	3.6	6.5	4.2	1.6	2.5	1.9	548.2	2,283	104.3
Danville	5.4	9.2	0.0	40.0	0.6	5.8	4.7	2.2	7.9	0.7	136.3	3,321	0.0
Fredericksburg	4.0	4.3	0.2	32.3	21.2	4.9	3.0	2.8	0.0	5.6	84.7	2,972	0.0
Hampton	5.6	3.4	0.1	39.1	1.3	5.3	5.2	5.9	8.5	2.6	309.3	2,296	0.0
Harrisonburg	1.6	4.6	0.1	52.9	0.6	4.6	9.0	2.6	0.4	2.5	6.2	115	0.0
Leesburg	0.0	23.2	0.1	0.0	0.0	16.9	21.4	12.1	1.1	0.0	124.3	2,299	16.8
Lynchburg	8.2	3.7	0.2	44.2	0.6	6.4	7.5	2.6	3.2	0.1	332.2	4,125	0.0
Manassas	0.7	5.4	0.0	55.7	1.9	7.1	11.0	0.2	2.1	2.2	110.0	2,674	0.0
Newport News	4.2	2.3	0.0	43.4	0.6	5.6	4.7	2.6	4.3	2.7	993.6	5,537	177.7
Norfolk	3.7	2.9	1.2	33.8	3.6	5.9	4.8	4.6	7.4	3.1	1,518.8	6,211	436.5
Petersburg	11.6	4.6	0.0	40.0	0.9	9.2	4.0	1.3	1.0	0.7	21.8	702	0.0
Portsmouth	4.6	1.3	0.1	34.2	2.2	6.6	4.7	2.7	5.6	3.5	589.7	6,218	17.1
Richmond	5.8	4.0	0.5	31.2	6.4	8.5	10.1	2.2	10.6	3.3	1,610.3	7,087	505.0
Roanoke	13.1	5.4	0.6	41.2	0.5	5.4	3.3	1.8	7.6	0.0	120.4	1,217	17.9
Salem	1.6	5.1	0.0	51.3	0.7	5.6	8.6	7.7	0.0	0.3	9.6	377	0.0
Staunton	6.4	7.9	0.5	40.7	8.0	6.6	6.2	2.7	1.8	0.0	56.2	2,311	0.0
Suffolk	3.2	10.5	0.0	44.7	0.7	6.3	3.7	2.5	5.0	0.0	628.7	6,977	169.6
Virginia Beach	3.2	5.9	0.5	46.1	3.6	5.2	8.2	7.4	1.8	1.2	1,484.0	3,299	35.5
Winchester	4.4	3.0	0.4	48.0	1.1	5.2	5.2	2.1	1.1	2.7	182.7	6,485	0.0
WASHINGTON	X	X	X	X	X	X	X	X	X	X	X	X	X
Auburn	0.0	10.8	0.0	0.0	0.5	19.3	36.9	14.5	0.3	1.5	69.3	852	4.7
Bellevue	0.0	19.7	0.0	0.0	0.0	10.1	19.9	14.7	6.0	4.0	284.6	1,959	0.0
Bellingham	0.0	10.9	1.6	0.0	6.3	14.3	17.5	8.3	2.8	2.5	106.3	1,194	10.6
Bothell	0.4	27.1	0.0	0.0	0.2	14.8	11.6	1.5	2.1	5.4	130.1	2,846	17.9
Bremerton	0.1	9.2	1.4	0.0	0.6	18.3	21.2	12.3	1.3	2.5	71.1	1,749	8.4
Burien	0.0	11.2	0.0	0.0	0.6	36.6	6.3	8.3	2.7	4.9	33.2	638	7.0
Camas	0.0	14.3	0.0	0.0	7.8	10.6	19.3	4.7	0.0	3.9	71.2	3,057	6.0
Des Moines	0.1	31.5	0.0	0.0	0.7	22.6	8.5	14.6	0.0	0.8	17.9	570	3.7
Edmonds	0.0	11.1	0.0	0.0	0.1	15.7	16.9	8.0	0.0	1.5	73.3	1,737	6.8
Everett	0.2	6.9	0.2	0.0	4.9	16.7	18.9	10.5	0.8	3.4	349.2	3,170	153.2
Federal Way	0.5	19.7	0.0	0.0	1.3	24.9	4.6	9.2	1.8	0.5	51.6	531	7.8
Issaquah	0.2	19.4	0.0	0.0	0.2	8.7	16.2	9.3	4.2	1.5	39.3	1,042	3.0
Kennewick	0.0	11.0	0.0	0.0	5.4	20.4	6.2	12.4	0.2	3.3	82.0	1,004	14.6
Kent	1.3	16.0	0.0	0.0	0.3	17.6	23.8	10.1	1.1	2.0	263.8	2,003	142.1
Kirkland	0.0	12.1	0.0	0.0	0.7	13.8	23.1	5.7	0.0	1.4	46.5	522	3.0
Lacey	0.0	11.2	0.0	0.0	0.5	17.0	29.0	9.9	0.0	1.1	37.8	762	7.8
Lake Stevens	0.0	22.7	0.0	0.0	0.2	40.0	7.4	2.6	6.2	4.2	18.2	554	0.9
Lakewood	0.7	28.9	0.0	0.0	0.4	40.0	6.2	4.1	2.6	0.9	12.5	207	4.6
Longview	0.0	8.0	0.0	0.0	0.3	19.3	29.8	3.8	2.2	1.5	60.1	1,599	1.3
Lynnwood	0.0	13.9	0.0	0.0	0.2	18.8	8.7	5.3	2.2	2.9	85.7	2,239	3.6
Maple Valley	0.2	25.1	0.0	0.0	0.0	23.1	0.5	13.1	4.3	1.7	7.6	291	0.5
Marysville	0.0	14.8	0.0	0.0	0.3	17.6	21.8	5.0	3.1	4.3	75.1	1,090	5.0
Mercer Island	0.3	7.7	0.0	0.0	5.2	13.8	19.0	7.6	5.1	2.9	33.5	1,302	1.3

1. Based on population estimated as of July 1 of the year shown.

STATE Place code	City	Land area[1] (sq. mi)	Population, 2021: Total persons 2021	Population, 2021: Rank	Population, 2021: Per square mile	Race 2020, Race alone[2] (percent): White	Race 2020, Race alone[2] (percent): Black or African American	Race 2020, Race alone[2] (percent): American Indian, Alaskan Native	Race 2020, Race alone[2] (percent): Asian	Race 2020, Race alone[2] (percent): Hawaiian Pacific Islander	Race 2020, Race alone[2] (percent): Some other race	Race 2020: Two or more races (percent)
		1	2	3	4	5	6	7	8	9	10	11
	WASHINGTON—Cont'd											
53 47245	Moses Lake	18.0	25,583	1,514	1,421.3	62.7	1.4	1.4	2.7	0.2	17.6	13.9
53 47560	Mount Vernon	12.3	35,404	1,124	2,878.4	61.0	1.0	1.8	3.7	0.5	17.6	14.3
53 51300	Olympia	18.2	55,919	699	3,072.5	73.8	3.2	1.2	6.7	0.7	3.2	11.2
53 53545	Pasco	34.0	78,871	459	2,319.7	45.1	1.7	1.4	2.1	0.3	32.3	17.1
53 56625	Pullman	10.9	32,827	1,205	3,011.7	69.6	3.4	0.7	10.7	0.4	4.1	11.0
53 56695	Puyallup	14.1	42,794	930	3,035.0	72.6	4.0	1.3	5.7	1.4	4.0	11.0
53 57535	Redmond	16.6	76,354	478	4,599.6	44.9	2.2	0.4	41.0	0.1	3.1	8.2
53 57745	Renton	23.5	105,179	304	4,475.7	41.9	10.1	0.9	26.1	0.8	8.5	11.6
53 58235	Richland	39.2	61,929	623	1,579.8	77.0	1.5	0.7	5.2	0.3	5.3	9.9
53 61115	Sammamish	20.4	66,630	570	3,266.2	52.6	1.3	0.2	35.8	0.1	1.4	8.5
53 62288	SeaTac	10.1	30,759	1,282	3,045.4	31.8	24.1	1.4	18.4	3.1	12.0	9.1
53 63000	Seattle	83.9	733,919	18	8,747.5	61.3	7.0	0.7	17.1	0.3	3.2	10.5
53 63960	Shoreline	11.6	57,918	683	4,992.9	62.0	6.4	0.9	16.0	0.4	3.9	10.4
53 67000	Spokane	68.8	229,071	96	3,329.5	79.3	2.7	1.9	2.8	1.2	2.4	9.7
53 67167	Spokane Valley	37.7	105,905	298	2,809.2	83.2	1.8	1.3	1.9	0.7	2.6	8.6
53 70000	Tacoma	49.7	219,205	103	4,410.6	57.4	10.3	1.8	9.2	2.0	6.3	13.0
53 72905	Tumwater	17.5	25,844	1,501	1,476.8	75.7	2.7	1.3	5.4	0.7	2.4	11.8
53 73465	University Place	8.3	34,900	1,141	4,204.8	61.9	9.1	0.7	10.9	1.2	3.1	13.1
53 74060	Vancouver	48.7	192,169	134	3,946.0	69.3	3.3	1.2	5.4	1.8	7.4	11.6
53 75775	Walla Walla	14.0	33,927	1,172	2,423.4	70.6	2.3	1.3	1.8	0.2	11.4	12.4
53 77105	Wenatchee	10.6	35,405	1,123	3,340.1	65.9	0.5	1.4	1.3	0.2	18.9	11.9
53 80010	Yakima	27.8	96,578	341	3,474.0	51.8	1.4	2.5	1.5	0.2	27.7	14.9
54 00000	WEST VIRGINIA	24,041.1	1,782,959	X	74.2	89.8	3.7	0.2	0.8	0.0	0.7	4.7
54 14600	Charleston	31.5	48,018	828	1,524.4	74.7	14.8	0.3	2.6	0.0	1.1	6.6
54 39460	Huntington	16.2	46,025	863	2,841.0	82.5	8.7	0.3	1.5	0.0	1.0	6.0
54 55756	Morgantown	10.2	29,219	1,340	2,864.6	82.9	4.6	0.2	3.7	0.1	1.3	7.1
54 62140	Parkersburg	11.8	29,403	1,327	2,491.8	91.0	2.0	0.3	0.5	0.0	0.7	5.5
54 86452	Wheeling	13.8	26,568	1,462	1,925.2	86.5	5.5	0.2	1.1	0.0	0.7	6.0
55 00000	WISCONSIN	54,167.4	5,895,908	X	108.8	80.4	6.4	1.0	3.0	0.0	3.1	6.1
55 02375	Appleton	24.8	74,854	491	3,018.3	80.1	2.9	0.9	6.4	0.1	3.2	6.5
55 06500	Beloit	17.3	36,609	1,085	2,116.1	60.0	14.5	1.0	1.6	0.1	11.4	11.3
55 10025	Brookfield	27.3	41,464	954	1,518.8	80.2	1.9	0.2	11.5	0.0	0.9	5.4
55 11950	Caledonia	45.2	25,229	1,532	558.2	84.2	3.3	0.4	1.7	0.0	2.4	7.9
55 19775	De Pere	12.0	25,335	1,527	2,111.3	87.9	1.9	1.3	2.1	0.1	1.4	5.2
55 22300	Eau Claire	32.9	69,441	543	2,110.7	85.9	1.5	0.6	5.7	0.1	1.1	5.1
55 25950	Fitchburg	34.9	30,674	1,290	878.9	65.3	10.9	0.8	5.0	0.0	8.5	9.5
55 26275	Fond du Lac	19.2	44,595	892	2,322.7	82.4	4.5	0.7	2.0	0.0	4.1	6.3
55 27300	Franklin	34.6	36,624	1,083	1,058.5	79.4	5.2	0.4	7.4	0.0	1.6	6.0
55 31000	Green Bay	45.5	107,015	290	2,352.0	66.6	5.5	4.4	4.4	0.1	8.4	10.6
55 31175	Greenfield	11.5	37,352	1,063	3,248.0	75.7	4.2	0.6	6.0	0.0	4.8	8.6
55 37825	Janesville	34.2	65,942	579	1,928.1	84.8	3.3	0.4	1.7	0.1	2.9	6.8
55 39225	Kenosha	28.3	99,286	331	3,508.3	67.9	10.8	0.5	1.9	0.1	7.3	11.5
55 40775	La Crosse	21.7	52,185	763	2,404.8	85.6	2.9	0.5	4.9	0.0	1.2	4.9
55 48000	Madison	79.6	269,196	81	3,381.9	71.0	7.4	0.5	9.5	0.1	3.8	7.8
55 48500	Manitowoc	17.8	34,547	1,155	1,940.8	82.9	2.4	0.7	5.0	0.0	2.6	6.4
55 51000	Menomonee Falls	32.9	38,906	1,019	1,182.6	84.1	3.8	0.3	6.1	0.0	0.8	5.0
55 51150	Mequon	46.3	25,200	1,535	544.3	85.7	3.1	0.2	4.7	0.0	1.1	5.1
55 53000	Milwaukee	96.2	569,330	31	5,918.2	36.1	38.6	0.9	5.2	0.0	9.0	10.1
55 54875	Mount Pleasant	33.9	27,646	1,405	815.5	77.3	7.8	0.5	2.4	0.0	3.6	8.3
55 55275	Muskego	31.6	25,242	1,529	798.8	92.6	0.3	0.2	1.2	0.0	0.8	4.9
55 55750	Neenah	9.4	27,525	1,413	2,928.2	88.0	1.8	0.7	2.3	0.1	1.5	5.8
55 56375	New Berlin	36.4	40,375	982	1,109.2	87.6	1.3	0.3	4.7	0.0	1.1	5.0
55 58800	Oak Creek	28.4	36,260	1,091	1,276.8	78.7	3.6	0.5	6.9	0.0	2.7	7.6
55 60500	Oshkosh	27.0	66,607	571	2,466.9	83.0	5.3	0.8	4.4	0.0	1.3	5.0
55 66000	Racine	15.5	77,127	470	4,975.9	51.5	23.9	0.7	0.8	0.0	10.4	12.7
55 72975	Sheboygan	15.6	49,931	799	3,200.7	72.3	3.3	0.6	11.1	0.0	4.8	7.9
55 77200	Stevens Point	17.2	25,692	1,508	1,493.7	85.6	2.7	0.6	4.8	0.0	1.3	4.9
55 78600	Sun Prairie	12.9	36,189	1,096	2,805.3	74.9	7.4	0.5	7.6	0.0	2.5	7.2
55 78650	Superior	36.6	26,561	1,463	725.7	87.7	1.8	2.1	0.9	0.1	0.6	6.7
55 84250	Waukesha	25.5	71,256	521	2,794.4	78.6	3.5	0.5	3.4	0.1	4.4	9.6
55 84475	Wausau	19.2	39,575	1,001	2,061.2	78.3	1.7	0.7	11.9	0.0	1.8	5.6
55 84675	Wauwatosa	13.2	47,752	835	3,617.6	82.7	6.0	0.2	3.5	0.0	1.1	6.4
55 85300	West Allis	11.4	59,484	653	5,217.9	73.4	6.3	1.3	2.6	0.0	6.0	10.4
55 85350	West Bend	15.5	31,727	1,247	2,046.9	90.0	1.8	0.4	1.1	0.0	1.5	5.2
56 00000	WYOMING	97,088.7	578,803	X	6.0	84.7	0.9	2.4	0.9	0.1	3.5	7.5
56 13150	Casper	26.6	58,656	669	2,205.1	86.1	1.1	1.4	0.9	0.1	2.8	7.6
56 13900	Cheyenne	32.3	65,051	588	2,014.0	79.4	2.7	1.2	1.5	0.2	4.4	10.5
56 31855	Gillette	23.2	32,884	1,199	1,417.4	85.3	0.6	1.5	0.9	0.1	4.8	6.8

1. Dry land or land partially or temporarily covered by water. 2. Hispanic or Latino persons may be of any race.

City	Percent Hispanic or Latino[1], 2020	Percent foreign born, 2016–2020	Age of population (percent), 2016–2020: Under 18 years	18 to 24 years	25 to 34 years	35 to 44 years	45 to 54 years	55 to 64 years	65 years and over	Median age, 2016–2020	Percent female, 2016–2020	Population: Census counts: 2010	Census counts: 2020	Percent change: 2010–2020	Percent change: 2020–2021
	12	13	14	15	16	17	18	19	20	21	22	23	24	25	26
WASHINGTON—Cont'd															
Moses Lake	36.3	10.2	29.2	9.6	14.9	11.2	12.6	7.6	15.0	32.4	53.1	20,340	25,401	24.9	0.7
Mount Vernon	33.7	16.4	25.5	9.2	15.7	11.3	10.0	11.7	16.7	34.7	50.3	31,722	35,232	11.1	0.5
Olympia	9.1	10.0	18.0	9.3	18.5	13.6	11.1	11.2	18.4	37.7	51.3	46,897	55,435	18.2	0.9
Pasco	57.5	21.4	33.3	9.7	16.0	13.5	9.9	8.3	9.2	29.7	49.4	62,161	77,579	24.8	1.7
Pullman	10.8	15.2	12.2	47.7	16.0	8.1	5.3	4.7	6.0	22.4	49.1	29,820	32,870	10.2	-0.1
Puyallup	9.8	9.0	22.3	7.3	16.4	12.9	13.8	12.4	14.9	38.3	51.9	37,244	42,985	15.4	-0.4
Redmond	7.2	40.6	22.9	6.3	22.2	17.6	11.5	9.2	10.2	34.5	49.5	54,511	73,375	34.6	4.1
Renton	15.5	27.8	21.4	8.1	18.1	15.8	13.8	11.3	11.5	36.3	49.8	91,929	106,966	16.4	-1.7
Richland	13.3	8.1	25.0	8.8	14.8	12.1	11.6	12.3	15.5	36.1	49.6	48,491	60,538	24.8	2.3
Sammamish	5.4	31.3	29.9	5.1	8.4	18.0	19.2	11.6	7.9	38.9	51.9	57,447	67,600	17.7	-1.4
SeaTac	19.4	37.6	23.7	7.4	19.0	15.5	11.6	11.2	11.7	35.0	45.6	26,903	31,402	16.7	-2.0
Seattle	8.2	19.4	14.5	10.3	24.7	15.5	12.2	10.3	12.5	35.2	49.4	608,660	735,157	20.8	-0.2
Shoreline	9.1	22.6	18.7	6.6	13.5	14.5	13.6	13.7	19.5	42.3	51.4	53,031	58,532	10.4	-1.0
Spokane	7.0	5.9	21.1	9.9	17.1	12.4	11.4	12.4	15.7	36.3	51.0	209,459	228,831	9.2	0.1
Spokane Valley	7.0	5.6	21.6	7.7	16.6	12.4	11.7	12.4	17.5	38.1	50.1	89,746	103,317	15.1	2.5
Tacoma	13.2	12.1	20.8	9.5	17.9	13.8	12.3	12.1	13.6	36.0	49.8	198,338	219,025	10.4	0.1
Tumwater	8.7	5.2	21.9	7.9	18.7	15.4	11.5	13.1	11.5	36.1	52.7	20,135	25,391	26.1	1.8
University Place	9.5	12.9	22.6	10.0	13.0	11.5	12.1	12.6	18.2	38.4	52.2	31,133	34,955	12.3	-0.2
Vancouver	16.0	13.6	22.3	8.7	15.8	13.2	11.9	11.9	16.2	37.1	51.2	167,167	190,810	14.1	0.7
Walla Walla	24.3	8.4	19.8	14.9	14.0	12.4	10.7	10.7	17.6	35.7	47.4	32,461	33,983	4.7	-0.2
Wenatchee	32.6	13.6	25.2	8.3	16.2	12.5	9.5	12.2	16.1	35.3	49.2	32,821	35,394	7.8	0.0
Yakima	48.5	17.0	28.2	10.1	13.6	12.8	10.5	9.8	15.0	33.6	51.0	91,285	96,873	6.1	-0.3
WEST VIRGINIA	1.9	1.6	20.2	8.8	11.9	12.0	12.9	14.3	19.9	42.7	50.6	1,853,008	1,793,716	-3.2	-0.6
Charleston	2.0	4.1	18.4	8.9	12.6	13.2	12.7	14.7	19.4	42.1	52.5	51,280	48,913	-4.6	-1.8
Huntington	2.1	2.3	17.9	18.5	13.1	11.1	11.7	11.3	16.5	35.6	52.9	49,312	46,645	-5.4	-1.3
Morgantown	4.1	8.3	9.8	42.0	15.5	7.8	7.5	8.0	9.4	24.2	45.9	28,497	29,150	2.3	0.2
Parkersburg	1.7	0.7	21.2	7.4	13.2	11.5	12.0	14.1	20.6	41.8	51.7	31,284	29,749	-4.9	-1.2
Wheeling	1.7	2.0	19.6	8.4	11.5	11.5	10.4	14.9	23.8	43.9	52.3	28,381	27,009	-4.8	-1.6
WISCONSIN	7.6	5.0	21.9	9.5	12.7	12.2	12.7	14.1	16.9	39.6	50.2	5,687,285	5,893,718	3.6	0.0
Appleton	7.3	6.4	23.8	9.8	14.2	12.9	12.5	11.7	15.2	36.5	50.6	72,584	75,315	3.8	-0.6
Beloit	21.3	9.2	25.7	11.8	12.9	11.6	11.4	12.4	14.2	34.6	51.7	37,023	36,470	-1.5	0.4
Brookfield	3.5	11.3	23.8	5.8	8.9	12.7	12.4	14.8	21.8	44.3	51.1	37,920	41,458	9.3	0.0
Caledonia	8.7	4.1	21.6	7.4	9.1	10.7	15.9	17.2	18.1	45.8	49.4	24,875	25,325	1.8	-0.4
De Pere	4.2	3.5	22.2	13.9	14.7	11.9	11.1	12.5	13.8	34.4	51.8	23,890	25,281	5.8	0.2
Eau Claire	3.3	4.7	18.0	20.7	15.1	11.4	9.9	10.8	14.0	32.2	51.4	66,237	69,291	4.6	0.2
Fitchburg	16.7	11.3	22.0	8.5	21.0	13.6	9.5	12.5	12.9	34.4	46.9	25,156	29,601	17.7	3.6
Fond du Lac	8.6	4.9	22.6	10.4	13.5	13.3	11.7	12.3	16.3	37.4	51.7	43,023	44,593	3.6	0.0
Franklin	6.7	7.5	20.4	6.8	11.0	14.0	13.2	15.9	18.6	43.4	49.4	35,462	36,818	3.8	-0.5
Green Bay	17.9	9.7	24.5	10.7	14.7	12.8	12.2	12.2	12.9	35.1	50.2	103,877	107,300	3.3	-0.3
Greenfield	13.8	8.2	17.2	5.6	15.4	12.7	12.2	14.8	22.1	44.1	52.3	36,753	37,793	2.8	-1.2
Janesville	7.2	3.4	23.0	7.8	13.2	13.5	12.2	13.1	17.0	38.8	51.5	63,667	65,631	3.1	0.5
Kenosha	19.7	9.0	24.6	10.3	13.5	13.5	12.6	12.2	13.3	36.5	51.3	99,274	99,882	0.6	-0.6
La Crosse	3.2	2.9	15.4	27.2	15.1	10.2	8.3	9.8	13.9	29.2	52.4	51,338	52,690	2.6	-1.0
Madison	8.7	11.9	16.1	21.0	19.4	12.2	9.7	9.6	12.0	31.2	50.5	233,413	268,414	15.0	0.3
Manitowoc	7.2	4.1	20.6	7.6	11.4	10.9	11.9	15.8	21.7	44.6	50.7	33,699	34,470	2.3	0.2
Menomonee Falls	3.2	5.2	23.1	6.0	10.6	13.1	13.5	14.1	19.6	42.0	52.8	35,625	38,466	8.0	1.1
Mequon	3.5	9.7	22.5	10.9	5.1	10.0	14.2	14.6	22.7	47.0	51.6	23,136	25,015	8.1	0.7
Milwaukee	20.1	10.2	26.1	11.8	17.3	12.6	10.9	10.6	10.5	31.4	51.7	594,503	577,235	-2.9	-1.4
Mount Pleasant	10.6	6.2	19.8	7.8	12.3	9.6	12.1	15.2	23.1	45.3	52.2	26,698	27,696	3.7	-0.2
Muskego	3.5	2.2	23.2	7.5	7.5	13.6	16.2	15.5	16.4	43.4	49.8	24,133	25,052	3.8	0.8
Neenah	4.8	2.5	26.3	6.7	14.6	11.7	13.2	12.6	15.0	37.1	51.9	25,500	27,330	7.2	0.7
New Berlin	4.5	6.2	19.4	6.8	10.3	12.2	13.9	15.8	21.6	46.4	49.9	39,607	40,395	2.0	0.0
Oak Creek	9.4	11.5	21.1	5.4	15.9	12.9	14.0	16.1	14.5	40.6	50.8	34,449	36,505	6.0	-0.7
Oshkosh	4.4	3.5	17.6	18.1	15.3	11.7	11.4	11.1	14.8	34.3	48.9	66,342	66,777	0.7	-0.3
Racine	24.2	6.1	28.0	9.0	13.1	13.6	11.6	11.9	12.8	34.9	50.6	78,559	77,775	-1.0	-0.8
Sheboygan	12.5	9.4	24.8	8.7	13.4	13.7	11.7	12.0	15.7	36.8	49.2	49,399	50,017	1.3	-0.2
Stevens Point	4.1	5.3	15.1	30.4	14.1	8.6	9.1	9.0	13.7	27.9	50.8	26,711	25,597	-4.2	0.4
Sun Prairie	6.1	6.5	25.3	7.3	14.1	15.8	13.1	10.7	13.9	37.0	50.0	29,539	36,147	22.4	0.1
Superior	2.1	3.4	20.2	10.8	14.9	13.5	12.6	12.2	15.7	37.4	51.4	27,229	26,722	-1.9	-0.6
Waukesha	14.0	7.6	20.0	12.5	15.3	13.0	11.8	13.1	14.3	36.3	51.1	71,224	71,405	0.3	-0.2
Wausau	4.1	6.8	22.3	9.2	14.7	12.5	10.7	13.3	17.1	38.0	51.6	39,299	39,831	1.4	-0.6
Wauwatosa	4.6	5.7	21.9	5.8	16.8	13.2	12.0	12.3	18.1	38.6	53.2	46,424	48,376	4.2	-1.3
West Allis	16.9	5.2	19.7	5.6	18.7	13.9	12.5	14.0	15.6	38.5	50.2	60,386	60,330	-0.1	-1.4
West Bend	4.9	2.1	22.2	7.6	12.6	14.7	12.3	13.2	17.4	39.4	51.5	31,186	31,731	1.7	0.0
WYOMING	10.2	3.3	23.2	9.2	13.5	12.6	11.4	13.6	16.4	38.0	49.0	563,775	576,851	2.3	0.3
Casper	9.5	1.9	24.0	8.5	14.6	13.7	11.1	12.7	15.4	36.9	51.0	55,311	59,072	6.8	-0.7
Cheyenne	16.3	2.8	21.3	8.3	17.1	12.0	11.9	12.6	17.0	37.5	49.6	59,531	65,096	9.3	-0.1
Gillette	10.3	1.8	30.6	9.0	16.6	12.5	10.0	12.2	9.0	31.5	48.6	31,419	33,408	6.3	-1.6

1. May be of any race.

City	Households, 2016–2020							Persons in group quarters, 2016–2020	Serious crimes known to police[2], 2020				Educational attainment, 2016–2020		
			Percent						Violent		Property			Attainment[4] (percent)	
	Number	Persons per household	Family	Married couple family	Female family	Non-family	One person		Number	Rate	Number	Rate	Population age 25 and over	High school graduate or less	Bachelor's degree or more
	27	28	29	30	31	32	33	34	35	36	37	38	39	40	41
WASHINGTON—Cont'd															
Moses Lake	8,283	2.80	63.6	40.3	18.5	36.4	31.6	215	87	354.8	872	3,555.7	14,352	42.1	22.6
Mount Vernon	12,679	2.74	67.8	49.9	12.0	32.2	26.5	797	70	191.7	1,109	3,037.3	23,195	39.5	24.4
Olympia	23,031	2.21	50.7	37.2	9.5	49.3	36.3	1,322	268	500.3	1,753	3,272.3	38,039	22.7	46.0
Pasco	22,174	3.33	76.0	54.0	15.9	24.0	19.6	509	183	237.8	1,351	1,755.2	42,279	48.4	19.8
Pullman	12,275	2.21	36.7	30.4	3.6	63.3	35.9	6,791	NA	NA	NA	NA	13,641	11.7	62.6
Puyallup	16,133	2.53	62.9	47.1	9.3	37.1	27.1	797	94	218.7	2,548	5,929.2	29,349	36.3	26.8
Redmond	27,083	2.50	65.9	57.8	5.6	34.1	24.7	325	74	99.8	1,742	2,349.2	48,082	10.7	71.8
Renton	39,157	2.58	61.8	41.8	12.4	38.2	26.3	672	348	338.3	4,342	4,221.4	71,828	33.0	35.0
Richland	22,382	2.55	64.1	48.2	10.5	35.9	29.0	247	164	276.2	1,553	2,615.8	38,017	21.2	43.5
Sammamish	21,599	3.02	86.8	77.5	6.2	13.2	10.0	103	17	25.4	442	660.9	42,414	8.1	75.1
SeaTac	10,372	2.70	60.2	37.9	10.8	39.8	32.9	1,053	141	481.5	1,394	4,760.6	20,052	43.6	21.8
Seattle	344,629	2.08	44.3	35.2	6.1	55.7	39.9	24,041	4,832	626.3	37,593	4,872.6	556,865	14.3	65.0
Shoreline	21,820	2.53	66.2	53.3	9.3	33.8	25.6	1,704	116	201.8	1,515	2,636.1	42,468	21.1	51.1
Spokane	93,075	2.28	55.9	38.5	12.3	44.1	34.2	7,231	1,341	599.9	11,514	5,151.1	151,128	29.1	31.9
Spokane Valley	41,459	2.37	60.5	44.3	10.6	39.5	31.2	862	342	334.1	4,370	4,269.0	70,120	34.0	24.6
Tacoma	86,563	2.42	57.5	39.5	12.4	42.5	32.7	6,481	1,856	843.2	12,123	5,507.4	150,424	35.3	30.2
Tumwater	9,272	2.51	63.7	46.3	13.6	36.3	24.7	155	63	257.2	613	2,502.8	16,418	21.7	36.7
University Place	13,351	2.51	65.5	50.8	9.2	34.5	27.3	212	117	340.7	904	2,632.6	22,693	25.1	42.0
Vancouver	73,427	2.46	59.4	43.3	11.2	40.6	30.3	2,420	884	474.1	6,709	3,598.5	126,099	33.2	30.0
Walla Walla	12,414	2.33	57.8	41.7	11.6	42.2	32.7	4,035	83	251.9	749	2,273.6	21,530	34.6	25.8
Wenatchee	13,427	2.49	61.5	43.1	10.6	38.5	32.3	807	67	194.1	570	1,651.0	22,783	41.6	25.3
Yakima	33,752	2.70	64.1	42.8	14.6	35.9	29.1	2,572	639	680.8	3,220	3,430.6	57,867	49.9	19.3
WEST VIRGINIA	734,235	2.40	64.1	48.4	10.8	35.9	30.2	47,206	6,352	355.9	24,976	1,399.4	1,283,869	52.4	21.3
Charleston	21,409	2.10	51.3	35.0	13.4	48.7	41.4	2,208	424	921.0	2,122	4,609.2	34,339	33.2	41.6
Huntington	19,520	2.21	46.8	31.4	11.8	53.2	40.4	3,069	368	823.6	1,642	3,674.7	29,362	41.5	29.3
Morgantown	10,851	2.43	42.8	29.8	7.5	57.2	36.5	4,583	48	156.0	636	2,066.6	14,907	27.0	54.5
Parkersburg	13,119	2.23	55.7	36.5	13.5	44.3	39.1	447	106	364.3	1,269	4,361.4	21,241	51.6	16.3
Wheeling	11,734	2.20	51.1	34.7	11.9	48.9	43.7	1,245	330	1,258.5	582	2,219.5	19,493	44.4	29.3
WISCONSIN	2,377,935	2.38	62.2	48.3	9.4	37.8	30.1	144,508	18,861	323.4	86,654	1,485.7	3,982,118	37.7	30.8
Appleton	29,729	2.40	62.8	48.9	9.7	37.2	30.6	2,483	198	266.6	1,155	1,555.5	49,128	34.7	33.6
Beloit	13,753	2.56	60.6	38.2	17.3	39.4	32.7	1,644	179	484.8	1,069	2,895.4	22,994	49.3	18.8
Brookfield	14,811	2.58	73.7	67.5	4.2	26.3	22.9	397	32	81.5	652	1,661.1	27,226	17.2	61.7
Caledonia	10,059	2.49	72.4	63.9	5.4	27.6	23.2	123	20	79.0	167	659.5	17,878	35.9	31.4
De Pere	9,770	2.36	66.6	51.0	10.5	33.4	26.1	1,961	27	107.6	164	653.6	15,978	26.1	39.3
Eau Claire	28,040	2.32	52.2	39.9	8.5	47.8	33.3	3,797	191	276.5	1,927	2,789.3	42,111	29.7	33.9
Fitchburg	13,076	2.23	56.0	40.7	11.3	44.0	33.1	926	83	263.6	541	1,718.4	20,870	19.1	56.8
Fond du Lac	17,479	2.32	58.8	45.7	8.4	41.2	34.5	2,408	134	309.5	878	2,027.9	28,763	42.9	23.1
Franklin	13,760	2.46	67.5	58.3	6.4	32.5	28.8	2,203	30	83.8	649	1,812.1	26,206	32.6	40.6
Green Bay	42,611	2.37	55.8	38.7	11.7	44.2	34.8	3,603	552	527.5	1,600	1,528.9	67,683	43.9	24.4
Greenfield	17,261	2.12	53.0	38.6	10.1	47.0	40.0	449	55	147.7	956	2,567.3	28,672	39.1	29.1
Janesville	27,302	2.33	59.3	42.7	11.9	40.7	34.0	894	145	224.2	1,392	2,152.1	44,549	39.5	25.2
Kenosha	38,416	2.51	61.5	40.5	14.6	38.5	31.1	3,383	391	391.0	1,443	1,442.9	64,925	40.9	25.7
La Crosse	21,239	2.21	43.4	28.8	8.7	56.6	39.2	4,657	131	255.8	2,236	4,366.2	29,572	31.9	36.5
Madison	111,832	2.20	45.3	35.0	7.2	54.7	37.3	11,786	842	320.5	7,301	2,778.8	162,679	18.0	58.5
Manitowoc	14,609	2.17	55.6	41.5	9.3	44.4	37.3	872	NA	NA	NA	NA	23,361	41.7	23.2
Menomonee Falls	15,397	2.43	66.9	57.8	6.7	33.1	29.1	188	NA	NA	NA	NA	26,684	26.4	45.2
Mequon	8,839	2.58	77.0	65.7	6.2	23.0	19.9	1,513	12	48.9	205	835.8	16,229	13.2	69.9
Milwaukee	229,227	2.51	53.4	26.9	20.6	46.6	37.4	16,291	9,407	1,596.8	16,074	2,728.5	367,665	46.7	24.6
Mount Pleasant	11,320	2.36	65.0	51.3	8.9	35.0	30.6	294	48	177.0	490	1,806.5	19,550	33.5	32.4
Muskego	9,564	2.61	74.9	66.8	5.0	25.1	22.1	89	8	31.7	210	832.1	17,382	30.4	38.1
Neenah	10,848	2.39	60.4	41.6	13.7	39.6	33.2	160	57	216.0	315	1,193.6	17,478	37.3	32.1
New Berlin	16,609	2.39	69.8	60.7	5.8	30.2	26.5	179	28	70.5	457	1,151.0	29,367	26.9	44.6
Oak Creek	15,348	2.36	62.0	48.1	10.8	38.0	28.8	75	49	134.2	749	2,051.9	26,691	33.4	36.5
Oshkosh	26,724	2.22	50.8	36.5	9.1	49.2	35.6	7,414	187	278.8	1,239	1,847.0	42,925	42.5	26.4
Racine	30,392	2.47	60.7	35.3	18.1	39.3	32.0	1,806	414	540.7	1,381	1,803.5	48,436	46.6	17.2
Sheboygan	20,227	2.34	55.1	40.2	9.6	44.9	36.4	861	157	328.4	832	1,740.1	32,004	44.7	22.1
Stevens Point	10,842	2.13	42.8	30.8	7.7	57.2	37.3	3,082	34	131.8	252	977.1	14,251	34.1	38.1
Sun Prairie	13,596	2.49	61.7	49.8	8.6	38.3	31.8	136	25	70.9	539	1,528.1	22,895	22.9	47.0
Superior	11,726	2.15	53.9	35.7	13.2	46.1	37.7	994	48	185.7	1,011	3,911.8	18,106	34.0	25.5
Waukesha	29,704	2.35	62.6	48.3	9.9	37.4	30.6	2,677	123	169.8	595	821.6	48,832	29.2	38.7
Wausau	17,254	2.18	54.1	38.7	11.2	45.9	35.7	995	174	452.0	560	1,454.8	26,483	38.9	28.4
Wauwatosa	20,474	2.32	59.0	46.8	8.9	41.0	33.7	693	67	138.8	1,092	2,262.5	34,842	18.1	59.1
West Allis	27,431	2.15	48.5	33.3	10.2	51.5	42.2	810	191	319.5	1,715	2,868.9	44,667	42.8	24.5
West Bend	13,706	2.28	60.9	47.8	9.2	39.1	34.3	403	80	253.1	513	1,623.3	22,174	35.1	30.3
WYOMING	233,231	2.43	64.0	52.0	7.9	36.0	28.8	14,293	1,364	234.2	9,379	1,610.6	392,819	35.0	28.2
Casper	24,850	2.30	59.5	44.2	11.0	40.5	33.0	1,185	124	212.9	1,659	2,848.4	39,329	33.3	26.5
Cheyenne	27,599	2.29	59.4	47.4	8.3	40.6	33.5	970	244	376.8	2,186	3,376.0	45,157	30.3	32.2
Gillette	11,936	2.68	70.5	54.7	10.0	29.5	23.2	482	62	193.2	617	1,922.5	19,611	42.2	19.8

2. Data for serious crimes have not been adjusted for underreporting. This may affect comparability between geographic areas and over time.
4. Persons 25 years old and over.

City	Money income, 2016–2020					Median earnings Full year, Full-time workers, 2016–2020			Housing units, 2016–2020				
	Households												
	Median household income	Percent with income less than $25,000	Percent with income of $200,000 or more	Median family income	Median non-family household income	All persons	Men	Women	Total	Occupied	Percent owner occupied	Median value[1] (dollars)	Median gross rent (dollars)
	42	43	44	45	46	47	48	49	50	51	52	53	54
WASHINGTON—Cont'd													
Moses Lake	60,136	19.7	2.5	67,865	35,046	47,932	53,967	43,871	9,203	8,283	59.8	188,000	965
Mount Vernon	63,194	18.3	4.4	76,984	38,540	45,618	51,345	38,652	13,120	12,679	62.3	308,900	1,056
Olympia	63,185	18.9	5.7	87,038	42,701	54,149	61,524	48,391	24,265	23,031	47.2	330,800	1,199
Pasco	64,756	15.6	5.7	72,444	37,253	42,912	48,726	39,926	23,126	22,174	69.5	222,000	927
Pullman	32,073	42.0	4.6	73,697	20,364	45,204	47,194	40,667	13,680	12,275	28.6	287,700	856
Puyallup	76,565	11.0	6.3	97,699	47,303	56,355	66,557	50,089	16,845	16,133	51.6	352,800	1,352
Redmond	132,770	8.2	27.4	157,526	86,635	112,730	128,279	86,568	28,606	27,083	50.1	788,500	2,009
Renton	79,824	11.9	9.9	92,794	59,333	58,157	61,168	54,865	40,922	39,157	52.7	442,600	1,612
Richland	77,981	11.3	9.4	99,769	54,462	62,384	75,326	54,298	23,663	22,382	64.9	283,200	1,128
Sammamish	181,464	4.4	45.3	198,039	93,634	129,782	151,031	94,979	22,142	21,599	85.9	878,000	2,395
SeaTac	66,131	11.8	3.8	80,183	48,904	47,240	48,314	45,493	11,010	10,372	48.9	338,000	1,364
Seattle	97,185	13.2	19.6	137,683	69,092	78,610	88,127	69,863	367,337	344,629	44.9	713,600	1,702
Shoreline	91,524	13.9	13.8	113,797	48,736	66,227	74,523	60,631	22,761	21,820	66.7	582,000	1,635
Spokane	52,600	22.0	4.0	68,630	34,061	44,444	49,043	41,556	99,705	93,075	56.0	205,500	905
Spokane Valley	56,351	19.6	3.2	70,367	34,158	45,081	48,177	41,393	43,681	41,459	57.8	226,800	969
Tacoma	64,457	17.3	5.4	81,572	45,077	51,612	53,265	49,125	91,813	86,563	53.6	311,700	1,253
Tumwater	76,676	13.6	4.9	94,195	42,686	61,989	66,113	57,562	9,604	9,272	57.3	312,600	1,266
University Place	77,832	11.5	9.8	95,342	46,780	58,358	68,276	51,200	14,120	13,351	58.5	387,800	1,250
Vancouver	63,617	15.7	5.0	72,790	46,316	49,832	52,679	44,603	76,559	73,427	51.7	318,200	1,289
Walla Walla	54,412	24.4	3.4	71,431	32,739	47,374	53,398	42,184	13,773	12,414	57.9	225,700	994
Wenatchee	56,962	19.7	4.3	70,892	35,884	41,081	45,870	37,235	14,207	13,427	55.5	273,100	951
Yakima	48,220	21.6	3.2	57,296	34,737	38,863	40,730	36,384	35,763	33,752	54.6	182,900	879
WEST VIRGINIA	48,037	26.6	3.1	61,707	26,825	42,479	49,512	36,219	893,615	734,235	73.7	123,200	732
Charleston	49,769	29.4	8.2	74,866	32,221	47,874	50,694	45,497	25,579	21,409	60.6	156,900	751
Huntington	33,012	39.2	2.7	49,708	21,769	35,360	41,586	31,650	24,554	19,520	51.1	100,300	727
Morgantown	42,474	36.2	5.7	81,341	21,873	44,922	43,622	47,763	12,575	10,851	44.4	215,000	840
Parkersburg	37,933	33.9	1.7	47,307	25,444	35,565	38,359	31,568	15,246	13,119	61.1	89,800	671
Wheeling	41,911	33.5	4.1	61,503	24,208	42,713	47,020	36,554	14,598	11,734	59.6	110,900	645
WISCONSIN	63,293	17.4	5.2	80,844	37,792	49,517	53,830	42,865	2,709,444	2,377,935	67.1	189,200	872
Appleton	61,475	16.6	4.6	76,791	40,197	46,837	51,509	41,686	30,873	29,729	65.8	157,700	796
Beloit	46,989	26.3	1.8	52,937	31,042	38,962	43,445	33,359	14,900	13,753	58.1	96,400	825
Brookfield	107,380	9.0	18.9	127,947	52,222	79,724	94,658	65,262	15,314	14,811	84.8	331,500	1,495
Caledonia	81,722	11.1	6.3	92,203	38,214	56,349	63,194	48,995	10,451	10,059	80.4	220,100	934
De Pere	73,972	13.1	3.6	85,933	45,383	51,442	57,397	39,897	10,055	9,770	61.9	188,800	883
Eau Claire	59,705	18.9	3.0	82,851	36,991	44,018	48,923	39,297	29,712	28,040	56.6	165,700	834
Fitchburg	76,240	13.2	13.7	99,828	55,683	55,531	62,465	52,587	13,493	13,076	50.6	323,400	1,098
Fond du Lac	54,587	19.9	2.7	70,061	33,970	44,320	49,304	38,856	19,085	17,479	58.1	128,500	761
Franklin	81,321	12.5	8.5	107,693	44,283	61,703	69,711	53,658	14,114	13,760	78.2	262,200	1,095
Green Bay	52,214	21.8	2.9	65,993	35,335	42,100	45,491	37,557	44,838	42,611	56.2	142,000	768
Greenfield	61,988	16.8	3.8	84,729	40,883	50,854	53,723	46,875	18,117	17,261	57.6	184,400	975
Janesville	55,914	21.3	2.2	70,805	33,656	46,193	50,058	42,126	28,254	27,302	65.5	151,400	874
Kenosha	56,113	21.2	3.6	70,037	35,237	44,605	50,199	39,683	41,371	38,416	57.4	160,900	923
La Crosse	46,438	26.9	3.3	66,928	32,206	40,908	43,614	37,319	22,724	21,239	45.5	150,500	820
Madison	67,565	17.1	7.3	96,502	47,601	53,033	56,711	48,925	116,810	111,832	47.7	262,400	1,147
Manitowoc	51,563	21.8	3.5	68,845	34,091	44,209	47,495	40,201	16,059	14,609	67.0	112,000	672
Menomonee Falls	86,555	10.3	12.3	111,122	42,685	65,137	75,083	56,456	15,982	15,397	74.6	264,800	1,129
Mequon	128,403	8.3	28.3	147,423	47,750	90,240	118,711	67,702	9,414	8,839	85.0	396,700	1,708
Milwaukee	43,125	30.0	2.2	51,170	31,698	40,816	42,944	38,008	256,856	229,227	40.7	128,300	866
Mount Pleasant	72,309	14.6	5.4	91,059	41,150	62,208	72,869	46,899	11,834	11,320	78.8	207,300	850
Muskego	95,472	7.2	9.9	114,474	44,003	70,288	73,387	66,862	9,897	9,564	86.1	304,400	1,201
Neenah	59,778	18.6	4.3	77,229	36,536	45,837	52,352	40,085	11,289	10,848	62.6	144,200	762
New Berlin	85,577	8.9	11.0	104,452	48,793	62,953	69,702	54,409	17,027	16,609	77.2	271,400	1,265
Oak Creek	75,657	11.1	5.5	95,464	54,342	60,017	65,358	52,924	15,693	15,348	62.3	238,100	1,115
Oshkosh	51,282	22.9	1.4	70,534	34,352	43,273	47,614	37,405	28,802	26,724	57.1	134,200	786
Racine	44,346	27.6	1.8	54,161	31,532	40,421	43,030	36,367	33,145	30,392	52.4	116,200	860
Sheboygan	52,088	18.7	1.4	63,636	34,020	43,844	48,861	37,547	21,819	20,227	58.8	121,600	708
Stevens Point	46,663	27.0	2.5	73,009	32,697	40,979	48,450	32,582	11,495	10,842	50.2	150,500	764
Sun Prairie	79,566	10.6	4.8	100,234	49,426	56,717	62,634	51,399	14,122	13,596	62.2	249,400	1,131
Superior	48,830	24.5	1.8	70,017	31,709	45,112	50,046	40,899	12,465	11,726	56.2	125,400	773
Waukesha	65,688	15.1	4.8	84,972	39,935	51,053	59,975	43,249	30,918	29,704	56.9	223,600	954
Wausau	47,438	24.1	3.6	64,580	31,914	40,870	44,357	37,724	18,606	17,254	54.3	121,100	767
Wauwatosa	84,306	14.0	10.5	109,112	48,941	66,415	73,936	59,660	21,714	20,474	63.4	251,300	1,121
West Allis	53,634	21.4	1.8	69,260	38,044	45,736	50,402	40,662	29,221	27,431	52.3	148,400	851
West Bend	64,879	16.7	3.1	82,751	35,459	49,262	53,403	42,378	14,171	13,706	65.5	183,300	864
WYOMING	65,304	17.0	5.0	81,290	37,385	50,154	58,120	40,139	278,495	233,231	71.0	228,000	853
Casper	59,412	17.8	5.3	78,108	39,787	48,767	55,545	40,388	27,437	24,850	67.3	213,900	842
Cheyenne	68,611	15.5	4.3	82,444	44,316	51,691	56,327	43,456	30,011	27,599	69.5	229,100	882
Gillette	73,867	16.7	3.6	84,157	42,833	52,217	63,875	39,304	13,950	11,936	71.8	217,400	830

1. Specified owner-occupied units

City	Commuting, 2016–2020[1]		Computer access[2], 2016–2020		Migration, 2016–2020		Civilian labor force, 2021				Civilian Employment, 2016–2020[4]			
	Percent		Percent						Unemployment[3]		Population age 16 and older		Population age 16 to 64	
	Drove alone	Mean travel time to work	With a computer in the house	With Internet access	Percent who lived in the same house one year ago	Percent who lived in another state or county one year ago	Total	Percent change 2020–2021	Total	Rate	Number	Percent in labor force	Number	Percent who worked full-year full-time
	55	56	57	58	59	60	61	62	63	64	65	66	67	68
WASHINGTON—Cont'd														
Moses Lake	79.0	18.3	89.4	81.2	83.8	5.9	12,047	-0.5	849	7.0	17,379	62.1	13,873	55.7
Mount Vernon	75.2	25.8	94.4	90.0	84.0	5.7	16,030	-2.9	1,040	6.5	27,399	61.9	21,486	49.8
Olympia	70.8	21.1	93.2	84.4	74.1	13.0	28,817	-2.1	1,448	5.0	44,424	62.3	34,817	47.5
Pasco	77.0	22.6	94.1	87.7	83.9	7.4	35,480	-0.2	2,399	6.8	52,279	68.1	45,476	51.3
Pullman	55.9	13.2	97.2	85.8	58.6	25.8	15,595	0.7	707	4.5	30,220	58.8	28,192	25.5
Puyallup	78.1	33.0	93.1	86.6	80.1	8.6	23,075	-1.0	1,335	5.8	33,601	65.5	27,374	53.6
Redmond	57.3	25.0	97.7	94.7	77.6	11.9	41,379	1.9	1,338	3.2	53,612	70.9	46,680	57.1
Renton	70.0	31.8	95.9	92.1	80.9	5.9	57,533	-0.8	2,916	5.1	82,282	71.3	70,528	55.6
Richland	79.9	19.8	95.3	90.4	82.0	8.0	30,732	-0.8	1,552	5.1	44,579	64.1	35,715	53.3
Sammamish	64.5	34.1	99.4	98.6	90.1	4.6	33,067	1.2	1,079	3.3	48,393	68.8	43,261	54.7
SeaTac	70.3	27.3	94.5	89.1	82.4	6.4	14,841	-4.1	1,056	7.1	22,658	71.6	19,267	50.7
Seattle	43.4	27.7	96.0	91.6	77.1	9.1	476,937	0.0	17,556	3.7	643,272	73.9	550,476	56.8
Shoreline	64.9	30.8	96.4	90.9	86.2	6.0	31,182	-0.5	1,402	4.5	47,325	65.2	36,261	53.9
Spokane	73.2	20.8	92.6	87.8	78.3	7.4	110,037	-2.0	6,202	5.6	177,265	62.2	142,906	48.0
Spokane Valley	79.1	20.1	92.0	85.1	80.7	6.7	52,744	-1.4	2,928	5.6	79,742	63.8	62,415	51.7
Tacoma	71.8	30.5	92.9	86.4	81.0	8.7	109,504	-1.9	6,994	6.4	175,267	64.9	146,022	51.1
Tumwater	75.9	20.4	94.2	90.6	80.2	7.2	13,254	-1.3	589	4.4	18,789	69.2	16,098	52.0
University Place	79.0	27.8	94.6	91.8	85.0	6.4	17,531	-1.0	860	4.9	26,837	62.4	20,722	51.7
Vancouver	74.9	25.3	94.5	89.0	79.0	8.7	93,713	0.5	5,394	5.8	145,963	64.4	116,399	50.3
Walla Walla	66.9	14.8	91.8	84.7	76.9	12.4	15,940	1.5	818	5.1	27,175	53.6	21,373	36.7
Wenatchee	78.4	17.7	90.9	85.1	83.0	8.4	19,315	0.3	1,098	5.7	26,223	63.5	20,725	50.8
Yakima	80.3	17.4	88.1	81.4	83.7	4.3	48,716	-1.9	3,046	6.3	69,908	60.1	55,808	46.4
WEST VIRGINIA	82.0	26.1	86.2	78.0	88.6	5.2	788,826	0.7	39,694	5.0	1,485,332	53.6	1,125,086	45.8
Charleston	74.8	17.1	89.0	80.8	85.0	6.4	22,113	-0.8	1,166	5.3	39,788	57.7	30,611	49.1
Huntington	72.7	19.1	86.7	72.2	81.5	8.8	19,666	-0.4	1,007	5.1	38,788	51.7	31,183	36.3
Morgantown	64.5	16.6	94.7	87.9	57.4	24.8	15,225	2.3	612	4.0	28,144	57.8	25,246	31.2
Parkersburg	77.0	16.8	83.4	75.8	87.3	3.4	12,061	0.2	701	5.8	24,194	50.6	18,062	41.4
Wheeling	80.1	19.0	80.8	70.7	86.8	7.7	12,424	-0.3	690	5.6	22,508	54.3	16,064	44.9
WISCONSIN	79.9	22.2	90.7	84.5	86.4	5.7	3,134,439	0.9	118,400	3.8	4,682,533	66.1	3,699,734	55.0
Appleton	80.7	18.7	91.5	87.4	86.8	7.9	39,849	0.5	1,282	3.2	58,626	68.9	47,411	55.2
Beloit	81.0	22.0	87.4	78.7	83.8	5.2	17,556	1.8	1,045	6.0	28,133	63.1	22,891	48.9
Brookfield	84.5	21.8	96.0	93.6	89.9	7.1	19,671	0.4	590	3.0	30,655	63.0	22,249	57.1
Caledonia	89.1	25.6	93.5	89.9	88.4	3.8	13,674	0.2	484	3.5	20,576	65.2	16,014	57.4
De Pere	82.1	17.2	94.7	91.2	83.3	9.1	13,757	0.4	442	3.2	20,420	69.1	16,979	53.2
Eau Claire	80.1	16.2	92.8	88.1	77.1	11.1	40,381	1.7	1,283	3.2	57,623	70.7	47,993	49.0
Fitchburg	79.3	20.5	97.0	92.5	83.3	7.5	17,681	2.7	512	2.9	24,033	70.2	20,160	63.9
Fond du Lac	82.0	17.3	88.3	80.2	82.3	7.2	22,976	1.1	838	3.6	34,199	65.1	27,214	52.0
Franklin	83.7	25.1	91.9	87.6	84.8	3.5	18,056	0.6	631	3.5	29,537	58.3	22,831	52.8
Green Bay	79.4	18.1	89.5	82.8	83.7	5.4	53,794	0.1	2,140	4.0	81,545	68.3	68,037	53.5
Greenfield	85.1	23.2	87.7	82.2	86.8	3.6	19,785	-0.2	842	4.3	31,436	65.0	23,239	62.5
Janesville	83.5	21.5	91.4	83.4	87.1	4.1	34,418	0.5	1,507	4.4	51,176	64.6	40,217	52.9
Kenosha	83.9	24.0	90.2	82.9	84.2	5.9	51,283	1.1	2,537	4.9	77,924	67.4	64,609	52.6
La Crosse	74.3	16.1	90.1	81.8	72.9	12.3	29,183	1.5	915	3.1	44,268	63.6	37,090	42.2
Madison	62.5	19.8	95.6	89.0	74.4	10.1	161,915	2.1	4,480	2.8	220,845	71.6	189,936	51.7
Manitowoc	81.9	15.5	88.9	83.6	87.6	3.7	16,046	0.3	607	3.8	26,751	60.2	19,670	55.0
Menomonee Falls	82.8	20.5	92.1	89.5	89.2	6.8	20,885	0.4	640	3.1	30,227	67.5	22,838	61.2
Mequon	76.2	23.6	94.7	92.5	89.0	9.2	12,238	1.2	350	2.9	19,686	59.0	14,164	51.6
Milwaukee	71.9	22.4	87.4	77.0	83.6	4.2	276,567	0.1	17,878	6.5	453,059	64.2	390,564	47.3
Mount Pleasant	83.7	22.4	91.6	87.1	90.5	4.7	14,415	0.3	540	3.7	22,077	60.9	15,835	54.5
Muskego	86.4	25.2	95.1	89.9	93.9	3.0	15,104	0.8	430	2.8	20,181	69.0	16,056	55.1
Neenah	82.5	17.8	91.5	86.8	85.6	6.1	14,311	0.4	461	3.2	19,952	68.5	16,027	58.4
New Berlin	86.6	23.3	94.8	90.8	91.8	5.2	21,693	0.1	672	3.1	32,811	65.0	24,203	60.5
Oak Creek	82.4	23.4	93.9	89.4	87.6	4.2	20,930	0.5	727	3.5	29,604	69.3	24,323	60.6
Oshkosh	81.4	17.8	92.0	85.6	75.6	10.2	34,895	0.8	1,180	3.4	56,292	62.3	46,402	46.3
Racine	80.6	23.4	90.2	82.4	82.7	4.6	35,100	0.3	2,250	6.4	57,929	62.5	48,070	47.7
Sheboygan	81.5	16.4	89.4	84.9	87.2	2.5	25,106	-0.5	903	3.6	37,451	67.4	29,882	56.8
Stevens Point	70.1	16.5	91.4	86.7	71.3	16.8	14,103	0.9	481	3.4	22,634	67.4	19,061	42.5
Sun Prairie	77.6	22.1	95.8	91.4	90.2	3.7	21,092	2.4	690	3.3	26,608	72.2	21,892	61.2
Superior	75.8	17.6	90.2	80.8	82.1	8.1	14,296	-1.4	550	3.8	21,567	66.1	17,434	51.8
Waukesha	81.0	21.5	93.7	89.5	83.7	8.1	41,668	0.3	1,415	3.4	60,011	71.2	49,667	55.7
Wausau	77.4	15.2	90.9	84.0	84.2	5.2	19,840	0.8	734	3.7	31,209	64.3	24,577	53.9
Wauwatosa	81.5	21.0	92.0	86.6	86.2	6.2	27,239	0.3	877	3.2	38,850	66.4	30,149	60.5
West Allis	82.2	21.5	86.5	79.7	86.2	3.6	33,113	-0.8	1,575	4.8	49,469	68.2	40,143	59.1
West Bend	84.0	24.2	90.9	86.5	85.3	5.3	16,818	0.2	580	3.4	25,420	68.5	19,910	61.0
WYOMING	77.4	17.9	93.1	85.5	83.3	7.3	290,404	-1.1	13,032	4.5	461,417	65.1	365,851	54.0
Casper	83.3	16.2	94.0	86.4	86.2	4.3	28,556	-2.5	1,719	6.0	45,909	69.7	36,956	58.0
Cheyenne	82.9	15.0	93.2	86.6	82.1	7.3	31,850	-1.6	1,314	4.1	51,982	64.1	41,091	59.4
Gillette	81.8	18.6	95.8	92.8	82.7	4.3	14,914	-5.0	861	5.8	23,600	70.4	20,661	58.6

1. Employed persons. 2. Households. 3. Percent of civilian labor force. 4. Persons 16 years old and over.

Table D. Cities — **Construction, Wholesale Trade, and Retail Trade**

City	Value of residential construction authorized by building permits, 2021			Wholesale trade[1], 2017				Retail trade[2], 2017			
	New construction ($1,000)	Number of housing units	Percent single family	Number of establishments	Number of employees	Sales (mil dol)	Annual payroll (mil dol)	Number of establish-ments	Number of employees	Sales (mil dol)	Annual payroll (mil dol)
	69	70	71	72	73	74	75	76	77	78	79
WASHINGTON—Cont'd											
Moses Lake	39,425	180	98.9	47	436	284.2	23.4	135	2,036	514.2	52.9
Mount Vernon	21,935	176	22.7	40	604	293.7	30.9	132	2,168	655.4	69.0
Olympia	59,974	263	50.2	47	329	265.6	21.2	362	5,504	1,662.3	161.8
Pasco	145,665	574	98.1	74	1,064	773.2	63.2	161	2,708	1,001.7	99.8
Pullman	65,014	358	13.1	10	177	128.8	7.7	50	1,209	312.5	28.9
Puyallup	35,588	103	98.1	42	571	502.8	30.5	216	5,482	2,233.9	200.7
Redmond	109,718	652	8.3	154	3,422	5,522.2	336.8	249	4,497	1,295.1	144.5
Renton	31,587	97	49.5	113	3,949	3,064.1	271.4	297	5,735	2,118.3	203.4
Richland	153,844	518	78.4	26	298	124.4	12.3	162	2,726	833.9	75.7
Sammamish	26,024	50	100.0	43	84	108.3	5.3	60	680	213.9	21.0
SeaTac	7,326	22	90.9	31	296	176.0	17.6	84	866	225.2	23.0
Seattle	1,927,983	11,980	2.2	1,041	19,093	17,790.2	1,341.2	2,502	39,883	60,443.5	1,782.3
Shoreline	193,687	983	16.3	31	124	62.9	6.3	128	2,759	995.7	98.2
Spokane	120,490	596	58.1	276	3,988	5,882.6	221.5	849	13,695	3,667.6	398.8
Spokane Valley	189,905	1,093	20.3	212	3,496	2,794.0	187.3	482	8,405	2,552.3	263.7
Tacoma	347,832	2,470	10.1	202	2,949	2,395.5	177.4	752	12,652	3,630.0	388.8
Tumwater	32,594	201	66.2	46	692	306.1	35.5	87	1,843	697.8	61.1
University Place	13,561	120	11.7	7	57	24.2	3.3	45	848	222.1	25.7
Vancouver	662,493	2,403	23.8	203	2,268	3,144.8	136.3	588	12,125	3,802.4	408.3
Walla Walla	26,064	156	32.1	30	161	85.1	7.6	132	1,505	353.7	42.4
Wenatchee	26,054	149	29.5	64	1,157	889.6	58.8	199	2,992	807.0	86.9
Yakima	62,632	450	32.7	103	2,417	1,523.0	113.0	344	5,794	1,960.2	181.9
WEST VIRGINIA	778,004	3,692	84.3	1,205	14,578	12,188.8	676.7	5,963	82,985	23,057.8	2,004.1
Charleston	1,702	9	77.8	101	1,097	929.9	55.3	302	5,318	1,348.5	127.6
Huntington	467	4	100.0	65	901	400.0	47.3	209	2,884	755.0	70.0
Morgantown	1,648	3	100.0	24	218	139.7	8.9	233	4,421	1,231.2	99.6
Parkersburg	652	3	100.0	39	357	132.6	13.7	183	3,194	974.8	88.2
Wheeling	13,542	86	2.3	57	1,099	3,863.6	47.4	138	1,595	412.8	39.1
WISCONSIN	5,985,631	25,444	51.9	5,934	104,382	81,566.3	6,129.1	18,908	317,668	91,763.8	8,273.7
Appleton	42,128	121	80.2	96	1,479	5,973.1	96.7	278	4,874	1,360.7	123.4
Beloit	8,813	55	100.0	19	352	230.8	26.2	104	1,761	540.0	45.4
Brookfield	61,726	303	5.9	109	1,689	984.7	113.0	271	5,303	1,065.6	135.5
Caledonia	NA	NA	NA	14	165	103.6	9.9	45	556	158.4	14.1
De Pere	15,081	52	84.6	43	1,034	591.9	61.6	64	1,327	308.8	30.1
Eau Claire	90,406	582	12.2	88	1,472	1,036.1	72.7	318	6,459	1,562.8	146.4
Fitchburg	87,438	371	33.7	28	1,002	568.7	57.0	52	999	269.4	28.0
Fond du Lac	13,796	103	24.3	47	858	577.2	54.4	197	4,289	1,237.1	110.5
Franklin	34,144	98	67.3	41	409	425.7	28.3	79	2,312	666.4	64.1
Green Bay	17,019	60	96.7	114	3,378	2,685.8	185.8	313	5,673	1,640.1	144.9
Greenfield	1,620	10	60.0	13	80	27.4	4.8	152	3,181	1,098.2	96.6
Janesville	65,431	308	44.8	71	1,740	1,273.7	95.3	276	6,749	1,609.4	199.2
Kenosha	43,576	418	6.5	53	897	1,334.0	87.0	290	9,394	4,528.0	272.9
La Crosse	14,901	102	17.6	56	1,406	2,316.7	76.7	243	4,846	1,200.2	116.9
Madison	554,833	3,626	9.0	271	5,246	3,744.1	313.8	946	19,081	6,336.3	530.7
Manitowoc	19,857	149	6.7	23	364	203.6	18.4	142	2,614	584.8	57.9
Menomonee Falls	63,988	204	48.0	90	1,597	844.0	104.9	124	2,867	812.6	74.8
Mequon	31,006	46	91.3	62	915	599.5	57.8	92	1,297	397.0	34.4
Milwaukee	28,055	204	13.7	439	11,197	6,788.3	825.4	D	D	D	D
Mount Pleasant	14,006	38	94.7	17	262	119.7	12.5	81	1,782	574.3	46.1
Muskego	16,652	36	88.9	30	352	98.0	21.7	42	808	186.5	19.3
Neenah	20,485	77	49.4	17	561	280.5	30.8	83	1,904	556.5	47.0
New Berlin	19,749	33	100.0	112	2,516	1,316.9	141.1	99	2,076	565.6	65.2
Oak Creek	10,975	31	67.7	39	2,298	1,576.2	161.6	88	2,244	680.0	52.5
Oshkosh	50,029	516	14.0	50	1,091	541.7	54.1	259	5,404	1,338.0	128.4
Racine	0	0	0.0	47	411	205.9	22.6	240	3,126	584.7	60.8
Sheboygan	9,305	91	7.7	42	889	586.6	42.3	171	3,226	830.5	79.9
Stevens Point	NA	NA	NA	24	372	180.9	17.1	113	1,947	563.3	48.5
Sun Prairie	NA	NA	NA	32	901	420.2	47.2	78	1,923	629.0	50.4
Superior	NA	NA	NA	38	652	978.5	33.7	117	2,027	591.6	57.7
Waukesha	NA	NA	NA	103	2,200	1,237.2	160.4	233	5,326	1,986.3	167.1
Wausau	NA	NA	NA	47	692	363.8	40.9	175	5,863	1,810.9	145.4
Wauwatosa	NA	NA	NA	56	1,110	519.5	60.0	291	5,783	1,144.0	135.3
West Allis	NA	NA	NA	99	2,156	1,409.2	136.1	228	4,008	1,175.5	119.7
West Bend	NA	NA	NA	29	218	95.9	9.4	132	2,525	771.3	65.2
WYOMING	1,058,126	2,706	79.7	696	5,967	6,061.0	342.4	2,583	29,786	9,124.4	852.8
Casper	25,364	126	51.6	92	1,039	2,442.9	63.7	291	4,198	1,158.9	119.8
Cheyenne	63,449	328	70.7	95	626	400.1	35.3	324	5,039	1,586.5	141.2
Gillette	13,463	37	100.0	60	699	413.8	46.6	151	2,171	675.4	64.8

1. Merchant wholesalers except manufacturers' sales branches and offices. 2. Establishments with payroll.

Table D. Cities — Real Estate, Professional Services, and Manufacturing

City	Real estate and rental and leasing, 2017				Professional, scientific, and technical services[1], 2017				Manufacturing, 2017			
	Number of establish-ments	Number of employees	Receipts (mil dol)	Annual payroll (mil dol)	Number of establish-ments	Number of employees	Receipts (mil dol)	Annual payroll (mil dol)	Number of establish-ments	Number of employees	Receipts (mil dol)	Annual payroll (mil dol)
	80	81	82	83	84	85	86	87	88	89	90	91
WASHINGTON—Cont'd												
Moses Lake	45	128	17.6	3.3	57	266	34.0	12.3	NA	NA	NA	NA
Mount Vernon	53	148	34.5	5.0	103	540	74.8	23.6	NA	NA	NA	NA
Olympia	109	425	123.1	18.0	D	D	D	D	NA	NA	NA	NA
Pasco	69	D	98.3	D	80	505	78.1	28.6	NA	NA	NA	NA
Pullman	43	252	34.8	6.4	41	273	30.2	12.9	NA	NA	NA	NA
Puyallup	112	431	193.2	20.0	118	885	94.4	49.1	NA	NA	NA	NA
Redmond	171	1,051	370.8	79.6	487	11,054	2,278.8	974.6	NA	NA	NA	NA
Renton	157	548	222.9	28.0	246	1,705	251.9	107.1	NA	NA	NA	NA
Richland	102	298	72.9	10.8	203	6,935	1,635.1	660.8	NA	NA	NA	NA
Sammamish	D	D	D	D	255	701	170.6	64.9	NA	NA	NA	NA
SeaTac	58	823	311.0	36.7	31	279	47.5	20.3	NA	NA	NA	NA
Seattle	2,133	12,440	3,881.3	779.8	5,375	82,213	18,758.2	7,648.8	NA	NA	NA	NA
Shoreline	84	268	145.5	12.8	128	516	65.6	25.6	NA	NA	NA	NA
Spokane	342	1,885	414.9	69.6	786	6,065	1,007.1	395.4	NA	NA	NA	NA
Spokane Valley	147	892	212.8	35.1	200	1,291	173.7	66.0	NA	NA	NA	NA
Tacoma	301	1,573	404.2	71.5	529	3,905	669.7	270.5	NA	NA	NA	NA
Tumwater	53	164	51.5	7.4	71	356	44.9	16.6	NA	NA	NA	NA
University Place	D	D	D	D	73	243	33.5	15.1	NA	NA	NA	NA
Vancouver	347	1,708	394.3	79.0	608	4,989	898.3	349.8	NA	NA	NA	NA
Walla Walla	44	154	29.3	6.2	81	412	52.6	20.1	NA	NA	NA	NA
Wenatchee	62	264	51.7	10.4	127	812	104.9	43.9	NA	NA	NA	NA
Yakima	163	746	132.9	24.7	215	1,522	235.9	89.6	NA	NA	NA	NA
WEST VIRGINIA	1,432	6,061	1,368.8	228.9	2,813	22,856	3,295.2	1,218.3	1,142	48,533	24,602.1	2,747.7
Charleston	129	607	176.3	26.7	368	3,580	684.9	231.0	NA	NA	NA	NA
Huntington	72	358	62.2	11.6	138	1,534	164.4	62.0	NA	NA	NA	NA
Morgantown	73	342	70.4	10.9	131	1,879	382.6	121.4	NA	NA	NA	NA
Parkersburg	48	212	52.3	7.7	80	524	67.2	24.7	NA	NA	NA	NA
Wheeling	48	D	38.4	D	128	1,957	259.6	102.6	NA	NA	NA	NA
WISCONSIN	4,956	27,163	5,908.1	1,105.8	11,553	106,041	18,879.6	7,306.9	8,837	455,538	171,896.3	25,180.6
Appleton	D	D	D	D	166	1,617	239.7	104.3	NA	NA	NA	NA
Beloit	19	141	75.3	9.7	41	1,084	28.7	102.1	NA	NA	NA	NA
Brookfield	111	1,494	232.0	64.2	314	4,513	933.3	417.8	NA	NA	NA	NA
Caledonia	12	54	12.5	1.7	35	133	12.4	6.2	NA	NA	NA	NA
De Pere	22	122	23.4	5.0	72	733	185.9	58.4	NA	NA	NA	NA
Eau Claire	96	541	81.3	17.5	151	1,328	189.1	74.7	NA	NA	NA	NA
Fitchburg	44	233	52.4	9.4	86	567	89.9	35.6	NA	NA	NA	NA
Fond du Lac	28	228	32.0	8.9	74	1,201	129.5	94.8	NA	NA	NA	NA
Franklin	29	130	26.8	4.1	61	416	72.4	19.3	NA	NA	NA	NA
Green Bay	87	637	132.3	26.8	212	2,075	365.3	134.1	NA	NA	NA	NA
Greenfield	44	198	52.7	8.4	77	707	60.8	31.2	NA	NA	NA	NA
Janesville	62	225	40.9	6.9	101	837	91.9	35.8	NA	NA	NA	NA
Kenosha	72	375	72.9	13.4	136	717	94.9	32.1	NA	NA	NA	NA
La Crosse	87	915	111.2	30.4	152	1,406	146.4	73.9	NA	NA	NA	NA
Madison	416	3,311	777.0	153.4	1,074	15,405	3,578.3	1,440.8	NA	NA	NA	NA
Manitowoc	D	D	D	D	53	400	62.2	20.2	NA	NA	NA	NA
Menomonee Falls	23	422	76.2	38.0	96	891	112.6	56.0	NA	NA	NA	NA
Mequon	D	D	D	D	148	823	163.5	63.0	NA	NA	NA	NA
Milwaukee	471	3,767	1,074.8	194.0	1,148	17,420	3,546.5	1,476.5	NA	NA	NA	NA
Mount Pleasant	27	135	24.0	4.8	59	414	50.1	26.0	NA	NA	NA	NA
Muskego	18	50	6.2	1.7	53	145	26.6	8.2	NA	NA	NA	NA
Neenah	24	167	95.8	7.8	50	562	52.5	43.7	NA	NA	NA	NA
New Berlin	39	125	45.7	5.7	122	2,110	399.7	83.7	NA	NA	NA	NA
Oak Creek	27	358	96.0	18.9	48	399	60.5	23.0	NA	NA	NA	NA
Oshkosh	60	366	66.1	12.0	95	1,604	704.5	79.1	NA	NA	NA	NA
Racine	D	D	D	D	101	657	73.4	36.5	NA	NA	NA	NA
Sheboygan	31	112	23.6	3.6	85	690	108.0	33.1	NA	NA	NA	NA
Stevens Point	27	122	19.2	3.6	61	451	71.2	24.6	NA	NA	NA	NA
Sun Prairie	38	155	36.9	6.0	89	516	86.3	29.4	NA	NA	NA	NA
Superior	31	D	21.5	D	58	365	30.4	15.1	NA	NA	NA	NA
Waukesha	58	539	138.8	16.1	170	1,218	218.6	83.2	NA	NA	NA	NA
Wausau	42	208	33.6	7.2	121	865	130.0	56.1	NA	NA	NA	NA
Wauwatosa	51	222	62.8	11.8	240	2,106	370.7	126.8	NA	NA	NA	NA
West Allis	50	255	75.6	11.6	86	863	157.2	63.4	NA	NA	NA	NA
West Bend	D	D	D	D	58	534	65.7	28.6	NA	NA	NA	NA
WYOMING	1,199	4,777	1,216.5	220.4	2,395	9,589	1,538.7	532.4	581	9,354	7,897.7	643.3
Casper	138	551	114.9	23.4	216	1,190	230.6	74.4	NA	NA	NA	NA
Cheyenne	145	577	167.3	27.2	520	2,272	337.7	125.4	NA	NA	NA	NA
Gillette	72	328	151.2	20.5	103	486	64.6	22.7	NA	NA	NA	NA

1. Establishments subject to federal tax.

Table D. Cities — **Accommodation and Food Services, Arts, Entertainment, and Recreation, and Health Care and Social Assistance**

City	Accommodation and food services, 2017				Arts, entertainment, and recreation[1], 2017				Health care and social assistance[1], 2017			
	Number of establish-ments	Number of employees	Receipts (mil dol)	Annual payroll (mil dol)	Number of establish-ments	Number of employees	Receipts (mil dol)	Annual payroll (mil dol)	Number of establish-ments	Number of employees	Receipts (mil dol)	Annual payroll (mil dol)
	92	93	94	95	96	97	98	99	100	101	102	103
WASHINGTON—Cont'd												
Moses Lake	83	1,471	87.7	24.8	10.0	208	10.2	3.7	103	2,159	251.8	88.2
Mount Vernon	94	1,312	77.2	24.4	16.0	359	15.3	6.3	151	4,991	626.7	277.9
Olympia	221	3,978	227.0	74.8	31.0	505	26.2	8.6	475	10,295	1,369.5	535.6
Pasco	105	1,625	96.1	26.5	D	D	D	D	126	1,987	190.0	90.1
Pullman	98	1,651	75.1	22.5	D	D	D	D	72	1,467	147.2	67.2
Puyallup	149	3,139	191.9	60.4	20.0	640	51.7	13.3	213	5,725	1,021.1	377.7
Redmond	295	5,942	509.0	169.0	37.0	692	38.2	13.8	250	3,359	434.0	164.4
Renton	282	4,099	327.5	91.8	24.0	904	487.2	275.7	362	8,124	1,233.6	559.9
Richland	156	3,019	182.7	55.6	32.0	652	23.9	8.9	242	5,653	818.5	326.1
Sammamish	40	658	45.4	13.5	23.0	463	21.0	8.7	99	700	64.2	27.1
SeaTac	113	3,690	452.8	124.6	3.0	599	23.9	8.0	42	1,090	108.9	31.0
Seattle	3,159	58,136	4,918.0	1,564.5	591.0	12,795	1,634.9	604.7	2,912	85,733	13,241.7	5,228.7
Shoreline	102	1,139	78.2	23.6	31.0	823	69.6	23.2	217	2,973	268.7	113.8
Spokane	642	12,036	702.7	233.6	95.0	1,696	82.3	29.7	956	29,351	3,805.7	1,483.1
Spokane Valley	226	3,918	269.4	75.9	32.0	463	26.4	8.6	374	7,637	779.2	361.9
Tacoma	541	9,576	600.3	193.6	77.0	2,714	323.4	84.3	673	27,464	4,362.3	1,778.2
Tumwater	71	1,107	66.0	19.5	11.0	231	12.0	4.2	105	1,179	108.3	46.5
University Place	40	697	35.5	11.6	D	D	D	D	100	1,095	85.2	35.2
Vancouver	494	8,677	556.8	168.0	62.0	1,091	61.5	17.8	693	15,603	1,793.9	753.9
Walla Walla	112	1,801	105.8	33.2	16.0	319	15.0	6.1	127	4,493	549.2	238.1
Wenatchee	129	1,974	119.7	37.9	19.0	245	10.2	3.6	154	5,506	854.5	373.2
Yakima	244	4,118	251.8	77.9	40.0	816	43.2	18.3	374	10,187	1,355.9	525.0
WEST VIRGINIA	3,614	68,102	4,069.1	1,075.6	775.0	6,681	487.7	107.9	4,869	132,627	15,236.9	5,844.2
Charleston	222	4,558	261.6	74.5	43.0	803	53.4	14.1	369	12,200	1,999.5	744.1
Huntington	189	3,616	166.3	51.1	28.0	561	19.4	6.9	NA	NA	NA	NA
Morgantown	225	4,566	212.9	60.3	31.0	279	14.9	3.9	135	10,407	1,409.0	527.8
Parkersburg	120	2,298	103.2	33.2	27.0	348	29.1	4.4	176	5,377	533.1	198.9
Wheeling	97	2,162	199.4	37.8	31.0	358	26.6	7.1	NA	NA	NA	NA
WISCONSIN	14,840	244,099	13,496.3	3,688.3	2,809.0	47,048	3,493.7	1,218.4	15,983	417,365	48,477.9	19,198.4
Appleton	217	4,163	206.4	58.9	31.0	1,106	37.8	14.0	296	9,061	1,093.1	476.7
Beloit	95	1,738	89.7	25.3	D	D	D	D	63	2,108	390.8	131.9
Brookfield	130	3,419	206.2	57.6	33.0	709	36.0	13.3	388	5,085	650.8	301.8
Caledonia	D	D	D	D	9.0	66	3.5	1.2	28	359	22.4	9.7
De Pere	70	1,062	44.9	13.4	D	D	D	D	51	850	68.8	34.1
Eau Claire	229	4,861	213.8	64.8	41.0	1,034	50.6	10.3	269	8,306	980.9	355.9
Fitchburg	45	984	53.1	15.3	19.0	403	14.2	4.5	59	2,084	189.7	78.1
Fond du Lac	116	2,144	104.4	28.9	19.0	473	32.1	6.4	199	5,515	753.8	264.6
Franklin	64	1,110	53.5	17.0	19.0	196	11.1	3.5	115	2,156	271.0	105.3
Green Bay	255	5,340	266.5	75.5	44.0	D	499.3	D	331	16,466	2,489.0	838.3
Greenfield	70	1,987	94.9	29.3	14.0	418	12.7	3.5	154	2,823	279.8	115.3
Janesville	165	3,467	167.9	46.2	27.0	436	20.4	6.6	186	5,385	709.8	301.4
Kenosha	229	4,304	204.6	58.9	23.0	495	30.3	7.4	345	7,213	737.8	313.3
La Crosse	227	4,549	212.9	62.8	45.0	912	36.1	10.6	186	9,192	1,144.5	496.7
Madison	808	17,393	960.2	292.7	156.0	2,474	159.4	49.6	741	39,689	5,638.7	2,305.9
Manitowoc	99	1,559	71.3	20.1	15.0	341	16.4	4.6	124	3,288	264.6	123.3
Menomonee Falls	72	1,570	78.6	23.9	22.0	486	18.3	6.2	82	4,159	457.9	189.1
Mequon	49	1,144	56.0	18.3	28.0	519	29.6	10.7	149	3,427	370.2	145.8
Milwaukee	1,229	26,656	1,947.3	483.9	164.0	6,049	829.5	354.9	1,744	61,852	7,646.2	2,756.2
Mount Pleasant	64	1,435	76.6	20.2	6.0	155	6.7	2.4	124	2,099	253.5	98.5
Muskego	42	643	28.9	8.6	11.0	105	6.6	2.0	39	642	58.2	23.9
Neenah	87	1,283	62.2	19.1	17.0	479	10.3	4.5	93	1,554	164.0	71.9
New Berlin	63	1,410	64.6	20.7	21.0	593	23.7	7.4	105	2,009	177.0	86.6
Oak Creek	73	1,672	84.8	23.6	12.0	80	3.3	1.1	71	714	68.3	29.1
Oshkosh	200	4,194	175.8	52.2	34.0	606	20.4	7.5	201	5,961	630.4	270.0
Racine	D	D	D	D	35.0	294	32.2	8.0	207	5,788	474.1	193.7
Sheboygan	140	2,347	116.0	34.5	22.0	491	19.9	7.0	196	4,863	612.2	238.1
Stevens Point	121	1,912	83.1	25.3	20.0	611	17.7	7.4	133	3,890	397.7	157.0
Sun Prairie	73	1,429	65.9	20.0	D	D	D	D	75	1,486	127.2	53.8
Superior	100	1,528	62.1	18.9	D	D	D	D	94	1,776	127.6	54.2
Waukesha	163	2,998	153.0	44.7	37.0	807	23.4	7.5	275	6,515	933.7	300.1
Wausau	117	2,122	100.9	29.7	27.0	476	19.1	6.3	232	7,274	1,108.3	401.6
Wauwatosa	155	3,902	200.0	62.8	26.0	674	32.9	9.6	384	12,197	1,526.6	570.3
West Allis	163	2,383	122.2	33.3	11.0	345	10.0	2.8	233	8,225	891.8	381.3
West Bend	72	1,479	66.3	18.0	18.0	459	13.6	5.3	120	1,658	129.0	51.9
WYOMING	1,839	27,248	1,946.0	556.4	445.0	4,791	384.3	107.2	2,001	33,540	3,871.9	1,657.4
Casper	158	3,086	170.9	52.2	35.0	327	19.5	6.0	317	5,458	731.8	306.5
Cheyenne	181	3,277	201.3	56.8	31.0	448	32.3	7.4	322	6,534	852.7	371.2
Gillette	99	1,713	89.4	28.0	16.0	148	6.1	2.0	107	2,083	274.8	119.8

1. Establishments subject to federal tax.

City	Other services[1]				Government employment and payroll, 2017								
						March payroll							
							Perent of total for:						
	Number of establish-ments	Number of employees	Receipts (mil dol)	Annual payroll (mil dol)	Full-time equivalent employees	Total (dollars)	Admin-istrative, judicial, and legal	Police and corrections	Fire protection	Highways and trans-portation	Health and welfare	Natural resources and utilities	Education and libraries
	104	105	106	107	108	109	110	111	112	113	114	115	116
WASHINGTON—Cont'd													
Moses Lake	66	271	25.8	6.8	193	1,114,960	7.5	25.8	13.1	2.8	9.1	22.9	0.0
Mount Vernon	83	352	39.4	11.9	210	1,455,600	14.6	29.7	19.8	8.6	4.7	16.0	4.5
Olympia	205	1,473	237.3	74.2	551	3,953,470	18.5	21.3	20.7	4.5	5.7	21.1	0.0
Pasco	D	D	D	D	296	1,995,450	11.3	31.5	27.9	6.9	0.0	20.5	0.0
Pullman	40	179	15.9	5.3	260	1,300,701	12.6	21.3	22.6	20.5	0.0	14.3	5.0
Puyallup	118	918	102.3	33.3	281	1,790,507	24.2	35.9	0.0	10.0	0.0	24.2	4.4
Redmond	162	1,043	113.0	41.2	663	4,945,324	26.5	18.0	28.4	2.9	0.0	16.7	0.0
Renton	189	1,039	102.9	34.8	925	6,233,220	9.2	38.4	20.7	6.2	0.6	14.9	0.0
Richland	89	553	61.3	19.1	479	3,366,979	11.0	18.5	16.9	1.6	1.3	33.2	1.7
Sammamish	37	182	14.6	5.1	102	675,663	21.7	0.4	0.0	22.6	20.2	22.4	0.0
SeaTac	73	836	110.5	31.6	115	755,800	40.7	0.8	0.0	24.5	3.0	16.1	0.0
Seattle	2,080	15,523	7,433.0	858.6	11,912	94,722,910	16.9	18.6	11.2	6.8	3.5	35.8	3.4
Shoreline	89	448	42.5	13.9	175	943,320	56.5	0.0	0.0	15.1	0.0	24.4	0.0
Spokane	458	2,736	306.3	86.0	2,145	13,755,462	13.5	23.9	20.9	6.7	0.9	26.0	2.9
Spokane Valley	207	1,477	163.7	52.6	90	563,427	64.4	0.0	0.0	21.1	0.0	14.5	0.0
Tacoma	453	3,393	438.0	123.6	3,566	27,168,562	11.2	12.0	13.6	9.5	2.5	44.6	1.9
Tumwater	64	401	42.1	12.9	188	1,294,050	20.3	21.0	26.9	11.0	0.0	16.1	0.0
University Place	60	262	24.6	8.4	48	380,073	66.6	0.0	0.0	29.5	0.0	3.9	0.0
Vancouver	404	2,443	366.9	81.0	1,065	6,647,181	12.7	25.6	25.6	6.2	0.0	20.3	0.0
Walla Walla	71	324	35.3	9.5	302	1,791,859	16.0	27.3	22.3	9.5	0.8	18.6	3.3
Wenatchee	109	452	55.9	14.7	155	925,754	11.9	32.3	0.0	6.7	5.1	14.0	0.0
Yakima	177	1,101	108.9	29.9	689	4,349,766	14.2	31.5	20.8	9.0	1.0	17.1	0.0
WEST VIRGINIA	2,524	14,894	1,896.8	465.2	X	X	X	X	X	X	X	X	X
Charleston	205	1,383	186.5	56.4	817	3,163,140	14.0	28.2	22.0	9.1	1.3	12.0	0.0
Huntington	86	503	70.4	15.8	322	1,195,342	11.3	39.6	27.3	4.2	2.0	7.7	0.0
Morgantown	81	652	183.9	21.8	440	1,827,342	5.9	24.3	13.4	11.1	0.0	35.1	3.6
Parkersburg	97	604	63.1	16.5	364	1,227,450	11.3	25.6	18.5	8.8	1.5	32.0	0.0
Wheeling	98	893	94.0	29.4	746	2,380,152	3.3	13.9	15.6	7.1	2.0	56.2	0.0
WISCONSIN	10,351	63,120	9,240.8	2,069.4	X	X	X	X	X	X	X	X	X
Appleton	139	1,292	140.5	49.0	648	3,496,019	10.3	25.2	17.1	7.8	4.2	15.7	6.3
Beloit	50	254	19.1	5.7	364	1,992,675	10.0	27.6	20.5	14.2	3.9	15.1	5.5
Brookfield	136	1,163	120.6	38.0	335	2,052,842	11.7	27.8	22.6	7.6	1.4	13.1	5.8
Caledonia	30	244	15.7	6.9	131	714,743	6.2	27.2	31.1	13.6	18.4	1.7	0.0
De Pere	41	313	31.4	7.4	148	854,071	17.6	32.6	21.8	9.0	2.9	13.2	0.0
Eau Claire	141	1,045	86.5	25.1	605	3,089,358	9.0	25.3	17.6	16.3	10.8	12.9	5.0
Fitchburg	41	471	45.7	16.5	190	974,003	18.2	37.1	14.6	5.1	3.0	7.7	7.2
Fond du Lac	92	634	58.6	16.5	335	1,792,502	8.0	28.0	22.7	13.6	1.5	14.1	7.1
Franklin	52	568	46.8	17.0	223	1,298,124	8.0	34.4	26.4	11.5	3.2	2.1	4.6
Green Bay	164	1,003	116.1	29.5	887	4,787,549	6.9	33.8	24.7	10.4	1.1	19.3	0.0
Greenfield	76	451	35.7	12.9	243	1,425,578	10.9	36.4	25.4	13.7	2.4	5.7	4.0
Janesville	121	685	56.5	15.8	564	2,898,547	7.2	25.2	21.3	14.1	4.1	12.4	12.7
Kenosha	153	1,037	77.9	25.4	830	4,343,227	5.8	28.2	22.2	10.6	2.7	18.1	7.6
La Crosse	121	989	126.6	36.4	613	2,798,236	11.4	21.5	19.2	15.4	0.0	13.8	8.5
Madison	645	5,782	1,189.3	262.0	2,789	13,351,958	8.7	28.1	15.4	21.6	1.9	11.0	4.1
Manitowoc	72	310	34.3	7.3	353	1,846,790	5.5	22.1	17.5	11.2	0.0	37.6	5.2
Menomonee Falls	71	672	48.1	15.8	91	437,223	16.8	35.8	15.3	11.3	3.3	9.5	6.8
Mequon	69	452	48.1	13.9	147	724,418	8.7	36.2	10.7	18.0	2.6	10.8	0.0
Milwaukee	846	6,350	2,493.6	245.4	6,507	37,635,419	7.8	42.5	16.2	7.4	4.0	14.5	2.9
Mount Pleasant	D	D	D	D	146	801,664	5.6	32.8	45.0	8.2	0.5	5.4	0.0
Muskego	51	243	15.6	5.6	120	672,448	13.7	46.5	0.0	16.0	3.8	11.8	7.4
Neenah	55	370	33.7	12.8	261	1,435,666	7.9	23.3	28.1	15.5	3.3	15.6	6.2
New Berlin	76	834	90.2	34.1	252	1,462,929	11.6	38.4	18.7	10.1	0.0	11.6	4.6
Oak Creek	50	303	24.5	7.9	286	1,625,666	11.4	31.8	22.3	8.7	2.1	14.7	2.8
Oshkosh	100	870	104.9	30.2	585	4,170,961	7.4	25.0	24.4	19.4	2.1	12.2	4.7
Racine	119	786	56.8	18.0	782	4,263,192	6.4	32.1	20.3	9.9	5.1	20.5	3.6
Sheboygan	100	523	38.8	11.8	432	2,262,569	7.3	27.6	19.5	15.5	2.1	18.2	5.8
Stevens Point	63	384	52.1	13.0	233	1,262,902	6.8	32.3	20.1	19.0	1.3	19.7	0.0
Sun Prairie	64	391	30.9	10.2	237	1,186,258	15.9	29.6	0.0	7.8	7.8	24.1	7.1
Superior	D	D	D	D	265	1,368,991	6.5	28.8	17.1	8.5	2.4	21.6	5.1
Waukesha	138	957	105.0	30.4	575	3,333,088	10.7	28.3	19.7	16.2	0.3	16.9	5.6
Wausau	75	425	53.6	12.7	314	1,558,210	11.7	30.0	21.8	22.6	3.6	7.8	0.0
Wauwatosa	104	808	148.1	29.7	410	2,437,615	9.3	30.2	28.9	11.1	3.8	9.4	4.0
West Allis	119	828	130.5	32.3	542	3,010,688	9.3	29.5	21.3	9.5	8.7	10.0	3.1
West Bend	84	582	41.6	13.7	234	1,051,988	12.4	34.5	19.9	6.5	0.9	15.2	5.4
WYOMING	1,368	6,245	931.2	221.4	X	X	X	X	X	X	X	X	X
Casper	160	826	116.8	29.0	496	2,420,062	12.8	27.5	16.6	7.0	1.7	28.3	0.0
Cheyenne	176	1,042	112.9	32.6	638	2,712,553	11.3	26.7	19.8	12.6	2.9	20.6	0.0
Gillette	86	475	77.8	23.1	303	1,429,261	20.3	28.0	0.0	4.0	0.0	28.0	0.0

1. Establishments subject to federal tax.

City	City government finances, 2017 — General revenue: Total (mil dol)	General revenue — Intergovernmental: Total (mil dol)	General revenue — Intergovernmental: Percent from state government	General revenue — Taxes: Total (mil dol)	General revenue — Taxes: Per capita[1] (dollars): Total	General revenue — Taxes: Per capita[1] (dollars): Property	General revenue — Taxes: Per capita[1] (dollars): Sales and gross receipts	General expenditure: Total (mil dol)	General expenditure — Per capita[1] (dollars): Total	General expenditure — Per capita[1] (dollars): Capital outlays
	117	118	119	120	121	122	123	124	125	126
WASHINGTON—Cont'd										
Moses Lake	36.9	1.4	84.3	18.2	780	282	476	32.9	1,411	7
Mount Vernon	47.9	2.8	92.6	23.8	677	212	429	48.5	1,379	150
Olympia	126.6	11.5	35.9	68.2	1,320	288	984	125.2	2,424	259
Pasco	83.7	5.0	79.2	37.8	519	109	387	73.8	1,013	126
Pullman	53.8	19.2	15.8	19.8	590	220	359	32.2	958	156
Puyallup	72.8	5.7	96.6	41.6	1,015	218	746	61.8	1,508	337
Redmond	185.4	25.0	35.3	98.5	1,518	369	1,022	163.0	2,512	562
Renton	253.4	57.8	30.8	111.4	1,092	364	670	198.6	1,948	240
Richland	97.0	11.9	53.5	51.3	906	298	562	100.1	1,766	163
Sammamish	88.7	3.5	66.2	49.0	755	422	232	46.9	722	128
SeaTac	61.9	13.1	53.4	41.7	1,425	500	882	55.1	1,882	504
Seattle	2,791.7	256.3	67.1	1,432.8	1,966	746	1,085	2,586.2	3,549	749
Shoreline	54.2	9.7	62.3	35.9	635	221	354	48.6	860	140
Spokane	411.8	42.1	62.2	171.7	790	318	446	404.4	1,860	278
Spokane Valley	59.5	12.0	93.4	42.9	439	117	298	61.2	627	191
Tacoma	584.1	62.6	36.7	224.1	1,050	349	656	560.1	2,625	341
Tumwater	47.8	1.8	99.1	27.3	1,191	389	775	40.5	1,762	238
University Place	28.5	6.8	100.0	16.0	479	121	321	29.9	895	256
Vancouver	284.4	29.9	49.8	143.3	794	249	506	239.2	1,326	217
Walla Walla	66.9	6.5	66.8	26.3	800	217	533	68.6	2,087	401
Wenatchee	48.3	5.8	72.5	25.7	750	98	620	36.3	1,060	127
Yakima	142.6	25.8	29.2	69.0	738	194	525	114.5	1,225	122
WEST VIRGINIA	X	X	X	X	X	X	X	X	X	X
Charleston	151.7	9.0	41.9	84.4	1,758	299	1,459	168.9	3,516	1,075
Huntington	70.6	6.4	38.9	30.7	657	126	532	73.0	1,562	18
Morgantown	65.2	1.6	40.9	27.9	902	187	715	63.4	2,048	578
Parkersburg	40.8	1.6	12.9	15.7	521	195	320	39.5	1,314	114
Wheeling	79.8	3.6	58.0	27.5	1,025	240	777	75.4	2,809	135
WISCONSIN	X	X	X	X	X	X	X	X	X	X
Appleton	109.9	32.9	58.2	46.1	619	554	59	111.6	1,498	325
Beloit	63.9	24.7	88.6	23.4	636	590	45	60.9	1,654	228
Brookfield	62.9	7.1	60.6	42.1	1,105	984	120	67.7	1,780	121
Caledonia	29.5	4.3	77.4	14.0	556	523	32	41.3	1,644	557
De Pere	33.0	4.4	91.4	15.0	599	564	32	38.2	1,525	488
Eau Claire	93.8	23.9	66.4	44.5	648	580	63	94.5	1,378	226
Fitchburg	39.1	5.0	84.8	27.1	918	878	40	37.8	1,281	387
Fond du Lac	61.0	15.6	68.2	27.3	640	576	60	58.0	1,358	165
Franklin	38.4	4.5	76.7	25.4	702	642	60	37.9	1,049	122
Green Bay	147.7	42.2	72.8	59.3	565	535	28	144.1	1,373	160
Greenfield	41.5	5.6	81.8	24.5	666	620	45	60.4	1,641	626
Janesville	90.4	18.7	60.4	41.0	637	576	60	109.5	1,702	522
Kenosha	146.4	31.1	73.3	81.9	821	777	41	129.9	1,302	158
La Crosse	101.1	25.7	78.4	47.6	920	820	81	94.8	1,833	332
Madison	481.5	105.0	66.8	246.0	962	874	83	423.1	1,654	173
Manitowoc	52.5	15.2	62.8	18.8	577	532	43	43.2	1,324	171
Menomonee Falls	51.2	4.7	93.6	31.0	828	708	121	57.9	1,547	173
Mequon	30.2	2.8	85.0	22.4	934	870	61	45.1	1,880	421
Milwaukee	940.5	378.3	76.2	286.3	482	454	28	1,116.7	1,881	235
Mount Pleasant	38.4	5.5	57.7	20.1	745	694	50	39.5	1,465	219
Muskego	25.8	3.1	90.3	13.7	550	526	22	33.9	1,356	173
Neenah	37.5	6.7	71.5	20.9	806	770	36	38.2	1,473	193
New Berlin	48.5	4.6	85.5	26.0	654	611	42	58.6	1,474	204
Oak Creek	47.8	10.2	93.6	25.5	704	593	106	59.4	1,637	456
Oshkosh	98.4	24.3	79.3	42.5	637	592	42	105.2	1,578	227
Racine	141.7	50.4	80.1	55.9	725	693	30	145.3	1,882	202
Sheboygan	61.7	19.8	84.6	27.6	570	491	69	62.9	1,302	129
Stevens Point	43.4	9.9	69.1	17.1	652	589	57	40.8	1,555	329
Sun Prairie	41.0	5.3	86.9	24.2	733	689	40	36.3	1,103	154
Superior	56.6	22.0	89.6	15.3	582	499	77	47.8	1,821	230
Waukesha	113.0	24.2	80.1	63.7	879	820	50	104.3	1,438	307
Wausau	56.4	13.8	85.6	30.0	776	719	47	65.2	1,684	572
Wauwatosa	76.9	10.3	65.6	45.7	952	876	68	92.5	1,927	439
West Allis	89.6	23.4	64.6	43.8	732	685	32	84.3	1,408	88
West Bend	37.9	6.8	77.3	23.6	747	688	52	32.4	1,029	110
WYOMING	X	X	X	X	X	X	X	X	X	X
Casper	109.5	52.4	65.1	11.7	202	98	90	121.0	2,092	543
Cheyenne	116.7	64.2	51.9	15.5	244	102	136	110.4	1,739	488
Gillette	101.0	65.0	73.3	4.1	127	99	28	67.6	2,098	414

1. Based on population estimated as of July 1 of the year shown.

Table D. Cities — **City Government Finances**

City	City government finances, 2017 (cont.)												
	General expenditure (cont.)												
	Percent of total for:										Debt outstanding		
	Public welfare	Highways	Parking facilities	Education	Health and hospitals	Police protection	Sewerage and sanitation	Parks and recreation	Housing and community development	Interest on debt	Total (mil dol)	Per capita[1] (dollars)	Debt issued during year
	127	128	129	130	131	132	133	134	135	136	137	138	139
WASHINGTON—Cont'd													
Moses Lake	0.0	10.8	0.0	0.0	5.4	18.2	18.7	12.3	0.8	2.5	30.0	1,286	2.7
Mount Vernon	0.1	13.4	0.0	0.0	0.4	14.9	33.2	2.3	1.1	3.3	38.6	1,096	3.2
Olympia	0.0	5.2	0.0	0.0	0.0	11.5	28.6	11.1	0.2	2.9	98.6	1,909	7.3
Pasco	0.0	7.0	0.0	0.0	8.0	19.2	11.7	9.1	1.6	1.8	67.7	930	8.6
Pullman	0.0	7.2	0.0	0.0	6.6	18.7	18.2	9.9	0.1	0.7	9.4	279	0.0
Puyallup	0.0	12.7	0.0	0.0	0.4	26.3	23.2	5.3	3.1	4.5	67.5	1,646	8.1
Redmond	0.0	14.0	0.0	0.0	4.2	12.8	18.9	7.6	1.2	1.5	136.5	2,105	31.0
Renton	0.6	11.2	0.0	0.0	0.4	12.9	26.1	6.5	1.0	3.5	144.1	1,413	8.9
Richland	0.0	9.2	0.0	0.0	3.5	11.4	14.8	5.3	4.8	1.8	196.5	3,469	12.1
Sammamish	0.0	20.6	0.0	0.0	0.5	14.1	7.6	17.7	1.9	0.3	2.8	43	0.1
SeaTac	1.3	30.4	0.0	0.0	0.7	17.6	2.5	3.3	1.6	0.4	4.5	152	0.7
Seattle	4.0	17.0	0.5	1.8	0.5	8.3	20.9	9.8	2.8	2.4	5,049.0	6,929	671.4
Shoreline	0.0	15.8	0.0	0.0	0.7	27.0	5.6	8.8	0.0	3.5	44.9	794	5.2
Spokane	2.3	11.2	0.0	0.0	0.3	14.1	32.5	7.1	1.0	2.0	408.0	1,877	34.7
Spokane Valley	0.1	27.3	0.0	0.0	0.7	30.8	2.9	4.7	3.3	0.7	20.0	205	8.4
Tacoma	0.0	9.7	0.7	0.0	0.8	15.3	22.2	3.0	3.0	4.8	1,703.7	7,983	197.3
Tumwater	0.0	14.9	0.0	0.0	0.0	14.6	23.8	6.1	2.4	1.8	19.1	833	1.6
University Place	0.0	58.3	0.1	0.0	0.4	12.0	0.0	3.4	3.3	7.0	42.0	1,256	19.7
Vancouver	0.0	13.8	0.7	0.0	0.4	16.9	14.0	7.1	3.0	2.8	180.5	1,000	9.3
Walla Walla	0.0	10.5	0.0	0.0	8.3	12.5	23.0	12.6	0.0	3.0	69.8	2,124	22.3
Wenatchee	3.2	14.7	0.0	0.0	0.6	17.7	14.7	11.7	2.4	2.7	38.2	1,117	9.0
Yakima	0.0	9.6	0.1	0.0	0.3	20.9	20.1	7.1	1.1	1.3	90.6	969	2.6
WEST VIRGINIA	X	X	X	X	X	X	X	X	X	X	X	X	X
Charleston	0.5	4.8	1.3	0.0	0.1	15.8	13.3	27.6	2.3	2.3	97.1	2,021	0.0
Huntington	0.6	4.1	1.2	0.0	0.1	17.9	26.3	5.0	3.1	0.1	35.7	764	1.2
Morgantown	0.3	9.4	3.4	0.0	0.0	13.5	35.5	7.0	0.6	2.1	187.8	6,064	73.6
Parkersburg	0.0	16.9	0.4	0.0	0.0	17.2	27.3	3.7	1.4	0.3	61.4	2,042	1.7
Wheeling	0.1	8.8	0.8	0.0	0.0	11.2	8.4	45.3	0.7	1.5	96.8	3,603	0.0
WISCONSIN	X	X	X	X	X	X	X	X	X	X	X	X	X
Appleton	0.6	23.6	1.6	0.0	1.0	15.9	11.9	10.3	0.4	6.6	167.6	2,249	57.7
Beloit	0.0	15.1	0.0	0.0	2.4	20.0	19.2	5.6	1.2	5.7	75.6	2,053	17.5
Brookfield	0.0	11.6	0.0	0.0	7.4	15.6	24.3	5.1	0.0	3.2	72.3	1,899	18.9
Caledonia	0.0	36.6	0.0	0.0	5.2	9.8	20.9	0.6	0.0	5.3	77.1	3,067	16.4
De Pere	0.0	28.8	0.0	0.0	1.2	12.3	23.0	6.3	0.2	3.3	33.5	1,338	7.1
Eau Claire	0.2	18.1	4.4	0.0	7.8	18.6	9.0	8.6	1.6	4.2	158.5	2,312	27.1
Fitchburg	0.1	15.7	0.0	0.0	1.3	21.2	10.1	7.1	0.0	3.5	47.4	1,604	9.7
Fond du Lac	0.0	16.8	0.7	0.0	6.7	17.7	19.1	4.6	1.0	8.6	153.9	3,606	6.1
Franklin	0.0	15.6	0.0	0.0	5.9	25.0	18.9	1.9	0.0	2.4	32.6	903	5.8
Green Bay	0.0	13.2	2.3	0.0	0.2	18.6	19.3	8.1	0.6	5.3	262.5	2,501	21.2
Greenfield	0.0	20.6	0.4	0.0	3.8	17.2	9.0	3.7	0.0	3.1	77.0	2,095	29.3
Janesville	0.6	16.2	0.1	0.0	3.1	12.8	18.5	4.6	3.2	2.3	112.9	1,756	28.7
Kenosha	0.0	13.5	0.0	0.0	8.9	22.3	11.8	6.5	8.1	5.8	111.1	1,113	20.7
La Crosse	0.0	14.6	7.6	0.0	0.4	15.5	9.1	11.5	4.9	2.2	63.5	1,227	15.7
Madison	0.0	13.6	2.2	0.0	3.2	17.3	10.8	9.9	10.2	5.5	906.4	3,543	152.3
Manitowoc	0.0	18.0	0.0	0.0	0.0	18.1	11.9	5.1	0.0	5.5	84.7	2,595	7.6
Menomonee Falls	0.0	15.9	0.0	0.0	5.0	16.2	31.7	2.3	0.0	5.0	94.8	2,535	19.9
Mequon	0.0	27.6	0.0	0.0	1.0	14.3	35.1	2.0	0.0	3.7	47.3	1,968	8.9
Milwaukee	0.0	13.6	2.2	0.0	2.1	28.3	8.0	0.3	2.9	4.3	1,507.0	2,538	492.0
Mount Pleasant	0.0	18.5	0.0	0.0	0.6	19.4	30.5	0.7	0.3	3.3	39.3	1,459	8.9
Muskego	0.0	15.9	0.0	0.0	0.1	16.6	39.8	4.5	0.0	3.7	37.6	1,505	8.7
Neenah	0.0	18.3	0.7	0.0	0.3	16.5	13.3	6.4	1.4	7.6	65.0	2,506	6.5
New Berlin	0.0	19.1	0.0	0.0	2.8	16.8	34.4	4.4	0.0	2.6	50.0	1,258	7.7
Oak Creek	0.0	16.6	0.0	0.0	9.4	18.3	13.4	4.1	0.0	5.1	115.1	3,173	33.9
Oshkosh	0.0	16.0	1.1	0.0	1.8	12.8	11.2	7.1	10.9	9.8	305.9	4,586	79.8
Racine	0.0	12.9	1.0	0.0	12.1	22.5	14.4	7.1	2.3	4.5	179.5	2,325	29.0
Sheboygan	0.0	13.4	0.7	0.0	1.9	22.5	14.2	4.5	3.6	3.3	56.0	1,158	16.3
Stevens Point	0.0	24.3	0.1	0.0	5.0	13.4	18.9	6.5	1.1	4.1	59.6	2,274	4.8
Sun Prairie	0.0	25.8	0.0	0.0	4.5	21.0	12.4	5.2	0.0	5.8	69.9	2,120	21.2
Superior	0.0	19.8	0.0	0.0	0.4	16.3	24.7	9.6	1.9	3.0	44.6	1,700	2.8
Waukesha	0.0	25.5	0.7	0.0	2.6	16.7	12.4	6.6	0.3	5.7	301.2	4,153	80.9
Wausau	0.0	23.3	3.2	0.0	4.8	14.4	8.4	16.0	1.4	2.4	75.1	1,939	27.4
Wauwatosa	0.0	15.6	0.1	0.0	11.0	16.7	8.8	1.4	0.9	3.9	126.1	2,627	19.4
West Allis	0.3	16.9	0.1	0.0	5.1	23.5	10.8	1.0	5.6	2.7	72.2	1,207	22.7
West Bend	0.0	14.6	0.0	0.0	2.0	24.4	13.6	9.4	0.9	6.0	63.7	2,020	7.5
WYOMING	X	X	X	X	X	X	X	X	X	X	X	X	X
Casper	1.2	13.1	0.0	0.0	1.3	13.4	18.9	17.5	0.1	0.2	15.8	273	0.0
Cheyenne	1.7	12.9	0.6	0.0	2.0	16.8	25.4	8.7	0.4	0.9	83.0	1,306	10.2
Gillette	0.0	12.9	0.0	0.0	0.8	11.7	10.3	4.0	1.3	0.4	158.6	4,925	5.4

1. Based on population estimated as of July 1 of the year shown.

PART E.

Congressional Districts of the 116th Congress

(For explanation of symbols, see page viii)

Congressional District Highlights and Rankings

Figure E-1. Median Household Income by Congressional District, 2016–2020

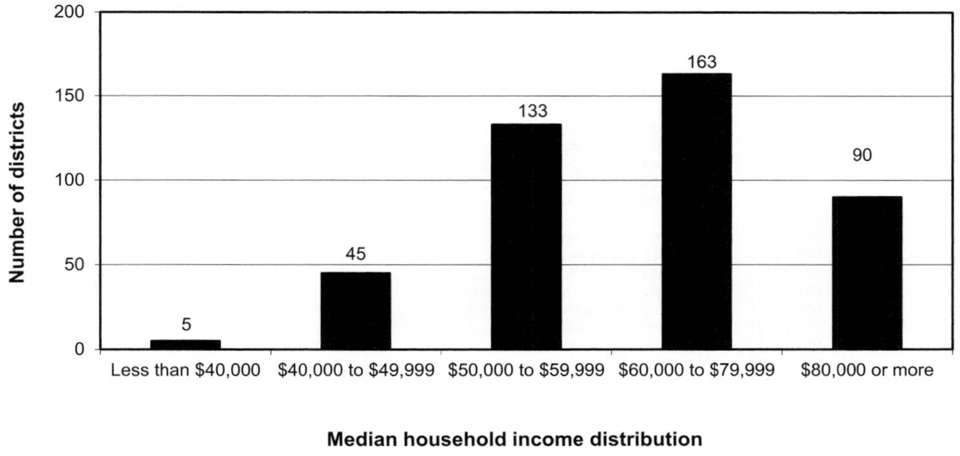

Every 10 years, the Census Bureau conducts a count to reapportion the seats in the U.S. House of Representatives. The House's 435 seats are divided among the 50 states. (The District of Columbia has no representative in Congress, although it has a nonvoting delegate.) The seats are reapportioned according to the population measured on April 1 of the census year in order to account for population changes among the states over the previous decade. The number of districts within a state may change after each decennial census, and the districts' boundaries may change more than once during a decade. The 116th Congress which convened in 2019 was the third to reflect the new boundaries based on the 2010 census. The Representatives of the 117th Congress are listed. Most of the data in Table E have been collected or updated for the 116th congress, but some sources were collected for the 115th congress or earlier. Boundary changes between the 114th and 115th congresses occurred in Florida, Minnesota, North Carolina, and Virginia.

As the state with the largest population, California had the most representatives with 53. Texas (36) and New York (27) were second and third largest, respectively. There were 7 states with just 1 representative: Alaska, Delaware, Montana, North Dakota, South Dakota, Vermont, and Wyoming. These states' representatives were considered "At Large," as they represented an entire state instead of a specific congressional district within the state.

Because the number of representatives is limited to 435, states with larger population growth add seats, while states with little or no growth lose seats. When the 113th Congress convened in January 2013, 8 states had more representatives in congress and 10 states had fewer. Based on the 2020 census, California, Illinois, Michigan, New York, Ohio, Pennsylvania, and West Virginia will lose one seat and Colorado, Florida, Montana, North Carolina, and Oregon will gain one seat while Texas will gain two seats.

As each decade progresses, population shifts alter the size of districts, leading up to the reapportionment of the next census. After the 2000 census, the population of each congressional district was about 645,000. Based on the 5-year data from 2016 to 2020, congressional districts average nearly 750,000 people. Montana's at-large congressional district had over a million people, while Delaware and South Dakota also had at-large seats with above-average populations. Texas's 22nd district is the largest apportioned congressional district in the United States with a population over 940,000 between 2016 and 2020. Rhode Island's two congressional districts have the smallest populations at 532,603 and 525,125. Congressional districts in Nebraska and West Virginia also have smaller populations. For years, Louisiana's 2nd district was the least populous congressional district in the nation due to outmigration after Hurricane Katrina.

While most of the congressional districts had about the same population size, they varied widely in other characteristics. In California's 33rd district, 96.1 percent of the residents were high school graduates, compared with just 58.7 percent in California's 40th district and 61.9 percent in California's 21st district. These two districts also had two of the lowest proportions of college graduates. In California's 21st district only 9.5 percent of residents had a college degree compared with 11.4 percent in California's 40th district. Texas's 29th district and 33rd districts also had low rates of college attainment with 10.9 percent and 12.0 percent of its residents, respectively, having a bachelor's degree or more.

The highest unemployment rates were found in New York's 15th district, Illinois's 2nd district, California's 16th district, and Michigan's 13th district, all at or over 11.0 percent. Three districts from California, two districts from Illinois and Michigan, and one district each from New York, Ohio, and Mississippi ranked among the 10 highest unemployment rates. Thirty-five congressional districts had 20 percent or more of their populations living in poverty. New York's 15th district had the highest poverty rate in the nation at 34.3 percent and the lowest median household income at $32,582 from 2016 to 2020. In California's 18th district, the median household income was $146,441, the highest in the nation. One hundred and twenty-four congressional districts had median household incomes exceeding $75,000 per year, while 5 districts had median household incomes below $40,000. The U.S. median household income between 2016 and 2020 was $64,994.

Congressional Districts of the 116th Congress of the United States

Selected Rankings

Population, 2016–2020			Land area, 2020			Population density, 2016–2020		
Population rank	State congressional district Representative	Population [col 2]	Land area rank	State congressional district Representative	Land area (square miles) [col 1]	Density rank	State congressional district Representative	Population density (per square mile) [col 3]
1	MT At large: Matthew M. Rosendale Sr. (R)	1,061,705	1	AK At-Large: Mary Peltola (D)	571,022	1	NY 13th: Adriano Espaillat (D)	74,723.1
2	DE: At-Large: Lisa Blunt Rochester (D)	967,679	2	MT At large: Matthew M. Rosendale Sr. (R)	145,550	2	NY 10th: Jerrold Nadler (D)	52,160.5
3	TX 22nd: Troy E. Nehls (R)	941,210	3	WY At-large Liz Cheney (R)	97,089	3	NY 15th: Ritchie Torres (D)	50,658.0
4	ID 1st: Russ Fulcher (R)	913,009	4	SD At-Large Dusty Johnson (R)	75,810	4	NY 12th: Carolyn B. Maloney (D)	48,763.4
5	Tx 10th: Michael T. McCaul (R)	904,588	5	NM 2nd: Yvette Herrell (R)	71,746	5	NY 9th: Yvette D. Clarke (D)	46,362.2
6	TX 26th: Michael C. Burgess (R)	901,361	6	OR 2nd: Cliff Bentz (R)	69,451	6	NY 7th: Nydia M. Velázquez (D)	44,702.9
7	TX 3rd: Van Taylor (R)	896,996	7	ND At-Large: Kelly Armstrong (R)	68,996	7	NY 8th: Hakeem S. Jeffries (D)	27,205.9
8	FL 9th: Darren Soto (D)	895,237	8	NE 3rd: Adrian Smith (R)	67,433	8	NY 6th: Grace Meng (D)	24,487.6
9	NC 12th: Alma S. Adams (D)	885,774	9	TX 23rd: Tony Gonzales (R)	58,059	9	NY 14th: Alexandria Ocasio Cortez (D)	24,031.5
10	TX 31st: John R. Carter (R)	884,928	10	NV 2nd: Mark E. Amodei (R)	55,898	10	CA 12th: Nancy Pelosi (D)	19,586.0
11	SD At-Large Dusty Johnson (R)	879,336	11	AZ 1st: Tom O'Halleran (D)	55,034	11	CA 34th: Jimmy Gomez (D)	15,407.0
12	TX 8th: Kevin Brady (R)	879,149	12	KS 1st: Tracey Mann (R)	52,542	12	NY 5th: Gregory W. Meeks (D)	14,796.1
13	NC 4th: David E. Price (D)	866,455	13	NV 4th: Steven Horsford (D)	51,010	13	NJ 8th: Albio Sires (D)	13,951.5
14	NC 2nd: Deborah K. Ross (D)	865,706	14	NM 3rd: Teresa Leger Fernandez (D)	44,966	14	PA 3rd: Dwight Evans (D)	13,647.7
15	VA 10th: Jennifer Wexton (D)	853,906	15	ID 2nd: Michael K. Simpson (R)	43,225	15	CA 37th: Karen Bass (D)	13,163.4
16	FL 16th: Vern Buchanan (R)	853,737	16	UT 2nd: Chris Stewart (R)	40,196	16	IL 4th: Jesus G. "Chuy" Garcia (D)	13,030.1
17	OR 1st: Suzanne Bonamici (D)	851,961	17	ID 1st: Russ Fulcher (R)	39,420	17	MA 7th: Ayanna Presley (D)	12,885.4
18	CO 1st: Diana DeGette (D)	843,348	18	TX 13th: Ronny Jackson (R)	38,351	18	CA 40th: Lucille Roybal-Allard (D)	12,280.0
19	OR 3rd: Earl Blumenauer (D)	843,221	19	OK 3rd: Frank D. Lucas (R)	34,116	19	PA 2nd: Brendan F. Boyle (D)	11,811.1
20	FL 10th: Val Butler Demings (D)	843,134	20	MN 7th: Michelle Fischbach (R)	33,429	20	IL 7th: Danny K. Davis (D)	11,564.9
21	AZ 5th: Andy Biggs (R)	842,222	21	AZ 4th: Paul A. Gosar (R)	33,220	21	NY 11th: Nicole Malliotakis (R)	11,240.3
22	ID 2nd: Michael K. Simpson (R)	841,358	22	CA 8th: Jay Olbernolte (R)	32,893	22	CA 46th: J. Luis Correa (D)	10,110.1
23	IA 3rd: Cynthia Axne (D)	841,226	23	CA 1st: Doug LaMalfa (R)	28,121	23	CA 43rd: Maxine Waters (D)	10,096.2
24	OR 5th: Kurt Schrader (D)	839,214	24	MN 8th: Pete Stauber (R)	27,909	24	NJ 10th: Donald M. Payne, Jr. (D)	10,001.4
25	CO 4th: Ken Buck (R)	837,275	25	TX 11th: August Pfluger (R)	27,835	25	NY 16th: Jamaal Bowman (D)	9,512.5
26	NV 3rd: Susie Lee (D)	835,738	26	ME 2nd: Jared F. Golden (D)	27,558	26	CA 44th: Nanette Diaz Barragan (D)	8,901.3
27	FL 19th: Byron Donalds (R)	834,988	27	TX 19th: Jodey C. Arrington (R)	25,836	27	NJ 9th: Bill Pascrell, Jr. (D)	7,907.3
28	GA 7th Carolyn Bourdeaux (D)	833,680	28	MI 1st: Jack Bergman (R)	25,029	28	CA 13th: Barbara Lee (D)	7,860.0
29	TX 35th: Lloyd Doggett (D)	830,798	29	WI 7th: Thomas P. Tiffany (R)	23,039	29	CA 29th: Tony Cárdenas (D)	7,754.1
30	OR 2nd: Cliff Bentz (R)	828,446	30	IA 4th: Randy Feenstra (R)	22,755	30	IL 5th: Michael Quigley (D)	7,718.4
31	AZ 7th: Ruben Gallego (D)	827,379	31	AR 4th: Bruce Westerman (R)	22,336	31	FL 24th: Frederica S. Wilson (D)	7,320.5
32	TX 21st: Chip Roy (R)	826,791	32	OK 2nd: Markwayne Mullin (R)	20,997	32	CA 38th: Linda T. Sánchez (D)	6,965.9
33	UT 4th: Burgess Owens (R)	825,680	33	UT 3rd: John R. Curtis (R)	20,074	33	IL 9th: Janice D. Schakowsky (D)	6,878.2
34	CO 6th: Jason Crow (D)	825,402	34	MO 8th:Jason T. Smith (R)	19,902	34	NV 1st: Dina Titus (D)	6,709.2
35	TX 12th: Kay Granger (R)	824,946	35	UT 1st: Blake D. Moore (R)	19,557	35	FL 27th: Maria Elvira Salazar (R)	6,610.5
36	TX 20th: Joaquin Castro (D)	823,263	36	AR 1st: Eric A. "Rick" Crawford (R)	19,280	36	NY 4th: Kathleen M. Rice (D)	6,522.9
37	CA 42nd: Ken Calvert (R)	822,515	37	WA 4th: Dan Newsome (R)	19,247	37	CA 32nd: Grace F. Napolitano (D)	5,692.6
38	OK 5th: Stephanie I. Bice (R)	821,362	38	MO 6th: Sam Graves (R)	18,198	38	CA 30th: Brad Sherman (D)	5,688.4
39	AR 3rd: Steve Womack (R)	820,935	39	OR 4th: Peter A. DeFazio (D)	17,273	39	CA 53rd: Sara Jacobs (D)	5,652.6
40	FL 4th: John H. Rutherford (R)	820,783	40	AZ 3rd: Raul M. Grijalva (D)	15,688	40	WA 7th: Pramila Jayapal (D)	5,549.8
41	CO 2nd: Joe Neguse (D)	817,394	41	MS 2nd: Bennie G. Thompson (D)	15,552	41	WI 4th: Gwen Moore (D)	5,514.2
42	TX 24rd: Beth Van Duyne (R)	813,614	42	WA 5th: Cathy McMorris Rodgers (R)	15,474	42	VA 8th: Donald S. Beyer, Jr. (D)	5,356.7
43	OR 4th: Peter A. DeFazio (D)	813,504	43	NY 21st: Elise M. Stefanik (R)	15,114	43	MN 5th: Ilhan Omar (D)	5,287.6
44	AZ 4th: Paul A. Gosar (R)	811,947	44	IL 15th: Mary E. Miller (R)	14,696	44	CA 48th: Michelle Steel (R)	4,937.3
45	CO 5th: Doug Lamborn (R)	811,504	45	LA 5th: Julia Letlow (R)	14,452	45	TX 7th: Lizzie Fletcher (D)	4,894.8
46	TX 2nd: Dan Crenshaw (R)	809,751	46	MO 4th: Vicky Hartzler (R)	14,407	46	AZ 9th: Greg Stanton (D)	4,811.1
47	MA 7th: Ayanna Presley (D)	808,106	47	KS 4th: Ron Estes (R)	14,315	47	FL 22nd: Vacancy	4,673.0
48	NC 7th: David Rouzer (R)	807,268	48	KS 2nd: Jake LaTurner (R)	14,144	48	TX 9th: Al Green (D)	4,663.9
49	AZ 6th: David Schweikert (R)	806,918	49	CA 2nd: Jared Huffman (D)	12,953	49	CO 1st: Diana DeGette (D)	4,448.1
50	OK 1st: Kevin Hern (R)	806,758	50	CA 4th: Tom McClintock (R)	12,837	50	CA 35th: Norma J. Torres (D)	4,433.0
51	AZ 8th: Debbie Lesko (R)	806,027	51	MS 3rd: Michael Guest (R)	12,755	51	CA 6th: Doris O. Matsui (D)	4,366.4
52	FL 15th: C. Scott Franklin (R)	805,103	52	LA 4th: Mike Johnson (R)	12,437	52	VA 11th: Gerald E. Connolly (D)	4,327.5
53	SC 1st: Nancy Mace (R)	804,679	53	IA 2nd: Mariannette Miller-Meeks(R)	12,261	53	TX 32nd: Colin Z. Allred (D)	4,195.9
54	TX 25th: Roger Williams (R)	804,296	54	KY 1st: James Comer (R)	12,084	54	CA 17th: Ro Khanna (D)	4,189.4
55	FL 14th: Kathy Castor (D)	802,492	55	IA 1st: Ashley Hinson (R)	12,049	55	TX 20th: Joaquin Castro (D)	4,118.9
56	TX 6th: Jake Ellzey (R)	802,430	56	MN 1st: Brad Finstad (R)	11,974	56	FL 23rd: Debbie Wasserman Schultz (D)	4,111.0
57	LA 1st: Steve Scalise (R)	802,133	57	KY 5th: Harold Rogers (R)	11,234	57	WA 9th: Adam Smith (D)	4,090.6
58	VA 11th: Gerald E. Connolly (D)	800,969	58	WI 3rd: Ron Kind (D)	11,117	58	AZ 7th: Ruben Gallego (D)	4,041.8
59	VA 1st: Robert J. Wittman (R)	800,745	59	MS 1st: Trent Kelly (R)	10,573	59	TX 29th: Sylvia R. Garcia (D)	3,944.0
60	TN 4th: Scott DesJarlais (R)	800,304	60	IL 18th: Darin LaHood (R)	10,515	60	NY 2nd: Andrew R. Garbarino (R)	3,928.7
61	VA 8th: Donald S. Beyer, Jr. (D)	800,273	61	AL 7th: Terri A. Sewell (D)	10,155	61	MI 9th: Andy Levin (D)	3,898.1
62	WA 7th: Pramila Jayapal (D)	798,799	62	AL 2nd: Barry Moore(R)	10,143	62	MI 14th: Brenda L. Lawrence (D)	3,715.2
63	NC 8th: Richard Hudson (R)	798,557	63	TX 4th: Pat Fallon (R)	10,131	63	MI 13th: Rashida Tlaib (D)	3,638.3
64	VA 7th: Abigail Davis Spanberger (D)	798,194	64	VA 5th: Bob Good (R)	10,031	64	CA 39th: Young Kim (R)	3,570.2
65	CO 7th: Ed Perlmutter (D)	797,811	65	CA 23rd: Kevin McCarthy (R)	9,902	65	OH 3rd: Joyce Beatty (D)	3,494.4
66	OH 3rd: Joyce Beatty (D)	797,029	66	PA 12th: Fred Keller (R)	9,896	66	TX 33rd: Marc A. Veasey (D)	3,483.3
67	MO 3rd: Blaine Luetkemeyer (R)	796,189	67	OK 4th: Tom Cole (R)	9,778	67	IL 8th: Raja Krishnamoorthi (D)	3,447.0
68	LA 6th: Garret Graves (R)	795,169	68	WV 3rd: Carol D. Miller (R)	9,746	68	CA 31st: Pete Aguilar (D)	3,423.2
69	TX 15th: Vicente Gonzalez (D)	794,094	69	PA 15th: Glen Thompson (R)	9,735	69	NJ 6th: Frank Pallone Jr. (D)	3,404.9
70	AZ 9th: Greg Stanton (D)	793,633	70	GA 2nd: Sanford D. Bishop Jr. (D)	9,631	70	PA 5th: Mary Gay Scanlon (D)	3,390.0
71	LA 2nd: Troy Carter (D)	793,342	71	TX 28th: Henry Cuellar (D)	9,379	71	HI 1st: Ed Case (D)	3,381.0
72	TX 7th: Lizzie Fletcher (D)	793,324	72	VT: At-large Peter Welch (D)	9,217	72	TX 18th: Sheila Jackson-Lee (D)	3,353.5
73	OK 4th: Tom Cole (R)	792,809	73	TN 7th: Mark E. Green (R)	9,161	73	CA 47th: Alan S. Lowenthal (D)	3,282.8
74	FL 20th: Sheila Cherfilus-McCormick (D)	791,022	74	TX 27th: Michael Cloud (R)	9,121	74	CA 28th: Adam B. Schiff (D)	3,260.1
75	FL 11th: Daniel Webster (R)	790,906	75	WA 3rd: Jaime Herrera Beutler (R)	9,118	75	NY 26th: Brian Higgins (D)	3,230.3

Congressional Districts of the 116th Congress of the United States

Selected Rankings

Percent Non-Hispanic White alone, 2016–2020			Percent Black alone, 2016–2020			Percent American Indian, Alaska Native alone, 2016–2020		
Non-Hispanic White alone rank	State congressional district Representative	Percent white [col 11]	Black rank	State congressional district Representative	Percent black [col 5]	American Indian Alaska Native rank	State congressional district Representative	Percent American Indian Alaska Native [col 6]
1	KY 5th: Harold Rogers (R)	95.2	1	TN 9th: Steve Cohen (D)	66.7	1	AZ 1st: Tom O'Halleran (D)	22.6
2	PA 15th: Glen Thompson (R)	94.3	2	MS 2nd: Bennie G. Thompson (D)	66.2	2	NM 3rd: Teresa Leger Fernandez (D)	18.5
3	OH 6th: Bill Johnson (R)	93.9	3	AL 7th: Terri A. Sewell (D)	62.8	3	OK 2nd: Markwayne Mullin (R)	17.5
4	ME 2nd: Jared F. Golden (D)	93.5	4	LA 2nd: Troy Carter (D)	61.5	4	AK At-Large: Mary Peltola (D)	14.6
5	WV 1st: David McKinley (R)	92.8	5	GA 13th: David Scott (D)	60.7	5	SD At-Large Dusty Johnson (R)	8.5
6	WV 3rd: Carol D. Miller (R)	92.6	6	GA 4th: Henry C. "Hank" Johnson Jr. (D)	60.3	6	NC 9th: Dan Bishop (R)	7.8
7	PA 14th: Guy Reschenthaler (R)	92.4	7	IL 2nd: Robin L. Kelly (D)	57.3	7	MT At large: Matthew M. Rosendale Sr. (R)	6.2
7	VT: At-large Peter Welch (D)	92.4	8	GA 5th: Nikema Williams (D)	56.6	8	OK 1st: Kevin Hern (R)	6.0
9	ME 1st: Chellie Pingree (D)	91.8	9	PA 3rd: Dwight Evans (D)	56.3	9	OK 3rd: Frank D. Lucas (R)	5.8
10	PA 12th: Fred Keller (R)	91.7	10	SC 6th: James E. Clyburn (D)	55.8	10	OK 4th: Tom Cole (R)	5.4
11	PA 13th: John Joyce (R)	91.2	11	MI 14th: Brenda L. Lawrence (D)	55.6	11	NM 2nd: Yvette Herrell (R)	5.2
11	WI 3rd: Ron Kind (D)	91.2	12	FL 20th: Sheila Cherfilus-McCormick (D)	53.9	11	ND At-Large: Kelly Armstrong (R)	5.2
13	NY 27th: Chris Jacobs (R)	91.0	12	MI 13th: Rashida Tlaib (D)	53.9	13	AZ 3rd: Raul M. Grijalva (D)	4.5
13	WI 7th: Thomas P. Tiffany (R)	91.0	14	OH 11th: Shontel M. Brown (D)	52.3	14	OK 5th: Stephanie I. Bice (R)	4.4
15	MN 8th: Pete Stauber (R)	90.9	15	MD 7th: Kweisi Mfume (D)	52.2	15	NM 1st: Melanie A. Stansbury (D)	4.3
15	TN 1st: Diana Harshbarger (R)	90.9	16	GA 2nd: Sanford D. Bishop Jr. (D)	52.0	16	AZ 9th: Greg Stanton (D)	3.0
17	MI 4th: John L. Moolenaar (R)	90.7	17	MD 4th: Anthony G. Brown (D)	51.9	17	MN 7th: Michelle Fischbach (R)	2.7
18	IN 6th: Greg Pence (R)	90.6	18	NJ 10th: Donald M. Payne, Jr. (D)	51.0	18	AZ 7th: Ruben Gallego (D)	2.6
19	MI 1st: Jack Bergman (R)	90.5	18	NY 8th: Hakeem S. Jeffries (D)	51.0	19	WA 4th: Dan Newsome (R)	2.5
20	IL 15th: Mary E. Miller (R)	90.4	20	IL 1st: Bobby L. Rush (D)	50.2	20	WI 8th: Mike Gallagher (R)	2.4
21	OH 16th: Anthony Gonzalez (R)	90.3	21	MO 1st: Cori Bush (D)	49.4	21	MI 1st: Jack Bergman (R)	2.3
22	OH 7th: Bob Gibbs (R)	90.1	22	NY 5th: Gregory W. Meeks (D)	48.0	21	MN 8th: Pete Stauber (R)	2.3
23	MO 3rd: Blaine Luetkemeyer (R)	89.9	23	FL 24th: Frederica S. Wilson (D)	47.4	21	WY At-large Liz Cheney (R)	2.3
24	NH 2nd: Ann M. Kuster (D)	89.8	24	NY 9th: Yvette D. Clarke (D)	46.5	24	NV 2nd: Mark E. Amodei (R)	2.2
25	MO 8th:Jason T. Smith (R)	89.7	25	VA 3rd: Robert C. "Bobby" Scott (D)	46.1	25	CA 2nd: Jared Huffman (D)	2.1
25	NY 21st: Elise M. Stefanik (R)	89.7	26	IL 7th: Danny K. Davis (D)	44.3	26	AZ 6th: David Schweikert (R)	1.9
27	MI 10th: Lisa McClain (R)	89.5	27	NC 1st: G. K. Butterfield (D)	43.5	26	OR 2nd: Cliff Bentz (R)	1.9
28	IN 7th: Larry Bucshon (R)	89.4	28	TX 30th: Eddie Bernice Johnson (D)	41.9	26	WA 6th: Derek Kilmer (D)	1.9
28	NH 1st: Chris Pappas (D)	89.4	29	VA 4th: A. Donald McEachin (D)	40.7	26	WI 7th: Thomas P. Tiffany (R)	1.9
30	KY 4th: Thomas Massie (R)	89.3	30	MD 5th: Steny H. Hoyer (D)	38.7	30	AZ 4th: Paul A. Gosar (R)	1.7
30	WV 2nd: Alexander X. Mooney (R)	89.3	31	TX 9th: Al Green (D)	37.4	30	CA 1st: Doug LaMalfa (R)	1.7
32	VA 9th: Morgan Griffith (R)	89.1	32	NC 12th: Alma S. Adams (D)	37.3	32	AZ 2nd: Ann Kirkpatrick (D)	1.5
33	PA 16th: Mike Kelly (R)	89.0	33	MD 2nd: C. A. Dutch Ruppersberger (D)	35.8	32	NC 11th: Madison Cawthorn (R)	1.5
34	WI 6th: Glenn Grothman (R)	88.4	34	MS 3rd: Michael Guest (R)	35.7	32	WA 5th: Cathy McMorris Rodgers (R)	1.5
35	IN 8th: Trey Hollingsworth (R)	88.3	35	NY 15th: Ritchie Torres (D)	35.5	35	UT 3rd: John R. Curtis (R)	1.4
36	IL 18th: Darin LaHood (R)	88.0	36	LA 5th: Julia Letlow (R)	35.2	36	CA 8th: Jay Olbernolte (R)	1.3
37	NY 23rd: Joseph Sempolinski (R)	87.9	37	GA 12th: Rick W. Allen (R)	34.9	36	CA 32nd: Grace F. Napolitano (D)	1.3
37	OH 15th: Mike Carey (R)	87.9	38	TX 18th: Sheila Jackson-Lee (D)	34.7	36	CA 34th: Jimmy Gomez (D)	1.3
39	OH 5th: Robert E. Latta (R)	87.8	39	OH 3rd: Joyce Beatty (D)	34.4	36	ID 1st: Russ Fulcher (R)	1.3
39	PA 9th: Daniel Meuser (R)	87.8	40	LA 4th: Mike Johnson (R)	34.3	36	ID 2nd: Michael K. Simpson (R)	1.3
41	MN 7th: Michelle Fischbach (R)	87.5	41	WI 4th: Gwen Moore (D)	33.7	36	KS 2nd: Jake LaTurner (R)	1.3
41	OH 14th: David P. Joyce (R)	87.5	42	NY 16th: Jamaal Bowman (D)	33.0	36	NE 1st: Mike Flood (R)	1.3
43	MN 6th: Tom Emmer (R)	87.4	43	AL 2nd: Barry Moore(R)	31.3	36	NV 1st: Dina Titus (D)	1.3
44	IA 1st: Ashley Hinson (R)	87.2	43	GA 8th: Austin Scott (R)	31.3	44	CA 16th: Jim Costa (D)	1.2
45	MI 7th: Tim Walberg (R)	87.1	45	IN 7th: André Carson (D)	30.3	44	CA 35th: Norma J. Torres (D)	1.2
45	MO 7th: Bill Long (R)	87.1	46	GA 1st: Earl L. "Buddy" Carter (R)	29.7	44	CA 50th: Darrell Issa (R)	1.2
47	TN 6th: John W. Rose (R)	87.0	47	NY 13th: Adriano Espaillat (D)	29.1	44	NC 8th: Richard Hudson (R)	1.2
48	KY 1st: James Comer (R)	86.9	48	MS 1st: Trent Kelly (R)	28.2	44	WA 1st: Suzan K. DelBene (D)	1.2
48	MO 6th: Sam Graves (R)	86.9	49	FL 10th: Val Butler Demings (D)	28.1	44	WA 10th: Marilyn Strickland (D)	1.2
50	OH 4th: Jim Jordan (R)	86.8	50	SC 7th: Tom Rice (R)	27.6	50	CA 3rd: John Garamendi (D)	1.1
51	NY 22nd: Claudia Tenney (R)	86.6	51	AL 1st: Jerry Carl (R)	27.5	50	CA 21st: David G. Valadao (R)	1.1
51	PA 17th: Conor Lamb (D)	86.6	52	PA 2nd: Brendan F. Boyle (D)	26.6	50	CA 23rd: Kevin McCarthy (R)	1.1
53	KY 2nd: Brett Guthrie (R)	86.4	53	SC 5th: Ralph Norman (R)	25.9	50	CA 36th: Raul Ruiz (D)	1.1
54	IA 4th: Randy Feenstra (R)	86.3	54	AL 3rd: Mike Rogers (R)	25.8	50	LA 1st: Steve Scalise (R)	1.1
55	WI 8th: Mike Gallagher (R)	86.2	55	GA 10th: Jody B. Hice (R)	25.5	50	MN 5th: Ilhan Omar (D)	1.1
56	MO 4th: Vicky Hartzler (R)	85.9	56	GA 3rd A. Drew Ferguson IV (R)	25.1	50	NV 4th: Steven Horsford (D)	1.1
56	WI 5th: Scott Fitzgerald (R)	85.9	57	MA 7th: Ayanna Presley (D)	24.7	50	OR 4th: Peter A. DeFazio (D)	1.1
58	NC 11th: Madison Cawthorn (R)	85.8	58	PA 5th: Mary Gay Scanlon (D)	24.5	50	UT 2nd: Chris Stewart (R)	1.1
59	MT At large: Matthew M. Rosendale Sr. (R)	85.6	59	LA 3rd: Clay Higgins (R)	24.4	50	WA 2nd: Rick Larsen (D)	1.1
60	TN 2nd: Tim Burchett (R)	85.4	59	TN 5th: Jim Cooper (D)	24.4	60	AL 1st: Jerry Carl (R)	1.0
61	MO 2nd: Ann Wagner (R)	85.2	61	SC 2nd: Joe Wilson (R)	24.2	60	AZ 5th: Andy Biggs (R)	1.0
62	OH 2nd: Brad R. Wenstrup (R)	84.8	62	LA 6th: Garret Graves (R)	24.0	60	AR 3rd: Steve Womack (R)	1.0
62	OH 8th: Warren Davidson (R)	84.8	63	MS 4th: Steven M. Palazzo (R)	23.4	60	CA 22nd: Connie Conway (R)	1.0
64	MA 8th: William R. Keating (D)	84.7	63	NC 8th: Richard Hudson (R)	23.4	60	CA 24th: Salud O. Carbajal (D)	1.0
65	MN 1st: Brad Finstad (R)	84.6	65	AR 2nd: J. French Hill (R)	22.9	60	CA 25th: Mike Garcia (R)	1.0
66	IA 2nd: Mariannette Miller-Meeks(R)	84.5	66	MD 3rd: John P. Sarbanes (D)	22.8	60	CA 40th: Lucille Roybal-Allard (D)	1.0
67	OH 12th: Troy Balderson (R)	84.3	67	KY 3rd: John A. Yarmuth (D)	22.5	60	MS 3rd: Michael Guest (R)	1.0
68	IN 4th: James R. Baird (R)	83.9	68	NC 4th: David E. Price (D)	22.3	68	AZ 8th: Debbie Lesko (R)	0.9
69	ND At-Large: Kelly Armstrong (R)	83.7	69	NC 13th: Ted Budd (R)	22.2	68	CA 4th: Tom McClintock (R)	0.9
69	PA 11th: Lloyd Smucker (R)	83.7	70	CA 37th: Karen Bass (D)	21.9	68	CA 26th: Julia Brownley (D)	0.9
71	WY At-large Liz Cheney (R)	83.6	71	MO 5th: Emanuel Cleaver (D)	21.7	68	CA 43rd: Maxine Waters (D)	0.9
72	AL 4th: Robert B. Aderholt (R)	83.2	71	OH 1st: Steve Chabot (R)	21.7	68	CA 51st: Juan Vargas (D)	0.9
73	NE 3rd: Adrian Smith (R)	83.1	73	TX 6th: Jake Ellzey (R)	21.6	68	GA 6th: Lucy McBath (D)	0.9
74	OR 4th: Peter A. DeFazio (D)	83.0	74	CA 43rd: Maxine Waters (D)	21.4	68	KS 4th: Ron Estes (R)	0.9
75	NY 19th: Patrick Ryan (D)	82.9	75	GA 7th Carolyn Bourdeaux (D)	21.3	68	ME 2nd: Jared F. Golden (D)	0.9

Congressional Districts of the 116th Congress of the United States

Selected Rankings

Asian or Pacific Islander rank	State congressional district Representative	Percent Asian or Pacific Islander [col 7]
Percent Asian or Pacific Islander alone, 2016–2020		
1	HI 1st: Ed Case (D)	57.9
2	CA 17th: Ro Khanna (D)	57.1
3	NY 6th: Grace Meng (D)	40.1
4	CA 27th: Judy Chu (D)	39.9
5	HI 2nd: Kaiali'I Kahele (D)	38.3
6	CA 15th: Eric Swalwell (D)	37.3
7	CA 14th Jackie Speier (D)	36.5
8	CA 12th: Nancy Pelosi (D)	32.7
9	CA 39th: Young Kim (R)	32.6
10	CA 19th: Zoe Lofgren (D)	30.2
11	CA 45th: Katie Porter (D)	26.3
12	CA 18th: Anna G. Eshoo (D)	25.2
12	WA 9th: Adam Smith (D)	25.2
14	CA 47th: Alan S. Lowenthal (D)	23.6
15	CA 13th: Barbara Lee (D)	21.9
16	CA 52nd: Scott H. Peters (D)	20.9
17	CA 32nd: Grace F. Napolitano (D)	20.0
18	CA 34th: Jimmy Gomez (D)	19.7
19	CA 48th: Michelle Steel (R)	19.4
20	TX 22nd: Troy E. Nehls (R)	19.2
20	VA 11th: Gerald E. Connolly (D)	19.2
22	NJ 6th: Frank Pallone Jr. (D)	19.1
23	NY 10th: Jerrold Nadler (D)	19.0
24	CA 7th: Ami Bera (D)	18.1
25	CA 6th: Doris O. Matsui (D)	18.0
26	NY 7th: Nydia M. Velázquez (D)	17.7
27	NJ 12th: Bonnie Watson Coleman (D)	17.6
28	NY 14th: Alexandria Ocasio Cortez (D)	17.5
29	NY 3rd: Thomas R. Souzzi (D)	17.3
30	TX 3rd: Van Taylor (R)	17.0
31	CA 38th: Linda T. Sánchez (D)	16.4
32	CA 11th: Mark Desaulnier (D)	15.8
32	VA 10th: Jennifer Wexton (D)	15.8
34	CA 33rd: Ted Lieu (D)	15.5
35	CA 9th: Jerry McNerney (D)	15.4
36	TX 24rd: Beth Van Duyne (R)	15.2
37	NY 5th: Gregory W. Meeks (D)	15.1
38	NV 3rd: Susie Lee (D)	15.0
39	GA 7th Carolyn Bourdeaux (D)	14.9
40	NY 11th: Nicole Malliotakis (R)	14.8
41	NY 12th: Carolyn B. Maloney (D)	14.5
42	CA 53rd: Sara Jacobs (D)	14.4
43	CA 46th: J. Luis Correa (D)	14.1
44	WA 7th: Pramila Jayapal (D)	14.0
45	CA 43rd: Maxine Waters (D)	13.9
46	IL 8th: Raja Krishnamoorthi (D)	13.5
46	NJ 9th: Bill Pascrell, Jr. (D)	13.5
48	CA 28th: Adam B. Schiff (D)	13.3
49	IL 9th: Janice D. Schakowsky (D)	13.2
50	CA 30th: Brad Sherman (D)	13.1
51	MN 4th: Betty McCollum (D)	13.0
52	MA 5th: Katherine Clark (D)	12.8
53	WA 1st: Suzan K. DelBene (D)	12.5
54	CA 3rd: John Garamendi (D)	12.3
55	GA 6th: Lucy McBath (D)	11.9
55	TX 9th: Al Green (D)	11.9
57	CA 5th: Mike Thompson (D)	11.8
57	VA 8th: Donald S. Beyer, Jr. (D)	11.8
59	MD 6th: David J. Trone (D)	11.5
60	IL 10th: Bradley Scott Schneider (D)	11.3
61	TX 7th: Lizzie Fletcher (D)	11.1
62	MA 7th: Ayanna Presley (D)	10.8
63	MI 11th: Haley M. Stevens (D)	10.7
63	NJ 5th: Josh Gottheimer (D)	10.7
63	NJ 7th: Tom Malinowski (D)	10.7
66	NJ 11th: Mikie Sherill (D)	10.6
66	WA 8th: Kim Schrier (D)	10.6
68	CA 37th: Karen Bass (D)	10.5
69	CA 42nd: Ken Calvert (R)	10.1
70	IL 6th: Sean Casten (D)	9.8
71	WA 2nd: Rick Larsen (D)	9.6
72	NJ 8th: Albio Sires (D)	9.5
73	CA 16th: Jim Costa (D)	9.4
73	NC 4th: David E. Price (D)	9.4
75	NV 1st: Dina Titus (D)	9.3

Hispanic rank	State congressional district Representative	Percent Hispanic [col 10]
Percent Hispanic or Latino,[1] 2016–2020		
1	CA 40th: Lucille Roybal-Allard (D)	88.0
2	TX 34th: Mayra Flores (R)	84.7
3	TX 15th: Vicente Gonzalez (D)	81.9
4	TX 16th: Veronica Escobar (D)	80.9
5	TX 29th: Sylvia R. Garcia (D)	78.9
6	TX 28th: Henry Cuellar (D)	77.9
7	FL 25th Mario Diaz-Balart (R)	75.6
8	CA 21st: David G. Valadao (R)	75.1
9	FL 27th: Maria Elvira Salazar (R)	72.0
10	CA 44th: Nanette Diaz Barragan (D)	71.0
11	CA 35th: Norma J. Torres (D)	70.5
12	CA 51st: Juan Vargas (D)	70.0
13	FL 26th: Carlos A. Gimenez (R)	69.9
14	TX 20th: Joaquin Castro (D)	69.4
15	TX 23rd: Tony Gonzales (R)	69.3
16	IL 4th: Jesus G. "Chuy" Garcia (D)	67.7
17	CA 29th: Tony Cárdenas (D)	67.6
18	TX 33rd: Marc A. Veasey (D)	66.8
19	NY 15th: Ritchie Torres (D)	65.7
20	CA 46th: J. Luis Correa (D)	65.6
21	AZ 7th: Ruben Gallego (D)	64.1
22	AZ 3rd: Raul M. Grijalva (D)	63.6
23	CA 16th: Jim Costa (D)	61.5
23	CA 38th: Linda T. Sánchez (D)	61.5
25	CA 41st: Mark Takano (D)	61.4
26	CA 32nd: Grace F. Napolitano (D)	61.2
27	CA 34th: Jimmy Gomez (D)	61.1
28	TX 35th: Lloyd Doggett (D)	60.9
29	NM 2nd: Yvette Herrell (R)	55.8
30	NY 13th: Adriano Espaillat (D)	54.4
31	CA 31st: Pete Aguilar (D)	54.2
32	NJ 8th: Albio Sires (D)	53.9
33	TX 27th: Michael Cloud (R)	53.7
34	CA 20th: Jimmy Panetta (D)	53.5
35	NM 1st: Melanie A. Stansbury (D)	50.4
36	CA 36th: Raul Ruiz (D)	49.3
36	NY 14th: Alexandria Ocasio Cortez (D)	49.3
38	CA 22nd: Connie Conway (R)	49.1
39	CA 43rd: Maxine Waters (D)	48.0
40	NV 1st: Dina Titus (D)	46.3
41	CA 26th: Julia Brownley (D)	45.8
42	CA 10th: Josh Harder (D)	44.7
43	TX 18th: Sheila Jackson-Lee (D)	43.4
44	CA 8th: Jay Olbernolte (R)	42.7
45	FL 9th: Darren Soto (D)	42.0
46	NM 3rd: Teresa Leger Fernandez (D)	41.4
47	CA 23rd: Kevin McCarthy (R)	41.1
48	FL 24th: Frederica S. Wilson (D)	41.0
49	CA 25th: Mike Garcia (R)	40.4
49	CA 42nd: Ken Calvert (R)	40.4
51	FL 23rd: Debbie Wasserman Schultz (D)	39.9
52	WA 4th: Dan Newsome (R)	39.7
53	NY 7th: Nydia M. Velázquez (D)	39.4
53	TX 30th: Eddie Bernice Johnson (D)	39.4
55	TX 11th: August Pfluger (R)	39.3
56	CA 19th: Zoe Lofgren (D)	39.2
57	TX 9th: Al Green (D)	39.1
58	CA 9th: Jerry McNerney (D)	38.8
59	CA 37th: Karen Bass (D)	38.7
59	NJ 9th: Bill Pascrell, Jr. (D)	38.7
61	TX 19th: Jodey C. Arrington (R)	37.5
62	CA 24th: Salud O. Carbajal (D)	36.6
63	CA 47th: Alan S. Lowenthal (D)	35.3
64	CA 53rd: Sara Jacobs (D)	34.0
65	CA 39th: Young Kim (R)	33.3
65	IL 3rd: Marie Newman (D)	33.3
67	TX 2nd: Dan Crenshaw (R)	33.1
68	CA 50th: Darrell Issa (R)	33.0
69	FL 14th: Kathy Castor (D)	31.8
70	NV 4th: Steven Horsford (D)	30.7
70	TX 7th: Lizzie Fletcher (D)	30.7
72	TX 21st: Chip Roy (R)	30.3
73	CA 3rd: John Garamendi (D)	30.1
74	CO 7th: Ed Perlmutter (D)	29.6
74	TX 5th: Lance Gooden (R)	29.6

Foreign-born rank	State congressional district Representative	Percent foreign born [col 13]
Percent foreign born, 2016–2020		
1	FL 25th Mario Diaz-Balart (R)	56.6
2	FL 27th: Maria Elvira Salazar (R)	54.5
3	NY 6th: Grace Meng (D)	50.7
4	CA 17th: Ro Khanna (D)	49.8
5	FL 26th: Carlos A. Gimenez (R)	48.1
6	NY 14th: Alexandria Ocasio Cortez (D)	45.1
7	NJ 8th: Albio Sires (D)	45.0
8	CA 34th: Jimmy Gomez (D)	44.6
9	FL 24th: Frederica S. Wilson (D)	43.9
10	NY 5th: Gregory W. Meeks (D)	42.8
11	CA 29th: Tony Cárdenas (D)	42.3
12	CA 40th: Lucille Roybal-Allard (D)	39.9
13	NJ 9th: Bill Pascrell, Jr. (D)	39.0
14	CA 27th: Judy Chu (D)	38.5
14	NY 9th: Yvette D. Clarke (D)	38.5
16	CA 28th: Adam B. Schiff (D)	38.3
17	CA 14th Jackie Speier (D)	37.9
18	CA 46th: J. Luis Correa (D)	37.8
19	FL 23rd: Debbie Wasserman Schultz (D)	37.3
20	CA 19th: Zoe Lofgren (D)	36.0
21	CA 32nd: Grace F. Napolitano (D)	35.3
22	CA 15th: Eric Swalwell (D)	35.2
22	NY 13th: Adriano Espaillat (D)	35.2
24	NY 15th: Ritchie Torres (D)	35.0
25	TX 9th: Al Green (D)	34.6
26	FL 20th: Sheila Cherfilus-McCormick (D)	34.4
27	NY 7th: Nydia M. Velázquez (D)	34.2
28	CA 44th: Nanette Diaz Barragan (D)	33.8
29	CA 12th: Nancy Pelosi (D)	32.9
29	TX 29th: Sylvia R. Garcia (D)	32.9
31	CA 30th: Brad Sherman (D)	32.6
32	NY 8th: Hakeem S. Jeffries (D)	32.5
33	CA 39th: Young Kim (R)	32.3
33	IL 4th: Jesus G. "Chuy" Garcia (D)	32.3
35	CA 51st: Juan Vargas (D)	32.1
35	MA 7th: Ayanna Presley (D)	32.1
37	CA 43rd: Maxine Waters (D)	31.9
38	TX 33rd: Marc A. Veasey (D)	31.4
39	VA 11th: Gerald E. Connolly (D)	31.3
40	NV 1st: Dina Titus (D)	31.1
41	CA 18th: Anna G. Eshoo (D)	30.9
42	CA 37th: Karen Bass (D)	30.8
42	NY 11th: Nicole Malliotakis (R)	30.8
44	NY 10th: Jerrold Nadler (D)	30.7
45	WA 9th: Adam Smith (D)	30.5
46	NJ 10th: Donald M. Payne, Jr. (D)	30.0
47	CA 38th: Linda T. Sánchez (D)	29.9
48	NY 16th: Jamaal Bowman (D)	29.8
48	TX 7th: Lizzie Fletcher (D)	29.8
50	CA 47th: Alan S. Lowenthal (D)	29.0
51	CA 35th: Norma J. Torres (D)	28.9
51	CA 45th: Katie Porter (D)	28.9
51	NJ 6th: Frank Pallone Jr. (D)	28.9
54	IL 8th: Raja Krishnamoorthi (D)	28.8
55	CA 21st: David G. Valadao (R)	28.3
55	FL 21st: Lois Frankel (D)	28.3
57	VA 8th: Donald S. Beyer, Jr. (D)	28.1
58	NJ 12th: Bonnie Watson Coleman (D)	28.0
59	FL 22nd: Vacancy	27.8
60	CA 13th: Barbara Lee (D)	26.6
61	NY 12th: Carolyn B. Maloney (D)	26.5
62	CA 11th: Mark Desaulnier (D)	25.9
63	IL 9th: Janice D. Schakowsky (D)	25.7
64	GA 7th Carolyn Bourdeaux (D)	25.6
65	FL 10th: Val Butler Demings (D)	25.4
66	TX 22nd: Troy E. Nehls (R)	25.3
67	CA 41st: Mark Takano (D)	25.2
68	CA 20th: Jimmy Panetta (D)	25.1
68	TX 24rd: Beth Van Duyne (R)	25.1
70	AZ 7th: Ruben Gallego (D)	24.9
71	MA 5th: Katherine Clark (D)	24.4
72	CA 48th: Michelle Steel (R)	24.3
72	IL 10th: Bradley Scott Schneider (D)	24.3
74	CA 16th: Jim Costa (D)	23.5
75	MD 8th: Jamie Raskin (D)	23.2

Congressional Districts of the 116th Congress of the United States

Selected Rankings

Percent under 18 years old, 2016–2020			Percent 65 years old and over, 2016–2020			Percent college graduates (bachelor's degree or more), 2016–2020		
Under 18 years old rank	State congressional district Representative	Percent under 18 years old [col 15 and 16]	65 years old and over rank	State congressional district Representative	Percent 65 years old and over [col 22 and 23]	College graduates rank	State congressional district Representative	Percent college graduates [col 27]
1	TX 15th: Vicente Gonzalez (D)	30.9	1	FL 11th: Daniel Webster (R)	36.6	1	NY 12th: Carolyn B. Maloney (D)	73.2
2	UT 4th: Burgess Owens (R)	30.8	2	FL 17th: W. Gregory Steube (R)	32.1	2	CA 33rd: Ted Lieu (D)	66.5
3	TX 33rd: Marc A. Veasey (D)	30.5	3	FL 19th: Byron Donalds (R)	31.8	3	CA 18th: Anna G. Eshoo (D)	64.6
4	TX 28th: Henry Cuellar (D)	30.4	4	AZ 4th: Paul A. Gosar (R)	28.0	4	GA 6th: Lucy McBath (D)	63.5
5	CA 21st: David G. Valadao (R)	30.3	5	FL 16th: Vern Buchanan (R)	26.7	5	VA 8th: Donald S. Beyer, Jr. (D)	63.4
5	UT 1st: Blake D. Moore (R)	30.3	6	FL 21st: Lois Frankel (D)	25.9	6	NY 10th: Jerrold Nadler (D)	62.8
7	TX 29th: Sylvia R. Garcia (D)	30.1	7	FL 18th: Brian J. Mast (R)	25.8	7	WA 7th: Pramila Jayapal (D)	62.4
8	CA 16th: Jim Costa (D)	29.8	8	FL 8th Bill Posey (R)	25.4	8	CA 12th: Nancy Pelosi (D)	60.6
9	UT 3rd: John R. Curtis (R)	29.5	9	FL 6th: Michael Waltz (R)	25.3	9	CA 17th: Ro Khanna (D)	60.0
10	AZ 7th: Ruben Gallego (D)	29.4	10	FL 12th: Gus M. Bilirakis (R)	24.4	10	DC: At-Large: Eleanor Holmes Norton (D)	59.8
11	TX 34th: Mayra Flores (R)	29.2	11	FL 13th: Vacancy	23.5	11	CA 52nd: Scott H. Peters (D)	59.6
12	WA 4th: Dan Newsome (R)	28.8	11	MI 1st: Jack Bergman (R)	23.5	12	MA 5th: Katherine Clark (D)	59.2
13	CA 22nd: Connie Conway (R)	28.6	13	NC 11th: Madison Cawthorn (R)	22.8	13	IL 5th: Michael Quigley (D)	56.9
14	TX 22nd: Troy E. Nehls (R)	27.8	14	MA 8th: William R. Keating (D)	22.2	13	VA 11th: Gerald E. Connolly (D)	56.9
14	TX 30th: Eddie Bernice Johnson (D)	27.8	15	CA 36th: Raul Ruiz (D)	22.0	15	MD 8th: Jamie Raskin (D)	56.3
16	CA 8th: Jay Olbernolte (R)	27.7	16	AZ 8th: Debbie Lesko (R)	21.9	16	CA 45th: Katie Porter (D)	56.1
17	CA 40th: Lucille Roybal-Allard (D)	27.6	17	CA 1st: Doug LaMalfa (R)	21.6	16	CO 2nd: Joe Neguse (D)	56.1
18	TX 23rd: Tony Gonzales (R)	27.4	17	SC 7th: Tom Rice (R)	21.6	16	NJ 11th: Mikie Sherill (D)	56.1
19	GA 7th Carolyn Bourdeaux (D)	27.3	19	AZ 2nd: Ann Kirkpatrick (D)	21.5	19	NC 4th: David E. Price (D)	55.9
19	NY 15th: Ritchie Torres (D)	27.3	20	CA 4th: Tom McClintock (R)	21.4	20	VA 10th: Jennifer Wexton (D)	55.8
21	CA 23rd: Kevin McCarthy (R)	27.1	20	FL 22nd: Vacancy	21.4	21	IL 9th: Janice D. Schakowsky (D)	55.6
21	TX 16th: Veronica Escobar (D)	27.1	20	PA 14th: Guy Reschenthaler (R)	21.4	22	TX 3rd: Van Taylor (R)	55.2
23	CA 10th: Josh Harder (D)	26.9	23	CA 2nd: Jared Huffman (D)	21.1	23	NJ 7th: Tom Malinowski (D)	54.7
24	CA 42nd: Ken Calvert (R)	26.8	23	OR 4th: Peter A. DeFazio (D)	21.1	24	NY 3rd: Thomas R. Souzzi (D)	54.4
24	UT 2nd: Chris Stewart (R)	26.8	25	ME 2nd: Jared F. Golden (D)	21.0	25	IL 6th: Sean Casten (D)	53.7
26	CA 9th: Jerry McNerney (D)	26.7	25	WV 3rd: Carol D. Miller (R)	21.0	26	MA 4th: Jake Auchincloss (D)	51.9
27	CA 41st: Mark Takano (D)	26.6	27	PA 13th: John Joyce (R)	20.9	27	CT 4th: James A. Himes (D)	51.7
27	CA 44th: Nanette Diaz Barragan (D)	26.6	28	PA 15th: Glen Thompson (R)	20.8	28	CA 13th: Barbara Lee (D)	50.9
29	VA 10th: Jennifer Wexton (D)	26.3	29	NY 3rd: Thomas R. Souzzi (D)	20.7	29	MO 2nd: Ann Wagner (R)	50.5
30	TX 26th: Michael C. Burgess (R)	26.2	29	OR 2nd: Cliff Bentz (R)	20.7	30	MN 3rd: Dean Philips (D)	50.4
31	AZ 3rd: Raul M. Grijalva (D)	26.1	31	VA 9th: Morgan Griffith (R)	20.6	31	CO 1st: Diana DeGette (D)	50.0
31	CA 25th: Mike Garcia (R)	26.1	31	WA 6th: Derek Kilmer (D)	20.6	32	TX 7th: Lizzie Fletcher (D)	49.8
31	CA 35th: Norma J. Torres (D)	26.1	33	FL 2nd: Neal P. Dunn (R)	20.5	33	MD 3rd: John P. Sarbanes (D)	49.7
34	ID 2nd: Michael K. Simpson (R)	26.0	33	MN 8th: Pete Stauber (R)	20.5	34	NJ 5th: Josh Gottheimer (D)	49.5
34	NE 2nd: Don Bacon (R)	26.0	33	TN 1st: Diana Harshbarger (R)	20.5	35	CA 14th Jackie Speier (D)	49.4
34	TX 5th: Lance Gooden (R)	26.0	36	VA 5th: Bob Good (R)	20.4	36	MA 8th: Stephen F. Lynch (D)	49.2
34	TX 31st: John R. Carter (R)	26.0	36	WI 7th: Thomas P. Tiffany (R)	20.4	37	MI 11th: Haley M. Stevens (D)	48.6
38	GA 13th: David Scott (D)	25.9	38	ME 1st: Chellie Pingree (D)	20.3	38	PA 4th: Madeleine Dean (D)	48.3
38	TX 6th: Jake Ellzey (R)	25.9	38	NY 19th: Patrick Ryan (D)	20.3	39	KS 3rd: Sharice Davids (D)	48.2
38	TX 18th: Sheila Jackson-Lee (D)	25.9	40	OH 14th: David P. Joyce (R)	20.2	40	MN 5th: Ilhan Omar (D)	48.0
41	IN 7th: André Carson (D)	25.8	41	OH 6th: Bill Johnson (R)	20.1	41	NY 17th: Mondaire Jones (D)	47.5
42	TX 3rd: Van Taylor (R)	25.7	41	PA 17th: Conor Lamb (D)	20.1	42	CA 15th: Eric Swalwell (D)	47.3
42	TX 9th: Al Green (D)	25.7	43	NJ 3rd: Andy Kim (D)	19.9	42	CA 28th: Adam B. Schiff (D)	47.3
44	CA 31st: Pete Aguilar (D)	25.6	43	NC 7th: David Rouzer (R)	19.9	42	NJ 12th: Bonnie Watson Coleman (D)	47.3
45	NC 2nd: Deborah K. Ross (D)	25.5	43	OH 16th: Anthony Gonzalez (R)	19.9	45	TX 24rd: Beth Van Duyne (R)	47.2
45	TX 20th: Joaquin Castro (D)	25.5	46	PA 8th: Matt Cartwright (D)	19.8	46	TX 21st: Chip Roy (R)	47.0
47	IN 3rd: Jim Banks (R)	25.4	47	PA 9th: Daniel Meuser (R)	19.7	47	IN 5th: Victoria Spartz (R)	46.9
47	MN 6th: Tom Emmer (R)	25.4	48	MN 7th: Michelle Fischbach (R)	19.6	48	MA 7th: Ayanna Presley (D)	46.6
47	OK 5th: Stephanie I. Bice (R)	25.4	48	NE 3rd: Adrian Smith (R)	19.6	49	TX 22nd: Troy E. Nehls (R)	46.5
47	Tx 10th: Michael T. McCaul (R)	25.4	50	AR 4th: Bruce Westerman (R)	19.5	50	MA 6th: Seth Moulton (D)	46.3
47	TX 11th: August Pfluger (R)	25.4	50	WV 1st:David McKinley (R)	19.5	50	PA 6th: Chrissy Houlahan (D)	46.3
52	KS 4th: Ron Estes (R)	25.3	52	PA 12th: Fred Keller (R)	19.4	52	CA 48th: Michelle Steel (R)	46.1
52	TX 36th: Brian Babin (R)	25.3	52	PA 16th: Mike Kelly (R)	19.4	52	CA 49th: Mike Levin (D)	46.1
54	AZ 5th: Andy Biggs (R)	25.2	52	VT: At-large Peter Welch (D)	19.4	54	IL 10th: Bradley Scott Schneider (D)	45.9
54	CA 51st: Juan Vargas (D)	25.2	55	MO 2nd: Ann Wagner (R)	19.3	55	TX 32nd: Colin Z. Allred (D)	45.6
54	IL 11th: Bill Foster (D)	25.2	55	NY 27th: Chris Jacobs (R)	19.3	56	CA 11th: Mark Desaulnier (D)	45.5
54	IL 14th: Lauren Underwood (D)	25.2	55	WV 2nd: Alexander X. Mooney (R)	19.3	57	AZ 6th: David Schweikert (R)	45.2
54	KS 3rd: Sharice Davids (D)	25.2	58	AZ 6th: David Schweikert (R)	19.2	57	TX 26th: Michael C. Burgess (R)	45.2
54	TX 7th: Lizzie Fletcher (D)	25.2	58	MI 4th: John L. Moolenaar (R)	19.2	59	GA 5th: Nikema Williams (D)	45.1
54	TX 8th: Kevin Brady (R)	25.2	60	AZ 1st: Tom O'Halleran (D)	19.0	60	CA 30th: Brad Sherman (D)	45.0
54	WI 4th: Gwen Moore (D)	25.2	60	HI 1st: Ed Case (D)	19.0	61	MN 4th: Betty McCollum (D)	44.6
62	NV 4th: Steven Horsford (D)	25.1	62	IL 15th: Mary E. Miller (R)	18.9	61	WA 1st: Suzan K. DelBene (D)	44.6
63	OK 1st: Kevin Hern (R)	25.0	62	IL 17th: Cheri Bustos (D)	18.9	63	CA 27th: Judy Chu (D)	44.4
63	TN 9th: Steve Cohen (D)	25.0	62	MD 1st: Andrew Harris (R)	18.9	64	WA 9th: Adam Smith (D)	44.2
63	TX 27th: Michael Cloud (R)	25.0	62	NJ 2nd: Jefferson Van Drew (R)	18.9	65	IL 7th: Danny K. Davis (D)	44.1
66	AK At-Large: Mary Peltola (D)	24.9	62	NY 23rd: Joseph Sempolinski (R)	18.9	66	NY 4th: Kathleen M. Rice (D)	43.7
66	TX 2nd: Dan Crenshaw (R)	24.9	67	CO 3rd: Lauren Boebert (R)	18.8	67	WI 2nd: Mark Pocan (D)	43.4
68	CO 6th: Jason Crow (D)	24.8	67	DE: At-Large: Lisa Blunt Rochester (D)	18.8	68	CO 6th: Jason Crow (D)	43.2
68	ID 1st: Russ Fulcher (R)	24.8	67	FL 25th Mario Diaz-Balart (R)	18.8	69	NJ 4th: Christopher H. Smith (R)	43.0
68	PA 2nd: Brendan F. Boyle (D)	24.8	67	IL 18th: Darin LaHood (R)	18.8	70	IL 14th: Lauren Underwood (D)	42.9
68	WA 8th: Kim Schrier (D)	24.8	67	MO 8th:Jason T. Smith (R)	18.8	70	TX 2nd: Dan Crenshaw (R)	42.9
72	CO 4th: Ken Buck (R)	24.7	67	NH 2nd: Ann M. Kuster (D)	18.8	72	GA 7th Carolyn Bourdeaux (D)	42.8
72	GA 4th: Henry C. "Hank" Johnson Jr. (D)	24.7	67	NJ 4th: Christopher H. Smith (R)	18.8	73	MD 6th: David J. Trone (D)	42.7
72	LA 3rd: Clay Higgins (R)	24.7	67	NY 22nd: Claudia Tenney (R)	18.8	74	CA 2nd: Jared Huffman (D)	42.5
72	MN 2nd: Angie Craig (D)	24.7	67	OH 13th: Tim Ryan (D)	18.8	74	CA 39th: Young Kim (R)	42.5

Congressional Districts of the 116th Congress of the United States

Selected Rankings

Median value of owner-occupied housing units, 2016–2020

Median value rank	State congressional district Representative	Median value (dollars) [col 43]
1	CA 18th: Anna G. Eshoo (D)	1,489,000
2	CA 33rd: Ted Lieu (D)	1,284,200
3	CA 12th: Nancy Pelosi (D)	1,165,300
4	CA 14th Jackie Speier (D)	1,089,000
5	CA 17th: Ro Khanna (D)	1,059,900
6	NY 10th: Jerrold Nadler (D)	1,049,300
7	NY 12th: Carolyn B. Maloney (D)	1,043,300
8	CA 28th: Adam B. Schiff (D)	865,200
9	CA 19th: Zoe Lofgren (D)	845,300
10	CA 15th: Eric Swalwell (D)	840,500
11	CA 48th: Michelle Steel (R)	812,600
12	CA 13th: Barbara Lee (D)	791,400
13	CA 37th: Karen Bass (D)	785,400
14	NY 7th: Nydia M. Velázquez (D)	768,800
15	CA 45th: Katie Porter (D)	763,100
16	CA 49th: Mike Levin (D)	741,800
17	CA 52nd: Scott H. Peters (D)	739,800
18	CA 27th: Judy Chu (D)	728,200
19	CA 11th: Mark Desaulnier (D)	702,500
20	CA 30th: Brad Sherman (D)	701,500
21	NY 9th: Yvette D. Clarke (D)	686,600
22	WA 7th: Pramila Jayapal (D)	674,100
23	CA 39th: Young Kim (R)	672,100
24	CA 2nd: Jared Huffman (D)	664,900
25	CA 34th: Jimmy Gomez (D)	640,500
26	NY 6th: Grace Meng (D)	638,200
27	NY 8th: Hakeem S. Jeffries (D)	633,700
28	NY 3rd: Thomas R. Souzzi (D)	633,100
29	CA 20th: Jimmy Panetta (D)	631,400
30	CA 47th: Alan S. Lowenthal (D)	619,000
31	CA 26th: Julia Brownley (D)	607,800
32	CA 24th: Salud O. Carbajal (D)	607,300
33	MA 5th: Katherine Clark (D)	589,900
34	NY 11th: Nicole Malliotakis (R)	587,800
35	CA 43rd: Maxine Waters (D)	586,700
36	VA 8th: Donald S. Beyer, Jr. (D)	574,700
37	CA 46th: J. Luis Correa (D)	560,000
38	NY 14th: Alexandria Ocasio Cortez (D)	556,900
39	CA 53rd: Sara Jacobs (D)	554,500
40	CA 5th: Mike Thompson (D)	553,500
41	CA 38th: Linda T. Sánchez (D)	541,600
42	MA 7th: Ayanna Presley (D)	537,500
43	CA 50th: Darrell Issa (R)	517,300
44	CA 29th: Tony Cárdenas (D)	515,300
45	WA 1st: Suzan K. DelBene (D)	514,600
46	VA 10th: Jennifer Wexton (D)	512,200
47	NY 13th: Adriano Espaillat (D)	509,900
48	CA 32nd: Grace F. Napolitano (D)	506,600
49	NY 4th: Kathleen M. Rice (D)	498,400
50	WA 9th: Adam Smith (D)	492,100
51	VA 11th: Gerald E. Connolly (D)	488,900
52	NY 5th: Gregory W. Meeks (D)	488,300
53	NY 17th: Mondaire Jones (D)	482,300
54	CA 25th: Mike Garcia (R)	479,100
55	NY 16th: Jamaal Bowman (D)	478,100
56	MA 6th: Seth Moulton (D)	475,500
57	MA 8th: Stephen F. Lynch (D)	461,500
58	CA 40th: Lucille Roybal-Allard (D)	459,800
59	MD 8th: Jamie Raskin (D)	458,500
60	NJ 11th: Mikie Sherill (D)	454,900
61	NJ 7th: Tom Malinowski (D)	454,400
62	CA 4th: Tom McClintock (R)	448,600
63	CA 42nd: Ken Calvert (R)	446,600
64	MA 4th: Jake Auchincloss (D)	441,400
65	CA 44th: Nanette Diaz Barragan (D)	438,600
66	NY 15th: Ritchie Torres (D)	431,500
67	NJ 5th: Josh Gottheimer (D)	429,100
68	CO 1st: Diana DeGette (D)	426,900
69	WA 8th: Kim Schrier (D)	409,800
70	NY 2nd: Andrew R. Garbarino (R)	403,100
71	OR 3rd: Earl Blumenauer (D)	401,300
72	NY 1st: Lee M. Zeldin (R)	400,700
73	CA 7th: Ami Bera (D)	399,700
74	WA 2nd: Rick Larsen (D)	399,300
75	OR 1st: Suzanne Bonamici (D)	395,800

Percent female-headed family households, 2016–2020

Female householder rank	State congressional district Representative	Percent with female householder [col 32]
1	NY 15th: Ritchie Torres (D)	34.0
2	NY 13th: Adriano Espaillat (D)	24.2
3	MS 2nd: Bennie G. Thompson (D)	23.4
4	CA 40th: Lucille Roybal-Allard (D)	23.1
5	TN 9th: Steve Cohen (D)	23.0
6	NY 5th: Gregory W. Meeks (D)	22.6
7	NY 8th: Hakeem S. Jeffries (D)	22.2
7	PA 2nd: Brendan F. Boyle (D)	22.2
9	CA 44th: Nanette Diaz Barragan (D)	22.1
10	MI 13th: Rashida Tlaib (D)	21.8
11	NJ 10th: Donald M. Payne, Jr. (D)	21.3
12	AL 7th: Terri A. Sewell (D)	20.7
13	TX 30th: Eddie Bernice Johnson (D)	20.3
14	AZ 7th: Ruben Gallego (D)	20.2
14	TX 33rd: Marc A. Veasey (D)	20.2
16	OH 11th: Shontel M. Brown (D)	19.9
17	CA 51st: Juan Vargas (D)	19.8
17	SC 6th: James E. Clyburn (D)	19.8
17	TX 9th: Al Green (D)	19.8
20	TX 18th: Sheila Jackson-Lee (D)	19.7
21	MI 14th: Brenda L. Lawrence (D)	19.6
21	TX 15th: Vicente Gonzalez (D)	19.6
23	NY 9th: Yvette D. Clarke (D)	19.5
24	TX 29th: Sylvia R. Garcia (D)	19.4
25	CA 16th: Jim Costa (D)	19.2
26	TX 34th: Mayra Flores (R)	19.1
27	CA 21st: David G. Valadao (R)	19.0
28	CA 43rd: Maxine Waters (D)	18.9
28	TX 28th: Henry Cuellar (D)	18.9
30	CA 35th: Norma J. Torres (D)	18.8
31	MO 1st: Cori Bush (D)	18.5
32	TX 16th: Veronica Escobar (D)	18.4
32	WI 4th: Gwen Moore (D)	18.4
34	CA 31st: Pete Aguilar (D)	18.2
35	NY 16th: Jamaal Bowman (D)	17.9
35	PA 3rd: Dwight Evans (D)	17.9
37	VA 3rd: Robert C. "Bobby" Scott (D)	17.8
38	CA 32nd: Grace F. Napolitano (D)	17.7
39	TX 20th: Joaquin Castro (D)	17.6
40	NC 1st: G. K. Butterfield (D)	17.5
40	OH 3rd: Joyce Beatty (D)	17.5
42	AZ 3rd: Raul M. Grijalva (D)	17.2
43	CA 41st: Mark Takano (D)	17.0
43	NJ 9th: Bill Pascrell, Jr. (D)	17.0
45	CA 46th: J. Luis Correa (D)	16.9
46	CA 38th: Linda T. Sánchez (D)	16.8
47	CA 29th: Tony Cárdenas (D)	16.4
48	NY 14th: Alexandria Ocasio Cortez (D)	16.3
48	TX 35th: Lloyd Doggett (D)	16.3
50	NV 1st: Dina Titus (D)	16.2
51	NY 7th: Nydia M. Velázquez (D)	16.0
52	NJ 8th: Albio Sires (D)	15.8
53	OH 9th: Marcy Kaptur (D)	15.6
54	MS 3rd: Michael Guest (R)	15.5
54	TX 23rd: Tony Gonzales (R)	15.5
54	VA 4th: A. Donald McEachin (D)	15.5
57	MS 4th: Steven M. Palazzo (R)	15.4
58	CA 6th: Doris O. Matsui (D)	15.3
58	NJ 1st: Donald Norcross (D)	15.3
58	PA 5th: Mary Gay Scanlon (D)	15.3
61	AL 2nd: Mary Peltola (D)	15.2
61	CA 9th: Jerry McNerney (D)	15.2
61	CA 22nd: Connie Conway (R)	15.2
64	CA 8th: Jay Olbernolte (R)	15.1
64	SC 7th: Tom Rice (R)	15.1
66	MI 5th: Daniel T. Kildee (D)	15.0
66	TX 27th: Michael Cloud (R)	15.0
68	NY 26th: Brian Higgins (D)	14.8
69	CA 34th: Jimmy Gomez (D)	14.7
70	MS 1st: Trent Kelly (R)	14.6
70	TX 5th: Lance Gooden (R)	14.6
72	NV 4th: Steven Horsford (D)	14.4
73	CA 23rd: Kevin McCarthy (R)	14.3
73	NC 12th: Alma S. Adams (D)	14.3
75	AR 2nd: J. French Hill (R)	14.2

Percent of households with one person, 2016–2020

One-person household rank	State congressional district Representative	Percent one-person households [col 33]
1	NY 12th: Carolyn B. Maloney (D)	46.4
2	DC: At-Large: Eleanor Holmes Norton (D)	45.1
3	PA 3rd: Dwight Evans (D)	43.3
4	IL 7th: Danny K. Davis (D)	42.6
5	GA 5th: Nikema Williams (D)	42.2
6	OH 11th: Shontel M. Brown (D)	41.8
7	NY 10th: Jerrold Nadler (D)	40.6
8	PA 18th: Michael F. Doyle (D)	39.5
9	MO 1st: Cori Bush (D)	39.2
10	MI 13th: Rashida Tlaib (D)	38.9
11	LA 2nd: Troy Carter (D)	38.5
12	WA 7th: Pramila Jayapal (D)	38.3
13	MN 5th: Ilhan Omar (D)	38.0
14	CA 12th: Nancy Pelosi (D)	37.6
15	TN 9th: Steve Cohen (D)	37.2
16	CO 1st: Diana DeGette (D)	37.1
17	AL 7th: Terri A. Sewell (D)	37.0
17	CA 28th: Adam B. Schiff (D)	37.0
19	NY 26th: Brian Higgins (D)	36.9
19	WI 4th: Gwen Moore (D)	36.9
21	IN 7th: André Carson (D)	36.8
21	MI 14th: Brenda L. Lawrence (D)	36.8
23	NY 13th: Adriano Espaillat	36.6
24	OH 9th: Marcy Kaptur (D)	36.3
25	FL 13th: Vacancy	36.1
26	SC 6th: James E. Clyburn (D)	35.7
27	MO 5th: Emanuel Cleaver (D)	35.5
28	CA 37th: Karen Bass (D)	35.3
29	FL 22nd: Vacancy	35.2
30	OH 13th: Tim Ryan (D)	35.1
31	IL 1st: Bobby L. Rush (D)	34.8
32	VA 8th: Donald S. Beyer, Jr. (D)	34.6
33	MD 7th: Kweisi Mfume (D)	34.5
34	KY 3rd: John A. Yarmuth (D)	34.4
35	IL 5th: Michael Quigley (D)	34.3
35	IL 9th: Janice D. Schakowsky (D)	34.3
35	NM 1st: Melanie A. Stansbury (D)	34.3
35	OH 3rd: Joyce Beatty (D)	34.3
39	AZ 2nd: Ann Kirkpatrick (D)	34.2
40	IL 13th: Rodney Davis (R)	34.1
41	AZ 9th: Greg Stanton (D)	34.0
41	CA 33rd: Ted Lieu (D)	34.0
43	TN 5th: Jim Cooper (D)	33.9
44	NV 1st: Dina Titus (D)	33.8
45	MI 9th: Andy Levin (D)	33.7
46	MA 7th: Ayanna Presley (D)	33.5
47	NY 20th: Paul Tonko (D)	33.4
48	IL 17th: Cheri Bustos (D)	33.3
49	IL 2nd: Robin L. Kelly (D)	33.1
50	NC 12th: Alma S. Adams (D)	33.0
51	OH 10th: Michael R. Turner (R)	32.9
52	FL 5th: Al Lawson (D)	32.5
52	ND At-Large: Kelly Armstrong (R)	32.5
54	CA 34th: Jimmy Gomez (D)	32.4
54	MS 2nd: Bennie G. Thompson (D)	32.4
54	NY 25th: Joseph D. Morelle (D)	32.4
57	FL 14th: Kathy Castor (D)	32.2
58	LA 4th: Mike Johnson (R)	32.1
58	NC 1st: G. K. Butterfield (D)	32.1
58	PA 17th: Conor Lamb (D)	32.1
61	CA 13th: Barbara Lee (D)	32.0
61	CA 36th: Raul Ruiz (D)	32.0
61	GA 2nd: Sanford D. Bishop Jr. (D)	32.0
64	RI 1st: David Cicilline (D)	31.9
64	TX 21st: Chip Roy (R)	31.9
66	IL 12th: Mike Bost (R)	31.8
66	NJ 10th: Donald M. Payne, Jr. (D)	31.8
68	FL 27th: Maria Elvira Salazar (R)	31.7
69	MI 5th: Daniel T. Kildee (D)	31.5
70	VA 4th: A. Donald McEachin (D)	31.4
70	VA 9th: Morgan Griffith (R)	31.4
72	MN 4th: Betty McCollum (D)	31.3
73	NY 8th: Hakeem S. Jeffries (D)	31.2
73	NY 9th: Yvette D. Clarke (D)	31.2
73	WV 1st:David McKinley (R)	31.2

Congressional Districts of the 116th Congress of the United States
Selected Rankings

Median household income, 2016–2020			Percent of persons below 65 years with no health insurance, 2016–2020			Percent of persons below the poverty level, 2016–2020		
Median income rank	State congressional district Representative	Median income (dollars) [col 47]	No health inurance rank	State congressional district Representative	Percent with no health insurance [col 59]	Poverty rate rank	State congressional district Representative	Poverty rate [col 49]
1	CA 18th: Anna G. Eshoo (D)	$146,441	1	TX 29th: Sylvia R. Garcia (D)	33.7		NY 15th: Ritchie Torres (D)	34.3
2	CA 17th: Ro Khanna (D)	$142,408	2	TX 33rd: Marc A. Veasey (D)	32.9		MI 13th: Rashida Tlaib (D)	28.2
3	VA 10th: Jennifer Wexton (D)	$132,276	3	TX 34th: Mayra Flores (R)	30.1		KY 5th: Harold Rogers (R)	25.9
4	NY 3rd: Thomas R. Souzzi (D)	$123,412	4	TX 15th: Vicente Gonzalez (D)	29.4		MS 2nd: Bennie G. Thompson (D)	25.9
5	CA 15th: Eric Swalwell (D)	$123,064	5	TX 28th: Henry Cuellar (D)	28.0		TX 34th: Mayra Flores (R)	25.8
6	CA 14th Jackie Speier (D)	$121,097	6	TX 9th: Al Green (D)	26.9		NY 13th: Adriano Espaillat (D)	24.9
7	CA 12th: Nancy Pelosi (D)	$120,697	7	TX 18th: Sheila Jackson-Lee (D)	24.9		TX 15th: Vicente Gonzalez (D)	24.8
8	NJ 11th: Mikie Sherill (D)	$119,624	8	TX 30th: Eddie Bernice Johnson (D)	23.2		GA 2nd: Sanford D. Bishop Jr. (D)	24.6
9	NJ 7th: Tom Malinowski (D)	$118,554	9	TX 5th: Lance Gooden (R)	22.4		AL 7th: Terri A. Sewell (D)	24.4
10	VA 11th: Gerald E. Connolly (D)	$117,382	10	OK 2nd: Markwayne Mullin (R)	22.1		OH 11th: Shontel M. Brown (D)	24.4
11	CA 33rd: Ted Lieu (D)	$115,408	11	TX 16th: Veronica Escobar (D)	21.7		CA 16th: Jim Costa (D)	24.1
12	NY 12th: Carolyn B. Maloney (D)	$114,058	12	TX 36th: Brian Babin (R)	21.2		PA 2nd: Brendan F. Boyle (D)	24.0
13	NY 4th: Kathleen M. Rice (D)	$113,902	13	AZ 7th: Ruben Gallego (D)	21.0		TN 9th: Steve Cohen (D)	23.9
14	VA 8th: Donald S. Beyer, Jr. (D)	$111,224	14	TX 23rd: Tony Gonzales (R)	20.9		CA 21st: David G. Valadao (R)	23.7
15	CA 45th: Katie Porter (D)	$111,197	15	TX 35th: Lloyd Doggett (D)	20.8		LA 2nd: Troy Carter (D)	23.1
16	MD 8th: Jamie Raskin (D)	$110,108	16	TX 27th: Michael Cloud (R)	20.6		SC 6th: James E. Clyburn (D)	23.0
17	NJ 5th: Josh Gottheimer (D)	$109,901	17	TX 1st: Louie Gohmert (R)	20.4		TX 29th: Sylvia R. Garcia (D)	23.0
18	CA 19th: Zoe Lofgren (D)	$109,530	18	NV 1st: Dina Titus (D)	20.3		AZ 7th: Ruben Gallego (D)	22.9
19	NY 2nd: Andrew R. Garbarino (R)	$108,089	19	TX 11th: August Pfluger (R)	19.8		LA 5th: Julia Letlow (R)	22.9
20	IL 6th: Sean Casten (D)	$106,701	20	TX 20th: Joaquin Castro (D)	19.4		NY 7th: Nydia M. Velázquez (D)	22.3
21	MA 4th: Jake Auchincloss (D)	$104,781	21	TX 13th: Ronny Jackson (R)	19.2		WI 4th: Gwen Moore (D)	22.2
22	MA 5th: Katherine Clark (D)	$104,727	22	TX 14th: Randy K. Weber Sr. (R)	18.8		PA 3rd: Dwight Evans (D)	22.0
23	MD 5th: Steny H. Hoyer (D)	$104,284	23	TX 19th: Jodey C. Arrington (R)	18.7		CA 34th: Jimmy Gomez (D)	21.9
24	NY 17th: Mondaire Jones (D)	$103,638	24	TX 32nd: Colin Z. Allred (D)	18.5		LA 4th: Mike Johnson (R)	21.9
25	WA 1st: Suzan K. DelBene (D)	$103,010	25	TX 7th: Lizzie Fletcher (D)	18.1		TX 18th: Sheila Jackson-Lee (D)	21.8
26	CA 52nd: Scott H. Peters (D)	$102,795	26	NJ 8th: Albio Sires (D)	17.7		TX 28th: Henry Cuellar (D)	21.8
27	NY 1st: Lee M. Zeldin (R)	$101,166	27	GA 9th: Andrew S. Clyde (R)	17.5		TX 33rd: Marc A. Veasey (D)	21.7
28	TX 3rd: Van Taylor (R)	$100,748	28	TX 4th: Pat Fallon (R)	17.4		WV 3rd: Carol D. Miller (R)	21.0
29	NY 10th: Jerrold Nadler (D)	$100,737	29	CA 34th: Jimmy Gomez (D)	17.3		NM 2nd: Yvette Herrell (R)	20.9
30	CA 11th: Mark Desaulnier (D)	$100,114	29	GA 2nd: Sanford D. Bishop Jr. (D)	17.3		MI 14th: Brenda L. Lawrence (D)	20.8
31	TX 22nd: Troy E. Nehls (R)	$99,747	29	TX 6th: Jake Ellzey (R)	17.3		NY 8th: Hakeem S. Jeffries (D)	20.3
32	GA 6th: Lucy McBath (D)	$99,516	32	OK 5th: Stephanie I. Bice (R)	16.8		OH 3rd: Joyce Beatty (D)	20.1
33	CA 48th: Michelle Steel (R)	$99,328	33	GA 4th: Henry C. "Hank" Johnson Jr. (D)	16.7		FL 24th: Frederica S. Wilson (D)	20.0
34	IL 14th: Lauren Underwood (D)	$98,672	34	TX 12th: Kay Granger (R)	16.6		IL 7th: Danny K. Davis (D)	20.0
35	WA 7th: Pramila Jayapal (D)	$97,596	35	IL 4th: Jesus G. "Chuy" Garcia (D)	16.5		CA 40th: Lucille Roybal-Allard (D)	19.9
36	MA 8th: Stephen F. Lynch (D)	$97,583	36	TX 8th: Kevin Brady (R)	16.4		NV 1st: Dina Titus (D)	19.9
37	CA 49th: Mike Levin (D)	$96,591	37	GA 14th: Marjorie Taylor Greene (R)	16.3		OH 9th: Marcy Kaptur (D)	19.7
38	MN 3rd: Dean Philips (D)	$96,454	38	GA 8th: Austin Scott (R)	16.2		NC 1st: G. K. Butterfield (D)	19.6
39	TX 26th: Michael C. Burgess (R)	$96,247	39	NC 11th: Madison Cawthorn (R)	16.1		TX 30th: Eddie Bernice Johnson (D)	19.6
40	CA 39th: Young Kim (R)	$95,636	40	CA 40th: Lucille Roybal-Allard (D)	16.0		GA 12th: Rick W. Allen (R)	19.3
41	MA 6th: Seth Moulton (D)	$94,965	40	OK 1st: Kevin Hern (R)	16.0		AZ 3rd: Raul M. Grijalva (D)	19.1
42	MD 3rd: John P. Sarbanes (D)	$93,724	42	GA 1st: Earl L. "Buddy" Carter (R)	15.9		MS 3rd: Michael Guest (R)	18.8
43	WA 8th: Kim Schrier (D)	$92,544	43	MS 2nd: Bennie G. Thompson (D)	15.8		GA 8th: Austin Scott (R)	18.7
44	PA 1st: Brian K. Fitzpatrick (R)	$92,187	43	TX 2nd: Dan Crenshaw (R)	15.8		OK 2nd: Markwayne Mullin (R)	18.7
45	PA 4th: Madeleine Dean (D)	$92,122	45	GA 7th Carolyn Bourdeaux (D)	15.7		TX 16th: Veronica Escobar (D)	18.7
46	NJ 12th: Bonnie Watson Coleman (D)	$91,433	45	OK 3rd: Frank D. Lucas (R)	15.7		GA 5th: Nikema Williams (D)	18.6
47	CA 42nd: Ken Calvert (R)	$91,349	47	SC 7th: Tom Rice (R)	15.6		TX 9th: Al Green (D)	18.6
48	VA 1st: Robert J. Wittman (R)	$91,248	47	TN 9th: Steve Cohen (D)	15.6		CA 51st: Juan Vargas (D)	18.5
49	NJ 4th: Christopher H. Smith (R)	$90,852	49	MS 4th: Steven M. Palazzo (R)	15.5		MO 8th:Jason T. Smith (R)	18.5
50	IL 5th: Michael Quigley (D)	$90,424	50	AZ 3rd: Raul M. Grijalva (D)	15.4		AZ 1st: Tom O'Halleran (D)	18.4
51	MN 2nd: Angie Craig (D)	$89,327	51	GA 12th: Rick W. Allen (R)	15.3		AR 1st: Eric A. "Rick" Crawford (R)	18.4
52	NY 18th: Sean Patrick Maloney (D)	$89,324	51	GA 13th: David Scott (D)	15.3		IN 7th: André Carson (D)	18.4
53	NJ 6th: Frank Pallone Jr. (D)	$89,001	53	TX 24rd: Beth Van Duyne (R)	14.9		MS 4th: Steven M. Palazzo (R)	18.4
54	CA 26th: Julia Brownley (D)	$88,064	54	MO 7th: Bill Long (R)	14.8		NM 3rd: Teresa Leger Fernandez (D)	18.4
55	MI 11th: Haley M. Stevens (D)	$88,023	54	NC 7th: David Rouzer (R)	14.8		MI 5th: Daniel T. Kildee (D)	18.3
56	PA 6th: Chrissy Houlahan (D)	$87,682	56	SC 6th: James E. Clyburn (D)	14.7		AR 4th: Bruce Westerman (R)	18.2
57	MD 4th: Anthony G. Brown (D)	$87,556	57	TX 17th: Pete Sessions (R)	14.5		IL 2nd: Robin L. Kelly (D)	18.2
58	CA 13th: Barbara Lee (D)	$87,295	58	OK 4th: Tom Cole (R)	14.4		LA 3rd: Clay Higgins (R)	18.1
59	MO 2nd: Ann Wagner (R)	$86,997	59	MO 8th:Jason T. Smith (R)	14.3		TX 35th: Lloyd Doggett (D)	18.0
60	CA 30th: Brad Sherman (D)	$86,710	59	NJ 9th: Bill Pascrell, Jr. (D)	14.3		CA 8th: Jay Olbernolte (R)	17.9
61	WA 9th: Adam Smith (D)	$86,397	61	AK At-Large: Mary Peltola (D)	14.2		KY 1st: James Comer (R)	17.9
62	HI 1st: Ed Case (D)	$86,203	61	NC 12th: Alma S. Adams (D)	14.2		VA 9th: Morgan Griffith (R)	17.9
63	MD 6th: David J. Trone (D)	$86,077	63	GA 5th: Nikema Williams (D)	14.1		MA 7th: Ayanna Presley (D)	17.8
64	IL 10th: Bradley Scott Schneider (D)	$85,567	64	CA 46th: J. Luis Correa (D)	14.0		CA 23rd: Kevin McCarthy (R)	17.6
65	NJ 3rd: Andy Kim (D)	$85,077	64	GA 11th: Barry Loudermilk (R)	14.0		TX 20th: Joaquin Castro (D)	17.6
66	CA 5th: Mike Thompson (D)	$84,399	66	Tx 10th: Michael T. McCaul (R)	13.9		AL 2nd: Barry Moore(R)	17.5
67	MN 6th: Tom Emmer (R)	$84,287	67	AZ 1st: Tom O'Halleran (D)	13.8		CA 44th: Nanette Diaz Barragan (D)	17.5
68	CA 27th: Judy Chu (D)	$83,765	67	MO 5th: Emanuel Cleaver (D)	13.8		SC 7th: Tom Rice (R)	17.5
69	CA 25th: Mike Garcia (R)	$83,267	67	TX 25th: Roger Williams (R)	13.8		CA 6th: Doris O. Matsui (D)	17.4
70	MA 3rd: Lori Trahan (D)	$83,233	70	CA 44th: Nanette Diaz Barragan (D)	13.7		MO 1st: Cori Bush (D)	17.4
71	VA 7th: Abigail Davis Spanberger (D)	$82,539	70	TX 21st: Chip Roy (R)	13.7		NY 26th: Brian Higgins (D)	17.3
72	CA 4th: Tom McClintock (R)	$81,951	72	WY At-large Liz Cheney (R)	13.6		TX 17th: Pete Sessions (R)	17.3
73	OR 1st: Suzanne Bonamici (D)	$81,705	73	NC 1st: G. K. Butterfield (D)	13.5		IL 13th: Rodney Davis (R)	17.1
74	Tx 10th: Michael T. McCaul (R)	$81,492	74	NC 5th: Virginia Foxx (R)	13.1		OH 13th: Tim Ryan (D)	17.1
75	CA 53rd: Sara Jacobs (D)	$81,447	74	NC 10th: Patrick T. McHenry (R)	13.1		CA 37th: Karen Bass (D)	16.9

Table E. Congressional Districts 116th Congress — **Land Area and Population Characteristics**

STATE District	Representative, 117th Congress	Land area,[1] 2020 (sq mi)	Population and population characteristics, 2016–2020												
					Race alone (percent)										
			Total persons	Per square mile	White	Black	American Indian, Alaska Native	Asian and Pacific Islander	Some other race (percent)	Two or more races (percent)	Hispanic or Latino[2] (percent)	Non-Hispanic White alone (percent)	Percent female	Percent foreign-born	Percent born in state of residence
		1	2	3	4	5	6	7	8	9	10	11	12	13	14

1. Dry land or land partially or temporarily covered by water. 2. May be of any race.

Table E. Congressional Districts 116th Congress — **Age and Education**

STATE District	Population and population characteristics, 2016–2020 (cont.)										Education, 2016–2020		
	Age (percent)											Attainment[2] (percent)	
	Under 5 years	5 to 17 years	18 to 24 years	25 to 34 years	35 to 44 years	45 to 54 years	55 to 64 years	65 to 74 years	75 years and over	Median age	Total Enrollment[1]	High school graduate or more	Bachelor's degree or more
	15	16	17	18	19	20	21	22	23	24	25	26	27

1. All persons 3 years old and over enrolled in nursery school through college and graduate or professional school. 2. Persons 25 years old and over.

Table E. Congressional Districts 116th Congress — **Households and Group Quarters**

STATE District	Households, 2016–2020						Total in group quarters, 2020	Persons in group quarters, 2020				
	Number	Average household size	Family households (percent)	Married couple family (percent)	Female family householder[1]	One person households (percent)		Correctional facilities for adults	Juvenile facilities	Skilled nursing facilities	College/ University student housing	Military quarters
	28	29	30	31	32	33	34	35	36	37	38	39

1. No spouse present.

Table E. Congressional Districts 116th Congress — **Housing and Money Income**

STATE District	Housing units, 2016–2020						Money income, 2016–2020		
		Occupied units						Households	
			Owner-occupied			Renter-occupied			
	Total	Occupied units as a percent of all units	Owner-occupied units as a percent of occupied units	Median value[1] (dollars)	Percent valued at $500,000 or more	Median rent[2]	Per capita income (dollars)	Median income (dollars)	Percent with income of $100,000 or more
	40	41	42	43	44	45	46	47	48

1. Specified owner-occupied units; $1,000,000 represents $1,000,000 2. Specified renter-occupied units.

Table E. Congressional Districts 116th Congress — **Poverty, Labor Force, Employment, and Social Security**

STATE District	Poverty, 2016–2020			Civilian labor force, 2016–2020			Civilian employment,[2] 2016–2020				Persons under 65 years of age with no health insurance, 2016–2020 (percent)	Social Security beneficiaries, December 2021		Supplemental Security Income recipients, December 2021
					Unemployment			Percent						
	Persons below poverty level (percent)	Families below poverty level (percent)	Percent of households receiving food stamps in past 12 months	Total	Total	Rate[1]	Total	Management, business, science, and arts occupations	Service, sales, and office	Construction and production		Number	Rate[3]	
	49	50	51	52	53	54	55	56	57	58	59	60	61	62

1. Percent of civilian labor force. 2. Persons 16 years old and over. 3. Per 1,000 resident population estimated in the 2016–2020 American Community Survey.

Table E. Congressional Districts 116th Congress — **Agriculture**

STATE District	Agriculture 2017									
		Land in farms			Value of products sold				Government payments	
	Number of farms	Acres	Average size of farm (acres)	Harvested crops (acres)	Total ($1,000)	Average per farm (dollars)	Percent from crops	Percent from livestock and poultry products	Total ($1,000)	Average per farm receiving payments (dollars)
	63	64	65	66	67	68	69	70	71	72

Table E. Congressional Districts 116th Congress — **Nonfarm Employment and Payroll**

STATE District	Private nonfarm employment and payroll, 2020												
		Employment										Annual payroll	
			Percent by selected industries										
	Number of establishments	Total	Manufacturing	Construction	Wholesale trade	Retail trade	Health care and social assistance	Finance and Insurance	Real estate and rental and leasing	Professional, scientific, and technical services	Information	Total (mil dol)	Average per employee (dollars)
	73	74	75	76	77	78	79	80	81	82	83	84	85

Table E. Congressional Districts 116th Congress — **Land Area and Population Characteristics**

STATE District	Representative, 117th Congress	Land area,[1] 2020 (sq mi)	Population and population characteristics, 2016–2020: Total persons	Per square mile	Race alone (percent): White	Black	American Indian, Alaska Native	Asian and Pacific Islander	Some other race (percent)	Two or more races (percent)	Hispanic or Latino[2] (percent)	Non-Hispanic White alone (percent)	Percent female	Percent foreign-born	Percent born in state of residence
		1	2	3	4	5	6	7	8	9	10	11	12	13	14
UNITED STATES		3,531,905.0	326,569,308	92.5	70.4	12.6	0.8	5.8	5.1	5.2	18.2	60.1	50.8	13.5	58.2
ALABAMA		50,647.0	4,893,186	96.6	67.5	26.6	0.5	1.4	1.5	2.4	4.4	65.2	51.7	3.4	69.3
District 1	Jerry Carl (R)	6,067.1	714,379	117.7	66.7	27.5	1.0	1.4	1.2	2.2	3.2	65.0	51.9	3.0	67.6
District 2	Barry Moore(R)	10,143.0	678,978	66.9	63.2	31.3	0.4	1.4	1.2	2.6	4.0	61.0	51.5	2.8	69.1
District 3	Mike Rogers (R)	7,543.5	713,404	94.6	68.7	25.8	0.3	2.0	1.1	2.1	3.1	67.0	51.5	3.2	64.5
District 4	Robert B. Aderholt (R)	8,888.9	687,640	77.4	86.5	7.0	0.8	0.6	2.4	2.7	6.7	83.2	50.9	3.6	74.1
District 5	Mo Brooks (R)	3,678.1	728,414	198.0	74.7	17.9	0.6	1.8	1.8	3.1	5.3	72.0	51.1	4.3	60.5
District 6	Gary J. Palmer (R)	4,171.6	708,092	169.7	77.2	16.2	0.3	1.7	2.0	2.6	4.9	74.8	51.7	4.3	71.0
District 7	Terri A. Sewell (D)	10,154.8	662,279	65.2	33.3	62.8	0.2	1.0	1.1	1.6	3.2	31.7	53.1	2.8	79.1
ALASKA		571,022.0	736,990	1.3	63.4	3.2	14.6	7.8	1.7	9.3	7.2	59.7	47.8	7.8	42.0
At Large	Mary Peltola (D)	571,022.0	736,990	1.3	63.4	3.2	14.6	7.8	1.7	9.3	7.2	59.7	47.8	7.8	42.0
ARIZONA		113,653.5	7,174,064	63.1	73.8	4.5	4.3	3.5	6.9	7.0	31.5	54.1	50.3	13.2	39.6
District 1	Tom O'Halleran (D)	55,034.2	772,404	14.0	63.1	2.6	22.6	1.7	4.0	6.0	23.3	48.1	49.4	6.0	52.2
District 2	Ann Kirkpatrick (D)	7,882.6	732,897	93.0	78.5	4.0	1.5	3.4	5.1	7.4	29.1	59.5	50.6	10.7	37.1
District 3	Raul M. Grijalva (D)	15,687.9	780,637	49.8	64.3	4.6	4.5	2.0	15.0	9.7	63.6	25.9	49.6	21.0	48.1
District 4	Paul A. Gosar (R)	33,220.3	811,947	24.4	85.7	1.8	1.7	1.4	4.2	5.2	20.4	72.6	49.7	7.8	28.7
District 5	Andy Biggs (R)	293.6	842,222	2868.6	81.5	3.6	1.0	5.0	3.4	5.6	18.4	69.3	51.2	10.1	36.4
District 6	David Schweikert (R)	625.1	806,918	1290.9	80.8	3.1	1.9	5.4	3.2	5.6	17.4	69.5	50.8	14.0	32.1
District 7	Ruben Gallego (D)	204.7	827,379	4041.9	58.9	9.9	2.6	2.7	15.9	10.1	64.1	20.0	50.0	24.9	48.7
District 8	Debbie Lesko (R)	540.1	806,027	1492.4	79.9	4.5	0.9	4.2	4.5	6.0	20.8	66.9	52.0	9.7	34.5
District 9	Greg Stanton (D)	165.0	793,633	4809.9	70.9	6.6	3.0	6.0	6.3	7.2	26.7	54.9	49.4	14.2	38.8
ARKANSAS		51,992.7	3,011,873	57.9	75.4	15.2	0.6	1.9	2.9	4.0	7.6	71.6	50.9	4.9	61.1
District 1	Eric A. "Rick" Crawford (R)	19,280.4	720,941	37.4	76.8	17.2	0.4	0.6	1.1	3.9	3.6	74.9	50.4	2.0	66.2
District 2	J. French Hill (R)	4,976.0	765,408	153.8	70.1	22.9	0.4	1.7	1.8	3.1	5.3	67.2	51.7	4.2	66.1
District 3	Steve Womack (R)	5,399.9	820,935	152.0	80.4	2.8	1.0	4.1	5.6	6.1	14.6	73.2	50.4	9.6	49.4
District 4	Bruce Westerman (R)	22,336.4	704,589	31.5	73.7	19.2	0.8	0.8	2.9	2.6	6.1	71.0	51.2	3.3	64.1
CALIFORNIA		155,858.6	39,346,023	252.4	56.1	5.7	0.8	15.2	14.3	7.9	39.1	36.5	50.3	26.6	56.0
District 1	Doug LaMalfa (R)	28,120.8	704,482	25.1	84.4	1.5	1.7	3.2	3.1	6.1	14.4	75.5	49.8	6.5	70.2
District 2	Jared Huffman (D)	12,952.6	714,171	55.1	78.2	1.5	2.1	4.0	7.2	7.0	17.9	70.0	50.6	13.0	60.7
District 3	John Garamendi (D)	6,184.6	746,967	120.8	64.5	6.4	1.1	12.3	6.9	8.9	30.1	46.1	50.0	18.3	61.8
District 4	Tom McClintock (R)	12,836.8	750,420	58.5	83.0	1.4	0.9	6.0	2.8	5.8	13.8	74.4	50.3	9.4	66.6
District 5	Mike Thompson (D)	1,730.6	724,984	418.9	60.5	6.2	0.7	11.8	12.9	7.9	28.6	48.8	51.2	20.7	59.9
District 6	Doris O. Matsui (D)	175.0	764,174	4366.7	48.2	12.4	0.7	18.0	11.1	9.6	28.5	35.7	51.0	22.9	60.2
District 7	Ami Bera (D)	548.9	762,260	1388.7	59.9	7.2	0.5	18.1	5.1	9.0	18.3	50.7	51.4	19.5	61.1
District 8	Jay Olbernolte (R)	32,893.0	729,399	22.2	70.0	7.8	1.3	3.9	7.9	9.0	42.7	41.6	49.7	13.8	66.7
District 9	Jerry McNerney (D)	1,251.0	775,716	620.1	51.0	9.1	0.6	15.4	10.6	13.3	38.8	32.6	50.8	21.9	65.1
District 10	Josh Harder (D)	1,820.3	757,213	416.0	67.4	3.5	0.8	8.5	10.1	9.7	44.7	40.0	50.1	20.2	67.5
District 11	Mark Desaulnier (D)	489.7	760,284	1552.6	54.7	7.7	0.4	15.8	12.3	9.0	27.6	43.8	51.0	25.9	54.3
District 12	Nancy Pelosi (D)	39.0	763,777	19584.0	47.2	5.2	0.4	32.7	7.2	7.2	14.6	42.1	48.7	32.9	39.2
District 13	Barbara Lee (D)	96.8	760,817	7859.7	40.4	16.2	0.8	21.9	12.2	8.5	21.9	34.3	51.4	26.6	49.7
District 14	Jackie Speier (D)	259.9	749,549	2884.0	42.1	2.9	0.5	36.5	10.6	7.5	23.1	33.2	50.4	37.9	46.8
District 15	Eric Swalwell (D)	598.2	788,527	1318.2	39.8	5.7	0.5	37.3	9.1	7.6	22.1	30.8	50.4	35.2	50.2
District 16	Jim Costa (D)	2,842.1	736,400	259.1	52.3	5.5	1.2	9.4	23.7	7.9	61.5	21.7	50.1	23.5	66.9
District 17	Ro Khanna (D)	185.4	776,763	4189.7	26.5	2.3	0.4	57.1	7.9	5.8	15.7	21.3	48.8	49.8	37.7
District 18	Anna G. Eshoo (D)	695.8	744,487	1070.0	60.0	2.1	0.4	25.2	5.6	6.7	16.3	51.6	50.2	30.9	46.6
District 19	Zoe Lofgren (D)	915.9	758,327	828.0	41.0	2.8	0.7	30.2	16.0	9.4	39.2	24.7	49.6	36.0	51.3
District 20	Jimmy Panetta (D)	4,875.2	736,750	151.1	57.2	2.1	0.7	5.7	26.9	7.4	53.5	36.2	49.7	25.1	58.5
District 21	David G. Valadao (R)	6,730.3	713,346	106.0	63.9	3.8	1.1	3.5	19.2	8.5	75.1	16.1	47.3	28.3	62.9
District 22	Connie Conway (R)	1,165.4	769,728	660.5	65.4	3.0	1.0	9.0	13.3	8.3	49.1	36.5	50.7	17.9	69.2
District 23	Kevin McCarthy (R)	9,901.5	748,143	75.6	68.1	6.3	1.1	5.4	10.7	8.4	41.1	43.7	49.4	14.4	69.7
District 24	Salud O. Carbajal (D)	6,882.3	736,030	106.9	76.1	1.8	1.0	4.9	7.6	8.5	36.6	53.5	49.7	17.5	61.3
District 25	Mike Garcia (R)	1,690.7	710,525	420.3	60.3	8.0	1.0	8.9	13.8	8.0	40.4	39.3	50.2	19.6	64.4
District 26	Julia Brownley (D)	938.9	724,221	771.4	75.7	1.9	0.9	6.7	6.2	8.7	45.8	42.8	50.4	21.9	59.5
District 27	Judy Chu (D)	699.9	711,767	1017.0	36.6	4.3	0.5	39.9	12.6	6.2	27.6	25.3	51.5	38.5	47.7
District 28	Adam B. Schiff (D)	218.5	712,193	3259.5	65.7	3.0	0.4	13.3	11.0	6.5	24.5	55.0	50.3	38.3	39.0
District 29	Tony Cárdenas (D)	92.3	715,422	7751.1	51.0	3.8	0.6	8.0	29.5	7.2	67.6	19.1	50.5	42.3	47.7
District 30	Brad Sherman (D)	135.9	773,221	5689.6	61.1	5.3	0.4	13.1	13.0	7.1	28.9	48.9	50.9	32.6	46.5
District 31	Pete Aguilar (D)	219.8	752,561	3423.8	54.7	10.2	0.7	8.2	17.2	9.0	54.2	25.0	50.9	20.6	65.7
District 32	Grace F. Napolitano (D)	124.3	707,305	5690.3	42.9	3.0	1.3	20.0	24.4	8.5	61.2	14.5	50.8	35.3	56.8
District 33	Ted Lieu (D)	288.7	708,972	2455.7	69.9	3.4	0.2	15.5	3.7	7.3	13.4	62.4	51.5	22.6	46.7
District 34	Jimmy Gomez (D)	47.7	734,546	15399.3	34.8	5.1	1.3	19.7	32.9	6.1	61.1	12.1	49.0	44.6	43.9
District 35	Norma J. Torres (D)	168.8	748,454	4434.0	42.4	6.4	1.2	7.8	32.2	10.0	70.5	13.5	50.0	28.9	62.4
District 36	Raul Ruiz (D)	5,915.0	755,516	127.7	64.1	4.9	1.1	3.8	18.5	7.7	49.3	39.8	49.9	21.1	56.3
District 37	Karen Bass (D)	55.3	727,449	13154.6	42.2	21.9	0.6	10.5	17.4	7.4	38.7	25.4	51.5	30.8	48.1
District 38	Linda T. Sánchez (D)	101.4	706,482	6967.3	40.5	4.0	0.8	16.4	31.0	7.2	61.5	16.1	51.1	29.9	61.8
District 39	Young Kim (R)	205.2	732,667	3570.5	48.1	2.4	0.6	32.6	9.9	6.4	33.3	28.9	50.8	32.3	55.3
District 40	Lucille Roybal-Allard (D)	57.7	708,362	12276.6	46.8	4.6	1.0	2.5	37.4	7.6	88.0	4.4	49.7	39.9	55.9
District 41	Mark Takano (D)	316.7	768,401	2426.3	43.5	8.9	0.7	6.7	33.4	6.8	61.4	21.1	50.4	25.2	63.0
District 42	Ken Calvert (R)	936.2	822,515	878.6	58.5	5.9	0.6	10.1	16.3	8.6	40.4	40.0	50.1	18.9	63.1
District 43	Maxine Waters (D)	72.1	727,766	10093.8	35.1	21.4	0.9	13.9	20.6	8.2	48.0	14.3	51.5	31.9	53.6
District 44	Nanette Diaz Barragan (D)	80.0	711,773	8897.2	40.4	15.0	0.8	6.5	29.6	7.7	71.0	6.3	51.0	33.8	58.2
District 45	Katie Porter (D)	330.6	781,871	2365.0	59.2	1.6	0.4	26.3	5.4	7.1	19.0	48.6	51.1	28.9	49.9
District 46	J. Luis Correa (D)	72.2	730,071	10111.8	49.8	1.9	0.7	14.1	26.5	7.0	65.6	16.9	49.8	37.8	52.8
District 47	Alan S. Lowenthal (D)	216.3	709,979	3282.4	50.7	7.1	0.5	23.6	11.7	6.3	35.3	31.2	50.5	29.0	56.1
District 48	Michelle Steel (R)	145.9	720,586	4938.9	64.0	1.3	0.4	19.4	8.2	6.7	21.0	54.1	50.7	24.3	53.1
District 49	Mike Levin (D)	553.5	741,671	1340.0	74.9	2.6	0.6	7.8	5.6	8.5	27.1	58.2	49.8	17.6	51.3
District 50	Darrell Issa (R)	2,789.6	748,893	268.5	73.3	2.6	1.2	5.8	8.1	9.0	33.0	54.0	50.4	19.1	56.4
District 51	Juan Vargas (D)	4,791.1	736,161	153.7	59.5	6.8	0.9	8.4	14.9	9.6	70.0	13.4	49.0	32.1	53.8
District 52	Scott H. Peters (D)	267.1	774,895	2901.1	64.8	3.1	0.4	20.9	3.6	7.2	15.1	56.1	49.3	23.1	42.9
District 53	Sara Jacobs (D)	136.1	769,064	5650.7	60.7	8.1	0.6	14.4	7.1	9.2	34.0	39.7	50.1	21.9	52.3

1. Dry land or land partially or temporarily covered by water. 2. May be of any race.

Table E. Congressional Districts 116th Congress — **Age and Education**

STATE District	Population and population characteristics, 2016–2020 (cont.)										Education, 2016–2020		
	Age (percent)											Attainment[2] (percent)	
	Under 5 years	5 to 17 years	18 to 24 years	25 to 34 years	35 to 44 years	45 to 54 years	55 to 64 years	65 to 74 years	75 years and over	Median age	Total Enrollment[1]	High school graduate or more	Bachelor's degree or more
	15	16	17	18	19	20	21	22	23	24	25	26	27
UNITED STATES	6.0	16.4	9.3	13.9	12.6	12.7	12.9	9.4	6.7	37.0	80,497,960	88.5	32.9
ALABAMA	6.0	16.4	9.3	13.1	12.2	12.8	13.4	10.0	6.9	37.7	1,168,551	86.9	26.2
District 1	6.1	16.7	8.4	12.9	11.9	12.5	13.6	10.7	7.1	38.5	160,520	87.8	25.5
District 2	6.0	16.4	9.3	13.4	12.2	12.7	13.1	10.0	7.1	37.2	158,459	85.9	23.6
District 3	5.9	16.0	10.7	12.9	12.1	12.9	13.0	10.0	6.5	37.2	182,430	85.8	23.2
District 4	6.1	16.6	8.0	12.1	12.0	13.2	13.7	10.8	7.5	39.5	150,148	83.1	18.1
District 5	5.7	16.1	9.0	13.3	12.2	13.5	13.8	9.6	6.9	38.4	177,406	88.6	33.2
District 6	6.3	17.0	7.8	13.0	13.5	13.2	13.0	9.6	6.6	38.2	170,472	91.1	37.3
District 7	6.0	15.5	12.3	14.3	11.3	11.6	13.1	9.5	6.5	34.2	169,116	85.6	21.7
ALASKA	7.1	17.8	9.5	16.1	12.8	12.0	12.8	8.1	3.8	34.1	180,787	93.1	30.0
At Large	7.1	17.8	9.5	16.1	12.8	12.0	12.8	8.1	3.8	34.1	180,787	93.1	30.0
ARIZONA	6.0	16.8	9.6	13.8	12.3	11.9	12.1	10.2	7.4	36.7	1,760,360	87.9	30.3
District 1	5.9	17.3	10.4	12.7	11.6	10.9	12.3	11.5	7.5	37.0	196,972	87.3	26.1
District 2	5.5	14.5	9.9	13.1	11.3	11.3	13.0	11.9	9.6	38.6	167,889	91.6	35.7
District 3	6.8	19.3	13.0	14.4	12.6	11.3	10.4	7.3	4.8	31.5	223,714	77.9	17.4
District 4	4.9	14.2	7.0	10.4	10.3	10.5	14.7	16.1	11.9	46.3	160,278	88.8	20.5
District 5	6.1	19.1	7.7	11.9	13.3	13.4	11.3	9.7	7.5	37.4	222,323	94.0	37.3
District 6	5.5	14.5	7.4	13.7	12.3	13.2	14.2	11.1	8.1	40.6	168,435	93.1	45.2
District 7	8.1	21.3	11.6	16.6	13.6	11.8	9.2	4.9	2.8	29.9	231,622	71.2	15.7
District 8	5.3	16.9	7.5	11.4	12.1	12.6	12.3	12.0	9.9	40.8	190,665	91.8	31.0
District 9	6.0	14.2	12.2	19.5	13.4	11.6	11.0	7.2	4.8	32.8	198,462	91.4	40.6
ARKANSAS	6.3	17.1	9.4	13.1	12.3	12.1	12.8	9.8	7.1	36.9	725,947	87.2	23.8
District 1	6.2	16.9	8.3	12.8	12.1	12.3	13.2	10.4	7.9	38.1	163,588	85.2	17.1
District 2	6.3	16.9	9.7	13.9	12.6	12.2	12.6	9.5	6.4	36.2	191,485	90.6	30.8
District 3	6.6	17.9	10.4	14.1	12.8	12.0	11.6	8.7	5.9	34.7	210,599	86.8	29.2
District 4	5.9	16.6	9.0	11.4	11.5	12.3	13.8	11.2	8.3	39.6	160,275	86.0	17.3
CALIFORNIA	6.1	16.7	9.5	15.2	13.3	12.8	12.0	8.3	6.0	35.6	10,331,447	83.9	34.7
District 1	5.2	14.6	9.5	12.2	11.0	11.3	14.6	12.9	8.7	40.3	162,117	90.3	25.2
District 2	4.9	15.0	7.8	10.8	12.1	13.5	14.9	12.9	8.2	43.1	163,465	91.1	42.5
District 3	6.3	17.0	12.0	14.4	12.0	11.8	11.9	8.7	6.0	34.5	213,558	85.4	26.6
District 4	5.0	15.7	6.9	10.8	12.2	13.0	15.1	12.6	8.8	43.0	168,766	93.8	35.2
District 5	5.4	14.8	8.6	13.4	12.9	12.5	14.2	10.8	7.3	39.4	167,755	88.1	33.3
District 6	6.9	17.2	9.1	18.0	13.5	11.3	11.5	7.5	5.0	33.4	203,207	85.3	30.0
District 7	6.0	17.4	8.0	13.7	13.4	13.5	12.6	9.0	6.4	36.9	197,836	90.6	33.9
District 8	7.7	20.0	9.6	13.8	12.2	11.3	12.1	8.1	5.3	33.1	196,324	83.2	17.1
District 9	6.6	20.1	9.8	13.4	13.0	12.1	11.9	7.8	5.3	34.2	217,988	81.8	21.4
District 10	7.0	19.9	9.3	14.3	12.8	12.5	11.4	7.5	5.3	33.4	211,104	81.3	18.2
District 11	5.8	16.1	8.0	13.2	13.4	13.6	13.1	9.7	7.1	38.6	187,617	88.7	45.5
District 12	4.6	8.6	6.5	24.5	16.2	13.0	11.3	8.5	6.9	37.9	130,334	89.1	60.6
District 13	5.6	12.9	9.8	18.7	14.8	12.3	11.5	8.8	5.7	36.1	189,862	87.4	50.9
District 14	5.3	14.0	7.7	15.4	14.4	13.7	13.1	9.3	7.2	38.4	176,758	89.4	49.4
District 15	5.8	17.1	6.9	14.0	15.3	14.6	12.6	8.0	5.6	37.9	199,681	90.2	47.3
District 16	8.3	21.5	11.0	15.6	12.4	10.8	9.8	6.4	4.3	30.0	226,074	68.9	13.1
District 17	6.4	14.7	7.5	19.3	15.5	13.4	11.2	6.6	5.6	35.4	187,117	91.8	60.0
District 18	5.4	16.3	7.6	13.6	13.6	14.6	13.0	8.5	7.4	38.7	193,334	94.4	64.6
District 19	5.9	16.7	9.4	15.1	14.1	13.5	11.9	7.9	5.5	35.9	205,972	82.0	37.4
District 20	6.4	17.9	11.8	13.8	12.7	11.8	11.6	8.4	5.6	34.4	215,715	77.7	29.5
District 21	8.0	22.3	11.2	15.7	13.2	11.2	9.2	5.4	3.6	30.3	215,740	61.9	9.5
District 22	7.6	21.0	9.6	14.8	12.6	11.3	10.3	7.4	5.4	31.9	232,520	82.8	26.0
District 23	7.0	20.1	9.1	14.8	12.8	11.6	11.6	7.8	5.2	33.4	214,749	83.2	21.7
District 24	5.6	14.9	15.4	12.8	11.3	10.8	12.2	9.8	7.4	35.0	214,044	86.0	35.5
District 25	6.7	19.4	9.1	13.1	12.6	14.1	12.9	7.3	4.9	35.2	203,859	85.6	28.7
District 26	5.9	17.4	9.4	13.5	12.3	12.9	13.0	8.9	6.6	36.6	189,803	84.5	34.1
District 27	5.5	13.7	7.7	14.0	13.2	14.3	13.6	9.5	8.6	40.0	171,743	86.3	44.4
District 28	4.5	10.9	6.9	19.9	15.0	14.0	12.8	8.8	7.1	39.1	141,442	88.9	47.3
District 29	5.9	17.0	10.0	17.2	14.2	13.2	11.2	6.9	4.6	34.3	190,267	70.9	21.3
District 30	5.6	14.2	8.1	15.4	14.1	14.1	13.0	8.5	6.9	38.3	186,521	89.2	45.0
District 31	6.9	18.7	10.4	16.5	12.8	12.5	11.1	6.7	4.4	32.4	218,006	81.4	24.7
District 32	5.6	16.1	10.5	14.8	13.0	13.3	12.4	8.3	5.9	35.6	186,707	77.6	23.3
District 33	5.0	14.0	9.0	14.1	13.3	14.0	13.2	9.6	7.8	40.3	176,643	96.1	66.5
District 34	5.7	14.0	10.1	20.3	14.8	12.7	10.3	6.7	5.4	34.2	174,895	69.9	29.5
District 35	6.7	19.4	11.5	15.7	14.0	12.5	10.1	6.2	3.8	31.7	223,631	73.7	17.3
District 36	5.5	16.1	7.8	12.3	11.5	11.9	12.9	11.9	10.1	41.5	169,636	81.3	22.2
District 37	5.3	13.4	10.7	19.6	14.0	12.5	11.2	7.4	5.8	34.2	179,156	81.5	40.9
District 38	5.8	16.3	9.8	14.6	13.2	12.9	12.0	8.3	6.8	36.2	182,765	81.3	24.8
District 39	6.0	15.9	9.2	13.7	12.3	13.6	13.9	9.0	6.4	37.5	196,168	90.0	42.5
District 40	6.8	20.8	11.1	16.3	13.4	13.0	9.4	5.6	3.5	30.7	214,892	58.7	11.4
District 41	6.8	19.8	12.6	15.9	13.1	12.0	9.9	6.1	3.9	30.8	233,870	77.3	18.8
District 42	6.9	19.9	8.8	13.8	13.7	13.1	11.6	7.1	5.2	34.4	239,080	87.8	26.9
District 43	7.0	16.7	9.1	16.0	13.8	13.1	11.9	7.3	5.4	34.7	191,443	78.3	28.3
District 44	7.0	19.6	10.5	15.6	13.2	12.4	10.9	6.4	4.3	32.2	201,340	66.0	14.4
District 45	6.0	15.6	9.3	13.7	13.4	14.5	12.3	8.7	6.5	37.4	218,770	94.0	56.1
District 46	6.4	17.7	11.3	17.3	13.6	12.7	10.5	6.1	4.6	32.7	208,208	70.0	21.0
District 47	5.8	15.5	9.3	15.8	13.5	13.8	12.8	8.0	5.6	36.6	184,726	82.3	33.8
District 48	5.1	14.0	7.6	14.1	12.5	14.4	14.3	10.1	7.9	41.0	166,996	90.0	46.1
District 49	6.4	17.0	9.8	13.2	12.7	13.4	12.5	8.8	6.3	35.7	187,893	90.9	46.1
District 50	6.7	17.3	8.9	13.6	12.7	12.6	13.1	8.8	6.3	36.3	196,426	87.9	30.0
District 51	6.8	18.4	11.2	16.5	13.1	11.8	10.4	6.9	5.2	31.9	206,777	72.3	16.1
District 52	5.8	13.7	9.8	17.9	13.8	12.6	11.6	8.6	6.2	35.5	196,787	94.9	59.6
District 53	5.8	13.7	10.4	18.9	14.2	12.1	11.5	7.8	5.5	35.0	201,360	90.4	39.3

1. All persons 3 years old and over enrolled in nursery school through college and graduate or professional school. 2. Persons 25 years old and over.

Table E. Congressional Districts 116th Congress — **Households and Group Quarters**

STATE District	Households, 2016–2020						Total in group quarters, 2020	Persons in group quarters, 2020				
	Number	Average household size	Family households (percent)	Married couple family (percent)	Female family house-holder[1]	One person households (percent)		Correctional facilities for adults	Juvenile facilities	Skilled nursing facilities	College/ University student housing	Military quarters
	28	29	30	31	32	33	34	35	36	37	38	39
UNITED STATES	122,354,219	2.60	65.3	48.1	12.3	28.0	8,239,016	1,967,297	88,115	1,627,046	2,792,097	328,372
ALABAMA	1,888,504	2.53	65.4	47.3	13.9	30.0	127,934	39,749	1,479	27,869	45,489	1,079
District 1	271,453	2.58	65.5	48.2	13.6	30.4	13,785	5,023	236	3,408	3,232	0
District 2	260,201	2.53	64.9	45.1	15.2	31.0	21,325	12,052	142	4,171	2,698	1,079
District 3	275,857	2.51	66.3	48.3	13.7	28.4	23,274	6,559	500	4,130	11,017	0
District 4	261,520	2.60	68.8	52.8	11.8	27.4	8,718	2,354	97	4,459	358	0
District 5	289,551	2.46	65.1	49.4	12.0	29.9	18,778	5,149	99	3,787	8,219	0
District 6	270,024	2.58	69.3	55.0	10.8	26.4	13,851	5,185	122	3,700	3,331	0
District 7	259,898	2.44	57.3	32.0	20.7	37.0	28,203	3,427	283	4,214	16,634	0
ALASKA	255,173	2.78	65.8	49.9	10.3	26.3	30,291	4,842	457	1,781	1,472	5,836
At Large	255,173	2.78	65.8	49.9	10.3	26.3	30,291	4,842	457	1,781	1,472	5,836
ARIZONA	2,643,430	2.65	65.1	47.5	12.1	27.5	160,269	64,154	2,331	21,938	38,945	4,284
District 1	264,539	2.79	68.1	49.0	13.5	25.4	27,635	12,206	164	1,664	10,286	0
District 2	308,521	2.31	58.4	43.3	10.5	34.2	18,828	7,488	203	4,096	1,005	2,809
District 3	247,090	3.05	71.7	46.6	17.2	21.4	24,180	13,531	168	1,111	8,210	0
District 4	325,329	2.41	65.4	52.8	8.4	28.0	24,876	18,560	200	1,522	1,937	781
District 5	299,272	2.80	71.8	57.7	9.8	22.4	6,461	5	439	1,823	438	0
District 6	332,973	2.41	62.1	47.7	9.9	30.3	6,348	136	304	2,527	71	0
District 7	249,563	3.27	67.5	38.0	20.2	24.5	20,892	7,664	285	1,029	7,766	0
District 8	296,864	2.67	70.2	56.1	10.0	24.3	15,328	4,524	238	4,921	1,608	694
District 9	319,279	2.44	53.7	35.7	12.3	34.0	15,721	40	330	3,245	7,624	0
ARKANSAS	1,170,544	2.50	65.8	48.2	13.1	28.7	82,518	27,079	1,248	19,266	26,887	741
District 1	284,939	2.43	66.3	47.3	14.0	28.8	25,999	15,497	176	5,700	3,428	0
District 2	300,155	2.49	63.2	45.0	14.2	31.0	17,892	3,210	357	4,531	7,285	741
District 3	310,840	2.59	67.4	51.8	11.0	25.8	18,567	1,762	281	4,103	9,666	0
District 4	274,610	2.49	66.3	48.6	13.3	29.4	20,060	6,610	434	4,932	6,508	0
CALIFORNIA	13,103,114	2.94	68.6	49.7	12.9	23.8	917,932	201,570	8,966	124,804	230,361	57,173
District 1	275,087	2.47	63.6	47.6	10.9	28.2	21,689	10,601	241	3,474	2,717	0
District 2	282,570	2.46	62.0	47.6	9.8	29.2	19,072	7,701	222	1,994	2,509	304
District 3	252,696	2.87	69.8	51.4	12.4	21.9	22,831	9,212	107	1,923	6,697	1,622
District 4	285,699	2.58	69.1	56.7	8.2	25.0	13,731	8,010	157	1,749	548	0
District 5	265,268	2.69	65.5	48.0	11.7	26.4	15,985	1,668	164	3,295	4,295	0
District 6	276,558	2.72	62.2	40.3	15.3	28.6	20,359	2,949	105	2,279	3,759	0
District 7	269,031	2.79	69.9	51.2	12.9	23.4	12,598	5,575	223	2,229	0	0
District 8	232,954	3.06	72.2	50.3	15.1	22.5	19,507	6,950	78	1,358	81	8,387
District 9	238,672	3.18	75.3	53.0	15.2	19.7	16,133	4,266	660	3,029	2,000	0
District 10	240,363	3.11	75.1	53.6	14.1	19.8	9,456	2,259	110	2,503	725	0
District 11	270,824	2.78	69.8	52.8	11.8	23.2	9,094	548	83	2,801	1,461	0
District 12	327,479	2.28	45.1	34.4	7.4	37.6	26,730	1,165	114	2,458	5,901	68
District 13	286,271	2.58	55.5	39.1	11.7	32.0	39,391	220	89	3,393	16,055	211
District 14	254,883	2.90	69.0	53.5	10.7	22.7	8,443	1,416	75	1,525	950	0
District 15	254,738	3.06	76.6	61.3	10.6	18.1	12,871	3,186	329	2,304	1,408	210
District 16	215,384	3.32	73.6	45.1	19.2	21.0	19,573	10,546	212	2,093	2,433	0
District 17	257,444	2.97	73.6	60.8	8.5	18.1	9,853	1,461	52	1,962	2,797	0
District 18	269,210	2.70	69.6	57.6	8.3	22.6	20,741	62	70	3,592	13,038	0
District 19	227,737	3.28	73.6	54.4	12.6	18.9	12,973	615	74	1,118	4,162	0
District 20	227,989	3.10	69.9	51.6	12.2	22.2	32,571	7,107	255	2,098	10,352	3,611
District 21	189,216	3.56	81.0	53.3	19.0	15.3	38,863	32,461	97	1,071	83	1,189
District 22	248,272	3.07	74.4	52.2	15.2	20.3	8,214	970	252	1,961	1,547	0
District 23	248,601	2.93	70.6	49.6	14.3	23.6	17,394	11,158	289	1,915	516	236
District 24	258,687	2.70	64.3	49.1	10.1	25.3	37,577	7,317	155	3,036	20,266	358
District 25	220,052	3.18	76.4	56.0	13.8	18.5	8,937	5,872	79	210	845	0
District 26	229,547	3.10	72.6	55.4	11.8	21.5	10,862	414	426	1,736	3,075	998
District 27	245,259	2.85	70.4	51.6	13.1	23.0	15,265	248	367	4,303	6,340	0
District 28	302,095	2.32	51.7	37.8	9.3	37.0	12,149	213	156	3,364	1,109	0
District 29	212,217	3.34	70.8	45.9	16.4	21.7	10,812	185	283	2,603	25	0
District 30	283,257	2.69	63.7	46.8	11.9	27.0	9,521	37	70	3,456	2,129	0
District 31	224,874	3.25	75.2	48.9	18.2	19.1	15,549	4,403	133	2,943	2,754	0
District 32	196,062	3.55	78.8	52.4	17.7	16.1	8,756	48	202	2,935	2,567	0
District 33	293,617	2.34	56.2	45.5	7.1	34.0	29,462	57	56	2,577	20,829	0
District 34	258,609	2.74	56.2	33.6	14.7	32.4	31,332	5,970	225	3,594	3,996	0
District 35	198,683	3.67	80.3	53.4	18.8	14.9	11,706	5,059	165	2,485	1,392	0
District 36	280,578	2.65	61.5	45.4	11.1	32.0	14,948	7,520	79	3,373	182	0
District 37	279,132	2.55	53.0	33.3	14.0	35.3	20,766	184	197	2,601	11,046	0
District 38	205,020	3.40	78.7	54.3	16.8	17.0	8,974	139	12	2,715	2,021	0
District 39	229,989	3.15	78.7	60.8	12.1	16.4	9,191	0	219	1,365	4,192	0
District 40	180,611	3.90	82.4	47.1	23.1	13.3	6,683	87	145	1,714	86	0
District 41	196,038	3.83	79.5	54.7	17.0	14.7	13,818	720	116	1,927	7,354	0
District 42	232,167	3.51	81.1	64.5	11.4	14.8	6,711	4,010	170	761	432	0
District 43	239,149	3.00	68.3	41.7	18.9	25.3	10,049	16	44	2,837	3,170	0
District 44	190,018	3.70	78.3	46.9	22.1	17.5	13,769	3,133	211	1,775	1,003	63
District 45	275,379	2.79	70.4	57.5	8.8	21.8	20,005	10	127	801	16,644	0
District 46	193,113	3.69	75.3	51.1	16.9	17.0	17,187	5,712	183	2,615	3,838	0
District 47	245,487	2.85	65.0	44.5	14.2	27.1	14,565	286	273	3,550	2,834	160
District 48	268,404	2.66	65.1	50.3	9.7	26.1	6,414	22	124	1,031	493	83
District 49	254,770	2.83	71.3	57.2	9.9	21.8	35,434	634	26	2,224	9,912	18,644
District 50	243,166	3.04	74.3	56.5	11.8	19.9	10,334	1,358	177	2,767	1,937	0
District 51	202,910	3.46	73.8	46.8	19.8	20.8	26,722	15,433	138	977	0	6,920
District 52	292,449	2.57	61.7	50.0	8.0	26.6	36,876	2,334	10	2,485	9,302	13,751
District 53	274,829	2.75	61.6	45.4	11.6	27.0	15,486	43	340	3,920	6,554	358

1. No spouse present.

Table E. Congressional Districts 116th Congress — **Housing and Money Income**

STATE District	Housing units, 2016–2020: Total	Housing units, 2016–2020: Occupied units: Occupied units as a percent of all units	Housing units, 2016–2020: Occupied units: Owner-occupied: Owner-occupied units as a percent of occupied units	Housing units, 2016–2020: Occupied units: Owner-occupied: Median value[1] (dollars)	Housing units, 2016–2020: Occupied units: Owner-occupied: Percent valued at $500,000 or more	Housing units, 2016–2020: Occupied units: Renter-occupied: Median rent[2]	Money income, 2016–2020: Per capita income (dollars)	Money income, 2016–2020: Households: Median income (dollars)	Money income, 2016–2020: Households: Percent with income of $100,000 or more
	40	41	42	43	44	45	46	47	48
UNITED STATES	138,432,751	88.4	64.4	229,800	16.0	1,096	35,384	64,994	31.0
ALABAMA	2,270,398	83.2	69.2	149,600	4.6	811	28,934	52,035	22.5
District 1	341,606	79.5	69.0	157,000	5.3	874	28,427	51,455	22.3
District 2	317,248	82.0	66.9	130,900	2.6	811	27,086	50,101	20.5
District 3	334,478	82.5	70.2	142,600	4.2	776	27,257	50,987	21.1
District 4	317,995	82.2	74.8	125,400	3.6	659	25,590	47,429	18.3
District 5	322,963	89.7	70.2	166,800	4.1	790	33,090	59,543	28.1
District 6	303,482	89.0	75.4	196,600	9.0	1,014	37,606	69,779	33.5
District 7	332,626	78.1	57.3	103,300	2.3	801	22,811	38,356	14.5
ALASKA	318,370	80.1	64.8	275,600	10.1	1,240	37,094	77,790	38.2
At Large	318,370	80.1	64.8	275,600	10.1	1,240	37,094	77,790	38.2
ARIZONA	3,040,595	86.9	65.3	242,000	11.4	1,097	32,340	61,529	27.7
District 1	343,885	76.9	71.4	194,700	8.2	975	26,755	56,448	24.0
District 2	352,292	87.6	63.2	199,100	7.7	913	32,957	55,389	23.9
District 3	275,815	89.6	64.5	167,700	2.6	955	22,002	51,963	19.3
District 4	411,087	79.1	75.6	214,300	7.4	951	29,539	54,385	21.5
District 5	338,314	88.5	74.2	304,700	12.6	1,368	38,237	80,388	40.0
District 6	372,184	89.5	66.1	364,700	31.5	1,244	48,490	76,013	38.0
District 7	268,945	92.8	47.5	188,200	3.4	992	20,690	48,574	17.4
District 8	329,347	90.1	74.7	266,600	7.9	1,319	34,296	71,960	33.3
District 9	348,726	91.6	48.7	291,200	15.7	1,148	37,719	63,416	29.4
ARKANSAS	1,379,778	84.8	65.8	133,600	3.4	760	27,724	49,475	19.8
District 1	345,050	82.6	66.1	107,600	1.9	697	24,523	44,325	15.8
District 2	344,116	87.2	63.8	154,300	4.2	838	30,855	53,439	23.5
District 3	343,911	90.4	62.9	164,000	5.1	804	30,703	55,258	24.1
District 4	346,701	79.2	71.0	102,100	2.2	674	24,128	43,861	15.5
CALIFORNIA	14,210,945	92.2	55.3	538,500	53.7	1,586	38,576	78,672	39.8
District 1	322,065	85.4	66.1	297,000	17.5	1,070	31,815	57,046	26.0
District 2	320,498	88.2	63.2	664,900	63.2	1,564	50,618	80,210	41.9
District 3	272,379	92.8	59.8	379,700	27.5	1,346	32,955	72,297	35.2
District 4	365,685	78.1	74.7	448,600	40.0	1,423	42,995	81,951	41.4
District 5	287,466	92.3	61.3	553,500	57.6	1,724	41,462	84,399	42.3
District 6	290,825	95.1	48.9	339,400	18.4	1,274	30,922	61,794	29.0
District 7	279,802	96.2	64.9	399,700	27.9	1,410	37,653	80,722	40.6
District 8	302,293	77.1	62.4	254,600	9.0	1,124	24,957	56,093	24.3
District 9	253,466	94.2	61.3	388,300	30.2	1,283	30,158	71,817	36.1
District 10	250,198	96.1	60.4	348,500	17.9	1,295	28,997	68,329	32.7
District 11	282,511	95.9	64.0	702,500	70.3	1,857	52,427	100,114	50.5
District 12	362,212	90.4	35.3	1,165,300	92.9	2,002	75,210	120,697	57.0
District 13	306,633	93.4	44.3	791,400	79.8	1,690	49,003	87,295	45.0
District 14	268,737	94.8	59.6	1,089,000	93.4	2,407	58,824	121,097	58.9
District 15	264,946	96.1	64.4	840,500	87.1	2,179	51,640	123,064	60.0
District 16	230,082	93.6	48.8	239,100	7.3	986	20,630	49,280	20.0
District 17	271,016	95.0	53.2	1,059,900	90.4	2,651	59,897	142,408	66.9
District 18	288,243	93.4	60.6	1,489,000	94.4	2,336	77,316	146,441	64.8
District 19	236,706	96.2	59.7	845,300	85.9	2,061	44,428	109,530	54.9
District 20	250,517	91.0	54.4	631,400	64.9	1,665	35,029	80,689	40.0
District 21	201,926	93.7	51.7	196,500	4.8	930	17,564	47,028	17.8
District 22	261,704	94.9	59.7	284,900	12.2	1,117	29,407	66,141	31.3
District 23	275,629	90.2	61.5	253,000	6.7	1,058	28,177	61,490	29.0
District 24	286,533	90.3	56.2	607,300	60.6	1,631	38,410	78,360	39.2
District 25	232,030	94.8	67.9	479,100	47.3	1,653	34,202	83,267	41.9
District 26	245,304	93.6	62.3	607,800	65.9	1,843	38,847	88,064	44.4
District 27	264,005	92.9	53.9	728,200	85.1	1,659	41,510	83,765	42.8
District 28	332,721	90.8	34.1	865,200	86.2	1,648	48,473	72,274	37.4
District 29	222,935	95.2	42.7	515,300	52.6	1,457	25,093	59,850	27.8
District 30	299,737	94.5	51.9	701,500	80.5	1,814	46,767	86,710	44.7
District 31	238,883	94.1	55.9	380,400	24.5	1,393	27,946	68,568	32.7
District 32	204,008	96.1	60.2	506,600	51.1	1,558	27,098	74,942	35.9
District 33	330,851	88.7	50.2	1,284,200	92.3	2,207	77,186	115,408	56.5
District 34	279,660	92.5	21.1	640,500	70.3	1,280	27,445	50,172	23.5
District 35	207,107	95.9	58.0	392,600	18.8	1,448	23,194	67,635	29.8
District 36	363,879	77.1	68.3	285,500	15.2	1,161	30,779	52,873	25.1
District 37	301,617	92.5	35.8	785,400	76.6	1,604	39,492	65,667	34.3
District 38	211,885	96.8	62.1	541,600	57.6	1,555	28,989	76,795	38.1
District 39	240,262	95.7	66.7	672,100	78.7	1,826	39,362	95,636	48.7
District 40	187,242	96.5	35.0	459,800	39.2	1,273	18,861	52,850	20.4
District 41	206,439	95.0	60.2	360,500	15.5	1,482	24,423	71,561	33.3
District 42	245,560	94.5	73.0	446,600	34.8	1,784	33,609	91,349	46.5
District 43	253,554	94.3	42.5	586,700	63.7	1,439	30,883	64,939	32.0
District 44	197,429	96.2	49.2	438,600	32.2	1,253	21,789	58,281	25.7
District 45	290,504	94.8	62.9	763,100	81.8	2,276	51,914	111,197	55.3
District 46	201,416	95.9	42.8	560,000	62.6	1,681	25,412	72,175	34.0
District 47	258,226	95.1	47.3	619,000	72.0	1,496	35,059	74,347	36.8
District 48	289,834	92.6	56.9	812,600	81.5	2,065	53,656	99,328	50.1
District 49	278,740	91.4	60.2	741,800	77.5	1,969	48,595	96,591	49.0
District 50	259,720	93.6	64.2	517,300	52.5	1,623	34,855	81,177	40.8
District 51	225,877	89.8	45.2	369,700	23.4	1,284	21,311	52,247	22.2
District 52	316,303	92.5	54.0	739,800	80.6	2,056	53,357	102,795	52.0
District 53	293,145	93.8	50.4	554,500	59.2	1,676	38,661	81,447	40.7

1. Specified owner-occupied units. 2. Specified renter-occupied units.

STATE District	Poverty, 2016–2020: Persons below poverty level (percent)	Poverty, 2016–2020: Families below poverty level (percent)	Poverty, 2016–2020: Percent of households receiving food stamps in past 12 months	Civilian labor force, 2016–2020: Total	Civilian labor force, 2016–2020: Unemployment: Total	Civilian labor force, 2016–2020: Unemployment: Rate[1]	Civilian employment,[2] 2016–2020: Total	Civilian employment,[2] 2016–2020: Percent: Management, business, science, and arts occupations	Civilian employment,[2] 2016–2020: Percent: Service, sales, and office	Civilian employment,[2] 2016–2020: Percent: Construction and production	Persons under 65 years of age with no health insurance, 2016–2020 (percent)	Social Security beneficiaries, December 2021: Number	Social Security beneficiaries, December 2021: Rate[3]	Supplemental Security Income recipients, December 2021
	49	50	51	52	53	54	55	56	57	58	59	60	61	62
UNITED STATES	12.8	9.1	11.4	164,759,496	8,870,516	5.4	155,888,980	39.5	38.7	21.8	10.2	63,660,190	194.9	7,694,877
ALABAMA	16.0	11.6	13.4	2,245,329	125,343	5.6	2,119,986	35.7	37.7	26.7	11.3	1,163,871	237.9	150,730
District 1	15.7	11.3	13.0	320,022	17,757	5.5	302,265	34.2	40.2	25.6	12.9	178,310	249.6	21,007
District 2	17.5	13.0	15.2	301,141	16,386	5.4	284,755	33.7	38.9	27.4	12.1	165,877	244.3	25,242
District 3	16.4	11.5	13.2	322,547	18,948	5.9	303,599	34.4	36.5	29.1	10.5	171,846	240.9	20,714
District 4	16.3	12.1	13.5	302,229	14,740	4.9	287,489	30.3	35.6	34.1	12.6	181,141	263.4	21,678
District 5	12.8	9.6	10.5	353,341	16,487	4.7	336,854	41.1	35.4	23.5	10.4	161,199	221.3	15,382
District 6	9.6	6.8	7.3	350,283	15,280	4.4	335,003	43.4	36.2	20.4	8.1	150,644	212.7	10,795
District 7	24.4	18.3	21.5	295,766	25,745	8.7	270,021	30.1	41.7	28.3	12.7	154,854	233.8	35,912
ALASKA	10.3	7.0	10.3	367,921	26,429	7.2	341,492	38.2	38.1	23.7	14.2	110,006	149.3	11,793
At Large	10.3	7.0	10.3	367,921	26,429	7.2	341,492	38.2	38.1	23.7	14.2	110,006	149.3	11,793
ARIZONA	14.1	10.1	10.5	3,415,201	199,358	5.8	3,215,843	37.6	42.6	19.8	12.7	1,449,120	202.0	114,812
District 1	18.4	12.9	13.3	315,178	24,766	7.9	290,412	34.5	43.3	22.2	13.8	177,018	229.2	16,890
District 2	13.9	9.5	11.2	336,226	21,030	6.3	315,196	41.5	42.8	15.7	9.7	188,824	257.6	14,057
District 3	19.1	15.3	18.5	364,251	27,628	7.6	336,623	26.0	45.9	28.1	15.4	128,426	164.5	18,867
District 4	12.5	8.5	9.9	318,130	20,291	6.4	297,839	32.2	45.4	22.3	12.1	253,176	311.8	11,694
District 5	7.6	5.6	4.9	420,279	19,129	4.6	401,150	45.3	39.6	15.1	8.9	154,250	183.1	6,903
District 6	10.4	7.4	5.7	427,211	18,917	4.4	408,294	46.4	39.4	14.2	9.9	156,985	194.5	7,800
District 7	22.9	19.2	21.1	401,733	25,451	6.3	376,282	24.4	45.9	29.7	21.0	86,936	105.1	20,789
District 8	8.7	5.7	6.4	372,429	18,384	4.9	354,045	40.2	42.0	17.8	9.0	194,902	241.8	8,426
District 9	14.2	9.7	7.6	459,764	23,762	5.2	436,002	43.2	41.1	15.7	12.5	108,603	136.8	9,386
ARKANSAS	16.1	11.8	11.7	1,381,452	71,704	5.2	1,309,748	34.9	37.8	27.3	9.9	709,191	235.5	98,939
District 1	18.4	13.7	15.0	314,463	20,702	6.6	293,761	30.8	37.7	31.6	9.4	185,478	257.3	30,236
District 2	14.6	10.7	10.2	369,043	17,219	4.7	351,824	39.9	38.7	21.4	9.0	169,116	220.9	25,124
District 3	13.7	9.5	8.2	397,249	16,052	4.0	381,197	37.0	37.1	25.9	11.2	167,019	203.4	16,738
District 4	18.2	13.4	13.8	300,697	17,731	5.9	282,966	29.8	37.9	32.3	9.7	187,578	266.2	26,841
CALIFORNIA	12.6	9.0	9.0	19,875,973	1,229,079	6.2	18,646,894	40.3	39.0	20.6	8.3	6,166,205	156.7	1,146,493
District 1	15.4	9.4	10.4	310,088	19,830	6.4	290,258	36.2	42.2	21.6	7.3	178,864	253.9	26,770
District 2	11.2	6.4	7.2	360,322	21,109	5.9	339,213	45.1	38.7	16.2	6.7	158,906	222.5	15,901
District 3	13.3	8.4	10.6	348,187	21,330	6.1	326,857	34.4	39.8	25.8	6.6	134,542	180.1	20,569
District 4	8.5	5.7	5.6	349,451	17,184	4.9	332,267	44.2	40.2	15.6	5.6	181,635	242.0	12,325
District 5	9.3	6.0	6.8	386,750	20,484	5.3	366,266	37.4	41.5	21.1	7.2	145,474	200.7	14,982
District 6	17.4	13.0	14.2	379,878	26,096	6.9	353,782	37.6	41.4	21.0	7.1	115,175	150.7	39,113
District 7	10.6	7.7	8.5	380,175	22,451	5.9	357,724	42.9	40.7	16.3	5.3	137,890	180.9	22,080
District 8	17.9	13.6	17.2	299,707	25,692	8.6	274,015	29.7	42.3	27.9	8.6	130,268	178.6	26,694
District 9	13.3	10.2	14.0	361,736	27,219	7.5	334,517	31.3	39.8	28.9	6.7	123,930	159.8	25,602
District 10	12.4	9.5	11.6	355,709	28,056	7.9	327,653	29.6	38.7	31.7	6.1	123,341	162.9	22,647
District 11	8.9	6.4	6.3	394,068	21,424	5.4	372,644	45.6	38.3	16.1	6.8	130,207	171.3	17,053
District 12	10.3	5.7	5.6	482,696	22,091	4.6	460,605	60.9	31.1	8.0	4.0	109,320	143.1	32,962
District 13	13.3	8.4	7.8	425,316	22,896	5.4	402,420	52.4	33.0	14.6	6.2	109,217	143.6	29,143
District 14	6.7	4.0	3.5	428,233	18,324	4.3	409,909	49.3	36.9	13.9	4.5	117,796	157.2	12,617
District 15	6.3	4.2	4.6	422,793	17,768	4.2	405,025	50.8	33.3	16.0	3.6	101,737	129.0	14,132
District 16	24.1	20.3	24.3	316,756	34,958	11.0	281,798	22.6	41.0	36.4	9.4	100,505	136.5	35,344
District 17	6.0	3.6	2.9	433,694	17,744	4.1	415,950	62.6	25.5	11.9	3.3	85,241	109.7	12,428
District 18	5.9	3.3	2.7	395,871	14,627	3.7	381,244	63.2	27.6	9.2	4.0	104,155	139.9	9,323
District 19	8.4	5.2	6.9	409,792	19,754	4.8	390,038	42.4	38.1	19.5	6.2	99,409	131.1	23,534
District 20	12.1	8.3	8.4	359,519	20,565	5.7	338,954	33.9	38.4	27.7	9.1	119,863	162.7	13,047
District 21	23.7	20.3	21.3	290,304	29,074	10.0	261,230	18.6	35.8	45.6	10.7	86,095	120.7	23,679
District 22	16.3	12.8	15.7	357,731	26,532	7.4	331,199	35.8	39.4	24.8	7.4	120,564	156.6	26,003
District 23	17.6	13.9	14.3	328,346	28,882	8.8	299,464	34.6	38.6	26.8	7.0	122,635	163.9	26,275
District 24	12.2	6.4	6.5	368,171	19,330	5.3	348,841	38.1	40.9	21.0	10.0	142,276	193.3	12,049
District 25	12.3	9.1	7.8	337,213	20,040	5.9	317,173	39.3	40.1	20.6	6.4	107,377	151.1	21,510
District 26	9.1	6.1	7.2	366,778	19,057	5.2	347,721	37.7	38.8	23.5	10.6	127,527	176.1	13,073
District 27	10.4	7.2	4.3	368,841	17,992	4.9	350,849	48.1	38.7	13.1	6.2	120,145	168.8	25,713
District 28	12.9	8.3	7.1	418,010	29,699	7.1	388,311	51.8	36.0	12.2	9.0	94,670	132.9	38,752
District 29	16.4	13.2	12.7	378,663	24,222	6.4	354,441	27.6	45.0	27.3	12.8	84,671	118.4	29,905
District 30	10.2	6.7	5.4	433,647	28,967	6.7	404,680	49.6	36.8	13.6	8.1	115,050	148.8	20,161
District 31	14.5	11.2	14.0	365,858	25,713	7.0	340,145	32.4	40.9	26.7	8.9	102,129	135.7	24,822
District 32	11.3	8.4	9.0	365,615	23,226	6.4	342,389	30.2	43.7	26.0	9.6	111,439	157.6	23,604
District 33	8.0	4.2	2.2	382,789	21,875	5.7	360,914	64.5	28.7	6.9	4.4	118,661	167.4	10,106
District 34	21.9	17.2	13.3	397,053	27,707	7.0	369,346	33.4	44.2	22.4	17.3	81,470	110.9	36,939
District 35	14.2	11.9	13.4	365,577	23,940	6.5	341,637	24.1	41.5	34.4	11.6	90,328	120.7	20,809
District 36	16.7	12.1	10.5	329,229	30,267	9.2	298,962	28.4	47.1	24.5	10.4	172,630	228.5	23,827
District 37	16.9	12.0	9.8	402,360	26,442	6.6	375,918	45.4	39.9	14.7	10.3	96,321	132.4	24,450
District 38	9.8	7.2	8.0	354,828	19,238	5.4	335,590	33.5	42.6	24.0	8.9	115,104	162.9	23,618
District 39	8.8	6.2	5.2	382,201	19,859	5.2	362,342	44.0	39.7	16.3	6.7	116,358	158.8	15,035
District 40	19.9	17.4	16.8	345,357	25,837	7.5	319,520	18.3	44.3	37.4	16.0	76,409	107.9	22,396
District 41	13.5	10.5	11.5	369,787	26,735	7.2	343,052	26.1	41.3	32.6	11.4	97,047	126.3	22,514
District 42	8.4	6.4	6.3	390,441	22,758	5.8	367,683	37.0	41.2	21.8	7.8	122,333	148.7	12,741
District 43	15.6	12.3	11.5	375,019	24,470	6.5	350,549	33.4	44.5	22.1	11.1	100,163	137.6	28,495
District 44	17.5	15.0	17.1	341,177	27,647	8.1	313,530	21.4	44.0	34.7	13.7	93,245	131.0	31,307
District 45	8.5	5.5	2.8	413,763	19,326	4.7	394,437	56.3	34.2	9.5	5.1	121,312	155.2	9,805
District 46	14.3	11.1	12.0	384,082	19,676	5.1	364,406	27.1	45.6	27.3	14.0	81,327	111.4	25,382
District 47	13.5	9.6	9.2	376,803	21,967	5.8	354,836	40.1	40.1	19.8	8.6	102,955	145.0	29,673
District 48	8.8	5.7	4.7	390,738	18,859	4.8	371,879	47.3	39.5	13.3	7.0	130,189	180.7	9,543
District 49	7.6	4.9	4.2	365,187	17,933	4.9	347,254	45.8	39.3	14.9	7.6	125,423	169.1	7,690
District 50	10.7	7.7	8.1	368,428	20,056	5.4	348,372	35.9	42.8	21.2	9.0	130,605	174.4	15,275
District 51	18.5	15.7	17.6	331,538	34,798	10.5	296,740	23.4	49.8	26.9	12.7	123,204	167.4	33,623
District 52	8.4	4.1	3.5	410,066	19,359	4.7	390,707	60.3	30.3	9.4	4.9	116,380	150.2	13,315
District 53	10.8	6.4	6.7	419,632	27,994	6.7	391,638	44.8	40.4	14.8	8.0	112,688	146.5	18,138

1. Percent of civilian labor force. 2. Persons 16 years old and over. 3. Per 1,000 resident population estimated in the 2016–2020 American Community Survey.

STATE District	Agriculture 2017									
	Number of farms	Land in farms			Value of products sold				Government payments	
		Acres	Average size of farm (acres)	Irrigated land (acres)	Total ($1,000)	Average per farm (dollars)	Percent from crops	Percent from livestock and poultry products	Total ($1,000)	Average per farm receiving payments (dollars)
	63	64	65	66	67	68	69	70	71	72
UNITED STATES	2,042,220	900,217,576	441	320,041,858	388,522,695	190,245	49.8	50.2	8,943,574	13,906
ALABAMA	40,592	8,580,940	211	2,205,766	5,980,595	147,334	20.3	79.7	134,654	8,892
District 1	2,928	652,956	223	227,241	310,410	106,014	76.8	23.2	15,572	16,762
District 2	8,100	2,095,530	259	504,145	1,514,029	186,917	18.4	81.6	43,478	11,103
District 3	5,232	1,104,479	211	215,369	813,111	155,411	20.1	79.9	13,810	7,955
District 4	11,374	1,639,238	144	473,554	2,172,299	190,988	8.7	91.3	24,234	6,379
District 5	5,927	965,903	163	459,776	519,220	87,602	43.1	56.9	14,741	7,456
District 6	2,580	399,443	155	81,843	217,477	84,293	16.4	83.6	4,185	6,707
District 7	4,451	1,723,391	387	243,838	434,050	97,517	19.2	80.8	18,634	8,615
ALASKA	990	849,753	858	31,877	70,459	71,171	42.1	57.9	2,091	9,293
At Large	990	849,753	858	31,877	70,459	71,171	42.1	57.9	2,091	9,293
ARIZONA	19,086	26,125,819	1,369	915,647	3,852,008	201,824	54.4	45.6	22,331	29,735
District 1	13,560	20,195,286	1,489	289,469	1,031,964	76,104	34.3	65.7	6,836	24,768
District 2	1,323	1,040,464	786	88,140	161,280	121,905	60	40	3,212	25,291
District 3	1,257	3,078,961	2,449	219,807	1,195,275	950,895	54.7	45.3	5,920	39,467
District 4	1,717	1,598,936	931	239,342	1,017,973	592,879	67.6	32.4	4,311	35,628
District 5	435	60,281	139	22,775	126,184	290,078	D	D	1,053	32,906
District 6	297	D	D	21,075	113,635	382,609	92	8	239	21,727
District 7	106	20,624	195	16,332	102,007	962,330	84	16	383	42,556
District 8	343	D	D	18,354	86,807	253,082	71.7	28.3	193	9,190
District 9	48	2,095	44	353	16,884	351,750	D	D	184	46,000
ARKANSAS	42,625	13,888,929	326	7,098,672	9,651,160	226,420	37.6	62.4	321,742	38,624
District 1	13,399	7,758,029	579	5,424,425	4,087,818	305,084	77.5	22.5	272,375	48,500
District 2	5,351	1,039,161	194	315,834	422,992	79,049	21.3	78.7	13,321	19,195
District 3	9,329	1,669,233	179	314,685	1,928,511	206,722	2.3	97.7	4,899	10,080
District 4	14,546	3,422,506	235	1,043,728	3,211,839	220,806	10.0	90.0	31,147	20,304
CALIFORNIA	70,521	24,522,801	348	7,857,512	45,154,359	640,297	73.9	26.1	127,938	24,112
District 1	7,949	3,690,258	464	650,694	1,471,521	185,120	81.2	18.8	17,554	27,300
District 2	4,847	1,983,379	409	121,953	1,206,957	249,011	56.6	43.4	2,866	14,697
District 3	5,761	2,222,919	386	1,075,534	2,524,704	438,241	92.6	7.4	27,813	31,356
District 4	5,025	1,537,953	306	149,086	783,366	155,894	70.6	29.4	5,706	16,444
District 5	3,616	502,424	139	106,858	889,982	246,123	89.6	10.4	2,234	17,591
District 6	95	7,723	81	7,171	14,672	154,442	99.6	0.4	232	38,667
District 7	714	134,035	188	30,374	186,365	261,015	63.7	36.3	860	18,696
District 8	830	405,833	489	25,014	160,823	193,763	31.2	68.8	1,370	42,813
District 9	3,034	682,651	225	417,973	1,881,357	620,091	74.8	25.2	5,136	24,226
District 10	4,282	881,704	206	463,869	2,915,414	680,853	56.4	43.6	5,996	18,855
District 11	230	105,382	458	19,726	36,383	158,187	77.0	23.0	332	15,091
District 12	9	89	10	5	452	50,222	D	D	D	D
District 13	35	D	D	34	2,608	74,514	12.6	87.4	D	D
District 14	121	24,065	199	2,329	48,318	399,322	98.3	1.7	D	D
District 15	409	138,780	339	6,969	34,387	84,076	76.5	23.5	194	7,462
District 16	3,710	1,394,781	376	800,605	4,460,128	1,202,191	54.7	45.3	10,377	27,094
District 17	60	D	D	541	11,233	187,217	97.5	2.5	D	D
District 18	492	63,346	129	10,962	195,998	398,370	99.3	0.7	18	3,600
District 19	612	268,704	439	14,521	197,717	323,067	92.1	7.9	490	16,897
District 20	2,210	1,901,631	860	338,292	4,831,405	2,186,156	98.4	1.6	1,925	12,419
District 21	4,578	2,751,011	601	1,718,981	9,790,565	2,138,612	62.0	38.0	18,580	24,609
District 22	3,428	771,371	225	483,801	3,124,957	911,598	60.9	39.1	8,611	28,703
District 23	2,800	1,981,120	708	419,024	2,438,036	870,727	87.9	12.1	4,921	24,605
District 24	4,091	1,708,370	418	237,661	2,708,747	662,123	97.4	2.6	5,168	17,227
District 25	403	36,030	89	7,779	53,359	132,404	D	D	64	6,400
District 26	1,814	193,157	106	69,560	1,128,887	622,319	99.5	0.5	743	16,152
District 27	124	3,062	25	989	24,781	199,847	99.3	0.7	43	14,333
District 28	93	1,488	16	67	965	10,376	72.2	27.8	D	D
District 29	75	1,341	18	686	12,735	169,800	98.7	1.3	D	D
District 30	47	1,864	40	1,529	15,037	319,936	99.7	0.3	D	D
District 31	177	6,904	39	2,458	19,407	109,644	99.5	0.5	124	24,800
District 32	49	804	16	211	15,520	316,735	99.7	0.3	D	D
District 33	101	5,819	58	1,248	9,241	91,495	98.7	1.3	D	D
District 34	12	151	13	13	54	4,500	100	0	D	D
District 35	168	10,073	60	3,962	207,967	1,237,899	13.0	87.0	310	34,444
District 36	961	185,512	193	106,983	649,142	675,486	86.7	13.3	1,502	34,930
District 37	13	D	D	31	169	13,000	D	D	D	D
District 38	37	179	5	98	5,583	150,892	D	D	D	D
District 39	81	5,324	66	649	10,590	130,741	95.7	4.3	300	50,000
District 40	5	D	D	21	617	123,400	100	0	D	D
District 41	413	29,236	71	9,848	57,385	138,947	87	13	16	1,778
District 42	1,178	45,409	39	24,697	212,078	180,032	38.4	61.6	101	11,222
District 43	27	1,709	63	330	8,044	297,926	D	D	139	46,333
District 44	36	188	5	118	21,704	602,889	D	D	D	D
District 45	82	26,333	321	3,066	41,076	500,927	99.9	0.1	3	1,000
District 46	17	D	D	91	4,874	286,706	D	D	D	D
District 47	28	9,985	357	214	5,939	212,107	99.3	0.7	D	D
District 48	28	2,641	94	704	20,354	726,929	99	1	3	1,000
District 49	813	21,797	27	7,962	174,311	214,405	90.9	9.1	13	2,167
District 50	3,783	153,781	41	37,897	597,859	158,038	94.4	5.6	542	12,044
District 51	697	563,066	808	470,449	1,908,532	2,738,209	66.5	33.5	3,641	32,509
District 52	214	7,688	36	2,821	19,376	90,542	93.3	6.7	D	D
District 53	107	3,830	36	1,054	12,679	118,495	98.8	1.2	D	D

STATE District	Private nonfarm employment and payroll, 2020												
		Employment										Annual payroll	
			Percent by selected industries										
	Number of establishments	Total	Manufacturing	Construction	Wholesale trade	Retail trade	Health care and social assistance	Finance and Insurance	Real estate and rental and leasing	Professional, scientific, and technical services	Information	Total (mil dol)	Average per employee (dollars)
	73	74	75	76	77	78	79	80	81	82	83	84	85
UNITED STATES	8,000,178	134,163,349	8.9	5.4	4.6	11.8	15.8	5.0	1.7	7.1	2.7	7,564,810	56,385
ALABAMA	100,955	1,777,495	14.9	5.2	4.2	12.8	15.3	3.9	1.3	6.4	1.7	81,317	45,748
District 1	16,135	243,986	11.1	7.3	4.6	15.3	13.6	3.1	1.8	5.0	1.5	10,733	43,991
District 2	14,142	218,228	12.6	4.5	5.3	14.5	17.2	3.3	1.2	4.5	1.3	8,998	41,231
District 3	11,896	188,103	22.2	4.4	3.4	15.4	14.7	2.4	1.2	3.0	1.0	7,000	37,216
District 4	12,537	198,766	28.3	4.3	3.7	13.8	15.8	3.0	0.9	2.0	1.1	7,555	38,010
District 5	15,508	284,681	15.3	4.5	3.3	12.7	15.2	2.4	1.0	18.0	1.9	15,001	52,694
District 6	16,582	265,760	6.7	6.8	4.3	14.9	13.6	7.8	1.6	5.2	3.6	13,724	51,639
District 7	13,580	304,428	16.6	5.5	5.4	8.6	20.2	4.8	1.8	3.8	1.5	15,501	50,918
ALASKA	21,184	266,063	4.8	6.2	3.3	12.5	19.5	2.7	1.8	7.6	2.4	16,331	61,380
At Large	21,184	266,063	4.8	6.2	3.3	12.5	19.5	2.7	1.8	7.6	2.4	16,331	61,380
ARIZONA	149,829	2,644,781	5.9	6.8	3.8	12.7	15.0	6.8	2.1	6.4	2.1	134,085	50,698
District 1	12,375	174,176	9.1	5.1	2.0	16.7	18.1	1.6	1.5	2.7	1.3	7,298	41,903
District 2	15,487	223,545	2.4	6.2	1.3	17.0	23.0	4.0	2.4	7.4	2.1	9,520	42,588
District 3	10,264	183,553	8.9	7.2	4.7	14.6	16.4	3.1	1.5	3.8	1.8	8,603	46,868
District 4	13,750	151,902	6.5	8.4	3.1	20.2	18.4	2.2	1.7	3.1	1.0	5,775	38,020
District 5	17,638	228,759	7.7	8.2	2.4	16.4	16.0	6.8	2.4	5.1	1.5	10,577	46,238
District 6	26,789	426,251	3.4	7.9	2.5	11.0	12.9	11.5	2.5	7.7	3.3	24,578	57,662
District 7	14,572	417,891	9.9	8.0	8.4	8.7	13.2	6.0	1.6	4.3	1.6	22,886	54,766
District 8	13,128	171,581	3.3	5.9	2.1	21.4	23.5	3.4	2.0	3.1	0.9	6,785	39,542
District 9	25,025	533,219	5.5	6.6	3.8	9.5	12.6	10.2	3.0	11.2	3.4	31,684	59,420
ARKANSAS	67,586	1,055,534	15.4	4.8	4.7	13.0	17.6	3.9	1.3	3.8	2.0	47,495	44,996
District 1	13,857	196,512	22.0	3.8	5.0	15.0	21.0	3.1	1.1	2.1	0.9	7,674	39,051
District 2	19,511	303,901	7.0	5.4	5.2	13.2	21.5	6.0	1.4	4.4	3.6	14,471	47,616
District 3	20,185	342,029	15.9	4.9	5.1	12.0	13.6	2.7	1.4	4.9	1.7	17,127	50,075
District 4	13,601	184,042	23.8	5.4	2.6	14.3	17.2	3.1	1.0	2.4	0.9	7,240	39,339
CALIFORNIA	981,369	15,710,859	7.4	5.5	5.2	10.7	13.7	4.1	2.0	8.4	4.7	1,132,426	72,079
District 1	15,788	180,308	6.6	7.0	3.2	17.3	21.5	3.5	1.4	4.2	1.4	8,002	44,382
District 2	22,006	236,390	7.7	7.4	4.3	14.8	16.3	3.4	2.3	6.4	3.1	14,304	60,509
District 3	12,532	184,140	8.9	8.4	6.0	15.7	16.1	2.8	1.6	3.8	1.7	9,272	50,352
District 4	19,985	246,344	3.6	10.5	2.3	14.3	14.6	5.6	2.7	5.8	2.1	13,295	53,969
District 5	17,630	245,845	12.5	9.3	4.1	13.1	18.7	2.5	1.6	3.9	1.2	14,430	58,696
District 6	16,588	295,538	4.0	7.4	6.0	10.8	19.1	2.8	2.0	7.0	1.9	16,750	56,676
District 7	14,897	227,407	5.1	7.8	2.3	13.7	15.5	9.4	2.0	9.7	2.5	14,367	63,176
District 8	10,118	123,911	5.0	5.8	1.3	18.6	18.8	1.6	2.4	2.7	1.2	4,806	38,786
District 9	11,657	176,780	7.7	8.0	5.8	13.4	17.6	3.5	1.8	2.9	1.0	9,019	51,018
District 10	13,142	207,246	12.2	5.9	5.5	16.3	16.0	2.1	1.2	3.6	1.0	10,078	48,629
District 11	17,729	241,678	4.2	7.4	3.5	14.0	18.3	6.8	2.2	7.7	1.8	15,495	64,114
District 12	33,030	706,632	1.1	3.3	2.3	6.6	10.2	9.0	2.7	18.9	12.3	90,859	128,580
District 13	20,154	321,355	6.2	6.4	4.5	9.4	17.6	4.2	1.8	9.9	3.9	23,916	74,423
District 14	19,845	412,334	6.2	4.9	4.9	9.2	8.6	3.7	1.8	10.1	18.1	60,036	145,600
District 15	17,992	314,865	8.1	8.6	7.7	9.5	12.2	3.9	1.6	12.2	7.6	26,258	83,395
District 16	9,493	167,382	15.3	6.2	6.5	11.6	18.8	1.6	1.6	2.5	1.5	7,693	45,960
District 17	21,679	627,274	15.8	4.6	11.1	5.5	6.0	2.1	1.1	13.8	9.9	100,905	160,862
District 18	21,995	431,680	2.8	2.8	2.6	8.6	17.1	3.5	1.5	14.2	17.5	63,501	147,103
District 19	14,604	232,707	7.4	8.1	4.4	9.5	11.0	2.5	2.1	11.8	6.4	18,705	80,382
District 20	16,709	214,918	7.7	6.2	5.5	16.0	15.6	2.1	1.7	5.7	1.4	10,399	48,384
District 21	7,227	116,188	16.3	5.2	7.8	16.7	11.5	1.1	1.2	1.5	0.9	5,150	44,329
District 22	15,517	227,601	7.8	6.4	3.7	16.3	19.2	4.4	1.9	4.3	1.2	10,082	44,298
District 23	12,790	186,022	4.9	7.1	3.5	13.8	20.7	2.9	1.8	5.0	1.8	8,869	47,676
District 24	21,070	259,202	8.1	6.4	3.7	13.0	15.5	2.6	2.0	7.0	3.9	13,879	53,546
District 25	13,563	169,595	9.4	7.4	4.0	15.9	14.3	2.0	1.9	8.9	1.4	8,105	47,793
District 26	19,669	251,653	9.2	5.8	5.8	14.4	14.9	5.4	1.8	8.8	2.3	15,092	59,971
District 27	23,587	259,700	2.1	2.3	2.7	11.4	19.7	6.6	2.1	10.5	1.9	14,379	55,370
District 28	28,983	345,912	3.8	3.4	2.3	10.8	19.1	2.7	3.1	7.4	10.7	22,457	64,921
District 29	13,549	174,553	13.4	8.5	6.3	11.9	20.5	1.8	2.9	3.3	2.3	8,758	50,174
District 30	33,835	363,181	5.1	4.4	3.3	11.2	17.5	6.3	2.6	7.0	10.3	22,976	63,263
District 31	14,434	261,300	7.5	5.2	4.4	13.8	22.1	3.0	1.4	3.4	2.1	12,594	48,197
District 32	16,077	254,331	14.8	5.0	9.4	12.5	16.0	3.1	1.7	4.4	1.2	12,776	50,234
District 33	44,017	528,535	5.5	1.8	2.7	9.4	12.4	4.6	3.4	14.1	10.0	45,268	85,649
District 34	24,869	348,375	3.8	2.0	7.9	6.5	14.2	7.9	2.6	12.5	2.2	24,289	69,722
District 35	14,969	293,033	10.9	6.8	11.2	13.2	10.7	1.7	1.3	2.1	1.2	14,952	51,024
District 36	13,440	181,910	3.6	6.6	1.9	18.5	17.2	1.6	2.4	2.8	1.4	6,924	38,064
District 37	23,432	283,193	2.8	1.9	2.8	9.4	13.6	4.1	3.9	11.8	12.6	23,785	83,989
District 38	15,525	252,182	12.1	5.7	13.8	13.0	15.1	2.2	1.5	4.0	1.3	12,304	48,788
District 39	21,520	272,014	9.9	8.2	10.9	11.2	9.4	6.5	1.8	4.7	1.4	14,133	51,958
District 40	11,798	221,161	19.2	2.8	15.0	11.2	11.9	1.5	1.3	1.9	0.8	10,133	45,818
District 41	11,429	213,802	8.6	8.4	5.5	13.9	14.3	1.9	1.5	3.0	1.2	9,506	44,461
District 42	13,589	178,255	10.4	15.3	7.0	13.2	12.6	1.8	1.5	4.3	1.0	8,022	45,004
District 43	16,219	309,541	10.8	2.9	6.4	10.0	12.5	2.0	2.4	6.3	2.2	17,507	56,560
District 44	9,316	165,480	17.9	6.8	11.3	9.8	10.3	1.0	1.2	2.0	1.4	8,456	51,102
District 45	28,651	445,902	9.2	5.8	7.8	7.5	9.5	7.2	4.2	13.5	4.9	36,562	81,995
District 46	18,663	398,558	9.9	8.0	5.9	7.2	14.4	4.7	2.0	5.4	1.0	20,091	50,408
District 47	16,850	243,427	8.2	5.6	5.3	11.4	17.1	5.5	2.1	6.0	1.8	12,544	51,530
District 48	27,148	341,010	6.7	5.1	4.8	13.1	12.8	6.6	3.9	10.1	1.7	22,059	64,688
District 49	23,534	296,883	10.3	5.4	5.9	11.6	13.1	2.5	2.3	13.7	1.9	18,777	63,246
District 50	17,377	214,419	7.4	13.4	3.8	16.0	12.8	1.9	1.6	4.2	1.0	9,418	43,926
District 51	11,007	147,274	10.0	5.2	6.6	21.3	16.3	2.3	1.7	3.2	1.7	5,901	40,067
District 52	31,166	561,365	7.6	5.0	3.8	7.7	8.0	6.6	2.6	17.8	4.2	42,878	76,381
District 53	17,525	251,733	3.2	6.2	1.6	11.4	30.1	4.3	2.4	7.3	0.9	13,354	53,050

STATE District	Representative, 117th Congress	Land area,[1] 2020 (sq mi)	Population and population characteristics, 2016–2020: Total persons	Per square mile	Race alone (percent): White	Black	American Indian, Alaska Native	Asian and Pacific Islander	Some other race (percent)	Two or more races (percent)	Hispanic or Latino[2] (percent)	Non-Hispanic White alone (percent)	Percent female	Percent foreign-born	Percent born in state of residence
		1	2	3	4	5	6	7	8	9	10	11	12	13	14
COLORADO		103,637.2	5,684,926	54.9	81.5	4.1	0.9	3.4	4.1	5.9	21.7	67.5	49.7	9.5	42.3
District 1	Diana DeGette (D)	189.6	843,348	4448.0	74.4	8.1	0.7	3.5	6.4	6.8	27.2	57.8	50.0	12.8	40.8
District 2	Joe Neguse (D)	7,538.2	817,394	108.4	88.8	0.9	0.6	3.3	1.7	4.6	10.8	81.7	49.4	7.1	35.8
District 3	Lauren Boebert (R)	49,729.7	752,192	15.1	86.9	1.0	2.3	1.0	4.2	4.6	24.9	69.9	49.7	5.8	48.7
District 4	Ken Buck (R)	38,101.1	837,275	22.0	87.3	1.4	0.7	2.6	3.0	5.0	22.4	70.9	49.3	8.1	48.0
District 5	Doug Lamborn (R)	7,265.8	811,504	111.7	79.9	5.9	0.8	2.7	3.5	7.2	16.6	70.2	49.0	6.4	32.3
District 6	Jason Crow (D)	473.7	825,402	1742.5	70.8	9.6	0.7	6.7	5.9	6.3	20.3	59.8	50.2	15.1	41.2
District 7	Ed Perlmutter (D)	339.1	797,811	2352.7	83.2	1.7	0.9	3.5	4.0	6.7	29.6	62.5	49.9	10.6	49.8
CONNECTICUT		4,842.4	3,570,549	737.4	74.2	10.7	0.3	4.6	5.4	4.8	16.4	66.0	51.2	14.6	54.4
District 1	John B. Larson (D)	675.4	709,090	1049.9	67.6	15.2	0.3	5.5	6.2	5.2	17.5	59.8	51.8	15.4	58.3
District 2	Joe Courtney (D)	1,988.1	701,886	353.0	85.0	4.1	0.4	3.4	2.6	4.6	8.9	80.5	49.8	7.2	56.2
District 3	Rosa L. DeLauro (D)	470.4	711,468	1512.5	70.5	14.8	0.2	4.5	5.6	4.3	16.3	62.6	51.9	13.4	61.1
District 4	James A. Himes (D)	460.8	736,148	1597.5	70.7	11.8	0.2	5.7	6.4	5.2	20.3	60.2	51.4	22.3	41.6
District 5	Jahana Hayes (D)	1,247.7	711,957	570.6	77.5	7.5	0.2	3.8	6.1	4.8	19.0	67.5	51.2	14.3	55.4
DELAWARE		1,948.6	967,679	496.6	67.4	22.0	0.4	4.1	2.3	3.9	9.4	61.5	51.7	9.4	44.3
At Large	Lisa Blunt Rochester (D)	1,948.6	967,679	496.6	67.4	22.0	0.4	4.1	2.3	3.9	9.4	61.5	51.7	9.4	44.3
DISTRICT OF COLUMBIA		61.1	701,974	11488.9	41.1	45.4	0.3	4.1	4.8	4.2	11.1	36.7	52.5	13.4	36.8
Delegate District (At Large)	Eleanor Holmes Norton (D)	61.1	701,974	11488.9	41.1	45.4	0.3	4.1	4.8	4.2	11.1	36.7	52.5	13.4	36.8
FLORIDA		53,652.2	21,216,924	395.5	71.6	15.9	0.3	2.8	3.3	6.0	25.8	53.4	51.1	20.8	35.9
District 1	Matt Gaetz (R)	4,018.3	785,773	195.5	75.9	13.2	0.4	2.8	2.1	5.5	6.8	72.5	49.7	5.7	38.8
District 2	Neal P. Dunn (R)	11,004.2	726,881	66.1	80.5	12.5	0.3	1.9	1.3	3.5	6.7	75.9	48.8	5.3	51.7
District 3	Kat Cammack (R)	3,565.7	747,806	209.7	73.6	16.3	0.2	3.5	1.5	4.9	10.5	66.6	50.6	7.8	50.4
District 4	John H. Rutherford (R)	1,569.7	820,783	522.9	78.8	9.5	0.3	4.7	2.0	4.7	9.0	73.1	50.8	10.8	40.3
District 5	Al Lawson (D)	3,820.0	737,321	193.0	43.8	47.3	0.3	2.6	2.0	4.1	8.7	38.6	51.5	7.4	60.1
District 6	Michael Waltz (R)	2,173.7	783,276	360.3	80.3	10.6	0.3	1.8	3.7	3.3	13.2	72.3	51.6	8.3	34.8
District 7	Stephanie N. Murphy (D)	392.7	775,811	1975.6	73.0	10.9	0.2	4.9	4.9	6.2	26.0	56.1	51.1	14.3	37.6
District 8	Bill Posey (R)	1,751.4	766,728	437.8	81.5	9.5	0.3	2.3	1.9	4.5	11.2	73.8	51.2	9.1	32.5
District 9	Darren Soto (D)	2,312.0	895,237	387.2	68.7	13.2	0.3	3.1	6.9	7.8	42.0	40.3	51.0	17.4	29.9
District 10	Val Butler Demings (D)	435.8	843,134	1934.7	52.3	28.1	0.2	5.4	6.7	7.3	29.5	34.7	51.4	25.4	35.1
District 11	Daniel Webster (R)	2,408.3	790,906	328.4	85.8	7.5	0.3	1.3	1.5	3.6	11.0	78.1	51.7	6.9	30.2
District 12	Gus M. Bilirakis (R)	858.3	788,853	919.1	85.3	5.2	0.3	2.9	1.6	4.7	13.6	75.9	52.0	11.0	32.2
District 13	Vacancy	181.7	736,584	4053.8	77.4	12.3	0.2	3.8	1.7	4.5	10.5	70.6	51.5	12.0	35.1
District 14	Kathy Castor (D)	276.0	802,492	2907.6	65.5	17.8	0.2	4.9	3.4	8.2	31.8	43.9	50.8	20.9	38.9
District 15	C. Scott Franklin (R)	1,088.1	805,103	739.9	71.9	14.7	0.3	3.0	4.1	6.0	24.0	56.1	51.2	13.1	41.3
District 16	Vern Buchanan (R)	1,294.7	853,737	659.4	80.7	9.2	0.3	2.3	3.2	4.3	17.6	68.8	51.8	13.3	31.1
District 17	W. Gregory Steube (R)	5,573.9	788,069	141.4	84.7	7.2	0.3	1.5	2.9	3.4	15.9	73.3	50.2	10.8	32.9
District 18	Brian J. Mast (R)	1,509.9	781,418	517.5	77.5	13.1	0.3	2.4	2.3	4.4	16.8	65.7	51.4	15.5	32.1
District 19	Byron Donalds (R)	747.5	834,988	1117.0	82.6	7.6	0.1	1.8	3.3	4.5	20.5	68.4	51.4	17.7	23.1
District 20	Sheila Cherfilus-McCormick (D)	2,159.1	791,022	366.4	34.7	53.9	0.3	2.7	2.6	5.9	24.4	17.5	51.5	34.4	43.2
District 21	Lois Frankel (D)	256.1	782,529	3055.6	72.0	15.8	0.2	2.8	3.3	5.8	25.0	54.4	51.4	28.3	27.5
District 22	Vacancy	163.7	765,204	4674.4	72.4	15.3	0.2	3.3	2.9	5.9	22.5	56.4	50.6	27.8	29.0
District 23	Debbie Wasserman Schultz (D)	186.8	768,038	4111.6	67.6	14.4	0.3	4.6	4.1	9.0	39.9	39.1	52.3	37.3	32.5
District 24	Frederica S. Wilson (D)	102.4	749,846	7322.7	38.9	47.4	0.2	1.3	5.4	6.8	41.0	11.1	51.0	43.9	41.9
District 25	Mario Diaz-Balart (R)	3,504.6	775,411	221.3	79.7	4.2	0.2	1.1	3.9	10.8	75.6	19.3	50.7	56.6	26.0
District 26	Carlos A. Gimenez (R)	2,184.4	771,373	353.1	71.8	11.0	0.3	1.9	4.5	10.5	69.9	16.9	51.2	48.1	35.6
District 27	Maria Elvira Salazar (R)	113.2	748,601	6613.1	75.8	4.9	0.2	2.1	4.4	12.6	72.0	20.8	50.9	54.5	29.1
GEORGIA		57,717.1	10,516,579	182.2	57.2	31.6	0.3	4.2	2.9	3.7	9.6	52.1	51.4	10.2	54.6
District 1	Earl L. "Buddy" Carter (R)	8,126.9	744,521	91.6	61.9	29.7	0.3	2.0	2.1	3.9	7.0	58.3	50.8	5.2	55.6
District 2	Sanford D. Bishop Jr. (D)	9,630.5	665,536	69.1	41.7	52.0	0.2	1.3	1.8	2.9	5.2	39.6	51.0	3.5	71.7
District 3	A. Drew Ferguson IV (R)	3,836.4	746,086	194.5	67.5	25.1	0.3	2.1	1.9	3.1	6.0	64.1	51.6	5.5	61.8
District 4	Henry C. "Hank" Johnson Jr. (D)	497.3	756,133	1520.5	26.1	60.3	0.3	5.5	3.7	4.0	9.4	22.1	52.6	16.6	47.3
District 5	Nikema Williams (D)	265.0	780,778	2946.3	32.4	56.6	0.4	4.7	2.4	3.6	7.0	29.1	52.0	9.0	52.0
District 6	Lucy McBath (D)	298.9	759,318	2540.4	66.0	13.8	0.9	11.9	2.5	4.9	12.3	58.7	50.7	21.5	33.4
District 7	Carolyn Bourdeaux (D)	392.9	833,680	2121.9	50.9	21.3	0.4	14.9	7.2	5.4	19.6	41.8	51.4	25.6	36.3
District 8	Austin Scott (R)	8,738.9	710,259	81.3	61.9	31.3	0.4	1.6	2.0	2.8	6.7	58.4	51.2	4.4	68.3
District 9	Andrew S. Clyde (R)	5,212.2	762,916	146.4	85.4	6.6	0.3	1.4	2.7	3.7	13.1	76.8	50.7	7.9	59.5
District 10	Jody B. Hice (R)	7,098.4	756,449	106.6	67.2	25.5	0.1	2.3	1.8	3.0	6.1	63.9	50.9	5.8	64.4
District 11	Barry Loudermilk (R)	1,070.1	777,408	726.5	71.6	16.9	0.2	3.6	3.4	4.2	11.3	65.4	51.1	11.8	45.3
District 12	Rick W. Allen (R)	8,211.5	729,203	88.8	57.5	34.9	0.2	1.9	2.2	3.3	6.4	54.3	50.8	4.4	66.4
District 13	David Scott (D)	714.3	770,115	1078.1	28.7	60.7	0.2	2.8	4.1	3.4	11.2	23.5	53.3	10.9	50.2
District 14	Marjorie Taylor Greene (R)	3,623.8	724,177	199.8	83.6	9.1	0.4	1.1	2.2	3.6	11.9	75.3	51.0	7.0	58.4
HAWAII		6,422.5	1,420,074	221.1	24.1	1.9	0.2	48.0	1.4	24.3	10.7	21.6	49.8	18.3	53.3
District 1	Ed Case (D)	209.0	706,681	3381.2	17.1	2.2	0.1	57.9	1.1	21.5	8.8	15.3	49.8	22.8	52.8
District 2	Kaiali'I Kahele (D)	6,213.5	713,393	114.8	31.1	1.5	0.4	38.3	1.7	27.0	12.7	27.8	49.8	13.9	53.8
IDAHO		82,645.2	1,754,367	21.2	88.4	0.7	1.3	1.6	3.8	4.3	12.7	81.4	49.9	5.9	46.4
District 1	Russ Fulcher (R)	39,420.4	913,009	23.2	88.3	0.6	1.3	1.4	4.0	4.4	11.3	82.7	50.0	4.8	42.2
District 2	Michael K. Simpson (R)	43,224.8	841,358	19.5	88.6	0.8	1.3	1.8	3.5	4.1	14.3	79.9	49.7	7.1	50.9
ILLINOIS		55,512.9	12,716,164	229.1	69.8	14.1	0.3	5.6	6.0	4.2	17.2	60.8	50.9	13.9	67.2
District 1	Bobby L. Rush (D)	258.3	705,263	2730.4	40.7	50.2	0.2	2.1	3.6	3.3	11.2	34.7	53.2	7.6	77.1
District 2	Robin L. Kelly (D)	1,080.6	692,805	641.1	34.8	57.3	0.1	0.8	4.0	2.9	14.3	26.0	53.3	6.9	76.8

1. Dry land or land partially or temporarily covered by water. 2. May be of any race.

Table E. Congressional Districts 116th Congress — **Age and Education**

STATE District	Population and population characteristics, 2016–2020 (cont.) Age (percent) Under 5 years	5 to 17 years	18 to 24 years	25 to 34 years	35 to 44 years	45 to 54 years	55 to 64 years	65 to 74 years	75 years and over	Median age	Education, 2016–2020 Total Enrollment[1]	Attainment[2] (percent) High school graduate or more	Bachelor's degree or more
	15	16	17	18	19	20	21	22	23	24	25	26	27
COLORADO	5.8	16.3	9.2	15.7	13.8	12.5	12.4	8.8	5.4	36.0	1,388,732	92.1	41.6
District 1	5.9	13.7	7.9	22.1	15.9	11.6	10.5	7.5	4.8	34.9	181,745	90.0	50.0
District 2	4.6	14.5	12.7	14.5	12.7	12.6	13.4	9.7	5.4	36.8	219,851	96.7	56.1
District 3	5.4	15.8	8.6	12.8	12.4	11.9	14.3	11.6	7.2	39.4	168,566	91.1	31.8
District 4	6.3	18.4	8.6	13.2	13.8	13.2	12.6	8.6	5.3	36.5	213,920	91.1	36.1
District 5	6.3	16.8	10.2	15.6	12.8	12.0	12.5	8.7	5.3	34.6	205,473	94.2	37.0
District 6	6.1	18.7	7.9	14.6	14.6	13.6	11.9	7.8	4.6	35.7	212,245	92.2	43.2
District 7	6.0	16.3	8.7	16.7	14.2	12.4	12.0	8.1	5.5	35.4	186,932	89.5	35.5
CONNECTICUT	5.1	15.5	9.7	12.4	11.9	13.9	14.3	9.7	7.6	39.4	888,200	90.9	40.0
District 1	5.3	15.3	8.8	13.3	12.3	13.4	14.0	9.7	7.9	39.1	170,437	90.0	38.0
District 2	4.6	14.4	11.3	11.9	11.1	13.8	15.1	10.4	7.6	39.8	171,213	93.1	36.3
District 3	4.9	14.5	10.7	13.9	11.8	13.2	13.8	9.7	7.5	38.1	180,406	91.6	37.3
District 4	5.5	17.4	9.0	11.4	12.6	14.6	13.8	8.7	7.0	39.0	198,260	90.3	51.7
District 5	5.3	15.7	8.7	11.7	11.7	14.0	14.9	10.0	7.9	40.8	167,884	89.9	36.7
DELAWARE	5.7	15.4	8.6	13.3	11.6	12.6	14.0	11.3	7.5	39.1	225,882	90.6	32.7
At Large	5.7	15.4	8.6	13.3	11.6	12.6	14.0	11.3	7.5	39.1	225,882	90.6	32.7
DISTRICT OF COLUMBIA	6.4	11.5	10.5	23.3	15.1	10.8	10.0	7.0	5.2	34.0	168,035	91.9	59.8
Delegate District (At Large)	6.4	11.5	10.5	23.3	15.1	10.8	10.0	7.0	5.2	34.0	168,035	91.9	59.8
FLORIDA	5.3	14.5	8.2	13.0	12.1	12.9	13.4	11.3	9.2	40.6	4,774,888	88.5	30.5
District 1	6.0	15.4	9.4	14.4	12.0	12.2	13.7	10.0	6.7	36.8	178,618	90.9	28.6
District 2	4.9	14.6	9.0	12.4	11.8	12.6	14.2	12.0	8.5	40.7	160,897	87.7	24.2
District 3	5.4	15.0	12.5	13.7	11.9	11.9	12.8	10.1	6.8	36.4	201,440	89.5	29.0
District 4	5.9	15.2	8.2	14.2	13.0	13.1	13.4	10.4	6.6	38.2	186,643	93.4	41.1
District 5	6.5	16.1	12.3	16.1	12.2	11.8	12.0	7.9	5.1	33.3	200,724	85.9	21.4
District 6	4.6	13.1	7.6	11.1	10.5	12.4	15.4	14.3	11.0	45.7	156,361	90.8	24.6
District 7	5.0	14.4	11.6	16.3	13.2	12.9	12.1	8.3	6.0	35.1	208,809	93.3	41.5
District 8	4.6	13.3	7.1	10.8	10.1	12.5	16.1	13.7	11.7	46.5	156,563	91.6	30.8
District 9	6.1	17.1	8.7	13.9	14.0	12.8	11.4	9.2	6.7	36.4	218,451	86.3	25.8
District 10	6.5	17.1	8.6	16.6	14.5	13.5	11.5	7.3	4.4	35.5	218,366	87.3	32.0
District 11	4.0	11.6	5.5	9.0	8.6	10.4	14.4	19.8	16.8	53.9	124,645	89.4	21.8
District 12	4.8	14.3	6.6	10.7	11.5	13.3	14.3	13.1	11.3	45.2	160,506	91.2	28.5
District 13	4.4	11.9	6.9	13.0	11.3	13.2	15.9	12.8	10.7	45.6	142,588	91.0	31.6
District 14	6.2	15.1	9.9	16.1	13.7	13.7	11.8	7.9	5.4	36.1	201,508	89.2	37.9
District 15	5.7	16.5	8.7	14.3	12.9	12.8	12.7	9.6	6.9	37.4	194,208	88.2	26.6
District 16	4.8	14.3	6.3	10.7	11.1	12.2	13.9	14.1	12.6	45.6	167,686	90.4	33.0
District 17	4.2	12.4	6.4	10.0	9.1	11.2	14.3	16.9	15.2	50.1	135,630	87.7	22.9
District 18	4.7	13.6	6.8	10.8	10.7	12.6	14.9	13.3	12.5	46.5	157,699	90.4	32.6
District 19	4.1	12.3	6.5	10.1	9.9	11.3	14.1	16.5	15.3	50.1	148,469	90.4	33.1
District 20	6.8	16.8	9.0	14.8	13.6	13.1	12.0	7.9	6.2	35.5	204,150	82.9	21.8
District 21	4.9	13.6	7.0	11.8	11.4	12.7	12.8	12.3	13.6	44.0	162,499	88.6	36.1
District 22	5.2	13.5	6.9	12.3	12.3	13.9	14.5	11.3	10.1	43.9	165,357	92.1	40.7
District 23	5.4	15.5	7.9	12.4	13.3	14.7	13.4	9.6	7.8	40.5	192,940	92.4	40.6
District 24	6.7	15.7	8.8	15.8	13.6	13.1	12.2	8.2	6.0	35.6	187,066	79.4	21.6
District 25	5.2	14.3	8.1	13.0	12.8	15.1	12.9	9.8	9.0	40.9	172,630	78.5	25.9
District 26	6.0	16.1	9.0	13.5	13.6	14.5	12.1	8.7	6.6	37.4	197,188	82.8	28.3
District 27	5.4	12.6	7.6	14.8	13.9	15.0	12.8	9.0	8.9	40.4	173,247	86.2	41.5
GEORGIA	6.2	17.6	9.6	13.9	13.1	13.3	12.3	8.5	5.3	35.5	2,743,653	87.9	32.2
District 1	6.7	16.7	9.9	15.3	12.6	11.9	12.1	9.2	5.8	34.4	187,412	88.6	26.3
District 2	6.3	17.2	10.6	13.6	12.0	11.8	12.9	9.4	6.4	34.9	173,652	83.5	18.4
District 3	5.9	18.0	9.3	12.7	12.5	13.7	12.8	9.3	5.9	37.1	190,313	88.6	28.1
District 4	6.6	18.1	8.9	14.5	13.6	13.7	12.9	7.6	4.1	34.5	205,453	88.7	32.4
District 5	5.9	14.5	12.1	20.0	13.8	11.9	10.2	7.1	4.4	32.8	208,668	90.1	45.1
District 6	6.1	18.0	6.8	13.3	14.9	15.2	12.7	8.1	5.0	37.5	194,170	94.3	63.5
District 7	6.7	20.6	8.7	12.6	15.2	14.8	11.1	6.7	3.8	35.1	239,697	88.9	42.8
District 8	6.2	17.4	9.9	13.6	12.4	12.3	12.6	9.2	6.3	35.7	180,545	86.4	22.9
District 9	5.6	16.8	8.9	11.7	11.8	13.4	13.3	11.2	7.4	40.1	177,423	83.5	24.3
District 10	5.7	17.5	11.9	12.3	12.3	13.3	12.3	9.2	5.7	36.2	210,240	87.9	27.9
District 11	5.9	17.3	9.4	14.6	13.6	14.3	12.1	8.0	4.7	35.8	200,251	91.7	42.4
District 12	6.4	17.1	11.3	14.2	12.4	11.9	12.4	8.8	5.6	33.8	190,252	85.0	22.1
District 13	6.8	19.1	8.9	13.9	14.0	14.4	11.7	7.5	3.9	34.2	209,605	89.2	29.6
District 14	6.1	18.2	8.7	12.8	13.0	13.9	12.4	9.0	5.9	37.0	175,972	82.2	18.8
HAWAII	6.2	15.1	8.5	14.3	12.7	12.1	12.8	10.4	8.0	37.9	318,529	92.5	33.6
District 1	5.9	14.0	8.4	15.1	13.1	12.4	12.1	10.1	8.9	38.0	160,346	91.9	36.9
District 2	6.6	16.1	8.7	13.4	12.2	11.7	13.4	10.8	7.1	37.9	158,183	93.1	30.1
IDAHO	6.5	18.8	9.4	13.1	12.7	11.5	12.3	9.6	6.2	35.9	456,826	91.3	28.7
District 1	6.2	18.6	8.5	12.3	12.5	12.1	12.7	10.5	6.6	37.4	227,619	91.6	27.3
District 2	6.9	19.1	10.3	14.0	12.8	10.8	11.7	8.6	5.8	34.2	229,207	90.9	30.2
ILLINOIS	5.9	16.5	9.2	13.8	12.9	12.9	13.0	9.1	6.6	37.0	3,166,891	89.7	35.5
District 1	5.9	16.7	9.6	13.3	11.9	12.7	13.5	9.4	6.9	36.2	181,199	89.7	30.1
District 2	6.1	17.8	9.8	12.6	11.9	13.0	13.1	9.0	6.5	35.9	178,346	88.7	23.7

1. All persons 3 years old and over enrolled in nursery school through college and graduate or professional school. 2. Persons 25 years old and over.

Table E. Congressional Districts 116th Congress — **Households and Group Quarters**

STATE District	Households, 2016–2020						Total in group quarters, 2020	Persons in group quarters, 2020				
	Number	Average household size	Family households (percent)	Married couple family (percent)	Female family house-holder[1]	One person households (percent)		Correctional facilities for adults	Juvenile facilities	Skilled nursing facilities	College/ University student housing	Military quarters
	28	29	30	31	32	33	34	35	36	37	38	39
COLORADO	2,137,402	2.60	63.6	50.0	9.1	27.7	126,848	32,307	1,525	21,379	38,819	12,999
District 1	339,423	2.44	50.3	37.2	8.9	37.1	16,817	3,352	193	2,936	4,445	0
District 2	317,900	2.50	61.3	51.5	6.1	26.4	27,846	1,268	46	2,997	20,193	0
District 3	294,453	2.50	63.3	49.5	9.4	29.7	15,760	3,130	256	3,390	5,858	0
District 4	294,488	2.78	71.5	58.4	8.7	22.9	18,861	9,533	207	3,282	3,647	0
District 5	302,655	2.58	67.7	53.9	9.4	25.1	30,012	10,263	478	2,881	1,789	12,665
District 6	292,875	2.79	69.3	53.7	10.6	23.9	7,161	2,235	124	2,659	36	334
District 7	295,608	2.66	63.8	48.0	10.5	27.4	10,391	2,526	221	3,234	2,851	0
CONNECTICUT	1,385,437	2.50	65.2	48.0	12.5	28.5	108,002	13,581	910	22,264	51,718	2,240
District 1	284,492	2.43	63.6	44.6	13.9	30.3	15,530	1,027	156	5,493	5,202	0
District 2	276,725	2.40	66.2	50.7	10.6	26.4	34,136	7,795	114	4,212	16,024	2,240
District 3	276,944	2.47	62.1	43.6	13.8	30.8	27,643	883	144	4,291	19,083	0
District 4	268,348	2.69	69.5	53.6	11.7	25.0	14,469	879	13	3,279	7,332	0
District 5	278,928	2.49	64.7	47.6	12.5	29.8	16,224	2,997	483	4,989	4,077	0
DELAWARE	370,953	2.54	65.5	48.0	12.7	28.1	22,745	4,801	114	4,585	11,045	93
At Large	370,953	2.54	65.5	48.0	12.7	28.1	22,745	4,801	114	4,585	11,045	93
DISTRICT OF COLUMBIA	288,307	2.30	42.8	26.1	13.3	45.1	40,682	2,278	315	2,727	23,802	818
Delegate District (At Large)	288,307	2.30	42.8	26.1	13.3	45.1	40,682	2,278	315	2,727	23,802	818
FLORIDA	7,931,313	2.62	64.5	46.9	12.7	28.6	464,583	149,333	4,203	112,610	114,794	11,953
District 1	300,202	2.51	65.6	49.0	12.2	27.3	31,716	12,352	323	4,930	4,134	7,343
District 2	280,665	2.43	64.8	49.3	11.1	29.1	44,293	29,730	186	5,109	7,896	114
District 3	277,234	2.57	61.5	44.5	12.6	30.5	38,403	16,873	243	4,876	13,391	0
District 4	314,445	2.56	66.0	51.9	9.8	27.0	17,343	1,302	169	6,448	4,064	3,690
District 5	279,247	2.52	58.1	33.4	19.4	32.5	28,882	15,306	225	3,394	5,241	0
District 6	312,779	2.47	64.3	48.8	10.6	28.7	18,956	3,070	297	5,885	6,402	21
District 7	291,851	2.58	62.6	46.0	11.9	27.6	28,106	770	185	4,000	21,127	0
District 8	301,921	2.51	63.2	49.9	9.3	30.9	9,550	1,651	233	3,782	1,799	135
District 9	289,225	3.07	72.1	50.7	15.0	21.7	9,692	4,715	108	3,047	642	0
District 10	281,411	2.97	68.3	46.8	15.6	23.6	10,397	2,216	180	2,926	2,034	0
District 11	333,726	2.32	66.2	53.2	9.3	28.5	17,225	11,545	125	4,074	43	0
District 12	315,688	2.47	64.7	49.6	11.1	29.6	11,055	2,079	68	5,042	2,298	0
District 13	311,657	2.31	55.2	40.2	10.7	36.1	17,288	2,783	221	6,857	2,156	71
District 14	309,209	2.55	58.2	39.3	13.8	32.2	21,588	1,257	212	3,887	12,954	350
District 15	284,725	2.78	67.3	48.6	13.2	25.2	15,333	3,192	298	2,997	5,926	0
District 16	332,823	2.54	65.3	51.8	9.9	28.7	15,262	2,773	115	7,365	1,207	12
District 17	309,443	2.49	66.2	53.1	9.3	27.8	19,984	12,597	281	4,494	117	0
District 18	304,931	2.54	65.2	50.8	10.5	28.8	11,347	3,539	132	4,236	482	24
District 19	333,345	2.47	63.8	51.7	8.5	30.3	15,456	2,069	156	6,258	4,671	55
District 20	254,904	3.04	66.0	37.5	21.2	27.7	12,688	5,402	117	3,633	17	9
District 21	302,089	2.57	62.2	46.2	11.3	31.1	8,685	0	11	5,134	290	0
District 22	313,038	2.41	56.9	42.7	10.1	35.2	12,437	1,746	126	3,897	5,133	0
District 23	282,570	2.70	65.7	48.2	12.8	28.5	4,045	142	23	1,849	1,068	0
District 24	245,575	2.99	65.3	35.1	22.3	28.9	12,599	2,579	22	2,979	3,518	0
District 25	251,299	3.04	74.3	50.3	16.6	20.6	9,670	3,206	92	1,418	924	0
District 26	232,698	3.25	77.7	51.7	18.4	17.1	13,313	6,421	34	1,365	2,895	100
District 27	284,613	2.59	61.0	42.1	12.9	31.7	9,270	18	21	2,728	4,365	29
GEORGIA	3,830,264	2.68	67.0	47.4	14.9	27.3	255,178	91,932	3,045	40,939	82,346	14,860
District 1	278,422	2.58	65.8	46.1	15.4	28.0	30,075	10,154	346	4,192	7,344	6,113
District 2	248,347	2.53	63.4	37.8	20.7	32.0	31,411	14,303	520	3,474	7,323	2,940
District 3	271,144	2.71	71.5	52.0	14.9	24.4	10,981	2,868	168	3,542	3,298	146
District 4	262,850	2.85	65.9	40.6	19.6	28.5	5,714	1,813	179	1,828	844	0
District 5	319,578	2.31	47.3	25.9	17.1	42.2	38,765	8,475	268	2,746	23,606	0
District 6	292,422	2.59	66.3	54.2	8.7	27.3	3,841	0	0	1,723	637	0
District 7	272,664	3.04	75.9	59.0	12.0	20.1	6,843	3,088	17	1,917	803	0
District 8	263,996	2.60	67.0	47.1	15.1	28.0	22,903	12,293	226	4,037	4,431	302
District 9	275,466	2.73	72.4	57.0	11.0	22.8	15,994	4,099	100	2,961	6,981	41
District 10	269,532	2.70	69.8	51.6	13.8	23.9	26,057	10,547	77	3,146	11,315	0
District 11	290,766	2.63	67.2	52.0	11.1	25.7	11,904	2,200	249	2,388	5,995	0
District 12	253,251	2.74	66.0	44.7	16.6	28.9	34,667	15,790	385	4,417	6,819	5,318
District 13	271,813	2.81	69.7	43.0	20.6	25.5	4,773	1,946	293	1,832	0	0
District 14	260,013	2.73	72.7	54.0	13.3	23.1	11,250	4,356	217	2,736	2,950	0
HAWAII	467,932	2.94	69.3	51.2	12.4	24.3	40,741	3,752	129	5,498	4,960	15,522
District 1	238,945	2.87	66.9	49.4	12.2	26.8	19,214	2,471	46	3,164	2,928	5,815
District 2	228,987	3.02	71.9	53.1	12.6	21.7	21,527	1,281	83	2,334	2,032	9,707
IDAHO	649,299	2.66	68.0	54.9	8.7	25.7	49,729	10,931	570	8,955	22,521	753
District 1	337,581	2.66	69.9	56.6	8.6	24.1	18,825	7,509	371	4,501	4,141	0
District 2	311,718	2.65	65.9	53.0	8.8	27.4	30,904	3,422	199	4,454	18,380	753
ILLINOIS	4,884,061	2.54	63.8	47.1	12.1	29.8	275,365	59,075	2,530	81,485	83,220	11,424
District 1	271,265	2.56	60.7	35.7	20.0	34.8	11,117	0	62	3,937	5,098	0
District 2	258,388	2.64	62.5	34.3	22.4	33.1	9,669	332	129	4,154	1,948	0

1. No spouse present.

STATE District	Housing units, 2016–2020: Total	Occupied units as a percent of all units	Owner-occupied units as a percent of occupied units	Median value[1] (dollars)	Percent valued at $500,000 or more	Renter-occupied: Median rent[2]	Money income, 2016–2020: Per capita income (dollars)	Households: Median income (dollars)	Households: Percent with income of $100,000 or more
	40	41	42	43	44	45	46	47	48
COLORADO	2,361,372	90.5	66.2	369,900	26.7	1,335	39,545	75,231	36.7
District 1	360,071	94.3	53.2	426,900	36.3	1,398	46,221	75,128	38.0
District 2	377,645	84.2	68.4	463,500	43.3	1,486	46,428	86,011	43.4
District 3	368,506	79.9	69.1	255,100	18.5	958	31,913	58,209	24.9
District 4	313,611	93.9	73.7	364,100	25.7	1,220	37,949	79,205	39.4
District 5	330,455	91.6	66.8	297,400	13.6	1,210	34,496	69,691	32.5
District 6	304,472	96.2	67.9	402,800	28.2	1,489	41,668	86,388	43.1
District 7	306,612	96.4	66.2	371,700	21.3	1,414	37,242	76,406	37.0
CONNECTICUT	1,521,199	91.1	66.1	279,700	16.8	1,201	45,668	79,855	40.5
District 1	307,338	92.6	64.3	240,000	6.1	1,127	40,924	76,056	38.1
District 2	307,911	89.9	71.8	254,400	8.7	1,133	41,570	80,744	40.0
District 3	304,143	91.1	62.2	260,000	8.2	1,223	39,413	72,887	36.7
District 4	291,020	92.2	65.2	505,500	50.4	1,533	63,226	101,143	50.9
District 5	310,787	89.7	66.9	272,500	12.2	1,125	42,528	75,297	38.4
DELAWARE	438,438	84.6	71.4	258,300	9.1	1,150	36,574	69,110	32.5
At Large	438,438	84.6	71.4	258,300	9.1	1,150	36,574	69,110	32.5
DISTRICT OF COLUMBIA	319,192	90.3	42.5	618,100	61.5	1,607	58,659	90,842	47.0
Delegate District (At Large)	319,192	90.3	42.5	618,100	61.5	1,607	58,659	90,842	47.0
FLORIDA	9,562,324	82.9	66.2	232,000	11.4	1,218	32,848	57,703	25.8
District 1	372,510	80.6	68.3	194,800	7.9	1,073	31,764	60,668	26.5
District 2	357,890	78.4	73.7	164,400	4.5	939	28,507	51,847	21.3
District 3	320,825	86.4	64.6	173,200	4.4	976	28,619	52,178	22.5
District 4	356,389	88.2	69.5	270,200	13.9	1,237	40,939	75,641	36.4
District 5	322,427	86.6	51.7	134,600	2.5	957	22,968	43,822	14.4
District 6	375,031	83.4	72.6	205,600	6.0	1,118	30,599	54,317	22.4
District 7	320,750	91.0	59.5	263,800	10.6	1,306	35,818	67,341	31.7
District 8	367,741	82.1	76.6	220,900	9.1	1,091	34,515	59,195	26.9
District 9	377,793	76.6	66.6	209,200	3.8	1,236	25,882	55,690	22.5
District 10	333,910	84.3	56.5	251,800	11.2	1,247	30,219	58,849	26.8
District 11	397,403	84.0	81.8	171,400	4.4	957	28,886	50,368	17.9
District 12	368,375	85.7	74.2	197,300	6.3	1,133	32,820	55,860	25.3
District 13	394,456	79.0	65.8	213,400	12.0	1,151	35,966	55,501	25.0
District 14	339,068	91.2	52.9	255,400	14.4	1,166	35,593	57,406	27.7
District 15	324,052	87.9	64.9	195,000	3.6	1,167	28,523	57,857	24.2
District 16	417,864	79.6	73.7	253,600	14.4	1,283	37,452	64,274	30.3
District 17	396,275	78.1	79.1	184,200	6.4	967	31,304	53,071	21.2
District 18	373,328	81.7	76.1	270,000	15.8	1,351	39,781	64,088	31.1
District 19	486,840	68.5	72.7	274,600	20.9	1,283	41,510	62,257	29.4
District 20	289,053	88.2	55.5	213,500	5.6	1,271	23,806	49,946	19.1
District 21	368,864	81.9	71.4	281,000	16.1	1,466	40,032	62,988	30.2
District 22	386,105	81.1	65.0	332,600	24.7	1,524	44,358	67,714	33.9
District 23	348,914	81.0	65.8	329,200	20.8	1,600	38,421	68,473	34.3
District 24	276,635	88.8	45.9	234,500	9.9	1,197	22,564	44,092	16.0
District 25	284,645	88.3	58.4	286,500	13.1	1,363	26,088	54,023	23.4
District 26	263,391	88.3	62.9	321,500	13.7	1,494	26,494	63,171	28.1
District 27	341,790	83.3	47.8	406,200	37.8	1,428	42,887	62,011	33.0
GEORGIA	4,329,675	88.5	64.0	190,200	8.8	1,042	32,427	61,224	28.3
District 1	328,027	84.9	61.2	166,700	7.4	1,003	29,365	54,772	23.6
District 2	302,252	82.2	55.8	110,400	1.9	766	22,812	40,595	15.8
District 3	296,174	91.5	70.1	182,400	5.6	975	32,186	65,076	29.7
District 4	284,085	92.5	61.4	174,200	3.6	1,144	28,604	59,808	26.1
District 5	369,062	86.6	45.8	229,900	19.8	1,154	39,703	57,586	28.3
District 6	311,747	93.8	65.3	393,900	31.4	1,410	54,281	99,516	50.3
District 7	284,208	95.9	68.5	274,500	10.8	1,342	35,613	80,096	40.3
District 8	307,071	86.0	64.6	130,800	2.9	800	26,162	50,150	21.1
District 9	338,615	81.4	74.8	195,300	8.1	860	29,549	59,198	25.6
District 10	307,303	87.7	69.6	187,900	6.3	881	29,928	59,490	27.3
District 11	311,855	93.2	65.3	267,300	14.3	1,251	41,833	78,832	39.0
District 12	307,918	82.2	63.1	128,900	2.7	810	25,596	49,091	20.2
District 13	293,278	92.7	63.4	172,500	3.2	1,131	28,994	63,305	26.7
District 14	288,080	90.3	70.2	150,300	3.3	778	26,443	54,634	22.4
HAWAII	546,571	85.6	60.3	636,400	65.7	1,651	37,013	83,173	41.4
District 1	267,529	89.3	56.6	694,800	72.9	1,696	39,311	86,203	43.4
District 2	279,042	82.1	64.1	580,300	59.0	1,587	34,737	80,253	39.7
IDAHO	737,411	88.1	70.8	235,600	9.4	887	29,494	58,915	24.5
District 1	382,762	88.2	74.1	255,600	10.4	924	29,953	60,698	25.4
District 2	354,649	87.9	67.1	211,800	8.3	861	28,996	56,968	23.6
ILLINOIS	5,373,385	90.9	66.3	202,100	9.5	1,038	37,306	68,428	33.3
District 1	306,227	88.6	60.8	194,600	4.3	987	30,710	57,466	27.8
District 2	297,341	86.9	61.6	135,100	1.9	978	27,052	53,158	22.8

1. Specified owner-occupied units. 2. Specified renter-occupied units.

Table E. Congressional Districts 116th Congress — **Poverty, Labor Force, Employment, and Social Security**

STATE District	Poverty, 2016–2020: Persons below poverty level (percent)	Poverty, 2016–2020: Families below poverty level (percent)	Poverty, 2016–2020: Percent of households receiving food stamps in past 12 months	Civilian labor force, 2016–2020: Total	Civilian labor force, 2016–2020: Unemployment: Total	Civilian labor force, 2016–2020: Unemployment: Rate[1]	Civilian employment,[2] 2016–2020: Total	Civilian employment,[2] 2016–2020: Percent: Management, business, science, and arts occupations	Civilian employment,[2] 2016–2020: Percent: Service, sales, and office	Civilian employment,[2] 2016–2020: Percent: Construction and production	Persons under 65 years of age with no health insurance, 2016–2020 (percent)	Social Security beneficiaries, December 2021: Number	Social Security beneficiaries, December 2021: Rate[3]	Supplemental Security Income recipients, December 2021
	49	50	51	52	53	54	55	56	57	58	59	60	61	62
COLORADO	9.8	6.1	7.2	3,079,769	142,722	4.6	2,937,047	43.5	37.4	19.1	9.0	925,084	162.7	69,926
District 1	11.1	7.7	7.4	499,798	20,933	4.2	478,865	49.4	35.3	15.4	10.0	108,535	128.7	14,480
District 2	9.8	3.8	4.2	466,236	21,478	4.6	444,758	50.5	35.0	14.5	6.7	135,384	165.6	4,588
District 3	13.2	9.0	11.0	375,988	20,702	5.5	355,286	35.8	40.8	23.3	12.2	166,646	221.5	13,554
District 4	8.6	5.7	7.2	439,413	19,195	4.4	420,218	41.1	36.2	22.7	8.1	138,406	165.3	8,693
District 5	10.0	6.7	8.8	391,397	22,632	5.8	368,765	42.2	39.5	18.3	8.5	142,299	175.4	10,483
District 6	7.2	4.7	5.6	457,284	19,723	4.3	437,561	43.4	37.9	18.6	8.5	113,458	137.5	9,135
District 7	8.8	5.7	6.5	449,653	18,059	4.0	431,594	39.5	38.5	22.0	9.2	120,356	150.9	8,993
CONNECTICUT	9.8	6.7	11.6	1,923,759	116,234	6.0	1,807,525	44.5	38.1	17.4	6.0	699,597	195.9	65,932
District 1	10.7	7.3	14.6	383,932	21,626	5.6	362,306	44.1	38.4	17.5	4.9	146,124	206.1	17,003
District 2	8.0	5.1	8.9	376,242	20,270	5.4	355,972	43.5	37.9	18.6	4.3	152,086	216.7	9,094
District 3	10.7	7.3	12.4	390,556	24,187	6.2	366,369	43.3	38.8	17.9	5.8	139,996	196.8	14,903
District 4	9.3	6.5	8.6	394,062	26,653	6.8	367,409	49.0	37.4	13.6	8.6	118,289	160.7	10,533
District 5	10.2	7.1	13.1	378,967	23,498	6.2	355,469	42.5	38.1	19.4	6.2	143,102	201.0	14,399
DELAWARE	11.4	7.7	10.6	485,206	28,334	5.8	456,872	40.8	38.8	20.4	7.1	229047	236.7	16,337
At Large	11.4	7.7	10.6	485,206	28,334	5.8	456,872	40.8	38.8	20.4	7.1	229047	236.7	16,337
DISTRICT OF COLUMBIA	15.5	11.3	12.2	411,398	29,290	7.1	382,108	65.5	28.1	6.4	4.1	83,228	118.6	24,191
Delegate District (At Large)	15.5	11.3	12.2	411,398	29,290	7.1	382,108	65.5	28.1	6.4	4.1	83,228	118.6	24,191
FLORIDA	13.3	9.4	13.2	10,240,825	556,113	5.4	9,684,712	36.4	43.9	19.7	15.6	4,909,642	231.4	559,875
District 1	12.1	8.4	11.1	360,235	19,586	5.4	340,649	36.7	43.7	19.6	13.9	183,244	233.2	16,607
District 2	14.1	9.5	13.2	314,799	17,424	5.5	297,375	36.4	41.5	22.1	14.5	191,559	263.5	19,247
District 3	17.1	10.7	12.8	346,941	20,339	5.9	326,602	39.3	41.8	18.9	12.6	168,355	225.1	19,284
District 4	8.7	5.8	6.7	420,278	17,132	4.1	403,146	44.6	38.8	16.6	11.2	175,793	214.2	11,780
District 5	22.0	15.9	22.1	353,546	25,344	7.2	328,202	31.5	46.1	22.3	14.1	139,808	189.6	27,785
District 6	12.7	8.0	12.1	351,961	17,502	5.0	334,459	33.0	46.2	20.8	15.9	246,225	314.4	17,074
District 7	11.9	8.1	9.4	422,092	19,791	4.7	402,301	44.8	40.5	14.7	11.9	133,370	171.9	13,553
District 8	11.1	7.4	9.6	347,110	18,533	5.3	328,577	39.5	41.3	19.2	13.6	233,787	304.9	14,526
District 9	13.7	10.8	16.5	431,020	23,564	5.5	407,456	31.9	45.1	22.9	14.6	192,582	215.1	27,401
District 10	14.5	11.5	16.6	452,987	26,785	5.9	426,202	34.7	45.8	19.5	16.0	128,472	152.4	22,274
District 11	12.8	8.7	11.4	281,478	18,290	6.5	263,188	30.8	46.9	22.3	16.4	333,225	421.3	16,989
District 12	11.2	7.7	10.6	357,558	20,240	5.7	337,318	40.4	42.7	17.0	13.8	220,066	279.0	15,699
District 13	12.4	7.8	10.3	372,974	19,396	5.2	353,578	39.7	43.2	17.1	14.5	189,395	257.1	17,733
District 14	15.5	10.9	14.7	428,965	23,269	5.4	405,696	40.9	42.0	17.1	14.3	128,048	159.6	25,218
District 15	13.3	9.8	12.6	396,357	19,751	5.0	376,606	35.7	42.7	21.7	14.1	167,722	208.3	22,035
District 16	10.7	7.3	8.4	388,120	19,760	5.1	368,360	37.0	43.6	19.4	15.1	238,374	279.2	12,429
District 17	12.9	8.8	10.7	309,974	17,810	5.7	292,164	29.3	45.0	25.7	17.9	265,366	336.7	14,644
District 18	10.5	7.0	8.7	369,244	17,599	4.8	351,645	37.2	44.1	18.7	15.3	213,467	273.2	11,980
District 19	10.8	7.1	7.4	366,793	16,985	4.6	349,808	33.9	45.9	20.2	17.6	247,367	296.3	11,903
District 20	18.4	14.6	22.1	405,908	30,180	7.4	375,728	28.2	49.1	22.7	20.1	123,816	156.5	22,617
District 21	11.0	7.7	9.0	383,103	22,659	5.9	360,444	36.4	46.2	17.4	18.4	191,155	244.3	10,256
District 22	10.5	7.3	8.0	403,314	22,476	5.6	380,838	41.1	42.7	16.2	15.9	154,608	202.0	11,141
District 23	10.3	7.7	9.0	404,556	21,374	5.3	383,182	43.5	42.2	14.3	12.5	133,924	174.4	16,113
District 24	20.0	15.9	29.1	377,406	29,063	7.7	348,343	26.5	49.2	24.4	23.8	122,551	163.4	46,028
District 25	15.2	12.3	24.1	395,916	16,166	4.1	379,750	28.3	44.5	27.2	20.8	139,577	180.0	41,128
District 26	14.6	12.1	21.5	390,134	18,043	4.6	372,091	32.7	45.9	21.4	17.8	125,207	162.3	39,823
District 27	13.9	10.4	18.6	408,056	17,052	4.2	391,004	42.6	40.6	16.9	15.7	122,579	163.7	34,608
GEORGIA	14.3	10.6	12.2	5,201,775	291,506	5.6	4,910,269	38.5	38.1	23.4	15.0	1,918,848	182.5	252,364
District 1	15.6	12.0	13.1	346,123	23,684	6.8	322,439	34.4	40.0	25.6	15.9	146,976	197.4	17,603
District 2	24.6	19.5	22.7	281,711	24,493	8.7	257,218	29.3	42.9	27.7	17.3	144,408	217.0	29,953
District 3	12.7	9.4	12.0	359,378	18,780	5.2	340,598	35.9	37.3	26.8	12.6	158,425	212.3	18,763
District 4	14.3	11.3	14.4	394,249	26,808	6.8	367,441	36.3	38.9	24.7	16.7	121,601	160.8	21,578
District 5	18.6	14.2	16.4	422,457	29,261	6.9	393,196	48.4	36.4	15.2	14.1	105,097	134.6	24,627
District 6	7.1	4.6	4.0	420,849	17,058	4.1	403,791	57.1	32.3	10.6	10.7	100,786	132.7	5,694
District 7	9.6	7.7	5.9	433,147	16,610	3.8	416,537	43.1	38.3	18.6	15.7	103,231	123.8	10,231
District 8	18.7	14.3	14.9	321,975	17,599	5.5	304,376	32.7	39.8	27.5	16.2	148,686	209.3	23,242
District 9	13.4	9.5	10.7	360,923	14,924	4.1	345,999	32.6	38.2	29.2	17.5	187,989	246.4	15,128
District 10	15.0	10.3	11.7	361,212	18,518	5.1	342,694	37.0	37.4	25.5	13.0	155,277	205.3	17,733
District 11	8.7	6.1	5.6	422,211	18,054	4.3	404,157	45.4	37.4	17.2	14.0	125,459	161.4	9,703
District 12	19.3	14.4	16.3	325,713	22,332	6.9	303,381	32.3	39.6	28.1	15.3	146,743	201.2	23,061
District 13	12.0	9.2	13.6	403,619	25,781	6.4	377,838	34.6	39.8	25.6	15.3	123,096	159.8	18,028
District 14	13.5	10.0	11.7	348,208	17,604	5.1	330,604	29.0	37.3	33.7	16.3	151,074	208.6	17,020
HAWAII	9.3	6.3	10.7	706,640	32,187	4.6	674,453	35.7	45.8	18.5	4.7	286,863	202.0	21,876
District 1	8.0	5.2	8.5	360,893	13,455	3.7	347,438	37.9	45.0	17.1	4.1	139,920	198.0	10,671
District 2	10.5	7.5	12.9	345,747	18,732	5.4	327,015	33.3	46.7	20.0	5.3	146,943	206.0	11,205
IDAHO	11.9	8.1	9.0	854,040	35,955	4.2	818,085	36.0	38.7	25.3	12.2	377,904	215.4	29,434
District 1	10.8	7.2	8.7	436,958	16,910	3.9	420,048	34.8	40.0	25.2	12.7	216,476	237.1	14,545
District 2	13.1	9.2	9.4	417,082	19,045	4.6	398,037	37.3	37.3	25.4	11.7	161,428	191.9	14,889
ILLINOIS	12.0	8.4	12.4	6,631,897	395,142	6.0	6,236,755	39.8	38.3	22.0	7.9	2,271,926	178.7	251,667
District 1	16.7	12.7	19.6	353,426	36,346	10.3	317,080	35.9	43.3	20.8	8.0	124,055	175.9	22,925
District 2	18.2	13.8	21.5	340,150	39,327	11.6	300,823	30.6	43.6	25.8	9.0	130,415	188.2	27,264

1. Percent of civilian labor force. 2. Persons 16 years old and over. 3. Per 1,000 resident population estimated in the 2016–2020 American Community Survey.

STATE District	Agriculture 2017									
		Land in farms			Value of products sold				Government payments	
	Number of farms	Acres	Average size of farm (acres)	Irrigated land (acres)	Total ($1,000)	Average per farm (dollars)	Percent from crops	Percent from livestock and poultry products	Total ($1,000)	Average per farm receiving payments (dollars)
	63	64	65	66	67	68	69	70	71	72
COLORADO	38,893	31,820,957	818	5,916,737	7,491,702	192,623	29.9	70.1	198,697	22,206
District 1	71	6,390	90	523	D	D	D	D	D	D
District 2	3,627	953,177	263	126,497	206,343	56,891	51.3	48.7	1,035	6,273
District 3	14,808	8,719,448	589	1,025,088	967,155	65,313	53.4	46.6	16,655	10,711
District 4	16,578	20,777,185	1,253	4,667,347	6,156,045	371,338	24.5	75.5	178,446	25,540
District 5	3,044	1,225,026	402	47,661	71,820	23,594	32.5	67.5	1,626	11,698
District 6	395	96,913	245	38,832	D	D	D	D	644	9,200
District 7	370	42,818	116	10,789	47,821	129,246	90.4	9.6	D	D
CONNECTICUT	5,521	381,539	69	122,074	580,114	105,074	72.4	27.6	1,850	7,551
District 1	720	41,976	58	17,349	88,995	123,604	97.0	3.0	202	7,481
District 2	2,501	171,834	69	60,637	290,026	115,964	61.6	38.4	869	7,364
District 3	560	22,760	41	8,099	30,317	54,138	D	D	322	11,500
District 4	336	49,386	147	2,989	32,355	96,295	41.5	58.5	10	1,667
District 5	1,404	95,583	68	33,000	138,421	98,590	D	D	446	6,758
DELAWARE	2,302	525,324	228	435,085	1,465,973	636,826	22.2	77.8	15,162	18,604
At Large	2,302	525,324	228	435,085	1,465,973	636,826	22.2	77.8	15,162	18,604
DISTRICT OF COLUMBIA	X	X	X	X	X	X	X	X	X	X
Delegate District (At Large)	X	X	X	X	X	X	X	X	X	X
FLORIDA	47,590	9,731,731	204	2,093,330	7,357,343	154,599	77.5	22.5	59,120	14,795
District 1	2,929	349,886	119	112,935	125,902	42,985	61.0	39.0	9,336	16,322
District 2	7,980	1,696,547	213	398,462	809,576	101,451	39.1	60.9	19,453	20,872
District 3	5,415	531,791	98	87,596	239,941	44,310	61.9	38.1	1,881	9,746
District 4	809	103,274	128	14,834	43,075	53,245	62.4	37.6	301	5,017
District 5	2,815	597,271	212	90,114	290,125	103,064	53.2	46.8	4,332	13,929
District 6	2,353	274,585	117	37,953	354,142	150,507	92.4	7.6	1,507	11,773
District 7	456	41,487	91	3,212	26,224	57,509	91.2	8.8	180	10,000
District 8	1,106	367,011	332	61,950	182,637	165,133	85.7	14.3	703	11,339
District 9	1,290	816,015	633	71,832	238,917	185,207	75.6	24.4	1,739	14,372
District 10	361	18,909	52	5,215	196,875	545,360	99.6	0.4	69	6,900
District 11	4,389	445,594	102	48,445	165,219	37,644	64.8	35.2	1,994	6,391
District 12	1,318	198,908	151	16,710	68,035	51,620	25.8	74.2	944	6,695
District 13	78	198	3	58	877	11,244	D	D	D	D
District 14	249	23,507	94	3,592	34,590	138,916	84.3	15.7	D	D
District 15	2,439	271,445	111	53,811	357,975	146,771	82.2	17.8	1,530	9,000
District 16	1,625	281,092	173	77,338	557,864	343,301	90.4	9.6	540	9,000
District 17	5,060	2,148,236	425	295,998	1,085,016	214,430	60.4	39.6	9,989	14,799
District 18	1,327	545,846	411	199,100	462,117	348,242	93.9	6.1	1,462	16,805
District 19	461	60,374	131	21,045	104,295	226,236	95.8	4.2	36	3,000
District 20	645	295,454	458	235,636	507,802	787,290	98.9	1.1	93	7,154
District 21	403	28,185	70	18,733	187,957	466,395	96.6	3.4	D	D
District 22	95	1,077	11	264	4,866	51,221	95.7	4.3	D	D
District 23	479	3,809	8	910	16,598	34,651	94.2	5.8	D	D
District 24	40	772	19	311	2,007	50,175	D	D	D	D
District 25	831	556,369	670	189,265	474,762	571,314	93.0	7.0	1,511	23,246
District 26	2,298	70,917	31	45,578	800,022	348,138	98.6	1.4	1,500	32,609
District 27	339	3,172	9	2,433	19,925	58,776	97.4	2.6	D	D
GEORGIA	42,439	9,953,730	235	3,628,707	9,573,252	225,577	34.2	65.8	247,428	18,310
District 1	2,271	444,632	196	144,495	285,752	125,827	63.5	36.5	5,441	11,985
District 2	5,565	2,604,471	468	1,196,536	1,835,745	329,873	61.5	38.5	96,196	31,406
District 3	3,547	473,893	134	73,710	386,470	108,957	12.2	87.8	2,164	5,116
District 4	236	19,841	84	3,114	2,128	9,017	54.6	45.4	60	4,615
District 5	37	3,697	100	101	216	5,838	49.1	50.9	97	8,083
District 6	96	3,153	33	323	1,399	14,573	43.5	56.5	D	D
District 7	191	11,824	62	2,645	15,251	79,848	81.1	18.9	20	2,000
District 8	6,410	2,070,355	323	924,328	1,416,022	220,908	64.0	36.0	68,008	22,692
District 9	6,825	670,548	98	151,029	2,238,033	327,917	3.3	96.7	8,570	5,343
District 10	5,529	1,116,120	202	235,447	921,978	166,753	19.6	80.4	12,584	9,717
District 11	969	103,747	107	20,615	97,670	100,795	18.5	81.5	1,105	7,367
District 12	6,001	1,866,526	311	733,828	1,293,651	215,573	51.9	48.1	47,457	19,522
District 13	313	17,735	57	2,715	2,894	9,246	58.9	41.1	26	1,733
District 14	4,449	547,188	123	139,821	1,076,043	241,862	4.5	95.5	5,700	5,449
HAWAII	7,328	1,135,352	155	84,767	563,802	76,938	74.0	26.0	8,362	12,631
District 1	252	12,158	48	3,152	32,162	127,627	91.2	8.8	53	2,524
District 2	7,076	1,123,194	159	81,615	531,641	75,133	72.9	27.1	8,309	12,963
IDAHO	24,996	11,691,912	468	4,576,077	7,567,440	302,746	42.4	57.6	129,605	21,306
District 1	12,254	4,107,446	335	1,325,074	1,577,768	128,755	48.8	51.2	34,226	16,969
District 2	12,742	7,584,466	595	3,251,003	5,989,671	470,073	40.7	59.3	95,379	23,458
ILLINOIS	72,651	27,006,288	372	22,701,382	17,009,972	234,133	81.4	18.6	521,229	10,727
District 1	186	61,309	330	58,228	38,288	205,849	92.4	7.6	198	3,536
District 2	1,119	419,020	374	395,183	295,161	263,772	91.3	8.7	2,900	6,416

STATE District	Private nonfarm employment and payroll, 2020												
		Employment										Annual payroll	
			Percent by selected industries										
	Number of establishments	Total	Manufac-turing	Construc-tion	Wholesale trade	Retail trade	Health care and social assistance	Finance and Insurance	Real estate and rental and leasing	Profes-sional, sci-entific, and technical services	Information	Total (mil dol)	Average per employee (dollars)
	73	74	75	76	77	78	79	80	81	82	83	84	85
COLORADO	175,965	2,510,726	5.2	7.2	4.1	11.3	13.2	5.0	2.1	8.7	3.8	145,130	57,804
District 1	31,589	533,304	3.6	5.2	4.8	8.1	12.4	5.8	3.0	10.7	3.5	35,779	67,090
District 2	31,733	380,032	9.0	6.1	4.6	12.4	12.0	2.7	2.3	11.0	5.2	23,095	60,771
District 3	26,666	264,450	4.9	9.4	2.8	14.9	18.2	2.9	2.7	4.6	1.5	11,272	42,626
District 4	21,472	260,447	9.4	11.5	3.8	14.5	13.1	3.7	1.7	6.3	3.2	13,638	52,363
District 5	21,142	279,503	4.6	6.3	2.2	12.8	16.2	4.8	1.7	9.3	3.3	13,544	48,457
District 6	21,775	349,049	2.6	6.6	5.4	11.8	15.5	8.5	1.7	8.3	8.1	22,425	64,247
District 7	20,734	299,756	5.8	11.4	4.9	13.3	12.4	5.7	1.7	8.4	2.0	15,302	51,048
CONNECTICUT	88,060	1,551,590	10.3	3.8	4.4	11.7	19.3	7.4	1.3	7.3	2.5	100,459	64,746
District 1	18,377	389,201	11.8	3.7	4.5	10.4	18.6	11.6	1.2	6.9	2.9	24,930	64,053
District 2	14,190	213,110	14.4	3.8	4.1	15.7	17.7	3.0	0.7	5.5	1.4	10,592	49,702
District 3	16,233	321,314	11.4	3.9	4.4	10.6	21.1	3.3	1.4	6.1	1.4	18,834	58,614
District 4	21,391	331,242	4.7	2.8	5.5	10.9	17.6	8.5	1.4	10.3	4.1	29,121	87,914
District 5	17,248	265,224	11.7	5.4	3.1	14.4	23.1	6.5	1.7	4.8	2.1	14,470	54,558
DELAWARE	27,472	422,044	7.0	5.6	4.4	13.0	17.8	9.7	1.5	7.8	1.7	25,115	59,508
At Large	27,472	422,044	7.0	5.6	4.4	13.0	17.8	9.7	1.5	7.8	1.7	25,115	59,508
DISTRICT OF COLUMBIA	24,083	543,174	0.2	1.8	0.6	4.3	13.5	3.8	2.1	19.8	5.3	45,850	84,411
Delegate District (At Large)	24,083	543,174	0.2	1.8	0.6	4.3	13.5	3.8	2.1	19.8	5.3	45,850	84,411
FLORIDA	591,046	9,084,079	3.6	5.4	3.7	12.3	13.2	4.4	2.1	6.2	1.9	440,383	48,479
District 1	18,570	232,053	3.5	6.8	2.6	17.0	16.5	6.1	2.5	7.4	1.2	9,851	42,452
District 2	15,587	177,304	6.6	6.5	3.1	17.3	18.5	3.2	1.9	6.8	1.8	7,423	41,868
District 3	17,217	236,599	5.8	5.8	3.5	17.1	24.6	3.0	1.7	4.7	1.7	9,721	41,085
District 4	26,322	405,412	4.0	6.6	5.0	11.9	14.6	9.6	1.9	7.4	1.6	19,777	48,783
District 5	15,041	238,665	5.8	7.8	4.5	14.8	14.4	5.2	1.7	5.2	2.9	11,417	47,835
District 6	18,209	200,429	5.6	7.2	2.4	18.3	17.7	3.4	2.0	5.1	1.8	7,681	38,321
District 7	25,848	375,677	2.6	7.6	3.6	12.3	15.2	8.4	2.0	10.2	3.9	20,118	53,551
District 8	19,374	241,091	7.4	6.9	2.2	15.8	17.2	2.8	1.9	9.9	1.6	11,169	46,327
District 9	16,065	221,254	5.0	6.4	2.7	16.3	13.8	3.0	3.5	4.5	1.5	8,528	38,546
District 10	25,563	541,415	4.3	4.8	4.8	12.0	8.2	1.8	3.6	5.8	2.5	23,814	43,984
District 11	13,467	156,712	5.1	9.2	1.9	19.2	24.3	2.4	3.4	3.0	1.8	5,891	37,589
District 12	18,037	186,877	4.6	6.9	2.6	19.8	20.3	4.9	1.8	7.3	1.2	7,589	40,609
District 13	22,730	330,149	7.8	5.3	3.3	12.8	19.2	7.2	2.1	6.8	2.9	17,007	51,514
District 14	26,908	458,092	3.0	5.8	4.5	9.4	15.3	9.5	2.2	11.3	2.7	26,092	56,958
District 15	17,717	290,997	5.9	8.0	6.2	15.2	14.1	6.6	1.7	5.3	2.1	13,300	45,704
District 16	23,013	253,299	5.4	8.0	3.7	18.2	17.4	3.2	2.4	6.0	1.5	11,073	43,717
District 17	14,825	147,781	6.1	9.2	3.2	21.3	19.8	2.7	2.0	3.5	1.3	5,699	38,561
District 18	23,664	247,023	3.9	6.7	2.7	15.9	17.7	3.2	2.0	7.0	1.5	11,806	47,794
District 19	27,794	333,530	2.6	10.5	3.2	17.7	16.1	2.7	3.3	5.4	1.5	15,030	45,064
District 20	18,931	274,070	5.9	8.6	8.1	13.5	15.2	3.3	2.1	6.1	4.3	14,279	52,099
District 21	23,483	214,593	1.5	6.7	2.2	16.9	19.9	3.1	2.8	6.3	1.9	9,450	44,038
District 22	35,502	375,705	2.7	5.8	4.8	13.1	13.8	5.4	2.8	10.2	2.8	19,979	53,178
District 23	28,258	314,390	1.7	4.1	4.6	18.5	12.6	4.5	2.6	6.9	3.3	15,415	49,030
District 24	18,272	226,172	5.1	3.7	7.4	14.1	23.2	2.8	2.2	6.3	1.4	11,077	48,977
District 25	28,194	352,238	5.9	6.5	11.2	12.3	9.4	4.0	1.8	4.8	3.4	16,522	46,905
District 26	17,104	141,465	2.6	7.8	5.1	19.7	14.2	3.6	2.7	5.2	1.0	5,305	37,499
District 27	33,937	357,950	0.8	2.7	2.1	12.6	16.0	7.2	2.8	12.3	2.3	21,438	59,891
GEORGIA	244,668	4,107,151	9.5	4.9	5.0	11.9	13.3	4.5	1.7	7.4	2.9	216,568	52,730
District 1	16,683	247,446	11.7	5.5	3.6	14.9	14.3	2.0	1.7	3.8	1.0	10,321	41,708
District 2	12,947	215,319	14.0	3.8	5.4	12.9	18.2	10.0	1.3	3.6	1.3	9,466	43,962
District 3	16,030	240,957	16.0	5.5	3.9	16.4	15.4	2.9	1.1	3.2	1.3	9,716	40,321
District 4	12,223	151,851	11.0	7.5	4.8	17.1	16.8	1.8	1.6	4.2	1.7	6,432	42,360
District 5	24,120	553,972	3.8	2.3	4.0	6.6	12.7	3.7	2.3	10.5	4.5	37,629	67,925
District 6	29,997	509,468	1.8	3.4	4.5	8.6	11.3	9.6	2.6	13.7	7.6	37,833	74,259
District 7	27,604	384,747	7.9	7.4	10.7	13.0	10.2	4.2	1.6	9.0	3.4	20,195	52,490
District 8	13,599	195,219	12.2	4.3	3.6	16.5	18.2	3.7	1.1	4.2	1.1	7,417	37,993
District 9	15,927	227,030	23.4	5.2	4.6	14.5	13.0	2.1	0.9	2.6	0.9	9,497	41,833
District 10	14,286	170,978	12.0	6.0	4.2	16.8	16.7	2.6	1.8	3.5	1.2	6,562	38,377
District 11	23,011	399,695	6.9	7.1	4.7	10.9	10.1	6.0	2.8	13.0	3.3	25,654	64,185
District 12	13,698	221,051	12.0	7.4	3.8	14.9	21.1	2.2	1.1	3.6	1.6	9,407	42,558
District 13	12,410	191,762	7.0	7.0	7.4	15.7	16.2	1.8	1.9	2.6	1.3	8,823	46,013
District 14	11,146	187,651	27.5	4.4	5.0	13.8	13.6	1.8	1.0	2.4	0.9	7,441	39,652
HAWAII	32,627	549,375	2.3	5.7	3.2	12.7	13.3	4.0	2.6	4.3	1.5	23,756	43,242
District 1	17,965	325,336	2.8	6.6	4.0	12.2	14.6	5.6	2.6	5.3	1.8	15,446	47,478
District 2	14,392	188,662	2.0	5.3	2.2	15.9	13.7	1.6	3.1	3.2	1.0	6,837	36,242
IDAHO	51,957	637,810	10.0	8.1	5.3	13.4	16.9	3.8	1.4	6.1	2.5	28,807	45,165
District 1	25,519	286,801	10.8	10.8	4.6	14.2	15.6	3.8	1.5	4.9	3.1	12,242	42,685
District 2	26,030	335,646	9.8	6.2	5.9	13.3	18.6	3.6	1.4	7.1	2.0	15,919	47,429
ILLINOIS	318,689	5,545,538	9.8	4.0	5.8	10.5	15.0	6.2	1.5	7.5	2.3	329,401	59,399
District 1	12,034	189,163	5.6	4.6	4.2	15.3	19.1	2.3	1.4	3.0	1.2	8,708	46,037
District 2	9,975	172,104	18.0	4.4	5.4	12.4	20.7	2.0	1.1	2.0	1.6	7,787	45,245

Table E. Congressional Districts 116th Congress — **Land Area and Population Characteristics**

STATE District	Representative, 117th Congress	Land area,[1] 2020 (sq mi)	Population and population characteristics, 2016–2020: Total persons	Per square mile	Race alone (percent): White	Black	American Indian, Alaska Native	Asian and Pacific Islander	Some other race (percent)	Two or more races (percent)	Hispanic or Latino[2] (percent)	Non-Hispanic White alone (percent)	Percent female	Percent foreign-born	Percent born in state of residence
		1	2	3	4	5	6	7	8	9	10	11	12	13	14
ILLINOIS—Cont'd															
District 3	Marie Newman (D)	236.9	708,422	2990.4	73.2	4.9	0.4	4.5	11.7	5.3	33.3	56.0	49.8	20.7	70.1
District 4	Jesus G. "Chuy" Garcia (D)	52.4	683,260	13039.3	53.6	4.1	0.6	4.0	29.6	8.2	67.7	23.4	49.9	32.3	54.0
District 5	Michael Quigley (D)	95.6	737,812	7717.7	78.0	3.0	0.2	7.6	5.9	5.3	19.8	66.9	50.5	21.1	55.1
District 6	Sean Casten (D)	378.7	723,356	1910.1	80.9	2.5	0.1	9.8	2.9	3.8	10.5	74.6	50.9	15.1	65.1
District 7	Danny K. Davis (D)	62.3	720,942	11572.1	36.4	44.3	0.2	8.0	7.0	4.1	16.6	29.1	52.0	14.5	61.5
District 8	Raja Krishnamoorthi (D)	205.7	708,921	3446.4	62.7	5.4	0.6	13.5	12.0	5.7	28.9	50.0	50.7	28.8	59.5
District 9	Janice D. Schakowsky (D)	105.4	724,967	6878.2	69.3	9.3	0.3	13.2	3.0	4.9	11.7	62.7	51.1	25.7	53.7
District 10	Bradley Scott Schneider (D)	299.8	705,705	2353.9	68.3	6.9	0.5	11.3	8.3	4.6	23.1	56.4	50.5	24.3	56.2
District 11	Bill Foster (D)	280.3	717,503	2559.8	64.4	11.1	0.4	8.3	9.3	6.5	27.9	50.2	50.7	19.4	64.8
District 12	Mike Bost (R)	5,008.0	690,097	137.8	77.4	16.9	0.2	1.3	1.1	3.1	3.7	75.4	50.6	2.5	68.1
District 13	Rodney Davis (R)	5,793.6	700,322	120.9	80.3	11.4	0.2	4.2	0.6	3.3	3.7	77.8	50.7	5.4	74.0
District 14	Lauren Underwood (D)	1,597.2	741,407	464.2	85.1	3.4	0.2	5.1	2.7	3.6	12.7	76.9	50.3	9.7	70.8
District 15	Mary E. Miller (R)	14,696.1	687,456	46.8	92.3	4.3	0.2	0.7	0.5	2.1	2.8	90.4	50.0	1.6	76.5
District 16	Adam Kinzinger (R)	7,916.3	691,553	87.4	88.4	4.0	0.1	1.5	2.7	3.2	10.4	81.9	50.1	5.2	76.9
District 17	Cheri Bustos (D)	6,930.3	675,779	97.5	80.5	12.0	0.3	1.4	1.9	3.9	9.2	74.9	50.6	4.8	72.0
District 18	Darin LaHood (R)	10,515.4	700,594	66.6	90.0	4.0	0.2	2.8	0.6	2.5	3.0	88.0	51.0	3.8	77.9
INDIANA		35,826.0	6,696,893	186.9	82.3	9.4	0.2	2.4	2.3	3.3	7.1	78.4	50.7	5.3	68.0
District 1	Frank J. Mrvan (D)	1,156.7	715,976	619.0	69.0	18.4	0.3	1.4	6.5	4.5	16.1	61.9	50.9	5.7	58.9
District 2	Vacancy	3,958.7	724,543	183.0	84.8	6.8	0.4	1.4	2.5	4.1	10.0	78.8	50.7	5.6	69.6
District 3	Jim Banks (R)	4,180.1	747,367	178.8	86.3	6.0	0.2	2.5	1.6	3.4	6.3	82.5	50.5	4.7	71.9
District 4	James R. Baird (R)	6,351.8	762,256	120.0	87.3	4.3	0.2	3.2	2.3	2.7	6.3	83.9	49.9	5.9	69.5
District 5	Victoria Spartz (R)	1,925.0	782,573	406.5	83.1	8.6	0.2	3.7	1.3	3.2	4.7	80.2	51.3	6.1	64.9
District 6	Greg Pence (R)	6,206.9	720,302	116.0	92.2	2.7	0.1	1.7	1.0	2.3	3.0	90.6	50.5	2.7	70.9
District 7	André Carson (D)	304.0	766,338	2520.8	57.1	30.3	0.2	3.8	4.2	4.4	11.5	51.0	51.6	10.3	66.6
District 8	Larry Bucshon (R)	7,255.5	719,258	99.1	90.9	4.4	0.1	1.2	1.0	2.4	2.7	89.4	50.2	2.5	75.2
District 9	Trey Hollingsworth (R)	4,487.3	758,280	169.0	90.5	2.9	0.2	2.6	0.9	2.8	3.5	88.3	50.7	4.0	65.1
IOWA		55,853.5	3,150,011	56.4	89.1	3.7	0.3	2.6	1.3	3.0	6.2	85.0	50.3	5.4	70.0
District 1	Ashley Hinson (R)	12,048.8	772,873	64.1	90.0	4.0	0.4	1.9	0.9	2.8	4.3	87.2	50.5	4.1	74.5
District 2	Mariannette Miller-Meeks(R)	12,261.0	782,527	63.8	88.5	4.4	0.2	2.6	1.2	3.1	5.9	84.5	50.4	5.3	67.5
District 3	Cynthia Axne (D)	8,788.9	841,226	95.7	87.1	4.5	0.2	3.6	1.4	3.1	7.1	82.3	50.6	6.9	66.8
District 4	Randy Feenstra (R)	22,754.8	753,385	33.1	91.1	1.8	0.5	2.4	1.5	2.8	7.3	86.3	49.8	5.2	71.6
KANSAS		81,758.6	2,912,619	35.6	83.0	5.7	0.8	3.1	2.7	4.8	12.1	75.3	50.2	7.0	59.4
District 1	Tracey Mann (R)	52,542.1	697,312	13.3	87.2	3.1	0.5	1.8	2.7	4.7	16.3	76.1	49.2	7.4	64.3
District 2	Jake LaTurner (R)	14,144.3	715,946	50.6	85.9	4.6	1.3	1.7	1.7	4.7	7.0	81.7	50.2	3.2	63.8
District 3	Sharice Davids (D)	757.5	774,850	1022.9	78.7	8.2	0.3	5.2	3.3	4.3	12.3	71.2	50.8	10.4	44.8
District 4	Ron Estes (R)	14,314.7	724,511	50.6	80.6	6.5	0.9	3.4	3.1	5.6	12.8	72.8	50.4	6.8	66.0
KENTUCKY		39,491.7	4,461,952	113.0	86.2	8.1	0.2	1.6	1.1	2.8	3.8	84.1	50.8	4.0	68.7
District 1	James Comer (R)	12,084.4	718,344	59.4	88.8	6.8	0.2	0.8	0.8	2.6	3.3	86.9	50.5	1.8	68.3
District 2	Brett Guthrie (R)	7,182.3	764,943	106.5	88.4	5.6	0.2	1.7	0.9	3.1	3.6	86.4	50.5	3.5	70.8
District 3	John A. Yarmuth (D)	319.7	744,444	2328.6	69.7	22.5	0.1	3.0	1.2	3.5	5.8	66.0	51.7	8.1	67.4
District 4	Thomas Massie (R)	4,373.9	763,817	174.6	91.2	3.4	0.1	1.3	1.3	2.7	3.5	89.3	50.3	3.2	60.7
District 5	Harold Rogers (R)	11,234.1	693,463	61.7	96.1	1.4	0.2	0.4	0.3	1.4	1.4	95.2	50.4	1.0	78.0
District 6	Garland "Andy" Barr (R)	4,297.3	776,941	180.8	83.9	8.6	0.2	2.2	1.8	3.3	4.9	81.4	51.2	5.7	67.8
LOUISIANA		43,210.3	4,664,616	108.0	61.2	32.2	0.6	1.8	1.6	2.7	5.2	58.3	51.2	4.1	78.0
District 1	Steve Scalise (R)	4,032.7	802,133	198.9	77.1	14.0	1.1	2.3	1.9	3.5	8.9	71.4	51.3	6.8	73.5
District 2	Troy Carter (D)	1,271.3	793,342	624.0	30.7	61.5	0.2	2.5	2.7	2.5	6.8	27.7	52.0	6.1	77.6
District 3	Clay Higgins (R)	6,984.2	785,605	112.5	69.6	24.4	0.4	1.5	1.0	3.0	4.1	67.1	51.2	3.1	83.6
District 4	Mike Johnson (R)	12,436.6	745,158	59.9	60.1	34.3	0.7	1.1	1.2	2.5	4.1	57.8	50.5	2.4	74.1
District 5	Julia Letlow (R)	14,452.4	743,209	51.4	60.9	35.2	0.4	0.7	0.8	1.9	2.5	59.6	50.4	1.7	81.0
District 6	Garret Graves (R)	4,033.1	795,169	197.2	68.9	24.0	0.5	2.3	1.7	2.6	4.6	66.3	51.6	4.4	78.3
MAINE		30,845.1	1,340,825	43.5	93.7	1.4	0.7	1.2	0.4	2.8	1.7	92.6	51.0	3.6	62.2
District 1	Chellie Pingree (D)	3,287.2	686,598	208.9	93.1	1.8	0.4	1.6	0.4	2.7	1.9	91.8	51.3	4.4	55.8
District 2	Jared F. Golden (D)	27,557.9	654,227	23.7	94.3	0.9	0.9	0.7	0.3	2.8	1.5	93.5	50.7	2.8	68.9
MARYLAND		9,711.1	6,037,624	621.7	54.2	29.9	0.3	6.4	4.7	4.5	10.3	50.2	51.5	15.2	47.4
District 1	Andrew Harris (R)	3,977.4	734,056	184.6	81.0	12.0	0.2	2.2	1.2	3.4	4.3	78.6	50.8	5.2	62.6
District 2	C. A. Dutch Ruppersberger (D)	348.7	768,582	2204.1	51.6	35.8	0.2	5.5	2.5	4.4	7.2	48.1	52.3	11.6	61.9
District 3	John P. Sarbanes (D)	304.5	756,291	2483.7	61.0	22.8	0.3	7.7	3.7	4.5	9.2	56.8	51.9	15.9	49.0
District 4	Anthony G. Brown (D)	297.8	755,373	2536.5	28.7	51.9	0.2	3.3	11.9	4.0	17.3	25.0	51.7	20.0	30.5
District 5	Steny H. Hoyer (D)	1,482.6	764,867	515.9	47.0	38.7	0.4	4.1	4.9	4.9	9.7	43.6	51.1	12.1	38.8
District 6	David J. Trone (D)	1,952.3	770,857	394.8	64.6	13.7	0.2	11.5	4.1	5.8	14.2	57.0	50.6	21.0	43.8
District 7	Kweisi Mfume (D)	488.2	717,953	1470.6	34.9	52.2	0.3	7.7	1.2	3.7	4.3	32.9	52.5	11.7	60.7
District 8	Jamie Raskin (D)	859.6	769,645	895.4	64.7	12.8	0.3	9.0	8.1	5.1	15.4	59.0	51.4	23.2	33.2
MASSACHUSETTS		7,800.9	6,873,003	881.1	76.6	7.5	0.2	6.8	4.2	4.8	12.0	70.8	51.5	16.9	60.2
District 1	Richard E. Neal (D)	2,350.1	727,193	309.4	82.8	6.4	0.2	2.2	3.5	4.9	18.7	71.3	51.8	7.5	65.8
District 2	James P. McGovern (D)	1,628.0	749,700	460.5	81.8	5.1	0.2	5.8	2.4	4.5	10.3	76.0	51.2	12.5	64.1
District 3	Lori Trahan (D)	757.6	768,471	1014.3	74.8	4.1	0.2	8.2	7.9	4.7	19.8	65.8	50.6	18.3	60.7
District 4	Jake Auchincloss (D)	668.3	760,391	1137.8	84.1	3.2	0.1	6.7	2.0	3.8	5.0	81.4	51.7	13.6	59.6
District 5	Katherine Clark (D)	265.1	771,266	2909.3	73.8	5.2	0.2	12.8	3.5	4.5	9.8	68.7	51.3	24.4	50.9
District 6	Seth Moulton (D)	526.9	773,421	1467.9	84.2	3.9	0.1	4.3	3.9	3.6	10.0	79.9	51.7	13.9	68.1
District 7	Ayanna Presley (D)	62.7	808,106	12888.5	48.8	24.7	0.4	10.8	6.6	8.7	22.2	40.3	51.4	32.1	41.1
District 8	Stephen F. Lynch (D)	326.0	770,058	2362.1	74.0	10.4	0.2	8.3	3.1	3.9	6.1	71.1	51.7	18.2	63.1
District 9	William R. Keating (D)	1,216.2	744,397	612.1	86.8	3.0	0.3	1.5	4.3	4.1	6.0	84.7	51.6	9.6	69.8

1. Dry land or land partially or temporarily covered by water. 2. May be of any race.

Table E. Congressional Districts 116th Congress — **Age and Education**

STATE District	Population and population characteristics, 2016–2020 (cont.)										Education, 2016–2020		
	Age (percent)											Attainment[2] (percent)	
	Under 5 years	5 to 17 years	18 to 24 years	25 to 34 years	35 to 44 years	45 to 54 years	55 to 64 years	65 to 74 years	75 years and over	Median age	Total Enrollment[1]	High school graduate or more	Bachelor's degree or more
	15	16	17	18	19	20	21	22	23	24	25	26	27
ILLINOIS—Cont'd													
District 3	6.3	17.7	8.1	12.9	13.2	13.0	13.4	8.8	6.4	37.2	180,818	86.4	29.4
District 4	6.3	17.7	9.7	18.4	15.1	12.1	10.4	6.3	4.0	33.5	176,443	75.8	26.9
District 5	6.0	12.8	8.8	21.6	14.9	12.2	10.9	7.4	5.5	35.2	161,428	92.7	56.9
District 6	5.7	17.4	7.8	11.2	12.3	14.6	14.8	9.4	6.5	39.9	187,351	95.2	53.7
District 7	5.7	13.3	10.0	21.1	13.7	11.3	11.3	8.1	5.3	33.6	166,978	87.2	44.1
District 8	6.4	17.0	8.4	14.7	14.0	13.0	12.5	8.4	5.7	36.6	174,085	87.1	34.3
District 9	6.1	14.8	8.1	13.8	13.0	13.6	13.2	9.4	8.1	39.6	179,121	91.9	55.6
District 10	5.8	17.6	9.7	11.9	12.6	13.3	13.4	8.9	6.8	37.1	179,846	89.7	45.9
District 11	6.2	19.0	9.5	13.0	14.2	13.7	11.7	7.6	5.1	35.4	193,375	87.6	36.5
District 12	5.9	16.2	8.7	13.2	12.3	12.5	13.9	9.9	7.3	38.3	164,439	90.5	24.3
District 13	5.3	14.3	15.3	12.9	11.2	11.5	13.1	9.4	7.2	35.5	201,969	92.4	31.3
District 14	5.7	19.5	8.1	10.8	13.5	15.0	13.5	8.4	5.6	38.9	201,361	94.1	42.9
District 15	5.9	16.4	8.0	12.1	12.0	12.4	14.3	10.5	8.4	39.9	152,915	90.3	20.6
District 16	5.6	16.4	9.5	11.9	11.8	12.9	13.9	10.3	7.7	39.3	165,350	90.5	23.2
District 17	6.0	16.2	8.8	12.2	11.7	12.2	14.1	10.7	8.2	39.1	152,202	88.6	19.9
District 18	5.9	16.6	8.5	12.0	12.3	12.4	13.5	10.4	8.4	39.6	169,665	94.0	33.0
INDIANA	6.2	17.3	9.9	13.1	12.3	12.5	13.0	9.2	6.5	36.5	1,654,841	89.3	27.2
District 1	5.9	17.0	8.7	12.6	12.8	12.7	13.9	9.8	6.8	37.9	166,726	90.1	24.0
District 2	6.6	18.0	9.5	12.5	11.7	12.3	12.9	9.5	6.9	36.5	177,873	86.4	22.8
District 3	6.9	18.5	8.9	13.0	11.9	12.2	13.0	9.2	6.4	35.8	180,734	88.3	24.0
District 4	5.9	16.8	12.5	12.6	12.0	12.3	12.7	8.9	6.4	35.3	208,017	90.8	27.5
District 5	6.1	17.7	8.2	13.2	13.4	13.4	12.7	9.0	6.3	37.4	193,577	94.5	46.9
District 6	5.7	16.4	10.0	11.9	11.7	13.1	13.7	10.0	7.5	38.8	166,473	89.4	22.5
District 7	7.6	18.2	9.8	16.7	13.0	11.7	11.6	7.0	4.6	32.7	196,726	84.2	25.7
District 8	5.9	16.4	9.5	12.5	11.8	12.4	14.0	10.2	7.4	38.6	167,623	89.5	22.0
District 9	5.7	15.9	11.5	12.9	12.5	12.6	13.1	9.5	6.3	37.0	197,092	90.3	27.1
IOWA	6.2	16.9	10.1	12.6	12.1	11.9	13.2	9.6	7.5	37.2	785,736	92.5	29.3
District 1	6.1	16.6	10.1	12.1	11.8	11.9	13.5	9.9	8.0	38.0	190,329	92.9	27.7
District 2	6.0	16.5	10.6	12.6	12.0	11.9	13.2	9.8	7.3	37.4	199,196	92.5	29.4
District 3	6.7	17.9	8.3	14.0	13.5	12.4	12.4	8.6	6.1	36.3	204,306	92.5	34.4
District 4	5.9	16.6	11.4	11.5	11.2	11.0	13.8	10.0	8.7	37.2	191,905	91.9	25.1
KANSAS	6.5	17.8	10.1	13.2	12.2	11.6	12.8	9.1	6.8	35.7	758,270	91.4	33.9
District 1	6.7	17.1	12.2	12.9	11.2	10.5	12.6	8.9	7.7	34.4	184,531	89.2	25.6
District 2	6.0	16.7	11.4	12.2	11.8	11.5	13.4	9.8	7.3	36.8	185,637	92.6	30.1
District 3	6.7	18.5	8.1	14.0	13.9	12.6	12.3	8.5	5.6	36.0	199,059	92.9	48.2
District 4	6.6	18.7	9.1	13.4	12.1	11.6	13.0	9.0	6.7	35.5	189,043	90.4	30.0
KENTUCKY	6.1	16.4	9.4	13.0	12.4	12.9	13.4	9.8	6.6	37.6	1,043,315	87.2	25.0
District 1	6.2	16.4	9.5	12.2	11.4	12.3	13.5	10.7	7.7	38.1	159,189	86.3	17.9
District 2	6.1	17.0	9.9	12.6	12.3	12.9	13.3	9.6	6.4	37.4	181,594	88.0	21.3
District 3	6.3	15.8	8.7	14.9	12.5	12.3	13.4	9.4	6.6	36.6	169,629	90.6	33.0
District 4	6.1	17.6	8.2	12.6	13.0	13.5	13.4	9.5	6.0	38.1	184,014	90.3	29.9
District 5	6.0	16.0	8.4	12.2	12.2	13.6	14.0	10.7	6.9	39.5	149,666	78.3	13.9
District 6	6.1	15.8	11.7	13.7	12.7	12.7	12.5	9.1	5.9	36.0	199,223	88.8	33.0
LOUISIANA	6.5	17.0	9.2	14.3	12.6	12.1	13.0	9.3	6.2	35.9	1,145,889	85.9	24.9
District 1	6.3	16.8	8.2	13.7	12.8	12.3	13.7	9.8	6.5	37.6	195,706	88.2	31.6
District 2	6.6	16.0	8.9	15.7	13.0	12.1	13.1	9.0	5.6	35.7	196,627	83.8	24.5
District 3	7.0	17.7	8.6	14.5	12.4	12.0	13.1	8.6	5.9	35.5	189,766	85.5	22.3
District 4	6.7	17.2	9.2	13.9	12.2	11.7	12.8	9.5	6.9	35.6	176,373	85.7	20.1
District 5	6.3	17.2	9.6	13.5	12.2	12.0	12.7	9.8	6.7	36.1	179,183	82.6	18.8
District 6	6.3	17.1	10.6	14.3	12.9	12.2	12.2	8.9	5.4	35.1	208,234	89.2	30.9
MAINE	4.8	13.9	8.0	12.0	11.5	13.5	15.8	12.2	8.4	43.4	278,782	93.2	32.5
District 1	4.7	13.9	7.9	12.5	11.8	13.4	15.4	11.9	8.4	42.6	142,152	94.3	39.3
District 2	4.8	13.9	8.1	11.5	11.1	13.4	16.0	12.6	8.4	44.3	136,630	92.1	25.3
MARYLAND	6.0	16.2	8.8	13.7	12.9	13.5	13.5	9.1	6.4	37.3	1,520,676	90.6	40.9
District 1	5.2	16.0	8.9	11.2	11.2	13.5	14.9	11.0	7.9	41.0	174,221	91.0	32.6
District 2	6.6	16.1	8.7	16.0	13.2	12.8	12.8	8.3	5.3	35.6	190,039	89.7	33.4
District 3	6.0	15.5	9.2	15.5	13.0	12.7	12.7	8.8	6.7	35.9	191,818	92.5	49.7
District 4	6.8	16.6	7.7	14.5	13.8	13.6	13.0	8.4	5.6	36.4	188,457	87.8	35.7
District 5	5.9	16.5	10.2	12.9	12.4	14.6	13.9	8.7	5.1	36.7	205,592	91.8	36.3
District 6	6.1	16.5	8.6	12.9	13.3	14.2	13.3	8.8	6.3	37.8	192,008	90.7	42.7
District 7	5.6	15.7	9.4	14.5	12.4	13.0	13.7	9.2	6.6	36.6	186,124	89.1	39.8
District 8	5.9	16.6	7.8	12.4	13.3	13.9	13.3	9.3	7.4	39.0	192,417	91.8	56.3
MASSACHUSETTS	5.2	14.6	10.1	14.3	12.3	13.3	13.6	9.5	7.0	38.0	1,702,976	91.1	44.5
District 1	5.1	15.0	10.1	12.3	11.2	13.1	14.6	10.7	7.8	40.0	171,835	88.5	30.6
District 2	4.8	14.9	12.5	12.5	11.8	13.6	13.9	9.3	6.5	37.9	204,075	91.9	40.1
District 3	5.7	16.6	9.1	13.2	12.9	13.8	14.2	8.6	5.8	37.7	192,871	89.4	39.0
District 4	5.0	16.8	9.3	11.6	12.2	14.8	13.8	9.5	7.0	40.0	198,454	93.4	51.9
District 5	5.6	13.9	9.6	15.4	13.4	13.2	12.7	8.9	7.1	37.5	194,840	93.9	59.2
District 6	5.4	14.9	8.5	11.9	11.7	14.4	14.9	10.3	7.9	41.2	175,763	92.9	46.3
District 7	5.1	11.4	15.4	23.6	12.9	10.6	9.8	6.4	4.7	31.4	234,395	85.9	46.6
District 8	5.4	13.8	8.1	16.6	12.9	13.2	13.6	9.1	7.2	38.0	174,820	92.4	49.2
District 9	4.7	14.2	8.2	10.8	10.8	13.7	15.3	12.9	9.3	43.9	155,923	91.2	36.5

1. All persons 3 years old and over enrolled in nursery school through college and graduate or professional school. 2. Persons 25 years old and over.

STATE District	Households, 2016–2020: Number	Average household size	Family households (percent)	Married couple family (percent)	Female family householder[1]	One person households (percent)	Total in group quarters, 2020	Persons in group quarters, 2020: Correctional facilities for adults	Juvenile facilities	Skilled nursing facilities	College/ University student housing	Military quarters
	28	29	30	31	32	33	34	35	36	37	38	39
ILLINOIS—Cont'd												
District 3	246,710	2.83	69.6	52.9	11.4	26.1	7,444	2,675	85	3,298	312	0
District 4	227,162	2.99	65.3	43.1	14.5	24.6	4,138	0	35	1,511	845	0
District 5	306,626	2.37	53.2	42.0	7.6	34.3	9,696	0	85	4,195	4,159	0
District 6	266,992	2.67	73.0	61.8	7.9	22.6	11,287	693	133	6,205	3,169	0
District 7	307,116	2.25	48.8	27.9	16.4	42.6	19,398	5,964	213	2,468	7,580	0
District 8	254,922	2.76	69.4	53.1	11.5	25.1	4,994	0	7	3,394	561	0
District 9	291,182	2.41	58.6	46.9	8.0	34.3	21,862	0	100	8,630	9,338	0
District 10	254,125	2.69	70.9	56.6	10.1	24.4	21,979	623	250	5,967	2,226	11,079
District 11	250,889	2.83	70.6	52.7	12.6	24.1	7,776	936	19	3,112	1,708	0
District 12	280,525	2.39	62.7	44.2	13.6	31.8	19,487	8,416	183	3,974	3,268	318
District 13	286,458	2.30	56.6	41.8	10.7	34.1	41,483	6,139	210	5,168	26,978	0
District 14	261,558	2.82	76.0	63.0	9.0	19.6	4,893	831	411	2,393	26	0
District 15	278,836	2.37	65.6	50.9	10.3	29.2	24,899	12,958	201	6,471	2,719	0
District 16	276,159	2.44	65.8	50.2	10.8	28.2	16,376	5,394	187	5,326	4,242	0
District 17	282,887	2.30	61.0	43.1	13.2	33.3	21,362	8,270	113	5,621	5,353	0
District 18	282,261	2.41	65.2	52.7	8.8	29.4	17,505	5,844	107	5,661	3,690	27
INDIANA	2,602,770	2.50	64.5	48.1	11.5	29.0	178,374	41,962	1,967	46,683	72,846	91
District 1	276,775	2.53	65.7	46.0	14.1	28.7	13,291	6,255	254	3,794	1,956	0
District 2	273,668	2.56	65.6	49.1	11.9	28.8	21,423	4,495	293	5,492	9,464	0
District 3	290,382	2.53	66.0	50.2	10.9	28.0	13,518	1,680	153	5,731	4,343	0
District 4	292,365	2.50	65.5	50.5	10.3	27.3	28,821	6,088	157	4,994	16,307	0
District 5	310,029	2.47	66.4	53.1	9.4	27.5	16,071	4,343	223	5,448	4,494	0
District 6	286,028	2.44	65.9	49.9	10.7	27.4	21,908	5,899	255	5,956	8,100	0
District 7	294,385	2.55	55.5	34.5	15.9	36.8	14,353	1,629	343	2,762	7,733	31
District 8	289,228	2.39	64.6	49.1	10.7	29.1	26,893	9,208	170	6,126	8,898	60
District 9	289,910	2.53	65.5	50.5	10.1	27.5	22,096	2,365	119	6,380	11,551	0
IOWA	1,273,941	2.40	62.9	49.6	9.1	29.8	98,558	13,064	1,325	28,369	46,412	31
District 1	312,589	2.39	63.5	50.6	8.6	29.5	24,630	2,308	241	7,625	12,251	31
District 2	314,189	2.41	62.8	49.2	9.4	29.4	25,650	4,872	271	6,447	12,164	0
District 3	333,441	2.47	63.1	48.7	10.1	29.4	16,483	3,218	335	5,568	4,987	0
District 4	313,722	2.30	62.0	49.8	8.1	30.8	31,795	2,666	478	8,729	17,010	0
KANSAS	1,141,985	2.48	64.6	50.5	9.8	29.1	86,940	18,204	707	20,370	30,358	5,754
District 1	275,867	2.42	63.0	50.2	8.6	30.4	32,126	5,630	80	6,461	12,839	5,024
District 2	285,525	2.41	63.5	49.6	9.5	29.5	27,671	6,951	306	4,776	12,872	350
District 3	298,335	2.58	67.2	53.1	9.9	26.7	8,751	1,458	114	4,136	601	0
District 4	282,258	2.52	64.4	48.7	11.2	30.0	18,392	4,165	207	4,997	4,046	380
KENTUCKY	1,748,053	2.48	65.2	48.0	12.2	28.7	124,909	38,346	1,090	25,822	40,025	5,020
District 1	282,993	2.44	65.9	49.9	11.2	28.9	24,494	7,912	147	4,924	4,760	3,760
District 2	293,595	2.53	67.4	50.7	11.5	26.5	19,360	4,814	166	3,957	7,397	1,260
District 3	307,368	2.37	58.6	39.5	14.2	34.4	15,702	2,134	252	4,584	5,595	0
District 4	285,501	2.62	68.7	52.5	11.2	25.6	15,432	7,567	96	4,104	1,476	0
District 5	271,288	2.47	68.1	50.1	12.7	27.7	24,796	12,051	362	4,569	5,530	0
District 6	307,308	2.45	63.1	46.2	12.3	28.7	25,125	3,868	67	3,684	15,267	0
LOUISIANA	1,751,956	2.59	63.7	43.4	15.5	30.7	124,123	51,241	1,050	24,180	32,772	2,707
District 1	303,528	2.60	65.4	48.1	13.1	29.0	15,056	1,479	177	3,569	7,719	44
District 2	296,598	2.60	55.8	30.7	20.1	38.5	21,063	7,671	258	2,905	6,410	374
District 3	297,642	2.60	66.3	46.7	14.3	27.8	9,003	3,359	126	4,018	485	0
District 4	286,306	2.52	63.1	42.6	15.5	32.1	19,433	9,627	119	5,374	1,600	1,753
District 5	272,564	2.55	64.8	43.1	16.7	30.8	42,853	27,227	332	5,167	6,279	536
District 6	295,318	2.66	67.2	48.9	13.4	26.1	16,715	1,878	38	3,147	10,279	0
MAINE	569,551	2.29	61.4	48.3	8.9	29.8	36,454	3,360	355	10,911	15,595	330
District 1	292,962	2.28	60.9	48.5	8.6	30.1	18,010	2,127	202	5,230	7,220	308
District 2	276,589	2.30	62.0	48.2	9.3	29.4	18,444	1,233	153	5,681	8,375	22
MARYLAND	2,230,527	2.64	66.3	47.6	14.0	27.5	125,505	27,040	1,008	29,252	46,179	2,464
District 1	278,540	2.57	69.8	54.5	11.0	24.7	15,885	4,708	164	3,674	4,649	0
District 2	287,666	2.60	64.8	42.7	16.7	28.6	16,661	6,808	171	3,699	3,633	771
District 3	290,429	2.54	62.3	46.4	12.0	29.7	15,602	302	124	3,620	9,589	116
District 4	270,886	2.77	65.8	41.9	17.7	28.5	6,589	660	43	2,799	66	295
District 5	264,704	2.82	71.1	51.8	14.6	23.7	19,521	570	83	3,492	13,365	409
District 6	278,087	2.69	70.2	53.1	12.4	24.5	19,884	10,794	199	4,134	1,687	125
District 7	275,508	2.52	58.4	35.5	18.8	34.5	20,064	2,578	171	3,880	9,980	0
District 8	284,707	2.67	68.5	55.1	9.1	25.5	11,299	620	53	3,954	3,210	748
MASSACHUSETTS	2,646,980	2.50	63.2	46.9	12.0	28.4	245,518	17,969	3,261	42,089	144,820	357
District 1	289,670	2.42	62.9	42.8	15.0	30.5	23,967	1,219	338	5,215	13,414	0
District 2	284,701	2.48	63.1	47.1	11.7	28.8	42,164	1,188	372	5,507	30,794	0
District 3	281,701	2.66	68.4	49.7	13.8	24.9	21,069	6,537	606	4,246	5,913	0
District 4	282,122	2.60	69.8	56.2	10.0	24.0	24,272	1,457	398	4,457	14,400	0
District 5	299,799	2.48	62.7	50.0	8.9	27.8	26,956	288	264	4,256	18,536	78
District 6	295,575	2.55	67.5	52.7	10.7	26.5	19,293	1,661	119	5,208	7,933	87
District 7	305,949	2.46	50.0	29.4	15.8	33.5	56,052	881	755	2,789	45,469	30
District 8	304,078	2.48	60.9	46.2	10.6	29.9	16,805	2,468	294	5,559	3,837	123
District 9	303,385	2.41	64.9	48.8	11.7	29.1	14,940	2,270	115	4,852	4,524	39

1. No spouse present.

Table E. Congressional Districts 116th Congress — **Housing and Money Income**

STATE District	Housing units, 2016–2020						Money income, 2016–2020		
		Occupied units						Households	
			Owner-occupied			Renter-occupied			
	Total	Occupied units as a percent of all units	Owner-occupied units as a percent of occupied units	Median value[1] (dollars)	Percent valued at $500,000 or more	Median rent[2]	Per capita income (dollars)	Median income (dollars)	Percent with income of $100,000 or more
	40	41	42	43	44	45	46	47	48
ILLINOIS—Cont'd									
District 3	262,708	93.9	75.0	238,100	8.2	1,052	34,145	73,152	36.1
District 4	248,536	91.4	48.3	253,500	9.6	1,060	27,641	59,793	27.0
District 5	330,956	92.6	55.9	363,800	29.8	1,407	56,143	90,424	45.8
District 6	279,567	95.5	79.6	330,900	21.1	1,380	52,078	106,701	54.2
District 7	353,102	87.0	41.6	289,600	22.5	1,241	45,618	64,171	34.5
District 8	267,577	95.3	67.5	233,600	4.6	1,268	34,442	76,550	35.5
District 9	314,775	92.5	61.2	350,700	25.4	1,210	48,432	77,821	40.6
District 10	270,057	94.1	70.1	276,400	22.8	1,219	46,661	85,567	43.9
District 11	264,235	94.9	71.0	223,900	7.2	1,288	36,590	80,435	39.8
District 12	324,759	86.4	67.9	114,200	1.7	775	29,324	53,061	22.8
District 13	325,023	88.1	64.0	126,400	1.9	806	30,623	54,091	23.8
District 14	273,538	95.6	82.4	270,100	7.4	1,261	43,624	98,672	49.8
District 15	317,776	87.7	75.2	108,100	1.7	681	29,425	55,696	23.0
District 16	300,959	91.8	72.0	144,300	2.0	841	31,974	63,107	27.8
District 17	322,572	87.7	67.3	103,300	1.7	721	27,695	50,713	19.3
District 18	313,677	90.0	75.3	150,000	2.6	789	35,876	67,418	31.1
INDIANA	2,903,720	89.6	69.5	148,900	3.6	844	30,693	58,235	24.5
District 1	309,921	89.3	71.2	163,800	3.4	889	31,038	60,796	27.1
District 2	310,576	88.1	71.6	135,300	3.0	793	27,911	55,566	21.9
District 3	324,370	89.5	73.0	138,400	3.5	765	29,068	57,731	22.1
District 4	320,046	91.4	70.6	152,400	2.5	838	30,381	60,919	25.9
District 5	336,073	92.3	70.8	210,000	9.4	995	42,313	74,413	37.4
District 6	318,029	89.9	72.6	132,700	2.4	762	29,021	56,952	22.2
District 7	335,857	87.7	52.9	126,900	2.2	885	26,045	46,963	17.9
District 8	324,313	89.2	71.6	127,300	2.2	748	29,060	54,158	21.2
District 9	324,535	89.3	71.3	161,400	3.2	873	30,780	60,297	25.6
IOWA	1,407,819	90.5	71.2	153,900	3.5	806	33,021	61,836	26.6
District 1	344,820	90.7	74.1	152,000	3.1	756	33,068	61,857	26.2
District 2	348,847	90.1	69.7	148,900	3.9	803	31,769	58,236	25.2
District 3	361,098	92.3	69.8	179,700	4.7	904	35,980	68,789	31.7
District 4	353,054	88.9	71.3	129,600	2.4	735	30,969	58,628	23.4
KANSAS	1,280,376	89.2	66.2	157,600	4.9	863	32,798	61,091	26.8
District 1	322,512	85.5	65.7	120,900	2.1	763	27,995	53,059	19.9
District 2	321,985	88.7	66.8	139,000	3.1	806	29,788	56,525	23.1
District 3	317,598	93.9	67.1	246,600	11.2	1,083	42,566	80,739	39.9
District 4	318,281	88.7	65.3	136,800	2.7	812	29,946	57,125	24.2
KENTUCKY	1,994,554	87.6	67.6	147,100	4.1	783	29,123	52,238	21.9
District 1	337,783	83.8	69.5	114,200	2.4	692	25,522	45,942	16.7
District 2	331,675	88.5	69.4	151,800	3.3	771	28,556	53,980	21.6
District 3	337,838	91.0	60.8	173,000	5.7	898	33,547	57,093	25.0
District 4	315,173	90.6	73.2	174,400	6.0	822	34,021	66,570	31.8
District 5	332,823	81.5	71.9	86,300	1.7	618	21,185	35,825	11.8
District 6	339,262	90.6	61.7	169,100	5.2	824	31,044	55,799	24.4
LOUISIANA	2,074,664	84.4	66.6	168,100	5.1	876	29,522	50,800	23.2
District 1	340,177	89.2	70.9	212,400	8.6	993	34,133	62,123	29.4
District 2	353,399	83.9	56.0	168,300	5.8	948	27,076	42,619	18.7
District 3	346,460	85.9	69.0	157,000	4.1	821	28,957	51,550	23.1
District 4	351,427	81.5	64.5	137,400	3.9	784	27,730	42,635	18.4
District 5	339,424	80.3	66.4	122,700	2.7	728	24,047	42,155	18.2
District 6	343,777	85.9	73.0	196,200	5.3	967	34,664	66,147	32.2
MAINE	746,793	76.3	72.9	198,000	7.3	873	33,774	59,489	25.6
District 1	362,467	80.8	71.8	254,400	11.2	1,023	38,044	68,389	31.0
District 2	384,326	72.0	74.0	151,600	3.2	760	29,293	51,585	20.2
MARYLAND	2,459,650	90.7	67.1	325,400	21.1	1,415	43,352	87,063	43.7
District 1	342,897	81.2	76.5	286,500	13.3	1,091	39,267	78,951	39.0
District 2	311,877	92.2	61.4	242,500	6.6	1,316	36,151	74,999	36.2
District 3	310,443	93.6	65.2	339,800	23.5	1,533	48,138	93,724	47.4
District 4	287,212	94.3	62.5	336,100	19.2	1,494	41,366	87,556	44.0
District 5	283,908	93.2	77.0	342,600	14.7	1,607	43,207	104,284	53.1
District 6	303,214	91.7	69.6	322,700	25.3	1,407	42,523	86,077	43.7
District 7	320,608	85.9	57.0	272,500	23.7	1,169	38,743	65,365	33.7
District 8	299,491	95.1	67.7	458,500	42.4	1,744	56,960	110,108	55.2
MASSACHUSETTS	2,913,009	90.9	62.5	398,800	34.3	1,336	45,555	84,385	43.0
District 1	321,882	90.0	65.4	229,300	5.8	922	33,650	61,444	29.8
District 2	305,439	93.2	64.4	293,300	13.2	1,093	38,319	74,432	37.8
District 3	295,983	95.2	64.2	361,000	25.2	1,233	41,120	83,233	42.4
District 4	296,370	95.2	72.5	441,400	41.6	1,366	55,489	104,781	52.7
District 5	315,309	95.1	59.5	589,900	62.2	1,755	56,532	104,727	52.6
District 6	311,291	95.0	70.3	475,500	44.6	1,400	48,901	94,965	48.3
District 7	329,757	92.8	33.8	537,500	54.3	1,678	41,490	73,201	38.3
District 8	325,499	93.4	62.1	461,500	42.9	1,651	51,285	97,583	49.3
District 9	411,479	73.7	71.9	380,500	28.3	1,028	42,538	76,031	38.4

1. Specified owner-occupied units. 2. Specified renter-occupied units.

Table E. Congressional Districts 116th Congress — **Poverty, Labor Force, Employment, and Social Security**

STATE District	Poverty, 2016–2020			Civilian labor force, 2016–2020			Civilian employment,[2] 2016–2020				Persons under 65 years of age with no health insurance, 2016–2020 (percent)	Social Security beneficiaries, December 2021		Supplemental Security Income recipients, December 2021
					Unemployment			Percent						
	Persons below poverty level (percent)	Families below poverty level (percent)	Percent of households receiving food stamps in past 12 months	Total	Total	Rate[1]	Total	Management, business, science, and arts occupations	Service, sales, and office	Construction and production		Number	Rate[3]	
	49	50	51	52	53	54	55	56	57	58	59	60	61	62
ILLINOIS—Cont'd														
District 3	10.2	7.9	10.4	358,205	23,073	6.4	335,132	34.5	39.4	26.0	9.5	119,745	169.0	11,627
District 4	14.4	11.7	16.1	369,234	22,420	6.1	346,814	30.3	41.2	28.5	16.5	76,655	112.2	16,163
District 5	7.9	5.2	5.9	449,725	18,538	4.1	431,187	53.3	33.4	13.3	7.3	97,286	131.9	10,501
District 6	4.8	3.2	4.1	396,458	16,592	4.2	379,866	50.8	35.2	13.9	4.6	124,921	172.7	5,236
District 7	20.0	15.3	20.0	388,722	35,229	9.1	353,493	50.0	35.7	14.3	8.6	98,049	136.0	29,816
District 8	8.7	6.5	9.9	393,559	18,100	4.6	375,459	36.3	38.6	25.2	10.7	110,791	156.3	7,621
District 9	10.6	6.5	8.8	382,795	16,519	4.3	366,276	52.6	34.6	12.8	8.0	125,179	172.7	15,945
District 10	8.4	5.9	8.9	368,799	18,741	5.1	350,058	43.9	37.0	19.1	9.1	116,507	165.1	9,413
District 11	8.6	6.5	11.1	391,219	20,742	5.3	370,477	37.2	38.3	24.5	8.7	106,055	147.8	8,061
District 12	15.8	11.2	16.1	330,362	19,212	5.8	311,150	33.1	41.8	25.1	6.9	149,801	217.1	18,361
District 13	17.1	9.9	13.3	349,184	18,913	5.4	330,271	39.4	39.7	20.9	5.1	140,573	200.7	14,953
District 14	5.4	3.9	5.6	401,315	17,225	4.3	384,090	43.6	36.8	19.6	4.5	127,318	171.7	5,064
District 15	13.2	9.4	13.6	328,239	15,879	4.8	312,360	32.4	36.8	30.8	7.1	159,579	232.1	13,546
District 16	11.4	7.6	11.6	355,125	21,055	5.9	334,070	31.7	38.5	29.8	5.6	152,983	221.2	8,926
District 17	16.6	12.3	17.8	326,646	22,322	6.8	304,324	29.6	40.6	29.8	7.1	156,791	232.0	17,803
District 18	9.6	6.2	8.8	348,734	14,909	4.3	333,825	41.0	37.5	21.5	5.1	155,223	221.6	8,442
INDIANA	12.9	8.9	9.3	3,379,544	159,865	4.7	3,219,679	35.1	36.7	28.2	9.4	1,388,573	207.3	124,019
District 1	14.1	10.8	11.2	346,850	21,985	6.3	324,865	32.5	39.0	28.4	7.8	154,197	215.4	15,389
District 2	13.3	9.6	9.0	359,032	16,669	4.6	342,363	30.8	36.4	32.7	12.3	151,245	208.7	12,326
District 3	11.4	8.3	8.5	380,013	16,743	4.4	363,270	31.5	35.3	33.2	11.9	155,722	208.4	12,367
District 4	11.6	7.0	7.1	388,609	15,682	4.0	372,927	35.4	35.0	29.7	7.9	154,384	202.5	10,517
District 5	8.5	6.1	5.9	417,336	15,871	3.8	401,465	48.5	35.3	16.2	6.8	149,564	191.1	10,050
District 6	13.4	9.1	9.9	358,275	15,210	4.2	343,065	33.2	36.6	30.3	9.3	170,785	237.1	14,290
District 7	18.4	13.7	14.7	386,770	24,406	6.3	362,364	32.9	39.4	27.7	11.9	123,650	161.4	22,707
District 8	13.4	9.4	9.6	354,806	15,695	4.4	339,111	31.9	37.3	30.8	8.9	166,322	231.2	14,457
District 9	12.3	7.5	7.6	387,853	17,604	4.5	370,249	36.6	37.0	26.4	7.6	162,704	214.6	11,916
IOWA	11.1	7.1	9.8	1,677,262	65,738	3.9	1,611,524	37.2	36.2	26.6	5.6	668,984	212.4	50,149
District 1	10.7	6.9	9.1	416,735	16,463	4.0	400,272	35.2	36.9	27.9	5.1	172,462	223.1	12,639
District 2	13.0	8.3	11.0	403,733	15,884	3.9	387,849	36.8	35.6	27.6	6.2	167,416	213.9	14,861
District 3	9.5	6.5	10.4	459,080	19,274	4.2	439,806	41.7	36.9	21.5	5.1	158,452	188.4	13,125
District 4	11.5	6.9	8.7	397,714	14,117	3.5	383,597	34.4	35.5	30.1	5.9	170,654	226.5	9,524
KANSAS	11.4	7.6	7.2	1,505,433	61,359	4.1	1,444,074	39.2	36.8	24.0	10.2	573,476	196.9	46,455
District 1	12.7	7.9	6.8	352,986	12,449	3.5	340,537	33.8	37.2	29.0	10.7	141,364	202.7	9,523
District 2	12.9	8.2	8.0	360,895	15,001	4.2	345,894	37.2	37.5	25.4	9.5	155,306	216.9	14,176
District 3	7.8	5.5	4.7	426,617	16,005	3.8	410,612	47.8	35.2	16.9	9.4	129,555	167.2	8,753
District 4	12.8	8.8	9.4	364,935	17,904	4.9	347,031	36.3	37.4	26.2	11.5	147,251	203.2	14,003
KENTUCKY	16.6	12.3	13.0	2,107,184	113,295	5.4	1,993,889	35.2	37.4	27.4	6.7	1,010,012	226.4	161,147
District 1	17.9	12.8	13.1	311,056	16,528	5.3	294,528	29.9	37.2	32.9	7.9	181,799	253.1	25,227
District 2	15.1	11.0	11.0	368,621	19,027	5.2	349,594	31.6	36.7	31.7	6.2	174,534	228.2	21,322
District 3	14.1	9.9	10.8	395,012	21,327	5.4	373,685	38.0	37.3	24.7	5.9	150,435	202.1	23,403
District 4	11.6	8.3	9.1	384,008	16,770	4.4	367,238	38.6	36.2	25.1	5.9	155,174	203.2	16,637
District 5	25.9	21.0	23.2	253,257	18,413	7.3	234,844	31.1	39.9	28.9	7.1	190,118	274.2	52,713
District 6	16.0	11.2	11.7	395,230	21,230	5.4	374,000	39.0	37.8	23.2	7.0	157,952	203.3	21,845
LOUISIANA	18.6	14.2	15.3	2,166,003	142,088	6.6	2,023,915	35.3	40.5	24.2	10.2	924,881	198.3	164,102
District 1	14.2	10.5	9.8	391,730	20,322	5.2	371,408	39.6	38.9	21.6	10.1	163,700	204.1	17,482
District 2	23.1	18.0	20.2	379,194	33,954	9.0	345,240	33.6	43.8	22.7	11.8	144,840	182.6	37,539
District 3	18.1	14.3	15.2	369,165	23,506	6.4	345,659	32.3	41.1	26.6	9.7	155,932	198.5	23,493
District 4	21.9	16.9	17.4	313,028	22,202	7.1	290,826	33.0	40.3	26.6	10.5	157,032	210.7	30,514
District 5	22.9	17.9	19.1	306,320	19,878	6.5	286,442	32.2	42.3	25.5	10.2	159,995	215.3	36,386
District 6	12.4	8.7	10.9	406,566	22,226	5.5	384,340	39.6	37.2	23.1	8.7	143,382	180.3	18,688
MAINE	11.1	6.7	12.6	704,226	28,442	4.0	675,784	38.8	38.5	22.8	9.5	359,152	267.9	34,899
District 1	9.0	5.4	9.6	379,095	12,962	3.4	366,133	42.5	37.3	20.2	7.9	175,126	255.1	13,113
District 2	13.3	8.1	15.7	325,131	15,480	4.8	309,651	34.4	39.9	25.8	11.2	184,026	281.3	21,786
MARYLAND	9.0	5.9	10.1	3,243,851	167,571	5.2	3,076,280	47.2	36.1	16.7	6.8	1,038,041	171.9	117,202
District 1	9.1	5.7	10.2	380,426	18,755	4.9	361,671	41.2	38.4	20.4	5.3	168,156	229.1	11,530
District 2	10.9	7.7	12.8	408,264	22,330	5.5	385,934	41.7	39.0	19.3	6.3	129,551	168.6	17,721
District 3	7.8	4.8	7.9	415,900	17,726	4.3	398,174	53.4	33.0	13.6	6.0	123,077	162.7	15,000
District 4	8.0	5.6	8.7	426,851	25,601	6.0	401,250	41.5	38.9	19.6	10.8	110,392	146.1	10,708
District 5	6.8	4.1	7.2	413,247	20,359	4.9	392,888	45.8	36.0	18.2	6.5	121,571	158.9	9,775
District 6	8.9	6.2	10.5	410,470	20,369	5.0	390,101	47.9	35.8	16.3	6.9	130,478	169.3	14,075
District 7	15.1	10.3	17.4	363,827	24,547	6.7	339,280	48.6	37.4	13.9	5.6	129,005	179.7	30,739
District 8	6.0	3.8	5.6	424,866	17,884	4.2	406,982	56.9	30.7	12.4	6.9	125,811	163.5	7,654
MASSACHUSETTS	9.8	6.6	11.6	3,809,494	193,769	5.1	3,615,725	48.0	36.1	15.9	3.2	1,295,088	188.4	172,887
District 1	13.3	9.4	18.1	370,292	21,147	5.7	349,145	38.6	40.2	21.2	3.4	169,855	233.6	35,469
District 2	10.4	6.5	12.1	404,939	20,240	5.0	384,699	45.0	36.8	18.2	2.6	143,160	191.0	18,937
District 3	9.8	6.9	13.7	419,407	23,288	5.6	396,119	43.8	36.6	19.6	3.7	137,266	178.6	21,819
District 4	6.4	4.3	8.0	416,756	17,878	4.3	398,878	54.0	32.6	13.4	2.2	140,203	184.4	10,599
District 5	7.5	4.6	6.0	444,815	19,786	4.4	425,029	58.6	30.8	10.6	3.2	121,237	157.2	10,188
District 6	7.4	5.0	8.7	430,985	18,456	4.3	412,529	49.1	36.0	14.9	2.6	154,329	199.5	13,000
District 7	17.8	13.0	17.4	482,068	31,866	6.6	450,202	49.8	38.1	12.2	4.4	91,248	112.9	31,754
District 8	7.5	5.2	9.2	449,153	22,085	4.9	427,068	51.2	35.1	13.7	2.7	138,212	179.5	14,126
District 9	8.6	5.9	11.0	391,079	19,023	4.9	372,056	39.2	39.9	20.9	3.8	199,578	268.1	16,995

1. Percent of civilian labor force. 2. Persons 16 years old and over. 3. Per 1,000 resident population estimated in the 2016–2020 American Community Survey.

Table E. Congressional Districts 116th Congress — **Agriculture**

STATE District	Agriculture 2017									
		Land in farms			Value of products sold				Government payments	
	Number of farms	Acres	Average size of farm (acres)	Irrigated land (acres)	Total ($1,000)	Average per farm (dollars)	Percent from crops	Percent from livestock and poultry products	Total ($1,000)	Average per farm receiving payments (dollars)
	63	64	65	66	67	68	69	70	71	72
ILLINOIS—Cont'd										
District 3	97	7,643	79	6,731	5,512	56,825	91.1	8.9	45	2,368
District 4	7	D	D	5	149	21,286	D	D	D	D
District 5	10	D	D	21	53	5,300	D	D	D	D
District 6	197	15,572	79	9,818	38,691	196,401	93.6	6.4	417	15,444
District 7	16	668	42	D	1,072	67,000	98	2	D	D
District 8	32	2,974	93	D	4,267	133,344	78.2	21.8	D	D
District 9	20	286	14	93	245	12,250	91	9	D	D
District 10	118	10,377	88	7,981	21,179	179,483	96.9	3.1	110	10,000
District 11	121	18,409	152	16,488	13,715	113,347	98.9	1.1	148	3,524
District 12	6,820	1,946,182	285	1,466,610	805,718	118,140	84.2	15.8	41,813	10,414
District 13	7,766	3,135,635	404	2,669,082	1,883,640	242,550	89.4	10.6	52,897	9,823
District 14	2,036	618,099	304	563,973	509,435	250,214	80.5	19.5	11,944	13,792
District 15	21,078	7,426,442	352	6,212,563	4,259,863	202,100	79.8	20.2	170,063	11,271
District 16	9,983	4,128,064	414	3,788,243	2,978,591	298,366	83.3	16.7	80,693	12,544
District 17	9,578	3,577,140	373	2,881,538	2,562,993	267,592	72.6	27.4	79,988	11,942
District 18	13,467	5,638,365	419	4,621,479	3,591,400	266,682	82.0	18.0	79,989	8,430
INDIANA	56,649	14,969,996	264	12,345,774	11,107,336	196,073	64.1	35.9	342,914	12,628
District 1	1,148	340,509	297	308,926	214,590	186,925	89	11	8,942	15,259
District 2	7,227	1,837,512	254	1,567,768	1,626,207	225,018	55.4	44.6	51,386	14,720
District 3	10,574	2,108,580	199	1,764,657	1,976,214	186,894	47.3	52.7	40,561	8,858
District 4	8,273	3,194,762	386	2,852,760	2,418,273	292,309	71.6	28.4	65,287	13,445
District 5	2,607	846,826	325	787,740	567,515	217,689	87.7	12.3	14,688	10,424
District 6	10,193	2,588,026	254	2,073,367	1,682,472	165,062	68.4	31.6	62,303	12,376
District 7	163	15,719	96	13,871	11,513	70,632	92	8	419	13,516
District 8	9,750	2,730,610	280	2,135,119	1,896,295	194,492	67.0	33.0	70,322	14,544
District 9	6,714	1,307,452	195	841,566	714,256	106,383	60.3	39.7	29,007	12,423
IOWA	86,104	30,563,878	355	24,347,862	28,956,455	336,296	47.8	52.2	682,995	11,146
District 1	21,735	6,684,219	308	5,250,747	6,067,485	279,157	50.2	49.8	156,577	9,697
District 2	19,439	5,982,719	308	4,032,959	4,288,086	220,592	50.2	49.8	144,109	11,010
District 3	11,923	4,582,245	384	3,312,351	2,634,857	220,989	65.9	34.1	95,406	12,633
District 4	33,007	13,314,695	403	11,751,805	15,966,026	483,716	43.2	56.8	286,904	11,716
KANSAS	58,569	45,759,319	781	21,837,465	18,782,726	320,694	34.4	65.6	509,205	14,089
District 1	27,977	29,850,908	1,067	13,748,148	14,276,677	510,300	28.6	71.4	368,435	17,621
District 2	19,374	7,619,877	393	4,210,470	2,184,002	112,729	63.1	36.9	59,851	6,569
District 3	1,128	202,593	180	127,288	73,657	65,299	81.5	18.5	971	3,996
District 4	10,090	8,085,941	801	3,751,559	2,248,390	222,833	41.9	58.1	79,947	13,596
KENTUCKY	75,966	12,961,784	171	5,474,346	5,737,920	75,533	44.3	55.7	126,697	7,502
District 1	21,346	4,852,908	227	2,696,597	3,093,230	144,909	47.9	52.1	76,262	9,436
District 2	19,839	3,134,196	158	1,336,434	1,157,083	58,324	51.3	48.7	36,761	7,633
District 3	190	10,644	56	2,639	5,100	26,842	85.6	14.4	56	7,000
District 4	11,807	1,645,348	139	555,968	316,984	26,847	62.5	37.5	4,898	4,230
District 5	11,110	1,472,160	133	350,486	244,748	22,030	34.5	65.5	3,322	2,579
District 6	11,674	1,846,528	158	532,222	920,776	78,874	19.5	80.5	5,398	3,512
LOUISIANA	27,386	7,997,511	292	3,314,955	3,172,978	115,861	65.0	35.0	177,399	22,822
District 1	1,724	380,822	221	57,206	71,150	41,270	55.9	44.1	251	12,550
District 2	412	269,457	654	103,019	70,301	170,633	94.4	5.6	330	10,313
District 3	5,682	1,812,789	319	565,038	505,329	88,935	77.2	22.8	50,916	24,562
District 4	7,211	1,572,422	218	430,884	728,780	101,065	25.0	75.0	23,611	17,860
District 5	9,960	3,395,715	341	1,894,297	1,548,447	155,467	77.7	22.3	96,718	24,149
District 6	2,397	566,306	236	264,511	248,972	103,868	71.9	28.1	5,574	17,364
MAINE	7,600	1,307,613	172	360,295	666,962	87,758	61.3	38.7	8,947	10,806
District 1	2,501	204,079	82	53,902	94,149	37,645	66.4	33.6	1,829	12,113
District 2	5,099	1,103,534	216	306,393	572,813	112,338	60.5	39.5	7,118	10,514
MARYLAND	12,429	1,990,122	160	1,290,212	2,472,806	198,955	38.3	61.7	44,410	12,471
District 1	5,298	1,147,145	217	812,238	1,915,054	361,467	33.5	66.5	32,857	14,181
District 2	143	7,808	55	2,261	7,223	50,510	71.1	28.9	111	11,100
District 3	183	14,350	78	7,991	11,926	65,169	83.0	17.0	249	20,750
District 4	129	5,728	44	2,148	8,721	67,605	96.6	3.4	10	2,500
District 5	1,878	182,049	97	89,237	73,022	38,883	79.5	20.5	2,353	8,715
District 6	2,462	330,277	134	179,485	237,611	96,511	38.3	61.7	2,972	7,375
District 7	653	79,254	121	45,853	55,821	85,484	86	14	1,092	11,258
District 8	1,683	223,511	133	150,999	163,428	97,105	53	47	4,767	10,641
MASSACHUSETTS	7,241	491,653	68	140,922	475,185	65,624	76.5	23.5	4,004	7,583
District 1	1,955	190,928	98	45,678	73,907	37,804	61.8	38.2	1,502	8,632
District 2	1,721	123,085	72	41,818	143,703	83,500	76.0	24.0	1,146	8,128
District 3	842	36,665	44	12,632	40,465	48,058	74.0	26.0	285	6,477
District 4	656	28,229	43	9,054	32,585	49,672	87.1	12.9	272	4,772
District 5	170	6,214	37	2,032	36,345	213,794	98.2	1.8	20	3,333
District 6	417	19,362	46	7,705	29,882	71,659	86.5	13.5	45	5,625
District 7	27	60	2	30	268	9,926	90.7	9.3	D	D
District 8	175	5,678	32	1,976	9,289	53,080	90.8	9.2	53	5,300
District 9	1,278	81,432	64	19,997	108,740	85,086	73.7	26.3	680	7,727

STATE District	Private nonfarm employment and payroll, 2020												
		Employment										Annual payroll	
			Percent by selected industries										
	Number of establishments	Total	Manufac-turing	Construc-tion	Wholesale trade	Retail trade	Health care and social assistance	Finance and Insurance	Real estate and rental and leasing	Profes-sional, sci-entific, and technical services	Information	Total (mil dol)	Average per employee (dollars)
	73	74	75	76	77	78	79	80	81	82	83	84	85
ILLINOIS—Cont'd													
District 3	15,948	228,468	11.7	4.7	5.3	12.7	13.7	2.2	1.3	4.4	0.9	10,731	46,970
District 4	11,220	138,670	14.9	3.5	7.3	16.7	14.7	3.3	1.3	3.2	1.0	6,063	43,722
District 5	23,388	372,392	7.3	4.0	4.9	9.8	13.9	3.5	2.7	5.7	1.9	20,103	53,985
District 6	25,345	386,031	8.8	4.5	6.3	11.0	13.7	7.1	1.4	8.0	2.9	23,177	60,040
District 7	30,255	884,569	2.9	1.7	3.0	4.4	13.1	15.5	2.2	19.1	5.3	83,660	94,578
District 8	24,029	409,638	13.5	5.7	11.5	9.4	9.5	4.8	1.8	6.7	3.3	24,701	60,299
District 9	20,344	298,895	6.9	3.0	4.1	11.1	24.0	3.1	1.9	5.6	1.7	16,902	56,549
District 10	21,552	366,109	10.9	3.2	12.1	10.0	14.0	6.2	1.3	10.2	1.4	29,204	79,769
District 11	17,032	294,289	9.0	5.0	8.3	13.8	13.8	3.0	1.3	4.9	1.4	14,865	50,510
District 12	14,007	211,877	12.7	4.8	4.3	15.2	19.5	3.1	1.1	4.0	1.1	9,046	42,695
District 13	14,893	237,454	7.9	4.6	4.2	13.3	22.7	4.4	1.7	4.3	2.2	10,718	45,138
District 14	18,173	196,443	13.1	8.4	5.6	14.5	11.8	2.9	1.3	5.7	1.0	9,419	47,946
District 15	14,905	204,194	19.9	4.6	5.7	12.1	18.3	3.6	0.8	2.2	1.2	8,281	40,555
District 16	14,815	230,783	20.4	5.5	4.3	13.9	15.4	3.1	0.8	2.9	1.2	10,493	45,466
District 17	14,054	256,701	15.4	4.1	4.2	10.9	19.6	3.6	0.8	3.8	1.2	13,852	53,963
District 18	15,705	250,012	10.5	4.6	6.3	15.1	14.8	11.3	0.9	3.6	1.4	11,693	46,770
INDIANA	148,724	2,821,903	18.1	5.2	4.5	11.6	16.0	3.8	1.3	4.7	1.5	133,253	47,221
District 1	14,937	249,245	14.4	6.6	3.7	14.3	19.3	2.3	1.2	3.5	1.0	11,381	45,663
District 2	15,817	324,101	34.0	3.8	4.8	10.7	12.8	2.4	0.9	2.6	1.3	14,572	44,962
District 3	17,756	334,023	26.8	4.9	5.0	11.6	16.0	3.5	1.0	2.7	1.3	15,208	45,530
District 4	15,535	274,915	22.1	5.3	4.1	15.4	15.3	2.1	1.1	2.7	0.9	11,585	42,141
District 5	22,517	410,776	6.5	4.8	5.0	10.6	15.9	7.7	1.9	9.4	2.1	21,383	52,056
District 6	14,241	239,814	22.3	4.5	4.1	12.6	17.1	2.7	0.8	3.8	1.1	10,440	43,532
District 7	15,367	353,238	8.9	6.7	5.6	8.3	18.1	4.4	2.4	5.9	2.8	20,631	58,406
District 8	16,168	284,755	20.4	6.2	4.2	12.3	17.9	3.1	1.1	3.8	1.2	12,736	44,725
District 9	15,627	251,616	17.8	6.1	3.5	15.4	17.5	3.1	1.2	2.8	1.2	10,177	40,445
IOWA	82,440	1,390,551	15.6	4.9	5.1	13.2	15.7	7.0	1.1	4.3	2.3	65,641	47,205
District 1	19,625	340,573	18.8	4.7	4.8	13.6	15.3	6.0	0.9	4.3	2.2	15,934	46,785
District 2	18,762	318,987	19.4	4.9	3.8	14.2	18.1	3.4	0.9	3.5	2.8	13,844	43,401
District 3	21,869	396,317	7.9	5.2	5.4	13.2	14.2	12.4	1.6	6.0	2.4	21,096	53,230
District 4	21,706	288,668	20.5	5.4	6.6	14.0	18.1	3.6	0.9	2.9	1.9	12,521	43,375
KANSAS	73,982	1,207,003	13.8	5.6	5.2	12.1	16.2	5.4	1.3	5.6	2.1	58,374	48,363
District 1	19,442	235,464	18.0	4.8	5.5	14.5	18.2	3.9	1.0	3.2	1.8	9,428	40,041
District 2	15,497	225,082	15.1	6.2	3.2	13.3	21.2	4.8	1.2	4.0	1.3	9,574	42,535
District 3	21,442	419,155	7.9	6.0	7.0	10.9	13.9	7.9	1.5	8.4	3.3	24,427	58,277
District 4	17,037	288,926	19.9	6.0	4.0	12.5	16.0	3.1	1.3	4.6	1.6	13,258	45,886
KENTUCKY	90,922	1,666,427	14.9	4.5	4.2	12.9	16.0	4.6	1.1	4.6	1.7	75,360	45,222
District 1	13,926	213,069	23.6	4.8	3.7	15.0	16.0	3.0	0.9	2.7	1.3	8,423	39,531
District 2	14,218	240,935	21.1	5.2	3.1	15.1	16.1	3.5	1.0	3.3	1.2	9,761	40,512
District 3	19,450	454,433	11.3	3.9	4.3	9.8	15.0	6.8	1.3	5.5	2.0	24,575	54,079
District 4	14,412	260,795	13.7	4.7	5.8	13.2	14.1	5.1	1.2	3.8	1.1	12,378	47,461
District 5	10,885	157,231	11.0	3.1	3.0	17.8	23.8	3.3	1.0	4.4	2.6	5,524	35,134
District 6	17,346	296,403	14.4	6.1	3.5	13.6	16.9	2.8	1.1	6.1	2.1	13,152	44,372
LOUISIANA	106,230	1,703,353	7.0	8.5	4.3	13.0	17.6	3.8	1.8	5.9	1.2	79,848	46,877
District 1	21,333	313,159	4.8	5.9	4.9	14.2	18.8	4.5	1.9	5.6	1.0	15,374	49,093
District 2	16,187	293,916	9.2	5.4	3.6	10.4	13.2	3.1	1.9	6.5	1.2	14,834	50,472
District 3	19,671	292,463	9.3	6.6	4.8	13.9	18.0	3.0	2.7	5.8	1.0	13,427	45,910
District 4	14,737	207,218	9.4	5.5	4.3	15.0	22.7	3.4	1.8	3.7	1.2	8,651	41,747
District 5	15,013	202,814	7.5	5.7	3.8	15.8	26.8	4.3	1.4	3.9	1.7	7,945	39,174
District 6	18,693	340,796	4.5	19.4	4.0	12.5	13.7	4.2	1.6	7.4	1.4	16,747	49,142
MAINE	41,646	520,969	9.9	5.3	3.5	15.7	21.5	5.5	1.4	4.6	2.0	24,650	47,317
District 1	23,815	311,183	9.6	5.0	3.5	14.8	21.1	6.0	1.6	5.2	1.8	15,424	49,564
District 2	17,468	204,904	10.6	5.9	3.2	17.4	22.5	4.4	1.3	3.5	2.2	8,883	43,353
MARYLAND	139,734	2,405,968	4.1	6.9	3.7	12.2	16.7	4.2	2.1	12.3	2.1	139,313	57,903
District 1	17,527	203,994	8.6	7.7	3.8	16.6	18.3	2.7	1.3	4.6	1.2	8,701	42,652
District 2	16,574	354,454	6.3	7.8	7.3	14.7	11.4	3.7	2.3	11.9	1.8	20,868	58,874
District 3	21,350	399,454	4.8	5.3	3.9	10.7	16.3	3.6	2.0	13.3	3.1	24,388	61,055
District 4	13,326	206,109	2.2	9.0	4.2	15.1	13.3	2.4	2.8	9.4	2.5	9,446	45,831
District 5	14,558	224,879	2.1	13.9	2.4	14.4	14.5	1.8	2.7	15.6	1.2	11,581	51,500
District 6	19,275	299,670	6.2	6.5	3.2	15.0	16.4	4.5	1.4	13.6	2.6	16,191	54,031
District 7	15,459	308,709	1.9	2.9	1.9	7.8	28.2	6.9	2.2	10.9	1.4	20,544	66,548
District 8	20,941	342,472	2.0	6.3	2.4	9.5	17.7	5.4	3.0	15.4	2.5	23,395	68,313
MASSACHUSETTS	179,456	3,390,833	6.9	4.6	4.4	10.8	18.4	5.5	1.6	9.6	3.7	242,545	71,530
District 1	15,789	257,772	10.8	4.7	3.5	12.7	23.9	4.4	1.4	4.0	1.2	11,889	46,121
District 2	16,774	291,363	9.4	4.2	4.2	13.2	22.0	5.0	1.1	5.8	1.2	14,714	50,499
District 3	16,830	293,984	16.0	5.4	6.0	10.3	18.1	3.4	1.1	9.3	3.1	20,998	71,426
District 4	20,922	354,042	8.5	4.4	7.3	12.5	16.2	3.7	1.8	5.7	2.9	22,262	62,879
District 5	21,011	407,418	3.6	4.6	4.4	9.1	13.9	3.7	1.6	14.8	5.7	31,616	77,600
District 6	21,653	369,304	11.8	5.8	4.8	12.9	18.0	3.2	1.2	8.5	5.1	24,663	66,782
District 7	17,588	553,870	1.7	1.9	2.4	6.8	20.6	5.6	1.9	12.8	5.2	51,130	92,315
District 8	25,101	547,732	3.5	5.0	3.7	9.3	17.1	12.0	2.4	13.2	4.4	48,306	88,193
District 9	23,048	249,237	6.3	8.2	3.6	18.0	21.4	2.8	1.4	4.7	1.4	11,888	47,696

Table E. Congressional Districts 116th Congress — **Land Area and Population Characteristics**

STATE District	Representative, 117th Congress	Land area,[1] 2020 (sq mi)	Population and population characteristics, 2016–2020: Total persons	Per square mile	Race alone (percent): White	Black	American Indian, Alaska Native	Asian and Pacific Islander	Some other race (percent)	Two or more races (percent)	Hispanic or Latino[2] (percent)	Non-Hispanic White alone (percent)	Percent female	Percent foreign-born	Percent born in state of residence
		1	2	3	4	5	6	7	8	9	10	11	12	13	14
MICHIGAN		56,608.2	9,973,907	176.2	77.6	13.6	0.5	3.2	1.3	3.8	5.2	74.5	50.8	6.9	76.3
District 1	Jack Bergman (R)	25,029.0	697,635	27.9	91.8	1.4	2.3	0.7	0.4	3.4	2.1	90.5	49.3	2.0	78.8
District 2	Bill Huizenga (R)	3,337.8	742,674	222.5	83.7	6.5	0.6	2.3	2.4	4.5	9.7	78.3	50.6	5.6	79.0
District 3	Peter Meijer (R)	2,630.8	747,357	284.1	82.5	8.0	0.3	2.1	2.3	4.8	7.9	78.2	50.0	5.6	77.7
District 4	John L. Moolenaar (R)	8,459.9	701,523	82.9	93.0	1.9	0.7	1.0	0.6	2.9	3.4	90.7	50.0	2.0	85.2
District 5	Daniel T. Kildee (D)	2,349.1	674,536	287.1	76.5	17.3	0.4	0.9	0.8	4.1	5.2	73.3	51.5	2.3	84.4
District 6	Fred Upton (R)	3,547.5	720,391	203.1	83.6	8.2	0.4	1.6	1.6	4.7	6.4	79.8	50.7	4.6	69.4
District 7	Tim Walberg (R)	4,228.2	706,645	167.1	90.3	4.2	0.4	1.1	0.7	3.3	4.6	87.1	49.9	2.9	74.0
District 8	Elissa Slotkin (D)	1,503.2	741,973	493.6	84.3	5.7	0.3	4.8	1.0	3.9	5.5	80.9	50.6	8.1	74.7
District 9	Andy Levin (D)	183.6	715,687	3898.1	76.4	14.1	0.3	4.9	0.7	3.6	2.7	74.6	51.2	11.4	75.9
District 10	Lisa McClain (R)	4,146.8	720,318	173.7	91.7	2.9	0.2	1.8	0.7	2.7	3.3	89.5	50.5	6.2	83.5
District 11	Haley M. Stevens (D)	419.1	733,525	1750.2	80.1	4.9	0.2	10.7	0.7	3.5	3.5	77.8	50.7	14.6	69.6
District 12	Debbie Dingell (D)	402.9	710,072	1762.4	77.4	11.0	0.3	5.7	1.5	4.2	5.9	73.7	51.0	12.3	68.5
District 13	Rashida Tlaib (D)	184.9	672,793	3638.7	37.2	53.9	0.5	1.5	3.3	3.6	8.2	33.3	52.2	7.9	76.3
District 14	Brenda L. Lawrence (D)	185.4	688,778	3715.1	33.4	55.6	0.3	5.3	1.8	3.6	4.6	31.0	52.4	10.4	71.5
MINNESOTA		79,626.6	5,600,166	70.3	81.6	6.4	1.0	5.0	2.1	3.9	5.5	79.0	50.2	8.4	67.6
District 1	Brad Finstad (R)	11,974.4	677,943	56.6	88.6	3.4	0.3	2.9	2.0	2.8	6.7	84.6	50.1	6.7	68.1
District 2	Angie Craig (D)	2,437.9	710,272	291.3	82.9	5.1	0.4	4.8	2.6	4.2	6.3	79.9	50.4	8.7	66.5
District 3	Dean Philips (D)	527.4	722,911	1370.7	77.7	8.1	0.3	7.9	2.0	4.0	4.4	75.6	51.0	12.2	62.0
District 4	Betty McCollum (D)	332.6	715,331	2150.7	68.9	10.2	0.6	13.0	2.2	5.1	6.9	65.4	51.1	13.9	61.5
District 5	Ilhan Omar (D)	135.7	717,702	5288.9	65.6	17.2	1.1	6.0	4.6	5.6	9.4	62.1	50.0	14.7	55.4
District 6	Tom Emmer (R)	2,880.6	720,083	250.0	88.9	3.9	0.3	2.6	1.2	3.0	3.1	87.4	49.7	5.0	77.3
District 7	Michelle Fischbach (R)	33,429.4	666,735	19.9	90.2	1.5	2.7	1.1	1.7	2.9	5.0	87.5	49.8	3.3	72.1
District 8	Pete Stauber (R)	27,908.6	669,189	24.0	92.0	1.1	2.3	0.8	0.6	3.2	1.9	90.9	49.3	1.8	78.5
MISSISSIPPI		46,924.0	2,981,835	63.5	58.0	37.7	0.5	1.0	1.1	1.7	3.2	56.4	51.6	2.3	71.6
District 1	Trent Kelly (R)	10,573.4	765,835	72.4	67.2	28.2	0.2	0.9	1.7	1.9	3.4	65.8	51.8	2.5	63.8
District 2	Bennie G. Thompson (D)	15,551.7	694,447	44.7	31.0	66.2	0.3	0.5	0.9	1.1	2.2	30.2	51.8	1.4	84.3
District 3	Michael Guest (R)	12,754.7	748,342	58.7	60.2	35.7	1.0	1.1	0.9	1.1	2.6	58.7	51.8	2.5	77.5
District 4	Steven M. Palazzo (R)	8,044.2	773,211	96.1	70.9	23.4	0.4	1.6	1.1	2.6	4.4	68.2	51.0	2.8	62.3
MISSOURI		68,746.5	6,124,160	89.1	81.3	11.4	0.4	2.2	1.3	3.5	4.3	78.8	50.9	4.2	66.1
District 1	Cori Bush (D)	225.4	725,037	3216.7	42.2	49.4	0.2	3.3	1.4	3.4	3.6	40.4	52.8	6.3	68.7
District 2	Ann Wagner (R)	465.7	762,478	1637.3	87.1	3.9	0.2	4.7	0.7	3.5	2.9	85.2	51.5	7.7	65.8
District 3	Blaine Luetkemeyer (R)	6,851.5	796,189	116.2	91.7	3.4	0.3	1.3	0.6	2.8	2.7	89.9	50.2	2.3	74.6
District 4	Vicky Hartzler (R)	14,406.9	771,796	53.6	88.4	4.6	0.5	1.8	0.9	3.8	4.1	85.9	50.1	3.3	63.0
District 5	Emanuel Cleaver (D)	2,425.3	773,768	319.0	67.7	21.7	0.3	2.2	3.7	4.4	9.2	63.2	51.5	6.0	60.3
District 6	Sam Graves (R)	18,198.1	775,367	42.6	89.4	4.2	0.3	1.7	1.1	3.3	4.3	86.9	50.5	3.0	64.8
District 7	Bill Long (R)	6,271.7	782,474	124.8	90.4	1.9	0.9	1.5	1.2	4.1	5.3	87.1	51.1	3.3	59.4
District 8	Jason T. Smith (R)	19,901.9	737,051	37.0	91.2	4.4	0.5	0.9	0.4	2.7	2.2	89.7	50.1	1.6	72.4
MONTANA		145,550.4	1,061,705	7.3	87.8	0.6	6.2	0.9	0.8	3.8	3.9	85.6	49.7	2.2	53.7
At Large	Matthew M. Rosendale Sr. (R)	145,550.4	1,061,705	7.3	87.8	0.6	6.2	0.9	0.8	3.8	3.9	85.6	49.7	2.2	53.7
NEBRASKA		76,817.9	1,923,826	25.0	85.3	4.8	0.9	2.6	2.5	3.9	11.2	78.3	50.1	7.4	64.8
District 1	Mike Flood (R)	8,877.7	649,058	73.1	86.9	2.9	1.3	2.8	2.0	4.1	9.7	80.7	49.7	7.3	66.3
District 2	Don Bacon (R)	506.9	675,243	1332.1	79.4	9.5	0.5	3.8	2.4	4.5	11.6	71.8	50.6	9.0	59.8
District 3	Adrian Smith (R)	67,433.3	599,525	8.9	90.3	1.4	0.9	0.9	3.3	3.2	12.3	83.1	50.0	5.7	68.7
NEVADA		109,860.5	3,030,281	27.6	62.1	9.3	1.2	9.0	10.8	7.5	28.9	48.2	49.8	19.4	26.8
District 1	Dina Titus (D)	104.5	701,019	6708.3	48.1	12.0	1.3	9.3	21.2	8.1	46.3	29.1	49.3	31.1	24.5
District 2	Mark E. Amodei (R)	55,897.6	725,776	13.0	76.9	2.1	2.2	4.7	8.0	6.2	23.0	65.3	49.1	12.4	31.8
District 3	Susie Lee (D)	2,848.9	835,738	293.4	63.6	7.9	0.5	15.0	5.4	7.5	17.8	54.0	50.5	18.5	22.8
District 4	Steven Horsford (D)	51,009.5	767,748	15.1	59.2	15.3	1.1	6.3	9.8	8.3	30.7	43.1	50.3	16.3	28.5
NEW HAMPSHIRE		8,953.8	1,355,244	151.4	92.0	1.6	0.2	2.7	0.6	2.9	3.9	89.6	50.4	6.1	41.0
District 1	Chris Pappas (D)	2,465.0	684,286	277.6	91.8	1.7	0.1	2.8	0.6	3.0	3.8	89.4	50.5	6.0	40.4
District 2	Ann M. Kuster (D)	6,488.8	670,958	103.4	92.2	1.4	0.2	2.6	0.6	2.9	4.0	89.8	50.4	6.1	41.5
NEW JERSEY		7,354.7	8,885,418	1208.1	65.5	13.4	0.3	9.7	6.4	4.8	20.4	54.7	51.1	22.7	52.0
District 1	Donald Norcross (D)	350.3	725,464	2071.0	66.8	17.1	0.2	5.3	6.2	4.4	14.2	61.5	51.7	9.7	55.4
District 2	Jefferson Van Drew (R)	2,094.2	712,096	340.0	73.3	12.4	0.4	3.8	5.4	4.7	16.7	64.8	50.9	10.0	60.2
District 3	Andy Kim (D)	898.3	740,858	824.7	78.7	11.1	0.1	3.9	2.1	4.1	8.7	73.9	51.2	8.9	61.5
District 4	Christopher H. Smith (R)	691.0	742,779	1074.9	83.8	6.3	0.1	4.1	2.8	2.9	11.0	77.4	51.4	11.9	59.6
District 5	Josh Gottheimer (D)	991.6	735,376	741.6	77.4	5.1	0.2	10.7	2.2	4.3	14.5	67.8	51.2	20.1	51.6
District 6	Frank Pallone Jr. (D)	215.3	733,029	3404.7	60.1	10.5	0.2	19.1	5.3	4.8	21.9	46.5	50.6	28.9	49.5
District 7	Tom Malinowski (D)	970.0	738,017	760.8	76.6	5.0	0.2	10.7	3.6	3.9	13.1	69.0	51.1	19.2	55.6
District 8	Albio Sires (D)	54.6	762,224	13960.1	52.3	10.3	0.5	9.5	19.3	8.2	53.9	25.4	50.0	45.0	35.4
District 9	Bill Pascrell, Jr. (D)	95.3	753,721	7908.9	57.1	9.8	0.2	13.5	12.3	7.0	38.7	36.9	51.4	39.0	42.5
District 10	Donald M. Payne, Jr. (D)	75.8	758,408	10005.4	27.3	51.0	0.3	7.3	8.8	5.3	20.8	18.8	52.1	30.0	48.3
District 11	Mikie Sherill (D)	506.2	735,124	1452.2	79.8	3.8	0.1	10.6	1.8	3.9	11.6	71.9	51.1	19.0	58.1
District 12	Bonnie Watson Coleman (D)	412.1	748,322	1815.9	54.9	17.2	0.4	17.6	5.8	4.1	18.4	45.2	51.1	28.0	46.9
NEW MEXICO		121,312.7	2,097,021	17.3	70.0	2.1	9.3	1.7	8.8	8.1	49.2	36.7	50.5	9.2	54.2
District 1	Melanie A. Stansbury (D)	4,600.9	699,637	152.1	70.6	2.7	4.3	2.6	10.5	9.3	50.4	38.4	51.1	10.1	54.3
District 2	Yvette Herrell (R)	71,746.2	700,971	9.8	77.4	1.9	5.2	1.0	6.5	7.9	55.8	35.5	49.7	11.3	50.7

1. Dry land or land partially or temporarily covered by water. 2. May be of any race.

Table E. Congressional Districts 116th Congress — **Age and Education**

STATE District	Population and population characteristics, 2016–2020 (cont.)										Education, 2016–2020		
	Age (percent)											Attainment[2] (percent)	
	Under 5 years	5 to 17 years	18 to 24 years	25 to 34 years	35 to 44 years	45 to 54 years	55 to 64 years	65 to 74 years	75 years and over	Median age	Total Enrollment[1]	High school graduate or more	Bachelor's degree or more
	15	16	17	18	19	20	21	22	23	24	25	26	27
MICHIGAN	5.7	16.0	9.6	12.9	11.7	13.0	14.0	10.1	7.1	38.4	2,400,867	91.3	30.0
District 1	4.5	13.8	8.6	10.7	10.4	12.2	16.3	13.7	9.8	45.3	140,976	93.0	26.9
District 2	6.2	17.2	10.3	13.4	11.9	11.9	13.1	9.3	6.7	36.3	184,034	91.3	27.2
District 3	6.3	17.3	9.3	14.1	12.5	12.5	13.1	8.9	6.1	36.1	184,385	91.8	32.9
District 4	5.1	15.3	10.7	11.4	11.1	12.7	14.5	11.2	8.0	40.5	166,321	91.7	22.6
District 5	5.8	16.1	8.3	12.3	11.4	12.8	14.7	10.8	7.9	39.8	151,866	90.2	20.1
District 6	5.9	16.5	10.7	12.3	11.6	12.2	13.6	10.2	7.0	37.7	177,943	91.0	28.9
District 7	5.4	16.1	8.5	11.6	11.7	13.4	14.8	10.9	7.4	40.9	162,208	92.4	25.8
District 8	5.3	16.1	12.4	12.0	11.9	13.5	13.6	9.5	5.8	37.3	207,566	94.9	41.8
District 9	5.5	14.3	8.0	15.9	12.1	13.1	14.2	9.7	7.3	38.1	151,715	90.8	31.7
District 10	5.1	16.2	7.7	11.1	11.7	14.7	15.4	10.8	7.5	42.4	160,648	91.7	24.7
District 11	5.3	16.0	7.8	12.0	12.6	14.3	15.1	10.0	6.9	40.6	175,569	95.2	48.6
District 12	5.7	15.1	13.6	14.8	11.4	12.4	12.2	8.9	5.9	34.0	207,641	91.0	36.4
District 13	7.2	17.4	9.5	14.7	11.8	12.6	12.7	8.3	5.7	34.2	167,102	83.5	17.0
District 14	6.5	16.3	8.9	14.7	11.6	12.5	13.0	9.3	7.2	35.9	162,893	88.3	32.7
MINNESOTA	6.3	17.0	8.9	13.6	12.7	12.4	13.4	9.1	6.7	37.3	1,392,298	93.4	36.8
District 1	6.2	16.9	10.1	12.5	11.9	11.5	13.5	9.5	8.0	37.6	172,552	92.2	30.2
District 2	6.3	18.4	8.4	12.4	13.6	13.5	13.3	8.3	5.7	37.0	183,515	94.9	40.1
District 3	6.1	17.6	6.2	12.5	13.4	14.0	14.3	9.4	6.5	39.2	177,201	95.7	50.4
District 4	6.6	17.0	9.3	15.3	12.5	11.9	12.7	8.6	5.9	35.1	187,711	92.2	44.6
District 5	6.7	13.8	10.7	20.7	13.8	10.8	11.0	7.3	5.3	33.7	177,300	91.6	48.0
District 6	6.5	18.9	9.3	12.3	13.4	13.3	13.1	8.0	5.1	36.5	189,347	94.3	31.0
District 7	6.4	17.2	8.8	11.2	11.3	11.4	14.3	10.5	9.1	39.2	156,837	92.3	22.9
District 8	5.3	15.7	8.5	11.1	11.3	12.2	15.4	11.9	8.6	42.2	147,835	93.6	24.5
MISSISSIPPI	6.2	17.5	9.8	12.9	12.4	12.3	12.8	9.5	6.4	36.3	754,722	85.3	22.8
District 1	6.0	17.7	9.9	12.5	12.6	12.8	12.6	9.4	6.5	36.8	194,476	84.9	21.5
District 2	6.5	18.2	9.9	13.0	12.2	11.8	13.1	9.5	6.1	35.0	182,643	82.3	19.8
District 3	6.1	17.0	10.0	13.1	12.4	12.2	12.8	9.6	6.7	36.4	189,752	86.2	27.1
District 4	6.3	17.3	9.3	13.2	12.6	12.4	13.0	9.5	6.4	36.8	187,851	87.6	22.4
MISSOURI	6.1	16.5	9.3	13.3	12.2	12.3	13.5	9.8	7.1	37.4	1,459,812	90.6	29.9
District 1	6.3	15.2	9.8	17.2	12.6	11.5	13.2	8.5	5.7	34.5	176,934	90.1	33.3
District 2	5.5	16.1	7.2	11.7	12.2	13.3	14.8	10.7	8.6	40.4	178,740	95.5	50.5
District 3	6.0	17.1	8.3	12.6	12.9	13.0	14.0	9.7	6.5	38.4	187,927	91.4	28.2
District 4	6.1	16.3	12.1	13.0	11.5	11.6	12.8	9.7	7.1	35.6	192,470	90.2	26.1
District 5	6.5	16.4	8.5	15.7	12.3	12.1	13.0	8.9	6.7	35.9	174,908	90.5	29.2
District 6	6.1	17.5	9.1	12.4	12.7	12.5	13.3	9.5	7.0	37.8	190,241	91.9	28.9
District 7	6.1	16.5	10.4	12.9	11.9	11.8	12.8	10.1	7.5	37.1	190,743	89.7	25.3
District 8	5.8	16.6	8.7	11.8	11.5	12.5	14.1	10.7	8.1	39.3	167,849	84.9	17.0
MONTANA	5.8	15.7	9.3	12.8	12.1	11.4	14.3	11.3	7.4	39.0	238,528	94.0	33.1
At Large	5.8	15.7	9.3	12.8	12.1	11.4	14.3	11.3	7.4	39.0	238,528	94.0	33.1
NEBRASKA	6.8	17.9	9.8	13.2	12.5	11.4	12.6	8.9	6.8	35.7	505,631	91.6	32.5
District 1	6.5	17.5	11.9	13.1	12.2	11.1	12.3	8.8	6.5	34.7	178,887	92.4	32.8
District 2	7.4	18.6	8.7	15.2	13.8	12.0	11.6	7.7	5.0	34.2	184,057	91.8	41.0
District 3	6.4	17.4	8.8	11.4	11.3	11.1	13.9	10.5	9.1	38.7	142,687	90.5	22.9
NEVADA	6.1	16.6	8.2	14.6	13.3	13.0	12.4	9.7	6.0	37.5	697,235	86.9	25.5
District 1	6.2	16.5	9.6	15.7	13.5	13.1	11.8	8.2	5.4	36.0	152,642	78.2	16.7
District 2	5.8	15.9	8.3	14.3	12.1	12.5	13.7	10.9	6.5	38.8	167,338	89.0	27.7
District 3	5.9	15.6	6.9	14.6	14.3	13.9	12.3	10.1	6.5	38.8	188,170	92.9	33.8
District 4	6.5	18.6	8.4	14.0	13.0	12.4	11.8	9.6	5.7	36.1	189,085	85.9	21.6
NEW HAMPSHIRE	4.7	14.4	9.3	12.5	11.4	14.0	15.6	10.9	7.2	41.7	301,741	93.3	37.6
District 1	4.6	14.3	9.7	12.9	11.6	13.9	15.5	10.5	6.9	41.1	153,833	93.4	38.1
District 2	4.8	14.3	8.9	12.1	11.4	14.1	15.7	11.3	7.5	42.3	147,908	93.1	37.0
NEW JERSEY	5.8	16.2	8.6	12.9	12.8	13.8	13.6	9.2	7.1	38.5	2,192,185	90.3	40.7
District 1	5.9	16.4	8.5	13.7	12.7	13.4	13.6	9.1	6.7	37.6	177,018	90.3	32.2
District 2	5.3	16.0	8.2	11.9	11.5	13.4	14.9	10.9	8.0	40.3	164,879	88.4	27.8
District 3	5.1	15.2	7.9	11.8	11.5	13.9	14.7	11.1	8.8	41.4	168,761	93.3	35.1
District 4	6.8	17.7	8.1	10.7	11.1	13.1	13.8	10.3	8.5	38.9	192,406	93.4	43.0
District 5	5.0	16.8	8.2	10.1	12.0	15.1	14.9	10.0	7.9	42.0	186,275	94.2	49.5
District 6	5.9	15.6	10.3	13.8	13.1	13.6	13.5	8.3	6.0	37.2	194,555	89.1	41.1
District 7	5.2	17.0	7.8	10.0	12.4	15.7	15.4	9.2	7.3	41.8	182,660	94.3	54.7
District 8	6.9	14.4	8.5	19.7	15.9	12.7	10.7	6.4	4.8	34.6	172,844	81.2	35.1
District 9	6.3	15.9	8.6	14.4	13.6	13.4	12.7	8.5	6.5	37.0	182,237	86.4	35.4
District 10	6.7	16.5	9.7	15.7	13.7	13.0	11.8	7.5	5.2	34.5	199,552	86.7	31.2
District 11	5.2	15.7	8.2	10.4	12.6	15.2	14.7	9.7	8.2	41.8	178,452	95.3	56.1
District 12	5.6	16.6	8.9	12.3	13.3	14.2	13.1	9.1	6.9	38.5	192,546	90.8	47.3
NEW MEXICO	5.9	17.2	9.5	13.5	12.1	11.4	13.0	10.4	7.0	36.6	526,666	86.5	28.1
District 1	5.5	15.8	9.0	14.6	12.7	12.0	13.4	10.2	6.7	37.4	170,998	89.3	34.4
District 2	6.4	18.1	10.8	13.0	11.6	10.8	12.2	10.0	7.2	34.9	182,625	82.2	21.8

1. All persons 3 years old and over enrolled in nursery school through college and graduate or professional school. 2. Persons 25 years old and over.

Table E. Congressional Districts 116th Congress — **Households and Group Quarters**

	Households, 2016–2020							Persons in group quarters, 2020				
STATE District	Number	Average household size	Family households (percent)	Married couple family (percent)	Female family house-holder[1]	One person households (percent)	Total in group quarters, 2020	Correctional facilities for adults	Juvenile facilities	Skilled nursing facilities	College/ University student housing	Military quarters
	28	29	30	31	32	33	34	35	36	37	38	39
MICHIGAN	3,980,408	2.45	63.5	46.9	11.8	29.9	221,716	54,748	2,179	44,179	83,931	90
District 1	296,643	2.27	62.7	50.2	8.2	30.4	23,742	8,297	69	4,317	6,944	47
District 2	279,861	2.58	68.1	52.8	10.5	25.4	19,815	5,448	139	3,818	7,850	0
District 3	283,238	2.57	66.6	51.1	10.6	26.7	21,190	8,012	344	2,868	6,270	0
District 4	277,326	2.43	65.5	51.1	9.6	27.6	26,705	11,039	266	3,925	8,880	0
District 5	286,282	2.32	62.5	41.7	15.0	31.5	7,914	677	308	2,919	691	0
District 6	285,776	2.47	65.4	49.6	11.0	27.4	12,107	292	83	3,058	6,759	0
District 7	279,428	2.44	66.5	51.5	10.1	27.8	23,333	12,439	137	3,649	4,942	0
District 8	284,410	2.53	64.7	51.9	8.8	27.4	21,235	779	169	2,429	15,989	0
District 9	301,721	2.35	59.4	42.2	12.4	33.7	4,923	536	36	3,075	0	0
District 10	287,965	2.47	68.1	54.2	9.6	26.8	8,271	2,845	48	3,237	45	43
District 11	291,884	2.49	67.1	55.3	8.2	27.4	7,620	0	114	3,187	2,496	0
District 12	280,068	2.46	59.2	43.4	11.1	31.1	24,369	2,229	25	2,421	18,482	0
District 13	269,191	2.46	55.3	27.3	21.8	38.9	10,712	420	293	1,965	3,525	0
District 14	276,615	2.45	57.3	32.4	19.6	36.8	9,780	1,735	148	3,311	1,058	0
MINNESOTA	2,207,988	2.48	63.6	50.3	9.0	28.8	138,293	16,672	1,351	37,952	45,260	0
District 1	271,984	2.41	64.6	51.6	8.3	28.1	23,233	3,859	134	5,730	8,814	0
District 2	265,904	2.63	70.5	56.7	9.6	23.6	11,375	827	126	3,601	4,333	0
District 3	282,121	2.55	68.1	55.7	8.8	26.0	7,058	181	77	3,663	704	0
District 4	272,961	2.55	60.7	45.5	10.8	31.3	21,007	2,376	77	4,467	8,699	0
District 5	302,948	2.30	49.0	34.9	9.9	38.0	24,430	890	126	5,240	9,658	0
District 6	259,947	2.72	71.0	58.1	8.4	22.1	13,830	3,230	234	2,661	4,805	0
District 7	272,693	2.38	64.2	51.9	7.9	30.3	17,273	831	242	6,967	4,686	0
District 8	279,430	2.32	63.0	50.1	8.3	29.6	20,087	4,478	335	5,623	3,561	0
MISSISSIPPI	1,116,649	2.59	66.3	44.7	17.0	29.2	93,671	30,745	758	20,323	32,502	2,762
District 1	282,214	2.65	68.3	49.0	14.6	27.3	19,895	3,450	214	4,863	9,469	368
District 2	256,076	2.59	63.7	35.2	23.4	32.4	28,804	13,376	172	5,183	8,899	33
District 3	284,758	2.54	65.5	46.4	15.5	29.8	24,637	8,569	267	6,057	7,595	151
District 4	293,601	2.57	67.5	47.4	15.4	27.8	20,335	5,350	105	4,220	6,539	2,210
MISSOURI	2,440,212	2.44	63.6	47.8	11.4	29.8	169,014	37,079	2,745	44,059	55,037	10,097
District 1	316,874	2.23	52.7	29.4	18.5	39.2	20,467	1,297	480	3,943	10,726	0
District 2	307,864	2.44	67.3	55.8	8.2	27.4	11,854	1,846	136	6,293	2,232	0
District 3	301,550	2.57	69.8	55.8	9.8	24.6	16,536	5,489	243	4,585	4,406	0
District 4	294,640	2.50	65.3	51.3	9.5	27.7	36,419	5,139	289	5,849	12,751	10,097
District 5	323,439	2.35	56.6	38.1	14.0	35.5	14,476	1,728	405	4,836	3,940	0
District 6	291,782	2.56	67.0	52.8	9.6	27.0	23,748	8,403	308	6,290	6,723	0
District 7	315,742	2.41	64.6	50.2	9.9	28.1	18,398	2,161	430	4,859	9,026	0
District 8	288,321	2.47	66.4	50.2	10.9	27.7	27,116	11,016	454	7,404	5,233	0
MONTANA	436,048	2.37	61.3	49.3	7.7	30.8	29,304	5,774	807	6,302	8,079	619
At Large	436,048	2.37	61.3	49.3	7.7	30.8	29,304	5,774	807	6,302	8,079	619
NEBRASKA	766,663	2.44	63.8	50.0	9.3	29.4	49,502	8,998	790	12,679	20,831	219
District 1	257,762	2.44	63.4	49.8	9.1	28.5	21,002	3,831	113	3,984	11,003	219
District 2	261,090	2.53	63.5	48.3	10.6	29.8	12,565	2,238	547	2,614	4,472	0
District 3	247,811	2.35	64.4	51.9	8.3	30.0	15,935	2,929	130	6,081	5,356	0
NEVADA	1,130,011	2.65	63.7	44.4	13.0	28.2	36,954	19,575	723	5,357	4,215	724
District 1	257,198	2.69	57.4	33.2	16.2	33.8	5,842	1,715	116	882	904	0
District 2	289,075	2.47	63.8	47.9	10.3	27.6	14,011	6,026	311	1,651	3,311	157
District 3	317,351	2.63	64.8	47.6	11.7	26.9	2,499	435	52	1,268	0	0
District 4	266,387	2.83	68.5	47.6	14.4	25.1	14,602	11,399	244	1,556	0	567
NEW HAMPSHIRE	539,116	2.44	65.2	52.2	8.6	26.7	42,735	4,395	415	9,363	22,883	0
District 1	274,522	2.42	64.5	51.3	8.8	26.8	18,959	933	179	5,019	10,661	0
District 2	264,594	2.45	65.9	53.2	8.4	26.5	23,776	3,462	236	4,344	12,222	0
NEW JERSEY	3,272,054	2.66	68.7	51.0	12.8	26.0	180,375	36,851	1,337	43,373	65,650	1,077
District 1	273,999	2.61	66.2	45.4	15.3	28.3	13,932	567	231	4,096	6,583	0
District 2	270,159	2.55	67.7	48.9	13.6	26.8	19,590	9,066	98	3,908	2,914	142
District 3	285,944	2.54	68.2	52.8	11.2	26.5	14,729	7,225	230	4,648	0	756
District 4	273,411	2.69	68.3	55.9	8.6	27.2	8,203	410	8	5,188	473	78
District 5	266,535	2.71	73.0	59.8	9.5	22.9	12,019	794	110	4,440	3,121	0
District 6	256,874	2.75	70.7	53.1	12.6	23.5	22,184	1,493	187	2,310	16,723	6
District 7	269,370	2.70	73.5	61.7	8.7	22.2	9,253	2,160	106	4,070	42	0
District 8	287,697	2.62	62.4	39.8	15.8	28.4	7,678	1,398	50	2,188	1,947	0
District 9	269,031	2.78	71.0	47.7	17.0	24.2	5,501	348	46	1,343	1,036	0
District 10	274,981	2.68	63.3	35.2	21.3	31.8	26,010	9,553	108	2,279	10,190	0
District 11	274,026	2.62	71.4	59.9	8.3	23.9	17,633	33	47	5,693	9,329	95
District 12	270,027	2.69	69.3	53.3	11.6	26.3	23,643	3,804	116	3,210	13,292	0
NEW MEXICO	792,755	2.59	62.7	43.0	13.7	31.0	42,850	14,807	752	6,176	9,436	2,831
District 1	281,695	2.45	58.6	39.1	13.4	34.3	11,581	1,908	204	2,592	2,805	693
District 2	252,521	2.69	65.4	45.8	13.5	28.6	20,966	9,731	309	1,822	4,639	1,642

1. No spouse present.

Table E. Congressional Districts 116th Congress — **Housing and Money Income**

STATE District	Housing units, 2016–2020						Money income, 2016–2020		
		Occupied units						Households	
			Owner-occupied			Renter-occupied			
	Total	Occupied units as a percent of all units	Owner-occupied units as a percent of occupied units	Median value[1] (dollars)	Percent valued at $500,000 or more	Median rent[2]	Per capita income (dollars)	Median income (dollars)	Percent with income of $100,000 or more
	40	41	42	43	44	45	46	47	48
MICHIGAN	4,611,913	86.3	71.7	162,600	5.0	892	32,854	59,234	26.4
District 1	451,706	65.7	79.0	148,000	5.4	718	29,958	52,480	19.3
District 2	322,737	86.7	75.0	164,600	3.3	871	29,406	60,728	24.8
District 3	305,268	92.8	73.3	176,100	5.2	883	33,135	64,059	28.5
District 4	351,886	78.8	78.1	131,300	2.1	742	29,172	53,585	21.4
District 5	330,976	86.5	71.1	108,100	2.2	763	27,652	47,747	18.5
District 6	332,480	86.0	72.5	160,400	5.5	800	31,277	57,413	24.8
District 7	309,285	90.3	77.6	162,500	3.7	841	32,490	62,612	26.8
District 8	304,028	93.5	73.4	230,800	7.5	965	39,048	74,904	37.0
District 9	320,362	94.2	70.5	162,500	5.2	991	36,469	63,023	28.2
District 10	318,184	90.5	80.9	195,900	4.0	892	34,546	67,189	31.5
District 11	306,633	95.2	76.6	259,600	11.3	1,136	46,761	88,023	44.6
District 12	298,819	93.7	64.7	163,600	5.9	1,035	35,091	62,489	29.5
District 13	332,162	81.0	54.2	79,400	1.3	853	21,642	37,601	12.9
District 14	327,387	84.5	55.8	134,700	6.3	968	31,699	49,537	23.3
MINNESOTA	2,458,030	89.8	71.9	235,700	8.9	1,010	38,881	73,382	35.1
District 1	295,186	92.1	74.0	180,200	5.1	828	34,371	66,004	29.0
District 2	275,560	96.5	77.5	277,600	9.0	1,175	41,731	89,327	44.3
District 3	294,028	96.0	75.0	316,000	19.4	1,316	52,475	96,454	48.8
District 4	286,016	95.4	65.0	257,900	10.2	1,089	39,538	74,059	36.8
District 5	318,647	95.1	53.2	251,400	11.5	1,101	40,881	68,727	33.2
District 6	274,079	94.8	80.0	250,700	6.8	978	37,311	84,287	40.6
District 7	334,907	81.4	75.2	165,600	4.6	720	31,404	59,870	24.3
District 8	379,607	73.6	78.0	181,500	5.0	792	32,031	60,014	25.7
MISSISSIPPI	1,330,867	83.9	68.8	125,500	3.0	789	25,444	46,511	18.8
District 1	334,512	84.4	71.8	132,700	2.7	783	25,931	50,629	20.0
District 2	313,682	81.6	61.7	93,100	2.0	708	21,473	37,410	13.6
District 3	337,352	84.4	72.1	131,900	4.3	818	27,706	48,554	21.6
District 4	345,321	85.0	68.9	141,600	2.7	852	26,338	49,110	20.1
MISSOURI	2,804,664	87.0	67.1	163,600	5.1	843	31,839	57,290	24.7
District 1	371,241	85.4	50.6	117,800	4.1	893	31,086	49,292	19.3
District 2	321,654	95.7	78.0	254,500	13.0	1,059	48,976	86,997	43.9
District 3	349,963	86.2	78.0	186,100	4.4	815	32,988	68,934	30.8
District 4	355,212	82.9	68.1	157,300	4.0	800	27,807	53,534	21.3
District 5	364,734	88.7	57.6	144,300	3.9	915	31,163	54,220	22.8
District 6	336,564	86.7	71.5	166,500	3.8	818	31,487	63,260	27.8
District 7	359,387	87.9	64.5	146,500	3.3	766	27,069	49,707	18.0
District 8	345,909	83.4	70.2	122,600	2.6	668	23,978	44,753	15.6
MONTANA	514,956	84.7	68.5	244,900	11.9	836	32,463	56,539	24.1
At Large	514,956	84.7	68.5	244,900	11.9	836	32,463	56,539	24.1
NEBRASKA	844,248	90.8	66.2	164,000	4.0	857	33,205	63,015	27.3
District 1	276,938	93.1	64.5	171,700	4.2	850	32,317	63,429	27.3
District 2	277,763	94.0	64.0	190,100	5.0	968	37,004	70,597	33.4
District 3	289,547	85.6	70.2	125,600	2.8	717	29,889	55,693	21.4
NEVADA	1,268,533	89.1	57.1	290,200	13.7	1,159	32,629	62,043	27.7
District 1	303,959	84.6	41.1	212,000	5.8	995	23,772	43,461	14.8
District 2	317,854	90.9	61.9	325,000	19.9	1,106	36,380	67,282	31.1
District 3	352,713	90.0	61.1	338,000	16.9	1,392	40,025	75,965	36.1
District 4	294,007	90.6	62.4	266,700	8.5	1,198	29,121	62,048	27.0
NEW HAMPSHIRE	638,611	84.4	71.2	272,300	10.7	1,145	41,234	77,923	38.1
District 1	324,100	84.7	70.2	284,900	12.7	1,174	42,062	78,400	38.9
District 2	314,511	84.1	72.3	259,200	8.8	1,107	40,390	77,432	37.6
NEW JERSEY	3,628,732	90.2	64.0	343,500	24.6	1,368	44,153	85,245	43.2
District 1	296,080	92.5	68.3	204,400	3.4	1,141	37,210	73,538	36.4
District 2	388,239	69.6	72.4	224,600	9.9	1,127	35,830	68,412	33.4
District 3	321,987	88.8	79.7	272,100	10.1	1,451	43,185	85,077	42.2
District 4	298,295	91.7	75.8	379,500	30.5	1,421	46,461	90,852	46.4
District 5	283,804	93.9	75.9	429,100	38.0	1,484	53,911	109,901	55.1
District 6	275,255	93.3	62.0	353,300	19.2	1,482	40,201	89,001	45.4
District 7	284,028	94.8	77.6	454,400	42.3	1,555	60,449	118,554	58.6
District 8	311,922	92.2	29.9	371,800	29.4	1,384	38,093	65,559	33.8
District 9	284,683	94.5	47.4	386,900	27.0	1,391	37,546	75,395	38.7
District 10	304,682	90.3	38.8	303,400	16.7	1,202	32,027	58,807	28.4
District 11	287,681	95.3	76.1	454,900	41.0	1,654	59,330	119,624	58.7
District 12	292,076	92.5	65.6	355,000	25.4	1,411	45,892	91,433	46.7
NEW MEXICO	943,568	84.0	68.0	175,700	6.4	857	27,945	51,243	21.9
District 1	307,401	91.6	64.3	201,800	6.4	883	31,069	53,599	23.6
District 2	316,885	79.7	68.7	138,500	3.1	776	24,417	46,729	19.2

1. Specified owner-occupied units. 2. Specified renter-occupied units.

Table E. Congressional Districts 116th Congress — **Poverty, Labor Force, Employment, and Social Security**

STATE District	Poverty, 2016–2020			Civilian labor force, 2016–2020			Civilian employment,[2] 2016–2020				Persons under 65 years of age with no health insurance, 2016–2020 (percent)	Social Security beneficiaries, December 2021		Supplemental Security Income recipients, December 2021
					Unemployment			Percent						
	Persons below poverty level (percent)	Families below poverty level (percent)	Percent of households receiving food stamps in past 12 months	Total	Total	Rate[1]	Total	Management, business, science, and arts occupations	Service, sales, and office	Construction and production		Number	Rate[3]	
	49	50	51	52	53	54	55	56	57	58	59	60	61	62
MICHIGAN	13.7	9.2	12.7	4,956,499	298,142	6.0	4,658,357	37.6	38.0	24.4	6.4	2,253,295	225.9	256,662
District 1	12.8	8.0	10.8	323,377	17,946	5.5	305,431	32.8	42.0	25.2	7.9	217,569	311.9	13,981
District 2	11.2	7.4	10.6	380,923	18,399	4.8	362,524	32.8	37.4	29.8	5.8	163,747	220.5	14,690
District 3	11.8	7.5	10.5	386,829	19,938	5.2	366,891	37.6	36.7	25.7	6.3	148,680	198.9	15,374
District 4	13.9	8.7	12.0	324,000	17,389	5.4	306,611	32.9	39.2	27.9	7.2	185,426	264.3	15,692
District 5	18.3	13.3	19.4	310,566	25,593	8.2	284,973	31.1	41.6	27.3	6.8	177,349	262.9	27,231
District 6	13.8	9.2	11.0	364,526	19,991	5.5	344,535	35.1	36.9	28.0	7.4	164,780	228.7	16,236
District 7	10.6	7.2	9.6	343,125	16,816	4.9	326,309	35.1	36.3	28.5	6.2	173,054	244.9	12,823
District 8	10.2	5.5	7.5	393,171	20,677	5.3	372,494	45.1	37.3	17.7	4.7	145,416	196.0	10,867
District 9	11.0	8.0	11.3	383,816	20,641	5.4	363,175	39.5	38.4	22.1	6.3	150,546	210.4	19,618
District 10	9.3	6.6	9.4	361,587	19,479	5.4	342,108	36.8	36.0	27.2	6.3	173,691	241.1	12,677
District 11	5.9	3.8	4.6	395,999	15,946	4.0	380,053	52.1	33.5	14.4	4.1	147,490	201.1	7,996
District 12	15.9	10.1	11.4	361,394	18,904	5.2	342,490	42.9	35.5	21.6	4.8	139,384	196.3	15,634
District 13	28.2	22.6	29.9	300,829	33,201	11.0	267,628	26.8	44.3	28.8	8.5	128,626	191.2	45,532
District 14	20.8	15.3	21.8	326,357	33,222	10.2	293,135	39.4	39.7	20.9	7.6	137,537	199.7	28,311
MINNESOTA	9.3	5.6	7.5	3,074,732	117,117	3.8	2,957,615	42.2	36.1	21.6	5.3	1,082,519	193.3	89,434
District 1	10.2	6.0	7.0	368,690	12,240	3.3	356,450	37.6	35.7	26.6	5.9	143,490	211.7	9,146
District 2	5.8	3.6	4.8	403,961	13,841	3.4	390,120	43.2	36.7	20.1	4.3	123,768	174.3	6,946
District 3	5.2	3.4	4.4	404,288	12,436	3.1	391,852	50.8	33.8	15.3	4.0	131,372	181.7	7,308
District 4	11.4	7.6	9.7	387,013	16,478	4.3	370,535	46.3	36.7	17.0	5.5	122,217	170.9	16,853
District 5	14.2	8.6	11.3	426,396	20,550	4.8	405,846	49.9	35.6	14.5	6.8	97,886	136.4	20,305
District 6	6.4	3.8	5.4	402,971	13,530	3.4	389,441	38.6	35.7	25.7	4.0	124,757	173.3	7,168
District 7	10.6	6.4	7.8	345,492	12,127	3.5	333,365	34.0	36.3	29.7	6.7	160,310	240.4	9,776
District 8	11.2	6.6	8.9	335,921	15,915	4.7	320,006	34.2	39.0	26.8	5.7	178,719	267.1	11,932
MISSISSIPPI	19.6	15.0	14.6	1,338,474	95,379	7.1	1,243,095	33.1	38.6	28.3	14.2	681,844	228.7	110,325
District 1	16.0	11.6	11.1	355,404	18,930	5.3	336,474	30.4	36.9	32.7	12.9	176,168	230.0	22,969
District 2	25.9	20.3	20.8	292,610	28,258	9.7	264,352	29.7	41.4	28.9	15.8	162,145	233.5	40,266
District 3	18.8	14.3	12.5	338,338	19,302	5.7	319,036	38.6	36.8	24.6	12.8	168,285	224.9	23,760
District 4	18.4	14.5	14.4	352,122	28,889	8.2	323,233	33.4	39.9	26.7	15.5	175,246	226.6	23,330
MISSOURI	13.0	8.9	10.5	3,071,591	138,673	4.5	2,932,918	37.9	38.7	23.4	11.2	1,329,084	217.0	131,148
District 1	17.4	13.0	16.3	386,689	23,756	6.1	362,933	39.9	42.0	18.2	11.2	133,048	183.5	26,049
District 2	5.2	3.3	3.2	407,251	13,138	3.2	394,113	51.6	34.7	13.7	4.8	163,986	215.1	5,927
District 3	8.7	6.2	7.2	412,527	16,171	3.9	396,356	36.5	38.0	25.5	8.3	178,496	224.2	10,434
District 4	14.8	9.3	10.2	363,037	16,471	4.5	346,566	35.8	38.1	26.1	12.6	169,873	220.1	15,274
District 5	14.5	10.6	11.3	408,607	19,927	4.9	388,680	36.1	40.1	23.8	13.8	150,430	194.4	18,874
District 6	10.5	6.7	7.4	389,220	14,819	3.8	374,401	37.3	36.4	26.4	9.8	161,980	208.9	11,416
District 7	15.2	10.0	11.8	380,730	16,881	4.4	363,849	33.4	41.5	25.1	14.8	182,535	233.3	17,069
District 8	18.5	13.0	16.3	323,530	17,510	5.4	306,020	30.3	39.3	30.4	14.3	188,736	256.1	26,105
MONTANA	12.8	7.7	9.3	542,584	22,541	4.2	520,043	37.5	39.7	22.8	10.2	248,513	234.1	16,921
At Large	12.8	7.7	9.3	542,584	22,541	4.2	520,043	37.5	39.7	22.8	10.2	248,513	234.1	16,921
NEBRASKA	10.4	6.6	8.1	1,034,886	35,114	3.4	999,772	38.8	37.1	24.1	9.5	360,240	187.3	28,763
District 1	10.6	6.4	7.7	350,924	11,784	3.4	339,140	38.7	37.4	23.9	8.9	119,174	183.6	8,815
District 2	9.6	6.2	8.4	368,891	14,085	3.8	354,806	43.8	37.8	18.4	9.6	108,040	160.0	11,475
District 3	11.0	7.3	8.3	315,071	9,245	2.9	305,826	33.2	36.1	30.8	10.1	133,026	221.9	8,473
NEVADA	12.8	9.0	11.6	1,525,262	100,222	6.6	1,425,040	30.9	48.1	21.1	13.0	571,841	188.7	54,728
District 1	19.9	15.4	19.7	352,313	27,902	7.9	324,411	19.6	57.2	23.2	20.3	113,650	162.1	18,017
District 2	10.7	6.5	9.6	374,762	19,534	5.2	355,228	34.2	40.7	25.1	11.5	155,465	214.2	10,046
District 3	8.6	5.8	6.3	440,749	26,576	6.0	414,173	38.1	47.3	14.5	8.9	156,046	186.7	9,813
District 4	12.9	9.9	12.3	357,438	26,210	7.3	331,228	29.2	48.0	22.8	12.0	146,680	191.1	16,852
NEW HAMPSHIRE	7.4	4.6	6.4	758,702	28,479	3.8	730,223	41.9	37.3	20.7	7.2	321,925	237.5	17,317
District 1	7.6	4.6	6.4	391,083	15,594	4.0	375,489	41.8	37.9	20.2	7.2	159,000	232.4	8,893
District 2	7.2	4.5	6.4	367,619	12,885	3.5	354,734	42.1	36.7	21.2	7.2	162,925	242.8	8,424
NEW JERSEY	9.7	7.0	8.4	4,698,414	271,795	5.8	4,426,619	44.2	37.4	18.5	8.8	1,652,973	186.0	167,599
District 1	10.9	7.8	10.4	386,934	24,270	6.3	362,664	40.8	39.3	19.8	6.8	146,255	201.6	19,156
District 2	12.1	8.7	10.7	352,509	26,321	7.5	326,188	35.1	43.3	21.7	8.2	172,209	241.8	17,678
District 3	6.2	4.1	4.8	383,100	20,568	5.4	362,532	42.4	39.8	17.8	5.6	178,918	241.5	9,754
District 4	8.5	5.4	5.2	368,933	18,865	5.1	350,068	46.0	38.9	15.0	6.1	164,204	221.1	7,328
District 5	5.1	3.6	3.7	394,337	19,693	5.0	374,644	50.3	35.7	14.0	5.6	143,078	194.6	8,289
District 6	9.7	7.1	7.6	387,977	21,769	5.6	366,208	44.6	35.2	20.2	8.6	120,600	164.5	13,049
District 7	4.7	3.2	3.3	403,990	18,155	4.5	385,835	53.6	33.4	13.0	4.9	131,839	178.6	5,838
District 8	15.1	11.7	14.2	429,547	24,279	5.7	405,268	37.1	37.0	25.9	17.7	89,717	117.7	23,221
District 9	13.2	10.7	13.9	398,639	22,320	5.6	376,319	38.0	37.8	24.2	14.3	123,652	164.1	16,771
District 10	16.6	13.9	16.6	393,902	32,859	8.3	361,043	35.9	43.2	20.9	12.7	108,968	143.7	26,468
District 11	4.2	2.7	2.8	405,853	19,026	4.7	386,827	55.2	32.9	11.9	4.6	140,846	191.6	5,541
District 12	9.3	6.3	7.0	392,693	23,670	6.0	369,023	49.3	33.5	17.2	8.6	132,687	177.3	14,506
NEW MEXICO	18.6	14.2	17.0	951,773	62,580	6.6	889,193	37.8	41.4	20.8	11.3	455,414	217.2	58,404
District 1	16.4	12.0	15.7	345,130	19,919	5.8	325,211	41.9	41.1	17.0	9.5	145,221	207.6	17,524
District 2	20.9	16.4	19.3	297,523	21,261	7.1	276,262	32.2	41.8	26.0	11.9	153,175	218.5	22,136

1. Percent of civilian labor force. 2. Persons 16 years old and over. 3. Per 1,000 resident population estimated in the 2016–2020 American Community Survey.

Table E. Congressional Districts 116th Congress — **Agriculture**

STATE District	Agriculture 2017									
		Land in farms			Value of products sold				Government payments	
	Number of farms	Acres	Average size of farm (acres)	Irrigated land (acres)	Total ($1,000)	Average per farm (dollars)	Percent from crops	Percent from livestock and poultry products	Total ($1,000)	Average per farm receiving payments (dollars)
	63	64	65	66	67	68	69	70	71	72
MICHIGAN	47,641	9,764,090	205	7,214,667	8,220,936	172,560	56.5	43.5	167,189	10,892
District 1	6,952	1,082,209	156	449,001	357,657	51,447	59.1	40.9	5,710	4,827
District 2	3,516	578,489	165	390,567	958,662	272,657	58.1	41.9	4,619	8,118
District 3	3,868	773,809	200	586,992	846,663	218,889	40.5	59.5	14,843	12,009
District 4	9,471	2,085,639	220	1,557,525	1,553,454	164,022	44.7	55.3	32,154	8,711
District 5	2,612	607,782	233	503,507	348,992	133,611	78.8	21.2	12,854	9,578
District 6	5,312	1,106,709	208	855,681	1,567,911	295,164	59.4	40.6	21,268	14,925
District 7	7,424	1,618,131	218	1,300,677	997,521	134,364	70.7	29.3	40,056	13,185
District 8	1,988	293,838	148	219,882	175,102	88,079	64.9	35.1	5,626	18,568
District 9	23	D	D	D	3,176	138,087	D	D	D	D
District 10	5,921	1,578,233	267	1,324,773	1,367,410	230,942	56.2	43.8	29,581	11,729
District 11	167	8,360	50	4,172	12,429	74,425	D	D	D	D
District 12	291	25,639	88	18,446	26,613	91,454	98.8	1.2	413	13,767
District 13	71	1,872	26	D	4,984	70,197	D	D	8	1,143
District 14	25	D	D	136	361	14,440	56.5	43.5	D	D
MINNESOTA	68,822	25,516,982	371	20,054,132	18,395,390	267,289	55.4	44.6	394,491	9,568
District 1	18,080	6,432,710	356	5,514,901	6,521,603	360,708	49.1	50.9	139,174	10,630
District 2	4,323	1,084,055	251	862,034	968,711	224,083	56.2	43.8	24,916	10,648
District 3	514	56,055	109	37,496	59,877	116,492	84.5	15.5	D	#VALUE!
District 4	306	26,745	87	20,368	18,073	59,062	D	D	374	5,194
District 5	24	1,241	52	875	5,449	227,042	D	D	D	D
District 6	5,231	981,166	188	719,093	927,726	177,352	47.0	53.0	8,131	4,055
District 7	30,340	14,905,007	491	11,889,723	9,079,273	299,251	61.9	38.1	213,860	9,993
District 8	10,004	2,030,003	203	1,009,642	814,678	81,435	39.1	60.9	7,721	3,575
MISSISSIPPI	34,988	10,415,136	298	4,174,210	6,195,969	177,088	37.0	63.0	213,785	14,986
District 1	9,940	2,535,334	255	815,727	741,685	74,616	51.9	48.1	38,445	7,803
District 2	8,921	4,904,171	550	2,870,319	2,405,086	269,598	71.4	28.6	147,529	27,936
District 3	9,886	2,098,567	212	369,795	2,283,032	230,936	5.4	94.6	21,401	7,317
District 4	6,241	877,064	141	118,369	766,165	122,763	8.6	91.4	6,410	5,658
MISSOURI	95,320	27,781,883	291	13,486,275	10,525,937	110,427	52.0	48.0	323,801	10,366
District 1	60	4,038	67	1,734	3,917	65,283	95.5	4.5	78	6,000
District 2	232	56,434	243	15,973	19,886	85,716	95.4	4.6	223	5,718
District 3	11,671	2,582,240	221	1,017,877	763,114	65,385	46.9	53.1	16,790	5,510
District 4	23,209	6,321,590	272	2,819,491	2,390,061	102,980	41.6	58.4	57,041	8,620
District 5	3,599	1,113,070	309	772,182	521,467	144,892	75.8	24.2	11,009	6,817
District 6	25,268	9,149,092	362	5,265,587	3,473,872	137,481	63.0	37.0	148,718	10,355
District 7	12,945	2,313,829	179	662,898	1,412,550	109,119	9.4	90.6	6,746	5,324
District 8	18,336	6,241,590	340	2,930,533	1,941,071	105,861	71.4	28.6	83,197	19,457
MONTANA	27,048	58,122,878	2,149	9,901,226	3,520,623	130,162	45.0	55.0	284,244	27,014
At Large	27,048	58,122,878	2,149	9,901,226	3,520,623	130,162	45.0	55.0	284,244	27,014
NEBRASKA	46,332	44,986,821	971	19,460,222	21,983,429	474,476	42.4	57.6	639,975	20,745
District 1	12,307	5,386,864	438	4,463,921	5,299,528	430,611	45.6	54.4	134,195	15,708
District 2	731	177,616	243	152,180	102,706	140,501	92.6	7.4	3,892	12,761
District 3	33,294	39,422,341	1,184	14,844,121	16,581,195	498,024	41.0	59.0	501,888	22,812
NEVADA	3,423	6,128,153	1,790	573,785	665,758	194,495	41.5	58.5	5,049	16,183
District 1	16	674	42	D	394	24,625	52	49	D	D
District 2	2,440	5,359,802	2,197	464,131	456,516	187,097	43.7	56.3	3,915	16,313
District 3	72	3,477	48	D	1,501	20,847	78	22	D	D
District 4	895	764,200	854	108,581	207,348	231,674	36.3	63.7	D	D
NEW HAMPSHIRE	4,123	425,393	103	85,793	187,794	45,548	57.4	42.6	3,494	11,344
District 1	1,429	114,081	80	21,437	43,425	30,388	65.6	34.4	1,243	12,186
District 2	2,694	311,312	116	64,356	144,369	53,589	54.9	45.1	2,251	10,927
NEW JERSEY	9,883	734,084	74	411,785	1,097,951	111,095	89.7	10.3	7,503	10,071
District 1	323	19,769	61	12,012	50,873	157,502	97.0	3.0	126	6,632
District 2	2,470	242,801	98	164,407	522,859	211,684	94.6	5.4	3,879	12,930
District 3	950	95,629	101	45,970	98,998	104,208	92.3	7.7	829	12,014
District 4	973	46,949	48	25,493	103,382	106,251	84.7	15.3	431	10,512
District 5	1,813	109,258	60	46,313	102,405	56,484	69.5	30.5	885	8,349
District 6	129	6,165	48	2,383	13,972	108,310	D	D	D	D
District 7	2,409	161,144	67	89,857	130,857	54,320	85.3	14.7	1,076	6,482
District 8	3	D	D	20	D	#VALUE!	D	D	D	D
District 9	10	77	8	55	D	#VALUE!	D	D	D	D
District 10	4	D	D	5	60	15,000	D	D	D	D
District 11	287	11,013	38	3,451	17,851	62,199	95	5	D	D
District 12	512	41,235	81	21,819	54,054	105,574	85.7	14.3	255	6,538
NEW MEXICO	25,044	40,659,836	1,624	806,138	2,582,343	103,112	25.2	74.8	63,660	18,436
District 1	2,270	1,912,502	843	20,328	62,931	27,723	30.0	70.0	2,343	16,385
District 2	9,762	20,343,252	2,084	390,375	1,562,618	160,072	30.7	69.3	25,845	19,580

STATE District	Private nonfarm employment and payroll, 2020												
		Employment										Annual payroll	
			Percent by selected industries										
	Number of establishments	Total	Manufac-turing	Construc-tion	Wholesale trade	Retail trade	Health care and social assistance	Finance and Insurance	Real estate and rental and leasing	Profes-sional, sci-entific, and technical services	Information	Total (mil dol)	Average per employee (dollars)
	73	74	75	76	77	78	79	80	81	82	83	84	85
MICHIGAN	221,060	4,000,120	15.0	4.1	4.6	11.7	16.1	4.5	1.4	7.3	1.7	201,871	50,466
District 1	19,550	211,220	13.6	6.5	2.9	16.8	19.2	3.8	1.4	3.2	1.4	8,615	40,789
District 2	16,849	338,451	27.7	4.6	6.0	11.9	11.5	2.5	0.9	3.3	0.9	15,431	45,592
District 3	16,072	316,039	20.3	4.2	5.7	9.4	16.9	4.6	1.2	4.9	1.6	15,955	50,485
District 4	13,318	190,803	16.2	6.4	3.4	16.5	17.0	3.5	1.5	3.8	1.2	8,074	42,314
District 5	13,079	213,094	12.7	4.4	4.7	14.5	23.0	3.0	1.3	3.4	1.1	9,306	43,672
District 6	14,431	238,108	21.6	4.6	4.3	13.0	15.6	3.1	1.6	4.8	0.8	11,460	48,129
District 7	12,796	205,158	22.1	4.1	3.8	13.3	14.7	4.2	0.9	4.2	1.4	9,415	45,892
District 8	16,200	239,157	11.1	5.4	3.1	14.2	18.2	6.5	1.6	6.1	2.0	10,813	45,214
District 9	17,454	280,684	13.9	4.0	5.4	11.7	20.0	2.3	2.1	12.2	1.6	14,561	51,877
District 10	14,860	216,390	28.1	6.0	3.5	15.5	12.8	2.2	1.0	6.5	0.9	9,736	44,991
District 11	24,202	488,887	9.9	3.9	7.4	11.5	12.2	6.3	1.4	15.1	2.3	30,623	62,638
District 12	15,583	304,789	11.1	2.6	3.4	12.6	20.6	3.3	1.2	10.1	2.5	17,370	56,989
District 13	10,217	222,392	13.1	2.7	4.2	9.9	21.8	1.0	1.2	3.0	1.4	11,646	52,367
District 14	15,597	338,468	5.5	3.6	4.3	7.2	18.9	13.0	2.8	12.3	3.2	22,741	67,187
MINNESOTA	150,819	2,738,254	11.5	4.9	5.3	11.1	17.6	6.2	1.4	6.8	2.2	155,205	56,680
District 1	16,754	304,203	17.2	4.0	2.9	12.4	18.8	3.0	0.9	13.9	1.8	14,777	48,577
District 2	17,083	283,245	12.7	6.2	5.6	13.5	13.5	5.1	1.2	4.1	2.8	14,442	50,987
District 3	23,494	481,190	13.0	4.4	6.9	11.5	12.3	9.0	2.2	7.7	2.3	31,844	66,177
District 4	17,840	364,360	8.6	3.7	5.2	9.8	20.7	6.1	1.5	5.1	2.4	21,218	58,233
District 5	21,158	528,217	5.9	4.1	4.2	6.3	19.5	9.0	1.8	9.2	3.2	36,939	69,932
District 6	17,288	237,546	16.1	10.1	5.1	14.9	15.9	3.0	1.0	3.2	1.0	11,004	46,322
District 7	19,021	232,796	19.1	5.2	6.4	14.8	21.9	3.6	0.7	2.9	1.3	9,713	41,721
District 8	17,445	215,474	9.2	5.6	2.7	15.5	25.6	3.2	1.1	3.5	1.3	9,047	41,987
MISSISSIPPI	58,897	949,927	15.5	4.8	4.0	14.3	18.5	3.4	1.0	3.2	1.4	38,104	40,113
District 1	14,749	241,947	22.4	3.5	4.4	14.8	15.2	2.8	0.9	2.2	1.1	8,946	36,974
District 2	12,196	182,974	16.8	4.0	4.2	14.1	20.0	2.8	1.0	2.4	1.3	7,083	38,710
District 3	17,282	269,665	10.7	5.6	5.0	13.7	21.4	4.7	1.3	4.0	2.0	11,683	43,325
District 4	14,255	231,411	14.5	5.8	2.2	15.8	18.0	3.1	1.1	3.3	1.0	9,536	41,207
MISSOURI	150,761	2,566,786	10.8	5.2	5.2	12.1	16.5	5.5	1.4	6.5	2.1	128,182	49,939
District 1	19,726	425,542	11.1	4.6	6.3	6.6	14.5	4.7	1.4	6.3	2.2	24,977	58,694
District 2	24,474	451,060	4.1	5.0	3.6	11.6	16.8	8.8	1.6	9.9	2.9	26,971	59,795
District 3	17,586	246,993	15.9	7.9	4.3	16.8	13.6	3.6	1.1	3.7	2.2	10,423	42,198
District 4	15,963	207,827	12.5	5.1	3.7	16.7	19.8	5.8	1.3	4.5	1.2	8,320	40,035
District 5	20,301	420,141	9.8	6.1	8.2	9.9	15.7	6.3	1.4	11.1	2.4	23,832	56,723
District 6	16,389	218,314	14.3	5.3	4.3	16.1	17.1	4.4	1.5	3.4	1.5	9,129	41,817
District 7	19,339	317,263	12.8	4.3	5.0	13.6	17.4	3.4	1.7	4.0	2.2	12,930	40,755
District 8	16,279	205,281	15.7	4.4	4.3	16.3	24.9	3.6	1.2	2.3	1.3	7,499	36,532
MONTANA	39,505	377,638	5.4	7.8	4.0	15.3	19.2	4.4	1.6	5.4	2.1	16,540	43,800
At Large	39,505	377,638	5.4	7.8	4.0	15.3	19.2	4.4	1.6	5.4	2.1	16,540	43,800
NEBRASKA	54,791	866,139	11.6	6.0	4.8	12.5	15.9	8.7	1.4	4.6	2.3	41,199	47,566
District 1	17,044	251,260	13.4	6.4	3.9	13.5	16.8	7.4	1.3	5.4	2.4	11,227	44,684
District 2	18,789	371,112	7.0	6.6	4.6	11.5	16.0	12.0	1.9	5.4	3.1	19,851	53,491
District 3	18,555	206,891	19.6	5.4	6.4	15.1	17.3	4.7	0.9	2.5	1.3	8,317	40,200
NEVADA	70,621	1,275,946	3.9	7.2	3.1	12.2	11.2	3.2	2.5	4.8	1.5	56,342	44,157
District 1	18,627	428,716	1.1	5.0	1.5	11.0	11.1	2.0	2.6	3.7	1.1	16,139	37,644
District 2	19,681	292,051	8.9	7.8	5.1	13.1	13.3	2.6	2.0	5.1	1.6	14,698	50,328
District 3	20,995	338,385	3.8	8.9	3.1	12.4	9.7	5.0	3.4	5.8	2.0	15,784	46,645
District 4	10,784	172,035	3.5	9.8	3.8	16.4	13.6	2.7	1.9	4.9	1.8	7,550	43,885
NEW HAMPSHIRE	38,350	621,263	10.6	5.0	3.9	15.7	15.8	4.7	1.4	5.8	2.6	33,455	53,850
District 1	19,919	309,203	10.4	5.3	4.0	16.0	15.3	6.4	1.7	5.9	3.1	16,988	54,941
District 2	17,964	272,309	12.5	5.3	3.9	17.5	18.6	2.6	1.1	5.8	2.4	14,036	51,544
NEW JERSEY	232,761	3,819,722	5.8	4.3	7.1	12.1	16.4	5.4	1.7	8.9	2.2	241,029	63,101
District 1	16,183	280,238	7.4	5.5	6.3	15.9	22.0	2.3	1.4	5.6	1.5	13,869	49,489
District 2	16,909	234,185	6.6	6.0	4.5	14.9	18.1	2.4	1.5	3.5	0.8	9,935	42,425
District 3	16,799	261,857	4.9	4.0	5.5	15.5	20.8	7.6	2.0	7.1	1.6	13,693	52,292
District 4	22,394	308,213	4.7	5.6	4.0	16.9	20.3	4.3	2.3	7.9	2.7	15,342	49,776
District 5	22,617	301,251	5.4	4.4	7.7	14.9	21.4	3.9	1.2	7.1	2.0	17,944	59,566
District 6	18,657	331,793	5.5	4.8	7.8	12.7	14.6	3.1	1.7	14.5	2.5	21,491	64,771
District 7	22,934	363,703	6.5	5.2	7.2	12.9	15.1	5.4	1.4	11.0	4.7	29,100	80,010
District 8	16,157	253,581	5.0	3.4	6.6	10.8	13.5	17.1	1.5	4.7	2.3	19,146	75,501
District 9	21,400	311,159	10.2	5.2	11.1	9.5	14.2	2.6	3.1	5.4	3.0	18,171	58,398
District 10	13,847	224,190	5.1	3.2	5.3	10.2	20.5	4.3	1.9	5.6	1.3	14,091	62,855
District 11	25,056	429,884	5.7	4.0	7.5	10.1	14.8	6.0	1.9	14.5	1.9	33,290	77,440
District 12	18,899	346,797	5.6	3.0	11.0	9.9	13.8	6.0	1.3	13.9	2.0	25,172	72,585
NEW MEXICO	43,587	651,756	4.3	6.7	3.1	14.0	19.7	3.9	1.5	9.2	1.6	28,386	43,554
District 1	16,252	281,145	4.6	7.6	4.0	12.6	19.3	4.2	1.5	11.7	2.2	12,866	45,761
District 2	12,831	177,174	4.3	7.3	2.5	15.4	20.9	3.3	1.6	4.2	1.1	7,019	39,615

Table E. Congressional Districts 116th Congress — **Land Area and Population Characteristics**

STATE District	Representative, 117th Congress	Land area,[1] 2020 (sq mi)	Population and population characteristics, 2016–2020: Total persons	Per square mile	Race alone (percent): White	Black	American Indian, Alaska Native	Asian and Pacific Islander	Some other race (percent)	Two or more races (percent)	Hispanic or Latino[2] (percent)	Non-Hispanic White alone (percent)	Percent female	Percent foreign-born	Percent born in state of residence
		1	2	3	4	5	6	7	8	9	10	11	12	13	14
NEW MEXICO—Cont'd															
District 3	Teresa Leger Fernandez (D)	44,965.6	696,413	15.5	61.9	1.6	18.5	1.5	9.4	7.2	41.4	36.2	50.8	6.2	57.6
NEW YORK		47,123.4	19,514,849	414.1	62.3	15.4	0.4	8.6	8.6	4.7	19.1	55.2	51.5	22.4	63.1
District 1	Lee M. Zeldin (R)	650.2	715,479	1100.4	84.2	5.4	0.2	4.3	2.2	3.8	15.1	73.7	50.8	12.5	78.7
District 2	Andrew R. Garbarino (R)	180.9	710,764	3929.0	72.9	9.9	0.3	3.8	8.4	4.6	24.8	59.8	50.8	17.6	74.8
District 3	Thomas R. Souzzi (D)	254.8	727,386	2854.7	71.9	3.0	0.3	17.3	4.1	3.4	11.3	66.2	51.4	22.6	69.4
District 4	Kathleen M. Rice (D)	110.7	722,351	6525.3	63.4	14.9	0.3	7.3	9.0	5.1	21.2	54.8	51.4	22.9	69.7
District 5	Gregory W. Meeks (D)	51.9	768,316	14803.8	17.1	48.0	0.5	15.1	13.6	5.6	19.0	11.0	52.3	42.8	49.5
District 6	Grace Meng (D)	29.8	729,584	24482.7	41.4	4.2	0.4	40.1	8.9	5.0	20.5	32.9	51.8	50.7	43.2
District 7	Nydia M. Velázquez (D)	16.1	721,505	44814.0	46.9	10.4	0.5	17.7	17.5	6.9	39.4	31.9	50.8	34.2	47.1
District 8	Hakeem S. Jeffries (D)	28.4	773,165	27224.1	30.1	51.0	0.3	5.9	7.7	5.0	17.7	24.5	54.5	32.5	52.6
District 9	Yvette D. Clarke (D)	15.5	720,840	46505.8	36.3	46.5	0.3	7.3	5.1	4.5	11.4	32.8	53.5	38.5	46.8
District 10	Jerrold Nadler (D)	14.0	732,646	52331.9	68.0	3.7	0.3	19.0	5.0	3.9	12.6	62.0	51.6	30.7	44.5
District 11	Nicole Malliotakis (R)	64.9	729,841	11245.6	67.7	8.0	0.2	14.8	5.2	4.1	17.4	58.2	51.5	30.8	62.1
District 12	Carolyn B. Maloney (D)	14.8	721,308	48737.0	70.6	5.3	0.3	14.5	4.6	4.8	14.1	63.4	52.5	26.5	41.7
District 13	Adriano Espaillat (D)	10.2	759,560	74466.7	26.1	29.1	0.7	4.8	31.0	8.4	54.4	14.4	52.6	35.2	47.1
District 14	Alexandria Ocasio Cortez (D)	28.6	686,868	24016.4	40.8	10.8	0.5	17.5	23.9	6.5	49.3	22.3	49.8	45.1	44.7
District 15	Ritchie Torres (D)	14.5	735,959	50755.8	15.8	35.5	0.7	2.2	38.2	7.6	65.7	2.7	52.9	35.0	51.6
District 16	Jamaal Bowman (D)	78.4	745,591	9510.1	42.9	33.0	0.5	5.5	12.4	5.6	26.7	34.4	53.1	29.8	55.6
District 17	Mondaire Jones (D)	382.6	740,776	1936.2	68.4	10.7	0.2	6.0	10.4	4.4	22.0	59.8	50.9	23.2	61.6
District 18	Sean Patrick Maloney (D)	1,354.1	724,007	534.7	75.2	9.9	0.3	3.2	6.3	5.1	17.8	67.0	50.3	12.6	69.8
District 19	Patrick Ryan (D)	7,937.2	697,087	87.8	86.9	4.6	0.2	1.6	2.4	4.2	8.0	82.9	49.9	6.5	74.8
District 20	Paul Tonko (D)	1,231.5	726,000	589.5	78.2	9.3	0.2	5.2	2.1	5.0	6.8	75.0	51.4	9.5	74.3
District 21	Elise M. Stefanik (R)	15,114.3	700,529	46.3	91.4	3.1	0.8	1.1	1.0	2.6	3.5	89.7	48.8	3.4	77.3
District 22	Claudia Tenney (R)	5,077.3	692,234	136.3	88.5	4.0	0.2	2.9	1.1	3.2	4.1	86.6	50.3	5.5	80.5
District 23	Joseph Sempolinski (R)	7,371.9	691,390	93.8	90.1	2.9	0.6	2.3	1.3	2.9	4.1	87.9	50.3	4.1	74.4
District 24	John Katko (R)	2,388.6	702,143	294.0	83.4	8.3	0.4	2.8	1.1	4.2	4.7	81.1	51.2	5.9	79.3
District 25	Joseph D. Morelle (D)	510.1	716,440	1404.5	73.9	15.6	0.3	3.9	2.2	4.2	9.4	69.1	51.9	8.7	73.2
District 26	Brian Higgins (D)	219.2	707,963	3229.8	70.5	17.6	0.4	4.6	2.6	4.2	6.9	67.9	52.3	8.5	78.7
District 27	Chris Jacobs (R)	3,972.9	715,117	180.0	92.5	2.7	0.6	1.0	1.0	2.2	2.8	91.0	50.0	3.3	85.2
NORTH CAROLINA		48,623.0	10,386,227	213.6	67.6	21.4	1.2	3.0	3.2	3.6	9.5	62.6	51.4	8.0	56.0
District 1	G. K. Butterfield (D)	5,871.5	760,016	129.4	46.8	43.5	0.8	2.1	3.0	3.8	9.2	42.1	52.4	7.4	64.5
District 2	Deborah K. Ross (D)	2,698.0	865,706	320.9	70.0	19.2	0.5	2.2	3.8	4.2	10.1	65.3	51.1	7.3	52.9
District 3	Gregory F. Murphy (R)	7,218.1	760,373	105.3	71.7	19.9	0.4	1.6	1.8	4.5	8.2	67.0	48.9	4.0	51.9
District 4	David E. Price (D)	732.4	866,455	1183.0	60.0	22.3	0.4	9.4	3.9	4.1	10.3	55.3	51.5	15.4	42.6
District 5	Virginia Foxx (R)	3,969.2	761,079	191.7	77.8	14.6	0.4	1.7	2.3	3.3	9.9	71.9	51.5	6.3	64.3
District 6	Kathy E. Manning (D)	3,910.8	777,809	198.9	70.3	20.4	0.4	1.9	3.7	3.3	10.3	64.8	51.8	7.1	63.4
District 7	David Rouzer (R)	5,946.9	807,268	135.7	74.0	18.4	0.8	0.9	2.7	3.2	9.7	67.9	51.5	5.8	59.4
District 8	Richard Hudson (R)	2,954.1	798,557	270.3	64.4	23.4	1.2	2.9	3.4	4.8	10.7	59.0	50.6	6.8	53.2
District 9	Dan Bishop (R)	3,874.7	788,078	203.4	64.3	19.0	7.8	3.2	2.7	3.1	7.9	59.9	51.4	7.6	56.5
District 10	Patrick T. McHenry (R)	2,590.3	765,741	295.6	80.3	12.0	0.3	1.9	2.4	3.1	6.8	76.7	51.8	4.9	63.9
District 11	Madison Cawthorn (R)	6,604.8	765,533	115.9	89.5	3.3	1.5	1.3	2.0	2.5	6.4	85.8	51.1	4.5	59.4
District 12	Alma S. Adams (D)	420.0	885,774	2109.0	45.1	37.3	0.4	5.9	7.1	4.1	15.3	38.9	51.9	16.6	41.5
District 13	Ted Budd (R)	1,832.2	783,838	427.8	68.3	22.2	0.4	3.6	2.2	3.3	8.2	63.6	51.9	8.3	59.2
NORTH DAKOTA		68,995.9	760,394	11.0	85.7	3.2	5.2	1.7	1.2	3.1	4.0	83.7	48.8	4.3	62.2
At Large	Kelly Armstrong (R)	68,995.9	760,394	11.0	85.7	3.2	5.2	1.7	1.2	3.1	4.0	83.7	48.8	4.3	62.2
OHIO		40,858.8	11,675,275	285.7	80.5	12.4	0.2	2.3	1.1	3.6	3.9	78.3	51.0	4.6	74.9
District 1	Steve Chabot (R)	686.7	747,788	1089.0	69.9	21.7	0.1	3.8	1.1	3.4	3.4	67.9	51.1	6.4	71.2
District 2	Brad R. Wenstrup (R)	3,221.4	729,324	226.4	86.2	8.4	0.2	1.7	0.6	2.9	2.2	84.8	51.3	3.1	74.3
District 3	Joyce Beatty (D)	228.1	797,029	3494.2	52.8	34.4	0.2	4.6	2.7	5.3	7.0	49.5	51.6	12.3	65.5
District 4	Jim Jordan (R)	4,665.4	710,636	152.3	89.4	5.0	0.2	1.0	0.8	3.6	4.1	86.8	50.0	1.9	82.5
District 5	Robert E. Latta (R)	5,626.1	722,437	128.4	90.7	2.8	0.2	1.4	1.5	3.3	5.6	87.8	50.9	2.8	79.1
District 6	Bill Johnson (R)	7,214.6	692,579	96.0	94.6	2.2	0.1	0.5	0.4	2.1	1.2	93.9	50.0	1.1	69.7
District 7	Bob Gibbs (R)	3,864.9	731,042	189.1	91.7	4.0	0.1	0.6	0.6	2.9	2.5	90.1	50.9	1.9	83.6
District 8	Warren Davidson (R)	2,449.4	732,249	299.0	87.3	5.9	0.1	2.1	0.9	3.7	3.6	84.8	50.9	4.2	74.3
District 9	Marcy Kaptur (D)	463.0	704,685	1522.0	72.7	16.2	0.4	1.8	3.2	5.7	11.3	67.2	51.3	4.9	75.4
District 10	Michael R. Turner (R)	1,129.4	723,673	640.8	75.5	16.8	0.2	2.4	1.1	4.1	3.1	73.8	51.6	4.8	69.5
District 11	Shontel M. Brown (D)	244.6	686,269	2805.7	39.3	52.3	0.2	2.5	1.6	4.1	4.5	37.1	53.3	5.5	73.7
District 12	Troy Balderson (R)	2,271.9	789,894	347.7	85.8	4.9	0.1	4.9	0.6	3.6	2.7	84.3	50.5	6.2	72.1
District 13	Tim Ryan (D)	894.0	705,582	789.2	81.5	11.7	0.2	2.1	0.7	3.8	3.4	79.6	51.5	3.6	76.5
District 14	David P. Joyce (R)	1,955.2	715,868	366.1	89.4	4.7	0.1	2.3	0.7	2.7	3.1	87.5	50.9	5.1	76.6
District 15	Mike Carey (R)	4,738.8	768,439	162.2	89.2	4.3	0.1	2.5	0.6	3.2	2.4	87.9	49.4	4.1	76.8
District 16	Anthony Gonzalez (R)	1,205.3	717,781	595.5	92.0	2.4	0.1	2.3	0.7	2.4	2.8	90.3	50.9	5.5	78.1
OKLAHOMA		68,596.6	3,949,342	57.6	71.1	7.3	7.7	2.4	2.8	8.7	10.9	64.9	50.5	6.0	60.7
District 1	Kevin Hern (R)	1,632.2	806,758	494.3	69.9	8.7	6.0	3.3	3.1	9.0	11.8	63.1	51.1	8.0	58.3
District 2	Markwayne Mullin (R)	20,996.5	749,583	35.7	65.4	3.2	17.5	0.9	1.7	11.4	5.6	62.9	50.3	2.3	61.2
District 3	Frank D. Lucas (R)	34,116.4	778,830	22.8	78.3	3.7	5.8	1.8	3.3	7.1	10.4	72.9	49.4	5.1	64.3
District 4	Tom Cole (R)	9,777.5	792,809	81.1	74.4	6.9	5.4	2.5	2.1	8.7	9.1	69.5	50.2	4.6	60.4
District 5	Stephanie I. Bice (R)	2,074.0	821,362	396.0	67.7	13.5	4.4	3.2	3.6	7.6	17.2	56.3	51.1	9.8	59.7
OREGON		95,995.9	4,176,346	43.5	82.6	1.9	1.1	4.9	3.4	6.2	13.2	74.9	50.4	9.8	45.9
District 1	Suzanne Bonamici (D)	3,007.1	851,961	283.3	77.5	1.8	0.7	8.8	4.4	6.7	14.9	69.4	50.4	14.8	43.1
District 2	Cliff Bentz (R)	69,451.2	828,446	11.9	88.7	0.7	1.9	1.3	2.3	5.1	14.2	79.0	50.1	5.9	44.7

1. Dry land or land partially or temporarily covered by water. 2. May be of any race.

Table E. Congressional Districts 116th Congress — **Age and Education**

STATE District	Population and population characteristics, 2016–2020 (cont.)										Education, 2016–2020		
	Age (percent)										Total Enrollment[1]	Attainment[2] (percent)	
	Under 5 years	5 to 17 years	18 to 24 years	25 to 34 years	35 to 44 years	45 to 54 years	55 to 64 years	65 to 74 years	75 years and over	Median age		High school graduate or more	Bachelor's degree or more
	15	16	17	18	19	20	21	22	23	24	25	26	27
NEW MEXICO—Cont'd													
District 3	5.7	17.7	8.6	12.8	12.1	11.6	13.4	11.0	7.1	37.7	173,043	87.7	27.8
NEW YORK	5.8	15.1	9.2	14.6	12.5	13.0	13.3	9.4	7.2	37.5	4,656,339	87.2	37.5
District 1	5.1	15.6	9.4	11.5	11.4	14.6	14.3	10.7	7.6	41.0	173,188	92.1	37.1
District 2	5.8	15.6	9.1	13.0	12.4	14.6	14.4	8.4	6.6	38.7	170,061	88.5	33.2
District 3	5.2	16.2	7.5	9.6	11.2	14.5	15.0	10.6	10.1	43.3	176,086	92.9	54.4
District 4	5.8	16.0	8.9	12.6	12.4	13.5	13.8	9.6	7.4	39.1	179,837	90.0	43.7
District 5	6.0	15.5	9.3	14.5	12.0	13.6	14.0	8.8	6.3	36.6	195,422	83.0	27.0
District 6	6.2	13.2	6.6	15.0	13.1	13.9	14.2	9.8	7.9	40.1	156,131	83.7	38.2
District 7	7.3	15.8	8.4	20.3	14.7	11.7	10.2	6.9	4.9	33.2	174,607	74.9	36.6
District 8	6.4	14.6	8.7	17.8	13.3	12.0	12.0	8.3	7.0	34.6	182,523	86.0	35.3
District 9	6.5	15.0	7.6	17.6	13.7	12.3	12.1	9.1	6.1	35.3	173,840	86.8	40.1
District 10	6.9	12.6	8.5	18.9	14.4	11.8	11.3	8.8	6.9	36.5	168,402	89.0	62.8
District 11	6.2	15.8	7.9	13.9	12.7	13.5	13.5	9.5	7.1	38.0	175,425	86.6	36.7
District 12	4.6	7.5	8.7	26.8	15.1	11.0	10.1	8.6	7.5	36.4	121,222	94.2	73.2
District 13	6.1	14.0	9.0	20.0	13.8	12.7	11.1	7.5	5.8	33.7	184,435	76.1	32.6
District 14	6.3	14.3	7.6	17.3	15.5	13.2	11.5	7.7	6.3	36.5	156,297	78.7	28.0
District 15	7.7	19.6	11.0	16.1	12.5	12.3	10.4	6.1	4.2	29.7	217,183	67.6	14.2
District 16	5.9	16.2	8.9	12.5	12.7	13.6	12.6	9.2	8.4	38.1	190,334	85.4	40.7
District 17	6.7	17.6	9.2	11.5	12.0	13.5	13.1	9.0	7.3	37.5	199,395	89.1	47.5
District 18	5.6	17.1	10.0	11.5	11.7	14.3	14.0	9.1	6.7	38.3	185,328	91.0	37.0
District 19	4.6	13.8	9.4	11.2	10.9	13.7	15.8	11.9	8.4	43.5	147,736	90.7	30.9
District 20	5.3	14.2	11.6	13.7	11.8	12.6	13.5	10.0	7.3	37.7	176,833	92.2	39.8
District 21	5.3	14.7	10.1	12.6	11.6	13.1	14.4	10.6	7.5	39.3	150,130	89.7	24.7
District 22	5.3	14.9	11.4	11.7	10.7	12.7	14.6	10.5	8.3	39.6	164,666	90.0	25.8
District 23	5.2	14.8	11.9	11.7	10.8	12.2	14.6	10.9	8.0	39.3	169,042	90.4	27.0
District 24	5.6	15.6	9.9	12.8	11.2	13.0	14.5	10.0	7.4	38.8	170,883	90.5	31.5
District 25	5.4	15.4	10.0	14.2	11.4	12.6	13.7	9.9	7.5	37.4	177,647	90.6	39.1
District 26	5.7	14.6	10.0	15.7	11.2	11.9	13.7	9.7	7.5	36.6	168,151	90.6	32.9
District 27	5.0	15.0	8.0	11.6	11.2	14.1	15.8	11.2	8.1	42.5	151,535	93.3	31.7
NORTH CAROLINA	5.8	16.4	9.5	13.4	12.6	13.2	13.0	9.8	6.5	37.4	2,521,615	88.5	32.0
District 1	5.7	15.3	11.1	14.2	11.9	12.1	13.2	9.8	6.7	36.2	192,661	85.2	29.4
District 2	6.4	19.1	7.5	12.0	14.0	14.7	12.4	8.7	5.2	37.7	228,245	91.0	37.4
District 3	6.2	15.3	12.0	13.6	11.2	11.4	13.0	10.4	6.9	34.5	172,530	89.0	24.8
District 4	5.7	15.8	11.7	16.6	14.4	13.2	11.1	7.1	4.3	34.1	241,212	93.1	55.9
District 5	5.2	15.6	10.2	12.0	11.5	13.4	13.8	10.6	7.6	39.5	182,194	86.5	27.0
District 6	5.7	16.8	8.6	11.6	11.9	13.9	14.0	10.4	7.3	39.9	184,041	86.6	25.5
District 7	5.4	15.3	9.1	11.9	11.8	12.4	14.2	12.4	7.5	40.4	180,669	88.0	27.2
District 8	6.7	17.3	9.8	14.5	12.6	12.3	11.9	8.8	6.1	34.1	202,371	89.8	27.6
District 9	6.0	18.7	8.3	11.4	12.9	14.5	12.9	9.0	6.2	38.2	202,311	88.3	35.3
District 10	5.4	15.6	8.0	12.3	12.1	13.7	14.1	11.2	7.5	40.9	164,923	87.4	25.7
District 11	4.8	14.0	7.8	11.4	11.3	13.1	14.6	13.3	9.5	43.7	152,125	87.6	26.5
District 12	6.8	16.8	9.8	18.5	15.0	13.0	10.3	6.3	3.5	33.0	225,198	89.0	41.4
District 13	5.5	16.2	9.7	13.1	11.9	13.8	13.1	9.8	7.0	38.5	193,135	88.5	29.7
NORTH DAKOTA	7.0	16.4	11.2	15.2	11.9	10.7	12.4	8.4	6.9	34.3	185,329	93.1	30.7
At Large	7.0	16.4	11.2	15.2	11.9	10.7	12.4	8.4	6.9	34.3	185,329	93.1	30.7
OHIO	5.9	16.3	9.1	13.2	11.9	12.7	13.8	9.9	7.2	38.0	2,771,293	90.8	28.9
District 1	6.6	17.4	9.7	13.7	12.1	12.6	13.1	8.8	6.0	35.5	191,343	91.5	36.3
District 2	5.9	16.5	7.6	13.7	12.5	12.9	14.0	9.8	7.2	38.5	161,432	90.3	32.7
District 3	7.5	16.9	11.1	18.6	13.1	11.3	11.1	6.5	4.1	32.0	210,201	88.0	29.1
District 4	5.9	16.4	8.9	11.9	12.0	12.8	14.3	10.4	7.4	39.7	164,815	91.0	18.9
District 5	5.9	16.6	9.7	12.2	11.5	12.3	14.1	10.1	7.6	38.5	177,266	93.3	27.3
District 6	5.2	15.6	7.8	11.4	11.4	13.1	15.3	11.6	8.5	41.9	144,937	89.0	16.9
District 7	6.0	17.4	8.1	11.5	11.6	12.9	13.9	10.6	7.9	39.5	164,589	88.9	21.4
District 8	6.1	17.2	10.3	11.7	11.8	12.7	13.4	9.7	7.0	37.7	183,951	91.0	25.5
District 9	6.0	15.9	9.2	14.5	11.8	12.6	13.7	9.7	6.7	37.3	162,134	87.8	23.5
District 10	6.0	15.8	9.8	13.6	11.5	12.1	13.5	10.1	7.6	37.0	181,631	91.1	30.5
District 11	6.1	15.3	9.9	14.5	11.2	11.9	14.0	9.6	7.4	36.3	167,920	88.4	28.7
District 12	6.1	17.1	8.6	12.9	13.5	13.6	12.7	9.3	6.2	37.7	197,873	93.8	42.4
District 13	5.3	14.3	10.4	13.3	11.2	12.5	14.3	10.7	8.1	39.3	158,107	90.3	23.5
District 14	5.2	16.0	7.5	10.7	11.5	13.6	15.3	11.6	8.6	42.5	157,502	92.4	35.2
District 15	5.7	15.9	9.4	14.7	13.0	13.3	12.9	9.0	6.2	37.1	185,780	91.4	33.1
District 16	5.3	15.7	8.0	11.6	11.4	13.3	14.8	11.2	8.7	41.4	161,812	93.8	34.9
OKLAHOMA	6.6	17.6	9.7	13.8	12.5	11.7	12.4	9.1	6.6	35.5	992,436	88.6	26.1
District 1	6.9	18.1	8.7	14.4	12.9	12.0	12.2	8.7	6.2	35.3	202,372	90.1	30.8
District 2	6.2	17.2	8.8	12.1	11.6	12.1	13.4	10.7	8.0	38.5	171,942	86.1	17.7
District 3	6.3	17.7	10.5	13.1	12.3	11.4	12.6	9.1	6.9	35.7	200,559	88.5	23.4
District 4	6.0	17.2	11.3	14.0	12.7	11.5	12.3	8.9	6.2	34.8	206,009	90.3	26.4
District 5	7.3	18.1	9.0	15.4	12.9	11.5	11.9	8.2	5.6	34.1	211,554	87.6	31.9
OREGON	5.5	15.3	8.7	14.2	13.4	12.3	13.0	10.7	6.9	38.5	948,174	91.1	34.4
District 1	5.7	16.2	8.2	15.2	14.6	13.0	12.3	9.0	5.8	37.0	201,460	92.6	42.2
District 2	5.6	15.9	7.6	12.7	12.0	11.7	13.9	12.5	8.2	40.6	175,108	89.7	26.6

1. All persons 3 years old and over enrolled in nursery school through college and graduate or professional school. 2. Persons 25 years old and over.

Table E. Congressional Districts 116th Congress — **Households and Group Quarters**

STATE District	Households, 2016–2020						Total in group quarters, 2020	Persons in group quarters, 2020				
	Number	Average household size	Family households (percent)	Married couple family (percent)	Female family house-holder[1]	One person households (percent)		Correctional facilities for adults	Juvenile facilities	Skilled nursing facilities	College/ University student housing	Military quarters
	28	29	30	31	32	33	34	35	36	37	38	39
NEW MEXICO—Cont'd												
District 3	258,539	2.65	64.4	44.4	14.2	29.9	10,303	3,168	239	1,762	1,992	496
NEW YORK	7,417,224	2.55	63.0	44.0	14.0	29.8	608,783	62,707	5,113	111,115	226,149	5,649
District 1	249,909	2.79	71.4	57.1	9.9	23.4	20,271	598	125	4,961	9,904	10
District 2	225,709	3.12	75.4	57.6	12.4	20.2	7,553	0	111	2,420	272	0
District 3	253,192	2.82	74.9	62.5	8.7	21.7	12,934	0	164	5,612	2,835	14
District 4	237,721	2.99	75.7	57.6	13.4	20.3	12,496	577	84	3,730	4,401	35
District 5	232,637	3.24	75.5	45.3	22.6	20.9	16,622	214	157	4,919	2,777	0
District 6	268,643	2.69	67.2	49.5	12.4	27.1	8,184	0	40	3,295	1,240	0
District 7	257,614	2.75	60.7	38.8	16.0	26.4	13,399	3,502	54	1,215	1,470	0
District 8	300,840	2.51	59.8	31.5	22.2	31.2	18,320	0	98	4,200	2,329	0
District 9	284,750	2.50	60.4	35.3	19.5	31.2	12,371	0	212	2,640	703	0
District 10	314,389	2.26	49.6	39.4	7.1	40.6	32,188	833	50	1,695	17,957	0
District 11	262,414	2.75	71.0	52.3	13.7	24.8	9,630	0	63	3,271	1,198	62
District 12	364,349	1.91	39.3	31.4	5.7	46.4	31,450	540	85	1,478	14,819	0
District 13	291,619	2.55	54.1	23.4	24.2	36.6	22,379	146	42	4,331	3,758	0
District 14	239,693	2.80	64.6	40.6	16.3	27.9	15,277	3,786	65	4,496	2,207	0
District 15	256,867	2.78	65.4	23.6	34.0	30.2	28,341	0	104	1,845	3,248	0
District 16	277,365	2.62	65.2	41.8	17.9	30.7	17,113	29	239	6,910	5,252	0
District 17	249,862	2.88	72.3	57.4	10.7	23.1	20,690	1,948	482	4,745	7,302	0
District 18	255,212	2.74	70.0	54.9	11.2	24.5	28,950	5,428	385	3,169	9,997	1,250
District 19	274,214	2.40	63.4	48.3	10.0	29.7	37,089	8,799	562	4,627	12,469	0
District 20	297,170	2.34	57.7	41.7	11.8	33.4	31,722	832	542	5,159	19,412	0
District 21	280,872	2.35	63.6	47.9	10.5	28.6	36,056	12,332	269	3,960	10,660	4,278
District 22	277,553	2.38	62.2	46.0	11.3	30.3	34,857	4,523	278	7,148	19,230	0
District 23	282,872	2.30	61.1	45.8	10.5	30.7	39,408	5,102	292	5,017	24,003	0
District 24	284,220	2.36	61.6	44.3	12.3	30.2	29,290	2,801	169	6,018	16,231	0
District 25	294,682	2.34	59.6	41.6	13.9	32.4	27,419	1,042	219	5,107	15,686	0
District 26	309,548	2.22	54.9	35.4	14.8	36.9	20,886	585	82	4,111	11,947	0
District 27	293,308	2.36	65.3	51.5	9.5	28.4	23,888	9,090	140	5,036	4,842	0
NORTH CAROLINA	4,031,592	2.51	65.1	47.9	12.8	28.7	285,522	59,099	2,119	48,719	109,150	36,715
District 1	301,542	2.40	60.7	38.5	17.5	32.1	32,656	10,959	204	4,486	12,786	0
District 2	310,785	2.76	73.9	58.2	11.6	21.8	9,980	3,365	85	2,660	2,520	0
District 3	297,319	2.43	66.6	50.5	11.9	27.7	38,697	6,990	127	3,681	898	25,254
District 4	336,166	2.48	59.8	45.3	10.8	30.4	30,804	4,339	56	2,209	21,437	0
District 5	304,931	2.41	64.1	48.3	11.6	30.1	25,700	4,974	201	4,011	14,741	0
District 6	305,649	2.50	67.4	49.2	13.5	27.7	16,209	2,776	171	3,866	7,150	0
District 7	321,712	2.45	64.2	48.0	11.9	29.5	16,446	5,849	68	3,104	4,061	661
District 8	298,020	2.60	67.0	49.2	13.7	28.0	20,545	2,924	423	3,359	1,977	10,800
District 9	287,573	2.69	70.3	52.9	13.0	25.7	16,211	6,522	65	3,683	4,920	0
District 10	303,052	2.48	64.5	47.4	11.8	29.5	16,798	2,846	119	5,726	5,219	0
District 11	315,474	2.38	65.4	50.9	10.4	29.0	17,906	3,779	282	4,814	5,406	0
District 12	339,656	2.57	58.5	39.5	14.3	33.0	15,209	1,584	113	2,273	9,122	0
District 13	309,713	2.46	65.4	46.2	14.0	28.6	28,361	2,192	205	4,847	18,913	0
NORTH DAKOTA	320,873	2.29	59.0	47.6	7.5	32.5	26,250	2,571	172	7,785	11,282	739
At Large	320,873	2.29	59.0	47.6	7.5	32.5	26,250	2,571	172	7,785	11,282	739
OHIO	4,717,226	2.41	62.6	45.5	12.3	30.9	299,628	67,080	2,398	85,112	111,646	330
District 1	297,416	2.44	62.7	44.3	13.8	30.5	22,186	4,753	194	5,326	9,388	0
District 2	300,567	2.39	63.1	47.2	11.6	30.5	10,523	774	87	7,155	770	0
District 3	311,470	2.49	55.9	32.6	17.5	34.3	24,592	2,067	52	2,173	17,312	0
District 4	281,504	2.42	65.2	48.8	11.2	28.9	25,278	13,388	145	5,390	4,858	0
District 5	292,705	2.41	64.8	50.4	9.6	28.9	17,053	866	77	6,022	8,615	0
District 6	275,857	2.43	65.6	50.2	10.3	29.5	20,537	9,748	179	5,789	3,292	0
District 7	284,526	2.52	67.8	52.5	10.7	27.1	13,257	906	362	5,914	3,977	0
District 8	280,708	2.55	67.3	51.4	11.0	26.5	17,281	1,426	88	5,389	9,237	0
District 9	304,086	2.27	55.9	34.4	15.6	36.3	14,167	1,470	166	4,502	4,938	60
District 10	303,007	2.30	60.6	42.5	13.5	32.9	21,603	1,690	121	5,663	11,935	270
District 11	307,663	2.15	51.4	26.7	19.9	41.8	21,518	2,522	351	5,464	8,191	0
District 12	298,333	2.59	67.9	54.3	9.6	25.9	17,665	5,859	102	4,279	6,017	0
District 13	302,948	2.26	57.8	38.9	13.9	35.1	21,167	4,531	140	4,495	9,999	0
District 14	289,564	2.43	66.1	53.0	9.2	28.3	11,287	2,417	19	5,928	1,039	0
District 15	294,083	2.51	65.0	50.3	10.0	27.9	29,351	14,405	248	4,903	8,592	0
District 16	292,789	2.41	66.2	53.5	8.5	28.5	12,163	258	67	6,720	3,486	0
OKLAHOMA	1,493,569	2.57	65.3	48.1	12.2	29.0	117,304	38,455	1,260	23,752	35,150	6,665
District 1	313,057	2.55	63.9	47.0	12.0	30.3	13,464	1,388	172	4,255	4,834	0
District 2	285,320	2.55	68.3	49.8	12.8	27.5	23,279	10,429	371	5,421	4,500	12
District 3	284,172	2.63	66.5	51.3	10.7	28.2	33,167	14,809	181	4,792	10,702	701
District 4	296,206	2.58	66.2	49.4	11.7	27.6	28,912	6,702	313	4,836	9,224	5,952
District 5	314,814	2.55	62.1	43.5	13.7	31.0	18,482	5,127	223	4,448	5,890	0
OREGON	1,642,579	2.49	63.0	48.3	10.1	27.4	96,930	20,434	1,486	14,441	25,364	145
District 1	326,358	2.57	65.3	51.7	9.4	26.0	14,603	3,956	349	2,116	3,447	85
District 2	330,941	2.44	65.6	50.1	10.5	26.4	19,130	9,425	192	3,091	2,038	0

1. No spouse present.

Table E. Congressional Districts 116th Congress — **Housing and Money Income**

STATE District	Housing units, 2016–2020: Total	Housing units, 2016–2020: Occupied units: Occupied units as a percent of all units	Occupied units: Owner-occupied: Owner-occupied units as a percent of occupied units	Owner-occupied: Median value[1] (dollars)	Owner-occupied: Percent valued at $500,000 or more	Renter-occupied: Median rent[2]	Money income, 2016–2020: Per capita income (dollars)	Households: Median income (dollars)	Households: Percent with income of $100,000 or more
	40	41	42	43	44	45	46	47	48
NEW MEXICO—Cont'd									
District 3	319,282	81.0	71.3	191,800	9.5	912	28,357	52,660	23.0
NEW YORK	8,362,971	88.7	54.1	325,000	30.7	1,315	40,898	71,117	36.0
District 1	312,539	80.0	81.1	400,700	30.5	1,838	46,730	101,166	51.2
District 2	240,489	93.9	82.8	403,100	22.3	1,774	42,439	108,089	54.5
District 3	270,228	93.7	82.3	633,100	67.2	1,922	62,427	123,412	59.3
District 4	250,153	95.0	78.0	498,400	49.6	1,786	48,392	113,902	56.6
District 5	248,341	93.7	56.9	488,300	46.8	1,456	30,466	76,306	37.4
District 6	290,834	92.4	47.1	638,200	63.1	1,649	34,971	70,694	35.0
District 7	280,018	92.0	23.0	768,800	78.1	1,510	36,852	63,974	34.0
District 8	326,521	92.1	33.6	633,700	68.3	1,371	34,332	58,878	30.5
District 9	308,061	92.4	30.3	686,600	69.7	1,435	37,666	64,635	33.2
District 10	366,658	85.7	32.0	1,049,300	84.9	1,948	77,566	100,737	50.9
District 11	284,931	92.1	58.1	587,800	62.2	1,463	37,019	78,735	40.7
District 12	443,184	82.2	27.7	1,043,300	84.4	2,268	95,376	114,058	56.2
District 13	313,455	93.0	10.8	509,900	50.9	1,267	29,526	46,570	22.2
District 14	264,734	90.5	31.9	556,900	56.7	1,565	29,356	62,988	29.2
District 15	268,706	95.6	9.5	431,500	35.5	1,138	17,843	32,582	11.5
District 16	291,639	95.1	50.5	478,100	47.1	1,440	46,866	75,001	39.1
District 17	265,105	94.3	66.7	482,300	46.5	1,680	50,052	103,638	52.0
District 18	280,698	90.9	70.6	315,400	18.5	1,317	42,995	89,324	45.2
District 19	367,843	74.5	73.1	212,400	7.5	973	35,748	65,877	31.6
District 20	336,450	88.3	59.8	221,400	5.6	1,034	38,534	70,506	34.6
District 21	379,121	74.1	70.3	151,700	4.5	856	31,170	59,058	25.2
District 22	325,883	85.2	70.1	123,700	2.3	768	30,433	57,414	24.0
District 23	345,993	81.8	69.2	111,700	2.8	792	29,420	54,138	21.4
District 24	319,992	88.8	67.8	140,000	2.4	861	33,322	61,396	27.8
District 25	317,773	92.7	62.7	151,200	2.7	948	35,164	61,516	29.1
District 26	344,707	89.8	59.4	136,400	3.2	829	31,767	52,796	22.7
District 27	318,915	92.0	76.9	165,600	4.1	829	36,667	67,705	32.0
NORTH CAROLINA	4,687,122	86.0	65.7	182,100	7.7	932	31,993	56,642	25.1
District 1	348,718	86.5	58.0	150,900	4.5	860	27,718	47,009	19.9
District 2	337,944	92.0	74.2	230,900	8.9	979	35,830	73,565	36.6
District 3	388,133	76.6	65.5	165,400	4.8	898	28,474	53,153	20.7
District 4	366,518	91.7	56.9	290,900	16.1	1,193	42,147	76,451	37.8
District 5	369,918	82.4	68.5	156,900	4.9	776	29,144	50,083	20.1
District 6	339,962	89.9	69.6	154,900	5.6	779	29,857	53,515	23.0
District 7	401,028	80.2	68.7	172,100	7.3	888	29,919	52,578	21.8
District 8	346,184	86.1	65.1	168,600	4.7	922	29,131	55,544	23.2
District 9	320,051	89.9	72.2	213,300	13.4	920	37,445	64,457	32.2
District 10	349,472	86.7	68.1	165,100	6.9	817	28,990	51,889	21.0
District 11	405,071	77.9	72.6	178,100	6.9	774	28,750	49,951	19.3
District 12	368,596	92.1	52.6	219,500	10.5	1,171	35,384	63,457	29.6
District 13	345,527	89.6	64.4	168,200	6.3	863	30,818	54,171	22.8
NORTH DAKOTA	376,597	85.2	62.5	199,900	5.8	828	36,289	65,315	29.6
At Large	376,597	85.2	62.5	199,900	5.8	828	36,289	65,315	29.6
OHIO	5,217,090	90.4	66.3	151,400	3.7	825	32,465	58,116	25.3
District 1	327,092	90.9	61.7	175,300	7.1	832	35,679	62,488	30.3
District 2	329,551	91.2	67.3	162,800	5.9	818	36,289	61,573	29.0
District 3	341,112	91.3	46.3	143,600	2.8	938	27,021	50,777	19.1
District 4	311,652	90.3	71.2	132,400	2.2	739	29,213	57,000	22.2
District 5	315,461	92.8	72.7	146,400	2.3	761	33,124	62,037	26.4
District 6	322,996	85.4	74.8	117,700	1.9	683	27,376	50,613	18.5
District 7	309,413	92.0	74.1	150,200	2.8	742	29,354	58,946	24.0
District 8	305,573	91.9	70.2	156,900	2.6	827	31,158	62,662	27.3
District 9	352,701	86.2	58.4	109,300	2.7	767	27,904	46,338	17.8
District 10	336,686	90.0	62.4	137,000	2.4	823	32,167	56,257	24.5
District 11	363,006	84.8	48.7	98,100	4.1	793	29,922	40,179	17.2
District 12	322,551	92.5	71.4	229,500	7.7	968	40,083	77,048	38.6
District 13	337,585	89.7	63.9	105,300	1.1	757	27,381	47,550	17.0
District 14	312,862	92.6	77.4	187,900	5.4	910	39,479	70,585	33.2
District 15	319,823	92.0	68.9	182,400	5.3	968	34,460	67,364	31.0
District 16	309,026	94.7	75.4	174,300	3.1	885	37,938	70,976	33.0
OKLAHOMA	1,740,972	85.8	66.1	142,400	4.0	818	29,873	53,840	22.7
District 1	350,863	89.2	62.7	159,700	4.8	876	35,345	58,084	26.3
District 2	358,984	79.5	71.5	110,000	3.0	686	24,559	45,165	15.9
District 3	339,167	83.8	70.7	132,100	3.1	762	27,674	53,724	22.5
District 4	337,277	87.8	65.9	150,000	2.8	847	29,811	59,180	24.7
District 5	354,681	88.8	60.4	154,500	6.3	865	31,493	54,297	24.1
OREGON	1,788,855	91.8	62.8	336,700	21.4	1,173	35,393	65,667	30.6
District 1	348,275	93.7	62.1	395,800	28.0	1,382	41,099	81,705	40.7
District 2	377,106	87.8	66.0	276,400	16.5	977	30,942	57,156	23.8

1. Specified owner-occupied units. 2. Specified renter-occupied units.

Table E. Congressional Districts 116th Congress — **Poverty, Labor Force, Employment, and Social Security**

STATE District	Poverty, 2016–2020: Persons below poverty level (percent)	Poverty, 2016–2020: Families below poverty level (percent)	Poverty, 2016–2020: Percent of households receiving food stamps in past 12 months	Civilian labor force, 2016–2020: Total	Civilian labor force, 2016–2020: Unemployment: Total	Civilian labor force, 2016–2020: Unemployment: Rate[1]	Civilian employment,[2] 2016–2020: Total	Civilian employment,[2] 2016–2020: Percent: Management, business, science, and arts occupations	Civilian employment,[2] 2016–2020: Percent: Service, sales, and office	Civilian employment,[2] 2016–2020: Percent: Construction and production	Persons under 65 years of age with no health insurance, 2016–2020 (percent)	Social Security beneficiaries, December 2021: Number	Social Security beneficiaries, December 2021: Rate[3]	Supplemental Security Income recipients, December 2021
	49	50	51	52	53	54	55	56	57	58	59	60	61	62
NEW MEXICO—Cont'd														
District 3	18.4	14.2	16.2	309,120	21,400	6.9	287,720	38.4	41.5	20.2	12.4	157,018	225.5	18,744
NEW YORK	13.6	10.0	14.3	10,009,209	570,570	5.7	9,438,639	42.6	40.5	16.8	6.3	3,680,521	188.6	583,442
District 1	6.7	4.5	5.4	370,792	17,066	4.6	353,726	42.2	39.9	18.0	4.8	156,242	218.4	9,045
District 2	6.1	4.1	6.4	391,705	18,006	4.6	373,699	38.1	42.0	19.9	5.0	137,395	193.3	8,837
District 3	5.3	3.6	3.8	368,256	14,729	4.0	353,527	53.4	35.7	10.9	3.9	149,671	205.8	6,743
District 4	5.8	4.1	4.7	384,077	15,744	4.1	368,333	45.3	39.4	15.3	5.5	139,674	193.4	8,902
District 5	10.8	8.2	15.9	395,122	29,143	7.4	365,979	31.3	47.5	21.2	8.4	115,546	150.4	26,383
District 6	11.8	9.6	10.3	376,572	18,686	5.0	357,886	39.7	43.2	17.0	10.1	123,253	168.9	18,117
District 7	22.3	18.8	23.7	368,627	22,807	6.2	345,820	42.6	42.2	15.2	9.2	88,996	123.3	29,208
District 8	20.3	16.1	24.3	380,560	28,483	7.5	352,077	41.9	42.9	15.2	6.7	113,212	146.4	44,631
District 9	15.6	12.2	20.3	374,852	23,927	6.4	350,925	45.7	41.2	13.1	7.4	105,372	146.2	27,496
District 10	14.8	11.1	10.8	406,509	20,189	5.0	386,320	61.3	31.1	7.6	5.1	104,823	143.1	19,045
District 11	12.1	9.5	13.8	353,264	18,782	5.3	334,482	42.0	41.0	17.0	5.7	132,386	181.4	26,243
District 12	10.0	5.8	6.1	458,627	19,615	4.3	439,012	69.6	25.9	4.5	4.5	105,891	146.8	12,971
District 13	24.9	22.5	28.8	393,952	36,299	9.2	357,653	38.2	47.1	14.7	8.9	111,490	146.8	50,801
District 14	13.7	10.8	16.3	360,217	22,177	6.2	338,040	31.0	46.9	22.1	11.9	96,607	140.6	17,425
District 15	34.3	30.4	45.1	321,517	37,582	11.7	283,935	20.6	59.1	20.2	9.7	98,026	133.2	66,389
District 16	11.8	8.8	14.5	377,268	25,182	6.7	352,086	43.3	42.1	14.6	6.9	127,348	170.8	20,282
District 17	10.3	6.5	7.6	379,250	21,056	5.6	358,194	48.5	37.8	13.6	6.1	130,550	176.2	9,324
District 18	9.3	6.1	7.7	366,971	17,247	4.7	349,724	41.8	40.0	18.1	5.2	139,638	192.9	11,228
District 19	11.8	7.6	9.8	348,616	18,043	5.2	330,573	38.7	39.5	21.8	6.1	172,770	247.8	14,011
District 20	11.1	6.9	10.8	386,704	19,490	5.0	367,214	45.9	38.8	15.4	3.8	156,253	215.2	17,742
District 21	12.7	8.5	13.5	328,574	16,669	5.1	311,905	35.4	41.0	23.7	5.6	177,659	253.6	18,535
District 22	14.5	9.7	14.9	334,653	18,778	5.6	315,875	37.6	40.6	21.8	4.7	169,121	244.3	20,686
District 23	15.2	9.4	14.2	331,299	17,039	5.1	314,260	37.6	38.2	24.2	6.6	170,108	246.0	18,527
District 24	13.9	9.8	13.7	353,189	19,512	5.5	333,677	39.6	40.2	20.2	4.6	160,278	228.3	19,253
District 25	14.3	9.9	14.8	372,857	19,979	5.4	352,878	45.7	38.3	16.0	3.9	160,294	223.7	25,358
District 26	17.3	12.4	18.3	359,678	19,372	5.4	340,306	39.4	42.9	17.8	3.9	156,948	221.7	26,936
District 27	8.3	5.5	8.4	365,501	14,968	4.1	350,533	40.0	37.4	22.6	3.7	180,970	253.1	9,324
NORTH CAROLINA	14.0	10.0	12.0	5,112,231	278,344	5.4	4,833,887	38.9	37.7	23.4	12.6	2,202,898	212.1	221,382
District 1	19.6	14.6	17.5	363,756	24,774	6.8	338,982	37.8	37.6	24.6	13.5	174,617	229.8	28,357
District 2	9.9	7.1	9.2	435,287	22,969	5.3	412,318	45.1	35.5	19.5	10.5	123,344	142.5	9,372
District 3	13.8	10.2	13.2	331,461	22,537	6.8	308,924	34.1	40.4	25.5	13.0	177,645	233.6	17,656
District 4	10.2	5.8	6.4	487,960	19,573	4.0	468,387	53.9	33.4	12.7	9.5	153,841	177.6	12,946
District 5	16.1	10.8	11.6	366,782	19,380	5.3	347,402	36.2	37.9	25.9	13.1	187,246	246.0	17,936
District 6	15.0	11.5	13.7	378,456	19,938	5.3	358,518	34.5	37.5	28.0	12.6	155,846	200.4	19,050
District 7	16.1	11.1	13.5	376,023	20,866	5.5	355,157	34.2	40.0	25.8	14.8	208,736	258.6	18,232
District 8	14.1	10.5	12.2	362,940	22,200	6.1	340,740	35.6	39.1	25.4	11.5	153,991	192.8	19,290
District 9	13.8	10.5	13.8	375,500	20,708	5.5	354,792	42.5	35.5	22.0	10.6	154,406	195.9	17,710
District 10	13.8	10.0	12.6	375,745	21,036	5.6	354,709	33.5	38.1	28.4	13.1	188,501	246.2	14,594
District 11	14.0	9.5	10.6	359,169	16,800	4.7	342,369	32.6	40.8	26.6	16.1	223,714	292.2	15,580
District 12	12.4	9.0	9.9	503,295	25,075	5.0	478,220	42.3	38.1	19.6	14.2	116,680	131.7	15,097
District 13	14.5	10.7	12.4	395,857	22,488	5.7	373,369	35.9	38.2	25.9	12.2	184,331	235.2	15,562
NORTH DAKOTA	10.5	6.2	6.6	414,440	12,861	3.1	401,579	38.3	37.1	24.7	8.5	140,668	185.0	8,005
At Large	10.5	6.2	6.6	414,440	12,861	3.1	401,579	38.3	37.1	24.7	8.5	140,668	185.0	8,005
OHIO	13.6	9.6	12.6	5,917,459	313,829	5.3	5,603,630	37.6	38.0	24.4	7.3	2,409,265	206.4	297,360
District 1	13.7	9.4	11.6	384,372	20,726	5.4	363,646	42.6	37.8	19.6	6.3	134,987	180.5	18,713
District 2	13.0	9.4	11.8	369,689	16,593	4.5	353,096	41.5	36.7	21.8	6.4	151,749	208.1	20,080
District 3	20.1	15.7	15.7	424,000	26,467	6.2	397,533	36.5	41.0	22.5	11.0	105,139	131.9	27,441
District 4	11.8	8.5	11.1	350,890	16,722	4.8	334,168	30.0	35.8	34.2	6.6	160,432	225.8	14,498
District 5	10.2	6.5	8.4	378,287	16,867	4.5	361,420	35.1	35.4	29.5	5.6	157,982	218.7	10,282
District 6	15.0	10.9	15.0	314,589	17,314	5.5	297,275	30.1	38.8	31.0	8.2	174,430	251.9	22,504
District 7	11.6	8.1	11.2	361,457	15,823	4.4	345,634	32.2	37.4	30.4	10.4	164,310	224.8	13,933
District 8	11.4	7.6	10.4	367,772	17,670	4.8	350,102	34.8	37.8	27.4	6.7	150,543	205.6	14,409
District 9	19.7	15.1	19.2	358,080	26,794	7.5	331,286	32.5	41.3	26.1	7.9	143,507	203.6	28,608
District 10	14.9	10.7	13.1	358,359	21,340	6.0	337,019	39.2	38.8	22.0	7.3	149,492	206.6	18,757
District 11	24.4	18.9	24.2	335,360	33,045	9.9	302,315	38.1	42.6	19.3	7.1	135,572	197.5	38,391
District 12	8.9	5.7	8.4	412,056	14,339	3.5	397,717	47.5	35.3	17.3	6.1	146,780	185.8	13,352
District 13	17.1	12.8	16.3	356,274	23,433	6.6	332,841	31.1	42.4	26.5	7.4	164,485	233.1	25,746
District 14	8.3	5.6	7.2	372,044	16,893	4.5	355,151	41.9	36.3	21.8	6.9	165,142	230.7	9,597
District 15	11.6	7.5	10.5	393,974	15,526	3.9	378,448	42.4	36.0	21.6	6.1	139,646	181.7	13,882
District 16	7.0	4.5	5.8	380,256	14,277	3.8	365,979	42.4	36.2	21.4	6.5	165,069	230.0	7,167
OKLAHOMA	15.3	11.2	12.6	1,874,598	95,441	5.1	1,779,157	35.6	39.1	25.3	16.9	813,941	206.1	94,181
District 1	13.7	10.4	11.4	409,330	21,750	5.3	387,580	38.1	39.4	22.5	16.0	157,199	194.9	17,801
District 2	18.7	14.3	16.5	316,831	18,992	6.0	297,839	30.3	39.0	30.7	22.1	186,952	249.4	25,502
District 3	15.0	10.3	11.0	362,795	16,130	4.4	346,665	33.7	38.4	28.0	15.7	161,878	207.8	14,065
District 4	13.0	9.0	10.9	380,517	18,984	5.0	361,533	37.0	38.8	24.2	14.4	160,768	202.8	16,024
District 5	16.1	12.2	13.3	405,125	19,585	4.8	385,540	37.5	40.0	22.5	16.8	147,144	179.1	20,789
OREGON	12.4	7.8	15.0	2,130,784	116,297	5.5	2,014,487	40.4	38.3	21.3	7.9	910,086	217.9	85,300
District 1	9.0	5.7	10.3	458,472	19,945	4.4	438,527	45.4	35.8	18.9	6.4	150,192	176.3	11,658
District 2	13.2	8.9	17.6	388,711	23,024	5.9	365,687	34.9	41.0	24.1	9.2	217,526	262.6	17,633

1. Percent of civilian labor force. 2. Persons 16 years old and over. 3. Per 1,000 resident population estimated in the 2016–2020 American Community Survey.

STATE District	Agriculture 2017									
	Number of farms	Land in farms			Value of products sold				Government payments	
		Acres	Average size of farm (acres)	Irrigated land (acres)	Total ($1,000)	Average per farm (dollars)	Percent from crops	Percent from livestock and poultry products	Total ($1,000)	Average per farm receiving payments (dollars)
	63	64	65	66	67	68	69	70	71	72
NEW MEXICO—Cont'd										
District 3	13,012	18,404,082	1,414	395,435	956,793	73,532	15.9	84.1	35,472	17,825
NEW YORK	33,438	6,866,171	205	3,581,095	5,369,212	160,572	39.3	60.7	59,106	9,162
District 1	466	25,862	55	16,618	199,192	427,451	90.1	9.9	76	6,333
District 2	42	432	10	120	2,985	71,071	81.0	19.0	D	D
District 3	78	4,488	58	2,845	26,075	334,295	87.7	12.3	D	D
District 4	7	207	30	22	95	13,571	100	0	D	D
District 5	X	X	X	X	X	X	X	X	X	X
District 6	3	D	D	D	58	19,333	D	D	D	D
District 7	3	D	D	3	D	D	D	D	D	D
District 8	5	6	1	6	34	6,800	100	0	D	D
District 9	11	14	1	14	6,641	603,727	D	D	D	D
District 10	3	3	1	3	14	4,667	100	0	D	D
District 11	6	D	D	D	D	D	D	D	D	D
District 12	X	X	X	X	X	X	X	X	X	X
District 13	4	8	2	4	31	7,750	100	0	D	D
District 14	X	X	X	X	X	X	X	X	X	X
District 15	X	X	X	X	X	X	X	X	X	X
District 16	4	D	D	6	122	30,500	100.0	0.0	D	D
District 17	64	3,607	56	456	5,688	88,875	88.5	11.5	D	D
District 18	834	97,545	117	41,571	101,205	121,349	76.6	23.4	472	6,841
District 19	4,978	893,753	180	386,911	453,031	91,007	47.5	52.5	4,562	5,894
District 20	1,144	153,570	134	77,467	117,643	102,835	52.4	47.6	680	4,533
District 21	5,867	1,422,164	242	667,428	987,044	168,237	20.5	79.5	6,091	6,945
District 22	4,325	857,969	198	394,978	472,075	109,150	25.6	74.4	4,719	5,157
District 23	8,113	1,647,668	203	854,912	1,065,088	131,282	35.9	64.1	15,512	9,066
District 24	2,543	572,957	225	352,684	699,584	275,102	39.9	60.1	6,333	11,349
District 25	392	69,264	177	42,514	49,178	125,454	89.2	10.8	1,757	23,427
District 26	80	12,569	157	4,774	8,567	107,088	98.9	1.1	D	D
District 27	4,466	1,104,024	247	737,743	1,174,577	263,004	42.5	57.5	18,827	14,482
NORTH CAROLINA	46,418	8,430,522	182	4,407,160	12,900,674	277,924	29	71	107,565	10,746
District 1	3,443	1,424,052	414	837,774	1,284,852	373,178	51.6	48.4	33,934	18,676
District 2	2,882	560,837	195	320,561	728,529	252,786	61.9	38.1	3,999	5,448
District 3	3,031	1,258,543	415	978,038	1,722,737	568,372	40.4	59.6	27,850	18,805
District 4	877	84,981	97	31,708	50,145	57,178	65.9	34.1	519	3,437
District 5	6,957	787,246	113	262,330	1,059,940	152,356	20	80	1,938	3,101
District 6	5,825	740,881	127	239,786	713,084	122,418	26.2	73.8	2,135	2,986
District 7	4,208	1,182,179	281	703,243	3,901,879	927,253	17	83	15,606	11,052
District 8	3,054	428,078	140	177,235	617,584	202,221	20.6	79.4	3,163	6,817
District 9	2,964	742,381	250	443,241	1,767,017	596,160	14.6	85.4	9,531	12,065
District 10	3,954	379,387	96	134,064	370,291	93,650	23.6	76.4	3,028	4,420
District 11	5,778	457,986	79	111,024	327,908	56,751	50.1	49.9	2,837	3,422
District 12	174	9,981	57	4,609	D	D	D	D	131	10,917
District 13	3,271	373,990	114	163,547	D	D	D	D	2,894	9,810
NORTH DAKOTA	26,364	39,341,591	1,492	23,976,011	8,234,102	312,324	81.1	18.9	467,034	22,770
At Large	26,364	39,341,591	1,492	23,976,011	8,234,102	312,324	81.1	18.9	467,034	22,770
OHIO	77,805	13,965,295	179	10,190,952	9,341,225	120,059	58.1	41.9	351,125	12,301
District 1	1,198	104,683	87	72,291	61,864	51,639	92.5	7.5	2,766	17,731
District 2	5,788	971,188	168	561,643	351,574	60,742	72.2	27.8	23,903	11,729
District 3	112	10,036	90	8,336	18,150	162,054	98.2	1.8	286	11,440
District 4	9,520	2,277,947	239	1,977,190	1,777,616	186,724	63.8	36.2	82,104	14,059
District 5	10,683	2,913,459	273	2,607,814	2,094,949	196,101	63.3	36.7	86,759	11,594
District 6	12,271	1,662,328	135	605,518	480,616	39,167	40.8	59.2	10,283	6,967
District 7	10,030	1,332,469	133	848,892	1,093,721	109,045	39.2	60.8	24,540	10,825
District 8	6,086	1,139,909	187	972,960	1,323,050	217,392	41	59	30,802	9,952
District 9	522	75,694	145	63,632	57,816	110,759	94.8	5.2	2,273	9,883
District 10	1,876	386,147	206	323,254	240,924	128,424	86.6	13.4	14,157	17,521
District 11	108	1,849	17	570	1,573	14,565	93.5	6.5	140	12,727
District 12	4,556	698,970	153	494,043	438,440	96,234	61.7	38.3	14,830	12,008
District 13	1,285	99,455	77	55,420	44,477	34,612	61.7	38.3	1,129	7,428
District 14	3,432	337,648	98	187,729	217,096	63,256	75.1	24.9	2,394	6,435
District 15	7,093	1,612,792	227	1,164,067	763,351	107,620	82.8	17.2	48,785	17,479
District 16	3,245	340,721	105	247,593	376,008	115,873	29.3	70.7	5,974	10,555
OKLAHOMA	78,531	34,156,290	435	7,812,594	7,465,512	95,065	20.3	79.7	232,018	11,248
District 1	3,313	588,647	178	182,107	110,733	33,424	49.2	50.8	2,543	6,218
District 2	29,177	7,890,823	270	1,392,848	2,290,737	78,512	11.2	88.8	25,153	5,613
District 3	28,506	19,928,136	699	5,158,149	4,192,913	147,089	23.7	76.3	164,878	13,484
District 4	13,511	5,008,747	371	969,680	797,804	59,048	23.8	76.2	37,282	12,272
District 5	4,024	739,937	184	109,810	73,324	18,222	30.4	69.6	2,162	4,590
OREGON	37,616	15,962,322	424	2,965,392	5,006,821	133,103	65.6	34.4	92,406	22,918
District 1	5,086	342,106	67	178,334	581,142	114,263	85.9	14.1	3,347	8,973
District 2	13,969	13,669,551	979	2,031,807	2,404,429	172,126	55	45	81,710	28,244

STATE District	Private nonfarm employment and payroll, 2020												
		Employment										Annual payroll	
			Percent by selected industries										
	Number of establishments	Total	Manufac-turing	Construc-tion	Wholesale trade	Retail trade	Health care and social assistance	Finance and Insurance	Real estate and rental and leasing	Profes-sional, sci-entific, and technical services	Information	Total (mil dol)	Average per employee (dollars)
	73	74	75	76	77	78	79	80	81	82	83	84	85
NEW MEXICO—Cont'd													
District 3	14,104	181,693	4.0	5.2	2.1	15.7	20.4	3.3	1.5	9.7	1.1	7,879	43,363
NEW YORK	537,369	8,617,513	4.7	4.5	4.0	10.6	20.8	6.3	2.2	7.9	3.6	601,878	69,844
District 1	23,109	246,132	7.3	8.6	5.7	16.1	22.5	2.9	1.0	6.4	1.3	13,787	56,015
District 2	20,638	260,136	11.3	9.8	7.9	13.6	17.1	2.5	1.2	5.3	1.7	13,099	50,356
District 3	29,963	397,669	3.3	4.9	6.2	10.4	24.8	7.7	2.2	7.8	1.9	26,344	66,245
District 4	24,524	276,582	2.4	5.9	2.9	14.0	24.8	4.8	1.6	7.2	1.5	13,479	48,735
District 5	11,713	168,863	1.7	5.1	2.1	11.8	22.4	1.4	1.8	2.0	0.8	7,634	45,210
District 6	18,931	190,471	2.2	6.8	3.0	12.2	42.4	3.3	2.4	3.7	1.1	7,629	40,054
District 7	22,846	257,889	3.3	6.2	4.6	10.5	31.0	3.2	2.8	5.4	1.8	10,848	42,064
District 8	12,165	162,660	1.8	2.8	3.1	13.7	37.6	2.1	2.2	2.5	2.1	6,337	38,959
District 9	13,229	131,377	1.0	2.9	1.5	11.1	47.9	1.6	3.0	3.3	2.0	5,536	42,142
District 10	38,949	851,937	1.0	2.3	2.5	6.4	13.6	12.4	2.5	12.0	9.0	83,874	98,451
District 11	16,299	176,046	0.9	7.1	1.9	16.8	36.3	2.7	1.4	3.4	1.3	7,479	42,482
District 12	66,634	1,592,168	1.0	2.7	4.2	6.0	10.8	12.7	3.7	15.4	8.5	195,989	123,095
District 13	10,296	163,880	0.2	1.6	0.4	9.4	50.3	1.3	3.1	2.2	1.4	10,186	62,154
District 14	12,353	161,080	2.6	10.9	3.5	9.7	28.1	1.9	2.3	1.8	1.3	7,708	47,853
District 15	9,242	142,023	3.3	4.4	7.8	12.7	33.8	1.1	3.2	1.7	1.2	6,387	44,969
District 16	15,949	175,235	3.0	9.4	2.4	15.7	22.7	2.0	3.7	3.5	1.8	8,320	47,481
District 17	26,322	353,097	3.4	5.8	5.2	10.8	24.2	5.7	1.9	7.1	2.0	25,673	72,708
District 18	19,362	228,482	7.3	6.1	5.5	16.8	20.8	2.5	1.7	5.7	1.8	10,892	47,672
District 19	16,636	168,839	8.0	6.0	3.0	16.3	22.8	3.4	1.1	3.4	1.4	6,851	40,579
District 20	18,777	342,181	7.7	4.5	3.8	12.3	20.5	5.2	1.4	9.0	2.5	18,671	54,564
District 21	14,991	179,630	11.5	5.4	2.6	18.7	22.9	2.5	1.2	2.7	1.7	7,392	41,151
District 22	13,721	221,457	13.2	3.5	3.3	14.4	21.7	4.8	0.9	4.4	1.7	9,340	42,175
District 23	13,808	219,593	14.0	3.8	2.9	14.1	18.7	2.6	1.1	4.4	1.5	9,442	42,997
District 24	15,863	279,024	10.2	4.6	5.3	13.4	19.8	4.0	1.5	6.3	2.0	13,278	47,587
District 25	16,869	349,462	10.1	3.9	4.5	11.4	21.1	3.6	1.9	7.1	2.8	16,949	48,501
District 26	17,092	353,698	8.1	3.2	5.2	11.1	20.1	8.5	1.5	7.0	1.6	16,782	47,446
District 27	16,106	213,343	17.9	6.4	4.4	18.3	14.9	2.4	1.3	3.4	1.1	9,576	44,883
NORTH CAROLINA	240,760	3,962,754	11.3	5.7	4.9	12.6	15.8	5.3	1.5	6.1	2.3	199,256	50,282
District 1	14,418	252,577	13.2	4.4	3.0	11.6	24.3	4.4	1.2	4.9	1.8	11,990	47,471
District 2	17,221	241,521	11.4	7.0	6.2	14.4	17.7	2.8	1.2	4.5	4.3	11,657	48,264
District 3	16,388	188,562	9.8	6.5	2.7	19.3	16.6	2.9	2.4	3.8	1.3	6,861	36,385
District 4	26,764	527,277	3.5	5.4	6.7	10.4	12.3	5.7	1.8	15.5	4.5	34,388	65,219
District 5	16,421	265,403	13.2	5.2	4.4	14.3	15.4	5.0	1.3	3.7	1.1	11,944	45,004
District 6	14,050	231,000	20.1	6.4	3.8	12.8	21.7	2.2	0.7	2.4	1.1	9,384	40,624
District 7	17,872	225,935	11.3	6.7	3.4	17.0	17.6	3.2	1.8	3.8	2.2	9,491	42,006
District 8	14,856	217,806	10.9	5.9	2.8	17.5	18.9	2.0	1.4	4.0	1.2	8,377	38,462
District 9	17,805	254,274	14.7	6.9	3.8	13.3	14.6	6.2	1.4	4.6	1.3	12,542	49,325
District 10	19,194	307,283	18.3	6.3	4.6	12.9	18.6	1.9	1.3	2.9	0.9	12,930	42,078
District 11	17,184	218,222	19.1	6.1	3.8	16.3	16.9	2.0	1.1	2.6	1.2	8,237	37,744
District 12	26,672	570,660	4.5	5.1	6.1	8.4	11.3	12.6	2.0	7.4	4.1	38,120	66,800
District 13	21,016	368,366	15.4	4.9	6.4	11.6	14.4	3.7	1.5	4.3	1.4	17,047	46,278
NORTH DAKOTA	24,510	355,103	7.9	6.8	6.3	13.6	18.5	5.2	1.6	5.1	2.0	17,814	50,167
At Large	24,510	355,103	7.9	6.8	6.3	13.6	18.5	5.2	1.6	5.1	2.0	17,814	50,167
OHIO	249,857	4,978,720	13.5	4.1	4.7	11.3	17.5	5.1	1.3	5.3	2.0	246,555	49,522
District 1	16,876	410,545	10.8	4.5	5.1	8.7	18.8	6.7	1.4	7.5	3.1	26,111	63,600
District 2	15,740	271,772	9.9	4.5	5.2	12.9	17.0	5.8	1.4	7.6	2.3	13,518	49,739
District 3	15,720	398,352	5.2	4.8	4.7	10.1	21.1	7.6	2.2	5.9	1.8	22,234	55,814
District 4	13,971	270,502	29.4	4.4	4.1	11.0	15.2	2.0	0.7	4.3	1.0	12,239	45,247
District 5	15,909	299,987	23.2	4.4	3.9	12.3	15.0	3.0	0.9	3.7	1.1	13,635	45,452
District 6	12,508	172,585	15.0	5.2	3.2	14.8	21.0	2.5	1.2	2.5	0.8	6,637	38,457
District 7	14,174	222,395	23.2	6.0	4.7	14.3	17.7	2.2	0.9	2.7	1.0	9,060	40,739
District 8	13,859	254,819	19.6	4.3	6.8	12.0	12.9	5.1	1.1	3.3	0.9	11,614	45,578
District 9	12,889	235,859	18.2	4.3	4.9	11.7	17.7	3.7	1.5	3.2	1.2	11,478	48,665
District 10	14,742	301,814	11.8	3.5	3.4	11.9	21.5	4.3	1.3	8.4	2.6	14,772	48,945
District 11	17,724	417,966	8.1	3.2	4.5	8.5	28.1	5.7	1.6	7.9	1.9	25,623	61,304
District 12	18,256	343,437	8.7	3.6	3.2	10.8	19.0	9.7	1.1	6.2	2.2	17,827	51,908
District 13	14,279	242,731	13.7	4.5	4.5	15.8	20.4	1.9	1.4	2.9	1.5	9,983	41,127
District 14	19,613	334,320	18.3	4.2	7.7	11.8	12.6	6.2	1.8	5.3	1.5	17,828	53,325
District 15	14,367	247,970	11.5	4.2	4.9	13.9	14.6	4.7	1.9	5.1	2.4	11,178	45,078
District 16	18,125	308,569	13.0	4.0	4.6	15.0	16.1	4.2	1.1	4.6	5.5	13,308	43,128
OKLAHOMA	93,595	1,405,824	9.3	5.5	4.3	13.0	16.0	4.2	1.4	5.6	1.8	64,020	45,539
District 1	21,736	381,190	11.8	5.5	4.3	11.4	14.8	4.1	1.4	6.5	2.6	19,024	49,907
District 2	13,006	161,993	14.6	4.7	3.4	15.6	24.1	3.4	0.8	2.7	1.3	5,978	36,904
District 3	16,986	193,358	12.5	7.5	4.8	15.0	14.0	3.7	1.5	3.9	1.5	7,657	39,602
District 4	16,778	216,472	7.9	5.8	2.7	17.2	17.8	3.6	1.7	5.1	1.3	8,365	38,643
District 5	24,561	397,782	5.4	5.4	5.5	12.0	16.1	5.1	1.6	6.4	1.9	19,349	48,643
OREGON	118,927	1,664,087	10.7	6.5	4.6	12.9	16.0	3.9	2.0	6.0	2.2	88,360	53,098
District 1	23,931	406,030	14.1	6.5	6.0	11.4	12.0	4.0	2.3	6.9	2.8	27,050	66,620
District 2	24,975	275,751	10.6	6.5	3.1	16.1	18.3	2.8	1.7	4.0	1.9	11,757	42,635

Table E. Congressional Districts 116th Congress — **Land Area and Population Characteristics**

STATE District	Representative, 117th Congress	Land area,[1] 2020 (sq mi)	Population and population characteristics, 2016–2020: Total persons	Per square mile	Race alone (percent): White	Black	American Indian, Alaska Native	Asian and Pacific Islander	Some other race (percent)	Two or more races (percent)	Hispanic or Latino[2] (percent)	Non-Hispanic White alone (percent)	Percent female	Percent foreign-born	Percent born in state of residence
		1	2	3	4	5	6	7	8	9	10	11	12	13	14
OREGON—Cont'd															
District 3	Earl Blumenauer (D)	1,074.5	843,221	784.8	76.9	5.1	0.9	8.1	2.6	6.4	11.6	69.9	50.4	13.1	43.3
District 4	Peter A. DeFazio (D)	17,272.9	813,504	47.1	87.3	0.8	1.1	2.7	2.4	5.8	8.2	83.0	50.6	5.2	46.7
District 5	Kurt Schrader (D)	5,190.2	839,214	161.7	82.9	1.0	0.9	3.3	4.9	6.9	17.1	73.7	50.7	9.7	51.8
PENNSYLVANIA		44,742.1	12,794,885	286.0	79.4	11.1	0.2	3.5	2.4	3.4	7.6	75.7	51.0	7.0	71.8
District 1	Brian K. Fitzpatrick (R)	638.4	709,715	1111.7	84.5	4.0	0.1	6.1	2.0	3.3	5.5	81.4	50.9	10.5	64.9
District 2	Brendan F. Boyle (D)	62.8	741,380	11805.4	46.1	26.6	0.4	8.3	13.6	5.0	26.2	37.5	51.9	18.0	63.3
District 3	Dwight Evans (D)	52.8	721,131	13657.8	32.6	56.3	0.3	5.8	1.4	3.5	4.7	30.5	53.4	9.3	65.6
District 4	Madeleine Dean (D)	476.9	730,845	1532.5	78.9	9.6	0.1	6.6	1.5	3.4	5.3	75.7	51.2	10.1	71.1
District 5	Mary Gay Scanlon (D)	211.8	717,928	3389.7	63.3	24.5	0.2	7.0	1.6	3.4	4.7	61.2	52.2	12.4	69.6
District 6	Chrissy Houlahan (D)	912.8	731,115	801.0	79.3	6.4	0.2	4.6	4.2	5.4	15.5	71.8	51.0	10.1	62.9
District 7	Susan Wild (D)	856.9	730,122	852.1	79.0	7.4	0.3	3.2	4.4	5.8	19.5	68.7	50.9	10.0	57.8
District 8	Matt Cartwright (D)	2,666.9	694,063	260.3	85.1	5.9	0.2	2.0	3.1	3.8	12.3	78.5	50.5	7.2	62.3
District 9	Daniel Meuser (R)	3,294.6	705,602	214.2	91.1	2.6	0.1	1.1	2.7	2.4	7.2	87.8	50.0	3.1	81.0
District 10	Scott Perry (R)	1,080.2	736,031	681.4	78.2	11.4	0.2	3.9	2.2	4.0	8.7	73.9	51.0	6.9	69.3
District 11	Lloyd Smucker (R)	1,503.0	735,086	489.1	88.9	3.7	0.1	2.0	2.2	3.1	9.0	83.7	50.9	4.5	70.1
District 12	Fred Keller (R)	9,895.9	696,809	70.4	93.2	2.2	0.1	1.8	0.6	2.1	2.5	91.7	49.9	2.9	77.1
District 13	John Joyce (R)	6,020.1	695,441	115.5	93.3	3.0	0.1	0.6	0.8	2.2	3.4	91.2	50.1	2.3	77.0
District 14	Guy Reschenthaler (R)	2,847.5	685,084	240.6	93.3	3.1	0.0	0.9	0.3	2.3	1.4	92.4	50.8	1.7	83.7
District 15	Glen Thompson (R)	9,734.7	677,288	69.6	95.1	2.0	0.1	0.7	0.3	1.7	1.5	94.3	49.0	1.5	85.3
District 16	Mike Kelly (R)	3,311.5	684,242	206.6	90.4	4.6	0.1	1.2	0.7	3.0	2.7	89.0	50.8	2.7	80.1
District 17	Conor Lamb (D)	882.8	709,873	804.1	87.4	5.9	0.1	3.0	0.8	2.8	1.7	86.6	51.3	4.8	78.2
District 18	Michael F. Doyle (D)	292.5	693,130	2369.7	73.3	18.2	0.2	4.1	0.7	3.4	2.6	71.9	52.0	6.4	76.5
RHODE ISLAND		1,033.9	1,057,798	1023.1	79.0	6.5	0.4	3.5	5.6	4.9	15.9	71.4	51.4	14.0	56.4
District 1	David Cicilline (D)	268.5	532,603	1983.6	74.6	8.8	0.4	3.6	6.9	5.8	18.6	66.0	51.6	17.3	50.2
District 2	James R. Langevin (D)	765.4	525,195	686.2	83.5	4.3	0.4	3.4	4.3	4.1	13.1	76.9	51.1	10.7	62.7
SOUTH CAROLINA		30,064.3	5,091,517	169.4	66.5	26.4	0.3	1.7	2.0	3.0	5.8	63.4	51.5	5.2	55.6
District 1	Nancy Mace (R)	1,549.6	804,679	519.3	73.2	18.4	0.2	2.0	2.5	3.5	6.6	69.9	51.5	6.2	41.8
District 2	Joe Wilson (R)	3,022.3	724,704	239.8	68.5	24.2	0.3	2.1	1.7	3.1	5.9	65.0	51.6	5.1	52.0
District 3	Jeff Duncan (R)	5,269.0	698,745	132.6	76.0	18.2	0.3	1.0	1.8	2.7	5.4	73.2	51.0	3.8	64.6
District 4	William R. Timmons IV (R)	1,299.7	739,881	569.3	72.1	18.2	0.3	2.8	3.0	3.7	8.5	67.8	51.5	7.8	55.1
District 5	Ralph Norman (R)	5,505.9	729,840	132.6	67.8	25.9	0.4	1.6	1.3	3.0	4.7	65.1	51.6	4.2	54.6
District 6	James E. Clyburn (D)	8,063.3	662,925	82.2	38.0	55.8	0.3	1.2	2.1	2.6	5.2	35.6	51.1	4.3	68.7
District 7	Tom Rice (R)	5,354.5	730,743	136.5	67.0	27.6	0.5	1.1	1.6	2.2	4.4	64.6	52.1	4.4	55.4
SOUTH DAKOTA		75,809.6	879,336	11.6	83.6	2.1	8.5	1.5	0.8	3.4	4.1	81.3	49.6	4.0	63.7
At Large	Dusty Johnson (R)	75,809.6	879,336	11.6	83.6	2.1	8.5	1.5	0.8	3.4	4.1	81.3	49.6	4.0	63.7
TENNESSEE		41,232.5	6,772,268	164.2	76.7	16.7	0.3	1.9	1.5	2.9	5.6	73.4	51.2	5.1	59.6
District 1	Diana Harshbarger (R)	4,143.6	720,629	173.9	93.3	2.3	0.3	0.9	0.8	2.5	3.9	90.9	51.0	2.9	61.6
District 2	Tim Burchett (R)	2,322.0	754,370	324.9	88.3	6.0	0.2	1.7	1.0	2.8	4.4	85.4	51.3	4.6	58.3
District 3	Chuck Fleischmann (R)	4,570.3	736,098	161.1	84.0	10.5	0.3	1.4	1.0	2.8	4.2	81.4	51.1	3.7	62.5
District 4	Scott DesJarlais (R)	5,985.0	800,304	133.7	83.1	9.4	0.2	1.9	1.6	3.7	6.9	78.6	50.7	5.3	59.8
District 5	Jim Cooper (D)	1,248.3	773,359	619.5	66.0	24.4	0.2	3.3	2.6	3.6	9.6	59.7	51.7	11.7	50.5
District 6	John W. Rose (R)	6,475.3	786,772	121.5	89.7	4.8	0.3	1.1	1.4	2.7	4.6	87.0	50.7	3.5	61.3
District 7	Mark E. Green (R)	9,161.2	789,106	86.1	83.0	9.9	0.4	2.3	1.0	3.4	5.4	79.5	50.4	4.2	51.8
District 8	David Kustoff (R)	6,846.1	708,450	103.5	74.2	19.8	0.3	2.2	1.0	2.5	3.5	72.2	51.3	3.9	65.7
District 9	Steve Cohen (D)	480.7	703,180	1462.8	25.4	66.7	0.2	1.9	3.5	2.3	7.4	22.3	53.0	6.1	66.2
TEXAS		261,267.8	28,635,442	109.6	69.2	12.1	0.5	5.0	6.2	7.0	39.4	41.4	50.3	16.8	59.7
District 1	Louie Gohmert (R)	7,869.1	722,673	91.8	75.0	17.3	0.4	1.2	2.2	3.9	17.8	61.5	51.2	7.6	71.0
District 2	Dan Crenshaw (R)	309.1	809,751	2619.7	62.6	12.7	0.4	8.0	9.7	6.6	33.1	43.9	50.4	20.5	52.3
District 3	Van Taylor (R)	480.9	896,996	1865.2	64.9	9.8	0.4	17.0	2.3	5.6	15.0	54.7	50.8	22.2	42.1
District 4	Pat Fallon (R)	10,131.2	765,400	75.5	79.3	10.3	0.8	1.4	3.7	4.5	14.6	70.5	50.6	6.6	66.6
District 5	Lance Gooden (R)	5,044.4	758,131	150.3	71.7	15.3	0.6	2.1	4.5	5.7	29.6	50.8	49.6	14.2	66.0
District 6	Jake Ellzey (R)	2,148.8	802,430	373.4	61.9	21.6	0.4	5.1	5.1	5.8	23.6	46.9	51.5	13.7	59.0
District 7	Lizzie Fletcher (D)	162.1	793,324	4894.0	59.2	15.2	0.5	11.1	7.4	6.6	30.7	40.0	51.2	29.8	44.9
District 8	Kevin Brady (R)	6,054.8	879,149	145.2	79.3	8.6	0.4	3.0	3.0	5.7	23.6	62.6	49.3	12.4	58.5
District 9	Al Green (D)	165.8	773,209	4663.5	33.3	37.4	0.2	11.9	11.5	5.7	39.1	10.4	51.4	34.6	49.3
District 10	Michael T. McCaul (R)	5,072.2	904,588	178.3	68.1	11.4	0.5	6.2	8.0	5.8	28.9	51.1	50.2	16.8	56.4
District 11	August Pfluger (R)	27,834.6	778,607	28.0	81.6	4.0	0.6	1.1	6.7	6.0	39.3	53.9	49.6	9.3	69.9
District 12	Kay Granger (R)	1,441.5	824,946	572.3	76.1	8.6	0.6	3.6	5.2	5.9	24.0	60.9	51.2	10.4	59.9
District 13	Ronny Jackson (R)	38,350.8	712,033	18.6	83.0	5.5	0.8	2.1	3.4	5.2	27.7	62.3	49.0	9.4	66.2
District 14	Randy K. Weber Sr. (R)	2,448.3	757,773	309.5	68.6	19.3	0.4	3.1	3.1	5.5	25.8	50.0	49.5	10.4	67.2
District 15	Vicente Gonzalez (D)	7,804.2	794,094	101.8	74.8	1.9	0.2	1.2	11.0	10.8	81.9	14.4	50.5	21.9	65.4
District 16	Veronica Escobar (D)	710.9	740,915	1042.2	69.7	3.6	0.5	1.6	12.3	12.3	80.9	13.0	50.5	22.5	58.4
District 17	Pete Sessions (R)	7,650.9	790,135	103.3	72.5	12.9	0.4	5.0	2.9	6.2	26.6	53.2	50.4	11.8	66.0
District 18	Sheila Jackson-Lee (D)	235.5	789,793	3353.7	44.8	34.7	0.4	4.2	8.9	7.0	43.4	16.4	49.9	22.6	59.3
District 19	Jodey C. Arrington (R)	25,835.8	731,230	28.3	79.6	6.2	0.7	1.7	5.9	6.0	37.5	52.9	49.4	8.2	72.2
District 20	Joaquin Castro (D)	199.9	823,263	4118.4	72.7	5.2	0.8	3.6	6.5	11.3	69.4	20.4	50.5	14.6	65.8
District 21	Chip Roy (R)	5,921.0	826,791	139.6	81.9	3.7	0.4	3.5	3.5	6.9	30.3	59.8	50.9	9.7	57.4
District 22	Troy E. Nehls (R)	1,033.7	941,210	910.5	55.7	14.3	0.4	19.2	3.7	6.7	26.1	38.0	50.4	25.3	50.8
District 23	Tony Gonzales (R)	58,058.9	767,109	13.2	76.1	3.6	0.9	1.7	9.0	8.7	69.3	24.0	49.3	16.9	64.4
District 24	Beth Van Duyne (R)	263.6	813,614	3086.5	60.5	12.7	0.5	15.2	5.4	5.7	24.6	44.5	50.8	25.1	44.3
District 25	Roger Williams (R)	7,622.5	804,296	105.5	80.2	7.4	0.4	3.5	2.6	5.9	19.8	66.6	49.9	7.7	57.6

1. Dry land or land partially or temporarily covered by water. 2. May be of any race.

Table E. Congressional Districts 116th Congress — **Age and Education**

STATE District	Population and population characteristics, 2016–2020 (cont.)										Education, 2016–2020		
	Age (percent)											Attainment[2] (percent)	
	Under 5 years	5 to 17 years	18 to 24 years	25 to 34 years	35 to 44 years	45 to 54 years	55 to 64 years	65 to 74 years	75 years and over	Median age	Total Enrollment[1]	High school graduate or more	Bachelor's degree or more
	15	16	17	18	19	20	21	22	23	24	25	26	27
OREGON—Cont'd													
District 3	5.3	14.0	8.0	18.0	16.2	13.2	11.7	8.7	5.0	37.3	191,745	91.7	42.4
District 4	4.9	13.8	11.3	12.5	11.5	11.2	14.0	12.6	8.5	40.0	187,728	91.8	28.1
District 5	5.9	16.7	8.7	12.8	12.7	12.3	13.1	10.8	7.1	38.3	192,133	90.0	32.0
PENNSYLVANIA	5.5	15.2	9.0	13.2	11.7	12.9	14.1	10.3	8.0	39.3	2,908,512	91.0	32.3
District 1	4.8	15.7	7.9	11.2	11.8	14.4	15.7	10.6	8.0	42.3	158,744	94.0	42.4
District 2	7.5	17.3	8.2	16.8	13.0	12.0	11.9	7.7	5.4	33.7	180,991	82.0	22.6
District 3	5.8	12.6	11.7	21.7	12.0	10.7	11.4	8.0	6.2	32.7	185,348	89.8	41.1
District 4	5.5	15.9	7.8	12.6	12.6	13.4	14.2	10.0	8.0	39.9	172,712	94.4	48.3
District 5	5.9	16.4	9.6	13.6	12.3	12.7	13.3	9.1	7.1	36.7	182,794	91.8	38.4
District 6	5.8	17.5	9.2	12.1	12.2	13.7	13.5	9.3	6.8	38.3	186,213	91.4	46.3
District 7	5.3	16.0	9.5	12.5	11.9	13.1	13.8	10.1	7.8	38.9	173,700	90.2	31.0
District 8	5.1	14.7	8.8	12.1	11.3	13.5	14.7	11.2	8.6	41.7	148,420	90.5	25.2
District 9	5.0	14.8	8.8	11.6	11.5	13.5	14.9	11.1	8.6	41.8	148,732	89.6	22.0
District 10	5.8	15.9	8.6	13.3	12.2	13.0	13.8	10.0	7.4	38.6	166,956	91.6	32.2
District 11	6.3	16.9	8.4	12.9	11.5	12.7	13.4	10.0	8.1	38.4	162,467	87.0	27.6
District 12	5.1	14.5	12.3	11.5	10.6	12.5	14.1	10.9	8.5	39.5	166,248	89.8	23.9
District 13	5.1	15.0	8.1	11.4	11.3	13.3	14.9	11.7	9.2	42.5	141,814	89.7	21.0
District 14	4.9	14.1	7.9	11.2	11.2	13.6	15.8	12.2	9.2	43.8	137,585	93.0	27.7
District 15	4.8	13.8	9.2	11.6	10.9	13.3	15.4	11.7	9.1	42.9	136,277	91.4	21.2
District 16	5.3	15.2	9.4	11.8	11.2	12.9	14.9	11.0	8.4	40.9	153,038	91.8	27.8
District 17	5.4	14.6	6.3	13.3	12.3	12.9	15.2	11.3	8.8	41.5	146,098	95.4	42.3
District 18	5.1	12.7	10.8	16.7	11.3	11.3	13.9	10.0	8.3	36.9	160,375	94.0	39.1
RHODE ISLAND	5.2	14.3	10.5	13.9	11.7	13.2	14.1	9.7	7.5	38.3	255,231	89.2	35.0
District 1	5.5	14.7	10.3	14.5	11.6	13.1	13.6	9.4	7.4	37.3	131,777	86.8	35.5
District 2	4.8	13.8	10.7	13.3	11.9	13.3	14.6	10.2	7.6	39.3	123,454	91.5	34.6
SOUTH CAROLINA	5.7	16.0	9.2	13.1	12.1	12.6	13.3	10.8	6.9	38.0	1,187,922	88.3	29.0
District 1	5.8	15.6	7.9	14.5	12.7	12.4	13.0	11.2	6.9	38.0	179,881	93.0	40.8
District 2	5.9	16.9	9.1	13.2	12.4	13.1	13.4	9.8	6.3	37.2	170,739	90.8	34.5
District 3	5.6	16.0	9.9	12.0	11.6	12.9	13.6	10.9	7.5	38.7	166,778	84.9	23.8
District 4	6.0	16.8	9.0	14.0	12.4	12.9	12.6	9.7	6.5	37.2	179,339	88.7	33.0
District 5	5.9	17.2	8.3	12.3	12.7	13.5	13.2	10.4	6.5	38.7	169,413	88.0	25.3
District 6	5.7	14.9	13.1	14.5	11.6	11.1	12.7	10.1	6.3	34.6	166,691	84.7	21.3
District 7	5.2	15.1	7.7	11.8	11.3	12.7	14.7	13.8	7.8	42.6	155,081	87.0	22.0
SOUTH DAKOTA	6.8	17.7	9.5	13.1	11.9	11.0	13.3	9.7	7.0	36.3	216,402	92.2	29.3
At Large	6.8	17.7	9.5	13.1	11.9	11.0	13.3	9.7	7.0	36.3	216,402	92.2	29.3
TENNESSEE	6.0	16.3	9.1	13.8	12.5	13.0	13.1	9.8	6.6	37.5	1,560,968	88.2	28.2
District 1	5.0	14.7	8.3	11.7	11.6	13.8	14.4	12.0	8.5	42.4	144,295	86.1	21.0
District 2	5.4	15.1	10.5	12.8	11.9	13.1	13.4	10.5	7.3	38.5	176,679	89.7	32.2
District 3	5.5	15.3	8.0	13.0	12.0	13.3	14.1	10.9	7.8	40.4	157,760	87.6	24.9
District 4	6.2	16.9	10.0	13.5	13.0	13.0	12.5	9.1	5.9	36.3	192,129	88.0	24.1
District 5	6.6	14.4	9.6	19.5	13.6	11.9	11.8	7.7	4.9	34.3	177,772	89.3	40.6
District 6	5.8	16.6	8.1	12.3	12.4	13.5	13.6	10.7	7.1	39.3	173,152	87.6	23.8
District 7	6.4	18.2	8.7	13.1	13.1	13.3	12.4	8.9	5.9	36.6	196,353	89.5	31.1
District 8	5.8	17.3	8.2	11.4	12.5	13.4	13.9	10.6	7.1	39.6	167,769	89.5	30.1
District 9	7.4	17.6	10.3	16.4	12.1	11.8	11.9	7.7	4.8	32.1	175,059	86.6	25.2
TEXAS	7.0	18.8	9.8	14.7	13.6	12.4	11.2	7.5	5.0	33.9	7,719,304	84.4	30.7
District 1	6.5	17.8	10.0	12.8	11.8	11.7	12.5	9.7	7.2	36.1	181,710	85.0	21.9
District 2	6.9	18.0	8.8	16.3	14.6	12.6	11.3	7.3	4.0	33.9	214,614	89.0	42.9
District 3	6.0	19.7	8.2	12.7	15.9	15.0	11.2	6.9	4.2	36.3	253,143	94.2	55.2
District 4	6.2	18.1	8.3	11.9	12.4	12.8	13.2	10.0	7.0	38.0	185,748	88.1	23.8
District 5	7.3	18.7	8.9	13.6	13.0	12.8	11.8	8.1	5.6	35.0	191,256	81.9	20.5
District 6	6.4	19.5	9.9	13.9	13.4	13.2	11.7	7.5	4.5	33.9	223,590	88.5	30.4
District 7	7.3	17.9	7.7	16.8	14.9	12.6	11.1	7.1	4.6	34.3	209,408	89.4	49.8
District 8	6.4	18.8	9.0	12.9	13.8	13.2	12.1	8.5	5.2	36.6	231,758	88.3	31.9
District 9	7.3	18.4	10.4	16.6	13.8	12.3	10.7	6.5	4.0	32.6	215,778	78.9	25.9
District 10	7.0	18.4	8.2	15.1	14.9	12.7	11.3	7.6	4.8	35.1	237,637	90.5	41.0
District 11	7.2	18.2	9.5	14.5	12.0	11.0	11.9	8.9	6.7	34.3	194,529	83.5	22.5
District 12	7.0	17.7	9.0	15.5	13.6	12.2	12.1	7.9	5.1	34.9	211,955	89.1	32.1
District 13	6.6	18.0	9.7	13.7	12.4	11.6	12.5	8.9	6.6	35.3	174,976	84.6	21.2
District 14	6.3	17.8	8.9	14.0	13.2	12.5	13.1	8.5	5.7	36.3	188,103	86.9	24.9
District 15	8.5	22.4	10.6	13.9	13.0	11.2	9.1	6.5	4.8	29.8	241,532	71.8	20.6
District 16	7.5	19.6	11.4	15.3	12.4	11.4	10.3	6.9	5.4	30.7	225,177	80.9	25.9
District 17	6.6	16.5	14.8	15.5	12.6	11.3	10.5	7.3	5.1	31.5	240,129	87.3	32.3
District 18	7.5	18.4	10.5	17.7	14.0	11.8	10.3	6.1	3.6	32.1	210,524	77.9	24.5
District 19	6.8	17.9	13.4	14.1	12.2	10.5	11.0	7.8	6.1	32.3	207,601	83.3	24.2
District 20	7.1	18.4	11.7	16.6	13.5	11.5	10.0	6.7	4.5	31.2	231,723	82.2	24.9
District 21	5.5	14.3	10.5	15.3	13.4	12.3	12.4	9.9	6.4	37.1	197,767	93.6	47.0
District 22	7.0	20.8	7.9	12.5	15.6	14.0	11.2	7.1	3.8	35.3	280,358	91.2	46.5
District 23	7.3	20.1	9.8	14.1	13.2	12.1	10.3	7.8	5.4	33.0	210,883	77.5	23.4
District 24	6.5	16.4	7.8	17.5	14.9	13.7	11.9	6.8	4.3	35.1	196,203	90.8	47.2
District 25	6.0	17.7	9.5	13.4	14.0	13.0	12.3	8.7	5.3	36.2	205,020	91.3	39.9

1. All persons 3 years old and over enrolled in nursery school through college and graduate or professional school. 2. Persons 25 years old and over.

Table E. Congressional Districts 116th Congress — **Households and Group Quarters**

STATE District	Households, 2016–2020: Number	Households, 2016–2020: Average household size	Households, 2016–2020: Family households (percent)	Households, 2016–2020: Married couple family (percent)	Households, 2016–2020: Female family householder[1]	Households, 2016–2020: One person households (percent)	Total in group quarters, 2020	Persons in group quarters, 2020: Correctional facilities for adults	Persons in group quarters, 2020: Juvenile facilities	Persons in group quarters, 2020: Skilled nursing facilities	Persons in group quarters, 2020: College/ University student housing	Persons in group quarters, 2020: Military quarters
	28	29	30	31	32	33	34	35	36	37	38	39
OREGON—Cont'd												
District 3	338,297	2.44	56.5	42.3	9.9	30.1	21,493	1,461	198	3,028	5,434	0
District 4	332,902	2.39	61.2	46.6	10.0	28.3	24,226	1,026	286	2,526	10,864	34
District 5	314,081	2.62	66.8	51.2	10.7	25.7	17,478	4,566	461	3,680	3,581	26
PENNSYLVANIA	5,106,601	2.42	63.7	47.4	11.7	29.8	404,096	81,297	4,476	90,797	176,483	57
District 1	271,717	2.57	71.5	57.8	9.4	23.4	10,638	792	415	5,589	1,401	0
District 2	264,057	2.76	62.3	33.2	22.2	30.7	16,859	4,079	202	2,842	5,720	0
District 3	304,812	2.26	46.0	23.6	17.9	43.3	29,357	1,537	102	3,032	19,696	0
District 4	282,784	2.52	68.4	55.2	9.7	26.2	18,251	4,393	382	5,776	3,904	0
District 5	266,763	2.60	65.5	45.2	15.3	29.4	23,877	2,390	314	3,910	15,041	0
District 6	270,699	2.63	69.6	54.3	11.3	24.2	18,499	612	275	4,206	9,849	0
District 7	276,604	2.56	67.6	50.0	12.4	25.8	22,591	1,576	215	6,371	12,601	0
District 8	277,618	2.42	63.8	46.3	12.3	30.5	22,489	7,226	290	5,261	6,805	0
District 9	278,820	2.42	66.2	50.3	10.5	27.6	26,061	8,918	301	6,069	8,087	0
District 10	295,670	2.40	63.9	48.1	11.9	29.5	23,657	6,271	111	5,101	9,025	20
District 11	278,822	2.59	70.4	56.9	9.4	23.9	15,784	696	102	7,857	5,453	0
District 12	273,311	2.41	65.0	51.3	8.9	27.9	36,826	5,923	172	4,689	23,896	0
District 13	283,162	2.37	66.4	52.3	9.7	28.2	22,546	7,876	271	4,962	7,034	0
District 14	291,642	2.28	64.0	50.0	9.9	30.5	17,410	4,789	128	4,246	5,871	0
District 15	280,249	2.30	64.2	50.7	8.7	29.8	33,222	15,890	457	5,271	8,683	0
District 16	283,568	2.31	63.1	47.6	10.9	30.4	28,449	6,100	520	5,827	13,434	15
District 17	310,104	2.26	62.0	49.1	9.3	32.1	11,342	78	127	5,027	3,487	22
District 18	316,199	2.11	51.1	35.4	11.9	39.5	26,238	2,151	92	4,761	16,496	0
RHODE ISLAND	414,730	2.45	62.2	44.5	13.0	30.6	45,755	3,082	341	9,133	25,919	1,219
District 1	206,971	2.47	61.3	42.1	14.1	31.9	24,192	640	148	5,674	13,059	1,219
District 2	207,759	2.43	63.1	47.0	11.8	29.3	21,563	2,442	193	3,459	12,860	0
SOUTH CAROLINA	1,961,481	2.53	65.3	47.1	13.9	29.1	138,603	31,693	1,537	22,638	51,443	17,441
District 1	310,345	2.56	65.9	52.1	10.3	27.4	14,430	387	175	2,659	2,872	6,377
District 2	280,474	2.51	66.8	48.9	13.8	27.8	14,070	815	139	3,205	741	7,444
District 3	270,004	2.51	67.1	49.4	13.1	27.6	23,069	5,063	364	3,335	12,347	0
District 4	285,010	2.53	66.5	49.1	12.8	28.1	17,708	2,983	227	4,020	8,542	0
District 5	278,936	2.57	67.6	49.2	13.4	28.3	13,091	4,097	302	2,847	3,983	290
District 6	251,453	2.47	57.8	33.8	19.8	35.7	40,148	14,196	288	3,343	16,430	3,330
District 7	285,259	2.51	64.7	45.2	15.1	29.8	16,087	4,152	42	3,229	6,528	0
SOUTH DAKOTA	347,878	2.43	62.9	49.4	9.0	30.6	32,153	6,709	598	8,107	8,979	857
At Large	347,878	2.43	62.9	49.4	9.0	30.6	32,153	6,709	598	8,107	8,979	857
TENNESSEE	2,639,455	2.51	65.4	48.2	12.7	28.6	156,422	47,728	2,088	32,882	55,024	1,413
District 1	294,526	2.39	65.6	49.1	11.5	29.1	15,611	4,099	284	3,269	5,611	0
District 2	302,242	2.44	64.5	50.0	10.3	28.9	20,082	2,136	175	3,795	10,945	0
District 3	296,412	2.42	64.6	48.7	11.6	29.9	15,077	4,223	148	4,575	4,364	20
District 4	295,323	2.66	69.9	52.5	12.0	23.8	17,037	5,135	99	3,455	6,359	0
District 5	320,066	2.35	55.6	38.7	12.6	33.9	25,916	4,752	156	2,746	15,112	0
District 6	300,505	2.58	70.7	55.1	10.5	24.7	13,237	5,280	141	3,720	2,964	0
District 7	287,996	2.68	71.3	56.4	11.0	24.2	19,512	9,475	410	4,439	2,809	1,321
District 8	269,814	2.56	70.8	54.2	12.3	25.4	17,516	7,255	449	4,248	4,379	12
District 9	272,571	2.52	56.5	28.5	23.0	37.2	12,434	5,373	226	2,635	2,481	60
TEXAS	9,906,070	2.83	69.0	50.2	13.7	25.3	606,045	248,764	7,645	102,213	147,089	34,376
District 1	257,901	2.70	69.5	51.1	13.9	25.4	24,191	7,824	181	4,850	9,206	0
District 2	294,298	2.72	67.0	51.1	11.3	26.6	9,103	2,331	122	2,070	3,392	0
District 3	318,388	2.80	73.1	60.1	9.3	22.0	6,470	900	77	2,109	3,106	0
District 4	277,506	2.70	71.4	54.7	12.3	24.6	17,014	8,450	0	4,537	3,245	0
District 5	257,706	2.85	71.5	51.4	14.6	24.0	23,757	18,442	31	3,483	487	0
District 6	271,773	2.92	73.5	54.2	14.1	22.1	9,853	725	112	2,891	5,533	0
District 7	306,186	2.59	64.5	48.0	11.8	29.3	3,592	0	0	2,611	0	0
District 8	301,885	2.81	73.3	59.3	10.0	21.7	31,315	24,836	111	2,028	3,639	0
District 9	266,879	2.89	67.4	40.6	19.8	27.3	3,454	0	37	2,047	228	0
District 10	320,827	2.78	68.6	54.7	9.8	24.5	16,692	1,984	449	3,690	7,263	0
District 11	276,702	2.74	67.5	51.1	11.7	27.6	18,190	7,869	418	3,519	2,352	1,339
District 12	298,182	2.72	67.3	51.0	11.9	26.6	16,574	6,177	96	3,831	4,050	361
District 13	259,825	2.61	68.0	51.2	11.6	27.6	30,404	16,107	471	4,275	3,688	4,200
District 14	275,816	2.63	67.6	49.2	13.7	27.0	28,306	22,624	275	3,091	1,064	26
District 15	233,079	3.34	77.9	52.6	19.6	18.4	14,615	10,164	234	2,241	1,225	0
District 16	245,983	2.95	71.3	46.8	18.4	24.7	15,195	4,695	114	1,826	1,182	5,864
District 17	289,563	2.62	62.4	44.9	13.1	28.8	37,341	7,641	564	4,953	22,772	0
District 18	276,040	2.78	63.3	37.0	19.7	29.9	26,209	9,977	359	1,174	10,436	0
District 19	263,351	2.62	64.7	47.4	12.5	27.9	36,121	18,584	238	4,009	10,288	350
District 20	258,813	3.13	65.4	42.0	17.6	27.6	14,834	0	17	2,033	3,529	8,211
District 21	329,330	2.46	59.2	46.9	8.7	31.9	22,216	442	564	3,741	7,358	4,194
District 22	304,456	3.07	80.0	65.2	10.6	16.6	5,441	2,923	166	1,469	0	0
District 23	234,460	3.19	74.7	53.8	15.5	22.2	23,016	16,324	738	3,118	1,249	613
District 24	321,146	2.52	62.4	47.8	10.6	30.7	3,890	7	15	2,302	768	0
District 25	284,790	2.70	70.2	56.6	9.9	23.3	35,386	11,875	191	3,557	12,189	4,676

1. No spouse present.

Table E. Congressional Districts 116th Congress — **Housing and Money Income**

STATE District	Housing units, 2016–2020						Money income, 2016–2020		
		Occupied units						Households	
			Owner-occupied			Renter-occupied			
	Total	Occupied units as a percent of all units	Owner-occupied units as a percent of occupied units	Median value[1] (dollars)	Percent valued at $500,000 or more	Median rent[2]	Per capita income (dollars)	Median income (dollars)	Percent with income of $100,000 or more
	40	41	42	43	44	45	46	47	48
OREGON—Cont'd									
District 3	358,522	94.4	57.9	401,300	31.4	1,297	39,191	71,652	35.2
District 4	358,534	92.9	63.2	265,100	11.9	1,004	30,174	54,164	22.4
District 5	346,418	90.7	64.8	332,800	20.1	1,150	35,237	67,908	32.0
PENNSYLVANIA	5,713,345	89.4	69.0	187,500	7.4	958	35,518	63,627	29.6
District 1	283,385	95.9	77.2	337,300	19.1	1,248	46,772	92,187	46.5
District 2	286,565	92.1	57.4	164,300	2.4	1,019	24,694	47,410	20.3
District 3	353,130	86.3	48.0	187,500	13.0	1,136	35,465	50,541	24.7
District 4	299,170	94.5	72.2	318,700	17.2	1,314	49,037	92,122	46.6
District 5	287,731	92.7	67.0	240,700	13.9	1,122	39,823	72,031	36.7
District 6	286,074	94.6	70.9	314,800	21.1	1,168	46,151	87,682	45.0
District 7	295,744	93.5	67.7	217,200	5.2	1,110	35,634	68,784	32.9
District 8	354,266	78.4	69.8	152,500	2.9	818	30,280	56,379	23.5
District 9	318,408	87.6	75.7	162,600	3.1	818	31,178	61,156	26.1
District 10	317,040	93.3	67.9	184,100	3.9	984	35,452	66,783	30.3
District 11	291,596	95.6	71.9	213,100	5.2	1,030	33,862	70,750	31.3
District 12	332,871	82.1	71.0	166,200	4.8	795	29,297	55,878	22.8
District 13	325,883	86.9	74.1	157,800	3.4	774	30,089	56,691	22.5
District 14	326,878	89.2	75.7	151,700	3.7	731	33,769	60,285	26.5
District 15	344,928	81.2	75.4	115,900	1.9	695	28,082	52,492	19.9
District 16	318,789	89.0	71.0	142,500	3.6	739	30,794	55,022	23.1
District 17	335,491	92.4	72.7	179,500	6.0	883	42,147	70,243	34.2
District 18	355,396	89.0	58.3	138,500	4.0	912	35,630	54,803	25.3
RHODE ISLAND	469,289	88.4	61.6	276,600	12.4	1,031	37,504	70,305	34.1
District 1	232,415	89.1	55.9	279,500	14.8	996	36,799	64,903	31.7
District 2	236,874	87.7	67.3	274,500	10.5	1,078	38,220	75,462	36.9
SOUTH CAROLINA	2,319,112	84.6	70.1	170,100	7.7	918	30,727	73,078	23.8
District 1	366,934	84.6	71.2	279,200	20.1	1,255	40,458	54,864	35.2
District 2	312,255	89.8	74.0	165,900	5.6	951	32,851	61,096	27.5
District 3	315,646	85.5	71.7	150,400	5.0	774	27,856	50,123	20.6
District 4	312,089	91.3	68.3	178,700	7.6	913	32,449	59,065	26.0
District 5	313,064	89.1	73.9	158,900	5.0	855	29,740	55,760	24.8
District 6	305,190	82.4	59.4	110,300	4.2	887	22,938	40,022	14.0
District 7	393,934	72.4	71.2	157,600	4.6	841	26,961	47,325	18.3
SOUTH DAKOTA	396,817	87.7	68.0	174,600	5.1	761	31,415	59,896	24.8
At Large	396,817	87.7	68.0	174,600	5.1	761	31,415	59,896	24.8
TENNESSEE	2,996,127	88.1	66.5	177,600	7.5	897	30,869	54,833	23.5
District 1	354,349	83.1	70.9	147,300	3.8	709	26,718	45,929	16.8
District 2	337,931	89.4	69.0	187,300	7.5	885	32,332	57,100	24.9
District 3	336,737	88.0	68.7	164,300	5.5	808	30,706	52,322	22.1
District 4	327,177	90.3	69.2	186,800	4.8	899	28,205	57,223	23.5
District 5	354,117	90.4	56.6	255,900	13.9	1,157	36,988	62,029	27.7
District 6	333,629	90.1	73.4	199,900	5.8	833	29,918	58,066	24.3
District 7	332,302	86.7	72.8	190,400	15.9	921	33,586	61,545	29.2
District 8	301,573	89.5	71.7	172,900	6.3	794	34,219	60,828	28.7
District 9	318,312	85.6	46.3	108,200	2.7	932	24,664	42,420	15.7
TEXAS	11,112,975	89.1	62.3	187,200	8.3	1,082	32,177	63,826	30.5
District 1	310,870	83.0	67.5	141,100	3.8	851	27,042	52,977	22.0
District 2	317,344	92.7	61.9	236,500	11.7	1,281	42,154	80,433	41.0
District 3	339,125	93.9	63.1	347,000	17.6	1,421	47,136	100,748	51.0
District 4	319,681	86.8	72.7	156,500	5.4	864	30,551	60,232	27.5
District 5	293,520	87.8	64.8	161,400	6.0	987	27,191	56,161	24.7
District 6	294,433	92.3	66.3	199,400	3.2	1,156	32,152	73,376	34.8
District 7	340,306	90.0	50.7	265,800	26.4	1,262	48,269	75,013	38.1
District 8	341,236	88.5	71.1	224,300	11.6	1,167	37,442	75,741	38.7
District 9	293,782	90.8	47.2	151,200	2.2	1,041	23,783	50,632	19.3
District 10	353,633	90.7	67.6	258,400	13.8	1,256	38,768	81,492	41.1
District 11	338,113	81.8	70.2	156,700	6.2	979	32,025	61,817	29.1
District 12	325,321	91.7	63.3	213,700	8.0	1,155	35,888	73,095	35.4
District 13	308,768	84.1	67.2	119,900	3.2	837	27,826	54,433	23.2
District 14	323,947	85.1	66.4	169,700	4.0	996	32,756	65,011	32.3
District 15	267,550	87.1	68.2	111,500	2.2	799	20,547	48,029	21.3
District 16	269,240	91.4	60.8	134,200	1.5	862	23,407	50,016	20.3
District 17	331,342	87.4	56.6	188,000	5.1	1,027	29,539	56,681	26.5
District 18	308,044	89.6	48.6	151,200	8.5	1,013	27,923	49,250	22.7
District 19	305,716	86.1	61.7	122,100	2.7	889	26,829	52,838	22.7
District 20	278,903	92.8	55.8	153,700	1.6	1,007	24,639	54,147	22.8
District 21	368,954	89.3	58.2	304,400	18.9	1,238	43,621	74,619	37.1
District 22	323,725	94.0	74.2	278,200	10.1	1,336	41,296	99,747	50.7
District 23	268,894	87.2	72.4	139,000	6.3	920	26,289	57,748	26.2
District 24	345,407	93.0	48.0	301,000	19.2	1,254	44,563	78,388	38.8
District 25	325,099	87.6	70.2	271,100	22.6	1,168	40,153	76,155	38.7

1. Specified owner-occupied units. 2. Specified renter-occupied units.

Table E. Congressional Districts 116th Congress — **Poverty, Labor Force, Employment, and Social Security**

STATE District	Poverty, 2016–2020			Civilian labor force, 2016–2020			Civilian employment,[2] 2016–2020				Persons under 65 years of age with no health insurance, 2016–2020 (percent)	Social Security beneficiaries, December 2021		Supplemental Security Income recipients, December 2021
	Persons below poverty level (percent)	Families below poverty level (percent)	Percent of households receiving food stamps in past 12 months	Total	Unemployment		Total	Percent				Number	Rate[3]	
					Total	Rate[1]		Management, business, science, and arts occupations	Service, sales, and office	Construction and production				
	49	50	51	52	53	54	55	56	57	58	59	60	61	62
OREGON—Cont'd														
District 3	12.8	8.2	14.4	482,209	25,187	5.2	457,022	45.4	36.1	18.6	7.5	136,160	161.5	19,695
District 4	16.0	9.2	18.2	387,630	26,972	7.0	360,658	36.7	40.7	22.6	8.4	219,523	269.8	21,429
District 5	11.0	7.2	14.4	413,762	21,169	5.1	392,593	37.6	39.1	23.3	8.2	186,685	222.5	14,885
PENNSYLVANIA	12.0	8.1	13.1	6,558,087	351,248	5.4	6,206,839	39.9	37.8	22.3	6.7	2,878,165	224.9	335,583
District 1	5.6	3.6	5.8	393,582	16,485	4.2	377,097	46.3	35.4	18.3	4.9	158,077	222.7	8,116
District 2	24.0	20.2	29.6	348,009	31,398	9.0	316,611	32.2	45.0	22.8	10.0	112,309	151.5	43,489
District 3	22.0	16.4	21.3	375,803	31,554	8.4	344,249	50.2	37.9	11.9	7.1	122,188	169.4	45,866
District 4	5.8	3.8	5.6	402,080	18,022	4.5	384,058	51.0	34.2	14.8	4.2	148,883	203.7	7,507
District 5	12.0	8.5	13.7	374,573	25,136	6.7	349,437	44.1	39.0	16.9	6.4	135,399	188.6	19,872
District 6	9.4	6.3	9.6	390,504	19,013	4.9	371,491	47.8	34.4	17.9	6.4	140,044	191.5	12,764
District 7	10.9	7.7	12.4	378,872	20,763	5.5	358,109	37.2	38.4	24.4	6.6	165,759	227.0	16,404
District 8	13.4	10.0	16.5	342,588	19,752	5.8	322,836	32.8	41.2	26.0	6.7	175,920	253.5	19,520
District 9	10.5	7.1	11.1	354,561	16,579	4.7	337,982	32.5	36.9	30.6	7.1	177,155	251.1	12,999
District 10	10.0	6.9	10.2	385,816	16,835	4.4	368,981	39.9	37.9	22.2	5.9	160,393	217.9	16,688
District 11	8.3	5.2	8.0	387,281	14,384	3.7	372,897	35.6	36.3	28.1	11.8	162,113	220.5	10,865
District 12	13.3	7.8	11.4	334,601	14,740	4.4	319,861	34.3	36.8	29.0	9.0	168,128	241.3	13,863
District 13	11.0	7.3	12.8	339,641	15,239	4.5	324,402	31.8	37.9	30.3	8.0	182,637	262.6	15,393
District 14	10.8	7.3	14.6	339,805	18,169	5.3	321,636	36.4	38.4	25.2	4.5	187,955	274.4	19,377
District 15	12.8	8.1	14.2	320,881	18,024	5.6	302,857	31.4	38.1	30.5	6.5	184,806	272.9	17,049
District 16	13.2	9.0	16.1	334,382	18,392	5.5	315,990	35.6	39.8	24.7	6.2	176,529	258.0	21,208
District 17	7.3	4.6	8.9	381,983	16,186	4.2	365,797	47.3	36.2	16.5	3.9	169,748	239.1	12,498
District 18	14.9	9.7	15.1	373,125	20,577	5.5	352,548	45.9	39.2	15.0	5.4	150,122	216.6	22,105
RHODE ISLAND	11.6	7.8	14.8	566,403	31,263	5.5	535,140	40.5	40.1	19.4	5.1	230,763	218.2	31,170
District 1	13.3	9.4	16.3	279,613	16,421	5.9	263,192	39.3	40.4	20.3	5.9	111,605	209.5	17,425
District 2	9.8	6.3	13.2	286,790	14,842	5.2	271,948	41.8	39.8	18.4	4.2	119,158	226.9	13,745
SOUTH CAROLINA	14.7	10.5	11.2	2,448,315	135,484	5.5	2,312,831	35.8	39.4	24.8	12.5	1,215,646	238.8	109,771
District 1	9.9	6.7	5.5	405,561	16,617	4.1	388,944	42.4	38.4	19.2	11.1	175,315	217.9	8,677
District 2	12.1	8.9	10.4	359,449	19,930	5.5	339,519	40.7	37.9	21.4	11.0	156,187	215.5	11,692
District 3	15.9	10.9	11.9	324,912	18,059	5.6	306,853	33.5	36.7	29.8	12.6	178,228	255.1	13,976
District 4	12.3	8.7	8.8	376,352	16,692	4.4	359,660	37.2	37.7	25.1	12.3	161,877	218.8	14,757
District 5	13.6	10.1	11.1	348,566	20,288	5.8	328,278	34.1	38.6	27.3	11.1	172,157	235.9	16,643
District 6	23.0	16.7	18.5	303,160	22,395	7.4	280,765	28.6	43.4	28.0	14.7	150,142	226.5	23,731
District 7	17.5	13.1	13.8	330,315	21,503	6.5	308,812	30.7	44.3	25.1	15.6	221,740	303.4	20,295
SOUTH DAKOTA	12.8	8.0	8.7	463,888	16,281	3.5	447,607	37.3	38.1	24.6	11.3	189,232	215.2	14,060
At Large	12.8	8.0	8.7	463,888	16,281	3.5	447,607	37.3	38.1	24.6	11.3	189,232	215.2	14,060
TENNESSEE	14.6	10.6	12.6	3,324,691	177,361	5.3	3,147,330	36.3	38.4	25.4	11.5	1,503,361	222.0	166,783
District 1	16.6	12.1	14.0	329,447	19,739	6.0	309,708	31.7	41.4	26.9	13.0	206,346	286.3	20,817
District 2	13.1	9.0	10.7	378,754	17,280	4.6	361,474	38.3	39.9	21.8	10.1	179,280	237.7	16,843
District 3	14.4	10.5	13.9	349,738	19,128	5.5	330,610	35.6	37.6	26.7	11.4	182,552	248.0	19,773
District 4	13.2	9.6	11.3	403,335	19,139	4.7	384,196	32.3	37.4	30.3	11.5	171,403	214.2	16,670
District 5	14.0	10.2	9.5	442,963	20,554	4.6	422,409	43.4	36.9	19.6	12.9	119,470	154.5	15,254
District 6	12.6	9.1	10.8	381,108	16,323	4.3	364,785	34.3	37.9	27.8	10.1	194,091	246.7	15,548
District 7	11.7	8.6	10.7	360,500	18,417	5.1	342,083	39.2	36.5	24.2	9.6	165,809	210.1	14,788
District 8	12.9	9.5	12.8	330,892	16,860	5.1	314,032	39.1	36.3	24.6	9.6	165,515	233.6	17,487
District 9	23.9	19.1	20.5	347,954	29,921	8.6	318,033	30.4	42.0	27.6	15.6	118,895	169.1	29,603
TEXAS	14.2	10.9	11.5	14,214,242	752,884	5.3	13,461,358	37.8	38.9	23.3	19.5	4,475,805	156.3	607,873
District 1	16.7	12.3	13.8	330,297	19,200	5.8	311,097	31.8	39.5	28.7	20.4	157,808	218.4	19,993
District 2	10.6	7.8	7.0	437,013	21,716	5.0	415,297	46.4	34.9	18.6	15.8	108,780	134.3	13,131
District 3	6.3	4.3	2.6	488,660	19,971	4.1	468,689	55.5	33.9	10.5	11.2	110,488	123.2	8,073
District 4	12.7	9.3	11.0	359,846	16,476	4.6	343,370	33.8	39.7	26.5	17.4	167,120	218.3	18,247
District 5	13.7	10.7	11.9	358,229	17,838	5.0	340,391	30.4	40.4	29.2	22.4	133,674	176.3	15,990
District 6	9.6	7.2	8.8	425,105	20,586	4.8	404,519	37.2	39.1	23.8	17.3	121,582	151.5	12,285
District 7	11.1	8.5	7.2	427,718	21,415	5.0	406,303	48.6	35.1	16.3	18.1	94,809	119.5	11,031
District 8	10.2	7.4	7.3	418,374	19,482	4.7	398,892	40.2	37.6	22.3	16.4	150,370	171.0	13,376
District 9	18.6	15.5	17.6	402,397	29,478	7.3	372,919	29.9	44.3	25.9	26.9	95,972	124.1	24,720
District 10	8.8	6.1	6.8	479,409	23,473	4.9	455,936	46.9	34.9	18.2	13.9	130,550	144.3	10,564
District 11	12.1	8.8	9.0	373,650	18,050	4.8	355,600	31.5	38.6	29.9	19.8	149,333	191.8	14,314
District 12	9.5	6.7	8.4	430,759	18,848	4.4	411,911	40.2	37.9	21.9	16.6	132,455	160.6	13,218
District 13	14.5	10.9	11.2	338,568	14,311	4.2	324,257	30.8	39.2	30.0	19.2	135,757	190.7	12,605
District 14	13.1	10.1	12.3	354,583	20,503	5.8	334,080	36.3	37.7	26.0	18.8	136,219	179.8	17,011
District 15	24.8	21.6	24.2	342,418	22,403	6.5	320,015	29.3	44.6	26.2	29.4	115,378	145.3	27,476
District 16	18.7	16.0	18.8	335,023	21,028	6.3	313,995	33.7	45.2	21.1	21.7	123,394	166.5	24,093
District 17	17.3	11.6	10.1	396,056	18,085	4.6	377,971	39.7	38.3	21.9	14.5	123,365	156.1	15,531
District 18	21.8	18.8	19.4	393,265	27,897	7.1	365,368	31.8	40.1	28.1	24.9	97,230	123.1	24,987
District 19	16.5	10.9	12.2	346,377	15,074	4.4	331,303	34.0	40.2	25.9	18.7	127,282	174.1	15,042
District 20	17.6	13.8	15.9	411,533	26,568	6.5	384,965	33.5	45.2	21.3	19.4	119,067	144.6	19,837
District 21	10.6	6.3	4.8	447,131	18,291	4.1	428,840	48.6	37.6	13.8	13.7	158,231	191.4	11,165
District 22	7.4	5.8	6.1	480,010	25,992	5.4	454,018	53.2	32.1	14.7	12.3	120,421	127.9	11,993
District 23	16.4	13.9	16.0	346,913	18,612	5.4	328,301	31.3	41.2	27.5	20.9	138,157	180.1	20,130
District 24	7.2	5.2	4.5	479,246	17,970	3.7	461,276	47.2	36.3	16.5	14.9	97,511	119.8	7,135
District 25	9.9	6.6	6.7	391,807	18,309	4.7	373,498	45.3	34.1	20.6	13.8	145,059	180.4	10,477

1. Percent of civilian labor force. 2. Persons 16 years old and over. 3. Per 1,000 resident population estimated in the 2016–2020 American Community Survey.

STATE District	Agriculture 2017									
		Land in farms			Value of products sold				Government payments	
	Number of farms	Acres	Average size of farm (acres)	Irrigated land (acres)	Total ($1,000)	Average per farm (dollars)	Percent from crops	Percent from livestock and poultry products	Total ($1,000)	Average per farm receiving payments (dollars)
	63	64	65	66	67	68	69	70	71	72
OREGON—Cont'd										
District 3	2,807	90,555	32	31,975	239,212	85,220	88	12	146	3,650
District 4	9,064	1,280,043	141	388,197	628,301	69,318	63	37	3,910	9,799
District 5	6,690	580,067	87	335,079	1,153,738	172,457	74.2	25.8	3,294	10,073
PENNSYLVANIA	53,157	7,278,668	137	3,931,996	7,758,885	145,962	35.8	64.2	74,182	6,823
District 1	866	78,687	91	52,691	84,647	97,745	75.2	24.8	637	7,583
District 2	22	68	3	23	133	6,045	85.7	15	D	D
District 3	21	216	10	94	194	9,238	77.8	21.6	D	D
District 4	596	37,975	64	20,987	32,564	54,638	62.9	37.1	233	5,825
District 5	61	2,385	39	668	9,494	155,639	97.8	2.3	D	D
District 6	1,814	162,693	90	103,764	727,609	401,107	79.2	20.8	1,908	10,258
District 7	942	142,994	152	110,081	118,328	125,614	74	26	2,367	15,173
District 8	1,236	193,249	156	64,158	60,087	48,614	49.4	50.6	588	3,973
District 9	5,166	636,513	123	426,263	1,214,767	235,147	36.4	63.6	9,756	6,668
District 10	1,551	189,487	122	134,814	211,943	136,649	46.4	53.6	2,500	8,251
District 11	6,578	576,434	88	427,814	1,689,756	256,880	18.6	81.4	8,468	9,645
District 12	10,546	1,728,148	164	820,450	1,414,932	134,168	23	77	19,379	6,302
District 13	8,124	1,343,863	165	780,880	1,379,471	169,802	27.3	72.7	13,151	7,331
District 14	4,142	528,568	128	205,558	140,027	33,807	55.3	44.7	2,522	5,447
District 15	5,867	906,075	154	398,379	315,753	53,818	48.5	51.5	8,177	6,495
District 16	4,602	665,252	145	350,735	320,968	69,745	56.2	43.8	4,262	4,491
District 17	885	75,415	85	31,530	35,258	39,840	70.1	29.9	D	D
District 18	138	10,646	77	3,107	2,953	21,399	89.5	10.5	D	D
RHODE ISLAND	1,043	56,864	55	14,302	57,998	55,607	70.5	29.5	1,037	14,205
District 1	322	14,540	45	5,779	22,877	71,047	58.4	41.6	174	10,235
District 2	721	42,324	59	8,523	35,122	48,713	78.4	21.6	862	15,393
SOUTH CAROLINA	24,791	4,744,913	191	1,599,887	3,008,739	121,364	36.4	63.6	55,192	10,400
District 1	616	76,208	124	11,039	35,526	57,672	91	9	166	3,689
District 2	3,388	457,224	135	143,344	497,742	146,913	31.5	68.5	6,844	14,562
District 3	6,839	881,416	129	194,971	658,491	96,285	12.2	87.8	6,681	5,971
District 4	1,792	108,346	60	24,522	33,573	18,735	71.8	28.2	518	4,709
District 5	4,851	840,194	173	230,826	627,665	129,389	27	73	7,124	7,916
District 6	4,388	1,527,163	348	566,689	597,829	136,242	63.7	36.3	23,870	14,564
District 7	2,917	854,362	293	428,496	557,913	191,263	45.2	54.8	9,989	9,755
SOUTH DAKOTA	29,968	43,243,742	1,443	16,371,543	9,721,523	324,397	53.1	46.9	419,508	19,416
At Large	29,968	43,243,742	1,443	16,371,543	9,721,522	324,397	53.1	46.9	419,508	19,416
TENNESSEE	69,983	10,874,238	155	4,566,352	3,798,934	54,284	57.4	42.6	115,945	6,254
District 1	10,091	895,703	89	279,460	232,281	23,019	30.1	69.9	5,109	3,355
District 2	5,504	500,612	91	153,466	180,981	32,882	60.2	39.8	5,341	3,980
District 3	5,878	609,260	104	179,821	259,736	44,188	14.5	85.5	5,365	4,341
District 4	11,384	1,622,906	143	534,915	727,550	63,910	36.7	63.3	12,949	4,982
District 5	2,099	234,406	112	64,699	43,218	20,590	70.3	29.7	866	2,656
District 6	14,561	1,977,518	136	640,720	655,337	45,006	50.9	49.1	15,680	3,678
District 7	13,036	2,353,365	181	747,529	469,912	36,047	58.8	41.2	24,773	6,542
District 8	7,246	2,648,961	366	1,949,573	1,217,343	168,002	86	14	45,431	13,218
District 9	184	31,507	171	16,169	12,575	68,342	96.9	3.1	433	16,654
TEXAS	248,416	127,036,184	511	17,595,330	24,924,041	100,332	27.7	72.3	749,231	20,984
District 1	11,811	1,756,575	149	240,554	1,342,954	113,704	5	95	1,334	7,058
District 2	213	19,714	93	3,901	8,856	41,577	87.4	12.6	186	14,308
District 3	1,362	137,649	101	52,404	46,263	33,967	32.2	67.8	1,166	18,219
District 4	23,721	4,211,086	178	1,078,170	1,306,516	55,078	18.2	81.8	39,599	10,272
District 5	12,604	1,947,480	155	361,393	454,125	36,030	35.1	64.9	2,243	11,049
District 6	5,347	1,020,043	191	307,085	143,690	26,873	58.3	41.7	8,011	13,026
District 7	59	27,971	474	540	687	11,644	83.7	16.3	D	D
District 8	9,409	1,692,702	180	199,691	341,363	36,280	40	60	1,033	8,134
District 9	98	D	#VALUE!	1,267	1,442	14,714	57.5	42.6	35	5,833
District 10	14,829	2,529,360	171	363,629	371,304	25,039	45.5	54.5	16,927	19,569
District 11	20,886	15,547,323	744	1,502,355	1,239,636	59,352	34.9	65.1	55,547	14,203
District 12	5,962	762,005	128	76,555	85,465	14,335	19.5	80.5	513	5,830
District 13	19,229	22,289,498	1,159	3,647,588	8,790,318	457,139	14.9	85.1	214,954	29,277
District 14	3,586	835,042	233	106,179	103,019	28,728	50.1	49.9	15,268	44,000
District 15	8,984	3,792,508	422	387,448	372,617	41,476	60.5	39.5	10,272	11,834
District 16	358	83,720	234	12,446	20,176	56,358	96.8	3.2	D	D
District 17	15,795	3,896,462	247	774,561	1,056,334	66,878	20.4	79.6	16,618	14,772
District 18	118	D	D	1,051	5,875	49,788	51.6	48.4	D	D
District 19	14,252	15,108,704	1,060	4,440,380	4,845,855	340,012	34.6	65.4	209,918	25,706
District 20	170	13,030	77	1,924	1,380	8,118	57.5	42.5	8	2,000
District 21	8,076	2,999,190	371	62,516	96,177	11,909	24.4	75.6	3,402	7,162
District 22	1,787	342,738	192	119,119	103,549	57,946	80.1	19.9	6,691	25,249
District 23	9,676	27,813,527	2,874	447,435	831,884	85,974	45.2	54.8	19,770	17,875
District 24	165	32,948	200	3,550	2,799	16,964	57.9	42.1	45	5,000
District 25	14,207	3,944,915	278	572,672	463,442	32,621	28.1	71.9	16,336	12,615

Table E. Congressional Districts 116th Congress — **Nonfarm Employment and Payroll**

STATE District	Private nonfarm employment and payroll, 2020												
		Employment										Annual payroll	
			Percent by selected industries										
	Number of establishments	Total	Manufac-turing	Construc-tion	Wholesale trade	Retail trade	Health care and social assistance	Finance and Insurance	Real estate and rental and leasing	Profes-sional, sci-entific, and technical services	Information	Total (mil dol)	Average per employee (dollars)
	73	74	75	76	77	78	79	80	81	82	83	84	85
OREGON—Cont'd													
District 3	26,776	418,740	7.2	5.4	4.9	10.6	16.1	4.9	2.3	7.7	2.6	22,784	54,412
District 4	19,917	253,690	12.2	6.2	3.6	15.2	19.0	3.4	1.5	4.7	1.3	11,432	45,061
District 5	22,719	284,057	10.7	9.0	4.7	14.4	17.8	3.2	2.0	4.7	2.0	13,694	48,208
PENNSYLVANIA	302,018	5,574,417	9.9	4.6	4.5	11.8	19.7	5.3	1.2	6.0	1.9	294,187	52,775
District 1	21,695	303,805	12.0	6.2	7.2	14.0	19.7	3.3	1.1	6.4	1.3	14,735	48,502
District 2	11,130	190,901	7.0	3.6	4.8	13.9	32.5	1.4	1.0	2.0	0.6	8,437	44,198
District 3	16,070	415,690	0.9	0.9	1.0	5.5	24.0	6.8	1.8	12.1	4.6	28,831	69,357
District 4	23,191	472,009	7.5	5.6	5.2	10.6	16.6	8.3	1.4	9.2	2.9	33,084	70,093
District 5	16,380	321,217	4.7	4.3	3.4	10.7	20.3	5.1	1.7	3.8	1.8	17,425	54,246
District 6	18,945	349,732	8.2	4.0	5.5	10.9	17.9	10.0	1.9	8.3	3.2	24,250	69,340
District 7	16,665	322,747	10.4	3.6	6.6	13.3	21.8	3.2	1.0	4.0	1.3	16,436	50,926
District 8	15,255	260,019	11.6	3.6	4.4	14.9	19.9	4.0	0.9	3.9	1.3	10,788	41,490
District 9	13,518	225,352	20.2	4.1	4.6	13.3	18.9	2.3	0.6	2.5	1.3	9,918	44,012
District 10	17,704	387,317	8.8	4.8	4.6	12.5	18.3	5.4	1.1	5.6	1.3	19,254	49,711
District 11	16,611	298,822	16.8	8.3	6.5	13.8	15.5	3.1	1.0	5.0	0.9	13,466	45,065
District 12	14,924	211,850	16.3	4.5	3.0	14.9	19.9	2.7	1.1	3.5	1.6	8,565	40,431
District 13	14,333	222,764	15.5	4.8	3.6	13.8	20.8	2.4	0.7	3.3	1.3	8,855	39,750
District 14	15,956	247,865	11.9	8.1	5.3	13.3	17.1	2.1	1.1	4.3	1.7	11,518	46,467
District 15	14,793	198,807	18.7	4.0	2.9	15.6	20.9	3.3	0.8	2.5	1.0	7,595	38,201
District 16	15,991	263,932	18.0	3.8	3.7	13.1	21.9	3.9	0.9	3.0	1.3	10,609	40,196
District 17	18,977	337,881	7.6	6.8	4.8	13.3	16.6	3.7	1.3	7.3	1.8	16,655	49,292
District 18	18,548	436,046	3.5	3.9	2.2	8.2	22.0	9.8	1.3	8.5	2.6	26,196	60,077
RHODE ISLAND	28,586	445,846	8.8	4.6	4.6	11.1	19.5	7.2	1.2	5.2	1.6	22,497	50,459
District 1	13,374	212,387	8.3	4.6	4.3	9.4	18.8	8.4	1.3	5.1	0.9	10,403	48,980
District 2	14,875	226,305	9.6	4.7	4.9	13.1	20.8	6.0	1.2	4.7	2.2	11,628	51,383
SOUTH CAROLINA	113,383	1,986,776	12.5	4.6	3.8	12.8	12.9	4.0	1.4	5.1	1.8	86,817	43,697
District 1	21,285	259,067	4.7	5.0	2.0	17.6	14.0	3.2	2.5	6.8	3.3	11,046	42,636
District 2	14,186	224,590	10.6	5.1	4.0	17.2	14.2	2.8	1.1	4.3	2.3	9,339	41,584
District 3	11,676	180,727	27.0	4.5	4.3	14.4	13.2	2.3	0.8	3.5	0.7	7,617	42,149
District 4	19,797	375,525	16.0	4.5	5.0	11.5	12.9	3.8	1.2	6.5	2.1	17,588	46,835
District 5	12,907	206,951	19.5	5.5	4.0	13.9	11.1	4.9	1.2	5.7	1.4	9,107	44,004
District 6	15,570	280,796	13.3	5.9	6.0	10.4	15.5	5.5	1.6	6.3	2.2	13,664	48,662
District 7	17,229	249,633	10.5	5.1	3.1	17.2	19.7	2.8	2.5	3.0	1.1	9,606	38,482
SOUTH DAKOTA	27,236	364,440	12.5	6.0	5.3	14.2	20.1	6.9	1.1	3.8	1.7	16,585	45,507
At Large	27,236	364,440	12.5	6.0	5.3	14.2	20.1	6.9	1.1	3.8	1.7	16,585	45,507
TENNESSEE	140,905	2,760,605	12.1	4.5	4.4	11.6	15.8	4.9	1.4	4.6	1.7	133,052	48,197
District 1	14,033	245,346	18.3	4.2	2.6	15.5	16.1	3.0	1.5	2.0	1.3	9,896	40,336
District 2	16,466	306,905	9.2	4.9	5.1	12.9	15.8	4.5	1.5	4.8	1.9	13,694	44,618
District 3	14,788	293,382	18.7	4.6	2.9	12.1	15.5	5.8	0.9	6.4	1.4	13,929	47,479
District 4	13,793	255,451	22.1	3.9	3.9	14.3	12.2	3.5	1.1	3.1	1.3	10,862	42,521
District 5	21,965	490,628	5.2	5.3	4.8	8.2	17.6	5.2	1.8	5.7	2.9	27,695	56,448
District 6	14,393	216,670	19.1	5.4	4.1	14.8	14.9	3.2	1.2	3.4	1.1	8,643	39,891
District 7	16,331	253,436	10.2	5.2	3.3	12.9	17.4	7.0	1.5	5.4	2.5	13,570	53,546
District 8	14,950	256,967	13.5	4.3	4.7	12.4	21.2	4.2	1.8	4.3	1.0	11,945	46,483
District 9	13,380	333,646	6.3	4.0	7.8	9.9	14.3	2.8	1.5	3.7	1.2	17,923	53,718
TEXAS	618,272	11,210,906	7.4	6.6	4.7	11.9	14.4	5.2	1.9	7.0	2.4	613,149	54,692
District 1	16,878	261,690	13.5	5.8	4.1	13.7	18.7	3.4	1.4	4.5	1.4	11,126	42,515
District 2	21,739	359,772	8.9	9.7	6.9	12.3	8.8	4.8	2.3	7.0	1.5	19,135	53,187
District 3	24,592	446,707	3.8	4.0	4.4	11.5	13.1	14.5	1.9	11.4	4.4	31,014	69,428
District 4	14,973	208,726	19.1	5.8	3.2	15.6	19.5	3.1	1.0	3.7	1.2	8,532	40,879
District 5	13,140	194,212	13.6	10.5	4.8	15.5	15.0	2.1	1.8	2.4	1.2	7,650	39,391
District 6	15,315	249,799	13.1	6.4	5.8	14.6	14.9	4.8	1.5	3.5	1.5	11,083	44,367
District 7	25,971	463,979	2.0	5.1	3.8	10.8	10.6	6.3	3.4	11.9	2.9	35,251	75,974
District 8	16,717	236,855	5.9	7.4	4.5	14.8	13.1	3.3	1.8	6.6	1.8	15,133	63,891
District 9	13,238	328,206	4.7	4.4	5.5	7.3	35.5	2.1	1.5	7.4	1.8	20,268	61,753
District 10	22,435	351,541	8.2	6.7	4.6	15.1	11.3	3.1	2.4	9.0	3.7	18,599	52,907
District 11	19,782	282,634	6.4	7.9	6.1	13.2	12.0	2.9	2.7	3.4	1.2	14,839	52,503
District 12	19,246	357,657	11.7	6.0	4.5	13.1	15.5	5.4	1.4	5.6	1.6	19,925	55,709
District 13	16,229	220,930	14.7	6.1	4.8	14.7	17.8	4.3	1.3	2.6	1.4	9,654	43,697
District 14	14,134	238,675	12.2	10.3	3.1	14.7	15.6	3.3	2.4	4.9	0.8	12,485	52,310
District 15	12,300	198,634	6.3	3.5	4.4	16.6	27.3	3.4	1.2	3.1	2.1	6,630	33,379
District 16	14,140	236,637	6.8	4.9	4.1	14.3	20.0	3.3	1.6	3.7	3.5	7,996	33,792
District 17	15,500	276,625	11.9	7.6	3.9	12.6	13.8	4.7	1.6	7.0	2.1	13,552	48,992
District 18	17,516	417,000	7.6	6.4	10.0	5.9	7.3	3.7	1.8	9.6	1.8	32,661	78,324
District 19	16,936	244,098	6.5	6.6	5.1	14.6	19.7	4.3	1.6	3.4	1.8	10,043	41,144
District 20	12,177	266,292	3.3	3.4	2.3	16.1	16.2	10.8	1.4	7.6	2.2	11,397	42,799
District 21	28,795	487,354	2.5	5.8	3.4	9.8	15.6	8.4	2.5	11.5	4.1	29,803	61,152
District 22	18,986	243,969	5.4	6.9	3.3	19.4	17.1	3.1	1.6	6.0	1.6	10,419	42,708
District 23	12,032	184,739	6.3	13.1	3.2	15.3	14.2	3.6	1.9	3.1	1.0	7,549	40,865
District 24	29,685	748,785	4.5	5.5	6.3	7.6	7.1	8.9	2.3	10.0	4.5	50,387	67,292
District 25	20,103	245,353	6.8	6.9	3.6	13.3	16.6	4.1	2.8	7.7	3.8	13,675	55,738

Table E. Congressional Districts 116th Congress — **Land Area and Population Characteristics**

STATE District	Representative, 117th Congress	Land area,[1] 2020 (sq mi)	Population and population characteristics, 2016–2020: Total persons	Per square mile	Race alone (percent): White	Black	American Indian, Alaska Native	Asian and Pacific Islander	Some other race (percent)	Two or more races (percent)	Hispanic or Latino[2] (percent)	Non-Hispanic White alone (percent)	Percent female	Percent foreign-born	Percent born in state of residence
		1	2	3	4	5	6	7	8	9	10	11	12	13	14
TEXAS—Cont'd															
District 26	Michael C. Burgess (R)	908.0	901,361	992.7	74.3	8.6	0.5	7.6	3.1	5.9	18.8	61.7	50.7	13.4	49.3
District 27	Michael Cloud (R)	9,120.8	740,663	81.2	79.5	5.0	0.3	1.8	5.5	8.0	53.7	38.4	50.5	8.7	75.0
District 28	Henry Cuellar (D)	9,379.0	759,810	81.0	76.8	4.6	0.2	1.1	4.7	12.5	77.9	15.7	51.1	20.3	64.9
District 29	Sylvia R. Garcia (D)	187.6	739,994	3944.5	63.9	10.4	0.5	1.8	13.1	10.2	78.9	8.4	49.2	32.9	57.8
District 30	Eddie Bernice Johnson (D)	356.7	788,685	2211.1	43.5	41.9	0.2	2.1	5.8	6.4	39.4	15.2	51.3	17.1	64.0
District 31	John R. Carter (R)	2,154.8	884,928	410.7	71.6	11.7	0.4	5.8	3.1	7.4	25.0	54.4	50.5	11.3	50.6
District 32	Colin Z. Allred (D)	186.0	780,503	4196.3	64.8	14.1	0.4	8.9	5.7	6.0	26.2	47.8	50.9	22.3	50.0
District 33	Marc A. Veasey (D)	212.1	738,970	3484.1	56.6	16.1	0.5	2.5	17.4	7.0	66.8	13.7	49.7	31.4	55.7
District 34	Mayra Flores (R)	8,191.6	719,488	87.8	84.3	1.3	0.2	0.6	5.4	8.2	84.7	13.1	50.2	18.4	71.2
District 35	Lloyd Doggett (D)	594.8	830,798	1396.8	67.3	9.3	0.7	2.0	12.0	8.7	60.9	26.2	49.7	15.3	64.1
District 36	Brian Babin (R)	7,125.9	748,782	105.1	79.0	9.1	0.5	2.0	3.8	5.6	27.3	59.5	49.9	10.5	68.6
UTAH		82,376.8	3,151,239	38.3	85.1	1.2	1.1	3.3	5.1	4.2	14.2	77.9	49.6	8.4	61.8
District 1	Blake D. Moore (R)	19,557.4	773,796	39.6	88.9	1.0	0.9	1.9	3.0	4.2	12.9	80.9	49.4	5.6	65.1
District 2	Chris Stewart (R)	40,195.7	781,231	19.4	82.2	1.3	1.1	3.6	7.8	4.0	15.9	75.9	49.6	9.4	58.8
District 3	John R. Curtis (R)	20,073.9	770,532	38.4	89.2	0.8	1.4	2.6	1.9	4.0	10.8	81.8	49.8	7.5	60.0
District 4	Burgess Owens (R)	2,549.8	825,680	323.8	80.5	1.7	0.8	4.8	7.6	4.7	16.8	73.4	49.8	11.0	63.0
VERMONT		9,217.4	624,340	67.7	93.6	1.3	0.3	1.7	0.4	2.7	2.0	92.4	50.6	4.6	49.5
At Large	Peter Welch (D)	9,217.4	624,340	67.7	93.6	1.3	0.3	1.7	0.4	2.7	2.0	92.4	50.6	4.6	49.5
VIRGINIA		39,482.2	8,509,358	215.5	66.3	19.0	0.3	6.8	2.8	4.8	9.5	61.2	50.8	12.6	49.1
District 1	Robert J. Wittman (R)	4,211.6	800,745	190.1	71.5	16.2	0.3	3.6	3.3	5.2	10.5	65.9	50.2	9.7	49.3
District 2	Elaine G. Luria (D)	1,103.8	739,205	669.7	66.0	19.5	0.3	6.0	2.1	6.1	8.4	61.8	49.9	8.9	41.6
District 3	Robert C. "Bobby" Scott (D)	625.2	740,270	1184.1	43.5	46.1	0.3	2.8	2.0	5.3	6.8	40.6	51.7	5.9	55.4
District 4	A. Donald McEachin (D)	3,642.2	775,135	212.8	51.3	40.7	0.3	1.9	1.8	4.1	6.1	48.1	51.4	5.3	61.3
District 5	Bob Good (R)	10,030.7	739,280	73.7	74.6	19.3	0.2	1.9	0.9	3.0	4.0	72.1	51.3	4.5	64.0
District 6	Ben Cline (R)	5,929.0	756,347	127.6	82.0	11.1	0.2	2.0	1.1	3.5	5.7	78.7	51.4	5.4	63.7
District 7	Abigail Davis Spanberger (D)	3,118.3	798,194	256.0	69.2	17.8	0.2	5.5	3.1	4.2	7.5	65.6	51.4	9.9	55.3
District 8	Donald S. Beyer, Jr. (D)	149.4	800,273	5356.6	61.0	14.6	0.3	11.8	6.3	5.9	18.7	51.0	50.5	28.1	24.4
District 9	Morgan Griffith (R)	9,115.5	705,034	77.3	90.5	5.3	0.2	1.5	0.6	1.9	2.4	89.1	50.2	2.7	64.7
District 10	Jennifer Wexton (D)	1,371.4	853,906	622.7	67.4	7.2	0.2	15.8	3.2	6.1	13.9	59.1	49.9	22.6	36.1
District 11	Gerald E. Connolly (D)	185.1	800,969	4327.2	54.7	13.2	0.3	19.2	6.1	6.6	18.6	44.8	51.0	31.3	29.7
WASHINGTON		66,455.0	7,512,465	113.0	73.5	3.9	1.2	9.5	4.8	7.1	12.9	67.5	50.0	14.5	46.6
District 1	Suzan K. DelBene (D)	6,181.9	768,331	124.3	75.6	1.3	1.2	12.5	3.3	6.0	9.1	71.2	49.7	17.8	47.4
District 2	Rick Larsen (D)	1,019.0	753,529	739.5	74.7	3.4	1.1	9.6	4.2	7.0	11.6	69.4	50.3	15.2	47.5
District 3	Jaime Herrera Beutler (R)	9,117.7	743,780	81.6	84.8	1.5	0.9	4.1	2.6	6.2	9.9	79.3	50.5	8.7	40.9
District 4	Dan Newsome (R)	19,246.6	732,957	38.1	71.9	1.4	2.5	1.8	15.6	6.8	39.7	52.8	49.6	16.2	56.3
District 5	Cathy McMorris Rodgers (R)	15,473.5	724,483	46.8	86.5	1.6	1.5	2.9	2.0	5.5	6.9	82.9	50.2	5.7	52.8
District 6	Derek Kilmer (D)	6,902.3	719,626	104.3	80.1	3.4	1.9	4.6	2.2	7.8	7.9	75.9	49.6	6.6	48.0
District 7	Pramila Jayapal (D)	143.9	798,799	5551.1	70.6	4.7	0.5	14.0	3.0	7.3	8.1	67.0	49.9	18.1	38.6
District 8	Kim Schrier (D)	7,359.5	758,134	103.0	73.3	3.1	0.9	10.6	5.3	6.9	11.7	68.5	50.2	14.7	51.3
District 9	Adam Smith (D)	183.5	750,506	4090.0	48.0	11.6	0.7	25.2	6.6	7.8	12.8	43.7	49.4	30.5	37.8
District 10	Marilyn Strickland (D)	827.1	762,320	921.7	70.7	6.5	1.2	8.7	3.5	9.4	12.3	64.6	50.3	10.5	46.8
WEST VIRGINIA		24,041.2	1,807,426	75.2	92.5	3.6	0.2	0.8	0.5	2.4	1.6	91.5	50.6	1.6	69.1
District 1	David McKinley (R)	6,276.1	608,716	97.0	93.7	2.5	0.2	1.0	0.5	2.2	1.4	92.8	50.2	1.8	67.9
District 2	Alexander X. Mooney (R)	8,019.2	621,458	77.5	90.6	4.6	0.2	0.9	0.7	3.0	2.2	89.3	50.7	2.1	62.4
District 3	Carol D. Miller (R)	9,745.9	577,252	59.2	93.3	3.6	0.1	0.5	0.4	2.1	1.1	92.6	50.8	0.9	77.6
WISCONSIN		54,167.1	5,806,975	107.2	84.3	6.3	0.8	2.9	2.3	3.4	7.0	80.6	50.2	5.0	71.2
District 1	Brian Steil (R)	1,728.0	719,909	416.6	85.8	5.5	0.4	1.8	2.5	4.0	10.3	79.6	50.4	5.7	66.9
District 2	Mark Pocan (D)	4,536.9	768,381	169.4	84.7	4.3	0.4	4.4	2.1	4.1	6.7	81.0	50.2	7.1	64.5
District 3	Ron Kind (D)	11,117.4	723,425	65.1	92.7	1.3	0.5	2.3	1.0	2.3	2.9	91.2	49.6	2.7	71.3
District 4	Gwen Moore (D)	128.4	708,155	5515.2	48.3	33.7	0.5	4.5	7.6	5.4	17.6	40.8	51.7	9.9	66.6
District 5	Scott Fitzgerald (R)	1,891.0	727,631	384.8	89.5	2.4	0.3	3.1	1.7	3.0	6.1	85.9	50.9	4.9	76.4
District 6	Glenn Grothman (R)	4,919.3	714,867	145.3	91.4	1.9	0.4	2.6	1.2	2.5	4.8	88.4	49.5	3.8	78.3
District 7	Thomas P. Tiffany (R)	23,039.3	711,161	30.9	92.6	0.7	1.9	1.7	0.7	2.5	2.5	91.0	49.6	2.2	67.3
District 8	Mike Gallagher (R)	6,806.8	733,446	107.8	88.8	1.5	2.4	2.4	1.9	3.1	5.5	86.2	50.0	3.8	78.4
WYOMING		97,088.8	581,348	6.0	90.3	0.9	2.3	0.9	1.7	3.9	10.1	83.6	49.0	3.3	42.7
At Large	Liz Cheney (R)	97,088.8	581,348	6.0	90.3	0.9	2.3	0.9	1.7	3.9	10.1	83.6	49.0	3.3	42.7

1. Dry land or land partially or temporarily covered by water. 2. May be of any race.

Table E. Congressional Districts 116th Congress — **Age and Education**

STATE District	Population and population characteristics, 2016–2020 (cont.) Age (percent) Under 5 years	5 to 17 years	18 to 24 years	25 to 34 years	35 to 44 years	45 to 54 years	55 to 64 years	65 to 74 years	75 years and over	Median age	Education, 2016–2020 Total Enrollment[1]	Attainment[2] (percent) High school graduate or more	Bachelor's degree or more
	15	16	17	18	19	20	21	22	23	24	25	26	27
TEXAS—Cont'd													
District 26	6.5	19.7	9.0	13.6	15.2	14.7	11.1	6.6	3.7	35.1	262,871	93.0	45.2
District 27	6.6	18.4	9.3	13.3	12.4	11.7	12.4	9.3	6.6	35.6	183,343	83.1	20.1
District 28	8.2	22.2	10.4	13.3	12.8	11.6	9.8	6.8	4.9	30.7	229,001	74.2	19.7
District 29	8.4	21.7	10.7	15.1	13.4	12.1	10.0	5.5	3.0	30.6	211,827	63.0	10.9
District 30	7.3	20.5	9.9	15.7	13.1	11.8	11.2	6.6	3.9	31.5	218,981	78.8	22.5
District 31	7.0	19.0	9.2	14.9	15.0	12.6	10.3	7.5	4.7	34.0	238,765	92.3	36.3
District 32	6.8	16.4	9.1	17.0	13.8	13.0	11.7	7.3	4.9	35.0	195,435	87.9	45.6
District 33	8.2	22.3	10.8	15.4	13.4	11.9	9.2	5.6	3.3	30.1	209,541	61.9	12.0
District 34	7.9	21.3	10.9	12.7	12.0	11.4	9.8	7.7	6.2	30.9	206,626	70.4	16.5
District 35	7.1	17.5	11.2	18.3	14.4	11.4	10.2	6.2	3.7	32.2	218,656	80.2	23.9
District 36	6.7	18.6	8.8	13.4	12.6	12.9	12.6	9.0	5.6	36.1	183,136	84.7	19.4
UTAH	7.9	21.6	11.3	14.8	13.7	10.3	9.5	6.6	4.4	30.4	992,124	93.0	34.7
District 1	7.9	22.4	11.1	13.8	13.6	10.5	10.1	6.4	4.1	30.3	243,208	93.1	30.9
District 2	7.1	19.7	10.5	15.2	13.5	10.2	10.1	8.0	5.7	32.7	228,277	91.8	33.9
District 3	7.7	21.8	14.9	13.5	12.4	9.9	8.9	6.4	4.2	27.6	272,616	95.1	42.5
District 4	8.7	22.1	8.8	16.3	15.2	10.5	8.9	5.8	3.7	30.8	248,023	92.0	32.3
VERMONT	4.7	13.9	10.7	11.8	11.3	12.9	15.4	11.8	7.6	41.1	142,422	93.5	39.7
At Large	4.7	13.9	10.7	11.8	11.3	12.9	15.4	11.8	7.6	41.1	142,422	93.5	39.7
VIRGINIA	6.0	16.0	9.5	13.9	13.1	13.2	13.0	9.2	6.3	37.1	2,110,795	90.3	39.5
District 1	5.9	17.4	8.7	12.1	12.9	14.0	13.3	9.4	6.1	38.2	200,815	91.7	38.2
District 2	6.0	15.3	11.1	15.7	12.6	11.7	12.6	8.8	6.2	34.2	179,393	93.0	36.6
District 3	6.8	15.6	11.2	16.6	12.0	11.4	12.5	8.1	5.6	33.1	194,568	90.1	27.6
District 4	5.8	15.0	9.6	15.4	12.6	13.0	13.6	9.1	5.7	36.9	188,775	88.6	31.1
District 5	5.1	14.6	9.5	11.9	11.0	12.8	14.6	11.9	8.5	41.0	169,308	87.8	29.9
District 6	5.4	14.7	11.8	12.5	11.3	12.5	13.4	10.5	8.0	38.5	186,141	88.5	28.0
District 7	6.0	17.3	7.8	12.8	13.2	13.7	13.2	9.6	6.3	38.3	191,216	91.7	40.3
District 8	7.0	14.0	7.4	19.1	16.0	13.3	10.9	7.4	4.9	35.7	181,220	92.1	63.4
District 9	4.6	13.6	11.1	11.5	11.1	13.2	14.3	11.8	8.8	41.5	160,733	85.1	21.2
District 10	6.4	19.9	7.8	10.9	15.1	15.4	12.0	7.5	5.0	37.9	238,550	92.8	55.8
District 11	6.4	17.6	9.0	14.3	14.9	13.7	12.1	7.4	4.5	36.0	220,076	91.8	56.9
WASHINGTON	6.1	16.0	8.8	15.2	13.4	12.5	12.7	9.4	6.0	36.7	1,753,707	91.7	36.7
District 1	6.6	16.8	6.8	14.4	14.6	13.7	13.0	8.9	5.2	37.9	179,717	94.4	44.6
District 2	5.7	14.5	10.0	14.8	13.2	12.0	13.4	10.1	6.4	37.6	170,955	92.2	32.8
District 3	5.9	17.1	7.7	12.7	12.7	12.8	13.6	10.8	6.6	39.1	169,919	91.9	27.1
District 4	7.7	21.1	9.0	13.5	12.2	11.1	11.3	8.5	5.6	33.5	195,828	80.8	22.0
District 5	5.7	15.5	11.0	14.0	11.8	11.6	13.3	10.4	6.9	36.8	182,752	93.3	30.8
District 6	5.4	13.9	8.2	13.9	11.8	11.8	14.5	12.8	7.8	40.1	143,782	93.3	31.5
District 7	4.8	10.7	9.7	22.4	15.2	12.4	11.2	8.2	5.4	35.8	169,119	95.6	62.4
District 8	6.4	18.4	8.2	12.4	14.4	13.8	13.2	8.1	5.1	37.6	191,504	91.9	36.0
District 9	6.0	15.3	7.9	17.9	14.3	13.1	11.8	7.9	5.8	35.7	168,329	90.1	44.2
District 10	6.5	16.8	9.3	16.0	13.1	11.8	12.0	8.7	5.7	34.4	181,802	91.7	28.8
WEST VIRGINIA	5.3	14.9	8.8	11.9	12.0	12.9	14.3	11.8	8.1	41.3	378,326	87.6	21.3
District 1	5.1	14.0	10.6	12.4	11.8	12.7	13.9	11.4	8.1	40.0	134,656	90.1	23.9
District 2	5.4	15.6	7.5	11.9	12.2	13.4	14.5	11.6	7.7	41.7	126,954	88.5	22.3
District 3	5.3	15.0	8.1	11.4	12.1	12.6	14.4	12.5	8.5	42.1	116,716	84.1	17.5
WISCONSIN	5.7	16.3	9.5	12.7	12.2	12.7	14.1	9.8	7.0	38.5	1,393,087	92.6	30.8
District 1	5.4	17.0	8.0	11.9	12.4	13.8	14.9	10.0	6.7	39.9	168,098	92.3	30.0
District 2	5.8	15.4	11.9	14.5	12.9	12.1	12.5	9.0	5.9	35.7	201,324	94.8	43.4
District 3	5.4	15.5	12.7	11.8	11.3	11.9	13.9	10.2	7.4	38.0	184,953	93.0	26.8
District 4	7.3	17.9	10.9	16.6	12.6	11.3	11.3	7.3	4.8	31.9	193,977	86.5	28.7
District 5	5.3	15.7	8.3	12.1	12.4	13.4	14.8	10.1	8.0	40.1	166,891	94.8	38.3
District 6	5.4	15.7	8.8	11.6	11.9	13.1	14.9	10.6	7.9	40.6	161,183	93.1	27.3
District 7	5.4	16.2	7.0	10.6	11.4	13.0	16.1	11.9	8.5	43.7	147,655	92.5	24.2
District 8	5.7	16.8	8.1	12.1	12.2	13.2	14.6	10.0	7.1	39.7	169,006	93.0	27.0
WYOMING	6.1	17.1	9.2	13.5	12.7	11.4	13.6	10.0	6.4	37.3	145,076	93.6	28.2
At Large	6.1	17.1	9.2	13.5	12.7	11.4	13.6	10.0	6.4	37.3	145,076	93.6	28.2

1. All persons 3 years old and over enrolled in nursery school through college and graduate or professional school. 2. Persons 25 years old and over.

Table E. Congressional Districts 116th Congress — **Households and Group Quarters**

STATE District	Households, 2016–2020						Total in group quarters, 2020	Persons in group quarters, 2020				
	Number	Average household size	Family households (percent)	Married couple family (percent)	Female family house-holder[1]	One person households (percent)		Correctional facilities for adults	Juvenile facilities	Skilled nursing facilities	College/ University student housing	Military quarters
	28	29	30	31	32	33	34	35	36	37	38	39
TEXAS—Cont'd												
District 26	304,145	2.93	74.4	60.9	9.5	19.9	9,555	529	124	2,345	5,306	0
District 27	265,150	2.74	68.8	48.4	15.0	26.2	13,244	3,684	307	4,318	2,701	126
District 28	222,112	3.39	77.7	52.9	18.9	19.5	7,398	2,811	88	2,524	853	231
District 29	224,754	3.28	74.4	46.2	19.4	21.2	2,207	2	116	853	0	0
District 30	273,749	2.81	63.5	37.5	20.3	30.7	14,566	6,550	116	2,100	2,541	0
District 31	300,298	2.90	70.4	54.3	11.8	24.1	13,115	1,604	170	3,103	2,941	4,151
District 32	299,393	2.59	62.7	47.8	10.3	29.5	10,100	30	54	2,203	6,798	0
District 33	226,076	3.24	71.9	42.8	20.2	22.5	5,092	1,877	381	1,073	209	0
District 34	218,063	3.22	75.8	50.2	19.1	21.1	18,336	13,288	347	2,437	1,436	34
District 35	282,375	2.87	61.3	39.5	16.3	28.7	24,741	6,676	337	2,844	6,055	0
District 36	265,070	2.76	71.7	52.6	13.2	24.2	14,512	10,812	25	2,958	0	0
UTAH	1,003,345	3.09	74.4	60.9	9.0	19.5	55,465	10,680	2,350	7,358	23,887	412
District 1	246,151	3.11	76.3	62.4	9.1	18.5	10,052	1,326	448	1,825	4,243	412
District 2	266,281	2.88	69.0	56.1	8.4	24.0	17,814	3,729	832	1,998	6,715	0
District 3	234,333	3.22	77.8	66.0	8.0	16.0	17,350	326	631	1,296	12,753	0
District 4	256,580	3.19	75.0	59.9	10.4	19.2	10,249	5,299	439	2,239	176	0
VERMONT	262,852	2.28	59.8	47.2	8.6	30.7	24,901	1,219	166	3,608	16,195	0
At Large	262,852	2.28	59.8	47.2	8.6	30.7	24,901	1,219	166	3,608	16,195	0
VIRGINIA	3,184,121	2.60	66.0	50.2	11.5	27.5	236,646	57,014	2,038	36,195	92,450	29,880
District 1	283,755	2.76	72.8	58.9	9.8	22.5	14,037	4,160	103	2,486	3,725	2,324
District 2	279,691	2.51	67.3	50.4	12.3	25.9	28,606	1,813	101	2,186	5,788	17,290
District 3	287,441	2.48	62.0	39.3	17.8	31.1	24,153	2,643	217	3,492	11,878	4,182
District 4	291,577	2.55	61.3	41.3	15.5	31.4	38,740	15,897	179	3,028	11,584	5,404
District 5	293,043	2.42	65.1	48.7	11.9	28.8	28,753	9,867	130	4,949	12,276	0
District 6	293,164	2.46	63.6	47.6	11.4	29.7	34,813	3,717	147	5,754	22,566	0
District 7	295,003	2.67	70.6	55.0	11.4	24.2	11,635	5,087	637	3,703	197	0
District 8	323,347	2.45	55.3	43.4	8.2	34.6	6,782	521	39	2,599	896	680
District 9	282,502	2.38	62.2	47.7	10.5	31.4	34,344	11,703	301	4,557	16,337	0
District 10	281,697	3.01	78.0	65.8	8.4	17.7	5,359	1,011	115	2,135	1,269	0
District 11	272,901	2.91	70.1	55.8	9.8	23.4	9,424	595	69	1,306	5,934	0
WASHINGTON	2,905,822	2.53	64.5	50.1	9.7	26.7	160,207	26,677	1,532	25,856	41,091	16,811
District 1	284,618	2.67	71.7	59.8	7.5	21.2	7,416	2,576	199	1,317	980	0
District 2	295,960	2.50	63.5	49.4	9.6	26.3	12,762	686	155	2,312	4,023	2,090
District 3	282,693	2.61	68.0	53.0	10.0	24.6	6,987	1,184	251	1,593	148	0
District 4	250,401	2.89	71.7	52.2	13.3	22.8	12,981	3,984	103	2,054	391	0
District 5	289,546	2.40	62.3	47.9	9.9	28.7	30,215	5,381	145	4,706	13,755	556
District 6	293,222	2.38	63.6	49.7	9.5	28.2	23,278	7,804	103	3,330	1,886	5,698
District 7	365,257	2.12	47.5	38.3	6.1	38.3	27,959	876	91	4,140	14,043	204
District 8	273,012	2.75	72.9	58.3	9.6	20.3	6,993	347	194	1,955	1,124	0
District 9	286,242	2.58	62.8	46.5	10.7	27.4	12,958	2,648	186	2,239	2,615	0
District 10	284,871	2.62	67.2	50.1	12.0	24.9	18,658	1,191	105	2,210	2,126	8,263
WEST VIRGINIA	734,235	2.40	64.1	48.4	10.8	30.2	52,067	19,669	829	10,456	17,006	0
District 1	243,677	2.41	61.9	47.2	10.2	31.2	24,705	8,423	312	3,823	10,939	0
District 2	250,431	2.44	64.9	49.2	10.8	29.4	10,637	3,319	217	2,951	2,982	0
District 3	240,127	2.34	65.4	48.9	11.4	30.0	16,725	7,927	300	3,682	3,085	0
WISCONSIN	2,377,935	2.38	62.2	48.3	9.4	30.1	151,299	32,853	1,183	30,617	60,123	119
District 1	284,440	2.48	66.7	51.8	10.2	27.3	15,505	4,855	472	3,882	3,780	0
District 2	318,062	2.36	58.3	46.0	8.4	30.7	21,003	1,710	118	2,938	10,953	0
District 3	292,757	2.36	60.6	48.4	7.7	30.1	32,303	5,687	100	4,344	18,135	119
District 4	279,884	2.47	54.2	30.2	18.4	36.9	16,900	1,198	97	2,645	9,934	0
District 5	297,968	2.40	64.5	52.8	7.9	29.2	12,433	851	70	3,583	5,237	0
District 6	297,865	2.32	62.8	50.5	7.8	30.3	26,013	12,416	43	4,223	6,133	0
District 7	303,955	2.30	65.2	53.2	7.7	28.5	12,402	3,239	201	4,879	1,149	0
District 8	303,004	2.37	65.3	52.6	8.1	28.1	14,740	2,897	82	4,123	4,802	0
WYOMING	233,231	2.43	64.0	52.0	7.9	28.8	13,328	3,352	342	2,723	4,457	596
At Large	233,231	2.43	64.0	52.0	7.9	28.8	13,328	3,352	342	2,723	4,457	596

1. No spouse present.

Table E. Congressional Districts 116th Congress — **Housing and Money Income**

STATE District	Housing units, 2016–2020						Money income, 2016–2020		
		Occupied units						Households	
			Owner-occupied			Renter-occupied			
	Total	Occupied units as a percent of all units	Owner-occupied units as a percent of occupied units	Median value[1] (dollars)	Percent valued at $500,000 or more	Median rent[2]	Per capita income (dollars)	Median income (dollars)	Percent with income of $100,000 or more
	40	41	42	43	44	45	46	47	48
TEXAS—Cont'd									
District 26	319,859	95.1	70.9	290,300	13.1	1,332	42,658	96,247	48.7
District 27	320,678	82.7	64.9	149,600	3.9	992	28,117	56,877	25.3
District 28	251,358	88.4	70.2	130,600	2.1	883	21,614	51,818	21.9
District 29	247,488	90.8	53.0	117,700	1.4	945	19,396	47,194	16.6
District 30	296,690	92.3	51.5	150,200	3.6	1,106	25,126	51,980	21.0
District 31	325,358	92.3	63.1	244,100	6.8	1,155	34,651	75,585	37.0
District 32	325,739	91.9	55.9	269,200	21.4	1,272	47,151	77,710	39.7
District 33	247,994	91.2	48.5	117,800	1.5	965	18,727	45,539	14.0
District 34	266,310	81.9	67.1	86,200	1.6	749	18,968	42,014	16.5
District 35	307,038	92.0	51.8	168,700	2.3	1,100	25,727	53,755	21.6
District 36	311,510	85.1	72.1	152,400	3.0	974	30,703	62,581	30.5
UTAH	1,110,369	90.4	70.5	305,400	15.4	1,090	30,986	74,197	34.2
District 1	284,237	86.6	74.2	269,500	12.2	956	29,995	74,194	32.8
District 2	302,086	88.1	67.0	284,000	13.4	1,038	31,095	67,049	30.6
District 3	254,821	92.0	69.3	351,900	23.7	1,124	32,359	77,315	37.9
District 4	269,225	95.3	71.8	324,600	13.3	1,201	30,531	78,557	36.7
VERMONT	337,214	77.9	71.3	230,900	8.2	999	35,854	63,477	28.8
At Large	337,214	77.9	71.3	230,900	8.2	999	35,854	63,477	28.8
VIRGINIA	3,537,788	90.0	66.7	282,800	21.1	1,257	41,255	76,398	38.0
District 1	316,958	89.5	76.8	321,600	16.4	1,366	41,229	91,248	45.7
District 2	311,896	89.7	63.2	279,200	13.4	1,281	38,199	73,446	34.9
District 3	315,839	91.0	54.5	209,000	4.4	1,104	32,316	57,954	24.6
District 4	319,789	91.2	62.0	224,700	7.9	1,081	33,717	62,263	29.4
District 5	355,287	82.5	70.8	194,600	11.8	906	33,656	58,557	26.5
District 6	333,826	87.8	66.6	196,500	5.3	864	31,353	57,285	23.9
District 7	316,067	93.3	73.6	277,700	12.2	1,225	42,535	82,539	40.9
District 8	343,040	94.3	51.9	574,700	58.4	1,867	61,078	111,224	55.9
District 9	346,489	81.5	71.2	129,800	3.2	712	26,553	46,258	17.2
District 10	293,891	95.9	78.4	512,200	51.5	1,729	56,946	132,276	63.5
District 11	284,706	95.9	66.8	488,900	48.1	1,888	51,154	117,382	58.4
WASHINGTON	3,150,194	92.2	63.3	366,800	29.9	1,337	40,837	77,006	37.8
District 1	305,202	93.3	71.8	514,600	51.6	1,688	49,895	103,010	52.3
District 2	323,601	91.5	62.7	399,300	29.6	1,368	37,735	74,591	35.3
District 3	307,486	91.9	68.5	315,300	15.1	1,187	34,379	69,543	32.3
District 4	275,375	90.9	66.1	219,400	7.0	899	27,628	60,819	26.4
District 5	318,461	90.9	63.9	239,400	8.2	919	31,540	58,180	25.3
District 6	331,151	88.5	67.6	324,500	20.5	1,197	37,639	68,891	32.4
District 7	388,471	94.0	49.0	674,100	71.8	1,700	61,900	97,596	49.5
District 8	297,671	91.7	73.3	409,800	34.9	1,417	43,438	92,544	46.6
District 9	302,919	94.5	54.0	492,100	48.7	1,613	48,108	86,397	44.3
District 10	299,857	95.0	60.5	313,100	11.5	1,308	33,817	72,416	32.9
WEST VIRGINIA	893,615	82.2	73.7	123,200	2.3	732	27,346	48,037	19.1
District 1	291,031	83.7	72.5	125,300	2.8	727	28,430	50,195	20.6
District 2	301,042	83.2	75.1	150,100	2.3	792	29,566	53,227	22.7
District 3	301,542	79.6	73.3	98,200	1.8	691	23,814	40,913	14.2
WISCONSIN	2,709,444	87.8	67.1	189,200	5.5	872	34,450	63,293	27.7
District 1	310,059	91.7	70.7	215,100	5.9	930	35,529	69,400	32.3
District 2	336,876	94.4	62.6	244,400	8.3	1,044	38,783	71,155	33.3
District 3	329,799	88.8	69.2	167,000	3.7	796	30,978	59,034	23.9
District 4	310,472	90.1	44.5	144,600	3.8	872	27,276	47,062	18.5
District 5	314,346	94.8	69.8	244,200	8.4	968	41,675	75,266	36.2
District 6	329,309	90.5	71.0	169,700	5.1	784	34,295	63,036	26.6
District 7	425,704	71.4	76.3	166,000	4.4	750	32,552	59,113	23.8
District 8	352,879	85.9	72.0	172,600	3.8	790	34,027	64,822	27.6
WYOMING	278,495	83.7	71.0	228,000	9.7	853	34,415	65,304	29.1
At Large	278,495	83.7	71.0	228,000	9.7	853	34,415	65,304	29.1

1. Specified owner-occupied units. 2. Specified renter-occupied units.

Table E. Congressional Districts 116th Congress — **Poverty, Labor Force, Employment, and Social Security**

STATE District	Poverty, 2016–2020			Civilian labor force, 2016–2020			Civilian employment,[2] 2016–2020				Persons under 65 years of age with no health insurance, 2016–2020 (percent)	Social Security beneficiaries, December 2021		Supplemental Security Income recipients, December 2021
	Persons below poverty level (percent)	Families below poverty level (percent)	Percent of households receiving food stamps in past 12 months	Total	Unemployment Total	Unemployment Rate[1]	Total	Percent Management, business, science, and arts occupations	Percent Service, sales, and office	Percent Construction and production		Number	Rate[3]	
	49	50	51	52	53	54	55	56	57	58	59	60	61	62
TEXAS—Cont'd														
District 26	7.1	4.2	4.4	496,769	20,239	4.1	476,530	48.0	36.0	16.0	11.2	115,631	128.3	6,885
District 27	15.5	11.6	14.9	347,164	18,770	5.4	328,394	30.9	40.5	28.6	20.6	145,403	196.3	18,841
District 28	21.8	18.5	20.4	330,175	22,744	6.9	307,431	27.8	45.3	26.8	28.0	123,150	162.1	26,666
District 29	23.0	20.5	19.3	349,066	23,815	6.8	325,251	18.7	39.4	41.9	33.7	81,159	109.7	19,953
District 30	19.6	15.6	16.2	379,028	23,346	6.2	355,682	31.9	40.5	27.5	23.2	106,940	135.6	28,656
District 31	8.9	6.4	8.4	446,365	25,261	5.7	421,104	43.3	38.6	18.0	12.5	142,920	161.5	11,962
District 32	10.2	7.2	6.1	441,652	19,211	4.3	422,441	46.2	36.4	17.4	18.5	105,173	134.8	10,889
District 33	21.7	18.9	19.5	354,211	23,214	6.6	330,997	17.2	40.7	42.2	32.9	82,570	111.7	20,276
District 34	25.8	22.3	23.2	294,379	17,210	5.8	277,169	27.6	46.6	25.8	30.1	124,367	172.9	35,015
District 35	18.0	13.3	14.8	433,781	23,169	5.3	410,612	31.1	43.7	25.2	20.8	112,297	135.2	20,751
District 36	14.0	10.9	12.0	347,265	24,329	7.0	322,936	32.6	36.1	31.3	21.2	146,183	195.2	15,555
UTAH	9.1	6.3	6.2	1,595,452	57,829	3.6	1,537,623	39.7	38.6	21.7	10.0	438,581	139.2	30,647
District 1	8.7	6.2	6.9	384,997	12,295	3.2	372,702	36.9	37.8	25.2	8.7	107,224	138.6	7,506
District 2	10.8	7.0	6.9	392,680	15,163	3.9	377,517	38.9	38.4	22.7	12.4	129,919	166.3	8,705
District 3	9.7	6.5	5.3	389,523	14,158	3.6	375,365	43.6	39.7	16.7	8.5	100,212	130.1	6,123
District 4	7.5	5.4	5.8	428,252	16,213	3.8	412,039	39.4	38.6	22.0	10.3	101,226	122.6	8,313
VERMONT	10.8	6.4	10.6	341,487	12,845	3.8	328,642	43.1	36.0	20.9	4.9	157,587	252.4	14,533
At Large	10.8	6.4	10.6	341,487	12,845	3.8	328,642	43.1	36.0	20.9	4.9	157,587	252.4	14,533
VIRGINIA	10.0	6.8	7.9	4,382,484	202,745	4.6	4,179,739	45.3	36.2	18.5	9.6	1,598,078	187.8	151,173
District 1	6.8	4.5	6.0	413,014	18,084	4.4	394,930	45.0	36.6	18.4	8.6	152,171	190.0	8,764
District 2	8.5	6.0	6.3	359,326	16,775	4.7	342,551	42.0	38.9	19.1	9.1	136,312	184.4	10,132
District 3	14.7	11.2	13.1	366,198	24,217	6.6	341,981	35.6	41.0	23.4	11.0	140,237	189.4	21,073
District 4	13.4	8.8	11.7	395,580	23,470	5.9	372,110	38.8	39.7	21.4	9.7	151,091	194.9	21,290
District 5	13.1	8.8	10.1	351,187	14,510	4.1	336,677	39.3	36.9	23.8	10.2	188,855	255.5	16,937
District 6	12.8	8.0	9.6	378,001	17,100	4.5	360,901	35.2	40.1	24.7	10.5	178,441	235.9	16,240
District 7	7.5	5.2	6.3	421,314	18,755	4.5	402,559	44.7	37.3	18.0	8.9	158,523	198.6	10,883
District 8	7.6	5.3	3.9	474,979	17,439	3.7	457,540	60.0	29.2	10.9	10.1	84,890	106.1	7,608
District 9	17.9	11.2	12.7	307,058	15,614	5.1	291,444	34.0	39.1	27.0	10.5	199,928	283.6	23,166
District 10	4.1	2.7	3.4	464,199	16,618	3.6	447,581	56.3	31.4	12.3	7.6	113,741	133.2	6,023
District 11	6.3	4.3	3.8	451,628	20,163	4.5	431,465	55.8	32.3	11.8	9.6	93,889	117.2	9,057
WASHINGTON	10.2	6.5	11.1	3,848,596	188,562	4.9	3,660,034	42.7	35.9	21.3	7.2	1,413,306	188.1	141,346
District 1	6.5	4.0	6.6	404,410	17,566	4.3	386,844	50.7	31.0	18.3	5.4	124,961	162.6	7,128
District 2	9.7	6.0	10.1	391,100	17,571	4.5	373,529	37.7	38.6	23.7	7.6	149,093	197.9	13,360
District 3	10.5	6.9	13.6	358,092	19,795	5.5	338,297	35.9	38.2	25.9	7.2	169,403	227.8	16,243
District 4	14.4	10.7	17.3	337,497	19,544	5.8	317,953	31.9	34.5	33.6	12.7	134,236	183.1	16,353
District 5	13.5	7.8	14.8	348,032	19,668	5.7	328,364	38.8	40.4	20.9	6.5	165,572	228.5	19,010
District 6	10.4	6.4	11.9	329,088	16,794	5.1	312,294	39.0	38.7	22.2	6.8	180,652	251.0	15,951
District 7	9.1	4.5	6.5	497,289	19,793	4.0	477,496	60.7	29.5	9.8	5.3	110,301	138.1	11,894
District 8	7.6	5.2	8.4	395,127	17,343	4.4	377,784	41.5	36.0	22.5	6.0	127,157	167.7	10,356
District 9	10.1	6.7	11.4	417,291	19,304	4.6	397,987	45.7	36.0	18.3	7.8	105,343	140.4	14,629
District 10	10.6	7.5	12.6	370,670	21,184	5.7	349,486	36.1	39.9	24.0	7.0	146,588	192.3	16,422
WEST VIRGINIA	17.1	12.3	16.5	796,303	52,031	6.5	744,272	34.2	40.7	25.2	7.6	475,824	263.3	66,503
District 1	15.8	10.0	14.0	283,764	18,010	6.3	265,754	35.0	40.1	24.9	7.5	149,977	246.4	17,682
District 2	14.7	10.9	14.3	288,060	16,924	5.9	271,136	35.4	39.4	25.2	7.4	160,137	257.7	18,432
District 3	21.0	16.1	21.5	224,479	17,097	7.6	207,382	31.5	43.1	25.5	8.0	165,710	287.1	30,389
WISCONSIN	11.0	6.8	10.2	3,093,131	109,854	3.6	2,983,277	37.2	36.4	26.3	6.5	1,289,260	222.0	112,416
District 1	9.2	6.2	10.4	381,496	16,645	4.4	364,851	36.0	37.8	26.2	6.1	159,038	220.9	13,157
District 2	10.9	5.8	8.1	438,271	11,821	2.7	426,450	47.1	33.3	19.6	5.0	145,863	189.8	11,002
District 3	11.8	6.0	9.4	380,941	12,818	3.4	368,123	33.5	37.3	29.2	7.7	169,217	233.9	11,641
District 4	22.2	17.0	22.6	352,696	20,182	5.7	332,514	34.3	41.0	24.6	9.3	113,221	159.9	37,295
District 5	6.9	4.1	6.2	403,907	12,839	3.2	391,068	42.5	36.0	21.4	4.5	162,645	223.5	7,681
District 6	8.5	5.0	8.5	378,417	11,799	3.1	366,618	33.8	35.9	30.4	5.4	173,350	242.5	9,847
District 7	9.9	6.4	10.0	362,594	12,102	3.3	350,492	33.7	35.6	30.7	8.0	196,191	275.9	10,998
District 8	8.7	6.1	7.7	394,809	11,648	3.0	383,161	34.5	35.6	29.9	6.0	169,735	231.4	10,795
WYOMING	10.8	6.7	5.3	300,597	13,222	4.4	287,375	35.9	36.3	27.7	13.6	120,816	207.8	6,819
At Large	10.8	6.7	5.3	300,597	13,222	4.4	287,375	35.9	36.3	27.7	13.6	120,816	207.8	6,819

1. Percent of civilian labor force. 2. Persons 16 years old and over. 3. Per 1,000 resident population estimated in the 2016–2020 American Community Survey.

STATE District	Agriculture 2017									
		Land in farms			Value of products sold				Government payments	
	Number of farms	Acres	Average size of farm (acres)	Irrigated land (acres)	Total ($1,000)	Average per farm (dollars)	Percent from crops	Percent from livestock and poultry products	Total ($1,000)	Average per farm receiving payments (dollars)
	63	64	65	66	67	68	69	70	71	72
TEXAS—Cont'd										
District 26	3,405	379,288	111	109,449	135,031	39,657	26.8	73.2	1,967	9,106
District 27	12,006	4,509,855	376	1,246,336	1,211,354	100,896	56.1	43.9	54,669	28,533
District 28	7,866	4,740,139	603	201,075	266,700	33,905	28.7	71.3	7,328	14,092
District 29	118	1,957	17	176	2,006	17,000	89.2	10.8	D	D
District 30	339	30,440	90	8,664	24,115	71,136	94.4	5.6	343	14,913
District 31	4,972	1,029,430	207	316,810	191,223	38,460	54.8	45.2	10,186	14,326
District 32	268	24,824	93	6,903	4,973	18,556	47.4	52.6	149	49,667
District 33	105	3,913	37	1,382	595	5,667	86.1	13.8	D	D
District 34	8,728	4,198,181	481	742,909	891,631	102,158	47.6	52.4	22,756	21,488
District 35	1,119	279,641	250	55,770	50,929	45,513	76.2	23.8	1,015	11,154
District 36	6,786	987,386	146	141,443	109,757	16,174	54.5	45.5	10,717	50,552
UTAH	18,409	10,811,604	587	1,062,894	1,838,609	99,876	30.5	69.5	27,868	12,633
District 1	7,638	5,450,417	714	483,806	534,894	70,031	34.5	65.5	16,242	16,034
District 2	4,838	2,447,277	506	379,948	964,666	199,394	23.8	76.2	6,629	9,156
District 3	3,559	2,492,368	700	126,072	194,706	54,708	40.8	59.2	3,232	11,107
District 4	2,374	421,542	178	73,068	144,343	60,802	46.7	53.3	1,766	9,921
VERMONT	6,808	1,193,437	175	417,925	780,968	114,713	24	76	5,698	8,355
At Large	6,808	1,193,437	175	417,925	780,968	114,713	24	76	5,698	8,355
VIRGINIA	43,225	7,797,979	180	2,613,010	3,960,501	91,625	34.4	65.6	60,805	10,122
District 1	3,054	645,919	211	388,966	301,198	98,624	77.7	22.3	10,885	18,233
District 2	610	149,494	245	108,539	274,025	449,221	46.7	53.3	3,964	26,079
District 3	333	105,974	318	64,944	89,535	268,874	69.8	30.2	3,263	26,967
District 4	1,879	581,527	309	348,136	278,687	148,317	77.8	22.2	18,864	24,123
District 5	11,408	2,257,513	198	614,799	601,654	52,740	42.7	57.3	9,223	5,255
District 6	8,091	1,278,122	158	392,804	1,481,922	183,157	9.4	90.6	5,475	6,411
District 7	3,235	576,339	178	193,179	350,186	108,249	44.3	55.7	2,518	5,097
District 8	27	1,634	61	201	378	14,000	92.1	7.7	D	D
District 9	11,933	1,893,432	159	389,465	486,668	40,783	21.5	78.5	6,227	5,506
District 10	2,629	305,569	116	111,745	95,792	36,437	66	34	378	3,231
District 11	26	2,456	94	232	457	17,577	54.9	44.9	D	D
WASHINGTON	35,793	14,679,857	410	4,472,130	9,634,461	269,172	72.5	27.5	168,990	30,692
District 1	3,760	184,504	49	92,737	609,749	162,167	50	50	2,098	6,812
District 2	1,672	128,023	77	67,888	301,189	180,137	64.3	35.7	462	4,574
District 3	5,744	907,479	158	201,363	409,081	71,219	45.1	54.9	5,633	14,297
District 4	9,281	7,215,328	777	2,037,982	6,606,543	711,835	74.9	25.1	72,231	40,488
District 5	7,248	5,707,399	787	1,939,306	963,198	132,892	90.6	9.4	85,143	32,081
District 6	2,429	167,201	69	29,213	93,124	38,338	38.3	61.7	326	5,175
District 7	210	2,788	13	721	2,850	13,571	76.5	23.5	D	D
District 8	4,031	312,692	78	89,276	472,565	117,233	80.7	19.3	2,914	18,327
District 9	73	884	12	150	1,013	13,877	88.6	11.4	D	D
District 10	1,345	53,559	40	13,494	175,150	130,223	35.2	64.8	79	2,548
WEST VIRGINIA	23,622	3,662,178	155	736,151	754,279	31,931	20.3	79.7	9,094	4,853
District 1	9,112	1,317,106	145	271,231	155,397	17,054	21.1	78.9	D	D
District 2	8,567	1,406,851	164	298,139	437,526	51,071	16.5	83.5	3,636	4,722
District 3	5,943	938,221	158	166,781	161,355	27,150	29.8	70.2	D	D
WISCONSIN	64,793	14,318,630	221	9,234,611	11,427,423	176,368	35.6	64.4	126,583	4,609
District 1	2,798	574,614	205	472,422	470,615	168,197	D	D	13,871	10,871
District 2	9,579	2,086,402	218	1,403,770	1,652,129	172,474	39.3	60.7	30,032	5,925
District 3	18,254	4,142,195	227	2,319,178	2,783,186	152,470	40.8	59.2	31,987	3,951
District 4	39	310	8	136	3,019	77,410	D	D	D	D
District 5	3,120	647,716	208	495,739	686,285	219,963	39	61	5,237	4,007
District 6	7,975	1,753,113	220	1,333,881	1,724,547	216,244	33.4	66.6	16,772	4,706
District 7	15,205	3,428,587	225	1,960,317	2,249,708	147,958	33.3	66.7	13,222	2,949
District 8	7,823	1,685,693	215	1,249,168	1,857,935	237,496	22.2	77.8	15,462	4,217
WYOMING	11,938	29,004,884	2,430	1,544,826	1,472,113	123,313	21.6	78.4	30,218	14,410
At Large	11,938	29,004,884	2,430	1,544,826	1,472,113	123,313	21.6	78.4	30,218	14,410

STATE District	Private nonfarm employment and payroll, 2020												
		Employment										Annual payroll	
			Percent by selected industries										
	Number of establishments	Total	Manufacturing	Construction	Wholesale trade	Retail trade	Health care and social assistance	Finance and Insurance	Real estate and rental and leasing	Professional, scientific, and technical services	Information	Total (mil dol)	Average per employee (dollars)
	73	74	75	76	77	78	79	80	81	82	83	84	85
TEXAS—Cont'd													
District 26	17,518	257,623	6.3	6.9	4.9	13.7	11.9	6.4	2.2	4.8	1.8	12,601	48,914
District 27	15,809	245,456	9.5	9.7	4.5	14.7	18.5	3.0	2.1	4.3	1.1	10,643	43,362
District 28	11,758	176,550	2.4	4.7	3.6	17.9	23.7	3.5	1.3	2.4	0.8	5,751	32,573
District 29	10,841	213,510	14.5	13.4	7.2	11.8	6.4	2.4	1.6	5.8	0.9	10,958	51,325
District 30	14,129	343,635	5.2	3.3	4.5	8.4	15.5	5.9	3.1	12.0	4.3	25,122	73,106
District 31	17,626	275,250	5.7	7.8	2.7	16.1	17.8	4.5	1.4	9.1	2.5	14,554	52,875
District 32	22,719	372,046	5.8	4.7	2.5	10.9	16.5	7.8	3.9	8.4	4.1	23,384	62,851
District 33	12,982	297,961	16.0	10.3	10.4	8.6	13.0	2.0	1.6	3.5	1.2	14,447	48,487
District 34	10,863	179,948	3.8	2.9	2.6	16.0	34.5	3.3	1.4	2.5	1.5	5,371	29,849
District 35	16,874	335,689	7.7	7.2	6.6	13.6	11.9	2.7	1.9	5.0	3.3	15,272	45,496
District 36	13,190	263,480	16.3	12.2	3.6	11.0	10.0	2.0	1.7	8.6	0.6	15,374	58,350
UTAH	86,927	1,405,666	9.4	7.1	4.3	11.4	10.9	5.2	1.6	7.1	4.2	72,303	51,437
District 1	19,910	257,358	16.9	7.7	3.5	14.0	12.2	3.8	1.8	6.3	1.2	11,044	42,913
District 2	23,648	412,456	10.4	6.6	5.3	10.7	11.3	5.6	1.5	6.4	2.7	22,410	54,334
District 3	21,513	297,759	5.7	6.0	3.8	12.1	12.3	4.7	1.7	7.6	5.8	14,571	48,935
District 4	21,290	348,332	8.4	10.0	5.0	12.7	11.0	6.4	1.9	8.7	6.8	18,964	54,441
VERMONT	20,540	258,423	11.9	5.5	4.1	14.3	19.5	3.5	1.2	4.8	2.8	11,668	45,151
At Large	20,540	258,423	11.9	5.5	4.1	14.3	19.5	3.5	1.2	4.8	2.8	11,668	45,151
VIRGINIA	204,131	3,483,867	6.9	5.7	3.0	12.3	13.7	4.8	1.6	14.6	2.8	202,239	58,050
District 1	17,739	235,380	4.7	10.8	4.9	17.0	13.3	4.1	1.4	9.0	1.1	10,448	44,388
District 2	16,729	235,871	4.8	6.0	2.1	14.9	12.8	5.6	2.9	10.0	1.7	9,848	41,752
District 3	16,927	350,922	13.6	4.7	3.3	12.4	18.7	3.6	2.0	7.5	1.8	17,640	50,267
District 4	16,194	287,592	9.1	6.8	4.6	12.3	15.6	4.4	1.8	6.4	1.3	15,099	52,500
District 5	16,762	214,760	11.5	7.3	2.6	15.2	18.5	3.2	1.3	6.1	1.7	9,698	45,159
District 6	18,202	310,648	14.2	5.6	3.2	13.1	16.9	4.4	1.2	3.9	1.3	13,305	42,829
District 7	19,614	311,909	3.0	6.2	3.6	14.4	14.3	11.7	1.8	8.4	2.5	17,564	56,310
District 8	20,431	380,881	1.0	3.7	1.4	9.6	9.4	2.5	2.0	27.1	3.3	27,722	72,785
District 9	13,815	203,710	19.4	4.0	3.8	16.8	18.1	2.9	0.9	3.9	1.6	8,007	39,307
District 10	24,421	381,496	5.2	7.3	2.8	11.8	10.8	2.6	1.3	20.8	3.4	24,183	63,389
District 11	22,461	493,201	0.7	3.7	2.0	8.3	10.7	5.8	1.6	32.8	7.0	43,172	87,534
WASHINGTON	194,967	2,959,864	9.1	7.3	4.6	11.6	15.1	3.9	1.9	7.6	5.4	203,851	68,872
District 1	20,149	301,879	9.2	10.1	4.6	8.5	9.2	2.2	1.5	10.5	19.2	32,479	107,589
District 2	20,608	287,921	22.1	8.4	3.2	14.9	13.7	4.2	1.8	4.3	2.0	15,920	55,293
District 3	17,269	219,391	12.0	10.0	4.8	13.2	16.5	3.6	1.7	4.8	1.7	11,425	52,075
District 4	15,054	210,316	11.6	8.2	6.2	14.7	16.6	2.3	1.4	6.0	1.1	10,288	48,915
District 5	17,822	248,032	9.0	6.3	4.9	13.9	21.6	5.2	1.9	4.5	2.3	11,897	47,966
District 6	17,703	209,708	4.7	5.8	2.3	16.4	25.0	3.3	1.8	5.5	1.1	10,255	48,902
District 7	29,196	533,153	3.1	4.4	3.1	8.0	12.8	5.6	2.7	13.2	7.5	48,364	90,713
District 8	16,749	186,462	8.9	10.7	6.8	14.3	13.1	1.8	1.6	3.6	2.2	10,064	53,973
District 9	23,837	492,917	9.4	5.6	6.2	8.7	13.6	3.5	2.1	6.6	6.6	38,484	78,074
District 10	15,840	224,563	6.6	9.8	4.7	15.8	18.3	3.4	1.9	3.5	1.7	10,592	47,169
WEST VIRGINIA	35,323	542,148	8.7	4.5	3.3	14.6	24.8	3.1	1.2	4.5	1.4	22,840	42,128
District 1	12,558	204,824	9.2	4.2	3.0	14.2	25.6	2.8	1.0	4.7	1.3	8,970	43,796
District 2	11,878	177,877	10.1	5.2	3.8	14.6	22.4	3.4	1.3	4.5	1.5	7,538	42,379
District 3	10,522	149,151	7.1	4.1	3.1	16.3	28.1	2.2	0.9	3.5	1.5	5,792	38,835
WISCONSIN	141,326	2,599,347	18.1	4.8	4.9	11.9	16.0	5.6	1.1	4.4	2.1	131,210	50,478
District 1	15,499	266,343	20.5	4.8	5.8	16.5	13.5	2.2	1.0	2.7	1.0	12,224	45,894
District 2	19,474	384,679	11.6	5.0	4.7	11.8	16.6	7.3	1.4	8.4	5.2	21,532	55,973
District 3	16,777	282,046	18.7	4.5	3.9	13.5	17.3	5.1	0.9	2.6	1.7	12,588	44,630
District 4	13,578	312,082	10.6	2.2	4.7	6.9	21.0	9.5	1.5	5.7	2.7	18,155	58,175
District 5	21,270	410,704	15.9	5.3	6.8	12.0	15.5	5.2	1.4	4.7	1.7	22,018	53,610
District 6	16,654	315,537	27.7	5.3	3.7	11.3	14.1	3.7	0.9	3.5	1.0	15,303	48,498
District 7	19,047	256,273	24.1	5.1	3.7	14.0	18.5	4.0	0.7	2.3	1.0	11,159	43,545
District 8	18,377	324,179	22.3	6.1	4.6	12.2	13.7	5.1	0.8	3.3	1.5	15,697	48,419
WYOMING	21,770	206,266	5.1	9.1	3.6	14.5	16.1	3.4	2.2	5.2	1.9	10,107	49,002
At Large	21,770	206,266	5.1	9.1	3.6	14.5	16.1	3.4	2.2	5.2	1.9	10,107	49,002

APPENDIX A
GEOGRAPHIC CONCEPTS AND CODES

GEOGRAPHIC AREAS COVERED

County and City Extra presents data for states (Table A), states and counties (Table B), metropolitan areas (Table C), cities with populations of 25,000 or more in 2020 (Table D), and congressional districts (Table E).

STATES AND COUNTIES

Data are presented for each of the 50 states, the District of Columbia, and the United States as a whole. The states are arranged alphabetically and counties in Table B are arranged alphabetically within each state. Data are presented for 3,144 counties and county equivalents.

County equivalents

In Louisiana, the primary divisions of the state are known as parishes rather than counties. In Alaska, the county equivalents are the organized boroughs, together with the census areas that were developed for general statistical purposes by the State of Alaska and the U.S. Census Bureau. Four states—Maryland, Missouri, Nevada, and Virginia—have one or more incorporated places that are legally independent of any county and thus constitute primary divisions of their states. Within each state, independent cities are listed alphabetically following the list of counties. The District of Columbia is not divided into counties or county equivalents—data for the entire district are presented as a county equivalent. New York City contains five counties: Bronx, Kings, New York, Queens, and Richmond.

County changes since the 2010 census

- The independent city of Bedford, VA, changed to town status and was added to Bedford County, effective July 1, 2013.
- Wade Hampton Census Area, AK (02-270), changed its name and FIPS code to Kusilvak Census Area (02-158), effective July 1, 2015.
- Shannon County, SD (46-113), changed its name and FIPS code to Oglala Lakota County (46-102), effective May 1, 2015.
- Petersburg Borough, AK, was created from part of Petersburg Census Area and part of Hoonah-Angoon Census Area. Petersburg Borough retains the FIPS code 02-195, formerly used by Petersburg Census Area, effective January 3, 2013.
- Prince of Wales-Hyder Census Area, AK, added part of the former Petersburg Census Area, effective January 3, 2013.
- Valdez-Cordova Census Area, AK (02-261), was split to form two new census areas, effective January 2, 2019.
- Chugach Census Area, AK (02-063), was created from part of the former Valdez-Cordova Census Area (02-261), effective January 2, 2019.
- Copper River Census Area, AK (02-066), was created from part of the former Valdez-Cordova Census Area (02-261), effective January 2, 2019.

County changes since the 2000 census

- Broomfield County, CO, was created from parts of Adams, Boulder, Jefferson, and Weld counties, effective November 15, 2001. The boundaries of Broomfield County reflect the boundaries of the City of Broomfield legally in effect on that date.
- Clifton Forge, VA, formerly an independent city, became a town within Alleghany County, effective July 1, 2001.
- Effective June 20, 2007, the Skagway-Hoonah-Angoon Census Area in Alaska was divided into the Skagway Municipality and the Hoonah-Angoon Census Area.
- In May and June 2008, the Wrangell-Petersburg and Prince of Wales-Outer Ketchikan Census Areas in Alaska were dissolved and replaced by Wrangell City and Borough, Petersburg Census Area, and Prince of Wales Census Area. Some territory from the Prince of Wales Outer Ketchikan Census Area became part of the existing Ketchikan Gateway Borough.

METROPOLITAN AREAS

Table C presents data for 384 metropolitan statistical areas and 31 metropolitan divisions, which are located within the 11 largest metropolitan statistical areas. The metropolitan statistical areas are listed alphabetically, and the metropolitan divisions are listed alphabetically under the metropolitan statistical area of which they are components.

The U.S. Office of Management and Budget (OMB) defines metropolitan and micropolitan statistical areas according to published standards. The major purpose of defining these areas is to enable all U.S. government agencies to use the same geographic definitions in tabulating and publishing data. The general concept of a metropolitan or micropolitan statistical area is that of a core area containing a substantial population nucleus, together with adjacent communities that have a high degree of economic and social integration with the core.

New delineations of these core-based statistical areas (CBSAs) based on the 2010 census were released in February 2013 and updated in July 2015, August 2017, September 2018, and March 2020. Table C in this book uses these 2020 delineations for metropolitan areas and metropolitan divisions, reflecting no changes in metropolitan areas from the 2018 delineations. Micropolitan areas are not included in Table C. Many of the data items in Table C were released under the old scheme but have been aggregated from county data of the newly defined 2018 metropolitan areas, which results in a higher level of data suppression for those items. The September 2018 changes were far more substantial than those of previous years. Users should be aware of these changes. A complete list is included as Appendix D.

Appendix B lists the metropolitan areas and metropolitan divisions with their component counties and 2010 census populations and their 2020 estimated populations. Appendix C lists the metropolitan and micropolitan areas, together with their 2010 census populations and their 2020 estimated populations. Appendix C includes one new micropolitan area from the March 6, 2020, delineations.

Standard definitions of metropolitan areas were first issued in 1949 by the Bureau of the Budget (the predecessor of OMB), under the designation "standard metropolitan area" (SMA). The term was changed to "standard metropolitan statistical area" (SMSA) in 1959 and to "metropolitan statistical area" (MSA) in 1983. The term "metropolitan area" (MA) was adopted in 1990 and referred collectively to metropolitan statistical areas (MSAs), consolidated metropolitan statistical areas (CMSAs), and primary metropolitan statistical areas (PMSAs). The term "core-based statistical area" (CBSA) became effective in 2000 and refers collectively to metropolitan and micropolitan statistical areas.

The 2010 standards provide that each CBSA must contain at least one urban area of 10,000 or more population. Each metropolitan statistical area must have at least one urbanized area of 50,000 or more inhabitants. Each micropolitan statistical area must have at least one urban cluster of at least 10,000 but less than 50,000 people.

Under the standards, a metro area contains a core urban area of 50,000 or more population, and a micro area contains an urban core of at least 10,000 (but less than 50,000) population. Each metro or micro area consists of one or more counties and includes the counties containing the core urban area, as well as any adjacent counties that have a high degree of social and economic integration (as measured by commuting to work) with the urban core.

If specified criteria are met, a metropolitan statistical area containing a single core with a population of 2.5 million or more may be subdivided to form smaller groupings of counties referred to as "metropolitan divisions."

As of March 6, 2020, there were 384 metropolitan statistical areas and 543 micropolitan statistical areas in the United States. Table C includes the 384 metropolitan statistical areas and the 31 metropolitan divisions. The metropolitan areas and metropolitan divisions are listed in Appendix B with their 2010 census population counts. The metropolitan areas, metropolitan divisions, and micropolitan areas are listed in Appendix C with their 2010 census populations and their 2020 populations. Appendix D lists the many changes made to metropolitan areas with the 2018 delineations. In March 2020 a new delineation established Bluffton, IN, as a new micropolitan area.

The largest city in each metropolitan or micropolitan statistical area is designated a "principal city." Additional cities qualify if specified requirements are met concerning population size and employment. The title of each metropolitan or micropolitan statistical area consists of the names of up to three of its principal cities and the name of each state into which the metropolitan or micropolitan statistical area extends. Titles of metropolitan divisions are typically also based on principal city names, but in certain cases consist of county names. The principal city need not be an incorporated place if it meets the requirements of population size and employment. Usually such a principal city is a census designated place in decennial census data, but it is not included in most other data sources and is not in Table D (cities) in this volume.

In view of the importance of cities and towns in New England, the 2010 standards also provide for a set of geographic areas that are defined using cities and towns in the six New England states. These New England city and town areas (NECTAs) are not included in this volume.

Appendix B lists the 384 metropolitan statistical areas, together with their component metropolitan divisions, where appropriate, the component counties of each area, and their 2010 census populations. Appendix C provides the same information for the 384 metropolitan areas delineated in September 2018, and it also includes the 543 micropolitan statistical areas delineated in March 2020. Maps showing the metropolitan and micropolitan areas within each state can be found at https://www.census.gov/geographies/reference-maps/2020/geo/cbsa.html.

CITIES

Table D presents data for 1,561 cities with 2020 census populations of 25,000 or more. Corresponding data for states are also provided. The states are arranged alphabetically and the cities are ordered alphabetically within each state.

As used in this volume, the term "city" refers to places that have been incorporated as cities, boroughs, towns, or villages under the laws of their respective states. Towns in the New England states and New York are treated as minor civil divisions (MCDs) and are not included in the cities database. For Hawaii, data for the census designated places (CDPs) are included in the cities table, since the Census Bureau does not recognize any incorporated places in Hawaii. CDPs are delineated by the Census Bureau, in cooperation with states and localities, as statistical counterparts of incorporated places for purposes of the decennial census. CDPs comprise densely settled concentrations of population that are identifiable by name but not legally incorporated as places.

Appendix E lists the 1,561 cities followed by the county where each city is located. If a city includes portions of more than one county, the population in each part is specified.

A consolidated city is an incorporated place that has combined its government functions with a county or subcounty entity but contains one or more other semi-independent incorporated places that continue to function as local governments within the consolidated government. Each consolidated city contains a core city, the area of a consolidated city not included in another separately incorporated place. The census geographic term for this core is the "balance" of the consolidated city. Thus the "balance" is essentially the core city of the consolidated government. This volume includes the consolidated city data where possible, but some data sources include numbers only for the "balance," and others do not specify which entity is represented.

Consolidated cities included in this volume are Milford, CT; Athens-Clarke County, GA; Augusta-Richmond County, GA; Indianapolis, IN; Louisville-Jefferson County, KY; Butte-Silver Bow, MT; and Nashville-Davidson, TN.

Appendix E lists these seven consolidated cities, followed by the component places and their 2020 census populations.

On January 1, 2014, Macon, GA, consolidated with Bibb County. A small portion of Macon that was in Jones County was de-annexed. Data from years prior to 2015 represent the smaller Macon city rather than the consolidated Macon-Bibb County.

CONGRESSIONAL DISTRICTS

The congressional districts shown in this volume are the districts used for the election of the 116th Congress, which convened in January 2019. These are the districts that were established following the 2010 Census and are based on population data from that census. Data are shown for the 435 regular districts plus the District of Columbia, which has a non-voting delegate but no representative. Corresponding data for each state also are included. States are listed alphabetically and districts are listed numerically within each state. Maps showing congressional districts for the 116th Congress can be found at https://www.census.gov/geographies/reference-maps/2019/geo/cong-dist-116-wall.html.

GEOGRAPHIC CODES

Tables A, B, C, and D provide, in one or more columns at the beginning of the table, a geographic code or codes for each area.

In Table B (states and counties), a 5-digit state and county code is given for each state and county. The first 2 digits indicate the state; the remaining 3 represent the county. Within each state, the counties are listed in order, beginning with 001, with even numbers usually omitted. Independent cities follow the counties and begin with the number 510. In the second column of Table B, a 5-digit core-based statistical area (CBSA) code is given for those counties that are within metropolitan and micropolitan areas. In Table A, a 2-digit state code is provided. The state code is a sequential numbering, with some gaps, of the states and the District of Columbia in alphabetical order from Alabama (01) to Wyoming (56).

These codes have been established by the U.S. government as Federal Information Processing Standards and are often referred to as "FIPS codes." They are used by U.S. government agencies and many other organizations for data presentation. The codes are provided in this volume for use in matching the data given here with other data sources in which counties are identified by FIPS code. The metro area codes will also enable the user to identify the metro area of which a county is a component. Table C (metropolitan areas) provides the same metro area codes for each metropolitan area as well as metropolitan division codes where appropriate.

Table D (cities) provides, in the first column, a 7-digit state and place code. The first 2 digits identify the state and are the same as the FIPS codes described above. The remaining 5 digits are the place FIPS codes established by the U.S. government.

INDEPENDENT CITIES

The following independent cities are not included in any county; their data are presented separately in this volume.

MARYLAND
Baltimore (separate from Baltimore County)

MISSOURI
St. Louis (separate from St. Louis County)

NEVADA
Carson City

VIRGINIA

Alexandria	Manassas
Bristol	Manassas Park
Buena Vista	Martinsville
Charlottesville	Newport News
Chesapeake	Norfolk
Colonial Heights	Norton
Covington	Petersburg
Danville	Poquoson
Emporia	Portsmouth
Fairfax	Radford
Falls Church	Richmond
Franklin	Roanoke
Fredericksburg	Salem
Galax	Staunton
Hampton	Suffolk
Harrisonburg	Virginia Beach
Hopewell	Waynesboro
Lexington	Williamsburg

COUNTY TYPE

Table B (states and counties) provides, in the third column, a *county type* code that identifies each county by its metropolitan/nonmetropolitan status and its size. These are the "rural-urban continuum codes" developed by the Economic Research Service of the U.S. Department of Agriculture.

The 2013 rural-urban continuum codes form a classification scheme that distinguishes metropolitan counties by size and nonmetropolitan counties by degree of urbanization and proximity to metro areas. The standard OMB metro and nonmetro categories have been subdivided into 3 metro and 6 nonmetro categories, resulting in a 9-part county codification. This scheme was originally developed in 1974. The codes were updated in 1983, 1993, and 2003 and slightly revised in 1988. The 1988 revision was first published in 1990. This scheme allows researchers to break county data into finer residential groups, beyond metro and nonmetro, particularly for the analysis of trends in nonmetro areas that are related to population density and metro influence. The 2013 and 2003 rural-urban continuum codes are not directly comparable with the codes from previous years because of the new methodology used in developing the 2013 metropolitan areas.

Metropolitan counties

1. Counties in metro areas of 1 million population or more.
2. Counties in metro areas of 250,000 to 1 million population.
3. Counties in metro areas of fewer than 250,000 population.

Nonmetropolitan counties

4. Urban population of 20,000 or more, adjacent to a metro area.
5. Urban population of 20,000 or more, not adjacent to a metro area.
6. Urban population of 2,500 to 19,999, adjacent to a metro area.
7. Urban population of 2,500 to 19,999, not adjacent to a metro area.
8. Completely rural or less than 2,500 urban population, adjacent to a metro area.
9. Completely rural or less than 2,500 urban population, not adjacent to a metro area.

APPENDIX B
METROPOLITAN STATISTICAL AREAS, METROPOLITAN DIVISIONS, AND COMPONENTS
(as defined March 2020)

State/ County FIPS code	Core-based statistical area	Title and Geographic Components	2010 census population	2020 census population
10180		Abilene, TX Metro area	165,252	176,579
10180	48059	Callahan County	13,545	13,708
10180	48253	Jones County	20,192	19,663
10180	48441	Taylor County	131,515	143,208
10420		Akron, OH Metro area	703,196	702,219
10420	39133	Portage County	161,424	161,791
10420	39153	Summit County	541,772	540,428
10500		Albany, GA Metro area	154,033	148,922
10500	13095	Dougherty County	94,564	85,790
10500	13177	Lee County	28,295	33,163
10500	13273	Terrell County	9,507	9,185
10500	13321	Worth County	21,667	20,784
10540		Albany-Lebanon, OR Metro area	116,681	128,610
10540	41043	Linn County	116,681	128,610
10580		Albany-Schenectady-Troy, NY Metro area	870,713	899,262
10580	36001	Albany County	304,208	314,848
10580	36083	Rensselaer County	159,433	161,130
10580	36091	Saratoga County	219,598	235,509
10580	36093	Schenectady County	154,751	158,061
10580	36095	Schoharie County	32,723	29,714
10740		Albuquerque, NM Metro area	887,063	916,528
10740	35001	Bernalillo County	662,477	676,444
10740	35043	Sandoval County	131,621	148,834
10740	35057	Torrance County	16,380	15,045
10740	35061	Valencia County	76,585	76,205
10780		Alexandria, LA Metro area	153,918	152,192
10780	22043	Grant Parish	22,309	22,169
10780	22079	Rapides Parish	131,609	130,023
10900		Allentown-Bethlehem-Easton, PA-NJ Metro area	821,273	861,889
10900	34041	Warren County	108,642	109,632
10900	42025	Carbon County	65,244	64,749
10900	42077	Lehigh County	349,675	374,557
10900	42095	Northampton County	297,712	312,951
11020		Altoona, PA Metro area	127,117	122,822
11020	42013	Blair County	127,117	122,822
11100		Amarillo, TX Metro area	251,935	268,691
11100	48011	Armstrong County	1,901	1,848
11100	48065	Carson County	6,184	5,807
11100	48359	Oldham County	2,052	1,758
11100	48375	Potter County	121,078	118,525
11100	48381	Randall County	120,720	140,753
11180		Ames, IA Metro area	115,850	125,252
11180	19015	Boone County	26,308	26,715
11180	19169	Story County	89,542	98,537
11260		Anchorage, AK Metro area	380,821	398,328
11260	02020	Anchorage Municipality	291,836	291,247
11260	02170	Matanuska-Susitna Borough	88,985	107,081
11460		Ann Arbor, MI Metro area	345,163	372,258
11460	26161	Washtenaw County	345,163	372,258
11500		Anniston-Oxford, AL Metro area	118,526	116,441
11500	01015	Calhoun County	118,526	116,441
11540		Appleton, WI Metro area	225,667	243,147
11540	55015	Calumet County	48,981	52,442
11540	55087	Outagamie County	176,686	190,705
11700		Asheville, NC Metro area	424,863	469,015
11700	37021	Buncombe County	238,330	269,452
11700	37087	Haywood County	59,032	62,089
11700	37089	Henderson County	106,719	116,281
11700	37115	Madison County	20,782	21,193

State/ County FIPS code	Core-based statistical area	Title and Geographic Components	2010 census population	2020 census population
12020		Athens-Clarke County, GA Metro area	192,567	215,415
12020	13059	Clarke County	116,688	128,671
12020	13195	Madison County	28,167	30,120
12020	13219	Oconee County	32,831	41,799
12020	13221	Oglethorpe County	14,881	14,825
12060		Atlanta-Sandy Springs-Alpharetta, GA Metro area	5,286,718	6,089,815
12060	13013	Barrow County	69,356	83,505
12060	13015	Bartow County	100,092	108,901
12060	13035	Butts County	23,695	25,434
12060	13045	Carroll County	110,570	119,148
12060	13057	Cherokee County	214,381	266,620
12060	13063	Clayton County	259,630	297,595
12060	13067	Cobb County	688,065	766,149
12060	13077	Coweta County	127,369	146,158
12060	13085	Dawson County	22,382	26,798
12060	13089	DeKalb County	691,961	764,382
12060	13097	Douglas County	132,282	144,237
12060	13113	Fayette County	106,560	119,194
12060	13117	Forsyth County	175,484	251,283
12060	13121	Fulton County	920,445	1,066,710
12060	13135	Gwinnett County	805,286	957,062
12060	13143	Haralson County	28,775	29,919
12060	13149	Heard County	11,829	11,412
12060	13151	Henry County	203,777	240,712
12060	13159	Jasper County	13,894	14,588
12060	13171	Lamar County	18,311	18,500
12060	13199	Meriwether County	21,978	20,613
12060	13211	Morgan County	17,871	20,097
12060	13217	Newton County	99,967	112,483
12060	13223	Paulding County	142,397	168,661
12060	13227	Pickens County	29,404	33,216
12060	13231	Pike County	17,873	18,889
12060	13247	Rockdale County	85,169	93,570
12060	13255	Spalding County	64,109	67,306
12060	13297	Walton County	83,806	96,673
12100		Atlantic City-Hammonton, NJ Metro area	274,525	274,534
12100	34001	Atlantic County	274,525	274,534
12220		Auburn-Opelika, AL Metro area	140,287	174,241
12220	01081	Lee County	140,287	174,241
12260		Augusta-Richmond County, GA-SC Metro area	564,893	611,000
12260	13033	Burke County	23,326	24,596
12260	13073	Columbia County	124,016	156,010
12260	13181	Lincoln County	7,996	7,690
12260	13189	McDuffie County	21,867	21,632
12260	13245	Richmond County	200,594	206,607
12260	45003	Aiken County	160,129	168,808
12260	45037	Edgefield County	26,965	25,657
12420		Austin-Round Rock-Georgetown, TX Metro area	1,716,323	2,283,371
12420	48021	Bastrop County	74,217	97,216
12420	48055	Caldwell County	38,055	45,883
12420	48209	Hays County	157,103	241,067
12420	48453	Travis County	1,024,444	1,290,188
12420	48491	Williamson County	422,504	609,017
12540		Bakersfield, CA Metro area	839,621	909,235
12540	06029	Kern County	839,621	909,235
12580		Baltimore-Columbia-Towson, MD Metro area	2,710,598	2,844,510
12580	24003	Anne Arundel County	537,631	588,261
12580	24005	Baltimore County	805,324	854,535
12580	24013	Carroll County	167,141	172,891
12580	24025	Harford County	244,824	260,924
12580	24027	Howard County	287,123	332,317
12580	24035	Queen Anne's County	47,785	49,874
12580	24510	Baltimore city	620,770	585,708
12620		Bangor, ME Metro area	153,931	152,199
12620	23019	Penobscot County	153,931	152,199

METROPOLITAN STATISTICAL AREAS, METROPOLITAN DIVISIONS, AND COMPONENTS (as defined March 2020)—*Continued*

State/ County FIPS code	Core-based statistical area	Title and Geographic Components	2010 census population	2020 census population
12700		Barnstable Town, MA Metro area	215,880	228,996
12700	25001	Barnstable County	215,880	228,996
12940		Baton Rouge, LA Metro area	825,917	870,569
12940	22005	Ascension Parish	107,215	126,500
12940	22007	Assumption Parish	23,416	21,039
12940	22033	East Baton Rouge Parish	440,525	456,781
12940	22037	East Feliciana Parish	20,260	19,539
12940	22047	Iberville Parish	33,404	30,241
12940	22063	Livingston Parish	127,674	142,282
12940	22077	Pointe Coupee Parish	22,808	20,758
12940	22091	St. Helena Parish	11,205	10,920
12940	22121	West Baton Rouge Parish	23,785	27,199
12940	22125	West Feliciana Parish	15,625	15,310
12980		Battle Creek, MI Metro area	136,150	134,310
12980	26025	Calhoun County	136,150	134,310
13020		Bay City, MI Metro area	107,773	103,856
13020	26017	Bay County	107,773	103,856
13140		Beaumont-Port Arthur, TX Metro area	388,749	397,565
13140	48199	Hardin County	54,635	56,231
13140	48245	Jefferson County	252,277	256,526
13140	48361	Orange County	81,837	84,808
13220		Beckley, WV Metro area	124,914	115,079
13220	54019	Fayette County	46,049	40,488
13220	54081	Raleigh County	78,865	74,591
13380		Bellingham, WA Metro area	201,146	226,847
13380	53073	Whatcom County	201,146	226,847
13460		Bend, OR Metro area	157,728	198,253
13460	41017	Deschutes County	157,728	198,253
13740		Billings, MT Metro area	167,165	184,167
13740	30009	Carbon County	10,078	10,473
13740	30095	Stillwater County	9,096	8,963
13740	30111	Yellowstone County	147,991	164,731
13780		Binghamton, NY Metro area	251,724	247,138
13780	36007	Broome County	200,675	198,683
13780	36107	Tioga County	51,049	48,455
13820		Birmingham-Hoover, AL Metro area	1,061,039	1,115,289
13820	01007	Bibb County	22,915	22,293
13820	01009	Blount County	57,322	59,134
13820	01021	Chilton County	43,632	45,014
13820	01073	Jefferson County	658,567	674,721
13820	01115	St. Clair County	83,350	91,103
13820	01117	Shelby County	195,253	223,024
13900		Bismarck, ND Metro area	110,625	133,626
13900	38015	Burleigh County	81,308	98,458
13900	38059	Morton County	27,469	33,291
13900	38065	Oliver County	1,848	1,877
13980		Blacksburg-Christiansburg, VA Metro area	162,960	166,378
13980	51071	Giles County	17,286	16,787
13980	51121	Montgomery County	94,422	99,721
13980	51155	Pulaski County	34,857	33,800
13980	51750	Radford city	16,395	16,070
14010		Bloomington, IL Metro area	169,577	170,954
14010	17113	McLean County	169,577	170,954
14020		Bloomington, IN Metro area	159,535	161,039
14020	18105	Monroe County	137,962	139,718
14020	18119	Owen County	21,573	21,321
14100		Bloomsburg-Berwick, PA Metro area	85,555	82,863
14100	42037	Columbia County	67,299	64,727
14100	42093	Montour County	18,256	18,136
14260		Boise City, ID Metro area	616,566	764,718
14260	16001	Ada County	392,372	494,967
14260	16015	Boise County	7,027	7,610
14260	16027	Canyon County	188,922	231,105
14260	16045	Gem County	16,719	19,123
14260	16073	Owyhee County	11,526	11,913
14460		Boston-Cambridge-Newton, MA-NH Metro area	4,552,595	4,941,632
14460		Boston, MA Div 14454	1,888,025	2,054,736
14460	25021	Norfolk County	670,910	725,981
14460	25023	Plymouth County	494,932	530,819
14460	25025	Suffolk County	722,183	797,936
14460		Cambridge-Newton-Framingham, MA Div 15764	2,246,215	2,441,831
14460	25009	Essex County	743,082	809,829
14460	25017	Middlesex County	1,503,133	1,632,002
14460		Rockingham County-Strafford County, NH Div 40484	418,355	445,065
14460	33015	Rockingham County	295,204	314,176
14460	33017	Strafford County	123,151	130,889
14500		Boulder, CO Metro area	294,560	330,758
14500	08013	Boulder County	294,560	330,758
14540		Bowling Green, KY Metro area	158,613	179,639
14540	21003	Allen County	19,958	20,588
14540	21031	Butler County	12,697	12,371
14540	21061	Edmonson County	12,177	12,126
14540	21227	Warren County	113,781	134,554
14740		Bremerton-Silverdale-Port Orchard, WA Metro area	251,143	275,611
14740	53035	Kitsap County	251,143	275,611
14860		Bridgeport-Stamford-Norwalk, CT Metro area	916,904	957,419
14860	09001	Fairfield County	916,904	957,419
15180		Brownsville-Harlingen, TX Metro area	406,215	421,017
15180	48061	Cameron County	406,215	421,017
15260		Brunswick, GA Metro area	112,385	113,495
15260	13025	Brantley County	18,428	18,021
15260	13127	Glynn County	79,627	84,499
15260	13191	McIntosh County	14,330	10,975
15380		Buffalo-Cheektowaga, NY Metro area	1,135,614	1,166,902
15380	36029	Erie County	919,134	954,236
15380	36063	Niagara County	216,480	212,666
15500		Burlington, NC Metro area	151,155	171,415
15500	37001	Alamance County	151,155	171,415
15540		Burlington-South Burlington, VT Metro area	211,264	225,562
15540	50007	Chittenden County	156,535	168,323
15540	50011	Franklin County	47,759	49,946
15540	50013	Grand Isle County	6,970	7,293
15680		California-Lexington Park, MD Metro area	105,144	113,777
15680	24037	St. Mary's County	105,144	113,777
15940		Canton-Massillon, OH Metro area	404,425	401,574
15940	39019	Carroll County	28,834	26,721
15940	39151	Stark County	375,591	374,853
15980		Cape Coral-Fort Myers, FL Metro area	618,755	760,822
15980	12071	Lee County	618,755	760,822
16020		Cape Girardeau, MO-IL Metro area	96,270	97,517
16020	17003	Alexander County	8,238	5,240
16020	29017	Bollinger County	12,358	10,567
16020	29031	Cape Girardeau County	75,674	81,710

METROPOLITAN STATISTICAL AREAS, METROPOLITAN DIVISIONS, AND COMPONENTS (as defined March 2020)—*Continued*

State/ County FIPS code	Core-based statistical area	Title and Geographic Components	2010 census population	2020 census population
16060		Carbondale-Marion, IL Metro area	139,148	133,435
16060	17077	Jackson County	60,206	52,974
16060	17087	Johnson County	12,577	13,308
16060	17199	Williamson County	66,365	67,153
16180		Carson City, NV Metro area	55,269	58,639
16180	32510	Carson City	55,269	58,639
16220		Casper, WY Metro area	75,448	79,955
16220	56025	Natrona County	75,448	79,955
16300		Cedar Rapids, IA Metro area	257,948	276,520
16300	19011	Benton County	26,069	25,575
16300	19105	Jones County	20,636	20,646
16300	19113	Linn County	211,243	230,299
16540		Chambersburg-Waynesboro, PA Metro area	149,631	155,932
16540	42055	Franklin County	149,631	155,932
16580		Champaign-Urbana, IL Metro area	217,806	222,538
16580	17019	Champaign County	201,081	205,865
16580	17147	Piatt County	16,725	16,673
16620		Charleston, WV Metro area	277,985	258,859
16620	54005	Boone County	24,625	21,809
16620	54015	Clay County	9,384	8,051
16620	54035	Jackson County	29,214	27,791
16620	54039	Kanawha County	193,053	180,745
16620	54043	Lincoln County	21,709	20,463
16700		Charleston-North Charleston, SC Metro area	664,645	799,636
16700	45015	Berkeley County	178,373	229,861
16700	45019	Charleston County	350,128	408,235
16700	45035	Dorchester County	136,144	161,540
16740		Charlotte-Concord-Gastonia, NC-SC Metro area	2,243,963	2,660,329
16740	37007	Anson County	26,929	22,055
16740	37025	Cabarrus County	178,121	225,804
16740	37071	Gaston County	206,098	227,943
16740	37097	Iredell County	159,464	186,693
16740	37109	Lincoln County	78,014	86,810
16740	37119	Mecklenburg County	919,664	1,115,482
16740	37159	Rowan County	138,494	146,875
16740	37179	Union County	201,332	238,267
16740	45023	Chester County	33,159	32,294
16740	45057	Lancaster County	76,651	96,016
16740	45091	York County	226,037	282,090
16820		Charlottesville, VA Metro area	201,569	221,524
16820	51003	Albemarle County	98,998	112,395
16820	51065	Fluvanna County	25,742	27,249
16820	51079	Greene County	18,389	20,552
16820	51125	Nelson County	15,015	14,775
16820	51540	Charlottesville city	43,425	46,553
16860		Chattanooga, TN-GA Metro area	528,126	562,647
16860	13047	Catoosa County	63,925	67,872
16860	13083	Dade County	16,643	16,251
16860	13295	Walker County	68,738	67,654
16860	47065	Hamilton County	336,477	366,207
16860	47115	Marion County	28,222	28,837
16860	47153	Sequatchie County	14,121	15,826
16940		Cheyenne, WY Metro area	91,885	100,512
16940	56021	Laramie County	91,885	100,512
16980		Chicago-Naperville-Elgin, IL-IN-WI Metro area	9,461,537	9,618,502
16980		Chicago-Naperville-Evanston, IL Div 16984	7,148,308	7,267,535
16980	17031	Cook County	5,195,026	5,275,541
16980	17043	DuPage County	916,741	932,877
16980	17063	Grundy County	50,079	52,533
16980	17111	McHenry County	308,882	310,229
16980	17197	Will County	677,580	696,355
16980		Elgin, IL Div 20994	735,288	748,811
16980	17037	DeKalb County	105,162	100,420
16980	17089	Kane County	515,322	516,522
16980	17093	Kendall County	114,804	131,869
16980		Gary, IN Div 23844	708,117	718,663
16980	18073	Jasper County	33,481	32,918
16980	18089	Lake County	496,108	498,700
16980	18111	Newton County	14,239	13,830
16980	18127	Porter County	164,289	173,215
16980		Lake County-Kenosha County, IL-WI Div 29404	869,824	883,493
16980	17097	Lake County	703,400	714,342
16980	55059	Kenosha County	166,424	169,151
17020		Chico, CA Metro area	220,005	211,632
17020	06007	Butte County	220,005	211,632
17140		Cincinnati, OH-KY-IN Metro area	2,137,713	2,256,884
17140	18029	Dearborn County	50,027	50,679
17140	18047	Franklin County	23,098	22,785
17140	18115	Ohio County	6,098	5,940
17140	18161	Union County	7,516	7,087
17140	21015	Boone County	118,810	135,968
17140	21023	Bracken County	8,486	8,400
17140	21037	Campbell County	90,338	93,076
17140	21077	Gallatin County	8,586	8,690
17140	21081	Grant County	24,655	24,941
17140	21117	Kenton County	159,728	169,064
17140	21191	Pendleton County	14,874	14,644
17140	39015	Brown County	44,826	43,676
17140	39017	Butler County	368,136	390,357
17140	39025	Clermont County	197,366	208,601
17140	39061	Hamilton County	802,371	830,639
17140	39165	Warren County	212,798	242,337
17300		Clarksville, TN-KY Metro area	273,942	320,535
17300	21047	Christian County	73,940	72,748
17300	21221	Trigg County	14,327	14,061
17300	47125	Montgomery County	172,362	220,069
17300	47161	Stewart County	13,313	13,657
17420		Cleveland, TN Metro area	115,747	126,164
17420	47011	Bradley County	98,926	108,620
17420	47139	Polk County	16,821	17,544
17460		Cleveland-Elyria, OH Metro area	2,077,277	2,088,251
17460	39035	Cuyahoga County	1,280,114	1,264,817
17460	39055	Geauga County	93,405	95,397
17460	39085	Lake County	230,051	232,603
17460	39093	Lorain County	301,374	312,964
17460	39103	Medina County	172,333	182,470
17660		Coeur d'Alene, ID Metro area	138,466	171,362
17660	16055	Kootenai County	138,466	171,362
17780		College Station-Bryan, TX Metro area	228,668	268,248
17780	48041	Brazos County	194,861	233,849
17780	48051	Burleson County	17,187	17,642
17780	48395	Robertson County	16,620	16,757
17820		Colorado Springs, CO Metro area	645,612	755,105
17820	08041	El Paso County	622,253	730,395
17820	08119	Teller County	23,359	24,710
17860		Columbia, MO Metro area	190,398	210,864
17860	29019	Boone County	162,652	183,610
17860	29053	Cooper County	17,604	17,103
17860	29089	Howard County	10,142	10,151
17900		Columbia, SC Metro area	767,469	829,470
17900	45017	Calhoun County	15,178	14,119
17900	45039	Fairfield County	23,959	20,948
17900	45055	Kershaw County	61,594	65,403
17900	45063	Lexington County	262,453	293,991
17900	45079	Richland County	384,425	416,147
17900	45081	Saluda County	19,860	18,862

METROPOLITAN STATISTICAL AREAS, METROPOLITAN DIVISIONS, AND COMPONENTS (as defined March 2020)—*Continued*

State/ County FIPS code	Core-based statistical area	Title and Geographic Components	2010 census population	2020 census population
17980		Columbus, GA-AL Metro area	308,478	328,883
17980	01113	Russell County	52,963	59,183
17980	13053	Chattahoochee County	11,263	9,565
17980	13145	Harris County	31,994	34,668
17980	13197	Marion County	8,738	7,498
17980	13215	Muscogee County	190,570	206,922
17980	13259	Stewart County	6,060	5,314
17980	13263	Talbot County	6,890	5,733
18020		Columbus, IN Metro area	76,783	82,208
18020	18005	Bartholomew County	76,783	82,208
18140		Columbus, OH Metro area	1,902,008	2,138,926
18140	39041	Delaware County	174,172	214,124
18140	39045	Fairfield County	146,194	158,921
18140	39049	Franklin County	1,163,476	1,323,807
18140	39073	Hocking County	29,369	28,050
18140	39089	Licking County	166,482	178,519
18140	39097	Madison County	43,438	43,824
18140	39117	Morrow County	34,825	34,950
18140	39127	Perry County	36,037	35,408
18140	39129	Pickaway County	55,684	58,539
18140	39159	Union County	52,331	62,784
18580		Corpus Christi, TX Metro area	405,025	421,933
18580	48355	Nueces County	340,223	353,178
18580	48409	San Patricio County	64,802	68,755
18700		Corvallis, OR Metro area	85,581	95,184
18700	41003	Benton County	85,581	95,184
18880		Crestview-Fort Walton Beach-Destin, FL Metro area	235,870	286,973
18880	12091	Okaloosa County	180,824	211,668
18880	12131	Walton County	55,046	75,305
19060		Cumberland, MD-WV Metro area	103,272	95,044
19060	24001	Allegany County	75,047	68,106
19060	54057	Mineral County	28,225	26,938
19100		Dallas-Fort Worth-Arlington, TX Metro area	6,366,537	7,637,387
19100		Dallas-Plano-Irving, TX Div 19124	4,228,853	5,129,966
19100	48085	Collin County	781,419	1,064,465
19100	48113	Dallas County	2,367,430	2,613,539
19100	48121	Denton County	662,557	906,422
19100	48139	Ellis County	149,610	192,455
19100	48231	Hunt County	86,144	99,956
19100	48257	Kaufman County	103,348	145,310
19100	48397	Rockwall County	78,345	107,819
19100		Fort Worth-Arlington-Grapevine, TX Div 23104	2,137,684	2,507,421
19100	48251	Johnson County	150,956	179,927
19100	48367	Parker County	116,949	148,222
19100	48439	Tarrant County	1,810,664	2,110,640
19100	48497	Wise County	59,115	68,632
19140		Dalton, GA Metro area	142,233	142,837
19140	13213	Murray County	39,628	39,973
19140	13313	Whitfield County	102,605	102,864
19180		Danville, IL Metro area	81,625	74,188
19180	17183	Vermilion County	81,625	74,188
19300		Daphne-Fairhope-Foley, AL Metro area	182,265	231,767
19300	01003	Baldwin County	182,265	231,767
19340		Davenport-Moline-Rock Island, IA-IL Metro area	379,681	384,324
19340	17073	Henry County	50,483	49,284
19340	17131	Mercer County	16,434	15,699
19340	17161	Rock Island County	147,541	144,672
19340	19163	Scott County	165,223	174,669
19430		Dayton-Kettering, OH Metro area	799,280	814,049
19430	39057	Greene County	161,577	167,966
19430	39109	Miami County	102,503	108,774
19430	39113	Montgomery County	535,200	537,309

State/ County FIPS code	Core-based statistical area	Title and Geographic Components	2010 census population	2020 census population
19460		Decatur, AL Metro area	153,827	156,494
19460	01079	Lawrence County	34,337	33,073
19460	01103	Morgan County	119,490	123,421
19500		Decatur, IL Metro area	110,777	103,998
19500	17115	Macon County	110,777	103,998
19660		Deltona-Daytona Beach-Ormond Beach, FL Metro area	590,288	668,921
19660	12035	Flagler County	95,692	115,378
19660	12127	Volusia County	494,596	553,543
19740		Denver-Aurora-Lakewood, CO Metro area	2,543,608	2,963,821
19740	08001	Adams County	441,697	519,572
19740	08005	Arapahoe County	572,118	655,070
19740	08014	Broomfield County	55,861	74,112
19740	08019	Clear Creek County	9,073	9,397
19740	08031	Denver County	599,825	715,522
19740	08035	Douglas County	285,465	357,978
19740	08039	Elbert County	23,088	26,062
19740	08047	Gilpin County	5,449	5,808
19740	08059	Jefferson County	534,829	582,910
19740	08093	Park County	16,203	17,390
19780		Des Moines-West Des Moines, IA Metro area	606,474	709,466
19780	19049	Dallas County	66,139	99,678
19780	19077	Guthrie County	10,955	10,623
19780	19099	Jasper County	36,842	37,813
19780	19121	Madison County	15,681	16,548
19780	19153	Polk County	430,631	492,401
19780	19181	Warren County	46,226	52,403
19820		Detroit-Warren-Dearborn, MI Metro area	4,296,227	4,392,041
19820		Detroit-Dearborn-Livonia, MI Div 19804	1,820,473	1,793,561
19820	26163	Wayne County	1,820,473	1,793,561
19820		Warren-Troy-Farmington Hills, MI Div 47664	2,475,754	2,598,480
19820	26087	Lapeer County	88,316	88,619
19820	26093	Livingston County	180,964	193,866
19820	26099	Macomb County	841,039	881,217
19820	26125	Oakland County	1,202,384	1,274,395
19820	26147	St. Clair County	163,051	160,383
20020		Dothan, AL Metro area	145,640	151,007
20020	01061	Geneva County	26,781	26,659
20020	01067	Henry County	17,299	17,146
20020	01069	Houston County	101,560	107,202
20100		Dover, DE Metro area	162,350	181,851
20100	10001	Kent County	162,350	181,851
20220		Dubuque, IA Metro area	93,643	99,266
20220	19061	Dubuque County	93,643	99,266
20260		Duluth, MN-WI Metro area	290,636	291,638
20260	27017	Carlton County	35,386	36,207
20260	27075	Lake County	10,862	10,905
20260	27137	St. Louis County	200,229	200,231
20260	55031	Douglas County	44,159	44,295
20500		Durham-Chapel Hill, NC Metro area	564,193	649,903
20500	37037	Chatham County	63,485	76,285
20500	37063	Durham County	270,001	324,833
20500	37077	Granville County	57,538	60,992
20500	37135	Orange County	133,693	148,696
20500	37145	Person County	39,476	39,097
20700		East Stroudsburg, PA Metro area	169,841	168,327
20700	42089	Monroe County	169,841	168,327
20740		Eau Claire, WI Metro area	161,383	172,007
20740	55017	Chippewa County	62,502	66,297
20740	55035	Eau Claire County	98,881	105,710
20940		El Centro, CA Metro area	174,524	179,702
20940	06025	Imperial County	174,524	179,702

METROPOLITAN STATISTICAL AREAS, METROPOLITAN DIVISIONS, AND COMPONENTS (as defined March 2020)—*Continued*

State/ County FIPS code	Core-based statistical area	Title and Geographic Components	2010 census population	2020 census population
21060		Elizabethtown-Fort Knox, KY Metro area	148,331	155,572
21060	21093	Hardin County	105,537	110,702
21060	21123	Larue County	14,181	14,867
21060	21163	Meade County	28,613	30,003
21140		Elkhart-Goshen, IN Metro area	197,569	207,047
21140	18039	Elkhart County	197,569	207,047
21300		Elmira, NY Metro area	88,847	84,148
21300	36015	Chemung County	88,847	84,148
21340		El Paso, TX Metro area	804,109	868,859
21340	48141	El Paso County	800,633	865,657
21340	48229	Hudspeth County	3,476	3,202
21420		Enid, OK Metro area	60,580	62,846
21420	40047	Garfield County	60,580	62,846
21500		Erie, PA Metro area	280,584	270,876
21500	42049	Erie County	280,584	270,876
21660		Eugene-Springfield, OR Metro area	351,705	382,971
21660	41039	Lane County	351,705	382,971
21780		Evansville, IN-KY Metro area	311,548	314,049
21780	18129	Posey County	25,912	25,222
21780	18163	Vanderburgh County	179,701	180,136
21780	18173	Warrick County	59,689	63,898
21780	21101	Henderson County	46,246	44,793
21820		Fairbanks, AK Metro area	97,585	95,655
21820	02090	Fairbanks North Star Borough	97,585	95,655
22020		Fargo, ND-MN Metro area	208,777	249,843
22020	27027	Clay County	58,999	65,318
22020	38017	Cass County	149,778	184,525
22140		Farmington, NM Metro area	130,045	121,661
22140	35045	San Juan County	130,045	121,661
22180		Fayetteville, NC Metro area	481,011	520,378
22180	37051	Cumberland County	319,431	334,728
22180	37085	Harnett County	114,691	133,568
22180	37093	Hoke County	46,889	52,082
22220		Fayetteville-Springdale-Rogers, AR Metro area	440,121	546,725
22220	05007	Benton County	221,348	284,333
22220	05087	Madison County	15,723	16,521
22220	05143	Washington County	203,050	245,871
22380		Flagstaff, AZ Metro area	134,426	145,101
22380	04005	Coconino County	134,426	145,101
22420		Flint, MI Metro area	425,787	406,211
22420	26049	Genesee County	425,787	406,211
22500		Florence, SC Metro area	205,576	199,964
22500	45031	Darlington County	68,611	62,905
22500	45041	Florence County	136,965	137,059
22520		Florence-Muscle Shoals, AL Metro area	147,137	150,791
22520	01033	Colbert County	54,428	57,227
22520	01077	Lauderdale County	92,709	93,564
22540		Fond du Lac, WI Metro area	101,623	104,154
22540	55039	Fond du Lac County	101,623	104,154
22660		Fort Collins, CO Metro area	299,630	359,066
22660	08069	Larimer County	299,630	359,066
22900		Fort Smith, AR-OK Metro area	248,240	244,310
22900	05033	Crawford County	61,935	60,133
22900	05047	Franklin County	18,137	17,097
22900	05131	Sebastian County	125,740	127,799
22900	40135	Sequoyah County	42,428	39,281
23060		Fort Wayne, IN Metro area	388,626	419,601
23060	18003	Allen County	355,339	385,410
23060	18183	Whitley County	33,287	34,191
23420		Fresno, CA Metro area	930,507	1,008,654
23420	06019	Fresno County	930,507	1,008,654
23460		Gadsden, AL Metro area	104,429	103,436
23460	01055	Etowah County	104,429	103,436
23540		Gainesville, FL Metro area	305,076	339,247
23540	12001	Alachua County	247,337	278,468
23540	12041	Gilchrist County	16,941	17,864
23540	12075	Levy County	40,798	42,915
23580		Gainesville, GA Metro area	179,724	203,136
23580	13139	Hall County	179,724	203,136
23900		Gettysburg, PA Metro area	101,428	103,852
23900	42001	Adams County	101,428	103,852
24020		Glens Falls, NY Metro area	128,946	127,039
24020	36113	Warren County	65,692	65,737
24020	36115	Washington County	63,254	61,302
24140		Goldsboro, NC Metro area	122,661	117,333
24140	37191	Wayne County	122,661	117,333
24220		Grand Forks, ND-MN Metro area	98,464	104,362
24220	27119	Polk County	31,600	31,192
24220	38035	Grand Forks County	66,864	73,170
24260		Grand Island, NE Metro area	72,744	77,038
24260	31079	Hall County	58,611	62,895
24260	31093	Howard County	6,274	6,475
24260	31121	Merrick County	7,859	7,668
24300		Grand Junction, CO Metro area	146,733	155,703
24300	08077	Mesa County	146,733	155,703
24340		Grand Rapids-Kentwood, MI Metro area	993,663	1,087,592
24340	26067	Ionia County	63,901	66,804
24340	26081	Kent County	602,625	657,974
24340	26117	Montcalm County	63,342	66,614
24340	26139	Ottawa County	263,795	296,200
24420		Grants Pass, OR Metro area	82,719	88,090
24420	41033	Josephine County	82,719	88,090
24500		Great Falls, MT Metro area	81,326	84,414
24500	30013	Cascade County	81,326	84,414
24540		Greeley, CO Metro area	252,827	328,981
24540	08123	Weld County	252,827	328,981
24580		Green Bay, WI Metro area	306,241	328,268
24580	55009	Brown County	248,003	268,740
24580	55061	Kewaunee County	20,578	20,563
24580	55083	Oconto County	37,660	38,965
24660		Greensboro-High Point, NC Metro area	723,923	776,566
24660	37081	Guilford County	488,454	541,299
24660	37151	Randolph County	141,824	144,171
24660	37157	Rockingham County	93,645	91,096
24780		Greenville, NC Metro area	168,176	170,243
24780	37147	Pitt County	168,176	170,243
24860		Greenville-Anderson, SC Metro area	824,031	928,195
24860	45007	Anderson County	186,922	203,718
24860	45045	Greenville County	451,211	525,534
24860	45059	Laurens County	66,513	67,539
24860	45077	Pickens County	119,385	131,404
25060		Gulfport-Biloxi, MS Metro area	388,591	416,259
25060	28045	Hancock County	44,023	46,053
25060	28047	Harrison County	187,109	208,621
25060	28059	Jackson County	139,669	143,252
25060	28131	Stone County	17,790	18,333
25180		Hagerstown-Martinsburg, MD-WV Metro area	269,146	293,844
25180	24043	Washington County	147,417	154,705
25180	54003	Berkeley County	104,188	122,076
25180	54065	Morgan County	17,541	17,063

METROPOLITAN STATISTICAL AREAS, METROPOLITAN DIVISIONS, AND COMPONENTS (as defined March 2020)—*Continued*

State/ County FIPS code	Core-based statistical area	Title and Geographic Components	2010 census population	2020 census population
25220		Hammond, LA Metro area	121,109	133,157
25220	22105	Tangipahoa Parish	121,109	133,157
25260		Hanford-Corcoran, CA Metro area	152,974	152,486
25260	06031	Kings County	152,974	152,486
25420		Harrisburg-Carlisle, PA Metro area	549,444	591,712
25420	42041	Cumberland County	235,387	259,469
25420	42043	Dauphin County	268,126	286,401
25420	42099	Perry County	45,931	45,842
25500		Harrisonburg, VA Metro area	125,221	135,571
25500	51165	Rockingham County	76,321	83,757
25500	51660	Harrisonburg city	48,900	51,814
25540		Hartford-East Hartford-Middletown, CT Metro area	1,212,471	1,213,531
25540	09003	Hartford County	894,052	899,498
25540	09007	Middlesex County	165,672	164,245
25540	09013	Tolland County	152,747	149,788
25620		Hattiesburg, MS Metro area	162,418	172,231
25620	28031	Covington County	19,573	18,340
25620	28035	Forrest County	74,862	78,158
25620	28073	Lamar County	55,732	64,222
25620	28111	Perry County	12,251	11,511
25860		Hickory-Lenoir-Morganton, NC Metro area	365,794	365,276
25860	37003	Alexander County	37,182	36,444
25860	37023	Burke County	90,837	87,570
25860	37027	Caldwell County	83,058	80,652
25860	37035	Catawba County	154,717	160,610
25940		Hilton Head Island-Bluffton, SC Metro area	187,010	215,908
25940	45013	Beaufort County	162,219	187,117
25940	45053	Jasper County	24,791	28,791
25980		Hinesville, GA Metro area	77,929	81,424
25980	13179	Liberty County	63,585	65,256
25980	13183	Long County	14,344	16,168
26140		Homosassa Springs, FL Metro area	141,230	153,843
26140	12017	Citrus County	141,230	153,843
26300		Hot Springs, AR Metro area	95,999	100,180
26300	05051	Garland County	95,999	100,180
26380		Houma-Thibodaux, LA Metro area	208,185	207,137
26380	22057	Lafourche Parish	96,642	97,557
26380	22109	Terrebonne Parish	111,543	109,580
26420		Houston-The Woodlands-Sugar Land, TX Metro are	5,920,487	7,122,240
26420	48015	Austin County	28,412	30,167
26420	48039	Brazoria County	313,117	372,031
26420	48071	Chambers County	35,107	46,571
26420	48157	Fort Bend County	584,699	822,779
26420	48167	Galveston County	291,312	350,682
26420	48201	Harris County	4,093,176	4,731,145
26420	48291	Liberty County	75,643	91,628
26420	48339	Montgomery County	455,747	620,443
26420	48473	Waller County	43,274	56,794
26580		Huntington-Ashland, WV-KY-OH Metro area	370,899	359,862
26580	21019	Boyd County	49,534	48,261
26580	21043	Carter County	27,721	26,627
26580	21089	Greenup County	36,906	35,962
26580	39087	Lawrence County	62,448	58,240
26580	54011	Cabell County	96,295	94,350
26580	54079	Putnam County	55,489	57,440
26580	54099	Wayne County	42,506	38,982
26620		Huntsville, AL Metro area	417,593	491,723
26620	01083	Limestone County	82,786	103,570
26620	01089	Madison County	334,807	388,153
26820		Idaho Falls, ID Metro area	133,331	157,429
26820	16019	Bonneville County	104,294	123,964
26820	16023	Butte County	2,893	2,574
26820	16051	Jefferson County	26,144	30,891
26900		Indianapolis-Carmel-Anderson, IN Metro area	1,888,075	2,111,040
26900	18011	Boone County	56,641	70,812
26900	18013	Brown County	15,244	15,475
26900	18057	Hamilton County	274,557	347,467
26900	18059	Hancock County	70,060	79,840
26900	18063	Hendricks County	145,456	174,788
26900	18081	Johnson County	139,855	161,765
26900	18095	Madison County	131,637	130,129
26900	18097	Marion County	903,375	977,203
26900	18109	Morgan County	68,926	71,780
26900	18133	Putnam County	37,945	36,726
26900	18145	Shelby County	44,379	45,055
26980		Iowa City, IA Metro area	152,586	175,419
26980	19103	Johnson County	130,882	152,854
26980	19183	Washington County	21,704	22,565
27060		Ithaca, NY Metro area	101,592	105,740
27060	36109	Tompkins County	101,592	105,740
27100		Jackson, MI Metro area	160,233	160,366
27100	26075	Jackson County	160,233	160,366
27140		Jackson, MS Metro area	587,115	591,978
27140	28029	Copiah County	29,448	28,368
27140	28049	Hinds County	245,364	227,742
27140	28051	Holmes County	19,483	17,000
27140	28089	Madison County	95,203	109,145
27140	28121	Rankin County	142,052	157,031
27140	28127	Simpson County	27,500	25,949
27140	28163	Yazoo County	28,065	26,743
27180		Jackson, TN Metro area	179,711	180,504
27180	47023	Chester County	17,145	17,341
27180	47033	Crockett County	14,576	13,911
27180	47053	Gibson County	49,687	50,429
27180	47113	Madison County	98,303	98,823
27260		Jacksonville, FL Metro area	1,345,594	1,605,848
27260	12003	Baker County	27,115	28,259
27260	12019	Clay County	190,878	218,245
27260	12031	Duval County	864,253	995,567
27260	12089	Nassau County	73,310	90,352
27260	12109	St. Johns County	190,038	273,425
27340		Jacksonville, NC Metro area	177,801	204,576
27340	37133	Onslow County	177,801	204,576
27500		Janesville-Beloit, WI Metro area	160,325	163,687
27500	55105	Rock County	160,325	163,687
27620		Jefferson City, MO Metro area	149,820	150,309
27620	29027	Callaway County	44,331	44,283
27620	29051	Cole County	75,975	77,279
27620	29135	Moniteau County	15,605	15,473
27620	29151	Osage County	13,909	13,274
27740		Johnson City, TN Metro area	198,757	207,285
27740	47019	Carter County	57,383	56,356
27740	47171	Unicoi County	18,311	17,928
27740	47179	Washington County	123,063	133,001
27780		Johnstown, PA Metro area	143,695	133,472
27780	42021	Cambria County	143,695	133,472
27860		Jonesboro, AR Metro area	121,019	134,196
27860	05031	Craighead County	96,443	111,231
27860	05111	Poinsett County	24,576	22,965
27900		Joplin, MO Metro area	175,509	181,409
27900	29097	Jasper County	117,391	122,761
27900	29145	Newton County	58,118	58,648
27980		Kahului-Wailuku-Lahaina, HI Metro area	154,840	164,754
27980	15009	Maui County	154,840	164,754
28020		Kalamazoo-Portage, MI Metro area	250,327	261,670
28020	26077	Kalamazoo County	250,327	261,670

METROPOLITAN STATISTICAL AREAS, METROPOLITAN DIVISIONS, AND COMPONENTS (as defined March 2020)—*Continued*

State/ County FIPS code	Core-based statistical area	Title and Geographic Components	2010 census population	2020 census population
28100		Kankakee, IL Metro area	113,450	107,502
28100	17091	Kankakee County	113,450	107,502
28140		Kansas City, MO-KS Metro area	2,009,355	2,192,035
28140	20091	Johnson County	544,181	609,863
28140	20103	Leavenworth County	76,220	81,881
28140	20107	Linn County	9,656	9,591
28140	20121	Miami County	32,781	34,191
28140	20209	Wyandotte County	157,523	169,245
28140	29013	Bates County	17,047	16,042
28140	29025	Caldwell County	9,418	8,815
28140	29037	Cass County	99,500	107,824
28140	29047	Clay County	221,906	253,335
28140	29049	Clinton County	20,743	21,184
28140	29095	Jackson County	674,166	717,204
28140	29107	Lafayette County	33,369	32,984
28140	29165	Platte County	89,329	106,718
28140	29177	Ray County	23,516	23,158
28420		Kennewick-Richland, WA Metro area	253,328	303,622
28420	53005	Benton County	175,168	206,873
28420	53021	Franklin County	78,160	96,749
28660		Killeen-Temple, TX Metro area	405,308	475,367
28660	48027	Bell County	310,159	370,647
28660	48099	Coryell County	75,474	83,093
28660	48281	Lampasas County	19,675	21,627
28700		Kingsport-Bristol, TN-VA Metro area	309,493	307,614
28700	47073	Hawkins County	56,826	56,721
28700	47163	Sullivan County	156,800	158,163
28700	51169	Scott County	23,168	21,576
28700	51191	Washington County	54,961	53,935
28700	51520	Bristol city	17,738	17,219
28740		Kingston, NY Metro area	182,519	181,851
28740	36111	Ulster County	182,519	181,851
28940		Knoxville, TN Metro area	815,025	879,773
28940	47001	Anderson County	75,082	77,123
28940	47009	Blount County	123,098	135,280
28940	47013	Campbell County	40,723	39,272
28940	47093	Knox County	432,260	478,971
28940	47105	Loudon County	48,561	54,886
28940	47129	Morgan County	21,986	21,035
28940	47145	Roane County	54,208	53,404
28940	47173	Union County	19,107	19,802
29020		Kokomo, IN Metro area	82,748	83,658
29020	18067	Howard County	82,748	83,658
29100		La Crosse-Onalaska, WI-MN Metro area	133,658	139,627
29100	27055	Houston County	19,020	18,843
29100	55063	La Crosse County	114,638	120,784
29180		Lafayette, LA Metro area	466,733	478,384
29180	22001	Acadia Parish	61,787	57,576
29180	22045	Iberia Parish	73,087	69,929
29180	22055	Lafayette Parish	221,778	241,753
29180	22099	St. Martin Parish	52,122	51,767
29180	22113	Vermilion Parish	57,959	57,359
29200		Lafayette-West Lafayette, IN Metro area	210,310	223,716
29200	18007	Benton County	8,836	8,719
29200	18015	Carroll County	20,160	20,306
29200	18157	Tippecanoe County	172,803	186,251
29200	18171	Warren County	8,511	8,440
29340		Lake Charles, LA Metro area	199,640	222,402
29340	22019	Calcasieu Parish	192,772	216,785
29340	22023	Cameron Parish	6,868	5,617
29420		Lake Havasu City-Kingman, AZ Metro area	200,182	213,267
29420	04015	Mohave County	200,182	213,267
29460		Lakeland-Winter Haven, FL Metro area	602,073	725,046
29460	12105	Polk County	602,073	725,046
29540		Lancaster, PA Metro area	519,443	552,984
29540	42071	Lancaster County	519,443	552,984

State/ County FIPS code	Core-based statistical area	Title and Geographic Components	2010 census population	2020 census population
29620		Lansing-East Lansing, MI Metro area	534,684	541,297
29620	26037	Clinton County	75,364	79,128
29620	26045	Eaton County	107,761	109,175
29620	26065	Ingham County	280,891	284,900
29620	26155	Shiawassee County	70,668	68,094
29700		Laredo, TX Metro area	250,304	267,114
29700	48479	Webb County	250,304	267,114
29740		Las Cruces, NM Metro area	209,217	219,561
29740	35013	Dona Ana County	209,217	219,561
29820		Las Vegas-Henderson-Paradise, NV Metro area	1,951,268	2,265,461
29820	32003	Clark County	1,951,268	2,265,461
29940		Lawrence, KS Metro area	110,826	118,785
29940	20045	Douglas County	110,826	118,785
30020		Lawton, OK Metro area	130,288	126,652
30020	40031	Comanche County	124,098	121,125
30020	40033	Cotton County	6,190	5,527
30140		Lebanon, PA Metro area	133,597	143,257
30140	42075	Lebanon County	133,597	143,257
30300		Lewiston, ID-WA Metro area	60,893	64,375
30300	16069	Nez Perce County	39,270	42,090
30300	53003	Asotin County	21,623	22,285
30340		Lewiston-Auburn, ME Metro area	107,709	111,139
30340	23001	Androscoggin County	107,709	111,139
30460		Lexington-Fayette, KY Metro area	472,103	516,811
30460	21017	Bourbon County	20,008	20,252
30460	21049	Clark County	35,603	36,972
30460	21067	Fayette County	295,870	322,570
30460	21113	Jessamine County	48,580	52,991
30460	21209	Scott County	47,096	57,155
30460	21239	Woodford County	24,946	26,871
30620		Lima, OH Metro area	106,313	102,206
30620	39003	Allen County	106,313	102,206
30700		Lincoln, NE Metro area	302,157	340,217
30700	31109	Lancaster County	285,407	322,608
30700	31159	Seward County	16,750	17,609
30780		Little Rock-North Little Rock-Conway, AR Metro	699,790	748,031
30780	05045	Faulkner County	113,238	123,498
30780	05053	Grant County	17,842	17,958
30780	05085	Lonoke County	68,382	74,015
30780	05105	Perry County	10,444	10,019
30780	05119	Pulaski County	382,749	399,125
30780	05125	Saline County	107,135	123,416
30860		Logan, UT-ID Metro area	125,442	147,348
30860	16041	Franklin County	12,786	14,194
30860	49005	Cache County	112,656	133,154
30980		Longview, TX Metro area	280,007	286,184
30980	48183	Gregg County	121,747	124,239
30980	48203	Harrison County	65,640	68,839
30980	48401	Rusk County	53,309	52,214
30980	48459	Upshur County	39,311	40,892
31020		Longview, WA Metro area	102,408	110,730
31020	53015	Cowlitz County	102,408	110,730
31080		Los Angeles-Long Beach-Anaheim, CA Metro area	12,828,957	13,200,998
31080		Anaheim-Santa Ana-Irvine, CA Div 11244	3,008,989	3,186,989
31080	06059	Orange County	3,008,989	3,186,989
31080		Los Angeles-Long Beach-Glendale, CA Div 31084	9,819,968	10,014,009
31080	06037	Los Angeles County	9,819,968	10,014,009

METROPOLITAN STATISTICAL AREAS, METROPOLITAN DIVISIONS, AND COMPONENTS (as defined March 2020)—*Continued*

State/ County FIPS code	Core-based statistical area	Title and Geographic Components	2010 census population	2020 census population
31140		Louisville/Jefferson County, KY-IN Metro area	1,202,686	1,285,439
31140	18019	Clark County	110,222	121,093
31140	18043	Floyd County	74,579	80,484
31140	18061	Harrison County	39,366	39,654
31140	18175	Washington County	28,254	28,182
31140	21029	Bullitt County	74,308	82,217
31140	21103	Henry County	15,413	15,678
31140	21111	Jefferson County	741,075	782,969
31140	21185	Oldham County	60,356	67,607
31140	21211	Shelby County	41,971	48,065
31140	21215	Spencer County	17,142	19,490
31180		Lubbock, TX Metro area	290,889	321,368
31180	48107	Crosby County	6,056	5,133
31180	48303	Lubbock County	278,918	310,639
31180	48305	Lynn County	5,915	5,596
31340		Lynchburg, VA Metro area	252,654	261,593
31340	51009	Amherst County	32,354	31,307
31340	51011	Appomattox County	15,028	16,119
31340	51019	Bedford County	74,929	79,462
31340	51031	Campbell County	54,809	55,696
31340	51680	Lynchburg city	75,534	79,009
31420		Macon-Bibb County, GA Metro area	232,245	233,802
31420	13021	Bibb County	155,783	157,346
31420	13079	Crawford County	12,601	12,130
31420	13169	Jones County	28,668	28,347
31420	13207	Monroe County	26,167	27,957
31420	13289	Twiggs County	9,026	8,022
31460		Madera, CA Metro area	150,834	156,255
31460	06039	Madera County	150,834	156,255
31540		Madison, WI Metro area	605,466	680,796
31540	55021	Columbia County	56,859	58,490
31540	55025	Dane County	488,081	561,504
31540	55045	Green County	36,839	37,093
31540	55049	Iowa County	23,687	23,709
31700		Manchester-Nashua, NH Metro area	400,706	422,937
31700	33011	Hillsborough County	400,706	422,937
31740		Manhattan, KS Metro area	127,094	134,046
31740	20061	Geary County	34,356	36,739
31740	20149	Pottawatomie County	21,608	25,348
31740	20161	Riley County	71,130	71,959
31860		Mankato, MN Metro area	96,742	103,566
31860	27013	Blue Earth County	64,013	69,112
31860	27103	Nicollet County	32,729	34,454
31900		Mansfield, OH Metro area	124,474	124,936
31900	39139	Richland County	124,474	124,936
32580		McAllen-Edinburg-Mission, TX Metro area	774,764	870,781
32580	48215	Hidalgo County	774,764	870,781
32780		Medford, OR Metro area	203,204	223,259
32780	41029	Jackson County	203,204	223,259
32820		Memphis, TN-MS-AR Metro area	1,316,102	1,337,779
32820	05035	Crittenden County	50,907	48,163
32820	28033	DeSoto County	161,267	185,314
32820	28093	Marshall County	37,151	33,752
32820	28137	Tate County	28,872	28,064
32820	28143	Tunica County	10,778	9,782
32820	47047	Fayette County	38,439	41,990
32820	47157	Shelby County	927,682	929,744
32820	47167	Tipton County	61,006	60,970
32900		Merced, CA Metro area	255,796	281,202
32900	06047	Merced County	255,796	281,202
33100		Miami-Fort Lauderdale-Pompano Beach, FL Metro area	5,566,274	6,138,333
33100		Fort Lauderdale-Pompano Beach-Sunrise, FL Div 22744	1,748,146	1,944,375
33100	12011	Broward County	1,748,146	1,944,375
33100		Miami-Miami Beach-Kendall, FL Div 33124	2,497,993	2,701,767
33100	12086	Miami-Dade County	2,497,993	2,701,767
33100		West Palm Beach-Boca Raton-Boynton Beach, FL Div 48424	1,320,135	1,492,191
33100	12099	Palm Beach County	1,320,135	1,492,191
33140		Michigan City-La Porte, IN Metro area	111,466	112,417
33140	18091	LaPorte County	111,466	112,417
33220		Midland, MI Metro area	83,621	83,494
33220	26111	Midland County	83,621	83,494
33260		Midland, TX Metro area	141,671	175,220
33260	48317	Martin County	4,799	5,237
33260	48329	Midland County	136,872	169,983
33340		Milwaukee-Waukesha, WI Metro area	1,555,954	1,574,731
33340	55079	Milwaukee County	947,728	939,489
33340	55089	Ozaukee County	86,395	91,503
33340	55131	Washington County	131,885	136,761
33340	55133	Waukesha County	389,946	406,978
33460		Minneapolis-St. Paul-Bloomington, MN Metro area	3,333,628	3,690,261
33460	27003	Anoka County	330,858	363,887
33460	27019	Carver County	91,086	106,922
33460	27025	Chisago County	53,890	56,621
33460	27037	Dakota County	398,590	439,882
33460	27053	Hennepin County	1,152,385	1,281,565
33460	27059	Isanti County	37,810	41,135
33460	27079	Le Sueur County	27,701	28,674
33460	27095	Mille Lacs County	26,097	26,459
33460	27123	Ramsey County	508,639	552,352
33460	27139	Scott County	129,908	150,928
33460	27141	Sherburne County	88,492	97,183
33460	27163	Washington County	238,109	267,568
33460	27171	Wright County	124,697	141,337
33460	55093	Pierce County	41,029	42,212
33460	55109	St. Croix County	84,337	93,536
33540		Missoula, MT Metro area	109,296	117,922
33540	30063	Missoula County	109,296	117,922
33660		Mobile, AL Metro area	430,719	430,197
33660	01097	Mobile County	413,139	414,809
33660	01129	Washington County	17,580	15,388
33700		Modesto, CA Metro area	514,450	552,878
33700	06099	Stanislaus County	514,450	552,878
33740		Monroe, LA Metro area	204,487	207,104
33740	22067	Morehouse Parish	27,979	25,629
33740	22073	Ouachita Parish	153,734	160,368
33740	22111	Union Parish	22,774	21,107
33780		Monroe, MI Metro area	152,031	154,809
33780	26115	Monroe County	152,031	154,809
33860		Montgomery, AL Metro area	374,540	386,047
33860	01001	Autauga County	54,597	58,805
33860	01051	Elmore County	79,272	87,977
33860	01085	Lowndes County	11,296	10,311
33860	01101	Montgomery County	229,375	228,954
34060		Morgantown, WV Metro area	129,702	140,038
34060	54061	Monongalia County	96,184	105,822
34060	54077	Preston County	33,518	34,216
34100		Morristown, TN Metro area	136,858	142,709
34100	47057	Grainger County	22,656	23,527
34100	47063	Hamblen County	62,534	64,499
34100	47089	Jefferson County	51,668	54,683
34580		Mount Vernon-Anacortes, WA Metro area	116,892	129,523
34580	53057	Skagit County	116,892	129,523

METROPOLITAN STATISTICAL AREAS, METROPOLITAN DIVISIONS, AND COMPONENTS (as defined March 2020)—*Continued*

State/ County FIPS code	Core-based statistical area	Title and Geographic Components	2010 census population	2020 census population
34620		Muncie, IN Metro area	117,670	111,903
34620	18035	Delaware County	117,670	111,903
34740		Muskegon, MI Metro area	172,194	175,824
34740	26121	Muskegon County	172,194	175,824
34820		Myrtle Beach-Conway-North Myrtle Beach, SC-NC Metro area	376,575	487,722
34820	37019	Brunswick County	107,429	136,693
34820	45051	Horry County	269,146	351,029
34900		Napa, CA Metro area	136,535	138,019
34900	06055	Napa County	136,535	138,019
34940		Naples-Marco Island, FL Metro area	321,522	375,752
34940	12021	Collier County	321,522	375,752
34980		Nashville-Davidson--Murfreesboro--Franklin, TN Metro area	1,646,183	1,989,519
34980	47015	Cannon County	13,813	14,506
34980	47021	Cheatham County	39,110	41,072
34980	47037	Davidson County	626,558	715,884
34980	47043	Dickson County	49,650	54,315
34980	47111	Macon County	22,226	25,216
34980	47119	Maury County	80,932	100,974
34980	47147	Robertson County	66,319	72,803
34980	47149	Rutherford County	262,588	341,486
34980	47159	Smith County	19,150	19,904
34980	47165	Sumner County	160,634	196,281
34980	47169	Trousdale County	7,864	11,615
34980	47187	Williamson County	183,277	247,726
34980	47189	Wilson County	114,062	147,737
35100		New Bern, NC Metro area	126,808	122,168
35100	37049	Craven County	103,498	100,720
35100	37103	Jones County	10,167	9,172
35100	37137	Pamlico County	13,143	12,276
35300		New Haven-Milford, CT Metro area	862,442	864,835
35300	09009	New Haven County	862,442	864,835
35380		New Orleans-Metairie, LA Metro area	1,189,891	1,271,845
35380	22051	Jefferson Parish	432,576	440,781
35380	22071	Orleans Parish	343,828	383,997
35380	22075	Plaquemines Parish	23,035	23,515
35380	22087	St. Bernard Parish	35,897	43,764
35380	22089	St. Charles Parish	52,888	52,549
35380	22093	St. James Parish	22,101	20,192
35380	22095	St. John the Baptist Parish	45,810	42,477
35380	22103	St. Tammany Parish	233,756	264,570
35620		New York-Newark-Jersey City, NY-NJ-PA Metro area	18,896,277	20,140,470
35620		Nassau County-Suffolk County, NY Div 35004	2,832,996	2,921,694
35620	36059	Nassau County	1,339,880	1,395,774
35620	36103	Suffolk County	1,493,116	1,525,920
35620		Newark, NJ-PA Div 35084	2,146,271	2,280,061
35620	34013	Essex County	783,891	863,728
35620	34019	Hunterdon County	127,361	128,947
35620	34027	Morris County	492,281	509,285
35620	34037	Sussex County	148,936	144,221
35620	34039	Union County	536,464	575,345
35620	42103	Pike County	57,338	58,535
35620		New Brunswick-Lakewood, NJ Div 35154	2,340,425	2,489,367
35620	34023	Middlesex County	810,038	863,162
35620	34025	Monmouth County	630,362	643,615
35620	34029	Ocean County	576,546	637,229
35620	34035	Somerset County	323,479	345,361
35620		New York-Jersey City-White Plains, NY-NJ Div 35614	11,576,585	12,449,348
35620	34003	Bergen County	905,107	955,732
35620	34017	Hudson County	634,284	724,854
35620	34031	Passaic County	501,600	524,118
35620	36005	Bronx County	1,384,580	1,472,654
35620	36047	Kings County	2,504,721	2,736,074
35620	36061	New York County	1,586,381	1,694,251
35620	36079	Putnam County	99,654	97,668
35620	36081	Queens County	2,230,619	2,405,464
35620	36085	Richmond County	468,730	495,747
35620	36087	Rockland County	311,691	338,329
35620	36119	Westchester County	949,218	1,004,457
35660		Niles, MI Metro area	156,808	154,316
35660	26021	Berrien County	156,808	154,316
35840		North Port-Sarasota-Bradenton, FL Metro area	702,312	833,716
35840	12081	Manatee County	322,879	399,710
35840	12115	Sarasota County	379,433	434,006
35980		Norwich-New London, CT Metro area	274,070	268,555
35980	09011	New London County	274,070	268,555
36100		Ocala, FL Metro area	331,299	375,908
36100	12083	Marion County	331,299	375,908
36140		Ocean City, NJ Metro area	97,257	95,263
36140	34009	Cape May County	97,257	95,263
36220		Odessa, TX Metro area	137,136	165,171
36220	48135	Ector County	137,136	165,171
36260		Ogden-Clearfield, UT Metro area	597,162	694,863
36260	49003	Box Elder County	49,983	57,666
36260	49011	Davis County	306,492	362,679
36260	49029	Morgan County	9,469	12,295
36260	49057	Weber County	231,218	262,223
36420		Oklahoma City, OK Metro area	1,253,002	1,425,695
36420	40017	Canadian County	115,566	154,405
36420	40027	Cleveland County	255,990	295,528
36420	40051	Grady County	52,430	54,795
36420	40081	Lincoln County	34,274	33,458
36420	40083	Logan County	41,854	49,555
36420	40087	McClain County	34,503	41,662
36420	40109	Oklahoma County	718,385	796,292
36500		Olympia-Lacey-Tumwater, WA Metro area	252,260	294,793
36500	53067	Thurston County	252,260	294,793
36540		Omaha-Council Bluffs, NE-IA Metro area	865,347	967,604
36540	19085	Harrison County	14,937	14,582
36540	19129	Mills County	15,059	14,484
36540	19155	Pottawattamie County	93,149	93,667
36540	31025	Cass County	25,241	26,598
36540	31055	Douglas County	517,116	584,526
36540	31153	Sarpy County	158,835	190,604
36540	31155	Saunders County	20,778	22,278
36540	31177	Washington County	20,232	20,865
36740		Orlando-Kissimmee-Sanford, FL Metro area	2,134,399	2,673,376
36740	12069	Lake County	297,047	383,956
36740	12095	Orange County	1,145,957	1,429,908
36740	12097	Osceola County	268,685	388,656
36740	12117	Seminole County	422,710	470,856
36780		Oshkosh-Neenah, WI Metro area	167,000	171,730
36780	55139	Winnebago County	167,000	171,730
36980		Owensboro, KY Metro area	114,746	121,559
36980	21059	Daviess County	96,641	103,312
36980	21091	Hancock County	8,565	9,095
36980	21149	McLean County	9,540	9,152

METROPOLITAN STATISTICAL AREAS, METROPOLITAN DIVISIONS, AND COMPONENTS (as defined March 2020)—*Continued*

State/ County FIPS code	Core-based statistical area	Title and Geographic Components	2010 census population	2020 census population
37100		Oxnard-Thousand Oaks-Ventura, CA Metro area	823,398	843,843
37100	06111	Ventura County	823,398	843,843
37340		Palm Bay-Melbourne-Titusville, FL Metro area	543,372	606,612
37340	12009	Brevard County	543,372	606,612
37460		Panama City, FL Metro area	168,850	175,216
37460	12005	Bay County	168,850	175,216
37620		Parkersburg-Vienna, WV Metro area	92,667	89,490
37620	54105	Wirt County	5,714	5,194
37620	54107	Wood County	86,953	84,296
37860		Pensacola-Ferry Pass-Brent, FL Metro area	448,991	509,905
37860	12033	Escambia County	297,620	321,905
37860	12113	Santa Rosa County	151,371	188,000
37900		Peoria, IL Metro area	416,253	402,391
37900	17057	Fulton County	37,071	33,609
37900	17123	Marshall County	12,646	11,742
37900	17143	Peoria County	186,496	181,830
37900	17175	Stark County	5,992	5,400
37900	17179	Tazewell County	135,392	131,343
37900	17203	Woodford County	38,656	38,467
37980		Philadelphia-Camden-Wilmington, PA-NJ-DE-MD Metro area	5,965,677	6,245,051
37980		Camden, NJ Div 15804	1,251,021	1,287,639
37980	34005	Burlington County	448,730	461,860
37980	34007	Camden County	513,535	523,485
37980	34015	Gloucester County	288,756	302,294
37980		Montgomery County-Bucks County-Chester County, PA Div 33874	1,924,229	2,037,504
37980	42017	Bucks County	625,256	646,538
37980	42029	Chester County	499,133	534,413
37980	42091	Montgomery County	799,840	856,553
37980		Philadelphia, PA Div 37964	2,084,769	2,180,627
37980	42045	Delaware County	558,757	576,830
37980	42101	Philadelphia County	1,526,012	1,603,797
37980		Wilmington, DE-MD-NJ Div 48864	705,658	739,281
37980	10003	New Castle County	538,484	570,719
37980	24015	Cecil County	101,102	103,725
37980	34033	Salem County	66,072	64,837
38060		Phoenix-Mesa-Chandler, AZ Metro area	4,193,129	4,845,832
38060	04013	Maricopa County	3,817,365	4,420,568
38060	04021	Pinal County	375,764	425,264
38220		Pine Bluff, AR Metro area	100,289	87,751
38220	05025	Cleveland County	8,692	7,550
38220	05069	Jefferson County	77,456	67,260
38220	05079	Lincoln County	14,141	12,941
38300		Pittsburgh, PA Metro area	2,356,294	2,370,930
38300	42003	Allegheny County	1,223,303	1,250,578
38300	42005	Armstrong County	69,059	65,558
38300	42007	Beaver County	170,531	168,215
38300	42019	Butler County	183,880	193,763
38300	42051	Fayette County	136,601	128,804
38300	42125	Washington County	207,849	209,349
38300	42129	Westmoreland County	365,071	354,663
38340		Pittsfield, MA Metro area	131,274	129,026
38340	25003	Berkshire County	131,274	129,026
38540		Pocatello, ID Metro area	90,661	94,896
38540	16005	Bannock County	82,842	87,018
38540	16077	Power County	7,819	7,878
38860		Portland-South Portland, ME Metro area	514,108	551,740
38860	23005	Cumberland County	281,690	303,069
38860	23023	Sagadahoc County	35,287	36,699
38860	23031	York County	197,131	211,972
38900		Portland-Vancouver-Hillsboro, OR-WA Metro area	2,226,003	2,512,859
38900	41005	Clackamas County	375,996	421,401
38900	41009	Columbia County	49,353	52,589
38900	41051	Multnomah County	735,146	815,428
38900	41067	Washington County	529,862	600,372
38900	41071	Yamhill County	99,216	107,722
38900	53011	Clark County	425,360	503,311
38900	53059	Skamania County	11,070	12,036
38940		Port St. Lucie, FL Metro area	424,107	487,657
38940	12085	Martin County	146,852	158,431
38940	12111	St. Lucie County	277,255	329,226
39100		Poughkeepsie-Newburgh-Middletown, NY Metro area	670,280	697,221
39100	36027	Dutchess County	297,454	295,911
39100	36071	Orange County	372,826	401,310
39150		Prescott Valley-Prescott, AZ Metro area	211,017	236,209
39150	04025	Yavapai County	211,017	236,209
39300		Providence-Warwick, RI-MA Metro area	1,601,206	1,676,579
39300	25005	Bristol County	548,242	579,200
39300	44001	Bristol County	49,844	50,793
39300	44003	Kent County	166,109	170,363
39300	44005	Newport County	83,141	85,643
39300	44007	Providence County	626,781	660,741
39300	44009	Washington County	127,089	129,839
39340		Provo-Orem, UT Metro area	526,885	671,185
39340	49023	Juab County	10,246	11,786
39340	49049	Utah County	516,639	659,399
39380		Pueblo, CO Metro area	159,063	168,162
39380	08101	Pueblo County	159,063	168,162
39460		Punta Gorda, FL Metro area	159,967	186,847
39460	12015	Charlotte County	159,967	186,847
39540		Racine, WI Metro area	195,428	197,727
39540	55101	Racine County	195,428	197,727
39580		Raleigh-Cary, NC Metro area	1,130,493	1,413,982
39580	37069	Franklin County	60,563	68,573
39580	37101	Johnston County	168,878	215,999
39580	37183	Wake County	901,052	1,129,410
39660		Rapid City, SD Metro area	126,400	139,074
39660	46093	Meade County	25,440	29,852
39660	46103	Pennington County	100,960	109,222
39740		Reading, PA Metro area	411,570	428,849
39740	42011	Berks County	411,570	428,849
39820		Redding, CA Metro area	177,221	182,155
39820	06089	Shasta County	177,221	182,155
39900		Reno, NV Metro area	425,442	490,596
39900	32029	Storey County	4,013	4,104
39900	32031	Washoe County	421,429	486,492
40060		Richmond, VA Metro area	1,186,471	1,314,434
40060	51007	Amelia County	12,695	13,265
40060	51036	Charles City County	7,256	6,773
40060	51041	Chesterfield County	316,240	364,548
40060	51053	Dinwiddie County	28,012	27,947
40060	51075	Goochland County	21,692	24,727
40060	51085	Hanover County	99,850	109,979
40060	51087	Henrico County	306,756	334,389
40060	51097	King and Queen County	6,940	6,608
40060	51101	King William County	15,927	17,810
40060	51127	New Kent County	18,432	22,945
40060	51145	Powhatan County	28,069	30,333
40060	51149	Prince George County	35,715	43,010
40060	51183	Sussex County	12,070	10,829
40060	51570	Colonial Heights city	17,410	18,170
40060	51670	Hopewell city	22,591	23,033
40060	51730	Petersburg city	32,441	33,458
40060	51760	Richmond city	204,375	226,610

METROPOLITAN STATISTICAL AREAS, METROPOLITAN DIVISIONS, AND COMPONENTS (as defined March 2020)—*Continued*

State/ County FIPS code	Core-based statistical area	Title and Geographic Components	2010 census population	2020 census population
40140		Riverside-San Bernardino-Ontario, CA Metro area	4,224,948	4,599,839
40140	06065	Riverside County	2,189,765	2,418,185
40140	06071	San Bernardino County	2,035,183	2,181,654
40220		Roanoke, VA Metro area	308,666	315,251
40220	51023	Botetourt County	33,152	33,596
40220	51045	Craig County	5,175	4,892
40220	51067	Franklin County	56,128	54,477
40220	51161	Roanoke County	92,465	96,929
40220	51770	Roanoke city	96,910	100,011
40220	51775	Salem city	24,836	25,346
40340		Rochester, MN Metro area	206,888	226,329
40340	27039	Dodge County	20,087	20,867
40340	27045	Fillmore County	20,868	21,228
40340	27109	Olmsted County	144,268	162,847
40340	27157	Wabasha County	21,665	21,387
40380		Rochester, NY Metro area	1,079,704	1,090,135
40380	36051	Livingston County	65,206	61,834
40380	36055	Monroe County	744,394	759,443
40380	36069	Ontario County	108,099	112,458
40380	36073	Orleans County	42,890	40,343
40380	36117	Wayne County	93,751	91,283
40380	36123	Yates County	25,364	24,774
40420		Rockford, IL Metro area	349,431	338,798
40420	17007	Boone County	54,167	53,448
40420	17201	Winnebago County	295,264	285,350
40580		Rocky Mount, NC Metro area	152,368	143,870
40580	37065	Edgecombe County	56,539	48,900
40580	37127	Nash County	95,829	94,970
40660		Rome, GA Metro area	96,314	98,584
40660	13115	Floyd County	96,314	98,584
40900		Sacramento-Roseville-Folsom, CA Metro area	2,149,150	2,397,382
40900	06017	El Dorado County	181,058	191,185
40900	06061	Placer County	348,502	404,739
40900	06067	Sacramento County	1,418,735	1,585,055
40900	06113	Yolo County	200,855	216,403
40980		Saginaw, MI Metro area	200,169	190,124
40980	26145	Saginaw County	200,169	190,124
41060		St. Cloud, MN Metro area	189,093	199,671
41060	27009	Benton County	38,451	41,379
41060	27145	Stearns County	150,642	158,292
41100		St. George, UT Metro area	138,115	180,279
41100	49053	Washington County	138,115	180,279
41140		St. Joseph, MO-KS Metro area	127,319	121,467
41140	20043	Doniphan County	7,948	7,510
41140	29003	Andrew County	17,296	18,135
41140	29021	Buchanan County	89,191	84,793
41140	29063	DeKalb County	12,884	11,029
41180		St. Louis, MO-IL Metro area	2,787,751	2,820,253
41180	17005	Bond County	17,768	16,725
41180	17013	Calhoun County	5,089	4,437
41180	17027	Clinton County	37,762	36,899
41180	17083	Jersey County	23,010	21,512
41180	17117	Macoupin County	47,763	44,967
41180	17119	Madison County	269,298	265,859
41180	17133	Monroe County	32,949	34,962
41180	17163	St. Clair County	270,078	257,400
41180	29071	Franklin County	101,468	104,682
41180	29099	Jefferson County	218,722	226,739
41180	29113	Lincoln County	52,536	59,574
41180	29183	St. Charles County	360,495	405,262
41180	29189	St. Louis County	998,985	1,004,125
41180	29219	Warren County	32,539	35,532
41180	29510	St. Louis city	319,289	301,578
41420		Salem, OR Metro area	390,738	433,353
41420	41047	Marion County	315,338	345,920
41420	41053	Polk County	75,400	87,433
41500		Salinas, CA Metro area	415,059	439,035
41500	06053	Monterey County	415,059	439,035
41540		Salisbury, MD-DE Metro area	373,754	418,046
41540	10005	Sussex County	197,103	237,378
41540	24039	Somerset County	26,470	24,620
41540	24045	Wicomico County	98,733	103,588
41540	24047	Worcester County	51,448	52,460
41620		Salt Lake City, UT Metro area	1,087,808	1,257,936
41620	49035	Salt Lake County	1,029,590	1,185,238
41620	49045	Tooele County	58,218	72,698
41660		San Angelo, TX Metro area	112,968	122,888
41660	48235	Irion County	1,597	1,513
41660	48431	Sterling County	1,143	1,372
41660	48451	Tom Green County	110,228	120,003
41700		San Antonio-New Braunfels, TX Metro area	2,142,520	2,558,143
41700	48013	Atascosa County	44,923	48,981
41700	48019	Bandera County	20,487	20,851
41700	48029	Bexar County	1,714,781	2,009,324
41700	48091	Comal County	108,520	161,501
41700	48187	Guadalupe County	131,527	172,706
41700	48259	Kendall County	33,384	44,279
41700	48325	Medina County	45,993	50,748
41700	48493	Wilson County	42,905	49,753
41740		San Diego-Chula Vista-Carlsbad, CA Metro area	3,095,349	3,298,634
41740	06073	San Diego County	3,095,349	3,298,634
41860		San Francisco-Oakland-Berkeley, CA Metro area	4,335,593	4,749,008
41860		Oakland-Berkeley-Livermore, CA Div 36084	2,559,462	2,848,280
41860	06001	Alameda County	1,510,258	1,682,353
41860	06013	Contra Costa County	1,049,204	1,165,927
41860		San Francisco-San Mateo-Redwood City, CA Div 41884	1,523,701	1,638,407
41860	06075	San Francisco County	805,184	873,965
41860	06081	San Mateo County	718,517	764,442
41860		San Rafael, CA Div 42034	252,430	262,321
41860	06041	Marin County	252,430	262,321
41940		San Jose-Sunnyvale-Santa Clara, CA Metro area	1,836,951	2,000,468
41940	06069	San Benito County	55,265	64,209
41940	06085	Santa Clara County	1,781,686	1,936,259
42020		San Luis Obispo-Paso Robles, CA Metro area	269,597	282,424
42020	06079	San Luis Obispo County	269,597	282,424
42100		Santa Cruz-Watsonville, CA Metro area	262,350	270,861
42100	06087	Santa Cruz County	262,350	270,861
42140		Santa Fe, NM Metro area	144,232	154,823
42140	35049	Santa Fe County	144,232	154,823
42200		Santa Maria-Santa Barbara, CA Metro area	423,947	448,229
42200	06083	Santa Barbara County	423,947	448,229
42220		Santa Rosa-Petaluma, CA Metro area	483,861	488,863
42220	06097	Sonoma County	483,861	488,863
42340		Savannah, GA Metro area	347,597	404,798
42340	13029	Bryan County	30,215	44,738
42340	13051	Chatham County	265,127	295,291
42340	13103	Effingham County	52,255	64,769

METROPOLITAN STATISTICAL AREAS, METROPOLITAN DIVISIONS, AND COMPONENTS (as defined March 2020)—*Continued*

State/ County FIPS code	Core-based statistical area	Title and Geographic Components	2010 census population	2020 census population
42540		Scranton--Wilkes-Barre, PA Metro area	563,604	567,559
42540	42069	Lackawanna County	214,415	215,896
42540	42079	Luzerne County	320,906	325,594
42540	42131	Wyoming County	28,283	26,069
42660		Seattle-Tacoma-Bellevue, WA Metro area	3,439,808	4,018,762
42660		Seattle-Bellevue-Kent, WA Div 42644	2,644,586	3,097,632
42660	53033	King County	1,931,287	2,269,675
42660	53061	Snohomish County	713,299	827,957
42660		Tacoma-Lakewood, WA Div 45104	795,222	921,130
42660	53053	Pierce County	795,222	921,130
42680		Sebastian-Vero Beach, FL Metro area	138,028	159,788
42680	12061	Indian River County	138,028	159,788
42700		Sebring-Avon Park, FL Metro area	98,784	101,235
42700	12055	Highlands County	98,784	101,235
43100		Sheboygan, WI Metro area	115,512	118,034
43100	55117	Sheboygan County	115,512	118,034
43300		Sherman-Denison, TX Metro area	120,877	135,543
43300	48181	Grayson County	120,877	135,543
43340		Shreveport-Bossier City, LA Metro area	398,606	393,406
43340	22015	Bossier Parish	117,036	128,746
43340	22017	Caddo Parish	254,914	237,848
43340	22031	De Soto Parish	26,656	26,812
43420		Sierra Vista-Douglas, AZ Metro area	131,359	125,447
43420	04003	Cochise County	131,359	125,447
43580		Sioux City, IA-NE-SD Metro area	143,582	149,940
43580	19193	Woodbury County	102,175	105,941
43580	31043	Dakota County	21,006	21,582
43580	31051	Dixon County	6,003	5,606
43580	46127	Union County	14,398	16,811
43620		Sioux Falls, SD Metro area	228,264	276,730
43620	46083	Lincoln County	44,823	65,161
43620	46087	McCook County	5,618	5,682
43620	46099	Minnehaha County	169,474	197,214
43620	46125	Turner County	8,349	8,673
43780		South Bend-Mishawaka, IN-MI Metro area	319,203	324,501
43780	18141	St. Joseph County	266,914	272,912
43780	26027	Cass County	52,289	51,589
43900		Spartanburg, SC Metro area	284,304	327,997
43900	45083	Spartanburg County	284,304	327,997
44060		Spokane-Spokane Valley, WA Metro area	514,752	585,784
44060	53063	Spokane County	471,220	539,339
44060	53065	Stevens County	43,532	46,445
44100		Springfield, IL Metro area	210,170	208,640
44100	17129	Menard County	12,705	12,297
44100	17167	Sangamon County	197,465	196,343
44140		Springfield, MA Metro area	693,059	699,162
44140	25011	Franklin County	71,381	71,029
44140	25013	Hampden County	463,615	465,825
44140	25015	Hampshire County	158,063	162,308
44180		Springfield, MO Metro area	436,756	475,432
44180	29043	Christian County	77,414	88,842
44180	29059	Dallas County	16,769	17,071
44180	29077	Greene County	275,179	298,915
44180	29167	Polk County	31,130	31,519
44180	29225	Webster County	36,264	39,085
44220		Springfield, OH Metro area	138,339	136,001
44220	39023	Clark County	138,339	136,001
44300		State College, PA Metro area	154,005	158,172
44300	42027	Centre County	154,005	158,172
44420		Staunton, VA Metro area	118,496	125,433
44420	51015	Augusta County	73,753	77,487
44420	51790	Staunton city	23,745	25,750
44420	51820	Waynesboro city	20,998	22,196
44700		Stockton, CA Metro area	685,306	779,233
44700	06077	San Joaquin County	685,306	779,233
44940		Sumter, SC Metro area	142,434	136,700
44940	45027	Clarendon County	34,949	31,144
44940	45085	Sumter County	107,485	105,556
45060		Syracuse, NY Metro area	662,624	662,057
45060	36053	Madison County	73,452	68,016
45060	36067	Onondaga County	467,067	476,516
45060	36075	Oswego County	122,105	117,525
45220		Tallahassee, FL Metro area	368,771	384,298
45220	12039	Gadsden County	47,744	43,826
45220	12065	Jefferson County	14,761	14,510
45220	12073	Leon County	275,483	292,198
45220	12129	Wakulla County	30,783	33,764
45300		Tampa-St. Petersburg-Clearwater, FL Metro area	2,783,485	3,175,275
45300	12053	Hernando County	172,778	194,515
45300	12057	Hillsborough County	1,229,202	1,459,762
45300	12101	Pasco County	464,705	561,891
45300	12103	Pinellas County	916,800	959,107
45460		Terre Haute, IN Metro area	189,774	185,031
45460	18021	Clay County	26,888	26,466
45460	18121	Parke County	17,349	16,156
45460	18153	Sullivan County	21,475	20,817
45460	18165	Vermillion County	16,210	15,439
45460	18167	Vigo County	107,852	106,153
45500		Texarkana, TX-AR Metro area	149,194	147,519
45500	05081	Little River County	13,168	12,026
45500	05091	Miller County	43,462	42,600
45500	48037	Bowie County	92,564	92,893
45540		The Villages, FL Metro area	93,420	129,752
45540	12119	Sumter County	93,420	129,752
45780		Toledo, OH Metro area	651,435	646,604
45780	39051	Fulton County	42,698	42,713
45780	39095	Lucas County	441,815	431,279
45780	39123	Ottawa County	41,433	40,364
45780	39173	Wood County	125,489	132,248
45820		Topeka, KS Metro area	233,860	233,152
45820	20085	Jackson County	13,460	13,232
45820	20087	Jefferson County	19,108	18,368
45820	20139	Osage County	16,294	15,766
45820	20177	Shawnee County	177,943	178,909
45820	20197	Wabaunsee County	7,055	6,877
45940		Trenton-Princeton, NJ Metro area	367,485	387,340
45940	34021	Mercer County	367,485	387,340
46060		Tucson, AZ Metro area	980,263	1,043,433
46060	04019	Pima County	980,263	1,043,433
46140		Tulsa, OK Metro area	937,523	1,015,331
46140	40037	Creek County	69,992	71,754
46140	40111	Okmulgee County	40,062	36,706
46140	40113	Osage County	47,473	45,818
46140	40117	Pawnee County	16,570	15,553
46140	40131	Rogers County	86,914	95,240
46140	40143	Tulsa County	603,430	669,279
46140	40145	Wagoner County	73,082	80,981
46220		Tuscaloosa, AL Metro area	239,214	268,674
46220	01063	Greene County	9,039	7,730
46220	01065	Hale County	15,762	14,785
46220	01107	Pickens County	19,746	19,123
46220	01125	Tuscaloosa County	194,667	227,036

METROPOLITAN STATISTICAL AREAS, METROPOLITAN DIVISIONS, AND COMPONENTS (as defined March 2020)—*Continued*

State/ County FIPS code	Core-based statistical area	Title and Geographic Components	2010 census population	2020 census population
46300		Twin Falls, ID Metro area	99,596	114,283
46300	16053	Jerome County	22,355	24,237
46300	16083	Twin Falls County	77,241	90,046
46340		Tyler, TX Metro area	209,725	233,479
46340	48423	Smith County	209,725	233,479
46520		Urban Honolulu, HI Metro area	953,206	1,016,508
46520	15003	Honolulu County	953,206	1,016,508
46540		Utica-Rome, NY Metro area	299,329	292,264
46540	36043	Herkimer County	64,469	60,139
46540	36065	Oneida County	234,860	232,125
46660		Valdosta, GA Metro area	139,662	148,126
46660	13027	Brooks County	16,314	16,301
46660	13101	Echols County	4,023	3,697
46660	13173	Lanier County	10,077	9,877
46660	13185	Lowndes County	109,248	118,251
46700		Vallejo, CA Metro area	413,343	453,491
46700	06095	Solano County	413,343	453,491
47020		Victoria, TX Metro area	94,003	98,331
47020	48175	Goliad County	7,210	7,012
47020	48469	Victoria County	86,793	91,319
47220		Vineland-Bridgeton, NJ Metro area	156,627	154,152
47220	34011	Cumberland County	156,627	154,152
47260		Virginia Beach-Norfolk-Newport News, VA-NC Metro area	1,713,955	1,799,674
47260	37029	Camden County	9,980	10,355
47260	37053	Currituck County	23,547	28,100
47260	37073	Gates County	12,185	10,478
47260	51073	Gloucester County	36,859	38,711
47260	51093	Isle of Wight County	35,277	38,606
47260	51095	James City County	67,379	78,254
47260	51115	Mathews County	8,976	8,533
47260	51175	Southampton County	18,573	17,996
47260	51199	York County	65,191	70,045
47260	51550	Chesapeake city	222,311	249,422
47260	51620	Franklin city	8,578	8,180
47260	51650	Hampton city	137,464	137,148
47260	51700	Newport News city	180,955	186,247
47260	51710	Norfolk city	242,827	238,005
47260	51735	Poquoson city	12,159	12,460
47260	51740	Portsmouth city	95,526	97,915
47260	51800	Suffolk city	84,565	94,324
47260	51810	Virginia Beach city	437,903	459,470
47260	51830	Williamsburg city	13,700	15,425
47300		Visalia, CA Metro area	442,182	473,117
47300	06107	Tulare County	442,182	473,117
47380		Waco, TX Metro area	252,766	277,547
47380	48145	Falls County	17,863	16,968
47380	48309	McLennan County	234,903	260,579
47460		Walla Walla, WA Metro area	58,781	62,584
47460	53071	Walla Walla County	58,781	62,584
47580		Warner Robins, GA Metro area	167,626	191,614
47580	13153	Houston County	139,819	163,633
47580	13225	Peach County	27,807	27,981
47900		Washington-Arlington-Alexandria, DC-VA-MD-WV Metro area	5,649,688	6,385,162
47900		Frederick-Gaithersburg-Rockville, MD Div 23224	1,204,687	1,333,778
47900	24021	Frederick County	233,403	271,717
47900	24031	Montgomery County	971,284	1,062,061

State/ County FIPS code	Core-based statistical area	Title and Geographic Components	2010 census population	2020 census population
47900		Washington-Arlington-Alexandria, DC-VA-MD-WV Div 47894	4,445,001	5,051,384
47900	11001	District of Columbia	601,767	689,545
47900	24009	Calvert County	88,739	92,783
47900	24017	Charles County	146,564	166,617
47900	24033	Prince George's County	864,029	967,201
47900	51013	Arlington County	207,696	238,643
47900	51043	Clarke County	14,025	14,783
47900	51047	Culpeper County	46,688	52,552
47900	51059	Fairfax County	1,081,703	1,150,309
47900	51061	Fauquier County	65,228	72,972
47900	51107	Loudoun County	312,348	420,959
47900	51113	Madison County	13,306	13,837
47900	51153	Prince William County	402,009	482,204
47900	51157	Rappahannock County	7,506	7,348
47900	51177	Spotsylvania County	122,453	140,032
47900	51179	Stafford County	128,984	156,927
47900	51187	Warren County	37,450	40,727
47900	51510	Alexandria city	139,998	159,467
47900	51600	Fairfax city	22,554	24,146
47900	51610	Falls Church city	12,244	14,658
47900	51630	Fredericksburg city	24,178	27,982
47900	51683	Manassas city	37,799	42,772
47900	51685	Manassas Park city	14,243	17,219
47900	54037	Jefferson County	53,490	57,701
47940		Waterloo-Cedar Falls, IA Metro area	167,819	168,461
47940	19013	Black Hawk County	131,086	131,144
47940	19017	Bremer County	24,280	24,988
47940	19075	Grundy County	12,453	12,329
48060		Watertown-Fort Drum, NY Metro area	116,232	116,721
48060	36045	Jefferson County	116,232	116,721
48140		Wausau-Weston, WI Metro area	162,804	166,428
48140	55069	Lincoln County	28,743	28,415
48140	55073	Marathon County	134,061	138,013
48260		Weirton-Steubenville, WV-OH Metro area	124,455	116,903
48260	39081	Jefferson County	69,716	65,249
48260	54009	Brooke County	24,051	22,559
48260	54029	Hancock County	30,688	29,095
48300		Wenatchee, WA Metro area	110,887	122,012
48300	53007	Chelan County	72,460	79,074
48300	53017	Douglas County	38,427	42,938
48540		Wheeling, WV-OH Metro area	147,957	139,513
48540	39013	Belmont County	70,400	66,497
48540	54051	Marshall County	33,131	30,591
48540	54069	Ohio County	44,426	42,425
48620		Wichita, KS Metro area	623,061	647,610
48620	20015	Butler County	65,884	67,380
48620	20079	Harvey County	34,684	34,024
48620	20173	Sedgwick County	498,356	523,824
48620	20191	Sumner County	24,137	22,382
48660		Wichita Falls, TX Metro area	151,474	148,128
48660	48009	Archer County	9,061	8,560
48660	48077	Clay County	10,754	10,218
48660	48485	Wichita County	131,659	129,350
48700		Williamsport, PA Metro area	116,102	114,188
48700	42081	Lycoming County	116,102	114,188
48900		Wilmington, NC Metro area	254,879	285,905
48900	37129	New Hanover County	202,683	225,702
48900	37141	Pender County	52,196	60,203
49020		Winchester, VA-WV Metro area	128,452	142,632
49020	51069	Frederick County	78,269	91,419
49020	51840	Winchester city	26,223	28,120
49020	54027	Hampshire County	23,960	23,093

METROPOLITAN STATISTICAL AREAS, METROPOLITAN DIVISIONS, AND COMPONENTS (as defined March 2020)—*Continued*

State/ County FIPS code	Core-based statistical area	Title and Geographic Components	2010 census population	2020 census population
49180		Winston-Salem, NC Metro area	640,503	675,966
49180	37057	Davidson County	162,822	168,930
49180	37059	Davie County	41,221	42,712
49180	37067	Forsyth County	350,638	382,590
49180	37169	Stokes County	47,413	44,520
49180	37197	Yadkin County	38,409	37,214
49340		Worcester, MA-CT Metro area	916,763	978,529
49340	09015	Windham County	118,380	116,418
49340	25027	Worcester County	798,383	862,111
49420		Yakima, WA Metro area	243,240	256,728
49420	53077	Yakima County	243,240	256,728
49620		York-Hanover, PA Metro area	435,015	456,438
49620	42133	York County	435,015	456,438
49660		Youngstown-Warren-Boardman, OH-PA Metro area	565,782	541,243
49660	39099	Mahoning County	238,787	228,614
49660	39155	Trumbull County	210,332	201,977
49660	42085	Mercer County	116,663	110,652
49700		Yuba City, CA Metro area	166,898	181,208
49700	06101	Sutter County	94,756	99,633
49700	06115	Yuba County	72,142	81,575
49740		Yuma, AZ Metro area	195,750	203,881
49740	04027	Yuma County	195,750	203,881

APPENDIX C
CORE-BASED STATISTICAL AREAS (Metropolitan and Micropolitan), METROPOLITAN DIVISIONS, AND COMPONENTS (as defined March, 2020)

Core based statistical area	State/County FIPS code	Title and Geographic Components	2010 Census Population	2020 Census Population
10100		Aberdeen, SD Micro Area	40,602	42,287
10100	46013	Brown County, SD	36,531	38,301
10100	46045	Edmunds County, SD	4,071	3,986
10140		Aberdeen, WA Micro Area	72,797	75,636
10140	53027	Grays Harbor County, WA	72,797	75,636
10180		Abilene, TX Metro Area	165,252	176,579
10180	48059	Callahan County, TX	13,544	13,708
10180	48253	Jones County, TX	20,202	19,663
10180	48441	Taylor County, TX	131,506	143,208
10220		Ada, OK Micro Area	37,492	38,065
10220	40123	Pontotoc County, OK	37,492	38,065
10300		Adrian, MI Micro Area	99,892	99,423
10300	26091	Lenawee County, MI	99,892	99,423
10420		Akron, OH Metro Area	703,200	702,219
10420	39133	Portage County, OH	161,419	161,791
10420	39153	Summit County, OH	541,781	540,428
10460		Alamogordo, NM Micro Area	63,797	67,839
10460	35035	Otero County, NM	63,797	67,839
10500		Albany, GA Metro Area	153,857	148,922
10500	13095	Dougherty County, GA	94,565	85,790
10500	13177	Lee County, GA	28,298	33,163
10500	13273	Terrell County, GA	9,315	9,185
10500	13321	Worth County, GA	21,679	20,784
10540		Albany-Lebanon, OR Metro Area	116,672	128,610
10540	41043	Linn County, OR	116,672	128,610
10580		Albany-Schenectady-Troy, NY Metro Area	870,716	899,262
10580	36001	Albany County, NY	304,204	314,848
10580	36083	Rensselaer County, NY	159,429	161,130
10580	36091	Saratoga County, NY	219,607	235,509
10580	36093	Schenectady County, NY	154,727	158,061
10580	36095	Schoharie County, NY	32,749	29,714
10620		Albemarle, NC Micro Area	60,585	62,504
10620	37167	Stanly County, NC	60,585	62,504
10660		Albert Lea, MN Micro Area	31,255	30,895
10660	27047	Freeborn County, MN	31,255	30,895
10700		Albertville, AL Micro Area	93,019	97,612
10700	01095	Marshall County, AL	93,019	97,612
10740		Albuquerque, NM Metro Area	887,077	916,528
10740	35001	Bernalillo County, NM	662,564	676,444
10740	35043	Sandoval County, NM	131,561	148,834
10740	35057	Torrance County, NM	16,383	15,045
10740	35061	Valencia County, NM	76,569	76,205
10760		Alexander City, AL Micro Area	53,155	51,698
10760	01037	Coosa County, AL	11,539	10,387
10760	01123	Tallapoosa County, AL	41,616	41,311
10780		Alexandria, LA Metro Area	153,922	152,192
10780	22043	Grant Parish, LA	22,309	22,169
10780	22079	Rapides Parish, LA	131,613	130,023
10820		Alexandria, MN Micro Area	36,009	39,006
10820	27041	Douglas County, MN	36,009	39,006
10860		Alice, TX Micro Area	52,620	48,722
10860	48131	Duval County, TX	11,782	9,831
10860	48249	Jim Wells County, TX	40,838	38,891
10900		Allentown-Bethlehem-Easton, PA-NJ Metro Area	821,173	861,889
10900	34041	Warren County, NJ	108,692	109,632
10900	42025	Carbon County, PA	65,249	64,749
10900	42077	Lehigh County, PA	349,497	374,557
10900	42095	Northampton County, PA	297,735	312,951
10940		Alma, MI Micro Area	42,476	41,761
10940	26057	Gratiot County, MI	42,476	41,761
10980		Alpena, MI Micro Area	29,598	28,907
10980	26007	Alpena County, MI	29,598	28,907
11020		Altoona, PA Metro Area	127,089	122,822
11020	42013	Blair County, PA	127,089	122,822
11060		Altus, OK Micro Area	26,446	24,785
11060	40065	Jackson County, OK	26,446	24,785
11100		Amarillo, TX Metro Area	251,933	268,691
11100	48011	Armstrong County, TX	1,901	1,848
11100	48065	Carson County, TX	6,182	5,807
11100	48359	Oldham County, TX	2,052	1,758
11100	48375	Potter County, TX	121,073	118,525
11100	48381	Randall County, TX	120,725	140,753
11140		Americus, GA Micro Area	37,829	34,163
11140	13249	Schley County, GA	5,010	4,547
11140	13261	Sumter County, GA	32,819	29,616
11180		Ames, IA Metro Area	115,848	125,252
11180	19015	Boone County, IA	26,306	26,715
11180	19169	Story County, IA	89,542	98,537
11220		Amsterdam, NY Micro Area	50,219	49,532
11220	36057	Montgomery County, NY	50,219	49,532
11260		Anchorage, AK Metro Area	380,821	398,328
11260	02020	Anchorage Municipality, AK	291,826	291,247
11260	02170	Matanuska-Susitna Borough, AK	88,995	107,081
11380		Andrews, TX Micro Area	14,786	18,610
11380	48003	Andrews County, TX	14,786	18,610
11420		Angola, IN Micro Area	34,185	34,435
11420	18151	Steuben County, IN	34,185	34,435
11460		Ann Arbor, MI Metro Area	344,791	372,258
11460	26161	Washtenaw County, MI	344,791	372,258
11500		Anniston-Oxford, AL Metro Area	118,572	116,441
11500	01015	Calhoun County, AL	118,572	116,441
11540		Appleton, WI Metro Area	225,666	243,147
11540	55015	Calumet County, WI	48,971	52,442
11540	55087	Outagamie County, WI	176,695	190,705
11580		Arcadia, FL Micro Area	34,862	33,976
11580	12027	DeSoto County, FL	34,862	33,976

CORE-BASED STATISTICAL AREAS (Metropolitan and Micropolitan), METROPOLITAN DIVISIONS, AND COMPONENTS (as defined March, 2020)—*Continued*

Core based statistical area	State/ County FIPS code	Title and Geographic Components	2010 Census Population	2020 Census Population
11620		Ardmore, OK Micro Area	56,980	58,149
11620	40019	Carter County, OK	47,557	48,003
11620	40085	Love County, OK	9,423	10,146
11660		Arkadelphia, AR Micro Area	22,995	21,446
11660	05019	Clark County, AR	22,995	21,446
11700		Asheville, NC Metro Area	424,858	469,015
11700	37021	Buncombe County, NC	238,318	269,452
11700	37087	Haywood County, NC	59,036	62,089
11700	37089	Henderson County, NC	106,740	116,281
11700	37115	Madison County, NC	20,764	21,193
11740		Ashland, OH Micro Area	53,139	52,447
11740	39005	Ashland County, OH	53,139	52,447
11780		Ashtabula, OH Micro Area	101,497	97,574
11780	39007	Ashtabula County, OH	101,497	97,574
11820		Astoria, OR Micro Area	37,039	41,072
11820	41007	Clatsop County, OR	37,039	41,072
11860		Atchison, KS Micro Area	16,924	16,348
11860	20005	Atchison County, KS	16,924	16,348
11900		Athens, OH Micro Area	64,757	62,431
11900	39009	Athens County, OH	64,757	62,431
11940		Athens, TN Micro Area	52,266	53,276
11940	47107	McMinn County, TN	52,266	53,276
11980		Athens, TX Micro Area	78,532	82,150
11980	48213	Henderson County, TX	78,532	82,150
12020		Athens-Clarke County, GA Metro Area	192,541	215,415
12020	13059	Clarke County, GA	116,714	128,671
12020	13195	Madison County, GA	28,120	30,120
12020	13219	Oconee County, GA	32,808	41,799
12020	13221	Oglethorpe County, GA	14,899	14,825
12060		Atlanta-Sandy Springs-Alpharetta, GA Metro Area	5,286,728	6,089,815
12060	13013	Barrow County, GA	69,367	83,505
12060	13015	Bartow County, GA	100,157	108,901
12060	13035	Butts County, GA	23,655	25,434
12060	13045	Carroll County, GA	110,527	119,148
12060	13057	Cherokee County, GA	214,346	266,620
12060	13063	Clayton County, GA	259,424	297,595
12060	13067	Cobb County, GA	688,078	766,149
12060	13077	Coweta County, GA	127,317	146,158
12060	13085	Dawson County, GA	22,330	26,798
12060	13089	DeKalb County, GA	691,893	764,382
12060	13097	Douglas County, GA	132,403	144,237
12060	13113	Fayette County, GA	106,567	119,194
12060	13117	Forsyth County, GA	175,511	251,283
12060	13121	Fulton County, GA	920,581	1,066,710
12060	13135	Gwinnett County, GA	805,321	957,062
12060	13143	Haralson County, GA	28,780	29,919
12060	13149	Heard County, GA	11,834	11,412
12060	13151	Henry County, GA	203,922	240,712
12060	13159	Jasper County, GA	13,900	14,588
12060	13171	Lamar County, GA	18,317	18,500
12060	13199	Meriwether County, GA	21,992	20,613
12060	13211	Morgan County, GA	17,868	20,097
12060	13217	Newton County, GA	99,958	112,483
12060	13223	Paulding County, GA	142,324	168,661
12060	13227	Pickens County, GA	29,431	33,216
12060	13231	Pike County, GA	17,869	18,889
12060	13247	Rockdale County, GA	85,215	93,570
12060	13255	Spalding County, GA	64,073	67,306
12060	13297	Walton County, GA	83,768	96,673
12100		Atlantic City-Hammonton, NJ Metro Area	274,549	274,534
12100	34001	Atlantic County, NJ	274,549	274,534
12120		Atmore, AL Micro Area	38,319	36,757
12120	01053	Escambia County, AL	38,319	36,757
12140		Auburn, IN Micro Area	42,223	43,265
12140	18033	DeKalb County, IN	42,223	43,265
12180		Auburn, NY Micro Area	80,026	76,248
12180	36011	Cayuga County, NY	80,026	76,248
12220		Auburn-Opelika, AL Metro Area	140,247	174,241
12220	01081	Lee County, AL	140,247	174,241
12260		Augusta-Richmond County, GA-SC Metro Area	564,873	611,000
12260	13033	Burke County, GA	23,316	24,596
12260	13073	Columbia County, GA	124,053	156,010
12260	13181	Lincoln County, GA	7,996	7,690
12260	13189	McDuffie County, GA	21,875	21,632
12260	13245	Richmond County, GA	200,549	206,607
12260	45003	Aiken County, SC	160,099	168,808
12260	45037	Edgefield County, SC	26,985	25,657
12300		Augusta-Waterville, ME Micro Area	122,151	123,642
12300	23011	Kennebec County, ME	122,151	123,642
12380		Austin, MN Micro Area	39,163	40,029
12380	27099	Mower County, MN	39,163	40,029

CORE-BASED STATISTICAL AREAS (Metropolitan and Micropolitan), METROPOLITAN DIVISIONS, AND COMPONENTS (as defined March, 2020)—*Continued*

Core based statistical area	State/ County FIPS code	Title and Geographic Components	2010 Census Population	2020 Census Population
12420		Austin-Round Rock-Georgetown, TX Metro Area	1,716,289	2,283,371
12420	48021	Bastrop County, TX	74,171	97,216
12420	48055	Caldwell County, TX	38,066	45,883
12420	48209	Hays County, TX	157,107	241,067
12420	48453	Travis County, TX	1,024,266	1,290,188
12420	48491	Williamson County, TX	422,679	609,017
12460		Bainbridge, GA Micro Area	27,842	29,367
12460	13087	Decatur County, GA	27,842	29,367
12540		Bakersfield, CA Metro Area	839,631	909,235
12540	06029	Kern County, CA	839,631	909,235
12580		Baltimore-Columbia-Towson, MD Metro Area	2,710,489	2,844,510
12580	24003	Anne Arundel County, MD	537,656	588,261
12580	24005	Baltimore County, MD	805,029	854,535
12580	24013	Carroll County, MD	167,134	172,891
12580	24025	Harford County, MD	244,826	260,924
12580	24027	Howard County, MD	287,085	332,317
12580	24035	Queen Anne's County, MD	47,798	49,874
12580	24510	Baltimore city, MD	620,961	585,708
12620		Bangor, ME Metro Area	153,923	152,199
12620	23019	Penobscot County, ME	153,923	152,199
12660		Baraboo, WI Micro Area	61,976	65,763
12660	55111	Sauk County, WI	61,976	65,763
12680		Bardstown, KY Micro Area	43,437	46,738
12680	21179	Nelson County, KY	43,437	46,738
12700		Barnstable Town, MA Metro Area	215,888	228,996
12700	25001	Barnstable County, MA	215,888	228,996
12740		Barre, VT Micro Area	59,534	59,807
12740	50023	Washington County, VT	59,534	59,807
12780		Bartlesville, OK Micro Area	50,976	52,455
12780	40147	Washington County, OK	50,976	52,455
12860		Batavia, NY Micro Area	60,079	58,388
12860	36037	Genesee County, NY	60,079	58,388
12900		Batesville, AR Micro Area	53,911	55,209
12900	05063	Independence County, AR	36,647	37,938
12900	05135	Sharp County, AR	17,264	17,271
12940		Baton Rouge, LA Metro Area	825,905	870,569
12940	22005	Ascension Parish, LA	107,215	126,500
12940	22007	Assumption Parish, LA	23,421	21,039
12940	22033	East Baton Rouge Parish, LA	440,171	456,781
12940	22037	East Feliciana Parish, LA	20,267	19,539
12940	22047	Iberville Parish, LA	33,387	30,241
12940	22063	Livingston Parish, LA	128,026	142,282
12940	22077	Pointe Coupee Parish, LA	22,802	20,758
12940	22091	St. Helena Parish, LA	11,203	10,920
12940	22121	West Baton Rouge Parish, LA	23,788	27,199
12940	22125	West Feliciana Parish, LA	15,625	15,310
12980		Battle Creek, MI Metro Area	136,146	134,310
12980	26025	Calhoun County, MI	136,146	134,310
13020		Bay City, MI Metro Area	107,771	103,856
13020	26017	Bay County, MI	107,771	103,856
13060		Bay City, TX Micro Area	36,702	36,255
13060	48321	Matagorda County, TX	36,702	36,255
13100		Beatrice, NE Micro Area	22,311	21,704
13100	31067	Gage County, NE	22,311	21,704
13140		Beaumont-Port Arthur, TX Metro Area	388,745	397,565
13140	48199	Hardin County, TX	54,635	56,231
13140	48245	Jefferson County, TX	252,273	256,526
13140	48361	Orange County, TX	81,837	84,808
13180		Beaver Dam, WI Micro Area	88,759	89,396
13180	55027	Dodge County, WI	88,759	89,396
13220		Beckley, WV Metro Area	124,898	115,079
13220	54019	Fayette County, WV	46,039	40,488
13220	54081	Raleigh County, WV	78,859	74,591
13260		Bedford, IN Micro Area	46,134	45,011
13260	18093	Lawrence County, IN	46,134	45,011
13300		Beeville, TX Micro Area	31,861	31,047
13300	48025	Bee County, TX	31,861	31,047
13340		Bellefontaine, OH Micro Area	45,858	46,150
13340	39091	Logan County, OH	45,858	46,150
13380		Bellingham, WA Metro Area	201,140	226,847
13380	53073	Whatcom County, WA	201,140	226,847
13420		Bemidji, MN Micro Area	44,442	46,228
13420	27007	Beltrami County, MN	44,442	46,228
13460		Bend, OR Metro Area	157,733	198,253
13460	41017	Deschutes County, OR	157,733	198,253
13500		Bennettsville, SC Micro Area	28,933	26,667
13500	45069	Marlboro County, SC	28,933	26,667
13540		Bennington, VT Micro Area	37,125	37,347
13540	50003	Bennington County, VT	37,125	37,347
13620		Berlin, NH Micro Area	33,055	31,268
13620	33007	Coos County, NH	33,055	31,268
13660		Big Rapids, MI Micro Area	42,798	39,714
13660	26107	Mecosta County, MI	42,798	39,714
13700		Big Spring, TX Micro Area	35,012	34,860
13700	48227	Howard County, TX	35,012	34,860
13720		Big Stone Gap, VA Micro Area	45,410	39,817
13720	51195	Wise County, VA	41,452	36,130
13720	51720	Norton city, VA	3,958	3,687
13740		Billings, MT Metro Area	167,167	184,167
13740	30009	Carbon County, MT	10,078	10,473
13740	30095	Stillwater County, MT	9,117	8,963
13740	30111	Yellowstone County, MT	147,972	164,731
13780		Binghamton, NY Metro Area	251,725	247,138
13780	36007	Broome County, NY	200,600	198,683
13780	36107	Tioga County, NY	51,125	48,455

CORE-BASED STATISTICAL AREAS (Metropolitan and Micropolitan), METROPOLITAN DIVISIONS, AND COMPONENTS (as defined March, 2020)—*Continued*

Core based statistical area	State/ County FIPS code	Title and Geographic Components	2010 Census Population	2020 Census Population
13820		Birmingham-Hoover, AL Metro Area	1,061,024	1,115,289
13820	01007	Bibb County, AL	22,915	22,293
13820	01009	Blount County, AL	57,322	59,134
13820	01021	Chilton County, AL	43,643	45,014
13820	01073	Jefferson County, AL	658,466	674,721
13820	01115	St. Clair County, AL	83,593	91,103
13820	01117	Shelby County, AL	195,085	223,024
13900		Bismarck, ND Metro Area	110,625	133,626
13900	38015	Burleigh County, ND	81,308	98,458
13900	38059	Morton County, ND	27,471	33,291
13900	38065	Oliver County, ND	1,846	1,877
13940		Blackfoot, ID Micro Area	45,607	47,992
13940	16011	Bingham County, ID	45,607	47,992
13980		Blacksburg-Christiansburg, VA Metro Area	162,958	166,378
13980	51071	Giles County, VA	17,286	16,787
13980	51121	Montgomery County, VA	94,392	99,721
13980	51155	Pulaski County, VA	34,872	33,800
13980	51750	Radford city, VA	16,408	16,070
14010		Bloomington, IL Metro Area	169,572	170,954
14010	17113	McLean County, IL	169,572	170,954
14020		Bloomington, IN Metro Area	159,549	161,039
14020	18105	Monroe County, IN	137,974	139,718
14020	18119	Owen County, IN	21,575	21,321
14100		Bloomsburg-Berwick, PA Metro Area	85,562	82,863
14100	42037	Columbia County, PA	67,295	64,727
14100	42093	Montour County, PA	18,267	18,136
14140		Bluefield, WV-VA Micro Area	114,166	106,363
14140	51021	Bland County, VA	6,824	6,270
14140	51185	Tazewell County, VA	45,078	40,429
14140	54055	Mercer County, WV	62,264	59,664
14160		Bluffton, IN Micro Area	27,636	28,180
14160	18179	Wells County, IN	27,636	28,180
14180		Blytheville, AR Micro Area	46,480	40,685
14180	05093	Mississippi County, AR	46,480	40,685
14220		Bogalusa, LA Micro Area	47,168	45,463
14220	22117	Washington Parish, LA	47,168	45,463
14260		Boise City, ID Metro Area	616,561	764,718
14260	16001	Ada County, ID	392,365	494,967
14260	16015	Boise County, ID	7,028	7,610
14260	16027	Canyon County, ID	188,923	231,105
14260	16045	Gem County, ID	16,719	19,123
14260	16073	Owyhee County, ID	11,526	11,913
14300		Bonham, TX Micro Area	33,915	35,662
14300	48147	Fannin County, TX	33,915	35,662
14380		Boone, NC Micro Area	51,079	54,086
14380	37189	Watauga County, NC	51,079	54,086
14420		Borger, TX Micro Area	22,150	20,617
14420	48233	Hutchinson County, TX	22,150	20,617
14460		Boston-Cambridge-Newton, MA-NH Metro Area	4,552,402	4,941,632
14460		Boston, MA Division 14454	1,887,792	2,054,736
14460	25021	Norfolk County, MA	670,850	725,981
14460	25023	Plymouth County, MA	494,919	530,819
14460	25025	Suffolk County, MA	722,023	797,936
14460		Cambridge-Newton-Framingham, MA Division 15764	2,246,244	2,441,831
14460	25009	Essex County, MA	743,159	809,829
14460	25017	Middlesex County, MA	1,503,085	1,632,002
14460		Rockingham County-Strafford County, NH Division 40484	418,366	445,065
14460	33015	Rockingham County, NH	295,223	314,176
14460	33017	Strafford County, NH	123,143	130,889
14500		Boulder, CO Metro Area	294,567	330,758
14500	08013	Boulder County, CO	294,567	330,758
14540		Bowling Green, KY Metro Area	158,599	179,639
14540	21003	Allen County, KY	19,956	20,588
14540	21031	Butler County, KY	12,690	12,371
14540	21061	Edmonson County, KY	12,161	12,126
14540	21227	Warren County, KY	113,792	134,554
14580		Bozeman, MT Micro Area	89,513	118,960
14580	30031	Gallatin County, MT	89,513	118,960
14620		Bradford, PA Micro Area	43,450	40,432
14620	42083	McKean County, PA	43,450	40,432
14660		Brainerd, MN Micro Area	91,067	96,189
14660	27021	Cass County, MN	28,567	30,066
14660	27035	Crow Wing County, MN	62,500	66,123
14700		Branson, MO Micro Area	51,675	56,066
14700	29213	Taney County, MO	51,675	56,066
14720		Breckenridge, CO Micro Area	27,994	31,055
14720	08117	Summit County, CO	27,994	31,055
14740		Bremerton-Silverdale-Port Orchard, WA Metro Area	251,133	275,611
14740	53035	Kitsap County, WA	251,133	275,611
14780		Brenham, TX Micro Area	33,718	35,805
14780	48477	Washington County, TX	33,718	35,805
14820		Brevard, NC Micro Area	33,090	32,986
14820	37175	Transylvania County, NC	33,090	32,986
14860		Bridgeport-Stamford-Norwalk, CT Metro Area	916,829	957,419
14860	09001	Fairfield County, CT	916,829	957,419
15020		Brookhaven, MS Micro Area	34,869	34,907
15020	28085	Lincoln County, MS	34,869	34,907
15060		Brookings, OR Micro Area	22,364	23,446
15060	41015	Curry County, OR	22,364	23,446
15100		Brookings, SD Micro Area	31,965	34,375
15100	46011	Brookings County, SD	31,965	34,375

CORE-BASED STATISTICAL AREAS (Metropolitan and Micropolitan), METROPOLITAN DIVISIONS, AND COMPONENTS (as defined March, 2020)—*Continued*

Core based statistical area	State/ County FIPS code	Title and Geographic Components	2010 Census Population	2020 Census Population
15140		Brownsville, TN Micro Area	18,787	17,864
15140	47075	Haywood County, TN	18,787	17,864
15180		Brownsville-Harlingen, TX Metro Area	406,220	421,017
15180	48061	Cameron County, TX	406,220	421,017
15220		Brownwood, TX Micro Area	38,106	38,095
15220	48049	Brown County, TX	38,106	38,095
15260		Brunswick, GA Metro Area	112,370	113,495
15260	13025	Brantley County, GA	18,411	18,021
15260	13127	Glynn County, GA	79,626	84,499
15260	13191	McIntosh County, GA	14,333	10,975
15340		Bucyrus-Galion, OH Micro Area	43,784	42,025
15340	39033	Crawford County, OH	43,784	42,025
15380		Buffalo-Cheektowaga, NY Metro Area	1,135,509	1,166,902
15380	36029	Erie County, NY	919,040	954,236
15380	36063	Niagara County, NY	216,469	212,666
15420		Burley, ID Micro Area	43,021	46,268
15420	16031	Cassia County, ID	22,952	24,655
15420	16067	Minidoka County, ID	20,069	21,613
15460		Burlington, IA-IL Micro Area	47,656	45,297
15460	17071	Henderson County, IL	7,331	6,387
15460	19057	Des Moines County, IA	40,325	38,910
15500		Burlington, NC Metro Area	151,131	171,415
15500	37001	Alamance County, NC	151,131	171,415
15540		Burlington-South Burlington, VT Metro Area	211,261	225,562
15540	50007	Chittenden County, VT	156,545	168,323
15540	50011	Franklin County, VT	47,746	49,946
15540	50013	Grand Isle County, VT	6,970	7,293
15580		Butte-Silver Bow, MT Micro Area	34,200	35,133
15580	30093	Silver Bow County, MT	34,200	35,133
15620		Cadillac, MI Micro Area	47,584	48,725
15620	26113	Missaukee County, MI	14,849	15,052
15620	26165	Wexford County, MI	32,735	33,673
15660		Calhoun, GA Micro Area	55,186	57,544
15660	13129	Gordon County, GA	55,186	57,544
15680		California-Lexington Park, MD Metro Area	105,151	113,777
15680	24037	St. Mary's County, MD	105,151	113,777
15700		Cambridge, MD Micro Area	32,618	32,531
15700	24019	Dorchester County, MD	32,618	32,531
15740		Cambridge, OH Micro Area	40,087	38,438
15740	39059	Guernsey County, OH	40,087	38,438
15780		Camden, AR Micro Area	31,488	27,389
15780	05013	Calhoun County, AR	5,368	4,739
15780	05103	Ouachita County, AR	26,120	22,650
15820		Campbellsville, KY Micro Area	35,770	37,130
15820	21087	Green County, KY	11,258	11,107
15820	21217	Taylor County, KY	24,512	26,023

Core based statistical area	State/ County FIPS code	Title and Geographic Components	2010 Census Population	2020 Census Population
15860		Ca±on City, CO Micro Area	46,824	48,939
15860	08043	Fremont County, CO	46,824	48,939
15940		Canton-Massillon, OH Metro Area	404,422	401,574
15940	39019	Carroll County, OH	28,836	26,721
15940	39151	Stark County, OH	375,586	374,853
15980		Cape Coral-Fort Myers, FL Metro Area	618,754	760,822
15980	12071	Lee County, FL	618,754	760,822
16020		Cape Girardeau, MO-IL Metro Area	96,275	97,517
16020	17003	Alexander County, IL	8,238	5,240
16020	29017	Bollinger County, MO	12,363	10,567
16020	29031	Cape Girardeau County, MO	75,674	81,710
16060		Carbondale-Marion, IL Metro Area	139,157	133,435
16060	17077	Jackson County, IL	60,218	52,974
16060	17087	Johnson County, IL	12,582	13,308
16060	17199	Williamson County, IL	66,357	67,153
16100		Carlsbad-Artesia, NM Micro Area	53,829	62,314
16100	35015	Eddy County, NM	53,829	62,314
16140		Carroll, IA Micro Area	20,816	20,760
16140	19027	Carroll County, IA	20,816	20,760
16180		Carson City, NV Metro Area	55,274	58,639
16180	32510	Carson City, NV	55,274	58,639
16220		Casper, WY Metro Area	75,450	79,955
16220	56025	Natrona County, WY	75,450	79,955
16260		Cedar City, UT Micro Area	46,163	57,289
16260	49021	Iron County, UT	46,163	57,289
16300		Cedar Rapids, IA Metro Area	257,940	276,520
16300	19011	Benton County, IA	26,076	25,575
16300	19105	Jones County, IA	20,638	20,646
16300	19113	Linn County, IA	211,226	230,299
16340		Cedartown, GA Micro Area	41,475	42,853
16340	13233	Polk County, GA	41,475	42,853
16380		Celina, OH Micro Area	40,814	42,528
16380	39107	Mercer County, OH	40,814	42,528
16420		Central City, KY Micro Area	31,499	30,928
16420	21177	Muhlenberg County, KY	31,499	30,928
16460		Centralia, IL Micro Area	39,437	37,729
16460	17121	Marion County, IL	39,437	37,729
16500		Centralia, WA Micro Area	75,455	82,149
16500	53041	Lewis County, WA	75,455	82,149
16540		Chambersburg-Waynesboro, PA Metro Area	149,618	155,932
16540	42055	Franklin County, PA	149,618	155,932
16580		Champaign-Urbana, IL Metro Area	217,810	222,538
16580	17019	Champaign County, IL	201,081	205,865
16580	17147	Piatt County, IL	16,729	16,673

CORE-BASED STATISTICAL AREAS (Metropolitan and Micropolitan), METROPOLITAN DIVISIONS, AND COMPONENTS (as defined March, 2020)—*Continued*

Core based statistical area	State/ County FIPS code	Title and Geographic Components	2010 Census Population	2020 Census Population
16620		Charleston, WV Metro Area	278,009	258,859
16620	54005	Boone County, WV	24,629	21,809
16620	54015	Clay County, WV	9,386	8,051
16620	54035	Jackson County, WV	29,211	27,791
16620	54039	Kanawha County, WV	193,063	180,745
16620	54043	Lincoln County, WV	21,720	20,463
16660		Charleston-Mattoon, IL Micro Area	64,921	57,313
16660	17029	Coles County, IL	53,873	46,863
16660	17035	Cumberland County, IL	11,048	10,450
16700		Charleston-North Charleston, SC Metro Area	664,607	799,636
16700	45015	Berkeley County, SC	177,843	229,861
16700	45019	Charleston County, SC	350,209	408,235
16700	45035	Dorchester County, SC	136,555	161,540
16740		Charlotte-Concord-Gastonia, NC-SC Metro Area	2,243,960	2,660,329
16740	37007	Anson County, NC	26,948	22,055
16740	37025	Cabarrus County, NC	178,011	225,804
16740	37071	Gaston County, NC	206,086	227,943
16740	37097	Iredell County, NC	159,437	186,693
16740	37109	Lincoln County, NC	78,265	86,810
16740	37119	Mecklenburg County, NC	919,628	1,115,482
16740	37159	Rowan County, NC	138,428	146,875
16740	37179	Union County, NC	201,292	238,267
16740	45023	Chester County, SC	33,140	32,294
16740	45057	Lancaster County, SC	76,652	96,016
16740	45091	York County, SC	226,073	282,090
16820		Charlottesville, VA Metro Area	201,559	221,524
16820	51003	Albemarle County, VA	98,970	112,395
16820	51065	Fluvanna County, VA	25,691	27,249
16820	51079	Greene County, VA	18,403	20,552
16820	51125	Nelson County, VA	15,020	14,775
16820	51540	Charlottesville city, VA	43,475	46,553
16860		Chattanooga, TN-GA Metro Area	528,143	562,647
16860	13047	Catoosa County, GA	63,942	67,872
16860	13083	Dade County, GA	16,633	16,251
16860	13295	Walker County, GA	68,756	67,654
16860	47065	Hamilton County, TN	336,463	366,207
16860	47115	Marion County, TN	28,237	28,837
16860	47153	Sequatchie County, TN	14,112	15,826
16940		Cheyenne, WY Metro Area	91,738	100,512
16940	56021	Laramie County, WY	91,738	100,512
16980		Chicago-Naperville-Elgin, IL-IN-WI Metro Area	9,461,105	9,618,502
16980		Chicago-Naperville-Evanston, IL Division 16984	7,147,982	7,267,535
16980	17031	Cook County, IL	5,194,675	5,275,541
16980	17043	DuPage County, IL	916,924	932,877
16980	17063	Grundy County, IL	50,063	52,533
16980	17111	McHenry County, IL	308,760	310,229
16980	17197	Will County, IL	677,560	696,355
16980		Elgin, IL Division 20994	735,165	748,811
16980	17037	DeKalb County, IL	105,160	100,420
16980	17089	Kane County, IL	515,269	516,522
16980	17093	Kendall County, IL	114,736	131,869

Core based statistical area	State/ County FIPS code	Title and Geographic Components	2010 Census Population	2020 Census Population
16980		Gary, IN Division 23844	708,070	718,663
16980	18073	Jasper County, IN	33,478	32,918
16980	18089	Lake County, IN	496,005	498,700
16980	18111	Newton County, IN	14,244	13,830
16980	18127	Porter County, IN	164,343	173,215
16980		Lake County-Kenosha County, IL-WI Division 29404	869,888	883,493
16980	17097	Lake County, IL	703,462	714,342
16980	55059	Kenosha County, WI	166,426	169,151
17020		Chico, CA Metro Area	220,000	211,632
17020	06007	Butte County, CA	220,000	211,632
17060		Chillicothe, OH Micro Area	78,064	77,093
17060	39141	Ross County, OH	78,064	77,093
17140		Cincinnati, OH-KY-IN Metro Area	2,137,667	2,256,884
17140	18029	Dearborn County, IN	50,047	50,679
17140	18047	Franklin County, IN	23,087	22,785
17140	18115	Ohio County, IN	6,128	5,940
17140	18161	Union County, IN	7,516	7,087
17140	21015	Boone County, KY	118,811	135,968
17140	21023	Bracken County, KY	8,488	8,400
17140	21037	Campbell County, KY	90,336	93,076
17140	21077	Gallatin County, KY	8,589	8,690
17140	21081	Grant County, KY	24,662	24,941
17140	21117	Kenton County, KY	159,720	169,064
17140	21191	Pendleton County, KY	14,877	14,644
17140	39015	Brown County, OH	44,846	43,676
17140	39017	Butler County, OH	368,130	390,357
17140	39025	Clermont County, OH	197,363	208,601
17140	39061	Hamilton County, OH	802,374	830,639
17140	39165	Warren County, OH	212,693	242,337
17220		Clarksburg, WV Micro Area	94,196	90,434
17220	54017	Doddridge County, WV	8,202	7,808
17220	54033	Harrison County, WV	69,099	65,921
17220	54091	Taylor County, WV	16,895	16,705
17260		Clarksdale, MS Micro Area	26,151	21,390
17260	28027	Coahoma County, MS	26,151	21,390
17300		Clarksville, TN-KY Metro Area	273,949	320,535
17300	21047	Christian County, KY	73,955	72,748
17300	21221	Trigg County, KY	14,339	14,061
17300	47125	Montgomery County, TN	172,331	220,069
17300	47161	Stewart County, TN	13,324	13,657
17340		Clearlake, CA Micro Area	64,665	68,163
17340	06033	Lake County, CA	64,665	68,163
17380		Cleveland, MS Micro Area	34,145	30,985
17380	28011	Bolivar County, MS	34,145	30,985
17420		Cleveland, TN Metro Area	115,788	126,164
17420	47011	Bradley County, TN	98,963	108,620
17420	47139	Polk County, TN	16,825	17,544
17460		Cleveland-Elyria, OH Metro Area	2,077,240	2,088,251
17460	39035	Cuyahoga County, OH	1,280,122	1,264,817
17460	39055	Geauga County, OH	93,389	95,397
17460	39085	Lake County, OH	230,041	232,603
17460	39093	Lorain County, OH	301,356	312,964
17460	39103	Medina County, OH	172,332	182,470

CORE-BASED STATISTICAL AREAS (Metropolitan and Micropolitan), METROPOLITAN DIVISIONS, AND COMPONENTS (as defined March, 2020)—*Continued*

Core based statistical area	State/ County FIPS code	Title and Geographic Components	2010 Census Population	2020 Census Population
17500		Clewiston, FL Micro Area	39,140	39,619
17500	12051	Hendry County, FL	39,140	39,619
17540		Clinton, IA Micro Area	49,116	46,460
17540	19045	Clinton County, IA	49,116	46,460
17580		Clovis, NM Micro Area	48,376	48,430
17580	35009	Curry County, NM	48,376	48,430
17660		Coeur d'Alene, ID Metro Area	138,494	171,362
17660	16055	Kootenai County, ID	138,494	171,362
17700		Coffeyville, KS Micro Area	35,471	31,486
17700	20125	Montgomery County, KS	35,471	31,486
17740		Coldwater, MI Micro Area	45,248	44,862
17740	26023	Branch County, MI	45,248	44,862
17780		College Station-Bryan, TX Metro Area	228,660	268,248
17780	48041	Brazos County, TX	194,851	233,849
17780	48051	Burleson County, TX	17,187	17,642
17780	48395	Robertson County, TX	16,622	16,757
17820		Colorado Springs, CO Metro Area	645,613	755,105
17820	08041	El Paso County, CO	622,263	730,395
17820	08119	Teller County, CO	23,350	24,710
17860		Columbia, MO Metro Area	190,387	210,864
17860	29019	Boone County, MO	162,642	183,610
17860	29053	Cooper County, MO	17,601	17,103
17860	29089	Howard County, MO	10,144	10,151
17900		Columbia, SC Metro Area	767,598	829,470
17900	45017	Calhoun County, SC	15,175	14,119
17900	45039	Fairfield County, SC	23,956	20,948
17900	45055	Kershaw County, SC	61,697	65,403
17900	45063	Lexington County, SC	262,391	293,991
17900	45079	Richland County, SC	384,504	416,147
17900	45081	Saluda County, SC	19,875	18,862
17980		Columbus, GA-AL Metro Area	307,788	328,883
17980	01113	Russell County, AL	52,947	59,183
17980	13053	Chattahoochee County, GA	11,267	9,565
17980	13145	Harris County, GA	32,024	34,668
17980	13197	Marion County, GA	8,742	7,498
17980	13215	Muscogee County, GA	189,885	206,922
....	13259	Stewart County, GA	6,058	5,314
17980	13263	Talbot County, GA	6,865	5,733
18020		Columbus, IN Metro Area	76,794	82,208
18020	18005	Bartholomew County, IN	76,794	82,208
18060		Columbus, MS Micro Area	59,779	58,879
18060	28087	Lowndes County, MS	59,779	58,879
18100		Columbus, NE Micro Area	32,237	34,296
18100	31141	Platte County, NE	32,237	34,296

Core based statistical area	State/ County FIPS code	Title and Geographic Components	2010 Census Population	2020 Census Population
18140		Columbus, OH Metro Area	1,901,974	2,138,926
18140	39041	Delaware County, OH	174,214	214,124
18140	39045	Fairfield County, OH	146,156	158,921
18140	39049	Franklin County, OH	1,163,414	1,323,807
18140	39073	Hocking County, OH	29,380	28,050
18140	39089	Licking County, OH	166,492	178,519
18140	39097	Madison County, OH	43,435	43,824
18140	39117	Morrow County, OH	34,827	34,950
18140	39127	Perry County, OH	36,058	35,408
18140	39129	Pickaway County, OH	55,698	58,539
18140	39159	Union County, OH	52,300	62,784
18180		Concord, NH Micro Area	146,445	153,808
18180	33013	Merrimack County, NH	146,445	153,808
18220		Connersville, IN Micro Area	24,277	23,398
18220	18041	Fayette County, IN	24,277	23,398
18260		Cookeville, TN Micro Area	106,042	113,982
18260	47087	Jackson County, TN	11,638	11,617
18260	47133	Overton County, TN	22,083	22,511
18260	47141	Putnam County, TN	72,321	79,854
18300		Coos Bay, OR Micro Area	63,043	64,929
18300	41011	Coos County, OR	63,043	64,929
18380		Cordele, GA Micro Area	23,439	20,128
18380	13081	Crisp County, GA	23,439	20,128
18420		Corinth, MS Micro Area	37,057	34,740
18420	28003	Alcorn County, MS	37,057	34,740
18460		Cornelia, GA Micro Area	43,041	46,031
18460	13137	Habersham County, GA	43,041	46,031
18500		Corning, NY Micro Area	98,990	93,584
18500	36101	Steuben County, NY	98,990	93,584
18580		Corpus Christi, TX Metro Area	405,027	421,933
18580	48355	Nueces County, TX	340,223	353,178
18580	48409	San Patricio County, TX	64,804	68,755
18620		Corsicana, TX Micro Area	47,735	52,624
18620	48349	Navarro County, TX	47,735	52,624
18660		Cortland, NY Micro Area	49,336	46,809
18660	36023	Cortland County, NY	49,336	46,809
18700		Corvallis, OR Metro Area	85,579	95,184
18700	41003	Benton County, OR	85,579	95,184
18740		Coshocton, OH Micro Area	36,901	36,612
18740	39031	Coshocton County, OH	36,901	36,612
18780		Craig, CO Micro Area	13,795	13,292
18780	08081	Moffat County, CO	13,795	13,292
18820		Crawfordsville, IN Micro Area	38,124	37,936
18820	18107	Montgomery County, IN	38,124	37,936
18860		Crescent City, CA Micro Area	28,610	27,743
18860	06015	Del Norte County, CA	28,610	27,743

CORE-BASED STATISTICAL AREAS (Metropolitan and Micropolitan), METROPOLITAN DIVISIONS, AND COMPONENTS (as defined March, 2020)—*Continued*

Core based statistical area	State/ County FIPS code	Title and Geographic Components	2010 Census Population	2020 Census Population
18880		Crestview-Fort Walton Beach-Destin, FL Metro Area	235,865	286,973
18880	12091	Okaloosa County, FL	180,822	211,668
18880	12131	Walton County, FL	55,043	75,305
18900		Crossville, TN Micro Area	56,053	61,145
18900	47035	Cumberland County, TN	56,053	61,145
18980		Cullman, AL Micro Area	80,406	87,866
18980	01043	Cullman County, AL	80,406	87,866
19000		Cullowhee, NC Micro Area	54,252	57,226
19000	37099	Jackson County, NC	40,271	43,109
19000	37173	Swain County, NC	13,981	14,117
19060		Cumberland, MD-WV Metro Area	103,299	95,044
19060	24001	Allegany County, MD	75,087	68,106
19060	54057	Mineral County, WV	28,212	26,938
19100		Dallas-Fort Worth-Arlington, TX Metro Area	6,366,542	7,637,387
19100		Dallas-Plano-Irving, TX Division 19124	4,230,520	5,129,966
19100	48085	Collin County, TX	782,341	1,064,465
19100	48113	Dallas County, TX	2,368,139	2,613,539
19100	48121	Denton County, TX	662,614	906,422
19100	48139	Ellis County, TX	149,610	192,455
19100	48231	Hunt County, TX	86,129	99,956
19100	48257	Kaufman County, TX	103,350	145,310
19100	48397	Rockwall County, TX	78,337	107,819
19100		Fort Worth-Arlington-Grapevine, TX Division 23104	2,136,022	2,507,421
19100	48251	Johnson County, TX	150,934	179,927
19100	48367	Parker County, TX	116,927	148,222
19100	48439	Tarrant County, TX	1,809,034	2,110,640
19100	48497	Wise County, TX	59,127	68,632
19140		Dalton, GA Metro Area	142,227	142,837
19140	13213	Murray County, GA	39,628	39,973
19140	13313	Whitfield County, GA	102,599	102,864
19180		Danville, IL Metro Area	81,625	74,188
19180	17183	Vermilion County, IL	81,625	74,188
19220		Danville, KY Micro Area	53,174	54,889
19220	21021	Boyle County, KY	28,432	30,614
19220	21137	Lincoln County, KY	24,742	24,275
19260		Danville, VA Micro Area	106,561	103,091
19260	51143	Pittsylvania County, VA	63,506	60,501
19260	51590	Danville city, VA	43,055	42,590
19300		Daphne-Fairhope-Foley, AL Metro Area	182,265	231,767
19300	01003	Baldwin County, AL	182,265	231,767
19340		Davenport-Moline-Rock Island, IA-IL Metro Area	379,690	384,324
19340	17073	Henry County, IL	50,486	49,284
19340	17131	Mercer County, IL	16,434	15,699
19340	17161	Rock Island County, IL	147,546	144,672
19340	19163	Scott County, IA	165,224	174,669
19420		Dayton, TN Micro Area	31,809	32,870
19420	47143	Rhea County, TN	31,809	32,870
19430		Dayton-Kettering, OH Metro Area	799,232	814,049
19430	39057	Greene County, OH	161,573	167,966
19430	39109	Miami County, OH	102,506	108,774
19430	39113	Montgomery County, OH	535,153	537,309
19460		Decatur, AL Metro Area	153,829	156,494
19460	01079	Lawrence County, AL	34,339	33,073
19460	01103	Morgan County, AL	119,490	123,421
19500		Decatur, IL Metro Area	110,768	103,998
19500	17115	Macon County, IL	110,768	103,998
19540		Decatur, IN Micro Area	34,387	35,809
19540	18001	Adams County, IN	34,387	35,809
19580		Defiance, OH Micro Area	39,037	38,286
19580	39039	Defiance County, OH	39,037	38,286
19620		Del Rio, TX Micro Area	48,879	47,586
19620	48465	Val Verde County, TX	48,879	47,586
19660		Deltona-Daytona Beach-Ormond Beach, FL Metro Area	590,289	668,921
19660	12035	Flagler County, FL	95,696	115,378
19660	12127	Volusia County, FL	494,593	553,543
19700		Deming, NM Micro Area	25,095	25,427
19700	35029	Luna County, NM	25,095	25,427
19740		Denver-Aurora-Lakewood, CO Metro Area	2,543,482	2,963,821
19740	08001	Adams County, CO	441,603	519,572
19740	08005	Arapahoe County, CO	572,003	655,070
19740	08014	Broomfield County, CO	55,889	74,112
19740	08019	Clear Creek County, CO	9,088	9,397
19740	08031	Denver County, CO	600,158	715,522
19740	08035	Douglas County, CO	285,465	357,978
19740	08039	Elbert County, CO	23,086	26,062
19740	08047	Gilpin County, CO	5,441	5,808
19740	08059	Jefferson County, CO	534,543	582,910
19740	08093	Park County, CO	16,206	17,390
19760		DeRidder, LA Micro Area	35,654	36,549
19760	22011	Beauregard Parish, LA	35,654	36,549
19780		Des Moines-West Des Moines, IA Metro Area	606,475	709,466
19780	19049	Dallas County, IA	66,135	99,678
19780	19077	Guthrie County, IA	10,954	10,623
19780	19099	Jasper County, IA	36,842	37,813
19780	19121	Madison County, IA	15,679	16,548
19780	19153	Polk County, IA	430,640	492,401
19780	19181	Warren County, IA	46,225	52,403
19820		Detroit-Warren-Dearborn, MI Metro Area	4,296,250	4,392,041
19820		Detroit-Dearborn-Livonia, MI Division 19804	1,820,584	1,793,561
19820	26163	Wayne County, MI	1,820,584	1,793,561

CORE-BASED STATISTICAL AREAS (Metropolitan and Micropolitan), METROPOLITAN DIVISIONS, AND COMPONENTS (as defined March, 2020)—*Continued*

Core based statistical area	State/ County FIPS code	Title and Geographic Components	2010 Census Population	2020 Census Population
19820		Warren-Troy-Farmington Hills, MI Division 47664	2,475,666	2,598,480
19820	26087	Lapeer County, MI	88,319	88,619
19820	26093	Livingston County, MI	180,967	193,866
19820	26099	Macomb County, MI	840,978	881,217
19820	26125	Oakland County, MI	1,202,362	1,274,395
19820	26147	St. Clair County, MI	163,040	160,383
19860		Dickinson, ND Micro Area	24,982	34,591
19860	38007	Billings County, ND	783	945
19860	38089	Stark County, ND	24,199	33,646
19940		Dixon, IL Micro Area	36,031	34,145
19940	17103	Lee County, IL	36,031	34,145
19980		Dodge City, KS Micro Area	33,848	34,287
19980	20057	Ford County, KS	33,848	34,287
20020		Dothan, AL Metro Area	145,639	151,007
20020	01061	Geneva County, AL	26,790	26,659
20020	01067	Henry County, AL	17,302	17,146
20020	01069	Houston County, AL	101,547	107,202
20060		Douglas, GA Micro Area	50,731	51,378
20060	13003	Atkinson County, GA	8,375	8,286
20060	13069	Coffee County, GA	42,356	43,092
20100		Dover, DE Metro Area	162,310	181,851
20100	10001	Kent County, DE	162,310	181,851
20140		Dublin, GA Micro Area	65,299	65,165
20140	13167	Johnson County, GA	9,980	9,189
20140	13175	Laurens County, GA	48,434	49,570
20140	13283	Treutlen County, GA	6,885	6,406
20180		DuBois, PA Micro Area	81,642	80,562
20180	42033	Clearfield County, PA	81,642	80,562
20220		Dubuque, IA Metro Area	93,653	99,266
20220	19061	Dubuque County, IA	93,653	99,266
20260		Duluth, MN-WI Metro Area	290,637	291,638
20260	27017	Carlton County, MN	35,386	36,207
20260	27075	Lake County, MN	10,866	10,905
20260	27137	St. Louis County, MN	200,226	200,231
20260	55031	Douglas County, WI	44,159	44,295
20300		Dumas, TX Micro Area	21,904	21,358
20300	48341	Moore County, TX	21,904	21,358
20340		Duncan, OK Micro Area	45,048	42,848
20340	40137	Stephens County, OK	45,048	42,848
20420		Durango, CO Micro Area	51,334	55,638
20420	08067	La Plata County, CO	51,334	55,638
20460		Durant, OK Micro Area	42,416	46,067
20460	40013	Bryan County, OK	42,416	46,067
20500		Durham-Chapel Hill, NC Metro Area	564,273	649,903
20500	37037	Chatham County, NC	63,505	76,285
20500	37063	Durham County, NC	267,587	324,833
20500	37077	Granville County, NC	59,916	60,992
20500	37135	Orange County, NC	133,801	148,696
20500	37145	Person County, NC	39,464	39,097

Core based statistical area	State/ County FIPS code	Title and Geographic Components	2010 Census Population	2020 Census Population
20540		Dyersburg, TN Micro Area	38,335	36,801
20540	47045	Dyer County, TN	38,335	36,801
20580		Eagle Pass, TX Micro Area	54,258	57,887
20580	48323	Maverick County, TX	54,258	57,887
20660		Easton, MD Micro Area	37,782	37,526
20660	24041	Talbot County, MD	37,782	37,526
20700		East Stroudsburg, PA Metro Area	169,842	168,327
20700	42089	Monroe County, PA	169,842	168,327
20740		Eau Claire, WI Metro Area	161,151	172,007
20740	55017	Chippewa County, WI	62,415	66,297
20740	55035	Eau Claire County, WI	98,736	105,710
20780		Edwards, CO Micro Area	52,197	55,731
20780	08037	Eagle County, CO	52,197	55,731
20820		Effingham, IL Micro Area	34,242	34,668
20820	17049	Effingham County, IL	34,242	34,668
20900		El Campo, TX Micro Area	41,280	41,570
20900	48481	Wharton County, TX	41,280	41,570
20940		El Centro, CA Metro Area	174,528	179,702
20940	06025	Imperial County, CA	174,528	179,702
20980		El Dorado, AR Micro Area	41,639	39,054
20980	05139	Union County, AR	41,639	39,054
21020		Elizabeth City, NC Micro Area	54,114	53,573
21020	37139	Pasquotank County, NC	40,661	40,568
21020	37143	Perquimans County, NC	13,453	13,005
21060		Elizabethtown-Fort Knox, KY Metro Area	148,338	155,572
21060	21093	Hardin County, KY	105,543	110,702
21060	21123	Larue County, KY	14,193	14,867
21060	21163	Meade County, KY	28,602	30,003
21120		Elk City, OK Micro Area	22,119	22,410
21120	40009	Beckham County, OK	22,119	22,410
21140		Elkhart-Goshen, IN Metro Area	197,559	207,047
21140	18039	Elkhart County, IN	197,559	207,047
21180		Elkins, WV Micro Area	29,405	27,932
21180	54083	Randolph County, WV	29,405	27,932
21220		Elko, NV Micro Area	50,805	55,557
21220	32007	Elko County, NV	48,818	53,702
21220	32011	Eureka County, NV	1,987	1,855
21260		Ellensburg, WA Micro Area	40,915	44,337
21260	53037	Kittitas County, WA	40,915	44,337
21300		Elmira, NY Metro Area	88,830	84,148
21300	36015	Chemung County, NY	88,830	84,148
21340		El Paso, TX Metro Area	804,123	868,859
21340	48141	El Paso County, TX	800,647	865,657
21340	48229	Hudspeth County, TX	3,476	3,202

CORE-BASED STATISTICAL AREAS (Metropolitan and Micropolitan), METROPOLITAN DIVISIONS, AND COMPONENTS (as defined March, 2020)—*Continued*

Core based statistical area	State/ County FIPS code	Title and Geographic Components	2010 Census Population	2020 Census Population
21380		Emporia, KS Micro Area	36,480	34,751
21380	20017	Chase County, KS	2,790	2,572
21380	20111	Lyon County, KS	33,690	32,179
21420		Enid, OK Metro Area	60,580	62,846
21420	40047	Garfield County, OK	60,580	62,846
21460		Enterprise, AL Micro Area	49,948	53,465
21460	01031	Coffee County, AL	49,948	53,465
21500		Erie, PA Metro Area	280,566	270,876
21500	42049	Erie County, PA	280,566	270,876
21540		Escanaba, MI Micro Area	37,069	36,903
21540	26041	Delta County, MI	37,069	36,903
21580		Espa±ola, NM Micro Area	40,246	40,363
21580	35039	Rio Arriba County, NM	40,246	40,363
21640		Eufaula, AL-GA Micro Area	29,970	27,458
21640	01005	Barbour County, AL	27,457	25,223
21640	13239	Quitman County, GA	2,513	2,235
21660		Eugene-Springfield, OR Metro Area	351,715	382,971
21660	41039	Lane County, OR	351,715	382,971
21700		Eureka-Arcata, CA Micro Area	134,623	136,463
21700	06023	Humboldt County, CA	134,623	136,463
21740		Evanston, WY Micro Area	21,118	20,450
21740	56041	Uinta County, WY	21,118	20,450
21780		Evansville, IN-KY Metro Area	311,552	314,049
21780	18129	Posey County, IN	25,910	25,222
21780	18163	Vanderburgh County, IN	179,703	180,136
21780	18173	Warrick County, IN	59,689	63,898
21780	21101	Henderson County, KY	46,250	44,793
21820		Fairbanks, AK Metro Area	97,581	95,655
21820	02090	Fairbanks North Star Borough, AK	97,581	95,655
21840		Fairfield, IA Micro Area	16,843	15,663
21840	19101	Jefferson County, IA	16,843	15,663
21860		Fairmont, MN Micro Area	20,840	20,025
21860	27091	Martin County, MN	20,840	20,025
21900		Fairmont, WV Micro Area	56,418	56,205
21900	54049	Marion County, WV	56,418	56,205
21980		Fallon, NV Micro Area	24,877	25,516
21980	32001	Churchill County, NV	24,877	25,516
22020		Fargo, ND-MN Metro Area	208,777	249,843
22020	27027	Clay County, MN	58,999	65,318
22020	38017	Cass County, ND	149,778	184,525
22060		Faribault-Northfield, MN Micro Area	64,142	67,097
22060	27131	Rice County, MN	64,142	67,097
22100		Farmington, MO Micro Area	65,359	66,922
22100	29187	St. Francois County, MO	65,359	66,922
22140		Farmington, NM Metro Area	130,044	121,661
22140	35045	San Juan County, NM	130,044	121,661
22180		Fayetteville, NC Metro Area	481,061	520,378
22180	37051	Cumberland County, NC	319,431	334,728
22180	37085	Harnett County, NC	114,678	133,568
22180	37093	Hoke County, NC	46,952	52,082
22220		Fayetteville-Springdale-Rogers, AR Metro Area	440,121	546,725
22220	05007	Benton County, AR	221,339	284,333
22220	05087	Madison County, AR	15,717	16,521
22220	05143	Washington County, AR	203,065	245,871
22260		Fergus Falls, MN Micro Area	57,303	60,081
22260	27111	Otter Tail County, MN	57,303	60,081
22280		Fernley, NV Micro Area	51,980	59,235
22280	32019	Lyon County, NV	51,980	59,235
22300		Findlay, OH Micro Area	74,782	74,920
22300	39063	Hancock County, OH	74,782	74,920
22340		Fitzgerald, GA Micro Area	17,634	17,194
22340	13017	Ben Hill County, GA	17,634	17,194
22380		Flagstaff, AZ Metro Area	134,421	145,101
22380	04005	Coconino County, AZ	134,421	145,101
22420		Flint, MI Metro Area	425,790	406,211
22420	26049	Genesee County, MI	425,790	406,211
22500		Florence, SC Metro Area	205,566	199,964
22500	45031	Darlington County, SC	68,681	62,905
22500	45041	Florence County, SC	136,885	137,059
22520		Florence-Muscle Shoals, AL Metro Area	147,137	150,791
22520	01033	Colbert County, AL	54,428	57,227
22520	01077	Lauderdale County, AL	92,709	93,564
22540		Fond du Lac, WI Metro Area	101,633	104,154
22540	55039	Fond du Lac County, WI	101,633	104,154
22580		Forest City, NC Micro Area	67,810	64,444
22580	37161	Rutherford County, NC	67,810	64,444
22620		Forrest City, AR Micro Area	28,258	23,090
22620	05123	St. Francis County, AR	28,258	23,090
22660		Fort Collins, CO Metro Area	299,630	359,066
22660	08069	Larimer County, CO	299,630	359,066
22700		Fort Dodge, IA Micro Area	38,013	36,999
22700	19187	Webster County, IA	38,013	36,999
22780		Fort Leonard Wood, MO Micro Area	52,274	53,955
22780	29169	Pulaski County, MO	52,274	53,955
22800		Fort Madison-Keokuk, IA-IL-MO Micro Area	62,105	57,809
22800	17067	Hancock County, IL	19,104	17,620
22800	19111	Lee County, IA	35,862	33,555
22800	29045	Clark County, MO	7,139	6,634
22820		Fort Morgan, CO Micro Area	28,159	29,111
22820	08087	Morgan County, CO	28,159	29,111
22840		Fort Payne, AL Micro Area	71,109	71,608
22840	01049	DeKalb County, AL	71,109	71,608

CORE-BASED STATISTICAL AREAS (Metropolitan and Micropolitan), METROPOLITAN DIVISIONS, AND COMPONENTS (as defined March, 2020)—*Continued*

Core based statistical area	State/ County FIPS code	Title and Geographic Components	2010 Census Population	2020 Census Population
22860		Fort Polk South, LA Micro Area	52,334	48,750
22860	22115	Vernon Parish, LA	52,334	48,750
22900		Fort Smith, AR-OK Metro Area	248,208	244,310
22900	40135	Sequoyah County, OK	42,391	60,133
22900	05033	Crawford County, AR	61,948	17,097
22900	05047	Franklin County, AR	18,125	127,799
22900	05131	Sebastian County, AR	125,744	39,281
23060		Fort Wayne, IN Metro Area	388,621	419,601
23060	18003	Allen County, IN	355,329	385,410
23060	18183	Whitley County, IN	33,292	34,191
23140		Frankfort, IN Micro Area	33,224	33,190
23140	18023	Clinton County, IN	33,224	33,190
23180		Frankfort, KY Micro Area	70,706	75,393
23180	21005	Anderson County, KY	21,421	23,852
23180	21073	Franklin County, KY	49,285	51,541
23240		Fredericksburg, TX Micro Area	24,837	26,725
23240	48171	Gillespie County, TX	24,837	26,725
23300		Freeport, IL Micro Area	47,711	44,630
23300	17177	Stephenson County, IL	47,711	44,630
23340		Fremont, NE Micro Area	36,691	37,167
23340	31053	Dodge County, NE	36,691	37,167
23380		Fremont, OH Micro Area	60,944	58,896
23380	39143	Sandusky County, OH	60,944	58,896
23420		Fresno, CA Metro Area	930,450	1,008,654
23420	06019	Fresno County, CA	930,450	1,008,654
23460		Gadsden, AL Metro Area	104,430	103,436
23460	01055	Etowah County, AL	104,430	103,436
23500		Gaffney, SC Micro Area	55,342	56,216
23500	45021	Cherokee County, SC	55,342	56,216
23540		Gainesville, FL Metro Area	305,076	339,247
23540	12001	Alachua County, FL	247,336	278,468
23540	12041	Gilchrist County, FL	16,939	17,864
23540	12075	Levy County, FL	40,801	42,915
23580		Gainesville, GA Metro Area	179,684	203,136
23580	13139	Hall County, GA	179,684	203,136
23620		Gainesville, TX Micro Area	38,437	41,668
23620	48097	Cooke County, TX	38,437	41,668
23660		Galesburg, IL Micro Area	52,919	49,967
23660	17095	Knox County, IL	52,919	49,967
23700		Gallup, NM Micro Area	71,492	72,902
23700	35031	McKinley County, NM	71,492	72,902
23780		Garden City, KS Micro Area	40,753	42,453
23780	20055	Finney County, KS	36,776	38,470
23780	20093	Kearny County, KS	3,977	3,983
23820		Gardnerville Ranchos, NV Micro Area	46,997	49,488
23820	32005	Douglas County, NV	46,997	49,488
23860		Georgetown, SC Micro Area	60,158	63,404
23860	45043	Georgetown County, SC	60,158	63,404
23900		Gettysburg, PA Metro Area	101,407	103,852
23900	42001	Adams County, PA	101,407	103,852
23940		Gillette, WY Micro Area	60,424	61,045
23940	56005	Campbell County, WY	46,133	47,026
23940	56011	Crook County, WY	7,083	7,181
23940	56045	Weston County, WY	7,208	6,838
23980		Glasgow, KY Micro Area	52,272	54,771
23980	21009	Barren County, KY	42,173	44,485
23980	21169	Metcalfe County, KY	10,099	10,286
24020		Glens Falls, NY Metro Area	128,923	127,039
24020	36113	Warren County, NY	65,707	65,737
24020	36115	Washington County, NY	63,216	61,302
24060		Glenwood Springs, CO Micro Area	73,537	79,043
24060	08045	Garfield County, CO	56,389	61,685
24060	08097	Pitkin County, CO	17,148	17,358
24100		Gloversville, NY Micro Area	55,531	53,324
24100	36035	Fulton County, NY	55,531	53,324
24140		Goldsboro, NC Metro Area	122,623	117,333
24140	37191	Wayne County, NC	122,623	117,333
24180		Granbury, TX Micro Area	51,182	61,598
24180	48221	Hood County, TX	51,182	61,598
24220		Grand Forks, ND-MN Metro Area	98,461	104,362
24220	27119	Polk County, MN	31,600	31,192
24220	38035	Grand Forks County, ND	66,861	73,170
24260		Grand Island, NE Metro Area	72,726	77,038
24260	31079	Hall County, NE	58,607	62,895
24260	31093	Howard County, NE	6,274	6,475
24260	31121	Merrick County, NE	7,845	7,668
24300		Grand Junction, CO Metro Area	146,723	155,703
24300	08077	Mesa County, CO	146,723	155,703
24330		Grand Rapids, MN Micro Area	45,058	45,014
24330	27061	Itasca County, MN	45,058	45,014
24340		Grand Rapids-Kentwood, MI Metro Area	993,670	1,087,592
24340	26067	Ionia County, MI	63,905	66,804
24340	26081	Kent County, MI	602,622	657,974
24340	26117	Montcalm County, MI	63,342	66,614
24340	26139	Ottawa County, MI	263,801	296,200
24380		Grants, NM Micro Area	27,213	27,172
24380	35006	Cibola County, NM	27,213	27,172
24420		Grants Pass, OR Metro Area	82,713	88,090
24420	41033	Josephine County, OR	82,713	88,090
24460		Great Bend, KS Micro Area	27,674	25,493
24460	20009	Barton County, KS	27,674	25,493
24500		Great Falls, MT Metro Area	81,327	84,414
24500	30013	Cascade County, MT	81,327	84,414

CORE-BASED STATISTICAL AREAS (Metropolitan and Micropolitan), METROPOLITAN DIVISIONS, AND COMPONENTS (as defined March, 2020)—*Continued*

Core based statistical area	State/County FIPS code	Title and Geographic Components	2010 Census Population	2020 Census Population
24540		Greeley, CO Metro Area	252,825	328,981
24540	08123	Weld County, CO	252,825	328,981
24580		Green Bay, WI Metro Area	306,241	328,268
24580	55009	Brown County, WI	248,007	268,740
24580	55061	Kewaunee County, WI	20,574	20,563
24580	55083	Oconto County, WI	37,660	38,965
24620		Greeneville, TN Micro Area	68,831	70,152
24620	47059	Greene County, TN	68,831	70,152
24660		Greensboro-High Point, NC Metro Area	723,801	776,566
24660	37081	Guilford County, NC	488,406	541,299
24660	37151	Randolph County, NC	141,752	144,171
24660	37157	Rockingham County, NC	93,643	91,096
24700		Greensburg, IN Micro Area	25,740	26,472
24700	18031	Decatur County, IN	25,740	26,472
24740		Greenville, MS Micro Area	51,137	44,922
24740	28151	Washington County, MS	51,137	44,922
24780		Greenville, NC Metro Area	168,148	170,243
24780	37147	Pitt County, NC	168,148	170,243
24820		Greenville, OH Micro Area	52,959	51,881
24820	39037	Darke County, OH	52,959	51,881
24860		Greenville-Anderson, SC Metro Area	824,112	928,195
24860	45007	Anderson County, SC	187,126	203,718
24860	45045	Greenville County, SC	451,225	525,534
24860	45059	Laurens County, SC	66,537	67,539
24860	45077	Pickens County, SC	119,224	131,404
24900		Greenwood, MS Micro Area	42,914	38,337
24900	28015	Carroll County, MS	10,597	9,998
24900	28083	Leflore County, MS	32,317	28,339
24940		Greenwood, SC Micro Area	69,661	69,351
24940	45047	Greenwood County, SC	69,661	69,351
24980		Grenada, MS Micro Area	21,906	21,629
24980	28043	Grenada County, MS	21,906	21,629
25060		Gulfport-Biloxi, MS Metro Area	388,488	416,259
25060	28045	Hancock County, MS	43,929	46,053
25060	28047	Harrison County, MS	187,105	208,621
25060	28059	Jackson County, MS	139,668	143,252
25060	28131	Stone County, MS	17,786	18,333
25100		Guymon, OK Micro Area	20,640	21,384
25100	40139	Texas County, OK	20,640	21,384
25180		Hagerstown-Martinsburg, MD-WV Metro Area	269,140	293,844
25180	24043	Washington County, MD	147,430	154,705
25180	54003	Berkeley County, WV	104,169	122,076
25180	54065	Morgan County, WV	17,541	17,063
25200		Hailey, ID Micro Area	22,493	25,349
25200	16013	Blaine County, ID	21,376	24,272
25200	16025	Camas County, ID	1,117	1,077
25220		Hammond, LA Metro Area	121,097	133,157
25220	22105	Tangipahoa Parish, LA	121,097	133,157

Core based statistical area	State/County FIPS code	Title and Geographic Components	2010 Census Population	2020 Census Population
25260		Hanford-Corcoran, CA Metro Area	152,982	152,486
25260	06031	Kings County, CA	152,982	152,486
25300		Hannibal, MO Micro Area	38,948	38,880
25300	29127	Marion County, MO	28,781	28,525
25300	29173	Ralls County, MO	10,167	10,355
25420		Harrisburg-Carlisle, PA Metro Area	549,475	591,712
25420	42041	Cumberland County, PA	235,406	259,469
25420	42043	Dauphin County, PA	268,100	286,401
25420	42099	Perry County, PA	45,969	45,842
25460		Harrison, AR Micro Area	45,233	44,598
25460	05009	Boone County, AR	36,903	37,373
25460	05101	Newton County, AR	8,330	7,225
25500		Harrisonburg, VA Metro Area	125,228	135,571
25500	51165	Rockingham County, VA	76,314	83,757
25500	51660	Harrisonburg city, VA	48,914	51,814
25540		Hartford-East Hartford-Middletown, CT Metro Area	1,212,381	1,213,531
25540	09003	Hartford County, CT	894,014	899,498
25540	09007	Middlesex County, CT	165,676	164,245
25540	09013	Tolland County, CT	152,691	149,788
25580		Hastings, NE Micro Area	31,364	31,205
25580	31001	Adams County, NE	31,364	31,205
25620		Hattiesburg, MS Metro Area	162,410	172,231
25620	28031	Covington County, MS	19,568	18,340
25620	28035	Forrest County, MS	74,934	78,158
25620	28073	Lamar County, MS	55,658	64,222
25620	28111	Perry County, MS	12,250	11,511
25700		Hays, KS Micro Area	28,452	28,934
25700	20051	Ellis County, KS	28,452	28,934
25720		Heber, UT Micro Area	59,854	77,145
25720	49043	Summit County, UT	36,324	42,357
25720	49051	Wasatch County, UT	23,530	34,788
25740		Helena, MT Micro Area	74,801	83,058
25740	30043	Jefferson County, MT	11,406	12,085
25740	30049	Lewis and Clark County, MT	63,395	70,973
25760		Helena-West Helena, AR Micro Area	21,757	16,568
25760	05107	Phillips County, AR	21,757	16,568
25780		Henderson, NC Micro Area	45,422	42,578
25780	37181	Vance County, NC	45,422	42,578
25820		Hereford, TX Micro Area	19,372	18,583
25820	48117	Deaf Smith County, TX	19,372	18,583
25840		Hermiston-Pendleton, OR Micro Area	87,062	92,261
25840	41049	Morrow County, OR	11,173	12,186
25840	41059	Umatilla County, OR	75,889	80,075
25860		Hickory-Lenoir-Morganton, NC Metro Area	365,497	365,276
25860	37003	Alexander County, NC	37,198	36,444
25860	37023	Burke County, NC	90,912	87,570
25860	37027	Caldwell County, NC	83,029	80,652
25860	37035	Catawba County, NC	154,358	160,610

CORE-BASED STATISTICAL AREAS (Metropolitan and Micropolitan), METROPOLITAN DIVISIONS, AND COMPONENTS (as defined March, 2020)—*Continued*

Core based statistical area	State/ County FIPS code	Title and Geographic Components	2010 Census Population	2020 Census Population
25880		Hillsdale, MI Micro Area	46,688	45,746
25880	26059	Hillsdale County, MI	46,688	45,746
25900		Hilo, HI Micro Area	185,079	200,629
25900	15001	Hawaii County, HI	185,079	200,629
25940		Hilton Head Island-Bluffton, SC Metro Area	187,010	215,908
25940	45013	Beaufort County, SC	162,233	187,117
25940	45053	Jasper County, SC	24,777	28,791
25980		Hinesville, GA Metro Area	77,917	81,424
25980	13179	Liberty County, GA	63,453	65,256
25980	13183	Long County, GA	14,464	16,168
26020		Hobbs, NM Micro Area	64,727	74,455
26020	35025	Lea County, NM	64,727	74,455
26090		Holland, MI Micro Area	111,408	120,502
26090	26005	Allegan County, MI	111,408	120,502
26140		Homosassa Springs, FL Metro Area	141,236	153,843
26140	12017	Citrus County, FL	141,236	153,843
26220		Hood River, OR Micro Area	22,346	23,977
26220	41027	Hood River County, OR	22,346	23,977
26260		Hope, AR Micro Area	31,606	28,375
26260	05057	Hempstead County, AR	22,609	20,065
26260	05099	Nevada County, AR	8,997	8,310
26300		Hot Springs, AR Metro Area	96,024	100,180
26300	05051	Garland County, AR	96,024	100,180
26340		Houghton, MI Micro Area	38,784	39,407
26340	26061	Houghton County, MI	36,628	37,361
26340	26083	Keweenaw County, MI	2,156	2,046
26380		Houma-Thibodaux, LA Metro Area	208,178	207,137
26380	22057	Lafourche Parish, LA	96,318	97,557
26380	22109	Terrebonne Parish, LA	111,860	109,580
26420		Houston-The Woodlands-Sugar Land, TX Metro Area	5,920,416	7,122,240
26420	48015	Austin County, TX	28,417	30,167
26420	48039	Brazoria County, TX	313,166	372,031
26420	48071	Chambers County, TX	35,096	46,571
26420	48157	Fort Bend County, TX	585,375	822,779
26420	48167	Galveston County, TX	291,309	350,682
26420	48201	Harris County, TX	4,092,459	4,731,145
26420	48291	Liberty County, TX	75,643	91,628
26420	48339	Montgomery County, TX	455,746	620,443
26420	48473	Waller County, TX	43,205	56,794
26460		Hudson, NY Micro Area	63,096	61,570
26460	36021	Columbia County, NY	63,096	61,570
26500		Huntingdon, PA Micro Area	45,913	44,092
26500	42061	Huntingdon County, PA	45,913	44,092
26540		Huntington, IN Micro Area	37,124	36,662
26540	18069	Huntington County, IN	37,124	36,662
26580		Huntington-Ashland, WV-KY-OH Metro Area	370,908	359,862
26580	21019	Boyd County, KY	49,542	48,261
26580	21043	Carter County, KY	27,720	26,627
26580	21089	Greenup County, KY	36,910	35,962
26580	39087	Lawrence County, OH	62,450	58,240
26580	54011	Cabell County, WV	96,319	94,350
26580	54079	Putnam County, WV	55,486	57,440
26580	54099	Wayne County, WV	42,481	38,982
26620		Huntsville, AL Metro Area	417,593	491,723
26620	01083	Limestone County, AL	82,782	103,570
26620	01089	Madison County, AL	334,811	388,153
26660		Huntsville, TX Micro Area	67,861	76,400
26660	48471	Walker County, TX	67,861	76,400
26700		Huron, SD Micro Area	19,469	20,812
26700	46005	Beadle County, SD	17,398	19,149
26700	46073	Jerauld County, SD	2,071	1,663
26740		Hutchinson, KS Micro Area	64,511	61,898
26740	20155	Reno County, KS	64,511	61,898
26780		Hutchinson, MN Micro Area	36,651	36,771
26780	27085	McLeod County, MN	36,651	36,771
26820		Idaho Falls, ID Metro Area	133,265	157,429
26820	16019	Bonneville County, ID	104,234	123,964
26820	16023	Butte County, ID	2,891	2,574
26820	16051	Jefferson County, ID	26,140	30,891
26860		Indiana, PA Micro Area	88,880	83,246
26860	42063	Indiana County, PA	88,880	83,246
26900		Indianapolis-Carmel-Anderson, IN Metro Area	1,887,877	2,111,040
26900	18011	Boone County, IN	56,640	70,812
26900	18013	Brown County, IN	15,242	15,475
26900	18057	Hamilton County, IN	274,569	347,467
26900	18059	Hancock County, IN	70,002	79,840
26900	18063	Hendricks County, IN	145,448	174,788
26900	18081	Johnson County, IN	139,654	161,765
26900	18095	Madison County, IN	131,636	130,129
26900	18097	Marion County, IN	903,393	977,203
26900	18109	Morgan County, IN	68,894	71,780
26900	18133	Putnam County, IN	37,963	36,726
26900	18145	Shelby County, IN	44,436	45,055
26940		Indianola, MS Micro Area	29,450	25,971
26940	28133	Sunflower County, MS	29,450	25,971
26980		Iowa City, IA Metro Area	152,586	175,419
26980	19103	Johnson County, IA	130,882	152,854
26980	19183	Washington County, IA	21,704	22,565
27020		Iron Mountain, MI-WI Micro Area	30,591	30,505
27020	26043	Dickinson County, MI	26,168	25,947
27020	55037	Florence County, WI	4,423	4,558
27060		Ithaca, NY Metro Area	101,564	105,740
27060	36109	Tompkins County, NY	101,564	105,740
27100		Jackson, MI Metro Area	160,248	160,366
27100	26075	Jackson County, MI	160,248	160,366

CORE-BASED STATISTICAL AREAS (Metropolitan and Micropolitan), METROPOLITAN DIVISIONS, AND COMPONENTS (as defined March, 2020)—*Continued*

Core based statistical area	State/ County FIPS code	Title and Geographic Components	2010 Census Population	2020 Census Population
27140		Jackson, MS Metro Area	586,320	591,978
27140	28029	Copiah County, MS	29,449	28,368
27140	28049	Hinds County, MS	245,285	227,742
27140	28051	Holmes County, MS	19,198	17,000
27140	28089	Madison County, MS	95,203	109,145
27140	28121	Rankin County, MS	141,617	157,031
27140	28127	Simpson County, MS	27,503	25,949
27140	28163	Yazoo County, MS	28,065	26,743
27160		Jackson, OH Micro Area	33,225	32,653
27160	39079	Jackson County, OH	33,225	32,653
27180		Jackson, TN Metro Area	179,694	180,504
27180	47023	Chester County, TN	17,131	17,341
27180	47033	Crockett County, TN	14,586	13,911
27180	47053	Gibson County, TN	49,683	50,429
27180	47113	Madison County, TN	98,294	98,823
27220		Jackson, WY-ID Micro Area	31,464	34,961
27220	16081	Teton County, ID	10,170	11,630
27220	56039	Teton County, WY	21,294	23,331
27260		Jacksonville, FL Metro Area	1,345,596	1,605,848
27260	12003	Baker County, FL	27,115	28,259
27260	12019	Clay County, FL	190,865	218,245
27260	12031	Duval County, FL	864,263	995,567
27260	12089	Nassau County, FL	73,314	90,352
27260	12109	St. Johns County, FL	190,039	273,425
27300		Jacksonville, IL Micro Area	40,902	37,864
27300	17137	Morgan County, IL	35,547	32,915
27300	17171	Scott County, IL	5,355	4,949
27340		Jacksonville, NC Metro Area	177,772	204,576
27340	37133	Onslow County, NC	177,772	204,576
27380		Jacksonville, TX Micro Area	50,845	50,412
27380	48073	Cherokee County, TX	50,845	50,412
27420		Jamestown, ND Micro Area	21,100	21,593
27420	38093	Stutsman County, ND	21,100	21,593
27460		Jamestown-Dunkirk-Fredonia, NY Micro Area	134,905	127,657
27460	36013	Chautauqua County, NY	134,905	127,657
27500		Janesville-Beloit, WI Metro Area	160,331	163,687
27500	55105	Rock County, WI	160,331	163,687
27530		Jasper, AL Micro Area	67,023	65,342
27530	01127	Walker County, AL	67,023	65,342
27540		Jasper, IN Micro Area	54,734	55,887
27540	18037	Dubois County, IN	41,889	43,637
27540	18125	Pike County, IN	12,845	12,250
27600		Jefferson, GA Micro Area	60,485	75,907
27600	13157	Jackson County, GA	60,485	75,907
27620		Jefferson City, MO Metro Area	149,807	150,309
27620	29027	Callaway County, MO	44,332	44,283
27620	29051	Cole County, MO	75,990	77,279
27620	29135	Moniteau County, MO	15,607	15,473
27620	29151	Osage County, MO	13,878	13,274
27660		Jennings, LA Micro Area	31,594	32,250
27660	22053	Jefferson Davis Parish, LA	31,594	32,250
27700		Jesup, GA Micro Area	30,099	30,144
27700	13305	Wayne County, GA	30,099	30,144
27740		Johnson City, TN Metro Area	198,716	207,285
27740	47019	Carter County, TN	57,424	56,356
27740	47171	Unicoi County, TN	18,313	17,928
27740	47179	Washington County, TN	122,979	133,001
27780		Johnstown, PA Metro Area	143,679	133,472
27780	42021	Cambria County, PA	143,679	133,472
27860		Jonesboro, AR Metro Area	121,026	134,196
27860	05031	Craighead County, AR	96,443	111,231
27860	05111	Poinsett County, AR	24,583	22,965
27900		Joplin, MO Metro Area	175,518	181,409
27900	29097	Jasper County, MO	117,404	122,761
27900	29145	Newton County, MO	58,114	58,648
27940		Juneau, AK Micro Area	31,275	32,255
27940	02110	Juneau City and Borough, AK	31,275	32,255
27980		Kahului-Wailuku-Lahaina, HI Metro Area	154,834	164,754
27980	15009	Maui County, HI	154,834	164,754
28020		Kalamazoo-Portage, MI Metro Area	250,331	261,670
28020	26077	Kalamazoo County, MI	250,331	261,670
28060		Kalispell, MT Micro Area	90,928	104,357
28060	30029	Flathead County, MT	90,928	104,357
28100		Kankakee, IL Metro Area	113,449	107,502
28100	17091	Kankakee County, IL	113,449	107,502
28140		Kansas City, MO-KS Metro Area	2,009,342	2,192,035
28140	20091	Johnson County, KS	544,179	609,863
28140	20103	Leavenworth County, KS	76,227	81,881
28140	20107	Linn County, KS	9,656	9,591
28140	20121	Miami County, KS	32,787	34,191
28140	20209	Wyandotte County, KS	157,505	169,245
28140	29013	Bates County, MO	17,049	16,042
28140	29025	Caldwell County, MO	9,424	8,815
28140	29037	Cass County, MO	99,478	107,824
28140	29047	Clay County, MO	221,939	253,335
28140	29049	Clinton County, MO	20,743	21,184
28140	29095	Jackson County, MO	674,158	717,204
28140	29107	Lafayette County, MO	33,381	32,984
28140	29165	Platte County, MO	89,322	106,718
28140	29177	Ray County, MO	23,494	23,158
28180		Kapaa, HI Micro Area	67,091	73,298
28180	15007	Kauai County, HI	67,091	73,298
28260		Kearney, NE Micro Area	52,591	56,772
28260	31019	Buffalo County, NE	46,102	50,084
28260	31099	Kearney County, NE	6,489	6,688
28300		Keene, NH Micro Area	77,117	76,458
28300	33005	Cheshire County, NH	77,117	76,458
28340		Kendallville, IN Micro Area	47,536	47,457
28340	18113	Noble County, IN	47,536	47,457
28380		Kennett, MO Micro Area	31,953	28,283
28380	29069	Dunklin County, MO	31,953	28,283

CORE-BASED STATISTICAL AREAS (Metropolitan and Micropolitan), METROPOLITAN DIVISIONS, AND COMPONENTS (as defined March, 2020)—*Continued*

Core based statistical area	State/ County FIPS code	Title and Geographic Components	2010 Census Population	2020 Census Population
28420		Kennewick-Richland, WA Metro Area	253,340	303,622
28420	53005	Benton County, WA	175,177	206,873
28420	53021	Franklin County, WA	78,163	96,749
28500		Kerrville, TX Micro Area	49,625	52,598
28500	48265	Kerr County, TX	49,625	52,598
28540		Ketchikan, AK Micro Area	13,477	13,948
28540	02130	Ketchikan Gateway Borough, AK	13,477	13,948
28580		Key West, FL Micro Area	73,090	82,874
28580	12087	Monroe County, FL	73,090	82,874
28620		Kill Devil Hills, NC Micro Area	33,920	36,915
28620	37055	Dare County, NC	33,920	36,915
28660		Killeen-Temple, TX Metro Area	405,300	475,367
28660	48027	Bell County, TX	310,235	370,647
28660	48099	Coryell County, TX	75,388	83,093
28660	48281	Lampasas County, TX	19,677	21,627
28700		Kingsport-Bristol, TN-VA Metro Area	309,544	307,614
28700	47073	Hawkins County, TN	56,833	56,721
28700	47163	Sullivan County, TN	156,823	158,163
28700	51169	Scott County, VA	23,177	21,576
28700	51191	Washington County, VA	54,876	53,935
28700	51520	Bristol city, VA	17,835	17,219
28740		Kingston, NY Metro Area	182,493	181,851
28740	36111	Ulster County, NY	182,493	181,851
28780		Kingsville, TX Micro Area	32,477	31,390
28780	48261	Kenedy County, TX	416	350
28780	48273	Kleberg County, TX	32,061	31,040
28820		Kinston, NC Micro Area	59,495	55,122
28820	37107	Lenoir County, NC	59,495	55,122
28860		Kirksville, MO Micro Area	30,038	29,346
28860	29001	Adair County, MO	25,607	25,314
28860	29197	Schuyler County, MO	4,431	4,032
28900		Klamath Falls, OR Micro Area	66,380	69,413
28900	41035	Klamath County, OR	66,380	69,413
28940		Knoxville, TN Metro Area	814,914	879,773
28940	47001	Anderson County, TN	75,129	77,123
28940	47009	Blount County, TN	123,010	135,280
28940	47013	Campbell County, TN	40,716	39,272
28940	47093	Knox County, TN	432,226	478,971
28940	47105	Loudon County, TN	48,556	54,886
28940	47129	Morgan County, TN	21,987	21,035
28940	47145	Roane County, TN	54,181	53,404
28940	47173	Union County, TN	19,109	19,802
29020		Kokomo, IN Metro Area	82,752	83,658
29020	18067	Howard County, IN	82,752	83,658
29060		Laconia, NH Micro Area	60,088	63,705
29060	33001	Belknap County, NH	60,088	63,705
29100		La Crosse-Onalaska, WI-MN Metro Area	133,665	139,627
29100	27055	Houston County, MN	19,027	18,843
29100	55063	La Crosse County, WI	114,638	120,784
29180		Lafayette, LA Metro Area	466,750	478,384
29180	22001	Acadia Parish, LA	61,773	57,576
29180	22045	Iberia Parish, LA	73,240	69,929
29180	22055	Lafayette Parish, LA	221,578	241,753
29180	22099	St. Martin Parish, LA	52,160	51,767
29180	22113	Vermilion Parish, LA	57,999	57,359
29200		Lafayette-West Lafayette, IN Metro Area	210,297	223,716
29200	18007	Benton County, IN	8,854	8,719
29200	18015	Carroll County, IN	20,155	20,306
29200	18157	Tippecanoe County, IN	172,780	186,251
29200	18171	Warren County, IN	8,508	8,440
29260		La Grande, OR Micro Area	25,748	26,196
29260	41061	Union County, OR	25,748	26,196
29300		LaGrange, GA-AL Micro Area	101,259	104,198
29300	01017	Chambers County, AL	34,215	34,772
29300	13285	Troup County, GA	67,044	69,426
29340		Lake Charles, LA Metro Area	199,607	222,402
29340	22019	Calcasieu Parish, LA	192,768	216,785
29340	22023	Cameron Parish, LA	6,839	5,617
29380		Lake City, FL Micro Area	67,531	69,698
29380	12023	Columbia County, FL	67,531	69,698
29420		Lake Havasu City-Kingman, AZ Metro Area	200,186	213,267
29420	04015	Mohave County, AZ	200,186	213,267
29460		Lakeland-Winter Haven, FL Metro Area	602,095	725,046
29460	12105	Polk County, FL	602,095	725,046
29500		Lamesa, TX Micro Area	13,833	12,456
29500	48115	Dawson County, TX	13,833	12,456
29540		Lancaster, PA Metro Area	519,445	552,984
29540	42071	Lancaster County, PA	519,445	552,984
29620		Lansing-East Lansing, MI Metro Area	534,684	541,297
29620	26037	Clinton County, MI	75,382	79,128
29620	26045	Eaton County, MI	107,759	109,175
29620	26065	Ingham County, MI	280,895	284,900
29620	26155	Shiawassee County, MI	70,648	68,094
29660		Laramie, WY Micro Area	36,299	37,066
29660	56001	Albany County, WY	36,299	37,066
29700		Laredo, TX Metro Area	250,304	267,114
29700	48479	Webb County, TX	250,304	267,114
29740		Las Cruces, NM Metro Area	209,233	219,561
29740	35013	Do±a Ana County, NM	209,233	219,561
29780		Las Vegas, NM Micro Area	34,274	31,390
29780	35033	Mora County, NM	4,881	4,189
29780	35047	San Miguel County, NM	29,393	27,201
29820		Las Vegas-Henderson-Paradise, NV Metro Area	1,951,269	2,265,461
29820	32003	Clark County, NV	1,951,269	2,265,461

CORE-BASED STATISTICAL AREAS (Metropolitan and Micropolitan), METROPOLITAN DIVISIONS, AND COMPONENTS (as defined March, 2020)—*Continued*

Core based statistical area	State/ County FIPS code	Title and Geographic Components	2010 Census Population	2020 Census Population
29860		Laurel, MS Micro Area	84,823	83,613
29860	28061	Jasper County, MS	17,062	16,367
29860	28067	Jones County, MS	67,761	67,246
29900		Laurinburg, NC Micro Area	36,157	34,174
29900	37165	Scotland County, NC	36,157	34,174
29940		Lawrence, KS Metro Area	110,826	118,785
29940	20045	Douglas County, KS	110,826	118,785
29980		Lawrenceburg, TN Micro Area	41,869	44,159
29980	47099	Lawrence County, TN	41,869	44,159
30020		Lawton, OK Metro Area	130,291	126,652
30020	40031	Comanche County, OK	124,098	121,125
30020	40033	Cotton County, OK	6,193	5,527
30060		Lebanon, MO Micro Area	35,571	36,039
30060	29105	Laclede County, MO	35,571	36,039
30100		Lebanon, NH-VT Micro Area	218,466	221,211
30100	33009	Grafton County, NH	89,118	91,118
30100	33019	Sullivan County, NH	43,742	43,063
30100	50017	Orange County, VT	28,936	29,277
30100	50027	Windsor County, VT	56,670	57,753
30140		Lebanon, PA Metro Area	133,568	143,257
30140	42075	Lebanon County, PA	133,568	143,257
30220		Levelland, TX Micro Area	22,935	21,537
30220	48219	Hockley County, TX	22,935	21,537
30260		Lewisburg, PA Micro Area	44,947	42,681
30260	42119	Union County, PA	44,947	42,681
30280		Lewisburg, TN Micro Area	30,617	34,318
30280	47117	Marshall County, TN	30,617	34,318
30300		Lewiston, ID-WA Metro Area	60,888	64,375
30300	16069	Nez Perce County, ID	39,265	42,090
30300	53003	Asotin County, WA	21,623	22,285
30340		Lewiston-Auburn, ME Metro Area	107,702	111,139
30340	23001	Androscoggin County, ME	107,702	111,139
30380		Lewistown, PA Micro Area	46,682	46,143
30380	42087	Mifflin County, PA	46,682	46,143
30420		Lexington, NE Micro Area	26,370	26,004
30420	31047	Dawson County, NE	24,326	24,111
30420	31073	Gosper County, NE	2,044	1,893
30460		Lexington-Fayette, KY Metro Area	472,099	516,811
30460	21017	Bourbon County, KY	19,985	20,252
30460	21049	Clark County, KY	35,613	36,972
30460	21067	Fayette County, KY	295,803	322,570
30460	21113	Jessamine County, KY	48,586	52,991
30460	21209	Scott County, KY	47,173	57,155
30460	21239	Woodford County, KY	24,939	26,871
30580		Liberal, KS Micro Area	22,952	21,964
30580	20175	Seward County, KS	22,952	21,964
30620		Lima, OH Metro Area	106,331	102,206
30620	39003	Allen County, OH	106,331	102,206

Core based statistical area	State/ County FIPS code	Title and Geographic Components	2010 Census Population	2020 Census Population
30660		Lincoln, IL Micro Area	30,305	27,987
30660	17107	Logan County, IL	30,305	27,987
30700		Lincoln, NE Metro Area	302,157	340,217
30700	31109	Lancaster County, NE	285,407	322,608
30700	31159	Seward County, NE	16,750	17,609
30780		Little Rock-North Little Rock-Conway, AR Metro Area	699,757	748,031
30780	05045	Faulkner County, AR	113,237	123,498
30780	05053	Grant County, AR	17,853	17,958
30780	05085	Lonoke County, AR	68,356	74,015
30780	05105	Perry County, AR	10,445	10,019
30780	05119	Pulaski County, AR	382,748	399,125
30780	05125	Saline County, AR	107,118	123,416
30820		Lock Haven, PA Micro Area	39,238	37,450
30820	42035	Clinton County, PA	39,238	37,450
30860		Logan, UT-ID Metro Area	125,442	147,348
30860	16041	Franklin County, ID	12,786	14,194
30860	49005	Cache County, UT	112,656	133,154
30900		Logansport, IN Micro Area	38,966	37,870
30900	18017	Cass County, IN	38,966	37,870
30940		London, KY Micro Area	148,099	149,863
30940	21051	Clay County, KY	21,730	20,345
30940	21121	Knox County, KY	31,883	30,193
30940	21125	Laurel County, KY	58,849	62,613
30940	21235	Whitley County, KY	35,637	36,712
30980		Longview, TX Metro Area	280,000	286,184
30980	48183	Gregg County, TX	121,730	124,239
30980	48203	Harrison County, TX	65,631	68,839
30980	48401	Rusk County, TX	53,330	52,214
30980	48459	Upshur County, TX	39,309	40,892
31020		Longview, WA Metro Area	102,410	110,730
31020	53015	Cowlitz County, WA	102,410	110,730
31060		Los Alamos, NM Micro Area	17,950	19,419
31060	35028	Los Alamos County, NM	17,950	19,419
31080		Los Angeles-Long Beach-Anaheim, CA Metro Area	12,828,837	13,200,998
31080		Anaheim-Santa Ana-Irvine, CA Division 11244	3,010,232	3,186,989
31080	06059	Orange County, CA	3,010,232	3,186,989
31080		Los Angeles-Long Beach-Glendale, CA Division 31084	9,818,605	10,014,009
31080	06037	Los Angeles County, CA	9,818,605	10,014,009
31140		Louisville/Jefferson County, KY-IN Metro Area	1,202,718	1,285,439
31140	18019	Clark County, IN	110,232	121,093
31140	18043	Floyd County, IN	74,578	80,484
31140	18061	Harrison County, IN	39,364	39,654
31140	18175	Washington County, IN	28,262	28,182
31140	21029	Bullitt County, KY	74,319	82,217
31140	21103	Henry County, KY	15,416	15,678
31140	21111	Jefferson County, KY	741,096	782,969
31140	21185	Oldham County, KY	60,316	67,607
31140	21211	Shelby County, KY	42,074	48,065
31140	21215	Spencer County, KY	17,061	19,490

CORE-BASED STATISTICAL AREAS (Metropolitan and Micropolitan), METROPOLITAN DIVISIONS, AND COMPONENTS (as defined March, 2020)—*Continued*

Core based statistical area	State/ County FIPS code	Title and Geographic Components	2010 Census Population	2020 Census Population
31180		Lubbock, TX Metro Area	290,805	321,368
31180	48107	Crosby County, TX	6,059	5,133
31180	48303	Lubbock County, TX	278,831	310,639
31180	48305	Lynn County, TX	5,915	5,596
31220		Ludington, MI Micro Area	28,705	29,052
31220	26105	Mason County, MI	28,705	29,052
31260		Lufkin, TX Micro Area	86,771	86,395
31260	48005	Angelina County, TX	86,771	86,395
31300		Lumberton, NC Micro Area	134,168	116,530
31300	37155	Robeson County, NC	134,168	116,530
31340		Lynchburg, VA Metro Area	252,634	261,593
31340	51009	Amherst County, VA	32,353	31,307
31340	51011	Appomattox County, VA	14,973	16,119
31340	51019	Bedford County, VA	74,898	79,462
31340	51031	Campbell County, VA	54,842	55,696
31340	51680	Lynchburg city, VA	75,568	79,009
31380		Macomb, IL Micro Area	32,612	27,238
31380	17109	McDonough County, IL	32,612	27,238
31420		Macon-Bibb County, GA Metro Area	232,293	233,802
31420	13021	Bibb County, GA	155,547	157,346
31420	13079	Crawford County, GA	12,630	12,130
31420	13169	Jones County, GA	28,669	28,347
31420	13207	Monroe County, GA	26,424	27,957
31420	13289	Twiggs County, GA	9,023	8,022
31460		Madera, CA Metro Area	150,865	156,255
31460	06039	Madera County, CA	150,865	156,255
31500		Madison, IN Micro Area	32,428	33,147
31500	18077	Jefferson County, IN	32,428	33,147
31540		Madison, WI Metro Area	605,435	680,796
31540	55021	Columbia County, WI	56,833	58,490
31540	55025	Dane County, WI	488,073	561,504
31540	55045	Green County, WI	36,842	37,093
31540	55049	Iowa County, WI	23,687	23,709
31580		Madisonville, KY Micro Area	46,920	45,423
31580	21107	Hopkins County, KY	46,920	45,423
31620		Magnolia, AR Micro Area	24,552	22,801
31620	05027	Columbia County, AR	24,552	22,801
31660		Malone, NY Micro Area	51,599	47,555
31660	36033	Franklin County, NY	51,599	47,555
31680		Malvern, AR Micro Area	32,923	33,040
31680	05059	Hot Spring County, AR	32,923	33,040
31700		Manchester-Nashua, NH Metro Area	400,721	422,937
31700	33011	Hillsborough County, NH	400,721	422,937
31740		Manhattan, KS Metro Area	127,081	134,046
31740	20061	Geary County, KS	34,362	36,739
31740	20149	Pottawatomie County, KS	21,604	25,348
31740	20161	Riley County, KS	71,115	71,959
31820		Manitowoc, WI Micro Area	81,442	81,359
31820	55071	Manitowoc County, WI	81,442	81,359
31860		Mankato, MN Metro Area	96,740	103,566
31860	27013	Blue Earth County, MN	64,013	69,112
31860	27103	Nicollet County, MN	32,727	34,454
31900		Mansfield, OH Metro Area	124,475	124,936
31900	39139	Richland County, OH	124,475	124,936
31930		Marietta, OH Micro Area	61,778	59,771
31930	39167	Washington County, OH	61,778	59,771
31940		Marinette, WI-MI Micro Area	65,778	65,374
31940	26109	Menominee County, MI	24,029	23,502
31940	55075	Marinette County, WI	41,749	41,872
31980		Marion, IN Micro Area	70,061	66,674
31980	18053	Grant County, IN	70,061	66,674
32000		Marion, NC Micro Area	44,996	44,578
32000	37111	McDowell County, NC	44,996	44,578
32020		Marion, OH Micro Area	66,501	65,359
32020	39101	Marion County, OH	66,501	65,359
32100		Marquette, MI Micro Area	67,077	66,017
32100	26103	Marquette County, MI	67,077	66,017
32140		Marshall, MN Micro Area	25,857	25,269
32140	27083	Lyon County, MN	25,857	25,269
32180		Marshall, MO Micro Area	23,370	23,333
32180	29195	Saline County, MO	23,370	23,333
32260		Marshalltown, IA Micro Area	40,648	40,105
32260	19127	Marshall County, IA	40,648	40,105
32280		Martin, TN Micro Area	35,021	32,902
32280	47183	Weakley County, TN	35,021	32,902
32300		Martinsville, VA Micro Area	67,972	64,433
32300	51089	Henry County, VA	54,151	50,948
32300	51690	Martinsville city, VA	13,821	13,485
32340		Maryville, MO Micro Area	23,370	21,241
32340	29147	Nodaway County, MO	23,370	21,241
32380		Mason City, IA Micro Area	51,749	50,570
32380	19033	Cerro Gordo County, IA	44,151	43,127
32380	19195	Worth County, IA	7,598	7,443
32460		Mayfield, KY Micro Area	37,121	36,649
32460	21083	Graves County, KY	37,121	36,649
32500		Maysville, KY Micro Area	17,490	17,120
32500	21161	Mason County, KY	17,490	17,120
32540		McAlester, OK Micro Area	45,837	43,773
32540	40121	Pittsburg County, OK	45,837	43,773
32580		McAllen-Edinburg-Mission, TX Metro Area	774,769	870,781
32580	48215	Hidalgo County, TX	774,769	870,781
32620		McComb, MS Micro Area	40,404	40,324
32620	28113	Pike County, MS	40,404	40,324

CORE-BASED STATISTICAL AREAS (Metropolitan and Micropolitan), METROPOLITAN DIVISIONS, AND COMPONENTS (as defined March, 2020)—*Continued*

Core based statistical area	State/ County FIPS code	Title and Geographic Components	2010 Census Population	2020 Census Population
32660		McMinnville, TN Micro Area	39,839	40,953
32660	47177	Warren County, TN	39,839	40,953
32700		McPherson, KS Micro Area	29,180	30,223
32700	20113	McPherson County, KS	29,180	30,223
32740		Meadville, PA Micro Area	88,765	83,938
32740	42039	Crawford County, PA	88,765	83,938
32780		Medford, OR Metro Area	203,206	223,259
32780	41029	Jackson County, OR	203,206	223,259
32820		Memphis, TN-MS-AR Metro Area	1,316,100	1,337,779
.	28033	DeSoto County, MS	161,252	48,163
32820	28093	Marshall County, MS	37,144	185,314
32820	28137	Tate County, MS	28,886	33,752
32820	28143	Tunica County, MS	10,778	28,064
32820	47047	Fayette County, TN	38,413	9,782
32820	47157	Shelby County, TN	927,644	41,990
32820	47167	Tipton County, TN	61,081	929,744
32820	05035	Crittenden County, AR	50,902	60,970
32860		Menomonie, WI Micro Area	43,857	45,440
32860	55033	Dunn County, WI	43,857	45,440
32900		Merced, CA Metro Area	255,793	281,202
32900	06047	Merced County, CA	255,793	281,202
32940		Meridian, MS Micro Area	107,449	97,587
32940	28023	Clarke County, MS	16,732	15,615
32940	28069	Kemper County, MS	10,456	8,988
32940	28075	Lauderdale County, MS	80,261	72,984
33020		Mexico, MO Micro Area	25,529	24,962
33020	29007	Audrain County, MO	25,529	24,962
33060		Miami, OK Micro Area	31,848	30,285
33060	40115	Ottawa County, OK	31,848	30,285
33100		Miami-Fort Lauderdale-Pompano Beach, FL Metro Area	5,564,635	6,138,333
33100		Fort Lauderdale-Pompano Beach-Sunrise, FL Division 22744	1,748,066	1,944,375
33100	12011	Broward County, FL	1,748,066	1,944,375
33100		Miami-Miami Beach-Kendall, FL Division 33124	2,496,435	2,701,767
33100	12086	Miami-Dade County, FL	2,496,435	2,701,767
33100		West Palm Beach-Boca Raton-Boynton Beach, FL Division 48424	1,320,134	1,492,191
33100	12099	Palm Beach County, FL	1,320,134	1,492,191
33140		Michigan City-La Porte, IN Metro Area	111,467	112,417
33140	18091	LaPorte County, IN	111,467	112,417
33180		Middlesborough, KY Micro Area	28,691	24,097
33180	21013	Bell County, KY	28,691	24,097
33220		Midland, MI Metro Area	83,629	83,494
33220	26111	Midland County, MI	83,629	83,494
33260		Midland, TX Metro Area	141,671	175,220
33260	48317	Martin County, TX	4,799	5,237
33260	48329	Midland County, TX	136,872	169,983
33300		Milledgeville, GA Micro Area	55,149	52,534
33300	13009	Baldwin County, GA	45,720	43,799
33300	13141	Hancock County, GA	9,429	8,735
33340		Milwaukee-Waukesha, WI Metro Area	1,555,908	1,574,731
33340	55079	Milwaukee County, WI	947,735	939,489
33340	55089	Ozaukee County, WI	86,395	91,503
33340	55131	Washington County, WI	131,887	136,761
33340	55133	Waukesha County, WI	389,891	406,978
33380		Minden, LA Micro Area	41,207	36,967
33380	22119	Webster Parish, LA	41,207	36,967
33420		Mineral Wells, TX Micro Area	28,111	28,409
33420	48363	Palo Pinto County, TX	28,111	28,409
33460		Minneapolis-St. Paul-Bloomington, MN-WI Metro Area	3,333,633	3,690,261
33460	27003	Anoka County, MN	330,844	363,887
33460	27019	Carver County, MN	91,042	106,922
33460	27025	Chisago County, MN	53,887	56,621
33460	27037	Dakota County, MN	398,552	439,882
33460	27053	Hennepin County, MN	1,152,425	1,281,565
33460	27059	Isanti County, MN	37,816	41,135
33460	27079	Le Sueur County, MN	27,703	28,674
33460	27095	Mille Lacs County, MN	26,097	26,459
33460	27123	Ramsey County, MN	508,640	552,352
33460	27139	Scott County, MN	129,928	150,928
33460	27141	Sherburne County, MN	88,499	97,183
33460	27163	Washington County, MN	238,136	267,568
33460	27171	Wright County, MN	124,700	141,337
33460	55093	Pierce County, WI	41,019	42,212
33460	55109	St. Croix County, WI	84,345	93,536
33500		Minot, ND Micro Area	69,540	77,546
33500	38049	McHenry County, ND	5,395	5,345
33500	38075	Renville County, ND	2,470	2,282
33500	38101	Ward County, ND	61,675	69,919
33540		Missoula, MT Metro Area	109,299	117,922
33540	30063	Missoula County, MT	109,299	117,922
33580		Mitchell, SD Micro Area	22,835	23,417
33580	46035	Davison County, SD	19,504	19,956
33580	46061	Hanson County, SD	3,331	3,461
33620		Moberly, MO Micro Area	25,414	24,716
33620	29175	Randolph County, MO	25,414	24,716
33660		Mobile, AL Metro Area	430,573	430,197
33660	01097	Mobile County, AL	412,992	414,809
33660	01129	Washington County, AL	17,581	15,388
33700		Modesto, CA Metro Area	514,453	552,878
33700	06099	Stanislaus County, CA	514,453	552,878
33740		Monroe, LA Metro Area	204,420	207,104
33740	22067	Morehouse Parish, LA	27,979	25,629
33740	22073	Ouachita Parish, LA	153,720	160,368
33740	22111	Union Parish, LA	22,721	21,107
33780		Monroe, MI Metro Area	152,021	154,809
33780	26115	Monroe County, MI	152,021	154,809

CORE-BASED STATISTICAL AREAS (Metropolitan and Micropolitan), METROPOLITAN DIVISIONS, AND COMPONENTS (as defined March, 2020)—*Continued*

Core based statistical area	State/ County FIPS code	Title and Geographic Components	2010 Census Population	2020 Census Population
33860		Montgomery, AL Metro Area	374,536	386,047
33860	01001	Autauga County, AL	54,571	58,805
33860	01051	Elmore County, AL	79,303	87,977
33860	01085	Lowndes County, AL	11,299	10,311
33860	01101	Montgomery County, AL	229,363	228,954
33940		Montrose, CO Micro Area	45,712	47,553
33940	08085	Montrose County, CO	41,276	42,679
33940	08091	Ouray County, CO	4,436	4,874
33980		Morehead City, NC Micro Area	66,469	67,686
33980	37031	Carteret County, NC	66,469	67,686
34020		Morgan City, LA Micro Area	54,650	49,406
34020	22101	St. Mary Parish, LA	54,650	49,406
34060		Morgantown, WV Metro Area	129,709	140,038
34060	54061	Monongalia County, WV	96,189	105,822
34060	54077	Preston County, WV	33,520	34,216
34100		Morristown, TN Metro Area	136,608	142,709
34100	47057	Grainger County, TN	22,657	23,527
34100	47063	Hamblen County, TN	62,544	64,499
34100	47089	Jefferson County, TN	51,407	54,683
34140		Moscow, ID Micro Area	37,244	39,517
34140	16057	Latah County, ID	37,244	39,517
34180		Moses Lake, WA Micro Area	89,120	99,123
34180	53025	Grant County, WA	89,120	99,123
34220		Moultrie, GA Micro Area	45,498	45,898
34220	13071	Colquitt County, GA	45,498	45,898
34260		Mountain Home, AR Micro Area	41,513	41,627
34260	05005	Baxter County, AR	41,513	41,627
34300		Mountain Home, ID Micro Area	27,038	28,666
34300	16039	Elmore County, ID	27,038	28,666
34340		Mount Airy, NC Micro Area	73,673	71,359
34340	37171	Surry County, NC	73,673	71,359
34350		Mount Gay-Shamrock, WV Micro Area	36,743	32,567
34350	54045	Logan County, WV	36,743	32,567
34380		Mount Pleasant, MI Micro Area	70,311	64,394
34380	26073	Isabella County, MI	70,311	64,394
34420		Mount Pleasant, TX Micro Area	44,735	43,711
34420	48063	Camp County, TX	12,401	12,464
34420	48449	Titus County, TX	32,334	31,247
34460		Mount Sterling, KY Micro Area	44,396	46,977
34460	21011	Bath County, KY	11,591	12,750
34460	21165	Menifee County, KY	6,306	6,113
34460	21173	Montgomery County, KY	26,499	28,114
34500		Mount Vernon, IL Micro Area	38,827	37,113
34500	17081	Jefferson County, IL	38,827	37,113
34540		Mount Vernon, OH Micro Area	60,921	62,721
34540	39083	Knox County, OH	60,921	62,721
34580		Mount Vernon-Anacortes, WA Metro Area	116,901	129,523
34580	53057	Skagit County, WA	116,901	129,523
34620		Muncie, IN Metro Area	117,671	111,903
34620	18035	Delaware County, IN	117,671	111,903
34660		Murray, KY Micro Area	37,191	37,103
34660	21035	Calloway County, KY	37,191	37,103
34700		Muscatine, IA Micro Area	42,745	43,235
34700	19139	Muscatine County, IA	42,745	43,235
34740		Muskegon, MI Metro Area	172,188	175,824
34740	26121	Muskegon County, MI	172,188	175,824
34780		Muskogee, OK Micro Area	70,990	66,339
34780	40101	Muskogee County, OK	70,990	66,339
34820		Myrtle Beach-Conway-North Myrtle Beach, SC-NC Metro Area	376,722	487,722
34820	37019	Brunswick County, NC	107,431	136,693
34820	45051	Horry County, SC	269,291	351,029
34860		Nacogdoches, TX Micro Area	64,524	64,653
34860	48347	Nacogdoches County, TX	64,524	64,653
34900		Napa, CA Metro Area	136,484	138,019
34900	06055	Napa County, CA	136,484	138,019
34940		Naples-Marco Island, FL Metro Area	321,520	375,752
34940	12021	Collier County, FL	321,520	375,752
34980		Nashville-Davidson--Murfreesboro--Franklin, TN Metro Area	1,646,200	1,989,519
34980	47015	Cannon County, TN	13,801	14,506
34980	47021	Cheatham County, TN	39,105	41,072
34980	47037	Davidson County, TN	626,681	715,884
34980	47043	Dickson County, TN	49,666	54,315
34980	47111	Macon County, TN	22,248	25,216
34980	47119	Maury County, TN	80,956	100,974
34980	47147	Robertson County, TN	66,283	72,803
34980	47149	Rutherford County, TN	262,604	341,486
34980	47159	Smith County, TN	19,166	19,904
34980	47165	Sumner County, TN	160,645	196,281
34980	47169	Trousdale County, TN	7,870	11,615
34980	47187	Williamson County, TN	183,182	247,726
34980	47189	Wilson County, TN	113,993	147,737
35020		Natchez, MS-LA Micro Area	53,119	48,225
35020	22029	Concordia Parish, LA	20,822	18,687
35020	28001	Adams County, MS	32,297	29,538
35060		Natchitoches, LA Micro Area	39,566	37,515
35060	22069	Natchitoches Parish, LA	39,566	37,515
35100		New Bern, NC Metro Area	126,802	122,168
35100	37049	Craven County, NC	103,505	100,720
35100	37103	Jones County, NC	10,153	9,172
35100	37137	Pamlico County, NC	13,144	12,276
35140		Newberry, SC Micro Area	37,508	37,719
35140	45071	Newberry County, SC	37,508	37,719
35220		New Castle, IN Micro Area	49,462	48,914
35220	18065	Henry County, IN	49,462	48,914
35260		New Castle, PA Micro Area	91,108	86,070
35260	42073	Lawrence County, PA	91,108	86,070

CORE-BASED STATISTICAL AREAS (Metropolitan and Micropolitan), METROPOLITAN DIVISIONS, AND COMPONENTS (as defined March, 2020)—*Continued*

Core based statistical area	State/ County FIPS code	Title and Geographic Components	2010 Census Population	2020 Census Population
35300		New Haven-Milford, CT Metro Area	862,477	864,835
35300	09009	New Haven County, CT	862,477	864,835
35380		New Orleans-Metairie, LA Metro Area	1,189,866	1,271,845
35380	22051	Jefferson Parish, LA	432,552	440,781
35380	22071	Orleans Parish, LA	343,829	383,997
35380	22075	Plaquemines Parish, LA	23,042	23,515
35380	22087	St. Bernard Parish, LA	35,897	43,764
35380	22089	St. Charles Parish, LA	52,780	52,549
35380	22093	St. James Parish, LA	22,102	20,192
35380	22095	St. John the Baptist Parish, LA	45,924	42,477
35380	22103	St. Tammany Parish, LA	233,740	264,570
35420		New Philadelphia-Dover, OH Micro Area	92,582	93,263
35420	39157	Tuscarawas County, OH	92,582	93,263
35440		Newport, OR Micro Area	46,034	50,395
35440	41041	Lincoln County, OR	46,034	50,395
35460		Newport, TN Micro Area	35,662	35,999
35460	47029	Cocke County, TN	35,662	35,999
35580		New Ulm, MN Micro Area	25,893	25,912
35580	27015	Brown County, MN	25,893	25,912
35620		New York-Newark-Jersey City, NY-NJ-PA Metro Area	18,897,109	20,140,470
35620		Nassau County-Suffolk County, NY Division 35004	2,832,882	2,921,694
35620	36059	Nassau County, NY	1,339,532	1,395,774
35620	36103	Suffolk County, NY	1,493,350	1,525,920
35620		Newark, NJ-PA Division 35084	2,147,727	2,280,061
35620	34013	Essex County, NJ	783,969	863,728
35620	34019	Hunterdon County, NJ	128,349	128,947
35620	34027	Morris County, NJ	492,276	509,285
35620	34037	Sussex County, NJ	149,265	144,221
35620	34039	Union County, NJ	536,499	575,345
35620	42103	Pike County, PA	57,369	58,535
35620		New Brunswick-Lakewood, NJ Division 35154	2,340,249	2,489,367
35620	34023	Middlesex County, NJ	809,858	863,162
35620	34025	Monmouth County, NJ	630,380	643,615
35620	34029	Ocean County, NJ	576,567	637,229
35620	34035	Somerset County, NJ	323,444	345,361
35620		New York-Jersey City-White Plains, NY-NJ Division 35614	11,576,251	12,449,348
35620	34003	Bergen County, NJ	905,116	955,732
35620	34017	Hudson County, NJ	634,266	724,854
35620	34031	Passaic County, NJ	501,226	524,118
35620	36005	Bronx County, NY	1,385,108	1,472,654
35620	36047	Kings County, NY	2,504,700	2,736,074
35620	36061	New York County, NY	1,585,873	1,694,251
35620	36079	Putnam County, NY	99,710	97,668
35620	36081	Queens County, NY	2,230,722	2,405,464
35620	36085	Richmond County, NY	468,730	495,747
35620	36087	Rockland County, NY	311,687	338,329
35620	36119	Westchester County, NY	949,113	1,004,457
35660		Niles, MI Metro Area	156,813	154,316
35660	26021	Berrien County, MI	156,813	154,316

Core based statistical area	State/ County FIPS code	Title and Geographic Components	2010 Census Population	2020 Census Population
35700		Nogales, AZ Micro Area	47,420	47,669
35700	04023	Santa Cruz County, AZ	47,420	47,669
35740		Norfolk, NE Micro Area	48,271	48,744
35740	31119	Madison County, NE	34,876	35,585
35740	31139	Pierce County, NE	7,266	7,317
35740	31167	Stanton County, NE	6,129	5,842
35820		North Platte, NE Micro Area	37,590	35,791
35820	31111	Lincoln County, NE	36,288	34,676
35820	31113	Logan County, NE	763	716
35820	31117	McPherson County, NE	539	399
35840		North Port-Sarasota-Bradenton, FL Metro Area	702,281	833,716
35840	12081	Manatee County, FL	322,833	399,710
35840	12115	Sarasota County, FL	379,448	434,006
35860		North Vernon, IN Micro Area	28,525	27,613
35860	18079	Jennings County, IN	28,525	27,613
35900		North Wilkesboro, NC Micro Area	69,340	65,969
35900	37193	Wilkes County, NC	69,340	65,969
35940		Norwalk, OH Micro Area	59,626	58,565
35940	39077	Huron County, OH	59,626	58,565
35980		Norwich-New London, CT Metro Area	274,055	268,555
35980	09011	New London County, CT	274,055	268,555
36020		Oak Harbor, WA Micro Area	78,506	86,857
36020	53029	Island County, WA	78,506	86,857
36100		Ocala, FL Metro Area	331,298	375,908
36100	12083	Marion County, FL	331,298	375,908
36140		Ocean City, NJ Metro Area	97,265	95,263
36140	34009	Cape May County, NJ	97,265	95,263
36220		Odessa, TX Metro Area	137,130	165,171
36220	48135	Ector County, TX	137,130	165,171
36260		Ogden-Clearfield, UT Metro Area	597,159	694,863
36260	49003	Box Elder County, UT	49,975	57,666
36260	49011	Davis County, UT	306,479	362,679
36260	49029	Morgan County, UT	9,469	12,295
36260	49057	Weber County, UT	231,236	262,223
36300		Ogdensburg-Massena, NY Micro Area	111,944	108,505
36300	36089	St. Lawrence County, NY	111,944	108,505
36340		Oil City, PA Micro Area	54,984	50,454
36340	42121	Venango County, PA	54,984	50,454
36380		Okeechobee, FL Micro Area	39,996	39,644
36380	12093	Okeechobee County, FL	39,996	39,644
36420		Oklahoma City, OK Metro Area	1,252,987	1,425,695
36420	40017	Canadian County, OK	115,541	154,405
36420	40027	Cleveland County, OK	255,755	295,528
36420	40051	Grady County, OK	52,431	54,795
36420	40081	Lincoln County, OK	34,273	33,458
36420	40083	Logan County, OK	41,848	49,555
36420	40087	McClain County, OK	34,506	41,662
36420	40109	Oklahoma County, OK	718,633	796,292

CORE-BASED STATISTICAL AREAS (Metropolitan and Micropolitan), METROPOLITAN DIVISIONS, AND COMPONENTS (as defined March, 2020)—*Continued*

Core based statistical area	State/County FIPS code	Title and Geographic Components	2010 Census Population	2020 Census Population
36460		Olean, NY Micro Area	80,317	77,042
36460	36009	Cattaraugus County, NY	80,317	77,042
36500		Olympia-Lacey-Tumwater, WA Metro Area	252,264	294,793
36500	53067	Thurston County, WA	252,264	294,793
36540		Omaha-Council Bluffs, NE-IA Metro Area	865,350	967,604
36540	19085	Harrison County, IA	14,928	14,582
36540	19129	Mills County, IA	15,059	14,484
36540	19155	Pottawattamie County, IA	93,158	93,667
36540	31025	Cass County, NE	25,241	26,598
36540	31055	Douglas County, NE	517,110	584,526
36540	31153	Sarpy County, NE	158,840	190,604
36540	31155	Saunders County, NE	20,780	22,278
36540	31177	Washington County, NE	20,234	20,865
36580		Oneonta, NY Micro Area	62,259	58,524
36580	36077	Otsego County, NY	62,259	58,524
36620		Ontario, OR-ID Micro Area	53,936	56,957
36620	16075	Payette County, ID	22,623	25,386
36620	41045	Malheur County, OR	31,313	31,571
36660		Opelousas, LA Micro Area	83,384	82,540
36660	22097	St. Landry Parish, LA	83,384	82,540
36700		Orangeburg, SC Micro Area	92,501	84,223
36700	45075	Orangeburg County, SC	92,501	84,223
36740		Orlando-Kissimmee-Sanford, FL Metro Area	2,134,411	2,673,376
36740	12069	Lake County, FL	297,052	383,956
36740	12095	Orange County, FL	1,145,956	1,429,908
36740	12097	Osceola County, FL	268,685	388,656
36740	12117	Seminole County, FL	422,718	470,856
36780		Oshkosh-Neenah, WI Metro Area	166,994	171,730
36780	55139	Winnebago County, WI	166,994	171,730
36820		Oskaloosa, IA Micro Area	22,381	22,190
36820	19123	Mahaska County, IA	22,381	22,190
36830		Othello, WA Micro Area	18,728	20,613
36830	53001	Adams County, WA	18,728	20,613
36837		Ottawa, IL Micro Area	154,908	148,539
36837	17011	Bureau County, IL	34,978	33,244
36837	17099	LaSalle County, IL	113,924	109,658
36837	17155	Putnam County, IL	6,006	5,637
36840		Ottawa, KS Micro Area	25,992	25,996
36840	20059	Franklin County, KS	25,992	25,996
36900		Ottumwa, IA Micro Area	35,625	35,437
36900	19179	Wapello County, IA	35,625	35,437
36940		Owatonna, MN Micro Area	36,576	37,406
36940	27147	Steele County, MN	36,576	37,406
36980		Owensboro, KY Metro Area	114,752	121,559
36980	21059	Daviess County, KY	96,656	103,312
36980	21091	Hancock County, KY	8,565	9,095
36980	21149	McLean County, KY	9,531	9,152
37060		Oxford, MS Micro Area	47,351	55,813
37060	28071	Lafayette County, MS	47,351	55,813
37100		Oxnard-Thousand Oaks-Ventura, CA Metro Area	823,318	843,843
37100	06111	Ventura County, CA	823,318	843,843
37120		Ozark, AL Micro Area	50,251	49,326
37120	01045	Dale County, AL	50,251	49,326
37140		Paducah, KY-IL Micro Area	98,762	98,660
37140	17127	Massac County, IL	15,429	14,169
37140	21007	Ballard County, KY	8,249	7,728
37140	21139	Livingston County, KY	9,519	8,888
37140	21145	McCracken County, KY	65,565	67,875
37220		Pahrump, NV Micro Area	43,946	51,591
37220	32023	Nye County, NV	43,946	51,591
37260		Palatka, FL Micro Area	74,364	73,321
37260	12107	Putnam County, FL	74,364	73,321
37300		Palestine, TX Micro Area	58,458	57,922
37300	48001	Anderson County, TX	58,458	57,922
37340		Palm Bay-Melbourne-Titusville, FL Metro Area	543,376	606,612
37340	12009	Brevard County, FL	543,376	606,612
37420		Pampa, TX Micro Area	23,464	22,054
37420	48179	Gray County, TX	22,535	21,227
37420	48393	Roberts County, TX	929	827
37460		Panama City, FL Metro Area	168,852	175,216
37460	12005	Bay County, FL	168,852	175,216
37500		Paragould, AR Micro Area	42,090	45,736
37500	05055	Greene County, AR	42,090	45,736
37540		Paris, TN Micro Area	32,330	32,199
37540	47079	Henry County, TN	32,330	32,199
37580		Paris, TX Micro Area	49,793	50,088
37580	48277	Lamar County, TX	49,793	50,088
37620		Parkersburg-Vienna, WV Metro Area	92,673	89,490
37620	54105	Wirt County, WV	5,717	5,194
37620	54107	Wood County, WV	86,956	84,296
37660		Parsons, KS Micro Area	21,607	20,184
37660	20099	Labette County, KS	21,607	20,184
37740		Payson, AZ Micro Area	53,597	53,272
37740	04007	Gila County, AZ	53,597	53,272
37770		Pearsall, TX Micro Area	17,217	18,385
37770	48163	Frio County, TX	17,217	18,385
37780		Pecos, TX Micro Area	13,865	14,812
37780	48301	Loving County, TX	82	64
37780	48389	Reeves County, TX	13,783	14,748
37800		Pella, IA Micro Area	33,309	33,414
37800	19125	Marion County, IA	33,309	33,414

CORE-BASED STATISTICAL AREAS (Metropolitan and Micropolitan), METROPOLITAN DIVISIONS, AND COMPONENTS (as defined March, 2020)—*Continued*

Core based statistical area	State/ County FIPS code	Title and Geographic Components	2010 Census Population	2020 Census Population
37860		Pensacola-Ferry Pass-Brent, FL Metro Area	448,991	509,905
37860	12033	Escambia County, FL	297,619	321,905
37860	12113	Santa Rosa County, FL	151,372	188,000
37900		Peoria, IL Metro Area	416,255	402,391
37900	17057	Fulton County, IL	37,069	33,609
37900	17123	Marshall County, IL	12,640	11,742
37900	17143	Peoria County, IL	186,494	181,830
37900	17175	Stark County, IL	5,994	5,400
37900	17179	Tazewell County, IL	135,394	131,343
37900	17203	Woodford County, IL	38,664	38,467
37940		Peru, IN Micro Area	36,903	35,962
37940	18103	Miami County, IN	36,903	35,962
37980		Philadelphia-Camden-Wilmington, PA-NJ-DE-MD Metro Area	5,965,343	6,245,051
37980		Camden, NJ Division 15804	1,250,679	1,287,639
37980	34005	Burlington County, NJ	448,734	461,860
37980	34007	Camden County, NJ	513,657	523,485
37980	34015	Gloucester County, NJ	288,288	302,294
37980		Montgomery County-Bucks County-Chester County, PA Division 33874	1,924,009	2,037,504
37980	42017	Bucks County, PA	625,249	646,538
37980	42029	Chester County, PA	498,886	534,413
37980	42091	Montgomery County, PA	799,874	856,553
37980		Philadelphia, PA Division 37964	2,084,985	2,180,627
37980	42045	Delaware County, PA	558,979	576,830
37980	42101	Philadelphia County, PA	1,526,006	1,603,797
37980		Wilmington, DE-MD-NJ Division 48864	705,670	739,281
37980	10003	New Castle County, DE	538,479	570,719
37980	24015	Cecil County, MD	101,108	103,725
37980	34033	Salem County, NJ	66,083	64,837
38060		Phoenix-Mesa-Chandler, AZ Metro Area	4,192,887	4,845,832
38060	04013	Maricopa County, AZ	3,817,117	4,420,568
38060	04021	Pinal County, AZ	375,770	425,264
38100		Picayune, MS Micro Area	55,834	56,145
38100	28109	Pearl River County, MS	55,834	56,145
38180		Pierre, SD Micro Area	19,988	20,745
38180	46065	Hughes County, SD	17,022	17,765
38180	46117	Stanley County, SD	2,966	2,980
38220		Pine Bluff, AR Metro Area	100,258	87,751
38220	05025	Cleveland County, AR	8,689	7,550
38220	05069	Jefferson County, AR	77,435	67,260
38220	05079	Lincoln County, AR	14,134	12,941
38240		Pinehurst-Southern Pines, NC Micro Area	88,247	99,727
38240	37125	Moore County, NC	88,247	99,727
38260		Pittsburg, KS Micro Area	39,134	38,972
38260	20037	Crawford County, KS	39,134	38,972
38300		Pittsburgh, PA Metro Area	2,356,285	2,370,930
38300	42003	Allegheny County, PA	1,223,348	1,250,578
38300	42005	Armstrong County, PA	68,941	65,558
38300	42007	Beaver County, PA	170,539	168,215
38300	42019	Butler County, PA	183,862	193,763
38300	42051	Fayette County, PA	136,606	128,804
38300	42125	Washington County, PA	207,820	209,349
38300	42129	Westmoreland County, PA	365,169	354,663
38340		Pittsfield, MA Metro Area	131,219	129,026
38340	25003	Berkshire County, MA	131,219	129,026
38380		Plainview, TX Micro Area	36,273	32,522
38380	48189	Hale County, TX	36,273	32,522
38420		Platteville, WI Micro Area	51,208	51,938
38420	55043	Grant County, WI	51,208	51,938
38460		Plattsburgh, NY Micro Area	82,128	79,843
38460	36019	Clinton County, NY	82,128	79,843
38500		Plymouth, IN Micro Area	47,051	46,095
38500	18099	Marshall County, IN	47,051	46,095
38540		Pocatello, ID Metro Area	90,656	94,896
38540	16005	Bannock County, ID	82,839	87,018
38540	16077	Power County, ID	7,817	7,878
38580		Point Pleasant, WV-OH Micro Area	58,258	54,673
38580	39053	Gallia County, OH	30,934	29,220
38580	54053	Mason County, WV	27,324	25,453
38620		Ponca City, OK Micro Area	46,562	43,700
38620	40071	Kay County, OK	46,562	43,700
38700		Pontiac, IL Micro Area	38,950	35,815
38700	17105	Livingston County, IL	38,950	35,815
38740		Poplar Bluff, MO Micro Area	56,894	52,809
38740	29023	Butler County, MO	42,794	42,130
38740	29181	Ripley County, MO	14,100	10,679
38780		Portales, NM Micro Area	19,846	19,191
38780	35041	Roosevelt County, NM	19,846	19,191
38820		Port Angeles, WA Micro Area	71,404	77,155
38820	53009	Clallam County, WA	71,404	77,155
38860		Portland-South Portland, ME Metro Area	514,098	551,740
38860	23005	Cumberland County, ME	281,674	303,069
38860	23023	Sagadahoc County, ME	35,293	36,699
38860	23031	York County, ME	197,131	211,972
38900		Portland-Vancouver-Hillsboro, OR-WA Metro Area	2,226,009	2,512,859
38900	41005	Clackamas County, OR	375,992	421,401
38900	41009	Columbia County, OR	49,351	52,589
38900	41051	Multnomah County, OR	735,334	815,428
38900	41067	Washington County, OR	529,710	600,372
38900	41071	Yamhill County, OR	99,193	107,722
38900	53011	Clark County, WA	425,363	503,311
38900	53059	Skamania County, WA	11,066	12,036

CORE-BASED STATISTICAL AREAS (Metropolitan and Micropolitan), METROPOLITAN DIVISIONS, AND COMPONENTS (as defined March, 2020)—*Continued*

Core based statistical area	State/ County FIPS code	Title and Geographic Components	2010 Census Population	2020 Census Population
38920		Port Lavaca, TX Micro Area	21,381	20,106
38920	48057	Calhoun County, TX	21,381	20,106
38940		Port St. Lucie, FL Metro Area	424,107	487,657
38940	12085	Martin County, FL	146,318	158,431
38940	12111	St. Lucie County, FL	277,789	329,226
39020		Portsmouth, OH Micro Area	79,499	74,008
39020	39145	Scioto County, OH	79,499	74,008
39060		Pottsville, PA Micro Area	148,289	143,049
39060	42107	Schuylkill County, PA	148,289	143,049
39100		Poughkeepsie-Newburgh-Middletown, NY Metro Area	670,301	697,221
39100	36027	Dutchess County, NY	297,488	295,911
39100	36071	Orange County, NY	372,813	401,310
39150		Prescott Valley-Prescott, AZ Metro Area	211,033	236,209
39150	04025	Yavapai County, AZ	211,033	236,209
39220		Price, UT Micro Area	21,403	20,412
39220	49007	Carbon County, UT	21,403	20,412
39260		Prineville, OR Micro Area	20,978	24,738
39260	41013	Crook County, OR	20,978	24,738
39300		Providence-Warwick, RI-MA Metro Area	1,600,852	1,676,579
39300	25005	Bristol County, MA	548,285	579,200
39300	44001	Bristol County, RI	49,875	50,793
39300	44003	Kent County, RI	166,158	170,363
39300	44005	Newport County, RI	82,888	85,643
39300	44007	Providence County, RI	626,667	660,741
39300	44009	Washington County, RI	126,979	129,839
39340		Provo-Orem, UT Metro Area	526,810	671,185
39340	49023	Juab County, UT	10,246	11,786
39340	49049	Utah County, UT	516,564	659,399
39380		Pueblo, CO Metro Area	159,063	168,162
39380	08101	Pueblo County, CO	159,063	168,162
39420		Pullman, WA Micro Area	44,776	47,973
39420	53075	Whitman County, WA	44,776	47,973
39460		Punta Gorda, FL Metro Area	159,978	186,847
39460	12015	Charlotte County, FL	159,978	186,847
39500		Quincy, IL-MO Micro Area	77,314	75,769
39500	17001	Adams County, IL	67,103	65,737
39500	29111	Lewis County, MO	10,211	10,032
39540		Racine, WI Metro Area	195,408	197,727
39540	55101	Racine County, WI	195,408	197,727
39580		Raleigh-Cary, NC Metro Area	1,130,490	1,413,982
39580	37069	Franklin County, NC	60,619	68,573
39580	37101	Johnston County, NC	168,878	215,999
39580	37183	Wake County, NC	900,993	1,129,410
39660		Rapid City, SD Metro Area	126,382	139,074
39660	46093	Meade County, SD	25,434	29,852
39660	46103	Pennington County, SD	100,948	109,222
39700		Raymondville, TX Micro Area	22,134	20,164
39700	48489	Willacy County, TX	22,134	20,164
39740		Reading, PA Metro Area	411,442	428,849
39740	42011	Berks County, PA	411,442	428,849
39780		Red Bluff, CA Micro Area	63,463	65,829
39780	06103	Tehama County, CA	63,463	65,829
39820		Redding, CA Metro Area	177,223	182,155
39820	06089	Shasta County, CA	177,223	182,155
39860		Red Wing, MN Micro Area	46,183	47,582
39860	27049	Goodhue County, MN	46,183	47,582
39900		Reno, NV Metro Area	425,417	490,596
39900	32029	Storey County, NV	4,010	4,104
39900	32031	Washoe County, NV	421,407	486,492
39940		Rexburg, ID Micro Area	50,778	66,301
39940	16043	Fremont County, ID	13,242	13,388
39940	16065	Madison County, ID	37,536	52,913
39980		Richmond, IN Micro Area	68,917	66,553
39980	18177	Wayne County, IN	68,917	66,553
40060		Richmond, VA Metro Area	1,186,501	1,314,434
40060	51007	Amelia County, VA	12,690	13,265
40060	51036	Charles City County, VA	7,256	6,773
40060	51041	Chesterfield County, VA	316,236	364,548
40060	51053	Dinwiddie County, VA	28,001	27,947
40060	51075	Goochland County, VA	21,717	24,727
40060	51085	Hanover County, VA	99,863	109,979
40060	51087	Henrico County, VA	306,935	334,389
40060	51097	King and Queen County, VA	6,945	6,608
40060	51101	King William County, VA	15,935	17,810
40060	51127	New Kent County, VA	18,429	22,945
40060	51145	Powhatan County, VA	28,046	30,333
40060	51149	Prince George County, VA	35,725	43,010
40060	51183	Sussex County, VA	12,087	10,829
40060	51570	Colonial Heights city, VA	17,411	18,170
40060	51670	Hopewell city, VA	22,591	23,033
40060	51730	Petersburg city, VA	32,420	33,458
40060	51760	Richmond city, VA	204,214	226,610
40080		Richmond-Berea, KY Micro Area	97,588	106,864
40080	21065	Estill County, KY	14,672	14,163
40080	21151	Madison County, KY	82,916	92,701
40100		Rio Grande City-Roma, TX Micro Area	60,968	65,920
40100	48427	Starr County, TX	60,968	65,920
40140		Riverside-San Bernardino-Ontario, CA Metro Area	4,224,851	4,599,839
40140	06065	Riverside County, CA	2,189,641	2,418,185
40140	06071	San Bernardino County, CA	2,035,210	2,181,654
40180		Riverton, WY Micro Area	40,123	39,234
40180	56013	Fremont County, WY	40,123	39,234
40220		Roanoke, VA Metro Area	308,707	315,251
40220	51023	Botetourt County, VA	33,148	33,596
40220	51045	Craig County, VA	5,190	4,892
40220	51067	Franklin County, VA	56,159	54,477
40220	51161	Roanoke County, VA	92,376	96,929
40220	51770	Roanoke city, VA	97,032	100,011
40220	51775	Salem city, VA	24,802	25,346

CORE-BASED STATISTICAL AREAS (Metropolitan and Micropolitan), METROPOLITAN DIVISIONS, AND COMPONENTS (as defined March, 2020)—*Continued*

Core based statistical area	State/ County FIPS code	Title and Geographic Components	2010 Census Population	2020 Census Population
40260		Roanoke Rapids, NC Micro Area	76,790	66,093
40260	37083	Halifax County, NC	54,691	48,622
40260	37131	Northampton County, NC	22,099	17,471
40300		Rochelle, IL Micro Area	53,497	51,788
40300	17141	Ogle County, IL	53,497	51,788
40340		Rochester, MN Metro Area	206,877	226,329
40340	27039	Dodge County, MN	20,087	20,867
40340	27045	Fillmore County, MN	20,866	21,228
40340	27109	Olmsted County, MN	144,248	162,847
40340	27157	Wabasha County, MN	21,676	21,387
40380		Rochester, NY Metro Area	1,079,671	1,090,135
40380	36051	Livingston County, NY	65,393	61,834
40380	36055	Monroe County, NY	744,344	759,443
40380	36069	Ontario County, NY	107,931	112,458
40380	36073	Orleans County, NY	42,883	40,343
40380	36117	Wayne County, NY	93,772	91,283
40380	36123	Yates County, NY	25,348	24,774
40420		Rockford, IL Metro Area	349,431	338,798
40420	17007	Boone County, IL	54,165	53,448
40420	17201	Winnebago County, IL	295,266	285,350
40460		Rockingham, NC Micro Area	46,639	42,946
40460	37153	Richmond County, NC	46,639	42,946
40530		Rockport, TX Micro Area	23,158	23,830
40530	48007	Aransas County, TX	23,158	23,830
40540		Rock Springs, WY Micro Area	43,806	42,272
40540	56037	Sweetwater County, WY	43,806	42,272
40580		Rocky Mount, NC Metro Area	152,392	143,870
40580	37065	Edgecombe County, NC	56,552	48,900
40580	37127	Nash County, NC	95,840	94,970
40620		Rolla, MO Micro Area	45,156	44,638
40620	29161	Phelps County, MO	45,156	44,638
40660		Rome, GA Metro Area	96,317	98,584
40660	13115	Floyd County, GA	96,317	98,584
40700		Roseburg, OR Micro Area	107,667	111,201
40700	41019	Douglas County, OR	107,667	111,201
40740		Roswell, NM Micro Area	65,645	65,157
40740	35005	Chaves County, NM	65,645	65,157
40760		Ruidoso, NM Micro Area	20,497	20,269
40760	35027	Lincoln County, NM	20,497	20,269
40780		Russellville, AR Micro Area	83,939	83,644
40780	05115	Pope County, AR	61,754	63,381
40780	05149	Yell County, AR	22,185	20,263
40820		Ruston, LA Micro Area	46,735	48,396
40820	22061	Lincoln Parish, LA	46,735	48,396
40860		Rutland, VT Micro Area	61,642	60,572
40860	50021	Rutland County, VT	61,642	60,572
40900		Sacramento-Roseville-Folsom, CA Metro Area	2,149,127	2,397,382
40900	06017	El Dorado County, CA	181,058	191,185
40900	06061	Placer County, CA	348,432	404,739
40900	06067	Sacramento County, CA	1,418,788	1,585,055
40900	06113	Yolo County, CA	200,849	216,403
40940		Safford, AZ Micro Area	37,220	38,533
40940	04009	Graham County, AZ	37,220	38,533
40980		Saginaw, MI Metro Area	200,169	190,124
40980	26145	Saginaw County, MI	200,169	190,124
41060		St. Cloud, MN Metro Area	189,093	199,671
41060	27009	Benton County, MN	38,451	41,379
41060	27145	Stearns County, MN	150,642	158,292
41100		St. George, UT Metro Area	138,115	180,279
41100	49053	Washington County, UT	138,115	180,279
41140		St. Joseph, MO-KS Metro Area	127,329	121,467
41140	20043	Doniphan County, KS	7,945	7,510
41140	29003	Andrew County, MO	17,291	18,135
41140	29021	Buchanan County, MO	89,201	84,793
41140	29063	DeKalb County, MO	12,892	11,029
41180		St. Louis, MO-IL Metro Area	2,787,701	2,820,253
41180	17005	Bond County, IL	17,768	16,725
41180	17013	Calhoun County, IL	5,089	4,437
41180	17027	Clinton County, IL	37,762	36,899
41180	17083	Jersey County, IL	22,985	21,512
41180	17117	Macoupin County, IL	47,765	44,967
41180	17119	Madison County, IL	269,282	265,859
41180	17133	Monroe County, IL	32,957	34,962
41180	17163	St. Clair County, IL	270,056	257,400
41180	29071	Franklin County, MO	101,492	104,682
41180	29099	Jefferson County, MO	218,733	226,739
41180	29113	Lincoln County, MO	52,566	59,574
41180	29183	St. Charles County, MO	360,485	405,262
41180	29189	St. Louis County, MO	998,954	1,004,125
41180	29219	Warren County, MO	32,513	35,532
41180	29510	St. Louis city, MO	319,294	301,578
41220		St. Marys, GA Micro Area	50,513	54,768
41220	13039	Camden County, GA	50,513	54,768
41260		St. Marys, PA Micro Area	31,946	30,990
41260	42047	Elk County, PA	31,946	30,990
41400		Salem, OH Micro Area	107,841	101,877
41400	39029	Columbiana County, OH	107,841	101,877
41420		Salem, OR Metro Area	390,738	433,353
41420	41047	Marion County, OR	315,335	345,920
41420	41053	Polk County, OR	75,403	87,433
41460		Salina, KS Micro Area	61,697	60,038
41460	20143	Ottawa County, KS	6,091	5,735
41460	20169	Saline County, KS	55,606	54,303
41500		Salinas, CA Metro Area	415,057	439,035
41500	06053	Monterey County, CA	415,057	439,035

CORE-BASED STATISTICAL AREAS (Metropolitan and Micropolitan), METROPOLITAN DIVISIONS, AND COMPONENTS (as defined March, 2020)—*Continued*

Core based statistical area	State/ County FIPS code	Title and Geographic Components	2010 Census Population	2020 Census Population
41540		Salisbury, MD-DE Metro Area	373,802	418,046
41540	10005	Sussex County, DE	197,145	237,378
41540	24039	Somerset County, MD	26,470	24,620
41540	24045	Wicomico County, MD	98,733	103,588
41540	24047	Worcester County, MD	51,454	52,460
41620		Salt Lake City, UT Metro Area	1,087,873	1,257,936
41620	49035	Salt Lake County, UT	1,029,655	1,185,238
41620	49045	Tooele County, UT	58,218	72,698
41660		San Angelo, TX Metro Area	112,966	122,888
41660	48235	Irion County, TX	1,599	1,513
41660	48431	Sterling County, TX	1,143	1,372
41660	48451	Tom Green County, TX	110,224	120,003
41700		San Antonio-New Braunfels, TX Metro Area	2,142,508	2,558,143
41700	48013	Atascosa County, TX	44,911	48,981
41700	48019	Bandera County, TX	20,485	20,851
41700	48029	Bexar County, TX	1,714,773	2,009,324
41700	48091	Comal County, TX	108,472	161,501
41700	48187	Guadalupe County, TX	131,533	172,706
41700	48259	Kendall County, TX	33,410	44,279
41700	48325	Medina County, TX	46,006	50,748
41700	48493	Wilson County, TX	42,918	49,753
41740		San Diego-Chula Vista-Carlsbad, CA Metro Area	3,095,313	3,298,634
41740	06073	San Diego County, CA	3,095,313	3,298,634
41760		Sandpoint, ID Micro Area	40,877	47,110
41760	16017	Bonner County, ID	40,877	47,110
41780		Sandusky, OH Micro Area	77,079	75,622
41780	39043	Erie County, OH	77,079	75,622
41820		Sanford, NC Micro Area	57,866	63,285
41820	37105	Lee County, NC	57,866	63,285
41860		San Francisco-Oakland-Berkeley, CA Metro Area	4,335,391	4,749,008
41860		Oakland-Berkeley-Livermore, CA Division 36084	2,559,296	2,848,280
41860	06001	Alameda County, CA	1,510,271	1,682,353
41860	06013	Contra Costa County, CA	1,049,025	1,165,927
41860		San Francisco-San Mateo-Redwood City, CA Division 41884	1,523,686	1,638,407
41860	06075	San Francisco County, CA	805,235	873,965
41860	06081	San Mateo County, CA	718,451	764,442
41860		San Rafael, CA Division 42034	252,409	262,321
41860	06041	Marin County, CA	252,409	262,321
41940		San Jose-Sunnyvale-Santa Clara, CA Metro Area	1,836,911	2,000,468
41940	06069	San Benito County, CA	55,269	64,209
41940	06085	Santa Clara County, CA	1,781,642	1,936,259
42020		San Luis Obispo-Paso Robles, CA Metro Area	269,637	282,424
42020	06079	San Luis Obispo County, CA	269,637	282,424
42100		Santa Cruz-Watsonville, CA Metro Area	262,382	270,861
42100	06087	Santa Cruz County, CA	262,382	270,861

Core based statistical area	State/ County FIPS code	Title and Geographic Components	2010 Census Population	2020 Census Population
42140		Santa Fe, NM Metro Area	144,170	154,823
42140	35049	Santa Fe County, NM	144,170	154,823
42200		Santa Maria-Santa Barbara, CA Metro Area	423,895	448,229
42200	06083	Santa Barbara County, CA	423,895	448,229
42220		Santa Rosa-Petaluma, CA Metro Area	483,878	488,863
42220	06097	Sonoma County, CA	483,878	488,863
42300		Sault Ste. Marie, MI Micro Area	38,520	36,785
42300	26033	Chippewa County, MI	38,520	36,785
42340		Savannah, GA Metro Area	347,611	404,798
42340	13029	Bryan County, GA	30,233	44,738
42340	13051	Chatham County, GA	265,128	295,291
42340	13103	Effingham County, GA	52,250	64,769
42380		Sayre, PA Micro Area	62,622	59,967
42380	42015	Bradford County, PA	62,622	59,967
42420		Scottsbluff, NE Micro Area	38,971	37,893
42420	31007	Banner County, NE	690	674
42420	31157	Scotts Bluff County, NE	36,970	36,084
42420	31165	Sioux County, NE	1,311	1,135
42460		Scottsboro, AL Micro Area	53,227	52,579
42460	01071	Jackson County, AL	53,227	52,579
42500		Scottsburg, IN Micro Area	24,181	24,384
42500	18143	Scott County, IN	24,181	24,384
42540		Scranton--Wilkes-Barre, PA Metro Area	563,631	567,559
42540	42069	Lackawanna County, PA	214,437	215,896
42540	42079	Luzerne County, PA	320,918	325,594
42540	42131	Wyoming County, PA	28,276	26,069
42620		Searcy, AR Micro Area	77,076	76,822
42620	05145	White County, AR	77,076	76,822
42660		Seattle-Tacoma-Bellevue, WA Metro Area	3,439,809	4,018,762
42660		Seattle-Bellevue-Kent, WA Division 42644	2,644,584	3,097,632
42660	53033	King County, WA	1,931,249	2,269,675
42660	53061	Snohomish County, WA	713,335	827,957
42660		Tacoma-Lakewood, WA Division 45104	795,225	921,130
42660	53053	Pierce County, WA	795,225	921,130
42680		Sebastian-Vero Beach, FL Metro Area	138,028	159,788
42680	12061	Indian River County, FL	138,028	159,788
42700		Sebring-Avon Park, FL Metro Area	98,786	101,235
42700	12055	Highlands County, FL	98,786	101,235
42740		Sedalia, MO Micro Area	42,201	42,980
42740	29159	Pettis County, MO	42,201	42,980
42780		Selinsgrove, PA Micro Area	39,702	39,736
42780	42109	Snyder County, PA	39,702	39,736
42820		Selma, AL Micro Area	43,820	38,462
42820	01047	Dallas County, AL	43,820	38,462

CORE-BASED STATISTICAL AREAS (Metropolitan and Micropolitan), METROPOLITAN DIVISIONS, AND COMPONENTS (as defined March, 2020)—*Continued*

Core based statistical area	State/ County FIPS code	Title and Geographic Components	2010 Census Population	2020 Census Population
42860		Seneca, SC Micro Area	74,273	78,607
42860	45073	Oconee County, SC	74,273	78,607
42900		Seneca Falls, NY Micro Area	35,251	33,814
42900	36099	Seneca County, NY	35,251	33,814
42940		Sevierville, TN Micro Area	89,889	98,380
42940	47155	Sevier County, TN	89,889	98,380
42980		Seymour, IN Micro Area	42,376	46,428
42980	18071	Jackson County, IN	42,376	46,428
43020		Shawano, WI Micro Area	46,181	45,136
43020	55078	Menominee County, WI	4,232	4,255
43020	55115	Shawano County, WI	41,949	40,881
43060		Shawnee, OK Micro Area	69,442	72,454
43060	40125	Pottawatomie County, OK	69,442	72,454
43100		Sheboygan, WI Metro Area	115,507	118,034
43100	55117	Sheboygan County, WI	115,507	118,034
43140		Shelby, NC Micro Area	98,078	99,519
43140	37045	Cleveland County, NC	98,078	99,519
43180		Shelbyville, TN Micro Area	45,058	50,237
43180	47003	Bedford County, TN	45,058	50,237
43220		Shelton, WA Micro Area	60,699	65,726
43220	53045	Mason County, WA	60,699	65,726
43260		Sheridan, WY Micro Area	29,116	30,921
43260	56033	Sheridan County, WY	29,116	30,921
43300		Sherman-Denison, TX Metro Area	120,877	135,543
43300	48181	Grayson County, TX	120,877	135,543
43320		Show Low, AZ Micro Area	107,449	106,717
43320	04017	Navajo County, AZ	107,449	106,717
43340		Shreveport-Bossier City, LA Metro Area	398,604	393,406
43340	22015	Bossier Parish, LA	116,979	128,746
43340	22017	Caddo Parish, LA	254,969	237,848
43340	22031	De Soto Parish, LA	26,656	26,812
43380		Sidney, OH Micro Area	49,423	48,230
43380	39149	Shelby County, OH	49,423	48,230
43420		Sierra Vista-Douglas, AZ Metro Area	131,346	125,447
43420	04003	Cochise County, AZ	131,346	125,447
43460		Sikeston, MO Micro Area	39,191	38,059
43460	29201	Scott County, MO	39,191	38,059
43500		Silver City, NM Micro Area	29,514	28,185
43500	35017	Grant County, NM	29,514	28,185
43580		Sioux City, IA-NE-SD Metro Area	143,577	149,940
43580	19193	Woodbury County, IA	102,172	105,941
43580	31043	Dakota County, NE	21,006	21,582
43580	31051	Dixon County, NE	6,000	5,606
43580	46127	Union County, SD	14,399	16,811
43620		Sioux Falls, SD Metro Area	228,261	276,730
43620	46083	Lincoln County, SD	44,828	65,161
43620	46087	McCook County, SD	5,618	5,682
43620	46099	Minnehaha County, SD	169,468	197,214
43620	46125	Turner County, SD	8,347	8,673
43660		Snyder, TX Micro Area	16,921	16,932
43660	48415	Scurry County, TX	16,921	16,932
43700		Somerset, KY Micro Area	63,063	65,034
43700	21199	Pulaski County, KY	63,063	65,034
43740		Somerset, PA Micro Area	77,742	74,129
43740	42111	Somerset County, PA	77,742	74,129
43760		Sonora, CA Micro Area	55,365	55,620
43760	06109	Tuolumne County, CA	55,365	55,620
43780		South Bend-Mishawaka, IN-MI Metro Area	319,224	324,501
43780	18141	St. Joseph County, IN	266,931	272,912
43780	26027	Cass County, MI	52,293	51,589
43900		Spartanburg, SC Metro Area	284,307	327,997
43900	45083	Spartanburg County, SC	284,307	327,997
43940		Spearfish, SD Micro Area	24,097	25,768
43940	46081	Lawrence County, SD	24,097	25,768
43980		Spencer, IA Micro Area	16,667	16,384
43980	19041	Clay County, IA	16,667	16,384
44020		Spirit Lake, IA Micro Area	16,667	17,703
44020	19059	Dickinson County, IA	16,667	17,703
44060		Spokane-Spokane Valley, WA Metro Area	514,752	585,784
44060	53063	Spokane County, WA	471,221	539,339
44060	53065	Stevens County, WA	43,531	46,445
44100		Springfield, IL Metro Area	210,170	208,640
44100	17129	Menard County, IL	12,705	12,297
44100	17167	Sangamon County, IL	197,465	196,343
44140		Springfield, MA Metro Area	692,942	699,162
44140	25011	Franklin County, MA	71,372	71,029
44140	25013	Hampden County, MA	463,490	465,825
44140	25015	Hampshire County, MA	158,080	162,308
44180		Springfield, MO Metro Area	436,712	475,432
44180	29043	Christian County, MO	77,422	88,842
44180	29059	Dallas County, MO	16,777	17,071
44180	29077	Greene County, MO	275,174	298,915
44180	29167	Polk County, MO	31,137	31,519
44180	29225	Webster County, MO	36,202	39,085
44220		Springfield, OH Metro Area	138,333	136,001
44220	39023	Clark County, OH	138,333	136,001
44260		Starkville, MS Micro Area	57,924	61,714
44260	28105	Oktibbeha County, MS	47,671	51,788
44260	28155	Webster County, MS	10,253	9,926
44300		State College, PA Metro Area	153,990	158,172
44300	42027	Centre County, PA	153,990	158,172

CORE-BASED STATISTICAL AREAS (Metropolitan and Micropolitan), METROPOLITAN DIVISIONS, AND COMPONENTS (as defined March, 2020)—*Continued*

Core based statistical area	State/ County FIPS code	Title and Geographic Components	2010 Census Population	2020 Census Population
44340		Statesboro, GA Micro Area	70,217	81,099
44340	13031	Bulloch County, GA	70,217	81,099
44420		Staunton, VA Metro Area	118,502	125,433
44420	51015	Augusta County, VA	73,750	77,487
44420	51790	Staunton city, VA	23,746	25,750
44420	51820	Waynesboro city, VA	21,006	22,196
44460		Steamboat Springs, CO Micro Area	23,509	24,829
44460	08107	Routt County, CO	23,509	24,829
44500		Stephenville, TX Micro Area	37,890	42,545
44500	48143	Erath County, TX	37,890	42,545
44540		Sterling, CO Micro Area	22,709	21,528
44540	08075	Logan County, CO	22,709	21,528
44580		Sterling, IL Micro Area	58,498	55,691
44580	17195	Whiteside County, IL	58,498	55,691
44620		Stevens Point, WI Micro Area	70,019	70,377
44620	55097	Portage County, WI	70,019	70,377
44660		Stillwater, OK Micro Area	77,350	81,646
44660	40119	Payne County, OK	77,350	81,646
44700		Stockton, CA Metro Area	685,306	779,233
44700	06077	San Joaquin County, CA	685,306	779,233
44740		Storm Lake, IA Micro Area	20,260	20,823
44740	19021	Buena Vista County, IA	20,260	20,823
44780		Sturgis, MI Micro Area	61,295	60,939
44780	26149	St. Joseph County, MI	61,295	60,939
44860		Sulphur Springs, TX Micro Area	35,161	36,787
44860	48223	Hopkins County, TX	35,161	36,787
44900		Summerville, GA Micro Area	26,015	24,965
44900	13055	Chattooga County, GA	26,015	24,965
44940		Sumter, SC Metro Area	142,427	136,700
44940	45027	Clarendon County, SC	34,971	31,144
44940	45085	Sumter County, SC	107,456	105,556
44980		Sunbury, PA Micro Area	94,528	91,647
44980	42097	Northumberland County, PA	94,528	91,647
45000		Susanville, CA Micro Area	34,895	32,730
45000	06035	Lassen County, CA	34,895	32,730
45020		Sweetwater, TX Micro Area	15,216	14,738
45020	48353	Nolan County, TX	15,216	14,738
45060		Syracuse, NY Metro Area	662,577	662,057
45060	36053	Madison County, NY	73,442	68,016
45060	36067	Onondaga County, NY	467,026	476,516
45060	36075	Oswego County, NY	122,109	117,525
45140		Tahlequah, OK Micro Area	46,987	47,078
45140	40021	Cherokee County, OK	46,987	47,078
45180		Talladega-Sylacauga, AL Micro Area	82,291	82,149
45180	01121	Talladega County, AL	82,291	82,149
45220		Tallahassee, FL Metro Area	367,413	384,298
45220	12039	Gadsden County, FL	46,389	43,826
45220	12065	Jefferson County, FL	14,761	14,510
45220	12073	Leon County, FL	275,487	292,198
45220	12129	Wakulla County, FL	30,776	33,764
45300		Tampa-St. Petersburg-Clearwater, FL Metro Area	2,783,243	3,175,275
45300	12053	Hernando County, FL	172,778	194,515
45300	12057	Hillsborough County, FL	1,229,226	1,459,762
45300	12101	Pasco County, FL	464,697	561,891
45300	12103	Pinellas County, FL	916,542	959,107
45340		Taos, NM Micro Area	32,937	34,489
45340	35055	Taos County, NM	32,937	34,489
45380		Taylorville, IL Micro Area	34,800	34,032
45380	17021	Christian County, IL	34,800	34,032
45460		Terre Haute, IN Metro Area	189,764	185,031
45460	18021	Clay County, IN	26,890	26,466
45460	18121	Parke County, IN	17,339	16,156
45460	18153	Sullivan County, IN	21,475	20,817
45460	18165	Vermillion County, IN	16,212	15,439
45460	18167	Vigo County, IN	107,848	106,153
45500		Texarkana, TX-AR Metro Area	149,198	147,519
45500	48037	Bowie County, TX	92,565	12,026
45500	05081	Little River County, AR	13,171	42,600
45500	05091	Miller County, AR	43,462	92,893
45520		The Dalles, OR Micro Area	25,213	26,670
45520	41065	Wasco County, OR	25,213	26,670
45540		The Villages, FL Metro Area	93,420	129,752
45540	12119	Sumter County, FL	93,420	129,752
45580		Thomaston, GA Micro Area	27,153	27,700
45580	13293	Upson County, GA	27,153	27,700
45620		Thomasville, GA Micro Area	44,720	45,798
45620	13275	Thomas County, GA	44,720	45,798
45660		Tiffin, OH Micro Area	56,745	55,069
45660	39147	Seneca County, OH	56,745	55,069
45700		Tifton, GA Micro Area	40,118	41,344
45700	13277	Tift County, GA	40,118	41,344
45740		Toccoa, GA Micro Area	26,175	26,784
45740	13257	Stephens County, GA	26,175	26,784
45780		Toledo, OH Metro Area	651,429	646,604
45780	39051	Fulton County, OH	42,698	42,713
45780	39095	Lucas County, OH	441,815	431,279
45780	39123	Ottawa County, OH	41,428	40,364
45780	39173	Wood County, OH	125,488	132,248
45820		Topeka, KS Metro Area	233,870	233,152
45820	20085	Jackson County, KS	13,462	13,232
45820	20087	Jefferson County, KS	19,126	18,368
45820	20139	Osage County, KS	16,295	15,766
45820	20177	Shawnee County, KS	177,934	178,909
45820	20197	Wabaunsee County, KS	7,053	6,877

CORE-BASED STATISTICAL AREAS (Metropolitan and Micropolitan), METROPOLITAN DIVISIONS, AND COMPONENTS (as defined March, 2020)—*Continued*

Core based statistical area	State/ County FIPS code	Title and Geographic Components	2010 Census Population	2020 Census Population
45860		Torrington, CT Micro Area	189,927	185,186
45860	09005	Litchfield County, CT	189,927	185,186
45900		Traverse City, MI Micro Area	143,372	153,448
45900	26019	Benzie County, MI	17,525	17,970
45900	26055	Grand Traverse County, MI	86,986	95,238
45900	26079	Kalkaska County, MI	17,153	17,939
45900	26089	Leelanau County, MI	21,708	22,301
45940		Trenton-Princeton, NJ Metro Area	366,513	387,340
45940	34021	Mercer County, NJ	366,513	387,340
45980		Troy, AL Micro Area	32,899	33,009
45980	01109	Pike County, AL	32,899	33,009
46020		Truckee-Grass Valley, CA Micro Area	98,764	102,241
46020	06057	Nevada County, CA	98,764	102,241
46060		Tucson, AZ Metro Area	980,263	1,043,433
46060	04019	Pima County, AZ	980,263	1,043,433
46100		Tullahoma-Manchester, TN Micro Area	100,210	107,124
46100	47031	Coffee County, TN	52,796	57,889
46100	47051	Franklin County, TN	41,052	42,774
46100	47127	Moore County, TN	6,362	6,461
46140		Tulsa, OK Metro Area	937,478	1,015,331
46140	40037	Creek County, OK	69,967	71,754
46140	40111	Okmulgee County, OK	40,069	36,706
46140	40113	Osage County, OK	47,472	45,818
46140	40117	Pawnee County, OK	16,577	15,553
46140	40131	Rogers County, OK	86,905	95,240
46140	40143	Tulsa County, OK	603,403	669,279
46140	40145	Wagoner County, OK	73,085	80,981
46180		Tupelo, MS Micro Area	161,544	163,398
46180	28057	Itawamba County, MS	23,401	23,863
46180	28081	Lee County, MS	82,910	83,343
46180	28115	Pontotoc County, MS	29,957	31,184
46180	28117	Prentiss County, MS	25,276	25,008
46220		Tuscaloosa, AL Metro Area	239,207	268,674
46220	01063	Greene County, AL	9,045	7,730
46220	01065	Hale County, AL	15,760	14,785
46220	01107	Pickens County, AL	19,746	19,123
46220	01125	Tuscaloosa County, AL	194,656	227,036
46300		Twin Falls, ID Metro Area	99,604	114,283
46300	16053	Jerome County, ID	22,374	24,237
46300	16083	Twin Falls County, ID	77,230	90,046
46340		Tyler, TX Metro Area	209,714	233,479
46340	48423	Smith County, TX	209,714	233,479
46380		Ukiah, CA Micro Area	87,841	91,601
46380	06045	Mendocino County, CA	87,841	91,601
46420		Union, SC Micro Area	28,961	27,244
46420	45087	Union County, SC	28,961	27,244
46460		Union City, TN Micro Area	31,807	30,787
46460	47131	Obion County, TN	31,807	30,787
46500		Urbana, OH Micro Area	40,097	38,714
46500	39021	Champaign County, OH	40,097	38,714
46520		Urban Honolulu, HI Metro Area	953,207	1,016,508
46520	15003	Honolulu County, HI	953,207	1,016,508
46540		Utica-Rome, NY Metro Area	299,397	292,264
46540	36043	Herkimer County, NY	64,519	60,139
46540	36065	Oneida County, NY	234,878	232,125
46620		Uvalde, TX Micro Area	26,405	24,564
46620	48463	Uvalde County, TX	26,405	24,564
46660		Valdosta, GA Metro Area	139,588	148,126
46660	13027	Brooks County, GA	16,243	16,301
46660	13101	Echols County, GA	4,034	3,697
46660	13173	Lanier County, GA	10,078	9,877
46660	13185	Lowndes County, GA	109,233	118,251
46700		Vallejo, CA Metro Area	413,344	453,491
46700	06095	Solano County, CA	413,344	453,491
46780		Van Wert, OH Micro Area	28,744	28,931
46780	39161	Van Wert County, OH	28,744	28,931
46820		Vermillion, SD Micro Area	13,864	14,967
46820	46027	Clay County, SD	13,864	14,967
46860		Vernal, UT Micro Area	32,588	35,620
46860	49047	Uintah County, UT	32,588	35,620
46900		Vernon, TX Micro Area	13,535	12,887
46900	48487	Wilbarger County, TX	13,535	12,887
46980		Vicksburg, MS Micro Area	48,773	44,722
46980	28149	Warren County, MS	48,773	44,722
47020		Victoria, TX Metro Area	94,003	98,331
47020	48175	Goliad County, TX	7,210	7,012
47020	48469	Victoria County, TX	86,793	91,319
47080		Vidalia, GA Micro Area	36,346	35,640
47080	13209	Montgomery County, GA	9,123	8,610
47080	13279	Toombs County, GA	27,223	27,030
47180		Vincennes, IN Micro Area	38,440	36,282
47180	18083	Knox County, IN	38,440	36,282
47220		Vineland-Bridgeton, NJ Metro Area	156,898	154,152
47220	34011	Cumberland County, NJ	156,898	154,152
47240		Vineyard Haven, MA Micro Area	16,535	20,600
47240	25007	Dukes County, MA	16,535	20,600

CORE-BASED STATISTICAL AREAS (Metropolitan and Micropolitan), METROPOLITAN DIVISIONS, AND COMPONENTS (as defined March, 2020)—*Continued*

Core based statistical area	State/ County FIPS code	Title and Geographic Components	2010 Census Population	2020 Census Population
47260		Virginia Beach-Norfolk-Newport News, VA-NC Metro Area	1,713,954	1,799,674
47260	37029	Camden County, NC	9,980	10,355
47260	37053	Currituck County, NC	23,547	28,100
47260	37073	Gates County, NC	12,197	10,478
47260	51073	Gloucester County, VA	36,858	38,711
47260	51093	Isle of Wight County, VA	35,270	38,606
47260	51095	James City County, VA	67,009	78,254
47260	51115	Mathews County, VA	8,978	8,533
47260	51175	Southampton County, VA	18,570	17,996
47260	51199	York County, VA	65,464	70,045
47260	51550	Chesapeake city, VA	222,209	249,422
47260	51620	Franklin city, VA	8,582	8,180
47260	51650	Hampton city, VA	137,436	137,148
47260	51700	Newport News city, VA	180,719	186,247
47260	51710	Norfolk city, VA	242,803	238,005
47260	51735	Poquoson city, VA	12,150	12,460
47260	51740	Portsmouth city, VA	95,535	97,915
47260	51800	Suffolk city, VA	84,585	94,324
47260	51810	Virginia Beach city, VA	437,994	459,470
47260	51830	Williamsburg city, VA	14,068	15,425
47300		Visalia, CA Metro Area	442,179	473,117
47300	06107	Tulare County, CA	442,179	473,117
47340		Wabash, IN Micro Area	32,888	30,976
47340	18169	Wabash County, IN	32,888	30,976
47380		Waco, TX Metro Area	252,772	277,547
47380	48145	Falls County, TX	17,866	16,968
47380	48309	McLennan County, TX	234,906	260,579
47420		Wahpeton, ND-MN Micro Area	22,897	23,035
47420	27167	Wilkin County, MN	6,576	6,506
47420	38077	Richland County, ND	16,321	16,529
47460		Walla Walla, WA Metro Area	58,781	62,584
47460	53071	Walla Walla County, WA	58,781	62,584
47540		Wapakoneta, OH Micro Area	45,949	46,422
47540	39011	Auglaize County, OH	45,949	46,422
47580		Warner Robins, GA Metro Area	167,595	191,614
47580	13153	Houston County, GA	139,900	163,633
47580	13225	Peach County, GA	27,695	27,981
47620		Warren, PA Micro Area	41,815	38,587
47620	42123	Warren County, PA	41,815	38,587
47660		Warrensburg, MO Micro Area	52,595	54,013
47660	29101	Johnson County, MO	52,595	54,013
47700		Warsaw, IN Micro Area	77,358	80,240
47700	18085	Kosciusko County, IN	77,358	80,240
47780		Washington, IN Micro Area	31,648	33,381
47780	18027	Daviess County, IN	31,648	33,381
47820		Washington, NC Micro Area	47,759	44,652
47820	37013	Beaufort County, NC	47,759	44,652
47900		Washington-Arlington-Alexandria, DC-VA-MD-WV Metro Area	5,649,540	6,385,162
47900		Frederick-Gaithersburg-Rockville, MD Division 23224	1,205,162	1,333,778
47900	24021	Frederick County, MD	233,385	271,717
47900	24031	Montgomery County, MD	971,777	1,062,061
47900		Washington-Arlington-Alexandria, DC-VA-MD-WV Division 47894	4,444,378	5,051,384
47900	11001	District of Columbia, DC	601,723	689,545
47900	24009	Calvert County, MD	88,737	92,783
47900	24017	Charles County, MD	146,551	166,617
47900	24033	Prince George's County, MD	863,420	967,201
47900	51013	Arlington County, VA	207,627	238,643
47900	51043	Clarke County, VA	14,034	14,783
47900	51047	Culpeper County, VA	46,689	52,552
47900	51059	Fairfax County, VA	1,081,726	1,150,309
47900	51061	Fauquier County, VA	65,203	72,972
47900	51107	Loudoun County, VA	312,311	420,959
47900	51113	Madison County, VA	13,308	13,837
47900	51153	Prince William County, VA	402,002	482,204
47900	51157	Rappahannock County, VA	7,373	7,348
47900	51177	Spotsylvania County, VA	122,397	140,032
47900	51179	Stafford County, VA	128,961	156,927
47900	51187	Warren County, VA	37,575	40,727
47900	51510	Alexandria city, VA	139,966	159,467
47900	51600	Fairfax city, VA	22,565	24,146
47900	51610	Falls Church city, VA	12,332	14,658
47900	51630	Fredericksburg city, VA	24,286	27,982
47900	51683	Manassas city, VA	37,821	42,772
47900	51685	Manassas Park city, VA	14,273	17,219
47900	54037	Jefferson County, WV	53,498	57,701
47920		Washington Court House, OH Micro Area	29,030	28,951
47920	39047	Fayette County, OH	29,030	28,951
47940		Waterloo-Cedar Falls, IA Metro Area	167,819	168,461
47940	19013	Black Hawk County, IA	131,090	131,144
47940	19017	Bremer County, IA	24,276	24,988
47940	19075	Grundy County, IA	12,453	12,329
47980		Watertown, SD Micro Area	33,130	34,489
47980	46029	Codington County, SD	27,227	28,325
47980	46057	Hamlin County, SD	5,903	6,164
48020		Watertown-Fort Atkinson, WI Micro Area	83,686	84,900
48020	55055	Jefferson County, WI	83,686	84,900
48060		Watertown-Fort Drum, NY Metro Area	116,229	116,721
48060	36045	Jefferson County, NY	116,229	116,721
48100		Wauchula, FL Micro Area	27,731	25,327
48100	12049	Hardee County, FL	27,731	25,327
48140		Wausau-Weston, WI Metro Area	162,806	166,428
48140	55069	Lincoln County, WI	28,743	28,415
48140	55073	Marathon County, WI	134,063	138,013
48180		Waycross, GA Micro Area	55,070	55,967
48180	13229	Pierce County, GA	18,758	19,716
48180	13299	Ware County, GA	36,312	36,251
48220		Weatherford, OK Micro Area	27,469	28,513
48220	40039	Custer County, OK	27,469	28,513

CORE-BASED STATISTICAL AREAS (Metropolitan and Micropolitan), METROPOLITAN DIVISIONS, AND COMPONENTS (as defined March, 2020)—*Continued*

Core based statistical area	State/ County FIPS code	Title and Geographic Components	2010 Census Population	2020 Census Population
48260		Weirton-Steubenville, WV-OH Metro Area	124,454	116,903
48260	39081	Jefferson County, OH	69,709	65,249
48260	54009	Brooke County, WV	24,069	22,559
48260	54029	Hancock County, WV	30,676	29,095
48300		Wenatchee, WA Metro Area	110,884	122,012
48300	53007	Chelan County, WA	72,453	79,074
48300	53017	Douglas County, WA	38,431	42,938
48460		West Plains, MO Micro Area	40,400	39,750
48460	29091	Howell County, MO	40,400	39,750
48500		West Point, MS Micro Area	20,634	18,636
48500	28025	Clay County, MS	20,634	18,636
48540		Wheeling, WV-OH Metro Area	147,950	139,513
48540	39013	Belmont County, OH	70,400	66,497
48540	54051	Marshall County, WV	33,107	30,591
48540	54069	Ohio County, WV	44,443	42,425
48580		Whitewater, WI Micro Area	102,228	106,478
48580	55127	Walworth County, WI	102,228	106,478
48620		Wichita, KS Metro Area	623,061	647,610
48620	20015	Butler County, KS	65,880	67,380
48620	20079	Harvey County, KS	34,684	34,024
48620	20173	Sedgwick County, KS	498,365	523,824
48620	20191	Sumner County, KS	24,132	22,382
48660		Wichita Falls, TX Metro Area	151,306	148,128
48660	48009	Archer County, TX	9,054	8,560
48660	48077	Clay County, TX	10,752	10,218
48660	48485	Wichita County, TX	131,500	129,350
48700		Williamsport, PA Metro Area	116,111	114,188
48700	42081	Lycoming County, PA	116,111	114,188
48780		Williston, ND Micro Area	22,398	40,950
48780	38105	Williams County, ND	22,398	40,950
48820		Willmar, MN Micro Area	42,239	43,732
48820	27067	Kandiyohi County, MN	42,239	43,732
48900		Wilmington, NC Metro Area	254,884	285,905
48900	37129	New Hanover County, NC	202,667	225,702
48900	37141	Pender County, NC	52,217	60,203
48940		Wilmington, OH Micro Area	42,040	42,018
48940	39027	Clinton County, OH	42,040	42,018
48980		Wilson, NC Micro Area	81,234	78,784
48980	37195	Wilson County, NC	81,234	78,784
49020		Winchester, VA-WV Metro Area	128,472	142,632
49020	51069	Frederick County, VA	78,305	91,419
49020	51840	Winchester city, VA	26,203	28,120
49020	54027	Hampshire County, WV	23,964	23,093
49060		Winfield, KS Micro Area	36,311	34,549
49060	20035	Cowley County, KS	36,311	34,549
49080		Winnemucca, NV Micro Area	16,528	17,285
49080	32013	Humboldt County, NV	16,528	17,285
49100		Winona, MN Micro Area	51,461	49,671
49100	27169	Winona County, MN	51,461	49,671
49180		Winston-Salem, NC Metro Area	640,595	675,966
49180	37057	Davidson County, NC	162,878	168,930
49180	37059	Davie County, NC	41,240	42,712
49180	37067	Forsyth County, NC	350,670	382,590
49180	37169	Stokes County, NC	47,401	44,520
49180	37197	Yadkin County, NC	38,406	37,214
49220		Wisconsin Rapids-Marshfield, WI Micro Area	74,749	74,207
49220	55141	Wood County, WI	74,749	74,207
49260		Woodward, OK Micro Area	24,232	24,219
49260	40045	Ellis County, OK	4,151	3,749
49260	40153	Woodward County, OK	20,081	20,470
49300		Wooster, OH Micro Area	114,520	116,894
49300	39169	Wayne County, OH	114,520	116,894
49340		Worcester, MA-CT Metro Area	916,980	978,529
49340	25027	Worcester County, MA	798,552	116,418
49340	09015	Windham County, CT	118,428	862,111
49380		Worthington, MN Micro Area	21,378	22,290
49380	27105	Nobles County, MN	21,378	22,290
49420		Yakima, WA Metro Area	243,231	256,728
49420	53077	Yakima County, WA	243,231	256,728
49460		Yankton, SD Micro Area	22,438	23,310
49460	46135	Yankton County, SD	22,438	23,310
49620		York-Hanover, PA Metro Area	434,972	456,438
49620	42133	York County, PA	434,972	456,438
49660		Youngstown-Warren-Boardman, OH-PA Metro Area	565,773	541,243
49660	39099	Mahoning County, OH	238,823	228,614
49660	39155	Trumbull County, OH	210,312	201,977
49660	42085	Mercer County, PA	116,638	110,652
49700		Yuba City, CA Metro Area	166,892	181,208
49700	06101	Sutter County, CA	94,737	99,633
49700	06115	Yuba County, CA	72,155	81,575
49740		Yuma, AZ Metro Area	195,751	203,881
49740	04027	Yuma County, AZ	195,751	203,881
49780		Zanesville, OH Micro Area	86,074	86,410
49780	39119	Muskingum County, OH	86,074	86,410
49820		Zapata, TX Micro Area	14,018	13,889
49820	48505	Zapata County, TX	14,018	13,889

APPENDIX D
CHANGES TO METROPOLITAN AREAS IN THE DELINEATIONS OF OMB BULLETIN 18-04

A map of the core-based statistical areas from OMB Bulletin 18-04 is available at https://www2.census.gov/geo/maps/metroarea/us_wall/Sep2018/CBSA_WallMap_Sep2018.pdf?#

Albany, GA, lost Baker County
Albany-Lebanon, OR, has a new name
Ames, IA, added Boone County
Atlanta-Sandy Springs-Alpharetta, GA, has a new name
Baton Rouge, LA, added Assumption Parish
Beaumont-Port Arthur, TX, lost Newton County
Bend, OR, has a new name
Billings, MT, added Stillwater County and lost Golden Valley County
Birmingham-Hoover, AL, lost Walker County
Bismarck, ND, lost Sioux County
Blacksburg-Christiansburg, VA, has a new name and lost Floyd County
Bloomington, IL, lost De Witt County
Bremerton-Silverdale-Port Orchard, WA, has a new name
Buffalo-Cheektowaga, NY, has a new name
Carbondale-Marion, IL, added Johnson County
Champaign-Urbana, IL, lost Ford County
Charleston, WV, added Jackson and Lincoln counties
Charlotte-Concord-Gastonia, NC-SC, added Anson County, NC
The Chicago-Naperville-Evanston, IL Division, in the Chicago-Naperville-Elgin, IL-IN-WI Metro area, has a new name and new CBSA code; this Division lost Kendall County, which has been added to the Elgin, IL Division
Cincinnati, OH-KY-IN, added Franklin County, IN
Clarksville, TN-KY, added Stewart County, TN
Columbus, GA-AL, added Stewart and Talbot counties, GA
Corpus Christi, TX, lost Aransas County
The Fort Worth-Arlington, TX Division in the Dallas-Fort Worth-Arlington, TX Metro area, lost Hood and Somervell counties
Dayton-Kettering, OH, has a new name and a new CBSA code
Des Moines-West Des Moines, IA, added Jasper County
Duluth, MN-WI, added Lake County, MN
Durham-Chapel Hill, NC, added Granville County
Fayetteville, NC, added Harnett County
Fayetteville-Springdale-Rogers, AR, lost McDonald County, MO
Fort Smith, AR-OK, added Franklin County, AR, and lost Le Flore County, OK
Fort Wayne, IN, lost Wells County
Gainesville, FL, added Levy County
Grand Island, NE, lost Hamilton County
Grand Rapids-Kentwood, MI, has a new name and added Ionia County
Greenville-Anderson, SC, has a new name
Gulfport-Biloxi, MS, has a new name and added Stone County
Hagerstown-Martinsburg, MD-WV, added Morgan County, WV
Hattiesburg, MS, added Covington County
Hilton Head Island-Bluffton, NC, has a new name
Huntington-Ashland, WV-KY-OH, added Carter County, KY, and lost Lincoln County, WV
Jackson, MS, added Holmes County
Jackson, TN, added Gibson County
Kahului-Wailuku-Lahaina, HI, lost Kalawao County
Kalamazoo-Portage, MI, lost Van Buren County
Kingsport-Bristol, TN-VA, has a new name
Lafayette-West Lafayette, IN, added Warren County
Lansing-East Lansing, MI, added Shiawassee County
Longview, TX, added Harrison County
Louisville/Jefferson County, KY-IN, lost Scott County, IN, and Trimble County, KY
Lynchburg, VA, lost Bedford city, but it stayed in the Metro area because it was absorbed by Bedford County
Macon-Bibb County, GA, has a new name
Manhattan, KS, added Geary County
Memphis, TN-MS-AR, lost Benton County, MS
Miami-Fort Lauderdale-Pompano Beach, FL, has a new name, as do two of its three Divisions: Fort Lauderdale-Pompano Beach-Sunrise Division and West Palm Beach-Boca Raton-Boynton Beach Division
Minneapolis-St. Paul-Bloomington, MN-WI, lost Sibley County, MN
Mobile, AL, added Washington County
Monroe, LA, added Morehouse County
Morrison, TN, added Granger County
Naples-Marco Island, FL, has a new name
Nashville-Davidson-Murfreesboro-Franklin, TN, lost Hickman County
The New York-Newark-Jersey City, NY-NJ-PA, Metro Area lost the Dutchess County-Putnam County Division, with Dutchess County moving out of the Metro area to the new Poughkeepsie-Newburgh-Middletown, NY, Metro Area. The Newark, NJ-PA, Division, lost Somerset County. New Brunswick-Lakewood, NJ, was established as a new Division

with Middlesex, Monmouth, Ocean, and Somerset counties. The New York-Jersey City-White Plains, NY-NJ Division lost Orange County, NY, and Middlesex, Monmouth, and Ocean counties, NJ, but added Putnam County, NY

Olympia-Lacey-Tumwater, WA, has a new name

Panama City, FL, lost Gulf County

Peoria, IL, added Fulton County

Phoenix-Mesa-Chandler, AZ, has a new name

Pocatello, ID, added Power County

Prescott Valley-Prescott, AZ, has a new name

Poughkeepsie-Newburgh-Middletown, NY, is a new Metropolitan Area, consisting of Dutchess and Orange counties, which were previously in the New York Metropolitan Area

Raleigh-Cary, NC, has a new name

Rapid City, SD, lost Custer County

Richmond, VA, added King and Queen County

Sacramento-Roseville-Folsom, CA, has a new name

St. Louis, MO-IL, added the part of Sullivan city that is in Crawford County, MO

San Angelo, TX, added Sterling County

San Diego-Chula Vista-Carlsbad, CA, has a new name

San Francisco-Oakland-Berkeley, CA, has a new name, as do two of its Divisions: Oakland-Berkeley-Livermore and San Francisco-Redwood City-San Mateo

San Luis Obispo-Paso Robles, CA, has a new name

Santa Rosa-Petaluma, CA, has a new name

Scranton-Wilkes Barre, PA, has a new name

The Seattle-Bellevue-Kent, WA Division in the Seattle-Tacoma-Bellevue Metropolitan area has a new name

Sebring-Avon Park, FL, has a new name

Shreveport-Bossier City, LA, lost Webster Parish

Sioux City, IA-NE-SD, lost Plymouth County, IA

Spartanburg, SC, lost Union County

Spokane-Spokane Valley, WA, dopped Pend Oreille County

Springfield, MA, added Franklin County

Staunton, VA, has a new name

Stockton, CA, has a new name

Sumter, SC, added Clarendon County

Terre Haute, IN, added Parke County

Toledo, OH, added Ottawa County

Trenton-Princeton, NJ, has a new name

Tuscaloosa, AL, added Greene County

Twin Falls, ID, formerly a Micropolitan area, became a Metropolitan area consisting of Jerome and Twin Falls counties

Vallejo, CA, has a new name

Virginia Beach-Norfolk-Newport News, VA-NC, added Camden County, NC, and Southampton County and Franklin City, VA

Visalia, CA, has a new name

Walla Walla, WA, lost Columbia County

Warner Robins, GA, lost Pulaski County

The Frederick-Gaithersburg-Rockville, MD Division, in the Washington-Arlington-Alexandria, DC-VA-MD-WV Metropolitan area, has a new name and Division code, and the Washington-Arlington-Alexandria, DC-VA-MD-WV Division added Madison County, VA

Wausau-Weston, WI, added Lincoln County

Wichita, KS, lost Kingman County

APPENDIX E
CITIES BY COUNTY

The following table is arranged alphabetically by state. Under each state heading are listed all cities with a 2020 census population of 25,000 or more, along with their component counties and the population in each component.

State code	Place code	County code	Geographic Area Name	2020 census population
01			**ALABAMA**	5,024,279
01	00820		Alabaster city	33,360
01	00820	117	Shelby County	33,360
01	02956		Athens city	25,420
01	02956	083	Limestone County	25,420
01	03076		Auburn city	76,000
01	03076	081	Lee County	76,000
01	05980		Bessemer city	26,044
01	05980	073	Jefferson County	26,044
01	07000		Birmingham city	200,763
01	07000	073	Jefferson County	198,855
01	07000	117	Shelby County	1,908
01	19648		Daphne city	27,525
01	19648	003	Baldwin County	27,525
01	20104		Decatur city	57,851
01	20104	083	Limestone County	55
01	20104	103	Morgan County	57,796
01	21184		Dothan city	71,182
01	21184	045	Dale County	1,522
01	21184	067	Henry County	1
01	21184	069	Houston County	69,659
01	24184		Enterprise city	28,752
01	24184	031	Coffee County	28,140
01	24184	045	Dale County	612
01	26896		Florence city	39,783
01	26896	077	Lauderdale County	39,783
01	28696		Gadsden city	34,070
01	28696	055	Etowah County	34,070
01	35800		Homewood city	26,388
01	35800	073	Jefferson County	26,388
01	35896		Hoover city	92,651
01	35896	073	Jefferson County	66,016
01	35896	117	Shelby County	26,635
01	37000		Huntsville city	214,372
01	37000	083	Limestone County	4,403
01	37000	089	Madison County	209,966
01	37000	103	Morgan County	3
01	45784		Madison city	57,124
01	45784	083	Limestone County	11,260
01	45784	089	Madison County	45,864
01	50000		Mobile city	186,833
01	50000	097	Mobile County	186,833
01	51000		Montgomery city	200,567
01	51000	101	Montgomery County	200,567
01	55200		Northport city	31,119
01	55200	125	Tuscaloosa County	31,119
01	57048		Opelika city	31,039
01	57048	081	Lee County	31,039
01	59472		Phenix City city	38,819
01	59472	081	Lee County	6,786
01	59472	113	Russell County	32,033
01	62328		Prattville city	37,813
01	62328	001	Autauga County	35,895
01	62328	051	Elmore County	1,918
01	76944		Trussville city	26,160
01	76944	073	Jefferson County	24,176
01	76944	115	St. Clair County	1,984
01	77256		Tuscaloosa city	99,706
01	77256	125	Tuscaloosa County	99,706
01	78552		Vestavia Hills city	39,166
01	78552	073	Jefferson County	39,136
01	78552	117	Shelby County	30
02			**ALASKA**	733,391
02	03000		Anchorage municipality	291,247
02	03000	020	Anchorage Municipality	291,247
02	24230		Fairbanks city	32,744
02	24230	090	Fairbanks North Star Borough	32,744
02	36400		Juneau city and borough	32,255
02	36400	110	Juneau City and Borough	32,255
04			**ARIZONA**	7,151,502
04	02830		Apache Junction city	38,675
04	02830	013	Maricopa County	391
04	02830	021	Pinal County	38,284
04	04720		Avondale city	89,490
04	04720	013	Maricopa County	89,490
04	07940		Buckeye city	91,154
04	07940	013	Maricopa County	91,154
04	08220		Bullhead City city	41,403
04	08220	015	Mohave County	41,403
04	10530		Casa Grande city	53,891
04	10530	021	Pinal County	53,891
04	12000		Chandler city	276,330
04	12000	013	Maricopa County	276,330
04	22220		El Mirage city	35,858
04	22220	013	Maricopa County	35,858
04	23620		Flagstaff city	76,781
04	23620	005	Coconino County	76,781
04	23760		Florence town	25,428
04	23760	021	Pinal County	25,428
04	27400		Gilbert town	268,302
04	27400	013	Maricopa County	268,302
04	27820		Glendale city	248,345
04	27820	013	Maricopa County	248,345

CITIES BY COUNTY—*Continued*

State code	Place code	County code	Geographic Area Name	2020 census population
04	28380		Goodyear city	95,003
04	28380	013	Maricopa County	95,003
04	37620		Kingman city	32,680
04	37620	015	Mohave County	32,680
04	39370		Lake Havasu City city	57,204
04	39370	015	Mohave County	57,204
04	44270		Marana town	52,020
04	44270	019	Pima County	52,020
04	44270	021	Pinal County	0
04	44410		Maricopa city	58,442
04	44410	021	Pinal County	58,442
04	46000		Mesa city	504,500
04	46000	013	Maricopa County	504,500
04	51600		Oro Valley town	47,185
04	51600	019	Pima County	47,185
04	54050		Peoria city	191,052
04	54050	013	Maricopa County	191,052
04	54050	025	Yavapai County	0
04	55000		Phoenix city	1,607,739
04	55000	013	Maricopa County	1,607,739
04	57380		Prescott city	45,683
04	57380	025	Yavapai County	45,683
04	57450		Prescott Valley town	46,811
04	57450	025	Yavapai County	46,811
04	58150		Queen Creek town	59,590
04	58150	013	Maricopa County	50,223
04	58150	021	Pinal County	9,367
04	62140		Sahuarita town	34,222
04	62140	019	Pima County	34,222
04	63470		San Luis city	35,905
04	63470	027	Yuma County	35,905
04	65000		Scottsdale city	241,488
04	65000	013	Maricopa County	241,488
04	66820		Sierra Vista city	45,321
04	66820	003	Cochise County	45,321
04	71510		Surprise city	143,261
04	71510	013	Maricopa County	143,261
04	73000		Tempe city	179,765
04	73000	013	Maricopa County	179,765
04	77000		Tucson city	541,349
04	77000	019	Pima County	541,349
04	85540		Yuma city	95,814
04	85540	027	Yuma County	95,814
05			**ARKANSAS**	3,011,524
05	04840		Bella Vista city	30,202
05	04840	007	Benton County	30,202
05	05290		Benton city	35,011
05	05290	125	Saline County	35,011
05	05320		Bentonville city	54,120
05	05320	007	Benton County	54,120
05	10300		Cabot city	26,573
05	10300	085	Lonoke County	26,573
05	15190		Conway city	63,656
05	15190	045	Faulkner County	63,656
05	23290		Fayetteville city	93,582
05	23290	143	Washington County	93,582
05	24550		Fort Smith city	89,177
05	24550	131	Sebastian County	89,177
05	33400		Hot Springs city	38,053
05	33400	051	Garland County	38,053
05	34750		Jacksonville city	29,469
05	34750	119	Pulaski County	29,469
05	35710		Jonesboro city	78,524
05	35710	031	Craighead County	78,524
05	41000		Little Rock city	202,514
05	41000	119	Pulaski County	202,514
05	50450		North Little Rock city	64,633
05	50450	119	Pulaski County	64,633
05	53390		Paragould city	29,439
05	53390	055	Greene County	29,439
05	55310		Pine Bluff city	41,246
05	55310	069	Jefferson County	41,246
05	60410		Rogers city	69,753
05	60410	007	Benton County	69,753
05	61670		Russellville city	29,150
05	61670	115	Pope County	29,150
05	63800		Sherwood city	32,780
05	63800	119	Pulaski County	32,780
05	66080		Springdale city	87,441
05	66080	007	Benton County	12,127
05	66080	143	Washington County	75,314
05	68810		Texarkana city	29,314
05	68810	091	Miller County	29,314
06			**CALIFORNIA**	39,538,223
06	00296		Adelanto city	37,817
06	00296	071	San Bernardino County	37,817
06	00562		Alameda city	78,611
06	00562	001	Alameda County	78,611
06	00884		Alhambra city	83,001
06	00884	037	Los Angeles County	83,001
06	00947		Aliso Viejo city	52,174
06	00947	059	Orange County	52,174
06	02000		Anaheim city	347,015
06	02000	059	Orange County	347,015
06	02252		Antioch city	115,360
06	02252	013	Contra Costa County	115,360

CITIES BY COUNTY—*Continued*

State code	Place code	County code	Geographic Area Name	2020 census population
06	02364		Apple Valley town	75,913
06	02364	071	San Bernardino County	75,913
06	02462		Arcadia city	56,737
06	02462	037	Los Angeles County	56,737
06	03064		Atascadero city	29,794
06	03064	079	San Luis Obispo County	29,794
06	03162		Atwater city	31,819
06	03162	047	Merced County	31,819
06	03386		Azusa city	49,757
06	03386	037	Los Angeles County	49,757
06	03526		Bakersfield city	402,907
06	03526	029	Kern County	402,907
06	03666		Baldwin Park city	72,323
06	03666	037	Los Angeles County	72,323
06	03820		Banning city	29,528
06	03820	065	Riverside County	29,528
06	04030		Barstow city	25,433
06	04030	071	San Bernardino County	25,433
06	04758		Beaumont city	53,101
06	04758	065	Riverside County	53,101
06	04870		Bell city	33,656
06	04870	037	Los Angeles County	33,656
06	04982		Bellflower city	79,298
06	04982	037	Los Angeles County	79,298
06	04996		Bell Gardens city	39,556
06	04996	037	Los Angeles County	39,556
06	05108		Belmont city	28,313
06	05108	081	San Mateo County	28,313
06	05290		Benicia city	27,092
06	05290	095	Solano County	27,092
06	06000		Berkeley city	119,693
06	06000	001	Alameda County	119,693
06	06308		Beverly Hills city	32,782
06	06308	037	Los Angeles County	32,782
06	08058		Brawley city	26,443
06	08058	025	Imperial County	26,443
06	08100		Brea city	47,415
06	08100	059	Orange County	47,415
06	08142		Brentwood city	64,355
06	08142	013	Contra Costa County	64,355
06	08786		Buena Park city	84,173
06	08786	059	Orange County	84,173
06	08954		Burbank city	107,563
06	08954	037	Los Angeles County	107,563
06	09066		Burlingame city	31,374
06	09066	081	San Mateo County	31,374
06	09710		Calexico city	38,649
06	09710	025	Imperial County	38,649
06	10046		Camarillo city	70,797
06	10046	111	Ventura County	70,797
06	10345		Campbell city	44,080
06	10345	085	Santa Clara County	44,080
06	11194		Carlsbad city	114,972
06	11194	073	San Diego County	114,972
06	11530		Carson city	95,367
06	11530	037	Los Angeles County	95,367
06	12048		Cathedral City city	51,535
06	12048	065	Riverside County	51,535
06	12524		Ceres city	49,276
06	12524	099	Stanislaus County	49,276
06	12552		Cerritos city	49,683
06	12552	037	Los Angeles County	49,683
06	13014		Chico city	102,849
06	13014	007	Butte County	102,849
06	13210		Chino city	90,989
06	13210	071	San Bernardino County	90,989
06	13214		Chino Hills city	78,573
06	13214	071	San Bernardino County	78,573
06	13392		Chula Vista city	276,025
06	13392	073	San Diego County	276,025
06	13588		Citrus Heights city	88,018
06	13588	067	Sacramento County	88,018
06	13756		Claremont city	36,462
06	13756	037	Los Angeles County	36,462
06	14218		Clovis city	120,254
06	14218	019	Fresno County	120,254
06	14260		Coachella city	41,987
06	14260	065	Riverside County	41,987
06	14890		Colton city	53,945
06	14890	071	San Bernardino County	53,945
06	15044		Compton city	95,959
06	15044	037	Los Angeles County	95,959
06	16000		Concord city	125,389
06	16000	013	Contra Costa County	125,389
06	16350		Corona city	157,265
06	16350	065	Riverside County	157,265
06	16532		Costa Mesa city	111,915
06	16532	059	Orange County	111,915
06	16742		Covina city	51,373
06	16742	037	Los Angeles County	51,373
06	17568		Culver City city	40,795
06	17568	037	Los Angeles County	40,795
06	17610		Cupertino city	60,575
06	17610	085	Santa Clara County	60,575
06	17750		Cypress city	50,269
06	17750	059	Orange County	50,269

CITIES BY COUNTY—*Continued*

State code	Place code	County code	Geographic Area Name	2020 census population
06	17918		Daly City city	104,940
06	17918	081	San Mateo County	104,940
06	17946		Dana Point city	33,165
06	17946	059	Orange County	33,165
06	17988		Danville town	43,602
06	17988	013	Contra Costa County	43,602
06	18100		Davis city	66,796
06	18100	113	Yolo County	66,796
06	18394		Delano city	51,845
06	18394	029	Kern County	51,845
06	18996		Desert Hot Springs city	32,529
06	18996	065	Riverside County	32,529
06	19192		Diamond Bar city	55,226
06	19192	037	Los Angeles County	55,226
06	19766		Downey city	114,558
06	19766	037	Los Angeles County	114,558
06	20018		Dublin city	72,142
06	20018	001	Alameda County	72,142
06	20956		East Palo Alto city	30,050
06	20956	081	San Mateo County	30,050
06	21230		Eastvale city	69,849
06	21230	065	Riverside County	69,849
06	21712		El Cajon city	106,286
06	21712	073	San Diego County	106,286
06	21782		El Centro city	44,347
06	21782	025	Imperial County	44,347
06	21796		El Cerrito city	25,977
06	21796	013	Contra Costa County	25,977
06	22020		Elk Grove city	177,145
06	22020	067	Sacramento County	177,145
06	22230		El Monte city	109,554
06	22230	037	Los Angeles County	109,554
06	22300		El Paso de Robles (Paso Robles) city	31,513
06	22300	079	San Luis Obispo County	31,513
06	22678		Encinitas city	62,082
06	22678	073	San Diego County	62,082
06	22804		Escondido city	151,271
06	22804	073	San Diego County	151,271
06	23042		Eureka city	26,547
06	23042	023	Humboldt County	26,547
06	23182		Fairfield city	119,793
06	23182	095	Solano County	119,793
06	24638		Folsom city	79,036
06	24638	067	Sacramento County	79,036
06	24680		Fontana city	208,766
06	24680	071	San Bernardino County	208,766
06	25338		Foster City city	33,818
06	25338	081	San Mateo County	33,818
06	25380		Fountain Valley city	57,175
06	25380	059	Orange County	57,175
06	26000		Fremont city	232,084
06	26000	001	Alameda County	232,084
06	27000		Fresno city	542,161
06	27000	019	Fresno County	542,161
06	28000		Fullerton city	143,367
06	28000	059	Orange County	143,367
06	28112		Galt city	25,525
06	28112	067	Sacramento County	25,525
06	28168		Gardena city	61,069
06	28168	037	Los Angeles County	61,069
06	29000		Garden Grove city	172,144
06	29000	059	Orange County	172,144
06	29504		Gilroy city	59,669
06	29504	085	Santa Clara County	59,669
06	30000		Glendale city	196,841
06	30000	037	Los Angeles County	196,841
06	30014		Glendora city	52,610
06	30014	037	Los Angeles County	52,610
06	30378		Goleta city	32,753
06	30378	083	Santa Barbara County	32,753
06	31960		Hanford city	57,932
06	31960	031	Kings County	57,932
06	32548		Hawthorne city	88,255
06	32548	037	Los Angeles County	88,255
06	33000		Hayward city	163,635
06	33000	001	Alameda County	163,635
06	33182		Hemet city	89,855
06	33182	065	Riverside County	89,855
06	33308		Hercules city	26,045
06	33308	013	Contra Costa County	26,045
06	33434		Hesperia city	100,038
06	33434	071	San Bernardino County	100,038
06	33588		Highland city	57,083
06	33588	071	San Bernardino County	57,083
06	34120		Hollister city	41,702
06	34120	069	San Benito County	41,702
06	36000		Huntington Beach city	199,140
06	36000	059	Orange County	199,140
06	36056		Huntington Park city	55,005
06	36056	037	Los Angeles County	55,005
06	36294		Imperial Beach city	26,190
06	36294	073	San Diego County	26,190
06	36448		Indio city	89,127
06	36448	065	Riverside County	89,127
06	36546		Inglewood city	107,961
06	36546	037	Los Angeles County	107,961

CITIES BY COUNTY—*Continued*

State code	Place code	County code	Geographic Area Name	2020 census population
06	36770		Irvine city	305,313
06	36770	059	Orange County	305,313
06	37692		Jurupa Valley city	105,107
06	37692	065	Riverside County	105,107
06	39122		Lafayette city	25,426
06	39122	013	Contra Costa County	25,426
06	39220		Laguna Hills city	31,402
06	39220	059	Orange County	31,402
06	39248		Laguna Niguel city	64,519
06	39248	059	Orange County	64,519
06	39290		La Habra city	63,200
06	39290	059	Orange County	63,200
06	39486		Lake Elsinore city	70,366
06	39486	065	Riverside County	70,366
06	39496		Lake Forest city	86,070
06	39496	059	Orange County	86,070
06	39892		Lakewood city	82,727
06	39892	037	Los Angeles County	82,727
06	40004		La Mesa city	61,191
06	40004	073	San Diego County	61,191
06	40032		La Mirada city	47,831
06	40032	037	Los Angeles County	47,831
06	40130		Lancaster city	173,305
06	40130	037	Los Angeles County	173,305
06	40340		La Puente city	38,166
06	40340	037	Los Angeles County	38,166
06	40354		La Quinta city	37,600
06	40354	065	Riverside County	37,600
06	40704		Lathrop city	28,789
06	40704	077	San Joaquin County	28,789
06	40830		La Verne city	31,408
06	40830	037	Los Angeles County	31,408
06	40886		Lawndale city	31,895
06	40886	037	Los Angeles County	31,895
06	41124		Lemon Grove city	27,656
06	41124	073	San Diego County	27,656
06	41152		Lemoore city	26,989
06	41152	031	Kings County	26,989
06	41474		Lincoln city	49,808
06	41474	061	Placer County	49,808
06	41992		Livermore city	88,614
06	41992	001	Alameda County	88,614
06	42202		Lodi city	66,409
06	42202	077	San Joaquin County	66,409
06	42524		Lompoc city	44,398
06	42524	083	Santa Barbara County	44,398
06	43000		Long Beach city	466,302
06	43000	037	Los Angeles County	466,302
06	43280		Los Altos city	31,706
06	43280	085	Santa Clara County	31,706
06	44000		Los Angeles city	3,893,986
06	44000	037	Los Angeles County	3,893,986
06	44028		Los Banos city	45,287
06	44028	047	Merced County	45,287
06	44112		Los Gatos town	33,587
06	44112	085	Santa Clara County	33,587
06	44574		Lynwood city	67,139
06	44574	037	Los Angeles County	67,139
06	45022		Madera city	66,316
06	45022	039	Madera County	66,316
06	45400		Manhattan Beach city	35,610
06	45400	037	Los Angeles County	35,610
06	45484		Manteca city	83,678
06	45484	077	San Joaquin County	83,678
06	46114		Martinez city	37,206
06	46114	013	Contra Costa County	37,206
06	46492		Maywood city	25,191
06	46492	037	Los Angeles County	25,191
06	46842		Menifee city	102,654
06	46842	065	Riverside County	102,654
06	46870		Menlo Park city	33,785
06	46870	081	San Mateo County	33,785
06	46898		Merced city	86,141
06	46898	047	Merced County	86,141
06	47766		Milpitas city	80,275
06	47766	085	Santa Clara County	80,275
06	48256		Mission Viejo city	93,759
06	48256	059	Orange County	93,759
06	48354		Modesto city	218,471
06	48354	099	Stanislaus County	218,471
06	48648		Monrovia city	38,022
06	48648	037	Los Angeles County	38,022
06	48788		Montclair city	37,936
06	48788	071	San Bernardino County	37,936
06	48816		Montebello city	62,771
06	48816	037	Los Angeles County	62,771
06	48872		Monterey city	30,102
06	48872	053	Monterey County	30,102
06	48914		Monterey Park city	61,259
06	48914	037	Los Angeles County	61,259
06	49138		Moorpark city	36,344
06	49138	111	Ventura County	36,344
06	49270		Moreno Valley city	208,865
06	49270	065	Riverside County	208,865
06	49278		Morgan Hill city	45,558
06	49278	085	Santa Clara County	45,558

State code	Place code	County code	Geographic Area Name	2020 census population
06	49670		Mountain View city	82,592
06	49670	085	Santa Clara County	82,592
06	50076		Murrieta city	111,050
06	50076	065	Riverside County	111,050
06	50258		Napa city	79,276
06	50258	055	Napa County	79,276
06	50398		National City city	56,235
06	50398	073	San Diego County	56,235
06	50916		Newark city	47,947
06	50916	001	Alameda County	47,947
06	51182		Newport Beach city	85,411
06	51182	059	Orange County	85,411
06	51560		Norco city	25,960
06	51560	065	Riverside County	25,960
06	52526		Norwalk city	102,910
06	52526	037	Los Angeles County	102,910
06	52582		Novato city	53,130
06	52582	041	Marin County	53,130
06	53000		Oakland city	439,349
06	53000	001	Alameda County	439,349
06	53070		Oakley city	43,390
06	53070	013	Contra Costa County	43,390
06	53322		Oceanside city	174,352
06	53322	073	San Diego County	174,352
06	53896		Ontario city	175,518
06	53896	071	San Bernardino County	175,518
06	53980		Orange city	138,992
06	53980	059	Orange County	138,992
06	54652		Oxnard city	202,185
06	54652	111	Ventura County	202,185
06	54806		Pacifica city	38,655
06	54806	081	San Mateo County	38,655
06	55156		Palmdale city	169,913
06	55156	037	Los Angeles County	169,913
06	55184		Palm Desert city	51,163
06	55184	065	Riverside County	51,163
06	55254		Palm Springs city	44,561
06	55254	065	Riverside County	44,561
06	55282		Palo Alto city	68,724
06	55282	085	Santa Clara County	68,724
06	55618		Paramount city	53,828
06	55618	037	Los Angeles County	53,828
06	56000		Pasadena city	138,679
06	56000	037	Los Angeles County	138,679
06	56700		Perris city	78,786
06	56700	065	Riverside County	78,786
06	56784		Petaluma city	59,713
06	56784	097	Sonoma County	59,713
06	56924		Pico Rivera city	62,215
06	56924	037	Los Angeles County	62,215
06	57456		Pittsburg city	76,439
06	57456	013	Contra Costa County	76,439
06	57526		Placentia city	51,911
06	57526	059	Orange County	51,911
06	57764		Pleasant Hill city	34,595
06	57764	013	Contra Costa County	34,595
06	57792		Pleasanton city	80,421
06	57792	001	Alameda County	80,421
06	58072		Pomona city	151,554
06	58072	037	Los Angeles County	151,554
06	58240		Porterville city	62,607
06	58240	107	Tulare County	62,607
06	58520		Poway city	48,918
06	58520	073	San Diego County	48,918
06	59444		Rancho Cordova city	79,666
06	59444	067	Sacramento County	79,666
06	59451		Rancho Cucamonga city	174,628
06	59451	071	San Bernardino County	174,628
06	59514		Rancho Palos Verdes city	42,365
06	59514	037	Los Angeles County	42,365
06	59587		Rancho Santa Margarita city	48,119
06	59587	059	Orange County	48,119
06	59920		Redding city	93,559
06	59920	089	Shasta County	93,559
06	59962		Redlands city	73,004
06	59962	071	San Bernardino County	73,004
06	60018		Redondo Beach city	71,520
06	60018	037	Los Angeles County	71,520
06	60102		Redwood City city	84,234
06	60102	081	San Mateo County	84,234
06	60242		Reedley city	25,221
06	60242	019	Fresno County	25,221
06	60466		Rialto city	104,216
06	60466	071	San Bernardino County	104,216
06	60620		Richmond city	116,287
06	60620	013	Contra Costa County	116,287
06	60704		Ridgecrest city	27,918
06	60704	029	Kern County	27,918
06	62000		Riverside city	314,347
06	62000	065	Riverside County	314,347
06	62364		Rocklin city	71,571
06	62364	061	Placer County	71,571
06	62546		Rohnert Park city	44,330
06	62546	097	Sonoma County	44,330
06	62896		Rosemead city	51,268
06	62896	037	Los Angeles County	51,268

CITIES BY COUNTY—*Continued*

State code	Place code	County code	Geographic Area Name	2020 census population
06	62938		Roseville city	147,817
06	62938	061	Placer County	147,817
06	64000		Sacramento city	522,754
06	64000	067	Sacramento County	522,754
06	64224		Salinas city	163,687
06	64224	053	Monterey County	163,687
06	65000		San Bernardino city	221,898
06	65000	071	San Bernardino County	221,898
06	65028		San Bruno city	43,906
06	65028	081	San Mateo County	43,906
06	65042		San Buenaventura (Ventura) city	110,600
06	65042	111	Ventura County	110,600
06	65070		San Carlos city	30,743
06	65070	081	San Mateo County	30,743
06	65084		San Clemente city	64,409
06	65084	059	Orange County	64,409
06	66000		San Diego city	1,385,922
06	66000	073	San Diego County	1,385,922
06	66070		San Dimas city	34,939
06	66070	037	Los Angeles County	34,939
06	67000		San Francisco city	873,965
06	67000	075	San Francisco County	873,965
06	67042		San Gabriel city	39,611
06	67042	037	Los Angeles County	39,611
06	67056		Sanger city	26,635
06	67056	019	Fresno County	26,635
06	67112		San Jacinto city	53,946
06	67112	065	Riverside County	53,946
06	68000		San Jose city	1,014,545
06	68000	085	Santa Clara County	1,014,545
06	68028		San Juan Capistrano city	35,253
06	68028	059	Orange County	35,253
06	68084		San Leandro city	91,675
06	68084	001	Alameda County	91,675
06	68154		San Luis Obispo city	47,085
06	68154	079	San Luis Obispo County	47,085
06	68196		San Marcos city	94,914
06	68196	073	San Diego County	94,914
06	68252		San Mateo city	105,674
06	68252	081	San Mateo County	105,674
06	68294		San Pablo city	32,109
06	68294	013	Contra Costa County	32,109
06	68364		San Rafael city	61,287
06	68364	041	Marin County	61,287
06	68378		San Ramon city	86,426
06	68378	013	Contra Costa County	86,426
06	69000		Santa Ana city	310,538
06	69000	059	Orange County	310,538
06	69070		Santa Barbara city	88,730
06	69070	083	Santa Barbara County	88,730
06	69084		Santa Clara city	127,452
06	69084	085	Santa Clara County	127,452
06	69088		Santa Clarita city	229,213
06	69088	037	Los Angeles County	229,213
06	69112		Santa Cruz city	62,341
06	69112	087	Santa Cruz County	62,341
06	69196		Santa Maria city	109,903
06	69196	083	Santa Barbara County	109,903
06	70000		Santa Monica city	93,028
06	70000	037	Los Angeles County	93,028
06	70042		Santa Paula city	30,713
06	70042	111	Ventura County	30,713
06	70098		Santa Rosa city	178,155
06	70098	097	Sonoma County	178,155
06	70224		Santee city	60,075
06	70224	073	San Diego County	60,075
06	70280		Saratoga city	31,164
06	70280	085	Santa Clara County	31,164
06	70686		Seal Beach city	25,272
06	70686	059	Orange County	25,272
06	70742		Seaside city	32,385
06	70742	053	Monterey County	32,385
06	72016		Simi Valley city	126,487
06	72016	111	Ventura County	126,487
06	73080		South Gate city	92,971
06	73080	037	Los Angeles County	92,971
06	73220		South Pasadena city	27,001
06	73220	037	Los Angeles County	27,001
06	73262		South San Francisco city	66,119
06	73262	081	San Mateo County	66,119
06	73962		Stanton city	37,953
06	73962	059	Orange County	37,953
06	75000		Stockton city	320,759
06	75000	077	San Joaquin County	320,759
06	75630		Suisun City city	29,471
06	75630	095	Solano County	29,471
06	77000		Sunnyvale city	156,291
06	77000	085	Santa Clara County	156,291
06	78120		Temecula city	110,130
06	78120	065	Riverside County	110,130
06	78148		Temple City city	36,545
06	78148	037	Los Angeles County	36,545
06	78582		Thousand Oaks city	126,926
06	78582	111	Ventura County	126,926
06	80000		Torrance city	147,323
06	80000	037	Los Angeles County	147,323

CITIES BY COUNTY—*Continued*

State code	Place code	County code	Geographic Area Name	2020 census population
06	80238		Tracy city	93,356
06	80238	077	San Joaquin County	93,356
06	80644		Tulare city	68,880
06	80644	107	Tulare County	68,880
06	80812		Turlock city	72,645
06	80812	099	Stanislaus County	72,645
06	80854		Tustin city	80,142
06	80854	059	Orange County	80,142
06	80994		Twentynine Palms city	27,420
06	80994	071	San Bernardino County	27,420
06	81204		Union City city	70,650
06	81204	001	Alameda County	70,650
06	81344		Upland city	79,110
06	81344	071	San Bernardino County	79,110
06	81554		Vacaville city	102,675
06	81554	095	Solano County	102,675
06	81666		Vallejo city	126,035
06	81666	095	Solano County	126,035
06	82590		Victorville city	134,550
06	82590	071	San Bernardino County	134,550
06	82954		Visalia city	141,561
06	82954	107	Tulare County	141,561
06	82996		Vista city	98,484
06	82996	073	San Diego County	98,484
06	83332		Walnut city	28,522
06	83332	037	Los Angeles County	28,522
06	83346		Walnut Creek city	70,078
06	83346	013	Contra Costa County	70,078
06	83542		Wasco city	27,275
06	83542	029	Kern County	27,275
06	83668		Watsonville city	52,739
06	83668	087	Santa Cruz County	52,739
06	84200		West Covina city	109,772
06	84200	037	Los Angeles County	109,772
06	84410		West Hollywood city	35,848
06	84410	037	Los Angeles County	35,848
06	84550		Westminster city	91,089
06	84550	059	Orange County	91,089
06	84816		West Sacramento city	53,666
06	84816	113	Yolo County	53,666
06	85292		Whittier city	87,383
06	85292	037	Los Angeles County	87,383
06	85446		Wildomar city	36,914
06	85446	065	Riverside County	36,914
06	85922		Windsor town	26,307
06	85922	097	Sonoma County	26,307
06	86328		Woodland city	60,852
06	86328	113	Yolo County	60,852
06	86832		Yorba Linda city	68,460
06	86832	059	Orange County	68,460

State code	Place code	County code	Geographic Area Name	2020 census population
06	86972		Yuba City city	70,101
06	86972	101	Sutter County	70,101
06	87042		Yucaipa city	54,620
06	87042	071	San Bernardino County	54,620
08			**COLORADO**	5,773,714
08	03455		Arvada city	124,539
08	03455	001	Adams County	2,901
08	03455	059	Jefferson County	121,638
08	04000		Aurora city	386,241
08	04000	001	Adams County	47,540
08	04000	005	Arapahoe County	336,188
08	04000	035	Douglas County	2,513
08	07850		Boulder city	105,414
08	07850	013	Boulder County	105,414
08	08675		Brighton city	39,990
08	08675	001	Adams County	39,629
08	08675	123	Weld County	361
08	09280		Broomfield city	74,112
08	09280	014	Broomfield County	74,112
08	12415		Castle Rock town	73,012
08	12415	035	Douglas County	73,012
08	12815		Centennial city	108,353
08	12815	005	Arapahoe County	108,353
08	16000		Colorado Springs city	479,260
08	16000	041	El Paso County	479,260
08	16495		Commerce City city	62,477
08	16495	001	Adams County	62,477
08	20000		Denver city	715,522
08	20000	031	Denver County	715,522
08	24785		Englewood city	33,609
08	24785	005	Arapahoe County	33,609
08	24950		Erie town	30,230
08	24950	013	Boulder County	12,845
08	24950	123	Weld County	17,385
08	27425		Fort Collins city	168,972
08	27425	069	Larimer County	168,972
08	27865		Fountain city	29,848
08	27865	041	El Paso County	29,848
08	31660		Grand Junction city	65,733
08	31660	077	Mesa County	65,733
08	32155		Greeley city	108,935
08	32155	123	Weld County	108,935
08	41835		Lafayette city	30,792
08	41835	013	Boulder County	30,792
08	43000		Lakewood city	155,944
08	43000	059	Jefferson County	155,944
08	45255		Littleton city	45,644
08	45255	005	Arapahoe County	42,690
08	45255	035	Douglas County	642
08	45255	059	Jefferson County	2,312

CITIES BY COUNTY—*Continued*

State code	Place code	County code	Geographic Area Name	2020 census population
08	45970		Longmont city	100,119
08	45970	013	Boulder County	98,820
08	45970	123	Weld County	1,299
08	46465		Loveland city	76,677
08	46465	069	Larimer County	76,677
08	54330		Northglenn city	38,143
08	54330	001	Adams County	38,119
08	54330	123	Weld County	24
08	57630		Parker town	58,477
08	57630	035	Douglas County	58,477
08	62000		Pueblo city	111,925
08	62000	101	Pueblo County	111,925
08	77290		Thornton city	141,935
08	77290	001	Adams County	141,935
08	77290	123	Weld County	0
08	83835		Westminster city	116,375
08	83835	001	Adams County	71,233
08	83835	059	Jefferson County	45,142
08	84440		Wheat Ridge city	32,380
08	84440	059	Jefferson County	32,380
08	85485		Windsor town	32,758
08	85485	069	Larimer County	7,762
08	85485	123	Weld County	24,996
09			**CONNECTICUT**	3,605,944
09	08000		Bridgeport city	148,692
09	08000	001	Fairfield County	148,692
09	08420		Bristol city	60,783
09	08420	003	Hartford County	60,783
09	18430		Danbury city	86,550
09	18430	001	Fairfield County	86,550
09	37000		Hartford city	121,219
09	37000	003	Hartford County	121,219
09	46450		Meriden city	60,859
09	46450	009	New Haven County	60,859
09	47290		Middletown city	47,057
09	47290	007	Middlesex County	47,057
09	47515		Milford city (balance)	50,587
09	47515	009	New Haven County	50,587
09	49880		Naugatuck borough	31,593
09	49880	009	New Haven County	31,593
09	50370		New Britain city	74,217
09	50370	003	Hartford County	74,217
09	52000		New Haven city	133,924
09	52000	009	New Haven County	133,924
09	52280		New London city	27,641
09	52280	011	New London County	27,641
09	55990		Norwalk city	91,143
09	55990	001	Fairfield County	91,143
09	56200		Norwich city	40,018
09	56200	011	New London County	40,018
09	68100		Shelton city	40,872
09	68100	001	Fairfield County	40,872
09	73000		Stamford city	135,445
09	73000	001	Fairfield County	135,445
09	76500		Torrington city	35,484
09	76500	005	Litchfield County	35,484
09	80000		Waterbury city	114,446
09	80000	009	New Haven County	114,446
09	82800		West Haven city	55,560
09	82800	009	New Haven County	55,560
10			**DELAWARE**	989,948
10	21200		Dover city	39,614
10	21200	001	Kent County	39,614
10	50670		Newark city	31,314
10	50670	003	New Castle County	31,314
10	77580		Wilmington city	70,941
10	77580	003	New Castle County	70,941
11			**DISTRICT OF COLUMBIA**	689,545
11	50000		Washington city	689,545
11	50000	001	District of Columbia	689,545
12		12	**FLORIDA**	21,538,187
12	00950		Altamonte Springs city	46,335
12	00950	117	Seminole County	46,335
12	01700		Apopka city	54,897
12	01700	095	Orange County	54,897
12	02681		Aventura city	40,225
12	02681	086	Miami-Dade County	40,225
12	07300		Boca Raton city	96,358
12	07300	099	Palm Beach County	96,358
12	07525		Bonita Springs city	53,820
12	07525	071	Lee County	53,820
12	07875		Boynton Beach city	80,401
12	07875	099	Palm Beach County	80,401
12	07950		Bradenton city	55,423
12	07950	081	Manatee County	55,423
12	10275		Cape Coral city	194,979
12	10275	071	Lee County	194,979
12	11050		Casselberry city	28,791
12	11050	117	Seminole County	28,791
12	12875		Clearwater city	117,227
12	12875	103	Pinellas County	117,227
12	12925		Clermont city	43,040
12	12925	069	Lake County	43,040
12	13275		Coconut Creek city	57,818
12	13275	011	Broward County	57,818

State code	Place code	County code	Geographic Area Name	2020 census population
12	14125		Cooper City city	34,394
12	14125	011	Broward County	34,394
12	14250		Coral Gables city	49,495
12	14250	086	Miami-Dade County	49,495
12	14400		Coral Springs city	134,366
12	14400	011	Broward County	134,366
12	15475		Crestview city	27,480
12	15475	091	Okaloosa County	27,480
12	15968		Cutler Bay town	45,407
12	15968	086	Miami-Dade County	45,407
12	16335		Dania Beach city	31,772
12	16335	011	Broward County	31,772
12	16475		Davie town	105,719
12	16475	011	Broward County	105,719
12	16525		Daytona Beach city	71,681
12	16525	127	Volusia County	71,681
12	16725		Deerfield Beach city	86,873
12	16725	011	Broward County	86,873
12	16875		DeLand city	37,404
12	16875	127	Volusia County	37,404
12	17100		Delray Beach city	66,911
12	17100	099	Palm Beach County	66,911
12	17200		Deltona city	94,158
12	17200	127	Volusia County	94,158
12	17935		Doral city	75,803
12	17935	086	Miami-Dade County	75,803
12	18575		Dunedin city	36,074
12	18575	103	Pinellas County	36,074
12	21150		Estero village	37,127
12	21150	071	Lee County	37,127
12	24000		Fort Lauderdale city	182,817
12	24000	011	Broward County	182,817
12	24125		Fort Myers city	85,525
12	24125	071	Lee County	85,525
12	24300		Fort Pierce city	47,279
12	24300	111	St. Lucie County	47,279
12	25175		Gainesville city	139,835
12	25175	001	Alachua County	139,835
12	27322		Greenacres city	44,152
12	27322	099	Palm Beach County	44,152
12	28400		Haines City city	26,750
12	28400	105	Polk County	26,750
12	28452		Hallandale Beach city	41,211
12	28452	011	Broward County	41,211
12	30000		Hialeah city	223,017
12	30000	086	Miami-Dade County	223,017
12	32000		Hollywood city	153,061
12	32000	011	Broward County	153,061
12	32275		Homestead city	80,697
12	32275	086	Miami-Dade County	80,697
12	35000		Jacksonville city	949,577
12	35000	031	Duval County	949,577
12	35875		Jupiter town	61,100
12	35875	099	Palm Beach County	61,100
12	36550		Key West city	26,983
12	36550	087	Monroe County	26,983
12	36950		Kissimmee city	79,242
12	36950	097	Osceola County	79,242
12	38250		Lakeland city	111,881
12	38250	105	Polk County	111,881
12	39081		Lake Worth Beach city	42,175
12	39081	099	Palm Beach County	42,175
12	39425		Largo city	82,632
12	39425	103	Pinellas County	82,632
12	39525		Lauderdale Lakes city	35,955
12	39525	011	Broward County	35,955
12	39550		Lauderhill city	74,495
12	39550	011	Broward County	74,495
12	39875		Leesburg city	26,942
12	39875	069	Lake County	26,942
12	43125		Margate city	58,697
12	43125	011	Broward County	58,697
12	43975		Melbourne city	84,313
12	43975	009	Brevard County	84,313
12	45000		Miami city	442,265
12	45000	086	Miami-Dade County	442,265
12	45025		Miami Beach city	82,826
12	45025	086	Miami-Dade County	82,826
12	45060		Miami Gardens city	111,579
12	45060	086	Miami-Dade County	111,579
12	45100		Miami Lakes town	30,435
12	45100	086	Miami-Dade County	30,435
12	45975		Miramar city	134,676
12	45975	011	Broward County	134,676
12	48625		New Smyrna Beach city	30,233
12	48625	127	Volusia County	30,233
12	49425		North Lauderdale city	44,781
12	49425	011	Broward County	44,781
12	49450		North Miami city	60,250
12	49450	086	Miami-Dade County	60,250
12	49475		North Miami Beach city	43,645
12	49475	086	Miami-Dade County	43,645
12	49675		North Port city	75,175
12	49675	115	Sarasota County	75,175
12	50575		Oakland Park city	44,214
12	50575	011	Broward County	44,214

CITIES BY COUNTY—*Continued*

State code	Place code	County code	Geographic Area Name	2020 census population
12	50750		Ocala city	63,455
12	50750	083	Marion County	63,455
12	51075		Ocoee city	47,331
12	51075	095	Orange County	47,331
12	53000		Orlando city	307,674
12	53000	095	Orange County	307,674
12	53150		Ormond Beach city	43,159
12	53150	127	Volusia County	43,159
12	53575		Oviedo city	40,183
12	53575	117	Seminole County	40,183
12	54000		Palm Bay city	119,874
12	54000	009	Brevard County	119,874
12	54075		Palm Beach Gardens city	59,218
12	54075	099	Palm Beach County	59,218
12	54200		Palm Coast city	89,310
12	54200	035	Flagler County	89,310
12	54450		Palm Springs village	26,972
12	54450	099	Palm Beach County	26,972
12	54700		Panama City city	32,967
12	54700	005	Bay County	32,967
12	55125		Parkland city	34,664
12	55125	011	Broward County	34,664
12	55775		Pembroke Pines city	171,163
12	55775	011	Broward County	171,163
12	55925		Pensacola city	54,394
12	55925	033	Escambia County	54,394
12	56975		Pinellas Park city	53,116
12	56975	103	Pinellas County	53,116
12	57425		Plantation city	91,736
12	57425	011	Broward County	91,736
12	57550		Plant City city	39,794
12	57550	057	Hillsborough County	39,794
12	58050		Pompano Beach city	112,117
12	58050	011	Broward County	112,117
12	58575		Port Orange city	62,872
12	58575	127	Volusia County	62,872
12	58715		Port St. Lucie city	204,913
12	58715	111	St. Lucie County	204,913
12	60975		Riviera Beach city	37,606
12	60975	099	Palm Beach County	37,606
12	61500		Rockledge city	27,688
12	61500	009	Brevard County	27,688
12	62100		Royal Palm Beach village	39,048
12	62100	099	Palm Beach County	39,048
12	62625		St. Cloud city	58,973
12	62625	097	Osceola County	58,973
12	63000		St. Petersburg city	258,277
12	63000	103	Pinellas County	258,277
12	63650		Sanford city	60,795
12	63650	117	Seminole County	60,795
12	64175		Sarasota city	54,108
12	64175	115	Sarasota County	54,108
12	64825		Sebastian city	25,084
12	64825	061	Indian River County	25,084
12	69700		Sunrise city	97,313
12	69700	011	Broward County	97,313
12	70600		Tallahassee city	196,068
12	70600	073	Leon County	196,068
12	70675		Tamarac city	71,891
12	70675	011	Broward County	71,891
12	71000		Tampa city	382,769
12	71000	057	Hillsborough County	382,769
12	71150		Tarpon Springs city	25,138
12	71150	103	Pinellas County	25,138
12	71400		Temple Terrace city	26,684
12	71400	057	Hillsborough County	26,684
12	71900		Titusville city	48,791
12	71900	009	Brevard County	48,791
12	73900		Venice city	25,290
12	73900	115	Sarasota County	25,290
12	75812		Wellington village	61,854
12	75812	099	Palm Beach County	61,854
12	76500		West Melbourne city	25,877
12	76500	009	Brevard County	25,877
12	76582		Weston city	68,094
12	76582	011	Broward County	68,094
12	76600		West Palm Beach city	117,151
12	76600	099	Palm Beach County	117,151
12	78250		Winter Garden city	46,998
12	78250	095	Orange County	46,998
12	78275		Winter Haven city	50,247
12	78275	105	Polk County	50,247
12	78300		Winter Park city	29,784
12	78300	095	Orange County	29,784
12	78325		Winter Springs city	38,484
12	78325	117	Seminole County	38,484
13			**GEORGIA**	10,711,908
13	01052		Albany city	69,832
13	01052	095	Dougherty County	69,832
13	01696		Alpharetta city	65,852
13	01696	121	Fulton County	65,852
13	03440		Athens-Clarke County unified government (balance)	127,320
13	03440	059	Clarke County	127,320
13	04000		Atlanta city	498,602
13	04000	089	DeKalb County	40,258
13	04000	121	Fulton County	458,344

CITIES BY COUNTY—*Continued*

State code	Place code	County code	Geographic Area Name	2020 census population
13			Augusta-Richmond County consoli-	
	04204		dated government (balance)	202,123
13	04204	245	Richmond County	202,123
13	10944		Brookhaven city	55,143
13	10944	089	DeKalb County	55,143
13	12988		Canton city	32,951
13	12988	057	Cherokee County	32,951
13	13492		Carrollton city	27,118
13	13492	045	Carroll County	27,118
13	15172		Chamblee city	30,133
13	15172	089	DeKalb County	30,133
13	19000		Columbus city	206,922
13	19000	215	Muscogee County	206,922
13	21380		Dalton city	34,348
13	21380	313	Whitfield County	34,348
13	23900		Douglasville city	34,698
13	23900	097	Douglas County	34,698
13	24600		Duluth city	31,908
13	24600	135	Gwinnett County	31,908
13	24768		Dunwoody city	51,629
13	24768	089	DeKalb County	51,629
13	25720		East Point city	38,384
13	25720	121	Fulton County	38,384
13	31908		Gainesville city	42,339
13	31908	139	Hall County	42,339
13	38964		Hinesville city	35,265
13	38964	179	Liberty County	35,265
13	42425		Johns Creek city	82,499
13	42425	121	Fulton County	82,499
13	43192		Kennesaw city	33,001
13	43192	067	Cobb County	33,001
13	44340		LaGrange city	30,917
13	44340	285	Troup County	30,917
13	45488		Lawrenceville city	30,436
13	45488	135	Gwinnett County	30,436
13	48624		McDonough city	29,182
13	48624	151	Henry County	29,182
13	49008		Macon-Bibb County	157,346
13	49008	021	Bibb County	157,346
13	49756		Marietta city	60,969
13	49756	067	Cobb County	60,969
13	51670		Milton city	41,318
13	51670	121	Fulton County	41,318
13	55020		Newnan city	42,383
13	55020	077	Coweta County	42,383
13	59724		Peachtree City city	38,248
13	59724	113	Fayette County	38,248
13	59735		Peachtree Corners city	42,309
13	59735	135	Gwinnett County	42,309
13	62104		Pooler city	25,560
13	62104	051	Chatham County	25,560
13	66668		Rome city	37,719
13	66668	115	Floyd County	37,719
13	67284		Roswell city	92,892
13	67284	067	Cobb County	0
13	67284	121	Fulton County	92,892
13	68516		Sandy Springs city	108,134
13	68516	121	Fulton County	108,134
13	69000		Savannah city	148,095
13	69000	051	Chatham County	148,095
13	71492		Smyrna city	55,689
13	71492	067	Cobb County	55,689
13	72122		South Fulton city	107,524
13	72122	121	Fulton County	107,524
13	73256		Statesboro city	33,159
13	73256	031	Bulloch County	33,159
13	73704		Stockbridge city	28,944
13	73704	151	Henry County	28,944
13	73784		Stonecrest city	59,148
13	73784	089	DeKalb County	59,148
13	74180		Sugar Hill city	25,093
13	74180	135	Gwinnett County	25,093
13	77652		Tucker city	36,989
13	77652	089	DeKalb County	36,989
13	78324		Union City city	26,839
13	78324	121	Fulton County	26,839
13	78800		Valdosta city	55,485
13	78800	185	Lowndes County	55,485
13	80508		Warner Robins city	80,324
13	80508	153	Houston County	79,757
13	80508	225	Peach County	567
13	84176		Woodstock city	34,985
13	84176	057	Cherokee County	34,985
15			**HAWAII**	1,455,271
15	06290		East Honolulu CDP	50,922
15		003	Honolulu County	50,922
15	07470		Ewa Gentry CDP	25,707
15		003	Honolulu County	25,707
15	14650		Hilo CDP	44,186
15		001	Hawaii County	44,186
15	22700		Kahului CDP	28,219
15		009	Maui County	28,219
15	23150		Kailua CDP (Honolulu County),	40,514
15		003	Honolulu County	40,514
15	28250		Kaneohe CDP	37,430
15		003	Honolulu County	37,430

CITIES BY COUNTY—*Continued*

State code	Place code	County code	Geographic Area Name	2020 census population
15	51050		Mililani Town CDP	28,121
15		003	Honolulu County	28,121
15	62600		Pearl City CDP	45,295
15		003	Honolulu County	45,295
15	71550		Urban Honolulu CDP	350,943
15		003	Honolulu County	350,943
	79700		Waipahu CDP	43,485
		003	Honolulu County	
16		16	**IDAHO**	1,839,106
16	08830		Boise City city	235,670
16	08830	001	Ada County	235,670
16	12250		Caldwell city	59,985
16	12250	027	Canyon County	59,985
16	16750		Coeur d'Alene city	54,515
16	16750	055	Kootenai County	54,515
16	23410		Eagle city	30,471
16	23410	001	Ada County	30,471
16	39700		Idaho Falls city	65,413
16	39700	019	Bonneville County	65,413
16	46540		Lewiston city	34,193
16	46540	069	Nez Perce County	34,193
16	52120		Meridian city	118,099
16	52120	001	Ada County	118,099
16	54550		Moscow city	25,414
16	54550	057	Latah County	25,414
16	56260		Nampa city	100,252
16	56260	027	Canyon County	100,252
16	64090		Pocatello city	56,238
16	64090	005	Bannock County	56,238
16	64090	077	Power County	0
16	64810		Post Falls city	38,538
16	64810	055	Kootenai County	38,538
16	67420		Rexburg city	34,931
16	67420	065	Madison County	34,931
16	82810		Twin Falls city	51,593
16	82810	083	Twin Falls County	51,593
17			**ILLINOIS**	12,812,508
17	00243		Addison village	35,742
17	00243	043	DuPage County	35,742
17	00685		Algonquin village	29,719
17	00685	089	Kane County	8,206
17	00685	111	McHenry County	21,513
17	01114		Alton city	25,701
17	01114	119	Madison County	25,701
17	02154		Arlington Heights village	77,595
17	02154	031	Cook County	77,595
17	03012		Aurora city	180,688
17	03012	043	DuPage County	51,654
17	03012	089	Kane County	111,384
17	03012	093	Kendall County	5,953
17	03012	197	Will County	11,697
17	04013		Bartlett village	41,164
17	04013	031	Cook County	17,224
17	04013	043	DuPage County	23,844
17	04013	089	Kane County	96
17	04078		Batavia city	26,093
17	04078	043	DuPage County	0
17	04078	089	Kane County	26,093
17	04845		Belleville city	42,333
17	04845	163	St. Clair County	42,333
17	05092		Belvidere city	25,327
17	05092	007	Boone County	25,327
17	05573		Berwyn city	57,120
17	05573	031	Cook County	57,120
17	06613		Bloomington city	78,273
17	06613	113	McLean County	78,273
17	07133		Bolingbrook village	73,956
17	07133	043	DuPage County	1,469
17	07133	197	Will County	72,487
17	09447		Buffalo Grove village	43,225
17	09447	031	Cook County	13,798
17	09447	097	Lake County	29,427
17	09642		Burbank city	29,408
17	09642	031	Cook County	29,408
17	10487		Calumet City city	35,968
17	10487	031	Cook County	35,968
17	11332		Carol Stream village	39,849
17	11332	043	DuPage County	39,849
17	11358		Carpentersville village	37,946
17	11358	089	Kane County	37,946
17	12385		Champaign city	88,421
17	12385	019	Champaign County	88,421
17	14000		Chicago city	2,747,231
17	14000	031	Cook County	2,747,231
17	14000	043	DuPage County	0
17	14026		Chicago Heights city	27,519
17	14026	031	Cook County	27,519
17	14351		Cicero town	85,180
17	14351	031	Cook County	85,180
17	17887		Crystal Lake city	40,243
17	17887	111	McHenry County	40,243
17	18563		Danville city	29,214
17	18563	183	Vermilion County	29,214
17	18823		Decatur city	70,765
17	18823	115	Macon County	70,765
17	19161		DeKalb city	40,506
17	19161	037	DeKalb County	40,506

State code	Place code	County code	Geographic Area Name	2020 census population
17	19642		Des Plaines city	60,681
17	19642	031	Cook County	60,681
17	20591		Downers Grove village	50,230
17	20591	043	DuPage County	50,230
17	22697		Edwardsville city	25,354
17	22697	119	Madison County	25,354
17	23074		Elgin city	114,809
17	23074	031	Cook County	24,604
17	23074	089	Kane County	90,205
17	23256		Elk Grove Village village	32,769
17	23256	031	Cook County	32,769
17	23256	043	DuPage County	0
17	23620		Elmhurst city	45,713
17	23620	031	Cook County	10
17	23620	043	DuPage County	45,703
17	24582		Evanston city	79,035
17	24582	031	Cook County	79,035
17	28326		Galesburg city	30,139
17	28326	095	Knox County	30,139
17	29730		Glendale Heights village	33,241
17	29730	043	DuPage County	33,241
17	29756		Glen Ellyn village	28,872
17	29756	043	DuPage County	28,872
17	29938		Glenview village	48,769
17	29938	031	Cook County	48,769
17	30926		Granite City city	27,764
17	30926	119	Madison County	27,764
17	32018		Gurnee village	30,746
17	32018	097	Lake County	30,746
17	32746		Hanover Park village	37,444
17	32746	031	Cook County	20,037
17	32746	043	DuPage County	17,407
17	34722		Highland Park city	30,217
17	34722	097	Lake County	30,217
17	35411		Hoffman Estates village	52,460
17	35411	031	Cook County	52,460
17	35411	089	Kane County	0
17	36750		Huntley village	27,782
17	36750	089	Kane County	5,876
17	36750	111	McHenry County	21,906
17	38570		Joliet city	150,352
17	38570	093	Kendall County	14,055
17	38570	197	Will County	136,297
17	41183		Lake in the Hills village	29,000
17	41183	111	McHenry County	29,000
17	42028		Lansing village	29,038
17	42028	031	Cook County	29,038
17	44225		Lockport city	26,101
17	44225	197	Will County	26,101
17	44407		Lombard village	44,441
17	44407	043	DuPage County	44,441

State code	Place code	County code	Geographic Area Name	2020 census population
17	45694		McHenry city	27,123
17	45694	111	McHenry County	27,123
17	49867		Moline city	42,954
17	49867	161	Rock Island County	42,954
17	50647		Morton Grove village	25,269
17	50647	031	Cook County	25,269
17	51089		Mount Prospect village	56,749
17	51089	031	Cook County	56,749
17	51349		Mundelein village	31,603
17	51349	097	Lake County	31,603
17	51622		Naperville city	149,427
17	51622	043	DuPage County	97,987
17	51622	197	Will County	51,440
17	52584		New Lenox village	27,218
17	52584	197	Will County	27,218
17	53000		Niles village	31,014
17	53000	031	Cook County	31,014
17	53234		Normal town	53,585
17	53234	113	McLean County	53,585
17	53481		Northbrook village	35,237
17	53481	031	Cook County	35,237
17	53559		North Chicago city	30,173
17	53559	097	Lake County	30,173
17	54638		Oak Forest city	27,403
17	54638	031	Cook County	27,403
17	54820		Oak Lawn village	58,271
17	54820	031	Cook County	58,271
17	54885		Oak Park village	54,486
17	54885	031	Cook County	54,486
17	55249		O'Fallon city	32,360
17	55249	163	St. Clair County	32,360
17	56640		Orland Park village	58,648
17	56640	031	Cook County	58,288
17	56640	197	Will County	360
17	56887		Oswego village	34,607
17	56887	093	Kendall County	34,607
17	56887	197	Will County	0
17	57225		Palatine village	67,771
17	57225	031	Cook County	67,771
17	57875		Park Ridge city	39,645
17	57875	031	Cook County	39,645
17	58447		Pekin city	31,727
17	58447	143	Peoria County	0
17	58447	179	Tazewell County	31,727
17	59000		Peoria city	113,173
17	59000	143	Peoria County	113,173
17	60287		Plainfield village	44,733
17	60287	093	Kendall County	3,269
17	60287	197	Will County	41,464
17	62367		Quincy city	39,560
17	62367	001	Adams County	39,560

CITIES BY COUNTY—*Continued*

State code	Place code	County code	Geographic Area Name	2020 census population
17	65000		Rockford city	149,009
17	65000	141	Ogle County	0
17	65000	201	Winnebago County	149,009
17	65078		Rock Island city	37,159
17	65078	161	Rock Island County	37,159
17	65442		Romeoville village	39,873
17	65442	197	Will County	39,873
17	66040		Round Lake Beach village	27,294
17	66040	097	Lake County	27,294
17	66703		St. Charles city	33,091
17	66703	043	DuPage County	594
17	66703	089	Kane County	32,497
17	68003		Schaumburg village	78,691
17	68003	031	Cook County	78,691
17	68003	043	DuPage County	0
17	70122		Skokie village	67,775
17	70122	031	Cook County	67,775
17	72000		Springfield city	114,461
17	72000	167	Sangamon County	114,461
17	73157		Streamwood village	39,519
17	73157	031	Cook County	39,519
17	75484		Tinley Park village	55,922
17	75484	031	Cook County	48,219
17	75484	197	Will County	7,703
17	77005		Urbana city	38,530
17	77005	019	Champaign County	38,530
17	77694		Vernon Hills village	26,894
17	77694	097	Lake County	26,894
17	79293		Waukegan city	89,361
17	79293	097	Lake County	89,361
17	80060		West Chicago city	25,632
17	80060	043	DuPage County	25,632
17	81048		Wheaton city	53,718
17	81048	043	DuPage County	53,718
17	81087		Wheeling village	39,158
17	81087	031	Cook County	39,158
17	81087	097	Lake County	0
17	82075		Wilmette village	28,119
17	82075	031	Cook County	28,119
17	83245		Woodridge village	34,182
17	83245	031	Cook County	0
17	83245	043	DuPage County	34,159
17	83245	197	Will County	23
17	83349		Woodstock city	25,551
17	83349	111	McHenry County	25,551
18			**INDIANA**	6,785,528
18	01468		Anderson city	54,745
18	01468	095	Madison County	54,745
18	05860		Bloomington city	79,912
18	05860	105	Monroe County	79,912
18	08416		Brownsburg town	28,952
18	08416	063	Hendricks County	28,952
18	10342		Carmel city	99,777
18	10342	057	Hamilton County	99,777
18	14734		Columbus city	50,423
18	14734	005	Bartholomew County	50,423
18	16138		Crown Point city	34,439
18	16138	089	Lake County	34,439
18	19486		East Chicago city	26,314
18	19486	089	Lake County	26,314
18	20728		Elkhart city	54,044
18	20728	039	Elkhart County	54,044
18	22000		Evansville city	117,298
18	22000	163	Vanderburgh County	117,298
18	23278		Fishers city	99,053
18	23278	057	Hamilton County	99,053
18	25000		Fort Wayne city	263,852
18	25000	003	Allen County	263,852
18	25450		Franklin city	25,124
18	25450	081	Johnson County	25,124
18	27000		Gary city	68,982
18	27000	089	Lake County	68,982
18	28386		Goshen city	34,849
18	28386	039	Elkhart County	34,849
18	29898		Greenwood city	63,903
18	29898	081	Johnson County	63,903
18	31000		Hammond city	77,754
18	31000	089	Lake County	77,754
18	34114		Hobart city	29,713
18	34114	089	Lake County	29,713
18	36003		Indianapolis city (balance)	887,752
18	36003	097	Marion County	887,752
18	38358		Jeffersonville city	49,413
18	38358	019	Clark County	49,413
18	40392		Kokomo city	59,609
18	40392	067	Howard County	59,609
18	40788		Lafayette city	70,906
18	40788	157	Tippecanoe County	70,906
18	42426		Lawrence city	49,322
18	42426	097	Marion County	49,322
18	46908		Marion city	28,337
18	46908	053	Grant County	28,337
18	48528		Merrillville town	36,603
18	48528	089	Lake County	36,603
18	48798		Michigan City city	32,081
18	48798	091	LaPorte County	32,081
18	49932		Mishawaka city	51,201
18	49932	141	St. Joseph County	51,201

State code	Place code	County code	Geographic Area Name	2020 census population
18	51876		Muncie city	65,382
18	51876	035	Delaware County	65,382
18	52326		New Albany city	37,688
18	52326	043	Floyd County	37,688
18	54180		Noblesville city	69,517
18	54180	057	Hamilton County	69,517
18	60246		Plainfield town	34,771
18	60246	063	Hendricks County	34,771
18	61092		Portage city	37,934
18	61092	127	Porter County	37,934
18	64260		Richmond city	35,915
18	64260	177	Wayne County	35,915
18	68220		Schererville town	29,570
18	68220	089	Lake County	29,570
18	71000		South Bend city	103,675
18	71000	141	St. Joseph County	103,675
18	75428		Terre Haute city	58,621
18	75428	167	Vigo County	58,621
18	78326		Valparaiso city	34,154
18	78326	127	Porter County	34,154
18	82700		Westfield city	46,427
18	82700	057	Hamilton County	46,427
18	82862		West Lafayette city	44,332
18	82862	157	Tippecanoe County	44,332
18	86372		Zionsville town	30,605
18	86372	011	Boone County	30,605
19		19	**IOWA**	3,190,369
19	01855		Ames city	65,955
19	01855	169	Story County	65,955
19	02305		Ankeny city	67,892
19	02305	153	Polk County	67,892
19	06355		Bettendorf city	39,106
19	06355	163	Scott County	39,106
19	11755		Cedar Falls city	40,536
19	11755	013	Black Hawk County	40,536
19	12000		Cedar Rapids city	137,664
19	12000	113	Linn County	137,664
19	16860		Council Bluffs city	62,701
19	16860	155	Pottawattamie County	62,701
19	19000		Davenport city	101,728
19	19000	163	Scott County	101,728
19	21000		Des Moines city	214,137
19	21000	153	Polk County	213,927
19	21000	181	Warren County	210
19	22395		Dubuque city	59,639
19	22395	061	Dubuque County	59,639
19	38595		Iowa City city	74,373
19	38595	103	Johnson County	74,373
19	49485		Marion city	41,572
19	49485	113	Linn County	41,572
19	49755		Marshalltown city	27,610
19	49755	127	Marshall County	27,610
19	50160		Mason City city	27,353
19	50160	033	Cerro Gordo County	27,353
19	60465		Ottumwa city	25,528
19	60465	179	Wapello County	25,528
19	73335		Sioux City city	85,731
19	73335	149	Plymouth County	3
19	73335	193	Woodbury County	85,728
19	79950		Urbandale city	45,582
19	79950	049	Dallas County	11,779
19	79950	153	Polk County	33,803
19	82425		Waterloo city	67,453
19	82425	013	Black Hawk County	67,453
19	83910		West Des Moines city	68,717
19	83910	049	Dallas County	22,908
19	83910	121	Madison County	1
19	83910	153	Polk County	45,583
19	83910	181	Warren County	225
20			**KANSAS**	2,937,880
20	17800		Derby city	25,761
20	17800	173	Sedgwick County	25,761
20	18250		Dodge City city	27,803
20	18250	057	Ford County	27,803
20	25325		Garden City city	28,138
20	25325	055	Finney County	28,138
20	33625		Hutchinson city	40,068
20	33625	155	Reno County	40,068
20	36000		Kansas City city	156,602
20	36000	209	Wyandotte County	156,602
20	38900		Lawrence city	94,909
20	38900	045	Douglas County	94,909
20	39000		Leavenworth city	37,416
20	39000	103	Leavenworth County	37,416
20	39075		Leawood city	33,933
20	39075	091	Johnson County	33,933
20	39350		Lenexa city	57,425
20	39350	091	Johnson County	57,425
20	44250		Manhattan city	54,507
20	44250	149	Pottawatomie County	2
20	44250	161	Riley County	54,505
20	52575		Olathe city	141,238
20	52575	091	Johnson County	141,238
20	53775		Overland Park city	197,295
20	53775	091	Johnson County	197,295
20	62700		Salina city	46,868
20	62700	169	Saline County	46,868

CITIES BY COUNTY—*Continued*

State code	Place code	County code	Geographic Area Name	2020 census population
20	64500		Shawnee city	67,340
20	64500	091	Johnson County	67,340
20	71000		Topeka city	126,515
20	71000	177	Shawnee County	126,515
20	79000		Wichita city	397,070
20	79000	173	Sedgwick County	397,070
21			**KENTUCKY**	4,505,836
21	08902		Bowling Green city	72,524
21	08902	227	Warren County	72,524
21	17848		Covington city	41,058
21	17848	117	Kenton County	41,058
21	24274		Elizabethtown city	31,447
21	24274	093	Hardin County	31,447
21	27982		Florence city	31,830
21	27982	015	Boone County	31,830
21	28900		Frankfort city	28,641
21	28900	073	Franklin County	28,641
21	30700		Georgetown city	37,048
21	30700	209	Scott County	37,048
21	35866		Henderson city	28,013
21	35866	101	Henderson County	28,013
21	37918		Hopkinsville city	30,839
21	37918	047	Christian County	30,839
21	39142		Independence city	28,557
21	39142	117	Kenton County	28,557
21	40222		Jeffersontown city	28,904
21	40222	111	Jefferson County	28,904
21	46027		Lexington-Fayette urban county	322,570
21	46027	067	Fayette County	322,570
21	48006		Louisville/Jefferson County metro government (balance)	632,689
21	48006	111	Jefferson County	632,689
21	56136		Nicholasville city	31,112
21	56136	113	Jessamine County	31,112
21	58620		Owensboro city	60,205
21	58620	059	Daviess County	60,205
21	58836		Paducah city	26,538
21	58836	145	McCracken County	26,538
21	65226		Richmond city	34,716
21	65226	151	Madison County	34,716
22			**LOUISIANA**	4,657,757
22	00975		Alexandria city	45,407
22	00975	079	Rapides Parish	45,407
22	05000		Baton Rouge city	225,128
22	05000	033	East Baton Rouge Parish	225,128
22	08920		Bossier City city	62,722
22	08920	015	Bossier Parish	62,722

State code	Place code	County code	Geographic Area Name	2020 census population
22	13960		Central city	29,962
22	13960	033	East Baton Rouge Parish	29,962
22	36255		Houma city	33,368
22	36255	109	Terrebonne Parish	33,368
22	39475		Kenner city	66,474
22	39475	051	Jefferson Parish	66,474
22	40735		Lafayette city	122,018
22	40735	055	Lafayette Parish	122,018
22	41155		Lake Charles city	85,434
22	41155	019	Calcasieu Parish	85,434
22	51410		Monroe city	47,780
22	51410	073	Ouachita Parish	47,780
22	54035		New Iberia city	28,518
22	54035	045	Iberia Parish	28,518
22	55000		New Orleans city	383,997
22	55000	071	Orleans Parish	383,997
22	70000		Shreveport city	187,993
22	70000	015	Bossier Parish	2,904
22	70000	017	Caddo Parish	185,089
22	70805		Slidell city	28,699
22	70805	103	St. Tammany Parish	28,699
23			**MAINE**	1,362,359
23	02795		Bangor city	31,821
23	02795	019	Penobscot County	31,821
23	38740		Lewiston city	36,806
23	38740	001	Androscoggin County	36,806
23	60545		Portland city	68,402
23	60545	005	Cumberland County	68,402
23	71990		South Portland city	26,492
23	71990	005	Cumberland County	26,492
24			**MARYLAND**	6,177,224
24	01600		Annapolis city	40,788
24	01600	003	Anne Arundel County	40,788
24	04000		Baltimore city	585,708
24	04000	510	Baltimore city	585,708
24	08775		Bowie city	58,310
24	08775	033	Prince George's County	58,310
24	18750		College Park city	35,423
24	18750	033	Prince George's County	35,423
24	30325		Frederick city	78,062
24	30325	021	Frederick County	78,062
24	31175		Gaithersburg city	69,657
24	31175	031	Montgomery County	69,657
24	36075		Hagerstown city	43,489
24	36075	043	Washington County	43,489
24	45900		Laurel city	30,036
24	45900	033	Prince George's County	30,036

CITIES BY COUNTY—*Continued*

State code	Place code	County code	Geographic Area Name	2020 census population
24	67675		Rockville city	67,101
24	67675	031	Montgomery County	67,101
24	69925		Salisbury city	32,849
24	69925	045	Wicomico County	32,849
25			**MASSACHUSETTS**	7,029,917
25	00840		Agawam Town city	28,699
25	00840	013	Hampden County	28,699
25	01370		Amherst Town city	39,470
25	01370	015	Hampshire County	39,470
25	02690		Attleboro city	46,429
25	02690	005	Bristol County	46,429
25	03690		Barnstable Town city	48,923
25	03690	001	Barnstable County	48,923
25	05595		Beverly city	42,714
25	05595	009	Essex County	42,714
25	07000		Boston city	676,216
25	07000	025	Suffolk County	676,216
25	07740		Braintree Town city	39,168
25	07740	021	Norfolk County	39,168
25	08130		Bridgewater Town city	28,432
25	08130	023	Plymouth County	28,432
25	09000		Brockton city	105,652
25	09000	023	Plymouth County	105,652
25	11000		Cambridge city	117,779
25	11000	017	Middlesex County	117,779
25	13205		Chelsea city	40,615
25	13205	025	Suffolk County	40,615
25	13660		Chicopee city	55,576
25	13660	013	Hampden County	55,576
25	21990		Everett city	49,165
25	21990	017	Middlesex County	49,165
25	23000		Fall River city	93,938
25	23000	005	Bristol County	93,938
25	23875		Fitchburg city	41,945
25	23875	027	Worcester County	41,945
25	24960		Framingham city	72,342
25	24960	017	Middlesex County	72,342
25	25172		Franklin Town city	33,243
25	25172	021	Norfolk County	33,243
25	26150		Gloucester city	29,726
25	26150	009	Essex County	29,726
25	29405		Haverhill city	67,764
25	29405	009	Essex County	67,764
25	30840		Holyoke city	38,247
25	30840	013	Hampden County	38,247
25	34550		Lawrence city	89,152
25	34550	009	Essex County	89,152
25	35075		Leominster city	43,782
25	35075	027	Worcester County	43,782
25	37000		Lowell city	115,441
25	37000	017	Middlesex County	115,441
25	37490		Lynn city	101,238
25	37490	009	Essex County	101,238
25	37875		Malden city	66,353
25	37875	017	Middlesex County	66,353
25	38715		Marlborough city	41,838
25	38715	017	Middlesex County	41,838
25	39835		Medford city	59,662
25	39835	017	Middlesex County	59,662
25	40115		Melrose city	29,860
25	40115	017	Middlesex County	29,860
25	40710		Methuen Town city	53,026
25	40710	009	Essex County	53,026
25	45000		New Bedford city	101,044
25	45000	005	Bristol County	101,044
25	45560		Newton city	88,787
25	45560	017	Middlesex County	88,787
25	46330		Northampton city	29,549
25	46330	015	Hampshire County	29,549
25	46598		North Attleborough Town city	30,795
25	46598	005	Bristol County	30,795
25	52490		Peabody city	54,486
25	52490	009	Essex County	54,486
25	53960		Pittsfield city	43,917
25	53960	003	Berkshire County	43,917
25	55745		Quincy city	101,685
25	55745	021	Norfolk County	101,685
25	56000		Randolph Town city	34,995
25	56000	021	Norfolk County	34,995
25	56585		Revere city	61,878
25	56585	025	Suffolk County	61,878
25	59105		Salem city	44,501
25	59105	009	Essex County	44,501
25	62535		Somerville city	81,054
25	62535	017	Middlesex County	81,054
25	67000		Springfield city	155,913
25	67000	013	Hampden County	155,913
25	69170		Taunton city	59,359
25	69170	005	Bristol County	59,359
25	72600		Waltham city	64,994
25	72600	017	Middlesex County	64,994
25	73440		Watertown Town city	35,374
25	73440	017	Middlesex County	35,374
25	76030		Westfield city	40,795
25	76030	013	Hampden County	40,795

State code	Place code	County code	Geographic Area Name	2020 census population
25	77890		West Springfield Town city	28,843
25	77890	013	Hampden County	28,843
25	78972		Weymouth Town city	57,513
25	78972	021	Norfolk County	57,513
25	81035		Woburn city	40,934
25	81035	017	Middlesex County	40,934
25	82000		Worcester city	206,601
25	82000	027	Worcester County	206,601
26			**MICHIGAN**	10,077,331
26	01380		Allen Park city	28,629
26	01380	163	Wayne County	28,629
26	03000		Ann Arbor city	122,830
26	03000	161	Washtenaw County	122,830
26	05920		Battle Creek city	52,631
26	05920	025	Calhoun County	52,631
26	06020		Bay City city	32,655
26	06020	017	Bay County	32,655
26	12060		Burton city	29,680
26	12060	049	Genesee County	29,680
26	21000		Dearborn city	109,910
26	21000	163	Wayne County	109,910
26	21020		Dearborn Heights city	63,257
26	21020	163	Wayne County	63,257
26	22000		Detroit city	639,614
26	22000	163	Wayne County	639,614
26	24120		East Lansing city	47,127
26	24120	037	Clinton County	2,455
26	24120	065	Ingham County	44,672
26	24290		Eastpointe city	34,342
26	24290	099	Macomb County	34,342
26	27440		Farmington Hills city	83,991
26	27440	125	Oakland County	83,991
26	29000		Flint city	81,381
26	29000	049	Genesee County	81,381
26	31420		Garden City city	27,360
26	31420	163	Wayne County	27,360
26	34000		Grand Rapids city	198,487
26	34000	081	Kent County	198,487
26	36280		Hamtramck city	28,413
26	36280	163	Wayne County	28,413
26	38640		Holland city	34,242
26	38640	005	Allegan County	7,728
26	38640	139	Ottawa County	26,514
26	40680		Inkster city	26,066
26	40680	163	Wayne County	26,066
26	41420		Jackson city	31,505
26	41420	075	Jackson County	31,505
26	42160		Kalamazoo city	73,808
26	42160	077	Kalamazoo County	73,808
26	42820		Kentwood city	54,375
26	42820	081	Kent County	54,375
26	46000		Lansing city	112,954
26	46000	037	Clinton County	5
26	46000	045	Eaton County	5,019
26	46000	065	Ingham County	107,930
26	47800		Lincoln Park city	40,201
26	47800	163	Wayne County	40,201
26	49000		Livonia city	95,531
26	49000	163	Wayne County	95,531
26	50560		Madison Heights city	28,473
26	50560	125	Oakland County	28,473
26	53780		Midland city	42,543
26	53780	017	Bay County	159
26	53780	111	Midland County	42,384
26	56320		Muskegon city	37,519
26	56320	121	Muskegon County	37,519
26	59140		Norton Shores city	25,166
26	59140	121	Muskegon County	25,166
26	59440		Novi city	66,252
26	59440	125	Oakland County	66,252
26	59920		Oak Park city	29,580
26	59920	125	Oakland County	29,580
26	65440		Pontiac city	61,572
26	65440	125	Oakland County	61,572
26	65560		Portage city	48,846
26	65560	077	Kalamazoo County	48,846
26	65820		Port Huron city	29,038
26	65820	147	St. Clair County	29,038
26	69035		Rochester Hills city	76,293
26	69035	125	Oakland County	76,293
26	69420		Romulus city	25,157
26	69420	163	Wayne County	25,157
26	69800		Roseville city	47,714
26	69800	099	Macomb County	47,714
26	70040		Royal Oak city	58,217
26	70040	125	Oakland County	58,217
26	70520		Saginaw city	44,166
26	70520	145	Saginaw County	44,166
26	70760		St. Clair Shores city	58,893
26	70760	099	Macomb County	58,893
26	74900		Southfield city	76,579
26	74900	125	Oakland County	76,579
26	74960		Southgate city	30,000
26	74960	163	Wayne County	30,000
26	76460		Sterling Heights city	134,348
26	76460	099	Macomb County	134,348
26	79000		Taylor city	63,384
26	79000	163	Wayne County	63,384
26	80700		Troy city	87,316
26	80700	125	Oakland County	87,316

CITIES BY COUNTY—*Continued*

State code	Place code	County code	Geographic Area Name	2020 census population
26	82960		Walker city	25,159
26	82960	081	Kent County	25,159
26	84000		Warren city	139,407
26	84000	099	Macomb County	139,407
26	86000		Westland city	85,433
26	86000	163	Wayne County	85,433
26	88900		Wyandotte city	25,016
26	88900	163	Wayne County	25,016
26	88940		Wyoming city	76,574
26	88940	081	Kent County	76,574
27			**MINNESOTA**	5,706,494
27	01486		Andover city	32,624
27	01486	003	Anoka County	32,624
27	01900		Apple Valley city	56,246
27	01900	037	Dakota County	56,246
27	02908		Austin city	26,152
27	02908	099	Mower County	26,152
27	06382		Blaine city	70,293
27	06382	003	Anoka County	70,293
27	06382	123	Ramsey County	0
27	06616		Bloomington city	90,012
27	06616	053	Hennepin County	90,012
27	07948		Brooklyn Center city	33,824
27	07948	053	Hennepin County	33,824
27	07966		Brooklyn Park city	86,688
27	07966	053	Hennepin County	86,688
27	08794		Burnsville city	64,352
27	08794	037	Dakota County	64,352
27	10918		Chanhassen city	25,967
27	10918	019	Carver County	25,967
27	10918	053	Hennepin County	0
27	10972		Chaska city	27,828
27	10972	019	Carver County	27,828
27	13114		Coon Rapids city	63,660
27	13114	003	Anoka County	63,660
27	13456		Cottage Grove city	38,882
27	13456	163	Washington County	38,882
27	17000		Duluth city	86,645
27	17000	137	St. Louis County	86,645
27	17288		Eagan city	68,905
27	17288	037	Dakota County	68,905
27	18116		Eden Prairie city	64,375
27	18116	053	Hennepin County	64,375
27	18188		Edina city	53,563
27	18188	053	Hennepin County	53,563
27	18674		Elk River city	25,798
27	18674	141	Sherburne County	25,798
27	22814		Fridley city	29,568
27	22814	003	Anoka County	29,568
27	31076		Inver Grove Heights city	35,783
27	31076	037	Dakota County	35,783
27	35180		Lakeville city	69,654
27	35180	037	Dakota County	69,654
27	39878		Mankato city	44,417
27	39878	013	Blue Earth County	44,417
27	39878	079	Le Sueur County	0
27	39878	103	Nicollet County	0
27	40166		Maple Grove city	70,509
27	40166	053	Hennepin County	70,509
27	40382		Maplewood city	42,100
27	40382	123	Ramsey County	42,100
27	43000		Minneapolis city	428,403
27	43000	053	Hennepin County	428,403
27	43252		Minnetonka city	53,962
27	43252	053	Hennepin County	53,962
27	43864		Moorhead city	44,443
27	43864	027	Clay County	44,443
27	47680		Oakdale city	28,322
27	47680	163	Washington County	28,322
27	49300		Owatonna city	26,438
27	49300	147	Steele County	26,438
27	51730		Plymouth city	81,181
27	51730	053	Hennepin County	81,181
27	52594		Prior Lake city	27,624
27	52594	139	Scott County	27,624
27	53026		Ramsey city	27,682
27	53026	003	Anoka County	27,682
27	54214		Richfield city	37,074
27	54214	053	Hennepin County	37,074
27	54880		Rochester city	121,244
27	54880	109	Olmsted County	121,244
27	55726		Rosemount city	25,679
27	55726	037	Dakota County	25,679
27	55852		Roseville city	36,251
27	55852	123	Ramsey County	36,251
27	56896		St. Cloud city	68,774
27	56896	009	Benton County	7,073
27	56896	141	Sherburne County	6,495
27	56896	145	Stearns County	55,206
27	57220		St. Louis Park city	50,016
27	57220	053	Hennepin County	50,016
27	58000		St. Paul city	311,448
27	58000	123	Ramsey County	311,448
27	58738		Savage city	32,495
27	58738	139	Scott County	32,495
27	59350		Shakopee city	43,641
27	59350	139	Scott County	43,641

CITIES BY COUNTY—*Continued*

State code	Place code	County code	Geographic Area Name	2020 census population
27	59998		Shoreview city	26,952
27	59998	123	Ramsey County	26,952
27	71032		Winona city	26,030
27	71032	169	Winona County	26,030
27	71428		Woodbury city	75,163
27	71428	163	Washington County	75,163
28			**MISSISSIPPI**	2,961,279
28	06220		Biloxi city	49,523
28	06220	047	Harrison County	49,523
28	08300		Brandon city	25,100
28	08300	121	Rankin County	25,100
28	14420		Clinton city	28,047
28	14420	049	Hinds County	28,047
28	29180		Greenville city	29,658
28	29180	151	Washington County	29,658
28	29700		Gulfport city	72,961
28	29700	047	Harrison County	72,961
28	31020		Hattiesburg city	47,289
28	31020	035	Forrest County	40,713
28	31020	073	Lamar County	6,576
28	33700		Horn Lake city	26,772
28	33700	033	DeSoto County	26,772
28	36000		Jackson city	153,643
28	36000	049	Hinds County	153,268
28	36000	089	Madison County	371
28	36000	121	Rankin County	4
28	44520		Madison city	27,767
28	44520	089	Madison County	27,767
28	46640		Meridian city	35,001
28	46640	075	Lauderdale County	35,001
28	54040		Olive Branch city	39,784
28	54040	033	DeSoto County	39,784
28	54840		Oxford city	25,821
28	54840	071	Lafayette County	25,821
28	55760		Pearl city	27,027
28	55760	121	Rankin County	27,027
28	69280		Southaven city	54,640
28	69280	033	DeSoto County	54,640
28	74840		Tupelo city	37,843
28	74840	081	Lee County	37,843
29			**MISSOURI**	6,154,913
29	03160		Ballwin city	31,151
29	03160	189	St. Louis County	31,151
29	06652		Blue Springs city	58,648
29	06652	095	Jackson County	58,648
29	11242		Cape Girardeau city	39,345
29	11242	031	Cape Girardeau County	39,345
29	11242	201	Scott County	0

State code	Place code	County code	Geographic Area Name	2020 census population
29	13600		Chesterfield city	50,014
29	13600	189	St. Louis County	50,014
29	15670		Columbia city	125,691
29	15670	019	Boone County	125,691
29	24778		Florissant city	52,548
29	24778	189	St. Louis County	52,548
29	27190		Gladstone city	27,064
29	27190	047	Clay County	27,064
29	28324		Grandview city	26,211
29	28324	095	Jackson County	26,211
29	31276		Hazelwood city	25,505
29	31276	189	St. Louis County	25,505
29	35000		Independence city	123,028
29	35000	047	Clay County	0
29	35000	095	Jackson County	123,028
29	37000		Jefferson City city	42,969
29	37000	027	Callaway County	15
29	37000	051	Cole County	42,954
29	37592		Joplin city	51,719
29	37592	097	Jasper County	44,577
29	37592	145	Newton County	7,142
29	38000		Kansas City city	507,969
29	38000	037	Cass County	101
29	38000	047	Clay County	138,134
29	38000	095	Jackson County	316,324
29	38000	165	Platte County	53,410
29	39044		Kirkwood city	29,487
29	39044	189	St. Louis County	29,487
29	41348		Lee's Summit city	101,160
29	41348	037	Cass County	2,670
29	41348	095	Jackson County	98,490
29	42032		Liberty city	30,244
29	42032	047	Clay County	30,244
29	46586		Maryland Heights city	28,307
29	46586	189	St. Louis County	28,307
29	54074		O'Fallon city	91,390
29	54074	183	St. Charles County	91,390
29	60788		Raytown city	30,010
29	60788	095	Jackson County	30,010
29	64082		St. Charles city	70,384
29	64082	183	St. Charles County	70,384
29	64550		St. Joseph city	72,456
29	64550	021	Buchanan County	72,456
29	65000		St. Louis city	301,578
29	65000	510	St. Louis city	301,578
29	65126		St. Peters city	57,725
29	65126	183	St. Charles County	57,725
29	70000		Springfield city	169,767
29	70000	043	Christian County	2
29	70000	077	Greene County	169,765
29	75220		University City city	35,009
29	75220	189	St. Louis County	35,009

CITIES BY COUNTY—*Continued*

State code	Place code	County code	Geographic Area Name	2020 census population
29	78442		Wentzville city	44,559
29	78442	183	St. Charles County	44,559
29	79820		Wildwood city	35,467
29	79820	189	St. Louis County	35,467
30			**MONTANA**	1,084,225
30	06550		Billings city	117,077
30	06550	111	Yellowstone County	117,077
30	08950		Bozeman city	52,855
30	08950	031	Gallatin County	52,855
30	11397		Butte-Silver Bow (balance)	34,495
30	11397	093	Silver Bow County	34,495
30	32800		Great Falls city	60,506
30	32800	013	Cascade County	60,506
30	35600		Helena city	32,257
30	35600	049	Lewis and Clark County	32,257
30	50200		Missoula city	73,746
30	50200	063	Missoula County	73,746
31			**NEBRASKA**	1,961,504
31	03950		Bellevue city	64,208
31	03950	153	Sarpy County	64,208
31	17670		Fremont city	27,182
31	17670	053	Dodge County	27,182
31	19595		Grand Island city	53,083
31	19595	079	Hall County	53,083
31	21415		Hastings city	25,175
31	21415	001	Adams County	25,175
31	25055		Kearney city	33,695
31	25055	019	Buffalo County	33,695
31	28000		Lincoln city	291,114
31	28000	109	Lancaster County	291,114
31	37000		Omaha city	490,627
31	37000	055	Douglas County	490,627
32			**NEVADA**	3,104,614
32	09700		Carson City	58,639
32	09700	510	Carson City	58,639
32	31900		Henderson city	317,521
32	31900	003	Clark County	317,521
32	40000		Las Vegas city	641,825
32	40000	003	Clark County	641,825
32	51800		North Las Vegas city	262,678
32	51800	003	Clark County	262,678
32	60600		Reno city	263,436
32	60600	031	Washoe County	263,436
32	68400		Sparks city	108,772
32	68400	031	Washoe County	108,772
33		33	**NEW HAMPSHIRE**	1,377,529
33	14200		Concord city	43,694
33	14200	013	Merrimack County	43,694
33	18820		Dover city	32,758
33	18820	017	Strafford County	32,758
33	45140		Manchester city	115,555
33	45140	011	Hillsborough County	115,555
33	50260		Nashua city	91,405
33	50260	011	Hillsborough County	91,405
33	65140		Rochester city	32,518
33	65140	017	Strafford County	32,518
34			**NEW JERSEY**	9,288,994
34	02080		Atlantic City city	38,504
34	02080	001	Atlantic County	38,504
34	03580		Bayonne city	71,555
34	03580	017	Hudson County	71,555
34	05170		Bergenfield borough	28,345
34	05170	003	Bergen County	28,345
34	07600		Bridgeton city	26,759
34	07600	011	Cumberland County	26,759
34	10000		Camden city	72,001
34	10000	007	Camden County	72,001
34	10750		Carteret borough	25,308
34	10750	023	Middlesex County	25,308
34	13570		Cliffside Park borough	25,700
34	13570	003	Bergen County	25,700
34	13690		Clifton city	90,222
34	13690	031	Passaic County	90,222
34	19390		East Orange city	69,725
34	19390	013	Essex County	69,725
34	21000		Elizabeth city	137,316
34	21000	039	Union County	137,316
34	21480		Englewood city	29,313
34	21480	003	Bergen County	29,313
34	22470		Fair Lawn borough	34,940
34	22470	003	Bergen County	34,940
34	24420		Fort Lee borough	40,206
34	24420	003	Bergen County	40,206
34	25770		Garfield city	32,662
34	25770	003	Bergen County	32,662
34	28680		Hackensack city	45,977
34	28680	003	Bergen County	45,977
34	32250		Hoboken city	60,675
34	32250	017	Hudson County	60,675
34	36000		Jersey City city	292,412
34	36000	017	Hudson County	292,412

CITIES BY COUNTY—*Continued*

State code	Place code	County code	Geographic Area Name	2020 census population
34	36510		Kearny town	42,165
34	36510	017	Hudson County	42,165
34	40350		Linden city	43,717
34	40350	039	Union County	43,717
34	41100		Lodi borough	26,207
34	41100	003	Bergen County	26,207
34	41310		Long Branch city	31,661
34	41310	025	Monmouth County	31,661
34	46680		Millville city	27,789
34	46680	011	Cumberland County	27,789
34	51000		Newark city	310,876
34	51000	013	Essex County	310,876
34	51210		New Brunswick city	55,443
34	51210	023	Middlesex County	55,443
34	55950		Paramus borough	26,661
34	55950	003	Bergen County	26,661
34	56550		Passaic city	70,466
34	56550	031	Passaic County	70,466
34	57000		Paterson city	159,674
34	57000	031	Passaic County	159,674
34	58200		Perth Amboy city	55,414
34	58200	023	Middlesex County	55,414
34	59190		Plainfield city	54,609
34	59190	039	Union County	54,609
34	60900		Princeton	31,026
34	60900	021	Mercer County	31,026
34	61530		Rahway city	29,538
34	61530	039	Union County	29,538
34	63000		Ridgewood village	25,985
34	63000	003	Bergen County	25,985
34	65790		Sayreville borough	45,315
34	65790	023	Middlesex County	45,315
34	74000		Trenton city	90,857
34	74000	021	Mercer County	90,857
34	74630		Union City city	68,512
34	74630	017	Hudson County	68,512
34	76070		Vineland city	61,305
34	76070	011	Cumberland County	61,305
34	79040		Westfield town	31,004
34	79040	039	Union County	31,004
34	79610		West New York town	52,798
34	79610	017	Hudson County	52,798
35			**NEW MEXICO**	2,117,522
35	01780		Alamogordo city	31,358
35	01780	035	Otero County	31,358
35	02000		Albuquerque city	564,563
35	02000	001	Bernalillo County	564,563
35	12150		Carlsbad city	32,241
35	12150	015	Eddy County	32,241
35	16420		Clovis city	38,324
35	16420	009	Curry County	38,324
35	25800		Farmington city	46,684
35	25800	045	San Juan County	46,684
35	32520		Hobbs city	40,508
35	32520	025	Lea County	40,508
35	39380		Las Cruces city	111,507
35	39380	013	Dona Ana County	111,507
35	63460		Rio Rancho city	103,977
35	63460	001	Bernalillo County	5
35	63460	043	Sandoval County	103,972
35	64930		Roswell city	48,539
35	64930	005	Chaves County	48,539
35	70500		Santa Fe city	87,497
35	70500	049	Santa Fe County	87,497
36			**NEW YORK**	20,201,249
36	01000		Albany city	99,345
36	01000	001	Albany County	99,345
36	03078		Auburn city	26,868
36	03078	011	Cayuga County	26,868
36	06607		Binghamton city	48,007
36	06607	007	Broome County	48,007
36	11000		Buffalo city	278,302
36	11000	029	Erie County	278,302
36	24229		Elmira city	26,379
36	24229	015	Chemung County	26,379
36	27485		Freeport village	44,479
36	27485	059	Nassau County	44,479
36	29113		Glen Cove city	28,313
36	29113	059	Nassau County	28,313
36	32402		Harrison village	28,652
36	32402	119	Westchester County	28,652
36	33139		Hempstead village	59,113
36	33139	059	Nassau County	59,113
36	38077		Ithaca city	31,853
36	38077	109	Tompkins County	31,853
36	38264		Jamestown city	28,643
36	38264	013	Chautauqua County	28,643
36	39853		Kiryas Joel village	32,996
36	39853	071	Orange County	32,996
36	42554		Lindenhurst village	27,150
36	42554	103	Suffolk County	27,150
36	43335		Long Beach city	34,968
36	43335	059	Nassau County	34,968
36	47042		Middletown city	30,421
36	47042	071	Orange County	30,421

CITIES BY COUNTY—*Continued*

State code	Place code	County code	Geographic Area Name	2020 census population
36	49121		Mount Vernon city	73,693
36	49121	119	Westchester County	73,693
36	50034		Newburgh city	28,931
36	50034	071	Orange County	28,931
36	50617		New Rochelle city	79,996
36	50617	119	Westchester County	79,996
36	51000		New York city	8,804,190
36	51000	005	Bronx County	1,472,654
36	51000	047	Kings County	2,736,074
36	51000	061	New York County	1,694,251
36	51000	081	Queens County	2,405,464
36	51000	085	Richmond County	495,747
36	51055		Niagara Falls city	48,709
36	51055	063	Niagara County	48,709
36	53682		North Tonawanda city	30,528
36	53682	063	Niagara County	30,528
36	55530		Ossining village	27,693
36	55530	119	Westchester County	27,693
36	56979		Peekskill city	25,377
36	56979	119	Westchester County	25,377
36	59223		Port Chester village	31,673
36	59223	119	Westchester County	31,673
36	59641		Poughkeepsie city	31,490
36	59641	027	Dutchess County	31,490
36	63000		Rochester city	211,233
36	63000	055	Monroe County	211,233
36	63264		Rockville Centre village	25,977
36	63264	059	Nassau County	25,977
36	63418		Rome city	32,138
36	63418	065	Oneida County	32,138
36	65255		Saratoga Springs city	28,143
36	65255	091	Saratoga County	28,143
36	65508		Schenectady city	67,000
36	65508	093	Schenectady County	67,000
36	70420		Spring Valley village	33,062
36	70420	087	Rockland County	33,062
36	73000		Syracuse city	147,363
36	73000	067	Onondaga County	147,363
36	75484		Troy city	50,760
36	75484	083	Rensselaer County	50,760
36	76540		Utica city	65,263
36	76540	065	Oneida County	65,263
36	76705		Valley Stream village	40,685
36	76705	059	Nassau County	40,685
36	81677		White Plains city	59,555
36	81677	119	Westchester County	59,555
36	84000		Yonkers city	211,237
36	84000	119	Westchester County	211,237
36			**NORTH CAROLINA**	10,439,388
37	01520		Apex town	58,797
37	01520	183	Wake County	58,797
37	02080		Asheboro city	26,954
37	02080	151	Randolph County	26,954
37	02140		Asheville city	94,539
37	02140	021	Buncombe County	94,539
37	09060		Burlington city	57,346
37	09060	001	Alamance County	55,505
37	09060	081	Guilford County	1,841
37	10740		Cary town	174,754
37	10740	037	Chatham County	3,716
37	10740	183	Wake County	171,038
37	11800		Chapel Hill town	61,326
37	11800	063	Durham County	2,905
37	11800	135	Orange County	58,421
37	12000		Charlotte city	874,541
37	12000	119	Mecklenburg County	874,541
37	12860		Clayton town	26,323
37	12860	101	Johnston County	26,323
37	12860	183	Wake County	0
37	14100		Concord city	105,186
37	14100	025	Cabarrus County	105,186
37	14700		Cornelius town	31,432
37	14700	119	Mecklenburg County	31,432
37	19000		Durham city	283,547
37	19000	063	Durham County	283,144
37	19000	135	Orange County	134
37	19000	183	Wake County	269
37	22920		Fayetteville city	208,871
37	22920	051	Cumberland County	208,871
37	25300		Fuquay-Varina town	34,152
37	25300	085	Harnett County	0
37	25300	183	Wake County	34,152
37	25480		Garner town	31,163
37	25480	183	Wake County	31,163
37	25580		Gastonia city	80,367
37	25580	071	Gaston County	80,367
37	26880		Goldsboro city	33,107
37	26880	191	Wayne County	33,107
37	28000		Greensboro city	297,899
37	28000	081	Guilford County	297,899
37	28080		Greenville city	87,882
37	28080	147	Pitt County	87,882
37	31060		Hickory city	43,279
37	31060	023	Burke County	79
37	31060	027	Caldwell County	32
37	31060	035	Catawba County	43,168
37	31400		High Point city	113,887
37	31400	057	Davidson County	6,662
37	31400	067	Forsyth County	80
37	31400	081	Guilford County	107,135
37	31400	151	Randolph County	10

CITIES BY COUNTY—*Continued*

State code	Place code	County code	Geographic Area Name	2020 census population
37	32260		Holly Springs town	41,251
37	32260	183	Wake County	41,251
37	33120		Huntersville town	61,403
37	33120	119	Mecklenburg County	61,403
37	33560		Indian Trail town	40,079
37	33560	179	Union County	40,079
37	34200		Jacksonville city	73,339
37	34200	133	Onslow County	73,339
37	35200		Kannapolis city	53,145
37	35200	025	Cabarrus County	42,878
37	35200	159	Rowan County	10,267
37	35600		Kernersville town	26,481
37	35600	067	Forsyth County	25,973
37	35600	081	Guilford County	508
37	41960		Matthews town	29,429
37	41960	119	Mecklenburg County	29,429
37	43480		Mint Hill town	26,468
37	43480	119	Mecklenburg County	26,462
37	43480	179	Union County	6
37	43920		Monroe city	34,551
37	43920	179	Union County	34,551
37	44220		Mooresville town	50,205
37	44220	097	Iredell County	50,205
37	44520		Morrisville town	29,633
37	44520	063	Durham County	207
37	44520	183	Wake County	29,426
37	46340		New Bern city	31,116
37	46340	049	Craven County	31,116
37	55000		Raleigh city	467,592
37	55000	063	Durham County	1,555
37	55000	183	Wake County	466,037
37	57500		Rocky Mount city	54,351
37	57500	065	Edgecombe County	15,422
37	57500	127	Nash County	38,929
37	58860		Salisbury city	35,567
37	58860	159	Rowan County	35,567
37	59280		Sanford city	30,227
37	59280	105	Lee County	30,227
37	64740		Statesville city	28,120
37	64740	097	Iredell County	28,120
37	67420		Thomasville city	27,147
37	67420	057	Davidson County	26,623
37	67420	151	Randolph County	524
37	70540		Wake Forest town	47,625
37	70540	069	Franklin County	1,510
37	70540	183	Wake County	46,115
37	74440		Wilmington city	115,955
37	74440	129	New Hanover County	115,955
37	74540		Wilson city	47,941
37	74540	195	Wilson County	47,941

State code	Place code	County code	Geographic Area Name	2020 census population
37	75000		Winston-Salem city	249,443
37	75000	067	Forsyth County	249,443
38			**NORTH DAKOTA**	779,094
38	07200		Bismarck city	73,651
38	07200	015	Burleigh County	73,651
38	19620		Dickinson city	25,656
38	19620	089	Stark County	25,656
38	25700		Fargo city	125,830
38	25700	017	Cass County	125,830
38	32060		Grand Forks city	59,022
38	32060	035	Grand Forks County	59,022
38	53380		Minot city	48,353
38	53380	101	Ward County	48,353
38	84780		West Fargo city	38,733
38	84780	017	Cass County	38,733
38	86220		Williston city	29,158
38	86220	105	Williams County	29,158
39			**OHIO**	11,799,448
39	01000		Akron city	190,534
39	01000	153	Summit County	190,534
39	03464		Avon Lake city	25,269
39	03464	093	Lorain County	25,269
39	03828		Barberton city	25,185
39	03828	153	Summit County	25,185
39	04720		Beavercreek city	46,507
39	04720	057	Greene County	46,507
39	07972		Bowling Green city	30,630
39	07972	173	Wood County	30,630
39	09680		Brunswick city	35,440
39	09680	103	Medina County	35,440
39	12000		Canton city	70,947
39	12000	151	Stark County	70,947
39	15000		Cincinnati city	310,242
39	15000	061	Hamilton County	310,242
39	16000		Cleveland city	373,091
39	16000	035	Cuyahoga County	373,091
39	16014		Cleveland Heights city	45,306
39	16014	035	Cuyahoga County	45,306
39	18000		Columbus city	905,672
39	18000	041	Delaware County	14,578
39	18000	045	Fairfield County	10,891
39	18000	049	Franklin County	880,203
39	19778		Cuyahoga Falls city	51,109
39	19778	153	Summit County	51,109
39	21000		Dayton city	138,310
39	21000	057	Greene County	0
39	21000	113	Montgomery County	138,310

CITIES BY COUNTY—*Continued*

State code	Place code	County code	Geographic Area Name	2020 census population
39	21434		Delaware city	41,252
39	21434	041	Delaware County	41,252
39	22694		Dublin city	49,359
39	22694	041	Delaware County	4,251
39	22694	049	Franklin County	40,735
39	22694	159	Union County	4,373
39	25256		Elyria city	52,738
39	25256	093	Lorain County	52,738
39	25704		Euclid city	49,628
39	25704	035	Cuyahoga County	49,628
39	25914		Fairborn city	34,488
39	25914	057	Greene County	34,488
39	25970		Fairfield city	44,936
39	25970	017	Butler County	44,936
39	25970	061	Hamilton County	0
39	27048		Findlay city	40,078
39	27048	063	Hancock County	40,078
39	29106		Gahanna city	35,749
39	29106	049	Franklin County	35,749
39	29428		Garfield Heights city	29,786
39	29428	035	Cuyahoga County	29,786
39	31860		Green city	27,477
39	31860	153	Summit County	27,477
39	32592		Grove City city	41,276
39	32592	049	Franklin County	41,276
39	33012		Hamilton city	63,386
39	33012	017	Butler County	63,386
39	35476		Hilliard city	37,132
39	35476	049	Franklin County	37,132
39	36610		Huber Heights city	43,341
39	36610	109	Miami County	5,649
39	36610	113	Montgomery County	37,692
39	39872		Kent city	27,813
39	39872	133	Portage County	27,813
39	40040		Kettering city	57,743
39	40040	057	Greene County	736
39	40040	113	Montgomery County	57,007
39	41664		Lakewood city	50,848
39	41664	035	Cuyahoga County	50,848
39	41720		Lancaster city	40,522
39	41720	045	Fairfield County	40,522
39	43554		Lima city	36,175
39	43554	003	Allen County	36,175
39	44856		Lorain city	65,340
39	44856	093	Lorain County	65,340
39	47138		Mansfield city	47,540
39	47138	139	Richland County	47,540
39	47754		Marion city	35,971
39	47754	101	Marion County	35,971
39	48160		Marysville city	25,324
39	48160	159	Union County	25,324
39	48188		Mason city	34,787
39	48188	165	Warren County	34,787
39	48244		Massillon city	32,148
39	48244	151	Stark County	32,148
39	48790		Medina city	25,969
39	48790	103	Medina County	25,969
39	49056		Mentor city	47,435
39	49056	085	Lake County	47,435
39	49840		Middletown city	51,033
39	49840	017	Butler County	47,253
39	49840	165	Warren County	3,780
39	54040		Newark city	49,913
39	54040	089	Licking County	49,913
39	56882		North Olmsted city	32,409
39	56882	035	Cuyahoga County	32,409
39	56966		North Ridgeville city	35,370
39	56966	093	Lorain County	35,370
39	57008		North Royalton city	31,292
39	57008	035	Cuyahoga County	31,292
39	61000		Parma city	81,047
39	61000	035	Cuyahoga County	81,047
39	62148		Perrysburg city	25,068
39	62148	173	Wood County	25,068
39	66390		Reynoldsburg city	41,091
39	66390	045	Fairfield County	1,099
39	66390	049	Franklin County	29,771
39	66390	089	Licking County	10,221
39	70380		Sandusky city	25,065
39	70380	043	Erie County	25,065
39	71682		Shaker Heights city	29,400
39	71682	035	Cuyahoga County	29,400
39	74118		Springfield city	58,940
39	74118	023	Clark County	58,940
39	74944		Stow city	34,491
39	74944	153	Summit County	34,491
39	75098		Strongsville city	46,449
39	75098	035	Cuyahoga County	46,449
39	77000		Toledo city	270,726
39	77000	095	Lucas County	270,726
39	77588		Troy city	26,308
39	77588	109	Miami County	26,308
39	79002		Upper Arlington city	36,810
39	79002	049	Franklin County	36,810
39	80892		Warren city	39,217
39	80892	155	Trumbull County	39,217
39	83342		Westerville city	39,160
39	83342	041	Delaware County	9,230
39	83342	049	Franklin County	29,930
39	83622		Westlake city	34,283
39	83622	035	Cuyahoga County	34,283

State code	Place code	County code	Geographic Area Name	2020 census population
39	86548		Wooster city	26,780
39	86548	169	Wayne County	26,780
39	86772		Xenia city	25,408
39	86772	057	Greene County	25,408
39	88000		Youngstown city	60,774
39	88000	099	Mahoning County	60,772
39	88000	155	Trumbull County	2
40			**OKLAHOMA**	3,959,353
40	04450		Bartlesville city	37,197
40	04450	113	Osage County	5
40	04450	147	Washington County	37,192
40	06400		Bixby city	28,700
40	06400	143	Tulsa County	28,515
40	06400	145	Wagoner County	185
40	09050		Broken Arrow city	113,730
40	09050	143	Tulsa County	93,358
40	09050	145	Wagoner County	20,372
40	23200		Edmond city	94,498
40	23200	109	Oklahoma County	94,498
40	23950		Enid city	51,327
40	23950	047	Garfield County	51,327
40	37800		Jenks city	26,017
40	37800	143	Tulsa County	26,017
40	41850		Lawton city	90,537
40	41850	031	Comanche County	90,537
40	48350		Midwest City city	58,459
40	48350	109	Oklahoma County	58,459
40	49200		Moore city	63,308
40	49200	027	Cleveland County	63,308
40	50050		Muskogee city	36,989
40	50050	101	Muskogee County	36,989
40	52500		Norman city	127,224
40	52500	027	Cleveland County	127,224
40	55000		Oklahoma City city	681,387
40	55000	017	Canadian County	77,164
40	55000	027	Cleveland County	78,337
40	55000	109	Oklahoma County	525,811
40	55000	125	Pottawatomie County	75
40	56650		Owasso city	38,415
40	56650	131	Rogers County	4,219
40	56650	143	Tulsa County	34,196
40	66800		Shawnee city	31,300
40	66800	125	Pottawatomie County	31,300
40	70300		Stillwater city	47,901
40	70300	119	Payne County	47,901
40	75000		Tulsa city	412,458
40	75000	113	Osage County	5,826
40	75000	131	Rogers County	42
40	75000	143	Tulsa County	406,555
40	75000	145	Wagoner County	35
41			**OREGON**	4,237,256
41	01000		Albany city	56,412
41	01000	003	Benton County	9,174
41	01000	043	Linn County	47,238
41	05350		Beaverton city	97,521
41	05350	067	Washington County	97,521
41	05800		Bend city	99,126
41	05800	017	Deschutes County	99,126
41	15800		Corvallis city	59,696
41	15800	003	Benton County	59,696
41	23850		Eugene city	174,753
41	23850	039	Lane County	174,753
41	26200		Forest Grove city	26,172
41	26200	067	Washington County	26,172
41	30550		Grants Pass city	39,205
41	30550	033	Josephine County	39,205
41	31250		Gresham city	114,507
41	31250	051	Multnomah County	114,507
41	34100		Hillsboro city	106,448
41	34100	067	Washington County	106,448
41	38500		Keizer city	39,408
41	38500	047	Marion County	39,408
41	40550		Lake Oswego city	40,786
41	40550	005	Clackamas County	38,148
41	40550	051	Multnomah County	2,635
41	40550	067	Washington County	3
41	45000		McMinnville city	34,319
41	45000	071	Yamhill County	34,319
41	47000		Medford city	85,828
41	47000	029	Jackson County	85,828
41	52100		Newberg city	25,447
41	52100	071	Yamhill County	25,447
41	55200		Oregon City city	37,466
41	55200	005	Clackamas County	37,466
41	59000		Portland city	652,089
41	59000	005	Clackamas County	843
41	59000	051	Multnomah County	649,601
41	59000	067	Washington County	1,645
41	61200		Redmond city	33,315
41	61200	017	Deschutes County	33,315
41	64900		Salem city	175,432
41	64900	047	Marion County	145,932
41	64900	053	Polk County	29,500
41	69600		Springfield city	62,360
41	69600	039	Lane County	62,360
41	73650		Tigard city	54,832
41	73650	067	Washington County	54,832
41	74950		Tualatin city	27,958
41	74950	005	Clackamas County	3,163
41	74950	067	Washington County	24,795
41	80150		West Linn city	27,376
41	80150	005	Clackamas County	27,376

CITIES BY COUNTY—*Continued*

State code	Place code	County code	Geographic Area Name	2020 census population
41	82800		Wilsonville city	26,594
41	82800	005	Clackamas County	24,523
41	82800	067	Washington County	2,071
41	83750		Woodburn city	26,030
41	83750	047	Marion County	26,030
42			**PENNSYLVANIA**	13,002,700
42	02000		Allentown city	126,092
42	02000	077	Lehigh County	126,092
42	02184		Altoona city	43,997
42	02184	013	Blair County	43,997
42	06064		Bethel Park municipality	33,573
42	06064	003	Allegheny County	33,573
42	06088		Bethlehem city	75,710
42	06088	077	Lehigh County	19,801
42	06088	095	Northampton County	55,909
42	13208		Chester city	32,718
42	13208	045	Delaware County	32,718
42	21648		Easton city	28,027
42	21648	095	Northampton County	28,027
42	24000		Erie city	94,823
42	24000	049	Erie County	94,823
42	32800		Harrisburg city	50,090
42	32800	043	Dauphin County	50,090
42	33408		Hazleton city	29,896
42	33408	079	Luzerne County	29,896
42	41216		Lancaster city	57,842
42	41216	071	Lancaster County	57,842
42	42168		Lebanon city	26,764
42	42168	075	Lebanon County	26,764
42	50528		Monroeville municipality	28,640
42	50528	003	Allegheny County	28,640
42	54656		Norristown borough	35,783
42	54656	091	Montgomery County	35,783
42	60000		Philadelphia city	1,603,797
42	60000	101	Philadelphia County	1,603,797
42	61000		Pittsburgh city	303,160
42	61000	003	Allegheny County	303,160
42	61536		Plum borough	27,153
42	61536	003	Allegheny County	27,153
42	63624		Reading city	95,097
42	63624	011	Berks County	95,097
42	69000		Scranton city	76,110
42	69000	069	Lackawanna County	76,110
42	73808		State College borough	39,848
42	73808	027	Centre County	39,848
42	85152		Wilkes-Barre city	44,498
42	85152	079	Luzerne County	44,498
42	85312		Williamsport city	27,764
42	85312	081	Lycoming County	27,764

State code	Place code	County code	Geographic Area Name	2020 census population
42	87048		York city	44,810
42	87048	133	York County	44,810
44			**RHODE ISLAND**	1,097,379
44	19180		Cranston city	82,935
44	19180	007	Providence County	82,935
44	22960		East Providence city	47,228
44	22960	007	Providence County	47,228
44	49960		Newport city	25,330
44	49960	005	Newport County	25,330
44	54640		Pawtucket city	75,842
44	54640	007	Providence County	75,842
44	59000		Providence city	190,284
44	59000	007	Providence County	190,284
44	74300		Warwick city	82,976
44	74300	003	Kent County	82,976
44	80780		Woonsocket city	43,322
44	80780	007	Providence County	43,322
45			**SOUTH CAROLINA**	5,118,425
45	00550		Aiken city	31,800
45	00550	003	Aiken County	31,800
45	01360		Anderson city	29,170
45	01360	007	Anderson County	29,170
45	07210		Bluffton town	28,121
45	07210	013	Beaufort County	28,121
45	13330		Charleston city	150,522
45	13330	015	Berkeley County	15,268
45	13330	019	Charleston County	135,254
45	16000		Columbia city	137,300
45	16000	063	Lexington County	588
45	16000	079	Richland County	136,712
45	25810		Florence city	39,970
45	25810	041	Florence County	39,970
45	29815		Goose Creek city	45,533
45	29815	015	Berkeley County	45,533
45	30850		Greenville city	70,633
45	30850	045	Greenville County	70,633
45	30985		Greer city	35,367
45	30985	045	Greenville County	25,611
45	30985	083	Spartanburg County	9,756
45	34045		Hilton Head Island town	38,191
45	34045	013	Beaufort County	38,191
45	48535		Mount Pleasant town	90,668
45	48535	019	Charleston County	90,668
45	49075		Myrtle Beach city	35,868
45	49075	051	Horry County	35,868
45	50875		North Charleston city	115,113
45	50875	015	Berkeley County	0
45	50875	019	Charleston County	86,728
45	50875	035	Dorchester County	28,385

CITIES BY COUNTY—*Continued*

State code	Place code	County code	Geographic Area Name	2020 census population
45	61405		Rock Hill city	73,905
45	61405	091	York County	73,905
45	68290		Spartanburg city	38,567
45	68290	083	Spartanburg County	38,567
45	70270		Summerville town	50,933
45	70270	015	Berkeley County	5,424
45	70270	019	Charleston County	2,542
45	70270	035	Dorchester County	42,967
45	70405		Sumter city	43,420
45	70405	085	Sumter County	43,420
46			**SOUTH DAKOTA**	886,667
46	00100		Aberdeen city	28,510
46	00100	013	Brown County	28,510
46	52980		Rapid City city	74,194
46	52980	103	Pennington County	74,194
46	59020		Sioux Falls city	192,683
46	59020	083	Lincoln County	36,170
46	59020	099	Minnehaha County	156,513
47			**TENNESSEE**	6,910,840
47	03440		Bartlett city	57,791
47	03440	157	Shelby County	57,791
47	08280		Brentwood city	45,377
47	08280	187	Williamson County	45,377
47	08540		Bristol city	27,178
47	08540	163	Sullivan County	27,178
47	14000		Chattanooga city	181,234
47	14000	065	Hamilton County	181,234
47	15160		Clarksville city	166,634
47	15160	125	Montgomery County	166,634
47	15400		Cleveland city	47,263
47	15400	011	Bradley County	47,263
47	16420		Collierville town	51,198
47	16420	157	Shelby County	51,198
47	16540		Columbia city	41,556
47	16540	119	Maury County	41,556
47	16920		Cookeville city	34,438
47	16920	141	Putnam County	34,438
47	27740		Franklin city	83,347
47	27740	187	Williamson County	83,347
47	28540		Gallatin city	44,352
47	28540	165	Sumner County	44,352
47	28960		Germantown city	41,256
47	28960	157	Shelby County	41,256
47	33280		Hendersonville city	61,756
47	33280	165	Sumner County	61,756
47	37640		Jackson city	68,211
47	37640	113	Madison County	68,211
47	38320		Johnson City city	70,588
47	38320	019	Carter County	1,342
47	38320	163	Sullivan County	829
47	38320	179	Washington County	68,417
47	39560		Kingsport city	55,444
47	39560	073	Hawkins County	2,713
47	39560	163	Sullivan County	52,731
47	40000		Knoxville city	190,011
47	40000	093	Knox County	190,011
47	41200		La Vergne city	38,783
47	41200	149	Rutherford County	38,783
47	41520		Lebanon city	38,204
47	41520	189	Wilson County	38,204
47	46380		Maryville city	31,765
47	46380	009	Blount County	31,765
47	48000		Memphis city	632,207
47	48000	157	Shelby County	632,207
47	50280		Morristown city	30,585
47	50280	063	Hamblen County	30,581
47	50280	089	Jefferson County	4
47	50780		Mount Juliet city	39,354
47	50780	189	Wilson County	39,354
47	51560		Murfreesboro city	152,437
47	51560	149	Rutherford County	152,437
47	52006		Nashville-Davidson metropolitan government (balance)	689,504
47	52006	037	Davidson County	689,504
47	55120		Oak Ridge city	31,389
47	55120	001	Anderson County	27,747
47	55120	145	Roane County	3,642
47	69420		Smyrna town	53,138
47	69420	149	Rutherford County	53,138
47	69420	187	Williamson County	0
47	70580		Spring Hill city	50,021
47	70580	119	Maury County	16,661
47	70580	187	Williamson County	33,360
48			**TEXAS**	29,145,505
48	01000		Abilene city	124,797
48	01000	253	Jones County	5,289
48	01000	441	Taylor County	119,508
48	01924		Allen city	104,786
48	01924	085	Collin County	104,786
48	02272		Alvin city	27,110
48	02272	039	Brazoria County	27,110
48	03000		Amarillo city	200,904
48	03000	375	Potter County	101,938
48	03000	381	Randall County	98,966
48	04000		Arlington city	394,218
48	04000	439	Tarrant County	394,218

CITIES BY COUNTY—*Continued*

State code	Place code	County code	Geographic Area Name	2020 census population
48	05000		Austin city	959,549
48	05000	021	Bastrop County	0
48	05000	209	Hays County	934
48	05000	453	Travis County	898,328
48	05000	491	Williamson County	60,287
48	05372		Balch Springs city	27,717
48	05372	113	Dallas County	27,717
48	06128		Baytown city	83,698
48	06128	071	Chambers County	4,863
48	06128	201	Harris County	78,835
48	07000		Beaumont city	114,586
48	07000	245	Jefferson County	114,586
48	07132		Bedford city	49,965
48	07132	439	Tarrant County	49,965
48	08236		Big Spring city	26,274
48	08236	227	Howard County	26,274
48	10768		Brownsville city	186,611
48	10768	061	Cameron County	186,611
48	10912		Bryan city	85,461
48	10912	041	Brazos County	85,461
48	11428		Burleson city	47,807
48	11428	251	Johnson County	38,625
48	11428	439	Tarrant County	9,182
48	13024		Carrollton city	133,348
48	13024	085	Collin County	676
48	13024	113	Dallas County	51,336
48	13024	121	Denton County	81,336
48	13492		Cedar Hill city	49,175
48	13492	113	Dallas County	48,549
48	13492	139	Ellis County	626
48	13552		Cedar Park city	77,646
48	13552	453	Travis County	7,576
48	13552	491	Williamson County	70,070
48	14920		Cibolo city	32,279
48	14920	029	Bexar County	0
48	14920	187	Guadalupe County	32,279
48	15364		Cleburne city	31,136
48	15364	251	Johnson County	31,136
48	15976		College Station city	118,180
48	15976	041	Brazos County	118,180
48	15988		Colleyville city	26,084
48	15988	439	Tarrant County	26,084
48	16432		Conroe city	89,148
48	16432	339	Montgomery County	89,148
48	16468		Converse city	27,677
48	16468	029	Bexar County	27,677
48	16612		Coppell city	43,002
48	16612	113	Dallas County	41,982
48	16612	121	Denton County	1,020
48	16624		Copperas Cove city	36,224
48	16624	027	Bell County	0
48	16624	099	Coryell County	35,325
48	16624	281	Lampasas County	899

State code	Place code	County code	Geographic Area Name	2020 census population
48	17000		Corpus Christi city	317,929
48	17000	007	Aransas County	0
48	17000	273	Kleberg County	0
48	17000	355	Nueces County	317,929
48	17000	409	San Patricio County	0
48	17060		Corsicana city	24,825
48	17060	349	Navarro County	24,825
48	19000		Dallas city	1,304,442
48	19000	085	Collin County	51,887
48	19000	113	Dallas County	1,224,075
48	19000	121	Denton County	28,474
48	19000	257	Kaufman County	3
48	19000	397	Rockwall County	3
48	19624		Deer Park city	34,503
48	19624	201	Harris County	34,503
48	19792		Del Rio city	34,688
48	19792	465	Val Verde County	34,688
48	19972		Denton city	141,123
48	19972	121	Denton County	141,123
48	20092		DeSoto city	56,155
48	20092	113	Dallas County	56,155
48	21628		Duncanville city	40,721
48	21628	113	Dallas County	40,721
48	21892		Eagle Pass city	28,392
48	21892	323	Maverick County	28,392
48	22660		Edinburg city	99,678
48	22660	215	Hidalgo County	99,678
48	24000		El Paso city	678,587
48	24000	141	El Paso County	678,587
48	24768		Euless city	61,089
48	24768	439	Tarrant County	61,089
48	25452		Farmers Branch city	36,019
48	25452	113	Dallas County	36,019
48	26232		Flower Mound town	75,859
48	26232	121	Denton County	75,217
48	26232	439	Tarrant County	642
48	27000		Fort Worth city	918,377
48	27000	121	Denton County	16,961
48	27000	251	Johnson County	0
48	27000	367	Parker County	1,252
48	27000	439	Tarrant County	900,164
48	27000	497	Wise County	0
48	27648		Friendswood city	41,218
48	27648	167	Galveston County	30,501
48	27648	201	Harris County	10,717
48	27684		Frisco city	200,675
48	27684	085	Collin County	119,305
48	27684	121	Denton County	81,370
48	28068		Galveston city	53,585
48	28068	167	Galveston County	53,585
48	29000		Garland city	246,132
48	29000	085	Collin County	165
48	29000	113	Dallas County	245,965
48	29000	397	Rockwall County	2

CITIES BY COUNTY—*Continued*

State code	Place code	County code	Geographic Area Name	2020 census population
48	29336		Georgetown city	66,964
48	29336	491	Williamson County	66,964
48	30464		Grand Prairie city	196,272
48	30464	113	Dallas County	125,014
48	30464	139	Ellis County	22
48	30464	439	Tarrant County	71,236
48	30644		Grapevine city	50,651
48	30644	113	Dallas County	0
48	30644	121	Denton County	0
48	30644	439	Tarrant County	50,651
48	30920		Greenville city	28,187
48	30920	231	Hunt County	28,187
48	31928		Haltom City city	46,120
48	31928	439	Tarrant County	46,120
48	32312		Harker Heights city	32,997
48	32312	027	Bell County	32,997
48	32372		Harlingen city	71,802
48	32372	061	Cameron County	71,802
48	35000		Houston city	2,302,792
48	35000	157	Fort Bend County	42,358
48	35000	201	Harris County	2,253,695
48	35000	339	Montgomery County	6,739
48	35000	473	Waller County	0
48	35528		Huntsville city	45,769
48	35528	471	Walker County	45,769
48	35576		Hurst city	40,442
48	35576	439	Tarrant County	40,442
48	35624		Hutto city	27,605
48	35624	491	Williamson County	27,605
48	37000		Irving city	256,793
48	37000	113	Dallas County	256,793
48	38632		Keller city	45,792
48	38632	439	Tarrant County	45,792
48	39148		Killeen city	152,570
48	39148	027	Bell County	152,570
48	39352		Kingsville city	25,408
48	39352	273	Kleberg County	25,408
48	39952		Kyle city	45,752
48	39952	209	Hays County	45,752
48	40588		Lake Jackson city	28,212
48	40588	039	Brazoria County	28,212
48	41212		Lancaster city	41,290
48	41212	113	Dallas County	41,290
48	41440		La Porte city	35,137
48	41440	201	Harris County	35,137
48	41464		Laredo city	255,181
48	41464	479	Webb County	255,181
48	41980		League City city	114,426
48	41980	167	Galveston County	111,899
48	41980	201	Harris County	2,527
48	42016		Leander city	59,345
48	42016	453	Travis County	9,239
48	42016	491	Williamson County	50,106
48	42508		Lewisville city	111,676
48	42508	113	Dallas County	1,312
48	42508	121	Denton County	110,364
48	43012		Little Elm city	46,361
48	43012	121	Denton County	46,361
48	43888		Longview city	81,760
48	43888	183	Gregg County	79,359
48	43888	203	Harrison County	2,401
48	45000		Lubbock city	257,180
48	45000	303	Lubbock County	257,180
48	45072		Lufkin city	34,148
48	45072	005	Angelina County	34,148
48	45384		McAllen city	142,242
48	45384	215	Hidalgo County	142,242
48	45744		McKinney city	195,057
48	45744	085	Collin County	195,057
48	46452		Mansfield city	72,654
48	46452	139	Ellis County	480
48	46452	251	Johnson County	4,760
48	46452	439	Tarrant County	67,414
48	47892		Mesquite city	150,308
48	47892	113	Dallas County	150,145
48	47892	257	Kaufman County	163
48	48072		Midland city	132,448
48	48072	317	Martin County	41
48	48072	329	Midland County	132,407
48	48096		Midlothian city	35,183
48	48096	139	Ellis County	35,183
48	48768		Mission city	85,868
48	48768	215	Hidalgo County	85,868
48	48804		Missouri City city	74,244
48	48804	157	Fort Bend County	68,512
48	48804	201	Harris County	5,732
48	50256		Nacogdoches city	32,213
48	50256	347	Nacogdoches County	32,213
48	50820		New Braunfels city	90,136
48	50820	091	Comal County	68,965
48	50820	187	Guadalupe County	21,171
48	52356		North Richland Hills city	69,968
48	52356	439	Tarrant County	69,968
48	53388		Odessa city	114,368
48	53388	135	Ector County	110,559
48	53388	329	Midland County	3,809
48	56000		Pasadena city	151,955
48	56000	201	Harris County	151,955
48	56348		Pearland city	125,944
48	56348	039	Brazoria County	111,898
48	56348	157	Fort Bend County	5,916
48	56348	201	Harris County	8,130

CITIES BY COUNTY—*Continued*

State code	Place code	County code	Geographic Area Name	2020 census population
48	57176		Pflugerville city	65,678
48	57176	453	Travis County	65,512
48	57176	491	Williamson County	166
48	57200		Pharr city	79,779
48	57200	215	Hidalgo County	79,779
48	58016		Plano city	285,900
48	58016	085	Collin County	280,366
48	58016	121	Denton County	5,534
48	58820		Port Arthur city	55,610
48	58820	245	Jefferson County	55,530
48	58820	361	Orange County	80
48	59696		Prosper town	30,225
48	59696	085	Collin County	24,026
48	59696	121	Denton County	6,199
48	61796		Richardson city	117,973
48	61796	085	Collin County	39,150
48	61796	113	Dallas County	78,823
48	62828		Rockwall city	47,283
48	62828	397	Rockwall County	47,283
48	63284		Rosenberg city	38,279
48	63284	157	Fort Bend County	38,279
48	63500		Round Rock city	119,519
48	63500	453	Travis County	1,934
48	63500	491	Williamson County	117,585
48	63572		Rowlett city	62,543
48	63572	113	Dallas County	55,053
48	63572	397	Rockwall County	7,490
48	64064		Sachse city	27,142
48	64064	085	Collin County	9,937
48	64064	113	Dallas County	17,205
48	64472		San Angelo city	100,006
48	64472	451	Tom Green County	100,006
48	65000		San Antonio city	1,434,270
48	65000	029	Bexar County	1,434,262
48	65000	091	Comal County	0
48	65000	325	Medina County	8
48	65516		San Juan city	35,329
48	65516	215	Hidalgo County	35,329
48	65600		San Marcos city	67,290
48	65600	055	Caldwell County	3
48	65600	187	Guadalupe County	0
48	65600	209	Hays County	67,287
48	66128		Schertz city	41,997
48	66128	029	Bexar County	5,748
48	66128	091	Comal County	1,634
48	66128	187	Guadalupe County	34,615
48	66644		Seguin city	29,419
48	66644	187	Guadalupe County	29,419
48	67496		Sherman city	43,625
48	67496	181	Grayson County	43,625
48	68636		Socorro city	34,276
48	68636	141	El Paso County	34,276
48	69032		Southlake city	31,289
48	69032	121	Denton County	719
48	69032	439	Tarrant County	30,570

State code	Place code	County code	Geographic Area Name	2020 census population
48	70808		Sugar Land city	111,046
48	70808	157	Fort Bend County	111,046
48	72176		Temple city	81,938
48	72176	027	Bell County	81,938
48	72368		Texarkana city	36,234
48	72368	037	Bowie County	36,234
48	72392		Texas City city	51,898
48	72392	071	Chambers County	0
48	72392	167	Galveston County	51,898
48	72530		The Colony city	44,437
48	72530	121	Denton County	44,437
48	74144		Tyler city	105,735
48	74144	423	Smith County	105,735
48	74492		University Park city	25,078
48	74492	113	Dallas County	25,078
48	75428		Victoria city	65,643
48	75428	469	Victoria County	65,643
48	76000		Waco city	137,948
48	76000	309	McLennan County	137,948
48	76816		Waxahachie city	40,925
48	76816	139	Ellis County	40,925
48	76864		Weatherford city	30,630
48	76864	367	Parker County	30,630
48	77272		Weslaco city	40,165
48	77272	215	Hidalgo County	40,165
48	79000		Wichita Falls city	102,498
48	79000	485	Wichita County	102,498
48	80356		Wylie city	57,602
48	80356	085	Collin County	54,727
48	80356	113	Dallas County	1,431
48	80356	397	Rockwall County	1,444
49			**UTAH**	3,271,616
49	01310		American Fork city	33,422
49	01310	049	Utah County	33,422
49	07690		Bountiful city	45,811
49	07690	011	Davis County	45,811
49	11320		Cedar City city	35,078
49	11320	021	Iron County	35,078
49	13850		Clearfield city	31,908
49	13850	011	Davis County	31,908
49	16270		Cottonwood Heights city	33,681
49	16270	035	Salt Lake County	33,681
49	20120		Draper city	50,510
49	20120	035	Salt Lake County	47,213
49	20120	049	Utah County	3,297
49	20810		Eagle Mountain city	43,760
49	20810	049	Utah County	43,760
49	34970		Herriman city	55,312
49	34970	035	Salt Lake County	55,312

CITIES BY COUNTY—*Continued*

State code	Place code	County code	Geographic Area Name	2020 census population
49	36070		Holladay city	32,024
49	36070	035	Salt Lake County	32,024
49	40360		Kaysville city	32,902
49	40360	011	Davis County	32,902
49	40470		Kearns metro township	36,825
49	40470	035	Salt Lake County	36,825
49	43660		Layton city	81,759
49	43660	011	Davis County	81,759
49	44320		Lehi city	76,107
49	44320	049	Utah County	76,107
49	45860		Logan city	52,673
49	45860	005	Cache County	52,673
49	47290		Magna metro township	29,327
49	47290	035	Salt Lake County	29,327
49	49710		Midvale city	36,057
49	49710	035	Salt Lake County	36,057
49	50150		Millcreek city	63,899
49	50150	035	Salt Lake County	63,899
49	53230		Murray city	50,743
49	53230	035	Salt Lake County	50,743
49	55980		Ogden city	86,830
49	55980	057	Weber County	86,830
49	57300		Orem city	98,070
49	57300	049	Utah County	98,070
49	60930		Pleasant Grove city	37,817
49	60930	049	Utah County	37,817
49	62470		Provo city	114,189
49	62470	049	Utah County	114,189
49	64340		Riverton city	45,402
49	64340	035	Salt Lake County	45,402
49	65110		Roy city	39,420
49	65110	057	Weber County	39,420
49	65330		St. George city	95,284
49	65330	053	Washington County	95,284
49	67000		Salt Lake City city	198,746
49	67000	035	Salt Lake County	198,746
49	67440		Sandy city	97,430
49	67440	035	Salt Lake County	97,430
49	67825		Saratoga Springs city	37,783
49	67825	049	Utah County	37,783
49	70850		South Jordan city	77,661
49	70850	035	Salt Lake County	77,661
49	71070		South Salt Lake city	26,382
49	71070	035	Salt Lake County	26,382
49	71290		Spanish Fork city	42,663
49	71290	049	Utah County	42,663
49	72280		Springville city	35,335
49	72280	049	Utah County	35,335
49	74810		Syracuse city	32,110
49	74810	011	Davis County	32,110
49	75360		Taylorsville city	60,552
49	75360	035	Salt Lake County	60,552
49	76680		Tooele city	35,670
49	76680	045	Tooele County	35,670
49	81960		Washington city	28,087
49	81960	053	Washington County	28,087
49	82950		West Jordan city	117,190
49	82950	035	Salt Lake County	117,190
49	83470		West Valley City city	140,571
49	83470	035	Salt Lake County	140,571
50			**VERMONT**	643,077
50	10675		Burlington city	44,890
50	10675	007	Chittenden County	44,890
51			**VIRGINIA**	8,631,393
51	01000		Alexandria city	159,467
51	01000	510	Alexandria city	159,467
51	07784		Blacksburg town	44,268
51	07784	121	Montgomery County	44,268
51	14968		Charlottesville city	46,553
51	14968	540	Charlottesville city	46,553
51	16000		Chesapeake city	249,422
51	16000	550	Chesapeake city	249,422
51	21344		Danville city	42,590
51	21344	590	Danville city	42,590
51	29744		Fredericksburg city	27,982
51	29744	630	Fredericksburg city	27,982
51	35000		Hampton city	137,148
51	35000	650	Hampton city	137,148
51	35624		Harrisonburg city	51,814
51	35624	660	Harrisonburg city	51,814
51	44984		Leesburg town	48,307
51	44984	107	Loudoun County	48,307
51	47672		Lynchburg city	79,009
51	47672	680	Lynchburg city	79,009
51	48952		Manassas city	42,772
51	48952	683	Manassas city	42,772
51	56000		Newport News city	186,247
51	56000	700	Newport News city	186,247
51	57000		Norfolk city	238,005
51	57000	710	Norfolk city	238,005
51	61832		Petersburg city	33,458
51	61832	730	Petersburg city	33,458
51	64000		Portsmouth city	97,915
51	64000	740	Portsmouth city	97,915

CITIES BY COUNTY—*Continued*

State code	Place code	County code	Geographic Area Name	2020 census population
51	67000		Richmond city	226,610
51	67000	760	Richmond city	226,610
51	68000		Roanoke city	100,011
51	68000	770	Roanoke city	100,011
51	70000		Salem city	25,346
51	70000	775	Salem city	25,346
51	75216		Staunton city	25,750
51	75216	790	Staunton city	25,750
51	76432		Suffolk city	94,324
51	76432	800	Suffolk city	94,324
51	82000		Virginia Beach city	459,470
51	82000	810	Virginia Beach city	459,470
51	86720		Winchester city	28,120
51	86720	840	Winchester city	28,120
53			**WASHINGTON**	7,705,281
53	03180		Auburn city	87,351
53	03180	033	King County	77,300
53	03180	053	Pierce County	10,051
53	05210		Bellevue city	152,045
53	05210	033	King County	152,045
53	05280		Bellingham city	91,231
53	05280	073	Whatcom County	91,231
53	07380		Bothell city	48,184
53	07380	033	King County	28,993
53	07380	061	Snohomish County	19,191
53	07695		Bremerton city	43,886
53	07695	035	Kitsap County	43,886
53	08850		Burien city	52,121
53	08850	033	King County	52,121
53	09480		Camas city	26,095
53	09480	011	Clark County	26,095
53	17635		Des Moines city	32,891
53	17635	033	King County	32,891
53	20750		Edmonds city	42,852
53	20750	061	Snohomish County	42,852
53	22640		Everett city	110,723
53	22640	061	Snohomish County	110,723
53	23515		Federal Way city	101,131
53	23515	033	King County	101,131
53	33805		Issaquah city	40,103
53	33805	033	King County	40,103
53	35275		Kennewick city	83,943
53	35275	005	Benton County	83,943
53	35415		Kent city	136,750
53	35415	033	King County	136,750
53	35940		Kirkland city	92,247
53	35940	033	King County	92,247
53	36745		Lacey city	53,442
53	36745	067	Thurston County	53,442
53	37900		Lake Stevens city	35,601
53	37900	061	Snohomish County	35,601
53	38038		Lakewood city	63,666
53	38038	053	Pierce County	63,666
53	40245		Longview city	37,861
53	40245	015	Cowlitz County	37,861
53	40840		Lynnwood city	38,583
53	40840	061	Snohomish County	38,583
53	43150		Maple Valley city	28,078
53	43150	033	King County	28,078
53	43955		Marysville city	70,683
53	43955	061	Snohomish County	70,683
53	45005		Mercer Island city	25,792
53	45005	033	King County	25,792
53	47245		Moses Lake city	25,401
53	47245	025	Grant County	25,401
53	47560		Mount Vernon city	35,232
53	47560	057	Skagit County	35,232
53	51300		Olympia city	55,435
53	51300	067	Thurston County	55,435
53	53545		Pasco city	77,579
53	53545	021	Franklin County	77,579
53	56625		Pullman city	32,870
53	56625	075	Whitman County	32,870
53	56695		Puyallup city	42,985
53	56695	053	Pierce County	42,985
53	57535		Redmond city	73,375
53	57535	033	King County	73,375
53	57745		Renton city	106,966
53	57745	033	King County	106,966
53	58235		Richland city	60,538
53	58235	005	Benton County	60,538
53	61115		Sammamish city	67,600
53	61115	033	King County	67,600
53	62288		SeaTac city	31,402
53	62288	033	King County	31,402
53	63000		Seattle city	735,157
53	63000	033	King County	735,157
53	63960		Shoreline city	58,532
53	63960	033	King County	58,532
53	67000		Spokane city	228,831
53	67000	063	Spokane County	228,831
53	67167		Spokane Valley city	103,317
53	67167	063	Spokane County	103,317
53	70000		Tacoma city	219,025
53	70000	053	Pierce County	219,025
53	72905		Tumwater city	25,391
53	72905	067	Thurston County	25,391
53	73465		University Place city	34,955
53	73465	053	Pierce County	34,955

State code	Place code	County code	Geographic Area Name	2020 census population
53	74060		Vancouver city	190,810
53	74060	011	Clark County	190,810
53	75775		Walla Walla city	33,983
53	75775	071	Walla Walla County	33,983
53	77105		Wenatchee city	35,394
53	77105	007	Chelan County	35,394
53	80010		Yakima city	96,873
53	80010	077	Yakima County	96,873
54			**WEST VIRGINIA**	1,793,716
54	14600		Charleston city	48,913
54	14600	039	Kanawha County	48,913
54	39460		Huntington city	46,645
54	39460	011	Cabell County	42,886
54	39460	099	Wayne County	3,759
54	55756		Morgantown city	29,150
54	55756	061	Monongalia County	29,150
54	62140		Parkersburg city	29,749
54	62140	107	Wood County	29,749
54	86452		Wheeling city	27,009
54	86452	051	Marshall County	345
54	86452	069	Ohio County	26,664
55			**WISCONSIN**	5,893,718
55	02375		Appleton city	75,315
55	02375	015	Calumet County	11,313
55	02375	087	Outagamie County	62,567
55	02375	139	Winnebago County	1,435
55	06500		Beloit city	36,470
55	06500	105	Rock County	36,470
55	10025		Brookfield city	41,458
55	10025	133	Waukesha County	41,458
55	11950		Caledonia village	25,325
55	11950	101	Racine County	25,325
55	19775		De Pere city	25,281
55	19775	009	Brown County	25,281
55	22300		Eau Claire city	69,291
55	22300	017	Chippewa County	2,185
55	22300	035	Eau Claire County	67,106
55	25950		Fitchburg city	29,601
55	25950	025	Dane County	29,601
55	26275		Fond du Lac city	44,593
55	26275	039	Fond du Lac County	44,593
55	27300		Franklin city	36,818
55	27300	079	Milwaukee County	36,818
55	31000		Green Bay city	107,300
55	31000	009	Brown County	107,300
55	31175		Greenfield city	37,793
55	31175	079	Milwaukee County	37,793
55	37825		Janesville city	65,631
55	37825	105	Rock County	65,631
55	39225		Kenosha city	99,882
55	39225	059	Kenosha County	99,882
55	40775		La Crosse city	52,690
55	40775	063	La Crosse County	52,690
55	48000		Madison city	268,414
55	48000	025	Dane County	268,414
55	48500		Manitowoc city	34,470
55	48500	071	Manitowoc County	34,470
55	51000		Menomonee Falls village	38,466
55	51000	133	Waukesha County	38,466
55	51150		Mequon city	25,015
55	51150	089	Ozaukee County	25,015
55	53000		Milwaukee city	577,235
55	53000	079	Milwaukee County	577,235
55	53000	131	Washington County	0
55	53000	133	Waukesha County	0
55	54875		Mount Pleasant village	27,696
55	54875	101	Racine County	27,696
55	55275		Muskego city	25,052
55	55275	133	Waukesha County	25,052
55	55750		Neenah city	27,330
55	55750	139	Winnebago County	27,330
55	56375		New Berlin city	40,395
55	56375	133	Waukesha County	40,395
55	58800		Oak Creek city	36,505
55	58800	079	Milwaukee County	36,505
55	60500		Oshkosh city	66,777
55	60500	139	Winnebago County	66,777
55	66000		Racine city	77,775
55	66000	101	Racine County	77,775
55	72975		Sheboygan city	50,017
55	72975	117	Sheboygan County	50,017
55	77200		Stevens Point city	25,597
55	77200	097	Portage County	25,597
55	78600		Sun Prairie city	36,147
55	78600	025	Dane County	36,147
55	78650		Superior city	26,722
55	78650	031	Douglas County	26,722
55	84250		Waukesha city	71,405
55	84250	133	Waukesha County	71,405
55	84475		Wausau city	39,831
55	84475	073	Marathon County	39,831
55	84675		Wauwatosa city	48,376
55	84675	079	Milwaukee County	48,376
55	85300		West Allis city	60,330
55	85300	079	Milwaukee County	60,330
55	85350		West Bend city	31,731
55	85350	131	Washington County	31,731

CITIES BY COUNTY—*Continued*

State code	Place code	County code	Geographic Area Name	2020 census population
56			**WYOMING**	576,851
56	13150		Casper city	59,072
56	13150	025	Natrona County	59,072
56	13900		Cheyenne city	65,096
56	13900	021	Laramie County	65,096
56	31855		Gillette city	33,408
56	31855	005	Campbell County	33,408
56	45050		Laramie city	31,317
56	45050	001	Albany County	31,317

The following consolidated cities are included in Table D. They are listed here with their 2020 census populations followed by the separate entities that make up the consolidated city. Data from the American Community Survey include only the "balance", the major city of each consolidated city.

State code	Consolidated City code	Place code	Geographic Area Name	2020 census population
09	47500	0	Milford consolidated city	52,059
09	47500	47515	Milford city (balance)	50,587
09	47500	88050	Woodmont borough	1,472
13	03436	0	Athens-Clarke County unified government	128,671
13	03436	03440	Athens-Clarke County unified government (balance)	127,320
13	03436	09068	Bogart town	153
13	03436	83728	Winterville city	1,198
13	04200	0	Augusta-Richmond County consolidated government	206,607
13	04200	04204	Augusta-Richmond County consolidated government (balance)	202,123
13	04200	09040	Blythe city	692
13	04200	38040	Hephzibah city	3,792
18	36000	0	Indianapolis city	897,123
18	36000	36003	Indianapolis city (balance)	887,752
18	36000	13492	Clermont town	1,377
18	36000	16156	Crows Nest town	67
18	36000	16336	Cumberland town	2,491
18	36000	34420	Homecroft town	750
18	36000	48456	Meridian Hills town	1,771
18	36000	54612	North Crows Nest town	41
18	36000	65556	Rocky Ripple town	651
18	36000	72232	Spring Hill town	95
18	36000	80234	Warren Park town	1,486
18	36000	84374	Williams Creek town	428
18	36000	85742	Wynnedale town	214
21	48003	0	Louisville/Jefferson County metro government	782,969
21	48003	48006	Louisville/Jefferson County metro government (balance)	632,689
21	48003	01504	Anchorage city	2,499
21	48003	02656	Audubon Park city	1,435
21	48003	03376	Bancroft city	503
21	48003	03556	Barbourmeade city	1,218
21	48003	05068	Beechwood Village city	1,275
21	48003	05392	Bellemeade city	905
21	48003	05464	Bellewood city	342
21	48003	07858	Blue Ridge Manor city	788
21	48003	09532	Briarwood city	445
21	48003	09847	Broeck Pointe city	247
21	48003	10162	Brownsboro Farm city	638
21	48003	10198	Brownsboro Village city	307
21	48003	12066	Cambridge city	161
21	48003	16395	Coldstream city	1,292
21	48003	18270	Creekside city	307
21	48003	18766	Crossgate city	221
21	48003	22204	Douglass Hills city	5,454
21	48003	22474	Druid Hills city	299
21	48003	27262	Fincastle city	844
21	48003	28342	Forest Hills city	439
21	48003	31348	Glenview city	592
21	48003	31402	Glenview Hills city	375
21	48003	31420	Glenview Manor city	207
21	48003	31870	Goose Creek city	300
21	48003	32523	Graymoor-Devondale city	2,862
21	48003	32986	Green Spring city	711
21	48003	36102	Heritage Creek city	1,207
21	48003	36374	Hickory Hill city	119
21	48003	36865	Hills and Dales city	143
21	48003	37576	Hollow Creek city	798
21	48003	37630	Hollyvilla city	516
21	48003	38170	Houston Acres city	495
21	48003	38814	Hurstbourne city	4,681
21	48003	38818	Hurstbourne Acres city	1,954
21	48003	39304	Indian Hills city	2,856
21	48003	40222	Jeffersontown city	28,904
21	48003	42598	Kingsley city	396
21	48003	43900	Langdon Place city	870
21	48003	46540	Lincolnshire city	138
21	48003	48558	Lyndon city	10,989
21	48003	48648	Lynnview city	946
21	48003	49800	Manor Creek city	240
21	48003	50412	Maryhill Estates city	181
21	48003	51193	Meadowbrook Farm city	114
21	48003	51258	Meadow Vale city	725
21	48003	51294	Meadowview Estates city	179
21	48003	51978	Middletown city	9,701
21	48003	52842	Mockingbird Valley city	177
21	48003	53328	Moorland city	433
21	48003	54660	Murray Hill city	563
21	48003	56550	Norbourne Estates city	437
21	48003	56730	Northfield city	1,000
21	48003	56928	Norwood city	379
21	48003	57658	Old Brownsboro Place city	374
21	48003	59322	Parkway Village city	620
21	48003	61554	Plantation city	826
21	48003	62370	Poplar Hills city	380
21	48003	63264	Prospect city	4,527
21	48003	65208	Richlawn city	415
21	48003	65766	Riverwood city	489
21	48003	66486	Rolling Fields city	719
21	48003	66504	Rolling Hills city	932
21	48003	67944	St. Matthews city	17,551
21	48003	67998	St. Regis Park city	1,435
21	48003	69384	Seneca Gardens city	672
21	48003	70284	Shively city	15,635
21	48003	72138	South Park View city	0
21	48003	72770	Spring Mill city	293
21	48003	72790	Spring Valley city	673
21	48003	74064	Strathmoor Manor city	352
21	48003	74082	Strathmoor Village city	683
21	48003	75190	Sycamore city	167
21	48003	75963	Ten Broeck city	94
21	48003	76380	Thornhill city	184
21	48003	80913	Watterson Park city	1,002
21	48003	81372	Wellington city	565
21	48003	81624	West Buechel city	1,367
21	48003	82164	Westwood city	574
21	48003	83208	Wildwood city	280
21	48003	83784	Windy Hills city	2,427
21	48003	84486	Woodland Hills city	731
21	48003	84576	Woodlawn Park city	944
21	48003	84891	Worthington Hills city	1,562
30	11390	0	Butte-Silver Bow	35,133
30	11390	11397	Butte-Silver Bow (balance)	34,495
30	11390	77650	Walkerville town	638
47	52004	0	Nashville-Davidson metropolitan government	715,884
47	52004	52006	Nashville-Davidson metropolitan government (balance)	689,504
47	52004	04620	Belle Meade city	2,898
47	52004	05140	Berry Hill city	2,104
47	52004	27020	Forest Hills city	5,028
47	52004	29920	Goodlettsville city	11,413
47	52004	54780	Oak Hill city	4,878
47	52004	63140	Ridgetop city	59

APPENDIX F
SOURCE NOTES AND EXPLANATIONS

The following documentation is provided in the order in which items appear in the tables. Internet addresses are provided for the sources of the data. Some of the links refer to the specific data tables. Others provide information about the general data source.

TABLE A—STATES

Table A presents 355 items for the United States as a whole, for each individual state, and for the District of Columbia. The states are presented in alphabetical order.

LAND AREA, Items 1 and 4

Source: U.S. Census Bureau—2020 U.S. Gazetteer Files
https://www.census.gov/geographies/reference-files/time-series/geo/gazetteer-files.html

Land area measurements are shown to the nearest square mile. Land area includes dry land and land temporarily or partially covered by water, such as marshlands, swamps, and river floodplains. The 2020 land areas have been aggregated from the counties as listed in the 2020 Gazetteer files.

POPULATION AND COMPONENTS OF CHANGE, Items 2–4, 31—41

Source: U.S. Census Bureau—Decennial Censuses and Population Estimates
https://www.census.gov/programs-surveys/popest.html
https://www.census.gov/programs-surveys/decennial-census/data/datasets.2010.html

The population data for 2021 are Census Bureau estimates of the resident population as of July 1, 2021.

The population data for 2000, 2010, and 2020 are from the decennial censuses and represent the resident population as of April 1 of those years.

The change in population between 2010 and 2020 is made up of (a) natural increase—births minus deaths, and (b) net migration—the difference between the number of persons moving into a particular state and the number of persons moving out of the state. Net migration is composed of internal and international migration.

POPULATION AND POPULATION CHARACTERISTICS, Items 5–23 and 45–63

Source: U.S. Census Bureau—Population Estimates and 2020 Experimental American Community Survey
https://www.census.gov/programs-surveys/popest.html
https://www.census.gov/programs-surveys/acs
https://www.census.gov/programs-surveys/acs/data/experimental-data.html

Data on age, sex, race, and Hispanic origin are from the Population Estimates program. Median age and data on place of birth are from the 2020 American Community Survey, a nationwide continuous survey designed to replace the long form questionnaire used in previous censuses. All 2020 ACS data in Table A are from the Experimental Data, the only 1-year ACS data released for 2020, only available at the state level.

The concept "race alone or in combination" includes people who reported a single race alone (e.g., Asian) and people who reported that race in combination with one or more of the other major race groups (e.g., White, Black or African American, American Indian and Alaska Native, Native Hawaiian and Other Pacific Islander, and Some Other Race). The "race alone or in combination" concept, therefore, represents the maximum number of people who reported as that race group, either alone, or in combination with another race(s).

The sum of the four individual race alone or in combination categories in this book may add to more than the total population because people who reported more than one race were tallied in each race category. In this book, the Asian group has been combined with the Native Hawaiian and Other Pacific Islander group, causing double-counting of persons who identify with both groups. This is especially pronounced in Hawaii.

Data on race were derived from answers to the question on race that was asked of all persons. The concept of race, as used by the Census Bureau, reflects self-identification by respondents according to the race or races with which they most closely identify. These categories are sociopolitical constructs and should not be interpreted as being scientific or anthropological in nature. Furthermore, the race categories include both racial and national origin groups.

The **White** population is defined as persons who indicated their race as White, as well as persons who did not classify themselves in one of the specific race categories listed on the questionnaire but entered a nationality such as Irish, German, Italian, Lebanese, Near Easterner, Arab, or Polish.

The **Black** population includes persons who indicated their race as "Black or African American" as well as persons who did not classify themselves in one of the specific race categories but reported entries such as African American, Afro American, Kenyan, Nigerian, or Haitian.

The **American Indian or Alaska Native** population includes persons who indicated their race as American Indian or Alaska Native, as well as persons who did not classify themselves in one of the specific race categories but reported entries such as Canadian Indian, French-American Indian, Spanish-American Indian, Eskimo, Aleut, Alaska Indian, or any of the American Indian or Alaska Native tribes.

The **Asian and Pacific Islander** population combines two census groupings: **Asian** and **Native Hawaiian or Other Pacific Islander**. The **Asian** population includes persons who indicated their race as Asian Indian, Chinese, Filipino, Japanese, Korean, Vietnamese, or "Other Asian," as well as persons who provided write-in entries of such groups as Cambodian, Laotian, Hmong, Pakistani, or Taiwanese. The **Native Hawaiian or Other Pacific Islander** population includes persons who indicated their race as "Native Hawaiian," "Guamanian or Chamorro," "Samoan," or "Other Pacific Islander," as well as persons who reported entries such as Part Hawaiian, American Samoan, Fijian, Melanesian, or Tahitian.

The **Hispanic population** is based on a question that asked respondents "Is this person Spanish/Hispanic/Latino?" Persons marking any one of the four Hispanic categories (i.e., Mexican, Puerto Rican, Cuban, or other Spanish) are collectively referred to as Hispanic.

Age is defined as age at last birthday (number of completed years since birth), as of April 1 of the census year.

The **female** population is shown as a percentage of total population.

The **median age** is the age that divides the population into two equal-size groups. Half of the population is older than the median age and half is younger. Median age is based on a standard distribution of the population by single years of age and is shown to the nearest tenth of a year.

The **foreign-born** population includes all persons who were not U.S. citizens at birth. Foreign-born persons are those who indicated they were either a U.S. citizen by naturalization or were not a citizen of the United States. Neither the census nor the American Community Survey asked about immigration status. The population surveyed included all persons who indicated that the United States was their usual place of residence. The foreign-born population consists of immigrants (legal permanent residents), temporary migrants (students), humanitarian migrants (refugees), and unauthorized migrants (persons illegally residing in the United States).

Percent born in state of residence is shown as a percentage of total population.

IMMIGRANTS, Item 24

Source: Department of Homeland Security, U.S. Citizenship and Immigration Services
https://www.dhs.gov/immigration-statistics/yearbook

The number of immigrants by state of intended residence is summarized from the administrative records of the Citizenship and Immigration Services. This information is compiled from immigrant visas and forms granting legal permanent resident status.

An **immigrant** is an alien admitted to the United States as a lawful permanent resident. Immigrants are those persons lawfully accorded the privilege of residing permanently in the United States (**i.e., immigrants who receive a "green card"**.) They may be newly arrived individuals who were issued immigrant visas by the Department of State overseas, or they may be U.S. residents who were admitted to permanent resident status in 2017 by the U.S. Citizenship and Immigration Services.

HOUSEHOLDS, Items 25–30 and 64–68

Source: U.S. Census Bureau—2010 1-year and 2020 Experimental American Community Survey
https://www.census.gov/programs-surveys/acs
https://www.census.gov/programs-surveys/acs/data/experimental-data.html

A **household** includes all of the persons who occupy a housing unit. Persons not living in households are classified as living in group quarters. A housing unit is a house, an apartment, a mobile home, a group of rooms, or a single room occupied (or, if vacant, intended for occupancy) as separate living quarters. Separate living quarters are those in which the occupants live separately from any other persons in the building and have direct access from the outside of the building or through a common hall. The occupants may be a single family, one person living alone, two or more families living together, or any other group of related or unrelated persons who share living quarters. The number of households is the same as the number of year-round occupied housing units.

A **family** includes a householder and one or more other persons living in the same household who are related to the householder by birth, marriage, or adoption. All persons in a household who are related to the householder are regarded as members of his or her family. A **family household** may contain persons not related to the householder; thus, family households may include more members than families do. A household can contain only one family for the purposes of census tabulations. Not all households contain families, as a household may comprise a group of unrelated persons or one person living alone. Families are classified by type as either a "married couple family" or "other family" according to the presence of a spouse.

The category **female family householder** includes only female-headed family households with no spouse present.

POPULATION PROJECTIONS, Items 42–44

Source: U.S. Census Bureau—Population Projections Branch
https://census.gov/programs-surveys/popproj/guidance.html

Projections are estimates of the population for future dates. They illustrate plausible courses of future population change based on assumptions about future births, deaths, international migration, and domestic migration. Projected numbers are based on an estimated population consistent with the most recent decennial census as enumerated. The Census Bureau does not have a current set of state population projections and currently has no plans to produce them. This volume includes projections released in 2005, based on the 2000 census. The Census Bureau notes that these projections should be used with caution because population trends may have changed substantially since their release.

HOUSING, Items 69–88

Source: U.S. Census Bureau—2010 1-year and 2020 Experimental American Community Survey
https://www.census.gov/programs-surveys/acs
https://www.census.gov/programs-surveys/acs/data/experimental-data.html

Housing data for 2010 and 2020 are from the American Community Survey, a nationwide continuous survey designed to replace the long form questionnaire used in previous censuses. A sample of households is surveyed to provide estimates. All 2020 ACS data in Table A are from the Experimental Data, the only 1-year ACS data released for 2020, only available at the state level.

A **housing unit** is a house, apartment, mobile home or trailer, group of rooms, or single room occupied or, if vacant, intended for occupancy as separate living quarters. Separate living quarters are those in which the occupants do not live and eat with any other person in the structure and which have direct access from the outside of the building or through a common hall. For vacant units, the criteria of separateness and direct access are applied to the intended occupants whenever possible. If that information cannot be obtained, the criteria are applied to the previous occupants.

The occupants of a housing unit may be a single family, one person living alone, two or more families living together, or any other group of related or unrelated persons who share living arrangements. Both occupied and vacant housing units are included in the housing inventory, although recreational vehicles, tents, caves, boats, railroad cars, and the like are included only if they are occupied as a person's usual place of residence.

A housing unit is classified as **occupied** if it is the usual place of residence of the person or group of persons living in it at the time of enumeration, or if the occupants are only temporarily absent (away on vacation). A household consists of all persons who occupy a housing unit as their usual place of residence.

Housing cost, as a percentage of income, is shown separately for owners with mortgages, owners without mortgages, and renters. Also shown is the percentage of mortgaged owners and renters who pay 30 percent or more of household income on selected monthly costs. Rent as a percent of income is a computed ratio of gross rent and monthly household income (total household income divided by 12). Selected owner costs include utilities and fuels, mortgage payments, insurance, taxes, etc. In each case, the ratio of housing cost to income is computed separately for each housing unit. The housing cost ratios for half of all units are above the median shown in this book, and half are below the median. Median monthly housing costs divides the monthly housing costs distribution into two equal parts, one-half of the cases falling below the median monthly housing costs and one-half above the median.

Median value is the dollar amount that divides the distribution of specified owner-occupied housing units into two equal parts, with half of all units below the median value and half above the median value. Value is defined as the respondent's estimate of what the house would sell for if it were for sale. Data are presented for single-family units on fewer than 10 acres of land that have no business or medical office on the property.

Median rent divides the distribution of renter-occupied housing units into two equal parts. The rent concept used in this volume is gross rent, which includes the amount of cash rent a renter pays (contract rent) plus the estimated average cost of utilities and fuels, if these are paid by the renter. The rent is the amount of rent only for living quarters and excludes any business or other space occupied. Single-family houses on lots of 10 or more acres of land are excluded.

Substandard units are occupied units that are overcrowded or lack complete plumbing facilities. For the purposes of this item, "overcrowded" is defined as having 1.01 persons or more per room. Complete plumbing facilities include hot and cold piped water, a flush toilet, and a bathtub or shower. These facilities must be located inside the housing unit, but do not have to be in the same room.

Different house includes all people 1 year old and over who, a year earlier, lived in a different house or apartment from the one they occupied at the time of interview.

COMPUTER AND INTERNET USE, Items 89–92

Source: U.S. Census Bureau—American Community Survey, 2020 Experimental Estimates
https://www.census.gov/programs-surveys/acs
https://www.census.gov/programs-surveys/acs/data/experimental-data.html

The **computer use** question asked if anyone in the household owned or used a computer and included four response categories for a desktop/laptop, smartphone, tablet or other portable, wireless computer, or some other type of computer. Respondents could select all categories that applied.

Another question asked if any member of the household accesses the **internet**. "Access" refers to whether or not someone in the household uses or connects to the internet, regardless of whether or not they pay for the service. Respondents were to select only ONE of the following choices:

- Yes, with a subscription to an Internet service—This category includes housing units where someone pays to access the Internet through a service such as a data plan for a mobile phone, a cable modem, DSL or other type of service. This will normally refer to a service that someone is billed for directly for Internet alone or sometimes as part of a bundle.
- Yes, without a subscription to an Internet service—Some respondents may live in a city or town that provides free Internet services for their residents. In addition, some colleges or universities provide Internet services. These are examples of cases where respondents may be able to access the Internet without a subscription.
- No Internet access at this house, apartment, or mobile home—This category includes housing units where no one connects to or uses the Internet using a paid service or any free services.

BUILDING PERMITS, Items 93–95

Source: U.S. Census Bureau—Building Permits Survey
https://www.census.gov/construction/bps/

These figures represent private residential construction authorized by building permits in approximately 20,000 places in the United States. Valuation represents the expected cost of construction as recorded on the building permit. This figure usually excludes the cost of on-site and off-site development and improvements, as well as the cost of heating, plumbing, electrical, and elevator installations.

National, state, and county totals were obtained by adding the data for permit-issuing places within each jurisdiction. These totals thus are limited to permits issued in the 20,000 place universe covered by the Census Bureau and may not include all permits issued within a state. Current surveys indicate that construction is undertaken for all but a very small percentage of housing units authorized by building permits.

Residential building permits include buildings with any number of housing units. Housing units exclude group quarters (such as dormitories and rooming houses), transient accommodations (such as transient hotels, motels, and tourist courts), "HUD-code" manufactured (mobile) homes, moved or relocated units, and housing units created in an existing residential or nonresidential structure.

MANUFACTURED HOUSING UNITS, Item 96

Source: U.S. Census Bureau—Manufactured Housing Survey
https://www.census.gov/data/tables/time-series/econ/mhs/shipments.html

The Manufactured Housing Survey (MHS) is conducted by the U.S. Census Bureau and sponsored by the Department of Housing and Urban Development (HUD). MHS produces monthly regional estimates of the average sales price of new manufactured homes and more detailed annual estimates including selected characteristics of new manufactured homes. In addition, MHS produces monthly estimates of homes shipped to each state.

A manufactured home is defined as a movable dwelling, 8 feet or more wide and 40 feet or more long, designed to be towed on its own chassis, with transportation gear integral to the unit when it leaves the factory, and without need of a permanent foundation. These manufactured homes include multi-wides and expandable manufactured homes. Excluded are travel trailers, motor homes, and modular housing.

BIRTHS AND DEATHS, Items 97–103

Source: U.S. Centers for Disease Control and Prevention, National Center for Health Statistics
https://www.cdc.gov/nchs/data/nvsr/nvsr70/nvsr70-08-508.pdf
https://www.cdc.gov/nchs/data/nvsr/nvsr70/nvsr70-17.pdf

The registration of births, deaths, and other vital events in the United States is primarily a state and local function. The civil laws of every state provide for continuous and permanent birth and death registration systems. Through the National Vital Statistics System, the National Center for Health Statistics (NCHS) obtains data on births and deaths from the registration offices of each state, New York City, and the District of Columbia.

Birth and death statistics are limited to events occurring during the year. The data are by place of residence and exclude events for nonresidents of the United States. Births or deaths occurring outside the United States are excluded.

Birth and death rates represent the number of births and deaths per 1,000 resident population enumerated as of April 1 for decennial census years and estimated as of July 1 for other years.

Figures for infant deaths include deaths of children under 1 year of age but exclude fetal deaths. The infant death rate is per 1,000 live births.

The rates of almost all causes of disease, injury, and death vary by age. Age adjustment is a technique for "removing" the effects of age from crude rates, in order to allow meaningful comparisons across populations with different underlying age structures. For example, comparing the crude death rate in Florida to that of California is misleading, since the relatively older population in Florida will lead to a higher crude death rate. For such a comparison, age-adjusted death rates are preferable.

The population estimates were developed by the Census Bureau's Population Division using a traditional cohort component method. Starting with a basic population from the 2000 census, each component of population change—births, deaths, domestic migration, and international migration—is estimated separately for each birth cohort by sex, race, and Hispanic or Latino origin.

Age-adjusted rates are calculated by applying the age-specific rates of various populations to a single standard population. In this volume, the standard population is 2000. Beginning in 2003, The Centers for Disease Control and Prevention switched to the year 2000, after many years of using the year 1940 as the standard population for age-adjusted death rates.

PERSONS LACKING HEALTH INSURANCE, Items 104–105

Source: U.S. Census Bureau—American Community Survey, 2020 Experimental Estimates
https://www.census.gov/programs-surveys/acs
https://www.census.gov/programs-surveys/acs/data/experimental-data.html

These estimates are from the American Community Survey, an ongoing nationwide survey that is conducted throughout the year. About 250,000 addresses per month receive the ACS. Respondents are asked whether each household member is currently covered (by specific types of health coverage) at the time of interview. The 2013 estimates were the first to use the ACS. Prior year estimates were based on the Annual Social and Economic Supplement (ASEC) of the Current Population Survey (CPS).

Those lacking coverage are the percentage of the population of each state who were not covered by private health plans purchased directly or provided by an employer, Medicaid, Medicare, or military health care.

MEDICARE BENEFICIARIES, Item 106

Source: U.S. Department of Health and Human Services, Centers for Medicare and Medicaid Services
https://data.cms.gov/summary-statistics-on-beneficiary-enrollment/medicare-and-medicaid-reports

The Centers for Medicare and Medicaid Services (CMS) administers Medicare, which provides health insurance to persons 65 years old and over, persons with permanent kidney failure, and certain persons with disabilities. Original Medicare has two parts: Hospital Insurance and Supplemental Medical Insurance. In recent years, Medicare has been expanded to include two new programs: Medicare Advantage plans and prescription drug coverage. Medicare Advantage Plans are health plan options that are approved by Medicare but run by private companies. Medicare prescription drug plans can be part of Medicare Advantage plans or stand-alone drug plans.

Persons who are eligible for Medicare can enroll in Part A (Hospital Insurance) at no charge, and can choose to pay a monthly premium to enroll in Part B. Most eligible persons are enrolled in Part A, and most enrollees in Part A are also enrolled in Part B (Supplemental Medical Insurance.) This table includes persons who were enrolled in both Part A and Part B during 2020.

Part B beneficiaries can choose to enroll in **Original Medicare**, a fee-for-service plan administered by the Centers for Medicare and Medicaid Services, or in a **Medicare Advantage** plan. Medicare Advantage plans include private fee-for-service plans, preferred provider organizations, health maintenance organizations, medical savings account plans, demonstration plans, and programs for all-inclusive care for the elderly.

The annual Medicare enrollment counts are determined using a person-year methodology. For each calendar year, total person-year counts are determined by summing the total number of months that each beneficiary is enrolled during the year and dividing by 12. Using this methodology, a beneficiary's partial-year enrollment may be counted in more than one category (i.e., both Original Medicare and Medicare Advantage).

CRIME, Items 107–110

Source: U.S. Federal Bureau of Investigation—Uniform Crime Reports
https://crime-data-explorer.app.cloud.gov/pages/downloads

Crime data are as reported to the Federal Bureau of Investigation (FBI) by law enforcement agencies and have not been adjusted for underreporting. This may affect comparability between geographic areas or over time.

Through the voluntary contribution of crime statistics by law enforcement agencies across the United States, the Uniform Crime Reporting (UCR) Program provides periodic assessments of crime in the nation as measured by offenses that have come to the attention of the law enforcement community. The Committee on Uniform Crime Records of the International Association of Chiefs of Police initiated this voluntary national data-collection effort in 1930. The UCR Program contributors compile and submit their crime data either directly to the FBI or through state-level UCR Programs.

Seven offenses, because of their severity, frequency of occurrence, and likelihood of being reported to police, were initially selected to serve as an index for evaluating fluctuations in the volume of crime. These serious crimes were murder and nonnegligent manslaughter, forcible rape, robbery, aggravated assault, burglary, larceny-theft, and motor vehicle theft. By congressional mandate, arson was added as the eighth index offense in 1979. The totals shown in this volume do not include arson.

In 2004, the FBI discontinued the use of the Crime Index in the UCR Program and its publications, stating that the Crime Index was driven upward by the offense with the highest number of cases (in this case, larceny-theft) creating a bias against jurisdictions with a high number of larceny-thefts but a low number of other serious crimes, such as murder and forcible rape. The FBI is currently publishing a violent crime total and a property crime total until a more viable index is developed.

In 2013, the FBI adopted a new definition of rape. Rape is now defined as, "Penetration, no matter how slight, of the vagina or anus with any body part or object, or oral penetration by a sex organ of another person, without the consent of the victim." The new definition updated the 80-year-old historical definition of rape which was "carnal knowledge of a female forcibly and against her will." Effectively, the revised definition expands rape to include both male and female victims and offenders, and reflects the various forms of sexual penetration understood to be rape, especially non-consenting acts of sodomy, and sexual assaults with objects. **Violent crimes** include four categories of offenses: (1) Murder and non-negligent manslaughter, as defined in the UCR Program, is the willful (non-negligent) killing of one human being by another. This offense excludes deaths caused by negligence, suicide, or accident; justifiable homicides; and attempts to murder or assaults to murder. (2) Rape is the penetration, no matter how slight, of the vagina or anus with any body part or object, or oral penetration by a sex organ of another person, without the consent of the victim. Assaults or attempts to commit rape by force or threat of force are also included; however, statutory rape (without force) and other sex offenses are excluded. (3) Robbery is the taking or attempting to take anything of value from the care, custody, or control of a person or persons by force or threat of force or violence and/or by putting the victim in fear. (4) Aggravated assault is an unlawful attack by one person upon another for the purpose of inflicting severe or aggravated bodily injury. This type of assault is usually accompanied by the use of a weapon or by other means likely to produce death or great bodily harm. Attempts are included, since injury does not necessarily have to result when a gun, knife, or other weapon is used, as these incidents could and probably would result in a serious personal injury if the crime were successfully completed.

Property crimes include three categories: (1) Burglary, or breaking and entering, is the unlawful entry of a structure to commit a felony or theft, even though no force was used to gain entrance. (2) Larceny-theft is the unauthorized taking of the personal property of another, without the use of force. (3) Motor vehicle theft is the unauthorized taking of any motor vehicle.

Rates are based on population estimates provided by the FBI. For some states, reporting is not sufficiently complete to be representative of the state as a whole. The FBI has estimated state totals for those states.

ELEMENTARY AND SECONDARY SCHOOL ENROLLMENT, Items 111 and 112

Source: U.S. Department of Education, National Center for Education Statistics—Common Core of Data
https://nces.ed.gov/ccd/elsi

Data on public school enrollment is from the Common Core of Data 2020–2021 survey. Public school enrollment includes pre-kindergarten through grade 12 and ungraded students. The student/teacher ratio is calculated by dividing the number of students in all schools by the number of full-time equivalent teachers employed by all schools and agencies.

EDUCATIONAL ATTAINMENT, Items 113–116

Source: U.S. Census Bureau—2010 1-year and 2020 Experimental American Community Survey
https://www.census.gov/programs-surveys/acs
https://www.census.gov/programs-surveys/acs/data/experimental-data.html

Data on **educational attainment** are tabulated for the population 25 years old and over. The data were derived from a question that asked respondents for the highest level of school completed or the highest degree received. Persons who had passed a high school equivalency examination were considered high school graduates. Schooling received in foreign schools was to be reported as the equivalent grade or years in the regular American school system. Vocational and technical training, such as barber school training; business, trade, technical, and vocational schools; or other training for a specific trade are specifically excluded.

High school graduate or more. This category includes persons whose highest degree was a high school diploma or its equivalent, and those who reported any level higher than a high school diploma.

Bachelor's degree or more. This category includes persons who have received bachelor's degrees, master's degrees, professional school degrees (such as law school or medical school degrees), and doctoral degrees.

LOCAL GOVERNMENT EDUCATION EXPENDITURES, Items 117 and 118

Source: U.S. Department of Education, National Center for Education Statistics—Common Core of Data
https://nces.ed.gov/ccd

Total expenditure for education includes provision or support of schools and facilities for elementary and secondary education. It encompasses instructional, support, and auxiliary services (school lunch, student activities, and community service) offered by public school systems. Retirement benefits paid to former education employees and interest payments are not included. Current expenditure includes all components of total expenditure except capital outlay. Expenditure data are obtained by the Census Bureau through its annual survey of government finances and are supplied to the National Center for Education Statistics (NCES). Current expenditure per student is current expenditure divided by the number of students enrolled. The number of students enrolled is based on an annual "membership" count of students on or about October 1.

NCES uses the Common Core of Data (CCD) Survey system to acquire and maintain statistical data from each of the 50 states, the District of Columbia, and the outlying areas. State education agencies compile and submit data for approximately 94,000 schools and 17,000 local school districts. Typically, this results in varying interpretation of NCES definitions and different record keeping systems, leading to large amounts of missing data for several states; this absence is reflected in the data in this publication. The numbers in Table A reflect imputations and adjustments as published in *Revenues and Expenditures for Public Elementary and Secondary Education: School Year 2018-2019 (Fiscal Year 2019)*

EXPORTS, Items 119–121

Source: U.S. Department of Commerce, International Trade Administration
https://www.census.gov/foreign-trade/statistics/state/origin_movement/index.html

The data on exports of goods by state of origin are based on the location of the exporter (the principal party responsible for exportation from the United States). Exporters are often intermediaries, so the data do not necessarily represent the states in which the goods were actually produced. The total includes re-exports of foreign goods.

INCOME AND POVERTY, Items 122–133

Source: U.S. Census Bureau—2020 Experimental American Community Survey
https://www.census.gov/programs-surveys/acs
https://www.census.gov/programs-surveys/acs/data/experimental-data.html

The data on income were derived from answers to questions which were asked of the population 15 years old and over. **Total income** is the sum of the amounts reported separately for wage or salary income; net self-employment income; interest, dividends, or net rental or royalty income or income from estates and trusts; Social Security or railroad retirement income; Supplemental Security Income (SSI); public assistance or welfare payments; retirement, survivor, or disability pensions; and all other income. Receipts from the following sources are not included as income: capital gains; money received from the sale of property (unless the recipient was engaged in the business of selling such property); the value of income "in kind" from food stamps, public housing subsidies, medical care, employer contributions for individuals, etc.; withdrawal of bank deposits; money borrowed; tax refunds; exchange of money between relatives living in the same household; and gifts and lump-sum inheritances, insurance payments, and other types of lump-sum receipts.

Earnings are defined as the sum of wage or salary income and net income from self-employment. "Earnings" represent the amount of income received regularly for people 16 years old and over before deductions for personal income taxes, Social Security, bond purchases, union dues, Medicare deductions, etc. An individual with earnings is one who has either wage/salary income or self-employment income, or both. Respondents who "break even" in self-employment income and therefore have zero self-employment earnings also are considered "individuals with earnings."

The median divides the earnings distribution into two equal parts: one-half of the cases falling below the median and one-half above the median. Median earnings is restricted to individuals 16 years old and over with earnings and is computed on the basis of a standard distribution.

Household income includes the income of the householder and all other individuals 15 years old and over in the household, whether or not they are related to the householder. Since many households consist of only one person, average household income is usually less than average family income. Although the household income statistics cover the past 12 months, the characteristics of individuals and the composition of households refer to the time of enumeration. Thus, the income of the household does not include amounts received by individuals who were members of the household during all or part of the past 12 months if these individuals no longer resided in the household at the time of interview. Similarly, income amounts reported by individuals who did not reside in the household during the past 12 months but who were members of the household at the time of interview are included. However, the composition of most households was the same during the past 12 months as at the time of interview.

Median income divides the income distribution into two equal parts, with half of all cases below the median income level and half of all cases above the median income level. For households and families, the median income is based on the distribution of the total number of households and families, including those with no income. Median income for households is computed on the basis of a standard distribution with a minimum value of less than $2,500 and a maximum value of $200,000 or more and is rounded to the nearest whole dollar.

For **family income**, the incomes of all household members 15 years old and over related to the householder are summed and treated as a single amount. Although the family income statistics cover the past 12 months, the characteristics of individuals and the composition of families refer to the time of interview. Thus, the income of the family does not include amounts received by individuals who were members of the family during all of part of the past 12 months if these individuals no longer resided with the family at the time of interview. Similarly, income amounts reported by individuals who did not reside with the family during the past 12 months but who were members of the family at the time of interview are included. However, the composition of most families was the same during the past 12 months as at the time of interview.

The **poverty status** data were derived from data collected on the number of persons in the household, each person's relationship to the householder, and the income data. The Social Security Administration (SSA) developed the original poverty definition in 1964, which federal interagency committees subsequently revised in 1969 and 1980. The Office of Management and Budget's (OMB) *Directive 14* prescribes the SSA's definition as the official poverty measure for federal agencies to use in their statistical work. Poverty statistics presented in American Community Survey products adhere to the standards defined by OMB in *Directive 14*.

The poverty thresholds vary depending on three criteria: size of family, number of children, and, for one- and two-person families, age of householder. In determining the poverty status of families and unrelated individuals, the Census Bureau uses thresholds (income cutoffs) arranged in a two-dimensional matrix. The matrix consists of family size (from one person to nine or more persons), cross-classified by presence and number of family members under 18 years old (from no children present to eight or more children present). Unrelated individuals and two-person families are further differentiated by age of reference person (under 65 years old and 65 years old and over). To determine a person's poverty status, the person's total family income in the last 12 months is compared to the poverty threshold appropriate for that person's family size and composition. If the total income of that person's family is less than the threshold appropriate for that family, then the person is considered poor or "below the poverty level," together with every member of his or her family. If a person is not living with anyone related by birth, marriage, or adoption, then the person's own income is compared with his or her poverty threshold. The total number of persons below the poverty level is the sum of persons in families

Poverty Thresholds for 2020 by Size of Family and Number of Related Children Under 18 Years

Size of family unit	Weighted average thresholds	Related children under 18 years								
		None	One	Two	Three	Four	Five	Six	Seven	Eight or more
One person (unrelated individual):	13,171									
Under age 65	13,465	13,465								
Aged 65 and older	12,413	12,413								
Two people:	16,733									
Householder under age 65	17,413	17,331	17,839							
Householder aged 65 and older	15,659	15,644	17,771							
Three people	20,591	20,244	20,832	20,852						
Four people	26,496	26,695	27,131	26,246	26,338					
Five people	31,417	32,193	32,661	31,661	30,887	30,414				
Six people	35,499	37,027	37,174	36,408	35,674	34,582	33,935			
Seven people	40,406	42,605	42,871	41,954	41,314	40,124	38,734	37,210		
Eight people	44,755	47,650	48,071	47,205	46,447	45,371	44,006	42,585	42,224	
Nine people or more	53,905	57,319	57,597	56,831	56,188	55,132	53,679	52,366	52,040	50,035

Source: U.S. Census Bureau.

and the number of unrelated individuals with incomes below the poverty level in the last 12 months. The average poverty threshold for a four-person family was $26,496 in 2020.

The data on **poverty status of households** were derived from answers to the income questions. Since poverty is defined at the family level and not the household level, the poverty status of the household is determined by the poverty status of the householder. Households are classified as poor when the total income of the householder's family in the previous 12 months is below the appropriate poverty threshold. (For nonfamily householders, the person's income is compared with the appropriate threshold.) The income of persons living in the household who are unrelated to the householder is not considered when determining the poverty status of a household, nor does their presence affect the family size in determining the appropriate threshold. The poverty thresholds vary depending upon three criteria: size of family, number of children, and, for one- and two-person families, age of the householder.

Poverty status of children by **family type** is the percentage of children living in that particular type of family that has a family income below the poverty threshold based on family size and composition.

PERSONAL INCOME AND EARNINGS, Items 134–158

Source: U.S. Bureau of Economic Analysis, Regional Economic Accounts https://www.bea.gov/data/economic-accounts/regional#state

Total personal income is the current income received by residents of an area from all sources. It is measured before deductions of income and other personal taxes but after deductions of personal contributions for Social Security, government retirement, and other social insurance programs. It consists of **wage and salary disbursements** (covering all employee earnings, including executive salaries, bonuses, commissions, payments-in-kind, incentive payments, and tips); various types of supplementary earnings, such as employers' contributions to pension funds (termed "other labor income" or "supplements to wages and salaries"); proprietors' income; rental income of persons; dividends; personal interest income; and government and business transfer payments.

Proprietors' income is the monetary income and income-in-kind of proprietorships and partnerships (including the independent professions), and the income of tax-exempt cooperatives. **Dividends** are cash payments by corporations to stockholders who are U.S. residents. **Interest** is the monetary and imputed interest income of persons from all sources. **Rent** is the monetary income of persons from the rental of real property, except the income of persons primarily engaged in the real estate business; the imputed net rental income of owner-occupants of nonfarm dwellings; and the royalties received by persons.

Transfer payments are income for which services are not currently rendered. They consist of both government and business transfer payments. Government transfer payments include payments under the following programs: Federal Old-Age, Survivors, and Disability Insurance ("Social Security"); Medicare and medical vendor payments; unemployment insurance; railroad and government retirement; federal- and state-government-insured workers' compensation; veterans' benefits, including veterans' life insurance; food stamps; black lung payments; Supplemental Security Income; and Temporary Assistance for Needy Families. Government payments to nonprofit institutions, other than for work under research and development contracts, are also included. Business transfer payments consist primarily of liability payments for personal injury and of corporate gifts to nonprofit institutions.

Per capita personal income is based on resident population estimated as of July 1 of the year shown.

Personal tax payments include taxes paid by individuals to federal, state, and local governments. Personal taxes include individual income taxes, estate and gift taxes, motor vehicle license taxes, and personal property taxes. Personal contributions to social insurance ("Social Security taxes") are not included, nor are sales taxes.

Disposable personal income equals personal income less personal tax payments. It is a measure of the income available to persons for spending or saving.

Earnings cover wage and salary disbursements, other labor income, and proprietors' income. The data for earnings obtained from the Bureau of Economic Analysis (BEA) are based on place of work. In computing personal income, BEA makes an "adjustment for residence" to earnings based on commuting patterns; thus, personal income is presented on a place-of-residence basis.

Farm earnings include the income of farm workers (wages and salaries and other labor income) and farm proprietors. Farm proprietors' income includes only the income of sole proprietorships and partnerships. Farm earnings estimates are benchmarked to data collected in the Census of Agriculture and the revised Department of Agriculture state totals of income and expense items.

Goods-related industries include mining, construction, and manufacturing. **Service-related** and other industries includes private-sector earnings in forestry, related activities, and other; utilities; transportation and warehousing; information; wholesale trade; retail trade; finance and insurance; real estate and rental and leasing; and services, which includes professional, scientific, and technical services; management of companies and enterprises; administrative and waste services; educational services; health care and social assistance; arts, entertainment, and recreation; accommodation and food services; and other services, except public administration. Government earnings include all levels of government. Industries are categorized under the North American Industry Classification System (NAICS), and are not directly comparable to years prior to 2002.

GROSS STATE PRODUCT, Item 159

Source: U.S. Bureau of Economic Analysis, Regional Economic Accounts https://www.bea.gov/data/economic-accounts/regional#state

Gross state product (GSP) for a state is derived as the sum of gross state product originating in all industries in the state. In concept, an industry's GSP, referred to as its "value added," is equivalent to its gross output (sales or receipts and other operating income, commodity taxes, and inventory changes) minus its intermediate inputs (consumption of goods and services purchased from other industries or imported from other countries). As such, it is often referred to as the state counterpart to the nation's gross domestic product (GDP). In practice, GSP estimates are measured as the sum of distributions by industry of the components of gross domestic income—that is, the sum of the costs incurred (such as compensation of employees, net interest, and indirect business taxes) and the profits earned in production.

SOCIAL SECURITY AND SUPPLEMENTAL SECURITY INCOME, Items 160–162

Source: U.S. Social Security Administration
https://www.ssa.gov/policy/docs/statcomps/oasdi_sc
https://www.ssa.gov/policy/docs/statcomps/ssi_sc

Social Security beneficiaries are persons receiving benefits under the Old-Age, Survivors, and Disability Insurance Program. These include retired or disabled workers covered by the program, their spouses and dependent children, and the surviving spouses and dependent children of deceased workers.

Supplemental Security Income (SSI) recipients are persons receiving SSI payments. The SSI program is a cash assistance program that provides monthly benefits to low-income aged, blind, or disabled persons.

Data are as of December of the year shown.

CIVILIAN EMPLOYMENT, Items 163–166

Source: U.S. Census Bureau—2020 Experimental American Community Survey
https://www.census.gov/programs-surveys/acs
https://www.census.gov/programs-surveys/acs/data/experimental-data.html
https://www2.census.gov/programs-surveys/acs/tech_docs/code_lists/2018_ACS_Code_Lists.pdf?#

The data on occupation were derived from answers to questions that were asked of all persons 15 years old and over who had worked in the past 5 years. **Occupation** describes the kind of work the person does on the job. For employed persons, the data refer to the person's job during the previous week. For those who worked two or more jobs, the data refer to the job at which the person worked the greatest number of hours. For unemployed persons, the data refer to their last job. The American Community Survey uses the occupational classification system that was developed for the 2000 census and modified in 2002 and again in 2010. This system consists of 539 specific occupational categories for employed persons arranged into 23 major occupational groups. This classification was developed based on the *Standard Occupational Classification (SOC) Manual: 2010*, published by the Executive Office of the President, Office of Management and Budget.

CIVILIAN LABOR FORCE AND UNEMPLOYMENT, Items 167–171

Source: U.S. Bureau of Labor Statistics—Local Areas Unemployment Statistics
https://www.bls.gov/lau/#tables

Data for the civilian labor force are the product of a federal-state cooperative program in which state employment security agencies prepare labor force and unemployment estimates under concepts, definitions, and technical procedures established by the Bureau of Labor Statistics (BLS). The **civilian labor force** consists of all civilians 16 years old and over who are either employed or unemployed.

Unemployment includes all persons who did not work during the survey week, made specific efforts to find a job during the prior four weeks, and were available for work during the survey week (except for temporary illness). Persons waiting to be called back to a job from which they had been laid off and those waiting to report to a new job within the next 30 days are included in unemployment figures.

PRIVATE NONFARM EMPLOYMENT AND EARNINGS, Items 172–183

Source: U.S. Bureau of Labor Statistics—Current Employment Survey
https://www.bls.gov/ces/#tables

Data for private nonfarm employment and earnings are compiled from payroll information reported monthly on a voluntary basis to the BLS and its cooperating state agencies. More than 350,000 establishments represent all industries except agriculture.

Employment is the annual average of monthly totals of persons who received pay for any part of the pay period including the 12th day of the month. Included are all full-time and part-time workers in nonfarm establishments. Not covered are government employees, proprietors, the self-employed, unpaid volunteers or family workers, farm workers, and domestic workers in households. The data by industry conform to the definitions established in the North American Industry Classification System (NAICS).

Earnings of **production workers** in **manufacturing** industries are derived from reports of gross payrolls and corresponding paid hours. Payroll is reported before deductions of any kinds. Total hours during the pay period include all hours worked (including overtime hours) and hours paid for holidays, vacations, and sick leave.

AGRICULTURE, Items 184–202

Source: U.S. Department of Agriculture, National Agricultural Statistics Service—2017 Census of Agriculture
https://www.nass.usda.gov/Publications/AgCensus/2017/index.php

The Census Bureau took a census of agriculture every 10 years from 1840 to 1920; since 1925, this census has been taken roughly once every 5 years. The 1997 Census of Agriculture was the first one conducted by the National Agricultural Statistics Service of the U.S. Department of Agriculture. Over time, the definition of a farm has varied. For recent censuses (including the 2017 census), a farm has been defined as any place from which $1,000 or more of agricultural products were produced and sold or normally would have been sold during the census year. Dollar figures are expressed in current dollars and have not been adjusted for inflation or deflation.

The term **producer** designates a person who is involved in making decisions for the farm operation. Decisions may include decisions about such things as planting, harvesting, livestock management, and marketing. The producer may be the owner, a member of the owner's household, a hired manager, a tenant, a renter, or a sharecropper. If a person rents land to others or has land worked on shares by others, he/she is considered the producer only of the land which is retained for his/her own operation. The census collected information on the total number of male producers, the total number of female producers, and demographic information for up to four producers per farm.

Government payments consists of direct payments as defined by the 2002 Farm Bill; payments from Conservation Reserve Program (CRP), Wetlands reserve Program (WRP), Farmable Wetlands Program (FWP), and Conservation Reserve Enhancement Program (CREP); loan deficiency payments; disaster payments; other conservation programs; and all other federal farm programs under which payments were made directly to farm producers, including those specified in the 2014 Agricultural Act (Farm Bill), including Agriculture Risk Coverage (ARC) and Price Loss Coverage (PLC).. Commodity Credit Corporation (CCC) proceeds, amounts from state and local government agricultural program payments, and federal crop insurance payments were not included in this category.

The acreage designated as **land in farms** consists primarily of agricultural land used for crops, pasture, or grazing. It also includes woodland and wasteland not actually under cultivation or used for pasture or grazing, provided that this land was part of the farm operator's total operation.

Land in farms is an operating-unit concept and includes all land owned and operated, as well as all land rented from others. Land used rent-free is classified as land rented from others. All grazing land, except land used under government permits on a per-head basis, was included as "land in farms" provided it was part of a farm or ranch. Land under the exclusive use of a grazing association was reported by the grazing association and included as land in farms. All land in Indian reservations used for growing crops or grazing livestock is classified as land in farms.

Irrigated land includes all land watered by any artificial or controlled means, such as sprinklers, flooding, furrows or ditches, sub-irrigation, and spreader dikes. Included are supplemental, partial, and preplant irrigation. Each acre was counted only once regardless of the number of times it was irrigated or harvested. Livestock lagoon waste water distributed by sprinkler or flood systems was also included.

Total cropland includes cropland harvested, cropland used only for pasture or grazing, cropland on which all crops failed or were abandoned, cropland in cultivated summer fallow, and cropland idle or used for cover crops or soil improvement but not harvested and not pastured or grazed.

Respondents were asked to report their estimate of the current market **value of land and buildings** owned, rented, or leased from others and rented and leased to others. Market value refers to the respondent's estimate of what the land and buildings would sell for under current market conditions.

The **value of machinery and equipment** was estimated by the respondent as the current market value of all cars, trucks, tractors, combines, balers, irrigation equipment, etc., used on the farm. This value is an estimate of what the machinery and equipment would sell for in its present condition and not the replacement of depreciated value. Share interests are reported at full value at the farm where the equipment and machinery are usually kept. Only equipment that was physically located at the farm on December 31, 2017, is included.

Market **value of agricultural products sold** by farms represents the gross market value before taxes and the production expenses of all agricultural products sold or removed from the place in 2017, regardless of who received the payment. It is equivalent to total sales and it includes sales by producers as well as the value of any share received by partners, landlords, contractors, and others associated with the operation. It includes value of organic sales, direct sales and the value of commodities placed in the Commodity Credit Corporation (CCC) loan program. Market value of agricultural products sold does not include payments received for participation in other federal farm programs. Also, it does not include income from farm-related sources such as customwork and other agricultural services, or income from nonfarm sources.

The value of crops sold in 2017 does not necessarily represent the sales from crops harvested in 2017. Data may include sales from crops produced in earlier years and may exclude some crops produced in 2017 but held in storage and not sold. For commodities such as sugarbeets and wool sold through a co-op that made payments in several installments, respondents were requested to report the total value received in 2017.

Organic farms are those that had organic production according to USDA's National Organic Program (NOP). Respondents reported whether their organic production was certified or exempt from certification and the sales from NOP produced commodities. Not included are farms that had acres transitioning into NOP production.

Farms with **internet access** are those that reported using personal computers, laptops, or mobile devices (e.g., cell phones or tablets) to access the internet. This can be done using services such as dial-up, DSL, cable modem, fiber-optic, mobile internet service for a cell phone or other device (tablet), satellite, or other methods. In 2017 respondents were also able to report connecting with an unknown service type, labeled as "Don't know" in the publication tables.

LAND USE, Items 203 to 205

Source: U.S. Department of Agriculture, Natural Resources Conservation Service—2015 National Resources Inventory https://www.nrcs.usda.gov/wps/portal/nrcs/main/national/technical/nra/nri

The National Resources Inventory (NRI) was conducted every five years between 1982 and 1997. Since 2000, NRI data have been gathered annually, using a more complex sampling design of core and rotational subsamples. It provides updated information on the status, condition, and trends of land, soil, water, and related resources on the Nation's non-federal lands. Non-federal lands include privately owned lands, tribal and trust lands, and lands controlled by State and local governments.

The 2015 NRI is based on a sample of about 800,000 locations throughout the United States (excluding Alaska and the District of Columbia). Acreages for federal land and total surface area are established through geospatial processes and administrative records. Total surface area of the contiguous United States is 1,944 million acres.

Federally-owned lands include military bases, national forests, wildlife refuges, parks, grassland game preserves, scenic waterways, wilderness areas, monuments, lakeshore, parkways, battlefields, Bureau of Land Management lands, and other federal lands.

The NRI **developed land** category includes (a) large tracts of urban and built-up land; (b) small tracts of built-up land of less than 10 acres; and (c) land outside of these built-up areas that is in a rural transportation corridor (roads, railroads, and associated rights-of-way). Urban and built-up areas consist of residential, industrial, commercial, and institutional land; construction sites; public administrative sites; railroad yards; cemeteries; airports; golf courses; sanitary landfills; sewage treatment plants; water control structures and spillways; other land used for such purposes; small parks (less than 10 acres) within urban and built-up areas; and highways, *railroads*, and other transportation facilities if they are surrounded by urban areas. Also included are tracts of less than 10 acres that do not meet the above definition but are completely surrounded by Urban and built-up land. Two size categories are recognized in the NRI: areas of 0.25 acre to 10 acres, and areas of at least 10 acres.

Rural land consists of four primary rural land types: forest, rangeland, cropland, and pasture.

Forest land is at least 10 percent stocked by single-stemmed woody species of any size that will be at least 4 meters (13 feet) tall at maturity. Also included is land bearing evidence of natural regeneration of tree cover (cut over forest or abandoned farmland) and not currently developed for non-forest use. Ten percent stocked, when viewed from a vertical direction, equates to an areal canopy cover of leaves and branches of 25 percent or greater. The minimum area for classification as forest land is 1 acre, and the area must be at least 100 feet wide.

Rangeland is composed principally of native grasses, grass-like plants, forbs or shrubs suitable for grazing and browsing, and introduced forage species that are managed like rangeland. This would include areas where introduced hardy and persistent grasses, such as crested wheatgrass, are planted and such practices as deferred grazing, burning, chaining, and rotational grazing are used, with little or no chemicals or fertilizer being applied. Grasslands, savannas, many wetlands, some deserts, and tundra are considered to be rangeland. Certain communities of low forbs and shrubs, such as mesquite, chaparral, mountain shrub, and pinyon-juniper, are also included as rangeland.

Cropland includes areas used for the production of adapted crops for harvest. Two subcategories of cropland are recognized: cultivated and non-cultivated. Cultivated land comprises land in row crops or close-grown crops, as well as other cultivated cropland; for example, hayland or pastureland that is in a rotation with row or close-grown crops. Non-cultivated cropland includes permanent hayland and horticultural cropland.

Pastureland is land managed primarily for the production of introduced forage plants for livestock grazing. Pastureland cover may consist of a single species in a pure stand, a grass mixture, or a grass-legume mixture. Management usually consists of cultural treatments: fertilization, weed control, reseeding, renovation, and control of grazing. For the NRI, this includes land that has a vegetative cover of grasses, legumes, and/or forbs, regardless of whether or not it is being grazed by livestock.

Other rural land includes farmsteads and other farm structures, field windbreaks, *barren land*, and *marshland*.

WATER CONSUMPTION, Item 206

Source: U.S. Geological Survey, National Water Use Information Program—2015 Water Use Data
https://www.usgs.gov/mission-areas/water-resources/science/water-use-united-states

Every five years, the U.S. Geological Survey compiles national water-use estimates. This volume includes the total fresh and saline water withdrawals for public water supplies expressed as million gallons per day. Estimate of withdrawals of ground and surface water are given for the following categories of use: public water supplies, domestic, commercial, irrigation, livestock, industrial, mining, and thermoelectric power. Only public water supply is included in this volume. Public supply refers to water withdrawn from ground and surface sources by public and private water systems for use by cities, towns, rural water districts, mobile-home parks, Native American Indian reservations, and military bases. Public-supply facilities provide water to at least 25 persons or have a minimum of 15 service connections. Water withdrawn by public suppliers may be delivered to users for domestic, commercial, industrial, and thermoelectric-power purposes, as well as to other public-water suppliers. Public-supply water is also used for public services (public uses)—such as pools, parks, and public buildings—and may have unaccounted uses (losses) because of system leaks or such non-metered services as firefighting, flushing of water lines, or backwashing at treatment plants. Some public-supply water may be used in the processes of water and wastewater treatment. Some public suppliers treat saline water before distributing the water. The definition of saline water for public supply refers to water that requires treatment to reduce the concentration of dissolved solids through the process of desalination or dilution.

MANUFACTURES, Items 207–216

Source: U.S. Census Bureau—2020 Annual Survey of Manufactures
https://www.census.gov/programs-surveys/asm.html

The Annual Survey of Manufactures (ASM) has been conducted annually every year since 1949, except for years ending in "2" and "7," at which time ASM data are included in the manufacturing sector of the Economic Census. The ASM provides statistics on employment, payroll, worker hours, payroll supplements, cost of materials, value added by manufacturing, capital expenditures, inventories, and energy consumption. It also provides estimates of value of shipments for over 1,400 classes of manufactured products. The Annual Survey of Manufactures includes approximately 50,000 establishments selected from the census universe of 350,000 manufacturing establishments.

The **all employees** number is the average number of production workers for the payroll periods including the 12th of March, May, August, and November plus the number of other employees in mid-March. Included are all persons on paid sick leave, paid holidays, and paid vacations during the pay period. Officers of corporations are included as employees, while proprietors and partners of unincorporated firms are excluded.

Payroll figures include the gross annual earnings of all employees on the payroll of operating manufacturing establishments. The definition, which is the same as the one used for calculating the federal withholding tax, includes all forms of compensation, such as salaries, wages, commissions, dismissal pay, bonuses, vacation and sick leave pay, and compensation-in-kind, prior to such deductions as employees' Social Security contributions, withholding taxes, group insurance, union dues, and savings bonds. The total includes salaries of officers of corporations; it excludes payments to proprietors or partners of unincorporated concerns. Also excluded are payments to members of armed forces and to pensioners carried on the active payrolls of manufacturing establishments.

Production workers include workers (up through the line-supervisor level) engaged in fabricating, processing, assembling, inspecting, receiving, storing, handling, packing, warehousing, shipping (but not delivering), maintenance, repair, janitorial and guard services, product development, auxiliary production for the plant's own use (for example, power plant), record keeping, and other services closely associated with these production operations at the establishment covered by the report. Employees above the working-supervisor level are excluded.

The number of production workers is for the payroll period including the 12th of March. Not included in this classification are all other employees, defined as non-production employees, including those engaged in factory supervision above the line-supervisor level.

Production worker hours cover annual hours worked or paid for at the manufacturing plant, including actual overtime hours (not straight-time equivalent hours). The data exclude hours paid for vacations, holidays, or sick leave when the employee is not at the establishment. Production wages represent all compensation paid to production workers.

Value added by manufacture is derived by subtracting the cost of materials, supplies, containers, fuel, purchased electricity, and contract work from the value of shipments (products manufactured plus receipts for services rendered). The result of this calculation is adjusted by the addition of value added by merchandising operations (the difference between the sales value and the cost of merchandise sold without further manufacture, processing, or assembly) plus the net change in finished goods and work-in-process between the beginning- and end-of-year inventories.

Value of shipments covers the received or receivable net selling values; free on board plant (excluding of freight and taxes), of all products shipped, both primary and secondary; and all miscellaneous receipts, such as receipts for contract work performed for others, installation and repair, sales of scrap, and sales of products bought and sold without further processing. Included are all items made by or for the establishments from material owned by it, whether sold, transferred to other plants of the same company, or shipped on consignment. The net selling value of products made in one plant on a contract basis from materials owned by another was reported by the plant providing the materials.

In the case of multi-unit companies, the manufacturer was asked to report the value of products transferred to other establishments of the same company at full economic or commercial value, including both the direct cost of production and a reasonable proportion of "all other costs" (including company overhead) and profit (interplant transfers).

The aggregate of the value of shipments figure for industry groups and for all manufacturing industries includes large amounts of duplications, as the products of some industries are used as materials by others. Estimates as to the overall extent of this duplication indicate that the value of manufactured products exclusive of such duplication (the value of finished manufactures) tends to approximate two-thirds of the total value of products reported in the census of manufactures.

Total cost of materials refers to direct charges actually paid or payable for items consumed or put into production during the year, including freight charges and other direct charges incurred by the establishment in acquiring these materials. It includes the cost of materials or fuel consumed, whether purchased by the individual establishment from other companies, transferred to it from other establishments of the same company, or withdrawn from inventory during the year. Included in this item are cost of parts, components, containers, etc.; cost of products bought and sold in the same condition; cost of fuels consumed for heat and power; cost of purchased electricity; and cost of contract work. Aggregate of total cost of materials and total value of shipments includes extensive duplication, since products of some industries are used as materials of others.

2017 ECONOMIC CENSUS: OVERVIEW, Items 217–308

Source: U.S. Census Bureau
https://www.census.gov/programs-surveys/economic-census.html

The Economic Census provides a detailed portrait of the nation's economy, from the national to the local level, once every five years. The 2017 Economic Census covers nearly all of the U.S. economy in its basic collection of establishment statistics. The 1997 Economic Census was the first major data source to use the North American Industry Classification System (NAICS); therefore, data are not comparable to economic data from prior years, which were based on the Standard Industrial Classification (SIC) system.

NAICS, developed in cooperation with Canada and Mexico, classifies North America's economic activities at two, three, four, and fivedigit levels of detail; the U.S. version of NAICS further defines industries to a sixth digit. The Economic Census takes advantage of this hierarchy to publish data at these successive levels of detail: sector (two-digit); subsector (three-digit); industry group (four-digit); industry (five-digit); and U.S. industry (six-digit). Information in Table A is at the two-digit level, with a few three- and four-digit items.

Several key statistics are tabulated for all industries included in this volume: number of establishments (or companies); number of employees; payroll; and a measure of output (sales, receipts, revenue, value of shipments, or value of construction work done).

Number of establishments. An establishment is a single physical location at which business is conducted. It is not necessarily identical with a company or enterprise, which may consist of one establishment or more. Economic Census figures represent a summary of reports for individual establishments rather than companies. For cases in which a census report was received, separate information was obtained for each location where business was conducted. When administrative records of other federal agencies were used instead of a census report, no information was available on the number of locations operated. Each Economic Census establishment was tabulated according to the physical location at which the business was conducted. The count of establishments represents those in business at any time during 2012.

When two activities or more were carried on at a single location under a single ownership, all activities were generally grouped together as a single establishment. The entire establishment was classified on the basis of its major activity and all of its data were included in that classification. However, when distinct and separate economic activities (for which different industry classification codes were appropriate) were conducted at a single location under a single ownership, separate establishment reports for each of the different activities were obtained in the census.

Number of employees. Paid employees consist of the fulltime and parttime employees, including salaried officers and executives of corporations. Included are employees on paid sick leave, paid holidays, and paid vacations; not included are proprietors and partners of unincorporated businesses. The definition of paid employees is the same as that used by the Internal Revenue Service (IRS) on form 941.

For some industries, the Economic Census gives codes representing the number of employees as a range of numbers (for example, "100 to 249 employees" or "1,000 to 2,499" employees). In this volume, those codes have been replaced by the standard suppression code "D".

Payroll. Payroll includes all forms of compensation, such as salaries, wages, commissions, dismissal pay, bonuses, vacation allowances, sickleave pay, and employee contributions to qualified pension plans paid during the year to all employees. For corporations, payroll includes amounts paid to officers and executives; for unincorporated businesses, it does not include profit or other compensation of proprietors or partners. Payroll is reported before deductions for Social Security, income tax, insurance, union dues, etc. This definition of payroll is the same as that used on IRS form 941.

Sales, shipments, receipts, revenue, or business done. This measure includes the total sales, shipments, receipts, revenue, or business done by establishments within the scope of the Economic Census. The definition of each of these items is specific to the economic sector measured.

CONSTRUCTION, Items 217–221

Source: U.S. Census Bureau—2017 Economic Census (See overview of 2017 Economic Census prior to Item 217)

The Construction sector (sector 23) comprises establishments primarily engaged in the construction of buildings and other structures, heavy construction (except buildings), additions, alterations, reconstruction, installation, and maintenance and repairs. Establishments engaged in the demolition or wrecking of buildings and other structures, the clearing of building sites, and the sale of materials from demolished structures are also included. This sector also contains those establishments engaged in blasting, test drilling, landfill, leveling, earthmoving, excavating, land drainage, and other land preparation. The industries within this sector have been defined on the basis of their unique production processes. As with all industries, the production processes are distinguished by their use of specialized human resources and specialized physical capital. Construction activities are generally administered or managed at a relatively fixed place of business, but the actual construction work can be performed at one or more different project sites. This sector is divided into three subsectors of construction activities: (1) building construction and land subdivision and land development; (2) heavy construction (except buildings), such as highways, power plants, and pipelines; and (3) construction activity by special trade contractors.

WHOLESALE TRADE, Items 222–226

Source: U.S. Census Bureau—2017 Economic Census (See overview of 2017 Economic Census prior to Item 217)

The Wholesale Trade sector (sector 42) comprises establishments engaged in wholesaling merchandise, generally without transformation, and rendering services incidental to the sale of merchandise. The wholesaling process is an intermediate step in the distribution of merchandise. Wholesalers are organized to sell or arrange the purchase or sale of (1) goods for resale (i.e., goods sold to other wholesalers or retailers), (2) capital or durable nonconsumer goods, and (3) raw and intermediate materials and supplies used in production.

Wholesalers sell merchandise to other businesses and normally operate from a warehouse or office. These warehouses and offices are characterized by having little or no display of merchandise. In addition, neither the design nor the location of the premises is intended to solicit walkin traffic. Wholesalers do not normally use advertising directed to the general public. Customers are generally first reached via telephone, inperson marketing, or by specialized advertising that may include internet and other electronic means. Followup orders are either vendorinitiated or clientinitiated, are usually based on previous sales, and typically exhibit strong ties between sellers and buyers. In fact, transactions are often conducted between wholesalers and clients that have longstanding business relationships.

This sector is made up of two main types of wholesalers: those that sell goods on their own account and those that arrange sales and purchases for others for a commission or fee.

(1) Establishments that sell goods on their own account are known as wholesale merchants, distributors, jobbers, drop shippers, import/export merchants, and sales branches. These establishments typically maintain their own warehouse, where they receive and handle goods for their customers. Goods are generally sold without transformation, but may include integral functions, such as sorting, packaging, labeling, and other marketing services.

(2) Establishments arranging for the purchase or sale of goods owned by others or purchasing goods on a commission basis are known as agents and brokers, commission merchants, import/export agents and brokers, auction companies, and manufacturers' representatives. These establishments operate from offices and generally do not own or handle the goods they sell.

Some wholesale establishments may be connected with a single manufacturer and/or promote and sell that particular manufacturer's products to a wide range of other wholesalers or retailers. Other wholesalers may be connected to a retail chain or a limited number of retail chains and only provide a variety of products needed by that particular retail operation(s). These wholesalers may obtain the products from a wide range of manufacturers. Still other wholesalers may not take title to the goods but act as agents and brokers for a commission.

Although, in general, wholesaling normally denotes sales in large volumes, durable nonconsumer goods may be sold in single units. Sales of capital or durable nonconsumer goods used in the production of goods and services, such as farm machinery, medium- and heavy-duty trucks, and industrial machinery, are always included in Wholesale Trade.

RETAIL TRADE, Items 227–235

Source: U.S. Census Bureau—2017 Economic Census (See overview of 2017 Economic Census prior to Item 217)

The Retail Trade sector (44–45) is made up of establishments engaged in retailing merchandise, generally without transformation, and rendering services incidental to the sale of merchandise.

The retailing process is the final step in the distribution of merchandise; retailers are, therefore, organized to sell merchandise in small quantities to the general public. This sector comprises two main types of retailers: store and nonstore retailers.

Store retailers operate fixed pointofsale locations, located and designed to attract a high volume of walkin customers. In general, retail stores have extensive displays of merchandise and use massmedia advertising to attract customers. They typically sell merchandise to the general public for personal or household consumption; some also serve business and institutional clients. These include establishments, such as office supply stores, computer and software stores, building materials dealers, plumbing supply stores, and electrical supply stores. Catalog showrooms, gasoline service stations, automotive dealers, and mobile home dealers are treated as store retailers.

In addition to retailing merchandise, some types of store retailers are also engaged in the provision of aftersales services, such as repair and installation. For example, new automobile dealers, electronic and appliance stores, and musical instrument and supply stores often provide repair services. As a general rule, establishments engaged in retailing merchandise and providing aftersales services are classified in this sector.

Nonstore retailers, like store retailers, are organized to serve the general public, although their retailing methods differ. The establishments of this subsector reach customers and market merchandise with methods, such as the broadcasting of "infomercials," the broadcasting and publishing of directresponse advertising, the publishing of paper and electronic catalogs, doortodoor solicitation, inhome demonstration, selling from portable stalls (street vendors, except food), and distribution through vending machines. Establishments engaged in the direct sale (nonstore) of products, such as home heating oil dealers and home-delivery newspaper routes are included in this sector.

The buying of goods for resale is a characteristic of retail trade establishments that distinguishes them from establishments in the Agriculture, Manufacturing, and Construction sectors. For example, farms that sell their products at or from the point of production are classified in Agriculture instead of in Retail Trade. Similarly, establishments that both manufacture and sell their products to the general public are classified in Manufacturing instead of Retail Trade. However, establishments that engage in processing activities incidental to retailing are classified in retail.

Industries in the **Motor Vehicle and Parts Dealers** subsector (441) retail motor vehicle and parts merchandise from fixed point-of-sale locations. Establishments in this subsector typically operate from a showroom and/or an open lot where the vehicles are on display. The display of vehicles and the related parts require little by way of display equipment. Personnel generally include both sales and sales support staff familiar with the requirements for registering and financing a vehicle as well as a staff of parts experts and mechanics trained to provide vehicle repair and maintenance services. Specific industries have been included in this subsector to identify the type of vehicle being retailed. Sales of capital or durable nonconsumer goods, such as medium and heavy-duty trucks, are always included in the Wholesale Trade sector. These goods are virtually never sold through retail methods.

Industries in the **Food and Beverage Stores** subsector (445) usually retail food and beverage merchandise from fixed point-of-sale locations. Establishments in this subsector have special equipment (e.g., freezers, refrigerated display cases, and refrigerators) for displaying food and beverage goods. They have staff trained in the processing of food products to guarantee the proper storage and sanitary conditions, as mandated by regulatory authority.

Industries in the **Clothing and Clothing Accessories Stores** subsector (448) retail new clothing and clothing accessories merchandise from fixed point-of-sale locations. Establishments in this subsector have similar types of display equipment, as well as employees who are knowledgeable regarding fashion trends and who can match styles, colors, and combinations of clothing and accessories to the characteristics and tastes of the customer.

Industries in the **General Merchandise Stores** subsector (452) retail new general merchandise from fixed point-of-sale locations.

Establishments in this subsector are unique in that they have the equipment and staff capable of retailing a large variety of goods from a single location. This includes a variety of display equipment and staff trained to provide information on many lines of products.

INFORMATION, Items 236–246

Source: U.S. Census Bureau—2017 Economic Census (See overview of 2017 Economic Census prior to Item 217)

The Information sector (51) comprises establishments engaged in the following processes: (1) producing and distributing information and cultural products, (2) providing the means to transmit or distribute these products as well as data or communications, and (3) processing data.

The main components of this sector are the publishing industries, including software publishing; the motion picture and sound recording industries; the broadcasting and telecommunications industries; and the information services and data processing industries.

For the purpose of NAICS, the transformation of information into a commodity that is produced and distributed by a number of growing industries is at issue. The Information sector groups three types of establishments: (1) those engaged in producing and distributing information and cultural products; (2) those that provide the means to transmit or distribute these products as well as data or communications; and (3) those that process data. Cultural products are those that directly express attitudes, opinions, ideas, values, and artistic creativity; provide entertainment; or offer information and analysis concerning the past and present. Included in this definition are popular, massproduced products, as well as cultural products that normally have a more limited audience, such as poetry books, literary magazines, or classical records. These activities were formerly classified throughout the existing national classifications. Traditional publishing was in manufacturing; broadcasting in communications; software production in business services; film production in amusement services; and so forth.

Industries in the **Publishing Industries, Except Internet** subsector (511) include establishments engaged in the publishing of newspapers, magazines, other periodicals, and books, as well as database and software publishing. In general, these establishments, which are known as publishers, issue copies of works for which they usually possess copyright. Works may be in one or more formats, including traditional print format, CDROM format, or proprietary electronic networks. Publishers may publish works originally created by others for which they have obtained the rights and/or works that they have created inhouse. Software publishing is included here because the activity (creation of a copyrighted product and bringing it to market) is equivalent to the creation process for other types of intellectual products.

In NAICS, publishing—the reporting, writing, editing, and other processes that are required to create an edition of a book or a newspaper—is treated as a major economic activity in its own right, rather than as a subsidiary activity to printing, which is a manufacturing activity. Thus, publishing is classified in the Information sector, while printing remains in the NAICS Manufacturing sector. In part, the NAICS classification reflects the fact that publishing increasingly takes place in establishments that are physically separate from the associated printing establishments. More crucially, the NAICS classification of book and newspaper publishing is intended to portray their roles in a modern economy—roles that do not resemble manufacturing activities.

Music publishers are not included in the Publishing Industries subsector, but can be found in the Motion Picture and Sound Recording Industries subsector. Reproduction of prepackaged software is treated in NAICS as a manufacturing activity; online distribution of software products is in the Information sector, and custom design of software to client specifications is included in the Professional, Scientific, and Technical Services sector. These distinctions arise because of the different ways that software is created, reproduced, and distributed.

The Information sector does not include products, such as manifold business forms. Information is not the essential component of these items. Establishments producing these items are included in subsector 323, Printing and Related Support Activities.

Industries in the **Motion Picture and Sound Recording Industries** subsector (512) group establishments involved in the production and distribution of motion pictures and sound recordings. While producers and distributors of motion pictures and sound recordings issue works for sale as traditional publishers do, the processes are different enough to warrant placing the establishments engaged in these activities in separate subsectors. Production is typically a complex process that involves several distinct types of establishments engaged in activities, such as contracting with performers, creating the film or sound content, and providing technical postproduction services. Film distribution is often to exhibitors, such as theaters and broadcasters, rather than to a wholesale or retail distribution chain. When the product is in a massproduced form, NAICS treats production and distribution as the major economic activity, rather than as a subsidiary activity to the manufacture of such products.

This subsector does not include establishments primarily engaged in the wholesale distribution of video cassettes and sound recordings, such as compact discs and audio tapes; these establishments are included in the Wholesale Trade sector. Reproduction of video cassettes and sound recordings that is carried out separately from establishments engaged in production and distribution is treated in NAICS as a manufacturing activity.

Industries in the **Broadcasting, except Internet** subsector (515) include establishments that create content or acquire the right to distribute and subsequently broadcast content. The industry groups (Radio and Television Broadcasting and Cable and Other Subscription Programming) are based on differences in the methods of communication and the nature of services provided. The Radio and Television Broadcasting industry group includes establishments that operate broadcasting studios and facilities for over-the-air or satellite delivery of radio and television programs, including entertainment, news, and talk programs. These establishments are often engaged in production and purchase of programs and generating revenues from the sale of air time to advertisers, as well as from donations, subsidies, and/or the sale of programs. The Cable and Other Subscription Programming industry group includes establishments that operate studios and facilities for the broadcasting of limited-format programs (such as news, sports, educational, and youth-oriented programs) that are typically narrowly-focused in nature; these programs are usually available on a subscription or fee basis. The distribution of cable and other subscription programming is included in subsector 517, Telecommunications.

Industries in the **Internet Publishing and Broadcasting and Web search portals** subsector (51913) consist of establishments primarily engaged in 1) publishing and/or broadcasting content on the Internet exclusively or 2) operating Web sites that use a search engine to generate and maintain extensive databases of Internet addresses and content in an easily searchable format (and known as Web search portals). The publishing and broadcasting establishments in this industry do not provide traditional (non-Internet) versions of the content that they publish or broadcast. They provide textual, audio, and/or video content of general or specific interest on the Internet exclusively. Establishments known as Web search portals often provide additional Internet services, such as e-mail, connections to other web sites, auctions, news, and other limited content, and serve as a home base for Internet users.

Establishments that are *not* in this group include those primarily engaged in—

- Providing wired broadband Internet access using own operated telecommunications infrastructure—these are classified in Wired Telecommunications Carriers;
- Providing both Internet publishing and other print or electronic (e.g., CD-ROM, diskette) editions in the same establishment or using proprietary networks to distribute content—these are classified in Publishing Industries (except Internet) based on the materials produced;
- Providing Internet access via client-supplied telecommunications connections—these are classified in All Other Telecommunications;
- Providing streaming services on content owned by others—these are classified in Data Processing, Hosting, and Related Services;
- Wholesaling goods on the Internet—these are classified in Wholesale Trade;
- Retailing goods on the Internet—these are classified in Retail Trade;
- Operating stock brokerages, travel reservation systems, purchasing services, and similar activities using the Internet rather than traditional methods—these are classified with the more traditional establishments providing these services.

Industries in the **Telecommunications** subsector (517) include establishments that provide telecommunications and services related to that activity (e.g., telephony, including Voice over Internet Protocol (VoIP); cable and satellite television distribution services; Internet access; telecommunications reselling services). The Telecommunications subsector is primarily engaged in operating, maintaining, and/or providing access to facilities for the transmission of voice, data, text, sound, and video. A transmission facility may be based on a single technology or a combination of technologies. Establishments primarily engaged as independent contractors in the maintenance and installation of broadcasting and telecommunications systems are classified in sector 23, Construction.

Industries in the **Data processing, hosting, and related services** subsector (518) are establishments primarily engaged in providing infrastructure for hosting or data processing services. These establishments may provide specialized hosting activities, such as web hosting, streaming services or application hosting; provide application service provisioning; or may provide general time-share mainframe facilities to clients. Data processing establishments provide complete processing and specialized reports from data supplied by clients or provide automated data processing and data entry services.

UTILITIES, Items 247–252

Source: U.S. Census Bureau—2017 Economic Census (See overview of 2017 Economic Census prior to Item 217)

The Utilities sector (22) comprises establishments engaged in the provision of the following utility services: electric power, natural gas, steam supply, water supply, and sewage removal. Within this sector, the specific activities associated with the utility services provided vary by utility: electric power includes generation, transmission, and distribution; natural gas includes distribution; steam supply includes provision and/or distribution; water supply includes treatment and distribution; and sewage removal includes collection, treatment, and disposal of waste through sewer systems and sewage treatment facilities.

Excluded from this sector are establishments primarily engaged in waste management. These services are classified in subsector 562, Waste Management and Remediation Services, which also collect, treat, and dispose of waste materials; however, establishments in this subsector do not use sewer systems or sewage treatment facilities.

TRANSPORTATION AND WAREHOUSING, Items 252–256

Source: U.S. Census Bureau—2017 Economic Census (See overview of 2017 Economic Census prior to Item 217)

The Transportation and Warehousing sector (48–49) includes industries that provide transportation of passengers and cargo, warehousing and storage for goods, scenic and sightseeing transportation, and support activities related to modes of transportation. Establishments in these industries use transportation equipment or transportation related facilities as a productive asset. The type of equipment depends on the mode of transportation, which includes air, rail, water, road, and pipeline.

The transportation and warehousing sector distinguishes three basic types of activities: subsectors for each mode of transportation, a subsector for warehousing and storage, and a subsector for establishments providing support activities for transportation. In addition, there are subsectors for establishments that provide passenger transportation for scenic and sightseeing purposes, postal services, and courier services.

FINANCE AND INSURANCE, Items 257–261

Source: U.S. Census Bureau—2017 Economic Census (See overview of 2017 Economic Census prior to Item 217)

The Finance and Insurance sector (52) comprises establishments primarily engaged in financial transactions (transactions involving the creation, liquidation, or change in ownership of financial assets) and/or in facilitating financial transactions. Three principal types of activities are identified:

(1) Raising funds by taking deposits and/or issuing securities and, in the process, incurring liabilities. Establishments engaged in this activity use raised funds to acquire financial assets by making loans and/or purchasing securities. Putting themselves at risk, they channel funds from lenders to borrowers and transform or repackage the funds with respect to maturity, scale and risk. This activity is known as financial intermediation.

(2) Pooling of risk by underwriting insurance and annuities. Establishments engaged in this activity collect fees, insurance premiums, or annuity considerations; build up reserves; invest those reserves; and make contractual payments. Fees are based on the expected incidence of the insured risk and the expected return on investment.

(3) Providing specialized services facilitating or supporting financial intermediation, insurance, and employee benefit programs.

In addition, monetary authorities charged with monetary control are included in this sector.

REAL ESTATE AND RENTAL AND LEASING, Items 262–266

Source: U.S. Census Bureau—2017 Economic Census (See overview of 2017 Economic Census prior to Item 217)

The Real Estate and Rental and Leasing sector (53) comprises establishments primarily engaged in renting, leasing, or otherwise allowing the use of tangible or intangible assets, and establishments providing related services. The major portion of this sector comprises establishments that rent, lease, or otherwise allow the use of their own assets by others. The assets may be tangible, such as real estate and equipment, or intangible, such as patents and trademarks.

This sector also includes establishments primarily engaged in managing real estate for others, selling, renting, and/or buying real estate for others, and appraising real estate. These activities are closely related to this sector's main activity. In addition, a substantial proportion of property management is selfperformed by lessors.

The main components of this sector are the real estate lessors industries; equipment lessors industries (including motor vehicles, computers, and consumer goods); and lessors of nonfinancial intangible assets (except copyrighted works).

PROFESSIONAL, SCIENTIFIC, AND TECHNICAL SERVICES, Items 267–275

Source: U.S. Census Bureau—2017 Economic Census (See overview of 2017 Economic Census prior to Item 217)

The Professional, Scientific, and Technical Services sector (54) is made up of establishments that specialize in performing professional, scientific, and technical activities for others. These activities require a high degree of expertise and training. The establishments in this sector specialize according to expertise and provide services to clients in a variety of industries (and, in some cases, to households). Activities performed include legal advice and representation; accounting, bookkeeping, and payroll services; architectural, engineering, and specialized design services; computer services; consulting services; research services; advertising services; photographic services; translation and interpretation services; veterinary services; and other professional, scientific, and technical services.

This sector excludes establishments primarily engaged in providing a range of daytoday office administrative services, such as financial planning, billing and record keeping, personnel services, and physical distribution and logistics services. These establishments are classified in sector 56, Administrative and Support and Waste Management and Remediation Services.

Legal Services comprises establishments primarily engaged in offering legal services such as offices of lawyers, notaries, title abstract and settlement offices, and all other legal services such as patent agent services, paralegal services, and process serving services.

Accounting, Tax Preparation, Bookkeeping, and Payroll Services comprises establishments primarily engaged in providing services, such as auditing of accounting records, designing accounting systems, preparing financial statements, developing budgets, preparing tax returns, processing payrolls, bookkeeping, and billing.

Architectural, Engineering, and Related Services comprises establishments primarily engaged in offering (1) architectural services for residential, institutional, leisure, commercial, and industrial buildings and structures as well as for landscape purposes; (2) offering engineering services, including drafting services or building inspection services; (3) offering geophysical surveying and mapping services; (4) surveying and mapping services, except geophysical; and (5) offering testing laboratory services except medical and veterinary (the testing can occur in a laboratory or on-site).

Computer Systems Design and Related Services consists of establishments primarily engaged in providing expertise in the field of information technologies through one or more of the following activities: (1) writing, modifying, testing, and supporting software to meet the needs of a particular customer; (2) planning and designing computer systems that integrate computer hardware, software, and communication technologies; (3) onsite management and operation of clients' computer systems and/or data processing facilities; and (4) other professional and technical computerrelated advice and services.

HEALTH CARE AND SOCIAL ASSISTANCE, Items 276–289

Source: U.S. Census Bureau—2017 Economic Census (See overview of 2017 Economic Census prior to Item 217)

The Health Care and Social Assistance sector (62) consists of establishments that provide health care and social assistance services to individuals. The sector includes both health care and social assistance, because it is sometimes difficult to distinguish between the boundaries of these two activities. The industries in this sector are arranged on a continuum starting with those that provide medical care exclusively, continuing with those that provide health care and social assistance, and finishing with those that provide only social assistance. The services provided by establishments in this sector are delivered by trained professionals. All industries in the sector share this commonality of process—namely, labor inputs of health practitioners or social workers with the requisite expertise. Many of the industries in the sector are defined based on the educational degree held by the practitioners included in the industry.

In this volume, taxable and tax-exempt establishments are presented separately.

Excluded from this sector are aerobic classes, which can be found in subsector 713, Amusement, Gambling and Recreation Industries; and nonmedical diet and weight-reducing centers, which can be found in subsector 812, Personal and Laundry Services. Although these can be viewed as health services, they are not typically delivered by health practitioners.

Industries in the **Ambulatory Health Care Services** subsector (621) provide health care services directly or indirectly to ambulatory patients and do not typically provide inpatient services. Health practitioners in this subsector provide outpatient services, and facilities and equipment do not usually play the most significant part in this sector's production process.

Industries in the **Hospitals** subsector (622) provide medical, diagnostic, and treatment services, including physician, nursing, specialized accommodation, and other health services, to inpatients. Hospitals may provide outpatient services as a secondary activity. Many of the services provided by establishments in the Hospitals subsector require the use of specialized facilities and equipment, both of which form a significant and integral part of the production process.

ARTS, ENTERTAINMENT, AND RECREATION, Items 290–294

Source: U.S. Census Bureau—2017 Economic Census (See overview of 2017 Economic Census prior to Item 217)

The Arts, Entertainment, and Recreation sector (71) includes a wide range of establishments that operate facilities or provide services that meet the diverse cultural, entertainment, and recreational interests of their patrons. This sector is made up of: (1) establishments that are involved in producing, promoting, or participating in live performances, events, or exhibits intended for public viewing; (2) establishments that preserve and exhibit objects and sites of historical, cultural, or educational interest; and (3) establishments that operate facilities or provide services that enable patrons to participate in recreational activities or pursue amusement, hobby, and leisure time interests.

Some establishments that provide cultural, entertainment, or recreational facilities and services are classified in other sectors. Excluded from this sector are: (1) establishments that provide both accommodations and recreational facilities—such as hunting and fishing camps and resort and casino hotels—are classified in subsector 721, Accommodation; (2) restaurants and night clubs that provide live entertainment in addition to the sale of food and beverages are classified in subsector 722, Food Services and Drinking Places; (3) motion picture theaters, libraries and archives, and publishers of newspapers, magazines, books, periodicals, and computer software are classified in sector 51, Information; and (4) establishments that use transportation equipment to provide recreational and entertainment services, such as those operating sightseeing buses, dinner cruises, or helicopter rides, are classified in subsector 487, Scenic and Sightseeing Transportation.

ACCOMMODATION AND FOOD SERVICES, Items 295–300

Source: U.S. Census Bureau—2017 Economic Census (See overview of 2017 Economic Census prior to Item 217)

The Accommodation and Food Services sector (72) consists of establishments that provide customers with lodging and/or meals, snacks, and beverages for immediate consumption. The sector includes both accommodation and food services establishments because the two activities are often combined at the same establishment. Excluded from this sector are civic and social organizations, amusement and recreation parks, theaters, and other recreation or entertainment facilities providing food and beverage services.

Industries in the **Food Services and Drinking Places** subsector (722) prepare meals, snacks, and beverages to customer order for immediate onpremises and offpremises consumption. There is a wide range of establishments in these industries. Some provide food and drink only; while others provide various combinations of seating space, waiter/waitress services and incidental amenities, such as limited entertainment. The industries in the subsector are grouped based on the type and level of services provided. The industry groups are fullservice restaurants; limitedservice eating places; special food services, such as food service contractors, caterers, and mobile food services, and drinking places. Food services and drink activities at hotels and motels; amusement parks, theaters, casinos, country clubs, and similar recreational facilities; and civic and social organizations are included in this subsector only if these services are provided by a separate establishment primarily engaged in providing food and beverage services. Excluded from this subsector are establishments operating dinner cruises. These establishments are classified in subsector 487, Scenic and Sightseeing Transportation, because they utilize transportation equipment to provide scenic recreational entertainment.

OTHER SERVICES, EXCEPT PUBLIC ADMINISTRATION Items 301–308

Source: U.S. Census Bureau—2017 Economic Census (See overview of 2017 Economic Census prior to Item 217)

The Other Services, Except Public Administration sector (81) comprises establishments engaged in providing services not specifically categorized elsewhere in the classification system. Establishments in this sector are primarily engaged in activities such as equipment and machinery repairing, promoting or administering religious activities, grant making, and advocacy; this sector also includes establishments that provide dry-cleaning and laundry services, personal care services, death care services, pet care services, photofinishing services, temporary parking services, and dating services.

Private households that employ workers on or about the premises in activities primarily concerned with the operation of the household are included in this sector.

Excluded from this sector are establishments primarily engaged in retailing new equipment and performing repairs and general maintenance on equipment. These establishments are classified in sector 44–45, Retail Trade.

Industries in the **Repair and Maintenance** subsector (811) restore machinery, equipment, and other products to working order. These establishments also typically provide general or routine maintenance (i.e., servicing) on such products to ensure they work efficiently; this maintenance also helps prevent breakdowns and make certain repairs unnecessary.

The NAICS structure for this subsector brings together most types of repair and maintenance establishments and categorizes them based on production processes (i.e., on the type of repair and maintenance activity performed, and the necessary skills, expertise, and processes required for different repair and maintenance establishments). This NAICS classification does not delineate between repair services provided to businesses versus those provided to households. Although some industries primarily serve either businesses or households, separation by class of customer is limited by the fact that many establishments serve both types. Establishments that repair computers and consumer electronics products are examples of such overlap.

The Repair and Maintenance subsector does not include all establishments engaged in repair and maintenance. For example, a substantial amount of repair is done by establishments that also manufacture machinery, equipment, and other goods. These establishments are included in the Manufacturing sector in NAICS. In addition, the repairing of transportation equipment is often provided by or based at transportation facilities, such as airports and seaports; these activities are included in the Transportation and Warehousing sector.

A particularly unique situation exists with repair of buildings. Plumbing, electrical installation and repair, painting and decorating, and other constructionrelated establishments are often involved in performing installation or other work on new construction, while also providing repair services on existing structures. Although some establishments do specialize in repair, it is difficult to distinguish between these two types. Thus, all such establishments are included in the Construction sector.

Excluded from this subsector are establishments primarily engaged in rebuilding or remanufacturing machinery and equipment. These are classified in sector 31–33, Manufacturing. Also excluded are retail establishments that provide aftersale services and repair. These are classified in sector 44–45, Retail Trade.

Industries in the **Personal and Laundry Services** subsector (812) include establishments that provide personal and laundry services to individuals, households, and businesses. Services performed include personal care services, death care services, laundry and dry-cleaning services, and a wide range of other personal services, such as pet care (except veterinary) services, photofinishing services, temporary parking services, and dating services.

The Personal and Laundry Services subsector is by no means allinclusive of the activities that could be termed personal services (i.e., those provided to individuals rather than businesses). There are many other sectors and subsectors that provide services to persons. Establishments providing legal, accounting, tax preparation, architectural, portrait photography, and similar professional services are classified in sector 54, Professional, Scientific, and Technical Services; those providing job placement, travel arrangement, home security, interior and exterior house cleaning, exterminating, lawn and garden care, and similar support services are classified in sector 56, Administrative and Support and Waste Management and Remediation Services; those providing health and social services are classified in sector 62, Health Care and Social Assistance; those providing amusement and recreation services are classified in sector 71, Arts, Entertainment and Recreation; those providing educational instruction are classified in sector 61, Educational Services; those providing repair services are classified in subsector 811, Repair and Maintenance; and those providing spiritual, civic, and advocacy services are classified in subsector 813, Religious, Grantmaking, Civic, Professional, and Similar Organizations.

Industries in the **Religious, Grantmaking, Civic, Professional, and Similar Organizations** subsector (813) include establishments that organize and promote religious activities, support various causes through grant making, advocate various social and political causes, and promote and defend the interests of their members. This category includes only tax-exempt establishments.

The industry groups within the subsector are defined in terms of their activities, separately grouping establishments that provide funding for specific causes or for a variety of charitable causes, establishments that advocate and actively promote causes and beliefs for the public good, and establishments that have an active membership structure to promote causes and represent the interests of their members. Establishments in this subsector may publish newsletters, books, and periodicals for distribution to their membership.

GOVERNMENT EMPLOYMENT, Items 309–311

Source: U.S. Bureau of Economic Analysis—Regional Economic Accounts
https://www.bea.gov/data/economic-accounts/regional#state

Employment is measured as the average annual sum of full-time and part-time jobs. The estimates are on a place-of-work basis. Data for federal civilian employment include civilian employees of the Department of Defense. Military employment includes all persons on active duty status.

STATE GOVERNMENT EMPLOYMENT AND PAYROLL, Items 312–330

Source: U.S. Census Bureau—Annual Survey of Public Employment and Payroll
https://www.census.gov/programs-surveys/apes.html

The annual Survey of Public Employment and Payroll measures the number of federal, state, and local civilian government employees and their gross monthly payroll for March of the survey year for state and local governments and for the Federal Government.

The survey provides state and local government data on full-time and part-time employment, part-time hours worked, full-time equivalent employment, and payroll statistics by governmental function (i.e., elementary and secondary education, higher education, police protection, fire protection, financial administration, central staff services, judicial and legal, highways, public welfare, solid waste management, sewerage, parks and recreation, health, hospitals, water supply, electric power, gas supply, transit, natural resources, correction, libraries, air transportation, water transport and terminals, other education, state liquor stores, social insurance administration, and housing and community development).

Data have been collected annually since 1957. A census is conducted every five years (years ending in '2' and '7'). A sample of state and local governments is used to collect data in the intervening years. A new sample is selected every five years (years ending in '4' and '9').

State government employees include all persons paid for personal services performed, including persons paid from federally funded programs, paid elected or appointed officials, persons in a paid leave status, and persons paid on a per meeting, annual, semiannual, or quarterly basis. Unpaid officials, pensioners, persons whose work is performed on a fee basis, and contractors and their employees are excluded from the count of employees. **Full-time employees** are persons employed during the pay period to work the number of hours per week that represents regular full-time employment. Included are full-time temporary or seasonal employees who are working the number of hours that represent full-time employment. **Part-time employees** are persons paid on a part-time basis during the designated pay period. Included are those daily or hourly employees usually engaged for less than the regular full-time workweek, as well as any part-time paid officials. **Full-Time Equivalent employees** is a computed statistic representing the number of full-time employees that could have been employed if the reported number of hours worked by part-time employees had been worked by full-time employees. This statistic is calculated separately for each function of a government by dividing the "part-time hours paid" by the standard number of hours for full-time employees in the particular government and then adding the resulting quotient to the number of full-time employees.

Full-time payroll represents gross payroll amounts for the one-month period of March for full-time employees. **Part-time pay** represents gross payroll amounts for the one-month period of March for part-time employees. Gross payroll includes all salaries, wages, fees, commissions, and overtime paid to employees **before** withholdings for taxes, insurance, etc. It also includes incentive payments that are paid at regular pay intervals. It excludes employer share of fringe benefits like retirement, Social Security, health and life insurance, lump sum payments, and so forth.

Administration combines **Financial administration** and **Other government administration**. **Financial administration** includes activities concerned with tax assessment and collection, custody and disbursement of funds, debt management, administration of trust funds, budgeting, and other government-wide financial management activities. This function is not applied to school district or special district governments. **Other government administration** applies to the legislative and government-wide administrative agencies of governments. Included here are overall planning and zoning activities, and central personnel and administrative activities. This function is not applied to school district or special district governments.

Judicial and legal includes all court and court related activities (except probation and parole activities that are included at the "Correction" function), court activities of sheriff's offices, prosecuting attorneys' and public defenders' offices, legal departments, and attorneys providing government-wide legal service.

Police includes all activities concerned, with the enforcement of law and order, including coroner's offices, police training academies, investigation bureaus, and local jails, "lockups", or other detention facilities not intended to serve as correctional facilities.

Corrections includes activities pertaining to the confinement and correction of adults and minors convicted of criminal offenses. Pardon, probation, and parole activities are also included here.

Highways and transportation includes activities associated with the maintenance and operation of streets, roads, sidewalks, bridges, tunnels, toll roads, and ferries. Snow and ice removal, street lighting, and highway and traffic engineering activities are also included here. Also included are the operation, maintenance, and construction of public mass transit systems, including subways, surface rails, and buses, and the provision, construction, operation, maintenance; support of public waterways, harbors, docks, wharves, and related marine terminal facilities; and activities associated with the operation and support of publicly operated airport facilities.

Public welfare includes the administration of various public assistance programs for the needy, veteran services, operation of nursing homes, indigent care institutions, and programs that provide payments for medical care, handicap transportation, and other services for the needy.

Health includes administration of public health programs, community and visiting nurse services, immunization programs, drug abuse rehabilitation programs, health and food inspection activities, operation of outpatient clinics, and environmental pollution control activities.

Hospitals includes only government operated medical care facilities that provide inpatient care. Employees and payrolls of private corporations that lease and operate government-owned hospital facilities are excluded.

Social insurance administration includes the administration of unemployment compensation systems, public employment services, and the Federal Social Security, Medicare, and Railroad Retirement trusts.

Natural resources and parks includes activities primarily concerned with the conservation and development of natural resources (soil, water, energy, minerals, etc.) and the regulation of industries that develop, utilize, or affect natural resources, as well as the operation and maintenance of parks, playgrounds, swimming pools, public beaches, auditoriums, public golf courses, museums, marinas, botanical gardens, and zoological parks.

Utilities, sewerage, and waste management includes operation, maintenance, and construction of public water supply systems, including production, acquisition, and distribution of water to general public or to other public or private utilities, for residential, commercial, and industrial use; activities associated with the production or acquisition and distribution of electric power; provision, maintenance, and operation of sanitary and storm sewer systems and sewage disposal and treatment facilities; and refuse collection and disposal, operation of sanitary landfills, and street cleaning activities.

Elementary and secondary education and libraries includes activities associated with the operation of public elementary and secondary schools and locally operated vocational-technical schools. Special education programs operated by elementary and secondary school systems are also included as are all ancillary services associated with the operation of schools, such as pupil transportation and food service. Also included are the establishment and provision of libraries for use by the general public and the technical support of privately operated libraries. This category includes classroom teachers, principals, supervisors of instruction, librarians, teacher aides, library aides, and guidance and psychological personnel as well as school superintendents and other administrative personnel, clerical and secretarial staffs, plant operation and maintenance personnel, health and recreation employees, transportation and food service personnel, and any student employees.

Higher education includes state government degree granting institutions that provide academic training above grade 12. This includes persons engaged in teaching and related academic research as well as administrative, clerical, custodial, cafeteria, health personnel, noninstructional employees engaged in organized research, law enforcement personnel, and paid student employees.

STATE GOVERNMENT FINANCES, Items 331–350

Source: U.S. Census Bureau—State Government Finances https://www.census.gov/programs-surveys/gov-finances.html

Data are from an annual survey conducted by the Census Bureau and pertain to state government fiscal years ending on June 30, except for four states with other ending dates: Alabama and Michigan (September 30), New York (March 31), and Texas (August 31).

The state government finance data presented in this publication may differ from data published by state governments because the Census Bureau may be using a different definition of which organizations are covered under the term, "state government."

For the purpose of Census Bureau statistics, the term "state government" refers not only to the executive, legislative, and judicial branches of a given state, but it also includes agencies, institutions, commissions, and public authorities that operate separately or somewhat autonomously from the central state government but where the state government maintains administrative or fiscal control over their activities as defined by the Census Bureau.

Total **general revenue** includes all revenue except utility, liquor stores, and insurance trust revenue. All tax revenue and intergovernmental revenue, even if designated for employee-retirement or local utility purpose, are classified as general revenue.

Intergovernmental revenue covers amounts received from the federal government as fiscal aid, reimbursements for performance of general government functions and specific services for the paying government, or in lieu of taxes. It excludes any amounts received from other governments from the sale of property, commodities, and utility services.

Taxes consist of compulsory contributions exacted by governments for public purposes. However, this category excludes employer and employee payments for retirement and social insurance purposes, which are classified as insurance trust revenue; it also excludes special assessments, which are classified as non-tax general revenue. Sales and gross receipts taxes do not include dealer discounts, or "commissions" allowed to merchants for collection of taxes from consumers. General sales taxes and selected taxes on sales of motor fuels, tobacco products, and other particular commodities and services are included.

General government expenditure includes capital outlay, a major portion of which is commonly financed by borrowing. Government revenue does not include receipts from borrowing. Among other things, this distorts the relationship between totals of revenue and expenditure figures that are presented and renders it useless as a direct measure of the degree of budgetary "balance" (as that term is generally applied).

Direct general expenditure comprises all expenditures of the state governments, excluding utility, liquor stores, insurance trust expenditures, and any intergovernmental payments.

State government expenditure for **education** is mainly for the provision and general support of schools and other educational facilities and services, including those for educational institutions beyond high school. They cover such related services as student transportation; school lunch and other cafeteria operations; school health, recreation, and library services; and dormitories, dining halls, and bookstores operated by public institutions of higher education.

Health and hospitals expenditure includes health research; clinics; nursing; immunization; other categorical, environmental, and general health services provided by health agencies; establishment and operation of hospital facilities; provision of hospital care; and support of other public and private hospitals.

Highways expenditure is for the provision and maintenance of highway facilities, including toll turnpikes, bridges, tunnels, and ferries, as well as regular roads, highways, and streets. Also included are expenditures for street lighting and for snow and ice removal. Not included are highway policing and traffic control, which are considered part of police protection

Public safety expenditure includes police and correctional institution expenditures.

Public welfare expenditure covers support of and assistance to needy persons; this aid is contingent upon the person's needs. Included are cash assistance paid directly to needy persons under categorical (Old Age Assistance, Temporary Assistance for Needy

Families, Aid to the Blind, and Aid to the Disabled) and other welfare programs; vendor payments made directly to private purveyors for medical care, burials, and other commodities and services provided under welfare programs; welfare institutions; and any intergovernmental or other direct expenditure for welfare purposes. Pensions to former employees and other benefits not contingent on need are excluded.

Natural resources, parks, and recreation includes expenditures for conservation, promotion, and development of natural resources (soil, water, energy, minerals, etc.) and the regulation of industries which develop, utilize, or affect natural resources. It also includes the provision and support of recreational and cultural-scientific facilities, such as golf courses, playgrounds, tennis courts, public beaches, swimming pools, play fields, parks, camping areas, recreational piers and marinas, galleries, museums, zoos, botanical gardens, auditoriums, stadiums, recreational centers, convention centers, exhibition halls, community music, drama, and celebrations.

Debt outstanding includes all long-term debt obligations of the government and its agencies (exclusive of utility debt) and all interest-bearing, short-term (repayable within one year) debt obligations remaining unpaid at the close of the fiscal year. It includes judgments, mortgages, and revenue bonds, as well as general obligation bonds, notes, and interest-bearing warrants. This category consists of non-interest-bearing, short-term obligations; inter-fund obligations; amounts owed in a trust or agency capacity; advances and contingent loans from other governments; and rights of individuals to benefit from government-administered employee-retirement funds.

VOTING AND REGISTRATION, Items 351 and 352

Source: U.S. Census Bureau—Current Population Survey
https://www.census.gov/topics/public-sector/voting.html

These estimates are based on the November 2020 Voting and Registration Supplement to the Current Population Survey (CPS).

Voting rates are calculated using the voting-age population, which includes both citizens and noncitizens. The percentages in columns 351 and 352 are based on the citizen population. Statistics from surveys are subject to sampling and nonsampling error. The CPS estimate of overall turnout differs from the "official" turnout reported by the Clerk of the House of Representatives.

ELECTION STATISTICS, Items 353–355

Source: U.S. House of Representatives, Statistics of the Presidential and Congressional Election of November 3, 2020
https://history.house.gov/Institution/Election-Statistics/2020election

Election results show the percentage of the total vote cast for the Democratic and Republican candidates, as well as the combined percentage for all other candidates in the 2020 presidential election. This information was compiled by the Office of the Clerk, U.S. House of Representatives and published on February 26, 2021.

TABLE B—STATES AND COUNTIES

Table B presents 199 items for the United States as a whole, each individual state, and the District of Columbia; and every county, county equivalent, and independent city. The counties are presented in alphabetical order within each state, and the states are also presented in alphabetical order. Independent cities, which are found in Maryland, Missouri, Nevada, and Virginia, are placed in alphabetical order at the end of the list of counties for those states. The District of Columbia is included in Table B as both a county and a state. It is also included as a city in Table D.

LAND AREA, Items 1 and 4

Source: U.S. Census Bureau—2020 U.S. Gazetteer Files, https://www.census.gov/geographies/reference-files/time-series/geo/gazetteer-files.html

Land area measurements are shown to the nearest square mile. Land area is an area measurement providing the size, in square miles, of the land portions of each county.

POPULATION, Items 2–4

Source: U.S. Census Bureau—Population Estimates
https://www.census.gov/programs-surveys/popest.html

The population data are Census Bureau estimates of the resident population as of July 1 of the year shown. The ranks are shown for counties (including independent cities and the District of Columbia).

Demographic components of population change (births, deaths, and migration) are produced at the national, state, and county levels of geography. Additionally, housing unit estimates are produced for the nation, states, and counties.

Current data on births, deaths, and migration are used annually to calculate population change since the most recent decennial census and produce a time series of estimates of population, demographic components of change, and housing units. The annual time series of estimates begins with the most recent decennial census data and extends to the vintage year.

POPULATION AND POPULATION CHARACTERISTICS, Items 5–19

Source: U.S. Census Bureau—Population Estimates
https://www.census.gov/programs-surveys/popest.html

The concept of race, as used by the Census Bureau, reflects self-identification by persons according to the race or races with which they most closely identify. These categories are sociopolitical constructs and should not be interpreted as being scientific or anthropological in nature. Furthermore, race categories include both racial and national origin groups.

Beginning with the 2000 census, respondents were offered the option of selecting one or more races. This option was not available in prior censuses; thus, comparisons between censuses should be made with caution. In Table B, Columns 5 through 8 refer to individuals who identified with each racial category, either alone or in combination with other races. The estimates exclude persons of Hispanic or Latino origin from all race groups.

The sum of the four individual race alone or in combination categories in this book will often add to more than the total population because people who reported more than one race were tallied in each race category. In this book, the Asian group has been combined with the Native Hawaiian and Other Pacific Islander group, causing double-counting of persons who identify with both groups. This is especially pronounced in Hawaii.

The **White** population is defined as persons who indicated their race as White, as well as persons who did not classify themselves in one of the specific race categories listed on the questionnaire but entered a nationality such as Irish, German, Italian, Lebanese, Near Easterner, Arab, or Polish.

The **Black** population includes persons who indicated their race as "Black or African American" as well as persons who did not classify themselves in one of the specific race categories but reported entries such as African American, Afro American, Kenyan, Nigerian, or Haitian.

The **American Indian or Alaska Native** population includes persons who indicated their race as American Indian or Alaska Native, as well as persons who did not classify themselves in one of the specific race categories but reported entries such as Canadian Indian, French-American Indian, Spanish-American Indian, Eskimo, Aleut, Alaska Indian, or any of the American Indian or Alaska Native tribes.

The **Asian and Pacific Islander** population combines two census groupings: **Asian** and **Native Hawaiian or Other Pacific Islander**. The **Asian** population includes persons who indicated their race as Asian Indian, Chinese, Filipino, Japanese, Korean, Vietnamese, or "Other Asian," as well as persons who provided write-in entries of such groups as Cambodian, Laotian, Hmong, Pakistani, or Taiwanese. The **Native Hawaiian or Other Pacific Islander** population includes persons who indicated their race as "Native Hawaiian," "Guamanian or Chamorro," "Samoan," or "Other Pacific Islander," as well as persons who reported entries such as Part Hawaiian, American Samoan, Fijian, Melanesian, or Tahitian.

The **Hispanic population** is based on a question that asked respondents "Is this person Spanish/Hispanic/Latino?" Persons marking any one of the four Hispanic categories (i.e., Mexican, Puerto Rican, Cuban, or other Spanish) are collectively referred to as Hispanic.

Age is defined as age at last birthday (number of completed years since birth), as of April 1 of the census year.

The **female** population is shown as a percentage of total population.

POPULATION AND COMPONENTS OF CHANGE, Items 20–26

Source: U.S. Census Bureau—Decennial Censuses and Population Estimates
https://www.census.gov/programs-surveys/popest.html
https://www.census.gov/programs-surveys/decennial-census/data/datasets.2010.html
https://www.census.gov/programs-surveys/decennial-census/about/rdo/summary-files.html

The population data for 2010 and 2020 are from the decennial censuses and represent the resident population as of April 1 of those years.

For annual population estimates, the latest decennial census typically serves as the population estimates base, but the 2020 Census could not be adopted for this purpose due to several challenges resulting from the COVID-19 pandemic. As a result, the Population Estimates Program developed a process for integrating the following three data sources at varying levels of detail to produce what they refer to as the Blended Base:

- 2020 Census PL 94-171 Redistricting File: Nation, state, and county total population counts
- 2020 Demographic Analysis (DA) Estimates: National population estimates by age and sex
- Vintage 2020 Postcensal Population Estimates: Nation, state, and county population estimates by age, sex, race, Hispanic origin, and population universe

The components of change are based on Census Bureau estimates of the resident population as of July 1, 2020, using this Blended Base. The change in population between April 1, 2020, and July 1, 2021, is made up of (a) natural increase—births minus deaths, and (b) net migration—the difference between the number of persons moving into a particular area and the number of persons moving out of the area. Net migration is composed of internal and international migration.

For 2021 estimates, the data and methods were updated to manage the lag in available data for the start of the new decade and account for increased mortality and changes to natality from the COVID-19 pandemic. Specifically, the Census Bureau incorporated national provisional monthly estimates on births and deaths for all months of 2020 from the National Center for Health Statistics website. They assigned characteristics to these using distributions from the last year of final birth and death data available, 2019. For births, they also incorporated monthly total births for the nation in the first quarter of 2021 and used recent trends to project births for the second quarter of the year. For deaths, they had monthly total data through June 30, 2021, that included recent trends and patterns of excess mortality from the pandemic. The adjusted national births and deaths serve as controls for subnational vital events, resulting in an increase in deaths and decrease in births for numerous states and counties. Other than the national control, no methodological changes were made to the subnational birth or death estimates.

For the net international migration component for the 2020 estimates period (July1, 2019-June 30, 2020), the Census Bureau adjusted to account for the impact of the COVID-19 global pandemic. They typically update prior years in the time series for each vintage as newer data become available. However, 2020 American Community Survey (ACS) data were not available to use for this time period due to data quality concerns resulting from the COVID-19 pandemic, so they did not update the estimates for April 1, 2020–June 30, 2020, for the 2021 estimates. At the time of production, 2019 was the latest ACS file available for estimating international migration. To account for trends from July 1, 2020, to June 30, 2021, they used current data from the United States Department of Justice, Department of Homeland Security (Citizenship and Immigration Services), State Department (Bureau of Consular Affairs and Refugee Processing Center), and the Institute of International Education to adjust 2019 ACS estimates.

Because the 2021 population estimates are based on a model that begins with a national population estimate, the county components of change do not always exactly add up to the difference between the 2020 census population and the 2021 estimates.

HOUSEHOLDS, Items 27–31

Source: U.S. Census Bureau—American Community Survey, 2020 5-year Estimates
https://www.census.gov/programs-surveys/acs

A **household** includes all of the persons who occupy a housing unit. (Persons not living in households are classified as living in group quarters.) A housing unit is a house, an apartment, a mobile home, a group of rooms, or a single room occupied (or, if vacant, intended for occupancy) as separate living quarters. Separate living quarters are those in which the occupants live separately from any other persons in the building and have direct access from the outside of the building or through a common hall. The occupants may be a single family, one person living alone, two or more families living together, or any other group of related or unrelated persons who share living quarters. The number of households is the same as the number of year-round occupied housing units.

A **family** includes a householder and one or more other persons living in the same household who are related to the householder by birth, marriage, or adoption. All persons in a household who are related to the householder are regarded as members of his or her family. A **family household** may contain persons not related to the householder; thus, family households may include more members than families do. A household can contain only one family for the purposes of census tabulations. Not all households contain families, as a household may comprise a group of unrelated persons or of one person living alone. Families are classified by type as either a "married-couple family" or "other family," according to the presence or absence of a spouse.

The measure of **persons per household** is obtained by dividing the number of persons in households by the number of households or householders. One person in each household is designated as the householder. In most cases, this is the person (or one of the persons) in whose name the house is owned, being bought, or rented. If there is no such person in the household, any adult household member 15 years old and over can be designated as the householder.

The category **female family householder** includes only female-headed family households with no spouse present.

A nonfamily household consists of a householder living alone or with nonrelatives only. Column 31 shows one-person households as a percentage of all households.

GROUP QUARTERS, Item 32

Source: U.S. Census Bureau—Population Estimates
https://www.census.gov/programs-surveys/popest.html

The Census Bureau classifies all persons not living in households as living in group quarters; this category includes both the institutional and noninstitutional populations. The institutionalized population includes persons under formally authorized, supervised care or custody in institutions, such as correctional institutions, nursing homes, mental (psychiatric) hospitals, and juvenile institutions. The noninstitutionalized population includes persons who live in group quarters other than institutions, such as college dormitories, military quarters, and group homes. This volume includes the total number of persons in group quarters.

Due to complications in Group Quarters (GQ) data as a result of the COVID-19 pandemic, the 2021 estimate uses GQ data from the April 1, 2020, base and holds it constant forward to July 1, 2021.

DAYTIME POPULATION, Items 33 and 34

Source: U.S. Census Bureau—American Community Survey, 2020 5-year Estimates
https://www.census.gov/programs-surveys/acs

Daytime population refers to the number of persons who are present in an area or place during normal business hours, including workers. This can be contrasted with the "resident" population, which is present during the evening and nighttime hours. The daytime population estimate is calculated by adding the total resident population and the total workers working in the area/place, and then subtracting the total workers living in the area/place from that result. Information on the expansion or contraction experienced by different communities between their nighttime and daytime populations is important for many planning purposes, especially those concerning transportation, disaster, and relief operations.

The employment/residence ratio is a measure of the total number of workers working in an area or place, relative to the total number of workers living in the area or place. It is often used as a rough indication of the jobs-workers balance in an area/place, although it does not take into account whether the resident workers possess the skills needed for the jobs available in their particular area/place. The employment/residence ratio is calculated by dividing the number of total workers working in an area/place by the number of total workers residing in the area/place.

BIRTHS AND DEATHS, Items 35–38

Source: U.S. Census Bureau—Population Estimates
https://www.census.gov/programs-surveys/popest.html

The numbers of births and deaths are from the Census Bureau's Population Estimates Program. They represent the total number of live births and deaths occurring to residents of an area as estimated using reports from the National Center for Health Statistics

(NCHS) and the Federal-State Cooperative for Population Estimates (FSCPE). The rates measure births and deaths during the specified time period as a proportion of an area's population. Rates are expressed per 1,000 population estimated as of July 1. These numbers and rates do not represent the calendar year, but rather the year-long period ending on July 1.

For 2021 estimates, the data and methods were updated to manage the lag in available data for the start of the new decade and account for increased mortality and changes to natality from the COVID-19 pandemic. Specifically, the Census Bureau incorporated national provisional monthly estimates on births and deaths for all months of 2020 from the National Center for Health Statistics website. They assigned characteristics to these using distributions from the last year of final birth and death data available, 2019. For births, they also incorporated monthly total births for the nation in the first quarter of 2021 and used recent trends to project births for the second quarter of the year. For deaths, they had monthly total data through June 30, 2021, that included recent trends and patterns of excess mortality from the pandemic. The adjusted national births and deaths serve as controls for subnational vital events, resulting in an increase in deaths and decrease in births for numerous states and counties. Other than the national control, no methodological changes were made to the subnational birth or death estimates.

Rates for births and deaths are calculated by taking the component value between July 1 and June 30 for an estimate year, dividing by the average of the July 1 beginning and ending resident total populations for the estimate year, and then multiplying by one thousand.

PERSONS UNDER 65 WITH NO HEALTH INSURANCE, Items 39 and 40

Source: U.S. Census Bureau—Small Area Health Insurance Estimates
https://www.census.gov/programs-surveys/sahie.html

The Small Area Health Insurance Estimates (SAHIE) program develops model-based estimates of health insurance coverage for counties and states. This developmental program builds on the work of the Small Area Income and Poverty Estimates (SAIPE) program. The SAHIE program models health insurance coverage by combining survey data with population estimates and administrative records. These estimates combine data from administrative records, postcensal population estimates, and the decennial census with direct estimates from the American Community Survey to provide consistent and reliable single-year estimates. These model-based single-year estimates are more reflective of current conditions than multi-year survey estimates.

MEDICARE ENROLLMENT, Items 41—43

Source: U.S. Department of Health and Human Services, Centers for Medicare and Medicaid Services
https://data.cms.gov/summary-statistics-on-beneficiary-enrollment/medicare-and-medicaid-reports

The Centers for Medicare and Medicaid Services (CMS) administers Medicare, which provides health insurance to persons 65 years old and over, persons with permanent kidney failure, and certain persons with disabilities. Original Medicare has two parts: Hospital Insurance and Supplemental Medical Insurance. In recent years, Medicare has been expanded to include two new programs: Medicare Advantage plans and prescription drug coverage. Medicare Advantage Plans are health plan options that are approved by Medicare but run by private companies. Medicare prescription drug plans can be part of Medicare Advantage plans or stand-alone drug plans.

Persons who are eligible for Medicare can enroll in Part A (Hospital Insurance) at no charge, and can choose to pay a monthly premium to enroll in Part B. Most eligible persons are enrolled in Part A, and most enrollees in Part A are also enrolled in Part B (Supplemental Medical Insurance.) This table includes persons who were enrolled in either Part A or Part B or both in December 2021.

Part B beneficiaries can choose to enroll in **Original Medicare**, a fee-for-service plan administered by the Centers for Medicare and Medicaid Services, or in a **Medicare Advantage** plan. Medicare Advantage plans include private fee-for-service plans, preferred provider organizations, health maintenance organizations, medical savings account plans, demonstration plans, and programs for all-inclusive care for the elderly.

This table includes persons who were enrolled in December 2021 because the annual data for 2021 was not in the database at the time of production. The annual Medicare enrollment counts are determined using a person-year methodology. For each calendar year, total person-year counts are determined by summing the total number of months that each beneficiary is enrolled during the year and dividing by 12. Using this methodology, a beneficiary's partial-year enrollment may be counted in more than one category (i.e., both Original Medicare and Medicare Advantage).

COVID-19, Items 44-47

Source: U.S. Centers for Disease Control and Prevention, National Center for Health Statistics, COVID-19 Death Data and Resources, Ad Hoc County of Residence COVID-19 Deaths Counts, 2020 Provisional, and Covid Data Tracker, COVID-19 Vaccinations in the United States by County
https://www.cdc.gov/nchs/covid19/covid-19-mortality-data-files.htm
https://www.cdc.gov/coronavirus/2019-ncov/vaccines/distributing/about-vaccine-data.html

The Centers for Disease Control and Prevention (CDC) is continually monitoring the impact of the Corona Virus pandemic and the vaccination status of residents of the United States. This book includes measures that describe a specific point in time, extracted from the many CDC datasets that are constantly changing. For the most accurate and up-to-date data for a specific county or state, the CDC recommends that you visit the relevant state or local health department website.

The number and percent of deaths from COVID-19 represent the provisional count of deaths involving COVID-19 by United

States county of residence, from January 1, 2020, through December 31, 2020. The provisional counts for COVID-19 deaths are based on a current flow of mortality data in the National Vital Statistics System. National provisional counts include deaths occurring within the 50 states and the District of Columbia. These data come directly from death certificates filed at the state and local level.

The total number of people who were fully vaccinated as of April 2022 is shown along with the percentage of the estimated population in the county. Fully vaccinated people have had a second dose of a two-dose vaccine or one dose of a single-dose vaccine. They may also have had booster doses. Vaccination data represents all vaccine partners including jurisdictional partner clinics, retail pharmacies, long-term care facilities, dialysis centers, Federal Emergency Management Agency and Health Resources and Services Administration partner sites, and federal entity facilities.

CDC determines the number of people receiving at least one dose, the number of people who are fully vaccinated, and the number of people with a booster dose based on information *reported to CDC* on dose number, dose manufacturer, administration date, recipient ID, and date of submission. Because the method used to determine dose numbers needs to be applied across multiple jurisdictions with different reporting practices, CDC's dose number estimates might differ from those reported by jurisdictions and federal entities. People receiving doses are attributed to the jurisdiction in which they reside. For nearly 10 million people, the county of residence is unknown.

There are challenges in linking records when someone receives vaccine doses in different jurisdictions or from different providers. That person could receive different unique person identifiers for different doses. CDC may not be able to link multiple unique person identifiers for different jurisdictions or providers to a single person, and subsequent doses may appear to be a first dose when reported. Thus, CDC's data may over-estimate first doses and under-estimate subsequent doses.

Another issue that poses challenges to estimating doses administered is that different jurisdictions and providers use different reporting practices. As people receiving doses are attributed to the jurisdiction in which they reside, the reporting method might change between doses if they move to a different jurisdiction. Also, CDC may lack information about a person's residence. These issues can cause CDC's dose number estimates to differ from those reported by jurisdictions and federal entities.

EDUCATION—SCHOOL ENROLLMENT AND EDUCATIONAL ATTAINMENT, Items 48–51

Source: U.S. Census Bureau—American Community Survey, 2020 5-year Estimates
https://www.census.gov/programs-surveys/acs

Data on **school enrollment** are tabulated for the population 3 years old and over. Persons were classified as enrolled in school if they reported attending a "regular" public or private school (or college) during the three months preceding the interview. The instructions were to include only nursery school, kindergarten, elementary school, and schooling which would lead to a high school diploma or a college degree as regular school. The Census Bureau defines a public school as "any school or college controlled and supported by a local, county, state, or federal government." Schools primarily supported and controlled by religious organizations or other private groups are defined as private schools.

Data on **educational attainment** are tabulated for the population 25 years old and over. The data were derived from a question that asked respondents for the highest level of school completed or the highest degree received. Persons who had passed a high school equivalency examination were considered high school graduates. Schooling received in foreign schools was to be reported as the equivalent grade or years in the regular American school system.

Vocational and technical training, such as barber school training; business, trade, technical, and vocational schools; or other training for a specific trade are specifically excluded.

High school graduate or less. This category includes persons whose highest degree was a high school diploma or its equivalent, and those who reported any level lower than a high school diploma.

Bachelor's degree or more. This category includes persons who have received bachelor's degrees, master's degrees, professional school degrees (such as law school or medical school degrees), and doctoral degrees.

LOCAL GOVERNMENT EDUCATION EXPENDITURES, Items 52 and 53

Source: U.S. Department of Education, National Center for Education Statistics, Common Core of Data (CCD), "Local Education Agency (School District) Finance Survey (F-33) Data," 2018-2019, version 1a, Provisional
https://nces.ed.gov/ccd

Expenditures are for elementary and secondary education which includes prekindergarten through twelfth grade regular, special, and vocational education, as well as cocurricular, community service, and adult education programs provided by a public school system, including charter schools. The financial activities of these systems for all instruction, support service, and noninstructional activities are included

Current spending comprises current operation expenditure, payments made by the state government on behalf of school systems, and transfers made by school systems into their own retirement funds. Current operation expenditures include direct expenditure for salaries, employee benefits, purchased professional and technical services, purchased property and other services, and supplies. It includes gross school system expenditure for instruction, support services, and noninstructional functions. It excludes expenditure for debt service, capital outlay, and reimbursement to other governments (including other school systems).

Current expenditure per student is current expenditure divided by the number of students enrolled. The number of students enrolled is based on an annual "membership" count of students on or about October 1, collected by the National Center for Education Statistics on the Common Core of Data (CCD) agency universe file—"Local Education Agency (School District) Universe Survey."

MONEY INCOME, Items 54–57

Source: U.S. Census Bureau—American Community Survey, 2020 5-year Estimates
https://www.census.gov/programs-surveys/acs

Total money income is the sum of the amounts reported separately for wage or salary income; net self-employment income; interest, dividends, or net rental or royalty income or income from estates and trusts; Social Security or railroad retirement income; Supplemental Security Income (SSI); public assistance or welfare payments; retirement, survivor, or disability pensions; and all other income. Receipts from the following sources are not included as income: capital gains; money received from the sale of property (unless the recipient was engaged in the business of selling such property); the value of income "in kind" from food stamps, public housing subsidies, medical care, employer contributions for individuals, etc.; withdrawal of bank deposits; money borrowed; tax refunds; exchange of money between relatives living in the same household; and gifts, lump-sum inheritances, insurance payments, and other types of lump-sum receipts.

Money income differs in definition from personal income (item 62). For example, money income does not include the pension rights, employer provided health insurance, food stamps, or Medicare payments that are included in personal income.

Per capita income is the mean income computed for every man, woman, and child in a particular group. It is derived by dividing the aggregate income of a particular group by the resident population in that group as estimated in the American Community Survey. Per capita income is rounded to the nearest whole dollar.

Household income includes the income of the householder and all other individuals 15 years old and over in the household, whether or not they are related to the householder. Since many households consist of only one person, median household income is usually less than median family income. Although the household income statistics cover the 12 months preceding the interview, the characteristics of individuals and the composition of households refer to the date of interview. Thus, the income of the household does not include amounts received by individuals who were no longer residing in the household at the time of interview. Similarly, income amounts reported by individuals who did not reside in the household during all of the past 12 months but who were members of the household at the time of interview are included. However, the composition of most households was the same during those 12 months as it was at the time of interview.

Median income divides the income distribution into two equal parts, with half of all cases below the median income level and half of all cases above the median income level. For households, the median income is based on the distribution of the total number of households, including those with no income. Median income for households is computed on the basis of a standard distribution with a minimum value of less than $2,500 and a maximum value of $200,000 or more and is rounded to the nearest whole dollar. Median income figures are calculated using linear interpolation if the width of the interval containing the estimate is $2,500 or less. If the width of the interval containing the estimate is greater than $2,500, Pareto interpolation is used.

Income amounts have been adjusted for inflation to represent the final year of multi-year estimates, in this case 2016-2020 estimates. The constant-dollar figures are based on an annual average Consumer Price Index from the Bureau of Labor Statistics. Constant-dollar figures are estimates representing an effort to remove the effects of price changes from statistical series reported in dollar terms. However, the estimates do not reflect the price and cost-of-living differences that may exist between areas.

INCOME AND POVERTY, Items 58–61

Source: U.S. Census Bureau—Small Area Income and Poverty Estimates Program
https://www.census.gov/programs-surveys/saipe.html

The annual income and poverty estimates by county are constructed from statistical models that relate income and poverty to indicators based on summary data from federal income tax returns, data about participation in the Food Stamp program, and the previous census. A regression model predicts the number of people in poverty using county-level observations from the current year's American Community Survey (ACS) and administrative records and census data as the predictors. The 2005 estimates were the first to use the ACS. Prior year models were based on the Annual Social and Economic Supplement (ASEC) of the Current Population Survey (CPS). The ACS is a much larger survey than the ASEC, permitting income and poverty estimates based on a single year for many counties, Because of the differences between the two surveys, caution should be used when comparing these estimates with those from earlier years.

The **poverty status** data were derived from data collected on the number of persons in a household, each person's relationship to the householder, and income data. The Social Security Administration (SSA) developed the original poverty definition in 1964, which federal interagency committees subsequently revised in 1969 and 1980. The Office of Management and Budget's (OMB) *Directive 14* prescribes the SSA's definition as the official poverty measure for federal agencies to use in their statistical work. Poverty statistics presented in American Community Survey products adhere to the standards defined by OMB in *Directive 14*.

Poverty thresholds vary depending on three criteria: size of family, number of children, and, for one- and two-person families, age of householder. In determining the poverty status of families and unrelated individuals, the Census Bureau uses thresholds (income cutoffs) arranged in a two-dimensional matrix. The matrix consists of family size (from one person to nine or more persons), cross-classified by presence and number of family members under 18 years old (from no children present to eight or more children present). Unrelated individuals and two-person families are further differentiated by age of reference person (under 65 years old and 65 years old and over). To determine a person's poverty status, the person's total family income over the previous 12 months is compared with the poverty threshold appropriate for that person's family size and composition. If the total income of that person's family is less than the threshold

Poverty Thresholds for 2020 by Size of Family and Number of Related Children Under 18 Years

Size of family unit	Weighted average thresholds	Related children under 18 years: None	One	Two	Three	Four	Five	Six	Seven	Eight or more
One person (unrelated individual):	13,171									
Under age 65	13,465	13,465								
Aged 65 and older	12,413	12,413								
Two people:	16,733									
Householder under age 65	17,413	17,331	17,839							
Householder aged 65 and older	15,659	15,644	17,771							
Three people	20,591	20,244	20,832	20,852						
Four people	26,496	26,695	27,131	26,246	26,338					
Five people	31,417	32,193	32,661	31,661	30,887	30,414				
Six people	35,499	37,027	37,174	36,408	35,674	34,582	33,935			
Seven people	40,406	42,605	42,871	41,954	41,314	40,124	38,734	37,210		
Eight people	44,755	47,650	48,071	47,205	46,447	45,371	44,006	42,585	42,224	
Nine people or more	53,905	57,319	57,597	56,831	56,188	55,132	53,679	52,366	52,040	50,035

Source: U.S. Census Bureau.

appropriate for that family, then the person is considered poor or "below the poverty level," together with every member of his or her family. If a person is not living with anyone related by birth, marriage, or adoption, then the person's own income is compared with his or her poverty threshold. The total number of persons below the poverty level is the sum of persons in families and the number of unrelated individuals with incomes below the poverty level over the previous12 months.

PERSONAL INCOME AND EARNINGS, Items 62–83

Source: U.S. Bureau of Economic Analysis, Regional Economic Accounts
https://www.bea.gov/data/economic-accounts/regional#state
https://www.bea.gov/data/income-saving/personal-income-county-metro-and-other-areas

Total personal income is the current income received by residents of an area from all sources. It is measured before deductions of income and other personal taxes, but after deductions of personal contributions for Social Security, government retirement, and other social insurance programs. It consists of **wage and salary disbursements** (covering all employee earnings, including executive salaries, bonuses, commissions, payments-in-kind, incentive payments, and tips); various types of supplementary earnings, such as employers' contributions to pension funds (termed "other labor income" or "supplements to wages and salaries"); proprietors' income; rental income of persons; dividends; personal interest income; and government and business transfer payments.

Per capita personal income is based on the resident population estimated as of July 1 of the year shown. BEA uses the Census Bureau's July 1 population estimates which use the most recent census as a base starting point. For the 2020 per capita income, estimates derived from the 2020 census were not available at the county level, so the county population estimates are based on the 2010 census, while the state data use estimates that incorporate the 2020 census.

Proprietors' income is the monetary income and income-in-kind of proprietorships and partnerships (including the independent professions) and the income of tax-exempt cooperatives.

Dividends are cash payments by corporations to stockholders who are U.S. residents. **Interest** is the monetary and imputed interest income of persons from all sources. **Rent** is the monetary income of persons from the rental of real property, except the income of persons primarily engaged in the real estate business; the imputed net rental income of owner-occupants of nonfarm dwellings; and the royalties received by persons.

Transfer payments are income for which services are not currently rendered. They consist of both government and business transfer payments. Government transfer payments include payments under the following programs: Federal Old-Age, Survivors, and Disability Insurance ("Social Security"); Medicare and medical vendor payments; unemployment insurance; railroad and government retirement; federal- and state-government-insured workers' compensation; veterans' benefits, including veterans' life insurance; SNAP (Supplemental Nutrition Assistance Program, or food stamps); black lung payments; Supplemental Security Income; and Temporary Assistance for Needy Families. Government payments to nonprofit institutions, other than for work under research and development contracts, are also included. Business transfer payments consist primarily of liability payments for personal injury and of corporate gifts to nonprofit institutions.

Personal income differs in definition from money income (items 54–57). For example, personal income includes pension rights, employer-provided health insurance, food stamps, and Medicare. These are not included in the definition of money income.

Earnings cover wage and salary disbursements, other labor income, and proprietors' income.

The data for earnings obtained from the Bureau of Economic Analysis (BEA) are based on place of work. In computing personal income, BEA makes an "adjustment for residence" to earnings, based on commuting patterns; personal income is thus presented on a place-of-residence basis.

Farm earnings include the income of farm workers (wages and salaries and other labor income) and farm proprietors. Farm proprietors' income includes only the income of sole proprietorships and partnerships. Farm earnings estimates are benchmarked to data collected in the Census of Agriculture and the revised Department of Agriculture statistical totals of income and expense items.

Goods-related industries include mining, construction, and manufacturing.

Mining, Quarrying, and Extracting comprises establishments that extract naturally occurring mineral solids, such as coal and ores; liquid minerals, such as crude petroleum; and gases, such as natural gas. The term mining is used in the broad sense to include quarrying, well operations, beneficiating (e.g., crushing, screening, washing, and flotation), and other preparation customarily performed at the mine site, or as a part of mining activity.

The **Construction** sector comprises establishments primarily engaged in the construction of buildings or engineering projects (e.g., highways and utility systems). Establishments primarily engaged in the preparation of sites for new construction and establishments primarily engaged in subdividing land for sale as building sites also are included in this sector.

Manufacturing comprises establishments engaged in the mechanical, physical, or chemical transformation of materials, substances, or components into new products. The assembling of component parts of manufactured products is considered manufacturing, except in cases where the activity is appropriately classified in **Construction**.

Service-related and other industries include private-sector earnings in agricultural services, forestry, and fisheries; transportation and public utilities; wholesale trade; retail trade; finance, insurance, and real estate; and services. Government earnings include all levels of government.

The **Information** sector comprises establishments engaged in the following processes: (a) producing and distributing information and cultural products, (b) providing the means to transmit or distribute these products as well as data or communications, and (c) processing data.

Professional, Scientific, and Technical Services comprises establishments that specialize in performing professional, scientific, and technical activities for others. These activities require a high degree of expertise and training. The establishments in this sector specialize according to expertise and provide these services to clients in a variety of industries and, in some cases, to households. Activities performed include: legal advice and representation; accounting, bookkeeping, and payroll services; architectural, engineering, and specialized design services; computer services; consulting services; research services; advertising services; photographic services; translation and interpretation services; veterinary services; and other professional, scientific, and technical services.

The **Retail Trade** sector comprises establishments engaged in retailing merchandise, generally without transformation, and rendering services incidental to the sale of merchandise. The retailing process is the final step in the distribution of merchandise; retailers are, therefore, organized to sell merchandise in small quantities to the general public. This sector comprises two main types of retailers: store and nonstore retailers.

Store retailers operate fixed point-of-sale locations, located and designed to attract a high volume of walk-in customers. In general, retail stores have extensive displays of merchandise and use mass-media advertising to attract customers. In addition to retailing merchandise, some types of store retailers are also engaged in the provision of after-sales services, such as repair and installation.

Nonstore retailers, like store retailers, are organized to serve the general public, but their retailing methods differ. The establishments of this subsector reach customers and market merchandise with methods, such as the broadcasting of "infomercials," the broadcasting and publishing of direct-response advertising, the publishing of paper and electronic catalogs, door-to-door solicitation, in-home demonstration, selling from portable stalls (street vendors, except food), and distribution through vending machines. Establishments engaged in the direct sale (nonstore) of products, such as home heating oil dealers and home delivery newspaper routes are included here.

Finance and Insurance comprises establishments primarily engaged in financial transactions (transactions involving the creation, liquidation, or change in ownership of financial assets) and/or in facilitating financial transactions. Three principal types of activities are identified: raising funds by taking deposits and/or issuing securities and, in the process, incurring liabilities; pooling of risk by underwriting insurance and annuities; and providing specialized services facilitating or supporting financial intermediation, insurance, and employee benefit programs.

The **Real Estate and Rental and Leasing** sector comprises establishments primarily engaged in renting, leasing, or otherwise allowing the use of tangible or intangible assets, and establishments providing related services. The major portion of this sector comprises establishments that rent, lease, or otherwise allow the use of their own assets by others. The assets may be tangible, as is the case of real estate and equipment, or intangible, as is the case with patents and trademarks. This sector also includes establishments primarily engaged in managing real estate for others, selling, renting and/or buying real estate for others, and appraising real estate.

Health Care and Social Assistance comprises establishments providing health care and social assistance for individuals. The sector includes both health care and social assistance because it is sometimes difficult to distinguish between the boundaries of these two activities. The industries in this sector are arranged on a continuum starting with those establishments providing medical care exclusively, continuing with those providing health care and social assistance, and finally finishing with those providing only social assistance. The services provided by establishments in this sector are delivered by trained professionals. All industries in the sector share this commonality of process, namely, labor inputs of health practitioners or social workers with the requisite expertise. Many of the industries in the sector are defined based on the educational degree held by the practitioners included in the industry.

Government includes the executive, legislative, judicial, administrative and regulatory activities of Federal, state, local, and international governments. Also included are Government enterprises: government agencies that cover a substantial portion of their operating costs by selling goods and services to the public and that maintain separate accounts.

Industries are categorized under the North American Industry Classification System (NAICS), and are not comparable to years prior to 2002.

SOCIAL SECURITY AND SUPPLEMENTAL SECURITY INCOME, Items 84–86

Source: U.S. Social Security Administration
https://www.ssa.gov/policy/docs/statcomps/oasdi_sc
https://www.ssa.gov/policy/docs/statcomps/ssi_sc

Social Security beneficiaries are persons receiving benefits under the Old-Age, Survivors, and Disability Insurance Program. These include retired or disabled workers covered by the program, their spouses and dependent children, and the surviving spouses and dependent children of deceased workers.

Supplemental Security Income (SSI) recipients are persons receiving SSI payments. The SSI program is a cash assistance program that provides monthly benefits to low-income aged, blind, or disabled persons.

Data are as of December of the year shown.

HOUSING, Items 87–96

Source: U.S. Census Bureau—Population Estimates Program
Source: U.S. Census Bureau—American Community Survey, 2020 5-year Estimates
https://www.census.gov/programs-surveys/popest.html
https://www.census.gov/programs-surveys/acs

Housing data for 2021 are from the Population Estimates Program. Housing unit characteristics for 2016-2020 are from the American Community Survey.

A **housing unit** is a house, apartment, mobile home or trailer, group of rooms, or single room occupied or, if vacant, intended for occupancy as separate living quarters. Separate living quarters are those in which the occupants do not live and eat with any other person in the structure and which have direct access from the outside of the building or through a common hall.

The occupants of a housing unit may be a single family, one person living alone, two or more families living together, or any other group of related or unrelated persons who share living quarters. Both occupied and vacant housing units are included in the housing inventory, although recreational vehicles, tents, caves, boats, railroad cars, and the like are included only if they are occupied as a person's usual place of residence.

A housing unit is classified as occupied if it is the usual place of residence of the person or group of persons living in it at the time of enumeration, or if the occupants are only temporarily absent (away on vacation). A household consists of all persons who occupy a housing unit as their usual place of residence. Vacant units for sale or rent include units rented or sold but not occupied and any other units held off the market.

Median value is the dollar amount that divides the distribution of specified owner-occupied housing units into two equal parts, with half of all units below the median value and half of all units above the median value. Value is defined as the respondent's estimate of what the house would sell for if it were for sale. Data are presented for single-family units on fewer than 10 acres of land that have no business or medical offices on the property.

Median rent divides the distribution of renter-occupied housing units into two equal parts. The rent concept used in this volume is gross rent, which includes the amount of cash rent a renter pays (contract rent) plus the estimated average cost of utilities and fuels, if these are paid by the renter. The rent is the amount of rent only for living quarters and excludes amounts paid for any business or other space occupied. Single-family houses on lots of 10 or more acres of land are also excluded.

Housing cost as a percentage of income is shown separately for owners with mortgages, owners without mortgages, and renters. Rent as a percentage of income is a computed ratio of gross rent and monthly household income (total household income divided by 12). Selected owner costs include utilities and fuels, mortgage payments, insurance, taxes, etc. In each case, the ratio of housing cost to income is computed separately for each housing unit. The housing cost ratios for half of all units are above the median shown in this book, and half are below the median shown in the book.

Substandard units are occupied units that are overcrowded or lack complete plumbing facilities. For the purposes of this item, "overcrowded" is defined as having 1.01 persons or more per room. Complete plumbing facilities include hot and cold piped water, a flush toilet, and a bathtub or shower. These facilities must be located inside the housing unit, but do not have to be in the same room.

CIVILIAN LABOR FORCE AND UNEMPLOYMENT, Items 97–100

Source: U.S. Bureau of Labor Statistics—Local Area Unemployment Statistics
https://www.bls.gov/lau/#tables

Data for the civilian labor force are the product of a federal-state cooperative program in which state employment security agencies prepare labor force and unemployment estimates under concepts, definitions, and technical procedures established by the Bureau of Labor Statistics (BLS). The civilian labor force consists of all civilians 16 years old and over who are either employed or unemployed.

Unemployment includes all persons who did not work during the survey week, made specific efforts to find a job during the previous four weeks, and were available for work during the survey week (except for temporary illness). Persons waiting to be called back to a job from which they had been laid off and those waiting to report to a new job within the next 30 days are included in unemployment figures.

Table B includes annual average data for the year shown. The Local Area Unemployment Statistics data are periodically updated to reflect revised inputs, re-estimation, and controlling to new statewide totals.

CIVILIAN EMPLOYMENT, Items 101–103

Source: U.S. Census Bureau—American Community Survey, 2020 5-year Estimates
https://www.census.gov/programs-surveys/acs

Total employment includes all civilians 16 years old and over who were either (1) "at work"—those who did any work at all during the reference week as paid employees, worked in either their own business or profession, worked on their own farm, or worked 15 hours or more as unpaid workers in a family farm or business; or were (2) "with a job, but not at work"—those who had a job but were not at work that week due to illness, weather, industrial dispute, vacation, or other personal reasons.

The **occupational categories** are based on the occupational classification system that was developed for the 2000 census and revised in 2002 and 2010. This system consists of 539 specific occupational categories for employed persons arranged into 23 major occupational groups. This classification was developed based on the *Standard Occupational Classification (SOC) Manual: 2000*, published by the Executive Office of the President, Office of Management and Budget.

Column 102 includes the Management, business, science, and arts occupations category while Column 103 combines the Natural resources, construction, and maintenance occupations and the Production, transportation, and material moving occupations.

PRIVATE NONFARM EMPLOYMENT AND EARNINGS, Items 104–112

Source: U.S. Census Bureau—County Business Patterns
https://www.census.gov/programs-surveys/cbp.html

Data for private nonfarm employment and earnings are compiled from the payroll information reported monthly in the Census Bureau publication *County Business Patterns*. The estimates are based on surveys conducted by the Census Bureau and administrative records from the Internal Revenue Service (IRS).

The following types of employment are excluded from the tables: government employment, self-employed persons, farm workers, and domestic service workers. Railroad employment jointly covered by Social Security and railroad retirement programs, employment on oceanborne vessels, and employment in foreign countries are also excluded.

Annual payroll is the combined amount of wages paid, tips reported, and other compensation (including salaries, vacation allowances, bonuses, commissions, sick-leave pay, and the value of payments-in-kind such as free meals and lodging) paid to employees before deductions for Social Security, income tax, insurance, union dues, etc. All forms of compensation are included, regardless of whether they are subject to income tax or the Federal Insurance Contributions Act tax, with the exception of annuities, third-party sick pay, and supplemental unemployment compensation benefits (even if income tax was withheld). For corporations, total annual payroll includes compensation paid to officers and executives; for unincorporated businesses, it excludes profit or other compensation of proprietors or partners.

AGRICULTURE, Items 113–132

Source: U.S. Department of Agriculture, National Agricultural Statistics Service—2017 Census of Agriculture
https://www.nass.usda.gov/Publications/AgCensus/2017/index.php

Data for the 2017 Census of Agriculture were collected in 2018, but pertain to the year 2017.

The Census Bureau took a census of agriculture every 10 years from 1840 to 1920; since 1925, this census has been taken roughly once every 5 years. The 1997 Census of Agriculture was the first one conducted by the National Agricultural Statistics Service of the U.S. Department of Agriculture. Over time, the definition of a farm has varied. For recent censuses (including the 2017 census), a farm has been defined as any place from which $1,000 or more of agricultural products were produced and sold or normally would have been sold during the census year. Dollar figures are expressed in current dollars and have not been adjusted for inflation or deflation.

The term **producer** designates a person who is involved in making decisions for the farm operation. Decisions may include decisions about such things as planting, harvesting, livestock management, and marketing. The producer may be the owner, a member of the owner's household, a hired manager, a tenant, a renter, or a sharecropper. If a person rents land to others or has land worked on shares by others, he/she is considered the producer only of the land which is retained for his/her own operation. The census collected information on the total number of male producers, the total number of female producers, and demographic information for up to four producers per farm.

The acreage designated as **land in farms** consists primarily of agricultural land used for crops, pasture, or grazing. It also includes woodland and wasteland not actually under cultivation or used for pasture or grazing, provided that this land was part of the farm operator's total operation. Land in farms is an operating-unit concept and includes all land owned and operated, as well as all land rented from others. Land used rent-free is classified as land rented from others. All grazing land, except land used under government permits on a per-head basis, was included as "land in farms" provided it was part of a farm or ranch. Land under the exclusive use of a grazing association was reported by the grazing association and included as land in farms. All land in Indian reservations used for growing crops or grazing livestock is classified as land in farms.

Irrigated land includes all land watered by any artificial or controlled means, such as sprinklers, flooding, furrows or ditches, sub-irrigation, and spreader dikes. Included are supplemental, partial, and preplant irrigation. Each acre was counted only once regardless of the number of times it was irrigated or harvested. Livestock lagoon waste water distributed by sprinkler or flood systems was also included.

Total cropland includes cropland harvested, cropland used only for pasture or grazing, cropland on which all crops failed or were abandoned, cropland in cultivated summer fallow, and cropland idle or used for cover crops or soil improvement but not harvested and not pastured or grazed.

Respondents were asked to report their estimate of the current market **value of land and buildings** owned, rented, or leased from others, and rented and leased to others. Market value refers to the respondent's estimate of what the land and buildings would sell for under current market conditions. If the value of land and buildings was not reported, it was estimated during processing by using the average value of land and buildings from similar farms in the same geographic area.

The **value of machinery and equipment** was estimated by the respondent as the current market value of all cars, trucks, tractors, combines, balers, irrigation equipment, etc., used on the farm. This value is an estimate of what the machinery and equipment would sell for in its present condition and not the replacement or depreciated value. Share interests are reported at full value at the farm where the equipment and machinery are usually kept. Only equipment that was physically located at the farm on December 31, 2017, is included.

Market value of agricultural products sold by farms represents the gross market value before taxes and the production expenses of all agricultural products sold or removed from the place in 2017, regardless of who received the payment. It is equivalent to total sales and it includes sales by producers as well as the value of any share received by partners, landlords, contractors, and others associated with the operation. It includes value of organic sales, direct sales and the value of commodities placed in the Commodity Credit Corporation (CCC) loan program. Market value of agricultural products sold does not include payments received for participation in other federal farm programs. Also, it does not include income from farm-related sources such as customwork and other agricultural services, or income from nonfarm sources.

Organic farms are those that had organic production according to USDA's National Organic Program (NOP). Respondents reported whether their organic production was certified or exempt from certification and the sales from NOP produced commodities. Not included are farms that had acres transitioning into NOP production.

Farms with **internet access** are those that reported using personal computers, laptops, or mobile devices (e.g., cell phones or tablets) to access the internet. This can be done using services such as dial-up, DSL, cable modem, fiber-optic, mobile internet service for a cell phone or other device (tablet), satellite, or other methods. In 2017 respondents were also able to report connecting with an unknown service type, labeled as "Don't know" in the publication tables.

Government payments consist of direct payments as defined by the 2002 Farm Bill; payments from Conservation Reserve Program (CRP), Wetlands Reserve Program (WRP), Farmable Wetlands Program (FWP), and Conservation Reserve Enhancement Program (CREP); loan deficiency payments; disaster payments; other conservation programs; and all other federal farm programs under which payments were made directly to farm producers, including those specified in the 2014 Agricultural Act (Farm Bill), including Agriculture Risk Coverage (ARC) and Price Loss Coverage (PLC). Commodity Credit Corporation (CCC) proceeds, amount from State and local government agricultural program payments, and federal crop insurance payments were not included in this category.

WATER CONSUMPTION, Items 133–134

Source: U.S. Geological Survey, National Water-Use Information Program, Estimated Use of Water in the United States County-Level Data for 2015, version 1.0
https://www.usgs.gov/mission-areas/water-resources/science/water-use-united-states

Every five years, the U.S. Geological Survey compiles county-level water-use estimates. This volume includes the total fresh and saline withdrawals for public water supplies in 2015, expressed as million gallons per day. Estimate of withdrawals of ground and surface water are given for the following categories of use: public water supplies, domestic, commercial, irrigation, livestock, industrial, mining, and thermoelectric power.

Only public water supply is included in this volume. The number of gallons withdrawn per person is based on the county population in 2015. Public supply refers to water withdrawn from ground and surface sources by public and private water systems for use by cities, towns, rural water districts, mobile-home parks, Native American Indian reservations, and military bases. Public-supply facilities provide water to at least 25 persons or have a minimum of 15 service connections. Water withdrawn by public suppliers may be delivered to users for domestic, commercial, industrial, and thermoelectric-power purposes, as well as to other public-water suppliers. Public-supply water is also used for public services (public uses)—such as pools, parks, and public buildings—and may have unaccounted uses (losses) because of system leaks or such non-metered services as firefighting, flushing of water lines, or backwashing at treatment plants. Some public-supply water may be used in the processes of water and wastewater treatment. Some public suppliers treat saline water before distributing the water. The definition of saline water for public supply refers to water that requires treatment to reduce the concentration of dissolved solids through the process of desalination or dilution.

2017 ECONOMIC CENSUS: OVERVIEW, Items 135–166

Source: U.S. Census Bureau
https://www.census.gov/programs-surveys/economic-census.html

The Economic Census provides a detailed portrait of the nation's economy, from the national to the local level, once every five years. The 2017 Economic Census covers nearly all of the U.S. economy in its basic collection of establishment statistics. The 1997 Economic Census was the first major data source to use the new North American Industry Classification System (NAICS); therefore, data from this census are not comparable to economic data from prior years, which were based on the Standard Industrial Classification (SIC) system.

NAICS, developed in cooperation with Canada and Mexico, classifies North America's economic activities at two, three, four, and fivedigit levels of detail; the U.S. version of NAICS further defines industries to a sixth digit. The Economic Census takes advantage of this hierarchy to publish data at these successive levels of detail: sector (two-digit), subsector (three-digit), industry group (four-digit), industry (five-digit), and U.S. industry (six-digit). Information in Table A is at the two-digit level, with a few three- and four-digit items. The data in Table B are at the two-digit level.

Several key statistics are tabulated for all industries in this volume, including number of establishments (or companies), number of employees, payroll, and certain measures of output (sales, receipts, revenue, value of shipments, or value of construction work done).

Number of establishments. An establishment is a single physical location at which business is conducted. It is not necessarily identical with a company or enterprise, which may consist of one establishment or more. Economic Census figures represent a summary of reports for individual establishments rather than companies. For cases in which a census report was received, separate information was obtained for each location where business was conducted. When administrative records of other federal agencies were used instead of a census report, no information was available on the number of locations operated. Each Economic Census establishment was tabulated according to the physical location at which the business was conducted. The count of establishments represents those in business at any time during 2017.

When two activities or more were carried on at a single location under a single ownership, all activities were generally grouped together as a single establishment. The entire establishment was classified on the basis of its major activity and all of its data were included in that classification. However, when distinct and separate economic activities (for which different industry classification codes were appropriate) were conducted at a single location under a single ownership, separate establishment reports for each of the different activities were obtained in the census.

Number of employees. Paid employees consist of the fulltime and parttime employees, including salaried officers and executives of corporations. Included are employees on paid sick leave, paid holidays, and paid vacations; not included are proprietors and partners of unincorporated businesses. The definition of paid employees is the same as that used by the Internal Revenue Service (IRS) on form 941.

For some industries, the Economic Census gives codes representing the number of employees as a range of numbers (for example, "100 to 249 employees" or "1,000 to 2,499" employees). In this volume, those codes have been replaced by the standard suppression code "D".

Payroll. Payroll includes all forms of compensation, such as salaries, wages, commissions, dismissal pay, bonuses, vacation allowances, sickleave pay, and employee contributions to qualified pension plans paid during the year to all employees. For corporations, payroll includes amounts paid to officers and executives; for unincorporated businesses, it does not include profit or other compensation of proprietors or partners. Payroll is reported before deductions for Social Security, income tax, insurance, union dues, etc. This definition of payroll is the same as that used by on IRS form 941.

Sales, shipments, receipts, revenue, or business done. This measure includes the total sales, shipments, receipts, revenue, or business done by establishments within the scope of the Economic Census. The definition of each of these items is specific to the economic sector measured.

WHOLESALE TRADE, Items 135–138

Source: U.S. Census Bureau—2017 Economic Census (See overview of 2017 Economic Census prior to Item 135)

The Wholesale Trade sector (sector 42) comprises establishments engaged in wholesaling merchandise, generally without transformation, and rendering services incidental to the sale of merchandise. The wholesaling process is an intermediate step in the distribution of merchandise.

Wholesalers are organized to sell or arrange the purchase or sale of (1) goods for resale (i.e., goods sold to other wholesalers or retailers), (2) capital or durable nonconsumer goods, and (3) raw and intermediate materials and supplies used in production.

Wholesalers sell merchandise to other businesses and normally operate from a warehouse or office. These warehouses and offices are characterized by having little or no display of merchandise. In addition, neither the design nor the location of the premises is intended to solicit walkin traffic. Wholesalers do not normally use advertising directed to the general public. In general, customers are initially reached via telephone, inperson marketing, or specialized advertising, which may include the internet and other electronic means. Followup orders are either vendorinitiated or clientinitiated, are usually based on previous sales, and typically exhibit strong ties between sellers and buyers. In fact, transactions are often conducted between wholesalers and clients that have longstanding business relationships.

This sector is made up of two main types of wholesalers: those that sell goods on their own account and those that arrange sales and purchases for others for a commission or fee.

(1) Establishments that sell goods on their own account are known as wholesale merchants, distributors, jobbers, drop shippers, import/export merchants, and sales branches. These establishments typically maintain their own warehouse, where they receive and handle goods for their customers. Goods are generally sold without transformation, but may include integral functions, such as sorting, packaging, labeling, and other marketing services.

(2) Establishments arranging for the purchase or sale of goods owned by others or purchasing goods on a commission basis are known as agents and brokers, commission merchants, import/export agents and brokers, auction companies, and manufacturers' representatives. These establishments operate from offices and generally do not own or handle the goods they sell.

Some wholesale establishments may be connected with a single manufacturer and promote and sell that particular manufacturer's products to a wide range of other wholesalers or retailers. Other wholesalers may be connected to a retail chain or a limited number of retail chains and only provide the products needed by the particular retail operation(s). These wholesalers may obtain the products from a wide range of manufacturers. Still other wholesalers may not take title to the goods, but act instead as agents and brokers for a commission.

Although wholesaling normally denotes sales in large volumes, durable nonconsumer goods may be sold in single units. Sales of capital or durable nonconsumer goods used in the production of goods and services, such as farm machinery, medium- and heavy-duty trucks, and industrial machinery, are always included in Wholesale Trade.

The county table includes only **Merchant wholesalers, except manufacturers' sales branches and offices,** establishments primarily engaged in buying and selling merchandise on their own account. Included here are such types of establishments as wholesale distributors and jobbers, importers, exporters, own-brand importers/marketers, terminal and country grain elevators, and farm products assemblers.

RETAIL TRADE, Items 139–142

Source: U.S. Census Bureau—2017 Economic Census (See overview of 2017 Economic Census prior to Item 135)

The Retail Trade sector (44–45) is made up of establishments engaged in retailing merchandise, generally without transformation, and rendering services incidental to the sale of merchandise.

The retailing process is the final step in the distribution of merchandise; retailers are therefore organized to sell merchandise in small quantities to the general public. This sector comprises two main types of retailers: store and nonstore retailers.

Store retailers operate fixed pointofsale locations, located and designed to attract a high volume of walkin customers. In general, retail stores have extensive displays of merchandise and use massmedia advertising to attract customers. They typically sell merchandise to the general public for personal or household consumption; some also serve business and institutional clients. These include establishments such as office supply stores, computer and software stores, building materials dealers, plumbing supply stores, and electrical supply stores. Catalog showrooms, gasoline service stations, automotive dealers, and mobile home dealers are treated as store retailers.

In addition to retailing merchandise, some types of store retailers are also engaged in the provision of aftersales services, such as repair and installation. For example, new automobile dealers, electronic and appliance stores, and musical instrument and supply stores often provide repair services. As a general rule, establishments engaged in retailing merchandise and providing aftersales services are classified in this sector.

Nonstore retailers, like store retailers, are organized to serve the general public, although their retailing methods differ. The establishments of this subsector reach customers and market merchandise with methods including the broadcasting of "infomercials," the broadcasting and publishing of directresponse advertising, the publishing of paper and electronic catalogs, doortodoor solicitation, inhome demonstration, selling from portable stalls (street vendors, except food), and distribution through vending machines. Establishments engaged in the direct sale (nonstore) of products, such as home heating oil dealers and home-delivery newspaper routes are included in this sector.

The buying of goods for resale is a characteristic of retail trade establishments that distinguishes them from establishments in the Agriculture, Manufacturing, and Construction sectors. For example, farms that sell their products at or from the point of production are classified in Agriculture instead of in Retail Trade. Similarly, establishments that both manufacture and sell their products to the general public are classified in Manufacturing instead of Retail Trade. However, establishments that engage in processing activities incidental to retailing are classified in Retail Trade.

REAL ESTATE AND RENTAL AND LEASING, Items 143–146

Source: U.S. Census Bureau—2017 Economic Census (See overview of 2017 Economic Census prior to Item 135)

The Real Estate and Rental and Leasing sector (53) comprises establishments primarily engaged in renting, leasing, or otherwise allowing the use of tangible or intangible assets, and establishments providing related services. The major portion of this sector is made up of establishments that rent, lease, or otherwise allow the use of their own assets by others. The assets may be tangible, such as real estate and equipment, or intangible, such as patents and trademarks.

This sector also includes establishments primarily engaged in managing real estate for others, selling, renting, and/or buying real estate for others, and appraising real estate. These activities are closely related to this sector's main activity. In addition, a substantial proportion of property management is selfperformed by lessors.

The main components of this sector are the real estate lessors industries; equipment lessors industries (including motor vehicles, computers, and consumer goods); and lessors of nonfinancial intangible assets (except copyrighted works).

PROFESSIONAL, SCIENTIFIC, AND TECHNICAL SERVICES, Items 147–150

Source: U.S. Census Bureau—2017 Economic Census (See overview of 2017 Economic Census prior to Item 135)

The Professional, Scientific, and Technical Services sector (54) is made up of establishments that specialize in performing professional, scientific, and technical activities for others. These activities require a high degree of expertise and training. The establishments in this sector specialize in one or more areas and provide services to clients in a variety of industries (and, in some cases, to households). Activities performed include legal advice and representation; accounting, bookkeeping, and payroll services; architectural, engineering, and specialized design services; computer services; consulting services; research services; advertising services; photographic services; translation and interpretation services; veterinary services; and other professional, scientific, and technical services.

This sector excludes establishments primarily engaged in providing a range of daytoday office administrative services, such as financial planning, billing and record keeping, personnel services, and physical distribution and logistics services. These establishments are classified in sector 56, Administrative and Support and Waste Management and Remediation Services.

MANUFACTURING, Items 151–154

Source: U.S. Census Bureau—2017 Economic Census (See overview of 2017 Economic Census prior to Item 135)

The Manufacturing sector (31–33) is made up of establishments engaged in the mechanical, physical, or chemical transformation of materials, substances, or components into new products. The assembling of component parts of manufactured products is considered manufacturing, except in cases in which the activity is appropriately classified in the Construction sector. Establishments in the Manufacturing sector are often described as plants, factories, or mills, and characteristically use power-driven machines and materials-handling equipment. However, establishments that transform materials or substances into new products by hand or in the worker's home, and establishments engaged in selling to the general public products made on the same premises from which they are sold (such as bakeries, candy stores, and custom tailors) may also be included in this sector. Manufacturing establishments may process materials or contract with other establishments to process their materials for them. Both types of establishments are included in the Manufacturing sector.

The materials, substances, or components transformed by manufacturing establishments are raw materials that are products of agriculture, forestry, fishing, mining, or quarrying, or are products of other manufacturing establishments. The materials used may be purchased directly from producers, obtained through customary trade channels, or secured without recourse to the market by transferring the product from one establishment to another, under the same ownership. The new product of a manufacturing establishment may be finished (in the sense that it is ready for utilization or consumption), or it may be semifinished to become an input for an establishment engaged in further manufacturing. For example, the product of the alumina refinery is the input used in the primary production of aluminum; primary aluminum is the input used in an aluminum wire drawing plant; and aluminum wire is the input used in a fabricated wire product manufacturing establishment.

Data are included for counties with 500 or more employees in the Manufacturing sector.

ACCOMMODATION AND FOOD SERVICES, Items 155–158

Source: U.S. Census Bureau—2017 Economic Census (See overview of 2017 Economic Census prior to Item 135)

The Accommodation and Food Services sector (72) consists of establishments that provide customers with lodging and/or meals, snacks, and beverages for immediate consumption. This sector includes both accommodation and food services establishments because the two activities are often combined at the same establishment.

Excluded from this sector are civic and social organizations, amusement and recreation parks, theaters, and other recreation or entertainment facilities providing food and beverage services.

HEALTH CARE AND SOCIAL ASSISTANCE, Items 159–162

Source: U.S. Census Bureau—2017 Economic Census (See overview of 2017 Economic Census prior to Item 135)

The Health Care and Social Assistance sector (62) consists of establishments that provide health care and social assistance services to individuals. The sector includes both health care and social assistance because it is sometimes difficult to distinguish between the boundaries of these two activities. The industries in this sector are arranged on a continuum, starting with establishments that provide medical care exclusively, continuing with those that provide health care and social assistance, and finishing with those that provide only social assistance. The services provided by establishments in this sector are delivered by trained professionals. All industries in the sector share this commonality of process—namely, labor inputs of health practitioners or social workers with the requisite expertise. Many of the industries in the sector are defined based on the educational degree held by the practitioners included in the industry.

Excluded from this sector are aerobic classes, which can be found in subsector 713, Amusement, Gambling, and Recreation Industries; and nonmedical diet and weight-reducing centers, which can be found in subsector 812, Personal and Laundry Services. Although these can be viewed as health services, they are not typically delivered by health practitioners.

OTHER SERVICES, EXCEPT PUBLIC ADMINISTRATION Items 163–166

Source: U.S. Census Bureau—2017 Economic Census (See overview of 2017 Economic Census prior to Item 135)

The Other Services, Except Public Administration sector (81) comprises establishments engaged in providing services not specifically categorized elsewhere in the classification system. Establishments in this sector are primarily engaged in activities such as equipment and machinery repairing, promoting or administering religious activities, grant making, and advocacy; this sector also includes establishments that provide dry-cleaning and laundry services, personal care services, death care services, pet care services, photofinishing services, temporary parking services, and dating services.

Private households that employ workers on or about the premises in activities primarily concerned with the operation of the household are included in this sector.

Excluded from this sector are establishments primarily engaged in retailing new equipment and performing repairs and general maintenance on equipment. These establishments are classified in sector 44–45, Retail Trade.

NONEMPLOYER BUSINESSES, Items 167 and 168

Source: U.S. Census Bureau—Nonemployer Statistics https://www.census.gov/programs-surveys/nonemployer-statistics.html

Nonemployer Statistics is an annual series that provides subnational economic data for businesses that have no paid employees and are subject to federal income tax. The data consist of the number of businesses and total receipts by industry. Most nonemployers are self-employed individuals operating unincorporated businesses (known as sole proprietorships), which may or may not be the owner's principal source of income.

The majority of all business establishments in the United States are nonemployers, yet these firms average less than 4 percent of all sales and receipts nationally. Due to their small economic impact, these firms are excluded from most other Census Bureau business statistics (the primary exception being the Survey of Business Owners). The Nonemployers Statistics series is the primary resource available to study the scope and activities of nonemployers at a detailed geographic level.

BUILDING PERMITS, Items 169 and 170

Source: U.S. Census Bureau—Building Permits Survey

https://www.census.gov/construction/bps

These figures represent private residential construction authorized by building permits in approximately 20,000 places in the United States. Valuation represents the expected cost of construction as recorded on the building permit. This figure usually excludes the cost of on-site and off-site development and improvements, as well as the cost of heating, plumbing, electrical, and elevator installations.

National, state, and county totals were obtained by adding the data for permit-issuing places within each jurisdiction. Not all areas of the country require a building or zoning permit. The statistics only represent those areas that do require a permit. These totals thus are limited to permits issued in the 20,000 place universe covered by the Census Bureau and may not include all permits issued within a state. Current surveys indicate that construction is undertaken for all but a very small percentage of housing units authorized by building permits.

Residential building permits include buildings with any number of housing units. Housing units exclude group quarters (such as dormitories and rooming houses), transient accommodations (such as transient hotels, motels, and tourist courts), "HUD-code" manufactured (mobile) homes, moved or relocated units, and housing units created in an existing residential or nonresidential structure.

COUNTY AREA LOCAL GOVERNMENT EMPLOYMENT AND PAYROLL, Items 171–179

Source: U.S. Census Bureau—2017 Census of Governments

https://www.census.gov/programs-surveys/cog.html

These items include data for all local governments (i.e., counties, municipalities, townships, special districts, and school districts) located within the county. The Census of Governments identifies the scope and nature of the nation's state and local government sector; provides authoritative benchmark figures of public finance and public employment; classifies local government organizations, powers, and activities; and measures federal, state, and local fiscal relationships. The Employment component was mailed March 2017 to collect information on the number of state and local government civilian employees and their payrolls.

Government employees include all persons paid for personal services performed, including persons paid from federally funded programs, paid elected or appointed officials, persons in a paid leave status, and persons paid on a per meeting, annual, semi-annual, or quarterly basis. Unpaid officials, pensioners, persons whose work is performed on a fee basis, and contractors and their employees are excluded from the count of employees. **Full-Time Equivalent employees** is a computed statistic representing the number of full-time employees that could have been employed if the reported number of hours worked by part-time employees had been worked by full-time employees. This statistic is calculated separately for each function of a government by dividing the "part-time hours paid" by the standard number of hours for full-time employees in the particular government and then adding the resulting quotient to the number of full-time employees.

March payroll represents gross payroll amounts for the one-month period of March for full-time and part-time employees. Gross payroll includes all salaries, wages, fees, commissions, and overtime paid to employees **before** withholdings for taxes, insurance, etc. It also includes incentive payments that are paid at regular pay intervals. It excludes employer share of fringe benefits like retirement, Social Security, health and life insurance, lump sum payments, and so forth.

Administration and Judicial and Legal combines **Financial administration**, **Other government administration, and Judicial and Legal** activities. **Financial administration** includes activities concerned with tax assessment and collection, custody and disbursement of funds, debt management, administration of trust funds, budgeting, and other government-wide financial management activities. This function is not applied to school district or special district governments. **Other government administration** applies to the legislative and government-wide administrative agencies of governments. Included here are overall planning and zoning activities, and central personnel and administrative activities. This function is not applied to school district or special district governments. **Judicial and legal** includes all court and court related activities (except probation and parole activities that are included at the "Correction" function), court activities of sheriff's offices, prosecuting attorneys' and public defenders' offices, legal departments, and attorneys providing government-wide legal service.

Police and Corrections includes all activities concerned, with the enforcement of law and order, including coroner's offices, police training academies, investigation bureaus, and local jails, "lockups", or other detention facilities not intended to serve as correctional facilities. **Corrections** includes activities pertaining to the confinement and correction of adults and minors convicted of criminal offenses. Pardon, probation, and parole activities are also included here.

Fire protection includes local government fire protection and prevention activities plus any ambulance, rescue, or other auxiliary services provided by a fire protection agency. Volunteer firefighters, if remunerated for their services on a "per fire" or some other basis, are included as part-time employees.

Highways and transportation includes activities associated with the maintenance and operation of streets, roads, sidewalks, bridges, tunnels, toll roads, and ferries. Snow and ice removal, street lighting, and highway and traffic engineering activities are also included here. Also included are the operation, maintenance, and construction of public mass transit systems, including subways, surface rails, and buses, and the provision, construction, operation, maintenance; support of public waterways, harbors, docks, wharves, and related marine terminal facilities; and activities associated with the operation and support of publicly operated airport facilities.

Health and Welfare includes **Health, Hospitals, and Public welfare. Health** includes administration of public health programs, community and visiting nurse services, immunization programs, drug abuse rehabilitation programs, health and food inspection activities, operation of outpatient clinics, and environmental pollution control activities. **Hospitals** includes only government operated medical care facilities that provide inpatient care. Employees and payrolls of private corporations that lease and operate government-owned hospital facilities are excluded. **Public Welfare** includes the administration of various public assistance programs for the needy, veteran services, operation of nursing homes, indigent care institutions, and programs that provide payments for medical care, handicap transportation, and other services for the needy.

Natural resources and Utilities includes activities primarily concerned with the conservation and development of natural resources (soil, water, energy, minerals, etc.) and the regulation of industries that develop, utilize, or affect natural resources, as well as the operation and maintenance of **parks**, playgrounds, swimming pools, public beaches, auditoriums, public golf courses, museums, marinas, botanical gardens, and zoological parks. **Utilities, sewerage, and waste management** includes operation, maintenance, and construction of public water supply systems, including production, acquisition, and distribution of water to general public or to other public or private utilities, for residential, commercial, and industrial use; activities associated with the production or acquisition and distribution of electric power; provision, maintenance, and operation of sanitary and storm sewer systems and sewage disposal and treatment facilities; and refuse collection and disposal, operation of sanitary landfills, and street cleaning activities.

Education and libraries includes activities associated with the operation of public elementary and secondary schools and locally operated vocational-technical schools. Special education programs operated by elementary and secondary school systems are also included as are all ancillary services associated with the operation of schools, such as pupil transportation and food service. Also included are the establishment and provision of libraries for use by the general public and the technical support of privately operated libraries. This category includes classroom teachers, principals, supervisors of instruction, librarians, teacher aides, library aides, and guidance and psychological personnel as well as school superintendents and other administrative personnel, clerical and secretarial staffs, plant operation and maintenance personnel, health and recreation employees, transportation and food service personnel, and any student employees. Also included are any degree granting institutions that provide academic training above grade 12.

LOCAL GOVERNMENT FINANCES, Items 180–193

Source: U.S. Census Bureau—2017 Census of Governments https://www.census.gov/programs-surveys/cog.html

Data on local government finances are based on result of the 2017 Census of Governments. For each county area, the financial data comprise amounts for all local governments—not only the county government, but also any municipalities, townships, school districts, and special districts within the county. Statistics from governmental units located in two or more county areas are assigned to the county area containing the administrative office.

Revenue and expenditure items include all amounts of money received and paid out, respectively, by a government and its agencies (net of correcting transactions such as recoveries of refunds), with the exception of amounts for debt issuance and retirement and for loan and investment, agency, and private transactions.

Payments among the various funds and agencies of a particular government are excluded from revenue and expenditure items as representing internal transfers. Therefore, a government's contribution to a retirement fund that it administers is not counted as expenditure, nor is the receipt of this contribution by the retirement fund counted as revenue.

Total **general revenue** includes all revenue except utility, liquor stores, and insurance trust revenue. All tax revenue and intergovernmental revenue, even if designated for employee-retirement or local utility purpose, are classified as general revenue.

Intergovernmental revenue covers amounts received from the federal government as fiscal aid, reimbursements for performance of general government functions and specific services for the paying government, or in lieu of taxes. It excludes any amounts received from other governments from the sale of property, commodities, and utility services.

Taxes consist of compulsory contributions exacted by governments for public purposes. However, this category excludes employer and employee payments for retirement and social insurance purposes, which are classified as insurance trust revenue; it also excludes special assessments, which are classified as non-tax general revenue. Property taxes are taxes conditioned on ownership of property and assessed by its value. Sales and gross receipts taxes do not include dealer discounts, or "commissions" allowed to merchants for collection of taxes from consumers. General sales taxes and selected taxes on sales of motor fuels, tobacco products, and other particular commodities and services are included.

General government expenditure includes capital outlay, a major portion of which is commonly financed by borrowing. Government revenue does not include receipts from borrowing. Among other things, this distorts the relationship between totals of revenue and expenditure figures that are presented and renders it useless as a direct measure of the degree of budgetary "balance" (as that term is generally applied).

Direct general expenditure comprises all expenditures of the local governments, excluding utility, liquor stores, insurance trust expenditures, and any intergovernmental payments.

Local government expenditure for **education** is mainly for the provision and general support of schools and other educational facilities and services, including those for educational institutions beyond high school. They cover such related services as student transportation; school lunch and other cafeteria operations; school health, recreation, and library services; and dormitories, dining halls, and bookstores operated by public institutions of higher education.

Health and hospital expenditure includes health research; clinics; nursing; immunization; other categorical, environmental, and general health services provided by health agencies; establishment and operation of hospital facilities; provision of hospital care; and support of other public and private hospitals.

Police protection expenditure includes police activities such as patrols, communications, custody of persons awaiting trial, and vehicular inspection.

Public welfare expenditure covers support of and assistance to needy persons; this aid is contingent upon the person's needs. Included are cash assistance paid directly to needy persons under categorical (Old Age Assistance, Temporary Assistance for Needy Families, Aid to the Blind, and Aid to the Disabled) and other welfare programs; vendor payments made directly to private purveyors for medical care, burials, and other commodities and services provided under welfare programs; welfare institutions; and any intergovernmental or other direct expenditure for welfare purposes. Pensions to former employees and other benefits not contingent on need are excluded.

Highway expenditure is for the provision and maintenance of highway facilities, including toll turnpikes, bridges, tunnels, and ferries, as well as regular roads, highways, and streets. Also included are expenditures for street lighting and for snow and ice removal. Not included are highway policing and traffic control, which are considered part of police protection

Debt outstanding includes all long-term debt obligations of the government and its agencies (exclusive of utility debt) and all interest-bearing, short-term (repayable within one year) debt obligations remaining unpaid at the close of the fiscal year. It includes judgments, mortgages, and revenue bonds, as well as general obligation bonds, notes, and interest-bearing warrants. This category consists of non-interest-bearing, short-term obligations; inter-fund obligations; amounts owed in a trust or agency capacity; advances and contingent loans from other governments; and rights of individuals to benefit from government-administered employee-retirement funds.

GOVERNMENT EMPLOYMENT, Items 194–196

Source: U.S. Bureau of Economic Analysis—Regional Economic Accounts https://www.bea.gov/data/economic-accounts/regional#state

Employment is measured as the average annual sum of full-time and part-time jobs. The estimates are on a place-of-work basis. State and local government employment includes person employed in all state and local government agencies and enterprises. Data for federal civilian employment include civilian employees of the federal government, including civilian employees of the Department of Defense. Military employment includes all persons on active duty status.

INDIVIDUAL INCOME TAX RETURNS, Items 197–199

Source: U.S. Internal Revenue Service, Statistics of Income Program https://www.irs.gov/uac/soi-tax-stats-county-data-2019

The Revenue Act of 1916 mandated the annual publication of statistics related to "the operations of the internal revenue laws" as they affect individuals, all forms of businesses, estates. nonprofit organizations, trusts, and investments abroad and foreign investments in the United States. The Statistics of Income (SOI) division fulfills this function by collecting and processing data so that they become informative and by sharing information about how the tax system works with other government agencies and the general public. Publication types include traditional print sources, Internet files, CD-ROMs, and files sent via e-mail. SOI has an information office, Statistical Information Services, to facilitate the dissemination of SOI data.

SOI bases its county data on administrative records of individual income tax returns (Forms 1040) from the Internal Revenue Service (IRS) Individual Master File (IMF) system. Included in these data are returns filed during the 12-month period, January 1, 2020, to December 31, 2020. While the bulk of returns filed during the 12-month period are primarily for Tax Year 2019, the IRS received a limited number of returns for tax years before 2019 and these have been included within the county data.

Data do not represent the full U.S. population because many individuals are not required to file an individual income tax return. The address shown on the tax return may differ from the taxpayer's actual residence. State and county codes were based on the ZIP code shown on the return. Excluded were tax returns filed without a ZIP code and returns filed with a ZIP code that did not match the State code shown on the return.

SOI did not attempt to correct any ZIP codes on the returns; however, it did take the following precautions to avoid disclosing information about specific taxpayers: Excluded from the data are items with less than 20 returns within a county. Also excluded are tax returns representing a specified percentage of the total of any particular cell. For example, if one return represented 75 percent of the value of a given cell, the return was suppressed from the county detail. The actual threshold percentage used cannot be released.

Column 197 shows the number of returns. Column 198 shows the mean Adjusted Gross Income for the county and column 199 shows the mean income tax (line 14 on Form 1040) for the county.

TABLE C—METROPOLITAN AREAS

Table C presents 199 items for the 384 metropolitan statistical areas (MSAs) and 31 metropolitan divisions in the United States.

The metropolitan areas are presented in alphabetical order, and the metropolitan divisions are presented in alphabetical order within the appropriate metropolitan area. For some data items, the metropolitan area data have been aggregated from county data sources.

LAND AREA, Items 1 and 4

Source: U.S. Census Bureau—2020 U.S. Gazetteer Files https://www.census.gov/geographies/reference-files/time-series/geo/gazetteer-files.html

Land area measurements are shown to the nearest square mile. Land area is an area measurement providing the size, in square miles, of the land portions of each county.

POPULATION, Items 2–4

Source: U.S. Census Bureau—Population Estimates https://www.census.gov/programs-surveys/popest.html

The population data are Census Bureau estimates of the resident population as of July 1 of the year shown. The ranks are shown for metropolitan statistical areas, but exclude metropolitan divisions.

Demographic components of population change (births, deaths, and migration) are produced at the national, state, and county levels of geography. Additionally, housing unit estimates are produced for the nation, states, and counties.

Current data on births, deaths, and migration are used annually to calculate population change since the most recent decennial census and produce a time series of estimates of population, demographic components of change, and housing units. The annual time series of estimates begins with the most recent decennial census data and extends to the vintage year.

POPULATION AND POPULATION CHARACTERISTICS, Items 5–19

Source: U.S. Census Bureau—Population Estimates https://www.census.gov/programs-surveys/popest.html

The concept of race, as used by the Census Bureau, reflects self-identification by persons according to the race or races with which they most closely identify. These categories are sociopolitical constructs and should not be interpreted as being scientific or anthropological in nature. Furthermore, race categories include both racial and national origin groups.

Beginning with the 2000 census, respondents were offered the option of selecting one or more races. This option was not available in prior censuses; thus, comparisons between censuses should be made with caution. In Table C, Columns 5 through 8 refer to individuals who identified with each racial category, either alone or in combination with other races. The estimates exclude persons of Hispanic or Latino origin from all race groups. Because respondents could include as many categories as they wished, and because the columns refer to the percentage of the population, the total will often exceed 100 percent.

The **White** population is defined as persons who indicated their race as White, as well as persons who did not classify themselves in one of the specific race categories listed on the questionnaire but entered a nationality such as Irish, German, Italian, Lebanese, Near Easterner, Arab, or Polish.

The **Black** population includes persons who indicated their race as "Black or African American" as well as persons who did not classify themselves in one of the specific race categories but reported entries such as African American, Afro American, Kenyan, Nigerian, or Haitian.

The **American Indian or Alaska Native** population includes persons who indicated their race as American Indian or Alaska Native, as well as persons who did not classify themselves in one of the specific race categories but reported entries such as Canadian Indian, French-American Indian, Spanish-American Indian, Eskimo, Aleut, Alaska Indian, or any of the American Indian or Alaska Native tribes.

The **Asian and Pacific Islander** population combines two census groupings: **Asian** and **Native Hawaiian or Other Pacific Islander**. The **Asian** population includes persons who indicated their race as Asian Indian, Chinese, Filipino, Japanese, Korean, Vietnamese, or "Other Asian," as well as persons who provided write-in entries of such groups as Cambodian, Laotian, Hmong, Pakistani, or Taiwanese. The **Native Hawaiian or Other Pacific Islander** population includes persons who indicated their race as "Native Hawaiian," "Guamanian or Chamorro," "Samoan," or "Other Pacific Islander," as well as persons who reported entries such as Part Hawaiian, American Samoan, Fijian, Melanesian, or Tahitian.

The sum of the four individual race alone or in combination categories in this book will often add to more than the total population because people who reported more than one race were tallied in each race category. In this book, the Asian group has been combined with the Native Hawaiian and Other Pacific Islander group, causing double-counting of persons who identify with both groups. This is especially pronounced in Hawaii.

The **Hispanic population** is based on a complete-count question that asked respondents "Is this person Spanish/Hispanic/Latino?" Persons marking any one of the four Hispanic categories (i.e., Mexican, Puerto Rican, Cuban, or other Spanish) are collectively referred to as Hispanic.

Age is defined as age at last birthday (number of completed years since birth), as of April 1 of the census year.

The **female** population is shown as a percentage of total population.

POPULATION AND COMPONENTS OF CHANGE, Items 20–26

Source: U.S. Census Bureau—Decennial Censuses and Population Estimates https://www.census.gov/programs-surveys/decennial-census/data/datasets.2010.html https://www.census.gov/programs-surveys/popest.html

The population data for 2010 and 2020 are from the decennial censuses and represent the resident population as of April 1 of those years.

For annual population estimates, the latest decennial census typically serves as the population estimates base, but the 2020 Census could not be adopted for this purpose due to several challenges resulting from the COVID-19 pandemic. As a result, the Population Estimates Program developed a process for integrating the following three data sources at varying levels of detail to produce what they refer to as the Blended Base:

- 2020 Census PL 94-171 Redistricting File: Nation, state, and county total population counts
- 2020 Demographic Analysis (DA) Estimates: National population estimates by age and sex
- Vintage 2020 Postcensal Population Estimates: Nation, state, and county population estimates by age, sex, race, Hispanic origin, and population universe

The components of change are based on Census Bureau estimates of the resident population as of July 1 of 2020, using this Blended Base. The change in population between April 1, 2020, and July 1, 2021, is made up of (a) natural increase—births minus deaths, and (b) net migration—the difference between the number of persons moving into a particular area and the number of persons moving out of the area. Net migration is composed of internal and international migration.

For 2021 estimates, the data and methods were updated to manage the lag in available data for the start of the new decade and account for increased mortality and changes to natality from the COVID-19 pandemic. Specifically, the Census Bureau incorporated national provisional monthly estimates on births and deaths for all months of 2020 from the National Center for Health Statistics website. They assigned characteristics to these using distributions from the last year of final birth and death data available, 2019. For births, they also incorporated monthly total births for the nation in the first quarter of 2021 and used recent trends to project births for the second quarter of the year. For deaths, they had monthly total data through June 30, 2021, that included recent trends and patterns of excess mortality from the pandemic. The adjusted national births and deaths serve as controls for subnational vital events, resulting in an increase in deaths and decrease in births for numerous states and counties. Other than the national control, no methodological changes were made to the subnational birth or death estimates.

For the net international migration component for the 2020 estimates period (July 1, 2019–June 30, 2020), the Census Bureau adjusted to account for the impact of the COVID-19 global pandemic. They typically update prior years in the time series for each vintage as newer data become available. However, 2020 American Community Survey (ACS) data were not available to use for this time period due to data quality concerns resulting from the COVID-19 pandemic, so they did not update the estimates for April 1, 2020–June 30, 2020, for the 2021 estimates. At the time of production, 2019 was the latest ACS file available for estimating international migration. To account for trends from July 1, 2020, to June 30, 2021, they used current data from the United States Department of Justice, Department of Homeland Security (Citizenship and Immigration Services), State Department (Bureau of Consular Affairs and Refugee Processing Center), and the Institute of International Education to adjust 2019 ACS estimates.

Because the 2021 population estimates are based on a model that begins with a national population estimate, the county and metropolitan area components of change do not always exactly add up to the difference between the 2020 census population and the 2021 estimates.

HOUSEHOLDS, Items 27–31

Source: U.S. Census Bureau—American Community Survey, 2016-2020 5-year Estimates
https://www.census.gov/programs-surveys/acs

A **household** includes all of the persons who occupy a housing unit. (Persons not living in households are classified as living in group quarters.) A housing unit is a house, an apartment, a mobile home, a group of rooms, or a single room occupied (or, if vacant, intended for occupancy) as separate living quarters. Separate living quarters are those in which the occupants live separately from any other persons in the building and have direct access from the outside of the building or through a common hall. The occupants may be a single family, one person living alone, two or more families living together, or any other group of related or unrelated persons who share living quarters. The number of households is the same as the number of year-round occupied housing units.

A **family** includes a householder and one or more other persons living in the same household who are related to the householder by birth, marriage, or adoption. All persons in a household who are related to the householder are regarded as members of his or her family. A **family household** may contain persons not related to the householder; thus, family households may include more members than families do. A household can contain only one family for the purposes of census tabulations. Not all households contain families, as a household may comprise a group of unrelated persons or of one person living alone. Families are classified by type as either a "husband-wife family" or "other family," according to the presence or absence of a spouse.

The measure of **persons per household** is obtained by dividing the number of persons in households by the number of households or householders. One person in each household is designated as the householder. In most cases, this is the person (or one of the persons) in whose name the house is owned, being bought, or rented. If there is no such person in the household, any adult household member 15 years old and over can be designated as the householder.

The category **female family householder** includes only female-headed family households with no spouse present.

A nonfamily household consists of a householder living alone or with nonrelatives only. Column 31 shows one-person households as a percentage of all households.

GROUP QUARTERS, Item 32

Source: U.S. Census Bureau—Population Estimates
https://www.census.gov/programs-surveys/popest.html

The Census Bureau classifies all persons not living in households as living in group quarters; this category includes both the institutional and noninstitutional populations. The institutionalized population includes persons under formally authorized, supervised care or custody in institutions, such as correctional institutions, nursing homes, mental (psychiatric) hospitals, and juvenile institutions. The noninstitutionalized population includes persons who live in group quarters other than institutions, such as college dormitories, military quarters, and group homes. This volume includes the total number of persons in group quarters.

Due to complications in Group Quarters (GQ) data as a result of the COVID-19 pandemic, the 2021 estimate uses GQ data from the April 1, 2020, base and holds it constant forward to July 1, 2021.

DAYTIME POPULATION, Items 33 and 34

Source: U.S. Census Bureau—American Community Survey, 2020 5-year Estimateshttps://www.census.gov/programs-surveys/acs

Daytime population refers to the number of persons who are present in an area or place during normal business hours, including workers. This can be contrasted with the "resident" population, which is present during the evening and nighttime hours. The daytime population estimate is calculated by adding the total resident population and the total workers working in the area/place, and then subtracting the total workers living in the area/place from that result. Information on the expansion or contraction experienced by different communities between their nighttime and daytime populations is important for many planning purposes, especially those concerning transportation, disaster, and relief operations.

The employment/residence ratio is a measure of the total number of workers working in an area or place, relative to the total number of workers living in the area or place. It is often used as a rough indication of the jobs-workers balance in an area/place, although it does not take into account whether the resident workers possess the skills needed for the jobs available in their particular area/place. The employment/residence ratio is calculated by dividing the number of total workers working in an area/place by the number of total workers residing in the area/place.

BIRTHS AND DEATHS, Items 35–38

Source: U.S. Census Bureau—Population Estimates https://www.census.gov/programs-surveys/popest.html

The numbers of births and deaths are from the Census Bureau's Population Estimates Program. They represent the total number of live births and deaths occurring to residents of an area as estimated using reports from the National Center for Health Statistics (NCHS) and the Federal-State Cooperative for Population Estimates (FSCPE). The rates measure births and deaths during the specified time period as a proportion of an area's population. Rates are expressed per 1,000 population base on the average of the July 1 beginning and ending resident total population estimates. These numbers and rates do not represent the calendar year, but rather the year-long period ending on July 1.

PERSONS UNDER 65 WITH NO HEALTH INSURANCE, Items 39 and 40

Source: U.S. Census Bureau—Small Area Health Insurance Estimates https://www.census.gov/programs-surveys/sahie.html

The Small Area Health Insurance Estimates (SAHIE) program develops model-based estimates of health insurance coverage for counties and states. This developmental program builds on the work of the Small Area Income and Poverty Estimates (SAIPE) program. The SAHIE program models health insurance coverage by combining survey data with population estimates and administrative records. These estimates combine data from administrative records, postcensal population estimates, and the decennial census with direct estimates from the American Community Survey to provide consistent and reliable single-year estimates. These model-based single-year estimates are more reflective of current conditions than multi-year survey estimates. The metropolitan area estimates have been aggregated from the county estimates.

MEDICARE ENROLLMENT, Items 41–43

Source: U.S. Department of Health and Human Services, Centers for Medicare and Medicaid Services https://data.cms.gov/summary-statistics-on-beneficiary-enrollment/medicare-and-medicaid-reports/medicare-monthly-enrollment/data

The Centers for Medicare and Medicaid Services (CMS) administers Medicare, which provides health insurance to persons 65 years old and over, persons with permanent kidney failure, and certain persons with disabilities. Original Medicare has two parts: Hospital Insurance and Supplemental Medical Insurance. In recent years, Medicare has been expanded to include two new programs: Medicare Advantage plans and prescription drug coverage. Medicare Advantage Plans are health plan options that are approved by Medicare but run by private companies. Medicare prescription drug plans can be part of Medicare Advantage plans or stand-alone drug plans.

Persons who are eligible for Medicare can enroll in Part A (Hospital Insurance) at no charge, and can choose to pay a monthly premium to enroll in Part B. Most eligible persons are enrolled in Part A, and most enrollees in Part A are also enrolled in Part B (Supplemental Medical Insurance.) This table includes persons who were enrolled in either Part A or Part B or both in December 2021.

Part B beneficiaries can choose to enroll in **Original Medicare**, a fee-for-service plan administered by the Centers for Medicare and Medicaid Services, or in a **Medicare Advantage** plan.

Medicare Advantage plans include private fee-for-service plans, preferred provider organizations, health maintenance organizations, medical savings account plans, demonstration plans, and programs for all-inclusive care for the elderly.

This table includes persons who were enrolled in December 2021 because the annual data for 2021 was not in the database at the time of production. The annual Medicare enrollment counts are determined using a person-year methodology. For each calendar year, total person-year counts are determined by summing the total number of months that each beneficiary is enrolled during the year and dividing by 12. Using this methodology, a beneficiary's partial-year enrollment may be counted in more than one category (i.e., both Original Medicare and Medicare Advantage).

LAW ENFORCEMENT, Items 44–47

Source: U.S. Federal Bureau of Investigation—Uniform Crime Reports https://crime-data-explorer.app.cloud.gov/pages/downloads

Crime data are as reported to the Federal Bureau of Investigation (FBI) by law enforcement agencies. The Metropolitan Area numbers in this volume are from *Crime in the United States* and have been adjusted by the FBI to include estimates of areas that did not report. Where the FBI analysts determined that the numbers reflected underreporting or overreporting or other factors that made them unreliable, the numbers have not been included.

Through the voluntary contribution of crime statistics by law enforcement agencies across the United States, the Uniform Crime Reporting (UCR) Program provides periodic assessments of crime in the nation as measured by offenses that have come to the attention of the law enforcement community. The Committee on Uniform Crime Records of the International Association of Chiefs of Police initiated this voluntary national data collection effort in 1930. The UCR Program contributors compile and submit their crime data either directly to the FBI or through state-level UCR Programs.

Seven offenses, because of their severity, frequency of occurrence, and likelihood of being reported to police, were initially selected to serve as an index for evaluating fluctuations in the volume of crime. These serious crimes were murder and nonnegligent manslaughter, forcible rape, robbery, aggravated assault, burglary, larceny-theft, and motor vehicle theft. By congressional mandate, arson was added as the eighth index offense in 1979. The totals shown in this volume do not include arson.

In 2004, the FBI discontinued the use of the Crime Index in the UCR Program and its publications, stating that the Crime Index was driven upward by the offense with the highest number of cases (in this case, larceny-theft), creating a bias against jurisdictions with a high number of larceny-thefts but a low number of other serious crimes, such as murder and forcible rape. The FBI is currently publishing a violent crime total and property crime total until a more viable index is developed.

In 2013, the FBI adopted a new definition of rape. Rape is now defined as, "Penetration, no matter how slight, of the vagina or anus with any body part or object, or oral penetration by a sex organ of another person, without the consent of the victim." The new definition updated the 80-year-old historical definition of rape which was "carnal knowledge of a female forcibly and against her will." Effectively, the revised definition expands rape to include both male and female victims and offenders, and reflects the various forms of sexual penetration understood to be rape, especially nonconsenting acts of sodomy, and sexual assaults with objects.

Violent crimes include four categories of offenses: (1) Murder and nonnegligent manslaughter, as defined in the UCR Program, is the willful (nonnegligent) killing of one human being by another. This offense excludes deaths caused by negligence, suicide, or accident; justifiable homicides; and attempts to murder or assaults to murder. (2) Rape is the penetration, no matter how slight, of the vagina or anus with any body part or object, or oral penetration by a sex organ of another person, without the consent of the victim. Assaults or attempts to commit rape by force or threat of force are also included; however, statutory rape (without force) and other sex offenses are excluded. (3) Robbery is the taking or attempting to take anything of value from the care, custody, or control of a person or persons by force or threat of force or violence and/or by putting the victim in fear. (4) Aggravated assault is an unlawful attack by one person upon another for the purpose of inflicting severe or aggravated bodily injury. This type of assault is usually accompanied by the use of a weapon or by other means likely to produce death or great bodily harm. Attempts are included, since injury does not necessarily have to result when a gun, knife, or other weapon is used, as these incidents could and probably would result in a serious personal injury if the crime were successfully completed.

Property crimes include three categories: (1) Burglary, or breaking and entering, is the unlawful entry of a structure to commit a felony or theft, even though no force was used to gain entrance. (2) Larceny-theft is the unauthorized taking of the personal property of another, without the use of force. (3) Motor vehicle theft is the unauthorized taking of any motor vehicle.

Rates are based on population estimates provided by the FBI. For many of the metropolitan areas, the FBI has estimated violent and property crimes, adjusted to include areas that did not report and to correct for underreporting and overreporting, as published in the FBI's *Crime in the United States*. If a metropolitan area was not included in *Crime in the United States,* it is not included in Table C in this volume. The metropolitan area data includes police departments of counties and cities within the area.

EDUCATION—SCHOOL ENROLLMENT AND EDUCATIONAL ATTAINMENT, Items 48–51

Source: U.S. Census Bureau—American Community Survey, 2020 5-year Estimates https://www.census.gov/programs-surveys/acs

Data on **school enrollment** and educational attainment were derived from a sample of the population. Persons were classified as enrolled in school if they reported attending a "regular" public or private school (or college) during the three months prior to the survey. The instructions were to "include only nursery school, kindergarten, elementary school, and schooling which would lead to a high school diploma or a college degree" as regular school. The Census Bureau defines a public school as "any school or college controlled and supported by a local, county, state, or federal government." Schools primarily supported and controlled by religious organizations or other private groups are defined as private schools.

Data on **educational attainment** are tabulated for the population 25 years old and over. The data were derived from a question that asked respondents for the highest level of school completed or the highest degree received. Persons who had passed a high school equivalency examination were considered high school graduates. Schooling received in foreign schools was to be reported as the equivalent grade or years in the regular American school system.

Vocational and technical training, such as barber school training; business, trade, technical, and vocational schools; or other training for a specific trade are specifically excluded.

High school graduate or less. This category includes persons whose highest degree was a high school diploma or its equivalent, and those who reported any level lower than a high school diploma.

Bachelor's degree or more. This category includes persons who have received bachelor's degrees, master's degrees, professional school degrees (such as law school or medical school degrees), and doctoral degrees.

LOCAL GOVERNMENT EDUCATION EXPENDITURES, Items 52 and 53

Source: U.S. Department of Education, National Center for Education Statistics, Common Core of Data (CCD), "Local Education Agency (School District) Finance Survey (F33) Data," 2018-2019 v.1a, provisional
https://nces.ed.gov/ccd

Expenditures are for elementary and secondary Education which includes prekindergarten through twelfth grade regular, special, and vocational education, as well as cocurricular, community service, and adult education programs provided by a public school system. The financial activities of these systems for all instruction, support service, and noninstructional activities are included

Current Spending comprises current operation expenditure, payments made by the state government on behalf of school systems, and transfers made by school systems into their own retirement funds. Current operation expenditures include direct expenditure for salaries, employee benefits, purchased professional and technical services, purchased property and other services, and supplies. It includes gross school system expenditure for instruction, support services, and noninstructional functions. It excludes expenditure for debt service, capital outlay, and reimbursement to other governments (including other school systems).

Current expenditure per student is current expenditure divided by the number of students enrolled. The number of students enrolled is based on an annual "membership" count of students on or about October 1.

INCOME AND POVERTY Items 54–61

Source: U.S. Census Bureau—American Community Survey, 2020 5-year Estimates
https://www.census.gov/programs-surveys/acs

The data on income were derived from responses of a sample of persons 15 years old and over. **Total money income** is the sum of the amounts reported separately for wage or salary income; net self-employment income; interest, dividends, or net rental or royalty income or income from estates and trusts; Social Security or railroad retirement income; Supplemental Security Income (SSI); public assistance or welfare payments; retirement, survivor, or disability pensions; and all other income. Receipts from the following sources are not included as income: capital gains; money received from the sale of property (unless the recipient was engaged in the business of selling such property); the value of income "in kind" from food stamps, public housing subsidies, medical care, employer contributions for individuals, etc.; withdrawal of bank deposits; money borrowed; tax refunds; exchange of money between relatives living in the same household; and gifts, lump-sum inheritances, insurance payments, and other types of lump-sum receipts.

Money income differs in definition from personal income (item 62). For example, money income does not include the pension rights, employer provided health insurance, food stamps, or Medicare payments that are included in personal income.

Per capita income is the mean income computed for every man, woman, and child in a particular group. It is derived by dividing the aggregate income of a particular group by the resident population in that group in the survey year. Per capita income is rounded to the nearest whole dollar.

Household income includes the income of the householder and all other individuals 15 years old and over in the household, whether or not they are related to the householder. Since many households consist of only one person, median household income is usually less than median family income. Although the household income statistics cover the year preceding the survey, the characteristics of individuals and the composition of households refer to the date of the survey. Thus, the income of the household does not include amounts received by individuals who were members of the household during the year if these individuals were no longer residing in the household at the time of the survey. Similarly, income amounts reported by individuals who did not reside in the household during the year but who were members of the household at the time of the survey are included. However, the composition of most households was the same during the year as it was at the time of the survey.

Mean household income is the amount obtained by dividing the aggregate income of all households by the total number of households. Mean individual income is obtained by dividing the aggregate income of all individuals by the total number of persons age 15 and older. The mean is based on the distribution of the total number of households or individuals including those with no income. Mean income is rounded to the nearest whole dollar. Care should be exercised in using and interpreting mean income values for small subgroups of the population. Because the mean is influenced strongly by extreme values in the distribution, it is especially susceptible to the effects of sampling variability, misreporting, and processing errors. The median, which is not affected by extreme values, is, therefore, a better measure than the mean when the population base is small.

Income components were reported for the 12 months preceding the interview month. Monthly Consumer Price Indices (CPI)

factors were used to inflation-adjust these components to a reference calendar year (January through December). For example, a household interviewed in March 2012 reports their income for March 2011 through February 2012. Their income is adjusted to the 2012 reference calendar year by multiplying their reported income by 2012 average annual CPI (January-December 2008) and then dividing by the average CPI for March 2011–February 2012. However, the estimates do not reflect the price and cost-of-living differences that may exist between areas.

The **poverty status** data were derived from data collected on the number of persons in a household, each person's relationship to the householder, and income data. The Social Security Administration (SSA) developed the original poverty definition in 1964, which federal interagency committees subsequently revised in 1969 and 1980. The Office of Management and Budget's (OMB) *Directive 14* prescribes the SSA's definition as the official poverty measure for federal agencies to use in their statistical work. Poverty statistics presented in American Community Survey products adhere to the standards defined by OMB in *Directive 14*.

Poverty thresholds vary depending on three criteria: size of family, number of children, and, for one- and two-person families, age of householder. In determining the poverty status of families and unrelated individuals, the Census Bureau uses thresholds (income cutoffs) arranged in a two-dimensional matrix. The matrix consists of family size (from one person to nine or more persons), cross-classified by presence and number of family members under 18 years old (from no children present to eight or more children present). Unrelated individuals and two-person families are further differentiated by age of reference person (under 65 years old and 65 years old and over). To determine a person's poverty status, the person's total family income over the previous 12 months is compared with the poverty threshold appropriate for that person's family size and composition. If the total income of that person's family is less than the threshold appropriate for that family, then the person is considered poor or "below the poverty level," together with every member of his or her family. If a person is not living with anyone related by birth, marriage, or adoption, then the person's own income is compared with his or her poverty threshold. The total number of persons below the poverty level is the sum of persons in families and the number of unrelated individuals with incomes below the poverty level over the previous 12 months.

PERSONAL INCOME AND EARNINGS, Items 62–83

Source: U.S. Bureau of Economic Analysis, Regional Economic Accounts https://www.bea.gov/data/economic-accounts/regional#state

Total personal income is the current income received by residents of an area from all sources. It is measured before deductions of income and other personal taxes, but after deductions of personal contributions for Social Security, government retirement, and other social insurance programs. It consists of **wage and salary disbursements** (covering all employee earnings, including executive salaries, bonuses, commissions, payments-in-kind, incentive payments, and tips); various types of supplementary earnings, such as employers' contributions to pension funds (termed "other labor income" or "supplements to wages and salaries"); proprietors' income; rental income of persons; dividends; personal interest income; and government and business transfer payments.

Per capita personal income is based on the resident population estimated as of July 1 of the year shown.

Proprietors' income is the monetary income and income-in-kind of proprietorships and partnerships (including the independent professions) and the income of tax-exempt cooperatives. **Dividends** are cash payments by corporations to stockholders who are U.S. residents. **Interest** is the monetary and imputed interest income of persons from all sources. **Rent** is the monetary income of persons from the rental of real property, except the income of persons primarily engaged in the real estate business; the imputed net rental income of owner-occupants of nonfarm dwellings; and the royalties received by persons.

Transfer payments are income for which services are not currently rendered. They consist of both government and business transfer payments. Government transfer payments include payments under the following programs: Federal Old-Age, Survivors, and Disability Insurance ("Social Security"); Medicare and medical vendor payments; unemployment insurance; railroad and government retirement; federal- and state-government-insured workers' compensation; veterans' benefits, including veterans' life insurance; food stamps; black lung payments; Supplemental Security Income; and Temporary Assistance for Needy Families. Government payments to nonprofit institutions, other than for work under research and development contracts, are also included. Business transfer payments consist primarily of liability payments for personal injury and of corporate gifts to nonprofit institutions.

Personal income differs in definition from money income (items 54–57). For example, personal income includes pension rights, employer-provided health insurance, food stamps, and Medicare. These are not included in the definition of money income.

Earnings cover wage and salary disbursements, other labor income, and proprietors' income.

The data for earnings obtained from the Bureau of Economic Analysis (BEA) are based on place of work. In computing personal income, BEA makes an "adjustment for residence" to earnings, based on commuting patterns; personal income is thus presented on a place-of-residence basis.

Farm earnings include the income of farm workers (wages and salaries and other labor income) and farm proprietors. Farm proprietors' income includes only the income of sole proprietorships and partnerships. Farm earnings estimates are benchmarked to data collected in the Census of Agriculture and the revised Department of Agriculture statistical totals of income and expense items.

Goods-related industries include mining, construction, and manufacturing. **Service-related** and other industries include private-sector earnings in agricultural services, forestry, and fisheries; transportation and public utilities; wholesale trade; retail trade; finance, insurance, and real estate; and services. Government earnings include all levels of government. Industries are categorized under the North American Industry Classification System (NAICS), and are not comparable to years prior to 2002.

Poverty Thresholds for 2020 by Size of Family and Number of Related Children Under 18 Years

Size of family unit	Weighted average thresholds	Related children under 18 years								
		None	One	Two	Three	Four	Five	Six	Seven	Eight or more
One person (unrelated individual):	13,171									
Under age 65	13,465	13,465								
Aged 65 and older	12,413	12,413								
Two people:	16,733									
Householder under age 65	17,413	17,331	17,839							
Householder aged 65 and older	15,659	15,644	17,771							
Three people	20,591	20,244	20,832	20,852						
Four people	26,496	26,695	27,131	26,246	26,338					
Five people	31,417	32,193	32,661	31,661	30,887	30,414				
Six people	35,499	37,027	37,174	36,408	35,674	34,582	33,935			
Seven people	40,406	42,605	42,871	41,954	41,314	40,124	38,734	37,210		
Eight people	44,755	47,650	48,071	47,205	46,447	45,371	44,006	42,585	42,224	
Nine people or more	53,905	57,319	57,597	56,831	56,188	55,132	53,679	52,366	52,040	50,035

Source: U.S. Census Bureau.

SOCIAL SECURITY AND SUPPLEMENTAL SECURITY INCOME, Items 84–86

Source: U.S. Social Security Administration
https://www.ssa.gov/policy/docs/statcomps/oasdi_sc
https://www.ssa.gov/policy/docs/statcomps/ssi_sc

Social Security beneficiaries are persons receiving benefits under the Old-Age, Survivors, and Disability Insurance Program. These include retired or disabled workers covered by the program, their spouses and dependent children, and the surviving spouses and dependent children of deceased workers.

Supplemental Security Income (SSI) recipients are persons receiving SSI payments. The SSI program is a cash assistance program that provides monthly benefits to low-income aged, blind, or disabled persons.

Data are as of December of the year shown.

HOUSING, Items 87–96

Source: U.S. Census Bureau—Population Estimates Program
Source: U.S. Census Bureau—American Community Survey. 2020 5-year Estimates
https://www.census.gov/programs-surveys/popest.html
https://www.census.gov/programs-surveys/acs

Housing data for 2021 are from the Population Estimates Program. Housing unit characteristics for 2016-2020 are from the American Community Survey.

A **housing unit** is a house, apartment, mobile home or trailer, group of rooms, or single room occupied or, if vacant, intended for occupancy as separate living quarters. Separate living quarters are those in which the occupants do not live and eat with any other person in the structure and which have direct access from the outside of the building through a common hall.

The occupants of a housing unit may be a single family, one person living alone, two or more families living together, or any other group of related or unrelated persons who share living quarters. Both occupied and vacant housing units are included in the housing inventory, although recreational vehicles, tents, caves, boats, railroad cars, and the like are included only if they are occupied as a person's usual place of residence.

A housing unit is classified as occupied if it is the usual place of residence of the person or group of persons living in it at the time of enumeration, or if the occupants are only temporarily absent (away on vacation). A household consists of all persons who occupy a housing unit as their usual place of residence. Vacant units for sale or rent include units rented or sold but not occupied and any other units held off the market.

Value is the respondent's estimate of how much the property (house and lot, mobile home and lot (if lot owned), or condominium unit) would sell for if it were for sale. If the house was owned or being bought, but the land on which it sits was not, the respondent was asked to estimate the combined value of the house and the land. Owners of noncondominium multi-unit buildings who live in one of the building's units, like duplexes and small apartment buildings, should report the value of the building, the land, and any additional buildings on the same plot of land. For vacant units, value was the price asked for the property. Value was tabulated separately for all owner-occupied and vacant-for-sale and sold, not occupied housing units, as well as owner-occupied mobile homes.

Mortgage refers to all forms of debt where the property is pledged as security for repayment of the debt, including deeds of trust; trust deeds; contracts to purchase; land contracts; junior mortgages; and home equity loans.

Gross rent is the contract rent plus the estimated average monthly cost of utilities (electricity, gas, and water and sewer) and fuels (oil, coal, kerosene, wood, etc.) if these are paid by the renter (or paid for the renter by someone else). Gross rent is intended to eliminate differentials that result from varying practices with respect to the inclusion of utilities and fuels as part of the rental payment. The estimated costs of water and sewer, and fuels are reported on a 12-month basis but are converted to monthly figures for the tabulations.

Housing cost as a percentage of income is shown separately for owners with mortgages, owners without mortgages, and renters. Rent as a percentage of income is a computed ratio of gross rent and monthly household income (total household income in the past 12 months divided by 12). Selected owner costs include utilities and fuels, mortgage payments, insurance, taxes, etc. In each case, the ratio of housing cost to income is computed separately for each housing unit. The housing cost ratios for half of all units are above the median shown in this book, and half are below the median shown in the book.

CIVILIAN LABOR FORCE AND UNEMPLOYMENT, Items 97–100

Source: U.S. Bureau of Labor Statistics—Local Area Unemployment Statistics https://www.bls.gov/lau/#tables

Data for the civilian labor force are the product of a federal-state cooperative program in which state employment security agencies prepare labor force and unemployment estimates under concepts, definitions, and technical procedures established by the Bureau of Labor Statistics (BLS). The civilian labor force consists of all civilians 16 years old and over who are either employed or unemployed.

Unemployment includes all persons who did not work during the survey week, made specific efforts to find a job during the previous four weeks, and were available for work during the survey week (except for temporary illness). Persons waiting to be called back to a job from which they had been laid off and those waiting to report to a new job within the next 30 days are included in unemployment figures.

Table C includes annual average data for the year shown. The Local Area Unemployment Statistics data are periodically updated to reflect revised inputs, reestimation, and controlling to new statewide totals.

CIVILIAN EMPLOYMENT, Items 101–103

Source: U.S. Census Bureau—American Community Survey. 2020 5-year Estimates https://www.census.gov/programs-surveys/acs

Total employment includes all civilians 16 years old and over who were either (1) "at work"—those who did any work at all during the reference week as paid employees, worked in either their own business or profession, worked on their own farm, or worked 15 hours or more as unpaid workers in a family farm or business; or were (2) "with a job, but not at work"—those who had a job but were not at work that week due to illness, weather, industrial dispute, vacation, or other personal reasons.

The **occupational categories** are based on the occupational classification system that was developed for the 2000 census. This system consists of 509 specific occupational categories for employed persons arranged into 23 major occupational groups. This classification was developed based on the *Standard Occupational Classification (SOC) Manual: 2000*, published by the Executive Office of the President, Office of Management and Budget.

Column 102 includes the Management, business, science, and arts occupations category while Column 103 combines the Natural resources, construction, and maintenance occupations and the Production, transportation, and material moving occupations.

PRIVATE NONFARM EMPLOYMENT AND EARNINGS, Items 104–112

Source: U.S. Census Bureau—County Business Patterns https://www.census.gov/programs-surveys/cbp.html

Data for private nonfarm employment and earnings are compiled from the payroll information reported monthly in the Census Bureau publication *County Business Patterns*. The estimates are based on surveys conducted by the Census Bureau and administrative records from the Internal Revenue Service (IRS).

The following types of employment are excluded from the tables: government employment, self-employed persons, farm workers, and domestic service workers. Railroad employment jointly covered by Social Security and railroad retirement programs, employment on oceanborne vessels, and employment in foreign countries are also excluded.

Annual payroll is the combined amount of wages paid, tips reported, and other compensation (including salaries, vacation allowances, bonuses, commissions, sick-leave pay, and the value of payments-in-kind such as free meals and lodging) paid to employees before deductions for Social Security, income tax, insurance, union dues, etc. All forms of compensation are included, regardless of whether they are subject to income tax or the Federal Insurance Contributions Act tax, with the exception of annuities, third-party sick pay, and supplemental unemployment compensation benefits (even if income tax was withheld). For corporations, total annual payroll includes compensation paid to officers and executives; for unincorporated businesses, it excludes profit or other compensation of proprietors or partners.

AGRICULTURE, Items 113–132

Source: U.S. Department of Agriculture, National Agricultural Statistics Service—2017 Census of Agriculture https://www.nass.usda.gov/Publications/AgCensus/2017/index.php

Data for the 2017 Census of Agriculture were collected in 2018, but pertain to the year 2017.

The Census Bureau took a census of agriculture every 10 years from 1840 to 1920; since 1925, this census has been taken roughly once every 5 years. The 1997 Census of Agriculture was the first one conducted by the National Agricultural Statistics Service of the U.S. Department of Agriculture. Over time, the definition of a farm has varied. For recent censuses (including the 2017 census), a farm has been defined as any place from which $1,000 or more of agricultural products were produced and sold or normally would have been sold during the census year. Dollar figures are expressed in current dollars and have not been adjusted for inflation or deflation.

The term **producer** designates a person who is involved in making decisions for the farm operation. Decisions may include decisions about such things as planting, harvesting, livestock management, and marketing. The producer may be the owner, a member of the owner's household, a hired manager, a tenant, a renter, or a sharecropper. If a person rents land to others or has land worked on shares by others, he/she is considered the producer only of the land which is retained for his/her own operation. The census collected information on the total number of male producers, the total number of female producers, and demographic information for up to four producers per farm.

The acreage designated as **land in farms** consists primarily of agricultural land used for crops, pasture, or grazing. It also includes woodland and wasteland not actually under cultivation or used for pasture or grazing, provided that this land was part of the farm operator's total operation. Land in farms is an operating-unit concept and includes all land owned and operated, as well as all land rented from others. Land used rent-free is classified as land rented from others. All grazing land, except land used under government permits on a per-head basis, was included as "land in farms" provided it was part of a farm or ranch. Land under the exclusive use of a grazing association was reported by the grazing association and included as land in farms. All land in Indian reservations used for growing crops or grazing livestock is classified as land in farms.

Irrigated land includes all land watered by any artificial or controlled means, such as sprinklers, flooding, furrows or ditches, sub-irrigation, and spreader dikes. Included are supplemental, partial, and preplant irrigation. Each acre was counted only once regardless of the number of times it was irrigated or harvested. Livestock lagoon waste water distributed by sprinkler or flood systems was also included.

Total cropland includes cropland harvested, cropland used only for pasture or grazing, cropland on which all crops failed or were abandoned, cropland in cultivated summer fallow, and cropland idle or used for cover crops or soil improvement but not harvested and not pastured or grazed.

Respondents were asked to report their estimate of the current market **value of land and buildings** owned, rented, or leased from others, and rented and leased to others. Market value refers to the respondent's estimate of what the land and buildings would sell for under current market conditions. If the value of land and buildings was not reported, it was estimated during processing by using the average value of land and buildings from similar farms in the same geographic area.

The **value of machinery and equipment** was estimated by the respondent as the current market value of all cars, trucks, tractors, combines, balers, irrigation equipment, etc., used on the farm. This value is an estimate of what the machinery and equipment would sell for in its present condition and not the replacement or depreciated value. Share interests are reported at full value at the farm where the equipment and machinery are usually kept. Only equipment that was physically located at the farm on December 31, 2017, is included.

Market value of agricultural products sold by farms represents the gross market value before taxes and the production expenses of all agricultural products sold or removed from the place in 2017, regardless of who received the payment. It is equivalent to total sales and it includes sales by producers as well as the value of any share received by partners, landlords, contractors, and others associated with the operation. It includes value of organic sales, direct sales and the value of commodities placed in the Commodity Credit Corporation (CCC) loan program. Market value of agricultural products sold does not include payments received for participation in other federal farm programs. Also, it does not include income from farm-related sources such as customwork and other agricultural services, or income from nonfarm sources.

Organic farms are those that had organic production according to USDA's National Organic Program (NOP). Respondents reported whether their organic production was certified or exempt from certification and the sales from NOP produced commodities. Not included are farms that had acres transitioning into NOP production.

Farms with **internet access** are those that reported using personal computers, laptops, or mobile devices (e.g., cell phones or tablets) to access the internet. This can be done using services such as dial-up, DSL, cable modem, fiber-optic, mobile internet service for a cell phone or other device (tablet), satellite, or other methods. In 2017 respondents were also able to report connecting with an unknown service type, labeled as "Don't know" in the publication tables.

Government payments consist of direct payments as defined by the 2002 Farm Bill; payments from Conservation Reserve Program (CRP), Wetlands Reserve Program (WRP), Farmable Wetlands Program (FWP), and Conservation Reserve Enhancement Program (CREP); loan deficiency payments; disaster payments; other conservation programs; and all other federal farm programs under which payments were made directly to farm producers, including those specified in the 2014 Agricultural Act (Farm Bill), including Agriculture Risk Coverage (ARC) and Price Loss Coverage (PLC). Commodity Credit Corporation (CCC) proceeds, amount from State and local government agricultural program payments, and federal crop insurance payments were not included in this category.

WATER CONSUMPTION, Items 133–134

Source: U.S. Geological Survey, National Water-Use Information Program, Estimated Use of Water in the United States County-Level Data for 2015, version 1.0 https://www.usgs.gov/mission-areas/water-resources/science/water-use-united-states

Every five years, the U.S. Geological Survey compiles county-level water-use estimates. This volume includes the total fresh and saline withdrawals for public water supplies in 2015, expressed as million gallons per day. Estimate of withdrawals of ground and surface water are given for the following categories of use: public water supplies, domestic, commercial, irrigation, livestock, industrial, mining, and thermoelectric power. Only public water supply is included in this volume because the other categories had not been published in time for this book. The number of gallons withdrawn per person is based on the metropolitan area population in 2015 but the water is not necessarily used locally, providing an indicator of metropolitan areas that serve as major water sources.

Public supply refers to water withdrawn from ground and surface sources by public and private water systems for use by cities, towns, rural water districts, mobile-home parks, Native American Indian reservations, and military bases. Public-supply facilities provide water to at least 25 persons or have a minimum of 15 service connections. Water withdrawn by public suppliers may be delivered to users for domestic, commercial, industrial, and thermoelectric-power purposes, as well as to other public-water suppliers. Public-supply water is also used for public services (public uses)—such as pools, parks, and public buildings—and may have unaccounted uses (losses) because of system leaks or such non-metered services as firefighting, flushing of water lines, or backwashing at treatment plants. Some public-supply water may be used in the processes of water and wastewater treatment. Some public suppliers treat saline water before distributing the water. The definition of saline water for public supply refers to water that requires treatment to reduce the concentration of dissolved solids through the process of desalination or dilution.

2017 ECONOMIC CENSUS: OVERVIEW, Items 135–166

Source: U.S. Census Bureau
https://www.census.gov/programs-surveys/economic-census/library/publications.html

The Economic Census provides a detailed portrait of the nation's economy, from the national to the local level, once every five years. The 2017 Economic Census covers nearly all of the U.S. economy in its basic collection of establishment statistics. Release of the 2017 Economic Census data began in 2019 and was ongoing as this book was developed. Some sections are not available or are incomplete. All tables in this book use the metropolitan area definitions established in 2018, reflecting substantial changes from the previous definitions. Because the Economic Census data refer to 2017, there are no official datasets that use the new metropolitan area definition so the county data were aggregated for this book. Consequently, suppression at the county level resulted in less than complete totals in some areas. Users are encouraged to review the metropolitan area changes and consult the Census Bureau's website for specific metropolitan areas.

The 1997 Economic Census was the first major data source to use the new North American Industry Classification System (NAICS); therefore, data from this census are not comparable to economic data from prior years, which were based on the Standard Industrial Classification (SIC) system.

NAICS, developed in cooperation with Canada and Mexico, classifies North America's economic activities at two, three, four, and fivedigit levels of detail; the U.S. version of NAICS further defines industries to a sixth digit. The Economic Census takes advantage of this hierarchy to publish data at these successive levels of detail: sector (two-digit), subsector (three-digit), industry group (four-digit), industry (five-digit), and U.S. industry (six-digit). Information in Table A is at the two-digit level, with a few three- and four-digit items. The data in Tables B and C are at the two-digit level.

Several key statistics are tabulated for all industries in this volume, including number of establishments (or companies), number of employees, payroll, and certain measures of output (sales, receipts, revenue, value of shipments, or value of construction work done).

Number of establishments. An establishment is a single physical location at which business is conducted. It is not necessarily identical with a company or enterprise, which may consist of one establishment or more. Economic Census figures represent a summary of reports for individual establishments rather than companies. For cases in which a census report was received, separate information was obtained for each location where business was conducted. When administrative records of other federal agencies were used instead of a census report, no information was available on the number of locations operated. Each Economic Census establishment was tabulated according to the physical location at which the business was conducted. The count of establishments represents those in business at any time during 2002.

When two activities or more were carried on at a single location under a single ownership, all activities were generally grouped together as a single establishment. The entire establishment was classified on the basis of its major activity and all of its data were included in that classification. However, when distinct and separate economic activities (for which different industry classification codes were appropriate) were conducted at a single location under a single ownership, separate establishment reports for each of the different activities were obtained in the census.

Number of employees. Paid employees consist of the fulltime and parttime employees, including salaried officers and executives of corporations. Included are employees on paid sick leave, paid holidays, and paid vacations; not included are proprietors and partners of unincorporated businesses. The definition of paid employees is the same as that used by the Internal Revenue Service (IRS) on form 941.

For some industries, the Economic Census gives codes representing the number of employees as a range of numbers (for example, "100 to 249 employees" or "1,000 to 2,499" employees). In this volume, those codes have been replaced by the standard suppression code "D".

Payroll. Payroll includes all forms of compensation, such as salaries, wages, commissions, dismissal pay, bonuses, vacation allowances, sickleave pay, and employee contributions to qualified pension plans paid during the year to all employees. For corporations, payroll includes amounts paid to officers and executives; for unincorporated businesses, it does not include profit or other compensation of proprietors or partners. Payroll is reported before deductions for Social Security, income tax, insurance, union dues, etc. This definition of payroll is the same as that used by on IRS form 941.

Sales, shipments, receipts, revenue, or business done. This measure includes the total sales, shipments, receipts, revenue, or business done by establishments within the scope of the Economic Census. The definition of each of these items is specific to the economic sector measured.

WHOLESALE TRADE, Items 135–138

Source: U.S. Census Bureau—2017 Economic Census
(See overview of 2017 Economic Census prior to Item 135)

The Wholesale Trade sector (sector 42) comprises establishments engaged in wholesaling merchandise, generally without transformation, and rendering services incidental to the sale of merchandise. The wholesaling process is an intermediate step in the distribution of merchandise.

Wholesalers are organized to sell or arrange the purchase or sale of (1) goods for resale (i.e., goods sold to other wholesalers or retailers), (2) capital or durable nonconsumer goods, and (3) raw and intermediate materials and supplies used in production.

Wholesalers sell merchandise to other businesses and normally operate from a warehouse or office. These warehouses and offices are characterized by having little or no display of merchandise. In addition, neither the design nor the location of the premises is intended to solicit walkin traffic. Wholesalers do not normally use advertising directed to the general public. In general, customers are initially reached via telephone, inperson marketing, or specialized advertising, which may include the internet and other electronic means. Followup orders are either vendorinitiated or clientinitiated, are usually based on previous sales, and typically exhibit strong ties between sellers and buyers. In fact, transactions are often conducted between wholesalers and clients that have longstanding business relationships.

This sector is made up of two main types of wholesalers: those that sell goods on their own account and those that arrange sales and purchases for others for a commission or fee.

(1) Establishments that sell goods on their own account are known as wholesale merchants, distributors, jobbers, drop shippers, import/export merchants, and sales branches. These establishments typically maintain their own warehouse, where they receive and handle goods for their customers. Goods are generally sold without transformation, but may include integral functions, such as sorting, packaging, labeling, and other marketing services.

(2) Establishments arranging for the purchase or sale of goods owned by others or purchasing goods on a commission basis are known as agents and brokers, commission merchants, import/export agents and brokers, auction companies, and manufacturers' representatives. These establishments operate from offices and generally do not own or handle the goods they sell.

Some wholesale establishments may be connected with a single manufacturer and promote and sell that particular manufacturer's products to a wide range of other wholesalers or retailers. Other wholesalers may be connected to a retail chain or a limited number of retail chains and only provide the products needed by the particular retail operation(s). These wholesalers may obtain the products from a wide range of manufacturers. Still other wholesalers may not take title to the goods, but act instead as agents and brokers for a commission.

Although wholesaling normally denotes sales in large volumes, durable nonconsumer goods may be sold in single units. Sales of capital or durable nonconsumer goods used in the production of goods and services, such as farm machinery, medium- and heavy-duty trucks, and industrial machinery, are always included in Wholesale Trade.

The metropolitan area table includes only **Merchant wholesalers, except manufacturers' sales branches and offices,** establishments primarily engaged in buying and selling merchandise on their own account. Included here are such types of establishments as wholesale distributors and jobbers, importers, exporters, own-brand importers/marketers, terminal and country grain elevators, and farm products assemblers.

RETAIL TRADE, Items 139–142

Source: U.S. Census Bureau—2017 Economic Census (See overview of 2017 Economic Census prior to Item 135)

The Retail Trade sector (44–45) is made up of establishments engaged in retailing merchandise, generally without transformation, and rendering services incidental to the sale of merchandise.

The retailing process is the final step in the distribution of merchandise; retailers are therefore organized to sell merchandise in small quantities to the general public. This sector comprises two main types of retailers: store and nonstore retailers.

Store retailers operate fixed pointofsale locations, located and designed to attract a high volume of walkin customers. In general, retail stores have extensive displays of merchandise and use massmedia advertising to attract customers. They typically sell merchandise to the general public for personal or household consumption; some also serve business and institutional clients. These include establishments such as office supply stores, computer and software stores, building materials dealers, plumbing supply stores, and electrical supply stores. Catalog showrooms, gasoline service stations, automotive dealers, and mobile home dealers are treated as store retailers.

In addition to retailing merchandise, some types of store retailers are also engaged in the provision of aftersales services, such as repair and installation. For example, new automobile dealers, electronic and appliance stores, and musical instrument and supply stores often provide repair services. As a general rule, establishments engaged in retailing merchandise and providing aftersales services are classified in this sector.

Nonstore retailers, like store retailers, are organized to serve the general public, although their retailing methods differ. The establishments of this subsector reach customers and market merchandise with methods including the broadcasting of "infomercials," the broadcasting and publishing of directresponse advertising, the publishing of paper and electronic catalogs, doortodoor solicitation, inhome demonstration, selling from portable stalls (street vendors, except food), and distribution through vending machines. Establishments engaged in the direct sale (nonstore) of products, such as home heating oil dealers and home-delivery newspaper routes are included in this sector.

The buying of goods for resale is a characteristic of retail trade establishments that distinguishes them from establishments in the Agriculture, Manufacturing, and Construction sectors. For example, farms that sell their products at or from the point of production are classified in Agriculture instead of in Retail Trade. Similarly, establishments that both manufacture and sell their products to the general public are classified in Manufacturing instead of Retail Trade. However, establishments that engage in processing activities incidental to retailing are classified in Retail Trade.

REAL ESTATE AND RENTAL AND LEASING, Items 143–146

Source: U.S. Census Bureau—2017 Economic Census (See overview of 2017 Economic Census prior to Item 135)

The Real Estate and Rental and Leasing sector (53) comprises establishments primarily engaged in renting, leasing, or otherwise allowing the use of tangible or intangible assets, and establishments providing related services. The major portion of this sector is made up of establishments that rent, lease, or otherwise allow the use of their own assets by others. The assets may be tangible, such as real estate and equipment, or intangible, such as patents and trademarks.

This sector also includes establishments primarily engaged in managing real estate for others, selling, renting, and/or buying real estate for others, and appraising real estate. These activities are closely related to this sector's main activity. In addition, a substantial proportion of property management is selfperformed by lessors.

The main components of this sector are the real estate lessors industries; equipment lessors industries (including motor vehicles, computers, and consumer goods); and lessors of nonfinancial intangible assets (except copyrighted works).

PROFESSIONAL, SCIENTIFIC, AND TECHNICAL SERVICES, Items 147–150

Source: U.S. Census Bureau—2017 Economic Census (See overview of 2017 Economic Census prior to Item 135)

The Professional, Scientific, and Technical Services sector (54) is made up of establishments that specialize in performing professional, scientific, and technical activities for others. These activities require a high degree of expertise and training. The establishments in this sector specialize in one or more areas and provide services to clients in a variety of industries (and, in some cases, to households). Activities performed include legal advice and representation; accounting, bookkeeping, and payroll services; architectural, engineering, and specialized design services; computer services; consulting services; research services; advertising services; photographic services; translation and interpretation services; veterinary services; and other professional, scientific, and technical services.

This sector excludes establishments primarily engaged in providing a range of daytoday office administrative services, such as financial planning, billing and record keeping, personnel services, and physical distribution and logistics services. These establishments are classified in sector 56, Administrative and Support and Waste Management and Remediation Services.

MANUFACTURING, Items 151–154

Source: U.S. Census Bureau—2017 Economic Census (See overview of 2017 Economic Census prior to Item 135)

The Manufacturing sector (31–33) is made up of establishments engaged in the mechanical, physical, or chemical transformation of materials, substances, or components into new products. The assembling of component parts of manufactured products is considered manufacturing, except in cases in which the activity is appropriately classified in the Construction sector. Establishments in the Manufacturing sector are often described as plants, factories, or mills, and characteristically use power-driven machines and materials-handling equipment. However, establishments that transform materials or substances into new products by hand or in the worker's home, and establishments engaged in selling to the general public products made on the same premises from which they are sold (such as bakeries, candy stores, and custom tailors) may also be included in this sector. Manufacturing establishments may process materials or contract with other establishments to process their materials for them. Both types of establishments are included in the Manufacturing sector.

The materials, substances, or components transformed by manufacturing establishments are raw materials that are products of agriculture, forestry, fishing, mining, or quarrying, or are products of other manufacturing establishments. The materials used may be purchased directly from producers, obtained through customary trade channels, or secured without recourse to the market by transferring the product from one establishment to another, under the same ownership. The new product of a manufacturing establishment may be finished (in the sense that it is ready for utilization or consumption), or it may be semifinished to become an input for an establishment engaged in further manufacturing. For example, the product of the alumina refinery is the input used in the primary production of aluminum; primary aluminum is the input used in an aluminum wire drawing plant; and aluminum wire is the input used in a fabricated wire product manufacturing establishment.

Data are included for counties with 500 or more employees in the Manufacturing sector.

ACCOMMODATION AND FOOD SERVICES, Items 155–158

Source: U.S. Census Bureau—2017 Economic Census (See overview of 2017 Economic Census prior to Item 135)

The Accommodation and Food Services sector (72) consists of establishments that provide customers with lodging and/or meals, snacks, and beverages for immediate consumption. This sector includes both accommodation and food services establishments because the two activities are often combined at the same establishment.

Excluded from this sector are civic and social organizations, amusement and recreation parks, theaters, and other recreation or entertainment facilities providing food and beverage services.

HEALTH CARE AND SOCIAL ASSISTANCE, Items 159–162

Source: U.S. Census Bureau—2017 Economic Census (See overview of 2017 Economic Census prior to Item 135)

The Health Care and Social Assistance sector (62) consists of establishments that provide health care and social assistance services to individuals. The sector includes both health care and social assistance because it is sometimes difficult to distinguish between the boundaries of these two activities.

The industries in this sector are arranged on a continuum, starting with establishments that provide medical care exclusively, continuing with those that provide health care and social assistance, and finishing with those that provide only social assistance. The services provided by establishments in this sector are delivered by trained professionals. All industries in the sector share this commonality of process—namely, labor inputs of health practitioners or social workers with the requisite expertise. Many of the industries in the sector are defined based on the educational degree held by the practitioners included in the industry.

Excluded from this sector are aerobic classes, which can be found in subsector 713, Amusement, Gambling, and Recreation Industries; and nonmedical diet and weight-reducing centers, which can be found in subsector 812, Personal and Laundry Services. Although these can be viewed as health services, they are not typically delivered by health practitioners.

OTHER SERVICES, EXCEPT PUBLIC ADMINISTRATION Items 163–166

Source: U.S. Census Bureau—2017 Economic Census (See overview of 2017 Economic Census prior to Item 135)

The Other Services, Except Public Administration sector (81) comprises establishments engaged in providing services not specifically categorized elsewhere in the classification system. Establishments in this sector are primarily engaged in activities such as equipment and machinery repairing, promoting or administering religious activities, grant making, and advocacy; this sector also includes establishments that provide dry-cleaning and laundry services, personal care services, death care services, pet care services, photofinishing services, temporary parking services, and dating services.

Private households that employ workers on or about the premises in activities primarily concerned with the operation of the household are included in this sector.

Excluded from this sector are establishments primarily engaged in retailing new equipment and performing repairs and general maintenance on equipment. These establishments are classified in sector 44–45, Retail Trade.

NONEMPLOYER BUSINESSES, Items 167 and 168

Source: U.S. Census Bureau—Nonemployer Statistics https://www.census.gov/programs-surveys/nonemployer-statistics.html

Nonemployer Statistics is an annual series that provides subnational economic data for businesses that have no paid employees and are subject to federal income tax. The data consist of the number of businesses and total receipts by industry. Most nonemployers are self-employed individuals operating unincorporated businesses (known as sole proprietorships), which may or may not be the owner's principal source of income.

The majority of all business establishments in the United States are nonemployers, yet these firms average less than 4 percent of all sales and receipts nationally. Due to their small economic impact, these firms are excluded from most other Census Bureau business statistics (the primary exception being the Survey of Business Owners). The Nonemployers Statistics series is the primary resource available to study the scope and activities of nonemployers at a detailed geographic level.

BUILDING PERMITS, Items 169 and 170

Source: U.S. Census Bureau—Building Permits Survey https://www.census.gov/construction/bps

These figures represent private residential construction authorized by building permits in approximately 20,000 places in the United States. Valuation represents the expected cost of construction as recorded on the building permit. This figure usually excludes the cost of on-site and off-site development and improvements, as well as the cost of heating, plumbing, electrical, and elevator installations.

National, state, and county totals were obtained by adding the data for permit-issuing places within each jurisdiction. Not all areas of the country require a building or zoning permit. The statistics only represent those areas that do require a permit. These totals thus are limited to permits issued in the 20,000 place universe covered by the Census Bureau and may not include all permits issued within a state. Current surveys indicate that construction is undertaken for all but a very small percentage of housing units authorized by building permits.

Residential building permits include buildings with any number of housing units. Housing units exclude group quarters (such as dormitories and rooming houses), transient accommodations (such as transient hotels, motels, and tourist courts), "HUD-code" manufactured (mobile) homes, moved or relocated units, and housing units created in an existing residential or nonresidential structure.

METROPOLITAN AREA LOCAL GOVERNMENT EMPLOYMENT AND PAYROLL, Items 171–179

Source: U.S. Census Bureau—2017 Census of Governments https://www.census.gov/programs-surveys/cog.html

These items include data for all local governments (i.e., counties, municipalities, townships, special districts, and school districts) located within the metropolitan area. The Census of Governments identifies the scope and nature of the nation's state and local government sector; provides authoritative benchmark figures of public finance and public employment; classifies local government organizations, powers, and activities; and measures federal, state, and local fiscal relationships. The Employment component was mailed March 2012 to collect information on the number of state and local government civilian employees and their payrolls.

Government employees include all persons paid for personal services performed, including persons paid from federally funded programs, paid elected or appointed officials, persons in a paid leave status, and persons paid on a per meeting, annual, semiannual, or quarterly basis. Unpaid officials, pensioners, persons whose work is performed on a fee basis, and contractors and their employees are excluded from the count of employees. **Full-Time Equivalent employees** is a computed statistic representing the number of full-time employees that could have been employed if the reported number of hours worked by part-time employees had been worked by full-time employees. This statistic is calculated separately for each function of a government by dividing the "part-time hours paid" by the standard number of hours for full-time employees in the particular government and then adding the resulting quotient to the number of full-time employees.

March payroll represents gross payroll amounts for the one-month period of March for full-time and part-time employees. Gross payroll includes all salaries, wages, fees, commissions, and overtime paid to employees **before** withholdings for taxes, insurance, etc. It also includes incentive payments that are paid at regular pay intervals. It excludes employer share of fringe benefits like retirement, Social Security, health and life insurance, lump sum payments, and so forth.

Administration and Judicial and Legal combines **Financial administration**, **Other government administration, and Judicial and Legal** activities. **Financial administration** includes activities concerned with tax assessment and collection, custody and disbursement of funds, debt management, administration of trust funds, budgeting, and other government-wide financial management activities. This function is not applied to school district or special district governments. **Other government administration** applies to the legislative and government-wide administrative agencies of governments. Included here are overall planning and zoning activities, and central personnel and administrative activities. This function is not applied to school district or special district governments. **Judicial and legal** includes all court and court related activities (except probation and parole activities that are included at the "Correction" function), court activities of sheriff's offices, prosecuting attorneys' and public defenders' offices, legal departments, and attorneys providing government-wide legal service.

Police and Corrections includes all activities concerned, with the enforcement of law and order, including coroner's offices, police training academies, investigation bureaus, and local jails, "lockups", or other detention facilities not intended to serve as correctional facilities. **Corrections** includes activities pertaining to the confinement and correction of adults and minors convicted of criminal offenses. Pardon, probation, and parole activities are also included here.

Fire protection includes local government fire protection and prevention activities plus any ambulance, rescue, or other auxiliary services provided by a fire protection agency. Volunteer firefighters, if remunerated for their services on a "per fire" or some other basis, are included as part-time employees.

Highways and transportation includes activities associated with the maintenance and operation of streets, roads, sidewalks, bridges, tunnels, toll roads, and ferries. Snow and ice removal, street lighting, and highway and traffic engineering activities are also included here. Also included are the operation, maintenance, and construction of public mass transit systems, including subways, surface rails, and buses, and the provision, construction, operation, maintenance; support of public waterways, harbors, docks, wharves, and related marine terminal facilities; and activities associated with the operation and support of publicly operated airport facilities.

Health and Welfare includes **Health, Hospitals, and Public welfare. Health** includes administration of public health programs, community and visiting nurse services, immunization programs, drug abuse rehabilitation programs, health and food inspection activities, operation of outpatient clinics, and environmental pollution control activities. **Hospitals** includes only government operated medical care facilities that provide inpatient care. Employees and payrolls of private corporations that lease and operate government-owned hospital facilities are excluded. **Public Welfare** includes the administration of various public assistance programs for the needy, veteran services, operation of nursing homes, indigent care institutions, and programs that provide payments for medical care, handicap transportation, and other services for the needy.

Natural resources and Utilities includes activities primarily concerned with the conservation and development of natural resources (soil, water, energy, minerals, etc.) and the regulation of industries that develop, utilize, or affect natural resources, as well as the operation and maintenance of **parks**, playgrounds, swimming pools, public beaches, auditoriums, public golf courses, museums, marinas, botanical gardens, and zoological parks. **Utilities, sewerage, and waste management** includes operation, maintenance, and construction of public water supply systems, including production, acquisition, and distribution of water to general public or to other public or private utilities, for residential, commercial, and industrial use; activities associated with the production or acquisition and distribution of electric power; provision, maintenance, and operation of sanitary and storm sewer systems and sewage disposal and treatment facilities; and refuse collection and disposal, operation of sanitary landfills, and street cleaning activities.

Education and libraries includes activities associated with the operation of public elementary and secondary schools and locally operated vocational-technical schools. Special education programs operated by elementary and secondary school systems are also included as are all ancillary services associated with the operation of schools, such as pupil transportation and food service. Also included are the establishment and provision of libraries for use by the general public and the technical support of privately operated libraries. This category includes classroom teachers, principals, supervisors of instruction, librarians, teacher aides, library aides, and guidance and psychological personnel as well as school superintendents and other administrative personnel, clerical and secretarial staffs, plant operation and maintenance personnel, health and recreation employees, transportation and food service personnel, and any student employees. Also included are any degree granting institutions that provide academic training above grade 12.

LOCAL GOVERNMENT FINANCES, Items 180–193

Source: U.S. Census Bureau—2017 Census of Governments https://www.census.gov/programs-surveys/cog.html

Data on local government finances are based on result of the 2012 Census of Governments. For each metropolitan area, the data are aggregated from its component counties, and the financial data comprise amounts for all local governments—not only the county governments, but also any municipalities, townships, school districts, and special districts within the county. Statistics from governmental units located in two or more county areas are assigned to the county area containing the administrative office.

Revenue and expenditure items include all amounts of money received and paid out, respectively, by a government and its agencies (net of correcting transactions such as recoveries of refunds), with the exception of amounts for debt issuance and retirement and for loan and investment, agency, and private transactions.

Payments among the various funds and agencies of a particular government are excluded from revenue and expenditure items as representing internal transfers. Therefore, a government's contribution to a retirement fund that it administers is not counted as expenditure, nor is the receipt of this contribution by the retirement fund counted as revenue.

Total **general revenue** includes all revenue except utility, liquor stores, and insurance trust revenue. All tax revenue and intergovernmental revenue, even if designated for employee-retirement or local utility purpose, are classified as general revenue.

Intergovernmental revenue covers amounts received from the federal government as fiscal aid, reimbursements for performance of general government functions and specific services for the paying government, or in lieu of taxes. It excludes any amounts received from other governments from the sale of property, commodities, and utility services.

Taxes consist of compulsory contributions exacted by governments for public purposes. However, this category excludes employer and employee payments for retirement and social insurance purposes, which are classified as insurance trust revenue; it also excludes special assessments, which are classified as non-tax general revenue. Property taxes are taxes conditioned on ownership of property and assessed by its value. Sales and gross receipts taxes do not include dealer discounts, or "commissions" allowed to merchants for collection of taxes from consumers. General sales taxes and selected taxes on sales of motor fuels, tobacco products, and other particular commodities and services are included.

General government expenditure includes capital outlay, a major portion of which is commonly financed by borrowing. Government revenue does not include receipts from borrowing. Among other things, this distorts the relationship between totals of revenue and expenditure figures that are presented and renders it useless as a direct measure of the degree of budgetary "balance" (as that term is generally applied).

Direct general expenditure comprises all expenditures of the local governments, excluding utility, liquor stores, insurance trust expenditures, and any intergovernmental payments.

Local government expenditure for **education** is mainly for the provision and general support of schools and other educational facilities and services, including those for educational institutions beyond high school. They cover such related services as student transportation; school lunch and other cafeteria operations; school health, recreation, and library services; and dormitories, dining halls, and bookstores operated by public institutions of higher education.

Health and hospital expenditure includes health research; clinics; nursing; immunization; other categorical, environmental, and general health services provided by health agencies; establishment and operation of hospital facilities; provision of hospital care; and support of other public and private hospitals.

Police protection expenditure includes police activities such as patrols, communications, custody of persons awaiting trial, and vehicular inspection.

Public welfare expenditure covers support of and assistance to needy persons; this aid is contingent upon the person's needs. Included are cash assistance paid directly to needy persons under categorical (Old Age Assistance, Temporary Assistance for Needy Families, Aid to the Blind, and Aid to the Disabled) and other welfare programs; vendor payments made directly to private purveyors for medical care, burials, and other commodities and services provided under welfare programs; welfare institutions; and any intergovernmental or other direct expenditure for welfare purposes. Pensions to former employees and other benefits not contingent on need are excluded.

Highway expenditure is for the provision and maintenance of highway facilities, including toll turnpikes, bridges, tunnels, and ferries, as well as regular roads, highways, and streets. Also included are expenditures for street lighting and for snow and ice removal. Not included are highway policing and traffic control, which are considered part of police protection

Debt outstanding includes all long-term debt obligations of the government and its agencies (exclusive of utility debt) and all interest-bearing, short-term (repayable within one year) debt obligations remaining unpaid at the close of the fiscal year. It includes judgments, mortgages, and revenue bonds, as well as general obligation bonds, notes, and interest-bearing warrants. This category consists of non-interest-bearing, short-term obligations; inter-fund obligations; amounts owed in a trust or agency capacity; advances and contingent loans from other governments; and rights of individuals to benefit from government-administered employee-retirement funds.

GOVERNMENT EMPLOYMENT, Items 194–196

Source: U.S. Bureau of Economic Analysis—Regional Economic Accounts
https://www.bea.gov/data/economic-accounts/regional#state

Employment is measured as the average annual sum of full-time and part-time jobs. The estimates are on a place-of-work basis. The estimates are on a place-of-work basis. State and local government employment includes person employed in all state and local government agencies and enterprises. Data for federal civilian employment include civilian employees of the federal government, including civilian employees of the Department of Defense. Military employment includes all persons on active duty status.

INDIVIDUAL INCOME TAX RETURNS, Items 197–199

Source: U.S. Internal Revenue Service, Statistics of Income Program
https://www.irs.gov/uac/soi-tax-stats-county-data-2019

The Revenue Act of 1916 mandated the annual publication of statistics related to "the operations of the internal revenue laws" as they affect individuals, all forms of businesses, estates. non-profit organizations, trusts, and investments abroad and foreign investments in the United States. The Statistics of Income (SOI) division fulfills this function by collecting and processing data so that they become informative and by sharing information about how the tax system works with other government agencies and the general public. Publication types include traditional print sources, internet files, CD-ROMs, and files sent via e-mail. SOI has an information office, Statistical Information Services, to facilitate the dissemination of SOI data.

SOI bases its county data on administrative records of individual income tax returns (Forms 1040) from the Internal Revenue Service (IRS) Individual Master File (IMF) system. Included in these data are returns filed during the 12-month period, January 1, 2020, to December 31, 2020. While the bulk of returns filed during the 12-month period are primarily for Tax Year 2019, the IRS received a limited number of returns for tax years before 2019 and these have been included within the county data.

Data do not represent the full U.S. population because many individuals are not required to file an individual income tax return. The address shown on the tax return may differ from the taxpayer's actual residence. State and county codes were based on the ZIP code shown on the return. Excluded were tax returns filed without a ZIP code and returns filed with a ZIP code that did not match the State code shown on the return.

SOI did not attempt to correct any ZIP codes on the returns; however, it did take the following precautions to avoid disclosing information about specific taxpayers: Excluded from the data are items with less than 20 returns within a county. Also excluded are tax returns representing a specified percentage of the total of any particular cell. For example, if one return represented 75 percent of the value of a given cell, the return was suppressed from the county detail. The actual threshold percentage used cannot be released.

Column 197 show the number of returns. Column 198 shows the mean Adjusted Gross Income for the metropolitan area and column 199 shows the mean income tax (line 56 on Form 1040). for the county.

TABLE D—CITIES

Table D present 139 items of data for cities with populations of 25,000 or more at the time of the 2020 census.

LAND AREA, Items 1 and 4

Source: U.S. Census Bureau—2021 U.S. Gazetteer Files
https://www.census.gov/geographies/reference-files/time-series/geo/gazetteer-files.html

Land area measurements are shown to the nearest square mile. Land area is an area measurement providing the size, in square miles, of the land portions of each county.

POPULATION, Items 2-4

Source: U.S. Census Bureau—Population Estimates
https://www.census.gov/programs-surveys/popest.html

The population data are Census Bureau estimates of the resident population as of July 1 of the year shown.

POPULATION CHARACTERISTICS, Items 5–22

Source: U.S. Census Bureau—P.L. 94-171 Redistricting Data
Source: U.S. Census Bureau—American Community Survey 2020 5-year Estimates
https://www.census.gov/programs-surveys/decennial-census/about/rdo/summary-files.html
https://www.census.gov/programs-surveys/acs

Data on race and Hispanic origin are from the 2020 census redistricting data file.

Data on age, sex, and place of birth are from the 2020 5-year American Community Survey, a nationwide continuous survey designed to replace the long form questionnaire used in previous censuses.

Data on race were derived from answers to the question on race that was asked of all persons. The concept of race, as used by the Census Bureau, reflects self-identification by respondents according to the race or races with which they most closely identify. These categories are sociopolitical constructs and should not be interpreted as being scientific or anthropological in nature. Furthermore, the race categories include both racial and national origin groups.

In the 2020 census, respondents were offered the option of selecting one or more races. This option was not available prior to the 2000 census; thus, comparisons between censuses should be made with caution. In this table, Columns 5 through 10 refer to individuals who identified with one specific racial category, while Column 11 includes those who selected more than one race.

The **White** population is defined as persons who indicated their race as White, as well as persons who did not classify themselves in one of the specific race categories listed on the questionnaire but entered a nationality such as Irish, German, Italian, Lebanese, Near Easterner, Arab, or Polish.

The **Black** population includes persons who indicated their race as "Black or African American" as well as persons who did not classify themselves in one of the specific race categories but reported entries such as African American, Afro American, Kenyan, Nigerian, or Haitian.

The **American Indian or Alaska Native** population includes persons who indicated their race as American Indian or Alaska Native, as well as persons who did not classify themselves in one of the specific race categories but reported entries such as Canadian Indian, French-American Indian, Spanish-American Indian, Eskimo, Aleut, Alaska Indian, or any of the American Indian or Alaska Native tribes.

The **Asian** population includes persons who indicated their race as Asian Indian, Chinese, Filipino, Japanese, Korean,

Vietnamese, or "Other Asian," as well as persons who provided write-in entries of such groups as Cambodian, Laotian, Hmong, Pakistani, or Taiwanese.

The **Native Hawaiian or Other Pacific Islander** population includes persons who indicated their race as "Native Hawaiian," "Guamanian or Chamorro," "Samoan," or "Other Pacific Islander," as well as persons who reported entries such as Part Hawaiian, American Samoan, Fijian, Melanesian, or Tahitian.

Some Other Race includes all other responses not included in the "White," "Black or African American," "American Indian or Alaska Native," "Asian," and "Native Hawaiian or Other Pacific Islander" race categories described above. Respondents reporting entries such as multiracial, mixed, interracial, or a Hispanic, Latino, or Spanish group (for example, Mexican, Puerto Rican, Cuban, or Spanish) in response to the race question are included in this category.

Two or More Races. People may choose to provide two or more races either by checking two or more race response check boxes, by providing multiple responses, or by some combination of check boxes and other responses. The race response categories shown on the questionnaire are collapsed into the five minimum race groups identified by OMB, and the Census Bureau's "Some Other Race" category.

The **Hispanic population** is based on a separate question that asked respondents "Is this person Spanish/Hispanic/Latino?" Persons marking any one of the four Hispanic categories (i.e., Mexican, Puerto Rican, Cuban, or other Spanish) are collectively referred to as Hispanic.

The Hispanic origin question was placed before the race question and specific instructions indicated that both questions should be answered.

The **foreign-born** population includes all persons who were not U.S. citizens at birth. Foreign-born persons are those who indicated they were either a U.S. citizen by naturalization or were not a citizen of the United States. The foreign-born population consists of immigrants (legal permanent residents), temporary migrants (students), humanitarian migrants (refugees), and unauthorized migrants (persons illegally residing in the United States).

Age is defined as age at last birthday (number of completed years since birth), at the time of the interview. The American Community Survey also asked for the specific date of birth of the respondent. Both age and date of birth are used in combination to calculate the most accurate age at the time of the interview.

The **female** population is shown as a percentage of total population.

POPULATION CHANGE, Items 23–26

Source: U.S. Census Bureau—Decennial Censuses
Source: U.S. Census Bureau—Population Estimates
https://www.census.gov/programs-surveys/decennial-census/data/datasets.2010.html
https://www.census.gov/programs-surveys/popest.html

The population data for 2010 and 2020 are from the decennial censuses and represent the resident population as of April 1 of those years. They actually show the "estimates base" which reflects changes to the decennial census population from the Boundary and Annexation Survey (BAS) and other geographic program revisions, the application of disclosure avoidance techniques, or the incorporation of alternate data sources.

The data for 2021 are from the Census Bureau's Population Estimates Program and represent the estimated resident population as of July 1.

The change in population from 2010 to 2020 and from 2020 to 2021 is calculated from census data based on city boundaries as they existed in 2010 and 2020, respectively. No attempt was made to adjust the data to reflect boundary changes.

HOUSEHOLDS, Items 27–34

Source: U.S. Census Bureau—American Community Survey, 2020 5-year Estimates
https://www.census.gov/programs-surveys/acs

A **household** includes all of the persons who occupy a housing unit. (Persons not living in households are classified as living in group quarters.) A housing unit is a house, an apartment, a mobile home, a group of rooms, or a single room occupied (or, if vacant, intended for occupancy) as separate living quarters. Separate living quarters are those in which the occupants live separately from any other persons in the building and have direct access from the outside of the building or through a common hall. The occupants may be a single family, one person living alone, two or more families living together, or any other group of related or unrelated persons who share living quarters. The number of households is the same as the number of year-round occupied housing units.

A **family** includes a householder and one or more other persons living in the same household who are related to the householder by birth, marriage, or adoption. All persons in a household who are related to the householder are regarded as members of his or her family. A **family household** may contain persons not related to the householder; thus, family households may include more members than families do. A household can contain only one family for the purposes of census tabulations. Not all households contain families, as a household may comprise a group of unrelated persons or of one person living alone. Families are classified by type as either a "married couple family" or "other family," according to the presence or absence of a spouse.

A **Married-Couple Family** is a family in which the householder and his or her spouse are listed as members of the same household. The category **female family householder** includes only female-headed family households with no spouse present.

A **Nonfamily Household** includes a householder living alone or with nonrelatives only. Unmarried couples households, whether opposite-sex or same-sex, with no relatives of the householder present are tabulated in nonfamily households.

The measure of **persons per household** is obtained by dividing the number of persons in households by the number of households or householders. One person in each household is designated as the householder. In most cases, this is the person (or one of the persons) in whose name the house is owned, being bought, or rented. If there is no such person in the household, any adult household member 15 years old and over can be designated as the householder.

CRIME, Items 35–38

Source: U.S. Federal Bureau of Investigation—Uniform Crime Reports
https://crime-data-explorer.app.cloud.gov/pages/downloads

Crime data are as reported to the Federal Bureau of Investigation (FBI) by law enforcement agencies and have not been adjusted for underreporting. This may affect comparability between geographic areas or over time.

Through the voluntary contribution of crime statistics by law enforcement agencies across the United States, the Uniform Crime Reporting (UCR) Program provides periodic assessments of crime in the nation as measured by offenses that have come to the attention of the law enforcement community. The Committee on Uniform Crime Records of the International Association of Chiefs of Police initiated this voluntary national data collection effort in 1930. The UCR Program contributors compile and submit their crime data either directly to the FBI or through state-level UCR Programs.

Seven offenses, because of their severity, frequency of occurrence, and likelihood of being reported to police, were initially selected to serve as an index for evaluating fluctuations in the volume of crime. These serious crimes were murder and nonnegligent manslaughter, forcible rape, robbery, aggravated assault, burglary, larceny-theft, and motor vehicle theft. By congressional mandate, arson was added as the eighth index offense in 1979. The totals shown in this volume do not include arson.

In 2004, the FBI discontinued the use of the Crime Index in the UCR Program and its publications, stating that the Crime Index was driven upward by the offense with the highest number of cases (in this case, larceny-theft), creating a bias against jurisdictions with a high number of larceny-thefts but a low number of other serious crimes, such as murder and forcible rape. The FBI is currently publishing a violent crime total and property crime total until a more viable index is developed. This book includes the total Crime Index, as well as violent crime and property crime rates.

In 2013, the FBI adopted a new definition of rape. Rape is now defined as, "Penetration, no matter how slight, of the vagina or anus with any body part or object, or oral penetration by a sex organ of another person, without the consent of the victim." The new definition updated the 80-year-old historical definition of rape which was "carnal knowledge of a female forcibly and against her will." Effectively, the revised definition expands rape to include both male and female victims and offenders, and reflects the various forms of sexual penetration understood to be rape, especially nonconsenting acts of sodomy, and sexual assaults with objects.

Violent crimes include four categories of offenses: (1) Murder and nonnegligent manslaughter, as defined in the UCR Program, is the willful (nonnegligent) killing of one human being by another. This offense excludes deaths caused by negligence, suicide, or accident; justifiable homicides; and attempts to murder or assaults to murder. (2)) Rape is the penetration, no matter how slight, of the vagina or anus with any body part or object, or oral penetration by a sex organ of another person, without the consent of the victim Assaults or attempts to commit rape by force or threat of force are also included; however, statutory rape (without force) and other sex offenses are excluded. (3) Robbery is the taking or attempting to take anything of value from the care, custody, or control of a person or persons by force or threat of force or violence and/or by putting the victim in fear. (4) Aggravated assault is an unlawful attack by one person upon another for the purpose of inflicting severe or aggravated bodily injury. This type of assault is usually accompanied by the use of a weapon or by other means likely to produce death or great bodily harm. Attempts are included, since injury does not necessarily have to result when a gun, knife, or other weapon is used, as these incidents could and probably would result in a serious personal injury if the crime were successfully completed.

Property crimes include three categories: (1) Burglary, or breaking and entering, is the unlawful entry of a structure to commit a felony or theft, even though no force was used to gain entrance. (2) Larceny-theft is the unauthorized taking of the personal property of another, without the use of force. (3) Motor vehicle theft is the unauthorized taking of any motor vehicle.

Rates are based on population estimates provided by the FBI. If a city is not in the UCR database, or if the population total for the units aggregated was less than 75 percent of the city's population (as estimated by the Census Bureau), the total was not considered representative of the city as a whole and was not published.

EDUCATIONAL ATTAINMENT, Items 39–41

Source: U.S. Census Bureau—American Community Survey, 2020 5-year Estimates
https://www.census.gov/programs-surveys/acs

Data on **educational attainment** are tabulated for the population 25 years old and over. The data were derived from a question that asked respondents for the highest level of school completed or the highest degree received. Persons who had passed a high school equivalency examination were considered high school graduates. Schooling received in foreign schools was to be reported as the equivalent grade or years in the regular American school system.

Vocational and technical training, such as barber school training; business, trade, technical, and vocational schools; or other training for a specific trade are specifically excluded.

High school graduate or less. This category includes persons whose highest degree was a high school diploma or its equivalent, and those who reported any level lower than a high school diploma.

Bachelor's degree or more. This category includes persons who have received bachelor's degrees, master's degrees, professional school degrees (such as law school or medical school degrees), and doctoral degrees.

INCOME, Items 42–49

Source: U.S. Census Bureau—American Community Survey, 2020 5-year Estimates
https://www.census.gov/programs-surveys/acs

Total money income is the sum of the amounts reported separately for wage or salary income; net self-employment income;

interest, dividends, or net rental or royalty income or income from estates and trusts; Social Security or railroad retirement income; Supplemental Security Income (SSI); public assistance or welfare payments; retirement, survivor, or disability pensions; and all other income. Receipts from the following sources are not included as income: capital gains; money received from the sale of property (unless the recipient was engaged in the business of selling such property); the value of income "in kind" from food stamps, public housing subsidies, medical care, employer contributions for individuals, etc.; withdrawal of bank deposits; money borrowed; tax refunds; exchange of money between relatives living in the same household; and gifts, lump-sum inheritances, insurance payments, and other types of lump-sum receipts.

Household income includes the income of the householder and all other individuals 15 years old and over in the household, whether or not they are related to the householder. Since many households consist of only one person, median household income is usually less than median family income. Although the household income statistics cover the twelve months prior to the survey, the characteristics of individuals and the composition of households refer to the date of the interview. Thus, the income of the household does not include amounts received by individuals who were members of the household during all or part of the year if these individuals were no longer residing in the household at the time of the interview. Similarly, income amounts reported by individuals who did not reside in the household during full year but who were members of the household at the time of the interview are included. However, the composition of most households was the same during the year as it was at the time of the interview.

Income of Families. In compiling statistics on family income, the incomes of all members 15 years old and over related to the householder are summed and treated as a single amount.

Median income divides the income distribution into two equal parts, with half of all cases below the median income level and half of all cases above the median income level. For households, the median income is based on the distribution of the total number of households, including those with no income. Median income for households and families is computed on the basis of a standard distribution with a minimum value of less than $2,500 and a maximum value of $200,000 or more and is rounded to the nearest whole dollar. Median income figures are calculated using linear interpolation if the width of the interval containing the estimate is $2,500 or less. If the width of the interval containing the estimate is greater than $2,500, Pareto interpolation is used.

Income components were reported for the 12 months preceding the interview month. Monthly Consumer Price Index (CPI) factors were used to inflation-adjust these components to a reference calendar year (January through December). For example, a household interviewed in March 2017 reports their income for March 2016 through February 2017. Their income is adjusted to the 2017 reference calendar year by multiplying their reported income by 2017 average annual CPI (January-December 2017) and then dividing by the average CPI for March 2016-February 2017. In addition, the 5-year estimates are inflation-adjusted to the final year. However, the estimates do not reflect the price and cost-of-living differences that may exist between areas.

Earnings are defined as the sum of wage or salary income and net income from self-employment. "Earnings" represent the amount of income received regularly for people 16 years old and over before deductions for personal income taxes, Social Security, bond purchases, union dues, Medicare deductions, etc. An individual with earnings is one who has either wage/salary income or self-employment income, or both. Respondents who "break even" in self-employment income and therefore have zero self-employment earnings also are considered "individuals with earnings."

HOUSING, Items 50–54

Source: U.S. Census Bureau--American Community Survey, 2020 5-year Estimates
https://www.census.gov/programs-surveys/acs

A **housing unit** is a house, apartment, mobile home or trailer, group of rooms, or single room occupied or, if vacant, intended for occupancy as separate living quarters. Separate living quarters are those in which the occupants do not live and eat with any other person in the structure and which have direct access from the outside of the building through a common hall. For vacant units, the criteria of separateness and direct access are applied to the intended occupants whenever possible. If that information cannot be obtained, the criteria are applied to the previous occupants.

The occupants of a housing unit may be a single family, one person living alone, two or more families living together, or any other group of related or unrelated persons who share living quarters. Both occupied and vacant housing units are included in the housing inventory, although recreational vehicles, tents, caves, boats, railroad cars, and the like are included only if they are occupied as a person's usual place of residence.

A housing unit is classified as occupied if it is the usual place of residence of the person or group of persons living in it at the time of enumeration, or if the occupants are only temporarily absent (away on vacation). A household consists of all persons who occupy a housing unit as their usual place of residence. Vacant units for sale or rent include units rented or sold but not occupied and any other units held off the market.

A housing unit is **owner occupied** if the owner or co-owner lives in the unit, even if it is mortgaged or not fully paid for. The owner or co-owner must live in the unit and is usually the first person listed on the census or ACS questionnaire.

All occupied housing units that are not owner occupied, whether they are rented for cash rent or occupied without payment of cash rent, are classified as **renter occupied**.

Median value is the dollar amount that divides the distribution of specified owner-occupied housing units into two equal parts, with half of all units below the median value and half of all units above the median value. Value is defined as the respondent's estimate of what the house would sell for if it were for sale. Data are presented for single-family units on fewer than 10 acres of land that have no business or medical offices on the property.

Median rent divides the distribution of renter-occupied housing units into two equal parts. The rent concept used in this volume is gross rent, which includes the amount of cash rent a renter pays (contract rent) plus the estimated average cost of utilities and fuels, if these are paid by the renter. The rent is the amount of rent only for living quarters and excludes amounts paid for any business or other space occupied. Single-family houses on lots of 10 or more acres of land are also excluded.

COMMUTING, Items 55 and 56

Source: U.S. Census Bureau—American Community Survey, 2020 5-year Estimates https://www.census.gov/programs-surveys/acs

Means of transportation to work refers to the principal mode of travel or type of conveyance that a worker usually used to get from home to work during the reference week. This question was asked of people who indicated that they worked at some time during the reference week. People who used different means of transportation on different days of the week were asked to specify the one they used most often, that is, the greatest number of days. People who used more than one means of transportation to get to work each day were asked to report the one used for the longest distance during the work trip. The category, "Car, truck, or van," includes workers using a car (including company cars but excluding taxicabs), a truck of one-ton capacity or less, or a van. The category, "**Drove alone**," includes people who usually drove alone to work as well as people who were driven to work by someone who then drove back home or to a non-work destination. Column 55 shows those who drove alone as a percentage of all workers age 16 and older.

The question on **travel time to work** was asked of people who indicated that they worked at some time during the reference week, and who reported that they worked outside their home. Travel time to work refers to the total number of minutes that it usually took the worker to get from home to work during the reference week. The elapsed time includes time spent waiting for public transportation, picking up passengers in carpools, and time spent in other activities related to getting to work. Column 56 shows the mean travel time to work (in minutes), the average travel time that workers usually took to get from home to work (one way) during the reference week.

COMPUTER AND INTERNET USE, Items 57 and 58

Source: U.S. Census Bureau—American Community Survey, 2020 5-year Estimates https://www.census.gov/programs-surveys/acs

The **computer use** question asked if anyone in the household owned or used a computer and included four response categories for a desktop/laptop, smartphone, tablet or other portable, wireless computer, or some other type of computer. Respondents could select all categories that applied.

Another question asked if any member of the household accesses the **internet**. "Access" refers to whether or not someone in the household uses or connects to the internet, regardless of whether or not they pay for the service. Respondents were to select only ONE of the following choices:

- Yes, with a subscription to an Internet service—This category includes housing units where someone pays to access the Internet through a service such as a data plan for a mobile phone, a cable modem, DSL or other type of service. This will normally refer to a service that someone is billed for directly for Internet alone or sometimes as part of a bundle.
- Yes, without a subscription to an Internet service—Some respondents may live in a city or town that provides free Internet services for their residents. In addition, some colleges or universities provide Internet services. These are examples of cases where respondents may be able to access the Internet without a subscription.
- No Internet access at this house, apartment, or mobile home—This category includes housing units where no one connects to or uses the Internet using a paid service or any free services.

MIGRATION, Items 59 and 60

Source: U.S. Census Bureau—American Community Survey, 2020 5-year Estimates https://www.census.gov/programs-surveys/acs

Residence one year ago is used in conjunction with location of current residence to determine the extent of residential mobility of the population and the resulting redistribution of the population across the various states, metropolitan areas, and regions of the country. **Same house** includes all people 1 year old and over who, a year before the survey date, lived in the same house or apartment that they occupied at the time of interview.

The **percent who lived outside** current **county** includes all persons who did not live in their current county 1 year before the interview. However, they may have lived outside their current city but still in the same county.

CIVILIAN LABOR FORCE AND UNEMPLOYMENT, Items 61–64

Source: U.S. Bureau of Labor Statistics—Local Areas Unemployment Statistics https://www.bls.gov/lau/#tables

Data for the civilian labor force are the product of a federal-state cooperative program in which state employment security agencies prepare labor force and unemployment estimates under concepts, definitions, and technical procedures established by the Bureau of Labor Statistics (BLS). The civilian labor force consists of all civilians 16 years old and over who are either employed or unemployed.

Unemployment includes all persons who did not work during the survey week, made specific efforts to find a job during the previous four weeks, and were available for work during the survey week (except for temporary illness). Persons waiting to be called back to a job from which they had been laid off and those waiting to report to a new job within the next 30 days are included in unemployment figures.

Table D includes annual average data for the year shown. The Local Area Unemployment Statistics data are periodically updated to reflect revised inputs, reestimation, and controlling to new statewide totals.

EMPLOYMENT, Items 65–68

Source: U.S. Census Bureau—American Community Survey, 2020 5-year Estimates https://www.census.gov/programs-surveys/acs

The **civilian labor force** includes all civilian persons 16 years old and over who were either (1) "at work"—those who did any work at all during the reference week as paid employees, worked in either their own business or profession, worked on their own farm, or worked 15 hours or more as unpaid workers in a family farm or business; or were (2) "with a job, but not at work"—those who had a job but were not at work that week due to illness, weather, industrial dispute, vacation, or other personal reasons.

Full-year, Full-Time Workers includes people 16 to 64 years old who usually worked 35 hours or more per week for 50 to 52 weeks in the past 12 months.

BUILDING PERMITS, Items 69–71

Source: U.S. Census Bureau—Building Permits Survey https://www.census.gov/construction/bps

These figures represent private residential construction authorized by building permits in approximately 20,000 places in the United States. Valuation represents the expected cost of construction as recorded on the building permit. This figure usually excludes the cost of on-site and off-site development and improvements, as well as the cost of heating, plumbing, electrical, and elevator installations.

National, state, and county totals were obtained by adding the data for permit-issuing places within each jurisdiction. These totals thus are limited to permits issued in the 20,000 place universe covered by the Census Bureau and may not include all permits issued within a state. Current surveys indicate that construction is undertaken for all but a very small percentage of housing units authorized by building permits.

Residential building permits include buildings with any number of housing units. Housing units exclude group quarters (such as dormitories and rooming houses), transient accommodations (such as transient hotels, motels, and tourist courts), "HUD-code" manufactured (mobile) homes, moved or relocated units, and housing units created in an existing residential or nonresidential structure.

2017 Economic CENSUS: OVERVIEW, Items 72–107

Source: U.S. Census Bureau https://www.census.gov/programs-surveys/economic-census.html

The Economic Census provides a detailed portrait of the nation's economy, from the national to the local level, once every five years. The 2017 Economic Census covers nearly all of the U.S. economy in its basic collection of establishment statistics. The 1997 Economic Census was the first major data source to use the new North American Industry Classification System (NAICS); therefore, data from this census are not comparable to economic data from prior years, which were based on the Standard Industrial Classification (SIC) system.

NAICS, developed in cooperation with Canada and Mexico, classifies North America's economic activities at two, three, four, and fivedigit levels of detail; the U.S. version of NAICS further defines industries to a sixth digit. The Economic Census takes advantage of this hierarchy to publish data at these successive levels of detail: sector (two-digit), subsector (three-digit), industry group (four-digit), industry (five-digit), and U.S. industry (six-digit). Information in Table A is at the two-digit level, with a few three- and four-digit items. The data in Table D are at the two-digit level.

Several key statistics are tabulated for all industries in this volume, including number of establishments (or companies), number of employees, payroll, and certain measures of output (sales, receipts, revenue, value of shipments, or value of construction work done).

Number of establishments. An establishment is a single physical location at which business is conducted. It is not necessarily identical with a company or enterprise, which may consist of one establishment or more. Economic Census figures represent a summary of reports for individual establishments rather than companies. For cases in which a census report was received, separate information was obtained for each location where business was conducted. When administrative records of other federal agencies were used instead of a census report, no information was available on the number of locations operated. Each Economic Census establishment was tabulated according to the physical location at which the business was conducted. The count of establishments represents those in business at any time during 2002.

When two activities or more were carried on at a single location under a single ownership, all activities were generally grouped together as a single establishment. The entire establishment was classified on the basis of its major activity and all of its data were included in that classification. However, when distinct and separate economic activities (for which different industry classification codes were appropriate) were conducted at a single location under a single ownership, separate establishment reports for each of the different activities were obtained in the census.

Number of employees. Paid employees consist of the fulltime and parttime employees, including salaried officers and executives of corporations. Included are employees on paid sick leave, paid holidays, and paid vacations; not included are proprietors and partners of unincorporated businesses. The definition of paid employees is the same as that used by the Internal Revenue Service (IRS) on form 941. For some industries, the Economic Census gives codes representing the number of employees as a range of numbers (for example, "100 to 249 employees" or "1,000 to 2,499" employees). In this volume, those codes have been replaced by the standard suppression code "D".

Payroll. Payroll includes all forms of compensation, such as salaries, wages, commissions, dismissal pay, bonuses, vacation allowances, sickleave pay, and employee contributions to qualified pension plans paid during the year to all employees. For corporations, payroll includes amounts paid to officers and executives; for unincorporated businesses, it does not include profit or other compensation of proprietors or partners. Payroll is reported before deductions for Social Security, income tax, insurance, union dues, etc. This definition of payroll is the same as that used by on IRS form 941.

Sales, shipments, receipts, revenue, or business done. This measure includes the total sales, shipments, receipts, revenue, or business done by establishments within the scope of the Economic Census. The definition of each of these items is specific to the economic sector measured.

WHOLESALE TRADE, Items 72–75

Source: U.S. Census Bureau—2017 Economic Census (See overview of 2017 Economic Census prior to Item 72)

The Wholesale Trade sector (sector 42) comprises establishments engaged in wholesaling merchandise, generally without transformation, and rendering services incidental to the sale of merchandise. The wholesaling process is an intermediate step in the distribution of merchandise.

Wholesalers are organized to sell or arrange the purchase or sale of (1) goods for resale (i.e., goods sold to other wholesalers or retailers), (2) capital or durable nonconsumer goods, and (3) raw and intermediate materials and supplies used in production.

Wholesalers sell merchandise to other businesses and normally operate from a warehouse or office. These warehouses and offices are characterized by having little or no display of merchandise. In addition, neither the design nor the location of the premises is intended to solicit walkin traffic. Wholesalers do not normally use advertising directed to the general public. In general, customers are initially reached via telephone, inperson marketing, or specialized advertising, which may include the internet and other electronic means. Followup orders are either vendorinitiated or clientinitiated, are usually based on previous sales, and typically exhibit strong ties between sellers and buyers. In fact, transactions are often conducted between wholesalers and clients that have longstanding business relationships.

This sector is made up of two main types of wholesalers: those that sell goods on their own account and those that arrange sales and purchases for others for a commission or fee.

(1) Establishments that sell goods on their own account are known as wholesale merchants, distributors, jobbers, drop shippers, import/export merchants, and sales branches. These establishments typically maintain their own warehouse, where they receive and handle goods for their customers. Goods are generally sold without transformation, but may include integral functions, such as sorting, packaging, labeling, and other marketing services.

(2) Establishments arranging for the purchase or sale of goods owned by others or purchasing goods on a commission basis are known as agents and brokers, commission merchants, import/export agents and brokers, auction companies, and manufacturers' representatives. These establishments operate from offices and generally do not own or handle the goods they sell.

Some wholesale establishments may be connected with a single manufacturer and promote and sell that particular manufacturer's products to a wide range of other wholesalers or retailers. Other wholesalers may be connected to a retail chain or a limited number of retail chains and only provide the products needed by the particular retail operation(s). These wholesalers may obtain the products from a wide range of manufacturers. Still other wholesalers may not take title to the goods, but act instead as agents and brokers for a commission.

Although wholesaling normally denotes sales in large volumes, durable nonconsumer goods may be sold in single units. Sales of capital or durable nonconsumer goods used in the production of goods and services, such as farm machinery, medium- and heavy-duty trucks, and industrial machinery, are always included in Wholesale Trade.

The city table includes only **Merchant wholesalers, except manufacturers' sales branches and offices,** establishments primarily engaged in buying and selling merchandise on their own account. Included here are such types of establishments as wholesale distributors and jobbers, importers, exporters, own-brand importers/marketers, terminal and country grain elevators, and farm products assemblers.

RETAIL TRADE, Items 76–79

Source: U.S. Census Bureau—2017 Economic Census (See overview of 2017 Economic Census prior to Item 72)

The Retail Trade sector (44–45) is made up of establishments engaged in retailing merchandise, generally without transformation, and rendering services incidental to the sale of merchandise.

The retailing process is the final step in the distribution of merchandise; retailers are therefore organized to sell merchandise in small quantities to the general public. This sector comprises two main types of retailers: store and nonstore retailers.

Store retailers operate fixed pointofsale locations, located and designed to attract a high volume of walkin customers. In general, retail stores have extensive displays of merchandise and use massmedia advertising to attract customers. They typically sell merchandise to the general public for personal or household consumption; some also serve business and institutional clients. These include establishments such as office supply stores, computer and software stores, building materials dealers, plumbing supply stores, and electrical supply stores. Catalog showrooms, gasoline service stations, automotive dealers, and mobile home dealers are treated as store retailers.

In addition to retailing merchandise, some types of store retailers are also engaged in the provision of aftersales services, such as repair and installation. For example, new automobile dealers, electronic and appliance stores, and musical instrument and supply stores often provide repair services. As a general rule, establishments engaged in retailing merchandise and providing aftersales services are classified in this sector.

Nonstore retailers, like store retailers, are organized to serve the general public, although their retailing methods differ. The establishments of this subsector reach customers and market merchandise with methods including the broadcasting of "infomercials," the broadcasting and publishing of directresponse advertising, the publishing of paper and electronic catalogs, doortodoor solicitation, inhome demonstration, selling from portable stalls (street vendors, except food), and distribution through vending machines. Establishments engaged in the direct sale (nonstore) of products, such as home heating oil dealers and home-delivery newspaper routes are included in this sector.

The buying of goods for resale is a characteristic of retail trade establishments that distinguishes them from establishments in the Agriculture, Manufacturing, and Construction sectors. For example, farms that sell their products at or from the point of production are classified in Agriculture instead of in Retail Trade. Similarly, establishments that both manufacture and sell their products to the general public are classified in Manufacturing instead of Retail Trade. However, establishments that engage in processing activities incidental to retailing are classified in Retail Trade.

REAL ESTATE AND RENTAL AND LEASING, Items 80–83

Source: U.S. Census Bureau—2017 Economic Census (See overview of 2017 Economic Census prior to Item 72)

The Real Estate and Rental and Leasing sector (53) comprises establishments primarily engaged in renting, leasing, or otherwise allowing the use of tangible or intangible assets, and establishments providing related services. The major portion of this sector is made up of establishments that rent, lease, or otherwise allow the use of their own assets by others. The assets may be tangible, such as real estate and equipment, or intangible, such as patents and trademarks.

This sector also includes establishments primarily engaged in managing real estate for others, selling, renting, and/or buying real estate for others, and appraising real estate. These activities are closely related to this sector's main activity. In addition, a substantial proportion of property management is selfperformed by lessors.

The main components of this sector are the real estate lessors industries; equipment lessors industries (including motor vehicles, computers, and consumer goods); and lessors of nonfinancial intangible assets (except copyrighted works).

PROFESSIONAL, SCIENTIFIC, AND TECHNICAL SERVICES, Items 84–87

Source: U.S. Census Bureau—2017 Economic Census (See overview of 2017 Economic Census prior to Item 72)

The Professional, Scientific, and Technical Services sector (54) is made up of establishments that specialize in performing professional, scientific, and technical activities for others. These activities require a high degree of expertise and training. The establishments in this sector specialize in one or more areas and provide services to clients in a variety of industries (and, in some cases, to households). Activities performed include legal advice and representation; accounting, bookkeeping, and payroll services; architectural, engineering, and specialized design services; computer services; consulting services; research services; advertising services; photographic services; translation and interpretation services; veterinary services; and other professional, scientific, and technical services.

This sector excludes establishments primarily engaged in providing a range of daytoday office administrative services, such as financial planning, billing and record keeping, personnel services, and physical distribution and logistics services. These establishments are classified in sector 56, Administrative and Support and Waste Management and Remediation Services.

MANUFACTURING, Items 88–91

Source: U.S. Census Bureau—2017 Economic Census (See overview of 2017 Economic Census prior to Item 72)

The Manufacturing sector (31–33) is made up of establishments engaged in the mechanical, physical, or chemical transformation of materials, substances, or components into new products. The assembling of component parts of manufactured products is considered manufacturing, except in cases in which the activity is appropriately classified in the Construction sector. Establishments in the Manufacturing sector are often described as plants, factories, or mills, and characteristically use power-driven machines and materials-handling equipment. However, establishments that transform materials or substances into new products by hand or in the worker's home, and establishments engaged in selling to the general public products made on the same premises from which they are sold (such as bakeries, candy stores, and custom tailors) may also be included in this sector. Manufacturing establishments may process materials or contract with other establishments to process their materials for them. Both types of establishments are included in the Manufacturing sector.

The materials, substances, or components transformed by manufacturing establishments are raw materials that are products of agriculture, forestry, fishing, mining, or quarrying, or are products of other manufacturing establishments. The materials used may be purchased directly from producers, obtained through customary trade channels, or secured without recourse to the market by transferring the product from one establishment to another, under the same ownership. The new product of a manufacturing establishment may be finished (in the sense that it is ready for utilization or consumption), or it may be semifinished to become an input for an establishment engaged in further manufacturing. For example, the product of the alumina refinery is the input used in the primary production of aluminum; primary aluminum is the input used in an aluminum wire drawing plant; and aluminum wire is the input used in a fabricated wire product manufacturing establishment.

Data are included for cities with 500 or more employees in the Manufacturing sector.

ACCOMMODATION AND FOOD SERVICES, Items 92–95

Source: U.S. Census Bureau—2017 Economic Census (See overview of 2017 Economic Census prior to Item 72)

The Accommodation and Food Services sector (72) consists of establishments that provide customers with lodging and/or meals, snacks, and beverages for immediate consumption. This sector includes both accommodation and food services establishments because the two activities are often combined at the same establishment.

Excluded from this sector are civic and social organizations, amusement and recreation parks, theaters, and other recreation or entertainment facilities providing food and beverage services.

ARTS, ENTERTAINMENT, AND RECREATION, Items 96–99

Source: U.S. Census Bureau—2017 Economic Census (See overview of 2017 Economic Census prior to Item 72)

The Arts, Entertainment, and Recreation sector (71) includes a wide range of establishments that operate facilities or provide services that meet the diverse cultural, entertainment, and recreational interests of their patrons. This sector is made up of: (1) establishments that are involved in producing, promoting, or participating in live performances, events, or exhibits intended for public viewing; (2) establishments that preserve and exhibit objects and sites of historical, cultural, or educational interest; and (3) establishments that operate facilities or provide services that enable patrons to participate in recreational activities or pursue amusement, hobby, and leisure time interests.

Some establishments that provide cultural, entertainment, or recreational facilities and services are classified in other sectors. Excluded from this sector are: (1) establishments that provide both accommodations and recreational facilities—such as hunting and fishing camps and resort and casino hotels—are classified in subsector 721, Accommodation; (2) restaurants and night clubs that provide live entertainment in addition to the sale of food and beverages are classified in subsector 722, Food Services and Drinking Places; (3) motion picture theaters, libraries and archives, and publishers of newspapers, magazines, books, periodicals, and computer software are classified in sector 51, Information; and (4) establishments that use transportation equipment to provide recreational and entertainment services, such as those operating sightseeing buses, dinner cruises, or helicopter rides, are classified in subsector 487, Scenic and Sightseeing Transportation.

Table D includes only those establishments subject to federal tax.

HEALTH CARE AND SOCIAL ASSISTANCE, Items 100–103

Source: U.S. Census Bureau—2017 Economic Census (See overview of 2017 Economic Census prior to Item 72)

The Health Care and Social Assistance sector (62) consists of establishments that provide health care and social assistance services to individuals. The sector includes both health care and social assistance because it is sometimes difficult to distinguish between the boundaries of these two activities. The industries in this sector are arranged on a continuum, starting with establishments that provide medical care exclusively, continuing with those that provide health care and social assistance, and finishing with those that provide only social assistance. The services provided by establishments in this sector are delivered by trained professionals. All industries in the sector share this commonality of process—namely, labor inputs of health practitioners or social workers with the requisite expertise. Many of the industries in the sector are defined based on the educational degree held by the practitioners included in the industry.

Excluded from this sector are aerobic classes, which can be found in subsector 713, Amusement, Gambling, and Recreation Industries; and nonmedical diet and weight-reducing centers, which can be found in subsector 812, Personal and Laundry Services. Although these can be viewed as health services, they are not typically delivered by health practitioners.

OTHER SERVICES, EXCEPT PUBLIC ADMINISTRATION Items 104–107

Source: U.S. Census Bureau—2017 Economic Census (See overview of 2017 Economic Census prior to Item 72)

The Other Services, Except Public Administration sector (81) comprises establishments engaged in providing services not specifically categorized elsewhere in the classification system. Establishments in this sector are primarily engaged in activities such as equipment and machinery repairing, promoting or administering religious activities, grant making, and advocacy; this sector also includes establishments that provide dry-cleaning and laundry services, personal care services, death care services, pet care services, photofinishing services, temporary parking services, and dating services.

Private households that employ workers on or about the premises in activities primarily concerned with the operation of the household are included in this sector.

Excluded from this sector are establishments primarily engaged in retailing new equipment and performing repairs and general maintenance on equipment. These establishments are classified in sector 44–45, Retail Trade.

CITY GOVERNMENT EMPLOYMENT AND PAYROLL, Items 171–179

Source: U.S. Census Bureau—2017 Census of Governments https://www.census.gov/programs-surveys/cog.html

Data are assembled from the Census Bureau's Individual Units file from the 2017 Census of Governments. Because the Census Bureau has not reviewed the individual unit data as separate time series, caution must be exercised in their use and interpretation. Users are encouraged to review the tables on the Census Bureau's website. The Census Bureau has not sanctioned, conducted, or reviewed any analysis using the Individual Units data files and they may contain high levels of nonsampling error.

These items include data for municipal governments only. They do not include any special district government entities within the city. The Census of Governments identifies the scope and nature of the nation's state and local government sector; provides authoritative benchmark figures of public finance and public employment; classifies local government organizations, powers, and activities; and measures federal, state, and local fiscal relationships.

The Employment component was mailed March 2012 to collect information on the number of state and local government civilian employees and their payrolls.

Government employees include all persons paid for personal services performed, including persons paid from federally funded programs, paid elected or appointed officials, persons in a paid leave status, and persons paid on a per meeting, annual, semiannual, or quarterly basis. Unpaid officials, pensioners, persons whose work is performed on a fee basis, and contractors and their employees are excluded from the count of employees. **Full-Time Equivalent employees** is a computed statistic representing the number of full-time employees that could have been employed if the reported number of hours worked by part-time employees had been worked by full-time employees. This statistic is calculated separately for each function of a government by dividing the "part-time hours paid" by the standard number of hours for full-time employees in the particular government and then adding the resulting quotient to the number of full-time employees.

March payroll represents gross payroll amounts for the one-month period of March for full-time and part-time employees. Gross payroll includes all salaries, wages, fees, commissions, and overtime paid to employees **before** withholdings for taxes, insurance, etc. It also includes incentive payments that are paid at regular pay intervals. It excludes employer share of fringe benefits like retirement, Social Security, health and life insurance, lump sum payments, and so forth.

Administration and Judicial and Legal combines **Financial administration**, **Other government administration, and Judicial and Legal** activities. **Financial administration** includes activities concerned with tax assessment and collection, custody and disbursement of funds, debt management, administration of trust funds, budgeting, and other government-wide financial management activities. This function is not applied to school district or special district governments. **Other government administration** applies to the legislative and government-wide administrative agencies of governments. Included here are overall planning and zoning activities, and central personnel and administrative activities. This function is not applied to school district or special district governments. **Judicial and legal** includes all court and court related activities (except probation and parole activities that are included at the "Correction" function), court activities of sheriff's offices, prosecuting attorneys' and public defenders' offices, legal departments, and attorneys providing government-wide legal service.

Police and Corrections includes all activities concerned, with the enforcement of law and order, including coroner's offices, police training academies, investigation bureaus, and local jails, "lockups", or other detention facilities not intended to serve as correctional facilities. **Corrections** includes activities pertaining to the confinement and correction of adults and minors convicted of criminal offenses. Pardon, probation, and parole activities are also included here.

Fire protection includes local government fire protection and prevention activities plus any ambulance, rescue, or other auxiliary services provided by a fire protection agency. Volunteer firefighters, if remunerated for their services on a "per fire" or some other basis, are included as part-time employees.

Highways and transportation includes activities associated with the maintenance and operation of streets, roads, sidewalks, bridges, tunnels, toll roads, and ferries. Snow and ice removal, street lighting, and highway and traffic engineering activities are also included here. Also included are the operation, maintenance, and construction of public mass transit systems, including subways, surface rails, and buses, and the provision, construction, operation, maintenance; support of public waterways, harbors, docks, wharves, and related marine terminal facilities; and activities associated with the operation and support of publicly operated airport facilities.

Health and Welfare includes **Health, Hospitals, and Public welfare. Health** includes administration of public health programs, community and visiting nurse services, immunization programs, drug abuse rehabilitation programs, health and food inspection activities, operation of outpatient clinics, and environmental pollution control activities. **Hospitals** includes only government operated medical care facilities that provide inpatient care. Employees and payrolls of private corporations that lease and operate government-owned hospital facilities are excluded. **Public Welfare** includes the administration of various public assistance programs for the needy, veteran services, operation of nursing homes, indigent care institutions, and programs that provide payments for medical care, handicap transportation, and other services for the needy.

Natural resources and Utilities includes activities primarily concerned with the conservation and development of natural resources (soil, water, energy, minerals, etc.) and the regulation of industries that develop, utilize, or affect natural resources, as well as the operation and maintenance of **parks**, playgrounds, swimming pools, public beaches, auditoriums, public golf courses, museums, marinas, botanical gardens, and zoological parks. **Utilities, sewerage, and waste management** includes operation, maintenance, and construction of public water supply systems, including production, acquisition, and distribution of water to general public or to other public or private utilities, for residential, commercial, and industrial use; activities associated with the production or acquisition and distribution of electric power; provision, maintenance, and operation of sanitary and storm sewer systems and sewage disposal and treatment facilities; and refuse collection and disposal, operation of sanitary landfills, and street cleaning activities.

Education and libraries includes activities associated with the operation of public elementary and secondary schools and locally operated vocational-technical schools. Special education programs operated by elementary and secondary school systems are also included as are all ancillary services associated with the operation of schools, such as pupil transportation and food service. Also included are the establishment and provision of libraries for use by the general public and the technical support of privately operated libraries. This category includes classroom teachers, principals, supervisors of instruction, librarians, teacher aides, library aides, and guidance and psychological personnel as well as school superintendents and other administrative personnel, clerical and secretarial staffs, plant operation and maintenance personnel, health and recreation employees, transportation and food service personnel, and any student employees. Also included are any degree granting institutions that provide academic training above grade 12.

CITY GOVERNMENT FINANCES, Items 117–139

Source: U.S. Census Bureau—2017 Census of Governments
https://www.census.gov/programs-surveys/cog.html

Data are assembled from the Census Bureau's Individual Units file from the 2017 Census of Governments. Because the Census Bureau has not reviewed the individual unit data as separate time series, caution must be exercised in their use and interpretation. Users are encouraged to review the tables on the Census Bureau's website. The Census Bureau has not sanctioned, conducted, or reviewed any analysis using the Individual Units data files and they may contain high levels of non-sampling error.

Revenue and expenditure data are included in Table D for municipal governments only. The data do not include funds of any special district governments located in the city. For example, if a city's school district is a separate governmental unit, it is not included.

Total **general revenue** includes all revenue except utility, liquor stores, and insurance trust revenue. All tax revenue and intergovernmental revenue, even if designated for employee-retirement or local utility purpose, are classified as general revenue.

Intergovernmental revenue covers amounts received from other governments as fiscal aid in the form of shared revenues and grants-in-aid, as reimbursements for the performance of general government functions and specific services for the paying government (for example, care of prisoners or contractual research), or in lieu of taxes. It excludes any amounts received from other governments from the sale of property, commodities, and utility services. All intergovernmental revenue is classified as general revenue. Intergovernmental revenue from the state governments includes amounts originally from the federal government but channeled through the state.

Taxes consist of compulsory contributions exacted by governments for public purposes. However, this category excludes employer and employee payments for retirement and social insurance purposes, which are classified as insurance trust revenue. All tax revenue is classified as general revenue and comprises amounts received (including interest and penalties, but excluding protested amounts and refunds) from all taxes imposed by a government. Note that local government tax revenue excludes any amounts from shares of state-imposed and collected taxes, which are classified as intergovernmental revenue.

Property taxes are based on ownership of property and measured by its value. They include general property taxes related to property as a whole—real and personal, tangible or intangible—whether taxed at a single rate or at classified rates. Also included are taxes on selected types of property, such as motor vehicles or certain or all intangibles.

Sales and gross receipts taxes include "licenses" at more than nominal rates, based on volume or value of transfers of goods or services; taxes upon gross receipts or upon gross income; and related taxes based upon the use, storage, production (other than the severance of natural resources), importation, or consumption of goods. Dealer discounts "commissions," which are allowed to merchants for the collection of taxes from consumers, are excluded.

Total **general expenditure** includes all city expenditure other than specifically enumerated kinds of expenditure, including utility, liquor store, and employee-retirement and other insurance trust expenditures.

Capital outlays are direct expenditures for contract of force account construction or buildings, roads, and other improvements, and for purchases of equipment, land, and existing structures. They include amounts for additions, replacements, and major alterations to fixed work and structures. Expenditures for repair to such works and structures, however, is classified as current operation expenditure.

A major portion of capital outlay is commonly financed by borrowing, while governmental revenue does not include receipts from borrowing. Among other things, this distorts the relationship between the totals presented for revenue and expenditure and renders this relationship useless as a direct measure of the degree of budgetary "balance" (as that term is generally applied).

Public welfare expenditure covers support of and assistance to needy persons; this aid is contingent upon the person's needs. Included are cash assistance paid directly to needy persons; vendor payments made directly to private purveyors for medical care, burials, and other commodities and services provided under welfare programs; welfare institutions; and any intergovernmental or other direct expenditure for welfare purposes. Pensions to former employees and other benefits not contingent on need are excluded.

Highway expenditure is for the provision and maintenance of highway facilities, including toll turnpikes, bridges, tunnels, and ferries, as well as regular roads, highways, and streets. Also included are expenditures for street lighting and for snow and ice removal. Not included are highway policing and traffic control, which are considered part of police protection

Parking facilities include the construction, purchase, maintenance, and operation of public-use parking lots, garages, parking meters, and other distinctive parking facilities on a commercial basis.

Education is mainly for the provision and general support of schools and other educational facilities and services, including those for educational institutions beyond high school. Elementary and secondary education includes the provision of public kindergarten through high school education by local governments. It encompasses instructional, support, and auxiliary services (school lunch, student activities, and community services) offered by public school systems. Higher education consists of all local institutions of higher education.

Health expenditures include outpatient health services other than hospital care, such as public health administration; research and education; categorical health programs; treatment and immunization clinics; nursing; environmental health activities, such as air and water pollution control; ambulance service if provided separately from fire protection services; and other general public health activities, such as mosquito abatement. School health services provided by health agencies (rather than school agencies) are included here. Not included are sewage treatment operations, which are classified as part of sewerage and sanitation. **Hospital expenditures** include financing, construction, acquisition, maintenance and operation of hospital facilities, provision of hospital care, and support of public or private hospitals.

Police protection encompasses expenditures for the preservation of law and order, as well as for traffic safety. It includes police patrols and communications, crime prevention activities, detention and custody of persons awaiting trial, traffic safety, and vehicular inspection.

Sewerage and recreation include sanitary and storm sewers, sewage disposal facilities and services, and other government activities for such purposes. Street cleaning and the collection and disposal of garbage and other waste are also included.

Parks and recreation includes cultural and scientific activities, such as museums and art galleries; organized recreation, including playgrounds and playing fields, swimming pools, and bathing beaches; and municipal parks and special recreation facilities, such as auditoriums, stadiums, auto camps, recreation piers, and boat harbors.

Housing and community development includes city housing and redevelopment projects and the regulation, promotion, and support of private housing and redevelopment activities. Data from Arizona, Kentucky, Michigan, New Mexico, New York, and Virginia generally include municipal housing authorities. Housing authorities for other cities are usually classified as independent governments, and data from them are not included.

Interest on debt is the amount paid for the use of borrowed money.

Total **debt outstanding** is the total of debt obligations remaining unpaid on the date specified. **Debt issued during the year** is the amount of the outstanding debt that was recently borrowed.

TABLE E—CONGRESSIONAL DISTRICTS OF THE 116TH CONGRESS

Members of the House of Representatives are for the 117th Congress.

LAND AREA, Items 1 and 3

Source: U.S. Census Bureau—2020 U.S. Gazetteer Files, https://www.census.gov/geographies/reference-files/time-series/geo/gazetteer-files.html

Land area measurements are shown to the nearest square mile. Land area includes dry land and land temporarily or partially covered by water, such as marshlands, swamps, and river floodplains.

POPULATION, Items 2–3

Source: U.S. Census Bureau—American Community Survey
https://www.census.gov/programs-surveys/acs

The population data are estimates from the 2020 5-year American Community Survey.

POPULATION AND POPULATION CHARACTERISTICS, Items 4–24

Source: U.S. Census Bureau—American Community Survey
https://www.census.gov/programs-surveys/acs

Data on age, sex, race, Hispanic origin foreign-born residents, and percent born in state of residence are from the 2020 5-year American Community Survey.

Data on race were derived from answers to the question on race that was asked of all respondents. The concept of race, as used by the Census Bureau, reflects self-identification by people according to the race or races with which they most closely identify. These categories are sociopolitical constructs and should not be interpreted as being scientific or anthropological in nature. Furthermore, the race categories include both racial and national origin groups.

In Table E, Columns 4 through 8 refer to individuals who identified with each racial category alone, while column 9 includes persons who identified with two or more races.

The **White** population is defined as persons who indicated their race as White, as well as persons who did not classify themselves in one of the specific race categories listed on the questionnaire but entered a nationality such as Irish, German, Italian, Lebanese, Near Easterner, Arab, or Polish.

The **Black** population includes persons who indicated their race as "Black or African American" as well as persons who did not classify themselves in one of the specific race categories but reported entries such as African American, Afro American, Kenyan, Nigerian, or Haitian.

The **American Indian or Alaska Native** population includes persons who indicated their race as American Indian or Alaska Native, as well as persons who did not classify themselves in one of the specific race categories but reported entries such as Canadian Indian, French-American Indian, Spanish-American Indian, Eskimo, Aleut, Alaska Indian, or any of the American Indian or Alaska Native tribes.

The **Asian and Pacific Islander** population combines two census groupings: **Asian** and **Native Hawaiian or Other Pacific Islander**. The **Asian** population includes persons who indicated their race as Asian Indian, Chinese, Filipino, Japanese, Korean, Vietnamese, or "Other Asian," as well as persons who provided write-in entries of such groups as Cambodian, Laotian, Hmong, Pakistani, or Taiwanese. The **Native Hawaiian or Other Pacific Islander** population includes persons who indicated their race as "Native Hawaiian," "Guamanian or Chamorro," "Samoan," or "Other Pacific Islander," as well as persons who reported entries such as Part Hawaiian, American Samoan, Fijian, Melanesian, or Tahitian.

The **Hispanic population** is based on a question that asked respondents "Is this person Spanish/Hispanic/Latino?" Persons marking any one of the four Hispanic categories (i.e., Mexican, Puerto Rican, Cuban, or other Spanish) are collectively referred to as Hispanic.

The **Non-Hispanic White alone** number in Column 11 includes only those persons who were not Hispanic and whose race was "White only."

The **female** population is shown as a percentage of total population.

The **foreign-born** population includes all persons who were not U.S. citizens at birth. Foreign-born persons are those who indicated they were either a U.S. citizen by naturalization or were not a citizen of the United States. The foreign-born population consists of immigrants (legal permanent residents), temporary migrants (students), humanitarian migrants (refugees), and unauthorized migrants (persons illegally residing in the United States).

Percent born in state of residence is shown as a percentage of total population.

Age is defined as age at last birthday (number of completed years since birth).

EDUCATION—SCHOOL ENROLLMENT AND EDUCATIONAL ATTAINMENT, Items 25–27

Source: U.S. Census Bureau—American Community Survey
https://www.census.gov/programs-surveys/acs

Data on school enrollment and educational attainment were derived from a sample of the population. Persons were classified as enrolled in school if they reported attending a "regular" public or private school (or college) during the year. The instructions were to "include only nursery school, kindergarten, elementary school, and schooling which would lead to a high school diploma or a college degree" as regular school. The Census Bureau defines a public school as "any school or college controlled and supported by a local, county, state, or federal government." Schools primarily supported and controlled by religious organizations or other private groups are defined as private schools.

Data on **educational attainment** are tabulated for the population 25 years old and over. The data were derived from a question that asked respondents for the highest level of school completed or the highest degree received. Persons who had passed a high school equivalency examination were considered high school graduates. Schooling received in foreign schools was to be reported as the equivalent grade or years in the regular American school system.

Vocational and technical training, such as barber school training; business, trade, technical, and vocational schools; or other training for a specific trade are specifically excluded.

High school graduate or more. This category includes persons who have received a high school diploma or its equivalent, and those who reported any level higher than a high school diploma.

Bachelor's degree or more. This category includes persons who have received bachelor's degrees, master's degrees, professional school degrees (such as law school or medical school degrees), and doctoral degrees.

HOUSEHOLDS, Items 28–33

Source: U.S. Census Bureau—American Community Survey
https://www.census.gov/programs-surveys/acs

A **household** includes all persons who occupy a housing unit. (Persons not living in households are classified as living in group quarters.) A housing unit is a house, an apartment, a mobile home, a group of rooms, or a single room occupied (or, if vacant, intended for occupancy) as separate living quarters. Separate living quarters are those in which the occupants live separately from any other persons in the building and have direct access from the outside of the building or through a common hall. The occupants may be a single family, one person living alone, two or more families living together, or any other group of related or unrelated persons who share living quarters. The number of households is the same as the number of year-round occupied housing units.

A **family** includes a householder and one or more other persons living in the same household who are related to the householder by birth, marriage, or adoption. All persons in a household who are related to the householder are regarded as members of his or her family. A **family household** may contain persons not related to the householder; thus, family households may include more members than families do. A household can contain only one family for the purposes of census tabulations. Not all households contain families, as a household may comprise a group of unrelated persons or of one person living alone. Families are classified by type as either a "husband-wife family" or "other family," according to the presence or absence of a spouse.

The measure of **persons per household** is obtained by dividing the number of persons in households by the number of households or householders. One person in each household is designated as the householder. In most cases, this is the person (or one of the persons) in whose name the house is owned, being bought, or rented. If there is no such person in the household, any adult household member 15 years old and over can be designated as the householder.

The category **female family householder** includes only female-headed family households with no spouse present.

GROUP QUARTERS, Items 34–39

Source: U.S. Census Bureau— Redistricting Data Summary File (Public Law 94-171)
https://www.census.gov/programs-surveys/decennial-census/about/rdo/summary-files.html

The Census Bureau classifies all people not living in households as living in **group quarters**. There are two types of group quarters: institutional, including **correctional facilities**, **nursing homes**, and mental hospitals; and non-institutional, including **college dormitories**, **military quarters**, group homes, missions, and shelters.

HOUSING, Items 40–45

Source: U.S. Census Bureau—American Community Survey
https://www.census.gov/programs-surveys/acs

A **housing unit** is a house, apartment, mobile home or trailer, group of rooms, or single room occupied or, if vacant, intended for occupancy as separate living quarters. Separate living quarters are those in which the occupants do not live and eat with any other person in the structure and which have direct access from the outside of the building or through a common hall. For vacant units, the criteria of separateness and direct access are applied to the intended occupants whenever possible. If that information cannot be obtained, the criteria are applied to the previous occupants.

The occupants of a housing unit may be a single family, one person living alone, two or more families living together, or any other group of related or unrelated persons who share living quarters. Both occupied and vacant housing units are included in the housing inventory, although recreational vehicles, tents, caves, boats, railroad cars, and the like are included only if they are occupied as a person's usual place of residence.

A housing unit is classified as **occupied** if it is the usual place of residence of the person or group of persons living in it at the time of interview, or if the occupants are only temporarily absent (away on vacation). A household consists of all persons who occupy a housing unit as their usual place of residence. Vacant units for sale or rent include units rented or sold but not occupied and any other units held off the market.

A housing unit is **owner occupied** if the owner or co-owner lives in the unit, even if it is mortgaged or not fully paid for. The owner or co-owner must live in the unit and is usually the first person listed on the census questionnaire

All occupied housing units that are not owner occupied, whether they are rented for cash rent or occupied without payment of cash rent, are classified as **renter occupied**.

Median value is the dollar amount that divides the distribution of specified owner-occupied housing units into two equal parts, with half of all units below the median value and half of all units above the median value. Value is defined as the respondent's estimate of what the house would sell for if it was for sale. Data are presented for single-family units on fewer than 10 acres of land that have no business or medical offices on the property.

Median rent divides the distribution of renter-occupied housing units into two equal parts. The rent concept used in this volume is gross rent, which includes the amount of cash rent a renter pays (contract rent) plus the estimated average cost of utilities and fuels, if these are paid by the renter. The rent is the amount of rent only for living quarters and excludes amounts paid for any business or other space occupied. Single-family houses on lots of 10 or more acres of land are also excluded.

INCOME AND POVERTY, Items 46–51

Source: U.S. Census Bureau—American Community Survey
https://www.census.gov/programs-surveys/acs

The data on income were derived from responses of a sample of persons 15 years old and over. **Total money income** is the sum of the amounts reported separately for wage or salary income; net self-employment income; interest, dividends, or net rental or royalty income or income from estates and trusts; Social Security or railroad retirement income; Supplemental Security Income (SSI); public assistance or welfare payments; retirement, survivor, or disability pensions; and all other income. Receipts from the following sources are not included as income: capital gains; money received from the sale of property (unless the recipient was engaged in the business of selling such property); the value of income "in kind" from food stamps, public housing subsidies, medical care, employer contributions for individuals, etc.; withdrawal of bank deposits; money borrowed; tax refunds; exchange of money between relatives living in the same household; and gifts, lump-sum inheritances, insurance payments, and other types of lump-sum receipts.

Per capita income is the mean income computed for every man, woman, and child in a particular group. It is derived by dividing the aggregate income of a particular group by the resident population in that group. Per capita income is rounded to the nearest whole dollar.

Household income includes the income of the householder and all other individuals 15 years old and over in the household, whether or not they are related to the householder. Since many households consist of only one person, median household income is usually less than median family income.

The **poverty status** data were derived from data collected on the number of persons in a household, from questionnaire item 3, which provided data on each person's relationship to the householder, and questionnaire items 41 and 42, which were also used to derive the income data. The Social Security Administration (SSA) developed the original poverty definition in 1964, which federal interagency committees subsequently revised in 1969 and 1980. The Office of Management and Budget's (OMB) *Directive 14* prescribes the SSA's definition as the official poverty measure for federal agencies to use in their statistical work. Poverty statistics presented in American Community Survey products adhere to the standards defined by OMB in *Directive 14*.

Poverty thresholds vary depending on three criteria: size of family, number of children, and, for one- and two-person families, age of householder. In determining the poverty status of families and unrelated individuals, the Census Bureau uses thresholds (income cutoffs) arranged in a two-dimensional matrix. The matrix consists of family size (from one person to nine or more persons), cross-classified by presence and number of family members under 18 years old (from no children present to eight or more children present). Unrelated individuals and two-person families are further differentiated by age of reference person (under 65 years old and 65 years old and over). To determine a person's poverty status, the person's total family income over the previous 12 months is compared with the poverty threshold appropriate for that person's family size and composition. If the total income of that person's family is less than the threshold appropriate for that family, then the person is considered poor or "below the poverty level," together with every member of his or her family. If a person is not living with anyone related by birth, marriage, or adoption, then the person's own income is compared with his or her poverty threshold. The total number of persons below the poverty level is the sum of persons in families and the number of unrelated individuals with incomes below the poverty level over the previous 12 months. The average poverty threshold for a four-person family was $24,230 in 2014.

The data on participation in the Food Stamp Program are designed to identify households in which one or more of the current members received food stamps during the past 12 months. Once a food stamp household was identified, a question was asked about the total value of all food stamps received by the household during that 12-month period. The Food Stamp Act of 1977 defines this federally funded program as one intended to "permit low-income households to obtain a more nutritious diet." (From title XIII of P.L. 95-113, The Food Stamp Act of 1977, declaration of policy.) Providing eligible households with coupons that can be used to purchase food increases food purchasing power. The Food and Nutrition Service (FNS) of the U.S. Department of Agriculture (USDA) administers the Food Stamp program through state

Poverty Thresholds for 2020 by Size of Family and Number of Related Children Under 18 Years

Size of family unit	Weighted average thresholds	Related children under 18 years: None	One	Two	Three	Four	Five	Six	Seven	Eight or more
One person (unrelated individual):	13,171									
Under age 65	13,465	13,465								
Aged 65 and older	12,413	12,413								
Two people:	16,733									
Householder under age 65	17,413	17,331	17,839							
Householder aged 65 and older	15,659	15,644	17,771							
Three people	20,591	20,244	20,832	20,852						
Four people	26,496	26,695	27,131	26,246	26,338					
Five people	31,417	32,193	32,661	31,661	30,887	30,414				
Six people	35,499	37,027	37,174	36,408	35,674	34,582	33,935			
Seven people	40,406	42,605	42,871	41,954	41,314	40,124	38,734	37,210		
Eight people	44,755	47,650	48,071	47,205	46,447	45,371	44,006	42,585	42,224	
Nine people or more	53,905	57,319	57,597	56,831	56,188	55,132	53,679	52,366	52,040	50,035

Source: U.S. Census Bureau.

and local welfare offices. The Food Stamp program is the major national income support program to which all low-income and low-resource households, regardless of household characteristics, are eligible.

CIVILIAN LABOR FORCE, UNEMPLOYMENT, AND EMPLOYMENT, Items 52–58

Source: U.S. Census Bureau—American Community Survey
https://www.census.gov/programs-surveys/acs

The **civilian labor force** consists of all civilians 16 years old and over who are either employed or unemployed.

Unemployment includes all persons who did not work during the survey week, made specific efforts to find a job during the previous four weeks, and were available for work during the survey week (except for temporary illness). Persons waiting to be called back to a job from which they had been laid off and those waiting to report to a new job within the next 30 days are included in unemployment figures.

Total employment includes all civilians 16 years old and over who were either (1) "at work"—those who did any work at all during the reference week as paid employees, worked in either their own business or profession, worked on their own farm, or worked 15 hours or more as unpaid workers in a family farm or business; or were (2) "with a job, but not at work"—those who had a job but were not at work that week due to illness, weather, industrial dispute, vacation, or other personal reasons.

The **occupational categories** are based on the occupational classification system that was developed for the 2000 census. This system consists of 539 specific occupational categories for employed persons arranged into 23 major occupational groups. This classification was developed based on the *Standard Occupational Classification (SOC) Manual: 2010*, published by the Executive Office of the President, Office of Management and Budget.

PERSONS WITH NO HEALTH INSURANCE, Item 59

Source: U.S. Census Bureau—American Community Survey
https://www.census.gov/programs-surveys/acs

The percentage of persons under age 65 with no **health insurance** shows the percentage of the population of each congressional district who were not covered by private health plans purchased directly or provided by an employer, Medicaid, Medicare, or military health care.

SOCIAL SECURITY AND SUPPLEMENTAL SECURITY INCOME, Items 60–62

Source: U.S. Social Security Administration
https://www.ssa.gov/policy/docs/factsheets/cong_stats

Social Security beneficiaries are persons receiving benefits under the Old-Age, Survivors, and Disability Insurance Program. These include retired or disabled workers covered by the program, their spouses and dependent children, and the surviving spouses and dependent children of deceased workers.

Supplemental Security Income (SSI) recipients are persons receiving SSI payments. The SSI program is a cash assistance program that provides monthly benefits to low-income aged, blind, or disabled persons.

Data are as of December of the year shown.

AGRICULTURE, Items 63–72

Source: U.S. Department of Agriculture, National Agricultural Statistics Service—2017 Census of Agriculture
https://www.nass.usda.gov/Publications/AgCensus/2017/index.php

Data for the 2017 Census of Agriculture were collected in 2018, but pertain to the year 2017.

The Census Bureau took a census of agriculture every 10 years from 1840 to 1920; since 1925, this census has been taken roughly once every 5 years. The 1997 Census of Agriculture was the first one conducted by the National Agricultural Statistics Service of the U.S. Department of Agriculture. Over time, the definition of a farm has varied. For recent censuses (including the 2017 census), a farm has been defined as any place from which $1,000 or more of agricultural products were produced and sold or normally would have been sold during the census year. Dollar figures are expressed in current dollars and have not been adjusted for inflation or deflation.

The acreage designated as **land in farms** consists primarily of agricultural land used for crops, pasture, or grazing. It also includes woodland and wasteland not actually under cultivation or used for pasture or grazing, provided that this land was part of the farm operator's total operation. Land in farms is an operating-unit concept and includes all land owned and operated, as well as all land rented from others. Land used rent-free is classified as land rented from others. All grazing land, except land used under government permits on a per-head basis, was included as "land in farms" provided it was part of a farm or ranch. Land under the exclusive use of a grazing association was reported by the grazing association and included as land in farms. All land in Indian reservations used for growing crops or grazing livestock is classified as land in farms.

Harvested cropland includes land from which crops were harvested and hay was cut, land used to grow short rotation woody crops, Christmas trees, and land in orchards, groves, vineyards, berries, nurseries, and greenhouses. Land from which two or more crops were harvested was counted only once. Land in tapped maple trees was included in woodland not pastured.

Market value of agricultural products sold by farms represents the gross market value before taxes and the production expenses of all agricultural products sold or removed from the place in 2017, regardless of who received the payment. It is equivalent to total sales and it includes sales by producers as well as the value of any share received by partners, landlords, contractors, and others associated with the operation. It includes value of organic sales, direct sales and the value of commodities placed in the Commodity Credit Corporation (CCC) loan program. Market value of agricultural products sold does not include payments received for participation in other federal farm programs. Also, it does not include income from farm-related sources such as custom work and other agricultural services, or income from nonfarm sources.

Government payments consist of direct payments as defined by the 2002 Farm Bill; payments from Conservation Reserve Program (CRP), Wetlands Reserve Program (WRP), Farmable Wetlands Program (FWP), and Conservation Reserve Enhancement Program (CREP); loan deficiency payments; disaster payments; other conservation programs; and all other federal farm programs under which payments were made directly to farm producers, including those specified in the 2014 Agricultural Act (Farm Bill), including Agriculture Risk Coverage (ARC) and Price Loss Coverage (PLC). Commodity Credit Corporation (CCC) proceeds, amount from State and local government agricultural program payments, and federal crop insurance payments were not included in this category.

PRIVATE NONFARM EMPLOYMENT AND EARNINGS, Items 73–85

Source: U.S. Census Bureau—County Business Patterns
https://www.census.gov/programs-surveys/cbp.html

Data for private nonfarm employment and earnings are compiled from the payroll information reported monthly in the Census Bureau publication *County Business Patterns*. The estimates are based on surveys conducted by the Census Bureau and administrative records from the Internal Revenue Service (IRS).

The following types of employment are excluded from the tables: government employment, self-employed persons, farm workers, and domestic service workers. Railroad employment jointly covered by Social Security and railroad retirement programs, employment on oceanborne vessels, and employment in foreign countries are also excluded.

Annual payroll is the combined amount of wages paid, tips reported, and other compensation (including salaries, vacation allowances, bonuses, commissions, sick-leave pay, and the value of payments-in-kind such as free meals and lodging) paid to employees before deductions for Social Security, income tax, insurance, union dues, etc. All forms of compensation are included, regardless of whether they are subject to income tax or the Federal Insurance Contributions Act tax, with the exception of annuities, third-party sick pay, and supplemental unemployment compensation benefits (even if income tax was withheld). For corporations, total annual payroll includes compensation paid to officers and executives; for unincorporated businesses, it excludes profit or other compensation of proprietors or partners.